All Music Guide to

SOUL

The Definitive Guide to R&B and Soul

Edited by

Vladimir Bogdanov

John Bush

Chris Woodstra

Stephen Thomas Erlewine

AMG
All Media Guide

Backbeat Books

All Media Guide has created the world's largest and most comprehensive information databases for music, videos, DVDs, and video games. With coverage of both in-print and out-of-print titles, the massive AMG archive includes reviews, plot synopses, biographies, ratings, images, titles, credits, essays, and thousands of descriptive categories. All content is original, written expressly for AMG by a worldwide network of professional staff and freelance writers specializing in music, movies, and games. The AMG databases—**All Music Guide®, All Movie Guide®, and All Game Guide™**—are licensed by major retailers and Internet content sites and are available to the public through its websites (www.allmusic.com, www.allmovie.com, www.allgame.com) and through its series of books: *All Music Guide, All Music Guide to Rock, All Music Guide to Country, All Music Guide to Jazz, All Music Guide to Blues, All Music Guide to Electronica,* and *All Music Guide to Soul.*

All Media Guide 301 E. Liberty Street, Suite 400, Ann Arbor, MI 48104
T: 734/887-5600 F: 734/827-2492
www. allmediaguide.com email: feedback@allmediaguide.com

Published by **Backbeat Books**
600 Harrison Street, San Francisco, CA 94107
www.backbeatbooks.com
Email: books@musicplayer.com
An imprint of the Music Player Group
Publishers of *Guitar Player, Bass Player, Keyboard, EQ,* and other magazines
United Entertainment Media, Inc.
A CMP Information company

CMP
United Business Media

Distributed to the book trade in the U.S. and Canada by
Publishers Group West, 1700 Fourth Street, Berkeley, CA 94710

Distributed to the music trade in the U.S. and Canada by
Hal Leonard Publishing, PO Box 13819, Milwaukee, WI 53213

Cover Design: Wagner Design, Ann Arbor, MI
Text Composition: Interactive Composition Corporation

Library of Congress Cataloging-in-Publication Data

All music guide to soul : the definitive guide to the R&B and soul / edited by Vladimir Bogdanov, Chris Woodstra, and Stephen Thomas Erlewine.
p. cm. — (All music guide)
ISBN 0-87930-744-7 (alk. paper)
1. Soul music—Discography. 2. Rhythm and blues music—Discography. 3. Sound recordings—Reviews. I. Bogdanov, Vladimir, 1965– II. Woodstra, Chris. III. Erlewine, Stephen Thomas. IV. AMG all music guide series.

ML156.4.S6A45 2003
016.781644'0266—dc21

2003052270

Printed in the United States of America
05 06 07 5 4 3 2

Contents

How to Use This Book **iv**
Contributors **v**
Introduction **vii**
Style Descriptions **viii**

Artists **1**

A 1
B 27
C 107
D 175
E 213
F 233
G 268
H 292
I 330
J 345
K 382
L 403
M 436
N 490
O 501
P 517
Q 556
R 557
S 596
T 665
U 708
V 712
W 720
X 772
Y 773
Z 775
Various Artists 777

Essays **836**

Early Rhythm & Blues 836
Music Map: R&B Through Soul and Funk to Urban and Contemporary R&B 837
Independent Labels: The 1940s and 1950s 838
Doo Wop 839
Music Map 840
New Orleans R&B 839
Music Map 841
Brill Building Sound 841
Music Map 842
Girl Group 842
Music Map 843
Soul 844
Music Map 845
Motown 845
Music Map 846
Blue-Eyed Soul 847
Music Map 847
Philly Soul 848
Music Map 848
Psychedelic Soul 848
Funk 850
Music Map 850
Northern Soul 851
Go-Go 852
New Jack Swing 853
British Soul 854
The Minneapolis Sound 854
Neo-Soul 855
Gospel 856
Soul Jazz 857
Reggae 858
House 858

Essential Artists **860**
Essential Songs **864**
Index **868**

How to Use This Book

ARTIST NAME

VITAL STATISTICS: For groups, **f.** indicates date and place of formation; **db.** indicated date disbanded. For individual performers, date and place of birth (**b.**) and death (**d.**), if known, are given.

INSTRUMENT(S) / STYLE(S): Indicates the instruments played if the artist is an individual, followed by the styles of music associated with the performer or group.

BIOGRAPHY: A quick view of the artist's life and musical career. For major performers, proportionately longer biographies are provided.

ALBUM REVIEWS: These are the albums selected by our editors and contributors.

KEY TO SYMBOLS: ● ☆ ★

☆ ESSENTIAL RECORDINGS: Albums marked with a star should be part of any good collection of the genre. Often, these are also a good first purchase (filled star). By hearing these albums, you can get a good overview of the entire genre. These are must-hear and must-have recordings. You can't go wrong with them.

●★ FIRST PURCHASE: Albums marked with either a filled circle or a filled star should be your first purchase. This is where to begin to find out if you like this particular artist. These albums are representative of the best this artist has to offer. If you don't like these picks, chances are this artist is not for you. In the case of an artist who has a number of distinct periods, you will find an essential pick marked for each period. Albums are listed chronologically when possible.

ALBUM TITLE: The name of the album is listed in bold as it appears on the original when possible. Very long titles have been abbreviated, or repeated in full as part of the comment, where needed.

DATE: The year of an album's first recording or release, if known.

RECORD LABEL: Record labels indicate the current (or most recent) release of this recording. Label numbers are not included because they change frequently.

ALBUM RATINGS: ✦ TO ✦✦✦✦✦ In addition to the stars and circles used to distinguish exceptional noteworthy albums, as explained above, all albums are rated on a scale from one to five diamonds.

REVIEWERS: The name of each review's author is given at the end of the review.

The Blackbyrds

f. 1973, Washington, D.C., **db.** 1978

Group / Jazz-Pop, Jazz-Funk, Urban, Funk

The Blackbyrds were a jazz-funk group with thick R&B streaks running down their backs. Assembled by Donald Byrd in 1974, the group's original members—percussionist Pericles "Perk" Jacobs Jr., drummer Keith Killgo, keyboardist Kevin Toney, reeds player Allan Barnes, bassist Joe Hall, guitarist Barney Perry—were mined from Howard University's music department, where the doctor and jazz legend was an instructor. (Other key players included guitarist Orville Saunders and saxophonist/flute player Steve Johnson.) During the Blackbyrds' nearly decade-long existence, the group cut a handful of LPs (1973's *The Blackbyrds*, 1974's *Flying Start*, 1975's *City Life*, 1976's *Unfinished Business*, 1977's *Action*, 1980's *Better Days*); scored films (1975's *Cornbread, Earl and Me*); and supported artists like B.B. King, Mandrill, and Roberta Flack. "Walking in Rhythm," "Rock Creek Park," and "Happy Music" are their three best-known cuts; they have remained underground club classics, and they have been kept alive, in part, through sampling.

The group's catalog has been overhauled and reissued a number of times; multiple best-ofs have been released (Fantasy's *Greatest Hits* is the strongest and most thorough), and most of the group's full-length output has been put out on CD through two-fers. As far as outside activities were considered, Barney Perry released a solo album under the name Blair in 1978 (through his own Solar Sound imprint). The remaining members' involvements are far too extensive to list. *—Andy Kellman*

☆ **City Life** / Nov. 1975 / Fantasy ✦✦✦✦✦

The Blackbyrds—a jazz-funk outfit formed in a university class taught by jazz trumpeter Donald Byrd, who produced the albums and wrote most of the tunes—were more of an Earth, Wind & Fire-style horn band than a purist jazz crew, but few groups were better in their chosen style, and 1975's *City Life* is probably their best album. It's certainly their most successful, including the pop hit "Happy Music" and what has become their signature tune, a percolating Latin-flavored jam called "Rock Creek Park" that's one of the pinnacles of '70s jazz-funk. As on the bouncy title track, the lyrical content is minimal, a simple hypnotic chant, but the fluid interplay of the musicians, who are masters of the unison horn section and the polyrhythmic groove, is what's important about this music. Other highlights include the funky Southern-style soul of "Hash and Eggs" and the lyrical ballad "Love So Fine." This is often-sublime stuff ripe for rediscovery by fans of '70s funk, soul, and fusion. *—Stewart Mason*

Action / Sep. 1977 / Fantasy ✦✦✦

If you had to own only one album by the Blackbyrds then *Action* should be it. All the elements came together for the Donald Byrd protégés on this scintillating certified gold album, which originally was issued in fall 1977. The sinewy Top 20 R&B hit "Supernatural Feeling" has bits of wisdom implanted in between its poppin' funk grooves. The enticing "Soft and Easy" slid into the R&B Top 20 with an ease that's equal to the gentle spoken seduction that is woven throughout this make out classic. The exotic radio-aired LP track "Something Special" features the nimble noodling of future smooth jazz favorite, pianist Kevin Toney. "Dreaming About You" is the perfect track to unwind during. *Action* was later issued as one of two LPs that was included on a single CD (the other being the George Duke-produced *Better Days*) in 1994 by U.K. label Ace Records. *—Ed Hogan*

● **Night Grooves: The Blackbyrds' Greatest Hits** / Dec. 1978 / Fantasy ✦✦✦✦

Despite the fact that 1989's *Greatest Hits* rendered this earlier Fantasy compilation obsolete—*Greatest Hits* contains all seven songs found here, plus four others—Fantasy continued to keep this disc in circulation. This is a tighter and more discerning collection, sticking to the absolute essential material that Donald Byrd's protégés churned out during the '70s, but simple mathematics places its value below the later, more inclusive anthology. Those who want to dig deeper can start with any of the group's first four proper LPs; each one peaked in the Top Ten of *Billboard*'s jazz album chart, and they all have their charms beyond the singles. Anyone who bet on the Blackbyrds' material to die a disposable pop death must feel foolish now, as cuts like "Rock Creek Park," "Happy Music," and "Walking in Rhythm" remain completely unironic fixtures in the record crates of many house DJs. *—Andy Kellman*

Better Days / Dec. 1980 / Fantasy ✦✦

Those who know the Blackbyrds best by their 1977 gold LP *Action* may feel discombobulated by the group's 1980 album, *Better Days*. Part of the reason may come from the ever-changing nature of pop music. In just a few short years, radio play lists had become tighter and less eclectic. No longer under the mentorship of jazz trumpeter/ producer Donald Byrd, and wrapped in the dazzling string/horn arrangements of *Action* arranger Wade Marcus, the Blackbyrds' sound was less fluid and the band's considerable chops (musical skills) were held in check. Going a radio-friendly route under the aegis of producer George Duke, the soft, thumpin' "What We Have Is Right" made it to number 38 R&B (*Billboard*) and the midtempo groovin' stepper "Love Don't Strike Twice" brushed the lower half of the chart. Other highlights are the horn-laced stompin' title track and "Do It Girl" (which sounds something like a Con Funk Shun ballad). *Better Days* was teamed with *Action* on a 1994 single CD from U.K. label Ace Records. *—Ed Hogan*

Contributors

All Music Guide

Vladimir Bogdanov, President
Chris Woodstra, Vice President of Content Development, Editor-in-Chief

AMG Popular Music Department

Stephen Thomas Erlewine, Director of Content
John Bush, Senior Editor
Joslyn Layne, Associate Editor

Assistant Editors

Al Campbell
Andy Kellman
Greg McIntosh
Sean Westergaard
Tim Sendra
Stacia Proefrock
Heather Phares
MacKenzie Wilson

Copy Editing

Jason Birchmeier
Amy Cloud
Dana Rowader
Rachel Sprovtsoff-Mangus
Aaron Warshaw
Dave Lynch

Data Processing

Mark Donkers, Manager
Jonathan Ball
Matt Collar
Heather Humphrey
Jack "Lee" Isles
Zac Johnson
Aaron Latham
Corwin Moore
David Serra
Chris True
Donn Stroud
Rob Theakston

Contributors

Bret Adams
Greg Adams
Mark Allan
Rick Anderson
Jason Ankeny
Jon Azpiri
Jonathan Ball
Rodney Batdorf
Ashley S. Battel
Brian Beatty
George Bedard
Larry Belanger
Jason Birchmeier
Roxanne Blanford
Myles Boisen
Ross Boissoneau
Drago Bonacich
John Book
Rob Bowman
Sandra Brennan
Rick A. Bueche
Scott Bultman
Jeff Burger
John Bush
Nathan Bush
Bryan Buss
Al Campbell
Dean Carlson
Bil Carpenter
Troy Carpenter
Nate Cavalieri
Eugene Chadbourne
Ken Chang
James Chrispell
Paul Clifford
Paul Collins
Stephen Cook
Steve Cooper
William Cooper
François Couture
Rosalind Cummings-Yeates
Craig Curtice
Bill Dahl
Hank Davis
Tom Demalon
Mark Deming
Ron DePasquale
Charlotte Dillon
John Dougan
Travis Drageset
John Duffy
Jim Dunn
Paula Edelstein
Bruce Eder
Kurt Edwards
Brian Egan
Jason Elias
Michael Erlewine
Stephen Thomas Erlewine
Jim Esch
Colin Escott
Keith Farley
Kathleen C. Fennessy
Rob Ferrier
John Floyd
Michael Freedberg
Christina Fuoco
Robert Gabriel
Michael Gallucci
Chris Genzel
Richard S. Ginell
Daniel Gioffre
Joshua Glazer
Ryan Randall Goble
Nicholas Gordon
Bob Gottlieb
Thom Granger
Tom Graves
Adam Greenberg
Jo-Ann Greene
Matthew Greenwald
JT Griffith
Tim Griggs

Jason Gross
Donald A. Guarisco
Nikki Gustafson
Owen Guthrie-Jones
Tom Hallett
Char Ham
Andrew Hamilton
Shawn M. Haney
Amy Hanson
Craig Harris
Kelvin Hayes
Dan Heilman
Alex Henderson
Gary Hill
Larry Hoffman
Steve Hoffman
Ed Hogan
Hal Horowitz
Stephen Howell
Steve Huey
Eddie Huffman
Jaime Ikeda
Jack L.V. Isles
Vik Iyengar
Zac Johnson
Liana Jonas
John Jones
Thom Jurek
Justin M. Kantor
Andy Kellman
Chris Kelsey
Wade Kergan
Quint Kik
Nic Kincaid
Ashleigh Kittle
Cub Koda
Todd Kristel
Steve Kurutz
Lynda Lane
Ronnie D. Lankford, Jr.
Theresa E. LaVeck
Joslyn Layne
Dan LeRoy
Jonathan Lewis
Kip Lornell
Bret Love
Lars Lovén
John Lowe
Craig Lytle
Dennis MacDonald
Jason MacNeil
Brian Mansfield
Dave Marsh
Kingsley Marshall
Stewart Mason
Derrick Mathis
Joseph McCombs
Steven McDonald
Steve McMullen
Stephen Mercier
Bill Meredith
Jon Mojo Mills
Ted Mills
Mark Morgenstein
Michael G. Nastos
Dave Nathan
Opal Louis Nations
Jim Newsom
Chris Nickson
Ed.Nimmervoll
Jim O'Neal
Brian O'Neill
Michael Ofjord
Christine Ohlman
J.P. Ollio
Thom Owens
Richard Pack
Roch Parisien
Joe Pettit, Jr.
Heather Phares
Lindsay Planer
J. Poet
Bob Porter
Greg Prato
Stacia Proefrock
Jose F. Promis
Jon Pruett
Bruce Boyd Raeburn
Brian Raftery
Ned Raggett
Vince Ripol
Matthew Robinson
William Ruhlmann
Thomas Schulte
Jeff Schwachter
Linda Seida
Tim Sendra
Joshua David Shanker
Tim Sheridan
Earl Simmons
Douglas Siwek
Richard Skelly
Chris Slawecki
Jim Smith
Kerry Smith
Tim A. Smith
Don Snowden
Leo Stanley
Roger Steffens
Peter Stepek
Denise Sullivan
Kim Summers
Michael Sutton
Glenn Swan
Stanton Swihart
Sara Sytsma
David Szatmary
Jeff Tamarkin
Ben Tausig
Ken Taylor
Rob Theakston
Bryan Thomas
Dave Thompson
Bradley Torreano
Richie Unterberger
Victor W. Valdivia
Mark Vanderhoff
Jos Veestraeten
Joe Viglione
Brian Whitener
Jonathan Widran
Tony Wilds
MacKenzie Wilson
Rose of Sharon Witmer
Chris Woodstra
Jim Worbois
Ron Wynn
Scott Yanow
Curtis Zimmermann

Introduction

Soul music can be a serious business. Ask any soul record collector. For them, it's hardly a hobby. It's an obsession, a calling, something that consumes all their time and energy, while draining their wallet. It's not uncommon for a collector to spend thousands of dollars on a mere two-song *single*—songs they only know through reputation, not because they've heard them.

Time was, this kind of passion was the province only of those who had the time and inclination to scour flea markets, garage sales and record conventions, searching for that rare Southern soul side or slice of independent Chicago soul. If you were in that culture, it was fun and intoxicating. If you weren't, it seemed rather exclusionary. How could it not, when its denizens were willing to part with a significant portion of their salary for a single?

Fortunately, times have changed. There are still many collectors who only purchase vinyl, or only collect 45s, but this music has found its way outside of the collectors market, thanks to the legion of reissue labels that bring this great music to a wider audience through their sharply sequenced, lovingly prepared releases, and specialty stores like Chicago's Dusty Groove that specialize in making this superb music available for online purchase. Because of this, it's easier than ever to immerse yourself in this music, to hear the rarities that once were exclusive and to build rich collections without too much effort or money. Nevertheless, it still can be difficult to navigate through the stacks of reissues, not to mention the decades of great soul music. That's where the *All Music Guide to Soul* comes in.

Soul is the lifeblood of popular music. Sure, rock & roll started the revolution, but it wouldn't have existed without R&B, and ever since the rock era began, soul thrived concurrently, often shifting as fluidly as rock or pop. Like all popular music, it mirrored the times, adopting current sounds and styles, whether it was the elasticity of psychedelia or the gritty postmodern rhythms of hip-hop. Through it all, fans and critics alike often called it "soul." Sam Cooke's seductive croon was a far cry from the singer/songwriter Bill Withers, the jazzy Anita Baker or the exuberant dance beats of the New Edition, yet all have been tagged as soul over the years. This doesn't make soul music difficult to understand, of course, but when a term is that ubiquitous, it can be difficult to discern what the heart of the music actually is. As it turns out, it's easy to pin the golden age of the music. Like rock & roll, the foundation of R&B and soul is the music made in the late '50s, '60s and early '70s, when the music was developing, along with all of its styles and subsidiaries. Sure, plenty of great, transcendent music has been made since then—after all, Prince, Michael Jackson, disco, sampling and hip-hop were yet to come—but this is the heart of the music, and, appropriately, this also forms the heart of the *All Music Guide to Soul*.

This book uses that golden era as the foundation to an exploration of every offshoot and mutation of soul, from the jump blues that gave way to pile-driving juke-joint small R&B combos all the way to the neo-soul that currently fascinates serious listeners. Part of the reason for that is that there was a surplus of great music being made during that time. Yes, there are the hits that remain popular to this day—the endless stream of Motown hits, the phenomenal Otis Redding and Aretha Franklin albums, the silky smooth Spinners, the elegance of Curtis Mayfield, the great Ray Charles—and there are also singers cherished by serious fans, such as Don Covay and James Carr. But, in addition to that canon, there are countless regional hits, near-misses and completely unheard, yet brilliant, sides that could have been hits in an alternate universe. These, naturally, are the kind of things that drive the serious collectors to spend a significant portion of their salary on unheard records.

What's good for those of us who love the music but prefer to live on some modicum of a budget is that there's more of this music available now than ever, making this the best time to collect soul music. Nearly every major artist has all their albums, or at least comprehensive compilations, in print, and the same is true for cult favorites, as well as forgotten and unheard singers, whether it's Southern or Northern soul. And these newly discovered treasures are easier to hear now, thanks to the painstaking efforts of such reissue labels as Sundazed in the U.S. and Ace in the U.K. In fact, there's so much of this material—and so much of it has been on CD over the years—that it's hard to keep it straight without a book like this.

The *All Music Guide to Soul* is designed to help soul fans of all kinds find great music, whether it's a classic Marvin Gaye album, or a relatively obscure Oscar Toney Jr. album recently released on CD. Better still, it reveal something that even dedicated collectors might have missed, such as Castle/Sequel's terrific Invictus/Hot Wax reissue series of 1999, or Ace's continuing various artist compilations of great forgotten soul singles from the '50s and '60s. This book has all that, plus much much more: earthy New Orleans R&B, wild funk, obscure disco, effervescent dance-pop, smooth quiet storm and seductive neo-soul. It covers everything that has been called Soul over the years, and lets fans of any era easily explore other sounds. (There is one notable exception and that's rap and hip-hop, which will be chronicled in a forthcoming AMG book of its own, also scheduled for publication in 2003.)

Is this book complete? Of course not. New artists arrive every month and rare sides are discovered all the time, so there's a ceaseless stream of great music to discover (please be sure to check out our website www.allmusic.com for the latest releases and reissues). Nevertheless, the *All Music Guide to Soul* is filled with great artists and great records, making it an essential roadmap for all soul fans. Whenever you're digging through the crates at a local used record store or find yourself about to walk into Dusty Groove in Chicago, make sure this book is by your side, since it will help you find music you love—music that you'll be amazed you've never heard before now. – *Stephen Thomas Erlewine*

Style Descriptions

BEACH

Beach Music is uptempo, good-time pop-soul—in other words, it's party music. Appropriately, it received its name through its constant presence at parties on the eastern coast. After all, there really isn't a specific "beach music"—the partiers on the East Coast gave these pop/rock and soul songs the name because these were the records they played on the beach during the '60s. It was all high-energy pop and soul in the vein of Motown. Often, there were regional stars, such as General Johnson, and there were regional hits, but just as frequently national records were played locally. Although it had ceased to have national impact by the beginning of the '70s, beach music retained its popularity for decades, and it was still holding strong by the turn of the millennium.

BLACK GOSPEL

While many white musicians gravitated toward country, folk, and old-timey music to express their spirituality outside of traditional Christian hymns, Black Gospel music drew heavily upon the traditional spirituals that had been passed down from the days of slavery, picking up its more driving rhythmic emphasis from blues and early jazz. Composer and singer Rev. Thomas A. Dorsey crystallized the style in 1932 with his epochal "Take My Hand, Precious Lord," and went on to compose a great many songs that later became standards. When performed in the churches, the music was traditionally sung by a choir, with individual soloists sometimes taking the spotlight; this often happened in a form known as "call and response," in which either the choir or the soloist would repeat and/or answer the lyric which had just been sung by the other, with the soloist improvising embellishments of the melody for greater emphasis. As the music developed, these soloists became more and more virtuosic, performing with wild emotion (and, in the South, physicality) in order to properly express the spiritual ecstasy the music was meant to evoke. The small-group format was also prevalent, with major figures including the Five Blind Boys of Mississippi, the Soul Stirrers, the Swan Silvertones, and the Dixie Hummingbirds. As the years progressed, black gospel and black popular music influenced and borrowed from one another, reflecting the gradual change of emphasis toward R&B; black gospel also had an enormous impact on the development of soul music, which directed gospel's spiritual intensity into more secular concerns, and included a great many performers whose musical skills were developed in the church. As a recognizable style unto itself, black gospel music largely ceased to develop around the 1970s; progressing racial attitudes had helped black popular music reach wider audiences (and become more lucrative) than ever before, and tastes had turned towards the earthy hedonism of funk and the highly arranged, sophisticated Philly soul sound. The former wasn't quite appropriate for worship, and it wasn't all that practical to duplicate the latter in church services. However, the traditional black gospel sound survived intact and was eventually augmented by contemporary gospel (an '80s/'90s variation strongly influenced by latter-day urban R&B); plus, singers like Whitney Houston continued to develop within its ranks.

BLAXPLOITATION

Blaxploitation films appeared in the early '70s, in the wake of Melvin Van Peebles' groundbreaking independent film *Sweet Sweetback's Baadasssss Song*. Van Peebles' angry masterpiece was a serious, even dangerous work that established that raw, independent African-American films would find audiences. It also happened to have a funk soundtrack—appropriate, since funk was the cutting-edge music of the time. As it would turn out, *Sweet Sweetback* ushered in an era of filmmaking that wasn't nearly as serious as Van Peebles' movie. Quite quickly, his innovations were diluted and channeled into a genre called blaxploitation. Where *Sweet Sweetback* was serious as a heart attack, blaxploitation—with a few exceptions—was lightweight, telling tales of detectives, outlaws, pimps, and hustlers. It played to a broad audience, and it found it. And those films were given funk soundtracks, similar to *Sweet Sweetback*—filled with wah-wah guitars, big bass, and funky beats—but the newer soundtracks were richer and more diverse. Much of this music held up better than the films themselves, even in the case of *Superfly*, one of the better blaxploitation films of the time, where Curtis Mayfield's music was better than the film. As the movie genre died out in the late '70s, so did the music, but both the films and the soundtracks remained cult favorites well into the next century.

BLUE-EYED SOUL

Blue-Eyed Soul refers to soul and R&B music performed and sung by white musicians. The term first came into play during the mid-'60s, when acts like the Righteous Brothers had hits with soulful songs like "You Lost That Loving Feeling." Throughout the late '60s, blue-eyed soul thrived, as acts like the Rascals, the Box Tops, Mitch Ryder, Tony Joe White, and Roy Head had a series of hits. During the '70s, blue-eyed soul continued to be successful, as acts like Hall & Oates, Robert Palmer, Average White Band, Boz Scaggs, and David Bowie updated the formula.

BRILL BUILDING POP

Brill Building Pop applied the concept of professional songwriters in traditional pop to rock & roll. Numerous teams of professional songwriters worked at the Brill Building—a block of music publishing houses in New York City—writing songs for artists as diverse as the Coasters, the Drifters, the Shangri-Las, the Ronettes, Neil Sedaka, and Connie Francis. The songs were indebted not only to rock & roll and R&B, but also Tin Pan Alley pop, as the sophisticated lyrics and melodies proved. The productions on these early '60s records were also more sophisticated than most rock & roll records, featuring orchestras and bands with large rhythm and guitar sections. Though it fell out of favor after the British Invasion, both British and American pop/rock demonstrated an enormous debt to Brill Building pop for years to come.

BROWN-EYED SOUL

Much like Britain's Northern soul community, the Latino population of southern California fell for soul music and initially imported many of its favorite songs, but the community also fostered a fertile base of artists by the mid-'60s. Unlike the sound of boogaloo/Latin soul (based in New York City), early brown-eyed soul owed little to traditional Latin music and was rarely performed in Spanish. Instead, rock bands like Cannibal & the Headhunters ("Land of 1000 Dances") and Thee Midniters—inspired by '50s Latino rocker Ritchie Valens—earned national recognition playing anthemic rock & roll with an R&B edge. Smooth Chicago soul and Motown hits were big crowd favorites at dances during the early '60s (alongside a rare local sensation like Brenton Wood). When the East L.A. community began gradually moving from energetic R&B to romantic soul, the results were some of the sweetest soul music heard during the late '60s and '70s. Another wing of the brown-eyed soul crowd was influenced by Chicano, the Latino civil-rights movement emphasizing heritage and cultural pride. As a result, bands like War, Malo, El Chicano, and Tierra followed Latin-rock breakout Santana into the nation's cultural consciousness. Brown-eyed soul anthems kept edging the charts during the mid-'70s (a good example being Bloodstone's "Natural High"), but rarely breached the national radar after 1980. Rhino Records' three-volume series *Brown Eyed Soul: The Sound of East L.A.* remains the definitive document of all the imported hits and homegrown talent associated with the style.

CHICAGO SOUL

Of the three major hotbeds for soul music during the 1960s, Motown had the hits and Memphis had the grit. Unfortunately, Chicago's fertile soul community is often left off the map—and if it's recognized at all, it's mostly for the accomplishments of Curtis Mayfield, both as a member of the Impressions and later as a solo act. The Chicago Soul scene obviously fostered a variety of production styles, but its best-known hits—including "The Monkey Time" by Major Lance, "Get on Up" by the Esquires, "People Get Ready" by the Impressions, and "(Your Love Keeps Lifting Me) Higher and Higher" by Jackie Wilson—featured a sound based on laid-back yet effervescent soul, with sweet vocals and a stinging horn section. Though Mayfield is rightly the central figure in the rise of Chicago soul, considering his work as a songwriter and producer as well as bandleader and vocalist, producer/A&R man Carl Davis deserves just as much credit for development of the sound. Often in tandem with Mayfield, Davis' productions (first for OKeh and later for Brunswick and his own label, Dakar) created definitive hits for Major Lance, Jackie Wilson, Gene Chandler, the Chi-Lites, Barbara Acklin, and Tyrone Davis, among others. Though the Chicago sound continued on into the '70s, the collapse of many independent labels proved a tragic blow to the fortunes of many fine soul singers.

CLUB/DANCE

Club/Dance music comes in many different forms, from disco to hip-hop. Though there have been various dance crazes throughout the history of popular music, club/dance music became its own genre in the mid-'70s, as soul mutated into disco and whole clubs were devoted to dancing. In the late '70s, dance clubs played disco, but by the end of the decade, disco was mutating into a number of different genres. All of the genres were collected under the catch-all term "dance," though there were distinct differences between dance-pop, hip-hop, house, and techno, among other subgenres. What tied them all together was their emphasis on rhythm—in each dance subgenre, the beat remains all-important.

CONTEMPORARY GOSPEL

Contemporary Gospel is an updated, polished version of traditional gospel. Most of the material in contemporary gospel is newly written and the gospel choir has absorbed many innovations in soul music, both vocally and musically. On record, contemporary gospel often sounds similar to urban music.

CONTEMPORARY R&B

Contemporary R&B developed after years of urban R&B. Like urban, contemporary R&B is slickly produced, but many of the musicians—Maxwell, D'Angelo, Terence Trent D'Arby—are obsessed with bringing the grit, spirit, and ambitiousness of classic soul (Marvin Gaye, Stevie Wonder, Otis Redding) back to contemporary soul and R&B.

COUNTRY-SOUL

Country-Soul is a canny fusion of country and soul. Often, it results in the soulful, gospel-inflected interpretations of country songs. Ray Charles was the pioneer of this fusion, and ever since his groundbreaking recordings, the lines between country and soul were forever blurred.

DANCE-POP

Dance-Pop was an outgrowth of disco. Over a pounding, dance-club beat, there are simple, catchy melodies—dance-pop has more fully-formed songs than pure dance music. Dance-pop is primarily a producer's medium. The producer writes the songs and constructs the tracks, picking an appropriate vocalist to sing the song. These dance divas become stars, but frequently the artistic vision is the producer's. Naturally, there are some major exceptions—Madonna and Janet Jackson have had control over the sound and direction of their records—but dance-pop is music that is about image, not substance.

DEEP FUNK

Deep Funk is a term used to describe obscure funk recordings that appeal mostly to zealous collectors and groove fanatics. Like deep soul, the term deep funk can evoke the strongly African-American essence of the music, but deep funk also carries the connotation of a collector. It can be vocal or instrumental, but in most cases, it's about rhythm, groove, and musicianship, not songwriting. Deep funk rarely innovates within the form, generally taking its cues from the hard, lean brand of funk epitomized by James Brown and the Meters, or—depending on the level of musicianship—moving into jazzier, more improvisational territory. The revival of interest in deep funk is closely tied to the hip-hop movement in America, with its ravenous appetite for fresh sample material, and to the rare groove and Northern soul club scenes in Britain, which place a premium on rediscovering vintage American musical artifacts (in funky jazz and sweet-leaning soul, respectively). At its best, deep funk is about giving credit to the unfairly overlooked—discovering great grooves and tight combos that really did stack up musically. Although deep funk's true format is the vinyl single, labels like Goldmine, BBE, and Stones Throw, and compilers like Scottish DJ Keb Darge, helped bring the pleasures of the funky 45 into the CD age.

DEEP FUNK REVIVAL

Deep Funk Revival, naturally enough, grew out of a renewal of interest in deep (read: obscure) funk on both sides of the Atlantic, mostly among DJs and record collectors. Whether they were looking for fresh sample material or just a great overlooked dance groove, deep funk attracted a cultish underground audience, and it was only a matter of time before some funk fanatics started making new recordings in the style toward the tail end of the '90s. Deep funk revival records were sometimes vocal performances (most notably by veteran James Brown disciple Lee Fields), but most often they were instrumentals by combos who were interested purely in the art of the groove. Because it's rooted in a style that requires its audience to be fairly obsessive, deep funk revival usually tries to re-create the feel of its inspirations as closely as possible—the hard-driving grooves, the organic grit, even the lower-fidelity recording quality. The New York-based Desco label, the first devoted solely to deep funk revival, enhanced the illusion by creating playful hoaxes about the recording dates of their releases and the actual backgrounds of their groups. Desco attracted some attention during the late '90s before splitting into two new labels, Dap-Tone and the ultra-raw Soul Fire. Most deep funk revival artists were concentrated in this label family, though not all. Most called James Brown or the Meters their primary influences, but not all; in keeping with funk collectors' related tastes, deep funk revival also included stylistic offshoots into jazz-funk and Afro-beat. Moreover, some better-known contemporary artists have dabbled in revivalist deep funk as part of a more eclectic vision, including the Beastie Boys, their keyboardist Money Mark, and acid-jazz staples the James Taylor Quartet.

DEEP SOUL

Like Southern soul, Deep Soul is gritty, funky soul music that borrows equally from the fervor of Southern gospel and the hard-driving energy of R&B. It is distinguished by a passionate, gospel-tinged singer, punchy horns, chicken-scratch guitars, and tight rhythm sections. In deep soul, the singer tends to have more prominent gospel influences than those in Southern soul, but the music sounds essentially the same. Deep soul emerged in the '60s and it reigned until the end of the decade, when smoother Philadelphia soul became popular. In the '80s and '90s, deep soul resurfaced as a revivalist genre.

DISCO

Disco marked the dawn of dance-based popular music. Growing out of the increasingly groove-oriented sound of early '70s and funk, disco emphasized the beat above anything else, even the singer and the song. Disco was named after discotheques, clubs that played nothing but music for dancing. Most of the discotheques were gay clubs in New York, and the DJs in these clubs specifically picked soul and funk records that had a strong, heavy groove. After being played in the disco, the records began receiving radio play and respectable sales. Soon, record companies and producers were cutting records created specifically for discos. Naturally, these records also had strong pop hooks, so they could have crossover success. Disco albums frequently didn't have many tracks—they had a handful of long songs that kept the beat going. Similarly, the singles were issued on 12-inch records, which allowed for extended remixes. DJs could mix these tracks together, matching the beats on each song since they were marked with how fast they were in terms of beats per minute. In no time, the insistent, pounding disco beat dominated the pop chart, and everyone cut a disco record, from rockers like the Rolling Stones and Rod Stewart to pop acts like the Bee Gees and new wave artists like Blondie. There were disco artists that became stars—Donna Summer, Chic, the Village People, and KC & the Sunshine Band were brand names—but the music was primarily a producer's medium, since they created the tracks and wrote the songs. Disco lost momentum as the '70s became the '80s, but it didn't die—it mutated into a variety of different dance-based genres, ranging from dance-pop and hip-hop to house and techno.

DOO WOP

Doo Wop was one of the most popular genres of rock & roll and R&B in the late '50s. Doo wop artists were vocal groups, with each singer in the group taking a different part that interweaved with the other singers. Frequently, the backing vocalists sang nonsense words as rhythm, and the genre's name derives from this trait. Most doo wop groups started as a cappella bands, performing without instrumental accompaniment. The hit doo wop singles inspired countless teenagers to form their own a cappella groups, though many of them were never recorded. Despite its a cappella origins, few doo wop records were made without instrumental backing. Doo wop faded away in the early '60s, though its influence was felt throughout popular music in the following decades.

FREESTYLE

Often growing in tandem with contemporary styles like electro and house, Freestyle emerged in the twin Latin capitals of New York City and Miami during the early '80s. Freestyle classics like "I Wonder If I Take You Home" by Lisa Lisa & Cult Jam, "Let the Music Play" by Shannon, and "Party Your Body" by Stevie B relied on angular, synthesized beats similar to electro and early house, but also emphasized the romantic themes of classic R&B and disco. The fusion of mechanical and sensual proved ready for crossover during the period, and both Shannon and Lisa Lisa hit the Top 40 during 1984-1985. Freestyle also dovetailed nicely with the rise of dance-pop during the mid-'80s—Madonna's early producer and remixer, John Benitez (aka Jellybean), was also active in the freestyle community. By the end of the decade, a number of artists—Exposé, Brenda K. Starr, Trinere, the Cover Girls, India, and Stevie B—followed them into the pop or R&B charts. Even after popular success waned in the late '80s, though, freestyle moved to the underground as a vital stream of modern dance music alongside house, techno, and bass music. Similar to mainstream house, freestyle artists are usually (though by no means exclusively) either female vocalists or male producers. Newer figures like Lil Suzy, George Lamond, Angelique, Johnny O, and others became big stars in the freestyle community.

FUNK

Named after a slang word for "stink," Funk was indeed the rawest, most primal form of R&B, surpassing even Southern soul in terms of earthiness. It was also the least structured, often stretching out into extended jams, and the most Africanized, built on dynamic, highly syncopated polyrhythms. As such, it originally appealed only to hardcore R&B audiences. The groove was the most important musical element of funk—all the instruments of the ensemble played off of one another to create it, and worked it over and over. Deep electric basslines often served as main riffs, with an interlocking web of short, scratchy guitar chords and blaring horns over the top. Unlike nearly every form of R&B that had come before it, funk didn't confine itself to the 45-rpm single format and the classic verse/chorus song structure. Funk bands were just as likely to repeat a catchy chant or hook out of the blue, and to give different song sections equal weight, so as not to disrupt the groove by building to a chorus-type climax. In essence, funk allowed for more freedom and improvisation, and in that respect it was similar to what was happening around the same time in blues-rock, psychedelia, and hard rock (in fact, Jimi Hendrix was a major inspiration for funk guitar soloists). The roots of funk lay in James Brown's post-1965 soul hits, particularly "Papa's Got a Brand New Bag" (1965) and "Cold Sweat" (1967). Sly & the Family Stone, who started out as a soul band influenced by rock and psychedelia, became a full-fledged (albeit pop-savvy) funk outfit with 1969's *Stand!*. However, the record that officially ushered in the funk era was James Brown's epochal "Get Up (I Feel Like Being A) Sex Machine." The arrangement was spare, the groove hard-hitting, and Brown's lyrics were either stream-of-consciousness slogans or wordless noises. Brown followed it with more records over the course of 1970 that revolutionized R&B, and paved the way for the third artist of funk's holy trinity, George Clinton. Clinton's Parliament and Funkadelic outfits made funk the ultimate party music, not just with their bizarre conceptual humor, but their sheer excess—huge ensembles of musicians and dancers, all jamming on the same groove as long as they possibly could. Thanks to Sly, Brown, and Clinton, many new and veteran R&B acts adopted funk as a central style during the '70s. Funk gradually became smoother as disco came to prominence in the mid- to late '70s, and lost much of its distinguishing earthiness. However, it had a major impact on jazz (both fusion and soul-jazz), and became the musical foundation of hip-hop. Thanks to the latter, funk enjoyed a renaissance during the '90s, especially among white audiences who rushed to explore its original classics.

GIRL GROUP

Falling somewhere between traditional pop and R&B, the sound of the Girl Groups was one of the most popular rock & roll genres in the early '60s. Though there were strong elements of rock & roll and R&B in the music, the girl group sound was decidedly more polished than earlier forms of rock & roll. It was driven by producers and songwriters, who helped guided the groups and gave them material to sing. The vocalists had roots in gospel and R&B, while the songwriters and producers were schooled in traditional pop, which resulted in an exciting hybrid. The songs were innocent and yearning, with sweet, catchy melodies and driving backbeats. Though the girl groups faded away in the mid-'60s, they had a profound influence on pop/rock, particularly British Invasion acts like the Beatles.

GO-GO

Go-Go was a bass-heavy, funky variation of hip-hop that was designed for house parties. Lyrically, there was little of substance in go-go, but the main message was the beat, not the words. During the mid-'80s, go-go was quite popular within the rap and R&B underground, particularly around the DC area where it originated, but it never became a pop success; the closest it came to a crossover hit was in 1988, when EU—along with Trouble Funk, the definitive go-go band—had a moderate hit with "Da Butt," taken from Spike Lee's *School Daze*. During the late '80s and early '90s, go-go was supplanted by Miami bass music, which took the groove-oriented aesthetic of go-go, turned up the bass, and de-emphasized the already-slim lyrics.

HIP-HOP

In the terminology of rap music, Hip-Hop usually refers to the culture—graffiti-spraying, breakdancing, and turntablism in addition to rapping itself—surrounding the music. As a style however, hip-hop refers to music created with those values in mind. Once rap had been around long enough to actually have a history, hip-hop groups began looking back to old-school figures including MCs like Kurtis Blow and Whodini, and DJs like Grandmaster Flash and Afrika Bambaataa. In fact, the latter's Zulu Nation collective sprang up in the late '80s around two of the most notable hip-hop artists, De La Soul and A Tribe Called Quest. With rap music's mainstream breakout during the '90s, dozens of hip-hop artists pointed the way back to the old school, including underground rappers like Mos Def and Pharoahe Monch.

HOUSE

House music grew out of the post-disco dance club culture of the early '80s. After disco became popular, certain urban DJs—particularly those in gay communities—altered the music to make it less pop-oriented. The beat became more mechanical and the bass grooves became deeper, while elements of electronic synth pop, Latin soul, dub reggae, rap, and jazz were grafted over the music's insistent, unvarying four-four beat. Frequently, the music was purely instrumental and when there were vocalists, they were faceless female divas that often sang wordless melodies. By the late '80s, house had broken out of underground clubs in cities like Chicago, New York, and London, and had begun making inroads on the pop charts, particularly in England and Europe but later in America under the guise of artists like C+C Music Factory and Madonna. At the same time, house was breaking into the pop charts; it fragmented into a number of subgenres, including hip-house, ambient house, and most significantly, acid house (a subgenre of house with the instantly recognizable squelch of Roland's TB-303 bassline generator). During the '90s, house ceased to be cutting-edge music, yet it remained popular in clubs throughout Europe and America. At the end of the decade, a new wave of progressive house artists including Daft Punk, Basement Jaxx, and House of 909 brought the music back to critical quarters with praised full-length works.

JAZZ-FUNK

In its earliest incarnation during the mid-'60s, Jazz-Funk was an earthy amalgamation of jazz and funky Southern soul, also heavily influenced by the proto-funk innovations of Sly & the Family Stone. In that respect, it was fairly similar to soul-jazz, but where soul-jazz was often content to lay back in the groove, jazz-funk drove forward with a stronger, more pronounced backbeat, as well as a more explicit devotion to the Stax/Volt brand of soul music (sometimes reflected in cover versions of popular soul hits). Many early jazz-funk artists were organists, like Lonnie Smith, Reuben Wilson, Charles Earland, and Jack McDuff (some of whom crossed freely between jazz-funk and soul-jazz); other key figures included saxophonist Eddie Harris and vibraphonist Roy Ayers. As the grittier strain of soul metamorphosed into funk during the early '70s, and as fusion helped make funk rhythms a compelling way for some hard boppers to reconnect with their African-American audience, the crucial R&B component of jazz-funk shifted with the times. Artists like trumpeter Donald Byrd, flutist Bobbi Humphrey, and keyboardist Ronnie Foster crafted a sunny, breezy style by performing compositions which often simply resembled jazzy R&B, and drew from Philly soul as well as funk. Keyboardists like Herbie Hancock and Lonnie Liston Smith explored a spacier, more atmospheric brand of jazz-funk, while the artists on Creed Taylor's CTI label (most prominently Freddie Hubbard) were wrapped in a shinier, more polished production. Because of its emphasis on danceable, funky grooves, jazz-funk became highly popular in the British underground music scene (where it was known as "rare groove") when it was rediscovered during the mid- to late '80s; an updated version mixed with funk and hip-hop became known as acid jazz. For similar reasons, jazz-funk was also the style to which many American hip-hop artists turned when looking for ways to fuse jazz and rap; Roy Ayers, in particular, enjoyed a renaissance and reappraisal in both scenes. Plus, artists like Medeski, Martin & Wood helped revive the classic jazz-funk sound and bring it to newer, wider audiences in the '90s.

JUMP BLUES

Jump Blues refers to an uptempo, jazz-tinged style of blues that first came to prominence in the mid- to late '40s. Usually featuring a vocalist in front of a large, horn-driven orchestra or medium sized combo with multiple horns, the style is earmarked by a driving rhythm, intensely shouted vocals, and honking tenor saxophone solos—all of those very elements a precursor to rock & roll. The lyrics are almost always celebratory in nature, full of braggadocio and swagger. With less reliance on guitar work (the instrument usually being confined to rhythm section status) than other styles, jump blues was the bridge between the older styles of blues—primarily those in a small band context—and the big band jazz sound of the 1940s.

MEMPHIS SOUL

Memphis Soul isn't the same thing as Southern soul, which tends to be gritty and earthy. Memphis soul is a little more stylish, a little more uptown—but unlike other uptown soul genres, like Chicago soul, it rarely makes concessions to pop. And, while it is certainly smooth, it's not as light as sweet soul. It's stylish and funky, classy but soulful. The quintessential Memphis soul artist is Al Green, and his '70s label, Hi, was the quintessential Memphis soul label. Hi's chief sonic architect, Willie Mitchell, developed the sound in the late '60s, but perfected it in the early '70s as he worked closely with Green. Their recordings were ground-zero for Memphis soul, and it remains the yardstick by which the entire genre is judged.

MOTOWN

The Motown label crafted a uniform house sound so instantly identifiable that "Motown" unequivocally became a style unto itself. During the '60s, Berry Gordy Jr.'s Detroit label became the biggest independent in the music industry, thanks to its smooth, sophisticated blend of R&B and memorable pop melodies. At Motown, the pop side of the equation took on greater importance than ever before, which helped make the records accessible to a wider audience; their velvety elegance helped cement black popular music firmly into mainstream American culture. Motown often utilized the same core session musicians on their records, which helped lay the Motown sound's basic rhythmic foundation of bouncing bass and echoing drums. But their arrangements were frequently lush and elaborate, adding strings, horns, woodwinds, piano, extra percussion, or whatever else might enhance the music's urbane stylishness. This polished pop craftsmanship, when matched with the smoothly soulful vocals of the Motown artist roster, became ubiquitously popular during the early '60s, with songwriters like Smokey Robinson and the team of Eddie Holland, Lamont Dozier, & Brian Holland turning out one gem after another with almost assembly-line regularity. When Holland, Dozier & Holland left the label in a dispute over royalties, producer Norman Whitfield became a major figure at Motown, keeping the label in step with the harder, funkier direction much soul music was heading in. In 1970, the Jackson 5 became superstars with a funky bubblegum-soul that began to break away from established Motown formulas, and during the rest of the decade, performers like Marvin Gaye and Stevie Wonder took greater control of their own music, investing it with their own personalities and helping break up the standardized Motown blueprint. It's that blueprint, which brought artists like the Temptations, Four Tops, and Supremes stardom, that people mean when they describe music as "Motown."

NEO-SOUL

Though it's roughly analagous to contemporary R&B, Neo-Soul artists pay more devotion to the era of classic soul, often seeking a sound and a style of songwriting with few concessions to events in the music world post-1975. The work of Lauryn Hill, first in the Fugees and later with her 1998 solo debut *The Miseducation of Lauryn Hill*, proved very important to the neo-soul scene, as did the debut of Erykah Badu in 1997. Several more females made splashy debuts around the turn of the millennium, including Macy Gray, Jill Scott, India.Arie, and Alicia Keys, but only the latter broke through to broad stardom. Other figures pursuing the neo-soul sound include Raphael Saadiq, Remy Shand, Sunshine Anderson, Musiq, Peven Everett, and Jaguar Wright.

NEW JACK SWING

New Jack Swing evolved in the late '80s, when urban contemporary soul artists began incorporating hip-hop rhythms, samples, and production techniques into their sound. Some songs simply had hip-hop beats, others had rapped sections and sung choruses, but the overall result was an edgier, more street-oriented sound that seamlessly blended both the melodic qualities of soul and the funky rhythms of rap. It paved the way for the '90s soul, where the dividing line between rap and R&B was frequently indistinguishable.

NEW ORLEANS R&B

Primarily a piano- and horn-driven style, New Orleans R&B is the next step over from its more bluesier practitioners. There's a cheerful good-naturedness to the style that infuses the music with a good-time feel, no matter how somber the lyrical text. The music itself uses a distinctively "lazy" feel, with all of its somewhat complex rhythms falling just a hair behind the beat, making for what is known as "the sway." The vocals can run the full emotional gamut, from laid-back crooning to full-throated gospel shouting, while the horn lines provide a perfect droning backdrop. Enlivened by Caribbean rhythms, an unrelenting party atmosphere, and the distinctive "second-line" strut of the Dixieland music so indigenous to the area, there's nothing quite as intoxicating as the sound of Crescent City R&B.

NORTHERN SOUL

Northern Soul, for many, is a meaningless term because it doesn't refer to any specific kind of music. For many others, it's a term that means everything. Where most soul genres are named for either the region that the music where the music was created, or for the sound of the music, Northern soul is named after where the music was played—in dance clubs in northern Britain. During the early '70s, once the mods had run out of steam and prog rock was ruling the landscape, there were a handful of underground dance clubs that played nothing but '60s soul records, and they weren't any ordinary oldies. Instead, the DJs at these clubs were obsessive collectors, finding the most obscure American soul singles. Usually, these records sounded like Motown, Chicago soul, or New York soul, but they were records by unknown or underappreciated performers. These records were dubbed Northern soul because of the clubs. Northern soul continued to gain popularity until the mid-'70s, when punk and disco stole its thunder; however, it never really faded away. Some clubs remained open and there was still a collectors' market for the singles, and many rare singles were going for astonishingly high prices. Most importantly, many clubgoers, from Marc Almond to Bob Stanley and Pete Wiggs of St. Etienne, went on to form their own groups, which kept the spirit of Northern soul alive.

PHILLY SOUL

Philly Soul was one of the most popular forms of soul music in the early '70s. Building on the steady groove of Hi Records and Stax/Volt singles, Philly soul added sweeping strings, seductive horns, and lush arrangements to the deep rhythms. As a result, it was much smoother—even slicker—than the deep soul of the late '60s, but the vocals remained as soulful as any previous form of R&B. Philly soul was primary a producer's medium, as Kenny Gamble & Leon Huff and Thom Bell created the instrumental textures that came to distinguish the genre. That isn't to short-change the vocalists, since the Spinners, the O'Jays, Harold Melvin & the Blue Notes, and the Stylistics were among many fine soul singers with distinctive voices, but the sonic elements that made Philly soul distinctive were the creation of the producers. Gamble & Huff worked with the Delfonics, Archie Bell, Harold Melvin & the Blue Notes, and the O'Jays; Bell produced the Spinners and the Stylistics, among others. The highly produced sound of Philly soul paved the way for the studio constructions of disco and urban contemporary R&B.

POP-SOUL

Pop-Soul is soul music that has been polished slightly and given a commercially viable, crossover production. The vocals are still raw, but the material and the sound of the record could easily fit onto pop radio stations' playlists. Motown was the pioneering label of pop-soul, and through much of the '60s, it was one of the most popular pop music genres. In the '70s, pop-soul became slicker, and it eventually metamorphosed into disco.

PSYCHEDELIC SOUL

Psychedelic soul was born in the late '60s, as the chemically altered consciousness and trippy production techniques of psychedelic rock found their way into the soul music of the period. Its receptiveness to rock & roll made it a definite precursor of funk, whose hard-driving rhythms and use of electronics and instrumental effects owed much to the ground broken by psychedelic soul. The music was often state-of-the-art soul at its most celebratory, evoking the heady good times of a new, multifaceted cultural openness. But there was also a darker, sometimes even paranoid side to the music that reflected its uncertain social times, particularly the increasing militancy of the civil rights movement. The catalyst behind psychedelic soul was Jimi Hendrix, who cut his teeth on the R&B circuit before coming into his own as a mind- and genre-bending instrumentalist who spoke to both white and black listeners. Similarly eclectic but more firmly based in R&B were Sly & the Family Stone, a racially integrated outfit forged in the psychedelic hotbed of San Francisco. Meanwhile, the Temptations, under the auspices of producer/arranger Norman Whitfield, redefined themselves by cutting some of the finest psychedelic soul of the late '60s and early '70s. Psychedelic soul remained a part of R&B's cutting edge into the '70s, as many early funk artists—Curtis Mayfield, Earth, Wind & Fire, the Isley Brothers, etc.—made it a component of their sound. None did so more than George Clinton's Parliament-Funkadelic aggregate, whose bizarre, druggy humor and acid-tinged jamming were direct outgrowths of psychedelic soul.

QUIET STORM

In 1975, Smokey Robinson released a smooth, sensuous solo LP of romantic adult soul titled *A Quiet Storm*. The album eventually gave its name to a style and radio format that aimed to create very similar moods. Quiet Storm also drew inspiration from Marvin Gaye's lush *Let's Get It On* LP, the orchestrations of Philly soul, and the gentle, ultra-smooth recordings of Al Green. In a way, quiet storm was R&B's answer to soft rock and adult contemporary—while it was primarily intended for black audiences, quiet storm had the same understated dynamics, relaxed tempos and rhythms, and romantic sentiment. However, there was also an urbane sophistication and subdued soulfulness that marked quiet storm as unmistakably rooted in R&B. Some artists concentrated near-exclusively on the style, but most recorded more uptempo tracks in addition to the ballads that fit the requirements of the radio format. Quiet storm remained popular from the late '70s into the early '90s, when mainstream R&B took on a harder-edged hip-hop influence; as a result, quiet storm found virtually no new practitioners.

R&B

Evolving out of jump blues in the late '40s, R&B laid the groundwork for rock & roll. R&B kept the tempo and the drive of jump blues, but its instrumentation was sparer and the emphasis was on the song, not improvisation. It was blues chord changes played with an insistent backbeat. During the '50s, R&B was dominated by vocalists like Ray Charles and Ruth Brown, as well as vocal groups like the Drifters and the Coasters. Eventually, R&B metamorphosed into soul, which was funkier and looser than the pile-driving rhythms of R&B.

RETRO-SOUL

Retro-Soul is soul music that was made after the heyday of soul music had passed. Although deep soul had fallen out of the spotlight in the early '70s, there were a number of artists that never stopped singing in that raw style. In the mid-'80s, a small but dedicated audience for new recordings by such masters as Johnnie Taylor and Little Milton had developed, and labels like Ichiban and Malaco began releasing new albums by these artists. Soon, they had found new vocalists that performed in the same style, and by the early '90s the entire genre of retro-soul was flourishing.

ROCK & ROLL

In its purest form, Rock & Roll has three chords, a strong, insistent back beat, and a catchy melody. Early rock & roll drew from a variety of sources, primarily blues, R&B, and country, but also gospel, traditional pop, jazz, and folk. All of these influences combined in a simple, blues-based song structure that was fast, danceable, and catchy. The first wave of rock & rollers—Chuck Berry, Elvis Presley, Little Richard, Jerry Lee Lewis, Buddy Holly, Bo Diddley, Bill Haley, Gene Vincent, the Everly Brothers, and Carl Perkins, among many others—set the template for rock & roll that was followed over the next four decades. From the British Invasion, folk-rock, psychedelia, and through hard rock, heavy metal, glam rock, and punk, most subgenres of rock & roll initially demonstrated an allegiance to the basic structure of rock & roll. Though traditional rock & roll faded from the charts, there were always artists that kept the flame alive. Some, like the Rolling Stones and the Faces, adhered to the basic rules of traditional rock & roll but played the music fast and loose. Others, like proto-punk rockers the Velvet Underground, the New York Dolls, and the Stooges, kept the basic song structure, but played it with more menace. Still others, like Dave Edmunds and Graham Parker, became rock & roll traditionalists, writing and recording music that never wavered from the sound of the late '50s and early '60s. Although the term "rock & roll" came to refer to a number of different music styles in the decades following its inception, the essential form of the music never changed.

SMOOTH SOUL

Smooth Soul plays exactly like you'd expect—smooth, stylish, and romantic. It wasn't really pop-soul, which was as likely to be a dance number as a ballad, but it certainly had melodic hooks ideal for crossover play. Instead, it was romantic soul—the songs, the singing, and the productions all captured the right seductive mood. Yet, unlike the urban quiet storm that followed it, there was still some funk to the beats, which made it feel more like soul than pop. Al Green and the Spinners were among the best and most popular smooth soul artists.

SOUL

Soul music was the result of the urbanization and commercialization of R&B in the '60s. Soul came to describe a number of R&B-based music styles. From the bouncy, catchy acts at Motown to the horn-driven, gritty soul of Stax/Volt, there was an immense amount of diversity within soul. During the first part of the '60s, soul music remained close to its R&B roots. However, musicians pushed the music in different directions; usually, different regions of America produced different kinds of soul. In urban centers like New York, Philadelphia, and Chicago, the music concentrated on vocal interplay and smooth productions. In Detroit, Motown concentrated on creating a pop-oriented sound that was informed equally by gospel, R&B, and rock & roll. In the South, the music became harder and tougher, relying on syncopated rhythms, raw vocals, and blaring horns. All of these styles formed soul, which ruled the black music charts throughout the '60s and also frequently crossed over into the pop charts. At the end of the '60s, soul began to splinter apart, as artists like James Brown and Sly Stone developed funk, and other artists developed slicker forms of soul. Although soul music evolved, it never went away—not only did the music inform all of the R&B that came after it, there were always pockets of musicians around the world that kept performing traditional soul.

SOUL-BLUES

Perhaps one of the most modern forms of blues, Soul-Blues fuses disparate elements of black popular music to create a wholly urban amalgam of its own. Artists who wanted to move stylistically beyond the three-chord confines of conventional blues forms found the R&B strain of the 1950s and the Southern soul style of the mid-'60s far more to their creative liking. Soul-blues combines the best elements of the two and blends that with the standard blues band instrumentation—sometimes augmented with an R&B-styled horn section. The genre also provides more traditional blues artists with a style to visit on occasion, injecting some contemporary life into their recordings.

SOUL-JAZZ

Soul-Jazz, which was the most popular jazz style of the 1960s, differs from bebop and hard bop (from which it originally developed) in that the emphasis is on the rhythmic groove. Although soloists follow the chords as in bop, the basslines (often played by an organist if not a string bassist) dance rather than stick strictly to a four-to-the bar walking pattern. The musicians build their accompaniment around the bassline and, although there are often strong melodies, it is the catchiness of the groove and the amount of heat generated by the soloists that determine whether the performance is successful. Soul-jazz's roots trace back to pianist Horace Silver, whose funky style infused bop with the influence of church and gospel music, along with the blues. Other pianists who followed and used similar approaches were Bobby Timmons, Junior Mance, Les McCann, Gene Harris (with his Three Sounds), and Ramsey Lewis. With the emergence of organist Jimmy Smith in 1956 (who has dominated his instrument ever since), soul-jazz organ combos (usually also including a tenor, guitarist, drummer, and an occasional bassist) caught on, and soulful players became stars, including Brother Jack McDuff, Shirley Scott, Jimmy McGriff, Charles Earland, and Richard "Groove" Holmes, along with such other musicians as guitarists Grant Green and Kenny Burrell; tenors Stanley Turrentine, Eddie "Lockjaw" Davis, David "Fathead" Newman, and King Curtis; and altoist Hank

Crawford. Despite its eclipse by fusion and synthesizers in the 1970s, soul-jazz has stayed alive and made a healthy comeback in recent years.

SOUTHERN SOUL

Southern Soul is gritty, funky soul that borrows equally from the fervor of Southern gospel and the hard-driving energy of R&B. It is distinguished by a passionate, gospel-tinged singer, punchy horns, chicken-scratch guitars, and tight rhythm sections. Southern soul emerged in the '60s and reigned until the end of the decade, when smoother Philadelphia soul became popular. In the '80s and '90s, Southern soul resurfaced as a revivalist genre.

UPTOWN SOUL

Uptown Soul is an outgrowth of uptown blues. Like its predecessor, it has heavier production than its grittier Southern counterparts, complete with string sections, backing vocalists, and more sophisticated harmonies and chord progressions. It sounds more polished than its peers, with slicker production and smooth, crooning vocalists.

URBAN

Also known as urban contemporary, Urban was the term given to the R&B/soul music of the 1980s and '90s. Like quiet storm and Philly soul, both strong influences, urban was very smooth and polished, but while its romantic ballads fit well into quiet storm radio formats, urban also had room for uptempo, funky dance tracks, which usually boasted the same high-tech, radio-ready production and controlled yet soulful vocals. That's why, in spite of its name, urban didn't usually have the earthy grit associated with the term "soul music," preferring to tone down the raw emotion in favor of a slick refinement. Up until the late '80s, most urban music was highly pop-oriented, often in melody but nearly always in terms of production. A number of artists—like Janet Jackson, Billy Ocean, and Whitney Houston—crossed over from the R&B charts to the pop charts, although there were others like Freddie Jackson, Luther Vandross, Stephanie Mills, and LeVert whose R&B popularity never translated quite the same way. The urban landscape began to shift with the advent of hip-hop; producer and Guy member Teddy Riley crafted a fusion of the two, inserted occasional rap breaks, and dubbed it new jack swing. New jack made a superstar of Bobby Brown and proved greatly beneficial to his ex-New Edition mates as well. Urban and hip-hop continued to cross-pollinate during the early '90s, eventually resulting in a new hybrid tagged "hip-hop soul." There was still a side of urban that retained roots in quiet storm and adult contemporary, though, and regardless of which side of the spectrum they fell on, the songs were increasingly becoming showpieces for elaborate vocal technique. Partly owing to the steep decline of mainstream pop/rock in the wake of alternative, urban more or less dominated the pop singles charts for the latter half of the '90s, with major acts including Mary J. Blige, Toni Braxton, R. Kelly, Boyz II Men, SWV, and Blackstreet, among others.

A

Aaliyah (Aaliyah Haughton)

b. Jan. 16, 1979, New York, NY [Brooklyn], **d.** Aug. 25, 2001, Abaco, The Bahamas

Vocals / Urban, Contemporary R&B, Hip-Hop, Dance-Pop

Contemporary R&B singer Aaliyah (born Aaliyah Haughton) became an overnight sensation in 1994 with her debut album, *Age Ain't Nothing But a Number*, and its two hit singles, "Back & Forth" and "At Your Best (You Are Love)." Born in Brooklyn but raised in Detroit, she was influenced by an entertainment background—her mother was a singer and her uncle an entertainment lawyer once married to Gladys Knight. She appeared in concert with Knight at the age of 11, and released her first album just four years later. Paced by the Top Ten hits "Back & Forth" and "At Your Best (You Are Love)" (the latter an Isley Brothers cover), 1994's *Age Ain't Nothing but a Number* became a multi-platinum smash. She endured controversy near the end of the year, however, when news broke of her marriage at the age of 15 to her producer, R. Kelly.

After severing her ties with Kelly, Aaliyah resurfaced in 1996 with her second album, *One in a Million*. Collaborating with rising production stars Timbaland and Missy Elliott, Aaliyah pointed the way for the minimalist hip-hop of the late '90s with hits like "One in a Million" and "If Your Girl Only Knew." By the end of the decade, she'd made the move to film, starring in *Romeo Must Die* with Jet Li and agreeing to appear in the projected pair of sequels to *The Matrix*. Just one month after her self-titled third album appeared in 2001, though, she died in a private-plane crash while returning from a video shoot in The Bahamas. *—Stephen Thomas Erlewine*

Age Ain't Nothing But a Number / 1994 / Blackground ♦♦♦♦

Aaliyah has a pleasant voice, but the real reason the teenager's debut album, *Age Ain't Nothing but a Number*, was a hit is the radio-ready production courtesy of R. Kelly, her husband. Kelly wraps Aaliyah's voice in layers of lush synths and deep grooves, while adding songs that are frequently better than the ones on his own album, *12 Play*. *Age* may have its share of filler, but its singles are slyly seductive. *—Stephen Thomas Erlewine*

One in a Million / Aug. 27, 1996 / Blackground ♦♦♦♦♦

Aaliyah's second album doesn't necessarily prove that she is indeed *One in a Million* but it does showcase more depth and talent than her acclaimed debut. That's not only due to the greater variety of material on *One in a Million*, or to the way that her producers (Vincent Herbert, Jermaine Dupri, and many others) immaculately produce each track, but it is also due to the fact that Aaliyah's singing is smoother, more seductive, and stronger than before. It might not be the commercial juggernaut of *Age Ain't Nothin' but a Number*, but *One in a Million* is a more consistently satisfying album. *—Leo Stanley*

● **Aaliyah** / Jul. 17, 2001 / Blackground ♦♦♦♦♦

Aaliyah waited nearly five years to deliver her third album, but considering that she was essentially growing up—it was the equivalent of spending time in college—when she came back with an eponymous record in the summer of 2001, she came back strong. *Aaliyah* isn't just a statement of maturity and a stunning artistic leap forward, it is one of the strongest urban soul records of its time. Where such peers as Macy Gray and Jill Scott work too hard to establish their ties with classic soul, Aaliyah revels in the present, turning out a pan-cultural array of sounds, styles, and emotions. This sound is entirely unfamiliar—part of the pleasure is how contemporary it sounds—but she sounds just as comfortable within the sonicscapes of Timbaland as Missy Elliott and, possibly, less self-conscious. Aaliyah never oversings, never oversells the songs—this comes on easy and sultry, and there's a lot of substance here, in terms of the songwriting and the songs themselves. Urban albums rarely come any better than this, and there haven't been many records better than this in 2001, period. *—Stephen Thomas Erlewine*

I Care 4 U / Dec. 10, 2002 / Blackground ♦♦♦♦♦

Respecting the legacy of one of R&B's most important artists during the '90s, Universal and Blackground waited more than a year after her death to deliver a new Aaliyah release. Considering all the time that had gone by, however, fans could be forgiven for expecting an album of all-new material to compensate for the long drought. *I Care 4 U* actually balances a brief hits collection with a half-dozen new songs, most of the fresh material appearing only after a run-through of the hits from her three proper albums. There isn't too much to complain about concerning the hits selection; *I Care 4 U* touches on most of the highlights from her seven-year career: "Back & Forth" and "At Your Best (You Are Love)" from her first album, "One in a Million" and "Got to Give It Up" from 1996's *One in a Million*, and three tracks from 2001's *Aaliyah*. (Surely though, the compilers could've found room on this 14-track collection for a pair of her Top Ten greats, "If Your Girl Only Knew" and "The One I Gave My Heart To," or the *Romeo Must Die* hit "I Don't Wanna.") Of the new tracks, four of the six feature composer credits from Johnta Austin ("I Don't Wanna"), and his affectionate, smoky ballads are perfectly suited to Aaliyah's vocals. "Miss You," the presciently titled single, and "All I Need" don't have the edge of her classic Timbaland productions, but they stand up well—even when they're slotted next to the best songs of her career. Aaliyah was well ahead of her time during her brief career, and *I Care 4 U* hangs together well, the hits showing the power of her voice and the strength of her accompanying productions, while the new songs provide an intriguing look at where Aaliyah may have taken her career had she lived. *—John Bush*

Gregory Abbott

Vocals / Urban, Soul, Quiet Storm

Gregory Abbott's roots stem from Venezuela, his mother's homeland, and the island of Antigua, his father's homeland; making him a dual citizen of the small tropical island and the U.S., where he was born. His career as an award-winning singer, composer, producer, and musician began in New York City. While in New York City, his mother taught him to play piano and encouraged him to develop his vocal talents. At the age of eight, he sang in the famed St. Patrick's Cathedral Choir, with which he recorded an album as well as performing on television. In his college years, he majored in psychology and minored in music and dramatic arts. While pursuing undergraduate and graduate studies at Boston University, Berkeley, and Stanford, he helped pay his tuition by creating a band and playing locally. It was here he developed his own personal musical style.

Eventually, Gregory Abbott taught English at Berkeley, while maintaining his love and appreciation of music. He eventually decided to become a professional musician; build a studio; and apply his academic discipline to developing skills as a singer/songwriter, guitarist, composer, producer, keyboard player, and drummer. One of his first endeavors was an album for an independent label, which included Gregory Abbott performing a duet with Whitney Houston along with her mother, Cissy Houston, singing background vocals. He then produced a group on Atlantic Records by the name of EQ with famed chairman Ahmet Ertegun. Shortly after, Gregory Abbott released the single and album *Shake You Down*, shaking up the music industry with countless honors and awards. The platinum single became the fastest song in the history of BMI to reach one million airplays, and won BMI's Pop Song of the Year award as the most performed song.

Gregory Abbott's music has crossed every barrier imaginable. Gregory Abbott is noted for coining the term "groove ballad," his signature style, and when referring to him, music writers and critics alike have affectionately used the term "Wall Street soul." He is a favorite with the ladies for his sophisticated demeanor and intelligent green eyes. The soulful strength and intensity is what Gregory Abbott projects in his music and what people love. "Shake You Down" went to number one on the *Billboard* pop, R&B, adult contemporary, and dance singles charts, and was the number three Pop Song of the Year in the magazine's year-end review.

The seemingly endless list of awards continues. Gregory Abbott won two *Soul Train* music awards for Best Male Singer and Best New Artist. He was the star of the New York Music Awards, receiving four honors: Best R&B Album, Best Debut Album, Best R&B Vocalist, and the Rising Star Award. He walked away with two awards at Dick Clark's Black Gold ceremonies, another honor from the R&B Awards in Las Vegas, a NAACP Image award, and two awards from the annual CEBA Awards dinner (Communications Excellence Aimed at Black Audiences). His striking good looks made him a favorite of fashion photographers, appearing in numerous magazine layouts, including a six-page fashion spread in *Playboy*, and a feature on the ten sexiest male recording artists in *Playgirl*. In fact, one of the more frequent observations by Gregory Abbott fans is the sophistication and style he carries off so well. In Japan, he won first prize at the annual Tokyo Music Festival, and the Japanese were so impressed with his music that the title song of his second album, *I'll Prove It to You*, was featured on a Japanese movie soundtrack. In Belgium, he performed in a video with Princess Stephanie of Monaco, and in Portugal he delighted fans by doing interviews in their native language. He also recorded a duet with one of Brazil's most popular singers, Rosanna, and sang in both English and Portuguese. Gregory Abbott also had the unique opportunity to travel to Russia for a songwriters summit, MSLTW (Music Speaks Louder Than Words). An album was released on Epic Records, using songs written there, by 20 top American and Russian songwriters. This was done to encourage communication and friendship between the two countries. Among other songwriters were Cyndi Lauper, Brenda Russell, Diane Warren, Barry Mann, Mike Stoller, and Michael Bolton. The song Gregory Abbott created while there was performed by Spanish pop star Emmanuel.

Gregory Abbott's non-stop schedule continued at home in America where he recorded vocals for the *Bill Cosby Show*. His own Caribbean-influenced album *One World!*, which he said he recorded as a tribute to his parents, was internationally released. Gregory Abbott's soundtrack and television work has included *White Lion*, *Hearts Afire*, *Evening Shade*, starring Burt Reynolds; *Tap*, starring Gregory Hines and Sammy Davis Jr.; and *Living Single*, starring Queen Latifah; among many others. Gregory Abbott has always been highly noted for his songwriting abilities. "I started off as a songwriter, and I guess I'll always be that first," said Gregory Abbott. He has written for many, artists including EQ, Rosanna, Emmanuel, Mona Lisa, Ronnie Spector, Freda Payne, and songstress Jennifer Warnes for her hit single "Rock You Gently." *Eyes, Whispers, Rhythm, Sex*... appeared in 2000, offering a more groove-based sound than his previous efforts. *—Larry Belanger*

● **Shake You Down** / 1986 / Columbia ♦♦♦♦
This album has an even flow. All the tracks have that midtempo rhythm. The quality vocals, light production touches, and effervescent melodies are attractive attributes. Taking the music industry by storm, Gregory Abbott hit the charts with the title track, "Shake You Down," an exquisitely arranged number in which Abbott's adamant delivery was contrasted with caressing background vocals. The single stayed on the *Billboard* R&B charts for 27 weeks, claiming the number one spot; it was also number one on the pop charts. Though songs like "Say You Will" and "You're My Angel" are more appealing, the second release was "I Got the Feelin' (It's Over)." Not as seductive as its predecessor, it still has that refreshing, melodious flow. It crested at number five on the charts. There are no bona fide ballads on this album; "Magic" is the only dance cut. "Rhyme and Reason" is trimmed in a Caribbean rhythm, musically and vocally. The remainder of the album is seasoned with well-rounded, midtempo songs. The quality of the vocals and the overall arrangement of the songs are commendable. *—Craig Lytle*

I'll Prove It to You / 1988 / Columbia ♦♦♦
Gregory Abbott's follow-up LP to his gold *Shake You Down* album was *I'll Prove It to You.* Co-produced by Abbott and keyboardist Alan Palanker, it finds the vocalist in the same vein as his previous effort; merging '80s music technology with '50s doowop/early-'60s soul-tinged sensibility. The result is enchanting. Another single, "Let Me Be Your Hero," was more in the vein of "Shake You Down. The title track and "Runaway" are on his greatest-hits set, *Super Hits.* The New York-born singer issued an album of new material, *Eyes, Whispers, Rhythm, Sex...*, in 2000. *—Ed Hogan*

One World! / 1994 / Musik International ♦♦♦
Gregory Abbott is back with a quality album. The opening tune, "Seasons Change," is rich with calypso groove layered with his trademark smooth-as-silk vocals. Of the three cover songs on the album, the best is James Taylor's "Handyman." Abbott adds some funk and a unique depth and color to this great song. His version of Johnny Nash's "I Can See Clearly Now" comes off very similar to the original, with Abbott's vocals adding spice to the marvelous melody. He has a fabulous voice that has a powerful presentation of fluidity in its delivery. His version of Bill Withers' "Ain't No Sunshine," with its tremendous keyboard and sequencing, is awe-inspiring. The harmonics and dynamic punch in this number are amazing and spellbinding. Abbott also does a duet with Phoebe Snow on "Three Little Birds," which transcends the listener to a spiritual high. The live version of the hit song "Shake You Down" has the same wonderful groove as the original with a slightly increased vibrance. The album has an overall alluring appeal, with plenty of romantic lyrics and sensual vocals. *—Larry Belanger*

● **Super Hits** / Jul. 21, 1998 / Columbia/Legacy ♦♦♦♦
Gregory Abbott's best-of collection, *Super Hits*, is somewhat misleadingly named, since his only true "super hit" was his definitive, platinum-selling single "Shake You Down." Despite failing to have similar chart success with his subsequent efforts, this collection reaffirms how consistent his work is. Songs like "I Got the Feelin' (It's Over)," "Magic," and "Say You Will" also come from *Shake You Down* and share the '60s-soul-meets-'80s-technology vibe of the album's title track. While some of the synths and drum programs could sound a little cold and dated on their own, Abbott's warm voice and emotive falsetto lend an interesting contrast. "I'll Prove It to You," "Runaway," and "Prisoner" have a warmer, richer take on Abbott's signature sound, also evinced on more recent tracks such as "Two of a Kind" and "Unfinished Business." While *Super Hits* is a little short at ten songs, they are undoubtedly ten of the best from the first part of Abbott's career. *—Heather Phares*

Eyes, Whispers, Rhythm, Sex... / 2000 / Musik International ♦♦♦

Paula Abdul

b. Jun. 19, 1962, Los Angeles, CA
Vocals / Club/Dance, Adult Contemporary, Urban, Dance-Pop
In the wake of Madonna's success, many dance-pop divas filled the charts, but out of them all, Paula Abdul was the only one who sustained a career. The former L.A. Lakers cheerleader and choreographer began to make inroads in pop music when she was hired as an assistant dance director on the Jackson's Victory tour, which led to a job choreographing Janet Jackson's videos for *Control.* Abdul's work on Jackson's videos helped make the album a hit, making her a sought-after choreographer. After working on *The Tracey Ullman Show* and videos for ZZ Top, Duran Duran, and the Pointer Sisters, Abdul began a recording career, releasing her debut album, *Forever Your Girl*, in 1988. The first two singles drawn from the record were moderate hits, but the release of "Straight Up" at the end of the year made her a superstar. Staying at the top of the charts for three weeks, "Straight Up" began a string of six number one singles (with "The Way That You Love Me" recharting at number three in 1989) that ran through the summer of 1991.

Abdul's singles were hits not because her singing was exceptional—her voice is thin and transparent—but because she worked with savvy producers who had a knack for picking songs with solid pop and dance hooks. Abdul's spectacular big-budget videos helped push the sales of *Forever Your Girl* past seven million in the U.S. alone. While her second album, 1991's *Spellbound*, wasn't as successful, it still sold over three million copies and spent two weeks at number one.

After *Spellbound*, Abdul took a few years off. During that time, she successfully fought a lawsuit filed by a former backup singer who alleged it was she, not Abdul, who had sung on *Forever Your Girl.* Abdul released her third album, *Head Over Heels*, in the summer of 1995. *—Stephen Thomas Erlewine*

Forever Your Girl / Jun. 1988 / Virgin ♦♦♦♦
Singer/dancer/choreographer Paula Abdul hit the big time with the third single, "Straight Up," off this album, which sparked a string of hits that carried through to her follow-up. Despite having a slight voice, her voice is distinct and perfectly suited to this synthesized type of late-'80s dance-pop. "Cold Hearted" is insistent and catchy, "Forever Your Girl" is sweet and accessible, and "Opposites Attract" gives Abdul a chance to spar with the Wild Pair. There is some filler—"Next to You," for example—that doesn't age as well as the better material, but overall this is a consistent album with some great pop-dance songs. Unfortunately, as Abdul and her material matured, her audience waned. *—Bryan Buss*

Shut Up & Dance: Dance Mixes / 1990 / Virgin ♦♦
When a record company is intent on milking an urban contemporary or dance-pop artist's popularity for all it's worth but doesn't have any new material to release, the logical solution is an album of remixes. Paula Abdul was still extremely popular at the dawn of the 1990s when Virgin released this weak collection of dance-oriented remixes. "Straight Up," "Knocked Out," "Cold Hearted," and other songs first heard on *Forever Your Girl* were pretty forgettable to begin with, and these remixes make the material seem even more faceless and robotic than before. Abdul's detractors often argued that, like Milli Vanilli and New Kids on the Block, she was a perfect example of style and image over substance. And nowhere is that more painfully obvious than on *Shut Up and Dance.* With so much excellent dance music having come out in the early 1990s (everything from Black Box to Soul II Soul to Inner City), listeners would do well to pass on this CD. *—Alex Henderson*

Spellbound / May 1991 / Virgin ♦♦♦
The reason Paula Abdul was one of the handful of pop-dance artists of her time to actually have a career is that her production is so good that 10-15 years later it stands as the embodiment of late-'80s pop without being a parody of itself. And with this, her second album, she reinforces the upbeat personality she expressed on *Forever Your Girl* while showing growth as well. "Promise of a New Day," "Rock House," and John Hiatt's "Alright Tonight" are bouncy and joyous, much like some of the bright hits from her debut, but she adds a funky techno edge with "Vibeology," and "Will You Marry Me?" skates that thin line between sweet and precious. Additionally, Abdul adds better and more ballads to this CD. Smartly, her production team has put together sweeping, adult love songs (the hits "Rush Rush" and "Blowing Kisses in the Wind") that help give her strong crossover appeal to adult contemporary without alienating her original fan base. Not many artists hit the mark twice in terms of commercial and critical appeal, but Abdul was savvy enough to choose strong material (much of which was co-written by Abdul herself, Peter Lord, Sandra St. Victor, and V. Jeffrey Smith) and smart producers (including Lord, Smith, and Don Was). This was a safe follow-up to a massively successful debut, and surprisingly enough for a pop star, the baby steps she took toward becoming a respected artist were sure and solidly embraced. *—Bryan Buss*

Head Over Heels / Jun. 13, 1995 / Virgin ♦♦
Four years after the release of *Spellbound*, Paula Abdul returned with the sleek *Head Over Heels. Head Over Heels* doesn't sound all that different than her previous album; it incorporates a couple of current dance trends without ever letting the beats dominate the accessible pop melodies of the songs. Unfortunately, the songs are more well constructed than well written—all of the arrangements hide the fact that the songs usually lack strong hooks. That weakness is accentuated by the length of the album. Approaching nearly 70 minutes, *Head Over Heels* spends too much time with lesser songs. Abdul remains an engaging presence, even with her limited vocal talents, and the record's best songs—the slinky "My Love Is for Real," for instance—are more mature and seductive than her earlier works, showing that she has the possibility to grow old gracefully. *—Stephen Thomas Erlewine*

● **The Greatest Hits** / Sep. 26, 2000 / Virgin ♦♦♦♦
The only Paula Abdul album most listeners will need, *Greatest Hits* gathers *almost* all the singles from her first three albums in one place. The 16 tracks here include an amazing run of eight consecutive Top Ten hits, six of which reached number one, over a span of approximately three years (before more soulful, urban sounds began to conquer Abdul's audience). In most cases, the versions included are the seven-inch single edits, which often differed from the album cuts and are hence quite nice to have collected. The only questionable choice is that the Top 20 single "Will You Marry Me?" was left off in favor of an unnecessary "Megamix Medley," but it's hard to imagine most fans finding this anything more than a minor flaw. The songs still sound as slick and hyper-produced as ever, but they're also catchy and well-constructed, and it's no surprise they were hits in their era (which, nostalgia buffs will find, they evoke very well). All in all, a nicely executed package. *—Steve Huey*

Colonel Abrams

b. Detroit, MI
Vocals / Garage/House, Urban, House, Club/Dance
Detroit-born vocalist Colonel Abrams (his actual name) enjoyed moderate success in the late '80s, singing in a harsh, terse soul style while fitting his voice into a garage and house setting. Abrams was in the group Conservative Manor with his brother Morris in the late '60s, then sang lead vocals for 94 East in 1976. Their roster included Prince on guitar. Abrams later joined Surprise Package, a NJ group. He scored a mild hit in 1984 with the ballad "Leave the Message Behind the Door" for New York's Streetwise Records. The follow-up, "Music Is the Answer," was an international dance hit and earned him a deal with MCA in 1985. He had more success with the singles "Trapped," "I'm Not Gonna Let You," and "How Soon We Forget" in the late '80s, and also recorded a pair of LPs. Abrams' single "Bad Timing" was produced by Cameo's Larry Blackmon for the independent Horrus label in 1990. *—Ron Wynn*

Colonel Abrams / 1986 / MCA ♦♦♦♦♦
Colonel Abrams straddled the category of love man and disco dancer on his debut album (with a touch of the preacher thrown in), and he was rewarded with four R&B chart hits: "Trapped" (number 20), "The Truth" (number 78), "I'm Not Gonna Let You" (number seven), and "Over and Over" (number 68). All found the beat-heavy Abrams confidently emoting in a manly style borrowed from the young Teddy Pendergrass. *—William Ruhlmann*

You and Me Equals Us / 1987 / MCA ♦♦

About Romance / 1992 / RCA ♦♦♦

Make a Difference / May 23, 1996 / Dancefloor ♦♦♦♦

A gospel-influenced R&B/dance music belter with a big, booming voice, Colonel Abrams was compared to James "D-Train" Williams (of "You're the One for Me" and "Keep Giving Me Love" fame) more than anyone else in the 1980s. And when *Make a Difference* came out in 1996, D-Train was still a valid comparison. But Abrams was never a clone of anyone, and he always comes across as his own man on this excellent but underexposed CD. Abrams' roots were the soul and disco of the late '70s, a fact that's hard to miss on such intoxicating house-music delights as "I'm Caught Up," "99 1/2" and "As Quiet as It's Kept." Don't let the high-tech production fool you; Abrams' dance music is consistently mindful of disco's Northern soul roots. Though fast tempos and a club orientation dominate *Make a Difference*, "Get With You" reminds us how effective the singer can be on ballads. It's unfortunate that this disc isn't better known. *—Alex Henderson*

● **The Best of Colonel Abrams** / Mar. 21, 2000 / Universal Special Products ♦♦♦♦♦

As a vocalist whose career began to rise in the mid-'80s, Colonel Abrams, like many other full-bodied vocalists, began to be compared to the booming-voice archetype Teddy Pendergrass. Although the comparisons were justified, Abrams had his own persona. A lightning rod for romantic tumult, *The Best of Colonel Abrams* has him battling cheating women, interfering parents, and nosy townsfolk, all to great effect. This effort compiles the 11 tracks Abrams recorded for MCA during the post-disco/early-house era. On the best dance tracks, *The Best of Colonel Abrams* proves that he and co-writer/producer Marston Freeman were rhythm innovators of the highest order. The polyrhythmic "I'm Not Gonna Let You" has the classic '70s Philly beats replicated through a battery of synthesizers. On that track, Abrams sings in his patented halting, percussive style and he's shouting the top of his lungs throughout. "Trapped" has Abrams even more perplexed as he sings, "But I don't want your folks to/Turn me over to the hands of the law." Both tracks and "Speculation" have held extremely well and set the standard for the stylistically similar work that came shortly afterward. Although he is chiefly known for dance tracks, *The Best of Colonel Abrams* also proves that he is skillful with ballads as well. On the poignant "Table for Two" he only sings for a minute-plus and doesn't hit one false note. *The Best of Colonel Abrams* put a lot of his essential songs back into print and is a must for his fans. *—Jason Elias*

AC Black

f. Macon, GA

Group / Pop, Urban, Funk

Formed in the mid-'80s by identical twins Alvin and Calvin Black (their real last name is Waters), this Macon, GA, group was one of the last self-contained R&B groups, along with Mint Condition and Tony! Toni! Toné! However, AC Black was less successful. The group performed in Georgia and surrounding states, gaining a following based on their high energy choreographed performances. AC Black featured a powerfully soulful lead vocalist, Kelvin Jones, a talented multi-instrumentalist, Tracey Orr, and a keyboardist/programmer, Brian Haught. Signed by Taj/Motown Records, AC Black released their one and only album in 1989. The self-titled album featured a minor hit, "Funky Situation," but failed to reach a substantial audience. The group disappeared in the early '90s after performing around the Southeastern U.S. and Japan. *—Tim Griggs*

● **AC Black** / 1989 / Motown ♦♦

AC Black's self-titled debut album showcases impressive performances by lead singer Kelvin Jones and keyboardist/programmer Brian Haught; however, most of the material is not worthy of their considerable talents. The highlights are two ballads—"I Can't Wait" and "I'm Just a Man," featuring the soulful, but restrained vocals of Jones. However, another ballad—"Emotional Feelings"—and numerous funk songs, including "Race With Race" and "Irresponsible," fall flat. Saxophonist Gerald Albright performs a solo on "I'm Just a Man." *—Tim Griggs*

Ace Spectrum

f. New York, NY

Group / R&B

A New York City vocal group, Ace Spectrum never enjoyed any huge hits, although they were a decent soul ensemble. Henry "Red" Zant, Aubrey "Troy" Johnson, Elliot Isaac, and Rudy Gay comprised the lineup. They had one Top 20 R&B single, "Don't Send Nobody Else" in 1974, and also did a fine version of the song "Just Like in the Movies," though it didn't earn for them the same recognition it did for Bloodstone. *—Ron Wynn*

● **Inner Spectrum** / 1974 / Atlantic ♦♦♦♦

The quartet's first and most popular of three Atlantic Records albums. It contains their only hit, "Don't Send Nobody Else" (also recorded by the Dynamic Superiors) and a first-rate rendition of "Don't Let Me Be Lonely Tonight," along with the perky "If You Were There." Group members Aubrey Johnson and Henry Zant collaborated on "Pickup," "Me and My Love," and "I Don't Want to Play Around." Atlantic did the album a disservice by only rolling out one single before flinging out a second album. However, the group's revolving-door membership may have been the underlying reason. Ace Spectrum's—whose personnel changed every album—signature was variety; they employed multiple leads, which kept listening interesting. *—Andrew Hamilton*

Low Rent Rendevous / 1975 / Atlantic ♦♦♦

Just Like in the Movies / 1976 / Atlantic ♦♦♦♦

Johnny Ace (John Marshall Alexander)

b. Jun. 9, 1929, Memphis, TN, **d.** Dec. 25, 1954, Houston, TX

Vocals, Piano / R&B

The senseless death of young pianist Johnny Ace while indulging in a round of Russian Roulette backstage at Houston's City Auditorium on Christmas Day of 1954 tends to overshadow his relatively brief but illustrious recording career on Duke Records. That's a pity, for Ace's gentle, plaintive vocal balladry deserves reverence on its own merit, not because of the scandalous fallout resulting from his tragic demise.

John Marshall Alexander was a member in good standing of the Beale Streeters, a loosely knit crew of Memphis young bloods that variously included B.B. King, Bobby "Blue" Bland, and Earl Forest. Signing with local DJ David Mattis' fledgling Duke logo in 1952, the re-christened Ace hit the top of the R&B charts his very first time out with the mellow ballad "My Song." From then on, Ace could do no musical wrong, racking up hit after hit for Duke in the same smooth, urbane style. "Cross My Heart," "The Clock," "Saving My Love for You," "Please Forgive Me," and "Never Let Me Go" all dented the uppermost reaches of the charts. And then, with one fatal gunshot, all that talent was lost forever (weepy tribute records quickly emerged by Frankie Ervin, Johnny Fuller, Varetta Dillard, and the Five Wings).

Ace scored his biggest hit of all posthumously. His haunting "Pledging My Love" (cut with the Johnny Otis orchestra in support) remained atop *Billboard*'s R&B lists for ten weeks in early 1955. One further hit, "Anymore," exhausted Duke's stockpile of Ace masters, so they tried to clone the late pianist's success by recruiting Johnny's younger brother (St. Clair Alexander) to record as Buddy Ace. When that didn't work out, Duke boss Don Robey took singer Jimmy Lee Land, renamed him Buddy Ace, and recorded him all the way into the late '60s. *—Bill Dahl*

● **Memorial Album** / 1973 / MCA ♦♦♦♦♦

Johnny Ace inadvertently pioneered the rock & roll cliché of "live fast, die young, and leave a good-looking corpse." On Christmas day, 1954, Ace died at the age of 25 as a result of a self-inflicted gunshot wound he received while playing Russian Roulette backstage at a show in Houston, TX. Ace recorded a mere 21 songs in his lifetime, and not long after his death Duke Records prexy Don Robey compiled 12 of them on *Memorial Album*. Remarkably enough, the collection is not only still in print, but remains the only widely available Johnny Ace compilation (even though his entire body of work would fit on one CD). Ultimately, this album forged the sonic portrait of Johnny Ace that has survived to this day, and it's still a powerful and indelible set of songs, with Ace's smooth but unmistakably melancholy voice riding on a pillow of tape echo over the lazy shuffle of drums, organs, and vibraphones. While a more complete collection would seem to be in order, *Memorial Album* remains a satisfying collection of Ace's work, and nearly half a century after his passing, songs like "Pledging My Love," "The Clock," "Anymore," and others are still haunting and compelling listening. *—Mark Deming*

Barbara Acklin

b. Feb. 28, 1944, Oakland, CA, **d.** Nov. 27, 1998, Omaha, NE

Vocals, Songwriter / Chicago Soul, Pop-Soul, Soul, Northern Soul

A pop-soul vocalist in the vein of Dionne Warwick or Brenda Holloway, Barbara Acklin is best known for her R&B/pop hit "Love Makes a Woman" from the summer of 1968. The only child of Herman and Hazel Acklin, Barbara Jean Acklin was born February 28, 1944, in Oakland, CA; in 1948, the family moved to Chicago, IL. Like many great soul singers, Acklin honed her vocal skills in the church choir (in her case, at Big Zion Baptist Church) at an early age. As a teenager, she began singing in nightclubs while attending Dunbar Vocational High School. Upon graduation, she was hired as a secretary for local label St. Lawrence Records by her cousin, producer/saxophonist Monk Higgins (his release "Who Dun It" made the national R&B charts in 1966 and he co-produced Bobby "Blue" Bland's late-'70s/early-'80s ICA hits). Higgins recorded an Acklin single under the name Barbara Allen for his Special Agent label. Later, Higgins used Acklin as a background singer on his Chess Records sessions.

In 1966, Acklin began working as a receptionist for producer Carl Davis (Chi-Lites, Gene Chandler) at the Chicago branch office of Brunswick Records. Acklin hadn't forgotten her dream of becoming a recording star and persistently asked Davis to record her. Davis said that he would, but in the meantime he encouraged her to keep writing songs. Cornering Brunswick Records star Jackie Wilson, Acklin had him listen to a tune that she co-wrote with David Scott (formerly of the Five Du-Tones and the Exciters). Wilson liked it and passed it on to Davis. Recorded on August 8, 1966, and released September 1966, "Whispers (Gettin Louder)" went to number six R&B and number 11 pop in the fall of 1966. The album, *Whispers*, was released shortly afterward, thus setting the stage for Wilson's mid-'60s comeback and smoothing the way for his only number one R&B single, "(Your Love Keeps Lifting Me) Higher and Higher." To return the favor, Wilson helped Acklin secure a recording contract with Brunswick. Acklin's first chart success came from "Show Me the Way to Go," a duet with Chandler, reaching number 30 R&B in the spring of 1968. In July 1968, Acklin earned her signature song with the extremely catchy "Love Makes a Woman," which went to number three R&B and number 15 pop in August 1968. The song also won a BMI Award.

Another Chandler/Acklin duet followed in October 1968. "From the Teacher to the Preacher" reached number 16 R&B and number 57 pop. Acklin's next charting singles were "Just Ain't No Love," "Am I the Same Girl," "After You," "I Did It," "Lady Lady Lady," and "I Call It Trouble." Acklin's Brunswick albums are *Love Makes a Woman* (summer 1968), *Seven Days of Night* (1969), *Someone Else's Arms* (April 1970), *I Did It* (December 1970), *I Call It Trouble* (1973), and *Barbara Acklin's Greatest Hits* (April 4, 1995).

"Am I the Same Girl" has a peculiar history. The record's backing tracks were used as a basis for Young-Holt Unlimited's instrumental hit "Soulful Strut," with a piano in place of Acklin's vocals. Released before "Am I the Same Girl," "Soulful Strut" did better chartwise and sale-wise, going Top Ten R&B, number three pop, and selling over two million copies. In the meantime, Acklin was writing songs with fellow Brunswick signee Eugene Record of the Chi-Lites. The collaboration was fruitful. The sparse melancholy ballad "Have You Seen Her" settled at number one R&B and number three pop, earning the Chi-Lites their first gold record. Originally the last track on the Chi-Lites' album *(For God's Sake) Give More Power to the People*, "Have You Seen Her" was getting massive airplay on soul stations despite its unusually long-for-radio length of five minutes. In a bit of déjà vu, another Acklin song had smoothed the way for an act to score a career-defining hit. The Chi-Lites had their first number one pop single, "Oh Girl," in the spring of 1972. The ethereal ballad went to number one R&B for two weeks in June 1972. Other Acklin/Record compositions for the Chi-Lites were the effervescent "Stoned Out of My Mind" and the wonderfully poignant "Toby" (a double-sided hit single and the title track of a 1974 album). "That's How Long," a song written by Archie Powell and Tony Byrd, was on the flip side, making the record a double delight.

In 1974, Acklin departed Brunswick for Capitol Records. Her first single, "Raindrops," was a R&B hit in June of that year. The album, *A Place in the Sun*, released May 1975 and produced by Chicago soul mainstay Willie Henderson, contained two more singles: "Special Loving" and "Give Me Some of Your Sweet Love." Despite a promising start and critical acclaim, Capitol dropped Acklin from their artist roster. She continued to tour as both a solo artist and as a background singer with the Chi-Lites and other acts.

In 1990, Oakland, CA, rapper MC Hammer covered "Have You Seen Her" on his superstar-making second Capitol album, *Please Hammer, Don't Hurt 'Em*. The multi-platinum LP established a precedent for being the first best-selling rap album in history, selling millions of copies. Released as a single, "Have You Seen Her" quickly went gold, no doubt fattening the coffers of songwriters Acklin and Record. British pop group Swing Out Sister had a 1992 U.K. hit with "Am I the Same Girl."

In late 1998, Acklin was doing a phone interview with Chicago cable TV host Royce Glamour from her Omaha, NE, home. Acklin was excited about working on material for her new album, and she also noted that she had a bad cold. The following weekend, she was rushed to a hospital where she passed away from pneumonia on November 27, 1998. Acklin left behind a son, Marcus; a daughter who's an aspiring singer, Samotta; a granddaughter, Sheratta; loving friends and family; and a wealth of classic Chicago soul music. *—Ed Hogan*

● **Love Makes a Woman** / 1968 / Brunswick ✦✦✦✦✦
Always classy and elegant, Barbara Acklin's debut album, *Love Makes a Woman* could survive on the reputation of the title track alone. One of the premier recordings of writer/producer Carl Davis, "Love Makes a Woman" features the bright horns and relaxed rhythms that are hallmarks of his productions for the Brunswick label. Coupled with Acklin's tense, confident delivery, the results are one of pop-soul's true shining moments. Well written originals here, like "Be By My Side" and "Come and See Me Baby," more than stand up to covers from the Bacharach/David canon, making this one of the most solid soul debuts around. *—Wade Kergan*

Seven Days of Night / 1969 / Brunswick ✦✦✦✦✦
More excellent late-'60s soul from Brunswick's top female artist, this album includes "Just Ain't No Love" and "Am I the Same Girl," both R&B hits. *—Bill Dahl*

Someone Else's Arms / 1970 / Edsel ✦✦✦
Either there was a shortage of original material or Brunswick simply tried to present Barbara Acklin as an all-around performer. Why else would she remake four pop tunes and a Martha & the Vandellas song? Acklin and her beau Eugene Record only contributed four tracks, with one being the bland, vanilla "Someone Else's Arms." The album does have moments—the whooping, harmonic "After You" and "Is It Me" are pleasures—but "Quiet Night of Quiet Stars" and "More Today than Yesterday" leave a lot to be desired. She does a competent performance of "You've Been in Love Too Long," but adds nothing to the original version by the Vandellas. So what was the point? *—Andrew Hamilton*

I Did It / 1970 / Brunswick ✦✦✦
Four of these tracks—"Spinning Wheel," "After You," "He's Just a Little Guy," and "More Ways than One"—were on *Someone Else's Arms*, released some months earlier. "I Did It," a midtempo floater, is pleasant but fireless. Lulu's "To Sir, With Love," is cloned note for note, offering nothing new in delivery or arrangement. "Make the Man Love You" has a Southern soul flavor that's different for Barbara Acklin but more enjoyable than the bland pop rehashes. Brunswick should have ditched the remakes and combined the original songs from this and the previous LP for one good Acklin album instead of two mediocre ones. *—Andrew Hamilton*

I Call It Trouble / 1973 / Brunswick ✦✦✦✦
With the exception of "I'll Bake Me a Man" and "I Call It Trouble," which recalls the excitement of "Love Makes a Woman," this is simply a recycling of the songs on Barbara Acklin's two previous albums. This makes the third album appearance in a row for "He's Just a Little Guy" and "After You." Both were on Acklin's *Someone Else's Arm* and *I Did It* albums. Despite the repeats, this is far better than the two previous LPs. *—Andrew Hamilton*

A Place in the Sun / 1975 / Capitol ✦✦✦

● **Greatest Hits** / Apr. 4, 1995 / Brunswick ✦✦✦✦✦
When people think of Chicago soul, they normally think of Curtis Mayfield. It makes sense, for he truly was the godfather of that sound. However, there were quite a few other gifted practitioners, one of them being Barbara Acklin. Her Brunswick sides combined Stax funk and Motown sheen along with the overall polish of Philadelphia International Records. This collection collects her best work from her prime late-'60s/early-'70s period. Most of the hits, unfortunately, were regional smashes, which in itself is a travesty. "Love Makes a Woman" is beautiful light funk crossed with swing, incredibly well-played, and led by Acklin's soulful vocals, which are easily on a par with Martha Reeves. One of Acklin's biggest songs was "Am I the Same Girl," which ended up being an instrumental hit for the Young-Holt Trio under the title "Soulful Strut." As great as their version was, it was a bit of a crime, and the original version is included here in all its glory. The vocal version of the song became a hit in 1992 when revived by Swing Out Sister. Barbara Acklin's awesome legacy, though, is well-represented in this fine collection, which is a must for all fans of early-'70s urban soul and pop. *—Matthew Greenwald*

Love Makes a Woman/Seven Days of Night / Oct. 13, 1998 / Diablo ✦✦✦✦✦

Someone Else's Arms/I Did It/I Call It Trouble / 1999 / Diablo ✦✦✦

Brunswick Singles A's & B's / Oct. 18, 1999 / Edsel ✦✦✦✦✦
European recording companies appreciate Barbara Acklin more than American ones; her best compilations are mainly imports. This will become a collectors item because of its excellent theme. Diablo Records gathered all of Acklin's 12 solo Brunswick singles, A- and B-sides, for a zesty 25-song collection. "I Call It Trouble" served as the A-side to "Love You Are Mine Today," as well as the B-side to "I'm Gonna Bake Me a Man," so there are 25 tracks, not 26. Her duets with Gene Chandler are not included. The arranger embellishes Acklin's strong soprano with pushy brass and rhythm charts for a resounding, dynamic sound. Choice cuts: "Love Makes a Woman," "Just Ain't No Love," and "Am I the Same Girl" (whose rhythm track—sans Acklin's vocal—was released as "Soulful Strut" by the Young-Holt Trio) rock alongside some equally as infectious tunes that didn't get as much exposure. There are also some B-sides that were omitted from her Brunswick albums. A keeper. *—Andrew Hamilton*

20 Greatest Hits / Feb. 12, 2002 / Brunswick ✦✦✦✦✦

The Ad Libs

f. 1964, Newark, NJ

Group / Brill Building Pop, Girl Group

The Ad Libs were an early-'60s vocal group from NJ whose female lead vocals and male-voiced backing prefigured the jazzy doo wop singing style of several later groups, including Manhattan Transfer. They scored a major hit in early 1965 with "The Boy From New York City," written by John T. Taylor, a saxophone player who had worked with various big band groups as far back as the '30s.

By the early '60s, John T. Taylor had quit playing music and had turned his attention to teaching. During this time, he heard a young Hudson County quintet who were calling themselves the Creators. The group consisted of Hugh Harris, Danny Austin, James Wright, John Alan, and Chris Coles. By mid-1963, the Creators had released their first record on the TR label without any chart success. A single for the Phillips label, "I'll Stay Home," met the same fate a year later.

The group re-formed in 1964 in Newark, NJ. Dave Watt and Norman Doegan replaced departing members Wright, Alan, and Coles, and they added a female lead vocalist, Mary Ann Thomas. A new name was needed, and thereafter they began calling themselves the Ad Libs. By now, Taylor's jazz-inflected songwriting along with the Ad Libs' natural harmonies created a sound like no other group. This was best personified on the upbeat piano-driven bounce rhythm of Taylor's first demo with the group, "The Boy From New York City."

Taylor took the demo tape to Red Bird Records owners Jerry Leiber & Mike Stoller, who signed the group to their Blue Cat imprint. "The Boy From New York City" was released in December 1964 and by March 1965 the song had climbed to number eight on the pop charts and number six on the R&B charts. A few months later, in May 1965, the group followed up with "He Ain't No Angel" (written by Jeff Barry and Ellie Greenwich), which, despite its enduring sound, barely scratched the pop Top 100. The next two singles failed to reach their intended audience, and the Ad Libs were soon dropped from the Blue Cat roster. They continued to record for a number of labels, and three singles later the Ad Libs signed with Share Records of New York and recorded their last Top 40 hit, "Giving It Up" (number-34 R&B).

Various group changes were made over the next 20 years and there were a few more releases, but none had the success of "The Boy From New York City." Years later, in 1984, Taylor started Passion Records with the idea to record the Ad Libs again, and in the fall of 1988 he came up with the Johnny-Boy label for their "I Stayed Home (New Years Eve)," a follow-up to their biggest hit. In 1989 they released another seasonal 45, "Santa's on His Way." *—Bryan Thomas*

● **The Ad Libs & Friends** / Aug. 27, 1996 / Collectables ✦✦✦
The Ad Libs & Friends features recordings by the Ad Libs, who scored with "The Boy From New York City"; the Dixie Cups of "Iko Iko" and "Chapel of Love" fame; and three less successful Red Bird and World Artist recording groups: the Poets, the Butterflies, and the Charmettes. The Poets—Donald McPherson, Luther Simmons Jr., and Tony Silvester—who became the Insiders, then Main Ingredient, represent with "Merry Christmas Baby," the Butterflies do Ellie Greenwich and Jeff Barry's "Gee Baby Gee," while the interesting Charmettes wail about their "Sugar Boy." These 18 sweet mid-'60s Brill Building sounds revisit a time when music was sugar, spice, and everything nice. *—Andrew Hamilton*

Faye Adams

Vocals / R&B, East Coast Blues, Jump Blues, Traditional Gospel

The heavily gospel-influenced chanteuse scored three chart-topping R&B hits in 1953-1954. From Newark, NJ, Adams joined Joe Morris' band in 1952 as featured singer. A year later, she was a star, thanks to her moving ballad "Shake a Hand" on Al Silver's NY-based Herald label. The song has proven an R&B standard, covered by the likes of Little Richard and Ruth Brown. Two more number-one R&B hits followed in rapid succession: "I'll Be True" (covered by Bill Haley & His Comets) and "Hurts Me to My Heart." Adams later moved to Imperial, and stirred up some action with "Keeper of My Heart" in 1957, before returning to the church. *—Bill Dahl*

● **The Herald Recordings** / Apr. 20, 1990 / Collectables ✦✦✦✦✦
This brings together 14 of Adams' landmark recordings for the Herald label, kicking off with her gospel-oriented smash "Shake a Hand," still sounding fresh as it did back in 1953. Her other two hits for the label, "Hurts Me to My Heart" and "I'll Be True," are here along with fine non-charters like "Everyday," "Angels Tell Me," and a nice turn on "Anytime, Anyplace, Anywhere." Adams kept recording after Herald, trying to find another hit, and eventually moved back to gospel music, but these are the sides that defined her sound. *—Cub Koda*

Gayle Adams

Vocals / Urban

A Washington, D.C., vocalist who also worked as a comedian and even briefly raced cars, disco diva Gayle Adams enjoyed sporadic success in the early and mid-'80s. She signed with Prelude in 1980, and her subsequent LP, *Gayle Adams*, included the single "Stretch'in Out." She gained more attention in 1981 for the songs "Love Fever" and a remake of "Baby I Need Your Loving." Her last significant single was 1984's "I'm Warning You" for Mainline. *—Ron Wynn*

Gayle Adams / 1980 / Prelude ✦✦✦

Producers Willie Lester and Rodney Brown give Gayle Adams little to work with on this disco set. Only a remake of Theola Kilgore's "The Love of My Man" shows any vocal pipes. The best of the dancers, "Stretch'in Out" and "You Brought It on Yourself," are like Chinese meals—after you've heard them, you're still empty and hungry for something else. Two movers and shakers, "Plain Out of Luck" and "I Don't Want to Hear It," sound like you've heard them before—probably because the producers borrowed so much from other songs, especially on the latter, which sounds like Sister Sledge's "We Are Family." [A 1992 reissue on Unidisc, titled *Your Love Is a Life Saver*, added several extended remixes to the original program.] *—Andrew Hamilton*

Love Fever / 1982 / Prelude ✦✦✦

● **Gayle Adams/Love Fever** / Jun. 10, 1997 / Deep Beats ✦✦✦

The Deep Beats two-fer disc pairing 1980's *Gayle Adams* with 1982's *Love Fever* practically functions as her complete recordings for Prelude—though the missing tracks are the extended 12-inch mixes that most disco fans prize above any other. Still, both of Adams' biggest hits, "Stretch'in Out" and "Love Fever," are found here, along with her other solid performance, "Your Love Is a Life Saver." The rest of the tracks are par for the course or worse, most of them simple variations on forms heard on many a disco track previously. Far better to look for "Stretch'in Out" or "Love Fever" on compilations—*Prelude's Greatest Hits, Vol. 2* for the first, and the fourth volume of the same series for the latter. *—John Bush*

Johnny Adams

b. Jan. 5, 1932, New Orleans, LA, **d.** Sep. 14, 1998

Vocals / R&B, New Orleans R&B, New Orleans Blues, Soul, Retro-Soul, Soul-Blues

Renowned around his Crescent City homebase as "the Tan Canary" for his extraordinary set of soulfully soaring pipes, veteran R&B vocalist Johnny Adams tackled an exceptionally wide variety of material for Rounder in his later years—elegantly rendered tribute albums to legendary songwriters Doc Pomus and Percy Mayfield preceded forays into mellow, jazzier pastures. But then, Adams was never particularly into the parade-beat grooves that traditionally define the New Orleans R&B sound, preferring to deliver sophisticated soul ballads draped in strings. Early on he waxed some outstanding follow-ups for the Ric label, notably "I Won't Cry," "A Losing Battle" and "Life Is a Struggle."

After a prolonged dry spell, Adams resurfaced in 1968 with an impassioned R&B revival of the country standard "Release Me" for SSS that blossomed into a national hit. Even more arresting was his magnificent 1969 country-soul classic "Reconsider Me," his lone leap into the R&B Top Ten; in it, he swoops effortlessly up to a death-defying falsetto range to drive his anguished message home with fervor. Despite several worthy follow-ups ("I Can't Be All Bad" was another sizable seller), Adams never traversed those lofty commercial heights again. *—Bill Dahl*

Heart & Soul / 1969 / SSS ✦✦✦✦✦

This country-soul album, containing all of his hits from 1962-1968, was produced by Shelby Singleton. *—Richard Pack*

Christmas in New Orleans / 1975 / Ace ✦✦

● **Reconsider Me** / 1976 / Collectables ✦✦✦✦✦

This 22-song British compilation is the only place to find a decent cross-section of Adams' SSS sides, including his two biggest hits, the stately "Release Me" and the truly stunning "Reconsider Me." Not all of Adams' late-'60s waxings were ballads; "South Side of Soul Street" is a sizzling upbeat workout. But it's as a balladeer that Adams has always excelled; some of his finest soul senders are to be found right here. *—Bill Dahl*

Stand by Me / 1976 / Chelsea ✦✦✦

This is a relaxed, live-in-the-studio recording of standards. *—Richard Pack*

From the Heart / 1984 / Rounder ✦✦✦✦

First-class production by Scott Billington, a delicious Crescent City combo led by longtime cohort Walter "Wolfman" Washington on guitar and Alvin "Red" Tyler on tenor sax, and Adams' perennially luxurious pipes tab this as one of his finest contemporary outings. Nice song selection: The pens of Tony Joe White, Percy Mayfield, Sam Cooke, and Doc Pomus were all tapped. Johnny unfurls his "mouth trombone"—an uncanny vocal 'bone imitation—on Mayfield's "We Don't See Eye to Eye." *—Bill Dahl*

After Dark / Jul. 1985 / Rounder ✦✦✦

When Johnny Adams signed with Rounder in the mid-'80s, few outside the R&B/soul and blues world were aware of his skills or eclectic range. *After Dark* was Adams' second Rounder session. It included amazing covers of Doc Pomus' "I Don't Know You" and "Give a Broken Heart a Break," John Hiatt's "Lovers Will," and the Dan Penn/Chips Moman soul classic "Do Right Woman—Do Right Man." This was one of the first records on which Adams' wondrous voice, with its extensive range at the top and bottom, was both well-produced and effectively mastered and recorded. *—Ron Wynn*

Room With a View of the Blues / Apr. 1987-May 1987 / Rounder ✦✦✦✦✦

Although calling Johnny Adams a blues singer is far too confining, he's certainly among the finest to perform in that idiom. He's equally brilliant at slow or uptempo numbers, can effectively convey irony, heartache or triumph, and is a masterful storyteller. These ten blues numbers covered every emotional base, allowing Adams a chance to show his proficiency. With great support from an instrumental corps that included guitarists Walter "Wolfman" Washington and Duke Robillard, keyboardist Dr. John, and saxophonists Alvin "Red" Tyler and Foots Samuel, plus Ernie Gautreau on valve trombone, Adams didn't just cut a blues album, he made unforgettable blues statements. *—Ron Wynn*

Walking on a Tightrope / Mar. 1989-May 1989 / Rounder ✦✦✦✦

Whenever Johnny Adams does a repertory album, it's as much his own showcase as a forum for the spotlighted composer. Even Percy Mayfield's lyrically brilliant works didn't hamper Adams from displaying his special magic; his treatments on the session's ten tunes ranged from excellent to magnificent. Adams was gripping on "My Heart Is Hangin' Heavy," nicely bemused on "The Lover and the Married Woman" and convincing on the title track and "Danger Zone." Although he's done numerous Rounder vehicles, Adams hasn't yet turned in a dud. *—Ron Wynn*

● **I Won't Cry** / 1991 / Rounder ✦✦✦✦✦

Even on his earliest singles, Adams already had developed a velvety crooning style seemingly at odds with his raucous hometown. This 14-track collection of Adams' 1959-1963 work for Ric Records contains some stunning stuff, most of it in the big-voiced ballad mode (with an occasional nod to Ray Charles). "I Won't Cry," "A Losing Battle," and "Lonely Drifter" capture Adams' tender, mellifluous delivery beautifully. *—Bill Dahl*

Johnny Adams Sings Doc Pomus: The Real Me / 1991 / Rounder ✦✦✦✦

The late Doc Pomus was one of the top songwriters in the R&B/blues tradition while Johnny Adams was one of his favorite singers; their eventual matchup was quite logical. Pomus wrote a few new songs and worked with Adams on planning this Rounder CD up until his own death. Fortunately the project was not halted and resulted in an enjoyable set. Pomus' intelligent and universal lyrics perfectly fit Adams' style, which features flawless enunciation and an ability to sincerely convey a wide range of emotions. With hornlines arranged by Alvin "Red" Tyler, occasional brief solos contributed by pianist Dr. John and guitarist Duke Robillard, and top-notch singing by Johnny Adams, Doc Pomus' music is well served on a strong set of blues and ballads. *—Scott Yanow*

Good Morning Heartache / 1993 / Rounder ✦✦✦

Adams could sing the phone book and make it sound sweet, so his personalized rendition of the title track and several more jazz standards on this collection shouldn't come as too much of a surprise. Nevertheless, it's a long way from "Reconsider Me," and perhaps a bit too jazzy for some R&B fans. *—Bill Dahl*

The Verdict / 1995 / Rounder ✦✦

Fans of Adams' R&B dusties may not find everything on this jazz-based collection to their taste, but Adams' vocal ease within the jazz idiom is undeniable. Noteworthy sidemen include Harry Connick Jr., and Houston Person. *—Bill Dahl*

One Foot in the Blues / 1996 / Rounder ✦✦✦✦

Johnny Adams is renowned for his smoky but smooth voice, but *One Foot in the Blues* is as much a showcase for Lonnie Smith's Hammond B-3 organ, which sounds like a living, breathing creature. The spare, mostly live-in-the-studio production allows plenty of wide open sonic space for Smith's expressive organ (including his pulsating bass pedal), Ed Peterson's after-hours tenor sax, and Jimmy Ponder's gentle guitar fills. While Adams' most fervent champions thrill to his every note, others may find his singing mannered on the ballads that dominate this session, and his voice is certainly huskier than in the days when he earned the sobriquet "the Tan Canary." As the title suggests, the CD is only partly blues; Adams' other "foot" here, as on his previous '90s recordings, is placed squarely between the cabaret-jazz crooning of Johnny Hartman and the soul-pop styling of Lou Rawls. *—Steve Hoffman*

Man of My Word / Aug. 18, 1998 / Rounder ✦✦✦✦✦

Adams kept cranking out solo albums for the Rounder imprint and this one was the ninth such effort, finding him in tip-top shape vocally and in full command of his consummate powers. In addition to top-notch new material from Dan Penn ("It Ain't the Same Thing"), Carson Whitsett ("Bulldog Break His Chain"), Bobby Charles ("I Don't Want to Know") and Jonnie Barnett ("Going Out of My Mind Sale"), Adams takes on William Bell's "You Don't Miss Your Water," Brook Benton's "Looking Back" and Percy Sledge's "It Tears Me Up." Closing out the album is a duet with Aaron Neville on the gospel chestnut "Never Alone." *—Cub Koda*

The Immortal Soul of Johnny Adams / Apr. 20, 1999 / Aim ✦✦✦✦

There Is Always One More Time / Oct. 31, 2000 / Rounder ✦✦✦

There Is Always One More Time is a compilation of the recordings Johnny Adams made for Rounder Records in the 1980s and '90s. The compilation was put together by Scott Billington, who produced all of Adams' Rounder albums. In his liner notes, Billington acknowledges that he had never produced an R&B singer before, so it may not be surprising that he was quick to have Adams sing in styles other than R&B. It was precisely this eclecticism that caused fans and reviewers to reserve their judgment on the Rounder recordings, and Billington has carried it over to the compilation. Drawing from all the albums as well as discs by Ruth Brown and Alvin "Red" Tyler on which Adams guested, he emphasizes novelty material. With Brown, Adams is heard joshing his way through Willie Mabon's "I Don't Know"; "A Lot of Living to Do" (aka "A Lot of Livin' to Do"), on which Adams is accompanied by Harry Connick Jr. at the piano and on which he imitates a horn, is from the Broadway musical *Bye Bye Birdie*; "But Not for Me," also featuring a horn imitation, is the Gershwin standard; and "Never Alone" is an a cappella gospel tune. Of course, there are some bluesy numbers, such as "One Foot in the Blues," and several R&B songs. *There Is Always One More Time* is representative of Adams' later work in that it tries to broaden him stylistically. Clearly, he went along gamely with whatever

Billington brought him and added his soulful sound to it. But that didn't mean he did his best work. —*William Ruhlmann*

Released: A Memorial Album / Feb. 1, 2001 / RPM ♦♦♦

The chronological span of this anthology is given in its subtitle, "The Big Voice, The Big Songs 1968-1983." Unfortunately, the year of release is not given for individual songs in the track listing, although the (actually rather lengthy) liner notes do at least admit that the "latter half" of this CD covers 1976-1983. It can be reasonably inferred that the first half thus covers material starting in the late '60s and dating from no later than the mid-'70s, particularly as it definitely does include his 1968-1970 singles "Reconsider Me," "Release Me," and "I Won't Cry." It's the earlier half of the CD—probably mostly or wholly from the late '60s and early '70s, from the sound of things—that commands the most attention, comprising accomplished though not quite godhead Nashville soul. These cuts are a bit (but not much) poppier than deep Southern soul, crossing gospel, swamp pop, R&B, blues, and even some country, funk, and New Orleans influences in an easygoing, warm fashion. Adams' likable vocals, which convey passion without breaking out in a sweat, retain their charm on the later material, the arrangements ranging from decently down-home to too sweet and slick urban soul flourishes, particularly in the keyboards. —*Richie Unterberger*

Oleta Adams

b. Yakima, WA

Vocals, Piano / Contemporary Gospel, Adult Contemporary, Urban

The youngest daughter of a minister, Adams' first musical experience was in the choir of her father's church. Discovered by Tears For Fears while performing solo in a Hyatt Regency lounge in Kansas City, MO, she was featured prominently on their *Seeds of Love* album. Tears For Fears member Roland Orzabal produced her 1990 debut album, *Circle of One*, featuring the hit "Get Here." She was a 1991 Grammy nominee. Adams' other recordings include 1993's *Evolution*, 1995's *Movin' On*, and 1997's gospel outing *Come Walk With Me*. —*Scott Bultman*

• **Circle of One** / 1990 / Fontana ♦♦♦♦♦

At the time of the release of her debut, *Circle of One*, Oleta Adams was best known as the impassioned backing vocalist on Tears For Fears' 1989 album *The Seeds of Love*, most prominently featured on "Woman in Chains." About a decade later, she was best known for "Get Here," a gospel-tinged belter, later revived by one Justin Guarini as his showpiece on the 2002 phenomenon *American Idol*. This, of course, proves that even small hits have unexpected shelf life, and anybody that decides to go back to Adams' debut may not find anything quite as good—though the other single, "Rhythm of Life," comes close—it's nevertheless a high-class, quality contemporary R&B record that perhaps sounds a little bit too much like its year, but nevertheless is a solid adult-oriented R&B record from that year. —*Stephen Thomas Erlewine*

Evolution / 1993 / Fontana/Mercury ♦♦♦

After the success of her debut, Adams doesn't change the formula for her second album. Which isn't a bad thing—the stylish love ballads she sings are some of the best adult contemporary pop of the early '90s. —*Stephen Thomas Erlewine*

Movin' On / Nov. 1995 / Fontana/Mercury ♦♦♦

Movin' On is Oleta Adams' most straightforward and mainstream release to date. Considering that she is working with Whitney Houston and Mariah Carey's producers (Rich & Friedman and Vassal Benford, respectively), the shift in sound shouldn't come as much of a surprise. What is a surprise is how well Adams' subtle voice works in this setting, adding extra textures to the subdued arrangements. Unfortunately, that can't compensate for inconsistent material, but *Movin' On* remains a fine contemporary soul record. —*Stephen Thomas Erlewine*

Come Walk With Me / Jun. 17, 1997 / Harmony ♦♦♦

Although she always demonstrated a strong gospel influence, *Come Walk With Me* is Oleta Adams' first full-fledged religious album. Unsurprisingly, her singing shines throughout, but the record falls just short from being a powerhouse because the songs often meander, failing to hit upon a strong, memorable hook. Nevertheless, the album succeeds in being a moving modern gospel record because of Adams' passion and her remarkable voice. —*Rodney Batdorf*

• **The Very Best of Oleta Adams** / Sep. 1, 1998 / Mercury ♦♦♦♦

All the Love / Feb. 27, 2001 / Monarch ♦♦♦♦

The ADC Band

Group / Funk, Soul

A nine-member funk and soul aggregation co-led by Kaiya Matthews and Michael Judkins, the ADC Band recorded for Cotillion in the late '70s and early '80s. At their best, the cuts utilized the funk touches of Parliament/Funkadelic and Slave. The biggest hit was 1978's "Long Stroke," which made it to number six on the R&B charts. —*Ron Wynn*

Long Stroke / 1978 / Cotillion ♦♦

Talk That Suff / 1979 / Cotillion ♦♦♦

Although ADC Band was signed to Cotillion, which automatically stuffed them into the generic disco suit that many of their labelmates wore, they were actually laying down some pretty interesting funk-fueled songs, influenced not only by the Parliament/Funkadelic experience, but also by the slower grooves of War and the like. And, while it was 1978's *Long Stroke* that heralded their initial recognition, by the time *Talk That Stuff* was released less than a year later, people were primed. The band wouldn't disappoint, from the moment the pounding "Stank Machine" opened the album. "I Just Want to Hold You," meanwhile, is a superb down-tempo number, dominated by outstanding vocals and suburb horns, while the title track itself hinges around humorous repartee between Audrey Matthews (who also takes a turn behind the drum kit on "ADC Is Back") and James Maddock Jr. "At the Party," meanwhile, has a wonderful Sly Stone-inflected ambience. ADC Band was sorely overlooked both in the funk community and by the general public, the consequence of arriving too late in the day, and sounding too old school to be part of the then-happening crowd. Sad as that may be, the modern funk aficionado will be pleasantly surprised by the entire experience. —*Amy Hanson*

• **Renaissance** / 1980 / Cotillion ♦♦♦

As far as late-'70s/early-'80s funksters go, the ADC Band were never heavyweights—the outfit wasn't in a class with Parliament/Funkadelic, Cameo, Rick James, the Gap Band, or the Bar-Kays. One of ADC's main problems was the lack of a strong identity; if the band wasn't emulating Parliament/Funkadelic or Steve Arrington-era Slave, they were emulating Mass Production. Nonetheless, ADC did come up with some decent grooves here and there. When the East Coast band enjoyed a major hit with "Long Stroke" in 1978, they were often compared to Parliament/Funkadelic—and, to be sure, the P-Funk influence was quite strong in the beginning. But on their third album, *Renaissance*, a much better comparison would be Mass Production. With this 1980 LP, ADC ditch the P-Funk leanings and favor a very Mass Production-minded approach—which isn't surprising because *Renaissance* was produced, arranged, and written by three Mass Production members: saxophonist Gregory McCoy, trumpeter James Drumgole, and keyboardist Tyrone Williams. Further, all three of them play on the record. So not surprisingly, the Mass Production influence is impossible to miss on uptempo funk/dance workouts like "Tripwire" and "State of Shock"—and it is equally strong on the soul ballad "Everyday." In fact, ADC ends up sounding like a poor person's Mass Production, which isn't to say that *Renaissance* is a bad album. The material is generally likable and catchy, it just isn't remarkable or mind-blowing. Not an essential purchase, *Renaissance* is strictly for ADC's hardcore fans. —*Alex Henderson*

WeekEnd: Funky Friday / 1980 / Sue International ♦♦♦

Brother Luck / 1981 / Cotillion ♦♦♦

Roll With the Punches / 1982 / Cotillion ♦♦♦

Adeva

b. Patterson, NJ

Vocals / Garage/House, Club/Dance, Disco

House/R&B vocalist Adeva is known for her commanding diva vamps, but she also has a strong feeling for songs closer to gospel ballads. Born in NJ, Adeva first gained fame in Australia and Europe; her first three singles ("Respect," "Warning," and "I Thank You") all peaked at number 17 in the British charts during the first ten months of 1989. A collaboration with U.S. producer Paul Simpson in March of that year also yielded a number 22 hit in England. Her debut album *Adeva!* gained platinum and gold distinctions in Europe, and an American release did respectably, as did two subsequent albums, *Love or Lust?* and *It Should Have Been*. In 1995, dance heavyweight Frankie Knuckles selected her as featured vocalist on virtually all of his *Welcome to the Real World* album. Adeva's work after the Knuckles LP included a single with Hyper Go Go in 1996. —*John Bush*

• **Adeva!** / Jun. 18, 1990 / Capitol ♦♦♦♦

By the late '80s/early '90s, house music had become a major focus in dance clubs, but was hardly a high priority of either major record companies or "urban contemporary" radio. Adeva, one of the few house/R&B divas to record for a major label, specializes in "deep house"—a style that stresses vocal personality and makes the singer the focal point instead of the producer. Essentially, "deep house" is late-'70s disco/soul updated, and this self-titled debut leaves no doubt that the big-voiced Adeva's aggressive, gospel-influenced belting is a throwback to the days of Gloria Gaynor, Grace Jones, Linda Clifford and Loleatta Holloway. When Adeva tears into such exhilarating neo-disco fare as "Promises," "Love Is Special" and "In & Out of My Life," it's clear that "deep house" is, for all intents and purposes, soul music. This CD boasts two versions of her inspired remake of the Otis Redding/Aretha Franklin hit "Respect," one of which features British rapper Monie Love. Unfortunately, *Adeva!* enjoyed little exposure outside of dance circles, and black radio generally ignored her in favor of considerably less talented singers like Paula Abdul and Nia Peeples. —*Alex Henderson*

Love or Lust? / Oct. 28, 1991 / Capitol ♦♦♦♦

With *Love or Lust*, Adeva remained a well-respected figure in dance music circles thanks to such exuberant, heartfelt "deep house" as "I'm the One for You," "Don't Let It Show on Your Face," "Undercover Lover" and the anthemic "Independent Woman"—all of which boast full-bodied, gospel-influenced wailing that underscores house's soul music roots. Adeva's version of "Respect" has demonstrated her impressive ability to transform a '60s soul classic into modern house, and this time, she interprets the Gladys Knight & the Pips hit "It Should Have Been Me" with equally impressive results. Adeva doesn't embrace very many ballads, but her soulful performance on "Until You Come Back" proves that she definitely should. While the song isn't all that remarkable, the emotion Adeva invests in it indicates that she has the potential to become a first-rate ballad singer. Like its predecessor, *Love or Lust* was generally ignored by black radio. Clearly, Adeva is someone who deserves to be heard outside of dance clubs. —*Alex Henderson*

New Direction / Nov. 10, 1997 / Distinctive ♦♦♦

African Music Machine

f. New Orleans, LA

Group / Funk, Deep Funk, New Orleans R&B

The African Music Machine was an eight-piece funk outfit from New Orleans led by bassist/songwriter Louis Villery. They got their start as a house band for the Jewel/Paula label axis, playing on records by the likes of Fontella Bass, Little Johnny Taylor, Roscoe Robinson, Ted Taylor, Tommie Young, and singer/producer Bobby Patterson, among others. From 1972-1974, they cut several of their own singles for the Patterson-owned Soul Power subsidiary. Most of their work was done in a heavy, James Brown vein, sometimes with a bit of Creole influence mixed in. Their original 45s—including "Black Water Gold," "Tropical," and "The Dapp"—later became highly prized items among funk collectors, fetching outlandish prices; a compilation of singles, also titled *Black Water Gold*, was reissued in 2000. In 2001, Villery assembled a new version of the African Music Machine and released an eponymous album on Singular. *—Steve Huey*

● **African Music Machine** / 2001 / Singular ♦♦♦♦

Black Water Gold / 2001 / Soul Power ♦♦♦

There's nothing really wrong with this record. Which may be why, in the end, it fails to deliver. The group sounds exactly like who they are, a group of studio musicians, in this case the house band for Paula/Jewel. They make no mistakes, they lay down a hard, funky groove, but in the end, they simply underline the difference between those who are players and those who are artists. When you take the safe route and the steady paycheck, you give up something else, a crackle, a force, a burning belief and a desperate gladness at the chance to finally get your music over. These guys are fat. And happy. And that comes out the speakers. This isn't bad. Those mining for beats will find some here. But if asked why this is different, the answer must be that it simply isn't. *—Rob Ferrier*

After 7

f. 1988, Indianapolis, IN

Group / Urban, New Jack Swing, Soul

After 7 emerged in the '90s as a solid contemporary ensemble able to perform creditably in either vintage soul or modern new jack and urban styles. The Indianapolis trio includes brothers Melvin and Kevon Edmonds (the brothers of producer/performer Babyface) and Keith Mitchell (cousin of Babyface's longtime partner L.A. Reid). They signed with Virgin in 1989 and had immediate success with their LP *After 7*. Such songs as "Can't Stop" and "Heat of the Moment" were major winners on the urban and quiet storm circuit, and a remix of "Can't Stop" also attracted sizable dance attention. They recorded with Johnny Gill, then enjoyed another hit release in 1992, *Takin' My Time*. It included a sterling remake of the Originals' "Baby, I'm For Real." *—Ron Wynn*

After 7 / Aug. 22, 1989 / Virgin ♦♦♦♦

The debut album from this Indianapolis-based trio had success written all over it. Two thirds of the trio are the brothers of producer Kenneth "Babyface" Edmonds, and the other third is the cousin of Antonio "L.A." Reid; the two produced the majority of the album, which features three smash hits and a host of other likable tracks. The first smash single was "Heat of the Moment," a popular dance track that peaked at number five on the *Billboard* R&B charts. The second of the three hits was the number one single "Ready or Not," aided by Melvin Edmonds' vigorous vocals. However, the song is anchored by Kevon Edmonds' soaring natural tenor and the soothing melody that just sails along with the song's steady rhythm arrangement. The third smash single was "Can't Stop," also claiming the number one spot on the R&B charts; it's a laidback track with a catchy hook line, complemented by its new jack swing beat. The song's popularity increased with several remixes. One other single worth mentioning is "One Night," an urban adult contemporary composition that was never released; it showcases Melvin and Kevon in an impressive vocal exchange over a midtempo rhythm. *—Craig Lytle*

Takin' My Time / 1992 / Virgin ♦♦♦

An excellent vocal trio that combines state-of-the-art, uptempo new jack swing tunes with classic romantic ballads. After 7 had several chart hits culled from this release, doing particularly well with a remake of The Originals' "Baby, I'm For Real." The lead vocalist is a relative of producer and vocalist Babyface. *—Ron Wynn*

Reflections / Jul. 18, 1995 / Virgin ♦♦♦

Reflections was standard fare for After 7, but that is a good thing. Filled with romantic ballads and slick, funky dance numbers, the album demonstrates that the trio is one of the finest vocal groups of the mid-'90s. Both the production and the quality of the material is excellent, making *Reflections* as satisfying as After 7's previous two albums. *—Stephen Thomas Erlewine*

● **The Very Best of After 7** / Mar. 11, 1997 / Virgin ♦♦♦♦♦

The Very Best of After 7 gathers a dozen of the group's singles and album highlights, as well as hard-to-find and previously unreleased material. The collection kicks off with a new cover of Hall & Oates' soulful "Sara Smile" that's in keeping with the rest of After 7's smooth, lush style. Several of the group's best songs, including "Heat of the Moment," "Gonna Love You Right," and the hit single "Can't Stop," appear in remix form; it would've been nice to include the album versions of at least a couple of these tracks on the compilation as well. "Ready or Not," "Can He Love You Like This," and "'Till You Do Me Right" are some of the other standouts on the collection, emphasizing After 7's collaborations with Babyface and L.A. Reid. Though it's not as complete a retrospective as it could have been, *The Very Best of After 7* does a good job of expressing and defining the group's classic yet fresh take on urban music. *—Heather Phares*

Jewel Akens

b. Sep. 12, 1940, Houston, TX

Vocals / Doo Wop, R&B

Born September 12, 1940, in Houston, TX, Jewel Akens began singing in church as a child. He was also influenced by the blues joint in his neighborhood. In the late '40s, his family moved to Los Angeles. In his teens, Akens sang with a group called the Four Dots. Introduced to Eddie Cochran's manager Jerry Capehart, the group recorded a single for Freedom Records in 1959. Later Aikens and a friend, Eddie Daniels, recorded as Akens and Daniels for Capehart's Silver and Capehart labels. Eddie Cochran played guitar on these sides as well as Akens' sides for Crest. Akens did background vocals on releases by John Ashley ("Hot Rod Gang," "High School Caesar," "2001: A Space Odyssey"). The Four Dots also recorded singles for Liberty ("Don't Wake Up the Kids," "Peace of Mind"), Bullseye, and Dot Records ("My Dear"). In 1961, Aikens and Daniels recorded an Imperial single, "Boom a Lay" b/w "Hide & Seek," as the Astro-Jets.

Akens began recording for Herb Newman's Era Records with a group called the Turnarounds. Newman's teenaged son had written a nursery rhymish song about the birds and the bees and the label owner wanted Akens to record it. After some honing, "The Birds and the Bees" b/w "Tic Tac Toe" was issued and hit number three pop on *Billboard*'s charts in early 1965. Another nursery rhyme-influenced song, "Georgie Porgie" b/w "Around the Corner (From My House)" peaked at number 68 pop during spring 1965. His *The Birds and the Bees* LP was released that same year. Though Akens kept recording (singles:"It's the Only Way to Fly" b/w "Sure Know How to Hurt a Fella" on Era, "Blue Eyed Soul Brother" b/w "Why Do You Want to Go" on Paula, "It's a Sin to Tell a Lie" b/w "You Better Move On," and a cover of Thurston Harris' "Little Bitty Pretty One" b/w "Born a Loser" [both on Colgems]), "The Birds and the Bees" and "Georgie Porgie" were his only charting singles.

Akens later toured with the Monkees and produced the 1973 duet album by Ted Taylor and Little Johnny Taylor, *Super Taylors*, for Stan Lewis' Paula Records. Akens was still performing in the '90s. *—Ed Hogan*

The Birds and the Bees / 1965 / Era ♦♦♦

A smooth R&B singer ("Opportunity" with Eddie Daniels) with strong leanings toward pop material, Jewel Akens is best known for the title track of this retrospective, a worldwide hit for him. This CD combines his original 1965 Era album with three unreleased bonus tracks. *—Cub Koda*

● **The Very Best of Jewel Akens** / Oct. 23, 2001 / Collectables ♦♦♦♦

Much like Sam Cooke's material for RCA, *The Very Best of Jewel Akens* presents a singer reining in the flourishes of soul for the more measured approach of early-'60s pop—a combination that paid off successfully for Jewel Akens with his one major hit in 1964, "The Birds and the Bees," which made it to number three on the *Billboard* pop charts. Unlike Cooke, however, Akens relied upon others to write his material and many of the songs and productions here are fairly innocuous, which is a shame because "Tic Tac Toe," co-written by Akens, has the same haunting quality of Cooke's best work. And while the other material here doesn't stand out with the same clarity, Akens is still a commanding vocalist who brings a polished grace to his work, infusing it with song-stylist subtlety rather than church-house flash. *– Wade Kergan*

Gerald Albright

b. 1957, Los Angeles, CA

Sax (Tenor), Sax (Alto) / Urban, Crossover Jazz, Jazz-Pop, Smooth Jazz, Contemporary Jazz

Beginning in the late '80s, saxophone master Gerald Albright recorded numerous successful solo albums for Atlantic when he wasn't busy assisting an impressive, and mammoth, roster of popular R&B artists. Born in South Central Los Angeles, the saxophonist idolized James Brown and took much influence from Maceo Parker and Cannonball Adderley. He first made a name for himself within the music industry during the 1980s, when he became a highly requested session musician. His revered reputation resulted in a solo contract with Altantic Records. His first album for the label, *Just Between Us*, introduced him to the masses in 1987, and numerous albums resulted, including a best-of collection in 2001.

Albright's fame peaked in the early '90s, around the time he released *Live at Birdland West*, a brave album for the saxman showcasing his ability to play jazz as well as R&B. He moved from Atlantic to GRP in 2002 for the *Groovology* album, his first in over five years, and continued to maintain his busy schedule as a sessionman. Some of the more well-known artists he assisted during his career include Anita Baker, Quincy Jones, the Temptations, Phil Collins, Whitney Houston, and many, many more. *—Jason Birchmeier*

Just Between Us / 1987 / Atlantic ♦♦

Bermuda Nights / 1989 / Atlantic ♦

Dream Come True / Nov. 6, 1990 / Atlantic ♦♦

A talented saxman whose influences range from John Coltrane to soul jazz/hard bop players like David "Fathead" Newman and Hank Crawford, Gerald Albright showed just how much potential he has on 1991's superb *Live at Birdland West*. But sadly, most of his commercial recordings offer little evidence of his considerable improvisatory skills—*Dream Come True* being among the offenders. Designed primarily for commercial radio airplay, this pop/R&B/jazz CD is, for the most part, as dull as it is contrived. Instead of taking risks, Albright embraces a tired, cliché-ridden Najee-meets-George Howard formula on such forgettable cuts as "Say Yes," "Sweet Dreams" and the title song. Instead of interpreting Johnny Gill's 1990 R&B hit "My My My," Albright offers a pointless, robotic note-for-note cover. The only decent cut here is the uplifting "Growing With Each Other," which boasts a heartfelt vocal by gospel singer BeBe Winans. Albright is too strong a player to be recording albums this weak. *—Alex Henderson*

Live at Birdland West / 1991 / Atlantic ♦♦♦♦

Virtually all of saxophonist Gerald Albright's previous recordings were in the pop/R&B field, making this mostly straight-ahead session a major surprise. Albright, alternating between alto and tenor, plays quite well throughout this set, which is highlighted by versions of "Impressions," "Georgia on My Mind," and "Limehouse Blues." Tenorman Kirk Whalum helps out on three tracks, and Eddie Harris makes a guest appearance on "Bubblehead McDaddy." This is easily Gerald Albright's most rewarding session to date. *—Scott Yanow*

Smooth / Feb. 22, 1994 / Atlantic ♦♦♦

After a feisty live album recorded at Birdland gave this soulful saxman a chance to stretch his straight-ahead chops, the super cool side of Albright came back on this one. *Smooth* is indeed the operative word here, as this is a tasty if somewhat typical journey through the land of quiet storm and light funk. Albright's sharp, distinctive tone (bearing both melody and unexpected improvisations) heats up a too long series of pleasant but unremarkable melodies and grooves—the one instrumental exception being the blazing dual energy provided on "G & Lee" by the breezy guitar of Lee Ritenour. As background for those seductive night moves, the silky vocals by the likes of Howard Hewett and Will Downing are can't miss. Though Albright himself dazzles, more sax and less commercial slickness would make this a triumph rather than just another fine but generic rhythm and jazz effort. After you've heard his real jazz chops, the lack of a true traditional piece is a notable omission as well. *—Jonathan Widran*

Live to Love / 1997 / Atlantic ♦♦♦
Live to Love finds Gerald Albright returning to urban R&B, turning in an album of laid-back, polished soul and smooth jazz. Several vocalists, including Albright's daughter Selina, his longtime partner Will Downing, and the Whispers' Walter and Wallace Scott, contribute their skills to these well-crafted tracks. The vocal cuts form the core of *Live to Love*, making it more of interest to an urban audience than to fusion jazz fans, although there are a few instrumental interludes as well. However, the key thing distinguishing *Live to Love* is focus—Albright hasn't had such a consistently engaging set of songs in years, and that's what makes the album such a pleasure for fans of his work. *—Leo Stanley*

● **The Very Best of Gerald Albright** / Jun. 19, 2001 / Atlantic ♦♦♦♦♦
The liner notes for this can't-miss compilation, of a saxman who was putting the "smooth" into jazz long before radio called it that, promise some serious smackin'. These 11 tunes remind the serious rhythm and jazz fan that Albright's been doing that in powerful, soul-stirring ways since the late '80s. Albright was playing with Anita Baker when he signed to Atlantic and launched his diverse career with *Just Between Us* in 1987. Sultry tunes like "Bermuda Nights" and "In the Mood" helped define new adult contemporary radio (the maiden name of "smooth jazz") in the early days, but Albright never just wanted to be one thing. Just as his pop-jazz star was in full swing circa 1991, he took an exciting detour and put out the very straight-ahead-oriented disc *Live at Birdland West*, which only increased his popularity and respect with critics. There are no misses on this greatest-hits package, but the two most exciting cuts come from this date: an intense, highly improvisational "Georgia on My Mind" and jamming "Boss of Nova," which features powerful interaction between Albright's alto and Joe Sample's percussive piano chords (as Harvey Mason keeps perfect bossa time on the skins). The other must-hear collaboration is "G & Lee," featuring Lee Ritenour. The genre has become more competitive over the years with similar sounding saxmen, but Albright shows he's up to the challenge with the moody funk gem "When Morning Comes," the sole new track on the album. You could look at this as Atlantic just milking a great catalog, but be optimistic and say it's the perfect primer for those who are unfamiliar with one of the best saxmen in the business (and a welcome package for longtime fans too). *—Jonathan Widran*

Groovology / Jun. 18, 2002 / GRP ♦♦♦♦
Gerald Albright offers his listeners ten fresh musical concepts on his GRP label debut entitled *Groovology*, and they are musical concepts that have not been done to death. At the top of his game, this collection of songs gives Albright a marvelous opportunity to exhibit his multitude of musical skills, including composing, arranging, producing, and playing all four saxophone voices, in addition to several other instruments. Not exactly an easy task. Accompanied by a splendid roster of guest artists, Gerald Albright is sensitive, funky, grooving, smooth, and also demonstrates his irresistible rhythm and blues-inflected ballad work on such songs as "Bring a Lil' Love," "I Will Always Love You," and "I Need You." On "We Fall Down," Albright's blowing is subdued but in an unusually relaxed manner that is idiosyncratically smooth yet rooted in the R&B/gospel tradition. However, the top picks are "Old School Jam" and "Groovology" because of their memorable hooks and grooves. Excellent solos, vocals, and supportive arrangements make this one a keeper for Gerald Albright fans. *—Paula Edelstein*

Arthur Alexander

b. 1942, Florence, AL, **d.** Jun. 9, 1993, Nashville, TN
Vocals / Soul, Southern Soul, Country-Soul, Deep Soul
Arthur Alexander was one of the first true singing, songwriting stars of country-soul, a genre that wed Southern black R&B singers to songs written in a country format and played basically by white musicians. Alexander's "You Better Move On" (number 24, 1962) was the first hit to come out of Rick Hall's fledgling Muscle Shoals studio. Alexander's work was immediately appreciated by his peers in the business; those who have covered his tunes (self-penned or otherwise) read like a who's who from both sides of the Atlantic: "Anna" (the Beatles); "Soldiers of Love" (the Beatles and Marshall Crenshaw); "Burning Love" (Elvis Presley); and "Set Me Free" (Joe Tex, Esther Phillips, Percy Sledge). The Rolling Stones' cover of "You Better Move On" led to valuable contacts for Rick Hall, and the resulting business enabled him to build the new FAME studio. It was the start of the whole Muscle Shoals sound, and Alexander's career was one of its cornerstones. He went on, after a brief retirement, to record for both Warner Bros. and Buddah.

"Anna (Go to Him)," one of Alexander's best-known tunes, epitomizes the anguished, haunting tone of his music. From the onset, the heavily echoed piano and tortured vocal set a mood that is soulful, mysterious, a little spooky, and totally mesmerizing. His work is essential to any country-soul collection.

As Alexander began a comeback in 1993, he died of a heart attack. However, the album he completed before his death, *Lonely Just Like Me*, is a gentle record that is a fine way to end his career. Warner Bros. issued an Arthur Alexander retrospective anthology in 1994, featuring the early-'70s LP he recorded for them plus some unissued tracks. *—Christine Ohlman*

You Better Move On / 1962 / Dot ♦♦♦♦♦
Arthur Alexander was a wonderful deep soul and country-influenced singer. He could express the urgency and longing of a soul artist and tell a story with the sensitivity and innocence of a great country artist. The title track as well as the other cuts on this greatest-hits work were his finest from the '60s. "Anna" and "You Better Move On" were turned into bigger hits by the Beatles and the Rolling Stones. *—Ron Wynn*

Arthur Alexander / 1972 / Warner Bros. ♦♦♦
While Arthur Alexander made a name for himself as a songwriter and vocalist in the early '60s, he was best known for the hits other folks had enjoyed with his songs (among them the Beatles and the Rolling Stones), while his performing career hit an unfortunate slump by the end of the decade. Alexander been out of the public eye for a few years when he scored a deal with Warner Brothers and cut a self-titled album in 1972. Alexander had great faith in the project, which was produced by Tommy Cogbill and featured the cream of the Muscle Shoals studio players, along with songwriting contributions from Dan Penn, Donnie Fritts, and Alexander himself. Sadly, the album flopped in the marketplace, but a listen to the results confirms this was the fault of the promotion men, not the artists; hitting a midpoint between deep Southern soul and country-leaning funk, *Arthur Alexander* showed he had only grown stronger and more impressive as a singer over the decade, and his songs, built from simple stories of love and loss, never failed to hit the home truth (it's a wonder that no one was able to pitch tracks like "In the Middle of It All" or "Love's Where Life Begins" to some of the more imaginative country acts in Nashville—imagine George Jones wrapping his voice around either). Cogbill's production was rich but uncluttered with a deeply Southern feel, and the album won a richly deserved cult following among soul enthusiasts. After Alexander's unfortunate death in 1993, Warner Brothers released a retrospective CD, *Rainbow Road: The Warner Bros. Recordings*, which featured most of the cuts from the album, along with several single sides and unreleased tracks Alexander cut for the label; in either form, this is beautiful, heart-wrenching music that no one with a heart and a soul can walk away from without feeling its impact. *—Mark Deming*

Soldier of Love / 1987 / Ace ♦♦♦
Fourteen tracks from the '60s: half previously unissued, a few from his rare Dot LP, a couple of tracks from obscure 45s, and a fine, more sparsely produced alternate version of the title track. Although this isn't as exceptional as his best stuff, it's fairly solid, and while the material isn't top-notch, Arthur Alexander's oddly reserved and affecting vocals are uniformly strong. *—Richie Unterberger*

Lonely Just Like Me / 1993 / Elektra Nonesuch ♦♦♦♦
The final album from country-soul vocalist Arthur Alexander. It was like all his work—simple, unsophisticated, and sung with an earthy, direct intensity. This was part of the American Explorers series on Elektra/Nonesuch, and Alexander got some critical attention with his probing, often searing vocals. Unfortunately, he died just as this album was gaining some attention. *—Ron Wynn*

★ **The Ultimate Arthur Alexander** / Jun. 15, 1993 / Razor & Tie ♦♦♦♦♦
Arthur Alexander was one of the great overlooked figures of 1960s soul music. Alexander possessed a rich, emotive voice that was the perfect instrument for the lovelorn themes of Southern soul, and he was also an estimable songwriter—the Beatles covered his tune "Anna (Go to Him)," while the Rolling Stones recorded "You Better Move On." However, the themes of disappointment and bad luck that dominated Alexander's lyrics seemed to follow him in real life as well, and he never enjoyed the consistent chart success his fine recordings deserved. *The Ultimate Arthur Alexander* is a compilation that concentrates on Alexander's early- to mid-'60s recordings for Dot Records; unfortunately, his superb early-'70s work for Warner Bros. is ignored, as well as his comeback album, 1993's *Lonely Just Like Me* (which, with the sort of tragic irony that often popped up in Alexander's songs, was released to excellent reviews only a few months before his death). As a result, this album is a bit lacking as a proper retrospective of Alexander's work, but what's here is splendid; beautifully crafted and emotionally compelling, this is Southern soul at its best, with Alexander's songs and performances hitting the bull's-eye each time out. *The Ultimate Arthur Alexander* doesn't quite live up to its billing, but it is a fine retrospective of his formative work and a treat for anyone who loves deep soul. *—Mark Deming*

Rainbow Road: The Warner Bros. Recordings / Apr. 26, 1994 / Warner Archives ♦♦♦♦♦
Songwriter and vocalist Arthur Alexander was sorely neglected during his lifetime, despite possessing a stark, compelling voice and being among pop and soul's greatest storytellers. He remained on the outside, coming close but never attaining stardom. This CD features 15 fantastic songs, most from the great 1972 Warner Bros. album recorded in Memphis that Alexander thought would finally earn him that elusive smash. There are also some singles cut in Nashville as companion records to the Memphis session. The 15 tracks range from the hypnotic title cut and "In the Middle of It All" to the uptempo burners "You Got Me Knockin'" and "Burning Love." There's also a moving gospel number, "Thank God He Came." This disc is a wonderful tribute to an unjustly ignored artist. *—Ron Wynn*

The Monument Years / May 8, 2001 / Ace ♦♦♦
Between his most famous recordings in the first half of the 1960s, and his early-'70s album for Warner Brothers, Arthur Alexander kept sporadically active as a recording artist, putting out half a dozen singles on the Monument and Sound Stage 7 labels. None of these were hits, and as the original 45s are so hard to find, it remained a mysterious missing link in his career to most listeners. This CD rectifies that problem by collecting all of those singles, and adding 16 previously unreleased tracks that he cut in the last half of the 1960s and the early '70s. It's quite a useful service for fans, but it can't be denied that these performances aren't the high points of the fine soul singer/songwriter's career. The mix of soul, pop, and country forces at work in these sides is similar to those heard on Alexander's earlier efforts. However, the material, whether penned by Alexander or others, just isn't that outstanding, and sometimes sound like lesser reworkings of ideas

and riffs he'd plied more effectively in prior days. When Alexander covers a well-known song like "Spanish Harlem" or "Cry Like a Baby," he adds little to it; when he tries to be uncharacteristically funny and risqué on "I Want to Marry You," it's embarrassing. On the later stuff, the pop influences become more prominent, usually to the disadvantage of the music. His distinctive brand of somber soul, with his reserved and sad, vulnerable vocals, does shine through to a large degree, and those that have enjoyed his other releases will find much to appreciate. But it should not be regarded as a first or second choice for the Alexander neophyte. —*Richie Unterberger*

Tatyana Ali

Vocals / Urban

R&B singer Tatyana Ali began her performing career as a child actress co-starring on the hit sitcom *The Fresh Prince of Bel-Air.* Following the series' 1996 cancellation, she followed in the footsteps of co-star Will Smith and turned to music, debuting in 1998 with the smash summer single "Daydreamin'." Ali's debut album, *Kiss the Sky,* followed later that year. —*Jason Ankeny*

● **Kiss the Sky** / Aug. 25, 1998 / MJJ/Work ♦♦♦

History has often taught us that when an actor or actress decides to record an album, consumers had best be on their guard and proceed with caution. But in some cases, actors are also worthwhile singers. A case in point is Tatyana Ali, who is best known for playing Ashley on the NBC sitcom *The Fresh Prince of Bel-Air.* After establishing herself as an actress, Ali entered the urban contemporary field with *Kiss the Sky* (for which Will "The Fresh Prince" Smith is an executive producer). Although not fantastic and not very risk-taking, the collection of hip-hop-ish R&B/pop demonstrated that Ali was a decent singer along the lines of Janet Jackson. This isn't to say that the CD is as interesting as a Jackson album—in fact, most of the material is pretty routine. But *Kiss the Sky* does contain a few memorable selections, including the sexy "He Loves Me," the remorseful "Through Life Alone" and the caressing title song. Ali has the potential to make a consistently strong album, but she'll need the right input, guidance and direction. —*Alex Henderson*

All-4-One

f. California

Group / Urban, Contemporary R&B, New Orleans Blues

Comprised of Tony Borowiak, Jamie Jones, Delious Kennedy, and Alfred Nevarez, the Californian contemporary R&B vocal quartet All-4-One's 1994 debut album sailed into the Top Ten thanks to the enormous hit single "I Swear," which stayed at number one for 11 weeks. *My Brother's Keeper* followed in 1998, and a year later the group returned with *On and On.* —*Stephen Thomas Erlewine*

● **All-4-One** / 1994 / Blitzz/Atlantic ♦♦♦♦♦

All-4-One's self-titled debut proved that the quartet were exceptional vocalists, but the songs they sing often don't do them justice. Dividing their time between ballads and smooth dance-pop numbers, the group always sounds good, but they aren't charismatic enough to make weak material compelling. Nevertheless, when the group does have a good song—like the massive hit "I Swear"—the results are first-rate. —*Stephen Thomas Erlewine*

And the Music Speaks / 1995 / Blitzz/Atlantic ♦♦♦

All-4-One scored the biggest single of 1994 with "I Swear," a sweetly syrupy adult contemporary soul number. While they had a massive hit, they weren't able to carve out an identity with their debut album apart from "I Swear," so it was up to the follow-up, *And the Music Speaks* to establish the group as more than one-hit wonders and it partially succeeds. Musically, the album is stronger than the debut, featuring a better selection of songs. The group is more confident with their harmonies, showing off their gospel roots and still allowing themselves to get funkier than they have before. Nevertheless, the strength of the album remains in the ballads, where All-4-One can pull out all of their dramatic, romantic tricks, as they show on "I Can Love You like That" and "These Arms." Despite these highlights, the group never is as distinguished or as charismatic as Boyz II Men, the clear leaders of laid-back romantic '90s soul. Nevertheless, All-4-One have proven with *And the Music Speaks* that they are competent professionals, capable of turning out high-quality commercial soul on demand. —*Stephen Thomas Erlewine*

On and On / Aug. 4, 1998 / Blitzz/Atlantic ♦♦♦

All-4-One came crashing out of the gates in 1994, rocketing to the top of the charts with "I Swear." Its success was phenomenal—it stayed at the top of the charts for 11 weeks and inspired a contemporary country cover by John Michael Montgomery. It's hard to top that sort of success, which may be the reason why their second record, *And the Music Speaks,* seemed to vanish upon its 1995 release. That lack of success could be the reason why they waited four years to deliver their third record, *On and On.* Given the large gap between releases, it would seem as if *On and On* could offer a departure from the group's signature sound, or at least a maturation of sorts. As it turns out, it's cut from the same cloth as its predecessors. That is both for better and for worse. It certainly will satisfy fans thirsting for more the same sweet, well-polished adult contemporary and urban soul that graced the first two records, but it rarely shows any signs of progression. Even worse, there aren't many songs that are that memorable—all the parts are in place and the production is impeccable, but the songs just don't deliver strong melodies. That's not to say that it's a bad listen, since it makes for quite enjoyable background music, but after four years, fans may wonder if that's enough. —*Stephen Thomas Erlewine*

A41 / Jan. 22, 2002 / American Music Corp. ♦♦

From a self-titled album in 1994 to *A41* in 2002, All-4-One's problem has never been a lack of vocal prowess—the group's four members are, without question, highly talented singers. But having a great deal of talent and making the most of it are two different things, and on this 2002 release, All-4-One's members still have yet to make the most of their considerable skills. Like the group's previous releases, *A41* usually favors a very safe, middle-of-the-road blend of urban and adult contemporary. And true to form, All-4-One embraces a lot of syrupy ballads that are pleasant but unremarkable and lightweight. Gentle ballads like "Heaven Sent," "Before U, Without You, After U," "Not Ready 4 Goodbye," and the single "Beautiful As You" will likely please those who All-4-One won over with their 1994 smash "I Swear"; in fact, unchallenging, innocuous background music is exactly what some stressed-out and overworked Americans are looking for. But the group is capable of a lot more, and on this CD it is clear that All-4-One is resorting to formula instead of gambling with inspiration and taking chances. Nonetheless, *A41* has its moments. The funky, uptempo "Round and Round" is quite infectious, and the gospel-tinged "Between Us" (which is arguably the CD's best track) has an enjoyably Stevie Wonder-ish quality. Also noteworthy is a cover of Andy Gibb's 1977 hit "I Just Wanna Be Your Everything," which isn't as strong as the original version but is still likable. Is *A41* a bad album? Definitely not. But it isn't a great album either, and it's sad to see All-4-One settling for competent when their members are obviously capable of excellence. —*Alex Henderson*

All Saints

f. 1993, London, England, **db.** Feb. 2001

Group / Urban, Dance-Pop, Teen Pop, Adult Contemporary, House

Those unfamiliar with pop music would be forgiven for confusing All Saints with another hotly tipped music property, the Spice Girls. The four members of All Saints could have stood for Spice Girls body doubles in a lineup: two brunettes, one blonde, and one of West Indian descent. While the Spice Girls were always pure pop and barely musically functional, the members of All Saints, however, were songwriters and music aficionados with a softer, more intelligent image less tied to their looks than their music. The group came together in 1993 when Melanie Blatt and Shaznay Lewis began recording and writing.

Following a single for ZTT Records in 1995, the duo recruited native Canadian Nicky Appleton and, later, her big sister Natalie, to make All Saints a quartet. After the group recorded a demo of the song "I Know Where It's At," manager John Benson signed the girls to London Records and connected them with top-flight producers Nellee Hooper (Massive Attack, Björk) and Cameron McVey (Neneh Cherry). Fully recorded, "I Know Where It's At" hit number four on the British charts and crossed over throughout Europe and Asia.

By 1997, All Saints had reached the top spot with their second single, "Never Ever." The quartet released their self-titled debut album in November 1997 and began to grow in America as well, hitting the Top 40 with "I Know Where It's At." By 1998, their self-titled debut album was certified platinum in the U.S. and five-times platinum in the U.K. —*John Bush*

All Saints / Nov. 1997 / London ♦♦♦♦

As the first group of consequence to be saddled with the "new Spice Girls" tag, it would be reasonable to expect that All Saints would be cut-rate dance-pop without the weirdly magical charisma that made the Spices international phenomenons. It is true that All Saints lack the personality of the Spices, but they make up for that with musical skills. All four members have better voices than the Spices, and they all have a hand in writing at least one of the songs on their eponymous debut, with Shaznay taking the most writing credits. More importantly, they and their producers have a better sense of contemporary dance trends—there are real hip-hop and club rhythms throughout the record, and samples of Audio Two, the Rampage, and (especially) Steely Dan are fresh and inventive. But what really makes the record are the songs. The singles are the standouts, with the party-ready, Steely Dan-fueled "I Know Where It's At" and the extraordinary gospel-tinged "Never Ever" leading the way, but the covers are well-chosen (their take on "Under the Bridge" eclipses the Red Hot Chili Peppers', boasting a better arrangement and more convincing vocals) and the lesser songs are pleasantly melodic. Sure, there's some filler, but that should be expected on any dance-pop album. What counts is that the performances are fresh, the production is funky, and there are a handful of classic pop singles on the album, and you can't ask for much better than that from a dance-pop record, especially one from a group that almost beat the Spice Girls at their own game. —*Stephen Thomas Erlewine*

Saints & Sinners / Oct. 24, 2000 / London ♦♦♦

Whereas it took three albums for the Spice Girls to descend from unmatched cartoon pop to dreary two-step, All Saints got the job done in two. Except they substituted *Forever's* artless dodging with some sort of irksome middle-of-the-road, sub-salsa prancing about that's enough to cause worldwide *Tiger Beat* subscribers to torch themselves like Buddha monks. This is an album that's not afraid to title songs "Love Is Love"; an album that looks Gloria Estefan Latin pap in the face and gives it a big kiss on the lips. It's not that it's unpleasant hearing Shaznay, et al., careen off every chorus in those high-pitched coos, but for an unapologetic chart act there is an astonishing lack of tunes. It's unfortunate, since the swell of magical realism in "Pure Shores" is one of the finest, most spine-gushing pop moments of 2000. —*Dean Carlson*

● **All Hits** / Dec. 2001 / London ♦♦♦♦♦

All Saints weren't together that long, only two albums and a handful of singles, but that was enough to rack up a bunch of tabloid headlines, several celebrity romances (Shaznay with Damon Albarn, Nic B with Robbie Williams and Liam Gallagher), one skin-baring movie for the sisters Blatt, and several big U.K. hits (and a few minor U.S. hits). It might not be a lot for a hits collection, but it was enough as the 13-track collection *All Hits* proves. This is padded out a bit, with two '98 remixes (one of "Lady Marmalade," one of "War of Nerves"), the original hit version of the spectacular "Pure Shores," plus the "2 Da Beach U Don't Stop Remix," and it bends the rules by featuring "Twentyfourseven," a hit by Artful Dodger featuring Melanie Blatt's vocals, but that's not necessarily a bad thing (particularly in the case of "Twentyfourseven"), since this does consolidate the basic hits—"Pure Shores," "Never Ever," "Under the Bridge," "I Know Where It's At," "Black Coffee," "Bootie Call"—onto one disc. All Saints did make good albums—both of their records hold their own against the Spice Girls—but inevitably some will just want to hear the hits, and this does an excellent job of serving them up with style. *—Stephen Thomas Erlewine*

Lee Allen

b. Jul. 2, 1926, Sewanee, TN, **d.** Oct. 18, 1994, Los Angeles, CA

Saxophone / New Orleans R&B, R&B, Instrumental Rock

The blasting tenor saxophone of Lee Allen was every bit as integral a factor in the sizzling sound of the '50s New Orleans R&B as were the well-documented contributions of Fats Domino, Lloyd Price, and Little Richard. As a key member of the studio band at Cosimo's, Allen played his searing solos that sparked hundreds of Crescent City classics. Allen's wallpaper-peeling sax solos are instantly identifiable; check out Richard's "Slippin' and Slidin'" and "Tutti Frutti" for irrefutably exciting evidence.

But, despite his sax mastery, Allen failed to sustain a brief solo career. Signing with Al Silver's New York-based Ember label, he managed one decent-sized hit in 1958, the rocking instrumental "Walkin' With Mr. Lee," while the second-line scorcher "Boppin' at the Hop" inexplicably never received any national airplay.

When the New Orleans sound shifted to a funkier beat, Allen's muscular sound fell out of favor on the local recording scene. Nevertheless, Allen remained active until his death in 1994, touring extensively with Domino, as well as working with a variety of young rockers (including the Blasters) who revered his blistering sound. *—Bill Dahl*

● **Walkin' With Mr. Lee** / 1958 / Collectables ♦♦♦♦♦

New Orleans' favorite tenor sax player had a modest hit with the title track, a bouncy instrumental tailor-made for his honkin' style. The resulting album issued on the Ember label and a stray 45 are collected up here, a loose batch of blues, rockers, smoky jazz ballads, and jumpers. All of these are assigned quaint malt-shop titles like "Teen Dream," "Hot Rod Special," "Boppin' at the Hop," and "Bee Hive." But corny titles aside, here's some classic New Orleans blowing in a variety of settings, all of which work, making for a solid sax album that's grade-A listening all the way. *—Cub Koda*

The Rance Allen Group

b. Detroit, MI

Vocals / Contemporary Gospel, Black Gospel, Urban

Gospel singer Rance Allen founded the Rance Allen Group in Detroit in the 1960s and has fronted the band with his soulful, soaring vocals ever since. The traditionally trained black gospel group was the first traditional gospel group to incorporate rock, jazz, and soul into their music. They were harbingers for the contemporary Christian music movement popularized in the late '70s by Andrae Crouch, Amy Grant, and the Winans. The Rance Allen Group scored a Top 30 R&B hit in 1979 with "I Belong to You," one of two Stax singles that year to make the charts. The group's recordings for Gospel Truth, Capitol, and Stax proved quite popular among gospel audiences, and had some success attracting soul fans as well. Rance Allen continued singing, recording, and performing with his group up into the next millennium, releasing *Miracle Worker* with the Rance Allen Group in spring 2000. *—Bil Carpenter and Ron Wynn*

Straight from the Heart / 1972 / Stax ♦♦♦

Gospel singer Rance Allen enjoyed some crossover soul success in the early '70s, recording on Stax's Gospel Truth label. His explosive, soaring voice was especially effective on upper-register notes and inspirational ballads. This was one of his biggest albums, especially the single "I Belong to You." *—Ron Wynn*

★ **Soulful Experience** / 1975 / Stax ♦♦♦♦♦

A couple of decades before such stylistic melding would became popular among gospel artists, Rance Allen and his brothers merged the dynamics of soulful rhythms, gospel lyrics, and Rance's testimonial lead vocals. This effort was produced by acclaimed Stax alumnus David Porter, who also co-wrote seven of the selections. The highlight from this album is the proverbial lyric and stirring rhythms of "Ain't No Need of Crying." Rance's versatile vocals sail up and down the register from squeals and cries to riffs and sighs without forsaking solid, cohesive vocals throughout the verses and chorus. The gospel gem peaked on the *Billboard* R&B charts at 61 after a nine weeks. On "Talk That Talk," Rance utilizes his vast vocal repertoire to personify a riveting guitar. The Michigan native slows his delivery on the introspective "Just Found Me." The Allen brothers are consistently excellent on every selection. *—Craig Lytle*

I Feel Like Goin' On / 1980 / Stax ♦♦♦

Although not as smartly produced or containing compositions as memorable as some earlier releases, Rance Allen still generated some mild R&B attention with this LP, as well as the usual good response in gospel circles. But the Allen style was becoming more predictable and would soon lose favor as huge choirs and slick, urban contemporary-styled groups and artists began to dominate the modern gospel scene. *—Ron Wynn*

Ain't No Need of Crying / 1985 / Stax ♦♦♦♦♦

Rance Allen's brand of soul-tinged gospel was at its best on this release. The title track cracked the R&B charts, and Allen's soaring voice, coupled with the fine harmonies provided by his brothers—Tom, Steve, and Esau—as well as assistance from cousins Judy, Linda, and Annie Mendez, resulted in some arresting songs. *—Ron Wynn*

Best of the Rance Allen Group / 1988 / Stax ♦♦♦♦♦

Infusing traditional gospel music with Memphis soul, Detroit-based singer Rance Allen helped pave the way for the secularized gospel sound of the '80s and '90s. After signing with Stax in 1969, Allen and his group proceeded to bring their hip brand of gospel to the masses by scoring several chart hits and opening concerts for the likes of Isaac Hayes. This hits package covers the group's successful run in the '70s, spotlighting Allen's incredibly flexible and powerful voice (one listens to cuts like "Ain't No Need of Crying" and "Gonna Make It Alright" and it's easy to figure out where Prince picked up his misty falsetto from). The selections include Allen's biggest Stax hit, "I Got to Be Myself," the spiritually recharged cover "Just My Imagination (Just My Salvation)," and modern gospel pioneer James Cleveland's "That Will Be Enough for Me." Allen contributes a handful of slick and spirited groovers, like "I Give My All To You" and "I Belong to You," and even goes in for a little disco on another original, "Smile" (considering Allen's devout nature, it's hard to tell if the more commercial elements in the music came from him or hit-minded producers). A bit of unintentional humor also finds its way into the set, with the raucous cut "Hot Line to Jesus." This spirited collection makes Allen's love of the music plain and offers a fine introduction to both his work and to the "new," yet (historically speaking) ancient mix of religious and secular black music. *—Stephen Cook*

Let the Music Get Down in Your Soul / 1997 / Stax ♦♦♦

Rance Allen has always been one of the most innovative and summarily influential of all modern-day contemporary gospel artists. This 14-track collection of the Rance Allen Group's (which featured his brothers Steve on bass and Tom on drums) 1971-1975 tenure with Stax Records' Gospel Truth subsidiary is less of a greatest-hits primer than it is a nice cross-section of the mix of contemporary sounds Allen brought to gospel music during that time. Eight of the tracks ("Care," "You Need a Friend Like Mine," "Happy Needs Help," "Everybody's Talkin'," "I Don't Know What I'd Do," "The Jesus Thing," "Lonely Girl," and the title song, which goes on for almost nine minutes and features Rance's octave-jumping falsetto squeals) are previously unissued and do much to illustrate the high wire Allen walked in those early days of the contemporary gospel movement. On five of those unissued sides, Rance's voice is aided by a solid Stax rhythm section (Donald "Duck" Dunn on bass and Al Jackson Jr.), sounding as fresh and relevant as when they were laid down more than two decades ago. *—Cub Koda*

Allure

Group / Club/Dance, Urban

The New York-based urban soul vocal group Allure was the first band to be signed to Mariah Carey's Crave Records. Such connections ensured that Allure would be promoted well and that their eponymous 1997 debut would have cameos by such stars as Nas, LL Cool J, Raekwon, 112, Q-Tip, and Carey herself, but it didn't ensure that the record itself would be a blockbuster. Instead, the album was a moderate hit, suggesting the group's commercial potential instead of fulfilling it.

The roots of Allure lay in the early '90s, when Alia Davis, Lalisha McLean, and Akissa Mendez were studying at the LaGuardia High School for the Performing Arts in New York. When the girls decided to form a full-fledged group, they recruited Davis' friend Linnie Belcher, who was studying at the Julia Richmond High School. For the next two years, they rehearsed and practiced, eventually securing management connections which brought them to the attention of Poke, a member of the production team Track Masters. Poke worked with the unnamed group and soon signed them to Track Masters under the name Allure, and then helped the group sign with Crave Records.

Allure's debut single, "Head Over Heels," featured a rap by Nas and became a moderate R&B hit in April of 1997. The following month, the group's eponymous debut album was released. *—Stephen Thomas Erlewine*

● **Allure** / May 5, 1997 / Crave/Track Masters ♦♦♦

Allure's eponymous debut had the mixed blessing of being the first album on Mariah Carey's high-profile vanity label, Crave. Carey's clout certainly helped Allure to line up celebrity collaborators, from Nas and L.L. Cool J to Q-Tip and Carey, but it also meant that the album would be scrutinized in detail, which is unfair to any new vocal group. Allure does acquit itself well on their debut, singing with passion and flair—it's clear they have talent. They are somewhat undone by inconsistent material, yet there are several instances where the group makes a song their own, and that's what makes *Allure* a promising debut. *—Stephen Thomas Erlewine*

Sunny Days / Sep. 25, 2001 / MCA ♦♦♦

The year was 1997 and Allure's self-titled debut—with the chart-topping remake of Lisa Lisa & Cult Jam's "All Cried Out"—seemed to poise the R&B quartet for instant and sustained success. Alas, the band's then-label, Mariah Carey's Crave, folded and the girls found themselves shopping a new deal. Fast-forward to 2001. Allure has found a home on MCA, which released the group's sophomore release, *Sunny Days*. Within minutes of listening to the disc, audiences will think, This is like all the other girl-group R&B fare on the radio today. And it is. *Sunny Days* is rife with contemporary danceable grooves, guest flows, urban flavor, and several grab-the-Kleenex ballads. And what's wrong with this? Allure, at this stage of its career, doesn't need to redefine the genre. If it sits alongside Destiny's Child, then, for the time being, this is an accomplishment after the group's four-year studio-recording hiatus. To be sure, the band has matured. The songs—which address the usual: good-time partying, relationships, and self-respect, among other themes—sound more seasoned this go-round. Perhaps four years of trying to find their place in the musical arena has put some notches on the life belts (ouch!) of the Allure ladies. Also, their voices sound more robust and confident. There's some really nice harmonizing on the ballad "Never Let You Go." The album's first single release, "Enjoy Yourself," is a winning upbeat R&B dance jam in the style of Zane and old-school tracks. This song will have audiences dancing and having a good time whether in their living room, car, or on the dancefloor. Welcome back, Allure. Here's hoping for more sunny days. *—Liana Jonas*

Gerald Alston

b. Nov. 8, 1951, North Carolina

Vocals / Urban

Gerald Alston inherited some big soul shoes and filled them admirably for 17 years. The nephew of gospel great Johnny Fields and the son of Rev. J.B. Alston, the NC-born singer learned his trade in the church. As a teen he formed the New Imperials, a group that did both secular and religious music, calling themselves Gospel Jubilee when they appeared in churches. During a local appearance, the Manhattans borrowed some audio equipment from Alston's band. When they came to pick it up they heard him rehearsing with his band. They asked the 17-year-old to join them, and Alston took over as their lead singer in 1971. Alston remained until 1988, and the group enjoyed enormous success in the '70s and '80s. Their 1976 single "Kiss and Say Goodbye" was both a number one R&B and pop hit, the first (and only one) the band ever earned. They won a Grammy in 1980 for "Shining Star." Alston sang a duet with fledging vocalist Regina Belle in 1986, "Where Did We Go Wrong." The Bobby Womack-produced tune was Belle's debut. Alston signed with Motown in 1988. He didn't have much commercial luck as a solo act, though the releases *Gerald Alston* and *Open Invitation* were well-produced and wonderfully sung; *Always in the Mood* appeared in 1992. *—Ron Wynn*

• **Gerald Alston** / 1988 / Motown ✦✦✦✦✦

Open Invitation / 1990 / Motown ✦✦✦
Open Invitation was Manhattans lead singer Gerald Alston's Top 14 R&B follow-up to his self-titled solo debut. The opener, "Slow Motion," produced by Stan Sheppard and Jimmy Varner of By All Means fame, was a number three R&B hit in the fall of 1990. The second single, "Getting Back Into Love," went Top Six R&B. Not surprisingly, with Alston having sung on such classic slow jams as the platinum-selling "Kiss and Say Goodbye" and the gold smash "Shining Star," the album best succeeds when it's in ballad mode. "Don't You Know" has a nice doo wop-ish sway in its groove. The same could be said of sweet, romantic "Crazy," which is helmed by Commodores producer James Anthony Carmichael. "We're Still in Love" conveys a kind of charming "ol' skool" romantic vibe in both lyric and feel. Alston does a smooth, snappy remake of the Chuck Jackson hit "Any Day Now," produced by Levi Seacer Jr. *—Ed Hogan*

Always in the Mood / 1992 / Motown ✦✦✦✦✦
Former Manhattans lead vocalist Gerald Alston has emerged as one of the 1990s' best soul and love singers. His passionate, intense leads never lose their steam or conviction, he wisely avoids doing songs with rappers, and he doesn't let production gimmicks and studio trappings overwhelm his vocals. *—Ron Wynn*

First Class Only / Sep. 27, 1994 / Volcano ✦✦✦
Gerald Alston sounds as good as ever on *First Class Only*, but his material isn't worthy of his excellent singing. *—Stephen Thomas Erlewine*

The Ambassadors

f. Philadelphia, PA
Group / Philly Soul, Soul
The Ambassadors had but one small R&B hit in 1969, "I Really Love You," a dramatic ballad in the Philadelphia soul style with an ascending horn riff, co-written by Kenny Gamble. They did stay together long enough to do an album, *Soul Summit*, which featured several musicians—including Leon Huff (on piano) and Earl Young (drums)—who were instrumental to the Gamble-Huff productions that epitomized the peak of Philadelphia soul in the early '70s. The Ambassadors didn't project a ton of personality, but then again, personality wasn't the long suit of some other big Philadelphia soul acts; perhaps if they'd been given excellent material, they would have been far more successful. As it is, the rare *Soul Summit* LP, reissued on CD in 1998, is a notable find for those who love the Gamble-Huff sound and want an accomplished example that they might not have previously heard. *—Richie Unterberger*

• **Soul Summit** / 1969 / Arctic ✦✦✦
Although this is filled out with covers of "You've Lost That Lovin' Feelin'," "Yes I'm Ready," and "Can't Take My Eyes Off You," on the whole it's a solid and varied album of early Gamble/Huff-styled Philadelphia soul. Even though Gamble and Huff's own contributions were peripheral (Jimmy Bishop produced, Gamble co-wrote the small hit "I Really Love You," and Huff played piano), several musicians who would play in Gamble-Huff's house bands participated. The harmonies are lively, the arrangements (by Bobby Martin, who would also work with Gamble-Huff) satisfyingly busy, and the material a bit ordinary but serviceable. Philly soul fiends may consider it a lost nugget of sorts; the three non-LP bonus tracks on the CD reissue include a couple of raucous live cuts with a straighter R&B feel. *—Richie Unterberger*

Amerie

Vocals / Contemporary R&B, Urban
Singer Amerie is the daughter of a Korean mother and an African-American father who was a career military member. She grew up on bases from Alaska to Germany, meanwhile gaining an appreciation of the classical arts from her mother and of R&B music from her father. She studied dance from an early age and performed in talent contests throughout her youth. After her high school graduation, her family finally settled down in Virginia, while she began to attend Georgetown University, from which she later graduated with a degree in English and Fine Arts.

While living in Washington, D.C., she met producer Rich Harrison, who worked with such performers as Mary J. Blige, and began developing demos with him. They led to a deal with Rise Entertainment and, in turn, with Columbia Records. In the spring of 2002, Rise/Columbia released Amerie's debut single, "Why Don't We Fall in Love." By the time her first album, *All I Have*, appeared that July, the single had reached the Top 20 of the R&B/hip-hop charts and the Top 40 of the pop charts. *—William Ruhlmann*

• **All I Have** / Jul. 30, 2002 / Rise/Columbia ✦✦✦
The debut album by 22-year-old Amerie is basically a showcase for writer/producer Rich Harrison, who constructs a series of midtempo rhythm tracks and writes lyrics of romantic longing. Harrison's lack of originality is suggested by his inability even to come up with new song titles: Among the tracks here are newly written songs entitled "Need You Tonight," "Got to Be There," and even "I Just Died" (that's right, "in your arms"). Amerie has a pleasant-enough voice that she uses to express a tempered fervor and a degree of eroticism, but she seems to be just another modestly talented performer chosen mostly for her looks; record companies seem to be on an endless search for attractive young women of mixed racial heritage (apparently in hopes of demographic crossover) who can carry a tune, and this willing Georgetown graduate with a Korean mother and African-American father is just the latest in a long line. None of which is to say that she won't succeed (record companies make a lot of money taking such bets), but at least on the basis of her debut album, Amerie has nothing to recommend her beyond a fairly anonymous surface appeal. *—William Ruhlmann*

Kip Anderson

b. 193?, Anderson, SC
Vocals / Soul-Blues, Retro-Soul, Southern Soul, R&B
Without benefit of anything resembling a chart hit, Kip Anderson amassed an impressive Southern soul legacy spanning several decades. And how many other R&B artists were named after Rudyard Kipling, anyway?

Anderson continued to live in the same rural region of South Carolina where he grew up. The singer learned his way around his folks' upright piano as a youth, composing his first tune in 1959. Anderson later bounced from label to label, cutting "I Will Cry" for producer Bobby Robinson in 1963; "That's When the Crying Begins" for ABC-Paramount the following year; and several gems for Checker in 1965-66 (including one of his best-known numbers, "A Knife and a Fork," in Muscle Shoals under the supervision of Rick Hall and Gene "Daddy G" Barge). By 1969, Anderson was inked to Nashville-based Excello, where he waxed the impassioned deep soul gem "I Went Off and Cried."

Anderson's hearty vocal talents also popped up recently on Ichiban Records. He's cut two albums for the Atlanta firm—*A Dog Don't Wear No Shoes* and *A Knife and a Fork*—and contributed the jolliest track of all, "Gonna Have a Merry Christmas," to the label's 1994 anthology *Ichiban Blues at Christmas, Vol. 3*. *—Bill Dahl*

• **A Dog Don't Wear No Shoes** / 1992 / Ichiban ✦✦✦✦
A Dog Don't Wear No Shoes is an energetic latter-day record from Kip Anderson that proves that the vocalist has lost very little of his power or charisma over the years. All of the music is in the deep soul tradition and he doesn't alter the formula much at all, but with a vocalist as gritty and impassioned as Anderson, that doesn't matter. *—Thom Owens*

A Knife and a Fork / 1993 / Ichiban ✦✦✦
A Knife and a Fork is nearly a carbon copy of its predecessor, *A Dog Don't Wear No Shoes*, but that's not necessarily a bad thing. Though the material is slightly weaker than the previous album, Kip Anderson makes the weakest songs somewhat convincing with his wonderful voice. *—Thom Owens*

Sunshine Anderson

b. Charlotte, NC
Vocals / Neo-Soul, Contemporary R&B, Urban
Though she sang in musicals and talent shows throughout her childhood, Charlotte, NC, native Sunshine Anderson was discovered while she was waiting in line in a cafeteria at North Carolina Central University, where she earned a B. S. in criminal justice. A friend of producer/Soulife A&R Vice President Mike City heard Anderson humming while she waited and introduced her to City. After she graduated from college, Anderson moved to Washington, D.C., and took a government job in human resources, but eventually relocated to Los Angeles, where she worked with City on her 2001 debut album *Your Woman* and found a manager in critically-acclaimed singer Macy Gray. *—Heather Phares*

• **Your Woman** / Apr. 17, 2001 / Atlantic ✦✦✦
While too many pop and R&B divas rely on Mariah Carey-like vocal histrionics, Sunshine Anderson wins over fans with her understated maturity. The first single, "Heard It All Before," breathes new life into a typical R&B diva scenario of a jilted woman confronting her cheating lover. The guitar-based midtempo track "Lunch and Dinner" features smooth guitar and straightforward, earnest lyrics. *Your Woman* features some solid production by Mike City and Mark Spark, and rather than trying to overpower the music with her voice, Anderson has enough confidence to just go along for the ride. *—Jon Azpiri*

Lee Andrews & the Hearts

b. 1954, Goldsboro, NC
Group / Doo Wop, R&B, Philly Soul
One of the finest R&B vocal groups of the '50s, the Philadelphia-based Lee Andrews & the Hearts specialized in smooth ballads and were influenced by similar vocal acts like the Moonglows, the Orioles, the Drifters, the 5 Royales, the Five Keys, the Midnighters, and the Ravens, while lead vocalist Lee Andrews' influences were mostly solo artists like Bing Crosby, Frankie Laine, Frank Sinatra, and especially Nat King Cole. These two key influences—a harmonizing four-part vocal base with a strong but tender tenor voice leading the way—was the foundation of the Hearts' hard-to-beat sound.

The group scored three charting hits in the span of a single year (1957-1958). Their "Long Lonely Nights" (recorded for the tiny Mainline label) managed to barely beat the former Drifter Clyde McPhatter's version by a few chart points (number 45 to Clyde's number 49). It scored even higher on the R&B charts (number 11). At its peak, the group's next single for Mainline, "Teardrops," was picked up for wider distribution by Chess. It was their biggest hit, making it to at number 20 on the pop charts (on November 25, 1957), and by January 1958, it had jumped over to the R&B charts, where it ended up listing at number four. A third hit, "Try the Impossible" for the United Artists label, charted at number 33 on the pop charts (June 22, 1958).

Lee Andrews (b. Arthur Lee Andrew Thompson) was raised by a musical family in Goldsboro, NC. His father, Beechie Thompson, sang with the Dixie Hummingbirds. The Thompson family soon moved to Philadelphia, PA, when little Arthur Thompson was two. By the time he was a student at Bertram High School in 1952, Thompson had begun singing with four friends: Royalston "Roy" Calhoun (first tenor), Thomas "Butch" Curry (second tenor), James "Jimmy" McCalister (baritone), and John Young (bass). The quintet—from the neighborhood of 49th and Woodland in South Philly—first began calling themselves the Dreams and later, the Dreamers.

Between 1952 and 1954, the Dreamers rehearsed after school (often tutored on spirituals by Curry's aunt) and soon began incorporating R&B stylings into the mix. In early 1954, they visited the local WHAT radio station and danced in the studio adjacent to the DJ booth, where on-air personality Kae Williams held court. On one particular night, Williams asked a group of teens dancing in the next room about what local acts they liked and was told he should listen to the Dreamers. They later auditioned two Top Ten charters from previous decades and Williams was so awed by this unique assemblage that he offered to manage them on the spot.

In the spring of that year, Williams squired the Dreamers into Reco Arts Studio and cut two sides. The group then traveled with Williams to New York City and to the offices of Eddie Heller and Bobby Heller's Rainbow Records, a label so small it shared space with a Hell's Kitchen storefront known as Sonny's Deli. The two also ran a club in North Philly and had previously associated with Williams.

It was here that they learned there was already an act calling themselves the Dreamers and it was Jimmy McCalister who came up with the Hearts after spying a small plastic heart on a secretary's desk—actually Heller's wife. Since Thompson was to be featured on as the group's leader, he began shuffling his names around to come up with something he felt would sound better—and read better on the labels—than Arthur Thompson and the Hearts. He finally settled on calling himself by his two middle names and thus the name Lee Andrews & the Hearts was finally born.

The Hearts' first single was a version of the Orioles' then-charting "Maybe You'll Be There" (accompanied only by piano). It was issued in mid-May 1954 and received airplay in Philadelphia, but couldn't compete with the polished and established Orioles' version and sank like a stone. "The White Cliffs of Dover," their second single, was a better overall group performance but saw even less airplay activity. A third single from October 1954, "The Bells of St. Mary's," battled on the charts with a better-produced version of the same song by the Drifters. Williams obviously thought three tries was enough for Rainbow and pulled his group from the label.

By 1955, McCalister was Navy bound and soon replaced by Ted Weems, another neighbor from South Philly. As they were now high school grads they had to think of full-time employment. Lee Andrews and Roy Calhoun went to work at Gotham Record Distributors, hoping to also scored a chance to audition for owner Ivan Ballen's Gotham record label. When the group learned that their contract with Williams wasn't valid because they were all minors when they signed it, they reportedly asked Ballen to audition them. However, Ballen's main interest was gospel music and he kept putting the teens off until the very end of 1955 when he finally relented and gave them a listen. Liking what he heard, he signed Lee Andrews & the Hearts to Gotham on January 3, 1956. Soon they were recording at the label's studio, located at 626 Federal Street.

Their first single, the Davies-Heyman standard "Bluebird of Happiness," was released in May, but failed to become a hit. Their next single, the Andrews-penned "Lonely Room," was virtually a note-for-note copy of the Larks' 1952 Apollo single "In My Lonely Room," but managed to gather airplay throughout Pennsylvania, Delaware, and New Jersey. The group's last Gotham single, which listed Andrews as its songwriter—even though it was reportedly penned by one Rita Sherwood—was issued toward the end of 1956. "Just Suppose" also failed to chart.

The Hearts grew frustrated when they realized that many of their best efforts for the label hadn't even been released. In early 1957, they auditioned at Weems' home for Philadelphia (WDAS) and New York (WWOV) jock Jocko Henderson, who—along with partner Barry Golder—owned Mainline Record Distributors. The Hearts looked like the perfect vehicle to start up their long planned Mainline label. Before they could record, however, bass vocalist John Young left the act (moving to New York) and the group continued to fill the low-register position with a series of replacements, including their piano player Gerald Thompson, Tom Hackett, and, finally, Roy's brother Wendell Calhoun, aka "Breeze."

By mid-year, however, the group was pleased to discover that their song "Long Lonely Nights" had caught on and found a new audience. The tiny Mainline label responded by issuing a new recording of the Hearts doing the song; meanwhile, Atlantic Records had their ace Clyde McPhatter record the song, and to further complicate things, a group calling themselves "the Kings" covered the song as well for their Baton label. As it turned out, the Kings were actually the popular act the Ravens, who were then signed to Chess Records' affiliate label Argo. With all of these versions of the same song competing for airplay, it's a wonder that the race was a close one at all and while there's no doubt the Hearts recording could have hit the Top Ten pop charts without the fierce competition, it managed to barely beat the former Drifters' version by a few points (number 45 to Clyde's number 49). It scored even higher on the R&B charts: number 11. (The Hearts' can be consoled in the fact that their version has become the choice of oldies radio stations, while McPhatter's is now known only by hardcore collectors).

In November 1957, the Hearts' next single, "Teardrops," was picked up by Chess nationally, but in Philadelphia, it was released on the Argo affiliate as part of a distribution deal between Chess and Mainline. The song was an instant classic, eventually charted at its peak at number 20 on the pop charts (on November 25, 1957), but by January 6, 1958, it had jumped over to the R&B charts, and hit number four.

After two hits and getting shorted on royalties from Chess, Lee Andrews & the Hearts moved over to United Artists, where the group charted for the last time in 1958 with the typically polished "Try the Impossible." Jocko Henderson—managing the group at this point—finagled a deal in the Philadelphia area with the single, which ended up being released on his locally distributed Casino label (which was co-owned by Mickey Golder (Barry's brother). It charted at number 33 on the pop charts (June 22, 1958). The group never again charted on the R&B charts.

The group spent the rest of the year touring, which took its ultimate toll, breaking apart the band. Weems joined the army and Lee Andrews left the Hearts behind to go solo. He eventually surfaced on Swan Records for three singles with a then-uncredited group (later identified as the Neons. Those that remained began calling themselves the Five Hearts, a group consisting of Tommy White (lead), Roy and Wendell Calhoun and Butch Curry of the Hearts; and Eddie Custus (who recorded as one of the Superiors for Mainline). In 1959, the Five Hearts recorded "It's Unbelievable" for Arcade. The group's third disc jockey/manager, Hy Lit, got them signed to Chancellor Records, where yet another version of the group, now a quartet made up of Calhoun, Curry, Custus, and Sonny Gordon, actually re-recorded "It's Unbelievable" again. In February 1962, the group reunited briefly for "Together Again" (Gowen Records) with a lineup consisting of Lee Andrews, Curry, the Calhoun brothers, and Custus.

Lee then soloed again (if you can call a record with backgrounds by the Dreamlovers, Rick and the Masters, and various Hearts a solo) on "I'm Sorry Pillow" in December 1962, on Parkway. Meanwhile, the four singing Hearts recorded "Aisle of Love" for Guyden Records, in November 1962. When the single flopped, they split up.

By 1963, the Hearts had stopped ticking and their recordings became very collectable, so Grand Records struck a deal with Gotham and issued some of the group's old sides. Collectors' demand for more recordings prompted Lee to form a new Hearts group in the summer of 1966 with a few familiar names paired up with a few new ones: Booker, Mason, alongside new Hearts Robert Howard and Victoria McCalister. They recorded "You're Taking a Long Time Coming Back" which was issued on single by RCA. The group signed the dotted line with Crimson Records, and eventually wound up two singles later on Crimson's parent company, Lost Night, recording three original singles (an unusual move for this all-oldies reissue company) that were issued in 1968. By the time they did a live LP for Lost Night—recorded at a club in Fairless Hills, PA—the Hearts were Lee Andrews, Richard Howard, Richard Booker, and Tommy White.

Eventually, Andrews went into semi-retirement and opened a successful dress shop. In a 1971 interview he stated that he formed a new group called First Born and they were in the process of recording for Columbia, though no such record release ever took place. Andrews later re-emerged at the urging of producer friend Billy Jackson (the Tymes), who knew Lee's interests were now leaning in a 5th Dimension-style direction. Together, they formed Congress Alley with Booker, Jackie Andrews (Lee's wife), and Karen Brisco. This group managed two singles and an LP for Avco Embassy, but the releases weren't successful.

In 1981, Collectable Records unearthed the original first studio session tapes from Gotham and issued three singles, including yet another version of "Long Lonely Nights" which was lyrically different from the hit song, with just a piano accompaniment and crystal-clear harmonies. The oldies circuit revival of the '70s provided momentum for Lee to form one more Hearts, this one a family affair with Lee, his wife Jackie, son Ahmir, and daughter Dawn.

Roy Calhoun died in an apartment fire in 1979, Butch Curry became ill with multiple sclerosis, Wendell Calhoun remained in Philadelphia, and Ted Weems joined the Pheasants ("Out of the Mist," Throne) in 1963 and later had a group called Tribute, but had no other hits. *—Bryan Thomas*

● **Their Biggest Hits** / 1981 / Collectables ✦✦✦✦✦
A 12-song budget collection that nonetheless offers a nice cross-section of the group's early Gotham and later Chess material. Early takes like "The Fairest" and "The White Cliffs of Dover" are one step removed from being a cappella, with only sparse piano accompaniment to back up the gorgeous harmonies. The version of "Long Lonely Nights" is the later Chess hit version, pairing up nicely with their other smash for the label, "Teardrops," also included here. The transfers range from very clean to scratchy and are taken off old 78s, but the music stays top-notch throughout. *—Cub Koda*

Gotham Recording Sessions / Apr. 19, 1990 / Collectables ✦✦✦
Here are the early Gotham sides from this marvelous doo wop group. On the plus side, the material is top-notch, kicking off with the original pre-hit version of their classic "Long Lonely Nights" and including "Leona," "Strollin' Baby," "Girl Around the Corner," and two takes of "Lonely Room," most of them featuring only piano accompaniment. The downside of this set is the utter lack of liner notes, recording or publishing information—another cheap Collectables package; plus, some of the sides sound as if they were pulled from vinyl or acetates. Still, it's some top-notch doo wop by one of the classiest in the genre. *—Cub Koda*

For Collectors Only / 1995 / Collectables ✦✦✦✦✦
A meticulous, aptly-titled anthology of Lee Andrews & the Hearts' recordings, but if you're not knee-deep into them, one of their smaller collections will be easier on your Visa and should suffice. This is the whole kit and caboodle: 61-tracks of classic '50s doo wop, featuring previously unreleased songs, demos, and alternate versions, as well as every A- and B-side they released, from their debut "Maybe You'll Be There" on Rainbow Records (1954) to the beautiful "Island of Love" on Lost Nite Records (1968). The pioneering group influenced a slew of Philly vocal groups, including the original, pre-Teddy Pendergrass, Blue Notes and the Intruders. The Intruders redid the Hearts' most successful recording, "Teardrops," on their *Save the Children* album. *For Collectors Only* is a flowing gathering of smooth, classy doo wop at its best. *—Andrew Hamilton*

Teardrops: The Very Best of Lee Andrews & the Hearts / Apr. 2, 2002 / Collectables ✦✦✦✦
Lee Andrews & the Hearts scored only three hits, "Long Lonely Nights," "Tear Drops," and "Try the Impossible," in 1957-1958, so this collection contains plenty of the group's (and solo act Andrews') also-rans along with the successes. Liner notes author Marv Goldberg contributes an affectionate biography that traces the group's career, but doesn't help the consumer determine the sources of the actual recordings contained on the album, which is notable since Andrews & the Hearts re-recorded many of their songs. The sequencing, which jumbles up the chronology, doesn't help an understanding of the group's legacy, either. They recorded in standard doo wop style for the most part, for example, but when Andrews made solo recordings like "Can't Do Without You" in 1968, long after the doo wop era was over, he performed in a style that slavishly copied the Motown sound. Such a track can be jarring when it is preceded and followed by doo wop group recordings.

Collectables is to be commended for gathering together nearly an hour's worth of Andrews solo and Andrews & the Hearts recordings, many of which are fine examples of the doo wop style. But the release could have been better assembled and annotated. *—William Ruhlmann*

Ruby Andrews

b. Mar. 12, 1947, Hollandale, MS

Vocals / Chicago Soul, Soul

Ruby Andrews' tuneful late-'60s sides established her as a seductive Windy City soul singer. Andrews debuted on the Zodiac label in 1967 and scored her biggest seller, "Casanova (Your Playing Days Are Over)," the same year. Successful follow-ups on Zodiac included "You Made a Believer (Out of Me)" in 1969 and "Everybody Saw You" the next year. Andrews later cut some bluesy material for Ichiban, with the outrageous Swamp Dogg producing. *—Bill Dahl*

Black Ruby / 1972 / Zodiac ✦✦✦

Ruby Andrews' second album on Zodiac Records has many highs; it produced the minor hit "You Made a Believer Out of Me." Another cut, "Just Lovin' You," a 1968 midtempo romp with passionate wailing, has achieved cult status among European soul fans and to many makes this whole hard-to-find album worthwhile. Though Zodiac was based in Chicago, owner Ric Williams cut these tracks at Universal Studios in Memphis, TN, in an attempt to give the album Southern flavor. He didn't quite achieve his goal, as these sound like uptown cuts and not at all like what Carla Thomas was doing. Other picks include "(I Wanta Be) Whatever It Takes to Please You," "Overdose of Love," "My Love Is Comin' Down," and "Hound Dog." *—Andrew Hamilton*

Kiss This / 1991 / Ichiban ✦✦✦

Hip Shakin' Mama / Mar. 10, 1998 / Ripete ✦✦✦

● **Casanova (Your Playing Days Are Over)** / 2000 / Collectables ✦✦✦✦✦

Ruby Andrews, nee Ruby Stackhouse, reportedly had 16 singles and two albums on Zodiac Records, not to mention some smokers on ABC Records; so these dozen Zodiac sides are hardly definitive. Still, this disk is worth owning; although Ruby never got the respect she deserved, her liquid alto was very effective when matched with the right material. Ric Williams, the owner of Zodiac Records, accomplished such a matching on the infectious "Casanova (Your Playing Days Are Over)," which cracked *Billboard*'s R&B Top Ten at number nine. "Casanova 70," released three years later, failed to recapture the adulation of the original, but remakes of the Soul Brother Six's "I Guess That Don't Make Me a Loser" and Candace Love's "Uh! Uh! Boy That's a No No" are better than the originals. "Everybody Saw You," "You Can Run but You Can't Hide," and "Can You Get Away" set the table for more troubled Southern soul dramas by Andrews on ABC Records like "I Got a Bone to Pick With You" (not included here). *—Andrew Hamilton*

The Angels

f. 1961, Orange, NJ

Group / Girl Group, Pop

The Angels' 1963 number one hit, "My Boyfriend's Back," is one of the half-dozen or so archetypal girl group classics. Hand clap beats, sassy vocals, slightly campy lyrics, and an arrangement paced by wailing horns and streetcorner harmonies; it was a surefire hit and one that the group could never live up to, although they continued to record for some time.

The Angels had actually been around for a while before "My Boyfriend's Back," making the Top 20 in 1961 with the ballad "Till," and the Top 40 with a follow-up, "Cry Baby Cry." Featuring sisters Barbara and Phyllis Allbut, along with lead singer Linda Jansen, the group was at this time much more inclined toward lush doo wop, somewhat in the mold of Little Anthony & the Imperials. Jansen left near the end of 1962, to be replaced by Peggy Santiglia, who gave the trio a tougher sound. In 1963, they hooked up with the songwriting/production team of Feldman-Goldstein-Gottehrer (later to oversee the McCoys and the Strangeloves), who penned and produced material more in line with the Spectorian Wall of Sound gracing the airwaves at the peak of the girl group era.

"My Boyfriend's Back" was originally cut as a demo that music publishers hoped to shop to the Shirelles, but it turned out so well that it was released as an Angels single, after they had been freed from their prior contract to sign with Smash. Surprisingly, they would never make the Top 20 again, although they had minor hits with "Thank You and Goodnight," "I Adore Him," and "Wow Wow Wee (He's the Boy for Me)." They were decent, ebullient singers, the best of their efforts standing up well to other New York-produced groups like the Shirelles, but could never latch on to a tune as surefire as "My Boyfriend's Back" again, despite (or maybe because of) a steady supply of material from the Feldman-Goldstein-Gottehrer consortium. They worked often as session vocalists in the '60s, most notably on Lou Christie's "Lightnin' Strikes," and continued to record, unsuccessfully, throughout the '60s. *—Richie Unterberger*

My Boyfriend's Back / 1963 / Collectables ✦✦✦✦

The Angels were a typical one-hit wonder girl group with a better than typical one hit. The title track is so familiar that it scarcely commands comment, but there's a big falloff in familiarity between that and too much else that the trio ever did. This 14-song collection features their two other chart hits, "Cry Baby Cry" and "'Till," as well as a host of additional songs. "And the Angels Sing" has a pleasing mix of voices and bells, and their version of "Sentimental Journey" has a sweetly ethereal yet sultry quality about it and is highlighted by heavily trilled strings over the voices. Unfortunately, producer Gerry Granahan wasn't as creative with a lot of what else is here, and apart from the two early hits, and a relaxed rendition of "Cotton Fields," there's not a lot that stands out—"Thank You and Goodnight" does benefit from some soaring harmony singing, but that's about it. As a mid-priced collection, however, this may be all of the Angels that most interested parties require. *—Bruce Eder*

● **The Best of the Angels** / Jun. 18, 1996 / Polygram ✦✦✦✦✦

This is a 21-song anthology of cuts from the early and mid-'60s, with all the hits, including the pre-"My Boyfriend's Back" charters "'Till" and "Cry Baby Cry." Despite the spirited vocals, accomplished production, and occasional highlights like "Why Don't the Boy Leave Me Alone?," "World Without Love" (not the Lennon-McCartney song), the ska-flavored "Jamaica Joe," and the James Bond riffs of "Boy From Crosstown," nothing here lights up the room like "My Boyfriend's Back." It's certainly the best collection, though, for those who want to hear more from the group than what's available on various-artist oldies compilations. *—Richie Unterberger*

My Boyfriend's Back / Apr. 17, 1998 / PSM ✦✦✦

Polygram Special Markets' *My Boyfriend's Back* is a budget-line collection that contains a jumble of hits, lesser-known singles and album tracks. Much of the most interesting second-tier material remains on the full-length collection *The Best of the Angels*, but what is here is quite good. Not only is the title track featured, but so are three singles that didn't scale those heights ("I Adore Him," "Thank You and Goodnight," "Wow Wow Wee (He's the Boy for Me)"), plus curiosities like "Little Beatle Boy" and "He Is the Kissing Kind," both of which are quite interesting. For curious fans of "My Boyfriend's Back" that are on a tight budget, this isn't a bad choice, even if *The Best of the Angels* is a more illuminating listen than this. *—Stephen Thomas Erlewine*

Another Bad Creation

Group / New Jack Swing, Urban

Michael Bivins, a founding member of New Edition and part of the trio Bell Biv Devoe, struck commercial gold as the manager/producer of this Atlanta pre-teen quintet. Chris Sellers, Dave Shelton, Romell Chapman, and brothers Marliss and Demetrius Pugh landed a platinum release with *Coolin' at the Playground Ya' Know!* for Motown in 1991. Both "Iesha" and "Playground" were Top Ten pop and R&B singles. *—Ron Wynn*

● **Coolin' at the Playground Ya Know!** / 1991 / Motown ✦✦✦✦✦

This bit of kiddie R&B did well with its intended audience. Motown has revived itself in the 1990s through more concentrated marketing strategies and smarter, streetwise production. While they haven't been able to do as well with this group as Boyz II Men, Motown scored some points by recycling some Jackson 5 material and aiming at the audience forfeited by Bell Biv Devoe's move into adult territory. *—Ron Wynn*

It Ain't What U Wear It's How U Play It / Sep. 21, 1993 / Motown ✦✦✦

Aquarian Dream

f. 1976, **db.** 1979

Group / Disco, Funk, Soul

Aquarian Dream was an obscure but noteworthy 1970s soul/funk band that, despite its association with Norman Connors, was unable to score a hit. The band was formed in 1976, when Connors brought it to Buddah and produced its debut album, *Norman Connors Presents Aquarian Dream.* That year, Dream's lineup included lead singer Gloria Jones (not to be confused with the singer of the same name who sang the original version of "Tainted Love" in the 1960s), saxophonist Claude Bartee Jr. (who had a jazz background and had been a sideman for Grant Green, Pucho, and others), guitarist Pete Bartee, keyboardist Jacques Burvick, percussionist Mike Fowler, and drummer Jimmy Morrison (who shouldn't be confused with the Doors' lead singer). By the time Dream recorded its second album, *Fantasy*—which was also produced by Connors—some personnel changes had taken place. Jones and Fowler were gone, and newcomers included lead vocalist Sylvia Striplin, bassist Ernie Adams, percussionist Dave Worthy, and keyboardist Winston Daley. *Fantasy* found Dream moving from Buddah to Elektra; unfortunately, changing labels didn't help the band commercially. *Fantasy*'s sales were disappointing; so with its third album, *Chance to Dance* (1979), Dream severed its ties to Connors and switched to a much more disco-oriented approach. But the album didn't do any better than its predecessors, and Dream broke up in 1979. None of Dream's three album's have ever been reissued on CD. *—Alex Henderson*

● **Norman Connors Presents Aquarian Dream** / 1976 / Buddah ✦✦✦

In 1976, Norman Connors was hot in the R&B market. Having enjoyed major hits with "Valentine Love" and "You Are My Starship," the Philadelphia jazz improviser-turned-soul-star was being denounced as a sellout by jazz's hardcore while commanding a lot of respect in R&B circles. So when Connors produced Aquarian Dream's debut album, *Norman Connors Presents Aquarian Dream*, in 1976, it should have done well. However, this little-known LP was a commercial disappointment (by R&B standards) despite Connors' presence and despite the fact that the material is generally respectable. The album detours into instrumental jazz-funk on "East 6th Street," but for the most part, it favors a sleek, sophisticated soul-funk approach that could be described as Connors-meets-New Birth-meets-Earth, Wind & Fire. Dream has an impressive lead singer in Gloria Jones, whose gospel-influenced belting serves the band well on cuts that range from the exuberant yet sentimental "I'll Always Love You, T" and the mystical "Phoenix" to the gritty "Guitar Talk." Like Dream's two subsequent albums, *Norman Connors Presents Aquarian Dream* has long been out of print and it's unlikely that it will ever be reissued on CD, but it's worth obtaining if you're able to track down a copy. *—Alex Henderson*

Fantasy / 1978 / Elektra ✦✦

Aquarian Dream moved from Buddah to Elektra with their second album, *Fantasy.* With lead vocalist Gloria Jones having left the band, a new singer, Sylvia Striplin, was added. (Striplin would be gone by the third album, *Chance to Dance*). Despite changing labels and undergoing some personnel changes, however, Dream hadn't changed their sound much; this LP is fairly similar to its predecessor, *Norman Connors Presents Aquarian Dream.* Connors can take some of the credit for that—the producer knew how he thought Aquarian Dream should sound, and on sleek, Connors-produced material such as "Gentle

Thoughts," "Do You Realize," and the Earth, Wind & Fire-flavored "You're a Star," his guidance clearly serves the band well. Arguably, *Fantasy* is Aquarian Dream's finest album, but even so, it wasn't the commercial breakthrough that the band was hoping for. *—Alex Henderson*

Aquarian Dream / 1980 / Buddah ♦♦

Chance to Dance / 1980 / Elektra ♦♦

With Aquarian Dream's first two albums having bombed commercially, the band decided to shift gears and try something different on their third album, *Chance to Dance.* This LP marked the first time that an Aquarian Dream album wasn't produced by Norman Connors—Jeff Lane handled the production this time, and a new female vocalist, Connie Harvey, came on board as well. Disco was huge in 1979, so that year, Dream reasoned that the way to finally have a hit was to be as disco-minded as possible. Instead of continuing to sound like a cross between Connors, New Birth, and Earth, Wind & Fire, Dream goes for maximum disco appeal on uptempo numbers like "Big Boy," "Disco Juice," "Love Slave," and "Gettum Up and Dance." The result is an album that often sounds mechanical and insincere and isn't as strong as Dream's two previous albums—nothing on *Chance to Dance* is in a class with "You're a Star" from *Fantasy* or "I'll Always Love You, T" from *Norman Connors Presents Aquarian Dream.* However, the Chic-ish "Dirty Trick" is rather catchy, and the gritty "Why Can't We Do It Like We Used To" is an enjoyable funk item that employs guitarist Eddie Hazel of Parliament/Funkadelic fame. So while *Chance to Dance* is Dream's least impressive album, it has its moments. *—Alex Henderson*

The Aquatones

f. 1957, Valley Stream, Long Island, NY, **db.** 1962

Group / Doo Wop, R&B

The Aquatones started their musical career in 1956, the year of Elvis, as a rockabilly-slanted vocal and instrumental combo known as the Rhythm Kings. The lineup of Long Island teenagers featured Larry Vannatta on alto and tenor saxophones, Gene McCarthy on tenor sax and Dave Goddard on lead vocals and piano. 16-year-old Lynne Nixon from Malverne, Long Island, was soon added as a backup vocalist and occasional female lead. After winning a local high school talent contest, they were signed by small-time record label owner Lou Fargo as the Acquations. Because of the guys' penchant for wearing aqua-colored shirts on-stage with Lynne in a matching dress, the group soon changed their moniker to the Aquatones.

The group came to their first session with two originals: "She's the Only One for Me," a driving rocker sung by Goddard, and "You," a ballad with Nixon on lead vocals. Fargo cut two sessions to produce a master of "You," which became their biggest (and lone) hit in 1958. The record only got as high as number 21 on the national charts, but its longevity and enduring popularity (it was used in Martin Scorcese's *Mean Streets* and the TV show *I'll Fly Away*) have made it an evergreen. The group followed that sentimental ballad with several other good sides, but chart success proved elusive. The group went their separate ways (college, the draft, marriage, disillusionment) by 1962. In 1964, Fargo Records issued a full-length album on the group that quickly became a staple in cutout bins and is now a collector's item going for several hundred dollars. The Aquatones may have been one-hit wonders, but a wonderful hit it was. *—Cub Koda*

You / 199 / London ♦♦♦

"You," the Aquatones' lone 1958 chart hit, was a slow doo wop classic with a strong female lead vocal by a teenaged Lynne Nixon. This 21-track compilation of virtually everything this doo wop quartet ever recorded features all the tracks from their lone album for the small independent Fargo label. *—Cub Koda*

● **The Complete Recordings** / Oct. 3, 2000 / Preserved ♦♦♦♦♦

Sing for "You" / Relic ♦♦♦♦♦

One of the greatest female-lead doo wop singles of all time, "You" provided the New York-based Aquatones with their brief moment in the sun. This simply played and beautifully sung ballad only made it to the Top 20 nationally in 1958, but its appreciation as a white vocal group classic remains undiminished. On this collection, Relic has rounded up all the tracks from their lone album (now a solid collector's item) along with all the stray single tracks and an alternate version of the title track. Everything is aboard here, from Xeroxes of their lone hit (hoping that lightning would strike again) to uptempo offerings of all varieties, but the biggest surprise here is the rocking flip side of "You," "She's the Only One for Me," where piano man Dave Goddard rips a solid boogie while handling both the lead and bass vocal parts. The Aquatones may be a mere footnote in rock & roll history, but they remain a varied and musical one, nonetheless. Because they had the good fortune to record in New York City, some tracks appear here in true stereo. *—Cub Koda*

Tasmin Archer

b. Bradford, Yorkshire, England

Vocals, Composer / Adult Contemporary, Urban

British soul singer Tasmin Archer's silky voice on her debut album, *Great Expectations*, and hit single, "Sleeping Satellite," helped propel her toward massive media exposure in the U.K. and respectable success in the U.S. in 1993. Archer's music echoes the highly textured and polished dance-pop of Seal, yet it leans more toward straightforward pop, as evidenced by her 1994 collection of Elvis Costello covers, *Shipbuilding. Bloom* followed in 1996. *—Stephen Thomas Erlewine*

● **Great Expectations** / 1993 / Capitol ♦♦♦♦♦

Brit vocalist Tasmin Archer maps out some interesting terrain somewhere between Seal and Tracy Chapman on her debut *Great Expectations*—a layered, well-produced mix of acoustic and synthetic instrumentation overlaid with committed, soulful vocals. Lead track "Sleeping Satellite" was a hit in several parts of Europe, and it's a hypnotic, fashionably retro-psych-soul beauty. That track is backstopped by several more solid contenders, including a sombre-yet-vibrant "In Your Care," an emotionally honest "Ripped Inside," and the uncharacteristically forceful "Somebody's Daughter." While perhaps not living up to the album title, there are enough good ones (and one great one) here to make *Great Expectations* well worth investigating. *—Roch Parisien*

Shipbuilding / Mar. 8, 1994 / SBK ♦♦♦

Now here's an interesting move: British soul-pop singer Tasmin Archer followed up her debut album with this eight-track EP, which consists of live versions of three songs from her album, an alternate version of another, and four Elvis Costello covers. The result is revelatory in a couple of ways. First of all, Elvis Costello fans, upon hearing Archer's silky but muscular renditions of "Shipbuilding," "Deep Dark Truthful Mirror," "New Amsterdam," and the obscure "All Grown Up" may be surprised at how much easier it is to listen to someone other than Costello—a fine singer with a distinctly limited voice—sing them. Second of all, Archer fans will likely find that her originals pale somewhat in comparison to Costello's, both in lyrical and melodic terms. Her "When It Comes Down to It" is a sweet-natured tribute to her mother that never quite achieves melodic focus, and Archer has difficulty singing it in tune. "Steel Town" is similarly flawed. But none of the originals are bad; they're all fair to good, and the Costello covers are very powerful. Recommended. *—Rick Anderson*

Bloom / 1996 / EMI ♦♦♦♦♦

Tasmin Archer's second album (third if you count *Shipbuilding*, a lengthy EP marrying four exquisite Elvis Costello covers with three mediocre live tracks) is a huge step up from her promising but tentative solo debut, 1994's *Great Expectations.* That album suffered from the ministrations of too many producers, all of them seemingly with their own musical agendas and their eyes on the adult contemporary charts. In comparison, *Bloom* was produced by Mitchell Froom, whose sympathetic production brings out the more idiosyncratic elements of Archer's songwriting (as before, she co-wrote all of the tracks, mostly with guitarist John Hughes) and who quite wisely puts the focus squarely on Archer's richly expressive voice. The resulting tracks could be compared to Sarah McLachlan or possibly Froom's then-wife Suzanne Vega, with the single "One More Good Night Out With the Boys" clearly aimed at the same demographic that had made Sheryl Crow's "All I Wanna Do" a hit. Archer's sweetly introspective lyrics and mildly quirky melodic sense, however, keep *Bloom* from sounding like just more AAA radio fodder. *—Stewart Mason*

Premium Gold Collection / Aug. 8, 2000 / EMI ♦♦♦♦

India.Arie

b. Denver, CO

Vocals, Guitar (Acoustic) / Neo-Soul, Contemporary R&B, Urban

One of a handful of neo-classic soul artists to emerge following the late-'90s success of artists like D'Angelo and Lauren Hill, Atlanta's India.Arie stood poised at the beginning of 2001 to make a major impact. A studied songwriter and guitar player rooted in the R&B, soul, Motown, and blues of the past, but grounded in the post hip-hop urban world of today, .Arie's debut, *Acoustic Soul*, was rich with textured songs, kooks, and impressively mature lyrics considering the artist had only been writing songs for five years. Born in Denver, CO, to parents from Memphis and Detroit, music was always in .Arie's life. The family moved to Atlanta when India was 13 and after high school she began playing guitar at the encouragement of her mother. Involvement in the fertile Atlanta urban music scene led to the formation of an artist's collective called Groovement and an independent label, *EarthShare*, which released a compilation CD featuring .Arie's first songs. A second-stage slot on the 1998 Lilith Fair tour garnered major-label interest, but .Arie eventually signed with Motown after being assured of having full artistic control.

Work on *Acoustic Soul* dragged out over nearly two years, but .Arie's relentless pursuit of perfection and musical integrity yielded very pleasing results: as successful a graft of classic soul and modern hip-hop style productions yet attempted. The album's first single, "Video," received strong radio and club play early in the year, and the full-length followed in March. Just over a year later, India.Arie had completed her second record, *Voyage to India*, and it appeared in September 2002. *—John Duffy*

● **Acoustic Soul** / Mar. 27, 2001 / Motown ♦♦♦♦

As one of the most promising neo-classic soul artists yet to emerge in the past few years, India.Arie casts her lot with the best artist of her label's storied history, playing deeply introspective songs laced with glistening acoustic guitar, churchy organ, and smooth, supple beats. When she name-checks those artists no longer with us she claims as influences (Ma Rainey, Miles Davis, Karen Carpenter, Charley Patton, Stevie Ray Vaughan, Donny Hathaway, etc.) in three separate interludes, you have no doubt she is looking back as well as forward, even going so far as to invoke Sam Cooke's "A Change Is Gonna Come." But *Acoustic Soul* is at its best when the arrangements are deliberately modern. And despite the uniqueness of being a guitar-based R&B album, it is .Arie's thick, sandy voice that shares star billing with her exceptional lyrics. Betraying youthful vulnerability while at the same time projecting strength, confidence, and uncanny insight for a 25-year-old singer/songwriter, .Arie wraps herself effortlessly around the deep, funky sensuality of "Brown Skin," and stands tall in defiance of pop-fashion expectations on the irresistibly catchy "Video." The uplifting "Faith, Courage, Wisdom" rides along on a euphoric chorus, and the plainly autobiographical "Back to the Middle" recounts an emotional and spiritual coming of age. Without the many concrete references to the great R&B music of the past, *Acoustic Soul* would be a purely modern gem, but as .Arie is determined to pay her debts up front, it is much more, and that is admirable. *—John Duffy*

Voyage to India / Sep. 24, 2002 / Universal ♦♦♦♦

Despite an excellent debut, India.Arie still had much to prove with her second record. Several of her neo-soul compatriots, from D'Angelo to Erykah Badu to Macy Gray, had faltered with sophomore albums, and it appeared she may have already said everything she had to say on *Acoustic Soul.* That anticipation, and trepidation, is exactly what makes

Voyage to India such a beautiful surprise; it's a record that easily equals her debut, boasting better vocal performances but also better songwriting and accompanying production. As on her debut, there is a marked balance of organic and artificial: An acoustic guitar paces many tracks, though the edges are shorn off for a digital feel; the beats are often sampled, but there are still plenty of handclaps and fingersnaps; and the arrangements are simple yet obviously very polished. The improvement in her songwriting is most obvious from the first three tracks (after the short intro). The themes driving "Little Things" (keeping it simple), "Talk to Her" (the importance of honesty, warmth, and communication in relationships), and "Slow Down" (taking life one day at a time) certainly have been covered already, many times even, but India.Arie writes with a fresh perspective that makes it sound as though she's the first to broach the topic. And, finally, her delivery is the best of any neo-soul vocalist, barring only the incomparable Jill Scott, alternately earnest and playful and sexy and questing. It all adds up to one of the most glowing comebacks of the year (if she ever left), an important record whose stamp—the Motown logo—isn't the only thing it has in similarity with a classic LP by Marvin Gaye or Stevie Wonder. *—John Bush*

Jo Armstead

b. Oct. 8, 1944, Yazoo City, MS
Vocals, Songwriter / R&B, Soul
Singer/songwriter Jo Armstead's biggest hit was "Stone Cold Lover." She also co-wrote Ray Charles' number one R&B classic "Let's Get Stoned" with Ashford and Simpson, Ruby Andrews' Top Ten R&B smash "Casanova (Your Playing Days Are Over)," and Garland Green's gold single "Jealous Kind of Fella." Born Josephine Armstead on October 8, 1944, in Yazoo City, MS, she joined the Ike & Tina Turner Revue in 1961 singing background vocals as one of the Ikettes who had a 1962 number three R&B hit with "I'm Blue (The Gong-Gong Song)" on Atco Records. Relocating to New York City, she began collaborating with Nick Ashford and Valerie Simpson who were staff writers for the publishing branch of Scepter/Wand Records.

Other Armstead/Ashford/Simpson songs were "Too Hot to Hold," "The Shoe Won't Fit," and "The Real Thing" by Betty Everett on VeeJay; the latter was a 1965 number 20 R&B hit by Tina Britt on Eastern.

In 1967, Armstead moved to Chicago from New York and formed Giant Productions with her new husband, Mel Collins. The label, which issued releases on the Giant, Globe, and Gamma imprints, had offices at 56th and Maryland, then 81st and Cottage Grove. The artist roster included Ruby Andrews, Garland Green, Fenton Robinson, Little Jimmy Scott, Shirley Wahls, Smokey Smothers, and Armstead herself, recording as Joshie Jo Armstead or Jo Armstead. Their first hit, Carl Carlton's "Drop by My Place," was recorded in Detroit with arranger Mike Terry. Hollandale, MS, native Ruby Andrews' "Casanova (Your Playing Days Are Over)," released on Ric Williams' Zodiac label, hit number nine R&B in the summer of 1967. Armstead wrote, produced, and recorded the Terry-arranged "Stone Cold Lover," which went to number 28 R&B in spring 1968. Giant's sole million-selling single was Garland Green's "Jealous Kind of Fella," which was leased to MCA's Uni label and peaked at number five R&B on *Billboard*'s charts in summer 1969. By 1970, Giant was no longer active. Armstead returned to New York, but was back in Chicago by the late '80s, managing boxer Alonzo Ratliff.

Her other singles were "I've Been Turned On," "There's Not Too Many More," "I'm Gonna Show You" b/w "I've Been Turned On" or "Never Had It Like This," "This and That" b/w "No Better for Ya," and "Stumblin' Blocks, Steppin' Stones (What Took Me So Long)" as Joshie Jo Armstead and "Ride out the Storm," both on Stax subsidiary Gospel Truth. *—Ed Hogan*

● **Stone Good Lover** / Nov. 5, 1996 / Collectables ✦✦✦✦
A nice collection of Armstead's late-'60s and early-'70s hits. Highlights include "I've Been Turned On," "I Feel an Urge Coming On," "I'm Gonna Show You (How a Man Is Supposed to Be Treated)," and the title track. Armstead's early training with Ike & Tina Turner shines brightly on these tracks, and as a woman writing much of her own material, this distanced her from other R&B divas of the time. A hidden treasure. *—Cub Koda*

Vanessa Bell Armstrong

b. Oct. 2, 1953, Detroit, MI
Vocals / Contemporary Gospel, Urban
With a style reminiscent of Aretha Franklin, soulful Vanessa Bell Armstrong has been belting out R&B-flavored contemporary gospel since the '80s. A native of Detroit and mother of five, she got her start working with Dr. Mattie Moss Clark. She has since gone on to work in both gospel and secular music. She did the theme song for the television series *Amen*, where her links to Rev. Al Green (and ultimately to Rev. Claude Jeter) were evident. She's recorded urban contemporary ballads and lyrically neutral material for Jive, and done gospel for Muscle Shoals Sound Gospel and Onyx, subsidiaries of Malaco. Albums include the slickly produced *Something on the Inside* (1993) and *The Secret Is Out* (1995). Three years later, she released her first live album, *Desire of My Heart: Live*; a best-of collection appeared in 1999. *—Bil Carpenter and Ron Wynn*

Peace Be Still / 1984 / Benson ✦✦✦✦✦

Vanessa Bell Armstrong / 1987 / Jive/Novus ✦✦✦

Greatest Hits / 1990 / Muscle Shoals ✦✦✦✦

Wonderful One / 1990 / Jive/Novus ✦✦✦
While the songs range from spectacular to disapponting, Vanessa Bell Armstrong's singing is uniformly excellent on this '90 collection of crossover gospel and light, urban contemporary pop and R&B. Armstrong's declarative, assertive delivery and triumphant manner make the good songs great and the one or two great ones unforgettable. *—Ron Wynn*

Chosen / Jul. 1, 1991 / Onyx ✦✦✦

Something on the Inside / 1993 / Jive/Novus ✦✦✦

The Secret Is Out / 1995 / Verity ✦✦✦
On *The Secret Is Out*, Vanessa Bell Armstrong turns in one of her most straightforward gospel recordings, with all of the material being written and produced by John P. Kee, whose choir provides musical support. *—Stephen Thomas Erlewine*

Desire of My Heart: Live in Detroit / Apr. 28, 1998 / Verity ✦✦✦✦
Recorded live in Detroit, *Desire of My Heart: Live in Detroit* is an excellent record that captures the passion and soul at the heart of Armstrong's music. Supported by Pastor Marvin Winans and the Perfecting Praise Choir, as well as several family members, she runs through many of her best-known and popular songs. Often these versions eclipse the studio versions in terms of passion, making the record a must for Armstrong fans. *—Stephen Thomas Erlewine*

● **The Best of Vanessa Bell Armstrong** / Jun. 29, 1999 / Verity ✦✦✦✦
Verity's *The Best of Vanessa Bell Armstrong* collects 14 highlights from the recordings she made for Zomba Records, after she left Benson/Onyx. Musically, these songs are very close to urban contemporary, which means this is hardly traditional gospel. That, of course, won't matter to Armstrong's fans, since they already know that she's one of the leading lights of contemporary gospel, and this collection shows why. At times, the material doesn't quite match the standards of her earlier records, but the collection is still a good portrait of Armstrong at the peak of her powers and popularity, featuring such CCM classics as "Pressing On," "You Bring Out the Best in Me," "You Can't Take My Faith Away," "Father I Stretch," "Good News Blues," and "The Secret Is Out." *—Stephen Thomas Erlewine*

Brand New Day / Nov. 6, 2001 / Tommy Boy ✦✦✦
Contemporary gospel music veteran Vanessa Bell Armstrong sports a new musical attitude on her debut project for the Tommy Boy Gospel label, entitled *A Brand New Day*. Under the production guidance of brother duo Deitrick and Gerald Haddon, the project finds Armstrong involving herself in an area she has always shunned, songwriting, having shared the writing credits on four songs. The Haddon brothers give Armstrong a vibrant, more youthful feel through their production, which can be readily noticed through the rock-flavored, guitar-dominated, Tina Turner-sounding track "He's Real" and the hip-hop-juiced "Make a Way." The calypso-dominated "There's No Failure in God" features Armstrong performing a duet with her daughter, Melody Armstrong. Overall, this recording ushers in a brand new day for a reborn Vanessa Bell Armstrong. *—Tim A. Smith*

Ginny Arnell

Vocals / Girl Group
Ginny Arnell isn't exactly a household name among girl group acts in the manner of, say, Joanie Sommers or Little Peggy March, but she left her mark on the field with one song, "I Wish I Knew What Dress to Wear," which remains a classic of the genre for poignancy. Arnell's credits were actually fairly substantial—a one-time partner of Gene Pitney in a duo called Jamie & Jane, who recorded for American Decca around 1959—she resurfaced as a solo act on MGM Records in late 1963 with a pathetically self-deprecating single called "Dumb Head," co-written by David Hess and Camille Monte, which reached number 50 nationally.

In early 1964, she re-emerged with "I Wish I Knew What Dress to Wear," written by Gloria Shayne and Noel Regney under the aegis of producers Jim Vienneau and Danny Davis. It only reached number 130 on the charts in April of that year, but left a major impression on fans of the genre. Arnell's singing projected extraordinary depth of feeling, similar to Lesley Gore, and turned the seemingly superficial song into a moving mini-drama. Despite the lackluster chart placement of her two singles, the label had enough confidence in Arnell to release a complete LP on her, *Meet Ginny Arnell*, which led off with "I Wish I Knew What Dress to Wear" and included the earlier single. That was Arnell's last known major contribution as a recording artist. *—Bruce Eder*

● **Meet Ginny Arnell** / 1964 / MGM ✦✦✦✦

P.P. Arnold

b. 1946, Los Angeles, CA
Vocals / Uptown Soul, Soul
A soul vocalist who came from a family of gospel singers, Pat (P.P.) Arnold began singing as a four-year-old. She got her start backing Bobby Day before being invited to join the Ikettes, backing Ike & Tina Turner. Arnold toured with them in the '60s, including one stint with the Rolling Stones. Mick Jagger persuaded her to remain in London, and she later recorded for the Immediate label (then run by the Stones' manager Andrew Loog Oldham). Loog Oldham, Jagger, and Mike Hurst produced Arnold's debut LP, *The First Lady of Immediate*, in 1967, which included the single "The First Cut Is the Deepest," which was written by Cat Stevens and later popularized by Rod Stewart.

Arnold also had moderate success with the singles "The Time Has Come," "(If You Think) You're Groovy," and "Angel of the Morning" in the late '60s, though they were hits in England and Europe rather than America. Arnold was part of the cast for the play *Catch My Soul* in 1969, and subsequently acted in the television shows *Fame* and *Knots Landing*, plus Andrew Lloyd Webber's *Starlight Express*. Arnold re-entered the music world in the mid-'80s. She sang lead on a Boy George song for the film *Electric Dreams* in 1984 while on 10 Records. She worked with Dexter Wansel and Loose Ends on the single "A Little Pain," which she recorded as Pat Arnold. She then had another English hit with the single "Burn It Up" on the Rhythm King label. The Beatmasters later produced her song "Dynamite." *—Ron Wynn*

P.P. Arnold Collection / May 21, 1991 / Columbia ✦✦✦✦✦
This transplanted American R&B singer hits it big with achingly soulful ballads. A '60s curio and more, especially "The First Cut Is the Deepest." *—Bruce Eder*

● **The First Cut** / May 1998 / Castle ✦✦✦✦✦
Shortly after arriving in London, it wasn't long until the hip, young, beautiful singer Pat Arnold (who'd just quit the Ikettes) was approached by entrepreneur Loog Oldham to

record for his fledgling Immediate label. Britain—its musical artists in particular—had been won over by the soulful black sounds of America. The uptempo beat of Motown and Atlantic had increasingly been filling dancefloors, and even the Top 30; it was time for the one-time Tina Turner backup artist to stand up on her own. A wise move! Arnold's signing in late 1967 was perfect timing. *The First Cut* (originally released in 1998, now remastered and featuring two bonus tracks) pulls all of Arnold's Immediate material neatly together in one package—strangely, other than "The First Cut Is the Deepest" (1967) and "Angel of the Morning" (1968), few of these recordings dented the British Top 30. However, in retrospect, the perfect combination of husky-voiced American soul, U.K. mod beat, Bacharach-flavored balladry, and Oldham's obsession with the bombastic production techniques of his hero Phil Spector is a pleasure to hear and a wonderful hybrid. This material has a unique sound and feeling, which draws it apart from the "want to be" club soul acts that graced the nation throughout the period. From the ice-cold version of "The First Cut Is the Deepest" to the incredible Small Faces collaboration "(If You Think You're) Groovy," these 28 cuts of mid- to late-'60s cross-pollination are a wonderful example of what happened when America and England met. *—Jon "Mojo" Mills*

Arrested Development

f. 1988, Atlanta, GA, **db.** 1996

Group / Alternative Rap, Urban, Hip-Hop, Political Rap

One of the major success stories of 1992, Arrested Development was a progressive rap collective fusing soul, blues, hip-hop, and Sly and the Family Stone-influenced funk with political, socially conscious lyrics. The group was founded in the late '80s by rapper Speech and DJ Headliner, who decided to make the transition to a more positive, Afrocentric viewpoint after hearing Public Enemy. Arrested Development's debut album took its title from the amount of time it took the group to secure a record contract; *3 Years, 5 Months & 2 Days in the Life Of...* produced the hit single "Tennessee," a strongly spiritual track that hit the Top Ten and sparked the album to sell over four million copies. Its two follow-ups, "People Everyday" (a rewrite of Sly's "Everyday People") and "Mr. Wendal" did likewise. Accolades poured in; Arrested Development won Grammys for Best Rap Album and Best New Artist, and were named *Rolling Stone's* Band of the Year. The group returned one year later with *Zingalamaduni*, which some reviews hailed as a major work, though overall response was more ambivalent. In 1996, contrary to Speech's earlier assertion that the group would be around for ten or 12 years, Arrested Development officially broke up. Speech went solo, though his debut album failed to make an impact. *—Steve Huey*

● **3 Years, 5 Months & 2 Days in the Life Of...** / Mar. 24, 1992 / Chrysalis ✦✦✦✦✦

Arrested Development delivers an extremely witty and introspective work. Their speech in the arena of rap includes lyrical messages of hope, love, rain, politics, nature, religion, and evolution. The group's five members demonstrate their creative talents and ability to grab hold of and retain the listener. The record is strong and assertive throughout, with little space for weak spots, and is the perfect kind of release to reminisce back to the early 1990s. An album of spontaneity and energy, Arrested Development leaves their mark as an influential rap/hip-hop act during the 1990s college scene and beyond. *—Shawn M. Haney*

Unplugged / Mar. 1993 / Chrysalis ✦✦

Basically a live re-recording of *3 Years, 5 Months & 2 Days in the Life Of...* (minus their breakthrough hit, "Tennessee"), *Unplugged* breaks no new ground for Arrested Development. Eight of the 11 songs on the album are from their debut, and the three new tracks are slight. The album is filled out with remixes of seven tracks, which are the instrumental tracks with the vocals turned down (they are still slightly audible). Despite the fact that it doesn't offer anything not on *3 Years*, the album is an enjoyable listen. *—Stephen Thomas Erlewine*

Zingalamaduni / Jun. 14, 1994 / Chrysalis ✦✦✦

Arrested Development's proper follow-up to their smash debut doesn't stray too far from the rootsy Southern hip-hop that made *3 Years* a hit, but it doesn't ignite as frequently as its predecessor. While its best tracks, like "Mister Landlord" and "Prasin'," are the equal of "Mr. Wendal" or "People Everyday," there is no statement of purpose on the level of "Tennessee." The album is too unfocused to be as impressive as the debut, yet *Zingalamaduni* shows that the group is more than a one-hit wonder. *—Stephen Thomas Erlewine*

The Best of Arrested Development / Jun. 2, 1998 / EMI-Capitol Special Markets ✦✦✦✦

The Best of Arrested Development is part of EMI-Capitol Special Markets' excellent *Ten Best Series*, a budget-line series that features an artist's ten biggest hits in their original recorded versions. All of the group's seven charting R&B hits—"Tennessee," "People Everyday," "Revolution," "Mr. Wendal," "Natural," "Ease My Mind," and "United Front"—along with three album tracks, like "Fishin' 4 Religion" and "Give a Man a Fish" are here. Although the disc is not sequenced in chronological order, the very fact that all these hits are on one disc at such an affordable price makes *The Best of Arrested Development* a terrific choice for budget-minded casual fans. *—Stephen Thomas Erlewine*

Greatest Hits / Jul. 31, 2001 / EMI ✦✦✦✦

Released only in England/Europe, *Greatest Hits* rounds up pretty much anything that most Arrested Development fans could want from the band—which means that it leans pretty heavily on the first album, containing such hits as "Mr. Wendal" and "Tennessee," plus album cuts like "Fishin' 4 Religion" and the non-LP single "Revolution." There are also two unplugged cuts, which are OK, but the main problem with the collection is that the original version—or even the original single version—of "People Everyday" is not here, only the "Metamorphosis Radio Edit." This isn't enough to sink the collection, but it may be enough for some listeners to wait for a definitive anthology that contains all the original versions of the big hits. *—Stephen Thomas Erlewine*

● **Classic Masters** / Jan. 29, 2002 / Capitol ✦✦✦✦✦

For a brief, shining moment at the dawn of the '90s, it seemed that Arrested Development's debut *3 Years, 5 Months & 2 Days in the Life Of...* would have as lasting an impact as Nirvana's *Nevermind*, which also ruled the charts in 1992. As it turns out, *Nevermind* ushered in years of grunge, indie rock, and, sadly, terrible hard rock, but *3 Years* wound up as the last big gasp of alt-rap before it was subsumed by gangsta after *The Chronic*. As such, Arrested Development's music has dated slightly, sounding like its time rather than transcending it, as this edition of *Classic Masters* illustrates. As a collection, it's quite good, containing not just every one of the group's hits and singles, but a B-side ("Southern Fried Funk"), a few album tracks, and Speech's 1995 solo single, "Like Marvin Said (What's Goin' On)." Several singles stand the test of time and emerge as classics, particularly "Tennessee," while several sound a little too closely tied to their time, but overall this is an excellent overview of the last great Daisy-Age era alt-rap crew. *3 Years* remains definitive, but if you want a sampler, containing bits of *Zingalamaduni* plus *Revolution*, this is the one to get. *—Stephen Thomas Erlewine*

The Artistics

f. 1958, Chicago, IL, **db.** 1973

Group / Chicago Soul, Northern Soul, Soul

A Chicago R&B and soul group discovered by Major Lance, the Artistics were formed in 1958 at Marshall High School. They sang at the 1960 Democratic Convention and backed Lance before recording for OKeh in 1963. Original lead vocalist Robert Dobyne joined founding members Aaron Floyd, Curt Thomas, Laurence Johnson, and Jesse Bolian in 1963. Their early recordings for OKeh included the singles "Get My Hands on Some Lovin' " and "This Heart of Mine" in 1964 and 1965. Former El Dorado Marvin Smith replaced Dobyne in 1964. The Artistics joined Brunswick in 1966, and scored their biggest hit with "I'm Gonna Miss You," which was also the title of their debut album for the label. They had three more moderate hits for Brunswick in the late '60s and early '70s. Smith left in 1967, though he continued singing on studio recordings. Tommy Green and Fred Pettis also served as lead vocalists until the group disbanded in 1973. *—Ron Wynn*

Get My Hands on Some Lovin' / 1966 / OKeh ✦✦✦✦

This debut by Chicago's Artistics is one of their best. Marvin Smith, Jesse Bolian, Larry Johnson, and Aaron Floyd's harmonies sparkled over the rudimentary rhythm tracks punctuated by stabbing horns. The songs are endearing; "Patty Cake" has cute lyrics ("Patty cake, patty cake baker man/Bake me a sweetie pie/I don't care what nobody say, I'm gonna love her anyway"). They outdo Marvin Gaye on one of the Master's early releases, "Got to Get My Hands on Some Lovin'." The guys' most successful OKeh release, Barrett Strong's "This Heart of Mine," has a similar feel to the Spinners' "I'll Always Love You." There's a charm associated with this release that is absent on their later stuff on Brunswick. *—Andrew Hamilton*

I'm Gonna Miss You / 1967 / Brunswick ✦✦✦

Carl Davis, probably due to an increase in funds, added strings to the mix on the Artistics' Brunswick debut. While the violin section embellished their biggest hit, "I'm Gonna Miss You," and made it better, the results on other sides were less satisfying. The horns that so aptly complemented the songs on their OKeh album are missing in action. I would have preferred them on "Girl I Need You" over the syrupy, unnecessary strings; ditto for the falsetto-led "Glad I Met You." One of the best songs, the Billy Butler-written "Hope We Have," chugs along nicely without the excess baggage. Sonny Sanders, a former member of Motown's first male vocal group, the Satintones, did a fine job with the rhythm arrangements; the strings, however, weakened this production. *—Andrew Hamilton*

The Articulate Artistics / 1968 / Brunswick ✦✦✦

The annoying strings on *I'm Gonna Miss You* aren't around to clutter this time. A rhythm section dominates the Artistics' second Brunswick album; horns are sparingly used for seasoning. Chi-Lite lead singer and prolific writer Eugene Record contributes three songs from his stash. "Hard to Carry On," a Floyd Smith/Gerald Sims composition, dented the R&B charts, and "You Left Me" should have been a hit. Lead singer Marvin Smith's voice shifts from falsetto to tenor like a sticky transmission. "Trouble, Heartaches, and Pain" features some plucky guitar playing and a fine torch lead by Marvin. Generally, the Artistics' voices dwarf the average material. *—Andrew Hamilton*

I Want You to Make Life / 1969 / Brunswick ✦✦✦

What Happened / 1969 / Brunswick ✦✦✦✦

Six slammin' Artistics sides and four standards "artistically" sung make for some enjoyable listening. The Chi-Lites' "Price of Love" is sung in Marvin's natural voice, distinguishing it from the original falsetto version. Gary Jackson's "Yesterday's Girl" remains one of their more enduring recordings. The scorching "What Happened to the Love We Had" showcases Marvin Smith's unique, mercurial tenor. His reading of "I Wish You Love" rivals the late Eddie Kendricks' rendition from *The Temptations in a Mellow Mood*. A basement-deep bass accents a soulful version of "With These Hands." *—Andrew Hamilton*

Look Out / 1973 / Brunswick ✦✦

Look Out is the hardest LP by the Artistics to find. It was recorded on the rush to take advantage of two recent releases. "Make My Life Over," which ranks with the Chicagoans' finest efforts, and "It's Those Little Things That Count" led by an airy falsetto giving it a Philly sound. If the label didn't say the Artistics, I wouldn't be able to guess their identity. The same can be said for "Make My Life Over," and several other selections. Brunswick included some previously released tracks, including "I'm Gonna Miss You," their most popular recording which is led by Marvin Smith, and "Girl I Need You," featuring Smith's replacement, Tommy Green. "Being in Love," a floating midtempo number was first recorded by the Chi-Lites. If this is the first Artistic album you ever buy, and you're not familiar with their work, this enjoyable set will be confusing because of the plethora of lead singers from different eras. *—Andrew Hamilton*

- **The Best of the Artistics** / 1995 / Brunswick ✦✦✦✦
Discovered by Major Lance, the Artistics recorded many memorable sides. Rhythm tracks and sometimes strings comprised most of the instrumentation; horns were rarely used. "I'm Gonna Miss You" scored the biggest for the Chicago natives. This best-of features 15 sides of Chicago magic, the cream of their Brunswick output, including "Girl I Need You," "You Left Me," "Yesterday's Girl," and "I Want You to Make My Life Over." —*Andrew Hamilton*

I'm Gonna Miss You/The Articulate Artistics / Jun. 8, 2000 / Edsel ✦✦✦✦✦

Ashanti (Ashanti S. Douglas)

b. Glen Cove, NY

Vocals / Urban, Contemporary R&B

With hitmaker Irv Gotti at the helm, Ashanti blasted into the urban music scene in 2002, topping the charts with multiple singles at once. She quickly became a sensation, gracing the covers of magazines and dominating urban radio. Ashanti built her reputation with duets, where she would complement an already popular rapper—Ja Rule ("Always on Time"), Fat Joe ("What's Luv?"), the Notorious B.I.G. ("Unfoolish")—contrasting the tough-guy male perspective with her own. It didn't take the young vocalist long to make a name for herself though: Her debut album topped the *Billboard* album chart just as her debut solo single, the album's title track, was topping the Hot 100 chart. Her presence was inescapable.

Ashanti's overnight jump to superstardom followed that of Ja Rule, a similar urban music sensation helmed by Gotti. The New York producer took notice of Ashanti initially because of her beauty, dancing, and acting. She trained as a dancer at the Bernice Johnson Cultural Arts Center, learning a number of dance styles. She danced most notably in Disney's *Polly*, which starred Phylicia Rashad, and also appeared in a number of big-name music videos, in addition to other dance work. As an actress, she made a name for herself with roles in Spike Lee's *Malcolm X* and *Who's da Man* before that. The multi-talented vocalist was causing quite a stir, and Gotti did what he could to bring her into his Murder Inc fold. After showcasing her swooning voice on Big Pun's "How We Roll" and the *Fast and Furious* soundtrack—both in 2001—Gotti put Ashanti to work on her debut album, which he produced.

Success came quickly. A duet with Ja Rule, "Always on Time," hit number one on Billboard's Hot 100 chart in early 2002 just as a duet with Fat Joe, "What's Luv?," was creeping toward the same number one position. These two airplay-heavy singles, of course, set the stage perfectly for Ashanti's self-titled debut release. The album's lead single, "Foolish," raced up the Hot 100 chart, entering the Top Ten in March alongside "Always on Time" and "What's Luv?," giving her three Top Ten songs in the same week, including the number one and two positions; a quite spectacular feat. And then Ashanti's album debuted at number one on the album chart, selling an astounding 500,000-plus copies in its first week. With all this chart-topping, Ashanti set some sales records and her success continued. Gotti readied a remix of "Foolish," titled "Unfoolish," that featured the Notorious B.I.G. and again overtook urban radio, where no artist was more omnipresent throughout 2002 than Ashanti. —*Jason Birchmeier*

- **Ashanti** / Apr. 2, 2002 / Universal ✦✦✦
Young, pretty, sexy, stylish, and hip, Ashanti is everything a modern, post-hip-hop soul crooner should be. She looks the part, trucks with hitmakers—at the time her eponymous debut was released, she was featured on a hit single by Fat Joe—and even approximates Alicia Keys' visuals on the back cover. She can sing, but she's not showy; she never hyperventilates, she croons. Her first album sounds modern, with fairly fresh beats and lightly insistent hooks, and is just naughty enough to warrant a parental advisory sticker (though if you're just listening to this record, it's nigh on impossible to figure out where the objectionable lines are). So why doesn't *Ashanti* play as greater than the sum of its parts? Largely because it lacks distinctive material, in either terms of the actual songs or the production—and when that's combined with a singer who is good, yet not distinctive herself, the entire production sounds as if its treading water or providing nifty aural wallpaper. It's not bad by any means, and it has its moments, but at 17 tracks, including skits, it all becomes a blur. A pleasing blur, one that shows promise, but a blur all the same. —*Stephen Thomas Erlewine*

Ashford & Simpson

f. 1964

Group / Soul, Smooth Soul, Quiet Storm, Disco, Urban

Nickolas Ashford (b. May 4, 1942, Fairfield, SC) and Valerie Simpson (b. Aug 26, 1946, New York City) have two careers, as songwriters and as performers, with the former seemingly more important than the latter until the mid-'80s. The two met in 1964 and scored their first songwriting hit in 1966 with Ray Charles' recording of their "Let's Go Get Stoned." After a period at Scepter Records, they moved to Motown, where they wrote hits for the duo of Marvin Gaye and Tammi Terrell ("Ain't Nothing Like the Real Thing," "You're All I Need to Get By"). When Diana Ross left the Supremes for a solo career, Ashford & Simpson wrote "Reach Out and Touch Somebody's Hand" for her.

Their own performing career was launched in 1973 with *Keep It Comin'* on Motown and *Gimme Something Real* on Warner Bros. Their first success came in 1977 with the gold-selling *Send It*, which contained the Top Ten R&B hit "Don't Cost You Nothing." *Is It Still Good to Ya*, a second gold album, contained the number two R&B hit "It Seems to Hang On" in 1978. *Stay Free*, their third straight gold album, contained "Found a Cure," another R&B smash that also made the Top 40 on the pop chart. *A Musical Affair*, in 1980, featured the hit "Love Don't Make It Right," but was not as successful as previous efforts.

Meanwhile, Ashford & Simpson continued to work with other artists, scoring successes with Ross, Chaka Khan ("I'm Every Woman"), and Gladys Knight. Their own career saw a resurgence in 1984 with *Solid*, which went gold and produced the R&B number one "Solid" (number 12 on the pop charts), "Outta the World," and "Babies." During the late '80s and '90s, Ashford & Simpson continued to tour and record sporadically. —*William Ruhlmann*

Gimme Something Real / Oct. 1973 / Warner Bros. ✦✦
This album launched the soul duo Ashford & Simpson on a run of successful Warner Bros. albums. The title track and several other singles utilized the patented formula of gospel-tinged vocals; slick, polished backing; and alternately sentimental or earnest lyrics. —*Ron Wynn*

Keep It Comin' / 1973 / Motown ✦✦✦

I Wanna Be Selfish / Jul. 1974 / Warner Bros. ✦✦✦
Ashford & Simpson were in the midst of their hit string of Warner Bros. albums when they released this. They included bits and pieces of gospel-tinged R&B, disco, funk, and sophisticated pop, linking everything through their own energetic vocals and harmonies, plus skillful production and a good group of songs. —*Ron Wynn*

Come as You Are / Apr. 1976 / Warner Bros. ✦✦✦✦✦
One of Ashford & Simpson's best Warner Bros. albums, especially from a production standpoint. The mix between uptempo and slow, love songs and dance tunes was perfect, and their interaction had been honed to the point where each anticipated the other. Simpson's soaring vocals and Ashford's less-impressive but still strong support, plus their outstanding harmonizing, was at its peak. —*Ron Wynn*

So So Satisfied / Jan. 1977 / Warner Bros. ✦✦✦
The Ashford & Simpson sound has always been lush, sentimental, and soulful, yet subdued. That's the case on this 1977 release. The title cut was a moderate hit, and, as always, the sweeping strings, lyrics, and production were first-rate. Ashford & Simpson albums can get extremely sappy, and at times this one did as well. But they're also usually superbly performed and constructed, and this was no exception. —*Ron Wynn*

Send It / Sep. 1977 / Warner Bros. ✦✦✦✦
Send It is not only one of Ashford & Simpson's finest releases, it is also the album that made them major stars as vocalists. As songwriters and producers, the Nick Ashford/Valerie Simpson team had been providing major hits since the '60s—Gladys Knight & the Pips, Marvin Gaye (with Tammi Terrell), and Diana Ross are among the R&B/pop artists who had recorded their songs. But it wasn't until 1977's *Send It* that Ashford & Simpson's singing became as famous as their songwriting and producing. *Send It* was the first Ashford & Simpson album that went gold in the U.S., where over 500,000 copies were sold—and it isn't hard to see why it did so well. From the sentimental title song to more uptempo offerings like "By Way of Love's Express," "Top of the Stairs," and the funky "Don't Cost You Nothing" (a major hit), this album is excellent. *Send It* also includes the dance-oriented instrumental "Bourgie Bourgie," which became a vocal number when, in 1980, lyrics were added for a remake by Gladys Knight & the Pips. "Bourgie Bourgie" was a bigger hit for that group, although Ashford & Simpson's original version enjoyed a fair amount of exposure in dance clubs. Sleek, polished, and sophisticated, but not without grit, *Send It* is the essence of '70s Northern soul. If you only have a few Ashford & Simpson releases in your collection, the essential *Send It* should be one of them. —*Alex Henderson*

Is It Still Good to Ya / Aug. 1978 / Warner Bros. ✦✦✦✦✦
Having written many popular numbers for various artists over the years, the dynamic duo retain that same tradition for this project. The first release from this album was the midtempo "It Seems to Hang On." While each verse is conveyed in a soft texture, the chorus jumps with excitement and intrigue, as does the vamp. Prior to this album, the husband-and-wife team had just one prior R&B Top Ten hit ("Don't Cost You Nothing," number ten in 1978).This song had a stronger impact; it stayed on the charts for 17 weeks. But more importantly, it held the number two position on the *Billboard* R&B charts for five consecutive weeks. The title track was the follow-up single. With its mesmerizing intonation, Ashford & Simpson intensely deliver this classic R&B ballad with all the right ingredients. In spite of the beauty of the song, it only peaked at number 12 on the charts in as many weeks. The final release was "Flashback." Not nearly as inviting as its predecessors, this disco number peaked at number 70 after five weeks on the charts. Other notables are "Ain't It a Shame," "Get Up and Do Something," and "As Long As It Holds You." —*Craig Lytle*

Stay Free / Aug. 1979 / Warner Bros. ✦✦✦
The title track was spectacular, and the rest of the album was expertly produced, performed, and arranged. Ashford & Simpson dominated the '70s as few couples ever have in any era; they were the textbook blend of classic R&B energy and urban contemporary class and sophistication. Their best material was neither so generic that it lacked soul, nor so soulful that it couldn't attract a crossover audience. —*Ron Wynn*

A Musical Affair / Aug. 1980 / Warner Bros. ✦✦✦
The year 1980 was fairly eventful for Nick Ashford and Valerie Simpson. In addition to writing and producing Gladys Knight & the Pips' excellent *About Love*, the duo had a major hit of their own with the snappy "Love Don't Make It Right." Nonetheless, 1980's *A Musical Affair* didn't go down in history as one of Ashford & Simpson's essential albums. This vinyl LP isn't bad; most of the tracks are decent, and a few are excellent, most notably "Love Don't Make It Right," the melancholy "Get out Your Hankerchief," and the sentimental ballad "Happy Endings." But overall, *A Musical Affair* isn't exceptional—likable and pleasant, but not exceptional. After five-star treasures like 1977's *Send It*, 1978's *Is It Still Good to Ya*, and 1979's *Stay Free*, one greeted this record with high expectations; however, *A Musical Affair* falls short of the consistent excellence that had characterized some of their best late-'70s albums. Some might even go so far as to say that in 1980, Ashford & Simpson gave their best songs to Gladys Knight & the Pips, whose *About Love* is nothing to be ashamed of. Both commercially and creatively, that LP was the group's most successful album since 1974's *I Feel a Song*. In fact, the single ("Landlord") made it to number three on *Billboard*'s R&B singles chart. So Ashford & Simpson certainly did right by Gladys Knight & the Pips in 1980, even though their own 1980

album falls short of essential. *A Musical Affair* is only recommended to Ashford & Simpson's hardcore fans. *—Alex Henderson*

Performance / Sep. 1981 / Warner Bros. ✦✦✦

Street Opera / May 1982 / Capitol ✦✦

Ashford & Simpson came up with an intriguing tack for this early-'80s session: Take a contemporary situation and use a quasi-operatic format to illuminate it. The only problem came in the execution; the songs weren't up to the concept, although most weren't terrible. They were just good, faceless urban contemporary dance and love tunes, hardly the kind of transcendent things needed to make this worthy of operatic pretensions. *—Ron Wynn*

High-Rise / Aug. 1983 / Capitol ✦✦

Ashford & Simpson had come close to exhausting their creative quotient by the mid-'80s. Simpson still sang effectively, and Ashford harmonized and contrasted her nicely, but they'd stated and restated both their own situations and any variations on it four albums before. As a result, the feeling that you've heard it all once too often permeates this album. Not that their fans wouldn't want to listen once more, nor that what they had to say wasn't at times compelling; it's just that it no longer was special. *—Ron Wynn*

Solid / Oct. 1984 / Capitol ✦✦✦✦

Ashford & Simpson have always been the prime representatives in R&B of the joys of wedded bliss, and this extended valentine is their most consistent set as well as their biggest hit ever. *—William Ruhlmann*

Real Love / Aug. 1986 / Capitol ✦✦✦

Although not as successful as their mid-'70s dates, *Real Love* did include some emphatic harmonies and above-average compositions, as well as consistently exciting vocals. What hurt it was the lack of interest in classic R&B arrangements during the late '80s, and the failure of any one single to emerge as a major hit. *—Ron Wynn*

Solid Plus Seven / Jan. 13, 1987 / Capitol ✦✦✦

This wasn't one of their finest, although it adhered to the usual high-production standards. But it lacked the kind of resolute love songs, knockout rhythm tracks, or humorous slice-of-life pieces that separate great Ashford & Simpson material from good or merely competent cuts. There is not enough of the former and too much of the latter on this release. *—Ron Wynn*

Love or Physical / Feb. 1989 / Capitol ✦✦✦

Capitol Gold: The Best of Ashford & Simpson / Jun. 21, 1993 / Capitol ✦✦✦✦✦

Ashford & Simpson scored 33 entries on the R&B singles charts between 1973 and 1990, all but one of them on Warner Bros. or Capitol. This compilation licenses the two biggest hits from the duo's tenure at Warner, "It Seems to Hang On" and "Found a Cure," both of which hit the Top Ten, and features the eight Capitol titles that made the R&B Top 40—"Street Corner," "Love It Away," "High-Rise," "Solid," "Outta the World," "Babies," "Count Your Blessings," and "I'll Be There for You." There are also six tracks culled from the five Capitol albums, bringing the disc's time to over 71 minutes. In other words, this is about as comprehensive an overview of A&S's career as could be managed by one label on one disc. There are good biographical liner notes by compiler David Nathan. *—William Ruhlmann*

Been Found / 1996 / Hopsack & Silk ✦✦✦

After an extremely long time without a recording contract, this dynamic R&B husband and wife singing duo decided to create their own label. This time out, they decided to return with a friend, the poet Maya Angelou. This is far from their best material, but the concept itself makes this an interesting project. Throughout these 11 urban adult contemporary songs Ashford & Simpson weave their luminous harmonies around Angelou's distinctively gravel-voiced recitations. The title track is the most inviting and boasts a delicious chorus on the subject of finding true love that will last. Angelou opens "Where We Come From," a reflection on childhood, with heartfelt nostalgia that works very well with the song's construction. However, sometimes the hip-hop influence later in the set becomes overwhelming on cuts like "This Time It's Real" and "Made for Me"; moreover, the poems don't always snugly fit the songs, but seem to have been inserted for no reason other than the idea that each song should have one. Still, Ashford & Simpson's following will savor this set in spite of its flaws. *—Bil Carpenter*

Gospel According to Ashford & Simpson / Oct. 29, 1996 / Capitol ✦✦✦✦

A 15-song sampler of their 1980s work, leaning far more heavily on tracks from the first half of the decade, this includes the hits "I'll Be There for You," "Count Your Blessings," "Street Opera," and "Solid," although one of their biggest, "Outta the World," is strangely absent. More than just about any other single-artist compilation you could name, this is a definitive representation of how mainstream soul often sounded in the 1980s. Which is to say, it often sounded more like adult contemporary pop than soul. *—Richie Unterberger*

The Best of Ashford & Simpson / Aug. 17, 1999 / EMI-Capitol Special Markets ✦✦✦

This compilation features Ashford & Simpson cuts from *Street Opera*, *High-Rise*, *Solid*, and *Real Love*, their four Capitol albums. Some but not all of the duo's best recordings are included—Ashford & Simpson were on the downslide at Capitol, their albums were no longer going gold as they had at Warner Brothers, and hits were hard to come by. The best of this lot includes the upbeat "Solid," where they sing about the joys of their long-lasting relationship, and "Street Corner." Ashford & Simpson fans should unapologetically love this, but casual fans might want to go with a more complete best-of collection encompassing more of the duo's career. *—Andrew Hamilton*

● **The Very Best of Ashford & Simpson** / Jan. 15, 2002 / Rhino ✦✦✦✦✦

Rhino's 2002 release *The Very Best of Ashford & Simpson* comes very close to being a complete greatest hits, but it stumbles on a major point—it only contains two songs from the group's Capitol recordings from the early '80s, including the hit "Solid." The rest is devoted to the duo's Warner recordings of the '70s. This isn't a bad thing, actually, since Ashford & Simpson were at their creative peak then, and this collection also touches on their superb writing gig at Motown with an opening live medley. So, this hits nearly all the bases—but misses just enough to stop it from being definitive. Still, it's arguably the best Ashford & Simpson collection assembled, and it will satisfy many listeners looking for a collection like this. *—Stephen Thomas Erlewine*

Tyrone Ashley (Sammy Campbell)

b. Plainfield, NJ

Vocals / Club/Dance, R&B, Soul

Tyrone Ashley was born Sammy Campbell in Plainfield, NJ. He recorded under his birth name until 1971 when he cut a single for Phil-L.A. of Soul Records in Philadelphia. The Parliament, also from Plainsfield, competed with Campbell's group, the Del Larks, in talent shows and holiday festivals. the Del Larks formed around 1958 and consisted of Campbell, Ronald Taylor, James Anderson, Mert Matthews, and Raymond Davis. The hangout in Plainsfield was the Silk Palace, a barbershop owned by George Clinton and Parliament members; after work the local warblers woodshedded in the back room.

It was a toss up who would score a big hit first, Parliament or the Del Larks; they started recording around the same time but the Del Larks early recordings were the most popular. They hit locally around 1958-1959 with "Bubblegum Doll," and "Lady Love," on East West Records distributed by Atlantic; and enjoyed success as Sammy & the Del Larks with "I Will Never Forget" on Ea-Jay, and "Little Darling," on Stop Records. They messed up a chance to appear on *The Ed Sullivan Show* by talking loud and cursing in the audition room.

Campbell wrote and produced for George Blackwell's Smoke Records in Newark, NJ, for a year without pay. Blackwell never released any of Campbell's material, so Campbell supported himself by promoting shows. He formed his own label, Queen City Records, and released "SOS of Love," but it was the second "Job Opening" that built an aura around Campbell; it was a magnificent record, a two-part throbbing jam with a fantastic sax solo coloring part two. He only pressed 1,500 copies. Problems with Blackwell caused the record's demise; Blackwell released a competing version of "SOS" by the Del Larks under a bogus name, and had "Job Opening" squelched. The record later found love among Northern soul fanatics who snatched up thousands of bootleg copies.

Raymond Davis joined Parliament, Anderson developed an alcohol problem, and the Del Larks disbanded. Campbell sent a demo to Galaxy/Fantasy Records in Oakland, CA, and got a deal as Sam Campbell & the Bystanders. A Ray Shanklin production, "Hey La, Ya, Ya," a bluesy number, was his sole Galaxy release. He moved to Oakland, but it didn't help, the label didn't like his other songs; they wanted him to sing blues but Campbell preferred R&B.

Back East he struck a deal with Phil-L.A. of Soul Records, who released "Let Me Be Your Man" by Tyrone Ashley in 1971, his most successful record. It nested in the 30s on *Billboard*'s R&B chart for a few weeks, and sold around 50,000 copies, which disappointed Campbell; he swore it sold at least twice that amount. A second single, "Love Sweet Love," stiffed, and Campbell left the label, and concentrated on writing and producing other artists, but the big deal always eluded him.

Around 1975, Ian Levine found him, and as Tyrone Ashley he became one of the first American soul singers produced by Levine. He scored a minor hit in Britain with "Feet Start Movin'." Other singles didn't move as expected and Campbell returned to Plainsfield where he laid tracks in a shed behind his house that he transformed into a recording studio. All the original Del Larks have passed except Raymond Davis, who sang with Parliament for years and joined the Temptations in 1995 for a stint with the legends. Hot Productions released *Looks Like Love Is Here to Stay*, a CD of Campbell's Ian Levine sides as Tyrone Ashley, in 1995. You can find his cuts sprinkled on a variety of Hot Productions compilations. To date, no one has compiled the early Del Larks or Sam Campbell/Tyrone Ashley singles on one CD. *George Clinton and P-Funk: An Oral History*, edited by Dave Marsh, contains many interesting quotes by Sammy Campbell. *—Andrew Hamilton*

● **Looks Like Love Is Here to Stay** / Oct. 1995 / Hot ✦✦✦

A compilation of material which soul singer Tyrone Ashley recorded under the direction of Northern soul aficionado Ian Levine in the mid-'70s, *Looks Like Love Is Here to Stay* doesn't offer anything substantially different musically than Levine's other productions of the time for Evelyn Thomas, L.J. Johnson, and Doris Jones. Rather, Ashley's voice is the distinguishing factor. He employs similar delivery techniques (probably by order of Levine); but his actual tone and innate phrasing is more down-home soulful than the others'. The highlights here are the chugging "Feet Start Moving" and the charming disco title track. Otherwise, the tunes are pleasant, but rather trajectory—and certainly not up to the standards of Ashley's abilities. *—Justin M. Kantor*

The Astors

f. 1960, **db.** 1967

Group / Doo Wop, Soul, Southern Soul

One of Stax's less typical acts, the Astors recorded five singles for the label between 1961 and 1967; only "Candy" was a hit, making number 12 on the R&B chart (and smaller waves on the pop listings) in 1965. More doo wop-influenced than most Southern soul groups, the Astors actually found much of their audience in Philadelphia, a town that always favored soul harmony vocals. Rawer in presence and execution than most artists on the Stax roster, the Astors recorded too sporadically to establish a distinctive imprint. Their sides hold substantial interest for serious soul fans, though, as Steve Cropper, Isaac Hayes, Booker T. Jones, and guitarist Larry Lee (briefly a member of Jimi Hendrix's band) are among those who penned their material. All of their official sides made it to CD in 1996, on a disc that also featured recordings by a later, equally obscure Stax group, the Newcomers. *—Richie Unterberger*

● **The Astors Meet the Newcomers: Sweet Soul from Memphis** / 1996 / Stax ✦✦✦✦✦

The Astors actually only have 11 of the 20 tracks on this CD; the other nine belong to the Newcomers, a similarly obscure Stax soul group from later vintage. This has both sides of all five Astors singles, plus a live version of "Candy" (taken from the *Funky Broadway: Stax Revue Live at the 5/4 Ballroom* compilation). It's not typical of either Stax or Southern soul in general, but it's nice period soul nonetheless, the Astors' half of the program outshining the Newcomers by a long shot. *—Richie Unterberger*

Sweet Pea Atkinson

Vocals / R&B

Sweet Pea Atkinson was one of the vocalists for the Detroit R&B ensemble Was (Not Was). The group issued four LPs from 1981-1990, although there was nearly a five-year gap between their second release and their third in 1988. Atkinson later departed for a solo career. *—Ron Wynn*

• **Don't Walk Away** / 1982 / Island ✦✦✦

For all intents and purposes, this is a Was (Not Was) record: It features the band's lead singer, much of the material was written by Don and David Was (who also produced), and the tracks are played by "the Was (Not Was) Orchestra." Tracks like "Dance or Die" are typical of Was (Not Was)'s approach of ironic lyrics and dancefloor beats. Sweet Pea Atkinson proves a good frontman in the husky soul-man mold, especially when he's given more typical soul-pop fare like General Johnson's "Don't Walk Away" or the Bacharach/David chestnut "Anyone Who Had a Heart." But mostly this record has the same sarcastic undercurrent of most of Was (Not Was)'s product, especially "Girls Fall for Me," no matter how sincerely Atkinson sings lines like: "In the smart cafes/Husbands chain their wives to the tables/That enables me/To eat in peace once in a while." *—William Ruhlmann*

Atlantic Starr

f. 1976, White Plains, NY

Group / Soul, Funk, Quiet Storm, Disco, Urban, Adult Contemporary

Atlantic Starr was among the top urban contemporary acts of the '80s and fared well in the adult contemporary market as well, but their roots were '70s soul and funk. The East Coast outfit was formed in White Plains, NY, in 1976 by three brothers: lead singer/guitarist David Lewis, lead singer/keyboardist Wayne Lewis, and trombonist/percussionist Jonathan Lewis. After the Lewis Brothers hired lead singer Sharon Bryant, trumpeter William Sudderth, saxophonist Damon Rentie (who was replaced by Koran Daniels in 1981), bassist Clifford Archer, drummer Porter Carroll Jr., and percussionist/flutist Joseph Phillips, Atlantic Starr's original nine-person lineup was in place.

Influenced by '70s funk/soul bands like Earth, Wind & Fire, the Commodores, New Birth, and L.T.D., Atlantic Starr started playing around the northeastern U.S. They had only been together for about two years when they signed with A&M and started working with Bobby Eli, a well-respected producer/songwriter from Philadelphia. Produced by Eli in 1978, Atlantic Starr's self-titled debut album wasn't a mega-platinum blockbuster but did reasonably well and contained the funk hit "Stand Up" (which made it to number 16 on *Billboard*'s R&B singles chart).

Eli went on to produce the band's second album, *Straight to the Point*; while that 1979 release did OK, A&M knew that Atlantic Starr could be bigger. So in 1981, the band changed producers and enlisted James Carmichael for their third album, *Radiance*. It was a wise move; *Radiance* and its hit single "When Love Calls" established Atlantic Starr as a supergroup in the R&B market. It was on *Radiance* that the charismatic Bryant (who was featured on "When Love Calls") really blossomed as a singer and her lead vocals played a major role in the band's success. Carmichael went on to produce 1982's *Brilliance* (which contained the number two R&B single "Circles") and 1983's *Yours Forever*; the latter includes "Touch a Four Leaf Clover," another major hit featuring Bryant.

Although Bryant was never Atlantic Starr's only lead singer—Wayne and David Lewis also provided their share of lead vocals—she was a major asset. So it came as quite a disappointment when she left Atlantic Starr in 1984 to pursue a solo career. But all was not lost. The talented Barbara Weathers was hired as a replacement and 1985's *As the Band Turns*—Atlantic Starr's first post-Bryant album and sixth album overall—found the outfit unveiling a smaller lineup that consisted of Weathers, the Lewis Brothers, and Phillips. Sudderth, Daniels, Archer, and Carroll were all gone, but despite those personnel changes, Atlantic Starr was still distinctive and recognizable.

As the Band Turns, which contained the major hit "Secret Lovers," turned out to be Atlantic Starr's last album for A&M; in 1987, they moved to Warner Bros. and fared well with the album *All in the Name of Love* and the smash hit "Always." A syrupy adult contemporary ballad, "Always" reflected the Lewis Brothers' desire to have the type of crossover success that Whitney Houston and Lionel Ritchie had been enjoying in the '80s; they got their wish when "Always" soared to number one on both the pop and R&B charts.

After *All in the Name of Love*, Weathers left the band to pursue a solo career and was replaced by Porscha Martin, who was featured on 1988's *We're Movin' Up*. Martin was around for a few years before being replaced by Rachel Oliver (Atlantic Starr's fourth female vocalist) in the early '90s. Atlantic Starr's relationship with Warner Bros. ended after 1991's *Love Crazy*, and in 1994, the band recorded one album for Arista: *Time*. That album was a commercial disappointment and the single "I'll Remember You" only made it to the fifties on *Billboard*'s R&B and pop singles charts. *Time* (which was David Lewis' last album with the band) found a fifth female singer, Aisha Tanner, replacing Oliver. And when 1999's *Legacy* was distributed by the small, independent Street Solid label, Atlantic Starr unveiled yet another lineup—one that consisted of two Lewis Brothers (Wayne and Jonathan) as well as Oliver (who had returned and replaced Tanner) and a new male singer named DeWayne Woods. Although *Legacy* received very little attention, Atlantic Starr hung in there and was still performing for die-hard fans when the 21st century arrived. *—Alex Henderson*

Atlantic Starr / 1978 / A&M ✦✦✦

Atlantic Starr was still trying to get its sound together when this, its first album to the hit the charts, was released. The nine-piece band had an impressive showing on the *Billboard* R&B charts with "Stand Up" and "Keep It Comin'." The former, led by Wayne Lewis, is a hand-clapping affair with a humpin' funk groove. The latter, led by Sharon Bryant and David Lewis, is a decent effort. Respectively, they both peaked at 16 and 49 on the charts. "(I'll Never Miss) The Love I Never Had" is a notable number. David Lewis comes across with a more convincing delivery than on the other selections he is featured on. The most engaging number is "With Your Love I Come Alive," which showcases Porter Carroll Jr. on lead. His tenor is brawny yet agile and his delivery comes with an unrehearsed feel. Wayne Lewis' vocals were still in a developmental stage, and he had not yet grasped that imposing tone he would later master. *—Craig Lytle*

Straight to the Point / 1979 / A&M ✦✦✦

These days, most A&R people at major labels (as opposed to indies) no longer believe in honest-to-God artist development—if an artist's first album isn't a hit, he/she gets dropped. But back in the '70s, major label A&R people were, as a rule, a lot more patient. They were more likely to view the artist as a long-term investment, which is why three- or four-album contracts weren't uncommon—labels reasoned that if an artist's first or second album wasn't a hit, the third or fourth just might be. Atlantic Starr is a perfect example of a band that benefited from insightful, smart A&R. In the late '70s, Atlantic Starr was a diamond in the rough that needed to be developed—thankfully, A&M's A&R department was wise enough (and patient enough) to develop the East Coast outfit. One hears a lot of potential on Atlantic Starr's second album *Straight to the Point*, which Bobby Eli produced at Philadelphia's legendary Sigma Sound Studios. From the funky single "(Let's) Rock 'N' Roll" to the slick "Let the Spirit Move Ya" (which has a Euro-disco flavor) and the soul ballad "Losin' You," this 1979 release is a generally decent (if slightly uneven) sophomore effort. But it isn't fantastic or mind-blowing, and not until 1981's *Radiance* did Atlantic Starr really start to live up to its creative and commercial potential. In 1979, Atlantic Starr was like a student who was getting Bs and Cs on his/her report card but had the potential to bring home a lot of As—the potential for excellence was there, and thank God A&M helped the band make the transition from decent to excellent. Although not among Atlantic Starr's essential releases, *Straight to the Point* is an LP that hardcore fans will find interesting. *—Alex Henderson*

Radiant / 1981 / A&M ✦✦✦✦✦

Both creatively and commercially, *Radiant* was a major step forward for Atlantic Starr—and the person they can thank is James Carmichael. This 1981 release was the first album that Carmichael produced for the band, whose two previous LPs (*Atlantic Starr* in 1978 and *Straight to the Point* in 1979) were decent but not great. Atlantic Starr needed to get to the next level, and Carmichael obviously gave the White Plains, NY, combo the sort of guidance, direction, and constructive criticism it needed to make the transition from decent to excellent. *Radiant* gets off to an impressive start with the haunting single "When Love Calls," and the material that follows is equally strong. That is true whether Atlantic Starr is getting into sentimental soul ballads ("Am I Dreaming," "Send for Me") or tough, gritty funk ("Think About That," "Under Pressure"). One of the band's greatest assets on this LP is lead singer Sharon Bryant; Carmichael brings out the best in her, and she really soars on "When Love Calls," as well as "My Turn Now" and the hit "Am I Dreaming" (a male/female duet with fellow lead singer David Lewis). But Bryant isn't the only lead vocalist who excels on this record. David and Wayne Lewis are also fine singers; "Send for Me," in fact, boasts one of Wayne's most memorable performances. And once again, Carmichael deserves much of the credit—he pushed the Lewis Brothers to excel just as he pushed Bryant to excel. With Carmichael's help, *Radiant* went down in history as one Atlantic Starr's finest and most essential albums. *—Alex Henderson*

Brilliance / 1982 / A&M ✦✦✦✦

Atlantic Starr hit its commercial peak in the late '80s, when the bland, insipid adult contemporary ballad "Always" soared to number one on both the pop and R&B charts. That song put Atlantic Starr in the Whitney Houston/Lionel Richie realm—in other words, people who associate Atlantic Starr with "Always" think of them as a crossover act. But from an R&B standpoint (as opposed to a pop/adult contemporary standpoint), Atlantic Starr provided their best work in the early '80s, when Sharon Bryant was still on board and the East Coast residents were being produced by James Carmichael. Released in 1982, *Brilliance* was the second of three albums that Carmichael produced for Atlantic Starr—and it is also one of the band's finest and most essential releases. There is nothing not to like about this LP. The soul ballads "Your Love Finally Ran Out" and "Let's Get Closer" are excellent, and so are uptempo funk/dance numbers like "Sexy Dancer" and "Love Moves" (which features Wayne Lewis on lead vocals and has a Slave/Steve Arrington/Aurra type of appeal). *Brilliance*, however, is best known for Bryant's soaring performance on the smash hit "Circles," which is one of those songs that is great on the dancefloor but is equally appealing if you want to simply sit down and listen to it. Bryant also excels on the single "Love Me Down," which wasn't as big a hit as "Circles" (it reached number 14 on *Billboard*'s R&B singles chart), but is still a fine medium-tempo item. If you have only a casual interest in Atlantic Starr and only want to have a few of its albums in your collection, *Brilliance* should definitely be among them. *—Alex Henderson*

Yours Forever / 1983 / A&M ✦✦✦

Atlantic Starr's fifth album, *Yours Forever*, was lead singer Sharon Bryant's last album with the East Coast soulsters; it was also the last of three albums that James Carmichael produced for them. While 1981's *Radiant* and 1982's *Brilliance*—the two previous Atlantic Starr LPs that Carmichael had produced—were superb, this 1983 release is uneven. That isn't to say that *Yours Forever* is a bad album; none of the material is terrible. But this time, there aren't as many five-star gems. The songs that deserve to be exalted as gems range from the haunting smash "Touch a Four Leaf Clover" and the rock-tinged "Tryin" (both of which feature Bryant) to the dreamy title song (which finds David Lewis providing a memorable lead vocal). Unfortunately, *Yours Forever* also has its share of songs that are merely competent. Take "I Want Your Love," for example. This Chic-like sophisti-funk/dance number (which shouldn't be confused with the 1978 Chic hit that is also titled "I Want Your

Love") is pleasant enough, but it isn't in a class with "Circles," "When Love Calls," "Love Me Down," and other treasures that Carmichael had produced for Atlantic Starr in 1981 or 1982. For Atlantic Starr fans, hearing *Yours Forever* in 1983 was like receiving beer when you had grown accustomed to champagne—if *Radiant* and *Brilliance* were R&B feasts, *Yours Forever* is merely a snack. It isn't a disaster, but it doesn't live up to the consistently high standards that had characterized Atlantic Starr's previous work with Carmichael. Of the three albums that Carmichael produced for Atlantic Starr in the early '80s, *Yours Forever* is the least essential and the most inconsistent. *—Alex Henderson*

As the Band Turns / 1985 / A&M ♦♦♦♦

In the mid-'80s, a lot of downsizing was taking place in R&B. Many of the large soul/funk bands that had emerged in the '70s were going high-tech, which meant cutting way back on horns (or even eliminating them altogether) and emphasizing keyboards and drum machines. Atlantic Starr, like Cameo, felt that they had to do some serious downsizing in order to remain competitive. In 1983, they still had nine members; when *As the Band Turns* came out two years later, it was down to five. This 1985 release found Starr unveiling a new quintet lineup that consisted of Wayne Lewis on lead vocals and keyboards, David Lewis on lead vocals and guitar, Jonathan Lewis on keyboards and trombone (mostly keyboards), Joseph Phillips on percussion, and newcomer Barbara Weathers (who had replaced Sharon Bryant) on lead vocals. *As the Band Turns* was not only Starr's first post-Bryant album—it was also the first album they had recorded since parting company with producer James Carmichael (who had produced their last three LPs). This time, the producers included Wayne and David Lewis or Joey Gallo and Wardell Potts Jr. But despite all those changes, Starr was still quite recognizable. Most of the material is excellent, and that is true of everything from the dreamy "Silver Shadow" to the electro-funk gem "Freak-A-Ristic." Without question, Bryant's departure was a major loss for the band. But it wasn't a fatal blow, and Weathers shows herself to be a talented replacement on "Silver Shadow," as well as the ballads "If Your Heart Isn't in It" and "Secret Lovers" (a major hit). Arguably the last great album that Atlantic Starr provided in the '80s, *As the Band Turns* demonstrated that there could be life after Sharon Bryant for the East Coast outfit. *—Alex Henderson*

● **Secret Lovers: The Best of Atlantic Starr** / 1986 / A&M ♦♦♦♦♦

The 1986 compilation *Secret Lovers: The Best of Atlantic Starr* collects some of the group's biggest songs up to that point, including "If Your Heart Isn't in It," "When Love Calls," "Touch a Four Leaf Clover," and "Silver Shadow." As the title implies, this collection focuses on the softer, romantic side of Atlantic Starr's music rather than their funkier efforts; "Gimme Your Lovin'," "Stand Up," "One Love," and the compilation's title track helped define that side of their sound in the '80s. Though it's not a complete collection of Atlantic Starr's output, *Secret Lovers* benefits from its selective focus, making it a fine collection of the group's quiet storm moments from their time with A&M. *—Heather Phares*

All in the Name of Love / 1987 / Warner Bros. ♦♦♦

Classics, Vol. 10 / 1987 / A&M ♦♦♦♦♦

This collection gathers Atlantic Starr's A&M hits, which also include "Freak-A-Ristic," "Secret Lovers," and "If Your Heart Isn't in It." But the group scored its biggest smash after moving to Warner Bros., the R&B and pop chart-topping "Always." *—Ron Wynn*

We're Movin' Up / 1988 / Warner Bros. ♦♦♦

Prototype classy love ballads, dance-pop, urban contemporary production/arrangements, and one or two above-average leads. Atlantic Starr has shuttled personnel often but never tampered much with its basic formula. The group does it well, and there's little here that's disturbing, poorly performed, or routinely performed. Porscha Martin made a good replacement for Barbara Weathers, who was a good replacement for Sharon Bryant, and, well, you get the idea. *—Ron Wynn*

Love Crazy / 1991 / Reprise ♦♦♦

Time / 1994 / Arista ♦♦♦

● **Ultimate Collection** / Sep. 26, 2000 / Hip-O ♦♦♦♦♦

Atlantic Starr's *Ultimate Collection* lives up to its name, gathering hits that span the group's two-decade existence. From early singles such as "Stand Up," "When Love Calls," and "Touch a Four Leaf Clover" to their later hits like "Always," "My First Love," and "Masterpiece." With 18 tracks covering their years on A&M, Warner, and Reprise, this album is indeed the ultimate collection of Atlantic Starr's career highlights. *—Heather Phares*

Atmosfear

f. 1977, England

Group / Club/Dance, Disco, Jazz-Funk

Atmosfear's most significant contribution to disco was the slightly loony "Dancing in Outer Space," a track that has remained popular with underground disco fanatics since its release. A U.K.-based jazz-funk outfit, the group's members included bassist Lester Batchelor, lead guitarist Andy Sojka, rhythm guitarist Anthony Anoniou, and saxophonist Stewart Gawthorne. Formed by Sojka, a record shop owner, in 1977, the group made their official debut two years later with "Dancing in Outer Space," which found its niche in the underground dance scene after the group licensed it to MCA. The group went on to release a handful of singles throughout the '80s that failed to do as well as their debut. Two albums, 1981's *En Trance* and 1984's *First/Foremost*, were both released on the group's Elite label (the same label that launched the career of Level 42). A couple of retrospectives have appeared, including 1999's *Altered Slates*, a collection of remixes and reworkings from the likes of Francois K and Masters at Work. A year later, Sequel issued the lovingly packaged *Dancing in Outer Space*, a best-of. *—Andy Kellman*

● **Dancing in Outer Space** / 2000 / Castle ♦♦♦

This compiles the entirety of the material that Atmosfear released on the Elite label, an independent run by the band. Elite would later launch the career of Level 42, but DJs who spin classic disco know Elite as the label that spit out Atmosfear's "Dancing in Outer Space" (the title didn't seem nearly as hackneyed back then, before the days of sloth-hop-heavy chill-out comps), a jazz-funk instrumental with its intention firmly aimed at the dancefloor. Its raw production and slightly amateurish execution actually place it closer to post-punk groups that sprouted up around the same time or shortly thereafter—namely ESG and A Certain Ratio. It has more in common with those groups than Roy Ayers' "Running Away," for instance, but one listen to the song's loping bass line and spacious qualities will tell you why it remains a DJ favorite. Atmosfear would never match the song, but the remainder of what's compiled here maintains an adequate level of quality. 1982's "Xtra Special" nearly matches the title track; it sees the group moving into vocal terrain and sounds like a lost gem from early-'80s R&B station play lists. This is the group's definitive compilation. *—Andy Kellman*

Aurra

f. 1979, Ohio, **db.** 1985

Group / Urban

Centered around leader Steve Washington and singers Starleana Young and Curtis Jones, Aurra was an outgrowth of the NJ-based funk band Slave. They recorded a handful of albums during their late-'70s and early-'80s existence, with most of that output released on Salsoul. The group's membership shifted constantly, with most of the musicians having strong ties to Slave. Aurra helped take Salsoul into the '80s by recording dancefloor-friendly material with the help of synthesizers and programmed rhythms. While the bulk of Salsoul's early releases featured elaborate string sections, mostly live instrumentation, and thumping disco foundations, '80s projects such as Aurra took advantage of studio technology and appealed to club DJs and radio programmers alike by concentrating equally on traditional songcraft and dance rhythms.

Washington instigated Aurra as a family affair of sorts, using various friends and members of the Slave road crew to fill out the group's lineup; at various points, Aurra's personnel swelled to a dozen. In addition to the core of Washington, Young, and Jones, Aurra's membership included Mark Adams, Steve Arrington, Charles "Cedell" Carter, Philip Field, Buddy "Hanks" Henderson, Jennifer Ivory, Tom Lockett, William Young, and Mike Young. Washington helped Aurra score a contract with Salsoul, one of the premier disco labels.

Their self-titled 1980 debut was actually released on Dream, a subsidiary of Salsoul, but their next three albums—1981's *Send Your Love*, 1982's *A Little Love*, and 1983's *Live and Let Live*—were released on Salsoul proper. Around the time *Live and Let Live* was conceived and released, financial matters began to cause turmoil within the group. Young and Jones grew increasingly distrustful of Washington, and the tension became so great that a frustrated Washington left and offered to sell Aurra's trademark to Young and Jones. Washington ended up keeping the name—allegedly after Young and Jones failed to follow through on the offer—and recorded an Aurra record for Quest with new membership, including former Bride of Funkenstein Sheila Horne and Chaka Khan sibling Mark Stephens. Thanks to the legal protestations of Young and Jones, the record never saw the light of day.

Young and Jones recorded a fifth Aurra album after leaving Salsoul. Apparently, Salsoul's improprieties were another source of strife within the group. Released on Next Plateau, 1985's *Like I Like It* gave Aurra their first chart hit in the U.K, in the form of the title track. That was the last anyone would hear from Aurra in name. Weary of further legal hassles, Young and Jones continued under the name Déjà and scored a number two R&B chart hit in 1987 with "You and Me Tonight." Young split from Jones in 1988 and went solo; she released an album in 1991 and also did background vocal work for her husband, Kool & the Gang's J.T. Taylor. Jones continued Déjà with Mysti Day and released a second album under that name. *—Andy Kellman*

Aurra / 1980 / Salsoul ♦♦♦

For Slave fans, the release of spinoff group Aurra's self-titled debut in 1980 was a major event. While *Aurra* isn't the group's most essential release and wasn't their most commercially successful —1981's *Send Your Love* was the Aurra album that boasted the hit "Are You Single?"—it's a solid funk/soul outing that has Slave written all over it. Indeed, the strong Slave influence is impossible to miss on such addictive cuts as "Who Are You," "When I Come Home," and the single "In the Mood (To Groove)." Those who had appreciated the rock influence in some of Slave's material should have no problem getting into "Too Much," a funk-rock gem that, in an ideal world, would have been a hit single. In 1980, however, "Too Much" stood little chance of finding radio airplay because it was too rock-minded for black radio and too funky for AOR programmers. The most disco-flavored song on the LP is "Got to Get My Lady Back"; while Slave and Aurra's albums generally had more to do with funk and R&B than disco, this Shalamar-inflected item was clearly aimed at the disco crowd. *Aurra* wasn't a chartbuster, but among Slave's more hardcore devotees, it earned a lot of respect. *—Alex Henderson*

Send Your Love / 1981 / Salsoul ♦♦♦

A sextet, Aurra featured the vocals of Starleana Young and Curt Jones. Originally released in 1981, none of the set's nine cuts come in under four minutes, but then there are no nine-minute workouts either. The reggae-influenced "Kingston Lady" and their disjointed, disco hit "Are You Single?" are the most memorable selections. Every song is pleasant, but often indistinguishable from the rest; if your mind wanders you have to consult the track listing to check what tune is playing and which one you just heard. *—Andrew Hamilton*

A Little Love / 1982 / Salsoul ♦♦♦

Having created a stir with their debut, this eminently funky R&B combo was now ready to light the sky on fire. All fat bass and liquid guitar riffing, *A Little Love* was a nice combination of dirty and sweet, ballad and body-shaker. It was a smart concoction; the LP would give the band a Top Ten hit, while "Make up Your Mind" emerged a popular opener in its own right, giving Aurra their highest-ever chart hit. And it's no wonder. Among the best songs the duo ever recorded, "Make up Your Mind" was a complex slab of funked-up disco augmented by a superb classic rock guitar solo from Steve Washington, sandwiched within a fat bass line. But Aurra didn't let it go with that. "A Little Love" itself is a sweet song with a ferocious bite, the intro unleashing a heavy hook before the rest of the show, while "Thinking of You" remains the LP's best ballad. Stronger across some tracks than others, *A Little Love* is ultimately an uneven effort. However, when Aurra is in top form they are truly outstanding, and this LP is worth having because of that. *—Amy Hanson*

Live and Let Live / 1983 / Salsoul ✦✦

Like I Like It / 1985 / Ten ✦✦

● **Anthology** / Dec. 5, 1995 / Salsoul ✦✦✦✦
Aurra's double-disc *Anthology* is an extensive way of distilling the group's output—which encompasses five albums—into singles and strong non-single material. The Slave offshoot, featuring co-ed vocals from Starleana Young and Curtis Jones, only cracked the Top Ten of the black singles chart once ("Make up Your Mind," number six), and was a constant presence in the lower rungs of the charts from 1980 to 1982. Stylistically, the bulk of this material can be classified as post-disco and pre-house. There is club appeal in most everything the group recorded, with programming of drum machines and synthesizers often playing a greater role than live instrumentation. Unless you carried a technology phobia, the era during which Aurra recorded was an extremely exciting time, with brilliant extensions of '70s soul and disco music shooting across radio airwaves in several countries. Aurra helped bring Salsoul, a label known for its sweeping string arrangements and big sounds during the '70s, into the '80s with a bright sound that was just as melodic and frequently just as deeply emotional. No highlight from Aurra's most prolific period is left behind here. "Are You Single?" "Checking You Out," "Make up Your Mind," "A Little Love," and "In the Mood" are all here. Actually, there are too many inclusions; the essential material could be condensed into one disc. Until that definitive single-disc compilation rolls around, this will have to do. *—Andy Kellman*

The Best of Aurra / Jul. 1, 1999 / Charly ✦✦✦✦

Patti Austin

b. Aug. 10, 1948, New York, NY
Vocals / Quiet Storm, Urban, Adult Contemporary
A professional since the age of five, Patti Austin was a protégée of Dinah Washington and Sammy Davis Jr. A 1969 single for United Artists titled "Family Tree" cracked the R&B Top 50. Austin cut her debut LP, *End of a Rainbow*, for Creed Taylor's CTI label in 1976, followed by *Havana Candy* in 1977 and *Body Language* in 1980. She sang lead vocals for Japanese koto player Yutaka Yokokura on "Love Light" in 1978, did a duet with Michael Jackson on "It's the Falling in Love" for *Off the Wall*, and sang "The Closer I Get to You" on Tom Browne's album in 1979.

Austin dueted with George Benson on "Moody's Mood for Love" in 1980. She sang backgrounds for sessions by Houston Person, Noel Pointer, Ralph McDonald, Angela Bofill, and Roberta Flack. Austin did vocals on Quincy Jones' *The Dude* LP in 1981, and was featured on the hit "Razzamatazz." She inked a solo deal on Jones' Qwest label, and her 1982 LP *Every Home Should Have One* included the number one pop hit (number nine R&B) "Baby, Come to Me," which got widespread exposure via the ABC soap opera *General Hospital*. The follow-up single, "How Do You Keep the Music Playing," was the theme for the film *Best Friends*. Both songs paired Austin with James Ingram. She continued recording for Jones' Qwest label through the '80s, but couldn't recapture her pop or R&B success, despite working with several top producers, including Jam-Lewis in 1985.

Austin switched to GRP in 1990 and recorded *Love Is Gonna Getcha*, with the singles "Through the Test of Time" and "Good in Love." She subsequently recorded *Carry On* and *Live* in 1991 and 1992. *Street of Dreams* followed in 1999 and *On the Way to Love* appeared in summer 2001. Her lovely tribute to Ella Fitzgerald, *For Ella*, appeared in spring 2002. *—Ron Wynn*

End of a Rainbow / Feb. 1976 / CTI ✦✦✦

Havana Candy / Nov. 1977 / CTI ✦✦
CTI was having its troubles financially at the time. They recycled arrangements for all their artists and limited their budgets. Austin sang this undistinguished material with as much conviction as she could muster, but the general pallid air lingering over the production also affected her vocals. *—Ron Wynn*

Live at the Bottom Line / 1979 / Epic ✦✦✦
Patti Austin came closest on this late-'70s live set to transferring onto vinyl the qualities that made her an outstanding vocalist outside of the studio. There's more spontaneity, emotion, and charisma in the vocals on this album than on almost all her other releases combined; perhaps the nightclub setting inspired her, or, more likely, Austin was free to sing without any agendas, marketing strategies, or producers' visions being factored into the process. *—Ron Wynn*

Body Language / Jul. 1980 / CTI ✦✦
The fourth album Patti Austin cut for the CTI label wasn't much different from the previous three. It was a patchwork quilt: a little fusion, a little quasi-jazz, some urban contemporary material, and even a standard or two. She sang them all with ease and grace, although things were so smooth that they were almost comatose at times. Austin would later go on to score much bigger hits working with Quincy Jones, who at least injected enough hooks and tricks into his urban contemporary stuff to grab someone's attention. *—Ron Wynn*

Every Home Should Have One / Sep. 1981 / Qwest ✦✦✦
The talented Patti Austin launched a successful jazz album career on CTI by the mid-'70s. Working with Quincy Jones since 1976, *Every Home Should Have One* was her long-awaited solo album with Jones as a producer. The hit singles "Do You Love Me" and "Every Home Should Have One" are polished—pleasing but derivative. Rod Temperton—who did four songs here, including the smooth "The Genie"—comes up with a true gem, the classic Austin and James Ingram duet "Baby Come to Me." The most telling aspect of *Every Home Should Have One* isn't the L.A. pop/R&B Austin could do standing on her head, it's the most meditative offerings. A cover of Thom Bell and Linda Creed's "Stop, Look and Listen" gets an effortless treatment. The album-closing "The Island," with music from Ivan Lins and Vitor Martins and lyrics by Alan and Marilyn Bergman, seems best suited for Austin as she gives a sensual and flawless reading. *Every Home Should Have One* doesn't possess Quincy Jones' all-encompassing production style of albums like *The Dude* and George Benson's *Give Me the Night*. While this seems like a debut album, it's far from it, but it's a perfect introduction to Austin and her more pop-orientated work. *—Jason Elias*

In My Life / Jun. 1983 / CTI ✦✦✦

Patti Austin / Mar. 1984 / Qwest ✦✦✦
Patti Austin enjoyed good chart action and radio airplay with this mid-'80s release. A pair of singles, "Hot! In the Flames of Love" and "Star Struck," got both R&B and dance attention, while the album had some other competent uptempo material and a couple of good ballads. It wasn't her best on Qwest, but it was far from her worst. *—Ron Wynn*

Gettin' Away With Murder / Oct. 1985 / Qwest ✦✦✦
Patti Austin's third Qwest album was a reasonable success, making the Top 50 on the R&B chart and throwing off three R&B chart singles, "Honey for the Bees," "The Heat of Heat," and the title track. But you could tell it was supposed to do a lot better on the pop chart: Five heavyweight producers (Russ Titelman, Tommy LiPuma, Monte Moir, and Jimmy Jam and Terry Lewis), plus 14 songwriters, contributed to what was doubtless a big-budget production, and that means label head Quincy Jones was looking for a lot more in the way of crossover than a low chart ranking for "The Heat of Heat." In retrospect, the fault lies with all that high-priced help, while Austin gives her all in any guise they devise for her—sultry balladeer, disco diva, and pop princess. *—William Ruhlmann*

The Real Me / Aug. 1988 / Qwest ✦✦✦✦✦
And how! Austin tackles standards such as "Smoke Gets in Your Eyes" and "They Can't Take That Away from Me," and succeeds brilliantly. Her version of Comden, Green, and Bernstein's "I Can Cook, Too" is enough by itself to make this a pick. *—William Ruhlmann*

Love Is Gonna Getcha / Mar. 1990 / GRP ✦✦✦
With apologies to Dianne Reeves, Patti Austin has always quite simply been the best jack-of-all-genre singers on the planet, crossing effortlessly from jazz to pop and R&B with a voice that's so sweet, rich, and lovely, it can't help but warm the heart. On the heels of her 1988 masterpiece *The Real Me*, her GRP debut packs a wallop of festive uptempo tunes, lite funk pop, torchy message songs, passionate ballads, and breezy tenderness—all delivered with a truly Austin-tatious flair. Austin surrounds herself with some of pop jazz's best here, with GRP's 1990 roster well represented: Dave Grusin (whose production is flawless), Don Grusin (with whom she co-wrote the happy "Ooh Wee (The Carnival)"), Deborah Henson-Conant (whose harp adds punch to "In My Dreams"), Lee Ritenour, and Nelson Rangell (whose alto soars on the title cut). But as tantalizing as the music is, it is Austin who gives the collection wings with a powerful voice whose mood she so artfully modulates depending on the feel of the individual tune. Soft and tender on her own composition "In My Life," easy and lilting for "In My Dreams," and full of genuine excitement for "Through the Test of Time" and "Ooh Wee." An added bonus is the Oscar nominated "The Girl Who Used to Be Me," which gives Austin a chance to show her range, even if the tune is a bit schmaltzy. *—Jonathan Widran*

Live / Mar. 1992 / GRP ✦✦✦

That Secret Place / Apr. 1994 / GRP ✦✦✦
The veteran sweet-voiced singer's fourth GRP album is perhaps her most musically diverse, covering an ambitious range of material. While each successive album she's recorded over that period has given the versatile entertainer an opportunity to showcase different elements of her artistry, this album gives her the chance to highlight her skills as a vocal stylist and interpreter with few peers. There's the lilting, jazz-inflected title track (an homage to Miles Davis), the reggae-flavored "Captivated," and the poignant ballad "Somebody Make Me Laugh," just for starters. Other standouts include the wistful "Broken Dreams," a bebop finger-snappin' take on Thomas Dolby's zesty "Ability to Swing," and the gospel-flavored "Reach." She saves the best for last, however, with the classical-flavored "Stars in Our Eyes," a gorgeous and haunting look back at a failed relationship with subtle keyboard harmonies by Bob James. Austin can do it all herself, but she enjoys the camaraderie she shares on various cuts with Vesta, Mervyn Warren, Tata Vega, and Phil Perry. *—Jonathan Widran*

● **The Best of Patti Austin** / Jun. 28, 1994 / Columbia ✦✦✦✦✦
The Best of Patti Austin isn't quite what it appears to be. Instead of compiling her big early-'80s hits like "Baby, Come to Me" and "How Do You Keep the Music Playing," the 16-track collection features her lesser-known late-'70s material for CTI Records, where she had only one notable hit in 1977 with "Say You Love Me." Despite the lack of hits, the compilation is actually quite enjoyable, featuring graceful versions of hits as diverse as "More Today Than Yesterday," "You Don't Have to Say You're Sorry," "Lost in the Stars," "We've Got Tonight" and "Another Nail for My Heart." It may not be the definitive Austin collection, yet it remains a good introduction to her style. *—Stephen Thomas Erlewine*

The Ultimate Collection / Jun. 6, 1995 / GRP ✦✦✦✦
Patti Austin's honed vocal instrument (she's been singing since she was five) has nailed its share of hits, but not nearly enough for one of urban/soul/pop's better divas. Her clear, compelling soprano never gets tiring, even though she always keeps it in check. You don't

get vocal aerobics from Austin à la Chaka Khan or Whitney Houston; you get a smoldering fire that's in a class of its own. Duets with Johnny Mathis, George Benson, and Cleve Francis (the rare African-American country singer) spice this concise 12-song best-of, which is orchestrated by a who who's list of producers, including Thom Bell and Rod Temperton. Revered among the urban jazz set, Patti Austin deserves a bigger piece of the pop pie as well. *—Andrew Hamilton*

In & Out of Love / Oct. 13, 1998 / Concord Jazz ♦♦♦

Street of Dreams / Aug. 24, 1999 / Intersound ♦♦♦
Street of Dreams was designed as a project for Patti Austin to sing her favorite songs, regardless of genre. True, there are a couple of later songs here, usually including two co-written by Vaneese Thomas, but the heart of the album is in interpretations of "The Look of Love," "Street of Dreams," "Someone to Watch Over Me," "Till There Was You," "I Only Have Eyes for You," "For Once in My Life," and "IGY (What a Beautiful World)." Although the arrangements can get a little too clean and synthesized (much of the album sounds as if it was recorded with DX-7s), Austin is in terrific form throughout, breathing life into songs that have been recorded numerous times. It's a fine latter-day effort from a fine singer. *—Stephen Thomas Erlewine*

On the Way to Love / Jun. 26, 2001 / Warner Bros. ♦♦♦
After affiliations with CTI (1976-1980), Qwest (1981-1988), and GRP (1990-1994), Patti Austin, as she passed the age of 50, seemed to have moved permanently from the soul jazz divisions of major labels to independents like Concord Jazz (for whom she made *In & Out of Love* in 1998) and even more modest recording affiliations (her last album, *Street of Dreams*, was handled by Platinum Entertainment). It is therefore something of a surprise that she has landed back at Quincy Jones' Warner Bros.-distributed Qwest label for her 15th album, *On the Way to Love*. It's also good news, since a singer of Austin's talent (and there aren't many of those) deserves the exposure possible through major-label distribution. The question, of course, is what sort of commercial compromises it entails. The answer is that Qwest's vision for Austin, one she seems to endorse enthusiastically, is to take her right back to the kind of quiet storm/adult contemporary/smooth jazz approach that characterized most of her earlier Qwest releases in the 1980s. Paul Brown, Boney James' producer, has been brought in, and, not surprisingly, the saxophonist turns up on "If You Really Need Me Now," a track that also features Austin's old duet partner (and Qwest labelmate) James Ingram. Siedah Garrett, another Qwest stalwart, co-wrote the title song, and Austin herself contributed to the writing of three songs, among them "Love's Been Kind to Me Lately," an attractive pop song that, like many here, may be more welcome on contemporary jazz stations than anywhere else. The songs indulge in street argot here and there, but this is an upscale effort for the most part, music for middle-aged Terry McMillan fans who aren't *Waiting to Exhale* anymore, but still don't want to work up a sweat. It's not bad, but Austin can do much better. *—William Ruhlmann*

The Very Best of Patti Austin: The Singles (1969-1986) / Oct. 16, 2001 / Rhino ♦♦♦♦
Rhino's 2001 release *The Very Best of Patti Austin: The Singles (1969-1986)* lives up to the first part of its title, offering 17 songs, including all her big hits on both the pop and R&B charts. This means there's a heavy dose of her duets—most notably two cuts with James Ingram ("Baby, Come to Me," "How Do You Keep the Music Playing?"), but also a pair of cuts with Quincy Jones and one with Narada Michael Walden, along with all of her solo signatures. This, combined with fine remastering and song-by-song annotation from Austin herself, makes this the definitive Austin collection. *—Stephen Thomas Erlewine*

The CTI Collection / Sony/Connoisseur ♦♦♦♦
A British compilation, *The CTI Collection* gathers the highlights of Patti Austin's early career, specifically the work she did for CTI in the '70s and early '80s. Though this period of her career isn't exactly her best-known—1977's "Say You Love Me" was her biggest hit from this era—her CTI work is still worthwhile, using her clear, mellow voice in a variety of styles spanning pop, soul, disco, and funk. Beyond "Say You Love Me," which is included here, Austin succeeds on the lively "People in Love (Do the Strangest Things)," the jazzy "I Can't Stop," and the Austin-penned "Sweet Sadie the Savior," which is one of the best showcases for her vocal and emotional range from this point in her career. Though her work for CTI was a little glossy and undistinguished compared to the records she'd make with Quincy Jones a few years later, this collection is a good retrospective of this work, gathering the best singles and album tracks from her albums for that label. Aside from the inherent unevenness of the material, the only quirk about *The CTI Collection* is that it presents Austin's work in reverse chronological order, which makes it a little more difficult to trace her development as an artist. Still, this album covers her early career much more thoroughly than Columbia's *The Best of Patti Austin*, offering nearly twice as many tracks. Fans curious about Austin's first recordings and willing to pay import prices should enjoy *The CTI Collection*. *—Heather Phares*

Avant

b. 1978, Cleveland, OH

Vocals / Contemporary R&B, Urban, Trip-Hop

Hailed as the "new voice of ghetto soul" and acknowledged as the first act signed to NBA great Magic Johnson's Magic Johnson Music, Chicago native Avant's debut album, *My Thoughts* was issued by MCA Records on May 9, 2000. Around the same time, the 22-year old singer/songwriter was enjoying a Top Five *Billboard* R&B/Hip Hop hit single, "Separated." The video for the song was getting massive play on cable channels BET and The Box. Avant's style of modern soul owes heavily to fellow Chicago-based singer R.Kelly.

Originally, Avant's manager, Eric Payton, released "Separated" in January 1998 on his Payton Entertainment label. The single began getting airplay on the number one rated radio station WGCI in Chicago before eventually being included on the 1999 MCA compilation, *Summer Heat*. The singer/songwriter wrote "Separated" based on his feelings following a failed romantic relationship. Avant felt that The Lord had blessed him enough for being allowed to put his sadness down on paper. Emotional lyrics such as "listen baby, every time I see you I get a bad vibe/just thinking of someone else in between your thighs... I can't believe I stayed around that damn long... you did me wrong/I thought you were true" won the singer instant acclaim in his home city.

Recorded in Chicago, *My Thoughts* was produced by accomplished multi-instrumentalist Steve Huff. Huff and Avant's overall high-quality musicianship gives *My Thoughts* a refreshing depth. The cover of Rene & Angela's 1983 number 12 R&B ballad classic, "My First Love" stands out with a wonderfully swirling string arrangement by veteran Chicago arranger Tom Tom Washington, known previously as Tom Tom 84 and now as Tom Tom 2000. The slammin' song "Reaction" contains a rhythm guitar sample from Issac Hayes' 1974 number-14 R&B/number-71 Pop hit, "Wonderful." While some singers get too sexually graphic in their songs, Avant decides to leave it up to the listener's own libido and imagination on sensuous ballads such as "I Wanna Know," "Destiny" and "Ooh Aah," and on slammin' jams such as "Reaction" and "Serious." In 2002, he released *Ecstacy* on Johnson's subsidiary, a new album that featured production from Steve Huff again. *—Ed Hogan*

My Thoughts / May 9, 2000 / MCA ♦♦♦
R. Kelly proved to be one of the most influential male R&B vocalists of the '90s, and Avant certainly doesn't escape his influence on *My Thoughts*—the singer's debut album and the first album to come out on basketball icon Magic Johnson's MCA-distributed Magic Johnson Music. Like Chicago native Kelly, Avant is from the Midwest; his home town is Cleveland, and his connection to the Windy City includes his Chicago-based producer Steve "Stone" Huff and his Chicago-based manager Eric Payton, who is among this CD's executive producers. Kelly's influence, in fact, is impossible to miss on *My Thoughts*, a competent, if uneven, effort that Huff produced. Much of the material is routine urban contemporary fare, but on the album's best tracks, you can hear Avant's potential. Arguably the CD's best offering, "My First Love" is a remake of a Rene & Angela ballad that features female vocalist Ketara Wyatt and boasts a delicious '70s-like string arrangement by Tom Tom 2000. Also likable is the melancholy hit "Separated," the moody "This Time," and the candid "Let's Make a Deal," an Avant/Huff composition that finds the singer declaring that a relationship cannot be one-sided. If Avant's phrasing sometimes brings to mind Ronald Isley, it's no coincidence—the Isley Brothers are a major influence on Kelly, who is Avant's primary influence. This isn't to say that *My Thoughts* is in a class with the Isley Brothers' work, or even Kelly's albums. *My Thoughts* isn't mind-blowing, but it's decent more often than not and lets us know that Avant has potential. *—Alex Henderson*

● **Ecstasy** / Mar. 26, 2002 / MCA ♦♦♦
Creatively, Avant's sophomore album, *Ecstasy*, is a step forward for the Cleveland-based urban contemporary singer. This 2002 release isn't perfect—some of the tracks are routine and pedestrian. But *Ecstasy* contains more gems than *My Thoughts*, Avant's competent, if uneven, debut album of 2000. Some things haven't changed; *Ecstasy*, like *My Thoughts*, was produced by Steve "Stone" Huff and Avant still brings a strong R. Kelly influence to the table, which means that listeners are also hearing a strong Ronald Isley influence. (Ronald Isley, lead singer of the Isley Brothers, is among Kelly's primary influences.) *Ecstasy* is hardly a radical departure from *My Thoughts*; the main difference between the two albums is that this time Avant usually has stronger material to work with. The Midwesterner really soars on the bluesy "You Ain't Right" and he is equally impressive on the moody "One Way Street (a duet with the Gap Band's Charlie Wilson). Also quite memorable is "Six in da Morning," which should not be confused with Ice-T's 1986 gangsta rap classic but is a funky, hip-hop-minded jam along the lines of Kelly's "Fiesta." Showing his flexibility, Avant demonstrates that he is as comfortable with hip-hop-friendly funk as he is with romantic ballads and slow jams. Again, *Ecstasy* (which lists basketball icon Magic Johnson as one of its executive producers) isn't without its share of generic filler, but the CD doesn't have as much of it as *My Thoughts*—and for every minus that you can find on this release, there are three or four pluses. If you had to choose between *Ecstasy* and *My Thoughts*, this album would be a better investment. *—Alex Henderson*

The Average White Band

f. 1972, Scotland, **db.** 1982

Group / Funk, Soul, Quiet Storm

Their self-effacing name to the contrary, Average White Band was anything but—one of the few white groups to cross the color line and achieve success and credibility playing funk, with their tight, fiery sound also belying their Scottish heritage, evoking American R&B hotbeds like Detroit, Memphis, and Philadelphia instead. Singer/bassist Alan Gorrie, guitarists Hamish Stuart and Onnie McIntyre, tenor saxophonist Malcolm Duncan, keyboardist/saxophonist Roger Ball, and drummer Robbie McIntosh comprised the original Average White Band lineup.

Veterans of numerous Scottish soul and jazz groups, they made their debut in 1973 as the opening act at Eric Clapton's Rainbow Theatre comeback gig, soon issuing their debut LP, *Show Your Hand*, to little notice. After adopting the abbreviated moniker AWB, a year later the band issued their self-titled sophomore effort, topping the American pop charts with the Arif Mardin-produced instrumental "Pick Up the Pieces." The record's mammoth success was nevertheless tempered by the September 23, 1974, death of McIntosh, who died at a Hollywood party after overdosing on heroin. Ex-Bloodstone drummer Steve Ferrone replaced McIntosh for AWB's third album, 1975's *Cut the Cake*, which scored a Top Ten hit with its title track as well as two other chart entries, "If I Ever Lose This Heaven" and "School Boy Crush." (*Put It Where You Want It*, issued later that same year, was simply a retitled and repackaged *Show Your Hand*.) With 1976's *Soul Searching*, the group reclaimed the full Average White Band name, scoring their final Top 40 hit with "Queen of My Soul." Following the live *Person to Person*, they issued *Benny & Us*, a collaboration with soul legend Ben E. King. However, after subsequent outings, including 1978's *Warmer Communications*, 1979's *Feel No Fret*, and 1980's *Shine*, failed to recapture the energy of AWB's peak, the group dissolved in 1982, with Ferrone later joining Duran Duran and Stuart recording with Paul McCartney. Gorrie, Ball, and McIntyre reformed Average White Band in 1989, tapping vocalist Alex Ligertwood for their comeback effort *Aftershock*. Oft-sampled by hip-hop producers throughout the 1990s, the group continued touring prior to releasing *Soul Tattoo* in 1996. The live album, *Face to Face*, followed three years later. *—Jason Ankeny*

Show Your Hand / 1973 / MCA ✦✦✦

AWB / Aug. 1974 / Rhino ✦✦✦✦✦

After debuting with 1973's excellent but neglected *Show Your Hand* (later reissued as *Put It Where You Want It*), the Average White Band switched from MCA to Atlantic and hit big with this self-titled gem. Upon first hearing gutsy, Tower of Power-influenced funk like "Person to Person" and the instrumental "Pick Up the Pieces" (a number 1 R&B hit), many soul fans were shocked to learn that not only were they white—they were whites from Scotland. Like Teena Marie five years later, AWB embraced soul and funk with so much conviction that it was clear this was anything but an "average" white band. This album is full of treasures that weren't big hits but should have been—including the addictive "You Got It," the ominous "There's Always Someone Waiting" and a gutsy remake of the Isley Brothers' "Work to Do." When Rhino reissued *AWB* on CD in 1995, an edited live version of "Pick Up the Pieces" recorded at the 1977 Montreux Jazz Festival was added. (The full-length version had been included on Rhino's 1994 reissue of *Warmer Communications*). *—Alex Henderson*

Put It Where You Want It / Mar. 1975 / MCA ✦✦✦

Put It Where You Want It is a retitled reissue of the Average White Band's first album, *Show Your Hand* (1973). *— William Ruhlmann*

Cut the Cake / Jun. 1975 / Rhino ✦✦✦

In the informative liner notes that he wrote for Rhino's early-'90s reissue of *Cut the Cake*, writer A. Scott Galloway explains that this excellent album was recorded under less-than-ideal circumstances. The Average White Band's original drummer, Robbie McIntosh, died of a heroin overdose in 1974, and the surviving members were still in mourning when they started working on their third album, *Cut the Cake* (which originally came out on LP in 1975). Steve Ferrone, a black drummer from London, England, was hired as a replacement—ironically, he became the first black member of a Scottish soul/funk band that had a very African-American sound and a largely African-American following. Despite the fact that AWB's members still had McIntosh's death on their minds when they were writing and recording *Cut the Cake*, this isn't a depressing or consistently melancholy album—far from it. In fact, parts of the album are downright fun, especially uptempo funk gems like "School Boy Crush," "Groovin' the Night Away" and the hit title song (which made it to number 7 on *Billboard*'s R&B singles chart). *Cut the Cake* is also the album that gave us the ballad "Cloudy" (one of the more melancholy tracks) and AWB's version of "If I Ever Lose This Heaven," a smooth soul classic that was originally recorded by Quincy Jones in 1973. The song wasn't a chartbuster—it peaked at number 25 on *Billboard*'s R&B singles chart—but it did become a favorite among AWB fans and enjoyed a lot of exposure on quiet storm formats. AWB's members certainly don't sound like they're in mourning on *Cut the Cake*—if anything, they honor McIntosh's memory by showing their resilience and delivering one of their finest, most engaging albums. *—Alex Henderson*

Soul Searching / Jul. 1976 / Rhino ✦✦✦✦

AWB's artistic winning streak continued with its outstanding fourth album, *Soul Searching*. Interestingly, this wasn't an album that enjoyed a great deal of publicity or contained a lot of major hits. In fact, its biggest single, the dreamy "Queen of My Soul," only made it to number 21 on *Billboard*'s R&B albums chart. But thanks to the devoted following AWB had acquired since signing with Atlantic in 1974, *Soul Searching* went gold. Indeed, AWB aficionados were quite receptive to first-rate material ranging from the invigorating "I'm the One" to the hauntingly romantic "A Love of Your Own." By zeroing in on their strengths—hard-hitting funk and delightfully melodic soul—AWB saw to it that *Soul Searching* was every bit as rewarding as its predecessors. *—Alex Henderson*

Person to Person / Jan. 1977 / Rhino ✦✦✦

Scotland's Average White Band was in a celebratory mood on its third major-label release, the live double-album *Person to Person*. Following the crossover success of the band's self-titled debut and subsequent *Cut the Cake*, *Person to Person* presented the six-piece R&B/funk act stretching out on most of its hits. Lead vocalists Alan Gorrie and Hamish Stuart switch between guitar and bass chores throughout, and drive the opening title track and "Cut the Cake." The ballads "If I Ever Lose This Heaven" and "Cloudy" provide nice changes of pace; rhythm guitarist Onnie McIntyre and drummer Steve Ferrone shine on lesser-known gems like "I'm the One" and "Love Your Life." But the real prize of this collection is an 18-minute version of the Average White Band's biggest hit, the instrumental "Pick Up the Pieces." After the expected solos from the studio version by saxophonists Roger Ball and Malcolm "Molly" Duncan, McIntyre, Stuart, Gorrie, and Ferrone take extended leads in this masterpiece of editing—the track actually features different versions from four concert halls, all spliced together so that each musician could have the solo of his choice represented. A few walk-through versions ("T.L.C.," "School Boy Crush," and the Marvin Gaye hit "Heard It Through the Grapevine") away from being a classic, *Person to Person* still shows what a great live act this underrated band was in its heyday. *—Bill Meredith*

Benny & Us / Jul. 1977 / Atlantic ✦✦✦

Warmer Communications . . . and More / 1978 / Rhino ✦✦✦✦

When other soulsters were turning to flashy disco/pop arrangements in 1978, AWB wisely stuck with the type of smooth soul and unapologetically gritty funk that had put the band on the map. By 1980, AWB would, in fact, turn to straight-up disco. But on *Warmer Communications*, AWB's last truly great album, the funk still prevailed. From such sweaty funk as "Your Love Is a Miracle," "Big City Lights" and "Same Feeling, Different Song" to relaxed "slow jams" like "One Look Over My Shoulder (Is This Really Goodbye?)" and the ethereal "She's a Dream," *Warmer Communications* is the work of a band that was still being true to itself. In 1994, Rhino reissued this classic on CD and added two instrumental bonus tracks: the driving "McEwan's Export" and an extended live version of "Pick Up the Pieces" (recorded at the 1977 Montreux Jazz Festival in Switzerland) that boasts improvisatory solos by jazz greats like trumpeter Randy Brecker, tenor sax man Michael Brecker, alto sax man Sonny Fortune and flutist Herbie Mann. The inspired jam proves that the freedom of jazz and the immediacy of R&B can be a dynamic combination. *—Alex Henderson*

Feel No Fret . . . And More / 1979 / Rhino/Atlantic ✦✦✦

The once-magnificent Average White Band was suffering from both artistic and commercial decline by the end of the 1970s. Although decent, *Feel No Fret* is a mild disappointment when compared to such pearls as *Soul Searching* and *Cut the Cake*. There are some noteworthy songs here, including the congenial "Atlantic Avenue," the grinding "When Will You Be Mine," and a cover of "Walk on By" (previously recorded by Dionne Warwick, Isaac Hayes, and Gloria Gaynor). But on the whole, this CD (which boasts four likable, but not essential, bonus tracks first heard on the *Part VIII* LP) falls short of AWB's previously high standards. Only the more devoted AWB fans will want this album, the first AWB date since 1973's *Put It Where You Want It* (aka *Show Your Hand*) that didn't go gold. *—Alex Henderson*

Shine / May 1980 / Arista ✦✦

Cupid's in Fashion / 1982 / RCA ✦

Aftershock / 1989 / Track Record ✦

The Average White Band were down to a trio consisting of singer/bassist Alan Gorrie, guitarist/singer Onnie McIntyre, and saxophonist Roger Ball on *Aftershock*, the band's first new album in six years. The threesome brought in a lot of session players, however, starting with Alex Ligertwood, who sang on three songs, and Elliot Lewis, who handled keyboards and programming, and including such friends as Chaka Khan and the Ohio Players. Producer John Robie, known for his mechanistic dance tracks, emphasized Average White Band's traditional funk sound without finding an effective way to update it, resulting in an album that was faithful to the band's heyday but did not address its career decline. *— William Ruhlmann*

● **Pickin' Up the Pieces: The Best of Average White Band (1974–1980)** / Sep. 1, 1992 / Rhino ✦✦✦✦✦

Anyone who is seriously interested in '70s soul and funk should own at least three or four Average White Band albums. But if a person insists on allotting himself/herself only one AWB CD, this is the logical choice. All of the essential hits—everything from the sweaty funk of "Cut the Cake," "Pick Up the Pieces," and "School Boy Crush" to the unapologetically romantic "If I Ever Lose This Heaven"—is included. Though most of the selections were recorded when AWB was still very much in its prime, a few were made after the Scottish band had peaked. "Let's Go Round Again" (1980) finds AWB taking a glossy pop/disco approach that's hardly in a class with its earlier triumphs, but is likable enough. Most of the selections, however, aren't simply decent; they are excellent. *—Alex Henderson*

Live on the Test / Jan. 20, 1995 / Windsong ✦✦✦

Soul Tattoo / 1997 / Artful ✦✦✦

Long after the Average White Band disappeared from the charts, its impact was being felt. Hip-hop, urban contemporary and new jack swing artists sampled AWB's '70s classics to death in the late '80s and early to mid-'90s, and such retro acts as the Brand New Heavies wore AWB's influence like a badge of honor. When *Soul Tattoo* was released in mid-1997, AWB was a quintet consisting of longtime members Alan Gorrie (lead vocals, bass), Onnie McIntyre (guitar, vocals) and Roger Ball (sax) and newcomers Elliot Lewis (keyboards, lead vocals, bass and guitar) and Peter Abbott (drums, percussion). Although not in a class with *Cut the Cake* or *Soul Searching*, the album (AWB's first since 1989's *Aftershock*) is surprisingly good. Thankfully, the band makes no attempt to appeal to 1997's urban contemporary market, and material ranging from the invigorating, horn-driven funk of "Soul Mine," "Love Is the Bottom Line" and the instrumental "Oh, Maceo" to the laidback soul of "Back to Basics," "Welcome to the Real World" and "No Easy Way to Say Goodbye" sounds like it could have been recorded 20 years earlier. Longtime AWB fans will be glad to hear how well Gorrie's voice has held up, and they'll definitely find *Soul Tattoo* to be inspired and satisfying. *—Alex Henderson*

David Axelrod

b. Apr. 17, 1936, Los Angeles, CA

Producer / Jazz-Funk, Baroque Pop, Psychedelic Pop, Obscuro

A Grammy award-winning producer for Capitol Records who helmed dozens of great jazz, funk, and soul records during the 1960s and '70s (by everyone from Stan Kenton to Lou Rawls to the Electric Prunes to Cannonball Adderley), David Axelrod also forged a distinctive musical style while recording several of the most eccentric albums of the '70s. His sound, as immediately recognizable as it is sparse, combines cavernous, heavily miked drums with baroque orchestration (just a step away from overblown) and ahead-of-his-time themes ranging from the environment to heightened mental awareness.

Born in Los Angeles in 1936, Axelrod learned about arrangement and production largely on his own. He began working as a staff producer for the cool jazz labels Specialty and Contemporary, and led a pair of 1959 LPs—*Free for All* by Frank Rosolino and *The Fox* by Harold Land—that developed an earthy response to the trademarked light, airy sound of West Coast jazz.

By the mid-'60s, Axelrod had grown famous in soul and jazz circles for his excellent recording skills, including two of the finest performance albums of the era, Lou Rawls' *Live!* and Cannonball Adderley's *Mercy, Mercy, Mercy! Live at "The Club"* (the latter was actually a studio date). Both artists tapped him for studio work as well, and Rawls especially benefited by scoring no less than five pop hits during 1966-1967. Capitol rewarded one of its most successful producers just one year later, releasing Axelrod's solo debut, *Song of Innocence*. Based on the visionary, mystical poetry of William Blake (as was its follow-up *Songs of Experience*), the album sounded like nothing else from its era, with melodramatic strings tied to heavy, echoed breakbeats—often supplied by session-drummer supremo Earl Palmer. After *Songs of Experience*, Axelrod turned his attention to the growing plight of the environment with 1970's *Earth Rot*.

Even aside from his burgeoning solo career, Axelrod stayed busy as a producer during the '70s; he recorded several Cannonball Adderley LPs plus works by Gene Ammons and Joe Williams. After 1980's *Marchin'*, however, he took an extended hiatus from recording. Axelrod returned in 1993 with *Requiem: The Holocaust* on Capitol's Liberty subsidiary, and recorded a surprising tribute to roots music (*The Big Country*) two years later. After several big names in the dance community (including DJ Shadow) began sampling Axelrod grooves in the mid-'90s, Stateside released the retrospective *1968 to 1970: An Axelrod Anthology* in 1999. Album reissues appeared the following year, and Axelrod even recorded a remix of "Rabbit in the Headlights," originally by the DJ Shadow project UNKLE. *—John Bush*

Song of Innocence / 1968 / Ascension ✦✦✦✦✦

Producer, arranger, and engineer David Axelrod made his mark with Cannonball Adderley, Lou Rawls, and the Electric Prunes. He created recording dates—both live and in the studio—with crisp innovative production, forward-looking arrangements, and killer sound effects (the Prunes' weird "Mass in F Minor" is a case in point). No one, however, expected him to make his own records. Nonetheless, in 1968 his first concept work was issued under the EMI imprint. His inspiration was *Songs of Innocence*, English poet William Blake's watershed collection of poems; Axelrod set seven of them to music using a bevy of studio musicians and a lot of clout at the label. Using a rock orchestra, Axelrod created a suite that blended pop, rock, jazz, theater music, and R&B that has withstood the test of time, and has been revisited and sampled by electronica pioneers such as DJ Shadow and DJ Cam. Perhaps the best known tune of this mystical mixture is the jazzed out, slow groove of "Holy Thursday," with its bluesy bop piano lines and huger than huge string section playing a vamp from a Count Basie tune. Meanwhile, the rhythm section floats a steady, swinging rhythm to the guitars and brass who answer with dramatic harmonics centered around a complex yet elegant melodic, and the guitar itself screams overhead. It's a jazz boogaloo with classical overtones. And yes, it, and the rest of the album, sound as if it would be excessive and awful. This was visionary work in 1968, and, to commit heresy, withstands the test of time better than the Beatles *Sgt. Pepper's Lonely Hearts Club Band* album that allegedly inspired it. Axelrod's psychedelia is implied; its compositional form and feeling that drive him to celebrate the wildness and folly of youth with celebration and verve. And as a result, the music here sounds fresh, free of cynicism and hipper-than-thou posturing, remaining new each time it is heard. *Song of Innocence* made critics turn their heads in its day, regarding it as a visionary curiosity piece; today it's simply a great, timeless work of pop art that continues to inspire over three decades after its initial release. *—Thom Jurek*

Songs of Experience / 1969 / Ascension ✦✦✦✦✦

After the modicum of success he'd experienced with his debut, *Song of Innocence*, set to William Blake's epic suite of poems, composer, arranger, and producer David Axelrod turned to the British poet's *Songs of Experience* for inspiration in creating his follow-up album. Using eight of Blake's poems, Axelrod composed a suite that was less rock in its aim and more pop- and jazz-oriented in places, but overall a more orchestral work. Texturizing a symphony with percussive elements and the use of British and Irish folk song, as well as the stylistic inventions of fellow arranger Gerald Wilson for effect, Axelrod created a sobering, and, in places, even melancholy collage of song and lyrical styles that slid rather than drove home its point: That experience is a good but bittersweet teacher. Axelrod's compositions are positively literary here, lush and varied, using as much space as they do sound for dramatic and dynamic effect. His complex use of the various colors the horn section was capable of producing allowed him to create new palettes for the rock instrumentation. The centerpiece of the album is "The Human Abstract," a gently swinging, funky, bass-driven work that juxtaposes a strummed electric guitar playing augmented sevenths against an acoustic piano and a muted drone of horns. By the time the guitar enters for its solo, the strings have erected a space out of the ether for themselves to further shore up the orchestra's time-honored body against the wail of unrepentant youth. The tension in the tune is dramatic, colorful, and hued with as much red and yellow as there is blue and black. When the French horns and tuba state their case against the high-flying impetuousness of the restless spirit, a piano bridges the gap, whispering the melody's main theme in the center channel, whispering them both out into silence. Other notables are the positively majestic "The Divine Image," and the pastoral sadness in "A Little Girl Lost." Axelrod's meditations were getting darker with the times in 1969, but they hadn't yet reached the horrific potential for darkness that they would on 1970's *Earth Rot*. In 1969, Axelrod was still a musical contemplative searching for a sound that best exemplified not only his feelings but also the heady text he sought to sonically illustrate. He succeeded in spades. *—Thom Jurek*

Earth Rot / 1970 / Capitol ✦✦✦✦

After the sublime excess of his two takes on William Blake, with *Songs of Innocence* and *Songs of Experience*, David Axelrod went bonkers and issued the single weirdest record of his career that stands pretty much unparalleled more than 30 years later. *Earth Rot* is in effect a cantata for the planet, or, in Axe's own words "contemporary music with ancient yet timely words set to the theme of ecology." Those ancient yet timely words come from the book of Isaiah in the Bible and for a Navajo legend called "Song of the Earth Spirit." There's a nine-piece choir singing these texts, accompanied by a 15-piece orchestra that includes Ernie Watts, Earl Palmer, Willie Green, and Jack Kelso. Capitol's Studio B must have been humming with the mojo for these dates. Musically, each side is divided into four sections. Side one deals with the warnings themselves. Axelrod's musical begins by celebrating the earth's lorry and then indicting humans for messing it up. With gorgeous tings of flute and guitar, he underlines his upfront horn section with a shimmering grace. Side two contains the warnings themselves, and Philip Glass' chorus lines in his opera were influenced by Axelrod's, I swear. The half-step dissonances between pitches, the long lines, the glimmer of consonance as the music enters the front of the mix—here with Ernie Watts blowing like crazy. In all, though, for as dark as it was reputed to be at the time, this is a blissed-out album musically. Gorgeous, lush, and full of gentleness, if it weren't so strange, so completely out of synch with everything that came before and after it, there might be a context in which to give it a higher rating. Bottom line, though, is that he was never this consistent again. *—Thom Jurek*

Rock Messiah / 1972 / RCA ✦✦✦

Heavy Axe / 1975 / Fantasy ✦✦

Axelrod's reputation underwent an extraordinary reassessment in the late '90s, with his instrumental albums and work as an arranger coming to be considered innovative and *au courant* by some tastemakers. Even taking into account that this is just one of many records bearing the Axelrod imprint, one has to wonder if the rehabilitation is in fact unwarranted inflation. This is run-of-the-mill, largely instrumental soul-jazz-funk, split between Axelrod originals and covers of tunes by Stevie Wonder, Carly Simon, Vince Guaraldi, and Cannonball Adderley. It would be eminently suitable for background soundtrack music for 1970s films and made for TV movies, and while some such efforts can be good, in this context, that is *not* meant as praise. Do you really want to hear a watery fusion cover of "You're So Vain," with Stephanie Spruill's straining soul vocals? You're welcome to it. Although about a couple dozen musicians (including Adderley and Gene Ammons) take part in the string- and horn-drenched arrangements, really these aren't that creative. They sound more like quickly assembled, made-to-order filler music for video productions, the horns sometimes sounding rather like those of school marching bands, with touches of early-'70s-style electric keyboards and wah-wahing funk-rock guitars. There's an orgiastic wordless female vocal on "Mucho Chupar," if that's what you like. The entire album is contained on the Fantasy CD reissue *The Axelrod Chronicles*, which adds eight tracks from 1973-1974 that Axelrod produced and/or arranged on albums by Gene Ammons, Nat Adderley, Hampton Hawes, and Funk, Inc. *—Richie Unterberger*

Seriously Deep / 1975 / Polydor ✦✦✦

Strange Ladies / 1978 / MCA ✦✦

Marchin' / 1980 / MCA ✦✦

Requiem: The Holocaust / 1993 / Liberty ✦✦✦

The Big Country / 1995 / Liberty ✦✦✦

• **1968 to 1970: An Axelrod Anthology** / 1999 / Stateside ✦✦✦✦✦

Confounding dozens of vinyl-philes who'd paid hundreds of dollars for the original LPs, *1968 to 1970: An Axelrod Anthology* compiles 11 tracks from the first (and best) three albums released by David Axelrod, including the two-volume series devoted to William Blake (*Song of Innocence, Songs of Experience*) and the 1970 ecological nightmare, *Earth Rot*. Alongside those tracks are seven of Axelrod's best productions, for soul singers like Lou Rawls (the Buffalo Springfield's "For What It's Worth") and Letta as well as Cannonball Adderley and the psychedelic mystics known as the Electric Prunes. The solo Axelrod tracks are dreadfully spare, usually just cavernous drum pattern and occasional orchestral texture, but the songs have an odd power that grows over time. Overall, *1968 to 1970: An Axelrod Anthology* is quite preferrable to spending collectors' prices for the originals. *—John Bush*

The Axelrod Chronicles / May 30, 2000 / Fantasy ✦✦✦

The first half of this 16-track compilation is comprised of Axelrod's 1974 album *Heavy Axe* (which he arranged and conducted without playing any instruments); the final eight tracks are cuts from 1973-1974 that Axelrod produced and/or arranged on albums by Gene Ammons, Nat Adderley, Hampton Hawes, and Funk, Inc. Axelrod's reputation underwent an extraordinary reassessment in the late '90s, with his instrumental albums and work as an arranger coming to be considered innovative and *au courant* by some tastemakers. Even taking into account that *Heavy Axe* is just one of many records bearing the Axelrod imprint, one has to wonder if the rehabilitation is in fact unwarranted inflation. It's run-of-the-mill, largely instrumental soul-jazz-funk, split between Axelrod originals and covers of tunes by Stevie Wonder, Carly Simon, Vince Guaraldi, and Cannonball Adderley. It would be eminently suitable for background soundtrack music for 1970s films and made-for-TV movies, and while some such efforts can be good, in this context, that is *not* meant as praise. Do you really want to hear a watery fusion cover of "You're So Vain," with Stephanie Spruill's straining soul vocals? You're welcome to it. Although about a couple of dozen musicians (including Adderley and Gene Ammons) take part in the string- and horn-drenched arrangements, really these aren't that creative. They sound more like quickly assembled, made-to-order filler music for video productions, the horns sometimes sounding rather like those of school marching bands, with touches of early-'70s-style electric keyboards and wah-wahing funk-rock guitars. There's an orgiastic, wordless female vocal on "Mucho Chupar," if that's your bag. As for the bonus cuts with assorted other artists, these are mostly pretty blah fusion, bearing the stamp of bloated, too-slick circa 1973-1974 pop-jazz-rock production. Nat Adderley gets into moodily suave pop-soul vocals on "Quit It," which is about the best of the extras. *—Richie Unterberger*

David Axelrod / 2001 / Mo' Wax ♦♦♦♦

It was reasonable to look at the dark side of a "new album" equation by legendary L.A. composer/producer/arranger David Axelrod. After all, it is on Mo' Wax, and was recorded at their beckoning. Axelrod has been sampled by every hip and wannabe DJ in the Northern hemisphere, and he is an iconoclast. For all the buildup it's gotten, it seemed like it had to tank because more than ever, music fans are encouraged to drink the music hype Kool-Aid week after week—and consequently, there is less and less there. However, after hiding out for six long years, receiving—and cashing—check after check from hip-hop DJs who sampled his material to various ends, the nefarious Axelrod returns to the scene of his greatest glories, Capitol's Studio B, with a slew of his old musical gang in tow and wrestles a gem of an album from the jaws of antiquity. His first recording in six years is far from the storied excess of either 1993's *Requiem* or 1995's paean to country music, *The Big Country*. Instead, Axelrod has claimed seven songs from a recording begun for Reprise in 1969. It seems Axelrod had been tinkering about with the idea of writing an album based on Goethe's *Faust* for Reprise. His lead sheets had been written and the rhythm tracks were already recorded and put on acetates. For internal reasons at Warner Bros., the album never happened and the material was all but forgotten until Mo' Wax stepped in after hearing about the existence of the acetates. Seven of the nine tracks here come from those sessions. They have been reworked and adorned with orchestral textures. In addition there are two new tracks: "The Little Children," the album's opening salvo, is a collaboration between Axelrod and longtime co-producer H.P. Barnum and West Coast rapper MC Ras Kass; and the other, "Loved Boy," is a reunion between Axelrod and R&B singer Lou Rawls that closes the disc. The set opens with trembling violins and Jim Hughart's trademark singing bassline that foreshadows the entrance of a choir and bassoon as well as other orchestral tinges. When Ras Kass enters, a glorious medieval gothic mood has been established, and despite his rapping—no streetwise style either, he's speaking as the true dark side of the Pied Piper—the mood isn't sullied. The strings swell and pulse, with winds and choir voices in the background. A cello bows out a lament and the track erupts into a post-bop blues, with Lanny Morgan blowing alto. It's a stunning montage that leaves an eerie taste in the listener's mouth until the full-fried boogaloo of "Jimmy T" kicks in. Orchestral swells meet the Meters' street funk and are tied together by Bob Efford's baritone solo. As always, Howard Roberts plays the hell out of the guitar, making each note sting—especially as the choir enters, and Axelrod's longtime rhythm section of Carol Kaye on bass, Earl Palmer on drums, Gary Coleman on percussion, and Don Randi on piano is augmented by none other than Joe Sample on B-3. By track three, "Crystal Ball," with Roberts' guitar biting deeply into the orchestra to lead the charge on the lead sheets, listeners realize that it's not going to stop, that there is no fluke or bad cliché, in the set's all too brief 36 minutes. Track after track, Axelrod displays that he has a word tattooed on each hand: on the right, "Restraint"; on the left, "Excess." He employs them judiciously and with extreme prejudice; nothing is left to chance. You can feel the time he spent getting solid takes from virtually every musician here, creating a blend of pop, rock, jazz, classical, and blues that seamless fits into his catalog—particularly from the time period of 1968-1970. The stylistically elegant swirl of music styles, besotted with poetic excess and shining harmonic truth and beauty, is nearly dizzying. From soul to noirish jazz to baroque pomp and circumstance to vaudeville to R&B, Axelrod digs deep into the box to pry pearl after pearl with titles dedicated symbolically to friends and kindred spirits, like "The Shadow Knows" (for DJ Shadow as much as the old radio program), "The Dr. & the Diamond" (for Dre and producer Diamond), and "Jimmy T" (for James Tolbert). On "Loved Boy" Rawls delivers the vocal performance of his career. All raw and throaty, Rawls climbs over words that are emotionally searing and reaches deep into his heart for a delivery that comes immediately. It seems that Rawls was with Axelrod when the latter received the news that his son had died. Rawls lets the orchestra buoy him up and carry him through the grief into a space that only people who've been touched by this experience can know. The drama in the tune is from the singer, not the song; he turns it and turns it again, over and over in the silence until it cracks; he then pries it open, right from the arrangement, and whispers to what is left of the song until it gives up its secret grief and pain. With the trumpet into and the brass sparely touching the melody, Rawls holds everything in his hands and lets it all drop, effortlessly. Only Nina Simone, Mahalia Jackson, and Paul Robeson could touch this still point and make it move into another dimension the way Rawls does with Axelrod's charts. And suddenly, it's over, with nothing but a whisper of the CD spinning to a dead stop and silence. The certainty of joy and drama that existed three and a half minutes before has ceased to matter and everything is up in the air—endless questions and the answers that do come are too fragile to hold up. Why would anybody end a wild, swinging disc like this one with the song "Loved Boy"? It's a teetering question that sends the mind to search in despair for an answer, and the only one forthcoming is simply that Axelrod isn't just anybody; he's nobody, nobody but himself, that is, and this is reason enough for him to air his grief as honestly, gorgeously, and painfully in his arrangements and songs as he needs to. It is truly an unselfish act, too, because there is no place on an album like this one (or maybe any one) to place such a song—no place but the end, that is. The song is so heartbreakingly beautiful and moving that along with the best performances in Rawls' career, it is one of the most personal and poetically honest songs in Axelrod's repertoire. To have it at all after such a fine piece of emotionally and aesthetically satisfying art has already been presented to listeners is a gift beyond the scope of any musician, critic, or music fan to assess. *—Thom Jurek*

Roy Ayers

b. Sep. 10, 1940, Los Angeles, CA

Vibraphone / Soul-Jazz, Jazz-Funk, Fusion, Jazz-Pop

Once one of the most visible and winning jazz vibraphonists of the 1960s, then an R&B bandleader in the 1970s and '80s, Roy Ayers' reputation s now that of one of the prophets of acid jazz, a man decades ahead of his time. A tune like 1972's "Move to Groove" by the Roy Ayers Ubiquity has a crackling backbeat that serves as the prototype for the shuffling hip-hop groove that became, shall we say, ubiquitous on acid jazz records; and his relaxed 1976 song "Everybody Loves the Sunshine" has been frequently sampled. Yet Ayers' own playing has always been rooted in hard bop: crisp, lyrical, rhythmically resilient. His own reaction to being canonized by the hip-hop crowd as the "Icon Man" is tempered with the detachment of a survivor in a rough business. "I'm having fun laughing with it," he has said. "I don't mind what they call me, that's what people do in this industry."

Growing up in a musical family—his father played trombone, his mother taught him the piano—the five-year-old Ayers was given a set of vibe mallets by Lionel Hampton, but didn't start on the instrument until he was 17. He got involved in the West Coast jazz scene in his early twenties, recording with Curtis Amy (1962), Jack Wilson (1963-1967), and the Gerald Wilson Orchestra (1965-1966); and playing with Teddy Edwards, Chico Hamilton, Hampton Hawes and Phineas Newborn. A session with Herbie Mann at the Lighthouse in Hermosa Beach led to a four-year gig with the versatile flutist (1966-1970), an experience that gave Ayers tremendous exposure and opened his ears to styles of music other than the bebop that he had grown up with.

After being featured prominently on Mann's hit *Memphis Underground* album and recording three solo albums for Atlantic under Mann's supervision, Ayers left the group in 1970 to form the Roy Ayers Ubiquity, which recorded several albums for Polydor and featured such players as Sonny Fortune, Billy Cobham, Omar Hakim, and Alphonse Mouzon. An R&B-jazz-rock band influenced by electric Miles Davis and the Herbie Hancock Sextet at first, the Ubiquity gradually shed its jazz component in favor of R&B/funk and disco. Though Ayers' pop records were commercially successful, with several charted singles on the R&B charts for Polydor and Columbia, they became increasingly, perhaps correspondingly, devoid of musical interest.

In the 1980s, besides leading his bands and recording, Ayers collaborated with Nigerian musician Fela Anikulapo-Kuti, formed Uno Melodic Records, and produced and/or co-wrote several recordings for various artists. As the merger of hip-hop and jazz took hold in the early '90s, Ayers made a guest appearance on Guru's seminal *Jazzmatazz* album in 1993 and played at New York clubs with Guru and Donald Byrd. Though most of his solo records had been out of print for years, Verve issued a two-CD anthology of his work with Ubiquity and the first U.S. release of a live gig at the 1972 Montreux Jazz Festival; the latter finds the group playing excellent straight-ahead jazz, as well as jazz-rock and R&B. *—Richard S. Ginell*

Daddy Bug & Friends / Mar. 6, 1967-Dec. 11, 1969 / Atlantic ♦♦♦♦

During 1967-1969, vibraphonist Roy Ayers (a few years before he turned to disco music) recorded three excellent albums for Atlantic. This 1976 LP has selections from two of the records, plus a pair of selections ("In the Limelight" and "Virgo Vibes") that were previously unreleased. On the fine sampler, Ayers' sidemen include Herbie Hancock, Joe Henderson, Charles Tolliver, and Ron Carter. "Slow Motion," the latest selection (from Dec. 1969), hints at the commercial direction that Ayers would be emphasizing after 1970. *—Scott Yanow*

Stoned Soul Picnic / Jun. 20, 1968 / 32 Jazz ♦♦♦

Stoned Soul Picnic dates from the earlier part of Roy Ayers' career as a leader, before he delved heavily into R&B and funk fusions and instead concentrated more on soul-jazz grooves. Ayers leads a septet including such big names as pianist Herbie Hancock, altoist Gary Bartz, bassist Ron Carter, and flutist Hubert Laws. The Laura Nyro-penned title track foreshadows Ayers' later forays beyond the boundaries of pure jazz, and the group keeps the groove percolating nicely throughout, making *Stoned Soul Picnic* one of Ayers' better jazz-oriented outings. *—Steve Huey*

Daddy's Back / Mar. 11, 1969-Mar. 12, 1969 / Atco ♦♦

This has pop-soul and funk touches, but fine vibes solos. *—Ron Wynn*

Ubiquity / 1971 / Polydor ♦♦♦

This is the start of the Ubiquity phase; best of funk with R&B-jazz. *—Ron Wynn*

Live at the Montreux Jazz Festival / Jun. 20, 1972 / Verve ♦♦♦

Generally disregarded by jazz purists, Roy Ayers' *Live at the Montreux Jazz Festival* is nevertheless a thoroughly engaging set of funky jazz fusion. In fact, the album is one of the most sampled jazz records in hip-hop. Loops of this performance of "Everybody Loves the Sunshine" have appeared on tracks by A Tribe Called Quest, Brand Nubian, and several others. The original grooves on this album are just as funky as those the hip-hop artists have derived from it. In fact, Ayers is probably funkier and looser than the musicians that borrowed from him several years later. *Live at the Montreux Jazz Festival* is one of the core recordings of acid jazz, "rare grooves," and jazz hip-hop; it's a record that sounds better 20 years after its release than it did when it first appeared. *—Stephen Thomas Erlewine*

Coffy / 1973 / Polydor ♦♦♦♦

Virgo Red / 1973 / Polydor ♦♦♦♦

Change Up the Groove / 1974 / Polydor ♦♦

A Tear to a Smile / 1975 / Polydor ♦♦♦

Mystic Voyage / 1975 / Polydor ♦♦♦

Depending on who you talk to, 1975's *Mystic Voyage* is either a classic or an example of a talented musician lowering his standards in order to make more money. Many funk and soul aficionados consider *Mystic Voyage* a classic, and the album has been sampled extensively by hip-hop and acid jazz artists. But jazz snobs have about as much use for *Mystic Voyage* as they have for George Benson's *Breezin'* and Patrice Rushen's *Pizzazz*, both of which found artists who used to specialize in straight-ahead jazz burning up the *Billboard* charts with more commercial music. *Mystic Voyage* doesn't pretend to be jazz; its primary focus is R&B, and it must be judged by R&B standards instead of jazz standards. Judging *Mystic Voyage* by jazz standards is like ordering a pizza and complaining that it doesn't taste like Vietnamese food; pizza isn't supposed to resemble Vietnamese cuisine, and similarly, *Mystic Voyage* isn't meant to impress jazz's hardcore. The only tune on the album that has anything to do with jazz is the title track, a laid-back pop-jazz instrumental that became a favorite with the quiet storm crowd. But *Mystic Voyage* is dominated by vocal-oriented R&B, and that includes gritty funk items like "Funky Motion," "Evolution," and "Spirit of Doo Do," as well as Ashford & Simpson's mellow "Take All the Time You Need." Although *Mystic Voyage* is a favorite among Ayers fans, it isn't the best R&B-oriented album that he recorded in the 1970s—*Vibrations* and *Everybody Loves the Sunshine* are actually stronger and more essential. But it's definitely enjoyable and pleasing if you fancy 1970s soul and funk and aren't a jazz snob. *—Alex Henderson*

Everybody Loves the Sunshine / 1976 / Polydor ♦♦

Roy Ayers' had long made his shift into R&B/soul by 1976's *Everybody Loves the Sunshine.* His recordings of this period can be very hit and miss, and in this particular record, you get both. The title track, "Everybody Loves the Sunshine," is a quintessential song from the mid-'70s. While it might not have slammed the charts like Wild Cherry's "Play That Funky Music," it's still a revered classic. It evokes that feeling of sweltering concrete in Brooklyn where the only relief is the local fire hydrant. Entirely sung by a choir repeating the same lines throughout, the rhythm section rolls along with a perfectly looped laid-back groove. It moves along lazily, hypnotically, and sluggishly as the sun slows things down to the right speed and "folks get down in the sunshine." The rest of the album can be considered incidental, but still mildly interesting. *—Jack LV Isles*

Red, Black and Green / 1976 / Polydor ♦♦♦

Vibrations / 1976 / Polydor ♦♦♦

Whenever someone makes the transition from jazz instrumentalist to R&B singer, he/she is bound to be lambasted by jazz purists and denounced as a sellout. Roy Ayers was no exception—like George Benson, George Duke, and Patrice Rushen, Ayers was frequently attacked by jazz's hardcore in the late '70s for turning away from instrumental jazz and making vocal-oriented soul and funk his main focus. But what didn't interest jazz snobs excited R&B lovers, who found a lot to admire about *Vibrations* and other Ayers albums from that period. This 1976 LP boasted the moody hit "Searching," which has jazz overtones but is essentially an R&B song. Ayers and his band Ubiquity are also quite appealing on gems that range from the sweaty, driving funk of "One Sweet Love to Remember," "Moving Grooving," "Higher," and "Domelo (Give It to Me)," to mellow quiet storm numbers like "Baby, You Give Me a Feeling" and "Baby, I Need Your Love." With *Vibrations,* Ayers reminded us that jazz's loss was certainly soul/funk's gain. *—Alex Henderson*

Crystal Reflections / 1977 / Muse ♦♦♦

Let's Do It / 1978 / Polydor ♦♦

It's always regrettable when a talented jazz improviser puts jazz on the back burner, and that's exactly what Roy Ayers did when he made soul and funk his primary emphasis in the late '70s. As a jazz vibist, Ayers showed great potential in the '60s and early '70s, so it's understandable that jazz lovers were sorry to see him give up instrumental jazz. But when jazz purists claimed that Ayers' soul/funk output was worthless, they were dead wrong. The truth is that while *Let's Do It* doesn't have much to offer from a jazz standpoint, it's an excellent R&B outing. Ayers and Ubiquity are as appealing on the infectious funk hit "Freaky Deaky" as they are on "Kiss," "You Came Into My Life," and other examples of mellow, relaxed quiet storm music. While the LP's more mellow offerings have jazz overtones, it's important to realize that they're R&B tunes first and foremost—saying that something is jazzy is not the same as calling it jazz. *Let's Do It* isn't the place to go looking for either acoustic jazz or electric jazz-fusion, but it's well worth obtaining if you're interested in '70s soul/funk. *—Alex Henderson*

You Send Me / 1978 / Polydor ♦♦

With 1978's *You Send Me,* Roy Ayers added vocalist Carla Vaughn to his band Ubiquity. Vaughn, who is featured on several selections, never became a big name in the R&B world, but showed some promise on this LP. When she hits the high notes, Vaughn has a Deniece Williams-ish appeal—and she proves to be an asset to Ayers when she sings lead on "I Want to Touch You Baby," the hypnotic "Can't You See Me," and a lush remake of Sam Cooke's "You Send Me." While Cooke's original 1957 version was pure doo wop, Ayers' sexy interpretation has a lot of quiet storm appeal. The gems that *don't* feature Benson at all include the funky "It Ain't Your Sign, It's Your Mind" and the disco-influenced "Get on Up, Get on Down," which didn't receive much radio airplay, but enjoyed its share of dance club exposure. Like other albums that Ayers recorded in the late '70s, *You Send Me* won't interest jazz purists but is rightly considered a classic by soul and funk enthusiasts. *—Alex Henderson*

Love Fantasy / 1980 / Polydor ♦♦♦

In the early '70s, Ayers was the most successful jazz act for Polydor Records. With various producers and arrangers, Ayers' always did tuneful yet challenging tracks. His warm vibe playing earned equal jazz and R&B acclaim. The bass-heavy "Red, Black and Green" typifies the style. By 1976's masterful *Everybody Loves the Sunshine,* the balance tilted to more non-jazz presentation. *Love Fantasy* finds Ayers at three years of superstar status. Most of the precise jazz playing had been toned down as well as his vibraphone playing. Luckily for Ayers and his fans, he still possessed a great musical ear and frequent co-producer William Allen did the strong string arrangements. That being said, *Love Fantasy* frequently veers too wildly from the sublime to the ridiculous. The title track is a little too repetitive for even his fans. The dance tracks here are disposable. "Rock Your Roll" and "Baby Bubba" did nothing but help get those unfortunate phrases in the lexicon. At this point, Ayers' metier was making great romantic and sensual music. So much so he could attain that even on the midtempo, self-empowerment track "Believe in Yourself." *Love Fantasy* also has two of Ayers' best tracks. This album has two of his best romantic tracks. "Sigh (Feel the Vibration)" unfortunately has Ayers breathing heavily throughout the track. "Betcha Gonna" has strong bass and drum interplay and has Ayers playing the synth and singing too many come-ons to mention. Despite the *Love Fantasy*'s lack of jazz, fans of Ayers' late-'70s/early-'80s work will indeed enjoy this. *—Jason Elias*

No Stranger to Love / 1980 / Polydor ♦♦♦

When you obtained a Roy Ayers/Ubiquity album in the late '70s you could usually count on two things: the funk smokers would be gritty and infectious, and the quiet storm tunes would be mellow and seductive. *No Stranger to Love* was no exception. Ayers comes through with some sweaty, get-down funk grooves, including "Shack Up, Pack Up, It's Up (When I'm Gone)," "Slyde," and the hit single "Don't Stop the Feeling." The quiet storm audience was bound to appreciate soft, relaxed, jazzy items like "No Stranger to Love/Want You" and Ayers' remake of Bobby Caldwell's "What You Won't Do For Love." When *No Stranger to Love* came out in 1979, the Disco Era was still in effect, so it isn't surprising that Ayers adds a fair amount of disco gloss to "Don't Hide Your Love." Whether he's in shake-your-booty mode or lover-man mode, Ayers exited the '70s on a high note with this excellent LP. *—Alex Henderson*

Prime Time / 1980 / Polydor ♦♦♦

The second album by the two jazz artists together treads the same furrow as the first. Dominated by Roy Ayers' style, the eight tracks feature an array of artists including Miki Howard and Augie Johnson of Side Effect, Dawn Silva from the Brides of Funkenstein, and Mike & Brenda Sutton. Only two numbers qualify as ballads. Uptempo material rules this roost, highlighted by "You Make Me Feel Like Rockin'," the funky "Thank You, Thank You," "It Ain't Your Sign, It's Your Mind," and "Million Dollar Baby." Wayne Henderson's trombone gets a good workout on "Can You Dance." It's a competent album, but 180-degrees from their jazz roots, and not as engaging as its predecessor. *—Andrew Hamilton*

Africa, Center of the World / 1981 / Polydor ♦♦♦

Feelin' Good / 1981 / Polydor ♦♦

You Might Be Surprised / 1985 / Columbia ♦♦♦

When *You Might Be Surprised* came out in 1985, Roy Ayers wasn't having as many hits as he had enjoyed in the late '70s. The R&B landscape had changed a lot since the days of *Vibrations* (1976) and *You Send Me* (1978). Ayers knew that if he didn't want to be accused of sounding dated, he needed to appeal to the urban contemporary tastes of 1985, so on this album he manages to update his approach without being untrue to himself. The production (some of it by James Mtume, some of it by Ayers himself) is high-tech and hip-hop-influenced—synthesizers and drum machines are prominent, and there are few horns and no strings. But Ayers still sounds distinctive on material that ranges from the clever single "Programmed for Love," and the funky "Can I See You," to the playful title song (a duet with singer Jean Carn). The opener "Hot" has some Prince/Jesse Johnson/Morris Day influence, but without obscuring Ayers' own identity. This time, there are a few likable, if unremarkable, jazz/R&B/pop instrumentals, which include "Night Flyte" and "Virgo" (a tune that employs Branford Marsalis on tenor sax). *You Might Be Surprised* isn't among Ayers' essential albums, but all things considered, it was a respectable addition to his catalog. *—Alex Henderson*

● **Evolution: The Polydor Anthology** / 1995 / Polydor ♦♦♦♦♦

Evolution charts Roy Ayers' 12 years and 20 LPs with Polydor, a rich time where his gliding, loose-groove jazz-funk gained many fans—though perhaps fewer than it did 20 years later in the midst of the rare groove/acid jazz revival. During the 1970s, Ayers and his band, Ubiquity, progressed from political- and social-commentary funk to blaxploitation to disco to some surprisingly touching R&B ballads, and this two-disc set covers it all with grace and a smooth flow. Fans of hip-hop, groove music, funk, and jazz will all be able to find something to enjoy on the collection. Highlights include "We Live in Brooklyn Baby," "Evolution," "Running Away," and "Get on Up, Get on Down," among others. *—John Bush*

The Best of Roy Ayers: Love Fantasy / Feb. 4, 1997 / Polydor ♦♦♦♦

Vibist Roy Ayers' proto-acid-jazz is collected on this best-of compilation, which features performances of "Running Away," "Don't Stop the Feeling," "What You Won't Do for Love" and "Mystic Voyage." *—Jason Ankeny*

B

B2K

f. 2001

Group / Urban, Teen Pop, Dance-Pop

Urban boy band B2K broke into the pop market in early 2002 with "Uh Huh," a fun song driven by more-dance-than-hip-hop beats and a hot delivery, downright sexy for four young innocent-looking men. The single's success drew attention toward the group's self-titled debut album and group members Omarion, Raz-B, Lil Fizz, and J-Boog. Epic Records, the label that developed B2K, marketed Jhene in conjunction with the boy band. The young woman is Lil Fizz's cousin and toured with B2K in 2002. *—Jason Birchmeier*

● **B2K** / Mar. 12, 2002 / Epic ♦♦♦

Epic Records definitely did its homework before unleashing B2K into the pop market. The boy band of clean-cut and suave young black men is everything a marketing department dreams about: attractive teens-becoming-men who make the girls melt with a little bit of a rugged, tough-guy attitude and flashy clothes. Of course, there are also the dance beats that are as much dance-pop as hip-hop; in fact, you might even wager a bet that the many producers and songwriters on this album had been listening to a bit of Craig David and other British 2-step pop stars. Plus, the group members are capable singers as well, which is another bonus. Overall, with the girl-magnet looks, the trendy radio-ready production, and the limitless vocal hooks, Epic Records has all the makings of pop stardom in B2K, including a market-testing hit single in "Uh Huh" that set the stage for the group's debut album. *B2K*, a self-titled album, gets off to a good start, jumping right into some of its best songs—"Gots ta Be," "Understanding," and "Why I Love You"—before unleashing the album highlight, the aforementioned "Uh Huh." From there, the album gets progressively long-winded, running through 17 songs in total, none of them overly distinct. Of course, that's the nature of pop albums, particularly boy band albums, and B2K definitely follows in the grand tradition of its predecessors: Jagged Edge, Dru Hill, Blackstreet, and Bell Biv Devoe. *—Jason Birchmeier*

Pandemonium! / Dec. 10, 2002 / Epic ♦♦♦

Striking while the iron is hot, B2K has been very busy in 2002, and *Pandemonium!* is the group's fourth album release of the year, following their self-titled debut, a remix collection, and a holiday EP. The quartet is pictured on the cover, decked out in stylish black leather outfits, with the outstretched hands of fans reaching up to crotch level, which says a lot. Their fast rise to the top of the pop heap is also attested to by the advance single "Bump, Bump, Bump," which was produced, written, and arranged by R. Kelly, and which is co-billed to rapper P. Diddy. The song is typical of the rest of the album, with its slow tempo, contrast of acoustic guitar with thudding percussion, and repetitious choral parts. In the hands of their many writers and producers, B2K covers the usual concerns of male hip-hop music: lust ("Bump, Bump, Bump"); undying love ("One Kiss"); apology ("Sleepin'"); and, sung with the greatest feeling, accusations that the woman addressed is only interested in money ("Would You Be Here"). The writers are not shy about making use of the group's increased stature, notably on "Everything," in which one of the singers assures a woman that he still loves her even though he is now a big star, and he really wants to spend time with her, or at least talk to her on his cell phone, in between concerts and video shoots. Nor are the group's handlers hesitant to exploit the group's listeners by padding the album. "Why I Love You" is repeated from B2K's debut release, and an entire track, "Dog," is given over to singer Jhene, whose upcoming album is promoted with an insert in the CD jewel box. But then, this sort of album is more about marketing than music. *—William Ruhlmann*

Jon B. (Jon Buck)

b. Nov. 11, 1974, Rhode Island

Vocals, Producer, Multi Instruments, Songwriter / Urban, Contemporary R&B, Hip-Hop

Songwriter, producer, vocalist, and instrumentalist Jon B. brings a distinctive focus on smooth melodies to contemporary R&B. Proficient on keyboards, guitar, bass, and drums, he wrote and produced songs for such rap music legends as Toni Braxton, After 7, and Color Me Badd. Born in RI, and raised in CA, Jon B. was the son of a professor of music and a concert pianist.

Influenced by music found in his grandparents' record store, he began combining '70s soul with '90s hip-hop on his 1995 debut album, *Bonafide*. It sold more than one million copies and went gold. His second album, 1997's *Cool Relax*, continued the emphasis on classic hip-hop soul. He continued entertaining audiences, with several concert tours throughout the world. Aside from personal performances, he writes for popular artists including Toni Braxton and the rap group Az Yet. In the new millennium, Jon B. returned to form for a third record. *Pleasures U Like* was issued in spring 2001. *—Kim Summers*

Bonafide / 1995 / Epic ♦♦♦

● **Cool Relax** / Sep. 16, 1997 / Epic ♦♦♦♦

Although there are a couple of mediocre songs scattered across the album, Jon B.'s second album, *Cool Relax*, is a step forward for the urban soul singer. For much of the time, he's able to create a seductive, sexy fusion of classic soul and rhythmic, swinging '90s hip-hop. That alone makes *Cool Relax* enjoyable on a surface level, but the moments that really shine are when the music, production, tunes and songwriting all converge and result in an alluring romantic and bracingly modern soul. It doesn't happen all that often, but when it does, it makes the weaker moments worthwhile. *—Leo Stanley*

Pleasures U Like / Mar. 20, 2001 / Epic ♦♦♦

Pleasures U Like is Jon B.'s most consistent album to date. A cool, nighttime dance club vibe flows through the album. Not every song is a dance track; there are also a number of appealing ballads. The catchy midtempo "Don't Talk" glides along like Donell Jones' "U Know What's Up." The chugging "Sof'n Sweet" says "Don't just stand there/Break it down." The bass-heavy ballad "Overjoyed" is a duet between the singer and Faith Evans. Babyface co-wrote the languid, muted-trumpet-sprinkled "Lonely Girl." Other highlights are the acoustic guitar-laced "Tell Me," as well as the deliciously languid slow jams "Calling on You" and "Inside." *—Ed Hogan*

Are U Still Down: Greatest Hits / Mar. 26, 2002 / Epic ♦♦♦♦

Stevie B

b. Miami, FL

Vocals, Producer / Freestyle, Club/Dance, Urban, Dance-Pop, Soul

Singer, songwriter, and producer Stevie B was among the leading lights of the Miami dance music scene of the late '80s, later reaching the top of the pop charts with the mega-hit "Because I Love You (The Postman Song)." A native of south Florida, he worked a variety of dead-end jobs ranging from car-wash attendant to fast-food server before scoring his debut hit with 1987's "Party Your Body," which grew from a regional success to national club smash; it was also the title track of his 1988 debut LP, which went gold.

With 1989's *In My Eyes*, Stevie B launched his first Top 40 hit, "I Wanna Be the One"; its follow-up, "Love Me for Life," soon cracked the Top 40 as well. With 1990's "Because I Love You," he reached the pinnacle of his success, with the single's accompanying album *Love & Emotion* also generating a pair of Top 20 hits, "I'll Be By Your Side" and the title cut. However, with the subsequent rise of alternative rock, Stevie B's light dance-pop sound lost much of its mainstream appeal, and he never again recaped his previous success, with records including 1992's *Healing* and 1996's *Waiting for Your Love* appearing to little notice. *The Best of Stevie B* followed in 1998. *—Jason Ankeny*

In My Eyes / 1989 / Lefrak-Moelis ♦♦

The ersatz heartthrob songs never stopped coming from Stevie B on his 1989 follow-up to *Party Your Body*. While some found the cloying lyrics and heavy breathing on "Love Me for Life" and "Girl I Am Searching for You" moving, they struck others as overdone and phony. He did include "I Came to Rock Your Body" for variety, and "Children of Tomorrow" was ostensibly his version of a message song. *—Ron Wynn*

Party Your Body / 1988 / Lefrak-Moelis ♦♦

Miami pop/soul (heavy on the pop) vocalist Stevie B got a little attention with this late-'80s album on the LMR label (later picked up and distributed by RCA). He had the kind of coy, pseudo-charming voice that was ideal for overly sentimental material, and that was his focus. He loaded this album with that type of song, and came close to getting a hit with "Spring Love (Come Back to Me)." *—Ron Wynn*

● **The Best of Stevie B** / Sep. 1991 / Lefrak-Moelis ♦♦♦♦♦

Miami-based vocalist Stevie B was never more than a pleasant pop/soul type, although he scored a left-field number one hit in 1990 with "Because I Love You (The Postman Song)." That's included on this anthology, along with his other sentimental smashes, which included "I'll Be By Your Side" and "Love and Emotion." He could be painfully maudlin, but that seemed to be his stock-in-trade, as every Stevie B tune that ever made any noise was drenched in vapid schmaltz. *—Ron Wynn*

Baby Huey (James Ramey)

b. 1944, Richmond, IN, **d.** Oct. 28, 1970, Chicago, IL

Vocals / Soul, Chicago Soul, Psychedelic Soul

A locally beloved figure on the Chicago soul scene, Baby Huey never achieved quite the same renown outside of his hometown, despite an exciting live act and a record on Curtis Mayfield's Curtom label. Born James Ramey in Richmond, IN, in 1944, Baby Huey was literally an enormous stage presence: A glandular problem kept his weight around 350-400 pounds and beyond. He began performing in Chicago clubs in 1963 with his backing band the Babysitters and soon became a popular concert draw.

As the '60s wore on, Baby Huey's sound moved from energetic R&B into a more psychedelic brand of soul, with a vocal style that drew comparisons to Otis Redding. He signed with Curtom and recorded a debut album, *The Baby Huey Story: The Living Legend*, that featured several Curtis Mayfield songs (most notably the oft-sampled "Hard Times" and "Mighty Mighty Children"), plus a cover of Sam Cooke's "A Change Is Gonna Come." Sadly, Baby Huey didn't live to see it released; his weight and substance-abuse problems were exacting a steep toll on his body, and on October 28, 1970, he suffered a drug-related heart attack in a hotel room in Chicago. The album was released early the next year, and the Babysitters attempted to carry on for a while with a new lead singer, the still-teenaged Chaka Khan (she would, of course, go on to fame as the frontwoman of funk band Rufus shortly thereafter). In the years since, Baby Huey's lone LP has become a sought-after collectible among soul fanatics. *—Steve Huey*

● **The Baby Huey Story: The Living Legend** / 1971 / Curtom ♦♦♦

Baby Huey wasn't exactly a studio rat, so his recording story is short. The hefty soul singer with his ever-changing backing crew the Babysitters (Chaka Khan was once a member) was a popular attraction in Chicago's lounges. The excitement of his club act never transformed to records, the most accommodating tracks here are familiar ones, like Sam Cooke's "A Change Is Gonna Come" and a trio of Curtis Mayfield songs: "Mighty Mighty Children," "Hard Times," and "Running"; the other four songs are acquired tastes. *—Andrew Hamilton*

Babyface (Kenneth Edmonds)

b. Apr. 10, 1959, Indianapolis, IN

Vocals, Producer, Guitar, Keyboards / Adult Contemporary, Urban, Quiet Storm, Club/Dance

As a singer, producer, and songwriter, Babyface was an inescapable presence in virtually every major facet of pop music during the '90s. His own recordings helped rejuvenate the R&B tradition of the smooth, sensitive, urban crooner and made him a staple of urban contemporary radio. Yet their considerable success was eclipsed by his songwriting and production work for other artists, which linked him with some of the biggest stars and hit singles of the decade (and not just in the realm of R&B). You'd be hard pressed to name a '90s hitmaker with a track record more consistently successful and versatile than Kenny "Babyface" Edmonds.

Kenneth Edmonds was born April 10, 1959, in Indianapolis, and began playing in local R&B bands as a teenager. He served a stint in Bootsy Collins' backing unit (where he earned his nickname) and subsequently joined the funk outfit Manchild, which signed a record deal in 1977 and released three albums. After their breakup, Babyface and partner Antonio "L.A." Reid formed an urban funk group called the Deele in the early '80s, which scored a few sizable hits on the R&B charts. Babyface and Reid began producing and writing for other artists on the side, landing hits in Pebbles' "Girlfriend" and the Whispers' "Rock Steady"; following the Deele's third album in 1988, the duo left to continue their outside activities full-time, co-founding the LaFace label in 1989. Further hits followed in Bobby Brown's "Every Little Step," Sheena Easton's "The Lover in Me," and Karyn White's "The Way You Love Me" and "Superwoman," all of which performed well on both the pop and R&B charts.

Babyface had actually recorded a little-noticed solo album in 1986, titled *Lovers*, but with his newfound success having marked him as one to watch, his solo career now began in earnest. Released in 1987, *Tender Lover* caught fire, spinning off four singles over the next year, including the R&B chart smashes "It's No Crime" (number one) and "Whip Appeal" (number two; both also reached the pop Top Ten); the album also went double platinum. Now firmly established as a powerhouse, Babyface went on to co-write hits for Johnny Gill ("My, My, My," nominated for the Best R&B Song Grammy), Whitney Houston ("I'm Your Baby Tonight"), and Madonna ("Take a Bow"); his biggest success, however, came with Boyz II Men, whose recording of "End of the Road" became one of the longest-running number ones in pop history (the Babyface-penned follow-up "I'll Make Love to You" was also pretty successful in its own right). He was co-nominated for an Album of the Year Grammy for his production on *The Bodyguard* soundtrack and went on to work with artists like Celine Dion, Mariah Carey, Gladys Knight, Aretha Franklin, En Vogue, and Mary J. Blige. As if that weren't enough, LaFace had become a highly successful and lucrative imprint, breaking artists like Toni Braxton, TLC, OutKast, and Usher (often with input from Reid and Babyface).

It's no wonder Babyface wound up taking a break from his own career as a singer during the early '90s, releasing only a remix album, *A Closer Look*, in 1991. The proper follow-up to *Tender Lover* didn't appear until 1993; even so, *For the Cool in You* was an even bigger hit than its predecessor, going triple platinum and producing Babyface's first Top Five pop hit, the change-of-pace acoustic guitar ballad "When Can I See You Again" (which won him his first Grammy as a performer for Best Male R&B Vocal). In 1995, he scored another major success with the *Waiting to Exhale* soundtrack, not only producing it but scoring the film itself and writing nearly all of its songs, including the Whitney Houston smash "Exhale (Shoop, Shoop)." The same year, he won the first of three consecutive Grammys as Producer of the Year. Successes just kept coming in 1996; the guest-laden album *The Day* spawned another Top Ten pop/R&B hit in "Every Time I Close My Eyes," and he solidified his crossover credentials once and for all by winning a Grammy for Record of the Year as producer of Eric Clapton's "Change the World."

Encouraged by the success of *Waiting to Exhale*, Babyface and his wife, Tracey Edmonds, formed their own film production company, which debuted in 1997 with the acclaimed urban family comedy/drama *Soul Food* (Babyface, naturally, masterminded the soundtrack). The next year, he contributed lyrics to the animated musical *The Prince of Egypt*, which went uncredited on the soundtrack album. With the movies taking up more of his time, his next musical releases were quick one-offs: an *MTV Unplugged* album in 1997 and the seasonal *Christmas With Babyface* the next year. His production and songwriting activities continued, though he remained silent as a performer for a few years. In 2000, Epic released the best-of compilation *A Collection of His Greatest Hits*, marking the end of his tenure with the label; he had elected to move to Arista, where L.A. Reid was now a high-ranking executive. In 2001, Babyface released a new album, *Face2Face*, and also produced the punk-pop soundtrack for the film *Josie & the Pussycats*. *—Steve Huey*

Tender Lover / Jul. 1989 / Solar/Epic ♦♦♦♦♦

Babyface's second release yielded the first number one R&B hit of the 1990s while establishing Edmonds as a major personality and performer. He wrote or co-wrote much of the material and even played several instruments. It was a combination of slick production and nicely sung sentimental tributes and heartache ballads. [The 2001 CD reissue adds historical liner notes and three bonus tracks: a "Dub L.A." version of "Tender Lover," a 12" version of "Whip Appeal," and a 12-inch version of "My Kinda Girl."] *—Ron Wynn*

Lovers / Oct. 1987 / Solar/Epic ♦♦♦

On his debut album, Babyface sings with just enough earnestness to be soulful and just enough sophistication and slickness to avoid sounding too much like a throwback. [The 2001 CD reissue adds historical liner notes and three bonus tracks: a "Free Style Mix" of "Mary Mack," a "Jazz Lover's Mix" of "Lovers," and a 12-inch version of "If We Try."] *—Ron Wynn*

A Closer Look / Nov. 19, 1991 / Solar/Epic ♦♦♦♦

Babyface had established himself as both a performing and production star in the '90s. His alternately innocent, hurt, and disillusioned vocals were this decade's equivalent of the soul/love songs of the '70s and '80s. He can sing sentimental material, tender tunes, or seem angry and confused. His lyrics get overly coy, but they've struck many responsive chords among women in particular. It's not soul, but it's what many who never heard Sam Cooke think it is. *—Ron Wynn*

For the Cool in You / Aug. 1993 / Epic ♦♦♦♦

In late 1993 Babyface, who was at the top of his game as pop/R&B's hottest writer and producer, released his acclaimed solo album *For the Cool in You*. The album featured four hit singles, those being the title track, "Never Keeping Secrets," "And Our Feelings," and the song that went on to become his signature tune, "When Can I See You." In early 2001, the album was reissued with three bonus tracks, which do the album a great deal of service and widely expand its musical boundaries. "For the Cool in You" is served up with two additional mixes. One is the "Quiet Storm Vocal Mix," which, as the name implies, is a laid-back, mellow quiet storm groove. The other is the album's closer, the "Midnight Luv Instrumental Mix," which is a fine, mellow, jazzy way to close off the album. Finally, "When Can I See You" is served up with the "Urban Soul Basement Mix," which is a dance-house version of the song. This version may displease some of the song's original fans (it was an acoustic ballad in its original inception), but ultimately serves to expand the musical boundaries of the album. For a record that was originally pop/R&B, the reissue is a jazzier offering that includes house music and makes for a surprisingly good listen from start to finish. Also included are beefed-up liner notes, which include all of the original liner notes' artwork. *—Jose Promis*

The Day / Oct. 29, 1996 / Epic ♦♦♦♦♦

The Day was the first album Babyface released after being elevated into a virtually guaranteed hitmaker in the mid-'90s through his work with Whitney Houston, Boyz II Men, Madonna, and Mariah Carey, among many others. The album confirms his skill for subtle, inventive songwriting and accessible, polished yet soulful production. Babyface can straddle the line between hip-hop and traditional soul better than nearly any other artist, as evidenced by the hits he has orchestrated for other artists. On his own, he is still compelling—his voice is as smooth as silk, and nearly as seductive—but it doesn't quite have the force of personality as his greatest productions. Nevertheless, *The Day* qualifies as state-of-the-art mid-'90s soul, featuring a handful of terrific songs, and a lot of extremely pleasurable filler. [The 2001 CD reissue adds historical liner notes and three bonus tracks: remixes of "Everytime I Close My Eyes," "This Is for the Lover in You," and "Everytime I Feel the Groove," the last of which was previously unreleased and not found on the original album in any form.] *—Leo Stanley*

Kenny "Babyface" Edmonds & Manchild / Oct. 21, 1997 / Collectables ♦♦♦♦

Released in 1997, after Babyface became one of the most popular and successful producers in pop music, *Kenny "Babyface" Edmonds & Manchild* is a career-spanning compilation that covers all three albums by the '70s soul outfit. The group had only one hit—"Especially for You" in 1977—and, listening to this 17-track collection, it's easy to see why: they weren't very good. Manchild was certainly competent, and on a few songs Babyface suggests that he had the talent he eventually developed, but only diehard fans of the contemporary soul man—or fans of vocalist Reggie Griffin, who later launched a solo career—will need to explore this collection. *—Stephen Thomas Erlewine*

MTV Unplugged NYC 1997 / Nov. 25, 1997 / Epic ♦♦♦

Even though he's had several hits, Babyface is better-known as a producer and a songwriter than a performer, which may be the reason why he invited a number of musicians—including Stevie Wonder, Eric Clapton, and Jodeci's K-Ci & JoJo—to perform at the concert that resulted in *MTV Unplugged NYC 1997*. Babyface performs his solo hits and a selection of hits he has written for other artists, such as "Change the World" and "The End of the Road," delivering them all with a smooth authority that borders on slickness. And that slickness may alienate some listeners, preventing them from realizing how sturdy most of these songs are, or the suppleness of Babyface's voice. That fondness for MOR production and delivery has always been one of Babyface's primary weaknesses, surfacing even on a stripped-down live album such as this. Some fans will find this weakness excusable, but it's a little frustrating to hear that the live versions don't differ drastically from the studio cuts. It's interesting to hear him sing "The End of the Road," and since this contains many of his greatest hits, it may be of interest to some casual fans, but on the whole, *MTV Unplugged* is a disappointingly modest effort. *—Stephen Thomas Erlewine*

Christmas With Babyface / Oct. 27, 1998 / Epic ♦♦♦

● **A Collection of His Greatest Hits** / Nov. 14, 2000 / Epic ♦♦♦♦♦

As can be expected with a Babyface retrospective, the songs are top-notch and the production is excellent. At his peak in the mid-'90s, Babyface was arguably the American music industry's hottest producer/songwriter. He also established himself as a top-rate balladeer, as evidenced by the songs on this selection. "Everytime I Close My Eyes," "Never Keeping Secrets," and "When Can I See You" are quintessential slow-jam Babyface. His uptempo numbers, such as "It's No Crime" and the Shalamar cover, "This Is for the Lover in You," are just as engaging. However, despite the inclusion of some of his best ballads and uptempo hits, this album suffers from several glaring omissions, and leaves one hoping for a more complete product, or at least a second volume to complement what's lacking in this one. Glaring omissions include two hits from his *Tender Lover* album, those being "My Kinda Girl" and the title track. Incidentally, both those songs were remixed (and greatly improved) when released as singles, so their inclusion on this hits package would have been a huge bonus for the singer's fans. Other omissions include his hit duet with Pebbles, "Love Makes Things Happen," his hit duet with Toni Braxton, "Give U My Heart," early singles "Mary Mack" and "Lovers," later singles "And Our Feelings" and "Rock Bottom," as well as his hard-to-find duet with Lisa Stansfield, "Dream Away," and his Top Ten hit with protégé Jon B., "Someone to Love." Omitting those songs in favor of non-hit album tracks such as "Soon as I Get Home" seems a tad bewildering. For completists, this collection is thoroughly lacking, but for the casual listener, it's a pleasure nonetheless. As a final note, two new songs are included, "When Men Grow Old" and "Reason for Breathing," as well as a live, unplugged version of a hit he wrote for Eric Clapton, "Change the World." *—Jose Promis*

Love Songs / Aug. 7, 2001 / Epic ♦♦♦♦♦

Babyface is famed for his love songs, so it only makes sense that Epic released a collection of his finest, or at least most popular, love songs. This is not the same thing as a greatest hits and there are several big items that are missing, but since many of his very biggest songs were indeed love songs, this may be of interest to many fans. It captures his smooth essence quite well, while featuring such hits as "This Is for the Lover in You," "For the Cool in You," and "Whip Appeal." Not a definitive overview, and certainly not all of his best music, but a fine listen all the same. *—Stephen Thomas Erlewine*

Face2Face / Sep. 11, 2001 / Arista ♦♦♦♦♦

Babyface took his sweet time to deliver the sequel to *The Day*, a rare flop in his catalog, waiting nearly five years to release *Face2Face*. He wasn't exactly in seclusion, since he still worked relentlessly as a producer and songwriter, even masterminding the tremendous pop-punk soundtrack for the 2001 film *Josie & the Pussycats*. All this activity, combined with the subtleness of *The Day*, is in no way preparation for *Face2Face*, a gleaming, stylish platter of urban funk and smooth soul that is easily among his very best records. As Babyface's sense of craft deepens, he's become more assured with what he wants to do on his own records. Though he's dabbled in funk since the beginning of his career, the grooves here cut deeper and are flashier than ever before, and the sweet croon of his voice just makes them seem deeper. Then there are the ballads that he's always excelled at—they're just as good here, but they not only offer good contrast, they sound better in this context, surrounded by such exquisite dance numbers and grooves. Even if *Face2Face* fails to match the chart heights of, say, "Whip Appeal," Babyface has never been in better form, and from beginning to end, this record captures him at the peak of his powers. *—Stephen Thomas Erlewine*

Erykah Badu (Erykah Wright)

b. Feb. 26, 1972

Vocals / Contemporary R&B, Alternative Rap, Hip-Hop, Neo-Soul, Adult Alternative Pop/Rock, Urban

She grew up listening to '70s soul and '80s hip-hop, but Erykah Badu drew more comparisons to Billie Holiday upon her breakout in 1997, after the release of her first album, *Baduizm*. The grooves and production on the album are bass-heavy R&B, but Badu's languorous, occasionally tortured vocals and delicate phrasing immediately removed her from the legion of cookie-cutter female R&B singers. A singer/songwriter responsible for all but one of the songs on *Baduizm*, she found a number 12 hit with her first single "On & On," which pushed the album to number two on the charts.

Born Erykah Wright in Dallas in 1972, Badu attended a school of the arts and was working as a teacher and part-time singer in her hometown when she opened for D'Angelo at a 1994 show. D'Angelo's manager, Kedar Massenburg, was impressed with the performance and hooked her up with the singer to record a cover of the Marvin Gaye/Tammi Terrell duet "Precious Love." He also signed Badu to his recently formed Kedar Entertainment label, and served as producer for *Baduizm*, which also starred bassist Ron Carter and members of hip-hop avatars the Roots on several tracks. The first single, "On & On," became a number one R&B hit in early 1997, and *Baduizm* followed it to the top of the R&B album charts by March. Opening for R&B acts as well as rap's Wu-Tang Clan, Erykah Badu stopped just short of number one on the pop album charts in April. Her *Live* album followed later in the year. In 2000 she returned with her highly anticipated second studio album, *Mama's Gun*, which was co-produced by Badu, James Poyser, Bilal and Jay Dee and contained the hit single, "Bag Lady." *—John Bush*

● **Baduizm** / Feb. 11, 1997 / Kedar/Universal ♦♦♦♦

Erykah Badu's debut album, *Baduizm*, is an astonishing display of vocal virtuosity and musical vision. Badu has fashioned a variation of urban soul that is utterly modern yet thoroughly rooted in tradition. There are elements of Billie Holiday, blues, soul, and hip-hop in *Baduizm*, and she seamlessly fuses them together, creating music that is wise beyond her years. That doesn't mean that the album is flawless. Like many debut artists, Badu's reach occasionally exceeds her grasp, and several of the songs are a little too similar, but that doesn't prevent *Baduizm* from being a remarkable and refreshing debut. *—Leo Stanley*

Live / Nov. 18, 1997 / Kedar/Universal ♦♦♦

Conventional wisdom dictates that an artist should not release a live album as their second record, especially if it follows the debut by a matter of months. However, Erykah Badu is not a conventional artist and *Live* is not a conventional live album. While her debut, *Baduizm*, earned strong reviews and healthy sales, her concerts became equally popular and she became known as a powerhouse live performer. *Live* solidifies that reputation, delivering soulful, gritty versions of cuts from *Baduizm*, a few covers, and the spectacular new single, "Tyrone." Not only does it illustrate the depths of Badu's talents, but *Live* is as strong and captivating as *Baduizm*. *—Leo Stanley*

Mama's Gun / Oct. 31, 2000 / Kedar/Universal ♦♦♦♦

Since the arrival of Erykah Badu onto the nu soul scene back in 1997 with *Baduizm*, commercial music has stood up and taken notice with an onslaught of similar artists reaching comparable peaks of mainstream success. After taking some time off for introspection and to raise her son, Badu returns with *Mama's Gun*, which is a turning point for her in many ways. Gone are the cryptic "Baduizms" that glossed all over her first release, replaced with a more honestly raw Badu singing directly from her heart rather than her head. Sonically, Badu wades out into adventurous territories as well. From the Jimi Hendrix-inspired opening number to the closing ten-minute song suite, she develops fresh aspects of her sound, employing artists such as legendary jazz vibraphonist Roy Ayers, jazz trumpeter Roy Hargrove, Stephen Marley, and Roots drummer ?uestlove; she sought after producer Jay Dee as well. The results are consistently tasteful, which only helps to prove once again that Badu is miles ahead of the rest. *—Rob Theakston*

J.R. Bailey (James Bailey)

Vocals / R&B, Soul

J.R. Bailey, born James Bailey, is an R&B singer and songwriter. He was a member of the Cadillacs from 1956 to 1972 and scored five R&B singles hits under his own name between 1968 and 1975, the biggest of which was "After Hours" (number 29, 1973). He is also the author of the hits "Everybody Plays the Fool" by the Main Ingredient and "Love, Love, Love" by Donny Hathaway. *— William Ruhlmann*

● **Rockin,' Rollin' and Strollin'** / 1958 / Capitol ♦♦♦

Love and Conversation / 1977 / United Artists ♦♦♦

Philip Bailey

b. May 8, 1951, Denver, CO

Vocals, Percussion / Soul, Quiet Storm, Urban, Black Gospel, Contemporary Gospel

Philip Bailey first gained fame as the mesmerizing lead falsetto of '70s supergroup Earth, Wind & Fire. The singer/percussionist's four-octave range set a high standard for upper-range pop vocalists. Bailey's shimmering falsetto blended perfectly with Maurice White's charismatic tenor to help the group build a reputation for exciting, live shows (complete with feats of magic) and innovative recordings. Six-time Grammy winners Earth, Wind & Fire had 46 charting R&B singles, 33 charting pop singles including eight gold singles.

The group also won four American Music Awards and earned more than 50 gold and platinum albums. In 1982, while continuing his work with EWF, Philip signed a solo deal with Columbia, releasing his first solo LP *Continuation*. Then in October 1984, *Chinese Wall* was issued, an album Bailey co-produced with Phil Collins. The second single, "Easy Lover," a duet with Phil Collins, became a worldwide hit, earning Bailey his first gold solo record. After Bailey's 1986 album, *Inside Out*, he began making a name for himself in the gospel world, releasing four recordings on Word. Shortly after returning to the studio with Earth, Wind & Fire to record the band's Grammy-nominated *Millennium* Bailey collaborated with singer Brian McKnight and members of PM Dawn and Arrested Development to co-write and record another pop/R&B solo project, *Philip Bailey* (1994). A single from the LP, "Here With Me" charted number 66 R&B in early 1994. In 1998, his album *Life and Love* was released throughout Europe.

In 1999, Bailey took another stylistic turn and signed with Heads Up International released the enhanced CD, *Dreams*, a smooth jazz album that features a "who's who" of contemporary jazz artists, including Gerald Albright, Luis Conte, Everette Harp, Grover Washington Jr. and Pat Metheny. *—Ed Hogan*

Continuation / 1982 / Columbia ♦♦♦

Expatriate Earth, Wind & Fire vocalist Philip Bailey stepped out on his own with *Continuation*, his first solo recording. Here Bailey got to explore some less-cluttered grooves than in EWF, and he also sang in his natural tenor rather than being limited to his falsetto. "I Know" received some air and club play, but for the most part the disc was ignored. That's too bad, because several of the songs are engaging R&B. "Vaya (Go With Love)" is the best ballad (Bailey's supposed strength with Earth, Wind & Fire), but the concluding "The Good Guy's Supposed to Get the Girl" and "Your Boyfriend's Back" are the best matches of hook-filled melody and Bailey's soaring voice. *—Ross Boissoneau*

Chinese Wall / 1984 / Columbia ♦♦♦♦

At the time Philip Bailey persuaded Phil Collins to produce his second solo album, *Chinese Wall*, Collins was among the hottest pop stars in the world. The advantage to that, of course, is the exposure it affords, and after the merely modest success of his debut solo album, *Continuation*, Bailey needed the reflected glory. On the other band, it's hard to shine yourself in such a glare, and although Bailey's name was on the gold-selling hit single "Easy Lover," a duet with Collins that helped the album take off, it's Collins' singing and drumming that one remembers. Elsewhere, tunes like "Photogenic Memory" and "Walking on the Chinese Wall" better represent Bailey's ability to handle a variety of material from ballads to techno dance tracks with his elastic falsetto. Still, *Chinese Wall* was a gold-selling standoff that made Bailey a solo hitmaker without really establishing him on his own. *— William Ruhlmann*

The Wonders of His Love / 1985 / Word ✦✦
Philip Bailey's debut gospel album. *—William Ruhlmann*

Triumph / 1986 / Word ✦✦

Family Affair / 1989 / Word ✦✦

Inside Out / 1990 / Columbia ✦✦
Philip Bailey turned to Nile Rodgers to produce *Inside Out*, his follow-up to *Chinese Wall*, and though Rodgers didn't turn it into a dance record on the order of his old band, Chic (the sort of thing he did do to other clients), the result is no more than pedestrian black pop, which is why Bailey's secular solo career ran out of gas at this point and he willingly re-upped with the new edition of Earth, Wind & Fire. He didn't make another secular solo album for nine years. *—William Ruhlmann*

• **The Best of Philip Bailey: A Gospel Collection** / 1991 / Word ✦✦✦✦✦
This is a compilation album culled from Philip Bailey's three gospel albums, *The Wonders of His Love*, *Triumph*, and *Family Affair*. Bailey brings the same creamy pop production and warm falsetto singing to his inspirational work that he does to his solo albums and to Earth, Wind & Fire, although he is far gentler here (except when he's being religiously righteous on "Call to War"). Note that this is listed as the pick among his gospel albums, not his entire solo catalog. *—William Ruhlmann*

Philip Bailey / Mar. 29, 1994 / Zoo ✦✦✦
Philip Bailey's self-titled, seventh solo album features some admirable talent, including production by Chuckii Booker, Brian McKnight, and PM Dawn. The album includes a dozen well-produced, light funk tunes; however, there are no standout tracks as memorable as his earlier hit with Phil Collins, "Easy Lover," or his many great works with Earth, Wind & Fire. *—Tim Griggs*

Dreams / Jun. 22, 1999 / Heads Up International ✦✦✦
Legendary falsetto-voiced Earth, Wind & Fire vocalist Philip Bailey invites quite a guest list of smooth jazz stars to this party, which marks a strong adult contemporary turn from his solo gospel recordings. Although he never fails to keep his vocal textures front and center, each solid sax solo here is by another great—Everette Harp, Gerald Albright, Grover Washington Jr., and Kirk Whalum—and Peter White and George Duke spruce up many a harmony line. Randy Brecker even shows up, spinning his flugelhorn around the exotic, tropical Latin percussion textures on a bass-driven spin on "Moondance." When you're dealing with this kind of voice, both brilliant and so familiar from years in the urban world, obviously the recording's success rises and falls based on the material. And while Bailey's mostly going the passionate ballad route—he also covers Bread's "Make It With You" and Pat Metheny's dreamy "Something to Remind You"—his eagerness, cleverness, and sincerity in delivery help listeners forget that there's not much tempo change going on here. Eric Huber's vocal production, often contrasting Bailey's high notes with a lower vocal line before easing them together, is also sharp. While there's not much funk, the two glorious changes of pace are Bailey's twist into Bobby Caldwell territory on the quartet-flavored "Masquerade Is Over" and "Are We Doing Better Now," which sounds like classic Earth, Wind & Fire meeting a spacy, retro-soul-minded George Duke. A little more groove next time might be cool, but Bailey's still got enough of the old fire burning. *—Jonathan Widran*

Soul on Jazz / 2002 / Heads Up International ✦✦✦

Anita Baker

b. Jan. 26, 1958, Toledo, OH
Vocals / Quiet Storm, Adult Contemporary, Urban
With her classy, refined brand of romantic soul, Anita Baker was one of the definitive quiet storm singers of the '80s. Gifted with a strong, supple alto, Baker was influenced not only by R&B, but jazz, gospel, and traditional pop, which gave her music a distinctly adult sophistication. Smooth and mellow, but hardly lifeless, it made her one of the most popular romantic singers of her time.

Baker was born January 26, 1958, in Toledo, OH, and raised in nearby Detroit, where she grew up listening to female jazz singers like Sarah Vaughan, Nancy Wilson, and Ella Fitzgerald. At age 12, she began singing a gospel choir, and by age 16 she was performing with several local bands. In 1975, she successfully auditioned for Chapter 8, one of Detroit's most popular acts at the time; the group eventually signed with Ariola and released an album in 1979, but were immediately dropped when the label was acquired by Arista (which didn't care for Baker's vocals). Chastened, Baker worked low-paying jobs in Detroit and eventually found steady work as a receptionist at a law firm. In 1982, Otis Smith—an executive who'd worked with Chapter 8—contacted Baker about recording for his new label Beverly Glen. Happy with her employment benefits and skittish over the experience with Arista, Baker was reluctant at first, but eventually flew out to the West Coast to record her debut album, *The Songstress*, in 1983. Though it didn't gain quite enough exposure to become a hit, it did help Baker build a strong fan base through word-of-mouth and she was signed by Elektra in 1985.

Working with producer Michael J. Powell (an old Chapter 8 cohort), Baker released her major-label debut *Rapture* in 1986. It was a platinum, Grammy-winning smash, appealing to both urban and adult contemporary listeners and producing two all-time quiet storm classics in "Caught Up in the Rapture" and "Sweet Love." Baker toured the world in 1987 and her guest appearance on the Winans track "Ain't Got No Need to Worry" won a Grammy. Her equally stylish follow-up album, *Giving You the Best That I Got*, appeared in 1988, spawning more staples in the title track and "Just Because." "Giving You the Best That I Got" also won Baker two more Grammys, for Best Female R&B Vocal and Best R&B Song. For her third Elektra album, Baker decided to handle a greater share of the songwriting, hence the title *Compositions*, which was released in 1990 and featured even stronger jazz inflections than Baker's previous work (not to mention all live instruments).

Following *Compositions*, Baker took a break from recording and touring; after having her first son in 1993, she returned to the studio to craft *Rhythm of Love*, which was released in 1994. In the years that followed, Baker was mostly silent, despite her fans' clamoring for a jazz album; instead, she raised her family and became embroiled in contract disputes with Elektra, which eventually led her to move to Atlantic. She began working on a new album in 2000, but had to start over from scratch due to defective recording equipment that made the original tracks unsalvageable. *—Steve Huey*

The Songstress / Jun. 1983 / Elektra ✦✦✦✦✦
Trends in African-American music changed considerably between Anita Baker's first taste of national exposure in 1979 (when she was a member of Detroit soul band Chapter 8 and sang lead on the hit ballad "I Just Wanna Be Your Girl") and her debut solo album, *The Songstress*, in 1983. While 1979's black music charts were full of large funk bands, standup vocal harmony groups, and disco divas, rappers and techno-funksters like the System were very much in vogue in 1983. Instead of following trends, Baker excelled by doing what she does best: gospel-influenced, '70s-type soul/pop with jazz overtones. *The Songstress*, released by the small Beverly Glen label and reissued by Elektra, wasn't the mega-hit her next album, *Rapture*, would be. But the Sarah Vaughan-influenced singer began to build a following with such honest, heartfelt ballads and "slow jams" as "No More Tears," "You're the Best Thing Yet," and the caressing "Angel." A sweaty taste of gospel-drenched funk, the invigorating "Squeeze Me" is atypical of the ballad-oriented Baker—although she definitely shines at this faster tempo. Indeed, Baker's solo career was off to a most impressive start with *The Songstress*. For those who savored *Rapture* and *Giving You the Best That I Got*, *The Songstress* is also essential listening. *—Alex Henderson*

• **Rapture** / Mar. 1986 / Elektra ✦✦✦✦✦
Though Anita Baker got some airplay out of *The Songstress*, that promising solo debut didn't bring her financial security. In fact, Baker was earning her living as a legal secretary in her native Detroit when she signed with Elektra in the mid-'80s. Elektra gave her a strong promotional push, and the equally superb *Rapture* became the megahit that *The Songstress* should have been. To its credit, Elektra made her a major star by focusing on Baker's strong point—romantic but gospel-influenced R&B/pop ballads and "slow jams," sometimes with jazz overtones—and letting her be true to herself. *Rapture* gave Baker one moving hit after another, including "Sweet Love," "Caught Up in the Rapture," "Same Ole Love," and "No One in This World." Praising Baker in a 1986 interview, veteran R&B critic Steve Ivory asserted, "To me, singers like Anita Baker and Frankie Beverly define what R&B or soul music is all about." Indeed, *Rapture*'s tremendous success made it clear that there was still a sizeable market for adult-oriented, more traditional R&B singing. *—Alex Henderson*

Giving You the Best That I Got / Oct. 1988 / Elektra ✦✦✦✦
The sizable following that Baker acquired with *Rapture* proved quite receptive to the only slightly less appealing *Giving You the Best That I Got*—an album that's quite similar to its predecessors. Though not quite on a par with *The Songstress* or *Rapture*, *Best* is far superior to most of 1988's uninspired R&B releases. Instead of tampering with *Rapture*'s consistently romantic and mellow soul/pop approach, Elektra brought back that album's producer, Michael J. Powell, and kept her at the top of the charts with such sleek yet earthy fare as "Just Because" (whose harmonies bring to mind producers Jimmy Jam & Terry Lewis, but lack the hip-hop elements they're quick to employ), "Priceless," the haunting "Good Love," and the title song. Much of Baker's music has contained jazz overtones, but on the Brazilian-influenced, slightly bossa nova "Good Enough," Sarah Vaughan's influence becomes even more apparent—and indicates that she is making a tremendous mistake by not recording outright jazz. *—Alex Henderson*

Compositions / Jun. 1990 / Elektra ✦✦✦
On *Rapture* and *Giving You the Best That I Got*, Baker embraced a blend of technology and "real instruments"—a definite contrast to the completely high-tech approach of so much '80s and '90s R&B. But on *Compositions*, producer Michael J. Powell moved even closer to a '70s-like approach to R&B—recording Baker's vocals live in the studio, employing a live rhythm section and avoiding drum machines altogether. What stayed the same was the type of material. Once again, Baker rejects hip-hop, techno-funk, new jack swing, and other '80s/'90s black music styles in favor of a consistently relaxed soul/pop mood. Though there's a lot to admire here—including "No One to Blame," "Soul Inspiration," and "Whatever It Takes," a song Baker wrote with Gerald LeVert and Marc Gordon of LeVert—Baker's approach was beginning to sound like a formula in 1990. Clearly blessed with a magnificent range and lots of soul, Baker needs to experiment and take more risks. And one way to go just might be jazz. The torchy and captivating "Lonely" shows that she has the ability to record a first-rate jazz album (if Elektra would okay such a project for her). Imagine Baker backed by James Moody, Tom Harrell, Chick Corea, Ray Brown, and Grady Tate. *—Alex Henderson*

Rhythm of Love / Sep. 13, 1994 / Elektra ✦✦✦
As the 1990s progressed, Anita Baker was sounding more and more contrived. One hoped that someone with so appealing a voice would challenge herself and try something different—perhaps recording more standards or exploring straight-ahead jazz (which she's obviously quite capable of doing). But instead of gambling with inspiration and risking a decline in sales, Baker tends to play it safe and offers a disc that often sounds like formula at work. Though *Rhythm of Love* is a generally decent album and even contains a few gems (including the dusky "Wrong Man," the torchy "Sometimes I Wonder Why" and heartfelt interpretations of "My Funny Valentine" and "The Look of Love"), Baker is capable of a lot more. The diva gives the impression that she desperately needs to follow Natalie Cole's lead and get away from catering to radio. *—Alex Henderson*

• **The Best of Anita Baker** / Jun. 18, 2002 / Rhino ✦✦✦✦✦
Rhino's 2002 compilation *The Best of Anita Baker* contains all of her hits—both the pop crossovers and songs that were big only on the R&B charts. Many of these songs are

presented in their single edits, not the album versions, which is a plus, since these are the versions that were played on the radio. Although it is true that nothing Anita Baker did was ever as sublime as *Rapture*, she did continually turn out fine adult contemporary and urban soul ballads throughout the late '80s and early '90s, all of which are here, making this not just a good summary/introduction, but a nice disc of highlights for those searching for more than *Rapture*. *—Stephen Thomas Erlewine*

LaVern Baker (Delores Williams)

b. Nov. 11, 1929, Chicago, IL, **d.** Mar. 10, 1997, New York, NY [Manhattan]
Vocals / R&B, Jump Blues
LaVern Baker was one of the sexiest divas gracing the mid-'50s rock & roll circuit, boasting a brashly seductive vocal delivery tailor-made for belting the catchy novelties "Tweedlee Dee," "Bop-Ting-a-Ling," and "Tra La La" for Atlantic Records during rock's first wave of prominence.

Born Delores Williams, she was singing at the Club DeLisa on Chicago's South Side at age 17, decked out in raggedy attire and billed as "Little Miss Sharecropper" (the same handle that she made her recording debut under for RCA Victor with Eddie "Sugarman" Penigar's band in 1949). She changed her name briefly to Bea Baker when recording for OKeh in 1951 with Maurice King's Wolverines, then settled on the first name of LaVern when she joined Todd Rhodes' band as featured vocalist in 1952 (she fronted Rhodes' aggregation on the impassioned ballad "Trying" for Cincinnati's King Records).

LaVern signed with Atlantic as a solo in 1953, debuting with the incendiary "Soul on Fire." The coy, Latin-tempo "Tweedlee Dee" was a smash in 1955 on both the R&B and pop charts, although her impact on the latter was blunted when squeaky-clean Georgia Gibbs covered it for Mercury. An infuriated Baker filed suit over the whitewashing, but she lost. By that time, though, her star had ascended: Baker's "Bop-Ting-A-Ling," "Play It Fair," "Still," and the rocking "Jim Dandy" all vaulted into the R&B Top Ten over the next couple of years.

Baker's statuesque figure and charismatic persona made her a natural for TV and movies. She co-starred on the historic R&B revue segment on Ed Sullivan's TV program in November of 1955 and did memorable numbers in Alan Freed's rock movies *Rock, Rock, Rock* and *Mr. Rock & Roll*. Her Atlantic records remained popular throughout the decade: She hit big in 1958 with the ballad "I Cried a Tear," adopted a pseudo-sanctified bellow for the rousing Leiber & Stoller-penned gospel sendup "Saved" in 1960, and cut a Bessie Smith tribute album before leaving Atlantic in 1964. A brief stop at Brunswick Records (where she did a sassy duet with Jackie Wilson, "Think Twice") preceded a late-'60s jaunt to entertain the troops in Vietnam. She became seriously ill after the trip and was hospitalized, eventually settling far out of the limelight in the Philippines. She remained there for 22 years, running an NCO club on Subic Bay for the U.S. government.

Finally, in 1988, Baker returned stateside to star in Atlantic's 40th anniversary bash at New York's Madison Square Garden. That led to a soundtrack appearance in the film *Dick Tracy*, a starring role in the Broadway musical *Black & Blue* (replacing her ex-Atlantic labelmate Ruth Brown), a nice comeback disc for DRG (*Woke Up This Mornin'*), and a memorable appearance at the Chicago Blues Festival. Baker died on March 10, 1997. *—Bill Dahl*

LaVern / 1956 / Atlantic ✦✦✦

LaVern Baker / 1957 / Atlantic ✦✦✦✦✦
This includes her hits "Tweedlee Dee" and "Jim Dandy." Some formulaic material (like "Tra-La-La," an obvious attempt at recapturing "Tweedly Dee") is included, but there's some good stuff too. *—George Bedard*

LaVern Sings Bessie Smith / Jan. 27, 1958 / Atlantic ✦✦✦✦✦
This is an album that should not have worked. LaVern Baker (a fine R&B singer) was joined by all-stars from mainstream jazz (including trumpeter Buck Clayton, trombonist Vic Dickenson, tenor saxophonist Paul Quinichette and pianist Nat Pierce) for twelve songs associated with the great '20s blues singer Bessie Smith. Despite the potentially conflicting styles, this project is quite successful and often exciting. The arrangements by Phil Moore, Nat Pierce, and Ernie Wilkins do not attempt to re-create the original recordings; Baker sings in her own style (rather than trying to emulate Bessie Smith), and the hot solos work well with her vocals. *—Scott Yanow*

Blues Ballads / 1959 / Atlantic ✦✦✦
Before she became a successful rock & roll vocalist, Lavern Baker did straight jazz and gutbucket blues, and that's what she's singing here. These tunes didn't have any crossover appeal, but they're gritty, unpolished, and sung with the intensity and energy that made Baker's later material so memorable. *—Ron Wynn*

Precious Memories / Jun. 4, 1959 / Atlantic ✦✦✦
LaVern Baker sang gospel with passion, exuberance, and reverence on this 1959 session. She was backed by a small combo with the Alex Bradford Singers and sounded more magnificent and moving than at any time she had done jazz, blues, or R&B. *—Ron Wynn*

Saved / Dec. 4, 1959-Dec. 6, 1960 / Atlantic ✦✦✦
Here is early-'60s jazz and blues material by LaVern Baker. She returned in the '60s to the songs she had cut prior to her rock & roll success. There was an interesting crew of guest stars on these sessions, among them Phil Spector on guitar, Sticks Evans on bass drums, and Taft Jordan on trumpet. Baker had a hit with a single from some earlier sessions, "You're the Boss With Jimmy Ricks." This song was issued on a single, but there's no listing for any album. *—Ron Wynn*

See See Rider / 1963 / Atlantic ✦✦✦

Let Me Belong to You / 1970 / Brunswick ✦

Her Greatest Hits / 1971 / Atlantic ✦✦✦
This 14-track compilation album of songs LaVern Baker recorded for Atlantic Records between 1953 and 1962 was the most thorough best-of in her catalog from the time of its release until the appearance of *Soul on Fire* in 1991. That is not to say that it was consistently available—it went out of print in the 1970s—or that it constitutes a complete portrait of Baker's work for the label. Of her 19 pop hits on Atlantic, only seven are included; of her 20 Atlantic R&B hits, only eight are here. The album does include some of her biggest hits—"Tweedle Dee," "Jim Dandy," "I Cried a Tear," "Saved," "See See Rider"—but it must be considered a bare minimum, especially now in light of the far more complete *Soul on Fire*. *—William Ruhlmann*

LaVern Baker Live in Hollywood '91 / 1991 / Rhino ✦✦✦

★ **Soul on Fire: The Best of LaVern Baker** / 1991 / Atlantic ✦✦✦✦✦
One of R&B's earliest divas, LaVern Baker could grab hold of a song and belt it out with the best of them, whether she was singing bouncy, uptempo rock & roll or bluesy torch ballads. Baker's contributions to the rockin' and rollin' wing of '50s R&B were in a class with Atlantic labelmates Ruth Brown and the Clyde McPhatter-era Drifters, as the stellar 20-track compilation *Soul on Fire: The Best of LaVern Baker* proves. Baker had a muscular delivery and a commanding personality on record, so much so that her ravishing visual appeal wasn't even necessary (though it certainly didn't hurt). Here she bellows and growls her way through rock & roll standards like "Tweedlee Dee" (her first big hit), the oft-covered "Jim Dandy" (her only R&B chart-topper), and "See See Rider," not to mention Leiber & Stoller's gospel pastiche "Saved." But Baker was equally powerful on her slow numbers, turning in positively smoldering performances on the classics "Soul on Fire," "Play It Fair," "I Cried a Tear" (her biggest pop hit), and "I Waited Too Long," among others. Baker isn't as much of a household name as she probably ought to be, but *Soul on Fire* is required listening for anyone interested in the first waves of R&B and rock & roll. *—Steve Huey*

Woke Up This Mornin' / Apr. 1992 / DRG ✦✦✦
This is a credible comeback effort that spotlights Baker's still-seductive pipes on a program of mostly familiar standards—everything from the straight-ahead blues "Rock Me Baby" to the Stax-era "Knock on Wood" and "I Can't Turn You Loose" to the Bee Gees' "To Love Somebody" and Carole King's sappy "You've Got a Friend." Supple backing by a cadre of New York session aces—guitarist Cornell Dupree, drummer Bernard Purdie, keyboardist Paul Griffin, bassist Chuck Rainey—adds the proper grooves for each. *—Bill Dahl*

LaVern/LaVern Baker / Jul. 28, 1998 / Collectables ✦✦✦✦✦
This Collectables CD contains LaVern Baker's first two albums, *LaVern* and *LaVern Baker*, on disc. Both records are excellent—even if a couple of cuts fall a little flat, most of the material is first-rate and Baker is in terrific form, singing with power and grace. The remastering and packaging aren't quite up to the standard of the music itself, but serious Baker fans will want this disc regardless, since it contains so many fine recordings that aren't available anywhere else. *—Stephen Thomas Erlewine*

See See Rider/Blues Ballads / Jul. 28, 1998 / Collectables ✦✦✦✦✦
Like its companion disc *LaVern/LaVern Baker*, this Collectables CD contains two early LaVern Baker albums, *See See Rider* and *Blues Ballads*, on one disc. There are a couple of minor flaws with each album, but for the most part, they each are dominated by great songs and performances, illustrating what a terrific, powerful vocalist Baker was. The remastering and packaging aren't quite up to the standard of the music itself, but serious Baker fans will want this disc regardless, since it contains so many fine recordings that aren't available anywhere else. *—Stephen Thomas Erlewine*

Precious Memories/LaVern Sings Bessie Smith / Jul. 11, 2000 / Collectables ✦✦✦✦
Lavern Baker praises the Lord on one hand ("Journey to the Sky" and "Just a Closer Walk With Thee") and tributes Bessie Smith on the other ("Empty Bed Blues" and "Gimme a Pigfoot [And a Bottle of Beer]") on the same CD. Baker's splendid vocals and superlative productions and arrangements make this contrasting gospel and blues union work. *—Andrew Hamilton*

Mickey Baker

b. Oct. 15, 1925, Louisville, KY
Guitar / R&B, East Coast Blues, Rock & Roll
Of all the guitarists who helped transform rhythm & blues into rock & roll, Mickey Baker is one of the very most important, ranking almost on the level of Chuck Berry and Bo Diddley. The reason he isn't nearly as well known as those legends is that a great deal of his work wasn't issued under his own name, but as a backing guitarist for many R&B and rock & roll musicians. Baker originally aspired to be a jazz musician, but turned to calypso, mambo, and then R&B, where the most work could be found. In the early and mid-'50s, he did countless sessions for Atlantic, King, RCA, Decca, and OKeh, playing on such classics as the Drifters' "Money Honey" and "Such a Night," Joe Turner's "Shake Rattle & Roll," Ruth Brown's "Mama, He Treats Your Daughter Mean," and Big Maybelle's "Whole Lot of Shakin' Going On." He also released a few singles under his own name, and made a Latin jazz-tinged solo album, *Guitar Mambo*.

Baker's best work, though, was recorded as half of the duo Mickey & Sylvia. Their hit "Love Is Strange," as well as several other unknown but nearly equally strong tracks, featured Baker's keening, bluesy guitar riffs, which were gutsier and more piercing than most anything else around in the late '50s. Mickey & Sylvia split in the late '50s (though they recorded off and on until the middle of the next decade), and Baker recorded his best solo album, the all-instrumental *The Wildest Guitar*. In 1961, he took the male spoken part (usually assumed to be Ike Turner) on Ike & Tina Turner's first hit, "It's Gonna Work Out Fine." Shortly afterwards he moved to France, making a few hard-to-find solo records and working with a lot of French pop and rock performers, including Ronnie Bird, the best '60s French rock singer. He has recorded only sporadically since the mid-'60s. *—Richie Unterberger*

The Wildest Guitar / 1959 / Atlantic ✦✦✦✦✦
Despite Baker's well-deserved reputation as one of the most influential guitar players of early rock & roll, *The Wildest Guitar* was one of the few chances he really got to strut his stuff as a solo artist. This entirely instrumental set features keening, sharp, bluesy riffs in

much the same distinctive style that gained him fame on "Love Is Strange" and other tunes with Mickey & Sylvia. The choice of material, though, is a bit surprising, favoring some surprisingly cornball standards: "Third Man Theme," "Autumn Leaves," "Lullaby of the Leaves," and Cole Porter's "Night and Day." Baker (who also arranged the album) manages to invest all of these with a snazzy R&B feel and biting solos. And he does actually write four of the 12 tunes himself, on which he fashions the kind of straightforward R&B that one would more likely to expect. This is a pretty good showcase to hear Baker's unadorned virtuosity. But he's really better-appreciated within the context of stronger material, either as half of Mickey & Sylvia or on the innumerable '50s R&B cuts (many on Atlantic) that feature his session work. *—Richie Unterberger*

Mississippi Delta Dues / 1973 / Verve ♦♦♦♦
This is a complete departure from his landmark 1950s electric guitar work for Ray Charles and others. With acoustic bottleneck specialist Stefan Grossman at his side, and surprisingly backed by the London Strings Orchestra, the talented guitarist covers a variety of tunes by long-dead bluesmen. Excluding the two bonus tracks, this was previously released as *House of the Blues, Vol. 5* on the Blue Star label. *—Mark Allan*

Blues, Jazz & Rock Guitar: Legendary Mickey Baker / 1992 / Shanachie ♦♦♦♦
Mickey Baker, a veteran studio guitarist best known for the hit "Love Is Strange" that he had as half of Mickey & Sylvia has long been a very versatile player. Tiring of commercial work, in the mid-'70s he went to Europe where he explored his roots in blues, jazz, and rock & roll. This intriguing CD finds Baker (who is joined on some numbers by acoustic guitarist Stefan Grossman, bassist Alex Sanders, and drummer Martin Drew) in London, playing mostly blues with a few nods towards his other musical interests. The mostly instrumental music holds one's interest and shows that Baker was a diverse and talented guitarist who had something of his own to offer the music world. Recommended. *—Scott Yanow*

● **Rock With a Sock** / Jun. 28, 1994 / Bear Family ♦♦♦♦♦
This 28-track collection rounds up sessions guitar player Mickey Baker cut as a leader between 1952-1957 for such labels as Savoy, Rainbow, Groove, MGM, and Vik. Baker is best-known for his duets with Sylvia Robinson as Mickey & Sylvia as well as his incredibly prolific and influential session work. As a leader, Baker tried various styles from rock & roll ("I'm Tired") to mambo ("Guitar Mambo") to acoustic blues ("Love Me Baby") to acoustic doo wop ("Oh, Happy Day") to tough blues ("Down to the Bottom," "You Better Heed My Warning") to jump blues ("Rock With a Sock," which features some hot sax by Warren Luckey) to jazz ("Chloe," "Ghost of a Chance"), trying his hand at instrumentals and vocals and always delivering high-energy, high-quality music. There are no lost classics hidden away here, but it is nice to hear Baker get a chance to step out on his own and rock. Baker's guitar playing is almost always energetic and unrestrained and his laconic vocals are a lot of fun. He also shows a more serious side on a date for Vik in 1957. The four tracks (all of which were never issued) are calm jazz ballads that Baker plays gently and with a great deal of finesse and feeling, and they show he could have had a career as a jazz player if he had wanted. As a bonus, Bear Family adds five previously unreleased Mickey & Sylvia tracks to the end of the set. Four of the tracks are typical smooth and poppy Mickey & Sylvia fare, but "Can't Get You on the Phone" displays a slightly harder musical edge to go with their usual lighthearted lyrics and delivery. It is almost a shame that they included these tracks, as they take some of the focus off of Mickey Baker's solo work, but the tracks are of such a high quality that it doesn't detract from the listening pleasure one bit. Anyone with an interest in discovering the versatility of one of the great craftsmen and founding fathers of rock & roll should check out this CD. You'll soon be singing the praise of Mickey Baker to anyone who will listen. *—Tim Sendra*

The Ballads

f. 1961, Oakland, CA
Group / R&B, Vocal Pop
The Ballads were an Oakland, CA, vocal group that came together in 1961. The members were Nathan Robertson, Jon Foster, Rico Thompson, and Lesley LaPalma. Their Ventura single "God Bless Our Love" went to number eight R&B, number 65 pop in summer 1968. It would be their only charting single, though there were more records: "Gift of Love" b/w "I Wish I Knew," "Goodnight My Love" b/w "Hey Diddle Diddle," and "You're the One" b/w "Love You Yeah." Some of their tracks can be found on CD; The lush ballad "Wait" features a lead vocal very reminiscent of Teddy Pendergrass and can be found on the 1999 I.T.P. Records CD *Underground Oldies, Vol. 6*. *—Ed Hogan*

Sweet Soul Sensation / 196 / Famous Groove ♦♦♦

Florence Ballard

b. Jun. 30, 1943, Rosetta, MS, **d.** Feb. 22, 1976, Detroit, MI
Vocals / Soul, Motown
Florence Glenda Ballard was born June 30, 1943, in Rosetta, MS, but before the age of ten, her family moved to Detroit to take advantage of Detroit's booming job market. Florence built a reputation as a singer by taking music classes and singing in her school choir. By 14, she befriended the group the Primes (later to become the Temptations) and performed gigs with the trio at various Detroit venues. The Primes' manager, Milton Jenkins, encouraged Ballard to form a sister group to the Primes, so she recruited Mary Wilson, Betty McGlown (soon to be replaced with Barbara Martin), and Diane Earle (better known as Diana Ross).

After a one-off record for Lupine Records as well as occasional backing sessions for Motown, the Primettes signed to Motown, changed their name to the Supremes, and Martin left, transforming the group into a trio. After a series of flops, number one smashes became automatic, the pace became frantic, and Motown muddied the water by pushing Wilson and Ballard out of the limelight to spotlight on Ross. Ballard didn't take the snub well, but the breaker came when she tired of the relentless pace. She couldn't keep up, started drinking, and subsequently missed gigs causing her ejection from the group in 1967. After filing a lawsuit over royalties, she married former Motown chauffeur Thomas Chapman and through various connections inked appeared to be a promising deal with ABC.

George Kerr produced her first single, "It Doesn't Matter How I Say It", but radio play was almost nonexistent. She completed an album, ... *You Don't Have To*, which ABC left for dead and instead opted to release the more commercial "Love Ain't Love," but let it languish. Soon thereafter ABC soured on Ballard and didn't extend her contract. The penthouse in Manhattan Ballard had purchased with her album advance was let go and the birth of twins—Michelle and Nicole—added to financial problems. Ballard's lawsuit finally settled; however, the lawyer took the monies forcing her to file a suit against him. Conditions went from bad to abject, she lost her home and suffered the humiliation of welfare and public housing. The couple had another daughter in 1972, but the marriage was shaky with Ballard's finances depleted. Chapman fooled around, became abusive and eventually left the family, which sent Ballard into a deep depression that only alcohol and pills solaced. Finally, the second lawsuit settled and she received a large settlement in 1975. Ballard cleaned up and made another go at recapturing the stardom she once took for granted. An appearance at Detroit's Ford Auditorium gave her a needed boost; she reconciled with Chapman, purchased a new house, and performed on television. But the melancholy years, fueled by chemicals and alcohol, weakened her system causing a fatal cardiac arrest February 22, 1976—she was 32 years old. *—Andrew Hamilton*

● **The Supreme** / Sep. 18, 2001 / Spectrum ♦♦♦♦

Hank Ballard & the Midnighters (John H. Kendricks)

b. Nov. 18, 1927, Detroit, MI, **d.** Mar. 3, 2003, Los Angeles, CA
Vocals, Songwriter / R&B, Doo Wop
In the world of early rhythm & blues and doo wop, Hank Ballard was the very definition of earthiness. Though influenced by high-energy gospel vocal groups, Ballard's music with the Midnighters couldn't have been more diametrically opposed in terms of subject matter: His lyrics were filled with raunchy double entendres that left little to the imagination, pushing the envelope of what was considered acceptable in the '50s. His songs were sometimes banned on the radio, but that only made him an even bigger jukebox favorite among black audiences. Ballard's hard-driving, rhythmic style was also an underappreciated influence on the rawer side of R&B, particularly on a young James Brown; plus, his composition "The Twist"—recorded for a hit by Chubby Checker—became one of the biggest hits in rock & roll history.

Hank Ballard was born November 18, 1927 (according to his birth records) in Detroit, but moved to Bessemer, AL, as a young child following his father's death. There he began singing in church and when he returned to Detroit at age 15, he set about forming a doo wop group while working on the Ford assembly line. Around the same time, singers Henry Booth and Charles Sutton were organizing a doo wop outfit called the Royals, which reputedly at one time also featured Jackie Wilson and future Four Top Levi Stubbs; it eventually grew to include vocalists Lawson Smith and Sonny Woods, plus gritty guitarist Alonzo Tucker. Initially copying the smooth style of Sonny Til & the Orioles, the Royals were discovered by Johnny Otis in 1952 and signed with Federal Records. However, when Hank Ballard replaced Smith in 1953, they adopted a rougher, more hepped-up sound in keeping with Ballard's numerous original compositions and Clyde McPhatter influence. Ballard's first recording with the group was 1953's "Get It," which hit the Top Ten on the R&B charts, but it was the following year's ribald "Work With Me Annie" that really broke the group (they changed their name to the Midnighters around this time, to avoid confusion with the Five Royales). "Work With Me Annie" topped the R&B charts and nearly reached the pop Top 20, despite a number of radio stations refusing to air the song. It inspired a number of answer records and the Midnighters themselves entered the fray with the sequels "Annie Had a Baby" (another R&B chart-topper) and "Annie's Aunt Fannie." They also scored another major smash with the Ballard-penned "Sexy Ways," which solidified their reputation as R&B's most risqué act.

However, after the momentum of "Work With Me Annie" slowed, the Midnighters seemed at a loss as to how to recapture it. They went nearly three and a half years without another big hit, and with the decline in their fortunes came numerous personnel shifts. Lawson Smith returned to the fold to replace Sutton, Norman Thrasher replaced Sonny Woods, and Tucker's guitar post was taken first by Arthur Porter, then Cal Green. Ballard attempted to take his 1958 composition "The Twist" to Vee-Jay, which declined to release the version they recorded; King, Federal's parent label, issued it as the B-side of the Midnighters' R&B comeback ballad hit "Teardrops on Your Letter" in 1959. Still, "The Twist" gained some notice and found a fan in *American Bandstand* host Dick Clark, who brought the song to Chubby Checker's attention; the rest was history, as "The Twist" became the first song to hit number one during two completely separate chart runs. Ballard and the Midnighters benefited from the exposure, scoring their first Top Ten pop singles in 1960 with "Finger Poppin' Time" and "Let's Go, Let's Go, Let's Go." A few more R&B hits followed, generally dance-oriented songs in the vein of "The Twist," before the well dried up for a second time. The Midnighters gradually disintegrated and Ballard became a solo act; by the end of the '60s, he was working with longtime fan James Brown, who produced several singles for Ballard during the late '60s and early '70s. After a lengthy absence from music, Ballard re-formed the Midnighters during the mid-'80s, first as a female group, then male, and began touring once again. In 1990, Ballard received his due as an R&B innovator with his election into the Rock and Roll Hall of Fame. Thirteen years later, he died of throat cancer. *—Steve Huey*

Greatest Juke Box Hits / 1958 / King ♦♦♦♦♦
This includes all the "Annie" songs, "Sexy Ways"—some overlap with 20 hits. *—George Bedard*

Singin' & Swingin' / Jun. 1959 / King ♦♦♦♦♦
Vintage red-hot R&B, shouting vocals, and frenzied instrumentals. Hank Ballard led one of the finest R&B orchestras on the '50s circuit, and his King albums are masterpieces. His singing was usually steamy, his lyrics laden with innuendo, and he kept up a furious

pace throughout each album. This is one of about ten Ballard albums that have been reissued on CD and is certainly well worth getting in any configuration. *—Ron Wynn*

Mr. Rhythm & Blues (Finger Poppin' Time) / 1960 / King ♦♦♦

While Hank Ballard & the Midnighters scored their biggest hits in the mid-'50s ("Work With Me Annie," "Sexy Ways"), they certainly didn't stop making the charts and cutting quality sides in the years that followed. And while many newcomers will want to first check out one of the fine retrospectives available, like Rhino's *Sexy Ways: The Best of Hank Ballard & the Midnighters*, seasoned listeners will not be disappointed by this circa-1960 release on the group's longtime label, King. Featuring the Top Ten smash "Finger Poppin' Time" and the infectious "The Coffee Grind," *Mr. Rhythm & Blues* rolls out the group's patented blend of gospel, R&B, and pop on 12 quality tracks. *—Stephen Cook*

Spotlight on Hank Ballard / 1961 / King ♦♦♦

Hank Ballard should have titled one of his albums "Bad Dude." Nobody bites into lyrics like this legendary R&B/soul singer. Often imitated but rarely duplicated, Ballard rocks you unmercifully on fast numbers and causes heart palpitations on the slow stuff. You won't find some of these songs on other compilations, which makes it an essential. Originally issued on King records in 1961. *—Andrew Hamilton*

Twistin' Fools / May 1962 / King ♦♦♦

All the Hank Ballard twist songs are here; compare with Chubby Checker and draw your own conclusions. *—George Bedard*

20 Hits: All 20 of Their Chart Hits (1953–1962) / 1977 / King ♦♦♦♦♦

Along with proto-doo wop groups like the Orioles and Sun Records' many early-'50s blues artists, Hank Ballard & the Midnighters helped create rock & roll. And as Ray Charles' gospel and R&B blend would later lay the foundation for soul artists like Marvin Gaye and Aretha Franklin, Ballard's mixing of jump blues and holy-roller vocal intensity helped the likes of Elvis Presley and Chuck Berry become rock & roll's first stars. While at Detroit's Dunbar High, Ballard formed the Midnighters (originally the Royals) and eventually signed to King in 1953. The Midnighters' many chart hits for both King and its subsidiary Federal label are included on this solid retrospective of the group's '50s and early-'60s prime. Along with several Ballard originals like "Work With Me Annie," "Annie Had a Baby," "Finger Poppin' Time," and "The Twist" (later turned into a dance phenomenon by Chubby Checker), the album also finds the band ably handling Leiber & Stoller's evergreen "Kansas City" and Don Covay's "Twist"-wannabe "The Switch-A-Roo." A great introduction to Hank Ballard & the Midnighters' classic hits. *—Stephen Cook*

What You Get When the Gettin' Gets Good / 1985 / Charly ♦♦♦♦♦

What You Get When the Getting Gets Good is a best-of collection featuring "Finger Poppin' Time," "Work With Me Annie," "Let's Go, Let's Go, Let's Go," "The Twist," and "Annie Had a Baby." It's Detroit R&B at its best. *—Cub Koda*

Let 'em Roll / 1990 / Charly ♦♦♦♦♦

★ **Sexy Ways: The Best of Hank Ballard & the Midnighters** / Nov. 16, 1993 / Rhino ♦♦♦♦♦

Hank Ballard saw one of his songs ("The Twist") turned into a craze by an R&B singer without soul, saw his style expanded by singers like James Brown and Clyde McPhatter without much recognition, saw his joyously risqué mentality become the norm in rock & roll and R&B, but he never had the fame he was due. Sure, he had hits and is well known among most serious R&B/soul fans, but that stops just short of the iconic status that he deserves. And if any collection makes a case for his greatness, it's the superb 20-track overview *Sexy Ways: The Best of Hank Ballard & The Midnighters*, released on Rhino in 1993. Over the course of 20 tracks, the best of Ballard's singles for Federal and King (including one cut with the Royals) are unveiled, and years later, his music still sounds exuberant, salacious, impassioned and irresistible, among the best '50s R&B had to offer. It's a bit of shock to hear what a carnal punch this music still packs, decades after it was recorded. It's not just the clear sexuality of "Work With Me Annie," "Sexy Ways," "Annie's Aunt Fannie" or "Look at Little Sister" (the latter effectively cut by Stevie Ray Vaughan), but even "The Twist" is charged and vibrant with sensuality, something Chubby Checker's bland remake ignored. This is an undercurrent throughout these dance songs, and it's irresistible, but what's more stunning is the consistently brilliant songwriting, or perhaps the impassioned performances. Either way, this is brilliant, timeless music, transcending the pigeonhole of great '50s R&B to stand among some of the great pop music of the 20th century. *—Stephen Thomas Erlewine*

From Love to Tears / Oct. 13, 1998 / Pool Party ♦♦♦

One of R&B's best innovators is in fine voice on ten mostly uptempo tunes, but there are only a few real sparks: "(How Did We Get) From Love to Tears" with its gospel flavor, "Shake What Your Mama Gave Ya," "Women Are Made for Lovin'," and the slow, bluesy "Crazy to Be in Love With You." *—Andrew Hamilton*

The EP Collection . . . Plus / Sep. 12, 2000 / See for Miles ♦♦♦♦

See for Miles' *EP Collection*, like most of the series, is a greatest-hits collection from Hank Ballard containing almost all of his biggest hits, plus a bunch of notable B-sides and covers. There are a few nifty rarities here, but also a couple of obscurities that aren't all that interesting either (the instrumental "The Big Frog"), and just because there are a generous 24 tracks doesn't necessarily mean that this is preferable to tighter collections. All the same, it's a fine collection of Ballard's best recordings and, while Rhino's set may be preferable, you'll still understand Ballard's greatness if you get this instead. *—Stephen Thomas Erlewine*

Dancin' and Twistin' / Oct. 31, 2000 / Ace ♦♦♦

Since Ballard & the Midnighters remain most known for their mid-'50s R&B/early rock & roll hits, it has sometimes been overlooked that they actually reached their crossover pop peak in the early '60s. In 1960 and 1961, they had seven Top 40 hits in the pop charts, and two Top Ten hits with "Finger Poppin' Time" and "Let's Go, Let's Go, Let's Go." All of those hits are on this 24-song anthology, which is devoted almost exclusively to Ballard's 1960s output. Ballard's original version of "The Twist," recorded in 1958 (and a Top 30 hit in 1960, although Chubby Checker's cover went to number 1), is here, and its success laid the foundation for an endless series of dance records over the next few years. "The Coffee Grind," "The Continental Walk," "The Switch-A-Roo," "It's Twistin' Time," "Good Twistin' Tonight," "Do You Know How to Twist?," even "The Float": all are on board. (And how could one resist calling "The Float" a dance bound to be dead on the water, even if it did make number-10 R&B?) Ballard may have been more earthy, more funky, and more authentic in every way than Chubby Checker, but in this era he was really pursuing a similar formula: twist and dance records, the themes recycled ad infinitum. And it must be conceded that the formula, in Ballard's hands, wears out its welcome when the singles are heard bang right after each other. It's competent dance rock bridging 1950s R&B and early soul, without nearly enough variation or innovation to sustain interest. Really, "Finger Poppin' Time," "Let's Go, Let's Go, Let's Go," and "The Twist" are all you need to hear from this era, and you can probably find them on various-artists anthologies without breaking too heavy a sweat. *—Richie Unterberger*

The Very Best of Hank Ballard & the Midnighters / Oct. 9, 2001 / Collectables ♦♦♦

Though it bills itself *The Very Best of Hank Ballard & the Midnighters*, Collectables' compilation doesn't quite live up to that title, since it's missing several definitive singles, including "Sexy Ways," "Work With Me Annie," and "Annie Had a Baby." However, it does feature some of Ballard's more pop-oriented songs, such as "Teardrops on Your Letter," "Let's Go, Let's Go, Let's Go," "Finger Poppin' Time," and "The Twist." The inclusion of songs like "Work With Me Annie" would have made this album almost as good of a retrospective as *Sexy Ways: The Best of Hank Ballard & the Midnighters*; as it stands, it's just a decent collection of Ballard's mid-career work. *—Heather Phares*

Darrell Banks (Darrell Eubanks)

b. 1938, Mansfield, OH, **d.** Mar. 1970, Detroit, MI

Vocals / Soul

Born Darrell Eubanks in Mansfield, OH, in 1938, the gospel-voiced soul singer stepped out as Darrell Banks from the East Side of Buffalo, NY, where he lived since a toddler. He sang in church before going secular and wailing at local watering holes. He befriended Doc Murphy, a dentist whose nightclub the Revilot lounge was one of those "holes." A scorching song written by fellow Buffalo resident Donnie Elbert got Banks off and running. He hooked up with Lebron Taylor via some type of license agreement with Murphy; Taylor used the name of Murphy's Buffalo nightspot, Revilot, for the label, which debuted in 1966 with "Open the Door to Your Heart," the tune Elbert had written for his Buffalo buddy. The song scored an impressive number two R&B and number 27 pop showing in 1966, Banks' biggest ever. Banks followed with Marc Gordon and Frank Wilson's "Somebody Somewhere Needs You" (a Motown song that wasn't originally or ever recorded by a Motown artist). Ike & Tina Turner first did the catchy romp on Loma Records (really just Tina; Ike's nowhere on the record). Banks' rendition charted at number 34 R&B and number 55 pop and provided circuit work for the singer; it was his last chart record. The Revilot deal somehow switched to Atlantic Records' Atco division for two nonstarters: "Here Come the Tears" b/w "I've Got That Feelin'" and "Angel Baby (Don't Ever Leave Me)" b/w "Look Into the Eyes of a Fool," both in 1967.

Banks never issued an album on Revilot to commensurate the success of the hit single, but both Revilot singles were compiled on his 1967 Atco album *Darrell Banks Is Here!* Atco switched him in-house to Cotillion Records for a final release, "I Wanna Go Home," written by Fred Briggs (aka Coldwater Stone) and Don Davis, b/w "The Love of My Woman" in 1968. Changing cooks again, Banks signed with Stax Records' Volt division for two singles and an album issued in 1969. "I'm the One Who Loves," followed by the two-sided gem "Beautiful Feeling" and "No One Is Blinder (Than a Man in Love)," sold well but didn't create any overtime at Stax's pressing plants. Tragedy aborted Banks' recording output at seven singles and two albums. The man considered by many as soul's finest voice was shot dead March 1970 in Detroit by Aaron Bullock, an off-duty policeman who was seeing Banks' woman. *—Andrew Hamilton*

Darrell Banks Is Here! / 1967 / Atco ♦♦♦♦♦

Some superb deep soul from Darrell Banks, one of the better late-'60s stylists, especially on ballads. This was one of two tremendous albums issued featuring Banks' dramatic, gospel-tinged wailing. He was killed in an altercation in 1970, and these albums attracted more attention after his death than during his lifetime. *—Ron Wynn*

Here to Stay / 1969 / Volt ♦♦♦♦♦

More superb soul ballads and crying songs from Darrell Banks, who not only made some excellent singles but had done some songwriting and producing for Stax in the '60s. Sadly, he was killed before he ever attained the level of popularity and exposure that he merited. *—Ron Wynn*

The Lost Soul / 1997 / Goldmine ♦♦♦♦♦

The title hints of the inner soul of Darrell Banks, a concept that may be over some heads; a more appropriate title for this 27-song extravaganza would have been The Complete Darrell Banks. Often called the best pure soul singer ever by serious students of the genre (a statement that Howard Tate fans will argue vehemently), Banks' recording career was short and sweet aesthetically, but a controversial mess on the business side. The double CD contains every track from his two albums on Atlantic and Volt Records, plus unreleased tracks, an especially sweet treat for Banks' admirers. Only fault is the sloppy compilation, a few tracks are different from what came out originally; however, only devotees will know that. Until someone comes up with something better, or remaster these tracks via some new super sound, this CD has everything you ever wanted from the late Darrell Banks and then some. *—Andrew Hamilton*

- **Open the Door to Your Heart: The Best of Darrell Banks** / 2000 / Connoisseur Collection ✦✦✦✦✦

Darrell Banks is an underrated Northern soul belter best-known for the classic "Open the Door to Your Heart." His smooth sound with just a trace of grit is reminiscent of soul men like Freddie Scott and Garnet Mimms. This collection rounds up the entire album he recorded for the Atlantic subsidiary Atco in 1967, the fabulous *Darrell Banks Is Here*, plus six other tracks recorded around the same time. Four of the songs are previously unreleased, including the clunkily titled but super funky "I'm Knocking at Your Heart, Please Let Me In." This is solid soul all the way through; any fan of '60s soul will want some Darrell Banks in their collection. Until a reissue label like Sundazed or Ace gets on the ball and does a "complete recordings of Darrell Banks" set, this collection is just as good as the other Banks collection that has been released. Granted, it does have fewer tracks than the others, but it is probably easier to find and the sound quality is a slight improvement. *—Tim Sendra*

Homer Banks

b. Aug. 2, 1941, Memphis, TN

Producer, Composer, Vocals / Soul, Memphis Soul, Southern Soul

Composer and producer Homer Banks was one of the unsung heroes behind the rise of Stax Records; though a fine soul singer in his own right, he never recorded for the label, instead teaming with Bettye Crutcher and Raymond Jackson as We Three, the songwriting troika responsible for a number of the company's classic singles. Born August 2, 1941, in Memphis, Banks co-founded the gospel group the Soul Consolidators before joining the office staff of the local Satellite Studios, later re-christened Stax. He dwelled in relative anonymity during his early years with the company, although co-workers Isaac Hayes and David Porter proved instrumental in landing him a session with the Genie label, resulting in the 1965 release of Banks' debut single "Sweetie Pie." The much-imitated and oft-covered "A Lot of Love" followed on the newly-revived Minit imprint in 1966, and over the next two years Banks issued four more singles for the label—"60 Minutes of Your Love," "Lady of Stone," "Round the Clock Lover Man" and "(Who You Gonna Run To) Me or Your Mama?"—all to little notice outside of the Memphis area.

As his singing career floundered, he increasingly focused on writing, teaming with Crutcher and Jackson as We Three to author hits for Stax artists Johnnie Taylor ("Who's Making Love"), the Staple Singers ("Be What You Are," "If You're Ready (Come Go With Me)"), and Isaac Hayes ("[If Loving You Is Wrong] I Don't Want to Be Right"). In addition to producing sessions for the Soul Children and Albert King, Banks also wrote the Sam & Dave classic "I Can't Stand Up (For Falling Down)," later covered by Elvis Costello; his other hits include "Touch a Hand (Make a Friend)" and "Woman to Woman." In 1977, Banks cut the solo album *Passport to Ecstasy*, and following Stax's demise he worked for a number of labels, including TK and Malaco. *—Jason Ankeny*

- **Passport to Ecstasy** / 1977 / Warner Bros. ✦✦✦

Rose Banks

b. Mar. 21, 1945, Dallas, TX

Vocals, Keyboards / R&B, Soul

West Coast vocalist Rose Banks enjoyed sporadic success in the '70s and '80s. She signed with Motown in the mid-'70s and recorded the LP *Rose* in 1976. One single, "Whole New Thing," made the lower reaches of the R&B charts. Some 12 years later, Banks was one of the vocalists on Quincy Jones' LP *Back on the Block*. *—Ron Wynn*

- **Rose** / 1976 / Motown ✦✦

Sly Stone's little sister, Rose Stone-Banks' first and only Motown album showed promise. Only two singles were released. "Whole New Thing," the first single, was co-written by Jeffery Bowen who produced every track except one, "Right's Alright," a co-production with Hamp "Bubba" Banks, Rose's husband. The tune is typical of Bowen's synthesizer dominated, high energy tracks. Ex Family Stone members, brother Freddie Stone and Cynthia Robinson, supply their talents on guitar and trumpet respectively. Banks gets mellow on "Darling Baby," popularized by the Elgins, giving the slinky, pleading, doo-wopper a sweet updating. The Holland, Dozier, Holland classic was Rose's second and final single. Motown should have dropped the sizzling "I've Got to Make It on My Own," originally by the Spinners off of *New & Improved*; It's Banks' most spirited vocal and had the potential to make some noise. She remakes big brother Sly's "I Get High on You" to good effect only to have it languish on the LP. Politics probably caused Motown's disinterest, since the material is on point. Augmenting Freddie and Cynthia are David Walker (guitar), Rusty Allen (bass), Truman Thomas (keyboards) and Pat Rizzo (tenor sax). *—Andrew Hamilton*

The Bar-Kays

f. 1966, Memphis, TN, **db.** 1988

Group / Funk, Soul, Memphis Soul, Instrumental Rock, R&B

Initially a funky instrumental soul combo on Stax/Volt, the Bar-Kays were nearly destroyed when most of the band perished in the same plane crash that claimed Otis Redding. Amazingly, the Bar-Kays not only regrouped but prospered, evolving into a popular funk ensemble over the course of the '70s. They continued to score hits on the R&B charts through much of the '80s as well, making for a career longevity that no one would have predicted for Stax's formerly star-crossed number-two house band.

The Bar-Kays were formed in Memphis, TN, in 1966, growing out of a local group dubbed the Imperials. Modeled on classic Memphis soul instrumental outfits like the Mar-Keys and Booker T. & the MG's, the Bar-Kays originally included guitarist Jimmy King (not the famed bluesman), trumpeter Ben Cauley, organist Ronnie Caldwell, saxophonist Phalon Jones, bassist James Alexander, and drummer Carl Cunningham. Adopting a mutated version of their favorite brand of rum (Bacardi) as their name, the band started playing heavily around Memphis, and eventually caught the attention of Stax/Volt, which signed the sextet in early 1967. With help from house drummer Al Jackson Jr., the label began grooming the Bar-Kays as a second studio backing group that would spell Booker T. & the MG's on occasion. That spring, the Bar-Kays cut their first single, "Soul Finger," a playful, party-hearty instrumental punctuated by a group of neighborhood children shouting the title. "Soul Finger" reached the pop Top 20 and went all the way to number three on the R&B chart, establishing the Bar-Kays in the public eye (although the follow-up, "Give Everybody Some," barely scraped the R&B Top 40). Producer Allen Jones began to take an interest in the group and became their manager and mentor; even better, Otis Redding chose them as his regular backing band that summer.

Unfortunately, disaster struck on December 10, 1967. En route to a gig in Madison, WI, Redding's plane crashed into frozen Lake Monona. He, his road manager, and four members of the Bar-Kays were killed. Trumpeter Ben Cauley survived the crash, and bassist James Alexander had not been on the flight; they soon assumed the heavy task of rebuilding the group. Adding insult to injury, the third and final single released by the original lineup, a cover of the Beatles' "A Hard Day's Night," was virtually ignored. Nonetheless, with Allen Jones' help, Cauley and Alexander assembled a new Bar-Kays lineup featuring guitarist Michael Toles, keyboardist Ronnie Gordon, saxophonist Harvey Henderson, and drummers Roy Cunningham and Willie Hall. At first, their sound was similar to the original lineup, and they were used as the house band on numerous Stax/Volt recording sessions; they also backed Isaac Hayes on his groundbreaking 1969 opus *Hot Buttered Soul*. Still, they were unable to land a hit of their own, and Cunningham and Gordon both left the group in 1970; the latter was replaced on keyboards by Winston Stewart.

With 1971's *Black Rock* album, the Bar-Kays debuted their first-ever lead vocalist, Larry Dodson, and incorporated some of the psychedelic-inspired rock/funk fusions of Sly & the Family Stone and Funkadelic. After playing on Isaac Hayes' hit *Shaft* soundtrack, Cauley and Toles both joined his backing band permanently, and were replaced by trumpeter Charles "Scoop" Allen and guitarist Vernon Burch. This new lineup took a more mainstream funk direction, scoring a minor hit with a takeoff on Jimi Hendrix's "Foxy Lady" dubbed "Copy Cat." The follow-up, another good-humored goof on a recent hit, was "Son of Shaft," which in 1972 became the group's first Top Ten R&B hit since "Soul Finger." That summer, the Bar-Kays played a well-received set at Wattstax (the black answer to Woodstock), but it wasn't enough to keep their commercial momentum going, especially as Stax/Volt headed toward eventual bankruptcy in 1975.

Armed with new guitarist Lloyd Smith (who'd joined when Burch left in 1973), new drummer Michael Beard, and trombonist Frank Thompson, the Bar-Kays signed with Mercury in 1976 and began the most commercially productive phase of their career. Writing most of their own material and using more synthesizers, their label debut, *Too Hot to Stop*, was a hit, powered by the smash R&B single "Shake Your Rump to the Funk." The group consolidated their success by opening for George Clinton's P-Funk machine on an extensive tour, and that loose, wild aesthetic was now a more accurate reflection of the Bar-Kays' brand of funk, although they were more easily able to bridge into disco. Follow-up *Flying High on Your Love* (1977) was the band's first gold record, and *Money Talks*—a Fantasy reissue of some previously unreleased Stax material—produced another Top Ten hit in "Holy Ghost" the following year. Drummer Sherman Guy and keyboardist Mark Bynum subsequently joined the band, and a string of hit albums followed: 1979's *Injoy* (which featured the Top Five R&B hit "Move Your Boogie Body"), 1980's *As One*, 1981's *Nightcruising* (which spawned two hits in "Hit and Run" and "Freaky Behavior"), and 1982's *Propositions* (more hits in "Do It (Let Me See You Shake)" and "She Talks to Me With Her Body"). All of those albums, save for *As One*, went gold.

In 1983, Sherman Guy and Charles Allen left the group, presaging a more commercial direction in keeping with the urban sound of the early '80s. In 1984, *Dangerous* produced one of the group's biggest hits, "Freakshow on the Dancefloor," and a couple more R&B chart hits in "Dirty Dancer" and "Sex-O-Matic." Their sound was becoming derivative, however, and although the group kept recording for Mercury through 1989, the changing musical landscape meant that the hits dried up. By 1987, only Larry Dodson, Harvey Henderson, and Winston Stewart remained; that same year, Allen Jones died of a heart attack, and the group scored its last R&B Top Ten hit with "Certified True." When their contract with Mercury was up, the Bar-Kays called it quits with 1988's *Animal*. Dodson and original bassist James Alexander put together a short-lived new version of the Bar-Kays for the 1994 album *48 Hours*, released on the small Basix label. *—Steve Huey*

Soul Finger / 1967 / Rhino ✦✦✦✦✦

The Bar-Kays were being trained as a second generation Booker T. & the MG's, largely by MG drummer Al Jackson. *Soul Finger* was their first album, coming off the success of their debut single, the group-written title cut. The album is in the classic Memphis-soul instrumental vein; sparse arrangements, accentuated low-end, walloping snare drum, and slightly delayed backbeat with horns taking the place of vocals. *Soul Finger* was the only album made by this particular version of the group. *—Rob Bowman*

Gotta Groove / 1969 / Stax ✦✦✦

After the plane crash in December 1967, trumpeter Ben Cauley and bass player James Alexander regrouped, forming a second edition of the Bar-Kays. *Gotta Groove* was the new group's first release. Modelled on earlier Bar-Kays work, the album is totally instrumental, including covers of the Mar-Keys' "Grab This Thing" and the Beatles' "Yesterday" and "Hey Jude." No standout cuts but plenty of fine, hard-driving slices of Memphis instrumental soul. *—Rob Bowman*

Black Rock / Feb. 1971 / Volt ✦✦

Do You See What I See? / 1972 / Stax ✦✦

Some vigorous funk and an occasional soulful ballad by the Bar-Kays, who were re-establishing their funk credentials and rebuilding after recovering from the 1967 plane crash. This album included the title track and several other short, peppy vocal and instrumental numbers, although it wasn't as well-produced as some later '70s and '80s efforts. *—Ron Wynn*

Coldblooded / 1974 / Stax ✦✦✦

One of the albums that the Bar-Kays cut for Stax in the early '70s after they revamped the group following the disastrous late-'60s plane crash that killed all but two of the originals. The new lineup featured guitarist Lloyd Smith, drummer Michael Beard, vocalist John Colbert, trumpeter Charles Allen, saxophonist Harvey Henderson, and others. This was classic Southern funk, with gospel-tinged vocals, energetic horn tracks, and lyrics that ranged from down-home musings to urban admonitions. *—Ron Wynn*

Too Hot to Stop / Oct. 1976 / Mercury ✦✦✦✦✦
One of their best '70s dates, The Bar-Kays were in overdrive throughout this one. The title track was a huge hit, and the other uptempo tunes were equally fast-paced and tightly played. The few slow songs provided enough changes of pace to keep things varied. The horn charts, production, and arrangements were funk personified, although they were starting to add synthesized elements in anticipation of changes on the urban front. *—Ron Wynn*

Flying High on Your Love / Nov. 1977 / Mercury ✦✦✦✦
The Age of Aquarius may have fallen out of fashion, but "what's your sign" was still the ultimate pickup line at the end of the 1970s. Disco novelty band the Floaters had counted on that with their brash mid-1977 "Float On," and the Bar-Kays, of course, couldn't resist a little good-humored stroke, especially if it carried commercial punch as well. So, for the November release of their second Mercury LP, *Flying High on Your Love*, the inner sleeve featured the band's photos—complete with star signs. Jokes aside, the Bar-Kays delivered a juicy set of funk movers accented by disco beats and augmented by ballads. It was a tremendous mix. "Shut the Funk Up" is an overlooked gem, lost as the band sublimated their sound in the 1980s. A near-perfect disco song punctuated by the funky horn triumvirate of Charles "Scoop" Allen, Harvey "Joe" Henderson, and Frank "Captain Disaster" Thompson and dominated by vocalist Larry "D" Dodson's call to "get on up or just shut the funk up," it's immediately apparent that disco never sounded so good—or so funky. "Woman of the Night" and "Let's Have Some Fun" follow suit, while stomping the disco beat down with some pretty heavy funk riffing. But, of course, that's why the Bar-Kays were, and remained, so successful. They were fully committed to their funk forbears while never taking their eyes off the shifting musical climate. Thus, they were able to make the leap from funk to disco in a way that almost no other bands could match. The Bar-Kays' late-'70s sounds, then, were not one or the other, but a seamless blend of both. A fine mix and a glorious achievement. *—Amy Hanson*

Money Talks / Oct. 1978 / Stax ✦✦✦✦
Although the Bar-Kays stuck with the Stax Records until its demise in 1976, the label stopped releasing the group's recordings after 1973. However, when they re-emerged as a success on the Mercury label with hits like "Shake Your Rump to the Funk," some unreleased recordings they made between 1974 and 1976 were released as an album entitled *Money Talks*. Although this repackaging was obviously designed to cash in on the group's success, *Money Talks* stands up as a solid and consistent album in its own right. This material lays the groundwork for the Bar-Kays' post-Stax style by trading live-in-the-studio jams for a carefully produced sound and blending in standout pop hooks into the funky grooves. The best example is "Holy Ghost," a hard-grooving monster of a jam where elaborate horn arrangements dance around a thick synthesizer bass line as Larry Dodson lays down a salacious vocal about his lover's otherworldly romantic skills. It became a big R&B hit when released as a single in 1978 and was later sampled by M/A/R/R/S on their club classic "Pump Up the Volume." Other memorable tracks include the title track, a high-stepping tune that showcases the chops of the horn players, and "Mean Mistreater," an unlikely but effective Grand Funk Railroad cover that transforms the minimalist original tune into a spooky yet sexy mood piece built on some languid keyboard work. None of the other tracks are as strong as "Holy Ghost" (which is so good that it bookends the album in two versions), but they are all listenable and flow together surprisingly well as an album. All in all, *Money Talks* is a fine slab of vintage funk that will please anyone who loves old-school grooves. *—Donald A. Guarisco*

Light of Life / Dec. 1978 / Mercury ✦✦✦
In 1978 the Bar-Kays with *Light of Life* continued all that they'd begun on the previous year's *Flying High on Your Love*. Debuting a new ten-member lineup, the group offered up a heady blend of classic funk spun with thoroughly contemporary disco ethics. The only drawback to the Bar-Kays' sound was that such a rapid-fire release schedule was rendering their unique sound a little samey. What worked beautifully across one LP was less unique across the next and, by the third, was nearing the point of overkill. That said, there are still many, many fine moments on *Light of Life*. Their balladeering skills were improving and are showcased magnificently on "We're the Happiest People in the World" and, of course, they absolutely sparkled across the funk-fests: the effusive "Get up 'N' Do It" and "Give It Up," which carries nods to both Hamilton Bohannon's "Disco Stomp" and the iconoclastic "Theme From Shaft." Rush-released to compete with Fantasy's cash-in *Money Talks*, compiled from the band's late Stax-era recordings, *Light of Life* faltered some in its wake. Nevertheless, *Light of Life* still gave the band their fourth Top 20 hit as "Shine," while "Are You Being Real" furthered their longevity on the singles chart. *—Amy Hanson*

Injoy / Oct. 1979 / Mercury ✦✦✦✦
Its title a snazzy double play, the Bar-Kays' 1979 classic *Injoy* LP was the first and most successful of a quintet of albums that swept the band to the top of the charts and into the stratosphere of superstardom for half a decade. An energetic and primarily funk-driven set, *Injoy* was dominated by the supreme "Move Your Boogie Body," an eminently danceable, pop-friendly slab that cut the bass with strings, powered home the excellent vocals, added some Euro-disco synth, and soared into the Top Five to give the Bar-Kays their highest-to-date spot on the charts. But while that track may have captured the public heart, the bandmembers had even better tricks up their very flashy sleeves, powering through the classic funk of "More and More" and "Up in Here"—a song of unmitigated old-school proportions that reprises the Moroder-isms deep in the mix. Elsewhere, the band toned it down with several ballads, including "Girl I'm on Your Side" and "Running In and Out of My Life." With the Bar-Kays at the top of their form, there was little that could detract from this set. And, while *Injoy* just missed the top spot on the R&B chart, it still got a nation off the couch and onto the dancefloor. *—Amy Hanson*

As One / Nov. 1980 / Mercury ✦✦
Another in the Bar-Kays' monstrous string of hit LPs, 1980's *As One* unleashed one more blistering set upon a public who seemed unable to get enough of the band. As usual, the LP slammed into the Top Ten, down only slightly from the previous year's *Injoy*. And, reaching back to the graphics of 1978's *Light of Life*, the group again wrought a fine parody of Earth, Wind & Fire's space-age Egyptology for their cover. But, of course, it's what's inside that matters. And here, at least in part, the Bar-Kays wouldn't disappoint. Both the title track and "Boogie Body Land" are classic Bar-Kays funk behemoths, and even the LP's second charting single, "Body Fever," isn't bad, although it does pale markedly in comparison. Where the band falters, however, is across a few more-than-mediocre ballads—replete with very MOR crescendoed backing vocals. They were never at their best as a ballad band, and by 1980 perhaps they had run out of steam on that front. "Open Your Heart," meanwhile, is a cute little disco song—but there were so many disco acts doing it better. The Bar-Kays were on a real fencepost here, teetering between old and new before dropping wholeheartedly into more contemporary waters. However, their three previous LPs were all leaning toward the future as well—and were done much better. At the end of the day, perhaps a little time out would have been warranted. *—Amy Hanson*

Nightcruising / Nov. 1981 / Mercury ✦✦
By 1981, the Bar-Kays were firmly at the front of the synth-laden R&B pack that would come to dominate much of the scene. But, although they had left their Stax era chops behind, four albums into their Mercury career the band was still capable of flinging some fine funk your way. Best described, perhaps, as contemporary and more urban dance, *Nightcruising* showcased the band in fine form. Multiple lineup changes hadn't detracted too much from their overall proficiency, a seamless sound ineffably aided by their long-term relationship with producer Allen Jones. The sonics here are slick, bright, and punchy, and when the Bar-Kays are good they're nearly unstoppable, a trait best experienced across the hits "Hit and Run" and the deliciously lunatic "Freaky Behavior," which is packed with electronic antics and just a hint of Rick James styling. But there are other nice touches as well, particularly across the older school-styled "Touch Tone" and "Traffic Jam." Where the band stumbles, however, is across their ballads. They're nice enough to be sure, but listeners have never looked to the Bar-Kays to fill that void. And ultimately, it's this mishmash of style and intent that detracts from the overall package. Rather than try to please everyone, the band should stick to what they do best—thrill the grooves off a crowd. *—Amy Hanson*

Propositions / Nov. 1982 / Mercury ✦✦✦
Funk pioneers the Bar-Kays not only succeeded in stamping their own rock influence on the genre, but also influenced a generation of vocalists while keeping their own sense of sound intact. By the '80s, however, the band had traded in some of their traditional chops for a more electronic vibe, one which certainly gave nod to the younger generation of funkers coming up right behind them—Prince and Cameo's Larry Blackmon especially. This move to a wave groove is particularly evident on *Propositions*, although the band keeps three very distinctive styles going throughout the set. The majority of songs, however, are heavy on the synth, including the title track and "Tripping Out." "Do It (Let Me See You Shake)," meanwhile, had trappings that were pure Prince, and cracked the R&B Top Ten. To temper that tumultuous flow, the band also included two soul/rock ballads, "Anticipation" and "I Can't Believe You're Leaving Me." Both the old school "(Busted)" and "You Made a Change in My Life," meanwhile, returned the funk to full focus, while the band lets their real talents rip. *Propositions* definitely succeeded in its time and place. Bar-Kays fans from the '70s probably won't love it, but anyone who cut their teeth on the pop sounds of the mid-'80s should snap this up and enjoy the history lesson. *—Amy Hanson*

Dangerous / Apr. 1984 / Mercury ✦✦✦
Able to move with the times, bringing all the elements of the new breed into their sound, and keeping their funk roots intact while traversing the slippery slope of 1980s dance, the Bar-Kays scored another hit with 1984's massive *Dangerous* LP. Whittled down to a hefty octet for this outing, the Bar-Kays easily proved they were still up to their old tricks, smoothly updating their sound while continuing to take some well-intentioned and good-humored jabs at more than a few peers along the way. This now-traditional penchant, never meant to hurt and only done in homage, is perhaps best heard across the album's three hit singles. Not only was the monstrously sassy "Freakshow on the Dance Floor" an integral part of the film *Breakin'*, but the incorporated elements from Midnight Starr's "No Parking on the Dancefloor" were just evident enough to prove that the similarities were deliberate. Following on the heels of that hit came the midtempo groover "Dirty Dancer," which tongue-and-cheekily captured the essence of Michael Jackson's current "Billie Jean," leaving the synthed-out "Sexomatic" following quite happily in Prince's purple footsteps. And while it's true that these songs may well be the best elements of *Dangerous*, the band wasn't done yet—not by a long shot. The title track remains an outstanding sliver of smooth dance that seamlessly incorporates more than a few Euro-disco splashes into the mix. It's very much of its era, but still compellingly fresh nevertheless. Elsewhere, the band rounds out the relative frenzy with one single ballad, the well-intentioned "Lovers Should Never Fall in Love," capping off another effusive, energetic set. And although, at the time, it seemed as if the Bar-Kays were unstoppable, *Dangerous* would prove to be the band's last major hit—making this album one to savor. *—Amy Hanson*

Banging the Wall / Sep. 1985 / Mercury ✦✦

Contagious / Oct. 1987 / Mercury ✦✦

Animal / 1988 / Mercury ✦✦

• **The Best of the Bar-Kays** / 1988 / Stax ♦♦♦♦♦
While curiously overlooking the group's earliest hits ("Soul Finger" and "Knucklehead"), *The Best of the Bar-Kays* offers a worthwhile thumbnail portrait of the Bar-Kays' evolution from a neo-Booker T. & the MG's soul instrumental combo into one of the wilder funk ensembles of the 1970s. Focusing on the years 1968 (when the group's second lineup came together following the death of four members of the band in the same airplane crash that claimed Otis Redding) through 1975 (when the band left Stax), *The Best of the Bar-Kays* finds them bridging the gap between the R&B sounds of the 1960s and the 1970s, and gaining more than their share of attitude along the way. Highlights include a very Booker T.-influenced cover of "Midnight Cowboy," the funky and funny Isaac Hayes pastiche "Son of Shaft," a revved-up take on "Montego Bay," and the tight groove of "A.J. the Housefly." While not a complete overview of the Bar-Kays' career, *The Best of the Bar-Kays* is at least a strong starter, and should ideally be followed up by *The Best of Bar-Kays*, which concentrates on their work for Mercury. *—Mark Deming*

The Best of Bar-Kays / May 18, 1993 / Mercury ♦♦♦♦♦
When the Bar-Kays joined Mercury Records in 1976, they shifted musical styles slightly, veering away from the goofy yet funky soul instrumentals that defined their Stax singles and concentrating on loose, wild funk driven by fat basslines and whining synthesizers. Mercury's *The Best of Bar-Kays* captures the majority of the highlights from their '70s recordings for the label. Over the course of 16 tracks, the compilation features the majority of their Top Ten R&B hits—including "Shake Your Rump to the Funk," "Too Hot to Stop," "Move Your Boogie Body," and "Hit and Run"—as well as several fine album tracks like "Freakshow on the Dance Floor," "Shut the Funk Up," and "Sexomatic," which illustrate the depth of the group's musical skills. *—Stephen Thomas Erlewine*

Black Rock/Gotta Groove / 1994 / Stax ♦♦♦

48 Hours / Nov. 17, 1994 / Basix ♦♦♦♦♦
The always entertaining and delightful, but sometimes derivative Bar-Kays come up aces this time. Three hard funk tunes—"She Can Get It," the title track, and "Irresistible"—are as arresting as top-flight ballads like the seven-minute-plus "(If Loving You Is Wrong) I Don't Want to Be Right" and "If It Takes All Night," where Evelyn "Champagne" King adds a soulful vocal. The CD opens with "Introduction," a lazy wass-up telephone call by one Bar-Kay to another, the same spiel used in a popular commercial that first aired during the Y2K NFL Super Bowl, six years after this CD surfaced. They also include a "Mega Mix," a musical collage of the disc's dozen songs. *—Andrew Hamilton*

The Best of Bar-Kays, Vol. 2 / May 21, 1996 / Mercury ♦♦♦
Another scoop of mid-'70s–mid-'80s material from the Mercury era, for those with an interest in the band's slicker phase. It's pretty formulaic, but does include several R&B hits, such as "Spellbound," "Do It," "Boogie Body Land," "Let's Have Some Fun," "Dirty Dancer," "Your Place or Mine," "Sexomatic," and "She Talks to Me With Her Body," whose thematic concerns can be easily gleaned from the titles. *—Richie Unterberger*

The Ballads Collection / May 19, 1998 / Mercury ♦♦♦
The Ballads Collection contains 12 slow jams and seductive ballads from the Bar-Kays. James Alexander has helped compile the album, which means it features both surefire hits like "Flying High on Your Love" and album tracks. That very diversity makes it a worthwhile addition to the group's catalog, and the record should please anyone looking for a romantic Bar-Kays album. *—Stephen Thomas Erlewine*

Barbara & the Uniques

f. 1963, **db.** 1975
Group / Girl Group, Soul
In 1970, five years after her girl group the Duettes issued their last single, Barbara Livsey returned to recording with sister Gwen Livsey, and Doris Lindsey as Barbara & the Uniques. Livsey was half of the Duettes who recorded for One-derful, M-Pac, and Mar-V-Lus Records. This time she benefits from a crack Eugene Record production for their first release on New Chicago Sound Records, "There It Goes Again," in October 1970. New Chicago Sound was short lived and Arden Records entered the picture for national distribution; it became a solid entry on *Billboard*'s R&B chart, and the biggest single of Barbara Livsey's career. Two more Arden singles followed: but neither "You're Gonna Make Me Cheat On You" b/w "I'll Never Let You Go," nor "You Make Me Feel So Young Again" b/w "Take Me As I Am," 1971 products, came close to duplicating the success of "There It Goes Again."

In 1972, Abbot Records issued "He's Gone" b/w "Take Me as I Am," but it only received local play; discouraged, Gwen and Doris quit, but Barbara carried on as Barbara Blake & the Uniques (three male vocalists) on 20th Century Records in 1974. Their first release "Prize Possession" b/w "It's Not That Easy," stiffed; as did, "Teach Me" b/w "Everlasting Thrill." A final release "I Need Your Love So Bad" b/w "Let Me Down Easy," in 1975 never got recognized. When the 20th Century deal ended, Barbara Livsey-Blake called it quits, this time for good. She had been recording since 1963, giving it her all with only one R&B hit to show for her efforts. *—Andrew Hamilton*

Gene Barge (Daddy "G")

b. Norfolk, VA
Producer, Sax (Tenor), Sax (Alto) / Soul, R&B
Musician/arranger/producer Gene Barge had a pivotal role in the development of major recording artists such as Natalie Cole and Gary "U.S." Bonds and also seminal acts on Stax Records and Chess Records. In 1955 Barge cut his first single, "Country," for Chess Records' Checker label and started touring with Philadelphia vocal group the Turbans and Ray Charles. While on tour, Barge was hired by Chuck Willis' band. In New York, the band recorded Willis' major hit, "C. C. Rider." Barge recorded a few more sides with the Atlanta, GA, singer/songwriter for Atlantic Records, including "Dupree's Blues." Signing with Frank Guida's Legrand Records, Barge released an instrumental single, "A Night With Daddy G." Labelmate Bonds heard the record and with Barge's permission put lyrics to his music. Their collaboration created "Quarter to Three," a number one gold single. Barge and Bonds collaborated on hits from mid-1961 to late 1962 ("School Is In," "School Is Out," "Dear Lady Twist," "Twist Twist Senora," and "Copy Cat").

In 1964 Barge was hired as a producer, arranger, sax player, and musical contractor for Chess Records. Some of the artists with whom he was involved were Little Milton, Billy Stewart, the Dells, Fontella Bass, Koko Taylor, Muddy Waters, and the Radiants. Barge had a great rhythm section to work with: drummer Maurice White, bassist Louis Satterfield, guitarist Gerald Sims, and pianists Raynard Minor, Sonny Thompson, and Leonard Caston. Among those doing background vocals on the sessions was Andrea Davis (aka Minnie Riperton), who was signed to Chess as part of the girl group the Gems. Assigned to Chess' gospel section, Barge worked with the Soul Stirrers, Dr. Alex Bradford, Ruth Davis & the Davis Sisters, the Meditation Singers, the Violinaires, and Fontella's mother, Martha Bass. When Chess folded in 1971, Barge was hired by Al Bell of Stax Records for their gospel division, Gospel Truth. The label had hits with Rance Allen, Rev. Maceo Woods, Howard Lemon, Vern Gaines, Rev. T.L. Barrett, and the PUSH Choir with choir director Marvin Yancy.

Barge also did some independent production. One song, "Lord Don't Move the Mountain" by Inez Andrews (ABC-Peacock, 1972), was a major gospel hit that was put in regular rotation on soul stations. Stax ceased operations around 1974, and Barge began working with pianist Marvin Yancy, whom he had met earlier at Andrews' house. Yancy played on most on the Andrews sessions as well on the PUSH Choir albums that Barge supervised for Stax's gospel label. After doing some work with Yancy and his partner, Charles Jackson, on their group the Independents, Barge was hired to do demos with an unknown singer named Natalie Cole. Barge recorded the instrumental tracks for the demo at Universal Recording Studios. Jackson and Yancy wrote Cole's first hit, "This Will Be," at the end of her demo sessions. More number one R&B singles followed, including "Inseparable," "Sophisticated Lady (She's a Different Lady)," "I've Got Love on My Mind," and "Our Love." Barge won a Grammy for co-producing "Sophisticated Lady." *—Ed Hogan*

Dance With Daddy "G" / 1965 / Checker ♦♦♦
Arranger/producer Gene Barge comes up with one of the better albums by people who normally work behind the scenes: arrangers and session musicians. These albums were the vogue in the '60s despite the fact that none sold well. Maybe that's why they're not the vogue now. This one comes from a Chicago perspective and feature instrumental arrangements of "Fine Twine," "The Monkey Time," "Voice Your Choice," "The In Crowd," and "Twine Time." These jams swing, shuffle, and groove, also includes renditions of "Shake," "My Guy," and "The Way You Do the Things You Do." *—Andrew Hamilton*

• **Dance With Daddy "G" Plus . . .** / 1996 / See for Miles ♦♦♦♦
Saxman Gene Barge played with some of the finest R&B and soul artists of the '50s and '60s, including Chuck Willis, Gary "U.S." Bonds, and Andrea Davis (aka Minnie Riperton). This disc features his record from 1965, *Dance With Daddy "G,"* plus six previously unreleased tracks cut later in the decade. *Dance With Daddy "G" Plus . . .* finds Barge in the spotlight doing instrumental covers of hits like the Beatles' "I Feel Fine," the Temptations' "The Way You Do the Things You Do," and Major Lance's "The Monkey Time," as well as a few originals. The record is aimed at dancefloors, but sounds more like music to be played in supermarkets; Barge sounds very restrained for the most part and his backing group is playing soul by the numbers. Especially wrong is his cover of Bob Dylan's "Blowing in the Wind," which features some embarrassing female vocals along with Barge's less-than-inspiring playing. Much more successful are the bonus tracks. His take on the Lemon Pipers' "Green Tambourine" has some funky drums and nasty fuzz guitar to add some grit to his smooth sax sound. The other five tracks feature Barge on vocals as well as sax and are much more energetic and fun than *Dance With Daddy "G"*. He doesn't have the greatest voice and the songs he does aren't always great (see "Chippie the Hippie From Mississippi" for proof of that), but at least there is a little bit of soul invested. In fact, Barge's cover of the Music Explosion's "Little Bit of Soul" is the highlight of the disc, as the band takes the song at a loping tempo and some sassy backup singers goose Barge along. Despite the handful of fun tracks tacked on to the end, *Dance With Daddy "G" Plus . . .* is definitely a footnote to the history of soul and should only be sought out by fans of easy listening soul saxophone records. Otherwise, be sure to check out Barge's far superior work with Gary "U.S." Bonds. *—Tim Sendra*

J.J. Barnes (James Jay Barnes)

b. Nov. 30, 1943, Detroit, MI
Vocals / Northern Soul, Motown, R&B, Soul
J.J. Barnes' "Baby Please Come Back Home" (June 1967) jammed all over the Midwest, East Coast, South, and west of the Mississippi River. This was the 11th single and the sixth recording company (Groovesville) of Barnes' career. Barnes co-wrote most of his recordings; "Baby Please Come Back Home" was co-written with Don Davis, a guitarist, songwriter, producer, music publisher, and record label owner. Barnes sang the lyrics with so much pain that the single went to number nine on Billboard's R&B chart. Unofficially, it was number one at inner-city skating rinks—skaters loved rolling to its cool, slinky, mercurial rhythm and pinging accents.

James Jay Barnes, born November 30, 1943, in Detroit, MI, had more than 25 single releases after his big hit, but none duplicated its captivating aura, sales, or chart position. Barnes' gospel background (the Halo Gospel Singers) isn't apparent on his recordings; he came along at a time in Detroit when the city's blues and R&B bases were strong. His style emulated Southern soul singers; the session players in Detroit in the early '60s were R&B players and gave Barnes' records a Southern feel. Other Detroit singers with a similar sound include Joe Stubbs, Steve Mancha, Darrell Banks, Sammy Ward, and Lee Rogers.

In 1960, when he was 17, Barnes cut his first single, "My Love Came Tumbling Down" b/w "Won't You Let Me Know" for Kable Records. Mickay Records issued four singles by Barnes; the first, "Just One More Time" (1963), is sought after by Northern soul fanatics.

Scepter Records realized its potential and plucked it for national distribution, but the sales never amounted to much. He cut one record for Ring Records in 1964, "Poor Unfortunate Me" b/w "She Ain't Ready."

Ric-Tic Records issued Barnes' seventh record and followed it with three more, debuting with "Please Let Me In" in 1965; like many of Barnes' recordings it had a pronounced, four-on-the-floor beat—the beat that defined the early Northern soul sound. Initially, if a tune didn't have that beat, it wasn't played in Northern England's popular dance clubs. Inner-city teens hated the beat (it wasn't cool to dance to) and R&B disc jockeys rarely played these tunes. Still, his Ric-Tic debut sold better than previous singles. "Real Humdinger," its successor, charted at number 20 on the R&B chart and number 60 on the pop chart, but, despite these numbers, wasn't played in some cities, mainly because of its hokey beat. An update of the Beatles' "Day Tripper" became his most successful record at the time. "Say It" b/w "Deeper in Love" didn't stand a chance because Ed Wingate was in the process of selling Ric-Tic/Golden World Records lock, stock, and barrel to Motown. Barnes wasn't happy being Motown's property, and neither was his ex-Ric-Tic bud, Edwin Starr. Motown never released anything by Barnes. The company was more interested in his songwriting abilities and released at least two songs co-written by Barnes: "Show Me the Way" by Martha & the Vandellas (October 1967) and "Don't Make Hurting Me a Habit" by the Marvelettes (December 1968).

Motown released Barnes from his contract and he hooked up with Don Davis again, scoring the first time on Groovesville Records with "Baby Please Come Back Home." Its successor, "Now That I Got You Back" b/w "Forgive Me" (1967), a stomper and a pleader, threw a rod at number 44. The third, "Sweet Sherry," with the Originals harmonizing behind Barnes, didn't sell despite its immense charm. Then came "Easy Living" b/w "I've Lost You," with backing vocals by the Holidays, on the Groove City label, which sank upon release. A stint on Revilot Records resulted in four singles, including "Our Love Is in the Pocket," a popular Northern soul song. Barnes co-wrote his final Revilot single, "So Called Friends" (1969), with George Clinton (Parliament) and two unknown brothers by the last name of Taylor.

Buddah, Volt, Leo, Magic Touch, Perception, and Invasion Records issued Barnes' next five releases from 1969 to 1973. Perception issued the first J.J. Barnes album, *Born Again* (1973); the Perception sides didn't compare to earlier recordings, nor did what followed. Old friend Edwin Starr moved to England and became very popular; remembering Barnes, Starr arranged for his old buddy to come over and do a series of shows with him. This proved to be a lucrative move, as Barnes signed a deal with Contempo Records, a U.K. label, in the mid-'70s. Contempo cranked out seven undistinguished singles and an album, *Sara Smile*. Barnes released at least five more records. Albums include *Rare Stamps* on Volt Records, which features cuts by Barnes, Steve Mancha, and Darrell Banks; he also recorded an album on Motor City Records entitled *Try It One More Time*. *—Andrew Hamilton*

Rare Stamps / 1969 / Volt ♦♦♦

Rare Stamps is a compilation of Don Davis productions for J.J. Barnes and Steve Mancha (born Clyde Wilson). Despite spending most of their lives in Detroit, both have deep-soul roots and possess a gritty, earthy sound. Barnes is a favorite of Northern soul fanatics. His biggest hit, "Baby Please Come Back Home," and is a Marvin Gaye soundalike, a midtempo mover that was a favorite at roller-skating rinks. The Originals, of "Baby I'm For Real" fame, contribute as much as Barnes on "Sweet Sherry" but are not credited. Mancha has one of the most soulful voices ever recorded; he later went on to sing with 100 Proof (Aged in Soul). Tracks like "Don't Make Me a Storyteller," "Hate Yourself in the Morning," and "Just Keep on Loving Me" are nononsense nonfiction accounts of painful love affairs. [Note: Stax, via Fantasy Records, released *Don Davis Presents the Sound of Detroit: J.J. Barnes, Steve Mancha, & Darrell Banks*; this fine CD has, in addition to the Barnes/Mancha sides, the complete *Here to Stay* LP by the late Darrell Banks all on one disc.] *—Andrew Hamilton*

The Sound of Detroit / 1969 / Stax ♦♦♦♦♦

Sophisticated R&B wasn't the only thing that Detroit artists made in the '60s. Some performers whose music was deemed too raw for the Motown pop machine found their way to other labels like Stax. That was the case for the three artists featured on this anthology of Detroit soul: J.J. Barnes, Steve Mancha, and Darrell Banks, who also did some recording on Atlantic subsidiary Atco. Banks gets the bulk of the cuts here, 12 out of the 25, and displays a fine shouting style and energetic delivery. Barnes is especially effective on the mono cut "Got to Get Rid of You," while Mancha's "Don't Make Me a Storyteller" and "Just Keep on Loving Me" are prime country-soul workouts. *—Ron Wynn*

● **King of Northern Soul: The Very Best of J.J. Barnes** / Apr. 2, 1996 / Motorcity ♦♦♦♦♦

J. J. Barnes tracks produced by Ian Levine. These are not the real deals; they lack the production expertise and soulful feeling of his American-produced recordings. Levine helped write some new material and re-recorded some of Barnes' old songs like "Sweet Sherry," "Please Let Me In," "Real Humdinger," and "Our Love Is in the Pocket." A high cost for this 18-song compilation is ridiculous; it would be more palatable, considering its obvious weak points, if it were more reasonably priced. Listeners are advised to check out a CD of his original recordings and pass this one by. *—Andrew Hamilton*

The Groovesville Masters / 1997 / Goldmine ♦♦♦♦

You would think 38 tracks on two CDs would be definitive for an obscure soul singer, but not in this case. J.J. Barnes had three recordings that achieved a modicum of success in the States; two of them—"Day Tripper" and "the Errol Flynn"—didn't make this set because they're products of other labels. The biggest record he appeared on was "I'll Love You Forever" as a member of the Holidays, with Edwin Starr on lead and Barnes and Steve Mancha providing backing vocals. The three never toured as the Holidays; subsequent Holidays recordings had completely different members. Barnes' biggest, "Baby Please Come Back Home," is a Marvin Gaye sound-alike with a staccato beat, memorable lyrics, and Barnes' incessant pleading. An a cappella version, also included, is strictly filler. He recorded before this song, and cut many tunes after it, but never came up with another as good. "Sweet Sherry" features the Originals as much as Barnes; it's a lilting beauty that should have done better, but never surfaced in the States. Barnes is a big favorite with European soul lovers; his tunes usually fit the four-on-the-floor beat they love. "Please Let Me In," "Snowflakes," "Chains," "Now That I Got You Back," and "Our Love Is in the Pocket" are Northern soul classics. Produced by Don Davis. *—Andrew Hamilton*

Born Again, Again! / Sep. 9, 1997 / Sequel ♦♦♦♦

Born Again, Again! is a 1997 reissue of J.J. Barnes' 1973 album *Born Again*, which happened to be the first proper album he recorded (the rest had all been singles collections). Although there are some weak songs scattered throughout the album, it is a strong sweet soul album, illustrating that Barnes was one of the most underrated soul vocalists of his time. *—Leo Stanley*

H.B. Barnum

b. 1936, Houston, TX

Producer, Arranger, Piano, Keyboards / Soul

H.B. Barnum is primarily a producer and arranger with an enormous number of credits dating back to the 1950s and including everyone from the Miracles to Frank Sinatra. As an artist, he debuted with the album *The Big Voice of Barnum* in 1960. His instrumental "Lost Love" was a Top 40 hit in 1961. *—William Ruhlmann*

● **Big Hits from Detroit** / 1965 / Capitol ♦♦

In the mid-'60s, arrangers, road bandleaders, and session musicians released albums under their names of instrumental arrangements of popular hits. Earl Van Dyke, Gene Barge, and others attempted to cash in with these projects. Few realize that H. B. Barnum was one of Motown's most popular arrangers—he worked almost exclusively with Holland, Dozier, & Holland—this was before Motown credited arrangers on the labels, so this album of Motown hits comes natural for him. A nice try, but there's nothing remotely close to a hit among these 11 elevator specials that include "Baby I Need Your Loving," "My Guy," "Heat Wave," "Come See About Me," and "Hitch Hike." *—Andrew Hamilton*

Barrabás

f. 1970, Madrid, Spain, **db.** 1977

Group / Latin Rock, Disco, Club/Dance

Barrabás was a Spanish group formed in the early '70s by former Los Brincos leader Fernando Arbex. At its formation, Barrabás was a six-piece including Tito Duarte, Miguel Morales, Ricky Morales, Ignacio Egaña, and Joao Vidal. (Members changed occasionally; the most significant change occurred when vocalist José Luís Tejada was added to the lineup.) The Madrid-based group was equally influenced by funk and psychedelic rock, and they certainly took a cue from Santana. Throughout their career, they flirted with jazz-funk and disco; a handful of singles become club favorites in several countries. Their first album, 1972's *Wild Safari*, spawned "Woman," their biggest hit. After a self-titled 1977 album, the group disbanded. Arbex resurrected the group in the early '80s with a slightly revamped lineup; that group released another pair of albums before finally dissolving for good. Beware: two "compilations" released under the name Barrabás—*Grandes Exitos* and *Vive*—feature no original members of the group and are fraudulent. *—Andy Kellman*

● **Wild Safari** / 1972 / RCA/Disconforme ♦♦♦

Barrabás' debut is the one that put them on the map, thanks to the surprise club hit "Woman." The Latin group—who were pioneers in a sense with their blend of Latin, African, and American influences—was one of the first international groups to leave its mark on the disco circuit. To this day, the song remains popular with disco/house DJs who have studied the histories of '70s clubs like the Paradise Garage and the Loft. Nothing else from *Wild Safari* caught on like "Woman," but the remainder sets the tone for what would follow from the group throughout the '70s: a combination of rock, dance music, soul with Latin roots, and an equal love for traditional pop structures and instrumental workouts. *—Andy Kellman*

Power / 1973 / RCA ♦♦♦

Madrid's Barrabás followed the success of their debut—due in most part to "Woman," a surprise hit that found a home in several American discos—a year later with *Power*, an accomplished if unremarkable album that indicates the varied stylistic interests of the group. "Mr. Money" seems to temper the hard, organ-driven sound of Deep Purple with the rhythmic thrust of early Santana, but unlike those two groups, Barrabás pushes their guitars into the distance. After a pair of nondescript traditional rock numbers, the group temporarily slides into easy listening pop with "The Horse," an instrumental led by Tito Duarte's flute. Two of the album's strongest songs appear during the latter half. "Casanova"'s lyrics are a bit silly, but it shows the group's rhythm section at its dynamic and complex best, and the soft "Time to Love" closes the album out in a breezy fashion, displaying how Barrabás is at its best when it avoids aggressive rock trappings—here, the band sounds its most natural. *—Andy Kellman*

¡Soltad a Barrabás! / 1974 / RCA/Disconforme ♦♦♦

Heart of the City / Aug. 1975 / Atco ♦♦♦

Watch-Out / 1976 / Atco ♦♦♦

By sticking primarily to funk and disco, *Watch-Out* is one of Barrabás' most streamlined and consistent albums. The thematic content of "Swinger" leaves the song in the year it was recorded—a shame, since it contains some of Juan Vidal's wildest keyboard work (not to mention a guest performance from Herbie Mann on flute). "Week End" is one of the group's best songs, a low-key and simple groove anchored by a thick bassline from Miguel Morales; gorgeous string accents and floating vocals from some uncredited female vocalists add a melancholy flair to a song whose mood is belied by its title. One highlight that delivers on its title is "Sweet and Mellow," another cut that benefits from female vocalists. Once again, Barrabás shows that its best moments come when it lets things flow gracefully. When the band tries too hard and appears to be out to prove something, the results sound forced. Guitarist Ray Gomez and saxophonist Michael Brecker also guest on this decent album. *—Andy Kellman*

Barrabás / 1982 / RCA ✦✦✦

Bestial / 1982 / RCA ✦

Piel de Barrabás / 1982 / Disconforme Sl ✦✦

Forbidden / 1984 / RCA ✦✦

Keith Barrow

d. Oct. 22, 1983

Vocals / Disco

Singer Keith Barrow's signature tune is the smooth-as-silk Top 30 R&B ballad/ steppers favorite, "You Know You Wanna Be Loved." Another Barrow track, "Turn It Up" is a favorite among dancefloor aficionados. The Chicago native's mother is Rev. Willie Barrow of Rev. Jesse Jackson's Push Organization. In his teens, Barrow headed a gospel group called the Soul Shakers. Produced by MFSB guitarist/songwriter Bobby Eli, his Jewel LP, *Keith Barrow*, was issued in 1973. One track "Mr. Magic Man" got some attention.

Produced by Michael Stokes, "You Know You Wanna Be Loved" went to number-26 R&B on Billboard's chart in summer 1978. The *Physical Attraction* LP yielded two other disco hits, "Physical Attraction" and "Turn It Up," and is replete with sensuous slow jams, "Overnight Success," "Step Into My Garden" and "Free To Me." Another single, "Turn Me Up" b/w "Physical Attraction" (the U.K. single's B-side was the jubilant "Joyful Music") was a huge disco hit charting number-79 R&B in early 1979. His song, "Teach Me (It's Something About Love)"—a charting single for Blue Magic—can be found on Rhino's *Blue Magic's Soulful Spell: The Best of Blue Magic*. Switching to Capitol, Barrow recorded the 1980 album, *Just As I Am*.

At the age of 29, Keith Barrow died of complications from AIDS on October 22,1983. "Turn Me Up, Pt. 1" is on *Dancin' 'n' Disco*, issued by Sony Special Products on April 16, 1995. *—Ed Hogan*

● **Keith Barrow** / 1973 / Jewel/P-Vine ✦✦✦✦

Physical Attraction / 1979 / Columbia ✦✦✦

Producer Michael Stokes, who produced Enchantment, probably wanted to work with Eddie Kendricks. When that didn't happen, he settled for Keith Barrow, who had a similar falsetto; in fact, "Turn Me Up" sounds more than a little like "Boogie Down." The ballads, including "If It's Love That You're Looking For" and "You Know You Wanna Be Loved," are real pleasers. Disco forays like "Joyful Music" had the wheels but never made much impact, while "Physical Attraction" and "Garden of Love" are pleasant, midtempo soothers. *—Andrew Hamilton*

Claudja Barry

b. Jamaica

Vocals / Euro-Pop, Disco, Hi-NRG

Jamaica-born, Toronto-raised Claudja Barry was a disco singer of the late '70s and '80s after a stage career that included roles in *Hair* and *Catch My Soul*. Her biggest hit was "Boogie Woogie Dancin' Shoes" in 1979. *— William Ruhlmann*

● **Sweet Dynamite** / 1977 / Lollipop ✦✦✦✦✦

From the disco era to the 21st century, critics of dance music have often accused it of being mechanical and robotic. To be sure, this has been true of some producer-driven dance recordings, which might grab you with an infectious beat but are lacking in soul, warmth and vocal personality. However, a lot of dance music *has* been full of warmth and feeling, and Claudja Barry is a prime example. The singer's promising debut album, *Sweet Dynamite*, was a major hit in clubs, but all of the material holds up nicely away from the dancefloor. None of the songs come across as mechanical or insincere, and Barry is as soulful on the haunting, European-flavored "Love for the Sake of Love" as she is on the exuberant "Why Must a Girl Like Me" and the gritty title song, which has as much to do with soul and funk as it does with Euro-disco. Though Barry's vocals are the album's main focus, she lays out on "Live a Little Bit," an infectious instrumental that successfully fuses Euro-disco with African pop and reggae. Produced by Jürgen S. Korduletsch, this promising debut went down in history as a true dance classic and is among Barry's most essential albums. *—Alex Henderson*

Claudja / 1978 / Salsoul ✦✦✦

Claudja Barry's first album, *Sweet Dynamite*, was an incredibly tough act to follow—so tough that her sophomore effort would have been disappointing if it were anything less than a gem. Because *Claudja*, the singer's second album, falls short of the excellence of *Sweet Dynamite*, it does, in fact, seem mildly disappointing. This isn't to say that *Claudja* (which was again produced by Jürgen S. Korduletsch) is a bad album—it's generally decent, if uneven and less focused than its predecessor. Opting for diversity, *Claudja* isn't strictly a disco LP and lets us know that Barry has R&B and pop credentials as well as disco know-how. "Dancin' Fever" is a pedestrian disco number, but Barry has a real gem in the eerie, futuristic "Love Machine"; she's also in good form on cuts that range from the seductive "Sexy Talkin' Lover" to covers of the Motown classic "Take Me in Your Arms" and Johnny Otis' "Every Beat of My Heart" (which was a major hit for Gladys Knight & the Pips in the early 1960s). Again, *Claudja* isn't a bad album, but it isn't in a class with *Sweet Dynamite* and isn't among her more essential releases. *—Alex Henderson*

Boogie Woogie Dancin' Shoes / 1979 / Chrysalis ✦✦

Claudja Barry moved from Salsoul to Chrysalis with her third album, *Boogie Woogie Dancin' Shoes*, which found the dance diva continuing to work with German producer Jürgen S. Korduletsch. More focused than *Claudja* and almost as strong as *Sweet Dynamite*, this album has a lot going for it. *Boogie Woogie Dancin' Shoes* kicks into high gear with the infectious title song, which was Barry's biggest hit and found her appealing to commercial radio as well as dance clubs; she keeps the momentum going with appealing tracks that range from the erotic "Cold Fire" and the playful "Give It Up" to the exhilarating "Forget About You." A gutsy cover of the Staple Singers' "Heavy Makes You Happy" makes it clear that Barry is well aware of disco's soul roots, while the strong Caribbean flavor on "Nobody But You" underscores the singer's Jamaican heritage. *Boogie Woogie Dancin' Shoes* is an album that Barry can be proud of. *—Alex Henderson*

I Wanna Be Loved By You / 1979 / Lollipop ✦✦✦✦

The outright funkiness of "Give It Up," the third track on *I Wanna Be Loved By You*, is reason alone to invest in this 1979 set. A harmonious matrimony of soul, funk, and jazzy elements, the arrangement's in-the-pocket bassline, bright horns, and sneaky key change play perfect companion to Barry's fiery yet earnest vocal. But "Give It Up" is merely one facet of a very versatile set: Other highlights include the carnival-esque "Nobody but You," which mingles traditional Spanish rhythms with pop chords; the rocker "Cold Fire"; and the straightforward disco chomper "(Boogie Woogie) Dancing Shoes," a coolly catchy tune that remains the singer's biggest international hit. A close second to *Made in Hong Kong*, this album is only missing the quirkiness and spontaneity of the former; otherwise, it's still a thoroughly enjoyable listen for dancing or pleasure—minus the lack of depth that appeared in many other disco records of the time. *—Justin M. Kantor*

Feel the Fire / 1980 / Hot Productions ✦✦✦

Whether they were coming from Donna Summer, Dead or Alive, Gloria Gaynor or Chic, the best dance records have had more going for them than just a beat. Obviously, Gloria Gaynor's "I Will Survive," Chic's "Good Times," Dead or Alive's "You Spin Me Round" and Coldcut's "People, Hold On" were designed to get bodies moving on the dance floor, but they don't lose their appeal away from the dance floor and are great to sit down and listen to. Claudja Barry is another dance artist who believes that vocal personality is as important as the beat, which is why her fourth album, *Feel the Fire* is, on the whole, good for both listening and dancing. A varied and unpredictable outing, *Feel the Fire* gets off to a surprising start with the rock-influenced title song—in 1980, the last thing one expected to hear on one of Barry's albums was an aggressive rock guitar. But the surprise is a pleasant one, and Barry is just as appealing on Euro-disco items like "Stop, He's a Lover" and "One Night Queen." Things become more mechanical on "Wake Up and Make Love to Me," which is among the more forgettable songs on the album. Meanwhile, "Love Seemed So Easy Without You" is a pleasant R&B/pop ballad—not a gem, but a likable reminder that she is quite capable of singing ballads. *Feel the Fire* isn't perfect, but more often than not, it paints a favorable picture of Barry. *—Alex Henderson*

Made in Hong Kong / 1981 / Hot Productions ✦✦✦✦✦

Of all of Barry's output from the '70s through the '90s, 1981's *Made in Hong Kong* is the most eclectic and energetic. While earlier albums such as *Sweet Dynamite* and *The Girl Most Likely* offer solid rhythm-section arrangements, they often lack sturdy hooks and cohesive melodies. Here, there's no shortage of either cleverness or catchiness and, as a result, Barry sounds thoroughly into her performance. "Radio Action" relays the first-person tale of an aspiring band vying for airtime atop a swirl of Euro-synths, while guitar power chords and country-tinged background vocals converge on "Don't Talk to the Wind." Equally compelling, the funky, down-tempo "Take Me to the River" merges colorfully punctuated bass and percussion with twangy guitars, and "Love Control" forges ahead with a sterling dance-pop arrangement and buoyant vocals. Throughout the sequence, Barry shines with a sharp soprano that incorporates touches of jazz, opera, and rock into a unique whole. *Made in Hong Kong* is a delightful treat for not only Barry's dedicated dance fans, but also Top 40, rock, and soul pundits with an ear for something different. *—Justin M. Kantor*

I, Claudja / 1987 / Epic ✦✦

The Best of Claudja Barry / 1991 / Lollipop ✦✦✦

Many gifted disco divas, no matter how substantial, have had a hard time getting exposure outside of dance-music circles. A classic example is Claudja Barry, who first thrilled club hounds during the disco era and continued to excite them in the 1990s. Unlike Donna Summer, Barry never became the pop star she deserved to be. *The Best of Claudja Barry*, a fine compilation released by Canadian label Lollipop, ranges from the expressive Canadian singer's disco-era hits "Boogie Woogie Dancin' Shoes," the gritty "Sweet Dynamite" and the haunting "Love for the Sake of Love" to such '80s club smashes as "Radio Action" and the addictive "Work Me Over." While the Canadian singer's early material emphasizes horns and strings, her '80s output is very synthesizer-oriented. This collection illustrates an important fact: Disco hardly died with the '70s—it simply changed its name to "dance music" and went high-tech. *—Alex Henderson*

Dave Bartholomew

b. Dec. 24, 1920, Edgard, LA

Trumpet, Songwriter, Vocals / New Orleans R&B, Rock & Roll, R&B

Dave Bartholomew is the multi-talented figure behind a majority of classic New Orleans R&B of the '50s and the self-proclaimed inventor of the "Big Beat." Bartholomew has over 4000 songs in his enormous catalog and is responsible for arranging and producing timeless records by Shirley & Lee, Lloyd Price, Smiley Lewis, and especially Fats Domino. Bartholomew was born in Edgard, LA, on December 24, 1920. His first instruments were tuba and trumpet. He fronted several bands in the Crescent City before being drafted into the army. His military time brought scoring and arranging experience which came in handy following World War II.

After his stint in the service, Bartholomew returned to New Orleans and put together a group of musicians that would comprise the bedrock of R&B in the city, including saxophonists Alvin "Red" Tyler, Lee Allen, and drummer Earl Palmer. This became the band that backed up the majority of solo talent traveling through New Orleans.

Bartholomew led his first studio session under his own name in 1947 for Deluxe, but the label went out of business shortly thereafter and the sessions went unnoticed. In 1949, Bartholomew met Lew Chudd who was forming a new label, Imperial Records. Chudd hired Bartholomew as house arranger, bandleader, and talent scout, and he immediately started cranking out numerous hits through the '50s for Fats Domino, Shirley & Lee, Smiley Lewis, Earl King, Chris Kenner, Tommy Ridgely, Frankie Ford, Robert Parker, and a host of others. Bartholomew stayed with Imperial until the hits dried up in the mid-'60s, followed by short stays at Trumpet, Mercury, and his own Broadmoor label. In the '70s and '80s, he took various behind-the-scenes musical jobs while living off his many song royalties and formed a Dixieland jazz band that continues to play around the Crescent City. The '90s found Bartholomew being inducted into the Rock and Roll Hall of Fame in 1991 and releasing two discs: *Dave Bartholomew & the Maryland Jazz Band* in 1995 and *New Orleans Big Beat* three years later. *—Al Campbell*

Fats Domino Presents David Bartholomew / 1961 / Imperial ♦♦♦♦♦

New Orleans House Party / 1963 / Imperial ♦♦♦

In the Alley / 1991 / Charly ♦♦♦♦

Dave Bartholomew is best known for producing and arranging classic New Orleans R&B sides from the '50s, especially for Fats Domino. It's curious that success eluded him on sessions released under his own name. Recorded between 1949 and 1952, the jump blues tracks on *In the Alley* were originally released on Deluxe and King, separate from Bartholomew's work with the Imperial label. King signed Bartholomew as a name artist, and ten of this compilation's 20 tracks find him backed up by the Todd Rhodes Orchestra. The remaining tracks are credited to the Dave Bartholomew Orchestra and feature some of the greatest Crescent City R&B session men from the period, including drummer Earl Palmer, bassist Frank Fields, and pianist Salvador Doucette. Six of the titles, including the excellent "Basin Street Breakdown," are previously unissued takes. Also included is the original song for which Bartholomew is most widely known, though again not for his version of it: "My Ding-A-Ling," which became a huge hit for Chuck Berry in 1972. Bartholomew was more of a Louis Jordan-style vocalist than a Joe Turner blues shouter, and that influence is prevalent throughout this disc. While this is a highly recommended set, there are a few clunkers here and there, including a strained and soulless "Stormy Weather" and the lengthy call-and-response vamp "Lawdy Lawdy Lord, Pt. 1 & 2," which would have been sufficient concluding with part one. *—Al Campbell*

★ **The Spirit of New Orleans: The Genius of Dave Bartholomew** / 1993 / EMI ♦♦♦♦♦

Released as part of EMI's *Legends of Rock 'n' Roll* series in 1992, there has been no better retrospective of Dave Bartholomew's music than the double-disc set *The Spirit of New Orleans: The Genius of Dave Bartholomew.* That's partially because at 50 tracks, it's the most comprehensive collection ever assembled on Bartholomew, but its real genius is that it doesn't shine a spotlight solely on his solo recordings. Instead, those are interspersed among the numerous hits he wrote and produced for such New Orleans legends as Fats Domino, Smiley Lewis, Earl King, Bobby Mitchell, Snooks Eaglin, Shirley & Lee, Pee Wee Crayton, Tommy Ridgley, Chris Kenner, and many others (including sides by T-Bone Walker). There are plenty of classics here—"Stack a Lee," "Ain't It a Shame," "Bo Weevil," "I Hear You Knocking," "I'm Gonna Be a Wheel Someday," "One Night," "Come On, Pts. 1 & 2," "Walking to New Orleans," and "Trick Bag" among them—plus numerous singles and songs known only to collectors. There has since been a dynamite single-disc collection of Bartholomew recordings issued, but any serious collector of New Orleans music needs to have this, pure and simple. *—Stephen Thomas Erlewine*

1947–1950 / Jul. 10, 2001 / Classics ♦♦♦♦

☆ **The Big Beat of Dave Bartholomew: 20 of His Milestone Productions 1949-1960** / Mar. 12, 2002 / Capitol ♦♦♦♦♦

The last time EMI/Capitol's reissue division prepared a large reissue series of Imperial's rich catalog of New Orleans R&B it was in the early '90s, and Dave Bartholomew was given a generous double-disc set that showcased his productions, songwriting, and performing. That set was used as the basis for 2002's *The Big Beat of Dave Bartholomew,* a single-disc, 20-track collection (released as part of EMI/Capitol's *Crescent City Soul* series) that does the job of that double-disc somewhat better, largely because of its conciseness. With only 20 tracks to work with, the compilers are forced to put the best of the hits and cult favorites on one disc, and the results are dynamite. Apart from Smiley Lewis' hit "One Night" and Bartholomew's record-collector favorites "The Monkey" and "That's How You Got Killed Before," there aren't that many acknowledged classics here—there are songs better known by other performers (Smiley Lewis and Fats Domino's "I Hear You Knocking" and "Blue Monday" are performed by the respective other artist, Bobby Mitchell's "I'm Gonna Be a Wheel Someday" is better known by Fats), but much of this is known primarily to fanatics of the scene, and it's great that they're given an airing such as this. Perhaps there aren't songs that should have been hits, but many of these songs stand as excellent sides from the peak of New Orleans R&B and any serious collector should pick this disc up—even if they already own *The Spirit of New Orleans.* *—Stephen Thomas Erlewine*

Chris Bartley

b. Apr. 17, 1947, Harlem, New York City, NY

Vocals / Pop-Soul, Soul

Born in New York's Harlem in 1947 (some sources say 1949), Chris Bartley grew up practically in the shadow of the Apollo Theater and spent much of his childhood absorbing the sounds around him, both in his actual vicinity and on the radio. His greatest inspiration as a teenager was reportedly Frankie Lymon & the Teenagers, who came from his neighborhood and had scored huge hits in the middle/late '50s during the three years before Bartley formed his first group, the Soulful Inspirations, with William Graham, Henry Powell, Sam Nesbitt, and Ronald Marshall. The quintet underwent numerous personnel shifts and name-changes over the next six years, evolving into the Mindbenders (no relation to the U.K. group). At one point, Bartley and Marshall were performing as a duo and their big break came when they auditioned for Van McCoy. Rather than signing the group, however, McCoy signed Bartley to his newly formed Vando Records label.

Bartley and the label scored a Top 40 pop hit and a Top Ten R&B hit their first time out with the McCoy-authored "The Sweetest Thing This Side of Heaven," an achingly beautiful soul ballad. The song was successful enough to get Bartley national exposure and even some performing engagements in England and is one of the more fondly remembered one-shot soul hits of its period, but it was only a one-shot—he was never able to duplicate its success despite several tries, including the excellent Motown-styled "Baby It's Wonderful." He lasted long enough on Vando to get out an entire album, which was a good tour through the Van McCoy songbag going right back to the end of the 1950s. Bartley was signed to Buddah Records after McCoy shut down Vando in 1968, and he cut a version of McCoy's "Baby I'm Yours" for the new label, which also failed to chart. Bartley reportedly left the music business in the mid-'70s after his mother fell seriously ill, and hasn't been heard much from since, though "The Sweetest Thing This Side of Heaven" keeps turning up on '60s soul reissues and oldies playlists on radio and his Vandor sides have been reissued on a very good Collectables CD. *—Bruce Eder*

● **Sweetest Thing This Side of Heaven** / 1967 / Collectables ♦♦♦

A CD clone of Chris Bartley's 1967 LP on Van McCoy's Vando Records. Collectables Records tacked the extra song "Love Me Baby" on to make it a baker's dozen with McCoy writing and producing every track. Bartley scored the first time out with "Sweetest Thing This Side of Heaven," a lilting beauty caressed by Bartley's flowery falsetto. The follow-up, the Motown-ish, formulaic "Baby It's Wonderful," flopped, though it probably sounded like a straight hit in the recording studio booming from those big speakers. He's better on "You Get Next to My Heart," the third single, the lilting "Sittin' Pretty," where he displays a honey-soaked false voice, and "Hooked on You," a hard-edged uptempo number where he sings natural and falsetto. Oozing with love is a remake of the Spellbinders' "For You," one of McCoys' best floaters, and the uptempo "Gotta Tell Somebody (About My Baby)" shows he can jam with the right material. Regardless of the tempo, Bartley's always depicted as a love-struck romantic. *—Andrew Hamilton*

Fontella Bass

b. Jul. 3, 1940, St. Louis, MO

Vocals, Piano / Chicago Soul, Pop-Soul, Soul, Northern Soul, Beach

An explosive gospel and soul singer, Fontella Bass is the daughter of the great vocalist Martha Bass and sister of David Peaston, as well as ex-wife of Art Ensemble of Chicago trumpeter Lester Bowie. But none of that family history means as much as her own skills, which include a tremendous voice, great range, and distinctive delivery. Bass, who is also a fine pianist and organist, sang in several church choirs, as her mother was a member of Clara Ward's gospel troupe. She later moved into R&B, singing in Oliver Sain's band and working with Little Milton in the early '60s. Bass teamed with Bobby McClure for two duets on Checker in 1965. "Don't Mess Up a Good Thing" reached number five on the R&B charts and inched into the pop Top 40, while "You'll Miss Me When I'm Gone" got into the R&B Top 40. Bass' debut single as a solo act was her greatest: "Rescue Me" topped the R&B charts for a month, peaked at number four on the pop charts, and was among the era's finest soul singles. The follow-up, "Recovery," was better than it has been credited, and reached number 13.

Bass never again attained soul stardom, but remained busy in the ensuing years. She later sang with Bowie's group, the Art Ensemble of Chicago, and was featured on the LP *Les Stances a Sophie.* She was also been part of the gospel group From the Root to the Source and has reunited with Bowie on occasional projects. *—Ron Wynn*

The New Look / 1966 / Checker ♦♦♦

Free / 1972 / Varese ♦♦♦

An expanded version of her 1972 Paula album *Now That I Found a Good Thing,* Fontella Bass' *Free* adds a new version of her classic "Rescue Me" along with four B-sides: "It Sure Is Good," "I'm Leaving the Choice to You," "Home Wrecker," and "It's Hard to Get Back In." Bass wrote most of the songs included here herself—along with a few collaborative efforts with her then-husband Lester Bowie—and all the tracks showcase her dynamic, dramatic approach to soul. *—Heather Phares*

● **Rescued: The Best of Fontella Bass** / Mar. 10, 1992 / MCA/Chess ♦♦♦♦♦

"Rescue Me" might have been her only big hit, but Fontella Bass was a terrific gospel-influenced soul vocalist who cut several great sides for Checker/Chess Records in the mid-'60s. They might not have gotten the attention they deserved when they were released, but they have held up very well over the years. *Rescued: The Best of Fontella Bass* collects sixteen of her finest tracks, including "Rescue Me," three duets with Bobby McClure, and a previously unreleased song; it makes a convincing case that she should have had more hit singles than she did. *—Stephen Thomas Erlewine*

No Ways Tired / 1995 / Nonesuch ♦♦

Travellin' / Apr. 10, 2001 / Justin Time ♦♦♦

The musical diversity of vocalist Fontella Bass is front and center on *Travellin'.* Best known for her huge 1965 hit, "Rescue Me," Fontella Bass features a family affair with styles to spare. Brimming with soul, rhythm, blues, and instrumental jazz on ten very special compositions, this CD represents a delightful musical tapestry that features her son Bahnamous Bowie on keyboards, her brother and singer David Peaston singing mightily on the soul ballads "Special Lady" and "Round & Round," and her son-in-law Tracy Mitchell contributing his lead vocals, electric guitar, and acoustic guitar. Bass' deeply rooted gospel style shines through on the title track while the rousing "Walk With Me" and the black gospel-styled gems "It's Alright Now," "In the Garden," and "Thank You Lord" are so reverent that she will bring tears of joy to your eyes. Backed by a versatile rhythm section of Ptah Williams on piano, Jimmy Hinds on electric bass, and Curtis Fondren on drums, this label debut should firmly plant Fontella Bass in the mainstream of gospel-jazz. *—Paula Edelstein*

The Bee Gees

f. 1958, Brisbane, Australia, **db.** Jan. 21, 2003

Group / Pop/Rock, Soft Rock, Adult Contemporary, Disco, Baroque Pop, Psychedelic Pop

No popular music act of the 1960s, 1970s, 1980s, and 1990s experienced more ups and downs in their popularity than the Bee Gees, or drew more of a varied audience. Beginning in the mid- to late '60s as a kind of Beatles-lite ensemble, Barry Gibb and his fraternal twin brothers Robin and Maurice quickly developed as songwriters in their own right and perfected a strange mix of progressive-pop music. "New York Mining Disaster 1941," released in 1967, made the Top 20 in England and America, and established the pattern of the group's work for the next several years. "Massachusetts" was a chart-topper in England and, after a temporary break-up, 1970's "Lonely Days" became the group's first number one hit in America. Then, after hitting a trough in their popularity in the early '70s, the Bee Gees reinvented themselves with a heavily Americanized, R&B-flavored sound that emphasized high harmonies and funk rhythms. "Jive Talkin'" became their second American number one in 1975, and two years later, the group's soundtrack of a forthcoming movie called *Saturday Night Fever* led to three chart-topping hits: "Stayin' Alive," "How Deep Is Your Love," and "Night Fever."

It didn't last, nor did the Bee Gees' second wave of success. The group may have helped contribute to the end of the party with their own excesses, in particular their contribution to a multimillion-dollar film called *Sergeant Pepper's Lonely Hearts Club Band*, "inspired" (if that's the word) by the Beatles' album and songs. The youngest Gibb brother, Andy Gibb, had emerged as a star in his own right late in the 1970s and he fell even harder when the decade ended, eventually losing his life in 1988 at the end of a downward personal spiral.

The Bee Gees were virtually invisible for most of the mid-'80s as recording artists, though 1987's *E.S.P.* received a good reception around the world and the title track of 1989's *One* even generated a Top Ten U.S. single. Their induction into the Rock and Roll Hall of Fame in 1997 led to the release of *Still Waters*, and in 1998, they issued the second live album in their history, cut at their first concert appearance in ten years.

The Bee Gees remained active until the death of Maurice in January 2003. While receiving treatment for an intestinal blockage he suffered cardiac arrest and died at the age of 53. Following his death, Robin and Barry decided to cease performing as the Bee Gees. *—Bruce Eder*

Main Course / May 1975 / Polydor ✦✦✦✦✦

It may sound silly to call the 12th album by a group with an eight-year string of gold records behind them a "breakthrough," but that's what *Main Course* was. The group's first disco album—and, for many white listeners, the first disco album they ever purchased—*Main Course* marked a huge change in the Bee Gees' sound. The group's earlier LPs, steeped in a dense romantic balladry, were beautifully crafted but too serious for any but hardcore fans. *Main Course* had a few ballads, such as "Songbird" and "Country Lanes," but the writing was simpler, and the rest of it was made up of catchy dance tunes (heavily influenced by the Philadelphia-based soul music of the period), in which the beat and the texture of the voices and instruments took precedence over the words. The combination proved irresistible, and *Main Course*—driven by the singles "Jive Talkin'," "Nights on Broadway," and "Fanny (Be Tender With My Love)"—attracted millions of new listeners. It also repelled fans of the group's earlier style, which was a bit ironic. The disco numbers on *Main Course* displayed the same care and craftsmanship that had characterized, say, "First of May" or "Odessa." Barry Gibb's falsetto voice, introduced on this album, was startling at first, and became an object of ridicule in later years, but the slow break on "Nights on Broadway" and songs like "Fanny (Be Tender With My Love)" and "Baby As You Turn Away" were as exquisitely sung as "Lonely Days" or "How Can You Mend a Broken Heart," and they had the same sense of romantic drama, leavened by a layer of sheer fun; one had less of a sense that the singer was dealing with the love of a lifetime, so much as a conquest for the evening, which was in keeping with the sexual mores of the mid-'70s. And the spirit of fun was no accident—producer Arif Mardin, seeking to rescue the group's stagnating career, had gotten the Bee Gees to turn their talents in a musical direction that they'd always loved but never embraced. Barry, Robin, and Maurice Gibb had been fascinated by R&B and soul for years ("To Love Somebody" had been written for Otis Redding to sing), but, as white Britons—fearing they'd seem ridiculous—they had never adapted those sounds themselves. Not only didn't they seem ridiculous, but they took to it as easily as they'd absorbed the Beatles' harmony-based rock sounds in the late '60s. It was a liberating experience for the entire group—Blue Weaver, newly added to the lineup with an array of electronic keyboards and ideas that ended up shaping lots of the songs here; Alan Kendall, playing in a funky guitar style; and drummer Dennis Byron, playing more complicated patterns than he'd been asked to in years, were also delighted with the new direction, and they constituted the instrumental core of the band for the next six years. Years later, *Main Course* holds up as well as anything the group ever did, and with killer album cuts like "Wind of Change" (featuring a superb Joe Farrell tenor sax solo) and "Edge of the Universe" all over it, demands as much attention as any hits compilation by the group. *—Bruce Eder*

Children of the World / Sep. 1976 / Polydor ✦✦✦✦

The Bee Gees' second R&B album, *Children of the World*, had the advantage of being written and recorded while the group was riding a string of Top Ten singles and the biggest wave of public adulation in their history off of the *Main Course* album. The group felt emboldened, but was also hamstrung by the absence of producer Arif Mardin, whose services were no longer available to them now that RSO Records had severed its ties to Atlantic Records. So they produced it themselves, all six bandmembers doing their best to emulate what Mardin would have had them do, with assistance from Albhy Galuten and Karl Richardson. The result still sounds a lot like Mardin's production from the previous album, and the group was in very good form—stretching out not only on disco numbers like "You Should Be Dancing," but also delivering beautiful soul ballads such as "You Stepped Into My Life" and "Love So Right" on side one, while side two featured a last look back at the older, more romantic Bee Gees sound. The album was also somewhat experimental in its way, making more use of synthesizers in a pop music setting than had ever been heard on a mainstream, commercial long-player before; not all of it works, because the technology wasn't quite perfected yet, but "Boogie Child," "Love Me," and "The Way It Was," as well as the title track were quite daring on a production level in their time, for a group shooting for millions of sales. Overall, the album isn't quite as beguiling as *Main Course*, which was a liberating experiment from start to finish. *Children of the World* is beautifully sung, but the group's sound changed here as well, Barry Gibb's falsetto now dominating the vocals, with Robin and Maurice Gibb moved out of center stage. But it's still one of the most enjoyably lighthearted albums in the group's history, and the dance numbers foreshadowed their work on the *Saturday Night Fever* soundtrack. *—Bruce Eder*

☆ **Saturday Night Fever** / Nov. 1977 / RSO ✦✦✦✦✦

Every so often, a piece of music comes along that defines a moment in popular culture history: Johann Strauss' operetta *Die Fledermaus* did this in Vienna of the 1870s; Jerome Kern's *Show Boat* did it for Broadway in the 1920s; and the Beatles' *Sgt. Pepper* album did it for psychedelic music in the 1960s. *Saturday Night Fever*, although hardly as prodigious an artistic achievement as those precursors, was precisely that kind of phenomenon for the second half of the 1970s—ironically, at the time before its release, the disco boom had seemingly run its course, and seemed confined to primarily Europe and black culture and the gay underground in America. *Saturday Night Fever*, as a movie and an album, and a brace of hit singles off of it, suddenly made disco explode into mainstream, working-, and middle-class America with new immediacy and urgency, increasing its audience by five- or tenfold. The Bee Gees had written "Stayin' Alive" (then called "Saturday Night"), "Night Fever," "How Deep Is Your Love," "If I Can't Have You," and "More Than a Woman" for what would have been the follow-up album to *Children of the World*, when Robert Stigwood asked them in early 1977 to contribute songs to the soundtrack of a movie that he was financing, a low-budget picture called *Tribal Rites on a Saturday Night*. They obliged him by turning over the best of their new numbers to the project; the group's involvement even survived the decision by the original director, John Avildsen, that he didn't want their music in the film—instead, Stigwood fired him and brought in the very talented and much more agreeable John Badham, and the movie's title was changed to *Saturday Night Fever*. The Bee Gees' music stayed, and the result was the biggest-selling soundtrack album in history, a 25-million copy monster whose sales, even as a more expensive double-LP, dwarfed those of *Children of the World* and *Main Course*. Strangely enough, for all of the fixation of the movie and its audience on dancing, the Bee Gees' new songs were weighted equally toward ethereal ballads, which may be one reason for the soundtrack album's extraordinary appeal—it delivers what its audience expects in dance numbers, plus the soaring, lyrical romantic numbers that were, as with most ventures by the Gibb brothers in this area, virtually irresistible as music. Despite the presence of other artists, *Saturday Night Fever* is indispensable as a Bee Gees album, not just for its array of hit songs—which became the de facto soundtrack for the second half of the '70s—but because it showed the Gibb brothers as composers as well as artists, in recordings by Yvonne Elliman ("If I Can't Have You") and Tavares ("More Than a Woman"). And because it placed their music alongside the likes of Kool & the Gang and MFSB. In essence, the layout of the soundtrack release was the culmination of everything they'd been moving toward on an artistic level since the *Mr. Natural* album, and even the presence of David Shire's "Night on Disco Mountain" and "Salsation," and Walter Murphy's "A Fifth of Beethoven," didn't hurt, because these set up a surrounding ambience that made the Bee Gees' material work even better. Heard on CD as 79 continuous minutes of music, *Saturday Night Fever* comes off like an idealized commercial-free radio set of late-'70s dance music (and, in that regard, the decision to leave Rick Dees' "Disco Duck" off the soundtrack album was a good one for all concerned, except Mr. Dees). The album has been out several times on CD, including a Mobile Fidelity audiophile disc that's rarer than hen's teeth and a 1995 newly annotated audiophile edition from Polydor that's so sharp you can hear the glistening harps on Tavares' version of "More Than a Woman" and feel like you're almost in the bell of the clarinet during Ralph McDonald's "Calypso Breakdown." *—Bruce Eder*

Spirits Having Flown / Jan. 1979 / Polydor ✦✦✦✦✦

Spirits Having Flown is regarded today as something of a letdown, representing the tail-end of the Bee Gees' period of greatest success, perhaps because it preceded a two-year layoff that, in turn, heralded a decline in their fortunes. At the time, however, no one heard anything less than what they expected—beautiful slow dance numbers ("Too Much Heaven," "Love You Inside Out"), achingly gorgeous romantic numbers ("Reaching Out"), soaring ballads ("Spirits (Having Flown)"), and pounding dance-rock numbers ("Tragedy"). If a few songs on the LP's second side, like "Stop (Think Again)" or "Search, Find," weren't quite up to that high standard, even the latter song displayed dazzling interwoven vocals on the choruses (which were pretty infectious) that made the trip worthwhile. The record showcased the usual superb singing, and featured the most delicate and ambitious production and arrangements in their history. It may have lacked the spirit of freedom and experimentation found on *Main Course* or *Children of the World*, but in its place was a boldness that manifested itself not only in the singing, but also the most intricate and ambitious production and arrangements of the group's entire history. This was also the first Bee Gees album to get serious airplay on black radio stations, a major breakthrough for the trio and one of the last bits of unfinished business in the group's move into soul music, which also likely helped—along with three chart-topping singles, the major tour that followed, and the network television special in the wake of the tour—in propelling *Spirits Having Flown* to 35 million sales. *—Bruce Eder*

Greatest / Oct. 1979 / Polydor ✦✦✦✦✦

Greatest is a double-album, 20-song retrospective of the Bee Gees' late-'70s hits. All of the band's biggest disco-era hits—"Jive Talkin'," "Nights on Broadway," "Fanny (Be Tender with My Love)," "You Should Be Dancing," "Love So Right," "How Deep Is Your Love," "Stayin' Alive," "Night Fever," "Too Much Heaven," "Tragedy," "Love You Inside Out"—are included, as well as several fine album tracks and the group's version of Andy Gibb's "(Our Love) Don't Throw It All Away." Although it's a little too long for some casual fans, it remains an excellent overview of the Bee Gees' most commercially successful era. *—Stephen Thomas Erlewine*

★ **Their Greatest Hits: The Record** / Nov. 20, 2001 / Polydor ♦♦♦♦♦

Their Greatest Hits: The Record stands as the best Bee Gees hits package available, assembling both vital European and American hits from their early-'60s period all the way through to 2001. Disc one includes their major '60s and early-'70s hits, up to "You Should Be Dancing." Included are their major American hits, such as "New York Mining Disaster 1941," "Massachusetts," "To Love Somebody," "Lonely Days," "How Can You Mend a Broken Heart," "Jive Talkin'," "Nights on Broadway," and "Words," as well as major European hits, such as "World" and the gorgeous "Don't Forget to Remember." Also included on disc one is the former B-side "If I Can't Have You" (popularized, of course, by Yvonne Elliman). Disc two continues the formula, beginning with the cultural phenomenon that was "Stayin' Alive" and continuing with "How Deep Is Your Love," "Night Fever," "Too Much Heaven," "Tragedy," and "Love You Inside and Out." Disc two also includes Barry Gibb's hit duet with Barbra Streisand, "Guilty," as well as major European hits such as "You Win Again" and "For Whom the Bell Tolls," and later American hits such as "One," "Alone," and their superb 2001 single "This Is Where I Came In." As a bonus treat, the album includes four newly recorded versions of Bee Gees songs which became hits for other artists. These include "Emotion," which was popularized by Samantha Sang and later Destiny's Child; "Heartbreaker," which was a comeback smash for Dionne Warwick; the chart-topping "Islands in the Stream," which was a hit for Kenny Rogers and Dolly Parton; and "Immortality," a European hit for Celine Dion. A wonderful, stellar collection through and through from one of the rock era's biggest, brightest, most influential, and most exciting acts. As a final note, the European version of this collection includes two songs which were annoyingly left off the American version: "Jumbo" and "My World." *—Jose F. Promis*

Jimmy Bee (Jimmy Brunsen)

Vocals, Executive Producer / R&B

R&B singer Jimmy Bee was born Jimmy Brunsen, and started his career as a tenor singer in the New York doo wop outfit the Four Jays; he left in early 1954 (shortly before the group changed their name to the Regals and recorded for Aladdin). In 1956, he joined a reconstituted version of the Rhythm Aces, which recorded under various names: the Rockets, the Rocketeers, the Magic Notes, and the Planets. In 1958, they joined the Johnny Otis Show and toured with the blues/R&B bandleader, also supplying uncredited backing vocals on some of his recordings that year (including the smash "Willie and the Hand Jive"). With no success on their own, they soon disbanded, and Brunsen toured with the Billy Williams Revue from 1959-1963.

Adopting the name Jimmy Bee, he eventually got his shot as a solo artist, starting with a couple of singles for 20th Century Fox ("Talkin' 'Bout Me" and "If It Wasn't for Love") over 1966-1967. A one-off single in 1969 for Kimberly, "Wanting You" b/w "I Only Have Eyes for You," later became a sought-after item among soul collectors. Bee went on to record for Kent and Ala in the early '70s, and Calla and Cherry Red later in the decade. He eventually left singing to work as a record promoter for Arista. *—Steve Huey*

Jimmy Bee Live / 1973 / ALA ♦♦♦

The Beginning of the End

f. Nassau, The Bahamas

Group / Funk, Soul

One of the very few soul groups from Nassau, the Beginning of the End had one hit in 1971, the scintillating "Funky Nassau." They recorded an album of the same name that year, then dropped out of sight. *—Ron Wynn*

● **Funky Nassau** / 1971 / Alston ♦♦♦

Thirty years after its maiden voyage, *Funky Nassau* sails again on a digitally remastered CD. Their number 15 pop smash "Funky Nassau Pt. 1 and 2" is the cream of this hands-on production by the Bahamas natives. The nine cuts fuses island rhythms and American jazz/funk into a doable, choppy mixture featuring guitars, bass, drums, and scratch vocals. Misclassified as a disco band, the Beginning of the End served up breezy Phil Upchurch-esque sounds, with "Come Down" and "Surrey Ride" being prime examples. *—Andrew Hamilton*

Bell Biv DeVoe

f. 1988

Group / New Jack Swing, Urban, Hip-Hop

Bell Biv DeVoe was hatched in the minds of its members, New Edition's Ricky Bell, Michael Bivins, and Ronnie DeVoe, upon the departure of lead singer Bobby Brown in 1986. But it wasn't until after New Edition completed its supporting tour for the album *Heart Break* in 1988 that the trio gave in to the urgings of *Heart Break* producers Jimmy Jam and Terry Lewis and decided to chart its own course. Bell Biv DeVoe enlisted a variety of producers for its debut album, including Jam and Lewis and Public Enemy producers Hank and Keith Shocklee. The results were quite unlike anything in New Edition's repertoire: The beats were funkier, the lyrics and vocals were sexier, and the overall sound had a harder, hip-hop-tinged edge. The album's title track, "Poison," became a number three smash, and it was followed by the equally successful "Do Me!" and the R&B hits "B.B.D. (I Thought It Was Me)," "When Will I See You Smile Again?," and "Dope! (aka She's Dope!)." The album itself went on to sell over three million copies and was followed by a remix album the next year. Meanwhile, Bivins took some time off to assemble the so-called East Coast Family, discovering and producing debut albums for Another Bad Creation and Boyz II Men. *Hootie Mack*, Bell Biv DeVoe's second proper album, was released in 1993 but didn't make as much of an impact. In 1996, all three members of Bell Biv DeVoe participated in a reunion of New Edition. *—Steve Huey*

Poison / Mar. 1990 / MCA ♦♦♦♦

With so many faceless, soundalike albums having come out of the "new jack swing" hybrid in the late '80s and early- to mid-'90s, it's important to give credit to the form's more creative and imaginative figures. Along with Guy and Bobby Brown, Bell Biv DeVoe (a New Edition spinoff trio comprised of Ricky Bell, Michael Bivins, and Ronnie DeVoe) delivered some of new jack swing's most worthwhile material. A hard-edged, tough-minded blend of R&B/funk and hip-hop, *Poison* was (like Brown's *Don't Be Cruel*) a radical departure from the Jackson 5-influenced "bubblegum soul" for which New Edition was originally known. Defined by their urgency, rawness, and vitality, "Poison," "B.B.D. (I Thought It Was Me)?," "She's Dope!," and "Do Me!" are considered new jack swing classics and are indeed among the best the style has to offer. Taking a break from the CD's overall aggression, B.B.D. moves closer to New Edition's sound with the decent, though far from outstanding, ballads "When Will I See You Again" and "I Do Need You." While other "new jacks" were content to simply emulate Guy, the distinctive BBD deserves applause for daring to stake out its own territory. *—Alex Henderson*

WBBD-Bootcity! The Remix Album / 1991 / MCA ♦♦♦

Bell Biv DeVoe was all over "urban contemporary" radio in 1991, when MCA Records set out to milk the trio's tremendous popularity for all it was worth with this generally decent and likable, though far from outstanding, collection of remixes. The best remixes surprise us by adding something different and fresh to familar songs—and *WBBD Bootcity!: The Remix Album* (which is presented in the form of an "urban contemporary" radio program, and even includes an interview with BBD) doesn't add anything particularly memorable or interesting to "B.B.D. (I Thought It Was Me)?," "She's Dope!" and other major hits from the triple-platinum *Poison*. There are a few surprises, including a jazz-influenced version of "Do Me!" that is decidedly less forceful than the original version. But on the whole, *WBBD* takes a predictable, play-it-safe approach that fails to demonstrate how inventive remixes can be. This is a CD that only the most hardcore BBD fanatics should check out. *—Alex Henderson*

Hootie Mack / Jun. 1993 / MCA ♦♦♦

Hootie Mack not only keeps the same energetic vibe that made *Poison* a hit, but expands upon that base, adding a more street-oriented production that, at its best, is more sexy and funky than their debut. Unfortunately, the high points on this album aren't as numerous as those on *Poison*; not only that, but the good songs didn't receive much airplay, causing the album to drop off the charts quickly. *—Stephen Thomas Erlewine*

● **Best of Bell Biv DeVoe** / Sep. 26, 2000 / MCA ♦♦♦♦

On the one hand, Bell Biv DeVoe deserves a good best-of compilation—they were one of the freshest-sounding new jack swing acts to hit the charts during the style's early-'90s heyday. On the other hand, they only recorded two albums during that heyday (not counting a remix album), and their third wasn't released until after this 2000 compilation, *The Best of Bell Biv DeVoe*. Thus, listeners get five tracks from the group's blockbuster debut, *Poison*; six from their decent but less-inventive follow-up, *Hootie Mack*; the non-LP single "Gangsta"; and four tracks from the aforementioned remix album, *WBBD-Bootcity!*, including the otherwise-unavailable single "Word to the Mutha." Aside from *Hootie Mack*'s "Something in Your Eyes" (an R&B Top Ten), all of the group's biggest hits came from *Poison*—the crossover smashes "Poison" and "Do Me!," the R&B chart-topper "B.B.D. (I Thought It Was Me)?," and the R&B Top Tens "When Will I See You Smile Again?" and "She's Dope." As such, casual fans might be just as happy with the mid-priced compilation *20th Century Masters—The Millennium Collection*, which—even though it features fewer songs—still has all their major hits, and costs a few dollars less. But for more devoted fans who want a generous BBD compilation, *The Best of Bell Biv DeVoe* does have all their best moments in one place, and makes for an excellent summary of why they were important to the development of '90s R&B. *—Steve Huey*

BBD / Dec. 18, 2001 / Universal ♦♦♦

20th Century Masters—The Millennium Collection: The Best of Bell Biv DeVoe / May 21, 2002 / MCA ♦♦♦♦

New Edition spin-off group Bell Biv DeVoe is a good candidate for the kind of limited compilation that the discount-priced *20th Century Masters—The Millennium Collection* series provides. The trio broke four hits off their multi-platinum debut album, *Poison* (1990), one off their remix album, *WBBD—Bootcity!* (1991), a couple off their second album, *Hootie Mack* (1993), and a couple released independently. They're all here in chronological order, with a couple of album tracks and a remix of the hit "Do Me!" making up the 12 tracks. (Nothing from the 2001 reunion album *BBD* is included.) The recordings reveal the singers to be horny and self-referential as they make their way through the involved beats that dominate the musical tracks, a successful musical formula for early-'90s R&B. Their moment may have passed, but Bell Biv DeVoe's best is easily encapsulated here. *—William Ruhlmann*

The Bell Notes

f. Long Island, NY

Group / Vocal Pop, Doo Wop, Pop

The Bell Notes may not know it but they inspired Ray Tabano and Steven Tyler, who rocked with Aerosmith. At 14, the two frequented Tabano's father's bar in the Bronx and commanded the stage when the regular band took a break. The Bell Notes "I've Had It" was a staple of their impromptu act. The Long Island band consisted of Carl Bonura (lead, vocals, sax), John Casey (drums), Ray Ceroni (lead, vocals, guitar), Lenny Giambalvo (bass), and Peter Kane (piano). They signed with Time Records and hit with "I've Had It," which soared to number six in March of 1959. Four subsequent singles in 1959: "Old

Spanish Town" (number 76), "That's Right," "You're a Big Girl Now," and "White Buckskin Sneakers & Checkerboard Socks," did little to advance their careers. Time also released an EP which met with the same dismal results as the barrage of singles. They started 1960 with an Autograph Records release, "Little Girl in Blue," but found no takers, and enjoyed two other releases on Madison Records: "Shortin' Bread" (number 96) and "Friendly Star." In two years, they charted three times but only entered the Top 40 once. After a promising start, the Bell Notes disbanded in less than three years. In 1964, the Bell Notes were one of 64 rock artists honored with a Nu-Trading Rock n' Roll Trading Card, but unlike baseball cards the fad didn't catch on. *—Andrew Hamilton*

● **I've Had It: The Very Best of the Bell Notes** / Jul. 28, 1998 / Collectables ♦♦♦♦
I've Had It: The Very Best of the Bell Notes contains 18 tracks from the Northeastern rock & roll quintet from the late '50s. All of the group's singles for Time Records have been included on this collection, along with several songs that have never appeared on CD. For hardcore collectors of '50s party rock & roll, there are some cool cuts here, but for most listeners, this will be a curiosity barely worth exploring. *—Stephen Thomas Erlewine*

Archie Bell & the Drells

f. Houston, TX
Vocals, Songwriter / Soul, Philly Soul, Disco
Archie Bell & the Drells scored a left-field number one hit in 1968 with "Tighten Up," which epitomized the virtues of their music: funky, exuberant, danceable soul out for a rousing good time. Born in Henderson, TX, Bell grew up in Houston and began singing in church. In junior high, he joined a vocal group called Little Pop & the Fireballs, and formed the Drells in high school with friends James Wise, Huey "Billy" Butler, and Joe Cross (later replaced by Willie Pernell). The Drells won several local talent shows, performing a repertoire dominated by Chicago soul, and were discovered by local DJ Skipper Lee Frazier, who became their manager and producer. Bell & the Drells cut a single for Frazier's Ovid label, "She's My Woman," which became a regional hit in 1966.

Unfortunately, Bell was drafted in 1967. Before he was shipped overseas, he managed to record a few more tracks with the Drells, including the single "Dog Eat Dog." The B-side was a dance tune called "Tighten Up," the title of which came from Butler; backing the Drells was an instrumental R&B combo from Texas Southern University called the T.S.U. Toronados. Frazier was talked into playing "Tighten Up" on his radio show, and it became a smash hit in Houston, drawing the attention of Atlantic. With major-label distribution, "Tighten Up" took the country by storm in early 1968, hitting number one on both the pop and R&B charts. Bell learned of the song's success while recovering from wounds suffered in Vietnam, and with Atlantic requesting a full album, he began traveling to and from the States on leave.

Meanwhile, several promoters took advantage of Bell's absence to send fake Archie Bell & the Drells lineups out on the road. The real Bell was granted leave to tour with the Drells that summer, and after a show in New Jersey, the group was approached by a fledgling Philadelphia-based songwriting/production team, Kenny Gamble & Leon Huff. Bell & the Drells started recording heavily with the duo, a partnership that produced several more danceable R&B hits in "I Can't Stop Dancing," "Do the Choo-Choo," and "(There's Gonna Be A) Showdown" (the former two in 1968, the latter in 1969). Also in 1969, Butler left the group and was replaced by Lee Bell, Archie's brother, who became the Drells' choreographer.

In spite of the fact that Bell received his discharge from the Armed Forces and was finally free to pursue his career, "(There's Gonna Be A) Showdown" proved to be the last Top 40 pop hit he ever had. Bell & the Drells left Atlantic in 1970 and signed with the smaller Glades label, where they had a minor hit with "Dancing to Your Music." Overall, though, the Glades stint was disappointing, and in 1973 the group reunited with Gamble & Huff on their flourishing TSOP/Philadelphia International imprint. Working with producers like Bunny Sigler and McFadden & Whitehead, Bell & the Drells landed on the R&B charts with some regularity over the next few years, their still-danceable sound now a hybrid of lush Philly soul and disco. They had several substantial R&B hits from 1975-1976 with "I Could Dance All Night," "Soul City Walk," and "Let's Groove," all of which helped *Dance Your Troubles Away* become a Top Ten album on the R&B charts. Three follow-up albums through 1979 didn't prove quite as successful, however, and the Drells gave their last performance just before Christmas 1979. Bell subsequently cut a solo album, *I Never Had It So Good*, for Becket in 1981, and had a minor hit with "Anytime Is Right," but disappeared from the scene afterward. With a new set of Drells, Bell later became a staple of the East Coast's oldies-centered beach-music circuit. *—Steve Huey*

Tighten Up / May 1968 / Atlantic ♦♦♦
Released on the heels of their number one smash "Tighten Up," this album includes both parts of that classic along with an assortment of Southern soul grooves like "Knock on Wood" and "In the Midnight Hour." There's also a fine rendition of Sunny Ozuna's "Give Me Time." Two Archie Bell compositions, "When You Left Heartache Began" and "A Soldier's Prayer," show the soulful Texan's writing and singing skills; the latter initially appeared on Ovide Records in 1967 and "Tighten Up" followed on Ovide the same year. The group made two more recordings (not included here) for East West Records. Atlantic Records licensed and re-released "Tighten Up," which blew up while Bell was in the Army. Credit goes to the T.S.U. Toronados, the band accompanying Bell on "Tighten Up." *—Andrew Hamilton*

I Can't Stop Dancing / Jun. 1968 / Atlantic ♦♦♦
Archie Bell & the Drells follow their debut album on Atlantic with this hurried effort highlighted by Kenny Gamble & Leon Huff's "I Can't Stop Dancing" and "Do the Choo Choo." "(Sitting On) The Dock of the Bay" and "Monkey Time" are both predictable remakes. But Bell's soulful "Love Is Gonna Rain on You" is a smoldering, underappreciated slow jam, as is their remake of the Impressions' heart-busting "I've Been Trying." Archie Bell could moan and cry with the best of them. *—Andrew Hamilton*

There's Gonna Be a Showdown / Jul. 1969 / Atlantic ♦♦♦♦
The Houston vocal group's final LP for Atlantic Records is 28 minutes of merriment. Their next two appeared on Philadelphia International. This finale continued the good vibes established on their two previous Atlantic albums. Producers/writers Kenny Gamble and Leon Huff employ the same lighthearted production on the Drells as they did the Intruders. The joyous title track isn't about gang-banging, but a dancing confrontation that Gamble & Huff spice with a convoluted but infectious break. The cutesy, compelling "My Balloon Is Going Up" warms your heart for no apparent reason; it's just a good, happy sound. Speaking of the Intruders, "Girl You're Too Young," a Gamble, Archie Bell, and Thom Bell song, has the "Cowboys to Girls" guys written all over it; "Here I Go Again," another R&B hit, is more formulaic. "Houston, Texas" pays homage to Archie Bell & the Drells' hometown, but they didn't write it—non-Texans Gamble, Huff, and Bobby Martin did. Others deserving a shout-out include Archie Bell's "Mama Didn't Teach Me That Way," Mikki Farrow and Mervin and Melvin Steals' "Green Power," and the Steals' tutorial "Go for What You Know." As Mystro and Lyric, the Steals later wrote their biggest record, "Could It Be I'm Falling in Love," for the Spinners. *—Andrew Hamilton*

Dance Your Troubles Away / Dec. 1975 / Philadelphia International ♦♦♦
Seven good songs from the Houston, TX, natives. On, "I Won't Leave You Honey," and a song obviously written for the O'Jays, Archie proves he's a quality soul belter. "I Could Dance All Night" written by Bunny Sigler, Ron Tyson, and Alan Felder, is a pleasant midtempo, lilting dance ditty, the melody will have you humming along. Tyson co-wrote the two aforementioned tunes; he later joined the Temptations as the fourth replacement for Eddie Kendricks. Ricky Owens briefly replaced Damon Harris, whom Glenn Leonard replaced. A good party record, "Let's Groove," and "The Soul City Walk" stand tall. The Drells were: Lee Bell (Archies' brother,) James Wise, and Willie Pernell. *—Andrew Hamilton*

Where Will You Go When the Party's Over / 1976 / Philadelphia International ♦♦♦
Archie Bell & the Drells' second LP for Gamble & Huff's Philadelphia International label, *Where Will You Go When the Party's Over*, suffered low sales caused by a paradox. While the low-charting "Glad You Could Make It" was the album's first single, the thump-funkin' "Don't Let Love Get You Down" received massive radio play as an album track; oddly, the track was issued as a U.K. single in the mid-'80s. So without a high-charting single lead-in, the energetic Bunny Sigler-produced follow-up single, "Everybody Have a Good Time," only charted number 68 R&B in spring 1977. Edited down on some other greatest-hits and various-artist compilations, the track is represented in all its sensational, elongated glory on Rhino's *Tightening It Up: The Best of Archie Bell & the Drells*. Some of this LP's other tracks can also be found on various reissues from Sony, Westside/VCI, and others. *—Ed Hogan*

Hard Not to Like It / 1977 / Philadelphia International ♦♦♦♦
Of the four records Archie Bell & the Drells recorded for Gamble & Huff in the 1970s, *Hard Not to Like It* is arguably the strongest. Cut in 1977 at the height of disco fever, the Drells were certainly on the pulse of what was happening, as evidenced here. The set opens with "Glad You Could Make It," a slippery backbeat groover that walks the line between hard, funky soul and disco. With the keyboard sounds tipping it in the mirror-ball direction, the bassline and backbone-slipping rhythm push it in the other. And for those who attribute the disco handclap sound to Chic, better take a listen here first. "Disco Showdown" is one of the first appearances of the "disco duck," with a killer calypso rhythm and horn line that might at first seem out of place on a modern disco plate; give it another couple of seconds and it turns itself inside out and becomes a thumping, roiling-floor track, though it cuts back to the calypso melody for the refrain. "Disco Fever" and "On the Road" rely much more on the funk groove-nee Ohio Players and Sly. On "It's Hard Not to Like You," the Drells bring all the inherent contradictions into one tune: It's a soul tune with a gorgeous chorus and a shimmering stroll of a funky backbeat groove, but the bassline and the textures in the strings and keyboards are pure disco heat. The set closes with a ballad, oddly enough, "I've Been Missing You." This is a fine testament to the diversity of the Drells, as they deliver this with the same conviction they put into their amazing and unreleased version of "Patches." In all, this is a fine addition to the Drells' catalog, even a necessary one. *—Thom Jurek*

Strategy / 1979 / The Right Stuff ♦♦♦
On their last album for Gamble & Huff's Philadelphia International label, the Drells went wholeheartedly into the disco fold by 1979. The tension that existed on their previous two records, which slipped back and forth across the disco/funk divide, is gone here. Elements of Barry White's Love Unlimited Orchestra and the Miami Sound Machine are deeply enmeshed in these tunes to the degree that the Drells' individual identity disappears. The instrumental and textural confusion that is "I Can't Get Enough of Your Love" (not Barry White's) is a case in point: a honky tonk/R&B piano sidles up next to a swelling string section, a thumping bassline that may or not be a synthed one, soul singing background vocalists, and swelling verses, punctuated by horns and layered with keyboards—what a mess! The title track is a blatant White rip-off from any number of his hits at the time, with its shifting one-two bassline and gospelized call-and-response lines buried under stings and special effects of cosmic proportion. All of this is still forgivable, still listenable, maybe even pleasant, but it all goes out into the dumper with "Tighten Up at the Disco." This blatant attempt at a cash-in not only doesn't work, but it unforgivably mars a record that may have been a bit of a disappointment in a bright and shining career, but was not an offensive one. *—Thom Jurek*

I Never Had It So Good / 1981 / Becket ♦♦

● **Tightening It Up: The Best of Archie Bell & the Drells** / Aug. 16, 1994 / Rhino ♦♦♦♦♦
It could be assumed that Archie Bell & the Drells essentially did the same thing over and over again, since "Tighten Up" almost consigns them to the level of one-hit wonders, but

that's not an accurate assessment of their gifts. True, they often followed the same stylish, sunny, utterly infectious sound, but there was a lot more depth and variety there, as Rhino's terrific 20-track collection *Tightening It Up: The Best of Archie Bell & the Drells* illustrates. What it reveals to those who weren't playing close attention is that the group was one of the first great Philly soul outfits, recording a number of Gamble & Huff's early songs and providing a training ground for the seminal duo. Though the hits didn't come fast and furious, like they would later, they, Bell & the Drells, created some wonderful singles, highlighted by "(There's Gonna Be A) Showdown" and "A World Without Music." There's plenty of other terrific moments throughout this collection, which proves that Bell & the Drells were far more than a one-hit wonder—they were one of the great under appreciated soul outfits of their time. *—Stephen Thomas Erlewine*

Where Will You Go When the Party's Over/Hard Not to Like It/Strategy / Dec. 15, 1998 / WestSide ♦♦♦♦

Norma Jean Bell

Vocals, Saxophone, Percussion, Producer / Club/Dance, House, Jazz-House

Prior to becoming a valued fixture of the Detroit house scene, singer/saxophonist/percussionist/producer Norma Jean Bell earned her stripes as a hired gun for artists like Frank Zappa, Tommy Bolin, Narada Michael Walden, and Parliament. In the mid-'90s, Bell became a close associate of Kenny Dixon Jr. (Moodymann) and the two began working together on a fair portion of each other's output (Dixon began producing the bulk of Bell's tracks, while Bell provided sax and vocals on a number of Dixon's songs). Bell started her own label, Pandamonium, in 1996, but she also hooked up with Laurent Garnier's France-based F Communications label, which issued her first and most popular 12-inch (*I'm the Baddest Bitch*) that same year. Pandamonium got off the ground in short time, issuing material from Bell, Dewayne Davis, Sharon Jones, and Billy Lo. By the end of 1999, Bell had eight of her own 12-inch releases that ranged from swooning disco to thick funk. Some of the tracks from those releases were selected for *Come Into My Room*, a CD compilation released in 2001 by the U.K.-based Peacefrog imprint. *—Andy Kellman*

● **Come Into My Room** / Oct. 2001 / Peacefrog ♦♦♦♦

Since the mid-'90s, Norma Jean Bell has gradually transformed herself from a veteran saxophonist-for-hire (Frank Zappa, Tommy Bolin, Parliament, Raydio) to a label entrepreneur and house artist extraordinaire, releasing her works in 12-inch form on her Detroit-based Pandamonium label. The ten housequakes on *Come Into My Room*, a CD compilation released by the U.K.-based Peacefrog label in late 2001, dip into a mere fraction of the imprint's output, including NJB's scattered productions for France's F Communications and some previously unreleased material as well. These tracks—collaboratively served up with handiwork from Theo Parrish, K Hand, and primarily Kenny Dixon Jr.—are shoehorned into a palatable digest full of steam, sweat, and libidinal abandon. Shifting from gritty and fervid to soft and wet in the blink of an eye, NJB's productions flick away all competitors with effortless facility. This is all-purpose loose-limbed house with a foot in the past, the other in the present, and a tail feather in the future. The only problem with the disc is that something more exhaustive remains in order, as anyone who has been buying Pandamonium product from release one will tell you; to somewhat illustrate, the disc's refusal to offer multiple versions of songs means that the spectacular Moodymann mixes of "I'm the Baddest Bitch" and "Nobody Is Gonna Love You" are left off. This approach is presumably taken in service of album-like ebbs and flows—rather than assemble a haphazard splatter of highlights, the sequencing, the selection, and the wide-ranging variation of NJB's material were issues taken into painstaking consideration. [Significant footnote: The voice that peppers a handful of these tracks belongs to the Electrifying Mojo, the infamous Detroit radio DJ. Snippets of the man's voice are taken from his live interview with Prince, which took place after one of "the Purple One"'s 1985 performances at Cobo Hall, on the eve of his birthday.] *—Andy Kellman*

Thom Bell

b. 1941, Philadelphia, PA

Producer, Keyboards, Arranger / Philly Soul, Smooth Soul

In tandem with the visionary production team of Kenny Gamble & Leon Huff, arranger and producer Thom Bell was among the principal architects of the lush and seductive Philly soul sound, one of the most popular and influential musical developments of the 1970s. Born in Philadelphia in 1941, Bell studied classical piano as a youth; he joined Gamble's harmony group the Romeos in 1959, and by the age of 19 was working as a conductor and arranger for hometown hero Chubby Checker. Within months he began writing original material for Checker as well, eventually joining the singer's production company. When Checker's organization folded, Bell signed on as a session pianist with Cameo Records, where he first worked with the local soul group the Delfonics. When their manager Stan Watson formed the Philly Groove label in 1968, Bell came aboard as a producer, helming Delfonics classics like 1968's "La La Means I Love You" and 1970's "Didn't I Blow Your Mind This Time."

Bell's work with the Delfonics became immediately recognizable for its shimmering beauty and exquisite sweetness, and when he reunited with Gamble and new partner Leon Huff at their newly formed Philadelphia International Records, the classic Philly soul sound quickly began to take shape. Over the course of seminal releases like Jerry Butler's 1969 smash "Only the Strong Survive," Billy Paul's 1972 smash "Me and Mrs. Jones," and the Harold Melvin & the Blue Notes classic "If You Don't Know Me by Now," the Gamble-Huff production aesthetic—an intoxicating combination of sweeping strings, smoky horns, and insistent rhythms—emerged as the definitive soul sound of the early '70s, its success due in large part to Bell's impeccable arrangements. The team arguably reached their pinnacle working with the O'Jays, scoring a series of classic hits like "Back Stabbers," "Love Train," and "For the Love of Money" and drafting the blueprint for the rise of disco during the latter half of the decade.

By the mid-'70s Bell began moving away from the Philadelphia International sphere, branching out to produce records for the likes of Johnny Mathis (1973's *I'm Coming Home*) and the Spinners; the latter with whom he enjoyed a long and fruitful collaboration that included albums like 1974's *Mighty Love* and the following year's *Pick of the Litter*. In 1977, Bell also teamed with Elton John, although the sessions were soon aborted, with only three tracks released two years later. After producing two LPs for singer Deniece Williams during the early '80s, Bell assumed a low profile throughout the remainder of the decade, resurfacing only occasionally to appear on efforts by artists ranging from Phyllis Hyman to Chuck Mangione. He remained similarly quiet through the 1990s, his sporadic work schedule including sessions with the likes of James Ingram, Angela Winbush, and Earth, Wind & Fire. *—Jason Ankeny*

William Bell (William Yarborough)

b. Jul. 16, 1939, Memphis, TN

Vocals, Piano / Northern Soul, Soul, Country-Soul

A principal architect of the Stax-Volt sound, singer/composer William Bell remains best known for his classic "You Don't Miss Your Water," one of the quintessential soul records to emerge from the Memphis scene. Born William Yarborough on July 16, 1939, he cut his teeth backing Rufus Thomas, and in 1957 recorded his first sides as a member of the Del Rios. After joining the Stax staff as a writer, in 1961 Bell made his solo debut with the self-penned "You Don't Miss Your Water," an archetypal slice of country-soul and one of the label's first big hits. A two-year Armed Forces stint effectively derailed his career, however, and he did not release his first full-length album, *The Soul of a Bell*, until 1967, generating a Top 20 hit with the single "Everybody Loves a Winner"; that same year, Albert King also scored with another classic Bell composition, the oft-covered "Born Under a Bad Sign."

Bell's next solo hit, 1968's "A Tribute to a King," was a poignant farewell to the late Otis Redding; the R&B Top Ten hit "I Forgot to Be Your Lover" soon followed, and a series of duets with Judy Clay, most notably "Private Number," also earned airplay. In 1969, he relocated to Atlanta and set up his own label, Peachtree; the hits dried up as the next decade opened, but in 1977 Bell capped a major comeback with "Trying to Love Two," which topped the R&B charts. In 1985, he founded another label, Wilbe, and issued *Passion*, which found its most receptive audiences in the U.K. (although "I Don't Want to Wake Up Feeling Guilty," a duet with Janice Bullock, was a minor U.S. hit). In addition to subsequent LPs, including 1989's *On a Roll* and 1992's *Bedtime Stories*, in 1987 Bell was inducted into the Georgia Music Hall of Fame; that same year receiving the Rhythm & Blues Foundation's R&B Pioneer Award. *—Jason Ankeny*

★ **The Soul of a Bell** / 1967 / Stax ♦♦♦♦♦

William Bell's history illustrates just how singles-oriented soul was in the 1960s. Though he'd enjoyed a hit in 1961 with "You Don't Miss Your Water," it wasn't until 1967 that Stax finally released his first album, the magnificent *The Soul of a Bell*. From that classic and Bell's moderate hits "Never Like This Before" and "Everybody Loves a Winner" to heartfelt versions of "Do Right Woman, Do Right Man" and "I've Been Loving You Too Long," everything on this album (reissued on CD in 1991) illustrates the gospel-drenched richness of Southern soul. Meanwhile, the influence of Motown and the Four Tops is hard to miss on the riveting single "Eloise (Hang on in There)," which should have been a major hit, but surprisingly, never even charted. [The 2002 CD reissue adds alternate versions of "You Don't Miss Your Water" and "Any Other Way."] *—Alex Henderson*

Duets / 1968 / Stax ♦♦♦

In the late '60s, Bell recorded a number of male/female duets with partners Judy Clay, Carla Thomas, and Mavis Staples; the ones with Clay were the most successful, "Private Number" and "My Baby Specializes" becoming modest R&B hits. All of his duet projects are assembled here, along with three solo sides that he cut in the 1970s. It's not among Bell's most striking work, but it's decent pop/soul, closer to Motown in feel than a lot of Stax material. I don't know what the deal is, but the version of "My Baby Specializes" here, though credited to Bell and Clay, only seems to feature Clay, unless that's Bell adding an odd backup grunt here and there. *—Richie Unterberger*

Bound to Happen / 1969 / Stax ♦♦♦

Released in the wake of his biggest Stax hit, 1968's "I Forgot to Be Your Lover" (which, oddly, is not included on the album), *Bound to Happen* had some blockbuster elements: Booker T. Jones produced and arranged, the MG's played backup, and the Memphis Horns were used. Bell and Jones wrote much of the material together. Still, it's only a cut above pleasant journeyman soul, often with a sweeter feel than you'd expect from a Jones production. The high points are the small hit "My Whole World Is Falling Down" and Bell's version of "Born Under a Bad Sign," which he co-wrote with Jones, and which had already been a big hit for Albert King. The covers of Sly Stone's "Everyday People" and Jimmy Webb's "By the Time I Get to Phoenix," though, smack of filler. This has been paired with his 1971 album *Wow...* on a single-disc CD reissue. *—Richie Unterberger*

Wow... / 1971 / Stax ♦♦♦

Much of Bell's first '70s album was cut at Muscle Shoals, with background vocals layered in at a studio in Los Angeles and horns and strings recorded in Memphis. This kind of production by mail usually spells trouble, and while it didn't have a readily apparent impact upon the results, this doesn't count as one of Bell's more distinguished efforts. Part of the problem is that William himself wrote hardly any of the material, but the larger issue is that it's competent but unremarkable period soul with a slightly slicker than necessary execution—criticisms that could be leveled at the output of the Stax label as a whole by 1970. When it gets just a little more rootsy, as on his version of Eddie Floyd's "I'll Be Home," things are more satisfying. To add marketability to the LP, Bell's late-1968 Top Ten R&B hit "I Forgot to Be Your Lover," his biggest single for Stax, was added to the track list. This has been paired with his 1969 album *Bound to Happen* on a single-disc CD reissue. *—Richie Unterberger*

Phases of Reality / 1973 / Stax ♦♦♦

Many of Stax's releases in its final years were dull soul. But by the standards of the era, Bell's second-to-last Stax LP was an above-average affair that was more diverse than many such efforts of the time. The three songs he co-wrote with guitarist Horace Shipp Jr. were socially conscious tunes in a different bag than the straightforward romantic odes Bell usually purveyed. "Save Us" was indebted to Marvin Gaye's *What's Going On* era, with a Philly-influenced funk-soul groove, and "Fifty Dollar Habit" was, of course, about drug use. Elsewhere, Bell stuck mostly to love songs, self-penned and otherwise, getting into a pre-disco lope on the title track, sweet soul balladry on "What I Don't Know Won't Hurt Me" and "If You Really Love Him," and light reggae-influenced rhythms on "Lonely for Your Love." [The album is now available as part of a reissue that combines *Phases of Reality* and Bell's final Stax LP, 1974's *Relating*, onto a single CD.] *—Richie Unterberger*

Relating / 1974 / Stax ✦✦

Bell's final Stax LP was, other than a couple of bright spots, blandly sentimental mid-'70s sweet soul. It had more of an Al Green-Hi Records influence than other Bell-Stax releases, due in all probability to the contribution of horn arrangements and backup vocals by musicians who were also involved in Hi sessions. There was also co-production by Booker T. & the MG's drummer Al Jackson Jr., who was doing a lot of work for Hi at the time; Jackson and MG's bassist Duck Dunn also play on the record. There were a few low-charting R&B singles on the disc—"I've Got to Go on Without You," "Lovin' on Borrowed Time," and "Gettin' What You Want (Losin' What You Got)." None particularly deserved to do better, though "Gettin' What You Want" is a decent midtempo ballad. Actually, the star cut is "Nobody Walks Away From Love Unhurt," with its pin-prick, bluesy guitar licks. [The album is now available as part of a reissue that combines *Relating* and Bell's previous Stax LP, 1973's *Phases of Reality*, onto a single CD.] *—Richie Unterberger*

Comin' Back for More / Mar. 1977 / Razor & Tie ✦✦✦✦

Despite the appropriate title, *Comin' Back for More* is not merely a comeback album for William Bell; it is arguably the artistic and commercial peak of his entire career. During the 1960s, Bell was perhaps best-known as a songwriter, although his recorded tenure at Stax yielded several minor R&B hits, most notably the Top Ten "I Forgot to Be Your Lover," which later became a slightly retitled pop hit for Billy Idol. After switching to Mercury in the mid-'70s, Bell seemed to re-emerge out of nowhere with *Comin' Back for More*. The single "Tryin' to Love Two" became his only R&B chart-topper as well as his lone Top Ten pop success. Although 1970s R&B was overflowing with odes to infidelity (i.e., Billy Paul's "Me and Mrs. Jones"), "Tryin' to Love Two" was one of the few promiscuous songs to address the consequences beyond getting caught and ending up alone. Besides the additional strain on his time and finances, Bell reveals the psychological cost of fooling around when he bemoans: "It started out had lots of fun/But now it's got me on the run/This jumping in and out of bed/Keeps messing with my head." Shifting seamlessly from ominous bass and staccato guitar to the sweet sounds of muted horns and female background vocals, "Tryin' to Love Two" is a perfect marriage of music and lyrics. "Relax" is nearly as good, combining an irresistible rhythm (patterned after Archie Bell & the Drells' "Tighten Up") with a loving supplication designed to ease the mind of his virginal sweetheart. Bell's emotional sincerity transforms the potentially smarmy seduction into a reassuringly romantic entreaty. More evidence of Bell's artistic maturity surfaces on the spiritually profound update of his 1962 single "You Don't Miss Your Water," which features the inspirational saxophone of Eli Fountain. The somber resignation of "Just Another Way to Feel" also benefits greatly from Fountain's extended soloing, and all of the musicians assembled by Bell and co-producer/arranger Paul Mitchell contribute uniformly excellent performances throughout the album. If the serviceable remake of Smokey Robinson's "You've Really Got a Hold on Me" seems like an anticlimactic finale, it's probably due to the high quality of the preceding originals. It's not easy to upstage a legendary songwriter like Robinson, yet Bell accomplishes that unlikely feat in welcome fashion on *Comin' Back for More*. *—Vince Ripol*

It's Time You Took Another Listen / 1977 / Mercury ✦✦✦

This features William Bell's last major hit, "Easy Coming Out (Hard Going In)," which speaks of the ease of slipping out but the difficulty of returning home in the wee hours of the morning. The album's chocked with smooth Southern soul productions like "Yesterday I Lied, Today I Cried," "Satin Sheets," "Your Love Keeps Me Going," and "Hollywood Streetwalker." This LP is more polished than his Stax releases, a closer marriage to urban than traditional Memphis soul, but a solid commitment from Mercury was lacking. After two hits on two albums, Bell and Mercury parted company. *—Andrew Hamilton*

● **The Best of William Bell** / 1988 / Stax ✦✦✦✦✦

The Best of William Bell focuses on the singer's output from 1968-1974, covering the albums *Duets*, *Bound to Happen*, *Wow...*, *Phases of Reality*, and *Relating*. While his 1967 debut, *The Soul of a Bell*, may be his finest album, this collection compiles many of the highlights that followed, including his exquisite 1968 single "I Forgot to Be Your Lover." That same year, Bell cut a satisfactory set of *Duets* (1968) with Judy Clay, Carla Thomas, and Mavis Staples, three of which are featured here. By 1969, however, Bell was singing with increased confidence and, while the arrangements retained all the grand gestures of old, they seemed tougher somehow. That year, Bell released *Bound to Happen* (1969), displaying a harder edge on the funky "Born Under a Bad Sign." The material on *Wow...* (1971) benefited as well with female backing singers, solid drumming, and a host of strings framing fine vocal performances on "All for the Love of a Woman" and "Till My Back Ain't Got No Bone." Add the hit "I Forgot to Be Your Lover" and you have one of Bell's finest album sets. Further changes surfaced in 1973, with Bell adopting the cinematic funk stylings of Curtis Mayfield's *Superfly* on the pleading "Save Us." All of the material mentioned above is included on this Stax set. Still, no Bell best-of can be complete without his reading of the Otis Redding classic "I've Been Loving You Too Long" or Moman & Penn's "Do Right Woman, Do Right Man," let alone the singer's best-loved number: his very own "You Don't Miss Your Water." In lieu of the perfect William Bell package, however, this disc serves him well, demonstrating both the breadth of his vocal powers and his stylistic range. *—Nathan Bush*

On a Roll / 1989 / Wilbe ✦✦

William Bell, one of the classic Southern soul singers, tried to update his production and surroundings in the '80s while retaining his traditional sound. His albums for his own Wilbe label, particularly this late effort, were only partially successful. His singing was mostly solid, his material mostly undistinguished. *—Ron Wynn*

A Little Something Extra / 1992 / Stax ✦✦✦

A fine collection of Stax outtakes from the 1960s, *A Little Something Extra* features several tracks, including his smoldering version of "Will You Love Me Tomorrow?," that rival his original singles. *—Stephen Thomas Erlewine*

Greatest Hits, Vol. 2 / 1995 / Ichiban ✦✦✦✦

William Bell's gentlemanly, deep soul sound, like fine wine, gets better with age. The 11 cuts include re-recordings of some of his Stax Records hits. His marvelous duet with Judy Clay, "Private Number," remains a crown jewel in his discography, and the new version is just as playful. Bell proves he still has strong pipes on the stately "I Need Your Love So Bad," and his tribute to the late Otis Redding, "A Tribute to a King," is as significant now as it was in the '60s. "Easy Coming Out (Hard Going In)," and "Everybody Loves a Winner" are two excellent examples of R&B. And the forewarning message in "You Don't Miss Your Water," Bell's signature song, still rings true. A good CD from an overlooked soul singer. *—Andrew Hamilton*

Wow . . . /Bound to Happen / Apr. 1, 1997 / Stax ✦✦✦✦✦

Phases of Reality/Relating / 1999 / Stax ✦✦✦

Regina Belle

b. Jul. 17, 1964, Englewood, NJ

Vocals / Adult Contemporary, Urban, Soul

Regina Belle emerged as a prolific, consistently engaging vocalist on the urban contemporary scene. Born in NJ, Belle's early experience was in gospel, though she was also attracted to R&B during her childhood. She studied trombone, tuba, and steel drums, and at 12 won a school contest singing the Emotions' "Don't Ask My Neighbors." Belle sang in a New Jersey vocal group, and studied opera and jazz in college. New York DJ Vaughn Harper introduced her to the Manhattans, and she began working as their opening act. Belle recorded a duet with them, "Where Did We Go Wrong," that was produced by Bobby Womack in 1986. She earned a solo Columbia contract in 1987, and the single "Please Be Mine" earned both praise and a number two R&B hit. A follow-up single, "So Many Tears," also made the R&B Top 20, and the hit "Without You," pairing her with Peabo Bryson, was the only memorable thing about the film *Leonard, Part 6*. Her second LP, *Stay With Me*, secured her success, and she went on to earn more acclaim. Releasing *Passion* in 1993, she returned five years later with *Believe in Me*. *—Ron Wynn*

All By Myself / Jun. 1987 / Columbia ✦✦✦

Stay With Me / Aug. 1989 / Columbia ✦✦✦✦✦

Passion / Feb. 1993 / Columbia ✦✦✦✦

Gifted with a voice that illuminates with such vigor to convey life's most inspiring and harshest moments, Regina Belle presents an album that steadfastly utilizes her vocal attributes. The New Jersey native's first single was the sentimental number "If I Could," a timeless tune that reflects a parent's desire to make life as easy as possible for their offspring. It cracked the *Billboard* R&B Top Ten at number nine after 21 weeks on the charts. The follow-up single was "Dream in Color." Set to a gospel-seasoned rhythm track, Belle expresses the ambitions of the idealistic lyric with an uplifting delivery. It only managed to peak at number 63 after a mere nine weeks. There were no other releases, but every song here is worthy of chart attention. The majority of the songs are ballads and midtempo numbers. One would think that with the sultry singer's impressive history of chart activity, the record company would expend more time and effort on such a proven artist. As the title indicates, Belle extends much passion in each one of these songs. She's lacking nothing on any one of these performances and the material is appropriately suited to the songstress. The album begins with the ardent title track, "Passion," and concludes with the inspirational "One Love." From the jazzy blues to the soulful R&B and pop-oriented tunes, Belle's vocals are mesmerizing to the last note. *—Craig Lytle*

Reachin' Back / Sep. 5, 1995 / Columbia ✦✦

Regina Belle's *Reachin' Back* is a collection of 11 covers of classic R&B and soul songs, including numbers performed by Al Green and the Spinners. Since their definitive original performances have become part of the public's collective consciousness, it's unfair to hold Belle's interpretations in comparisons, since hers inevitably pale. Taken on their own terms, her versions are well-sung and well-produced, yet slightly uninspired. Fans might find it necessary, but *Reachin' Back* doesn't rank among her most distinguished efforts. *—Stephen Thomas Erlewine*

● **Baby Come to Me: The Best of Regina Belle** / Nov. 11, 1997 / Columbia/Legacy ✦✦✦✦

Regina Belle stands as one of the most underrated R&B singers to emerge in the late '80s. This collection is an adequate retrospective of the singer, although a couple of her key singles, "Please Be Mine" and her first duet with Peabo Bryson, "Without You," were left off in favor of a few non-hits. However, the collection clocks in at nearly 74 minutes, and the songs are featured in their full-length versions (most of them averaging five minutes in length, two over seven), so therefore this CD is nearly filled to capacity. Belle is a singer of sophisticated, jazz-infused quiet storm R&B, similar at times to Anita Baker, Oleta Adams, and Phyllis Hyman. She shines brightest on her signature song "Baby Come to Me." Other highlights on this set include the equally satisfying "So Many Tears" (complete with exquisite saxophone solos), the gorgeous "If I Could" (which should have been a much bigger hit than it was), her take on Teddy Pendergrass' "Love TKO," the Dianne

Warren-penned "All I Want Is Forever" (with James "J.T." Taylor), and her biggest hit to date, "A Whole New World (Aladdin's Theme)," again with Peabo Bryson. There is not too much information on the singer or the songs in terms of liner notes, but at least the chart positions of her hits are included. Save for the two omissions, this set provides a good representation of the singer's best work, and it will have to do until the day when a more complete, two-disc retrospective is issued. *—Jose Promis*

Believe in Me / Jun. 9, 1998 / MCA ♦♦♦♦
Recording the theme for Disney's *Aladdin* didn't have the same effect on Regina Belle's career as *Beauty and the Beast* had for Celine Dion's. With the exception of a pair of Top 40 pop hits ("Make It Like It Was," "If I Could") Belle's success was confined to the realm of R&B. Change was in the air, however, for her fifth and strongest release, *Believe in Me*. Aside from switching to MCA from Columbia and co-writing four of the songs herself, Belle manages to utilize slick, hip production and update her sound without forgetting the most important element: strong hooks and well-written tunes. Eric "E-Smooth" Hicks provides the production backdrop for eight of the album's tracks, giving Belle the strongest rhythmic push her music has ever had. After several easy-listening songs in her career, it's refreshing to hear her loosen up on the radio-ready likes of "Don't Let Go," "Baby Love," and the title track. Her ballads are also more R&B-flavored than ever, and Belle gives some of the laziest, sexiest vocals of her career on "I Got It" and "Come See About Me." Belle even recognizes that great production doesn't always have to be cluttered, illustrated on "I Gotch U" (written and produced by her brother, Bernard Belle; talent clearly runs in the family) and "Teach Me How to Live," both of which seduce in a gorgeously minimal setting. Another refreshing element is song length; while a lot of R&B music tends to run on for five minutes or more, only the final cut, "Be in Love Again" (coincidentally, the album's blandest composition), clocks in at that length; the rest of the songs are in the four-minute range or shorter, resulting in a breezy effect that inspires repeat listenings. Even a couple of less interesting pop tunes ("Never Should Have Let You Go," "Be in Love Again") aren't enough to weigh this project down. Filled with memorable hooks and irresistible grooves, *Believe in Me* finds Regina Belle at the top of her game. *—John Jones*

This Is Regina! / Oct. 23, 2001 / Peak ♦♦♦♦
This Is Regina follows in the traditional Regina Belle formula: lush, sophisticated quiet storm ballads, augmented by Belle's strong, warm, elegant, inviting vocals. The album steers clear of anything too adventurous, which is just fine, because Belle's fans have come to love her for her reliability as an old friend who returns every few years with a fresh set of new, yet familiar songs. The album begins with the pleasantly sexy "Oooh Boy," then leads into a several pretty ballads, notably the sweeping "From Now On," which recalls her American chart-topper "A Whole New World." Highlights include the funky, smooth, sexy "Don't Wanna Go Home Now," which could be safely classified as adult contemporary club music and recalls Koffee Brown's 2001 hit "After Party." "Johnny's Back" is an endearing, shuffling little tune about, well, Johnny coming home, and possesses a warm, adult innocence rare in popular music. The album also features a more modern-sounding tune, "La Da Di," which, for better or worse, brings to mind Destiny's Child and features a rap courtesy of MC Lyte. In short, save for a few left turns, this adequately titled album is pure Regina Belle and will undoubtedly please the sophisticated songstress' many fans. *—Jose F. Promis*

The Belmonts

f. 1960, New York, NY [The Bronx]
Group / Doo Wop
The history of the Belmonts is usually linked to that of their lead singer, Dion (born Dion DiMucci, July 18, 1939), with whom they had their biggest hits. In point of fact, however, the link up between Dion & the Belmonts actually lasted only two years, and the group existed (albeit briefly) prior to and a long after his time with them. Angelo D'Aleo (born February 3, 1940), first tenor; Fred Milano (born August 22, 1939), second tenor; and Carlo Mastrangelo (b. October 5, 1938), baritone; and Dion DiMucci were all friends from the area around Belmont Avenue in the Bronx, in N.Y.C. They attended Roosevelt High School and hung out together, and all of them sang; D'Aleo, Milano, and Mastrangelo began singing together and named themselves the Belmonts. As a trio, they recorded for the Mohawk label in 1957, making their debut with the song "Teenage Clementine," which came and went without notice. It was when Mastrangelo wrote a song of his own, "We Went Away," that was heard by Dion, that the quartet came together. It was recorded for Mohawk under the direction of conductor/arranger Hugo Montenegro (who had previously arranged an abortive debut single by Dion with a separate backing group), and the B-side got onto several local radio play lists.

The group moved to Laurie Records, newly founded by Bob Schwartz (who'd been a part-owner of Mohawk) and his brother Gene, and, with Dion as lead singer, cut their label debut with "I Wonder Why," which made it to number 22 on the pop charts, making them a hot act in New York and the Northeast. It was followed by a pair of hits, "No One Knows" and "Don't Pity Me," which peaked at 19 and 40, respectively. "A Teenager in Love" made number five, and further hits with "Where or When" and "When You Wish Upon a Star" elevated Dion & the Belmonts as a major national act. Dion DiMucci was clearly the star of the group, in presentation and billing, but the vocal talents of the group were displayed equally well, if not as prominently, on most of those hits and the tracks cut for their LPs. Their own musical tastes diverged somewhat from those of their lead singer, into jazz, pop ballads, and other areas, while Dion preferred harder rock & roll sounds and later gravitated toward blues.

In 1960, Dion decided to pursue a solo career and parted company with the Belmonts. The usual perception is that the group disappeared after this, but the truth is that the Belmonts continued to enjoy success for the first year after his departure. The trio remained with Laurie Records for one single, "We Belong Together," featuring Carlo Mastrangelo as lead singer, and then formed their own label—originally named Surprise, and then Sabrina, it was finally christened Sabina Records when those two earlier choices proved to belong to other companies. The label became active (as Surprise) in March of 1961 with the recording of "Tell Me Why," which rose to number 18 nationally. The follow-up record late that summer, "Don't Get Around Much Anymore," rose to a modest number 57, and the next release, "I Need Someone," only got to 75.

The Belmonts' fortunes picked up again with their Sabina single "Come on Little Angel," written by Ernie Maresca. Produced by Gerry Granahan, an established songwriter and recording star (as Dickie Do & the Don'ts), who also oversaw the operations of the company, the single got to number 28 during the summer of 1962. The group also made a bad miscalculation around this time when Maresca offered them the first crack at a song entitled "The Wanderer," and the Belmonts turned it down, only to see it become a massive hit—indeed, a signature tune—for Dion. A major lineup change then occurred, when a split developed within the group over their business affairs and the financial condition of Sabina Records; Mastrangelo exited the Belmonts in favor of trying to record solo for Laurie Records. The group carried on, replacing him with Frank Lyndon, and released their first LP, *Carnival of Hits*, late in 1962 to try and capitalize on "Come on Little Angel."

Sabina Records began diversifying its catalog slightly, releasing "Time to Dream," which was credited to Buddy Christie and Buddy Sheppard, with the Belmonts singing backup as "the Holidays." They also recorded material by a friend of theirs from the Bronx, Pete Barin, but the label couldn't seem to click with any records except those by the Belmonts themselves, and that was changing. By 1963, the Belmonts were not only struggling for a hit, and battling the woefully under-financed condition of their record label, but also changes in public taste. Dion had managed to keep his music current as a solo performer and racked up some huge hits in the process, through 1963, but the Belmonts, by the nature of their name and their harmony sound, seemed more dated. A brief revival in doo wop music in 1961 had been a godsend to the trio, in terms of bookings as well as record sales, and there'd been lots of work in New York and the surrounding area, at a time when they were just coming off of several big hits with Dion. By this time, there were other harmony-based groups out there recording and adding their own respective wrinkles to the music, including the Beach Boys and, closer to home, the East Coast-based Jay & the Americans and the Four Seasons, both of whom had a more commercial sound than the Belmonts. The sales of their own records began declining around this time, "Diddle-Dee-Dum" getting to number 53 and "Ann-Marie" to number 86 in 1963.

Sabina Records struggled on through a handful of additional releases by the Belmonts that never charted, and finally, in 1964, folded. The group moved to United Artists Records that year, and cut their final recordings from this part of their history there in 1966. The trio disbanded that year, although they were back together in 1967 on ABC Records with *Together Again*, an album that reunited them with Dion. The group remained active after this, cutting an album entitled *Summer Love* on the Dot Records label in 1969.

The group next became visible in the early '70s, amid the oldies boom. They cut an album for Buddah Records entitled *Cigars Acappela Candy*, on which they performed several classic oldies tracks and also applied their sound to contemporary hits like "My Sweet Lord" and "Na Na Hey Hey (Kiss Him Goodbye)." In 1972, however, they reunited with Dion for what proved to be the biggest single gig in their history, a performance at New York's Madison Square Garden, which was not only a sell-out event but also recorded for posterity and released as *Live at Madison Square Garden 1972*. Milano, Mastrangelo, and D'Aleo were the participants in that performance, which was reportedly released two different ways—the original Warner Bros. LP was heavily sweetened in the studio, where the subsequent reissues (including the Rhino CD) were made from untouched tapes from the original show. The Madison Square Garden show and its aftermath, which included performances together in 1973 as well, basically allowed all concerned to grab their moment of glory. Dion resumed his solo career, while the Belmonts continued working and got another LP of their own out in 1978, entitled *Cheek to Cheek*, and generated a nostalgia-laced hit in 1981 entitled "Let's Put the Fun Back in Rock & Roll," on which they were teamed with Freddy Cannon, another veteran of early '60s rock & roll. The group's vintage post-Dion work resurfaced on Relic Records and the Ace label from England, which has made it part of it's reasons for existence to reissue seemingly every available note of music by both Dion and the Belmonts, and as of 1996, Fred Milano remained active representing the Belmonts. *—Bruce Eder*

Laurie Sabina & United Artists Sides, Vol. 1 / Sep. 19, 1995 / Ace ♦♦♦♦♦
In their Dion-less career, the Belmonts were in an awkward place. The vocal-group doo wop they had sung with Dion was going out of style, and they tried on various approaches for size without getting much success with any of them. For all that, they were more successful than most 1960s doo wop acts, and this 30-track compilation of material from 1961-1966 has all half-dozen of their charting records, including their biggest and best, "Tell Me Why." At times, unfortunately, it is obvious that they're trying to imitate the stuff Dion was having solo success with at the time, as on "Come on Little Angel." The rest of the disc is inconsistent, and widely variable stylistically. "I Don't Know How to Cry" tries for an uptown New York R&B-pop sound; others are traditional slow doo wop ballads; "Have You Heard" is a midtempo ballad in the style of the Duprees; "Ann-Marie" is Beach Boys-influenced; "I Got a Feeling" is a Jay & the Americans cop; etc. There are occasional above-average tunes like the group original "I Confess," but most of the cuts are mediocre. Includes some previously unissued material, and three tracks they participated in as the backup group to Buddy Sheppard (billed as the Holidays). *—Richie Unterberger*

● **The Very Best of the Belmonts: Tell Me Why** / Oct. 22, 2002 / Collectables ♦♦♦♦♦
As Bill Dahl writes in his excellent liner notes, Dion says that he split from the Belmonts in 1961 because they wanted to take a smoother, more traditional musical approach and he wanted to introduce more strains of rock & roll and blues. But when the Belmonts got out on their own, they ended up following Dion's lead to such an extent that they might as well have stayed with him. This is clear from a listen to Collectables Records' 25-track collection of their 1961-1964 recordings for their own Sabina label, including the six singles they charted. True, they could offer their covers of songs associated with Duke Ellington ("Don't Get Around Much Anymore"), Bing Crosby ("AC-Cent-Tchu-Ate the Positive"), and Frank Sinatra ("This Love of Mine"). But many of their performances

sounded like copies of Dion hits, particularly "I Need Someone," a dead ringer for "Runaround Sue" that followed its appearance by months. Collectables focuses on the Belmonts' similarity to Dion by including several recordings on which they sang backup to Dion soundalikes. "So Wrong" and "Lookout for Cindy" feature lead vocals by Pete Barin, while Buddy Christie (aka Buddy Sheppard) takes the lead on "That Background Sound," "Now It's All Over," and "Time to Dream." The Belmonts themselves changed lead singers during this period, with Carlo Mastrangelo being replaced by Frank Lyndon, and since the sequencing mixes up the chronology, the tracks seem to be coming from several different Dion & the Belmonts copycat groups. Nevertheless, there are many enjoyable performances here (all but six of them in stereo), and this album will make a good addition to the collection of any Dion fan. *—William Ruhlmann*

Jesse Belvin

b. Dec. 15, 1932, San Antonio, TX, **d.** Feb. 6, 1960, Fairhope, AR

Vocals / Brown-Eyed Soul, R&B, Soul

While not nearly as well remembered by the general public as either Sam Cooke or Otis Redding, singer Jesse Belvin was in many regards a performer of equal stature whose career was also cut far too short by tragedy. At the time of his death, Belvin was moving in the much the same direction as Cooke (he was even on the same record label, although signed earlier), and was scoring and writing hits long before Redding ever cut a record. Jesse Lorenzo Belvin was born in San Antonio, TX, in 1932. When he was five, his family relocated to Los Angeles, and by age seven he was singing in church. He discovered R&B in his early teens, and in 1950 joined jazz saxophonist Big Jay McNeely's backing vocal quartet Three Dots & a Dash. Belvin's falsetto was placed up front in his debut release, 1950's "All the Wine Is Gone"; the response was so strong that on the group's next record, his name was placed directly under McNeely's on the B-side, "Sad Story." In 1952, Belvin and bandmate Marvin Phillips signed to Specialty. They cut four singles: The first three—"Baby Don't Go," "One Little Blessing," and "Love of My Life"—were credited to Jesse Belvin, and all failed to chart. The last, "Dream Girl," which featured Belvin on piano and vocals with Phillips on saxophone, was credited to Jesse & Marvin, and got to number two on the R&B charts in 1953.

Unfortunately, just as it looked like Belvin's career was going to take off, he was drafted. While home on leave, he wrote a song called "Earth Angel," inspired by a young white woman who lived near him. The song was subsequently recorded by a semiprofessional doo wop quartet called the Penguins and became one of the first R&B singles to cross over onto the pop charts, selling a million copies between late 1954 and early 1955. (A lawsuit later erupted over the authorship and origins of the song, which took almost two years to settle; Belvin was awarded one-third credit for the song, alongside the Penguins' Curtis Williams and a third singer who had a claim to writing it.)

Belvin was a prolific songwriter, but his business approach was rather cavalier. In a period in which millions of dollars were sometimes earned on a carefully protected copyright, Belvin wrote songs as a way of raising quick cash and often sold them outright to others for as little as 100 dollars. The result was dozens upon dozens of songs that Belvin was responsible for as writer and singer on the demo or guide track, few of which he actually received credit for. In 1956, he signed a long-term contract with Modern Records, and also continued to sing for other labels under assumed names, working in the background with other artists. Some of the Modern releases were credited to the Cliques, which was really Jesse Belvin and Eugene Church, but most were credited to Belvin alone. It was with Modern that he cut his most enduring record. "Goodnight My Love" had been written by producer George Mottola ten years earlier, but he had never been able to finish it; Belvin provided the lines for the bridge that completed the song, but asked for 400 dollars in lieu of co-authorship credit. Mottola didn't have it, but a colleague, John Marascalco, did, and put up the money, receiving co-authorship credit in the bargain. The song reached number seven on the R&B charts in 1956; curiously, the pianist on the recording was an 11-year-old session player making his recording debut named Barry White, who would emerge as a giant in his own right about two decades later. More important at the time, "Goodnight My Love" became the outro theme to Alan Freed's rock & roll radio show, heard by millions of young listeners every night.

Belvin cut ten singles for Modern, of which "Goodnight My Love" was far and away the most successful. In 1958, he was again on the move, recording for Knight, Class, and Jamie Records under his own name, as well as for the Aladdin label in association with the Sharptones. His biggest success that year, however, came through a group called the Shields, which had been formed by George Mottola to record on his own Tender label. Adding his voice to the mix, Belvin joined the group, which also included Frankie Ervin on lead and Johnny "Guitar" Watson on guitar. The Shields' only record with Belvin was "You Cheated," which had already been cut by a white group called the Slades; the Shields' version was the more successful, reaching number 15 on the pop charts in the summer of 1958.

Around this time, Belvin's career took a decided upswing, in part with help from his wife Jo Anne, a fine songwriter in her own right who became his manager and took charge of his career. One of the first results was getting him signed to RCA Records; his first big success for the new label came in April of 1959 with the Top 40 hit "Guess Who." He finished his first album, *Just Jesse Belvin*, later in the year, developing a more mature studio sound and a somewhat more sophisticated singing style as well. Like Sam Cooke, who would follow him on to RCA with similar goals a short time later, Belvin began to realize that he had the potential to cross over to adult white audiences while keeping his original fans as well. For its part, RCA saw in Belvin the potential for another Nat King Cole or Billy Eckstine: A powerful and charismatic performer; he had acquired the nickname "Mr. Easy" for his way with the ballads that increasingly made up his live sets.

In late 1959, with the encouragement of his wife and the support of producer Dick Pierce and arranger/conductor Marty Paich, Belvin went into the studio for three recording dates that yielded a dozen songs, among them intensely soulful covers of standards like "Blues in the Night," "In the Still of the Night," and "Makin' Whoopee." The band included Art Pepper on the sax and clarinet and Jack Sheldon on the trumpet, and the playing was extraordinary all the way around. Alas, Belvin never heard the finished album, *Mr. Easy*; on February 6, 1960, shortly after finishing a performance in Little Rock, AR, on a bill with Sam Cooke, Jackie Wilson, and Marv Johnson, Belvin and his wife were killed in a head-on auto collision. *Mr. Easy* was released later in 1960, his final testament and an enduring legacy. *—Bruce Eder*

Just Jesse Belvin / 1959 / RCA ♦♦♦

The next-to-last album made by R&B crooner/balladeer Jesse Belvin. It's part slick pop, part soulful R&B, although his sound has more of a Nat King Cole influence than gospel. Belvin's work merged the smooth, sophisticated West Coast sound with the more earthy southern approach. *—Ron Wynn*

Mr. Easy / Dec. 8, 1959 / RCA ♦♦♦♦♦

Some would argue that this album (reissued on CD in 1995) isn't really representative of Jesse Belvin's sound, coming at the very end of his life so that he couldn't follow it up and displaying a final mix that he never got to hear. But *Mr. Easy* is about as fine an album as any R&B singer ever cut in search of a mainstream audience and ought to be in every '50s vocal collection. Anyone who owns even one Sam Cooke CD should make it his or her business to buy it, and nobody who enjoys Nat King Cole, Frank Sinatra, or Billy Eckstine would be doing wrong, either. No, his voice wasn't as rich as Sinatra or Cooke's at either's best, but he knew how to use it, and he went further with this material than anybody had a right to, straddling the worlds of soul and popular music magnificently. By itself, the closing number, "The Very Thought of You," is worth the price of the disc, and isn't much easier to listen to than Cooke's "A Change Is Gonna Come," even if it is a very different kind of song. *—Bruce Eder*

The Unforgettable Jessie Belvin / 1960 / Crown ♦♦♦

Jesse Belvin's Best / 1966 / Camden ♦♦♦♦♦

Blues Balladeer / 1990 / Specialty ♦♦♦♦

The best of Jesse Belvin's early soul sides, dating between 1952 and 1958 (though principally done between 1952 and 1955) and originally released by Art Rupe's Specialty label and related imprints such as Recorded In Hollywood, including the Jesse & Marvin sides ("Dream Girl," and etc.). Even at this early date, Belvin was a master balladeer, able to gently coax the sultriest and most sensual meaning from any song, but he was also a master blues singer, as is evident from the 1952 B-side "My Love Comes Tumbling Down." The 24 tracks on this CD includes ten previously unreleased tracks, among them an outtake of Jesse & Marvin's "Dream Girl," and a group of Belvin demos, among them the beautiful, moody "Jesse's Blues" from early 1952. A large portion of the songs here were written by Belvin, although the latest tracks on the disc, dating from 1956 and 1958, are collaborations (none previously released) between Belvin and his wife Jo Ann, who was also responsible for forcing her husband to take a professional approach to the business side of songwriting. They're all well crafted, very romantic and sensual soul—"Let's Try Romance" and "Love of My Life" (the latter from late 1958) both bridge the gap to some degree between Belvin's early- and mid-'50s R&B sound and his move into a more romantic pop vein with his signing to RCA in 1958—"Come Back," by contrast, is a solid rock & roll number, complete with a very prominent guitar and drums, and with one more take to tighten up the playing might have become a classic of the genre. *—Bruce Eder*

● **Goodnight, My Love** / 1991 / Capitol ♦♦♦♦♦

Jesse Belvin's Modern Record legacy, from 1955-1957, 25 songs (including an alternate take of "Goodnight My Love") including an undubbed version of "Beware," a pair of previously unheard songs ("What Can I Do Without You," "I'll Make a Bet"), a compelling soulful cover of Sam Cooke's "You Send Me," and the previously overlooked single version of "Sad and Lonesome," as well as a sample ("Summertime") of the kind of pop standard that he would later master. Whether he's doing doo wop style or crooning, the voice is magnificent, and the overall sound is extremely powerful and points very much toward the sound that Belvin would arrive at before his death. This CD isn't easy to find—stores stock Flair/Virgin's B.B. King reissues more willingly—but it's worth tracking down or ordering. *—Bruce Eder*

Golden Classics / Apr. 22, 1997 / Collectables ♦♦♦♦♦

This 75-minute, 26-song collection of Jesse Belvin's last round of recordings on RCA, from 1958 until the very end of 1959, is even better coming from Collectables Records than it would have been if RCA had put it out, because Collectables also licensed "Girl of My Dreams" and "Goodnight My Love" from his Modern Records catalog to round it out. This compilation presents the final flowering of Belvin's tragically short career as a Nat King Cole-style pop singer. His voice is astonishingly rich and expressive with this repertory, turning light classics like "Secret Love" into the most soulful pop music you ever heard, and stretching out on numbers like "Ol' Man River" as well. Other highlights include "Zing! Went the Strings of My Heart" (done straight, not like the Coasters' version) and "Witchcraft," where he starts moving closer to Frank Sinatra than Nat King Cole (and it works, too), and the R&B hit "Funny," which made the R&B top 30 in early 1959. What is so extraordinary is that numbers like "Guess Who," "My Funny Valentine," and "Now You Know," all done complete with way-overblown angelic choruses more suited to Doris Day recordings of the period, are both transformed into superb soul ballads in Belvin's hands. All of that, plus the complete contents of the *Mr. Easy* album, make this one of the finest soul releases of its period, a vital Jesse Belvin document, and maybe the best release in the whole Collectables catalog to date. The only minor drawback is that the notes say a lot about Belvin's career, but almost nothing about his time at RCA or the sessions that yielded these songs, not even producer and arranger credits; plus, a tighter focus on the music at hand would have been nice. *—Bruce Eder*

Benet

f. 1984, **db.** 1993

Group / Urban

Benet (ba-nay) was the brother-sister vocal duo of Lisa and Eric Benet Jordan who released a self-titled debut on EMI Records around October 1992. The Milwaukeans worked with an impressive list of producers: Jeff Lorber (Art Porter), Bryan Loren (Shanice, Vesta, Mic Murphy), Robert Brookins (Stephanie Mills, Christopher Williams), Sami McKinney (Melba Moore, Patti LaBelle), and their cousin, George Nash Jr. There was stellar instrumental support from Lorber, Loren, Freddie Hubbard, Alec Milstein, Dave Koz, Les Pierce, Gary Meeks, and Paul Jackson Jr.

Benet started in 1984, when Eric Benet began writing songs with Nash. This led to them recording basement demos and sending them to record companies. A lot of them came back unopened, stamped not accepting unsolicited material. But they kept trying. After hooking up with Gerard Entertainment Group, a Milwaukee production firm, Eric began performing with a band called Gerard and Lisa with a band called Beat Crazy. They performed with the bands for three years. During their off days, they'd be recording in the Gerard facilities. It was a very intense time for them, tearing down the band gear because they had no roadies, then going into the studio early the next morning. After three years of recording demos, the duo felt that they had some pretty decent material. They attended the Jack the Rapper convention in Atlanta, an annual record business event. That year a contest was held—"Tracking With the Future Stars"—where about 500 to 1,000 demo tapes were narrowed down to 20 acts that would perform.

Benet was picked to be perform in front of an audience that included Keith Sweat, the O'Jays, Gerald LeVert, and other performers and producers. Afterwards, they were approached by a big-name producer who wanted to do one of their songs. But they rejected the offer, citing that they wanted to keep the songs for their act and not share any of the publishing. After thinking about the opportunity they had turned down, the duo felt really dumb. But it turns out that a producer from *The Sally Jessy Raphael Show* was there and wanted Benet to come on Raphael's show to help promote a show produced by their parent company, Multimedia. Record producer Sami McKinney saw Benet's appearance on *Sally Jessy Raphael* and contacted their management about doing some demos. When they were completed, McKinney took the demos to Capitol. The *Benet* album didn't chart and only had one chart single. Lisa Jordan went back into private life while Eric stuck with it until he got his breakthrough with the album *True to Myself*. *—Ed Hogan*

● **Benet** / 1992 / Capitol ♦♦♦♦

A solid debut from future star Eric Benet and his sister, Lisa. The first single, "Only Want to Be With You," and charted briefly on the R&B charts. The next single, "Rainy Days and Mondays," was a remake of the Carpenters' classic, and Benet does a sensitive and reverent cover with a poignant sax solo by Dave Koz. Producer/writer Sami McKinney contributes three excellent tracks: the midtempo, calypso-ish "Something Real," the forlorn, beautiful "Stranger Things Have Happened," and the lovely closing ballad, "Till We Meet Again." *Benet* is a strong collection of jazz-spiced urban music with a deserving spotlight on Eric and Lisa's beautiful vocal blend. *—Ed Hogan*

Eric Benet

Vocals / Contemporary R&B, Urban

Eric Benet is a contemporary gospel singer with heavy hip-hop and urban soul influences. As a teenager, Benet was in a vocal group called Benet with his sister and cousin. The group signed with Capitol and released an eponymous album in 1992 that went ignored. Eric went out as a solo artist shortly afterward, signing to Warner Bros. and releasing his debut album, *True to Myself*, in the fall of 1996. *A Day in the Life* followed in 1999, launching the R&B chart smash "Spend My Life With You." *—Stephen Thomas Erlewine*

True to Myself / Sep. 24, 1996 / Warner Bros. ♦♦♦♦

Eric Benet's debut album *True to Myself* elevates the singer to the front ranks of late-'90s retro-soul vocalists, yet the album suffers from inconsistent material. which prevents it from being a thoroughly impressive debut. As it stands, *True to Myself* is merely an appealing, promising collection of soul that usually straddles the line between classic and urban soul quite skillfully. *—Leo Stanley*

● **A Day in the Life** / Apr. 27, 1999 / Warner Bros. ♦♦♦♦

On his second album of urban adult contemporary, singer/songwriter Eric Benet scores with a series of mellow grooves and sizzling duets aimed at both the body and brain. *A Day in the Life* is sharper than contemporary R&B, keeping the arrangements and production simple, all the while nodding toward the genre's golden era of the '70s (which is also evident in the album's Toto and Kansas covers). Benet does, however, play the same loverman role on most of the songs here, never quite allowing them or his tranquil voice to stretch (and sometimes breathe). The best cuts, though—Toto's "Georgy Porgy" with Faith Evans and "Spend My Life With You" (featuring Tamia)—are velvety modern soul soaked in traditional sounds. *—Michael Gallucci*

George Benson

b. Mar. 22, 1943, Pittsburgh, PA

Guitar, Vocals / Smooth Jazz, Crossover Jazz, Contemporary Jazz, Jazz-Pop, Hard Bop, Quiet Storm

George Benson is simply one of the greatest guitarists in jazz history, but he is also an amazingly versatile musician, and that frustrates critics to no end who would paint him into a narrow bop box. He can play in just about any style—from swing to bop to R&B to pop—with supreme taste, a beautiful rounded tone, terrific speed, a marvelous sense of logic in building solos, and always, an unquenchable urge to swing. His inspirations may have been Charlie Christian and Wes Montgomery—and he can do dead-on impressions of both—but his style is completely his own. Not only can he play lead brilliantly, he is also one of the best rhythm guitarists around, supportive to soloists and a dangerous swinger, particularly in a soul-jazz format. Yet Benson can also sing in a lush soulful tenor with mannerisms similar to those of Stevie Wonder and Donny Hathaway, and it is his voice that has proved to be more marketable to the public than his guitar. Benson is the guitar-playing equivalent of Nat King Cole—a fantastic pianist whose smooth way with a pop vocal eventually eclipsed his instrumental prowess in the marketplace—but unlike Cole, Benson has been granted enough time after his fling with the pop charts to reaffirm his jazz guitar credentials, which he still does at his concerts. *—Richard S. Ginell*

The George Benson Cookbook / 1966 / Columbia/Legacy ♦♦♦

Giblet Gravy / 1968 / Verve ♦♦♦♦

No, you're not in Creed Taylor country yet, but you might as well be, for many of the ingredients that would garnish Benson's albums with Taylor are already present in this often enjoyable prototype. The immediate goal was to groom Benson as the next Wes Montgomery (who was about to leave Verve)—and so he covers hit tunes of the day ("Sunny," "Along Comes Mary," "Groovin' "), playing either with a big band plus voices or a neat quintet anchored by Herbie Hancock, and the sound is contoured to give his guitar a warm mellow ambience. But the eclectic Benson is his own man, as his infectious repeated-interval rhythm trademark tells us on his self-composed title track, and despite Tom McIntosh's mostly lame arrangements, George's work is always tasty and irresistibly melodic. *—Richard S. Ginell*

The Other Side of Abbey Road / 1970 / A&M ♦♦♦♦♦

Just three weeks after the U.S. release of the Beatles' swan song *Abbey Road*, Creed Taylor ushered Benson into the studio to begin a remarkably successful pop/jazz translation of the record (complete with a parody of the famous cover, showing George with guitar crossing an Eastern urban street). It is a lyrical album, with a hint of the mystery and a lot of the cohesive concept of the Beatles' original despite the scrambled order of the tunes. Benson is given some room to stretch out on guitar, sometimes in a bluesy groove, and there are more samples of his honeyed vocals than ever before (oddly, his voice would not be heard again by record buyers until he signed with Warner Bros.). Don Sebesky's arrangements roam freely from baroque strings to a full-throated big band, and Freddie Hubbard, Sonny Fortune and Hubert Laws get some worthy solo space. Yet for all its diversity, the record fits together as a whole more tightly than any other George Benson project, thanks to his versatile talents and the miraculous overarching unity of the Beatles' songs. One wonders if the Fab Four liked it, too. *—Richard S. Ginell*

★ **Beyond the Blue Horizon** / 1972 / Columbia/Legacy ♦♦♦♦♦

Having taken Benson along with him when he founded CTI, Creed Taylor merely leaves the guitarist alone with a small group on his first release. The payoff is a superb jazz session where Benson rises to the challenge of the turbulent rhythm section of Jack DeJohnette and Ron Carter, with Clarence Palmer ably manning the organ. Benson is clearly as much at home with DeJohnette's advanced playing as he was in soul/jazz (after all, he did play on some Miles Davis sessions a few years before), and his tone is edgier, with more bite, than it had been for awhile. The lyrical Benson is also on eloquent display in "Ode to a Kudu" (heard twice on the CD, as is "All Clear"), and there is even a somewhat experimental tilt toward Afro-Cuban-Indian rhythms in "Somewhere to the East." A must-hear for all aficionados of Benson's guitar. *—Richard S. Ginell*

White Rabbit / 1972 / Columbia ♦♦♦♦

For Benson's second CTI project, producer Creed Taylor and arranger Don Sebesky successfully place the guitarist in a Spanish-flavored setting full of flamenco flourishes, brass fanfares, moody woodwinds and such. The idea works best on "California Dreamin'" (whose chords are based on Andalusian harmonies), where, driven by Jay Berliner's exciting Spanish rhythm guitar, Benson comes through with some terrifically inspired playing. On "El Mar," Berliner is replaced by Benson's protégé Earl Klugh (then only 17) in an inauspicious—though at the time, widely-heralded—recorded debut. The title track is another winner, marred only by the out-of-tune brasses at the close, and in a good example of the CTI classical/jazz formula at work, Heitor Villa-Lobos' "Little Train of the Caipira" is given an attractive early-'70s facelift. Herbie Hancock gets plenty of nimble solo space on Rhodes electric piano, Airto Moreira contributes percussion and atmospheric wordless vocals, and Ron Carter and Billy Cobham complete the high-energy rhythm section. In this prime sample of the CTI idiom, everyone wins. *—Richard S. Ginell*

Body Talk / 1973 / Columbia ♦♦♦♦

With an eye and ear on what was happening on the soul charts—James Brown in particular—Benson made a decided swerve toward R&B on this release. Indeed the J.B.'s Pee Wee Ellis turns up as a big band arranger on three tracks, and he no doubt had a direct influence on the distinct JB groove of one of the non-big-band tunes, "Dance." It should come as no surprise by now that this formidable guitarist has no problem handling any kind of groove, although the mixed rhythm section of Jack DeJohnette, Ron Carter, electric pianist Harold Mabern, and percussionist Mobutu sometimes sends mixed messages. Earl Klugh has a few tasty moments on his own, and there are some reconnaissance flights back to the jazz side of George, which he handles with his usual confident aplomb. *—Richard S. Ginell*

Bad Benson / Oct. 13, 1974 / Columbia ♦♦♦

The CTI formula of long tracks tastefully decorated and shaped takes firm hold here, though George Benson, apropos the title, makes sure that the flavor of funky soul/jazz is the dominant one. With the help of the relentless rhythm guitar of Phil Upchurch, Benson produces some relentless riffing of his own on "Take Five"; indeed, on several cuts he flaunts his prowess as a rhythm soloist. Alas, arranger Don Sebesky is not in one of his more inventive moods; "Summer Wishes, Winter Dreams" is an outright attempt to evoke Wes Montgomery's last albums, and it falls flat—and there are a few times when Benson himself seems to be on automatic pilot. Nice, but there's better Benson out there. [The CD reissue offers two extra numbers.] *—Richard S. Ginell*

Breezin' / 1976 / Warner Bros. ♦♦♦

All of a sudden, George Benson became a pop superstar with this album, thanks to its least representative track. Most of *Breezin'* is a softer-focused variation of Benson's

R&B/jazz-flavored CTI work, his guitar as assured and fluid as ever with Claus Ogerman providing the suave orchestral backdrops and his crack then-working band (including Ronnie Foster on keyboards and sparkplug Phil Upchurch on rhythm guitar) pumping up the funk element. Yet it is the sole vocal track (his first in many years), Leon Russell's "This Masquerade"—where George unveiled his new trademark, scatting along with a single-string guitar solo—that reached number ten on the pop singles charts and drove the album all the way to number one on the pop (!) LP charts. The attractive title track also became a minor hit single, although Gabor Szabo's 1971 recording with composer Bobby Womack is even more fetching. In the greater scheme of Benson's career, this is really not so much a breakthrough as it is a transition album; the guitar is still the core of his identity. *—Richard S. Ginell*

Good King Bad / 1976 / Columbia ✦✦✦✦✦
The R&B elements get stronger, the sound and mix are more attuned to the dancefloor, yet this brings out the best in George Benson's funky side. Thanks in part to the more rigid beat, Benson pares down his style to its rhythmic essentials, refusing to spray notes all over the place at random, and as a result, the record cooks and dances. His treatment of Vince Guaraldi's "Cast Your Fate to the Wind," hugely complemented by Joe Farrell's wistfully prancing flute, is a mini-masterpiece in the use of space, of hitting exactly the right stabbing note right in the pocket. Again, Creed Taylor turns to a James Brown alumnus, David Matthews, for arrangements, and he discreetly and wisely stays out of Bad George's way. Buy this one for "Cast Your Fate," but there is plenty more to savor here (the CD also includes "Hold On, I'm Comin'" as a bonus). *—Richard S. Ginell*

In Concert-Carnegie Hall / 1976 / CTI ✦✦✦

Weekend in L.A. / 1978 / Warner Bros. ✦✦✦✦
Recording live at Los Angeles' Roxy club—then a showcase for many of the hottest acts in pop—was just the tonic that Benson and his *Breezin'* band needed on this often jumping album. With unusually lively crowds (for a record industry watering hole) shouting encouragement, the band gets deep into the four-on-the-floor funk and Benson digs in hard, his rhythmic instincts on guitar as sharp as ever. The balance between vocals and instrumentals is about even—George's voice sounds more throaty and soul oriented than before—and amidst the new material, there is a revisit to a favored CTI-era instrumental, the lovely "Ode to a Kudu." This album also introduced "On Broadway," an extended stomping version of the Drifters' hit that has become Benson's climactic showstopper to this day. The only superfluous element is the after-the-fact addition of Nick De Caro's string synthesizer backdrop; the real Claus Ogerman-arranged thing would have been preferable if we must have strings. *—Richard S. Ginell*

Livin' Inside Your Love / 1979 / Warner Bros. ✦✦✦
The success of *Weekend in L.A.* no doubt prompted producer Tommy LiPuma and Warner Bros. to give Benson another double album (now on one CD)—and this, like its three Warners predecessors, also went Top Ten. It is also, alas, slicker, more romantic in mood and more bound by perceptions of formula than the others, fussed over in three different studios in earnest search of another hit single (the dance-tempo cover of L.T.D.'s "Love Ballad"). Most of the touring band, including Ronnie Foster, Ralph MacDonald and Phil Upchurch, is back, and Claus Ogerman's soft symphonic touch provides most of the backdrops, with Mike Mainieri supplying the orchestra on three tracks. Even at this point, the great guitarist is still given much room to burn—the balance between instrumentals and vocals remains close—and George comes up with some tasty stuff when the rhythm section pushes him on "Nassau Day" and "You're Never Too Far From Me." Ultimately there is just enough jazz content amidst the velvet soul to keep guitar buffs interested. *—Richard S. Ginell*

Give Me the Night / 1980 / Warner Bros. ✦✦✦✦✦
This is the peak of Benson's courtship of the mass market—a superbly crafted and performed pop album with a large supporting cast—and wouldn't you know that Quincy Jones, the master catalyst, is the producer. Q's regular team, including the prolific songwriter Rod Temperton and the brilliant engineer Bruce Swedien, is in control, and Benson's voice, caught beautifully in the rich, floating sound, had never before been put to such versatile use. On "Moody's Mood," Benson really exercises his vocalese chops and proves that he is technically as fluid as just about any jazz vocalist, and he become a credible rival to Al Jarreau on the joyous title track. Benson's guitar now plays a subsidiary role—only two of the ten tracks are instrumentals—but Q has him play terrific fills behind the vocals and in the gaps, and the engineering gives his tone a variety of striking, new, full-sounding timbres. The instrumentals themselves are marvelous: "Off Broadway" is a kick-driving, danceable track and Ivan Lins' "Dinorah, Dinorah" grows increasively seductive with each play. Benson should have worked with Quincy Jones from this point on, but this would be their only album together. *—Richard S. Ginell*

In Your Eyes / 1983 / Warner Bros. ✦✦
In search of more platinum, Benson turns to one-time Atlantic Records ace producer Arif Mardin for support. Yet Mardin's best days seemed to be behind him, as this mostly routine package of period R&B backbeats, synthesizer rhythm tracks and love songs indicates. Any competent soul vocalist could have fit in comfortably here. For jazz fans, Benson's albums at this point become a search for buried treasure, for his guitar time is extremely limited. But when you do encounter a Benson solo, hang on tight. "Love Will Come Again," otherwise a routine soul bumper, concludes with a magnificent solo in octaves that Wes Montgomery would have envied, breathtaking in its economy and swing. Also, check out the instrumental "In Search of a Dream" for proof that George could still burn. *—Richard S. Ginell*

20/20 / 1984 / Warner Bros. ✦✦
George Benson certainly is a good soul vocalist, fervently turning every phrase as if he meant every lovelorn syllable. Here, though, he is shackled by stale pop/soul sentiments and one hack arrangement after another, assembled in no less than 17 studios! Russ Titelman, who shows only a flickering awareness of George's huge talent, is the producer, spelled twice by the even more commercial Michael Masser. The only bright spots are the tense high-tech title track and—surprise—an elegant Basie-like treatment of "Beyond the Sea," and with several jazz luminaries in the all-star band and Frank Foster and Ralph Burns handling the chart. There is only one instrumental, "Stand Up," and it ain't much. *—Richard S. Ginell*

While the City Sleeps / 1986 / Warner Bros. ✦✦

Collaboration / 1987 / Warner Bros. ✦✦✦

Twice the Love / 1988 / Warner Bros. ✦✦

Tenderly / 1989 / Warner Bros. ✦✦✦✦✦

Big Boss Band / 1990 / Warner Bros. ✦✦✦✦
This project had its genesis back in 1983 with a Benson promise to Count Basie that he would record an album in his style, a promise partially fulfilled the following year with *20/20*'s "Beyond the Sea." Focusing on standards that steer commendably clear from tunes normally associated with Basie, Benson takes on the dual challenge of big band singer and lead guitarist and succeeds with authority in both roles. The robust playing of the Basie band under Frank Foster poses absolutely no problems for Benson's muscular guitar, for he punches out the notes and octaves in irresistibly swinging fashion (for prime mature Benson, check out "Basie's Bag"). As a vocalist, he sounds solid and debonair, blending well with Basie vocalist Carmen Bradford on "How Do You Keep the Music Playing." There are two deviations from the format, though. "Baby Workout" starts out as an electronic dance number, augmented by horns, that harkens back to his run of routine '80s albums. The sole Robert Farnon-arranged track, a lush orchestral treatment of "Portrait of Jennie" recorded in London, was salvaged from an aborted project that was promised back in 1988. Clearly Benson had wrestled control of his music from the accountants, and though the direction is conservative, it makes better use of his talents. *—Richard S. Ginell*

● **The George Benson Anthology** / Sep. 19, 2000 / Rhino ✦✦✦✦✦
George Benson's two-disc *Anthology* from Rhino ultimately manages to encapsulate Benson's career. These 32 tracks not only highlight the obligatory vocal pop hits "Turn Your Love Around," "Give Me the Night," and "On Broadway," but dish out a heavy dose of his early jazz recordings that followed in the footsteps of Wes Montgomery, and his many appearances throughout the years with Brother Jack McDuff, Lonnie Smith, Hubert Laws, Aretha Franklin, Jimmy Smith, Earl Klugh, and the Count Basie Orchestra. If you're only accustomed to Benson's pop/jazz crossover work, check out this definitive overview. *—Al Campbell*

Brook Benton (Benjamin Franklin Peay)

b. Sep. 19, 1931, Camden, SC, **d.** Apr. 9, 1988, New York, NY
Vocals / R&B, Soul
Silky smooth: that was Brook Benton's byword from his first record to his very last, as the singer parlayed his rich baritone pipes into seven number one R&B hits and eight Top Ten items. Stints on the gospel circuit preceded Benton's first secular session for OKeh in 1953, but his career didn't begin to take off until he teamed with writer/producer Clyde Otis. Benton co-wrote and sang hundreds of demos for other artists before frequent collaborator Otis signed his friend to Mercury; together they pioneered a lush, violin-studded variation on the standard R&B sound, which beautifully showcased Benton's intimate vocals.

Benton crashed the top spot on the R&B charts in early 1959 with his moving "It's Just a Matter of Time," then rapidly encored with three more R&B chart-toppers: "Thank You Pretty Baby," "So Many Ways," and "Kiddio." Pairing with Mercury labelmate Dinah Washington, their delightful repartee on "Baby (You've Got What It Takes)" and "A Rockin' Good Way" paced the R&B lists in 1960.

The early '60s were a prolific period for Benton, but he left Mercury a few years later and bounced between labels before reemerging with the atmospheric Tony Joe White ballad "Rainy Night in Georgia" on Cotillion in 1970. Benton later made a halfhearted attempt to cash in on the disco craze, but his hitmaking reign was at an end long before his death in 1988. *—Bill Dahl*

Brook Benton / 1959 / Staryday ✦✦✦

It's Just a Matter of Time / 1959 / Mercury ✦✦✦✦✦

Songs I Love to Sing / 1960 / Mercury ✦✦✦✦✦
Songs I Love to Sing by Brook Benton is a gorgeous array of 12 standards as interpreted by Benton and his collaborator, Clyde Otis. He does not sound like the Benton of his last hit, "Rainy Night in Georgia"; rather, the singer goes to the place where Nat King Cole reigned supreme. He sounds unbelievably like Cole on some of these tunes, the phrasing and vocal texture so similar it is amazing, perfectly surrounded by superb orchestration. The Rube Bloom/Johnny Mercer classic that charted for Glenn Miller two decades before this rendition, "Fools Rush In (Where Angels Fear to Tread)," went Top 25 in 1960 from *Songs I Love to Sing* and is indicative of the lush sounds found on this wonderful disc. Great singers from every era always have the urge to emulate their idols; Rod Stewart sprinkled his favorite songs over various albums, culminating in his 2002 concept disc *It Had to Be You... The Great American Songbook*. Like Stewart, Brook Benton was a singer/songwriter, though he was in a genre where the Frank Sinatra and Johnny Mathis types let others write the tunes they would bring to life. In this setting, Benton hits a home run; these recordings are a stunning display of his vocal prowess and understanding of the material. "September Song" should have been licensed for one of the Kurt Weil tribute albums, a decidedly different version than what Lou Reed uncovered for the *Lost in the Stars: The Music of Kurt Weil* '80s compilation. The uncredited and worthwhile liner notes on an LP jacket which has the singer leaning on a large gold harp give some insight;

Benton got the idea for this collection while convalescing in the hospital. Clyde Otis supervised the sessions and the orchestration, and it is all very beautiful, from the Gershwins' "They Can't Take That Away from Me" to Peggy Lee's "I Don't Know Enough About You." The album concludes with the hit "Fools Rush In (Where Angels Fear to Tread)," which Rick Nelson brought to the Top 15 three years after this, though there's no comparison whatsoever—Benton's rendition is classic, as is this very special record. *—Joe Viglione*

The Boll Weevil Song / 1961 / Mercury ✦✦✦

Singing the Blues / 1962 / Mercury ✦✦✦

Anthology / 1986 / Rhino ✦✦✦✦✦

Rhino's Brook Benton *Anthology* is a 23-track collection that hits all of the high points, not only including songs from his tenure with Mercury—"It's Just a Matter of Time," "So Many Ways," "Kiddio," "Baby (You've Got What It Takes)," "A Rockin' Good Way (To Mess Around and Fall in Love)," "The Boll Weevil Song," "Hotel Happiness"—but also his later hits on Cotillion Records, including "Rainy Night in Georgia." It's the only collection that covers such a wide range of material—the terrific *40 Greatest Hits* only features his Mercury recordings, which admittedly are his best work—and thereby gives a good overview of his entire career. *—Stephen Thomas Erlewine*

20 Golden Hits / 1986 / Deluxe ✦✦✦

40 Greatest Hits / 1989 / Mercury ✦✦✦✦✦

40 Greatest Hits is one of the most complete CD anthologies of Brook Benton's Mercury hits. The two-disc set includes every one of Benton's Top 100 pop hits, except for a Christmas single and a minor spoken-word hit. Everything else, including his two rock-oriented duets with Dinah Washington and smash hit "The Boll Weevil Song," is here. Benton's smooth Nat King Cole-influenced vocals are very white-sounding at times, but he was a pioneer in hiring black string players for his sessions, and his eclectic choices of material show that he was an artist with broad tastes and exceptional talent. His range is remarkable, spanning gospel, pop, country, rock & roll, and easy listening balladry, and his recordings were often crisply produced in the Nashville Sound-style by Shelby Singleton. Colin Escott wrote the liner notes for this package, which concludes with Benton's last major hit, "Rainy Night in Georgia." A cross-licensed collection could conceivably round up his remaining minor hits and be marginally more complete, but *40 Greatest Hits* is the ideal summary of Benton's peak years on the chart. *—Greg Adams*

This Is Brook Benton / 1989 / RCA ✦✦✦

Brook Benton recorded almost all of his hits for Mercury Records between 1959 and 1964. He then signed to RCA Victor, apparently with the intention of moving from the singles charts to the LP charts and becoming what they used to call an "all-around entertainer." At least, that's the impression you get from this 20-track, 55-minute compilation of Benton's 1965-1966 recordings for RCA. Backed by a full orchestra, Benton essays a set of pop standards—"Call Me Irresponsible," "A Nightingale Sang in Berkeley Square," "Unforgettable"—in what seems to be his bid to join the ranks of Nat King Cole and Billy Eckstine. (He really pulls out the stops trying to top Cole's definitive reading of "Unforgettable.") Benton acquits himself adequately, but his R&B material is preferable. This set contains only one song from the Benton-Clyde Otis songwriting partnership, the countryish "Mother Nature, Father Time," and, not coincidentally, that's the only singles chart entry to be found here, too. *—William Ruhlmann*

● **Endlessly: The Best of Brook Benton** / Jun. 16, 1998 / Rhino ✦✦✦✦✦

Twelve years after they released *Anthology*, arguably the definitive career-spanning Brook Benton collection, Rhino adapted the compilation for CD, releasing *Endlessly: The Best of Brook Benton*. *Endlessly* features three tracks less than *Anthology*, yet it doesn't suffer—it remains a nearly flawless overview of Benton's career, featuring all of his big hits plus many terrific lesser-known singles. Every one of his great singles—from "It's Just a Matter of Time," "Baby (You've Got What It Takes)," and "Kiddio" to "The Boll Weevil Song" and "Rainy Night in Georgia"—are here, in a more concise and accessible form than Mercury's double-disc *40 Greatest Hits*. That double-disc set remains an ideal choice for collectors, but less dedicated fans will find *Endlessly* to be essential. *—Stephen Thomas Erlewine*

The Essential Vik and RCA Victor Recordings / Jan. 30, 2001 / Taragon ✦✦✦

Brook Benton's *Essential Vik and RCA Victor Recordings* collects some of his best moments from his work on both of those labels, including "Break Her Heart," "If You Only Knew," "Your Love Alone," and "Only Your Love." Much of the collection dates to the mid-'60s, and tracks such as "Mother Nature, Father Time" and "Too Much Good Lovin' (No Good for Me)" trace the evolution of Benton's smooth, lush sound during that time. Though this period of his career didn't generate as many hits as his earlier or later years, *The Essential Vik and RCA Victor Recordings* proves that this era is just as enjoyable as his more famous work. *—Heather Phares*

Bert Berns

b. Nov. 8, 1929, New York, NY, **d.** Dec. 31, 1967, New York, NY

Producer, Arranger, Songwriter / Brill Building Pop, British Invasion, Soul

Bert Berns was one of the great rock and soul songwriters of the 1960s as well as a producer of note. He worked in the studio with the Drifters, Ben E. King, the Isley Brothers, and Solomon Burke. He wrote or co-wrote a raft of classics, including "Twist and Shout," the Drifters' "I Don't Want to Go on Without You," Burke's "Cry to Me" and "Everybody Needs Somebody to Love," Garnet Mimms' "Cry Baby" and "It Was Easier to Hurt Her," and "Hang on Sloopy." When writing and producing for soul artists, Berns was notable for his ability to combine the best of pop and R&B. As with the compositions of his sometimes writing partner Jerry Ragovoy, there was an earthy gospel and down-home soul feel that was surprising coming from the pen of a white New Yorker.

In the mid-'60s, Berns did some work in London with Lulu and Them, including the original version of his composition "Here Comes the Night," recorded by Lulu. In a move that could have been sloppiness or just the producer and Decca Records trying to fire on all cylinders, Berns produced covers by both Lulu and Them at around the same time; Them's superior version of this classic tune became the big hit. Although lead singer Van Morrison was already writing quality material for the group, Them recorded several other decent Berns songs in the mid-'60s, including "(It Won't Hurt) Half as Much," "I Gave My Love a Diamond," and "Go on Home Baby."

In 1965, Berns founded the Bang! label, with Atlantic executives Ahmet Ertegun, Nesuhi Ertegun, and Jerry Wexler as partners; "Bang" was just an acronym of their first initials (Jerry Wexler being considered "Gerald Wexler" for this purpose). In its brief existence, Bang! was very successful: recording pop-garage rock with the teenage McCoys, getting a Bo Diddley-derived hit with "I Want Candy" by the Strangeloves, and issuing Neil Diamond's first hit singles. Bang! also had a subsidiary, Shout!, for soul material, including releases by Freddie Scott and Erma Franklin, who did the original version of "Piece of My Heart" for the label. Morrison had been at loose ends after leaving Them in 1966 and recorded his first singles, and debut solo album, in New York with Berns as producer. This quickly yielded a big hit with "Brown Eyed Girl." Berns then unexpectedly died of a heart attack on December 31, 1967. *—Richie Unterberger*

The Heart and Soul of Bert Berns / Oct. 1, 2002 / Universal ✦✦✦✦

As Berns was an interesting and important figure in 1960s soul and pop/rock, this is a good idea for a compilation: songs that were produced (with one exception) by Berns and either written or co-written by him. The song selection is good as well, including the hits "Cry Baby" (Garnet Mimms), "Everybody Needs Somebody to Love" (Solomon Burke), "Twist and Shout" (the Isley Brothers), and "Piece of My Heart" (the original version, by Erma Franklin), as well as lesser-known goodies like Hoagy Lands' "Baby Come on Home," later recorded by Led Zeppelin. What's the big flaw here, then? It's the quantity, not the quality. A mere ten songs in the CD age? There was plenty more that could have been included, even assuming that licensing issues might have made some tracks off-base. There's no, for instance, "Hang on Sloopy" (the McCoys) or "Here Comes the Night" (Them). Nor are a bunch of interesting lesser-known, Berns-penned tracks by the likes of Mimms, Burke, and the Drifters represented. What's on the disc is good-to-great early- to mid-'60s music by a writer and producer who was more adept than almost anyone at combining pop with soul. But it just leaves you hungry for more instead of satisfying as much as it should. *—Richie Unterberger*

Chuck Berry

b. Oct. 18, 1926, St. Louis, MO

Vocals, Songwriter, Guitar / Rock & Roll

Of all the early breakthrough rock & roll artists, none is more important to the development of the music than Chuck Berry. He is its greatest songwriter, the main shaper of its instrumental voice, one of its greatest guitarists, and one of its greatest performers. Quite simply, without him, there would be no Beatles, Rolling Stones, Beach Boys, Bob Dylan, nor a myriad others. There would be no standard "Chuck Berry guitar intro," the instrument's clarion call to get the joint rockin' in any setting. The clippety-clop rhythms of rockabilly would not have been mainstreamed into the now standard 4/4 rock & roll beat. There would be no obsessive wordplay by modern-day tunesmiths; in fact, the whole history (and artistic level) of rock & roll songwriting would have been much poorer without him. Like Brian Wilson said, he wrote "all of the great songs and came up with all the rock & roll beats." Those who do not claim him as a seminal influence or profess a liking for his music and showmanship show their ignorance of rock's development as well as his place as the music's first great creator. Elvis may have fueled rock & roll's imagery, but Chuck Berry was its heartbeat and original mindset.

He was born Charles Edward Anderson Berry to a large family in St. Louis. A bright pupil, Berry developed a love for poetry and hard blues early on, winning a high school talent contest with a guitar-and-vocal rendition of Jay McShann's big band number, "Confessin' the Blues." With some local tutelage from the neighborhood barber, Berry progressed from a four-string tenor guitar up to an official six-string model and was soon working the local East St. Louis club scene, sitting in everywhere he could. He quickly found out that black audiences liked a wide variety of music and set himself to the task of being able to reproduce as much of it as possible. What he found they *really* liked—besides the blues and Nat King Cole tunes—was the sight and sound of a black man playing white hillbilly music, and Berry's showmanlike flair, coupled with his seemingly inexhaustible supply of fresh verses to old favorites, quickly made him a name on the circuit. In 1954, he ended up taking over pianist Johnny Johnson's small combo and a residency at the Cosmopolitan Club soon made the Chuck Berry Trio the top attraction in the black community, with Ike Turner's Kings of Rhythm their only real competition.

But Berry had bigger ideas; he yearned to make records, and a trip to Chicago netted a two-minute conversation with his idol Muddy Waters, who encouraged him to approach Chess Records. Upon listening to Berry's homemade demo tape, label president Leonard Chess professed a liking for a hillbilly tune on it named "Ida Red" and quickly scheduled a session for May 21, 1955. During the session the title was changed to "Maybellene" and rock & roll history was born. Although the record only made it to the mid-20s on the *Billboard* pop chart, its overall influence was massive and groundbreaking in its scope. Here was finally a black rock & roll record with across-the-board appeal, embraced by white teenagers and Southern hillbilly musicians (a young Elvis Presley, still a full year from national stardom, quickly added it to his stage show), which for once couldn't be successfully covered by a pop singer like Snooky Lanson on Your Hit Parade. Part of the secret to its originality was Berry's blazing 24-bar guitar solo in the middle of it, the imaginative rhyme schemes in the lyrics, and the sheer thump of the record, all signaling that rock & roll had arrived and it was no fad. Helping to put the record over to a white teenage audience was the highly influential New York DJ Alan Freed, who had been given part of the writers' credit by Chess in return for his spins and plugs. But to his credit, Freed was also the first white DJ/promoter to consistently use Berry on his rock & roll stage show extravaganzas at the Brooklyn Fox and Paramount theaters (playing to predominately white audiences); and when Hollywood came calling a year or so later, also made sure that Chuck appeared with him in *Rock! Rock! Rock!*, *Go, Johnny, Go!*, and *Mister Rock'n'Roll*. Within a years' time, Chuck had gone from a local St. Louis blues picker making 15 dollars a night to an overnight sensation commanding over a hundred times that, arriving at the dawn of a new strain of popular music called rock & roll.

The hits started coming thick and fast over the next few years, every one of them about to become a classic of the genre: "Roll Over Beethoven," "Thirty Days," "Too Much Monkey Business," "Brown Eyed Handsome Man," "You Can't Catch Me," "School Day," "Carol," "Back in the U.S.A.," "Little Queenie," "Memphis, Tennessee," "Johnny B. Goode," and the tune that defined the moment perfectly, "Rock & Roll Music." Berry was not only in constant demand, touring the country on mixed package shows and appearing on television and in movies, but smart enough to know exactly what to do with the spoils of a suddenly successful show business career. He started investing heavily in St. Louis area real estate and, ever one to push the envelope, opened up a racially mixed nightspot called the Club Bandstand in 1958 to the consternation of uptight locals. *These* were not the plans of your average R&B singers who contented themselves with a wardrobe of flashy suits, a new Cadillac, and the nicest house in the black section. Berry was smart with plenty of business savvy and was already making plans to open an amusement park in nearby Wentzville. When the St. Louis hierarchy found out that an underage hat-check girl Berry hired had also set up shop as a prostitute at a nearby hotel, trouble came down on Berry like a sledgehammer on a fly. Charged with transporting a minor over state lines (the Mann Act), Berry endured two trials and was sentenced to federal prison for two years as a result.

He emerged from prison a moody, embittered man. But two very important things had happened in his absence. First, British teenagers had discovered his music and were making his old songs hits all over again. Second, and perhaps most important, America had discovered the Beatles and the Rolling Stones, both of whom based their music on Berry's style, with the Stones' early albums looking like a Berry song list. Rather than being resigned to the has-been circuit, Berry found himself in the midst of a worldwide beat boom with his music as the centerpiece. He came back with a clutch of hits ("Nadine," "No Particular Place to Go," "You Never Can Tell"), toured Britain in triumph, and appeared on the big screen with his British disciples in the groundbreaking *T.A.M.I. Show* in 1964. Berry had moved with the times and found a new audience in the bargain and when the cries of "yeah-yeah-yeah" were replaced with peace signs, Berry altered his live act to include a passel of slow blues and quickly became a fixture on the festival and hippie ballroom circuit. After a disastrous stint with Mercury Records, he returned to Chess in the early '70s and scored his last hit with a live version of the salacious nursery rhyme, "My Ding-a-Ling," yielding Berry his first official gold record. By decade's end, he was as in demand as ever, working every oldies revival show, TV special, and festival that was thrown his way. But once again, troubles with the law reared their ugly head and 1979 saw Berry headed back to prison, this time for income tax evasion. Upon release this time, the creative days of Chuck Berry seemed to have come to an end. He appeared as himself in the Alan Freed bio-pic, *American Hot Wax*, and was inducted into the Rock and Roll Hall of Fame, but steadfastly refused to record any new material or even issue a live album. His live performances became increasingly erratic, with Berry working with terrible backup bands and turning in sloppy, out-of-tune performances that did much to tarnish his reputation with younger fans and oldtimers alike.

In 1987, he published his first book, *Chuck Berry: The Autobiography*, and the same year saw the film release of what will likely be his lasting legacy, the rockumentary *Hail! Hail! Rock 'N' Roll*, which included live footage from a 60th-birthday concert with Keith Richards as musical director and the usual bevy of superstars coming out for guest turns. But for all of his off-stage exploits and seemingly ongoing troubles with the law, Chuck Berry remains the epitome of rock & roll, and his music will endure long after his private escapades have faded from memory. Because when it comes down to his music, perhaps John Lennon said it best, "If you were going to give rock & roll another name, you might call it 'Chuck Berry'." *—Cub Koda*

After School Session / 1958 / Chess ♦♦♦♦♦

While Chuck Berry's first album, *After School Session*, featured only one hit single, the Top Ten "School Day," several of the songs became rock & roll standards, including "Too Much Monkey Business," "No Money Down," and "Brown Eyed Handsome Man." *After School Session* also featured a couple of stylistic variations, including the calypso-flavored "Havana Moon" and the straight blues of "Wee Wee Hours." *—Stephen Thomas Erlewine*

One Dozen Berrys / 1958 / Chess ♦♦♦♦♦

Chuck Berry's second album is ever so slightly more sophisticated than its predecessor. Although *One Dozen Berrys* is hooked around a pair of hit singles, "Sweet Little Sixteen" and "Rock & Roll Music," most of what's here doesn't really sound too much like either of those songs—rather, the other ten tracks each constitute a close-up look at some individual component of the types of music that goes into brewing up the Chuck Berry sound. Thus, the slow instrumental "Blue Feeling" is a look at the blues sound that Berry initially proposed to bring to Chess Records; "How You've Changed" presents him in a slow ballad, singing in a manner closer to Nat King Cole than to any rock & roller of the era; and "Lajaunda" shows off his love of Latin music. "Rocking at the Philharmonic" is a rippling guitar/piano workout, a compendium of the sounds that lay beneath those hit singles, and a killer showcase not only for Berry, but also for Lafayette Leake at the ivories, and also a decent showcase for Willie Dixon's bass playing. "Oh Baby Doll" is a return to the beat of "Maybellene," this time carrying a lyric that's more sensual (in a bluesy sense) than rollicking fun, though it comes out that way amid the pounding beat and Berry's crunchy, angular guitar solo. "Guitar Boogie" is yet another guitar instrumental, one of four on this album, leading one to wonder if he was running short of first-rate lyrics in mid-1957, amid his frantic pace of recording and touring—no matter, for the piece is a killer track, a pumping, soaring working out for Berry's guitar that had some of the most impressive pyrotechnics that one was likely to hear in 1957; what's more, the track was good enough to form the template for Jeff Beck's more ornate adaptation, "Jeff's Boogie," from the 1966 album *Roger the Engineer* (aka *The Yardbirds* aka *Over Under Sideways Down*). The best of the album's tracks is easily "Reelin' & Rockin'," which is also just about the dirtiest song that Berry released in all of the 1950s (and for many years after that), essentially a blues-boogie recasting, on a more overt level, of the extended feats of sexual intercourse alluded to in Bill Haley's "Rock Around the Clock." The one totally weird track here is "Low Feeling," which is nothing but "Blue Feeling" doctored in the studio by Leonard and Phil Chess, slowed down to half speed and edited to create a 12th track—doing that to the original was bad enough, but sticking it on the same LP with the original was downright bizarre. And the album's closer, "It Don't Take But a Few Minutes," is a reminder of just how much Berry owed to country music for his sound, and explains, to anyone coming in late, how he could have been mistaken for a white hillbilly in those early days, based on the sound of this song and "Maybelene." *—Bruce Eder*

☆ **Chuck Berry Is on Top** / 1959 / Chess ♦♦♦♦♦

If you had to sweat all of Chuck Berry's early albums on Chess (and some, but not all, of his subsequent greatest-hits packages), this would be the one to own. The song lineup is exemplary, cobbling together classics like "Maybellene," "Carol," "Sweet Little Rock & Roller," "Little Queenie," "Roll Over Beethoven," "Around and Around," "Johnny B. Goode" and "Almost Grown." With the addition of the Latin-flavored "Hey Pedro," the steel guitar workout "Blues for Hawaiians," "Anthony Boy" and "Jo Jo Gunne," this serves as almost a mini-greatest hits package in and of itself. While this may be merely a collection of singles and album ballast (as were most rock & roll LPs of the 1950s and early '60s), it ends up being the most perfectly realized of Chuck Berry's career. *—Cub Koda*

Rockin' at the Hops / 1960 / Chess ♦♦♦

New Juke Box Hits / 1961 / Chess ♦♦♦

Chuck Berry's fifth Chess Records album, *New Juke Box Hits*, was recorded and released in the midst of the legal difficulties that would put him in jail the following year. That distraction seems to have kept him from composing top-flight material, while the attendant publicity adversely affected his record sales, such that the album contained no hits. The included single was "I'm Talking About You," later successfully recorded by the Rolling Stones, and the album also contained "The Thirteen Question Method" and "Don't You Lie to Me," worthy minor entries in the Berry canon. Elsewhere, Berry filled out the record covering others' hits—Nat King Cole's "Route 66," B.B. King's "Sweet Sixteen," Little Richard's "Rip It Up." The result is a good rock & roll set, but not in the same league with Berry's earlier albums. *— William Ruhlmann*

☆ **St. Louis to Liverpool** / 1964 / Chess ♦♦♦♦♦

This album puts the lie to the popular myth that Chuck Berry's music started to fade away around the same time that the Beatles, the Rolling Stones, et al. emerged covering his stuff. His songwriting is as strong here as ever—side one is packed with now-familiar fare like "Little Marie" (a sequel to "Memphis, Tennessee"), "No Particular Place to Go," "Promised Land," and "You Never Can Tell," but even filler tracks like "Our Little Rendezvous" and "You Two" are among Berry's better album numbers, the latter showing off the slightly softer pop/R&B side to his music that many listeners forget about. Side two includes a bunch of tracks, including the hard-rocking "Go Bobby Soxer" and the even better "Brenda Lee," the slow blues "Things I Used to Do" (with a killer guitar break), and the instrumentals "Liverpool Drive" and "Night Beat," one fast and the other slow, that never get reissued or compiled anywhere. The sound on the 1984 reissue LP is excellent, and it's a lot easier to find than an original album. *—Bruce Eder*

Chuck Berry's Golden Decade / 1967 / Chess ♦♦♦♦♦

Chuck Berry's Golden Hits / 1967 / Mercury ♦

Berry's first release for Mercury Records was this collection of re-recordings—done at a faster tempo, and in stereo—of his Chess hits. The songs are perfectly fine, but that's the best that can be said for this release. The playing, though perfectly competent, lacks the rough roadhouse ambience of the originals, and the stereo sound is an unnecessary distraction. *—Bruce Eder*

The London Sessions / 1972 / Chess ♦♦♦

One-half of this album is a studio recording featuring Ian McLagan and Kenny Jones of the Faces. The other half is a live recording from the Lancaster Arts Festival in Coventry, England, featuring performances of "My Ding-a-Ling" and "Reelin' and Rockin'" that, in edited form, became the first hit singles for Chuck Berry in many years. ("My Ding-a-Ling" went gold and hit number 1.) This gold-selling, Top Ten album represents Berry's commercial, if not artistic, peak. *— William Ruhlmann*

★ **The Great Twenty-Eight** / 1982 / Chess ♦♦♦♦♦

This is the place to start listening to Chuck Berry. *The Great Twenty-Eight* was a two-LP, single CD compilation that emerged during the early '80s, amid a brief period in which the Chess catalog was in the hands of the Sugar Hill label, a disco-oriented outfit that later lost the catalog to MCA. It has proved to be one of the most enduring of all compilations of Berry's work. Up until the release of this disc, every attempt at a compilation had either been too sketchy (the 1964 *Greatest Hits* album on Chess) or too demanding for the casual listener (the three *Golden Decade* double-LP sets), and this was the first set to find a happy medium between convenience and thoroughness. Veteran listeners will love this CD even if they learn little from it, while neophytes will want to play it to death. All of the cuts come from Berry's first nine years in music, including all of the major singles as well as relatively minor hits such as "Come On" (which was more significant in the history of rock & roll in its cover version performed by the Rolling Stones as their debut release). The sound is decent throughout (surprisingly, except for "Come On," which has some considerable noise), although it is considerably outclassed by the most recent round of remasterings. In the decades since its release, there have been more comprehensive collections of Berry's work, but this is the best single disc, if one can overlook the relatively lo-fi digital sound. *—Bruce Eder*

Rock 'n' Roll Rarities / 1986 / Chess ♦♦♦♦♦
On this follow-up to *The Great Twenty-Eight*, the songs are familiar, but the versions are not. Delving into the Chess Records archives, producer Steve Hoffman has come up with 20 tracks, many in unreleased or unusual versions. Some are demos, some are stereo recordings of songs usually heard in mono. Hoffman has remixed many of them, bringing up the '50s and '60s sound quality to near-'80s standard. Start with *The Great Twenty-Eight*, but come to this collection for interesting new ways to hear the old Berry favorites. *—William Ruhlmann*

More Rock & Roll Rarities From the Golden Era of Chess Records / Aug. 1986 / Chess ♦♦♦
This second volume of producer Steve Hoffman's discoveries in the Chess Records vaults features some less-prominent Chuck Berry tunes, again in the form of demos, unreleased alternate takes, and stereo remixes. Listeners are getting into collector territory here, but there are still some enjoyable examples of the Berry repertoire. *—William Ruhlmann*

Hail! Hail! Rock 'N' Roll / 1987 / MCA ♦♦♦
This is the soundtrack to a documentary film chronicling a concert held to celebrate Chuck Berry's 60th birthday. The band was led by Keith Richards and featured Berry's regular pianist, Johnnie Johnson, Richards' regular pianist, Chuck Leavell, Rolling Stones sax player Bobby Keys, bassist Joey Spampinato from NRBQ, and drummer Steve Jordan from Richards' solo band. The guests included Robert Cray, Linda Ronstadt, Eric Clapton, Julian Lennon, and Etta James. Berry was ragged-voiced but enthusiastic, the band had spirit, and the guests, even if they were sometimes unlikely, were sincere. The best way to hear Berry's music is to obtain the original recordings, of course, but as a souvenir of the Taylor Hackford film, this is an enjoyable romp through the catalog. *—William Ruhlmann*

☆ **The Chess Box** / 1988 / Chess ♦♦♦♦♦
Over the course of three compact discs, *The Chess Box* contains most of the highlights from Chuck Berry's career, including all of the hit singles. In addition to the familiar items, which are all included here, there are numerous tracks that are lesser-known but equally as good. That's particularly true on the stellar first two discs, where album tracks, B-sides, and forgotten singles like "Downbound Train," "Drifting Heart," "Havana Moon," "Betty Jean," "Bye Bye Johnny," "Down the Road a Piece," and "The Thirteen Question Method" get equal space with "Maybellene," "Thirty Days," "No Money Down," "Roll Over Beethoven," "Too Much Monkey Business," "Brown Eyed Handsome Man," "School Day," "Rock & Roll Music," "Sweet Little Sixteen," "Johnny B. Goode," and "Carol." Some serious fans, however, also found disc one, and especially the earlier songs on that disc, to be very controversial; part of the intrinsic nature of Berry's music was the sheer noisiness of the songs—tracks like "Maybellene," "Thirty Days," "You Can't Catch Me," and "Brown Eyed Handsome Man" insinuated themselves into listeners' consciousness over the radio and on the jukebox with their sheer raucous, in-your-face sound (frequently near overload). But at the time *The Chess Box* was done, the philosophy about CD mastering was to clean up the noise in original recordings whenever it was too pronounced, lest the "hot" digital sound make the track too harsh. [Note: this "problem" especially afflicted "Layla" by Derek & the Dominos, so much so that the producers of the Clapton box remixed the song.] Thus, the first 15 or so tracks on the first disc of *The Chess Box* may sound too "clean," lacking some of the raw edge from their vinyl editions. On the plus side, the detail revealed—every note, and even the action on the guitar on the opening of "Roll Over Beethoven"—is always interesting, and occasionally fascinating, and it is difficult to complain too loudly about hearing Johnnie Johnson's or Lafayette Leake's piano, or Willie Dixon's upright bass in such sharp relief. Additionally, for many years this set had the only undistorted CD version of "Come On"—a relatively minor Berry song, but one that provided the Rolling Stones with their debut release—that you could find, but potential purchasers should also be aware of the compromise in the sound. That caveat aside, the programming manages to get in most of the best album cuts, including tracks like Berry's hot cover of "House of Blue Lights" and the "Memphis Tennessee" "sequel" "Little Marie," though not quite enough material from 1964-1965. And toward the end of the set, the quality of the material begins to sag a bit, but there are still forgotten gems like "Tulane" that prove Berry's songwriting hadn't completely dried up. The now out of print *Great Twenty-Eight* collection remains the definitive single CD hits collection, and the audio quality on MCA's two-CD *Anthology*, released a dozen years later, is superior, but *The Chess Box* offers a flawed but near essential overview of his work for any serious fan, either of Chuck Berry or rock & roll. *—Bruce Eder*

Missing Berries / Jul. 1990 / Chess ♦♦♦
The third and final collection of Chuck Berry rarities from the Chess Records vaults, *Missing Berries* concentrates on Berry's blues recordings, which were never quite as captivating as his rock & roll, yet they're fascinating for devoted fans. *—Stephen Thomas Erlewine*

☆ **His Best, Vol. 1** / Mar. 25, 1997 / Chess ♦♦♦♦♦
Strictly focusing on his single tracks in a chronological manner, this first of two volumes in MCA's Chess 50th Anniversary collection hits all the high spots of Chuck's career up to 1958. It also serves as the first compilation to really showcase Berry's development as a songwriter over the first three years of his massive crossover success, including the seldom-anthologized "Downbound Train" (perhaps the darkest and most demonic ditty he ever recorded) juxtaposed against his car songs ("Maybellene," "You Can't Catch Me"), his calculated and carefully crafted instant classics for the 1950s teenage market ("Reelin' and Rockin'," "Sweet Little Sixteen," "School Day") and his celebrations of the music itself ("Rock and Roll Music," "Johnny B. Goode," "Roll Over Beethoven"). There's a ton of great music here (with a second companion volume to complete the picture) and for a big chunk of what makes Chuck Berry perhaps rock & roll's original triple-threat package (singer, songwriter, and its first guitar hero), there's much here to tip the scales in its favor to recommend this volume as a first-time purchase. [Note: This collection and its companion volume now take the place of the single disc *The Great Twenty Eight*, which is now out of print.] *—Cub Koda*

☆ **His Best, Vol. 2** / May 20, 1997 / Chess ♦♦♦♦♦
Picking up where the first volume left off, *His Best, Vol. 2* runs through Chuck Berry's best-known singles in 1958 with "Sweet Little Rock and Roller" and runs through 1972, when he inexplicably had his first number one record with "My Ding-a-Ling." In addition to hits like "Let It Rock," "Little Queenie," "Almost Grown," "Nadine," "No Particular Place to Go," "You Never Can Tell," and "Promised Land," there are lesser-known gems like "Jo Jo Gunne," making it more than just a rote greatest-hits collection. No matter how good the two-part *His Best* series is—and for fans that don't want to spring for *The Chess Box*, it's the best way to assemble a reasonably comprehensive Chuck collection—it's still a shame that Chess decided to delete the flawless single-disc compilation *The Great Twenty-Eight* in favor of this series. *—Stephen Thomas Erlewine*

The Latest & the Greatest/You Never Can Tell / 1998 / BGO ♦♦♦♦
The value of this two-on-one CD from England's Beat Goes On Records is greater than the sum of its parts—most of the important tracks here can be found on either the Chuck Berry box or one of the individual MCA-Chess CDs, but they sound infinitely better here, in new late-'90s transfers, than they do on MCA's mid-'80s digital editions. And "good" in this case means they're clean but mean, crisp but raunchy, not like the over-cleaned up versions off of the Chess Box's first disc. The notes are a bit vague as far as the origins of the two LPs are concerned—they were patchwork creations from recent singles and old U.S. album tracks, done specifically for the British market by Pye Records—but the sound makes up for those shortcomings. *—Bruce Eder*

★ **Anthology** / Jun. 27, 2000 / Chess ♦♦♦♦♦
Falling squarely between the 71-track triple-disc *Chess Box* and numerous single-album distillations of Chuck Berry's hits, most notably *The Great Twenty-Eight*, is this 2000-released, chronologically compiled double-disc set. Its 50 tunes include all of Berry's seminal Chess hits plus key album tracks like "Beautiful Delilah," "Jo Jo Gunne," and "Jaguar & Thunderbird" that were influential but never cracked the charts. The 20-page booklet features a fascinating, extensive essay that provides crucial insights into Berry's work as well as rare pictures and track-by-track personnel listing. Since virtually all of Berry's essential work was done for the Chess label, now part of the Universal empire, there's no reason to decry the lack of anything from Berry's Mercury years, even though those tracks are now owned by the same company and could have been included, especially tacked onto disc two that times out at a relatively conservative 64 minutes. But with a lineup like this, who's complaining? Berry is the undisputed father of rock & roll and his music, much of it blues based and in a few cases like "Havana Moon" even Caribbean inspired, remains timeless as well as inspirational decades after it was recorded. The joys of discovering forgotten, relatively obscure cuts like "Come On" or "I'm Talking About You," both of which are easily on par with any of his more popular hits, is one of life's little bonuses. Berry's lyrics remain intriguingly descriptive, and the remastered sound brings these songs alive with every instrument, especially Willie Dixon's dynamic, jazzy stand-up bass clearly defined. The savvy track selection makes this a better, more consistent listen than the bulky box and stands as the best introduction to one of the most significant pop musicians of 20th century music and the single most important rock & roller ever. *—Hal Horowitz*

Richard Berry

b. Apr. 11, 1935, Extension, LA, **d.** Jan. 23, 1997
Vocals, Keyboards / R&B, Rock & Roll
If for no other reason than that he was the original writer and performer of "Louie Louie" (itself based on "El Loca Cha Cha" by Rene Touzet), Richard Berry holds a permanent place of honor in the history of rock & roll. Beyond that, though, Berry was an important, if secondary, figure of the early- and mid-'50s Los Angeles R&B scene. As a teenager with the Flairs and as a solo act, Berry recorded quite a few singles that demonstrated his versatility with ballads, novelty songs, and even Little Richard-styled numbers. His facility with deep-voiced comic material was a clear forerunner of the Coasters, and in fact he was the uncredited lead singer on Leiber & Stoller's "Riot in Cell Block #9," recorded by the Robins (later to mutate into the Coasters). He took another uncredited vocal as Ella James' deep-voiced sparring partner on "Roll With Me, Henry," one of the biggest R&B hits of the mid-'50s. Berry originally recorded "Louie Louie" in 1956; the record was a regional hit in several West Coast cities, but no more than that.

Berry's recording career petered out in the late '50s, though he remained an active performer. In the early '60s, several Northwest bands seized upon "Louie Louie" as cover material, scoring sizable regional hits; finally, in 1963 the Kingsmen broke the song nationally, reaching number two. In the decades since then, "Louie Louie" became one of the most oft-covered rock standards of all time; there probably exists well over 1,000 versions. The song was investigated by the FBI and inspired parades and campaigns to adopt it as the official song of the state of Washington. The original version ironically remains extremely difficult to find, appearing only on obscure compilations (the Berry version on Rhino's *Louie Louie* anthology is a re-recording). For Berry there was a happy ending—in the late '80s he regained the rights to his song that he had lost many years ago. *—Richie Unterberger*

Richard Berry and the Dreamers / 1963 / Crown ♦♦♦
Richard Berry sang lead on the Robins' (later the Coasters) "Riot in Cell Block #Nine." On the two standout tracks on this record, he tells the rest of that story. Berry gets into all kinds of trouble on "Next Time" as the song concludes with the judge declaring, "You're

gonna jail right now!" On "The Big Break," Berry follows up "Riot" as he and his friend Snake carry out the prison break. The remainder of this record is undistinguished doo wop, lacking Berry's sense of humor and deep-voiced rap. *—J.P. Ollio*

• **Get Out of the Car** / 1982 / Flair ✦✦✦✦✦
Twenty songs from the mid-'50s, both solo and with the Flairs. Chuck Berry wrote or co-wrote most of the tunes, which are solid if somewhat generic R&B on the verge of rock & roll, occasionally treading into doo wop territory. He's most memorable on the uptempo, comic-jiving numbers, with a sardonic and sassy tone that pointed the way for the Coasters. This doesn't have "Louie Louie" or any of the late-'50s material he recorded for the Flip label, which is available on the hard-to-find Swedish import *Louie Louie*. *—Richie Unterberger*

Daddy Daddy / 1995 / P-Vine ✦✦✦
This 23-track disc—a mixture of drags, ups, and novelties—doesn't do justice to Richard Berry's prolific career as a southern California recording artist. But it beats a blank. Berry made solo, group, and duet recordings—a whole slew of them. "Louie Louie," his most significant song, isn't represented, nor is "Have Love Will Travel." A complete package of Berry's efforts would take a multiple-disc box set. This one features solo efforts and outings with the Flairs and the Dreamers. If you didn't reside in southwest U.S.A. when these dropped, you probably never heard any of these local/regional-ish recordings. But Berry was as influential as Bo Diddley, and if Diddley's in the Rock and Roll Hall of Fame, then Berry and singers like Billy Stewart should be too. This Japanese import satisfies the hunger pains somewhat. Besides, "Daddy, Daddy," "Baby Darling," "Look out Miss James," "Get Out of the Car," and "Yama Yama, Pretty Mama" are hard to find. *—Andrew Hamilton*

Beverly & Duane

Group / Disco
Beverly Wheeler and Duane Williams were a '70s disco duo who made one self-titled album in 1979 and two R&B chart singles, "Glad I Gotcha Baby" and "Living in a World." *—William Ruhlmann*

• **Beverly & Duane** / 1978 / Ariola ✦✦✦

The Big Bopper (Jiles Perry Richardson)

b. Oct. 24, 1930, Sabine Pass, TX, **d.** Feb. 3, 1959, Clear Lake, IA
Vocals / Rock & Roll
Legendary as one of the three rock greats to die in the tragic 1959 Clear Lake, IA, plane crash that also claimed the lives of Buddy Holly and Ritchie Valens, the Big Bopper (born Jiles Perry Richardson) had just established himself as a rock hitmaker with the rollicking "Chantilly Lace." Born in the heart of Taxas, Richardson grew up in Beaumont and changed his first name to Jape. He broke into show biz as a DJ over KTRM radio, where he coined the nickname the Big Bopper. He began recording for Mercury in 1957, his animated baritone scaling pop play lists the next year with "Chantilly Lace"—easily his top seller—and the equally raucous novelty "Big Bopper's Wedding." Richardson wrote "White Lightning," a huge country hit for George Jones, and Johnny Preston's number-one smash "Running Bear." *—Bill Dahl*

Chantilly Lace / 1958 / Mercury ✦✦✦
An apparent CD reissue of the Big Bopper's 1958 LP (though, if the liner notes on Rhino's best-of are accurate, it's missing at least a couple of songs that were on the original vinyl version). The 19-track Rhino compilation has all of these songs, although *Chantilly Lace* is apt to retail for a lower price. Which begs the question: If you're enough of a collector to want some Big Bopper on CD, why settle for half as many tracks just to save a few bucks? *—Richie Unterberger*

• **Hellooo Baby!: The Best of the Big Bopper, 1954–1959** / 1989 / Rhino ✦✦✦✦✦
Hellooo Baby!: The Best of the Big Bopper, 1954-1959 is a single-CD compilation of the Big Bopper's finest, including "Chantilly Lace," "Little Red Riding Hood," and "Big Bopper's Wedding." It's wild and fun. *—Cub Koda*

Big Maybelle (Maybelle Louise Smith)

b. May 1, 1924, Jackson, TN, **d.** Jan. 23, 1972, Cleveland, OH
Vocals / New York Blues, Jump Blues, R&B, East Coast Blues
Her mountainous stature matching the sheer soulful power of her massive vocal talent, Big Maybelle was one of the premier R&B chanteuses of the 1950s. Her deep, gravelly voice was as singular as her recorded output for OKeh and Savoy, which ranged from down-in-the-alley blues to pop-slanted ballads. In 1967, she even covered ? & the Mysterians' "96 Tears" (it was her final chart appearance). Alleged drug addiction leveled the mighty belter at the premature age of 47, but Maybelle packed a lot of living into her shortened lifespan.

Born Mabel Louise Smith, the singer strolled off with top honors at a Memphis amateur contest at the precocious age of eight. Gospel music was an important element in Maybelle's intense vocal style, but the church wasn't big enough to hold her talent. In 1936, she hooked up with Memphis bandleader Dave Clark; a few years later, Maybelle toured with the International Sweethearts of Rhythm. She debuted on wax with pianist Christine Chatman's combo on Decca in 1944, before signing with Cincinnati's King Records in 1947 for three singles of her own backed by trumpeter Hot Lips Page's band.

Producer Fred Mendelsohn discovered Smith in the Queen City, re-christened her Big Maybelle, and signed her to Columbia's OKeh R&B subsidiary in 1952. Her first OKeh platter, the unusual "Gabbin' Blues" (written by tunesmith Rose Marie McCoy and arranger Leroy Kirkland) swiftly hit, climbing to the upper reaches of the R&B charts. "Way Back Home" and "My Country Man" made it a 1953 hat trick for Maybelle and OKeh. In 1955, she cut a rendition of "Whole Lot of Shakin' Goin' On" a full two years before Louisiana piano pumper Jerry Lee Lewis got his hands and feet on it. Mendelsohn soon brought her over to Herman Lubinsky's Savoy diskery, where her tender rendition of the pop chestnut "Candy" proved another solid R&B hit in 1956. Maybelle rocked harder than ever at Savoy, her "Ring Dang Dilly," "That's a Pretty Good Love," and "Tell Me Who" benefiting from blistering backing by New York's top sessioneers. Her last Savoy date in 1959 reflected the changing trends in R&B; Howard Biggs' stately arrangements encompassed four violins. Director Bert Stern immortalized her vivid blues-belting image in his documentary *Jazz on a Summer's Day*, filmed in color at the 1958 Newport Jazz Festival.

Maybelle persevered throughout the '60s, recording for Brunswick, Scepter (her "Yesterday's Kisses" found her coping admirably with the uptown soul sound), Chess, Rojac (source of "96 Tears"), and other labels. But the good years were long gone when she slipped into a diabetic coma and passed away in a Cleveland hospital in 1972. *—Bill Dahl*

The OKeh Sessions / Oct. 8, 1952-Mar. 21, 1955 / Epic ✦✦✦✦✦
A reissue of a reissue, here's the Charly version of a Columbia vintage compilation of Maybelle's best OKeh sides. It covers everything from sassy numbers like "Gabbin' Blues" and "One Monkey Don't Stop No Show" to ballads like "Ain't No Use" and "You'll Be Sorry" to the original version of the soon-to-be rock & roll classic "Whole Lot of Shakin' Going On." Superlative liner notes from Peter Guralnick put her story in perfect perspective and makes this one the collection to beat. *—Cub Koda*

Candy / May 14, 1956-Nov. 26, 1957 / Savoy Jazz ✦✦✦✦✦
The belter moved over to Newark, NJ-based Savoy midway through the decade and continued to prosper: "Candy," "Ramblin' Blues," and the intense "Blues Early, Early" rate with her finest cuts. "Ring Dang Dilly" and "Tell Me Who" rock with the seemingly effortless swing peculiar to New York's R&B scene at the time, thanks to the presence of saxists Warren Luckey and Jerome Richardson and guitarists Mickey Baker and Kenny Burrell, among others. *—Bill Dahl*

Blues, Candy and Big Maybelle / 1958 / Savoy Jazz ✦✦✦
Two vinyl albums of Maybelle's Savoy recordings on one compact disc makes for a nice 28-track retrospective of her prime work. First up is the album originally issued as *Blues, Candy and Big Maybelle*, a chunk of session work from 1956-1957, with a three-song date from 1959 to round things up. Her takes on "Rockhouse," "Ramblin' Blues," and the title track are the big tickets here. The second anthology, titled simply *Big Maybelle*, features her recordings from 1956-1959, with the balance of it leaning toward her later output for the label. A 1957 session with Kenny Burrell on guitar yields interesting stabs at "White Christmas" and "Silent Night," while a 1959 session finds her big voice framed with a string section on a great read of "Until the Real Thing Comes Along." A very underrated singer, Big Maybelle is a total delight and deserves a much wider hearing. *—Cub Koda*

Saga of the Good Life and Hard Times / 1966-1969 / Rojac ✦✦✦
A mix of soul and blues from her last sessions is sung with despair. *—Richard Pack*

The Last of Big Maybelle / 1973 / Muse ✦✦
This may be late in her career recordings, chock full of wah-wah pedals and other dated devices, but make no mistake about it, this is Big Maybelle still singing her heart out on each and every track. Moving effortlessly between rockers, R&B ballads, pop lightweights, Hank Williams country, and the blues, Big Maybelle's voice inhabits this material with a warmth and husk that most female singers today can only hint at. Not the place to start, but a good place to end up. *—Cub Koda*

• **The Complete OKeh Sessions 1952–55** / 1994 / Epic/Legacy ✦✦✦✦✦
Maybelle's entire OKeh output—26 tracks—including her three R&B chart items, "Whole Lotta Shakin' Goin' On," and the risqué slow blues "I'm Getting 'Long Alright." "Gabbin' Blues," her 1952 OKeh debut smash, is a humorous dialogue between Maybelle and gossiping rival Rosemarie McCoy, the tune's co-writer. Maybelle was no mere copyist; her sandpapery vocals stood in sharp contrast to the many interchangeable thrushes then populating the R&B world. Great support from New York session wizards such as tenor saxist Sam "The Man" Taylor and guitarist Mickey Baker throughout. *—Bill Dahl*

The Very Best of Big Maybelle: That's All / Jan. 5, 1998 / Collectables ✦✦✦
Collectables' *The Very Best of Big Maybelle: That's All* features 12 songs that she recorded for Sceptor Records in the '60s. This wasn't the most particularly distinguished period of Maybelle's career, and this collection doesn't put it in perspective, leaving out some of the best records she made for the label, including the minor hit "Yesterday's Kisses." That said, this does have its moments—enough to make it worthwhile to dedictated soul collectors willing to sort the wheat from the chaff. It just isn't a definitive collection, not even of her Scepter recordings. *—Stephen Thomas Erlewine*

Travis Biggs

Keyboards, Producer / Soul
Travis Biggs was a keyboardist who worked with Isaac Hayes during the late '70s, a period that found Hayes flirting with disco. Biggs also released two spacy, synth-driven LPs of his own during that era: 1976's *Challenge*, on *TB&C*, and 1979's *Solar Funk*, on MCA subsidiary Source. He is best remembered for the much-sampled cut "Tibetan Serenity." *—Steve Huey*

• **Challenge** / 1976 / TB&C ✦✦✦✦

Solar Funk / 1979 / MCA ✦✦✦

Edwin Birdsong

Organ, Keyboards / Funk, Fusion, Urban
An underrated organist, Edwin Birdsong worked with numerous artists in varied musical situations. His background was in gospel; Birdsong was the son of a minister and grew up in a strict fundamentalist environment. He joined the Los Angeles Community Choir, where he met such artists as Merry Clayton, Billy Preston, and D.J. Rogers, and eventually served in Vietnam. Birdsong later played in clubs in Germany, entertaining service personnel. After moving to New York, he headed a trio that played blues and jazz. Birdsong attended the Manhattan School of Music and Juilliard as a composition major.

He later played with the Youth Symphony Orchestra before signing with Polydor in 1971. He issued two albums of funk, rock, fusion, and jazz, *What It Is* and *Supernatural*, in 1972 and 1973. Birdsong issued one album for Bamboo, *Dance of Survival*, in 1975, then recorded *Edwin Birdsong* for Philadelphia International in 1979, which included the single "Phiss-Phizz." But Birdsong had more success teaming with vibist/vocalist Roy Ayers. The two co-wrote the songs "Running Away" and "Freaky Deaky," and Birdsong co-produced Ayers' LPs *Vibrations*, *Lifeline*, and *Let's Do It*. They also collaborated on productions and songs for the group Eighties Ladies. Birdsong recorded the singles "Perfect Love" in 1984 and "Son of a Rapper Snapper" in 1985 for Salsoul, and continued session work with many artists, including Stevie Wonder. *—Ron Wynn*

What It Is / Jan. 1972 / Polydor ✦✦✦

● **Super Natural** / 1973 / Polydor ✦✦✦✦✦
If you ever wondered where Lenny Kravitz got his thing, search no further. This album from the early '70s is shockingly ahead of its time; drenched in odd keyboard hues and stinging layers of guitar, this is the blueprint for the black rock that followed. This is a record that works on a whole lot of levels. If you dig Funkadelic and its immediate progeny, this is something you simply need to hear. *—Rob Ferrier*

Edwin Birdsong / 1979 / Philadelphia International ✦✦✦✦

Funtaztik / 1981 / Salsoul ✦✦✦

Black Ivory

f. New York, NY [Harlem]
Group / Soul, Smooth Soul, Disco
Leroy Burgess, Stuart Bascombe, and Russell Patterson were Black Ivory, an exceptional and occasionally brilliant soul group from Harlem that recorded throughout the '70s and returned sporadically during the decades following. The trio developed out of the late '60s as a group called the Mellow Sounds and were eventually taken under the wing of Patrick Adams. Adams had been in a group called the Sparks, but he developed his skills as a songwriter, arranger, and producer with Black Ivory.

Adams scraped together all the money he possibly could in order to have the group record their first single, "Don't Turn Around." Adams took the demo to several unimpressed labels before hitting Today Records. That label had a very different opinion and signed the group on the strength of the recording. "Don't Turn Around," written by Adams, became a Top 40 hit on the R&B chart, hitting number 38 in 1971. Black Ivory had their first taste of success. Not only that, but Today offered Adams—still a teenager at the time—an A&R position.

Another batch of singles that charted in the Top 40 supported the trio's first LP, 1972's *Don't Turn Around*. The album remained on the charts for nearly five months and peaked at number 13, an impressive feat for an album released on a small independent. The group's hot streak was capped off that year with a second album, *Baby, Won't You Change Your Mind*. That album spawned another series of singles and topped out at number 26. Today went through financial troubles and the group, unhappy about unpaid royalties, ended up riding out the last year of their contract.

Once the contract with Today ran out, Black Ivory joined the Kwanza label for a brief spate. "What Goes Around (Comes Around)," written and produced by the Akines-Bellman-Drayton-Turner team, hit the lower rung of the R&B chart. The group's popularity was on a steady wane when they signed to Buddah, a label with a bigger budget, but further attempts at gaining back that degree of popularity from early on failed. Furthermore, Adams was no longer producing the group and was apparently out of the picture entirely. Burgess left the group on good terms in 1977 to focus on a number of projects. However, he temporarily returned a year later to give the group its most spectacular song, the disco classic "Mainline." Leonard Adams, the group's manager at the time, called the departed Burgess and asked if he had any songs to give to the group, who was preparing to make another album. It just so happened that Burgess had two songs written that were originally intended for a project that didn't reach fruition. So he provided those two songs, "Mainline" and "Hustlin' (You Gotta Be Dancin')," and wound up returning to the group briefly to provide arrangements and backup vocals for those songs. "Mainline" became the group's best-known song and an extremely beloved one on dancefloors.

By the dawn of the '80s, Black Ivory was no more. The name was resurrected by Patterson in the mid-'80s, who partnered with David Hart and Lenny Adams. As one can guess, the fact that two-thirds of the original group wasn't involved left the new Black Ivory hamstrung. This incarnation did not last long. However, Bascombe, Patterson, and Burgess hooked up again in the early 2000s to play sporadic dates. Burgess had long since become a cult legend as one of the primary instigators of house music. Under a gaggle of pseudonyms, Burgess was behind an even greater number of disco and boogie cuts that fans of melodic dance music continue to enjoy. He continued to collaborate on and off with Patrick Adams, another pioneer—and a primary influence—who arranged, produced, wrote, and played instruments on several seminal recordings. Patterson also worked a little with Burgess in the intervening years, contributing vocals to the spectacular Salsoul singles released in 1981 under the name Logg. *—Andy Kellman*

Don't Turn Around / 1972 / Today ✦✦✦

Baby, Won't You Change Your Mind / 1972 / Today ✦✦✦
A more even affair than their first LP. Patrick Adams' songs and productions are as impressive as the vocals. Leroy Burgess' angelic falsetto carries the title track, gliding over Stuart Bascombe and Russell Patterson's arresting harmonies. "Time Is Love" is irresistible, the lyrics are paralyzing—"Love is remembered after the wine, it locks your heart and intoxicates your mind." Some quality mid- and uptempo numbers rounds this satisfying package. *—Andrew Hamilton*

Feel It / 1976 / Buddah ✦✦✦
After a four-year absence, and minus producer Patrick Adams, *Feel It*, produced by Robert John, Mike Gately and Black Ivory, ranks as good or better than the previous two. Heavy on ballads, this offering contains three sides written by group members Leroy Burgess, Stuart Bascombe, and Russell Patterson: "Warm Inside," "Your Eyes Say Goodbye," and the disco-oriented "Daily News." The cream, however, is John & Gately's "Will We Ever Come Together," a vastly underrated ballad. *—Andrew Hamilton*

Black Ivory / 1977 / Buddah ✦✦✦

Hangin' Heavy / 1979 / Unidisc ✦✦✦✦

Heavy Heavy / 1980 / Buddah ✦✦✦

Don't Turn Around: A Golden Classics Edition / 1994 / Collectables ✦✦✦
This New York City group attained a strong following in the '70s and were the one of the best falsetto-led groups proficient in ballads. This 1993 set compiles tracks from there first two albums, both released in 1972. Unlike the Phil Perry-led Montclairs, who often seemed on the verge of nervous collapse, Black Ivory was a little more poised and polished. Despite the level of skill of Leroy Burgess' falsetto and the close harmonies of Stuart Bascombe and Russell Patterson, the group was patently hit or miss. "Don't Turn Around" and "Time Is Love" both exemplify the sweetness and haunting sound of the group. The phenomenal self-pity classic "I'll Find a Way" has the great and funny lyric "I'm the loneliest man in town." Not surprisingly, this has its fair share of duds. Tracks "Wishful Thinking," "Loveland," and "I Keep Asking You Questions" are well sung but faceless. The odd "Our Future" doesn't even feature singing, but "super-cool" conversation that was an unfortunate given for most R&B groups in the early '70s. For fans, all of these songs and more are known, but this set also includes something different. The group's best known song, "You & I," shows up here in a newer version with telltale late-'80s synths. While not as strong as the original, it won't make a fan snap the CD in two. Like many '90s *Golden Classic Editions*, this isn't a greatest hits, but individual album efforts. Regardless what the title is, this is worth picking up. *—Jason Elias*

Battle of the Bands: Round One / Aug. 19, 1997 / Sequel ✦✦✦✦
Round One of Sequel's *Battle of the Bands* is uneven track-wise; Black Ivory does 12 tracks and Odds & Ends eight. New Yorkers Leroy Burgess, Stuart Bascombe, and Russell Patterson were Black Ivory, and Philadelphians' Wanda and Larry Butler and Jim Grant (siblings) were Odds & Ends. The Black Ivory cuts were culled from their first two Perception/Today albums, and 99.9 percent of the plums made the set: "Don't Turn Around," "Spinning Around," "Time Is Love," "You and I," "We Made It," and "Find the One Who Loves You." Sequel's only mistake was omitting "No ifs, ands, Buts" and including "Our Future," an idiotic idea swiped from the Five Stairsteps and Cubie's "New Dance Craze"; the snapping-contest track was originally intended for child prodigy Lucky Peterson. The outnumbered Odds & Ends land some heavy blows; it's easy to see why many think of them as a female group. Wanda Butler, a honey-voiced singer who could lullaby the baby-from-hell to dreamland, handles the leads accompanied by her high-singing brothers; on some tracks additional female voices were used for sweetening. Listening to Odds & Ends is a pleasure. An update of Deon Jackson's "Love Makes the World Go Round" bests the original, as does a makeover of "Apples, Peaches, Pumpkin Pie" (Jay & the Techniques); "Give Me Something" shuffles sweetly, and the slow, rapturous "Talk That Talk" is a grade-A ballad. The trio contributed material as well, including the uptempo "Foot Track" and "Let Me Try," an icy beat ballad. *—Andrew Hamilton*

● **Spinning Around: The Today Sessions** / Apr. 24, 2001 / Castle ✦✦✦✦
Built around Leroy Burgess' sugary leads and Stuart Bascombe and Russell Patterson's close harmonies, Black Ivory's Today recordings dripped with emotion, but their drama went virtually unnoticed outside the tri-state area from New York City down through New Jersey to Philadelphia. Via CD magic, Castle delivers their first two albums in one package. The misleading title has you thinking there were three LPs; however, "Spinning Around" and "Baby, Won't You Change Your Mind" were both on the *Baby, Won't You Change Your Mind* album. This disk is crammed with heart crushers aplenty, including the already mentioned along with "Don't Turn Around," "Time Is Love," "Wishful Thinking," "Find the One Who Loves You," and "You and I." Castle even included their excellent "We Made It," which dropped after their first two albums were compiled; it's a nice bonus, a ballad on which Burgess forsakes his falsetto and sings *au naturel*. *—Andrew Hamilton*

Black Merda

f. Mississippi
Group / Funk, Soul, Deep Funk
Black Merda was a funky rock combo with a significant debt to Jimi Hendrix, mixing fuzz-toned, psychedelic blues-rock with folky acoustic passages and contemporary late-'60s soul. Featuring guitarists Anthony and Charles Hawkins, bassist Veesee L. Veasey, and drummer Tyrone Hite, the group got its start in Mississippi but traveled to Chicago to record for Chess, issuing a self-titled debut album in 1967. The following year they were linked to Fugi, another psychedelic soul group who released their debut album on Chess, Mary, *Don't Take Me on No Bad Trip*. Some account say the bands were one and the same, others list Black Merda simply as producers. Shortening their name to Mer-Da, the group returned in 1971 with *Long Burn the Fire*, a funkier outing for Janus that bore a likeness to early Funkadelic. *—Steve Huey*

● **Long Burn the Fire/Black Merda** / Jun. 18, 1996 / Funky Delicacies ✦✦✦✦
Both of Black Merda's studio LPs, 1967's self-titled debut and its 1971 follow-up, *Long Burn the Fire*, are included on this two-fer, making it an easy and inexpensive way to track down their back catalog. *—Jason Ankeny*

Black Nasty

f. 1972, Detroit, MI
Group / Funk
Black Nasty was a little-known but decent group in the early-'70s Detroit funk scene, following the path of the Parliament/Funkadelic crowd in mixing rock, psychedelic, soul, and funk influences. They recorded a fair album for Stax that was released in 1973, but wasn't a heavy seller. After losing their contract with Stax (which would soon go out of

business anyway) in 1975, they changed into different R&B acts that would have a little more commercial success.

Black Nasty's mentor was Johnnie Mae Matthews, a singer who owned several independent Detroit R&B labels, including Northern, Reel, Audrey, Jam, Art, Big Hit, and Tank. Matthews also recorded more than two dozen singles under her own name. Though none were notable successes, she continued her involvement in the artistic side of the music business by encouraging her drummer son, Artwell, when he formed a band in the mid-'60s with his cousin, bassist Mark Patterson, and friends. Originally called Raw Integrated Funk, there were prominent rock elements at the outset (Ted Nugent was an early member), but under the influence of Johnnie Mae Matthews, they broadened their style to include more R&B. After putting out a cover of the Supremes' "You Keep Me Hanging' On" on Tank, they were signed to Stax, for which they recorded three singles and an album between 1971 and 1974. The Stax sessions (all of the singles also appeared on the album) were produced by Johnnie Mae Matthews and Bonny "Mack" Rice, the minor but noted Detroit soul singer. Rice had recommended Black Nasty to Stax after starting work at the label as a songwriter.

While their records were more promise than payoff, the album did have an interesting mix of funk with hard rock guitar, soul ballads on which Johnnie Mae Matthews' teenage daughter Audrey took lead, and some socially conscious compositions that reflected black urban life of the early '70s. After the album made little impact, Stax dropped Black Nasty, which changed their name to Nazty and recorded a couple of singles for Excello. After some personnel changes, the group became ADC Band, getting an R&B Top Ten hit with "Long Stroke" in 1978 and recording as late as the mid-'80s. *—Richie Unterberger*

Talking to the People / 1973 / Stax ✦✦✦✦

Like Rare Earth and early Funkadelic, Black Nasty took a very rock-minded approach to Detroit soul and funk—probably *too* rock-minded for many program directors at black radio. And at the same time, Black Nasty was too funky and soul-oriented for FM rock radio. So Black Nasty fell through the cracks in the early- to mid-'70s, although it enjoyed some commercial success after evolving into the ADC Band and recording the major funk hit of 1978, "Long Stroke." The band's only album as Black Nasty, *Talking to the People*, was a commercial disappointment but a creative triumph. Those who savored the Motor City funk/rock experiments of Rare Earth and early Funkadelic will find a lot to admire about gritty, hard-edged smokers like "Nasty Soul," "Getting Funky Round Here," and the single "Black Nasty Boogie" (which brings to mind John Lee Hooker's work with Canned Heat). To its credit, Black Nasty has no problem turning around and providing silky, mellow slow jams such as "Rushin' Sea" and "I Must Be in Love," both of which feature singer Audrey Matthews. It is Nasty's other lead singer, Terrance Ellis, who handles the more uptempo gems. Originally a vinyl LP, *Talking to the People* was reissued on CD in 1999. *—Alex Henderson*

Bill Black

b. Sep. 17, 1926, Memphis, TN, **d.** Oct. 21, 1965, Memphis, TN

Bass / Memphis Soul, Instrumental Rock

Bill Black had two distinct phases of his career in which he made a notable mark on early rock & roll music: first as the rockabilly bass player for Elvis Presley and then as a bandleader of Bill Black's Combo, which scored numerous instrumental hits in the early '60s. Such is the way of the world that his most artistically important contributions, as one-third of the rockabilly trio that Elvis Presley fronted at the beginning of his career, brought him much less commercial reward than the far less remarkable hit records under his own name.

Black first recorded for Sun Records in early 1954 as a member of a country band, Doug Poindexter and the Starlite Wranglers, which also included guitarist Scotty Moore. That group issued just one single for Sun, but that was enough to make the talents of Black and Moore known to Sun head Sam Phillips, who put the pair together with Elvis Presley. Under the billing of Elvis Presley, Scotty, and Bill, they put out five records on Sun in 1954 and 1955, which are usually acknowledged as some of the finest rockabilly records ever done and Presley at his most youthfully uninhibited. Black was an important part of the early Presley sound with his slap stand-up bass and ebullient on-stage manner.

Black and Moore continued to work with Presley until 1958, leaving his band in large part due to disputes over financial terms. Black and Moore had taken one-quarter of the royalties at the outset of Presley's career, but even after Presley had rocketed to stardom with RCA starting in 1956, they were on a mere 200 dollars/week wage. Although Moore would eventually work with Presley again, Black never did, joining a Memphis group that evolved into Bill Black's Combo in 1959. Their instrumental "Smokie," released late that year, made the Top Ten.

Bill Black's Combo stuck to the formula of "Smokie" for many of their subsequent singles: a basic shuffle beat, simple bluesy R&B riffs, and some rinky-dink organ and smoky saxophone lines on top. They weren't too imaginative, but they were quite successful, placing eight singles in the Top 40 between 1959 and 1962, including "White Silver Sands," "Josephine," "Don't Be Cruel," "Blue Tango," and "Hearts of Stone." Their sales were greatly boosted by the suitability of their instrumental rock for background music at bars, clubs, and diners, with many of their discs placed in jukeboxes. They were still charting in the Top 100 as late as 1964, the year they also toured with the Beatles during the British stars' first nationwide American tour.

Black, sadly, developed a brain tumor and died in 1965, shortly before his 40th birthday and before rock historians had a chance to allow him to tell his side of the Elvis Presley story. *—Richie Unterberger*

Greatest Hits/Plays Chuck Berry / 1988 / Hi ✦✦✦✦

Two Bill Black albums from the mid-'60s, *Greatest Hits* and *Plays Chuck Berry*, were reissued on one CD by Hi Records in 1995. Although each record has its share of weak spots, they remain infectious and enjoyable, and this disc is worth seeking out for any hardcore fan of Black. *—Stephen Thomas Erlewine*

Let's Twist Her/The Untouchable Sound / 1992 / Hi ✦✦✦

Bill Black's Combo Goes West/Plays the Blues / Nov. 20, 1995 / Hi ✦✦✦

Hi Masters / Sep. 15, 1998 / Hi ✦✦✦

The Wonderful Feeling/Movin' / Feb. 13, 2001 / Hi ✦✦✦

• **The Best of Bill Black's Combo: The Hi Records Years** / Apr. 10, 2001 / Capitol ✦✦✦✦

These 18 songs, from 1959-1964, should be all anyone needs of this extremely popular instrumental group. Indeed, people tend to forget just how popular these fellows were back in the early '60s: all but two of these cuts made the Top 100, and six made the Top 20 in 1959-1961 alone. It's still surprisingly samey-sounding all at once, though, most of the cuts anchored by a walking R&B shuffle beat, often embellished by honking sax and chintzy organ. It was the Bill Doggett ("Honky Tonk") format, diluted somewhat for the pop audience, and tethered to very basic bluesy riffs that didn't vary too much over the years. For that reason, these must have been better to hear back in the day on actual honky tonk jukeboxes than on greatest-hits compilations one after the other. When there's some change in the tempo, as on "Blue Tango" and "Tequila," it comes as a relief. The collection is enhanced by Colin Escott's lengthy and learned historical liner notes. *—Richie Unterberger*

James Black

b. Feb. 1, 1940, New Orleans, LA, **d.** Aug. 30, 1988, New Orleans, LA

Drums / Mainstream Jazz, Funk, Jazz-Funk

Though he's little known outside of New Orleans and never recorded an album under his own name, drummer James Black was a Crescent City legend capable of performing everything from complex modernist jazz to gritty funk. An accomplished composer as well, Black had a reputation for being an irascible bandleader, intimidating with his personality just as much as his skill. Born in New Orleans on February 1, 1940, Black soaked up the city's trademark "second line" rhythms from a young age, and by the early '60s was already doing session work for the likes of Fats Domino. His main interest was jazz, however, and he played in a group with the young Ellis Marsalis on piano and Nat Perrilliat on sax. Nat Adderley (along with brother Cannonball) used all three on his 1962 session *In the Bag*, to which Black contributed two compositions. The following year, Marsalis cut an underrated album of modern jazz called *Monkey Puzzle*; this time out Black handled four of the seven compositions, including the intricate 5/4 piece "Magnolia Triangle," which ranks as perhaps his greatest work. Black went on to play with Yusef Lateef and Lionel Hampton in the mid-'60s, although his career was interrupted by a stint in the Angola State Penitentiary (during which time he actually played in a prison band with blues pianist James Booker and saxophonist Charles Neville).

In the late '60s, Black paid the bills with R&B gigs around New Orleans, and in 1968 caught on at the Scram label as a house drummer. He played on Eddie Bo's "Hook and Sling," helping to make it one of the great New Orleans funk singles, and soon took his place alongside Smokey Johnson and the Meters' Ziggy Modeliste as one of the city's top funky drummers. Meanwhile, he continued to play jazz on the side as part of Ellis Marsalis' band ELM Music Company; they took up residency at Lu and Charlie's beginning in 1972 and became local favorites. During the '70s, Black also led his own group, the James Black Ensemble, which often featured his longtime girlfriend "Sister Mary" Bonette on vocals. He attempted several times to record a full-length album, including once for the Sound of New Orleans label and another time at Allen Toussaint's studio, but the sessions never progressed beyond a few tracks. Black continued performing in New Orleans into the '80s, still playing with Ellis Marsalis (as well as Marsalis' then-teenage pupil, Harry Connick Jr.); he also served as the drummer for the 1982 Marsalis Family album *Fathers and Sons*. Black died of a drug overdose on August 30, 1988.

In 2002, the Night Train label assembled a compilation of mostly unreleased tracks, many from Black's aborted LP sessions; *I Need Altitude: Rare & Unreleased New Orleans Jazz and Funk, 1968-1978* ran the gamut from heavy funk and psychedelic soul to soul-jazz, and featured several of the drummer's own vocals. In the spring of 2003, Ellis and Wynton Marsalis presented a program of Black compositions as part of the *Jazz at Lincoln Center* series. *—Steve Huey*

• **I Need Altitude: Rare & Unreleased New Orleans Jazz & Funk 1968–1978** / 2002 / Night Train ✦✦✦

The Blackbyrds

f. 1973, Washington, D.C., **db.** 1978

Group / Jazz-Pop, Jazz-Funk, Urban, Funk

The Blackbyrds were a jazz-funk group with thick R&B streaks running down their backs. Assembled by Donald Byrd in 1974, the group's original members—percussionist Pericles "Perk" Jacobs Jr., drummer Keith Killgo, keyboardist Kevin Toney, reeds player Allan Barnes, bassist Joe Hall, guitarist Barney Perry—were mined from Howard University's music department, where the doctor and jazz legend was an instructor. (Other key players included guitarist Orville Saunders and saxophonist/flute player Steve Johnson.) During the Blackbyrds' nearly decade-long existence, the group cut a handful of LPs (1973's *The Blackbyrds*, 1974's *Flying Start*, 1975's *City Life*, 1976's *Unfinished Business*, 1977's *Action*, 1980's *Better Days*); scored films (1975's *Cornbread, Earl and Me*); and supported artists like B.B. King, Mandrill, and Roberta Flack. "Walking in Rhythm," "Rock Creek Park," and "Happy Music" are their three best-known cuts; they have remained underground club classics, and they have been kept alive, in part, through sampling.

The group's catalog has been overhauled and reissued a number of times; multiple best-ofs have been released (Fantasy's *Greatest Hits* is the strongest and most thorough), and most of the group's full-length output has been put out on CD through two-fers. As far as outside activities were considered, Barney Perry released a solo album under the name Blair in 1978 (through his own Solar Sound imprint). The remaining members' involvements are far too extensive to list. *—Andy Kellman*

The Blackbyrds / Oct. 1973-Oct. 1974 / A&M ✦✦✦✦✦

This amazing album is the product of six full-time Howard University students taking the direction of department head and jazz great Donald Byrd into the Fantasy Studios along with the aid of production wizard Larry Mizell. The result is some of the finest groove-oriented jazz music ever recorded. The rhythm section of Joe Hall on bass and Keith Killgo on drums provides a tight foundation for the Blackbyrds to enhance any dancefloor with their soulful explorations. With Kevin Toney supplying beautiful keyboard work and Barney Perry hitting listeners up with his chicken-scratch guitar, the skeletal framework for what could be called optimistic funk was firmly established by this debut record. Recommended songs include "Do It, Fluid," "Reggins," and "Summer Love," although the overall consistency of quality tracks on *The Blackbyrds* is reason enough to give the album a complete listen. *—Robert Gabriel*

Flying Start / Nov. 1974 / Fantasy ✦✦✦✦
For their second album, *Flying Start*, the Blackbyrds whipped up yet another healthy menu of proto-disco music. Complete with crispy drum breaks, relentless basslines, chicken-scratch guitar, majestic horns, and meandering clavinet, their dance-oriented brand of funky jazz is captured at its finest on tracks such as "The Baby," "Blackbyrds' Theme," and "Spaced Out." Meanwhile, breezier songs such as "Love Is Love," "Walking in Rhythm," and "April Showers" express the more melodic side of the Blackbyrds' repertoire. Produced by Howard University professor and jazz legend Donald Byrd, the album represents an accessible rather than experimental version of jazz fusion, a style that later became wholly embraced by proponents of hip-hop culture. *—Robert Gabriel*

Cornbread, Earl and Me / Jun. 1975 / Fantasy ✦✦
The Blackbyrds provided the soundtrack for the 1975 blaxploitation film *Cornbread, Earl and Me*, which featured the movie debut of Larry Fishburne. Composed entirely by Donald Byrd, it's serviceable, routine soul-jazz background film music, varying between funk/jazz/rock vamps (such as the Sly Stone-styled instrumental workout "The One-Eye Two-Step"), snazzy jazzy bits for action scenes, and sentimental orchestrated interludes. There are also occasional vocal numbers in a pedestrian mid-'70s soul/jazz/rock mode, such as the "Cornbread" theme. It's an incidental addition to the Blackbyrds catalog. In 2001, it was paired on a single-CD reissue on Prestige with another blaxploitation soundtrack, Charles Earland's *The Dynamite Brothers*. *—Richie Unterberger*

☆ **City Life** / Nov. 1975 / Fantasy ✦✦✦✦✦
The Blackbyrds—a jazz-funk outfit formed in a university class taught by jazz trumpeter Donald Byrd, who produced the albums and wrote most of the tunes—were more of an Earth, Wind & Fire-style horn band than a purist jazz crew, but few groups were better in their chosen style, and 1975's *City Life* is probably their best album. It's certainly their most successful, including the pop hit "Happy Music" and what has become their signature tune, a percolating Latin-flavored jam called "Rock Creek Park" that's one of the pinnacles of '70s jazz-funk. As on the bouncy title track, the lyrical content is minimal, a simple hypnotic chant, but the fluid interplay of the musicians, who are masters of the unison horn section and the polyrhythmic groove, is what's important about this music. Other highlights include the funky Southern-style soul of "Hash and Eggs" and the lyrical ballad "Love So Fine." This is often-sublime stuff ripe for rediscovery by fans of '70s funk, soul, and fusion. *—Stewart Mason*

Unfinished Business / Nov. 1976 / Fantasy ✦✦✦

Action / Sep. 1977 / Fantasy ✦✦✦
If you had to own only one album by the Blackbyrds then *Action* should be it. All the elements came together for the Donald Byrd protégés on this scintillating certified gold album, which originally was issued in fall 1977. The sinewy Top 20 R&B hit "Supernatural Feeling" has bits of wisdom implanted in between its poppin' funk grooves. The enticing "Soft and Easy" slid into the R&B Top 20 with an ease that's equal to the gentle spoken seduction that is woven throughout this make out classic. The exotic radio-aired LP track "Something Special" features the nimble noodling of future smooth jazz favorite, pianist Kevin Toney. "Dreaming About You" is the perfect track to unwind during. *Action* was later issued as one of two LPs that was included on a single CD (the other being the George Duke-produced *Better Days*) in 1994 by U.K. label Ace Records. *—Ed Hogan*

● **Night Grooves: The Blackbyrds' Greatest Hits** / Dec. 1978 / Fantasy ✦✦✦✦
Despite the fact that 1989's *Greatest Hits* rendered this earlier Fantasy compilation obsolete—*Greatest Hits* contains all seven songs found here, plus four others—Fantasy continued to keep this disc in circulation. This is a tighter and more discerning collection, sticking to the absolute essential material that Donald Byrd's protégés churned out during the '70s, but simple mathematics places its value below the later, more inclusive anthology. Those who want to dig deeper can start with any of the group's first four proper LPs; each one peaked in the Top Ten of *Billboard*'s jazz album chart, and they all have their charms beyond the singles. Anyone who bet on the Blackbyrds' material to die a disposable pop death must feel foolish now, as cuts like "Rock Creek Park," "Happy Music," and "Walking in Rhythm" remain completely unironic fixtures in the record crates of many house DJs. *—Andy Kellman*

Better Days / Dec. 1980 / Fantasy ✦✦
Those who know the Blackbyrds best by their 1977 gold LP *Action* may feel discombobulated by the group's 1980 album, *Better Days*. Part of the reason may come from the ever-changing nature of pop music. In just a few short years, radio play lists had become tighter and less eclectic. No longer under the mentorship of jazz trumpeter/producer Donald Byrd, and wrapped in the dazzling string/horn arrangements of *Action* arranger Wade Marcus, the Blackbyrds' sound was less fluid and the band's considerable chops (musical skills) were held in check. Going a radio-friendly route under the aegis of producer George Duke, the soft, thumpin' "What We Have Is Right" made it to number 38 R&B (*Billboard*) and the midtempo groovin' stepper "Love Don't Strike Twice" brushed the lower half of the chart. Other highlights are the horn-laced stompin' title track and "Do It Girl" (which sounds something like a Con Funk Shun ballad). *Better Days* was teamed with *Action* on a 1994 single CD from U.K. label Ace Records. *—Ed Hogan*

● **Greatest Hits** / Jul. 21, 1989 / Fantasy ✦✦✦✦✦
When Donald Byrd embraced soul and funk in the 1970s, some jazz players and critics didn't hesitate to lambast the trumpeter and label him a sellout. But while it's always sad to see a great improviser put his improvisatory skills on the back burner, the fact is that many of the Byrd's more commercially successful recordings were highly creative. Like Byrd's own '70s dates, the albums he produced for the Blackbyrds are best described as soul and funk with jazz overtones. Anyone who seriously followed the black music scene of the mid-'70s has heard many of the songs on this CD, which range from the dreamy "Walking in Rhythm" to invigorating funk hits like "Happy Music," "Do It Fluid" and "Rock Creek Park" (a suggestive gem that many rappers have sampled). The jazz influence is especially strong on the instrumental "Gut Level" and the peaceful "Summer Love," which has slightly Pharoah Sanders-ish qualities. But it must be stressed that this band had more to offer from an R&B standpoint than a jazz standpoint. For lovers of '70s R&B, this is a collection to savor. *—Alex Henderson*

City Life/Unfinished Business / 1995 / BGP ✦✦✦✦✦
This 1999 reissue combines two of the Blackbyrds' classic albums, *City Life* from 1975 and *Unfinished Business* from 1976, on a single 74-minute CD. To be sure, "classic" isn't a word that many jazz purists have used to describe the albums—when Donald Byrd produced them, bop's hard-liners were denouncing the Clifford Brown-influenced trumpeter as a shameless sellout and insisting that he should have stuck to straight-ahead acoustic jazz. But then, the Blackbyrds weren't going after jazz purists—their music was soul, funk, and disco with jazz overtones, and the people who bought their albums were more likely to be into Earth, Wind & Fire and Tower of Power than Sonny Stitt or Art Blakey. Unlike Stevie Wonder, Gil Scott-Heron, Marvin Gaye, the O'Jays, and Curtis Mayfield, the Blackbyrds didn't get into a lot of heavy sociopolitical messages; their forte was party music, and it is that escapist, feel-good mindset that defines the infectious hits "Happy Music" and "Rock Creek Park" (both from *City Life*) as well as memorable album tracks such as the mellow "Love So Fine" from *City Life* and the insistently funky "Party Land" from *Unfinished Business*. Calling this music escapist isn't saying that it's faceless or mechanical—far from it. The Blackbyrds' party-time lyrics may not have been challenging, but musically, the band was creative, risk-taking, and distinctive. Even though they were primarily a soul/funk/disco outfit, the Blackbyrds came from jazz backgrounds—and that jazz influence often works to their creative advantage on this excellent reissue. *—Alex Henderson*

At the Movies / Mar. 30, 2001 / Prestige ✦✦
This single-CD reissue pairs two blaxploitation soundtracks by different artists: 1975's *Cornbread, Earl and Me*, composed by Donald Byrd and performed by the Blackbyrds, and 1973's *The Dynamite Brothers*, composed and performed by Charles Earland. *Cornbread, Earl and Me*, which featured the movie debut of Larry Fishburne, is serviceable, routine soul-jazz background film music, varying between funk-jazz-rock vamps (such as the Sly Stone-styled instrumental workout "The One-Eye Two-Step"), snazzy jazzy bits for action scenes, and sentimental orchestrated interludes. There are also occasional vocal numbers in a pedestrian mid-'70s soul-jazz-rock mode, such as "The Cornbread Theme." It's an incidental addition to the Blackbyrds catalog. *The Dynamite Brothers* was one of the most obscure blaxploitation movies. Although there were some soul-jazz elements in the score, it also reflected the move among many musicians from that background into funk, fusion, and rock territory in the early- to mid-'70s, particularly in the synthesizers by Patrick Gleeson. It often sounds like the kind of music you might have heard from a band warming up a crowd for a Miles Davis concert of the time. It's suitably slightly spaced soul-funk-fusion, atmospheric but not too heavy on remarkable compositional ideas. Gleeson does come up with some eerie wavering, high-pitched effects and squiggles on his ARP 2600 and Pro Soloist synths, and Earland gets down with some real earthy, extended bluesy soloing on "Shanty Blues." Earland switches from organ to soprano sax on the most avant-garde and dissonant outing, the eight-minute "Snake." *—Richie Unterberger*

J. Blackfoot (John Colbert)

b. 1947, Greenville, MS
Vocals / Soul, R&B
J. Blackfoot was the lead singer of the Soul Children, the Memphis-based group that scored 15 R&B hits between 1968 and 1978. Colbert launched a solo career as J. Blackfoot with the single "Taxi," which climbed into the R&B Top Ten in 1984. *—William Ruhlmann*

● **City Slicker** / Dec. 1983 / Sound Town ✦✦✦✦✦
J. Blackfoot's debut solo LP, *City Slicker*, is a concept album based on that age-old theme, the country boy's experiences when he comes to the city. Blackfoot isn't embarrassed to borrow heavily from Stevie Wonder's "Livin' for the City" for the album-opening "The Way of the City," and it's a good indication of what's to come: Blackfoot, with his gruff voice, is a forceful soul belter, but he's not exactly original. Nevertheless, in 1983 it was pleasant to hear someone hewing so closely to the soul sound of the late '60s and early '70s, and Blackfoot scored a Top Ten R&B hit with the smooth "Taxi" from this album, which also made a respectable showing on the R&B LP chart. *—William Ruhlmann*

U-Turn / Jul. 1987 / Edge ✦✦✦
Former Soul Children member, J. Blackfoot's *U Turn* album contains some fine deep soul. The soulful "Tear Jerker" is credited to J. Blackfoot, but Ann Hines is featured on this eye-wetting Homer Banks/Lester Snell song; Blackfoot can be heard on the chorus vocalizing the hook. Larry Johnson, Ann Hines, Bertram Brown (ex-Newcomers and Kwick), and

Jabbo (ex-Tempree) supply backing vocals. Homer Banks' "Bad Weather" is Southern-fried soul at its finest, the clever lyrics and heart-touching vocals marry well. Instrumentation is sparse—only a rhythm section—which is good; horns and strings would have muddied this beauty. *—Andrew Hamilton*

Loveaholic / 1991 / Basix ♦♦♦

At His Best / Apr. 6, 1999 / Basix ♦♦♦

Some of J. Blackfoot's classic tales include a new rendition of his memorable "Taxi" as "Taxi 95," the woeful "I Was So Hurt Inside, I Stood on the Sidewalk and Cried," his too-accommodating "Let Me Put You Up for a Night" (said the fox to the hen), and "Loveaholic," a cry for passion. Blackfoot handles the stressful lyrics with confidence and gets jubilant on "Until Then"—a duet with Lynn White—romantic on "Now Is the Time," and ready to rumble on "May the Best Man Win." *—Andrew Hamilton*

Having an Affair / Oct. 26, 1999 / Basix ♦♦♦

Blackstreet

f. 1994, **db.** 1999

Group / New Jack Swing, Club/Dance, Urban, Hip-Hop

Teddy Riley, one of the most innovative and successful R&B producers of the '80s and '90s, formed Blackstreet in 1994 with Chauncey Hannibal, Levi Little, and David Hollister. Under Riley's direction, Blackstreet's smooth fusion of pop, R&B, and hip-hop became an across-the-board hit upon its release. *Another Level*, featuring the monster hit "No Diggity," followed in 1996, and in 1999 the group returned with *Finally*. *—Stephen Thomas Erlewine*

Blackstreet / 1994 / Interscope ♦♦♦

Teddy Riley is an impeccable craftsman and genius of sorts, not to mention a trendsetter. In releasing so much product, however, his music can also occasionally descend into a pedestrian, formulaic version of new jack swing, the production style he himself invented, fine-tuned, and perfected. That pitfall plays out intermittently on Blackstreet's debut album. Some of the music and vocal harmonies blend together or sound like new jack retreads, and a handful of the songs are so commercially savvy and obviously directed toward the mainstream public that it is hard to wholly enjoy them. Some of the songs, too, are less than fully formed, consisting of just a single melody or groove that exists for the sole purpose of moving feet and/or giving the quartet an excuse to harmonize. More often, however, Blackstreet hits the spot with a sleek and inventive progression on the new jack template, sharpening and filling out the sound that Guy made famous. Riley makes sure the beats are hip-hop savvy and the bass is booming, and then slathers squealing synthesizer lines all over them. Frankly, he is not technically a fantastic singer, at least in comparison to his three harmonizing mates, but his voice has such a distinctive character that it has always been entirely ingratiating, making up in expressiveness for any lack in range or virtuosity. The songs on which he takes lead invariably stand out the most and tend to be the most appealing cuts. The glue on the album, though, is the tight four-part harmony singing of Blackstreet, and it leads to some brilliantly catchy R&B tracks, songs that easily stood out in the mid-'90s urban soul crowd. *—Stanton Swihart*

• **Another Level** / Sep. 9, 1996 / Interscope ♦♦♦♦

Powered by the massive hit single "No Diggity," *Another Level* is arguably the finest album created by Teddy Riley, the leader of Blackstreet. Riley has masterminded an album that blends street-level rhythms with urban soul and pop crossover potential, adding two new members—Eric Williams and Mark Middleton—to the lineup in order to position Blackstreet as an heir to the classic R&B vocal group tradition. The realignment works, since the group sounds fuller and more eclectic with the two added voices. But the key to the success of *Another Level* is Riley's songwriting, which is by and large catchy and inventive, whether he is writing ballads or party jams. *Another Level* sags a bit halfway through—it's hard to sustain interest for a nearly 70 minute album—but it has enough strong moments to make it an enjoyable listen. *—Stephen Thomas Erlewine*

Finally / Mar. 23, 1999 / Interscope ♦♦♦

The title is a not-so-subtle admission that it took a little longer than expected for Blackstreet's third album to hit the shelves. Delays are commonplace in pop music, but they're not welcome, since part of the game is capitalizing on recent successes—in this case, that would have been "No Diggity," a Teddy Riley masterpiece that broke Blackstreet big. *Finally* didn't arrive quickly enough to expand on that success, but it feels as if it could have followed shortly after *Another Level*, since Riley doesn't really expand their sound that much on the third record. That's not to say it isn't enjoyable, since Riley knows how to make infectious funk and seductive ballads. He also knows that cameos sell a record, and he's loaded this disc with appearances from celebrities like Stevie Wonder and Janet Jackson. It's fun to hear the guests appear, but it takes away from Blackstreet somewhat, especially since the guests are the only noteworthy things on a few cuts. Nevertheless, there's no discounting Riley's skills, and he delivers some dynamic grooves and soothing slow jams throughout the record. They're not radically different from those on *Another Level*, but in a way, they don't need to be. At their best, Riley and Blackstreet are among the best '90s new jack soul has to offer, and there's just enough of the group at their best on *Finally* to make it worth the wait. *—Stephen Thomas Erlewine*

Otis Blackwell

b. 1931, New York, NY [Brooklyn], **d.** May 6, 2002, Nashville, TN

Songwriter, Piano / East Coast Blues, Urban Blues, Rock & Roll, R&B

Few 1950s rock & roll tunesmiths were as prolifically talented as Otis Blackwell. His immortal compositions include Little Willie John's "Fever," Elvis Presley's "Don't Be Cruel" and "All Shook Up," Jerry Lee Lewis' "Great Balls of Fire" and "Breathless," and Jimmy Jones' "Handy Man" (just for starters). Though he often collaborated with various partners on the thriving '50s New York R&B scene (Winfield Scott, Eddie Cooley, and Jack Hammer, to name three), his songwriting style is identifiable.

In 1952, Blackwell parlayed a victory at an Apollo Theater talent show into a recording deal with veteran producer Joe Davis for RCA, switching to Davis' own Jay-Dee logo the next year. He was fairly prolific at Jay-Dee, enjoying success with the throbbing "Daddy Rollin' Stone." From 1955 on, though, Blackwell concentrated primarily on songwriting. "Fever," co-written by Cooley, was Blackwell's first winner (he used the pen name of John Davenport, since he was still contractually obligated to Jay-Dee).

Blackwell never met Elvis in person, but his material traveled a direct pipeline to the rock icon; "Return to Sender," "One Broken Heart for Sale," and "Easy Question" also came from his pen. Dee Clark ("Just Keep It Up" and "Hey Little Girl"), Thurston Harris, Wade Flemons, Clyde McPhatter, Brook Benton, Ben E. King, the Drifters, Bobby Darin, Ral Donner, Gene Vincent, and plenty more of rock's primordial royalty benefited from Blackwell's compositional largess before the British Invasion forever altered the Brill Building scene. *—Bill Dahl*

All Shook Up / 1995 / Shanachie ♦♦♦♦

Blackwell's "comeback" album, originally cut in 1976 for Herb Abramson's Inner City label, is a successful effort at reclaiming the songs of his that made people like Elvis, Jerry Lee Lewis ("Great Balls of Fire," "Breathless"), Dee Clark ("Hey Little Girl"), et al. famous. For some listeners this album won't offer any real revelation, alas—the backings seem a little too smooth (one suspects that the original demos on "Fever," "All Shook Up," etc., had some rough edges that made them more interesting). They're all played well, however, and Blackwell's singing is impeccable. Anyone else might be accused of mimicking Elvis' style on "All Shook Up" and related numbers, except that history tells us different, and the performances are genuine and honest. Blackwell shows off a surprisingly wide range, most notably on the lullaby "Sleep Is Just Around the Corner" and the ballad "Clinging to a Dream," all of which makes this far more than just an Elvis Presley-related curio. Also included is Blackwell's credible rendition of "Searchin'," a song authored by his contemporary rivals Leiber & Stoller. *—Bruce Eder*

• **Otis Blackwell 1953–55** / Nov. 28, 1995 / Flyright ♦♦♦♦♦

The British Flyright logo has neatly compiled all 17 known titles that Otis Blackwell cut for Jay-Dee, including "Daddy Rollin' Stone" and the equally ominous "On That Power Line," and four sides with a killer New York combo featuring tenor sax wailer Sam "The Man" Taylor and guitarist Mickey Baker. *—Bill Dahl*

Billy Bland

b. Apr. 5, 1932, Wilmington, NC

Vocals / Rock & Roll, R&B, Soul

Billy Bland had a one-shot hit in 1960 with "Let the Little Girl Dance" (number seven), a pop-R&B-early soul mixture very much in the same mold as records from the period by Jackie Wilson, right down to the Latinate "Lonely Teardrops" rhythm. Some of his other singles were in the same style, but Bland (not to be confused with the unrelated Bobby "Blue" Bland) was actually a pretty versatile vocalist, also purveying R&B, Bo Diddley-styled rock & roll, urban blues, and dance-craze early-'60s rock. He recorded often for Old Town from the mid-'50s through 1963, but though his range was wide, his quality was not. He was a competent journeyman no matter what his genre, never finding another song with the pop hooks of "Let the Little Girl Dance." Or writing one: though he didn't pen "Let the Little Girl Dance," he wrote much of his own material.

Bland began singing shortly after moving to New York in the late '40s, and made his first records for Imperial in New Orleans in the mid-'50s, as a member of the Bees. They did an early version of Dave Bartholomew's naughty "My Ding-a-Ling" (eventually a hit for Chuck Berry), although when the Bees did it, it was titled "Toy Bell." (It can now be found on the box set *Crescent City Soul: The Sound of New Orleans 1947-1974*). Bland went solo in 1955, however, beginning his lengthy association with the New York-based Old Town label. "Let the Little Girl Dance" was almost an accident: It was being recorded by Titus Turner, and Bland showed him how to do it in the studio. Unknown to Bland, his demonstration was recorded by Henry Glover, and became the hit, with guitar ace Mickey Baker playing on the session.

Bland tried to vary the "Let the Little Girl Dance" pop-R&B sound on various singles, and also ride the bandwagons of other rock trends, with no success, and made his final Old Town disc in 1963. After his retirement from his full-time music career, Bland spent his time running a soul food restaurant in Harlem. *—Richie Unterberger*

• **Let the Little Girl Dance** / Jan. 1, 2000 / Ace ♦♦♦

Featured here are 29 songs recorded by Bland for Old Town between 1955 and 1963, with five tracks that were unissued at the time, including an alternate (but similar) take of "Let the Little Girl Dance." Bland and Old Town tried a variety of strategies evident over the course of the disc. There are more sub-Jackie Wilson imitations with the "Lonely Teardrops" rhythm ("You Were Born to Be Loved"). There are also fair Bo Diddley-derived tunes ("Chicken in the Basket" is not just a derivation, but an imitation); down-home electric blues with Sonny Terry and Brownie McGhee as accompanists ("Chicken Hop"); uptempo urban jump blues-R&B ("Grandma Gave a Party," "The Fat Man"); doo wop; faux New Orleans sounds ("Momma Stole the Chicken"); and sub-twist, early-'60s dance-craze rock ("Do the Bug With Me"). It's almost an unwitting primer of black music in the 1950s and early 1960s as it turned into R&B, rock, and soul. The material, however, is on the by-numbers side, and Bland is a likable but undistinguished singer. Some points of interest are "Uncle Bud," (like "Chicken Hop") which features just-out-of-the-country electric blues that probably has Sonny Terry on guitar (the composer credit is "S. Terry"); the little-known and unmemorable Gene Pitney tune "Harmony"; and "I Spend My Life Loving You," which was co-written by Bland and J. Mack, though sounds like it *could* be mistaken for a Gene Pitney composition. *—Richie Unterberger*

Bobby "Blue" Bland

b. Jan. 27, 1930, Rosemark, TN

Vocals, Leader / Electric Texas Blues, Soul-Blues, Texas Blues, Retro-Soul, R&B, Soul

Bobby "Blue" Bland earned his enduring blues superstar status the hard way: without a guitar, harmonica, or any other instrument to fall back upon. All Bland had to offer was his magnificent voice, a tremendously powerful instrument in his early heyday, injected with charisma and melisma to spare. Just ask his legion of female fans, who deem him a sex symbol to this day. Most of Bland's savage Texas blues sides during the mid- to late '50s featured the slashing guitar of Clarence Hollimon, notably "I Smell Trouble," "I Don't Believe," "Don't Want No Woman," "You Got Me (Where You Want Me)," and the torrid "Loan a Helping Hand" and "Teach Me (How to Love You)." But the insistent guitar riffs guiding Bland's first national hit, 1957's driving "Farther Up the Road," were contributed by Pat Hare, another vicious picker who would eventually die in prison after murdering his girlfriend and a cop. Later, Wayne Bennett took over on guitar, his elegant fretwork prominent on Bland's Duke waxings throughout much of the '60s. The gospel underpinnings inherent to Bland's powerhouse delivery were never more apparent than on the 1958 outing "Little Boy Blue," a vocal *tour de force* that wrings every ounce of emotion out of the grinding ballad. He steered into smoother material as the decade turned—the seminal mixtures of blues, R&B and primordial soul "I Pity the Fool," the Brook Benton-penned "I'll Take Care of You," and "Two Steps from the Blues" were tremendously influential to a legion of up-and-coming Southern soulsters. *—Bill Dahl*

Blues Consolidated / May 1958 / Duke ✦✦✦✦✦

An album split between Bobby "Blue" Bland and his *Blues Consolidated* touring partner, Junior Parker, featuring great early-'50s sides by these two Houston-based performers. *—Cub Koda & Hank Davis*

Like Er Red Hot / 1960 / Duke ✦✦✦

This anthology presents a cross section of early Duke/Peacock hits. *—Bill Dahl*

☆ **Two Steps From the Blues** / 1961 / MCA ✦✦✦✦✦

Without a doubt, *Two Steps From the Blues* is the definitive Bobby "Blue" Bland album and one of the great records in electric blues and soul-blues. In fact, it's one of the key albums in modern blues, marking a turning point when juke joint blues were seamlessly blended with gospel and Southern soul, creating a distinctly Southern sound where all of these styles blended so thoroughly it was impossible to tell where one began and one ended. Given his Memphis background, Bobby "Blue" Bland was perfectly suited for this kind of amalgam as envisioned by producer/arranger Joe Scott, who crafted these wailing horn arrangements that sounded as impassioned as Bland's full-throated, anguished vocals. It helped, of course, that the songs were uniformly brilliant. Primarily from the pen of Deadric Malone, along with Duke head Don Robey and Scott (among others), these are the tunes that form the core of Bobby "Blue" Bland's legend and the foundation of soul-blues: "Two Steps From the Blues," "I Don't Want No Woman," "Cry, Cry, Cry," "I'm Not Ashamed," "Lead Me On," "Little Boy Blue"—songs so good they overshadow standards like "St. James Infirmary." These are songs that blur the division between Ray Charles soul and Chess blues, opening the doors for numerous soul and blues sounds, from Muscle Shoals and Stax through the modern-day soul-bluesman. Since this, like many blues albums from the late '50s/early '60s, was a collection of singles, it's possible to find the key tracks, even the entire album, on the numerous Bobby "Blue" Bland collections released over the years, but this remains an excellent, essential blues album on its own terms—one of the greatest ever released. *—Stephen Thomas Erlewine*

Call on Me / 1963 / MCA ✦✦✦✦✦

Ain't Nothing You Can Do / 1964-1965 / MCA ✦✦✦✦

This features fine, soulful mid-'60s sides, including the title track, "Loneliness Hurts," and a cathartic reading of the soul classic "Blind Man." *—Cub Koda & Hank Davis*

The Soul of the Man / 1966 / MCA ✦✦✦✦✦

Like his two other seminal '60s titles on the Duke label, *Here's the Man* and *Two Steps From the Blues*, Bobby "Blue" Bland's *The Soul of the Man* features the powerful and gravelly voiced singer mixing it up with a bluesy, soul-tinged blend of swingers and slower, after-hours material. While the uptempo blues "Reach Right Out" finds Bland vocally playing it cool, ballad cuts like "I Can't Stop" show him seamlessly working his dynamic range of hushed tones and throaty cries. Bland's varied approach is reflected in the album's diverse material, which includes the Stax-inspired groover "Back in the Same Old Bag"; a driving, horns-aplenty instrumental "Soul Stretch"; and the breezy, Northern soul sounding gem "Let's Get Together." Adding to the album's appeal are fine covers of the Jimmy Witherspoon standard "Ain't Nobody's Business If I Do" and Peggy Lee's signature tune "Fever." Bland's longstanding musical director Joe Scott provides his standard mix of tight rhythmic backing and urbane horn and guitar charts, perfectly framing the singer's robust voice with a toasty and slightly rough-hewn backdrop. While *The Soul of the Man* is essential listening for Bland fans, it also serves as a fine introduction to the great blues singer's catalog. *—Stephen Cook*

Here's the Man! / 1969 / Duke ✦✦✦

Here's the Man! contains recordings Bland cut for the Duke label in the early '60s. It has the same intensity and variety of his late-'50s breakthrough album, *Two Steps From the Blues*, and mimics that album's program of big band-blues swingers, straight blues, and ballads. Bland displays his vocal power throughout *Here's the Man!* using his volcanic, guttural delivery to easily work through Joe Scott's galvanizing arrangements, especially on "Twistin' Up the Road" and "Turn on Your Love Light." He shows stylistic flexibility as well, expertly handling both T-Bone Walker's after-hours classic "Stormy Monday Blues" and the honky tonk-style ballad "You're the One (That I Adore)." In the '70s, Bland would even record an entire album of country standards. Along with Little Milton, Bland took the swinging, soulful blues of Roy Brown and B.B. King and updated it to fit the more polished, yet no less driving soul sound that was emerging around 1960; *Here's the Man!* is a prime document of Bland's explorations. Since it is out of print, though, look for these fine tracks on Bland's many MCA compilations. *—Stephen Cook*

His California Album / 1973 / BGO ✦✦✦

This is his first for ABC/Dunhill in 1973 after more than two decades with Duke (Robey's still represented, though, under his songwriting alias of Deadric Malone on four cuts, including the album's biggest hit, "This Time I'm Gone for Good"). Producer Steve Barri contemporized Bland by having him cover Leon Russell's "Help Me Make It Through the Day," Luther Ingram's "(If Loving You Is Wrong) I Don't Want to Be Right," and Gladys Knight & the Pips' "I've Got to Use My Imagination." *—Bill Dahl*

☆ **The Best of Bobby "Blue" Bland** / 1974 / MCA ✦✦✦✦✦

There have been many Bobby "Blue" Bland collections over the years, and 1974's *The Best of Bobby "Blue" Bland* has been eclipsed by several of them in terms of comprehensiveness and completeness. Still, in terms of a listening experience, this is one of the great blues greatest-hits collections, providing 12 of Bland's greatest songs, including "I Smell Trouble," "I Pity the Fool," "Cry, Cry, Cry," "Turn on Your Love Light," "Farther Up the Road," and "Stormy Monday." Best of all, there are only three tunes that overlap with his seminal *Two Steps From the Blues*, which makes this an excellent supplement to that album, as well as a great, concise introduction to this blues titan. *—Stephen Thomas Erlewine*

Dreamer / 1974 / BGO ✦✦✦

Barri's slightly antiseptic production style and Michael Omartian's arrangements weren't the equivalent of Joe Scott's immaculate collabrations with Bland, but this 1974 album's "Ain't No Love in the Heart of the City" and a meaty "I Wouldn't Treat a Dog (The Way You Treated Me)" were both huge hits. *—Bill Dahl*

Woke up Screaming / 1974 / Duke ✦✦✦✦✦

This is a 16-track import anthology of Bland's earliest Duke sides from 1952-1957, at which point the *Blues Consolidated* album takes over. *—Hank Davis*

Together Again . . . Live / 1976 / Impulse! ✦✦

This not-so-exciting second Bobby "Blue" Bland and B.B. King pairing was recorded in Los Angeles Coconut Grove. There were more show business theatrics and less solid, soulful blues vocalizing than on their acclaimed debut, but there were still enough good moments to make it acceptable. *—Ron Wynn*

Members Only / 1985 / Malaco ✦✦✦

After some fairly soporific early-'80s releases for MCA, this album re-energized Bland's recording fortunes. The Larry Addison-penned title track caught on with blues-soul fans, making it to the middle reaches of the R&B charts as a single. *—Bill Dahl*

Blues You Can Use / 1987 / Malaco ✦✦✦

Blues You Can Use could have accurately been titled *Blues and Soul You Can Use* because it offers a generous dose of R&B along with straight-ahead electric blues. But then, that title wouldn't have been as catchy. More important than the title, of course, is the music itself—and Bobby "Blue" Bland is in decent form on this album, which came out when the singer was 56 or 57. To be sure, *Blues You Can Use* isn't in a class with Bland's classic Duke output of the 1950s and 1960s—and his voice is undeniably thinner than it was in his younger days. But Bland demonstrates that he could still be expressive and charismatic on 12-bar ditties like "I've Got a Problem" and "For the Last Time" as well as laid-back soul numbers such as "Restless Feelin's," "There's No Easy Way to Say Goodbye" and the tear-jerker "Let's Part as Friends." Produced by Malaco founders Tommy Couch Sr. and Wolf Stephenson, *Blues You Can Use* isn't essential. But it's enjoyable, and it's a good example of the fact that Malaco often did well by Bland in the 1980s and 1990s. *—Alex Henderson*

Midnight Run / 1989 / Malaco ✦✦✦

When Bobby "Blue" Bland was recording for Malaco in the 1980s and 1990s, many blues experts asserted that he was past his prime—and they were right. Bland had done his best work for Duke in the 1950s and 1960s, and his voice wasn't what it once was. But the blues/soul singer was still capable of delivering a worthwhile album, and he still had a loyal fan base. In fact, the singer was a consistent seller for Malaco, which could generally be counted on to give him good or excellent material to work with. Recorded when Bland was in his late fifty's, *Midnight Run* isn't remarkable but is generally decent. The production of Tommy Couch and Wolf Stephenson is rock solid, and Bland is soulful and satisfying on the amusing "Take Off Your Shoes," the reggae-influenced title song and arrangements of Bill Withers' "Ain't No Sunshine" and the Mel & Tim hit "Starting All Over Again." Although casual listeners would be better off with a collection of Bland's Duke material, *Midnight Run* is a CD that his hardcore fans will enjoy. *—Alex Henderson*

The 3B Blues Boy—The Blues Years: 1952–59 / 1991 / Ace ✦✦✦

25-track compilation of bluesy material that Bland recorded for Duke between 1952 and 1959. Bland had previously released a few sides for Chess and Modern in the early '50s, but these sides represent the era in which he began to find his voice. It still catches him at a relatively early stage in his development, concentrating on jump blues-oriented material, sometimes with horn sections, showing the considerable influence of B.B. King. There's some sharp guitar on these sides (including some by Roy Gaines, who also played with Chuck Willis and Hound Dog Thornton), and the vocals are full and confident, if a bit overripe. But neophytes should begin with his early- and mid-'60s sides, when his blend of blues and soul reached a much higher level of maturity. *—Richie Unterberger*

The Voice: Duke Recordings 1959–69 / 1991 / Ace ✦✦✦✦✦

A 26-track compilation of Duke sides from Bland's peak decade (1959-1969). MCA's two-volume *The Duke Recordings* covers this period in greater depth, and will be more readily available to most North American consumers. On its own terms, though, it's an excellent collection. Contains most of his biggest R&B hits ("Turn on Your Love Light,"

"Stormy Monday Blues," "Call on Me," "Ain't Nothing You Can Do"), as well as some cuts that didn't make it onto *The Duke Recordings*. *—Richie Unterberger*

☆ **I Pity the Fool: The Duke Recordings, Vol. 1** / 1992 / MCA ✦✦✦✦✦
Everything the young Bland waxed for Duke between 1952 and the 1960 date that produced "Cry, Cry, Cry" and the R&B-laced "Don't Cry No More." From 1955 on, this is uniformly seminal stuff, Bland's vocal confidence growing by the session and buttressed by the consistently innovative riffs and solos of guitarists Clarence Hollimon, Wayne Bennett (he's amazing on a torrid "You Did Me Wrong"), Roy Gaines and Pat Hare. "Farther Up the Road," the exotic ballad "Hold Me Tenderly," "Little Boy Blue," and the title track are but few of the two-disc collection's many standouts. No blues fan should be minus this set! *—Bill Dahl*

Years of Tears / 1993 / Malaco ✦✦✦✦
Perhaps no artist has flourished at Malaco more than Bobby "Blue" Bland. Bland's animated, raw voice, though not as wide-ranging, still has a character and quality unmatched in blues, soul or vintage R&B. This CD is his finest for the label since *Members Only*. The opening number "Somewhere Between Right & Wrong" has a simmering track, Bland's mournful, explosive leads, tasty organ, tight drumming, and on-the-money lyrics from composers Johnny Barranco and Jackson. It sets the stage for nine additional country-tinged and bluesy soul tunes, including three from Frederick Knight, who also produced his compositions. It's not his Duke material, but it's close enough to satisfy. *—Ron Wynn*

☆ **Turn on Your Love Light: The Duke Recordings, Vols. 1-2** / 1994 / MCA ✦✦✦✦✦
Picking up right where the first volume left off and continuing into 1964, this two-disc compilation (50 tracks!) showcases one of Bland's most appealing periods at Duke. Joe Scott was experimenting boldly with his protégé's repertoire, his brass-powered arrangements urging Bland to increased heights of incendiary energy on "Turn on Your Love Light" and "Yield Not to Temptation" (driven by future James Brown drummer Jabo Starks's funky traps) and advanced sophistication levels for the honey-smooth "Share Your Love With Me" and "That's the Way Love Is." Bennett's crackling blues licks invest "Stormy Monday Blues," "The Feeling Is Gone," and "Black Night" with T-Bone-derived tradition, while Bland handles Charlie Rich's "Who Will the Next Fool Be" with just the right amount of bluesy resignation. *—Bill Dahl*

Sad Street / Oct. 24, 1995 / Malaco ✦✦
Malaco's well-oiled, violin-enriched studio sound fits Bland's laid-back contemporary approach just fine these days (even if his voice admittedly ain't what it used to be). With top-flight songwriters George Jackson, Robert Johnson, and Sam Mosley contributing material to the project, the results are agreeable if less than earthshaking. Why Bland chose to cover Rod Stewart's "Tonight's the Night" remains a mystery, however. *—Bill Dahl*

That Did It!: The Duke Recordings, Vol. 3 / Jun. 18, 1996 / MCA ✦✦✦
That Did It! is the third and final installment in MCA's series of double-disc compilations of Bobby "Blue" Bland's Duke recordings. This set collects everything he recorded between 1965 and 1972, including two unreleased tracks and several alternate takes. Although the music on *That Did It!* isn't quite as strong as the songs on the first two installments of the series, it does collect a full 16 singles that have never appeared on an album before, as well as featuring several top-notch album tracks. For Bland fans, the collection remains a necessary purchase—this is Bland's final set of essential recordings. *—Thom Owens*

★ **Greatest Hits, Vol. 1: The Duke Recordings** / Jun. 16, 1998 / Duke/Peacock ✦✦✦✦✦
This single-disc compilation cherry-picks through MCA's three two-disc anthology sets and puts together 16 tracks of essential Bland, starting with 1957's "Farther Up the Road" and ending up with his 1969 reading of Big Joe Turner's "Chains of Love." It gathers up all the biggies: "Turn on Your Lovelight," "I Pity the Fool," "Stormy Monday Blues," "Call on Me," "I'll Take Care of You," and the transfers are exemplary. While it obviously leaves off a few of the early favorites—"Little Boy Blue" is almost inexcusable in its absence—this and its companion volume will be the best introduction for anyone wanting to explore the Bobby "Blue" Bland collection. *—Cub Koda*

Greatest Hits, Vol. 2: The ABC/Dunhill/MCA Recordings / Jul. 14, 1998 / MCA ✦✦✦✦✦
Subtitled *The ABC/Dunhill/MCA Recordings*, this picks up the last tenure of Bland working under the corporate MCA umbrella. With tunes aboard from various albums and singles, this 16-track collection covers the highlights from his 1970s period, with only 1982's "Recess in Heaven" falling outside the time frame. Bland was a much different vocalist by now, and if anything, these tracks, some of them flirting outright with disco, spearheaded the easy-listening-blues style that he still spearheads. Highlights include "This Time I'm Gone for Good," an uncharacteristically funky "Goin' Down Slow," "I Wouldn't Treat a Dog (The Way You Treated Me)," "Ain't No Love in the Heart of the City," "Yolanda" and Bland's own "The Soul of a Man." Experiments with country show up on "Today I Started Loving You Again" and "I Hate You," and yet Bland's duet with B.B. King on Louis Jordan's "Let the Good Times Roll" still shows that his blues roots were always close at hand. Not the place to start, but his last hurrah before going over to Malaco, and a solid collection to investigate nonetheless. *—Cub Koda*

Blues & Ballads / May 18, 1999 / MCA ✦✦✦
A 16-track collection that draws on his Duke and Dunhill recordings from the '60s, '70s, and '80s. Kicking off with the 1960 single "I've Been Wrong So Long" (featuring barn-burning guitar work from Wayne Bennett) and continuing right to the Al Bell productions from the early '80s, Bland's seamless command of the material at hand makes for a smooth listening ride all the way. A perfect companion set to any greatest-hits collection you might want to assemble. *—Cub Koda*

☆ **The Anthology** / Jun. 5, 2001 / MCA ✦✦✦✦✦
As the quintessential chitlin circuit R&B/blues star, Memphis-based singer Bobby "Blue" Bland's career has been relatively well-documented on CD. Still, until this 2001 double set, all 25 of his Top Ten R&B hits have not been available in one package. *The Anthology* is still not a complete career overview though, as it ends in 1982 before his prolific years at Malaco. It does, however, cover a remarkably prolific 30-year period, starting with his first recordings for Duke in 1952 and touching base at Dunhill and MCA, all conveniently located under the current Universal Music label umbrella. Die-hard fans of Bland during this period likely own the three double-disc sets MCA released in the mid-'90s but, for those who don't need the warts-and-all treatment yet want something more in depth than skimpy single-disc collections, this is certainly the way to go. Soul expert Bill Dahl's excellent liner notes provide anecdotes along with the major events that shaped Bland's life and ultimately these recordings. The 16-page book lists detailed and comprehensive individual track information, noting specific musicians on each of the 50 cuts. The overall effect is startling in its consistency. Bland's style and voice are immediately identifiable throughout, and the songwriting—even on the later tracks—typically suits his grits-and-honey approach. A previously unreleased live eight-minute 1973 version of "This Time I'm Gone for Good," which demonstrates how effectively Bland extended his songs in concert, is the only collectable track here, but this chronologically arranged set is not geared toward that segment of the audience. Sonically, *The Anthology* is the best this material has ever sounded, with the '60s songs absolutely stunning in their remastered definition. While he experienced a significant career resurgence in the '80s, which is where this sets stops, these are the classic songs that form the basis of any serious blues collection. As such, it's an essential document of one of America's most talented, and creative, blues singers. *—Hal Horowitz*

Marcie Blane

b. May 21, 1944, Brooklyn, NY
Vocals / Girl Group
A singer who crossed the teen idol sound with a light girl group flavor, Marcie Blane had one huge hit, "Bobby's Girl," which made number three in late 1962. The single was saccharine, but incessantly catchy, with its low tremeloed guitar riffs; doofy male "You're not a kid anymore!" backup interjections; and Blane's wholesome vocals, preceded by some melodramatic spoken lines. She released about half a dozen other singles on the Seville label, several written, like "Bobby's Girl," by the Klein-Hoffman team. None were hits, though, and none were remarkable, falling into the most lightweight sector of the girl group trend. *—Richie Unterberger*

● **Marcie Blane Together With Tracey Dey** / Missing ✦✦✦
This hard-to-find, probably unauthorized CD combines 12 tracks by Blane with 13 by the even more obscure 1960s girl group-style vocalist Tracey Dey. Nothing else has the hooks that made "Bobby's Girl" (which is here, of course) a hit, and Blane's slight, girlish voice doesn't make the material into anything more than it is. If you're a huge 1960s girl group/girl singer fan, though, it's certainly representative of the sound of an era, with production that fairly screams 1962-1963—not quite part of the teen-idol era, but not quite as modern as Phil Spector (or even the Shirelles) either. "She'll Break the String" and "After the Laughter" are the only tunes that would even cut the ice as items on compilations of decent or half-decent overlooked girl-group recordings; the rest are pretty meaningless. Tracey Dey's half of the CD, incidentally, is considerably better, with some fairly good obscure girl group-style singles (such as "I Won't Tell"), which could tip the balance in favor of purchase if you collect this genre. *—Richie Unterberger*

Mary J. Blige

b. Jan. 11, 1971, New York, NY [The Bronx]
Vocals / Hip-Hop, Urban, Club/Dance, Contemporary R&B
When her debut album, *What's the 411?*, hit the street in 1992, critics and fans alike were floored by its powerful combination of modern R&B with an edgy rap sound that glanced off of the pain and grit of Mary J. Blige's Yonkers, NY, childhood. Called alternately the new Chaka Khan or new Aretha Franklin, Blige had little in common stylistically with either of those artists, but like them helped adorn soul music with new textures and flavors that inspired a whole generation of musicians. With her blonde hair, self-preserving slouch and combat boots, Blige was street-tough and beautiful all at once, and the record company execs who profited off of her early releases did little to dispel the bad-girl image that she earned as she stumbled through the dizzying first days of her career. As she exorcised her personal demons and softened her style to include sleek designer clothes, she remained a hero to thousands of girls growing up in the same kinds of rough places she came from.

Blige reinvented her career again and again by shedding the bad habits and bad influences that kept her down; by the time her fourth album, *Mary*, was released in 1999, she had matured into an expressive singer able to put the full power of her voice behind her music, while still reflecting a strong urban style. With her fifth album, *No More Drama*, it wasn't just Blige's style that shone through the structures set up for her by songwriters and producers, it was her own vision—spiritual, emotional, personal, and full of wisdom, and reflected an artist who was comfortable with who she was and how far she had come.

Born in the Bronx on January 11, 1971, Blige spent the first few years of her life in Savannah, GA, before moving with her mother and older sister to the Schlobam housing projects in Yonkers, NY. Her rough life there produced more than a few scars, physical and otherwise, and Blige dropped out of high school her junior year, instead spending time doing her friends' hair in her mother's apartment and hanging out. When she was at a local mall in White Plains, NY, she recorded herself singing Anita Baker's "Caught Up in the Rapture," into a karaoke machine. The resulting tape was passed by Blige's stepfather to Uptown Records' CEO Andre Harrell. Harrell was impressed with Blige's voice and signed her to sing backup for local acts like Father MC. In 1991, however, Sean "Puffy" Combs took Blige under his wing and began working with her on *What's the 411?*, her debut album. Combs had a heavy hand in *What's the 411?*, along with producers Dave Hall, Mark Morales, and Mark Rooney, and the stylish touches that they added to Blige's unique vocal style created a stunning album that bridged the gap between R&B and rap in a way that no female singer had before. Uptown tried to capitalize on the success of *What's the 411?* by issuing a remixed version of it a year later, but it was only a modest success creatively and commercially.

Her 1995 follow-up, *My Life*, again featured Combs' handiwork, and if it stepped back stylistically from its urban roots by featuring less of a rap sound, it made up for it with its subject matter. *My Life* was full of ghetto pathos and Blige's own personal pain shone through like a beacon. Her rocky relationship with fellow Uptown artist K-Ci Hailey likely contributed to the raw emotions on the album. The period following the recording of *My Life* was also a difficult time professionally for Blige as she severed her ties with Combs and Uptown, hired Suge Knight as a financial advisor and signed with MCA.

1997's *Share My World* marked the beginning of Blige's creative partnerships with Jimmy Jam and Terry Lewis. The album was another hit for Blige and debuted at number one on the *Billboard* charts. Critics soured somewhat on its more conventional soul sound, but Blige's fans seemed undaunted. By the time her next studio album, *Mary*, came out in 1999, the fullness and elegance of her new sound seemed more developed, as Blige exuded a classic soul style aided by material from Elton John and Bernie Taupin, Stevie Wonder, and Lauryn Hill. *Mary* made it obvious that the ghetto fabulous style and more confrontational aspects of her music were gone, while the emotive power still remained.

That power also helped carry the more modern-sounding 2001 release, *No More Drama*, a deeply personal album that remained a collective effort musically yet reflected more of Blige's songwriting than any of her previous efforts. The Mary J. Blige on *No More Drama* seemed miles away from the flashy kid on *What's the 411?*, yet it was still possible to see the path through her music that produced an older, wiser, but still expressive artist. *—Stacia Proefrock*

● **What's the 411?** / 1992 / MCA ✦✦✦✦✦

Mary J. Blige's debut album, *What's the 411?*, was a revolution in disguise. Like her new jack predecessors, Blige combined R&B with hip-hop, but unlike Guy and Bobby Brown, her music was more seductive and sly. More importantly, she sounds grittier and more real than most new jack swingers or female R&B vocalists. Blige can slip between singing and rapping with ease, which is partially the reason why *What's the 411?* is so successful. It doesn't hurt that her collaborators, from Grand Puba to Sean "Puffy" Combs, help construct backing tracks that are both melodic, relentlessly funky, and sexy. *—Stephen Thomas Erlewine*

My Life / 1994 / MCA ✦✦✦✦

Perhaps the single finest moment in Sean "Puffy" Combs' musical career has been the production on this, Mary J. Blige's second proper album. The production is not exactly original, and there is evidence here of him borrowing wholesale from other songs. The melodic sources this time around, though, are so expertly incorporated into the music that they never seem to be intrusions, instead playing like inspired dialogues with soulsters from the past, connecting past legacies with a new one. This certainly isn't your parents' (or grandparents') soul. But it is some of the finest modern soul of the '90s, backing away to a certain extent from the hip-hop/soul consolidation that Blige introduced on her debut album. The hip-hop part of the combination takes a few steps into the background, allowing Blige's tortured soul to carry the album completely, and it does so with heartwrenching authority. *My Life* is, from beginning to end, a brilliant, wistful individual plea of desire. Blige took a huge leap in artistry by penning almost everything herself (the major exception being Norman Whitfield's "I'm Going Down") in collaboration with co-producers Combs and multi-instrumentalist Chucky Thompson, and everything seems to leap directly from her gut. Blige's strain is sleekly modern and urban, and the grit in it comes from being streetwise and thoroughly realistic about the travails of life. *My Life*, nevertheless, emanates from some deep, dark place where both sadness and happiness cohabitate and turn into one single, beautiful sorrow. *—Stanton Swihart*

Share My World / Apr. 22, 1997 / MCA ✦✦✦✦

The hype that surrounded Mary J. Blige in the beginning was simply ridiculous. When *What's the 411?* was released in 1992, she was exalted as "the new Chaka Khan"— a definite exaggeration, considering how uneven that debut album was. But Blige did show promise, and by the time she recorded her third album, *Share My World*, she had developed into a fairly convincing soul/urban singer. Her strongest and most confident effort up to that point, *Share* had much more character, personality, and honesty than most of the assembly line fare dominating urban radio in 1997. For all their slickness, emotive cuts like "Get to Know You Better," "Love Is All We Need," and "Keep Your Head" left no doubt that Blige was indeed a singer of depth and substance. Although high tech, the production of everyone from R. Kelly (with whom she duets on the inviting "It's On") and Babyface to Jimmy Jam and Terry Lewis doesn't come across as forced or robotic, but, in fact, is impressively organic. With *Share My World*, Blige definitely arrived. *—Alex Henderson*

The Tour / Jul. 28, 1998 / MCA ✦✦✦

The hype that surrounded Mary J. Blige in 1992 was definitely excessive, and those who exalted her as the "new Chaka Khan" did both Khan and Blige an unforgivable disservice (few could live up to such a title). But as the 1990s progressed, Blige really did evolve into one of the decade's most appealing R&B vocalists, and she's in good to excellent form on *The Tour*, which was recorded on her *Share My World* Tour of 1997-1998. The very fact that a live urban contemporary album came out in the late 1990s was quite surprising; after all, R&B had become so technology-driven and studio-oriented that few R&B artists even bothered to make live albums anymore. But Blige was an exception, and she proves herself capable of taking it to the stage on passionate versions of such hits as "My Life," "Mary Jane (All Night Long)," "Reminisce," and "Mary's Joint." Blige could have done without the male bandmember who tries to function as her on-stage cheerleader, but even so, this is an impressive release that her followers will want. *—Alex Henderson*

Mary / Aug. 17, 1999 / MCA ✦✦✦✦

Perhaps it was inevitable that Mary J. Blige would mature, toning down the raunchier elements of her persona that have been evident since her debut, while repositioning herself as a classicist soul singer. Even so, the sheer classiness of *Mary*, her fourth album, may come as a bit of a surprise. Blige made a conscious effort to create an album that recalled the classic dawning days of quiet storm yet worked as a unified, cohesive album. That meant that the more overt hip-hop elements have been subdued in favor of '70s soul. There's still grit in the music, but it's been glossed over with a polished production, and she now favors sophisticated songs, including material from such writers as Stevie Wonder, Bacharach & David, Lauryn Hill, and Elton John & Bernie Taupin. Some of these writers were collaborators and others contributed songs outright, but the amazing thing about the end result belongs to nobody else but Blige. It's different, to be sure, but still her—and it's a rewarding, engaging way to mature. Blige's voice is richer and her skills have deepened, and her new songs, while not as streetwise, are worthy of her talents. Consequently, *Mary* is a thoroughly winning album. *—Stephen Thomas Erlewine*

No More Drama / Aug. 28, 2001 / MCA ✦✦✦✦

Listeners of Mary J. Blige's seasoned and confident fifth studio release will have zero problems remembering the album's title, *No More Drama*. An urban-sounding vocal sample that sings, "Mary J. Blige, no more drama," plays throughout the length of the 17-track disc. This very well may be the first time such a tactic has been used in contemporary music; generally a vocal sample repeats throughout the course of only one song, but because the fare on *No More Drama* is so good, this recurring vocal sample is as subtle and congruent as a consistent drum hit. Blige has come a long way since 1992's breakthrough, *What's the 411?*, and that's made very clear on this solid disc. The singer/songwriter has blossomed into an all-out R&B diva—with a hip-hop edge—full of soul and command. Her songs on this recording exude the wisdom of a woman who's seen it all and has found her center. And she will no longer tolerate drama, pettiness, and overall crap. In 2001's crop of R&B singers, Blige's voice was truly inimitable. It's husky, strong, soulful, and full of maturity. Make no mistake, though, this lady can still flow like no one's business; just check out the bouncy album-opener "Love." In fact, many of the record's cuts are standout moments. For instance, only Blige has the balls to write and pull off a song called "PMS," a soulful and bluesy number that describes, in detail, this condition inherent to the female experience. And while she also explores themes of love, Blige's disc is essentially a journey through her personal evolution and spirituality. The final cut, "Testimony," best summarizes the album's theme: finding what's real in life. And for Blige, that's self-love and God. To her credit, Blige has a killer instinct for penning lyrics that people can relate to and creating gritty, thick, and soul-infused R&B fare. (She does get some help on this disc from such R&B and hip-hop heavyweights as Missy Elliot, Jimmy Jam, and Terry Lewis, among others.) Her music is more than heard, it is felt, and audiences would be hard-pressed to not surrender to her groove. Interestingly, many of Blige's peers sing about drama, but not this artist—not anymore. [*No More Drama* was re-released in early 2002 with a handful of different tracks.] *—Liana Jonas*

Dance for Me / Jul. 22, 2002 / MCA International ✦✦✦

Yes, *Dance for Me* is another remix album from a hip-hop/urban artist, following hot on the heels of high-profile remix releases from P. Diddy and others. But unlike any other mainstream artist, Mary J. Blige has the range and energy of the best disco divas, plus the exquisite taste of any dance scenester—both of which combine to make *Dance for Me* one of the best, most innovative remix albums of recent vintage. Included are remixes from producers like Junior Vasquez, Hex Hector, and Barry Harris (from Thunderpuss), who've done dozens of remixes for artists like Blige in the past, and easily display a flair for giving her songs the natural settings they deserve. "No More Drama," the title track from her full-length of 2001, particularly shines after getting treated by Thunderpuss. Tweaked out to nearly ten minutes with no sign of stretch-marks, the song becomes a multi-part epic in the hands of Blige, freestyling like the best dance vocalists of *any* era, from Loleatta Holloway to La India. "Family Affair," the Dr. Dre production (originally) with the lyric that spawned this album's title, boasts a chunky, classic-disco rework from Spanish Fly, while Vasquez and Hector give their inclusions the high-energy synthetics of hard house. Al B. Rich offers some variety (and a nod to dance taste-makers) with a 2-step groove for "Never Been," and the last track—Blige's 1999 cover of the seminal disco anthem "Let No Man Put Asunder" by First Choice—ends it on a high note, proving to anyone who's curious that, no matter who invented the remix, Mary J. Blige is her generation's most artistic diva. *—John Bush*

Bloodstone

f. 1962, Kansas City, MO

Group / Brown-Eyed Soul, Funk, Soul

Bloodstone was a key group in creating the shift from the R&B and soul group concepts of the '50s and '60s to the funk and black rock ideas of the '70s and afterward. The group began in Kansas City, while the original members were in high school, as an a cappella doo wop group, the Sinceres, around 1962. They evolved with the decade, and by 1968 were ensconced in Las Vegas, playing lounges like many other soul minor leaguers (Sonny Charles & the Checkmates, most notoriously). From there, they went to Los Angeles and did the unexpected: They learned to play instruments and became a band (like the Clash and Steely Dan, they never did settle on a permanent drummer).

In fact, Bloodstone was a very good funk-soul group using the Hendrix-derived licks of Charles Love and Willis Draffen against multiple percussion ideas to underpin a vocal blend that still owed its soul to gospel and doo wop. (If this makes you think of the Isley Brothers of "That Lady," you're on the right track.) Bloodstone received no record company interest in L.A., however, so at the advice of its manager, the group relocated to London in 1971. There, they teamed up with Mike Vernon, founder of the Blue Horizon label, who'd made his bones producing an album with the great Chicago pianist Otis

Spann; white blues acts like Fleetwood Mac and Savoy Brown; and early Euro-rock with Focus. Vernon took Bloodstone into the studio and by early 1973, its debut single, "Natural High," had cracked the R&B and pop Top Ten, becoming the group's defining song.

Vernon produced the first five Bloodstone albums, which garnered seven Top 20 R&B singles, almost all of which made the pop Top 40. The group was a big concert draw, and its album sold well, if not spectacularly. Somehow, all of this was parlayed into a 1975 film deal. *Train Ride to Hollywood* is arguably the funniest picture of the whole '70s blaxploitation film boom, derived in equal parts from the Marx Brothers and such early spoofs as *The Palm Beach Story* and *International House*. Somehow, amidst the slapstick and the reefer jokes, Bloodstone wedges in a fairly complete history of black vocal harmony music from the Mills Brothers to the Coasters to their own bad selves. They do it even better on the soundtrack album. (All of the Vernon-produced Bloodstone albums contain versions of '50s and '60s oldies.)

The group then faded from popular view, despite a brief stint at Motown, until the early '80s, when it hooked up with the Isley Brothers' T-Neck and scored a commercially and artistically successful album, *We Go a Long Way Back*, produced by the Brothers. The title track returned them to the R&B Top Ten in 1982, but although several other T-Neck singles charted, the group's recording career essentially ended there. Nevertheless, this heartland group had made a significant mark and can lay fair claim to being one of the first to figure out its particular era's future. *—Dave Marsh*

Bloodstone / 1972 / Decca ✦✦✦

Natural High / 1973 / Decca ✦✦✦

Bloodstone's finest song was the title cut, a triumphant bit of wailing soul that remains a favorite among ballad fans. It momentarily put the Kansas City-cum-Los Angeles group Bloodstone into the spotlight. The remainder of the early-'70s album was decent, but it didn't really matter since no one played anything except the single anyhow. *—Ron Wynn*

I Need Time / 1974 / London ✦✦

This features some above-average funk and soul propelled by drummer Steve Ferrone, who was later recruited by the Average White Band. Bloodstone were among the best harmonizers on the '70s soul/R&B circuit, and their production utilized the falsetto lead against two background voices in an exceptional manner. *—Ron Wynn*

Unreal / 1974 / London ✦✦✦✦

The first ten tracks here came from the second Bloodstone album, *Unreal*; the last five are from *Bloodstone*, the 1972 U.K. release that mostly parallels *Natural High* in the States. "Outside Woman" was the hit but the point is the blend of rock and soul. Wayne Edwards' notes are superb. *—Dave Marsh*

Riddle of the Sphinx / 1975 / London ✦✦

This is the final album before Steve Ferrone left to join the Average White Band, and also the last charting album for Bloodstone for seven years. The title cut was straightforward R&B/funk, while the rest of the album blended the band's usual emphatic ballads with upbeat, hard-edged funk and soul. *—Ron Wynn*

Train Ride to Hollywood / 1976 / London ✦✦✦✦✦

This is the soundtrack to their 1975 movie. It didn't make the charts, but it's nevertheless one of the best soul-funk-rock fusions of its era, spanning a blend of material that includes versions of "As Time Goes By," "Yakety Yak," "Money," and "Toot! Toot! Tootsie (Goodbye)." The originals are solid, especially Willis Draffen's "Go to Sleep" and the band's rollicking "Rock & Roll Choo Choo." Notes are sloppy, discographical detail non-existent or this would rate half a notch higher. *—Dave Marsh*

We Go a Long Way Back / 1982 / T Neck ✦✦

Bloodstone came back from a lengthy period off the charts with this early-'80s work. The title track was one of its finest slow tunes in several years, while the other cuts, especially the uptempo ones, were produced and arranged well enough to get Bloodstone back on urban radio. *—Ron Wynn*

Bloodstone's Greatest Hits / 1985 / Columbia ✦✦✦

Natural High / Jul. 16, 1996 / Rhino ✦✦✦✦✦

The bulk of this is their debut album from 1972, featuring everything from a Bo Diddley medley to gospel-bred harmonies to Hendrix-derived guitar licks. Plus the hit, a beautiful fusion of all the above in the form of a sweet 'n' dreamy soul ballad. The best early-'70s Isley Brothers album that the Isley Brothers didn't make themselves. (And believe me, there were plenty trying.) This reissue includes a previously uncollected 1972 single ("Girl (You Look So Fine)"/"Judy, Judy") and four outtakes, including a bizarre yet respectful "Little Green Apples." The annotation by Wayne Edwards is superb, and the discography complete. *—Dave Marsh*

The Ultimate Collection / Aug. 27, 1996 / ITP ✦✦✦✦✦

This is one for the time capsule or at least a permanent slot in the CD changer. Heart-rendering soul music by one of its best purveyors, buoyed by two excellent falsetto singers—silky smooth Charles McCormick and the exciting Henry Williams—Bloodstone's music is absolutely compelling. This excellent compilation features new songs, rekindled versions of their own hits, and stunning remakes. Renditions of Tower of Power's "You're Still a Young Man," Linda Jones' "Hypnotized," the Drewvells' "Tell Him" (as "Tell Her"), and the Fuzz's "I Love You for All Seasons" are unexpected, delightful surprises. Traditionalists and purists will quibble that "Natural High," "We Go a Long Way Back," "Outside Woman," "Never Let You Go," and some others are recuts, rather than the originals, but the voices and the songs are as riveting as ever. *—Andrew Hamilton*

● **The Very Best of Bloodstone** / May 5, 1997 / Rhino ✦✦✦✦✦

Bloodstone's stomping ground was Kansas City by way of Los Angeles and England, but the soul outfit sounded more like it was from Detroit by way of Philadelphia. While Motor City groups like the Temptations and the Dramatics were a major influence on Bloodstone, these soulsters also did some of their best work when they were thinking more along the lines of the Moments, the Stylistics and Blue Magic. A fine illustration of Bloodstone's flexibility, this 1997 release spans 1972-1982 and ranges from heavenly Thom Bell-ish ballads like "Natural High," "Outside Woman" and "Give Me Your Heart" to such funky, Detroit-minded smokers as "Take These Chains" and "Tell It to My Face." *Very Best* also gives us everything from the cutesy "My Little Lady" to the overlooked gem "Little Linda," which describes a young woman's addiction to hard drugs. The slicker, more disco-ish cuts (including "Train Ride") aren't as strong as some of the other material, but even at its second and third best, Bloodstone was enjoyable. And at its best, the group was outstanding. *—Alex Henderson*

We Go a Long Way Back: Greatest Hits / Jan. 5, 1998 / Collectables ✦✦✦✦

The Blossoms

f. 1954, Los Angeles, CA

Group / Girl Group

The Blossoms were a female vocal group formed at Fremont High School in Los Angeles in 1954 as the Dreamers and consisting of Fanita James (nee Barrett), Gloria Jones, and the twin sisters Nanette and Annette Williams. They recorded for Flair Records in 1954. By 1957, Nanette Williams had been replaced by Darlene Wright, who later took the name Darlene Love. They did extensive session work, and Love and James were members of producer Phil Spector's studio group Bob B. Soxx & the Blue Jeans. Love also recorded with Spector under her own name and as part of the Crystals. The Blossoms had one pop chart entry in 1961 with "Son-In-Law," an answer record to Ernie K-Doe's hit "Mother-In-Law." Later, the Blossoms—by now consisting of Love, James, and Jean King—were regular backup singers on the pop music television series *Shindig* in 1965. In 1967, they scored an R&B singles chart entry with "Good, Good Lovin'." There were more personnel changes and a string of singles on several labels. In 1972, the Blossoms recorded the album *Shockwave*. *—William Ruhlmann*

● **Shockwave** / 1972 / MGM ✦✦✦

Blowfly (Clarence Reid)

b. Feb. 14, 1945, Cochran, GA

Vocals / Blaxploitation, Funk

Blowfly is the X-rated alter ego of Clarence Reid, a songwriter/producer who had quite a bit of success under his own name in the '70s, writing and producing hits for Gwen MacRae, KC & the Sunshine Band, Betty Wright, and others while on the staff at the preeminent Florida disco label of the era, TK Records. It's as Blowfly that Reid is best remembered in certain circles, though. The Redd Foxx of the Southern soul circuit, Blowfly specializes in dirty parodies of current soul and pop hits; his over two dozen albums, almost all of them recorded live in the studio with the ambience of a liquor-fueled all-night party, are an entertaining mixture of filth and wit that's neither too disgusting to be funny nor too refined to be dirty.

Born in Cochran, GA, on Valentine's Day, 1945, Reid got his nickname in the early '60s when his grandmother caught the adolescent singing dirty lyrics to a popular hit and proclaimed that her grandchild was "nastier than a blowfly." Reid moved to the more dirty-word-friendly climes of Miami in the mid-'60s and hooked up with producer and label owner Henry Stone. Under his own name, Reid released several solid albums of straight R&B, and had several chart singles, starting with 1969's Top Ten soul hit "Nobody but You Babe," for Stone's Alston and TK imprints.

Reid never lost his knack for filthying up Top 40 hits, though, and after a few years of performing his parodies for friends and co-workers, Reid resurrected his adolescent nickname and went in the studio after hours with some studio musician buddies in 1970 and recorded Blowfly's debut album, *The Weird World of Blowfly*. Of course, Stone's labels couldn't touch the results, so Reid pressed the album on his own Weird World imprint, housing it in a bizarre homemade-looking sleeve featuring Reid standing on a trash can in a comically hideous monster mask, a pair of homemade wings, a blue sweater with "BF" printed on it in yellow and a pair of tighty-whiteys and knee socks, holding a rubber chicken in one hand and clawing at two large-Afro'ed nude women kneeling before him. A weird world indeed.

Sold on the same semi-underground circuit that traded in Rudy Ray Moore's Dolemite albums and other cultural oddities, the Blowfly records were massively popular. Although it was an open secret from the beginning that Blowfly was Clarence Reid, Reid always appeared in some sort of elaborate and/or strange costume on the record sleeves. His reticence to be publicly identified as Blowfly stemmed not only from his religious upbringing—despite his dirty mouth, Reid is a devout Christian who forswears liquor and cigarettes and has worked as a minister—but from the criminal prosecution that Reid's latter-day buddies 2 Live Crew found out about the hard way. Stores have been prosecuted for carrying Blowfly albums in some communities, and Reid was sued by the then-president of ASCAP, Stanley Adams, after Blowfly parodied Adams' jazz standard "What a Difference a Day Makes" as "What a Difference a Lay Makes."

Reid released Blowfly records under a variety of label names through the '70s, '80s, and '90s, collaborating with like-minded folks like 2 Live Crew and even Flea from the Red Hot Chili Peppers. Blowfly is enough of a cultural icon that he even recorded his own holiday single in the mid-'70s. Of course, the songs were called "Jingle Fuckin' Bells" and "Queer for the New Year," but this is Blowfly we're talking about here, not Bing Crosby. Blowfly also starred in the low-budget documentary *The Twisted World of Blowfly* in 1991, and several of his albums were reissued on CD through the '90s, capped by *The Best of Blowfly: Analthology* in 1996. *—Stewart Mason*

The Weird World of Blowfly / 1971 / Hot Productions ✦✦✦✦

Recorded live in the studio, *The Weird World of Blowfly* has the ambience of an after-hours party. In the tradition of older albums by similar (though tamer) acts like Doug Clark & Hot Nuts, *The Weird World of Blowfly* starts with his theme song, "Weird World," and then moves through 14 sexual and scatological parodies of popular soul and pop hits of the time, interspersed with good-humored, rambling introductions. So is it funny? Some will undoubtedly find the whole enterprise juvenile and distasteful, and frankly, a couple of the parodies are a little too obvious to be clever (surely sixth graders around the world have written songs like "Shittin' on the Dock of the Bay"), but most of the album is really very funny, for those who like this sort of thing. The 1995 reissue adds three tracks to the original LP (first released on Clarence Reid's own Weird World label), including both sides of a celebrated mid-'70s holiday single, "Jingle Fuckin' Bells" and "Queer for the New Year," along with, oddly enough, a clean single released under Reid's own name in 1974, "Fonky Party." *—Stewart Mason*

Porno Freak / 1977 / Hot Productions ♦♦♦

Blowfly's Disco Party / 1978 / Weird World ♦♦♦

Oldies But Goodies / 1978 / Weird World ♦♦♦♦♦

Here are raunchy-beyond-belief sendups of *American Bandstand*, with every song you ever loved from the '50s ("Ten Commandments of Sex," "F**k Around the Clock," etc.), raped, pillaged, and plundered in the bargain. *—Cub Koda*

Zodiac Party / 1978 / Weird World ♦♦♦

Blowfly's Party / 1980 / Weird World ♦♦♦♦

Electronic Banana / 1984 / Oops! ♦♦♦

On Tour '86 / 1986 / Oops! ♦♦♦

For President / 1988 / Oops! ♦♦♦♦♦

The sheer lunacy of X-rated comedian Blowfly running for any political office, let alone the presidency, provides an entertaining hook for this often-outrageous release. *—Ron Wynn*

The Twisted World of Blowfly / 1990 / Oops! ♦♦♦

This features some inspired philosophy delivered in terms ranging from confused to bizarre to obscene. Longtime urban/ghetto comedian Blowfly entered the '90s in style. Suddenly he was getting publicity from the same image-conscious types who'd once relegated his humor to the underground. He even appeared on a Big Daddy Kane record, and people suddenly realized that there was a host of black comic observers who never got a chance to showcase their wares in comedy clubs or for major labels. *—Ron Wynn*

The Best of Blowfly: Analthology / Aug. 20, 1996 / Pandisc ♦♦♦

Reviewing a Blowfly album is a bit like discussing a porno film; you pretty much know what the dirty parts are going to be like at the outset, so the real question is: Does the work in question have any redeeming artistic merit? Clarence Reid, the semi-respectable creative mind behind the outrageously freaky persona of Blowfly, knows more than a little about making a solid R&B record, and once you get past the mega-filthy lyrics and titles like "Hole Man" and "Porno Freak," you can usually find some solid soul and funk grooves on the best Blowfly records. However, *The Best of Blowfly: Analthology* for the most part reflects the less-than-ideal state of old school R&B these days. While the original Blowfly albums on Weird World Records exuded the gloriously drunken ambience of an after-hours party gone nasty, *Analthology* consists of mid-'90s re-recordings of Blowfly's underground hits, with synthesizers and drum machines often replacing the live rhythm sections that conjured up the good groove behind Blowfly's classic albums (please remember "classic" is a relative term). Reid's performances are still enthusiastically filthy, and the jokes are just as funny as they've ever been (decide for yourself if that's good or bad), but the cleaner surfaces of the digital-friendly production make for a less-enjoyably dirty experience, sort of like the difference between a vintage adult movie shot on film and a modern porn quickie produced on videotape. Longtime Blowfly fans will be glad to hear the king of smut funk is still in solid form, but anyone looking for a real Blowfly greatest-hits disc ought to dig up *The Worst of Blowfly*, a collection of vintage Weird World material. *—Mark Deming*

● **The Worst of Blowfly** / Oct. 15, 1996 / Hot Productions ♦♦♦♦

The Worst of Blowfly is an aptly titled collection only if one thinks of the word "worst" in the sense of (to use one of the man's favorite words) "nastiest." This 1996 compilation, with tracks that stretch back over a quarter century to some of Clarence Reid's earliest recordings under his foulmouthed Blowfly persona, is for those who find Doug Clark & Hot Nuts too prim: These 20 songs are pure Southern gutbucket funk with absolutely filthy—and usually hilarious—lyrics. Titles like "Spearmy Night in Georgia" and "She Sucks on My Dick" say it all, yet there's a playfulness and good humor to these songs that keep them from being merely crude. Reid doesn't have a hateful bone in his body, and so there's no anger or spite in Blowfly's songs, just a schoolboy's glee in naughtiness for its own sake. It also helps that thanks to Reid's other career as a straight R&B singer, producer, and arranger, he has always been able to get ace musicians for his Blowfly sessions, with the result that songs like "Funky Party" work just as well as groove thangs. *—Stewart Mason*

The Blue Jays

f. 1961, Venice, CA, **db.** 1962

Group / Doo Wop

The Blue Jays perfectly represent the transitional era between '50s R&B and the '60s soul era by singing doo wop-styled songs with a gospelly lead vocal. They are best known for their 1961 Top 40 hit "Lovers Island," which many consider to be the last hit record in true doo wop style. The Los Angeles-based vocal quartet–Leon Peels, Van Richardson, Alex Manigo, and Leonard Davidson (aka "Len" and "Tree Tall Len")—came together in the suburb of Venice, CA, in 1961. Following an appearance at an amateur show at the Fox Theater in Venice, the group were put in touch with country singer Werly Fairburn, who signed them to his Milestone label. Milestone's roster consisted mostly of rockabilly bands and had already achieved some success with the Paradons ("Diamonds and Pearls").

The Blue Jays' first single "Lovers Island," written by Peels and Manigo, seemed almost like a throwback to an earlier time in vocal group music. Though it was not a big seller like other vocal act singles of the time by groups like the Jive Five or the Dreamlovers—it charted in the pop Top 40 at number 31 and performed well on the local L.A. R&B charts—it served as a beautiful swan song for the doo wop era. Milestone also released an album pairing the Paradons with the Blue Jays.

The group followed their hit with singles like "Tears Are Falling" (1961) and "The Right to Love" (1962), but nothing came of them and the group broke up in early 1962. Leon Peels later recorded a number of singles—including "On a Magic Island"—for Whirlybird Records, backed by the Hi-Tensions. *—Bryan Thomas*

● **The Bluejays Meet the Paradons** / Jul. 28, 1998 / Collectables ♦♦♦♦♦

Collectables' *The Bluejays Meet the Paradons* is a bit of a treasure trove for doo wop collectors. The title is a little misleading: The Bluejays dominate the proceedings—14 of the 18 tracks are theirs—and they're a better vocal group than the Paradons, who nevertheless have an extraordinary single with "Diamonds and Pearls." Since it's the first time most of the material here has been released on CD, the disc will be of interest to hardcore doo wop collectors, especially since the Bluejays have a couple of sides that are quite nice. *—Stephen Thomas Erlewine*

Blue Magic

f. 1973, Philadelphia, PA

Group / Quiet Storm, Soul, R&B

Blue Magic, an R&B vocal quintet whose members were Theodore Mills, Vernon Sawyer, Wendell Sawyer, Keith Beaton, and Richard Pratt, was formed in Philadelphia and signed to Atlantic Records in 1973. They hit the Top 40 of the R&B singles chart with their first three 45s before breaking through and crossing over with "Sideshow," released in April 1974, which went gold, topped the R&B charts, and became a Top Ten pop hit. "Three Ring Circus," their next single, made the R&B Top Ten and the pop Top 40. Blue Magic had two more R&B chart singles in 1975 and four in 1976 before suffering a career slump, but they returned with R&B chart singles in 1981 and 1983 and made a comeback album, *From Out of the Blue*, in 1989. *—William Ruhlmann*

Blue Magic / Feb. 1974 / Atco ♦♦♦♦

In the '70s, Philadelphia's most famous soul empire was Kenny Gamble & Leon Huff's Philadelphia International Records, home of the O'Jays, the Intruders, Harold Melvin & the Blue Notes, the Three Degrees, and Billy Paul. But the Thom Bell/Linda Creed school of Philly soul was also huge thanks to heavyweights like the Stylistics and the Delfonics. When Blue Magic hit big in 1974, their smooth, polished sound owed a lot to the Bell/Creed school; this incredibly promising debut album finds the Philly vocal group wearing their Stylistics/Delfonics/Moments heritage like a badge of honor. But the LP also demonstrates that Blue Magic was a fine group in their own right. The single that put Blue Magic on the map was "Sideshow," a hit ballad that is as clever as it melancholy. "Sideshow" describes a circus, but not an ordinary circus—a circus in which all of the attractions are noteworthy because of their terrible luck when it comes to romantic relationships. The tune is simply brilliant; like so many great blues and country gems, "Sideshow" finds a very witty way to talk about romantic disappointments. But even though "Sideshow" is one of Philly soul's all-time classics, it isn't the only song that makes this LP worth owning. The rest of the album is also superb, and that includes the snappy "Look Me Up," as well as dreamy, gossamer ballads like "Spell" and "What's Come Over Me" (which Blue Magic revisited on a 1975 remake that features singer Margie Joseph). All of the albums that Blue Magic recorded in the '70s are worth hearing, but this 1974 debut is arguably the finest and most essential of the bunch. *—Alex Henderson*

The Magic of the Blue / 1975 / Atco ♦♦♦

13 Blue Magic Lane / Sep. 1975 / Atco ♦♦♦

Mystic Dragons / Sep. 1976 / Atco ♦♦♦♦

Heavily influenced by the Delfonics and the Stylistics, Blue Magic was best known for smooth, dreamy, gossamer treasures like "Sideshow," "What's Come Over Me," "Spell," and "Three Ring Circus." Blue Magic epitomized the sweeter side of Philadelphia soul, and R&B lovers associated the vocal quintet with romantic ballads and slow jams—not tough, gritty funk. So it came as a major surprise when, in 1976, Blue Magic opened its fourth album, *Mystic Dragons*, with the very funky and very danceable "Freak-N-Stein." That infectious opener demonstrated that the Philadelphians were quite capable of handling funk, and they are every bit as inspired on the equally funky "Mother Funk." Also surprising is the exuberant "Rock N Roll Revival," which blends R&B with rock and is hardly the sort of tune one expected Blue Magic to record in 1976. But the group doesn't abandon ballads and slow jams on this Bobby Eli-produced LP—those who cherish its sweetly romantic side should have no problem getting into "Summer Snow," "To Get Love," or "Making Love to a Memory." Although not as essential as 1974's *Blue Magic* or 1975's *13 Blue Magic Lane*, *Mystic Dragons* is a solid, rewarding effort that offers its share of surprises. *—Alex Henderson*

Message / 1978 / Atco ♦♦♦♦

Blue Magic's 1978 Atco/Atlantic LP *Message* was produced by Skip Scarborough (Earth, Wind & Fire, LTD's "Love Ballad," Creative Source) and is a favorite of soft soul enthusiasts. Most of the LP's songs were co-written by the group. An album that's definitely on the mellow side, one reason for its lack of huge commercial success may have been that it was released at the height of disco. No matter, the LP brims with great make-out music: the majestic ballads "Still in Love With You," "Sweet Woman," the samba-flavored "Can't Get You off My Mind," and the glockenspiel *clop, clop*-laced slow jam "Lady in My World of Love." Blue Magic picks up the tempo a bit on the optimistic "Message." Those who loved the group's two gold singles, "Sideshow" and "Three Ring Circus," won't be disappointed. The slick and swift "I Waited" from the LP is included on the 1996 Rhino CD, *Soulful Spell: The Best of Blue Magic*. *—Ed Hogan*

The Magic of the Blue: Greatest Hits / 1986 / Atco ♦♦♦

● **The Best of Blue Magic: Soulful Spell** / Jan. 23, 1996 / Rhino ♦♦♦♦
Released in 1996, *The Best of Blue Magic: Soulful Spell* typified the pros and cons of compiling a set from one of '70s R&B's best acts. It should be easy. During its 1972-1989 run, Blue Magic always had a fierce and devoted fan base and at least 30 essential songs to choose from. The thing that weighs this set down is the omission of quite a few of those tracks. However, the majority of what's here can't be argued with. "Sideshow," "What's Come Over Me," and "Look Me Up" are all powered by Ted Mills' uncommonly strong falsetto and Norman Harris' earthy yet ethereal productions. This set offers essential tracks from 1975's great *13 Blue Magic Lane*. "Loneliest House on the Block," "Haunted By Your Love," and "Chasing Rainbows" are all suitably creepy and sweeping. If anything makes this CD less than great, it's the single edits of album favorites like "Spell," "Look Me Up," and "Chasing Rainbows." The diminishing quality of the post-1975 work doesn't help either. "Teach Me (It's Something About Love)," and "Freak-N-Stein" are as deplorable as the core tracks are sublime. The Philip Bailey co-written EWF clone, "I Waited," the retro "Land of Make-Believe," and the synth-heavy "Magic #" are all textbook flops. Fans will note that essentials like "You Don't Have to Tell Me Goodbye" and 1989's "It's Like Magic" didn't make it here. Sure, most of the work here is great, but a few key inclusions would have made it definitive. *—Jason Elias*

The Blues Brothers

Group / Retro-Soul, Soul
Whether celebrated as a sincere tribute or derided as a tongue-in-cheek put-on, the Blues Brothers—Joliet Jake and his silent brother Elwood—was among the most popular groups of the late '70s; what started as a skit on the hit NBC television sketch comedy series *Saturday Night Live* quickly snowballed to become a true phenomenon, complete with hit records, a sold-out concert tour, and even a feature film. Clad in vintage black suits, narrow ties, fedoras, and omnipresent wrap-around sunglasses, the Blues Brothers delivered spirited renditions of classic soul hits in the tradition of the signature Stax-Volt sound; purists may still cringe, but if nothing else the group deserves credit for introducing any number of soul and blues classics to a new generation of listeners while also allowing some of the most gifted session men in the business a chance to shine on-stage and on screen.

According to "Don Kirshner" (actually *Saturday Night Live* bandleader Paul Shaffer in disguise), the Blues Brothers' history was as follows: "In 1969, Marshall Checker, of the legendary Checkers Records, called me on a new blues act that had been playing in the small, funky clubs on Chicago's South Side.... Today they are no longer an authentic blues act, but have managed to become a viable commercial product." In reality, however, vocalist Jake and harpist Elwood Blues were music lovers John Belushi and Dan Aykroyd, two of *SNL*'s brightest stars who created their respective aliases in early 1976 to warm up crowds before performances of the hit series. The Blues Brothers made their national TV debut with Belushi and Aykroyd outfitted in the bee costumes they often wore for another sketch, performing (naturally enough) Slim Harpo's "I'm a King Bee," and in the months to follow they grew in popularity, appearing on the program with increasing regularity.

The Blues Brothers' band included top Memphis session men like guitarist Steve Cropper and bassist Donald "Duck" Dunn, who together appeared on many of the original Stax label recordings of songs in the group's repertoire; later incarnations also featured notables like bluesman Matt "Guitar" Murphy. While opening for comedian Steve Martin in Los Angeles in 1978, the Blues Brothers recorded their debut live LP, *Briefcase Full of Blues*; the album quickly went platinum, launching Top 40 hit covers of "Soul Man" and "Rubber Biscuit." They also toured in 1980 to promote their feature-length movie, *The Blues Brothers*, a sprawling musical comedy featuring cameos by everyone from Cab Calloway to Aretha Franklin, as well as their second LP, *Made in America*; two more Top 40 hits—"Gimme Some Lovin'" and "Who's Making Love"—appeared that same year.

In 1981, *The Best of the Blues Brothers* was released, further solidifying their massive popularity; however, on March 5, 1982, Belushi died in Hollywood of an accidental drug overdose, and the Blues Brothers' saga was effectively over. Or so it seemed; as the movie remained a cult favorite and old *Saturday Night Live* sketches continued to run in syndication, the group's "legend" continued to grow, and, in 1988, Cropper, Dunn, Murphy, and other players re-formed the Blues Brothers Band for a world tour, often backing singer Eddie Floyd. In 1992, they even cut a new LP, *Red White and Blues*, which featured a guest appearance from Aykroyd/Elwood. Around the same time, Aykroyd also mounted his House of Blues franchise, an international chain of upscale blues joints; he, actor John Goodman, and Belushi's brother Jim also appeared on occasion in a new Blues Brothers lineup. Finally, in 1998 a second movie, *Blues Brothers 2000*, was released to negative reviews and poor box office returns. *—Jason Ankeny*

Briefcase Full of Blues / Dec. 1978 / Atlantic ♦♦♦♦
"The Blues Brothers" began as an affectionate joke-cum-tribute to R&B music, and taken in that spirit it retained its entertainment value, even after this live album topped the charts, sold two million copies, and produced hit singles in "Rubber Biscuit" and "Soul Man." The guardians of popular music have always been entirely too reverent and humorless, however, and it wasn't long before they were leveling charges of rip-off against the Brothers and complaining that John Belushi couldn't sing as well as Otis Redding. So what? No one seems to have noticed that Belushi was as obsessive about citing his sources as Frank Sinatra is about naming his arrangers—you'd have thought those critics would have appreciated the footnotes. The beneficiaries of Belushi's encomiums didn't mind the increased exposure or the renewed royalty checks ("I suggest you buy as many blues albums as you can," Belushi told the audience), and even today, what comes across in these performances is the sincerity of feeling—that and some tasty playing from a top-notch band. *—William Ruhlmann*

Blues Brothers [Original Soundtrack] / Jun. 1980 / Atlantic ♦♦♦
Comic actors John Belushi and Dan Aykroyd received a lot of flak for their Blues Brothers shtick—mostly for the albums, not 1980's beloved classic film. But they should be given credit for exposing many people—including this reviewer—to the music of blues and R&B veterans. *The Blues Brothers* soundtrack was released on Atlantic Records. On the surface this doesn't seem unusual, since the Blues Brothers' Atlantic debut, *Briefcase Full of Blues*, was a number one album; but the movie was released by Universal, and its parent company, MCA, passed on the soundtrack. The rollicking remake of the Spencer Davis Group's "Gimme Some Lovin'" was a hit, featuring an arrangement notable for the horn section that replaces Steve Winwood's rumbling organ work. Ray Charles has a good time with "Shake a Tail Feather," and he's helped out by Jake and Elwood Blues (Belushi and Aykroyd, respectively). The cover of Solomon Burke's "Everybody Needs Somebody to Love" is a lot of fun, thanks to the great overall rhythm and Elwood's lightning-fast stage rap, while James Brown and the Reverend James Cleveland Choir provide a blast of gospel music on "Old Landmark." Aretha Franklin's "Think" is explosive, and Cab Calloway's "Minnie the Moocher" is slyly irresistible. Charles, Brown, Franklin, and Calloway all have small roles in the film, yet so does John Lee Hooker, but he's not represented here. *—Bret Adams*

The Best of the Blues Brothers / Dec. 1981 / Atlantic ♦♦♦

● **The Definitive Collection** / 1992 / Atlantic ♦♦♦♦
It isn't exactly difficult to scoff at the Blues Brothers—beginning your musical career as a sketch on *Saturday Night Live* is not the best way to develop artistic credibility, and while Elwood Blues wasn't too shabby a harp player, his brother, Joliet Jake, sang only marginally better than that guy who used to impersonate Joe Cocker on late-night television. But no one ever bought a Blues Brothers album expecting a life-changing musical experience—these guys were there to put on a show, and putting on a great show is just what they did. It helped that Dan Aykroyd and John Belushi obviously loved the music, and they knew how to put together a killer band (any fan with the vision to hire Steve Cropper, Donald "Duck" Dunn, Steve Jordan, and Matt "Guitar" Murphy" to cover classic blues and R&B deserves credit for good taste, if nothing else). *The Definitive Collection* pulls together highlights from the band's debut live album, *Briefcase Full of Blues*, as well as cuts from the soundtrack to *The Blues Brothers* movie (including contributions from Ray Charles and Aretha Franklin) and the second, rather less-remembered live set *Made in America*. Anyone who buys this without owning a decent Otis Redding or Sam & Dave set first ought to be ashamed of themselves, but as a one-stop overview of the work of two dedicated R&B fans having a great time playing the songs they love, you could hardly do better than *The Definitive Collection*. Play it loud and dance a lot—John would have wanted it that way. *—Mark Deming*

Red, White & Blues / 1992 / Turnstyle ♦♦
Steve Cropper, Donald "Duck" Dunn, Matt "Guitar" Murphy, "Blue Lou" Marini, and Alan "Mr. Fabulous" Rubin were all members of the all-star band that backed John Belushi and Dan Aykroyd in their Blues Brothers incarnation between 1978 and 1980. Here, they reorganized with a few more players, notably singer Larry "T" Thurston, as the Blues Brothers Band. The music (mostly new songs) was in the Blues Brothers' familiar uptempo R&B style, Elwood Blues made a cameo appearance, and the playing was session-man-hot, but of course it just wasn't the same without Joliet Jake, who had gone to that great roadhouse in the sky ten years before. *—William Ruhlmann*

The Blues Brothers Complete / May 2, 2000 / Atlantic ♦♦♦♦
The title of *The Blues Brothers Complete* pretty much says it all; the double-disc, 35-track collection contains everything Jake and Elwood Blues recorded during the peak of their career. The catch is that the compilation was only released by EastWest/Atlantic's Australian division, therefore, it's hard to find outside of Australia. But, for hardcore fans, it's worth tracking down since it has every track from *Briefcase Full of Blues*, the soundtrack to *The Blues Brothers* (including the selections sung by Cab Calloway, James Brown, and Aretha Franklin), and *Made in America*, plus "I Ain't Got You," which was only on *The Best of the Blues Brothers*, and "From the Bottom," which was the B-side of the "Soul Man" single. In other words, it's everything. Some may laugh that anyone would want the complete works of the Blues Brothers who were often considered a joke (especially by blues purists), but in hindsight, these recordings don't sound bad at all. How could they when Belushi and Aykroyd were backed by a world-class studio band. And, a lot can be said for enthusiasm. No, Belushi wasn't the greatest vocalist, and neither was his brother, but he had true love and passion for this music, which translates in his performances. The result may not match the original recordings they strove to replicate, but they're fun and they undoubtedly introduced many listeners to the original artists. Strangely, that's the reason why they hold up fairly well; they were labors of love and that love is apparent throughout the recordings, from the truly impeccable song selection (they did have good taste) to the enthusiastic performances. *—Stephen Thomas Erlewine*

Eddie Bo (Edwin J. Bocage)

b. Sep. 20, 1930, New Orleans, LA
Vocals, Piano / R&B, New Orleans R&B, Deep Funk
A sorely underappreciated veteran of the New Orleans R&B scene, singer/songwriter/producer/pianist Eddie Bo evolved into one of the city's foremost funk players during the late '60s and early '70s, although he never had a national hit commensurate with his musical standing. Born Edwin Joseph Bocage on September 20, 1930, Bo was raised in the Algiers and Ninth Ward sections of New Orleans by a musical family; uncles Peter and Charles and cousin Henry all played in post-WWI jazz orchestras (including A.J. Piron's), and his mother was a pianist in the Professor Longhair style. Bo served in the Army after high school, and returned to New Orleans to study at the Grunewald School of Music, where he discovered bebop pianists like Art Tatum and Oscar Peterson. He started playing around the jam-heavy New Orleans jazz scene, but soon discovered that R&B was more popular and accessible, not to mention better-paying. He joined the house band at Club Tijuana under the name Spider Bocage, and later formed the Spider Bocage

Orchestra, a professional backing band that supported many prominent blues and R&B artists of the day, including Ruth Brown, Earl King, Lloyd Price, Big Joe Turner, Smiley Lewis, and Guitar Slim.

Bo cut his first record in 1955 for the Ace label, and would go on to release more singles than any other New Orleans artist save Fats Domino. One of his singles for Apollo, the local hit "I'm Wise," was later adapted by Little Richard into the hit "Slippin' and Slidin'." In addition to those labels, Bo also recorded a few singles for Chess and Checker, but did the majority of his '50s work for the small New Orleans label Ric, scoring regional hits like "Every Dog Has Its Day" and "Tell It Like It Is"; his "My Dearest Darling" was also covered for a hit by Etta James. In 1961, the dance-craze tune "Check Mr. Popeye" became the closest thing to a national hit he'd had yet, selling well in the South and Northeast; however, competing versions by Chubby Checker and Huey "Piano" Smith diminished its chart performance. During this period, Bo also produced records by numerous local artists; his credits include work with Irma Thomas, Chris Kenner, and Johnny Adams, among others.

New Orleans R&B took a commercial downturn during the '60s, and Bo was largely relegated to cutting records for a long string of small local labels, most of which weren't distributed nationally. As the '60s wore on, Bo's piano style not only got funkier, but brought back more and more of his jazz training, creating a distinctive sound that helped lay the groundwork for New Orleans' own brand of funk (along with artists like the Meters and Willie Tee). His biggest hit, "Hook & Sling, Pts. 1 & 2," was recorded for Scram and reached the Top 40 on the R&B charts in 1969. By this time, however, Bo was tired of being at the music industry's mercy for his livelihood; he subsequently formed his own Bo-Sound label and in 1971 scored another hit with "Check Your Bucket." Other early-'70s sides for Bo-Sound, such as "Pass the Hatchet," cemented Bo's future standing as a lost funk treasure.

Bo worked in music only sporadically after the early '70s, instead setting up his own renovation business, although he did record two self-produced albums, *Another Side of Eddie Bo* and *Watch for the Coming*, in the late '70s. He recorded with the Dirty Dozen Brass Band during the late '80s, when he also toured Europe. In the '90s, Bo resurrected his Bo-Sound label and released a series of albums that included *Eddie Bo and Friends*, *Back Up This Train*, and *Nine Yards of Funk*. In 1999, he was featured in the PBS documentary *River of Song*. He continued to tour internationally, and also gigged frequently in his hometown, most often at Tipitina's. *—Steve Huey*

● **Check Mr. Popeye** / 1988 / Rounder ♦♦♦♦♦

Here is engaging early-'60s New Orleans R&B from a prolific pianist, with a classic title track that spawned a local "Popeye" dance craze. *—Bill Dahl*

I Love to Rock 'N' Roll / 1994 / Famous Groove ♦♦♦♦

There is no sessionography, no discography, no indication of when the 29 tracks on Famous Groove's Eddie Bo compilation *I Love to Rock 'N' Roll* were recorded, but it's clear that these are all from the early and mid-'50s, prior to his stint at RIC in 1959. Most of them come from his time with Apollo, along with singles earlier and later. It would have been nice to have more detail in the notes, but this provides a thorough overview of his pre-hit years, while serving up some raw, stinging R&B and blues, as well as some sweet ballads. Though there are a couple of cuts that fall flat over the course of the collection, much of this is top-drawer New Orleans R&B, whether it's rocking or swinging (witness "I'm Wise," an easy swinger that Little Richard turned into the hard-charging "Slippin' and Slidin'"). There's a heavier blues element here than a lot of New Orleans R&B, which helps give it some depth, and the surprising variety in the material—ballads, mambos, rockers, swing, and shuffles—will make up for the low fidelity and slightly uneven material. All of this makes *I Love to Rock 'N' Roll* a good choice for those serious about their New Orleans R&B, even if it doesn't have the hits of "Check Mr. Popeye" or 1969's "Hook & Sling." *—Stephen Thomas Erlewine*

Hook & Sling / Feb. 27, 1997 / Funky Delicacies ♦♦♦♦♦

A mover and shaker behind the New Orleans music scene, Eddie Bo had regional success in the late '50s with piano stroll-era novelties like "Check Mr. Popeye," but hit his stride a decade later with a brand of funk and soul that could only have originated in his hometown. "Hook & Sling" was an R&B hit in 1969, propelled by Bo's good-natured exhortations and the undeniable groove from drummer James Black. The follow-up single, "(If It's Good to You) It's Good for You," did not achieve the same kind of chart success but is just as tough. *Hook & Sling* collects Bo's output for a number of small New Orleans labels, as well as tracks previously unreleased. Primarily heavy funk instrumentals, with plenty of wah wah guitars and drum breaks, there are connections to Bo's musical past, including "Love Has Been Good" and "Come to Me," two blues-based ballads that lean hard on Bo's piano. Despite the contrasting styles, *Hook & Sling*'s material is impressively strong throughout, including good advice on love ("Check Your Bucket" and dance crazes "The Thang"). This is a life-changing release from the vaults. *—Kurt Edwards*

Bob & Earl

Group / Soul, R&B

Bob & Earl had already recorded under a myriad of pseudonyms during their careers before they were a duo; both "Bob"s (the first was Bobby Byrd, aka Bobby Day, and his replacement was Bobby Relf) and "Earl" (Earl Nelson) were key players in L.A.'s doo wop and R&B vocal scene in the mid- to late '50s. Today, Bob & Earl are best remembered for their minor-key rumbler "Harlem Shuffle," which provided the listener with instructional R&B dance moves for an accompanying dance also called the Harlem Shuffle. Their vocal interplay presaged Stax Records' Sam & Dave. When "Harlem Shuffle" was originally released, it climbed into the lower rungs of the American Top Forty (number 36 Cashbox/ number 44 *Billboard*), but the song achieved its biggest chart success when it was re-released in 1969, becoming a Top Ten U.K. hit.

Bobby Byrd (b. July 1, 1932, in Fort Worth, TX) was the first "Bob," although he is better known today for writing three early rock & roll classics between 1957 and 1958. He had been one of the founders of the Famous Flames in 1950, a prolific group—along with the Robins, they were one of the grandfather doo wop groups in L.A.—who waxed singles for Recorded in Hollywood, Specialty, Lucky, Swingtime, Money, and other labels before the group finally had their first major hit, "Buzz, Buzz, Buzz," a number 18 pop hit for Ebb Records in 1958.

By 1957, however, Byrd (under his new name, Bobby Day) had cut the original version of his self-penned "Little Bitty Pretty One" for Class Records. When a nearly identical cover version by Thurston Harris (featuring the Sharps) beat Byrd's original to the punch and turned out to be a huge hit—it was Harris' one and only Top Ten R&B and pop hit for Aladdin—Byrd switched gears and started a solo career, using the name Bobby Day. One theory about where the new last name came from is that Class Records' "Googie" Rene (owner Leon Rene's son, and the label's A&R director and producer) suggested it. Regardless of how he got the new moniker, Day bounced back with a hit of his own, "Rockin' Robin," which topped the R&B charts in 1958. Day waxed a few more hits for Class, including "That's All I Want" and "The Bluebird, the Buzzard and the Oriole" in 1959. It was during this time that Earl Nelson formed the first incarnation of Bob & Earl. Nelson (b. September 8, 1928, in Lake Charles, LA) had also been an original member of the Hollywood Flames; that's him singing lead on "Buzz, Buzz, Buzz." By 1960, however, after a stint on Atco, the Flames eventually ended up on Edsel, at which point Nelson and Day ventured off to form Bob & Earl on their own. Day left Bob & Earl before they produced any hits, however, and Nelson soon re-configured the group with a second "Bob," Bobby Relf.

Relf had already led several L.A.-based acts in his career, including the Laurels and the Upfronts (featuring Barry White), and was also a replacement member of the Hollywood Flames after Byrd had left to join up with Nelson. Relf had also called himself "Valentino" for his short-lived group Valentino & the Lovers, an early-'60s group formed with the vocalists who had auditioned but had not been chosen to be in the lineup of Little Caesar & the Romans. Incidentally, White had also been a member of Valentino & the Lovers, singing bass and doubling on piano. The duo recorded several singles for various L.A.-based labels, but their lone hit was "Harlem Shuffle," a dance number punctuated by trumpet blasts and echo-laden percussion. It was arranged by a young Barry White, who played piano. Produced by Fred Smith (a talented R&B songwriter who had previously written hits with partner Cliff Goldsmith and produced the Olympics among others), "Harlem Shuffle" was originally released in the U.S. on the Marc label in 1963. It climbed into the low end of the American Top 40 in 1964 before slipping off the charts.

However, the duo failed to follow up with any additional hits and soon were splitting for solo careers. Nelson began recording solo tracks under a bunch of aliases, including Jay Dee, Earl Cosby, and Chip Nelson, but his biggest success was as Jackie Lee (Jackie was Earl's wife's name and Lee his own middle name), for another popular R&B dance cut in 1965, "The Duck," for the Mirwood label. A year after "Harlem Shuffle" slid off the charts, Nelson was touring the U.S. (with Barry White on drums). Relf waxed singles under the names Bobby Garrett and Bobby Valentino.

"Harlem Shuffle" was re-released in 1969, and became a Top Ten U.K. hit (number seven pop). Since its 1963 debut, the song has seen numerous cover versions, including those by the Righteous Brothers, Edgar Winter, Wayne Cochran, and the Rolling Stones, who revived it in 1986 for their *Dirty Work* LP. In 1968, the song appeared on blue-eyed soul singer Danny Wagner's album, *The Kindred Soul of Danny Wagner*; Barry White produced the album. The original "Bob" Bobby Byrd passed away on July 15, 1990. *—Bryan Thomas*

● **Harlem Shuffle** / 1966 / Sue ♦♦♦♦♦

Bob & Earl were Bobby Relf and Earl Nelson. Relf replaced Nelson's former partner, Bobby Byrd, who worked with him in James Brown's Famous Flames. That duo cut songs for various labels, but hadn't clicked as an act. The new Bob & Earl struck gold with this single, which made it to the Top 50 when it was issued in 1963. *—Ron Wynn*

Bob & Earl / 1969 / Crestview ♦♦♦

A curious album that has the feel of a thrown-together exploitation LP—there's no indication of when the tracks were recorded, although an educated guess would put the era in the mid-'60s. It's serviceable period soul with a slight uptown production feel, but not outstanding. The version of "Harlem Shuffle" here is *not* the original, but an instrumental rendition with a faster tempo and fuzz guitars. *—Richie Unterberger*

The Bobbettes

f. 1955, New York, NY [Harlem], **db.** 1974

Group / Girl Group, R&B

The Bobbettes were among the first successful girl groups of the rock era; in a field dominated by male artists, their 1957 hit "Mr. Lee" not only cracked the pop Top Ten, but also hit number one on the R&B charts. Originally dubbed the Harlem Queens, the group teamed sisters Emma and Jannie Pought with Laura Webb, Helen Gathers, and Reather Dixon; first meeting in 1955 while singing in the glee club at Harlem's P.S. 109, soon the girls were appearing at the Apollo Theater's legendary amateur nights, and through manager James Dailey, they landed a contract with Atlantic. Inspired by one of their school teachers, the Bobbettes' debut "Mr. Lee" appeared in mid-1957 and was also their biggest hit. four Atlantic follow-ups failed to chart, and after issuing the ballad "You Are My Sweetheart" in 1959, the group left the label for the Triple-X imprint. There, "I Shot Mr. Lee"—a song recorded for but rejected by Atlantic—began to climb the charts, forcing Atlantic to release their own version and effectively killing the single's momentum; although the subsequent "Have Mercy Baby" and "Dance With Me Georgie" both emerged as minor hits, in 1960 the Bobbettes moved to End Records, cutting the standard "Teach Me Tonight." 1962's "I Don't Like It Like That," an answer song to the Chris Kenner hit "I Like It Like That," was the group's last chart entry, although they continued recording for a series of labels—most notably Diamond and Mayhew—through 1974, touring oldies circuits in years to follow. *—Jason Ankeny*

● **Mr. Lee & Other Big Hits** / 1989 / Revival ♦♦♦

Angela Bofill

b. 1954, New York, NY [The Bronx]

Vocals / Urban

This Bronx native sang with Ricardo Morrero & the Group and the Dance Theater of Harlem chorus before her 1978 debut. With her strong, distinctive alto, she has carved a niche as an outstanding interpreter of soul ballads. Between 1978 and 1984, Bofill had consistent success on the R&B charts, with six albums making the Top 40 (five of which made the Top 100 on the pop charts as well), including two, *Angel of the Night* (1979) and *Too Tough* (1983), that made the Top Ten. During this period, she also placed seven singles in the R&B Top 40, with "Too Tough" making the Top Ten. Bofill's career cooled off after 1984, but she returned to the R&B charts with *Intuition* (1988), *I Wanna Love Somebody* (1993), and *Love in Slow Motion* (1996). *—Bil Carpenter*

Angie / 1978 / GRP ✦✦✦

Angela Bofill temporarily became the hot Latin pop singer in the late '70s with her debut for GRP. It was a smart blend of glossy urban contemporary, light jazz, and fusion; Bofill's voice had enough sophistication to sound sleek and enough Flora Purim influence to attract interest from jazz, Latin, and urban contemporary audiences. It scored three mild hits and got the then-fledging GRP label some vital sales. *—Ron Wynn*

Angel of the Night / Oct. 1979 / GRP ✦✦✦✦

Angela Bofill proved herself extremely adroit at doing Latin, jazz, and R&B with equal finesse on her debut, *Angie*. *Angel of the Night* is the highly anticipated sophomore set originally released on GRP when it was distributed on Arista. With such a comfortable style well suited to Bofill's voice, this doesn't veer that far away from the work on the first album. The first track, the immediately classic "I Try," is beautifully sung, dramatic, and offers no false moments. The title track is just as effective in a gentle and lilting way. *Angel of the Night*'s producers David Grusin and Larry Rosen, who also worked on Jon Lucien's 1973-1975 albums, cover some ambitious territory with a rich-voiced, quirky singer here as well. The epic "The Voyage" has the producers' sense of drama, a perfect match for Bofill's deliberate delivery, which is oddly though sweetly reminiscent of Lucien. "What I Wouldn't Do (For the Love of You)" and "The Feelin's Love" bring her to a more customary, sleek R&B material with her trademark vocals making them even better. The only thing that qualifies as a miss is a disco-style take on Thom Bell and Linda Creed's "People Make the World Go 'Round." It's not that bad, though. *Angel of the Night* is one of Bofill's finest and most charming albums. Any fan of sophisticated late-'70s R&B/Latin jazz need to have this in their collection. *—Jason Elias*

Something About You / Nov. 1981 / Arista/BMG Heritage ✦✦✦✦

Angela Bofill enjoyed surprising commercial success with her first two albums, *Angie* and *Angel of the Night*, produced by contemporary jazz executives Dave Grusin and Larry Rosen for their GRP label, distributed by Arista. She then jumped to Arista proper (causing some bad blood with GRP) to try for a deliberate jazz-pop crossover on her third album, which was produced by Narada Michael Walden and shepherded by Arista president Clive Davis, who took an executive producer credit. Davis canvassed the publishing world for likely hit songs, then Walden put together a studio team to create a smooth, sophisticated sound that would, it was hoped, work for pop, R&B, and adult contemporary radio as well as setting feet moving in the discos. In practice, it didn't work out that way. The title track, with a lush disco arrangement, arrived as a single after disco had faded, though it, like second single "Holdin' out for Love," a professional song by professional songwriters Cynthia Weil and Tom Snow, managed to peak in the R&B Top 40. With those calling cards, the album was able to register only a Top 20 R&B/Top 100 pop showing, not as high as *Angel of the Night*, as Bofill's contemporary jazz fans deserted her in droves for her commercial sellout. This is a shame, since, however compromised its goals, much of *Something About You* is effective early-'80s pop-jazz, and Bofill sings powerfully throughout. Particularly impressive are the ballads "Break It to Me Gently" and "Time to Say Goodbye." The 2002 reissue adds four bonus tracks. "Love Light" and "Rhythm of Your Mind" were actually cut by Grusin and Rosen during the *Angel of the Night* sessions, while "Never Wanna Be Without Your Love" is a duet with Walden and there is a Spanish version of "Holdin' out for Love." *—William Ruhlmann*

Too Tough / Jan. 1983 / Arista ✦✦✦✦✦

Angela Bofill scored one of her biggest dance and R&B hits with the title track. It had a great hook, excellent production, and good arrangement, and her vocal was the ideal mix of aggressive, enticing, and defiant. There were also two good songs done in an opposite fashion, "Is This a Dream" and "I Can See It in Your Eyes." This was arguably the best Bofill production done by Narada Michael Walden. *—Ron Wynn*

Teaser / Nov. 1983 / Arista ✦✦✦

Angela Bofill never reached her pinnacle as an artist. While her talents as a writer, singer and producer were excellent, the forces directing her career made some questionable decisions, and this album is a good example. This album, more than any other, lacks quality production. Although Narada Michael Walden is known for producing great crossover tunes, he comes up short on this project. Every selection, save the ballad "I'm on Your Side," is uptempo, and an imitation of the next. The project is just shy of shoddy as the music inundates Bofill's attempts to vocally salvage some lackluster songs. "I'm on Your Side" is the only bright spot, and it sealed the Top 20 on the *Billboard* R&B charts. As it was upon its release, this song remains a standard within the R&B genre. *—Craig Lytle*

Let Me Be the One / Nov. 1984 / Arista ✦✦

• **The Best of Angela Bofill** / Aug. 1986 / Arista ✦✦✦✦✦

1986's *The Best of Angela Bofill* collects the biggest hits and definitive album tracks of her career up to that point, including "I'll Try," "Time to Say Goodbye," and "This Time I'll Be Sweeter." For the most part the collection concentrates on the smooth, soulful ballads with which Bofill made her name, although there are a few of her more uptempo tracks, like "What I Wouldn't Do (For the Love of You)" and "Let Me Be the One," for variety's sake. Strangely, the collection doesn't include "Too Tough," one of her biggest hits for Arista, opting instead for "Tonight I Give In" from that album. Still, despite the collection's brevity, *The Best of Angela Bofill* does give a good, concise idea of the sound and songs that made Bofill one of the best urban songstresses of the '70s and '80s. *—Heather Phares*

Love Is in Your Eyes / 1991 / Capitol ✦✦

Angela Bofill tried a little of everything on this early-'90s date. There's some pop, some urban contemporary, some light fusion, and even a little Latin. None of it did very well, but it showed her versatility. Her voice had a deeper, richer, more experienced quality than when she debuted in the late '70s. Unfortunately, she found that the new generation wasn't aware of her past hits, nor were they that attuned to the fresh material. *—Ron Wynn*

Love in Slow Motion / 1996 / Shanachie/Cachet ✦✦✦

• **The Definitive Collection** / Jun. 15, 1999 / Arista ✦✦✦✦

Over the course of 17 songs, *The Definitive Collection* covers most of Angela Bofill's best-known singles and album tracks, including "I Try," "This Time I'll Be Sweeter," "Angel of the Night," and "Let Me Be the One." This collection also includes several worthwhile songs that didn't make it onto her previous retrospective, *The Best of Angela Bofill*, such as "Too Tough," "Baby I Need Your Love," "Ain't Nothing Like the Real Thing," and "Can't Slow Down." As with the other collection, the emphasis is still on Bofill's earliest work; while she did indeed record many of her definitive songs during that time, some tracks from her more recent albums would have been a welcome addition for completeness' sake. Even though this compilation still isn't a total look at Bofill's artistry, *The Definitive Collection* does offer the most comprehensive look at her work available. *—Heather Phares*

Bohannon

f. 1972

Group / Disco, Funk, Soul, Deep Funk

Drummer Hamilton Bohannon (b. March 7, 1942) was among the top bandleaders, percussionists, and producers in '70s disco/dance music. Bohannon grew up in Newman, GA, and was drumming in a high school band while an elementary school student. After earning a music degree from Atlanta's Clark College, he was hired as a drummer by Stevie Wonder, and moved to Detroit, where he was a bandleader and arranger for Motown tours until he joined Dakar/Brunswick in 1972. Bohannon perfected his formula of heavy, thudding bass accents and aggressive rhythms while recording for Dakar. He had several songs that were successful club records, but only mild R&B hits, among them "South African Man," "Foot Stompin' Music," "Disco Stomp," and "Bohannon's Beat."

He moved to Mercury in the late '70s, and scored a major hit with "Let's Start the Dance" in 1978, Bohannon's only Top Ten R&B release. The song featured vocalist Carolyn Crawford. He subsequently produced Crawford's solo release, "Coming on Strong," that same year, and continued working with her into the '80s. Bohannon kept recording for Mercury, though barely getting light chart action, in 1979 and 1980. He started Phase II Records in 1980, and recorded there until 1984. Bohannon introduced another vocalist, Liz Lands, on a remake of the Originals' "Baby, I'm for Real," which was included on the 1980 LP *One Step Ahead*. He signed with MCA in 1984 and recorded several albums. His 1989 release *Here Comes Bohannon* featured another fresh female voice, Altrinna Grayson. *—Ron Wynn*

Stop & Go / 1973 / Dakar ✦✦✦

Keep on Dancin' / 1974 / Dakar ✦✦✦

Bohannon / 1975 / Dakar ✦✦✦✦

Insides Out / 1975 / Dakar ✦✦✦

Mighty Bohannon / 1975 / Dakar ✦✦✦

Dance Your Ass Off / 1976 / Dakar ✦✦✦

This album lives up to its title; truly a dance album to the last beat. Hamilton Bohannon concocts a never-ending groove on this seven-song set. Three songs share a similar looping bass line and special effects; the other four share a close resemblance to their respective rhythmic attributes. Notwithstanding, all selections offer that pumped-up beat and enticing aria. On a few tracks, Bohannon injects some faintly urgent vocals. With this being his last recording for Dakar, no songs from this album charted. However, "The Groove I Feel" is a good pick. *—Craig Lytle*

Phase II / 1977 / Mercury ✦✦✦

With one foot firmly embedded in the monstrous disco movement and the other continuing to tickle the jazz sensibilities, Hamilton Bohannon's *Phase II* was yet another blissfully orchestrated funk exploration in what some could say was becoming a series. And like the other albums before it, *Phase II* wouldn't earn any glittering feathers on anyone's cap; its one break-away single, the captivating "Bohannon's Disco Symphony," only came to rest at number 67 on the R&B charts. It wasn't until the following year's "Let's Start the Dance" that he would crack the Top Ten—for the first and last time. What made *Phase II* most interesting is that the album became a reunion of sorts for Bohannon. With guest appearances by old bandmates Melvin Ragin and Ray Parker Jr., a spark was ignited and duly kindled across the set. "Isn't It a Beautiful Morning" was an odd blend of disco guitar surrounded by what only could be described as music for a never-ending elevator ride. It's bizarrely bad, yet incredibly compelling. Elsewhere, Bohannon and company get their groove on across the slightly smarmy and *Shaft*-like opener, "Andrea," and the instrumental "Moving Fast." It was the funk-affected "Just Doing My Thang," though, with its great background vocals and punchy arrangement, that hit the high point in this set. That Hamilton Bohannon is an incredibly gifted musician is a fact; that he got sideswiped by disco is another. This album certainly wouldn't knock your socks off, but still it's an easy listener and as wallpaper it's quite magnificent. *—Amy Hanson*

Bohannon's Best / 1978 / London ♦♦♦♦

On My Way / 1978 / Mercury ♦♦♦

Summertime Groove / Jun. 1978 / Mercury ♦♦♦

Drummer/bandleader/vocalist Hamilton Bohannon's *modus operandi* was shuffling, syncopated grooves that made you boogie to the beats. "Summertime Groove" exemplifies the Bohannon sound, as does the funky, potent "Let's Start the Dance," featuring Carolyn Crawford on vocals. "Me and the Gang," "The Street Dance," and the lesser of the rump-shakers, "Listen to the Children Play," continue the party atmosphere. This is pure uncut boogie music. The only ballad is a wistful winner titled "I Wonder Why." As innovative as Bohannon's sound was, it never really captured the fancy of record buyers and only enjoyed a cult following. *—Andrew Hamilton*

Music in the Air / Mar. 1980 / Mercury ♦♦♦

Bohannon albums carbon each other: all have shuffling grooves, heavy rhythms, and quality ballads; the only things that change are the personnel and the song titles. Liz Lands replaces Carolyn Crawford as the feature vocalist on this release. Both recorded at Motown and, despite making good records, failed to scale the charts at Hitsville U.S.A. Lands' vocals elevate *Music in the Air* above the mediocre level. Lands has an amazing vocal range that reminds me of a singing flute. She does an admirable job on the Originals' classic "Baby I'm For Real"; her finest moment occurs on "Thoughts and Wishes," a song with jazz roots—her soprano soars to crystal-shaking heights as she rips into the lyrics. As always, Bohannon has some dance grooves to shake your booty too; "The Funk Walk," "The Hammer" and "Feel Like Dancin'" will get you up and down on the dance floor. *—Andrew Hamilton*

● **The Very Best of Bohannon** / Nov. 21, 1995 / Rhino ♦♦♦♦♦

Led by former Stevie Wonder drummer Hamilton Bohannon, Bohannon was one of the leading disco/funk bands of the mid-'70s. Many of their dance club classics and all of their biggest hits are included on the 14-track *The Very Best of Bohannon*, which was compiled by Bohannon himself. It is the most thorough retrospective of the band ever assembled and it's likely there will never be a collection as thorough as this. *—Stephen Thomas Erlewine*

Foot Stompin' Music / Oct. 13, 1998 / Edsel ♦♦♦♦

Gary "U.S." Bonds (Gary Anderson)

b. Jun. 6, 1939, Jacksonville, FL

Vocals / Rock & Roll, R&B

After moving to the Norfolk, VA, area in the mid-'50s, young Gary Anderson began plying his vocal wares, first in church, later with a local group called the Turks. When he was not yet 21, he was approached by local record producer Frank Guida to join his tiny Legrand label. Guida changed Anderson's name to U.S. Bonds, hoping the first release would get extra airplay by disc jockeys mistaking it for a public-service announcement. The result was the classic "New Orleans," combining rock-combo raunch with impassioned, scorched soul-singing that set the stage for all that would follow. Guida double- and triple-tracked Bonds' voice and the resulting murky production gave all the hits (including "Quarter to Three," "School Is Out," and "Dear Lady Twist") a party-in-outer-space quality all their own. Though he kept recording, making a couple of excellent solo albums in the early '80s with the help of Bruce Springsteen, Bonds shifted his focus after those releases to dotting the landscape of oldies shows the world over, singing the songs that made him famous. *—Cub Koda*

Dance 'Til Quarter to Three / 1961 / Legrand ♦♦

Bonds' debut album was a typical LP for the era: a few hits ("Quarter to Three," "New Orleans," "School Is Out") surrounded by tunes not far removed from the style of the singles, but not nearly as memorable. At least this one was mostly comprised of original material, written by producer Frank Guida, Bonds, and saxophonist Gene Barge, with a few others pitching in. The calypso and Caribbean beats that found their way into several Bonds singles crop up with some frequency; "Please Forgive Me," "Don't Go to Strangers," and "I Know Why Dreamers Cry" are doo wop/R&B ballads in a more traditional vein than Bonds' usual approach; and "Not Me" would be covered for a hit by the Orlons in 1963. The album was reissued, together with Bonds' second LP (1962's *Twist Up Calypso*), on a single-CD compilation by Ace in 1998, although this CD substitutes the original version of "Please Forgive Me" (the B-side of "New Orleans") for the one that was re-recorded for the LP. *—Richie Unterberger*

Twist Up Calypso / 1962 / Legrand ♦♦♦

The success of "Dear Lady Twist" (included here) inspired an entire album of songs derived from calypso music. Bonds and producer Frank Guida, it must be said, didn't do it halfway: almost everything here employs prominent calypso beats, and in addition to covers of the calypso tunes "Day-O" and "Mama Look a Booboo," several of the originals are obviously based on calypso riffs (such as "A Woman Is Smarter"). Bonds pulls off his task with genuine exuberance—the arrangements are considerably hotter and more indebted to the "party" sounds of his hits than the filler on his first LP—though as usual it's the hits, "Twist, Twist Senora!" and the fabulous "Dear Lady Twist," that stand out. The album was reissued, together with Bonds' first LP (1961's *Dance 'Til Quarter to Three*), on a single-CD compilation by Ace in 1998. *—Richie Unterberger*

Meets Chubby Checker / 1981 / EMI ♦♦

This short album gives over one side to four of Chubby Checker's biggest hits of the early '60s, and the other to four of Gary "U.S." Bonds' hits of the same era. These are the original artists, but they don't sound like the original recordings. *— William Ruhlmann*

The Star / 1981 / ♦♦♦

This is a four-song, 45 rpm, 10-inch import EP of material that Gary "U.S." Bonds recorded with producer Jerry Williams Jr. between 1968 and 1970. It reveals Bonds to be a good, bluesy wailer of a vocalist, although there's nothing here that matches his best work. (All four songs later were included on the Rhino Records album *Certified Soul.*) *— William Ruhlmann*

Dedication / Apr. 1981 / Razor & Tie ♦♦♦

Bruce Springsteen played guitar, sang a duet, wrote three songs, and co-produced and co-arranged four on Gary "U.S." Bonds' comeback album, recorded 20 years after his heyday. Springsteen also lent his backup group, The E Street Band, while E Street guitarist Miami Steve (Van Zandt) also contributed a song and produced the bulk of the record. The result, naturally, sounds like a Bruce Springsteen and the E Street Band album with lead vocals by Gary "U.S." Bonds. Bonds' elastic tenor, heard in much greater clarity than it ever was in his early years, has just enough grit to be soulful, and he puts across the pop-soul tunes Springsteen and Van Zandt have constructed for him effectively. He also tackles the Beatles' "It's Only Love" and Bob Dylan's "From a Buick 6," and sings Jackson Browne's "The Pretender" as if the lyric was devoid of irony. It's an enjoyable album that does nothing to change the notion that Bonds as a recording artist essentially conforms himself to the intentions of his producer, whether that's Frank Guida, Jerry Williams Jr., or Bruce Springsteen. *— William Ruhlmann*

On the Line / Jun. 1982 / Razor & Tie ♦♦♦

On the Line, Gary "U.S." Bonds' second comeback album under the sponsorship of Bruce Springsteen, was even more of a Springsteen record than its predecessor. This time, Springsteen wrote seven of the 11 songs, co-produced all of them with Miami Steve (Van Zandt) and again lent the E Street Band for the sessions. While there were no Springsteen masterpieces here, the rock & roll revival style of the material, similar to that on *Dedication*, made it, in effect, the follow-up to Springsteen's *The River* album, albeit with a different vocalist. And that vocalist was, if anything, more expressive than the author—on a song like "Out of Work," one of Springsteen's blue-collar anthems, Bonds sang with the conviction of a journeyman who knows what work is and what it's like not to have it. *— William Ruhlmann*

Standing in the Line of Fire / 1984 / Phoenix ♦♦

For the album's title track, Gary "U.S." Bonds turned to Little Steven (Van Zandt), who wrote, arranged, played lead guitar, and produced it, some of the same tasks he had undertaken for Bonds' previous two albums. As a result, the performance had much of the drive of the anthemic songs on Little Steven's solo albums. For the rest, on which he was co-billed with his backup band, the American Men, Bonds was for the first time his own boss, and he proved he could come up with sturdy rock & roll songs, although nothing to match his early hits or the songs Bruce Springsteen wrote for him in the early '80s. *— William Ruhlmann*

Greatest Hits / ♦♦♦♦♦

Gary "U.S." Bonds' '80s comeback with "This Little Girl" and *Dedication* inspired many repackagings of his '60s recordings in different countries. This 14-track French collection featured seven of Bonds' eight single hits from 1960-1962 (the omission is "Seven Day Weekend"), plus flops like "Not Me" and "Take Me Back to New Orleans," all with brief explanatory notes from producer Frank Guida. Most interesting is Bonds' final '60s chart entry, "Copy Cat," which name-checks competitors like Chubby Checker and Freddy Cannon. But as this collection demonstrates, nobody copies Gary "U.S." Bonds as closely as he does himself—most of the songs are essentially remakes of his biggest hit, "Quarter to Three." *— William Ruhlmann*

Warning: For Health's Sake Restrict Play Three Times Daily / ♦♦♦

Warning: For Health's Sake Restrict Play Three Times Daily is a compilation of Gary "U.S." Bonds' early material on producer Frank Guida's Legrand label. There has been some remixing, and some tracks are presented in stereo, but songs like "Quarter to Three," "School Is Out," "School Is In," and "Seven Day Weekend" sound much as they did on singles in the early '60s. Those are the only hits among the 13 tracks, although Bonds and Guida retain a party atmosphere throughout and one gets a greater sense of their overall style than a singles collection would provide. [Although the album does not bear a copyright date, it appears to have been released circa 1983, if only because Little Walter, who wrote the liner notes, recalls working on the tracks with Guida during Thanksgiving week 1982.] *— William Ruhlmann*

The School of Rock 'N' Roll: Best of Gary "U.S." Bonds / Apr. 1990 / Rhino ♦♦♦♦♦

In the early '60s, nobody made noisier, crazier sounding rock & roll party records than U.S. Bonds, with records rife with massive amounts of echo and good times galore. The crudeness of Frank Guida's production techniques is undeniable; overdub upon overdub are lopped on top of each other until the original band track is buried under a muck of tape hiss and echo, a swirling pool of party noise that is unabated. Why Guida and Bonds were so successful with this formula, milking it for all it was commercially worth, is here to be investigated on this single-disc 18-track collection. The big hits are here: "Quarter to Three," "New Orleans," "School Is In," "School Is Out" (although the last two are missing the spoken intros that graced the original singles), "Dear Lady Twist," "Twist Twist Senora," and "Not Me." But curiously left out are several powerful tracks, most notably "Trip to the Moon," to make room for lesser tracks from later in Bonds's career. This is still the best overview available though, until somebody does a better retrospective or decides to reissue the original Legrand album. *—Cub Koda*

The Best of Gary "U.S." Bonds / Jun. 1996 / EMI ♦♦♦

This ten-track compilation is *not* really the best of Gary "U.S." Bonds; it's the best of the material he recorded during his early-'80s comeback. It has tracks from the *Dedication* and *On the Line* albums (including the hits "This Little Girl" and "Out of Work"), as well as previously unreleased live 1981 versions of a couple of his '60s hits ("New Orleans" and "Quarter to Three"). *—Richie Unterberger*

• **The Very Best of Gary "U.S." Bonds: Original Legrand Masters** / Aug. 11, 1998 / Varese ✦✦✦✦✦
The title to this 16-track collection has more than its share of quirks and wrinkles. 14 tracks are duplicated with Rhino's 1990's *The Best of Gary "U.S." Bonds*, making it a negligible buy for anyone who already owns the latter compilation. All the chart hits are here, including "New Orleans," "Quarter to Three," "School Is Out" (again with the original intro clipped off, same as the Rhino comp), "School Is In," "Twist Twist Senora," and "Dear Lady Twist." New to this collection are the inclusion of "Gettin' a Groove," "Copy Cat," and "I Dig This Station." The latter two items grazed the bottom of the charts, hence their inclusion, but leaving off strong album and single material like "Trip to the Moon," "I Know Why Dreamers Cry," "Mixed Up Faculty," and "Cecelia" to make room for the second go round of non-charters like "Take Me Back to New Orleans," "Having So Much Fun," "Where Did the Naughty Little Girl Go," and "I Want To Holler (But the Town's Too Small)" makes this a less than stellar supplement to the Rhino package. But it's a decent alternative, leaving a half of a compilation's worth of material between the two best-of's. *—Cub Koda*

Dance 'Til Quarter to Three/Twist Up Calypso / Sep. 29, 1998 / Ace ✦✦✦

Bone Thugs-N-Harmony

f. 1993, Cleveland, OH
Group / Gangsta Rap, Urban, G-Funk, Hip-Hop
When Bone Thugs-N-Harmony first exploded on the rap scene in 1994 with their fast rhymes, harmonious choruses, ominous G-funk, and gangsta attitude, no one knew whether the uncanny Cleveland group were for real or if they were a novelty success. After all, at this point in time, few rap groups outside of New York or California had been able to prove themselves on a commercial level. And Bone Thugs-N-Harmony leapfrogged cult success, instantly rising to the top of the charts with their summer 1994 anthem "Thuggish Ruggish Bone." By the time their first full-length album, *E 1999 Eternal*, dropped a year later, it not only debuted at number one but also proved to be one of the decade's most important and enduring albums. While other rap groups struggled to break away from the clichés first forged by NWA, Public Enemy, Boogie Down Productions, 2 Live Crew, and LL Cool J in the late '80s, Bone Thugs-N-Harmony was one of the few groups able to carve out their own stylistic niche, an inimitable myriad of urban sounds with a strong ghetto attitude. Yet following the unprecedented success of *E 1999 Eternal* and, more so, the Grammy-winning success of "Tha Crossroads," Bone struggled to meet unreasonable expectations and also struggled with redundancy, having realized their apparent summit on their debut album. Yet even if the group was unable to repeat their success, they remained a vital group, as few were able to bite on their signature style. *—Jason Birchmeier*

Creepin on ah Come Up / Jun. 1994 / Ruthless/Epic ✦✦
When this brief EP first debuted in 1994, few rap groups had been able to attain success that weren't from either California or New York. By end of the decade, this wouldn't be the case, but when *Creepin on Ah Come Up* put the unlikely midwestern city of Cleveland on the rap map (as NWA did for L.A. and Master P for the South), Bone Thugs-N-Harmony had done more than just release a great record—they opened the doors for other non-New York and non-California groups. Besides this underlying importance, it's also important to recognize the other ways this EP proved to be so innovative. First of all, R&B had been integrated into rap in the late '80s, thanks mostly to Teddy Riley, but no one had ever brought the vocal harmony of R&B to gangsta rap, a genre still in its infantile years circa 1994. So when "Thuggish Ruggish Bone" became an unprecedented commercial hit (eventually followed by "Tha Crossroads"), Bone Thugs-N-Harmony weren't merely soaking up the spotlight, but actually functioning as minor innovators. Besides their first hit, a song that still stands as one of their best, this EP also features another harmonious gangsta rap classic, "For Tha Love of Money," featuring Eazy-E, the notorious West Coast rapper responsible for signing the group to his label, Ruthless. Besides these two hits, the rest of the EP is fairly mediocre, merely foreshadowing the splendid follow-up full-length, *E 1999 Eternal*, a classic album that proved that Bone Thugs-N-Harmony were more than a novelty. *—Jason Birchmeier*

E 1999 Eternal / Jul. 25, 1995 / Ruthless/Epic ✦✦✦✦
Following the surprise success of their summer 1994 "Thuggish Ruggish Bone," Bone Thugs-N-Harmony returned a year later with their first full-length album, instantly dismissing any notion that the group was a one-hit wonder. From the opening "Da Introduction" to the closing moments of "Shotz to tha Double Glock," there are few weak moments, as DJ U-Neek's smoked-out, gloomy G-funk kept the mood ominous while the Bone Thugs traded off fast-paced, harmonious rhymes and joined together for melodic choruses; in sum, it was a stunning confluence of modified gangsta rap and R&B conventions that never sound derived. Lurking beneath the group's vocal harmonies and DJ U-Neek's synth melodies is a dark and harsh album that paints a dim yet alluring view of ghetto life. Where "Mr. Ouija 2" and "Shotz to tha Double Glock" spoke of street violence, songs such as "Mr. Bill Collector" and "No Shorts, No Losses" spoke of ghetto greed, and "Buddah Lovaz" and "Budsmokers Only" spoke of a celebratory passion for marijuana; other songs such as "Crossroads" and "Eternal" alluded to the group's bleak view of the world. In other words, this is a well-rounded, perfect rap album: It crafts a unique style for itself, features a few catchy hits, covers all the essential gangsta rap themes, and doesn't include any filler. Actually, it is such a perfect rap album that succeeding Bone Thugs albums were initially received with disappointment as they were unable to compare to the flawless *E 1999 Eternal*. *—Jason Birchmeier*

The Art of War / Aug. 5, 1997 / Ruthless/Epic ✦✦✦
The double-disc album was the bane of mid-'90s hip-hop. Single-disc albums tended to be over-long in the first place, but double-discs were even worse, since it required artists incapable of successfully filling out a 70-minute disc to produce *twice* as much music. And it wasn't a question of the two-disc set being an artistic statement—as if the rappers had so much to say they couldn't contain themselves to one disc—it was purely a commercial decision, so they could take home more royalties. It could be argued the first two double-disc rap albums by 2Pac and the Notorious B.I.G. justified their length, since they were hip-hop giants, and the Wu-Tang Clan's *Wu-Tang Forever* more than justified its length with vision, depth and variety. However, Bone Thugs-N-Harmony's double-disc *Art of War* can only qualify as an exercise in pure indulgence. Unlike the aforementioned artists, Bone doesn't posess either a lyrical or musical vision; their most distinctive trademark, whiny "soulful" sung vocals alternating with ragga-inflected raps, was lifted from Snoop Dogg and Dre productions. While the group is capable of producing a catchy single, they don't have the personality to sustain an album, much less a double-disc set. By the end of the second disc, they have repeated all of their ideas at least five times apiece, and only a few of those ideas resulted in actual songs in the first place. Even hardcore fans will find *Art of War* to be an endurance test. As the cliché says, it's a double album that would have made an excellent single disc—and in this case, that means a standard 45-minute record, not a 70-minute CD. *—Stephen Thomas Erlewine*

• **The Collection, Vol. 1** / Nov. 17, 1998 / Ruthless/Epic ✦✦✦✦
Bone Thugs-N-Harmony had only released two albums and an EP, plus a handful of side projects, when they released *Collection, Vol. 1* in the fall of 1998. Usually, that would be the sign of a ripoff, but since their albums have been notoriously uneven, this functions as a useful summary for both casual and hardcore fans alike, since it contains all of their best songs, from "Thuggish Ruggish Bone" and "For Tha Love of Money" to "1st of Tha Month" and "Tha Crossroads." It also contains their cover of N.W.A's "Fuck tha Police," previously only available on a tribute album. It may be of interest to collectors, but it's a weak cover, and is the only thing marring this otherwise fine compilation. *—Stephen Thomas Erlewine*

The Collection, Vol. 2 / Nov. 14, 2000 / Ruthless/Epic ✦✦

Thug World Order / Oct. 29, 2002 / Ruthless/Epic ✦✦✦
Bone Thugs-N-Harmony is a good example of a group that has become little more than a brand name as its various members devote more of their time to solo projects. *Thug World Order* is only their fourth proper album in seven years, although many solo albums and recordings by other configurations have emerged during the period. By now, however, every album by the group seems like a reunion effort, their last one being dubbed *BTNHResurrection*, while, on this album, one of the members mutters unconvincingly, "I ain't gonna say we back, 'cause we never left. . . . " The group's musical approach hasn't changed much, its raps offset by vocal harmonies and its musical beds anchored by samples as surprising as Phil Collins' "Take Me Home." Lyrically, their concerns are also much the same, extending from boasting and reflections on life in the 'hood to complaints about low-quality drugs ("Bad Weed Blues") and the duplicitousness of women with whom they have had sex ("Not My Baby"). But their attention seems distracted, especially when they interrupt the proceedings with commercials for their upcoming solo projects, and the album's disappointing initial commercial reception suggested that their audience wasn't paying close attention, either. *—William Ruhlmann*

Boney M.

f. 1976, Germany
Group / Disco, Euro-Dance
Although they never had much success in America, the Euro-disco group Boney M. was a European phenomenon during the '70s. After German record producer Frank Farian (born in 1942) recorded the single "Baby Do You Wanna Bump?" (which was successful in Holland and Belgium), he created Boney M. to support the song, bringing in four West Indian vocalists who had been working as session singers in Germany—Marcia Barrett (born in 1948, St. Catherines, Jamaica), Liz Mitchell (born in 1952, Clarendon, Jamaica), Maizie Williams (born in 1951, Monserrat, West Indies), and Bobby Farrell (born in 1949, Aruba, West Indies). "Daddy Cool" reached the U.K. Top Ten in February 1977, followed in April by a remake of Bobby Hebb's "Sunny." In July, "Ma Baker" just missed the U.K. number one spot, and "Belfast" hit the Top Ten in December. In 1978, Boney M. was at the height of their popularity with "Rivers of Babylon"/"Brown Girl in the Ring," which became the second-biggest selling single in U.K. chart history. "Rivers of Babylon" also was Boney M.'s only U.S. Top 40 hit. Boney M's album, *Nightflight to Venus*, also topped the U.K. charts. In October 1978, "Rasputin" became another U.K. Top Ten hit, followed by the seasonal chart-topper "Mary's Boy Child"/"Oh My Lord," which became the fifth-biggest selling single in U.K. history. In March 1979, "Painter Man" hit the U.K. Top Ten, followed in May by "Hooray! Hooray! It's a Holi-Holiday." In September, the album *Oceans of Fantasy* hit number one. Farian went on to create the late-'80s dance sensation Milli Vanilli. *—Stephen Thomas Erlewine*

Take the Heat Off Me / 1976 / Atco ✦✦✦
This long-player marked the album debut of one of the world's most successful disco groups, Boney M. Although they never found much success in the United States, they were a phenomenon overseas during the late '70s and this album makes it easy to understand why. They were the right group at the right time—their unique combination of rocksteady disco rhythms and infectious bubblegum pop hooks created a sound that anyone in any country could easily grasp and find appealing. Some may find the Boney M. sound to be too sweet, but the group's soulful vocals subtly add a little grit into the mix to keep the music from drifting off into the ether. The big hits from this album were "Sunny," a pulsating, string-drenched update of Bobby Hebb's pop-soul classic, and "Daddy Cool," a relentless groove that combines staccato violin stabs, mariachi horns, and an aggressive drum attack to create an irresistibly catchy dance-pop ditty. The other tracks offer a similar mix of poppy originals and odd covers: "Got a Man on My Mind" combines reggae rhythms and choral vocals to great effect and Boney M.'s cover of Bob Marley's "No Woman, No Cry" may seem preposterous in concept but works thanks to its effective combination of soulful vocals and slick instrumentation. "Baby Do You Wanna

Bump," the only song that strays from the pop song format, drags noticeably, but the high quality of the surrounding tunes makes up for this flaw. *Take the Heat Off Me* won't win any new fans to the disco cause, but it remains an effective and likable slice of Euro-disco at its most effervescent. *—Donald A. Guarisco*

Love for Sale / 1977 / Atlantic ✦✦✦

Nightflight to Venus / 1978 / Sire ✦✦✦

This 1978 album finds producer/Svengali Frank Farian starting to push his pop-disco attraction Boney M. into new and interesting musical territory. The songs are still very much disco tracks with an emphasis on bubblegum pop hooks, but Farian works some interesting musical flavors into the mix: "Painter Man" (a cover of a track by mod rockers Creation) effectively pits a series of heavy, distorted hard rock guitar riffs against its danceable beat, and "Brown Girl in the Ring" adds some distinctive steel drums into its rhythmic calypso-pop mixture. However, the oddest and most unusual and interesting combination of musical elements arrives with "Rasputin," a tribute to the legendary Russian historical figure that uses balalaikas to create its textured rhythm guitar hook. *Nightflight to Venus* also spawned a major international hit with "Rivers of Babylon," which mixes religious lyrics and a folk song melody with a pronounced beat to create an instantly accessible pop hymn. The other tracks include a few less than colorful moments ("Never Change Lovers in the Middle of the Night" could have been performed by any disco outfit), but *Nightflight to Venus* is an overall success thanks to the group's strong harmonies and the slick production from Farian, which keeps everything moving at a fast clip. The end result is one of the strongest albums in the Boney M. catalog, and a treat for anyone who likes dance music that is sugary sweet. *—Donald A. Guarisco*

Oceans of Fantasy / 1979 / Hansa/BMG Ariola ✦✦✦

The Magic of Boney M.: 20 Golden Hits / 1980 / Musicrama ✦✦✦✦✦

A 20-track hits compilation, *The Magic of Boney M.: 20 Golden Hits* is a fair accounting of the band's biggest chart smashes, with a few extra goodies thrown in for fun. A club staple in Europe and the U.K., the band also had a fair amount of success in the United States, although, good as they could be, they remained for the most part on the fringe. Better across their hits than on albums proper, Boney M. kick off this well-paced collection with the classic reggae spiritual "Rivers of Babylon" before diving to the opposite end of the spectrum with the slightly sinister stylings of "Daddy Cool"—"Do you know who your sugar daddy is?" Other side one highlights are the outstanding and gleefully overwrought "Rasputin" and "Ma Baker." "El Lute," on the other hand, doesn't work within the formula and sounds more sub-MOR ABBA than anything else, negating the golden-hits tag. Included, too, are the now classic "Brown Girl in the Ring" and "My Friend Jack." The latter, originally performed by British band Smoke in 1967, was probably better in its initial airing—maybe. And it just wouldn't be a true Boney M. experience without one or two of their holiday hits. We are rewarded with both "Mary's Boy Child" and the less-than-stellar "Hooray Hooray, It's a Holi-Holiday." Now all that's needed is a domestic 12-inch hits collection. *—Amy Hanson*

Boonoonoonoos / 1981 / Atlantic ✦✦✦

Christmas Album / Nov. 23, 1981 / Hansa ✦✦✦

10,000 Light Years / 1984 / MCI ✦✦

Eye Dance / 1985 / MCI ✦✦

● **The Greatest Hits** / Mar. 19, 2002 / RCA ✦✦✦✦✦

At long last a U.S. Boney M collection has been issued, featuring all 16 of the quartet's biggest U.K. hits (including all of their U.K. Top 40 hits and their four charted U.S. hits). The group scored a massive run of hits in Europe, but in the U.S. only "Rivers of Babylon," based on Psalms 137:1 and featuring the oldest lyric on a charted record (according to Joel Whitburn's *Top Pop Singles* book), managed to crack the American Top 40. Highlights include the disco hit "Ma Baker," the bizarre but infectious "Rasputin" (a dance song about, of all things, the mysterious Russian monk), the "Fernando"-ish "El Lute," their version of "No Woman No Cry," and the song they will probably be best remembered for, "Mary's Boy Child/Oh My Lord," one of the U.K.'s biggest-selling singles ever (along with "Rivers of Babylon.") Unfortunately, this album features nothing as far as liner notes are concerned, and only one picture of the group, rendering them as somewhat anonymous entities behind Frank Farian's production machine, best (and notoriously) remembered as the force behind Milli Vanilli. By no means complete, this collection provides a good introduction to Boney M. for American audiences, especially those who enjoy 1970s dance music, Europop, and ABBA. Finally, the collection ends with a decent 2001 remix of "Daddy Cool" and a "Mega Mix," although it would have been nice to see other singles, such as "Bahama Mama" or "I See a Boat on the River." *—Jose F. Promis*

The Bonne Villes

f. 1964

Group / R&B, Soul

The Bonne Villes were one of the better white R&B-based acts to record for the Winston-Salem-based Justice label. A sextet consisting of Donald W. Cartner (drums), Curtis "Buzzy" Cobb (sax, organ), Butch "Carl F." Steele (bass), Nelson M. Bradshaw (lead guitar), James Alan Lovette (lead vocals), and Gary Howe (vocals), they made their way across frat parties and local clubs from their native Salisbury on out, playing early- to mid-'60s R&B; mostly covers of songs by the Drifters, James Brown, Wilson Pickett, etc., spiced with occasional originals in a similar vein by Jim Lovette. They had a fairly sophisticated vocal attack, and their instrumental skills were up to the repertory they chose; witness Steele's attack on the bass on their cover of "96 Tears." *—Bruce Eder*

● **Bringing It Home** / 1967 / Collectables ✦✦✦

This is not a bad representation of the band's strengths, a collection of 11 tracks, mostly covers of R&B and rock & roll standards. The singing isn't up to the task of the most sophisticated material, including "Bring It on Home to Me," but the group does have a cohesive sound. Their originals simply don't hold up, however, and lackluster numbers like "Helping Hand" and "Who's Afraid of Virginia Woolf" pale next to "My Girl," "Under the Boardwalk," or "96 Tears." *—Bruce Eder*

Booker T. & the MG's

f. 1962, Memphis, TN, **db.** 1971

Group / Soul, Southern Soul, Instrumental Rock, R&B

As the house band at Stax Records in Memphis, Booker T. & the MG's may have been the single greatest factor in the lasting value of that label's soul music—not to mention Southern soul as a whole. Their tight, impeccable grooves can be heard on classic hits by Otis Redding, Wilson Pickett, Carla Thomas, Albert King, and Sam & Dave, just to name the very most prominent examples. For that reason alone, they would deserve their spot in Rock and Roll's Hall of Fame. But in addition to their formidable skills as a house band, on their own they were one of the top instrumental outfits of the rock era, cutting classics like "Green Onions," "Time Is Tight," and "Hang 'em High."

The anchors of the Booker T. sound were Steve Cropper, whose slicing, economic riffs influenced tons of other guitar players, and Booker T. Jones himself, who provided much of the groove with his floating organ lines. In 1960, Jones started working as a session man for Stax, where he met Cropper. Cropper had been in the Mar-Keys, famous for the 1961 instrumental hit "Last Night," which laid out the prototype for much of the MG's (and indeed Memphis soul's) sound with its organ-sax-guitar combo. With the addition of drummer Al Jackson and bassist Lewis Steinberg, they became Booker T. & the MG's. In a couple years or so, Steinberg would be replaced permanently by Donald "Duck" Dunn, who, like Cropper, had also played with the Mar-Keys.

The band's first and biggest hit, "Green Onions" (number three, 1962), came about by accident. Jamming in the studio while fruitlessly waiting for Billy Lee Riley to show up for a session, they came up with a classic minor-key, bluesy soul instrumental, distinguished by its nervous organ bounce and ferocious bursts of guitar. For the next five years, they'd have trouble recapturing its commercial success, though the standard of their records remained fairly high, and Stax's dependence upon them as the house band ensured a decent living.

In the late '60s, the MG's really hit their stride with "Hip Hug-Her," "Groovin'," "Soul-Limbo," "Hang 'em High," and "Time Is Tight," all of which were Top 40 charters between 1967 and 1969. As a band that featured two blacks and two whites playing as tightly together as possible, they also set a somewhat under-appreciated example of both how integrated, self-contained bands could succeed, and how both black and white musicians could play funky soul music. As is the case with most instrumental rock bands, their singles contained their best material, and they're best appreciated via anthologies. But their albums were not inconsequential, and occasionally ambitious (they did an entire instrumental version of the Beatles' *Abbey Road*, which they titled *McLemore Avenue* in honor of the location of Stax's studios).

Though they'd become established stars by the end of the decade, the group began finding it difficult to work together, not so much because of personnel problems, but because of logistical difficulties. Cropper was often playing sessions in Los Angeles, and Jones was often absent from Memphis while he finished his music studies at Indiana University. The band decided to break up in 1971, but were working on a reunion album in 1975 when Al Jackson was tragically shot and killed by a burglar in his Memphis home. The remaining members have been active as recording artists and session musicians since, Cropper and Dunn joining the Blues Brothers for a while in the late '70s.

The MG's got back into the spotlight in early 1992 when they were the house band for an extravagant Bob Dylan tribute at Madison Square Garden. More significantly, in 1993 they served as the backup band for a Neil Young tour, one which brought both them and Young high critical marks. The following year, they released a comeback album, arranged in much the style of their vintage '60s sides, which proved that their instrumental skills were still intact. Like most such efforts, though, it ultimately failed to recreate the spark and spontaneity it so obviously wanted to achieve. *—Richie Unterberger*

Green Onions / Oct. 1962 / Atlantic ✦✦✦✦✦

There's not a note or a nuance out of place anywhere on this record, which was 35 of the most exciting minutes of instrumental music in any category that one could purchase in 1962 (and it's no slouch four decades out, either). "I Got a Woman" is the single best indicator of how superb this record is and this band was—listening to this track, it's easy to forget that the song ever had lyrics or ever needed them, Booker T. Jones' organ and Steve Cropper's guitar serving as more-than-adequate substitutes for any singer. Their version of "Twist and Shout" is every bit as satisfying. Even "Mo' Onions," an effort to repeat the success of "Green Onions," doesn't repeat anything from the earlier track except the tempo, and Jones and Cropper both come up with fresh sounds within the same framework. "Behave Yourself" is a beautifully wrought piece of organ-based blues that gives Jones a chance to show off some surprisingly nimble-fingered playing, while "Stranger on the Shore" is transformed into a piece of prime soul music in the group's hands. "Lonely Avenue" is another showcase for Jones' keyboard dexterity, and then there's the group's cover of Smokey Robinson's "One Who Really Loves You," with a ravishing lead performance by Jones on organ and Cropper's guitar handling the choruses. Just when it seems like the album has turned in all of the surprises in repertory that it could reasonably deliver, it ends with "Comin' Home Baby," a killer jazz piece on which Steve Cropper gets to shine, his guitar suddenly animated around Jones' playing, his quietly trilled notes at the crescendo some of the most elegant guitar heard on an R&B record up to that time. *—Bruce Eder*

Soul Dressing / 1965 / Atlantic ✦✦✦

Assembled mostly from (non-hit) 1963-1965 singles, this is solid stuff, but a notch below their peak collections. The best tracks ("Soul Dressing," "Tic-Tac-Toe," "Can't Be Still") are usually included on their best-of anthologies, but "Plum Nellie," featuring some ferocious, cutting-edge solos by Cropper and Jones, is an overlooked highlight. *—Richie Unterberger*

And Now . . . Booker T. and the MG's / 1966 / Rhino ♦♦♦

In the Christmas Spirit / Oct. 1966 / Atlantic ♦♦♦

Hip Hug-Her / Jun. 1967 / Rhino ♦♦♦♦♦

A great album cover and songs like "Groovin'," "Soul Sanction," "Double or Nothing," and the classic title track are just the beginning of the wealth of terrific Memphis soul available on this album. *—Stephen Thomas Erlewine*

Get Ready / 1968 / Atlantic ♦♦♦

Doin' Our Thing / Apr. 1968 / Rhino ♦♦♦

Rhino once again put together a classy reissue from the vaults of Atlantic Records. Highlights from this solid album include the title track, "Let's Go Get Stoned," and "You Keep Me Hanging On." *—Stephen Thomas Erlewine*

Soul Limbo / Oct. 1968 / Stax ♦♦♦

This 1968 album found the Memphis instrumental group running through the usual batch of then-current soul hit covers ("La La Means I Love You," "Be Young, Be Foolish, Be Happy"), pop tunes ("Eleanor Rigby," "Foxy Lady") and hits like "Hang 'em High" and the title track in their own trademark style. Most interesting are the tracks where Booker T. switches over to piano and the band suddenly becomes a very jazzy outfit, like "Willow Weep for Me" and "Over Easy." One of the better albums in their discography. *—Cub Koda*

☆ **The Best of Booker T. & the MG's** / Nov. 1968 / Atlantic ♦♦♦♦♦

The Stax Records catalog ended up partially in the hands of Atlantic Records and partially with Fantasy Records, and the dividing point is 1968. That's why there are two Booker T. & the MG's hits compilations. This one, *The Best Of. . .*, presents the material owned by Atlantic. There are 12 tracks, covering the group's popular instrumental hits from "Green Onions" in the summer of 1962 to "Groovin'" in the summer of 1967. Booker T. and the MG's scored some of their biggest hits, including "Hang 'em High" and "Time Is Tight," in 1968-1969, and for those you will have to look to the Stax/Fantasy *Greatest Hits*, originally released in October 1970. Just to be confusing, in 1991 Fantasy released an album called *The Best Of* that again contains only the later material. (Rhino's *Very Best Of* finally combined the two eras.) *—William Ruhlmann*

Uptight / Dec. 1968 / Stax ♦♦♦

The soundtrack to the 1968 Jules Dassin movie of the same name, the album reflects, through the score of Booker T. Jones, the story of a young black man living in the ghetto during the turbulent time after the assassination of Martin Luther King Jr. Containing the hit single "Time Is Tight," the songs move from soft and contemplative ("Children, Don't Get Weary") to driving and urgent ("Run Tank Run"). Though not one of their better albums, Uptight does contain the always exemplary musicianship that the MG's brought to a record and it pre-dates both the *Superfly* and *Shaft* soundtracks by three years. *—Steve Kurutz*

The Booker T. Set / May 1969 / Stax ♦♦♦

Here is a fine collection featuring the great soul quartet putting their spin on classic numbers, ranging from Cliff Nobles' "The Horse" to Motown, Beatles, Isley Brothers, and even some in-house songs like Eddie Floyd's "I've Never Found a Girl (To Love Me Like You Do)." The original lineup is in fine form, particularly drummer Al Jackson Jr. This was reissued on CD in 1989. *—Ron Wynn*

McLemore Avenue / 1970 / Stax ♦♦♦

Though Booker T. & the MG's had always been more of a singles act, they made a series of respectable long-players throughout the 1960s as well, culminating in the fine *Melting Pot* from 1971. Prior to recording that album, however, they assembled this Beatles homage, tackling an entire album from the Liverpool quartet. Rather than stroll down the *Abbey Road* they pay tribute to, however, organist Booker T. Jones, guitarist Steve Cropper, bassist Donald "Duck" Dunn, and drummer Al Jackson Jr. strut down *McLemore Avenue*, the funky Memphis location of the equally legendary Stax studios. Most of the songs are arranged in a fluid medley style, maintaining the suite-like feel that unified the original. The results often veer toward a sort of funky muzak. Imagine, if you will, the sort of tunes you might have heard piped into the Stax offices or renditions offered up by a late-night lounge act. Following the introductory pairing of "Golden Slumbers" and "Carry That Weight," the quartet flexes its combined muscle on "The End," a performance complete with soloing from Cropper and heated organ bursts from Jones. It's all over far too quickly, however, lapsing into George Harrison's "Something" and bringing up the main problem with *McLemore Avenue*. As the backing band behind countless Stax classics, rhythm, rather than melody, has always been the MG's' strong suit. Thankfully, the *Abbey Road* material balances the schmaltzy sentimentality of tracks like "Golden Slumbers" and "Here Comes the Sun" with the tougher grooves of "The End" and "Come Together": songs that lend themselves much better to the MG's' approach. The quartet may have been better off stretching out on a few of these tracks, rather than rendering the bulk of the album. As it is, *McLemore Avenue* remains a curio for Booker T. and Beatles fans alike. *—Nathan Bush*

Melting Pot / Jan. 1971 / Stax ♦♦♦♦♦

Melting Pot could be the most well-realized of all the albums by Booker T. & the MG's, a smooth and soulful, yet expansive 35 minutes of all originals, the latter in sharp contrast to their exploration of the Beatles' *Abbey Road* album material on their preceding album. And the irony was that it was their swan song. Booker T. Jones, in particular, was increasingly unhappy working at Stax/Volt Records, owing his feelings to management and structural changes at the company, and also felt the need to change the group's formula somewhat. Steve Cropper was playing lots of session work that was keeping him from recording in Memphis as well, and the result was an album recorded mostly in New York City, far away from Stax/Volt and largely built on the group's (especially Jones') best impulses. That said, *Melting Pot* managed to be a sort of back-to-the-roots effort in the sense that they were back to doing originals, but was also a strikingly more expansive record, with Jones in particular playing with an almost demonic intensity and range, backed ably by Donald "Duck" Dunn's rocksteady bass in particular. There were a few other touches, such as the wordless chorus on "Kinda Easy Like" and extended running times, showing the group stretching out on much larger musical canvases. *—Bruce Eder*

Memphis Sound / 1975 / Stax ♦♦♦

Evergreen / May 1975 / Epic ♦♦

Union Extended / 1976 / Stax ♦♦

Universal Language / 1977 / Asylum ♦♦

The Best of Booker T. & the MG's / 1986 / Stax ♦♦♦

Somewhat confusingly, this disc is titled identically to a CD on Atlantic that concentrates on their earlier material. This 17-cut disc draws from 1967-1971, and includes three of their four Top 20 pop hits: "Soul Limbo," "Hang 'em High," and "Time Is Tight." This perhaps lacks a bit of the edge of their mid-'60s recordings, concentrating on loping, relaxed grooves more than biting, incisive chops. The standard remains pretty high, though, with the interplay between Steve Cropper's guitar, Booker T. Jones' organ, and the rhythm section never less than telepathic. Most of the material is original, but even on the covers of period pop hits—including unlikely versions of "Something," "Eleanor Rigby," and "Mrs. Robinson"—the group is soulful and tight. This is perhaps better music for background and party listening than anything else, but within those confines it's quite good. *—Richie Unterberger*

That's the Way It Should Be / May 24, 1994 / Columbia ♦♦♦

Booker T. & the MG's do what they do very well. What they do is present a spare, funky sound in which each instrument, drums (here played by Steve Jordan or James Gadson), bass, guitar, and organ, is heard distinctly, playing medium-tempo melodies with slight variations. Precision is a key, and the result, while impressive, is anything but showy. Seventeen years since their last outing, the group exhibits the same qualities and the same limitations it did in its heyday. *—William Ruhlmann*

★ **The Very Best of Booker T. & the MG's** / Jun. 21, 1994 / Rhino ♦♦♦♦♦

This 16-song CD, clocking in at 46 minutes, is the second-best, and the handiest and most easily affordable, compilation available on Booker T. & the MG's. It's not remotely as comprehensive as Fantasy Records' three-CD set (although this disc does have two tracks, "Booker-Loo" and "Slum Baby," that don't appear on the triple-CD set) but is more comprehensive and better representative of their work (and offers better sound) than either Fantasy's single-disc best-of or the old Atlantic Records' best-of compilation. The collection does jump around a bit across history in the course of covering the years 1963-1971, bouncing between late-'60s singles and album tracks and odd early/mid-'60s tracks. "Booker-Loo," one of the pieces unique to this set, features some very crunchy rhythm guitar and flamboyant organ work in its intro, before Steve Cropper takes center stage with an unusually flashy lead guitar solo spot. "Slum Baby," from three years later, features a much smoother and funkier sound. "Slim Jenkins' Place" shows off Booker T. Jones' piano skills as well as his organ playing, and all of it is marked by virtuoso playing. The collection also makes a strong case for the band's members as composers—hits like "Hang 'em High" come off beautifully, especially in the crisply remastered version presented here, which brings out every nuance in the organ and guitar-dominated rendition of Dominic Frontiere's theme from the Clint Eastwood movie of that name. But originals like the majestic, soaring "Time Is Tight" and the lyrical, playful "Soul-Limbo" are great pieces of pop-soul composition as well, and stand up just as well to repeated listening. Buy the triple-disc set if it's in your budget, but at less than one-third of the cost, this collection shouldn't be dismissed for its compactness and range. *—Bruce Eder*

Play the Hip Hits / 1995 / Stax ♦♦♦♦

This British-made archeological dig through the Stax archives is a major addition to the Booker T. & the MG's discography, a compilation of 25 cover tunes recorded on the wing and never released anywhere. In the course of backing the Stax roster's recording sessions, this tightly interlocked musical machine worked so efficiently that there was frequently plenty of studio time left over—and not wanting to put it to waste, the quartet would come up with head arrangements of anything that happened to be on their minds. They're not fooling around or jamming aimlessly, either; these are all polished, concise, thought-out, radio-play-length performances that are at the very least up to the level of the filler on their mid-'60s albums. All but one of the titles ("Fannie Mae") are new to the MG's canon, and many will be surprising, like Petula Clark's hit "Downtown," retrofitted for a driving Memphis soul stew treatment, or the transformation almost beyond recognition of "You Are My Sunshine." The down-home soul workout of the Beatles' "Day Tripper" is especially effective, digging into the tune's blues roots, and Willie Dixon's "Spoonful" gets a deep-pile backwoods tread. Most revealing are the MGs' re-interpretations of two Sam & Dave hits on which they played: "Soul Man" sounds starkly stripped-down, shifting the balance of power over to Booker T.'s organ, and "When Something Is Wrong With My Baby" spotlights Steve Cropper's dignified guitar. It's doubtful, though, that there were any lost-long potential hit singles in this batch; nothing leaps out at you with the originality of, say, "Green Onions," "Soul Limbo," or the inspired cover of "Groovin'." *—Richard S. Ginell*

Time Is Tight / Oct. 6, 1998 / Stax ♦♦♦♦♦

A three-CD, 65-song box set that includes all their hits from 1962 through 1971, in addition to numerous LP tracks and failed singles; the third disc is devoted entirely to previously unreleased live material (most from 1992-1994) and rarities. Greatest-hits compilations will serve the needs of all but intense Booker T. and Stax fans. However, if you really dig their instrumental sound, this is a fine package. It might skip an odd worthy track from their catalog, but basically has just about everything deserving of attention, concentrating more on their original compositions than their covers. Some of the more obscure selections, like their jazzy 1967 LP cut "Pigmy" and their inventive 1969 cover of "Lady Madonna," are overlooked standouts. A number of sides here, like "Burnt Biscuits," "Fannie Mae," "Sunday Sermon," "MG Party," and the moody, dignified "Meditation," were never on album before. Other oddities fans will want to know about is a live medley of James Brown material from 1968, Albert King doing "Born Under a Bad Sign" with them live (also from 1968), a hit 1965 single ("Hole in the Wall") released under the name "the Packers," and "Booker's Theme," which was only available on the 1969 Stax various-artists sampler *Soul Explosion*. The 1992-1994 live cuts (all previously unreleased), with various drummers in place of the late Al Jackson, show the band in decent though not amazing form, including a ten-minute jam on "Time Is Tight" and a version of "(Sittin' On) The Dock of the Bay" with Neil Young on vocals. The booklet contains extensive liner notes by Stax Records authority Rob Bowman. *—Richie Unterberger*

Chuckii Booker

b. 1966, Los Angeles, CA

Keyboards, Synthesizer / Urban

A very capable musician, Chuckii Booker was prominent on the urban contemporary front as an instrumentalist, bandleader, songwriter, and performer. Born in Los Angeles, he was proficient on guitar and drums by age 14, but for a while preferred graphic art to music. His godfather, Barry White, signed him to a deal with White's production company in 1984, but Booker left after White failed to issue an LP he recorded. He joined Tease, and played keyboards with them for three years. Booker began to earn his reputation as a producer after this, working with C.J. Anthony, White, Geoffrey Williams, and Lalah Hathaway. He also recorded as an instrumentalist with Vanessa Williams, Troop, and Kool & the Gang, and toured with Janet Jackson as her musical director on the *Rhythm Nation* tour. Booker has also recorded as a solo act for Atlantic, including *Niice 'n Wiild* in 1992. *—Ron Wynn*

Chuckii / May 1989 / Atlantic ♦♦♦

Some nice soul, synthesized R&B, and urban contemporary ballads, with just the right blend of hip-hop flavored snippets, samples, and production. The former keyboardist for Tease, Chuckii Booker also proved a solid vocalist, not overly gifted but able to effectively deliver the slow songs and punctuate the uptempo tunes. *—Ron Wynn*

● **Niice 'n Wiild** / Sep. 1992 / Atlantic ♦♦♦♦♦

Chuckii Booker is chasing black lovermen such as Luther Vandross and Michael Jackson, putting major emphasis on the bass drum (well, it would be a bass drum if everything weren't programmed), and singing in an emotive tenor. Dancefloors and boudoirs are given equal emphasis in the tempos. An experienced session man, Booker knows most black styles of the last 25 years and presents them efficiently (in the album's second half, he even throws in some George Clinton-like funk and a copy of James Brown, complete with shouts of "J.B.'s!"), the exception being rap/hip-hop, which he ignores. In those long stretches when his predecessors are between albums, there is plenty of room for him to sneak in with an acceptable substitute like the number one hit "Games." But nothing about his second album suggests he would be any real competition head to head. *—William Ruhlmann*

James Booker

b. Dec. 17, 1939, New Orleans, LA, **d.** Nov. 8, 1983, New Orleans, LA

Vocals, Piano / Boogie-Woogie, Acoustic New Orleans Blues, Piano Blues, New Orleans R&B, New Orleans Blues

Certainly one of the most flamboyant New Orleans pianists in recent memory, James Carroll Booker III was a major influence on the local rhythm & blues scene in the '50s and '60s. Booker's training included classical instruction until age 12, by which time he had already begun to gain recognition as a blues and gospel organist on radio station WMRY every Sunday. By the time he was out of high school he had recorded on several occasions, including his own first release, "Doing the Hambone," in 1953. In 1960, he made the national charts with "Gonzo," an organ instrumental, and over the course of the next two decades played and recorded with artists as varied as Lloyd Price, Aretha Franklin, Ringo Starr, the Doobie Brothers, and B.B. King. In 1967, he was convicted of possession of heroin and served a one-year sentence at Angola Penitentiary (referred to as the "Ponderosa"), which took the momentum out of an otherwise promising career. The rediscovery of "roots" music by college students during the '70s (focusing primarily on "Fess" by Professor Longhair) provided the opportunity for a comeback by 1974, with numerous engagements at local clubs like Tipitina's, The Maple Leaf, and Snug Harbor. As with "Fess," Booker's performances at the New Orleans Jazz & Heritage Festivals took on the trappings of legendary "happenings," and he often spent his festival earnings to arrive in style, pulling up to the stage in a rented Rolls Royce and attired in costumes befitting the "Piano Prince of New Orleans," complete with a cape. Such performances tended to be unpredictable: he might easily plant some Chopin into a blues tune or launch into a jeremiad on the CIA with all the fervor of a "Reverend Ike-meets-Moms Mabley" tag-team match.

Booker's left hand was simply phenomenal, often a problem for bass players who found themselves running for cover in an attempt to stay out of the way; with it he successfully amalgamated the jazz and rhythm & blues idioms of New Orleans, adding more than a touch of gospel thrown in for good measure. His playing was also highly improvisational, reinventing a progression (usually his own) so that a single piece would evolve into a medley of itself. In addition, he had a plaintive and seering vocal style which was equally comfortable with gospel, jazz standards, blues, or popular songs. Despite his personal eccentricities, Booker had the respect of New Orleans' best musicians, and elements of his influence are still very much apparent in the playing of pianists like Henry Butler and Harry Connick Jr. *—Bruce Boyd Raeburn*

King of the New Orleans Keyboard / 1976 / Junco Partner ♦♦♦♦♦

A spectacular date by a great New Orleans pianist whose personal difficulties prevented him from both a long life and sustained career achievement. James Booker was cited as an inspiration by everyone from Dr. John to Harry Connick Jr., and played with an array of performers, from Lloyd Price to Aretha Franklin, B.B. King, Ringo Starr, and the Doobie Brothers. He seamlessly fused a blues base, jazz touches, and an R&B/gospel feeling, and this was among his best (and few) recordings. *—Ron Wynn*

Junco Partner / Oct. 22, 1976 / Hannibal ♦♦♦♦♦

This solo disc by arguably the most brilliant of New Orleans' resplendent pianists shows off all the edge and genius he possessed. There may be moments on other discs of slightly more inspired playing (and this is arguable), but for a whole disc this one stands far from the crowd. You can hear some of the most awe-inspiring playing here that reflects the extremely broad background that he could, and did, draw from. You can hear his classical training and the brilliance of his interpretive skills in "Black Minute Waltz." He follows this with a version of Leadbelly's "Good Night Irene," which shows off his raucous bordello style of playing and voice. The disc goes on showing off the eclectic variety of influences that make up this man's music. This disc also displays the man's prodigious composing and arranging talents. Though he was regarded as eccentric and crazy, even by New Orleans' accepting standards (he was a flamboyant, black substance abuser, and a homosexual, who spent time both in Angola State Prison and a mental institution), he was considered a musical genius and thus given a certain amount of leeway. Very informative notes by Booker himself (some insight), Joe Boyd (the producer), and George Winston on Booker and his styling. An absolute must if you like New Orleans music. *—Bob Gottlieb*

New Orleans Piano Wizard: Live! / Nov. 27, 1977 / Rounder ♦♦♦♦

Why so much of what pianist/vocalist James Booker recorded in the 1970s didn't surface until the '90s is a mystery, but that's secondary compared to the greatness routinely presented on this CD. It contains nine Booker selections which he performed at the 1977 Boogie Woogie and Ragtime Piano Contest held in Zurich. His relentless, driving style, ability to switch from a hard-hitting tune to a light, soft one without skipping a beat, and wild mix of sizzling keyboard licks and bemused, manic vocals is uniformly impressive. It's a bit short for a CD at 37 minutes, but it has so much flamboyant music and singing that it shouldn't be missed. *—Ron Wynn*

★ **Classified** / Oct. 18, 1982+Oct. 20, 1982 / Rounder ♦♦♦♦♦

While there has suddenly been a flood of CDs featuring masterful New Orleans keyboard wizard and vocalist James Booker, his best release arguably remains *Classified*. The 12-track set was a landmark album, as Booker displayed every facet of his distinctive style. He did uptempo blues, quasi-classical, rock and R&B, making them all sound easy while performing frequently awesome keyboard feats. His "Professor Longhair Medley: Bald Head/Tipitina" pays homage to a legend while also demonstrating how much farther Booker's pianistic skills had developed. While his vocals sometimes aren't the equal of his brilliant playing, they're never less than effective and are sometimes almost frightening in their intensity. *—Ron Wynn*

Spiders on the Keys / 1993 / Rounder ♦♦♦

This aptly named disc showcases James Booker's piano playing; his stretches and runs are breathtaking in their fluidity. This disc (along with its Rounder partner, *Resurrection of the Bayou Maharajah*) was culled from some 60 or so hours of tapes that John Parsons recorded at the Maple Leaf Bar from 1977 to 1982. The main difference in the music on the two discs is that this one is purely instrumental. In fact listen to this version of "Papa Was a Rascal," and then listen to the rendition on *Resurrection*, and what you have is two almost entirely different entities. This disc is made up roughly of what might be called piano bar standards, such as "Sunny Side of the Street" and "Eleanor Rigby," but regardless of how many times you have heard this fare, Booker manages to make each song sound fresh and vital. A special debt of gratitude must go to both Scott Billington and John Parsons for the care taken with this recorded legacy. *—Bob Gottlieb*

Resurrection of the Bayou Maharajah / Jul. 22, 1993 / Rounder ♦♦♦♦

For a man of such talent and influence, New Orleans piano legend James Booker is amazingly underrecorded. This disc, along with its partner (*Spiders on the Keys*) offer up some measure of what the folks of the Big Easy might have heard if they caught James Booker on one of his "on" nights (he was a known drug user and inconsistent in his playing). He is at his best here (recorded at the Maple Leaf between 1972-1982), focused and intense in his playing, wildly passionate on both keyboards and vocals. Some songs are repeated on the companion disc, but each treatment makes the songs new again, so that even his standards are always fresh and vital. Sheer genius at the keyboards and unrestrained, heartfelt vocals on such highlights as Fats Domino's "All By Myself," "The Fat Man," and "St. James Infirmary." *—Bob Gottlieb*

Gonzo: More Than All the 45's / Jun. 11, 1996 / Night Train ♦♦♦♦

Numerous discs are available featuring the eccentric and tragic New Orleans R&B pianist James Booker usually performing solo, recorded during live gigs from the 1970s and early '80s. This disc provides an amazing collection of the earliest Booker on piano and organ backed by a full band. Booker made his recording debut in 1954 with the Imperial single "Doing the Hambone," backed with "Thinking About My Baby." During the next few years he would release equally exciting, although sporadic, singles on Chess, Ace, Peacock, and Duke, supported by some of New Orleans finest R&B musicians, including the sax section of Lee Allen, Robert Parker, and Red Tyler, drummer Earl Palmer, and bassist Frank Fields. The 1956 Chess singles "You're Near Me" and "Heavenly Angel" find Booker paired up on doo wop vocal duets with Arthur Booker (no relation). The remaining tracks are scorching dance numbers tied in with novelty/twist themes with catchy names such as "Teenage Rock," "Gonzo" (providing a national hit), "Cool Turkey," "The Duck," "The Crown," and "Beale Street Popeye." This is exceptional New Orleans R&B that provides an important piece of the James Booker musical puzzle. *—Al Campbell*

Lost Paramount Tapes / Mar. 11, 1997 / DJM ♦♦♦

This is a disc made by one of the best piano players to come out of New Orleans, James Booker, playing with an all-star band of New Orleans musicians, most of whom Booker befriended during his days with Dr. John. The music sparkles, all the more amazing because it was recorded live in the L.A. area with no overdubs in 1973, and is just being released in 1997 because it was lost for 20 years. This disc hits a groove and does not quit, shifting from straight-ahead blues to an R&B beat, drifting into some complex Caribbean rhythms, moving off into some jazz riffs, but all the time maintaining the original blues feel it started with. All the players get to shine, but it is definitely James Booker's disc. *—Bob Gottlieb*

A Taste of Honey / 2000 / Night Train ✦✦✦
New Orleans pianist James Booker is captured live on these previously unreleased 1977 solo tracks recorded in the Crescent City. Many of these titles were standards in Booker's repertoire and similar versions have previously been released on disc by Rounder. Spread out over two discs are multiple versions of "A Taste of Honey," "Junko Partner," "Please Send Me Someone to Love," and "Tico Tico/Papa Was a Rascal." The revealing "Classified ('Version 1')" contains almost ten minutes worth of the bizarre rants Booker became known for on "bad" nights. While it provides insight into the unfortunate mental condition of this brilliant pianist, it becomes thoroughly depressing with repeated listening. Throughout his career, Booker consistently demonstrated a capacity to provide emotional renditions of these songs no matter how many times he had played them or what his mental shape happened to be at the time. This disc doesn't provide any revelatory renditions of these songs; it simply uncovers another sampling of this genius of New Orleans piano. *—Al Campbell*

Taka Boom (Yvonne Stevens)

b. 1954, Chicago, IL
Vocals / Disco
The sister of Chaka Khan, vocalist Yvonne Stephens forged a new identity by combining the Swahili word for "love of my people" ("Taka") with a last name derived from her ex-husband's occupation (demolitions expert). She worked alongside Khan locally in their hometown of Chicago until Chaka joined Rufus, and Taka moved to Los Angeles. Boom was a session vocalist in the early '70s, singing with the Gap Band and Carl Carlton, as well as being a member of George Clinton's Brides of Funkenstein. She served as lead vocalist for Undisputed Truth in 1975, then signed as a solo singer with Ariola. Her debut LP, *Taka Boom*, was released in 1979, and the single "Night Dancing" became her only R&B Top 20 hit (at 20). She later switched to Mirage, and made the LP *Climate for Love* in 1985. "Middle of the Night" got some attention as a single, but the LP went nowhere. After moving to London in the mid-'90s, she did session work and consistent live appearances. *—Ron Wynn*

• **Taka Boom** / May 1979 / Ariola ✦✦✦✦
With an impressive array of musical history under her belt, from the black power band Shades of Black she formed with her sister Chaka Khan in the late '60s, to her work with Parliament and her stint with Norman Whitfield's Undisputed Truth, Taka Boom's solo work was undoubtedly shaped by those dazzling moments. Striking out on her own, Boom took all these experiences and influences and brought them to delightful fruition on her 1979 eponymous debut. Backed by an impressive array of musicians that included her husband, tenor saxophonist John "Boom" Brumbach; her sister; and her brother, Aurra's Mark Stevens, among others, Boom crafted a punchy, joyful, and spirited blend of pure disco, funk fire, and good old R&B that edged her just into the Top 50. *Taka Boom*, in turn, spawned two successful singles, the disco-driven "Red Hot" and the percussion- and horn-led "Night Dancin'," which dipped into the Top 20. Lighter disco-inclined pop, both songs are good, but are also reflective of what made a hit at the end of the decade. Where Boom is at her best, though, is across those songs which are now forgotten, most notably the deeply funky "Dance Baby Dance," which features blistering horns and bass, and its cousin, "Dance Like You Do at Home," which is equally funk-heavy. Also interesting is the blues-inflected "Troubled Waters," which showcases Boom's vocal range to its best advantage across moody instrumentation. *Taka Boom* is a marvelous debut from a highly talented musician, who unfortunately has always been relegated to the annals of fringe, too often cast aside as Chaka Khan's sister. This LP still proves any nay-sayers wrong, though, and is a wonderful addition to any funk collection. *—Amy Hanson*

Boomerang / 1983 / Calibre ✦✦✦

The Bop Chords

f. 1955, **db.** 1957
Group / Doo Wop
Harlem's the Bop Chords formed in 1955 in the same building where the Ladders, Channels, and Willows got their start. Lead vocalist Ernest Harriston, William Dailey, Ken Hamilton, Leon Ivey, and Morris Smarr had all sung with other neighborhood groups, and Hamilton had recorded with the Five Wings earlier in the year on a tribute to Johnny Ace that was issued by King. The Bop Chords recorded for Holiday in 1956, and the midtempo "Castle in the Sky" was a local and regional hit. Their second single, "When I Woke Up This Morning," also did well on the East Coast, but internal clashes over song content and wardrobe soon caused lineup defections and changes. Dailey and Smarr left and were replaced by Skip Boyd and Peggy Jones, their first female vocalist. They recorded "Why" in 1957, then disbanded. Harriston did background vocals for Shep & the Limelites and recorded "We Need Love" for Asnes in 1962 as Ernie Johnson. A new edition of the Bop Chords resurfaced in 1971, with lead vocalist Johnson, Hamilton, Boyd, and Ivey. They never recorded, but were a popular attraction at various New York locations and oldies shows in the '70s. *—Ron Wynn*

• **Jackie & the Starlites Meet the Bopchords: Golden Classics** / Collectables ✦✦✦✦✦

Earl Bostic

b. Apr. 25, 1913, Tulsa, OK, **d.** Oct. 28, 1965, Rochester, NY
Sax (Alto) / R&B, Soul-Jazz
Alto saxophonist Earl Bostic was a technical master of his instrument, yet remained somewhat underappreciated by jazz fans due to the string of simple, popular R&B/jump blues hits he recorded during his heyday in the '50s. Born Eugene Earl Bostic in Tulsa, OK, on April 25, 1913, Bostic played around the Midwest during the early '30s, studied at Xavier University, and toured with several bands before moving to New York in 1938. There he played for Don Redman, Edgar Hayes, and Lionel Hampton, making his record debut with the latter in 1939. In the early '40s, he worked as an arranger and session musician, and began leading his own regular large group in 1945. Cutting back to a septet the next year, Bostic began recording regularly, scoring his first big hit with 1948's "Temptation." He soon signed with the King label, the home of most of his biggest jukebox hits, which usually featured a driving, heavy, R&B-ish beat and an alto sound that could be smooth and romantic or aggressive and bluesy.

In 1951, Bostic landed a number one R&B hit with "Flamingo," plus another Top Ten in "Sleep." Subsequent hits included "You Go to My Head" and "Cherokee." Bostic's bands became important training grounds for up-and-coming jazzmen like John Coltrane, Blue Mitchell, Stanley Turrentine, Benny Golson, Jaki Byard, and others. Unfortunately, Bostic suffered a heart attack in the late '50s, which kept him away from music for two years. He returned to performing in 1959, but didn't record quite as extensively; when he did record in the '60s, his sessions were more soul-jazz than the proto-R&B of old. On October 28, 1965, Bostic suffered a fatal heart attack while playing a hotel in Rochester, NY. *—Steve Huey*

For You / 1956 / Deluxe ✦✦✦✦✦
Although primarily known as a smoothly raucous R&B bandleader, Earl Bostic has jazz credentials that go deep, with records that reveal a technique as good as Charlie Parker's. While Parker made history, and the honker "walked the bar," Bostic still deserves kudos for producing some of the most urbane early-'50s jump blues. And, like Art Blakey after him, he should be remembered for mentoring a slew of up-and-coming hard bop stars—at various times his roster included John Coltrane, Benny Golson, Tommy Turrentine, Blue Mitchell, Stanley Turrentine, and Teddy Charles. In the post-bebop era where jazz combos dominated, many of these musicians might have missed invaluable lessons in ensemble playing and soloing economy that swing era musicians learned routinely in the big band-rich '30s. The outfits of Bostic, King Kolax, and Johnny Otis helped fill the gap, and this particular Bostic album, with its super-tight arrangements and incredible playing, proves the point. Coltrane might not be heard working out an early version of his "sheets of sound," but there's a wealth of top-quality material to be heard. Hits like "Sleep" and "Cherokee" (one of Bostic's best solo vehicles) only make "misses" like the nostalgic, after-hours rendition of "Smoke Gets in Your Eyes" and the heavenly swinging "Night and Day" that much more of a treat. A definite must for fans who like a little pop in their jazz and R&B mix. *—Stephen Cook*

Alto-Tude / 1957 / King ✦✦✦
Here is another in the series of releases by alto saxophonist Earl Bostic issued by King in the late '50s. Although some, this one included, have dubious sound quality, Bostic's alto solos are uniformly excellent, regardless of material. *—Ron Wynn*

Dance Time / 1957 / King ✦✦✦✦✦
These are mostly uptempo instrumental R&B, pop, and dance/novelty tunes delivered with style and flair by the great Earl Bostic. He was among the finest honking saxophonists, and King kept pumping out collections of his singles throughout the '50s. *—Ron Wynn*

Invitation to Dance / 1957 / King ✦✦
This was pretty pro forma—very similar in selections, sound, pace, and style to several other dance/R&B/novelty albums King issued that year. This also wasn't the best material Bostic ever recorded in this vein. *—Ron Wynn*

Let's Dance With Earl Bostic / 1957 / King ✦✦✦

Bostic Rocks / Dec. 18, 1957-Dec. 19, 1957 / King ✦✦✦
This is an unusual set in that the music was recorded twice, once in mono in 1957 and then again in stereo two years later. Adding to the confusion is the fact that both albums have the same title and are listed as King 571. As it turns out, both albums are worth getting, since there are differences in tempos and interpretations. The brilliant altoist Earl Bostic (the most popular saxophonist of the 1950s) is joined by a five-piece rhythm section, including vibraphonist Wallace Snow, guitarist Tony Rizzi, and drummer Earl Palmer, for such swing-era hits as "Southern Fried," "Jersey Bounce," "Air Mail Special," "Honeysuckle Rose," and the slightly later "Night Train." Bostic's joyful sound and obvious control of his horn uplift these fairly basic performances. *—Scott Yanow*

Alto Magic in Hi-Fi / 1958 / King ✦✦✦✦✦

C'Mon and Dance With Earl Bostic / 1958 / King ✦✦✦
Altoist Earl Bostic was at the height of his fame during the era when he recorded the dozen titles heard on this melodic and spirited, R&B-oriented set. Four selections match the virtuosic saxophonist with organist Bill Doggett, while others use ten-piece bands. Although such sidemen as Benny Golson and Teddy Edwards on tenors, guitarist Barney Kessel, and even altoist Benny Carter are present, Bostic takes virtually all of the solo space. Highlights of the enjoyable but not essential LP include "Avalon," "Laura," "Indiana," and "Mambolino." *—Scott Yanow*

Showcase of Swinging Dance Hits / 1958 / King ✦✦✦
Perhaps his best rocking and uptempo instrumental pop and R&B material. This album was aimed at the jukebox market and weighted toward the hottest, most furiously played cuts in the Bostic repertoire. Bostic was as technically accomplished as any alto saxophonist in his era, but he wasn't able to show that while on King. This album was one of the few times that he was able to really show his skills on uptempo material. *—Ron Wynn*

Dance Music from the Bostic Workshop / Oct. 10, 1958-Dec. 3, 1958 / King ✦✦✦
Includes an astonishing display of sax technique over a torrid R&B beat on the breathtaking "Up There in Orbit." *—Bill Dahl*

● **All His Hits** / Jan. 1, 1996 / King ✦✦✦✦
This definitive recording is not entirely made of altoist Earl Bostic's hits; in fact, "Arrivederci Roma" was never previously released. However, virtually all of Bostic's best-selling numbers are here, including the two-part "That's the Groovy Thing," "Flamingo," "Sleep," and "845 Stomp," plus later tunes taken from albums. 1964's "Walk on the Wild Side" is from Bostic's final King record, cut a year before his death. Listeners wanting to be introduced to Earl Bostic's popular R&B-ish music cannot do better than picking up this album. *—Scott Yanow*

EP Collection / Jun. 23, 1999 / See for Miles ✦✦✦✦
British label See for Miles continues its high-quality *EP Collection* series with a fine look at smooth jump blues star Earl Bostic's prime material. Focusing on the alto saxophonist's circa-1950 work, the 26-track mix includes several complete EP sets with plenty of hits ("Flamingo," "Cherokee") and "B-side" nuggets ("Wrap It Up," "Cracked Ice"). These primarily were released by R&B indie King and feature such contemporary and future jazz stars as Blue Mitchell, Benny Golson, Teddy Edwards, and Jimmy Cobb. Whether sweet ballad or honking swinger, Bostic is all tempered power and polished blowing on this essential release. *—Stephen Cook*

The EP Collection, Vol. 2 / Feb. 13, 2001 / See for Miles ✦✦✦✦

David Bowie (David Robert Jones)

b. Jan. 8, 1947, Brixton, England
Vocals, Saxophone, Keyboards, Guitar / Experimental Rock, Proto-Punk, Pop/Rock, Glam Rock, Prog-Rock/Art Rock, Hard Rock, Blue-Eyed Soul
The cliché about David Bowie says he's a musical chameleon, adapting himself according to fashion and trends. While such a criticism is too glib, there's no denying that Bowie demonstrated remarkable skill for perceiving musical trends at his peak in the '70s. After spending several years in the late '60s as a mod and as an all-around music-hall entertainer, Bowie reinvented himself as a hippie singer/songwriter. Prior to his breakthrough in 1972, he recorded a proto-metal record and a pop-rock album, eventually redefining glam-rock with his ambiguously sexy Ziggy Stardust persona. Ziggy made Bowie an international star, yet he wasn't content to continue to churn out glitter-rock.

By the mid-'70s, he developed an effete, sophisticated version of Philly soul that he dubbed "plastic soul," which eventually morphed into the eerie avant-pop of 1976's *Station to Station.* Shortly afterward, he relocated to Berlin, where he recorded three experimental electronic albums with Brian Eno. At the dawn of the '80s, Bowie was still at the height of his powers, yet following his blockbuster dance-pop album *Let's Dance* in 1983, he slowly sank into mediocrity before salvaging his career in the early '90s. Even when he was out of fashion in the '80s and '90s, it was clear that Bowie was one of the most influential musicians in rock, for better and for worse. Each one of his phases in the '70s sparked a number of subgenres, including punk, new wave, goth-rock, the New Romantics, and electronica. Few rockers ever had such lasting impact. *—Stephen Thomas Erlewine*

David Live / 1974 / Rykodisc ✦✦
The supporting tour for *Diamond Dogs* was supposed to be a theatrical extravaganza, yet as he headed out on the road, David Bowie became infatuated with Philly soul and changed his entire approach to reflect his new interest, as well as his backing band in the process. As a result, the double-album *David Live* captures Bowie in transition, as he moves from glam-rock to plastic soul. The set list draws heavily from *Ziggy Stardust*-era songs, yet a few surprises, like a stilted cover of "Knock on Wood" and an inspired version of "All the Young Dudes," a song Bowie gave Mott the Hoople. Since Bowie's attempts at soul are a little awkward at this stage, *David Live* is primarily of interest as a historical document, yet there's enough good material to make it worthwhile for fanatics. *—Stephen Thomas Erlewine*

Young Americans / 1975 / Virgin ✦✦✦
Bowie had dropped hints during the *Diamond Dogs* tour that he was moving toward R&B, but the full-blown blue-eyed soul of *Young Americans* came as a shock. Surrounding himself with first-rate sessionmen, Bowie comes up with a set of songs that approximate the sound of Philly-soul and disco, yet remain detached from their inspirations; even at his most passionate, Bowie sounds like a commentator, as if the entire album was a genre exercise. Nevertheless, the distance doesn't hurt the album—it gives the record its own distinctive flavor, and its plastic, robotic soul helped inform generations of synthetic British soul. What does hurt the record is a lack of strong songwriting. "Young Americans" is a masterpiece, and "Fame" had a beat funky enough that James Brown ripped it off, but only a handful of cuts ("Win," "Fascination," "Somebody Up There Likes Me") come close to matching their quality. As a result, *Young Americans* is more enjoyable as a stylistic adventure, than as a substantive record. [The 1991 CD has three bonus tracks, including the terrific outtake "Who Can I Be Now?"] *—Stephen Thomas Erlewine*

Station to Station / 1976 / Virgin ✦✦✦✦✦
Taking the detached plastic soul of *Young Americans* to an elegant, robotic extreme, *Station to Station* is a transitional album that creates its own distinctive style. Abandoning any pretense of being a soulman, yet keeping rhythmic elements of soul, Bowie positions himself as a cold, clinical crooner and explores a variety of styles. Everything from epic ballads and disco to synthesized avant-pop is present on *Station to Station,* but what ties it together is Bowie's cocaine-induced paranoia and detached musical persona. At its heart, *Station to Station* is an avant-garde, art rock album, most explicitly on "TVC15" and the epic sprawl of the title track, but also on the cool crooning of "Wild Is the Wind" and "Word on a Wing," as well as the disco stylings of "Golden Years." It's not an easy album to warm to, but its epic structure and clinical sound were an impressive, individualistic achievement, as well as a style that would prove enormously influential on post-punk. *—Stephen Thomas Erlewine*

Let's Dance / 1983 / Virgin ✦✦✦
After summing up his maverick tendencies on *Scary Monsters,* David Bowie aimed for the mainstream *Let's Dance.* Hiring Chic bassist Nile Rodgers as a co-producer, Bowie created a stylish, synthesized post-disco dance music that was equally informed by classic soul and the emerging New Romantic subgenre of New Wave, which was ironically heavily inspired by Bowie himself. *Let's Dance* comes tearing out of the date, propulsed by the skittering "Modern Love," the seductively menacing "China Girl" and the brittle funk of the title track. All three songs became international hits, and for good reason—they are catchy, accessible pop songs that have just enough of an alien edge to make them distinctive. However, that careful balance is quickly thrown off by a succession of pleasant but unremarkable plastic soul workouts. "Cat People" and a cover of Metro's "Criminal World" are relatively strong songs, but the remainder of the album indicates that Bowie was entering a songwriting slump. However, the three hits were enough to make the album a massive hit, and their power hasn't diminished over the years, even if the rest of the record sounds like an artifact. *—Stephen Thomas Erlewine*

Tonight / 1984 / Virgin ✦✦
On the basis of *Tonight,* it appears that David Bowie didn't have a clear idea of how to follow the platinum success of *Let's Dance.* Instead of breaking away from the stylized pop of "Let's Dance" and "China Girl," Bowie delivers another record in the same style. Apart from the single "Blue Jean," none of the material equals the songs on *Let's Dance,* but that didn't stop *Tonight* from becoming another platinum success. Nevertheless, the record stands as one of the weakest albums Bowie ever recorded. *—Stephen Thomas Erlewine*

Never Let Me Down / 1987 / Virgin ✦✦
Bowie broke away from the mainstream pop of *Tonight* with 1987's *Never Let Me Down,* turning out a jumbled mix of loud guitar rockers and art-rock experiments, like the failed "Glass Spider." While it's not as consistent as *Tonight,* it's far more interesting, with the John Lennon homage of the title track being one of his most underrated songs. *—Stephen Thomas Erlewine*

★ **Changesbowie** / Mar. 1990 / Rykodisc ✦✦✦✦✦
Changesbowie is a CD greatest-hits collection that revamps the original *Changesonebowie* by adding selections from Bowie's late-'70s and early-'80s albums. Consequently, it functions as a definitive single-disc introduction to David Bowie, featuring all of his major hits from "Space Oddity," "Changes," "Ziggy Stardust," "Jean Genie," and "Rebel Rebel" to "Heroes," "Ashes to Ashes," "Let's Dance," "Modern Love," and "Blue Jean." One complaint: It wasn't necessary to substitute the "Fame '90" remix for the original to hook completists, since it is inferior and was already issued as a separate single. *—Stephen Thomas Erlewine*

Black Tie White Noise / Oct. 1993 / Virgin ✦✦✦
A fitfully successful comeback effort by Bowie, *Black Tie White Noise* works best when he subtly tries to update his sound. When he duets with Al B. Sure! on the title track and does a tepid remake of Cream's "I Feel Free," the modernization of soul and glam sounds forced, which never happens on the house beats of "Jump They Say" or the moving reworking of Morrissey's "I Know It's Gonna Happen Someday." Unfortunately, the good songs—and the best material here is easily his best since *Scary Monsters*—are obscured by the filler and ill-conceived dance experimentations. Had it been trimmed by five or six songs, the album could indeed have brought him back to the top of the charts. *—Stephen Thomas Erlewine*

☆ **Singles: 1969–1993** / Nov. 16, 1993 / Rykodisc ✦✦✦✦✦
Taking *Changesbowie* one step further, *Singles: 1969-1993* collects all of David Bowie's biggest hits while picking up such overlooked gems as "Drive-in Saturday" and "Loving the Alien." The comprehensiveness and quality of the songs make *Singles* the best Bowie compilation available; fans will be pleased with the inclusion of the complete lyrics to all of the songs on this two-disc set. *—Stephen Thomas Erlewine*

The Box Tops

f. 1966, Memphis, TN, **db.** Feb. 1970
Group / Sunshine Pop, Blue-Eyed Soul, Pop
During their brief lifespan, the Box Tops earned a reputation as one of the best blue-eyed soul groups of the '60s, even if their recorded legacy wasn't as large or consistent as, say, the Righteous Brothers or the Rascals. Today they're remembered not only for their smashes "The Letter" and "Cry Like a Baby," but as the launching pad for singer Alex Chilton, who went on to become one of rock's most revered cult figures thanks to his groundbreaking power pop unit Big Star. In his teenage years, Chilton was an amazingly gritty Memphis soul belter akin to an American version of the Spencer Davis Group's Stevie Winwood. The Box Tops' music also encompassed touches of pop and psychedelia, although the group's own lack of control over it eventually led to their split-up.

The Box Tops began life as the Devilles, a white R&B group featuring guitarists Gary Talley and John Evans, bassist Bill Cunningham, and drummer Danny Smythe. After the band's local popularity blossomed, teenage singer Alex Chilton joined up, and the Devilles quickly caught the attention of songwriters/producers Chips Moman and Dan Penn, who were on the lookout for a Stevie Winwood-type white soul singer. Changing their name to the Box Tops to avoid confusion with a different group of the same name, they signed with Bell Records and began recording at Moman's Memphis-based American Studio. The first single the group cut, "The Letter," rocketed to the top of the charts in 1967, not only spending four weeks at number one but ending up as *Billboard* magazine's number one single of the year. (Chilton was all of 16 at the time.) With a hit on their hands, Penn began to exert more control over the group; in the wake of "The Letter," he frequently used session musicians on the Box Tops' recordings, sometimes replacing the whole band behind Chilton, sometimes just individual members. Frustrated,

Evans and Smythe both left the band to return to school in early 1968, and were replaced by Rick Allen (ex-Gentrys) and Tom Boggs, respectively.

The follow-up to "The Letter," "Neon Rainbow," didn't do nearly as well, but the Box Tops managed another massive hit in 1968 with the Dan Penn/Spooner Oldham tune "Cry Like a Baby," which went to number two on the pop charts. Although a couple of minor hits followed in "I Met Her in Church" and "Choo Choo Train," Chilton was rapidly growing dissatisfied with the inconsistency of the material the Box Tops were handed (which was clear on the three LPs the group had released through 1968). As a result, Chilton was chafing at Penn's extreme reluctance to allow him to record his own original compositions. By the time of the Box Tops' fourth and final LP, 1969's *Dimensions* (an attempt to make a more cohesive album), Penn had bowed out and moved on to other projects. Several Chilton songs appeared on *Dimensions*, including "I Must Be the Devil," and the group had one last minor hit with "Soul Deep." Cunningham subsequently departed, also to go back to school, and the Box Tops began to disintegrate. When their contract expired in February 1970, they officially disbanded, and Chilton moved to Greenwich Village for a while. Not finding the creative hospitality he'd hoped for, Chilton soon returned to Memphis and joined an Anglo-pop outfit run by his friend Chris Bell; they morphed into Big Star, one of the most revered and mercurial bands in power pop (or, for that matter, underground rock & roll) history. *—Steve Huey*

The Letter/Neon Rainbow / 1967 / Sundazed ✦✦✦

It has since been revealed that most of the music on the Box Tops' records—with the exception of (ironically) "The Letter"—was done by session men. Even as early as the first album, this method cut both ways. It ensured a Southern soul professionalism that the young band likely couldn't have conjured on their own, but also worked against the development of a solid group identity, particularly as Alex Chilton was allowed to record very little of his own material. In fact, there are no Chilton songs on this debut, a spotty affair showing every indication of having been assembled very quickly in the wake of "The Letter" soaring to number one. Although "The Letter" author Wayne Carson Thompson and the Dan Penn-Spooner Oldham team wrote most of the songs, their blue-eyed soul compositions are surprisingly journeyman, with nothing nearly as outstanding as "The Letter," save maybe the follow-up hit "Neon Rainbow." Chilton's vocals are strong and, for the most part, as gritty as those on "The Letter." Has there every been another case in pop history when a teenager sounded like a wizened adult at the outset of his career, but his voice became higher and more youthful in subsequent years? The 2000 Sundazed reissue adds four bonus tracks: the mono single versions of "The Letter" and "Neon Rainbow," the routine non-LP 45 track "Turn on a Dream," and the previously unreleased "Georgia Farm Boy." The last of these, a plaintive country-soul tune, is credited to "Newbury," presumably Mickey Newbury (the liner notes don't give a first name or initial). *—Richie Unterberger*

Cry Like a Baby / 1968 / Sundazed ✦✦✦

Searching for a hit to follow up the widely successful "The Letter," and at the end of their creative rope, in a burst of inspiration, songwriters Dan Penn and Spooner Oldham came up with the title track to this album within hours of the scheduled recording session. The song, a perfect slice of blue-eyed soul, subsequently became a hit for the Alex Chilton-fronted Box Tops. The rest of the album builds off of "Cry Like a Baby," but with less success. Songs like "The Trouble With Sam" and "Weeping Analeah" foreshadow the British Invasion style that Chilton would employ with Big Star, but the melody lines and instrumentation lack the gritty authenticity found on *The Letter*. And the normally outstanding writing team of Penn and Oldham, responsible for such soul classics as "Do Right Woman" and "A Woman Left Lonely," seems to have softened up their approach in order to make the Box Tops sound more pop. All in all, with the exception of "Cry Like a Baby," an album that could've potentially contained some real gems just doesn't. The 2000 Sundazed reissue adds five bonus tracks: the mono 45 version of "Cry Like a Baby," three non-LP songs from singles, and the previously unreleased "Take Me to Your Heart." *—Steve Kurutz*

Non-Stop / 1968 / Sundazed ✦✦✦

The Box Tops—or more precisely Alex Chilton and producer Dan Penn—were treading water on the third album to be churned out under the group's name in less than a year. The usual blue-eyed soul dominates the program, without anything on the order of "Cry Like a Baby" or "The Letter," although with "I Met Her in Church," Penn and songwriting partner Spooner Oldham were probably trying for something on that level. Sometimes the moods are a bit on the bluesy side ("Choo Choo Train," "Rock Me Baby"), at others on a gentler and poppier one ("Rollin' in My Sleep"). For the first time Chilton had the opportunity to write an LP track, and with "I Can Dig It," he brought out his most gravelly voice for an average midtempo soul belter. That's nothing compared with "Yesterday Where's My Mind," in which he sounds like he's trying to out-gravel the most sandpaper-voiced white singer of the era, Tim Rose; in fact, the track bears more than a passing similarity to "Morning Dew," one of the songs Rose interpreted on his debut album. "Sandman," a luscious ballad by the composer of "The Letter," Wayne Carson Thompson, is the most interesting little-known cut. Overall, though, this, like all of the Box Tops' albums, is a middling product with its share of filler. [The 2000 reissue on Sundazed adds five bonus tracks: two of them mono single versions (of "Choo Choo Train" and "I Met Her in Church"), the others from non-LP 45s. Those non-LP items include a Randy Newman cover ("Let Me Go") on which Chilton sounds like Paul Jones of Manfred Mann, and another of Chilton's earliest self-penned numbers, the soul-pop ballad "Since I Been Gone."] *—Richie Unterberger*

Dimensions / 1969 / Sundazed ✦✦✦

There were mild signs of artistic progression and evolution on the Box Tops' final album. For the first time, Dan Penn was not involved in the record (as either producer or songwriter), and Alex Chilton was allowed no less than three original compositions. A couple of these clearly hinted at an original songwriting voice. "I Must Be the Devil" was a wrenching, grind-it-out blues/soul ballad worthy of the mid-'60s Animals, and "(The) Happy Song" was an uncharacteristic (for the Box Tops) wistful Dylanesque tune (Dylan's "I Shall Be Released" was covered elsewhere on the LP). Closing the record was a pointless, nine-minute "Rock Me Baby," which the group had already recorded (in a much shorter version) on *Nonstop*. The rest of the album consisted mostly of the journeyman soul-pop that people had come to expect from Box Tops long-players, though "Soul Deep" (by the composer of "The Letter," Wayne Carson Thompson) gave the group their last big hit. The 2000 Sundazed reissue has five bonus tracks, including the mono single versions of "Soul Deep" and "Sweet Cream Ladies, Forward March," as well as two non-LP cuts from 45s, "King's Highway" and the Chilton-penned "I See Only Sunshine." There's also a previously unissued cut, "Lay Your Shine on Me." *—Richie Unterberger*

Greatest Hits / 1982 / Rhino ✦✦✦✦✦

A classic example of Rhino Records' early strength in excellent, straightforward single-artist reissues, the Box Tops' *Greatest Hits* is genuinely as much Box Tops as all but the most ardent (pun intended) fan will require. All of the Memphis group's singles are included, from the hits "The Letter" and "Cry Like a Baby" to lesser-selling but equally beloved blue-eyed soul gems like "Soul Deep" and "Neon Rainbow." The compilers also include a nice cross-section of B-sides and album tracks, like the gospel-tinged shouter "I Met Her in Church" and a weird but wonderful psych-soul nugget with a New Orleans-style second-line rhythm (complete with tuba) called "Sweet Cream Ladies Forward March." Other rarities include "The Happy Song," one of the few Box Tops tracks penned by lead singer Alex Chilton, and "Mi Sento Felice," which is "Cry Like a Baby" in extraordinarily poor phonetic Italian. *—Stewart Mason*

The Ultimate Box Tops / 1988 / Warner Bros. ✦✦✦✦

● **The Best of the Box Tops: Soul Deep** / Oct. 1, 1996 / Arista ✦✦✦✦✦

Who would be interested in a compilation devoted to a two-hit wonder, albeit a very good two-hit wonder? In the case of the Box Tops, there are actually several answers: oldies fans, blue-eyed soul devotees, and Big Star fans interested in the early development of bandleader Alex Chilton. At 18 tracks, *The Best of the Box Tops: Soul Deep* is the most extensive compilation of the blue-eyed soul group's output, featuring all of their singles and pretty much all of their best album cuts. Their LPs were erratic at best, since producer Dan Penn didn't always expend A-list material on the group; plus, up until the end, he refused to allow budding songwriter Chilton to record original contributions. *Soul Deep* is a vastly preferable way to hear the Box Tops' best moments, and it proves that when they were handed the right songs, they were an excellent pop-oriented blue-eyed soul group, easily ranking with the more renowned Righteous Brothers or Rascals. Like the latter group, they flirted with psychedelia on some of their poppier numbers (most notably "Sweet Cream Ladies, Forward March"), which contrasts sharply with the occasional return to down-home, rootsy soul. Chilton fanatics are treated to some of his earliest originals—the gritty blues "I Must Be the Devil," the straightforward period pop of "The Happy Song," and a couple more. Even if nothing is quite as striking as the group's two big hits, "The Letter" and "Cry Like a Baby," there's enough here to make *The Best of the Box Tops: Soul Deep* worth the time of fans with a serious interest. *—Steve Huey*

Boyz II Men

f. 1988, Philadelphia, PA

Group / New Jack Swing, Adult Contemporary, Urban, Club/Dance

According to no less an authority than the RIAA, Boyz II Men are the most commercially successful R&B group of all time. They've sold ludicrous numbers of records and been involved in three of the longest-running number-one pop singles in history, and they've done it as a unit of equals. In fact, their four-part harmonies blend so smoothly that most of the general public would be hard pressed to name any of the group's individual members. And that's no reflection on their skill as singers; Boyz II Men were among the first male urban soul artists to adopt the sort of hyper-technical melodic embellishments that were popularized by virtuosic divas like Whitney Houston and Mariah Carey. Their early music was indebted to new jack swing, but the group quickly found their forte in lush, soulful ballads, where their harmonies could be showcased to greatest effect. Boyz II Men may never duplicate their incredible run of success during the first half of the '90s, but that's a near-impossible task for anyone, even with the broad-based appeal of their clean-cut romantic image.

Boyz II Men were formed in 1988 at Philadelphia's High School of the Creative and Performing Arts. Founding members Nathan Morris and Marc Nelson had been singing together for several years, but had trouble keeping a group together simply due to members graduating. Things finally stabilized when they hooked up with Wanya Morris, Shawn Stockman, and bass vocalist Michael McCary; calling themselves Unique Attraction, the quintet performed a well-received Valentine's Day show for their school, and developed a repertoire that leaned heavily on New Edition songs (one of which, "Boys to Men," gave them their name). Their big break came in 1989, when they snuck backstage at a Bell Biv DeVoe concert and wowed group member Michael Bivins (also formerly of New Edition, and a budding music entrepreneur) with an a cappella version of New Edition's "Can You Stand the Rain." Bivins offered them a deal right there, but Nelson would not stick around to be part of it; personality conflicts led to his departure soon after (he later resurfaced as a member of Az Yet).

Down to a quartet, Boyz II Men entered the studio to record their debut album, *Cooleyhighharmony*, for the legendary Motown Records. Backed by the new jack production then in vogue, they dubbed their sound "hip-hop doo wop," though as a vocal-harmony group they were more indebted to R&B of the '60s and '70s. *Cooleyhighharmony* was released in 1991, and its first single, the uptempo dance track "Motownphilly," rocketed up the charts, going Top Five pop and number one R&B on its way to platinum sales. The a cappella ballad "It's So Hard to Say Goodbye to Yesterday," a cover of a song from the film *Cooley High*, also hit the pop Top Five and topped the R&B charts, and went gold. Meanwhile, the album won a Grammy for Best R&B Vocal Performance by a Duo or Group. Boyz II Men joined MC Hammer's *Too Legit to Quit* tour in 1992, but tragedy struck when tour manager Khalil Roundtree was shot and killed in Chicago; the group rededicated "It's So Hard to Say Goodbye to Yesterday" to him.

The tragedy notwithstanding, Boyz II Men had had an extremely auspicious beginning to their career. Still, nothing could have foreshadowed the group's Midas touch over the next few years. Briefly entering the studio in between concert gigs, Boyz II Men cut a smooth Babyface ballad called "End of the Road" for the soundtrack of the Eddie Murphy film *Boomerang*. Released as a single, it became not just a blockbuster, but one of the biggest hits in history; it spent 13 weeks at number one on the pop charts, an incredible run that broke the record of 11 weeks Elvis Presley had held ever since 1956 with the double-sided single "Don't Be Cruel"/"Hound Dog." "End of the Road" won a slew of awards and cemented Boyz II Men's star status beyond any doubt; while crafting their next album during 1993, the group released a couple of placeholders: a Top Five cover of the Five Satins doo wop classic "In the Still of the Nite," from the TV-movie *The Jacksons: An American Dream*, and the holiday album *Christmas Interpretations*. (Also that year, Whitney Houston's "I Will Always Love You" broke "End of the Road"'s record with 14 weeks at number one.)

The post-"End of the Road" buzz helped make Boyz II Men's next album, *II*, an instant smash when it arrived in 1994, even though it didn't include "End of the Road." Produced by the likes of Babyface and Jimmy Jam & Terry Lewis, rather than Bivins (who wanted to concentrate on developing new artists), *II* debuted at number one on its way to sales of over 12-million copies. The first single, "I'll Make Love to You" (also penned by Babyface), raced up the charts and wound up tying Houston's short-lived record, with 14 weeks of its own at number one—a staggering feat in itself, made all the more amazing by the fact that the group had already set the record once. Moreover, the follow-up single "On Bended Knee" actually replaced "I'll Make Love to You" at number one for a six-week run of its own; only Elvis and the Beatles had ever replaced themselves at number one. "Thank You" was a relative flop, not quite making the pop Top 20, but "Water Runs Dry" returned them to the Top Five, falling one slot short of number one.

Boyz II Men spent much of 1995 touring the U.S. and beyond in support of *II*, and also opened their own recording studio. They spent some time recording collaborations with other artists: Wanya Morris duetted with Brandy on the hit "Brokenhearted," and the whole group sang on Michael Jackson's "History" and LL Cool J's "Hey Lover." The biggest one, however, was a song done with Mariah Carey called "One Sweet Day." Featuring two of the biggest chart powerhouses in the industry, "One Sweet Day" was virtually a guaranteed blockbuster, and it went on to spend 16 weeks at number one on the pop charts, debuting there in December 1995; it was the *third* such record-setting single of Boyz II Men's career.

Over the group's objections, Motown released a piece of cash-in product titled *The Remix Collection* in late 1995; in retaliation, Boyz signed a distribution deal with Sony, not Motown, for their new vanity label Stonecreek. It was the beginning of a souring relationship that only worsened upon the release of Boyz II Men's next album, *Evolution*, in 1997. The record started out strong, debuting at number one and sending "4 Seasons of Loneliness" to the same position on the singles charts; its Top Ten follow-up, "A Song for Mama," gave Boyz II Men their record-setting seventh platinum single. However, Motown was unable to throw its full promotional muscle behind the record (perhaps because of their transition to a new label president), meaning that *Evolution* didn't have nearly the shelf life of *II*, selling only two-million copies. It didn't help that critics were less than enthusiastic, questioning the album's title since the music itself was more of the same. The group was also forced to postpone parts of their supporting tour when Wanya Morris developed a benign polyp on his vocal cords. He recovered fully, though, and in early 1999, amid major record-company mergers, the group got their contract transferred from Motown to Universal. For their next album, the group assumed greater control over songwriting and production, handling a greater share of each by themselves. The resulting record, *Nathan Michael Shawn Wanya*, was released in 2000, and while it received better reviews than *Evolution*, it continued the group's downward commercial slide, only going gold and producing a smaller-scale hit in "Pass You By." The group subsequently signed with Arista Records. In summer 2002, Boyz II Men kept with their sophisticated approach for the aptly titled release *Full Circle*. —*Steve Huey*

Cooleyhighharmony / Apr. 30, 1991 / Motown ♦♦♦♦♦
Boyz II Men's retro sound dominated the 1991 pop and R&B marketplaces, with their singles "It's So Hard to Say Goodbye to Yesterday" and "Motownphilly" hitting the Top Ten on both charts. The album eventually sold over five million copies and put Boyz II Men at the forefront of a movement returning the emphasis in black popular music to vocal harmonies and a cappella interaction. —*Ron Wynn*

● **II** / Aug. 30, 1994 / Motown ♦♦♦♦♦
With their second album, Boyz II Men assured their place at the top of the charts, as well as history. "I'll Make Love to You," the album's first single, stayed on the top of the charts for over two months, only to be unseated by "On Bended Knee," the album's second single. Not surprisingly, *II* is a carefully constructed crowd pleaser, accentuating all of the finest moments from their hit debut. While there are some high-energy dance tracks, the album's main strength is its slower numbers, where the group's vocals soar. —*Stephen Thomas Erlewine*

The Remix Collection / 1995 / Motown ♦♦♦

Evolution / Sep. 23, 1997 / Motown ♦♦♦
Evolution is supposed to capture Boyz II Men in full maturity, but it sounds surprisingly similar to their blockbuster, *II*. Like that album, *Evolution* relies on ballads, downplaying the group's dance-pop side. There are still several uptempo numbers on the record, but it's clear that the group and their producers were more concerned with smooth ballads like "4 Seasons of Loneliness" and "A Song for Mama," which they deliver with typical grace. However, Boyz II Men's signature sound is beginning to sound like a formula, especially since the group fails to offer any new twists on their trademark hip-hop doo-wop. There's enough strong material on *Evolution* to satisfy Boyz II Men's large fan base, but they will truly need to evolve on their fourth album in order to stay viable. —*Stephen Thomas Erlewine*

Nathan Michael Shawn Wanya / Sep. 12, 2000 / Universal ♦♦♦♦
Even if Boyz II Men's third album *Evolution* didn't rival *II* in terms of commercial clout, the group was still inescapable. Every male urban vocal group that reached the pop and R&B charts were clearly indebted to the quartet's stylish blend of old-school harmony, post-Aretha hyper-vocalizing, and lite hip-hop beats. The group returned to action in the fall of 2000 with *Nathan Michael Shawn Wanya*, a nearly eponymous title for their first full-fledged adult album. And, as adults, they've made sure they're responsible for their own music—at least one member (usually all) has songwriting credits for all but two of the album's 14 songs, and the group is credited with all but four of the album's productions. Usually, when a popular group seizes control of their reins in such a dramatic fashion, the result is muddled to say the least, but a remarkable thing happens here—the group succeeds. True, they don't expand on the formula they developed on *II*, but they do fulfill the expectations that album set. There are no unexpected twists or turns, just the standard lush ballads and swinging hip-hop soul, but it delivers both sonically *and* substantively. Not every cut on the record is a standout, but even the average cuts are pleasant, and the best of the batch are either seductive or effortlessly danceable. Also, the group is beginning to cut back on their vocal histrionics, resulting in a record that is truly their most mature yet. It might not be their best—it doesn't have the powerhouse singles of *II*—but Boyz II Men make up for it by demonstrating that they can do much of this on their own, and still sound like the standard-bearers for urban soul. —*Stephen Thomas Erlewine*

Legacy: The Greatest Hits Collection / Oct. 30, 2001 / Universal ♦♦♦♦♦
Released a decade into Boyz II Men's enormously successful career and a year after another best-of collection, *Ballad Collection*, *Legacy: The Greatest Hits Collection* puts all the quartet's hits on one disc. Songs like "Motownphilly" and "End of the Road" were phenomenons during their reign atop the *Billboard* charts, and many of the other songs here were nearly as ubiquitous at various points in the '90s. Boyz II Men's success simmered out a bit toward the latter end of the '90s, but that doesn't mean they weren't performing great songs. Even if singles like "Song for Mama" didn't dominate the airwaves like the group's early-'90s hits, they're still amazing. Not surprisingly, *Legacy* focuses on Boyz II Men's first two albums—*Cooleyhighharmony* and *II*—and not so much on *Evolution* and *Nathan Michael Shawn Wanya*. Overall, this best-of is a great place to get all of Boyz II Men's hits if you're not one of the millions of people who bought the original LPs. —*Jason Birchmeier*

Full Circle / Jun. 11, 2002 / Arista ♦♦♦
Boyz II Men grew up with 2000's *Nathan Michael Shawn Wanya*, providing a really fine, mature urban soul album, but not many noticed, so it was time for another new start in 2002. They left Motown and signed with Arista, where Antonio "L.A." Reid had successfully set up shop, breaking new acts and re-establishing old ones—with the latter clearly in mind when he executive produced Boyz II Men's *Full Circle*, with the Boyz handling production duties. Everybody involved apparently decided that the best way to bring the boyz into the 2000s is by hedging their bets: offering a little of the stilted, early-'80s funk-influenced hip-hop that marked modern soul, while offering a lot of adult contemporary balladry. Although the group doesn't delve too hard into funk, it still doesn't mesh particularly well together, especially since the material, while well-sung as ever, isn't particularly distinguished. That doesn't mean it's bad—the album is pleasant enough as it spins—but it's simply not that memorable, which is quite a disappointment after the very, very nice *Nathan Michael Shawn Wanya*. —*Stephen Thomas Erlewine*

Tiny Bradshaw

b. Sep. 23, 1905, Youngstown, OH, **d.** Nov. 26, 1958, Cincinnati, OH
Vocals, Drums, Piano, Leader / Jump Blues, Swing, R&B
Tiny Bradshaw really had a two-part career, in the 1930s in swing and from the mid-'40s on as a best-selling R&B artist. He majored in psychology at Wilberforce University but chose music as his career. Bradshaw sang early on with Horace Henderson's Orchestra (in addition to playing drums), Marion Hardy's Alabamians, the Savoy Bearcats, the Mills Blue Rhythm Band, and Luis Russell. In 1934, he put together his own orchestra and they recorded eight spirited numbers for Decca later that year. A decade of struggle lie ahead and, when Bradshaw's big band recorded again, in 1944, the music was more R&B and jump-oriented. The majority of Bradshaw's recordings were cut during 1950-1954, although there would be one session apiece made in 1955 and 1958. All of his post-1947 output was made for King including the seminal "Train Kept A-Rollin'" in 1951. For several decades, that song became a staple of numerous garage bands along with notable recorded versions by the Yardbirds in the '60s and Aerosmith in the '70s.

In 1954, Bradshaw suffered the first of two strokes, the second would be two years later. He spent the next few years recovering in a Florida hospital. In the meantime, King tried to keep his name from disappearing altogether by releasing a single made up of previous sessions. By early 1958, Bradshaw slowly returned to touring and leading his band. A final single was released by King, "Bushes" backed with "Short Shorts," which failed to gain any interest. Essentially Tiny Bradshaw's career was over. The record-buying public, led by teenagers, had already discovered Little Richard, Chuck Berry, and Elvis. While trying to make the transistion to the rock & roll market, Bradshaw passed away of a third stroke on November 26, 1958, at his home in Cincinnati. He was 53 years old. Bradshaw is remembered not only as a fine jump blues shouter, but a bandleader who employed some of the greatest jazz players as sidemen along the way including Shad Collins, Russell Procope, and Happy Caldwell (all in 1934); Sonny Stitt (who recorded with Bradshaw in 1944); Big Nick Nicholas; Red Prysock; Bill Hardiman; and Sil Austin. —*Scott Yanow & Al Campbell*

• **Breakin' Up the House** / 1950-1952 / Charly ♦♦♦♦♦

Here are sixteen of Tiny Bradshaw's biggest and hardest-swinging King label waxings from 1950-1952, notably "The Train Kept A-Rollin'," "Well, Oh Well," "Two Dry Bones on the Pantry Shelf," "Walkin' the Chalk Line," and the jiving title item. Unfortunately, the torrid big band-styled instrumental arrangements that also defined Bradshaw's output are nowhere to be found on this collection. *—Bill Dahl*

The Great Composer / 1959 / King ♦♦♦

This domestic CD collection duplicates one of the popular jump blues bandleader's early albums from the King catalog. *—Bill Dahl*

Walk That Mess!: The Best of the King Years / Dec. 15, 1998 / WestSide ♦♦♦♦

EP Collection . . . Plus / Dec. 14, 1999 / See for Miles ♦♦♦♦

Another excellent entry in See for Miles' EP series, here are 24 of Bradshaw's sides for the King label pulled from various extended-play 45 albums along with five bonus tracks. By and large, it's a wild collection of honkin' sax-driven big band sides that trot the fine line between big band stomps and jump blues rockers with a few stray pop things (the corny "Butterfly") thrown in to round things out. An excellent introduction to this highly underrated bandleader's work. *—Cub Koda*

Johnny Bragg

b. Jan. 18, 1926, Nashville, TN

Vocals / Doo Wop, R&B

Johnny Bragg came to the music business by a stranger route than most other artists. When he formed his first group and began to write songs, he was doing serious time in a Tennessee prison for rape. Falsely accused of numerous counts of the crime at the age of 16 and convicted at 17, Bragg had already begun serving six sentences of 99 years each when he began singing. The court had ordered that he serve his sentences consecutively. While singing with a group of other inmates he called the Prisonaires, and with a decade of time served already under his belt, he came to the attention of a reform-minded governor and eventually to the notice of Sam Phillips, who recorded Bragg on his Sun label. Many evenings, Bragg and his fellow bandmates left prison walls behind to perform at concerts held in such esteemed venues as the governor's mansion. Bragg and the Prisonaires also sang on television. Their list of appearances also included the home of Al Gore Sr. All the while they were performing, they were held under armed guard before being transported back to their tiny cells.

In retrospect, it seems Bragg might not have received the big musical break with Phillips if he hadn't also gotten one of the worst breaks of his life by being wrongly accused and convicted. *Just Walkin' in the Rain*, a book about Bragg and his group of musical prisoners written by Jay Warner, was published in 2001 by Renaissance Books. A CD titled *The Johnny Bragg Story: Just Walkin' in the Rain* was also issued that year by Relentless. Bragg led the Prisonaires during the 1950s. Later he sang with two other groups, the Solotones and the Marigolds, who recorded on the label Excello. He also recorded as a solo act for ElBeJay and Tree Music in 1959. His greatest claim to fame, however, came when he wrote the best-selling "Just Walkin' in the Rain." Bragg and the Prisonaires first recorded the song in 1953. Three years later, Johnnie Ray's version soared up the charts, barely missing the top spot. Jim Reeves also made a cover of the song. BMI acknowledged Bragg with honors in 1988 when the number of times "Just Walkin' in the Rain" had been played on the radio topped a million.

While Bragg surely got a bad break when he was sent off to prison, the periods of his life that bracket his time behind bars weren't much easier. A native of Nashville, he was blind from the time of his birth in 1926. His affliction suddenly disappeared when he was around the age of six or seven. His teen years were marked by small-time scrapes with local authorities. Bragg eventually was released from prison when Tennessee's governor, before leaving office, commuted his sentence early in 1959. Bragg landed back in jail a few more times before finally leaving prison life behind for good in 1977. *—Linda Seida*

• **The Johnny Bragg Story: Just Walkin' in the Rain** / Feb. 13, 2001 / Madacy ♦♦♦

The music contained on this disc is as compelling as the stories that are behind it. Both bear out the old saying that truth is stranger than fiction. Fiction has certain rules it has to obey, and it has to be "believable," while there are no constraints or regulations whatsoever on the truth. This music is from the seminal stages of rock & roll, and this group is straight from the Tennessee State Penitentiary system, thanks to a Governor who appreciated music. This group was not just released, but still incarcerated and having to go back there each night after the recording sessions, which for the most part were done at Sun Studios, the same studio where Elvis Presley, Johnny Cash, Carl Perkins, and all those other pioneers made their starts. Rumor has it that Elvis and Johnny Bragg became a great admirer of the work the other was doing and often traded musical ideas. They did sing with each other at various state functions of the time. This is work that is reminiscent of some of the recordings of the Ink Spots, Louis Jordan, and the Mills Brothers, and yet at times has the raw energy of the early Elvis and Hank Williams. The fact that we have it is due to the forward thinking of the Governor of Tennessee at the time, Frank Clement (a story in his own right). The music comes from the harmonies of the gospel groups, the street corners, and all the music that was available on the radio at the time. Music that stretched the whole gamut, all the way from the groups previously mentioned to Perry Como, and all the pioneers at the Grand Ole Opry. The man who put it all together was Johnny Bragg, who never sang until he was falsely incarcerated for rape. Stories held in abeyance, this is music that should not be missed, and contained here is the original version of "Just Walkin' in the Rain," and this version is capable of bringing tears to your eyes. This is rock & roll at its most primal. *—Bob Gottlieb*

Brainstorm

f. 1976, Detroit, MI

Group / Funk, Urban

A Detroit '70s funk band, Brainstorm recorded for Tabu in the late '70s. They started in 1976, and one of their members, Renell Gonsalves, was the son of longtime Ellington sax great Paul Gonsalves. Other bandmembers were vocalist Belita Karen Woods, Charles Overton, Jeryl Bright, Larry H. Sims, Gerald Kent, Trenita Womack, E. Lamont Johnson, and Willie Wooten. They made a good inspirational/message track in 1977, "Wake Up and Be Somebody," but enjoyed their biggest hit later that year in "Lovin' Is Really My Game." It reached number 14 on the R&B charts. They never scored another one. *—Ron Wynn*

Stormin' / 1977 / RCA ♦♦♦

This nine-member R&B band's debut album release for Tabu features some upbeat, dance-oriented numbers. The energetic, soulful vocals of Belita Woods stand supreme. The two single releases were the socially uplifting "Wake Up and Be Somebody" and the incessantly groovin' "Lovin' Is Really My Game." The former has some Latin undertones on top of atypical R&B rhythms, and the latter is more disco-seasoned. The vocal prowess of Woods is admirable as she unleashes the lyric with her urgent vocal appeal. The expedient numbers clipped the R&B charts at number 48 and number 14, respectively. The irony of this project is that the most popular song on it was never released. "This Must Be Heaven" is a highly sought-after composition, as is this album. Set in a romantic, utopian mood, the ballad gracefully builds to a jovial climax. This song is a quiet storm classic. *—Craig Lytle*

• **Journey to the Light** / 1978 / CBS ♦♦♦♦

Although Brainstorm's debut album, *Stormin'*, didn't make the Motor City outfit a huge name in R&B, it did contain a number 14 R&B hit ("Lovin' Is Really My Game") and indicated that Brainstorm was a band to watch out for. There was reason to believe that Brainstorm might go on to become huge, but regrettably, its sophomore effort, *Journey to the Light*, was a commercial disappointment. The LP didn't provide any major hits, and the only people who bought it were Brainstorm's hardcore followers. Regardless, *Journey to the Light* is generally excellent. Brainstorm had a gem of a lead singer in Belita Woods, who really soars on tunes that range from Stevie Wonder's funky "Every Time I See You, I Go Wild!" to the quite storm pearl "If You Ever Need to Cry" and the jazzy, Roy Ayersish "Brand New Day." Nor are the lead vocals of Trenita Womack (who is featured on the slow jam "Loving Just You") and Deon Estus anything to complain about. One can speculate on the reasons why *Journey to the Light* wasn't as commercially successful as *Stormin'*—some would argue that none of the songs had as much disco and dancefloor appeal as "Lovin' Is Really My Game." At any rate, this is an album that should have done a lot better. *—Alex Henderson*

Funky Entertainment / 1979 / Tabu ♦♦♦

It's often been said that if an R&B act didn't have a lot of dancefloor appeal in the late '70s, it could forget about being commercially successful. That isn't necessarily true; Frankie Beverly's Maze, just to give one example, was never a dancefloor favorite—and yet, all of its late-'70s albums went gold. Nonetheless, having disco appeal certainly didn't hurt. When Brainstorm's second album, *Journey to the Light*, failed to sell, some people reasoned that it was due to a shortage of uptempo material. So with its third and final album, *Funky Entertainment*, the Detroit band decided to go for maximum disco appeal and make uptempo songs a top priority. While *Journey to the Light* was primarily an album for listening, *Funky Entertainment* is very dance-oriented. In fact, the ballad "You Put a Charge in My Life" is the only thing on the LP that isn't aimed at the dancefloor. Obviously, Brainstorm was hoping for another "Lovin' Is Really My Name"—nothing on this LP is in a class with that hit, although exuberant tunes like "Popcorn," "Hot for You," and "A Case of the Boogie" are mildly catchy, if unremarkable and contrived, examples of late-'70s disco/funk. *Funky Entertainment* wasn't a big seller, but it did enjoy some exposure in dance clubs. At the same time, there were die-hard Brainstorm fans who felt that by neglecting ballads, slow jams, and quiet storm material, the Motor City residents were selling themselves short creatively. And, to be sure, *Funky Entertainment* is the least-essential and least-memorable of Brainstorm's three albums. *—Alex Henderson*

The Brand New Heavies

f. 1985, London, England

Group / Club/Dance, Acid Jazz, Urban, House, Hip-Hop, Alternative Rap, Alternative Dance

Pioneers of the London acid jazz scene, the Brand New Heavies translated their love for the funk grooves of the 1970s into a sophisticated sound which carried the torch for classic soul in an era dominated by hip-hop. Formed in 1985 by drummer/keyboardist Jan Kincaid, guitarist Simon Bartholomew, and bassist/keyboardist Andrew Levy—longtime school friends from the London suburb of Ealing—the Brand New Heavies were originally an instrumental unit inspired by the James Brown and Meters records its members heard while clubbing the rare groove scene in vogue at the moment. The trio soon began recording their own music, gaining enormous exposure when their demo tracks were spun at the influential Cat in the Hat Club.

Eventually adding a brass section, the Brand New Heavies built a cult following throughout the London club circuit, surviving the shift which saw the rare groove scene fade in the wake of acid house. After an earlier recording deal with Cooltempo yielded the single "Got to Give," the Heavies—now including vocalist Jay Ella Ruth—signed with the fledgling indie label Acid Jazz; recorded on a budget of just 8,000 pounds, the group's self-titled LP appeared in 1990 to strong critical acclaim, resulting in a licensing deal with the American company Delicious Vinyl. With Ruth now out of the band, Delicious Vinyl hand-picked N'dea Davenport as her successor, insisting the Heavies re-record tracks from their debut for their first U.S. effort, also an eponymous release which appeared in 1992.

After scoring at home with "Dream Come True" and "Stay This Way," the single "Never Stop" soon landed on the American R&B charts, with the Heavies the first British group to accomplish such a feat with a debut single since Soul II Soul several years earlier; a subsequent New York performance augmented by rappers Q-Tip (A Tribe Called Quest) and MC Serch (3rd Bass) inspired the group to begin absorbing hip-hop, and that summer they cut *Heavy Rhyme Experience, Vol. 1*, an album including guest appearances by rappers including Main Source, Gang Starr, Grand Puba, and the Pharcyde. 1994's *Brother Sister*, which went platinum in Britain, was Davenport's last recording with the Heavies before beginning a solo career; she was replaced by singer Siedah Garrett in time for 1997's *Shelter*. Two years later, the group reappeared with a British best-of album entitled *Trunk Funk: The Best of the Brand New Heavies*; the title was recycled the following year for an American compilation, *Trunk Funk Classics 1991-2000*, which featured a new song recorded with Davenport. *—Jason Ankeny*

Brand New Heavies / Feb. 20, 1990 / Acid Jazz ✦✦✦✦✦
Many of the artists who were part of Britain's soul scene of the late '80s/early '90s, including Soul II Soul, Lisa Stansfield and Caron Wheeler, took a high-tech, neo-soul approach, combining '70s-influenced R&B and disco with elements of hip-hop. The equally impressive Brand New Heavies, however, used technology sparingly, stressed the use of real instruments, and were unapologetically retro and '70s-sounding through and through. Drawing on such influences as the Average White Band and Tower of Power, the Heavies triumph by sticking with the classic R&B approach they clearly love the most. The band has a jewel of a singer in N'dea Davenport, who is characteristically expressive on "Dream Come True" and "Stay This Way." Real horns—not synthesizers made to sound like horns—enrich those gems as well as the sweaty vocal funk of "People Get Ready" and "Put the Funk Back in It" and the jazz-influenced instrumental "BNH." While this fine album enjoyed cult hit status, it was sadly ignored by American urban contemporary radio. [The 1992 version released by Acid Jazz includes one less song—"Gimme One of Those"—than the Delicious Vinyl release.] *—Alex Henderson*

Heavy Rhyme Experience, Vol. 1 / Aug. 3, 1992 / Delicious Vinyl ✦✦✦✦
Between their debut and full-fledged second album, Brand New Heavies released an album of collaborations with some of the brightest stars in hip-hop, such as Gang Starr, Grand Puba, and Main Source. *Heavy Rhyme Experience, Vol. 1* actually works better than their debut, since the rappers bring a gritty street credibility to the group's lush R&B; at its best, the album stands as a splendid fusion of jazz, soul, and hip-hop. *—Stephen Thomas Erlewine*

Brother Sister / Mar. 22, 1994 / Delicious Vinyl ✦✦✦
This album finds the BNH heading back to the groove-driven, horn-splashed, hand-clapping funk of their debut album, with N'dea Davenport stepping back into her role as diva/lead vocalist. Following the string of distinguished rappers who made BNH's sophomore album a brave if not wholly successful attempt to infuse rap with the energy of live instruments, Davenport delivers the consistency that was missing from that effort. Repeated listens show this album to be catchier than it initially seems (as long as one avoids "Fake," tone of the most irritating songs in a long time), and when the BNH really lock into a groove, as they do on "Keep Together," the title track, and the instrumental "Snake Hips," they surely do put the funk back in it. *—Peter Stepek*

Excursions, Remixes & Rare Grooves / 1995 / Delicious Vinyl ✦✦✦
Since the Brand New Heavies were always more club-centric than their contemporaries, it shouldn't come as a surprise that their remix effort, *Excursions: Remixes & Rare Groove*, is entertaining. Nevertheless, it is a bit of a surprise that it's as cohesive as it is, considering that it contains a selection of remixes, rare tracks, and new songs. It still pales somewhat to the clearly focused studio efforts, but there are enough gems to make it necessary for hardcore Heavies fans. *—Stephen Thomas Erlewine*

Original Flava / 1995 / Hollywood ✦✦✦
The Brand New Heavies' fusion of retro funk and energetic jazz propelled their eponymous 1991 debut to levels of artistic and commercial success that subsequently eluded them on solid follow-ups like *Brother Sister*. Unsurprisingly, when the choice was made to mine their early sessions for unreleased material, the resulting compilation became the group's most consistently enjoyable effort since *The Brand New Heavies*. The bulk of *Original Flava* was recorded in 1990, around the same time N'dea Davenport contributed her dynamic vocals to the versions of "Never Stop" and "Dream Come True," which bolstered the debut. Lead singer/songwriter/keyboardist/drummer Jan Kincaid doesn't have Davenport's pipes, but his understated croon and light touch successfully recast "Never Stop" in a lounge-jazz arrangement that retains only the seductive bass line from his Top Five R&B hit. "Dream Come True" is one of three inclusions recorded with Linda Muriel for Chrysalis in 1988, and she invests her co-composition with an emotional intensity equal to Davenport's interpretation. Elsewhere, the band flexes its improvisational muscle on the Crusaders-inspired "Country Funkin'" and the adventurous live version of "Headhunters," which features Gerard Presencer on trumpet. As with other Heavies compilations, one could fuss over the missed opportunity to gather non-album favorites such as their U.K. Top 20 version of "Midnight at the Oasis," but the adherence to earlier tracks results in a cohesiveness not often experienced on collections of demos or outtakes. Unlike most assemblages of its type, *Original Flava* does not need to be programmed to sequence a few highlights; it is exceptionally engaging from start to finish. *— Vince Ripol*

Shelter / May 13, 1997 / Delicious Vinyl ✦✦✦
By the time the Brand New Heavies released *Shelter* in 1997, urban R&B was shifting toward the more organic grooves that they helped pioneer in the early '90s. Although the Heavies were into acid jazz as well, they smoothed over many of the experimental elements of their music in the mid-'90s, leaving behind a seductive, earthy, and jazzy variation of urban soul. That provided the foundation for *Shelter*, their first album featuring Siedah Garrett as lead singer. Garrett's smooth voice helps push the band toward more conventional territory, yet their songwriting is stronger than most of the contemporaries, and their sound is funkier and more convincing. While there are no standout singles on *Shelter*, it's a uniformly engaging listen, illustrating that the Brand New Heavies are one of the great underrated urban R&B bands of the '90s. *—Leo Stanley*

In Tha Beginning . . . / Aug. 17, 1999 / Music Club ✦✦✦✦
A collection including nine of the ten tracks from the Brand New Heavies' self-titled debut album, plus three tracks recorded live in Tokyo, *In Tha Beginning...* is a fresh look at the acid jazz group's first recordings. Entrenched in England's rare-groove scene at the time, the Brand New Heavies were a tight unit that fused dexterous instrumental jazz-funk with just a touch of P-Funk bounce for club audiences. The results, on "Dream Come True," "People Get Ready" and the instrumental highlight "BNH," are great examples of acid jazz. It's a shame that the track "Never Stop" was deleted from the original program. *—Keith Farley*

● **Trunk Funk Classics: 1991–2000** / Oct. 17, 2000 / Rhino ✦✦✦✦
Trunk Funk Classics: 1991-2000 is the first Brand New Heavies best-of available domestically in the U.S. Not to be confused with the similarly titled British release *Trunk Funk: Best of the Brand New Heavies*, the American version doesn't feature all of the group's U.K. chart singles ("Midnight at the Oasis" and "You Are the Universe" are missing), but it does give more airtime to the Heavies' collaborations with American rappers, including Main Source, the Pharcyde, Mos Def, and Q-Tip. There's also a newly recorded track, "Finish What You Started," which temporarily reunites the group with longtime vocalist N'dea Davenport; wisely, it's also the 1991-1994 Davenport era that's most heavily drawn upon for the collection. It may not be *entirely* comprehensive, but *Trunk Funk Classics* does cover the essence of the Brand New Heavies, and just as importantly, it's a consistently infectious listen. *—Steve Huey*

Brandy (Brandy Norwood)

b. Feb. 11, 1979, McComb, MS
Vocals / Urban, Dance-Pop, Club/Dance
Though still in her teens, singer Brandy was among the biggest and brightest new stars to emerge during the 1990s; a multimedia sensation, she was a success not only on the pop and R&B charts, but also on television. Born in McComb, MS, in 1979, Brandy Norwood was raised in California, first attracting attention singing with area youth groups. From there she moved on to a series of television award shows and specials, and later co-starred in the short-lived ABC sitcom *Thea*. Brandy's self-titled debut LP appeared in 1994, launching a series of hits, among them "I Wanna Be Down," "Baby," and "Brokenhearted"; by now a major star, she returned a year later with the blockbuster "Sittin' Up in My Room," a cut from the soundtrack to the film *Waiting to Exhale*. "Missing You," from the soundtrack to 1996's *Set It Off*, was also a hit, but instead of immediately releasing a follow-up LP, Brandy returned to acting, starring in the acclaimed UPN sitcom *Moesha* and also appearing in the title role of the 1997 Disney telefilm *Cinderella*, one of the biggest success stories of the television season. Her long-awaited sophomore album, *Never Say Never*, was finally issued in mid-1998. *—Jason Ankeny*

● **Brandy** / Sep. 27, 1994 / Atlantic ✦✦✦✦
This teenage R&B singer hit the Top Ten late in 1994 with "I Wanna Be Down," a representative track from her solid debut album. Brandy knows her way around a hip-hop beat, layering tender-tough vocals over spare arrangements like a lower-key Janet Jackson or a more stripped-down Mary J. Blige. Good songs and crisp production make Brandy a moody, moving success. *—Eddie Huffman*

Never Say Never / Jun. 9, 1998 / Atlantic ✦✦✦✦
Shortly after the release of her eponymous debut in 1995, Brandy became a star. Not only did the album sell well, but she starred on UPN's *Moesha* and Disney's made-for-TV *Cinderella*, all before she released her second album, *Never Say Never*, in 1998. Needless to say, there was much more riding on the second record than the debut and, fortunately, she follows through with *Never Say Never*, delivering an album that rivals her first. Brandy wisely decides to find a middle ground between Mariah Carey and Mary J. Blige—it's adult contemporary with a slight streetwise edge. As with most adult contemporary albums, the record is bogged down by some filler, but Brandy's delivery has improved and her subdued vocals can make mediocre material sound convincing. Still, what make *Never Say Never* a winning record are quality songs and production. The smooth Monica duet "The Boy Is Mine" and the tripped-out "Top of the World" (which features a rap from Mase) are two examples of what Brandy can achieve when everything's in the right place, and they help make *Never Say Never* a better, more adventurous record than her debut. *—Stephen Thomas Erlewine*

Full Moon / Mar. 5, 2002 / Atlantic ✦✦✦✦
Brandy built her stardom on a few well-timed singles, but she never really delivered albums that fulfilled her promise as a front-woman. *Full Moon*, her third album, comes the closest to being a full-fledged, well-rounded album, as well as establishing a personality as a singer. That's not to say this album is as fiercely independent or adventurous as Aaliyah's last album, or even efforts by Blu Cantrell and Toya, but it's the most assured, risky album Brandy has yet recorded, the one that suggests that she is more than an appealing young personality who is as effective on record as she is on made-for-TV movies. *Full Moon* still has some flaws common to contemporary urban soul records—namely, it's too lengthy, filled with songs that are just there to ensure that the album runs close to 70 minutes, giving some listeners the impression they're getting more bang for their buck; apart from that, the record can be a little too even-keeled and samey—but it's professionally performed and expertly pitched at the mainstream, with just enough beats to make it seem fresh, yet those very rhythms are polished but always enough to keep the entire enterprise safe and non-threatening. That, of course, means that *Full Moon* is perched perfectly between the interesting and the mundane and is in equal parts either.

Since she's pushing slightly harder to be mature, it's a little more mature and consistent than her previous albums, but each step forward feels measured and calculated—not necessarily a bad thing, but something that's noticeable as the album stretches on and on over its 17 tracks. There are plenty of moments here that are seductively smooth and even the filler goes down smoothly, but when it's finished, Brandy seems no more distinctive than she did when it started, so it's no wonder that even its triumphs seem muted. *—Stephen Thomas Erlewine*

Brass Construction

f. 1968, Brooklyn, NY, **db.** 1985

Group / Disco, Funk, Soul

Vocalist/instrumentalist Randy Muller was at the helm of two pivotal East Coast funk and disco aggregations in the '70s and '80s. One was Brass Construction; the other was Skyy. Muller, a vocalist and instrumentalist who doubled on keyboards and flute, organized the band with drummer Larry Payton, trumpeters Wayne Parris and Morris Price, lead guitarist Joe Arthur, vocalist/conga player Sandy Billups, saxophonists Michael Grudge and Jesse Ward, and bassist Wade Williamston. Their 1975 debut, produced by Jeff Lane, went platinum and contained two dancefloor anthems in "Movin'" and "Changin'." *Brass Construction II, III, IV,* and *V* mined the same territory, though only the single "Ha Cha Cha (Funktion)" in 1977 and "L-O-V-E-U" in 1978 came close to attaining similar commercial heights. They recorded for United Artists until 1980, then moved to Liberty and recorded for them until 1983. Muller became their producer in the early '80s, and he shifted their emphasis into a heavily synthesized direction. They continued on Capitol from 1983 to 1985, but couldn't regain their past momentum. The group's vintage hits were remixed and reissued internationally by EMI's Syncopate label in the late '80s, and Brass Construction reappeared on England's charts in 1988. *—Ron Wynn*

Brass Construction / Apr. 1975 / United Artists ✦✦✦✦

Some bands enjoy their greatest success with their first release, and this Brooklyn-based funk ensemble is a good example. Their first single was the chart-topping "Movin'." Aside from the verse being chanted in unison, this aggressively paced dance number, with its catchy, melodious hook line, utilizes reeds and brass, complemented by keyboard and synthesizer solos from bandleader Randy Muller. The single moved its way to the number one spot on the R&B charts, the group's only chart-topper out of 17 singles that reached the charts, and one of two to ever crack the Top Ten. The follow-up single, "Changin'," has a similar arrangement at a slightly slower tempo. The melody is not seductive like its predecessor. Seeming to be more of a musical exhibition and less dance-oriented, it still managed to peak at number 24 on the charts. While the group's music is centered around its horns, the majority of the songs from this album feature vocals throughout the verses and choruses. Adding their social awareness to the mix on a couple tracks, all numbers are consistent with the album's dance/funk appeal. *—Craig Lytle*

Brass Construction 2 / 1976 / United Artists ✦✦✦

Brass Construction leader Randy Muller took the group in a wider direction on their sophomore effort, *Brass Construction 2* issued in December 1976. Their second LP was still funky, horn-punctuated disco; it just wasn't non-stop funky disco as their gold self-titled debut. Adding more Latin/Afro Cuban rhythms, they had a Top 10 R&B hit with the first single "Ha Cha Cha." It also introduced the Irving Spice Strings, who give the urgent radio-aired "Screwed" a swirling, almost tipsy feel. The LP also had mellow tracks. "The Message" is almost inspirational in its theme. Both it and its flipside, the seriously funky "What's On Your Mind(Expression)" received airplay with "..Mind" becoming the source sampling material for several rap and hip-hop artists in the '80s and '90s. *Brass Construction 2*, the band's second gold album is also a testament to their influence on the acid jazz movement of the '90s. Some of the LP's cuts are on the 1993 Capitol CD, *The Best of Brass Construction: Movin' & Changin'*, the 1991 CD *Golden Classics* and some are covered on *Live*—both are from Collectables. *—Ed Hogan*

Brass Construction 3 / 1977 / United Artists ✦✦✦

The danger signs were already in view. They had no standout single on their third release, and they were beginning to recycle the funk tracks and arrangements. The bandmembers maintained their high standards, but not even their playing could completely salvage the album. Brass Construction's condition echoed disco's. *—Ron Wynn*

Brass Construction 4 / 1978 / United Artists ✦✦

Brass Construction's recording career got off to an impressive start with its self-titled debut album of 1976, and the funk-disco outfit kept the creative momentum going with its sophomore effort, *Brass Construction II.* But by 1977's *Brass Construction III*, the band was going downhill. Released in 1978, the disappointing *Brass Construction IV* has its moments but usually sounds mechanical and uninspired—most of the time, Brass Construction comes across as a band that is merely going through the motions. The album's decent offerings include the sleek "Starting Tomorrow" (which contains elements of the Philadelphia International sound) and the mellow soul ballad "Sweet as Sugar." But on "Get Up," "One to One," "Pick Yourself Up," and other unimaginative tracks, Brass Construction's funk-disco formula is sounding tired and worn out. And "Perceptions (What's the Right Direction)," another weak track, incorporates elements of the Ohio Players' sound without being nearly as creative. Definitely not in a class with Brass Construction's first two albums, *Brass Construction IV* is for completists and no one else. *—Alex Henderson*

Brass Construction 5 / 1979 / United Artists ✦✦✦

When *Brass Construction 5* came out in 1979, one greeted the LP with skepticism. 1977's *Brass Construction III* was very uneven, and 1978's disappointing, uninspired *Brass Construction IV* was the funk-disco outfit's weakest album ever. So people didn't have very high hopes for Brass Construction's fifth album. But Randy Muller and his associates pleasantly surprised their fans with this enjoyable LP, which finds them sounding revitalized. A definite improvement over *Brass Construction IV*, this 1979 release boasts some of the combo's most infectious grooves since *Brass Construction II.* If Brass Construction's decline in 1977 and 1978 had caused you to lose faith in the band, confident jams like "Get Up to Get Down," "It's Alright," and "Music Makes You Feel Like Dancing" made it clear that it wasn't time to give up on Muller and company just yet. As enjoyable as *Brass Construction 5* is, the album falls short of essential and isn't quite in a class with *Brass Construction* or *Brass Construction II.* Nonetheless, it's a likable record that restored many listeners' faith in Brass Construction. *—Alex Henderson*

Brass Construction 6 / 1980 / United Artists ✦✦

Arguably their least-interesting album. Brass Construction was due for an overhaul and clearly showed it throughout this release. The production and some of the arrangements were still acceptable, but there was no energy in the playing and even less in the lyrics or vocals. *—Ron Wynn*

Attitudes / 1982 / Liberty ✦✦

Some needed changes were evident on this release. Producer Randy Muller moved Brass Construction away from horn-driven disco/funk and toward the synthesizer-dominated, heavily syncopated sound that was now ruling R&B and dance music. He restored a little lost luster, as the single "Can You See the Light" got some urban and dance radio airplay, and the band was no longer missing in action. *—Ron Wynn*

Conversations / 1983 / Capitol ✦✦✦

Brass Construction continued to avoid the scrap heap, turning out another better-than-expected album. There were two more good singles in "Walkin' the Line" and "We Can Work It Out," and the production, arrangements, instrumental support, and vocals were all more inspired than they had been in the past. *—Ron Wynn*

Renegades / 1984 / Capitol ✦✦

Conquest / 1985 / Capitol ✦

Golden Classics / Sep. 12, 1991 / Collectables ✦✦✦✦✦

● **The Best of Brass Construction: Movin' & Changin'** / Nov. 2, 1993 / EMI ✦✦✦✦✦

Brass Construction's unique take on jazz, funk, and even disco (which would come to full fruition with vocalist Randy Muller's project, Skyy) are revisited on *The Best of Brass Construction: Movin' & Changin'.* All of the hits are included, with some lesser-known early career tracks thrown in for a fair sense of historical perspective. While these earlier tracks are somewhat of a nuisance to trudge through (especially as there are a few obscure earlier numbers that could have been equally effective on the compilation), they are pardoned by hearing their signature anthems in their full remastered glory. If this is your first time exploring the magical funk of Brass Construction, your best bet would be to seek out *Get Up to Get Down: Brass Construction's Funky Feeling.* *—Rob Theakston*

● **Get Up to Get Down: Brass Construction's Funky Feeling** / Jun. 3, 1997 / Capitol ✦✦✦✦✦

Undoubtedly, the Brooklyn-based Brass Construction was one of the most respected instrument-driven soul machines of the '70s and early '80s. While the more funk-heavy, groove-laden tracks (as well as half the tracks on this compilation) are on *The Best of Brass Construction: Movin' & Changin', Get Up to Get Down* captures the full range of Brass Construction's capabilities as a powerhouse band by highlighting some amazing pop songwriting and album material, not just the band's extended jam workouts. Later releases from the '80s are also highlighted, making this by far the most complete collection on the market capturing their entire career. *—Rob Theakston*

Brass Fever

f. 1975, Los Angeles, CA

Group / Funk, Hard Bop, Bop

Formed in Los Angeles in 1975, Brass Fever was a short-lived group of session players that recorded two instrumental jazz-funk albums for ABC: 1975's *Brass Fever* and 1976's *Time Is Running Out.* Brass Fever was an appropriate name for the group, which employed no less than five trombonists on its first album and four on its second. Brass Fever wasn't a full-time gig for any of the participants, who included guitarist Lee Ritenour, trombonist George Bohanon, and trumpeter Oscar Brashear—it was merely a side sproject for them. One of the things that most of the participants had in common was the fact that they could handle jazz and R&B equally well; they were the sort of versatile guys who would have been capable of improvising with Chick Corea one minute and backing Aretha Franklin the next. They weren't bop snobs, and they were heavily influenced by the Crusaders (as opposed to the Jazz Crusaders). Although full of busy, well-known musicians, Brass Fever itself was quite obscure. *Brass Fever* and *Time Is Running Out* received very little attention, and in 1976, the band called it quits. *—Alex Henderson*

● **Brass Fever** / 1975 / ABC/Impulse ✦✦✦

It's safe to say that the vast majority of people who were listening to jazz in the 1970s never heard of Brass Fever. Neither of its albums (*Brass Fever* in 1975 and *Time Is Running Out* in 1976) received much attention. Nonetheless, the band boasted an all-star lineup—some of the participants on this self-titled debut album include John Handy (alto sax), Oscar Brashear (trumpet), Lee Ritenour (guitar), Buddy Collette (flute), and drummer Shelly Manne. And there are no less than five trombonists (Kai Winding, Frank Rosolino, Garnett Brown, George Bohanon, and Charlie Loper), which explains why the outfit is called Brass Fever. Such a lineup could have easily delivered a first-rate bop album, but this out of print LP isn't straight-ahead jazz. Brass Fever's focus is very accessible jazz funk à la the Crusaders, and a groove-oriented approach prevails on Jimmy Smith's "Back at the Chicken Shack" as well as LaBelle's "Lady Marmelade" and Donovan's "Sunshine Superman." These days, NAC artists like Najee and Kenny G would simply perform note-for-note covers of LaBelle and Donovan tunes—Brass Fever, however, interprets these songs and uses them as a vehicle for honest-to-God improvisation. That isn't to say that any of the performances would appeal to a bop snob; again, Brass Fever is unapologetically funky, and this very enjoyable LP (which is the band's most essential release) is strictly for those who like their jazz laced with lots of R&B. *—Alex Henderson*

Time Is Running Out / 1976 / ABC ✦✦✦

In an ideal world, both of Brass Fever's LPs—*Brass Fever* from 1975 and *Time Is Running Out* from 1976—would be reissued back-to-back on a single CD. But that is unlikely to happen because there isn't much of a demand for the out of print albums. So the only thing to do is search for them at a place that sells a lot of 1970s vinyl. *Brass Fever* is the more essential of the two; *Time Is Running Out* is uneven but does have its moments. The title track has little to do with jazz—it's an infectious soul/disco vocal number featuring the Jones Girls. But most of the time, Brass Fever offers instrumental jazz-funk versions of major R&B and rock hits, including the Jackson Five's "Dancing Machine" and the Doobie Brothers' "Takin' It to the Streets." Although Esmond Edwards tends to overproduce, participants like guitarist Lee Ritenour and trumpeter Oscar Brashear still manage to get in some inspired solos. However, Brass Fever doesn't fare as well on a forgettable arrangement of Toots & the Maytals' ska/reggae classic "Pressure Drop," and its cheesy remake of Bob Dylan's "Mr. Tambourine Man" is pure elevator Muzak. But *Time Is Running Out* has more plusses than minuses, although Brass Fever's first LP is definitely more consistent. *—Alex Henderson*

Tamar Braxton

Vocals / Contemporary R&B

The youngest of the Braxton sisters, singer Tamar Braxton has a solid background in R&B, gospel, and pop thanks to her heritage: Her father is a Methodist minister; her mother an amateur opera singer; and her eldest sister, Toni, needs no introduction. As with the rest of her singing siblings, Tamar grew up surrounded by music at home and at church. Along with her sisters Trina and Towanda, Tamar performed in the Braxtons and released the 1996 debut album *So Many Ways*; a tour as Toni's backup singers also raised the group's prominence. In 1999, Tamar explored both the gospel and pop sides of her sound, appearing on T.D. Jakes' *Sacred Love Songs* before releasing her solo debut, *Ridiculous*, on DreamWorks the following spring. *—Heather Phares*

● **Ridiculous** / Nov. 2, 1999 / DreamWorks ✦✦✦

This solo debut from Toni Braxton's younger sister, Tamar is both impressive and enjoyable. It features a fitting mix of soulful ballads and upbeat rhythm tracks, replete with mellow harmonies and sassy backbeats. Tamar collaborates with top-notch producers Jermaine Dupri and Tricky Stewart to create a smooth, radio-friendly sound along the lines of Mariah Carey and Christina Aguilera. While not in possession of a vocal range as refined as her sister Toni, Tamar hits her own mark on standout tracks "If You Don't Wanna Love Me," "Tonight," and "Get None." This recording is primarily a quiet display of Tamar's competence at present day rhythm & blues with some contemporary hip-hop flavor thrown in. If it wasn't such an all-around good listen, it would certainly be worthy of recognition on the basis of its professional presentation alone. *—Roxanne Blanford*

Tamar / May 2, 2000 / MCA ✦✦✦

Toni Braxton

b. Oct. 7, 1967, Severn, MD

Vocals / Adult Contemporary, Urban, Contemporary R&B

Toni Braxton was one of the most popular and commercially female R&B singers of the '90s, thanks to her ability to straddle seemingly opposite worlds. Braxton was soulful enough for R&B audiences, but smooth enough for adult contemporary; sophisticated enough for adults, but sultry enough for younger listeners; strong enough in the face of heartbreak to appeal to women, but ravishing enough to nab the fellas. Wielding such broad appeal, Braxton managed to score not one, but *two* albums that sold over eight-million copies; naturally, they were accompanied by a long string of hit singles on the pop and R&B charts, one of which—"Un-Break My Heart"—ranks among the longest-running number-one pop hits of the rock era.

Toni Braxton was born in Severn, MD, on October 7, 1967. The daughter of a minister, she was raised mostly in the strict Apostolic faith, which prohibited not only all popular culture, but also pants in women's wardrobes. Encouraged by their mother, an operatically trained vocalist, Braxton and her four sisters began singing in church as girls; although gospel was the only music permitted in the household, the girls often watched *Soul Train* when their parents went shopping. Braxton's parents later converted to a different faith, and eased their restrictions on secular music somewhat, allowing Braxton more leeway to develop her vocal style; because of her husky voice, she often used male singers like Luther Vandross, Stevie Wonder, and Michael McDonald as models, as well as Chaka Khan. Braxton had some success on the local talent-show circuit, continuing to sing with her sisters, and after high school studied to become a music teacher. However, Braxton soon dropped out of college after she was discovered singing to herself at a gas station by songwriter Bill Pettaway (who co-authored Milli Vanilli's "Girl You Know It's True"). With Pettaway's help, Braxton and her sisters signed with Arista Records in 1990 as a group dubbed simply the Braxtons.

The Braxtons released a single in 1990 called "The Good Life," and while it wasn't a hit, it caught the attention of L.A. Reid and Babyface, the red-hot songwriting/production team who had just formed their own label, LaFace (which was associated with Arista). Braxton became the first female artist signed to LaFace in 1991, and the following year she was introduced to the listening public with a high-profile appearance on the soundtrack of Eddie Murphy's *Boomerang*. Not only did her solo cut "Love Shoulda Brought You Home" become a substantial pop and R&B hit, but she also duetted with Babyface himself on "Give U My Heart." Anticipation for Braxton's first album ran high, and when her eponymous solo debut was released in 1993, it was an across-the-board smash, climbing to number one on both the pop and R&B charts. It spun off hit after hit, including three more Top Ten singles in "Another Sad Love Song," "Breathe Again," and "You Mean the World to Me," plus the double-sided R&B hit "I Belong to You"/"How Many Ways." With eventual sales of over eight-million copies, *Toni Braxton*'s run of popularity lasted well into 1995. By that time, Braxton had scored Grammys for Best New Artist and Best Female R&B Vocal ("Another Sad Love Song") in 1994, and tacked on another win in the latter category for "Breathe Again" in 1995.

To tide fans over until her next album was released, Braxton contributed "Let It Flow" to the Whitney Houston-centered soundtrack of *Waiting to Exhale* in 1995. Again working heavily with L.A. Reid and Babyface, Braxton released her second album, *Secrets*, in the summer of 1996, and predictably, it was another enormous hit. The first single, "You're Makin' Me High," was Braxton's most overtly sexual yet, and it became her biggest pop hit to date; however, its success was soon eclipsed by the follow-up single, the Diane Warren-penned ballad "Un-Break My Heart." "Un-Break My Heart" was an inescapable juggernaut, spending an amazing 11 weeks on top of the pop charts (and even longer on the adult contemporary charts). Further singles "I Don't Want To" and "How Could an Angel Break My Heart" weren't quite as successful (not that that's an indictment), but that didn't really matter; by then *Secrets* was well on its way to becoming Braxton's second straight eight-million-seller. In 1997, she picked up Grammy awards for Best Female Pop Vocal and Best Female R&B Vocal (for "Un-Break My Heart" and "You're Makin' Me High," respectively).

Toward the end of 1997, Braxton filed a lawsuit against LaFace Records, attempting to gain release from a contract she felt was no longer fair or commensurate with her status. When LaFace counter-sued, Braxton filed for bankruptcy, a move that shocked many fans (who wondered how that could be possible, given her massive sales figures) but actually afforded her protection from further legal action. Braxton spent most of 1998 in legal limbo, and passed the time by signing on to portray Belle in the Broadway production of Disney's *Beauty and the Beast* (a role originally held by erstwhile teen queen Deborah Gibson). Braxton and LaFace finally reached a settlement in early 1999, and the singer soon began work on her third album. *Heat* was released in the spring of 2000, and entered the charts at number two, matching the highest position held by *Secrets*. Lead single "He Wasn't Man Enough" was a Top Ten hit (and an R&B chart-topper), although the follow-ups "Just Be a Man About It" (a duet with Dr. Dre) and "Spanish Guitar" didn't sustain the album's momentum as well as one might have expected. A brisk seller out of the box, *The Heat* eventually cooled off around the two-million mark; a disappointing showing compared to her previous efforts, despite yet another Grammy win for Best Female R&B Vocal ("He Wasn't Man Enough").

In 2001, Braxton made her feature film debut in the ensemble comedy *Kingdom Come*, and married Mint Condition keyboardist Keri Lewis; by the end of the year, they had a baby boy. Braxton also released her first holiday album, *Snowflakes*. In early 2002, Braxton appeared in the VH1 movie *Play'd*, and announced that she was beginning work on a new album. *—Steve Huey*

● **Toni Braxton** / Jul. 1993 / La Face ✦✦✦✦✦

Toni Braxton is both an elegant and earthy songstress, nicely balancing those seemingly divergent sentiments on her self-titled debut disc. Braxton's husky, enticing voice sounds hypnotic on "Breathe Again," dismayed on "Another Sad Love Song" and disillusioned on "Love Shoulda Brought You Home." But she's never out of control, indignant or so anguished and hurt that she fails to retain her dignity. It's a sign of how great the Babyface/L.A. Reid production team was that they didn't settle for a defining mood; they presented Braxton with enough diverse emotional settings to hold the interest of urban contemporary males and females. *—Ron Wynn*

Secrets / Jun. 18, 1996 / La Face ✦✦✦✦✦

Toni Braxton's second album, *Secrets*, follows through on the promise of her eponymous debut. Like her first album, the majority of *Secrets* was co-produced by Babyface and his partner L.A. Reid, while the material is divided between songs written by outside songwriters like R. Kelly, Tony Rich, and Diane Warren and originals by Braxton and Babyface. Braxton and Babyface's collaborations are the highlights of the album, combining rich melodies and gorgeous choruses with subtle, clever lyrics that are never laced with clichés. Nearly equalling the original numbers are contributions by Tony Rich ("Come on Over Here") and R. Kelly ("I Don't Want To"); with these tracks, both musicians demonstrate why they are considered two of the top songwriters in '90s R&B and soul. *Secrets* does have a couple of weak moments. The numbers produced by David Foster are too predictable in their slick commercial appeal, but Braxton manages to infuse the songs with life and passion that elevates them beyond their generic confines. And her vocal talent is what unites *Secrets* and makes it into a first-rate contemporary R&B collection. Braxton is a singer who can cross over into the smooth confines of adult contemporary radio without losing or betraying the soul that lies at the foundation of her music, and her talent burns at its brightest on *Secrets*. *—Stephen Thomas Erlewine*

The Heat / Apr. 25, 2000 / La Face ✦✦✦✦

Toni Braxton went through a lot in the years separating her star-making *Toni* and her 2000 comeback *The Heat*. Yes, she became a star, but she also went through a painful bankruptcy that delayed her sequel for years. Fortunately, you wouldn't be able to tell that there was so much behind-the-scenes drama from *The Heat*—it's a confident, assured, sexy effort that reaffirms Braxton's status as one of the finest contemporary mainstream soul singers. She may not be as street-smart as Mary J. Blige, nor does she push the boundaries of the genre the way TLC does, but she has a full, rich voice that instantly lends her songs a sense of maturity and sensuality, especially since she never, ever oversings or misjudges her material. And, while that material can occasionally be a little generic, much of *The Heat* is built on solid ballads and smoldering, midtempo dance numbers. Producers as diverse as Babyface, Rodney Jerkins, Daryl Simmons, Teddy Bishop, and David Foster are responsible for various tracks on the album, which is typical for a big-budget, superstar release like this, but rarely are the tracks quite as consistent and cohesive as they are here. The skittering beats of "He Wasn't Man Enough" and "Gimme Some" are every bit as effective as the simmering title track or ballads "I'm Still Breathing" and "Spanish Guitar"—or "Just Be a Man About It," an instant classic telephone break-up song, with Dr. Dre playing the wayward lover breaking the news to Ms. Braxton. True, *The Heat* slightly runs out of momentum toward the end, but there aren't many dull spots on the record—it's all stylish, sultry, seductive, appealing urban contemporary soul that confirms Braxton's prodigious talents. *—Stephen Thomas Erlewine*

More Than a Woman / Nov. 19, 2002 / Arista ✦✦✦✦
If there's any problem with *More Than a Woman*, Toni Braxton's fourth album, it's that its so consistent, so much a continuation of its predecessor, *Heat*, that it may be hard to pinpoint distinctive characteristics. Unlike that album, it lacks a single as undeniable as "He Wasn't Man Enough," yet much of this album is in a similar sexy spirit. It also doesn't have any ballads as seductive as "Unbreak My Heart." In fact, few of the songs stand out, yet that doesn't mean they're bland or generic. They're simply cut from the same cloth and fit well together, particularly since they're given a nice, stylish production that's rarely flashy. The same could be said for Braxton's performance, since it's assured and sensual, but never strutting. And that may be the problem with the record for some—it's confident but not brassy, never overwrought. Unlike many diva dance-pop albums of 2002, it never tries too hard, so it was easy to overlook it, but it was easily one of the most satisfying listens of its kind released that year, and another fine record by Toni Braxton. *—Stephen Thomas Erlewine*

Brenda & the Tabulations

f. 1966, Philadelphia, PA
Group / Pop-Soul, Disco, Soul
Among the better Philadelphia soul groups of the '60s and '70s, Brenda & the Tabulations made some fine heartache ballads, particularly "Dry Your Eyes" and "Right on the Tip of My Tongue." The original lineup was lead singer Brenda Payton, Jerry Jones, Eddie Jackson, and Maurice Coates. Bernard Murphy joined in 1969. They became a trio in 1970, featuring Payton, Pat Mercer, and Deborah Martin. "Dry Your Eyes" was their biggest hit, reaching number eight on the R&B chart and number 20 pop in 1967. They continued recording for Dionn until 1969, then Top & Bottom from 1970 to 1973, followed by stints with Epic and Chocolate City. "Right on the Tip of My Tongue" returned them to prominence in 1971, peaking at number ten R&B, and the follow-up, "A Part of You," was number 14 that same year. The group enjoyed some sporadic success on the disco circuit in the late '70s with the LP *I Keep Coming Back for More*. The single "Let's Go All the Way (Down)" attracted some international and club interest. *—Ron Wynn*

• **Dry Your Eyes** / 1967 / Dionn ✦✦✦
As was the custom for the day, Brenda & the Tabulations' debut album was overstuffed with familiar cover versions, which were done respectably; actually, the sultry, drawn-out reading of "Summertime" is really good, as is the calypso-ish take of the Marvelettes' "Forever." There are also a few more originals by the Brenda Payton-Maurice Coates team responsible for "Dry Your Eyes," including the low-charting single "Just Once in a Lifetime"; this has a similar marriage of doo wop-type vocals with the lush orchestration for which Philadelphia soul was famous. The album had yet two more small soul hits in "Stay Together Young Lovers" and Smokey Robinson's "Who's Loving You?" The CD reissue adds two bonus tracks, including "When You're Gone," a minor 1968 hit in which the vibes and trembling violins brought the group closer to the mainstream of symphonic Philly soul production. *—Richie Unterberger*

Brenda & The Tabulations / 1971 / Top & Bottom ✦✦✦✦
Sadly, the groups' first and only album on Top & Bottom Records dropped before the release of their biggest record on the label, "Right on the Tip of My Tongue." Still, you have airy soul delights like "The Touch of You," a good seller in many R&B markets that features an endearing whisper/vocal from Brenda Payton. The more rhythmic "And My Heart Sang (Tra La La)" didn't fare as well, and nothing else on the LP ever surfaced. Crafty remakes of "Don't Make Me Over," "California Soul," and "Someday We'll Be Together" get the soft soul treatment that exemplified Philly soul before the arrival of the harder-edged Philadelphia International sound, which obliterated everything that came before it. *—Andrew Hamilton*

Right on the Tip of My Tongue / Apr. 25, 2000 / Jamie/Guyden ✦✦✦✦✦
Unfortunately original release information is not given with this package. But it can safely be deduced that this includes most or all of the tracks from their eponymous 1970 Top & Bottom LP, as well as some non-LP singles ("Right on the Tip of My Tongue" and "A Part of You") and one previously unreleased track, "Sha Na Na—He Loves Me." Basically, then, it's a survey of their 1969-1971 Top & Bottom output, entirely produced by Van McCoy. The Brenda & the Tabulations/Van McCoy collaboration marked a real high-water mark in Philly soul that deserves wider historical recognition. Certainly there was little, if any, soul produced in the city outside the Gamble-Huff and Thom Bell empires that was of such a high standard. Philly sweet soul was rarely more melodic than this, probably due in large measure to McCoy's songwriting and arrangements, which went heavy on the graceful strings and flutes. Brenda Payton and her group do a lot on their part, though, putting across the songs without overdoing it. A half-dozen R&B hits are here: the title track (also a pretty big pop hit), "The Touch of You," "And My Heart Sang (Tra La La)," "A Part of You," the one stab at social consciousness ("A Child No One Wanted"), and a remake of "Don't Make Me Over." There's not much filler—an unusual condition for soul-pop artists of the time—although the one unissued tune, "Sha Na Na—He Loves Me," is a giggly throwaway. *—Richie Unterberger*

Jackie Brenston

b. Aug. 15, 1930, Clarksdale, MS, **d.** Dec. 15, 1979, Memphis, TN
Vocals, Saxophone / Jump Blues, R&B, Electric Memphis Blues
Determining the first actual rock & roll record is a truly impossible task. But you can't go too far wrong citing Jackie Brenston's 1951 Chess waxing of "Rocket 88," a seminal piece of rock's fascinating history with all the prerequisite elements firmly in place: practically indecipherable lyrics about cars, booze, and women; Raymond Hill's booting tenor sax, and a churning, beat-heavy rhythmic bottom.

Sam Phillips, then a fledgling in the record business, produced "Rocket 88," Brenston's debut waxing, in Memphis. The singer/saxist was backed by Ike Turner's Kings of Rhythm, an aggregation that Brenston had joined the previous year. Turner played piano on the tune; Willie Kizart supplied dirty, distorted guitar. Billed as by Jackie Brenston & His Delta Cats, "Rocket 88" drove up to the top slot on the R&B charts and remained there for more than a month. But none of his Chess follow-ups sported the same high-octane performance, though "Real Gone Rocket" was certainly a deserving candidate.

Brenston's slide from the spotlight was swift. After a few more Chess singles stiffed (including a duet with Edna McRaney, "Hi-Ho Baby"), Brenston reunited with Turner in 1955, holding down the baritone sax chair until 1962. He cut a series of terrific sides fronting Turner's Kings of Rhythm along the way: "Gonna Wait for My Chance" and "Much Later" for Federal in 1956, "You've Got to Lose" for Chicago's Cobra label in 1958 (also doing session work there with Otis Rush and Buddy Guy), and "You Ain't the One" for Sue in 1961. After a final single for Mel London's Mel-Lon imprint, Brenston was through; he worked as a truck driver and showed little interest in reliving his glory years. *—Bill Dahl*

• **Rocket 88** / 1991 / Charly ✦✦✦✦✦
If Brenston's "Rocket 88" was in actuality the very first rock & roll record, as many experts claim, the rest of his brief Chess legacy adds up to quite a definitive rockin' statement. Among these 16 sides dating from 1951-1953 are his amazing sequel "My Real Gone Rocket," which probably rocks even harder than "Rocket 88" as Ike Turner pounds the keys; "Tuckered Out," the evocative "Fat Meat Is Greasy" (one of several items only out in Japan before the advent of this British CD), and seven sides Brenston cut in Chicago without Sam Phillips to guide him, nor Turner's Kings of Rhythm to back him up. Great stuff. *—Bill Dahl*

Brick

f. 1972, Atlanta, GA, **db.** 1981
Group / Disco, Funk
Brick was an Atlanta band that created a successful merger of funk and jazz in the '70s they called "dazz." Brick's roster included lead vocalist/saxophonist/flutist Jimmy Brown; guitarist/bassist/vocalist Regi Hargis; lead singer Ray Ransom, who doubled as a bassist/keyboardist/percussionist; and Eddie Irons, who did lead vocals and played drums and keyboards. They recorded "Music Matic" for Main Street in 1976, before signing to the CBS-distributed label Bang. Their first Bang single, "Dazz," topped the R&B charts and was number-three pop in 1976, and they continued on Bang until 1982. Brick scored two more huge hits in 1977, "Dusic" and "Ain't Gonna' Hurt Nobody," each with a chunky, propulsive beat and catchy, light pop-jazz refrain. Their last Top Ten R&B hit was "Sweat (Til You Get Wet)" in 1981. *—Ron Wynn*

Good High / 1976 / Bang ✦✦✦✦
The debut album from the Atlanta-based funk aggregate spawned three singles and a host of soul numbers. The first single from the album was "Music Matic," a smooth yet funky composition in which the group expresses the lyric in unison, augmented by Jimmy Brown's commendable flute and sax solos. The second single was "Dazz," which was defined by the group in the chorus as "disco jazz." With Regi Hargis' twanging guitar and Brown's long-winded sax riffs, the catchy hook line caught on across the nation and the song claimed the number-one spot on the R&B charts for four consecutive weeks (it reached number three on the pop side). "Can't Wait" is set in a looping sci-fi rhythm through the verses before segueing to a hopping groove. Brown's refreshing saxophone work can be heard on the instrumental cuts "Southern Sunset," whose title provides a good setting, and "Sister Twister." Having a fetish for jazz, the self-contained quintet glimmer on this extended jazz composition, which includes funky basslines. The third single, "That's What It's All About," the only ballad featured on the album, has an soft melody and encouraging lyric delivered by Brown's husky baritone. Every song is complemented by Brown's impressive horn exhibition and the group's overall musical ability. *—Craig Lytle*

Brick / 1977 / Bang ✦✦✦✦
Brick's second album release on the Bang imprint had the Atlanta-based funk ensemble standing on solid ground. "Dusic" came charging onto the charts and dancefloors nationwide, and for good reason. With falsetto-layered vocals and a gritty, soulful backing track, "Dusic" worked its way to number two on the R&B charts. With lead vocals sung in unison, "Ain't Gonna Hurt Nobody" came right behind it with plenty of locomotion and stamina. The single popped the Top Ten at number seven inside of 15 weeks. The self-contained band had to its credit the reed and brass virtuoso Jimmy Brown. On "Happy," Brown improvises his way through each verse, switching from one reed instrument to brass and back again—an outstanding horn exhibition on this appropriately titled number. The entire album is superb. *—Craig Lytle*

Stoneheart / 1979 / Bang ✦✦✦
Brick's first two albums, *Good High* in 1976 and *Brick* in 1977, were equally superb. So in 1979, one greeted the Atlanta funksters' third album, *Stoneheart*, with very high hopes. But unfortunately, this vinyl LP is a minor disappointment. *Stoneheart* isn't terrible; "Raise Your Hands" and "Magic Woman" are decent funk items, and "To Me" is a likable soul ballad. Meanwhile, "We'll Love" is a pleasant pop-jazz instrumental that quiet storm enthusiasts could get into. But none of the material is mind-blowing; nothing on this uneven record is in a class with "Dazz," "Music Matic," "Dusic," or "Ain't Gonna Hurt Nobody." *Stoneheart* is an LP that simmers, but unlike *Good High* and *Brick*, never burns and never explodes. This album is strictly for collectors and Brick's most hardcore fans. *—Alex Henderson*

Waiting on You / 1980 / Bang ✦✦✦
After setting the funk world on fire with 1976's *Good High* and 1977's *Brick*, the Atlanta-based Brick seemed to be running out of steam on 1979's competent but unremarkable *Stoneheart*. Gratefully, Brick's fourth album, *Waiting on You*, was an improvement. Fans who found *Stoneheart* to be uneven and mildly disappointing were pleased to discover that Brick is more inspired and focused on this 1980 LP. Without question, Brick sounds rejuvenated on energetic, infectious funk smokers like "Free," "Get Started," "Sweet Lips," and "Push, Push." And the band is equally appealing on the romantic soul ballad "Let Me Make You Happy." As much as *Waiting on You* has going for it, the record isn't quite as strong as *Good High* or *Brick*, both of which are classics. But it's certainly superior to *Stoneheart*, and it demonstrated that Brick was still quite capable of being exciting. *—Alex Henderson*

Summer Heat / 1981 / Bang ✦✦✦
Although best remembered for their chart-topping 1976 single "Dazz," Brick nevertheless carved a nice niche for themselves in the annals of jazzy funk and the release of their final album, *Summer Heat*, saw them exit the stage in a blaze of glory. Under the nimble fingers of producer Ray Parker Jr., they hashed together a solid set. And while Parker may now be better-known for penning the hit theme song to 1984's *Ghostbusters* soundtrack, he is better known in funk circles for his earlier unions with Barry White, Rufus, Bobby Womack, and Herbie Hancock among others. It is this rich musical portfolio that helped Brick reach back to their own halcyon days to create such a superb sound. The urgent "Sweat (Till You Get Wet)" is pure early era Brick, packed with solid horn breaks, sexy guitars, and jamming bridge. As a single, the song deservedly returned the band back in the Top Ten. "Wide Open" also reins in the beat enough to create an instant party. But, although we know that Brick can stand alone with energetic funk fests, the band also proves themselves equally proficient and comfortable with a mellower mood. Both "Sea Side Vibes" and the Ray Parker Jr.-penned "Babe" are effective soul ballads. And, even though Brick disbanded not long after *Summer Heat*, they managed to cap a musical canon with panache. Not many bands can claim that feat. *—Amy Hanson*

● **The Best of Brick** / Jun. 13, 1995 / Epic/Bang ✦✦✦✦✦
This 1995 Epic release is easily the best introduction to the Atlanta-based group's unique fusion of funk, disco, and improvisational soul. With only one pronounced omission—their later 1981 hit "Sweat (Till You Get Wet)"—*The Best of Brick* covers all the major points of the group's short but influential seven-year recording career—with a decided focus on their first two records. This is a fresh look at a group whose influence has remained steady over the past two decades. *—Rob Theakston*

The Brides of Funkenstein

f. 1978, **db.** 1980
Group / Funk, Urban
During his heyday as a bandleader and organizer, George Clinton had several elements of his Parliament/Funkadelic empire signed with record labels. The Brides of Funkenstein were a female group who accompanied his other bands on tours. They recorded for Atlantic from 1978 to 1980. While Chaka Khan's sister Taka Boom was once a member, the group's roster on the Atlantic sessions included Lynn Mabry and Dawn Silva. They also got assistance from the Dramatics' Ron Banks and Larry Demps. The single "Disco to Go" was number seven on the R&B charts in 1978; it was their lone hit, although the song "Never Buy Texas From a Cowboy" was probably their most interesting record. *—Ron Wynn*

● **Funk or Walk** / 1978 / Atlantic ✦✦✦✦
Much like Prince in the 1980s, George Clinton had a long list of disciples in the late '70s. Clinton's P-Funk empire wasn't only Parliament/Funkadelic, it also included Bootsy's Rubber Band, Fred Wesley & the Horny Horns, and two female groups: Parlet and the Brides of Funkenstein. The latter recorded two albums in the late '70s, the first of which is the good to excellent *Funk or Walk*. In addition to producing or co-producing everything on the LP, Clinton co-wrote most of the material. So not surprisingly, *Funk or Walk* tends to be very Clinton-flavored. But the record is surprisingly diverse, and Clinton keeps things unpredictable. "Birdie," "Amorous," and the infectious opener "Disco to Go" (which Clinton wrote and produced with Bootsy Collins) are all very Parliament-like, but the jazz-influenced "Nappy" isn't unlike something Dr. Buzzard's Original Savannah Band would have done. The melancholy "Just Like You" is a conventional soul ballad, and the glossy "When You're Gone" would have been appropriate for a Silver Convention album. On *Funk or Walk*, the Brides' two-woman lineup consists of Dawn Silva and Lynn Mabry, both demonstrating that they have no problem handling the variety of things that Clinton sends their way. *—Alex Henderson*

Never Buy Texas From a Cowboy / 1979 / Atlantic ✦✦
George Clinton guided and directed a new Brides of Funkenstein lineup on the group's second and final album, *Never Buy Texas From a Cowboy*. This time, the Brides were a trio instead of a duo. Dawn Silva was still on board, but Lynn Mabry was gone, and Silva's new allies were Sheila Horn and Jeanette McGruder. With the new Silva/Horn/McGruder lineup in place, the Brides delivered a sophomore effort that is as unpredictable as their first album, *Funk or Walk*. "Smoke Signals" (which Clinton wrote and produced with Bootsy Collins) and "Party Up in Here" are very Parliament-like, which is to be expected. But "I'm Holding You Responsible" and the 15-minute title song find the Brides delivering an unlikely mixture of Chic and P-Funk, and "Didn't Mean to Fall in Love" isn't P-Funk at all. The only tune on the LP that Clinton didn't produce or co-produce, "Didn't Mean to Fall in Love" is a romantic northern soul item along the lines of First Choice, the Three Degrees, or Honey Cone. Like *Funk or Walk*, *Never Buy Texas From a Cowboy* contains its share of surprises, and it demonstrates that the Brides of Funkenstein did the right thing by being unpredictable. *—Alex Henderson*

Live at the Howard Theatre 1978 / Apr. 23, 1996 / Sequel ✦✦✦

Alicia Bridges

b. Jul. 15, 1953, Atlanta, GA
Vocals / Disco, Hi-NRG, Dance-Pop, Soul
Disco diva Alicia Bridges scored big in 1978 with her chart-topping hit "I Love the Nightlife." It was her biggest moment in music, making her self-titled debut a definite part of the feel-good disco scene of the late '70s. The blues-tinged "Diamond in the Rough" and "Broken Woman" were mildly successful, but Bridges never regained her disco reign. Two more albums followed—1979's *Play It as It Lays* and 1984's *Hocus Pocus*—but those failed to gain recognition despite some disco threads transitioning into the new wave scene of the early '80s. Bridges wasn't entirely forgotten. Nearly 20 years later, electronic dance gurus "Little" Louie Vega and Kenny "Dope" Gonzalez of the house act Masters at Work revamped "I Love the Nightlife for the campy flick *The Last Days of Disco*. *—MacKenzie Wilson*

Alicia Bridges / 1978 / Polydor ✦✦
Almost immediately awarded the honoraria of one-hit wonder for her smash "I Love the Nightlife (Disco Round)," Alicia Bridges pretty much reached the high point of her career in one glorious moment. That title has endured a complete change in sonic landscape, remaining a staple of retro hits packages, while Bridges herself can still be counted as one of the queens of disco. And it's certainly that one track which drives her eponymous 1978 debut. The combination of light rhythm, light strings, disco attitude, and Bridges' own throaty cry of "action" sent the single to the top of the charts, and the front of the play list at clubs across the nation. But the catch is that that's the LP's one trick—the rest of *Alicia Bridges* flows downhill in a deluge of one-dimensionality that's hard to ignore. She repeats her initial testiness across both the minor chart hit "Body Heat," while adding a proto-Heart-ian rock ethic to "Diamond in the Rough." Elsewhere, the slower-tempoed "In the Name of Love" utilizes some very patchy backing vocals, while "High Altitudes" is nearly a cappella until the guitar kicks in. Both put Bridges firmly on the strata of the lesser nightclub circuit, and neither hides the fact that she hasn't got a lot of vocal range. Despite the utter glory of the hit, there's not enough to keep even the most rabid listener occupied across two sides. Keep this slab of vinyl pristine and spin "I Love the Nightlife (Disco Round)" indefinitely. *—Amy Hanson*

Play It as It Lays / 1979 / Polydor ✦✦
It's unfortunate that Alicia Bridges' commercial success was so short-lived, for there's much more to her output than 1978's "I Love the Nightlife (Disco Round)." This overlooked sophomore set features an impressive cast of session musicians, including the Tower of Power horns and background vocalists Rhodes-Chalmers-Rhodes. Bridges and writing partner Susan Hutcheson prove they are apt in a number of styles, ranging from the gutsy soul of "Learned to Dance Too Soon" to the fiery rock of "What Would You Do if Your Heart Stopped Beating Tonight?" Vocally, Bridges covers wide terrain, too: She's sassy on "Under the Cover of Darkness," lighthearted and sultry on the cool "So Cozy," and mellow on the fine jazz arrangement of "Cheap Affairs." Meanwhile, tunes like "Rex the Robot" and "Learned to Dance..." effectively blend disco elements with straight-ahead rock and funk ingredients. More adventurous and better-produced than her self-titled debut (which wasn't bad at all), this is a must-have for any Bridges fan. *—Justin M. Kantor*

Hocus Pocus / 1984 / Second Wave ✦✦
Bridges tried to fit in with '80s rock trends on this independently released set. Employing lots of synthesizers and various chant-like background voices, many numbers have interesting melodic elements but get quite repetitive. The pouty lyrics of "Bullets Don't Talk" and "I Regret It" aren't helped out by vacuous arrangements that are over-produced; and a reworking of "Under the Cover of Darkness" (originally on 1979's *Play It As It Lays*) is a far cry in quality from the original. Thankfully, Bridges' adept vocals save the day in a few instances—but overall, this set lives up to its name a little too literally. *—Justin M. Kantor*

● **I Love the Nightlife** / Mar. 22, 1999 / Universal ✦✦✦✦✦
Though this budget disc is merely a reordered reissue of Bridges' stellar 1978 debut, it's the only full-length CD of her work available, making it a wise investment for any fans of '70s rock and/or disco. Unquestionably a "Diamond in the Rough," the versatile singer/songwriter moves from the jazzy pop-soul of "Break Away" to the gutsy rock & roll of "Body Heat" (a minor pop hit in early 1979) to the mellow pop-disco fusion she's eternally known for, "I Love the Nightlife (Disco Round)." Lyrically, her scope is equally impressive, with the specialty being hardships brought upon by society's standards. "Self Applause" pertains to vanity as a mask over emotion, "Diamond in the Rough" explores the sacrifice of social exile for a true relationship, and "High Altitude" travels through an individual plane of freedom, away from disconcerting pressures. In addition to Bridges' combination of genre defiance and lyrical frankness, her unique vocal personality—seemingly influenced by everyone from Joe Cocker to Diana Ross—is superbly represented throughout. The only drawback to this CD is the skimpy packaging, which includes none of the original liner notes or musician and production credits. *—Justin Kantor*

Larry Bright (Julian Ferebee Bright)

b. Aug. 17, 1934, Norfolk, VA
Guitar / Rock & Roll
Larry Bright was born Julian Ferebee Bright in Norfolk, VA, on August 17, 1934. His stepfather, a Navy man, nicknamed him "little Larry." The Bright family moved frequently around the South, finally settling in Corpus Christi, TX, where Bright learned to play the guitar. He was exposed to a musical diet comprised mainly of southern Texas blues, which later influenced everything he ever played or wrote. Bright moved to Southern California for his own somewhat brief stint in the Navy (he was released on a Section 8) and quickly established a reputation as both a dynamic guitarist and a performer with a penchant for odd behavior. He began jamming in the local clubs, including the Sea Witch, where, in 1959, he was scouted by producer Joe Saraceno (the Ventures, the Marketts),

who invited Bright to lay down some tracks at Western Recorders. Once in the studio, Bright, inspired by Muddy Waters' "mojo song" (he didn't know the title) decided to make up a mojo song of his own: "Mojo Workout." After local black-owned Tide Records picked it up, the track received heavy airplay on KGFJ, the major R&B station in L.A. Jim Randolph, a black disc jockey at the station, thought Bright was a black artist and pushed him heavily. The song went on to hit number one on the black music charts in June 1960, and also charted, barely, on the Hot 100 at number 90.

After the Tide label refused to advance him any royalties (he intended to purchase a new suit for an upcoming *American Bandstand* appearance), Bright signed another recording contract, this one with Rendezvous Records. Tide found out and sued Rendezvous, retrieving the master tapes for a number of singles (Rendezvous, meanwhile, released Bright's "Twinkie Lee" single under the name Pete Roberts). Bright continued to record for Tide and released several more singles, including "Bloodhound," "One Ugly Child" (later covered by the Downliners Sect), and a great version of Andre Williams' "Bacon Fat." Tide later leased his contract to Del-Fi Records, which was already handling their national distribution. Del-Fi impresario Bob Keane attempted to have Bright cash in on the surf music craze of 1963, recording various surf and hot rod instrumentals, Johnny Rivers-style teen rock, and a Goffin-King penned dance number ("When I Did the Mashed Potatoes With You").

Bright continued to remain a fixture on the Sunset Strip scene and toured as the only white blues performer on an otherwise all-black tour headlined by Chuck Berry. He later worked with Lou Rawls and Roy Clark, and developed a bizarre friendship with Elvis Presley, who wanted to hire Bright as his guitarist, but eventually declined because of Bright's drinking problem. Bright remains an unknown due to his poor business dealings, legal problems, and alcohol-fueled madness. In 1995, Del-Fi collected most of his singles for a collection called *Shake That Thing!* —*Bryan Thomas*

● **Shake That Thing!** / Apr. 29, 1997 / Del-Fi ✦✦✦✦✦

Del-Fi gives listeners, on one CD, sides from nearly half of Larry Bright's entire discography of singles. Five other non-released tracks are included. The sum is proof that voodoo-loving Bright was a talented and dynamic guitarist and vocalist. It would be a shame to see him forgotten in this era of CD revisitations. Listening to this collection, it is no surprise that Bright first charted at number one on the black music chart in 1960. The Texas-born musician soaked up the "chitlin circuit" sounds of the time and let their power shape his own style. Listen to him work through "Bacon Fat," "Maybelline," and "New Orleans." Apparently, one of the many strikes against this hard-drinking, superstitious performer was his own lack of confidence in covering songs. Nothing but surety and competence comes across on these tracks, though. His inspirations are apparent in his original material, too. Listen to "When I Did the Mashed Potatoes With You"; it is all about the Drifters' "Save the Last Dance for Me." Bright caught the shining sparks from the magic sounds of his day, and his music still works wonders. The effect was immediate. Many tracks are jumping with sax. This sounds like Wrecking Crew great Plas Johnson. The entire Bright story is told in Del-Fi's ten-page booklet. While his history is in the text, the compiled tracks are an exciting slice through the beginnings of rock & roll. His monkey paw may never have brought him wide fame and fortune, but his rockers are more than most guitar hands can conjure. —*Thomas Schulte*

Double Standards / 2002 / Clean Music ✦✦

The music on this set is not strictly jazz, and in fact it is pretty deep in the funk. Larry Bright's drums are mixed up front and are not too subtle. Guitarist Frank Gambale and keyboardist Hakon Graf have a few good spots in a rockish vein but a couple raps and some weak R&B-ish vocals, along with forgettable material, sink this run-of-the-mill effort. —*Scott Yanow*

Brighter Side of Darkness

f. 1972, Chicago, IL, **db.** 1974

Group / Soul

This Chicago group of mostly high school students didn't enjoy a lengthy tenure, but made the marvelous wailing ballad "Love Jones" in 1972. It was a gold record and number-three R&B hit, and remains among classic soul one-hit wonders. Their lead singer Darryl Lamont was 12; other members were Ralph Eskridge, Randolph Murph, and Larry Washington. The follow-up, "I Owe You Love," barely made the R&B Top 50, and they were soon only a memory. Both songs were issued on 20th Century Records. —*Ron Wynn*

Love Jones / 1973 / 20th Century ✦✦✦✦

Other than the Jackson Five's early Motown releases, and the excellent Curtis Mayfield-produced debut by the Five Stairsteps, the Brighter Side of Darkness' *Love Jones* is one of the best teen albums ever. Twelve-year-old lead singer Darryl Lamont, like Michael Jackson, sounds like Frankie Lymon reincarnated. His youthful voice crosses age barriers. "I Owe You Love," "Can I Come Over," and the million-selling title track are all must-hear soul gems. —*Andrew Hamilton*

Jimmy Briscoe & the Little Beavers

Group / Soul, Smooth Soul

Jimmy Briscoe, Stanford Stansberry, Kevin Barnes, Maurice Pulley, and Robert Makins were the original Jimmy Briscoe & the Little Beavers. Bobby Finch replaced Makins in 1977. The Jersey City, NJ-based group debuted with a version of Frankie Lymon & the Teenagers' "Why Do Fools Fall in Love" on Atlantic Records the fall of 1971. Paul Kyser, their manager and mentor, produced the side and its flip, "Sugar Brown."

Atlantic never issued anything else on them; their follow-up, "Together, Together (We'll Make a Way)," appeared on J City Records the following year. Six well-received releases—from 1973 to 1976—followed on the Pi Kappa label, including local/regional favorites "My Ebony Princess," "Where Were You," and "I Only Feel This Way When I'm Near You." But nothing sold enough to merit an appearance on the nationally syndicated *Soul Train* television program.

When Finch joined they dropped the "Little" and became Jimmy Briscoe & the Beavers. They cut the rousing disco cut "Invitation to the World" on Wanderick Records in 1977; Kyser did a licensing deal with TK Records, but the additional clout didn't make the record take off as expected. A final release, the spacy "Into the Milky Way," mixed by Bobby Guttadaro, bounced out on Salsoul Records the summer of 1979. When it didn't cause a stampede to record outlets, the group disbanded and pursued other endeavors. —*Andrew Hamilton*

Jimmy Briscoe & the Little Beavers / Aug. 5, 1993 / Collectables ✦✦✦

The only missing element in this CD discography of Jimmy Briscoe & the Little Beavers' career is the Atlantic Records single "Why Do Fools Fall in Love" b/w "Sugar Brown" (9/1971) cut prior to these 19 tracks on J City, Pi Kappa, Wanderick, and Salsoul Records. The Jersey group led by Jimmy Briscoe (lead, first tenor, second tenor) also featured Stanford Stansberry's hard-edged second tenor/baritone at times. They cut good records, but nothing fantastic, and rarely got played outside the New Jersey/New York area. Furthermore, the name denotes a kiddie group and didn't help matters, which is a shame because they recorded some good material that merited attention. Some of their better moments include "Forever," a consummate wedding song; the contagious "Rockin' and Dancing"; "Together We'll Find the Way"; the romantic "My Ebony Princess"; and "My Fallen Angel," a love-happy, uptempo song with energetic vocals. —*Andrew Hamilton*

Johnny Bristol

b. Feb. 3, 1939, Morgantown, NC

Producer / Soul, Smooth Soul, Motown

Though born in Morgantown, NC, vocalist, composer, and producer Johnny Bristol began his career in Detroit and was a longtime force at Motown from 1961 to 1973. Bristol teamed with Jackey Beavers doing duets for Gwen Gordy's Tri-Phi label in Detroit during the early '60s. They cut the original version of "Someday We'll Be Together," which was remade by Diana Ross & the Supremes in 1969. Bristol was the session's producer, and also the male voice doing harmony.

Bristol was professionally and personally part of Motown, as he married Iris Gordy, and was also Harvey Fuqua's writing and production partner for several years. They co-produced Junior Walker & the All-Stars' remake of "How Sweet It Is" in 1966, then co-wrote and produced "What Does It Take." Bristol wrote and/or produced songs for Diana Ross, Marvin Gaye and Tammi Terrell, Smokey Robinson, David Ruffin, Edwin Starr, Michael Jackson, Gladys Knight & the Pips, Martha Reeves, Jimmy Ruffin, the Spinners, the Four Tops, and Stevie Wonder. "Ain't No Mountain High Enough," "25 Miles," "Help Me Make It Through the Night," "I Don't Want to Do Wrong," and "Yester-Me, Yester-You, Yesterday" were some of the songs featuring Bristol's input. He signed with MGM as a solo artist in 1974. His first single, "Hang on in There Baby," was his biggest; it was number-two R&B and number-eight pop that year. Bristol enjoyed two more sizable hits for MGM, "You And I" and "Leave My World" in 1974 and 1975.

He moved to Atlantic in 1976, and scored his last hit with "Do It to My Mind," a number-five R&B record. The Osmonds also had a number one record in England with Bristol's "Love Me For a Reason." Bristol remade "Hang on in There Baby" as a duet with Alton McClain for Polydor in 1980, and did another duet with Amii Stewart titled "My Guy/My Girl" for Handshake. He recorded for England's Motorcity label, and scored a British hit with "Man Up in the Sky" in 1989. His last entry was "Come to Me" for Whichway in 1991. Bristol was also productive as a writer and producer in the '70s and '80s; Tavares, Buddy Miles, Tamiko Jones, Real Thing, O.C. Smith, and Margie Joseph recorded his compositions in the '70s, and Bristol produced a Four Tops remake of "I'm Ready for Love" in 1985, briefly returning to Motown. —*Ron Wynn*

Hang on in There Baby / 1974 / MGM ✦✦✦✦

The prolific Johnny Bristol made his name at Motown as a writer and producer of tracks like Diana Ross & the Supremes' "Someday We'll Be Together," a song he co-wrote years before. In 1974, he did a successful production assignment for Boz Scaggs and made his solo debut for MGM. In short order, Bristol created an intriguing persona with a patented wry vocal delivery. The title track is a sensual masterpiece that all but summed up his lyrical metier. The infinitely playable and smooth "You and I" is just as good. "I Got Cha Number," also on Scaggs' *Slow Dancer*, has Scaggs coming on to do some fun harmony vocals, but tracks like "Memories Don't Leave Like People Do" and "Love Me for Reason" are so-so efforts. This is prime '70s L.A. R&B/pop with Bristol's sure production hand and arrangements by H.B. Barnum. Players include David T. Walker and his singular guitar fills. Despite the lack of plentiful great tracks, any album with both "Hang on in There Baby" and "You and I" is more than worth your time. —*Jason Elias*

Feeling the Magic / 1975 / MGM ✦✦

Bristol's Creme / 1976 / Ariola ✦✦

● **Best of Johnny Bristol** / 1978 / Polydor ✦✦✦✦✦

Smooth, romantic songs from songwriter/producer/singer Johnny Bristol. The best of his Polydor years include heartfelt originals from Bristol's pen like "You and I," "Love Me for a Reason," chart stepper "Do It to My Mind," and his big hit, "Hang on in There Baby." —*Andrew Hamilton*

Strangers / 1978 / Polydor ✦✦✦✦

Bristol's finest since he broke from Motown's apron strings with the *Hang on in There* album, but Polydor skimped on promotion and it went unnoticed. Bristol's unheralded singing shines on "Strangers in Dark Corners," "I'm Waiting on Love," and "If You Ever Need Somebody." His diction and vocal tone are remarkable and keeps whatever he sings interesting. "When the Fire Is Burning" is the only clunker, the rest are comparable to his best solo work with the common denominator being Bristol's fluid, effortless singing. —*Andrew Hamilton*

Free to Be Me / 1981 / Hanza/Handshake ✦✦✦

Brother to Brother

Group / Soul, Funk

St. Louis native Michael Burton formed Brother to Brother with studio musicians Billy Jones, Frankie Prescott, and Yogi Horton in the mid-'70s. They enjoyed success with a good cover of Gil Scott-Heron's "In the Bottle" in 1974, scoring a number nine R&B hit. It was the only one of their releases for Turbo that made any impact. *—Ron Wynn*

- **In the Bottle** / 1974 / Turbo ♦♦♦♦

Let Your Mind Be Free / 1976 / Turbo ♦♦♦

As far as '70s funk bands go, Brother to Brother was never a major-league act. If Parliament/Funkadelic, the Ohio Players, L.T.D., Earth, Wind & Fire, Graham Central Station, the Commodores, Tower of Power, and the Bar-Kays constituted funk's major leagues, you would have to call the lesser-known Brother to Brother a minor-league act. That isn't to say that Brother to Brother didn't come up with its share of worthwhile grooves; *Let Your Mind Be Free* is a competent but uneven funk/soul outing from 1976. Although nothing mind-blowing occurs, the band's sound is a likable, if undeveloped, mixture of Sly Stone, the Ohio Players, and the pre-J.T. Taylor Kool & the Gang. "Leavin' Me," the single "Chance With You," and the title track are gritty funk numbers, while the jazzy, hypnotic "Visions" would please the acid jazz crowd. And "Take My Love," which Brother to Brother guitarist Billy Jones co-wrote with Sylvia Robinson, is a decent Northern soul item. "Chance With You" enjoyed some radio airplay, but even so, *Let Your Mind Be Free* didn't go very far commercially. This LP has been out of print since the late '70s, and it is most unlikely that the album will ever be reissued on CD. *—Alex Henderson*

The Brothers Johnson

f. 1975, Los Angeles, CA

Group / Pop/Rock, Funk, Soul

Guitarist/vocalist George Johnson and bassist/vocalist Louis Johnson formed the band Johnson Three Plus One with older brother Tommy and their cousin Alex Weir while attending school in Los Angeles. When they became professionals, the band backed such touring R&B acts as Bobby Womack and the Supremes. George and Louis Johnson later joined Billy Preston's band, and wrote "Music in My Life" and "The Kids and Me" for him before leaving his group in 1973.

Quincy Jones hired them to play on his LP *Mellow Madness*, and recorded four of their songs, including "Is It Love That We're Missing?" and "Just a Taste of Me." Jones took them on a Japanese tour, then produced their debut LP, *Look Out for #1*, after they signed with A&M, which was also his label at the time (1976). They scored a number-one R&B and number-three pop hit with "I'll Be Good to You," and enjoyed R&B chart toppers in 1977 and 1980 respectively with "Strawberry Letter 23" and "Stomp!," while sustaining a consistent hit presence via such songs as "Get the Funk Out Ma Face" and "Runnin' for Your Lovin." Jones remade "I'll Be Good to You" in 1989 with Ray Charles and Chaka Khan on his *Back on the Block* release.

The Brothers earned platinum records for *Look Out for #1* and *Right on Time*. Jones produced both of these, along with their third and fourth LPs, *Blam!!* and *Light Up the Night*. The group produced its single "The Real Thing" in 1981. It reached number 11 on the R&B charts, and the Brothers had another hit with "Welcome to the Club" in 1982. They started doing separate ventures; Louis Johnson played bass on Michael Jackson's *Thriller* LP and recorded a gospel album, while George Johnson worked with Steve Arrington. Leon Sylvers produced their mid-'80s return LP *Out of Control*; it didn't equal their past success, but got them another R&B hit with "You Keep Coming Back" in 1984. They recorded *Kickin'* in 1988, and co-wrote "Tomorrow" with Siedah Garrett for Jones' *Back on the Block* in 1989. *—Ron Wynn*

Look Out for #1 / 1976 / A&M ♦♦♦♦

The Brothers Johnson first earned national recognition as recording artists by singing the sensuously funky midtempo number "Is It Love That We're Missin'," featured on Quincy Jones' album *Mellow Madness*. The dynamic duo maintains that same groove on this, its debut release for A&M Records. The first single was the moderate number "I'll Be Good to You," which is soothing like a ballad but inducing like a liquid funk cut. The guitar tandem landed on top of the R&B charts with this gold-selling single. They returned to the Top Five with the bona fide funk jam "Get the Funk Out Ma Face," which peaked at number four. Their remake of the Beatles' classic "Come Together" comes with a soulful twist. Aside from this remake, the Brothers co-wrote every other song on this album, including the untarnished instrumental "Tomorrow," which later became a number one single for Quincy Jones' *Back on the Block*. This album is consistent throughout. *—Craig Lytle*

Right on Time / 1977 / A&M ♦♦♦♦♦

Potentially viewed as something of a warm-up for Quincy Jones before producing Michael Jackson's wildly successful *Off the Wall* and *Thriller* albums, the Brothers Johnson's first two releases spawned hits like "I'll Be Good to You" and brought George and Louis Johnson to a mass audience of their own. (Louis, in fact, would go on to play bass on those first two sessions by the King of Pop.) As with the Jackson discs, Jones creates a seamless mix of pop and funk on the Brothers sophomore release *Right on Time*, helping to create the group's second chart-topper "Strawberry Letter 23" as well the equally effervescent, minor R&B hit "Runnin' for Your Lovin'." With Earth, Wind & Fire's airy dancefloor hits in mind, the Brothers also deliver polished funk tracks like "Right on Time" and "Never Leave You Lonely," as well as more pop-friendly material like "Free Yourself, Be Yourself" and "Love Is." And with one of the best jazz arrangers in the business behind the board, the Brothers couldn't forgo some instrumentals here as well, specifically the breezy, funk-in-a-quiet-storm number "'Q'" and the less intriguing, synthesizer jam "Brother Man." An enjoyable and even infectious collection that, in its sophistication, certainly avoids being just some sort of dry run for Jones. *—Stephen Cook*

Blam!! / 1978 / A&M ♦♦♦♦

In the late '70s and early '80s, funk could be divided into two main categories: hardcore funk (which included Rick James, Graham Central Station, Cameo, the Gap Band, the Bar-Kays, and George Clinton's Parliament/Funkadelic empire) and the lighter, softer sophisticated funk ("sophisti-funk" for short) of Rufus & Chaka Khan, the Average White Band, the Whispers, Heatwave, Chic, Dynasty, and Teena Marie. Before the arrival of J.T. Taylor in 1979, Kool & the Gang were the epitome of hardcore funk—and once he arrived, they epitomized sophisti-funk (which was also called "uptown funk"). Another group that epitomized sophisti-funk was the Brothers Johnson, whose third album, *Blam!!*, demonstrates that funk can be sleek and gritty at the same time. This 1978 classic is full of definitive examples of sophisti-funk; if you're a lover of that style, tracks like "Ain't We Funkin' Now" (a major hit), "Mista' Cool," "Ride-O-Rocket," and the title song are required listening. Equally strong are the mellow ballad "It's You, Girl" and the pop-jazz instrumental "Streetwave," both of which were well-received by quiet storm enthusiasts. The person the Brothers Johnson can thank for this album being so consistent is producer Quincy Jones, who really knew how to bring out the best in the group. A former jazz musician who shifted his focus to R&B/pop in the 1970s, Jones can be a real perfectionist. It was Jones who, in 1982, produced the best selling album of all time (Michael Jackson's *Thriller*), and he rarely let the Brothers Johnson settle for second best. As a result, *Blam!!* is excellent from start to finish. *—Alex Henderson*

Light Up the Night / 1980 / A&M ♦♦♦♦

Light Up the Night marked the end of an era for the Brothers Johnson—it was the last of four albums that Quincy Jones produced for the Los Angeles siblings, and it was the last time a Brothers Johnson album was truly excellent instead of merely decent. When Jones was producing the Brothers Johnson's albums from 1976-1980, he gave them something their subsequent albums lacked—consistency. Even though George and Lewis Johnson recorded some decent material after *Light Up the Night*, none of their post-Jones albums had the type of consistency that Jones gives this 1980 release. The album gets off to an impressive start with the major hit "Stomp!" (a definitive example of the smooth, sleek brand of funk that was termed sophisticated funk in the late '70s and early '80s), and the tracks that follow are equally memorable. From the sleek sophisti-funk of "You Make Me Wanna Wiggle," "This Had to Be" (which was co-written by Michael Jackson and employs him as a background vocalist), and the title song to the tender R&B/pop ballads "Treasure" and "All About the Heaven," *Light Up the Night* is without a dull moment. *—Alex Henderson*

Winners / 1981 / A&M ♦♦

From 1975-1980, the Brothers Johnson enjoyed a very lucrative association with producer Quincy Jones—one that brought them both creative and commercial success. And when that association ended after their fourth album, *Light Up the Night*, their popularity faded. Released in 1981, *Winners* was the first Brothers Johnson album that Jones didn't produce—and it was also their first disappointing album. This isn't to say that *Winners*, which they produced themselves, is a disaster; most of the material is decent. "In the Way," "Caught Up," "Do It for Love," and the single "The Real Thing" (a number-11 R&B hit) are pleasant, likable songs, but they aren't great songs—and when the Johnson siblings had Jones' guidance and direction, they had no problem providing albums that were excellent instead of merely decent. None of the tunes are terrible, but none of them are in a class with "Strawberry Letter 23," "I'll Be Good to You," or "Ain't We Funkin' Now." Definitely not one of the Brothers Johnson's essential releases, *Winners* is only recommended to completists. *—Alex Henderson*

Blast!: The Latest and the Greatest / 1983 / A&M ♦♦♦

When artists are anxious to release some new material but don't have enough of it for a full-length album, their options range from providing EPs to assembling combined new material/greatest-hits packages. The Brothers Johnson favored the latter option in 1982, when they offered four new songs and five previously released hits on the LP *Blast!: The Latest and the Greatest*. The problem with latest/greatest combinations is that they seem confused—*Blast!* isn't a greatest-hits package in the true sense, but it isn't an album of nothing but new material either. In an ideal world, the Brothers Johnson would come out with two releases in 1982—the four new songs ("Welcome to the Club," "Funk It," "I'm Giving You All of My Love," and "The Great Awaking") should have ended up on an EP, and the Quincy Jones-produced smashes ("Get the Funk Out Ma Face," "Strawberry Letter 23," "Ain't We Funkin' Now," "Stomp!" and "I'll Be Good to You") should have been placed on a separate "Best of the Brothers Johnson" LP. The four new songs aren't bad, but they aren't exceptional and don't belong on a greatest-hits package. *Blast!* is an example of problematic packaging, and it is an LP that only completists need to own. *—Alex Henderson*

Out of Control / 1984 / A&M ♦♦

Although they were nearly a decade on from their '70s heyday, the Brothers Johnson, with Leon Sylvers at the production helm, still managed to set a few grooves on fire among the heavy, heady crop of synthesized R&B that flooded the adult contemporary market. There's an interesting interplay between the strong bass and vocals, supported by a smattering of guitar and a markedly slow tempo, which ensured that the single "You Keep Me Coming Back" would power into the R&B Top 20. Much of *Out of Control* follows through with much the same attitude, with nary a true funk-fueled jam to be found. Some of the duo's original intent survives on "I Came Here to Party" and the title track, but such stompers are few and far between, merely filling space in between the ballads and soft soul numbers which dominate the set, leaving the smart "Dazed" to fall somewhere in between. *Out of Control* probably won't thrill the socks off the Brothers' funk fans, but there are still moments which merit a closer listen. And despite the soft sonics which proliferate, the Brothers Johnson certainly proved they were worthy of their staying power, while so many of their peers fell soundly by the wayside. *—Amy Hanson*

Kickin' / 1988 / A&M ✦✦
Re-emerging from what had turned into a four-year hiatus, the Brothers Johnson hoped to repeat earlier successes with 1988's Kickin'. Unfortunately for the duo, however, their smooth brand of slick R&B had, by that time, been severely scaled back in favor of new flavors and grooves, with their original style fully co-opted by a whole new crop of young hipsters. The portents were poor from the outset, as they previewed the album with the groove-laden, jangly hooked assault of the Irene Cara co-penned "Kick It to the Curb." The single bombed despite its catchy melody, and set a sour scene for the rest of the record—which is a shame because there was certainly follow-up material aplenty on board. "Ball of Fire" uses remarkably raunchy guitar licks to sublimate sweet backing vocals and synthesized horn flourishes in what emerges a remarkably funky groove, while the pseudo ballad "Real Love" falls well into appealing puppy love territory. Elsewhere, the band cover Curtis Mayfield's "We Must Be in Love" with aplomb and try their hand at something completely different on the sparse and futuristic closer "Party Avenue." Overall, however, there isn't really anything to criticize on *Kickin'*, nor is there much to recommend it either. The Brothers Johnson are still in a good groove, but it is scattershot across so many styles that it just winds up distracting. *—Amy Hanson*

● **Greatest Hits** / Jun. 18, 1996 / A&M ✦✦✦✦✦
Coming to prominence toward the tail end of the funk era (the late '70s), the Brothers Johnson boasted a polished, state-of-the-art studio sound that took into account the rise of disco in black pop, not to mention the synthesizer. Early on, they also had an important ally in producer Quincy Jones, who masterminded their first four albums; not surprisingly, those turned out to be their most successful, though they continued to record through the first half of the '80s, often producing themselves. *Greatest Hits* throws in a few of those '80s cuts for good measure, but concentrates mostly on their prime years with Jones, which produced the classic singles "I'll Be Good to You," the psychedelic "Strawberry Letter 23," and "Stomp!"; all three hit number one on the R&B charts, and "Get the Funk Out Ma Face" also made the Top Ten. *Greatest Hits* also includes a number of fine lesser singles over its 15 tracks, including "Ain't We Funkin' Now," "Runnin' for Your Lovin'," "Free and Single," and "Light Up the Night," as well as the Grammy-winning instrumental "Q." It also gathers a couple of their bigger '80s hits, "The Real Thing" and "You Keep Me Comin' Back," though it leaves off 1982's "Welcome to the Club," which just missed the R&B Top Ten. Even so, *Greatest Hits* still stands as a near-definitive Brothers Johnson compilation; it's certainly all that casual fans will need, and it serves the needs of most funk fanatics pretty nicely as well. *—Steve Huey*

Brothers of Soul

Group / Brown-Eyed Soul, Urban, Motown
The Brothers of Soul was a vocal trio composed of Fred Bridges, Richard Knight, and Bobby Eaton, which released several singles in a smooth, uptown, Motown-derived vein. Their biggest hit was 1968's "I Guess That Don't Make Me a Loser," released on Boo Records, which scraped the lower reaches of the R&B Top 40. It has since become a soul collectible, and also gained the group a following among the Latino community in Southern California. Some of their other single releases included "Can't Get You Off of My Mind," "The Love I Found in You," and "Candy." Bridges, Knight, and Eaton also worked as a songwriting team, most prominently for Ruby Andrews during the late '60s. By the mid-'70s, the Brothers of Soul had broken up; Eaton became a session singer, while Bridges and Knight continued on as songwriters, getting a couple of compositions recorded by the Four Tops. The 1995 Collectables compilation *I Guess That Don't Make Me a Loser* reissued 14 Brothers of Soul sides on CD. *—Steve Huey*

● **I Guess That Don't Make Me a Loser** / 1995 / Collectables ✦✦✦

Bobby Brown

b. Feb. 5, 1969, Boston, MA
Vocals / New Jack Swing, Club/Dance, Urban, Dance-Pop
One of the brightest R&B stars of the late '80s and early '90s, Bobby Brown was the man who popularized new jack swing, a blend of classic soul, urban synth-funk, and hip-hop rhythms that often featured rap breaks in between the conventionally melodic verses and choruses. Guy's Teddy Riley may have been new jack's greatest innovator, but Brown was its greatest hitmaker, crossing over to pop audiences with his blockbuster *Don't Be Cruel* album and thus making new jack swing the dominant trend in R&B through the early '90s (which, in turn, helped kick start the solo careers of his former bandmates in New Edition). As R&B tastes changed, Brown became better known for his private life than his music; a sometimes rocky marriage to Whitney Houston and a series of run-ins with the law kept him in the tabloid headlines for most of the '90s, even though he wasn't actually recording much music.

Bobby Brown was born February 5, 1969, in Boston, and began singing with Roxbury schoolmates Michael Bivins and Ricky Bell in 1978. The group developed into New Edition and, after a few talent show wins, were discovered by producer Maurice Starr. Starr signed the group to his label and co-authored their debut hit "Candy Girl," which helped get New Edition a deal with MCA. After a few years of teen stardom, Brown longed to move on to an adult solo career, and left New Edition in 1986. He released his debut solo album, *King of Stage*, in 1987, and while it didn't make a name for Brown as a pop star, it did spawn a major R&B hit in the ballad "Girlfriend." Overall, though *King of Stage* gave little indication that Brown was about to become a breakout star on the cutting edge of modern R&B.

For his follow-up, Brown sought a more distinctive musical identity in the budding new jack swing movement. He enlisted the emerging production/songwriting team of L.A. Reid and Babyface to handle the majority of the record, with new jack pioneer Teddy Riley coming on board in a limited capacity as well. The result, *Don't Be Cruel*, was a state-of-the-art, star-making affair. Released in the summer of 1988, the record produced Brown's first pop Top Ten hit in the title track, but really started to take off when the driving statement of purpose "My Prerogative" went all the way to number one toward the end of the year (and managed to work the word "prerogative" into a catchy hook). From there, *Don't Be Cruel* just kept spinning off hits: the ballad "Roni," the dance tune "Every Little Step" (which showed off Brown's rapping skills), and another ballad "Rock Wit'cha" all hit the Top Ten in 1989, with the former two both making it all the way to number three. *Don't Be Cruel* topped the album charts and sold a whopping seven-million copies, making Brown a superstar. In 1990, he was tapped to provide the theme song for *Ghostbusters II* and responded with the number-two smash "On Our Own," another rap/R&B mixture; he also contributed a rap to friend Glenn Medeiros' number-one pop hit "She Ain't Worth It." Brown was so popular at this point that even his 1990 remix album *Dance!... Ya Know It!* went platinum.

And then, somehow, the momentum began to slow. Countless other artists expanded on the new jack swing blueprint, with many of Brown's former New Edition colleagues at the forefront: Bell Biv Devoe, Johnny Gill, and Ralph Tresvant. Moreover, *Don't Be Cruel* made L.A. Reid and Babyface into hot commodities, and their sound was all over the airwaves. Just before his new album *Bobby* was released in the summer of 1992, Brown married superstar diva Whitney Houston, who sang the duet "Something in Common" on the new record. *Bobby*'s lead single "Humpin' Around" was a smash on both the pop and R&B charts, reaching the Top Five on the former. However, *Bobby* didn't sustain the momentum of *Don't Be Cruel*; perhaps it didn't stand out from the pack the way *Don't Be Cruel* had in 1988, or perhaps white audiences were too preoccupied with grunge. Whatever the reason, sales of *Bobby* topped out at around two-million copies, despite several more R&B hits in "Good Enough," "Get Away," and "That's the Way Love Is." In 1993, Georgia police arrested Brown for an overly suggestive stage performance, an incident that would prove to be the first of many legal difficulties for Brown over the next few years.

In 1995, Brown was arrested after a brawl in a Disney World nightclub, in which a patron who allegedly made a pass at a woman in Brown's party had his ear at least partially torn off. (Charges were later dropped when Brown settled out of court.) Several months later, Brown was charged with battery in Los Angeles after allegedly kicking a hotel security guard who tried to halt a party in Brown's room (he was sentenced to two years' probation). The same year, Brown checked himself into the Betty Ford Clinic to battle drug and alcohol problems. However, in August 1996, he wrecked Houston's leased Porsche while speeding in Florida; reportedly, his blood-alcohol level was twice the legal limit. In the midst of all this chaos, Brown found time to record with the fully reunited New Edition, whose comeback album *Home Again* entered the charts at number one that fall. Brown toured with the group, but departed for good when the tour was over. Meanwhile, the tabloids were having a field day over Brown and Houston's rumored marital problems; in 1997, Brown was accused of spousal abuse when Houston suffered a cut on her cheek during a yachting trip, although both Brown and Houston denied the reports.

Also in 1997, Brown released his fourth solo album, *Forever*, a commercial disappointment which failed to even break the Top 50. In the summer of 1998, Brown was arrested for sexual battery stemming from an alleged incident in the Beverly Hills Hotel, although no charges were filed for lack of evidence. He served five days in a Florida jail stemming from his drunk-driving incident, and after spending time in rehab, he was arrested again for allegedly having shown up at the jail drunk. Brown reportedly violated his probation by testing positive for cocaine several times; while those charges were dropped, he was sentenced to 75 days in jail for refusing to take another drug test in the summer of 2000. Upon his release, Brown began working in earnest on a new album, which was derailed for a time when he suffered a seizure in the summer of 2001, reportedly from heat exhaustion and dehydration. It wasn't until 2002 that he really came back into the media spotlight, following a duet with Ja Rule he was captured by the police for marijuana possession and driving without a license after a routine stop for speeding. *—Steve Huey*

King of Stage / 1987 / MCA ✦✦✦
Bobby Brown's style was still fairly close to that of his comrades in New Edition when he recorded his first solo effort, *King of Stage*—an album giving little indication of the hard-edged, aggressive "new jack swing" that was only two years away on *Don't Be Cruel*. While comparisons to his subsequent work are inevitable, *Stage* is a generally decent, though not breathtaking, album that stands on its own merit—and one that proves that there was indeed life outside of New Edition for the singer/rapper. Although Cameo leader Larry Blackmon, who serves as producer on "Girl Next Door," "Spending Time" and "Baby, I Wanna Tell You Something," brings an undeniably Cameo-ish element to these high-tech funk smokers, Brown's individuality comes through loud and clear. But as enjoyable as the Blackmon-produced tracks are, top honors must go to "Seventeen"—a riveting account of a teenage mother who turns to drugs and prostitution—and the unapologetically sentimental, '70s-like soul ballad "Girlfriend." Brown sounds like he's going through the motions on the Rick James-ish "Your Tender Romance" and the lackluster ballad "Spending Time," but thankfully, *Stage* has more strengths than weaknesses. *—Alex Henderson*

Don't Be Cruel / 1988 / MCA ✦✦✦✦
Don't Be Cruel was to Bobby Brown what *Control* was to Janet Jackson—a tougher, more aggressive project that shed his "bubble gum" image altogether and brought him to a new artistic and commercial plateau. With "My Prerogative" and the title song, Brown became a leader of new jack swing—a forceful, high-tech blend of traditional soul singing and rap/hip-hop that's also associated with Guy and Brown's New Edition colleagues, Bell Biv DeVoe. Brown had been a strong advocate of rap since his days with New Edition, and on *Cruel*, he did even more rapping than before. But for all the tough-mindedness he exhibited on his "new jack" hits, the charismatic Bostonian hadn't lost his love of sentimental, old-fashioned R&B romanticism—and he definitely excels in that area on his hits "Every Little Step," "Roni," and "Rock Wit'cha." Much of *Cruel* was produced by the ubiquitous production/songwriting duo L.A. Reid & Babyface, who've often been accused (and rightly so) of taking a formulaic, cookie-cutter approach to R&B. But here, their work is never less than inspired. *—Alex Henderson*

Dance!... Ya Know It! / 1990 / MCA ♦♦
Cynics tend to dismiss remix albums as cheap exploitation and opportunism on the part of labels. But when the remixing is handled by inventive DJs, they definitely have their pleasures. *Dance!... Ya Know It!* obviously fueled by MCA Records' desire to cash in on the enormous success of Bobby Brown's *Don't Be Cruel*, is neither one of the better nor one of the worst remix albums available. While the primary focus is material from *Cruel*—including the hard and rugged new jack swing of "My Prerogative" and "Don't Be Cruel" and the vulnerable romanticism of "Roni," "Every Little Step" and "Rock Wit' Cha"—Brown's debut solo album, *King of Stage* is represented by remixes of "Seventeen," "Girl Next Door" and "Baby, I Wanna Tell You Something." Much of the remixing is done by hit R&B producers L.A. Reid & Babyface, who are far from adventurous and fail to add anything really new, interesting or significant to the songs. Though an enjoyable release and one that works well enough as a "best of," *Dance!... Ya Know It!* is hardly essential listening for those who already own *Stage* and *Cruel*. —*Alex Henderson*

Bobby / 1992 / MCA ♦♦♦
Brown's follow-up to the groundbreaking *Don't Be Cruel* isn't as innovative or consistent as his previous album, but that doesn't mean it's without any charms; the singles "Humpin' Around," "Good Enough," and "Get Away" are strong and memorable, which almost makes the abundance of filler forgivable. —*Stephen Thomas Erlewine*

Remixes N the Key of B / 1993 / MCA ♦♦

Forever / Nov. 4, 1997 / MCA ♦♦♦
Bobby Brown began to spiral out of control after *Bobby*, his follow-up to the blockbuster *Don't Be Cruel*, failed to match its predecessor's success. Instead of being famous for his music, Brown became famous for being Whitney Houston's husband, often landing in the tabloids for his bad behavior. He began to rehabilitate his image with New Edition's 1996 reunion album, *Home Again*, but he didn't make a big impact on the record, and neither of the album's two hit singles featured him on lead vocals. His weak presence on *Home Again* left many questions about his musical vitality in the late '90s unanswered, giving his 1997 comeback record *Forever* the duty of re-establishing him as a preeminent contemporary soul artist. Brown struggles to prove his vitality on *Forever*, turning out a series of impeccably produced ballads and dance numbers, but it's not an entirely successful record. Often, it sounds like he's trying too hard, especially since many of the songs just aren't that interesting. Still, when he has the right song, such as the single "Feelin' Inside," he invests it with charisma and charm, turning it into irresistible urban soul. Unfortunately, those moments don't come often enough on *Forever*. —*Stephen Thomas Erlewine*

● **Greatest Hits** / Sep. 26, 2000 / MCA ♦♦♦♦
Although the bulk of Bobby Brown's most important work is featured on *Don't Be Cruel*, he was a fairly consistent singles artist throughout most of his solo career (that is, when he actually recorded). *Greatest Hits* doesn't feature anything from 1997's lackluster *Forever*, but that's entirely forgivable; the 14 tracks that are here include an amazing 11 Top Ten R&B hits, six of which went to number one, and eight of which also reached the pop Top Ten. Brown's hit duets with Glenn Medeiros ("She Ain't Worth It") and wife Whitney Houston ("Something in Common") are also included, although there's nothing from his first or second go-rounds with New Edition. However, there doesn't need to be—the body of work presented on *Greatest Hits*, while not completely uniform in style or production, is arguably the catchiest urban pop-soul of its time. There are a few silky ballads, but Brown's real bread and butter is slamming, uptempo new jack dance-pop. On those numbers, Brown is the total urban contemporary package, able to stick with the melody, improvise around it, or throw in credible raps that complement the hard-hitting hip-hop-derived beats. He may not be a technical master, but Brown's understanding of how to construct a tight, catchy single makes *Greatest Hits* an essential purchase for even the most casual fans of late-'80s/early-'90s R&B. —*Steve Huey*

Charles Brown

b. Sep. 13, 1922, Texas City, TX, **d.** Jan. 21, 1999, Oakland, CA
Vocals, Piano / Urban Blues, West Coast Blues, Piano Blues
How many blues artists remained the absolute top of their game after more than a half century of performing? One immediately leaps to mind: Charles Brown. His incredible piano skills and laidback vocal delivery remained every bit as mesmerizing as it was way back in 1945, when his ultra-mellow, jazz-inflected sound invented an entirely new blues genre for sophisticated postwar revelers. Classically trained on the ivories, Brown recorded his first single "Drifting Blues" as head of the Blazers. After the single hit number two on the R&B charts, the band remained popular during the late '40s until Brown opted to go solo. Recording for Aladdin, he visited the R&B Top Ten no less than ten times from 1949 to 1952, retaining his mournful, sparsely arranged sound for smashes like the chart-topping "Trouble Blues."

Brown's mellow approach failed to make the transition to rock's brasher rhythms though, and he soon faded from national prominence. Occasionally recording without causing much of a stir during the '60s and '70s, Brown began to regroup by the mid-'80s with a well-received album (1986's *One More for the Road*) and the support slot on a Bonnie Raitt tour. His successful comeback included over half-a-dozen albums recorded for Alligator, Bullseye Blues and Verve; Brown passed away on January 21, 1999." —*Bill Dahl*

Blues and Other Love Songs / 1992 / 32 Jazz ♦♦♦
This Charles Brown session from early 1992 finds the singer sounding just as natural as he did in the early '50s. *Blues and Other Love Songs* was originally released on Muse records and is available as a budget title from the excellent reissue label 32 Jazz. Brown is in a typically soulful mood, crooning like a gritty modern day Nat King Cole. Backing up the piano and vocals of Brown are soul-groove saxophonist Houston Person, whose smoky tenor chops were an excellent match for Brown's blues. Danny Caron on guitar, Ruth Davies on bass, and Gaylord Birch round out the rhythm section. These ten tracks consist of five originals and five covers featuring a brief version of Thelonious Monk's "Round Midnight," showing off Brown's ability to play straight jazz. Person is also heard with Brown on the 32 jazz reissue *Lost and Found*, which combines the albums *Sweet Slumber* and *Wildflower* on one disc. —*Al Campbell*

Someone to Love / 1992 / Bullseye Blues ♦♦♦
Bonnie Raitt, who played such an integral role in Brown's successful comeback, guests on two tracks on the pianist's *Bullseye Blues* encore, which isn't quite the *tour de force* that his previous outing was but is eminently solid nonetheless. Danny Caron and Clifford Solomon once again shine in support of their leader. —*Bill Dahl*

☆ **The Complete Aladdin Recordings of Charles Brown** / 1994 / Mosaic ♦♦♦♦♦
Every single brilliant side—some 109 in all—that this elegant, tremendously influential pianist cut for the Mesner brothers' Philo and Aladdin imprints from 1945 to 1956 is housed in this lavishly produced five-disc box set. Mosaic's customary attention to detail is evident in the packaging and the sound; Brown's brilliance makes the entire box a delight, from his earliest sessions with the Three Blazers through his hitmaking run as a solo star during the late '40s and early '50s. The genesis of the entire West Coast club blues style resides in this box; its expense is well worth it. —*Bill Dahl*

Just a Lucky So and So / Jan. 24, 1994 / Bullseye Blues ♦♦♦

★ **Driftin' Blues: The Best of Charles Brown** / Sep. 1, 1995 / Collectables ♦♦♦♦♦
Originally put out by EMI in 1992, this roundup of Charles Brown's 1945-1956 Aladdin sides is essential listening for all R&B fans—and that goes for jazz and pop lovers as well. Sticking mostly to an exquisite after-hours mode, Brown delivers one smooth blues gem after another until this 20-track disc comes to a close. Backed for the most part by guitarist Johnny Moore & his Three Blazers, Brown effortlessly lays down such standouts as the title track, "Black Night," and "Get Yourself Another Fool." Yes, the mood here is evocative of Nat Cole's classic trio sides, but Brown and Moore—unlike Cole—infuse their lush surroundings with a healthy dose of sophisticated West Coast blues. Capped off with the original version of Brown's classic Yuletide cut "Merry Christmas Baby," *Driftin' Blues* is the perfect way to get cozy with this venerable blues performer. —*Stephen Cook*

Honey Dripper / Nov. 5, 1996 / Verve ♦♦♦♦
"Soothing" is not a word normally associated with blues, but its the word that best captures the experience of listening to Charles Brown, and *Honey Dripper* is no exception. Listening to it is like sipping a fine bottle of cognac. Seventy-two years old at the time of this recording session, Brown sounds agile, almost ageless. Indeed, time seems to stand still when he plays and sings in that same understated, urbane manner he popularized with Johnny Moore's Three Blazers back in the 1940s. Like his other recordings this decade, *Honey Dripper* features Brown's regular working combo, led by guitarist Danny Caron and including saxophonist Clifford Solomon. The songs range from straight-ahead blues to jazz ballads, with some straddling the line. —*Steve Hoffman*

1944–1945 / Mar. 25, 1997 / Classics ♦♦♦♦♦
This Classics CD features pianist/vocalist Charles Brown on his first 22 recordings, when he was a sideman with guitarist Johnny Moore's Three Blazers. Brown already sounded quite distinctive, and as it turned out, the 21st song ("Drifting Blues") was his biggest hit. The music, due to the instrumentation (a trio/quartet with bassist Eddie Williams and sometimes Oscar Moore on second guitar), is a bit reminiscent at times of the Nat King Cole Trio, but it had a special soul and feeling of its own. Frankie Laine makes a couple of early appearances, but Brown takes care of the bulk of the vocals, and there are also eight excellent instrumentals. Recommended. —*Scott Yanow*

1946 / Feb. 3, 1998 / Classics ♦♦♦♦
With the great success of the slow blues ballad "Driftin' Blues," Johnny Moore's Three Blazers emphasized laid-back material on record after record in 1946, looking for another hit. Ironically the main star of virtually all of the records, pianist-vocalist Charles Brown, was given second billing if he was mentioned at all, while guitarist Moore (who is joined by bassist Eddie Williams) was often mistaken as the singer. Brown would stick with Moore into 1947 and was largely responsible for the group's success. The second Classics CD to reissue all of the trio's recordings includes 23 enjoyable titles that mostly have a sameness to them in tempo and mood. All are vocal showcases for Brown except for the two-part "Warsaw Concerto" and "Nutmeg," the lone instrumentals. A worthwhile set but not as essential a release as the earlier volume in this series. —*Scott Yanow*

So Goes Love / May 12, 1998 / Verve ♦♦♦
Like his previous two efforts for Verve, *These Blues* and *Honey Dripper*, *So Goes Love* doesn't really offer anything new from Charles Brown, but that's hardly a bad thing. Again, he serves up a collection of appealing, laid-back blues that often drifts into jazz territory. The repertoire is a tad too predictable ("Stormy Monday," "Sometimes I Feel Like a Motherless Child"), but the performances are so lovely that there's no reason to complain. *So Goes Love* is hardly the first album to pick up if you're beginning a Brown collection, but once you've been introduced to his charms, it's quite welcome. —*Stephen Thomas Erlewine*

Blue Over You: The Ace Recordings / Oct. 26, 1999 / WestSide ♦♦♦
An entire album of unissued Charles Brown, recorded for Johnny Vincent's Ace label between 1959 and 1960, yields a treasure trove of tracks in this collection. There are nice remakes of "Black Night" and "Driftin' Blues," but even better are tracks like "Please Come Home for Christmas, blues ballads like "Blue Over You," and the old standard "There Is No Greater Love." Many tracks recorded in extreme late-'50s stereo make for fascinating listening to go along with some fascinating music. —*Cub Koda*

1946–1947 / Mar. 14, 2000 / Classics ♦♦♦♦♦
The 24 selections on this Classics CD (their third Charles Brown release) were all recorded by Johnny Moore's Three Blazers, a trio consisting of guitarist Moore, bassist Eddie Williams, and the real star, pianist-vocalist Charles Brown. The final three numbers add Moore's brother, Oscar Moore (formerly with the Nat King Cole Trio), on second guitar. Unlike with their earlier pre-"Driftin' Blues" material, the emphasis is generally on slower tempos with Brown having a vocal on every selection. Most notable is the hit version of "Merry Christmas Baby"; other highlights include "Was I to Blame for Falling in Love With You," "Huggin' Bug," "St. Louis Blues," "Juke Box Lil," and "New Orleans Blues." The Blazers' style, a more bluish version of the Nat King Cole Trio, is always pleasing. However, since Charles Brown was getting very little recognition for his talents (audience members often thought that he was Johnny Moore!), he would not be sticking around in the group much longer. *—Scott Yanow*

1947–1948 / Apr. 3, 2001 / Classics ♦♦♦♦
Although the 24 selections on this CD have been reissued under pianist/vocalist Charles Brown's name, he is actually the featured sideman with Johnny Moore's Three Blazers, a band also including guitarists Johnny Moore and Oscar Moore, plus bassist Eddie Williams. However, putting it under Brown's name is only fitting because he has vocals on all but one of the selections (the instrumental "Scratch Street") and is the most impressive soloist. These performances, cut for the small L.A.-based Exclusive label, are mostly little-known (making them formerly rare collector's items), and the set overall has more tempo and mood variation than the earlier classics; the band was not trying as hard to duplicate the success of "Driftin' Blues." Recommended. *—Scott Yanow*

1948–1949 / May 7, 2002 / Classics ♦♦♦
Pianist/singer Charles Brown left Johnny Moore's Three Blazers in 1948 since Brown's vocals were chiefly responsible for the group's success, but he was receiving no credit; people thought that he was Johnny Moore. His first 24 records as a leader, with Chuck Norris or Tiny Mitchell on guitar and bassist Eddie Williams, are reissued on this disc. The music was all recorded for the Aladdin label and nine of the selections were previously unreleased. "Trouble Blues" and "Get Yourself Another Fool" were minor hits. The main problem with the music is that virtually every song is at the same medium-slow tempo, so listening to this set straight through can be a little tedious. But it is very good to have this formerly rare material available in such comprehensive form. *—Scott Yanow*

1949–1951 / Jan. 21, 2003 / Classics ♦♦♦♦

Chuck Brown & the Soul Searchers

f. Washington, D.C.
Vocals / Go-Go, Soul
Washington, D.C., bandleader, performer, and songwriter Chuck Brown has been a prominent figure on the city's go-go scene since the late '70s. Brown & the Soul Searchers have also been one of the rare go-go acts to gain national attention, even though it was short-lived. The Soul Searchers included trombonist/keyboardist John "J.B." Buchanan, trumpeter Donald Tillery, saxophonist/flutist Leroy Fleming, bassist Jerry Wilder, percussionist Gregory Gerran, organist Curtis Johnson, keyboardist Skip Fennell, drummer Ricardo Wellman, and guitarist LeRon Young. They vaulted into the spotlight with "Busting Loose," the top R&B single for four consecutive weeks at the end of 1978. Its fabulous arrangement; exuberant horn work; and arresting, terse vocals made the band momentary celebrities. But the follow-up, "Game Seven," flopped, and they were soon back on the go-go circuit. They had one more flirtation with the spotlight in 1984, as the single "We Need Some Money (Bout Money)" reached number 26 amid predictions that go-go was ready to explode into the mainstream. It didn't happen, but Brown remained active. He tried again in 1991 with *'90s Goin' Hard* for Goff. A documentary on the Washington, D.C., go-go scene appeared in 2002 and prominently featured Brown and his music. *—Ron Wynn*

• **Bustin' Loose** / 1979 / Valley Vue ♦♦♦♦♦
In the 1980s many of go-go's supporters insisted that it was going to become as big as rap. Regrettably, that never happened. Go-go was huge in Washington, D.C., where a Chuck Brown or Rare Essence show was as big a deal as a George Clinton concert, and a go-go release could be as impressive a seller as the latest Rick James record. But nationally, only a few go-go songs became major hits: E.U.'s "Da Butt" was huge in 1988, and Chuck Brown soared to the top of the R&B charts in 1978 with the insanely funky "Bustin' Loose." Brown and his band, the Soul Searchers, showed a great deal of promise on this debut album, which James Purdie produced at the famous Sigma Sound Studios in Philadelphia. The title song is one of go-go's all-time classics, and anyone with a taste for sweaty, hard-driving funk will also find a lot to love about "If It Ain't Funky" and "I Gotcha Now." But not everything on the album is aggressive. Even though Brown is best known for his gutbucket funk grooves, "Could It Be Love" and an inspired cover of the Jerry Butler/Gamble & Huff pearl "Never Gonna Give You Up" demonstrate that he has no problem handling romantic ballads and slow jams. It isn't surprising that the album's slower tracks are so heavily influenced by Philly soul. After all, Sigma Sound is where the O'Jays, the Intruders, Blue Magic, Teddy Pendergrass, the Stylistics, Billy Paul, and countless others recorded their biggest hits. Most of *Bustin' Loose*, however, isn't typical of recordings made at Sigma; the majority of the material is pure go-go, and *Bustin' Loose* went down in history as one of go-go's most essential releases. *—Alex Henderson*

Funk Express / 1980 / Source ♦♦♦
Although not as strong as 1978's *Bustin' Loose*, 1980's *Funk Express* is a generally decent and occasionally excellent LP that was produced by Wayne Henderson. Hard bop fans, of course, know Henderson as a founding member of the Jazz Crusaders; but in the 1970s, he moved away from straight-ahead acoustic jazz and became a lot more commercial. Whether he was producing Ronnie Laws and Side Effect from 1975-1977 or Chuck Brown & the Soul Searchers in 1980, it was clear that Henderson's days as a full-time bop trombonist were a thing of the past. *Funk Express* isn't among Brown's essential releases, and it didn't contain a big national hit like *Bustin' Loose*'s title song. But it fared well in the Washington, D.C./Baltimore area and has its share of infectious go-go grooves, which include "In the Pocket," "Come on and Boogie," and "Sticks and Stones" (a tune that combines go-go with elements of George Clinton's P-Funk sound). Not all of the songs are go-go-minded; "Who Are You" and Henderson's "Time Has No Ending" are romantic soul ballads, and the LP takes a mildly jazzy turn with a remake of the Crusaders' 1976 hit "Keep That Same Old Feeling." For casual listeners, *Bustin' Loose* would be a better choice than *Funk Express*, although Brown's hardcore fans will find this album enjoyable. *—Alex Henderson*

Unadorned / 1983 / Grandma Katherine's ♦
Forget about the District of Columbia go-go king. Instead, Chuck Brown spends his time playing a long-winded, tinkling piano that's as exciting as navigating a utility company's voice mail menu. Judging by the titles—"Judgment Day," "The Value of Life," and "Kigali: Tears for the Children"—this was meant to be a deep, profound collection. But after listening to a few of the 17 tracks you're not going to want to participate in Brown's indulgences anymore; you'll want to (and will) eject this droning collection from your player to the trash can. Don't play it for the first time in your car—you'll fling it right out the window. Never purchase a Chuck Brown CD without knowing the content beforehand. *—Andrew Hamilton*

Go Go Swing Live / 1986 / Future Sound ♦♦♦♦
If you're ever in the position of deciding whether to buy a studio or live recording by Chuck Brown, opt for the live disc every time; Brown's bounty of sounds marry and flow much better in a live setting. On this live capture, the multi-talented Washington, D.C., native's transitions from go-go to swing, jazz, blues, and R&B, are smooth as butter. Standouts include "It Don't Mean a Thing," "Woody Woodpecker," a fantastic rendition of "Harlem Nocturne," and the old calypso tune "Run Joe," which Brown milks for nearly nine minutes. Other entertaining pleasers are Brown's adaptations of Stevie Wonder's "Boogie on Reggae Women" ("Boogie on Go Go Woman"); Sly Stone's "Family Affair," and Duke Ellington's "Take the a Train" ("Take the Go Go Train"), which features Brown's goofy but effective scatting. *—Andrew Hamilton*

Any Other Way to Go? / 1987 / Rhythm Attack ♦♦♦♦
Best known for their ferocious live gigging, Chuck Brown & the Soul Searchers' recorded catalog often falls by the wayside. But still, live shows aside, their albums remain one of the strongest and best chronicles of Washington, D.C.'s go-go sound. And *Any Other Way to Go?*, coming as the scene's spark was dying, is an excellent, tight masterpiece—easily as good as anything released in the frenzy of the genre's early days. Brown and his crew, alongside Trouble Funk and Rare Essence, constantly threatened to break the genre nationally during the 1980s without much luck. But, because this music and these songs fell so far below the radar at the time—they were never completely co-opted by mainstream music—they remain as vibrant as they ever were at the time of issue. And even at the end of go-go's party, the man who created the genre made sure this album was packed with goodies. Full of funk breaks, prominent drumbeats, and inspired raps, *Any Other Way to Go?* delivers. From the opening "Run Joe," an outstanding go-go-fied calypso, to "Go-Go Drug Free" and "Do That Stuff," Brown & the Searchers keep the groove moving. But Brown wasn't ready to stop there. He added a fresh trio of Sly Stone covers and put his own spin on them. The resulting "Stormy Monday," "Be Bumpin Fresh," and especially "Family Affair" are outstanding. Easily as good as their 1979 proto go-go smash *Bustin' Loose*, *Any Other Way to Go?* certainly capped a genre in ultimate style. Chuck Brown & the Soul Searchers are a vital, vibrant reminder of how good music could be in an era often remembered for such little substance. *—Amy Hanson*

This Is a Journey . . . Into Time / 1991 / Raw Venture ♦♦♦

Other Side / 1992 / Liaison ♦♦♦

Hah Man / 1994 / Liaison ♦♦♦

Your Game: Live at the 9:30 Club Washington, D.C. / May 15, 2001 / Raw Venture ♦♦♦♦
Even an avid R&B fan may not be familiar with go-go music of the 1970s. The unique polyrhythmic style blended horns, bass, and keyboard and eventually became the forerunner to '80s groups like E.U. and Trouble Funk as well as the Miami bass music of the '80s and '90s. While his unique sound has lived on, Chuck Brown, one of the genre's originators, has had relatively little commercial success, except for his 1978 hit "Bustin' Loose." Recorded in January 2001 in front of a lively hometown crowd in Washington, D.C., *Your Game: Live at the 9:30 Club* is an attempt to shed some light on Brown's influential work. Brown brings his fans plenty of funk in "Wind Me Up Chuck/Hoochie Coochie Man" and "Walk to the Witches Castle." He also brings his unique take on '70s classics such as Herbie Hancock's "Chameleon" and the Stylistics' "People Make the World Go Round." While *Your Game: Live at the 9:30 Club* is unlikely to make Brown a household name, it is an excellent introduction to the genre of go-go music. *—Jon Azpiri*

Put Your Hands Up / Aug. 20, 2002 / Raw Venture ♦♦♦♦
Recorded live at D.C.'s 9:30 club, this energetic double-disc celebration of go-go music features plenty of funky vamping, call-and-response chants, and party atmosphere. It starts, appropriately enough, with E.U. 's "Let the Party Begin." E.U. continues its bass-heavy workout with a cover of "I Want You Back" featuring guest vocalist Maleisha Rashad and several other songs, including their hit "Da Butt," that seamlessly maintain the band's funk-shaking groove. Back Yard and 911 keeps things moving for the rest of the first disc, and the latter band even contributes a five-and-a-half-minute ballad, "Ready for Love." Chuck Brown takes over on the second disc. It's evident from his first track, "Mister Magic," that his sound is somewhat different from the three preceding groups; the

inclusion of a trumpeter (Brad Clements), saxophonist (Bryan Mills), and trombonist (Jim McFalls) in his band gives it more of a jazz-funk feel. Nonetheless, his music fits quite comfortably with the first disc of this album; even his rendition of "Family Stone" fits right into the go-go groove. Granted, this cover version illustrates the limitations of Brown's approach—it completely lacks the original's sense of tension of drama and tension, which were sacrificed to maintain the go-go grooves—but it still sounds good. This track is followed by a few more, including "Back Up Against the Wall" featuring Andre "Whiteboy" Johnson, a cover of Missy Elliott's "Get Ur Freak On" featuring Little Benny, and a concluding 11-and-a-half-minute medley. This double album provides a good overview of go-go music; it should appeal to fans of the genre, who are probably already familiar with some of the names here, and to newcomers who won't to learn more about it. However, it is a rather long album (the two discs run for a combined total of nearly two hours) and not recommended to people with limited tolerance for repetition, since that it one of the characteristics of the genre. *—Todd Kristel*

James Brown

b. May 3, 1933, Macon, GA

Vocals, Piano, Organ, Leader, Arranger / Soul, Funk, R&B, Blaxploitation

"Soul Brother Number One," "the Godfather of Soul," "the Hardest Working Man in Show Business," "Mr. Dynamite"—those are mighty titles, but no one can question that James Brown has earned them more than any other performer. Other singers were more popular, others were equally skilled, but few other African-American musicians have been so influential on the course of popular music. And no other musician, pop or otherwise, put on a more exciting, exhilarating stage show; Brown's performances were marvels of athletic stamina and split-second timing.

Through the gospel-impassioned fury of his vocals and the complex polyrhythms of his beats, Brown was a crucial midwife in not just one, but two revolutions in American black music. He was one of the figures most responsible for turning R&B into soul; he was, most would agree, *the* figure most responsible for turning soul music into the funk of the late '60s and early '70s. Since the mid-'70s, he's done little more than tread water artistically; his financial and drug problems eventually got him a controversial prison sentence. Yet in a sense his music is now more influential than ever, as his voice and rhythms were sampled on innumerable rap and hip-hop recordings, and critics have belatedly hailed his innovations as among the most important in all of rock or soul.

Brown's rags-to-riches-to-rags story has heroic and tragic dimensions of mythic resonance. Born into poverty in the South, he ran afoul of the law by the late '40s on an armed robbery conviction. With the help of singer Bobby Byrd's family, Brown gained parole, and started a gospel group with Byrd, changing their focus to R&B as the rock revolution gained steam. The Flames, as the Georgian group was known in the mid-'50s, were signed by Federal/King, and had a huge R&B hit right off the bat with the wrenching, churchy ballad "Please, Please, Please." By now the Flames had become James Brown & His Famous Flames, the charisma, energy, and talent of Brown making him the natural star attraction.

All of Brown's singles over the next two years flopped, as he sought to establish his own style, recording material that was obviously derivative of heroes like Roy Brown, Hank Ballard, Little Richard, and Ray Charles. In retrospect, it can be seen that Brown was in the same position as dozens of other R&B one-shots; talented singers in need of better songs, or not fully on the road to a truly original sound. What made Brown succeed where hundreds of others failed was his superhuman determination, working the chitlin circuit to death, sharpening his band, and keeping an eye on new trends. He was on the verge of being dropped from King in late 1958 when his perseverance finally paid off, as "Try Me" became a number-one R&B (and small pop) hit, and several follow-ups established him as a regular visitor to the R&B charts.

Brown's style of R&B got harder as the '60s began, as he added more complex, Latin- and jazz-influenced rhythms on hits like "Good Good Lovin'," "I'll Go Crazy," "Think," and "Night Train," alternating these with torturous ballads that featured some of the most frayed screaming to be heard outside of the church. Black audiences already knew that Brown had the most exciting live act around, but he truly started to become a phenomenon with the release of *Live at the Apollo* in 1963. Capturing a James Brown concert in all its whirling-dervish energy and calculated spontaneity, it reached number two in the album charts, an unprecedented feat for a hardcore R&B LP.

Live at the Apollo was recorded and released against the wishes of the King label. It was these kinds of artistic standoffs that led Brown to seek better opportunities elsewhere. In 1964, he ignored his King contract to record "Out of Sight" for Smash, igniting a lengthy legal battle that prevented him from issuing vocal recordings for about a year. When he finally resumed recording for King in 1965, he had a new contract that granted him far more artistic control over his releases.

Brown's new era had truly begun, however, with "Out of Sight," which topped the R&B charts and made the pop Top 40. For some time, Brown had been moving toward more elemental lyrics that threw in as many chants and screams as words, and more intricate beats and horn charts that took some of their cues from the ensemble work of jazz outfits. "Out of Sight" wasn't called funk when it came out, but it had most of the essential ingredients. These were amplified and perfected on 1965's "Papa's Got a Brand New Bag," a monster that finally broke Brown to the white audience, reaching the Top Ten. The even more adventurous follow-up, "I Got You (I Feel Good)," did even better, making number three.

These hits kicked off Brown's period of greatest commercial success and public visibility. From 1965 to the end of the decade, he was rarely off the R&B charts, often on the pop listings, and all over the concert circuit and national television, even meeting with Vice President Hubert Humphrey and other important politicians as a representative of the black community. His music became even bolder and funkier, as melody was dispensed with almost altogether in favor of chunky rhythms and magnetic interplay between his vocals, horns, drums, and scratching electric guitar (heard to best advantage on hits like "Cold Sweat," "I Got the Feelin'," and "There Was a Time"). The lyrics were now not so much words as chanted, stream-of-consciousness slogans, often aligning themselves with black pride as well as good old-fashioned (or new-fashioned) sex. Much of the credit for the sound he devised belonged to (and has now been belatedly attributed) his top-notch supporting musicians, such as saxophonists Maceo Parker, St. Clair Pinckney, and Pee Wee Ellis; guitarist Jimmy Nolen; backup singer and longtime loyal associate Bobby Byrd; and drummer Clyde Stubblefield.

Brown was both a brilliant bandleader and a stern taskmaster, leading his band to walk out on him in late 1969. Amazingly, he turned the crisis to his advantage by recruiting a young Cincinnati outfit called the Pacemakers, featuring guitarist Phelps "Catfish" Collins and bassist Bootsy Collins. Although they only stayed with him for about a year, they were crucial to Brown's evolution into even harder funk, emphasizing the rhythm and the bottom even more. The Collins brothers, for their part, put their apprenticeship to good use, helping define '70s funk as members of the Parliament/Funkadelic axis.

In the early '70s, many of the most important members of Brown's late-'60s band returned to the fold, to be billed as the J.B.'s (they also made records on their own). Brown continued to score heavily on the R&B charts throughout the first half of the 1970s, the music becoming even more and more elemental and beat-driven. At the same time, he was retreating from the white audience he had cultivated during the mid- to late '60s; records like "Make It Funky," "Hot Pants," "Get on the Good Foot," and "The Payback" were huge soul sellers, but only modest pop ones. Critics charged, with some justification, that the Godfather was starting to repeat and recycle himself too many times. It must be remembered, though, that these songs were made for the singles/radio/jukebox market and not meant to be played one after the other on CD compilations (as they are today).

By the mid-'70s, Brown was beginning to burn out artistically. He seemed shorn of new ideas, was being out-gunned on the charts by disco, and was running into problems with the IRS and his financial empire. There were sporadic hits, and he could always count on enthusiastic live audiences, but by the 1980s, he didn't have a label. With the explosion of rap, however, which frequently sampled vintage J.B. records, Brown was now hipper than ever. He collaborated with Afrika Bambaataa on the critical smash single "Unity," and re-entered the Top Ten in 1986 with "Living in America." Rock critics, who had always ranked Brown considerably below Otis Redding and Aretha Franklin in the soul canon, began to reevaluate his output, particularly his funk years, sometimes anointing him not just as Soul Brother Number One, but as *the* most important black musician of the rock era.

In 1988, Brown's personal life came crashing down in a well-publicized incident in which he was accused by his wife of assault and battery. After a year skirting hazy legal and personal troubles, he led the police on an interstate car chase after allegedly threatening people with a handgun. The episode ended in a six-year prison sentence that many felt excessive; he was paroled after serving two years.

It's probably safe to assume that Brown will not make any more important recordings, although he continues to perform and release new material like 1998's *I'm Back*. Yet his music is probably more popular in the American mainstream today than it has been since the 1970s, and not just among young rappers and samplers. For a long time his cumbersome, byzantine discography was mostly out of print, with pieces available only on skimpy greatest-hits collections. A series of exceptionally well-packaged reissues on PolyGram has changed the situation; the *Star Time* box set is the best overview, with other superb compilations devoted to specific phases of his lengthy career, from '50s R&B to '70s funk. *—Richie Unterberger*

Please Please Please / 1959 / Polydor ♦♦♦

Though James Brown & His Famous Flames had scored an R&B Top 10 hit in 1956 with "Please, Please, Please," and Brown's next nine singles for Federal Records flopped until "Try Me," his third single of 1958, scored. That was when King Records (Federal's parent label) assembled this, Brown's debut album, out of some of those singles sessions. You can hear the sound of a group and its enthusiastic singer looking for a hit, sometimes in the rock & roll of "Chonnie-On-Chon" (1957) or the 1956 B-side "I Feel That Old Feeling Coming On," sometimes by remaking "Please, Please, Please" under another name, such as "I Don't Know" (1956), sometimes by tackling Coasters-like novelty material such as "That Dood It" (1958), sometimes by aping the smooth Sam Cooke, as on the 1958 B-side "That's When I Lost My Heart," and once by rewriting "My Bonnie (Lies Over The Ocean)" as the 1958 B-side "Baby Cries Over The Ocean." Only the two hits were really memorable, but the album presented the sound of a major star-to-be in search of his sound. *—William Ruhlmann*

Try Me! / 1959 / King ♦♦♦

When James Brown & His Famous Flames finally scored a second hit with their 11th single, "Try Me," King Records constructed this 16-track LP, including the hit along with both sides of three of its follow-ups, "I Want You So Bad"/"There Must Be a Reason," "I've Got to Change"/"It Hurts to Tell You," and "Got to Cry"/"It Was You"; the B-side of a fourth follow-up, "Don't Let It Happen to Me"; the 1957 single "Can't Be the Same"/"Gonna Try"; the 1957 B-sides "I Won't Plead No More" and "Messing With the Blues"; the B-side of Brown's first hit ("Please Please Please"), "Why Do You Do Me"; and three other stray tracks. The earliest work especially sounded more like that of a doo wop group rather than that of a gritty R&B solo singer. None of it measured up to "Try Me," but you could see what Brown had been aiming at, and if the set list comprised what were in effect James Brown's greatest flops, circa 1959, it demonstrated that he possessed as much promise as fervor. [*Try Me!* was reissued in 1964 under the title *The Unbeatable James Brown: 16 Hits*.] *—William Ruhlmann*

Think / 1960 / Polydor ♦♦♦

James' third album (his first for King), gets a straight-up reissue on compact disc, right down to the booklet featuring both original covers on either side—a nice touch. This is 1960 James Brown, moving from King's Federal subsidiary to the parent label with the hits "Bewildered," "If You Want Me," "You've Got the Power," "I'll Go Crazy," "Baby You're Right" (co-written with Joe Tex), and "I'll Never, Never Let You Go." Although Brown's albums would soon be interchangeable, the same cuts reappearing again and again, this is one of his better efforts as well as a pivotal point in his career. *—Cub Koda*

The Amazing James Brown / 1961 / King ♦♦♦♦
Well on his way to becoming Soul Brother Number One, James Brown's recordings are exhilarative, which can be attributed to his urgent delivery. His uptempo numbers illuminate the Georgia native's trademark baritone, while his ballads are impressively as smooth as silk. The two singles to see chart action from this album are "Just You and Me, Darling" and "Lost Someone." The former has that locomotive rhythm and chanting background vocals complemented by the Godfather's wailing cry—vintage James Brown. The latter, a pleading ballad, has its tender moments charged with Brown's weeping sighs. His ability to bring excitement to his upbeat songs goes without saying, but his serenading side is as majestic as some of the best melodramatic groups of the day. He goes from his stalwart vocals to a silky tone. This album houses quite a few of those recordings. *—Craig Lytle*

James Browns Presents His Band & Five Other Great Artists / Oct. 1961 / King ♦♦♦♦
James Brown on organ, along with Henry Moore, Hank Marr, Clifford Scott, Jimmy Forrest, and Herb Hardesty, explodes on 12 scorching R&B instrumentals. King Records reissued these same tracks, the same year (1961), under the same catalog number as *Jump Around*. "Hold It" b/w "The Scratch," a "Night Train" sound-alike, was the first single; it was followed by "Suds," "Cross Firing" (the B-side of "Lost Someone"), and "Night Train." These tracks have held up well and are as invigorating as ever. A sax, Brown's organ, and a bop-influenced bass dominate. Four of these tracks are available on the CD *Soul Pride: The Instrumentals (1960-69)*. *—Andrew Hamilton*

Shout & Shimmy / 1962 / King ♦♦♦
On an album named after the R&B Top 40 title hit and featuring the 1961 Top Ten R&B hit "I Don't Mind," James Brown & His Famous Flames can be heard making music in the variety of styles—blues, Little Richard-style rock, doo wop—out of which they eventually would develop the James Brown funk sound of the mid-'60s. (Actually, the music is older than the copyright date, since King cobbled the LP together from non-charting singles and B-sides dating back to 1958.) It's a more primitive sound than they would later achieve, but remains infectious. [*Shout & Shimmy* was reissued in 1963 under the title *Excitement—Mr. Dynamite*.] *—William Ruhlmann*

Tours the U.S.A. / 1962 / King ♦♦♦
This material from 1961 and 1962 includes several instrumentals. *—George Bedard*

★ **Live at the Apollo** / Jan. 1963 / Polydor ♦♦♦♦♦
In 1963, James Brown had earned a handful of hits on the R&B charts and had won a reputation as one of the most dynamic performers in the nation, but he hadn't yet made a record that reflected the full range of his musical personality or his magnetic stage presence. *Live at the Apollo* killed these two birds with one smoking hot platter; while this performance predates the brittle but powerful funk grooves which would later make Brown the most sampled man in show business and focuses on his earlier and (relatively) more conventional hits, the building blocks of his pioneering sound are all here in high-octane live versions of "I'll Go Crazy," "Think" and especially the frantic closing performance of "Night Train," while the ten-minute-plus rendition of "Lost Someone" captures the sound of Brown baring his soul with an almost unbearable intensity, which drives the audience into a manic chorus of shouts and screams. Brown's band (which at this time included Bobby Byrd and St. Clair Pinckney) is in stellar form, tight as a fist (especially the horn section) and supporting their leader with both strength and subtlety, but Brown is truly the star of this show, and by the end of these thirty-two minutes, no one will doubt that James really was the Hardest Working Man in Show Business (and this without even seeing him dance!), and his communication with his audience is nothing short of astounding. While James Brown would later make more amazing music in the studio, *Live at the Apollo* left no doubt in anyone's mind that he was a live performer without peer, and that his talent could communicate just as strongly on tape as in person; a watershed album, both for James Brown and for the burgeoning soul music movement. *—Mark Deming*

Prisoner of Love / Sep. 1963 / King ♦♦♦
In the wake of James Brown's first substantial pop hit, "Prisoner of Love," King rushed out this LP, as usual drawing upon old singles ("Try Me," "Lost Someone," "Bewildered"), B-sides ("Waiting in Vain," the organ instrumental "[Can You] Feel It [Part 1]"), and Brown's then-current single, "Signed, Sealed, and Delivered" (not the Stevie Wonder song). The idea seemed to be to put together a collection in the medium-tempo, string-filled, lovelorn style of the hit, so there was a lot of pleading on this record. Brown would always be more interested in the dancefloor than the bedroom, but he was a convincing romantic beggar, so the album's loose concept held together. *—William Ruhlmann*

Pure Dynamite! Live at the Royal / Feb. 1964 / King ♦♦♦♦♦
It has only eight songs, it's less than half an hour long, and two of the songs are studio tracks with overdubbed audience noise. It's not nearly as well-known as his live '60s albums recorded at the Apollo, but *Pure Dynamite!*, recorded live at Baltimore's Royal Theater in 1963, is nearly as good. This is decidedly more raucous than his 1962 *Live at the Apollo*, with the balance leaning toward uptempo ravers like "Shout and Shimmy," "Signed, Sealed, and Delivered," and the set-closing "Good Good Lovin'," all of which are positively kinetic. To break up the pace, there are some R&B torch ballads, including the song without which no James Brown show was complete, "Please, Please, Please." It's also fair to say that the recording quality is primitive, even more so than on his 1962 Apollo gig; the vocals are a bit hollow, and the audience occasionally overwhelms the music with its noisy enthusiasm. Somehow, it doesn't matter much. The performances are so energetic that you can't help getting caught up in the excitement. *—Richie Unterberger*

Showtime / Apr. 1964 / Smash ♦♦
A transition album. James Brown's contract with King Records had a few more legs, and the Godfather of Soul was handicapped in what he could wax for Smash Records, his new label. Hence, an album of remakes enhanced—or marred—by overdubbed applause. Some apparently don't have a problem with overdubbed applause, judging from the lofty prices record collectors ask and get for a copy. Brown does his best retooling on Louis Jordan's "Caledonia," "Ain't Nobody Here But Us Chickens," and "Somebody Changed the Lock on My Door," but the canned applause causes flashbacks to '60s sitcoms. *—Andrew Hamilton*

Out of Sight / Sep. 1964 / Smash ♦♦♦
Smash Records first released this collection in 1964 when James Brown made his highly publicized moved from the King label. An odd album; outside of a few funky numbers, the material consists of standards—songs more commonly sung by Frank Sinatra and Nat King Cole, such as "I Wanna Be Around," "Mona Lisa," "Come Rain or Shine," "Nature Boy," and others. Brown does a good job; the man could actually sing ballads—in the '50s and early '60s he made a reputation singing about love changes and could make you cry with his touching deliveries. But this was 1964, and Brown had a brand-new thing in the form of "Out of Sight," a horn-blaring, rhythmic dancefloor jam that he implodes on. For some reason, Smash put "Maybe the Last Time," one of Brown's best songs, on the flip side, but it was so dominant that it surfaced and became a staple of his concerts. Only three other cuts funk: "Somethin' Else," an early version of "I Got You," and "Good Rockin' Tonight." *—Andrew Hamilton*

Papa's Got a Brand New Bag / Aug. 1965 / Polygram ♦♦♦

James Brown Plays James Brown: Yesterday and Today / Nov. 1965 / Smash ♦♦

Mighty Instrumentals / 1966 / King ♦♦♦

I Got You (I Feel Good) / Jan. 1966 / King ♦♦♦
At the start of 1966, James Brown was at his peak as a crossover star, having hit the pop Top Ten twice in a row in the last six months, first with "Papa's Got a Brand New Bag," and then with his biggest-ever pop success, "I Got You (I Feel Good)." But Brown was a singles artist almost exclusively; for him, LPs simply constituted a different configuration in which to re-sell his singles. So, his '60s LPs consisted of his current hit plus previously released singles tracks. *The I Got You (I Feel Good)* LP was no exception: Leading off with the title track, it included songs that dated back to 1959's "Good, Good Loving." Of course, some of these tracks, such as "Lost Someone," "Night Train," and "Think," were among Brown's classics, so the collection on the whole is appealing, even if arbitrary. *—William Ruhlmann*

James Brown Plays New Breed / Mar. 1966 / Smash ♦♦♦

It's a Man's Man's Man's World / Aug. 1966 / King ♦♦♦
In the early '60s, James Brown tended to release two vocal albums a year, one in the summer and one in the winter. Each album was keyed to Brown's latest hit single, with the remainder of the record made up of previous Brown recordings; Brown did not record LPs as such. As late as mid-1966, this was still the case, and this album differed only in that it featured not only the title track, an R&B number one/pop Top Ten hit, and its B-side, "Is It Yes or Is It No?," but also an earlier 1966 single, "Ain't That a Groove (Part 1 and Part 2)," along with eight oldies, such as "Bewildered" and "I Don't Mind" (two 1961 singles). As such, there was slightly more contemporary material here than usual, but at the same time, Brown's evolution into his funk period was beginning to make the juxtapositions of new and old material more jarring. *—William Ruhlmann*

Handful of Soul / Nov. 1966 / Smash ♦♦♦

Presenting the James Brown Show / Jan. 1967 / Smash ♦♦♦
Amazingly, no one has reissued this '60s original on CD. It represents the exciting *James Brown Show* of the mid-'60s supporting acts. Baby Lloyd opens like a ball of fire with "I Can't Get No Satisfaction" and "The Dog"; Vicki Anderson follows with two Motown classics: "Don't Mess With Bill" and "Nowhere to Run," and the Jewels, from Washington, D.C., radiate on "This Is My Story" and a roof-ripping "Something's Got a Hold on Me." James Crawford finishes with four cuts and the James Brown Orchestra takes you home with a reprise of "Satisfaction." The Godfather accompanies his protégés on the organ; the only artist omitted here from his live shows of this era is Elsie "TV Mama" Mae, a whopping 350-pound blues singer who electrified crowds with a sidesplitting rendition of "All of Me." *—Andrew Hamilton*

Sings Raw Soul / Mar. 1967 / Polydor ♦♦♦
Brown's '60s studio albums were often assembled with all the care and attention to sequencing of a grocery list, mixing disparate tracks that were frequently recorded years apart. *Raw Soul* is no exception, setting propulsive early funk like "Let Yourself Go" next to oldies retreads, concert recordings, slickly produced pop-soul ballads, and filler instrumentals. There *is* some excellent music: "Bring It Up," "Let Yourself Go," "Don't Be a Dropout," and "Money Won't Change You" (both parts of the last title are included) were all early funk hits, and are all on the *Star Time* box. Most of the rest is okay, but inessential unless you're building a complete JB library, the clear highlight being a frenetic 1966 live funk number, "Tell Me That You Love Me," that fades out at the height of its sub-two-minute frenzy. Reissued on CD in 1996. *—Richie Unterberger*

James Brown Plays the Real Thing / Jun. 1967 / Smash ♦♦♦
James Brown's new deal with Smash Records gave him the creative freedom to pump out instrumentals as well as vocals. The funky soul singer is as funky an organist as he is a singer. He lays down gritty renditions of popular hits: "Jimmy Mack," "Bernadette," "Funky Broadway," and "I Never Loved a Man the Way I Love You." He cops a cool groove on Cannonball Adderley's "Mercy, Mercy, Mercy" and a couple of solid originals, such as "Peewee's Groove in D," which showcase saxophonist Alfred "Pee Wee" Ellis. *—Andrew Hamilton*

Cold Sweat / Aug. 1967 / King ♦♦♦♦♦
If "Cold Sweat" was a revolutionary single in 1967, clearly pointing the way to funk music, the *Cold Sweat* LP at least promised to be something new in James Brown's catalog

as well. Where Brown's albums had been collections containing his current single and miscellaneous older tracks, this one proclaimed on its cover, "All New," "Great Songs," "Never In," "An Album." This was not quite true. While half of the tracks had been recorded during the first half of 1967, the other half (though previously unreleased) dated from 1964. That wasn't the main problem with the album, though. Having taken a giant step forward with "Cold Sweat," Brown spent the rest of the album stepping back, covering standards such as "Nature Boy" and "Mona Lisa" (associated with Nat King Cole), "Fever" (Little Willie John), "Stagger Lee" (Lloyd Price), and other oddities, including "I Loves You Porgy" from *Porgy & Bess*. Brown was never anybody's idea of a smooth ballad singer, and this material was all the more incongruous when packaged with his most remarkable slab of funk yet. *—William Ruhlmann*

James Brown Presents His Show of Tomorrow / 1968 / King ♦♦

Soul Party / 1968 / Polydor ♦♦♦

A Thinking About Little Willie/A Few Nice Things / 1968 / King ♦♦♦♦

I Can't Stand Myself When You Touch Me / Mar. 1968 / King ♦♦♦

This is the Japanese Polydor CD replica of the original 1968 James Brown King album *I Can't Stand Myself*. The majority of these tracks have been reissued elsewhere, which makes this a luxury purchase mainly for the most avid Brown collector. Containing the album's 12-track original playing order (sorry, no bonus cuts) and cover art including the Vox advertisement urging, "Kids stay in school and play better." The music is unquestionably some of the funkiest recorded by Brown. "I Can't Stand Myself When You Touch Me," "There Was a Time," "Get It Together," and the instrumentals "Funky Soul #1," "The Soul of J. B.," and, from the pen of Brown's mentor Little Willie John, "Need Your Love So Bad." *—Al Campbell*

I Got the Feelin' / Apr. 1968 / Polydor ♦♦♦

James Brown Plays Nothing But Soul / Aug. 1968 / King ♦♦♦

Live at the Apollo / Aug. 1968 / Polydor ♦♦♦♦♦

As a whole, this double album is pretty erratic—there are a bunch of torchy R&B ballads that were somewhat anachronistic in light of the explosive funk innovations Brown was unleashing in the studio during this time, and some of those funk hits are reprised here in super-brief versions that seem to cut off before they have a chance to get started. On the other hand, some of it is as essential as anything else Brown ever recorded. In particular, the 20-minute medley of "Let Yourself Go/There Was a Time/I Feel All Right/Cold Sweat" is a magnificent, seamless ball of energy, a landmark performance in the evolution of soul and funk. Other highlights are "Bring It Up" and an 11-minute "It's a Man's, Man's, Man's World." *—Richie Unterberger*

James Brown Sings Out of Sight / Sep. 1968 / Polydor ♦♦♦

Brown actually recorded this album in 1964, during his brief alliance with Smash; a court injunction from King Records prevented its release at the time, and it wasn't issued until four years later. Despite the presence of the groundbreaking title track, it's not as funky a set as you might expect. Most of the numbers are surprisingly conservative reworkings of pop standards and R&B oldies, with decidedly non-funky arrangements (by Sammy Lowe) that often employ strings and large bands. High points are "Maybe the Last Time," a gospel-ish R&B throwback, and an interesting, jazzy take on "I Got You" that predates the much more celebrated 1965 hit version. Reissued on CD in 1996. *—Richie Unterberger*

Say It Loud, I'm Black and I'm Proud / Mar. 1969 / Polydor ♦♦♦

Although historical evaluations of Brown's work during the last half of the '60s tend to focus on the innovative funk of his biggest hit singles, his repertoire—both live and on record—in fact remained pretty versatile. Like his other '60s studio albums, *Say It Loud* is more R&B/pop-conscious than a lot of listeners would expect, mixing the funky monsters "Say It Loud I'm Black and I'm Proud" and "Licking Stick" with soul ballads. It's a notch above similar albums from earlier in the decade, however, in that the slow numbers are usually gritty slow burns that eschew syrupy orchestration. Reissued on CD in 1996, it includes a couple of minor hits ("Goodbye My Love" and "I Guess I'll Have to Cry, Cry, Cry") that don't turn up on the *Star Time* box set. Reissued on CD in 1996. *—Richie Unterberger*

Gettin' Down to It / May 1969 / Polydor ♦♦

It's a Mother / Aug. 1969 / Polydor ♦♦♦

The Popcorn / Aug. 1969 / Polydor ♦♦♦

Ain't It Funky / Jan. 1970 / King ♦♦

Sex Machine / Aug. 1970 / Polydor ♦♦♦♦♦

A double live outing from Brown's seminal 1970 J.B.'s lineup, including Bootsy Collins, Clyde Stubblefield, Fred Wesley, Maceo Parker, Bobby Byrd, and many more. While it's a cut below *Love Power Peace* in documenting this lineup live, Brown and his band still smoke, tearing into extended versions of funk classics like "Sex Machine" (nearly eleven minutes), "Brother Rapp," "Give It Up Or Turnit-a Loose," and "Mother Popcorn," plus a healthy quotient of earlier soul material sprinkled in between. *—Steve Huey*

Sho Is Funky Down Here / Apr. 1971 / King ♦♦

Hot Pants / Aug. 1971 / Polydor ♦♦♦

Brown left his label King after 12 successful, if not always peaceful, years. *Hot Pants* marks his first effort for Polydor, a bigger outfit that was able to give him a larger budget, better presentation, and, most importantly, artistic freedom. The original set of the J.B.'s with Bootsy Collins had dissolved, and Brown and his newer band had only been together for a few months. Although the original J.B.'s were more rock-based and fiery, *Hot Pants* proves that the reformed band was more ductile. It was at this point where trombonist Fred Wesley became the bandleader and the band became even more efficient than the earlier group. The leisurely "Blues and Pants" has a great bass pattern from Fred Thomas and Wesley's sly horn charts. "Can't Stand It" is a busier take on the 1968 hit "I Can't Stand Myself." The most recognizable track is the title song, though the version heard here is less potent than the complete take (featured on "Escape-ism," the early-'90s CD reissue of *Hot Pants*, clocking in at 19-plus minutes). While that might be cause for alarm for some, it is truly instructive. The track goes to the bridge, stays there, and has great studio chatter between Brown and his band and solos from Wesley and saxophonist St. Clair Pinckney. This album features only four tracks and is basically Brown getting acquainted with his new band, but the camaraderie makes it worth listening to. *—Jason Elias*

Revolution of the Mind / Dec. 1971 / Polydor ♦♦♦

Subtitled "Recorded Live at the Apollo, Vol. III," *Revolution of the Mind* presents a 1971 James Brown concert performance, which means the set list is given over largely to the singles Brown had released over the previous couple of years, including "Give It Up or Turnit a Loose," "Super Bad," and "Make It Funky," all of them groove tunes with chanted slogans for lyrics, plus a medley of slightly less recent hits and the occasional real oldie, such as "Try Me." Brown concentrates on communicating with his audience, generating female screams, for example, when he comes out against dieting "'cause the more you got, the more I want." On the one hand, this can be considered indulgent—Brown spends the nearly 13 minutes of "Make It Funky" introducing the band by asking each member where he's from—on the other hand, the aural evidence suggests it went over better in the theater than it does in your living room. That wasn't true of the first *Live at the Apollo*, though. [Initially released as a double-LP, *Revolution of the Mind* was reissued on CD in 1993.] *—William Ruhlmann*

Soul Brother No. 1 / 1971 / Polydor ♦♦

Super Bad / 1971 / King ♦♦♦

There It Is / Jun. 1972 / Polydor ♦♦♦♦♦

Brown's Polydor debut, *Hot Pants*, was nothing more than an inferior remake of the title track baited with a batch of half-baked vamps. *There It Is*, his second Polydor studio album, was a marked improvement. Not that he put much into this one either. This 1972 effort collected five of his best early-'70s tracks and mixed in minimal filler. "Talkin' Loud and Sayin' Nothing" and "There It Is (Parts 1 and 2)," with its bebop-style horns, were both innovative and hard driving to a fault. The hilarious "I'm a Greedy Man," with its hypnotic bass and help from Bobby Byrd, has Brown firing off such witticisms as "I'm a greedy man / yes I are" and "Taking care of my business/now run tell that." Brown wasn't all fun and games on this one. "King Heroin," an eerie, laid-back jazz offering, has him reciting chilling poetry about the ills of the drug. "Public Enemy #1 (Pt. 1)" attempts to re-create the same message. By "Public Enemy #2 (Pt. 2)" he is doing nothing but connecting the same dots and screaming himself hoarse to little effect. Although by this point Brown was best known for his dance tracks, he still had a way with a ballad. "Who am I," a song that had been kicking around his oeuvre for aeons, gets a strong arrangement and has Brown giving an impassioned performance. Like many of his '70s albums, *There It Is* was out of circulation for close to 20 years until it was reissued on CD in mid-'90s. It's well worth picking up. *—Jason Elias*

Get on the Good Foot / Nov. 1972 / Polydor ♦♦♦♦

In an era where Brown went on to make three studio doubles, *Get on the Good Foot* was the first. This 1972 album finds Brown having great chemistry with both his newer J.B.'s and the New York session players. The title track is particularly stunning. "Get on the Good Foot" was so off-the-cuff and nonpareil, he couldn't have replicated the formula even if he wanted to. "I Got a Bag of My Own," on the other hand, sounds forced and synthetic. Although Brown was known for his new product, this album has him recycling some of his King singles. Doing so-so remakes of "Cold Sweat" and "Ain't It a Groove" could be taken as an attempt for Brown to ease some of his old catalog to his new label. It was a nice try, but you should stick with the originals. Not surprisingly, *Get on the Good Foot* does have its share of throwaway cuts. "Recitation By Hank Ballard" is a spoken-word effort with Ballard extolling his buddy's virtues as well as giving unsolicited advice about the perils of showbiz. "Dirty Harri," a lukewarm instrumental, goes nowhere fast for all of its six-plus minutes. The 1995 CD reissue offered a track that was previously available only on the international release, the warm "I Know It's True," which hearkens back to Brown's '60s-ballad style as he turns in a genuinely affecting performance. Although *Get on the Good Foot* only managed to yield two hits, the album is one of his more varied and fun efforts. *—Jason Elias*

Black Caesar / Feb. 1973 / Polydor ♦♦♦

After Isaac Hayes kicked his career into high gear with the popular and influential score for *Shaft*, and Curtis Mayfield managed the same feat with *Superfly*, seemingly every major soul star of the early 1970s ended up doing music for a blaxploitation film, and James Brown was certainly no exception. Brown sang the title tune for Larry Cohen's idiosyncratic black crime film *Black Caesar*, as well as performing ten other pieces for the movie's soundtrack (most written by Brown in collaboration with Fred Wesley); Barry Devorzon's lead-off cut, "Down and Out In New York City," sets up the picture's story, while most of the other five vocal cuts reflect the film's narrative in one way or another (although "Make It Good To Yourself" seems to be here mainly because of it's high funk quotient, and on "Mama Feelgood," Brown appropriately hands the vocal chores over to Lynn Collins). Like most soundtrack albums of the period, *Black Caesar* sounds rather scattershot, especially when the music is divorced from the film's narrative, and this isn't one of Brown's stellar albums of the 1970s; however, there are several top-notch tracks, especially the much-sampled "The Boss", the potent "Make It Good to Yourself," and the melodramatic "Mama's Dead," and Fred Wesley's superb horn charts, Jimmy Nolen's percussive guitar, and Jabo Starks' dead-on-the-one drumming make even the weaker instrumental cuts worth a quick listen (though just try to imagine a chase scene cut to something with the power of "Mother Popcorn"—now THAT would be a movie!). *—Mark Deming*

Slaughter's Big Rip-Off / Jul. 1973 / Polydor ♦♦♦

James Brown was extremely busy in 1973. Not only did he continue to release two-plus albums a year, he was also producing and writing for the J.B.'s, plus other acts. During the early '70s Brown was still doing great work, but not much of it shows up here. While the earlier *Black Caesar* soundtrack found Brown engaged enough to offer great tracks, particularly, "The Boss" and "Down and Out in New York City," this one, also a soundtrack, finds him preoccupied. The swaggering and slick title track kicks things off here. "Trying to Get Over" and "Big Strong" both fall into the traps of bad movie music. Since an album of Brown doing chase themes seems horrifying, *Slaughter's Big Rip-Off* does offer more. Throughout this effort he recycles some of his classic tracks; the oddly titled "Happy for the Poor" is actually a Latinized version of the J.B.'s 1971 single, "Gimme Some More." He goes back even further for his own 1970 classic, "Brother Rapp," which makes an appearance and has the "live" crowd removed. While it's unclear why he would resort to such odd song choices, he had one more shocker in store. "Sexy, Sexy, Sexy" uses the exact backing track from his 1967 hit "Money Won't Change You," with new vocals and lyrics on top. The sad part is that it works too well. While *Slaughter's Big Rip-Off* proved that he wasn't going to be a soundtrack innovator, the idea of Brown in the film-scoring business has its own appeal. *—Jason Elias*

The Payback / Dec. 1973 / Polydor ♦♦♦♦♦

Originally released in 1973 as a sprawling two-LP set, *The Payback* was one of James Brown's most ambitious albums of the 1970s, and also one of his best, with Brown and his band (which in 1974 still included Fred Wesley, Maceo Parker, St. Clair Pinckney, Jimmy Nolen and Jabo Starks) relentlessly exploring the outer possibilities of the James Brown groove. Stretching eight cuts out over the space of nearly 73 minutes, *The Payback* is long on extended rhythmic jamming, and by this time Brown and his band had become such a potent and nearly telepathic combination that the musicians were able pull out lengthy solos while still maintaining some of the most hypnotic funk to be found anywhere, and on the album's best songs—the jazzy "Time Is Running Out Fast," the relentless "Shoot Your Shot," the tight-wound "Mind Power," and the bitter revenge fantasy of the title cut—the tough, sinuous rhythms and the precise interplay between the players is nothing short of a wonder to behold. And even the album's lower-key cuts (such as the lovelorn "Doing the Best That I Can" and "Forever Suffering") sink their hooks into the listener and pull you in; quite simply, this is remarkable stuff, and even Brown's attempts at lyrical relevance (which were frankly getting a bit shaky at this point in his career) are firmly rooted enough to sound convincing. *The Payback* turned out to be one of James Brown's last inarguably great albums before he hit a long fallow streak in the mid- to late '70s, but no one listening to this set would ever imagine that this was the work of an artist (or a band) about to run out of gas. *—Mark Deming*

Hell / Jul. 1974 / Polydor ♦♦♦♦♦

Brown's early-'70s run of classic singles and good-to-great albums is still impressive. *Hell* was the double album released a year after the gold selling *The Payback*. To some, the title might put this effort in the realm of kitsch, but in many ways *Hell* was one of Brown's strongest albums. The album was the pinnacle of his work as the Minister of the Super New New Heavy Funk. From the tough and nimble Latin rhythms of "Coldblooded," and "Sayin' It and Doin' It" to the title track, all are prime pre-disco Brown. "My Thang" is probably as hard and unrelenting as he got without spontaneously combusting. The biggest surprise of *Hell* is that no matter how odd the song choices seemed, practically everything worked, excluding a few key songs of course. Both "When the Saints Go Marching In" and "Stormy Monday" don't belong in James Brown's catalog, let alone the same album. Ballad-wise, Brown fares better. "These Foolish Things Remind Me of You" has him getting all warm and fuzzy as he inexplicably throws in an "I'm hurt, I'm hurt" for good measure. That song, as well as the weepers "A Man Has to Go to the Cross Road Before He Finds Himself" and "Sometime," were produced by David Matthews who could always get good ragged yet poised vocals from Brown. Although Brown did roll snake eyes on all of side three, he did leave *Hell* on a good note. "Papa Don't Take No Mess" is laid-back, funky jazz that's worth each of its 13-plus minutes. Despite a few detours, *Hell* is worth listening to. *—Jason Elias*

Reality / 1974 / Polydor ♦

By this point Brown's insane schedule was catching up to him. He seemingly had singles or albums coming out on a weekly basis, and *Reality* finds him at an artistic impasse. Released in late 1974, *Reality* was one of the few of his '70s albums recorded entirely in NY, with and without the J.B.'s. The title track has him complaining about something or another with the background singers goading him on with, "The Godfather, sing it James Brown." The best thing about the song is David Sanborn's sax solo near the fade. "Funky President" is one of Brown's most underrated songs and manages to hit the lyrical messages. "All for One" misses by a mile. In retrospect it was foolish to except a "fun" album from Brown during this time. He seemed to view America as a doomed nation, and considered the gas shortage, Watergate, and unemployment lines as signs of the coming apocalypse. A hint of sadness and ennui cloaks over the album. "The Twist" (his own song, not Chubby Checker's), is a lightweight funk offering and a red flag that he was hitting a serious writer's block. Other signs of desperation were apparent as well, like his cutesy cover of the always hideous "Don't Fence Me In" or "Who Can I Turn To," with Brown's final whines on the song akin to fingernails screeching a chalkboard. Including some sped-up dance tracks and his worst ballads on record, *Reality* was proof that Brown could indeed turn in an album that was a real downer. *—Jason Elias*

Sex Machine Today / May 1975 / Polydor ♦

The most innovative R&B artist of the late '60s and early '70s, James Brown had fallen well behind the curve by 1975 when he tried to retread an old hit with *Sex Machine Today*. "I admit we wasn't as funky as we used to be, but we was tryin' harder," he muttered at the top of side two, and it was a painfully accurate admission. Brown was at a peak of self-mythologizing; his name appeared on the LP label four times, accompanied by the sobriquets "the Godfather of Soul" and "Minister of New New Super Heavy Funk." But his legendary band had fragmented and he seemed to have run out of ideas. It wasn't enough to call your music "disco soul," let out a howl, and shout, "Sex machine!" every few minutes. Once, Brown had led funk music in new directions, but now he seemed to be doing the best he could just to borrow others' styles and invoke old glories. *—William Ruhlmann*

Everybody's Doin' the Hustle & Dead on the Double Bump / Sep. 1975 / Polydor ♦♦

Despite its ludicrous title, *Everybody's Doin' the Hustle & Dead on the Double Bump* found James Brown making more of an effort to connect with current musical trends and create coherent song structures than he had on the previous *Sex Machine Today*. The album, in essence, consisted of Brown's two moderately successful R&B singles of the period, "Hustle!!! (Dead on It)" and "Superbad, Superslick," filled out with remakes—"Papa got a brand new bag," Brown noted at one point. But the reliance on keyboard textures was new for Brown, and he sounded more enthusiastic, especially in interplay with saxophonist Maceo Parker, than in recent efforts. This wasn't great Brown, by any means, but it suggested he wasn't quite through yet. *—William Ruhlmann*

Hot / 1976 / Polydor ♦♦♦

Get Up Offa That Thing / Jul. 1976 / Polydor ♦♦♦

During the disco era of the late '70s, James Brown didn't have as many major hits as he enjoyed in the 1950s, 1960s, and early '70s. But he was still coming up with some captivating funk grooves, and his late-'70s output should not be ignored. Although 1976's *Get Up Offa That Thing* falls short of essential, it's a focused, rewarding LP that has a lot going for it. The title song, a sweaty funk gem, became a hit, and almost as appealing are "I Refuse to Lose" and "Can't Take It With You." These tracks follow the funk principle that Brown perfected in the 1960s: find an addictive groove and work it to death. Meanwhile, the romantic "You Took My Heart" is closer to smooth Northern soul than the type of raw Southern-style soul Brown is best known for. And "Home Again" is a 12-bar blues number with jazz leanings; the tune would have been perfect for a Jimmy Witherspoon session. Again, this LP isn't quite essential, but it's easily recommended to seasoned Brown fans. *—Alex Henderson*

Bodyheat / Dec. 1976 / Polydor ♦♦

Bodyheat is a low-key effort filled with ballads and female backup vocals. "Woman," set to the tune of "It's a Man's, Man's, Man's World," recasts that song's message. "Got a new kiss," Brown says in the seductive "Kiss in 77," and he also covers "What the World Needs Now Is Love," extending the romantic tone. "James Brown—A New Sound," reads the album jacket, and in his liner notes, Brown signs himself, "With the feeling of a new beginning...a new sound." The heat, clearly, is supposed to generate a Phoenix-like rebirth for Brown, which it didn't quite succeed in doing, perhaps because the "new sound" turned out to be suspiciously close to that of Earth, Wind & Fire. *—William Ruhlmann*

Mutha's Nature / 1977 / Polydor ♦♦

On *Mutha's Nature*, James Brown returned to a bass-heavy groove sound with a new J.B.'s band, which made for a funkier result than on recent albums, but he still wasn't coming up with slogans to match those of old—"Give Me Some Skin" and "If You Don't Give a Dogone About It" just didn't rank with "Say It Loud, I'm Black and I'm Proud." And given that Brown largely buried his vocals in the mix, it wouldn't have been easy to tell if he did have something to say. (One time you could hear him, though, was on a cover of Gershwin's "Summertime" that Brown rewrote into a vaguely religious/environmentalist message song.) Brown hadn't been humbled by his recent lack of commercial success: "the King, as you've named me, has come back to set our musical record straight again like Beethoven, Bach, Brahms, and now Brown," he wrote in his liner notes. But the accomplishments didn't match the rhetoric. *—William Ruhlmann*

Jam/1980's / Mar. 1978 / Polydor ♦♦

The mid- to late '70s were commercially difficult for Brown. Key members of his band the J.B.'s left, most going to Parliament/Funkadelic. By the mid-'70s, Brown began to slide down to the lowest regions of the charts. The whole disco era took Brown by surprise, and in response he often came to the party testy, often making music that was too fast and one-dimensional to dance to. 1978's *Jam/1980's* was a welcome change and a chance for him to steal back horn riffs from the Brecker Brothers and the Average White Band. This was his first album in years where Brown was in good spirits (all the way through, that is). Through much trial and error (Brown's albums from 1975-1977), he finally attained a sense of nonchalance and actually revamped the way he thought about rhythm. On most of the cuts, the bass is elastic and the drums are an afterthought. "Jam," while good, is the type of showbizzy funk he did in the '80s and beyond. The album does get better. "The Spank," with its wry horn chart and bass heavy mix, is the heart of this effort. The rest of the cuts adhere to the not great song but great groove mentality. No one's ever going to know what Brown's intention on "Eyesight" was about, but the easy off-time shuffle of "Nature" will still pack a dancefloor. The dance or bust mentality of *Jam/1980's* may be a little monotonous. In fact, Brown's heartfelt tribute to Elvis Presley, "Love Me Tender," the single B-side to "The Spank," should have been included here. This effort is proof that Brown's good work didn't stop with *The Payback*. *—Jason Elias*

Take a Look at Those Cakes / Dec. 1978 / Polydor ♦♦♦

James Brown helpfully offers his own review of this album on the back of the LP jacket: "*Take a Look at Those Cakes* is my greatest since *The Payback*," he writes. Never trust an artist to rate his or her own work. The (near) title track, "For Goodness Sakes, Look at Those Cakes," is Brown's 11-minute tribute to the female derrière, but it doesn't match such classics of the somewhat limited genre as "Shake Your Booty." It does have a percolating rhythm track, however, indicating that Brown is at least keeping up with dance music trends. Still, whatever the never-humble Brown may have thought, this album did not represent a comeback. —*William Ruhlmann*

The Original Disco Man / Jul. 1979 / Polydor ✦✦✦✦
This effort finds Brown staking claim to a genre that he was indisputably partially responsible for. But by the late '70s, Brown as an innovator of rhythm was having a difficult time getting hits. As singles like "The Spank" and "Take a Look at Those Cakes" failed to set the charts ablaze, Brown—and probably his label—felt some changes should be made. *The Original Disco Man* pairs him with Muscle Shoals producer Brad Shapiro and is one of those rare efforts that gets better with each play. Shapiro was one of the more in-demand producers with Jackie Moore, Millie Jackson, and Joe Simon among the most famous of his credits. But it took Brown to take his sound to another level. For this effort, Shapiro has complete control and had a hand in all of the album's five original tracks. If Brown felt remorse that he didn't offer nary a song or lyric, he didn't let on. In fact *The Original Disco Man* finds Brown animated and invigorated, due in part to the band. Featuring such luminaries as bassist David Hood and Roger Hawkins on drums, the players here are better than any latter-day J.B.'s Brown could piece together. "It's Too Funky in Here" is chock full of Brown's growls, grunts, and non sequiturs. Musically, like the rest of the album, it's more of Shapiro's mix of soul/disco rather than of a replication of Brown's production style. Brown sounds right at home on this effort. "Star Generation," a track filled with dancy bass patterns and country guitar fills, has him making magic from lyrics as simple as "watch him rock." Although the masterful title track is a little self-congratulatory, Brown certainly was due. As the backup girls sing the suitably flattering chorus, Brown screams, "You tell 'em you tell 'em." That song in particular proves that Shapiro was one of the best producers Brown had worked with. As a Southern disco effort and a Brown album, *The Original Disco Man* more than gets the job done. —*Jason Elias*

People / Mar. 1980 / Polydor ✦✦
In early 1980, James Brown had an R&B singles-chart entry with the ballad "Regrets," which served as the leadoff track and only respectable tune on this mediocre album of disco retreads. The low point was "That's Sweet Music," which found Brown paying tribute to all forms of pop music, from Loretta Lynn to "new wave rock." You could blame songwriter, arranger, and producer Brad Shapiro instead of Brown this time, but whoever was responsible, Brown's music continued to deteriorate. —*William Ruhlmann*

Soul Syndrome / Dec. 1980 / Rhino ✦✦✦
By 1980 James Brown was slightly adrift. His 1979 album, *The Original Disco Man*, failed to light a commercial fire, and its follow-up, *People*, seemed to fly into the cutout bins. Brown cut his losses and left Polydor—his home for over a decade—for one album for Henry Stone's T.K. While this doesn't have Brown bubbling over with innovation, he still provided a more substantial alternative to disco. The first track, "Rapp Payback (Where Iz Moses?)," at first is a clumsy attempt at trying to get praise from the burgeoning rap scene as he sings, "I know you heard of Master Gee / But you didn't hear nothing / About J.B." It then merges into a sped-up version of "The Payback," which would be blasphemous if it didn't rock like nobody's business. The off-the-cuff remake of "Mashed Potatoes" has Brown reuniting with Bobby Byrd as he calls out "taters." Shortly afterward they both go through a travelogue of cities and states like it's "Night Train" all over again. *Soul Syndrome* has Brown at least a little more chipper, but he was still bereft of ideas. The inane "Funky Men" would be garbage if it weren't for a reggae/funk guitar riff and a Latin horn arrangement. The cautionary "Smokin' and Drinkin'" only perks up when Brown begins to cough for close to a minute on the fade. The last track, like most of *Soul Syndrome*, wasn't overly concerned with the future as he closes with an instrumental of "Honky Tonk." Although this isn't essential, *Soul Syndrome* finds Brown engaged and that always makes for a potent product. —*Jason Elias*

Nonstop! / Apr. 1981 / Polydor ✦✦✦
By the time of this release, James Brown and Polydor had parted ways, and Brown was recording for T.K. Records. Thus, this is a contractual obligation release, the last album on Brown's ten-year Polydor deal, and it is perfunctory, consisting of rhythmic remakes of Brown evergreens with titles like "Popcorn 80s" and "Super Bull/Super Bad." Released with zero promotion, it sank without a trace, Brown's first album in memory not even to make the R&B charts. —*William Ruhlmann*

Mean on the Scene / 1982 / Audio Fidelity ✦✦✦
In the late '70s and early '80s, no dance club was more loved and more hated than New York's Studio 54. The club's critics denounced it as pretentious, phony, overrated, elitist, exclusionary, and anti-working class—and, to be sure, it was all of those things. How elitist was Studio 54? So elitist that on occasion, major disco and R&B artists that it had booked had a hard time getting inside. But one artist who got inside without a problem was James Brown, who filled Studio 54 to capacity when he performed there in 1980. Released in 1982, *Mean on the Scene* documents the Godfather's appearance at the infamous club, where he performs a handful of songs from the 1950s, 1960s, and 1970s and is backed by a tight band. This LP isn't in a class with *Live at the Apollo* or the live double-LP *Sex Machine*; nonetheless, Brown is in fine form on two gems from the late '70s ("Get Up Offa That Thing" and "It's Too Funky in Here") as well as "Please, Please, Please," "Cold Sweat," and "Get on the Good Foot." Although not essential, *Mean on the Scene* is worth obtaining if you're a diehard Brown collector. —*Alex Henderson*

Bring It On! / 1983 / Churchill/Augusta ✦✦✦
James Brown moved to another small Southern independent label for his first studio album in three years. The title track was an attempt to return to the funk of an earlier time, but elsewhere Brown contented himself to cover old standards: "Tennessee Waltz," "The Night Time Is the Right Time," and "Your Precious Love" (which he filled with nostalgic reminiscences). Clearly, he remained a talented performer, and just as clearly he didn't have any idea what to do as a recording artist. —*William Ruhlmann*

Roots of a Revolution / 1984 / Polydor ✦✦✦✦✦
A double-CD retrospective of 1956-1964 recordings that charts Brown's progress from doo wop and Little Richard-influenced R&B to the verge of his groundbreaking mid-'60s funk. It doesn't include his biggest hits of the era (which are found on *Star Time*), but these are by and large equally exciting. Many fine overlooked R&B hits and B-sides are included like "Shout and Shimmy," "I've Got Money," the gospel-influenced "Oh Baby Don't You Weep," and "Maybe the Last Time," which inspired the Rolling Stones' "The Last Time." —*Richie Unterberger*

The CD of JB / 1985 / Polydor ✦✦✦✦✦
Polydor Records put a tentative toe into the emerging CD stream in 1985 and enjoyed surprising commercial success with this 56-minute, 18-song James Brown sampler. Rather than taking the standard greatest-hits approach, compiler Cliff White mixed familiar hits with rarities and even unreleased material, a shortened version of the later boxed-set formula. So, along with number one R&B hits like "Papa's Got a Brand New Bag," "Super Bad," and "Mother Popcorn," one heard a previously unreleased version of "It's a Man's World," two years older than the better-known one, and "I Got You," an early version of "I Got You (I Feel Good)," culled from the withdrawn *Out of Sight* LP. The effect, especially for a first-time listener, was to whet the appetite for more, though *The CD of JB* was more a highlights disc than a thorough anthology. —*William Ruhlmann*

Dead on the Heavy Funk (74–76) / 1985 / Polydor ✦✦✦✦✦
An excellent anthology spotlighting Brown's mid-'70s funk singles and extended jams. It's now been supplanted by other anthologies and greatest-hits collections on CD. But if you can find the vinyl, it's worth getting. —*Ron Wynn*

In the Jungle Groove / 1986 / Polydor ✦✦✦✦✦
In the Jungle Groove was one of the first (and still one of the best) collections of James Brown's transitional and hard-hitting soul/funk workouts from 1969-1971. While the first few numbers here feature Brown sidemen who were in on his mid-'60s hits, the majority feature the original J.B.'s outfit that helped the singer forge several extended and funk-defining sides during 1970. Faced with a walkout by his old band, Brown partially formed the J.B.'s out of the New Dapps from Cincinnati, taking aboard brothers Phelps "Catfish" Collins on guitar and William "Bootsy" Collins on bass; many of those ex-band members, namely drummer Clyde Stubblefield, saxophonist St. Clair Pinckney, and trombonist Fred Wesley, would eventually return to flesh out the J.B.'s lineup. The one constant was vocalist and organist Bobby Byrd, who had been with Brown since the singer's start in 1956. The incredible grooves Bootsy Collins and Stubblefield laid down here would become manna for hip-hop DJs over 15 years later, with the album's "Funky Drummer (Bonus Beat Reprise)" becoming one of the supreme breakbeats of all time. Filling out the collection are the very soulful pre-J.B.'s tracks "It's a Brand New Day" (tenor saxophonist Maceo Parker's only appearance on the disc) and the original "Funky Drummer," as well as the post-Bootsy cut "Hot Pants (She's Got to Use What She's Got to Get What She Wants)." All the numbers here are as in the pocket as you will ever hear in soul and funk. And while many of these tracks are found on various packages like Polydor's *Funk Power* and *Foundations of Funk*, *In the Jungle Groove* has the upper hand with its unequaled coverage of Brown's transformation from Soul Brother Number One to funk originator. —*Stephen Cook*

James Brown's Funky People / 1986 / Polydor ✦✦✦✦
The first in the wildly popular three-disc series, *James Brown's Funky People* is an outstandingly chunky collection that spotlights some of the many talented musicians associated with James Brown and his early- to mid-'70s People Records imprint. The material comprising this disc is split primarily between the J.B.'s, Fred Wesley both with and without the J.B.'s, and one of funk's original divas, Lyn Collins. "Gimme Some More," "Pass the Peas," "Givin' Up Food for Funk (Part 1)," and "Hot Pants Road" are the J.B.'s' offerings, spectacular studio recordings that highlight some of the band's best material for the label—material which at the time was often passed over in favor of their "proper" James Brown recordings. Fred Wesley, meanwhile, weighs in with the CD-only long version of "Damn Right, I Am Somebody (Parts 1 & 2)," before joining the J.B.'s on three more tracks, including the epic "(It's Not the Express) It's the J.B.'s Monaurail (Part 1)." This particular song, credited to the New J.B.'s, was recorded during one of the more traumatic times in the James Brown camp and, when compared to the other classics on this CD, doesn't have the same spark or fire. And if anyone questioned the odd spelling in the title, the band's request that if you don't know what a monorail is "check out Seattle" clears up any doubt. The Lyn Collins tracks feature a mono version of "Mama Feelgood" and the outstanding "Think (About It)," a song that would become an iconoclastic symbol of the funk era, heavily sampled by over 40 artists during the 1980s and 1990s. Included, too, is the bonus "Same Beat (Part 1)," recorded by Wesley and the J.B.'s on September 7, 1973, in New York. —*Amy Hanson*

The CD of JB II / 1987 / Polydor ✦✦✦✦✦
An excellent follow-up package that includes various James Brown hits from both the soul and funk eras, beginning with "Cold Sweat" and continuing into the '70s. It's also not as vital since the issue of the 1991 boxed set, but contains several fine songs. —*Ron Wynn*

Motherlode / 1988 / Polydor ✦✦✦✦
During the mid- and late '80s, after Brown and Polydor parted ways, the label began to reissue his work, some of which had been out of print for close to a decade. *Motherlode* is one of the finest compilations. Coming a few years after *In the Jungle Groove*, a compilation effort that culled some of Brown's harder-edged 1969-1971 tracks, this covers

1969-1973 and has the smoothness of a regular release effort. By this point, *Motherlode* producers Cliff White and Tim Rogers began to know more about Brown's "classic" work than he did and could do compilations where the tracks were all potent. This set starts off with an explosive live take of "There It Is" recorded at the Apollo in 1972. 1969's "She's the One" with his late-'60s orchestra has great guitar work from both Jimmy "Chank" Nolen and Alphonso "Country" Kellum. Since most of the tracks here weren't hits, or were even released, it provides a fresh interpretation of Brown's production style and the skills of his players. "Untitled Instrumental" features Brown's rock and psychedelic-influenced unit, with included guitarist Phelps Collins and his brother, Bootsy Collins, and his singular bass skills. The heart of this CD, however, is "People Drive Your Funky Soul." Originally on *Slaughter's Big Rip-Off* in a too brief 3:50 version, *Motherlode* brings the entire take to the public for the first time. The track, which manages to subtly cross reggae with bebop, again features Brown with his 1971-1975 band and it exhibits their chemistry and the band's unbelievable versatility. Although *Motherlode* has been lost in the shuffle due to a plethora of other compilations, this is still illuminating and enjoyable. *—Jason Elias*

Santa's Got a Brand New Bag / 1988 / Rhino ✦✦✦✦✦
Compiled from three Christmas LPs and various singles released by the "Santa of Soul" between 1966-1970, this 16-track collection includes one of James Brown's most over-the-top scream-fests on "Let's Make Christmas Mean Something this Year," while he gets loose and funky with "Soulful Christmas." Others have tried, but nobody can beat the Godfather of Soul on his ballad "Sweet Little Baby Boy," and nobody but the "Man who put the 'wet' in sweat" can pull off "Santa Claus Go Straight to the Ghetto." This is as essential as it gets. *—Dennis MacDonald*

James Brown's Funky People, Pt. 2 / Feb. 1988 / Polydor ✦✦✦✦
The second volume of material compiled from Brown's People Records label isn't quite as strong as the first, as it reaches for more obscurities—but those obscurities can be interesting, especially Brown's collaboration with Hank Ballard on "From the Love Side." Again, Brown wrote (or co-wrote), arranged, and produced much of the material, appearing on vocals several times, and the J.B.'s are featured heavily, whether as a unit or with individual members stepping out as solo acts. The highlights are Bobby Byrd's two 1971 R&B hits, "I Know You Got Soul" and "Hot Pants—I'm Coming, Coming, I'm Coming"; also featured are Marva Whitney, Lyn Collins, and Fred Wesley, among others. *—Steve Huey*

I'm Real / Jun. 1988 / Scotti Bros. ✦✦✦
A couple of years after Brown's return to the pop Top Ten with "Living in America," he decided to take a further shot at updating his sound with the help of the production team of Full Force. Despite the title's suggestion that Brown had regained his creative vitality, though, *I'm Real* is mostly a showcase for the writing and production of Full Force; Brown receives only one writing credit and one co-writing credit. Of course, since it's James Brown, some of the material is still worth hearing, but it's also clear why his comeback fizzled so quickly. *—Steve Huey*

Messing With the Blues / 1990 / Polydor ✦✦✦
Although he is most famous for his innovations in soul and funk music, James Brown never lost sight of his blues and R&B roots. His albums often placed surprisingly rootsy covers of old chestnuts alongside his groundbreaking polyrhythmic workouts. This double CD compiles thirty of the bluesiest items from his vast recorded legacy. Cut between 1957 and 1985, most of the tracks actually date from the '60s; many of these, in turn, were laid down in the early part of the decade, when J.B. was gradually evolving from his more conventional beginnings. The artists whose songs are covered here read like a *Who's Who* of R&B pioneers: Louis Jordan, Roy Brown, Memphis Slim, Ivory Joe Hunter, Fats Domino, Chuck Willis, Little Willie John, Billy Ward, Guitar Slim, and Bobby "Blue" Bland. It's quite an instructive insight into Brown's not-always-visible roots. It would be fair to say that this does not rank among his most exciting material, finding him in a smoother and more conventional style than his most innovative work. It is nonetheless always entertaining and accomplished, with Brown's love for this material shining through strongly in his committed interpretations. Especially intriguing are an 11-minute cover of Chuck Willis' "Don't Deceive Me" and a two-part, blues-based rap vamp from the early '70s, "Like It Is, Like It Was (The Blues)." The disc includes several unreleased cuts, alternate takes, and unedited versions of previously released songs. *—Richie Unterberger*

☆ **Star Time** / May 7, 1991 / Polydor ✦✦✦✦✦
When the four-disc *Star Time* box was released in 1991, James Brown's catalog sorely needed an overhaul; much of it was out of print, and what was available was hardly befitting of his magnitude. *Star Time* got everything right: it put Brown's hugely influential career into striking perspective, helping to complete his critical renaissance, and the richness of its music set a standard for box sets in general. It was no easy task to balance Brown's lengthy, multi-part funk workouts with the need to include all of his most significant tracks, and the compilers did an excellent job in deciding when and when not to truncate ("Cold Sweat," for example, *must* be heard in its entirety). There's nothing from *Live at the Apollo* (which should be experienced start to finish), and his last hurrah on the pop charts, "Living in America," is missing, but these 71 tracks cover all the other high points, and make an eloquent case for Brown as the greatest R&B artist of all time. Disc one covers Brown's early R&B years, when his pleading intensity helped lay the groundwork for soul music. Disc two, however, is where his genius truly crystallizes—it basically chronicles the birth of funk, as Brown gradually discards song structure in favor of working hard grooves; it also offers a picture of Brown's emergence as a bandleader and spokesman for black pride. Disc three features Brown's hardest funk, including his much-revered material with the Bootsy Collins band. Disc four traces Brown's later creative decline, yet he duplicated his former glories often enough to make this disc a surprisingly solid listen; plus, his massive impact on hip-hop is underlined on the last track, the Afrika Bambaataa duet "Unity." *Star Time* paved the way for several other excellent compilations which highlighted different parts of Brown's vast legacy, but as the definitive retrospective of one of the most important musicians of the 20th century (black or otherwise), it has yet to be equaled. *—Steve Huey*

Love Over-Due / Jul. 23, 1991 / Scotti Bros. ✦✦✦
Some recent James Brown, much of it delivered with fire and fury but little substance. Brown hasn't had a major hit since "I'm Real" in 1988, and there's nothing on this collection that seems like it will end the cold streak. *—Ron Wynn*

● **20 All-Time Greatest Hits!** / Oct. 22, 1991 / Polydor ✦✦✦✦✦
While Brown's 30-track *Solid Gold* collection would be the first-pick introductory disc if it made it to CD, this fine hits package certainly won't disappoint Brown neophytes looking for a way in. Covering his prime stretch from the late '50s through the early '70s, *20 All-Time Greatest Hits!* includes early R&B milestones ("Please, Please, Please"), epochal '60s sides ("Papa's Got a Brand New Bag, Pt. 1"), and latter-day funk classics ("Papa Don't Take No Mess, Pt. 1"). And that's not to mention such perennials as "Mother Popcorn," "Hot Pants," "Cold Sweat," and "Think." Start your Brown obsession here. *—Stephen Cook*

Is Back / 1992 / Hollywood ✦✦
Some recent James Brown material that just doesn't come close to equaling the quality of his past work. There's little that's hit material, and even less that longtime fans of Brown will treasure. It's good that he's still able to record, but someone should find him some good songs before turning him loose. *—Ron Wynn*

Universal James / 1992 / Scotti Bros. ✦✦✦
Given that samples of James Brown records constitute the very foundations of hip-hop, then in theory it wouldn't seem to be necessary to update the Godfather's sound one whit to help him score a hit record within the rap community. Yet 1992's *Universal James* is just that—a slick, ultra-commercial update of the James Brown aesthetic, complete with pale hip-hop beats which themselves are merely watered-down imitations of Brown's own groundbreaking peak material. From the opening track "Can't Get Any Harder" onward, the songs strain for rap credibility; instead of allowing Brown to find his own groove, the production constricts him, tailoring the music to what were the moment's prevailing trends. As a consequence, *Universal James* sounded dated within moments of its release. Time has not been any kinder. *—Jason Ankeny*

The Greatest Hits of the Fourth Decade / Apr. 14, 1992 / Scotti Bros. ✦✦✦
Collecting Brown's 1980s hits that didn't make it onto *Star Time*, *Greatest Hits of the Fourth Decade* shows that the period was not among his most creatively fertile, even with the monster hit "Living in America." Still, the disc does pick the best tracks from a dry spell, making it a nice supplement to the box set. *—Stephen Thomas Erlewine*

Love Power Peace / Jun. 23, 1992 / Polydor ✦✦✦✦✦
James Brown with the then newly-formed J.B.'s—the maestro's second great band, including Bootsy Collins, Phelps Collins, Jabo Starks, Bobby Byrd, and Fred Wesley. *Live at the Apollo* had caught James Brown, the '50s gospel/R&B singer; *Love Power Peace* captures James the funkster. In the early '70s Brown turned up the funk, recording such litanies for black America as "Ain't It Funky Now," "Sex Machine," "Give It Up or Turn It Loose," "Super Bad," "Get Up, Get Into It, Get Involved," and "Soul Power." They're all here, along with revved-up, white-hot versions of the early- and middle-period classics. Brown had planned to release this as a triple album in 1971. When several band members left shortly after it was recorded, Brown switched from King to Polydor Records, leading him to scrap it and record a new studio album instead. In 1992, Polygram decided to make the recording available for the first time. *—Rob Bowman*

Soul Pride: The Instrumentals (1960–69) / Mar. 23, 1993 / Polydor ✦✦✦✦✦
Everyone knows how hot James Brown's bands were, but not everyone's aware that he and his sidemen recorded lots of instrumental sides in the '60s. Originally scattered haphazardly over many out-of-print singles and albums, *Soul Pride* brings together the best of this work into one cohesive and chronological package. These cuts are nearly equal in power to J.B.'s vocal performances. Not only does the band cook on most of these insinuating vamps, but you can also hear the evolution of the man's sound from gritty R&B to tight-as-a-drum soul to free-form funk. Soul Brother Number One himself plays organ and adds unpredictable shouts and screams on most of these tracks. But the chief stars are sidemen like Maceo Parker, Fred Wesley, and Pee Wee Ellis, who broke new ground with their compulsive counterpoint riffs. This fiery two-disc, 36-track box set contains over two hours of music, as well as a few non-LP B-sides and previously unreleased tracks. *—Richie Unterberger*

James Brown's Funky Christmas / 1995 / Polydor ✦✦✦
At his superstar peak in the 1960s and early '70s, Brown tried to appeal to several constituencies on his many LPs, and the Christmas market was not neglected. Indeed, for a while he was on a regular schedule—this 17-track compilation includes selections from seasonal albums cut by J.B. in 1966, 1968, and 1970. Good Christmas rock & soul is somewhat of an oxymoron, but if you want some, you're better off with this than most anything else. The songs usually boast the funk-driven arrangements that were typical of his prime work, and Brown's performances are satisfyingly committed. That's not to say the material itself is on par with his best classics; it isn't. In fact it's rather variable—"Go Power at Christmas Time" is a hot slice of 1970 J.B. funk, but some of the poppy cuts with strings are a bit weak and forgettable. All power to J.B., though, for investing the holiday season with a smidgen of social consciousness on "Santa Claus Go Straight to the Ghetto." *—Richie Unterberger*

Live at the Apollo 1995 / 1995 / Scotti Bros. ✦✦✦

☆ **Foundations of Funk: A Brand New Bag, 1964–1969** / Mar. 19, 1996 / Polydor ✦✦✦✦✦
There are several worthy James Brown compilations. But this is the one, more than any other, that presents his most fertile and innovative soul and funk material. From 1964's "Out of Sight" through 1969's "Mother Popcorn," this was Brown at the apex of his

creativity, turning soul into funk in the mid-'60s, then pushing the rhythm even more to the forefront. Most of his hit singles from this five-year explosion of white heat are on this 27-track, two-CD set, including "Out of Sight," "Papa's Got a Brand New Bag," "I Got You (I Feel Good)," "Say It Loud—I'm Black and I'm Proud," and "Cold Sweat." There are some minor omissions that could be questioned (the absence of the studio version of "Bring It Up," for instance), and big James Brown fans will already have the lion's share of tracks, on the *Star Time* box and other releases. It does, however, contain minor but significant bonuses: an alternate take of "Cold Sweat," a previously unreleased live medley of "Out of Sight" and "Bring It Up," and a previously unreleased live version of "Licking Stick—Licking Stick." There are also longer versions of "I Don't Want Nobody to Give Me Nothing" (ten minutes!), "I Got the Feelin'," "The Popcorn," and "Brother Rapp" that were edited when they were prepared for official release. *—Richie Unterberger*

Funk Power 1970: A Brand New Thang / Jun. 4, 1996 / Polydor ♦♦♦♦♦
The period during which Brown was backed by the original J.B.'s (with Bootsy and Phelps Collins) was extremely brief, lasting only a year. But it was also an extremely important and influential phase of Brown's career, when he moved from soul-funk to hard funk, stretching out the grooves and putting more stress on the bottom than ever before. This 78-minute disc is the cream of his recordings from the Bootsy Collins era. The nine tracks (the tenth is a brief public-service announcement) include some of his core funk workouts—"Get Up I Feel Like Being a Sex Machine" (two versions), "Super Bad," "Give It Up or Turn It Loose," "Talkin' Loud and Sayin' Nothing," "Get Up, Get Into It, Get Involved," and "Soul Power." It's not for those who find Brown's funk phase too monotonous, and indeed the grooves do get a bit similar when experienced all at once. But it's unquestionably the best of Brown's '70s recordings, and indeed some of the hardest funk ever waxed by anyone at any time. As a bonus, the CD has previously unreleased complete versions of "Soul Power" (12 minutes) and "Talkin' Loud and Sayin' Nothing" (14 minutes), as well as a previously unreleased version of "There Was a Time." *—Richie Unterberger*

Make It Funky—The Big Payback: 1971–1975 / Jul. 23, 1996 / Polydor ♦♦♦♦♦
While the first half of the 1970s saw Brown's sales and art start to slowly decline, at their best he and the J.B.'s remained capable of generating a lot of heat. Record-wise it was a very erratic period, especially on his albums, which makes this two-and-a-half-hour double-disc compilation of his best material from the era especially welcome. Besides his biggest hits from the time ("Make It Funky," "Get on the Good Foot," "The Payback," "Funky President"), it has a number of high-charting R&B 45s that didn't make it onto the *Star Time* box. Familiar hits are sometimes presented in their full unedited mega-versions (12 minutes of "Make It Funky," 14 of "Papa Don't Take No Mess"), and there are also a few previously unreleased outtakes and alternate versions. It's only a disappointment relative to the towering accomplishments of his 1960s and early-'70s classics. On its own terms, it's excellent funk, if rather homogenous taken all at once, with occasional departures from the formula, like "Down and Out in New York City," with its poppy woodwinds. *—Richie Unterberger*

★ **JB40: 40th Anniversary Collection** / Oct. 8, 1996 / Polydor ♦♦♦♦♦
Brown's catalog was in a shambles for years, but the CD age has reversed the situation to such an extent that you now have a wide variety of greatest-hits options to choose from. On the whole, this might be the best buy, cramming 40 of his biggest hit singles from 1956-1979 onto two discs. It's perhaps a little too weighted toward the '70s (which comprise all of disc two), and some decent moderate-size hits are omitted, like "Oh Baby Don't You Weep," "Bring It Up," and "Get It Together." But it does have the core classics. If you don't want to spring for the *Star Time* box, but want more than a single-disc collection, this is the one to have. *—Richie Unterberger*

Dead on the Heavy Funk, 1975–1983 / May 12, 1998 / Polydor ♦♦♦
The last in Polydor's series of double-disc James Brown anthologies, *Dead on the Heavy Funk 1975-1983*, is inarguably the weakest. By the late '70s, all the great musicians that populated J.B.'s band had left, leaving him with a competent band that largely recycled old funk and tried its hand at disco. Most of their records were uneven, yet every once in a while they brought it all together and worked a good groove, even if they tended to let it go on a bit too long. *Dead on the Heavy Funk* has all those moments, as well as some less successful moments, extended mixes, previously unreleased takes and live cuts, plus the independent single "Bring It On ... Bring it On." It's an effective summary of these eight years, containing all of the good moments without disguising Brown's artistic decline. For hardcore fans, it's worth exploring, but most listeners—especially ones who loved his groundbreaking '60s funk—will be satisfied by the sampling of this material on the classic box set *Star Time*. *—Stephen Thomas Erlewine*

Say It Live & Loud: Live in Dallas 1968 / Aug. 11, 1998 / Polygram ♦♦♦♦
When James Brown was exalted as the "Hardest Working Man In Show Business," it wasn't just some empty hype that a publicist dreamed up—few singers in any genre were more workaholic or perfectionist. The Godfather of Soul demanded a lot from himself and a lot from his musicians, on whom he could be notoriously hard. Those who were lucky enough to see him live usually got what they paid for and then some, and he certainly goes that extra mile on *Say It Loud & Live: Live in Dallas 1968*. Though a few of these performances had come out on various 1990s anthologies, most of them remained in the can until the release of this CD in 1998. The Godfather is in excellent form on sweaty versions of 1960s hits like "Say It Loud—I'm Black And I'm Proud" (which had just come out as single), "Cold Sweat," "I Got the Feeling" and "There Was a Time," as well as a medley of his '50s classics "Try Me," "Lost Someone" and "Bewildered." Brown was at his creative and commercial peak, and his five-star band boasted such dynamos as guitarist Jimmy Nolen, trombonist Fred Wesley and saxmen Maceo Parker, St. Claire Pinckney and Alfred "Pee Wee" Ellis. It's too bad that most of these red-hot performances went unreleased for 30 years. *—Alex Henderson*

I'm Back / Nov. 17, 1998 / Mercury ♦♦♦
Since 1976's *Get Up Offa That Thing*, Brown has been existing on comebacks, near-misses, and embarrassments, no matter how ultimately substantive and profitable they turned out to be. His work had been re-evaluated by the early '80s, but his newer work, primarily his album output, including 1992's *Universal James*, has been uneven and substandard. Although *I'm Back* isn't a masterwork of cohesion, it proves the artist's viability, and that's more than enough. This set starts off with a hip-hop, synth-based version of "Can't Stand It." It should be appalling, but it's not. Throughout most of the album, Brown runs headlong into newer production values and remixes, and comes out generally unscathed. "Funk on Ah Roll" shows up in three versions, the best being "Funk on Ah Roll (S Class Club Mix)." The track has Brown singing, "Bring back the funk"—and it does, sampling a few of his hard-edged '70s tracks in an inventive manner. The tracks devoid of studio wizardry fare less well. Brown phones in "What It Takes," a bland duet reworking of Brook Benton and Dinah Washington's "Baby (You've Got What It Takes)," giving two people a chance to turn over their graves for the price of one. A potent remake of "Papa's Got a Brand New Bag" has St. Clair Pinckney doing a great, old-timey, honking sax riff. The uncomfortably astute, slightly anachronistic, early-'90s styled "Break Away" has Brown sounding off to fans who attempt to flee him, only to return his patently, screaming-loud R&B. *I'm Back* does have its share of duds, but it mostly shows Brown in command and still a viable presence. *—Jason Elias*

James Brown's Funky People, Pt. 3 / Jun. 13, 2000 / Polygram ♦♦♦♦
James Brown's Funky People, Pt. 3 collects more funky tracks from Brown's early '70s People label, which included Vicki Anderson, Hank Ballard & the Dapps, Lyn Collins, and the Dee Felice Trio. The album opens with the hard-to-find "rock" version of Brown's "Talkin' Loud and Sayin' Nothin'," which was withdrawn within days of its release, and also includes a previously unreleased, undubbed version of Fred Wesley & the J.B.s' "Blow Your Head." Rare singles such as Sweet Charles' "Hang out & Hustle" and Beau Dollar's "Who Knows" complete this collection, which consists entirely of songs that have never appeared on CD before. *—Heather Phares*

Ballads / Oct. 17, 2000 / Polydor ♦♦♦
For good reason, much emphasis has been placed on the exhilarating revolutionary uptempo funk classics recorded by the Godfather of Soul James Brown, but his earliest hits were actually R&B ballads. This Polydor package highlights 18 tracks that capture the energy and passion of songs like "It's a Man's, Man's, Man's World," "Prisoner of Love," and "If I Ruled the World." Even when strings are incorporated, Brown never becomes smothered by the arrangement and always fulfills the pleading bittersweet message that may have been lost with another performer. *Ballads* is a set that will satisfy any James Brown fan containing 13 original single mixes available on CD for the first time, including the rarely heard string sections on "Try Me," "Lost Someone," and "Bewildered." *—Al Campbell*

Live at the Apollo, Vol. II [Deluxe Edition] / Jun. 26, 2001 / Polydor ♦♦♦♦
If the purpose of the "Deluxe Edition" of *Live at the Apollo, Vol. II* is to make the best even better, the mission is more than accomplished. Not only has the original running time been increased by over half an hour—re-creating an entire performance, but also the sound, is likewise all encompassing and complete. According to Alan Leeds—tour director of the James Brown show in the late '60s—by 1968 Brown was honored with the distinction of selling one million concert tickets during his various appearances at the famed Apollo Theatre. The first volume of *Live at the Apollo [1963]* captures the R&B fury that would single-handedly define the soul music genre. While this volume reveals Brown's updated stage show, it more importantly offers another prolific observation into the future of R&B—funk. It would be nearly two years before Brown would discover the likes of Bootsy Collins and ultimately form the J.B.'s. However, as *Live at the Apollo, Vol. II* testifies, "Soul Brother Number One" is already submerging his band into more extended musical tangents, bobbing and weaving within a tight framework. This yields exciting new readings of familiar classics such as "It's a Man's, Man's, Man's World." Not only does Brown brilliantly incorporate the track "Lost Someone"—recalling the extended workout given on *Live at the Apollo [1963]*—Brown's percussive, heart-attack inducing call-and-response will leave even the most unflappable enthusiast slack jawed. This "expanded edition" also incorporates soloists, as well as other featured musicians who were often part of Brown's revue. Included on this release are previously unissued performances by Bobby Byrd ("Sweet Soul Music") and the James Brown Band ("Caravan"). The sonic brilliance on this double-disc set is visually matched in the 28-page liner notes booklet. Replete with newly published photos and memorabilia circa Brown's 1967 spring and summer tours, the booklet also features essays from Allen Leeds and percussionist Ahmir Khalib Thompson, aka ?uestlove. *—Lindsay Planer*

Jocelyn Brown

b. Nov. 25, 1950, Kingston, NC

Vocals / Club/Dance, Urban, Disco, House, Contemporary R&B

Jocelyn Brown comes from a musical family: her aunt, Barbara Roy, sang in the female group Ecstasy, Passion and Pain (EPP). Her grandmother, mother, two aunts, and a cousin all sang. Brown spent her preschool years with her grandmother in Kinston, NC. Her aunt's success with EPP provided the inspiration for Brown to spread her own musical wings. Beginning in church and singing with various gospel choirs out of Brooklyn, Brown built up a solid following, becoming a favored soloist at her uncle's church in Washington, D.C.

Gradually, Brown left gospel for secular music—disco in particular—singing with local bands like Machine and Kleer. She was a member of Monty Rock's pseudo-soul group Disco Tex and the Sex-O-Lettes, who scored with "Get Dancing," and Musique, who waxed "Keep on Jumpin'" and the risqué "Push Push in the Bush." Brown was traveling all over the world doing what she loved best—singing. At home she worked with producer Greg Diamond on different projects, including the group Change, which featured a male vocalist by the name of Luther Vandross. She kept busy touring with Change and doing studio and live background vocals for a laundry list of artists, eventually including Lou Reed, Roberta Flack, Mick Jagger, Dan Hartman, Bette Midler, George Benson, and Culture Club. When the members of Change disbanded, Brown started recording with other groups like Inner Life on Salsoul Records, where she soloed on a superlative disco version of "Ain't No Mountain High Enough" and established herself on the dance club circuit. All the while, she kept her bank account afloat by doing session work throughout the late '70s and early '80s. Around 1982, she worked in the movie *Divine Madness*, starring Bette Midler. Returning east, she waxed "Caught Up in a One Night Love Affair," a very popular number in New York's disco clubs like Studio 54, Paradise Garage, the Fever, Harlem World, and Bond's International.

In the fall of 1983, Brown teamed with her sister Annette and wrote "Somebody Else's Guy," her most popular recording to date; it reached the number two position of *Billboard*'s black singles chart and number 13 in the U.K.—Brown was truly a disco diva. She has appeared on Manu Dibango's *Soul Makossa* LP; cut "Ego Maniac" and "Whatever Satisfies You" (produced by Hubert Eaves III); waxed sides as a duet with Kym Mazelle in "No More Tears (Enough Is Enough)" and "Love Me the Right Way"; recorded "Riding on the Wings" with Motiv 8; and appeared in concert with Roy Ayers and Ray Gaskins (her cousin) overseas. Another cousin, La Rita Gaskins, is a singer and musician in NY; Ray Gaskins resides in London and is a noted saxophonist, songwriter, and producer. Brown continues to write songs with her sister Annette, who also helps manage her family members' creative activities. Like her brother, Brown lives in London (since 1990) and continues to be in demand. *—Andrew Hamilton*

Essential Dancefloor Artists, Vol. 6 / Apr. 20, 1996 / Sequel ✦✦✦✦

● **Moment of My Life: Jocelyn Brown Anthology** / Nov. 30, 1999 / EMI ✦✦✦✦

Moment of My Life is an admirable attempt at summarizing Jocelyn Brown's prolific career as one of the preeminent disco/dance vocalists from the '70s through the '90s, covering solo material and tracks she fronted for groups and producers like Musique, Inner Life, Salsoul Orchestra, Cerrone, Joe Bataan, and Masters at Work. The one problem with this disc's desire to cover as much ground as possible is the fact that radio edits are often favored over superior full-length and extended versions; both Larry Levan's mix of "Ain't No Mountain High Enough" and François Kevorkian's mix of "Keep on Jumpin'," for instance, are sacrificed in order to cover more ground. The blame can be placed on Brown more than the compilers; it's her fault for being responsible for bringing life to such a plentiful amount of excellent songs throughout the course of her career—it's all but impossible to do her service within the confines of one compact disc. A proper anthology of Brown's mark on dance music would require the space of several discs and dozens of licensing nightmares, but *Moment of My Life* does just fine for the time being, tying up enough classics to provide an excellent starter kit. *—Andy Kellman*

Maxine Brown

b. Apr. 27, 1932, Kingstree, SC

Vocals / Uptown Soul, Pop-Soul, R&B, Soul

Although she never had many hits, Maxine Brown was one of the most underrated soul and R&B vocalists of the '60s. During the '60s she released a series of singles for Nomar and Wand, with only a couple of songs—"All in My Mind," "Funny," "Something You Got," "Oh No Not My Baby"—managing to become either pop or R&B hits. Despite her lack of hits, Brown is acknowledged as one of the finest R&B vocalists of her time, capable of delivering soul, jazz, and pop with equal aplomb.

Born in Kingstree, SC, Brown began singing as child, singing with two New York-based gospel groups when she was a teenager. In 1960, she signed with the small Nomar label, who released the smooth soul ballad "All in My Mind" late in the year. The single became a hit, climbing to number two on the R&B charts (number 19 pop), and it was quickly followed by "Funny," which peaked at number three. Brown was poised to become a star, and she moved to ABC-Paramount in 1962, but she left the label within a year without scoring any hits. She signed to the New York-based, uptown soul label Wand in 1963. Brown recorded her best work at Wand, having a string of moderate hits for the label over the next three years. Among these were Carole King/David Goffin song "Oh No Not My Baby," which reached number 24 on the pop charts; "It's Gonna Be Alright"; and the Chuck Jackson duets "Something You Got," "Hold on I'm Coming," and "Daddy's Home." Part of the reason Brown didn't receive much exposure is that the label focused much of their attention on Dionne Warwick, leaving Maxine Brown to toil in semi-obscurity.

In 1969, she left Wand and signed with Commonwealth United, where she had the minor hits "We'll Cry Together" and "I Can't Get Along Without You." In 1971, she moved to Avco Records, but all of her recordings for the label went ignored and she faded away over the course of the decade. *—Stephen Thomas Erlewine*

The Fabulous Sound of Maxine Brown / 1962 / Wand ✦✦✦✦✦

This features some sizzling, sensual laments, ballads, and love songs from Maxine Brown, who was emerging as a secular vocalist in the early '60s after being a star in gospel. The album contained two hits in "All in My Mind" and "Funny," although it was more a collection of Scepter/Wand singles than a unified project. *—Ron Wynn*

Spotlight on Maxine Brown / 1964 / Wand ✦✦✦

This disc collected ten songs that appeared on 1963-1965 singles, along with a couple ("Gotta Find a Way" and "Wonder What My Baby's Doing Tonight") that made their first appearance on this LP. As it happens, it does have much of her best work from that era, although all but two of the tracks are on her finest anthology, *Oh No Not My Baby: The Best of Maxine Brown* (on a Kent CD). In addition, the entire album is available on another Kent release, which combines *Spotlight on Maxine Brown* and all but two songs from her 1967 Wand LP *Greatest Hits* onto one CD, with the addition of eight rare and previously unissued bonus tracks. So while *Spotlight on Maxine Brown* is a good pop-soul album on its own merits, it makes far more sense to seek out one of the Kent anthologies mentioned above than to get the original Wand LP. *—Richie Unterberger*

Maxine Brown's Greatest Hits / 1967 / Wand ✦✦✦✦

We'll Cry Together / 1969 / United ✦✦✦

● **Oh No Not My Baby: The Best of Maxine Brown** / 1990 / Kent ✦✦✦✦✦

This 28-song CD is undoubtedly the best compilation of this underrated soul singer's work, featuring many of her '60s singles and several tunes from the era that were unreleased until the '80s. This disc draws from her recordings for the Wand label between 1963 and 1967, when Brown was at her artistic peak. Of course the hit title track is a highlight, but there are no clunkers in this excellent collection of overlooked '60s pop-soul, featuring the New York "uptown" production that also graced the records of fellow Wand/Scepter artists like Dionne Warwick and Chuck Jackson. Brown was one of the most versatile soul divas of the '60s, showing the influence of Brill Building pop, girl groups, Motown, and even Stax soul and supper-club ballads. As with a similar artist like Betty Everett, this versaility has worked against her in some ways. Neither full-fledged pop nor unabashedly soul, her work cannot be easily pigeonholed into a certain soul genre, and has cost her the respect that some purists reserve for "deep" soul singers. But her work holds up well. Collectors should be aware that this disc doesn't include any of the records she cut in the early '60s before joining Wand; the version of her 1961 Top 20 hit "All in My Mind" here is from a live 1964 release, not the original single. *—Richie Unterberger*

● **Greatest Hits** / 1995 / Tomato ✦✦✦✦✦

This 23-track best-of has a lot of overlap with the British import *Oh No Not My Baby*; both cover her mid-'60s period with Wand, and each has some songs not on the other. There's not a crucial difference between the pair, but the nod probably goes to the import, which has more songs and better sound. In its favor, this compilation includes five of her duets with Chuck Jackson, none of which are on the other CD (although the duets don't rank among her best material). It also has a studio version of "All in My Mind," rather than the live one on the British anthology. *—Richie Unterberger*

Something You Got: The Best of Chuck Jackson & Maxine Brown / 1996 / Ichiban/Soul Classics ✦✦✦

All 20 of the duet tracks that Maxine Brown and Chuck Jackson recorded for the Wand label between 1965 and 1967 are here, comprising the entirety of their two albums for the company. It's reasonable pop-soul, but not nearly as memorable as the best male-female soul duets of the era (like the ones by Marvin Gaye and various Motown partners, or by Otis Redding and Carla Thomas). Highlights are the early compositions by the Jo Armstead-Nick Ashford-Valerie Simpson team, including a version of "Let's Go Get Stoned" that was recorded (though not released) before Ray Charles' more famous hit rendition. *—Richie Unterberger*

Spotlight on Maxine Brown/Greatest Hits / Aug. 29, 2000 / Kent ✦✦✦✦

A confusing release that seems to have tried to both sweep up rarities for the completist and offer something approximating a greatest-hits package, the result being, of course, that everyone's a bit unsatisfied. Basically, the idea was to combine all the songs from her 1965 LP *Spotlight* (actually largely a collection of 1963-1965 singles) and her 1967 LP *Greatest Hits* (which duplicated five tracks from *Spotlight*) onto one CD, adding eight rare bonus tracks. Those additional cuts are taken from non-LP mid-'60s recordings and a couple of previously unissued items. There are two problems with that concept. The first is that no less than 15 of the 28 tracks also appear on another Kent release, the fine anthology *Oh No Not My Baby: The Best of Maxine Brown*, which many of the people considering buying any Brown reissue are likely to have already. The second is that this CD actually does not include "All in My Mind" and "Funny," which—if the cover art of *Greatest Hits*, complete with track listing, reproduced on the cover of this two-fer is to be believed—were on the original 1967 *Greatest Hits* LP. That's an uncommon gaffe for Ace/Kent to make, but from all appearances that's what happened. Now, certainly this is still a fine pop-soul disc from one of the best pop-soul vocalists. Of the material on *Spotlight On/Greatest Hits* not on that other Kent collection, it ranges from good—the bluesy "You Upset My Soul," an odd cover of the Beatles' "We Can Work It Out," the brassy 1966 single "Anything You Do Is Alright," a nice interpretation of the pop standard "When I Fall in Love"—to unmemorable. *—Richie Unterberger*

25 All Time Greatest Hits / Aug. 13, 2002 / Varese ✦✦✦✦✦

There was more than one Maxine Brown greatest-hits collection prior to this 2002 release, and no doubt there will be others in the future. On its own merits, though, it does a good job of assembling her best-known material, focusing on her mid-'60s recordings for Wand, which yielded the bulk of her best and highest-selling sides. One small advantage this does have over prior collections, such as Kent's fine *Oh No Not My Baby: The Best of Maxine Brown*, is that it does include her two key pre-Wand hits released on Nomar in 1961, in their original versions: "All in My Mind" and "Funny" (the versions on *Oh No Not My Baby* are later re-recordings). Otherwise, it's mostly top of the line mid-'60s pop-soul, including her biggest and best singles of the era: "Oh No Not My Baby," "Ask Me," "One Step at a Time," and "It's Gonna Be Alright," as well as good non-hits like "One in a Million," "Gotta Find a Way," "Put Yourself in My Place," and "Since I Found You." There aren't any of her recordings with Chuck Jackson, which might miff some fans, as some of those singles charted. But really, those duets weren't up to the standard of her best solo work, so it's not a significant flaw in focus. It's not a major gaffe, but two songs identified as previously unissued—"Baby Cakes" and "Slipping Through My Fingers," both bearing the songwriting credit of Otis Redding—have in fact shown up on previous Brown compilations, the first on *Oh No Not My Baby*, the second on Tomato's *Maxine Brown's Greatest Hits*. *—Richie Unterberger*

Nappy Brown (Napoleon Brown Goodson Culp)

b. Oct. 12, 1929, Charlotte, NC

Vocals / Jump Blues, R&B

Nobody sounded much like Nappy Brown during the mid-'50s. Exotically rolling his consonants with sing-song impugnity (allegedly, Savoy Records boss Herman Lubinsky thought Brown was singing in Yiddish), bellowing the blues with gospel-inspired ferocity, Brown rode rock & roll's first wave for a few glorious years before his records stopped selling. But in the early '80s, Brown seemingly rose from the dead to stage a comeback bid. Now he's ensconced once again as a venerable blues veteran who'll stop at nothing (including rolling around the stage in sexual simulation) to enthrall his audience. Brown brought hellfire intensity to his blues-soaked Savoy debut, "Is It True," but it was "Don't Be Angry" the next year that caused his fortunes to skyrocket. The sizzling rocker sported loads of Brown's unique vocal gimmicks and a hair-raising tenor sax solo by Sam "The Man" Taylor, becoming his first national smash. Novelty-tinged upbeat items such as "Little by Little" and "Piddily Patter Patter" defined Nappy's output, but his throat-busting turn on the 1957 blues "The Right Time" remains a highlight of his early heyday. After decades away from the limelight, Nappy resurfaced in 1984 with a very credible album for Landslide Records, *Tore Up*. —*Bill Dahl*

That Man / Mar. 31, 1954-Aug. 21, 1961 / Swift ♦♦♦♦♦

That Man collects 17 songs Nappy Brown recorded for Savoy Records between 1954 and 1961, including "The Right Time," "Down in the Alley," and "Is It True." The compilation spotlights his lesser-known recordings, not his hits, but these songs are every bit as good as his more popular material from the same era. —*Thom Owens*

Don't Be Angry! / Feb. 1, 1955-Oct. 4, 1956 / Savoy Jazz ♦♦♦♦♦

Rolling his consonants like a crazed cantor, shouter Nappy Brown brought a gospel-imbued fervor to his rocking mid-'50s R&B that few of his peers could match. Backed by some of New York's finest sessioneers, Brown roars 16 of his best early Savoy sides on this essential purchase. "Don't Be Angry," "Just a Little Love," "Open Up That Door," and "Bye Bye Baby" rate with his hottest jump efforts, "I Cried like a Baby" and "It's Really You" are hair-raising blues, and "Little by Little" rides a bouncy, pop-accessible groove. Now where's volume two?? —*Bill Dahl*

I Done Got Over / Feb. 26, 1983-Apr. 1983 / Stockholm ♦♦

I Done Got Over features some good vocal performances from Nappy Brown, but this album—which essentially runs through his '50s hits, with a couple new tracks thrown in for good measure—is one of his lesser works. Brown is supported by the Roosters, a stiff Swedish band who can't get the music cooking. Consequently, Brown never puts forth much of an effort. The result is a disappointingly uninspired record. —*Thom Owens*

Tore Up / Aug. 1984 / Alligator ♦♦♦

After too many years during which he was missing and presumed forever lost in action, Brown returned to prominence with this very credible album, cut with backing by guitarist Tinsley Ellis and the Heartfixers and originally issued on the tiny Landslide logo. He reprises his salacious blues "Lemon Squeezin' Daddy" and rolls his R's like the good old days on dusties by Little Walter, the Midnighters, Howlin' Wolf, and even Bob Dylan and the Allmans. —*Bill Dahl*

Something Gonna Jump out the Bushes / Apr. 1987 / Black Top ♦♦♦♦

Ultra-solid support from guitarists Anson Funderburgh, Eugene Ross, Ronnie Earl, and Earl King and Black Top's superb house horn section make this Dallas-cut set Brown's best contemporary album to date. His lusty shouting style works well on covers of the Dominoes' "Have Mercy Baby," the "5" Royales' title track, a pair of Earl King-penned numbers, and Robert Ward's "Your Love Is Real." —*Bill Dahl*

● **Night Time Is the Right Time** / Jul. 18, 2000 / Savoy Jazz ♦♦♦♦♦

Night Time Is the Right Time is a two-disc collection of 36 gems recorded by R&B singer Nappy Brown. With one foot grounded in the blues and the other stepping toward soul, Brown's mid- to late-'50s recordings are exciting and impressive. The first disc, with classics like "Don't Be Angry," "That Man," and "Two-Faced Woman (And a Lyin' Man)," is probably the best. The tight arrangements, filled with saxophone, piano, and electric guitar, place Brown's voice in the best light. He shouts, croons, and bends words playfully on upbeat numbers like "Just a Little Love" and "Piddily Patter Patter." While his voice is distinctive, it is the exuberant punch of his delivery that keeps his music vibrant some forty years after it was recorded. Even slower numbers, such as "Is that Really You?," find Brown building a soulful intensity, or the "slow burn" as it was called. There are several songs like "I've Had My Fun" on the second disc that fall more comfortably into the blues category. These are fine recordings, but straight R&B seemed to work best for his style. It should also be noted that whatever you call his music—R&B, soul, jump blues—much of it would have fit comfortably into '50s rock & roll, though it is certainly rawer and more exciting than the average Top 40 radio. This is fine R&B and a good collection for Brown fans. A great place to learn more about the roots of soul music. —*Ronnie Lankford, Jr.*

Peter Brown

b. Jul. 11, 1953, Blue Island, IL

Vocals, Keyboards, Percussion / Pop, Funk, Disco

Peter Brown first came to fame with the first million-selling 12-inch dance single, "Do Ya Wanna Get Funky With Me." Brown was a pioneer in home recording, having recorded his seminal hit in his bedroom. (His '70s-era home recording studio is pictured on the cover of Westside/DNA's *Get Funky With Me: The Best of the TK Years*.) He also co-wrote Madonna's 1985 pop hit, "Material Girl," with Peter Rans. Born July 11, 1953, in Blue Island, IL, Brown, started playing drums in his teens and later began experimenting with his four-track reel-to-reel tape recorder in his bedroom studio. The singer/keyboardist/producer was signed to Drive Records, a subsidiary of Henry Stone's TK Records. His first album for the label, *A Fantasy Love Affair*, was produced by Cory Wade, who had helped Brown get the record deal. The percolating "Do Ya Wanna Get Funky With Me" went to number-three R&B, number-18 pop on *Billboard*'s charts in summer 1977. Another Drive LP, *Stargazer* yielded "Crank It Up (Funk Town), Pt. 1." His 1983 RCA LP, *Back to the Front* included the charting single, "Baby Gets High." Brown's 1984 Columbia LP, *Snap* included the sly rock/dance classic "Zie Zie Won't Dance," the dub reggae-sounding "Hot Flash," the driving, swirling horn-laced "Electric Shoes," the dream-like "Double or Nothing," and the pumping single, "They Only Come Out at Night." In September 1999, Brown's *Chasing Fireflies* was released by Orchard and in November 1999, UK label Resurgence issued Brown's *Party in the Rain* CD. —*Ed Hogan*

A Fantasy Love Affair / 1978 / Drive ♦♦♦

Thanks to "Do You Wanna Get Funky With Me," a million-selling crossover disco single that lit up the black singles, club play, and pop singles charts, Peter Brown's debut album for TK Disco offshoot Drive, *A Fantasy Love Affair*, also placed high, reaching number six on the black albums chart. Though "Do You Wanna Get Funky With Me" and "Dance With Me" are clearly intended for clubs, the remainder of the album also shows flashes of a less-cynical Steely Dan in songs like "A Fantasy Love Affair" and "It's True What They Say About Love." The other half of the album is well-crafted by multi-instrumentalist Brown, if nondescript. [Collectables remastered the album for CD release in 1998 with no bonus tracks.] —*Andy Kellman*

Stargazer / 1979 / TK ♦♦♦

When Peter Brown excelled in the 1970s and 1980s, he *really* excelled; "Do You Wanna Get Funky With Me?," "Fantasy Love Affair," "Overnight Sensation," and "Dance With Me" are disco-funk classics. But unfortunately, the Chicagoan didn't excel as often as he should have. Brown's albums tend to be uneven and unfocused, and that's definitely the case with his second LP, *Stargazer*. This 1979 release contains a few gems, including the passionate "It's Alright," the mysterious "Leadmeon," and the hell-raising hit "Crank It Up." But most of the tunes are merely competent. Brown, who wrote or co-wrote all of the songs and produced *Stargazer* with Cory Wade, had the potential to record an album that was great all the way through. But *Stargazer* isn't such an album; it's a generally decent record, but Brown was capable of a lot more. —*Alex Henderson*

Back to the Front / 1983 / TK ♦♦♦

To hear some disco haters tell it, disco died with the 1970s. But that's hardly true, disco was alive and well throughout the 1980s and 1990s, only it was being called dance music and dance-pop instead of disco. Released in 1983, *Back to the Front* demonstrated that there was still a market for the type of disco-funk that put Peter Brown on the map in 1977 with the dancefloor classic "Do You Wanna Get Funky With Me?" This vinyl LP, which contains the dance hits "Overnight Sensation" and "Baby Gets High," isn't much different from Brown's late-'70s recordings; he was still providing plenty of disco-funk in 1983, although the term disco was no longer in vogue. Like *Fantasy Love Affair* and *Stargazer* in the late '70s, *Back to the Front* is uneven. It contains a few gems, "Overnight Sensation" and "Baby Gets High" are excellent, but most of the material is merely adequate. Brown never recorded an album that was superb from start to finish, and like his other LPs, *Back to the Front* is usually competent but is only great on occasion. —*Alex Henderson*

● **Get Funky With Me: The Best of the TK Years** / May 19, 1998 / WestSide ♦♦♦♦

This compilation covers the hitmaking years of Peter Brown, a musician who had some notable dance music hits in the late '70s and early '80s on the Miami-based TK Records label. This label is best known as the home of funky disco acts like K.C. & the Sunshine Band and Jimmy "Bo" Horne, but Brown's work took a different tack. The songs on *Get Funky With Me: The Best of the TK Years* pursue slick, carefully crafted sound that has more to do with studio-driven dance acts like Chic. Like Prince, Brown recorded the majority of his instrumentation on his own in a home studio and added frills like orchestration and backup vocals later. The result is a sound that feels lush yet has a hand-crafted touch: "Dance With Me" is a bouncy disco outing that blends sprightly strings with an insistent bass-driven groove, and "Do You Wanna Get Funky With Me" is a reggae-tinged slice of dance funk that features Brown trading vocals with a brassy female chorus over a sumptuous production full jazzy horns and percolating synthesizers. There is also the occasional ballad; the standout is "Without Love," which layers hymn-like vocals over a track that marries subtle strings to dreamy synthesizer hooks. *Get Funky With Me: The Best of the TK Years* also throws in a pair of modern remixes, both of which lack the handcrafted charms of the original tunes. Overall, the songs presented here are lightweight (especially in the lyrical department) but this is forgivable because they were obviously intended as fun, lighthearted dance music. More importantly, his music triumphs over such shortcomings because he has an undeniable knack for crafting hooks and layering them in a hypnotic fashion: for instance, "Can't Be Love—Do It to Me Anyway" weaves minimalist keyboard riffs and chant-like vocal hooks into an entrancing synth pop epic. All in all, *Get Funky With Me: The Best of the TK Years* is a solid disco collection that is well worth a spin for anyone who has enjoyed Brown's hits. —*Donald A. Guarisco*

Roy Brown

b. Sep. 10, 1925, New Orleans, LA, **d.** May 25, 1981, San Fernando, CA

Vocals, Songwriter, Piano, Leader / Jump Blues, R&B, West Coast Blues

When you draw up a short list of the R&B pioneers who exerted a primary influence on the development of rock & roll, respectfully place singer Roy Brown's name near its very top. His seminal 1947 DeLuxe Records waxing of "Good Rockin' Tonight" was immediately ridden to the peak of the R&B charts by shouter Wynonie Harris and subsequently covered by Elvis Presley, Ricky Nelson, Jerry Lee Lewis, and many more early rock icons (even Pat Boone). In addition, Brown's melismatical pleading, gospel-steeped delivery impacted the vocal styles of B.B. King, Bobby "Blue" Bland, and Little Richard (among a plethora of important singers). Clearly, Roy Brown was an innovator—and from 1948-1951, an R&B star whose wild output directly presaged rock's rise.

Born in the Crescent City, Brown grew up all over the place: Eunice, LA (where he sang in church and worked in the sugarcane fields); Houston, TX; and finally Los Angeles by age 17. Back then, Bing Crosby was Brown's favorite singer—but a nine-month stint at a Shreveport, LA, nightclub exposed him to the blues for the first time. He conjured up "Good Rockin' Tonight" while fronting a band in Galveston, TX. Ironically, Harris wanted no part of the song when Brown first tried to hand it to him. When pianist Cecil Gant heard Brown's knockout rendition of the tune in New Orleans, he had Brown sing it over the phone to a sleepy DeLuxe boss, Jules Braun, in the wee hours of the morning. Though Brown's original waxing (with Bob Ogden's band in support) was a solid hit, Harris' cover beat him out for top chart honors.

Roy Brown didn't have to wait long to dominate the R&B lists himself. He scored 15 hits from mid-1948 to late 1951 for DeLuxe, ranging from the emotionally wracked crying blues of "Hard Luck Blues" (his biggest seller of all in 1950) to the party-time rockers "Rockin' at Midnight," "Boogie at Midnight," "Miss Fanny Brown," and "Cadillac Baby." Strangely, his sales slumped badly from 1952 on, even though his frantic "Hurry Hurry Baby," "Ain't No Rockin' No More," "Black Diamond," and "Gal From Kokomo" for Cincinnati's King Records rate among his hottest house rockers.

Brown was unable to cash in on the rock & roll idiom he helped to invent, though he briefly rejuvenated his commercial fortunes at Imperial Records in 1957. Working with New Orleans producer Dave Bartholomew, then riding high with Fats Domino, Brown returned to the charts with the original version of "Let the Four Winds Blow" (later a hit for Domino) and cut the sizzling sax-powered rockers "Diddy-Y-Diddy-O," "Saturday Night," and "Ain't Gonna Do It." Not everything was an artistic triumph; Brown's utterly lifeless cover of Buddy Knox's "Party Doll"—amazingly, a chart entry for Brown—may well be the worst thing he ever committed to wax (rivaled only by a puerile "School Bell Rock" cut during a momentary return to King in 1959).

After a long dry spell, Brown's acclaimed performance as part of Johnny Otis' troupe at the 1970 Monterey Jazz Festival and a 1973 LP for ABC-BluesWay began to rebuild his long-lost momentum. But it came too late; Brown died of a heart attack in 1981 at age 56, his role as a crucial link between postwar R&B and rock's initial rise still underappreciated by the masses. *—Bill Dahl*

Mighty Mighty Man! / 1993 / Ace ✦✦✦✦✦
Mighty Mighty Man! is another British import that really delivers the rocking goods. This time zeroing in on Brown's 1953-1959 King sides exclusively, the 22-cut CD shows that Brown actually picked up his tempos to meet rock's rise head on. The clever sequel "Ain't No Rocking No More," "Black Diamond," "Gal from Kokomo," and "Shake 'Em Up Baby" rate with his hottest rockers, with great support from a crew of Crescent City stalwarts. *—Bill Dahl*

★ **Good Rocking Tonight: The Best of Roy Brown** / 1994 / Rhino ✦✦✦✦✦
An unassailable 18-cut cross section of the monstrously popular and influential New Orleans jump blues shouter's sides for the DeLuxe, King, and Imperial labels that spans 1947-1957 and takes in his seminal "Good Rocking Tonight" (where it all began!), "Rockin' at Midnight," "Boogie at Midnight," and "Love Don't Love Nobody"; the almost unbearably tortured "Hard Luck Blues"; and the unbelievably raunchy two-parter "Butcher Pete." Looking for the origins of rock? Here they are! *—Bill Dahl*

The Complete Imperial Recordings / Jun. 20, 1995 / Capitol ✦✦✦
In the mid-'50s Brown, like many other early R&B pioneers, was a bit lost at sea amid the rock & roll explosion. From 1956 to 1958, he recorded these 20 tracks for Imperial under the direction of legendary New Orleans R&B producer Dave Bartholomew. Brown and Bartholomew were attempting to update Brown's jump blues/R&B hybrid with a lot of Fats Domino-type Crescent City influence on these sides. The results weren't bad, but with Bartholomew co-writing most of the tunes and using local musicians like saxophonist Lee Allen, Brown sounded more like a journeyman New Orleans R&B singer than an innovative, bluesy forefather of rock & roll. There were a couple of commercial successes; his cover of Buddy Knox's "Party Doll" made the R&B Top 20, and "Let the Four Winds Blow" actually made the pop Top 40, although Fats Domino would have much greater success with the same song when he covered it a few years later. Diluted by occasional pop and rock influences, as well as a substandard variation of "Good Rockin' Tonight," this compilation shouldn't be the first Brown on your shelf. But for those who want to go a little further, it's packaged very well, with thorough liner notes and seven previously unissued cuts. *—Richie Unterberger*

Ruth Brown (Ruth Weston)

b. Jan. 12, 1928, Portsmouth, VA
Vocals / Jump Blues, R&B

They called Atlantic Records "the house that Ruth built" during the 1950s, and they weren't referring to the Sultan of Swat. Ruth Brown's regal hitmaking reign from 1949 to the close of the '50s helped tremendously to establish the New York label's predominance in the R&B field. Later, the business all but forgot her—she was forced to toil as domestic help for a time—but she returned to the top, her status as a postwar R&B pioneer (and tireless advocate for the rights and royalties of her peers) recognized worldwide. Young Ruth Weston was inspired initially by jazz chanteuses Sarah Vaughan, Billie Holiday, and Dinah Washington. She ran away from her Portsmouth home in 1945 to hit the road with trumpeter Jimmy Brown, whom she soon married. A month with bandleader Lucky Millinder's orchestra in 1947 ended abruptly in Washington, D.C., when she was canned for delivering a round of drinks to members of the band. Cab Calloway's sister Blanche gave Ruth a gig at her Crystal Caverns nightclub and assumed a managerial role in the young singer's life. DJ Willis Conover dug Brown's act and recommended her to Ahmet Ertegun and Herb Abramson, bosses of a fledgling imprint named Atlantic.

Unfortunately, Brown's debut session for the firm was delayed by a nine-month hospital stay caused by a serious auto accident en route to New York that badly injured her leg. When she finally made it to her first date in May of 1949, she made up for lost time by waxing the torch ballad "So Long" (backed by guitarist Eddie Condon's band), which proved to be her first hit.

Brown's seductive vocal delivery shone incandescently on her Atlantic smashes "Teardrops in My Eyes" (an R&B chart-topper for 11 weeks in 1950), "I'll Wait for You" and "I Know" in 1951, 1952's "5-10-15 Hours" (another number-one rocker), the seminal "(Mama) He Treats Your Daughter Mean" in 1953, and a tender Chuck Willis-penned "Oh What a Dream" and the timely "Mambo Baby" the next year. Along the way, Frankie Laine tagged her "Miss Rhythm" during an engagement in Philly. Brown belted a series of her hits on the groundbreaking TV program *Showtime at the Apollo* in 1955, exhibiting delicious comic timing while trading sly one-liners with MC Willie Bryant (ironically, ex-husband Jimmy Brown was a member of the show's house band).

After an even two-dozen R&B chart appearances for Atlantic that ended in 1960 with "Don't Deceive Me" (many of them featuring hell-raising tenor sax solos by Willis "Gator" Jackson, who many mistakenly believed to be Brown's husband), Brown faded from view. After raising her two sons and working a nine-to-five job, Brown began to rebuild her musical career in the mid-'70s. Her comedic sense served her well during a TV sitcom stint co-starring with McLean Stevenson in *Hello, Larry*, in a meaty role in director John Waters' 1985 sock-hop satire film *Hairspray*, and during her 1989 Broadway starring turn in *Black and Blue* (which won her a Tony Award).

There were more records for Fantasy in the '80s and '90s (notably 1991's jumping *Fine and Mellow*), and a lengthy tenure as host of National Public Radio's "Harlem Hit Parade" and "BluesStage." Brown's nine-year ordeal to recoup her share of royalties from all those Atlantic platters led to the formation of the nonprofit Rhythm & Blues Foundation, an organization dedicated to helping others in the same frustrating situation. Factor in all those time-consuming activities, and it's a wonder Ruth Brown has time to sing anymore. But she does (quite royally, too), her pipes mellowed but not frayed by the ensuing decades that have seen her rise to stardom not once, but twice. *—Bill Dahl*

Ruth Brown Sings Favorites / 1956 / Atlantic ✦✦✦
Ruth Brown had extensive gospel and jazz roots, which Atlantic honed to perfection, turning her into an R&B queen. These songs aren't quite the same, but they show her full stylistic range and also how powerful and strong her voice was in the '50s. *—Ron Wynn*

Ruth Brown / 1957 / Atlantic ✦✦✦
Here is Ruth Brown at her stinging, assertive, bawdy best, doing the sizzling, innuendo-laden R&B that helped make Atlantic the nation's prime independent during the early days of rock & roll. There's also plenty of equally fiery, hot musical accompaniment, with Willis Jackson sometimes featured on tenor sax. *—Ron Wynn*

Late Date With Ruth Brown / Jan. 27, 1959-Feb. 5, 1959 / Atlantic ✦✦✦✦
This is a good after-hours, smoky blues and R&B session featuring Ruth Brown in prime form. Nobody, male or female, sang with more spirit, sass, and vigor than Brown during the '50s, and this session reminded those who had forgotten that Brown could also hold her own with sophisticated material as well as sexy stuff. *—Ron Wynn*

Gospel Time / 1962 / Polygram ✦✦✦

Along Comes Ruth / Apr. 12, 1962 / Philips ✦✦✦
A good, but not essential, early-'60s session showing that both Ruth Brown and her brain trust were about to run dry. She still had the powerhouse vocals, but there are fewer inspiring songs, and by the end of side two Brown is getting by on energy alone. *—Ron Wynn*

Ruth Brown '65 / 1964 / Mainstream ✦✦✦
Ruth Brown '65 was an underrated, nicely produced mid-'60s album putting Ruth Brown more in the blues and interpretive mode that she moved away from during the hit years. She can still belt out numbers, but also shows some wit and some flourishes that were sacrificed for impact when she was doing rock & roll. *—Ron Wynn*

Fine Brown Frame / Jun. 18, 1968+Jul. 2, 1968 / Koch International ✦✦
In the late '60s, veteran singer Ruth Brown recorded two albums with the Thad Jones/Mel Lewis Orchestra, but neither one was all that classic. She sounds fine, though the big band has little to do except be supportive. The opening "Yes Sir, That's My Baby" is pretty weak, and "Sonny Boy" certainly did not need to be revived. Much better are "Trouble in Mind," "Black Coffee" and "Fine Brown Frame," but Ruth Brown's earlier (and later) recordings are superior to this historical curiosity. *—Scott Yanow*

Black Is Brown and Brown Is Beautiful / 1969 / DCC ✦✦
Veteran R&B/jazz singer Ruth Brown is in strong voice for this audiophile CD reissue but she occasionally goes over the top. The Gary McFarland arrangements for an expanded rhythm section (with guitarist Eric Gale) and the Howard Roberts Chorale are quite predictable and the material has few surprises except for a soulful version of "Yesterday." Closer to soul than to jazz, the set is enjoyable enough but nothing happens to raise it above the average album of the period. Ruth Brown has recorded more significant music elsewhere. *—Scott Yanow*

Have a Good Time / Jun. 10, 1988-Jun. 11, 1988 / Fantasy ✦✦✦✦
Ruth Brown, a top-selling artist in the 1950s, endured over two decades of relative obscurity before she began to be noticed again in 1988. Recorded live at the Cinegrill in Hollywood, Brown is assisted by a fine quintet (which includes tenor great Red Holloway, altoist Charles Williams and organist Bobby Forrester) for fresh remakes of some of her hits, along with some newer material. All of Brown's Fantasy CDs feature a mature singer still in her prime. Highlights of this particular release (her debut for the label) include "Gee Baby, Ain't I Good to You," "Teardrops From My Eyes," "When I Fall in Love" and "Mama He Treats Your Daughter Mean." *—Scott Yanow*

★ **Miss Rhythm (Greatest Hits and More)** / 1989 / Rhino ✦✦✦✦✦
Before Aretha Franklin was exalted as the Queen of Soul, Ruth Brown was dubbed "Miss Rhythm"—and with good reason. A gritty, aggressive belter with an impressive range and a powerhouse of a voice, Brown was the top female R&B singer of the early to mid-'50s, and would directly or indirectly have an influence on such greats as Etta James and

LaVern Baker. A two-CD set ranging from Brown's early hits to engaging obscurities and rarities, *Miss Rhythm* offers a fine overview of her Atlantic years. Early hits like "Mama, He Treats Your Daughter Mean," "Teardrops From My Eyes," "Mambo Baby," and "5-10-15 Hours" point to the fact that a lot of early R&B was essentially blues at a fast tempo. The set also reminds of early R&B's connection to jazz—in fact, classics like 1949's "So Long" (her first single) and "Have a Good Time" are examples of first-class torch singing. There are numerous Brown albums that are well worth acquiring, but for those interested in exploring her early music for the first time, *Miss Rhythm* is an excellent place to start. *—Alex Henderson*

Blues on Broadway / Jun. 12, 1989-Jun. 13, 1989 / Fantasy ✦✦✦✦✦
Ruth Brown was starring on Broadway in *Black and Blue* when she recorded her second Fantasy set. The emphasis is on ancient standards (mostly from the 1920s) that predated Brown's rise as an R&B star in the 1950s. Assisted by trumpeter Spanky Davis, tenorman Red Holloway, trombonist Britt Woodman, a rhythm section led by pianist/organist Bobby Forrester and (on three numbers) altoist Hank Crawford, Brown makes such songs as "Nobody Knows You When You're Down and Out," "If I Can't Sell It, I'll Keep Sittin' on It" and "Am I Blue" sound as if they were written for her. *—Scott Yanow*

Fine and Mellow / Apr. 1, 1991-Aug. 13, 1991 / Fantasy ✦✦✦✦
Nice contemporary effort with a strongly swinging R&B flavor running throughout. Ruth Brown goes back to the '40s (Louis Jordan's "Knock Me a Kiss," Dinah Washington's "Salty Papa Blues") and '50s (Brook Benton's "It's Just a Matter of Time," Jackie Wilson's "I'll Be Satisfied," the Lula Reed/Ray Charles dirge "Drown in My Own Tears") for much of the disc, paying loving tribute to her main lady Billie Holiday with the tasty title cut and delivering a pair of Duke Ellington numbers along the way. *—Bill Dahl*

Songs of My Life / Aug. 20, 1993 / Fantasy ✦✦✦
Before Ruth Brown became an R&B and rock legend in the '50s, she was a jazz, blues, and gospel stylist. She shows that aspect of her talent on *The Songs of My Life*, a fine set produced by guitarist Rodney Jones, who also did the arrangements and conducted the backing band. While she displays her timing, interpretive skills, and still-impressive delivery and enunciation throughout, Brown also demonstrates on her rendition of Eric Clapton's "Tears in Heaven" that she retains an interest in and awareness of contemporary songs that fit her style. Ruth Brown proves that it's not the song or the lyric but the singer who makes a tune work. *—Ron Wynn*

Live in London / Jan. 23, 1996 / Jazz House ✦✦✦

★ **The Best of Ruth Brown** / Jun. 18, 1996 / Rhino ✦✦✦✦✦
For those who want a cheaper and more concise collection of her best Atlantic cuts than the two-CD *Miss Rhythm*, this superb 23-track CD has the cream of her '50s work, including no less than 19 Top Ten R&B singles. Charting her evolution from her jazzy debut, "So Long," through jump blues and early rock & roll, it also adds a bonus of two previously unissued live cuts from 1959. *—Richie Unterberger*

R+B = Ruth Brown / Jan. 20, 1997-Feb. 28, 1997 / Bullseye Blues ✦✦✦✦
Ruth Brown's lengthy career has taken her from the Apollo Theater to Broadway. One of the original R&B superstars, she has emerged on the other side as one of the genre's most beloved singers. On this outing, producer Scott Billington returns Brown to her roots in the company of a superb New Orleans band, surrounds her with stellar arrangements of new and old songs, and just lets her rip. The kickoff track, "That Train Don't Stop Here," finds her in a bluesy groove with a lengthy rap at the end that extends the running time to almost seven minutes. Tunes like "In Another World," "Too Little Too Late," and "Break It to Me Gently" mine classic soul ballad territory, while Brown's jazzy side comes to the fore on "Sold My Heart to the Junkman" and "Love Letters." In the blues department, fine versions of Ivory Joe Hunter's "False Friend Blues" and Willie Mabon's "I Don't Know" strengthen the song selection, while Brown teams up with Bonnie Raitt on a conversational "Outskirts of Town." On the last tune, Sarah Brown's "Can't Get Excited," Ruth Brown starts out militant and winds up flirtatious, making a fitting closer for this great little album. Brown is in fine form here, and this is one terrific modern-day roots recording. *—Cub Koda*

You Don't Know Me/Touch Me in the Morning / Oct. 25, 1997 / Indigo ✦✦✦✦

Good Day for the Blues / Mar. 2, 1999 / Bullseye Blues ✦✦✦
At age 70, Ruth Brown was still in full command of her powers when she cut this beaut of an album in 1998. Fueled by an all-star band featuring Duke Robillard on guitar and New Orleans session stalwarts like James Singleton on bass, keyboardist Davell Crawford, alto saxophonist Ray Moore and a core group that also serves as her touring group, this record was cut live with all the musicians (including a full horn section) playing at once with no overdubs, a throwback to her recording modus operandi at Atlantic back in the 1950s. The songs are first rate, featuring new compositions from soul tunesmith Dan Penn ("Can't Stand a Broke Man," "Be Good to Me Tonight"), torchy ballads ("Never Let Me Go," "A Lover Is Forever," "The Richest One," "I Believe I Can Fly" and "True"), riotous spoken word fables ("Cabbage Head" and "H.B.'s Funky Fable"), and solid rhythm numbers ("Hangin' by a Shoestring," "Ice Water in Your Veins"), all expertly played and sung. Far from being on the downhill side of things, Brown demonstrated that there was still plenty of gas left in the tank when she cut this one. *—Cub Koda*

Ruth Brown/Miss Rhythm / Jun. 22, 1999 / Collectables ✦✦✦✦
Comprised of two prior Atlantic collections, this 26-track disc features the cream from Brown's hitmaking stretch for the label during most of the '50s. Along with such smashes as "(Mama) He Treats Your Daughter Mean," "Lucky Lips," and "Teardrops From My Eyes," there are plenty of minor gems to be had like "Somebody Touched Me" and "I Can See Everybody's Baby." And adding a bit of '50s pop verve, there are rockin' novelties like the Bobby Darin-penned "This Little Girls Gone Rockin'" and Leiber & Stoller's "I Can't Hear a Word You Say" (all told, the Coasters' hitmaking duo contribute three cuts to the mix). Along with a balanced mix of A- and B-sides, the disc features a support crew that includes tenor saxophonists Budd Johnson and Willis Jackson, trumpeter Taft Jordan, guitarist Mickey Baker, and drummer Connie Kay. This Collectables title might not beat out Rhino's two-disc retrospective, but it certainly will suit those in the market for a less-exhaustive introductory collection. *—Stephen Cook*

Here's That Rainy Day / Oct. 12, 1999 / Garland ✦✦✦
"Lush" usually isn't the first word that comes to mind when you think of Ruth Brown—earthy, gritty, funky, and soulful, certainly, but not lush. However, lush is exactly the word that describes this reissue, which finds the influential vocalist joined by a huge string orchestra. On *Here's That Rainy Day*, Brown's lavish backing includes no less than 17 violins as well as four violas, three cellos, a variety of horns, and a rhythm section. Not a typical Brown project, *Here's That Rainy Day* is, for the most part, an album of jazz-influenced pre-rock pop. Brown provides some exuberant blues shouting on Nellie Lutcher's "He's a Real Gone Guy," but overall, *Here's That Rainy Day* is very much a pop album. In fact, Brown's performances of "Whispering Grass," "Porgy," and the title song aren't unlike Dinah Washington's commercial pop output of the 1950s. Far from essential, *Here's That Rainy Day* isn't recommended to casual listeners. But hardcore collectors will find it to be an interesting departure for the singer. *—Alex Henderson*

Shirley Brown

b. Jan. 6, 1947, West Memphis, AR
Vocals / Southern Soul, R&B, Soul, Club/Dance, Urban
Born January 6, 1947, in West Memphis, the Browns moved to St. Louis, MO, when Shirley was very young. Cutting her teeth in church, at the age of ten, she earned a reputation in gospel circles throughout the city for delivering powerful solos. In her late teens, she concentrated on secular music and sung with many of the city's soul singers. Her first recordings, produced by Oliver Sain, did nothing nationally but made some noise locally. "I Ain't Gonna Tell" and "Love Is Built on a Strong Foundation" found their way to Memphis R&B stations, giving Brown the impetus, with the help of manager Albert King, to tryout and secured a deal with Stax Records. Brown had the last hit for Stax before the label folded. On November 14, 1974, "Woman to Woman" topped the R&B chart for two weeks.

Luck and timing caused her finest moment in music to occur, writers James Banks, Eddie Marion, and Henderson Thigpen wanted newly signed Inez Foxx ("Mockingbird") to cut the trend-setting love triangle. But, Foxx turned it down, suggesting the long rap on the beginning made it more suitable for Issac Hayes. After "Woman," she released two more singles on Stax's Truth label: "It Ain't No Fun" and "It's Worth a Whippin'," but Stax was on its last leg, and the doors to the theater at 926 East McLemore closed forever in 1975. She signed with Arista Records in 1977, her first single "Blessed Is the Woman (With a Man Like Mine)" didn't light up the charts. Neither did two other Arista singles: "Givin' Up" and "I Can't Move No Mountains." A self titled Arista album suffered the same fate as the singles. Brown's next label, 20th Century, released "You Got to Like What I Do" in 1980 but it didn't sell and the label lost interest. The previous year Stax/Fantasy released an LP of unreleased cuts, *The Real Feeling*. A deal with Sound Town resulted in the LP *Intimate Storm*, and one single, "Leave the Bridges Standing," in 1984. Two years later, "Shootin' a Blank" on Chelsea Avenue bombed, as did a single on Black Diamond Records, "If This Is Goodbye."

At this point, Shirley couldn't buy a hit. She may have gotten discouraged, but she never quit. Despite waxing only one bona fide hit in her career, Shirley Brown still records for Malaco Records, a label she joined in 1978. She's had six albums released, including a compilation LP. She also does clubs in the South and it's a safe bet that "Woman to Woman" remains her most requested song. *—Andrew Hamilton*

● **Woman to Woman** / 1974 / Stax ✦✦✦✦✦
Woman to Woman is Shirley Brown's first album and finds the singer settling in nicely to a set of slow ballads, all soaked with an ache that the singer seems born to convey. The title track is the song most associated with the singer and one of the great love-triangle melodramas of the '70s, sparking a series of answer songs, the best of which is Barbara Mason's "From His Woman to You." While not a song cycle like Millie Jackson's *Caught Up*, which took the cheating subgenre to its extreme, *Woman to Woman* does create an insular feeling, wrapping the listener in a string of indirectly related emotional contexts. From the intimacy of "So Glad to Have You" to the more direct "Between You and Me" and all points between, *Woman to Woman* displays all the good and bad complexities that soul singers found at the dark end of the street. *— Wade Kergan*

Shirley Brown / 1977 / Arista ✦✦✦

Fire & Ice / 1978 / Malaco ✦✦✦
While some of her labelmates at Malaco (including Johnnie Taylor and Latimore) have continued to record the type of straight-up soul music they embraced in the 1970s, Shirley Brown's Malaco CDs of the late '80s and '90s have found her trying to balance soul and urban contemporary considerations, with mixed results. Decent but uneven, the singer's Malaco releases have fallen short of the excellence of her classic Stax recordings. A case in point is *Fire & Ice*. The CD does contain a few gems, including the sexy "Take Me to Your Heart," the gritty "Sowed to the Wind" and the moving duet with Bobby Womack, "Ain't Nothin' Like the Lovin' We Got." But much of the material, although likable enough, isn't as strong as it could be. Brown is capable of a lot more. *—Alex Henderson*

For the Real Feeling / 1979 / Stax ✦✦✦
When Fantasy acquired the Stax catalog in 1977 and decided to revive the label, one of the artists who recorded for the new Stax was Shirley Brown. Unfortunately, the new Stax didn't get very far—though Fantasy has fared well with reissues of Stax's 1968-1975 output, none of the albums that came out on the new Stax in the late '70s were big sellers. But while *For the Real Feeling* suffered from disappointing sales, its material was generally decent and sometimes excellent. Produced by David Porter (who co-wrote many

Stax smashes with Isaac Hayes) and Lester Snell Jr., *For the Real Feeling* came out on a label that was famous for Memphis soul but often sounds like it could have been recorded for Philadelphia International. Indeed, Porter and Snell seem to be taking some hints from Gamble & Huff and their disciples on disco-influenced items like "Move Me—Move Me," "Hang on Louie," and "When, Where and What Time"—Brown's Aretha Franklin-influenced vocals are tough and gritty, but the production is very sleek, clean, and orchestrated. The producers don't turn Brown into an all-out dancefloor diva à la Gloria Gaynor, Linda Clifford, or Loleatta Holloway, although the influence of Northern soul/disco is certainly there. *—Alex Henderson*

Timeless / 1990 / Malaco ♦♦♦

Joy & Pain / 1993 / Malaco ♦♦♦

Diva of Soul / May 1, 1995 / Malaco ♦♦♦♦♦

The similarity between Brown's style and that of '80s-era Aretha Franklin is undeniable. That is certainly not the worst thing to say about a singer, but it reveals a lack of originality in her material. The blues and soul workouts here are competent but unremarkable, and the production is tinny. *—Tim Sheridan*

The Soul of a Woman / Oct. 28, 1997 / Malaco ♦♦♦♦♦

Shirley Brown scored back in the day with "Woman to Woman," but she's hardly past her prime; in fact, this soulful, gritty collection proves most definitely that Ms. Brown is in her stride. Producers Wolf Stephenson, Bobby Manual, Richard Cason, and Shirley herself help make this 11-track CD a force to be reckoned with—one devastating, deep-soul drama after another. The first track, "Why You Want to Love Me Like That," is so satisfying you'll take awhile to hear the rest of the CD, 'cause you'll keep repeating this track. Buoyed by the Muscle Shoals Horns and a crack rhythm section, Brown's bell-clear vocals could stir the dead. There isn't a loser in the bunch; especially inviting are "Female Player," "Don't Go Lookin' for My Man" (which includes a rap), "You Left a Good Woman for a Good Time," and "I Caught You With Your Pants Down." As Ken Hawkins, a DJ in Cleveland during the '60s, used to say, "if you don't like this, you got a hole in your soul." *—Andrew Hamilton*

Veda Brown

Vocals / Soul

Virtually nothing is known about Veda Brown, one of the lesser-known singers on Stax's roster in the early '70s. She did manage to crack the lower regions of the charts with two of her four singles on the label, "Short Stopping" and the ballad "Don't Start Lovin' Me." Brown was one of several talented but minor singers that could be found in the Stax empire alone, and while her work there is decent characteristic early-'70s Stax soul, there's not enough to indicate that she necessarily deserved a wider berth. After a couple of subsequent singles on the Raken label, nothing was heard from her again. *—Richie Unterberger*

● **Private Numbers** / 1993 / Stax ♦♦♦♦♦

Judy Clay has ten of the 18 tracks on this CD, the remainder belonging to Veda Brown, an even more obscure late-period Stax female soul belter. Clay's work for the label was gutsier in general than the sides she waxed during the same time for Atlantic, although only one of them made any chart impact, "Private Number" (a duet with William Bell). Including six solo turns and four duets with Bell, the material compiled here (all from 1968-1969) is solid, but doesn't catch fire that often. The best cuts are the just-a-bit-bluesy "Private Number," the pop-inflected deep soul ballad "It's Me" (penned by Isaac Hayes and David Porter), and a far more overlooked gem, "Children, Don't Get Weary," a minor-keyed, sparsely produced gospel-soul hybrid. On the latter track, Clay lets loose to a greater degree than she ever had before, or would ever do again. *—Richie Unterberger*

Brownstone

f. 1993, Los Angeles, CA

Group / Club/Dance, Urban

Smooth and silky R&B group Brownstone formed in Los Angeles in 1993 around the trio of Mimi, Nicci, and Maxee. Their debut single "Pass the Lovin'" performed respectably on the R&B charts, but the follow-up "If You Love Me" became a big hit, reaching the Top Ten of the pop charts and pushing Brownstone's first album, *From the Bottom Up*, into platinum territory. Additional singles "Grapevyne" and "I Can't Tell You Why" (an Eagles cover) also did well, though Mimi was forced to leave the group in 1995 due to health problems; she was replaced by Kina Cosper. Brownstone released their second album, *Still Climbing*, in June 1997. *—John Bush*

From the Bottom Up / 1995 / MJJ Music ♦♦♦

The L.A.-based R&B vocal trio Brownstone released its first album *From the Bottom Up* (on Michael Jackson's label) in 1995. A solid debut, *From the Bottom Up* showcases the group's considerable vocal talents, but Brownstone is somewhat distinctive in that the group's members also had a hand in writing their own material. Predictably, the album's songs alternate between R&B funk workouts and slinky slow jams, but the vocals rise above the material, making the album a delightful listen. The opener, "Party Wit' Me," gets things off to a funky start, and the hip-shakers "Pass the Lovin'" and "True to Me" prove Brownstone, unlike many R&B vocal groups, doesn't rely too heavily on ballads. Fortunately, the album's slow numbers are just as strong as the more uptempo material; the group's Gospel influences are evident in the album's hit single, "If You Love Me" (a slow-burning slice of R&B vocal heaven) and especially in the slow, sad "Don't Cry for Me." Brownstone's unlikely cover of the Eagles' hit ballad "I Can't Tell You Why" is one of the album's most successful tracks, as is the beautiful, piano-led "Half of You." *From the Bottom Up* is somewhat undermined by an overabundance of producers (of the album's 12 tunes, the group uses no less than ten producers/production teams), but this doesn't take away from the quality of the songs and the solid vocal performances. *—William Cooper*

● **Still Climbing** / Jun. 24, 1997 / MJJ Music ♦♦♦

Brownstone's second album, *Still Climbing*, suffers from the same inconsistent songwriting that plagued their debut *From the Bottom Up*, yet that isn't a fatal flaw. There are as many strong singles on *Still Climbing* as on the debut, and Brownstone sounds stronger and more confident on the record, making it an enjoyable, if tentative, step forward. *—Stephen Thomas Erlewine*

Don Bryant

b. Apr. 4, 1942, Memphis, TN

Vocals, Songwriter / Memphis Soul, Soul-Blues, Soul

Best known as a staff songwriter under Willie Mitchell at Hi Records, and as the husband of Hi star Ann Peebles, Don Bryant was also a fine, underappreciated singer in his own right. Bryant was born in Memphis on April 4, 1942; his father Edward sang with a gospel group called the Four Stars of Harmony, and Bryant himself began singing in church at age five. In 1955, he and four brothers formed their own gospel group, the Five Bryant Brothers, which soon switched to doo wop under the name the Quails. Not long after, Bryant joined several high school friends in another doo wop group, the Four Canes, who were named after their manager, local DJ D. Cane Cole. When the group split with Cole, Bryant changed their name to the Four Kings, and they caught the attention of trumpeter/bandleader Willie Mitchell, who began performing with them around the Memphis club scene. Through Mitchell, Bryant got his original composition "Is There Someone Else on Your Mind" recorded by the "5" Royales, and made his first solo recording in 1964 with a cover of Chris Kenner's "I Like It Like That."

Over the next five years, Bryant recorded several duets with Marion Brittnam and numerous cover songs, the latter of which constituted his first full-length LP, 1969's *Precious Soul* (issued on Hi). However, his behind-the-scenes career soon became more lucrative, specifically when Mitchell assigned him to work with new Hi signee Ann Peebles. No longer the label's focal point, Bryant resisted at first, but quickly discovered a creative and personal chemistry with Peebles that blossomed into a relationship in 1972 and marriage two years later. In the meantime, Bryant co-wrote a number of Peebles' signature songs, including "I Can't Stand the Rain" and "99 Pounds"; his success led to a staff songwriting position, where he penned material for other Hi stars like Al Green, Syl Johnson, O.V. Wright, and Otis Clay. Of necessity, his own recording career flagged during the '70s. When Hi's heyday ended, Bryant and Peebles both took a hiatus from the music industry; Bryant returned briefly in 1986 to record a self-released gospel album, *What Do You Think About Jesus*. When Peebles returned to recording during the '90s, Bryant again assisted with songwriting and musical backup. In 2000, he recorded another gospel album, *It's All in the Word*. *—Steve Huey*

● **The Singles Collection** / Jan. 16, 1996 / Hi ♦♦♦♦

The 1996 release *The Singles Collection* is the best single-disc overview of Don Bryant's Hi recordings. On the subsequent double-disc *Complete Don Bryant on Hi Records*, the sheer volume of material made his work seem generic. Distilled to 20 highlights, he sounds better—a solid journeyman vocalist, capable of turning out thoroughly enjoyable, bluesy Southern soul. This isn't as easy to find as 1998's *Hi Masters*—which, at 15 tracks, offers less, but is still a good substitute—but it stands as the best Bryant comp assembled for CD. It's the one that argues the case for his talents most effectively. *—Stephen Thomas Erlewine*

Hi Masters / Sep. 15, 1998 / Hi ♦♦♦♦

● **The Complete Don Bryant on Hi Records** / May 16, 2000 / Hi ♦♦♦♦

Released in 2000, *The Complete Don Bryant on Hi Records* stands as the most extensive compilation of Don Bryant's key material yet assembled—which is appropriate, considering the title. At two discs and 52 tracks, it's a bit much for anybody but serious fans, since Bryant favored generic—albeit enjoyable—Southern soul during his stint at Hi. This isn't a bad thing, since the Hi band and producers always managed to turn out exceedingly listenable sides, but it does wear thin over the course of two discs for anybody but serious soul fans. Those are the listeners advised to purchase this; the rest are better off with either single disc collection, *Hi Masters* or *Singles Collection*. *—Stephen Thomas Erlewine*

Peabo Bryson

b. Apr. 13, 1951, Greenville, SC

Vocals / Adult Contemporary, Urban

Vocalist Peabo Bryson was among the premier silky-voiced soul artists who emerged as the softer, more sophisticated urban contemporary sound became dominant in the '70s and '80s. Bryson, who was born in Greenville, SC, sang with Al Freeman & the Upsetters in 1965, and was in the group Moses Dillard & the Tex-Town Display from 1968 to 1973. He was a producer and composer for Atlanta's Bang Records in the early '70s, and sang in Michael Zager's Moon Band. His self-titled debut LP and several singles were recorded for Bang's subsidiary company Bullet, among them "Do It With Feeling," "Underground Music," "It's Just a Matter of Time," "Just Another Day," and "I Can Make It Better." All were moderate R&B hits. Bryson moved to Capitol in 1978, where his first album, *Reaching for the Sky*, went gold, and the title track was a number-six R&B hit. He remained in the Moon Band until 1979, departing after "I'm So Into You" spent two weeks as the nation's number-two R&B hit in 1978.

Bryson continued a prolific career as both lead act and duet participant. He made hit duets with Natalie Cole, Roberta Flack, Melissa Manchester, and Regina Belle. Bryson recorded for Capitol until 1984, when he switched to Elektra, and enjoyed more success with "If Ever You're in My Arms Again." He moved to Columbia in 1991, issuing *Can You Stop the Rain*; subsequent efforts include 1994's *Through the Fire* and 1999's *Unconditional Love*. He also enjoyed more acclaim making duets with Belle. *—Ron Wynn*

Peabo / Sep. 1976 / Bang/Bullet ♦♦♦
Peabo, released in 1976, is the first album from the talented singer. Even by his mid-twenties, Bryson had the clear and singular tenor and the mix of strength and vulnerability. Not yet an established lothario, the best tracks here deal mostly with regret and bittersweet emotions. Bryson wrote or co-wrote all of the tracks and serves as producer. On the first song, the country-styled "Just Another Day," Bryson reviews a going nowhere relationship as he sings "I guess I'll stay and see the end/Imagine I was here/For a while" with the perfect balance of restraint and self-pity. The emotional and melody rich "I Can Make It Better" has Bryson giving his best performance here. *Peabo* also has uptempo tracks, although he's not as proficient at them as he is the ballads. "Smile" and "Underground Music" are skilled, but his metier is no doubt songs with a slower pace. The bittersweet "Lovely Lady" is close to the work he would subsequently do for Capitol. Recorded with the "LA Rhythm Section," the track features a dramatic string arrangement from Gene Page and another smooth and assured vocal from Bryson. The last track, "God Is on Our Side," has Bryson skillfully putting across his message without making it boring. *Peabo* was recorded at four different recording studios and employed esteemed session players and singers including Ray Parker Jr., David T. Walker, Luther Vandross, and Cissy Houston. *Peabo* is a great debut and offers a few of his most loved songs. *—Jason Elias*

Reaching for the Sky / Jan. 1978 / Capitol ♦♦♦♦♦
Here is Peabo Bryson's first great album and the vehicle that established him as a favorite of urban contemporary audiences. He was still officially working with Michael Zager's Moon Band. This was his Capitol debut, and the title track became Bryson's first R&B Top Ten hit. The album also went gold and signaled that it was only a matter of time before Bryson would split from the Zager band. *—Ron Wynn*

Crosswinds / Nov. 1978 / Capitol ♦♦♦♦♦
This is a great album, one of Peabo Bryson's first smash efforts. His vocals were at their most expressive and soulful, and the production didn't subordinate his singing to the orchestrations or arrangements. The title track was an R&B Top 40 hit, and the album yielded a second solid song in "She's a Woman." *—Ron Wynn*

We're the Best of Friends / Nov. 1979 / Capitol ♦♦♦
This features another hit album for Bryson, and one of his many successful collaborations with female vocalists. Natalie Cole's career had hit a dry spell, and she piggybacked on Bryson's hit status. But the two proved to be quite effective partners, although he was in much better vocal shape than she was at the time. His soaring leads often nearly evaporated her complementary lines, but the album still worked. It also got the pair two hits in the songs "Gimme Some Time" and a cover of Bobby Caldwell's "What You Won't Do for Love." *—Ron Wynn*

Paradise / Apr. 1980 / Capitol ♦♦

Live & More / Dec. 1980 / Atlantic ♦♦♦

Turn the Hands of Time / Feb. 1981 / Capitol ♦♦

I Am Love / Nov. 1981 / Capitol ♦♦♦
On this album, Peabo Bryson still retains some of the appeal that made him a favorite among R&B lovers. The title track is the first song on the A-side, and rightly so, as it hooks you in immediately. Its comforting, moody chord changes are pleasantly engaging. Bryson's pleading vocals are convincing, even in their mournful tone. This song was not a release, but it did receive radio airplay and remains a Quiet Storm standard. There were two featured singles: "Let the Feeling Flow" and "There's No Guarantee" are both moderately paced ballads with a commercial feel; the former is a more dynamic song. While Bryson's lead vocals roar throughout the body of the song, his background vocalist Terry Dukes stands just as tall in the vamp, where the two exchange vocal ad libs. The song also enjoyed more chart success than its companion; it peaked at number six on the *Billboard* R&B charts after 20 weeks. "There's No Guarantee" fell 30 positions short of its predecessor at number 36 after only nine weeks on the charts. While "Impossible" conveys a pop texture during its inception, it slowly transcends into a spirited R&B number with much gospel influence. To be known for Quiet Storm savvy, the SC native has some rhythmic uptempo numbers that hold their own. Bryson's overall ability to inflict his vocal prowess upon a song remains prominent on this album. *—Craig Lytle*

Don't Play With Fire / Nov. 1982 / Capitol ♦♦♦
Peabo Bryson got three chart singles from this album and stayed high atop the urban contemporary and R&B charts. He still wasn't hitting the peaks he routinely climbed in the late '70s, but was maintaining his status as a hit act and romantic idol. *—Ron Wynn*

Born to Love / Jul. 1983 / Capitol ♦♦♦
Bryson hit his '80s peak with this hugely successful duet album with Roberta Flack. It did the same thing for her that his album with Natalie Cole had done in the late '70s; Flack was revived as an urban stylist. The single "Tonight I Celebrate My Love" was all over the airwaves and even used on a soap opera. It made it into the pop Top 20 and reached the number five spot on the R&B charts. *—Ron Wynn*

Straight from the Heart / May 1984 / Elektra ♦♦♦♦♦
A good mix of slow- and uptempo tunes, including the definitive Bryson ballad "If Ever You're in My Arms Again." *— William Ruhlmann*

● **Collection** / Jun. 1984 / Capitol ♦♦♦♦♦
Released in 1984, *Collection* covers the basics of Peabo Bryson's peak hitmaking years at Capitol, featuring his hits between 1978 and 1983. Later collections, such as 2001's *Anthology*, covered more ground and featured many more songs, but for a snapshot of his peak—containing such hits as "I'm So Into You," "You're Lookin' Like Love to Me," "We Don't Have to Talk (About Love)" and his classic Roberta Flack duet "Tonight I Celebrate My Love"—this works very, very well indeed. *—Stephen Thomas Erlewine*

Take No Prisoners / Jun. 1985 / Elektra ♦♦♦
In the wake of his ascension into the pop Top Ten with the ballad "If Ever You're in My Arms Again," Peabo Bryson might have been expected to try to consolidate that success with his follow-up record. And indeed, *Take No Prisoners*, produced by such crossover veterans as Arif Mardin and Tommy LiPuma and featuring such pop songwriters as Barry Mann, Cynthia Weil, and Tom Snow, may have seemed like a try for that. But Elektra led off its singles releases with the light, uptempo title track, and followed with another, "There's Nothin' out There," apparently in a move to solidify Bryson's R&B base. Neither of those songs found much success, however, and the potential crossover ballads, such as "Love Always Finds a Way" and "She's Over Me," never got off side two and onto the airwaves. As a result, the album represented a missed opportunity for Bryson, even though he sang with his usual assurance, the material was of good quality, and the production was sympathetic. *— William Ruhlmann*

Quiet Storm / Oct. 1986 / Elektra ♦♦
A prototype album for late-'80s urban contemporary music. Bryson made some overproduced, effectively sung ballads and a few decent uptempo tracks, and the results were disappointing but mildly successful. The album did get extensive publicity and support, but there were no hits. *—Ron Wynn*

Can You Stop the Rain / Jun. 1991 / Columbia ♦♦♦
Having returned to Capitol Records for 1989's *All My Love* and enjoyed a career uptick, Peabo Bryson moved again to Columbia Records, where he completed his comeback to the commercial status he had enjoyed in the early '80s. Bryson seemed to have reconciled himself to the public's view of him as primarily a balladeer, and he delivered the goods, especially on the title track, a number-one R&B hit, and on the Cynthia Weil/Barry Mann tune "Closer Than Close," which also hit the R&B Top Ten. (Bryson helped his own cause considerably by involving himself in the writing and production of five of the 11 songs.) The album topped the R&B charts, and although Bryson still had trouble crossing over to the pop charts, it was his biggest seller in seven years. The album's success, however, was quickly overshadowed by Bryson's soundtrack work, as he placed hits from the *Beauty and the Beast* and *Aladdin* scores in the charts later in 1991 and 1992. *—William Ruhlmann*

● **I'm So Into You: The Passion of Peabo Bryson** / Jun. 3, 1997 / Capitol ♦♦♦♦♦
I'm So Into You: The Passion of Peabo Bryson is a terrific overview of the smooth soul singer's late-'70s and early-'80s hits, featuring the majority of his Top Ten R&B hits for Capitol Records ("Reaching for the Sky," "I'm So Into You," "Let the Feeling Flow," "Gimme Some Time"), plus his hit duets with Roberta Flack ("Tonight I Celebrate My Love for You") and Natalie Cole ("Love Will Find You," "Let's Fall in Love/You Send Me"). *—Stephen Thomas Erlewine*

Unconditional Love / Apr. 27, 1999 / Private Music ♦♦♦
Peabo Bryson carved a lucrative recording/entertaining career as one of the leading exponents of sophisticated or mature R&B. He still exudes a highbrow persona on this late-'90s CD, excelling on "Did You Ever Know," "Ain't No Body" (the old Rufus song), the umpteenth rendition of Leon Russell's "A Song for You," "The Gift" (a duet with Roberta Flack), and "Light the World," with Deborah Gibson. Pure Peabo, but it carbons previous albums and is only essential to a completist. *—Andrew Hamilton*

Anthology / 2001 / Capitol ♦♦♦♦♦
This double-disc set compiles 30 of Peabo Bryson's highest-charting—as well as best-loved—R&B and pop/soul classics. Bryson's smooth tenor vocals epitomize the late '70s and '80s quiet storm genre of laid-back sexy soul music. *Anthology* highlights both Bryson's hits as a solo artist, as well as his highly regarded and memorable duets. Additionally, by cross-licensing songs from other labels, *Anthology* is easily the most comprehensive overview of Bryson's work available. While this set is drawn primarily from his albums on Capitol Records in the mid- to late '70s and '80s, the set begins with a trio of songs—"Underground Music," "Just Another Day," and "I Can Make It Better" from Bryson's debut on the Atlanta, GA-based Bang label. His lengthy relationship with Capitol began in earnest with *Reaching for the Sky*—represented on this collection by the Top Ten title track, among several others. Bryson's tremendous crossover appeal ensured that pop and R&B radio were always mere minutes away from either one of Bryson's solo hits or his numerous duets. The album that broke Bryson nationally was a volume with co-vocalist Natalie Cole titled *We're the Best of Friends*. Included from that release are the hits "Gimmie Some Time" and "What You Won't Do for Love." The instantly recognizable "Tonight I Celebrate My Love" is one of the three duets underscoring the special chemistry between Bryson and Roberta Flack. While no substitute for her late partner Donny Hathaway, Bryson certainly rekindles the flame. Another notable duet on *Anthology* is "Lovers After All," featuring co-vocalist Melissa Manchester. The track stands as the *only* highlight on her otherwise forgettable *For the Working Girl* album in 1980. *Anthology* features a 12-page liner notes booklet including an essay by David Nathan as well as detailed track information. *—Lindsay Planer*

B.T. Express

f. 1973, New York, NY [Brooklyn], **db.** 1981
Group / Disco, Funk
This funk-disco group was formed by Jeff Lane in Brooklyn during the '70s. They started in 1972 as the King Davis House Rockers, and later were called the Brooklyn Trucking Express. The roster consisted of saxophonist/vocalist Bill Risbrook, percussionist Dennis Rowe, guitarist Rick Thompson, saxophonist/flutist Carlos Ward, keyboardist Michael Jones (Kashif), lead guitarist/vocalist Wesley Hall, drummer Leslie Ming, bassist, organist and vocalist Louis Risbrook, and vocalist Barbara Joyce Lomas. Their debut LP *Do it ('Til You're Satisfied)* had two number-one R&B and Top Ten pop hits in the title cut and

"Express." Subsequent LPs yielded two more R&B Top Ten singles, "Give It What You Got/Peace Pipe" in 1975 and "Can't Stop Groovin' Now, Wanna Do It Some More" in 1976.

After 1977's "Shout It Out," which cracked the R&B Top 20 (number 12), the group slumped with the album *Shout!* They were off the charts until 1980. They made a slight comeback that year with *B.T. Express 1980*, though only the single "Give Up the Funk (Let's Dance)" made it into the Top 40 (number 24). They later recorded for Record Shack, Earthtone, and King Davis, but couldn't duplicate their earlier success. Kashif scored hits as a producer, performer, and composer in the '80s. *—Ron Wynn*

Do It ('Til You're Satisfied) / Nov. 1974 / Roadshow ✦✦✦✦

Do It ('Til You're Satisfied) features two million sellers by the New York natives; the title track and "Express" are funky, irresistible disco gems. Produced by Jeff Lane and mixed by Tom Moulton, the two dancefloor classics features hypnotic basslines, handclaps on alternate beats, and the coolest congas on the planet, all combined with masterfully mixed guitars, saxophones, flutes, strings, Barbara Joyce Lomas' blaring lead, Louis Risbrooks' bass vocal retorts, and Richard Thompson's support vocals. Lane was never able to repeat the tightness of the two tracks on subsequent albums or even on this one. "If I Don't Turn You On" and "Do You Like It" come close, but "Once You Get It," "Do It," "This House Is Smoking," and "Mental Telepathy" do not. Good, because of the two classics, but a greatest-hits collection would be even better. *—Andrew Hamilton*

Non-Stop / Jul. 1975 / Roadshow ✦✦✦✦✦

When one thinks of the cultural contributions that Brooklyn's African-American neighborhoods made in the 1980s and 1990s, the people who immediately come to mind range from director Spike Lee to major rappers (the Fat Boys, Big Daddy Kane, MC Lyte, Biz Markie, among many others) to soul/urban contemporary singer James "D-Train" Williams. But back in the 1970s, Brooklyn was known for its disco-minded brand of funk. Brooklyn funk wasn't the kind of hardcore funk that you expected from James Brown, George Clinton's P-Funk empire (Parliament/Funkadelic, Bootsy Collins, the Brides of Funkenstein, etc.), the Gap Band, Rick James, or the Ohio Players—it was funk-disco, and Brooklyn outfits like B.T. Express, the Crown Heights Affair, and Skyy were huge in the clubs (especially black clubs). When B.T. Express' second album, *Non-Stop*, came out in 1975, Scepter assumed that it would fare well in dance clubs—and sure enough, club DJs went wild over this record. However, *Non-Stop* contained some major radio hits as well, including "Peace Pipe" and "Give It What You Got" (both of which reached number five on *Billboard*'s R&B singles chart). Meanwhile, "Still Good, Still Like It" and "Discotizer" are among that tracks that weren't big radio hits but grabbed the attention of club jocks. The LP's only ballad is a cover of the Burt Bacharach/Hal David favorite "Close to You"; although B.T. Express' version is pleasant enough, the fact remains that romantic ballads were never its strong point. Uptempo material is what defines *Non-Stop* and makes it one of the band's finest, most essential albums. *—Alex Henderson*

Energy to Burn / May 1976 / Columbia ✦✦✦✦✦

B.T. Express' third album, *Energy to Burn*, marked two firsts for the Brooklyn residents: It was their first album for Columbia, and it marked the arrival of keyboardist Michael Jones, aka Kashif. Not that Kashif's arrival was a major event for R&B fans of 1976, the year in which this album came out. It wasn't until 1981, when Kashif wrote "I'm in Love" for Evelyn "Champagne" King, that he became famous as a producer/songwriter—and his first solo album didn't come out until 1983. Besides, *Energy to Burn* (which was lead singer Barbara Joyce's last album with B.T. Express) doesn't sound anything like the smooth, sophisticated urban contemporary music that Kashif wrote or produced for King, George Benson, Howard Johnson, Melba Moore, and others in the early 1980s; this LP is state-of-the-art B.T. Express. Although the band's work was uneven in the late 1970s and early 1980s, *Energy to Burn* is generally excellent. Those who had grooved to B.T. Express' two previous albums weren't disappointed by hypnotic funk-disco smokers like "Can't Stop Groovin' Now," "Wanna Do It Some More" (which reached number six on *Billboard*'s R&B singles charts), "Depend on Yourself," and the title song (which was only a number-37 R&B hit but was a favorite in clubs). One of the album's most unorthodox tracks is "Herbs," an instrumental that successfully fuses B.T. Express' trademark funk-disco sound with the sort of sweet reggae that prevailed in Jamaica during the rocksteady era. And not surprisingly, the album's least inspired track is a cover of Gamble & Huff's "Now That We've Found Love"—romantic ballads and slow jams were never B.T. Express' strong point. But other than that, *Energy to Burn* is one of the band's strongest albums. *—Alex Henderson*

Function at the Junction / May 1977 / Columbia ✦✦✦

When lead vocalist Barbara Joyce left B.T. Express after its third album, *Energy to Burn*, the Brooklyn combo didn't search for another female singer—instead, it decided to carry on as an all-male outfit. Joyce was an appealing, talented singer, but losing her was hardly a fatal blow for B.T. Express. Unlike the Commodores, L.T.D., or Earth, Wind & Fire, B.T. Express never went out of its way to push a superstar vocalist—its 1970s albums were about the overall sound of the band, not any particular singer. *Function at the Junction* was B.T. Express' first post-Joyce LP, but it isn't much different from the New Yorkers' three previous albums. With Jeff Lane (the guy who produced Brass Construction in the 1970s) producing, B.T. Express continue to mine the same funk-disco waters on club-friendly tracks like "Expose Yourself," "We Got It Together," and "Funky Music." Overall, this is a decent record, although it is mildly uneven and falls short of the excellence of B.T. Express' previous releases. And that isn't because of Joyce's departure; Columbia was bringing in more and more outside songwriters, which made its post-1976 albums inconsistent and less focused. Columbia assumed that those outside songwriters would be an asset, but they turned out to be something of a distraction. Nonetheless, *Function at the Junction* has more pluses than minuses, and is worth hearing if you're among B.T. Express' hardcore fans. *—Alex Henderson*

Shout! / Feb. 1978 / Columbia ✦✦

If you notice some similarities between B.T. Express and Brass Construction, it's no coincidence. B.T. Express was a major influence on Brass Construction, and the same guy who produced all of Brass Construction's 1970s albums (Jeff Lane) also produced B.T. Express' first four albums: 1974's *Do It ('Til You're Satisfied)*, 1975's *Non-Stop*, 1976's *Energy to Burn*, and 1977's *Function at the Junction*. Released in 1978, *Shout!* was the first B.T. Express album that Lane didn't produce. Instead, B.T. Express produced this LP with guitarist/songwriter Billy Nichols, who wasn't an actual member but had been writing songs for the band since 1974. It was Nichols who wrote B.T. Express' first major hit, "Do It ('Til You're Satisfied)." So he had a strong feeling for its music, and *Shout!* (which was Kashif's last album with the band) isn't a radical departure from the four B.T. Express albums that Lane produced. However, this is an uneven, disappointing record. "Shout It Out" (which reached number 11 on Billboard's R&B singles chart) is a funk-disco gem, and the sociopolitical "Look at the People" is a catchy message song. But much of the material is merely average. Tracks like "Shake It Off," "I Want You With Me," and "You Got Something" aren't terribly inspired or memorable, and point to the fact that B.T. Express was running out of steam in 1978. So not surprisingly, a lot of people who bought the "Shout It Out" single opted to pass on the *Shout!* LP, which is strictly for completists. *—Alex Henderson*

B.T. Express 1980 / May 1980 / Excalibre ✦✦✦

In the 1970s, it wasn't uncommon to find a funk band that was entirely self-contained—all of the producing, writing, and arranging was done by actual bandmembers, not outsiders. B.T. Express, however, was never totally self-contained; even its first major hit, "Do It ('Til You're Satisfied)," was written by someone who wasn't an official member: guitarist Billy Nichols. But it is safe to say that B.T. Express was more self-reliant in the beginning than it was in the early 1980s; at that point, Columbia was bringing in so many outside songwriters and additional musicians that the Brooklynites were becoming less distinctive. Depending on the band, outside influence can be either a positive or a negative—in some cases, it can revitalize a band. B.T. Express, however, recorded its most essential albums when it was more self-reliant. Produced by Morrie Brown, this 1980 release is full of songs that weren't written or even co-written by B.T. Express members and employs its share of extra musicians (mostly keyboardists). *B.T. Express 1980* is a mixed bag; although it isn't good to hear B.T. Express losing its identity, most of the material is decent—"Takin' Off," "Funk Theory," and "Heart of Fire" are enjoyable, infectious funk-disco items even though they lack that distinctive B.T. Express sound of the 1970s. Meanwhile, the single "Give Up the Funk (Let's Dance)," which made it to number 24 on the R&B singles chart, is more recognizable as a B.T. Express tune. Some of the material is pretty generic, but overall, *B.T. Express 1980* isn't a bad record—in fact, it's an improvement over 1978's disappointing *Shout!* Nonetheless, *B.T. Express 1980* is the work of a band that was four years past its prime, and the LP is only recommended to completists and hardcore collectors. *—Alex Henderson*

Golden Classics / Sep. 19, 1991 / Collectables ✦✦✦✦✦

B.T. Express exploded on the funk-disco scene in the mid-'70s with back-to-back number-one R&B hits, "Do It ('Til You're Satisfied)" and "Express," both of which also cracked the pop Top Ten. "Give It What You Got/Peace Pipe" was another big hit, but the group had peaked by the late '70s. This collection includes these three smashes, plus other respectable numbers. They were never great singers, but were a good funk ensemble. *—Ron Wynn*

● **The Best of B.T. Express** / May 27, 1997 / Rhino ✦✦✦✦✦

Although B.T. Express didn't have that many major radio hits, the New Yorkers' extremely danceable funk reigned supreme in the clubs (especially black clubs). "Do It ('Til You're Satisfied)," "Peace Pipe," "Shout It Out" and "Express" are among the handful of jams on this engaging 15-song CD that were actually sizable hits on black radio; most of the other songs, however, don't fit that description. But play this collection for anyone who DJ'd in a black club in the 1970s, and chances are they'll know most of the material. Express, a major influence on East Coast units like the Brass Construction and Mass Production, was very much a party band, and addictive album tracks like "This House Is Smokin'" and "Once You Get It" found their way to club turntables without ever coming out as singles. Although pleasant enough, a cover of Burt Bacharach & Hal David's "Close to You" shows that ballads were never the Express' strong point (which is truly ironic, given that one of its members, Kashif, would become known as a top R&B love man in the 1980s). And the 1980 recordings "Stretch" and "Does It Feel Good" are pretty generic, but on the whole, this disc is something funksters should savor. *—Alex Henderson*

Bull & the Matadors

f. Chicago, IL

Group / Pop-Soul, R&B, Soul

Bull & the Matadors were a Chicago-based group consisting of James Lafayette Parks (aka Jamell Bull Parks), Milton Hayes, and James Otis Love. (Another group named Bull & the El Capalaras recorded for Bell Records in 1971-1972 but are a different crew.) Bull & the Matadors scored in 1968 on Toddlin' Town Records with "The Funky Judge," a raucous, hard-edge novelty with a sinister beat; the minor hit created by Andre Williams and Leo Hutton was a great party record. The follow-up, "Move With the Groove," never ignited. Len Ron Hanks, who later teamed with Zane Grey to compose "Back in Love Again," co-wrote the song with Charles Nealey and Karl Tareleton. Parks, Hayes, and Love wrote both sides of "You Decide" b/w "Love Come Down," but the 1969 issue flopped also, and they faded from the scene. *—Andrew Hamilton*

Vernon Burch

b. Washington, D.C.

Guitar / Soul

Washington, D.C., guitarist Vernon Burch spent two years backing the Delfonics as a teen sensation. He was 13 when he joined them. He later played with the Stairsteps, and then with the Bar-Kays for four years. Burch began recording for United Artists in 1975, and later for Columbia, Chocolate City, and Spector. Only the singles "Changes (Messin' With My Mind)" in 1975 and "Do It to Me" in 1981 made it into the R&B Top 20. Burch probably gained more recognition and exposure for his role in the film *Hollywood Nights* in 1980, playing Marvin Gaye. *—Ron Wynn*

I'll Be Your Sunshine / 1975 / United Artists ✦✦✦
When an 18-year-old Vernon Burch launched his solo career in the mid-'70s, those who knew him for his four years with the Bar-Kays tended to assume that his solo output would be similar. But *I'll Be Your Sunshine*, the singer/guitarist's first solo effort, doesn't sound anything like his work with the Bar-Kays (which was a Memphis soul band before reinventing itself as a hardcore funk band). Instead, Burch brings a strong Stevie Wonder influence to this 1975 LP, which finds him co-producing and doing almost all of the writing. Burch's phrasing as a vocalist underscores his appreciation of Wonder, and his composing is obviously Wonder-influenced on originals that range from the haunting ballad "Dreamin'" to funky offerings like "Ain't Gonna Tell Nobody" and the single "Changes (Messin' With My Mind)." But being Wonder-influenced isn't the same as being a clone; as much as he admires the artist's singing and writing, Burch still comes across as his own man. *I'll Be Your Sunshine* falls short of remarkable, but it was a solid and decent solo debut for the former Bar-Kays member. *—Alex Henderson*

● **When I Get Back Home** / 1976 / Columbia ✦✦✦✦
Vernon Burch was only 21 when, in 1977, he moved from United Artists to Columbia for his second solo album, *When I Get Back Home*. Creatively, there were no signs of a sophomore slump on this LP; in fact, *When I Get Back Home* is the singer/guitarist's strongest, most consistent album. Burch's writing and co-writing are impressive throughout the LP, and that is true on gritty funk items like "Ghetto Penthouse" and the single "Sexasonic," as well as more laid-back offerings such as "Mr. Sin," "Bye, Bye, Baby," and "Paradise." The Washington, D.C., native brings a healthy appreciation of Stevie Wonder to all of the material, but he never sounds like he's actually trying to emulate Wonder—Burch is his own person and has a recognizable style of his own. Unfortunately, creative success doesn't necessarily mean commercial success, and *When I Get Back Home* wasn't the big hit it should have been. Even though Burch had a gem of a single in "Sexasonic," this LP fell through the cracks. But that doesn't erase the fact that *When I Get Back Home* is Burch's most essential album. *—Alex Henderson*

Love-A-Thon / 1978 / Chocolate City ✦✦

Get Up / 1979 / Chocolate City ✦✦✦
In the late '70s and early '80s, some people argued that Vernon Burch had made a big mistake by leaving the Bar-Kays. At the time, the Bar-Kays were huge. A combo that was originally known for Memphis soul had successfully reinvented itself as a hardcore funk band, and its albums of the period were doing a lot better than Burch's solo efforts. Naturally, some people couldn't help but wonder if Burch would have been better off sticking around for smashes like "Holy Ghost" and "Shake Your Rump to the Funk." But he didn't want to spend his entire career as the Bar-Kays' guitarist; he was determined to see what he could accomplish on his own. Recorded in 1979, *Get Up* was Burch's second album for Chocolate City/Casablanca and his fourth solo album overall. This LP, which marked the first time he worked with producer/drummer James E. Gadson, was a departure from his previous releases in that it found him emphasizing dance-oriented material. "Once Again in My Life" is the record's only ballad, and Burch is obviously going after the disco crowd on uptempo dance items like "Arrogant Lady," "Never Can Find the Way (Hot Love)," and "Dr. Do It Good." Even the familiar "Try a Little Tenderness" (a major hit for Otis Redding in the 1960s) gets the disco-funk treatment. *Get Up* isn't a masterpiece, but it's generally enjoyable—and it was an improvement over 1978's *Love-A-Thon*. *—Alex Henderson*

Steppin' Out / 1980 / Chocolate City ✦✦

Playing Hard to Get / 1982 / Spector ✦✦

Leroy Burgess

b. New York, NY [Harlem]
Vocals, Keyboards, Producer, Multi Instruments / Club/Dance, Disco, Urban, Funk
Flip through any old stack of underground disco and boogie vinyl released between the late '70s and mid-'80s. If Leroy Burgess isn't in the credits of at least one of the first 50 scanned, consider it a fluke. He had his hand in so many recording sessions that even devout fans had trouble keeping tabs on his activities. Each release—some by short-lived studio projects, others by full-blown groups—was either aided or carried by Burgess, a multi-instrumentalist, vocalist, producer, arranger and songwriter who made a significant impact on dance music. Even if Burgess never had a single note of his voice recorded, his value to black music (including the birth of house) would be firmly in place. But it's his supremely expressive gospel-steeped baritone that has earned him most of the attention.

Born and raised in Harlem, Burgess sang in church choirs and was tutored by Herbie Jones, a Duke Ellington and Billy Strayhorn associate; apart from that, his musical knowledge was picked up informally through his mother (a one-time opera singer) and the infrequent meet-ups with his uncle, arranger/producer Thom Bell. He cut his teeth in the late '60s as one third of the Mellow Souls, a group that evolved into Black Ivory. Their debut single, "Don't Turn Around," hit the Top 40 of the R&B chart. Burgess departed in 1977, after three ballad-heavy LPs. However, a temporary return yielded "Mainline," a disco classic.

"Mainline" was a turning point in Burgess' career. That and "Weekend," a song given to former Black Ivory manager/arranger/producer/songwriter Patrick Adams for his Phreek album, kicked off a flurry of projects. Releases by Bumblebee Unlimited, Inner Life, Dazzle, the Fantastic Aleems, Universal Robot Band and Change featured Burgess' handiwork in various capacities, as did material from solo artists such as Rick James, Fonda Rae, Venus Dodson, Ben E. King and Eddie Kendricks. Needless to say, Burgess was in demand.

In the middle of all this work, Burgess also found time to lead a couple projects. An impromptu session with two frequent partners, James Calloway and Sonny Davenport, birthed Convertion's "Let's Do It"—a sweet midtempo single full of oddball synth sounds and Burgess' ever-beaming vocals. Convertion continued as Logg and delivered a horribly overlooked self-titled LP on Salsoul in 1981. The album spawned three singles—including "I Know You Will," remixed by Larry Levan—that exemplify the era that followed disco and predated house. Amazingly, "I Know You Will" registered at a lowly number 81 on the dance chart.

Burgess' output was reduced to a slow pace by the end of the '80s. His inability to become a household name can be attributed to his happiness with anonymity and the fact that most of his releases came out on very small labels. Still, there isn't a single history-aware house DJ who doesn't know his or her Leroy Burgess. In 2002, Soul Brother tied up several loose ends in his discography by issuing two spectacular retrospectives. *—Andy Kellman*

● **Anthology, Vol. 1: The Voice** / Feb. 2002 / Soul Brother ✦✦✦✦✦
As house producer Ashley Beedle states in the liner notes, "If James Brown is the godfather of funk then surely Leroy Burgess deserves the same title for his badass disco boogie." No single disc could possibly put a full perspective on the career of Burgess, a writer, producer, instrumentalist, and vocalist who has been smack in front of some of the best disco and boogie to have inspired people to cut a rug or shed a tear in life-affirming joy. The title of this package, *Anthology, Vol. 1: The Voice*, thankfully gives the promise of further strides to put Burgess' deep discography back into circulation and to lasso rare gems from someone who operated as/with so many names that only die-hard fans were able to keep tabs on him throughout the better part of two decades. This focuses on his Logg project for Salsoul and his partnership with Taharqa and Tunde-Ra Aleem for the Aleems' Nia imprint, and it also includes the A-side of a proper solo single for Salsoul and a previously unreleased cut. The three Logg jams—"You've Got That Something," "I Know You Will," "Dancing Into the Stars"—are presented in their extended mixes and make for the highlights of these highlights. These co-productions between Burgess and Greg Carmichael continue to complement sunny Saturday afternoons and activate sweat-drenched dancefloors over 20 years after their committal to tape. Burgess' boundless energy is funneled through that expressive voice of his that goes straight to the heart ("expressive" in this case should be capitalized, italicized, and underscored). If there's any indication as to how deep Burgess' discography runs, this disc doesn't include two of his hottest, best-known cuts: Black Ivory's "Mainline" and Convertion's "Let's Do It." Bring on round two. Quick! *—Andy Kellman*

Anthology, Vol. 2: The Producer / Sep. 2002 / Soul Brother ✦✦✦✦
There's really no point in paying any mind to Soul Brother's admirable attempt at separating Leroy Burgess' work as a producer from his work as a vocalist. As one can determine from a glance at the credits, Burgess often produced and sang on the same song—not to mention that he often wrote, arranged, and played keyboards. Regardless, this second volume proves that the first hardly cleared out the top drawer; perhaps the biggest testament of all to Burgess' status as a disco/boogie legend is the fact that neither disc contains Universal Robot Band's "Barely Breaking Even," a favorite of many Burgess freaks and unaware club-goers alike. This second volume does show the man in more of a behind-the-scenes light, as he often isn't the lead vocalist. Still, it's nearly impossible to play favorites; just about every selection is full of the ingredients that Burgess' associations became known for. Black Ivory's "Mainline," written by Burgess for another project but eventually given to the group he departed from, temporarily brought him back into the group for one of the most heavenly disco singles recorded. Though accounts seem to differ on whether it was Burgess or Bob Blank who produced Fonda Rae's "Over Like a Fat Rat," it's a simple but incredibly infectious tune aided by crisp production and Burgess' background vocals. Class Action's version of "Weekend," a song written by Burgess and Black Ivory bassist James Calloway (and one of the first Sleeping Bag releases), arguably tops Phreek's original with squelch-squirt synths, delirious keyboard stabs, and some wonderful high-hat/handclap combinations. High Frequency's "Summertime" is one of several buried gems unearthed here, recorded by Burgess with the Aleems. It's as great as any other summer-themed song, replete with a string vamp that Burgess admittedly copped from John Williams' *Jaws* score. Yet another essential compilation. One listen to anything here is likely to make your day. *—Andy Kellman*

Keni Burke (Kenneth M. Burke)

b. Sep. 28, 1953, Chicago, IL
Bass, Vocals, Songwriter / Urban, Funk, Soul
Keni Burke has a three-decade career that includes singing with the Five Stairsteps and being a top session musician. Born Kenneth M. Burke on September 28, 1953, in Chicago, he first tasted musical stardom in his teens as a member of the family group the Five Stairsteps. The Chicago-based group was dubbed "the First Family of Soul" because of their successful five-year chart run. Initially a teenage five-member brothers-and-sister vocal group made up of the offspring of Betty and Clarence Burke, the Five Stairsteps featured lead singer Clarence Jr., Alohe, James, Dennis, and 13-year-old Kenneth.

In the spring of 1970, the group released their sole certified million-seller and biggest pop hit, "O-o-h Child." The following year, the group resurfaced as the Stairsteps with two charting Buddah singles: "Didn't It Look So Easy" and "I Love You.... Stop!" Billy Preston introduced the Stairsteps to the Beatles, and the group signed with George Harrison's Dark Horse label distributed by A&M Records. An album, *2nd Resurrection*, was released in February 1976, produced by Billy Preston, Robert Margouleff, and the Stairsteps. "From Us to You" was the group's biggest hit since "O-o-h Child," peaking at number-ten R&B in early 1976.

After the Stairsteps disbanded, Keni remained with Dark Horse as a solo artist. His self-produced debut solo LP, *Keni Burke*, was released in August 1977. He also became an in-demand session bass player, playing with dozens of artists including Sly & the Family Stone, Natalie Cole, Billy Preston, the Four Tops, Curtis Mayfield, Dusty Springfield, Diana Ross, and Gladys Knight.

In 1981, Burke got a new solo album deal with RCA Records. The self-produced LP *You're the Best* included the jubilant "Let Somebody Love You" and the title track as singles. His next RCA album, 1982's *Changes*, yielded his biggest solo hit, the inspiring "Risin' to the Top." The second *Changes* single, the pumpin' "Shakin'," has DJs and dance/funk music collectors scouring used record bins.

Burke also worked as a writer/producer with the O'Jays, the Jones Girls, the Whispers, the Whitehead Brothers, Keith Sweat, George Howard, Peabo Bryson, Bill Withers, and Perri, among others. After meeting Expansion Records executive Ralph Tee at a Berwick Soul Weekender, Burke signed with the Sony-distributed U.K. label. *Nothin' But Love* was his first album for the label and was released March 1998. The first 12-inch single was "I Need Your Love" with vocals by Burke's son, Osaze Burke, but the flip side, the mellow "Indigenous Love," became a hit with the steppers crowd. *—Ed Hogan*

You're the Best / 1982 / RCA Victor ✦✦✦

Keni Burke is the youngest of the original Five Stairsteps and the only one still seriously involved in music. *You're the Best*, a fine effort, never reached first base. RCA pushed "Let Somebody Love You" and the title track, but neglected tracks like the chugging, stop-and-go "Night Riders," pumped by spirited backing vocals, and "Gotta Find My Way Back to Your Heart," a dramatic ballad that Burke composed with Bill Withers. "Never Stop Loving Me," a Burke/Curtis Mayfield composition, has the same texture and sweetness of a Mayfield solo, while "Paintings of Love" is pure, unbridled Burke, sung in a soft, introspective voice that gels with the poetic lyrics. *—Andrew Hamilton*

● **Changes** / Apr. 1982 / BMG ✦✦✦

Pristinely recorded at Philadelphia's legendary Sigma Sound Studios and initially issued in April 1982, Keni Burke's second RCA LP, *Changes*, yielded the classic "Risin' to the Top." A favorite among both the steppers and hip-hop crowd, it was written by Burke, Allan Felder, and former Chic member Norma Jean Wright. It's on numerous compilations including Rhino's *Smooth Grooves After Hours* issued in January 2000. The track has been sampled by numerous artists including Mary J. Blige ("Love No Limit") and Doug E. Fresh ("Keep Risin' to the Top"). Other highlights are the crucially chuggin' "Shakin'," the midtempo ballad "One Minute More" (another steppers favorite), and the sparse, floating sl-o-o-w jam "Who Do You Love." Burke, keyboardist Dean Gant, and former Average White Band drummer Steve Ferrone were quite a rhythm section. *Changes* was issued on CD by RCA/BMG with two bonus tracks from *You're the Best* and reissued by BMG Japan on both CD and vinyl in 1995. Burke's next album was 1998's *Nothing but Love*. *—Ed Hogan*

Nothin' But Love / 1998 / Expansion ✦✦✦

A master of *real* modern soul, music vet Keni Burke (the Five Stairsteps, "Risin' to the Top,") breaks an almost two-decade hiatus with this charming album for U.K. label Expansion Records (Sony/3MW).The set cleverly combines '90s music technology with classic songwriting. "Indigenous Love," which has a bassline similar to "Risin' to the Top," took off with the steppers set. It's also represented with an instrumental reprise. Other highlights are the sweet slow jam "This Dedication," the Philly soul-flavored "I Get Off on You," and "Tell Me You Want My Love." The midtempo midnight groover "Give Me a Chance" has a sly, sensuous bassline. The earnest ballad "I Can Give You Plenty Love" says "tell me what you want and I'll come running." A fine set, yet fans of the one-time A-list session bassist may be taken aback from the absence of the instrument. Those looking for a wide showcase for Burke's "badd" bass-playing skills should check out his earlier efforts: *Keni Burke*, *You're the Best*, and *Changes*, as well as his sides with Bill Withers, D.J. Rogers, Narada Michael Walden, and Billy Preston, among many others. *—Ed Hogan*

Solomon Burke

b. Mar. 21, 1936, Philadelphia, PA

Vocals / Soul, Deep Soul, Southern Soul, Country-Soul

While Solomon Burke never made a major impact upon the pop audience—he never, in fact, had a Top 20 hit—he was an important early soul pioneer. On his '60s singles for Atlantic, he brought a country influence into R&B with emotional phrasing and intricately constructed, melodic ballads and midtempo songs. At the same time, he was surrounded with sophisticated "uptown" arrangements and provided with much of his material by his producers, particularly Bert Berns. The combination of gospel, pop, country, and production polish was basic to the recipe of early soul. While Burke wasn't the only one pursuing this path, not many others did so as successfully. And he, like Otis Redding and Wilson Pickett, was an important influence upon the Rolling Stones, who covered Burke's "Cry to Me" and "Everybody Needs Somebody to Love" on their early albums.

Burke came by his gospel roots even more deeply than most soul stars. He was preaching at his family's Philadelphia church, and hosting his own gospel radio show, even before he'd reached his teens. He began recording gospel and R&B sides for Apollo in the mid- to late '50s. Like several former gospel singers (Aretha Franklin, Wilson Pickett), he was molded into a more secular direction when he signed with Atlantic in the 1960s.

Burke had a wealth of high-charting R&B hits in the early half of the '60s, which crossed over to the pop listings in a mild fashion as well. "Just Out of Reach," "Cry to Me," "If You Need Me," "Got to Get You Off My Mind," "Tonight's the Night," and "Goodbye Baby (Baby Goodbye)" were the most successful of these, although unlike Franklin or Pickett, he wasn't able to expand his R&B base into a huge pop following as well. He left Atlantic in the late '60s, and spent the next decade hopping between various labels, getting his biggest hit with a cover of Creedence Clearwater Revival's "Proud Mary" in 1969, and recording an album in the late '70s with cult soulster Swamp Dogg as producer.

In the 1980s and 1990s, Burke became one of the most visible living exponents of classic soul music, continuing to tour and record albums in a rootsy, at times gospelish style. Although these were critically well received, their stylistic purity also ensured that their market was primarily confined to roots music enthusiasts, rather than a pop audience. His live show—and later recorded work—is a favorite of those who want to experience a soul legend with his talents and stylistic purity relatively intact. Burke's 2002 release *Don't Give Up on Me* was hailed as a major comeback for the legendary soulman. Great songwriters like Elvis Costello, Dan Penn, Nick Lowe, and Tom Waits contributed songs and Joe Henry produced the album. which has been compared to Johnny Cash's landmark album *American Recordings*. *—Richie Unterberger*

Solomon Burke / 1962 / Kenwood ✦✦✦

The early hits that made Solomon Burke a new force on the soul scene. His quavering delivery, robust sound, and huge presence had both the emphatic earnestness of gospel and the celebratory spirit of soul. Burke strained, roared, sighed, and exploded on his early hits, telling masterful stories and making each song a total experience. *—Ron Wynn*

Solomon Burke's Greatest Hits / 1962 / Atlantic ✦✦✦

Solomon Burke's booming, magnificent vocals and dramatic approach were particularly effective on a string of great early-'60s tracks. The lyrics, production, and setting blended soul and country elements, and Burke was the ideal singer to convey the two genres' similarities. This includes the epic tracks "Everybody Needs Somebody to Love" and "Just Out of Reach (Of My Empty Arms)." *—Ron Wynn*

If You Need Me / 1963 / Atlantic ✦✦✦

This early Solomon Burke album is named for the opening cut, his take on Wilson Pickett's "If You Need Me," which was a successful single for Burke, almost reaching number one on the R&B charts. Recorded between late 1959 and early 1963, these mostly midtempo songs find Burke's somewhat gritty pleas at home in sultry, bluesy surroundings ("Send Me Some Loving") and sweetened up for the occasional exotica-tinged arrangement ("Tonight My Heart She Is Crying"). It's unfortunate that the sound was not remastered for the late-'90s reissue by Sequel. *—Joslyn Layne*

Rock 'n' Soul / 1964 / Atlantic ✦✦✦

Solomon Burke's first album for Atlantic Records features three bona fide hits and other treats done as only the soulful, preaching singer with croon-ability can. He defies pigeonholing. Nobody ever talks of what range Burke sings in because it doesn't matter. Like Michael Jordan or Allen Iverson on the basketball court, Burke makes you feel like he's capable of anything and everything in the studio. *—Andrew Hamilton*

I Wish I Knew / 1968 / Atlantic ✦✦✦

I Wish I Knew, Solomon Burke's final album for longtime home label Atlantic, is a desperate mix of R&B oldies, sappy contemporary tunes and a scurrying search for style in the storm. Burke was in the middle of a cultural revolution when this album was made; soul music now crashed with such sonic force to keep up with pop's psychedelic trippings that Burke's blend of Sam Cooke-like cooing and Sunday-morning fervor seemed a bit quaint. The seasoning of *I Wish I Knew* is misguided at best. There's a forced "grooviness" to the tunes that makes them dusty relics of their era and a somewhat desolate end to a golden age of R&B. Burke sounds fine throughout (his singing, in fact, is nearly as fervent as it was on the previous year's treasure *King Solomon*), but aside from "I Wish I Knew (How It Would Feel to Be Free)," too much of the album stinks of period goo. (Later reissued by Koch with *King Solomon*.) *—Michael Gallucci*

King Solomon / 1968 / Atlantic ✦✦✦

Solomon Burke's last flash of R&B genius sparked on his penultimate Atlantic album, *King Solomon*, a smooth blend of soul crooning and passionate wailers that may represent Burke at his vocal peak. Finding himself surrounded by Summer of Love shenanigans, Burke retaliated with a solid collection of songs that defined the '60s soul movement—heartbreak and celebration of the heart wrapped in tight, three-minute packages. The best songs here—"Take Me (Just As I Am)," "Keep a Light in the Window," "Baby, Come on Home," "Detroit City," "Someone Is Watching" and "Party People"—were all released as singles and all resonate with an ardor that verges on spiritual. *King Solomon* could very well be Burke's best album. It's one last gasp of vital R&B breath before subpar material and lackluster performances drowned his commercial career for good. (Later reissued on Koch with *I Wish I Knew*.) *—Michael Gallucci*

Proud Mary / 1969 / Bell ✦✦✦

Burke kept pace with changing soul and rock trends fairly well on this album, which has a funkier, bluesier deep soul feel than his more famous early- and mid-'60s Atlantic material. That feel didn't come about by total accident, of course; the album was recorded at Muscle Shoals, where he could sing with the area's esteemed session musicians, rather than the uptown New York players he'd worked with at Atlantic. There's a bit of a sense of Burke following the crowd rather than blazing his own path, and the song selection is a bit unimaginative (not that this was an unusual happenstance on soul albums), with covers of "These Arms of Mine," "I'll Be Doggone," "That Lucky Old Sun," and "What Am I Living For." Still, even those are given respectable readings, and Burke also tackles a couple of songs Dan Penn co-penned, in addition to waxing one of his own, "How Big a Fool (Can a Fool Be)," which has that thin electric sitar-guitar hybrid sound peculiar to some pop-soul discs of the era. The album was reissued on CD under the title *Proud Mary: The Bell Sessions* by Sundazed in 2000, with the addition of seven bonus cuts from 1969-1970 singles and outtakes. *—Richie Unterberger*

Electronic Magnetism / 1972 / Polydor ✦✦✦

I Have a Dream / 1974 / Dunhill ✦✦✦

Back to My Roots / 1975 / Chess ✦

Music to Make Love By / 1975 / Chess ✦✦
This is not a good album. It's doubtful that any of the participants involved in *Music to Make Love By*, from the rhythm track "designers" to the spiritual consultants to Solomon Burke himself, remember making this album. Perhaps that was their intention, to craft a work that would ease into the background as the listeners became more involved with other matters at hand, in which case the album is a resounding success. And who could argue that a man with 21 kids doesn't know something about romance? There is always something redeeming about a Solomon Burke release, and his Barry White-inspired rap on "Music to Make Love By, Pts. 1 & 2" is worth a low-priced admission. *—Kurt Edwards*

Lord We Need a Miracle / 1979 / Savoy ✦✦✦
One-time boy preacher Solomon Burke returned to his gospel roots on this earth-shaking date. There's nothing secular about anything here, from the lyrics to Burke's impassioned, heartfelt cries, shouts, and roars. The only problem was that he'd been away from gospel so long that many in the church community didn't take this album seriously. *—Ron Wynn*

Sidewalks, Fences & Walls / 1979 / Infinity ✦✦✦✦✦

Soul Alive! / 1985 / Rounder ✦✦✦✦
For pure soul testifying, no one compares to Solomon Burke. He earned his title—"King of Soul"—by bringing the gospel fervor of the Southern preacher to his performances, and no recording proves his command over an audience quite like *Soul Alive!* Recorded in 1983 in Washington, D.C., the set proves Burke had lost little from his '60s heyday; he works through nearly all of his hits, spurring on the concert-goers as though *they* were the ones performing instead of him—in fact, some of the women are heard screaming so often they should've been credited. Burke shines most when leading the faithful through "I Can't Stop Loving You," pausing for a lengthy monologue before reprising the song and leading into a devastating finish. Elsewhere he works through deeply felt country-blues-gospel fusions like "I Almost Lost My Mind," "Take Me (Just as I Am)," "He'll Have to Go," and "Down in the Valley." [Originally released by Rounder in 1985, *Soul Alive!* made a re-appearance in 2002, a double-disc edition including two shows from his stand at the Phoenix 1 club.] *—John Bush*

A Change Is Gonna Come / 1986 / Rounder ✦✦✦✦✦
While he wasn't scoring chart hits anymore, Burke hadn't lost any of his prowess by the mid-'80s. He cut one of the decade's great soul statements for Rounder in 1985. It's available on CD, and should be a revelation for anyone unaware of Burke's singing and performing zeal. His oral narratives were as smashing and memorable as his vocals, and the assembled band included a super three-piece horn section led by alto, tenor and baritone saxophonist Foots Samuel. This was no nostalgia trip, but a contemporary soul journey that retains its appeal years after its initial release. *—Ron Wynn*

You Can Run But You Can't Hide / 1987 / Mr. R&B ✦✦✦✦✦
You Can Run but You Can't Hide collects 20 tracks from Burke's formative years at Apollo, recorded between 1955-1959. The material tends to be more pop-oriented than his classic Atlantic sides, but his singing is nearly as impressive as it is on his hits. *—Stephen Thomas Erlewine*

The Bishop Rides South / 1988 / Charly ✦✦✦✦✦
When Solomon Burke left Atlantic, he signed with New York City's Bell Records. Bell wisely sent Burke down to Muscle Shoals. Two 1969 hits, covers of "Uptight Good Woman" and "Proud Mary," resulted, along with a slew of classic Southern soul covers. *—Rob Bowman*

Homeland / 1990 / Rhino ✦✦✦

Home in Your Heart: The Best of Solomon Burke / Apr. 21, 1992 / Rhino ✦✦✦✦✦
Of the great stars of the 1960s soul movement, Solomon Burke isn't as well-remembered as many of his peers, most likely because he had relatively minor success in the crossover marketplace (never scoring a Top 20 pop hit), and he faded from view on the R&B charts by the early '70s. But if Burke's impact was somewhat narrow, it was also quite deep; he was hugely popular in the deep south, a potent live attraction across the country, and (after Ray Charles) one of the first major attractions at Atlantic Records, who helped define the label's signature polished-but-deeply soulful sound. Burke also had, quite simply, one of the finest voices in popular music, a rich and resonant instrument that possessed a churchy authority that was the ideal match for his material, which balanced the pleasures of the flesh with the price of transgression. While Burke made solid albums after leaving Atlantic, his tenure at that label remains his strongest and most rewarding period, and *Home in Your Heart: The Best of Solomon Burke* is a superbly compiled and annotated two-disc set that cherrypicks 40 superb selections from Burke's Atlantic archive, including the epochal "Everybody Needs Somebody to Love," "Just out of Reach (Of My Two Empty Arms)," "Cry to Me," "The Price," "If You Need Me," and many more. Someday, some archivist should go through Burke's long out-of-print sides for MGM, Bell, Chess, Dunhill, and other labels and create a compilation that will fill in the gaps of Burke's "lost years" before his re-emergence in the mid-'80s, but for the meantime *Home in Your Heart: The Best of Solomon Burke* remains the best place to start exploring his body of work, and it's a remarkable collection of Southern soul at its finest. *—Mark Deming*

Let Your Love Flow / 1993 / Shanachie ✦✦✦✦
Jerry Williams (Swamp Dogg) produced an excellent late-'70s soul session for the legendary Solomon Burke on the tiny Infinity Records label. Williams mixed upbeat numbers with a pronounced Afro-Latin beat and confessional country/soul tunes, emphasizing Burke's trademark song sermons. The music was much too raw and rural for the pseudo-sophisticated big-city radio set, but Southern soul loyalists treasured it. Shanachie's CD reissue includes two bonus cuts, and its digital sound displays the strength, clarity, and power of Burke's voice. Shanachie gets high praises for reissuing the album, but low marks for the horrendous misspelling of Burke's name all over the CD. *—Ron Wynn*

Live at House of Blues / 1994 / Black Top ✦✦✦✦✦
The big, brassy band that backs Solomon Burke on this live set enhances and never overshadows his powerful vocals and God given charisma. Opening with "Everybody Needs Somebody to Love," he gets the crowd in a festive mood before slinking into a strong three-song medley comprising "If You Need Me"/"Tonight's the Night"/"I Almost Lost My Mind." He displays his preaching skills on "Cruel World" and you can almost see the collection plate being passed. "Candy/Candy Rap" begins with a big band arrangement, the sound is bold and brassy, then lightens with Burke's "Candy Rap." He excels on "Got to Get You Off My Mind," another one of Burke's hits from back-in-the-day. In fact the only glaring omission from his *King Solomon* era is the bewitching "Somebody's Watching You." On the three or so blues tunes he does, if you close your eyes, you'll think it was a female singing, as he sings in a higher key on blues tunes. Burke, a true character, closes this enjoyable performance with Roy Brown's classic "Good Rockin' Tonight." *—Andrew Hamilton*

★ **The Very Best of Solomon Burke** / Feb. 3, 1998 / Rhino ✦✦✦✦✦
The Very Best of Solomon Burke is an excellent 16-track collection that features his biggest hits from 1961-1968, including "Just Out of Reach (Of My Two Open Arms)," "Cry to Me," "Down in the Valley," "I'm Hanging Up My Heart for You," "If You Need Me," "You're Good for Me," "Goodbye Baby (Baby Goodbye)," and "Everybody Needs Somebody to Love." All of his best-known songs in their hit versions are available on this concise, affordable disc, not always in strict release order but still an education in and of themselves—the tracks all come from the first generation original single masters, many of which were remixed or even shunted aside in favor of re-recorded versions for his albums during the 1960s, including his greatest-hits and best-of collections. The producers spent the time to track down those long-unused and forgotten originals for this, their first authentic representation on CD. Additionally, the 16th song is a true diamond among the R&B treasures here—the June 1968 single "Soul Meeting" cut by the Soul Clan, which consisted of Burke, Arthur Conley, Don Covay, Ben E. King, and Joe Tex, the super-session product of a short-lived experiment in raising money for the black community. This is the only appearance of this Don Covay-authored track on CD, and makes this release essential even for those who already own the 1992 double-CD set *Home in Your Heart*. *—Stephen Thomas Erlewine & Bruce Eder*

If You Need Me/Rock 'n' Soul / Jul. 28, 1998 / Collectables ✦✦✦✦✦

I Wish I Knew/King Solomon / Jan. 19, 1999 / Koch International ✦✦✦✦

Proud Mary: The Bell Sessions / Jul. 18, 2000 / Sundazed ✦✦✦
This is a somewhat spruced-up version of Burke's 1969 *Proud Mary* album, containing all of the songs from that LP, and adding seven bonus cuts from 1969-1970 singles and outtakes. Burke kept pace with changing soul and rock trends fairly well on *Proud Mary*, which has a funkier, bluesier deep soul feel than his more famous early- and mid-'60s Atlantic material. That feel didn't come about by total accident, of course; the record was recorded at Muscle Shoals, where he could sing with the area's esteemed session musicians, rather than the uptown New York players he'd worked with at Atlantic. There's a bit of a sense of Burke following the crowd rather than blazing his own path, and the song selection is a bit unimaginative (not that this was an unusual happenstance on soul albums). Still, even those are given respectable readings, and Burke also tackles a couple of songs Dan Penn co-penned, in addition to waxing one of his own, "How Big a Fool (Can a Fool Be)," which has that thin electric sitar-guitar hybrid sound peculiar to some pop-soul discs of the era. The bonus tracks are pretty interesting, including previously unissued covers of Bob Dylan's "The Mighty Quinn" and Sam Cooke's "Change Is Gonna Come," along with some non-LP singles that showed Burke absorbing (as he had on the *Proud Mary* album) some contemporary rock influences. His own "The Generation of Revelations," a 1969 single, made some fashionable lyrical bows to the counterculture; an odd 1970 single matched a post-Elvis Presley cover of "In the Ghetto" with the gospel rock of "God Knows I Love You," written by the unusual songwriting team of Delaney Bramlett and "In the Ghetto" composer Mac Davis. *—Richie Unterberger*

Don't Give Up on Me / Jul. 23, 2002 / Fat Possum ✦✦✦✦✦
It's a sad irony that in the 1980s and '90s, many of the great artists of soul and R&B suffered musically at the hands of those who professed to love them the most. After soul had dropped off the major-label radar in favor of hip-hop and new jack sounds, a number of smaller companies stepped forward to record veteran artists who were still giving their all on the road, but for every truly inspired release from labels such as Malaco, Bullseye, or Alligator, there were a dozen others which featured rote, generic production and arrangements that attempted to recapture the thrilling sound of soul's glory days without coming within driving distance of conjuring their ineffable magic. Solomon Burke was one of the greatest talents of '60s soul, whose strong, burnished voice resonated with a churchy fervor that could speak volumes about either triumph or hurt, but while he continued to record regularly through the '70s, '80s and '90s and always sounded splendid, the records themselves often weren't much to write home about, with Burke using his gifts to prop up second-rate material or re-record tunes he'd performed definitively in the past. So it's good news indeed to report that Burke's new album, *Don't Give Up on Me*, is nothing short of revelatory, a superb set which presents "the King of Rock and Soul" at the very top of his form. Singer and songwriter Joe Henry produced the set, and rather than trying to replicate the sound of a vintage Jerry Wexler session, he's taken a very different approach, going for a spare and open sound, with nothing but a subdued rhythm section, a guitar, and an organ (the latter played by Rudy Copeland, who performs the same honors at the church where Burke preaches) accompanying Burke on most of these 11 songs. Henry also put out a call for material worthy of Burke's gifts, and a number of

his better-known fans responded, including Bob Dylan, Tom Waits, Van Morrison, Elvis Costello, Brian Wilson, and Nick Lowe, all of whom contributed songs to the project. But for all the songwriting starpower on deck, the focus is squarely on Solomon Burke throughout, and he proves he's lost none of the power, force, or dramatic intensity of his glory days. Henry's low-key production captures the nooks and crannies of Burke's voice, and he delivers a performance worthy of a great actor on each cut, from the deep soul of "Don't Give Up on Me" and the blues-based swagger of "Stepchild" to the inspired tall tales of "Diamond in Your Mind" and the near-operatic passion of "The Judgement." His voice is in superb shape, too, sounding no less powerful at age 66 than he did in his glory days, and with a depth of emotion and gift for phrasing that's only grown with the passage of time. In many ways, *Don't Give Up on Me* most closely resembles Johnny Cash's superb *American Recordings*, in that the spare simplicity of the album's presentation reveals the rich complexities of the singer's gifts as they've rarely been allowed in the past; while it's a very different kettle of fish from his classic sides for Atlantic in the 1960s, *Don't Give up on Me* leaves no doubt that Solomon Burke is still one of the finest voices of his time, and anyone who has ever been moved by the power of soul music needs to hear this album. *—Mark Deming*

Harold Burrage

b. Mar. 30, 1931, Chicago, IL, **d.** Nov. 26, 1966, Chicago, IL

Vocals, Piano / R&B, Soul

Pianist Harold Burrage started out singing blues and R&B during the 1950s and ended up as a linchpin of the emerging Chicago soul sound of the '60s; he made recordings in both styles and more than a few idiomatic shades in between. Burrage mentored young soul singers Otis Clay and Tyrone Davis, but never had a chance to see them fully blossom; he died young in 1966.

Burrage debuted on wax in 1950 with a jumping "Hi-Yo Silver" for Decca with Horace Henderson's band in support. Singles for Aladdin and States preceded one of his most prolific studio periods with Eli Toscano's Cobra imprint. In 1956, Burrage cut the amusing "You Eat Too Much" for Cobra, backed by a solid combo featuring guitarist Wayne Bennett and bassist Willie Dixon. Jody Williams added stinging guitar to Burrage's 1957 Cobra offering "Messed Up," while "Stop for the Red Light," his third Cobra 45, was a novelty complete with auto-wreck sound effects. "Betty Jean," his last Cobra single, is unabashed rock & roll, with Otis Rush on guitar. Burrage also served as a session pianist for the firm, backing up Magic Sam and Charles Clark.

After a romping 1960 effort for Vee-Jay, "Crying for My Baby," Burrage revamped his vocal approach considerably when recording rather prolifically for One-derful's M-Pac! subsidiary during the early to mid-'60s. There he sang in a very credible soul style, enjoying his only national R&B hit in 1965 with the driving "Got to Find a Way" (later revived by one of Burrage's protégés, Otis Clay). *—Bill Dahl*

• **Messed Up: Complete Cobra Recordings** / Jun. 26, 2002 / WestSide ✦✦✦✦✦

Messed Up only showcases one facet of the late piano-playing singer's multi-faceted discography, but it's one of the most fascinating—his 1956-1958 stay at Chicago's Cobra Records. Under Willie Dixon's supervision, Burrage recorded in a variety of styles—rockin' blues ("Satisfied," the amusing "You Eat Too Much"), novelty stuff ("Stop for the Red Light," complete with crashing sound effects reminiscent of Nervous Norvus), and straight-ahead rock & roll ("Betty Jean"). *—Bill Dahl*

The Bus Boys

f. Los Angeles, CA

Group / Bar Band, Album Rock, Pop/Rock, Rock & Roll

The Bus Boys were a Los Angeles-based rock & roll band made up of five African-Americans and a Hispanic who played satirically upon their ethnic origins in songs with titles like "There Goes the Neighborhood." They were formed in the late '70s with a lineup of brothers Brian O'Neal (keyboards, vocals) and Kevin O'Neal (bass, vocals), Gus Louderman (vocals), Mike Jones (keyboards, vocals), Victor Johnson (guitar), and Steve Felix (drums). Essentially a novelty act, they nevertheless impressed listeners with their energetic bar band rock. They reached their peak of national exposure when they appeared in the 1982 Eddie Murphy film *48 Hrs.* Their two Arista albums reached the charts, as did the 1984 single "Cleanin' Up the Town," which was featured in the film *Ghostbusters.* *—William Ruhlmann*

• **Minimum Wage Rock & Roll** / 1980 / Arista ✦✦✦✦✦

In the 1950s, rock & roll started out as black music, but you wouldn't have guessed that to pick up Rolling Stone or Creem in the early '80s—by that time, rock was almost exclusively the province of skinny white guys, and black artists were only to be found on the R&B charts, as if Chuck Berry, Little Richard, and Jimi Hendrix had never happened. So if there was more than a bit of novelty in the music of the Bus Boys, that's not to say that what they were doing wasn't important or necessary—as one of the first African-American groups to emerge to national prominence in the new wave scene, the Bus Boys were willing to embrace the contradictions and confront the stereotypes that faced black musicians playing what had come to be known as "white" music. If some of the jokes are a bit forced, they're also pretty funny, especially "There Goes the Neighborhood" ("The whites are moving in!/They'll bring their next of kin!") and "KKK" ("Gonna join the Ku Klux Klan/And play in a rock & roll band"), while the music was certainly prescient, blending straight-ahead rock & roll and old-school R&B with George Clinton-esque absurdity and harmonies and new wave synthesizer squeals at a time when Prince was just edging into similar territory (and well before Cameo dropped the B-52's-ish *Alligator Woman*). Meanwhile, "Minimum Wage" and "D-Day" faced universal anxieties with honesty and bitter humor, and the band plays with fire and enthusiasm throughout. Not exactly up there with Bad Brains, *Minimum Wage Rock & Roll* is still smart and enthusiastic rock & roll that's unafraid to take chances; too bad the Bus Boys never managed another album this strong. *—Mark Deming*

American Worker / 1982 / Arista ✦✦✦

In 1980, the Bus Boys sent shock waves through the music world with their song "KKK," which found members of a mostly African-American band singing that they wanted to "join the Ku Klux Klan and play in a rock & roll band." Of course, no one in the Bus Boys really aspired to be a Klansman—they were actually ridiculing institutional racism and asserting that if African-Americans were good enough to pay taxes and fight in the Vietnam War, they shouldn't be excluded from any part of the American dream, including the white-dominated rock & roll field. Unfortunately, a few simpletons took their lyrics out of context and assumed that the Bus Boys were self-hating blacks, but to anyone with half a brain, it was clear where they were coming from. After using shock value and humor to get their anti-racism, pro-working-class message across on their first album, *Minimum Wage Rock & Roll*, the Bus Boys brought an equally sociopolitical agenda to their sophomore effort, *American Worker.* This likable, if uneven, LP ranges from political offerings like "American Workers," "I Get Lost," and the reggae-influenced "Opportunity" to less provocative, more mainstream pop/rock fare such as "Last Forever" and "Heart and Soul." Regrettably, this 1982 release was the Bus Boys' last album on Arista (they wouldn't record another album until the late '80s, when they shifted their focus from rock to synth-funk/urban contemporary). The Bus Boys had a lot of potential, and it's unfortunate that they didn't fully live up to it. But despite their imperfections, *Minimum Wage Rock & Roll* and *American Worker* are fun albums that deserve credit for taking some risks and making some sociopolitical statements that needed to be made. *—Alex Henderson*

Money Don't Make No Man / 1988 / Voss ✦✦

Sam Butera

b. Aug. 17, 1927, New Orleans, LA

Bandleader, Vocals, Saxophone / Cocktail, New Orleans Jazz, Rock & Roll, R&B

Sam Butera spent much of his career leading Louis Prima's band, but his career continued long after Prima's death, coming to include sounds and styles far beyond Prima's brand of New Orleans jazz. A rock, R&B, and jazz legend, Butera is a towering crossover figure at the saxophone and as a bandleader.

He was born in New Orleans to Italian-American parents. His father Joseph owned a butcher shop in a black section of the city, and played the guitar and the concertina in his spare time. At a wedding he was taken to at age seven, Sam Butera first saw and heard a saxophone, and, with his father's blessings, asked to take lessons. He studied the clarinet at school but eventually returned to the sax, and at age 18 was featured in *Look* magazine (*Life*'s major competitor) as one of the top young jazzmen in the country. He got a gig with Ray McKinley right out of high school, and also played with the bands of Tommy Dorsey and Joe Reichman. His major influences in those years included Charlie Ventura, Lester Young, Gene Ammons, Charlie Parker, and Big Jay McNeely; he seemed to gravitate naturally to swing and bebop. Ultimately, however, the biggest influence on his playing was Lee Allen, a member of Paul Gayten's band, with which he frequently played.

Butera formed his own group—inspired by Gayten's band—after returning to New Orleans, and they quickly began a four-year engagement at the 500 Club, which was owned by Louis Prima's brother. His sound reflected a vast range of influences, including modern jazz and R&B, and in 1951 Butera cut a pair of raunchy R&B instrumental sides that might have figured in the early history of white rock & roll if only they'd gotten out at the time. He also had a featured spot in a Woody Herman concert that yielded both a chance for a new tour and a recording contract with RCA. The resulting sessions in the fall of 1953 gave Butera a chance to rock out in an alternately soft and sweet, or hard and playful manner. There weren't any significant sales, but RCA had him back in early 1954 for a series of sessions of its R&B-oriented Groove label (home of Piano Red, amongst others), and his version of "I Don't Want to Set the World on Fire" was a modest regional hit.

He played some R&B shows, including a celebrated tour as part of Alan Freed's first East Coast rock & roll showcase, and Butera's loud, wild sax sound won him an enthusiastic following. By 1955, however, he was back doing jazz with Ella Fitzgerald and Louie Bellson. He finally hooked up with Louis Prima and spent the next 20 years leading his band, the Witnesses. Butera's own record releases were cut short, with only a handful of his Groove sides (including a vocal performance, "Giddyap Baby") ever issued at the time. Butera achieved financial security over the next 20 years working for Prima, and only then, in the mid-'70s, began re-emerging as a performer in his own right. *—Bruce Eder*

• **Hot New Orleans Nights** / 1989 / Bear Family ✦✦✦✦✦

Nineteen tracks cut by Sam Butera for RCA between September 1953 and July 1954. Highlights include the hot rocking "Chicken Scratch," "Shine the Buckle," "Sam's Clan," and "Easy Rocking," the superb vocal performance "Giddyap Baby," the sultry yet raunchy "Ooh," and the soft, soulful "Sam's Reverie," adapted from a piece by Debussy. *—Bruce Eder*

Billy Butler

b. Jun. 7, 1945, Philadelphia, PA

Vocals / Chicago Soul, Northern Soul, Soul

The younger brother of Jerry Butler, Billy Butler wasn't nearly as well known as his sibling, but recorded some fine Chicago soul in the '60s. Recording for OKeh under producer Carl Davis, Butler's mid-'60s singles were quite similar to labelmates Major Lance's and (less obviously) Curtis Mayfield's as stellar examples of the finest features of the Chicago soul sound. Similar to Motown in its full, brassy production, the Chicago brand was earthier, with stronger tinges of gospel, doo wop, and Latin influences. Nor was Butler terribly similar to his brother, Jerry, with a punchier, more uptempo sound.

With backing group the Enchanters, Billy recorded consistently fine singles for OKeh from 1963 to 1966, scoring R&B hits with "I Can't Work No Longer" (1965) and "Right Track" (1966). Butler left OKeh after 1966 and recorded for a variety of labels, denting the R&B charts with the singles "Get on the Chase" (1969) and "Free Yourself" (1971). A songwriter of note, he contributed material to fellow Chicago soul greats Major Lance, Gene Chandler, and his brother, Jerry. *—Richie Unterberger*

Sugar Candy Lady / 1977 / Sequel ♦♦♦
Billy Butler, brother of Jerry and author of one of the greatest songs in soul music history—"I Stand Accused"—is one of the unluckiest men in the history of recorded music. Despite his phenomenal abilities and in-the-cut songs, the earmarks of his career were false starts, record company politics and double-dealing, and being in the right place at the wrong time. This 1977 album, his first for Curtis Mayfield's Curtom label, is a mixed bag. Ballads such as "I Know the Feeling Well," the two-part "Alone at Last," and "I'm Gonna Make Her Mine" offer portraits of Butler as a solid singer, writer, and arranger. His guitar playing, like Terry Callier's and Curtis Mayfield's, is also highly individualistic and expressive. The midtempo tracks, such as "Feel the Magic," "She's Got Me Singing," and "The Saga of Sadie Lee," are among the finest in Chicago soul, with their Philly-influenced grooves and solid Northern soul bridges. But on the title track, "Play My Music," and "My Love for You Grows," Butler's flirtation with disco feels far too formulaic, like pandering to the genre to make an impact. Alas, these three tracks—one that opens and another that closes the album—mar what could have been a mid-'70s classic. *—Thom Jurek*

Right Track: The Very Best Of and More / 1995 / Mar ♦♦♦♦♦
Marginal, the import label of release for the lengthy, quasi-legal nuggets series *Soul Cargo* as well as an excellent Billy Stewart collection, did Chicago soul fans yet another favor with this collection, a bulked-up version of the former *Right Track: The Very Best Of.* Adding eight more tracks makes it function as a complete-on-OKeh compilation, featuring both sides of each single plus all of Butler's 1966 LP *Right Track.* Thanks to his sweet voice and the songwriting/production expertise of Curtis Mayfield, Billy Butler's songs were right next to the Impressions in terms of quality, and quite a few of these ("Found True Love," "My Sweet Woman") haven't been anthologized as much as they deserve. Fans of the early Impressions as well as good-time Chicago soul perennials like Major Lance or Bob & Earl will find much to love here, including "(You Make Me Think) You Ain't Ready" and "(I've Got a Feeling) You're Gonna Be Sorry." The early singles are much more enjoyable than the album tracks; OKeh was aiming Butler at the same audience that picked up on Major Lance's "Monkey Time," resulting in a few novelties like "Boston Monkey." With just a few exceptions, though, Butler's recordings for OKeh were of a very high quality. *—John Bush*

● **The Class of Mayfield High: The Brunswick/Dakar Recordings** / 1999 / WestSide ♦♦♦♦♦
This is one hell of a release! United Kingdom's WestSide Records compiles the best Brunswick/Dakar sides from Billy Butler, Major Lance, and Otis Leavill. Only a couple did anything on the pop chart; most were lower-echelon R&B hits, not because of their substance, but because of scant promotion and a finicky public. The title signifies that the artists began their careers by recording Curtis Mayfield songs; none of these selections, however, are Mayfield compositions or productions. Billy explodes on "I'll Bet You," a popular R&B recording and remake of the early George Clinton song "Help Yourself," an in-your-face fast-tempo dancer, and "Careless Heart," a heartfelt ballad that Butler croons like his big brother, Jerry. Lance's sides—"Sweeter as the Days Go By," "Since You Been Gone," and "Follow the Leader"—wallowed in obscurity and received more recognition in Europe than in the States. His selections are completely different from Curtis Mayfield's productions; they're also more Southern than Chicago soul. Otis Leavill is featured on 13 songs, the largest collection of his recordings ever assembled. His tunes include the only hits: "I Love You," and "Love Uprising." The sides contain surprise remakes of the Artistics' "Glad I Met You," "Why, Why, Why," and an early Chi-lites recording "I'm So Jealous." There are eight songs by Butler and six by Lance to go with Leavill's baker's dozen. *—Andrew Hamilton*

Jerry Butler

b. Dec. 8, 1939, Sunflower, MS
Vocals / Soul, R&B, Chicago Soul, Uptown Soul, Pop-Soul, Northern Soul
Jerry Butler's career spans four decades; he recorded more than 50 albums and his voice is one of the most distinguished voices in all of music. As soulful as ever, yet smooth as ice, his nickname "The Ice Man" epitomizes his demeanor—and sound. In spite of his status as a true music icon, he remains humble. Butler moved from Sunflower, MS, to Chicago, IL, at the age of three during the mass migration of blacks from the South to the North. (He grew up in an area which is now known as the Cabrini-Green Housing Projects.)

Butler acquired his initial music lessons as a young boy while a member of the church choir in Chicago. Curtis Mayfield, who was three years younger, was also a member of the same choir. The two befriended each other and began a collaboration that would have an everlasting impact on music. The twosome joined up with brothers Arthur and Richard Brooks and Sam Gooden to form the R&B group the Roosters. In fact, the Brooks brothers, Gooden, and a female had migrated to Chicago from Tennessee, and were called the Roosters & a Chick. But when Butler and Mayfield joined them, the group became simply the Roosters. In 1957, the quintet's name was changed to Jerry Butler & the Impressions. Butler scored his first hit with the Impressions in 1958 with the timeless ballad "For Your Precious Love." (He'd written the lyrics to the song when he was just 16.)

That same year Butler and the Impressions cordially split, and Butler began his solo career. He released his first single, "Lost," on the Abner label. It peaked at number 17 on the *Billboard* R&B charts. Jumping over to Vee-Jay in late 1960 where his career blossomed, Butler had his first hit as a solo artist with "He Will Break Your Heart." The single popped to the top of the charts at number one and stayed there for seven consecutive weeks. In 1961, Butler bounced back with two Top Ten singles: "Find Another Girl" and "I'm a Telling You." In 1967, he signed with Mercury and teamed up with the production duo of Kenny Gamble & Leon Huff. His work with these two master producers and songwriters resulted in some classic recordings, including the outstanding album *The Ice Man Cometh.* The album featured one superb track after another, including two number-one singles ("Hey, Western Union Man," "Only the Strong Survive") and two Top Ten singles ("Never Give You Up," "Are You Happy"). Always known for being a crooner, "Hey, Western Union Man" revealed to many that Butler was more than capable of singing uptempo songs.

In 1971, Gamble & Huff formed their own label and subsequently Butler formed a creative workshop to help provide material for his forthcoming albums. Material that did not make his albums, he marketed to other artists. In the spring of 1971, Butler hit the Top Ten with the number-eight single "If It's Real What I Feel," which was written by Chuck Jackson (the younger brother of Rev. Jesse Jackson). Butler continued his hit-making tradition with "Ain't Understanding Mellow," a classic soul-ballad duet with Brenda Lee Eager that peaked at number three on the *Billboard* R&B charts. Butler scored a number-six single with Eager with a remake of the Carpenters' "(They Long to Be) Close to You" and a solo hit with a remake of the O'Jays' "One Night Affair," which was also his last song to crack the Top Ten.

Never one to categorize singers because he believes that a singer is a singer—not based on genre, but on a person's mere ability to sing—Butler himself covered several styles of music during his lengthy music career. He had many highs in his career; ranging from sharing the spotlight with such greats as Aretha Franklin to being the chairman of the board for the Rhythm and Blues Foundation (a non-profit organization). Butler also became a force in another field: politics. In the mid-'80s, he was a significant campaign supporter of Chicago's first black mayor Harold Washington. A short time later, Butler himself became the Cook County (IL) Commissioner and by the late '90s he was a Chicago City Alderman. When the great Jerry Butler is not lobbying for his constituents, he can be found on-stage giving one of his spine-chilling performances with Ice Man-cool delivery. *—Craig Lytle*

Jerry Butler, Esq. / 1959 / Abner ♦♦
After leaving the Impressions and scoring a hit with "Lost," Jerry Butler recorded his debut LP, *Jerry Butler, Esq.*, for the Abner label. And just as he's pictured on the cover (looking rather elegant with a cane in his hand), Butler's strong voice and impassioned delivery is more '50s supper-club pop than juke-joint soul, in a similar vein to Ben E. King and the Drifters. The material fits as well, with versions of "September Song" and "Come Back My Love" complementing "Lost," plus a reworking of his recent Impressions hit, "For Your Precious Love." Though the accompanying strings and vocal chorus pour it on just a bit too much, Butler has little trouble swinging effortlessly over the top. *—John Bush*

He Will Break Your Heart / 1960 / Vee-Jay ♦♦♦♦
Jerry Butler's sophomore effort, and his first recorded for Vee-Jay, is more suited to his talents than his debut. True, there are several tracks packed with an over-reaching orchestra, similar to *Jerry Butler, Esq.* Still, the addition of old friend Curtis Mayfield as a co-composer (and backing vocalist) for four tracks gives an edge to Butler's grand, sweeping performances. Three Butler/Mayfield tracks—the title song, "The Gift of Love," and "I Found a Love"—are the highlights here, along with Butler's own "Sweet Was the Wine." As usual, the strings and vocal choruses aren't much of a stumbling block to Jerry Butler's gentle swing and powerful voice. *—John Bush*

Love Me / 1961 / Fontana ♦♦♦

Folk Songs / 1963 / Vee-Jay ♦♦♦
An interesting concept, and some liberties are being taken with the term "folk." Butler, normally a supper-club/sophisticated soul vocalist, tackles some earthier, simpler material and does a reasonably good job. Still, it's clear on many numbers that these aren't his type of songs. *—Ron Wynn*

Need to Belong / 1963 / Vee-Jay ♦♦♦

The Soul Artistry of Jerry Butler / 1967 / Mercury ♦♦♦
Mercury Records tried to make Jerry Butler Johnny Mathis with a baritone—a lofty goal that didn't quite exalt the Chicago crooner to a high level of pop achievement but did demonstrate that Butler was more than just a chitlin-circuit soldier. The tone of *The Soul Artistry of Jerry Butler* is classy and pop-ish; Mercury was looking for MOR plays. Still, Butler's uptown soul comes through, maybe a little more mellow but as real as ever. He's in fine voice throughout, especially on "I'm Gonna Make You Love Me" and "I Dig You Baby," a minor hit. This marked the beginning of Butler's association with Kenny Gamble; the Philly songwriter/producer co-wrote "I'm Gonna Make You Love Me" and "You Don't Know What You Got Until You Lose It." *—Andrew Hamilton*

Gift of Love / 1968 / Sunset ♦♦♦

The Soul Goes On / 1968 / Mercury ♦♦♦

Souled Out / 1968 / Upfront ♦♦♦♦
A tight compilation of classic Butler, featuring the early Curtis Mayfield compositions "He Will Break Your Heart," "I'm A-Telling You," and the mysterious "Isle of Sirens"; Curtis shadows Butler's lead on some tracks. His debut with the Impressions, "For Your Precious Love," is stark and exquisitely executed. "You Can Run But You Can't Hide" was a favorite on R&B stations, and "Make It Easy on Yourself" enhanced Butler's reputation as a premier soul crooner with crossover power. *—Andrew Hamilton*

The Ice Man Cometh / Nov. 1968 / Mercury ♦♦♦♦♦
The Ice Man Cometh, Jerry Butler's most successful LP, was the first full-album work from the production team Kenneth Gamble & Leon Huff. It marks an excellent collaboration, the first time R&B production techniques reached a level of maturity and elegance capable of fully complementing one of the smoothest vocalists in soul history. The Top Ten singles "Hey, Western Union Man" and "Only the Strong Survive" weren't just popular radio hits, but great performances displaying how far the R&B/soul crowd had progressed from the novelty-laden '50s. Thanks to Butler and Gamble/Huff, the sound proved incredibly influential, both in the short term (Elvis Presley was definitely listening and cut a very similar "Only the Strong Survive" one year later) and the long term (Gamble & Huff's Philly Intl. label ruled the mid-'70s R&B world with the same sound). Here's where it coalesced. *—John Bush*

Ice on Ice / Aug. 1969 / Mercury ♦♦♦
Ice on Ice didn't yield as many hits as its predecessor (*The Ice Man Cometh*), but for fans of mature uptown soul and smooth string-laden productions, it's yet another success. The Butler-Gamble-Huff triumvirate began right where they'd left off less than a year earlier, and occasionally upped the energy level, as on the highlight "Been a Long Time." True, there's nothing on *Ice on Ice* up to the level of "Only the Strong Survive" or "Hey, Western Union Man," but it's a great place to go for more of Jerry Butler's smooth, confident approach to late-'60s soul. *—John Bush*

Jerry Butler Sings Assorted Sounds . . . / 1971 / Mercury ♦♦♦
In the early '70s, Jerry Butler founded a songwriting workshop in his native Chicago. *Jerry Butler Sings Assorted Sounds . . .* offers some of the tracks from a batch of newer writers and features the brash Chicago production style slightly updated. Compared to his Gamble-Huff efforts, the arrangements here aren't as emotionally fulfilling and the lyrics aren't as apt. Without that high standard, it took a while for Butler to adjust commercially and musically. This effort reflects the adjustment period. The first track, "How Did We Lose It," has a good bassline and an acid guitar solo. On this effort, Butler enlisted the help of a rising new writer and arranger, Donny Hathaway, who arranged three tracks here. The best, the melodic "Special Memory," is warm track that features Hathaway's earthy piano and an animated vocal from Butler. "If It's Real What I Feel," a duet with Brenda Lee Eager, has a playful arrangement and there is plenty of chemistry between the two. The album's last track, "Do You Finally Need a Friend," has a challenging melody and a dramatic arrangement that helps Butler give a multi-layered and nuanced vocal. *Jerry Butler Sings Assorted Sounds . . .* is an album of near greatness, but it can't help but pale in comparison to the efforts done with Gamble & Huff. *—Jason Elias*

The Sagittarius Movement / 1971 / Mercury ♦♦♦
Sagittarius Movement is icier than Butler's two ice-titled albums (*Ice Man Cometh* and *Ice on Ice*) that Kenny Gamble & Leon Huff produced. The songs are products of Butler's Songwriting Workshop with Butler's endearing duet with Brenda Lee Eager, "Ain't Understanding Mellow," written by Homer Talbert and Horsholt Polk—the *pièce de résistance*; the quiet storm staple surely inspired Rick James' even more dramatic "Fire and Desire," which he recorded with Teena Marie some years later. Original copies aren't aplenty; a copy in good condition will set you back about 50 bucks. *—Andrew Hamilton*

Spice of Life / 1972 / Mercury ♦♦♦
Spice of Life is a double album during an era when they were rare, especially for solo R&B acts. The first track, "What's So Good About It (You're My Baby)," is a middling ballad that oddly mixes the thoughts of a recent Vietnam veteran with a declaration of love. The Flamingos classic "I Only Have Eyes for You" is taken at a faster pace but strays too far from the song's singular melody. The effort's best original ballad, the mandolin-filled "That's the Way It Was (That's the Way It Is)," has Butler turning in an emotional performance. Carole King's "So Far Away," with its adventurous arrangement, is nearly as good with Butler's ad-libs and tone, bringing poignancy to the track. By the middle of *Spice of Life*, it is clear the ideas are either poorly conceived or too lengthy. The Philly-styled "I Need You" has great backing but a barely-there premise. Frequent duet partner Brenda Lee Eager shows up for "You Can't Always Tell" and a cover of "(They Long to Be) Close to You." Despite the rambling, Butler brings *Spice of Life* to a close with a warm take on Burt Bacharach and Hal David's unsung gem "All Kinds of People." Despite Butler's best intentions, this would have worked better as a single album. *—Jason Elias*

The Love We Have, the Love We Had / 1973 / Mercury ♦♦♦
Jerry Butler and Brenda Lee Eager's voices weave together seamlessly on this fine exhibition of male/female duet singing. The warblers climbed the charts with "Ain't Understanding Mellow" (number three R&B); they nearly cast the spell again accompanied by Chicago's best musicians, eight songs from Butler's Songwriting Workshop, and two killers from Motown. In the spotlight are the pair's rendition of "The Love We Had (Stays on My Mind)," popularized by the Dells; an update of Marvin Gaye and Tammi Terrell's "If This Love Was Mine"; "As the Seasons Change"; "Can't Understand It"; and "How Long Will It Last." And they rock hard on Holland, Dozier, & Holland's "Take Me in Your Arms (Rock Me for a Little While)." While nothing's as mesmerizing as "Ain't Understanding Mellow," this set begs for CD exposure, along with other Butler/Eager tracks. *—Andrew Hamilton*

Power of Love / 1973 / Mercury ♦♦♦

Love's on the Menu / 1976 / Motown ♦♦♦

Suite for the Single Girl / 1977 / Motown ♦♦♦
Jerry Butler's second release for Motown, like his best efforts, exudes maturity, intelligence, and warmth. The best tracks here are quintessential "singers songs" that oddly haven't been covered elsewhere. On the album's biggest track "I Wanna Do It to You," Butler blunted the song's request with a "like you did it to me." Whether he meant "relations" or a neatly crafted affirmation, the song was his biggest hit in close to four years. The title track is a skilled and well-crafted lament, co-written by Butler and started off with his "Brown paper bags are telephone pages / Books on life as seen by sages / Yet she can't understand." One would be hard-pressed to find a more pessimistic ballad for unattached women. Butler didn't let up in his role as armchair psychologist: "Music in Her Dreams" has him singing the praises of a woman who has to put her love of singing on hold. "Only Pretty Girls," perhaps the richest and most subtle of the bunch, completed the "Unfulfilled Women Trilogy" with a perfect match of commiserate tone and subdued arrangement. This being a late-'70s effort, Butler also had to do his time on the dance-floor, and "You Gotta Believe in Me" benefits from a good bass line and Butler's charm. *Suite for the Single Girl* was the most successful album during his three-year stint with Motown. *—Jason Elias*

Soul Workshop / 1986 / Charly ♦♦♦♦♦
This excellent Charly disc offers up 22 sides from Jerry Butler's time at the Vee-Jay label during 1960-1967. Butler would go on to score more smashes on Mercury during the late '60s and early '70s, but his prime material may well be found here with cuts like "He Will Break Your Heart," "Find Another Girl," and "I Stand Accused." Less soul-symphonic than his Philly/Mercury work for Gamble & Huff, Butler's Vee-Jay tracks feature more of the romantic, late-'50s sound of his early Impressions sides (Butler's big hit with the Impressions, "For Your Precious Love," is included here). The MOR sophistication is particularly well essayed on his amazing versions of Bacharach's "Make It Easy on Yourself" and "Message to Martha." None of his fine duets with Betty Everett are to be found, but this is a small complaint considering the wealth contained herein. *—Stephen Cook*

★ **The Best of Jerry Butler** / 1987 / Rhino ♦♦♦♦♦
Still the only compilation to range through Jerry Butler's entire career on the pop charts, Rhino's *The Best of Jerry Butler* offered a lot of tracks (especially for the mid-'80s) and remains the best place to hear the full scope of Chicago's smoothest soul singer. The 18-tracker begins fittingly with his first hit, the sweet ballad "For Your Precious Love," recorded during the brief time in 1958 when he led the Impressions—later to find even more pop success on their own than Butler would. During the early '60s, though, Jerry Butler was one of the most popular artists in Chicago soul, paced by his big Vee-Jay singles: "He Will Break Your Heart," "I'm a Telling You," the sublime Burt Bacharach production "Make It Easy on Yourself," and his biggest hit of the era, the Betty Everett duet "Let It Be Me." The compilation then skips ahead to close out with three hits from his years in Philadelphia with Mercury, the Gamble-Huff hits "Never Give You Up," "Hey, Western Union Man," and "Only the Strong Survive." Anyone with more than a passing interest in Chicago soul would do better with separate sets for his Vee-Jay and Mercury years (*The Sweetest Soul* and *Iceman: The Mercury Years*, respectively), but *The Best of Jerry Butler* is a great choice for listeners wanting only the best. *—John Bush*

Time & Faith / 1992 / Ichiban ♦♦
Jerry Butler was 52 when, in 1992, he recorded *Time & Faith*. At that point in his life, the Iceman was no longer a full-time singer—he was putting most of his energy into politics and held the title of Cook County Commissioner in his native Chicago. But while he had placed music on the back burner, Butler hadn't given it up altogether. *Time & Faith* is the work of an artist who was past his prime, both commercially and creatively, but it isn't a bad album—and even though the Iceman's voice wasn't what it was in the 1960s and 1970s, he's still likable. *Time & Faith* is fairly unpredictable; while "Trying to Break the Habit" is a bluesy soul number, the ballads "I Was Right About You" and "You're the Only One" are essentially adult contemporary. The Impressions graduate also turns his attention to everything from reggae-pop (Jimmy Cliff's "Sitting in Limbo") to country-pop (Willie Nelson's "Angel Flying Too Close to the Ground"). Despite being generally decent, *Time & Faith* isn't for the casual listener who would be much better off with a collection of Butler's classic Vee-Jay or Mercury output. But if you're a collector or a die-hard fan, this little-known CD is worth searching for. *—Alex Henderson*

Iceman: The Mercury Years / Feb. 4, 1992 / Mercury ♦♦♦♦
Iceman: The Mercury Years compiles 44 tracks from the talented Butler's mostly successful 1965-1974 stint at the label. Despite his hits and classics with the label, he didn't start off with gangbusters there. He did steady himself somewhat with "I Dig You Baby" and "Mr. Dream Merchant." Just as his fortunes seemed to be drifting downward, Butler rebounded by 1967. *Iceman: The Mercury Years* makes no bones about its unabashed emphasis on Butler's work with Kenny Gamble, Leon Huff, and Thom Bell. Not surprisingly, the tracks included prove the point. The big hits—including "Only the Strong Survive," "Hey, Western Union Man," and "A Brand New Me"—lose nothing in a greatest-hits format. Still, some of the lesser-known songs from *Ice on Ice* and *The Iceman Cometh* certainly weren't the best choice for this compilation. Away from Gamble & Huff and back in Chicago, Butler's early-'70s work was typified by the strong and dramatic sounds of the area. Interestingly enough, this set gets its most interesting and instructive moments centering on Butler's Mercury decline. Songs like "Special Memory," "How Did We Lose It," and "If It's Real" aren't great, but certainly retain their strength among the better-known tracks. While his 1973 hit duet, "Ain't Understanding Mellow," is included, other great tracks of the period, like "That's the Way It Was (That's the Way It Is)" and his great cover of Carole King's "So Far Away," didn't make it here. All in all, *Iceman: The Mercury Years* does offer great songs, but the original albums might be more sufficient. *—Jason Elias*

The Ice Man Cometh / 1993 / Vee-Jay ♦♦♦♦♦
Jerry Butler's elegant, soulful vocals got their first exposure on Vee-Jay, both in a group setting when he was leader of the Impressions and later in a string of wonderful solo tunes. Butler could turn old pop songs like "Moon River" into sterling triumphs, and although his sound was always smooth, it never lacked strength or conviction. The 25 numbers on this reissue include numbers that he made anthems, like "I Stand Accused" and "Make It Easy on Yourself," plus three early Impressions songs; his huge duet hit with Betty Everett, "Let It Be Me"; and many other excellent efforts. *—Ron Wynn*

Jerry Butler, Esq./He Will Break Your Heart / Sep. 26, 2000 / Collectables ♦♦♦

Aware of Love/Need to Belong / Oct. 17, 2000 / Collectables ♦♦♦

Moon River/Delicious Together / Oct. 17, 2000 / Collectables ♦♦♦

The Sweetest Soul / Feb. 9, 2001 / RPM ♦♦♦♦
This is a very good British anthology covering Butler's Vee-Jay era, the 26 tracks including all of his major solo hits with the label in the first half of the 1960s: "He Will Break Your Heart," "Moon River," "Find Another Girl," "I'm a Telling You," "Make It Easy on Yourself," and "Need to Belong." There's also the bonus of his big 1958 hit with the Impressions, "For Your Precious Love," although his huge 1964 duet smash with Betty

Everett, "Let It Be Me," is absent. It's not just a recycling of the material found on the most comprehensive U.S. retrospective of Butler's Vee-Jay period, *The Iceman*; almost half of these songs are not found on the American counterpart. That's an important distinction, since some of the cuts only on *The Sweetest Soul* are notable, such as the fine 1964 ballad "Giving Up on Love," and a few songs that Curtis Mayfield wrote or co-wrote. Unfortunately the original release dates are not given for all of the songs in the track listings and liner notes, and some of the non-hit tracks are much less memorable than Butler's best efforts for Vee-Jay. But these are the only small reservations that apply to this quality early soul disc. *—Richie Unterberger*

The Philadelphia Sessions / Oct. 9, 2001 / Mercury ✦✦✦✦✦

Here's a sensible, good-value thematic reissue, a blast of fresh air in an era where sometimes any excuses seem to be getting made to put out the same material over and over. Both of the late-'60s albums on which Butler collaborated with the Kenny Gamble & Leon Huff production team, *The Iceman Cometh* and *Ice on Ice*, are combined on a single CD, with the addition of three other tracks from the era (which originally appeared on the LPs *Mr. Dream Merchant* and *You and Me*) featuring the same Butler-Gamble-Huff combination. Thus it isolates, on one solid package, the short-lived time in which Butler, working with Gamble & Huff, successfully enhanced the early Philadelphia soul sound, and vice versa. *The Iceman Cometh*, the (slightly) earlier of the pair of albums, is the one that will grab listeners' attention more, as it has the hits "Never Give You Up," "Hey, Western Union Man," and "Only the Strong Survive." But really, *Ice on Ice* isn't far behind in quality, featuring "A Brand New Me," which some listeners might be more familiar with from Dusty Springfield's version. It was the equal of its predecessor in sophisticated production, too, sometimes introducing the electric sitar-like sounds that became vogue throughout soul music for a while. The consistently sentimental stories might be a little overwhelming all at once. But overall these sessions are highlights of slick-yet-not-too-slick early Philly soul production, and ones in which the artist (Butler) is as much a creative contributor as Gamble & Huff. The CD also adds historical liner notes by author Craig Werner. *—Richie Unterberger*

Bobby Byrd (Bobby Day)

b. Aug. 15, 1934, South Carolina

Vocals, Piano, Organ / Funk, Soul, Deep Funk

As a long-running right-hand man, Bobby Byrd performed an invaluable function in the James Brown Show, warming up the crowds as a solo singer, then retreating to the sidelines as a member of the Famous Flames, Brown's backup vocal group. Indeed, without Byrd, James Brown may have never made it out of Georgia: in the early '50s, Byrd and his family sponsored Brown's parole from prison, and Byrd gave Brown a spot in his vocal group, the Flames (which, of course, Brown eventually took over and relegated to the background). Like many of Brown's close associates and support musicians, Byrd got a chance to record his own records under Brown's direction, releasing numerous Brown-produced singles between the early '60s and early '70s. Some of these were even modest R&B hits—"We're in Love" (1965) and "I Need Help (I Can't Do It Alone)" (1970) were the biggest, making the R&B Top 20. Brown's backing musicians (and sometimes Brown himself) often figured heavily in the arrangements, and unsurprisingly the tracks often sounded like James Brown records featuring a different vocalist.

The unfortunate problem was that Byrd was an average, even nondescript soul singer, sounding much more like a poor person's Sam & Dave than a facsimile of Soul Brother Number One. The records were often fine, the early-'70s hard funk singles in particular (which usually featured the J.B.'s cook), but you can't help wondering if they might sound a lot better with J.B. himself on the front line. Still, fans of the James Brown groove will find a lot to like in Byrd's best recordings, in much the same way as they'll enjoy the *James Brown's Funky People* series of recordings that J.B. oversaw (but did not sing lead on). Certainly Eric B. & Rakim thought so, reworking one of Byrd's best singles (1971's "I Know You Got Soul") so faithfully that legal action ensued. After splitting from Brown in 1973, Byrd recorded sporadically and performed often (particularly in Europe), releasing *On the Move* in 1994. *—Richie Unterberger*

Live in the Stuffenbau / 1991 / East Side ✦✦✦

On the Move / 1994 / Instinct ✦✦✦✦

Often called "the Godfather's Godfather," Bobby Byrd found the young James Brown a home and a job so he could get out of doing time in a juvenile detention center, then served as his bandleader and arranger until 1970. Not only that, but Byrd wrote more than 40 of Brown's biggest hits, including "Sex Machine," "Talkin' Loud and Sayin' Nothing," and "I Know You Got Soul." Unfortunately, Byrd never received proper credit for much of his work, which is why he remains a relative unknown to this day. Fortunately, a small label in Europe (where Byrd has a much bigger following) rescued him from obscurity for this comeback solo LP, his first since the early '70s. With a little help from his family—wife Vicki Anderson and daughter Carleen Anderson of Young Disciples fame on backup vocals, sons Tony Byrd and Bart Anderson on drums and organ, and godson Jerry Preston on bass—and his friends (the Tower of Power horns and the Godfather himself, who co-wrote two songs here), Byrd sounds just as funky as ever, stirring up a steaming pot of sweat-soaked funk. On cuts like "Try It Again," "Sayin' It & Doin' It Is Two Different Things," and "I Got It (It's Been a Long Time Comin')," Byrd and company deliver the groovin' goods in a way James Brown has largely failed to do since his '70s heyday, leaving little doubt that Byrd was the man behind much of the Godfather's magic. *—Bret Love*

● **The Bobby Byrd Got Soul: The Best of Bobby Byrd** / Aug. 22, 1995 / Polydor ✦✦✦✦✦

As is the case with the J.B.'s and other James Brown protégés, Bobby Byrd's legacy is spread over numerous out-of-print, difficult-to-find vinyl records. So this 22-song retrospective, which gathers numerous singles and a couple of previously unreleased tracks spanning 1964 to 1973, is a welcome consolidation of his most significant work into one package. Solid stuff, covering both standard soul from the '60s and hard funk (usually featuring the J.B.'s) from the early '70s, though it sounds a lot more like a James Brown record with a different vocalist than a Bobby Byrd record that happens to benefit from James Brown's backing crew. Brown produced (and occasionally contributed to) all of the recordings here, and duets with Bobby on the 1968 single "You've Got to Change Your Mind." *—Richie Unterberger*

Donald Byrd (Donaldson Toussaint L'Ouverture II)

b. Dec. 9, 1932, Detroit, MI

Trumpet / Crossover Jazz, Hard Bop, Fusion, Jazz-Funk, Funk, Smooth Soul

In the late '50s and early '60s, Donald Byrd carved out a niche for himself as one of the most adept hard boppers of his generation. Never a wildly original player, Byrd nevertheless captured the tenor of his times as a solid, clean-toned, lyrical improviser in the manner of contemporaries like Clifford Brown and Freddie Hubbard. In the mid-'50s, he recorded for the Prestige, Riverside, Blue Note, and Savoy labels (among others), both as a leader and as a sideman. Following stints with the likes of Max Roach, Art Blakey, and Sonny Rollins, Byrd co-led a band with baritone saxophonist Pepper Adams from 1958-1961. After releasing a number of fine straight-ahead Blue Note albums throughout the '60s, in the '70s his music took a decidedly commercial turn. Byrd recorded a number of heavily produced, pop-oriented albums on which his horn was subjugated by disco-fied vocals and string sections. In the '80s and '90s, Byrd returned to his jazz roots, recording with peers such as Joe Henderson and Bobby Hutcherson, and with younger musicians like Kenny Garrett and Mulgrew Miller. *—Chris Kelsey*

Fancy Free / May 9, 1969-Jun. 6, 1969 / Blue Note ✦✦✦

Fancy Free, released in 1969, marked the beginning of Donald Byrd's move away from hard bop, staking out fusion-flavored territory that—at this juncture—owed more to Miles Davis than the R&B-dominated jazz-funk Byrd would embrace several years down the road. Recorded just a few months after Davis' *In a Silent Way*, *Fancy Free* finds Byrd leading a large ensemble prominently featuring Frank Foster on tenor, Lew Tabackin or Jerry Dodgion on flute, and several percussionists. But the most important piece of the puzzle is Duke Pearson's electric piano, the first time Byrd utilized the instrument. Pearson dominates the texture of the group sound, which makes the entirety of the session seem farther outside the realm of funky hard bop than it actually is. However, that's not to say that *Fancy Free* isn't a clear break with Byrd's past—especially the two Byrd originals that open the album. The title track—which later became one of Byrd's more covered compositions—contrasts Pearson's spacy musings with a busy, funky percussion groove, and there's a loose, open feel to the improvisations that breaks with hard bop conventions. The warm ballad "I Love the Girl" has a similarly airy feel, and at eight and a half minutes, is the shortest cut; clearly Byrd wanted an open framework for exploration. The other two numbers are more traditional hard bop compositions by former Byrd students, which—although funky and full of improvisations—can't help but feel more tethered than their predecessors. Still, even if it isn't his most adventurous fusion outing, *Fancy Free* is the rare Donald Byrd album that holds appeal for rare-groove fanatics and traditionalists alike. *—Steve Huey*

Kofi / 1969-1970 / Blue Note ✦✦✦✦

Kofi was extracted from some of last Blue Note sessions of the 1960s before Byrd's ventures into soul fusion territory. The playing here is no less than stellar, with seasoned veterans such as Ron Carter and Airto Moreira giving Byrd more than ample support to stretch out and soulfully foreshadow elements of future recordings. Lew Tabackin easily shares the spotlight with his beautiful flute passages on the title track, while Frank Foster and the rest of the supporting group complement Byrd's playing with a grace that emulates the early chemistry between the early Miles Davis groups of the early '60s. The subtle relaxed tones of this album make it truly one of the essential releases in Byrd's catalog, not only from a historical standpoint (his future collaborations with the Mizell brothers would take him to an entirely different plane of thought), but from a casual listening standpoint as well. *—Rob Theakston*

Electric Byrd / May 15, 1970 / Blue Note ✦✦✦✦✦

Donald Byrd's transitional sessions from 1969-1971 are actually some of the trumpeter's most intriguing work, balancing accessible, funky, Davis-style fusion with legitimate jazz improvisation. *Electric Byrd*, from 1970, is the best of the bunch, as Byrd absorbs the innovations of *Bitches Brew* and comes up with one of his most consistent fusion sets of any flavor. Byrd leads his largest fusion group yet (ten to 11 pieces), featuring many of his cohorts of the time (including Jerry Dodgion, Lew Tabackin, and Frank Foster on various woodwinds). Most important are electric pianist Duke Pearson, who once again dominates the arrangements, and percussionist Airto Moreira, who in places lends a strong Brazilian feel that predates *Return to Forever*. Moreira also contributes one of the four compositions, "Xibaba," which starts out as an airy Brazilian tune but morphs into a free-form effects extravaganza; the rest are Byrd originals that prove equally imaginative and diverse. The Brazilian-tinged opener "Estavanico" has a gentle, drifting quality that's often disrupted by jarring dissonances. There's also the shifting—and sometimes even disappearing—slow groove of "Essence," and the hard-edged, bop-based funk of "The Dude." Much of the album has a spacy, floating feel indebted to the psychedelic fusion of *Bitches Brew*; it's full of open-ended solo improvisations, loads of amplification effects, and striking sonic textures. The arrangements are continually surprising, and the band never works the same groove too long, switching or completely dropping the underlying rhythms. So even if it wears its influences on its sleeve, *Electric Byrd* is indisputably challenging, high-quality fusion. It's also the end of the line for jazz purists as far as Donald Byrd is concerned, which is perhaps part of the reason the album has yet to receive its proper due. *—Steve Huey*

Ethiopian Knights / Aug. 25, 1971-Aug. 26, 1971 / Blue Note ✦✦✦

Right from the stop-start bass groove that opens "The Emperor," it's immediately clear that *Ethiopian Knights* is more indebted to funk—not just funky jazz, but the straight-up James Brown/Sly Stone variety—than any previous Donald Byrd project. And, like a true funk band, Byrd and his group work the same driving, polyrhythmic grooves over and over, making rhythm the focal point of the music. Although the musicians do improvise, their main objective is to keep the grooves pumping, using their solos more to create texture than harmonic complexity. That's why jazz purists began to detest Byrd with this album (though the follow-ups certainly cinched it); in truth, even though *Ethiopian Knights* did move Byrd closer to R&B, it's still more jazz than funk, and didn't completely foreshadow his crossover. The dense arrangements and lo-o-o-ng workouts (two of the three tracks are over 15 minutes) are indicative of Byrd's continued debt to Miles Davis, in particular the bevy of live double LPs Davis issued in the early '70s. Byrd again leads a large ensemble, but with mostly different players than on his recent sessions; some come from the group assembled for Bobby Hutcherson's *Head On* album, others from the Jazz Crusaders. That's part of the reason there are fewer traces of hard bop here, but it's also clear from the title that Byrd's emerging Afrocentric consciousness was leading him—like Davis—to seek ways of renewing jazz's connection to the people who created it. Even if it isn't quite as consistent as *Kofi* and *Electric Byrd*, *Ethiopian Knights* is another intriguing transitional effort that deepens the portrait of Byrd the acid jazz legend. *—Steve Huey*

★ **Black Byrd** / Apr. 3, 1972-Apr. 4, 1972 / Blue Note ♦♦♦♦♦
Purists howled with indignation when Donald Byrd released *Black Byrd*, a full-fledged foray into R&B that erupted into a popular phenomenon. Byrd was branded a sellout and a traitor to his hard bop credentials, especially after *Black Byrd* became the biggest-selling album in Blue Note history. What the elitists missed, though, was that *Black Byrd* was the moment when Byrd's brand of fusion finally stepped out from under the shadow of his chief influence, Miles Davis, and found a distinctive voice of its own. Never before had a jazz musician embraced the celebratory sound and style of contemporary funk as fully as Byrd did here—not even Davis, whose dark, chaotic jungle-funk stood in sharp contrast to the bright, breezy, danceable music on *Black Byrd*. Byrd gives free rein to producer/arranger/composer Larry Mizell, who crafts a series of tightly focused, melodic pieces often indebted to the lengthier orchestrations of Isaac Hayes and Curtis Mayfield. They're built on the most straightforward funk rhythms Byrd had yet tackled, and if the structures aren't as loose or complex as his earlier fusion material, they make up for it with a funky sense of groove that's damn near irresistible. Byrd's solos are mostly melodic and in-the-pocket, but that allows the funk to take center stage. Sure, maybe the electric piano, sound effects, and Roger Glenn's ubiquitous flute date the music somewhat, but that's really part of its charm. *Black Byrd* was state-of-the-art for its time, and it set a new standard for all future jazz/R&B/funk fusions—of which there were many. Byrd would continue to refine this sound on equally essential albums like *Street Lady* and the fantastic *Places and Spaces*, but *Black Byrd* stands as his groundbreaking signature statement. *—Steve Huey*

Street Lady / Jun. 13, 1973-Jun. 15, 1973 / Blue Note ♦♦♦
Not so much a fusion album as an attempt at mainstream soul and R&B, *Street Lady* plays like the soundtrack to a forgotten blaxploitation film. Producer/arranger/composer Larry Mizell conceived *Street Lady* as a concept album to a spirited, independent prostitute, and while the hooker with a heart of gold concept is a little trite, the music uncannily evokes an urban landscape, circa the early '70s. Borrowing heavily from Curtis Mayfield, Isaac Hayes and Sly Stone, Donald Byrd and Mizell have created an album that is overflowing with wah-wah guitars, stuttering electric pianos, percolating percussion, soaring flutes, and charmingly anemic, tuneless vocals. It's certainly not jazz, or even fusion, but it isn't really funk or R&B, either—the rhythms aren't elastic enough, and each of the six songs are simply jazzy vamps without clear hooks. But the appeal of *Street Lady* is how its polished neo-funk and pseudo-fusion sounds uncannily like a jive movie or television soundtrack from the early '70s—you can picture the Street Lady, decked out in polyester, cruising the streets surrounding by pimps with wide-brimmed hats and platform shoes. And while that may not be ideal for jazz purists, it's perfect for kitsch and funk fanatics. *—Stephen Thomas Erlewine*

Stepping into Tomorrow / Nov. 1974-Dec. 1974 / Blue Note ♦♦♦
The follow-up to 1974's *Street Lady*, *Stepping into Tomorrow* is one of those albums disgruntled jazz lovers may hate, but it definitely helped Byrd continue his crossover success. Tacitly ethnocentric and experimental, the album shows great chemistry between artist and producer (the Mizell brothers, Fonce and Larry). The title track, with its chanted vocals and skilled support playing, provided an atmosphere for Byrd to offer some emotive and complex riffs. On that track, as well as the comforting "Design a Nation," Byrd trades solos with alto saxophonist Gary Bartz. "Think Twice" has a mellifluous bridge that has warm keyboard playing from Jerry Peters and Larry Mizell. But despite the good tracks, there is far too much filler. "Rock and Roll Again" does neither and features James Carter's loved or hated whistled solos. "You Are the World," however, is another strong track and has that classic Mizell production style. The last track, "I Love the Girl," closes this effort on a ho-hum note. Although it isn't going to make any short list of straight-ahead jazz classics, *Stepping into Tomorrow* is a solid example of the Blue Note's early-'70s commercial sound. *—Jason Elias*

Places and Spaces / Aug. 1975-Sep. 1975 / Blue Note ♦♦♦
Reuniting with Larry Mizell, the man behind his last three LPs, Donald Byrd continues to explore contemporary soul, funk and R&B with *Places and Spaces*. In fact the record sounds more urban than its predecessor, which often played like a Hollywood version of the Inner City. Keeping the Isaac Hayes, Curtis Mayfield, and Sly Stone influences of *Street Lady*, *Places and Spaces* adds elements of Marvin Gaye, Earth, Wind & Fire, and Stevie Wonder, which immediately makes the album funkier and more soulful. Boasting sweeping string arrangements, sultry rhythm guitars, rubbery bass, murmuring flugelhorns and punchy horn charts, the music falls halfway between the cinematic neo-funk of *Street Lady* and the proto-disco soul of Earth, Wind & Fire. Also, the title *Places and Spaces* does mean something—there are more open spaces within the music, which automatically makes it funkier. Of course, it also means that there isn't much of interest on *Places and Spaces* for jazz purists, but the album would appeal to most fans of Philly soul, lite funk and proto-disco. *—Stephen Thomas Erlewine*

Caricatures / Apr. 1976-May 1976 / Blue Note ♦♦♦
One of his last efforts with the Mizell production team was definitely not his most critically acclaimed, but *Caricatures* continued Byrd's commercial winning streak that started years previous with 1969's *Kofi* and such '70s Blue Note classics as *Places and Spaces*, *Black Byrd*, and *Street Lady*. His last release for the label was no exception to the formula set forth from the previously mentioned albums. One of *Caricatures* strongest features is the level of musicianship from start to finish. Byrd recruited some of the top '70s soul-jazz musicians, such as Gary Bartz, Alphonse Mouzon, David T. Walker, and future '80s R&B hitmaker Patrice Rushen, to help complement the musicianship laid down by Byrd and the Mizell brothers. The atmosphere is light and soulful, with musicians bouncing off one another for ideas that shift closer towards R&B while maintaining a sense of jazz ideals. While there is no truly memorable anthemic release or hit to speak of, *Caricatures* serves its primary purpose of being a jazz fusion record to make both people dance and purists wince at the notion that jazz can fuse with other elements and achieve success. *—Rob Theakston*

Thank You . . . For F.U.M.L. (Funking Up My Life) / Jul. 1978 / Elektra ♦♦
This album was Byrd's debut for Elektra/Asylum and a return to the charts after the demise of Blue Note Records. After taking a brief hiatus from recording, Byrd got right back in the business of commercial jazz/R&B while the purists again recoiled in horror. During the '70s, he was one of the leaders at making intelligent, R&B-based jazz with high selling albums, *Black Byrd* and *Places And Spaces*, both produced by Larry Mizell and Fonce Mizell. *Thank You . . . For F.U.M.L. (Funking Up My Life)* has Byrd producing himself, taking disco much too seriously and straying too far from his jazz roots. Although this does feature his 125th Street Orchestra, which included Wah Wah Watson, Ed Watkins, and Gregory Phillinganes, they paled in comparison to his 1972-1975 bands. The disco-fied "In Love With Love" isn't even suited for Byrd's trumpet blaring in the background. The other dance tracks, "Have You Heard the News?" and the title track, almost take a scientific approach to disco, and to that end there's little spontaneity. Byrd did much better with the melodically challenging songs on the album. Tracks like the assured "Your Love Is My Ecstasy" and the sharp, midtempo "Loving You" has him animated and playing recondite and rewarding notes. By the album's last song, "Close Your Eyes and Look Within," it's clear that the relative lightweight nature of *Thank You . . . For F.U.M.L. (Funking Up My Life)* wasn't going to bring out the best in him or the listener. *—Jason Elias*

Blue Breakbeats / Jun. 16, 1998 / Blue Note ♦♦♦

C

The Cadets

f. Los Angeles, CA, **db.** 1958

Group / Doo Wop, R&B

This West Coast group used two names for recording sessions. They called themselves the Jacks when doing dates for Modern and the Cadets on RPM. They began as a gospel group during the late '40s in Los Angeles. Ted Taylor, Aaron Collins, Lloyd McCraw, and Will "Dub" Jones were the original lineup, and the Cadets were among the more popular bands doing R&B covers. The Cadets' lone hit was "Stranded in the Jungle," which they recorded for Modern as the Jacks in 1956. It peaked at number-eight R&B and number-15 pop. Davis and Collins would later join the Flares in 1961, while Taylor would enjoy solo success as a blues, soul, and gospel vocalist. Jones joined the Coasters in 1958 and remained there for over a decade. Collins' sisters, Betty and Rose, also recorded for Modern/RPM as the Teen Queens. *—Ron Wynn*

Rockin' n' Reelin' / 1957 / Crown ✦✦✦✦✦

Yes, those rockin' and reelin' Cadets were also those jumping Jacks, and vice versa; a simple side-by-side comparison of the cover of this and the cover of *Jumpin' With the Jacks* (their original and sole album for Crown) confirms that it's obviously the same group. The general idea was that all the smooth ballad material would be issued as the Jacks and all the uptempo sides would be issued under the Cadets' banner. And that's pretty much the edict that's largely offered here, with only the bluesy "So Will I" and covers of "Fools Rush In," Johnnie & Joe's "I'll Be Spinning," and—improbably enough—"Heartbreak Hotel" heading into doo wop ballad territory. The rest of the album consists of first-rate covers (how the group got on the charts in the first place, covering the Jayhawks' "Stranded in the Jungle" as the Cadets and the Feathers' "Why Don't You Write Me" as the Jacks) of Peppermint Harris' "I Got Loaded," "Smack Dab in the Middle," the Marigolds' "Rollin' Stone," the Willows' "Church Bells May Ring," and the Dominoes' "Sixty Minute Man," here presented with the cleaned-up title change "Dancin' Dan." This is one of the all-time great doo wop albums, wacky behind-the-scenes rock & roll record-company chicanery and all. *—Cub Koda*

The Cadets Meet the Jacks / 1958 / Ace ✦✦✦✦

Recording frequently as the Jacks, the Cadets produced some of the greatest doo wop rockers of the '50s, many of which are featured here as companions to 1956's huge novelty hit, "Stranded in the Jungle." Blessed with one of doo wop's most distinctive vocalists in Dub Jones, the disc also features many of the Cadets' best covers, including Nappy Brown's "Don't Be Angry" and an English version of the French cabaret hit "Hands Across the Table." Some great originals include the sweaty "Baby Ya Know" and "Let's Rock 'n' Roll," one of the era's awesome lost anthems. *—Jim Smith*

The Cadets / 1966 / Crown ✦✦✦

● **Stranded in the Jungle** / Dec. 1, 1995 / P-Vine ✦✦✦✦

Though the similarly titled Japanese compilation on P-Vine offers two more tracks, Ace's *Stranded in the Jungle* gets the nod since it's found more often and has better liner notes. The first of two Cadets/Jacks collections from the label, *Stranded in the Jungle* focuses on the Cadets' recordings for Modern/RPM from late 1954 ("Don't Be Angry") to December 1957 ("Ring Chimes," their last single for RPM). (The second volume, *Why Don't You Write Me,* concerns itself mostly with Jacks singles from the same years.) Paced by the rollicking Top 20 story song "Stranded in the Jungle," the Cadets recorded plenty of fine material, and all of it sounded great thanks to the arrangements of Maxwell Davis and the supervision of Modern vice pres Joe Bihari (one of the four Biharis who put in time at the label). The Cadets also did covers or answer songs that rocked just as hard as the originals: just check out the "Work With Me Henry" answer song "Annie Met Henry," or "Dancin' Dan," a cover (in all but the name) of "Sixty Minute Man." "I'll Be Spinning" shows the group sounding great when playing it straight as well, and compiler Walter DeVenne wisely added to the program a couple of Jacks songs cut from the same cloth ("Love Bandit"). Prime doo wop at its most exuberant and fun. *—John Bush*

Why Don't You Write Me / Dec. 1, 1995 / Ace ✦✦✦

The Cadillacs

f. 1953, Harlem, NY, **db.** 1962

Group / Doo Wop

Earl Carroll, LaVerne Drake, and Robert Phillips were already singing together in the early '50s as the Carnations, whose lineup also included "Cub" Gaining. Carroll and Phillips were nearly as close as brothers, Carroll having been taken in by Phillips' family after the death of his own mother. The group—based in New York's Harlem in the area around 131st St. and Seventh and Eighth Avenues—had an energetic approach to music, but somewhat threadbare harmonies, and they were popular at dances held at the local public school they all attended. Their main influence was the Orioles, whose slow romantic numbers went over very well with the group members and the audiences of the period. Carroll's own musical roots included gospel, specifically the Five Blind Boys, the Swanee Quintet, and the Soul Stirrers, but also R&B vocal outfits such as the Clovers, the Ravens, the Swallows, and the Five Keys.

The Carnations were heard in a performance at Public School 43 by Lover Patterson, a one-time associate of the Orioles who had organized a group called the Five Crowns (whose 1958-era membership would become the new Drifters, of "There Goes My Baby" fame), who was impressed enough with their singing to introduce the group to Esther Navarro, a secretary for the Shaw Artist Agency who also wrote songs.

The audition itself brought about changes in the Carnations' lineup. Baritone Bobby Phillips wanted to switch to bass, partly to see if the novelty value of a 5' 4" bass singer would have some value (most basses were big guys), but Cub Gaining didn't like the idea and quit before the audition. Patterson replaced him with James "Poppa" Clark of the Five Crowns and Johnny "Gus" Willingham. It was this group—Earl Carroll (lead tenor), LaVerne Drake (tenor), James Clark (tenor), Johnny Willingham (baritone), and Bobby Phillips (bass)—that auditioned for Navarro. They were duly signed but had to give up their name, as the Carnations was already being used by a professional outfit. The Cadillacs was chosen for its association with automotive elegance and to separate the group from the spate of bird and flower names that were common among singing groups.

The group brought a pair of songs, Navarro's "Gloria" and Patterson's "I Wonder Why," to Jubilee Records, an independent outfit owned by former bandleader Jerry Blaine. Their first single was in stores by the end of July 1954, and it proved to be a regional success, with strong sales on the East Coast from Baltimore to Boston, especially (no surprise) in New York. Patterson's more uptempo "I Wonder Why" had more success than the more restrained and romantic "Gloria." By the time of the release of the group's second single, "Wishing Well," issued later that summer, the lineup had changed, with James Clark and Johnny Willingham replaced by baritone Earl Wade and tenor Charles "Buddy" Brooks. The group experienced modest success during the latter part of 1954 and early 1955, and then they had their breakthrough record, "Speedo." There have been several stories associated with the origins of the song, all of which surround Earl Carroll's attributes: Carroll has claimed that it originated with a nickname he got as a child, but also said that the beat and background were influenced by the group's appreciation of a Regals song called "Got the Water Boiling." Esther Navarro, whose name is signed to the song as writer, claimed at the time that it derived from Carroll's derisive nickname "Speedy," earned by his slow-moving demeanor; she claimed that he said to her, "They often call me Speedy but my real name is Mr. Earl."

The song was recorded in September of 1955, and released in October of that year. It became a monster hit, but only after laying dormant for weeks. The turning point came when Cleveland-based disc jockey Alan Freed booked the group onto his Christmas show at the Academy of Music. The group by that time was completely professional, and had added dance routines choreographed by Cholly Atkins, who later trained most of the Motown acts in their stage presentations. The group swept the board during the two weeks of appearances in the Freed show, which, itself was a major turning point in the history of rock & roll. There had been showcases of that kind going on for several years, but mostly before black audiences; the Freed show broke the theater's box-office record, and in the process drew in a major contingent of white teenagers.

"Speedo" finally broke out in early December, and it entered the *Billboard* pop charts before it reached the R&B charts, something that had never happened before with an R&B single. The music industry began taking notice not only of this phenomenon, but also of the Cadillacs. The song rode the charts for four months, well into 1956, by which time the Cadillacs were established as one of the top R&B groups in the country. They also had a membership change early in that year, with Jimmy Bailey replacing founding member LaVerne Drake. Their attempts at a follow-up hit failed despite some initial encouraging signs from the trade papers, but this didn't slow their momentum on-stage; they remained one of the most heavily and prominently booked groups among the package tours that were the norm, and the bookings were still good into the late winter of 1957.

Unfortunately, nothing was that straightforward for the group itself. At some point, they split with Esther Navarro, and the group also split into two rival sets of Cadillacs. Earl Carroll led the Original Cadillacs, as they became known—consisting of Carroll, Charles Brooks, Bobby Phillips, and Earl Wade—while Navarro had Jimmy Bailey leading Bobby Spencer, Bill Lindsay, and Waldo "Champ Rollow" Champen under the name the Cadillacs. The groups both continued recording, both on Jubilee (which was caught in the middle of the dispute), and effectively canceled each other out.

Navarro's Bailey-led Cadillacs (who only recorded once officially, doing "My Girlfriend" in May of 1957) went on the road in an abortive attempt to carry on, but they were pulled out of the late-1957 package tour before it was half over. By November of 1957, the two groups had made a sort of peace: Champ Rollow and Bill Lindsay were out, and Carroll, Bailey, Brooks, Phillips, and Wade were working together in the studio as the Cadillacs. Brooks was soon replaced by Bobby Spencer, but there were other changes as well: Earl Carroll was pushed into the background of the group's vocals by Jimmy Bailey and Bobby Spencer. Of course, it didn't matter that much, because in their search for a sound that would sell, the group had changed into a comedic doo wop outfit in the mold of the Coasters, specializing in humorous novelty numbers. They hardly resembled the outfit that Earl Carroll had co-founded in the early '50s.

The sad thing, in some respects, is that this worked. They were back on the national charts for the first time in over two years in October of 1958 with "Peek-A-Boo," a sort of "Yakety Yak"-type number that made the Top 40 and gave the group a new lease on life as a concert attraction. Having succeeded once with a comic novelty tune, they mined this vein again with a pair of singles, "Jay Walker" and "Please Mr. Johnson." Both were recorded early in 1959 and featured (in very effective performances) in the 1959 Alan Freed-starring jukebox classic *Go Johnny Go*, which also featured Jimmy Clanton, Sandy Stewart, Chuck Berry, Jackie Wilson, Eddie Cochran, Ritchie Valens, and Jo-Ann Campbell.

The group's string of hits had ended, however. Earl Carroll left the group that he had founded in 1959; the Cadillacs kept working for a few more years, recording unsuccessfully for a number of labels before packing it in during the early '60s. Carroll fared reasonably well, however, remaining in music and eventually joining the Coasters in 1961, where he remained for more than 20 years. He later re-formed the Cadillacs, with Bobby Phillips the only other veteran member of the group, and he kept the new group going throughout the 1980s and into the 1990s, even doing a well-received comeback record early in the '90s. *—Bruce Eder*

The Fabulous Cadillacs / 1957 / Jubilee ♦♦♦

Crazy Cadillacs / 1959 / Jubilee ♦♦♦

The Cadillacs Meet the Orioles / 1961 / Collectables ♦♦♦♦♦

A classic doo wop album featuring one group well known for novelty tracks and another that was among the earliest creators of the genre. Some wonderful jump tunes, silly songs, and romantic ballads. *—Ron Wynn*

Twisting With the Cadillacs / 1962 / Jubilee ♦♦♦

★ **The Best of the Cadillacs** / 1990 / Rhino ♦♦♦♦♦

Although completists will have to have the multi-disc set on Collectables, for the rest of their listeners, this seldom championed but nonetheless superlative single-disc compilation will more than fill the bill. At 18 tracks, a few collectors' favorites are understandably absent ("Wishing Well," "Jaywalkin'"), but *all* of the major and minor hits are well aboard, clearly showcasing the groups' ability to tackle everything from beautiful ballads ("Gloria," "The Girl I Love") to jump numbers ("Speedo," "My Girl Friend") to Coaster-style novelties ("Peek-a-Boo," "Please, Mr. Johnson") and do it all with style, grace, and choreography that *burned*. Covering their stint with Josie Records from 1954 to 1960 in a straight chronological fashion with excellent liner notes from John Neilson, this particular compilation offers great value for the bread and should be one of your very first stops in assembling a definitive doo wop collection. The Cadillacs were one of the first and one of the very best, and here's where you go to dig their basic message before proceeding further. *—Cub Koda*

The Complete Josie Sessions / 1995 / Bear Family ♦♦♦♦♦

This box is really the CD descendant of Murray Hill Records' early-'80s-era LP set, which included lots of outtakes. It seems like complete and absolute overkill to put out four CDs on a vocal quintet that only ever charted two songs ("Speedoo," "Peek-A-Boo") nationally, and, yet... it works. But, if you like '50s R&B, doo wop music, or generally just good singing, there's so much here to listen to that will delight you that the package suddenly seems reasonable. The Cadillacs' secret was the sheer variety of their music—they started out working in a slow romantic vein, and eventually hit it big with one of the fastest-rocking vocal numbers of the period, but they also sang blues (with solid backing, including some fine guitar work) like "(That's) All I Need." Their last sides are still finely sung, but aren't romantic—rather, they began moving toward comedic and satiric pieces such as "Please Mr. Johnson" and "Jaywalker." The diversity is entertaining in itself, and the only real objection that one could have is the presence of different versions of the same songs. Even these are very interesting, such as the slower alternate version of "Speedoo," which would never have been a hit but does reveal more about the song itself. The sessionography is also a big help in sorting out precisely who was in the group at any given moment after their early sides. *—Bruce Eder*

Terry Callier

b. May 24, 1945, Chicago, IL

Vocals, Guitar / Folk-Jazz, Chicago Soul, Singer/Songwriter, Soul

For far too long, folk-jazz mystic Terry Callier was the exclusive province of a fierce but small cult following; a singer/songwriter whose cathartic, deeply spiritual music defied simple genre categorization, he went all but unknown for decades, finally beginning to earn the recognition long due him after his rediscovery during the early '90s. Born in Chicago's North Side—also home to Curtis Mayfield, Jerry Butler, and Ramsey Lewis—and raised in the area of the notorious Cabrini Green housing projects, Callier began studying the piano at the age of three, writing his first songs at the age of 11, and regularly singing in doo wop groups throughout his formative years. While attending college, he learned to play guitar, eventually setting up residency at a Chicago coffeehouse dubbed the Fickle Pickle and in time coming to the attention of Chess Records arranger Charles Stepney, who produced Callier's debut single "Look at Me Now" in 1962.

In 1964, Callier met Prestige label producer Samuel Charters, and a year later they entered the studio to record his full-length bow *The New Folk Sound of Terry Callier*; upon completion of the session, however, Charters traveled to Mexico with the master tapes in tow, and the album went unreleased before finally appearing to little fanfare in 1968. Undaunted, Callier remained a fixture of the Windy City club scene, and in 1970 he and partner Larry Wade signed on with his boyhood friend Jerry Butler's Chicago Songwriters Workshop. There they composed material for local labels including Chess and Cadet, most notably authoring the Dells' 1972 smash "The Love We Had Stays on My Mind." The song's success again teamed Callier with Stepney, now a producer at Cadet, and yielded 1973's *Occasional Rain*, a beautiful fusion of folk and jazz textures which laid the groundwork for the sound further explored on the following year's *What Color Is Love?* Despite earning strong critical notices and building up a devoted fan base throughout much of urban America, Callier failed to break through commercially, and after 1975's *I Just Can't Help Myself* he was dropped by Cadet; in 1976, he also suffered another setback when Butler closed the Songwriters Workshop. Upon signing to Elektra's Jazz Fusion imprint at the behest of label head Don Mizell, Callier resurfaced in 1978 with the lushly orchestrated *Fire on Ice*; with the follow-up, 1979's *Turn You to Love*, he finally cracked the pop charts with the single "Sign of the Times," best known as the longtime theme for legendary WBLS-FM disc jockey Frankie Crocker. He even appeared at the Montreux Jazz Festival. However, when Mizell exited Elektra, Callier was quickly dropped from his contract; after a few more years of diligent touring, he largely disappeared from music around during the early '80s; a single parent, he instead accepted a job as a computer programmer, returning to college during the evenings to pursue a degree in sociology.

Despite essentially retiring from performing, Callier continued composing songs, and in 1991 he received a surprise telephone call from fan Eddie Piller, the head of the U.K. label Acid Jazz. Piller sought permission to re-release Callier's little-known, self-funded single from 1983, "I Don't Want to See Myself (Without You)"; seemingly overnight, the record became a massive success on the British club circuit, and the singer was soon flown to Britain for a pair of enormously well-received club dates. In the coming months, more gigs followed on both sides of the Atlantic, and in 1996, Callier even recorded a live LP, *TC in DC*. In 1997, he teamed with British singer Beth Orton, another of his most vocal supporters, to record a pair of tracks for her superb EP *Best Bit*; the following year, Callier also released his Verve Forecast debut *Timepeace*, his first major-label effort in close to two decades. *LifeTime* followed in 1999. *Alive*, which captured a show at London's Jazz Cafe in 2000, followed in summer 2001. *—Jason Ankeny*

The New Folk Sound of Terry Callier / 1965 / BGP ♦♦♦♦

The New Folk Sound of Terry Callier was not released until 1968, about three years after the project was originally completed; while the long delay almost certainly crippled the momentum of Callier's fledgling career, the impact on the music itself was at most minimal—while not the singer's best album, it's his most timeless and inviting, adhering closely to the folk stylings addressed by the title while largely ignoring the mystical jazz dimensions which texture his later material. Surprisingly, none of the album's eight songs are originals, relying instead on traditional tunes like "900 Miles" and "Cotton Eyed Joe"; while Callier's spiralling acoustic guitar lines and the use of two bassists (Terbour Attenborough and John Tweedle) reflect his admiration of John Coltrane, *New Folk Sound* is for the most part stark and simple, possessed of a subtle grace which spotlights his remarkably moving vocals to excellent effect—it's a debut which holds all the promise fulfilled by his classic recordings for Cadet. *—Jason Ankeny*

● **Occasional Rain** / 1972 / Cadet ♦♦♦♦♦

Recorded more than six years after *The New Folk Sound*, this was the first album to feature Terry Callier's unusual hybrid sound. The combination of a rich baritone voice and his unique blues/folk/jazz songwriting are met by just a touch of Andy Williams' zim, making *Occasional Rain* the best of his albums from the early '70s. Often prone to expansive, wandering melodies, Callier has written a tightness into most of the songs here that would generally be abandoned on the records to follow. Two of his most recognizable songs, "Ordinary Joe" and "Lean on Me," make their appearance and are joined by fragments of "Go 'Head On," which are interspersed throughout and provide a conceptual framework for the album as a whole. Highly accessible, this album conjures an intimate and relaxed mood, perfect for that lazy weekend morning. *—Joshua David Shanker*

What Color Is Love / Mar. 1973 / Cadet ♦♦♦♦♦

Like the artist himself, the music on this brilliant album defies all categories, embracing Callier's wide range of influences and experiences. Callier's musical kaleidoscope is filled with funk, rock, folk, jazz and even classical influences. "Dancing Girl" opens the album with Charles Stepney's majestic orchestration. This opus is the album's pinnacle, moving with soft intensity toward soul-stirring crescendos. Songs like "What Color Is Love" and "Ho-Tsine Mee (A Song of the Sun)," an elegant anti-war prayer of confusion, somehow avoid clichés or take them to another level. "You Goin' to Miss Your Candyman" was made popular by Urban Species when they sampled it on "Listen" in the early 1990s, and not surprisingly, it sounds better in its original form. No matter where you turn, Callier's passionate voice captures the sweeping drama of the human condition. A lost romantic amidst "concrete front yards," this album is a must-have for any music connoisseur. *—Ryan Randall Goble*

I Just Can't Help Myself / 1975 / MCA ♦♦♦♦♦

Terry Callier's third and final album for the Cadet label is the most soulful and supple of the bunch—Marvin Gaye's classic Motown LPs from the same early 1970s period serve as a good reference point, both in their richly-detailed arrangements as well as their thoughtful political and social messages. Despite its contemporary feel, however, much of the material on *I Just Can't Help Myself* dates back several years—both the powerful "Alley-Wind Song" and the John Coltrane tribute "Can't Catch the Trane" were initially recorded during the 1969 sessions which later comprised the *First Light* collection, while the graceful reading of Duke Ellington's "Satin Doll" was and would remain a long-standing highlight of Callier's live set. Under the circumstances, then, the cohesive beauty and power of *I Just Can't Help Myself* is all the more remarkable—possessed of a subtlety and shading absent from his other Cadet dates, the disc simmers with quiet intensity, its underlying confidence and serenity occasionally giving way to moments of soul-searching angst. Certainly Callier's later records have much to recommend them, but the conclusion of his Cadet stint was nevertheless the end of an era—he never reached quite the same peaks again. *—Jason Ankeny*

Fire on Ice / 1978 / Elektra ♦♦♦

Fire on Ice is easily the most confounding album of Terry Callier's career. While it's true that his Elektra recordings are not regarded as highly as the Cadet material, it may be time to critically re-evaluate them for their considerable worth and innovation. That said, it's hard to know whom to blame for making a mess of what was arguably a solid album. It's not the slick arrangements—done by longtime Callier cohort Richard Evans, nor is it the personnel, which includes tenor saxophonists Eddie Harris, Fred Jackson, guitarists Phil Upchurch and Larry Wade, and backing vocalist Minnie Ripperton. Callier's own songs are, for the most part, clean bedrock, deep Chicago soul slicked up for the onrushing disco age. The funky soul edge is fine on tunes like "Be a Believer," and "Holdin' on to Your Love." And the slippery, shimmering synth on the ballads like "Butterfly" works because Callier's slightly smoky sweet voice caresses his accompaniment. As strings waft in to the center of the mix, swelling up above the other instruments, you can hear where Evans and Don Mizell got carried away trying to carry Callier into Salsoul orchestra territory. Combine that with complete filler material like "Disco in the Sky" and the overwrought loungey smooth disco jazz of "I Been Doin' Alright, Part II (Everything's Gonna Be Alright)" and you see the schizophrenic influence of trying to accomplish too many things at once with Callier's awesome voice and tender lyrics. But given the fact that he wrote the lyrics to "Disco in the Sky" means he's not infallible. And who told Wade he could write a song on his own? "Love to Love" is just a staggeringly bad piece of disco garbage. Still, two of Callier's most moving tracks are here, the stunningly poetic "African Violet," with a melody as spare and haunting as anything Callier ever composed and a vocal workout that lasts over seven minutes it joins the list of his epics. The disc closes with the well-intentioned and phenomenally written "Martin St. Martin." Again, Evans' large horn and string sections with an artificial rhythm track mar what is a very powerful song—it's one Callier still does live with an acoustic guitar and it never ceases to blow audiences away. *Fire on Ice* is far from Callier's most compelling record, but, nonetheless, has its own quark strangeness and charm. *—Thom Jurek*

Turn You to Love / 1979 / Elektra ✦✦✦✦

This is easily Terry Callier's most underrated album. Chalk it up to the slick arrangement, jazzy charts, and funky rhythms in the heat of the disco era, but the year after Callier missed the boat with *Fire on Ice*, he was back with a slicker, shinier record. But, unlike its predecessor, it has no fat in the songwriting department. Leaving Richard Evans' production behind, Callier and Don Mizell enlisted Sonny Burke to produce, arrange, and conduct the large band. Callier handled a lot of the guitar work himself but he did have help from stalwart Larry Wade, his songwriting partner, and Tommy Tedesco. Also in the house was Motown's Randy Dunlap—courtesy of Smokey Robinson—and horn heroes Ernie Watts and Fred Wesley. The song selection here is impeccable, from the hard, growling gospel funk of "Sign of the Times" to the serpentine love song "Pyramids of Love" and a pair of awesome covers: Smokey's "Still Water (Love)" and Becker and Fagen's "Do It Again." On the former, Callier reaches deep into his mellifluous tenor bag for all the soul crooning gospel he can muster, to chilling effect. On the latter, the snaky, complex rhythms are accentuated and the horn section soars above the dense, heavily layered pumped uptempo mix. Callier gets to hang back and enunciate, slipping his down and dirty funky tip on the lyrics. But the greatest surprise on the album is Callier re-recording his classic, "Occasional Rain." With a shimmering, sparse string section accompanying his acoustic guitar, Callier sings half an octave lower than the original as ghostly bells slip through the center of the mix. Every two bars or so another instrument is added, but the gauzy texture of the mix holds throughout. The listener keeps holding her breath waiting for a string section crescendo—given how polished these proceedings are—to wash over her, but it never comes, thank God. The set ends with the weakest, but nonetheless very soulful track on the album, "A Mother's Love." It's sentimental, but, given how sincerely Callier delivers his lyrics, it comes off as sincere, not hackneyed. This is a gorgeous set that showcases an entirely different side of Callier than the legends note. He is every bit as fine an R&B singer as he is a folksy soul singer. The man's voice and his sincerity know no limits and this disc is a perfect testament to his genius. *—Thom Jurek*

TC in DC / Oct. 8, 1996 / Premonition ✦✦✦

This is an interesting live concert of folk music featuring guitarist-singer Terry Callier in a trio with bassist Eric Hochberg and percussionist-vocalist Penn McGee. Callier wrote all but one of the pieces and is the main star throughout although McGee's background vocals are also an asset. The music is heartfelt, well-performed, and has enough variety to hold one's interest. Although influenced a little by jazz, this falls more into the folk area and should interest fans of singer/songwriters and the folk music revival of the 1960s. *—Scott Yanow*

First Light: Chicago 1969–1971 / 1998 / Premonition ✦✦✦✦✦

Despite the lag between the 1965 recording of his debut album *The New Folk Sound of Terry Callier* and his 1972 sophomore effort *Occasional Rain*, Callier was far from inactive—in addition to regularly playing on the Chicago club circuit, he also cut a series of extraordinary demos which have finally surfaced almost three decades later as *First Light*. In the nine studio tracks which comprise the collection—a superb 1971 solo benefit date is also included—it's possible to hear the foundations of the aesthetic perfected on his classic Cadet recordings of the mid-'70s; on early renditions of songs like "Ordinary Joe" and "Alley Wind Song," all the pieces are already in place, as the haunted soulfulness of Callier's vocals blends perfectly with waves of acoustic folk guitar and subtle jazz textures. "Can't Catch the Trane," a tribute to his hero John Coltrane, barrels forward with appropriate locomotive force, spurred on by an incendiary tenor sax solo, while "Lean on Me" is beautifully delicate, a ballad of remarkable warmth and tenderness. Essential stuff. *—Jason Ankeny*

TimePeace / Jan. 27, 1998 / Verve ✦✦✦✦

Where has Terry Callier been all of our lives? Outside of the lucky few collectors fortunate enough to possess copies of his 1968 debut *The New Folk Sound of Terry Callier* and the series of brilliant records he cut for the Cadet label during the mid-'70s, the Chicago singer/songwriter has otherwise slipped through the cracks of contemporary music; his resurrection has been a long time in coming, and *TimePeace* is indeed well worth the wait. Long ago tagged with the label "folk-jazz," Callier's music eludes easy description; cosmic and spiritual, it also bears the influence of gospel and soul, yet synthesizes its disparate elements in unprecedented and breathtaking ways. Sparked by Callier's spiralling guitar leads, highlights like "Lazarus Man" and "Java Sparrow" seem to tap a higher consciousness, his yearning vocals channeling unfathomable power; the stark opener "Ride Suite Ride" matches the grace of Curtis Mayfield with the poignancy of Nick Drake, while "Coyote Moon" captures an ethereal yet pastoral beauty best likened to extraterrestrial country music. It's wonderful to have Callier back again—we need him now more than ever. *—Jason Ankeny*

● **Essential: The Very Best Of** / May 4, 1998 / Universal ✦✦✦✦✦

Terry Callier's trio of records for Cadet during the early '70s—*Occasional Rain*, *What Color Is Love*, and *I Just Can't Help Myself*—were among the most intriguing, refreshing, and neglected work of any R&B *or* folk artist during the '70s. In yet another case of the title not fitting the collection, *Essential: The Very Best Of* doesn't collect the best tracks from those records very well, but since over half of these tracks are previously unreleased songs from the period, it makes this of much more interest for fans than anyone else. Only four of the songs here are really Cadet must-haves ("Occasional Rain," "Ordinary Joe," "Dancing Girl," and "Just as Long as We're in Love"), leaving the rest as intriguing curiosities that anyone with a passing interest in Terry Callier should definitely hear. *—John Bush*

LifeTime / Sep. 6, 1999 / Talkin' Loud ✦✦✦

While it was perhaps inevitable that *LifeTime* would fail to recapture the cathartic intensity of Terry Callier's comeback effort *TimePeace*—a remarkably pure expression of a soul and spirit finally granted freedom after years trapped in limbo—it's nevertheless surprising how many comparatively few peaks the album actually does reach. Brian Bacchus' slick production, which often teeters precariously close to overkill on *TimePeace*, tumbles completely over the edge here—songs like "Holdin' On," "When the Music Is Gone," and "Fix the Blame" are rendered with so much gloss they seem trapped in amber, while the reggae-lite "Comin' up From Babylon" is as ill-conceived as the attempts at disco which marred Callier's records for Elektra two decades earlier. It's hardly shocking that *LifeTime's* most memorable moments are also its most unaffected ones, allowing Callier's remarkable voice and exquisite guitar the space to breathe—the supple, sensual opener "When My Lady Danced" is vintage folk-jazz, while "Sunset Boulevard" offers a potent reminder that no one sings this kind of protest soul with quite so much wisdom and compassion. Best of all is "Love Can Do," a shimmering duet with Beth Orton that is as rich and resonant as any of their past collaborations. *—Jason Ankeny*

Live at Mother Blues: 1964 / Feb. 15, 2000 / Premonition ✦✦✦✦

Recorded in front of a hometown Chicago crowd and predating the sessions for his debut studio LP *The New Folk Sound of Terry Callier* by about a year, *Live at Mother Blues: 1964* captures Callier's folk-jazz hybrid in its embryonic stages, documenting the genesis of his signature aesthetic in its most intimate and natural setting. Accompanied by a pair of bassists (John Tweedle and Terbour Attenborough) in imitation of John Coltrane, Callier subverts traditional material like "Drill Ye Tarriers," "The Gambler Song," and "Lizzy Mae," sticking close to the original melodies but expanding the songs in structure and scope by favoring extended instrumental passages and vocal improvisations; the opener, a cover of the Nat Adderley/Oscar Brown Jr. composition "Work Song," comes closest to capturing a true marriage of folk and jazz in its spare, slow-burning intensity. Even this early in his development, Callier is in full command of his skills—his soulful vocals simmer with gospel-like passion, and his guitar work is hypnotic and intricate, navigating the dual bass backdrops with serpentine dexterity. *—Jason Ankeny*

Alive / May 8, 2001 / Mr. Bongo ✦✦✦✦✦

Speak Your Peace / 2002 / Mr. Bongo ✦✦✦✦✦

When Terry Callier returned to the music scene as an active participant in 1998, after 20 years in self-imposed exile, he jumped headlong into the recording and touring process. His first two recordings, the fine *TimePeace* and the less-than-satisfying *LifeTime*, both had songs worthy of anything Callier ever wrote during the 1960s or 1970s. The live album, *Alive* on Mr. Bongo from 2001, is a testament to that. But finding a producer who could properly illustrate the vast subtleties in Callier's work, which effortlessly blurs the boundaries between jazz, pop, soul, and poetry, proved difficult in the studio. On *Speak Your Peace*, Callier has found the perfect working mates in Jean-Paul "Bluey" Maunick and Marc Mac (from 4Hero), two men who understand that his work is more about nuance than statement, sense impression than solid image, poetry than prose. Callier's glorious voice and wonderfully fluid acoustic guitar are front and center in the mixes of both men. Mac accents the skeletal angle of Callier's compositions, as on "Monuments of Mars." He underscores them with gentle rhythms, ambient sounds, well-placed strings, hand drums, and space, allowing the poetic, moral message of Callier's vision to come through unimpeded. Maunick's production techniques, as evidenced on all but three of the album's tracks, ranges; there are the shimmering drum loops on "Running Around," propped by scenic strings and a heavier bassline, that bring Callier's voice to a level above the instrumentation—and this is fine since he sings with such an authority that it doesn't have to be imposing, so there's no overkill. And then there's the single, "Brother to Brother," which Callier co-wrote with Paul Weller, who joins him in a duet. Everything on the track is spare, full of space and ambience, until the end, where the two voices entwine and a keyboard pulls the rhythm section toward the front. "Caravan of Love" could have been written by Curtis Mayfield and performed by MFSB with backing vocals by Hall & Oates. Yeah, it's that good. As for Callier's compositions, they're stronger than ever. Quoting his words in the context of a review is to belittle their achievement in that they are inextricably wedded to his musical frameworks. (Let's just say that if all pop music were as profound, we would all be activists working for peace and harmony.) The upshot is that this is easily the most seamlessly beautiful and wonderfully consistent recording he's made since his return. There are 14 tracks of ethereal, moving soul, groove, and poignancy that would (or at least should) make Bob Dylan and Smokey Robinson cry. *Speak Your Peace* rates with Callier's Cadet work in its vision, articulation, and execution. Indeed, on this recording one can hear, in the grain of his voice, a plea for wholeness that could only come from profound heartbreak. *—Thom Jurek*

Calloway

f. 1988, Cincinnati, OH

Group / Club/Dance, Urban

Formed by trumpeter Reginald and trombone player Vincent Calloway (both respected producers) after they left Midnight Star in the late '80s, Calloway's first single "I Wanna Be Rich" hit number two on the pop charts, a better showing than Midnight Star had made in a dozen years. The track was their major hit, followed only by "Sir Lancelot" and the title track from their 1990 debut album *All the Way*. Calloway returned two years later with *Let's Get Smooth*, but the album proved their last. The brothers continued working, with Teddy Pendergrass, Pieces of a Dream and Bootsy Collins, among others. *—John Bush*

All the Way / 1990 / Solar ✦✦✦

Let's Get Smooth / Feb. 10, 1992 / Solar ✦✦✦

● **Let's Get Smooth: The Best of Calloway** / Jun. 4, 2002 / Castle ✦✦✦

This 15-track retrospective gathers the highlights from Calloway's two early-'90s albums, *All the Way* and *Let's Get Smooth*. The collection ranges from new jack-meets-quiet storm ballads like "Let's Get Smooth"—which appears in both interlude form and in its original version—"Sugar Free," and "I Want You," to melodic, poppy songs such as "I Wanna Be Rich," to the harder-edged, relatively funky "Sir Lancelot," "Freaks Compete," and "Work Hard." Calloway proves that it's almost equally adept at each side of its sound, but a slight facelessness pervades most of the material. All of the tracks here sound good, which makes sense since the group is the brainchild of two producers, but it lacks that extra something that could make its music truly outstanding. The smooth, lush productions that the Calloway brothers come up with give a slight edge to their group's romantic side; even on its covers, Calloway sounds more in its element doing "La La La (Means I Love You)" than "Family Affair." Despite the somewhat generic quality of the material here, *Let's Get Smooth: The Best of Calloway* is a thoughtfully assembled collection that fans will appreciate, especially since the group's albums are out of print. *—Heather Phares*

Calypso King & the Soul Investigators

f. Helsinki, Finland

Group / Deep Funk Revival, Funk, Soul, Acid Jazz

When New York retro-funk label Desco shut its doors, co-founder Phillipe Lehman started up a new label, Soul Fire, which was dedicated to releasing only the sort of rough, raw, lower-fidelity funk Lehman preferred. Calypso King & the Soul Investigators were the first band to issue a full-length album on Soul Fire, and like many of the groups in Lehman's orbit, their origins were unlikely: a Meters/J.B.'s/MG's-styled instrumental funk band from Helsinki, Finland. All the members played in other bands; guitarist Pete Toikkanen was in a garage rock group called the Paisley, while organist Antti Maattanen, bassist Sami Kantelinen, and drummer Jukka Sarapaa all played in Mood (aka Maor Presto). Forming in 1998, the group issued a couple of 45s before hooking up with Lehman; after a debut single on Soul Fire in 2000, "Compin' and Smokin'," they recorded their debut full-length, *Soul Strike!* which was released in 2001. The Soul Investigators subsequently recorded for their own Timmion label with a newly added horn section, featuring trumpeter Eero Savela, trombonist Erno Haukkala, and saxophonist Lasse Tolvanen. *—Steve Huey*

● **Soul Strike!** / Mar. 27, 2001 / Soul Fire ✦✦✦✦✦

The first non-vinyl release from New York's mighty, vinyl-only Soul Fire label is actually the third issue from Calypso King & the Soul Investigators. The first was a scorching funk 45 that is not included here and has sold out its press run. While funk has as many schools and persuasions as rock or jazz, this music should be immediately recognizable to anyone whose groove taste runs to the Meters or early-'70s James Brown. All instrumental, the sound is fat, in mono, and greasier than beans and fatback. Driven by a Hammond B-3 and a riff-based lead guitar, both drummer and bassist hold down a smoking, overdriven groove for the front-line instruments to engage in basic, but nonetheless dazzling, chops pyrotechnics. Take "Ma-Gee" for instance: The B-3 is in maximum overload, guitars twin the bass line, and the drummer—there are no credits given—plays a second line rhythm crisscrossed with a 12-bar blues. As the organ goes into a meltdown solo away from the riff, the guitar picks it up, grinding, grinding, grinding it down, sharpening it to a fine slash through the rhythm section before taking a minimal solo, and then coming back full-force with the B-3. On "Some Funk," the groove is backbone-slipping in its dark recesses of excessive groovalicious ecstasy. This is the deep nasty, ready for fingerpoppin' mommas and daddies to slip into the middle of the mix and turn the dancefloor out. And it just keeps goin'! There isn't a weak second in 12 tracks! In sum, this may be the finest party record released in the past 20 years. If you're still having trouble deciding if this is for you, try taking Maceo Parker's rhythm section and marrying it to Jack McDuff's organ playing through the Meters' versions of Northern soul and funk jams. Soul Fire is a label worth checking out, with other full-lengths on the way and a 45 rpm series that's to die for. One warning though: Don't play this disc if you're trying to wind everybody down and send them home with a nice groove in their bonnets. This mutha will crank up the bash anew and send bodies flailing onto whatever serves as a dancefloor. *—Thom Jurek*

Cameo

f. 1974, New York, NY

Group / Quiet Storm, Urban, Funk

An outlandish, in-your-face stage presence, a strange sense of humor, and a hard-driving funk sound that criss-crossed a few musical boundaries earned Cameo countless comparisons to Parliament/Funkadelic in their early days. However, Cameo eventually wore off accusations of being derivative by transcending their influences and outlasting almost every single one of them. Throughout the '70s and '80s, the group remained up with the times and occasionally crept ahead of them, such that they became influences themselves upon younger generations of R&B and hip-hop acts. By the time the group's popularity started to fizzle in the late '80s, a series of R&B chart hits—ranging from greasy funk workouts to synthesized funk swingers to dripping ballads—was left in their wake. Further separating Cameo from their forebears, they didn't have a diaper-clad guitarist. Instead, they had a codpiece-wearing lead vocalist.

That vocalist was Larry Blackmon. In 1974, the ex-Juilliard student and New York City club-goer instigated a funk band with a membership of 13 called the New York City Players. Blackmon, Tomi Jenkins, and Nathan Leftenant formed the group's nucleus. The Casablanca label signed the group to their Chocolate City offshoot, and shortly after that, the group changed its name to Cameo. Their excellent debut album, 1977's *Cardiac Arrest*, was highlighted by four singles. Three of those hit the *Billboard* R&B chart: "Rigor Mortis" (number 33), "Funk Funk" (number 20), and "Post Mortem" (number 70). Although the group was clearly inspired by elder funk groups like Parliament, Funkadelic, and the Ohio Players, *Cardiac Arrest* made Cameo's case for belonging in the same division an open-and-shut one.

In an attempt to keep the ball rolling, 1978 saw the release of Cameo's second and third albums. Neither *We All Know Who We Are* nor *Ugly Ego* were as solid as the debut, but the group's singular characteristics were becoming increasingly evident. The winding, horn-punctuated "It's Serious" (from *We All Know Who We Are*) narrowly missed the Top 20 of the R&B chart, while "Insane" (from *Ugly Ego*) dipped just inside it, peaking at number 17. The best halves of these two albums would've made a fine sophomore LP.

Released in 1979 and featuring a disco-fied re-visiting of *Cardiac Arrest*'s "Find My Way" and the magnificently funky and slightly loony number three chart hit "I Just Want to Be," *Secret Omen* was stacked with fine album cuts and brought Cameo back as a group that excelled in the LP format. "Sparkle" was one of their best ballads, a sinewy number that hit the Top Ten. Five albums released between 1980 and 1983 (*Cameosis, Feel Me, Knights of the Sound Table, Alligator Woman, Style*) brought about a slight dip in quality on the album front. Despite an abundance of filler on each record, none of those albums were strict disappointments, delivering hot Top 20 R&B singles like "Shake Your Pants," "We're Goin' Out Tonight," "Keep It Hot," "Freaky Dancin'," "Just Be Yourself," "Flirt," and "Style."

One of the most significant ripples in Cameo's time line came during that period, in 1982, when they packed up and set up shop in Atlanta. Pared down to a quintet and located in a less hectic city, the group became bigger fish in a smaller pond. Blackmon even started his own label, Atlanta Artist. The label's first LP, *Style*, also marked a significant shift in sound, with synthesizers taking on a pronounced role. Paydirt was struck with 1984's *She's Strange*; the title cut, a late-night slithery smolder, topped the R&B chart and eclipsed the Top 50 of the pop chart, kicking off a remarkable three-album run that made Cameo one of the most popular groups of the '80s. *Single Life* and *Word Up!*, released respectively in 1985 and 1986, continued the hot streak. The singles from those two albums—"Attack Me With Your Love," "Single Life," "Word Up," "Candy," and "Back and Forth"—held down the Top Five plateau of the R&B chart. "Word Up" even went to number six on the pop chart, giving them their biggest bite of the mainstream. The song was everywhere.

What goes up must come down, and that's exactly what happened to Cameo. Despite the fact that two more singles—"Skin I'm In" and "I Want It Now"—scaled up to number five on the R&B chart, neither *Machismo* nor *Real Men Wear Black* performed well as albums. After 1991's *Emotional Violence*, the group's profile was lowered significantly, but they did tour sporadically to the delight of hardcore fans as well as plenty of misguided people who thought Cameo was all about "Word Up" and nothing more. Notably, Blackmon spent a few years of the '90s at Warner Bros., as the vice president of A&R. Cameo's presence continued to be felt throughout the early 2000s, not only through extensive sample use and less tangible influences upon younger artists and producers. Several retrospectives have kept the group's music alive: Mercury's 1993 compilation *The Best of Cameo* is an excellent point of entry. Mercury's *12" Collection & More*, released in 1999, covers the group's best dancefloor moments. 2002's spectacular *Anthology*, a double-disc set also released by Mercury, covers a lot of ground and does the group justice as a total package. *—Andy Kellman*

Cardiac Arrest / 1977 / Mercury ✦✦✦✦✦

In 1977, one of funk's most promising debuts came from Cameo, whose first album, *Cardiac Arrest*, made it crystal clear that Larry Blackmon's outfit was a force to be reckoned with. If you were into hard, tough funk in 1977, it was impossible not to be excited by Cameo's debut. This excellent LP contains a romantic soul ballad ("Stay By My Side") as well as the original version of "Find My Way," which is the sort of smooth yet funky disco-soul that groups like the Trammps and Double Exposure were known for in the late '70s. But for the most part, this is an album of aggressive, unapologetically gritty funk. On classics like "Rigor Mortis," "Funk, Funk," and "Post Mortem," one can pinpoint Cameo's influences—namely, Parliament/Funkadelic, the Ohio Players, and the Bar-Kays. But at the same time, these gems demonstrate that even in 1977, Cameo had a recognizable sound of its own. And ultimately, Cameo would become quite influential itself. For funk lovers, *Cardiac Arrest* is essential listening. Period. *—Alex Henderson*

We All Know Who We Are / 1977 / Mercury ✦✦✦

Cameo's second album, *We All Know Who We Are*, is uneven, but it has its moments, both in the quiet storm field ("Why Have I Lost You") and the disco-funk category ("It's Serious"). Much of the record sounds like filler, but the best moments illustrate that Cameo is beginning to grow and refine their own sound. *—Stephen Thomas Erlewine*

Ugly Ego / 1978 / Casablanca ♦♦♦
Another great funk treatise, with the first-rate, uptempo tune "Insane" and a decent romantic song, "Give Love a Chance." They were slowly moving toward a new sound, although the influence of classic horn-driven funk bands like the Ohio Players and the Bar-Kays is still prominent. *—Ron Wynn*

Secret Omen / 1979 / Rebound ♦♦♦♦♦
Cameo never recorded a bad album, but it did record some uneven ones. One such LP was 1978's *Ugly Ego*, which was generally decent but fell short of the excellence of Cameo's superb debut album, *Cardiac Arrest*. But if *Ugly Ego* led some people to believe that Cameo might be slipping, the band's fourth album, *Secret Omen*, put that idea to rest. Released in 1979, *Secret Omen* is among Cameo's most essential releases. Everything on this album is a winner; anyone who appreciates sweaty, gutsy, horn-powered funk would have a hard time not loving "I Just Want to Be" (a major hit) and equally gritty gems like "New York," "Macho," and "The Rock." Meanwhile, a remake of "Find My Way" (previously heard on 1977's *Cardiac Arrest*) is even more disco-minded than the original version. Disco was never Cameo's specialty, but because disco was so huge in 1979, it made sense to revisit "Find My Way." And although "Find My Way" is atypical of Cameo on the whole, it's still a great song. Equally impressive is the hit soul ballad "Sparkle"; even though Larry Blackmon and friends are best known for uptempo songs, they recorded their share of memorable ballads in the 1970s and 1980s. *Secret Omen* is recommended to anyone with even a casual interest in late-'70s funk. *—Alex Henderson*

Cameosis / Apr. 1980 / Mercury ♦♦♦♦
The big single on *Cameosis*, the stimulating "Shake Your Pants," provokes body moves from the animated group vocals to the rump-shakin' groove. The vivacious number "We're Going out Tonight" is a man's salute to his lady. Larry Blackmon and Tomi Jenkins sing in unison throughout the body of the song, with first tenor Wayne Cooper soaring in the vamp. The group puts a different twist on a remake of their own "Why Have I Lost You." Tomi Jenkins imparts a compassionate rap in the intro before crooning his way through the imaginative lyric, where Wayne Cooper reaches one climax after another. Like the original version, it, too, never graced the charts but found a home on radio. The sleeper on this album is "I Care for You." Anthony Lockett took the vocal lead on this tear-jerking ballad, in which a man tolerates his woman's questionable behavior. From Lockett's execution to the song's overall arrangement, this is a must-listen. *—Craig Lytle*

Feel Me / Oct. 1980 / Casablanca ♦♦♦
Cameo has been known for so many funk grooves—like this album's featured single, "Keep It Hot"—that their plush ballads are seldom recognized. The title track, "Feel Me," was one of those classic gems. Guitarist Anthony Lockett assumes lead vocal duties on this charming number. As Lockett patiently and gently caresses the lyric, his wholesome, amplifying tenor exudes a plea for that elusive intimacy. (Anthony Lockett would soon exit the group for gospel music.) "Better Days," also a ballad, has less musical attire; it's trimmed with primarily a rhythm section and Cameo's trademark horn arrangement and cooing background vocals. Preceded by an improvising piano solo, "Is This the Way" finds its stride with a rapid, percussive groove and a socially conscious message. *—Craig Lytle*

Knights of the Sound Table / 1981 / Casablanca ♦♦♦
As Cameo continued to hone their sound, they found themselves in the position not only of having to bridge a musical gap, but also needing to follow up a smash album. Following on the heels of 1980's massive *Cameosis*, which created a signature vibe and set the band up for truly massive early success, it's surprising that *Knights of the Sound Table* would lose strength. But it did. The band was exhausted, only coming off the road long enough to record the album before heading straight back out again. *Knights of the Sound Table* plays through like a transitional album—and it falters at times because of it. Even though the band remained bound to their funk roots, they were tweaking them within a very different framework—a 1980s pre-wave wave. The set is divided into two very distinct camps, then, booty shaking funk and saccharine ballads. When it's good, it's tremendous. "Knights by Night" is strong and very typically Cameo, while "Don't Be So Cool" leans more into an '80s frame of mind. The marvelous "Freaky Dancin'" pulled out ahead of the pack and was rewarded with a number three spot on the R&B charts for its efforts, while two other tracks, the funky "I Like It" and "Feel Me," would also chart. Where the band weakened was across their ballads. "I'll Always Stay" and "I Never Knew" feel more like filler than anything else, while "The Sound Table" is a poke at disco—too long after the genre left the dancefloor. Despite such serious wobbles, though, the set is cohesive enough to forgive its failings, the sound of a band keeping their past alive while stretching their wings toward the future. *—Amy Hanson*

Alligator Woman / 1982 / Casablanca ♦♦♦
Dropping the Parliament-esque, *Mothership*-era theatrics, and the multitude of band-members that comprised 1981's *Knights of the Sound Table* tour, Cameo's Larry Blackmon scaled the band back to a less financially prohibitive number and returned to the studio to record what would be the band's last effort for longtime label Chocolate City. The mighty *Alligator Woman*, released in spring 1982, marked the quintet's final foray into the annals of the deep funk that had signposted much of their material so far. A continuation, but extension of the otherworldly synthesis which blended old-school sounds with new technology, the LP emerged a peerless hybrid, giving Cameo another Top Ten hit for their collection. Both "Be Yourself" and "Soul Army" are deep slabs of funk, heavily steeped in the band's own past, with the former driven by harmonized vocals and groovy guitar, and the latter dominated by Blackmon's distinctive vocals. Elsewhere, the lively "Flirt," a Top Ten hit, is a sassy exercise in tricky pop, while the title track proves a heady mix of all of the above. Included, too, are the less interesting ballads "Secrets of Time" and "For You" but, despite such occasional stumbles, *Alligator Woman* was a remarkably cohesive and energetic outing for the new-look band. It also proved a perfect bridge for the gap between the antics of *Knights* and Cameo's forthcoming exploits, later in the decade. *—Amy Hanson*

Style / 1983 / Atlanta Artists ♦♦♦

She's Strange / 1984 / Casablanca ♦♦♦♦
By 1984, African-American popular music had become extremely high-tech. The horn-powered funk bands that were huge in the 1970s were out of style, and young audiences were demanding hip-hop, electro-funk, and urban contemporary—not horn bands that sounded like the Ohio Players or Tower of Power circa 1975. Horn bands were still in vogue only in the home of the go-go explosion: Washington, DC. But these changes in the marketplace didn't hurt Cameo; both commercially and creatively, 1984's *She's Strange* was a winner. Thankfully, Cameo leader Larry Blackmon isn't afraid to try different things on this excellent album. The mysterious title song (a major hit) and the socio-political "Talking Out the Side of Your Neck" find Cameo responding to hip-hop's popularity by including a lot of rapping, while "Lé Ve Toi!" is very rock-minded—it's still funk, but funk laced with lots of rock. "Tribute to Bob Marley" is a reggae gem that salutes the Jamaican legend, and "Hangin' Downtown" is a smooth, jazzy number with a definite quiet storm appeal. When *She's Strange* soared up *Billboard*'s R&B albums chart, one had to admire Cameo's durability. Other bands that had emerged in the 1970s were hurting, but with *She's Strange*, Cameo had no problem maintaining both its freshness and its popularity. *—Alex Henderson*

Single Life / 1985 / Casablanca ♦♦♦♦
In the late '70s and very early '80s, Cameo was the epitome of a horn-driven funk band. Like Parliament/Funkadelic (a major influence), the Ohio Players, Earth, Wind & Fire, the Commodores, Tower of Power, and so many other bands that defined funk in the '70s, Cameo was famous for its horn section. But when horn bands went out of style and urban contemporary audiences started craving synth-funk and electro-funk, Cameo leader Larry Blackmon was determined to change with the times and remain on the charts. Thus, the Cameo of 1985's *Single Life* is a lot more high-tech than the Cameo of 1978's *We All Know Who We Are* or 1980's *Cameosis*. Blackmon felt that the market called for a downsized Cameo, which is why the Cameo he leads on this LP is a trio consisting of Tomi Jenkins, Nathan Leftenant, and himself. *Single Life* isn't devoid of horns, but the horn players are strictly guests—not actual Cameo members—and the group's sound is built around synthesizers and electric bass. Some funk fans missed the old horn-powered Cameo, but *Single Life* had no problem appealing to urban contemporary audiences. Although not quite as essential as 1986's *Word Up!*, this album is generally excellent. The infectious title song was a major hit, and Cameo is equally impressive on other synth-funk offerings like "I've Got Your Image" and "Attack Me With Your Love." Much to Blackmon's credit, the album is fairly diverse and unpredictable. "A Good-Bye" is more of a rock ballad than an R&B ballad, while "Little Boys, Dangerous Toys" is a political reggae gem inspired by the Cold War and the nuclear arms race. And one of the album's best songs is "Urban Warrior," a fun yet idealistic rap tune about a hip-hopper who travels the world partying and promoting world peace. *Single Life* was a welcome addition to Cameo's catalog. *—Alex Henderson*

Word Up! / 1986 / Mercury ♦♦♦♦♦
Many of the funk bands that were big in the 1970s had a hard time surviving in the 1980s, especially if they were horn bands. Having a killer horn section was something that a lot of 1970s funk outfits prided themselves on, and it was no fun when, in the 1980s, they were told that their horns sound dated and that urban contemporary audiences only wanted to hear synthesizers, sequencers, and drum machines. But Cameo, unlike many funk bands that emerged in the late '70s, really thrived in the 1980s. Lead singer/producer Larry Blackmon insisted on changing with the times, and he did so by making Cameo more high-tech and seeing to it that albums like 1985's *Single Life* and 1986's *Word Up!* were relevant to the urban contemporary and hip-hop scenes. Nonetheless, Cameo still sounded like Cameo; *Word Up!*, in fact, is one of its best albums. The wildly infectious title song was a major hit, and Cameo is equally captivating on other funk treasures that include "Fast, Fierce and Funny," "Back and Forth," and "Candy." To the young urban contemporary and hip-hop fans who bought *Word Up!* in 1986, Cameo's funk was fresh and cutting edge; and at the same time, slightly older fans that Cameo had won over in the late '70s were still buying its records. Both commercially and creatively, *Word Up!* was a major triumph for Cameo. *—Alex Henderson*

Machismo / 1988 / Atlanta Artists ♦♦♦
In the late '80s, most of the great funksters who had emerged in the 1970s knew that their best days were behind them. Sure, many of them were receiving royalty checks when young hip-hoppers sampled their classic recordings (assuming that they had kept their publishing rights), but they were no longer seeing their names at the top of the charts. But Cameo was another story. Unlike other horn bands that were formed in the 1970s, Cameo had no problem reinventing itself as a high-tech, downsized, hip-hop-influenced synth-funk/urban contemporary trio. 1986's *Word Up!*, in fact, is one of Cameo's finest and most essential albums. *Word Up!* was an incredibly tough act to follow, and the album that followed it, 1988's *Machismo*, isn't as strong or as consistent. *Machismo* isn't a bad album; a few of the tunes are excellent, including "Skin I'm In" (a poignant commentary on racism), the rock-influenced "Promiscuous," and the jazz-minded "In the Night" (which features the late jazz trumpet innovator Miles Davis). But *Machismo* isn't as successful when Cameo tries to recycle *Word Up!*; there can only be one *Word Up!*, and when Larry Blackmon and his colleagues try to recycle it, they end up sounding formulaic. But while *Machismo* isn't among Cameo's essential releases, it has more plusses than minuses and fared well among its hardcore fans. *—Alex Henderson*

Emotional Violence / Aug. 1991 / Reprise ♦♦♦

• **The Best of Cameo** / May 18, 1993 / Mercury ✦✦✦✦✦
Larry Blackmon and his Cameo mates ruled funk's domain for over a decade. Cameo evolved from its origins as a horn-based and dominated ensemble into a synthesizer-oriented group that still featured sturdy basslines and exuberant vocals, but was in tune with urban and black America's new sensibility. These 14 selections range from the formative cuts "Rigor Mortis," "Shake Your Pants," and "It's Over" to the definitive "Word Up," "Candy," and "Back and Forth." Blackmon's alternately sneering, defiant, and aggressive vocals were the constant from Cameo's beginnings in the 1970s to their emergence as funk's reigning champions in the 1980s. *—Ron Wynn*

The Best of Cameo, Vol. 2 / May 21, 1996 / Mercury ✦✦✦✦✦
Here are fifteen songs and 78 minutes for those who want a little more than what's on sale on *The Best of Cameo.* It spans their whole career, and includes R&B hits like "Freaky Dancin'," "Keep It Hot," "Be Yourself," "Insane," "We're Going Out Tonight," "Feel Me," and "Alligator Woman" (the definite highlight, even if it wasn't one of their highest charters). Nona Hendryx guests on "Don't Be So Cool," and Miles Davis does the same for "In the Night." *—Richie Unterberger*

Anthology / Jun. 18, 2002 / Mercury ✦✦✦✦
Mercury's Cameo *Anthology* supersedes the two single-disc *Best of Cameo* volumes issued in the mid-'90s with a lengthy two-CD set that comprehensively chronicles the group's tenure on the Chocolate City and Atlanta Artists labels in the 1970s and '80s and just into the '90s. More casual fans may want to stick with the discount-priced *20th Century Masters—The Millennium Collection: The Best of Cameo* best-of, since this is a band best remembered for one particularly successful phase of a long career, the mid-'80s, when their new wave-influenced funk style led to the chart-topping R&B and Top Ten pop hit "Word Up." On *Anthology,* you don't get to that point in Cameo's story until 12 tracks into the second disc. What you do get is 23 of their 26 Top 40 R&B hits, beginning with 1977's "Rigor Mortis" and ending with 1990's "I Want It Now." (Inexplicably, one of the omissions is the 1988 Top Five R&B hit "You Make Me Work.") Along the way, Cameo can be heard to evolve from a Parliament/Funkadelic-style freeform funk band into a more disciplined unit that often sounds very similar to Earth, Wind & Fire, notably on the tracks "We're Goin' out Tonight" (1980) and "Feel Me" (1981). With "Freaky Dancin'," which appropriately opens the second disc, however, bandleader Larry Blackmon is starting to bring in his own interpretation of rock's new wave in the form of more aggressive playing while maintaining the funk feel, and by 1984's "She's Strange" he had found a sound for his band that would push them to a new level of popularity. That success would prove relatively short-lived, but by the time Cameo faded from the top of the charts in the early '90s they had built up quite a library of dance-oriented R&B, and most of the best of it is here. *—William Ruhlmann*

G.C. Cameron

b. Franklin Country, MS
Vocals / Motown, Soul
Soul singer G.C. Cameron is a veteran of more than 30 years in the music business and also is famous for his high-energy lead on the Spinners' "It's a Shame." He was born in a small township in Franklin County, MS, but his family moved to Detroit in 1955 when he was young. After a Marine stint, which included servitude in Vietnam, Cameron was chosen by the Spinners to replace Chico Edwards, adding a new lead voice to the group. With Cameron in the fold, Motown's producers found the Spinners more interesting and heavyweights like Stevie Wonder started writing and producing for them.

Motown released "It's a Shame" on June 6, 1970, and watched it scale the charts to number-14 pop and become the Spinners' biggest hit to date. But the group was fed up with Motown's treatment. It was apparent Motown wasn't ever going to take them seriously and they made plans to leave. Cameron, however, had become romantically involved with Gwen Gordy (Berry Gordy's sister) and stayed with Motown. But Cameron wasn't concerned; Motown was going to make him a star, or so he thought. The company placed him on its Mowest label for a series of singles that went nowhere.

Uneasiness reared: The Spinners with Philippe Wynne were making an unprecedented run with Top Ten hits and good-selling albums, yet Cameron couldn't make the charts. He was switched to the Motown label for his other recordings, including "No Matter Where" (1973) and "Let Me Down Easy" (1973), neither of which sold well. His first solo LP, *Love Songs & Other Tragedies* (1974), followed; a second LP, the self-titled *G.C. Cameron* (1976), was preceded by "If You're Ever Gonna Love Me" (1975). The next single, "It's So Hard to Say Goodbye to Yesterday," (1975) was perfect, but for Boyz II Men, not Cameron. "Dream Lady" (1976) and "You're What's Missing in My Life" (1977), which was also the title of his third album, issued in 1977 and which followed the same dismal road as previous efforts. Motown issued *Rich Love, Poor Love* by G.C. & Syreeta in 1977 and put out one single from the album, "Let's Make a Deal." Two years later, Syreeta scored with Billy Preston on "With You I'm Born Again."

Cameron left the company after the pair with Syreeta failed and his romance with Gwen Gordy soured. When "I've Got My Second Wind," a duet with Tata Vega off her *Givin' All My Love* album (1981), came out, Cameron was long gone. The talented, multi-voice singer (every producer who worked with him found a different sound) recorded off and on for a bunch of little labels from 1977 on; his most significant recording was *Give Me Your Love* (1983) for Malaco Records in Jackson, MS (sort of a homecoming for Cameron). *—Andrew Hamilton*

Love Songs & Other Tragedies / 1974 / Motown ✦✦✦

G.C. Cameron / 1976 / Motown ✦✦✦

• **You're What's Missing in My Life** / 1977 / Motown ✦✦✦✦✦
Produced by Brian Holland, this was Cameron's best work, with lush orchestration on the title track and "This Will Make You Dance." *—Rick A. Bueche*

Give Me Your Love / 1983 / Malaco ✦✦✦
Former Spinners lead singer and Motown solo artist G.C. Cameron returned to his Mississippi roots in the early '80s, relocating to the state and signing with the Jackson based company Malaco. This album was unfortunately too Southern, and too rural in its production and sensibility to get any shot on urban contemporary radio stations. It did get some regional attention, and also showed that Cameron's soulful sound hadn't lost its edge. *—Ron Wynn*

The Very Best of the Motorcity Recordings / Sep. 17, 1996 / Hot Productions ✦✦✦✦
G.C. Cameron's career never got on track. After a scintillating start with the Spinners ("It's a Shame"), he neglected to follow them to Atlantic Records. A vocal chameleon, he's at his best impersonating others; just take five records by Cameron by five producers and you'll think you were listening to five different singers. When Smokey Robinson produced him ("Don't Wanna Play Pajama Games"), everyone thought it was Robinson singing and someone had typed the wrong name on the label. On "We'll Have It Made" (produced by Stevie Wonder), he mimics Dennis Edwards. *The Very Best of the Motorcity Recordings* is a compilation of 16 latter-day recordings from Cameron, half of the tracks co-written by the singer himself with producer Ian Levine. "Right of Way" is a midtempo love song propelled by his strong tenor, while "Come Back to Me" is a yearning ballad and "Good Times Up Ahead" rocks with a solid Northern groove. But "Straight in the Eye" has a hokey, klutzy beat. His falsetto glows on the Temptations' "Just My Imagination" and "Too Busy Thinking About My Baby" showcases his rough tenor, and he sounds better than the Spinners on "I'll Be Around." A remake of "It's a Shame" highlights his vocal dexterity. He mimics Marvin Gaye on "You're All I Need to Get By," a duet with Martha Reeves. This isn't the best of Cameron by any means—the tracks lack Motown's punch but Cameron's vocal gymnastics keep you listening. *—Andrew Hamilton*

Tevin Campbell

b. 1978, Texas
Vocals / New Jack Swing, Urban
There's some dispute over who actually discovered Texas child sensation Tevin Campbell. Some accounts credit flutist Bobbi Humphrey, while much of the publicity material credits Quincy Jones. It's assured that Campbell first came to the notice of music fans just after his 11th birthday in late 1989 when he appeared on Jones' LP *Back on the Block* and was featured on "Tomorrow (A Better You, Better Me)," which hit number one on the R&B charts in June 1990. With his high, flexible tenor, Campbell recalled an earlier Jones protégé, Michael Jackson. Later that year, he appeared in Prince's *Graffiti Bridge* film singing "Round and Round," which Prince wrote for him and which became a gold single. Next, in the summer of 1991, he appeared on the soundtrack to *Boyz in the Hood* singing "Just Ask Me To," a Top Ten R&B hit. All of this set the stage for his debut album, 1991's *T.E.V.I.N.,* which went platinum and spawned two R&B chart-toppers, "Tell Me What You Want Me to Do" and "Alone with You," as well as the R&B Top Five hit "Goodbye." *I'm Ready,* released two years later, did even better, going double platinum and featuring three R&B chart hits—the number one "Can We Talk," "I'm Ready," which went Top Five, and "Always in My Heart," which reached the Top Ten. But 1996's *Back to the World* was a sales disappointment, and 1999's *Tevin Campbell* did even worse. A compilation package was issued in early 2001. *—Ron Wynn & William Ruhlmann*

• **T.E.V.I.N.** / Nov. 19, 1991 / Qwest/Warner Bros. ✦✦✦✦✦
If *T.E.V.I.N.* had been recorded by an adult instead of a teenager, the album would still be impressive, but the fact that Tevin Campbell was only fourteen years old when this was made makes it all the more amazing. Campbell's voice is remarkably expressive, able to handle both ballads and uptempo dance tracks without losing confidence. When he has the right material—like the hit single, Prince's "Round and Round"—the results are flawless; if the material is weak, he's merely enjoyable. *—Stephen Thomas Erlewine*

I'm Ready / Oct. 26, 1993 / Qwest/Warner Bros. ✦✦✦✦
Tevin Campbell emerged as a true soul singer with *I'm Ready,* his second album. The Texas native had the good fortune of working with some of the best producers and writers in the business to construct an excellent work. The first single, "Can We Talk," was written and produced by Babyface and his longtime partner, Daryl Simmons. Behind a percussive rhythm track and a sensuous melody, Campbell patiently steps into the lyric, but soon bows to an urgent cry. The infectious chorus has a timeless ring and there's no secret as to why it held the number one spot on the R&B charts for three consecutive weeks. "I'm Ready," the title track, isn't as explosive as its predecessor, though both songs have a resemblance. The two singles to follow were "Always in My Heart" and "Don't Say Goodbye Girl." The former romances the heart with its comforting melody and supplicating lyric, while the latter is a midtempo number with a romantic lyric insulated with a pop texture. Prince, whose credit is listed as Paisley Park, also gives the project a funky edge with the unreleased numbers "Uncle Sam" and the grooving ballad "Shhh." There is much to savor on this album. *—Craig Lytle*

Back to the World / Jun. 25, 1996 / Qwest/Warner Bros. ✦✦✦✦
Back to the World is where Tevin Campbell returns as a man, ready to prove that he is no longer the child prodigy of yesteryear. For the most part, he succeeds in establishing himself as a vocalist of prodigious talents and significant worth. Of course, it was clear even in his earliest recordings that he was something special—a vocalist that could sing with a sweet, easy grace but remain soulful and not cloying in the slightest. No matter how Campbell tries to phase out that sweetness on *Back to the World*—after all, one of the first steps of maturity is to shed your childhood affectations—he retains that appealing quality, which makes the album all the more endearing. That's not to say that the uptempo cuts don't work. On the contrary—they are state-of-the-art pieces, thanks to the talents of producers like Puffy Combs, whose "I Need You" is a highlight. But the key to the record's success is how Campbell grows and matures without sacrificing his gift for pure sweet contemporary soul. *Back to the World* is proof positive that the teen idol is now a man. *—Leo Stanley*

Tevin Campbell / Feb. 23, 1999 / Qwest/Warner Bros. ✦✦✦
Dig the slow jams: This young R&B singer kicks out some easy beats and infectious hooks with the help from the likes of Wyclef Jean, Quincy Jones and Stevie J. Check out hip

tracks like "Never Again" and "For Your Love." Granted, some of the material doesn't rise above the standard vocal grandstanding, but there are signs of great things to come. *—Tim Sheridan*

The Best of Tevin Campbell / Jan. 30, 2001 / Qwest/Warner Bros. ♦♦♦
When a record company has a successful artist who has scored enough hits to justify a compilation of them, it waits until the artist is between regular album releases and positions the compilation in a prime buying season such as the fall. Then it tries to persuade the artist to contribute a new track or two so that a single can be released and even long-time fans can be given an incentive to buy the collection. On the other hand, when a record company has an artist whose career as a hitmaker appears to be over, it compiles a hits album and tosses it into the marketplace in a barren season, such as the dead of winter, preparatory to deleting the artist's regular albums from the catalog. Unfortunately, the second situation, not the first, is the case with the youthful R&B singer Tevin Campbell. But note that *The Best of Tevin Campbell* does not even do its subject justice. There's a reason why it isn't called *Greatest Hits*, and that's the omission of some of Campbell's most popular recordings. Though his first hit, "Tomorrow (A Better You, Better Me)" from the Quincy Jones album *Back on the Block*, was released on Qwest, it's not here, and neither is "Just Ask Me To" (from the *Boyz in the Hood* soundtrack), another Qwest release. Strangest of all, "Alone With You," one of Campbell's biggest hits, is also missing. Instead, there are five album-only tracks from the singer's first three albums. As a result, *The Best of Tevin Campbell* is inadequate as a collection of his most successful recordings, which, in the overall context of the release, is adding insult to injury. *—William Ruhlmann*

Cannibal & the Headhunters

f. Los Angeles, CA
Group / Latin Rock, Brown-Eyed Soul, Frat Rock, Garage Rock, Rock & Roll
Cannibal & the Headhunters were one-hit wonders, but what a hit to have, if you're only going to have one: "Land of 1000 Dances." The group was also one of the first Mexican-American rock bands to have a national hit record, courtesy of that same tune. Founded by Frankie Garcia—who reportedly earned his nickname "Cannibal" as a boy when he bit an opponent during a fight—with Robert Jaramillo and Joe Jaramillo of East L.A. in the mid-'60s, the group grew out of a number of earlier bands, including the Rhythm Playboys and the Romanos. The Headhunters' version of "Land of 1000 Dances," written by Chris Kenner and Fats Domino, was issued on the Rampart label in early 1965 and peaked at number 30 on the charts, which got the group booked supporting the Beatles, among many other bands. Wilson Pickett later had the biggest hit version of the same song, reaching number ten, but dozens, perhaps hundreds, of versions were issued. The group's next single didn't do much, but the *Land of 1000 Dances* album did chart in mid-1965. The group later moved to Columbia's Date Records imprint (home of the Zombies' "Time of the Season"), and at the end of the 1960s they signed with Capitol Records, but found no more success. After a decade of doing oldies shows, Garcia and his then-current group of Headhunters called it quits in 1978, although he has since led other versions of the group in shows on the oldies circuit. *—Bruce Eder*

● **Golden Classics** / Nov. 5, 1996 / Collectables ♦♦♦♦♦
A really solid dance album, and a great '60s party album, sparked by a lot more than just "Land of 1000 Dances." Among the 16 tracks here (which includes a version of "La Bamba" and covers of "My Girl," "Shotgun," and "The Boy From New York City"), there's not a bad number to be found. The sound quality is excellent, and the notes are pretty thorough as well, and since it's unlikely that even Bear Family would do a box set on the group, this is probably as good as it's going to get. *—Bruce Eder*

Ace Cannon

b. May 5, 1934, Grenada, MS
Session Musician, Saxophone, Instrumental / Memphis Soul, Nashville Sound/Countrypolitan, Country-Pop, R&B, Soul
One of Nashville's premier session men from the late '50s through the early '70s, alto saxophonist Ace Cannon began playing at the age of ten and signed with Sun Records during the early days of rock & roll. He performed with Billy Lee Riley and Brad Suggs but then in 1959 joined the original Bill Black Combo, recording for the Hi label. He stayed with the band until 1961, when he made his solo chart debut with the instrumental "Tuff," which made it to the country Top 20. This in turn was followed by a Top 40 hit, "Blues (Stay Away From Me)," and a minor hit for the Santos label, "Sugar Blues." He had two more hits in the mid-'60s with "Cotton Fields" and "Searchin'," both recorded for Hi. A decade later, he became the subject of the 1974 documentary film, *Ace's High*. After moving to Nashville in the mid-'70s, Cannon's version of "Blue Eyes Crying in the Rain" became a minor hit and was nominated for the Best Country Instrumental Performance Grammy that year. Cannon continued to perform into the '90s and frequently toured with such legends of early rock & roll as Carl Perkins. *—Sandra Brennan*

Aces High/Plays the Great Show Tunes / Nov. 20, 1995 / Hi ♦♦♦♦
Two early albums from Ace Cannon, *Aces High* and *Plays the Great Show Tunes*, were reissued on one CD by Hi Records in 1995. Although each record has its share of weak spots, they remain infectious and enjoyable, and this disc is worth seeking out for any hardcore fan of Cannon or early-'60s rock & roll and R&B. *—Stephen Thomas Erlewine*

Tuff Sax/Moanin' Sax / Nov. 20, 1995 / Hi ♦♦♦
Two early albums from Ace Cannon, *Tuff Sax* (1962), was reissued with, *Tuff Sax* (1963), on one CD by Hi Records in 1995. Although each record has its share of weak spots, they remain infectious and enjoyable examples of early-'60s rock & roll and R&B. Both albums have been out of print for years, so their reappearance on disc is welcome. *—Stephen Thomas Erlewine*

The Best of Ace Cannon / Nov. 19, 1996 / Curb ♦♦♦
The Best of Ace Cannon contains pleasant but unexceptional '90s re-recordings of Ace Cannon's biggest hits, including "Tuff" and "Blue Eyes Crying in the Rain," plus versions of standards like "Tennessee Waltz" and "Georgia on My Mind." *—Stephen Thomas Erlewine*

● **The Best of Ace Cannon: The Hi Records Years** / Apr. 10, 2001 / Hi ♦♦♦♦
On this 18-song best-of, the chronological and stylistic breadth is a little—not much—greater than you'd suspect, starting with his biggest single, 1961's "Tuff," and going all the way up to 1971. Most of the time, the saxophonist was content to grind out slow to medium shuffles with repetitive riffs and simple R&B-pop hooks, occasionally using organ, much in the style of his labelmates Bill Black's Combo (with whom Cannon sometimes played sax). Like Black, Cannon's singles were good jukebox fare, sometimes selling a lot to the specific jukebox market even when they didn't chart. (And often they didn't chart; only three singles besides "Tuff" made the Top 100, all of them included here.) The formula was simplistic and sometimes monotonous, especially when piled right after the other. However, his grooves were tight, and in the unavoidable Cannon-Black comparisons, Cannon comes out on top, simply because his instrumentals were more soulful and just a bit grittier. Toward the end of the 1960s, too, he unexpectedly got into a tougher bag that was explicitly derivative of fellow Memphians Booker T. & the MG's, but was actually pretty well done. It made for an improved sound, anyway, on cuts like "Funny (How Time Slips Away)," the downright funky "Soul for Sale," and "If I Had a Hammer" (yes, the old Peter, Paul & Mary folk hit). The 1971 cover of Joe Liggins' "Drunk" is, again unexpectedly, quite creditable funk, and only number here to feature vocals, done in a suitably phlegmy manner. *—Richie Unterberger*

Freddy Cannon (Frederico Anthony Picariello)

b. Dec. 4, 1940, Lynn, MA
Vocals / Rock & Roll
In looking back over the history of rock & roll, the sad fact remains that very few of its original practitioners stayed true to its original big beat vision. Some made a handful of brilliant sides before broader horizons—television or the movies—beckoned. Others were rockers in name only, pop singers who couldn't wait to shimmy into a tuxedo, trading in stomp 'n' shout hysteria for the more "respectable" future of dispensing supper-club schmaltz. But Freddy Cannon was a true believer, a rocker to the bone. He made rock & roll records—great *noisy* rock & roll records and *all* of them were infused with a gigantic drum beat that was an automatic invitation to shake it on down anyplace there was a spot to dance. Cannon remained true to the beat and made some really great *fun* rock & roll records in the bargain.

Because of the time frame he enjoyed his biggest successes in—the late '50s to the mid-'60s—Cannon is wrongly lumped in with the "Bobbies and Frankies" that proliferated during that era. But a quick listen to any of his finest records quickly dispels any preconceived notions of him being a pretty-boy teen-idol no-talent. Cannon could genuinely rock, and on two of his very best records—"Tallahassee Lassie" and "Buzz-Buzz-a-Diddle-It"—he supplies his own electric rhythm guitar, with his scrappy work on the latter record being particularly effective. His records were masterminded by producers Bob Crewe and Frank Slay, all well-constructed discs with every thump of the big beat and every vocal "woo" out of Cannon perfectly placed and timed for maximum impact. Hits like "Way Down Yonder in New Orleans," "Action," and "Palisades Park" may be "slicker" records than the two mentioned above, but they still possess an enormous vitality and commitment to rock & roll; few others could bring an old chestnut like "Way Down Yonder in New Orleans" into the modern age with a straight face. Cannon's immense energy and contagious style make these noisy, very exciting records well worth investigating.

He was born Frederico Anthony Picariello in 1940 and grew up in the nearby Boston suburb of Lynn, MA. Young Freddy soaked up the R&B of Big Joe Turner and the jump blues of bands like Buddy Johnson on the radio. But it was the guitar music of Chuck Berry that made the most lasting impression. Like most American teenagers at the time, Freddy went in search of the new music, which wasn't plentiful back then. He soon threw his lot in—playing rhythm guitar and singing—with a group called the Spindrifts and cut his first record, a local almost-hit called "Cha-Cha-Do." After the group's 15 minutes of local fame had evaporated, Cannon formed his first rock & roll band, Freddy Karmon & the Hurricanes. With himself on rhythm guitar, another guy on sax taking most of the leads, a piano man, and a distant relative keeping the beat, Freddy had his first big beat combo.

One afternoon, he arrived home and his mother instructed him to grab his guitar; she had written a poem that she wanted him to set to music. The poem was called "Rock and Roll Baby," which Freddy put to a stomping Chuck Berry beat and three-chord rock & roll progression. A quickie solo demo eventually found its way into the hands of indie producer Bob Crewe and his partner, Frank Slay. Slay and Crewe rewrote the tune's verses and had Freddy Karmon & the Hurricanes go into a Boston studio and cut the new version as "Tallahassee Lassie." It was Freddy's first solo record, his first hit, and the first record under his new name: Freddy Cannon. It was also the birth of a whole new style, a style that belonged to Cannon and his producers, lock, stock, and excitement galore.

Following a formula of cutting tunes that named cities or states in the title, Cannon re-stormed the charts with records like "Okefenokee," "Way Down Yonder in New Orleans," "Chattanooga Shoe Shine Boy," and "Muskrat Ramble." It is "Palisades Park," however, that remains his most enduring hit. Later chart entries like "Humdinger," "Transistor Sister," "If You Were a Rock and Roll Record," and "Teen Queen of the Week" showed that Cannon kept bringing the energy and the big beat at a time when most male singers were insipidly crooning. After leaving Swan with the height of Beatlemania lurking right around the corner, Cannon kept on rocking, extending his hit streak over to Warner Brothers with records like "Abigail Beecher," "Beechwood City," "The Dedication Song," and providing the theme for Dick Clark's *Where the Action Is!* *—Cub Koda*

● **The Best of Freddy "Boom Boom" Cannon** / Nov. 21, 1995 / Rhino ♦♦♦♦♦
The definitive collection. Twenty tracks, 17 of them Top 100 singles, including "Tallahassee Lassie," "Way Down Yonder in New Orleans," "Palisades Park," "Abigail Beecher," and

"Action," as well as a rare 1958 single by Spindrift. The other selections really aren't up to the level of the best hits, despite occasional raw detours like "Buzz Buzz A-Diddle-It" and the odd novelty "If You Were a Rock and Roll Record," with the immortal line, "If you were a rock and roll record, I know they'd sell a million of you." *—Richie Unterberger*

EP Collection / Aug. 11, 1999 / See for Miles ✦✦✦✦

See for Miles' *EP Collection* is something more than an average greatest-hits collection, since it contains the songs that made the flip side of British EPs—which means these are B-sides, covers, and album tracks, and will not likely be of interest to anybody who already isn't a Freddy Cannon fan. If you are so, this is pretty fun, especially for collectors who are looking for some of the relative rarities here. If you're not a collector, but are pretty dedicated, this has its charms, since it gives a good idea what Cannon's records sounded like at the time. Rhino's and Varese's collections remain the best bet for most fans, but if you'd like a hits collection with quirks, this is a good choice. *—Stephen Thomas Erlewine*

Palisades Park: The Very Best of Freddy Cannon 1959–1963 / May 2, 2000 / Varese ✦✦✦✦

The Explosive!/Happy Shades of Blue Plus / Sep. 11, 2001 / See for Miles ✦✦✦

Freddy Cannon/Action! . . . Plus / Sep. 11, 2001 / See for Miles ✦✦✦

Freddy Cannon was one the most energetic performers of the teen idol era, and the vigor he displayed on-stage, whether live or lip-syncing, came across on his studio work as well. Taking no prisoners, Cannon blasts through these 28 tracks, which were recorded after his glory years of "Palisades Park," etc. Backed by a who's who of studio musicians, including Leon Russell on keyboards and James Burton on guitar, Cannon gives it up on the frantic upbeat material featuring Cannon-ized renditions of James Brown's "Papa's Got a Brand New Bag," Chuck Berry's "Too Much Monkey Business," the Beatles' "She Loves You," and Tommy Tucker's "High Heel Sneakers." Also included are a few of Cannon's hits from this era, such as "Let Me Show You Where It's At" and "Abigail Beecher." Freddy "Boom Boom" Cannon—the singer you didn't want to miss when Dick Clark announced he was going to perform on *American Bandstand*—rises again on this CD. *—Andrew Hamilton*

Where the Action Is: The Very Best, 1964-1981 / May 7, 2002 / Varese ✦✦✦

Most of Cannon's best-known, and best, hits were done for Swan Records in the late '50s and early '60s. This CD can't help but suffer in comparison, focusing on his post-Swan career, a period that saw him land just two big hits ("Abigail Beecher" and "Action," both here, naturally). All but two of these 18 tracks came out between 1964-1970, a time in which Cannon's brand of everyman teen idol rock became increasingly irrelevant. This compilation's chief drawback is not so much its unfashionability as the general running-in-place mediocrity of its mainstream pop/rock, though Cannon did attack everything with his customary let's-have-a-good-wholesome-time energy. "Abigail Beecher," though, was about as good as it got, the songs often sounding unmemorably similar to each other in their slick teen rock production. Some slight surf/hot rod influences impinge on songs like "All American Girl," "Let Me Show You Where It's At," and "Beachwood City"; "In My Wildest Dreams" sounded like Gary Lewis, perhaps unsurprisingly, as Leon Russell (who also worked with Lewis) arranged. By the late '60s the ideas were getting more contrived, like a remake of "Rock Around the Clock," "Beautiful Downtown Burbank" (based around a running joke on the *Laugh-In* TV show), and the medley of some his old hits that passed for "Charged-Up, Turned-Up Rock-n-Roll Singer"; the 1974 single "Rock & Roll ABC's" wasn't any improvement. Three of the songs, including a 1967 remake of "Rockin' Robin," were previously unreleased. *—Richie Unterberger*

Blu Cantrell

Vocals / Contemporary R&B, Urban

As she grew up in Providence, R.I., with her five siblings, Blu Cantrell was toted from one jazz performance to another to watch her mother sing. From that point forward, she knew what she wanted to do, and began auditioning for vocal gigs and displaying her dynamic alto at talent shows. On a visit to Atlanta in 2000, Cantrell played her demo tape for A&R executive Tab and producer C. Stewart (aka Tricky) of RedZone Entertainment. They were so impressed that they immediately provided studio work to the young singer, and she sang backgrounds for artists including Gerald LeVert, Faith Evans, Puff Daddy, and Aaron Hall. Meanwhile, Cantrell began recording tracks for what would ultimately become her first full-length album. Upon hearing the cut "Till I'm Gone," L.A. Reid, the CEO and president of Arista Records, signed Cantrell. Before the release of the full-length, the single "Hit 'Em Up Style (Oops!)" occupied the number two position on the Hot 100 list. The buzz was out and Cantrell was invited to perform on national television programs. Her full-length debut, 2001's *So Blu*, reached the Top Ten on the album charts. Two years later, Cantrell let her sassy side go with the release of *Bittersweet*. *—Stephen Howell*

● **So Blu** / Jul. 31, 2001 / Arista ✦✦✦✦✦

The summer of 2001 turned out to be a golden age for urban soul and contemporary R&B, as the strained credibility of such over-achievers as Jill Scott and the careering of Destiny's Child gave way to such stellar records as the emergence of Alicia Keys and the re-emergence of Aaliyah. Plus, the debut of Blu Cantrell, whose *So Blu* is a wonderfully fresh recasting of contemporary soul and R&B mores. Of the aforementioned trio, this is the most conventional, but it still sounds vibrant, thanks not just to Cantrell's impassioned vocals, but how the songs and productions are wrapped in contemporary mores but delivered as if they were classic. This is a record that maintains its momentum from beginning to end, punctuated by such fine singles as "Hit 'Em Up Style (Oops!)," and even though those singles remain the standouts, even the album tracks showcase the depth of Cantrell's considerable talents. *—Stephen Thomas Erlewine*

The Capitols

f. 1962, Detroit, MI, **db.** 1969

Group / Soul, Pop-Soul, Beach

The energetic Detroit-based Capitols capitalized on mid-'60s R&B dance fever with one of the most memorable entries of the genre, "Cool Jerk." Successful local producer Ollie McLaughlin signed the trio—lead singer Sam George, Donald Norman (who wrote most of the group's material under his real surname of Storball), and Richard Mitchell—to his Karen logo, and the irresistible "Cool Jerk" made them an overnight sensation. After a couple more chart entries later that year, the trio faded quickly. George was murdered on March 17, 1982. *—Bill Dahl*

Dance the Cool Jerk / 1966 / Atco ✦✦✦

An exciting trio who stepped as good as they sang. Ollie McLaughlin did a good job producing this on the rush. Most of the 12 cuts are remakes done in the Capitols' uptempo, fresh style. A pounding bass/drum beat and a rollicking piano dominates "Cool Jerk;" Donald Norman, Richard Mitchell and lead singer, Sam George—the Capitols—ride the heavy beat telling the world about a new dance called the "Cool Jerk." The same formula was used on the Rascals' "Good Lovin" and Jimmy Reed's "I Got My Mojo Working." The guys had a way with slow tunes too. "Hello Stranger," "My Girl" and Deon Jackson's "Love Makes the World Go Round," are pleasant enough to keep you listening, though they lack the magic of the originals. McLaughlin tried to give the trio a deeper sound by having them do "In the Midnight Hour," and "Please Please Please," but this clearly wasn't the direction the trio should have been going. *—Andrew Hamilton*

We Got a Thing That's in the Groove / 1966 / Atco ✦✦✦

This fast-playing vinyl (29 minutes) is over before you realize it. Most selections are remakes of popular jams "Hold on I'm Comin'," "Knock on Wood," fellow Detroiter Darrell Banks' "Open the Door to Your Heart" and Lee Dorsey's "Working in a Coal Mine." More relaxed updates include a less than riveting version of "When a Man Loves a Woman," a watered-down "Let's Go Get Stoned" and a needless rendition of the Troggs' "Wild Thing." The title track is what the title implies; the successor to "Cool Jerk" explodes from the speakers for more than two minutes of nonstop jamming. Producer Ollie McLaughlin mimics the groove on "It's Googaloo Time," while the nondescript "Tired Running from You" is one of the LP's scarce ballads. File this one under "party records." *—Andrew Hamilton*

● **Golden Classics** / Jan. 17, 1990 / Collectables ✦✦✦✦

Collectables' *Golden Classics* edition on the Capitols is the only compilation available of this Detroit soul trio, and though nothing else here can touch the dance anthem "Cool Jerk," there's still a lot to love for fans of mad '60s soul. There's also only five tracks that overlap with their two 1966 LPs (*Dance the Cool Jerk* and *We Got a Thing That's in the Groove*), most of the tracks here coming from singles recorded later in the '60s, just before their breakup in 1969. "Cool Jerk" follow-ups "We Got a Thing That's in the Groove" and "It's Googaloo Time" sound almost as good as the prototype, while the Capitols' cover of the James Brown scorcher "Please Please Please" is worthy of J.B. himself. The rest are one-note novelties like "Ain't That Terrible," which inanely references dances of the time, mixed with a few covers (Ray Charles' "Let's Go Get Stoned"). *—John Bush*

The Capris

f. 1957, Ozone Park, NY

Group / Doo Wop

Not to be confused with the Philadelphia group of the same name, the New York City Capris were a white doo wop group. Although strongly associated with the 1950s rock & roll sound, the two records they are best known for, "There's a Moon out Tonight" and "Morse Code of Love," didn't become hits until the '50s were over.

The group originally formed in 1957 in the borough of Queens, NY, when all were teenagers. The original lead was Nick Santamaria (aka Santo), Mike Mincelli (first tenor), Steve Reina (second tenor), Vinny Narcardo (baritone), and John Apostol (bass). In selecting their name, the guys were apparently unfamiliar with the Philadelphia group that had preceded them by a few years. By 1958, the group had attracted the attention of some independent record producers, and were soon in the studio cutting an original ballad called "There's a Moon out Tonight" that was picked up for release by Planet, a small New York City label. Unfortunately for the Capris though, Planet was not able to effectively promote the record and it became an almost instant obscurity.

Soon thereafter, the group members all went their separate ways, and one would think that's where the story would end. But for the Capris, things took a different and interesting turn. By 1960, much of what was being passed off to teenagers as rock & roll, was polished pop with a beat, lacking the original vitality of what had preceded it in the mid-'50s. Discerning and disgruntled teenagers were looking backward, and radio programs were starting to focus on "oldies," even though these "oldies" may have been released only two or three years earlier. As luck would have it, the Capris record made the national charts and stayed there for over three months. With a national hit on their hands, the Capris reunited but were dissolving again by 1963. The group continued on, but the next big event in the history of the Capris came 20 years later.

In 1982 the group went into the studio to record a new album. Besides doing covers of some doo wop classics, the Capris also included a couple of original tunes. One of these was a song called "Morse Code of Love." The tune sounded like it came right out of the late '50s. It was released as a single in 1982, backed with "There's a Moon out Again." And the song got even more exposure when the Manhattan Transfer decided to cover it. Over the years, "Morse Code of Love" has only grown in popularity and has become one of the most requested tunes on "oldies" type radio stations. Once again the Capris scored a home run with a 1950s sound that touched the heartstrings of the listeners and evoked the spirit of a time when life was simpler. *—Jim Dunn*

There's a Moon out Again! / 1982 / Ambient Sound ✦✦✦

Recorded in 1982, live to two-track, here's a perfect example of what a great modern-day doo wop album should be. *—Cub Koda*

There's a Moon out Tonight / 1982 / Collectables ♦♦♦♦

Nick Santo's anguished, innocent-sounding lead on "There's a Moon Out Tonight" became a hit some three years after the song was originally issued. By this time they had disbanded, but regrouped in a hurry trying to milk the hit. This album collects ten tunes they cut for Planet, most of them superior to "There's a Moon Out Tonight," but none of them able to duplicate that song's success. *—Ron Wynn*

Morse Code of Love / Nov. 30, 1992 / Collectables ♦♦♦

- **There's a Moon out Tonight: The Very Best of the Capris** / Jan. 25, 2000 / Collectables ♦♦♦♦

The Capris were known for the wonderful "There's a Moon out Tonight," one of the great doo wop songs of all time, a song so lovely and delicate that it remains the standard for love songs. They never had another song as good as that—few bands do—but they had a number of fine romantic doo wop ballads, all collected on Collectables' *There's a Moon out Tonight: The Very Best of the Capris.* Be warned—this is still the province of dedicated doo wop fans, since there really aren't any cuts that could legitimately be called lost treasures, but for those who love the sound and the Capris in particular, this delivers some nice tunes. *—Stephen Thomas Erlewine*

The Capris

Group / R&B

Preceding the New York City Capris by three to four years, the Philadelphia Capris were an interesting teenage R&B vocal ensemble. The group's style, reflecting their youth, was more enthusiastic than polished. Nonetheless, on at least one recording they were able to achieve a certain musical magic that would guarantee them being remembered almost 50 years later. Featuring the lead female vocals of Renee Hinton, the Capris' recording of "God Only Knows" assured their place in the hearts of 1950s vocal group harmony lovers. When it formed in 1953 the group was originally an all-male quintet, comprised of Ruben Wright, Charlie Stroud, Eddie Warner, Harrison Scott, and Bobby Smart. The members all hailed from South and West Philadelphia and were in their mid-teens. Besides singing, Wright was also a talented piano player and songwriter who wrote several of the songs the group would eventually record. His piano work is also featured prominently in the Capris' recordings. Wright seemed to be equally at home with ballad stylings or uptempo jump tunes. By the end of 1953, Stroud, who had been handling lead vocals with the group, was gone. By now though, Wright and his cohorts were more aware of the competitive musical scene around them, and were looking for a replacement that would help their group to stand out from their peers. They found that person when their paths crossed with Renee Hinton. Not long after, under the direction of their new manager Sidney Goldstein, the Capris signed to Gotham Records, a Philadelphia label owned by Ivin Ballen.

For their first release, Ballen chose "God Only Knows," an original ballad by the group. The success of the disc also opened up a variety of local performance opportunities for the group. In fact, it did well enough to prompt another R&B cover version by the Crystals (male group) issued on Deluxe in January 1955. But their newly found success was to be short-lived. As was the fate of many groups of the day, the military beckoned, and in 1955 Wright and the other Capris answered the call. Trying to piggy back on the success of their first outing, Gotham issued two follow-up singles by the group in late 1954 and early 1955 that quickly fizzled out.

In 1958, the Capris tried again. With the fellows back from the service, they gave it one more try for Ballen on his Twentieth Century label. But their release of "My Weakness" was also ill-fated, and with that the group called it a day. In subsequent periods of renewed interest in "oldies," "God Only Knows" would find new groups of listeners to appreciate it once again. Besides their released material, the Capris recorded several other tracks for Gotham which have now been made available on a number of CDs. *—Jim Dunn*

- **Gotham Recording Stars** / Mar. 6, 1990 / Collectables ♦♦♦♦♦

The Capris should not be confused with their Italian counterparts, whose name was spelled similarly. This African-American group was from Philadelphia and didn't score any hits during their mid-'50s tenure on Gotham. This album includes their one near-hit, "God Only Knows," plus several good to excellent singles that weren't issued while they were recording for Gotham from 1954 to 1958. *—Ron Wynn*

1954–1958 / Nov. 28, 1995 / Flyright ♦♦♦♦

Chuck Carbo

Vocals / New Orleans R&B, R&B

The mellifluous vocal tones of Chuck Carbo was a principal ingredient in the success of the Spiders, the premier R&B vocal group around New Orleans during the 1950s. He mounted a strong comeback bid as a smooth solo artist, cutting two albums for Rounder: *Drawers Trouble* in 1993 and 1996's *The Barber Blues.*

The gospel-steeped Carbo (whose actual first name is Hayward) and his brother Chick (real first name: Leonard) shared frontman duties for the Spiders, whose hits for Imperial included the two-sided smash "I Didn't Want to Do It"/"You're the One," a ribald "I'm Slippin' In" in 1954, and "Witchcraft" (later covered by Elvis Presley) the next year. Imperial's main man in the Crescent City, Dave Bartholomew, produced the quintet's 1954-1956 output, as well as writing many of their best numbers (notably a risqué "The Real Thing"). Carbo cut a few 45s under his own name for Imperial, Rex, and Ace after going solo; Chick waxed 45s of his own for Atlantic, Vee-Jay, and Instant.

Chuck Carbo never stopped performing entirely, although he made his living as a lumber truck driver when gigs got scarce. In 1989, he scored a local hit with his cover of Jeannie & Jimmy Cheatham's "Meet Me With Your Black Drawers On." It was reprised on *Drawers Trouble,* a comeback set reuniting Carbo with pianists Mac "Dr. John" Rebennack and Edward Frank. *The Barber's Blues* ensured Carbo's return to the spotlight with two more Cheatham copyrights and a second-line "Hey, Mardi Gras! (Here I Am)." *—Bill Dahl*

- **Drawers Trouble** / 1993 / Rounder ♦♦♦♦

Veteran New Orleans R&B singer Carbo proves he's a capable front man even without the presence of his '50s vocal group, the Spiders, on this infectious comeback set. With Crescent City vet Edward Frank handling piano and arranging duties, Carbo smoothly intones a mostly original lineup of songs (Jeannie & Jimmy Cheatham's lascivious standard "Meet Me With Your Black Drawers On" being one of the few exceptions). Dr. John contributes his considerable skills on keyboard and guitar to the project. *—Bill Dahl*

The Barber's Blues / 1996 / Rounder ♦♦♦

Ex-Spiders lead Carbo returns with a Rounder encore that eschews Dr. John but brings back Edward Frank as co-producer and pianist. Some of the selections are a little on the hackneyed side (a permanent moratorium on "Everyday I Have the Blues," please!), but Carbo's second line-based "Hey, Mardi Gras! (Here I Am)," the title item, and a easy-on-the-ears reprise of the Cheathams' "Don't Boogie With Your Black Drawers On" hit the spot. *—Bill Dahl*

Mariah Carey

b. Mar. 27, 1970, New York, NY

Vocals / Urban, Adult Contemporary, Club/Dance, Dance-Pop

The best-selling female performer of the 1990s, Mariah Carey rose to superstardom on the strength of her stunning five-octave voice; an elastic talent who moved easily from glossy ballads to hip-hop-inspired dance-pop, she earned frequent comparison to rivals Whitney Houston and Celine Dion, but did them both one better by composing all of her own material. Born in Long Island, NY, on March 27, 1970, Carey moved to New York City at the age of 17—just one day after graduating high school—to pursue a music career; there she befriended keyboardist Ben Margulies, with whom she began writing songs. Her big break came as a backing vocalist on a studio session with dance-pop singer Brenda K. Starr, who handed Carey's demo tape to Columbia Records head Tommy Mottola at a party. According to legend, Mottola listened to the tape in his limo while driving home that same evening, and was so immediately struck by Carey's talent that he doubled back to the party to track her down.

After signing to Columbia, Carey entered the studio to begin work on her 1990 self-titled debut LP; the heavily promoted album was a chart-topping smash, launching no less than four number one singles: "Vision of Love," "Love Takes Time," "Someday," and "I Don't Wanna Cry." Her overnight success earned Grammy awards as Best New Artist and Best Female Vocalist, and expectations were high for Carey's follow-up, 1991's *Emotions.* The album did not disappoint, as the title track reached number one—a record fifth consecutive chart-topper—while both "Can't Let Go" and "Make It Happen" landed in the Top Five. Carey's next release was 1992's *MTV Unplugged* EP, which generated a number-one cover of the Jackson 5's "I'll Be There"; featured on the track was backup singer Trey Lorenz, whose appearance immediately helped him land a recording contract of his own.

In June 1993, Carey wed Mottola—some two decades her senior—in a headline-grabbing ceremony; months later she released her third full-length effort, *Music Box,* her best-selling record to date. Two more singles, "Dreamlover" and "Hero," reached the top spot on the charts. Carey's first tour followed and was widely panned by critics; undaunted, she resurfaced in 1994 with a holiday release titled *Merry Christmas,* scoring a seasonal smash with "All I Want for Christmas Is You." 1995's *Daydream* reflected a new artistic maturity; the first single, "Fantasy," debuted at number one, making Carey the first female artist and just the second performer ever to accomplish the feat. The follow-up, "One Sweet Day"—a collaboration with Boyz II Men—repeated the trick, and remained lodged at the top of the charts for a record 16 weeks.

After separating from Mottola, Carey returned in 1997 with *Butterfly,* another staggering success and her most hip-hop-flavored recording to date. *#1's*—a collection featuring her 13 previous chart-topping singles as well as "The Prince of Egypt (When You Believe)," a duet with Whitney Houston effectively pairing the two most successful female recording artists in pop history—followed late the next year. With "Heartbreaker," the first single from her 1999 album *Rainbow,* Carey became the first artist to top the charts in each year of the 1990s; the record also pushed her ahead of the Beatles as the artist with the most cumulative weeks spent atop the Hot 100 singles chart.

However, the 2000s weren't as kind to Carey. After signing an 80 million dollar deal with Virgin—the biggest record contract ever— in 2001 she experienced a very public personal and professional meltdown that included rambling, suicidal messages on her website; an appearance on *TRL* where, clad only in a T-shirt, she handed out Popsicles to the audience; and last but not least, the stupendously awful movie *Glitter* and its attendant soundtrack (which was also her Virgin Records debut). Both the film and the album did poorly critically as well as commercially, with *Glitter* making just under 4 million dollars in its total U.S. gross and the soundtrack struggling to make gold sales. Following these failures, Virgin and Carey parted ways early in 2002, with the label paying her 28 million dollars. That spring, she found a new home with Island/Def Jam, where she set up her own label, MonarC Music. In December, she released her ninth album, *Charmbracelet.* *—Jason Ankeny*

Mariah Carey / May 1990 / Columbia ♦♦♦

This extremely impressive debut is replete with smooth-sounding ballads and uplifting dance/R&B cuts. Carey convincingly seizes many opportunities to display her incredible vocal range on such memorable tracks as the popular "Vision of Love" (featured during her television debut on *The Arsenio Hall Show,* an appearance noted by many as her formal introduction to stardom), the energetic "Someday," and the moody sounds of the hidden treasure "Vanishing." With this collection of songs acting as a springboard for future successes, Carey establishes a strong standard of comparison for other breakthrough artists of this genre. *—Ashley S. Battel*

Emotions / Sep. 1991 / Columbia ♦♦♦

A strong follow-up to Carey's self-titled debut album, *Emotions* puts to rest any concern of a "sophomore jinx." The same mix of dance/R&B/ballads that gave Carey's debut such tremendous auditory appeal can be found with equal strength on this release, indicating that placing firm belief in the notion of "Why fool with success?" may, in fact, have its merits. Most notably, the gospel influences of "If It's Over" (with music co-written by Carole King), the yearning cries for a lost love in "Can't Let Go," and the catchy, upbeat title track, all serve to send the listener on a musical journey filled with varying emotions. However, the one emotion that prevails upon completion of the album is definitely a positive one—satisfaction! *—Ashley S. Battel*

MTV Unplugged [EP] / Mar. 1992 / Columbia ♦♦♦

This live performance is the perfect peek into the life of rising pop/soul vocal sensation Mariah Carey at a youthful and innocent age in an intimate, acoustic setting. Throughout this performance, recorded live for MTV's *Unplugged*, Carey is quite electric and charismatic within her vocal presence and succeeds in enlightening the already engaged audience from the get-go. The audience certainly feels the warmth and sincerity of Carey's lyrical messages of longing, loss, friendships, and love. Carey's supporting cast of gifted group musicians back her up with soulful melodiousness, spontaneity, and enriching percussion. Gradually, the power and esteem of these tales lift to new heights and remain at a peak with the breathtaking, moment-making performance of "I'll Be There," a charming song first cut by the Jackson 5. All and all, this is an inspiring event, though still simple enough for the listener to catch those musical places that need to be polished. "Can't Let Go," Carey's radio single for the album, makes it as the seventh and final track, though the cameras are shut off for the *Unplugged* episode. Certainly, this is a record of hope, virtue, and the possibilities of newfound love. *—Shawn M. Haney*

Music Box / Sep. 1993 / Columbia ♦♦♦♦

Mariah Carey has been stung by critical charges that she's all vocal bombast and no subtlety, soul or shading. Her solution was to make an album in which her celebrated octave-leaping voice would be downplayed and she could demonstrate her ability to sing softly and coolly. Well, she was partly successful; she trimmed the volume on *Music Box*. Unfortunately, she also cut the energy level; Carey sounds detached on several selections. She scored a couple of huge hits, "Hero" and "Dreamlover," where she did inject some personality and intensity into the leads. Most other times, Carey blended into the background and let the tracks guide her, instead of pushing and exploding through them. It was wise for Carey to display other elements of her approach, but sometimes excessive spirit is preferable to an absence of passion. *—Ron Wynn*

Daydream / Oct. 3, 1995 / Columbia ♦♦♦♦♦

Mariah Carey certainly knows how to construct an album. Positioning herself directly between urban R&B with tracks like "Fantasy" and adult contemporary with songs like "One Sweet Day," a duet with Boyz II Men, Carey appeals to both audiences equally because of the sheer amount of craft and hard work she puts into her albums. *Daydream* is her best record to date, featuring a consistently strong selection of songs and a remarkably impassioned performance by Carey. A few of the songs are second-rate—particularly the cover of Journey's "Open Arms"—but *Daydream* demonstrates that Carey continues to perfect her craft and that she has earned her status as an R&B/pop diva. *—Stephen Thomas Erlewine*

Butterfly / Sep. 16, 1997 / Columbia ♦♦♦♦

Upon its release, *Butterfly* was interpreted as Mariah Carey's declaration of independence from her ex-husband (and label president) Tommy Mottola, and to a certain extent, that's true. *Butterfly* is peppered with allusions to her troubled marriage and her newfound freedom, and the music is supposed to be in tune with contemporary urban sounds instead of adult contemporary radio. Nevertheless, it feels like a Mariah Carey album, which means that it's a collection of hit singles surrounded by classy filler. What is surprising about *Butterfly* is the lack of uptempo dance-pop. Apart from the Puffy Combs-produced "Honey," *Butterfly* is devoted to ballads, and while they are all well-crafted, many of them blend together upon initial listening. Subsequent plays reveal that Carey's vocals are sultrier and more controlled than ever, and that helps "Butterfly," "Break Down," "Babydoll" and the Prince cover "The Beautiful Ones" rank among her best; also, the ballads do have a stronger urban feel than before. Even though *Butterfly* doesn't have as many strong singles as *Daydream*, it's one of her best records, illustrating that Carey is continuing to improve and refine her music, which makes her a rarity among her '90s peers. *—Stephen Thomas Erlewine*

● **#1's** / Nov. 17, 1998 / Columbia ♦♦♦♦♦

Protest as she may—and she does, claiming in the liner notes that *#1's* is "not a greatest hits album! It's too soon, I haven't been recording long enough for that!"—it's hard to view *#1's*, Mariah Carey's first compilation, as anything other than a greatest-hits album. Carey was fortunate enough to have nearly every single she released top the pop charts. Between 1990's "Vision of Love" and 1998's "My All," all but four commercially released singles ("Anytime You Need a Friend," "Can't Let Go," "Make It Happen," "Without You") hit number one, with only a handful of radio-only singles ("Butterfly," "Breakdown") making the airwaves, not the charts. That leaves 12 big hits on *#1's*, all number ones. Since Carey's singles always dominated her albums, it comes as no surprise that *#1's* is her best, most consistent album, filled with songs that represent state-of-the-art '90s adult contemporary and pop-oriented urban soul. That said, it isn't a perfect overview—a couple of good singles are missing because of the self-imposed "#1 rule"; plus, the Ol' Dirty Bastard mix of "Fantasy" is strong, but fans familiar with the radio single will be disappointed that the chorus is completely missing on this version. The album is also padded with a personal favorite (her Brian McKnight duet "Whenever You Call," taken from *Butterfly*) and three new songs—the Jermaine Dupri-produced "Sweetheart," the Whitney Houston duet "When You Believe" (taken from *The Prince of Egypt* soundtrack), and "I Still Believe," a remake of a Brenda K. Starr tune—which are all fine, but not particularly memorable. Still, that's hardly enough to bring down a thoroughly entertaining compilation that will stand as her best record until the "official" hits collection is released. *—Stephen Thomas Erlewine*

Rainbow / Nov. 2, 1999 / Columbia ♦♦♦

Mariah Carey claims *Rainbow*, her first album since divorcing Tommy Mottola, "chronicles my emotional roller coaster ride of the past year," but less subjective listeners could be forgiven for viewing it as simply another Mariah Carey album. After all, all the elements are in place—the crossover dance hits, the ballads, the cameos, the hip producers, the weird cover choice from the early '80s. But dig a little deeper, and her words ring true. *Rainbow* is the first Carey album where she's written personal lyrics, and allusions to her separation from Mottola are evident throughout the album, even if it doesn't really amount to the "story" she mentions in the liner notes. As appropriate for any introspective album, it's a bit ballad heavy, which makes *Rainbow* seem a little samey. Yet that's not the only reason the record has a weird sense of déjà vu, since this follows the same formula as its two predecessors, distinguished primarily by her newfound fondness for flashing flesh. That repetition isn't necessarily a problem, since she does formula very well, managing to appeal to both housewives as well as B-boys. *Rainbow* proves that she can still pull off that difficult balancing act, but it's hard not to be a little disappointed that she'd didn't shake the music up a little bit more—after all, it would have been a more effective album if the heartbreak, sorrow, and joy that bubbles underneath the music were brought to the surface. *—Stephen Thomas Erlewine*

Glitter / Sep. 11, 2001 / Virgin ♦♦

It wasn't supposed to be this way. Mariah Carey's first album for Virgin Records was supposed to be a triumph, an album that confirmed her status as pop's reigning diva, while serving as the soundtrack to a film that proved her crossover status was every bit as potent as that of her unexpected arch-rival Jennifer Lopez. Instead, *Glitter* proved to be an utter meltdown—the pop equivalent of Chernobyl. It's hard not to sympathize with everybody involved, actually, from Mariah herself, to all the musicians and producers involved in this and the film, plus the label that shelled out millions of dollars for a proven quantity that suddenly stopped delivering the goods. Because *Glitter* is a catastrophe—it captures Mariah on a downturn of creativity and popularity, just when she needs to shine the brightest, and then it was paired with an extremely public emotional breakdown, highlighted by a bizarre appearance on *TRL*, where she was seemingly dressed only in a T-shirt and handing out Popsicles, plus a scarily suicidal message posted and then quickly deleted from her website. Poor Mariah! Poor Virgin! Who could have predicted this pop perfect storm? And, when you're seeing it unfold, or listening to it unspool, it's hard not to be shocked by the miscalculation of every aspect of *Glitter*. Superficially, it's not that all far removed from her last Columbia album, *Rainbow*, but if that record illustrated the freeing effect of her divorce from Tommy Motolla, this album shows that Mariah needs some guiding force, something to keep her on track. Otherwise, she sinks into formless ballads, covers of early-'80s funk tunes that sound exactly like the originals, hip-hop funk that plays plastic and stiff. This touches on everything Mariah tried before, but nothing works—not the oversinging, not the sentimental, not the desperate attempts for street cred. If she indeed was paranoid about Lopez's career and success, as certain tabloid reports indicated, she shouldn't have made a record that seems to ape *On the 6* the way that album slavishly followed prime Mariah. It's an embarrassment, one that might have been easier to gawk at if its creator wasn't so close to emotional destruction at the time of release. *—Stephen Thomas Erlewine*

Charmbracelet / Dec. 3, 2002 / Island ♦♦

If it didn't follow *Glitter*, the gold standard for diva implosions in the early 21st century, Mariah Carey's *Charmbracelet* would simply be her worst album, but since it was rushed out in late 2002 in an effort to mask that disaster, to treat it as if it never happened, it achieves a special kind of grandeur—it's a botched attempt to restore a career after a botched attempt at a crossover. Of course, the Carey party line, including her new label Island (who has sponsored her vanity imprint, MonarC), claims her lone Virgin album, *Glitter*, shouldn't be considered an official Mariah album since it was a soundtrack, but not only does that theory not hold water (perhaps *Purple Rain* shouldn't be considered a Prince album, then?), it signals that everybody realizes that *Glitter* wasn't just a disaster, but that her whole ghetto-fabulous trip of the late '90s eroded her core MOR audience. So, with *Charmbracelet*, the backpedalling is immediately evident, from the demure photos gracing the artwork (the tight shorts of *Rainbow* are long gone) and the first single/opening track "Through the Rain," a slow ballad designed as "Vision of Love" meets "Hero." Mariah is back in the adult contemporary camp, no longer trying to prove that she's real. She hasn't completely abandoned hip-hop, but whenever it rears its head on *Charmbracelet*, it's utterly jarring, whether it's Jay-Z's and Freeway's guest spots on "You Got Me," the club-ready groove of "You Had Your Chance" (built on the same bass line as "Nuthin' but a G Thang"), or the blatant rewrite of Cam'ron's "Oh Boy" on "Boy (I Need You)" (he may endorse it with a cameo, yet the sampled vocal hook remains singularly annoying no matter how its presented), or the crackling vinyl used as ambient noise on "Irresistible," or the distracting use of dripping water as percussion on "I Only Wanted." Weirdly enough, even these detours are nothing more than flourishes—window-dressing on songs that remain firmly in the middle of the road, since that's where the sales are, or at least where Mariah's aging fan base is. This, of course, is not a problem, since she's done hip-hop-influenced dance tunes and ballads very well before. What is a problem is that there are no good songs on this record outside of Def Leppard's power ballad classic "Bringin' on the Heartbreak," which isn't even covered all that well. What is a greater problem is that Mariah's voice is shot, sounding in tatters throughout the record. Whenever she sings, there's a raspy whistle behind her thin voice and she strains to make notes throughout the record. She cannot coo or softly croon, nor can she perform her trademark gravity-defying vocal runs. Her voice is damaged, and there's not a moment where it sounds strong or inviting. That alone would be disturbing, but since the songs are formless and the production bland—another reason why the hip-hop announces itself, even though it's nowhere near as pronounced as it has been since *Butterfly*—her tired voice becomes the only thing to concentrate on, and it's a sad, ugly thing, making an album that would merely have been her worst into something tragic. *—Stephen Thomas Erlewine*

Carl Carlton

b. 1953, Detroit, MI

Vocals / Funk, Soul

Detroit native Carl Carlton began recording for Lando Records in the late '60s as Little Carl Carlton. His first single was "I Love True Love." When a later single, "Competition Ain't Nothing," started to take off in the summer of 1968, the single was picked up by Don Robey's Back Beat Records. Carlton scored some minor chart hits for Back Beat in the late '60s and early '70s, with "46 Drums—1 Guitar," "Oh Mary How I Got Over," "I Can Feel It," and "Drop By My Place." When Robey sold his Duke Peacock/Back Beat labels to ABC Records in 1972, a compilation album of Carlton's singles was released, *You Can't Stop a Man in Love*.

Former Temptation David Ruffin was a friend of Carlton. After listening to one of Ruffin's albums, Carlton got excited about one song, "Everlasting Love." Carlton wasn't aware that the song was previously a Top Ten hit for Robert Knight in 1967. In spite of the song's previous success, the first Carlton single on ABC was "I Wanna Be Your Main Squeeze" with a low-key version of "Everlasting Love" on the flip. After given a more disco-friendly arrangement by Nashville's Papa Don Schroder, "Everlasting Love" garnered Carlton his first Top Ten pop hit in 1974. An album, *Everlasting Love*, produced by Bob Monaco (Rufus, Three Dog Night), was released. 1975 saw Carlton traveling to Philadelphia to work with producer/songwriter Bunny Sigler. The resultant album, *I Wanna Be With You*, weakly charted despite the release of three singles: "Ain't Been No One Before You," "Ain't Gonna Tell Nobody (About You)," and "Live for Today, Not for Tomorrow."

For a year and a half, Carlton had to wait until his contract with ABC lapsed until he could do anymore recording. He resurfaced in late 1977 with a Mercury single, "You You," and continued to perform around Detroit. Veteran soul singer Leon Haywood flew Carlton to California and worked with him in his recording studio. Getting him a singles deal with the label that he was signed to, 20th Century, Haywood produced a cover of his own "This Feeling's Rated Xtra" with a James Ingram tune, "Fighting in the Name of Love," on the B-side. It charted briefly, doing well enough for 20th Century to release the next single, "She's a Bad Mama Jama." It earned Carlton a gold record in 1981, staying at number two for eight weeks straight. An album, *Carl Carlton*, was released. His next was *The Bad C.C.* (RCA), which included a catchy synth-heavy cover of the Four Tops' "Baby I Need Your Loving." 1986 saw the release of Carlton's sixth album, *Private Property* (Casablanca). It is safe to say that Carlton wanted and needed a hit. So one can probably excuse the title track and first single for being a "Mama Jama" clone. It did the trick, landing in the upper half of the R&B charts. *—Ed Hogan*

You Can't Stop a Man in Love / 1973 / Back Beat ✦✦

Everlasting Love / 1974 / ABC ✦✦✦

Carl Carlton began his recording career as Little Carl Carlton in his native Detroit in 1964 on Lando Records. One of his early sides, "Nothing No Sweeter Than Love," a Northern soul favorite, can be found on the 1999 Life on Mars/BMG CD *Cream of Vintage Soul, Vol.1* and on *Popcorn's Detroit Soul Party*. His cover of "Everlasting Love" (a hit for Robert Knight) was his pop breakthrough in fall 1974. That track and its slow-burn flip side, "I Wanna Be Your Main Squeeze," was produced by Papa Don (James & Bobby Purify's "I'm Your Puppet"). The rest of the album, produced by Bob Monaco, consists mostly of cleverly arranged remakes. The follow-up singles were "Morning, Noon and Night" and "Smokin' Room." Carlton also performs a cover of "La La Song," written by Leon Heywood, who wrote and produced his sole gold single, "She's a Bad Mama Jama." ["Everlasting Love" is on *Duke-Peacock's Greatest Hits, Party Starter Level 1: The Classics, Pure Disco, Vol. 2, Soul Hits of the 70s: Didn't It Blow Your Mind, Vol. 13*, and *ABC's of Soul, Vol. 2: Classics From the ABC Records Catalog 1969-1974* among others.] *—Ed Hogan*

I Wanna Be With You / 1975 / ABC ✦✦

● **Drop By My Place** / 1988 / Charly R&B ✦✦✦✦✦

Without another Carl Carlton roundup to be found, Charly's excellent *Drop By My Place* automatically qualifies as the first-disc choice for newcomers. The 16 tracks were cut between 1968-1975 during Carlton's early prime. Contending with frequent Stevie Wonder comparisons—early on he was labeled "The 12-Year Old Wonder" to riff off of Wonder's own "12-Year Old Genius" tag—Carlton made his own dent in the R&B and pop charts with a mix of lean '60s soul and slicker pop gems in the Philly International mold. This collection takes it all in with Northern soul treats like "Drop By My Place" and bump beat and electric piano sides such as the Rufus cover "Smokin' Room." The album also includes one of Carlton's biggest pop successes in the proto-disco track "Everlasting Love" (this was before "She's a Bad Mama Jama," which is not included here, went number two in 1981) and such gritty funk as "Two Timer" and the Bunny Sigler-produced psycho-soul closer "Wild Child." Throughout, Carlton navigates the varied musical terrain nicely with his supple, high-toned pipes. Topped off with more fine production work by Bob Monaco and Papa Don Schroeder & Tommy Cogbill, *Drop By My Place* will certainly please soul fans looking for some rare-groove gold. *—Stephen Cook*

The Carltons

f. Washington, DC

Group / Chicago Soul, Soul

The Carltons—James Leon Diggs, Larry Bell, and Jerry Norris—from Washington, D.C., were Chess Records' answer to the Impressions. A&R director Billy Davis was so enamored with Diggs' songwriting skills that he signed them to a deal, even though Diggs was already contracted to Chess with Richard Dunbar as the Knight Brothers. They sounded totally different—the Knight Brothers sang emotionally gripping, down-home soul with heavy gospel overtones, while the Carltons' breezy, soulful sounds were reminiscent of second-tier Impressions.

Andy Mack's early 1964 single on Chess, "Later Than You Think" b/w "Do You Wanna Go," featured the Carltons. It flopped, but the Carltons issued their first single, "Ooo Baby" b/w "Can't You Hear the Beat," in May 1964. Diggs shifted between both acts depending on who had something going on. Neither ever caught fire, so there was never a conflict. "Hey Mr. Lonesome" b/w "Easy Livin'" (September 1964) was their most successful single, but it was a turntable hit: the units sold didn't equal the radio action.

Chess issued the Carltons' singles on their Argo subsidiary; the final one appeared the same month (October 1964) as the Knight Brothers' first single, which was recorded in Chicago. Previous 45s were cut in D.C. and New York. "I'm a Man" b/w "Keep on Hoping" is the only Carltons single that Diggs didn't write (besides Andy Mack's—Shena DeMell and Sugar Pie DeSanto co-wrote both sides, with Billy Davis collaborating on the A-side). The single failed to do anything, and the Carltons resigned; ironically, the Knight Brothers' "Temptations 'Bout to Get Me," issued the same month as the Carltons swan single, was the duo's biggest record. Diggs sang with the Starfires on two late-'50s singles on Decca Records. *—Andrew Hamilton*

Jean Carn (Sarah Jean Perkins)

b. Columbus, GA

Vocals / Philly Soul, Soul

Singer Jean Carne's career has had various incarnations, as well as a slight name change similar to Dionne Warwick's (adding an "e" to the end of her last name as Warwick did for a short time). Born Sarah Jean Perkins in Columbus, GA, she was raised in Atlanta. She began singing gospel music in the church choir at age four; she also took piano lessons and learned the clarinet and bassoon. Carne won a music scholarship to Morris Brown College and began her recording career in 1969 with her husband, keyboardist Doug Carn, on the Black Jazz label, where she was one of the last vocalists to work with jazz legend Duke Ellington before his death.

Carne popped up several times during the early- to mid-'70s, singing with Earth, Wind & Fire on two albums, recording several times with Norman Connors, and reaching the charts via George Duke's hit single "Reach for It." In 1977, Carne was signed to Kenneth Gamble & Leon Huff's Philadelphia International Records; her debut album, *Jean Carn*, was a classy affair that merged the best of '70s soul and jazz with solid songwriting and tight instrumental support (MFSB, Instant Funk). The debut single "Free Love" went to number-23 R&B. Though the follow-up single didn't chart, several of the album's tracks received considerable radio airplay, and some tracks made the disco charts. In June 1978, her second album for the label was released; *Happy to Be With You* included the hit single "Don't Let It Go to Your Head."

Carn's final Philadelphia International album, 1980's *When I Find You Love*, was more of a return conceptually (musically and sonically) to *Jean Carn*. Produced by Dexter Wansel, the album rates as one of Carne's best efforts. The smooth and halting "My Love Don't Come Easy" peaked at number-35 R&B. Released in August 1981, Carne's *Sweet and Wonderful* featured a remake of the Spinners' "Love Don't Love Nobody," which went to number-35 R&B. Carne moved to Motown Records in 1982, making her label debut with the album *Trust Me*. The single "If You Don't Know Me By Now," a cover of the Harold Melvin & the Blue Notes hit with backing vocals by the Temptations, went to number 49 R&B.

By 1986, Carne signed to Omni Records; *Closer than Close* was released in July of that year and the title track that went to number one R&B. Her 1988 album *You're a Part of Me* included a hit cover of Aretha Franklin's "Ain't No Way." Carne later signed with Place One Entertainment, which reunited her with former Omni Records president Steve Bernstein, with her *Love Lessons* album being distributed by PPI/Peter Pan. Carne continues to tour with Connors, among others, and makes her home in Atlanta. *—Ed Hogan*

Jean Carn / 1977 / Philadelphia International ✦✦✦

Jean Carn's self-titled debut for Gamble & Huff's Philadelphia International Records could be subtitled "Philly soul at its best." Released during the era of emerging sophisticated soul-formatted FM radio stations, *Jean Carn* provided perfectly suited singles, the wise R&B hit "Free Love," and format-friendly, radio-aired LP tracks: the airy ballads "No Laughing Matter," "I'm in Love Again," and the jazzy "You Are All I Need." "Free Love," "Time Waits for No One," "You Got a Problem," and the second single "If You Wanna Go Back" were all long-running hits on *Billboard*'s Hot Disco charts. This album was issued as a Sony Music Japan CD reissue and also paired with *Happy to Be With You* on a late-'90s two-album single CD from the U.K. label VCI/Westside. Some of the LPs tracks can be found on the 1999 Capitol CD, *Closer Than Close: The Best of Jean Carn* and on the 1998 Recall CD, *The Best of Jean Carn & the Jones Girls*. *—Ed Hogan*

Happy to Be With You / Jun. 1978 / The Right Stuff ✦✦✦✦

The transformation of Jean Carn from jazz vocalist to mainstream artist continues on her second Philadelphia International LP, originally released in 1978. She does an interesting remake of hubby Doug Carn's "Revelation/Infant Eyes." The most successful track, "Don't Let It Go to Your Head," missed the R&B Top 20 by more than 30 rungs, despite its enormous charm. "There's a Shortage of Good Men" and "You Can't Come Back Now" are dancefloor fillers, while the ballads are beauties, especially "Together Once Again" and Jean's classy rendition of Debby Boone's "You Light Up My Life." *—Andrew Hamilton*

When I Find You Love / 1980 / Philadelphia International ✦✦✦✦✦

Issued in late 1979, *When I Find You Love* comes closest to the breath and depth of Jean Carn's self-titled dazzling debut for Gamble & Huff's Philadelphia International Records. Touting the production talents of Dexter Wansel, Jack Faith, and the duo of Jerry Butler & John L. Usry, its tracks scored on many different levels. "My Love Don't Come Easy," with its come-hither groove, was a mid-charting R&B favorite. "What's on Your Mind," "Give It Up," and particularly "Was There All It Was" became dance club hits. Other highlights include the sweepingly romantic "Lonely Girl in a Cold Cold World," the gentle, quiet title track, and the radio-aired album cut "Start the Fire." The album was reissued as a 1999 WestSide two-LP single CD (*When I Find You Love/Sweet and Wonderful*), and some of its tracks appear on *Closer Than Close: The Best of Jean Carn, The Best of Jean Carn & the Jones Girls, First Ladies of Philadelphia Soul*, and *Greatest Hits of Philadelphia: 1976-1986*. *—Ed Hogan*

Trust Me / 1982 / Motown ✦✦✦

Closer Than Close / 1986 / Omni ✦✦✦✦

The Best of Jean Carn & the Jones Girls / Sep. 15, 1998 / Recall ✦✦✦
When this was released in 1998 there were few sufficient compilations available for either artist's work on Phliadelphia International. The English label Recall decided to do a two-CD set with Jean Carn and the Jones Girls each getting one disc of material. Despite the often-arbitrary selections, this does offer great work. This set arguably has a better time capturing the sensual voiced Carn than the work of the Jones Girls. Classics like "Don't Let It Go to Your Head" and "My Love Don't Come Easy" are both brilliant mixes of her warmth and sexuality and the glossy though not overproduced style the label was known for. The best ballad here, "When I Find You Love," co-written by then labelmate Jerry Butler, is one of Carn's most poignant performances. The omissions of both "You Are All I Need" and "Don't Say No (To Love)" diminishes the set's appeal. The same could be said for the Jones Girls portion of this effort. Although this set teeters on the edge of clutter, the individual tracks more than stand up. The group's essential tracks "Dance Turned Into a Romance" and "Nights Over Egypt" are included here. But what didn't make the list presents a problem. R&B and quiet storm necessities like their remake of the Stylistics "Children of the Night" and "My Melody" oddly didn't make the list. The inclusion of "Get as Much Love as You Can," "Life Goes On," and "I Close My Eyes" almost makes up for it. The subtle mix and the totality of the songs included make this recommended. *—Jason Elias*

● **Closer Than Close: The Best of Jean Carn** / Jun. 8, 1999 / Capitol ✦✦✦✦
These 16 prime cuts represent the best of Jean Carn's career. Her most successful record, the floating "Closer Than Close," written by Terry Price and Brandi Wells, and produced by Grover Washington Jr. for Omni Records, didn't stop until it hit the top of the R&B charts on August 2, 1986, where it remained for two weeks. This collection also includes her duet with Michael Henderson, "Valentine Love," and moving remakes of "If You Don't Know Me By Know," "Love Don't Love Nobody," and "Isn't No Way." The popular "Don't Let It Go to Your Head" and "Free Love" are on board, as well as a rare O'Jays production: the emotional "My Love Don't Come Easy." *—Andrew Hamilton*

Barbara Carr (Barbara Crosby)

b. Jan. 9, 1941, St. Louis, MO
Vocals / Soul-Blues, Chicago Soul, Retro-Soul
Folks only familiar with her more recent work may be mildly surprised that alluring singer Barbara Carr recorded for Chess back in 1966. Carr's "Don't Knock Love" was a delicious slice of Chicago soul arranged by Phil Wright that got dusted off and released by Chess a second time in 1970 when she came back to the company and cut "Think About It Baby" (written, arranged, and produced by St. Louis saxist Oliver Sain). After a lengthy fallow period, Carr returned with an infectious "Good Woman Go Bad" for (presumably) her own Bar-Car logo. Carr also did a credible job on "Messin' With My Mind," a George Jackson number that both Otis Clay and Clarence Carter have also cut. Stan Lewis' Shreveport-based Paula Records later issued an album of Carr material from this era that deftly mixes blues and soul genres. *—Bill Dahl*

● **Good Woman Go Bad** / Oct. 18, 1994 / Paula ✦✦✦✦✦
Barbara Carr had a number of good Chess singles during the late '60s, but she never received the opportunity to record a full album for the label. She didn't make a full-length album until the '90s, when all kinds of underappreciated blues veterans were given a second chance. Carr was one of the more deserving of that breed, as *Good Woman Go Bad* proves. She's a dynamic, energetic vocalist who invests true passion to even mediocre songs. Unfortunately, there are a few too many average tunes on the record, but Carr saves the day with her storming performances. *—Thom Owens*

Footprints on the Ceiling / Mar. 4, 1997 / Ecko ✦✦✦✦

Bone Me Like You Own Me / May 5, 1998 / Ecko ✦✦✦✦
Adults only please! Barbara Carr's hot, risqué Southern soul tales are too explicit for the kiddies and will shock most adults. The titles—"Long on Talk, Short on Love," "Bone Me Like You Own Me," and "If the Lord Keeps the Thought of You out of Mind, I'll Keep Your Booty out of My Bed"—speak volumes. On "Livin' a Lie," Carr is miserable because her husband supplies but doesn't satisfy; she's totally off the wall on "Bit Off More Than You Could Chew" and "Show Me No Mercy." Every song is delivered in Barbara's tough-as-nails style, and she's ably assisted by a crack production crew. *—Andrew Hamilton*

What a Woman Wants / May 11, 1999 / Ecko ✦✦✦

James Carr

b. Jun. 13, 1942, Coahoma County, MS, **d.** Jan. 7, 2001
Sax (Tenor), Vocals / Soul, Deep Soul, Southern Soul, Country-Soul
One of the greatest pure vocalists that deep Southern soul ever produced, James Carr is often mentioned in the same breath as Otis Redding, Percy Sledge, and Aretha Franklin in terms of the wrenching emotional power in his delivery. Or at least he is by hardcore soul aficionados; despite producing several classic R&B singles and some of the most intense country-soul ever waxed, Carr never achieved the pop crossover success that could have made him a household name, and his material wasn't always as distinctive as that of Stax artists like Redding or Sam & Dave. Ultimately, though, Carr's greatest obstacle was himself: he was plagued for much of his life by severe depression that made pursuit of a career—or, for that matter, even single recording sessions—extraordinarily difficult, and derailed his occasional comeback attempts.

James Carr was born June 13, 1942, in Coahoma County, MS, near Clarksdale; his father, a minister, moved the family to Memphis when Carr was very young. Carr began singing in church at age nine, and performed with several area gospel groups in his teenage years, including the Harmony Echoes (though not, as legend had it, the Soul Stirrers). Both Carr and Echoes manager Roosevelt Jamison had been harboring ambitions for careers in secular music, and the two began looking for a solo deal for Carr in 1963. Stax turned him down, but in late 1964 he caught on with Goldwax, a Memphis label started by Quinton Claunch (who'd earlier co-founded Hi Records) that, in its early days, also featured O.V. Wright (with whom Carr had sung in the Redemption Harmonizers). Over the next couple of years, Carr cut several singles that ranged from Motown-ish pop to soul-blues, searching for the best stylistic match for his richly expressive baritone.

Carr finally hit in 1966 with the country-soul ballad "You Got My Mind Messed Up," a Top Ten R&B hit that earned him comparisons to Otis Redding. It kicked off the prime period of Carr's recording career, and among his next few singles was his clear-cut masterpiece "Dark End of the Street." Given a tortuously intense performance by Carr, "Dark End of the Street" was a bleak tale of adultery that marked the first songwriting collaboration between Dan Penn & Chips Moman; although the song was recorded by the likes of Aretha Franklin, Clarence Carter, Linda Ronstadt, and the Flying Burrito Brothers, Carr's original version still stands as definitive. Featuring other hit singles like the Redding-esque "Love Attack" and the exquisite "Pouring Water on a Drowning Man," Carr's 1966 debut LP *You Got My Mind Messed Up* is also considered a classic by many Southern soul collectors.

Despite Carr's first flush of success on the R&B charts over 1966-1967, things were not looking up. Carr signed on with Phil Walden, Otis Redding's manager, in 1966, but without Roosevelt Jamison around (he'd served as Carr's caretaker just as much as his manager), Carr found himself unable to deal with the stress of touring; he frequently wandered off alone and got lost. By 1968, his mental state had deteriorated greatly, making even recording sessions a challenge. He was able to complete a second LP, 1968's *A Man Needs a Woman*, but in Muscle Shoals for his last Goldwax session in 1969, he simply sat at the microphone and stared into space, singing only one song (the Bee Gees' "To Love Somebody"). Not long afterward, Goldwax went bankrupt; wary of the singer's instability, Capitol rescinded an offer to buy out his contract, and although Carr signed with Atlantic, he released only one single in 1971.

In 1977, Carr released one single on the small River City label, which was run by Roosevelt Jamison. Two years later, he undertook a tour of Japan that started off well; however, at the Tokyo gig, Carr—apparently having taken too many anti-depressants—stood motionless at the microphone as though in a hypnotic trance. He returned to Memphis, where he lived with his sister (in between institutionalizations), and spent much of the '80s barely conscious of the world around him. With medication, his condition improved to the point where Jamison and Quinton Claunch cut an album with him in 1991 for a revived Goldwax. The record, *Take Me to the Limit*, received mixed reviews, although its very existence was an achievement in itself. Carr was even able to return to the road, touring the blues circuits in America and Europe. In 1994, he released another album on Claunch's new Soultrax label, titled *Soul Survivor*. Unfortunately, Carr was soon diagnosed with lung cancer, and spent several years battling the disease before finally succumbing on January 7, 2001. *—Steve Huey*

☆ **You Got My Mind Messed Up** / 1966 / Vivid Sound ✦✦✦✦✦
If ever there was a soul singer who rivaled Otis Redding's raw, deep emotional sensuality, it was James Carr, and the proof is in the pudding with *You Got My Mind Messed Up*. Carr was one of the last country-soul singers to approach any chart given to him as if it was a gift from God. Carr was Redding's rival in every respect if for no other reason than the release of this, his debut album recorded in 1966. The 12 songs here, many of them covered by other artists, are all soul classics merely by their having been sung and recorded by Carr. Among them is the Baker/McCormick smash "Pouring Water on a Drowning Man," George Jackson's "Coming Back to Me Baby," a handful of tracks by O.B. McLinton, including "Forgetting You" and the title track, and the Chips Moman/Dan Penn hit "Dark End of the Street." And while it's true that few have ever done bad versions of the song because of the phenomenal writing, there is only one definitive version, and that one belongs to Carr. In his version he sings from the territory of a heart that is already broken but enslaved both to his regret and his desire. This is a love so pure it can only have been illicit. When he gets to the beginning of the second verse, and intones "I know time is gonna take its toll," he's already at the end of his rope, he knows that desire that burns like this can only bring about ruin and disaster, and it is precisely since it cannot be avoided that his repentance is perhaps accepted by the powers that would try him and judge him. He holds the arrangement at bay, and unlike some versions, Carr keeps his composure, making it a true song of regret, remorse, and a love so forbidden yet so faithful that it is worth risking not only disgrace and destruction for, but also hell itself. As the guitar cascades down the fretboard staccato, he can see the dark end of the street and holds it as close to his heart as a sacred and secret memory. By the album's end with the title track, listeners hear the totality of the force of Memphis soul. With Steve Cropper's guitar filling the space in the background, Carr offers a chilling portrait of what would happen to him in the future. Again pleading with the beloved in a tone reminiscent of a church-singer hell, he's in the church of love. He pleads, admonishes, begs, and finally confirms that the end of this love is his insanity, which was a chilling prophecy given what happened to Carr some years later. This is one of *the* Memphis soul records of the mid-'60s, full of rough-hewn grace, passion, tenderness, and danger. A masterpiece. *—Thom Jurek*

A Man Needs a Woman / 1968 / Vivid Sound ✦✦✦✦✦
Along with his other original Goldwax LP, *You Got My Mind Messed Up*, James Carr's *Man Needs a Woman* represents one of the high watermarks of Southern soul music. And beyond his tonal resemblance to Otis Redding, Carr was as distinct a voice as the genre

ever produced. Compilations on both Kent (*Complete Goldwax Singles*) and Razor & Tie (*The Essential James Carr*) are certainly good places to start, but this LP might be even a better introductory title, especially considering the likelihood one will want to obtain all of Carr's prime late-'60s work. Whether Carr revels in the uptempo soul of "I'm a Fool for Your" or stops the presses on sanctified slow-burners like "You've Got My Mind Messed Up" and the Dan Penn & Chips Moman-penned classic "Dark End of the Street," the intensity never falters. *—Stephen Cook*

Take Me to the Limit / 1991 / Goldwax ♦♦♦

James Carr's comeback, on a resurrected Goldwax label. It doesn't quite live up to his '60s stuff—maybe nothing could—but it is good, contemporary Southern soul in the classic vein, and it's great to have him back. *—Christine Ohlman*

Soul Survivor / May 24, 1994 / Ace ♦♦♦♦

Looking back over ten years since it was released, James Carr's *Soul Survivor* seems like an unjustly overlooked recording. While it's true that it isn't one of his Goldwax masterpieces, it is nonetheless a hell of a record. For purists who need either a Muscle Shoals or Stax/Volt rhythm section to make it authentic, the slicker 1990s production elements will seem like a travesty. For those who understand that music needs to evolve to be essentially itself, this recording will feel like seeing a lily bloom in the desert. The bottom line is that this is still deep soul music; *Soul Survivor* transcends time, arrangements, instrumentation, and click tracks; it triumphs over virtually everything else in the neighborhood—from the 1990s to the present—and rises above it all to become a work of art in and of itself because James Carr is in phenomenal shape. The title track is worth the price of admission alone in that it tells Carr's own story: the tales of terror and mental and physical illness and the long bouts of bad luck touched by brief moments of victory followed by more loss. Through it all, his ability to deliver the song remains, untouched by time or circumstance. And if that isn't enough, try skipping to track three, "Put Love First," with its deep, heart-worn message and amazing backing choruses by Brown & Brown, where the saxophones come from deep in the pocket and wind around Carr's baritone and hold it fast to a lyric that is as affirming as it is wrenching. To tell about the rest is superfluous; this record is a necessary addition to many modern soul collections and to any library with Carr's work in it. Pick up the CD reissue of *You Got My Mind Messed Up* and then go for this, play 'em back to back, you won't be sorry. *—Thom Jurek*

★ **The Essential James Carr** / Feb. 21, 1995 / Razor & Tie ♦♦♦♦♦

When the soul era of the mid-'60s was in full bloom, for a period of three years James Carr was the maker of some of its mightiest music. His warm, soulful voice could make the reading of virtually anything he touched (even his version here of the Bee Gees' "To Love Somebody") a transcendent event. He is also the mystery man of the genre, unlettered and imbued with an almost childlike innocence, disappearing for a decade after these recordings were made with charges of mental instability cropping up whenever his name is mentioned. But music this special doesn't come without a price and certainly Carr paid that price, not unlike the gospel singers who influenced him who sometimes sang themselves to death right on-stage. But the music will always win out, because personal problems aside, the music James Carr made is as deep as Southern soul music gets, on an equal par with the best of a Sam Cooke or an Otis Redding. Tracks like "You've Got My Mind Messed Up," "Pouring Water on a Drowning Man" and his masterpiece, "The Dark End of the Street" are all justifiable classics of the genre, and this 20-track collection is where you go to get the big picture on an artist who deserves a much wider hearing. *—Cub Koda*

Complete Goldwax Singles / Oct. 9, 2001 / Kent ♦♦♦♦♦

All 28 songs from Carr's 1964-1970 Goldwax singles are here, which is enough to make it a fair bid for a good best-of compilation, although it doesn't have everything he recorded. About half of the songs on this British import are not on the most well-known American CD compilation of Carr's work, *The Essential James Carr*, and those tracks are consistent with the level of his other Goldwax recordings, although they don't include anything on the level of "The Dark End of the Street" or "Pouring Water on a Drowning Man." This disc is particularly valuable for filling in some of his earliest 1964-1966 sides, which have a very slightly poppier and more uptempo bent than his most esteemed songs. "That's What I Want to Know"'s groove is pretty Motown-ish, for instance, while "I Can't Make It" and "Only Fools Run Away" have Marvelettes-like chirping in the background. The 1970 funk update of "Row, Row Your Boat" isn't much to cheer about, though. There are plenty who will argue the point, but this doesn't quite live up to Carr's billing as the greatest '60s deep soul singer; Otis Redding (who Carr resembles in some respects) was better, and others had better and more imaginative material. It's good, certainly, and recommended to fans of artists like Redding who are looking for similar stuff that doesn't get played on the radio anymore. *—Richie Unterberger*

★ **You Got My Mind Messed Up [Bonus Tracks]** / Aug. 20, 2002 / Kent ♦♦♦♦♦

This CD reissue of Carr's first album, 1967's *You Got My Mind Messed Up*, doubles the length of that LP with no less than 12 bonus tracks, all of them rare and unreleased. *You Got My Mind Messed Up* is a fine '60s Memphis soul album, even if, in the manner of many LPs of the time, it's largely built around previously released singles. Indeed, ten of the 12 songs drawn from the original *You Got My Mind Messed Up* LP also show up on Carr's Ace compilation *The Complete Goldwax Singles*, though there is a difference in that eight of those ten songs are presented on this CD in new stereo mixes, where *The Complete Goldwax Singles* used the original mono masters. (If you're keeping a scorecard on such matters, the only songs on the *You Got My Mind Messed Up* reissue *not* to benefit from new stereo mixes are "Coming Back to Me Baby," "She's Better Than You," and the LP-only cut "I Don't Want to Be Hurt Anymore.") "Pouring Water on a Drowning Man," "Coming Back to Me Baby," "You Got My Mind Messed Up," and naturally "The Dark End of the Street" are the hits that will be the most familiar items on the disc, though the other songs taken from the original LP are pretty sturdy Southern deep soul as well and varied to include other kinds of material than the tortured ballads for which Carr's most known. Hardcore fans will be most interested, naturally, in the dozen bonus cuts, four of them previously unreleased, the others drawn from obscure reissue LPs and CDs. In the absence of firm dates, the compilers opted to try to guess which of these rarities date from the earlier part of Carr's Goldwax career and split off the earlier half for this compilation, saving the rest for a subsequent CD reissue of Carr's lone other Goldwax LP, *A Man Needs a Woman*. These additional tracks, unsurprisingly, aren't up to the level of the cuts from the original *You Got My Mind Messed Up* LP. But they're still respectable outings worth a listen, sometimes a little more explicitly influenced by (or at least similar to) Otis Redding, as on the cover of "These Arms of Mine" and the uptempo "There Goes My Used to Be," though the incomplete version of "Sock It to Me—Baby!" is atypical and not suited to Carr's chief strengths. The four previously unreleased cuts include a cover of the Rascals' "Love Is a Beautiful Thing," as well as alternate vocal versions of "Life Turned Her That Way" and "A Losing Game." *—Richie Unterberger*

Sister Wynona Carr

b. Aug. 23, 1924, Cleveland, OH, **d.** May 12, 1976, Cleveland, OH

Vocals / Black Gospel, Traditional Gospel, Jump Blues, R&B

Though largely unrecognized during her own lifetime, singer and composer Sister Wynona Carr was among the truly pioneering artists of gospel's golden era; while her music—sophisticated and sensual, distinguished by lyrics of rare metaphorical depth and a progressive sound drawing heavily on jazz and blues—was simply too radical for contemporary listeners, in hindsight she stands as one of the great innovators of her day. In early 1949 Carr traveled to Los Angeles to record her first Specialty label session; her debut 78, pairing the swinging "Each Day" with the torch-like ballad "Lord Jesus," served as an immediate indication of her versatility. Her next studio date was a revolutionary session which yielded "I'm a Pilgrim Traveler"—a reworking of the blues standard "St. James Infirmary"—as well as "I Heard the News (Jesus Is Coming Again)," which updated the 1948 secular hit "Good Rockin' Tonight." Other material, like the Carr original "Our Father," suggested a strong jazz influence; however, while all of the tracks recorded during the session promised to push the singer into new stylistic directions, Specialty apparently felt the songs were all too daring, and none of them were released.

Despite all of the frustration and setbacks, Carr forged on; she toured relentlessly, but did not go back into the studio until mid-1952. With "The Ball Game," a vividly metaphorical tale of a showdown between Jesus and Satan, she finally scored a major gospel hit, yet her career continued to flounder—another two years passed prior to her next session. Although she recorded rarely, Carr nevertheless remained a highly prolific songwriter, composing poetic, topical material often inspired by headlines of the day; she cut dozens of demos for Specialty, and ironically enough earned more money from sales of her sheet music than from her actual recordings. *—Jason Ankeny*

Jump Jack Jump! / 1955 / Specialty ♦♦♦♦♦

This 24-track set covers Carr's R&B tunes, with many unissued but fine tunes such as "If These Walls Could Speak," "Finders Keepers," and "Weather Man" finally getting out of the vault. The CD also includes her trademark upbeat, sassy songs, "Jump Jack Jump," "Boppity Bop (Boogity Boop)," "Ding Dong Daddy" and "Nursery Rhyme Rock." Thematic variety wasn't her label's strong suit when it came to material, and they might have done better with more numbers like "Please Mr. Jailer" and "It's Raining Outside" and a few less boogies and jump pieces. *—Ron Wynn*

★ **Dragnet for Jesus** / 1992 / Specialty ♦♦♦♦♦

A must for every fan of soul gospel, *Dragnet for Jesus* compiles all of the gospel songs—many (previously) unreleased—that Wynona Carr recorded for the Specialty label. Spanning 1949 to 1954, are many of Carr's original compositions including "I'm a Pilgrim Traveler" and "Nobody but Jesus," as well as her efforts at incorporating pop culture into God's message with the sports-themed "15 Rounds for Jesus" and her most-recognized song, "The Ball Game." The title track is based around a popular TV show of the time, *Dragnet*, opening with a detective office scene. But don't imagine that Carr was making light of, or trying to secularize, the message of salvation. One listen to her earnest, soulful voice and there's no doubt that the woman's heart was in it. Imagine the smoke-and-scotch hoarse edge of Janis Joplin's voice, pour Aretha Franklin's soulful inflections all over it, and you're close to the powerful delivery of Wynona Carr. Carr was, in fact, the gospel choir director of Rev. C. L. Franklin's church (Aretha's father) when Aretha was young. Most of the song's feature a quartet of piano, bass, drums, and either organ or guitar, with Carr usually on the piano. At the end of the disc is a bonus of two demos and a live recording of her leading the previously mentioned church choir in a stunning, hair-raising arrangement of "Our Father." With her out-of-this-world sultry voice, Carr incorporated blues and jazz elements and popular themes, yet she never really took off with the gospel audiences. Regardless, she remains one of the leading ladies of gospel. *—Joslyn Layne*

Paul Carrack

b. Apr. 22, 1951, Sheffield, Yorkshire, England

Vocals, Keyboards, Piano / Blue-Eyed Soul, Pop/Rock, Soft Rock, Adult Contemporary

Paul Carrack was pop music's ultimate journeyman. A vocalist and keyboardist who enjoyed considerable success over the course of his lengthy career while in the service of bands ranging from Ace to Squeeze to Mike + the Mechanics, his finest work often came at the expense of his own identity as a performer; indeed, of the many big hits on which the unassuming singer was prominently featured, only one, 1987's "Don't Shed a Tear," bore his own name. He first hit the charts after writing and singing Ace's debut single "How Long," a number-three hit in the U.S. during 1975. After the group disbanded in 1977, Carrack resurfaced in Roxy Music before releasing his solo debut, 1980's *Nightbird*. He next joined Squeeze, assuming lead vocal duties on the hit "Tempted." Once again, he attempted to forge a solo career with the 1982 LP *Suburban Voodoo*, and cracked the U.S. Top 40 with "I Need You." In 1985 he joined Genesis' Mike Rutherford in his side project Mike + the Mechanics, singing on the hits "Silent Running" and "All I Need Is a Miracle." Subsequently, his third solo album *One Good Reason* proved to be by far his most popular effort to date, with the single "Don't Shed a Tear" reaching the Top Ten. After his 1989 solo LP *Groove Approved*, Carrack split time between Mike + the Mechanics and Squeeze during the '90s. The solo album *Blue Views* appeared in 1996, followed in 1997 by *Beautiful World*. *—Jason Ankeny*

Suburban Voodoo / Aug. 1982 / Epic ✦✦✦
With *Suburban Voodoo*, Paul Carrack re-launched his solo career following a successful stint with Squeeze that produced a hit with his lead vocal on "Tempted." By this point, Carrack was playing with Nick Lowe, who produced *Suburban Voodoo*, and the album sounds very much like a Lowe album with Carrack singing. That's all to the good, though, since Carrack's supple voice is well-suited to Lowe's updated '60s rock & roll style. Carrack scored his first solo Top 40 hit with "I Need You," but that was one of the slighter tracks on an unusually tuneful album. *—William Ruhlmann*

One Good Reason / Nov. 1987 / Chrysalis ✦✦

Groove Approved / Oct. 1989 / Chrysalis ✦✦✦
After pulling four singles off of 1987's *One Good Reason*, Paul Carrack looked to be on the verge of finally establishing himself as a solo star. Instead, he stumbled with the follow-up, *Groove Approved*, a solid, workman-like collection that featured only one Top 40 number in "I Live by the Groove." One suspects that this had less to do with the album's real commercial potential than with upheavals in the record company, which was being sold by its founders to EMI during this period. Yet, afterward, Carrack went back to working with Squeeze and Mike + the Mechanics, putting his solo career on hold. *—William Ruhlmann*

● **Twenty-One Good Reasons: The Paul Carrack Collection** / Jan. 25, 1994 / Chrysalis ✦✦✦✦✦
A nifty idea for a compilation, *Twenty-One Good Reasons: The Paul Carrack Collection* gathers not only Carrack's solo hits, but all the major songs by other artists on which he sang lead: Ace's Top Five smash "How Long," Squeeze's new wave classic "Tempted," Mike + the Mechanics' "Silent Running" and the number one ballad "The Living Years," and two duets with country singer Carlene Carter from her 1981 album *Blue Nun*. As such, it's the definitive overview of Carrack's career. If you're a somewhat anonymous journeyman, you don't stick around as long as Carrack has, or participate in so many different projects, without demonstrating your versatility. Carrack shows himself to be comfortable with bright, bouncy pop, post-new wave roots rock, smooth adult contemporary, and sentimental ballads. But his true forte is the sort of blue-eyed soul that became popular in the post-Hall & Oates era. His clear, soulful pipes are already in evidence on the four selections culled from his tenure with Ace, which bridges into the Squeeze and Carter songs, and then into 12 selections culled from his solo albums. There are a couple of fine Nick Lowe co-writes in "I Live on a Battlefield" and the early hit "I Need You," plus a fine cover of Jackie DeShannon's folk-rock classic "When You Walk in the Room." The high point is Carrack's terrific 1988 Top Ten hit "Don't Shed a Tear," a catchy, modern blue-eyed soul track that fit comfortably into Top 40, adult contemporary, *and* mainstream rock radio, and even landed him some MTV airplay. Even if Carrack's production is far more synthetic than one usually associates with the term "soul," he proves himself quite a solid stylist over the course of this surprisingly ingratiating collection. *—Steve Huey*

Carter Brothers

Group / Electric Blues, Soul, Soul-Blues
This electric blues act with a soul bent recorded for Jewel Records, among other labels. Roman Carter (lead vocals, bass), Albert Carter (guitar), and Jerry Carter (vocals, piano) came from Garland, AL, and began recording in 1964 for producer/songwriter Duke Coleman's local label. Stan Lewis' Jewel Records licensed a pair of their singles, of which "Southern Country Boy" got to number 21 on the R&B charts nationally. They never cut an album, but before splitting up in 1967 (when Albert and Jerry Carter were said to have been drafted) the trio recorded more than a dozen single sides, which might make a great album someday. Lead singer Roman Carter, who also cut solo singles for Jewel, endured as a solo performer over the next 30 years and was given an award as Best Male Blues Vocalist at the Fifth Annual Real Blues Awards, sponsored by *Real Blues Magazine* in 1999. *—Bruce Eder*

● **Blues on Tour: 1965–1969** / Jun. 26, 2002 / WestSide ✦✦✦✦
The Carter Brothers (Roman, Albert, and Jerry) played a stripped-down, primitive, blues-infused brand of soul. Or is that a soul-infused brand of blues? They certainly straddled the line between blues and soul, and made some rough-and-ready singles for the Jewel label in the mid-'60s. All seven of them are included on this set, plus 15 previously unreleased tracks and seven alternate takes. Some of the highlights are the wild and rollicking "Do the Flo Show"; the soul-strutting "I Don't Care," which features some truly wonderful bad guitar playing; the funky "What You Say Big Mama"; and the Stax-styled "Anything for You Baby." The unreleased tracks are all just as good as the singles that actually came out, in some cases better. The alternate tracks aren't that much different than the released takes to make including them anything special. If you are a fan of soul-blues or blues-soul, the Carter Brothers are definitely worth investigating, and this disc gives you all they've got. *—Tim Sendra*

Clarence Carter

b. Jan. 14, 1936, Montgomery, AL
Vocals, Guitar, Keyboards / Deep Soul, Southern Soul, Soul
A blind soul singer whose numerous hits of the late '60s and early '70s epitomized the Muscle Shoals R&B sound, Carter hit the big time with his Atlantic single "Patches" (1970) and won a lasting place in the annals of Southern soul with others like "Slip Away" and "Too Weak to Fight." In 1977, Carter broke out of a dry spell with the Venture album *Let's Burn*, featuring a track called "Workin' (On a Love Building)," which set the theme for much of what was to follow: robust, lascivious lovemaking boasts. More recent tracks such as his salacious reworking of Tampa Red's "Love Me With a Feeling" and the jukebox favorite "Strokin'" (too risqué for some radio stations) further solidified the carnal Carter image. Still primarily a soul/R&B singer, Carter has incorporated more hard blues elements in his music recently than in the Muscle Shoals days, despite his new and unblues-minded penchant for playing and programming all the instruments on his albums. *—Jim O'Neal*

This Is Clarence Carter / 1968 / Atlantic ✦✦✦✦✦
Here is fine country-soul, blues, and humorous/novelty tracks by Clarence Carter, then at his peak both artistically and musically. He didn't score any big hits from this album, but played with the exuberance and earthy charisma that marked his biggest Atlantic hits. *—Ron Wynn*

The Dynamic Clarence Carter / 1969 / Atlantic ✦✦✦✦✦
Clarence Carter was churning out classic Southern soul in the late '60s. Everything—from soap opera-ish tales of deprivation to sexually suggestive boasts, country-soul ballads, and uptempo wailers—clicked. This isn't so much an album as a string of great singles, all of them sung with fire, conviction, and passion. *—Ron Wynn*

Testifyin' / 1969 / Atlantic ✦✦✦

Patches / 1970 / Atlantic ✦✦✦

Real / 1974 / ABC ✦✦✦

Let's Burn / 1977 / Venture ✦✦✦
This features fine Southern soul, light blues, and humorous, bawdy cuts from Clarence Carter. The single "Working on a Love Building" got some national attention, as did the title cut. The production was minimal, but Carter's gritty, earnest vocals were consistently effective. *—Ron Wynn*

Mr. Clarence Carter in Person / 1981 / Venture ✦✦✦

Messin' With My Mind / 1985 / Ichiban ✦✦

Touch of Blues / Dec. 1989 / Ichiban ✦✦✦✦
Not as blues-oriented as some might think, *Touch of Blues* focus primarily on the thing Clarence Carter had been known for since the 1960s: earthy, unpretentious Southern-style soul music. To be sure, the CD does contain more 12-bar blues material than Carter usually embraced, including "It's a Man Down There" and heartfelt versions of T-Bone Walker's "Stormy Monday" and B.B. King's "Rock Me Baby." But R&B is dominant, and Carter's followers (a great many of them in the South) were quite receptive to such good-humored, lighthearted soul as "Why Do I Stay Here (And Take This Shit from You)" and the risque "Kiss You All Over." One medium that wasn't at all receptive to *Touch of Blues* was urban contemporary radio, which has pretty much ignored Carter's Ichiban recordings. But thankfully, Carter has enough of a following to do okay without urban radio's support. *—Alex Henderson*

Between a Rock and a Hard Place / 1990 / Ichiban ✦✦✦
Clarence Carter entered the 1990s sounding very much like he had in the 1960s. While the O'Jays, Gladys Knight and other soul survivors had turned to urban contemporary songs in the '80s, Carter refused to change his style. Though *Between a Rock and a Hard Place* and other albums he's done for Ichiban Records have their share of keyboards and synthesizers, there's no mistaking the fact that the Montgomery, Alabama native's forte was still Southern-style soul music. Though the album isn't quite on a par with *Touch of Blues*, a 54-year-old Carter demonstrates that his powers hadn't decreased on down-home offerings like "Pickin' Em Up, Layin' Em Down," "If You See My Baby" and the humorous "Things Ain't like They Used to Be." A remake of Carter's '60s hit "Too Weak to Fight" pales in comparison to the original version, but gratefully, this CD has more strengths than weaknesses. *—Alex Henderson*

The Dr.'s Greatest Prescriptions: The Best of Clarence Carter / 1992 / Ichiban ✦✦✦✦
As long as Clarence Carter has been recording first-class soul music, it isn't surprising that more than one compilation is titled *The Best of Clarence Carter*. This particular compilation spotlights his work for Ichiban Records, a small Atlanta-based label that has also recorded Curtis Mayfield, the Chi-Lites, Eddie Floyd and quite a few other soul veterans. One of Ichiban's best selling artists, Carter has pretty much rejected high-tech urban contemporary sounds and stuck with the type of earthy Southern soul that's been his forte since the 1960s. In fact, this CD underscores the fact that his Ichiban output is almost as strong as his classic Atlantic recordings. The best known track here is Carter's risque hit "Strokin'," but he's equally adept at everything from the smooth "I Was in the Neighborhood" to the good-natured "Kiss You All Over" to the blues smoker "Love Me with a Feeling." Most of Carter's Ichiban discs are well worth hearing, but for those unfamiliar with his work for that label, this collection can serve as an engaging introduction. *—Alex Henderson*

● **Snatching It Back** / 1992 / Rhino ✦✦✦✦✦
Among the great soul artists who recorded for Atlantic Records during the 1960s, Clarence Carter was one of the few who left the label at the peak of his fame; while he'd previously enjoyed a handful of minor hits, "Patches," his biggest crossover hit, broke in 1970, a year before Carter moved on to ABC, while Carter had his greatest latter-day success recording for Southern soul revival label Ichiban. *Snatching It Back* is a compilation that collects 21 classic sides from Carter's tenure at Atlantic, and by focusing strictly on his output for one label, this set misses the mark as a career retrospective (they could have at least tacked on Carter's lascivious jukebox classic "Strokin'" in the name of a more complete picture). But *Snatching It Back* does a superlative job of skimming the

cream of Carter's Atlantic sides, which for the most part do represent his strongest work, and Carter's passionate, room-filling vocals and clean, blues-flavored guitar figures shine on each song, from the sentimental tale of "Patches" and the lover's lament "Slip Away" to the sassy "Tell Daddy" and "Makin' Love (At the Dark End of the Street)," which amusingly predates his more provocative material for Ichiban. *Snatching It Back* is a few notches short of the definitive Clarence Carter collection, but you could hardly ask for a better summation of his Atlantic material. *—Mark Deming*

Loneliness & Temptation/A Heart Full of Song / 1996 / Edsel ✦✦✦

Patches/The Dynamic Clarence Carter / Jun. 6, 2000 / Collectables ✦✦✦✦

Mel Carter

b. Apr. 22, 1939, Cincinnati, OH

Vocals / Soul

Mel Carter was soul music at its most vanilla, if indeed he could be characterized as a soul singer at all. Although he did record for Sam Cooke's SAR label in the early '60s, by the time he reached his commercial peak with Imperial in the middle of the decade, he was specializing in middle-of-the-road pop ballads. These actually charted considerably higher on the easy listening charts than the pop ones, his biggest smash being the Top Ten pop hit "Hold Me, Thrill Me, Kiss Me" (1965), an update of a composition that predated the rock era. He had a couple of other Top 40 entries over the next year ("Band of Gold" and "(All of a Sudden) My Heart Sings"), as well as a few other big easy listening sellers, sounding at times like a more nervous and slightly uptempo Johnny Mathis. "Hold Me, Thrill Me, Kiss Me" is the song he'll be remembered for, enduring as an oft-played radio oldie for decades after its release. *—Richie Unterberger*

When a Boy Falls in Love / 1963 / Derby ✦✦✦✦

This rare album fetches at least $350 in mint condition. Its contents are the epitome of love songs, all eloquently performed by Mel Carter, Mr. Velvety Tenor. "After the Parting the Meeting is Sweeter," "Hold Me," "When I Fall in Love," and Sam Cooke's "When a Boy Falls in Love" are a few examples of the heartfelt romantic treats on the set. Wink Martindale—the perennial game show host—adds value to the LP with his liner notes. *—Andrew Hamilton*

● **The Best of Mel Carter** / Jun. 1996 / EMI ✦✦✦✦✦

At only ten songs and 24 minutes, this is a bit skimpy, but it does include his Imperial chart singles from the mid-'60s. "Hold Me, Thrill Me, Kiss Me" is the natural highlight, and one that may be best appreciated via its appearance on compilations. *—Richie Unterberger*

The Cascades

f. San Diego, CA

Group / Doo Wop

An intriguing vocal group from San Diego, the Cascades sang in a light, pop-oriented style, but managed a Top Ten R&B hit in 1963, "Rhythm of the Rain" on Valiant. It was written by guitarist/lead singer John Gummoe, who joined fellow vocalists Eddie Snyder, David Stevens, David Wilson, and David Zabo. They also became a major attraction in England and Australia. They followed "Rhythm of the Rain" with "Shy Girl" and "Last Leaf," but neither duplicated their earlier success. "My First Day Alone" flopped, and the group moved to RCA. But they never again scored a hit, despite recording for Charter, Liberty, Arwin, Smash, Probe, UNI, London, and Can Base. They continued until the early '70s. *—Ron Wynn*

● **The Very Best of the Cascades** / Oct. 20, 1998 / Taragon ✦✦✦✦✦

The Cascades began aboard a Navy ship in the early '60s, writing songs and cutting demos on cheap equipment. After pounding on some in Hollywood, they saw their first release on the tiny Valiant label in 1962, which is where this compilation of the group's best begins. Both sides of their debut disc, "There's a Reason" and "Second Chance," set the squeaky-clean tone of this retrospective. The Cascades were pure vanilla ice cream in their harmony approach; so much so that when they were recording their hit, "Rhythm of the Rain," at the Gold Star Studios, producer Phil Spector asked them if they were cutting a demo for Ricky Nelson! Although only "Shy Girl," "The Last Leaf," and "A Little Like Lovin'" made the charts, but all the group's best performances from their run at Valiant and later at RCA Victor are aboard in this solid little compilation. As an extra bonus, this 19-track collection also sports five previously unreleased masters from the RCA vaults recorded in 1963, a prime year for the group. For a supposed one-hit wonder, the Cascades had a lot of great music to show for their efforts nonetheless. *—Cub Koda*

Alvin Cash (Alvin Welch)

b. Feb. 15, 1939, St. Louis, MO, **d.** Nov. 21, 1999

Vocals / Soul, Funk

Alvin Cash was born Alvin Welch, February 15, 1939, in St. Louis, MO, to a large family. One of eight children, Alvin formed a song and dance group with three of his brothers, doing tap and soft shoe. He attended Summers High in St. Louis with future R&B luminaries Luther Ingram, Billy Davis (Fifth Dimension), and Anna Mae Bullock (Tina Turner).

In 1961, Alvin and three of his brothers moved to Chicago, IL, seeking a record deal, but had to dance for tips their first few years in the Windy City. Former Fortune and Motown artist/songwriter/producer Andre Williams, who worked for One-derful/Mar-V-Lus/M-Pac Records whenever he and Berry Gordy disagreed, caught the newly named Crawlers' act and invited them to the studio to chant over a dance track he'd written (with Verlie Rice) called "Twine Time." It was in the same format as Williams' 1957 hit "Bacon Fat," a funky instrumental augmented by chants and sayings, and was a take-off of the Five Du-Tones' "Woodbine Twine." "Twine Time" surprised everybody by zooming to number 14 on the pop chart in February 1965. On the label the artist was listed as Alvin Cash & the Crawlers, though it's unclear if his brothers participated in the recording; but his band, the Nightlighers, did.

The Nightlighters changed their name to the Crawlers and accompanied Alvin Cash on gigs, eventually changing again to the Registers. Cash abandoned his siblings after a few records and went solo. His post-"Twine" recordings never measured up commercially, though many were far better recordings; the most successful was "The Philly Freeze," which reached number 49. Subsequent releases—"The Barracuda," "Mr. Penquin," "Unwind the Twine," and "The Philly Freeze"—hit the R&B charts, but weren't pop successes. He recorded many tributes to pugilist Muhammad Ali, including an LP *Alvin Cash Does the Greatest Hits of Muhammad Ali.* Cash appeared in the Buddy Holly movie as a member of the Five Satins and in a few black action films including *Petey Wheatstraw* and *Black Jack.* The flamboyant dancer/entertainer, known in Chicago's blues clubs for his colorful lavender, pink, and yellow outfits, succumbed to stomach and ulcer problems on November 21, 1999. *—Andrew Hamilton*

● **Twine Time** / 196 / Ma-V-Lus ✦✦✦✦✦

Gritty, funky Andre Williams-produced grooves featuring Alvin Cash's slick/talk vocals exhorting you to throw down on "Shake a Tail Feather," his biggest hit "Twine Time," and its follow up "Barracuda." This debut LP is fleshed out with "Twine Time" revisited—"Do It One More Time," a clone: "Twine Awhile," and solid dance jams like "Hawk Eye Bump," "Burn Just a Hair," and "You Shot Me Through the Grease." *—Andrew Hamilton*

Cashmere

f. 1982

Group / Club/Dance, Urban, Dance-Pop, Soul, Hip-Hop

After being the featured tenor and falsetto lead in the R&B group Heaven & Earth, Dwight Dukes ventured out and started Cashmere, a dance- and club-oriented group with R&B roots. The group included keyboardist McKinley Horton, drummer Daryl Burgee, and fellow Heaven & Earth vocalist Keith Steward. Primarily focusing on the vocal talents of Dukes, Cashmere had four singles that surfaced on the R&B charts between 1983 and 1985. During the group's brief presence in the music industry, even though they recorded only three albums, there was personnel change on each album, with Dukes remaining at the forefront. *—Craig Lytle*

● **The Best of Cashmere** / Jun. 18, 1996 / Hot Productions ✦✦✦✦

Cashmere was one of the several '80s R&B groups who could deliver an extension of '70s smooth soul one moment and then turn around and carry the torch for disco with a programming-heavy club track. During the group's three-album career, they hit the *Billboard* charts a few times but never quite reached the heights of like-minded groups such as Imagination, Shalamar, and Midnight Star. Hot Productions' *The Best of Cashmere* includes those singles that charted—"Do It Anyway You Wanna," "Try Your Lovin'," "Can I," and "We Need Love"—and it also gathers nine other songs that wrap up pretty much all of the group's finest album moments. Energetic should've-been-hit-singles like "Fascination," "Keep Me Up," and "Someone Like You" round out the compilation and help make it more than a curiosity for die-hard '80s R&B fanatics. *—Andy Kellman*

The Casinos

f. 1958, Cincinnati, OH

Group / Beach, Doo Wop, Soft Rock

The Casinos were an anomaly when they reached the Top Ten in early 1967 with "Then You Can Tell Me Goodbye," a slow-dance smoocher with a swelling organ that was a throwback to the sound of the early '60s. So were the group themselves, both in their doo wop-flavored close-harmony sound and their well-groomed, conservative appearance. The music wasn't bad, though, with a romantic white soul groove that would fit well with the Southeastern beach music scene, although the Casinos were actually from Cincinnati. They recorded a bunch of other singles for Fraternity in the '60s, some in a similar group harmony mold, others in a more updated, upbeat soul-pop vein, but never approached the success of "Then You Can Tell Me Goodbye" again. *—Richie Unterberger*

● **The Best of the Casinos: Then You Can Tell Me Goodbye** / Mar. 11, 1997 / Varese ✦✦✦✦✦

Gene Hughes & the Casinos are best known for their lone hit, the enduring "Then You Can Tell Me Goodbye," but this 14-track compilation shows that the Cincinnati band had more to offer than just one well sung and arranged tune. Doo wop fans will be thrilled with the first two tracks: their first record from 1962, the impossibly rare "Do You Recall" (sung by original lead singer J.T. Sears and sounding like it was cut at least five years earlier) and "Too Good to Be True," which features the guitar work of Lonnie Mack. By the fourth entry, the first appearance of the original long mono version of "Then You Can Tell Me Goodbye," the set veers into mid-'60s lounge-soul, the sound that suited the band the best and which remained pretty well intact through two tracks cut in 1980, "Wisdom of a Fool" and "You Belong to Me." If you're looking to add the tune to your collection and you want a whole lot more in the same vein, this is the one to get. *—Cub Koda*

The Castelles

f. USA

Group / Doo Wop

The Castelles recorded little more than a dozen songs during their prime years of 1953-1955, yet they remain one of the best-loved vocal groups from Philadelphia for serious R&B collectors. Founded by George Grant (lead), Ronald Everett (bass), Anthony Octavius (first tenor), William Taylor (baritone), and Frank Vance (second tenor, guitar) in 1949, the group's members had grown up together in west Philadelphia during the mid-'40s. Their idols included acts like the Orioles, the Ink Spots, the Clovers, and the Four Buddies. When they first got together, however, they created a sound that had no parallel with any of those groups, highlighted by George Grant's exquisite high-tenor lead.

The group began singing together at the local YMCA, when the members were no more than 12 or 13 years old, and none of them thought of turning professional. Singing was a lark until Frank Vance wrote a song, "My Girl Awaits Me," inspired by the pop hit "Heavenly Father," and they made an amateur demo and played it back at a local record store. The owner of the record store, Herb Slotkin, and his helper, Jerry Ragavoy (later to play a major role as a writer and producer), heard the song and decided to record the Castelles.

They were signed to Slotkin's Grand Records in 1953, and cut their first sides on August 4 of that year, "My Girl Awaits Me" b/w "Sweetness," the former sung by Grant and the latter by Octavius. That first record sold 100,000 copies as a regional hit and made it to number six in Cashbox's listings for the Newark, NJ, market. It was also a major hit in Philadelphia, Washington, D.C., and Baltimore. Their second single, "The Silver Ring," rose to number ten on the group's hometown R&B chart, and three more singles followed. There were membership changes along the way, as William Taylor left to be replaced by Walt Miller, but the group kept selling records locally and throughout the Middle Atlantic states.

After the group's sixth and last release for Grand Records in late 1955 (a recording of "Heavenly Father," which brought their history full circle, as this was the song that had inspired "My Girl Awaits Me"), the group was signed to Atlantic Records. Their two singles for the company's Atco imprint in 1956 were failures, however, and the Castelles disbanded after Vance and Everett left. George Grant continued to perform and record occasionally in association with other groups, and in 1969 his career turned back to his roots when he became a member of one of the various lineups of the Ink Spots, one of the groups that inspired him as a boy.

The Castelles' 15 songs meld a sweet, romantic innocence with extraordinarily precise and elegant singing. Grant's vocals come across like those of a more mature and controlled (but equally beguiling) Frankie Lymon, and also prefigure the work of Smokey Robinson. They were not an a cappella group, despite all of that vocal talent, and their best sides feature some surprisingly gritty guitar, courtesy of Frank Vance, as well as chiming piano accompaniment and raw saxophone. Their later Grand singles include some novelty tunes that take a little getting used to, but most of their work is special and unique right to the end with "Heavenly Father," as fine a rendition of the song as it has ever received. *—Bruce Eder*

● **Sweetness** / Jan. 1, 1996 / Relic ✦✦✦✦✦
The 15 songs here are virtually all worthwhile listening, and not just for '50s R&B fanatics—if you like Smokey Robinson & the Miracles, this is also a disc worth owning. The originals, including "Sweetness" and "My Girl Awaits Me," are extraordinarily beautiful compositions and recordings, and even the covers of standards like "Over the Rainbow" are worthwhile. "Heavenly Father" is worth the price of the CD by itself, and Donn Fileti's notes answer lots of questions about the history of the group and its members. *—Bruce Eder*

The Jimmy Castor Bunch

b. Jun. 2, 1943, New York, NY
Vocals, Saxophone / Funk
A master of novelty/disco funk, saxophonist Jimmy Castor started as a doo wop singer in New York. He wrote and recorded "I Promise to Remember" for Wing With the Juniors in 1956, a group whose roster included Al Casey Jr., Orton Graves, and Johnny Williams. Castor replaced Frankie Lymon in the Teenagers in 1957 before switching to sax in 1960. He appeared on several soul-jazz and Afro-Latin sessions and had a solo hit with "Hey Leroy, Your Mama's Callin' You" on Smash in 1966. Castor also played sax on Dave "Baby" Cortez's hit "Rinky Dink."

He formed the Jimmy Castor Bunch in 1972 and signed with RCA. Their first release, *It's Just Begun*, launched Castor's next phase with the song "Troglodyte (Cave Man)." It was a Top Ten R&B and pop smash. Castor continued the trend in 1975 with "The Bertha Butt Boogie" and later recorded "E-Man Boogie," "King Kong," "Bom Bom," and "Amazon." The Castor band included keyboardist/trumpeter Gerry Thomas, bassist Doug Gibson, guitarist Harry Jensen, conga player Lenny Fridle Jr., and drummer Bobby Manigault. Thomas left to join the Fatback band. Castor recorded as a solo performer from 1976 until 1988. He had one of his bigger hits in many years with a 1988 revival of "Love Makes a Woman," which paired him with disco diva Joyce Sims. Castor had his own label, Long Distance, in the '80s. *—Ron Wynn*

Hey Leroy / 1967 / Smash ✦✦✦✦✦
Long before Jimmy Castor became a successful humorist and funkmeister, he scored a Latin hit with "Hey Leroy, Your Mama's Callin' You," a smoothly performed bit of samba with jazz touches by Castor. It was such a hit that he issued an entire album of similar tunes, none of which did anywhere near as well as the single, which cracked the R&B Top 20 (number 16) and pop Top 40 (number 31). *—Ron Wynn*

It's Just Begun / 1972 / RCA ✦✦✦
This 1972 outing set the tone for the Jimmy Castor Bunch's 1970s success through an effective and distinctive mix of funk, pop hooks, social commentary, and gonzo comedy. *It's Just Begun* also helped the group score a million-selling crossover hit single with "Troglodyte." This memorably whacked-out funk jam is built on an infectious fuzz-guitar hook and features Castor detailing the romantic adventures of a caveman who meets up with Bertha Butt, a comic character that would continue to appear on his albums for many years to come. The album also included a b-boy favorite in its title track, a salsa-inflected funk excursion whose breakbeats continued to be spun by DJs well into the 1980s. Beyond these favorites, the group knocks out a relentless stream of thick, funky grooves as Jimmy Castor tackles everything from morality ("You Better Be Good (Or the Devil Gon' Getcha)") to philosophy ("L.T.D.," which stands for life, truth, and death). To add variety, Castor also throws in "My Brightest Day," a sweet, horn-accented ballad, and "I Promise to Remember," an updated slice of doo wop that Castor originally penned for Frankie Lymon & the Teenagers. The album's all-things-to-all-people sense of ambition occasionally overwhelms the final product: for instance, "Creation," the dissonant orchestral instrumental that bookends the album, doesn't really have any reason to be there. Despite these quibbles, *It's Just Begun* is an important and influential release from a sadly underrated group and well worth a listen for anyone interested in the roots of 1970s funk. *—Donald A. Guarisco*

Phase Two / 1972 / RCA ✦✦✦
After scoring success on both the pop and R&B charts in 1972 with *It's Just Begun*, the Jimmy Castor Bunch knocked out another album in the same vein before the year ended. *Phase Two* adheres closely to the previous album's formula, right down to using an orchestral instrumental for its intro and epilogue. As a result, parts of it feel like a re-tread: the standout example of this problem is "Luther the Anthropoid (Ape Man)," which sports a nice groove but is a merely a thinly veiled rewrite of "Troglodyte." Despite some uninspired moments like this, *Phase Two* makes up for the problem with tight arrangements and an infectiously funky performance from the band. "Say Leroy (The Creature From the Black Lagoon Is Your Father)" mixes Latin rock with frenzied funk-rock breaks to create a punchy tune that gave the band another pop hit and "When?" is an effective, fuzz guitar-drenched trip through the woes of ghetto life. The most unusual and interesting of these cuts is "Tribute to Jimi: Purple Haze/Foxy Lady," a novel medley that layers the vocal melody and lyrics of "Foxy Lady" over the tune of "Purple Haze." The album also does well in its softer moments: "Paradise" is a pleasantly harmonized ballad and the band's saxophone-led instrumental take on "The First Time Ever I Saw Your Face" is quite pretty. Overall, *Phase Two* lacks the strong crossover appeal and original material that made *It's Just Begun* such a standout album, but it will definitely appeal to fans of that album. *—Donald A. Guarisco*

The Everything Man / 1973 / RCA ✦✦✦
A Junior Walker-style mix for *The Everything Man*, Jimmy Castor abandoned Bertha Butt and Luther & the Troglodytes for a smooth urban/adult contemporary album of seven instrumentals and four tunes with vocals. There are a couple of band originals mixed in with covers spanning the pop galaxy—written by Redbone's Lolly Vegas, Lou Reed, Stevie Wonder, Thom Bell, and David White of the obscure Crystal Mansion—that gives the group a chance to explore all sorts of melodic structure. Redbone's "Maggie" gets a wonderful instrumental take, and someone finally found a way to do a clean version of Lou Reed's "Walk on the Wild Side" without censoring the rock & roll animal—just leave all the lyrics off the disc. Castor has a good voice, and though "Heaven Kissed" and "Goodbye My Lover" are decent, it's the wailing sax on "Love Train" which makes more of an impact. There is a nice version of the Crystal Mansion near-hit, "The Thought of Loving You," an amazing song which even the Manhattan Transfer embraced. The Jimmy Castor Bunch's soulful arrangement, courtesy of Gerry Thomas, adds elegance, and Castor's vocal stays true to Dave White Tricker's innocence on the original. The funky title track works well, but the band lays back a bit too much, the emphasis going to Jimmy Castor's sax. Sometimes, "the bunch" frustrates because you know they are capable of exploding but opt for playing it safe. The result is a very good album of excellent songs which could have been much more if they had just taken a few risks. *—Joe Viglione*

Butt of Course / 1975 / Atco ✦✦✦
The Jimmy Castor Bunch weren't among the more consistent funk/soul bands of the '70s, but they were good for some goofy, wacky novelty items now and then. One of the goofiest and wackiest was 1974's "The Bertha Butt Boogie," which was essentially a sequel to 1972's "Troglodyte (Cave Man)" and had some laughs at the expense of people who lived in ancient times. For all its silliness, "The Bertha Butt Boogie" is quite infectious; it is also among the more successful tunes on this album. Like other Castor Bunch releases, *Butt of Course* is wildly uneven—which isn't to say that this funk/soul/disco LP from 1974 doesn't have its moments. "E-Man Boogie," with its strong Kool & the Gang influence, is almost as infectious as "The Bertha Butt Boogie" (although not as wacky). Nor is the funky "Potential" anything to be ashamed of. But some of the other tracks are downright embarrassing. "Hallucinations" is a lame attempt at psychedelic pop, while the syrupy ballad "One Precious Word" is a dreadful attempt to emulate the Stylistics. And the Castor Bunch's mostly instrumental, mildly jazzy covers of the Stylistics' "You Make Me Feel Brand New" and Elton John's "Daniel" are nothing more than elevator muzak—this is the sort of the fluff that Kenny G and Richard Elliott would end up playing in the '80s and '90s. Without a doubt, *Butt of Course* is very much a mixed bag. Those who have only a casual interest in the Castor Bunch's '70s output would do well to skip this erratic LP and look for a greatest-hits package; nonetheless, there are some die-hard Castor fans and soul collectors who will want to hear *Butt of Course* despite its flaws. *—Alex Henderson*

E Man Groovin' / 1976 / Atco ✦✦✦✦
The Jimmy Castor Bunch scored with a few novelty hits and sought to continue the trend with this well-rounded LP, but the trend had passed and this good production failed to reach its projected sales. The novelty special on this one, "Dracula," isn't up to the standards of past nonsensical efforts like "Leroy! Your Mama's Calling." This is unfortunate because the other jams, particularly the ballads and midtempo numbers, are marvelous executions of funk/jazz. A remake of the Spinners' "I Don't Want to Lose You" features a crying sax and emotive vocals; the midtempo numbers—"Space Age," "Mellow Groove," and "Everything Is Beautiful"—are creditable and instantly likable. Groovy stuff. *—Andrew Hamilton*

● **The Everything Man: The Best of the Jimmy Castor Bunch** / Nov. 21, 1995 / Rhino ✦✦✦✦✦
Some music is just so immediately full of the groove and desire to dance that anyone who doesn't or can't must be dead, if still breathing. Jimmy Castor is a master of same, and if the slightly overheated claims in the knowledgeable and appreciative liner notes for this excellent compilation making him second only to James Brown might be a bit much in cold print, the music is its own best argument for his quality. Starting with his great Latin/soul hit "Hey Leroy, Your Mama's Callin' You" and concluding with an item from

his doo wop days in the '50s, "I Promise to Remember," *Everything Man* covers whole eras of American popular music with style and skill. The two numbers that sealed his fame and reputation into the hip-hop era are unsurprisingly here: the Latin funk monster "It's Just Begun," with one of the deepest basslines in creation and a fantastic mid-song percussion breakdown, and "Troglodyte," with its freakish, wigged-out spoken word intro. Bertha Butt of the Butt Sisters makes her first legendary appearance here, while the snarling guitar and grunting bass perfectly match Castor's rasped, hilarious shaggy dog tale about caveman love. Those are just two highlights of a well-chosen and brilliantly mastered set, with many guest appearances from Bertha and Leroy both (the deep grunt of "Bertha Butt Boogie," "The Return of Leroy, Pt. 1," and so forth). Castor's penchant for bizarro covers is discussed but not included among the cuts—presumably all for the better, given selections like "You Light Up My Life"—but his sharp take on Redbone's "Maggie" does make the grade. Other great cuts include the vocal tradeoffs on "Potential" between Castor and his bandmembers, the monster stomp and shake of "Supersound," and the upbeat, salsa-tinged "Bom Bom." *—Ned Raggett*

● **16 Slabs of Funk** / Mar. 19, 2002 / RCA ✦✦✦✦✦
BMG Heritage's 2002 collection *16 Slabs of Funk* doesn't cover as much ground as Rhino's 1995 set *The Everything Man*, concentrating on his early '70s work for RCA Records. This means there are crucial tracks missing—no "Hey Leroy, Your Mama's Callin' You," no "Bertha Butt Boogie," no "Supersound" to mention the most obivious tunes missing in action (this isn't even counting a sampling of his earlier doo wop material tacked onto the Rhino set). So, this really isn't the first place to turn if you want to hear the Jimmy Castor Bunch, if you want all the best stuff on one disc. However, if you want to dig deeper into his funky prime, this is necessary, since it contains just three tracks from the Rhino comp, with the remaining 13 being wildly funny, wildly funky jams that may be silly, but for sheer enjoyment, it falls just below Parliament in its flamboyant goofiness. *—Stephen Thomas Erlewine*

The Cellos

f. 1955, New York, **db.** 1958

Group / Doo Wop, Novelty, R&B

The Cellos' singing was as smooth as the sound of their instrumental namesake. Formed at Charles Evans Hughes High School on West 18th Street in Manhattan, the Cellos were Alvin Williams (bass), Billy Montgomery (first tenor), Alton Campbell (ballad lead), Bobby Thomas (baritone), and Cliff Williams (second tenor); their inspirations were the Heartbeats, the Cleftones, the Harptones, and the Coasters. Alvin Williams wrote their original material, including a number called "Rang Tang Ding Dong (I'm the Japanese Sandman)" that so impressed the engineer on their first demo session, Lewis Merenstein (who later produced Thelonious Monk, Art Farmer, and Van Morrison), that he brought it to Apollo Records, which was owned by his uncle. The group got a contract from that demo, and had their first session in January of 1957.

"Rang Tang Ding Dong" b/w "You Took My Love" reached number 62 on the *Billboard* national chart during a ten-week run, a promising beginning; the song was covered by the likes of Chuck Miller ("House of Blue Lights") and Ray Stevens. This was a feat the group was never able to repeat. The Cellos were extremely versatile, capable of delivering soaring, dreamily ethereal harmony numbers ("You Took My Love") or scorching, funny novelty songs ("Juicy Crocodile") with equal aplomb. Few groups had their range, and even fewer an in-house songwriter of Williams' caliber; between them, they made some gorgeous and memorably funny doo wop and R&B records. But they never managed to connect nationally, despite their receiving the blessing of tastemaker Alan Freed and a featured spot at one of his Brooklyn Paramount shows.

Undaunted, their management got them booked onto national tours, and some of their records got decent airplay. The sales didn't follow suit, however, and by the end of 1958 the group had called it quits, although Alvin Williams remained in the business for a few more years. *—Bruce Eder*

The Best of the Cellos on Apollo / 198 / Relic ✦✦✦✦
The sound quality is a little shaky, but the material is so good that one can forgive slight deficiencies. There are fourteen songs here including an interrupted outtake (take 16, yet) of "Rang Tang Ding Dong," "Juicy Crocodile," an outtake of their final single, the hard-rocking "What the Matter for You," and a couple of other lost tracks, as well as the issued sides. *—Bruce Eder*

● **Rang Tang Ding Dong** / 1992 / Relic ✦✦✦✦✦
This is an excellent CD compilation of all their best Apollo sides, including unreleased material. It contains the title cut, plus "Juicy Crocodile," "The Be Bop Mouse," and "You Took My Love." *—Cub Koda*

Cerrone (Jean-Marc Cerrone)

b. 1952, Paris, France

Producer, Drums / Club/Dance, Disco, Euro-Dance, House

Jean-Marc Cerrone was one of the most influential disco producers in Europe during the 1970s and early '80s, eclipsed only by Giorgio Moroder. Born in Paris in 1952, he studied music as a child and won his first post as the orchestra leader at a Parisian club at the age of 18. After additional work with the French producer Barclay during the early '70s, he released his first solo album, *Love in C-Minor*, in 1976. The title track proved a massive European hit and worked its way into the American Top 40 as well. Although he only placed one more single in the U.S., Cerrone stayed popular on his native continent over the course of a career spanning a dozen albums. *—John Bush*

Love in C Minor / 1976 / Malligator ✦✦✦✦✦
Though it's barely half an hour long, Cerrone's album debut is a masterful sample of midtempo disco with an eye towards production prowess instead of chart potential. The full-length includes a 15-minute version of the hit title track, plus a cover of the old Los Bravos hit "Black Is Black." *—John Bush*

Cerrone's Paradise / 1977 / Barclay ✦✦✦✦✦
Over the years, the sophomore curse has plagued many talented artists, who showed considerable promise on their debut albums but failed to make good on that promise when they recorded their second albums. Gratefully, that wasn't a problem for Cerrone, whose sophomore album, *Cerrone's Paradise*, only strengthened his reputation in the Euro-disco field. This 1977 outing is similar to Cerrone's 1976 debut, *Love in C Minor*, but without sounding like musical recycling. On the original LP version of this album, the 16-minute title song took up all of side one, just as *Love in C Minor*'s first side was devoted entirely to its title song. But "Cerrone's Paradise" is a fine orchestral Euro-disco work in its own right, and the slick but funky piece is far from a carbon copy of "Love in C Minor." Euro-disco fans also found a lot to admire about "Take Me" and "Time for Love," the songs that Cerrone co-wrote for side two of the original *Cerrone's Paradise* LP. While the exuberant "Take Me" was a club favorite, "Time for Love" is an unexpected quiet storm/R&B slow jam. Unexpected because the fans Cerrone acquired with *Love in C Minor* assumed that everything on his second album would be aimed at the dancefloor. Today, Cerrone's Euro-disco arrangements sound extremely dated, after only a few notes, one can easily tell that *Cerrone's Paradise* was recorded in the late '70s. But then, dated isn't necessarily a bad thing, if you hold a particular era in high regard, dated can actually be a good thing. And for those who hold the disco era in high regard, *Cerrone's Paradise* is among the classics of its time. *—Alex Henderson*

● **Cerrone 3: Supernature** / 1977 / Malligator ✦✦✦✦✦
Recorded during the summer of 1977, the ambitious *Supernature* was a surprising departure from Cerrone's two previous albums, *Love in C Minor* and *Cerrone's Paradise*. Those who expected the Parisian producer/composer/drummer to come up with another happy, sexy party record had a major surprise when they discovered that Cerrone's third album is a moody, conceptual effort that could be described as the Euro-disco equivalent of a horror or science fiction movie. But Cerrone doesn't go for pure shock value, and the lyrics are never gruesome or graphic. *Supernature*, although entertaining, has a social conscience. If the album has a dominant theme, it's that scientists should proceed with caution if they are going to experiment and mess around with nature. This isn't to say that *Supernature* is consistently dark and depressing; "Love Is Here" and "Love Is the Answer" are fairly optimistic and assert that negativity doesn't have to prevail. Some Cerrone fans applauded him for providing such a risk-taking album, while others longed for the totally escapist Cerrone of *Love in C Minor* and *Cerrone's Paradise*. But *Supernature* fared well in Europe, and the excellent album explodes the myth that Euro-disco cannot be challenging. *—Alex Henderson*

Cerrone IV: The Golden Touch / 1978 / Barclay ✦✦✦✦
When Cerrone started recording his fourth album, *The Golden Touch*, fans were anxious to see what he would come up with. Would the project be as conceptual and ambitious as *Supernature*, or would Cerrone return to the happy, completely escapist party vibe of *Love in C Minor* and *Cerrone's Paradise*? Without question, *Supernature* was a tough act to follow, and Cerrone knew better than to try to turn his fourth album into *Supernature: Part II*. This excellent 1978 release is as strong as *Supernature*, although quite different. A departure from *Supernature*'s moody horror/sci-fi ambiance, *The Golden Touch* is the lush Euro-disco album that fans of *Love in C Minor* and *Cerrone's Paradise* were hoping for—but with a twist. The lyrics aren't entirely escapist; "Je Suis Music" addresses socio-political concerns while winning the listener over with its irresistible groove. And on "Look for Love" and "Music of Life," Cerrone provides the type of uplifting, motivational love is the answer message that Earth, Wind & Fire is known for. A fine addition to Cerrone's catalog, *The Golden Touch* is among the finest Euro-disco efforts of 1978. *—Alex Henderson*

Cerrone V: Angelina / 1979 / Malligator ✦✦✦

Cerrone 6 / 1980 / Malligator ✦✦✦

The Best of Cerrone / Jan. 9, 1990 / Malligator ✦✦✦✦
Cerrone was a dominant Euro-disco act in the mid-'70s. His music accented both disco's strengths (multi-layered arrangements; a driving, at times almost overbearing beat; and sophisticated strings) and weaknesses (a stifling lyrical sameness and arrangement/production formula that could quickly grow wearisome). But only Gino Soccio and Georgio Moroder rivaled Cerrone in this style of disco. *—Ron Wynn*

Chairmen of the Board

f. 1969, Detroit, MI, **db.** 1976

Group / Pop-Soul, Soul, Smooth Soul

Best-known for the stuttering number three single "Give Me Just a Little More Time," the Chairmen of the Board were one of the smoothest and most popular soul acts to emerge from Detroit in the early '70s. Although their time at the top of the R&B charts was brief—their first Top 10 arrived in 1970, their last in 1973—they recorded a handful of '70s soul classics, all distinguished by the high, trembling vocals of General Norman Johnson, who also wrote the bulk of the group's material.

Born and raised in Norfolk, VA, Johnson began singing in the church choir when he was a child, eventually forming his first vocal group, the Humdingers, when he was 12. During high school, he formed the Showmen, and in his senior year, the group recorded the rock & roll tribute, "It Will Stand." The single scraped the pop and R&B charts in 1961, and Johnson stayed with the Showmen for the next seven years, releasing a series of singles on Minit and Swan Records that became regional hits. By the end of the group's career, they had become staples on the beach music circuit on the East Coast. Johnson decided to leave the group for a solo career in 1968, eventually working his way to Detroit, MI, where he signed with former-Motown producers and songwriters Holland-Dozier-Holland's fledgling Invictus record label. Johnson formed a group with former Showman Danny Woods; ex-Stone Soul Children Harrison Kennedy; and Eddie Curtis, who formerly sang with Lee Andrews & the Hearts and Huey Smith & the Clowns. Originally, the group was called the Gentlemen, but they quickly changed their name to the Chairmen of the Board.

The Chairmen of the Board's first single, "Give Me Just a Little More Time," was an instant hit, reaching number three on the pop charts and number-eight R&B in early 1970, putting Invictus on the map. Two other singles, "(You've Got Me) Dangling on a String" and "Everything's Tuesday," followed, which established them as R&B chart contenders, but they failed to climb past 38 on the pop charts. Although the subsequent "Pay to the Piper" reached number 13 on pop, it was their last Top 40 hit. Between 1971 and 1974, the Chairmen of the Board received more support from the R&B audience, with songs like "Chairman of the Board" (1971) and "Finder's Keepers" (1973) reaching the Top Ten.

Despite this constant stream of singles, the band stopped recording in 1971, which led to a temporary breakup. The following year, they re-formed and toured throughout the Southeast beach music circuit, where their singles were continually regional hits. Although the Chairmen were having trouble reaching the charts, Johnson's songs became hits for the likes of Clarence Carter ("Patches"), Freda Payne ("Bring the Boys Home"), and Honey Cone, who had no less than three hits—"Want Ads," "Stick Up," "One Monkey Don't Stop No Show"—with his compositions.

The Chairmen of the Board continued touring and releasing albums until 1976, when they disbanded, with each member releasing solo albums. Johnson and Woods continued performing under the Chairmen name for a short time before Johnson moved to Arista in the late '70s. He had a handful of hits for the label, all of which demonstrated contemporary disco influences, before reuniting with Woods as the Chairmen in the early '80s. Over the next two decades, the duo regularly toured the Southeast to much success. *—Stephen Thomas Erlewine*

The Chairmen of the Board / Apr. 1970 / Invictus ♦♦♦♦

The explosive "Give Me Just a Little More Time" had Four Tops written all over it. From the in-your-face vocals, the insatiable beat, and spirited backing, the song was a bona fide, can't-miss hit. A rousing "You Got Me Dangling on a String" again features General Johnson's (formerly of the Showmen) unusual, quivering lead on another song that seem tailored for the Tops. The country-influenced "Patches" is the most interesting song here; it was later recorded by Clarence Carter, becoming one of his biggest hits. The group's versatility is showcased, as each member—General Johnson, Danny Woods, Eddie Curtis, and Harrison Kennedy—leads at least one song. The problem is, each has a different agenda: Woods is hardcore R&B, Curtis likes '60s easy listening, Kennedy is a rocker, and General Johnson is General Johnson. The assorted leads give the album a quilting effect. *—Andrew Hamilton*

In Session / Oct. 1970 / Invictus ♦♦♦

Another good release by the hand-picked group, "Chairmen of the Board" is a rocking, swaggering slice of braggadocio where the lead boasts about his mastery over his woman. "Everything Tuesday" is one of the lyrically clever concoctions that Invictus/Hot Wax became known for; a good snappy beat didn't hurt matters either. "Pay to the Piper" provides an excellent vehicle for soul singer extraordinaire Danny Woods to display his vocal prowess; Woods could belt 'em out with the best of them. Due to the popularity of Clarence Carter's remake, the original "Patches" is included on the group's second LP as well as the first. "When Will She Tell Me She Needs Me" is definitive General Johnson; Johnson sounds like he's being choked as he sings the aching lyrics. Good tunes are in abundance on *In Session*, as "All We Need Is Love" and "Hanging on to a Memory" are additional gems. *—Andrew Hamilton*

Bittersweet / Mar. 1972 / Invictus ♦♦♦

After the departure of Eddie Custus, the Chairmen of the Board found themselves pared down to a trio for their 1972 release *Bittersweet*. This turned out to be a blessing in disguise because it allowed the group to eliminate the middle-of-the-road ballad covers that Custus favored and resulted in their most consistent overall album to date. The impressive "Men Are Getting Scarce" provides the album with an energetic opener and its combination of wah-wah guitar and pulsing keyboards isn't too far from the funky, message-oriented soul sound that the Temptations were scoring with at the time. Other notable tunes on this album include the title track, a breakup ballad with an unusual but effective slow-fast-slow structure, and "Working on a Building of Love," an infectious uptempo tune that blends a piano-pounding, gospel-tinged melody with a clever lyric worthy of Smokey Robinson. However, the album's finest moment is "I'm on My Way to a Better Place," a spiritual ballad built on a soaring, string-laden melody that features an intensely moving vocal performance from General Johnson. The other tunes don't command the attention as strongly as the songs mentioned here, but each is well-crafted and adds to the album's smooth, consistent feel. The result lacks the consistent, high level of inspiration to be judged a masterpiece but it will definitely please anyone who enjoys the Chairmen of the Board's hits. *—Donald A. Guarisco*

Skin I'm In / Oct. 1974 / Invictus ♦♦♦♦

For what would be their final album, the Chairmen of the Board teamed up with producer Jeffrey Bowen to create an album that was radically different from all of their previous output. Instead of the Motown-styled harmony soul that earned the group their pop-chart success, *Skin I'm In* was built on a psychedelic funk-rock sound that was very close to the music George Clinton was exploring around the same time. A look at the album's credits reveals why the album sounds like this: the backup band includes several members of Funkadelic and Parliament, including Bernie Worrell and Eddie Hazel. The result is a surprisingly effective combination of pop-soul hooks and funky grit: "Everybody Party All Night" pits smooth harmonies against a staccato wah-wah guitar hook to create an energetic, rhythmic slice of soul and "Finders Keepers" weaves punchy horn charts into its soulful keyboard-driven melody to create a funky toe-tapper of a tune. The album's centerpiece is an epic cover of Sly Stewart's "Life and Death" that blends the song's pulsating melody with flowery instrumental passages built of Mellotron and synthesizer. The album balances this funk-rock attack with lovely ballads on the album's second side, including a heartbreakingly soulful cover of "Only Love Can Break a Heart." In the end, *Skin I'm In* is so different from past efforts that it may alienate fans of the Chairmen of the Board's early hits but it is definitely a worthwhile listen for fans of funk music, especially those who love Funkadelic and Parliament. *—Donald A. Guarisco*

● **Greatest Hits** / Jan. 9, 1992 / Fantasy ♦♦♦♦♦

When hit songwriters/producers Holland-Dozier-Holland left Motown Records and founded Hot Wax/Invictus, there was plenty of cause for optimism. And, to be sure, the labels had their share of Motown-ish "uptown soul" hits courtesy of the Honey Cone, 100 Proof (Aged in Soul), Freda Payne and Laura Lee. Another one of the company's strong points was the Chairmen of the Board, a vocal harmony group that, like the Four Tops at Motown, could be gritty and sweet at the same time. Lead singer General Norman Johnson, in fact, had a Levi Stubbs-like quality. Though not quite on a par with HDH's work with the Tops, enjoyably Detroit-sounding hits like "Dangling on a String," "Give Me Just a Little More Time" and "Pay to the Piper" showed that the team's knack for finding memorable, hook-laden soul-pop hadn't gone away. The group gets away from its Four Tops-influenced approach on the arresting "Try My Love on for Size" and the surprisingly bluesy "Chairman of the Board," a moderate hit. Unfortunately, the Chairmen's success—like that of Hot Wax/Invictus—was short-lived. *—Alex Henderson*

Bittersweet/Skin I'm In / 1999 / Sequel ♦♦♦♦

The Chairmen of the Board/In Session / 1999 / Sequel ♦♦♦♦

Everything's Tuesday: The Best of Chairmen of the Board / Nov. 7, 2000 / Invictus ♦♦♦♦♦

The Chairmen of the Board scored a slew of soul-pop gems for Invictus Records. The group was initially billed to feature four lead singers: stuttering/shaky-voiced General Johnson, hard soul-singing Danny Woods, acid rockish Harrison Kennedy, and smooth R&B/soul crooner Eddie Custus. Johnson quickly became the dominant lead, with Woods ("Pay to the Piper") a distant second; Kennedy and Custus led songs occasionally—always album cuts—and Custus was the first to exit the group. This 22-song Import compilation is an essential collection of the Chairmen of the Board's prime cuts. They missed some very nice B-sides (i.e., "When Will She Tells Me She Needs Me"), but track for track you won't find a better bundle of their hits, including "Give Me Just a Little More Time," the title track, "Patches," "You've Got Me Dangling on a String," and later singles "Elmo James," "Finders Keepers," and "Everybody Party All Night." *—Andrew Hamilton*

The Chakachas

f. Belgium

Group / Funk, Soul

Best-known for their near-pornographic funk classic "Jungle Fever," the Chakachas were actually a group of Belgian-based studio musicians. Led by Gaston Boogaerts, who served as the group's arranger, the Chakachas first appeared during the early '60s, recording a playful mixture of Latin music, jazz, and European-style exotica. By the time Polydor released the *Jungle Fever* album in the U.S. in 1972, they'd updated that foundation with a heavier funk groove. The title cut—a down-and-dirty, stop-start funk instrumental punctuated by heavy breathing and orgasmic female moans—went Top Ten for the group's only American hit. "Jungle Fever" played more to dance-club patrons than radio listeners, which helped it endure into the disco years; it was also heavily sampled by the hip-hop generation. The remainder of the group's history is difficult to trace; it's been suggested that they—or at least some of their personnel—also recorded as El Chicles and backed singer Nico Gomez (who wrote one of the songs included on *Jungle Fever*). It is known that they hired a Latin band from NY called Barrio to pose as the Chakachas for an American tour in the wake of "Jungle Fever." *—Steve Huey*

Los Chakachas / 1961 / RCA Victor ♦♦♦

The Chakachas are best known for the sultry funk classic "Jungle Fever," but their typical sound, even on the *Jungle Fever* album, is evident on 1961's *Los Chakachas*. (There is also a very rare album with a mask on the jacket and maybe others.) The group is Belgian though led by a Spanish drummer and Cuban singer. Significantly, the Belgians account for a sound and cheesiness that is very close to the Francis Bay Big Band's Latin efforts. Both bands occasionally prove their mettle, however. The percussion and vocalizing (in whatever form) is irreverent and unserious; the order of the day is mid-'60s fun. But the songs are well chosen. "Mucho Tequila" is a page from the Champs' book. Better is "Negra Mi Cha Cha Cha," an update of an obscure RCA track by Facundo Rivera (from the 1955 *Cha Cha Cha* compilation by RCA Victor). It is hard to imagine a better vocal cha cha cha than the Rivera version, but *Los Chakachas* get points for taste and bravery. *—Tony Wilds*

● **Jungle Fever** / 1972 / Polydor ♦♦♦♦

A triumph of European attempts at Latin music, *Jungle Fever* is notable for more than the classic funk-with-grunts of the title track. Since the earlier *Los Chakachas* the percussion, arrangements, and singing have greatly improved. "Un Rayo del Sol" is an example of a song in their typical style which really approaches perfection. "Eso Es El Amor" is another update of an old standard. "Harlem Nocturne" is a mildly interesting instrumental choice. A truly modern cha cha cha, "Ay Mulata" mixes up the funk and jazz riffs with a soulful chorus. *—Tony Wilds*

The Chambers Brothers

f. 1954, Lee County, MS, **db.** 1972

Group / Psychedelic, Soul, Psychedelic Soul

Like their West Coast contemporaries Sly and the Family Stone, the Chambers Brothers shattered racial and musical divides to forge an incendiary fusion of funk, gospel, blues, and psychedelia that reached its apex with the perennial 1968 song "Time Has Come Today." The Chambers siblings—bassist George, guitarist Willie, harpist Lester, and guitarist Joe, all of whom contributed vocals—were born and raised in Lee County, MS; the products of an impoverished sharecropping family, the brothers first polished their vocal harmonies in the choir of their Baptist church, a collaboration which ended after George was drafted into the army in 1952. Following his discharge he relocated to Los Angeles, where the other Chambers brothers soon settled as well; the foursome began performing gospel and folk throughout Southern CA in 1954, but remained virtually unknown until appearing in New York City in 1965. The addition of white drummer Brian Keenan not only made the Chambers Brothers an interracial group, but pushed their music closer to rock & roll; a well-received appearance at the Newport Folk Festival further enhanced their growing reputation, and they soon recorded their debut LP, *People Get Ready*.

As the Chambers Brothers toured rock clubs (including the famed Fillmore in San Francisco) and R&B venues (most notably the Apollo Theatre) alike, their music increasingly embraced elements of both; after recording 1968's *Shout!* for the Vault label, the group signed to Columbia to issue *The Time Has Come*, scoring a major pop hit with the title track, an 11-minute psychedelic soul epic in its original album incarnation. The follow-up, *A New Time—A New Day*, yielded another Top 40 hit, a cover of the Otis Redding's classic "I Can't Turn You Loose," but subsequent efforts including 1969's *Love, Peace & Happiness* and 1970's *Live at Fillmore East* failed to maintain the commercial momentum. Upon completing 1972's *Oh My God!*, the Chambers Brothers disbanded, only to reunite two years later for *Unbonded*. *Right Move* appeared in 1975, and although no new studio records were forthcoming, the group regularly performed live in the decades to follow, with the brothers also pursuing individual projects; the Chambers Family Choir, a gospel group including the siblings' own children, remained a priority as well. *—Jason Ankeny*

People Get Ready / 1965 / One Way ♦♦♦

The first of a handful of early live albums by the group, recorded in concert at the Ash Grove in Los Angeles and the Unicorn in Boston in 1965. The Chambers Brothers were purely an R&B outfit at the time (their psychedelic stylings being a couple of years in the future), and a good one, although they're a little bit surer on the more basic blues than on some of the R&B that they cover—their renditions of Jimmy Reed's material seem more inspired than their performance of the Valentinos' old hit "It's All Over Now," although to their credit their rendition of the latter sounds nothing like the Rolling Stones' then-current cover of the same song. The group also does a beautiful job of harmonizing on Curtis Mayfield's "People Get Ready," and shows a command of the poppier side of rock & roll on "Call Me," a group original with a catchy "Hang on Sloopy"-style central riff. This album, like its companion release, *Now*, is a good low-cost introduction to the Chambers Brothers, who show that, even at this early date in their history, they were a commanding and exciting presence on-stage. *—Bruce Eder*

The Chambers Brothers Now / 1966 / Vault ♦♦♦

The Time Has Come / Nov. 1967 / Columbia/Legacy ♦♦♦♦♦

This, the Chambers Brothers' coming-of-age record, was a well-timed and even better executed exercise in modern record-making. The brothers had recorded several excellent gospel-folk sides on a few labels (including CBS) in the mid-'60s. They were darlings of the folk set, and even sang backup on a few unreleased Bob Dylan sessions in 1965. By 1967, they were at loose ends. Having demoed a slightly demented song called "Time Has Come Today" that year, the group entered the studio with producer David Rubinson, who was fresh from some critical acclaim after recording Moby Grape. The resulting album and subsequent title-track hit were huge successes, especially on FM radio. The rest of the album shows the brothers not just embracing the psychedelic trends, but also redefining their R&B leanings. Fabulous. The 2000 CD reissue on Columbia/Legacy adds three 1966-1967 non-LP B-sides, as well as the first single version of "Time Has Come Today," which is substantially different from the familiar one on the album. *—Matthew Greenwald*

A New Time—A New Day / Sep. 1968 / Columbia ♦♦♦

Love, Peace & Happiness / Dec. 1969 / GNP Crescendo ♦♦♦

The brothers seemed to really believe in the title track's message, and they earned style points by including white drummer Brian Keenan, making them one of the few racially mixed American bands. This album, originally released as a double LP, is half studio and half live. The studio sides reflect the message with titles such as "Have a Little Faith" and "To Love Somebody." But the brothers lose their way in covers of songs by the Bee Gees and Marvin Hamlisch, and the epic title track never coheres like "Time Has Come Today." The live sides are better, with stronger material, including "I Can't Turn You Loose" and "People Get Ready." The boys have some fun with the encore, a barbershop medley. *—Mark Allan*

New Generation / 1970 / Columbia ♦♦♦

Eschewing their normal frenzied mix of soul and rock, the brothers package their socially uplifting messages more in James Brown-style funk than usual. They produce the album themselves and their ambition often exceeds their grasp. String orchestrations by band members Brian Keenan and Joe Chambers clutter an already-busy mix. The title track is the kind of extended rave-up that seems to be on every one of their albums. "Going to the Mill" closes the session with a straightforward, and welcome, shot of gospel. *—Mark Allan*

● **Time Has Come: The Best of the Chambers Brothers** / Oct. 15, 1996 / Columbia/Legacy ♦♦♦♦♦

As the Chambers Brothers' albums could be erratic and/or excessive, this 16-track best-of, covering their 1966-1970 prime, is a most welcome distillation of their career highlights. Focusing mostly on their late-'60s singles (some of them non-LP), it also includes a live rendition of "Wade in the Water" and a rejected, even more psychedelicized, 1966 version of their signature tune, "Time Has Come Today." By concentrating on the band's most economic and soulful outings, this disc is the most effective compilation of their gospel-soul-psychedelia. *—Richie Unterberger*

Chambers Brothers Now/People Get Ready / Jun. 23, 1999 / Repertoire ♦♦♦

Now! Live / Jun. 29, 1999 / One Way ♦♦♦

Champaign

f. 1981, Champaign, IL

Group / Quiet Storm, Adult Contemporary, Urban, Soul

Champaign took its name from its home city of Champaign, IL. The group was an interracial septet comprising singers Pauli Carman and Rena Jones, guitarist Howard Reeder, keyboardists Michael Day and Dana Walden, bassist Michael Reed, and percussionist Rocky Maffitt. They hit a commercial peak with their 1981 debut album, *How 'Bout Us*, whose title track was a hit single (Top Five in the U.K. and on the U.S. R&B chart). Follow-ups included *Modern Heart* (1983) (which includes the Top Ten R&B hit "Try Again") and *Woman in Flames* (1984), featuring the R&B Top Ten hit "Off and On Love." *—William Ruhlmann*

● **How 'Bout Us** / Jan. 1981 / Columbia ♦♦♦♦♦

This is smooth, well-crafted pop-R&B topped by the creamy vocals of Pauli Carman and Rena Jones. This debut is a pop hybrid that sounds very promising, although the group never followed through adequately. *—William Ruhlmann*

Modern Heart / Mar. 1983 / Columbia ♦♦

Champaign, a soul vocal group who downplayed the fact that it were among the rare early-'80s interracial acts, had scored a big hit in 1981 with the single "How 'Bout Us." But for some reason, the band didn't get a second album out fast enough to keep things moving, in part because of intra-group problems. By the time its second album came around, people had forgotten about the band and soul was again struggling, as the early-'80s revival had begun petering out. This wasn't a bad album, but it was almost completely ignored. *—Ron Wynn*

Woman in Flames / Oct. 1984 / Columbia ♦♦

The interracial soul group Champaign staged a comeback of sorts with this self-produced 1984 album. The group got its third R&B Top Ten hit with the song "Off and On Love," and lead vocalist Pauli Carman got enough mileage from the hit single to leave for a short-lived solo career. *—Ron Wynn*

Champaign IV / 1991 / Malaco ♦♦♦

Champaign had huge hits with 1981's "How 'Bout Us" and 1983's "Try Again," but by the late 1980s, the Illinois group was struggling. So Champaign turned to the same Jackson, MS-based label that had been a refuge for Johnnie Taylor, Denise LaSalle, Latimore and other soul veterans: Malaco. In 1990, Champaign signed with Malaco and recorded *IV*, its first album since 1984's *Woman In Flames*. Lead singer Pauli Carman had been recording as a solo artist, and returned to the band for this decent but not earth-shattering release. Instead of jumping on the new jack swing bandwagon and adding an abundance of rapping, Champaign pretty much sticks with the type of pop-flavored R&B it had been recording since the early 1980s. Although Champaign uses a lot of keyboards and drum machines, R&B/adult contemporary tunes like "Belong," "Teardrops Fall" and "Trials of the Heart" aren't much different from the songs Champaign had done for its Columbia debut almost ten years earlier. The production is high-tech, but the writing is pretty much the same. *IV* was ignored by urban contemporary radio, and adult contemporary radio wasn't very responsive either. *—Alex Henderson*

Nolan Chance (Charles Davis)

b. Nov. 11, 1939, Louisiana

Vocals / Doo Wop, Soul

Nolan Chance was a fixture on the music scene in Chicago for years; a singer of considerable talent who, by virtue of bad timing and business situations beyond his control, never quite got the right break at the right time to achieve some of the recognition that he might have deserved. He was born Charles Davis in Louisiana in 1939, and was raised in Chicago after his family moved there in the early '40s. In his early teens, he formed an R&B vocal group with some friends at Lyons Township High School, and they did well enough to get an opening spot on a bill with Freddie King. In 1959, he joined the vocal group the Trinidads, who left behind a recorded legacy of one unsuccessful single, "When We're Together."

Davis spent his early-'60s career as a member of the Turbo Jets, and then the Dukays. He was recruited into the latter group in 1962 as the successor to Gene Chandler, following the latter's exit in the wake of the success of the single "Duke of Earl." The group failed to hit with any of the records they cut during Davis' year-long tenure, however, and by 1963 he was gone from the Dukays and singing with the Artistics.

In 1964, Davis signed to the Constellation label, taking the name Nolan Chance. His debut for the label was "She's Gone," a ballad that attracted considerable attention and did well on numerous local charts, even though it failed to register nationally. His next record, "Just Like the Weather," was well-received but had the bad fortune to appear just as Constellation was starting to collapse.

Chance didn't record again until the end of the 1960s, when Eddie Thomas signed with the Curtom label. He cut the single "I'll Never Forget You," which became a sufficiently popular R&B hit to get Chance back into touring and performing. The fit between Chance and Curtom should have been a natural, in view of the fact that the label later became home to Gene Chandler, the man he'd replaced in the Dukays, but the relationship with the label didn't last. He was produced by Thomas—who departed Curtom in 1970—during 1972 for the Scepter label, on the single "Sara Lee." As with his experience on Constellation, however, Chance's timing was bad; Scepter, which had once been a very successful New York-based R&B label, was declining rapidly, and folded soon after, and "Sara Lee" never sold what it could have. *—Bruce Eder*

Gene Chandler (Eugene Dixon)

b. Jul. 6, 1937, Chicago, IL

Vocals / Chicago Soul, Pop-Soul, Northern Soul, Soul, Uptown Soul, Brown-Eyed Soul

Gene Chandler is remembered by the rock & roll audience almost solely for the classic novelty and doo wop-tinged soul ballad "Duke of Earl"; the unforgettable opening chant of the title leading the way, the song was a number-one hit in 1962. He's esteemed by soul fans as one of the leading exponents of the '60s Chicago soul scene, along with Curtis Mayfield and Jerry Butler. Born Eugene Dixon, he was a member of the doo wop group the Dukays and "Duke of Earl" was actually a Dukays recording; Dixon was renamed Gene Chandler and the single bore his credit as a solo singer. Chandler never approached the massive pop success of that chart-topper (although he occasionally entered the Top 20), but he was a big star with the R&B audience with straightforward midtempo and ballad soul numbers in the mid-'60s, many of which were written by Curtis Mayfield and produced by Carl Davis. Chandler's success became more fitful after Mayfield stopped penning material for him, although he enjoyed some late-'60s hits and had a monster pop and soul smash in 1970 with "Groovy Situation." His last successes were the far less distinguished disco- and dance-influenced R&B hits "Get Down" (1978) and "Does She Have a Friend?" (1980). *—Richie Unterberger*

Just Be True / 1964 / Collectables ♦♦♦

Led by the title track, Gene Chandler's biggest hit of the '60s after "Duke of Earl," *Just Be True* is a set of period soul tracks including "You Threw a Lucky Punch" (an answer record to Mary Wells' "You Beat Me to the Punch") and the lame "Duke of Earl" knockoff "Walk on With the Duke." Chandler's wonderful voice raises all this material to a level unimagined by any but the half-dozen best soul singers out there. [The Collectables reissue includes four bonus tracks.] *—John Bush*

Live at the "Regal" / 1965 / Charly ♦♦♦

Bill "Bunky" Sheppard's Constellation label released this live set by the Duke of Earl in 1965. Driven by the massive R&B hit "Rainbow 65," the set has its moments. *Live at the Regal* features three of Gene's greatest ballads: "What Now," "Just Be True," and "God Bless Our Love." Curtis Mayfield penned four of the nine selections, including Major Lance's "Monkey Time," a song Gene wanted to record but producer Carl Davis had already promised to Lance. He really cuts loose on "Soul Hootenanny" and Billy Butler's "A Song Called Soul." Gene, always knocked for his inability to stay on key, doesn't disprove that argument here. Still, you can't deny the Duke's energy and charisma. [Collectables did us a favor by reissuing Gene Chandler's only live recording in 1994 in CD format.] *—Andrew Hamilton*

Gene Chandler / 1967 / Checker ♦♦♦

The Girl Don't Care / 1967 / Brunswick ♦♦♦♦♦

One of Chandler's best, chock full of midtempo grooves, succulent ballads and jump tunes like "Good Times." Curtis Mayfield's "Nothing Can Stop Me" is spiced with punchy horns and choral backing vocals for Gene to play his cool, swaggering tenor against. The pain in his voice is undeniable on "Here Come the Tears," where he literally cries the agonizing lyrics. He gets philosophical on "The Girl Don't Care," an intense ballad that always seems too short. This could almost pass for a greatest-hits LP, since at least six of the selections were released as A-sides. "Fool for You," as well as the others mentioned above, got their share of plays on soul stations, and all should have been bigger hits. The B-sides occupy most of side two and are just a couple of notches below the plug sides. It's amazing how overlooked and underappreciated these gems were. *—Andrew Hamilton*

There Was a Time! / 1968 / Brunswick ♦♦♦♦

Gene Chandler's second LP for Brunswick suffers from comparisons to its predecessor, but consider how difficult it must have been to top an album padded with several tracks previously released as Constellation singles. The two singles here, "Those Were the Good Old Days" and "There Was a Time," are as good as anything he'd recorded for the label. Though the titles evoke similar themes, they're radically different songs. The first is (as expected) a good-time nostalgia tune with a sweet female chorus, but the second is a torrid horn-driven salute to the best dances of recent years; one looks back to the heady Chicago soul of the Impressions, while the other looks ahead to the increasingly intense urban funk of Curtis Mayfield. Chandler again displays an amazing mastery of voice control, adding brilliant tossed-off vocals between lines on the choruses. He also shows off his growing compositional skills by co-writing half of the songs here, including the highlights "Blind Heart," "Teacher Teacher," and "Laughter to Tears." The production is a bit too polished for his occasionally gritty voice, but *There Was a Time* is nevertheless an excellent LP. *—John Bush*

The Two Sides of Gene Chandler / 1969 / Brunswick ♦♦♦

For Gene Chandler's third Brunswick LP, there are a few of the usual evocative soul showcases: "Can I Change My Mind?," "Familiar Footsteps," and "If You Would Love Me." The balance of *The Two Sides of Gene Chandler* presents him as a '60s pop standard bearer, covering hits from the canon like "This Guy's in Love With You," "Eleanor Rigby," Bobby Goldsboro's "Honey," Dinah Washington's "This Bitter Earth," and the Tin Pan Alley chestnut "Yesterdays." Chandler performs these well—he's a professional, after all—but it's difficult to escape the impression that Brunswick was just pushing material in hopes of a hit. The "funky" alternate reading of "Eleanor Rigby" isn't very adventurous, and the originals end up sounding much better than any of the covers. *—John Bush*

The Gene Chandler Situation / 1970 / Mercury ♦♦♦♦

This is slick Chicago soul from 1970, and includes the smash "Groovy Situation." *—Bill Dahl*

Gene & Jerry: One & One / 1971 / Mercury ♦♦♦

Gene Chandler achieved a million in sales with Mel & Tim ("Backfield In Motion") on his Bamboo label and some minor R&B hits with Simtec & Wylie on his Mr. Chand setup. Both acts were unknown until Chandler's discovery, yet they made the charts. What would two-name artists do? That prospect energized this project, which at first glance appeared to be an LP of Simtec & Wylie and Mel & Tim leftovers. ("Mail Call Time" and "I Found That I Was Wrong" appeared on Mel & Tim's *Good Guys Only Win in the Movies* album.) But actually, they all pooled their talent to come up with material and production ideas to make *Gene & Jerry: One & One* a success. However, other than "Ten and Two (Take This Woman off the Corner)," a minor R&B hit about prostitution and johns, nothing else scored; its subject matter was out of character for Butler anyway. Another single, "You Just Can't Win (By Making the Same Mistakes)," didn't bust a grape. Ironically, both Simtec & Wylie and Mel & Tim had bigger hits on smaller labels—go figure. Despite its dismal sales, this is a good album of uptown male duets by two of soul's greatest. *—Andrew Hamilton*

Get Down / 1979 / 20th Century ♦♦

When You're #1 / 1979 / 20th Century ♦♦

After a brief hiatus, Chandler signed to producer Carl Davis' Chi-Sound, a subsidiary of 20th Century Fox, and got back in the business of making hits. His 1978 single and album *Get Down* was one of the biggest surprises of the disco era, a time that got many R&B talents back on the charts. This album is the follow-up. *When You're #1* doesn't boast a hit as big as "Get Down," but it's not for lack of trying. The first track, the polyrhythmic and flashy "That Funky Disco Rhythm" has Chandler extolling the virtues of disco with lines like "You're gonna go where the music wants to take you." It's no doubt corny but Chandler seems to be singing it in all seriousness. The busy title track co-written by Chandler has him signing about battling disco dancing kids. With lyrics like "Jimmy turned and twisted as the ladies watched him dance," the whole thing seems a bit fatuous. Although dancing was a major concern during the time, he also had time for a ballad or two. Both "I'll Remember You" and "Stay Here in My Heart" are hampered by their uneventful lyrics and arrangements. The best one, "Do What Comes So Natural" has that melodic Chicago sound that hit its peak in the late '70s/early '80s and an animated vocal from Chandler. If anything, the lingering success of *Get Down* prevented this effort from being a big hit. For fans of Chandler and the updated Chicago sound, this is well worth looking into. *—Jason Elias*

Gene Chandler '80 / 1980 / 20th Century ♦♦♦

First, the good: "Does She Have a Friend for Me?" explodes from the speakers with a catchy beat, good lyrics, and a top-notch production—yet it failed to achieve what 20th Century Fox Records and "Get Down" did for him earlier. Now the bad: This was Chandler's fourth and final LP for the label, and the other tracks are most likely rejects from other sessions. Another remake of his "Rainbow," aptly titled "Rainbow 80," is limp compared to both the live "Rainbow 65" and the original on Vee-Jay Records. "All About the Paper" is all right, but the Dells' version is better. Try to get "Does She Have a Friend for Me?" on a compilation disc and skip this one. *—Andrew Hamilton*

Here's to Love / 1981 / 20th Century ♦♦♦

Gene Chandler's tenure at 20th Century Fox Records had about run its course by the time of this LP. A couple of disco hits were the highlights of his Fox experience. *Here's to Love* is a nice parting shot for Eugene Dixon, known professionally as Gene Chandler, but who will always be the Duke of Earl. "I'm Attracted to You" failed as a single, and rightfully so; it's a good album cut, but there were stronger tunes to release. "I've Got to Meet Her" is classic Gene Chandler, an emotional tale of a love triangle written by James Thompson that Chandler dramatizes, accompanied by some hitting female backing vocals. On his 20th Century Fox albums, Chandler always included one of his earlier R&B hits; this time it's Billy Butler's "God Bless Our Love" that gets updated. His best vocal performance is wasted on an OK song, "Almost All the Way to Love," the most pop-sounding selection here. He gets introspective on a Sam Dees composition entitled "For the Sake of the Memories"; the song is not one of Dees' best. The bouncy "Almost Daylight" has commercial appeal, but it's too cute a song for Chandler. *—Andrew Hamilton*

● **Nothing Can Stop Me: Gene Chandler's Greatest Hits** / Aug. 30, 1994 / Varese Sarabande ♦♦♦♦♦

This 20-track CD is the only collection that has all of his most popular recordings, from "Duke of Earl" through his soul hits for Constellation, Vee-Jay, Checker, Mercury, and Chi-Sound, spanning 1962 to 1980 (all but three tracks were released before 1968). Some fans might prefer *The Duke of Earl*, which focuses on his Vee-Jay years, but this has a much wider breadth, and includes "Groovy Situation." Curtis Mayfield wrote eight of the songs, although they frankly don't fully measure up to the Chicago soul he was writing for his own group, the Impressions, at the time. *—Richie Unterberger*

The Duke of Earl / Jul. 14, 1995 / Prime Cuts ♦♦♦♦

The sound quality isn't top-notch, but this budget-priced CD contains the Chicagoan's classic early-'60s work for Vee-Jay and Constellation Records. *—Bill Dahl*

The Soul of Gene Chandler / Jun. 18, 1996 / Brunswick ♦♦♦♦

A collection of Gene's Brunswick sides, 20 tracks of lively productions by producer Carl Davis. None of these sides made an impact on the pop chart and did only fair on the R&B chart, which is perplexing. Tunes like "Good Times," the romping, confident "Nothing Can Stop Me," his duet with Barbara Acklin "From the Teacher to the Preacher," "Fool For You," and the soulful "Here Comes the Tears" should have been much bigger. This is not definitive Chandler, but the 20 tracks are a good helping of some of his better recordings that were victimized by poor promotion. *—Andrew Hamilton*

Duke of Soul: The Brunswick Years / Oct. 27, 1998 / Edsel ♦♦♦♦♦

Edsel's 20-track summation of Gene Chandler's short career at Brunswick Records (1966 through 1969) hits all of the obvious high points: "Nothing Can Stop Me," "(Gonna Be) Good Times," "Here Comes the Tears," "There Was a Time," "Those Were the Good Old Days," "Cowboys to Girls," and "You Can't Hurt Me No More." Perhaps wisely, the compilers completely bypassed his inferior final album for Brunswick, *The Two Sides of*

Gene Chandler. Though there's still a lot of quality material from the period for which space didn't allow, *Duke of Soul: The Brunswick Years* is an excellent study of one of the most underrated soul singers of the '60s. [Since the two-disc set—*The Brunswick Years 1966-69,* also known as *The Girl Don't Care/There Was a Time/Two Sides of Gene Chandler*—includes all three of Chandler's original Brunswick LPs, and can be found at a relatively inexpensive price, some listeners may find it worthwhile to bypass this greatest-hits volume and spring for the complete set instead.] *—John Bush*

Gene Chandler '80/Here's to Love / Jun. 22, 1999 / WestSide ♦♦♦

Get Down With the Get Down / Sep. 14, 1999 / WestSide ♦♦♦
This is a handy collection of 15 of Gene Chandler's disco-era cuts (many of them previously unissued) for Carl Davis' Chi-Sound label, recorded between 1978 and 1983. The fact that the disc opens with the eight-minute 12" version of "Get Down" and the smoother "Does She Have a Friend for Me?" should be all the selling points that this CD needs for fans, but the producers have also included Chandler's demo version of "Get Down," a short, stripped-down rendition with more of a jazz feel. Not much of the rest actually comes up to the standard of those highlights—"Skate (aka Miss Crazy Legs)" is nothing to write home about, apart from the fact that it's almost a rap song, "I'll Be There," a duet with Barbara Acklin, is the best of the previously unissued cuts, and "I'll Make the Living if You Make the Loving Worthwhile" holds up well enough, but apart from the two established hits, most of the rest is of purely historical and archival interest, diverting but not essential. *—Bruce Eder*

The Brunswick Years: 1966–1969 / Oct. 26, 1999 / WestSide ♦♦♦♦
Give this one high marks—it's the most comprehensive assemblage of Gene Chandler's Brunswick sides ever, and includes six duets with Barbara Acklin all on two shiny, durable compact discs. Chandler's solo sides represent three complete albums fattened with a few singles that didn't make it to an LP. The Acklin duets are the best from their album together. High notes include "Nothing Can Stop Me," "I'm Just a Fool for You," "Here Come the Tears," "Good Times," "The Girl Don't Care," and remakes of James Brown's "There Was a Time," and the Intruders' "Cowboys to Girls." *—Andrew Hamilton*

The Best of Gene Chandler: The Duke of Earl / Oct. 17, 2000 / Collectables ♦♦♦♦
Here are early Gene Chandler sides, many recorded with the Dukays, including the immortal "Duke of Earl." Feature tracks include "Walk on With the Duke," which was a total bust although it is interesting in retrospect, as it was the answer to "Duke of Earl"; the original studio cut of "Rainbow"; the stark and magnificent "Man's Temptation"; an answer to Mary Wells' "You Beat Me to the Punch" via "You Threw a Lucky Punch"; a remake of the Temptations' "Check Yourself," where Chandler outdoes Paul Williams who led the original; and a whole slew of Dukays tracks when Chandler toiled with them. *—Andrew Hamilton*

Change

Group / Urban, Disco
Change was a studio group formed by Italian producer Jacques Fred Petrus containing European and American musicians, including leaders Paolo Gianolio (guitar) and David Romani (bass). The group is most notable for featuring Luther Vandross on lead vocals on their first two albums. Later, the group based itself in New York with singers James Robinson and Deborah "Crab" Cooper, the latter going on to join C&C Music Factory. In 1998, the Rhino label released the definitive retrospective *Very Best of Change.* *—Steve Huey*

The Glow of Love / 1980 / Warner Bros. ♦♦♦♦♦
To Change's detractors, the studio group was nothing more than a poor man's Chic. But knowledgeable disco and R&B enthusiasts knew better; Change wasn't a carbon copy of Chic any more than jazz great Chet Baker was a clone of Miles Davis. Without question, Change was heavily influenced by the Nile Rodgers/Bernard Edwards sound; nonetheless, Change had an energy of its own, and anyone who seriously listened to its first album, *The Glow of Love,* could easily tell the difference between Chic and Change (just as serious jazz fans can tell the difference between Baker's trumpet playing and Davis'). Produced by Jacques Fred Petrus and arranged by David Romani and Paolo Gianolio, this 1980 debut is a disco/R&B masterpiece. The playful opener "A Lover's Holiday" is Change's best-known song, but the group is just as captivating on the sassy "It's a Girl's Affair" and the passionate "Angel in My Pocket." Meanwhile, Luther Vandross is featured on "Searching" and the dreamy, laid-back title song, which became a quiet storm favorite and demonstrates that not everything Change recorded was aimed at the dancefloor. In 1980, Vandross had yet to provide his first solo album, although many of the people who heard his performances on those two gems agreed that a solo career was inevitable; and sure enough, his first big solo hit, "Never Too Much," came out the following year. Excellent from start to finish, *The Glow of Love* is Change's most essential album. *—Alex Henderson*

Miracles / 1981 / Atlantic ♦♦♦
Miracles was Italian dance band Change's first album without lead vocals by a prestardom Luther Vandross. Much ado was made about James Robinson taking over the lead vocal duties, including unfair comparisons. Lost in the discussion was the fact that *Miracles* is a very good album. Of course, there are strong Chic influences (they were one of the hottest acts around at the time), but taken on their own merit, Change could jam with the best of them. The chugging, thumpin' "Paradise" went to number-seven R&B in spring 1981. The soul-tugging "Heaven of My Life" was the third single. Its flip side was the mellow "Miracles," a loving ode from a father to his daughter. Other highlights are the dreamy second single "Hold Tight," the smooth radio-aired "Your Move," and the sweet ballad "Stop for Love." Some 20 years later, R&B singer Tamia sampled several cuts. Some of the LP's tracks can be found on *Very Best of Change.* *—Ed Hogan*

Sharing Your Love / 1982 / London ♦♦♦
The second and final album that featured lead vocalist James Robinson. Change continued scoring hits with "The Very Best in You," while the uptempo tunes clicked in the clubs and the slow songs got urban contemporary airplay. The group had toured successfully in 1981 and that momentum continued into 1982. *—Ron Wynn*

This Is Your Time / 1983 / Atlantic ♦♦

Change of Heart / 1984 / Atlantic ♦♦
Jimmy Jam and Terry Lewis produced the bouncy danceable hit title track (similar in groove to Zapp's "More Bounce to the Ounce"), as well as the serene, atmospheric "Say You Love Me Again" and "You Are My Melody"; all can be found on *Very Best of Change.* The bulk of the album was written and produced by Timmy Allen, including the charting follow-up, the sly and funky "It Burns Me Up," and the quirky "Lovely Lady." *—Ed Hogan*

Turn on Your Radio / 1985 / Atlantic ♦
The once-dominant disco group Change enjoyed its final hit with this 1985 album. The lineup had changed radically from the days when Luther Vandross or James Robinson were providing exciting, soulful leads. The leads throughout this session, even on the lone successful single, "Let's Go Together," were more efficient than distinctive. The group's founder, Jacques Fred Petrus, returned to the production helm and recycled the arrangements that once made the group a major act. *—Ron Wynn*

● **Very Best of Change** / Jun. 30, 1998 / Rhino ♦♦♦♦♦
Showcasing a youthful Luther Vandross prior to his solo jaunts, *Very Best of Change* surveys the high points of the group's four-record career. This compilation does a very adequate job of chopping away at the filler found on each of its individual records and focuses not only on the hits, but the stronger album tracks that might have gone unnoticed. Early house music fans will find Change's attention to strong melodies and arrangements on par with many of its contemporaries (D Train, Aurra), but with a slightly sleeker R&B/Italo-disco edge. Fans of the group might find the notable absence of cult disco hit "Angel in My Pocket" irritating, but if you are only seeking out the hits then look no further than this compilation. *—Rob Theakston*

Miracles/Change of Heart / Nov. 19, 2002 / Spy ♦♦♦

Changing Faces

Group / Urban, Hip-Hop, Club/Dance
Changing Faces is a New York-based urban soul vocal duo much in the vein of similar all-female bands like TLC and SWV. The group blended soulful, gospel-tinged vocals with slick contemporary production and slight hip-hop influences.

Cassandra Lucas (b. East Harlem, NY) and Charisse Rose (b. Bronx, NY), the two members of Changing Faces, met each other while studying at New York's Music and Art High School. Following their high school graduation, the two went their separate ways, with Lucas studying sociology at Hunter College and Rose studying criminal justice at John Jay. Although both women were pursuing degrees, they hadn't given up on music and frequently performed as session musicians, singing demos, jingles, and background vocals. Within a few years, the two met again when they were hired as the touring supporting vocalists for Sybil.

Lucas and Rose stayed with Sybil for two years before deciding to team together as Changing Faces. The pair returned to New York, where they worked at a dermatologist's office in Manhattan during the day while recording demos at night with producer Dinky Bingham. Despite the long hours working on the demo, it wasn't a tape that led the group to Big Beat Records; it was the fact that they were heard by Kenny Smoove, head of Big Beat subsidiary Spoiled Rotten, as they sang on the street. A week later, the group had signed to the label, which was a subsidiary of Atlantic, and they had begun recording their debut.

Changing Faces' first two singles—"Stroke You Up" and "Foolin' Around"—were written and produced by R. Kelly, the hottest urban producer of the mid-'90s. The two singles reached the R&B Top Ten in late 1994, with "Stroke You Up" peaking at number three on the pop charts as well. Changing Faces' eponymous debut was released in 1995 and went gold on the strength of the two hits, even if the third single, "Keep It Right There," stalled at number 49.

Changing Faces returned in 1997 with their second album, *All Day All Night.* Kelly produced "G.H.E.T.T.O.U.T.," the first single from the album, and it was their biggest hit to date, reaching number one on the R&B charts and number-eight pop. Their third release, *Visit Me,* followed three years later. *—Stephen Thomas Erlewine*

Changing Faces / 1995 / Spoiled Rotten ♦♦♦♦♦
Changing Faces' recording career was off to a pleasant, if less than spectacular, start with this self-titled debut album. The name Changing Faces alluded to changing trends in 1990s R&B, which was moving away from hard-driving, hard-edged new jack swing and toward a smoother, softer type of medium-tempo groove. In fact, pretty much everything on this CD (which was produced by R. Kelly, Heavy D, Kenny "K-Smoove" Kornegay, and Devante Swing, among others), favors a medium tempo—the New York duo doesn't inundate the listener with either ultra-slow ballads or fast, danceable material. Cassandra Lucas and Charisse Rose, collectively Changing Faces, are competent singers—and while slow jams like "Thoughts of You," "Movin' On," and "Come Closer" are neither mind-blowing nor distinctive, they're likable enough. Not surprisingly, "Foolin' Around" and "Stroke You Up" (both written and produced by R. Kelly) became major hits—Kelly was huge in 1995, and his Isley Brothers-meets-hip-hop approach was very much in-demand. Even though this slick debut isn't a gem, it let listeners know that Changing Faces had potential. *—Alex Henderson*

● **All Day, All Night** / Jun. 10, 1997 / Atlantic ♦♦♦♦♦
Changing Faces' second album, *All Day, All Night,* finds the group working a musical territory similar to their debut, namely smooth urban R&B with light hip-hop influences.

Although the group's material is wildly uneven, the production is stylish and their vocals are strong, making the weak moments tolerable and the best songs quite attractive. *—Leo Stanley*

Visit Me / Oct. 10, 2000 / Atlantic ✦✦✦✦
The third album from the sister duo of Changing Faces brings about more of a mature attitude and a sheer presentation of urban beats and classic R&B grooves. On *Visit Me*, Cassandra Lucas and Charisse Rose deliver another dose of sassy wit and hellcat rhythms. The 15-song set list featured on *Visit Me* is slightly vibrant, although production credits from crooner R. Kelly boast the shimmering title cut and sultry "Stroke You Up." However, things get spicy with rapper Queen Pen's collaboration on "Ain't Got Me." It's nasty, and Changing Faces' strong femininity is full-fledged. They do not hide anything, and that serves for a brash delivery alongside fellow female artists such as Toni Braxton, Whitney Houston, and Lil' Kim. *—MacKenzie Wilson*

Bruce Channel

b. Nov. 28, 1940, Jacksonville, TX
Vocals / Rock & Roll
Bruce Channel's "Hey Baby"—a classic one-shot, number-one hit from 1962—is one of the many records proving that, during a period in which rock has sometimes been characterized as near death, the form was continuing to evolve in unexpected and delightful ways. An irresistible midtempo shuffle from the first few bars of homespun harmonica (played by Delbert McClinton), it was a seemingly effortless blend of rock, blues, country, and Cajun beats, featuring Channel's lazy, drawling vocals and an instantly catchy tune. It was perhaps too much of a natural; Channel could never recapture the organic spontaneity of the track, failing to re-enter the Top 40 despite many attempts.

The Texan had written "Hey Baby" around 1959 with his friend Margaret Cobb, and had already been performing the tune for a couple of years before recording it amidst a series of demos for Fort Worth producer Major Bill Smith. First released locally on Smith's label, it was picked up for national distribution by Smash. Channel would continue to write most of his own material (sometimes in collaboration with Cobb) for a series of moderately enjoyable follow-ups that echoed the riffs of "Hey Baby" too closely.

McClinton played his immediately identifiable harmonica on several of these, and made his own contribution to rock history in 1962, when he was touring as a member of Channel's band in Britain. On one of their shows, they were supported by a then-unknown Liverpool group, the Beatles, who had yet to cut their first record. John Lennon was smitten by McClinton's style of playing, and picked up some pointers that he put to use on the Beatles' very first single, "Love Me Do"; in fact, McClinton's influence can be easily detected in Lennon's harmonica playing on many early Beatles tracks from 1962 and 1963. Channel did get another Top 20 hit in Britain in 1968, "Keep On," which was written by Wayne Carson Thompson (famous for penning the Box Tops' "The Letter"). Nothing else clicked in a big way on either side of the ocean, and by the late '70s he was working in Nashville as a songwriter. *—Richie Unterberger*

● **Hey! Baby** / 1962 / Collectables ✦✦✦✦
Here's Bruce's original Smash album, recorded hot on the heels of the title hit, along with the bonus of the follow-up single, "Number One Man." The album filler all features Delbert McClinton's harmonica, which added the signature sparkle to "Hey! Baby" (the track that made John Lennon want to pick up a harp), with credible renditions of "Baby, It's You," "Chantilly Lace," Jivin' Gene's "Breakin' Up Is Hard to Do," "Ain't Got No Home," Roy Orbison's "Dream Baby," and Elvis' "Love Me," probably all staples of his then-current stage act. For a quickie album, this is a marvelously cohesive-sounding effort, and a nice souvenir of early-'60s Texas rock & roll/pop. *—Cub Koda*

Goin' Back to Louisiana / 1964 / Sonet ✦✦

Hey Baby! / 1990 / Teenager ✦✦✦✦
Here are nineteen of his vintage sides, many mining the same Cajun/Tex-Mex/shuffle groove as "Hey Baby," sometimes simply rewriting the song sideways by inserting or mildly modifying its key riffs. It's still highly enjoyable stuff, just too derivative of his one great hit to qualify him as a true original. McClinton plays harmonica on several of the tracks, and also wrote one of them, "My Baby"; the LP also includes his 1968 British hit "Keep On." The sound and liner notes aren't that great; this interesting early exponent of Southern swamp rock deserves a more carefully packaged retrospective on CD. *—Richie Unterberger*

The Channels

f. 1955, New York, NY
Group / Doo Wop
While never having a run of hits, the Channels were among the most popular East Coast doo wop ensembles. Larry Hampden, Billy Morris, and Edward Doulphin were charter members of the Channels, who formed in 1955. They started with two part-time members, but then absorbed lead vocalist Earl Michael Lewis and Clifton Wright from the Lotharios. Lewis became their principal songwriter and he penned their best-known hit, "The Closer You Are." The Channels also brought a fresh style to doo wop singing with their practice of opening a verse in five-part harmony, then having Lewis sing lead in the bridge. Later releases like "The Gleam in Your Eye" and "I Really Love You" were superbly performed, but never got the push needed for national recognition. They later recorded for Gone, Fury, Port, Hit, Enjoy, and Groove with numerous personnel changes. *—Ron Wynn*

● **Greatest Hits** / 1990 / Relic ✦✦✦✦
The Channels (surprisingly) never reached the charts, so *Greatest Hits* isn't an accurate title—maybe "Greatest Regional Hits" would've been a better choice—but everything else about this Relic collection is done thoughtfully and well. The disc includes each of the 16 sides the group recorded over five years with Bobby Robinson's labels (Whirlin' Disc and Fury), including East Coast favorites like "The Closer You Are" and "The Gleam in Your Eye." The Channels never moved far from that rich, midtempo supper-club sound, but with the talent displayed on most of these tracks, the lack of variety hardly sounds like a liability. Other highlights are "My Love Will Never Die," a gorgeous 1959 ballad from their second stint with Robinson (after two years misspent with George Goldner), and "Stay as You Are," with a stunning harmony falsetto. Though it's more obscure than the *New York's Finest* collection on Collectables (filed under Earl Lewis & the Channels), this one has two extra tracks. *—John Bush*

The Chantels

f. 1956, New York, NY [The Bronx], **db.** 1970
Group / Girl Group, Doo Wop, R&B, Harmony Vocal Group
One of the very first girl groups, the Chantels are best-known for their 1957 hit "Maybe." Between 1957 and 1963, the trio racked up a number of hit singles, but none of them was ever as popular as "Maybe," which came to be regarded as one of the definitive singles of the genre.

All five members of the Chantels—Arlene Smith, Lois Harris, Sonia Goring, Jackie Landry, and Rene Minus—met as children, when they sang in the choir of Saint Anthony of Padua, a Bronx-area school. Arlene Smith was the leader of the quintet. Smith wrote all of the group's early material and she was the one who convinced the other girls—whose age ranged between 14 and 17 at the time—to audition for Richard Barrett, a record producer and a member of the doo wop group the Valentines. Barrett signed the band to End Records and produced the Chantels' first single, a Smith song called "He's Gone." Released in the summer of 1957, the single peaked at number 71. However, the group's second single—another Smith composition called "Maybe"—was a smash hit, peaking at number two on the R&B charts and number 15 on the pop charts in early 1958. "Maybe" sold more copies than its chart position suggests; the single was pirated by several other small record labels and none of those sales were tallied for the final chart position.

For the next year, the Chantels tried in vain to deliver a follow-up as successful as "Maybe." Two hit singles—"Every Night (I Pray)" and "I Love You So"—followed on End Records, but the label dropped them after a handful of other records failed to make an impact. Around that time, Smith left the group to pursue a solo career and Harris had left the group. The Chantels didn't replace either singer and continued as a trio.

In the summer of 1959, the group supported Richard Barrett on his single, "Summer's Love," which peaked at number 29 on the R&B charts. In 1961, the Chantels signed with Carlton Records, where they had two minor pop hits: "Look in My Eyes" and "Well, I Told You." Carlton dropped the group the following year and the band moved to Ludix, where they had a minor hit with "Eternally" in the spring of 1963.

The Chantels continued performing until the end of the decade; they officially disbanded in 1970. A few years later, Arlene Smith re-formed the Chantels, recruiting four new members; the other original members all retired from the entertainment business. Smith continued to lead various incarnations of the Chantels into the '90s. When she wasn't touring the oldies circuit with the Chantels, Smith worked as a schoolteacher. *—Stephen Thomas Erlewine*

The Chantels / 1958 / Collectables ✦✦✦
Originally released by End in 1958, this fine reissue collects the Chantels' smash "Maybe," along with their follow-up attempts to that hit. With Richard Barrett and George Goldner producing, they created a majestic sound with only spare instrumentation (usually piano, bass and drums) and the power of Arlene Smith's passionate voice. *—J.P. Ollio*

We Are the Chantels / 1958 / End ✦✦✦
The first LP ever issued on the End label was a natural product of the success of "Maybe," one of the great ballads to come out of the rock & roll boom and one of the most beloved R&B singles ever to emanate from the orbit of label owner George Goldner. For the album, all Goldner did was assemble the two sides of each of the existing six Chantels singles, but it's still a pretty impressive body of music, a fact that makes it a tribute to producer Richard Barrett. "Maybe" is the best song here, to be sure, with a career-making performance by Arlene Smith, but the rest of the album is not to be ignored: "The Plea" (co-authored by Smith and Barrett), which offers shimmering backing vocals by the group and a memorably passionate lyric; the radiant "Come My Little Baby," with its exquisite chorus and a honking sax solo thick enough to cut with a knife; the bluesy "Congratulations," with its "lead" bass instrumental arrangement; the ethereal ballads "Prayee," "He's Gone," and "I Love You So"—even Richard Barrett's attempt to emulate "Maybe," "Every Night (I Pray)," is worth hearing as a refinement and expansion of the hit. [Note: This album was originally released as *We Are the Chantels*, with an image of the five-member group on the cover; such were the racial sensitivities of the time, however, that it was withdrawn and reissued in 1959 with the same catalog number and the title *The Chantels*, packaged in a more innocuous cover depicting two white teenagers standing next to a jukebox.] *—Bruce Eder*

The On Tour (The Look in My Eyes) / 1961 / Carlton ✦✦✦

There's Our Song Again / 1962 / End ✦✦✦
The second End Records album by the Chantels, released after they'd switched labels, was assembled mostly from existing singles. It's a more sophisticated record, reflecting the fact that its songs date from 1959-1961 rather than 1957-1959. The actual personnel singing on much of this record, however, is a matter of conjecture (apart from a pair of songs that unquestionably feature Arlene Smith), but the appeal of the music is a given. "Never Let Go" is the catchiest song here, a bouncy and memorable tune wrapped around a lovely and spirited performance, but everything here is accessible. If there is a flaw other than the disjointed personnel, which leaves a somewhat confusing array of singers and sounds to sort through, it's that the recordings themselves are softening somewhat, and moving toward sophisticated pop ("C'est Si Bon") rather than sticking with pure R&B or early rock & roll. *—Bruce Eder*

For Collectors Only / 1988 / Collectables ♦♦♦

- **The Best of the Chantels** / May 1990 / Rhino ♦♦♦♦♦

The Chantels were rock & roll's first great female group. This 18-track best-of gathers all of their important recordings for George Goldner's End label, along with some rarities amongst the hits. In addition to the smashes "Maybe," "He's Gone," and "Every Night," the set also includes their work with Richard Barrett and their one-off single backing Willie Wilson, issued as the Tunemasters. An interesting chapter of the distaff side of rock & roll history. *—Cub Koda*

The Look in My Eyes: The Best of Carlton & Ludix Years / Oct. 21, 1997 / Collectables ♦♦♦

The Chantels' story is usually told in terms of Arlene Smith's involvement with the group, and little is said of their work after her departure, following their being dropped by End Records. This disc covers their lesser-known but equally beguiling early 1960s sides for the Carlton and Ludix labels, when their lead singer was Annette Smith. The material is palpably different from the classic Chantels' sound, mostly because the early '60s weren't the late '50s—R&B had grown more sophisticated, a shift reflected in producer Richard Barrett's use of string arrangements on "Look in My Eyes" and its even prettier B-side, "Glad to Be Back," which heralded a new Chantels sound. Even the hard-rocking "Well I Told You" features a tasteful and effective use of an orchestra, buried very deep in the mix but just audible enough to add extra color to the uptempo piece. The reconstituted Chantels kept their string going for close to another year, getting serious radio play on "Here It Comes Again" and cutting perhaps their prettiest vocal performance in George Gershwin's "Summertime," when Carlton Records ran into financial trouble, and they were forced to jump to Ludix, where they succeeded again with the single "Eternally." The later Barrett-composed songs are upbeat dance numbers that anticipate the sound that he would later perfect with the Three Degrees. The Chantels were, by the middle of the decade, one of the more sophisticated female R&B outfits of their era. That's the side profiled here, and it's worth hearing, even if it isn't quite the groundbreaking work of the original group. The CD is nicely programmed. *—Bruce Eder*

We Are the Chantels/There's Our Song Again / Jun. 9, 1998 / WestSide ♦♦♦♦

The Chanters

f. Queens, NY

Group / R&B

The Chanters, from Queens, NY, sounded like Frankie Lymon & the Teenagers, but the similarities ended there—the group never enjoyed any fame and had only one hit (and that occurred after they had called it quits). The members were Larry Pendergrass, Elliot Green, Fred Paige, Bud Johnson, and Bobby Thompson. Johnson's father, Bud Johnson Sr. (who composed "Since I Fell for You" and recorded during the '40s and '50s for Decca and Mercury) tutored the group and wrote lavish arrangements for their singles. He also used his influence and contacts to get the Chanters a deal with Deluxe Records in 1958.

Their first record, the bona fide rocker "My, My Darling," languished, as did subsequent singles: "Row Your Boat," "Five Little Kisses," and "No, No, No" (as Bud Johnson & the Chanters), all released in 1958. They left Deluxe to record "For Sentimental Reasons" as the Voices Five on Craft Records in 1959, their last time in the studio, but not their last release. In 1961, Deluxe reissued "No, No, No" a second time, and this time backed it with bucks; it became the Chanters first chart record at number-41 pop, and number-nine R&B. Though Deluxe released two more Chanters singles, the group had disbanded and never benefited from their hit record.

The guys splintered in many directions. Life was good for Bud Johnson Jr., for awhile: He married, had kids, and worked as a computer programmer. But drugs caused him to lose it all, and home became Queens, NY's notorious LaFrak City Apartments. (His son is Albert Johnson, aka Prodigy, half of the rap duo Mobb Deep.) Alas, Johnson Jr., never kicked his addiction and died in 1996 from AIDS. *—Andrew Hamilton*

- **Golden Classics** / Sep. 24, 1996 / Collectables ♦♦♦♦♦

If you didn't know better, these 18 infectious tracks would have you thinking that the Chanters were one of the late-'50s/early-'60s' top groups. Despite an abundance of skills, however, nothing clicked for the Queens, NY, natives. They never sold many records and only enjoyed a small following. Kiddie tenor Larry Pendergrass was a virtual clone of Frankie Lymon; a more mature tenor did the honors on "Angel Darling," a quality slow doo wop, but Pendergrass handled most leads. Crack arrangements by Bud Johnson elevated their recordings (style-wise) above those of their contemporaries, and you'll love all of these charming, contagious romps and ballads (except possibly "On the Alamo," an odd, campy tune with dumb lyrics). Prime movers include "No, No, No," "Five Little Kisses," "Row Your Boat," "At My Door," "My, My Darling," and the strong MOR updates "Over the Rainbow" and "For Sentimental Reasons." *—Andrew Hamilton*

Chapter 8

f. 1972, Detroit, MI, **db.** 1989

Group / Quiet Storm, Soul

This Detroit group is best known as the band that helped launch Anita Baker's career. The original group was founded by Michael Powell and David Washington in 1972. They backed the Detroit Emeralds until Powell and Washington added vocalist Rick Means and Carolyn Crawford. Crawford was later replaced by Barbara Love. When Love departed, Washington added Baker, whom he had heard singing background with the Osmoses, another local group. Means had left by the time Chapter 8 signed with Ariola in 1979. Baker and Gerald Lyles split lead vocals, with Powell, Derek Dickson, Allen E. Nance, Courtien Hale, Scott Guthrie, Van Cephus, and Washington completing the lineup. Their debut LP, *Chapter 8*, was released in 1979, but Ariola promptly dropped them. Baker moved on to solo fame. By their second LP in 1985 for Beverly Glenn, Valerie Pinkson was alternating on lead vocals with Lyles, while keyboardist Vernon Falls joined veterans Hale, Washington, and Powell. *This Love's for Real* didn't garner any hits, but was a solid soul and funk outing. The lineup remained intact for their third release, *Forever*, in 1988 for Capitol. Powell produced it, but it also didn't sell and Capitol also dropped them. Powell has emerged as a successful producer, scoring hits on songs produced for Baker and Regina Belle. Various Chapter 8 musicians have also recorded with Baker, Peabo Bryson, David Peaston, and James Ingram. *—Ron Wynn*

- **Chapter 8** / 1979 / Varese Sarabande ♦♦♦

Before she gained fame as a solo star, Anita Baker was the lead singer of Chapter 8. Their self-titled album was the most popular, spawning four hit singles, including "I Just Wanna Be Your Girl." *—Jonathan Ball*

Forever / 1988 / Capitol ♦♦

Charlene (Charlene Marilynn D'Angelo)

b. Jun. 1, 1950, Hollywood, CA

Vocals / Motown, Pop, Soft Rock, Urban

Her mom christened Charlene (born June 1, 1950, in Hollywood, CA), Charlene Marilynn D'Angelo. Who would have thought a recording career with Motown, years later, would twist and turn more than a Rubik's Cube? She signed to the label in 1973, when she was 23 years old, as Charlene Duncan. Her first single, "All That Love Went to Waste," came in January 1974, sandwiched between Edwin Starr's "Ain't It Hell Up in Harlem" and the Jackson Five's "Dancing Machine.

She next appeared on Motown's Prodigal label three years later with "It Ain't Easy Comin' Down," which was credited to Charlene, though an album issued the same month had Charlene Duncan on the spine (confusingly, it was titled *Charlene*). Another album, *Songs of Love* from May 1977, was a repackaging of the previous album with a new version of one song, "I've Never Been to Me," this time missing a spoken bridge. Issued as her third single, it became the most successful to date with a number 97 showing on the charts. She released one more single on Motown, 1980's "I Won't Remember Ever Loving You," but then was dropped until 1982, when "I've Never Been to Me" became a radio hit. Motown re-recorded the song with the deleted spoken bridge—which preached about abortion and unborn children—and it soared to number three on the pop chart in 1982.

Unfortunately, Charlene was never able to follow up her lucky break with another hit. "Used to Be," a duet with Stevie Wonder, notched at number 46 in 1982, though it was her last chart entry. Lack of hits, however, didn't prevent Motown from emptying its vaults of Charlene tracks. Her third LP, *I've Never Been to Me*, came out in March 1982, and again one month later with a different cover. *The Sky Is the Limit* dropped in January 1983, and *Hit and Run Lover* appeared a year and a half later. Her recording of "Fire" appeared on *The Last Dragon* soundtrack from the movie of the same name, but after leaving Motown again in 1985, she seemingly dropped from the face of the earth. *—Andrew Hamilton*

- **I've Never Been to Me** / 1982 / Motown ♦♦♦♦♦

Bobby Charles (Robert Charles Guidry)

b. Feb. 21, 1938, Abbeville, LA

Songwriter, Vocals / New Orleans R&B, Traditional Cajun

More successful as a songwriter than a singer, Bobby Charles was nonetheless an important contributor to Louisiana music in both respects. He authored several hits for key artists in the early days of rock & roll (including Bill Haley and Fats Domino), and although he recorded mostly in obscurity, he emerged as one of the founding fathers of swamp pop.

Robert Charles Guidry was born February 21, 1938, in the Cajun-country town of Abbeville, LA, and grew up listening to traditional Cajun music. As a teenager, he discovered rock & roll and rhythm & blues, and began singing with a band called the Cardinals, who performed at local dances. During this period, he wrote a song called "See You Later, Alligator," which particularly impressed a Crowley, LA, record-store owner who happened to know Chess Records founder Leonard Chess. The young singer auditioned over the phone and was rewarded with a recording session at the legendary Cosimo's studio in New Orleans. After hearing the single version of "See You Later, Alligator," Chess signed Guidry (by some accounts, not realizing he was a white Cajun) and soon shortened his name to the less regional Bobby Charles. Chess released "See You Later, Alligator" as Charles' debut single in 1955, and he toured behind it after graduating from high school. While it connected with R&B audiences, the song didn't become a big pop hit until 1956, when Bill Haley covered it for a national best-seller. Charles scored another minor hit that year with "Time Will Tell," and stayed with Chess through 1957, recording R&B singles that even at this stage were already infused with a Cajun musical sensibility.

In 1958, Charles moved to Imperial and cut several more singles through the next year. Although he was silent for a few years after cutting a one-off cover of "Goodnight Irene" for Farie in 1959, Charles' reputation as a songwriter continued to grow. In 1960, Fats Domino took "Walking to New Orleans" into the Top Ten, and Clarence "Frogman" Henry did likewise early the following year with "(I Don't Know Why I Love You) But I Do." Charles subsequently recorded sides for Hub City (1963), Jewel (1964), and Paula (1965), by which time he was experimenting with country music.

With little commercial success of his own, Charles drifted away from the music business for a while. He returned in 1972 on the Bearsville label and cut a self-titled album (his first full-length) that was co-produced by the Band's Rick Danko. In fact, the majority of the Band appeared on the record as supporting musicians, as did Dr. John, David Sanborn, and Amos Garrett. In spite of considerable critical acclaim, *Bobby Charles* didn't sell very well, and after recording with Paul Butterfield in 1973, a disenchanted Charles again retreated from music. He appeared with the Band in their 1976 concert film *The Last Waltz*, joining them on-stage for one song of their final performance. The following year, he returned to Bearsville and recorded another album with Spooner Oldham on piano, but the project was never released.

Charles kept quiet for most of the next decade, returning in 1986 with a couple of singles on the Rice n' Gravy label, plus a European-only album called *Clean Water* in

1987. In the meantime, his songs had been recorded by numerous artists from the worlds of blues, rock, country, and soul; a partial list includes Joe Cocker, Delbert McClinton, Lou Rawls, Ray Charles, Tom Jones, Kris Kristofferson, Rita Coolidge, Etta James, Junior Wells, Clarence "Gatemouth" Brown, Bo Diddley, David Allan Coe, and even UB40. In 1995, Charles signed with the Canadian blues and roots label Stony Plain and released a new album, *Wish You Were Here Right Now*, which consisted of sessions from 1992-1993 plus selections from a 1984 jam session at Willie Nelson's studio. In addition to Nelson, guests included Neil Young, Fats Domino, and slide ace Sonny Landreth. A follow-up, *Secrets of the Heart*, appeared in 1998, but Charles returned to rural Cajun country to live the quiet life, supported by his songwriting royalties; he also became a local environmental activist. His excellent *Bobby Charles* album has been reissued several times (including once in 1988 under the title *Small Town Talk*, its most famous composition). *—Steve Huey*

- **Bobby Charles** / 1972 / Stony Plain ✦✦✦✦✦

Hooking up with the Band, specifically Rick Danko and their producer John Simon, was one of the smartest moves Bobby Charles ever made. His subsequent eponymous album on Bearsville not only gave him a bigger audience, but led to the perfect production for his sly, subtle blend of New Orleans R&B, rock & roll, and country. Partially, that's because the production is fuller, richer than his sides for Chess, Jewel, and Paula, boasting not just some grit, but a sweetness on ballads like "I Must Be in a Good Place Now," a tune every bit as good as those from the singer/songwriters who dominated the charts in 1972. This gives the album an earthier quality than anything else he recorded; it also makes the album feel like a perfect companion piece to other roots rock albums from the time like, of course, the Band. Still, there's a special charm to this record, largely because while it sounds contemporary, it retains Charles' mellow vibe and his sharp songwriting. The songs come on slow—"Street People," "He's Got All the Whiskey," and "Small Town Talk" all slowly unwind—but the slow build is friendly, welcoming you into the song. This isn't lazy music, but it takes its time and it's better for it; it's perfect music for a hot summer afternoon. It's a true hidden gem of blue-eyed soul, Southern R&B, and early '70s roots rock (and early-'70s singer/songwriterism, for that matter). *—Stephen Thomas Erlewine*

- **Chess Masters** / 1986 / Chess ✦✦✦✦✦

Bobby Charles is a rare talent, an eccentric whose eccentricities were subtle and charming, not as pronounced as many of the rock & roll and R&B wildmen. As such, he's been ignored by all but aficio nados of New Orleans R&B over the years, even after such prominent exposure as his featured slot on the Band's Last Waltz. This status as a perennial cult act means that his work was rarely available consistently, and this 1986 vinyl collection *Chess Masters* remains the only time his Chess recordings have been collected. In other words, they've never made it to CD, apart from the superb 1995 set *Chess New Orleans*, which had the bulk of Charles' singles for the label. For collectors, that remains the way to track the material down (although that set has since gone out of print, unfortunately), but this collection proves that it should be heard on its own terms, since his exceptional songwriting talents, sly laidback delivery, and rollicking rhythms music rank him among the best New Orleans has offered. Plus, his Chess recordings offered not just his definitive "See You Later Alligator," but the hardest rocking music he ever made. *—Stephen Thomas Erlewine*

Wish You Were Here Right Now / 1995 / Stony Plain ✦✦✦

Secrets of the Heart / Jan. 27, 1998 / Stony Plain ✦✦✦✦

Hopefully, this disc will prevent the writer of such songs as "Walking to New Orleans," "See You Later Alligator," "I Can't Quit You," and "The Jealous Kind" from being known only as a songwriter. Bobby Charles is a writer of superb talent and stylistic versatility. This disc includes the R&B smash for Delbert McClinton, "I Can't Quit You," the south of the border "Angel Eyes," the "loungey" (in the best sense) "But I Do," and the second-line soul of "Party Town" standing out; several new tracks, like "You" and "I Don't Want to Know," have the potential to join the ranks of Charles classics. To bring out the best in these songs, he has received the support of a stellar cast of players from New Orleans and beyond, who treat the songs with the respect that their writer deserves. There are no mediocre songs on this disc; some may not be to your taste, but each is well crafted and performed with care. There is also a bonus at the end of the disc after a two-minute pause—a better-than-average interview that lasts about 15 minutes. It's nice the first time, but it is a pain when it comes up on shuffle mode. *—Bob Gottlieb*

Walking to New Orleans (The Jewel & Paula Recordings 1964–1965) / Dec. 12, 2000 / WestSide ✦✦✦✦✦

Bobby Charles could write a hit, as "Walking to New Orleans" and "See You Later Alligator" proved, but he wasn't necessarily the one to *have* the hit. Others would come along and record perfect, definitive versions of the songs, while Charles remained behind the scenes—or, perhaps more accurately, down in New Orleans, recording singles for independent labels without ever breaking out of the region. It's not that hard to see why he remained a local favorite, not a star. He had a relaxed delivery that was too idiosyncratic and laid-back, something that was perfect for New Orleans and R&B connoisseurs back then, and right now, which is why WestSide is offering *Walking to New Orleans (The Jewel & Paula Recordings 1964-1965)*. These are the sides that are often overlooked in Charles' career—he had more success with Chess in the '50s; his Band-sponsored Bearsville record in 1972 brought him to a new audience—but they're as good as anything he ever did. This has a light, easy touch, not just in his delivery but in the nimble rhythms and the no-frills production (never gritty, always friendly). Some of the sides are a little generic but in a good way: They deliver what they should. But the best is smart, funny, warm New Orleans R&B that anyone who truly loves the genre should seek out. *—Stephen Thomas Erlewine*

Ray Charles (Ray Charles Robinson)

b. Sep. 23, 1930, Albany, GA

Vocals, Piano, Leader / Soul, Country-Soul, Jazz Blues, R&B, Piano Blues, Urban Blues, Pop-Soul

Ray Charles was the musician most responsible for developing soul music. Singers like Sam Cooke and Jackie Wilson also did a great deal to pioneer the form, but Charles did even more to devise a new form of black pop by merging '50s R&B with gospel-powered vocals, adding plenty of flavor from contemporary jazz, blues, and (in the '60s) country. Then there is his singing; his style is among the most emotional and easily identifiable of any 20th century performer, up there with the likes of Elvis and Billie Holiday. He's also a superb keyboard player, arranger, and bandleader. The brilliance of his 1950s and 1960s work, however, can't obscure the fact that he's made few classic tracks since the mid-'60s, though he's recorded often and tours to this day.

Blind since the age of six (from glaucoma), Charles studied composition and learned many instruments at the St. Augustine School for the Deaf and the Blind. His parents had died by his early teens, and he worked as a musician in Florida for a while before using his savings to move to Seattle in 1947. By the late '40s, he was recording in a smooth pop/R&B style derivative of Nat King Cole and Charles Brown. He got his first Top Ten R&B hit with "Baby, Let Me Hold Your Hand" in 1951. Charles' first recordings have come in for their fair share of criticism, as they are much milder and less original than the classics that would follow, although they're actually fairly enjoyable, showing strong hints of the skills that were to flower in a few years.

In the early '50s, Charles' sound started to toughen as he toured with Lowell Fulson, went to New Orleans to work with Guitar Slim (playing piano on and arranging Slim's huge R&B hit, "The Things That I Used to Do"), and got a band together for R&B star Ruth Brown. It was at Atlantic Records that Ray Charles truly found his voice, consolidating the gains of recent years and then some with "I Got a Woman," a number-two R&B hit in 1955. This is the song most frequently singled out as his pivotal performance, on which Charles first truly let go with his unmistakable gospel-ish moan, backed by a tight, bouncy horn-driven arrangement.

Throughout the '50s, Charles ran off a series of R&B hits that, although they weren't called "soul" at the time, did a lot to pave the way for soul by presenting a form of R&B that was sophisticated without sacrificing any emotional grit. "This Little Girl of Mine," "Drown in My Own Tears," "Hallelujah I Love Her So," "Lonely Avenue," and "The Right Time" were all big hits. But Charles didn't really capture the pop audience until "What'd I Say," which caught the fervor of the church with its pleading vocals, as well as the spirit of rock & roll with its classic electric piano line. It was his first Top Ten pop hit, and one of his final Atlantic singles, as he left the label at the end of the '50s for ABC.

One of the chief attractions of the ABC deal for Charles was a much greater degree of artistic control of his recordings. He put it to good use on early-'60s hits like "Unchain My Heart" and "Hit the Road Jack," which solidified his pop stardom with only a modicum of polish attached to the R&B he had perfected at Atlantic. In 1962, he surprised the pop world by turning his attention to country & western music, topping the charts with the "I Can't Stop Loving You" single, and making a hugely popular album (in an era in which R&B/soul LPs rarely scored high on the charts) with *Modern Sounds in Country & Western Music*. Perhaps it shouldn't have been so surprising; Charles had always been eclectic, recording quite a bit of straight jazz at Atlantic, with noted jazz musicians like David "Fathead" Newman and Milt Jackson.

Charles remained extremely popular through the mid-'60s, scoring big hits like "Busted," "You Are My Sunshine," "Take These Chains From My Heart," and "Crying Time," although his momentum was slowed by a 1965 bust for heroin. This led to a year-long absence from performing, but he picked up where he left off with "Let's Go Get Stoned" in 1966. Yet by this time Charles was focusing increasingly less on rock and soul, in favor of pop tunes, often with string arrangements, that seemed aimed more at the easy listening audience than anyone else. Charles' influence on the rock mainstream was as apparent as ever; Joe Cocker and Steve Winwood in particular owe a great deal of their style to him, and echoes of his phrasing can be heard more subtly in the work of greats like Van Morrison.

One approaches sweeping criticism of Charles with hesitation; he's an American institution, after all, and his vocal powers have barely diminished over the years. The fact remains, though, that his work since the late '60s on record has been very disappointing. Millions of listeners yearned for a return to the all-out soul of his 1955-1965 classics, but Charles had actually never been committed to soul above all else. Like Aretha Franklin and Elvis Presley, his focus is more upon all-around pop than many realize; his love of jazz, country, and pop standards is evident, even if his more earthy offerings are the ones that truly broke ground and will stand the test of time. He's dented the charts (sometimes the country ones) occasionally, and can command devoted international concert audiences whenever he feels like it. For good or ill, he ensured his imprint upon the American mass consciousness in the 1990s by singing several ads for Diet Pepsi™. The CD era has seen several excellent packages that focus on various chronological/thematic phases of the legend's career. *—Richie Unterberger*

Ray Charles / Jul. 1957 / Atlantic ✦✦✦

These are animated soul and R&B recordings, although the rock & roll links are pretty obvious as well. The songs, vocals, arrangements, and production are great; only the sound quality falters. But they can also be obtained on many other anthologies with far superior sound. *—Ron Wynn*

The Great Ray Charles / 1957 / Atlantic ✦✦✦

This set is rather unusual, for it is strictly instrumental, allowing Ray Charles a rare opportunity to be a jazz-oriented pianist. Two selections are with a trio (bassist Oscar Pettiford joins Charles on "Black Coffee"), while the other six are with a septet taken from his big band of the period. Key among the sidemen are David Newman (soloing on both tenor and alto) and trumpeter Joseph Bridgewater; highlights include Quincy Jones' "The Ray," "My Melancholy Baby," "Doodlin'," and "Undecided." Ray Charles should have recorded in this setting more often in his later years. *—Scott Yanow*

Soul Brothers / 1958 / Atlantic ♦♦♦♦
By the time this album was cut, Ray Charles was already an established rhythm & blues star, fortified with the recording of his 1955 hit "I Got a Woman." He joined up with Milt Jackson two years later for a session that merges the soul styling of Charles with the jazz orientation of Jackson. Although some discographies have it the other way around, this is really a Charles event and thus there is a play list consisting mostly of songs he composed and certainly music that he was comfortable playing, with a nice balance between soul, blues, and straight-up jazz. Apparently, one objective of this album was to demonstrate that Charles' talent extended beyond vocals and piano. Here he is heard as more than a fair-to-middling alto sax player, as well as dabbling with the electric piano, and he doesn't sing on this edition of the session. The set kicks with a slow-dragging version of Leroy Carr's "How Long, How Long Blues," where Charles plays both alto sax and piano at the same time, obviously through the use of dubbing, with Skeeter Best's guitar getting in some significant licks. This track is as close to pure soul as one can get within a jazz context. Charles also used this occasion to establish himself as a swinging bop pianist as he and Jackson trade fours and eights on "Cosmic Ray," underscored by drum breaks by Connie Kay. "Charlesville" is devoted entirely to Charles' pianism with just the rhythm section in tow. Jackson sits this one out. An excellent session by two masters of their art. *—Dave Nathan*

Ray Charles at Newport / Jul. 5, 1958 / Atlantic ♦♦♦♦♦
For his appearance at the Newport Jazz Festival on July 5, 1958, Charles pulled out all the stops, performing raucous versions of "The Right Time," "I Got a Woman," and "Talkin' 'Bout You." [This album was reissued in 1973 as a two-record set, packaged with *Ray Charles in Person* under the title *Ray Charles Live*.] *—William Ruhlmann*

Yes, Indeed!! / Oct. 1958 / Atlantic ♦♦♦

The Genius of Ray Charles / 1959 / Atlantic ♦♦♦♦♦
Some players from Ray Charles' big band are joined by many ringers from the Count Basie and Duke Ellington bands for the first half of this program, featuring Charles belting out six songs arranged by Quincy Jones. "Let the Good Times Roll" and "Deed I Do" are highlights, and there are solos by tenorman David "Fathead" Newman, trumpeter Marcus Belgrave and (on "Two Years of Torture") tenor Paul Gonsalves. The remaining six numbers are ballads, with Charles backed by a string orchestra arranged by Ralph Burns (including "Come Rain or Come Shine" and "Don't Let the Sun Catch You Cryin'"). Ray Charles' voice is heard throughout in peak form, giving soul to even the veteran standards. *—Scott Yanow*

What'd I Say / May 28, 1959 / Atlantic ♦♦♦
At a concert held at Herndon Stadium in Atlanta on May 28, 1959, Ray Charles turns in a blistering version of "What'd I Say" and takes on the big band era with versions of Tommy Dorsey's "Yes Indeed!" and Artie Shaw's "Frenesi," not to mention performances of "The Right Time" and "Tell the Truth." [This album was reissued in 1960 under the title *Ray Charles in Person* and again in 1973 as a part of a two-record set, packaged with *Ray Charles at Newport* under the title *Ray Charles Live*.] *—William Ruhlmann*

Genius + Soul = Jazz / 1960 / DCC ♦♦♦
One of the best early-'60s examples of soul/jazz crossover, this record, like several of his dates from the period, featured big-band arrangements (played by the Count Basie band). This fared better than some of Charles' similar outings, however, if only because it muted some of his straight pop aspirations in favor of some pretty mean and lean, cut-to-the-heart-of-the-matter Hammond B-3 organ licks. Most of the album is instrumental and swings pretty vivaciously, although Charles does take a couple of vocals with "I'm Gonna Move to the Outskirts of Town" and "I've Got News for You." Yet one of those instrumentals, a cover of the Clovers' "One Mint Julep," would give Charles one of his most unpredictable (and best) early-'60s hits. In 1997, it was combined with the much later *My Kind of Jazz* album (from 1970) onto a single-disc CD reissue by Rhino. *—Richie Unterberger*

The Genius Hits the Road / 1960 / Rhino ♦♦♦
In keeping with his jazz/pop crossover ambitions, Charles decided to record a concept album of sorts with a dozen songs devoted to various parts of the U.S.—"Alabamy Bound," "Georgia on My Mind," "Moonlight in Vermont," "California, Here I Come," "Blue Hawaii," etc. The crossover vibe is further heightened by the brassy big-band arrangements, and material from the likes of Al Jolson and Hoagy Carmichael. It sounds a bit corny now, with an in-your-face gung-ho cheer. But it did what Charles wanted it to do, reaching the Top Ten of the album charts, and spinning off a big hit with "Georgia on My Mind." The 1997 CD reissue on Rhino adds seven bonus tracks from 1956-1972 that also had a travel/geographic theme, and the best of these are actually the highlights of the record, most notably "Hit the Road Jack," "Lonely Avenue," and his cover of Hank Snow's "I'm Movin' On." *—Richie Unterberger*

Ray Charles in Person / May 1960 / Atlantic ♦♦♦♦♦
At a concert held at Herndon Stadium in Atlanta on May 28, 1959, Ray Charles turns in a blistering version of "What'd I Say" and takes on the big band era with versions of Tommy Dorsey's "Yes Indeed!" and Artie Shaw's "Frenesi," not to mention performances of "The Right Time" and "Tell the Truth." [This album is a reissue of *What'd I Say*; it was reissued in 1973 as part of a two-record set, packaged with *Ray Charles at Newport* under the title *Ray Charles Live*.] *—William Ruhlmann*

The Genius After Hours / 1961 / Rhino ♦♦♦♦♦
Taken from the same three sessions as *The Great Ray Charles* but not duplicating any of the performances, this set casts Charles as a jazz-oriented pianist in an instrumental setting. Brother Charles has five numbers with a trio (three songs have Oscar Pettiford on bass) and jams on three other tunes ("Hornful Soul," "Ain't Misbehavin'," and "Joy Ride") with a septet arranged by Quincy Jones; solo space is given to David "Fathead" Newman on tenor and alto and trumpeter Joseph Bridgewater. Fine music—definitely a change of pace for Ray Charles. *—Scott Yanow*

Soul Meeting / 1961 / Atlantic ♦♦♦

Ray Charles and Betty Carter / Jun. 13, 1961-1966 / ABC/Paramount ♦♦♦♦
This pairing of two totally idiosyncratic vocalists acquired legendary status over the decades in which it had been out of print. But the proof is in the listening, and frankly it doesn't represent either artist's best work. There is certainly a powerful, often sexy rapport between the two—Charles in his sweet balladeering mode, Carter with her uniquely keening, drifting high register—and they definitely create sparks in the justly famous rendition of "Baby, It's Cold Outside." The main problem is in Marty Paich's string/choir arrangements, which too often cross over the line into treacle, whereas his charts for big band are far more listenable. Moreover, Charles' sweetness can get a bit cloying too, although some of the old grit emerges on "Takes Two to Tango." On the CD reissue—remixed by Charles himself—Dunhill adds the great, rare B-side to the "Unchain My Heart" single, "But on the Other Hand Baby," and two excellent if unrelated album cuts, "I Never See Maggie Alone" (1964) and "I Like to Hear It Sometime" (1966). *—Richard S. Ginell*

The Genius Sings the Blues / Oct. 1961 / Atlantic ♦♦♦♦♦
This features down-home, anguished laments and moody ballads were turned into triumphs by Ray Charles. He sang these songs with the same conviction, passion, and energy that made his country and soul vocals so majestic. This has not turned up in the reissue bins. *—Ron Wynn*

Do the Twist With Ray Charles! / Nov. 1961 / Atlantic ♦♦♦
Here is a low-budget compilation of early Ray Charles material. The songs are great, but better-mastered versions and more complete packages are available on other labels. *—Ron Wynn*

☆ **Modern Sounds in Country & Western Music** / Apr. 1962 / Rhino ♦♦♦♦♦
Less modern for its country-R&B blend (Elvis Presley & company did it in 1955) and lushly produced C&W tone (the Nashville sound cropped up in the late '50s) than for its place as a high-profile crossover hit, *Modern Sounds in Country & Western* fit right in with Ray Charles' expansive musical ways while on the Atlantic label in the '50s. In need of even more room to explore, Charles signed with ABC-Paramount and eventually took full advantage of his contract's "full artistic freedom clause" with this collection of revamped country classics. Covering a period from 1939 to the early '60s, the 12 tracks here touch on old-timey fare (Floyd Tillman's "It Makes No Difference to Me Now"), honky tonk (three Hank Williams songs), and early countrypolitan (Don Gibson's "I Can't Stop Loving You"). Along with a Top Ten go at Eddy Arnold's "You Don't Know Me," the Gibson cover helped the album remain at the top of the pop charts for nearly three months and brought Charles international fame. Above a mix of swinging big band charts by Gerald Wilson and strings and choir backdrops from Marty Paich, Charles' intones the sleepy-blue nuances of country crooners while still giving the songs a needed kick with his gospel outbursts. No pedal-steel or fiddles here, just a fine store of inimitable interpretations. *—Stephen Cook*

☆ **Modern Sounds in Country & Western Music, Vol. 2** / Oct. 1962 / Rhino ♦♦♦♦♦
Having struck the mother lode with *Vol. 1* of this genre-busting concept, "Brother Ray," producer Sid Feller, and ABC-Paramount went for another helping and put it out immediately. The idea was basically the same—raid the then-plentiful coffers of Nashville for songs and turn them into Ray Charles material with either a big band or a carpet of strings and choir. This time, though, instead of a random mix of backgrounds, the big band tracks—again arranged by Gerald Wilson in New York—went on side one, and the strings/choir numbers—again arranged by Marty Paich in Hollywood—were placed on side two. Saleswise, it couldn't miss, but, more importantly, *Vol. 2* defied the curse of the sequel and was just as much of an artistic triumph as its predecessor, if not as immediately startling. Charles' transfiguration of "You Are My Sunshine" sets the tone, and, as before, there's a good quota of Don Gibson material; "Don't Tell Me Your Troubles" becomes a fast gospel rouser and "Oh Lonesome Me" a frantic big band number. Paich lays on the '50s and early-'60s Muzak with an almost gleeful, over-the-top commercial slickness that with an ordinary artist would have been embarrassing. But the miracle is that Charles' hurt, tortured, soulfully twisting voice transforms the backgrounds as well as the material; you believe what he's singing. It appealed across the board, from the teenage singles-buying crowd to adult consumers of easy listening albums and Charles' core black audience—and even those who cried "sellout" probably took some secret guilty pleasures from these recordings. While Charles didn't get a number one chartbuster à la "I Can't Stop Loving You" out of this package, "Sunshine" got up to number seven, and "Take These Chains From My Heart," with its Shearing-like piano solo and big string chart, made it to number eight—which wasn't shabby at all. *—Richard S. Ginell*

Ingredients in a Recipe for Soul / Jul. 1963 / ABC ♦♦♦♦
Although it was a big commercial success, reaching number two on the LP charts, this record would typify the erratic nature of much of Charles' '60s output. It's too eclectic for its own good, really, encompassing pop standards, lowdown blues, Mel Tormé songs, and after-hours ballads. The high points are very high—"Busted," his hit reworking of a composition by country songwriter Harlan Howard, is jazzy and tough, and one of his best early-'60s singles. And the low points are pretty low, especially when he adds the snow-white backup vocals of the Jack Halloran Choir to "Over the Rainbow" and "Ol' Man River." A number of the remaining cuts are pretty respectable, like the tight big band arrangement of "Ol' Man Time" and the ominously urbane "Where Can I Go?" In 1997, it was paired with the 1964 LP *Have a Smile With Me* on a two-for-one CD reissue on Rhino, with the addition of historical liner notes. *—Richie Unterberger*

Sweet & Sour Tears / Mar. 1964 / Rhino ♦♦♦
One of a series of ultra-loose concept albums Charles cut in the '60s, this one dedicated entirely to songs with titles or lyrical references to crying and tears. It's an excuse for Ray to choose his usual varied menu of upbeat jumpers, slow countrified weepers, and

proudly saccharine pop standards. The production, as one might fear, also tends to the lachrymose side on the slow tunes, with the thick strings and backup vocals straight out of TV variety shows. One is almost tempted to think that Charles was toying with audience expectations by mixing unabashedly sentimental slow tunes with the far more bluesy, satisfying, and upbeat numbers, such as "Don't Cry, Baby" and "Baby, Don't You Cry," as well as his surprisingly brassy, punchy treatment of "Cry Me a River." These outings have always played much better with critics than the gloppy pop tunes, and for good reason—they are much better. The Rhino CD reissue adds seven bonus tracks from throughout his early career (1956-1971) that also tapped into the "crying" motif. These threaten to steal the show from the *Sweet & Sour Tears* album it's supposedly embellishing, including the Bacharach-David penned 1964 single "I Wake Up Crying," the smoldering 1966 album track "No Use Crying," and the 1956 R&B chart-topper "Drown in My Own Tears," next to which much of the rest of the program sounds positively hokey. *—Richie Unterberger*

Have a Smile With Me / 1964 / ABC/Paramount ✦✦

The idea behind this LP was to offer a lighthearted sequel to its quasi-concept predecessor, *Sweet & Sour Tears*. There's nothing wrong with the idea of letting Charles just kick back and have fun, but "The Thing" and "The Man with the Weird Beard" transcend the boundaries of humor into silliness and, worse, stupidity. On the other hand, he also turns out a good jazzy version of Hank Williams' "Move It on Over" (the record's highlight), and manages to swing through fairly superficial fare like "Ma (She's Making Eyes at Me)" and "Two Ton Tessie" with solid flair. It was another inconsistent '60s set, the shortage of top-notch tunes disguised by a flimsy concept, though he elevates the material with soulful vocals and good arrangements, particularly when the Raelettes back him up (as they do on half the tracks). In 1997, it was paired with the 1963 LP *Ingredients in a Recipe for Soul* on a two-for-one CD reissue on Rhino, with the addition of historical liner notes. *—Richie Unterberger*

Live in Concert / Jan. 1965 / ABC ✦✦✦

This classic 1964 recording by Ray Charles includes 12 vintage tracks performed to perfection. His voice is in great shape, and the recording by Wally Heider is a marvel for its day; all the instruments are placed nicely with Charles' voice out front where it belongs. There's a slinky version of "Hallelujah I Love Her So," the musicians creating nice little changes behind Charles' soulful nuances. The singer tells us Miss Lillian Ford of the Raelettes "helps out" on "Don't Set Me Free"; it's a duet and a nice change of pace. Rick Ward's tacky liner notes fail to say who is backing up the singer at The Shrine Auditorium in Los Angeles, except for David "Fathead" Newman credited with the tenor solo on "Swing a Little Taste," the opening track. Not to be confused with the 1973 re-release *Ray Charles Live*, which is comprised of 1958 and 1959 concerts, this album is called *Live in Concert*, and is Charles in Los Angeles after a Japanese tour in 1964. "What I'd Say" and a nice version of "Margie" are here, along with a six-minute take on "I Gotta Woman." For the finale he has the Ray Charles Choir come out to help close the show with a marching-band version of "Pop Goes the Weasel." The 12 tracks are priceless Ray Charles, especially the reinvention of "You Don't Know Me," stirringly different from his timeless hit version but just as impressive. Excellent photos by Ray Hearne, especially the cover profile. *—Joe Viglione*

Country & Western Meets Rhythm & Blues / Aug. 1965 / ABC/Paramount ✦✦✦

This is a partially successful revisiting by Charles of his country sessions of the early '60s. These songs weren't quite as transcendent as those on the prior dates, but he showed once again that the lines between country, R&B, and soul weren't as rigid as many in the various camps thought. *—Ron Wynn*

Crying Time / Feb. 1966 / ABC/Paramount ✦✦✦

Ray's Moods / Jul. 1966 / ABC/Paramount ✦✦✦

A Portrait of Ray / Mar. 1968 / ABC/Tangerine ✦✦✦

Love Country Style / 1970 / ABC/Tangerine ✦✦✦

While this legendary performer's fourth trip to the country & western well starts strongly with "If You Were Mine" and his version of the Johnny Cash standard "Ring of Fire," the album as a whole doesn't come close to his Olympian standards. Some of the arrangements by Sid Feller are better suited for the unrelated (and unworthy) Ray Charles Singers. For a much more satisfying slice of the Genius doing country music his way, listen instead to either of his *Modern Sounds in Country and Western Music* volumes. *—Mark Allan*

My Kind of Jazz / Apr. 1970 / Tangerine ✦✦✦✦

This LP came seemingly out of the blue as a showcase for the Ray Charles big band, spawning two little-known sequels later on in the '70s. It's a roaring, solid band, too, playing jazz standards like "This Here," "The Sidewinder," "Bluesette," and "Senor Blues," comfortable at slow, loping tempos as well as in the rousers, with excellent mainstream soloists (none of whom are identified) and good conventional charts (also uncredited). The sole exception to the pattern—and a hit single in its own right—is a catchy, funky Charles gospel/blues called "Booty Butt," where Charles adds multi-tracked gospel moans for his sole vocal contribution, and the band chimes in only on the very last chord. Clearly, the title and the appalling lack of credits say volumes about Charles' reputation as a control freak; this is his kind of jazz and nobody else's. In 1997, it was combined with the much earlier *Genius + Soul* album onto a single-disc CD reissue by Rhino. *—Richard S. Ginell & Richie Unterberger*

Volcanic Action of My Soul / Apr. 1971 / ABC/Tangerine ✦✦✦

Only Ray Charles and a select few could make a dirty blues like "Feel So Bad" soulful against the backdrop of an orchestra and a lavish arrangement. But he does just that throughout this 1971 release that comes with a poem by Julian Bond, credited here as the Bishop of Atlanta. The larder of mostly remakes includes "Wichita Lineman," "Something," "The Long and Winding Road," and a bluesy "What Am I Living For." Charles works his magic; but after listening to his gritty vocals on these slick charts, you'll be longing for a previously unreleased Ray Charles in Muscle Shoals session (if there ever was one) to be uncovered in a vault. *—Andrew Hamilton*

A Message From the People / Apr. 1972 / ABC/Tangerine ✦✦✦

My Kind of Jazz, Number 2 / 1973 / Tangerine ✦✦✦

A great, though poorly distributed, session on Charles' own Tangerine label. It was his return to the combo jazz of the early '60s, and he showed that he could still play it with authority. Charles owns all the Tangerine masters, and hasn't as of yet opted to reissue these, so it's doubtful that this will emerge again anytime soon. *—Ron Wynn*

Ray Charles Live / May 1973 / Atlantic ✦✦✦✦✦

A repackaging of *Ray Charles in Newport* and *Ray Charles in Person* presents concerts from 1958 and 1959 that found Charles in peak form, performing some of his best-known R&B hits. *—William Ruhlmann*

Porgy & Bess / Oct. 1976 / RCA Victor ✦✦✦

Charles and Cleo Laine duet on the songs from George Gershwin's opera, in a version arranged and conducted by Frank DeVol (who provides extra instrumentals) and produced by Norman Granz. The material is perfect for the performers, and they give it an effective, if unstudied, treatment. *—William Ruhlmann*

True to Life / Oct. 1977 / Atlantic ✦✦✦

Love & Peace / Sep. 1978 / Atco ✦✦

Here, unfortunately, is one of several examples of why Ray Charles has been such a frustrating record-maker over the last quarter of the 20th century at least. His powers of expression as a vocalist and keyboardist are undiminished on the second album of his return to the Atlantic fold; he could still squeeze some soul out of anything. But his ability to choose great, good, or even merely appropriate material had deserted him—and so we hear nowhere ballads ("She Knows"), stale song ideas ("You 20th Century Fox"), empty, poorly arranged and paced rousers ("We Had It All"), and political statements that fall flat ("A Peace That We Never Before Could Enjoy," "Give the Poor Man a Break")—nothing that even this prodigious talent can save, and all treated to a veiled, raucous mix. Other than the team of arrangers (Harry Goodnight, Roger Newman, Larry Mahoberack), there are no musician credits nor any notes. Ultimately the blame for this uninteresting record must go to the producer, the co-engineer, the lead keyboardist, and the singer—who are all one and the same person. *—Richard S. Ginell*

Ain't It So / Sep. 1979 / Atlantic ✦✦✦

Here is one of the better albums from Charles' second sojourn at Atlantic in the '70s. Here, he gives listeners an uptempo version of Irving Berlin's "What'll I Do," and similarly revamps such standards as "Some Enchanted Evening" and "Blues in the Night." *—William Ruhlmann*

Wish You Were Here Tonight / 1983 / Columbia ✦✦✦

One of Columbia's "Best of Times" specials, this features Ray Charles doing nice, sometimes above average, country-pop and countrypolitan, plus some nondescript filler. This isn't one of his better releases, or the label's. *—Ron Wynn*

Do I Ever Cross Your Mind? / Apr. 1984 / Columbia ✦✦✦

This is a fairly typical example of Charles' '80s period doing country music in Nashville, which is to say respectable performances that aren't a patch on his '60s country-crossover material. The title track was a minor country hit single and the album made the lower reaches of the country LP chart. But Charles remains an eclectic; some of the material fits better into the pop and R&B categories than it does country. *—William Ruhlmann*

Friendship / Aug. 1984 / Columbia ✦✦

Ray Charles was cutting decent-to-competent light country material in Nashville during the mid-'80s. His still-gripping voice and masterful timing and delivery kept things from getting too disturbing, but these songs were a far cry from either his magnificent soul/R&B or his groundbreaking early-'60s country. They were mostly polite, sedate, occasionally humorous duets with such country stars as George Jones, Mickey Gilley, Merle Haggard, Janie Fricke, and Hank Williams Jr. *—Ron Wynn*

From the Pages of My Mind / Jul. 1986 / Columbia ✦✦✦

Another light country and countrypolitan outing from Ray Charles. These mid-'80s albums were miles removed from the earthiness and intensity he brought to his revolutionary '60s country dates. They're pleasant and often entertaining, but hardly vital. *—Ron Wynn*

Greatest Hits, Vol. 1 / 1987 / DCC ✦✦✦✦✦

The first of two DCC compilations to collect the best of Brother Ray's 1960s stint at ABC-Paramount Records, when he flew off in a dozen different stylistic directions. Included on this 20-track disc are Charles' immortal rendering of "Georgia on My Mind," and the sinuously bluesy "Unchain My Heart," the Latin-beat instrumental "One Mint Julep," personalized remakes of the country standards "Born to Lose," "Your Cheating Heart," and "Crying Time," and his exultant rendition of the soulful "Let's Go Get Stoned." *—Bill Dahl*

Greatest Hits, Vol. 2 / 1987 / DCC ✦✦✦✦✦

More seminal performances from the '60s ABC catalog of the Genius (DCC split the classics evenly between the two discs, making both of them indispensable). His beloved "Hit the Road Jack" (one of several Percy Mayfield copyrights dotting Charles' repertoire), the daring country crossover "I Can't Stop Loving You," an electric-piano powered "Sticks and Stones," a wise "Them That Got," and a wonderfully mellow "At the Club" rank with the 20-song disc's standouts (though versions of the Beatles' "Yesterday" and the corny "Look What They Done to My Song, Ma" end the set on a bummer note). *—Bill Dahl*

Genius After Hours/Great Ray Charles / Jul. 7, 1987 / Rhino/Atlantic ♦♦♦

☆ **Greatest Country and Western Hits** / 1988 / DCC ♦♦♦♦♦

Greatest Country and Western Hits is a 17-track compilation dating from DCC's early CD reissues of Ray Charles' post-Atlantic catalog. It's a fine distillation of Charles' two *Modern Sounds in Country & Western Music* albums, from which all of its selections are culled. At one time, this would have been an excellent addition to any basic Charles collection. Now that Rhino has acquired the rights to the whole of Charles' catalog, this compilation is long out of print, but certainly worth picking up if you run across a used copy. Otherwise, the original *Modern Sounds in Country & Western Music* albums remain the best-available introduction to Charles' country material, unless Rhino eventually releases a compilation of highlights from its four-disc box set *The Complete Country & Western Recordings 1959-1986*. *—Steve Huey*

Just Between Us / 1988 / Columbia ♦♦

Here is some late-'80s Charles light pop, countrypolitan, and other good to below-average material. Charles sings with the usual strong touches, but he can't salvage much of this stuff. It's designed for those who want everything he's ever done. Otherwise, it won't merit much mention in his extensive legacy. *—Ron Wynn*

Anthology / 1989 / Rhino ♦♦♦♦♦

This is perhaps the best single CD collection of Ray Charles' '60s and '70s ABC-Paramount material. They've also been issued on two separate anthologies, but for someone who only wants the essential items, this disc has them all over its 20 tracks. *—Ron Wynn*

Seven Spanish Angels & Other Hits / 1989 / Columbia ♦♦

This is a collection of what the label considered Charles' best cuts from his mid-'80s countrypolitan and country pop sessions, none of which were that great. The title track was a mildly entertaining duet between Charles and Willie Nelson. *—Ron Wynn*

Soul Brothers/Soul Meeting / 1989 / Atlantic ♦♦♦♦♦

This brings together all of the extant takes recorded for two albums that Milt Jackson made with Ray Charles for Atlantic in 1957 and 1958. With Oscar Pettiford, Connie Kay, and Kenny Burrell in the various lineups, this is bluesy jazz in a laid-back manner; it surprised many hardcore R&B fans when these albums were originally issued. Jackson moves from vibes to piano, and even guitar (on "Bag's Guitar Blues"), while Ray jumps between piano and alto sax on these sessions. A rare glimpse of Charles' jazz soul coming up for air. *—Cub Koda*

Would You Believe? / Oct. 16, 1990 / Warner Bros. ♦♦♦

Here is some early-'90s Ray Charles material that ranges from enjoyable to entertaining to forgettable. His voice retains its drama, intensity, and flair, but he's extending himself less and less (at least on album) and not finding the kind of material that his talents merit. *—Ron Wynn*

☆ **The Birth of Soul** / 1991 / Atlantic ♦♦♦♦♦

The title isn't just hype—this absolutely essential three-disc box is where soul music first took shape and soared, courtesy of Ray Charles' church-soaked pipes and bedrock piano work. Brother Ray's formula for inventing the genre was disarmingly simple: he brought gospel intensity to the R&B world with his seminal "I Got a Woman," "Hallelujah I Love Her So," "Leave My Woman Alone," "You Be My Baby," and the primal 1959 call-and-response classic "What'd I Say." There's plenty of brilliant blues content within these 53 historic sides: Charles' mournful "Losing Hand," "Feelin' Sad," "Hard Times," and "Blackjack" ooze after-hours desperation. No blues collection should be without this boxed set, which comes with well-researched notes by Robert Palmer, a nicely illustrated accompanying booklet, and discographical info aplenty. *—Bill Dahl*

The Birth of a Legend / 1992 / Valley Vue ♦♦♦♦♦

Of all the countless compilations that have been stitched together of Ray Charles' early sides for Jack Lauderdale's Swing Time Records, this two-disc box is the only CD package that treats these enormously important works with the reverent respect that they deserve (meaning decent mono sound quality instead of murky electronic reprocessed stereo dubbed from vinyl, cogent liner notes, and full discographical annotation). This is where the genius began, imitating Charles Brown at the very start (1949) and sounding like nobody but Brother Ray by 1952 (when he defected to Atlantic and hit the real big time). There are 41 tracks in all. *—Bill Dahl*

Blues + Jazz / 1993 / Rhino ♦♦♦♦♦

Another easy access point for Charles' seminal Atlantic catalog. This two-disc set is evenly split between his bluesiest sides on the first disc and a selection of his greatest jazz sides on disc two (gorgeously showcasing the sax work of David "Fathead" Newman on several pieces). Charles was a masterful blues purveyor; his "I Believe to My Soul" is simultaneously invested with heartbreak and humor, while the earlier "Sinner's Prayer," "The Sun's Gonna Shine Again," and the gospel-based "A Fool for You" emanate both hope and deep pain. *—Bill Dahl*

The Early Years / 1994 / Fat Boy ♦♦♦

In the late '40s and early '50s, Charles recorded several dozen sides for the Swingtime/Downbeat label, 30 of which are presented here. As has been noted many times by critics, these usually found Charles in a Nat King Cole swing-blues groove that was much smoother than the gritty R&B/soul he'd record for Atlantic in the later '50s; the influence of urban blues balladeer Charles Brown is also evident. Some critical essays, in fact, may lead you to believe that this work is trivial, but while it's undeniably derivative, it's enjoyable on its own terms, and not without strong hints of the searing soulfulness that was to come. Some of the selections are delivered with such refined polish that it doesn't even sound like Charles. But on the more anguished and fast-tempoed cuts in particular, you can hear him starting to arrive at the phrasing and emotion that would flower in the mid-'50s. Unfortunately, like most Tomato reissues, the sound is substandard; even assuming that the master tapes can't be located, a better job was probably possible, and a couple of cuts even duplicate skips from the vinyl. Exact dates and songwriting credits are also missing, although Pete Welding's essay does at least discuss the material on the discs in some detail, unlike many of Tomato's liner notes. *—Richie Unterberger*

Ain't That Fine / May 10, 1994 / Drive Archive ♦♦♦♦

Although the exact recording dates are not given, this reissue CD from the budget Drive Archive label is quite historical. The 14 selections are taken from Ray Charles' first sessions and they generally feature the pianist/vocalist in a trio with guitar and bass. Heavily influenced at the time by both Charles Brown and Nat King Cole, Charles is almost unrecognizable on these jazz-oriented pre-Atlantic rarities; two of the songs feature him with a larger group. Highlights include "Ain't That Fine," "You Always Miss the Water When the Well Runs Dry," "Don't Put All Your Dreams in One Basket" and "Baby Won't You Please Come Home." *—Scott Yanow*

★ **The Best of Ray Charles: The Atlantic Years** / Jul. 19, 1994 / Rhino ♦♦♦♦♦

Taking one of the most interesting bodies of work in the history of American music and trying to narrow it down to one 20-song compact disc would seem to be the sort of project that's doomed to failure, and there's little arguing that this collection of Ray Charles' classic Atlantic Records sides merely skims the surface of some of the most groundbreaking music in the history of R&B. But that's not to say that the surface in question isn't quite satisfying, and as an introduction to Charles' most crucial period of creative growth, *The Best of Ray Charles: The Atlantic Years* offers nearly all the hits, some choice lesser-known cuts, and an admirably accurate representation of his creative arc from this period, starting with rough-and-tumble jump blues such as "It Should've Been Me" and "Greenback" and growing into heartfelt but sophisticated proto-soul masterpieces like "What'd I Say" and "Drown in My Own Tears." One disc simply isn't enough to tell Ray Charles' full musical story from this period, but what is here is all top-shelf stuff, and the selection and sequence of this collection should please both longtime fans looking for a portable sampler and neophytes easing their way into Ray's Atlantic catalog. The mastering and packaging is done with Rhino's typical degree of care, and besides, who wouldn't enjoy a disc with "I Got a Woman," "Hallelujah, I Love Her So," "Lonely Avenue," "Night Time (Is the Right Time)," and "This Little Girl of Mine" on it? *—Mark Deming*

Strong Love Affair / Jan. 30, 1996 / Warner Bros. ♦♦

Once he signed to Warner Bros., Ray Charles adopted the '90s superstar schedule, releasing an album every three years. *Strong Love Affair*, the third of them (now on Quincy Jones' custom label, Qwest), is a self-production that finds Charles performing his usual mix of blues, R&B, and pop on a set of newly written songs. The material is serviceable, if generic, but what matters is Charles' typically expressive vocal performance. At 65, Charles may no longer be able to surprise us, but he doesn't seem ready to retire, and if new recordings from him risk redundancy and irrelevance, at their best they nevertheless can represent Charles as well as his earlier, revolutionary work. *Strong Love Affair* never tries to conform Charles to anything other than his eclectic self, and it never gets in his way. *—William Ruhlmann*

Complete Swing Time & Down Beat Recordings 1949-1952 / Feb. 21, 1997 / Night Train ♦♦♦

The light blues and jazz of Ray Charles' early recordings were heavily influenced by Nat King Cole, and Charles frequently recorded in a similar trio format. His sound changed dramatically soon after he signed to Atlantic in 1952: His singing became more forceful and confident, and his rock 'n' soul performances were unlike anything he had done earlier for the Swing Time or Down Beat labels. Night Train's two-disc set collects 45 of Charles' rare recordings for the aforementioned independent labels, including several alternate takes, all of which find him in an imitative mode that pales beside his later trailblazing sides. It is interesting to hear a reserved Ray Charles croon his way through these arrangements, many of which are frankly lackluster despite the presence of supporting players like Stanley Turrentine (a situation not improved by the slightly murky sound quality and sometimes wobbly pitch of the source material). As a historical document, this is a comprehensive look at Charles' early output, with session information and cursory notes, but without songwriting or publishing information. Buyers looking for early, raw R&B won't find it here, but serious devotees of Ray Charles will appreciate this archival release. *—Greg Adams*

Genius + Soul = Jazz/My Kind of Jazz / Jun. 10, 1997 / Rhino ♦♦♦♦♦

Ingredients in a Recipe for Soul/Have a Smile With Me / Aug. 19, 1997 / Rhino ♦♦♦

Genius & Soul: The 50th Anniversary Collection / Sep. 16, 1997 / Rhino ♦♦♦♦♦

As the first comprehensive, multi-label box set assembled on Ray Charles, the five-disc, 101-song *Genius & Soul: The 50th Anniversary Collection* is an extensive overview of one of the greatest musicians of the 20th century. Charles produced a body of work so rich and diverse that even five CDs only scratches the surface of his accomplishments. None of his instrumentals are on *Genius & Soul*, nor are his jazz and traditional pop efforts spotlighted. Instead, the box traces the evolution of his career, as he moves from an R&B pioneer to a mainstream pop crooner to a country-pop vocalist to a contemporary soul singer. Charles was a gripping, captivating vocalist, capable of making even bland music sound vital, but the fact is, his '70s and '80s recordings pale in comparison to his seminal '50s and '60s sides. Which means that the set becomes less compelling as it reaches the fifth disc, but the first three and a half discs are filled with timeless music that remains exciting, vital and altogether wondrous. *—Stephen Thomas Erlewine*

Ray Charles and Betty Carter/Dedicated to You / 1998 / Rhino ♦♦♦♦♦

Standards / Mar. 3, 1998 / Rhino ♦♦♦♦

Standards is a 17-track collection of Ray Charles' versions of classic pop songs, culled from recordings he made for Atlantic, ABC/Paramount, ABC/TRC and Crossover/Atlantic between 1959 and 1977. There are a handful of hits—"Georgia on My Mind,"

"Ruby," "That Lucky Old Sun," "Without Love (There Is Nothing)," "Makin' Whoopee"—but the collection concentrates on little-known album tracks and live cuts. Although the steady stream of repackages from Rhino can be a little overwhelming, the idea behind *Standards* is attractive, and it's executed well—it's nice to have all these songs on one collection, even if the live cuts can be a little distracting. Certainly, anyone looking for a collection of mellow ballads from Charles will not be disappointed by this set. *—Stephen Thomas Erlewine*

Duets / May 19, 1998 / Rhino ✦✦✦✦

Duets is such a terrific idea for a Ray Charles compilation, it's a wonder it hasn't been done before. Charles is always compelling as a solo vocalist, but he's also an exceptional duet partner, shaping his performance to that of his partners. He also sang with an exceptionally talented and diverse array of vocalists, from Betty Carter to George Jones. Both of those singers are featured, along with such luminaries as Margie Hendrix, Aretha Franklin, B.J. Thomas, Willie Nelson, Johnny Cash, Lou Rawls, Gladys Knight and Chaka Khan, on *Duets*, which draws from his Atlantic, ABC/Paramount, Columbia and Warner recordings. By covering so much ground, the compilation is a little uneven—the hard soul of "(The Night Time Is) The Right Time" doesn't necessarily jibe with the glossy pop-funk of "I'll Be Good to You"—but it's tied together by the simple fact that nearly all the performances are first-rate. The compilers have included some familiar items, such as "Summertime" and "Take Two to Tango," but they concentrate on forgotten gems. As a result, it's a compilation that will appeal to both casual and serious fans alike, especially considering that it's available at a very reasonable price. *—Stephen Thomas Erlewine*

Instrumentals / Jun. 2, 1998 / Rhino ✦✦✦✦

Rhino's *Instrumentals* features 16 instrumentals Ray Charles recorded between 1953 and 1970, culled from ten different albums for a variety of labels. These don't just feature Charles on the piano or organ—there are several cuts that feature him on the saxophone. Since it's divided between small-group and big-band sessions, the collection winds up being a little incoherent, but there's enough great music here to make such complaints quibbles—for anyone who's only familiar with his hits and vocal cuts, it offers a valuable look into an often-neglected side of Charles' work. *—Stephen Thomas Erlewine*

Complete Country & Western Recordings 1959–1986 / Oct. 27, 1998 / Rhino ✦✦✦✦

Ray Charles' explorations into country music were no mere dalliance. They have their genesis in "I'm Movin' On," the last record he made for Atlantic before moving on to ABC Paramount in 1960. But it was with the enormously successful *Modern Sounds in Country & Western* series of albums in 1962 (and the career making single "I Can't Stop Lovin' You") that made their mark, crossing over genre boundaries that were unthinkable at the time. An African-American doing hillbilly music was not a first, nor were uptown arrangements of hillbilly songs, but here was the Genius of Soul validating the music of the white working class, plain and simple. He was putting his own spin to it (hence the *Modern Sounds*), not merely a black voice singing Gene Autry songs, investing them with pain, emotion, and sorrow. It was an unprecedented achievement, both commercially and artistically, and now—decades later—it's viewed as just another genre-bender in the grand Ray Charles tradition. But this 92-track, four-CD box set is the first to gather them all in one place and view it as a consistent piece of work spread over a career as a stylist that's second to none. The first disc combines both volumes of the *Modern Sounds* albums; the rest of the anthology moves through singles, various returns to the concept over the years, and stray tracks from his later stretch at Columbia to spice it all up. This multi-disc set contains some very special music, nicely packaged—a moment in American music well worth investigating. *—Cub Koda*

Love Songs / Jan. 19, 1999 / Rhino ✦✦✦

Ray Charles has sung thousands of songs and many of them were love songs. For the compilers of Rhino's *Love Songs*, the ones that mattered are classics. Yes, there are a couple of unexpected inclusions that are thrilling, such as Leon Russell's "A Song for You," but for the most part it's standards like "I Can't Stop Loving You," "Come Rain or Come Shine," "Baby It's Cold Outside," "Georgia on My Mind," "You Are My Sunshine," "How Deep Is the Ocean" and "Till There Was You." True, there aren't too many big hits here, but that's all right, since every performance is superb. Since it spans so many years, the collection feels a little disjointed in places, but it will still satisfy fans looking for a strong collection of some of Charles' finest love songs. *—Stephen Thomas Erlewine*

★ **Ultimate Hits Collection** / Mar. 16, 1999 / Rhino ✦✦✦✦✦

James Brown may be "the hardest working man in show business," Aretha Franklin may be the Queen of Soul, but as *Ultimate Hits Collection* proves, the most apt nickname in all of music may belong to Ray Charles: the Genius. Forget for a moment that fitting all of Charles' hits on a mere two CDs is not remotely possible. Almost any Ray Charles greatest-hits compilation is going to be excellent, and this one is better than most, if only because it's two-discs long. *Ultimate Hits Collection* follows the path of Charles' work as it cruises through the genres he so richly influenced: R&B, pop, jazz, blues, and country. The standard favorites are here from Charles' repertoire, but what sets this compilation apart are the lesser-known tracks. "Mess Around" and "Hide Nor Hair" are certainly not as popular as "Hit the Road Jack," but they are no less enjoyable. The most welcome inclusion is Charles' version of the country classic "You Don't Know Me," which is often left off of other Charles retrospectives. Of the multitude of duets he has recorded, two appear here. "Seven Spanish Angels" with Willie Nelson and "I'll Be Good to You" with Quincy Jones and Chaka Khan are fine choices, but adding "Baby Grand" with Billy Joel could have pushed the collection from great to superb. The liner notes are lengthy and compelling, featuring some great photos, and the packaging, with each disc in its own jewel box, is functional. The sound quality is also superb, considering some of the recordings were almost 50 years old at the time of this release. *—Mark Vanderhoff*

The Very Best of Ray Charles / Mar. 14, 2000 / Rhino ✦✦✦✦

This 16-track budget package hits all the high notes of Brother Ray's rise to greatness. Starting in the '50s with classic Atlantic sides like "I've Got a Woman," "Hallelujah I Love Her So," "Night Time (Is the Right Time)," and "What'd I Say," the set also includes his landmark ABC country sides of the '60s ("I Can't Stop Loving You," "Georgia on My Mind"), finishing up with a duet with Willie Nelson on "Seven Spanish Angels." A perfect introduction to an American musical treasure. *—Cub Koda*

The Very Best of Ray Charles, Vol. 2 / Sep. 19, 2000 / Rhino ✦✦✦✦

Another round of great tracks compiled in typical Rhino fashion: the best recordings of the best tracks by some of the best artists. Chock-full of soul, this compilation features "Brother Ray" classics like "Hide Nor Hair," "Take These Chains From My Heart," and the one-two punch of the Beatles' "Yesterday" and "Eleanor Rigby." The only complaint about this fine collection is that the first volume really packed in the well-known songs, leaving volume two with what almost feels like second-string hits. A fine second step into the world of Ray Charles' music, especially for the price. *—Zac Johnson*

Blues Is My Middle Name / Feb. 27, 2001 / King Jazz ✦✦✦

The liner notes admit few details about the origins of these dozen songs, except to say that it's a "largely, previously unreleased selection of blues flavored tracks," and that they were recorded during Charles' stint at the independent Warwick imprint before he forged that fruitful relationship with Atlantic Records. It's certain that these do come from the early, pre-Atlantic years of Charles' career, even though about half of the titles appear on pre-Atlantic Charles compilations like *The Birth of a Legend* and *Complete Swing Time & Down Beat Recordings 1949-1952*. Charles' early discography is murky enough that it may be that even Ray Charles biographers couldn't say for sure which of these selections have never before appeared anywhere. Regardless, it's a slice of his early sessions, when he was trying out various blends of swing jazz, R&B balladry, and jump blues, though he had yet to find the raw soulful rock/R&B sound that launched him to greatness at Atlantic. It suffers mostly in comparison to his famous work; on its own merits it's decent, if derivative and erratic, formative R&B. At times there are strong hints at the grittiness that would flavor his classic work, as on "I'm Gonna Drown (Misery in My Heart)," "Hey Now," and the uptempo, raucous "Kissa Me Baby." At other times it's too polite jazz-blues, with his voice almost unrecognizably thin and restrained. *—Richie Unterberger*

Ray Charles Sings for America / Sep. 3, 2002 / Rhino ✦✦✦

The theme of this collection is, in large part, songs of patriotism, about specific American places, or testaments to the American spirit. Still, you do get the sense that the concept's rather vague, or at least has been applied pretty liberally in order to snag 20 songs that could fill up a collection to appeal to the national mood at the time of its release (about a year after September 2001). "Let It Be" and "Imagine," for instance, are classic songs, but (even leaving aside that they were written by Englishmen) how exactly do they embody the American character? Likewise, "That Lucky Old Sun" and "Over the Rainbow" might be venerated American songs, but they doesn't plug into a specifically American viewpoint as readily as, for instance, "New York's My Home" or even his cover of "Abraham, Martin and John." It's better to treat this as something of a ride through Ray Charles' take on Americana, which goes through country music, popular standards, gospel, covers of rock hits, and not a whole lot of the hard-driving soul for which he's most esteemed. It's an erratic set, spanning the early '60s to the inevitable 2001-2002 re-recording of "God Bless America," featuring Slash and Billy Preston, with six of the songs (including the equally inevitable "America the Beautiful") hailing from his 1972 album *A Message From the People*. Some of it's excellent, like "New York's My Home," the cover of Percy Mayfield's "The Danger Zone," and "Carry Me Back to Old Virginny"; some of it's fair; and the 1970s material, which comprises the bulk of the disc, too often tends toward the overly sentimental in both song selection and production. *—Richie Unterberger*

Tina Charles

Vocals / Disco, Hi-NRG

Session vocalist Tina Charles was no stranger to music by the time she partnered with Martin Jay in 5000 Volts, in 1975, to score the international hit "I'm on Fire." Charles and Jay already had some time together under their belts in the little-remembered band Northern Lights, while she also released a string of unsuccessful singles for CBS during 1969-1970: "Nothing in the World," "In the Middle of the Day," "Good to Be Alive," and "Bo-Bo's Party." Another early outfit, Wild Honey, cut a brace of 45s for Gordon Mills' MAM label during 1971-1972. Solo again by 1974, Charles signed with Bell and released "One Broken Heart for Sale," while also working as a vocalist for the *Top of the Pops* series of hit cover albums; she appears on around a dozen volumes in the redoubtable series, recorded between 1973-1975.

In 1975, Charles reunited with her old Northern Lights partner Martin Jay as Airbus. When their debut single "Bye Love" was flipped by their U.K. imprint Philips (which also christened them the more electrifying 5000 Volts), the B-side "I'm on Fire" became a major worldwide hit. More importantly, it brought her to the attention of the singularly named, and fast-rising disco producer Biddu.

Having already struck disco gold with Carl Douglas' massive hit, "Kung Fu Fighting," Biddu approached Charles and had her cut the solo single "You Set My Heart on Fire." Released on CBS (her permanent home through the 1970s), the single didn't do anything in the charts; undeterred, they promptly rebounded with the monumental disco anthem "I Love to Love (But My Baby Just Loves to Dance)." Reaching number one on the U.K. singles charts in February 1976, the track also emerged a minor hit in the U.S., where it fared better in the discos than in the mainstream slipstream. With Biddu working magically behind the scenes, Charles brought yet another single, "Love Me Like a Lover," into the U.K. charts that year. Backed by a band that included future Buggles Trevor Horn and Geoff Downes, Charles released her first LP that summer. *Dance Little Lady* brought a further two singles into the Top Ten at the end of 1976, the number six hit "Dance Little

Lady Dance" and the number-four smash "Dr Love." In total, Charles spent a remarkable 42 weeks on the U.K. chart in 1976 alone.

The following year was just as fruitful—she recorded two more LPs, *Rendezvous* and *Heart 'N Soul*, and three of her singles were chart smashes: "Rendezvous"; a medley of "Love Bug" and the oldie "Sweets for My Sweet" hit in 1977; but the most notable was the following year's cover of fellow-Biddu stablemate Jimmy James' hit "I'll Go Where Your Music Takes Me." Charles' star, though, appeared to be on the decline as disco gave way to a different kind of hedonism all together. Despite continuing to release singles during 1978, she began sinking from sight. A 1980 LP, *Just One Smile*, also failed to make any mark whatsoever. Charles returned to the British charts just one more time, with a 1986 remix of "I Love to Love." *—Amy Hanson*

Dance Little Lady / 1976 / CBS ✦✦✦

If Tina Charles' debut album was the sound of an uncertain vocalist wed to an over-ambitious producer, then her sophomore effort, 1976's *Dance Little Lady*, evens up the match. Both the title track, which gave her a U.K. number-six hit in August, and the smarmy-but-smart follow-up, "Dr. Love," brought Charles success on the singles chart, while both "Fallin' in Love With a Boy" and "When You Got Love" could easily have followed them. The highlights of the album, however, are two tracks that you might ordinarily have dreaded to encounter on a Biddu-fired disco album, the hauntingly traditional "Amazing Grace" and the old Billy Fury smash "Halfway to Paradise." In both cases, Charles finds a singing voice that far surpasses her familiar strained shriek, with "Paradise," in particular, a masterpiece of gentle cajoling that barely needs the strings to nudge it along. Elsewhere, *Dance Little Lady* hangs around precisely the same dance-floors that the bulk of Charles' career was built around, light and insubstantial disco flashed by the occasional catchy chorus. It was a competent brew, of course. But now you know she could do better. *—Amy Hanson*

I Love to Love / 1977 / Columbia ✦✦

● **Greatest Hits** / 1978 / CBS ✦✦✦

Though her regular albums all have their inspired moments, there really is only one direction in which the aspiring Tina Charles fan really needs to go—and this is it. This 1978 *Greatest Hits* spans, across 13 tracks, most of Charles' U.K. and European hits, including the still precious "You Set My Heart on Fire," which was a Top Three hit in Sweden months before her own British public started buying the follow-up. That, of course, was "I Love to Love," which opens this collection with a still-dazzling flamboyance. No matter that producer Biddu's arrangement owed so much to Barry White and MFSB, nor that the record established a musical precedent that Charles was never to break away from. Still it is easy to see how effortlessly it swept the globe. Moving deeper into the collection, a handful of generally well-chosen album tracks pad out the hits—"It's Time for a Change" was a welcome inclusion from *Dance Little Lady*, while "Sweets for My Sweet" was certainly the pick from *Rendezvous*. In fact, the only major criticism of the album is that, in its desire to portray Charles in a light that the average hits fan would find favorable, it leaves her looking even more one-dimensional than she actually was. She did love to love, of course. But she liked to do other things as well. *—Amy Hanson*

Just One Smile / 1980 / CBS ✦✦

The Very Best of Tina Charles / May 16, 2000 / Summit ✦✦✦

Fans were dished up a real treat with the 2000 release of *The Very Best of Tina Charles*. A comprehensive foray into the singer's 1976/1977-era material, this collection spans her hits and misses, and then adds even more besides. Taking the title track, Charles' 1976 smash "I Love to Love (But My Baby Loves to Dance)," and reaching out from there, it's a snappy spin through the best of her canon, from the earliest hits, "Dance Little Lady Dance" and "Dr. Love," and continuing on through the Biddu-fired passions of "I'll Go Where Your Music Takes Me" and "Love Bug." And that's just the hits. A host of other Charles cuts makes up the rest of this 18-track album, including the often-forgotten "You Set My Heart on Fire," "World of Emotions," and a cover of First Choice's 1973 hit "Smarty Pants." Although there are a few glaring omissions, most notably 1976's "Disco Fever," and although the end of the 1970s are woefully forgotten, *The Very Best of Tina Charles* makes up for it with a few more notable covers, including distinctive interpretations of Carly Simon's "You're So Vain" and Freda Payne's "Band of Gold." Thus, while it could have been far more complete in terms of its scope, this compilation is by far the best-available collection of Charles' unique body of work, one that will surely allow fans to finally file away their scratchy, old vinyl copies of their favorite songs. *—Amy Hanson*

The Charts

f. 1956, **db.** 1958

Group / Doo Wop, R&B

The Charts' 1957 hit "Deserie" endures as a doo wop classic, despite the fact that it failed to chart. Formed in 1956, the Harlem-born group—led by lead vocalist Joseph Grier and featuring Leroy Binns, Ross Buford, and Glenmore Jackson—were managed by musician Les Cooper, a native of Norfolk, VA, who had previously been a member of the Empires and the Whirlers, and by the mid-'50s was already a longtime scenemaker on New York's doo wop scene.

Cooper scored the Harlem quintet a contract with Danny Robinson's Everlast imprint and they recorded their only hit, "Deserie," the following year. It was covered by the Blue Angels for Del-Fi's Selma imprint on the West Coast. After a few more 45s for Everlast, the Charts disbanded in 1958. Cooper eventually cut a hit single with his own group, the Soul Rockers, in 1962. The vocal A-side was "Dig Yourself," but the major hit was the instrumental B-side, "Wiggle Wobble," which featured a prominent King Curtis-styled tenor sax performance by former-Charts lead singer Grier. *—Bryan Thomas*

● **Greatest Hits** / 1981 / Collectables ✦✦✦✦✦

The Charts are remembered—if at all—by their one hit, the doo wop classic "Deserie," which charted nationally twice, some 30 years apart. The group only made five singles, and all ten sides are here on this budget collection. The subsequent follow-ups that didn't click like "Deserie" still show a group that was equally adept at both ballads and uptempo material, like "Zoop," "Dance Girl," and "All Because of Love." Vocal-group fans, here's a one-stop shopping package that fires on all cylinders. *—Cub Koda*

Oliver Cheatham

b. 1948, Detroit, MI

Songwriter, Vocals / R&B, Funk, Soul

Singer Oliver Cheatham worked with fellow Detroiters Al Hudson and One Way and had a Top 40 R&B hit with the dance classic "Get Down Saturday Night" on MCA Records. Written by Cheatham and One Way multi-instrumentalist Kevin McCord, the jubilant "Get Down Saturday Night" made it to number 37 on the R&B chart in spring 1983. The follow-up single was the solid midtempo groover "Bless the Ladies," which featured a softly singing female chorus repeating: "bless the ladies / bless the girls / what would you do without us in this world." Cheatham's other charting singles included the Top 40 R&B hit "S.O.S," "Celebrate Our Love," and two duets with Jocelyn Brown: "Turn Out the Lights" and "Mindbuster." Other Oliver Cheatham singles were "Mama Said," "Put a Little Love in Your Heart," "Things to Make U Happy," and "Wish on a Star." *—Ed Hogan*

● **Saturday Night** / 1983 / MCA ✦✦✦

Chubby Checker (Ernest Evans)

b. Oct. 3, 1941, Philadelphia, PA

Vocals / Rock & Roll, R&B

Chubby Checker was the unrivaled king of the rock & roll dance craze; although most of the dances his records promoted—the Pony, the Fly, and the Hucklebuck, to cite just three—have long since faded into obscurity, his most famous hit, "The Twist," remains the yardstick against which all subsequent dancefloor phenomena are measured. Born Ernest Evans on October 3, 1941, in Philadelphia, he worked in a local poultry shop while in high school, and while on the job often entertained customers by singing and cracking jokes. His workplace antics helped win an audition with the local Cameo-Parkway label, who signed the fledgling singer in 1959; at the suggestion of no less than Dick Clark's wife, the portly youth was re-christened Chubby Checker, the name a sly reference to Fats Domino.

Checker's first single, "The Class," showcased his skills as an impressionist; while the record became a minor novelty hit, none of its immediate follow-ups were successful. In 1960, however, he recorded "The Twist," a cover of a 1958 Hank Ballard & the Midnighters B-side; Checker's rendition de-emphasized the original's overtly sexual overtones, focusing instead on the song's happy-go-lucky charms. The single rocketed to number one during the autumn of 1960, remaining on the charts for four months; some time after it dropped off, it slowly returned to prominence, and in late 1961 it hit number one again; the only record ever to enjoy two stays at the top more than a year apart. After "The Twist" first made Checker a superstar, he returned to the top in 1961 with "Do the Pony"; that same year, he also reached the Top Ten with "Let's Twist Again," which ensured the dance's passage from novelty to institution.

In addition to 1961's "The Fly," Checker's other Top Ten hits included three 1962 smashes: "Slow Twistin'," "Limbo Rock," and "Popeye the Hitchhiker." He even starred in a pair of feature films, *Twist Around the Clock* and *Don't Knock the Twist*. In total, Checker notched 32 chart hits before the bubble burst in 1966; as interest in dance novelties dwindled, he briefly turned to folk music, and became a regular on the nightclub circuit. From the 1970s onward, he was a staple of oldies revival tours; in 1982, more than a decade after his last studio LP, he signed with MCA and issued the disco-inspired *The Change Has Come*, scoring a pair of minor hits with the singles "Running" and "Harder Than Diamond." In 1988, Checker returned to the Top 40 for the first time in a quarter century when he appeared on the Fat Boys' rap rendition of "The Twist," and he continued touring regularly throughout the decade to follow. *—Jason Ankeny*

Chubby Checker / 1960 / Parkway ✦✦✦

Twist With Chubby Checker / Oct. 1960 / Parkway ✦✦✦✦

Listening to *Twist With Chubby Checker* is similar to listening to a Chuck Berry record—after a few minutes, you realize that the songs are just a series of variations on the same chord progressions with different lyrics. However, you also realize that the charisma of the performer is substantial enough to make such an enterprise interesting and, in fact, fun to listen to. Checker's bread and butter number, "The Twist" is likely to be the only song most listeners will recognize on the album, but that doesn't mean they won't enjoy hearing the rest of it. The record's back cover implores listeners to "put this ablum on from the beginning to the groovy end and go!!!" Indeed. *—Brian Egan*

Let's Twist Again / Sep. 1961 / Parkway ✦✦✦

Twistin' Round the World / 1962 / Golden Guinea ✦✦✦

Don't Knock the Twist [Soundtrack] / May 1962 / Parkway ✦✦✦

● **Chubby Checker's Greatest Hits** / Nov. 1972 / London ✦✦✦✦✦

In 1972, when nostalgia for late-'50s and early-'60s rock & roll was bringing Chuck Berry and others back into the charts, Allen Klein's ABKCO Records obtained the rights to reissue Chubby Checker's Cameo-Parkway singles on this 15-track hits LP. Checker actually had many more hits than just "The Twist" and "Let's Twist Again," and this LP presents his other dance tunes—"Pony Time," "The Fly," "Limbo Rock"—and several of his later, less successful singles when he was trying to branch out into a sort of Harry Belafonte-style folk approach. But the heart of the collection is still the early-'60s dance tunes, which demonstrate that, while Checker was not a great rocker, he still, like Freddy Cannon and Gary "U.S." Bonds, was one of the people keeping the flame of rock & roll flickering between the time Buddy Holly's plane went down in Iowa and the day the Beatles flew in from London. [Released on LP, this album is long out of print, and it is listed as Checker's "pick" album because, as of 1995, there is no in-print album containing his original hits.] *—William Ruhlmann*

The Checkmates, Ltd.

f. Fort Wayne, IN

Group / Pop-Soul, Soul

A '60s soul group, the Checkmates, Ltd. scored with one big hit, 1969's "Black Pearl." They were fronted by Sonny Charles, who later scored a big hit in the early '80s as a solo act. The group earned some attention for its integrated roster; other members were Bobby Stevens, Harvey Trees, Bill Van Buskirk, and Marvin Smith. They were from Fort Wayne, IN, and were a discovery of Nancy Wilson. They disbanded from 1970 to 1974, then returned for another shot and issued "All Alone by the Telephone" in 1976 for Polydor, which flopped. *—Ron Wynn*

Live at Caesars Palace / 1967 / Capitol ✦✦✦

● **Love Is All I Have to Give** / 1969 / A&M ✦✦✦✦

"Black Pearl" is one of the great Phil Spector productions, a phenomenal song with his extraordinary sound. That being said, it would be easy to try to dismiss this excellent album and focus just on the hit. That's the wonderful paradox of *Love Is All We Have to Give* by the Checkmates, Ltd. and Sonny Charles. Charles only re-scratched the Top 40 once (and that in 1983), but it is this album which showcases his major voice. The Leiber & Stoller composition "I Keep Forgettin'" has that sound from the 1966 Billy Stewart hit version of Gershwin's "Summertime" without the scat singing. Spector's remake of his own 1961 classic for Ben E. King, "Spanish Harlem," fits perfectly here, while "Proud Mary," the simple John Fogerty title, becomes a gospel *tour de force* falling somewhere between Tina Turner and the Edwin Hawkin Singers. The indomitable Perry Botkin Jr., who would hit seven years later with "Nadia's Theme" (aka "The Young & the Restless"), arranges and conducts side one with assistance from Dee Barton. Side two is another kettle of fish. Barton arranges Spector's adaption of "The Hair Anthology Suite" from the play *Hair*, most notably the material made famous by the 5th Dimension ("Age of Aquarius"/"Let the Sunshine In"). Though both artists probably tracked it around the same time—the 5th Dimension hitting in March and "Black Pearl" hitting in May 1969—there is none of the life here that Marilyn McCoo, Billy Davis Jr., and their group put into their first number one hit. Like a classic Spector 45, this album has one side that is totally inspired and brilliant, and a flip that won't get as many spins. All in all, it's a very important, and largely forgotten, bridge in Spector's catalog and his only hit in America on A&M, the same label he brought the Ronettes and Ike & Tina Turner's classic "River Deep, Mountain High." *—Joe Viglione*

Bobby Stevens & the Checkmates, Ltd. / 1971 / Rustic ✦✦

Cherelle (Cheryl Week Norton)

b. 1958, Los Angeles, CA

Vocals / Urban, Contemporary R&B

Cherelle hit number one R&B with "Everything I Miss at Home" written and produced by Jimmy Jam and Terry Lewis. Her other hits with the duo include "I Didn't Mean to Turn You On," "When I Look in Your Eyes," and a couple of debuts with Alexander O' Neal—"Saturday Love" and "Never Knew Love Like This."

Born Cheryl Week Norton in 1958 in Los Angeles, CA, her cousin is singer Pebbles. When her family moved to Detroit, MI, she met bassist/singer Michael Henderson who had hits with Norman Conners ("Valentine Love," a number ten hit duet with Jean Carn and "You Are My Starship," a number four summer 1976 hit). In 1977, Henderson was recording his gold album *In the Night-Time* ("Take Me I'm Yours," "In the Night-Time") and invited Cheryl to the studio. She come there in the evenings after she'd finished working at the bank. She became Cherelle because her boss would be stressed because she was always late for work. She'd yell, "Cher—relle, you're late!"

Cherelle went on tour with Michael Henderson and Luther Vandross. Later, she recorded a demo that came to the attention of Tabu Records owner Clarence Avant. Her attorney father negotiated the recording contract with Avant's label that was distributed by A&M Records. Teamed with producers/songwriters Jimmy Jam and Terry Lewis, who had hits with Tabu recording act the S.O.S. Band, Cherelle began to have a steady stream of hits: *Fragile* from summer 1984 produced the singles "I Didn't Mean to Turn You On" and the popular radio-aired "When I Look in Your Eyes"; *High Priority* had the number two R&B hit "Saturday Love," a duet with labelmate Alexander O' Neal.

Jam & Lewis decided to apply a concept LP format for Cherelle's third album like they'd used for O'Neal's Hearsay album, *Affair*. The concept was the songs would be based around a romantic relationship that went bad. The LP's first single was another Cherelle/O'Neal duet, "Never Knew Love Like This," which parked at number-two R&B for two weeks on *Billboard*'s charts in early 1988. The duo decided that "Everything I Miss at Home" should have a jazz piano lounge feel to it. It went to number-one R&B in late 1988. *Affair*, which went to number-15 R&B in late 1988, also yielded "Affair," a number-four R&B hit, in early 1989.

Her last charting LP, *The Woman That I Am*, with production by Narada Michael Walden, boasted "Never in My Life," "Tears of Joy," "Still in Love With You," and a cover of Carla Thomas' "Gee Whiz."

Cherelle appears on LPs by Alexander O' Neal ("In the Middle"/"Your Precious Love" from his 1993 LP *Love Makes No Sense* and "Baby Come to Me" from 1997's *Lovers Again*) and Pebbles ("Always" from her gold *Always* album and on her 1995 *Straight From My Heart* album).

Cherelle resurfaced in 1999 with her *The Right Time* CD. *—Ed Hogan*

● **High Priority** / Oct. 1986 / Tabu ✦✦✦✦✦

Cherelle's light, wispy, occasionally whiny soprano proved quite popular with '80s urban audiences, especially women. Her second album included a monster single, "Saturday Love," that was dominated by duet partner Alexander O'Neal, but marked the start of what became a profitable union. The song almost made it to the top, peaking at number two and turning the album into a smash. It also yielded a decent follow-up hit in "Artificial Heart," which reached number 18. Cherelle later appeared on O'Neal's debut album *Alexander O'Neal*. *—Ron Wynn*

The Best of Cherelle / Oct. 11, 1995 / Tabu ✦✦✦✦

Ava Cherry

Vocals / Disco, Dance-Pop, Soul, Urban

Ava Cherry (aka Black Barbarella) was raised in Chicago. The singer/model grew up loving Motown, Aretha Franklin, and Gladys Knight, but a four-year stint with rock star David Bowie would forever change her musical direction. From 1974 to 1978, as part of a backing trio comprising Robin Clark and Luther Vandross, she performed on-stage and in the studio with Bowie, appearing on some his most-acclaimed albums. Lovers as well, Cherry and Bowie remained friends throughout the years. The experience spoiled Cherry; she traveled all over the world, sang before crowds of 50,000 people, and mingled with superstars like John Lennon, the Rolling Stones, and others.

After she split with Bowie, Cherry returned home to Chicago where a friend introduced her to Curtis Mayfield. Curtom/RSO Records released her first album, *Spend the Night*, in a snug disco/soul bag and didn't use any of the hard rock songs she'd written. The Curtom album didn't do as well as anticipated and Cherry returned to Bowie's camp. Her second album followed in 1983 on Capitol Records, but *Streetcar Named Desire* went unnoticed. When Vandross started blowing up, she joined him in 1986 and was heard on the *Any Love* album onward. In 1987, her second Capitol LP, *Picture Me*, dropped with little celebrity or sales. However, along with Lisa Fischer and Kevin Owens, Cherry contributed to making Luther Vandross a top draw in urban music. The group didn't just sing behind Vandross; they executed some classy stepping and dance routines that always wowed the patrons. In 1997, J-Bird made her *Spend the Night* album available on CD. *—Andrew Hamilton*

Ripe!!! / 1980 / RSO ✦✦✦

● **Spend the Night** / May 20, 1997 / J-Bird ✦✦✦

A brief six-song CD originally released in the '70s, and reissued by J-Bird Records on CD, by ex-cover girl and ex-David Bowie backing singer Ava Cherry. The title track, co-written by Cherry, is a slow, vamping, romantic tune that's pleasant but unspectacular. "If You Want My Lovin'" chugs along like a freight train carrying a shipment of cardboard boxes: if it arrives on time, fine; if not, who really cares; the longer you listen the more mundane it gets, the chugging beat never changing once in nearly five minutes. Another Cherry composition, "You Are," has a little more going for it, with its eerie, floating feel and Cherry's feathery, sensual vocal. A remake of Patrice Rushen's "Forget Me Nots" is more pleasing than Rushen's bouncy, cutesy original; Cherry's rendition is slower, sexier, and more soulful, her husky vocal making the song a bona fide keeper. She tries hard, but "Gimme Gimme" never rises above the filler level no matter how long they stretch it out. "Say" has a dark, hypnotic bass line that makes it instantly likable; the lyrics are a romantic plea, and the backing singers ooh and ahh in all the right places. Cherry keeps busy as one of Luther Vandross' backing singers, sharing the stage with Lisa Fischer and Kevin Owens. *—Andrew Hamilton*

Neneh Cherry (Neneh Mariann Karlsson)

b. Mar. 10, 1964, Stockholm, Sweden

Vocals / Dance-Pop, Pop-Rap, Alternative Dance, Club/Dance, Urban, Alternative Rap

The stepdaughter of jazz trailblazer Don Cherry, vocalist Neneh Cherry forged her own groundbreaking blend of pop, dance, and hip-hop which presaged the emergence of both alternative rap and trip-hop. She was born Neneh Mariann Karlsson on March 10, 1964, in Stockholm, Sweden, the daughter of West African percussionist Amadu Jah and artist Moki Cherry. Raised by her mother and her trumpeter stepfather in both Stockholm and New York City, Cherry dropped out of school at age 14, and in 1980 she relocated to London to sing with the punk group the Cherries.

Following brief flings with the Slits and the Nails, she joined the experimental funk outfit Rip Rig + Panic, and appeared on the group's albums *God* (1981), *I Am Cold* (1982), and *Attitude* (1983). When the band broke up, Cherry remained with one of the spin-off groups, Float Up CP, and led them through one album, 1986's *Kill Me in the Morning*. The band proved short-lived, however, and Cherry began rapping in a London club, where she earned the attention of a talent scout who signed her to a solo contract. Her first single, "Stop the War," railed against the invasion of the Falkland Islands.

After attracting some notice singing backup on the The's "Slow Train to Dawn" single, she became romantically and professionally involved with composer and musician Cameron McVey, who, under the alias Booga Bear, wrote much of the material that would comprise Cherry's 1989 debut LP *Raw Like Sushi*. One song McVey did not write was "Buffalo Stance," the album's breakthrough single; originally tossed off as a B-side by the mid-'80s pop group Morgan McVey, Cherry's cover was an international smash which neatly summarized the album's eclectic fusion of pop smarts and hip-hop energy.

A pair of hits—the eerie "Manchild" and "Kisses on the Wind"—followed, but shortly after the record's release Cherry was sidelined with Lyme disease, and apart from a cover of Cole Porter's "I've Got You Under My Skin" for the 1990 *Red Hot + Blue* benefit album, she remained silent until 1992's *Homebrew*. A more subdued collection than *Raw Like Sushi*, it featured cameos from Gang Starr and R.E.M.'s Michael Stipe; as well as writing and production assistance from Geoff Barrow, who layered the track "Somedays" with the same distinct trip-hop glaze he later perfected as half of the duo Portishead. While the album was not as commercially successful as its predecessor, Cherry returned to the charts in 1994 duetting with Youssou N'Dour on the global hit "Seven Seconds." After another lengthy layoff spent raising her children, she resurfaced with the atmospheric *Man* in 1996. *—Jason Ankeny*

● **Raw Like Sushi** / May 1989 / Virgin ✦✦✦✦✦

Those arguing that the most individualistic R&B and dance music of the late '80s and early- to mid-'90s came out of Britain could point to Neneh Cherry's unconventional *Raw Like Sushi* as a shining example. An unorthodox and brilliantly daring blend of R&B, rap, pop, and dance music, *Sushi* enjoyed little exposure on America's conservative, urban, contemporary radio formats, but was a definite underground hit. Full of personality, the singer/rapper is as thought-provoking as she is witty and humorous when addressing relationships and taking aim at less-than-kosher behavior of males and females alike. Macho homeboys and Casanovas take a pounding on "So Here I Come" and the hit "Buffalo Stance," while women who are shallow, cold-hearted, or materialistic get lambasted on "Phoney Ladies," "Heart," and "Inna City Mamma." Cherry's idealism comes through loud and clear on "The Next Generation," a plea to take responsibility for one's sexual actions and give children the respect and attention they deserve. *—Alex Henderson*

Homebrew / Oct. 27, 1992 / Virgin ♦♦♦♦♦

Neneh Cherry doesn't get into the studio nearly often enough. Three years passed before the British singer/rapper came out with a second album. Thankfully, she more than lived up to the tremendous promise of *Raw Like Sushi* on the equally magnificent and risk-taking *Homebrew.* Cherry shows no signs of the dreaded sophomore slump—everything on the CD is a gem. She triumphs with a seamless and unorthodox blend of hip-hop, R&B, dance music, and pop, and on "Money Love" and "Trout," the presence of R.E.M.'s Michael Stipe brings rock to the eclectic mix. As humorous as Cherry can be, her reflections on relationships and social issues are often quite pointed. While "Money Love" decries the evils of materialism, the moving "I Ain't Gone Under Yet" describes an inner-city woman's determination not to be brought down by the poverty and drugs that surround her. And "Twisted" is about keeping yourself sane in a world gone insane. Unfortunately, *Homebrew* wasn't the commercial breakthrough Cherry was more than deserving of. *—Alex Henderson*

Man / 1996 / Hut ♦♦♦

Neneh Cherry, the critically acclaimed singer/songwriter and rapstress who burst onto the scene in 1989 with the mega-hit "Buffalo Stance," did not even see the release of her third album, *Man,* in the United States. This set differs from her previous efforts in that there is absolutely no rap to be found anywhere on the disc, and all of the songs are slow-burning, midtempo alt-rock numbers, as opposed to anything remotely resembling dance or rap (though there are some hip-hop styled beats). There are really no immediate hits on this album, although it includes the international chart-topping duet with Youssou N'Dour, "7 Seconds," as well as several other highlights, including "Woman," "Hornbeam," and "Everything." Also included here is a tribute cover she recorded of Marvin Gaye's "Trouble Man." The album is a high-quality collection of alt-rock womens' anthems, at times bluesy, at times folksy, and much more akin to her previous rock-leaning effort *Homebrew* than her breakthrough *Raw Like Sushi.* The songs have an organic, earthy feel, in tune with the Lilith Fair alternative-style musical movement going on at the time. A good deal of alterna-sexual references are found, especially considering some of the song titles (first single "Kootchi" and "Beastiality," to mention two). A solid album, but definitely not very commercial. Still, it should have been given a chance in the U.S. market, especially given her previous track record. *—Jose Promis*

The Chi-Lites

f. 1959, Chicago, IL, **db.** 1983

Group / Soul, Smooth Soul, Chicago Soul, Psychedelic Soul

One of the most popular smooth soul groups of the early '70s didn't hail from Philadelphia or Memphis, the two cities known for sweet, string-laden soul. Instead, the Chi-Lites were from Chicago, a town better known for its gritty urban blues and driving R&B. Led by vocalist Eugene Record, the Chi-Lites had a lush, creamy sound distinguished by their four-part harmonies and layered productions. During the early '70s, they racked up 11 Top Ten R&B singles, ranging from the romantic ballads "Have You Seen Her" and "Oh Girl" to protest songs like "(For God's Sake) Give More Power to the People" and "There Will Never Be Any Peace (Until God Is Seated at the Conference Table)." All the songs featured Record's warm, pleading tenor and falsetto, and the majority of the group's hits were written by Record, often in collaboration with other songwriters like Barbara Acklin.

The Chi-Lites had been around for nearly a decade before they finally had a hit in the late '60s. Eugene Record, Robert Lester, and Clarence Johnson formed the doo wop group the Chanteurs in the late '50s, and they released one single on Renee Records in 1959. Shortly afterward, Creadel "Red" Jones and Marshall Thompson, who had sung with the Desideros, teamed with the trio to form the Hi-Lites. Over the next four years, the Hi-Lites released a number of singles on local labels. In 1964, they changed their name to Marshall & the Chi-Lites, adding the "C" as tribute to their hometown Chicago. By the end of the year, Johnson left the group and the remaining quartet truncated their name to the Chi-Lites. Over the next four years, the group continued to perform and release independent singles, with Record slowly emerging as the group's lead singer, songwriter, and producer.

In 1968, the Chi-Lites signed with the large Chicago indie label Brunswick Records, and early the following year "Give It Away" became their first national hit single, reaching number ten on the R&B charts. Despite the moderate success of "Let Me Be the Man My Daddy Was," the group wasn't able to deliver another big hit until "Are You My Woman? (Tell Me So)" climbed into the R&B Top Ten in early 1971, beginning a string of ten Top Ten hits that ran intermittently over the next four years. The follow-up to "Are You My Woman?," "(For God's Sake) Give More Power to the People," was their first pop hit, setting the stage for a pair of slow, soulful ballads, "Have You Seen Her" and "Oh Girl," which both reached number one on the R&B charts; the latter was a number-one pop hit, as well. in the spring of 1972.

Shortly after the release of the hit "Stoned Out of My Mind," the Chi-Lites began to splinter in 1973, when Jones left the group and was replaced by Stanley Anderson, who was quickly replaced by Willie Kensey. The revamped lineup had three Top Ten R&B hits—"Homely Girl," "There Will Never Be Any Peace (Until God Is Seated at the Conference Table)," and "Toby"—before they replaced Kensey with Doc Roberson. Shortly afterward, Brunswick became involved in serious financial problems, which prevented the label from promoting the group's record. Frustrated, Record left the band to become a solo recording artist for Warner Bros. The remaining trio, augmented by David Scott and Danny Johnson (who was replaced by Vandy Hampton in 1977), signed with Mercury, but none of their singles were hits.

The original lineup of the Chi-Lites re-formed in 1980, and the group began recording for Eugene Record's label, Chi-Sound. Although their first singles were more successful than their Mercury Records, they didn't have a genuine hit until 1982, when "Hot on a Thing (Called Love)" reached number 15. The following year, they moved to Larc Records, where they had their final Top Ten hit with "Bottoms Up." Late that year, Creadel Jones retired and the group continued to tour as a trio throughout the remainder of the decade. Record left the group in 1990 to record as a solo artist. He was replaced by Anthony Watson. By the early '90s, Jones had re-joined the group, and this version of the Chi-Lites became a regular on the oldies and soul circuit during the '90s. *—Stephen Thomas Erlewine*

Give It Away / 1969 / Brunswick ♦♦♦♦

After nearly a decade of plugging away in the Chicago soul scene, the Chi-Lites finally reached the charts in 1969 with the effervescent Top Ten R&B hit "Give It Away." Hot on its heels followed this debut LP, a strong one thanks to the composing/performing/producing dynamo Eugene Record as well as the steady hand of producer Carl Davis. "24 Hours of Sadness" is a copycat of their first hit, but just as enjoyable a performance and just as sparkling a production, while "Let Me Be the Man My Daddy Was" is a sweet ballad that avoids the expected melodramatic pitfalls. The group's runthrough of several Motown nuggets ("My Whole World Ended," "I Heard It Through the Grapevine," "I'm Gonna Make You Love Me") is also surprisingly successful, with Record's crystal falsetto on the former making for a nice translation of David Ruffin's original. The quartet got a little groovy for "That's My Baby for You," and though a few of the other album tracks are distinctly inferior, the Chi-Lites' first full-length was a bright spot for Chicago soul. *—John Bush*

I Like Your Lovin' (Do You Like Mine?) / 1970 / Victor ♦♦♦

In need of a full-length to package the Chi-Lites' latest single around, Brunswick released the obligatorily titled *I Like Your Lovin' (Do You Like Mine)* in mid-1970, even though only three new songs were available for inclusion. After the title track hit, the solid sound-alike "Are You My Woman? (Tell Me So)," and a forlorn "Trouble's A-Comin'," some uncreative compiling resulted in an LP padded out with nearly all of 1969's *Give It Away.* (The liner notes admitted sheepishly that a suitable subtitle would be "highlights by the Chi-Lites.") Though unobservant fans were doubtless rudely awakened after a single spin, *I Like Your Lovin' (Do You Like Mine)* certainly isn't a bad record—the best songs from the first album are right here, buttressed by two more hit singles by a group that started slowly but had really started cooking by 1970. [Thanks go to Edsel for the 1999 reissue *Give It Away/I Like Your Lovin'/(For God's Sake) Give More Power to the People*, which collected all 21 tracks making up the Chi-Lites' first three albums.] *—John Bush*

(For God's Sake) Give More Power to the People / 1971 / Brunswick ♦♦♦♦♦

Though they boasted one of the sweetest voices in soul music with Eugene Record, the Chi-Lites broke away from that format—thankfully, only slightly—for 1971's *(For God's Sake) Give More Power to the People.* Influenced by the growing social consciousness of soul music during the early '70s (especially Sly & the Family Stone and the solo debut of fellow Chicagoan Curtis Mayfield), Record wrote a pair of songs (the title track and "We Are Neighbors") evoking not only deep frustration but also a plea for hope and unity that challenging times demanded. It certainly didn't hurt that both were monster productions with raw, aggressive synthesizers, intense lead vocals, and some of the strongest, loudest harmonizing ever heard on a soul record. Doubly ironic and doubly fortunate too, that *(For God's Sake) Give More Power to the People* also featured a pair of the Chi-Lites' sweetest soul ballads, "Have You Seen Her?" and "I Want to Pay You Back," plus the excellent strollers "Love Uprising" and "You Got Me Walkin'." The Chi-Lites weren't exactly album artists, but *(For God's Sake) Give More Power to the People* was a powerful example of early-'70s soul and the best record they ever released. *—John Bush*

Greatest Hits / 1972 / Brunswick ♦♦♦♦♦

A Lonely Man / 1972 / Brunswick ♦♦♦♦♦

Behind the talents of Eugene Record, the Chi-Lites presented an impeccable album featuring one gem after another. Not losing any steam from their previous album, the Chi-Lites plugged another number one song, the universally appealing "Oh Girl," which also claimed the number one spot on the pop charts. "Coldest Days of My Life" came with a placid arrangement and peaked at number eight, and "Lonely Man" was a humble extension of "Have You Seen Her." From the testimonial "Living in the Footsteps of Another Man" to the midtempo "Being in Love" to the ballad "Love Is," the Chi-Lites were flawless with this effort. Record is masterful with his articulation of the lyric; he stays in control of his vocals. His penmanship is phenomenal and his production skills are irreproachable. The only socially charged number is a remake of the Marvin Gaye classic "Inner City Blues (Make Me Wanna Holler)," and it's done with skillful execution. *—Craig Lytle*

The Chi-Lites / 1973 / Brunswick ♦♦♦

The ingenious creativity of Eugene Record was the driving force behind the Chi-Lites, and on this album Record maintained the same savvy. The first single was ironically the last song on the album, "Stoned Out of My Mind." This midtempo number is introduced with a animated string arrangement which yields to Record's colorful falsetto as he addresses the spellbinding lyric. The string arrangement re-surfaces throughout the song. The single reached the number-two spot on the *Billboard* R&B charts after 16 weeks. The follow-up single was the rockin' "I Found Sunshine." Paced by a thick, electric guitar, Record strolls his way through this cheerful number. It cracked the top 20 at 17 after 14 weeks. The third single was "Homely Girl," which resembles a country tune accented by horn antics heard in a big top circus or carnival. The lyric and Record's delivery enhance an already impressive arrangement. It climbed all the way to number three on the *Billboard* R&B charts inside 17 weeks. Record's penmanship and production skills can only be commended. Aside from the mature lyrical content on most of his work, Record was also a master at taking riddle-like lyrics and conveying a sound message as well. "Go Away Dream" is a good example. With its pretentious lyric and sprightly rhythm, Record tailors the single with a splendid string and horn arrangement (as he does with "Stoned Out of My Mind"). Record utilizes his undeviating falsetto once again on this fairytale-based single. From his harmonious vocal arrangements to his exquisitte string and horn arrangements, Record makes every selection here worthy. *—Craig Lytle*

A Letter to Myself / 1973 / Brunswick ♦♦♦
Not as riveting as some of their earlier efforts, and too pop for die-hard Chi-Lites fans. Besides the R&B hit "I Write a Letter to Myself," there's not much to write about. "Just Two Teenage Kids in Love" is way too long. Too much filler, not enough thrillers. *—Andrew Hamilton*

Half a Love / 1974 / Brunswick ♦♦♦♦
A good but hitless Chi-Lite album, *Half a Love* was released by Brunswick only in the United Kingdom. Songs include "I Never Had It So Good (And Felt So Bad)," a dramatic ballad similar to "Lonely Man," but more reserved; the bouncy, infectious "Living in the Footsteps of Another Man"; and the Stylistics-sounding "I'm Not a Gambler." Lead Eugene Record does his best on "Half a Love," "Here I Am," and "It's Time for Love," but all songs lack the grip and pull normally associated with a Chi-Lite song. Lovers of Record's feather tenor will enjoy the sweet, cloying "Ain't Too Much of Nothing," "I'm Gonna Make You Love Me," and "Go Away Dream." *—Andrew Hamilton*

Toby / 1974 / Edsel ♦♦♦
The title track, "Toby," should have made this LP financially viable, but as enchanting and beautiful as it is, the tale was morbid (Toby gets killed) and it didn't burn any rubber on the charts. The insightful "There Will Never Be Any Peace (Until God Is Seated at the Conference Table)" was also expected to do some serious damage, but didn't fare as well as "Toby." Both were excellent examples of lead singer, writer and producer Eugene Record's immense creativity. A remake of Roberta Flack's "First Time (Ever I Saw Your Face)" rivaled the original. The public didn't think much of this release, as it only dented *Billboard*'s Top 200 LP Chart at number 181. *—Andrew Hamilton*

Greatest Hits, Vol. 2 / 1975 / Brunswick ♦♦♦

Heavenly Body / 1980 / 20th Century ♦♦
The Chi-Lites made a comeback in 1980, signing with Carl Davis' Chi-Sound label. Eugene Record returned, and this debut album under that contract even got them some renewed attention for the first time in years. The single "Heavenly Body" got some airplay and chart action, and they appeared on *Soul Train* that year. *—Ron Wynn*

Me & You / 1981 / 20th Century ♦♦♦
Throughout the early '70s, the Chi-Lites were one of the leading R&B and pop groups. But by the latter part of the decade, Eugene Record left the group for a solo career at Warner Bros. The Chi-Lites lost members, gained new ones, and did two albums for Mercury. This is the follow up to the group's 1980 *Heavenly Body* album that brought back the best incarnation of Record, Creadel Jones, Robert Lester, and Marshall Thompson. This effort was even more successful than its predecessor. During this time the group began to center on dancefloor material rather than heartfelt ballads. Since Record's ballads weren't great shakes at the time, it's a compromise his fans could live with. The best song on the album, "Whole Lot of Good Good Lovin'," is reggae tinged, filled with steel drums, great harmonizing, and Jones' bass runs. Like many people signed to Chi-Sound, remakes were in order. The Chi-Lites do a version of their classic "Oh Girl" here, but most of the longing had dissipated. The rollicking "Get Down With Me" has a good Stevie Wonder style bridge, as Record shamelessly says, "You're special effects are so real." His lascivious nature works even better on one track. The big hit, the smooth and kinetic "Hot on a Thing (Called Love)" has great, punchy horns. "Never Speak to a Stranger" is a dramatic and effective ballad where Record hits some nice falsetto notes. *Me & You*, produced by Record and Carl Davis is another strong effort from the group. *—Jason Elias*

☆ **Greatest Hits** / 1992 / Rhino ♦♦♦♦♦
One of Chicago's finest, the Chi-Lites blazed bright during the late '60s and early '70s, with several soul and pop hits that have retained their luster through the years. Amidst a sea of slick Philly International smashes and late gold from Stax, Hi, and Motown, the Chi-Lites found their niche with the smooth grit of singer and frontman Eugene Record's nicely layered charts. Showing their wide-ranging touch, the band ably handles a mix of quiet storm ballads ("Have You Seen Her," "Oh, Girl"), topical funk ("(For God's Sake) Give More Power to the People"), and summery convertible classics ("Stoned Out of My Mind"). With Rhino's 18-track hits collection taking in these and several other of the group's Brunswick label highlights, there's plenty of rich harmonies, tasty instrumental work, and vintage beats to go around. It is an essential soul package. *—Stephen Cook*

Sweet Soul Music / Nov. 2, 1995 / Charly ♦♦♦
Sweet Soul Music is a two-fer without the title. These 15 songs originally made up the Chi-Lites' two 20th Century Fox albums: *Heavenly Body* (1980) and *Me & You* (1981). A down period, the only song that made a significant chart showing was the herky-jerky, hiccupping "Hot on a Thing (Called Love)." Overall, the product was good; however, the commitment to promoting on a grand scale just wasn't there. And if "Have You Seen Her" and "Oh Girl" sound different, it's because they are; as with Gene Chandler, who also recorded for 20th Century, producer Carl Davis updated one of the artists' classics on each album. Each is extended time-wise from the original million-sellers. A good buy for the Chi-Lites' completist—all six of their 20th Century Fox singles' are included, including B-sides. *—Andrew Hamilton*

Live! / Feb. 20, 1996 / Super Power ♦♦♦

Inner City Blues / Jun. 4, 1996 / Brunswick ♦♦♦
Add the Chi-Lites' name to the growing list of recording artists who have been repackaged to death. At least Brunswick didn't title this a "best-of" or "Greatest Hits" collection. This is a sprinkling of hits surrounded by album cuts and B-sides with no defining thread. Many of these songs feature Eugene Record singing in his soft, innocent, juvenile-ish falsetto; ironically, his most popular recordings in that voice ("Stoned Out of My Mind" and "Give It Away") were omitted. He also sang in a harder falsetto and his normal register. Examples of his light, airy sounds include "Ain't Too Much of Nothing," "Love Uprising," "Let Me Be the Man My Daddy Was," "12th of Never," "Go Away Dream" and "Love Is." He uses a harder, more intense falsetto on the street-corner favorite "What Do I Wish For" and the jammin' "I Like Your Lovin'." Robert "Squirrel" Lester leads a very ordinary sounding "Inner City Blues." The drama filled "Lonely Man" is the most popular Chi-Lite cut here. *—Andrew Hamilton*

Greatest Hits, Vol. 2 / Oct. 15, 1996 / Rhino ♦♦♦
Greatest Hits, Vol. 2 picks up where Rhino's first volume of Chi-Lites' *Greatest Hits* left off, compiling all of the group's lesser-known R&B hit singles. The compilation contains recordings that the group made between 1968 and 1981 for the record labels Dakar, Brunswick, Mercury, and Chi-Sound. Though there are a few gems on the record—including "I Like Your Lovin' (Do You Like Mine)," "A Lonely Man," and "You Got to Be the One"—the material on *Greatest Hits, Vol. 2* by and large pales to the songs on the first collection, yet fans of the group's smooth soul sound will find several cuts to treasure on this album. *—Stephen Thomas Erlewine*

Give It Away/I Like Your Lovin/(For God's Sake) Give More Power to the People / Jan. 29, 1999 / Diablo ♦♦♦♦

★ **20 Greatest Hits** / Oct. 23, 2001 / Brunswick ♦♦♦♦♦
Besides being one of the most dynamic acts on the soul circuit of the late '60s and early '70s, the Chi-Lites also had an enviable range, which took them from intelligent protest firestorms like "(For God's Sake) Give More Power to the People" and "We Are Neighbors" to the velvet-smooth ballads "I Want to Pay You Back" and "Have You Seen Her." (Even more impressive then, that each of those four excellent songs first appeared on the same album, 1971's *(For God's Sake) Give More Power to the People.*) Largely self-contained as a group (frontman Eugene Record penned and produced much of their material), the Chi-Lites hit with some of the greatest soul tracks of the '70s, and they've never sounded better than they do on *20 Greatest Hits.* Though Brunswick's design and packaging leave much to desire (the cover makes it look like this compilation dates from the medieval ages of the CD medium), everything that really counts is done perfectly. All of the hits, and a few solid album tracks, are presented in chronological order, while the sound quality is the best yet. There's always room for one quibble, though; the version of "The Coldest Days of My Life" heard here isn't the full version, as on Brunswick's previous *Greatest Hits.* *—John Bush*

Chic

f. 1977, New York, NY
Group / Disco, Funk, Dance-Pop
There can be little argument that Chic was disco's greatest band; and, working in a heavily producer-dominated field, they were most definitely a *band.* By the time Chic appeared in the late '70s, disco was already slipping into the excess that eventually caused its downfall. Chic bucked the trend by stripping disco's sound down to its basic elements; their funky, stylish grooves had an organic sense of interplay that was missing from many of their overproduced competitors. Chic's sound was anchored by the scratchy, James Brown-style rhythm guitar of Nile Rodgers and the indelible, widely imitated (sometimes outright stolen) bass lines of Bernard Edwards; as producers, they used keyboard and string embellishments economically, which kept the emphasis on rhythm. Chic's distinctive approach not only resulted in some of the finest dance singles of their time, but also helped create a template for urban funk, dance-pop, and even hip-hop in the post-disco era. Not coincidentally, Rodgers and Edwards wound up as two of the most successful producers of the '80s.

Nile Rodgers and Bernard Edwards first met in 1970, when both were jazz-trained musicians fresh out of high school. Edwards had attended New York's High School for the Performing Arts and was working in a Bronx post office at the time, while Rodgers' early career also included stints in the folk group New World Rising and the Apollo Theater house orchestra. Around 1972, Rodgers and Edwards formed a jazz-rock fusion group called the Big Apple Band. This outfit moonlighted as a backup band, touring behind smooth soul vocal group New York City in the wake of their 1973 hit "I'm Doin' Fine Now." After New York City broke up, the Big Apple Band hit the road with Carol Douglas for a few months, and Rodgers and Edwards decided to make a go of it on their own toward the end of 1976. At first they switched their aspirations from fusion to new wave, briefly performing as Allah & the Knife Wielding Punks, but quickly settled into dance music. They enlisted onetime LaBelle drummer Tony Thompson and female vocalists Norma Jean Wright and Alfa Anderson, and changed their name to Chic in summer 1977 so as to avoid confusion with Walter Murphy & the Big Apple Band (who'd just hit big with "A Fifth of Beethoven").

Augmented in the studio by keyboardists Raymond Jones and Rob Sabino, Chic recorded the demo single "Dance, Dance, Dance (Yowsah, Yowsah, Yowsah)" and shopped it around to several major record companies, all of which declined it. The small Buddah label finally released it as a 12 inch in late 1977, and as its club popularity exploded, Atlantic stepped in, signed the group, and re-released the single on a wider basis. "Dance, Dance, Dance" hit the Top Ten, peaking at number six, and made Chic one of the hottest new groups in disco. Chic scrambled to put together their self-titled first album, which spawned a minor follow-up hit, "Everybody Dance," in early 1978. At this point, Wright left to try her hand at a solo career (with assistance from Rodgers and Edwards), and was replaced by Luci Martin. It was a good time to come on board; "Le Freak," the first single from sophomore album *C'est Chic*, was an out-of-the-box smash, spending five weeks on top of the charts toward the end of 1978 and selling over four-million copies (which made it the biggest-selling single in Atlantic's history). Follow-up "I Want Your Love" reached number seven, cementing the group's new star status, and *C'est Chic* became one of the rare disco albums to go platinum.

1979's *Risqué* was another solidly constructed LP that also went platinum, partly on the strength of Chic's second number-one pop hit, "Good Times." "Good Times" may not have equaled the blockbuster sales figures of "Le Freak," but it was the band's most imitated track: Queen's number-one hit "Another One Bites the Dust" was a clear rewrite, and the Sugarhill Gang lifted the instrumental backing track wholesale for the first commercial rap single, "Rapper's Delight," marking the first of many times that Chic grooves would be recycled into hip-hop records. Also in 1979, Rodgers and Edwards took on their first major outside production assignment, producing and writing the Sister Sledge smashes "We Are Family" and the oft-sampled "He's the Greatest Dancer." This success, in turn, landed them the chance to work with Diana Ross on 1980's *Diana* album, and they wrote and produced "Upside Down," her first number-one hit in years, as well as "I'm Coming Out."

The disco fad was fading rapidly by that point, however, and 1980's *Real People* failed to go gold despite another solid performance by the band. Changing tastes put an end to Chic's heyday, as Rodgers and Edwards' outside production work soon grew far more lucrative, even despite aborted projects with Aretha Franklin and Johnny Mathis. Several more Chic LPs followed in the early '80s, with diminishing creative and commercial returns, and Rodgers and Edwards disbanded the group after completing the lackluster *Believer* in 1983. Later that year, both recorded solo LPs that sank without a trace. Hungry for acceptance and respect in the rock mainstream (especially after accusations that *they* had ripped off Queen instead of the other way around), both Rodgers and Edwards sought out high-profile production and session work over the rest of the decade. Rodgers produced blockbuster albums like David Bowie's *Let's Dance*, Madonna's *Like a Virgin*, and Mick Jagger's *She's the Boss*. Edwards wasn't as prolific as a producer, but did join the one-off supergroup the Power Station along with Tony Thompson as well as Robert Palmer and members of avowed Chic fans Duran Duran; he later produced Palmer's commercial breakthrough *Riptide*. Edwards also worked with Rod Stewart (*Out of Order*), Jody Watley, and Tina Turner, while Rodgers' other credits include the Thompson Twins, the Vaughan Brothers, INXS, and the B-52's comeback *Cosmic Thing*.

Rodgers and Edwards re-formed Chic in 1992 with new vocalists Sylvester Logan Sharp and Jenn Thomas, and an assortment of session drummers in Thompson's place; they toured and released a new album, *Chic-Ism*. In 1996, the reconstituted Chic embarked on a tour of Japan; sadly, on April 18, Edwards passed away in his Tokyo hotel room due to a severe bout of pneumonia. Rodgers continued to tour occasionally with a version of Chic, and, in 1999, his Sumthing Else label issued a recording of Edwards' final performance with the band, *Live at the Budokan*. *—Steve Huey*

Chic / 1977 / Atlantic ♦♦♦

When Chic's self-titled debut album came out in 1978, many rock critics gave it very negative reviews and failed to see just how rhythmically and harmonically exciting Chic's blend of funk, soul, and Euro-disco was. But one critic who often gave Chic favorable coverage was Don Waller, who hit the nail on the head when he exalted the band as "an uptown version of Booker T. & the MG's." It was a most insightful analogy—Chic's music was a lot sleeker than Booker T. & the MG's raw, instrumental Memphis soul, but like Booker T., the Niles Rodgers/Bernard Edwards team turned out some of the most infectious and influential R&B party grooves of their era. Although not quite as strong as Chic's next two albums—*C'est Chic* and *Risqué*—would be, this highly enjoyable album put the group on the map commercially thanks to the infectious hits "Dance, Dance, Dance" and "Everybody Dance." Some rock critics saw *Chic* as just another faceless disco production, but, in fact, the opposite is true—with this album, Chic fashioned a very distinctive and recognizable sound that proved to be as influential in its era as Booker T. & the MGs were in theirs. The sound that Chic established with this album was one that everyone from Queen and ABC to Sister Sledge, the Sugarhill Gang, and Madonna would benefit from. *—Alex Henderson*

C'est Chic / 1978 / Atlantic ♦♦♦♦♦

Released in 1978, just as disco began to peak, *C'est Chic* and its pair of dancefloor anthems, "Le Freak" and "I Want Your Love," put Chic at the top of that dizzying peak. The right album at the right time, *C'est Chic* is essentially a rehash of *Chic*, the group's so-so self-titled debut from a year earlier. That first album also boasted a pair of floor-filling anthems, "Dance Dance Dance" and "Everybody Dance," and, like *C'est Chic*, it filled itself out with a mix of disco and ballads. So, essentially, *C'est Chic* does everything its predecessor did, except it does so masterfully: each side similarly gets its timeless floor-filler ("Le Freak," "I Want Your Love"), quiet storm come-down ("Savoir Faire," "At Last I Am Free"), feel-good album track ("Happy Man," "Sometimes You Win"), and moody album capper ("Chic Cheer," "[Funny] Bone"). Producers Bernard Edwards and Nile Rodgers were quite a savvy pair and knew that disco was as much a formula as anything. As evidenced here, they definitely had their fingers on the pulse of the moment, and used their perceptive touch to craft one of the few truly great disco albums. In fact, you could even argue that *C'est Chic* very well may be *the* definitive disco album. After all, countless artists scored dancefloor hits, but few could deliver an album this solid, and nearly as few could deliver one this epochal as well. *C'est Chic* embodies everything wonderful and excessive about disco at its pixilated peak. It's anything but subtle with its at-the-disco dancefloor mania and after-the-disco bedroom balladry, and Edwards and Rodgers are anything but whimsical with their disco-ballad-disco album sequencing and pseudo-jet-set Euro poshness. Chic would follow *C'est Chic* with "Good Times," the group's crowning achievement, but never again would Edwards and Rodgers assemble an album as perfectly calculated as *C'est Chic*. *—Jason Birchmeier*

Risqué / 1979 / Atlantic ♦♦♦♦

Chic was very much in its prime when it recorded its third album, *Risqué*, which contained hits that ranged from "My Feet Keep Dancing" and "My Forbidden Lover" to the influential "Good Times." That feel-good manifesto is one of the first songs that comes to mind when one thinks of the disco era and the Jimmy Carter years, but Chic's popularity certainly wasn't limited to the disco crowd. The fact that "Good Times" became the foundation for both the Sugarhill Gang's "Rapper's Delight" and Queen's "Another One Bites the Dust" tells you a lot—it underscores the fact that Chic was influencing everyone from early rappers to art rockers. A group that many rock critics were so quick to dismiss was having an impact in many different areas. From hip-hoppers to new wavers in London and Manchester, *Risqué* was considered primary listening. And *Risqué* is impressive not only because of its uptempo cuts, but also because of slow material that includes the lush "A Warm Summer Night" and the dramatic ballad "Will You Cry (When You Hear This Song)." *Risqué* is definitely among Chic's essential albums. *—Alex Henderson*

Real People / 1980 / Atlantic ♦♦♦

In the early '80s, Chic's influence on other artists was hard to miss. Change, Fantasy, Luther Vandross, the Talking Heads, Grace Jones and Queen were among the many artists who were incorporating elements of the Chic sound. It was ironic and quite amusing to hear some members of the "Death to Disco!" brigade blaring Queen's "Another One Bites the Dust" on their car stereos during the summer of 1980, for that funk-rock ditty was obviously based on "Good Times." But Chic itself was seeing its popularity start to fade, and fans were realizing that the group had reached its creative peak in the late '70s. Like other albums that Chic recorded in the early '80s, *Real People* is competent but less than essential. Diehard fans will find that while "Rebels Are We," "I Got Protection" and "Chip off the Old Block" are likable and catchy, they aren't in a class with "Good Times" or "Le Freak." This is a decent album, but it's also the work of a group that was past its prime. *—Alex Henderson*

Take It Off / 1981 / Atlantic ♦♦♦

In 1981, a lot of rock & rollers were claiming that the disco era was officially over. Disco, of course, never really died—a lot of the dance-pop, house music, Hi-NRG, and Latin freestyle that was recorded in the '80s and '90s was essentially disco—but as far as many of the radio stations and record company A&R men of 1981 were concerned, disco was dead. And that was bad news for Chic, a group closely identified with the disco era. Even though a lot of Chic's work had as much to do with funk and soul as it did with the Euro-disco sound, Chic was unable to live down its reputation as a disco group. But Nile Rodgers and Bernard Edwards gave it a try with 1981's *Take It Off*, an admirable, if uneven, project that finds the group downplaying the Euro-disco elements. With R&B and funk as the foundation, Chic tries to branch out by incorporating elements of pop-rock on "Your Love Is Canceled," and jazz on "Flash Back" and "So Fine" (which shouldn't be confused with the "So Fine" that Kashif produced for R&B singer Howard Johnson in 1982). In fact, a few of Rodgers' guitar solos give the impression that he'd been listening to a lot of Wes Montgomery. But as likable as the LP is, it didn't contain a major hit—the single "Stage Fright" only made it to #34 on *Billboard*'s R&B singles chart. And for a group that had enjoyed #1 pop and R&B smashes only two and three years earlier, that was certainly disappointing. *—Alex Henderson*

Tongue in Chic / 1982 / Atlantic ♦♦♦

None of the albums that Chic recorded from 1980 to 1983 can be called essential, and none of them are in a class with *C'est Chic* or *Risqué*. Even so, they were generally respectable, and they didn't deserve to be ignored. When *Tongue in Chic* came out in 1982, the only people who were still buying Chic's albums were its most diehard fans. Black radio no longer seemed to be interested, which is ironic because the R&B charts of the early '80s were full of Chic-influenced groups (Change, High Fashion, Fantasy, among many others). Although *Tongue In Chic* isn't among the group's best albums and didn't contain any radio hits, it isn't a bad album either. "Hangin'," "Chic (Everybody Say)," and "I Feel Your Love Comin' On," demonstrated that Nile Rodgers and Bernard Edwards were still quite capable of providing infectious R&B/funk grooves, and "City Lights" almost sounds like an example of early house music—which isn't all that surprising when you consider that Marshall Jefferson and many other house icons were major Chic fans. *—Alex Henderson*

Believer / 1983 / Atlantic ♦♦♦

If Prince and Shalamar—two artists who made their recording debuts in the late '70s—could be relevant to the urban contemporary scene of 1983 and even cross over to pop-rock/new wave audiences, why not Chic? Nile Rodgers and Bernard Edwards hoped that Chic could, which is why 1983's *Believer* finds the group updating its sound with generally appealing, if uneven, results. Using a lot more keyboards and drum machines and favoring a more high-tech production style, Rodgers and Edwards sound like they're trying hard to live down their reputation as a late-'70s disco act. Urban contemporary considerations are strong, and some of the songs might have reached pop-rock and new wave audiences with the right promotion. The infectious "Party Everybody" contains more rapping than singing, and acknowledges hip-hop's popularity, which is appropriate considering how often hip-hoppers have sampled Chic over the years. And even though *Believer* falls short of being a gem, you have to admire Chic's ability to update its approach while continuing to sound incredibly distinctive. But the LP didn't contain any hit singles, and *Believer* would be Chic's last album for Atlantic. Chic broke up in 1985, although they reunited for 1992's uneven *Chic-ism* and 1999's superb *Live at the Budokhan* (neither of which were big sellers). The ironic thing is that while Rodgers and Edwards were very much in demand as producers during the '80s (when Rodgers produced such superstars as Duran Duran, Madonna, David Bowie, and the B-52's, and Edwards worked with the

Power Station, Rod Stewart, Robert Palmer, and Jody Watley, among others), Chic itself never returned to the top of the charts. *—Alex Henderson*

Dance, Dance, Dance: The Best of Chic / Nov. 5, 1991 / Atlantic ♦♦♦♦♦
You think disco was nothing more than assembly line funk and freeze-dried beats? Then you need to step into the crisp grooves and walloping boogie found on this stunning collection of Chic's '70s recordings. Such hits as "Good Times," "Dance Dance Dance," and "Le Freak" used the stylistic innovations of James Brown and Sly Stone as a blueprint for a new era of funk. Bernard Edwards' basslines are so provocative they seem to talk, while Nile Rodgers' skeletal guitar runs hark back to Steve Cropper's slashing style. Sure, the songs don't say much. Sure, the dance mixes collected here ramble on after about six minutes. But once you step into these grooves—grooves that influenced an entire generation of artists from David Byrne to Prince—you will realize that these were indeed good times. *—John Floyd*

Chic-Ism / Mar. 3, 1992 / Warner Bros. ♦♦
"Doin' That Thing to Me" contains a reference to the mythological wizard Merlin in its lyrics. By some strange twist of nature, mythology was certainly at work when those reviewing *Chic-Ism* on its release in 1992 dismissed it purely because Chic were old hats. In actuality, the worst thing about it is the cover. *Chic-Ism* certainly isn't likely to make album of the century listings, but as Chic albums go, it's fine if a tad '80s, which is to be expected as it was recorded only two years into the '90s. What were critics expecting of Chic—synthesizers à la Kraftwerk? Kicking in with the infectious "Chic Mystique," a little too long at six and a half minutes, it's pretty much business as usual. This leads into "Your Love" and "Jusagroove," both keeping pace before slowing down for "One and Only One." "In It to Win It" is a perfect update of their New York disco-funk style, a recipe that bands like the Brand New Heavies emulated in later years. The last stretch of the album includes "High," a beauty that is close enough a slowed down "Good Times." "MMFTCF (Make My Funk the Chic Funk)" and a better edited reprise of "Mystique" conclude. *—Kelvin Hayes*

The Best of Chic, Vol. 2 / Nov. 10, 1992 / Rhino ♦♦♦♦♦
Filling out the gaps left by the first volume, *The Best of Chic, Vol. 2* proves with its collection of album tracks and singles that Chic was not merely a great disco band, but was a great band, period. *—Stephen Thomas Erlewine*

★ **The Very Best of Chic** / Mar. 14, 2000 / Rhino ♦♦♦♦♦
To the rock critics who dismissed Chic's music as disposable and mindless back in the late '70s: it might seem like a stretch to say that Nile Rodgers and Bernard Edwards had as great an impact as Gamble & Huff, George Clinton, and the folks at Stax Records. But in fact, Chic's music *was* that influential—and its disco/funk/soul innovations would be having an impact long after the '70s ended. From Madonna, Change, and Queen, to Duran Duran, Soul II Soul, and ABC—new wave, hip-hop, house, European Hi-NRG, Latin freestyle, and acid jazz—you could write a book about all the artists who have been influenced by Chic. This collection, which came out in 2000 and spans 1977-1982, is full of grooves that prove to be anything but disposable. Most of Chic's essential hits are provided, including "Good Times," "Le Freak," "Dance, Dance, Dance," "I Want Your Love," and "Everybody Dance." Less than essential, but still likable and decent, are early '80s recordings such as "Rebels Are We" from *Real People*, and "Stage Fright" from *Take It Off*. By 1980, Chic wasn't having as many hits and was feeling the sting of the death-to-disco movement. But disco never really died—it simply changed its name to dance music and evolved into such forms as Hi-NRG, Latin freestyle and house. When that happened, Chic's long-lasting influence was impossible to miss—you could say that Chic's influence lasted a lot longer than Chic itself. For those who need a concise introduction to Chic's legacy and want to hear some of R&B's most influential grooves, *The Very Best of Chic* is highly recommended. *—Alex Henderson*

The Chicago Gangsters

f. Ohio

Group / Funk, Disco, Smooth Soul, Ballads

Despite their name, the Chicago Gangsters were originally from Ohio, consisting of brothers James, Sam, Chris, and Leroy McCant. Their sound ranged from heavy funk and disco to sweet, smooth soul balladry. They adopted the name Chicago Gangsters after catching on with the Gold Plate label, where they worked with prolific songwriter/arranger Richard Evans and a number of Chicago's top studio musicians. Their debut LP, *Blind Over You*, was released in 1975 and contained the slamming funk of "Gangster Boogie," as well as a minor hit cover of "I Choose You," which Willie Hutch had originally recorded as the love theme to the film *The Mack*. The title track of their 1976 sophomore album *Gangster Love* was another minor hit, and also the first 12-inch single their label ever issued. 1977's "I'm an Outlaw" was their last single for Gold Plate; a year later, they cut "Windy City Boogie" for RCA. Dropping the "Chicago" part of their name, the Gangsters subsequently signed with Heat and recorded a third album, *Life Is Not Easy Without You*, in 1979. They continued on into the early '80s before disbanding. "Gangster Boogie" became a massively popular sample item for hip-hoppers and breakbeat aficionados, most prominently appearing on L.L. Cool J's hit "Mama Said Knock You Out"; their first album was eventually reissued as *Gangster Boogie*. *—Steve Huey*

● **Gangster Boogie** / 1975 / Gold Plate ♦♦♦♦

Gangster Love / 1976 / Gold Plate ♦♦♦

El Chicano

f. Los Angeles, CA

Group / Latin Rock, Brown-Eyed Soul, Soul

Over the years, El Chicano has often been compared to Santana and, to be sure, there are a lot of parallels. Both are from California (although different parts of the state), both are led by Mexican-Americans, both have recorded in English as well as in Spanish, and both have favored a very eclectic and unpredictable mixture of rock, soul, funk, jazz, blues, and Afro-Cuban salsa. Further, there is no getting around the fact that El Chicano (whose Spanish name means "the Chicano" or "the Mexican-American") has been heavily influenced by Carlos Santana's outfit. Nonetheless, El Chicano has a style of its own and Santana isn't the band's only influence. Over the years, El Chicano has been affected by everyone from Chicano soulsters like Cannibal & the Headhunters and Thee Midniters to Latin soul-jazz favorite Pucho to salsa heavyweights such as Tito Puente, Ray Barretto, and Mongo Santamaria.

El Chicano's members were not only affected by the Mexican-American experience, they were also well aware of what Cuban and Puerto Rican musicians were doing on the East Coast and in the Caribbean. El Chicano, which was originally called the V.I.P.'s, was founded in East Los Angeles (a heavily Mexican-American area) in the late '60s. The band's original members included co-founder/leader Bobby Espinosa (organ, electric keyboards, acoustic piano, vocals), Freddie Sanchez (bass, vocals), Mickey Lespron (lead guitar, vocals), Andre Baeza (congas), and John De Luna (drums). Along the way, El Chicano had more than its share of personnel changes; members who didn't join until the '70s included Ersi Arvizu (lead vocals), Hector "Rudy" Regalado (timbales, vocals), Max Garduno (congas), Danny Lamonte (drums), Brian Magness (bass), Joe Perreira (bass), Jerry Salas (lead vocals, guitar), Rudy Salas (guitar), and Steve Salas (lead vocals), among others. (The Salas brothers went on to join another East L.A. band, Tierra, which was an El Chicano spinoff and is best-known for its hit 1980 cover of the Intruders' Philadelphia soul ballad "Together").

After creating a buzz in East L.A. in the late '60s, El Chicano signed with MCA in 1970 and recorded its debut album, *Viva Tirado*. The instrumental title song, which was written by jazz pianist Gerald Wilson, was released as a single and became El Chicano's biggest hit; the recording reached number 28 on *Billboard*'s pop singles chart and number 20 on its R&B singles chart. On regional L.A. charts, "Viva Tirado" spent about 12 weeks at number one. "Viva Tirado" (which was inspired by Mexican bullfighter Jose Ramon Tirado) was a rarity; in the '60s and '70s, one rarely saw any type of jazz instrumental—straight-ahead, fusion, soul-jazz, or otherwise—climbing that high up the national *Billboard* charts. When a jazz instrumental became a hit single in the pop or R&B markets, it was the exception instead of the rule.

While the "Viva Tirado" single didn't make El Chicano national superstars—they were never as big as Santana—the band did acquire a loyal cult following and was especially popular in the Mexican-American neighborhoods of the southwestern U.S. After the *Viva Tirado* LP, El Chicano went on to record several more albums for MCA, including 1971's *Revolucion*, 1972's *Celebration*, 1973's *El Chicano*, 1974's *Cinco*, 1975's *The Best of Everything*, and 1976's *Pyramid of Love & Friends*. El Chicano's second biggest hit came in 1973 when MCA released the brown-eyed soul classic "Tell Her She's Lovely" as a single. Nationally, the tune (which features Jerry Salas on lead vocals) wasn't a major hit; "Tell Her She's Lovely" only reached number 40 on *Billboard*'s pop singles chart and number 98 on the magazine's R&B singles chart. But in Mexican-American neighborhoods, the song was huge—among Chicano Baby Boomers, "Tell Her She's Lovely" was as popular as War's big '70s hits. El Chicano's contract with MCA ended in 1976; that year, the band recorded its first post-MCA album, *This Is... El Chicano*, for the independent Shady Brooke label (where the L.A. residents enjoyed more creative control than they had during their six years at MCA).

The band's next LP, *Look of Love*, was released on Musidisc in 1977; then in the early '80s, El Chicano briefly recorded for Columbia, which released the romantic blue-eyed soul tune "Do You Want Me" as a single in 1983. Although not a national chart-buster, the song became a minor hit (primarily in Mexican-American areas). El Chicano didn't do a lot of recording in the '80s or '90s, but the band made a long overdue return to the studio with 1998's *Painting the Moment*. Released on Thump, that CD marked the return of original lead guitarist Mickey Lespron, who had not recorded with El Chicano since the '70s. *—Alex Henderson*

Viva Tirado / 1970 / MCA ♦♦♦

Revolucion / 1971 / Kapp ♦♦♦

El Chicano / 1973 / MCA ♦♦♦♦

Cinco / 1974 / MCA ♦♦♦

● **Viva El Chicano! Their Very Best** / 1976 / MCA ♦♦♦♦
One of Latin rock's most restless, dynamic groups, El Chicano recorded furious Latin jams and gorgeous pop ballads, covering everyone from Van Morrison to Les Baxter to Ray Barretto, and recording some solid original material as well. Though it includes only ten songs, *Viva El Chicano! Their Very Best* weighs in at nearly 50 minutes, and tells El Chicano's story quite well. It begins with "Viva Tirado," their biggest hit (one that hit the jazz, pop *and* R&B charts), a groovy re-engineering of the boogaloo grooves of Willie Bobo and Pucho & His Latin Soul Brothers with great interplay between organ and guitar. "The Latin One" gained a degree of fame after being used in the 1997 gangster film *Donnie Brasco*, and the group's cover of "Brown Eyed Girl" illustrates their way with a tender ballad. "Tell Her She's Lovely," though, is the cornerstone of the group's career and this collection as well, with great group vocals and a breezy summer-day soul arrangement. With none of the group's original albums available, *Viva El Chicano! Their Very Best* is still the best place to investigate one of the best groups of the '70s Latin rock explosion. *—John Bush*

Chicano Chant / Aug. 12, 1997 / MCA ♦♦♦♦
El Chicano was never an easy band to categorize. Were they Latin rock, brown-eyed soul, funk, jazz fusion, or salsa? Truth be told, the Los Angeles combo offered all of those things. And while comparisons to Santana—an equally adventurous Mexican-American outfit from a different part of CA—were inevitable, El Chicano had an energy of their own. This collection, which MCA assembled in 1997, looks back on the band's early-'70s heyday. *Chicano Chant* isn't really a best-of because some essential tracks are missing—most notably, the hit "Tell Her She's Lovely," which only reached number 40 on the pop singles chart but became a favorite in Mexican-American neighborhoods. Nonetheless, the tracks

that MCA does offer are excellent, and the majority of them are Afro-Cuban-flavored jazz fusion instrumentals. The most famous is El Chicano's hit 1970 version of pianist Gerald Wilson's "Viva Tirado"; however, lovers of '70s jazz fusion will also find a lot to admire about "Viva La Raza," "El Grito," and "Juntos," all of which are quite loose and free-spirited. Meanwhile, "El Cayuco" is an infectious cha cha along the lines of Tito Puente's "Oye Como Va" (a major hit for Santana in the early '70s), Ray Barretto's "Cocinando," or Poncho Sanchez's "Sonando." Although the cha cha beat was created in Cuba, "El Cayuco" demonstrates that you don't have to be Cuban to take advantage of it. Two of the vocal-oriented and less-jazz-minded tracks are "Sabor a Mi" (a romantic Latin-style bolero) and El Chicano's arrangement of "Gringo in Mexico." But instrumental jazz fusion is the thing that dominates this rewarding CD. *—Alex Henderson*

The Chiffons

f. 1960, New York, NY [The Bronx], **db.** 1972

Group / Brill Building Pop, Girl Group, Pop

One of the best early-'60s New York girl groups, combining sassiness and innocence on several of the style's greatest classics. The Chiffons had some singles under their belt when they reached number one with "He's So Fine," whose classic "doo-lang, doo-lang" riff was appropriated by George Harrison in 1970 for his own chart-topper, "My Sweet Lord" (Harrison was subsequently ordered to pay substantial damages to the original publishers, though he always claimed the resemblance was unintentional). Their follow-up, Goffin-King's "One Fine Day," was just as good, featuring killer piano riffs from King herself. Actually cut as a Little Eva track, the Chiffons' vocal was substituted, resulting in a Top Five hit. There were a couple other memorable hits—"I Have a Boyfriend" and the Motown-influenced "Sweet Talkin' Guy"—and interesting misfires like the Martha & the Vandellas-inspired "The Real Thing," as well as some singles issued under an alter ego, the Four Pennies. The group recorded quite a bit of material during the '60s, much of it derivative. *—Richie Unterberger*

The Chiffons / 1963 / Laurie ✦✦✦

One Fine Day / 1963 / Laurie ✦✦✦

Flips, Flops & Rarities / 1986 / Impact ✦✦✦

At a bargain-basement price you get 16 Chiffons tracks you've probably never heard before. Among the bounty are B-sides, releases that stiffed, demos, tracks that never emerged, and quickly pulled promo releases. To keep the hits going, their recording company tried the sweet-singing ladies on a variety of cuts, including obvious knockoffs like "Up on the Bridge," the wolf-warning "He's a Bad One," and whimsical numbers like "Lucky Me." Some experimentation took place and a few tracks display their voices in full bloom. But on the whole these tracks lacked oomph. Die-hard Chiffons aficionados, however, will appreciate the effort. *—Andrew Hamilton*

● **16 Golden Classics** / Apr. 18, 1990 / Collectables ✦✦✦✦✦

At one time the best and most readily available Chiffons compilation on the market, Collectables' *16 Golden Classics* has since gone out of print. If you can find a copy, it still makes a fine summary of the girl group's career, adding plenty of lesser-known recordings to their three big hits: the number one "He's So Fine" and the Top Tens "One Fine Day" and "Sweet Talkin' Guy." Those songs all rank as girl group classics, but there are other fine performances here as well. Minor chart hits "I Have a Boyfriend," "When the Boy's Happy (The Girl's Happy Too)," "Sailor Boy," and others capture the innocence and feminine longing of their (distinctly pre-feminist) era. With *16 Golden Classics* now very difficult to find, hardcore girl group fanatics are directed for the time being to the Remember label's 2001 compilation *One Fine Day*, which features a whopping 26 tracks. *—Steve Huey*

The Chimes

f. 1959, **db.** 1964

Group / Doo Wop

There may well have been hundreds of groups during the 1950s that used the name the Chimes. Only the quintet from Brooklyn—Lenny Cocco (lead), Pat DePrisco (first tenor), Richard Mercado (second tenor), Joseph Croce (baritone), Pat McGuire (bass)—ever made the charts, however, or became more than local stars.

Lenny Cocco, the son of a Brooklyn accordion player, organized the group in the mid-'50s, and their first record was a vocal arrangement of the old Tommy Dorsey hit "Once in a While," which was issued on the Tag label. The quintet scored right out of the box as that record reached number 11, which led to a follow-up record, a recording of the 1930s standard "I'm in the Mood for Love." By 1962, they were cutting songs under the name Lenny & the Chimes. They left Tag Records in 1963, jumping first to Metro and then to Laurie, before releasing a single, "Two Times," on Vee-Jay in 1964. The group broke up in 1964 amid the onslaught of the British invasion and the collapse of Vee-Jay, but they have reformed, usually as Lenny & the Chimes, in various configurations for oldies shows since the early '70s. *—Bruce Eder*

● **The Chimes Meet the Videls** / 1995 / Collectables ✦✦✦

Here are eleven songs by the Chimes, including their two chart entries, "Once in a While" (and its two different B-sides, "Summer Nights" and "Oh How I Love You So," of which the latter is the stronger, with a catchier melody and arrangement) and "I'm in the Mood for Love." The sound is clean and the textures of the harmony vocals and the backing instruments are revealed in very fine detail. Their version of "Let's Fall in Love" is a revelation, a languid, radiant slow ballad interpretation of a song usually taken at a much faster tempo by everyone from Frank Sinatra to the Three Stooges. "Dream Girl," by contrast, is more in the vein of a doo wop novelty number. "Paradise," written by Lenny Cocco, is uncomfortably close to "This Magic Moment," in content and arrangment, right down to the choruses and the string playing, although it is pleasant enough on its own terms. The CD is rounded out by six songs by the Videls. *—Bruce Eder*

The Chips

f. 1956, Brooklyn, NY

Group / Doo Wop

The Chips had one record released from August 1956 to April 1980, "Rubber Biscuit," an outrageous novelty song that failed to crack the pop Top 40 but did well along the East Coast. Raised in the Bedford-Stuyvesant area of Brooklyn, the Chips formed in 1956; the members were Charles Johnson (lead), Sammy Strain (first tenor), Shedwick Lincoln (second tenor), Nathaniel Epps (baritone), and Paul Fulton (bass). They created the novelty and its flip "Oh My Darling" while attending a school for delinquent teens. Josie Records thought it had something and released the nutty ditty. After a few appearances at some major R&B venues, the group disbanded; Josie never released another recording by them, though some members enjoyed more success with other groups: Fulton sung with the Velours and the Poets, Lincoln with the Invitations, and Johnson with the Platters. And Sammy Strain had enjoyed an illustrious career with the Fantastics, Little Anthony & the Imperials, and the O'Jays. In 1979, "Rubber Biscuit" enjoyed another stint of success when the Blues Brothers remade it for a Top 40 hit. The Chips promptly regrouped in 1980—minus Sammy Strain, who had connected with the O'Jays—and recorded "Everyone's Laughing," their first single in 24 years. *—Andrew Hamilton*

Chocolate Genius

Group / Adult Alternative Pop/Rock, Contemporary R&B, Pop-Soul

Chocolate Genius is the brainchild of Marc Anthony Thompson, an eclectic singer/songwriter who released two solo albums under his own name during the '80s. Thompson was born in Panama, raised in California, and later moved to New York, where he became involved in the downtown avant-garde scene. When his solo career (which included albums in 1984 and 1989) hit a dead end, Thompson made that downtown scene his focal point, most notably recording with guitarist Marc Ribot in the mid-'90s. Thompson originally conceived Chocolate Genius as a reclusive, self-important alter ego, but the joke soon turned into a full-fledged recording project.

The Chocolate Genius supporting band was a loose, free-floating collective of Thompson's downtown cronies, including Ribot, cellist Jane Scarpantoni (plus several other ex-Lounge Lizards); keyboardist John Medeski and bassist Chris Wood of Medeski, Martin & Wood; guitarist (and fellow singer/songwriter) Chris Whitley, and ex-Living Colour guitarist Vernon Reid, among others. Thompson's debut as Chocolate Genius was *Black Music*, released in 1998. Its eclectic fusion of genre-bending R&B (Sly Stone, Prince, Stevie Wonder), jazz experimentation, and indie singer/songwriter depression (Mark Eitzel, Elliott Smith, Tom Waits) drew many favorable reviews, and earned the auteur behind Chocolate Genius a spot in the emerging neo-soul movement. In the wake of *Black Music*, Thompson scored the film *Urbania* and the theatrical production *A Huey P. Newton Story*, among several other side projects. In 2001, he returned with a second Chocolate Genius album, the acclaimed *Godmusic*. *—Steve Huey*

Black Music / Jul. 14, 1998 / V2 ✦✦✦✦

That Marc Anthony Thompson went nearly a decade between releases says something about both record companies' perception of what, indeed, black music is and the realities of a business situation where the individual approach is the least likely thing to get any cohesive support. Happily, *Black Music* found Thompson on top of his game thanks to his talent and wide-ranging tastes, which have a clear echo in the reach of the album. He may start with a Dixieland jazz-meets-folk number and end with a hidden acoustic rendition of the fantastic slow-burn soul "Half a Man," but in between he tries just about anything that takes his fancy. Comparisons were made to similarly genre-elusive singer/songwriters like Prince and Jeff Buckley upon *Black Music*'s release, but Thompson is his own man through and through. His voice tackles ranges from falsetto to gravelly blues and comes up trumps, while his ear for hooks and varying approaches skip between greasy R&B to acoustic, art rock-tinged introspection—it's not too surprising after listening to songs like "Stupid Again" to learn that he's a Radiohead fan. If there's a weakness to *Black Music*, it's that Thompson's strong enough to avoid sounding like an aimless dabbler, but at points can't really make his syntheses stand out as well as could be hoped. When he hits, though, he hits hard. "My Mom," a tender, harrowing reflection on the ravages of time on memory and personal connection, has both the lyrical and musical impact to matter, with Thompson's husky singing backed by acoustic plucking, low strings, and the softest of rhythms. Other strong points include "Safe and Sound," with its rising, anthemic build suddenly shifting into a roughly recorded drum jam without missing a step, and the moody-yet-pretty crawl of "Hangover Nine," one of several moments on the album where he showcases his fine sax abilities. *—Ned Raggett*

● **Godmusic** / Aug. 7, 2001 / V2 ✦✦✦✦✦

Chocolate Genius (aka Marc Anthony Thompson) may be getting lumped in with nu-soul brethren like Bilal and D'Angelo, but his sound is far more unclassifiable than that of your average R&B crooner. Take "For One More Look at You," the first proper track off his second LP, for instance. With its spacy atmosphere, subtle strings, melodic piano accents, textural percussion, and so-breathy-they're-barely-there vocals, the song sounds more like a long-lost outtake from Talk Talk's *Laughingstock* than the sizzling sex-you-up innuendo we've come to associate with the genre. And yeah, maybe "Love" crosses the line into sappy sentimentality, but when the man's got world-class musicians like guitarists Marc Ribot and Chris Whitley and bassist Chris Wood kicking out the slow jams behind him, you're willing to grant him a bit more leeway. Besides, Thompson's songwriting more than makes up the difference, veering from the alt-rock anthem of "My Endless Fall" to the psychedelic folk of "Bossman Piss (In My Lemonade)" to the haunting Peter Gabriel balladry of "To Serve You," like Prince before he contracted a crippling case of musical diarrhea. Though far less inconsistent than his debut, *Godmusic* still isn't quite the genre-hopping classic you suspect Chocolate Genius may yet have in him, but it's good enough to move him near the top of the neo-soul class. *—Bret Love*

The Chocolate Jam Co.

Group / Quiet Storm, Disco, Funk, Soul

Whether he was playing jazz or R&B, drummer Leon "Ndugu" Chancler spent much of his career in a sideman role. But the Los Angeles resident was in the driver's seat in 1979 and 1980, when he led an obscure, short-lived soul/funk outfit he called the Chocolate Jam Co. It's safe to say that the vast majority of R&B fans have never even heard of the combo, which was assembled by Chancler in 1979 and signed with Epic that year. The Chocolate Jam Co. (whose influences included Earth, Wind & Fire, Roy Ayers and Chancler employer George Duke) only recorded two albums: 1979's *The Spread of the Future* and 1980's *Do I Make You Feel Better?*, both of which were produced by Chancler and found him writing or co-writing all of the material. The LPs also gave Chancler an opportunity to do a lot of lead singing, which was unusual for him because he was a drummer first and foremost. Unfortunately, neither LP received much attention and both of them went out of print in the early '80s. *—Alex Henderson*

- **The Spread of the Future** / 1979 / Epic ✦✦✦

Best known for his association with keyboardist George Duke, drummer/composer Leon "Ndugu" Chancler was one of those musicians who had both jazz and soul credentials in the 1970s and 1980s. Chancler was well aware of the fact that soul was a lot more profitable, and his R&B side prevailed when, in 1979 and 1980, he led an obscure outfit called the Chocolate Jam Co. The list of musicians Chancler employs on the Company's first album, *The Spread of the Future*, is a long one—some of the participants include Duke, Earth, Wind & Fire guitarist Al McKay, saxman Don Myrick, and trumpeter Oscar Brashear. In addition to producing the LP and writing or co-writing all of the songs, Chancler tries his hand at singing and provides many of the lead vocals (along with Virginia Ayers and Leo Miller). Understandably, people tend to be skeptical when drummers become vocalists, but Chancler is a competent singer even though he isn't a great one. And *The Spread of the Future* is an enjoyable LP even though it isn't a masterpiece. The material ranges from gritty, aggressive funk ("Looking Glass," "A Chocolate Jam") to romantic, polished soul ("Just as You Are"). Earth, Wind & Fire is a prominent influence, as are George Duke and Roy Ayers. *The Spread of the Future* received very little attention, which is why it went out of print in the early '80s. But the LP is worth looking out for if you find yourself in a place that sells a lot of old R&B vinyl. *—Alex Henderson*

Chocolate Milk

f. 1974, Memphis, TN, **db.** 1983

Group / Funk, Soul

A New Orleans funk and soul ensemble that enjoyed moderate success in the mid-'70s, Chocolate Milk recorded for RCA from 1975 to 1983. Their roster included lead vocalist Frank Richard, saxophonist Amandee Castenell, trumpeter Joe Foxx, keyboardist Robert Dabon, guitarist Mario Tio, and drummer Dwight Richards. Their best songs were uptempo and/or light dance/novelty numbers such as "Action Speaks Louder Than Words" in 1975, "Girl Callin'" in 1978, and "Blue Jeans" in 1981. All were Top 20 R&B hits; they also tried ballads and heartache tunes, but Richard wasn't as confident or effective on those. *—Ron Wynn*

Chocolate Milk / 1976 / RCA ✦✦✦

Comin' / 1977 / RCA ✦✦✦

We're All in This Together / 1977 / RCA ✦✦

Hipnotism / 1980 / RCA ✦✦✦

Blue Jeans / 1982 / RCA ✦✦

- **Ice Cold Funk: The Greatest Grooves of Chocolate Milk** / Apr. 7, 1998 / Razor & Tie ✦✦✦✦

Ice Cold Funk: The Greatest Grooves of Chocolate Milk is a definitive 12-track overview of the New Orleans funk band, featuring all of their charting hits—"Action Speaks Louder Than Words," "How About Love," "Comin'," "Girl Callin'," "Say Won'tcha," "Groove City," "Hey Lover," "Blue Jeans," "Let's Go All the Way," "Take It Off," and "Who's Getting It Now"—plus a couple of album tracks. *—Stephen Thomas Erlewine*

The Choice Four

Group / Disco, Soul

The Choice Four was a nice harmonizing soul group from Washington, D.C., whose records deserved a better fate. They recorded for RCA in the mid-'70s, but were never able to score a breakout hit, despite making some very moving, nicely sung ballads. Lead singer Bobby Hamilton was an above-average stylist, and was effectively supported by Ted Maduro, Pete Marshall, and Charles Blagmore. Maduro and Marshall were former members of the Love Tones, and Blagmore of the Stridels. Unfortunately, none of their singles ever cracked the R&B Top 40. *—Ron Wynn*

The Finger Pointers / 1975 / RCA ✦✦✦

On Top of Clear / 1976 / RCA ✦✦✦

- **The Very Best of the Choice Four** / Feb. 22, 2000 / Koch International ✦✦✦✦

This 17-track collection has its ups, no downs, but some mundane areas. If you're familiar with David Ruffin's three Van McCoy-produced albums, you'll recognize "I'm Gonna Walk Away From Love," "The Finger Pointers," "Just Let Me Hold You for a Night," and "Ready, Willing and Able," all initially done by the Choice Four and redone by Ruffin, who makes the originals sound like demos. This disc includes their debut (and arguably best recording) "I Need Your Love to Keep Me Warm" and a stellar rendition of McCoy's "When You're Young and in Love." McCoy used the group's tenor too much, he did everything bel canto style, showing little emotion. Choice Four's falsetto singer is more exciting especially on "This Time It's for Real," a song with a Delfonics-ish feel; "You're So Right for Me," a sweet floater; and "Besides Me," a tune that sounds like the Stylistics' post-Thom Bell stuff. McCoy's other protégées, Faith, Hope & Charity are featured prominently on some tracks. Koch omitted two disco tunes: "Hey, What's That Dance You're Doing" and "A Time for Celebration," as well as their final recording, "You're My Peace of Mind," a tune Ruffin also redid and took to another level. *—Andrew Hamilton*

The Chords

f. 1951, New York, NY [The Bronx], **db.** 1960

Group / Doo Wop, R&B

The Chords—Carl and Claude Feaster (lead and baritone), Jimmy Keyes (first tenor), Floyd "Buddy" McRae (second tenor), and Ricky Edwards (bass)—formed in 1951 in the Bronx, but weren't discovered until three years later, when they were spotted singing in a subway station, a performance that ultimately landed them a recording contract with Atlantic Records.

Jerry Wexler, Atlantic's top talent A&R man, had the Chords cover a Patti Page hit, "Cross Over the Bridge" (it was also covered by the Flamingos for Chance), but it was the B-side, "Sh-Boom," a swinging R&B vocal tune with a catchy intro made up of seemingly nonsensical syllables ("shh-boom, shh-boom, yadda da da yadda da da da da da") that caused considerably more commotion.

"Sh-Boom" is supposed to have been titled after the threat of an atom bomb explosion which, in the midst of Cold War posturing in 1954, was a very real topic on the public's mind. However, this demented ditty also included the surreally optimistic message that everything was ultimately fine and as the rest of the lyrics suggested, "life could be a dream." By the end of June 1954, "Sh-Boom" had climbed up the charts nationwide, charting on both the R&B (number five) and pop (number two) lists, a nearly unprecedented feat for its time. For all practical purposes—along with the Crows' 1953 hit "Gee" (another upbeat B-side hit that DJs flipped over)—"Sh-Boom" introduced the white audience to black R&B music for the first time.

Not everyone thought the song was a precursor of good things to come. Peter Potter, host of TV's popular *Juke Box Jury*, was seemingly aghast at the state of this then-new trend in pop music and attacked "Sh-Boom" asking if anyone would remember the admittedly demented ditty in five, let alone 20 years time and whether any record label would even think to re-release it in the future. (The answers to his rhetorical questions were, of course, yes and yes.)

The songwriters were deluged by music publishing companies wanting to buy the rights to "Sh-Boom" in order to reap huge potential earnings (the group quickly came to an agreement with Hill & Range). Soon there were cover versions hitting radio stations across the country simultaneously with the Chords' original single. Some were memorable and some otherwise, including a countrified take by the Billy Williams Quartet for Coral, and most notably, the Crew Cuts' version for Mercury.

The Chords soon appeared on TV shows (still an invention not yet in many American homes), but were knocked for a loop when they learned there was a more-obscure group already using the name Chords. They were forced to change their name to the Chordcats. Subsequent Atlantic record ads noted that their group was the creators and originators of "Sh-Boom," even though the Canadian Crew Cuts' paler pop version by then had knocked the Chords' R&B-styled version off the charts.

Atlantic later moved the Chords over to their new Cat Records subsidiary, releasing numerous additional singles which mostly failed to chart. A last-gasp attempt to resurrect the act came in mid-1955 when the group renamed themselves the Sh-Booms after their one big hit. The group went through several personnel changes during the late '50s, recording a handful of forgettable records for Vik Records in 1957, and eventually returned to Atlantic in 1960 for one last recording before slipping away into the ether. *—Bryan Thomas*

- **The Best of the Chords** / Cat ✦✦✦✦

Chris Clark

b. 1946, Los Angeles, CA

Vocals / Motown, Northern Soul, Soul

Along with Bobby Darin and Rare Earth, Chris Clark was one of a relative handful of white artists signed to Motown Records; she also went a good deal farther with the company in her creative career than any other white artist (and most artists, period) who ever recorded there. The Los Angeles-born Clark was discovered by Motown CA talent representative Hal Davis (who had also pointed Brenda Holloway their way), who arranged an audition for her with Berry Gordy in Detroit. Gordy hated the songs on her demo but loved her voice, and she was signed to Motown at age 18. Clark was wise beyond her years, especially in the ways of music, having spent a big part of her youth around jazz musicians. Her voice was suited to the harder, bluesier side of R&B, and Gordy gave her one of the raunchier singles ever to come out of the label, "Do Right Baby, Do Right," as her debut. The two started writing songs together, including "I Want to Go Back There Again," and she ended up just as involved on the creative side of the business as the performing side, assisting and advising Gordy in his work on behalf of several artists' careers. Additionally, the two were involved personally for years.

Her own biggest hit, released in 1966 on the Motown subsidiary VIP label, was "Love's Gone Bad," authored by Holland-Dozier-Holland, which reached number 41 on the R&B chart and went to number 105 in the pop listings. That led to her first LP, *Soul Sounds*, released in 1967; as much a compilation of singles as a real album, it contained the hit as well as "Do Right Baby, Do Right," her killer rendition of "Day By Day or Never," and Clark's version of Smokey Robinson's "From Head to Toe." Although she never made a deep or lasting impression in America—where her race and sound, as well as her interracial romance with Gordy, touched on some very raw and sensitive issues—Clark was embraced in England, where audiences dubbed her "the White Negress" and meant it as a compliment. She was responsible for a string of good singles that weren't hits, among them "I Want to Go Back There Again" and "Whisper You Love Me Boy." She was also an imposing figure on-stage, six feet tall and platinum blonde; between the looks and the voice she might've been America's Dusty Springfield, although she never had the kind of chart action that Springfield did.

In 1969, Gordy decided to put Clark's abilities to use behind the scenes by making her vice president in charge of the record label's new film division. It was in this capacity that she grabbed a little chunk of the glory from the one major hit spawned by Motown's jump into movies; with Terence McCloy and Susan DePasse, she co-authored the screenplay for *Lady Sings the Blues* and snagged an Academy Award nomination. Clark also had a talent for photography, which she used on behalf of numerous Motown artists, and became an executive at the company. She was in charge of the company's creative affairs from 1981 until 1989, when she left Motown. Clark later recorded for the Motorcity label. *—Bruce Eder*

- **Soul Sounds** / 1967 / Motown ✦✦✦

Unissued on CD to date, this out-of-print album contains the blue-eyed soul singer's Holland-Dozier-Holland stomper "Love Gone Bad" and the righteous "Do Right Baby, Do Right." Clark has more heart than voice and more soul than skill but can work it on the right material. She wails on Berry Gordy's "Day By Day or Never" (also recorded by Bobby Taylor & the Vancouvers), Frank Wilson and Marc Gordon's "Sweeter As the Days Go By," the whimsical "I Want To Go Back There Again," and Mickey Gentile and Jennie Lambert's "Born to Love You Baby." *—Andrew Hamilton*

Dee Clark (Delecta Clark)

b. Nov. 7, 1938, Blythesville, AR, **d.** Dec. 7, 1990, Smyrna, GA

Vocals / R&B, Soul, Chicago Soul

Dee Clark was a solid R&B vocalist who had some huge hits in the late '50s and early '60s. The Arkansas-born singer moved to Chicago as a child and was in the Hambone Kids with Sammy McGrier and Ronny Strong. They recorded for OKeh in 1952; the next year Clark sang with the Goldentones. This group later became the Kool Gents, then recorded as the Delegates for Vee-Jay in 1956. Clark went solo in 1957 and in 1958 enjoyed his first smash with "Nobody for You," an Abner release that reached number-three R&B and just missed the Top 20 on the pop charts. He continued a string of R&B winners with "Just Keep It Up," "Hey Little Girl," and "How About That" for Abner in 1959 and 1960. Clark teamed with guitarist Phil Upchurch to write "Raindrops" in 1961, his signature tune. The song peaked at number-three R&B and number-two pop, and was his last major hit. Clark continued performing through the '60s, '70s, and '80s, but never again was a factor, though "Raindrops" remains a staple on oldies radio. *—Ron Wynn*

- **Rain Drops** / 1993 / Vee-Jay ✦✦✦✦✦

Dee Clark was one of the most adaptable R&B vocalists of the '50s and early '60s, as this 25-song reissue shows. He did songs in a Little Richard mode, an Afro-Latin setting, and also performed ballads, novelty tunes ("Kangaroo Hop"), and covers ("Cupid"). Clark's gem was "Raindrops," a song with enough drama, hooks, and appeal to nearly top both the pop and R&B charts. It was his biggest hit, but not his only fine number. There are many cuts, such as "Nobody but You," "What Kind of Fool," and the newly issued "Bring Back My Heart," that equal or even top the tune that made him famous. *—Ron Wynn*

Golden Classics / Nov. 5, 1996 / Collectables ✦✦✦✦

Not exactly a greatest-hits package, but an interesting blend of three of Dee's biggest hits on Vee-Jay (a nice stereo mix of "Raindrops" kicks things off) with a generous helping of his later sides for Constellation. These sides capture Clark moving toward a proto-soul style, with tracks like "Crossfire Time," "I'm Going Home," "Warm Summer Breezes," and "Heartbreak" showing the depth of Clark's vocal range on ballads, soul grinders, and jazz-tinged material. Lots of great Vee-Jay sides MIA on this, but a nice companion once you track the earlier sides down. *—Cub Koda*

Take Care of Business: The Constellation Masters 1963–66 / Aug. 11, 1998 / WestSide ✦✦✦

Subtitled "The Constellation Masters 1963-66," this picks up the second phase of Clark's solo career after his hit-making days at Vee-Jay. These sides find him moving in a more soulful direction, making hard Southern and Motown-inflected soul with the best of them on "Crossfire Time," "I'm Going Home," "Come Closer" and "That's My Girl." Although material like "Heartbreak," "I Ain't Gonna Be a Fool," "Warm Summer Breezes," and "I Don't Need (Nobody Like You)" were top-flight, Clark couldn't score a hit during his three years with Constellation chronicled here. But the lack of hits still yields a 17-track feast of brand-name mid-'60s Chicago soul music, played and sung with a professional flair that's unmistakably Dee Clark. Other highlights include "T.C.B.," "She's My Baby," "Hot Potato" and a live two-part workout on "Nobody But You" that makes a fitting closer to this set. *—Cub Koda*

Dee Clark/How About That / Sep. 26, 2000 / Collectables ✦✦✦✦

You're Looking Good/Hold On, It's Dee Clark / Oct. 17, 2000 / Collectables ✦✦✦

Judy Clay (Judy Lee)

b. St. Paul, NC

Vocals / R&B, Soul

A talented journeywoman soul singer, Judy Clay (born Judy Lee) joined the Drinkard Singers gospel group (who also included Cissy Houston) in the late '50s. Like many singers who started with gospel, she moved to soul in the '60s, releasing a string of non-hit singles for the Ember and Scepter labels that are esteemed by British Northern soul fans today; she also sang backup vocals for soul singers like Wilson Pickett and Solomon Burke. In the late '60s, she briefly teamed with Billy Vera to form what may have been the first interracial recording duo, recording an album and a couple minor hit singles, "Storybook Children" and "Country Girl-City Man (Just Across the Line)." Her other recordings with Stax and Atlantic in the late '60s (which included a 1969 session at Muscle Shoals Sound) produced a hit R&B duet with William Bell, "Private Number," and a minor hit solo single, "Greatest Love." She continued to work as a backup vocalist in the '70s with Aretha Franklin and Ray Charles, among others. Struck with a brain tumor in 1979, she returned to gospel music shortly after her recovery. *—Richie Unterberger*

- **Featuring Storybook Children & Greatest Love** / 1995 / Ichiban/Soul Classics ✦✦✦✦✦

Eleven of these 19 tracks are actually taken from her duet recordings with Billy Vera, including "Storybook Children" and "Country Girl-City Man (Just Across The Line)," most of the 1968 *Storybook Children* LP, and the 1969 non-LP single "Reaching For The Moon"/"Tell It Like It Is." The CD also has eight songs that Clay recorded on her own for Atlantic and Stax in the late '60s (most at the Muscle Shoals Sound Studio) which are generally more impressive than her duets with Vera, sporting a much earthier soul sound. Six of those solo tracks are from singles never available on album; two were previously unreleased. *—Richie Unterberger*

Bluesoul Belles, Vol. 4: The Scepter and Musicor Recordings / Oct. 9, 2001 / WestSide ✦✦✦✦

Otis Clay

b. Feb. 11, 1942, Waxhaw, MS

Vocals, Leader / Soul, Chicago Soul, Deep Soul, Soul-Blues, R&B

Otis Clay made most of his best-known records in Memphis during the early '70s, but he's still universally hailed as Chicago's deep soul king. In a city filled to overflowing with legendary blues artists, Clay has become the proud standard-bearer for Chicago's enduring soul tradition.

Like so many of his contemporaries, Clay's intense vocal style reflects a gospel background. He made the secular jump in 1965, signing with Chicago's One-derful Records and issuing a series of gospel-tinged soul records that were a lot grittier than the customary Windy City soul sound. Clay inaugurated Atlantic's Cotillion subsidiary in 1968 with a supercharged cover of the Sir Douglas Quintet's "She's About a Mover," produced by Rick Hall in Muscle Shoals shortly before the singer joined forces with Hi Records boss Willie Mitchell. With the relentlessly driving Hi Rhythm Section in tow, Clay waxed his biggest seller in 1972, "Trying to Live My Life Without You," later covered very successfully by Bob Seger.

Although Clay's tenure on Hi may have been his most commercially potent, he steadily recorded and gigged in the years following. He is a genuine hero in Japan, where he's recorded two sizzling live albums filled with the churning grooves, punchy horns, and searing vocals that inevitably characterize the best deep soul—no matter where it's recorded. *—Bill Dahl*

I Can't Take It / 1977 / Hi ✦✦✦

Soul Man: Live in Japan / Oct. 22, 1983 / Bullseye Blues ✦✦✦✦✦

Thankfully, Otis Clay is an artist who refused to change with the times. When the R&B audience embraced disco and, later, urban contemporary, the hard-edged belter wisely stuck with the type of raw, unapologetically Southern-sounding soul that put him on the map. Though he calls Chicago home, Clay's approach has always shouted "Memphis!" in no uncertain terms. A 41-year-old Clay was clearly very much his prime when this magnificent live date was recorded in 1983. Sparing no passion on such treasures as "Holding on to a Dying Love" and Al Green's "Here I Am (Come and Take Me)," Clay illustrates why his small yet devoted following holds him in such high regard. One of the most pleasant surprises is the ballad "Love Don't Love Nobody." While the Spinners' excellent hit version boasted a sleek Philly soul production, Clay takes the gem straight to Memphis. *—Alex Henderson*

I'll Treat You Right / 1992 / Bullseye Blues ✦✦✦✦✦

The Gospel Truth / 1993 / Blind Pig ✦✦✦

Otis Clay demonstrates how secular roots music can walk hand in the hand with fervent gospel on *The Gospel Truth.* While the sentiment and lyrics are purely devotional, Clay doesn't cast off his blues and soul background, which steeps this material in gritty, instrumental truth. *—Roch Parisien*

The 45's / Nov. 20, 1995 / Hi ✦✦✦✦

Otis Clay was a great Southern soul singer, singing in an era when the productions were sweeter than his earthy voice. He was also on a label that had a superstar in Al Green and another hitmaker in Ann Peebles, so he never got as far on the charts as he may have on another label—or as far as he could have gotten a few years earlier, when full-throated singers like Wilson Pickett, Otis Redding, and, to a lesser extent, James Carr, were having big pop hits. Clay never hit the pop charts and never broke the Top 20 on the R&B charts, but as this rock-solid collection of 14 singles proves, he consistently delivered great music on his sides for Hi. Foremost among those is the undeniable "Trying to Live My Life Without You," and perhaps the other songs aren't as transcendent as that, but they're all strong Southern soul, pushed over the edge by Clay's passionate performances and the grittiest production to come out of Hi (the closest they came to Stax). *The 45s* is certainly not a complete overview of Clay's work for the label (as 2000's *The Complete Otis Clay on Hi Records* is, nor is it as comprehensive as the 1996 collection *The Best of Otis Clay,* but at 14 tracks, it's concise, punchy and plays as good as any classic vinyl hits collection, and is an excellent sampler in its own right. *—Stephen Thomas Erlewine*

Best of Otis Clay: The Hi Records Years / Jul. 23, 1996 / Hi ✦✦✦✦✦

Best of the Hi Records Years is an excellent collection of Otis Clay's early-'70s heyday, featuring such songs as "If I Could Reach Out" and the classic "Trying to Live My Life Without You." Although these recordings aren't quite as gritty as his singles for One-derful! and Cotillion Records, the tight Hi rhythm section keeps things at a steady, sexy groove, so they are nevertheless excellent and deeply soulful and are arguably his best work, making this compilation an essential addition to any comprehensive '70s soul collection. *—Stephen Thomas Erlewine*

This Time Around / Mar. 25, 1998 / Bullseye Blues ✦✦✦✦

The idea of teaming Clay with his original Hi Records producer Willie Mitchell serves up a winner on *This Time Around,* an album filled with solid songwriting and great playing. Cash McCall's tunesmithing talents are served up on "You Never Miss Your Water" and "That's How It Is (Slap Some Sense In Me)," the latter being a remake of Otis' single on One-derful back in 1967. The backing musicians all have long pedigrees in Memphis soul music circles, either working at Stax or with producer Mitchell. The result is one sensational album capturing an artist in the prime of his soulful art. Other highlights include "You're the One I Choose," "When Hearts Grow Cold," "I Can Handle It," "That's How It Is" and the title track. Otis Clay may have started singing and recording some 30-odd years ago, but he's never sounded more in command of his talent. *—Cub Koda*

Hi Masters / Sep. 15, 1998 / Hi ✦✦✦✦✦

● **The Complete Otis Clay on Hi Records** / Mar. 7, 2000 / Hi ✦✦✦✦✦
Hi Records put Otis Clay's soul-dripping, gruff vocals to good use, but the company's real promotional efforts revolved around Al Green. Hence, Clay's recordings, like Syl Johnson, Don Bryant, and Ann Peeble's, got the scraps. This two-CD import, however, captures the essence of one of Memphis' finest Southern soul singers and will get you up to speed. Clay left it all in the studio, so every track is stellar. The picks are any song written by Bryant; Clay's remake of Jackie Moore's "Precious, Precious," "I Die a Little Everyday," the Bobby Womack-ish "I Didn't Know the Meaning of Pain," "The Woman Don't Live Here No More," Mack Rice's "Pussy Footing Around" and "House Ain't a Home (Without a Woman)." Sandra Chalmers, Judy Rodman, and Karen Taylor's voices sweeten every track they touch. A classic collection of Southern soul. *—Andrew Hamilton*

Willie Clayton

b. Mar. 29, 1955, Indianola, MS
Vocals / Retro-Soul, Chicago Soul, Soul-Blues
As long as he's been recording (from 1969 through the 2000s), one might think that Willie Clayton is an old geezer. No way—he was just past the age of 40 when he hit his commercial stride with a couple of blues-soul albums for Ace that sold well to the Southern market (where the two interrelated idioms have never been deemed mutually exclusive). After his debut single for Duplex, "That's the Way Daddy Did," went nowhere, Clayton left Mississippi for Chicago in 1971. Like his older Windy City compatriots Otis Clay and Syl Johnson, the young singer ended up contracted to Hi Records in Memphis, where he worked with producer Willie Mitchell and the vaunted Hi rhythm section. Hi issued a series of fine Clayton efforts on its Pawn subsidiary, including "I Must Be Losin' You," "It's Time You Made Up Your Mind," and "Baby You're Ready," but none of them hit.

Finally, in 1984, Clayton enjoyed a taste of soul success when his "Tell Me" (produced by General Crook) and "What a Way to Put It" for Compleat Records nudged on to the R&B charts. *Let's Get Together*, Clayton's 1993 album for Johnny Vincent's Ace logo, was a smooth soul-blues hybrid dominated by originals but titled after Al Green's immortal hit. *Simply Beautiful*, his Ace follow-up, found Clayton mixing dusties by Rev. Al, Aretha Franklin, and Arthur Crudup with his own stuff. *It's About Love* followed in 1999. *—Bill Dahl*

Feels Like Love / 1992 / Ichiban ✦✦✦
It seems like he's been around forever, but this is Willie Clayton's solo debut. The emotive soul singer is still a well-kept secret north of the Mason-Dixon Line and west of the Mississippi River. You got a hole in your soul if you can't get into Clayton's heart-on-the-sleeve, gut-wrenching renditions of David Ruffin's "Walk Away From Love" and Bobby Womack's "That's the Way I Feel About You." His resonant, razor-edged tenor also does supreme justice to seven originals. To single out a few would be dogging the rest; they're all top-shelf, direct declarations, requests, and whiskey-induced flights in fantasy, of which "Suspended Animation" is but one example. *—Andrew Hamilton*

Let's Get Together / 1993 / Ace ✦✦✦
Here is contemporary Southern deep soul with a strong taste of blues underlying. The clever "Three People (Sleeping in My Bed)" and "Back Street Love Affair," along with the self-penned "Feels like Love" and "Let Me Love You," are attractive showcases for Clayton's warm, assured vocal delivery. *—Bill Dahl*

Simply Beautiful / 1994 / Ace ✦✦✦
This is more of the same—Clayton's intimate confident vocals framed in terms midway between deep soul and contemporary blues. His own "Lose What You Got" and "Crazy for You" rate highly, along with Frank Johnson's "Love Stealing Ain't Worth Stealing" and the singer's delicate revival of Al Green's title cut. *—Bill Dahl*

No Getting over Me / 1995 / Ichiban ✦✦✦✦✦
Worth the price of admission for Clayton's soulful remake of country crooner Ronnie Milsap's title track alone—but there's plenty more contemporary deep soul to be found on this exceptionally solid set. *—Bill Dahl*

● **Chicago Soul Greats** / Jul. 18, 1995 / Hi ✦✦✦✦

At His Best / Nov. 21, 1995 / Ichiban ✦✦✦
You can pick any one of the sensational Willie Clayton's CDs at random and come up with a winner every time. *At His Best* is not a greatest-hits compilation; the title signifies Clayton at his best, or in his best voice. His golden tenor is like a Porsche engine: well-tuned, powerful, and smooth as Jack Daniels. You forget the originals when Clayton remakes a song, and he does many here, excelling on timeless deep soul classics like "I've Been Loving You Too Long," "Open the Door to Your Heart," "Shining Star," "In the Mood," and the Independents' "Leaving Me." There are also two choking compositions by Sam Dees: "What a Way to Put It" and "So Tied Up." *—Andrew Hamilton*

Ace in the Hole / Feb. 13, 1996 / Ace ✦✦✦✦
The most consistent and satisfying of Clayton's contemporary output for Johnny Vincent's reactivated Ace imprint, thanks to top-flight soul-blues items like "Hurt by Love" and "My Baby's Cheating on Me," the Bob Jones-penned "Equal Opportunity" and "Bartender's Blues," and the singer's own "Happy." *—Bill Dahl*

Something to Talk About / Jun. 2, 1998 / Avanti ✦✦✦
Since 1992, Willie Clayton has recorded a steady stream of excellent albums comprising Southern soul, R&B, and blues. *Something to Talk About*, while less essential than previous efforts, continues the amazing string. The 14 songs here are mostly originals—quite different from previous releases, where his engaging tenor enhanced a slew of remakes. Laid-back but effective, the standouts include "Mine All Mine," "One Last Kiss," "Are You Married," the title track, and "Heart of the City," though you won't be unhappy with any of these. *—Andrew Hamilton*

The Cleftones

f. 1955, Jamaica, Queens, NY, **db.** 1964
Group / Doo Wop
Formed in Queens, NY, in 1955, the Cleftones consisted of five friends from Jamaica High School—Herb Cox (lead), Warren Corbin (bass), Charlie James (first tenor), William McClain (baritone), and Berman Patterson (second tenor). Originally signed to Gee, the group released its first single, "You Baby You," late in 1955; an uptempo doo wop song, the record became a regional hit. "Little Girl of Mine," the Cleftones' second single, broke nationally, charting at number-eight R&B and number-57 pop in 1956; two other similar singles, "Can't We Be Sweethearts" and "String Around My Heart," were released the same year, yet they failed to attract national attention. "See You Next Year," a ballad the group recorded in 1957, did not earn the group an audience outside of New York.

Two years later, McClain left the group and was replaced by Gene Pearson from the Rivileers. Patricia Spann was also added to the Cleftones' lineup that year, which helped nudge the band away from traditional group-oriented doo wop harmonies and toward a vocal sound that was dominated by the lead vocals. In 1961, the Cleftones realized the potential of the sound with their smash hit version of the standard "Heart & Soul"; it became the group's biggest hit, reaching number 18 on both pop and R&B charts. Later that year, the group had another hit with "For Sentimental Reasons," but the band had reached a peak with "Heart and Soul" and were never able to reach those heights again. The Cleftones broke up in 1964, three years after their greatest success. *—Stephen Thomas Erlewine*

Heart & Soul / 1961 / Gee ✦✦✦

For Sentimental Reasons / 1962 / Gee ✦✦✦

● **The Best of the Cleftones** / 1991 / Rhino ✦✦✦✦✦

Heart & Soul/For Sentimental Reasons / Jun. 9, 1998 / WestSide ✦✦✦✦✦
This compilation brings together both Cleftones albums recorded for Gee, Rama and Roulette Records between 1956 and 1961. *Heart & Soul* originally consisted of new tracks recorded in stereo along with old mono masters rechanneled in fake stereo; this reissue keeps the actual stereo masters in place and replaces the fakes with the original mono masters. All of their early hits, including the anthemic "Little Girl of Mine," are here along with six new sides from 1961. *For Sentimental Reasons* utilizes the last of the group's '50s masters ("Hey Babe" and "What Did I Do That Was Wrong"), but the entire album was recorded in real stereo and presented that way here. Both albums are also presented back to back in their original running order. A great package on this seminal doo wop group. *—Cub Koda*

Clarence Clemons

b. Jan. 11, 1942, Norfolk, VA
Saxophone, Vocals / Pop/Rock, Rock & Roll
A saxophonist and vocalist who was a member of Bruce Springsteen's backup group, the E Street Band, from 1973 to 1989. Clemons has released several solo albums and scored a duet hit with Jackson Browne, "You're a Friend of Mine." *—William Ruhlmann*

Rescue / Oct. 1983 / Columbia ✦✦
As Bruce Springsteen labored over the album that would become *Born In The U.S.A.*, E Street Band tenor saxophonist Clarence Clemons took the opportunity to create this busman's holiday, fronting a septet he called the Red Bank Rockers. The group's lead singer was John "J.T." Bowen, a gruff-voiced shouter in the tradition of Wilson Pickett, and Clemons assembled such songwriters as Ellie Greenwich and Desmond Child to put together a set of neo-'60s R&B ravers. Also included was Springsteen's "Savin' Up," on which the Boss played rhythm guitar. Of course, Clemons himself played lots of sax in the rock & roll style of King Curtis and Steve Douglas. The album suggested that the Rockers might be a good band to catch on a hot night in Red Bank. But it didn't make anyone mistake Clemons for anything other than a talented sideman. *—William Ruhlmann*

The Chief / 1984 / Rooster Blues ✦✦✦

● **Hero** / Nov. 1985 / Columbia ✦✦✦✦
Narada Michael Walden produces most of this album by Mokshagun Clarence Clemons, known to the world as the Big Man. His unmistakable saxophone that lifted many a Bruce Springsteen tune sounds like it was lifted right out of a Phil Spector session on *Hero*. "You're a Friend of Mine" by Jeffrey Cohen and Narada has Jackson Browne dueting on the lead vocal with Clemens and his then-girlfriend, Daryl Hannah, on backing vocals. The same songwriting duo comes up with "Temptation," a hooky, smart, mid-'80s thick-pop sound with Booker T. Jones again on keyboards. For "It's Alright With Me Girl" it's the very hip Jonzun Crew backing up Clemons: Michael Jonzun, Gordon Worthy, guitarist Tony "Rocks" Cowan, Maurice Starr on bass, and Princess Loria on vocals, with stunning dynamic switches from Narada Michael Walden to Michael Jonzun in a flash. Clemons and Jonzun put "It's Alright With Me Girl" together, and it's a shame there aren't four or five more of these collaborations. One oddity on the album is the closing to side one, the Arthur Baker-produced remake of the Walker Brothers' hit "The Sun Ain't Gonna Shine Anymore," with Stu Kimball from Face to Face and Phil Spector singer Darlene Love. The title track, which kicks off side two, is a tremendous song about being a lover and a friend. "Crossin' the Line" works, as does "Kissin' on You," where Clemons' nickname, the Big Man, is one of the hooks. The leadoff track with Jackson Browne went Top 20 in 1985, four years before his first go-round with the E-Street Band was concluding. It's great to see a musician step from the shadows of a legend and make a mark on his own, and Clarence Clemons does that remarkably well here. This is a record where dropping

names means something, because the names are allowed to do what is expected of them. It's a beautiful work that will appeal to those who never found the Boss all that exciting. Of course, it might appeal to Springsteen fans as well. *—Joe Viglione*

Night With Mr. C / Aug. 1989 / Columbia ✦✦
The problem with Clarence Clemons' third solo album was apparent on the first cut, a remake of Gary "U.S." Bonds' "Quarter to Three." The song was one Clemons frequently played in Bruce Springsteen's E Street Band, in a faithful rendition of the original. But here Clemons turned rapper over a synthesizer backing, retaining only the chorus, and even then changing "Daddy G" to "Mr. C." Similar modernizing was applied to classics like "Shotgun" and "Twistin' the Night Away," and if one wasn't as offended by the originals (which tended toward bland jazz-fusion), neither was one impressed. Things didn't improve when Clemons began reciting the poetry of his guru, Sri Chinmoy. It was hard to imagine who the audience was supposed to be for this record—those who remembered "Quarter to Three" wouldn't like such a radical treatment, and rap fans weren't likely to be convinced, either. As it turned out, there was no audience for *A Night With Mr. C*, which didn't sell well enough to make the charts. *—William Ruhlmann*

Peacemaker / 1995 / Zoo ✦✦
You are likely to find this instrumental album in either the Jazz or New Age sections of the record store. Tenor saxophonist Clarence Clemons creates attractive mood music that matches an unusually smooth sax sound (especially for him) with a variety of percussion instruments so broad that the list of them in the album's booklet concludes "...and some other stuff we can't pronounce or spell." It makes for an eclectic selection of music appropriate for the all usual new age functions, from meditation to cooking. *—William Ruhlmann*

Rescue/Hero / Aug. 28, 2001 / Collectables ✦✦✦

Cleopatra

Group / Teen Pop, Urban, Dance-Pop
Cross the Spice Girls with Hanson and you get Cleopatra, a teen trio from Manchester, England, comprised of three of the Higgins sisters—oldest sibling Zainam, third child Yonah, and second-oldest Cleopatra, who in addition to lending the group its name also assumed lead vocal duties on all of their songs, most of which the sisters co-wrote. The offspring of session singer Christine Higgins, the trio was inspired by everything from gospel to trip-hop to classic soul. After winning a local talent contest, they were signed to a management contract, then spent six years performing around the U.K. before being signed to the British division of Warner Bros. Records in early 1997. They released two top five singles, "Cleopatra's Theme" and "Life Ain't Easy," followed by their Top 20 debut album *Comin' Atcha* in the spring of 1998. The album then spun off two more British chart singles, a Top Five cover of the Jackson 5's "I Want You Back" and the Top 40 "A Touch of Love." In the U.S., the group was picked up by Madonna's Maverick label. "Cleopatra's Theme" reached the pop Top 40 as well as the R&B charts, and "Life Ain't Easy" also made both charts, while *Comin' Atcha* spent a few months in the lower half of the album charts. With their mother and their youngest sister Terry, the group launched its own comedy/variety show on British television, which was a ratings success. Their second album, *Steppin' Out*, was released in August 2000. *—Jason Ankeny & William Ruhlmann*

Comin' Atcha / Jun. 30, 1998 / Warner Bros. ✦✦✦
Cleopatra's debut album *Comin' Atcha* has a few weak spots, but that should be expected from any dance-pop album. What is surprising is that the cuts that work are so enjoyable. It's easy to be suspcious of a group that feels like a genetically engineered hybrid of Hanson and the Spice Girls, but the three sisters in Cleopatra have a spunky charm that makes their light dance-pop and urban ballads enjoyable. There's enough filler on the album to make it a frustrating listen but the best moments—namely singles like "Cleopatra's Theme"—make the dull spots worthwhile. *—Stephen Thomas Erlewine*

● **Steppin' Out** / Aug. 22, 2000 / Warner Bros. ✦✦✦
Still all under the age of 20, the three Higgins sisters who perform under the name of second oldest sibling Cleopatra have come a long way from Manchester on their second album. With 1998's *Comin' Atcha*, which featured three top five hits in the U.K., they were part of the teen-pop wave started by the Spice Girls two years earlier. But though they got some attention in the U.S., including a Top 40 entry for "Cleopatra's Theme," the American market didn't quite know what to make of a black trio that didn't sound like R&B. *Steppin' Out* answers that confusion by moving the group in an R&B/hip-hop direction without sacrificing their teen-pop approach. Employing a variety of production teams including Cutfather & Joe, and Jimmy Jam & Terry Lewis, and recording at various U.S. and U.K. locations as well as in Norway and Denmark, Cleopatra has come up with an album of 11 potential singles, most of them in a familiar dance-pop style. "Nobody Said," the lone holdout from Manchester writer-producers Tim Scrafton & Kenny Hayes, is a ballad containing self-help advice, while Jam & Lewis' "Who's Your Woman," anchored by a striking single-note keyboard pattern, has an inventive sound. But for the most part, whether they're in Scandinavia, England, or America, the trio is singing harmless romantic pop (typical titles: "Take Me Now," "Come and Get Me") over light dance tracks. The weak spot is actually the vocals. Even though their mother Christine is credited with "additional vocals" on every track (she even gets her own section for her thank-yous in the characteristically lengthy acknowledgments section of the album's booklet), the sisters, led by Cleopatra herself, are not distinctive singers capable of giving this trite material any depth or particularity. In 1998, you had to say that Cleopatra was no Spice Girls; in 2000, you'd have to add that they're no Destiny's Child, either. *—William Ruhlmann*

Linda Clifford

b. 1944, Brooklyn, NY
Vocals / Soul, Quiet Storm, Disco
A former Miss New York State, Brooklyn vocalist Linda Clifford parlayed a jazz background, booming voice, and sassy manner into disco and R&B/urban contemporary stardom in the '70s and '80s. She sang with the Jerico Jazz Singers and led her own trio in the '60s before switching to R&B and pop. She made a little noise on Paramount, then signed with Curtis Mayfield's Curtom label. Clifford got her first hit in 1978 with "Runaway Love," a song that peaked at number three on the R&B charts. The highly stylized "If My Friends Could See Me Now" was a club favorite that same year. Her next hit was a duet with Mayfield, "Between You Baby and Me," a much more soulful number in 1979 that peaked at number 14. She continued recording for RSO, Capitol, and Red Label in the '80s, but didn't recapture her former success. During the early '90s, she did some tracks produced by Rick Gianatos, but failed to find any label to release them. *—Ron Wynn*

Linda / 1977 / Warner Bros. ✦✦✦
This album is the debut outing for Linda Clifford, Curtom Records' answer to Donna Summer. Although Clifford would soon become a well-known disco diva through hits like her over-the-top remake of "If My Friends Could See Me Now," this set is a surprisingly low-key affair that downplays disco grooves for a more soul-oriented sound. The standout dance tracks are "You Can Do It," a self-determination anthem set to a sultry, midtempo groove, and "From Now On," a Bunny Sigler composition that pits a clavinet-driven beat against glossy orchestrations to create an ideal disco showcase for Clifford's gospel-tinged vocals. The other material is mostly covers of pop and soul hits, including Stevie Wonder's "If It's Magic" and the Bee Gees' "Be Tender With My Love." The best of these covers is Clifford's doo wop take on Rod Stewart's "Tonight's the Night," a clever remake that provides a good vehicle for her brassy vocal persona. However, the presence of all these covers points up the big problem with this album: its reliance upon covers keeps it from establishing a strong persona for its star attraction. *Linda*'s overall power is also diminished by the fact that Clifford often attacks the songs with a little too much enthusiasm: the heartbroken ballad "You Gotta Tell Her" would have benefited more from a subtle, vulnerable vocal performance instead of the full-throated gospel wail that Clifford gives it. Despite these problems, *Linda* boasts an appealingly slick production by ex-Motown staffer Gil Askey and clearly highlights the promise that would soon be realized on her future hits. *—Donald Guarisco*

If My Friends Could See Me Now / 1978 / Curtom ✦✦✦✦
For Linda Clifford's second album, producers Gil Askey and Curtis Mayfield wisely left behind the overabundance of cover tunes that weighted down her debut outing to concentrate on original material. The result is *If My Friends Could See Me Now*, the opus that earned Clifford her disco diva status. The first side of the album represents her finest recorded work. It starts with a bang via the title track, which transforms this classic show tune from *Sweet Charity* into a driving slice of orchestrated disco. It provides an ideal vehicle for Clifford's brassy vocal persona and is further sweetened by expert call and response support from the Jones Girls on backup vocals. From there, the album downshifts into a gentler mood with "You Are, You Are," a Curtis Mayfield song that combines a lovely midtempo groove with some spacy synthesizer effects and romantic-devotion lyrics that are given emotional heft by Clifford's vocal conviction. The *coup de grâce* is provided by "Runaway Love," a funky, Latin-accented dressing down of an unfaithful lover that intersperses its silky rhythms with spoken word bits in a Millie Jackson-styled feminist vein. Unfortunately, the second side doesn't hold up quite as well. The flamenco-flavored "Broadway Gypsy Lady" gets the toes tapping, but the other tunes feel like filler: they are solidly crafted and professionally performed, but lack the distinctive lyrical and musical hooks that made the first side such a treat. Despite this unevenness, *If My Friends Could See Me Now* is listenable all the way through and remains Clifford's shining hour on record. *—Donald A. Guarisco*

Here's My Love / 1979 / RSO ✦✦✦

Let Me Be Your Woman / 1979 / RSO ✦✦✦
After the success of *If My Friends Could See Me Now*, Linda Clifford continued in a similar vein with this lavishly produced album. *Let Me Be Your Woman* was even more directly aimed at the dancefloor than her previous outings and was released in two versions, a single album edition with edited tracks and a deluxe edition that stretched the album's tracks to cover four sides' worth of vinyl (the latter is the one reviewed here). It starts well with "Hold Me Close," a Curtis Mayfield-penned song that effectively pits the hypnotic chant of the title against a strong, percussive groove, and the title track, a melodramatic orchestrated ballad that Clifford pulls off through an impressively emotional performance. After that, *Let Me Be Your Woman* suffers from the same inconsistency that dogged Clifford's previous outings and the fact that it is a double album makes this problem more pronounced. The biggest examples of this problem are "Don't Give It Up," a pseudo-feminist dance track with a ranting tone that becomes especially ludicrous when stretched to nine minutes, and "Sweet Melodies," a midtempo track that endlessly spins its wheels in search of the strong hooks that it lacks. The album picks up at the end with an over-the-top uptempo remake of Simon & Garfunkel's "Bridge Over Troubled Water," but wading through four padded sides of material to get to it is too much to ask from anyone except the most devoted fan. Ultimately, *Let Me Be Your Woman* is too taxing a listen for the casual pop music fan but its stronger moments will still hold appeal for disco historians. *—Donald A. Guarisco*

I'm Yours / 1980 / RSO ✦✦✦
Linda Clifford's final outing on the Curtom label found her teamed up with fellow soul artist Isaac Hayes as her producer. The pairing fit like a glove and resulted in *I'm Yours*, Clifford's strongest and most consistent album since *If My Friends Could See Me Now*. It also produced two notable hits for Clifford. The first was "Shoot Your Best Shot," a string-laden disco epic that benefited from one of Hayes' trademark dramatic arrangements. It perfectly captured the combination of gloss and groove that typified Clifford's best songs and she rose to the occasion with a sassy yet carefully controlled performance that helped make the song a disco favorite. The album's other big hit was "Red Light," a song also

featured on the soundtrack of *Fame*. This bouncy midtempo groover features Clifford convincingly laying down the law for a woman who is trying to steal her man and it skillfully creates a danceable groove through a tasty combination of slap-bass and an energetic horn arrangement. The non-hits don't jump out as strongly as these two, but they are easy on the ears: A great example is "I Want to Get Away With You," a sleek ballad that finds Clifford dipping into the low end of her vocal range to create a convincing imitation of Isaac Hayes' vocal style. The one real downside of the album is that some of songs drag on a little too long, but this shortcoming is made up for by Hayes' hook-laden arrangements (listen closely for the electric guitar riff that snakes its way in and out of "It Don't Hurt No More") and the fact that Clifford sings these songs with the kind of soulful emotion that was lacking on *Here's My Love*. These two factors make *I'm Yours* a necessity for Linda Clifford fans and a solid listen for fans of the disco sound. *—Donald A. Guarisco*

The Right Combination / 1980 / RSO ✦✦
A marvelous duet album between Linda Clifford, a disco diva before the term was commonly used, and Chicago soul vocalist/producer/performer/composer Curtis Mayfield. The album included two chart hits in "I Just Wanna Wanna" and "Love's Sweet Sensation." It also convinced any doubters that Clifford could sing earnest, straight soul as well as pop and disco. *—Ron Wynn*

Sneakin' Out / 1985 / Red Label ✦✦

Greatest Hits / Nov. 28, 1989 / Curtom ✦✦✦✦✦
Those who were quick to malign disco because of the genre's excesses were oblivious to an important fact: not all disco was created equal. And in fact, when disco was mindful of its soul roots, the results could be thrilling. This was definitely true of Linda Clifford, a big-voiced diva who was among the most captivating singers of the disco era. The biggest hit song on this CD is the campy, Vegas-like "If My Friends Could See Me Now," which is enjoyable enough, but is far from her best offering. For better demonstrations of how captivatingly soulful Clifford could be, get into "Runaway Love," "Shoot Your Best Shot" and "Don't Give It Up"—all of which effectively combine disco's slickness and polish with the fire and intensity of classic soul music. Sadly, Clifford faded into obscurity after the disco era. *—Alex Henderson*

Let Me Be Your Woman/Here's My Love / Aug. 15, 2000 / Sequel ✦✦✦

• **Runaway Love: The Singles Anthology** / Oct. 31, 2000 / Sequel ✦✦✦✦
This impressive collection focuses on the top disco artist at Curtom Records, Linda Clifford. While she may not be as well-remembered as Donna Summer, this compilation shows that Clifford created plenty of solid disco epics during her late-'70s/early-'80s chart tenure. *Runaway Love: The Singles Anthology* collects all of the songs released as singles during Clifford's time at Curtom, and further sweetens the package by including a couple of 12-inch mixes that helped her become a dancefloor favorite. Dynamic hits like "If My Friends Could See Me Now" and "Shoot Your Best Shot" remain as elegant and danceable as ever, but the real surprises are the rare non-album singles that open the package: "(It's Gonna Be) A Long Hard Winter" has an intriguingly Motown-styled sound that Clifford never tried again during her Curtom days, and "Turn the Key Softly" is a classy, sweetly orchestrated heartbreak ballad that should have been a hit. This compilation also includes "Between You Baby and Me" and "Love's Sweet Sensation," two tracks from the duet albums that Clifford recorded with Curtis Mayfield. Both songs mix the doo wop elements that characterized Mayfield's hits with the Impressions with a slick, glossy '70s production style to create delightful soul songs with a retro edge. To make the package even more enticing, the people at Castle Music have also thrown in *I'm Yours*, Clifford's 1980 Isaac Hayes-produced outing, as a bonus disc. All in all, *Runaway Love: The Singles Anthology* is a generous and well-assembled package that will cover both the needs of the casual listener and the hardcore Clifford fan. *—Donald A. Guarisco*

George Clinton

b. Jul. 22, 1941, Kannapolis, NC
Producer, Vocals, Keyboards, Synthesizer / Funk, Urban
The mastermind of the Parliament/Funkadelic collective during the 1970s, George Clinton broke up both bands by 1981 and began recording solo albums, occasionally performing live with his former bandmates as the P Funk All-Stars. Born in Kannapolis, NC, on July 22, 1941, Clinton became interested in doo wop while living in NJ during the early '50s. He formed the Parliaments in 1955, based out of a barbershop back room where he straightened hair. The group had a small R&B hit during 1967, but Clinton began to mastermind the Parliaments' activities two years later. Recording both as Parliament and Funkadelic, the group revolutionized R&B during the '70s, twisting soul music into funk by adding influences from several late-'60s acid heroes: Jimi Hendrix, Frank Zappa, and Sly Stone. The Parliament/Funkadelic machine ruled black music during the '70s, capturing over 40 R&B hit singles (including three number ones) and recording three platinum albums.

By 1980, George Clinton began to be weighed down by legal difficulties arising from Polygram's acquisition of Parliament's label, Casablanca. Jettisoning both the Parliament and Funkadelic names (but not the musicians), Clinton signed to Capitol in 1982 both as a solo act and as the P Funk All-Stars. His first solo album, 1982's *Computer Games*, contained the Top 20 R&B hit "Loopzilla." Several months later, the title track from Clinton's *Atomic Dog* EP hit number one on the R&B charts; it stayed at the top spot for four weeks, but only managed number 101 on the pop charts. Clinton stayed on Capitol for three more years, releasing three studio albums and frequently charting singles—"Nubian Nut," "Last Dance," "Do Fries Go With That Shake"—in the R&B Top 40. During much of the three-year period from 1986 to 1989, Clinton became embroiled in legal difficulties (resulting from the myriad royalty problems latent during the '70s with recordings of over 40 musicians for four labels under three names). Also problematic during the latter half of the '80s was Clinton's disintegrating reputation as a true forefather of rock; by the end of the decade, however, a generation of rappers reared on P Funk were beginning to name check him.

In 1989, Clinton signed a contract with Prince's Paisley Park label and released his fifth solo studio album, *The Cinderella Theory*. After one more LP for Paisley Park (*Hey Man, Smell My Finger*), Clinton signed with Sony 550. His first release, 1996's *T.A.P.O.A.F.O.M.* ("the awesome power of a fully operational mothership"), reunited the funk pioneer with several of his Parliament/Funkadelic comrades from the '70s. Clinton's *Greatest Funkin' Hits* (1996) teamed old P Funk hits with new-school rappers such as Digital Underground, Ice Cube, and Q-Tip. [See Also: Parliament, Funkadelic] *—John Bush*

• **Computer Games** / Nov. 5, 1982 / Capitol ✦✦✦✦✦
In the late '70s George Clinton helmed a massive empire bound to eventually decline—which it did, in a rather ugly manner. Once he finally distanced himself in the early '80s from the massive kinetic force that was Parliament/Funkadelic and signed a solo contract with Capitol, he suddenly seemed rejuvenated in terms of creativity and enthusiasm. This freewheeling disposition comes across clearly on *Computer Games*, his first solo album. Of course, calling this a true solo album isn't exactly true, since Bootsy Collins, Gary Shider, and Walter "Junie" Morrison all play a role in the album's success. Still, you get the sense that Clinton is firmly in control of this album, something you can't honestly say about the latter-day Parliament and Funkadelic records, and this sense makes the album quite revealing. Above anything, Clinton turns here to the early-'80s vogue for synthesizers and drum machines that would later become staples of hip-hop and techno production. This fetish for new studio technology still in its primitive stage gives the album a slightly stiff feeling, as the humans are replaced by machines, a very different style of funk. It's this proto-techno funk that colors the album's better moments, particularly "Atomic Dog," "Loopzilla," and the title track. If you're expecting the freewheeling style of his earlier work, you may be disappointed by the confined feeling of Clinton's '80s work. Ultimately, this album ends up being by far the best of Clinton's solo career, with nearly every song having its own character and its own strengths, while latter albums struggled to come up with anything as inventive or effective. Furthermore, no successive album has anything remotely as catchy as "Atomic Dog," a song that Clinton himself could never duplicate no matter how hard he tried on his next three albums. *—Jason Birchmeier*

You Shouldn't-Nuf Bit Fish / Dec. 1983 / Capitol ✦✦✦
When George Clinton rebounded with *Computer Games*, an album met with unanimous acclaim, it seemed as if his already long-winded career was about to enter a new era of inspired creativity. *You Shouldn't-Nuf Bit Fish* surfaced a year later in 1983, though, and whatever momentum Clinton had garnered quickly dissipated. From the Pedro Bell artwork to the ensemble of contributors to the early-'80s synth-drum aesthetic, *You Shouldn't-Nuf Bit Fish* seemed a fitting follow-up upon initial inspection, though there was one glaring difference between the two albums—quality. *Computer Games* had been stacked with great songs; *You Shouldn't-Nuf Bit Fish* clearly wasn't. It's hard to pinpoint exactly what makes the songs of lesser quality: Clumsy attempts at rapping, a lack of effective hooks, awkward attempts to make primitive drum machines funky, a brief running length, and just plain bad songwriting all figure into the album's failure as an adequate follow-up, with none being any worse than the other. "Nubian Nut" stands as Clinton's first attempt at rapping, a truly jarring moment best forgotten. In fact, only "Quickie" is worth bothering with here, a Walter "Junie" Morrison song carried largely by Andre Williams' great guitar riff. Overall, the songs on this album are just plain bad. It's that simple, leaving one to ask the inevitable question: What happened? Well, the answer may lie in Bell's cryptic artwork, where an enigmatic statement alludes to the fact that this album is comprised of leftovers from the *Computer Games* sessions. Whether or not this is indeed the case, *You Shouldn't-Nuf Bit Fish* marked a turning point in Clinton's briefly ignited solo career, a turn toward quick oblivion. *—Jason Birchmeier*

Some of My Best Jokes Are Friends / Jul. 1985 / Capitol ✦✦✦
With technology having taken over R&B in a major way by the mid-'80s, George Clinton made a point of "updating" his P Funk by being much more high tech and using keyboards, drum machines, and sequencers extensively. On his third "solo album," *Some of My Best Jokes Are Friends*, Clinton even recruits Britain's very technology-oriented new waver Thomas Dolby to help with the production on a few cuts. *Jokes* is far from his best effort, and sometimes comes across as forced and unnatural. But the CD definitely has its strong points, including the addictive "Bodyguard," the eerie "Bangladesh," and the antiwar protest songs "Bullet Proof" and "Thrashin'." With Parliament and Funkadelic, Clinton often had fun making strong social and political statements in a subliminal fashion—this time, however, he's much more direct. Despite its strengths, *Jokes* is an album that only Clinton's most devoted followers should invest in—those exploring his innovations for the first time would do much better to purchase one of his classic Parliament or Funkadelic albums of the '70s (or, for that matter, his first "solo album" *Computer Games*). *—Alex Henderson*

Mothership Connection (Live from the Summit, Houston, Texas) / 1986 / Capitol ✦✦
Credited to George Clinton Parliament Funkadelic, *The Mothership Connection (Live from the Summit, Houston, Texas)* is a discount-priced, six-track mini-LP consisting of one side devoted to a 24-minute soundtrack to a video of the same name, backed with three previously released Clinton studio tracks. A sprawling, often impressive concert recording featuring the immense Mothership Connection organization under George Clinton's reign. This set was perhaps the only time any album conveyed the sense of spectacle, chaos, wild humor, and musical mayhem that were routinely on display during their live shows. *—Ron Wynn*

R&B Skeletons in the Closet / Apr. 1986 / Capitol ✦✦✦✦✦
A definite improvement over the uneven *Some of My Best Jokes Are Friends*, the considerably more focused and confident *R&B Skeletons in the Closet* is one of George Clinton's strongest solo efforts. The P-Funkster continues using technology extensively, but this time, his blend of technology and "real instruments" sounds much more natural. Though not quite in a class with Parliament classics like *Mothership Connection* or

Funkentelechy Vs. the Placebo Syndrome or Funkadelic treasures ranging from *Cosmic Slop* to *Uncle Jam Wants You*, *Skeletons* is a superb collection that's well worth acquiring. The CD kicks into high gear with the wildly infectious "Hey Good Lookin'" and maintains that high level of excitement on such driving, sweaty funk treasures as "Do Fries Go With That Shake?" and the appropriately titled "Intense" and the title song. Clinton's eccentricity and outrageous sense of humor serve him well on "Electric Pygmies" and "Mix-Master Suite," an unorthodox, quirky, and cinematic ode to hip-hop drawing on everything from jazz to classical music to Western movies. Many of Clinton's longtime associates are on hand to help make this album the artistic success it is, including saxman Maceo Parker, trombonist Fred Wesley, and the ever-amusing Bootsy Collins. *—Alex Henderson*

The Cinderella Theory / Aug. 1989 / Paisley Park ♦♦♦

On his first album for Prince's Paisley Park record label, George Clinton's willingness to experiment with samplers and hip-hop (including guest appearances by such artists as Chuck D. and Flavor Flav of Public Enemy) resulted in a slightly inconsistent record, but it has more than enough truly fine songs to make *The Cinderella Theory* rank among his best solo albums. *—Stephen Thomas Erlewine*

Sample Some of Disc, Sample Some of DAT / Jan. 1993 / AEM ♦♦♦

Concerned about the huge strides being made in the development of samplers, and the ways in which artists were being sampled by everyone from rappers to plunderphonic collage artists, George Clinton hit on the idea of creating legal, low-cost sample discs based on excerpts from his vast archives. The catch here is that if you use one or more samples from this disc, then you sign over a portion of your royalties to Clinton and company. A good idea, on the surface, but the actual royalty schedule involved was close to heinous, leaving samplers preferring to shell out a hundred dollars or more for license-free discs. This initial disc has some interesting flaws, too, in that the track listing on the inner sleeve has no reference whatsoever to the actual tracks, an error that causes quite a bit of confusion. Finally, the samples (full mixes to solo instrument tracks) represent a more or less ho-hum selection from the vaults. *—Steven McDonald*

Hey Man, Smell My Finger / Oct. 1993 / Paisley Park ♦♦♦♦

Hey Man, Smell My Finger is everything a great George Clinton album should be—conceptually disjointed, overlong, silly, sloppy, and funky as hell. Thankfully, the music here is his best since *Computer Games*, and the album proves just how responsible he is for much of the music of the 1990s, as the irresistible single "Paint the White House Black" illustrates with its numerous cameos. *—Stephen Thomas Erlewine*

George Clinton With Parliament / Apr. 16, 1995 / Music Merchant ♦♦

Apparently, the superb archival Parliament release *First Thangs* was released without George Clinton's approval or input. How else to explain this release, which cannibalizes half the tracks on that album, sequences them out of order, and retains the superb liner notes from that anthology, which make references to tracks that are not on this release? Add a contemporary photo of Clinton on the cover, and what results is guaranteed to confuse and irritate consumers. To be fair, the music—recorded during the sessions for the first Parliament album, *Osmium*, in 1970—is worth hearing. "Fantasy Is Reality" is a gospel-tinged song with psychedelic overtones, and "Breakdown," a hard rock number with fiery lead guitar work from Eddie Hazel, is as superb as anything Parliament and Funkadelic released officially. It is also true that *First Thangs* suffered from poor distribution upon its release. Still, it would have been more of a treat for fans if the entire album had simply been reissued, rather than a portion (the remaining tracks appear on *Tamurinillis*). Fans who want to hear this music might make do with this release, but really should expend the effort to track down *First Thangs* instead. *—Victor W. Valdivia*

T.A.P.O.A.F.O.M. (The Awesome Power of a Fully Operational Mothership) / Jun. 1996 / 550 Music/Epic ♦♦

The Awesome Power of a Fully Operational Mothership is the first George Clinton album to show signs of a Dr. Dre G-funk influence. Where his previous album, *Hey Man, Smell My Finger*, was pretty much nothing but standard P-funk, *Awesome Power* slows the beat down just like Dre does on *The Chronic*. The difference is, Dre actually works those grooves into songs where Clinton just lets the funk meander. He doesn't even try to write songs—he operates under the belief that ceaseless jamming and randomly interjected vocals constitues a good groove. And it does, when given the right source material and musicians. On *Awesome Power*, Clinton has neither. The musicians may have all played with various incarnations of Parliament, but they sound tired and bored on the album—there isn't a single instant when they latch on to a good groove. And what that means is this: On *Awesome Power*, George Clinton sounds more out of touch with contemporary funk and R&B than he ever has. *—Stephen Thomas Erlewine*

Greatest Funkin' Hits / Oct. 29, 1996 / Capitol ♦♦♦

Greatest Funkin' Hits has something of a misleading title. It implies that all of George Clinton's biggest solo hits, in their original forms, are featured on this compilation. Instead, *Greatest Funkin' Hits* takes Clinton's best-known songs—not just solo hits like "Atomic Dog" and "Do Fries Go With That Shake," but also Parliament/Funkadelic songs like "Flashlight," "Mothership Connection," "Knee Deep" and "Bop Gun"—and presents them in remixed forms. Sometimes, the remixes are good—Coolio's take on "Atomic Dog" is fun, and Ice Cube's appearance on "Bop Gun (One Nation)" is terrific—but often, the remixes are perfunctory and uninspired, making the album a tedious listening experience. Most importantly, it should not be considered in any way as a greatest-hits album—it's simply another in a long line of pointless Clinton-associated remix albums. *—Leo Stanley*

Greatest Hits / May 9, 2000 / Capitol ♦♦♦♦

George Clinton's solo output of the 1980s and 1990s wasn't as consistent as his work with Parliament/Funkadelic in the 1970s—nonetheless, the P Funk innovator has had his share of inspired moments as a solo artist, and some of his best solo recordings are united on this collection. Released in 2000, *Greatest Hits* spans 1976-1986 and draws on such solo albums as *Computer Games*, *You Shouldn't-Nuf Bit Fish*, *Some of My Best Jokes Are Friends*, and *R&B Skeletons in the Closet*. The oldest recording is the bonus track, a live Parliament/Funkadelic medley of "Let's Take It to the Stage" and "Do That Stuff" from a 1976 Houston show; most of the selections, however, come from Clinton's Capitol solo albums of 1982-1986. Not surprisingly, the CD opens with "Atomic Dog," Clinton's best-known and most essential solo hit. And the Right Stuff's other choices are also wise ones, including "Do Fries Go With That Shake?," "Cool Joe," "Loopzilla," "Hey Good Lookin'," and the quirky rap item "Nubian Nut." *Greatest Hits* isn't the last word on George Clinton's solo career, but if you need a concise introduction to the funkmeister's Capitol efforts of the 1980s, it's the logical place to go. *—Alex Henderson*

Cloud One

f. New York

Group / Disco, Club/Dance

The studio-bound disco unit Cloud One made its debut in 1976 with the spectacular "Atmosphere Strut," a drifting, blissed-out nugget of underground disco that featured a repeated female vocal refrain of "We're gonna fly/Fly away." More importantly, what made the song stand out from everything else released at the time was the wild synthesizer line from producer and arranger Patrick Adams, who—as with dozens of other short-lived disco acts shamelessly chucked into obscurity—helmed the group. The nine-minute single was also the inaugural release on P&P, the first of several small labels run by Adams and partner Peter Brown.

Several Cloud One singles followed throughout the late '70s on P&P-affiliated labels, such as Queen Constance, Golden Flamingo, Heavenly Star, and Sound of New York. The *Atmosphere Strut* LP, released in 1976, compiled some of the group's 12" material (the LP included a seven-minute edit of the dizzying "Disco Juice," another Adams classic). *Funky Disco Tracks of Cloud One*, an EP, was issued in 1978. A second LP, called *Happy Music*, appeared in 1979. Another Cloud One gem that's worth mentioning is "Patti Duke," a spacy number full of bizarro Moog manipulations and clusters of hand percussion that, when sped up, would probably sound like one of the hottest go-go tracks ever recorded. Thankfully, Cloud One's recorded works haven't been too difficult to come by. The Unidisc label issued *Atmosphere Strut* on CD in 1996, while M.I.L. Multimedia put out *The Best of Cloud One* two years later. The U.K.-based Counterpoint label has also provided a major service for those attempting to track down songs released by P&P and its offshoots; in 1997, the *Disco Juice* compilation was released and a second volume followed in 2002. Four Cloud One songs were included between the two discs. *—Andy Kellman*

Cloud One / 1977 / P&P ♦♦♦♦

Since the disco underground communicated through the 12-inch format, containing A-sides and B-sides that almost always surpassed the several-minute mark, full-length albums were a rarity. Cloud One's self-titled album (reissued on CD in the mid-'90s as *Atmosphere Strut*, and then included in its entirety on both *The Best of Cloud One* and *The Very Best of Cloud One*) is one exception to the rule. As with the remainder of Cloud One's material, each song on this LP was produced and arranged by Patrick Adams, a remarkably prolific cult legend whose name should be just as instantly recognized in dance music circles as Giorgio Moroder and Arthur Baker's. Not only was Adams an incredibly talented figure behind the boards (and a label operator on top), but he also revolutionized synth playing—no one before, during, or since has played the synthesizer like him. *Cloud One* is one of several testaments to these facts, containing a handful of classic disco cuts that remain in DJ crates decades after being recorded. "Atmosphere Strut" and "Disco Juice" (the latter in a different mix from its longer, more popular counterpart) have the highest profile of these six songs. Both are euphoric but completely distinct from one another. "Atmosphere Strut" is a nine-minute drift carried by a light, winding groove, a repeated refrain of "We're gonna fly, fly away," crazy synth squiggles, human handclaps, and incidental exclamations of delight. "Disco Juice" is downright colossal; with its humid, nocturnal feel; shimmering strings; taut bassline; and a dazed, wordless refrain, it practically forces anyone within earshot to involuntarily twirl in a state of bliss. The delirious "Spaced Out," the smooth/easy "Dust to Dust," and the jubilant closer "Doin' It All Night Long" put a cap on this brilliant album. *—Andy Kellman*

Funky Disco Tracks of Cloud One / 1978 / Queen Constance ♦♦♦

The Best of Cloud One / Sep. 15, 1998 / M.I.L. Multimedia ♦♦♦♦

In 1998, the M.I.L. Multimedia label issued *The Best of Cloud One*, which simply paired *Cloud One* with *Funky Disco Tracks of Cloud One* while adding Queen Yahna's "Ain't It Time," a stray nugget from the house of P&P (one of Patrick Adams and Peter Brown's labels). Although it's bizarre to call this disc *The Best of Cloud One*, someone getting into the group for the first time is in good hands because just about everything of note is here, save for "Patti Duke" (available on Counterpoint's *Disco Juice*) and "Don't Let Me Pass This Rainbow By" (available on BBE's *Disco Spectrum 2*). Some of the most brilliant underground disco can be found on this disc. *—Andy Kellman*

● **The Very Best of Cloud One** / 2000 / 21st Century ♦♦♦♦

The Very Best of Cloud One, released by 21st Century Music in 2000, includes *The Best of Cloud One* in its entirety and adds a second disc of productions related to Patrick Adams & Peter Brown, the two arrangers, producers, writers, and musicians responsible for several short-lived Harlem-based record labels in the '70s and '80s. It's not the easiest Cloud One disc to track down, but it is the one to get. Not only does it offer *Cloud One* and *Funky Disco Tracks of Cloud One* in full, but the second disc includes a handful of excellent rarities. Karisma's "Got You Dancing" (with the great Jocelyn Brown on vocals), Johnson Products' "Johnson Jumpin'," Little Scott's "Going to a Disco Tonight," and the remix of Cloud One's "Atmosphere Strut" add plenty of value to an already value-packed compilation. Those who find themselves smitten with the work of Adams & Brown should also hunt down both volumes of Counterpoint's *Disco Juice*, which anthologize more of the dynamic duo's work released through their labels. *—Andy Kellman*

The Clovers

f. 1946, Washington, D.C.

Group / Doo Wop, R&B

The Clovers occupy an exalted place in the history of R&B, if not in the minds of many listeners, other than hard-core devotees of the music's history—the Drifters tend to eclipse them, by virtue of their longer history and the string of hits that the later incarnation of that group had during the 1960s. The truth is that the Clovers not only started earlier than any other act on Atlantic, but they also scored more hits in their six years there than any other R&B act in the label's history.

The group's origins, like those of so many R&B vocal outfits, goes back to the members' middle teenage years. Tenor/baritone Harold "Hal" Lucas, tenor Billy Shelton, and bass Robert Woods were students at Armstrong High School in Washington, D.C., during the mid-'40s when they formed a trio led by Lucas, who also came up with the name the Clovers. A fourth member, John "Buddy" Bailey, another tenor, joined up and eventually became their lead singer, while Lucas started singing baritone. Their early sound was influenced by the likes of such professional outfits of the era as the Orioles and the Ravens.

The history of R&B isn't easily contained within the boundaries of the post-World War II era, when it began gathering popularity. The Clovers took shape over the next few years, as Woods departed to be replaced by Matthew McQuater, and Shelton was succeeded by Harold Winley, and a fifth member, in the guise of guitarist Bill Harris, joined in 1949. During these years, their repertory was largely drawn from the records and set lists of the Orioles and the Ravens, but as the 1950s dawned, the group had begun to embrace a harder, edgier brand of R&B, with less restraint in their embellishments. They were discovered while playing a club in Washington by Baltimore-based entrepreneur Lou Krefetz, who got them onto a small label called Rainbow Records, where they made their debut with "Yes Sir, That's My Baby." It was Ahmet Ertegun, the founder of the then new label, who interceded and, after getting the group onto his label, started feeding them rougher, more rhythm-oriented material, including the first song Ertegun ever wrote, "Don't You Know I Love You"—according to Nick Tosches, that single was also the first record by an R&B quartet to incorporate a saxophone solo (by Frank Culley) into its structure; the record became a number-one R&B hit during the summer of 1951 and heralded a new era in popular music, serving as the template for a decade of R&B hits. Indeed, there are those who identify that record as the very first identifiable rock & roll single.

The group was put in the hands of producer/songwriter Jesse Stone (aka Charles Calhoun), who, with Ertegun, directed them further into this new territory that they suddenly found themselves trailblazing. In April of 1952, "One Mint Julep" became a number two single, and they followed that up in July with "Ting-A-Ling," which also got to number-two. The Clovers' fortunes continued until Bailey was drafted during the summer of 1952, and the group didn't see any significant success again until the summer of 1953 when "Good Lovin'" charted at number two with Charlie White, late of Billy Ward's group the Dominoes. They charted again at number three in the spring of 1954 with "Lovey Dovey," and then Billy Mitchell came in as lead singer for "Your Cash Ain't Nothin' But Trash." That single was only a relatively modest hit during the summer of 1954, but it was useful on a whole different level, getting the group a berth in the pioneering rock & roll/R&B short feature *Rock 'n' Roll Revue*. Beginning in 1955, with Bailey's discharge from the army, he and Mitchell served as joint lead singers in the group.

The Clovers switched to a ballad style in 1955 with the release of "Blue Velvet," which was a modest success at number 14 on the R&B listings. Their next single, "Devil or Angel," the latter an "over-the-transom" submission by an amateur songwriter named Blanche Carter, got to number three, but that marked the end of their run of hits on Atlantic. Ironically, it was those last two singles—which were really the least representative of their sound of any of their hits—became their best-known singles, getting the widest airplay, though their version of "Devil or Angel" was later eclipsed by Bobby Vee's recording. Following its release, as the rock & roll boom solidified around white performers, guitar-based acts, and novelty tunes, the Clovers experienced a downturn in their fortunes. They ceased charting singles and after two more years of attempts at reviving their sales, Atlantic released the bluesy sleeper classic "Down in the Alley" (1957), one of the raunchiest songs of its period ever aimed at a mainstream audience, which even had the temerity to project its lustful observations slowly.

Rather than retreat, the act, with the encouragement of their manager, Lou Krefetz, grew bolder. He organized a new label, Poplar Records, and had the Clovers record an entire LP, an extraordinary opportunity for a group that wasn't riding high on the charts at the time—even the Drifters had never recorded an actual LP at the time, their albums being compilations of previously recorded singles. The group scored with the LP and its accompanying single, "Pennies From Heaven," and it looked as though they might pull out of their ongoing commercial slump. Fate then took a hand as Krefetz was offered the opportunity to become the head of sales for United Artists Records, a newly organized label that had the money of one of the top studios in Hollywood behind them. The manager accepted the offer and was able to fold the Clovers, along with their recordings for Poplar, into the larger company. Krefetz next linked the group up with Jerry Leiber & Mike Stoller, the result being the biggest pop hit in the group's history, in the form of "Love Potion No. 9," sung by Billy Mitchell, and peaked at number 23 (which, oddly enough, was the same slot it occupied on the R&B charts).

Alas, this was to be the group's last success. They never found another producer as effective as Leiber & Stoller, much less Ertegun or Stone, and even when they returned to work with Stone, they were unable to find a way back to the charts; even re-recording their old hits, such as "One Mint Julep," failed to attract any listeners. By 1961, the group had parted company with United Artists, and soon they were grasping at straws commercially, spiraling down in a series of contracts with ever smaller and weaker labels, losing Matthew McQuater in the process. The group splintered, with Billy Mitchell and Harold Lucas reorganizing the lineup with a pair of members from another group, the Bachelors, James "Toy" Walton and Robert Russell. They made a brief return to Atlantic in 1961 without any resulting rebound in sales, and after that, the group's situation became complicated by the existence of rival incarnations—along with Mitchell's outfit was a group called (at times) "the Fabulous Clovers," led by Bailey. Roosevelt "Tippie" Hubbard succeeded Mitchell, leading a quartet called "Tippie and the Clovers," who cut sides for Leiber & Stoller's Tiger label, among them "Bossa Nova Baby," a number that was even an embarrassment to Elvis Presley when he did it.

By the dawn of the rock & roll revival at the turn of the 1960s into the 1970s, the Clovers' situation had become at least as complicated as that of the Drifters, with multiple groups claiming the name in various performing venues and recording situations. None of it really mattered by then, as the recordings had assumed a life of their own, separate from any performances by survivors or pretenders. The group was honored by the Rhythm-and-Blues Foundation in 1988 with a Pioneer Award, given to surviving members Bailey, McQuater, Lucas, and Winley, and thanks to the CD boom, their classic Atlantic sides have been more readily available since the 1990s than they've been at any time since the mid-'50s, Rhino Records keeping two different hits compilations in print while Collectables Records has reissued their two Atlantic LPs on a single CD. *—Bruce Eder*

The Clovers / 1956 / Atlantic ✦✦✦✦

Dance Party / 1959 / Atlantic ✦✦✦

In Clover / 1959 / United Artists ✦✦✦

Love Potion No. 9: The Best of the Clovers / Sep. 2, 1991 / EMI America ✦✦✦✦✦

Love Potion No. 9: The Best of the Clovers features their later sides for United Artists including the classic title track. *—Cub Koda*

☆ **Down in the Alley: The Best of the Clovers** / Oct. 1, 1991 / Rhino/Atlantic ✦✦✦✦✦

This 21-song compilation covers the six-year history of one of history's most important R&B groups at Atlantic Records. All of the Clovers' charting singles are represented (albeit not in release order), along with notes indicating their chart history. For the uninitiated, this is where R&B started as a popular phenomenon, from a group that was incredibly consistent for its six years on the label. The material is representative of R&B as it sounded at its point of origin, and at its most well-defined and powerful, an unerring jump band beat melded with elements of urban blues and superb quartet singing, all of which were a new musical phenomenon when the Clovers brought it to the charts in 1951. Moreover, one hears the basis in these early tracks for Atlantic's subsequent move into R&B vocals with the Drifters and the Coasters, the sound of these early sides highlighted by very powerful sax and electric guitar accompaniment and the stomping beat one would expect out of a roadhouse band. From "Don't You Know I Love You" through "Ting-A-Ling," "Crawlin'," "Hey, Miss Fannie," and "Lovey Dovey," right into the middle of the decade, this CD moves from one jewel-like R&B-cum-rock & roll classic to the next, and the only complaint that one could reasonably have is that there isn't a complete compilation of the Clovers' work on Atlantic, from Rhino, Collectables, or Sequel. *—Bruce Eder*

The Clovers / 1997 / Sequel ✦✦✦✦

The Clovers' 1956 debut album has been remastered and augmented by ten additional cuts, including overlooked B-sides, early singles that were bypassed for the original LP, and a surprisingly jazzy outtake of "Your Cash Ain't Nothin' But Trash." Those forgotten sides have been well-preserved, and are as worthy of a hearing as any of the songs that did make it onto the original long-player. "Skylark," the slow ballad side of their first Atlantic single (and their first hit), was a reworking of the Earl Hines/Billy Eckstine version from a decade earlier, and sounds almost like a lost Ink Spots track. "Needless" is the kind of soaring ballad that the Clovers did beautifully, but which was overshadowed on the radio and on jukeboxes by their uptempo numbers. "Comin' On" is a slow blues with a sax solo that skirts effectively between hot and languid. "One Mint Julep" (possibly the best-selling record in the group's output), "Good Lovin'," "I Confess," "The Feeling Is So Good," and "Down in the Alley" are out and out rockers, the latter featuring a hot, brittle guitar solo that should have made it a rock & roll standard in its own time (yet, somehow, the song never charted). "Your Cash Ain't Nothin' But Trash" is a more swinging version of the released song and well worth hearing in this rendition. The production on the CD is very good, and the notes are thorough, although they do have some spelling and editing errors. *—Bruce Eder*

★ **Very Best of the Clovers** / Feb. 3, 1998 / Rhino ✦✦✦✦✦

The Very Best of the Clovers is an excellent 16-track collection that features their biggest hits from 1951-1959, including "Don't You Know I Love You," "Fool, Fool, Fool," "One Mint Julep," "Ting-A-Ling," "I Played the Fool," "Hey, Miss Fannie," "Good Lovin'," "Lovey Dovey," "Little Mama," "Your Cash Ain't Nothin' But Trash," "Blue Velvet," "Devil or Angel" and "Love Potion No. 9." All of the group's best-known songs in their hit versions are available on this concise, affordable disc, which makes for an ideal introduction to this legendary R&B group. *—Stephen Thomas Erlewine*

The Clovers/Dance Party / Jul. 28, 1998 / Collectables ✦✦✦✦

This collectables' CD contains two of the Clovers' early albums, *The Clovers* and *Dance Party*, on one compact disc. Although *Dance Party* is a little uneven, it contains a number of great songs, and *The Clovers* is absolutely terrific, filled with classics like "Lovey Dovey," "Ting-A-Ling," "Blue Velvet" and "Devil or Angel." Most listeners will be satisfied eitherAtlantic's *Down in the Alley* or Rhino's *The Very Best of the Clovers*, but anyone who wants to dig a little deeper should pick this up, despite its shakey packaging and sound. *—Stephen Thomas Erlewine*

Anthology / Aug. 4, 1998 / Ripete ✦✦✦

The pride and joy of Washington, D.C., this smooth R&B/doo wop group ranks as the genres' most successful messengers, enjoying a string of hits—from 1951 to 1958—for Atlantic Records. Ahmet Ertegun, Atlantic's owner, wrote eight of their first nine singles. This is not a definitive collection; some hits are included (e.g., "Lovey Dovey," "Devil or Angel," "Down in the Alley," and "One Mint Julep"), but many others—including "Ting-A-Ling," "I Played the Fool," and "Little Mama"—are not. While 21 tracks don't do the

Clovers' vast repertoire justice, the CD is titled *Anthology* and you expect a collection skewered with hits rather than two takes of the obscure "Squeeze Box." Not conforming to its title, however, makes this collection valuable. You're getting renditions of "Don't Play That Song," "Going Home to Jesus," and irresistibles like "Let's Get Loose" and "You Sexy Thing"—cuts you rarely find on one package. They're out there on the morass of Clovers compilations but are usually scattered among various discs. *—Andrew Hamilton*

Club Nouveau

f. 1986, Sacramento, CA

Group / Club/Dance, Urban, Disco, Dance-Pop, Soul

Club Nouveau formed in Sacramento in 1986, including Jay King, Denzil Foster, Thomas McElroy, Samuelle Pratter, and Valerie Watson. King was the creative force behind the hit "Rumours" by the Timex Social Club in 1986, and formed King Jay Records for Club Nouveau. They made some good disco-flavored and funk tunes, and had four consecutive hits in 1986 and 1987: "Jealousy," "Situation #9," a cover of Bill Withers' "Lean on Me," and "Why You Treat Me So Bad." The last two both reached the number-two spot on the R&B charts. But, in 1988, at the height of their popularity, McElroy, Pratter, and Foster left the group, and were replaced by David Agent and Kevin Irving. Their final recordings for Tommy Boy/Warner Bros. didn't sustain the momentum, and they subsequently disbanded. *—Ron Wynn*

● **Life, Love & Pain** / 1986 / Warner Bros. ♦♦♦♦♦

The funky, dance-oriented R&B act Club Nouveau stormed onto the musical scene in late 1986 with *Life, Love, & Pain.* Half the songs on this eight-title set received some form of airplay, but none matched the success of their lighthearted, reggae/hip-hop remake of the Bill Withers classic "Lean on Me," which topped the American pop charts for two weeks in 1987. The follow-up, "Why You Treat Me So Bad," only peaked at number 39 on the pop charts (but fared much better on the R&B charts), yet has enjoyed an equally long (if not longer) shelf life. By the end of the '90s, "Why You Treat Me So Bad" had already been sampled into two of the decade's biggest hip-hop hits: "I Got Five on It" by Luniz and "Satisfy You" by Puff Daddy and R. Kelly. The album also featured "Jealousy," which was a remake/answer song to Timex Social Club's 1986 Top Ten hit "Rumours," and the R&B hit "Situation #9." The album closes with "Pump It Up," which is a reprise of "Lean on Me." Club Nouveau never again came close to matching the success of this album or its singles. There are a few compilations on Club Nouveau, but to capture the spirit of the band at their best, go with *Life, Love, & Pain. —Jose F. Promis*

Under a Nouveau Groove / 1986 / Warner Bros. ♦♦♦

Here are some entertaining, if very derivative, urban contemporary dance-pop, R&B, and ballads. Club Nouveau had only hit, a cover of Bill Withers' "Lean on Me," and, by the time of this album, had virtually exhausted an already lightweight bag of tricks. This album was more interesting as a barometer of late-'80s production trends than for the songs or performances. *—Ron Wynn*

A New Beginning / 1992 / Quality ♦♦

By the time the 1990s rolled around, much of the urban contemporary world had pretty much given up on Jay King and assumed that his career was over and done with. Club Nouveau had lost too many key members (most notably, Denzil Foster and Thomas McElroy, who were busy working with En Vogue and others), and it seemed doubtful that King's band would make a comeback. But in 1992, King gave it a shot with *A New Beginning,* which unveiled a new Club Nouveau lineup. The CD didn't do much commercially, and it's hardly in a class with *Life, Love, & Pain* or even *Listen to the Message.* But *A New Beginning* does have its moments, including the reassuring "I'll Be There" (not to be confused with the Jackson 5 hit), the troubling "Mary," and a spirited remake of the Edwin Hawkins Singers' gospel favorite "Oh, Happy Day." The album is slightly better than some skeptics might think, although it's definitely the work of someone who was past his prime. Only completists will find *A New Beginning* to be of interest. *—Alex Henderson*

Greatest Hits / Nov. 20, 2001 / Thump ♦♦♦♦

Club Nouveau's *Greatest Hits* collection compiles many of the group's best-known songs from the '80s, including "Rumors," "Jealousy," "Situation #9," and "Lean on Me." The album is somewhat brief, featuring only 12 songs, but it compensates for its lack of quantity by offering a succinct listening experience with few lulls. *—Jason Birchmeier*

The Coasters

f. Feb. 1956, Los Angeles, CA, **db.** 1972

Group / Doo Wop, Rock & Roll, R&B

The Coasters were one of the few artists in rock history to successfully straddle the line between music and comedy. Their undeniably funny lyrics and on-stage antics might have suggested a simple troupe of clowns, but Coasters records were no mere novelties—their material, supplied by the legendary team of Jerry Leiber & Mike Stoller, was too witty, their arrangements too well-crafted, and the group itself too musically proficient. That engaging and infectious combination made them one of the most popular early R&B/rock & roll acts, as well as one of the most consistently entertaining doo wop/vocal groups of all time.

The Coasters grew out of a successful Los Angeles doo wop group called the Robins, which had been recording since 1949 and working with Leiber & Stoller since 1953. Atlantic Records acquired the Robins in 1955, when the Leiber & Stoller composition "Smokey Joe's Cafe" was becoming too big a hit for their small Spark label to handle; its success scored the duo an independent contract with Atlantic as producers and composers. Amid uncertainties over their new major-label arrangement, the Robins split up that fall; lead tenor Carl Gardner (a more recent addition) and bass Bobby Nunn formed a new group, the Coasters (named for their West Coast base), which maintained the Leiber & Stoller association—an extremely wise move. The initial Coasters lineup was completed by baritone Billy Guy (a gifted comic vocalist) and second tenor Leon Hughes, with guitarist Adolph Jacobs figuring prominently on their recordings through 1959. Their first single, "Down in Mexico," became a Top Ten R&B hit in 1956, epitomizing the sort of humorous story-song Leiber & Stoller were perfecting. The Coasters hit again in 1957 with the double-sided smash "Young Blood"/"Searchin'," both sides of which reached the pop Top Ten. The follow-ups weren't as successful, and it was decided that both the group and Leiber & Stoller would move their operations to New York, where Atlantic was based. As a result, Nunn and Hughes left the group in late 1957, to be replaced respectively by bass Will "Dub" Jones (ex-Cadets, of "Stranded in the Jungle" fame) and second tenor Obie Jessie (for a very short period), then Cornell Gunter (ex-Flairs).

The Coasters' first recording in New York was 1958's "Yakety Yak," which featured King Curtis on tenor sax. Its witty, slice-of-life lyrics about a teenager being hassled by his parents struck a resounding chord, and "Yakety Yak" became the Coasters' first number-one pop hit that summer, topping the R&B charts as well. "Charlie Brown," which cast Jones in the title role of class clown (and immortalized him with the catch-phrase, "why's everybody always pickin' on me?"), hit number two on both the pop and R&B charts in 1959, firmly establishing the Coasters' widespread crossover appeal. More hits followed: the Western-themed "Along Came Jones," "Poison Ivy," "Shoppin' for Clothes," and the group's final Top 30 hit, 1961's burlesque-dancer tribute "Little Egypt."

Following "Little Egypt," Gunter departed, to be replaced by Earl "Speedo" Carroll (of the Cadillacs). Other personnel shifts ensued over the next few years, especially as the hits dried up; even more discouragingly, Leiber & Stoller left Atlantic in 1963. The Coasters parted ways with Atlantic in early 1966, signing with Columbia's Date subsidiary and reuniting with Leiber & Stoller for a time. Although they charted several times, no more hits were forthcoming, given the radically different musical climate; their last chart single was a 1971 cover of "Love Potion No. 9" (by which time Gardner was the only remaining original member), and their last new release came with a 1976 version of "If I Had a Hammer." Since then, numerous different Coasters lineups have toured the oldies circuit; Gardner's holds the legal claim to legitimacy, but Gunter, Guy, Jones, Nunn, *and* Hughes all led differing lineups at one point or another. Nunn died of a heart attack in 1986, one year before the Coasters became the first vocal group inducted into the Rock and Roll Hall of Fame. Gunter was murdered in Las Vegas in 1990, and Jones passed away in early 2000. *—Steve Huey*

The Coasters / 1958 / Atco ♦♦♦♦

Coastin' Along / 1961 / Atco ♦♦♦

Coast Along With the Coasters / 1962 / Atco ♦♦♦

The Ultimate Coasters / 1986 / Warner Bros. ♦♦♦♦♦

This is a well-done single-disc anthology, the best collection that's available on one package. This doesn't provide the overview available on the Rhino two-disc set, but it's certainly the best one to get for someone who only wants the hits and doesn't want to pay too much for them. *—Ron Wynn*

☆ **50 Coastin' Classics: Anthology** / Nov. 24, 1992 / Rhino ♦♦♦♦♦

Although it may well be too much for the casual fan, this double CD is easily the best Coasters retrospective ever assembled. Besides featuring every one of their hits, it also contains nine strong tunes cut in the mid-'50s by the Robins, who evolved into the Coasters after some personnel changes. As for the enticing obscurities, "Three Cool Cats" and "Besame Mucho" were cut by the Beatles on unreleased recordings in the early '60s, and "Ain't That Just like Me" would be a small hit for the Searchers. "Down in Mexico" and "Brazil" are cool R&B/Latin melodramas, and "Shoppin' for Clothes," "What About Us," and "That Is Rock & Roll" are half-forgotten vignettes of youthful independence that stack up against the best songs of Jerry Leiber & Mike Stoller, who wrote most of the group's material. Indeed, there's little difference in quality between the hits and the B-sides on this comp, either in the group's matchless ensemble R&B/comedy vocals or Leiber/Stoller's witty songwriting. The accompanying booklet features comments on most of the tracks by Leiber & Stoller themselves. *—Richie Unterberger*

★ **The Very Best of the Coasters** / 1993 / Rhino ♦♦♦♦♦

The Coasters were the 1950s' (and early rock's) dominant novelty/comic R&B ensemble, benefiting from Jerry Leiber & Mike Stoller's lyrical wit and inspired production. They weren't simply proficient clowns; the Coasters were a skilled vocal unit whose talents were utilized on slice-of-life narratives, prophetic youth manifestos, and even an occasional teen anthem, as well as the prototype humorous vehicles "Yakety Yak" and "Poison Ivy." Although Rhino has already given them the deluxe two-disc treatment, consumers who either don't want that much Coasters material or prefer only the hits are nicely served by this 18-track anthology. It contains every major release, plus valuable lesser-known selections such as "Shoppin' for Clothes" and "What About Us." *—Ron Wynn*

Wayne Cochran

b. Thomson, GA

Vocals / Pop-Soul, Roots Rock

The outlandish Wayne Cochran—wild outfits, high snow-white pompadour—and his musical odyssey began in 1955 with his first band. By 1963, after a move to Macon, GA, and numerous personnel changes, the outfit became known as Wayne Cochran & the C.C. Riders ("Cochran's Circuit Riders"). Inspired by James Brown and his relentless touring schedule, Cochran purchased an old bus and hit the road. The group took its high-octane show all over the South and Midwest before settling in Miami for an extended stay as the house band at the Barn (aka "the House of Soul"). By this time, the C.C. Riders also had horns to accompany its boogie rhythm section and Cochran's over-the-top vocals. He was a big favorite at the Barn, and stars such as Jackie Gleason caught his shows regularly. (The enterprising soul singer even wrote a cookbook while in Miami entitled *Wayne Cochran's Soul Recipes.*)

He cut his first record, "My Little Girl," on Scottie in 1959. Cochran cut two singles for Gala in the early '60s ("Funny Feeling" and "Liza Jane") before moving on to Confederate ("Linda Lu") and the Aire label ("Cindy Marie"). He obviously loved cutting songs titled with women's names and the trend continued on King Records with "Little Orphan Annie." He also redid his own "Last Kiss," (which he wrote) for his second King single; while "Last Kiss" didn't do much for Cochran, it exploded for J. Frank Wilson & the Cavaliers, who reached number two on the pop charts with it in 1964.

All the singing—at the top of his lungs—along with the usual musical excesses reduced his once-mighty voice to a fraction of what it was. By the time he started appearing on national television shows, the Wayne Cochran that thrilled throngs in Southern pits and Midwest holes was all show, the voice practically gone, so he ratcheted up the live shows with as much gloss as he could. Significant singles included a remake of Bob & Earl's "Harlem Shuffle," which bubbled onto the pop singles chart, and "Sleepless Nights." Wayne Cochran & the C. C. Riders had a Miami reunion in Miami on July 26, and on August 1, 2001, in Hollywood, FL. The C. C. Riders were many, and even included renown jazz bassist Jaco Pastorius at one time. Cochran went through years of turmoil before becoming a born-again Christian and pastor; he started a ministry in 1981. *—Andrew Hamilton*

Wayne Cochran! / 1968 / Chess ✦✦✦
This is the debut album from Mr. Blue-Eyed Soul, Wayne Cochran. Cochran was a sight, a large white man with James Brown moves, sporting a big pompadour. He traveled all year crossing the country on his bus with a big band that included a young Jaco Pastorious on bass. He took time off to record for Chess this album consisting of rehashes of R&B recordings. Cochran, a bona fide soul man, jams on Bobby McClure's "Peak of Love," the Temptations' "Get Ready," Sam & Dave's "You Don't Know Like I Know," and the smoldering "You Can't Judge a Book By the Cover." Mildly successful, it cracked the pop albums chart in 1968 but hit a wall at number 167. *—Andrew Hamilton*

Joe Cocker (John Robert Cocker)

b. May 20, 1944, Sheffield, Yorkshire, England
Vocals / Pop/Rock, Soft Rock, Blues-Rock, Adult Contemporary
After starting out as an unsuccessful pop singer (working under the name Vance Arnold), Joe Cocker found his niche singing rock and soul in the pubs of England with his superb backing group, the Grease Band. He hit number one in the U.K. in November 1968 with his version of the Beatles' "A Little Help From My Friends." His career really took off after he sang that song at the Woodstock festival in August 1969. A second British hit came with a version of Leon Russell's "Delta Lady" in the fall of 1969 (by then, Russell was Cocker's musical director) and both of his albums, *With a Little Help From My Friends* (April 1969) and *Joe Cocker!* (November 1969), went gold in America.

In 1970, his cover of the Box Tops' hit "The Letter" became his first U.S. Top Ten. Cocker's first peak of success came when Russell organized the "Mad Dogs & Englishmen" tour of 1970, featuring Cocker and over 40 others, and resulting in a third gold album and a concert film. Subsequent efforts were less popular, and problems with alcohol (both on-stage and off-) reduced Cocker's once-powerful voice to a croaking rasp. But he returned to the U.S. Top Ten with the romantic ballad "You Are So Beautiful" in 1975 and topped the charts in a duet with Jennifer Warnes on "Up Where We Belong," the theme from the 1982 film *An Officer and a Gentleman.* He has survived, still charting into the '90s, albeit with less frequency than he did in the '70s and '80s. He also continued to work throughout the new millennium. *No Ordinary World* was his first release since 1997's *Across from Midnight. Respect Yourself* appeared in 2002. *—Cub Koda & William Ruhlmann*

With a Little Help From My Friends / Apr. 1969 / A&M ✦✦✦✦✦
The album that foisted Joe Cocker on an unsuspecting public is full of tasteful, raucous covers, Cocker's trademark hysterical vocals, and outstanding studio backing by pros like Jimmy Page and Steve Winwood. *—Tom Graves*

Joe Cocker! / Nov. 1969 / A&M ✦✦✦✦
Joe Cocker's first three A&M albums form the bedrock of a career that spans over three decades. While Cocker certainly wasn't always in top form during this stretch—thanks to alcohol problems and questionable comeback moves in the '80s and '90s—his early records did inform the classic pub rock sound later credited to proto-punk figures like Graham Parker and Brinsley Schwarz. On those early records, Cocker mixed elements of late-'60s English blues revival recordings (John Mayall, et al.) with the more contemporary sounds of soul and pop; a sound fused in no small part by producer and arranger Leon Russell, whose gumbo mix figures prominently on this eponymous release and the infamous *Mad Dogs & Englishmen* live set. Russell's sophisticated swamp blues aesthetic is felt directly with versions of his gospel ballad "Hello, Little Friend" and Beatles-inspired bit of New Orleans pop—and one of Cocker's biggest hits—"Delta Lady." Following up on the huge success of an earlier cover of "With a Little Help From My Friends," Cocker mines more Beatles gold with very respectable renditions of "She Came in Through the Bathroom Window" and "Something." And rounding out this impressive set are equally astute takes on Dylan's "Dear Landlord," Leonard Cohen's "Bird on the Wire," and John Sebastian's "Darling Be Home Soon." Throughout, Cocker gets superb support from his regular backing group of the time, the Grease Band. A fine introduction to the singer's classic, late-'60s and early-'70s period. *—Stephen Cook*

Mad Dogs & Englishmen / Aug. 1970 / A&M ✦✦✦✦✦
A superb document of Cocker's high-energy 1970 tour, it included about a zillion musicians and hangers-on. All the goods are here, and many consider this Cocker's last great moment. *—Tom Graves*

I Can Stand a Little Rain / Aug. 1974 / A&M ✦✦✦
With *I Can Stand a Little Rain,* Joe Cocker returned to interpreting songs instead of essaying his original songs. As usual, there are a couple of highlights, but a couple of awkward choices prevent the album from being as effective as *Joe Cocker!* or *Mad Dogs & Englishmen. —Stephen Thomas Erlewine*

Jamaica Say You Will / Aug. 1975 / A&M ✦✦

Luxury You Can Afford / Aug. 1978 / A&M ✦✦✦

Sheffield Steel / May 22, 1982 / Island ✦✦✦
Joe Cocker's sole Island album found him backed by some of Jamaica's finest. Again, balancing reggae with rockin' soul, Joe found many good tunes to cover, among them, Jimmy Cliff's "Many Rivers to Cross," Steve Winwood's "Talking Back to the Night," Jimmy Webb's "Just Like Always," and Bob Dylan's "Seven Days." But while these and the rest of the record make for fine listening, there were no hits, and thus, Joe moved on. A good one. *—James Chrispell*

Civilized Man / May 1984 / Capitol ✦✦

Unchain My Heart / Oct. 1987 / Capitol ✦✦

One Night of Sin / Aug. 1989 / Capitol ✦✦

Live! / May 1990 / Capitol ✦✦✦

Night Calls / Jul. 6, 1992 / Capitol ✦✦✦
Cocker's rep has always been as a superb interpreter of other people's material. For *Night Calls*, the Sheffield native peaks with the opening track—a memory-engraving rendition of the Bryan Adams/Diane Warren-penned "Feels Like Forever." It's the higher profile songs that ultimately disappoint on *Night Calls.* Cocker eventually works up a lather toward the end of "You've Got to Hide Your Love Away," but it never reaches the standard of other Beatles classics in his repertoire ("With a Little Help From My Friends," "She Came in Through the Bathroom Window"). The biggest let-down is the lack of commitment projected on Elton John's "Don't Let the Sun Go Down on Me." Still, even slumming Cocker sounds more real and soulful than, say, Michael Bolton in his wildest dreams. *—Roch Parisien*

The Best of Joe Cocker / Mar. 16, 1993 / Capitol ✦✦✦✦✦
Although Cocker's Capitol material wasn't as consistent as his A&M work, this compilation successfully distills the highlights, including the splendid "When the Night Comes," onto a single CD. *—Stephen Thomas Erlewine*

Have a Little Faith / Sep. 8, 1994 / 550 Music/Epic ✦✦✦

Long Voyage Home / Nov. 21, 1995 / A&M ✦✦✦✦✦
Long Voyage Home: The Silver Anniversary Collection is nearly the definitive Joe Cocker anthology, covering his recording career from the late '60s to the mid-'90s, featuring material from all the labels he recorded for—A&M, Elektra, Island, and Capitol. After an early single from 1964 (a version of the Beatles' "I'll Cry Instead"), the set skips ahead to his late-'60s recordings with his Mad Dogs & Englishmen troupe. From there, the collection doesn't miss many of Cocker's greatest hits or favorite album tracks. In addition to the familiar tracks, there are a handful of unreleased cuts that are tantalizing for the collector; casual fans will find them of marginal interest. *—Stephen Thomas Erlewine*

● **The Anthology** / Aug. 17, 1999 / A&M ✦✦✦✦✦
A&M's double-disc *Anthology* may be too much for casual fans that just want the hits, but anyone else will find this exhaustive 37-track chronicle of Joe Cocker's prime years definitive. The first disc concentrates on his first three albums, buttressed by a rare 1964 single of the Beatles' "I'll Cry Instead" and his 1970 non-LP single "The Letter"/"Space Captain." Disc two features highlights of all the albums he recorded between 1972 and 1982, selecting not only hits, but key album tracks. The end result is a collection that is concise and definitive. It may be missing such latter-day hits as "When the Night Comes" and doesn't cover as much ground as the box set *Long Voyage Home*, but anyone looking for a comprehensive collection of Cocker's classic recordings will be satisfied by *Anthology. —Stephen Thomas Erlewine*

Bill Coday

b. May 10, 1942, Coldwater, MS
Vocals / Soul-Blues, Soul, Pop-Soul, Quiet Storm, Urban
Soul singer Bill Coday first came to fame with the hit single "Get Your Lies Straight" during the early spring of 1971. Signed to Crajon Productions, owned by the husband and wife team of Bill and Denise Jones (who recorded under the name Denise LaSalle and scored a 1971 gold single, "Trapped by a Thing Called Love"), Coday was the perfect vehicle for LaSalle's blues-oriented R&B songs. Born May 10, 1942, in Coldwater, MS, Coday began his singing career as a teenager, performing in juke joints around Blytheville, Arkansas, with a band that included Son Seals.

In 1961, he relocated to Chicago, IL, donning the name Chicago Willie. LaSalle spotted the singer while he was performing at the Black Orchid club. She teamed him with Memphis, TN, soul music producer Willie Mitchell whom she often worked with on her releases for Detroit, MI's Westbound label and for those of other Crajon artists (the Sequins' hits "Hey Romeo" and "The Third Degree"). Mitchell went on to have hits with another Chicago singer, Syl Johnson, and gold and platinum-laced success with Al Green on Hi Records. Coday's first Crajon singles, "Sixty Minute Teaser" and "I Get High on Your Love," were regional hits. The third single, "Get Your Lies Straight," proved to be the breakthrough, going to number-14 R&B on *Billboard*'s charts in early 1971. On the flipside was "You're Gonna Want Me." As was the custom on a fast-selling national record, the independently-distributed Crajon leased Coday's single to the much larger Galaxy label, a subsidiary of Berkeley, CA's Fantasy Records, for wider distribution. The follow-up, issued on Galaxy, the Denise LaSalle song "When You Find a Fool, Bump His Head," made it to number-48 R&B in summer 1971. There were other Galaxy singles, but none charted nationally.

Coday enjoyed a regional hit on Crajon with "I'm Back to Collect" in the first half of 1973. Some of his Galaxy/Crajon releases can be found on the compilations *All Night Long They Played the Blues* (1992), *Bad Bad Whiskey* (1993)—both from U.K. label Ace Records—and an '80s collection of Coday's Crajon singles on Japanese label Vivid Sounds. In 1973, he signed with Epic Records and the single "I Don't Want to Play This Game" was issued. It was later included on the 1975 Epic compilation *Lost Soul*, reissued as a 1994 CD by Sony Legacy.

In 1984, Coday began to tour with Denise LaSalle as her opening act. He began recording again after several years away from the studio. Signing with Memphis-based label Ecko Records, his first release was the appropriately titled *Sneakin' Back* album. The tracks "Her Love Is Good Enough to Put in Collard Greens," "I Can Move the Hoochie Coochie Man," "Doctor Thrill Good," and a remake of "Get Your Lies Straight" became favorites with blues lovers and blues-formatted radio stations. His second Ecko CD, *Can't Get Enough*, included "In the Room Next to the Room" and "Not a Word" with labelmate Barbara Carr. Coday's third Ecko CD, 1999's *Put Me in the Mood*, gave his fans more of his tasty blend of spicy, bluesy Southern soul. *—Ed Hogan*

Sneakin' Back / 1995 / ECD ♦♦♦

Put Me in the Mood / Feb. 9, 1999 / Ecko ♦♦♦

● **Memories** / Jul. 11, 2000 / Ecko ♦♦♦

A fine Southern soul album by Bill Coday featuring a tribute to the late Johnnie Taylor entitled "We're Gonna Miss You Johnnie." He details his lovemaking technique in a raunchy, backwoods blues number called the "Bo Hawg Grind," but expresses sincere sentiments on "My Outside Woman" not about his wife, but about his outside woman. Coday exhibits shades of Ike Turner (pre Tina) on "It's a Blues Thang," a driving uptempo jump. He becomes Mr. Nasty on "Moans, Groans and Grunts" and Daddy Blues on "Backhills Country Juke Joint"—two tunes from previous albums. On the lilting "When This Dance Is Over," Coday gets as mainstream as he can on a grabber that can be appreciated by everybody. *—Andrew Hamilton*

Cold Blood

f. 1968, USA, **db.** 1976

Group / Latin Rock, Funk, Soul

A San Francisco-based R&B band originally formed by guitarist Larry Field as the "New Invaders" in the wake of the Summer of Love, Cold Blood had the key elements of strong female vocalist, a fine guitarist, and a powerful horn section. After successful gigs at Golden Gate Park and at the Fillmore, they were signed by impresario Bill Graham to his new San Francisco Records label, on which they released their self-titled debut in 1969. Four more albums followed over the next five years—in fact, later efforts boasted the production and musical contributions of Steve Cropper—but all were hamstrung by Graham's underhanded distribution deals with Columbia and Atlantic.

Though the debut's single "You've Got Me Humming" crawled up to number 52 on the American charts, Cold Blood seemed doomed to labor in the shadow of bands like Tower of Power, Chicago, and especially Janis Joplin. The latter comparison became endemic among critics; for although the blues belter joined Field's band as its youngest member—she had formerly been, of all things, a childhood national rollerskating champion—her magnetic stage presence established her as the band's central force. Eventually, the band billed itself as Lydia Pense With Cold Blood, and even released an album simply titled *Lydia*. Joplin sensed a kindred soul; after screaming at Cold Blood for scooping her on a blistering cover of "Piece of My Heart," she warmed to Pense enough to give her a swig of Southern Comfort.

After hitting increasingly lower tier venues in San Francisco by the late '70s, Cold Blood disbanded for most of the next decade; Pense focused her energies on child rearing. By the late '80s, the band slowly awoke from its long sleep, and they began regular features on California's festival and fair circuit. A 1998 return to their Fillmore stomping ground brought out the band's faithful. *—Paul Collins*

Cold Blood / 1969 / San Francisco Sound ♦♦♦♦

Cold Blood was one of the Bay Area's non-psychedelic contributions to pop music in the late '60s and early '70s. Their R&B-influenced combination of rock, blues, and jazz stood out from the guitar-driven acid rock bands most identified with that scene. After establishing themselves at dancehalls such as the Avalon or Bill Graham's Winterland Ballroom, Cold Blood became one of the first acts signed to Graham's Fillmore record label—which was named after another one of his venerable venues. Their 1969 self-titled debut—although somewhat contained in comparison to their live shows—is a good representation of their soulful, horn-driven funk. One of the major reasons for the band's success is the unadulterated and otherwise raw vocal style of Lydia Pense. The album features a mixture of dramatic ballads—such as the medley of "I'm a Good Woman" and "Let Me Down Easy"—as well as full-blown R&B rave-ups on the cover of Sam & Dave's "You Got Me Hummin'" or their freewheeling version of "I Just Want to Make Love To You." Keyboardist Raul Matute's contribution, "If You Will," is a perfect vehicle for Pense's vocals as it glides between licks from lead guitarist Larry Fields and the five-piece brass section. Inevitable comparisons have been made between Pense, Janis Joplin, and Lynn Hughes—of another San Fran rock and soul combo, Stoneground. However, there is a smoky scintillation to Pense's approach—particularly potent on the gospel-tinged opener, "I Wish I Knew How It Would Feel to Be Free"—that is downplayed or altogether lacking from her contemporaries. This intangible quality would become increasingly pronounced and evident on Cold Blood's follow-up LP, the classic *Sisyphus* (1971). [In 2001 Collectables reissued this album along with *Sisyphus* as part of two LPs on one CD collection. Although marred by sloppy mastering, it is recommended as the only place to hear this album in its entirety.] *—Lindsay Planer*

Sisyphus / 1970 / San Francisco Sound ♦♦♦♦

Sisyphus—Cold Blood's second release for Bill Graham's San Francisco label—was a shift to a more aggressive and decidedly funkier sound. Taking their cues as much from James Brown's J.B.'s as from their Bay Area contemporaries and labelmates Tower of Power, *Sisyphus* is a much more cohesive and concentrated effort compared to their 1969 eponymous debut. The infusion of strong original material certainly did not hurt either—as five of the disc's six tracks are credited as original band compositions. From the opening edgy/uptempo instrumental "Shop Talk," the change in Cold Blood's direction is evident. This extended jam showcases the entire ensemble—sans vocalist Lydia Pense—including the band's latest addition, Sandy McKee (drums/percussion). The track also features notable assistance from original Santana bandmember Chepito Areas (congas/timbales). The driving rhythms are punctuated by the three-piece brass section, whose contributions are infinitely less obtrusive, especially during the dramatic segue into "Funky on My Back"—one of Cold Blood's most definitive compositions. Highlighted by Pense's dramatic and sensual vocals, the track recalls the laid-back, soulful style of their first album. Another throwback is the slightly gospel-influenced cover of "Your Good Thing"—originally performed by Stax diva Mable John—which also features background vocals from the Pointer Sisters. The second half of *Sisyphus* consists of uptempo groovers "Too Many People," "Understanding," and "I Can't Stay," which is not only the hardest-rocking track on the disc, it also features a lead vocal from percussionist McKee. The song actually comes off sounding like an early Santana cut rather than anything else on the album. This probably has to do more with the frenetically inspired fretwork of Larry Fields than the absence of Pense. *—Lindsay Planer*

First Taste of Sin / 1972 / Reprise ♦♦♦

Founding guitarist Larry Field left before this album was recorded, resulting in an emphasis on keyboardist Raul Matute and sax player Danny Hull. The result is, surprisingly, somewhat tighter playing by the band, with the horn section reined in to provide percussive punches on guitar and keyboard-driven songs. The Escovedos drop in to provide Latin percussion on such funk monsters as "Down to the Bone," and the band sounds both confident and aggressive in the tightly wound rave-up of "All My Honey." The album takes a unusual turn toward soulfully bittersweet blues on "You Had to Know"; while the song takes entirely too long to resolve, it's still an admirable showcase for Lydia Pense's bruised vocals. Trumpeter Max Haskell also steps in to provide vocals on a couple tracks, but they're an unavoidable letdown after the explosive power of Pense's singing. *—Paul Collins*

Thriller! / 1973 / Reprise ♦♦♦

Lydia / 1974 / Warner Bros. ♦♦

Lydia Pense and Cold Blood / 1976 / ABC ♦♦♦

A slight improvement over *Lydia* from two years earlier, this album suffers from uneven material. Since the highlights are by outsiders—"Drink the Wine" by Nicholas Ashford & Valerie Simpson, and "Blinded By Love" by Allen Toussaint—the fault clearly lies with the band's own material. It's too bad, because singer Lydia Pense still sounds great seven years after the band's debut album, and Cold Blood has rarely sounded as comfortable with its preferred white funk sound. The Al Kooper-penned "I Love You More Than You'll Ever Know" gives the sultry Pense a chance to lay out and wrap herself around a slow groove for a change. *—Mark Allan*

● **The Best of Cold Blood** / 1995 / GNP ♦♦♦♦♦

Aside from an almost-ran in "You Got Me Hummin'," Cold Blood never really had any hits to speak of, so assembling a best-of is less a matter of picking hit singles than of individual taste. As such, this is a decent compilation of this San Francisco workhorse. It's also the only release readily available on CD, probably because it's all most listeners will need. It includes all of their debut album, as well as some of their better later tracks like "Lo and Behold." Cold Blood stayed true to its female-belter and brass-band blues formula throughout its career, with the result that this retrospective coheres as an album in its own right. *—Paul Collins*

Cold Blood/Sisyphus / Jul. 31, 2001 / Collectables ♦♦♦

Vintage Blood: Live! 1973 / Oct. 9, 2001 / Dig Music ♦♦♦

Natalie Cole

b. Feb. 6, 1950, Los Angeles, CA

Vocals, Piano / Quiet Storm, Adult Contemporary, Urban, Soul

The daughter of jazz and pop legend Nat King Cole, Natalie Cole has forged a successful career in two phases, doing R&B/urban contemporary and then jazz-based pop. She made her stage debut at age 11 and sang in college. Cole met the writing and producing team of Chuck Jackson and Marvin Yancy in 1973, but didn't produce albums with them until later. The next year they collaborated on some sessions that were recorded at Curtis Mayfield's Curtom studios in Chicago. These helped her land a deal with Capitol, and she teamed with Jackson/Yancey for a string of hit albums and singles from 1975 until 1983 that yielded five number-one R&B hits including "This Will Be," "Inseparable," "Our Love," and "I've Got Love on My Mind." She scored more hits with "Jump Start," "I Live for Your Love," and "Over You" in 1987, and "Pink Cadillac," a cover of a Bruce Springsteen tune, in 1988, and then made her stylistic shift. Cole eased into the transition with "When I Fall in Love," a number her father recorded in 1957. It was included on her 1987 LP, *Everlasting*. She fully embraced the move with the 1991 LP *Unforgettable with Love*, earning Grammy awards and landing a number-one pop album that eventually sold over five million copies. *—Ron Wynn*

Inseparable / 1975 / Capitol ♦♦♦♦♦

When Natalie Cole's debut album, *Inseparable*, came out in 1975, many fans of her late father hoped that she would follow his lead and embrace jazz and pre-rock pop. But *Inseparable* doesn't sound anything like a Nat King Cole session, and it wasn't until 1991's *Unforgettable* that Natalie Cole recorded the sort of project her father would have recorded. In the 1970s, she was essentially an R&B singer, and the person she was compared to more than anyone was Aretha Franklin. Some reviewers also compared Cole to Chaka Khan, which made sense because Khan certainly didn't escape Franklin's influence either. To be sure, Cole brings a definite Franklin influence to this promising debut album; her admiration for the Queen of Soul comes through on the joyous, gospel-drenched "This Will Be" and the hit ballads "I Can't Say No" and "Inseparable" as well as funky album tracks like "Something for Nothing" and "How Come You Won't Stay Here." But as strong as Franklin's influence is, Cole never fails to sound like her own person. By the end of the 1970s, it was clear that Cole wasn't a soul purist—and not surprisingly, she picked up a lot of adult contemporary and quiet storm fans along the way. But *Inseparable* (which Capitol reissued on CD in the early 1990s) is among Cole's most soul-oriented albums, and it is also one of her most essential. *—Alex Henderson*

Natalie / 1976 / One Way ♦♦♦♦

In 1976, Nat King Cole fans were still hoping that his 26-year-old daughter Natalie would provide an album of standards and pre-rock pop. But R&B fans had a different agenda: They hailed her as "the next Aretha Franklin" and wanted her to stick to gritty, gospel-drenched soul music. Cole, however, didn't see herself as a soul purist any more than she saw herself as a female version of her late father, although her first few albums were quite soul-oriented. From a soul standpoint, Cole's second album, *Natalie*, is among her strongest releases. Those who like Cole as a robust, big-voiced soul shouter weren't disappointed by Franklin-influenced offerings like "Touch Me," "Keep Smiling," and the funky hit "Sophisticated Lady (She's a Different Lady)," which shouldn't be confused with the Duke Ellington standard. But Cole brings jazz overtones to the exuberant "Mr. Melody" (another major hit), and she detours into torch singing on the ballad "Good Morning, Heartache," which Billie Holiday defined in 1946. It wasn't until 1991's *Unforgettable* that Cole recorded the sort of project her father would have recorded—for the first 15 or 16 years of her recording career, she avoided his type of music. But occasionally, the Natalie Cole of the 1970s and 1980s showed her appreciation of jazz, standards, and pre-rock pop—and her pleasing interpretation of "Good Morning, Heartache" is a perfect example. Nonetheless, R&B is her primary focus on the excellent *Natalie*, which was produced by Chuck Jackson and Marvin Yancy. *—Alex Henderson*

Thankful / 1977 / One Way ♦♦♦

Thankful could be subtitled the finest hour for Natalie Cole and the songwriting/production duo of Chuck Jackson and Marvin Yancy. The album flows from track to track. It boasts the beautiful number one R&B/Top Ten pop million-selling ballad "Our Love," as well as radio-aired tracks: the rousing, gospel-ish "Be Thankful," "Just Can't Stay Away," the lushly orchestrated torch number "Ain't Nothing Stronger Than Love," and the smooth tropical-flavored "La Costa." The driving, dramatic-themed "Annie Mae" became a steppers favorite. *Thankful* went platinum and was later issued both as a high-quality audiophile pressing from Mobile Fidelity and as a 1996 CD from One Way. [Some of the LP's tracks are on *The Collection*, the 1995 EMI-Capitol CD *I've Got Love on My Mind, This Will Be: Natalie Cole's Everlasting Love*, and the HOL CD *Sophisticated Lady*.] *—Ed Hogan*

Unpredictable / 1977 / Capitol ♦♦♦♦

For many artists, a title like *Unpredictable* is nothing but empty rhetoric—anyone who relies on tired, worn-out formulas (something many artists do) is hardly unpredictable. But Natalie Cole was, in fact, fairly unpredictable in the 1970s. She started out as pretty much a straight-up soul singer but was picking up her share of quiet storm and adult contemporary fans by the end of the decade. Released in 1977, *Unpredictable* was the third album that the Chuck Jackson/Marvin Yancy team produced for her. Most of the songs were written by Jackson/Yancy, including the major hits "I'm Catching Hell" (a confessional ballad) and "I've Got Love on My Mind." However, Cole does some writing herself, contributing "Your Eyes" and the quiet storm item "Peaceful Living"—and the exuberant feel-good anthem "Party Lights" was written by keyboardist Tennyson Stephens. Without question, Jackson and Yancy get high marks for being consistent. They saw to it that 1975's *Inseparable* and 1976's *Natalie* were excellent, and they also make sure that *Unpredictable* is a highly rewarding addition to Cole's catalog. *—Alex Henderson*

Natalie Live! / 1978 / One Way ♦♦♦♦♦

Regrettably, most of the R&B artists who emerged in the '70s never recorded official live albums—and bootlegs aren't an option in most cases because bootleggers usually stick to rock and pop. Natalie Cole fans, however, were given a pleasant surprise when, in 1978, Capitol provided the double-LP *Natalie Live!* This excellent release contains the highlights of two concerts: one at the Universal Amphitheater in Universal City, CA (a Los Angeles suburb), in August 1977, and the other at the Latin Casino in Cherry Hill, NJ (near Philadelphia), in March 1978. Backed by solid bands, Cole is inspired and passionate on performances of gems from *Inseparable* ("I Can't Say No," "This Will Be," and the title song) and *Natalie* ("Sophisticated Lady"), as well as *Unpredictable* ("I've Got Love on My Mind," "Party Lights") and *Thankful* ("Our Love" and "Lovers"). Cole also surprises us with a few covers that weren't on any of her studio LPs, including a sweaty version of "Cry Baby" and a totally unexpected performance of the Beatles' "Lucy in the Sky With Diamonds." That psychedelic classic might seem like an odd choice for Cole, but the tune actually works quite well for her. Besides, Cole never claimed to be a soul purist—she never swore off rock or pop, and some of the gems that she performs have jazz overtones (including "Lovers" and "Mr. Melody"). One could nitpick about the absence of the enchanting, Brazilian-flavored "La Costa," which drove quiet storm programmers wild. But all things considered, *Natalie Live!* is an exciting document of the singer's live performances of the late '70s. *—Alex Henderson*

I Love You So / 1979 / One Way ♦♦♦

If, in 1979, anyone still had illusions about Natalie Cole being a hardcore soul purist, they were shattered by *I Love You So*. Although this is primarily an R&B effort, Cole laces her R&B with a big dose of pop. And that isn't necessarily a bad thing, because most of the material is solid and enjoyable. Those who like Cole as gritty, funky soul shouter should appreciate "You're So Good," but she also gets into everything from sleek disco ("I Love You So") and a Fleetwood Mac cover ("Oh, Daddy") to a commercial R&B/adult contemporary blend ("Who Will Carry On"). Meanwhile, "Your Lonely Heart" (a Cole original that also appeared on her *We're the Best of Friends* album with Peabo Bryson) is the sort of pop-country ballad that wouldn't be out of place at a Dolly Parton or Reba McEntire session. *I Love You So* isn't among Cole's essential releases, but it's a satisfying effort that underscores her ability to successfully tackle a variety of musical styles. *—Alex Henderson*

We're the Best of Friends / 1979 / One Way ♦♦♦

Peabo Bryson was never a hardcore soul purist; he's someone to listen to if you like your R&B laced with lots of pop and adult contemporary. So when Capitol united Natalie Cole with Bryson for this duet album in 1979, you can be certain that the label had its eye on both the R&B charts and the pop charts. And Capitol wasn't disappointed by the LP's performance; *We're the Best of Friends* was black enough for R&B and quiet storm stations, but pop enough for adult contemporary audiences. On the whole, this slick album isn't mind-blowing, but most of the tracks are pleasant—and that is true of "I Want to Be Where You Are" and the hit single "Gimme Some Time," as well as the title song. Arguably, the best thing on the record is Cole and Bryson's remake of Bobby Caldwell's "What You Won't Do for Love," an obvious choice for quiet storm formats in 1979. Also noteworthy is a medley of Harold Arlen's "Let's Fall in Love" and Sam Cooke's "You Send Me," which was arranged by the late Nelson Riddle. Although the two songs are from different eras (the '30s and the late '50s), they prove compatible. *We're the Best of Friends* isn't one of Cole's more essential efforts, but it's a decent outing that her hardcore fans appreciated. *—Alex Henderson*

Don't Look Back / 1980 / One Way ♦♦

Natalie Cole entered the '80s with *Don't Look Back*, which Marvin Yancy produced with Gene Barge. This LP marked the first time that Chuck Jackson didn't co-produce one of Cole's studio albums, and it was also the first time that one of her albums was uneven and disappointing. *Don't Look Back* does contain a few enjoyable tracks, including two adult contemporary ballads ("Beautiful Dreamer" and the major hit "Someone That I Used to Love") and an interpretation of the standard "Stairway to the Stars." Arranged by Nelson Riddle, the latter has nothing to do with R&B or adult contemporary—it's vocal jazz, and Cole's scat singing is right out of Ella Fitzgerald and Sarah Vaughan. In the early '80s, Cole was still unwilling to take the plunge and record an album that emphasized jazz or jazz-based pre-rock pop; she was still fearful of people thinking that she was trying to ride on her late father's coattails. Nonetheless, she did record the occasional standard in the late '70s and early '80s—and when she did, it was clear that she was making a big mistake by not recording more of them. *Don't Look Back* has its moments, although most of the time, Cole is saddled with mediocre, pedestrian material and sounds uninspired. Definitely not one of the singer's more consistent efforts, *Don't Look Back* is strictly for completists. *—Alex Henderson*

Happy Love / 1981 / One Way ♦♦

I'm Ready / 1983 / Epic ♦♦

Dangerous / 1985 / Modern ♦♦

A lackluster production job hurt this project and it failed to live up to what Natalie Cole's fans had come to expect from her—this, despite an accompanying cast of musicians, singers, engineers, and producers that reads like a who's who of studio rats. A trio of pulsating beaters, "Billy the Kid Next Door," "Opposites Attract," and "Your Car (My Garage)" are nearly there, but are missing something you can't quite put your finger on. The self-assured "Nobody's Soldier" possesses similar qualities to her Capitol hits, but doesn't sustain them to the finish line. The best ballad, "A Little Bit of Heaven," doesn't captivate like "I'm Catching Hell." Singers who had great chart runs find that their new recordings are often compared to past successes; such is the case here. From an unknown this would be a good debut, but from Cole it's disappointing. Her greatness is not evident on any of the CD's nine tracks. Nothing makes you say, "Wow!" *—Andrew Hamilton*

Everlasting / 1987 / Elektra ♦♦♦

Everlasting was one of Natalie Cole's best '90s albums. The title track was written and produced by the hit production duo of Jerry Knight & Aaron Zigman. Produced by the Calloways (Midnight Star), the number-two R&B hit "Jump Start" is a slab of slammin' squishy funk with some parts sounding like "No Parking on the Dance Floor." Burt Bacharach & Carole Bayer Sager contribute the smooth "Split Decision" and the lightly swinging "In My Reality." Cole gives one of her best performances, covering one of her famous father's classics on the Marcus Miller-produced "When I Fall in Love." She also skillfully covers Bruce Springsteen's "Pink Cadillac." Cole co-wrote and co-produced the light samba-tinged "More Than the Stars," which is in the same vein as "La Costa," from *Thankful*. *Everlasting* was issued on CD in June 1991. *—Ed Hogan*

The Collection / 1988 / Capitol ♦♦♦♦

This contains the finest soul and sophisticated pre-rock pop tracks from Cole's days at Capitol (1975-1981). Cole made some superb singles in her early days, especially "This Will Be" and "Inseparable." At the same time, she laid the foundation for the early-'90s change that would surprise those who slept on "Mr. Melody" or "I've Got Love on My Mind." Her voice was actually more suited for these songs than the soul numbers, which were as much production and arranging triumphs as vocal victories. *—Ron Wynn*

Unforgettable: With Love / Sep. 10, 1991 / Elektra ♦♦♦♦

A major change of direction for Natalie Cole, *Unforgettable* found the singer abandoning the type of R&B/pop she'd been recording since 1975 in favor of jazz-influenced pre-rock pop along the lines of Nat King Cole's music. It was a surprising risk that paid off handsomely—both commercially and artistically. Nay-sayers who thought that so radical a change would be commercial suicide were proven wrong when the outstanding *Unforgettable* sold a shocking five million units. Quite clearly, this was an album Cole was dying to make. Paying tribute to her late father on "Mona Lisa," "Nature Boy," "Route 66" and other gems that had been major hits for him in the 1940s and early '50s, a 41-year-old Cole sounds more inspired than she had in well over a decade. On the title song, overdubbing was used to make it sound as though she were singing a duet with her father—dishonest perhaps, but certainly enjoyable. Thankfully, standards and pre-rock pop turned out to be a primary direction for Cole, who was a baby when the title song became a hit for her father in 1951. *—Alex Henderson*

Snowfall on the Sahara / Jun. 22, 1999 / Elektra/Asylum ✦✦✦✦
With *Unforgettable*, Natalie Cole refashioned herself as a modern interpreter of the classic American songbook. Once that album turned into a blockbuster, she saw no reason to return to contemporary pop or R&B. Over the course of the '90s, she released a series of faithful, sophisticated, traditional pop albums, all to diminishing artistic and commercial returns. With *Snowfall on the Sahara*, she pulls back from her classic pop routine and she does so with style. She doesn't abandon her role as a torch songstress, but this time she updates it, not only through Phil Ramone's production but through her selection of songs. This time around, the classics are contemporary—"A Song for You," "Corrina," "Everyday I Have the Blues," "Gotta Serve Somebody" (complete with a new verse, written by Bob Dylan especially for Cole)—and she also performs some forgotten tunes and newer songs, along with her fine co-written original title track. Ramone pretty much keeps things in a soulful adult contemporary mold, with the occasional unexpected flourish (such as the trip-hop intro to "Corrina") popping up here and there. Even with such clean radio-ready production, *Snowfall on the Sahara* is hardly a conventional adult contemporary record; it plays like a nightclub revue from a classic pop vocalist, only with modernized arrangements and songs. Such subtle deviations from formula results in a surprisingly satisfying record. By balancing the form of traditional pop with strong material and modernized production, *Snowfall on the Sahara* illustrates adult pop needs to be neither predictable or devoid of substantive songs. *—Stephen Thomas Erlewine*

● **Greatest Hits, Vol. 1** / Nov. 7, 2000 / Elektra ✦✦✦✦
In 1988 Natalie Cole was enjoying great success with her recording career. Her comeback album, *Everlasting*, proved to be a smash, and had provided her with several big hits. Among those was her version of Bruce Springsteen's "Pink Cadillac." The third single from the album, it was revamped into a powerful dance song—much improved from the original, lackluster album version. It was that dance mix which propelled the song into the Top Five, making it the biggest hit of her career. Imagine the disappointment when, upon hearing her 2000 collection *Greatest Hits, Vol. 1*, one realizes the version on this album is the original album mix, not the version that became a hit! This long-awaited greatest-hits album, released to coincide with a television movie and a biography, has 19 tracks. In the U.S., Natalie Cole scored 18 Hot 100 pop hits up to the time of the album's release, so an all-inclusive album of her chart hits would have been a realistic possibility. As it goes, many of her bigger hits—"Jump Start," "Sophisticated Lady," "Someone That I Used to Love"—are not on this album. Her earlier hits, among them "Mr. Melody" and "Our Love," are included as live recordings. Also, there is heavy emphasis on selections from her 1999 album *Snowfall on the Sahara*. All this leads one to hope that any complementary volume to this one will include the studio versions of her hits. As an additional note, this collection boasts two new songs, "Angel on My Shoulder" and "Livin' for Love," plus the soundtrack-only single "A Smile Like Yours." True, the songs are good and the album is a pleasure to the ear. One only wishes that the extra step would have been taken to assemble the correct versions of her hits, and that a second volume will follow. *—Jose Promis*

Mitty Collier

b. Jun. 21, 1941, Birmingham, AL
Vocals / Soul, Chicago Soul, Northern Soul
Singer Mitty Collier is best known for her sensual orchestrated ballad "I Had a Talk With My Man," a 1964 Chess single, which ironically wasn't her highest-charting single. A later single, "Sharing You," was a Top Ten R&B hit. "...Man" has been covered by Dusty Springfield (*Anthology*, 1997), Shirley Brown (*Timeless*, 1991), Inez Foxx (*Memphis & More*, 1996), and Marva Wright (*Marvalous*, 1995), among others.

Born June 21, 1941, in Birmingham, AL, Mitty Collier sang in church as a teen and toured with the Hayes Ensemble, a gospel group. While in college, Collier started singing R&B in local clubs. While visiting her brother in Chicago in the summer of 1959, a former instructor suggested that she enter talent shows. Winning WGES DJ Al Benson's Talent Contest at the legendary Regal Theater for six weeks straight, she was offered a record contract by Ralph Bass of Chess Records in 1960.

Her first charting single was an answer record to Little Johnny Taylor's "Part Time Love," a number-one R&B smash in summer 1963. Collier's "I'm Your Part Time Love" b/w "Don't You Forget It" hit number-20 R&B in fall 1963. Her next hit became her signature song. Inspired in part by gospel great James Cleveland's "I Had a Talk With God Last Night" and produced by Chess staff producer Billy Davis, "I Had a Talk With My Man" b/w "Free Girl (In the Morning)" hit number-three R&B on *Cashbox Magazine*'s R&B chart in fall 1964. Another hit inspired by Cleveland ("No Cross No Crown"), "No Faith, No Love" b/w "Together," peaked at number-29 R&B in early 1965.

Collier's other Chess singles were "Come Back Baby" b/w "Ain't That Love," the local hit "For My Man" b/w "Help Me," "Sharing You" b/w "Walk Away," "Watching and Waiting" b/w "Like Only Yesterday," "That'll Be Good Enough" b/w "Git Out," and "You're the Only One" b/w "Do It With Confidence." In 1969, Collier signed with Peachtree Records of Atlanta, GA and released the singles "True Love Never Comes Easy" and "You Hurt So Good" b/w "I Can't Lose." Her other releases are the single "Let Them Talk" and the U.K. CD *Shades of Genius*.

In 1972, Collier left secular music and began singing gospel music. In the '90s, she was a minister at a church in Chicago. Mitty Collier had a feature story in issue number 66 of *Goldmine Magazine*. *—Ed Hogan*

● **Shades of a Genius** / 1965 / Chess ✦✦✦✦
Collier's Chess album is an above-average mid-'60s soul LP, particularly for an artist that never had a big pop hit. Collier's voice is deeper and more gospel-inflected than that of most woman soul singers of the period. She favors slower material than most soul vocalists did as well, as on her most famous recording, "I Had a Talk with My Man Last Night" (included here); Ray Charles stands out as an influence, as three of his songs are covered. She proves capable on swinging medium-tempo belters too, as on the imaginatively arranged version of "My Babe," which sounds here more like gospel-soul than the electric blues tune as popularized by Little Walter. It's quality, varied soul, not simply collector marginalia despite Collier's obscurity. The top-flight Chess soul production—frequent tasteful brass and strings, yet also some earthy numbers with tough bluesy licks—sometimes recalls the sound of Etta James' recordings from the same era. [The 1998 British CD reissue expands the program considerably to 22 tracks, although there's an inexcusable absence of annotation explaining the origins of the cuts.] *—Richie Unterberger*

Bootsy Collins

b. Oct. 26, 1951, Cincinnati, OH
Bass, Vocals / Funk
Bootsy (born William Collins, October 26, 1951, Cincinnati) is a funk/R&B bassist/singer/bandleader. He formed his first group, the Pacesetters, in 1968, featuring Phelps "Catfish" Collins (his brother; guitar), Frankie "Kash" Waddy (drums), and Philippe Wynne. From 1969 to 1971, the group functioned as James Brown's backup band and was dubbed the J.B.'s. In 1972, Bootsy joined George Clinton's Parliament/Funkadelic. He launched Bootsy's Rubber Band as a spin-off of P Funk in 1976, the band including his brother Phelps, Waddy, Joel "Razor Sharp" Johnson (keyboards), Gary "Mudd-Bone" Cooper (drums), and Robert "P-Nut" Johnson (vocals), along with "the Horny Horns." (He was sometimes billed alone as Bootsy, and sometimes as William "Bootsy" Collins.)

Signing to Warner Bros., he enjoyed the first of his 15 R&B singles-chart entries in 1976 with "Stretchin' Out (In a Rubber Band)." His most successful singles were "The Pinocchio Theory" (1977) and the chart-topping "Bootzilla" (1978). He also released six albums on Warners through 1982, including the gold-sellers *Ahh ... the Name Is Bootsy Baby!* (1977) and *Bootsy? Player of the Year* (1978), then took a six-year recording hiatus, and returned on Columbia in 1988 with the appropriately named *What's Bootsy Doin'?* In 1989, Bootsy was a member of the Bootzilla Orchestra on Malcolm McLaren's album *Waltz Dancing*. In 1990, Bootsy was a featured guitarist and bassist with the dance music trio Deee-Lite. Bootsy's New Rubber Band released *Blasters of the Universe* on August 2, 1994. *Straight Outta "P" University* followed four years later. *—William Ruhlmann*

Stretchin' Out in Bootsy's Rubber Band / Apr. 1976 / Warner Bros. ✦✦✦✦✦
Arguably, William "Bootsy" Collins was to 1970s P-funk what Snoop Doggy Dogg was to 1990s gangsta rap—a quirky, goofy, highly colorful figure who was as funky as he was entertaining. The very sound of Snoop's voice is amusing, and the same goes for Collins. But for all their eccentricity, neither Snoop nor Collins are mere novelty artists. If you removed all the humorous banter from *Stretchin' Out in Bootsy's Rubber Band*, it would still be an album of ultra-funky grooves. Released in 1976, this LP found a 24-year-old Collins launching his solo career after having been employed by James Brown and George Clinton. Collins produced his solo debut with Clinton, and not surprisingly, the Parliament/Funkadelic influence is impossible to miss on P-funk gems like "Psychoticbumpschool" and the hits "I'd Rather Be With You" and "Stretchin' Out (In a Rubber Band)." But this album also made it clear that Collins was very much his own man; in fact, he was Clinton's most distinctive disciple and inevitably became influential himself. All of the albums that Collins provided in the late '70s are worth owning, but *Stretchin' Out in Bootsy's Rubber Band* is among his most consistent and his most essential. *—Alex Henderson*

Ahh ... The Name Is Bootsy, Baby! / Jan. 1977 / Warner Bros. ✦✦✦✦✦
Bootsy Collins' debut solo album, *Stretchin' Out in Bootsy's Rubber Band*, was an extremely tough act to follow, but thankfully, there are no signs of a sophomore slump (either creatively or commercially) on his second album, *Ahh ... The Name Is Bootsy, Baby!* Most P-funk addicts consider this 1977 LP essential listening, and it isn't hard to see why they feel that way. Everything on the album is excellent; that is true of uptempo smokers like "The Pinocchio Theory" and the title song as well as slow, moody, eerie offerings such as "What's a Telephone Bill?" and "Munchies for Your Love." The lyrics are consistently humorous and clever, the grooves are consistently infectious. You can think of *Ahh ... The Name Is Bootsy, Baby!* as a meeting of the funk minds—Collins produced this record with his mentor, George Clinton, who co-wrote all of the material. So Clinton has a lot of input and gives *Ahh ... The Name Is Bootsy, Baby!* the distinctive P-funk sound that Parliament/Funkadelic was known for. But at the same time, he encourages Collins' originality—Bootsy's Rubber Band sounds like a Parliament/Funkadelic spin-off (which is exactly what it was), but not a Parliament/Funkadelic clone. Without question, *Ahh ... The Name Is Bootsy, Baby!* is essential listening for lovers of hard 1970s funk. *—Alex Henderson*

Bootsy? Player of the Year / Feb. 1978 / Warner Bros. ✦✦✦✦✦
Released in 1978 at the height of P-funk mania, *Bootsy? Player of the Year* finds Bootsy definitely not short on quality material, despite his affiliation with the numerous P-funk-affiliated projects being churned out at this time. In fact, this album finds Bootsy at his peak; his previous two albums may have their share of brilliant moments and were no doubt filled with great ideas, melodies, and funk, but here he seems to have finally perfected his songwriting—never again in his career would his songs sound so fully realized. There really isn't a song on the album that doesn't deserve accolades for one reason or another. The uptempo songs—"Bootsy?," "Bootzilla," "Roto-Rooter"—rate as some of the most dance-worthy P-funk material ever released, each song clocking in over five minutes and chock full of elastic basslines. And with only these three hard funk songs, this album

isn't weighed down with over-exuberance. The abundance of down-tempo funk ballads—"May the Force Be With You," "Very Yes," and "As In (I Love You)"—helps maintain a healthy sense of balance, providing a breather from the sweaty dancefloor moments. And, even more importantly, these sappy love songs remain brilliant anomalies in the otherwise ballad-free P-funk canon. Then there is "Hollywood Squares," a song that teeters somewhere between a dance song and a ballad, sometimes picking up the pace and getting sweaty, other times slowing things down to a crooning pace. As mentioned, every song here deserves recognition; "Hollywood Squares" and "May the Force Be With You" really stand out among the rest, though; "Bootzilla" may have been the album's big hit, but, unlike these two songs, it's a fairly formulaic dance song for Bootsy, albeit infectiously formulaic with remarkable rhythm and an extra dose of kookiness. *—Jason Birchmeier*

This Boot Is Made for Fonk-N / Jul. 1979 / Warner Bros. ✦✦✦

If there's one album where Bootsy's output suddenly went from brilliant songwriting to tired retreads, it's *This Boot Is Made for Fonk-N.* His three preceding albums were near-perfect, each employing a healthy balance of manic dancefloor funk and laid-back bedroom funk, as well as a plethora of catchy hooks and timeless melodies. With *This Boot Is Made for Fonk-N*, though, something went wrong for Bootsy. The funk remained, but the songwriting simply lacked both imagination and inspiration. None of the six songs are incredibly unique; the album's three standout songs—"Under the Influence of a Groove," "Bootsy Get Live," and "Jam Fan (Hot)"—essentially co-opt the kooky funk of "Bootzilla" from a year before, with long meandering jams anchored by some vocal hooks and over-filled with Bootsy's crazed charisma. In fact, Bootsy's persona crosses the line from comedic to self-parody many times on this album. Up until now he's been content letting Gary "Mudd-Bone" Cooper handle most of the vocals, but here he just can't keep himself away from the microphone. Besides the lack of fresh ideas, songs, originality, and tact on Bootsy's part, the album sorely lacks down-tempo moments. The ballad "Oh Boy Gorl" just isn't enough, and since the other songs rate as some of the most relentlessly dancefloor-oriented epic funk jams released by this group, some relaxing moments are definitely in need. So, in sum, Bootsy's output isn't quite up to par here. Unfortunately, it would only sink lower on successive releases. Yet as easy as it is to criticize this album for not measuring up to its predecessors, it's still filled with great funk jams—sprawling rather than focused, manic rather than mannered. It's definitely far from a poor album, but undeniably not as well-crafted as Bootsy's first three. *—Jason Birchmeier*

Ultra Wave / Nov. 1980 / Warner Bros. ✦✦✦

The Rubber Band doesn't seem to have been functioning at this point, so *Ultra Wave* is a "solo" Bootsy album, not that the sound is distinguishable. In fact, the problem here is not that there's too much Bootsy, it's that there's not enough. All albums that emerge from The P Funk Mothership deliver the funk by definition, but what separates the good and great ones from the merely OK ones is an individual vision, whether it's P Funk leader George Clinton's or Bootsy's. On *Ultra Wave*, there are tracks that could fit easily not only on any other P Funk album, but also on those of P Funk's more diluted competitors, the Ohio Players, say, or even Earth, Wind And Fire. "Is That My Song?" asks one title, and it's a fair question. *—William Ruhlmann*

The One Giveth, The Count Taketh Away / May 1982 / Warner Bros. ✦✦✦

One of the final albums before Bootsy Collins took a break from bandleading and returned to doing mostly session work. There were more entertaining numbers than dreary ones, and Collins and company had their final chart singles during 1982. *—Ron Wynn*

• **Back in the Day: The Best of Bootsy** / Aug. 9, 1994 / Warner Bros. ✦✦✦✦✦

Can it get any better? If aliens came down needing to know what funk was all about, in all its talented, embrace-anything-and-everything, screw with your head and get your butt down glory, then this is a prime candidate for what to give them. The man, his voice, his bass, the backing of a prime core band including his guitarist brother Catfish, Fred Wesley, and Maceo Parker leading the brass—beautiful, hilarious, and just plain great. This one-disc collection could easily be a two-disc or more if one wanted to include every last highlight from Collins' up-down-all-around career—his work with James Brown alone is beyond the bomb—but when it comes to solo work, this is as perfect a place to start as any. Drawing mostly on the albums done with the active help of George Clinton in the late '70s, *Back in the Day* is a model for what a good compilation should be. Sound is excellent throughout, while full details on who plays what and where, along with where everything came from in the first place, all appear in exhaustive detail. The liner notes, meanwhile, come from longtime funk road manager (Brown, Prince, plenty of others) Alan Leeds, explaining every step of Collins' wonderful story. Collins himself gets in a great concluding bit of thanks and message that's a joy to read, and needless to say the photos of him in his sunglassed late-'70s star-bass-guitar glory abound. And the music? "Bootzilla," "Stretchin' Out (In a Rubber Band)," and "Pinocchio Theory" are just three jam masterpieces of many. A couple of fine rarities flesh things out; "What So Never the Dance," recorded in 1971 when Collins' band was still known as the House Guests, is a great slice of greasy, J.B.-tinged funk. "Body Slam!" shows him getting to grips with electro nicely, while "Scenery," originally a B-side ballad, has him doing his loveman-goes-nuts deal at the end. A fierce 1976-era live take on "Psychoticbumpschool," with the Horny Horns in full blow, wraps up this fantastic collection. *—Ned Raggett*

Keepin' Dah Funk Alive 4-1995 / 1995 / Rykodisc ✦✦

Fresh Outta "P" University / 1997 / Mercury ✦✦✦

Like most latter-day Bootsy albums, *Fresh Outta "P" University* doesn't offer any surprises—it's another sprawling collection of funky in all its incarnations, from deep soul to disco—but since Collins and his backing band deliver it with such energy, style and professionalism, these 22 songs are entertaining and infectious. Only long-time Collins fanatics will have the need to acquire this record—casual fans, after all, will need the classic uncut funk of the '70s—but they will be pleasantly surprised by the album, which is one of his stronger releases of the '90s. [*Fresh Outta "P" University* is also available in an import release.] *—Stephen Thomas Erlewine*

Live in Louisville 1978 / 1999 / Disky ✦✦✦✦

Glory B da' Funk's on Me!: The Bootsy Collins Anthology / Jun. 5, 2001 / Rhino ✦✦✦✦✦

Bootsy Collins has rightfully received accolades as funk's second officer (after George Clinton—and it should be third after James Brown and Clinton). For decades he has been sampled by every rapper from Snoop Dogg to OutKast, and virtually created the bass sound that made the Red Hot Chili Peppers a household name and that created a career for Les Claypool. Yet, his most influential sound emanated not from his tenure with James Brown or P Funk, but his own Rubber Band, and until now that wooly, wild, and surreal unit has never been properly anthologized—until now. Rhino, in their usual thorough, crazy fashion, have directed the folks at the Warner archives and have created a massive, drop-the-bomb two-disc set that sets the record straight. This may not be no disco but it sho' 'nuff is some mean foolin' around. Sorry. Got carried away. In the middle of "Psychotic Bumpschool," the refrain David Byrne ripped off for "Life During Wartime" rears its beautiful, black, sassy head and introduces itself. The tune wraps itself around your head with that bass up front and as nasty and greasy as a lube job on a vintage Ford. Released in 1976 and recorded at P Funk's home studio, United Sound in Detroit with Clinton, this is just one of four tunes from *Stretchin' Out in Bootsy's Rubber Band*, Collins' debut.

And where else but Detroit? This was the place Collins developed his deep-space bass with the P Funk organization and was encouraged by Papa Funk to go out on his own—with George producing, of course. Also from this revolutionary slab of Roman-orgy pleasure psychoses are "Stretchin' Out (In a Rubber Band)," "I'd Rather Be With You," and "Vanish in Our Sleep," all co-written with Clinton. These are the four singles issued from the LP which hit number ten on the R&B charts and number 56 on the pop charts. Three of the four charted. Some of the cats helping out on this date were guitarists Michael Hampton and Garry Shider, Phelps Collins, and a horn section that included Fred Wesley and the Brecker Brothers. Next up we get five tracks from Bootsy's breakthrough album, *Ahh... The Name Is Bootsy Baby*, with space dub sounds that rivaled anything ever spliced together by Scratch Perry. And there are no lower ones in recorded bass history than on this heavyweight funk & roll soul record. The title track is a co-write with Clinton and Maceo Parker, who joins the cast of the first album along with P Funk keyboard-king Bernie Worrell. This is the funk jam disc, where everything comes off including the damn lid: excess, dirty grooves and that low-ridin' bass come steamin' out of the speakers into meltdown territory. The horns meet the rhythm section in a devilish groove and about a hundred voices act as a chorus to phony crowd noise but who gives a shit? It jams! The crazy thing is, it is toppled by the very next cut, "Pinocchio Theory." From the center of Planet FONK, Bootsy and Clinton weave together the pumped up bass, stretched to its thumbed limit and add some obnoxious keyboards that push the tune over the limit. If it weren't for the chorus, which becomes the tune's lyric body, the whole thing would disintegrate. "Munchies for Your Love," "What's a Telephone Bill?," and the killer freaky soul of "Can't Stay Away" close out the selections from an album that reached number one on the R&B chart and number 16 on the pop charts. With the groove throne firmly established, and P Funk beginning to move the funk into disco territory, Bootsy was the undisputed king of the genre until Rick James toppled him a few years later. Rhino has closed out disc one and opened disc two with four tracks, with "Roto-Rooter" and "Very Yes" from the man's next chart-topping success, *Bootsy? Player of the Year.* If you don't know about "Roto-Rooter," you should. This is acid-drenched funk at its most extreme. Sweet vocals exaggerated to an extreme are held in check by a bass that pops the groove into their faces. It's an elongated synth-string freakout that's a tribute to bonin'. One can hear Jamaican soul in the backbeat and the fill rhythms. And the distorted vocals stretch out across both channels and drive the keyboards and Bootsy's strings into overdrive, going out in a freakout of noisy effects and detuned bass overload.

Disc two slides and slithers its way into deeper, weirder, freakier territory, sampling cuts from no less than five recordings, including the mutation of Bootsy's Rubber Band into the Sweat Band. Lineups change very little from recording to recording, and Clinton is on board for all of them, but there are different backing vocalists and characters like Detroit's Larry Fratangelo and Jeanette Washington added to the mix. Of course we have the anthem of late-'70s freak funk, "Bootzilla"—which if you haven't heard, drop your TV dinner and go to a record store right now because you've been indoors waaay too long. But there are also offerings that wouldn't be so readily noticed: "She Jam" and "Jam Fan (Hot)." These were singles or B-sides from *This Boot Is Made for Fonk-N*, which charted at number six on the R&B chart and number 52 in the pop charts (hopeless squares those pop fans). But in 1979 the climate was changing; James had hit the scene, Prince had made his mark, and disco was on its way to the hell it so richly deserved. By the time we hear the tracks from *Ultra-Wave*, issued in 1980, we can see Bootsy's moment had slipped from the skyline. Even with massive jams like "F-Encounter" and "Mug Push," the set only reached number 30 on the R&B list and failed to crack the Top 50 in pop. The killer single "Freak to Freak," with a dual bassline and whomping-ass keyboard bass—for a three-bass hit—only marked 26 at R&B, and was Bootsy's first non-Warner record in six years. Clinton used his CBS deal to issue the single and album on Uncle Jam. Collins was playin' Rick James' game and losing; even though he did it far better, he was considered old-school by the funk-buying public, and white kids—other than Detroiters and Ohioans—had yet to encounter the Super FONK. Five of the last six tracks are taken from the criminally underrated *The One Giveth, the Count Taketh Away*, which slipped to 18 in the R&B charts and failed to crack the Hot 100 in *Billboard*'s pop bible. What is baffling is that this may be Collins' strongest, most individual music. Cuts like "Countrakula," "Landshark" (no relation to Frank Zappa's), and "Shine-O-Myte" are so far out in the zone they're close encounters of a tenth kind. The entire set ends with a 12-inch mix of the classic "Body Slam," and coincidentally, the listener is exhausted, dragged through the stratosphere to the pit of soul & roll to the elevated plateaus of the funk kingdom. This collection is every bit as necessary as the Funkadelic singles compilation, Parliament's *Chronicles and First Thangs* collection, and the James Brown *20 Greatest Hits* comp. This is the shit that got kickin' and keeps on tickin' over 30 years after the original bomb was dropped. *—Thom Jurek*

Lyn Collins

b. Jun. 12, 1948, Abilene, TX
Vocals / Soul, Funk, Deep Funk
Nicknamed the "Female Preacher," Lyn Collins was discovered in the early '70s along with her relatives Bootsy and Phelps Collins by James Brown, who was making the transition to the hardest funk phase of his career. Lyn Collins was born June 12, 1948, in Abilene, TX, where she grew up; she began singing in her teens, waxing a tune called "Unlucky in Love" at age 14, and married a man who served both as her manager and as the local promoter for the James Brown Revue. Collins sent Brown a demo tape and he responded by essentially putting her on standby in 1970, when Marva Whitney left the Revue. Former vocalist Vicki Anderson elected to rejoin, however, so Brown instead invited Collins to come to Georgia for a recording session in early 1971, which produced the single "Wheel of Life."

By the end of that year, Anderson was ready to leave again, and Collins officially joined the James Brown Revue. In 1972, Brown's People Records label released Collins' self-penned single "Think (About It)"; produced by Brown, it became her first and biggest hit, made her the most commercially successful female singer in Brown's camp, and was later sampled for the main vocal hook in the party rap classic "It Takes Two" by Rob Base & DJ E-Z Rock. Collins' first full-length album, also titled *Think (About It)*, was released later in the year. Collins continued to record singles for Brown through 1973, also fulfilling her heavy touring commitments as a member of the Revue. Collins' second album, *Check It Out if You Don't Know Me By Now*, was released in 1975. She eventually became a backup session vocalist, also appearing on the soundtracks of the film *Dr. Detroit* and the TV series *Fame*.

Around the late '80s/early '90s, Collins attempted a comeback as a dance-club diva, recording the house single "Shout" for Belgium's ARS label, and a self-penned track called "Break Your Heart" for an Italian label. In 1993, Collins' profile was given a boost by female dancehall reggae singer Patra, who invited Collins to perform on her hit remake of "Think (About It)"; partly due to the resulting interest, her two official albums were reissued in England and Holland. In addition, Collins' work has appeared on Polydor compilations like *James Brown's Funky People* and *James Brown's Original Funky Divas*, as well as the bootleg singles comp *Female Preacher*, she continues to tour and perform, most notably at the European Jazz/Funk Festival (in both 1998 and 1999) and the Montreux Jazz Festival. *—Steve Huey*

● **Think (About It)** / 1972 / Polydor ✦✦✦✦
At the time of the release of *Think (About It)* in 1972, Lyn Collins had been a member of James Brown's performing revue for about two years. Her full-throated voice had earned her the nickname "the Female Preacher" and a shot to record her own album. Of course, the Godfather was in the producer's chair, writing four of the nine tracks, directing the J.B.'s as they laid down their usual funky grooves, and liberally adding vocals throughout. The title track is the main point of interest here; from Collins' throat-ripping vocals to the track's nasty groove to Brown's background interjections, this is a killer. (Rob Base & DJ E-Z Rock later sampled the track for their rap classic "It Takes Two"). The rest of the record is a little uneven: "Just Won't Do Right" is a good doo wop-ish ballad with some churchy organ and great vocals by Collins and Brown, "Wheels of Life" is a nice little groover that sounds like vintage Aretha Franklin, and "Women's Lib" is a very slow ballad that lets Collins show off her anguished yowl of a vocal to its fullest. Where the album stumbles is on the covers of familiar songs. Her versions of Bill Withers' "Ain't No Sunshine" and the Gamble & Huff classic "Never Gonna Give You Up" are mediocre, and worst of all is her leaden take on "Fly Me to the Moon." Still, the record is worth tracking down for hardcore James Brown or funky soul fans. The less devoted should look for "Think (About It)" on one of the many compilations on which it appears. *—Tim Sendra*

Check Me Out If You Don't Know Me by Now / 1975 / Polydor ✦✦✦✦
Here is a sterling effort from one of James Brown's most talented finds. Wearing the producer's hat, Brown showcases the "Female Preacher" on songs and styles from standards to funk to Southern and Philly soul. On the funk tip you have "Rock Me Again & Again & Again & Again" and "How Long Can I Keep It Up." Collins injects soul and sweat into the standards "A Foggy Day" and "Try a Little Tenderness"; shows her southern roots on "Put It on the Line"; and pays homage to the sound of Philadelphia on a quality remake of "Back Stabbers" and a dramatic five-minute-plus rendition of "If You Don't Know Me by Now." *—Andrew Hamilton*

Color Me Badd

f. 1990, Oklahoma City, OK, **db.** 1998
Group / New Jack Swing, Club/Dance, Urban
This vocal quartet formed as high school students in Oklahoma City before relocating to New York. They proved adept at both churning dance tunes and sincere ballads. Signing to Giant Records, they broke through in 1991 with their performance of "I Wanna Sex You Up" on the soundtrack of *New Jack City*. Released as a single, the song topped the R&B charts, went Top Five pop, and enjoyed double-platinum sales. They followed it with the gold-selling "I Adore Mi Amor," which hit number-one on both the pop and R&B charts. The singles set the stage for the first Color Me Badd album, *C.M.B.*, which sold over three million copies and spawned the gold-selling number-one pop hit "All 4 Love" as well as the Top 20 singles "Thinkin' Back" and "Slow Motion." Color Me Badd's next single was another movie soundtrack song, "Forever Love" from *Mo' Money*, their sixth consecutive single to reach the Top 20. They finished 1992 second only to Boyz II Men as the top pop singles act of the year. After slating fans' thirst for a new album with the remix collection *Young, Gifted & Badd—The Remixes*, the group issued their second album of new material, *Time and Chance*, in November 1993. It featured two Top 20 pop singles, the title track (which also made the R&B Top Ten) and "Choose," and went gold, but that was a commercial disappointment after the enormous success of the first album. *Now & Forever* (1996) gave Color Me Badd a final Top 20 pop single in "The Earth, the Sun, the Rain," but it barely registered in the charts. The group switched to Sony for a final album, *Awakening*, but its commercial failure led them to disband. *—Ron Wynn & William Ruhlmann*

● **C.M.B.** / 1991 / Giant ✦✦✦✦✦
The urban contemporary market can be incredibly fickle. While Color Me Badd was the toast of the urban world in 1991, the interracial quartet was all but forgotten a few years later. In the age of videos, Badd's image proved very marketable (for a while, anyway). But in general, its songs were far from remarkable, and its singing wasn't great by any means. This debut album—which soared to triple-platinum sales thanks to some very aggressive marketing on the part of veteran music industry exec Irving Azoff's Giant Records—does have its moments, including the hit slow jams "I Adore Mi Amor" and "I Wanna Sex You Up" (which samples rapper Slick Rick in a rather clever fashion). But most of the songs are pedestrian and generic. There's little or nothing to distinguish cliché-ridden numbers like "Roll the Dice" or "Heartbreak" from the countless other new jack swing songs flooding the market in the early '90s. And all the "cool videos" in the world can't erase the CD's many weaknesses. *—Alex Henderson*

Young, Gifted & Badd / 1992 / Giant ✦✦

Now & Forever / 1996 / Giant ✦✦

● **The Best of Color Me Badd** / Aug. 22, 2000 / Giant ✦✦✦✦
Two years after Color Me Badd broke up in the wake of the commercial failure of *Awakening*, Giant Records assembled this compilation. The title *The Best of Color Me Badd* instead of Greatest Hits, signals that it is not a simple collection of the group's chart singles. In fact, of their nine Top 40 pop hits, six are included, among them the major hits "I Wanna Sex You Up," "I Adore Mi Amor," and "All 4 Love." (The missing titles are "Slow Motion," "Forever Love," and "Time and Chance.") The other half of the disc consists of B-sides (the R&B chart entry "Color Me Badd"), album tracks (among them a cover of the 1973 Skylark hit "Wildflower" produced and arranged by David Foster, who was in Skylark), and rarities ("Got 2 Have U" from the *Beverly Hills 90210* TV soundtrack and "Where Lovers Go," previously available only as a Japanese bonus track). The result is a reasonable sampler of Color Me Badd's work. "We're not a fad," they sang on "Color Me Badd," but they were, breaking five top 20 hits off their 1991 debut album, the triple-platinum *C.M.B.*, and going straight downhill from there. Picking up from New Edition and especially New Kids on the Block, who were subsiding just as they emerged, Color Me Badd, along with Boyz II Men, was the teen-oriented male vocal group of their day, complete with hype, videos, silly haircuts, and four interweaving mediocre tenor voices. It is no coincidence that, just as they themselves were slipping below the radar, descendants like Backstreet Boys and N'Sync were just coming on. But unlike the so-called "boy bands" that came after them (how can they be bands if they don't play instruments?), they were R&B-influenced rather than Euro-centric, even to the point of being an integrated group, and they incorporated a broader range of musical styles into their sound. They were also more overtly sexual ("I Wanna Sex You Up"), even if "Sexual Capacity," one of the album tracks included here, proves to be a confession of limited capacity when you examine the lyrics. The characteristic they shared with both their predecessors and followers, however, is that they were essentially image-based, a bunch of reasonably attractive, modestly talented young men more important for their pinup value than their musical accomplishments, and so they remain on this compilation. That means the likely audience for *The Best of Color Me Badd* is women in their mid-twenties at the turn of the century who are already looking back nostalgically on junior high school. *—William Ruhlmann*

The Commodores

f. 1967, Tuskegee, AL
Group / Quiet Storm, Urban, Funk, Soul
Known for such hits as "Just to Be Close to You," "Easy," and "Brickhouse," to name a few, the Commodores were one of the top bands during their long tenure at Motown. The group is credited with seven number-one songs and a host of other Top Ten numbers on the *Billboard* charts. They also have a vast music catalog that has generated more than 50 albums, and the recordings continue to be in demand.

The members of the Commodores, all of whom attended Tuskegee Institute in AL, came together as a result of two groups disbanding: the Mystics and the Jays. Initially formed to simply play music as a pastime and to meet girls, the lineup consisted of William King (trumpet), Thomas McClary (guitar), Ronald LaPread (bass), Walter "Clyde" Orange (drums), Lionel Richie (saxophone), and Milan Williams (keyboards). The members nearly went stir-crazy trying to pick a name for the group, but to no avail. As a last resort, Orange gave King a dictionary and told him to pick a name, and that name was the Commodores. With the only learned musician in the group being Clyde Orange, the Commodores began spreading their music throughout their regional base, which included Tuskegee, Montgomery, and Birmingham, AL. After experiencing success in securing dates in their own backyard, the band ventured to New York City for a gig at the Smalls Paradise club. They were told, in so many words by the club owner, that their sound was not happening. However, a short time later the self-contained band was called back to the club to fill-in for a last minute cancellation. That night the Tuskegee alumni performed before a standing-room-only crowd. Most of the crowd were friends and family of the band. Unaware of the planned crowd, the owner booked the band for two more weeks.

The Commodores association with Motown was a result of the group touring with the Jackson 5. That opportunity occurred in 1971 when the group was told to be in New York City for an audition. The members did not know the audition was for the Jackson 5 tour until two weeks later when they were selected for the tour. They toured with the Jackson 5 for two-and-one-half years, and their presence on that tour ultimately solidified a deal with Motown. Their first release on Motown was the uptempo instrumental dance cut "Machine Gun." Written by Milan Williams, the song gave the group immediate attention with its Top Ten outing (*Billboard* number seven, 15 weeks). That number was followed by the Top 20 single "I Feel Sanctified," which lead to their third single and first number-one record in "Slippery When Wet." Inside of 17 weeks, the AL-based septet was rocking the radio waves with their Southern funk spiced with an animated vocal delivery, courtesy of Lionel Richie and Clyde Orange.

In September of 1976, they released "Just to Be Close to You," their second number one single and a number-seven pop hit. The Top Ten hit "Fancy Dancer" followed, and then came "Easy." Different from their other tunes, "Easy" was very serene and not nearly as soulful or funky as the band's other tunes. Nonetheless, it claimed the number-one spot on the charts, and it paved the way for the style of ballads the group would later be known for. However, soul and funk was still very much present in spite of the benevolent rhythms of "Easy." This was demonstrated with the release of what would become the group's anthem, "Brickhouse." The arrangement and candid vocal lead by Clyde Orange is complemented by the evenly saturated percussive and rhythmic attack. It cracked the Top Ten at number four. The irony is that "Brickhouse" was the last song recorded for the group's self-titled album. Two consecutive number-one singles would follow: the dance cut "Too Hot Ta Trot" and the placid number "Three Times a Lady." And then there was "Still." The last number one for the group with Richie as a member.

In 1981, Richie recorded "Endless Love" with Diana Ross. The song peaked at number one for seven and nine weeks respectively on the *Billboard* R&B and pop charts. The success of the single was a prelude to the success Richie would relish upon his exit from the group, which occurred in 1982. But before his departure, the band had a string of hits which included "Old Fashion Love," "Lady (You Bring Me Up)," and "Oh No." However, the Commodores had many songs that were not singles and never charted, but were and remain favorites among many. The most notable being "Zoom." A simmering ballad in which Richie patiently sails through the utopian lyric; truly an R&B classic. In the absence of Richie, the group courted the talents of tenor J.D. Nicholas (formerly of Heatwave) and would go on to release its biggest hit. That occurred on January 15, 1985, when "Nightshift" was released. Penned by Clyde Orange, the song pays to tribute to the late soul singers Marvin Gaye and Jackie Wilson. Orange and Nicholas' co-led the nostalgic number which navigated its way to the top spot on the charts and stayed there through four consecutive weeks; it also won the group its only Grammy.

The Commodores left Motown in 1985. The group's split with label was a matter of principle, which the group could not forsake. Motown gave a commitment to releasing the group's album prior to Richie's solo release. However, the label did not honor the commitment and proceeded to release Richie's project. Consequently, the group signed with Polydor in the same year and had another swing at the Top Ten with "Goin' to the Bank" (*Billboard* R&B, number two, 20 weeks). *—Craig Lytle*

Machine Gun / Jul. 1974 / Motown ✦✦✦

Before the Commodores started having major adult contemporary hits like "Three Times a Lady," "Easy," and "Still," they were happy to be a full-time funk/soul band. The Southerners became increasingly pop-minded in the late '70s, but when their debut album, *Machine Gun*, came out in 1974, their music was unapologetically gritty. This was, without question, a very promising debut—Lionel Richie and his allies really hit the ground running on sweaty funk items like "Young Girls Are My Weakness," "The Bump," "Gonna Blow Your Mind," and the single "I Feel Sanctified." These songs aren't funk-pop or sophisticated funk—they're hardcore funk. What you *won't* find on *Machine Gun* are a lot of sentimental love ballads. In the late '70s, the Commodores became as famous for their ballads as they were for their funk and dance material, but believe it or not, there are no ballads to be found on this consistently funky, mostly uptempo debut. As much as this LP has going for it, *Machine Gun* isn't the Commodores' best or most essential album. *Machine Gun* is rewarding, but their subsequent albums *Caught in the Act* (1975), *Movin' On* (1975), and *Hot on the Tracks* (1976) are even stronger. *—Alex Henderson*

Caught in the Act / Feb. 1975 / Motown ✦✦✦✦✦

The sophomore slump wasn't a problem for the Commodores. The band's first album, *Machine Gun*, was quite promising, but its sophomore album, *Caught in the Act*, is even stronger. This superb 1975 LP, which the Commodores produced and arranged with James Carmichael, is more diverse than its mostly uptempo predecessor. There are plenty of uptempo funk gems; anyone with a taste for hard, sweaty 1970s funk won't be disappointed by "Look What You've Done to Me," "Wide Open," or the hit "Slippery When Wet," which soared to number one on *Billboard*'s R&B singles chart and urges unfaithful husbands to give up their adulterous ways. But *Caught in the Act*, unlike *Machine Gun*, doesn't neglect slower material; "You Don't Know That I Know" and "This Is Your Life" are first-rate soul ballads. Excellent from start to finish, *Caught in the Act* is among the Commodores' finest albums. *—Alex Henderson*

Movin' On / Oct. 1975 / Motown ✦✦✦✦✦

R&B purists have often argued that the Commodores did their most essential work before 1977. It was in 1977 that they crossed over to the pop/adult contemporary audience in a major way with "Easy," and subsequent hits like 1978's "Three Times a Lady" and 1979's "Still" (both of which reached number one on *Billboard*'s pop singles charts) certainly weren't the work of R&B snobs. Of course, Lionel Richie never claimed to be an R&B purist, although it is safe to say that the Commodores were still a hardcore funk/soul band when their third album, *Movin' On*, came out in 1975. From an R&B standpoint (as opposed to a pop or adult contemporary standpoint), this is one of their most essential releases. Those who love hard, gutsy 1970s funk can't go wrong with horn-powered gems like "Mary, Mary," "(Can I) Get a Witness," "Gimme My Mule," and "Hold On"; however, the song that *Movin' On* is best remembered for is the laid-back, gospel-drenched hit "Sweet Love." Written by Richie, "Sweet Love" is one of those secular soul tunes that isn't really gospel but borders on it; when Richie belts out the lyrics, "You got to keep on searching/harder/day by day," you feel like you're in the front row during an AME church service. And even though *Movin' On* is an LP that R&B purists rave about (rightly so), you can't say that it was ignored by pop audiences—"Sweet Love" was a number-two R&B hit, but it also reached number five on *Billboard*'s pop singles chart. *—Alex Henderson*

Hot on the Tracks / Jun. 1976 / Motown ✦✦✦✦✦

1976's *Hot on the Tracks* was the Commodores' fourth album, and it was also the last album they recorded before becoming a major crossover act. From 1977 on, the Commodores were as big among pop and adult contemporary audiences as they were with R&B audiences. That isn't to say that pop fans ignored them before 1977; "Just to Be Close to You," the single that *Hot on the Tracks* is best known for, reached number seven on *Billboard*'s pop singles chart as well as number one on its R&B singles chart. The album itself made it to number one on *Billboard*'s R&B albums chart, while climbing to number 12 on its pop albums chart. Nonetheless, this is an R&B record first and foremost, and the Commodores never sound like they're going out of their way to be pop. R&B purists should have no problem with "Just to Be Close to You," which is very much a soul ballad and doesn't have the adult contemporary appeal of subsequent hits like "Three Times a Lady," "Easy," and "Still." Nor should they have any problem with hardcore funk treasures such as "Fancy Dancer" (a number-nine R&B hit), "Come Inside," "Let's Get Started," and the quirky "Quick Draw." For those who prefer the Commodores' hardcore funk and soul over their crossover material, *Hot on the Tracks* is recommended without hesitation. *—Alex Henderson*

Zoom / 1977 / Motown ✦✦✦

Commodores / Mar. 1977 / Motown ✦✦✦✦

Commodores Live! / Oct. 1977 / Motown ✦✦✦✦

From Midwestern funk bands to Philadelphia vocal groups, the 1970s were a great time for R&B concerts. Now for the bad news: The vast majority of R&B artists who were active in the 1970s never recorded official live albums. And much to the dismay of many serious soul collectors, R&B bootlegs were practically nonexistent; 1970s bootleggers were mainly interested in rock. So a valuable part of music history—1970s R&B concerts—wasn't nearly as well documented as it should have been. Nonetheless, there are some excellent documents of live 1970s R&B, including Earth, Wind & Fire's *Gratitude*, War's *War Live*, Parliament's *P-Funk Earth Tour*, and this two-LP set by the Commodores (which reached number two on *Billboard*'s R&B albums chart and number three on its pop albums chart). Recorded in Atlanta and Washington, D.C., during their 1977 tour, *Live!* has no problem capturing the excitement of the Commodores on-stage in their heyday. The band is as inspired on hardcore funk ("Brick House," "Fancy Dancer," "Slippery When Wet," "Come Inside") as it is on ballads and slow jams ("Just to Be Close to You," "Sweet Love," and "Easy"). The only studio offering is "Too Hot Ta Trot," a gritty funk gem that was released as a single and soared to number one on *Billboard*'s R&B singles chart. This superb double LP is undeniably essential and is recommended to anyone with even a casual interest in the Commodores. *—Alex Henderson*

Natural High / May 1978 / Motown ✦✦✦

The Commodores' sixth studio album, *Natural High*, is best known for the ballad "Three Times a Lady," which became a staple of adult contemporary radio and reached number one on both the pop and R&B charts. "Three Times a Lady" was their first number one pop hit, and Lionel Richie was being recognized as a major crossover star. Not everyone liked "Three Times a Lady"—some people found the song to be much too sappy, and R&B purists argued that the Commodores were watering their music down. But even if "Three Times a Lady" isn't your cup of tea, *Natural High* still has a lot to offer R&B fans. "X-Rated Movie," "Such a Woman," and "I Like What You Do" are exhilarating examples of hardcore funk, and those who appreciate artists like Heatwave and the Brothers Johnson will find a lot to admire about "Fire Girl" and "Flying High" (both of which are sleek examples of the sophisticated funk style). Meanwhile, "Say Yeah" (featuring Richie) is a first-rate R&B slow jam. Whatever your opinion of "Three Times a Lady"—whether you love it or hate it—the fact is that *Natural High* has more plusses than minuses and was a generally respectable, if imperfect, addition to the Commodores' catalog. *—Alex Henderson*

Midnight Magic / Jul. 1979 / Motown ✦✦✦

When the Commodores' seventh studio album, *Midnight Magic*, came out in 1979, one could safely assume that the LP would contain at least one adult contemporary ballad. And sure enough, *Midnight Magic* contains the ballad "Still," which was a number-one pop hit (as well as a number-one R&B hit) and became a staple on adult contemporary radio. The sappy ballad (which features Lionel Richie) wasn't without its detractors, who felt that the Commodores had become too much of a slick crossover act. But even if "Still" doesn't excite you, the rest of the album isn't bad. "Wonderland" (a number-21 R&B hit) is an enjoyable R&B slow jam, and fans of sophisticated funk (as opposed to hardcore funk) should appreciate "You're Special," "Gettin' It," and the disco-minded title song. "Sexy Lady" is the only thing on the LP that can honestly be described as hardcore funk; most of the uptempo tunes favor the type of sophisticated funk that the Brothers Johnson, Rufus/Chaka Khan, and Heatwave were known for in the late '70s. Next to "Still," the album's best-known track is "Sail On," which reached number eight on *Billboard*'s R&B singles chart (and number four on its pop single chart) despite the fact that it is essentially a pop-country song. Some R&B purists saw "Sail On" as a blatant example of how watered down the Commodores had become, but it's still a charming and likable tune—one that wouldn't have been out of place on a Dolly Parton or Glen Campbell LP. *Midnight Magic* isn't one of the Commodores' essential releases, and R&B purists are advised to stick to the band's pre-1977 albums. Nonetheless, this is a generally decent, if uneven, record that has more strengths than weaknesses. *—Alex Henderson*

Heroes / Jun. 1980 / Motown ♦♦♦

From 1974 until the end of the '70s, the Commodores enjoyed kicking out the hits. As the 1980s rolled in, the Commodores did not lose much steam as they scored their first Top Ten hit of the decade with the midtempo beauty "Old Fashion Love." From the flattering lyric to the zestful groove, the splendid selection is complemented by Lionel Richie's colorful delivery. It peaked at number eight on the *Billboard* R&B charts. "Heroes" extols everyday people for their feats and courage and checked in at 27 after 11 weeks on the charts. The former Tuskegee collegians were not known to do gospel, but the self-contained sextet scored big with "Jesus Is Love." Richie's prayerful message and pleading cries are solidified with a lyric and melody that complement one another. The song's popularity is far greater than what the charts reflected (number 37). "Wake Up Children" and "Mighty Spirit" are two other inspirational selections. *—Craig Lytle*

In the Pocket / Jun. 1981 / Motown ♦♦♦

In 1980 and 1981, many people in the music world suspected that Lionel Richie would soon be leaving the Commodores to pursue a solo career—and sure enough, he officially became a full-time solo artist in 1982. *In the Pocket*, released in 1981, turned out to be his final album with the group. Not surprisingly, Richie dominates the album, singing lead on everything from adult contemporary ballads like "Lucy" and "Oh No" (a number-four pop/number-five R&B smash) to the sophisticated funk of "Why You Wanna Try Me" and the Top Five R&B favorite "Lady (You Bring Me Up)." Walter Orange and Thomas McClary also contribute some lead vocals, but the album's best-known songs are the ones that feature Richie. While *In the Pocket* doesn't contain a lot of hardcore funk à la "Brick House" or "Slippery When Wet," the sleeker, smoother sophisti-funk style is well represented by "Why You Wanna Try Me" and "Lady (You Bring Me Up)," as well as "Saturday Night" and "Keep on Taking Me Higher." Overall, *In the Pocket* isn't great—"Lady (You Bring Me Up)" is certainly a gem, although the rest of the material is merely decent. But while *In the Pocket* isn't among the Commodores' essential releases, it was still a pleasant way for Richie to end his association with the Southern band. *—Alex Henderson*

Commodores 13 / Sep. 1983 / Motown ♦♦♦

For the Commodores, losing Lionel Richie in 1982 was a lot like L.T.D. losing Jeffrey Osborne and Rose Royce losing Gwen Dickey—it was a severe blow, although not a fatal one. In fact, the Commodores had a few major hits after Richie's departure, including "Nightshift" (a number-one R&B/number-three pop smash) in 1984 and "Goin' to the Bank" in 1986. Released in 1983, *Commodores 13* was the band's first post-Richie album as well as its first album without producer James Carmichael (who had been working with the Commodores since 1974). This LP came out around the same time as Richie's second solo album, *Can't Slow Down*, which sold over eight-million copies in the U.S. alone. *Commodores 13* didn't do nearly that well, although it's a generally decent, if uneven, record that had a number-20 R&B hit in "Only You." The lead vocals are handled by Walter Orange, Thomas McClary, and the Mean Machine's Harold Hudson, who was an interim vocalist rather than an official full-time vocalist. Not surprisingly, the Commodores cover both their R&B bases and their pop bases, getting into everything from sleek keyboard funk ("Touchdown," "Nothing Like a Woman") to adult contemporary ballads ("Only You"). Meanwhile, "Ooo Woman You," which McClary co-wrote with Melissa Manchester, is a catchy pop/rock number. Is *Commodores 13* a masterpiece? No. This release isn't in a class with essential treasures like 1976's *Hot on the Tracks* or 1977's *The Commodores*. But it isn't a bad album, and it indicated that there could be life after Lionel Richie for the Commodores. *—Alex Henderson*

Nightshift / Jan. 1985 / Motown ♦♦♦

The Commodores made one final stab at regaining R&B glory when Lionel Richie and producer/arranger James Anthony Carmichael both left in the mid-'80s. J.D. Nicholas became their lead singer, and Dennis Lambert assumed production duties. They rebounded temporarily when "Nightshift" leaped out of an otherwise ordinary album to become a Grammy-winning R&B and pop smash. It stayed atop the R&B charts for a month and peaked at number-3 pop. Unfortunately, it was also the end for Thomas McClary, who left the group once the album had run its course. It was their next-to-last hit and basically the end for the band, although they continued for a couple more years. *—Ron Wynn*

United / Oct. 1986 / Polydor ♦♦

Rock Solid / 1988 / Polydor ♦♦

● **The Ultimate Collection** / Mar. 25, 1997 / Motown ♦♦♦♦♦

Widely acknowledged as the top band during their tenure at Motown, the Commodores were one of the bands that kept Berry Gordy's mythical hit machine on top of the commercial R&B game. Especially during a tumultuous period in Motown's history, where artists were changing creative direction (much to Gordy's chagrin) and others were fleeing for other opportunities at labels elsewhere. Amidst all of the drama, the Commodores persevered and made some of the most potent hits of the label's entire catalog. Mapping the evolution of the band primarily from the mid-'70s to mid-'80s, *The Ultimate Collection* spares no expense in thoroughly covering many of the group's high points, free of traditional greatest-hits filler. Funk-heavy stompers are pared next to some of Lionel Richie's most beautifully penned ballads, showcasing the unbelievable depth and production skills the group had during their heyday. Those wishing to get a fuller scope historically of the evolution of the group would be better-served to check out the double-disc *Anthology* set Motown issued in 2001. But for those looking solely for the hits, stay where you are. This is the most comprehensive collection of the Commodores' hits you are likely to find in print. *—Rob Theakston*

Anthology / Sep. 25, 2001 / Motown ♦♦♦♦♦

There were essentially two Commodores—the funk machine of the early '70s that kicked out such classics as "Machine Gun" and "Brick House," then the Lionel Richie-led smooth soulsters that glided to the top of the charts with such cuts as "Easy" and "Three Times a Lady." Motown's 2001 double disc collection *Anthology* very nearly splits those two phases in half, with the funk on the first disc and the balladeering on the second, with the important flaw of "Easy" showing up as the final number of the first disc. This is a bit of a hiccup in sequencing, but if the collection is just seen as sheer music, this satisfies, since it contains all the big hits—both pop crossovers and R&B smashes—along with some lesser-known sides and album tracks. For some, it may be a bit much, but for the serious fan, this is the set to get. *—Stephen Thomas Erlewine*

Con Funk Shun

f. 1972, Memphis, TN, **db.** 1988

Group / Quiet Storm, Funk

Con Funk Shun was formed by high-school classmates Michael Cooper and Louis "Tony" McCall, along with Karl Fuller, Paul "Maceo" Harrell, Dennis Johnson, Cedric Martin, and Danny "Sweet Man" Thomas, when they moved to Memphis together. All of them had been playing together since their high-school days in Vallejo, CA. Felton Pilate, also from Vallejo, joined the group after his band, a local rival, disbanded.

In the early '70s, the group was a backup band for the Soul Children with the name Project Soul. And when they weren't on the road with the Soul Children, they were creatively working with various Stax staff writers. In the mid-'70s, Project Soul made an effort to become a headliner, but they met dead-ends and little success. However, they found good fortune at Audio Dimensions, a Memphis recording studio owned by producer Ted Sturges. Around this time, he group named itself after the title of one of their instrumentals, "Con Funk Shun." During their three-year stint at Audio Dimensions, Sturges, besides owning the studio, was also Con Funk Shun's producer. Their association resulted in the group's first album, *Organized Con Funk Shun*.

As their sound developed, Pilate and Cooper emerged as the primary lead vocalists. Around the time their first album for Crankshaft Productions, Inc. was being recorded, the eighth member, MC and technician Dennis Johnson, left the group to attend seminary in California. By 1976, the group signed to Mercury, where they remained for ten years. Their first hit for Mercury was "Ffun," written by Michael Cooper as a tribute to the R&B/funk band Brick. One of the premiere party funk bands of its time, they also began recording ballads and instrumental tracks by the early '80s. Aside from being the primary musicians on all their albums, Con Funk Shun also contributed to each of their albums as writers, arrangers, and/or producers.

Burnin' Love, the septet's last album with Mercury, was recorded without their long-time musical center, Felton Pilate, who left the group in 1986 to become a successful producer. (Pilate eventually became the musical force behind MC Hammer.) Melvin Carter, a frequent collaborator of Con Funk Shun, joined the group upon Pilate's exit, and that same year Michael Cooper left for a solo career. Con Funk Shun disbanded after their last album with Mercury, but reunited in the '90s, and began performing at festivals and concerts around the world. *—Craig Lytle*

Organized Con Funk Shun / 1973 / Pickwick ♦♦♦

Being that this was Con Funk Shun's first album, it set the stage for what was to come during their reign as a premier R&B group. During this time, the group was under contract to the Memphis-based Crankshaft Productions, Inc. and under the direction of Ted Sturges. The album covers everything from funk to R&B/soul to jazz; "Love in Me" offers a spirited alto sax and melodious guitar rhythms, blended smoothly with the velvet vocals of Michael Cooper and Felton Pilate. "Love in Me" segues into the horn exhibition of "Seascape," featuring Pilate, Karl Fuller and Paul Harrell; the track is jazzy, mellow and soulful, but set in a ballad tempo. However, the featured ballad on the album is "Do You Really Know What Love Is For." Lyrically speaking, the song is a good indication that Con Funk Shun was a young group with maturity destined for success; the track is complemented by a young Felton Pilate, whose tenor nurtures the song graciously. *—Craig Lytle*

The Memphis Sessions / 1973 / 51 West/CBS ♦♦♦

During Con Funk Shun's three-year stay in Memphis, they spent long hours in the studio working with their first producer, Ted Sturges, at his Audio Dimensions Studio. From the hours invested in the recording studio, Con Funk Shun assembled a host of songs recorded in 1973 and appropriately named the collection *The Memphis Sessions*. From this album came the song that reflected the group's name; ironically, it is a rather short composition. The septet recorded the Marvin Gaye classic "You Sure Love to Ball" in the same year Gaye did; Con Funk Shun's rendition is a crafty blend of R&B and jazz featuring Felton Pilate's subtle, flowing falsetto tenor and Michael Cooper's vocal ad lib and jazzy guitar rhythms on the vamp. "The Way It Should Be (Felton's Song)" is a beautiful wedding song paced by piano chords; Pilate expresses compassion in each lyric and delivers a heartfelt performance in the end. On "Another World," Pilate's vocals are complemented by Paul Harrell's soulful saxophone and riffing flute solos, while Cooper lends his scintillating guitar rhythms. *—Craig Lytle*

Con-Funk-Shun / 1976 / Mercury ♦♦♦

This self-titled 1976 release was Con Funk Shun's first album for Mercury/Polygram, and it came at a time when the northern California funk/soul outfit was still obscure—not until 1977's *Secrets* did Con Funk Shun become well-known in the R&B world. Although mildly uneven and not in a class with subsequent gems like *Secrets* and *Candy*, *Con-Funk-Shun* isn't a bad album. In 1976, the band still had some growing and developing to do. But it did have a recognizable sound—which is certainly a plus—and one hears some potential on tracks that range from the snappy "Sure Feels Good to Me" and the Gamble & Huff-influenced "Nothing to Lose By Trying" to the glossy disco instrumental, "Foley Park." As a rule, Con Funk Shun wasn't a disco band—it was a funk/soul band that branched out into urban contemporary in the 1980s. But "Foley Park" is the type of disco number that would have worked for the Crown Heights Affair or T-Connection. Overall, this LP's uptempo funk and dance offerings are decent (if less than remarkable), and so are Northern soul-style ballads like "Never Be the Same" and "Another World." But here's the thing: Con Funk Shun's members had way too much talent to settle for merely decent. Felton Pilate and his colleagues needed to take it to the next level—both creatively and commercially—and they did exactly that the following year. With 1977's *Secrets*, Con Funk Shun enjoyed its big commercial breakthrough and made the transition from decent to excellent. You might say that this out of print LP was the calm before the storm. Although not among Con Funk Shun's essential releases and not recommended to casual listeners, this record is interesting if you're among the funksters' hardcore fans. *—Alex Henderson*

Secrets / 1977 / Mercury ♦♦♦
Con Funk Shun's second album for Phonogram/Mercury, *Secrets* catapulted the group to national acclaim. The Vallejo, CA, natives presented a balance of songs featuring the smash single "Ffun," which hit the top of the R&B charts, and also made the pop Top 40. That single was followed by "Confunkshunizeya"; with a catchy hook and swinging horns, it peaked at number 31. With the success of these two singles, the septet's name became popular among R&B lovers. Even though there were just two singles that charted from this album, any one of the tracks from this diverse collection could have easily made it to the charts. The title track is a laid-back, midtempo composition; "Indian Summer Love" is an uptempo instrumental utilizing the synthesizer technology of its day. Also, there are a few mellow compositions on this album, the first being "Who Has the Time," a social indictment of the public-at-large featuring Felton Pilate's resonating tenor. "Tears in My Eyes" showcases Pilate and Michael Cooper in an emotionally charged lyric. And "I'll Set You Out O.K." highlights Cooper's tenor and Pilate's falsetto in unison, rounded out by Paul Harrell's jazzy saxophone. *—Craig Lytle*

Loveshine / 1978 / Mercury ♦♦♦
With some endearingly mellow grooves, CA's Con Funk Shun continued to capitalize on their easy blend of soulful funk and disco across 1978's *Loveshine*. The band was enjoying their ascendancy to the spotlight on the back of their number one hit "Ffun," and used that momentum to power this new LP into the Top 40. Leaning more toward disco-inflected soul than the more classic jazzed funk of their earlier material, yet retaining the funky backbeat, Con Funk Shun swaggered through a slick set punctuated by the hits "So Easy" and "Shake and Dance With Me." Elsewhere, the catchy horn-heavy strains of "When the Feeling's Right" were proof that the band was not going to be any flash in the pan—their quiet storm was here to stay. The contrasting style of the traditional ballad "I Think I Found the Answer," meanwhile, is a fine highlight of the band's overall range, although they slip with the middle of the road "Wanna Be There." With a plethora of instrumentation to complete the picture, including guest percussion from Sheila Escovedo, who would later emerge as the Prince protégée Sheila E., *Loveshine* is a gem of its era. And while purists may best love their early-'70s Soul Children *Wattstax*-era material, *Loveshine* kicked off their next incarnation in style, and gave the band the momentum that kept them firmly in the charts for nearly a decade. *—Amy Hanson*

Candy / 1979 / Mercury ♦♦♦♦
What a difference a few years can make. When Con Funk Shun joined the Mercury/Polygram roster with a self-titled LP in 1976, the Northern Californians were still finding their way. They weren't well known, and despite their tremendous potential, they had yet to make the transition from decent to excellent. But when *Candy* came out in 1979, Con Funk Shun had come to be regarded as funk royalty—and deservedly so. *Candy*, which was the band's fourth album for Mercury, is a gem. This LP contains some excellent love songs; "Not Ready" and the hit single "Let Me Put Love on Your Mind" are fine examples of smooth, romantic '70s soul ballads. But Con Funk Shun was best known for hard, tough, gutsy funk, and there is plenty of that on *Candy* (which was co-produced by Skip Scarborough). Some people no doubt bought *Candy* after hearing "Let Me Put Love on Your Mind" on the radio, but most Con Funk Shun fans acquired the record because of sweaty funk jams like "Chase Me," "Main Slice," "Da Lady," and the title song. From the expressive lead vocals of Michael Cooper and Cedric Martin to Con Funk Shun's killer horn section, all of the pieces fall into place nicely on *Candy*. By the mid-'80s, Con Funk Shun had gone high-tech—in other words, more synthesizers and drum machines and fewer horns. But in 1979, horn-driven funk bands were still in vogue in the R&B world, and Con Funk Shun was a perfect example of one. Synthesizers were being used in soul and funk, although R&B had yet to go totally electronic. *Candy* went down in history as one of Con Funk Shun's best albums, and it is isn't hard to understand why. *—Alex Henderson*

Spirit of Love / 1980 / Mercury ♦♦♦
Continuing their association with veteran producer Skip Scarborough and riding high on the success of their prior albums, Con Funk Shun maintains that stride on this album with the funk/dance track "Got to Be Enough." With an energized introduction incorporating their trademark horns, Michael Cooper storms through the verses, while Felton Pilate accentuates the chorus with his high-flying falsetto. Penned by Cooper and Pilate, the single peaked on the *Billboard* R&B charts at number eight after an 18-week run. The credible, yet less popular dance track "Happy Face" slipped into the *Billboard* R&B Top 100 Singles chart at number 87. On a more serene note, they followed that single up with "By Your Side," a dulcet, easy flowing composition led by Pilate's consoling vocals, peaking at number 27 on the *Billboard* R&B charts. "All Up to You," a momentum building song, and "Honey Wild," did not grace the charts, although they are two splendid ballads. Both songs are complemented by Pilate's vocal creativity. This album exceeded sales of 500,000. *—Craig Lytle*

Touch / 1980 / Mercury ♦♦♦
This album starts off with the funk groove "Too Tight," which peaked at number eight on the *Billboard* R&B charts. Complemented by the swinging horn intro, the lyrics and the vocals are an enticement to the dancefloor. It's followed by another dance-flavored track, "Lady's Wild," which features a catchy hook and a party ad lib. Two mellowed-out numbers in "Give Your Love to Me" and "Can't Say Goodbye" never made the charts. The former offers jazzy interlude solos by Michael Cooper (rhythm guitar) and Felton Pilate (trombone), and the latter is a quiet storm favorite. *—Craig Lytle*

Con Funk Shun 7 / 1981 / Mercury ♦♦♦
Con Funk Shun entitled this album *Con Funk Shun 7* to commemorate the seven members in the group and to acknowledge that the number seven represents renaissance—rebirth, the emergence of something new. The featured track is the R&B Top 20 hit "Bad Lady," with Michael Cooper hovering over the track with his husky tenor. The album has a horde of songs that could have received airplay and chart action. Specifically, "Promise You Love" is a song that transcends several genres of music. It's a ballad that begins with a bass-driven intro, which segues into a bluesy pre-verse rhythm and ultimately settles down into a vintage R&B groove. The track features Michael Cooper and Felton Pilate, with Cooper adding a passionate monologue ad lib in the vamp. But this album was fueled by the the ballad "Straight from the Heart." The song speaks for itself. It's beautifully written and arranged, led by Felton Pilate's supplicating falsetto and Michael Cooper's compassionate tenor. Though the single was not a mega seller and was also preceded by "(Let Me Put) Love on Your Mind" from a previous album, it set the stage for a string of unreleased and uncharted ballads to follow. Moreover, the group experimented with a little rock on the track "California One," featuring Pilate on vocals and his rock-flavored electric guitar. *—Craig Lytle*

To the Max / 1983 / Mercury ♦♦♦

Fever / 1984 / Mercury ♦♦♦

Electric Lady / 1985 / Mercury ♦♦♦

Burnin' Love / 1988 / Mercury ♦♦

● **The Best of Con Funk Shun** / 1993 / Mercury ♦♦♦♦
Con Funk Shun's brand of funk was polished with spirited horns, titillating guitar rhythms and ear-pleasing vocals. These 17 tracks encompass the group's tenure at Mercury beginning with their first charted single "Sho' Feels Good to Me," and also including six Top Ten singles, three Top 20 singles and a horde of Top 30 hits. Of the many gems found on this compilation album, two that never charted are "Love's Train" and "All Up to You," both Quiet Storm classics. Also included in this package are liner notes by Harry Weinger, chronicling the reign of funk the self-contained septet had on the music industry. All numbers feature the lead vocals of Felton Pilate and Michael Cooper. *—Craig Lytle*

The Best of Con Funk Shun, Vol. 2 / May 21, 1996 / Mercury ♦♦♦
This features a mix of LP cuts and moderate-to-big R&B hits, the most famous of those being the novelty "Electric Lady," and "Too Tight" (presented here in an extended version). *—Richie Unterberger*

Ballads Collection / May 19, 1998 / Mercury ♦♦♦♦
Michael Cooper and Felton Pilate compiled *The Ballads Collection*, a selection of 12 romantic numbers the group have recorded over the years. The collection not only features singles like "(Let Me Put) Love on Your Mind" and "Baby I'm Hooked (Right Into Your Love)," it also has album tracks, making it an ideal choice for any listener looking for a romantic Con Funk Shun collection. *—Stephen Thomas Erlewine*

Arthur Conley

b. Jan. 4, 1946, Atlanta, GA
Vocals, Horn / Soul, Deep Soul, Southern Soul
A protégé of Otis Redding and, like Redding, a musical disciple of Sam Cooke, Conley co-wrote (with Redding) and sang "Sweet Soul Music," one of the true anthems of the '60s. Based on Cooke's "Yeah, Man," the record was sweet and hot at the same time, with a readily identifiable horn intro and lyrics that immortalized the soul stars of the day. Conley, although signed to Atco, toured overseas with the Stax/Volt Revue and later joined the Soul Clan with Atlantic labelmates Wilson Pickett, Solomon Burke, Don Covay, Ben E. King, and Joe Tex. He has lived in Holland for a number of years, where he appeared on television and radio programs and runs an independent record label. *—Christine Ohlman*

Sweet Soul Music / 1967 / Atco ♦♦♦♦♦
The title track is a real killer! Conley sounds young but assured, and the Otis Redding production is solid throughout. Includes "Let Nothing Separate Us" and "I Can't Stop." *—Christine Ohlman*

Shake Rattle & Roll / 1967 / Atco ♦♦♦

Soul Directions / 1968 / Atco ♦♦♦

More Sweet Soul / 1969 / Atco ♦♦♦♦♦
This wasn't an album in the classic sense but a collection of singles, as were many soul LPs in the '60s. But Conley's exuberance and spirit are so infectious that it overcomes the fact that much of this is second-level soul at best and clichéd filler at worst. *—Ron Wynn*

● **Sweet Soul Music: The Best of Arthur Conley** / 1995 / Ichiban/Soul Classics ♦♦♦♦♦
Conley was ultimately a minor soul performer, but he made his share of decent records. Aside from "Sweet Soul Music," most of them have been inaccessible until this 22-song compilation of 1965-1970 material. There's no getting around the fact that "Sweet Soul

Music" towers above his other efforts, but Conley was a decent exponent of Southern soul. This includes all seven of his chart singles, cuts from several albums, and half a dozen songs from non-LP singles. Conley sometimes sounded like a watered-down Otis Redding (particularly in his later years), and some of his later singles were trendy and slight (like "Aunt Dora's Love Soul Shack" and the cover of "Ob-La-Di, Ob-La-Da"). There are some good unheralded performances here, though, particularly on the pre-"Sweet Soul Music" singles; Conley emotes more heavily than would be his wont in later times, aided by material supplied by ace songwriters Dan Penn and Spooner Oldham. *—Richie Unterberger*

Norman Connors

b. Mar. 1, 1947, Philadelphia, PA

Drums, Producer, Leader / Smooth Jazz, Quiet Storm, Crossover Jazz, Jazz-Funk, Urban, Post-Bop, Fusion

Like Roy Ayers, George Benson, and Patrice Rushen, Norman Connors is best known for his major R&B hits, but started out as a jazz improviser. The drummer/composer was born and raised in Philadelphia, where he lived in the same neighborhood as Bill Cosby and became interested in jazz when he was only a child. As a kid in elementary school, Connors was exposed to jazz extensively thanks to such schoolmates as drummer Lex Humphries and the younger brother of bassist and Jazz Messenger-to-be Spanky DeBrest. Connors was in junior high when he began sneaking into jazz clubs and sat in for Elvin Jones at a John Coltrane gig. At 13, he first got to meet his idol, Miles Davis, and started expressing his admiration for the famous trumpeter by dressing like him. Connors went on to study music at Philly's Temple University and the Juilliard School of Music in New York. Gigs with Jackie McLean, Jack McDuff and Sam Rivers followed, and he was first recorded as a sideman when Archie Shepp employed him on his 1967 Impulse! session *Magic of JuJu*.

After touring with Pharoah Sanders and playing on several of his albums, Connors signed with Buddah's Cobblestone label in 1972 and recorded his first album as a leader, *Dance of Magic*. A few more jazz-oriented Cobblestone and Buddah dates followed, and it was in 1975 that Connors made R&B his main priority with *Saturday Night Special* (which included the number-ten soul hit "Valentine Love"). The rest of the 1970s found Connors featuring R&B singers prominently (including Michael Henderson, Jean Carn, and the late Phyllis Hyman) and scoring such R&B hits as "We Both Need Each Other," "Once I've Been There," and the lovely "You Are My Starship." Connors, who signed with Arista in 1977, wasn't as popular or as visible in the 1980s, although, in the 1990s, he would make a comeback by signing with Motown's MoJazz label and focusing on both urban contemporary and crossover. *—Alex Henderson*

Dance of Magic / Mar. 1973 / Sequel ✦✦✦✦

Dark of Light / 1973 / Buddah ✦✦✦

This is in the stone groove of earlier Connors delights—New York club music, the nexus where disco and jazz collided and gave birth to a brassy sort of funk. Players abound here: Herbie Hancock, Cecil McBee, Gary Bartz, and Stanley Clarke, to name but a few. Soon after this, Connors had some hits and started making records he figured his "public" wanted to hear. *—Rob Ferrier*

Slewfoot / Apr. 1975 / Kama Sutra/Buddah ✦✦✦

1975's *Slewfoot* continues Norman Connors' diversification into jazz-funk and brassy R&B with mostly positive results. Surrounded as usual by an all-star personnel—including but not limited to vocalist Jean Carn, bassist Ron Carter, pianist Lonnie Liston Smith, tenor saxophonist Gary Bartz, horn player Eddie Henderson, and flutist Hubert Eaves III—Connors tears through a mostly hard-driving set of songs. Carlos Garnett's "Mother of the Future" leads off the album as a frenetic jazz-funk workout and offers each instrumentalist a chance to flex muscles; Carn is particularly hot, while Elmer Gibson's electric piano runs highlight the latter half of the song. Henderson's "Dreams" and a gorgeous reworking of Coltrane's "Welcome" (Carn takes another spotlight) are the only reprieves from the upbeat slant. The remainder is dotted with decent but slightly innocuous funk and fusion instrumentals that are occasionally punctuated by bold horn charts (Richard Clay's "Back on the Street," Elmer Gibson's "Chuka," Connors' "Jump Street"). Not one of Connors' best, but it does have its moments. *—Andy Kellman*

Saturday Night Special / Feb. 1976 / Sequel ✦✦✦

Connors' strong *Saturday Night Special* is most notable for "Valentine Love," a Top Ten black singles hit. The romantic ballad, a duet between Michael Henderson and Jean Carn, arrived in time for February 14 and also peaked on the Top 100 of the pop chart. One can't help but feel that the whole LP is truly Carn's show, as she contributes her rich voice to a number of stylistically varied numbers. Whether belting out in front of industrial-strength funk fusion ("Saturday Night Special"; watch out for Reggie Lucas' needling guitar solo here), sliding through breezy jazz (a rendition of Jobim's "Dindi"), or slipping into some ethereal colorings (a take on Herbie Hancock's "Maiden Voyage"), Carn proves herself to be an extremely versatile vocalist, equally adept with each approach. "Skin Diver," penned by Harry "We Live in Brooklyn, Baby" Whitaker and Dwight Carson, is the best of the lot—a slowly simmering number that features Carn at her soaring best. Hancock contributes piano to "Kwasi," a painfully brief fusion cut that begins with a two-minute Connors drum solo and ends after another two minutes, just when it begins to really cook. *—Andy Kellman*

You Are My Starship / 1977 / Buddah ✦✦✦

Early on, Connors didn't have the accolades bestowed on contemporaries like Billy Cobham or Tony Williams. Connors simply didn't possess their chops in the jazz idiom. But in a genre closer to R&B, and as an assembler of talent, Connors was in a league all his own. *Slewfoot* provided Connors all he needed to do in the "serious" vein, with tracks like "Mother of the Future." *You Are My Starship* has the sound of previous albums coming to fruition. The atmospheric title track represents a classic in the genre, with Michael Henderson's smooth vocals and bass playing, plus a solo on soprano sax by Gary Bartz. Connors does a masterful, slowed-down remake of the Stylistics' "Betcha By Golly Wow" with Phillis Hyman's bittersweet and romantic vocal. Hyman and Henderson duet on "We Both Need Each Other," and it shows genuine sexual chemistry between the two. Even though this was released in 1976, Connors was still having difficulties letting go of the old sound, as the Latin-styled but aimless "Just Imagine" proved. Connors put a good gloss on the often-recondite "The Creator Has a Master Plan (Peace)." *You Are My Starship* has some great work, and it's only one or two songs away from being truly essential. *—Jason Elias*

Romantic Journey / 1977 / Buddah ✦✦✦

When Norman Connors made the transition from jazz albums to commercially successful R&B-oriented dates, the drummer found himself being lambasted repeatedly in jazz press (something Roy Ayers, Patrice Rushen, George Duke and George Benson could also relate to). Myopic jazz critics trashed *Romantic Journey* simply because it contains so much R&B/pop, as opposed to judging its merits as an R&B/pop-oriented album. Though not as strong as its predecessor, *You Are My Starship*, this decent offering has its strong points, including Philip Mitchell's vocal on the haunting "Destination Moon" and Eleanore Mills' performance on a likable cover of the Stylistics' "You Are Everything." Although R&B/pop is dominant, *Romantic Journey* does have two noteworthy jazz instrumentals—the Return to Forever-influenced title song and an interpretation of Pharoah Sanders' "Thembi." Connors' ultra-slick version of Gato Barbieri's "Last Tango In Paris" is a little too Muzak-like and sounds like producer Creed Taylor at his most calculated, but *Journey*'s strengths outweigh its weaknesses. *—Alex Henderson*

This Is Your Life / 1978 / Buddah ✦✦✦✦

The follow-up to the successful *Romantic Journey*, *This Is Your Life* was Connors' first album for Arista and found him doing the same great, intelligent music that had placed him at the top of the list of true jazz/R&B innovators. His self-production debut, the record was done in the same style of his high-selling late-'70s efforts. Although Connors was highly regarded as a sideman with Pharoah Sanders, among others, jazz/R&B was definitely his metier. The title track is a delicate rendering of a contemplative Jimmy Webb tune, powered by an emotional vocal from Eleanor Mills. As a producer, Connors was unabashed about his R&B skills and the execution comes across more confident and defined. The melodic "Say You Love Me" has Connors stepping out on lead vocals; unlike many other jazz artists turned singers, Connors' lack of great pipes provided a good juxtaposition to flawless backing track (having Jean Carn on backing vocals didn't hurt either). *This Is Your Life*, more than any of his albums of the time, skillfully balanced his R&B and jazz offerings. The cover of Herbie Hancock's "Butterfly" has a phenomenal and dramatic arrangement with vocals from Mills and James Robinson. The last track, "The Creator," doesn't fare half as well but it's not enough to dim the virtues of this effort. *This Is Your Life* is not only one of Connors' strongest, but also one of the genre's best. *—Jason Elias*

Invitation / 1979 / Buddah ✦✦

Take It to the Limit / 1980 / BMG ✦✦✦

Drummer and stellar lineup assembler Norman Connors landed on Arista for *Take It to the Limit*, an album that continued the man's embrace of smooth R&B and gradual abandonment of jazz. The roster here is extremely lengthy; not only is there a group numbering at about a dozen that's dubbed the Starship Orchestra, but there's well over 30 *other* (!) guests who pop in and out of the mix in various capacities. Both the title track (featuring Adaritha on vocals) and "Melancholy Fire" (Glenn Jones) rightfully cracked the Top 30 of the black singles chart, but a small clutch of other gems deserved similar achievements. "I Don't Need Nobody Else," sung by Al Johnson (arranger and conductor of half the album's cuts), sparkles brightly, while Adaritha's "Justify" is just as gorgeous as the album's hit singles. One minor disappointment is Leon Ware's set-closing "Everywhere Inside of Me," which falls toward the sappy side. One major dud is a plonking cover of Steely Dan's "Black Cow," which has inexplicably shown up on a number of Connors anthologies. Six out of eight ain't bad by any stretch. *—Andy Kellman*

Mr. C / 1981 / Arista ✦✦✦

Mr. C saw Norman Connors descend from chart action a little too soon, as it boasts a handful of cuts that should've performed well. Only "She's Gone," the leadoff number featuring Connors on vocals, registered on the black singles chart. Like the remainder of the record's first side, "She's Gone" sees Connors moving into synthesized sounds and rhythm programming—if he hadn't lost the jazz purists through his jazz-funk and fusion cuts of the mid- to late '70s, they were surely completely gone after hearing this material. Suffice to say, this album has more in common with Cameo and D Train than Sam Rivers and John Coltrane. The first half is a straight-up party record, full of brisk arrangements and tugging melodic hooks. Despite the heavy use of electronics, this record employed another laundry list of guest musicians, including Marion Meadows, Pee Wee Ford, and Paulinho Da Costa. Most of these people are present on the album's second side, which moves back into the jazzy, smooth R&B favored by Connors on albums like *This Is Your Life* and *Take It to the Limit*. Lovers of both electrified and lush early-'80s R&B should not overlook this one. *—Andy Kellman*

Passion / 1988 / Capitol ✦✦

Saturday Night Special/You Are My Starship / 1992 / Sequel ✦✦✦

Remember Who You Are / 1993 / Motown ✦✦✦✦

Norman Connors' first set since 1988's successful *Passion*, *Remember Who You Are* has the drummer/composer not only successfully updating his trademark sound but also broadening his production skills. This effort is his first for MoJazz, distributed by Motown. Connors does an equal amount of originals and covers throughout the recording. He reunites with one of his best vocalists, Phyllis Hyman, for the poignant and well-orchestrated title track. "You and I," featuring a great vocal from Angela Bofill, is reminiscent of Connors' classic sound and melodic changes. Not all of the covers work, though. Spencer Harrison hams it up on the always tricky "Lush Life," but he makes up for it on the solid cover of "A Song for You." The biggest surprise here is Connors' take on Herbie Hancock's "Tell Me a Bedtime Story"—the track features a charismatic, full-bodied lead from Eve Cornelious, who also co-wrote the added lyrics. The production and arrangement stay true to the song's whimsical nature, and an ultrasmooth acoustic piano solo from Patrice Rushen is featured. There is also some good instrumental work on *Remember Who You Are*. The moody and atmospheric "Only When She Cries" has a keyboard solo from Jacques Burvick and fine tenor sax from Marion Meadows. John Coltrane's classic "Naima" gets the first-class treatment. A few of the tracks in the contemporary jazz/R&B vein, "I Can't Wait Till I See You Again" and "Just Like This" (featuring Denise Stewart), are skilled enough not to be disconcerting. *Remember Who You Are* shows Connors truly on his game; the album is another one of his fulfilling efforts. *—Jason Elias*

Very Best of Norman Connors / 1998 / BMG ✦✦✦✦
Throughout the latter half of the '70s and the early '80s, drummer Norman Connors was rather successful as a crossover solo artist who slowly shed his jazz roots to the point where he was making electronics-heavy, dancefloor-aimed R&B. He's often regarded as having been more skilled at assembling guest lineups than anything else, and by judging the roster of talent that adorned those records, it's hard to disagree with that observation. Connors never produced a bona fide masterpiece, but each album he released during the period covered by *The Very Best of Norman Connors* presented at least a handful of moments that ranged from good to phenomenal. This disc focuses on the cuts that impacted the black singles chart, while throwing in some choice album selections and a couple hits from Connors' brainchild, Aquarian Dream. It provides a good introduction to newcomers, but its selection is questionable with some of the non-singles. Despite this, it's one of the better anthologies of the man's work available. *—Andy Kellman*

● **The Best of Norman Connors: Melancholy Fire** / Apr. 27, 1999 / Razor & Tie ✦✦✦✦
This excellent 1999 set is an overview of drummer and producer Connors' 1975-1988 work. During the mid-'70s to the '80s he was leader of the fusion of jazz and R&B during its most influential and successful era. Unlike other compilations on similar artists, *The Best of Norman Connors: Melancholy Fire* centers on what made Connors such a popular and enduring artist and zeroes in on his skill as a bandleader and a hitmaker. After the relative failure of his early '70s efforts, Connors finally attained the jazz/R&B mix that suited him best. Tracks like "You Are My Starship," "Valentine Love," and "Betcha by Golly Wow" with its poignant reading from Phyllis Hyman, created the blueprint for Connors' sophisticated and emotional productions. Although most are familiar with Jean Carn, Phyllis Hyman, the collection also highlights many other of Connors' vocalists. Eleanor Mills' soulful and precise vocals can be heard on the flawless cover of Jimmy Webb's "This Is Your Life" and the funky and refined "Wouldn't You Like to See." By the late '70s, and perhaps due to lessened jazz content, Connors' hitmaking acumen began to wane. Tracks like "Invitation" and "Handle Me Gently" lack the necessary jazz quotient and challenging melodic sense of his earlier work. The masterful 1980 title track, featuring Glenn Jones, is more in line with Connors' production gifts. This album is one of a handful of compilations that doesn't attempt to rewrite history with unreleased tracks and failed experiments. This set is a necessity for Connors fans and lovers of intelligent jazz and R&B. *—Jason Elias*

June Conquest

b. Chicago, IL
Vocals / Soul
June Conquest is both an extraordinary, and extraordinarily (and undeservedly) obscure soul singer. During the early '60s, she released a pair of singles, "Almost Persuaded" under her own name, and a duet with a man known only as the Demon on "The Only Way to Correct a Mistake (Is to Make One)." She was based in Houston around the time of the latter record, which, like its predecessor, failed to chart, and have since become choice collector's items. By 1966, Conquest was based in Chicago and signed to Curtis Mayfield's short-lived Windy C label, where she only cut one single, "Take Care." Mayfield obviously had a lot of faith in her ability, signing her to Curtom when he organized the company in 1968. Her single "What's This I See" was the first record ever issued by the new label and became a serious local hit in Chicago. Despite this encouraging start, however, Conquest's solo recording career never took off.

She next appeared a year later in a duet setting. The idea had been to team Conquest with Sam Cooke's brother L.C. Cook, who was a pretty formidable soul singer in his own right, but he didn't make the sessions. Instead, Donny Hathaway, who had never before cut records outside the setting of the Mayfield Singers or as a backup singer on various Windy C and Curtom sides, stepped in. It was the start of an auspicious career, but not for Conquest. Donny & June, as they were billed, didn't tear the charts up with "I Thank You," "Just Another Reason," or their remake of "What's This I See," but the sound they got anticipated Hathaway's subsequent celebrated duets with Roberta Flack. Indeed, the single "I Thank You," which went almost unnoticed in 1969, finally came into its own three years later, reaching number 41 on the R&B listings and number-94 pop when it was reissued in the wake of Hathaway's success with Flack. It wasn't enough to rescue Conquest's recording career, however; she never cut another record and later gave up singing. *—Bruce Eder*

The Continental IV

f. Pennsylvania
Group / Soul
The Continental IV were a beloved soul quartet of the early '70s, and among the finest units featuring the "sweet" falsetto sound. Lead Freddie Kelly didn't get either the plaudits or hits of the Delfonics' William Hart, Blue Magic's Ted Mills, the Moments' Harry Ray, or the Stylistics' Russell Tompkins Jr., but he had an equally arresting, ethereal falsetto. Kelly, Ronnie and Larry McGregor, and Anthony Burke recorded for the Jay Walking label. Their 1971 single "Day By Day (Every Minute of the Hour)" remains a ballad favorite, though it only reached number 19 on the soul charts. Latter-day soul vocalist Chuck Stanley covered it in the late '80s. The Continental IV's singles have been reissued on a Collectables CD, *Dream World*. *—Ron Wynn*

● **Dream World** / 1989 / Collectables ✦✦✦✦✦
Ten singles cut by the smooth PA-based soul group for Jay Walking Records, produced by Bobby Martin. The best known song here is "Day By Day (Every Minute of the Hour)," which was a Top 20 R&B hit during the summer of 1971, and "I Don't Have You," which had earlier scraped the Top 50 in R&B. The sounds here are surprisingly sophisticated, not just in the singing but the backing arrangements, which include a beautiful extended sax and volume pedal guitar section on "Nite Moods." Freddie Kelly's falsetto lead and Anthony Burke's rich baritone form an exquisite pairing in the opening bars "I Don't Have You Baby," and it's difficult to understand overall how a group like this could not have scored more hits, except perhaps that they had the bad fortune to be cutting music in Philadelphia just when the city was filled with talented R&B groups, all making records at exactly the same time. *—Bruce Eder*

The Contours

f. 1958, Detroit, MI
Group / Frat Rock, Motown, R&B, Soul
The Contours are widely remembered for their 1962 smash "Do You Love Me?," one of the early hits that helped put Motown on the map. Yet they aren't always associated with their contribution to the label; they were one of the roughest, hardest R&B groups Berry Gordy ever signed, and their sound simply didn't resemble the smooth, sophisticated blueprint that later became Motown's trademark. Nor did their stage presence; in contrast to the slick choreography and wardrobe of Motown's signature artists, the Contours were all wild, irrepressible energy, leaping and sliding all over the stage and even doing the splits. As a result, they fell out of favor once Motown got its crossover-friendly hit factory up and running, and never duplicated the success of their first hit.

Formed in Detroit in 1958, the Contours originally began life as a quartet called the Blenders. Lead singer Billy Gordon, Billy Hogg, Sylvester Potts, and Joe Billingslea were soon joined by Hubert Johnson, a cousin of the legendary Jackie Wilson, as well as guitarist Huey Davis. Changing their name to the Contours, the group landed an audition with Berry Gordy's fledgling Motown label. Gordy was not impressed and told them to try again in a year, and they enlisted Jackie Wilson's aid in honing their act. Wilson personally recommended the group to Gordy, who finally relented and signed them up in 1961. The Contours' first single "Whole Lotta Woman" sank without a trace, and Gordy nearly dropped them until Wilson once again interceded on their behalf. The move paid off handsomely when Gordy offered them a chance to cut "Do You Love Me?," a song originally intended for the Temptations, who couldn't quite nail down the rough and rowdy feel Gordy wanted. Released in 1962, "Do You Love Me?" zoomed straight to the top of the R&B charts in just a few short weeks, peaking at number three on the pop side.

Although the Contours were riding high thanks to their hit and their exciting live act, they found the momentum difficult to maintain. They were able to score a follow-up hit, "Shake Sherrie," in 1963, and ran off a string of R&B Top 40 singles over 1965-1966: "Can You Jerk Like Me?," the Top Ten "The Day When She Needed Me," the Smokey Robinson-penned "First I Look at the Purse," and "Just a Little Misunderstanding." Despite the often high quality of those singles, the Contours simply weren't getting the attention—either from the label or the public—that Motown's top stars were, and their sound was more of an anomaly at Hitsville than ever. By this time, the original quintet was no longer intact; new members included Joe Stubbs, brother of the Four Tops' Levi Stubbs, and Dennis Edwards, who went on to replace David Ruffin in the Temptations.

The Contours had their last charting single in 1967 with "It's So Hard Being a Loser"; Billingslea and Potts subsequently led versions of the group on the oldies circuit during the '70s and '80s. Sadly, Johnson committed suicide in 1981, and wasn't around to witness the 1988 revival of "Do You Love Me?" thanks to the wildly popular film *Dirty Dancing*. Billingslea, Potts, and their new cohorts hit the oldies circuit with renewed vigor, and also cut the album *Running in Circles* for U.K. Motown revivalist Ian Levine's Motorcity label in 1990. Stubbs passed away in 1998, and guitarist Davis did likewise in 2002. *—Steve Huey*

Do You Love Me / 1962 / Motown ✦✦✦
The first LP released on Gordy Records is also the Contours' first and only regular album release on Motown; a later collection also titled *Do You Love Me* was a greatest-hits compilation. This is worth a few bucks if you can find a copy. Three cuts were released on the Motown label before they were switched to Gordy ("The Stretch," "Funny," and "Whole Lotta Woman"); all stiffed. On Gordy, the group enjoyed their biggest hit the first time out in "Do You Love Me." "You Better Get In Line," a slick dance number, died as the flip of "Shake Sherrie." A lively "You Must Be Love" has Billy Gordon swapping leads with Joe Billingslea. "Shake Sherrie" has a looping beat, a wandering baritone sax, and incredulous vocals from Gordon, Billingslea, Sylvester Potts, Billy Hogg, and Hubert Johnson. The rest suffer from a lack of identity; neither the group nor Motown had defined their sound when these were cut. *—Andrew Hamilton*

The Very Best / Feb. 20, 1996 / Hot Productions ✦
Drop any image you have of the Contours' Motown sound or this "very best" CD—including late-period recordings for Ian Levine's Motorcity label—will be that much more disappointing. The two original members, Sylvester Potts and Joe Billingslea, played minor roles in regards to lead singing for the original group, so their presence doesn't authenticate the sound. Contouring with Potts and Billingslea are Darryl Nunlee, Arthur Hinson, and Charles Davis. Listening to this will have you longing for some good handclaps, a definitive bass, a kicking drummer, and a sense of urgency in the singers. *—Andrew Hamilton*

- **The Very Best of the Contours** / Mar. 23, 1999 / Motown ♦♦♦♦

The first CD best-of compilation for the Contours actually takes the exact same ten tracks that were available on the *Do You Love Me* album and adds five more, most of which are of secondary interest. Regardless, it's a decent overview of a minor but good Motown act. "Do You Love Me" will always be their calling card, but "Shake Sherrie," "First I Look at the Purse," "It Must Be Love" and "Can You Do It" are well worth hearing for anyone who wants to hear the Motown sound at its rawest and most raucous. Smokey Robinson's "That Day When She Needed Me" and the 1961 doo wop single "Funny" show an unexpectedly mellow side of the group. The 1966-1967 sides, "Just a Little Misunderstanding" and "It's So Hard Being a Loser" find them being steered toward a slicker, Temptations-like direction; indeed, future Temp, Dennis Edwards, sings lead on the latter cut. *—Richie Unterberger*

A New Direction / Apr. 25, 2000 / Orchard ♦♦

The Controllers

f. 1965, Fairfield, AL
Group / Urban, Soul
Alabama soul belters the Controllers began as the Epics in 1965. They became the Soul Controllers in 1970, and finally the Controllers. Reginald and Larry McArthur, Lenard Brown, and Ricky Lewis formed the lineup, and were especially effective on heartache ballads, though they also did competent uptempo dance numbers. They relocated to Miami in the late '70s and began recording for Juana. Frederick Knight produced some of their material, including the 1977 debut LP *Somebody's Gotta Win, Somebody's Gotta Lose.* They enjoyed moderate success with other Juana singles and LPs, though both "Heaven Is Only One Step Away" and "We Don't" were outstanding performances. They moved to MCA in 1984. Stevie Wonder made a guest appearance on harmonica for their first MCA single, "Crushed," which reached number 30 on the R&B charts. Their biggest MCA hit was "Stay," which peaked at number 12 in 1986. They moved to Capitol in 1988, issuing *Just in Time* that year. *—Ron Wynn*

- **In Control** / 1977 / Collectables ♦♦♦♦

The Controllers were among the most underrated and overlooked '70s soul groups. They didn't generate nearly as much publicity or have as much crossover success as fellow AL performers the Commodores, but their slow songs were far more earthy and explosive. Their reflective "Somebody's Gotta Win," eloquently and passionately delivered by lead singer Reginald McArthur, stands tall amongst the set's more Southern-flavored offerings. This album was a solid hit with R&B and Southern soul audiences, and still retains plenty of power. Collectables later reissued this album as part of their *Golden Classics* series. *—Ron Wynn & Andrew Hamilton*

For the Love of My Woman / 1980 / MCA ♦♦♦

Some marvelous deep soul and above-average uptempo numbers from the sorely overlooked Controllers. Their MCA albums languished due to poor promotion, but they deserved a much better fate. This had some excellent love tunes, notably "My Secret Fantasy" and "Sleeping Alone." But as they did with Little Milton and Bobby "Blue" Bland, MCA simply couldn't or wouldn't put enough muscle behind the group's songs. *—Ron Wynn*

Stay / 1986 / MCA ♦♦♦

Just in Time / 1989 / Capitol ♦♦♦

Clear View / Jul. 22, 1997 / Malaco ♦♦♦

L.C. Cook

Vocals, Songwriter / Soul, R&B, Black Gospel
The younger brother of Sam Cooke, L.C. Cook was also a singer, although he achieved his greatest prominence on paper, as a songwriter, thanks to his more famous brother's tangled contractual relationships. L.C. Cook (the "e" being absent from the family's spelling of the name) was born two years after Sam, the fifth of ten children of the Rev. Charles Cook and his wife Annie May. The entire family was musical, steeped in gospel, and while Sam was the most obvious potential star, L.C. was also a budding singer while still a young boy. In the late '30s, Sam organized a group called the Singing Children with two of his sisters, which L.C. later joined to make a gospel quartet. The two sang together in the family quintet the Singing Children, and later in the Nobleairs, and achieved some success together in the late '40s as members of the Highway Q.C.'s. They stopped singing together when L.C.'s older brother was recruited into the ranks of the Soul Stirrers in 1951.

In 1956, Cook joined the Chicago-based R&B vocal group the Magnificents, which had been formed by Johnny Keyes not much more than a year earlier. At the time, the Magnificents recorded for Vee-Jay Records and were enjoying huge success with their half-million selling single "Up on the Mountain." Cook also began recording, cutting the single "I Need Your Love" for Chess Records. In 1960, he signed with his brother's newly-formed SAR Records label. Cook recorded several singles for SAR, but despite the uncanny similarities between his and Sam Cooke's voice, his early efforts were all failures. The closest that L.C. Cook ever came to even a modest hit at SAR was also his first not to be produced by Sam. "The Wobble" and "Put Me Down Easy," both written by Sam Cooke and recorded by his brother in 1963, failed to chart, but at least had a run at success, particularly the former, a novelty dance tune. Ironically, Cooke had a major chart hit with a song—Chester "Howlin' Wolf" Burnett's "Little Red Rooster"—that L.C. Cook rejected as a single for himself. In the wake of Sam Cooke's death in late 1964, L.C. Cook announced plans for a tribute, and he continued to perform and record, but his career never ascended to anything resembling his brother's, as a singer or songwriter.

Strangely enough, L.C. Cook's greatest visibility also took place in tandem with his brother's songwriting. During the late '50s, Sam Cooke found himself trapped in an interlocking array of recording and publishing contracts that weren't going to take him anywhere. "You Send Me," "You Were Made for Me," "Win Your Love for Me," "I Don't Want to Cry," and "That's All I Need to Know" ended up credited to L.C. Cook in order to prevent them, as Sam Cooke compositions, from falling into the hands of the latter's earlier publishers. After Sam Cooke's death, he toured with the Upsetters, and announced planned recordings of his own, including a tribute to his brother, but by the end of the 1960s L.C. Cook had receded into the background. L.C. Cook tried to make the same sort of jump from gospel to popular music that his brother had done. He was never in the right place, with the right song, however, despite a powerful voice of his own. *—Bruce Eder*

Little Joe Cook

b. 1922, Philadelphia, PA
Vocals / Doo Wop, R&B
Little Joe Cook has had at least three successful music careers in one lifetime. One of the most durable singers ever to come out of Philadelphia, Cook sang gospel and R&B, fostered a few dance crazes, and organized at least one successful girl group in his career.

Joe Cook was born in Philadelphia in 1922, and by 1934 at age 12, had organized his own gospel group, the Evening Star Quartet. With his falsetto voice, winning personality, and dazzling musical instincts, he was a popular local figure in Philadelphia when he started recording in 1949. He later had his own radio show in Philadelphia and in the early '50s, he decided to make the jump to R&B, which was booming at the time. He organized the Thrillers with Farrie Hill (second lead), Richard Frazier (tenor), Donald Burnett (baritone), and Henry Pascal (bass), and by 1956 they had a contract with OKeh, the R&B imprint of Columbia Records. Their first single "Do the Slop," released that year, became a regional hit in NY and Philadelphia, and got enough action to justify an appearance at the Apollo Theater in Harlem. The Slop was one of two dances that Little Joe Cook introduced (the other was the Bicycle Bounce), and made him one of the top R&B figures in Philadelphia. It sold well enough to justify further efforts on their behalf by OKeh, which was trying to get in on the rock & roll boom.

The group's second single, "Peanuts," released in 1957, featured Cook's piercing falsetto voice as the lead. It was catchy and distinctive enough to get the group an appearance on *American Bandstand.* Little Joe & the Thrillers became one of the first R&B groups to score a national hit through television exposure; the single was propelled, with help from *Bandstand* and host Dick Clark, to number 23 nationally, and it sold in huge numbers. This was to be the Thrillers' only national hit; they tried to score a second time with "The Echoes Keep Calling Me," a faster-paced number that put Cook's falsetto out in front again, but the record never charted. OKeh kept releasing Little Joe & the Thrillers' records until 1961, with "I Love You for Sentimental Reasons," which ended their contract. The group recorded one single for 20th Century Records before disappearing. (Ironically, the OKeh label that they'd left behind vanished into inactivity around the same time).

During the early '60s, Cook organized a girl group with his daughters, eventually called the Sherrys, who charted with one record before a couple of marriages and a change in management forced them out of the business. Little Joe Cook remained an active performer in Boston, and "Do the Slop" and "Peanuts" are still remembered as two of the most beguiling of R&B-cum-rock & roll hits of the late '50s. *—Bruce Eder*

The Golden Classics: Little Joe & the Thrillers Meet the Schoolboys / 1991 / Collectables ♦♦♦

Nice mixture of novelty tunes, down-home blues, R&B, doo wop, and jump material featuring the lightly regarded but good vocalist Little Joe Cook & the Schoolboys, not a great singing group but a solidly professional one. If this is still in print, it's well worth hearing. *—Ron Wynn*

Lady From the Beauty Shop / 1996 / Beantown ♦♦♦

- **A Blast From the Past: The Legendary Little Joe Cook & The Thrillers** / 1997 / Beantown ♦♦♦♦

The Top 25 song from 1957, "Peanuts," leads off this majestic 32-song compilation released by Little Joe Cook's own Beantown International in 1997. This generous disc is a very easy listen for fans of rock & roll, R&B, pop, and American music. The falsetto on "Peanuts" inspired Frankie Valli; in fact, the Four Seasons recorded the tune, although it was credited to another songwriter on their disc (and other covers as well, for a very long time). After a lengthy battle, Cook has set the record straight. A true pioneer, the 14-page booklet that comes with the CD is chock full of photos and information. Alternate takes of "Cherry," "This I Know," "Please Don't Go," and "Peanuts" are here, along with the "Peanuts" sequel, "The Echoes Keep Calling Me," Cook's rendition of "For Sentimental Reasons," and his classic version of "Stay." Although Cook did not enjoy the recognition of a record based on his style, "Stay" has been a staple in his live show for four decades. Everything on this collection has vintage sound, and really on-target performances. Cook's voice and songs deserved a wider audience over the years—his influence on the Sherrys, his student Tammi Montgomery (who became Marvin Gaye's partner, Tammi Terrell), and Garnet Mimms & the Enchanters can be heard throughout these mostly two-minute songs. And that's part of the fun of this disc. "Let's Do the Slop," not the latter-day song by Moogy Klingman, with its jungle beat, and "Public Opinion"'s soulful preaching help make *A Blast From the Past* a textbook that is as much fun as it is informative. There were 16 titles on the vinyl released 17 years prior to this, all included here, with 16 different titles and alternate takes. Both the vinyl and CD were re-mastered by famous Boston disc jockey Little Walter DeVenne; the vinyl also includes Allen Day liner notes absent from the CD, which is a good reason to seek out both. *—Joe Viglione*

Sam Cooke (Sam Cook)

b. Jan. 22, 1931, Clarksdale, MS, **d.** Dec. 11, 1964, Los Angeles, CA
Vocals / Soul, R&B, Black Gospel
Sam Cooke was the most important soul singer in history—he was also the inventor of soul music, and its most popular and beloved performer in both the black and white communities. Equally important, he was among the first modern black performers and composers to attend to the business side of the music business, and founded both a record label and a publishing company as an extension of his careers as a singer and composer. Yet, those business interests didn't prevent him from being engaged in topical issues,

including the struggle over civil rights, the pitch and intensity of which followed an arc that paralleled Cooke's emergence as a star—his own career bridged gaps between black and white audiences that few had tried to surmount, much less succeeded at doing, and also between generations; where Chuck Berry or Little Richard brought black and white teenagers together, James Brown sold records to white teenagers and black listeners of all ages, and Muddy Waters got young white folkies and older black transplants from the South onto the same page, Cooke appealed to all of the above, and the parents of those white teenagers as well—yet he never lost his credibility with his core black audience.

In a sense, his appeal anticipated that of the Beatles, in breadth and depth. He was born Sam Cook in Clarksdale, MS, on January 22, 1931, one of eight children of a Baptist minister and his wife. Even as a young boy, he showed an extraordinary voice and frequently sang in the choir in his father's church. During the middle of the decade, the Cook family moved to Chicago's South Side, where the Reverend Charles Cook quickly established himself as a major figure in the religious community. Sam and three of his siblings also formed a group of their own, the Singing Children, in the 1930s. Although his own singing was confined to gospel music, he was aware and appreciative of the popular music of the period, particularly the melodious, harmony-based sounds of the Ink Spots, whose influence could later be heard in songs such as "You Send Me" and "For Sentimental Reasons." As a teenager, he was a member of the Teen Highway QCs, a gospel group that performed in churches and at religious gatherings. His membership in that group led to his introduction to the Soul Stirrers, one of the top gospel groups in the country, and in 1950 he joined them.

If Cooke had never recorded a note of music on his own, he would still be remembered today in gospel circles for his work with the Soul Stirrers. Over the next six years, his role within the group and his prominence within the black community rose to the point where he was already a star, with his own fiercely admiring and devoted audience, through his performances on songs like "Touch the Hem of His Garment," "Nearer to Thee," and "That's Heaven to Me." The group was one of the top acts on Art Rupe's Specialty Records label, and he might have gone on for years as their most popular singer, but Cooke's goal was to reach audiences beyond the religious community, and beyond the black population, with his voice. This was a tall order at the time, as the mere act of recording a popular song could alienate the gospel listenership in an instant; singing for God was regarded in those circles as a gift and a responsibility, and popular music, rock & roll, and R&B were to be abhorred, at least coming from the mouth of a gospel singer; the gap was so great that when a blues singer such as Blind Gary Davis became "sanctified" (that is, found religion) as the Rev. Gary Davis, he could still sing and play his old blues melodies, but had to devise new words, and he never sang the blues words again.

He tested the waters of popular music in 1956 with the single "Lovable," produced by Bumps Blackwell and credited under the name Dale Cooke so as not to attract too much attention from his existing audience. It was enough, however, to get Cooke dropped by the Soul Stirrers and their record label, but that freed him to record under his real name. The result was one of the biggest selling singles of the 1950s, a Cooke original entitled "You Send Me," which sold over two million copies on the tiny Keen Records label and hit number one on both the pop and R&B charts. Although it seems like a tame record today, "You Send Me" was a pioneering soul record in its time, melding elements of R&B, gospel, and pop into a sound that was new and still coalescing at the time.

Cooke was with Keen for the next two years, a period in which he delivered up some of the prettiest romantic ballads and teen pop singles of the era, including "For Sentimental Reasons," "Everybody Loves to Cha Cha Cha," "Only Sixteen," and "(What A) Wonderful World." These were extraordinarily beautiful records, and in between the singles came some early album efforts, most notably *Tribute to the Lady*, his album of songs associated with Billie Holiday. He was unhappy, however, with both the business arrangement that he had with Keen and the limitations inherent with recording for a small label—equally to the point, major labels were knocking on Cooke's door, including Atlantic and RCA Records; Atlantic, which was not yet the international conglomerate that it later became, was the top R&B-oriented label in the country and Cooke almost certainly would have signed there and found a happy home with the company, except that they wanted his publishing, and Cooke had seen the sales figures on his songs, as well as their popularity in cover versions by other artists, and was well aware of the importance of owning his copyrights.

Thus, he signed with RCA Records, then one of the three biggest labels in the world (the others being Columbia and Decca), even as he organized his own publishing company, Kags Music, and a record label, SAR, through which he would produce other artists' records—among those signed to SAR were the Soul Stirrers, Bobby Womack (late of the Valentinos, who were also signed to the label), former Soul Stirrers member Johnny Taylor, Billy Preston, Johnnie Morisette, and the Simms Twins.

Cooke's RCA sides were a strangely schizophrenic body of work, at least for the first two years. He broke new ground in pop and soul with the single "Chain Gang," a strange mix of sweet melodies and gritty, sweaty sensibilities that also introduced something of a social conscience to his work—a number-two hit on both the pop and R&B charts, it was his biggest hit since "You Send Me" and heralded a bolder phase in his career. Singles like bluesy, romantic "Sad Mood," the idyllic romantic soul of "Cupid," and the straight-ahead dance tune "Twistin' the Night Away" (a pop Top Ten and a number one R&B hit), and "Bring It on Home to Me" all lived up to this promise, and also sold in huge numbers. But the first two albums that RCA had him do, *Hits of the Fifties* and *Cooke's Tour*, were among the lamest LPs ever recorded by any soul or R&B singer, comprised of washed-out pop tunes in arrangements that showed almost none of Cooke's gifts to their advantage.

In 1962, Cooke issued *Twistin' the Night Away*, a somewhat belated "twist" album that became one of his biggest-selling LPs. He didn't really hit his stride as an LP artist, however, until 1963 with the release of *Night Beat*, a beautifully self-contained, dark, moody assembly of blues-oriented songs that were among the best and most challenging numbers that Cooke had recorded up to that time. By the time of its release, he was mostly identified through his singles, which were among the best work of their era, and had developed two separate audiences, among white teen and post-teen listeners and black audiences of all ages. It was Cooke's hope to cross over to the white audience more thoroughly, and open up doors for black performers that, up to that time, had mostly been closed—he had tried playing the Copa in NY as early as 1957 and failed at the time, mostly owing to his inexperience, but in 1964 he returned to the club in triumph, an event that also yielded one of the most finely recorded live performances of its period. The problem with the Copa performance was that it didn't really represent what Sam Cooke was about in full—it was Cooke at his most genial and non-confrontational, doing his safest repertory for a largely middle-aged, middle-class white audience; they responded enthusiastically, to be sure, but only to Cooke's tamest persona.

In mid-1963, however, Cooke had done a show at the Harlem Square Club in Miami that had been recorded. Working in front of a black audience and doing his "real" show, he delivered a sweaty, spellbinding performance built on the same elements found in his singles and his best album tracks, combining achingly beautiful melodies and gritty soul sensibilities. The two live albums sum up the split in Cooke's career and the sheer range of his talent, the rewards of which he'd finally begun to realize more fully in 1963 and 1964.

The drowning death of his infant son in mid-1963 had made it impossible for Cooke to work in the studio until the end of that year. During that time, however, with Allen Klein now managing his business affairs, Cooke did achieve the financial and creative independence that he'd wanted, including more money than any black performer had ever been advanced before, and the eventual ownership of his recordings beginning in November of 1963—he had achieved creative control of his recordings as well, and seemed poised for a breakthrough. It came when he resumed making records, amid the musical ferment of the early '60s. Cooke was keenly aware of the music around him, and was particularly entranced by Bob Dylan's song "Blowin' in the Wind," its treatment of the plight of black Americans and other politically oppressed minorities, and its success in the hands of Peter, Paul & Mary—all of these factors convinced him that the time was right for songs that dealt with more than twisting the night away.

The result was "A Change Is Gonna Come," perhaps the greatest song to come out of the civil rights struggle, and one that seemed to close and seal the gap between the two directions of Cooke's career, from gospel to pop. Arguably his greatest and his most important song, it was an artistic apotheosis for Cooke. During this same period, he had also devised a newer, more advanced dance-oriented soul sound in the form of the song "Shake." These two recordings heralded a new era for Cooke and a new phase of his career, with seemingly the whole world open to him.

None of it was to be. Early in the day on December 11, 1964, while in Los Angeles, Cooke became involved in an altercation at a seedy motel, with a woman guest and the night manager, and was shot to death while allegedly trying to attack the manager. The case is still shrouded in doubt and mystery, and was never investigated the way the murder of a star of his stature would be today. Cooke's death shocked the black community and reverberated far beyond—his single "Shake" was a posthumous Top Ten hit, as were "A Change Is Gonna Come" and the *At the Copa* album, released in 1965. Otis Redding, Al Green, and Solomon Burke, among others, picked up key parts of Cooke's repertory, as did white performers, including the Animals and the Rolling Stones. Even the Supremes recorded a memorial album of his songs, which is now one of the most sought-after of their original recordings, in either LP or CD form.

His reputation survived, at least among those who were smart enough to look behind the songs—to hear Redding's performance of "Shake" at the Monterey Pop Festival, for example, and see where it came from. Cooke's own records were a little tougher to appreciate, however. Listeners who heard those first two, rather poor RCA albums, *Hits of the Fifties* and *Cooke's Tour*, could only wonder what the big deal was about, and several of the albums that followed were uneven enough to give potential fans pause. Meanwhile, the contractual situation surrounding Cooke's recordings greatly complicated the reissue of his work—Cooke's business manager, Allen Klein, exerted a good deal of control, especially over the songs cut during that last year of the singer's life. By the 1970s, there were some fairly poor, mostly budget-priced compilations available, consisting of the hits up through early 1963, and for a time there was even a television compilation out there, but that was it. The movie *National Lampoon's Animal House* made use of a pair of Cooke songs, "(What A) Wonderful World" and "Twistin' the Night Away," which greatly raised his profile among college students and younger baby-boomers, and Southside Johnny & the Asbury Jukes made almost a mini-career out of reviving Cooke's songs (most notably "Having a Party," and even part of "A Change Is Gonna Come") in concert.

In 1984, *The Man and His Music* went some way to correcting the absence of all but the early hits in a career-spanning compilation, but since the mid-'90s, Cooke's final year's worth of releases have been separated from the earlier RCA and Keen material, and is in the hands of Klein's ABKCO label. Finally, in the late '90s and beyond, RCA, ABKCO, and even Specialty (which still owns Cooke's gospel sides with the Soul Stirrers) each issued comprehensive collections of their portions of Cooke's catalog. *—Bruce Eder*

Cooke's Tour / 1960 / RCA ✦✦

Sam Cooke's debut album for RCA was a fundamentally flawed attempt to shoehorn his singing into a safe, MOR pop concept album, showcasing songs about different parts of the world. The strings and harps are almost overpowering and, given what Cooke should have been singing for his first LP for the label, are doubly inappropriate. The repertory is about as safe as can be, including "Jamaica Farewell," "South of the Border," "Bali Ha'i," "Arrivederci, Roma," and "London by Night"—the only surprise is Earl Robinson's "The House I Live In," which was associated with Josh White and Frank Sinatra and, in its own way, was part of the 1940s roots of the modern Civil Rights movement. Cooke would later get a lot more topical and soulful. *—Bruce Eder*

Hits of the Fifties / Aug. 1960 / RCA ✦✦✦

Sam Cooke's second RCA album is mostly a missed opportunity, in terms of representing much about Sam Cooke as an artist or singer—having him cover pop hits of the previous decade wasn't a terrible idea on its face, but Cooke was still getting accustomed to working at RCA, and he wasn't inspired by the material or the way it was chosen, and the result is an album aimed at what the label thought the white teenage market was all about (and what the company thought the parents of those kids would be most comfortable with them buying from a black recording artist), that's a lot less interesting than some of the singles, including "Chain Gang" and "Wonderful World," that he was doing around the same time. His versions of hits associated with Nat King Cole, Johnnie Ray, and the Platters should have made for a more interesting record. *Hits of the Fifties* is still an improvement over its immediate predecessor, *Cooke's Tour*, but it's also one of the records that for many years—in the absence of his best material being available—blighted Cooke's reputation as a soul singer. *—Bruce Eder*

Swing Low / 1960 / RCA ♦♦♦

My Kind of Blues / 1961 / RCA ♦♦♦♦♦

Twistin' the Night Away / Apr. 1962 / RCA Victor ♦♦♦

This was one of Cooke's more successful LPs, only his second ever to chart (the first was his 1957 debut long-player), and from here on, all of his albums would sell in serious numbers. *Twistin' the Night Away* remains one of Cooke's most accessible records, despite the fact that it was a "twist" album, aimed by the producers at cashing in on that craze, and Cooke was shoehorned into doing numbers like "Camptown Twist," "Twistin' in the Kitchen With Dinah," and "Twistin' in the Old Town," as well as his version of Hank Ballard's "The Twist." Around them, the singer is at his most soulful, exciting, and passionate, on the bluesy "Somebody Have Mercy"; the romantic lament "Somebody's Gonna Miss Me"; the ebullient "Sugar Dumpling"; the achingly beautiful, yearning "A Whole Lot of Woman"; the soaring "Soothe Me" (with Lou Rawls); and the slow dance number "Movin' and Groovin'." One of the great dance albums of its period, but a brilliant soul album as well, which is why it holds up 40 years later. *—Bruce Eder*

☆ **Live at the Harlem Square Club, 1963** / 1963 / RCA ♦♦♦♦♦

For anyone who thought they knew Sam Cooke's music based on the hit singles, this disc will be a revelation. This is the real Sam Cooke, doing a sweaty, raspy soulful set at the Harlem Square Club in North Miami, FL, on Jan. 12, 1963, backed by King Curtis and his band, a handful of local musicians, and Cooke's resident sidemen, guitarist Cliff White and drummer Albert "June" Gardner. To put it simply, it's one of the greatest soul records ever cut by anybody, outshining James Brown's first live album from the Apollo Theater and easily outclassing Jackie Wilson's live record from the Copa. Cooke's pop style is far removed from the proceedings here, which have the feel of being virtually a secular sermon. The record opens with the frantic, desperate chant-like "Feel It," followed by a version of "Chain Gang" that has all of the gentling influences of the single's string accompaniment stripped from it—Cooke's slightly hoarse voice only adds to the startling change in the song, transformed from a piece of pop-soul into an in-your-face ode to freedom and release. "Cupid," perhaps the most sweetly textured song that Cooke cut during the 1960s, gets the full soul treatment, with horns and Curtis' sax up front and Cooke imparting an urgency here that's only implied in the studio rendition. "Twistin' the Night Away" gets two hot King Curtis sax solos, the highlights of a pounding, rippling performance with a beautifully vamped extended ending (with the drums, bass, and White's guitar wrapping themselves ever tighter around the central riff) that never would have made it to the floor of the Copa. "Somebody Have Mercy" leads into a long vamp by Cooke, a brief, soaring quotation from "You Send Me" that could easily have been a high point in sheer intensity—and then Cooke and the band crank the tension and the spirits several notches higher with the greatest version of "Bring It on Home to Me" ever done by anybody. It all ends with a version of "Having a Party" that manages to be both soothing and wrenching at the same time, Cooke luxuriating in every nuance as the crowd joins in singing, reaching a higher pitch to the gently swinging tune, the drums kicking in harder, the rhythm guitar rising up, and Curtis' sax and the horns rising up slowly while Cooke goes on with his singing, which is more like preaching and the group sounds like it could play the riff all night. It's one of the cruel ironies of the recording business that this unique and extraordinary concert recording went unreleased for almost 22 years, in favor of the more polished (but also more antiseptic and duller) *Sam Cooke at the Copa*. *—Bruce Eder*

☆ **Night Beat** / Aug. 1963 / ABKCO ♦♦♦♦♦

Saddled with soaring strings and vocal choruses for maximum crossover potential, Sam Cooke's solo material often masked the most important part of his genius—his glorious voice—so the odd small-group date earns a special recommendation in his discography. Thankfully, Cooke's voice took center stage on this admirably low-key session from February 1963, recorded in Los Angeles with a quartet of studio veterans. Unlike so many session crews and producers of the time, these musicians gave him plenty of space and often simply framed Cooke's breathtaking vocals. (On one of the best tracks here, "Lost and Lookin'," he's barely accompanied at all; only bass and cymbals can be heard far in the background.) The results are wonderful—except for his early Soul Stirrers sides, *Night Beat* is the best place to marvel at one of the two or three best voices of the century. The songs are intimate blues, most taken at the pace of a late-night stroll, but despite the dark shading and heart-rending tempos, Cooke's voice is so transcendent it's difficult to become depressed while listening. Cooke also wrote three of the songs, including the excellent "Mean Old World," and rendered the traditional "Nobody Knows the Trouble I've Seen" practically unfamiliar with his own re-arrangement. Cooke also stretches out on a pair of jump blues classics, "Little Red Rooster" and "Shake, Rattle and Roll," summoning some honest grit for the former and putting the uptown swing into the latter. He also allows some solo space, from Barney Kessel's simple, unadorned solo on "Get Yourself Another Fool" to Billy Preston's playful organ vocalizing on "Little Red Rooster." If Sam Cooke had lived longer, there would've been several more sessions like this, but *Night Beat* is an even richer treasure for its rarity. *—John Bush*

Ain't That Good News / 1964 / RCA Victor ♦♦♦♦

The last of his studio albums released in his lifetime, Sam Cooke's *Ain't That Good News* offers a lot of superb material, pointing in several directions that, alas, were to go largely unexplored. The central number is, of course, the earth-shattering "A Change Is Gonna Come," with its soaring gospel sound and the most elaborate production of any song in Cooke's output. The rousing though less substantial title track also came out of a gospel tradition, as does Cooke's treatment of "Tennessee Waltz," which is one of his finest adaptations of contemporary pop material. "Falling in Love" was the work of Harold Battiste, an old friend of Cooke's who had recently re-entered his orbit and was partly responsible for encouraging the singer in exploring the New Orleans sound that was evident on "Rome Wasn't Built in a Day" and "Meet Me at Mary's Place." And then there's "Good Times," a bittersweet, introspective party number, and the pensive successor to "Twistin' the Night Away." There are a few moments where the spell is almost broken by the intrusion of what seems like pop material, but even Cooke's version of "The Riddle Song" is worth owning, as a glimpse of how he could turn a folk song into a something so quietly soulful that its origins disappeared. With the exception of "Another Saturday Night," which had been released as a single early in the previous year, *Ain't That Good News* comprised the first material that Cooke had recorded in the six months following the drowning death of his 18-month-old son Vincent; it was also the first album that Cooke recorded and released under his new contract, which gave him greater freedom in choosing repertory and sidemen than he'd ever had, and so it offered a lot of pent-up emotional and musical expression, and, as it turned out, was tragically unique in the singer's output. As a result of that same contract, control over it and all subsequently released material moved to ABKCO records and Cooke's manager, Allen Klein, and most of its contents were subsequently repackaged on the 2002 *Keep Movin' On* compilation. *—Bruce Eder*

Sam Cooke at the Copa / Oct. 1964 / ABKCO ♦♦♦

For decades, *Sam Cooke at the Copa* was a frustrating record. One of a handful of live albums by any major soul artist of its era, it captured Cooke in excellent voice, and was well-recorded—it just wasn't really a "soul" album, except perhaps in the tamest possible definition of that term. Playing to an upscale, largely white supper-club audience, in a very conservatively run venue where he had previously failed to impress either patrons or the management, Cooke toned down his performance and chose the safest material with which he could still be comfortable. In place of songs like "Feel It," "Bring It on Home to Me," or even "Cupid," which were part of his usual set, he performed numbers like "The Best Things in Life Are Free," "Bill Bailey," and "When I Fall in Love" here. True, his renditions may be the versions of any of those songs that any R&B fan will like best, but that's all that can be said for them, and they're a poor substitute for what's not here—not just the songs that he didn't do, but the intense, sweaty presentation, as much a sermon as a concert, the pounding beat, and the crowd being driven into ever more frenzied delight. All of that is missing here, and for decades fans had to content themselves with the contradiction of a beautifully executed but very flat concert. The release of *Live at the Harlem Square Club* solved that problem, giving us a real Sam Cooke concert and one of the great soul albums of all time. *Sam Cooke at the Copa* is still worth hearing as a document of what he was trying to do at one point in his career, crossing over to an older, more upscale white audience. It has some nice moments, such as "Twistin' the Night Away," "Frankie and Johnny," "Try a Little Tenderness," "This Little Light of Mine" and his performance of Dylan's "Blowin' in the Wind" (all of which, if he'd done his usual set, we likely wouldn't have), but it's hardly an essential purchase. *—Bruce Eder*

Shake / Jan. 1965 / RCA ♦♦♦

Sam Cooke had been killed the previous month with a current single, "Shake," ready for release. A brilliant uptempo song with dazzling vocal acrobatics and a great beat, it was issued less than two weeks after Cooke's death and soared into the Top Ten, but there was no accompanying LP, and Cooke had not left behind enough unissued studio material to create one. Instead, starting within days of Cooke's death in order to get this album out for January of 1965, RCA reached back as far as six years, to Cooke's sides for Specialty records and the Keen label ("Win Your Love for Me," "Comes Love"), up through songs from early 1964's *A Change Is Gonna Come* album and the handful of numbers he'd finished late in the year. They threw on the shortened single version of "A Change Is Gonna Come," as edited for the B-side of "Shake," to create the first in an ever-weaker series of pastiche albums in Cooke's catalog. This actually isn't a bad selection of material, and some of what's here was among his latest sides, thus representing some facet of where his music was heading during his last year alive, in what amounted to an unfinished career in an unfinished life, in an unsettled time. It's just not a terribly relevant album in terms of anything it says about Cooke's music, apart from its diversity over time. Most of the material on this album has reappeared in more recent years on either *The Man Who Invented Soul* box or the *Keep Movin' On* CD. *—Bruce Eder*

The 2 Sides of Sam Cooke / 1970 / Specialty ♦♦♦♦♦

This 12-song release splits its time between Cooke's early gospel sides as a member of the Soul Stirrers ("The Last Mile of the Way," "Were You There," "Touch the Hem of His Garment") and his early attempts at crossing over into pop music, including "Lovable," which was originally issued under the name of Dale Cooke to avoid upsetting his gospel fans. A major highlight is "Jesus Gave Me Water," Sam's first recording, done when he was 19 years old. Top-notch liner notes from Barret Hansen (aka Dr. Demento) make this a great little package well worth checking out. The CD is a straight-up reissue of the original vinyl album from 1970. *—Cub Koda*

★ **The Man and His Music** / Feb. 1986 / RCA ♦♦♦♦♦

When this 28-song compilation (two LPs/one CD) originally appeared, it was the first serious exploration of Sam Cooke's catalog ever done. What's more, a lot of care went into the selection, if not the packaging—despite the fact that it has no annotation, or even release dates on its 28 songs, *The Man and His Music* is still the only comprehensive single-volume collection of the hits and highlights of Cooke's career from the mid-'50s to his last sides in 1964. What's more, it's out of print, and it is likely to be the last such compilation that we'll ever see, because in the years since its release, the ownership of Cooke's post-1963 sides (comprising his most advanced and ambitious soul recordings) shifted from RCA to ABKCO, and the chances are next to nonexistent that either company will ever license its portion of Cooke's catalog to the other. There are better-sounding collections and better-annotated collections, to be sure, and fuller collections—in 2000, RCA issued *The Man Who Invented Soul*, a four-CD that goes deeper into Cooke's output from 1958 through 1963; and in 2002, ABKCO issued *Keep Movin' On*, a single-disc compilation covering Cooke's 1964 sides, including his final hits. But *The Man and His Music* is the only Sam Cooke compilation that covers all of the major phases of his career, from his gospel work with the Soul Stirrers through all of the early pop hits and his move into soul music, culminating with his final classic soul sides. The Soul Stirrers' classic "Touch the Hem of His Garment" slides effortlessly into and through sides like "You Send Me" and "Chain Gang," to the early soul numbers like "Nothing Can Change This Love," "Rome Wasn't Built in a Day," and the achingly beautiful "Just for You," to "Having a Party" and the wrenching balladry of "Sad Mood," and through to the transcendent final sides, the rousing "Shake" and the Civil Rights "A Change Is Gonna Come" (the latter showing up for the first time in decades, and the first of only two times on CD, in its full-length version). There are better collections with all of these songs and more on them, but none handier than this in presenting every facet of Cooke's work—the only flaw, if there is one, is the absence of one of the better tracks off of the Harlem Square live album. *—Bruce Eder*

His Earliest Recordings / 1991 / Specialty ♦♦♦♦♦

For fans only familiar with Sam Cooke's later secular blockbusters, this fine Specialty disc of classic Soul Stirrers sides is essential listening. Taking over for powerhouse lead R.H. Harris in 1950, Cooke proceeded to take gospel singing to new heights with the Stirrers, showing a level of grace in his phrasing and tone not often heard before. He also penned many of their most popular songs, including such standouts as "Mean Old World," "Touch the Hem of His Garment," and "Nearer to Thee." And while his pop hits ("You Send Me," "Having a Party," "Chain Gang," etc.) are incredible, it's these early gospel sides that many believe to be his best. While the debate goes on, do yourself a favor and check out this amazing collection. *—Stephen Cook*

The SAR Records Story / 1994 / ABKCO ♦♦♦♦♦

Sam Cooke's SAR Records Story is a double-disc set presenting material recorded for the legendary soul singer's own SAR label from 1959-1965, much of it produced by Cooke himself and including a few of his rough, unreleased demos. The first disc covers the label's religious side, with a multitude of cuts from Cooke's former group the Soul Stirrers (now with Jimmie Outler on lead vocals), plus a generous helping of songs by R.H. Harris & His Gospel Paraders and the Womack Brothers. The second disc covers essentially the same gospel-derived soul territory but with a secular bent, featuring future stars Bobby Womack (with the Valentinos), Billy Preston, and Johnnie Taylor, plus L.C. Cook, Johnnie Morisette, the Simms Twins, and Mel Carter. All in all, it's an excellent look at a lesser-known portion of Cooke's career, and there's some great, underappreciated music to boot. *—Steve Huey*

The Rhythm and the Blues / Oct. 24, 1995 / RCA ♦♦♦♦

From the title, you might infer that this 20-track compilation—taken from early-'60s sessions, and principally composed of LP-only cuts—aims to showcase Cooke's most soulful side. That's true to some degree, but this isn't his funkiest stuff; for that, look to *Live at the Harlem Square Club 1963*, or even his most uptempo singles. Most of this is in fact suave pop/R&B, the emphasis sometimes falling on the pop, with lightly swinging, jazzy arrangements and some orchestration. Cooke didn't write most of the material here, and while "Little Red Rooster" (a hit single) represents the earthiest extreme that the CD touches upon, there are also quite a few songs that were originally performed by jazz/popsters from the '20s, '30s, and '40s. Certainly these are decent offerings; Cooke's a great singer and interpreter, and the arrangements are smooth without being overdone. But it's neither Cooke at his very best (the hits compilation *Man and His Music* is much better) or his grittiest (that honor belongs to *Harlem Square*). It does restore much of his better obscure material to wide availability and is recommended to those who have the above-mentioned albums and want more Cooke, although the 1963 LP *Night Beat* (reissued on CD in 1995) is a bluesier and better one to check out first. *—Richie Unterberger*

★ **Greatest Hits** / Feb. 24, 1998 / RCA ♦♦♦♦♦

Although it isn't as sublime as the definitive *The Man and His Music, Greatest Hits* still does a good job of rounding up the majority of Sam Cooke's biggest pop hits. Ironically, it doesn't have enough gospel or R&B cuts, skipping over such essentials as "Touch the Hem of His Garment," "Ain't That Good News" and "A Change Is Gonna Come" in favor of such pop hits as "Sugar Dumpling." However, it has just enough songs that aren't on *The Man and His Music* to make it worth exploring for fans who haven't been able to hear some of this material before, since some of these songs have been out of print for years. Nevertheless, the curious and the novice should be aware that this is not a good introduction to Sam Cooke, because it doesn't provide a full portrait of his career and it overlooks too many necessary songs. *—Stephen Thomas Erlewine*

☆ **The Man Who Invented Soul** / Sep. 26, 2000 / RCA ♦♦♦♦♦

This set is near essential to fans of Sam Cooke, despite the fact that it contains none of his gospel recordings for Specialty Records or any of the work from the final year of his career (owned by ABKCO Records). Scattered every few minutes across this four-disc collection are reminders of just how far ahead of all existing musical forms Cooke was, creating sounds that stretched the definitions of song genres as they were understood and created completely new categories. Indeed, he was so successful that it's easy to underestimate the impact and importance of many of his early triumphs. "You Send Me," which opens this set, may seem today like the safest, tamest pop music, but in 1957 it was a genre-bending single, a new kind of R&B/pop music hybrid and one that quietly shook the foundations of the music business when it hit number one. Disc one offers a fresh appreciation of the best of the early Keen Records sides, drawing on the best of nearly two years of singles and the strongest of Cooke's LP tracks in the best account to date of his early career in popular music. Disc two begins Cooke's RCA years, and the quality of his singles, which clearly and easily bridge the gap between genres, races, and generations, improves dramatically. The development of Cooke's writing and singing and his growing confidence and range culminate with disc four, which encompasses the *Night Beat* album and Cooke's live performance from the Harlem Square Club. The sound is extraordinary throughout, expansive, rich-textured, and vividly detailed; a choice earlier CD release, *The Man and His Music*, by comparison, sounds thin and tinny. *—Bruce Eder*

Keep Movin' On / Jan. 15, 2002 / ABKCO ♦♦♦♦♦

This 23-song CD stands in Sam Cooke's output roughly where those four posthumous LPs (beginning with *Dock of the Bay*) stand in Otis Reddings catalog, with the major difference that Cooke's work included far fewer leftovers and sides that were justified simply by being available—he seemed to throw a special effort into almost everything that ever recorded, and that goes double for this disc's content, which encompasses the final year of his recording career. This was a period in which he explored several promising musical directions and broke through both to an extraordinarily sophisticated synthesis of his gospel roots with topical songwriting within a pop context. Listeners won't find his most popular songs—"You Send Me," "Chain Gang," "Only Sixteen," etc.—here, a result of the split control of his catalog between RCA and ABKCO, but they will find his most important and influential songs. Cooke was inactive in the studio for a significant chunk of 1963, following the drowning death of his infant son, and when he resumed work late in the year it was under a new contract that was to ultimately give control and ownership of his recordings to him (or, as events worked out, his manager, Allen Klein). Represented here is his foray into a New Orleans sound, on "Basin Street Blues" etc., which he'd never explored before—and which he shaped his own way—as well as his poignant recording of "The Riddle Song," which (according to Peter Guralnick's notes) was a way of his coming to terms musically with the death of his son; and "Good Times," the somber-toned party song of Cooke's that the Rolling Stones chose to cover, and the equally pensive and compelling "Another Saturday Night," a relic of the first half of 1963 that fits equally well with this later material. On any other R&B collection, all of those tracks would be perceived as extraordinarily fine records, but Cooke himself raised the bar so high during the final months of his career, that they pale next to the most important of his songs: "Shake," which embodied a harder, more visceral soul sound than Cooke had ever embraced before; and "A Change Is Gonna Come." The latter, written by Cooke in the wake of his hearing Bob Dylan's "Blowin' In The Wind," seemed to tie up his origins as a gospel singer with all that he had learned and experienced in the ensuing decade and, channeled through the topical subject of civil rights, became his greatest musical achievement—not his biggest hit, or his best known song even today, but his most accomplished piece of composition, singing, and recording. Cooke never had a chance to follow up either, and died before he could even assess the impact of either song—ironically, it was Otis Redding (who died almost three years later to the day) that took them into his repertory most successfully, and kept them out there, on record and, in the case of "Shake," on-stage as well; so this disc not only brings us to the final, magnificent phase of Cooke's career, but also shows the door that he opened for Otis Redding et al. *Keep Movin' On* should probably not be the only Sam Cooke compilation that a neophyte fan should buy, mostly because it covers only his late career and leaves out a lot of essential material, but it is an absolutely essential companion (along with the *Harlem Square Club* live disc) to the current RCA greatest hits disc or the 4-CD *Man Who Invented Soul* set, finishing the story that they start. Most of what's here was never on CD before and hasn't been available on vinyl in the US since the 1960s, and even the tracks that have been out before are improved so significantly in the quality of their transfer to CD, that they're like new releases, and they're accompanied by superb annotation. *—Bruce Eder*

The Complete Specialty Recordings of Sam Cooke / Oct. 15, 2002 / Specialty ♦♦♦♦♦

They were known as the Soul Stirrers when they did the 1951-1957 recordings on this three-CD, 84-song collection. It's billed to Sam Cooke with the Soul Stirrers, though, as it's the ultimate collection of sides he recorded as a member of the group for Specialty Records, along with seven tentative secular pop/rock sides he did for the label as a solo singer in 1956. Cooke doesn't sing lead on all of the Soul Stirrers' tracks, though there are plenty of his leads to hear throughout the set; he shares lead duties with Paul Foster, although by the end of his time in the outfit, Cooke was taking most of the solo leads. There's also one cut, "All Right Now," on which Cooke shares lead with Rev. Julius Cheeks (two alternate versions of the song are also on the set). Even if Cooke isn't always the solo lead, however, he's a big presence on all of these sides, which represent both an important summary of his career prior to achieving pop stardom and a major body of gospel music. While much of the material is traditional (with Cooke contributing some originals), the arrangements do evolve, including some drums, organ, piano, bass, and electric guitar at various points. The link between gospel, R&B, and rock & roll becomes evident to more secular-minded listeners, sometimes strikingly so in Cooke's phrasing, which, even on songs as far back as 1953 ("I'd Give Up All My Sins and Serve the Lord"), contained clear antecedents to his vocals on his first breakthrough pop hit, "You Send Me." Naturally those antecedents are heard strongest on the seven 1956 solo cuts that represented his first pop ventures, and although these are on the innocuous side, they're enjoyable foreshadowings of his rock & roll years. Numerous alternate takes and three 1955 live songs (with good sound) complete the most comprehensive portrait of Cooke's gospel years. Note, though, that the version of "I'll Come Running Back to You"—a Top 20 entry in the wake of "You Send Me"—lacks the overdub on the hit single. *—Richie Unterberger*

Cookie & the Cupcakes

f. 1955, Lake Charles, LA

Group / Swamp Blues, Swamp Pop, R&B, Soul

Cookie & the Cupcakes were among the first to blend Cajun music with rock & roll to create the musical hybrid known as swamp pop. The eight-piece band reached its peak in 1959 when their lively dance tune "Mathilda" reached number 47 on the *Billboard* charts. Although they subsequently toured as the opening act for Jerry Lee Lewis and Fats Domino, Cookie & the Cupcakes mostly played in the TX/LA region, with many performances in New Orleans hotel clubs.

Launching their career as the house band at the Moulin Rouge Club in Lake Charles, LA, in 1953, Cookie & the Cupcakes began performing "Mathilda" in 1957. Although they approached numerous record labels, they failed to spark interest until radio station KAOK agreed to let the band use their studios to record the song. Initially released by George Khoury, who sold thousands of copies on his Khoury label, the song was leased for national distribution to Judd Phillips, the brother of Sun Records owner Sam Phillips. Cookie & the Cupcakes were also the supporting band for Phil Phillips' hit "Sea of Love." In January 1995, the group was inducted into the Music Hall of Fame at the Musical Heritage Exhibit of the Museum of the Gulf Coast. —*Craig Harris*

● **By Request** / 1993 / Jin ✦✦✦✦✦

Cookie & the Cupcakes were among the most popular rock and roll artists in LA during the early '50s. They infused their R&B and rock material with a loping swamp-pop flavor, performing both inspired covers and their own soulful originals. This CD reissue contains 20 Cupcake numbers, among them hard-rocking covers of "Honey Hush," "Betty and Dupree" and "Feel So Good." The group was also skilled at heartache tunes, as they showed on "I've Been So Lonely" and "I've Cried." Cookie & the Cupcakes kept things simple, doing short, exuberant dance fare or fervent slow ballads. This disc provides a comprehensive portrait of their music. —*Ron Wynn*

The Cookies

f. 1953, Brooklyn, NY, **db.** 1963

Group / Brill Building Pop, Girl Group

The Cookies essentially had two histories as distinctly different groups (with one member in common) that existed for two years at a time, six years and an entire decade apart in styles and sounds. The original Cookies were Margie Hendrix, Ethel "Earl-Jean" McCrea, and Pat Lyles, who started singing together in Brooklyn in the early '50s, made their recording debut on the Lamp imprint of Aladdin Records in 1954, and were signed to Atlantic Records in 1955 by producer/songwriter Jesse Stone. This lineup enjoyed a Top Ten hit on the R&B charts in 1956 with the single "In Paradise," and backed Chuck Willis and Joe Turner on various sessions during that same period. They ceased to exist as the Cookies when Ray Charles, who was also signed to Atlantic, transformed them into the Raelettes. They spent the next six years working under that name until 1962, when a new version of the Cookies emerged in New York, with Earl-Jean McCrea joining newcomers Dorothy Jones and Margaret Ross.

That lineup began doing sessions at the Brill Building, specifically at Aldon Music, behind Tony Orlando and Neil Sedaka, among others, cutting demos and generally becoming part of the company's basic operation. It was McCrea, for example, who suggested Little Eva as a babysitter to a married pair of songwriters working at the Brill Building (Carole King & Gerry Goffin) who ended up using the babysitter's dancing and singing skills to create "The Locomotion." The single put Aldon's spinoff label, Dimension Records, on the map and the Cookies sang backup on that record, the success of which finally earned them some sessions of their own in 1962. In recent years, Goffin and King have both criticized the group for its "soft" sound, but this overlooks the sultriness of their singing—with a sharp arrangement, as on the 1962 singles "Chains," which hit number 17 on the pop charts in the fall of 1962, "Girls Grow Up Faster Than Boys" (number 33 in early 1963), and "Don't Say Nothin' Bad About My Baby" (number seven in early 1963), the combination was unbeatable. Even their lesser material, such as the rather prosaic rendition of "On Broadway," is pleasant, and a few songs, such as "I Never Dreamed," have a soaring, ethereal quality that's a joy to hear, even 40 years later.

In point of fact, the Cookies did have a more lyrical sound and less of the hard, soulful feel most of the black girl groups of the period had. They could have sounded more "white" than many Motown groups of the same period, but it wasn't a sound that could compete and, absent the most solid songs, the trio had run out their string by 1964. However, they earned a special place in pop music history when the Beatles added "Chains" to their repertory and ended up recording it on their first LP, *Please Please Me*, in 1963; there were the Cookies, right along with other American influences on the group, including the Shirelles, the Miracles, and Arthur Alexander.

Following their breakup, Earl-Jean McCrea, working under the name Earl-Jean, had a solo recording career that started on a promising note in the summer of 1964 with "I'm Into Something Good." Unfortunately for her, the song was picked up by Herman's Hermits and charted in the Top Ten in their version the following fall, eclipsing the original record and the artist herself. —*Bruce Eder*

Don't Say Nothin' Bad About the Cookies / 1991 / Teenager ✦✦✦✦

This import compilation includes the hits "Chains" and "Don't Say Nothin' Bad About My Baby," and is jammed with obscure Goffin-King tunes. The problem is, most of them aren't anywhere nearly as good as the the two hits the team penned for the Cookies or their work with other girl groups. It does include the obscure gem "Girls Grow Up Faster Than Boys," a sassy cut that's as good as the hits. —*Richie Unterberger*

● **The Complete Cookies** / 1994 / Sequel ✦✦✦✦

Apparently, Gerry Goffin & Carole King saddled the Cookies with songs they couldn't place on other artists. Maybe they should have called them "the Dumpies." Occasionally magic occurred, as it did on "Chains," and their signature song "Don't Say Nothing Bad About My Baby." But others like "Girls Grow Up Faster Than Boys," "Randy," and "They're Jealous of Me," are less than memorable. A remake of the Drifters' "On Broadway," is one of few substantive songs on the CD, but if you're a fan of the Cookies, Goffin & King, or the Brill Buildings' songwriters, you'll find this CD essential; if not, this disc isn't for you. It's a piece of nostalgia, definitive, but it's not for everyone. —*Andrew Hamilton*

Les Cooper

b. Mar. 15, 1931, Norfolk, VA

Vocals / Rock & Roll, R&B

A longtime denizen of New York's doo wop scene, Cooper's only major hit was the 1962 instrumental "Wiggle Wobble." The Norfolk, VA, native was a member of the Empires and the Whirlers, and managed the Charts, before signing with Danny Robinson's Everlast imprint and cutting a vocal called "Dig Yourself" with his band, the Soul Rockers. Ironically, it was the flip side (a pounding instrumental called "Wiggle Wobble," featuring prominent King Curtis-styled tenor sax by ex-Charts lead singer Joe Grier) that gave Cooper his only chart ride. Follow-up efforts included the similar "Let's Do the Boston Monkey" for Enjoy. —*Bill Dahl*

● **Wiggle Wobble** / 1963 / Collectables ✦✦✦✦✦

"Wiggle Wobble," with its definitive growling R&B tenor sax courtesy of Joe Grier, was the only hit that Les Cooper had, but the good-natured fun of that song is present in almost all of the 12 sides on *Wiggle Wobble*. More than half of the songs here are instrumentals, but Cooper gets a chance to shine on tunes like "Dig Yourself" and "Owee Baby." A prime document of early-'60s soul, when the lines between R&B and soul weren't yet defined. — *Wade Kergan*

Ruth Copeland

b. Durham, England

Vocals / Funk, Urban

A blues folksinger born in Durham, England, Ruth Copeland first came to attention after marrying Jeffrey Bowen, a staff producer at Motown. When Bowen followed songwriters Holland-Dozier-Holland over to their own Invictus label in 1970, Copeland was one of his first signings as she joined the fledgling vocal group New Play to become the label's first white performer.

Collaborating with Edith Wayne and future P Funk producer Ron Dunbar, Copeland wrote "Music Box," New Play's debut single, and the second ever Invictus release. However, the group broke up soon after its release and Copeland began planning for a solo career. She also struck up an unlikely partnership with George Clinton and became a massively influential force on Parliament's debut album, 1971's *Osmium*. Not only did she co-produce the sessions, she also wrote what remain two of the most bizarre (and decidedly unfunky) songs in that band's entire repertoire, the haunting "Little Old Country Boy" and "The Silent Boatman." Two further songs, "Come in Out of the Rain" (co-written with Clinton) and "Breakdown" (with Clinton and Clyde Wilson) appeared as Parliament singles in 1971 and 1972.

Copeland's partnership with Clinton naturally flowed into her solo career. Viewed today as a virtual twin of *Osmium*, her *Self Portrait* debut featured contributions from Eddie Hazel, Lucius Ross, Bernie Worrell, Billy "Bass" Nelson, Tiki Fulwood, and Clinton himself, while the co-writes included a new version of the epic "The Silent Boatman.

Late 1971 brought the release of Copeland's second album, *I Am What I Am*, recorded with many of the same musicians as its predecessor, only now they were her own band. In an odd twist, Hazell, Worrell, Fulwood, and Nelson had all quit Parliament/Funkadelic, but remained together to back Copeland, first in the studio and then on tour as she promoted the album. The tour was a success; the shows were solid and the audiences receptive. Unfortunately, Copeland quickly found herself in an uncomfortable position. Touring as support to Sly Stone, she took to introducing her band as Funkadelic—much to the headliner's annoyance. The last straw came when she allowed the band to take one of her encores. Stone insisted she either leave the tour or lose the band. She lost the band.

Following her solo success in 1971 and 1972, Copeland faded from the spotlight. She would re-emerge briefly in 1976 with her third album, *Take Me to Baltimore*, but it did little and she once more retreated into shadow. —*Amy Hanson*

Self Portrait / 1971 / Invictus ✦✦

One of the poorest albums that George Clinton was ever involved with. Ruth Copeland couldn't decide whether she was a pop, folk, funk, or a soul singer. She was closer to folk than anything, but her weak voice even had trouble putting across material in that genre. Her songs bordered on the esoteric-absurd. Opinions differ, but some favorite tunes are "Gift of Me," done a cappella; "Your Love Been So Good to Me," a rocker accented by Eddie Hazel's acid lead guitar; and "I Got a Thing for You Daddy," the closest thing to the Parliament/Funkadelic sound here. "The Music Box" as a single release isn't bad, it's just boring, but others like "Thanks for the Birthday Card," "William in the Night" (ugh), and "Bel Di (One Fine Day)" will have you scratching your head and possibly breaking this record. —*Andrew Hamilton*

I Am What I Am / 1971 / Invictus ✦✦✦

● **Self Portrait/I Am What I Am** / Jul. 8, 1997 / Deep Beats ✦✦✦✦

Self-Portrait/I Am What I Am contains Ruth Copeland's first two albums on one disc. Copeland was a talented vocalist that was capable of anything from R&B and hot funk to folky pop. Her material didn't always match her talents, but she was supported by a tight, exciting band (Eddie Hazel plays on her blistering version of "Gimme Shelter") that helps make this two-fer of interest to '70s funk fetishists. —*Stephen Thomas Erlewine*

The Cordells

f. Los Angeles, CA

Group / R&B, Soul

Along with the original Harold Melvin & the Bluenotes, the Dreamlovers, and others, the Cordells were one of Philadelphia's pioneering R&B groups. The members were Jimmy Ellis, (lead), Earl Young (bass), Val Walker, and Russell Boston, all from the Broad & Lehigh area of North Philly. They recorded "Please Don't Go"/"Believe in Me," for

Bullseye Records in 1958 and didn't get the opportunity again until 1961 when "The Best of My Heart"/"Laid Off," fell on Bargain Records. Neither side was more than a local play and while the group kept busy doing local gigs and built a little reputation around town, nothing really happened for them.

Later in 1961, Ellis, Young, Walker, and Boston became the Whirlwinds and had releases on Guyden and Phillips Records. Ellis and Young later, after many attempts, found a modicum of success with the Trammps, noted for the quintessential disco hit "Disco Inferno." In addition, Young became a sought after session musician and recorded with Ron Baker and Norman Harris as Baker, Harris, & Young. *—Andrew Hamilton*

Cornelius Brothers & Sister Rose

f. 1971, Dania, FL

Group / Funk, Soul

A Florida family group, Cornelius Brothers & Sister Rose had a brief moment in the sun in 1972, with their self-titled United Artists LP. They scored two pop hits in "Too Late to Turn Back Now" and "Treat Her Like a Lady," and the album cracked the pop LP chart at number 29. They actually fared better with general audiences than R&B and soul fans, who found their arrangements, harmonies, and style lacking grit and intensity. They enjoyed one more mild hit in "Don't Ever Be Lonely (A Poor Little Fool Like Me)." But their two hits are among the most requested songs of the early '70s that air on oldies stations. *—Ron Wynn*

Cornelius Brothers & Sister Rose / 1972 / United Artists ✦✦✦

Big Time Lover / 1974 / United Artists ✦✦✦

● **Story of Cornelius Brothers & Sister Rose:** / Oct. 29, 1996 / Capitol ✦✦✦✦✦

This group's story is very much one of the songs overwhelming the singers: "Too Late to Turn Back Now" and "Treat Her Like a Lady" are remembered because of their catchy, AM-friendly melodies, not the performers' talents. It's true that the singers never came out with anything else as good, as this compilation of 1972-1976 material (including both of those monster hits, as well as some smaller ones and two previously unreleased cuts) demonstrates. But if you can adjust your expectations to accept that these aren't strikingly distinctive talents such as the O'Jays or the Spinners, you'll find some decent period "sweet" soul here. Songwriter and lead singer Eddie Cornelius had a knack for hooks that owed more to pop than R&B, though the soul never got quite as "sweet" as those of the Philly groups, with a bit of mild Sly or Jacksons influence popping up here and there. That helps render the verdict of: lightweight but enjoyable collection, by a minor but likable act. *—Richie Unterberger*

● **Classic Masters** / Jan. 29, 2002 / Capitol ✦✦✦✦✦

Cornelius Brothers & Sister Rose's edition of Capitol's *Classic Masters* series finds the smooth soul group in prime form. Their hits are here—"Treat Her Like a Lady," "Too Late to Turn Back Now," "Don't Ever Be Lonely"—along with some singles that only made an impact on the R&B charts, as well as a few album tracks. The three big singles are undoubtedly the best songs here, with some of the secondary material running toward a supper club feel, but even the weaker moments have a pleasant sound reminiscent of the hits—pleasant enough, it should satisfy most fans who like the sound of the hits as much as the songs. This, along with the fairly shrewd selection, make this collection one of the better Cornelius Brothers & Sister Rose compilations yet released. *—Stephen Thomas Erlewine*

The Corporation

Group / R&B, Soul

The Corporation—not to be confused with the 1969 Capitol Records act—was the name used by the songwriter/producer/arranger collective behind the early Motown hits of the Jackson 5, including their three consecutive number-one pop hits: "I Want You Back," "ABC," and "The Love You Save." The members were Motown founder Berry Gordy, Freddie Perren, Fonce Mizell, and Deke Richards. Some believe the Corporation was created to keep the identities of the creative team secret so that Motown wouldn't have more contentious superstars to deal with. (Around the time the Corporation was formed, Motown was in litigation with their former hitmaking trio Holland-Dozier-Holland.)

Shortly after moving to CA, pianist Perren and bassist Mizell met guitarist Richards, who had been a part of another Motown collective, the Clan. While working on song ideas, the trio came up with "I Wanna Be Free," which was suggested by Motown label president Berry Gordy as good for the teenage group he'd just signed. The song evolved into "I Want You Back." The track date included Perren and Mizell on piano, bassist Wilton Felder of the Crusaders, guitarists David T. Walker and Louis Shelton, Don Peake doubling the bassline, and drummer Gene Pello.

Perren was a former schoolteacher, so it's appropriate that the Jackson 5's next hit was "ABC." It became the group's second consecutive number-one single, topping the R&B chart and holding down the top spot of its pop chart for two weeks in the spring of 1970. "The Love You Save" used the same elements from the groups's last two number one records (the super-charged youthful energy of the brothers, the interplay between Michael and Jermaine, Tito's kid-bass voice, and top L.A. session musicians) and it *also* hit number one on R&B and pop. Though the Corporation weren't responsible for the Jackson 5's fourth consecutive number one single, "I'll Be There," they had a strong presence on the group's *Third Album*. The follow-up to "I'll Be There" was the Corporation's "Mama's Pearl," which stayed at number-two R&B/pop for two weeks in early 1971. The Jackson 5's 1971 album *Maybe Tomorrow* was produced by the Corporation.

Perren, Mizell, and Richards planned to release albums as the Corporation, but that never happened. Mizell and Perren worked on tracks by Edwin Starr and scored the soundtrack of the 1973 Fred Williamson/American International movie *Hell Up in Harlem*. But all three went on to have impressive careers. Freddie Perren produced post-Smokey hits on the Miracles ("Do It Baby," "Don't Cha Love It," "Love Machine, Pt. 1"), the Sylvers, Peaches & Herb, and Tavares. Mizell produced L.T.D. with lead vocals by Jeffrey Osborne (number one hit "Love Ballad") and A Taste of Honey (number-one hit "Boogie Oogie Oogie"), and Deke Richards had a hit with the Jackson 5's "Corner of the Sky" and went on to work with Black Oak Arkansas and Diana Ross. *—Ed Hogan*

The Corsairs

f. 1961, La Grange, NC

Group / Doo Wop, R&B

The Corsairs originated from La Grange, NC, releasing seven records as the Corsairs, and one as Landy McNeil & the Corsairs, the first on Smash, and the rest on Tuff Records. Their lineup consisted of three brothers, Jay, James, and Moses Uzzell, and cousin George Wooten. As the Gleems they sang at all the local functions and made their way north to the NJ/NY area, and were discovered harmonizing in a Newark, NJ, night spot by Abner Spector. Spector later hit with "Sally Go Round the Roses" by the Jaynetts. The family affair debuted on Smash as the Corsairs with "Time Waits" b/w "It Won't Be A Sin" in 1961, but it went unnoticed. For their second release Spector switched them to Tuff Records where they scored with "Smokey Places," which nearly cracked the pop Top Ten, settling at number 12 in 1961. Chess Records distributed this and their subsequent Tuff recordings. They followed with "I'll Take You Home" b/w "Sittin' on Your Doorstep" in 1962, a fine recording that stalled at number 62.

They kept releasing singles until 1964, but "Dancing Shadows," "At the Stroke of Midnight," "Stormy (It's Almost)," and "Save a Little Monkey" did next to nothing. A versatile group, all three brothers sang lead, their recordings bridged the gap between '50s doo wop and '60s R&B. They released their final recording in 1964, "The Change in You," b/w "On the Spanish Side," as Landy McNeil & the Corsairs, but the sound had stagnated and didn't stand a chance against current favs' like "My Girl," "Baby I Need Your Loving," and other mid-'60s sounds. *—Andrew Hamilton*

Dave "Baby" Cortez (David Cortez Clowney)

b. Aug. 13, 1938, Detroit, MI

Organ, Piano / Instrumental Rock, Soul

Though hardly a soulful, bluesy master like Jimmy Smith or dashing experimentalist like Larry Young, organist Dave "Baby" Cortez made his mark in the '50s,'60s, and '70s as a capable, often clever soloist and pop instrumentalist. His flair for catchy melodies, riffs, and hooks resulted in a number-one pop and number-five R&B hit with "The Happy Organ" in 1959. Cortez had another double winner in 1962 with "Rinky Dink," this one peaking at number-nine R&B and number-ten pop. Before his instrumental success, Cortez recorded for Ember as David Clowney in 1956, and was in the Pearls from 1955 to 1957. He landed one other song on the R&B Top 50, "Someone Has Taken Your Place," in 1973 for All Platinum. His other songs were recorded for Clock and Chess. There has been no domestic reissue of Cortez's songs, but there are import anthologies available. *—Ron Wynn*

The Happy Organ / 1959 / Collectables ✦✦✦

Rinky Dink / Sep. 1962 / Chess ✦✦✦

● **Happy Organs Wild Guitars & Piano Shuffles** / Mar. 1, 1994 / Ace ✦✦✦

Presented here are 25 songs recorded by Cortez, mostly or entirely, for Clock between 1958 and 1961—mostly or entirely because although each track is grouped into a "New York 1958-1961" discography, a couple of them are given the dates 1965 on the CD track listing; the three dated 1993 are presumably unreleased outtakes from the era (although they are not precisely identified as such). The real question is: do you need to hear anything else besides his number-one hit (and this album's opener) "The Happy Organ"? For almost everyone, the answer is no. The other songs are average R&B-based rockers, sometimes given a lift above similar generic instrumental fare from the era by Cortez's zippy organ and some sharp guitar (much or all of which was probably played by Jimmy Spruill, who did the guitar solo on "The Happy Organ"). The majority is instrumental, with Cortez occasionally adding vocals that are either perfunctory, or that fall within the ordinary, early black vocal group style (as on "Love Me as I Love You"). Otherwise, this is for instrumental rock fans only, although Cortez deserves credit for popularizing the organ as a rock instrument. The moody reading of "Summertime" isn't bad, and when he and the band get a little less restrained on "Tootsie," it seems possible that he could have influenced the sound of 1960s soul-rockers who used the organ, like Booker T. & the MG's. Cortez's low-charting, soundalike follow-up to "The Happy Organ," "The Whistling Organ," is included, but his only other big hit, "Rinky Dink" (1962), is not, as it was done for Chess. *—Richie Unterberger*

3 on 1: Organ Shindig/Tweetie Pie/In Orbit / Nov. 1995 / Sequel ✦✦

This disc brings together three of Cortez's little-known albums for the Roulette label: *Organ Shindig*, *In Orbit*, and *Tweetie Pie*. As several tracks on *Organ Shindig* were repeated on the later *Tweetie Pie* album, this CD pares the three albums down to the actual 27 tracks that appeared with no duplication. By and large, it's Cortez running through the hits of the early and mid-'60s (when all these were recorded) in his usual, powerful B-3 style. The *In Orbit* album features much more original material, but the entire disc consists of top-flight Hammond organ workouts that haven't dated at all, no matter what material he's working with. Highly recommended. *—Cub Koda*

The Counts

f. 1971, **db.** 1976

Group / Funk, Soul, Deep Funk

In the early '70s, the boundaries of black pop became more fluid. Soul and funk could intermingle with jazz, hard rock, psychedelia, and singer/songwriting. The Counts were not one of the more exceptional outfits that brewed these influences together; for one thing, they never stuck to any one mixture long enough for listeners to get a handle on the group. They were, however, emblematic of the currents sweeping through R&B at the time, even if they were hardly as innovative as, say, Funkadelic, or Marvin Gaye in his *What's Going On* period. Offering both vocal and instrumental tracks, the group could lay down loping, jazzy instrumental grooves heavy on the sax and organ. In a heartbeat, they could switch gears into spacy novelties like "Flies Over Watermelon!" and "The Munchies." In between there were some sweet soul ballads, and even a sop to the mainstream with a cover of Carole King's "Jazzman."

Originally a Detroit-based sextet, the Counts' first LP was an instrumental outing on Cotillion, with noted Michigan producer Ollie McLaughlin taking the co-writing credits on all of the songs. A few years later, the group moved to Atlanta, paring down to a quartet by the time they recorded the *Love Sign* album for the Aware label in 1973. An expanded lineup recorded the *Funk Pump* album for the same company in 1975; the two Aware albums formed the basis for CD reissues of the Counts' work in the mid-'90s, when their brand of soul-funk-jazz was becoming hip again. *—Richie Unterberger*

• **What's Up Front That Counts** / Sep. 1971 / Westbound ✦✦✦✦

Shortchanged by Westbound records in favor of the Ohio Players and Funkadelic, the Counts were a good band that didn't hang around long enough to sniff gold. "Rhythm Changes" dropped as a single while this LP, their first, incubated. The credit read "the Fabulous Counts," but by time the album emerged, they were simply the Counts. "Thinking Single" was the first 45 from the completed album, but "What's Up Front," a studio monster comprising eight minutes of stoner funk; the staccato-ish "Rock of Lies"; and "What's It All About," a lurching beat-ballad, were better choices. Style-wise, the Counts exhibited shades of the Ohio Players but were nowhere near as identifiable. Like the Bar-Kays, but to a much greater degree, the Counts didn't have a definitive style. But that hardly kept them from jamming their butts off, as they do on this disk. *—Andrew Hamilton*

Love Sign / 1973 / Aware ✦✦

Funk Pump / 1974 / Aware ✦✦✦

Golden Classics / 1993 / Collectables ✦✦✦

With just four pieces, the Counts sounded bigger. The Detroit quartet presented a variety of sounds that made them impossible to peg or name in a blindfold test. You never knew what to expect from them: a ballad, funk, fusion, Southern soul, uptown—you name it, they did it. Their versatility hampered their careers; successful recording artists tend to have one definitive sound and the Counts jumped all over the place. These 14 tracks may seem like a good overview from a band with few hits, but the disc misses the mark by not including some of their more commercial, albeit not very successful, tracks. Some of the jazzy selections are soothingly sweet, but nothing screams *essential!* *—Andrew Hamilton*

It's What's in the Groove / 1996 / Southbound ✦✦✦

Twenty tracks from 1973-1975, drawn from their *Love Sign* (1973) and *Funk Pump* (1975) albums, with a few stray odds and ends added. It's worth hearing if you want to check out something far more eclectic than the sweet soul that ruled the radio back then, yet considerably less weird than the Parliament-Funkadelic axis. *—Richie Unterberger*

Don Covay (Donald Randolph)

b. Mar. 24, 1938, Orangeburg, SC

Vocals / Soul, Deep Soul, Southern Soul

An R&B and soul songwriting great, Don Covay compositions have been recorded by everyone from the Rolling Stones to Jimi Hendrix, Gladys Knight to Wilson Pickett, and many others. Covay was the son of a Baptist preacher. He sang in his family's gospel group, the Cherry-Keys, as a youngster. Covay was born in Orangeburg, SC, but grew up in Washington, D.C., and joined the Rainbows alongside Marvin Gaye, John Berry, and Billy Stewart in the '50s. Covay also performed as a solo singer with Little Richard, who recorded Covay as Pretty Boy on the Atlantic release "Bip Bop Bip." Covay had moderate success with the single "Pony Time," which he co-wrote with Berry, for the Arnold label in 1960.

He began to hit his stride in 1964. Besides fronting Don Covay & the Goodtimers, he wrote "Mercy Mercy," "Sookie Sookie," and "See Saw," and had tunes recorded by Gene Chandler and Aretha Franklin. Covay did both blues and soul numbers for the Janus and Mercury labels in the '70s. His biggest hit as a performer was "See Saw," which made it to number five on the R&B charts in 1965. But his most electrifying number was 1973's "I Was Checkin' Out While She Was Checkin' In," which made it to number six. Covay was also part of the short-lived Soul Clan, with Solomon Burke, Arthur Conley, Ben E. King, and Joe Tex in 1968. Their collaboration "Soul Meeting" made it to number 34, but wasn't quite the elaborate or explosive number everyone had envisioned.

Covay made one LP for Gamble & Huff's Philadelphia International label in 1976, but *Travelin' in Heavy Traffic* proved a disappointment. Covay recorded for Newman in 1980, and got his last chart single with "Badd Boy." (Some of his singles were reissued on a 1994 Mercury release, *Checkin' in With Don Covay.*) An all-star gathering that included Ron Wood, Robert Cray, Bobby Womack, Iggy Pop, Peter Wolf, King, Todd Rundgren, Billy Squier, and Jimmy Witherspoon recorded a tribute album to Covay in 1993. After regaining his strength following many years of poor health, Covay finally returned to the studio and recorded *Adlib* in 2000.*—Ron Wynn*

See Saw / 1966 / Atlantic ✦✦✦✦✦

Don Covay rides his most creative crest as a solo artist with this hearty collection of songs. The settings are simplistic for Atlantic Records, which recorded similar artists in lusher settings. But rawness is what makes these recordings arresting. A guitarist as well as a singer, Covay's pickings aren't buried in the mix, and you don't need a Geiger counter to detect the grooves. Most impressive are "See Saw," "Mercy Mercy," "Sookie, Sookie," and "Boomerang," a call to dance with the feeling of Major Lance singing a Curtis Mayfield song. On "Fat Man," you wonder if he's singing about his old Washington, D.C., buddy Billy Stewart. The two began their careers with the Rainbows. *—Andrew Hamilton*

House of Blue Light / 1969 / Atlantic ✦✦✦✦✦

This album, credited to Don Covay and the Jefferson Lemon Blues Band, is not only a great record on its own terms, but it's sort of a black parallel/precursor to a few blues-rock LPs by white artists that sold a hell of a lot more copies around the same time. On the one hand, it's as solid a blues album as anyone associated with R&B was making in 1969 and contains some of the best guitar-based blues on Atlantic this side of that one-off Blind Willie McTell record that they did at the end of the '40s. The guitar blues, interspersed with some organ-based numbers, mixes with Covay's whooped and hollered vocals like someone caught a performance at some roadhouse 20 miles from nowhere in Mississippi—except that it's perfectly recorded, like someone sneaked Atlantic producer Herb Abramson and a late-'60s tape unit into a roadhouse 20 miles from nowhere. But the repertory ranges wider than that description would lead one to believe, from standards like "Key to the Highway" and "But I Forgive You Blues" to a brace of Covay originals, including the jaunty "Four Women," the soulful "Homemade Love" (which manages to be smooth, raw, and cute, all in six minutes), and two parts of "House of Blue Lights"—not the Freddie Slack/Don Raye song popularized by the Andrews Sisters, Merrill Moore, and Chuck Berry, but, rather, a mournful lament akin thematically and in tempo to the original "House of the Rising Sun," only more intense and serious. The organ, mouth harp, and guitar textures achieved on that seven-minute song ripple and shimmer as though lifted and slowed down from the Rolling Stones' "Street Fighting Man," while "But I Forgive You Blues" goes back to '20s and early-'30s basics (and is really cool, with the guitars isolated on one channel so you can appreciate the playing up close and personal). Much of the album sounds like the sonic and spiritual blueprint for *Let It Bleed* and *Exile on Main Street* and parts of *Layla & Other Assorted Love Songs.* Reissued in 2002 by the Sepiatone label in state-of-the-art sound and worth tracking down at twice the price they're charging (which is about what a vinyl copy would cost if you did find one). *—Bruce Eder*

Country Funk / 1970 / Polydor ✦✦✦

Superdude / 1973 / Mercury ✦✦✦

Don Covay hadn't seen a lot of chart activity since the '60s, and this is the soul singer/writer's comeback album. Single releases "Overtime Man," "I Was Checkin' Out While She Was Checkin' In," and "Somebody's Been Enjoying My Home" were all worthy of high recognition, but only "I Was Checkin'," a classic about a guy cheating on his woman while she's cheating on him at the same motel, made any real noise. "Leave Him, Pts. 1-2" is another good gritty track, but Mercury spoiled it by putting the first part on the A-side and the second on the B-side, which doesn't make a whole lot of sense. On the positive side, Covay breathes new life into "Money (That's What I Want)." The recording quality is slicker and better engineered than his earlier stuff, and there are more musicians, but the raw charm of "See Saw" and "Mercy Mercy" is missing. This is the mature, been-through-the-mill Don Covay, whose singing about adultery and promiscuity has a Southern/uptown soul feel. *—Andrew Hamilton*

Hot Blood / 1975 / Mercury ✦✦✦

Don Covay recorded with the Rainbows, the Soldier Boys, the Goodtimers, the Soul Clan, and solo as Pretty Boy, and his recording career experienced a mini-revival via his first Mercury album, *Superdude. Hot Blood* was supposed to continue the roll and take Covay to even higher planes. He even managed to get his old friends the Isley Brothers to contribute some liner notes. Things look promising when "It's Better to Have (And Don't Need)" started picking up airplay on R&B stations; the gritty soul tune remains vibrant these days on numerous websites and still screams with passion. But a second (and Covay's final) Mercury single, "Rumble in the Jungle," a play on the name of Muhammad Ali and George Foreman's celebrated boxing match, didn't live up to its title and hardly created a stir, let alone any rumblings. Then Mercury inexplicably dropped the ball, wasting tracks like "A Mind Is a Terrible Thing to Waste," "What's Good to You (Don't Have to Be Good for You)," the title track, and "Sexy Lady." *—Andrew Hamilton*

Travelin' in Heavy Traffic / 1976 / Philadelphia International ✦✦

★ **Mercy Mercy: The Definitive Don Covay** / Oct. 19, 1994 / Razor & Tie ✦✦✦✦✦

To many R&B fans, Don Covay is better-remembered as a songwriter than as a vocalist, which isn't difficult to understand given the fact his tunes were covered by everyone from Wilson Pickett and Aretha Franklin to the Rolling Stones and Steppenwolf. But this certainly shortchanges his skills as a frontman; if Covay wasn't a brilliant vocalist, he was a highly expressive one, and he was able to move from rough-and-ready soul shouters like "Take This Hurt off Me" to heartfelt ballads such as "A Woman's Love" without missing a step or losing a bit of his dynamic presence in the process (and he certainly knew how to make the most of his own songs, no small feat given the many interpretations of his biggest hits). *Mercy Mercy: The Definitive Don Covay* compiles 23 songs (nearly all of which Covay wrote or co-wrote as well as sang), which span his career from the early '60s (the frantic "Bip Bob Bip" and "Pony Time," later a hit for Chubby Checker) to the mid-'70s (the hard-driving "No Tell Motel" from a 1976 session for Philadelphia International). *Mercy Mercy: The Definitive Don Covay* is a thorough career overview of an truly underappreciated artist, and certainly the best place to begin examining his recordings. *—Mark Deming*

"Ooh! My Soul" (The Rockin' Years) / Official ✦✦✦✦✦

The liner notes give only a few sketchy career details and little about the actual tracks on this 26-track compilation, which is probably unauthorized. But it can be safely assumed that it covers roughly the mid-'50s to the mid-'60s, as it reaches way back to some sides he did as a member of the Rainbows, and all the way up to "See Saw" and "Mercy, Mercy." Only a half dozen or so of the tracks are on Razor & Tie's *Mercy Mercy* collection, so this goes a lot further into the roots of one of soul music's most interesting journeymen. It's erratic but fun, and in a way serves as a mini-primer on African-American rock through the mid-'60s, including doo wop; obvious Little Richard imitations, some very rawly performed and recorded; early 1960s dance tunes along the lines of Hank Ballard, like "Pony Time" and "The Fat Man"; a Ben E. King cop, "See About Me" (covered by Gladys Knight and the Pips); and, ultimately, early quality soul in which Covay found a more distinct songwriting voice. Unfortunately this doesn't have some good mid-'60s tracks like "Please

Do Something" and "Sookie Sookie" (though those are on *Mercy Mercy*). Strange and very debatable assertion from the liner notes: "The very best song that the Jimi Hendrix Experience ever played was 'Mercy Mercy.'" *—Richie Unterberger*

The Cover Girls

f. 1986, New York

Group / Freestyle, Urban, Dance-Pop

This NY female dance/pop trio was the project of music promoter Sal Abbatiello and had a revolving lineup of vocalists, starting with Louise "Angel" Sabater, Sunshine Wright, and Caroline Jackson. This version of the group had three minor R&B chart hits in 1987. By the time of their 1989 Capitol album *We Can't Go Wrong*, Wright was replaced by Margo Urban. This lineup scored a number-eight pop hit in the album's title track. For the 1992 release *Here It Is*, Abbatiello replaced Urban and Sabater with Evelyn Escalera and Michelle Valentine, and by 1996's *Satisfy* none of the original Cover Girls remained. Instead, vocal duties were handled by a new trio of vocalists, Damie, Gayle, and Shelia, on this effort. *—Heather Phares*

Show Me / 1987 / Fever ✦✦✦✦

The original members of the Cover Girls (Louise "Angel" Sabater, Sunshine Wright, and Caroline Jackson) weren't fantastic singers; their voices were undeniably thin. But then, no one honestly believed that they were the next Martha & the Vandellas. Despite their obvious limitations as singers, the Cover Girls made some memorable contributions to Latin freestyle—in fact, their debut album, *Show Me*, is among freestyle's most important releases. Boasting such producers as Andy "Panda" Tripoli, Louis Martinee (the brains behind Expose), and Little Louie Vega, *Show Me* is full of infectious, Latin-flavored dance-pop grooves that no freestyle enthusiast should be without. "Inside Outside," "Because of You," "One Night Affair" (not to be confused with the Gamble & Huff classic), and the hit title track are, without question, some of freestyle's most essential recordings. Meanwhile, the unexpected and very retro "That Boy of Mine" finds the NY trio recalling the girl group sound of the early '60s. *Show Me* contains a few mediocre tunes, but they are the exception instead of the rule. All things considered, *Show Me* is an album that anyone with even a casual interest in freestyle should own. *—Alex Henderson*

We Can't Go Wrong / Aug. 30, 1989 / Capitol ✦✦✦

This manufactured group of rotating vocalists had success with this album due to the strong singles "We Can't Go Wrong," "All That Glitters Isn't Gold," and "My Heart Skips a Beat." The rest of the album is by-the-numbers filler, however; not that it's not enjoyable, it's just not very interesting. In some ways, the trio sounded dated even when their singles were first being released, and, where Paula Abdul embodies '80s music even in the 21st century, the Cover Girls were parodies at the time—even the cover of this album looked bargain bin when it was first released. The marketing, the production, and the writing ("I don't know what to do/I'm so in love with you") weren't up to the fight for more prominence for the Cover Girls, which is unfortunate, because when Louise "Angel" Sabater, Margo Urban, and Caroline Jackson Calister are allowed to shine, they're good. There's a simple quality to their voices that gives "We Can't Go Wrong" a particularly plaintive tone, and the mindful "All That Glitters Isn't Gold" is undeniable. Those two cuts are strong enough to make the album somewhat worthwhile, but much of the rest of the material is weak despite some unquestionably catchy hooks (notably "Once Upon a Time" and "Cute," which, despite being too precious, isn't as bad as you'd expect from the title). The positive aspects are that the group was part of the freestyle movement of the late '80s and, despite the adolescent lyrics of cuts like "Nothing Could Be Better" or "That Boy of Mine," the Cover Girls sound like a '60s girl group, and girl groups throughout the decades have never been much about maturity (think the Shangri-Las or the Crystals)—they've been about boys, love, and fun. So though their pop careers waned after this album, the girls are in good company. *—Bryan Buss*

Here It Is / 1992 / Epic ✦✦✦✦

By the time this pioneering freestyle trio's third album release rolled around, the group had undergone three lineup changes, and it had become clear that the name the Cover Girls was more of a marketing concept than a real, live group. It's hard to know exactly which member is doing what, given that the credits fail to mention leads and—most importantly—the "unseen" backing vocalists that seem to be supporting the girls on nearly every track. The 12-inch for the driving "Funk Boutique," which had been released in single form a year and a half before this album saw the light of day, even credited producer Tony Moran and long-time session vocalist Debbe Cole with background vocals—their voices are still heard prominently here, but aren't mentioned. Many different vocal shades and colors are found on the choruses of various tracks, but there's no clue as to who helped the trio. It cannot be denied that dance is a producer-driven genre, and despite the shadiness of non-crediting found here, the grooves are smokin', and the powerhouse lead vocals by Michelle Valentine and Evelyn Escalera are dynamite in the context. *Here It Is* begins with the deceptively morose "Wishing on a Star," a cover of the 1978 Rose Royce hit. Valentine displays ample soul and tenderness with her vocals, turning in a performance which surpasses the vitality of the original and resulted in a number-nine pop hit. Meanwhile, Escalera, whose voice is remarkably similar, throws down defiantly on "Still Miss You," a spicy brew of freestyle, house and traditional Latin elements. Nearly every other cut on the album lives up to the one before it. The melodically soulful "Always" may be midtempo, but its seeping bassline, coy guitar effects and varied percussion fills make it an inimitable club number; the relentless "If You Want My Love (Here It Is)" has a jazzy vibe via its quasi-horn arrangement and is lyrically contagious; and the saucy "That Feeling" merges James Brown-esque samples and hip-hop beats with a house bassline, a memorable R&B melody and an irresistible vocal arrangement. The charming melody and fairy-tale lyrics of "Thank You," the album's other ballad, provide a nice balance toward the middle of the album. *Here It Is* is an essential piece for freestyle stalwarts and any fans of '90s club music. *—Justin Kantor*

● **Greatest Hits** / Jul. 14, 1998 / Warlock ✦✦✦✦✦

Deborah Cox

Vocals / Contemporary R&B, House, Dance-Pop, Club/Dance, Urban

A native of Toronto, Deborah Cox began singing for TV commercials at age 12, also entering various talent shows with her mother's help. She performed in nightclubs as a teenager, and around this time, she also began to write her own material with the help of writer, producer, and future romantic interest Lascelles Stephens. Much like Whitney Houston, with whom she is often compared vocally as well, Cox was discovered, shortly after graduating from high school, by Arista Records president Clive Davis. Davis recruited some of the top names in R&B to provide Cox with material for her 1995 debut, including Babyface, Dallas Austin, and Keith Crouch, but Cox herself co-wrote her first hit single, "Sentimental," with Austin and bass player Colin Wolfe, along with three other tracks on the album. *Deborah Cox, Vol. 2* followed in 1998, launching the R&B chart-topper "We Can't Be Friends." *—Steve Huey*

● **Deborah Cox** / Sep. 12, 1995 / Arista ✦✦✦✦

Like Whitney Houston and Mariah Carey, Deborah Cox straddles the line between soul and pop, appealing to adult contemporary and R&B fans in equal measures. She is a confident and stylish singer, but her self-titled debut is helped by considerably by the powerhouse producers work behind the scenes. Featuring tracks produced by Babyface, Dallas Austin, and Daryl Simmons among others, the record is filled with immaculately crafted dance-pop and ballads. Not all of the songs are up to the production standards, however. Like many singers in her genre, Deborah Cox is only as good as her material, and the songs on their debut are uneven. She shines on the hit "Sentimental" and several other cuts, including "Never Gonna Break My Heart Again" and the poppy "Who Do U Love," but nearly half of the record consists of undistinguished material. Nevertheless, the best songs on the album suggests that Cox has the potential to develop into a star. *—Stephen Thomas Erlewine*

One Wish / Sep. 15, 1998 / Arista ✦✦✦✦

Arista set out to make a huge star of Deborah Cox. Her first album scored a couple of moderate hits, but with her second they were poised to turn the burgeoning belter into a new Whitney Houston. That didn't quite happen, but the set did make her into a considerable star, thanks in part to her monster cross-format smash "Nobody's Supposed to Be Here." An interesting thing happened the year before this album's release. Cox recorded a song for the *Money Talks* soundtrack, "Things Just Ain't the Same." The song was not a big hit initially, but a dance mix picked up steam in clubs across the U.S., and after several months turned into a huge dance smash, which in turn opened the singer to a whole new audience almost unexpectedly. Therefore, the first official single from *One Wish*, "Nobody's Supposed to Be Here," was released as an R&B ballad to urban radio stations, and as a revved-up club anthem to pop stations and club DJs. The song was a smash, spending countless weeks atop the R&B charts and eight weeks at number two on the U.S. pop charts, cementing the singer's newfound broad appeal. That feat wasn't repeated, although the album scored another Top Ten pop hit with dramatic ballad "We Can't Be Friends," a duet with labelmate R.L. of the group Next. The album's musical spectrum was varied, ranging from the typical cheating man song popular at the time (the second single, "It's Over Now," which, in a remixed version, topped the dance charts), to safe middle-of-the-road, adult contemporary fare ("Couldn't We" and the beautiful "One Day You Will"), funky R&B tunes (one of the set's highlights, "One Wish"), and club anthems, including the dance mix of "Things Just Ain't the Same." Cox's voice, a powerhouse unto itself, sounds just as effective and very sweet when she's not belting out a tune Whitney Houston-style (evident on "I Won't Give Up"). The album also includes a bonus track, which is a hip-hop mix of the set's midtempo opener "September." A good album, which includes a couple of quintessential 1990s dance hits, and a prime example of Arista's incomparable marketing savvy. *—Jose Promis*

The Morning After / Nov. 5, 2002 / J-Records ✦✦✦

Randy Crawford

b. Feb. 18, 1952, Macon, GA

Vocals / Soul, Urban, Smooth Jazz

Randy Crawford's initial notoriety came from her fiery vocal on "Street Life," a 1979 song matching her with the Crusaders that was included on the soundtrack for Burt Reynolds' film *Sharky's Machine*. Crawford was born in Macon and grew up in Cincinnati; she worked in clubs as a teen, accompanied by her father. Crawford was lead vocalist in a group that included bassist Bootsy Collins before touring as George Benson's opening act in 1972. Cannonball Adderley invited her to sing on his LP *Big Man*. Crawford recorded "Don't Get Caught in Love's Triangle," a song produced by Johnny Bristol, during a short stay on the label. She soon moved to Warner Bros., and after "Street Life," recorded and toured Europe with the Crusaders. Crawford was tabbed Most Outstanding Performer at the 1980 Tokyo Music Festival.

She remained with Warner Bros. through the '80s and early '90s, but was unable to score either a big R&B hit or major crossover smash, despite having one of the most readily identifiable voices and distinctive approaches of any contemporary female vocalist. She's been more successful overseas, particularly in England, where such singles as "Knockin' on Heaven's Door," "Rainy Night in Georgia," and "Last Night at Danceland" have gotten universal acclaim. *—Ron Wynn*

Miss Randy Crawford / 1977 / Warner Bros. ✦✦✦✦

Randy Crawford's charming debut was produced by Bob Montgomery (Bobby Goldsboro, Billy Sherrill) with some tracks having a slight country-ish/Southern soul feel to them. Its a perfect showcase for Crawford's interpretive skill.The singer makes the Don

Henley/Glenn Frey song "Desperado" and the Mack Gordon/Harry Warren standard "At Last," her own. The former and her erotically charged take on Paul Kelly's "Under the Influence of You" received airplay on R&B/soul-formatted FM stations. *Miss Randy Crawford* was a tasty precursor for what was to come. *—Ed Hogan*

Raw Silk / 1979 / Warner Bros. ✦✦✦

• **Now We May Begin** / 1980 / Warner Bros. ✦✦✦✦
The Crusaders produced this '80 album, one of the better Randy Crawford sets. The song "Last Night At Danceland" was a hit, while the album cut "One Day I'll Fly Away" got widespread radio airplay and did well in the international market. Crawford's quivering delivery and eclectic nature has made it difficult for record companies to target and market her material; this was one of the few times she penetrated the urban contemporary and R&B markets. *—Ron Wynn*

Secret Combination / 1981 / Warner Bros. ✦✦✦
Randy Crawford made even more noise on the urban contemporary and R&B front in 1981 with this album, one of her most successful ever from a chart and hit standpoint. The title track and the album cut "Rio De Janeiro Blue" were well-received. She continued smartly blending jazzy pop, slick ballads, and earnest, anguished numbers like her cover of "Rainy Night in Georgia." *—Ron Wynn*

Windsong / 1982 / Warner Bros. ✦✦✦
This is another strong album for Randy Crawford; the song "Imagine" remains one of the best R&B covers/versions around, while "One Hello" did well in Europe and made it to the charts, as did "Imagine," although it broke later in America. Crawford sang with consistency and character on every number. *—Ron Wynn*

Nightline / 1983 / Warner Bros. ✦✦✦
Here is a nice combination of jazzy, sophisticated ballads, a few harder-hitting numbers, and some heartache material. The title track made it to the Top 30 on the R&B chart, and Crawford was a popular attraction on the urban contemporary and upscale R&B concert circuit. *—Ron Wynn*

Abstract Emotions / 1986 / Warner Bros. ✦✦✦
Randy Crawford continued her run of good '80s albums, generating more R&B chart hits with this 1986 release, plus an international smash with "Almaz." The album even reached Britain's Top 20, while two of its singles were moderate American successes. *—Ron Wynn*

The Very Best of Randy Crawford / 1994 / Alex ✦✦✦✦
If Randy Crawford was a car, she would be a fully loaded Lexus. Compiling a best of album by Crawford is easy, you simply make sure you include "Street Life" and "Knockin' on Heaven's Door," then you pick at least 12 more songs from her array of albums; any 12, it doesn't matter which ones you choose cause she doesn't make bad tracks, everything she does is first class. Recent Crawford best-ofs omit "Cigarette in the Rain," and this one doesn't have "Give Me the Night" or "Your Precious Love" but makes up for the omissions with sterling renditions of "Rainy Night in Georgia" and "I Stand Accused"—a wash. Crawford's remarkable voice croons, caresses, teases, and pleases on 18 gems, four more than you'll find on *The Best of Randy Crawford*. *—Andrew Hamilton*

• **Best of Randy Crawford** / Apr. 1996 / Warner Bros. ✦✦✦✦✦
The Best of Randy Crawford highlights her jazzy urban R&B hits, including "Street Life," "Give Me the Night" and the Al Jarreau duet "Your Precious Love," among many others. Nearly all of her finest moments are included, making the compilation the perfect introduction to Crawford's career. *—Stephen Thomas Erlewine*

Creative Source

f. 1972, Los Angeles, CA
Group / Funk, Soul
The Los Angeles-based quintet Creative Source seemingly appeared out of nowhere in the early '70s to score with a funky disco rendition of Bill Withers' "Who Is He (And What Is He to You)." The group, comprised of Barbara Berryman, Barbara Lewis, Don Wyatt, Steve Ranagan, and Celeste Rose, was managed by Fifth Dimensions' Ron Townsend and two of the members were seasoned vets. Lewis sang with the Los Angeles Elgins on their Lummtone recordings, while Wyatt performed with a pair of late-'50s groups (the Fortunes and the Colts) and also sang in Nat King Cole's background group for a spell.

Mike Stokes produced their first and most successful album, 1974's *Creative Source*, released on Sussex Records (also Withers' label at the time). The *Migration* album followed later in 1974, but failed to spawn anything major despite Skip Scarborough's exquisite vocal arrangements. Creative Source's other significant singles were "You Can't Hide Love" (the Earth, Wind & Fire ditty), "You're Too Good to Be True," and "I Just Can't See Myself Without You."

Wrongly labeled by many as strictly disco and funk, Creative Source could mellow out with the best of them, such as Withers' "Let Me in Your Life," a floating beauty, and "You're Too Good to Be True," where the male lead sounds like a cross between Tyrone Davis and Jerry Butler. Polydor issued their final two albums (*Pass the Feelin' On* and *Consider the Source*), which were as compelling as the Sussex productions, but a lack of promotion and public indifference caused them both to fizzle. With little backing and no label after Polydor, Creative Source drifted back into basic Southern CA nine-to-five living. *—Andrew Hamilton*

• **... And More** / Feb. 4, 1997 / Polygram ✦✦✦✦✦
This smooth-singing quintet faded after four woefully underappreciated albums on Sussex and Polydor Records. The choicest picks from those LPs appear on this veiled best-of collection. Blessed with a sultry female lead and a male that possessed a baritone like Jerry Butler's (only rangier), this Los Angeles-based group was something special. They deliver a peppy, jazzy version of "You Can't Hide Love" that's totally different from Earth, Wind & Fire's. Bill Withers' songs are like magical elixirs to Creative Source. They excel on his mellow "Let Me Into Your Life," where the male lead slides effortlessly from baritone up to falsetto, and the hypnotic "Who Is He and What Is He to You," which flows like Moret for more than 11 minutes; the LP also contains the shorter radio edit. Steppenwolf's "Magic Carpet Ride" and Skylark's "Wildflower" get classy, designer makeovers. Special kudos to the imaginative arrangements, especially Brad Shapiro's tantalizing horn charts. *—Andrew Hamilton*

The Crests

f. 1956, **db.** 1960
Group / Doo Wop
One of the most successful integrated doo wop groups, the Crests waxed the classic ballad "16 Candles" in 1959. Formed in 1956, they began recording the next year for Joyce, where they inched onto the pop lists with "Sweetest One." Moving to the brand-new Coed logo, Johnny Maestro's (b. May 7, 1930) warm tenor made "16 Candles" a national smash, and pop/R&B hybrids like "The Angels Listened In" and "Step by Step" also did well. Maestro went solo in 1960, scoring the next year with "Model Girl" on Coed, while the Crests attempted to survive on their own. Maestro eventually reclaimed stardom as leader of Brooklyn Bridge, an 11-piece aggregation that hit with "Worst That Could Happen" in 1968. *—Bill Dahl*

The Crests Sing All Biggies / 1960 / Sundazed ✦✦✦
This features eloquent crooning by the Crests, starting with their fourth single, "Sixteen Candles." Three previous singles (two on Joyce and one on Coed Records) didn't make the cut. But then, the title is *The Crests Sing All Biggies*, and that they do, taking you down Crest Lane with "Six Nights a Week," "The Angels Listened In," "In the Still of the Night," and a shimmering "Earth Angel." Crests fans will bristle at the omissions, but they'll appreciate having these 16 timeless doo wops and Bob Hyde's informative liner notes in one package. *—Andrew Hamilton*

• **The Best of the Crests Featuring Johnny Maestro** / 1990 / Rhino ✦✦✦✦✦
Rhino's *The Best of the Crests Featuring Johnny Maestro* is a generous 18-track collection that contains all of the doo wop group's greatest hits, along with a selection of singles, B-sides, and album tracks that prove that the Crests were one of the finest outfits of their time. There may not be any earth-shaking revelations among the songs that didn't make the charts, but there is certainly a bunch of fine music, and this is worth the time of any serious doo wop fan. *—Stephen Thomas Erlewine*

Greatest Hits / Apr. 19, 1990 / Collectables ✦✦✦
This 18-track collection compiles the notable sides Johnny Maestro and the Crests recorded for the NY-based Coed label. Although their debut single—the doo wop collector favorite "My Juanita," originally released on the Joyce label—isn't aboard, all of their biggies like the classic "16 Candles," "Six Nights a Week," "The Angels Listened In," "A Year Ago Tonight," "Step By Step," and "Trouble in Paradise" more than pick up the slack. The transfers are excellent, many of them amazingly in true stereo. There's a reason that this mixed group of four African-Americans and a white Italian lead singer is so revered by doo wop collectors, and here's where you find their legacy. *—Cub Koda*

For Collectors Only / Aug. 26, 1994 / Collectables ✦✦✦✦✦
This is a 40-song overview of the Crests, one of R&B's first integrated groups (lead vocalist Johnny Maestro is white). Though racially mixed, listeners were never conscious of that when listening to their music because Maestro's feel for doo wop was genuine. His leads were as extraordinary as any in the business. Not an original member, Maestro joined when they debuted on Joyce Records in 1957 as a quintet with Patricia Vandross (Luther Vandross' older sister); Vandross left before the Coed recordings, reducing the Crests to quartet. Prior to the Crests, Maestro sang with Tony Orlando in another integrated group. The 40 tracks are almost a complete discography of their glory years on Coed Records from 1958 to 1961, and the tunes aren't in chronological order. Their most noted singles—"16 Candles," "Six Nights a Week," and "The Angels Listened In"—are here, along with stimulating remakes like "Earth Angel" and "I Remember (In the Still of the Night)." Their final Coed recording is missing, which makes the "for collectors only" tag dubious. (Nothing before the Joyce sides or after Coed made this collection either.) Maestro left after Coed, but some members regrouped and recorded on Selma and Trans Atlantic Records. Maestro failed as a solo artist and as Johnny Maestro & the Crests on Parkway Records with the Tymes backing him, before happier times with Brooklyn Bridge. *—Andrew Hamilton*

Steve Cropper

b. Oct. 21, 1941, Willow Spring, MO
Guitar, Producer / Soul, Funk, Electric Blues, Modern Electric Blues
Probably the best-known soul guitarist in the world, Cropper came to prominence in the early '60s, first with the Mar-Keys ("Last Night"), then as a founding member of Booker T. & the MG's. A major figure in the Southern soul movement of the '60s, Cropper made his mark not only as a player and arranger (most notably on classic sides by Otis Redding, Sam & Dave, and Wilson Pickett) but as a songwriter as well, co-writing the classic "In the Midnight Hour." After the breakup of the MG's, Cropper spent most of the '70s producing Jeff Beck and Mitch Ryder, among others. In the '80s, he rode the classic Stax sound (which he helped shape) back to popularity with a new audience when actors John Belushi and Dan Aykroyd tapped him for service in the Blues Brothers, a *Saturday Night Live* skit that stretched into several albums and a movie. *—Cub Koda*

Jammed Together / 1969 / Stax ✦✦✦

• **With a Little Help from My Friends** / 1971 / Stax ✦✦✦✦
After years of being a team player, Steve Cropper got to make a solo album for the label he helped put on the map, Stax Records (actually their Volt subsidiary). As you might figure, it turned out as an instrumental soul album, and a darn good one, too. It's a bona fide Telecaster-soaked dance workout, with Steve turning in signature versions of "Land of a

Thousand Dances," "99 1/2" (which features a particularly nasty period fuzz guitar), "Funky Broadway," "Boo-Ga-Loo Down Broadway," "In the Midnight Hour," and original instrumentals like "Crop Dustin'" and the closer "Rattlesnake." A solid and soulful little side project that holds up quite well years later. *—Cub Koda*

Playing My Thang / 1980 / MCA ✦✦

Crown Heights Affair

f. New York, NY [Brooklyn]

Group / Disco, Soul

A good band that cut several fine funk and disco songs during the '70s, Crown Heights Affair enjoyed a regional hit with "Super Rod" in 1973. Lead vocalist Phillip Thomas, saxophonist Bert Reid, guitarist Raymond Reid, guitarist/vocalist William Anderson, trumpeter James "Ajax" Baynard, vocalist/drummer Raymond Rock, keyboardist Howie Young, and bassist/vocalist Muki Wilson were the original lineup. They switched from RCA to Dee-Lite, and remained there until 1983. Their 1975 release "Dreaming a Dream" was an international smash, reaching the number-five position on the R&B charts and scoring with club audiences everywhere. It was their biggest hit, although their subsequent singles "Every Beat of My Heart," "Foxy Lady," and "Dancin'" all were Top 20 R&B hits.

Things slowed afterward, with "Dance Lady Dance" being their last major single in 1979. The group's fortunes suffered through a combination of the anti-disco backlash and decline of large funk and soul bands. The Reids finally left in 1986, but Crown Heights Affair continued recording. House music maven Marshall Jefferson remixed the 1989 single "I'll Do Anything." Ray Reid also teamed with Anderson to co-produce several dance music artists, among them Unlimited Touch, France Joli, and Trilark. *—Ron Wynn*

Do It Your Way / 1976 / De Lite ✦✦✦

With one foot in disco and the other in soul/funk, the Crown Heights Affair had a very recognizable sound that effectively combined grit and gloss. The Brooklyn residents could get funky, but it wasn't the type of hardcore, gutbucket funk that Parliament/ Funkadelic, Rick James, the Ohio Players, the Bar-Kays and the Gap Band were known for. And while Crown Heights Affair had plenty of disco appeal, it wasn't the type of Euro-disco that Cerrone, the Silver Convention and Donna Summer gave us. One of the band's best albums was *Do It Your Way*, which boasted the Top 20 R&B hit "Dancin'." While radio favored "Dancin'," clubs weren't about to play the single exclusively—club DJs considered the entire album fair game, and they knew that infectious album cuts like "Music Is the World," "Love Me" and "Searching for Your Love" could easily bring a dancefloor to life. Thankfully, Unidisc reissued *Do It Your Way* on CD in 1994. *—Alex Henderson*

Dream World / 1978 / Mercury ✦✦

The NY-born disco band Crown Heights Affair is best known for their Top Five R&B/Top 40 pop hit "Dreaming a Dream." On *Dream World*, the group combined the optimistic tone of that smash with a slightly heavier funk tone; though their trademark horn sound is still in tact, "Galaxy of Love" is a fun, brassy romp that retains some of the frothy flavor of "Dreaming" and was a Top Five hit in the U.K. The huge club hit "Say a Prayer for Two" has gospel-ish lead vocals, a driving bass similar to Brass Construction's "Movin'," and charted number-41 R&B in the fall of 1978. *—Ed Hogan*

Sure Shot / 1980 / Mercury ✦✦

Crown Heights Affair had a string of hits beginning with the number-five R&B/Top 40 hit "Dreaming a Dream" in the summer of 1975 and also including the Top 20 R&B hits "Every Beat of My Heart," "Foxy Lady,"—not the Jimi Hendrix classic—and "Dancin'." Though the title track of their 1980 LP *Sure Shot* managed to chart number 72 in the summer of 1980, it was an album track that garnered the most attention. The radio-aired smooth dance cut "Use Your Body and Soul" embodies both the band's upbeat sound, elements of Chic, and a get-up-and-dance rap break/interlude. *—Ed Hogan*

● **Dreams of De-Lite: Essential Crown Heights Affair** / Oct. 29, 1996 / Castle ✦✦✦✦✦

● **Striking Gold: The Best of Crown Heights Affair** / Apr. 22, 1997 / Deep Beats ✦✦✦✦

One of the first of many subsequent best-of CDs featuring the Crown Heights Affair, and it still kicks! While named after a lively, mostly urban section of Brooklyn, NY, the band has a disco/soul sound that occasionally gets raw, i.e., "Sure Shot" and some others. Highs include their signature "Dreamin' a Dream," which is as infectious as anything from the era, the explorative "Foxy Lady," "Far Out," "Love Ripoff," "Say a Prayer For You," and "Rock the World," an old-school rap joint. *—Andrew Hamilton*

The Crows

f. 1951, New York, NY, **db.** 1954

Group / Doo Wop

One of the first doo wop groups, one of the first so-called bird groups, and one of the first acts of any kind to score a bona fide rock & roll hit record, the Crows were among the more important one-shot artists in rock & roll history. Discovered at New York's Apollo Theater in 1952, the Crows were one of the many groups pioneering doo wop with their infectious, cheerful vocals and harmonies, use of nonsense syllables, and modified jump blues instrumental backing. Cut in 1953, "Gee," with its irresistible melody, naively enthusiastic street-corner singing, and Charlie Christian-like guitar solo, was far and away their best single. It was also their only successful one, although it needed almost a year to take off, reaching number 14 on the pop charts (and number two on the R&B charts) in early 1954. Recording about a half-dozen other 45s between 1952 and 1954, the group broke up with little fanfare only months after "Gee" fell off the hit parade. *—Richie Unterberger*

● **Gee, It's the Crows** / 1988 / Murray Hill ✦✦✦✦✦

Here are sixteen sides covering their complete output for the Jubilee and Rama labels between 1952 and 1954, including all their singles, as well as 45s on which they backed Fatman Humphries (as the 4 Notes) and Lorraine Ellis. It's a respectable mix of uptempo numbers and ballads that will appeal to few listeners besides doo wop aficionados. By far the best of the batch besides "Gee" is their final single, "Sweet Sue," a snazzy, uptempo cut with a thumping beat. "I Love You So," the flipside of "Gee," is also well-remembered by doo wop fans, and was covered a few years later by The Chantels. Includes detailed liner notes and discography. *—Richie Unterberger*

Strictly for the Birds: The Rama and Gee Recordings 1953-1956 / Feb. 8, 2000 / WestSide ✦✦✦✦✦

For the first time on CD, this brings together all the extant recordings by both of these groups: their complete output for George Goldner between 1953 and 1956. This 30-track collection, split evenly between the two groups, also includes five never before available alternate takes. The Crows were simply one of New York's seminal doo wop groups, and tracks like "Gee," "I Love You So," "Untrue," and "Miss You" are utterly charming in their basic crudity. The Wrens were more urbane and their takes on "Come Back My Love" and "Eleven Roses" are two of the many highlights in Goldner's vocal-group crown. As an absolutely essential piece of vocal group—and rock & roll—history, this is the real thing and then some. *—Cub Koda*

Arthur "Big Boy" Crudup

b. Aug. 24, 1905, Forest, MS, **d.** Mar. 28, 1974, Nassawadox, VA

Vocals, Guitar / Electric Delta Blues, Electric Blues, Delta Blues, R&B

Arthur Crudup may well have been Elvis Presley's favorite bluesman. The swivel-hipped rock god recorded no less than three of Big Boy's Victor classics during his seminal rockabilly heyday—"That's All Right Mama" (Elvis' Sun debut in 1954), "So Glad You're Mine," and "My Baby Left Me." Often lost in all the hubbub surrounding Presley's classic covers are Crudup's own contributions to the blues lexicon. He didn't sound much like anyone else, and that makes him an innovator, albeit a rather rudimentary guitarist (he didn't even pick up the instrument until he was 30 years old). Crudup pierced the uppermost reaches of the R&B lists during the mid-'40s with "Rock Me Mama," "Who's Been Foolin' You," "Keep Your Arms Around Me," "So Glad You're Mine," and "Ethel Mae." He cut the original "That's All Right" in 1946, but it wasn't a national hit at the time. In 1961, Crudup surfaced after a long layoff with an album for the Fire logo dominated by remakes of his early hits. Another lengthy hiatus preceded Delmark boss Bob Koester's following the tip of Big Joe Williams to track down the elusive legend (Crudup had drifted into contract farm labor work in the interim). Happily, the guitarist's sound hadn't been dimmed by Father Time: His late-'60s work for Delmark rang true. Finally, Crudup began to make some decent money, playing various blues and folk festivals for appreciative crowds for a few years prior to his 1974 death. *—Bill Dahl*

★ **That's All Right Mama** / 1992 / Bluebird ✦✦✦✦✦

If Arthur "Big Boy" Crudup had never made another fan in the course of his career than a certain young kid in Memphis, TN, his place in music history would still have been assured—Elvis Presley often cited Crudup as one of his favorite blues artists, and the future "King of Rock & Roll" recorded three of Crudup's songs ("That's All Right, Mama," "My Baby Left Me," and "So Glad You're Mine"), bringing them to a far wider audience then their original author would ever enjoy on his own. Anyone expecting to hear Elvis' primal influence on *That's All Right, Mama*, a compilation of 22 songs Crudup recorded for the RCA-affiliated Bluebird label between 1941 and 1954, might be a bit disappointed—for the most part, this is rough-and-ready rural blues, dominated by Crudup's big, boomy voice and simple but efficient guitar runs, though by the end of the disc, drums, electric guitars, and even saxophone have begun to creep into the mix, suggesting a stripped-down but high-powered Chicago blues combo. In short, this isn't rock & roll, or even R&B, but pure blues stuff, and it certainly makes clear that Presley's influences were a lot rawer and deeper than most folks would lead you to believe. *That's All Right, Mama* also reveals that Crudup deserves to be known as more than just the guy who Elvis liked—this is a tough but good-grooving blues collection that should please those who like their blues straight with no chaser. *—Mark Deming*

The Crusaders

f. 1960, Houston, TX, **db.** 1988

Group / Crossover Jazz, Hard Bop, Fusion, Soul-Jazz

Back in 1954, Houston pianist Joe Sample teamed up with high school friends tenor saxophonist Wilton Felder and drummer Stix Hooper to form the Swingsters. Within a short time, they were joined by trombonist Wayne Henderson, flutist Hubert Laws, and bassist Henry Wilson and the group became the Modern Jazz Sextet. With the move of Sample, Felder, Hooper, and Henderson to Los Angeles in 1960, the band (a quintet with the bass spot constantly changing) took on the name of the Jazz Crusaders. The following year they made their first recordings for Pacific Jazz and throughout the 1960s the group was a popular attraction, mixing together R&B and Memphis soul elements with hard bop; its trombone/tenor frontline became a trademark. By 1971, when all of the musicians were also busy with their own projects, it was decided to call the group simply the Crusaders so it would not be restricted to only playing jazz.

After a few excellent albums during the early part of the decade (with guitarist Larry Carlton a strong asset), the group began to decline in quality. In 1975, the band's sound radically changed when Henderson departed to become a full-time producer. 1979's "Street Life" was a hit, but also a last hurrah. With Hooper's decision to leave in 1983, the group no longer sounded like the Crusaders and gradually disbanded. In the mid-'90s, Henderson and Felder had a reunion as the Crusaders but in reality only Joe Sample has had a strong solo career. *—Scott Yanow*

Pass the Plate / May 1971 / Chisa ✦✦✦

The Jazz Crusaders dropped the "jazz" from their name after over a decade of popular recordings for the Pacific Jazz label, and they switched record companies for the first time. Although a little funkier than previously, there was no major change (at least immediately) in the group's sound. This somewhat obscure LP is comprised of tunes by trombonist Wayne Henderson (including the five-part, 15 1/2-minute "Pass the Plate"), keyboardist Joe Sample and drummer Stix Hooper. Original member Wilton Felder (on tenor and electric bass) completes the basic quartet which is joined by guitarist Arthur Adams. Good music although nothing all that memorable occurs. *—Scott Yanow*

Unsung Heroes / Aug. 1973 / MCA ♦♦♦

The music on this Crusaders set is quite pleasant, but unfortunately none of the original melodies are all that catchy or unique; a remake of "Hard Times" (which was recorded by David Newman back in 1960) is easily the most memorable cut and a revisit to Joe Sample's "Freedom Sound" from the early days of the Jazz Crusaders is under two minutes long. There are some good solos from the soulful tenor saxophonist Wilton Felder, trombonist Wayne Henderson, electric keyboardist Joe Sample and guitarist Larry Carlton but this CD reissue does not reach the heights (or have the strong material) of *1*. *—Scott Yanow*

Southern Comfort / 1974 / MCA ♦♦♦

The follow-up to 1973's *Unsung Heroes* was the first of the group's Blue Thumb efforts to be distributed by ABC Records. The label switch also coincided with the inclusion of lyrical guitarist Larry Carlton as a full-fledged member. Although much of *Southern Comfort* puts a gloss on ideas made definitive on earlier efforts, the complaints are minimal and this remains the most appealing, multi-faceted incarnation of the band. The first track, "Stomp and Buck Dance," is an offhanded and skilled approach to the group's patently earthy style. The insistent "The Well's Gone Dry" has the edginess of some of the better tracks on *Unsung Heroes*, and has Carlton doing great work on the bridge. Not surprisingly, it is Carlton's presence here that adjusts the band chemistry and makes the best of *Southern Comfort* even more so. The best track here, the poignant "When There's Love Around," has Carlton's guitar attaining the perfect sense of longing that meshes well with Joe Sample's trademark Fender Rhodes tones. The last tracks here are also in a thoughtful ballad vein: "Lilies of the Nile" has great horn work from Wilton Felder and Wayne Henderson, and the last track, "A Ballad for Joe (Louis)," is a heartfelt rumination on the death of the famed boxer, featuring Sample's inherent sense of melody. A good representation of the Crusaders' tasteful and intelligent playing, *Southern Comfort* is more than recommended to their fans. *—Jason Elias*

Scratch / 1974 / MCA ♦♦♦♦

Recorded live at the Roxy, *Scratch* was one of the Crusaders' best recordings, an extravaganza of jazz and funk with great soloing from the group on top of a set of excellent grooves. From the loose-limbed funk of "Scratch" to a restless, understated version of their live standard "Eleanor Rigby" (which they'd been performing live for over six years), the Crusaders displayed a command of R&B forms in a jazz context. Another cover, Carole King's "So Far Away," is betrayed by a muddy '70s arrangement and sound, but nothing else here fails to illustrate the excellence of the best R&B group in the jazz world. *—John Bush*

● **Chain Reaction** / 1975 / MCA ♦♦♦♦♦

One of the tastiest concoctions of the mid-'70s jazz-fusion era, *Chain Reaction* finds the Crusaders at the top of their form. The compositions are both accessible and memorable, and the playing is uniformly excellent. Guitarist Larry Carlton delivers some of his finest licks and funkified rhythm work. Wayne Henderson shows there is a place in fusion for the trombone. Wilton Felder does double duty, delivering smoking saxophone lines and funky bass riffs. Joe Sample's Fender Rhodes piano provides a solid chordal foundation and great solos. And the stickman, Stix Hooper, keeps the groove solid. The band employs a variety of rhythms and tempos, and gives the members plenty of room to strut their individual and collective stuff. In fact, "collective" may be the key word here, for this is the sound of a band, not just a group of guys thrown together for a recording session. *Chain Reaction* was one of the albums that helped lure young, rock and soul-oriented listeners over to check out the jazz side, and should not be missed by those interested in the more accessible, funky side of fusion. *—Jim Newsom*

Those Southern Knights / 1975 / MCA ♦♦♦

Deep in their prime period, the Crusaders reaffirm their affinity with the groove and rely entirely upon all six of their funky selves for their material. "My Mama Told Me So" and "Feeling Funky" contain the most infectious outcropping of the groove, while "Spiral" is OK, yet just a bit too frantic for the groove to thrive. "And Then There Was the Blues" is a laid-back, mildly funky jog at quite some length, where everyone gets a chance to solo extensively; essentially this is the old Jazz Crusaders frontline sound with a funky underbelly. "Til the Sun Shines" is an urbane Larry Carlton ballad with synthesized strings, quite different and to the point, but "Serenity" is a bore, a nothing idea stretched out for too long. The Crusaders' groove machine is still very much in gear, but the fuel is occasionally diluted. *—Richard S. Ginell*

☆ **Free as the Wind** / Dec. 1976 / MCA ♦♦♦♦♦

There's a terrific reason why the triple-CD Crusaders retrospective *The Golden Years* included six of *Free as the Wind*'s eight tracks—the material. Indeed, side one of the LP version may be the strongest single side of original tunes that the band ever put together. It opens with Joe Sample's driving, tense title cut, and flows flawlessly through Stix Hooper's subtly funky "I Felt the Love," Pops Popwell's infectiously finger-popping "The Way We Was" (a high point in the Crusaders' groove collection), and Larry Carlton's steamy vehicle for Wilton Felder, "Nite Crawler." Even the two tracks that the box set left out—the galvanic "Feel It," driven by Sample's clavinet and Hooper's tom-toms, and "River Rat"—are as funky as you can stand it. And from out of the blue, Sample concludes the album with a lovely, wistful tune that may have become a standard, "It Happens Everyday." When the material is this good, everything falls into place from there; the grooves are deeper, the soloing by all five Crusaders is more melodic and probing, and while Sample provides a few brass and string arrangements, this is just harmless decoration, neither a necessity nor a hindrance. This would be the Crusaders' high-water mark in the post-Wayne Henderson years, and it can stand tall with anything they've done. *—Richard S. Ginell*

Images / 1978 / MCA ♦♦♦

The Crusaders' sound had changed by 1978 due to the decision of trombonist Wayne Henderson to become a fulltime producer, and the gradual dominance of funky R&B rhythms. Although the band (which consisted of keyboardist Joe Sample, Wilton Felder on tenor and soprano, drummer Stix Hooper and for this LP guitarist Billy Rogers and bassist Pops Popwell) now had a more conventional instrumentation, its music remained infectious and at least to an extent influenced by jazz. However none of the seven group originals on this little-known date are all that memorable. *—Scott Yanow*

Street Life / 1979 / MCA ♦♦♦♦

Although the Crusaders could not have known it at the time, their recording of "Street Life" (which features a memorable vocal by Randy Crawford) was a last hurrah for the 20-year old group. Their recordings of the next few years would decline in interest until the band gradually faded away in the 1980s. However this particular set is well worth picking up for the 11-minute title cut and there is good playing by the three original members (Wilton Felder on tenor, soprano and electric bass, keyboardist Joe Sample and drummer Stix Hooper) along with guitarist Barry Finnerty; horn and string sections plus additional guitarists are utilized on Sample's commercial but listenable arrangements *—Scott Yanow*

Rhapsody and Blues / Mar. 1980 / MCA ♦♦

The Crusaders' follow-up to *Street Life* did not result in any additional hits (does anyone remember Bill Withers' vocal on "Soul Shadows?") and found the group's R&Bish music sounding closer to a formula. Each of the three remaining original Crusaders (Wilton Felder on tenor, soprano, alto and electric bass, keyboardist Joe Sample and drummer Stix Hooper), who are joined by an expanded rhythm setion, contribute at least one original apiece but the group's concept was starting to sound a bit tired. *—Scott Yanow*

At Their Best / Jul. 27, 1992 / Motown ♦♦♦

As a band, the Crusaders were always the most respected, as intelligence and earthiness permeated throughout their best work. The group—Joe Sample on keyboards, Wilton Felder on bass/saxophone, Wayne Henderson playing trombone, and drummer Stix Hooper—had been together for close to 15 years when all of the work on this album, *At Their Best*, was recorded. The title is somewhat misleading. These tracks were compiled from two 1970-1971 albums, *Old Socks, New Shoes* and *Pass the Plate*. Both efforts were released when Motown was distributing Chisa in the early '70s. During the time the Crusaders dropped the "Jazz" part of their name, and started to simplify, but not dumb down, their arrangements. *At Their Best* proves that even during this stylistic change the playing still was top-notch and influential. On the track "Listen and You'll See," Sample's judicious electric piano is heard throughout, as it became a hallmark of their '70s work. That track, as well an updated take of their own "Young Rabbits," also has the signature sound of both Felder and Henderson's emotive yet restrained horn playing. A lot of cover material shows up on *At Their Best*. Sly & the Family Stone's "Thank You (Falletin' Me Be Mice Elf Agin)" is quite close to the original and shows them having fun in a newer genre. The group even brings "Spanish Harlem" to life on a decidedly revamped and surprisingly exciting version. The collection finds the group no doubt doing good work, but the great work came before and after this. *—Jason Elias*

The Crusaders' Finest Hour / Jun. 27, 2000 / Verve ♦♦♦

After a career that spanned the '60s with a number of releases on Pacific Jazz records as the Jazz Crusaders, the beginning of the '70s found the band dropping the jazz moniker from their name and moving toward the more commercially accessible pop/R&B crossover audience. These nine selections are taken from seven albums originally released on the Blue Thumb and MCA labels recorded between 1971 and 1979 with a live cut featuring B.B. King from 1981. The Crusaders have a lot of material still available featuring both incarnations with this compilation containing a worthy sample from the second half of their career. For a closer inspection of the earlier Jazz Crusaders, seek out *Live at the Lighthouse 66* on Pacific Jazz. *—Al Campbell*

The Crystals

f. 1961, Brooklyn, NY, **db.** 1966

Group / Girl Group

Among aficionados of the girl group sound, there can't be five acts more beloved than the Crystals. Their best-known songs, which include "He's a Rebel," "Uptown," "Da Doo Ron Ron," "Then He Kissed Me," and "There's No Other Like My Baby," are among the finest examples of the best that American rock & roll had to offer in the period before the British Invasion.

The group was originally a quintet consisting of Barbara Alston, Dee Dee Kennibrew, Mary Thomas, Patricia Wright, and Myrna Gerrard, organized by Benny Wells while they were still in high school. Alston was Wells' niece, and although she later became known as their lead singer on many of their records, she was actually recruited as a backup singer by her uncle. Under Wells' guidance, they began performing in more of a pop vein, and one of the gigs that they got was cutting demos for the publisher Hill & Range, which brought them to the Brill Building in midtown Manhattan. It was there, while they were rehearsing, that they chanced to be heard by Phil Spector, who at that time was just starting up his own label, Philles Records. He was in the market for new talent and the Crystals—who, by that time, had lost Gerrard and added La la Brooks to their lineup as lead singer—were just what he was looking for, sort of. He liked their sound and their range, but he didn't initially like Brooks' voice and insisted on Alston taking the lead, somewhat reluctantly on her part.

In September of 1961, the slightly reconfigured group cut their first hit, "There's No Other Like My Baby," which rose to number 20 nationally. It was a promising beginning, putting the group, Spector, and his new label on the map. In early 1962, the Crystals recorded a Barry Mann/Cynthia Weil song called "Uptown." Alston's strong-yet-sensuous vocals enunciated lyrics that were as steeped in topical subject matter, especially about the frustrations of life in the ghetto, as they were in romance. Its production marked a major step forward in the making of rock & roll singles in its production, and heralded a newer, bolder era in pop music and R&B.

It was at this point, in the wake of "Uptown," that the history of the Crystals gets a little more complicated. It wasn't until June of 1962 that they had another single ready to go, and it engendered all kinds of problems that "Uptown" had avoided. If that song had gotten a serious lyric across with an elegant and quietly passionate setting, "He Hit Me (It Felt Like a Kiss)" (co-authored by Carole King and Gerry Goffin, no less) was the reverse, presenting a disturbing lyric about infidelity and the physical abuse of a woman by a man, in a dark, ominous manner. Radio stations simply wouldn't play it, and the public didn't like the song, period.

The following month, Spector was back in the studio running another Crystals session, except that this time it wasn't really the Crystals that he was recording, but Darlene Love. As the owner of the Crystals' name and, as their producer, possessing the right to record anyone he wanted (or *anything* he wanted) and label it as being from "the Crystals," he decided to forego any further battles over who should sing lead and forego using the group entirely for "He's a Rebel." A celebration of street-level machismo like no other, it was an upbeat number with gorgeous hooks and, with none of the baggage of its failed predecessor, became a number-one hit, as well as ingraining itself in pop culture history as a quintessential girl group classic. Darlene Love was the lead singer on the next hit by "the Crystals," "He's Sure the Boy I Love," as well.

It wasn't until early 1963 that the group again sang on one of their own records, "Da Doo Ron Ron," and by that time, Spector had accepted La la Brooks in lieu of Alston as lead singer. That record rose to number three in America and became their second biggest British hit, reaching the number-five spot in the U.K. That placement, along with the U.K. number-two position for "Then He Kissed Me" (which also got to number six in America), was very important, because at the time a lot of major British bands were about to break onto the charts at home, before coming to dominate American music a year later. "Da Doo Ron Ron" and "Then He Kissed Me" became among the most popular American rock & roll songs of the period in England, covered by all manner of acts on-stage and on-record.

The Crystals were in a seemingly enviable position, except for the fact that they and Spector were increasingly at odds. They'd been unhappy from the time when Spector began using their name on behalf of records made by Darlene Love. By 1964, they also perceived Spector's growing inattention; he had lately discovered a girl trio called the Ronettes on whose music and lead singer, Veronica Bennett, he was lavishing ever more of his time and energy. By 1964, following the failure of two consecutive genuine Crystals singles, the group—with Frances Collins replacing Wright—was no longer interested in working with Spector. The following year they bought out their contract and headed to the seemingly greener pastures of the Imperial label, where they found no success; by that time, the only girl groups that were still competitive in the music marketplace were associated with Motown.

By 1966, the Crystals had disbanded. Spector closed down Philles Records, and the resulting unavailability of their records except on the radio only raised the value of the old copies that were out there, and made his periodic reissues of the group's work that much more prized by fans. *—Bruce Eder*

• **The Best of the Crystals** / Sep. 22, 1992 / ABKCO ✦✦✦✦✦

Still the definitive Crystals retrospective nearly a decade after its release, ABKCO's *The Best of the Crystals* gathers their most beloved singles, including "Uptown," "He's a Rebel," "Da Doo Ron Ron," and "Then He Kissed Me"; the infamous withdrawn single "He Hit Me (It Felt Like a Kiss)"; and relatively obscure songs such as "What a Nice Way to Turn 17," "Look in My Eyes," and "I Wonder." The way the collection presents the Crystals' work in more or less chronological order helps trace the group's development and also allows somewhat lesser-known songs like "Heartbreaker," "Girls Can Tell," and "Another Country—Another World" more equal footing among the group's classic tracks. Though the *He's a Rebel* bootleg offers an even more complete collection of the group's output, *The Best of the Crystals* remains the best legitimate retrospective of their pioneering work. *—Heather Phares*

Phil Spector Wall of Sound, Vol. 3: The Crystals Sing Their Greatest Hits! / 1995 / Phil Spector International ✦✦✦

For a long time, the British Phil Spector International series was the only way you could pick up his classic early '60s productions. The Crystals volume covers all of the essential bases: the monster hits, worthy obscurities like "Please Hurt Me" and "No One Ever Tells You," and the controversial, withdrawn Goffin-King single, "He Hit Me." It's been superseded as the collection of choice by the 1992 ABKCO CD, *The Best of the Crystals*. As this import collection is out-of-print and difficult to find, all those looking for a definitive Crystals anthology should go for the ABKCO one instead. But if you already have this vinyl LP, it essentially duplicates the contents of the CD; audiophiles may differ on the matter, but I wouldn't say it's worth the $15 or so to "upgrade." *—Richie Unterberger*

He's a Rebel / 1997 / Marginal ✦✦✦✦✦

This 29-song bootleg compilation more or less matches the authorized Crystals collection from ABKCO for sound quality, perhaps denser and louder. But it also includes a much heftier selection of songs, among them the Crystals' version of "On Broadway" and the quintet's Christmas songs, and one of the rarest and most seldom heard of all Phil Spector productions—"The Screw (Let's Dance)." The latter song, for those unfamiliar, was something that Spector delivered to fulfill the provisions of a business arrangement with a partner he no longer wanted, and consists of the Crystals doing a rather fetching chorus ("Let's do it, come on and do it, to the right, to the left") to a boogie-woogie beat, accompanied by piano, drums, and bass, while Spector, sounding bored and surly, occasionally comes in announcing, "Do the screw," or "Let's dance the screw." No more than a handful of copies were ever pressed, since Spector never seriously intended that it be released, and the quality here is astonishingly good—it also reveals itself as the longest song Spector ever put into finished version in this era, a four-minute-plus joke. The whole disc is claimed to be Cedar-ized, and the noise reduction treatment hasn't hurt. There are no notes, but the cover art is cool. *—Bruce Eder*

The Crystals / Apr. 24, 2001 / Town Sound ✦

A trio version of the Crystals containing only harmony singer Dee Dee Kennibrew from the lineups that recorded the group's hits in the early '60s re-records those hits on this album. There were six Top 20 entries by the Crystals during 1961-1962—"There's No Other (Like My Baby)," "Uptown," "He's a Rebel," "He's Sure the Boy I Love" (the last two originally sung by Darlene Love & the Blossoms, actually), "Da Doo Ron Ron," and "Then He Kissed Me"—and, when the members of the current group dispose of them, they try other hits from the era associated with other singers, including "One Fine Day" (the Chiffons), "Today I Met the Boy I'm Gonna Marry" (Darlene Love), "Rescue Me" (Fontella Bass), and, in a "Club Mix," "Chapel of Love." The arrangements approximate those of the original recordings, though here they are played largely on synthesizers. *—William Ruhlmann*

The Cues

Group / Rock & Roll, R&B

The Cues were Atlantic Records' first (and most prominent) studio vocal group during rock & roll's infancy (circa 1954), but their real claim to fame was their backing support for R&B artists on the Atlantic roster. The Cues may have been the identifiable name by which they would later try and make their mark as a recording group, but during the formidable '50s they went by many different identities: Ruth Brown's "Rhythmakers," LaVern Baker's "Gliders," Big Joe Turner's "Blues Kings," Ivory Joe Hunter's "Ivory Tones," and Carmen Taylor's "Boleros."

The acknowledged mastermind behind this plan was Atlantic's house arranger and songwriting sessionman Jesse Stone, who would also work with the Drifters, the Clovers, Big Joe Hunter, and other Atlantic artists. Stone brought together two members of the recently disbanded group the Blenders—Abel DeCosta and lead singer Ollie Jones (originally a member of the Ravens)—and two other vocalists, Eddie Barnes and Robie Kirk (aka Winfield Scott on his songwriting credits).

In late 1954, Stone brought the Cues to the Messner Brothers' Aladdin Records and recorded for their Lamp subsidiary. Around this same time, they also recorded for RCA as the Four Students, releasing "So Near and Yet So Far" on the Groove label in mid-1955, and even turned up on Jubilee Records with a cover of the Platters' "Only You," all of which sunk without a trace.

While they had little success under their own name, the Cues continued to prosper behind the scenes, backing up LaVern Baker for "Tweedle Dee," Roy Hamilton on "Don't Let Go" (the first rock & roll hit to be recorded in stereo), and Nat King Cole for his many recordings on Capitol during the '50s (along with a group called the Four Knights). By late 1955, the Cues had added Jimmy Breedlove and moved from Atlantic to Capitol, where they recorded 12 songs aimed at the pop market. The first release was "Burn That Candle," which immediately took off, but unfortunately, Bill Haley & His Comets promptly recorded the song for Decca. It became a national hit, knocking the Cues version off the charts.

The group later joined Buck Ram's traveling "Happy Music" national tour and recorded four more singles for Capitol, but failed to find any success. By mid-1957, Breedlove had departed from the group. The Cues' next record, "Crazy Crazy Party," appeared on the Capitol subsidiary Prep. Alan Freed gave the song considerable airplay, which generated a little success on the sales charts, but it was a case of too little, too late. In 1960, they recorded one last song for Festival, a cover of the standard "Old Man River." Discographers have often claimed that the record was actually a re-working of the song by a reconstituted version of the Ravens (featuring Jimmy Ricks), while others claim that the Cues were doing a Ravens-style treatment of the tune. The group disbanded in the early '60s. *—Bryan Thomas*

• **Why** / 1991 / Bear Family ✦✦✦✦✦

Culture Club

f. 1981, London, England, **db.** 1986

Group / Pop/Rock, New Wave, Blue-Eyed Soul

Few new wave groups were as popular as Culture Club. During the early '80s, the group racked up seven straight Top 10 hits in the U.K. and six Top 10 singles in the U.S. with their light, infectious pop-soul. Though their music was radio-ready, what brought the band stardom was Boy George, the group's charismatic, cross-dressing lead singer. George dressed in flamboyant dresses and wore heavy makeup, creating a disarmingly androgynous appearance that created a sensation on early MTV. George also had a biting wit and frequently came up with cutting quips that won Culture Club heavy media exposure in both America and Britain. Although closely aligned with the New Romantics—they were both inspired by Northern soul and fashion—Culture Club had sharper pop sense than their peers and they consequently had a broader appeal. However, their time in the spotlight was brief. Not only could they not withstand the changing fashions of MTV, but the group was fraught with personal tensions, including Boy George's drug addiction. By 1986, the group had broken up, leaving behind several singles that rank as classics of the new wave era. *—Stephen Thomas Erlewine*

Kissing to Be Clever / 1982 / Virgin ✦✦✦✦

Kissing to Be Clever was the album that put Culture Club on the musical map. Incorporating pop, rock, dance, new wave, soul and Caribbean rhythms (an amalgamation of "cultures"), the result was a soulful, progressive pop outing which scored several landmark international hits and made a star out of the band's outrageous front man Boy George. A couple of tracks were European dance hits, but the first "official" single, "Do You Really Want To Hurt Me," was a simple masterpiece, resonating with an ache that harked back to the classic torch songs of yesteryear. Most of the other songs were quite different, with energetic beats and sometimes silly, campy themes ("Boy Boy I'm the Boy,"

"White Boys Can't Control It" and "White Boy"). The album scored two other major hits, the zippy and bouncy "I'll Tumble 4 Ya" and the gorgeous "Time (Clock of the Heart)." However, beware that "Time" is only on certain pressings of the album. When the album was issued on CD, and once the Epic label dissolved, the formerly color album cover had turned to black and white, and "Time" had been omitted, which is pretty ridiculous, considering the song was a huge number-two hit, and the album was then left with only nine tracks. Still, this set is a highlight of 1980s music, and set the stage for one of the decade's most loved and oft-remembered bands. *—Jose F. Promis*

Colour By Numbers / 1983 / Virgin ♦♦♦♦♦

Colour By Numbers was Culture Club's most successful album, and, undoubtedly, one of the most popular albums from the 1980s. Scoring no less than four U.S. hit singles (and five overseas), this set dominated the charts for a full year, both in the U.S. and in Europe. The songs were infectious, the videos were all over MTV, and the band was a media magnet. Boy George sounded as warm and soulful as ever, but one of the real stars on this set was backing vocalist Helen Terry, who really brought the house down on the album's unforgettable first single, "Church of the Poison Mind." This album also featured the band's biggest (and only number one) hit, the irresistibly catchy "Karma Chameleon," its more rock & roll Top Five follow-up "Miss Me Blind," and the fourth single (and big club hit), "It's a Miracle" (which also featured Helen Terry's unmistakable belting). Also here are "Victims," a big, dark, deep, and bombastic power ballad which was a huge hit overseas but never released in the U.S., and other soulful favorites such as "Black Money" and "That's the Way (I'm Only Trying to Help You)," where Boy George truly flexed his vocal muscles. The 1980s music was, in many cases, flamboyant, fun, sexy, soulful, colorful, androgynous, and carefree, and this album captured that spirit perfectly. A must for any collector of 1980s music, and the artistic and commercial pinnacle of a band which still attracts new fans years later. *—Jose Promis*

Waking Up With the House on Fire / 1984 / Virgin ♦♦

From Luxury to Heartache / 1986 / Virgin ♦♦

● **At Worst . . . The Best of Boy George and Culture Club** / Nov. 2, 1993 / Virgin ♦♦♦♦♦

The success of "The Crying Game" marked a comeback for Boy George, especially in the U.S., where his solo career had never taken hold beyond the dance clubs, and SBK (distributor of his label, Virgin) took advantage of his resurgence by compiling this 75-minute, 19-track album, which combines his former group Culture Club's biggest hits with selections from his solo work. The ten Culture Club tracks are of a piece, from 1982's "Do You Really Want to Hurt Me" (which here leads off with an ominous voice intoning, "Popularity breeds contempt") to "Love Is Love," which wasn't a hit, but is a better choice than the missing "The War Song," which was. The solo tracks are a more mixed batch, and not only because Top 40 U.K. hits like "Keep Me in Mind," "Sold," and "To Be Reborn" are missing. They often rely on loud percussion tracks that strand Boy George's tender tenor somewhere in the distance. He remains most effective on rhythmic ballads, whether "Do You Really Want to Hurt Me," "Everything I Own" (his chart-topping first U.K. solo hit), or "The Crying Game." *—William Ruhlmann*

Clifford Curry

b. Knoxville, TN

Vocals / Pop-Soul, Beach, Modern Electric Blues

Clifford Curry is a true soul survivor, a veteran of more than 45 years in music and still kicking. The Knoxville, TN, native joined the Echos while he still attended Austin High School in Knoxville; they had been around four years before Curry joined and backed Faye Adams on her number-one R&B smash "Shake a Hand." The revamped group cut two records as the renamed Five Pennies for Savoy Records ("Mr. Moon" and "My Heart Trembles" in 1955 and 1956 respectively) and also waxed unreleased sides for Herald Records. Royalties, money, and the lack of, caused the group to splinter in different directions. Curry and some other Knoxville cronies formed the Bingos, which cut a deal with Ernie Young's Excello Records. Excello issued the single on its Nasco subsidiary and renamed them the Hollyhocks; as before, nothing happened and the members disbanded into other ventures.

Curry found a stable gig with the Bubba Suggs Band in 1959, staying until 1964. The band played around their home base, Clarksville, TN, and backed up the major R&B acts that wheeled into their neck of the woods. He left after five years because Bubba couldn't vision much outside of Clarksville, neither could the other band members. Hit the road! Jack, you got to be kidding.

Returning to Knoxville, not exactly a music Mecca either, Curry went solo as Sweet Clifford. Revisiting Excello Records, Young recorded four sides on Curry, messing up the first single by crediting "Things Got to Get Better" as Clifford Sweet. Curry was furious, first from Bingos to Hollyhocks, now this crap. A follow-up got it right with the credit reading Sweet Clifford. The efforts stiffed, but that didn't deter Curry, he was in music for the duration.

He hooked up with some more Knoxville crooners—Luey & Duey Guy, Bob Adams, Jerry Johnson, and Wayne Cronin—to form the Fabulous Six. Curry had a fetish with six-man groups, his debut crew the Five Pennies, despite the name, was six-men strong: Curry, the Meyers Brothers—John, Herbert, and James—Charles Holloway, and Benjamin Washington. The Fabulous Six's single on the miniscule Ridgecrest label out of La Grange, GA, is so obscure that historians and discographers fail to include it in their encyclopedia-type guides to soul singles. As the Contenders, the same lineup cut "Mr. Dee Jay" on Blue Sky Records (1965), which didn't go. Curry tried his hand at songwriting (with Knoxville DJ Rob Galbraith) for others, with little success.

The association with Galbraith bared fruit in 1967, not with one of their songs, but the Galbraith hookup with Buzz Cason enabled Curry to cut a song Carson held the rights to, entitled "She Shot a Whole in My Soul." Carson produced and issued the record on Elf Records, which was distributed by Bell Records. Curry's biggest hit showed at number 95 pop and nearly entered the R&B Top 40 at number 45. Seven more Elf singles followed (from 1967–1969), along with three each on SSS, Caprice, and Abbott Records spanning 1970 to 1973, but none charted as high as "She Shot..." However, Curry's success as an entertainer spread to the Carolina Beaches, where the baritone became a prime showman for their musical events and a solid purveyor of Beach music, which is anything you can shag to and look cool doing it.

The popular Beach entertainer didn't record again until an association with Buddah Records in 1977 that resulted in two singles: "Body Shop" and "Moving in Circles." In 1980, he cut his first tune with the word "shag" in it; "Shag With Me" trailed by "Lets Have a Party" came out on Woodshed Records, the last title dropping in 1982. Two DJ-only singles for CC Records followed and then singles on Ripete and Compleat took him through 1985. While Clifford's recordings weren't chart busters, they got played in regions where he reigned as an entertainer of note and kept him busy. He never stopped recording; releasing music, contributing backing vocals on others albums, and doing commercials into the millennium. Collectables Records outdid themselves in 1995 by releasing a 20-song compilation CD of Curry's recordings, many from the numerous one-off labels he recorded for; Appaloosa Records issued *Clifford's Blues: The Provider* in 1996. The Knoxville native now lives in Nashville, TN, with his irons still in the fire, and is not to be confused with the Clifford Curry who sang with the Notations or the Clifford Curry who blew some notes with the Los Angeles-based Sly, Slick & Wicked. *—Andrew Hamilton*

The Provider / 1993 / Appaloosa ♦♦♦

This 1993 Appaloosa/Ichiban CD put Curry in blues territory, and it wasn't a memorable trip. Curry isn't a convincing blues vocalist; it doesn't help that several numbers aren't that great anyway, but he doesn't cut it singing straight blues. When he does get interesting lyrics, as on "Tall Oak Tree," his renditions lack impact and depth. As much as you want to root for Clifford Curry, he's simply not a blues artist. *—Ron Wynn*

● **She Shot a Hole in My Soul** / 1995 / Collectables ♦♦♦♦

This 20-song set brings together all of Clifford's recordings for Buzz Cason's Elf label. Classic late-'60s Southern R&B, these recordings vary widely from his earlier sides for Excello as "Sweet Clifford." Curry pleads and croons his way through classics like "East West North or South," "The Natives Are Restless Tonight," "Barkin' Up the Wrong Tree," "Leave Him to Me," and the title track. His turns on cover material like "Delta Dawn" and "Double Shot of My Baby's Love" put an original spin on these two old warhorses. A nice collection of this artist's best. *—Cub Koda*

Clifford's Blues / Jan. 22, 1996 / Appaloosa ♦♦♦

Cymande

f. West Indies

Group / Funk, Soul

Although underappreciated and woefully overlooked during their original tenure together, the fine early-'70s outfit Cymande (pronounced Sah-mahn-day) was one of the first to merge African rhythms with rock, funk, reggae, and soul. Comprised of members who hailed from such exotic locales as Guyana, Jamaica, and St. Vincent, the nine-man lineup (who were all entirely self-taught) contained Steve Scipio (bass), Ray King (vocals, percussion), Derek Gibbs (alto/soprano), Pablo Gonsales (congas), Joey Dee (vocals, percussion), Peter Serreo (tenor), Sam Kelly (drums), Mike Rose (alto, flute, bongos), and Patrick Patterson (guitar). The band issued a total of three releases: 1972's self-titled debut (which spawned one of their best-known songs, "The Message," peaking at number 22 on the domestic R&B charts in 1974), 1973's *Second Time Around*, and 1974's *Promised Heights*—before splitting up.

By the '90s, Cymande became the recipient of a strong cult following as another track from their debut, "Bra," was included on the soundtrack to Spike Lee's motion picture *Crooklyn*, and several of their songs were sampled by rap artists (including Raze, Master Ace, MC Solaar, De La Soul, DJ Kool, and the Fugees). Due to sudden interest in Cymande, a pair of compilations were issued—a British double CD titled *The Message* (which collected all three of their albums) and a 13-track collection, *The Soul of Rasta*. *—Greg Prato*

Cymande / 1973 / Collectables ♦♦♦♦

Invigorating head music done Rastafarian style by Cymande. "Zion I" is a spiritual chant put to music, setting the mood for *Cymande*. A laid-back "One More" lulls you into subliminal meditation before "Getting It Back" jolts you into some scintillating Jamaican funk fusion. There's a message in many of Cymande's cuts, with "Listen," and "Bra" (a recognition of the women's lib movement), the most inspiring. Both are sung with passion, and are skillfully executed; the former is slow and painstaking in its message, while "Bra" slaps you upside the head with a stirring sax solo and bass-fueled vamp. An air of supreme coolness permeates *Cymande*, unusual for a first effort written by members of the band. Cymande sounds like they have done this before; nowhere is this more evident than on the beautiful "Dove," a gorgeous concoction of lead guitar, tambourines, haunting backing vocals, and percussion, with the horns used as sparingly as table seasonings on a gourmet dish. Along with "Bra," the group's most popular cut is "The Message"—it's difficult keeping body parts still on this grooving mutha. All in all, *Cymande* is a marvelous collection that premiered a fine funk band. *—Andrew Hamilton*

Second Time Around / 1973 / Janus ♦♦♦

Cymande's second LP is captivating enough, but perhaps too political for the masses. Still, there've been few better fusions of reggae and jazz than *Second Time Around*. The spirited "Anthracite" is driven by horns on the chorus, a scorching sax solo, and a titillating flute. Flautist Mike Rose continues to captivate on the oddly titled "Willie Headache," which is far too mellow to cause listeners to grab for the Tylenol. Everything is centered around Steve Scipo's bubbly bass notes, a good example being "Trevorgus," in which the beat falls between midtempo and uptempo and everything (the horns, the rhythm, the chanting vocals) complements each other as if linked by an invisible chain. The group scintillates on "Fug," a rapid-fire mover and shaker that speaks of people dying because of greed and deceit. Cymande let their dreads down on this one—emoting, getting real, and performing like there's no tomorrow. Gotta give Pablo Gonsales a bone for his constant, creative work on the congas throughout; drummer Sam Kelly stays in the background, happy with his understated role and keeping it tight. Vocalist Ray King breaks off his best lead on the tempo changing "Bird," and Joey Dee assists vocally while patting on his conga set; Peter Serreo, and Derek Gibbs sax play sparkles like champagne from beginning to end. *—Andrew Hamilton*

Promised Heights / 1974 / Contempo ✦✦✦
On their final LP for Janus Records, *Cymande* continues the heavy message theme of *Second Time Around*. "Pon de Dungle" is about the secrets of life and love articulated over a lazy beat. "Equatorial Forest" is a multifaceted tune with a lightning tempo and sliding, accentuating horns, while the Curtis Mayfield-ish "Brothers on the Slide" has some commercial appeal. The flavorful "Changes" is like viewing a good oil painting; the slow moody instrumental has a meditating effect, and a soft, airy flute makes for an inconspicuous lead instrument. "Promised Heights," the title cut, is strong, and should have done better for Cymande. It has the lilt and beauty of earlier sides, the horn work is sensational and a nice sax solo scintillates. That same looping reggae beat is matched with meaningful lyrics and a positive, working-together theme on "Losing Ground." "The Recluse" has a great hook ("When will all the lights go, will they leave the blackest night") and features a nice romping beat spiced by sweeping horns. Cymande is a perfect example of music's universal appeal; despite not knowing 70 percent of what they're saying, you're still drawn into the sounds. *—Andrew Hamilton*

The Message / 1999 / Sequel ✦✦✦✦
It's hard to fathom why Cymande didn't follow in the paths of such early-'70s funk-rock hitmakers as War, Santana, and Curtis Mayfield straight up to the top of the charts. But for reasons unknown, the eight-member band wallowed in obscurity during their brief tenure together. This all changed years later, after the group developed a cult following in the '90s after several rap acts began prominently sampling the group, leading to great interest in the group's three studio albums issued during a mere two-year span, from 1973 to 1974. The only problem was, all three were long out of print and never issued on CD. But this all changed in 1999, when the British label Sequel Records (a division of Castle Music) issued the double-disc set, *The Message*. Weighing in at 32 tracks, the set contains all three of their albums (1973's self-titled debut, their sophomore effort, *Second Time Around*, and 1974's *Promised Heights*), as well as three tracks that were previously unissued the first time around. All three of their albums are incredibly consistent from beginning to end (with perhaps the rather tedious and predictable "Rastafarian Folk Song" being the only lowlight), as evidenced by such outstanding tracks as "One More," "Getting It Back," "Listen," "Dove," "Bra," "Willy's Headache," "For Baby Ooh," "Fug," "Bird," "Them and Us," and the collection's title track, among others. *The Message* may be hard to track down for folks outside of the U.K., but it will be well worth the hunt to discover this exceptional music. *—Greg Prato*

● **The Soul of Rasta** / Sep. 12, 2000 / Newhouse ✦✦✦✦✦
Like other underappreciated bands from the same era (the Velvet Underground, the Stooges, etc.), the multi-member funk band Cymande was virtually ignored during their short career, which spawned a trio of albums during the early '70s. But 20 years after their breakup, the group gained a large cult following, after countless modern-day rap acts began sampling bits from Cymande's tunes. With their three studio albums long out of print despite renewed interest, the Newhouse label assembled a 13-track best-of set in 2000, *The Soul of Rasta*, collecting the finest tracks of all three original releases. Although comparable at times to such bands as Santana and War (especially evident in the group's use of percussion), Cymande's music is a must-hear, as it's a fantastic blend of exotic and funky ensemble playing (the group included eight members), soulful vocals, and uplifting lyrics, the latter of which sometimes reflected their Rastafarian beliefs. All 13 tracks are standouts, but tops would have to be "Bra" (which was a popular radio hit in New York City when originally released), the groovy "The Message," the long and winding 11-minute track "Dove," and arguably the finest song on the collection, the soothing "Willy's Headache." *The Soul of Rasta* is an essential purchase for admirers of '70s funk and soul, but chances are it will lead to the purchase of the hard-to-find 1999 British import double-disc set *The Message*, which collects all three of the albums along with three previously unissued tracks. *—Greg Prato*

D

D Train

f. 1980, **db.** 1985

Group / Garage/House, Urban, Funk, Quiet Storm

D Train, an innovative duo that consisted of James "D-Train" Williams (vocals) and Hubert Eaves III (keyboards, bass, drums, arrangements, productions), recorded a clutch of electrified dance/R&B classics in the early '80s. From the release of their first single onward, Williams' voice was instantly recognizable for its power-packed, uplifting nature. Eaves' instrumental backing and production were extremely complementary to Williams' deliveries, punching out bold, intricate arrangements that were often livened up for the dancefloor by remixer extraordinaire Francois Kevorkian.

Williams and Eaves met while attending high school in Brooklyn, NY. Shortly after the '70s gave way to the '80s, they began recording together, using Williams' nickname—earned from his prowess on the football field—as their recording alias. They signed a contract with Prelude and released their first single, the brilliant "You're the One for Me," by the end of 1981. The song hit number one on the dance chart in early 1982 and kept that position for three weeks. Their somewhat spotty debut album followed later that year and included another spectacular track, the spirited "Keep On."

Music, D Train's second album, followed in 1983 and was supported with another batch of singles: "Keep Giving Me Love," "Are You Ready for Me," and Top 40 U.K. hit "Music" amongst them. *Something's on Your Mind*, the third and final album from the duo, spawned a Top Five R&B chart hit in the form of the title track. A couple of other singles from the album didn't do as well, but the group bowed out in fine fashion. They could've milked the sound of "You're the One for Me" for a long time, but they kept moving ahead and did the unexpected by incorporating elements inspired from other music forms. A list covers they recorded—Carole King's "So Far Away," Bacharach/David's "Walk on By," Mandel/Webster's "The Shadow of Your Smile"—hardly indicate the scope.

Williams and Eaves quit recording as D Train in 1985. Eaves' accomplishments did not go unnoticed; he began a busy second life as a valued session hand, working on records by Aretha Franklin, Whitney Houston, and Luther Vandross. Williams continued as a solo artist and notched three R&B chart hits during the latter half of the '80s. He also leant background vocals to several records throughout the following decade. *—Andy Kellman*

D Train / 1982 / Prelude ✦✦✦✦

Some of the most memorable and fresh-sounding R&B of the early to mid-'80s came from D Train, a group that had one foot in soul music and the other in urban contemporary. Blessed with a big, booming voice, lead vocalist James "D-Train" Williams was, in many respects, the epitome of the classic soul belter. Williams, like so many of the great soulsters of the 1960s and '70s, brought a strong gospel influence to secular lyrics and wasn't afraid to wear his heart on his sleeve. But in terms of production, Williams' partner, Hubert Eaves III, was very urban contemporary. When Eaves produced the duo's self-titled debut album in 1981 and 1982, he made sure that his distinctive keyboards were quite prominent. Horns and strings are employed, but keyboards are really the main instrument on funk gems like "You're the One for Me" (a major hit), "Keep On," and "Love Vibration." And keyboards are equally important on the ballads, which include the Philadelphia soul-influenced "Lucky Day" and an inspired remake of the Burt Bacharach/ Hal David favorite "Walk on By" (which had previously been recorded by Isaac Hayes, Dionne Warwick, and Gloria Gaynor). Many 1970s funk bands thought of horn sections as part of the main course and keyboards as a mere side dish—on this superb LP, it's just the opposite. Not that Eaves was alone in pushing R&B in a more keyboards-minded direction; anyone who listened to urban radio in 1982 realized that R&B producers in general were using more and more keyboards and synthesizers. From Eaves' attractive production to Williams' inspired singing and the duo's first-rate songwriting, *D Train* is a stunning debut all around. *—Alex Henderson*

Music / 1983 / Prelude ✦✦✦

D Train's second album for Prelude isn't on the level of their debut, as the amount of filler lessens the impact of the standouts, and none of the standouts match "You're the One for Me" or "Keep On." Both the title track and "Keep Giving Me Love" featured familiar sounds, but were different enough to keep the attention of fans of the duo's initial singles. James "D-Train" Williams' rich, booming baritone and Hubert Eaves III's bold production are just as unique as ever—when you hear a D Train song, there's no mistaking who it is. Like its predecessor, *Music* is loaded with upbeat numbers and throws in a ballad to show that Eaves is much better at crafting energetic material for dancefloors. When Unidisc issued the album on CD in the early '90s, they did everyone a favor by including an assortment of alternate mixes and radio edits. *—Andy Kellman*

Something's on Your Mind / 1984 / Prelude ✦✦✦

Released in 1984, *Something's on Your Mind* was the last of three albums that singer/composer James "D-Train" Williams and producer/keyboardist/composer Hubert Eaves III—together known as D Train—recorded for Prelude. In 1985, Williams and Eaves left the small NY-based label (which subsequently went out of business) and, although they continued to work together, Williams signed with Columbia as a solo artist in 1986. *Something's on Your Mind* isn't quite as essential as D Train's self-titled debut album of 1982, but it's still impressive. The moody yet funky title song became a major hit, and the duo is equally captivating on funk/dance offerings like "I'll Do Anything" and "Hustle and Bustle of the City" (which should have been released as a single). To its credit, the duo isn't afraid to try different things—"Thank You" finds Williams and Eaves detouring into reggae, while a brief performance of Carole King's "So Far Away" combines R&B with adult contemporary/soft rock elements. Eaves' keyboards played a prominent role on most of the duo's Prelude recordings, but on "So Far Away" Williams accompanies himself on acoustic guitar. Again, 1982's *D Train* is the group's most essential album, but this LP is also rewarding and is well worth having. *—Alex Henderson*

● **The Best of D Train** / Apr. 11, 1990 / Unidisc ✦✦✦✦

The most irritating thing about D Train's best-of is that it favors a remix of "You're the One for Me" over the superior, original album version. Most people have that exact song pop immediately into her or his head whenever the name D Train is brought up, so it's a shame to not have its definitive version available on something designed as a first-stop. Otherwise, *The Best of D Train* covers all the bases, including "Keep Giving Me Love," "Keep On," "Music," "Something's on Your Mind," and five others. This duo was one of the first and only to combine funk, soul, and gospel with electronic elements, and much of what they left behind remains powerful and fresh. They are one of the most exemplary post-disco/pre-house groups, and have remained influential within dance music for over two decades. *—Andy Kellman*

The Best of the 12" Mixes / Nov. 16, 1992 / Unidisc ✦✦✦

D'Angelo (Michael Eugene Archer)

b. Feb. 11, 1974, Richmond, VA

Vocals, Producer, Keyboards, Producer / Neo-Soul, Contemporary R&B, Urban

D'Angelo was one of the founding fathers and leading lights of the neo-soul movement of the mid- to late '90s, which aimed to bring the organic flavor of classic R&B back to the hip-hop age. Modeling himself on the likes of Marvin Gaye, Stevie Wonder, Prince, Curtis Mayfield, and Al Green, D'Angelo's influences didn't just come across in his vocal style—like most of those artists, he wrote his own material (and frequently produced it as well), helping to revive the concept of the R&B auteur. His debut album, *Brown Sugar*, gradually earned him an audience so devoted that the follow-up, *Voodoo*, debuted at number one despite a five-year wait in between.

Michael D'Angelo Archer was born February 11, 1974, in Richmond, VA, the son of a Pentecostal minister. He began teaching himself piano as a very young child, and at age 18, he won the amateur talent competition at Harlem's Apollo Theater three weeks in a row. He was briefly a member of a hip-hop group called I.D.U. and signed a publishing deal with EMI in 1991. His first major success came in 1994 as a writer/producer, helming the single "U Will Know" on the *Jason's Lyric* soundtrack; it featured a one-time, all-star R&B aggregate dubbed Black Men United. That helped lead to his debut solo album, 1995's *Brown Sugar*. Helped by the title track and a cover of Stevie Wonder's "Lady," *Brown Sugar* slowly caught on with R&B fans looking for an alternative to the hip-hop soul dominating the urban contemporary landscape; along with artists like Erykah Badu, Lauryn Hill, and Maxwell, D'Angelo became part of a retro-leaning, neo-soul revivalist movement. *Brown Sugar* received enormously complimentary reviews and sold over two million copies, and D'Angelo supported it with extensive touring over the next two years.

And then—not much of anything happened. D'Angelo took some time off to rest and split acrimoniously with his management; meanwhile, EMI went under, leaving his 1998 stopgap release *Live at the Jazz Cafe* out of print. On occasion, D'Angelo contributed a cover tune to a movie soundtrack, including Eddie Kendricks' "Girl You Need a Change of Mind" (*Get on the Bus*), the Ohio Players' "Heaven Must Be Like This" (*Down in the Delta*), and Prince's "She's Always in My Hair" (*Scream 2*). He also duetted with Lauryn Hill on "Nothing Really Matters," a cut from her Grammy-winning blockbuster *The Miseducation of Lauryn Hill*. Still, fans awaiting a proper follow-up to *Brown Sugar* remained frustrated—at first by no news at all, and then by frequent delays in the recording process and the scheduled release date. Finally, the special-guest-laden *Voodoo* was released in early 2000 and debuted at number one, an indication of just how large—and devoted—D'Angelo's fan base was. The extremely Prince-like lead single, "Untitled (How Does It Feel)," was a smash on the R&B charts and won a Grammy for Best Male R&B Vocal; likewise, *Voodoo* won for Best R&B Album. Reviews of *Voodoo* were once again highly positive, although a few critics objected to the looser, more atmospheric, more jam-oriented feel of the record, preferring the tighter songcraft of *Brown Sugar*. *—Steve Huey*

● **Brown Sugar** / 1995 / Capitol ✦✦✦✦✦

By the mid-'90s, most urban R&B had become rather predictable, working on similar combinations of soul and hip-hop, or relying on vocal theatrics on slow seductive numbers. With his debut album, *Brown Sugar*, the 21-year-old D'Angelo crashed down some of those barriers. D'Angelo concentrates on classic versions of soul and R&B, but unlike most of his contemporaries, he doesn't cut and paste older songs with hip-hop beats; instead, he attacks the forms with a hip-hop attitude, breathing new life into traditional forms. Not all of his music works—there are several songs that sound incomplete, relying more on sound than structure. But when he does have a good song—like the hit "Brown Sugar," Smokey Robinson's "Cruisin'," or the bluesy "Shit, Damn, Motherfucker," among several others—D'Angelo's wild talents are evident. *Brown Sugar* might not be consistently brilliant, but it is one of the most exciting debuts of 1995, giving a good sense of how deep D'Angelo's talents run. *—Stephen Thomas Erlewine*

Voodoo / Jan. 11, 2000 / Virgin ♦♦♦♦
Five years after his *Brown Sugar* album helped launch contemporary R&B, D'Angelo finally returned with his sophomore effort, *Voodoo*. His soulful voice is just as sweet as it was on *Brown Sugar*, though D'Angelo stretches out with a varied cast of collaborators, including trumpeter Roy Hargrove and guitarist Charlie Hunter, fellow neo-soul stars Lauryn Hill and Raphael Saadiq, and hip-hop heads like DJ Premier, Method Man & Redman, and Q-Tip. It must have been difficult to match his debut (and the frequent delays prove it was on his mind), but *Voodoo* is just as rewarding a soul album as D'Angelo's first. *—John Bush*

Dakota Moon

Group / Urban
Dakota Moon is an unusual urban R&B group, one that's equally influenced by Boyz II Men and '70s soft rock, such as Eric Clapton and James Taylor. The group is comprised of Ty Taylor (guitar, vocals), Ray Artis (bass, vocals), Malloy (percussion, vocals), and Joe Dean (guitar, vocals). Taylor and Artis were NY natives; Malloy and J Dean hailed from CA. The quartet met at a recording session in Los Angeles for producers Andrew Logan and Mike More. The musicians had such a chemistry that they decided to form a band. Taylor and Artis moved to Los Angeles, and Dakota Moon began to regularly play on the L.A. club circuit. Eventually, the head of Elektra Records, Sylvia Rhone, spotted the group in concert. Impressed, she offered the group a contract and they accepted. Before they made their debut album, they toured as Tina Turner's opening act in 1997. By the end of the year, they had recorded their debut with producers Logan and More. The resulting record, entitled *Dakota Moon*, was released in April 1998. *—Stephen Thomas Erlewine*

• **Dakota Moon** / Apr. 14, 1998 / Elektra ♦♦♦♦
Dakota Moon is a true rarity—an urban group that's closer to '70s soft-rock than quiet storm. Coming across like a cross between Boyz II Men and Eric Clapton ("Wonderful Tonight" and "Change the World," not "Layla"), Dakota Moon can sometimes err on the side of schmaltz, but there's a charm in their romantic convictions. Furthermore, the group rarely indulges in the vocal histrionics that mark many Boyz II Men successors, and they do have instrumental skill and a flair for sharp pop hooks. Not everything on their self-titled debut works, but the best moments, such as the single "A Promise That I Make," is urban soul of the highest order. *—Leo Stanley*

A Place to Land / Feb. 19, 2002 / Elektra ♦♦♦
Dakota Moon doesn't change too much on their second album, *A Place to Land*, again working with producer Andrew Logan and again going for a somewhat uncanny synthesis of early-2000s urban pop and '70s soft rock. The album-opening title track is perhaps the most typical Dakota Moon moment on the album, sounding like half Backstreet Boys and half Eagles. The foursome then go straight into their most sexually charged song on the album, "Keeps Me Comin' (Addiction)," an album highlight that seems a little out of character for this otherwise good-mannered group. Overall, there aren't too many surprises here. Dakota Moon may have not stormed up the *Billboard* charts with their debut album, but that album was generally seen as a success. So it's perhaps not that surprising that Dakota Moon tried to duplicate the success of their debut, working again with Logan as the producer and retaining that uncanny synthesis of early-2000s urban pop and '70s soft rock. *—Jason Birchmeier*

The Danleers

Group / Doo Wop, R&B, Soul
With their debut single "One Summer Night," the Danleers became one of the most successful vocal groups of the late '50s. Written by the group's songwriter/manager Danny Webb and recorded during their first recording session, the tune reached the pop Top Ten and sold over a million copies. The Danleers were one of many vocal groups that arose out of the street corners, playgrounds, and tenement hallways of Brooklyn. Originally a quintet, featuring lead singer Jimmy Weston, baritone singer Nat McCune, bass vocalist Roosevelt Mays, and tenors Johnny Lee and Will Ephraim, the band's sound was reinforced by the addition of Webb.

Initially released on the Amp-3 label, "One Summer Night" quickly became a local hit and attracted the attention of Mercury, who reissued the tune in June 1958. After performing at Alan Freed's Labor Day Extravaganza at the Brooklyn Fox Theater, the Danleers were invited to join Frankie Avalon, Bobby Darin, Eddie Cochran, Connie Francis, Dion & the Belmonts, Buddy Holly & the Crickets, Clyde McPhatter, and the Coasters in a nationally touring road show.

"One Summer Night" marked the last success for the Brooklyn-based group, however. After three attempts to recapture the momentum of "One Summer Night" failed, the group was dropped by Mercury. Reorganized, with different personnel, by Weston, the Danleers released two singles in the mid-'60s that failed to revive their early success. *—Craig Harris*

• **The Best of the Danleers: The Mercury Years** / Jul. 15, 1996 / Mercury ♦♦♦♦♦
Both sides of all four of their late '50s singles for Mercury (including their only chart hit, "One Summer Night") form the core of this 17-song compilation. It also has the two singles they recorded during a brief return visit to Mercury in 1964, four cuts from the late '50s that were previously unreleased in the US, and a couple songs from a 1958 session in which they backed Pearl Galloway. There's nothing else as good as "One Summer Night" on this compilation of average late '50s New York doo wop, the group proving themselves capable of handling uptempo numbers in addition to "One Summer Night"-type ballads. *—Richie Unterberger*

Danny & the Juniors

f. 1955, Philadelphia, PA, **db.** 1964
Group / Doo Wop, Rock & Roll
Danny & the Juniors shot straight to the top of the charts in early 1958 with their biggest hit ever, the gold-selling "At the Hop" (penned by the songwriting team of Dave White and John Madara), though they reached the charts again with eight more singles through 1963, notably the Top 40 charters "Rock and Roll Is Here to Stay," "Dottie," and "Twistin' U.S.A."

Danny Rapp (lead tenor), Frank Maffei (second tenor), Joe Terranova (baritone/bass), and Dave White Tricker (tenor) (aka Dave White) were four Philadelphia high school friends—all were born in 1940 or 1941—who formed an atypical late-'50s rock & roll dance combo, originally calling themselves the Juvenairs. Rapp—the group's leader—choreographed their dance steps and invented the routines that they performed during their sets. After playing after-school gigs and local shows as a foursome for a while, they later added saxophonist Lennie Baker to the lineup.

While still in high school in late 1957, they were working a record hop as the intermission entertainment, when a local businessman named John Madara spotted the band. Madara had an interest in rock & roll promotion and introduced them to a local songwriter and vocal coach named Artie Singer, who also ran his own label, Singular Records.

Singer auditioned the band and liked an original song White had written that captured the energetic spirit of rock & roll. It was called "Do the Bop." However, since the term "bop" was by then already out of fashion, he suggested that the song's title needed to be changed and helped them shape it into the hit we know today: "At the Hop." Singer also shortened the name of the group from the Juvenairs to the Juniors and had them cut a demo of "At the Hop" that he took around to play for local DJs. Working with producer Leon Huff, it took 13 takes in Reco-Art Studios in Philadelphia before Singer felt he had the goods from the group.

Singer played the song for Dick Clark, whose popular music show *American Bandstand* was broadcast live from their hometown of Philadelphia. Clark didn't have any immediate openings on the show, but as luck would have it, Little Anthony & the Imperials canceled an appearance soon thereafter and Clark asked Danny & the Juniors to fill in as replacements. "At the Hop" proved to be an immediate success. Singular quickly issued the song as the group's first single and it became a regional hit, selling 7,000 copies in one week in Philadelphia alone. Financially strapped, Singular Records later leased the record for 5,000 dollars to ABC Paramount. "At the Hop" proceeded to climb up the charts in December of 1957, reaching number one, where it remained for seven weeks.

Danny & the Juniors soon followed up with "Rock and Roll Is Here to Stay," another White-penned rocker, which also made the Top 20. The group toured with several of Alan Freed's traveling rock & roll shows and put two more songs into the Top 40. In the early '60s the group switched over to the Swan label and after their last song charted in 1963, Danny & the Juniors eventually parted ways.

Madara ended up running his own record store, located at 60th and Market Streets in Philly. He and White also went on to join the Spokesmen, whose minor hit "The Dawn of Correction" was an answer song to Barry McGuire's number-one charter, "Eve of Destruction." White also made a solo album for Bell Records, which was released in 1971 under the name David White Tricker. Lead vocalist Danny Rapp committed suicide in 1983. Saxophonist Lennie Baker went on to be a founding member of nostalgia act Sha-Na-Na).

Interesting side notes: years later, the motion picture American Graffiti featured a scene at a senior class dance with a band playing Danny & the Juniors' "At the Hop." The '50s-style band, calling themselves "Herby & the Heartbeats," were actually portrayed by Flash Cadillac & the Continental Kids (but were virtually the spitting image of Danny & the Juniors themselves). *—Bryan Thomas*

Back to the Hop: The Swan Recordings 1960–1962 / 1992 / Rollercoaster ♦♦♦
Subtitled "The Swan Recordings, 1960-1962," these sides come from the second part of the group's recording career, before the oldies circuit beckoned. This 27-track collection gathers together virtually everything the group left behind in the vaults, counting up alternate takes, issued singles and the like. Obviously, hit-making themes are mined continuously on here ("Back to the Hop," "Twistin' USA," "Twistin' England," "Twistin' Germany," "Twistin' Italy" and three other tracks with "twist" in the title) and over half the material has ties to various dance crazes like "The Pony Express" and "Doin' the New Continental Walk." Of special interest is their duet with Freddy Cannon on "Twistin' All Night Long" and their version of his "Talahassee Lassie." Not the most essential doo wop collection, but an interesting one nonetheless, illustrating a '50s group trying to keep pace with a changing marketplace and making some decent music in the bargain. *—Cub Koda*

• **Golden Classics Edition** / Apr. 22, 1997 / Collectables ♦♦♦♦
While it's easy to dismiss Danny & the Juniors as a one-hit wonder due to the mega-success of "At the Hop," this 20-track collection of their best sides makes a strong case them as a top-notch doo wop group at the dawn of rock's golden age. Combining their ABC-Paramount and Swan sides, tracks like "Sometimes," "Rock 'n' Roll Is Here to Stay," "Dottie," "In the Meantime," "Crazy Cave," "Sassy Fran," and "I Feel So Lonely" are Philly doo wop at its best, street accents intact. While it's true the group went to the well once too often in search of another hit, this is still marvelous period music that deserves a much wider hearing. *—Cub Koda*

Terence Trent D'Arby

b. Mar. 15, 1962, New York, NY

Vocals, Saxophone, Keyboards, Drums, Guitar, Producer / Pop/Rock, Urban, Contemporary R&B, Adult Alternative Pop/Rock

Terence Trent D'Arby emerged in 1987 amid a storm of publicity. Claiming his debut record was the best since *Sgt. Pepper's*, his brash arrogance captured headlines throughout the U.K., eventually winding their way back to America—which, ironically, is the exact opposite of how D'Arby conducted his career. During the early '80s, Terence Trent D'Arby was a soldier for the United States Army. While posted in Germany, he joined a funk band called Touch, which marked the beginning of his musical career. After leaving the Army, he moved to London, where he recorded the demo tape that led to his record contract with CBS. D'Arby's first single, "If You Let Me Stay," rocketed into the U.K. Top Ten upon its release. Its accompanying album, *Introducing the Hardline According to Terence Trent D'Arby*, was also a massive success, hitting number one and spending over a year in the top half of the chart.

D'Arby didn't have a major hit in the U.S. until 1988, when the sparse funk of "Wishing Well" hit number one. The ballad "Sign Your Name" followed it into the Top Five and *Introducing* ended up selling over two million copies. All of the success—both commercial and critical—had D'Arby poised as a major act, artistically and popularly. D'Arby's mix of soul, rock, pop, and R&B recalled Prince in its scope and sound, yet his sensibility was grittier and earthier. At least they were at first. By the time of his second album, 1989's *Neither Fish nor Flesh*, his ambitions were more nakedly pretentious. The record carried the weighty subtitle "A Soundtrack of Love, Faith, Hope & Destruction" and attacked many self-consciously important themes, including homophobia and environmental destruction. In addition to the self import of the lyrics, the music added a variety of new textures, from Indian drones to straight-ahead '50s R&B.

All of the added baggage was too much for his audience and *Neither Fish nor Flesh* dropped off the charts quickly, without so much as one hit single. It took D'Arby a full four years to record a new album. When *Terence Trent D'Arby's Symphony or Damn*—an album containing many of the same ideas as *Neither Fish nor Flesh*, only better executed—was released in 1993, it received favorable reviews, as well as some airplay on modern rock radio stations and MTV. It was enough for D'Arby to regain some credibility, yet it wasn't enough to make the album a hit. Two years later, he released *TTD's Vibrator*, which received the same fate as *Symphony or Damn*. —*Stephen Thomas Erlewine*

Introducing the Hardline According to Terence Trent D'Arby / 1987 / Columbia ♦♦♦♦

Introducing the Hardline According to Terence Trent D'Arby is a strong debut by this young, cocky Black British singer, who wrote virtually every note, played a multitude of instruments, and claimed that his was the most important album since the Beatles' *Sgt. Pepper*. Hits included "If You Let Me Stay," "Dance Little Sister," "Sign Your Name," and the number one "Wishing Well." His first album is a curious mixture of old and new styles. Although the production is quite modern, D'Arby shows his roots in the work of older artists, borrowing a page or two from Michael Jackson and Stevie Wonder, while James Brown appears to have had the strongest influence on D'Arby's stage presence. —*Rob Bowman*

Neither Fish nor Flesh / Oct. 1989 / Columbia ♦♦♦

Following the major success of his debut, Terence Trent D'Arby made the always-difficult sophomore effort more difficult. In addition to the brash declarations that preceded his first record, D'Arby made ultimately self-sabotaging demands upon his label, concerning *Neither Fish nor Flesh*'s promotion and release (to coincide with the competitive Christmas market). The challenging nature of the album didn't help matters. *Neither Fish nor Flesh* is a sprawling, overly ambitious work that incorporates Middle Eastern flavorings and even more of a gospel influence into his gritty mix of rock, R&B, and funk. Lyrically, D'Arby's pretensions run a bit wild, but the man does possess a voice that is a force to be reckoned with. Songs like the rousing, soulful "I'll Be Alright" and the sexy "To Know Someone Deeply Is to Know Someone Softly" are masterful. Other highlights include the breezy, Motown vibe of "Billy Don't Fall" (a song actually about AIDS) and the skeletal, fiery "This Side of Love." *Neither Fish nor Flesh* crashed upon release, but the album remains a compelling, if flawed, effort from a musician that has been one of the more baffling unfulfilled talents in recent memory. —*Tom Demalon*

● **Terence Trent D'Arby's Symphony or Damn** / May 11, 1993 / Columbia ♦♦♦♦♦

Falling halfway between the modern R&B of *Introducing the Hardline* and the extravagant *Neither Fish nor Flesh*, *Symphony or Damn* is Terence Trent D'Arby's most ambitious album yet. It's also his best, because it takes the fine songwriting of his debut and melds it to the sonic excesses of *Fish*. Sure, some of it is embarrassing (it's hard not to cringe during the "Welcome to My Monasteryo" declaration at the beginning of the album), but more often than not, D'Arby's experimentations succeed, and succeed grandly, at that. —*Stephen Thomas Erlewine*

TTD's Vibrator / Jun. 1, 1995 / Work ♦♦♦

Symphony or Damn was an impressive comeback for Terence Trent D'Arby, pulling together the melodic songcraft of his debut and the conceptual ambitions of *Neither Fish nor Flesh*. *TTD's Vibrator* follows the same pattern of *Symphony or Damn*, only without the songs to support the ambitions. —*Stephen Thomas Erlewine*

The Dartells

f. 1962, Oxnard, CA

Group / R&B

The Dartells formed in 1962 in Oxnard, CA, which is midway between Los Angeles and Santa Barbara. The members were: Doug Phillips (bass/vocals), Dick Burns (guitar), Gary Peeler (drums), Randy Ray (organist), and saxophonists Rich Peil and Corky Wilkie. They broke into the pop Top 20 their first time out with "Hot Pastrami" (1963), a reworking of Nat Kendricks & the Swans' "Mashed Potatoes." The Swans were James Brown's band and Kendricks was the drummer. Tom Ayers, who went on to bigger and better things, was the Dartells' manager, mentor, and producer. He got the hot local group a deal with Arlen Records in 1962 and the record started selling from day one. It became so popular that Dot Records picked it up and marketed it all the way to number-11 pop in 1963. An album titled after the song was hastily thrown together and the band briefly basked in its newfound success, which included a television appearance on *The Munsters*. The Dot deal was weird. Their follow-up and only other recording to make the pop 100, "Dance Everybody Dance" (number 99), came out on Arlen (Arlen 513) and Dot (Dot 16502). It seems Arlen must have released it first and when they started bubbling, Dot took over. The Viceroys, a band from Seattle, covered "Dartell Stomp," the flipside of "Hot Pastrami," but a third single, "Clap Your Hands," a cover of Montreal's Beau Marks original, did nothing. (The Beau Marks enjoyed a number-one hit in Canada and Australia with the song.) Shortly thereafter, the Dartells, who were 18–20 when they started, disbanded.

Tom Ayers went on to play bass in the Johnny Burnette Quintet. The Dartells' mentor also worked with the Sir Douglas Quintet, Ultra Violet, and Gene Vincent. He's most-known for bringing David Bowie to RCA Records. Ayers became a mover and shaker, working for Hanna-Barbara Productions, ABC, Columbia, United Artists, Kama Sutra, Buddha, and RCA Records. He passed May 30, 2000, in Shreveport, LA, at the age of 57. He was born in Sabine Parish, LA. Doug Phillips formed Now Concepts in the late '60s, but singles on ABC-Paramount and Atco Records were D.O.A. In 1971, he led the band Cottonwood, which cut a no-go album for ABC Records in 1971 entitled *Camaraderie*. Some other Dartells became members of Rain, a late-'60s recording group that shot blanks. —*Andrew Hamilton*

● **Hot Pastrami!** / 1963 / Dot ♦♦♦

On the heels on "Hot Pastrami" (a reworking of Nat Kendricks & the Swans' "Mashed Potatoes") comes this hastily assembled LP named after it. The Dartells' sound was dominated by energized organ playing riffs, frantic horns, and half-baked soul wails. The formula worked on "Hot Pastrami," a number-11 pop hit in 1963, but failed on everything else they ever did. This includes "Dartell Stomp," the B-side of their hit, which was covered by the Viceroys (not the L.A. doo wop group, but a band from Seattle), and watered-down but interesting remakes of Shep & the Limelights' "Daddy's Home" and James Brown's "Night Train." —*Andrew Hamilton*

Craig David

b. May 5, 1981, Southampton, England

Vocals, Producer / Contemporary R&B, Urban, Club/Dance, 2-Step/British Garage, Garage/House

R&B sensation Craig David was barely out of his teens when he took a hold of the U.K. pop circuit, twisted it around, and threw it back on its bum during fall 2000. This fresh-faced native of Southampton, England, was merely playing into his love of funkadelic hip-hop and crooning urban stylings when he started writing songs as a teenager. His love for Terence Trent D'Arby, Sisqo, and Donell Jones allowed him to put his creative love for art, culture, and history into a musical beat all his own. And the new millennium belonged to him and garage had been redefined.

Born Craig Ashley David on May 5, 1981, David was slicing and dicing ragga and R&B on the local station PCRS 106.5FM and found himself playing club gigs prior to rubbing elbows with some of music's finest. It was during this time he hooked with Artful Dodger's Mark Hill. After winning a national writing competition, Craig was more than ready to start producing with Hill. His big break came when he put his own additives on Damage's "I'm Ready," a B-side to "Wonderful Tonight." Soon thereafter he remixed his own version of Human League's "Human" and started himself a regular spot in area clubs during the weekends. "Rewind" was another underground smash, specifically a definitive move for David. His respect for Stevie Wonder, Faith Evans, and R. Kelly was most apparent, however his own vocal talent was beginning to shine. He and Hill's specialty show on Capital Radio provided another outlet for David to shape his musical work of genius. "Fill Me In" proved yet another hit, shooting straight to number one in summer 2000. David was now the youngest British male solo artist to have a number one single. He was 19 years old.

A deal with Wildstar Records in the U.K. sparked toward the end of the summer as "Re-Rewind" and "7 Days" gained praise in late November. A stateside agreement with Atlantic also led to more global hype. He had sold 3.5 million records worldwide and garage was finally becoming massive overseas and it was David's debut *Born to Do It* that was at the head.

But not all were pulling for this R&B prodigy. Aside from winning three awards at the MOBO's in October, Craig David walked away empty handed at the 2000 Brit Awards in February 2001. He was up for six nominations, including Best British Male Solo Artist, Best British Newcomer, and Best British Single for "7 Days," but industry politics fell into operation. Many mainstream stars came to David's defense, artists such as Elton John, U2, and Robbie Williams, professing their disgust for the ill recognition for David and his musical efforts in the past year. Death threats soon followed for the superstar in spring 2001 as he took the stage in a show in London. An anonymous caller claimed a soldier would injure David with tear gas and hand grenades. Still, his record sales continued to soar in the U.K. with sales of *Born to Do It* increasing over 100 percent after his dismal beginning months of 2001. He bombarded American Shores with a deal with Atlantic and released *Born to Do It* stateside in summer 2001. Mainstream radio flocked to him immediately. Missy Elliott, Beyoncé Knowles, and Usher called themselves fans.

The next year, things didn't simmer down for the now international pop star. Craig David returned with a sophomore effort *Slicker Than Your Average* in November 2002. This particular album saw a much grittier side from David. Debut single "What's Your Flava?" also became one of the year's hottest singles. —*MacKenzie Wilson*

● **Born to Do It** / Jul. 17, 2001 / Atlantic ♦♦♦♦

In his 2000 debut album, Craig David merges smooth-soul crooning with a cascade of glistening keyboards, circling guitars, and sophisticated rhythms. Displaying a healthy marriage of current R&B vocal stylings and U.K. club/dance fused beats, David's music skillfully evades feeling robotic and cold, while still sounding pristine and immaculate. As an artist who is in his late teens, he conjures up a personal and revealing work that delves into both his mature sound and youthful attitude. Co-writing and co-producing with Mark Hill of the British garage act the Artful Dodger, David wraps his scorching-cool vocals around a mellow attack of keyboards and drums, while distinctly focusing on romance, relationships, and clubbing. Guitars simmer on "7 Days," a day-by-day account of an adventurous first week with a woman he magically encounters while in a subway. In "Can't Be Messing 'Round," the performer's razor sharp vocals heat-seek while a keyboard hammers before being covered by a high-sounding whirlpool of strings. With the dance anthem "Time to Party," drums sting and a whispering guitar is faintly heard while he optimistically sings "Friday, payday/Ready to do the things we love." The lyrics do sometimes sound underdeveloped due to David's age, and the music can occasionally lack distinctiveness, yet those two factors do not hinder the celebratory power of *Born to Do It*. The album features an effortless presentation of limber and carefully articulated vocal talents by the singer that seamlessly glide through the polished collage of songs. *—Stephen Mercier*

Slicker Than Your Average / Nov. 19, 2002 / Atlantic ♦♦♦
The former British teen sensation kicked off his singing career with the stellar Grammy-nominated *Born to Do It*, which blended 2-step, R&B, and pop. With his second release, *Slicker Than Your Average*, Craig David shows a different side. While *Born to Do It* was filled with romantic lyrics, *Slicker Than Your Average* shares David's feelings about fame, with a small dose of his trademark love songs. On the title track, David takes a stab at those who criticize his "squeaky clean" image and musical style: "Now they're telling me that I'm too R&B/How I turned my back on the whole U.K. garage scene/Now they're stressing me when/I know there's so much more to see." Broken hearts and playing the field are prominent topics as well. Musically, *Slicker Than Your Average* is a collage of styles—dance ("What's Your Flava?," "Eenie Meenie," "Fast Cars") and 2-step ("2 Steps Back") as well as R&B/pop ballads ("World Filled With Love" and "Rise & Fall"). "Rise & Fall," a song featuring a guest vocal by Sting, is among the highlights on the album, as are "You Don't Miss Your Water ('Til the Well Runs Dry)," "What's Your Flava?," and the Beatlesque "World Filled With Love," which is filled with soaring harmonies. *Slicker Than Your Average* is stronger than the average sophomore effort, and it proves that Craig David's abilities are innate. *—Christina Fuoco*

Betty Davis (Betty Mabry)

b. 1945, Pittsburgh, PA
Vocals / Funk, Soul

A wildly flamboyant funk diva with few equals even three decades after her debut, Betty Davis combined the gritty emotional realism of Tina Turner, the futurist fashion sense of David Bowie, and the trend-setter flair of Miles Davis, her husband for a year. It's easy to imagine the snickers when a 23-year-old model married a famous musician twice her age, but Davis was no gold-digger; she turned Miles on to Jimi Hendrix and Sly Stone (providing the spark that led to his musical re-invention on *In a Silent Way* and *Bitches Brew*), then proved her own talents with a trio of sizzling mid-'70s solo LPs.

Born Betty Mabry in Pittsburgh, Davis began working as a model during the mid-'60s. She gained entrance into hipster musical circles very early on—her first writing credit, "Uptown" by the Chambers Brothers, came in 1967, before she'd turned 20. One year later, she met Miles Davis in New York, and they were married by the end of summer 1968. Though their marriage didn't survive the end of the decade, Betty Davis was tremendously influential on Miles, introducing him to psychedelic rock and even influencing his wardrobe. Miles' 1968 LP *Filles de Kilimanjaro* featured her on the cover, and he wrote the final track ("Mademoiselle Mabry") for her.

Miles divorced her in 1969, explaining later in his autobiography that she was "too young and wild" for him. (He also suspected her of an affair with Jimi Hendrix, an allegation she denies.) By the beginning of the '70s, Betty Davis began work on a set of songs, and tapped a host of great musicians to bring them to fruition: Gregg Errico and Larry Graham from Sly Stone's band, Michael Carabello from Santana, the Pointer Sisters, and members of the Tower of Power horn section. Her self-titled debut album finally appeared in 1973, and though it made no commercial impact at all, it was an innovative collection with plenty of blistering songs. Even more so than a soul shouter like Tina Turner, Davis was a singer for the feminist era, a take-no-prisoners sexual predator who screamed, yelled, grunted, purred, and cooed her way through extroverted material like "Anti Love Song," "Shoo-B-Doop and Cop Him," and "He Was a Big Freak." Religious groups protested many of her concert appearances (several were canceled), and radio outlets understandably refused to play her extreme work.

Davis hardly let up with her second and third albums, 1974's *They Say I'm Different* and 1975's *Nasty Gal*, but they too made little impact. Though she would've made an excellent disco diva, Betty Davis largely disappeared from the music scene afterward. An aborted 1979 session has been released on multiple occasions, once as *Crashin' From Passion* and also as *Hangin' out in Hollywood*. *—John Bush*

Betty Davis / 1973 / Vinyl Experience ♦♦♦♦♦
Betty Davis' debut was an outstanding funk record, driven by her aggressive, no-nonsense songs and a set of howling performances driven by a crack band to new heights of extroverted soul. Listeners wouldn't know it from the song's title, but for the opener, "If I'm in Luck I Might Get Picked Up," Davis certainly doesn't play the wallflower; she's a woman on the prowl, positively luring the men in and best of all, explaining exactly how she does it: "I said I'm wigglin' my fanny, I'm raunchy dancing, I'm-a-doing it doing it/This is my night out." "Game Is My Middle Name" begins at a midtempo lope, but really breaks through on the chorus, with the Pointer Sisters and Sylvester backing up each of her assertions. As overwhelming as Davis' performances are, it's as much the backing group as Davis herself that makes her material so powerful (and believable). Reams of underground cred allowed her to recruit one of the tightest rhythm sections ever heard on record (bassist Larry Graham and drummer Greg Errico, both veterans of Sly & the Family Stone), plus fellow San Francisco luminaries like master keyboardist Merl Saunders and guitarists Neal Schon or Douglas Rodriguez (both associated with Santana at the time). Graham's popping bass and the raw, flamboyant, hooky guitar lines of Schon or Rodriguez make the perfect accompaniment to these songs; Graham's slinky bass is the instrumental equivalent of Davis' vocal gymnastics, and Rodriguez makes his guitar scream during "Your Man My Man." It's hard to tell whether the musicians are pushing so hard because of Davis' performances or if they're egging each other, but it's an unnecessary question. Everything about Betty Davis' self-titled debut album speaks to Davis the lean-and-mean sexual predator, from songs to performance to backing, and so much the better for it. All of which should've been expected from the woman who was too wild for Miles Davis. *—John Bush*

They Say I'm Different / 1974 / Just Sunshine ♦♦♦♦♦
Betty Davis' second full-length featured a similar set of songs as her debut, though with Davis herself in the production chair and a radically different lineup. The openers, "Shoo-B-Doop and Cop Him" and "He Was a Big Freak," are big, blowsy tunes with stop-start funk rhythms and Davis in her usual persona as the aggressive sexual predator. On the title track, she reminisces about her childhood and compares herself to kindred spirits of the past, a succession of blues legends she holds fond—including special time for Bessie Smith, Chuck Berry, and Robert Johnson. A pair of unknowns, guitarist Cordell Dudley and bassist Larry Johnson, do a fair job of replacing the stars from her first record. As a result, *They Say I'm Different* is more keyboard-dominated than her debut, with prominent electric piano, clavinet, and organ from Merl Saunders, Hershall Kennedy, and Tony Vaughn. The material was even more extreme than on her debut; "He Was a Big Freak" featured a prominent bondage theme, while "Your Mama Wants Ya Back" and "Don't Call Her No Tramp" dealt with prostitution, or at least inferred it. With the exception of the two openers, though, *They Say I'm Different* lacked the excellent songs and strong playing of her debut; an explosive and outré record, but more a variation on the same theme she'd explored before. *—John Bush*

Nasty Gal / 1975 / MPC ♦♦♦♦

Hangin' out in Hollywood / Nov. 2, 1995 / Charly ♦♦
Listeners who haven't heard and loved Betty Davis' first two smokin' albums, *They Say I'm Different* and *Nasty Gal*, might appreciate this attempt to smooth the funky sister from Pittsburgh, PA. Those who *have* heard those releases might not be so inclined. Not only was BD hangin' out in Hollywood in 1979, she was Cadillac-ing it in the studios, forsaking the funk that made her a cult figure to wax these tracks that until recently were unreleased. Since she composed all the tunes you'd think she would be more into it, but she sounds disinterested. The front cover leads you to think this is similar to *They Say I'm Different*, since the same one graced that LP's back view, but the old adage about not judging a book by its cover rings true here. "Quintessence of Hip," "Crashin' From Passion," and "I Need a Whole Lotta Love" best represent the funk but the limp ballads are throwaways. These same tunes sequenced differently are also on a CD entitled *Crashin' From Passion*. *—Andrew Hamilton*

Crashin' From Passion / Feb. 20, 1996 / Razor & Tie ♦♦

● **Anti Love: The Best of Betty Davis** / 2000 / MPC ♦♦♦♦♦
Along with their welcome Betty Davis reissue campaign of 2000, MPC added a near-definitive hits compilation. Split into the "Sex Side" and the "Sleaze Side," *Anti Love* hits *most* of the major moments from funk's most outrageous performer (no small feat), including "Anti Love Song," "He Was a Big Freak," "If I'm in Luck I Might Get Picked Up," "Shoo-B-Doop and Cop Him," and her brash statement of purpose, "They Say I'm Different." Twelve tracks is mighty short for any digital-era collection, though, and it's missing a few high points (the title track from 1975's *Nasty Gal*, "Walkin Up the Road"). A solid first place to turn, but interested parties would do better to seek out the original full-lengths. *—John Bush*

Carl Davis

Producer / Chicago Soul, Soul

Producer and A&R man Carl Davis played a large part in Chicago soul of the '60s and '70s, although his contribution is usually unfairly overlooked by rock historians (as, indeed, Chicago soul as a whole is to some extent). As producer and A&R director for OKeh Records, he got hits with Major Lance that helped define the Chicago soul sound, as well as working on lesser-known but quality soul discs by Billy Butler and Walter Jackson. He also produced some notable records by soul stars Gene Chandler and Mary Wells.

After leaving his position at OKeh, Davis worked at A&R and production for Brunswick Records, which recorded the bulk of top Chicago soul in the late '60s and '70s. He helped revive, albeit briefly, Jackie Wilson's career by collaborating with him on earthier, more contemporary soul material than he had been getting in previous years, particularly on the hit "(Your Love Keeps Lifting Me) Higher and Higher." Brunswick also had memorable hits by Barbara Acklin ("Love Makes a Woman") and Young-Holt Unlimited's instrumental "Soulful Strut," which came about when the vocal track was stripped from a number Acklin had recorded, and the backing track issued on its own.

As the '60s turned into the '70s, Davis' greatest triumphs were with romantic records that have been pegged as "sweet soul" and "soft soul." Davis formed the Atlantic-distributed Dakar label in 1968, its biggest artist being Tyrone Davis, who had sensual hits with "Can I Change My Mind" and "Turn Back the Hands of Time." Back on Brunswick there were also harmony soul smashes by the Chi-Lites, one of the biggest soul vocal groups of the '70s. The prosperity of Chicago soul began to ebb after the mid-'70s, as did the profile of Davis (along with many other soul-specializing producers throughout the U.S.). *—Richie Unterberger*

Geater Davis

b. Jan. 29, 1946, Kountze, TX, **d.** Sep. 29, 1984, Dallas, TX
Vocals / Southern Soul, Soul

Geater Davis was one of the South's great lost soul singers, an impassioned stylist whose voice was a combination of sweetness and sandpaper grit. Comparable to the blues-drenched likes of Johnnie Taylor or, especially, Bobby "Blue" Bland, Davis wound up even more of a cult artist than deep soul peers like James Carr or O.V. Wright, having recorded mostly for small local labels during his prime. Davis was born in Kountze, TX, in 1946, and did the vast majority of his recording during the first half of the '70s, often writing or co-writing his own material and occasionally producing or playing guitar as well. He cut an album, *Sweet Woman's Love*, for the House of Orange label in 1971, and his cover of Jerry Butler & the Impressions' "For Your Precious Love" later became a favorite among British soul collectors. He went on to release singles for Luna ("I Don't Worry (About Jody)") and Ace ("Strange Situation," "Tired of Busting My Brain") before a longer spell with 77, where his output included "Long Cold Winter," "I'm Gonna Change" (recorded at Muscle Shoals), "I've Got to Pay the Price," and "Your Heart Is So Cold," among others. Unfortunately, Davis' records never sold very well, even in spite of heavy touring on the blues and chitlin circuits. He died of a heart attack on September 29, 1984; he was only 38 years old. In 1998, WestSide released *Sadder Shades of Blue: The Southern Soul Sessions 1971-76*, a compilation covering most of the labels for which he recorded (except House of Orange). *—Steve Huey*

- **Sadder Shades of Blue: The Southern Soul Sessions 1971–76** / Nov. 10, 1998 / WestSide ✦✦✦✦

The Spencer Davis Group

f. 1963, Birmingham, England, **db.** 1986

Group / British Invasion, Blue-Eyed Soul

His ferocious soul-drenched vocals belying his tender teenage years, Stevie Winwood powered the Spencer Davis Group's three biggest U.S. hits during their brief life span as one of the British Invasion's most convincing R&B-based combos. Guitarist Davis formed the band with Winwood on organ, his brother Muff Winwood on bass, and drummer Peter York. Signing on with producer Chris Blackwell, the quartet got their first hit (the blistering "Keep on Running") from another of Blackwell's acts, West Indian performer Jackie Edwards. After topping the British charts in 1965, the song struggled on the lower reaches of the US Hot 100.

The group's two hottest sellers were self-penned projects. "Gimme Some Lovin'" and "I'm a Man" were searing showcases for the adolescent Winwood's gritty vocals and blazing keyboards and the band's pounding rhythms. Although they burned up the charts even on the other side of the ocean in 1967, the quartet never capitalized on their fame with an American tour. At the height of their power, Winwood left to form Traffic, leaving Davis without his dynamic frontman. The bandleader focused on producing other acts, including a Canadian ensemble called the Downchild Blues Band during the early '80s. *—Bill Dahl*

Their First LP / 1965 / Fontana ✦✦✦

The group's first album is basically a reflection of their early repertoire and very heavy on the R&B/soul standards. Dominated by covers of Ike & Tina Turner, the Coasters, John Lee Hooker, Little Walter, Brenda Holloway, and others, only three of the tunes are original. Two of these are written by Stevie Winwood, the other by Spencer Davis; Winwood's midtempo soul number "It Hurts Me So" is easily the best of them. Winwood is in fine voice and the group is energetic, but this is neither as good as their best work nor nearly as good as the best British R&B albums of the era by competitors like Them and the Rolling Stones. It includes their first two British singles, "Dimples" and "I Can't Stand It." *—Richie Unterberger*

Autumn '66 / 1966 / Fontana ✦✦✦

At the peak of their popularity, the Spencer Davis Group's albums were considerably less impressive than their hits and a bit thin on imagination, although they were never less than competent. This, their third LP, relies heavily on soul covers, as well as a few oft-covered blues standards ("Midnight Special," "Mean Woman Blues," "Dust My Blues"). Highlights are their second British number-one hit "Somebody Help Me," the decent group original "High Time Baby," Winwood's organ-based instrumental "On the Green Light," and "When I Get Home," which (like "Somebody Help Me") was a hit in Britain, but not the U.S. *—Richie Unterberger*

I'm a Man / 1967 / United Artists ✦✦✦✦

Stevie Winwood and Muff Winwood had left the Spencer Davis Group just a few months before the summer 1967 release of their second U.S. album, which nonetheless was entirely comprised of songs done by the original lineup. Like their first U.S. album, *Gimme Some Lovin'*, it was a more or less arbitrary assortment of songs that had been recorded by the band at various points in the mid-'60s. And again, the big hit, "I'm a Man," was a classic soul-rock group original that outclassed everything else on the record. Otherwise it was standard British R&B-rock that varied from average to very good. The standouts were their covers of John Lee Hooker's "Dimples" and the relatively little-known American soul tunes "I Can't Stand It" and "Look Away." The cooking Stevie Winwood-penned instrumental "On the Green Light" had dynamic organ and blues guitar. The 2001 CD reissue on Sundazed adds add bonus tracks from the same era, including some of their best efforts: the percolating cover of "Watch Your Step," the anguished original blues ballad "Hey Darling," "Let Me Down Easy," "Strong Love," and the instrumental "Waltz for Lumumba," which anticipates Traffic with its unusual percussion and jazzy accents. *—Richie Unterberger*

With Their New Face On / 1967 / Repertoire ✦✦✦

The departure of Steve and Muff Winwood left the Spencer Davis Group at a bit of a loss. Hiring vocalist Eddie Hardin, the band regrouped and recorded *With Their New Face On*, a limp collection of instrumentals, half-hearted blues and mild pop. There's nothing offensive about *With Their New Face On*, but there's nothing of interest, either. It's not surprising that the group disbanded shortly after its release. *—Stephen Thomas Erlewine*

- **Golden Archive Series** / 1987 / Rhino ✦✦✦✦✦

Here is the best compilation of their best moments. 14 songs, including both of their U.S. hits, "I'm a Man" and "Gimme Some Lovin'"; the U.K. chart-toppers "Keep on Running" and "Somebody Help Me," the smaller U.K. hit "When I Come Home," and several fine R&B covers, all from 1964-1966. *—Richie Unterberger*

Eight Gigs a Week: The Steve Winwood Years / Apr. 22, 1996 / Island ✦✦✦✦✦

This two-CD, 51-song set covers virtually everything the group recorded with Steve Winwood in the lineup from 1964-1967. The gap between the band's best and worst material was considerable; quite a few of their R&B covers are surprisingly routine, and the occasional cuts that don't have Winwood on lead vocals are downright pedestrian. Because of this inconsistency, the general fan's better off with the Rhino best-of, if it can be found. If you want to get more, though, this is the first and last place to go, with all the hit singles, everything from their three albums, an early EP, some B-sides, and a couple of previously unissued tracks. And some of the obscure material is really good, whether in a straight R&B/blues or more soulful vein. Be aware that the version of "Gimme Some Lovin'" here is the less dynamic, original British mix, minus some backup vocals and percussion. *—Richie Unterberger*

- **Best of the Spencer Davis Group** / 1998 / EMI America ✦✦✦✦✦

This budget-priced 25-minute CD (part of Capitol's *Ten Best* series) has it all over EMI-America's late-'80s *Best of the Spencer Davis Group*, made from much better source tapes and priced about 20 percent lower. It only has ten songs on it, but those include "Gimme Some Lovin'," "Keep on Running," "I'm a Man," "When I Come Home," "Searchin'," and "Every Little Bit Hurts," exactly the songs that nine out of ten people who remember the Spencer Davis Group would want. "I'm a Man" evidently is making its first appearance in stereo on this CD, comes off better in mono, though it is interesting to hear the instrumental component of the song divided in this way. Surprisingly, the producers have also found room for one post-Steve Winwood-era track, the mildly psychedelic "Time Seller" (which sounds a little like an early ELO track) that slots in decently in this setting. *—Bruce Eder*

Thornetta Davis

Vocals / Alternative Pop/Rock, Soul

Detroit-born blues diva Thornetta Davis reluctantly began her career at the age of 15 when, on the encouragement of friends, she made her debut at an area talent show. After forming the vocal group Chanteuse to cover R&B hits by the Pointer Sisters and the Emotions, Davis did not discover the blues until 1986, when she became the backing vocalist for the Motor City band Lamonte Zodiac & the Love Signs, later renamed the Chisel Brothers. In 1991, she was recruited to sing backup for the funk-metal outfit Big Chief, appearing on their Sub Pop label LPs *Face* and *Mack Avenue Skull Game*. When the group disbanded, Davis was signed to Sub Pop as a solo performer; after assembling the majority of Big Chief as a backing unit, she recorded her 1996 debut *Sunday Morning Music*. *—Jason Ankeny*

- **Sunday Morning Music** / Oct. 15, 1996 / Sub Pop ✦✦✦✦

Working with her previous employers from Big Chief, specifically bassist Matt O'Brien, guitarist Phil Durr and drummer Mike Danner, turned out to be the perfect approach for Davis' solo debut. It's not quite Big Chief with a different lead singer, happily, with *Sunday Morning Music* showcasing her affinity for the blues while not losing the powerful punch of that band. Davis' singing is just wonderful—she's got a rich, warm voice that she doesn't show off with, avoiding pointless vocal high jumps and wails for confident, often soaring delivery. She can really turn it on when needed, and the results on "Helpless" and the hard-rocking "The Deal" are well worth it. There's one cover song, Stevie Wonder's "You Haven't Done Nothin'," which Davis does a great job on and then some (a duo between the two would be amazing). She splits the lyrical work with album producer Al Sutton, another Big Chief vet, both having a good ear for statements of love, heartbreak and inspiration that avoid warmed-over clichés. "Only One," a message to a departed partner, and "Sunday Morning," a reflective comparison of past beauty and hopes and present, grimmer realities delivered over a lovely acoustic guitar melody, are two standouts. Her backing bandmates, meanwhile, create excellent music for her to work with, touching on everything from full funk chops to, on the concluding "Come Go With Me," delightful retro-soul. Various guests stop by to make things almost a Detroit-area love-in, from keyboardist Chris Codish to Kid Rock, who creates the beat on the striking, passionate "Sunset," one of the album's best tracks. Black Crowes member Eddie Harsch also adds keys and clavinet at various points, easily slotting into the band's smoky sound. Through it all, Davis sounds on top of her game, and the whole album makes for a worthwhile, invigorating listen. *—Ned Raggett*

Tyrone Davis

b. May 4, 1938, Greenville, MS

Vocals / Soul, Chicago Soul, Smooth Soul, Pop-Soul

The king of romantic Chicago soul, Tyrone Davis' warm, aching vulnerability and stylish class made him especially popular with female soul fans during a lengthy hitmaking run that lasted throughout the '70s. Best known for the classics "Can I Change My Mind" and "Turn Back the Hands of Time," Davis was a versatile baritone singer who could handle everything from pop-soul to funk to bluesy chitlin circuit R&B, but smooth soul was his true bread and butter. Once Davis broke through in the late '60s, he never really stopped recording; although the R&B chart hits dried up by the early '80s, he was still going strong into the new millennium, decades after his first single was released.

Tyrone Davis was born May 4, 1938, in Greenville, MS; he spent most of his formative years in Saginaw, MI, and moved to Chicago in 1959, where he eventually found a job as a valet and chauffeur for bluesman Freddie King. He befriended the likes of Bobby "Blue" Bland, Little Milton, and Otis Clay, among others, and began to pursue his own singing career in the clubs on the city's West and South Sides. Singer/pianist Harold Burrage took Davis under his wing and helped him refine his craft, and the budding blues shouter got his first shot in 1965 on the Four Brothers label. His first single, "Suffer," was recorded under the name Tyrone the Wonder Boy and written and produced by Burrage, as was the follow-up "Good Company." Unfortunately, Burrage passed away in late 1966, and after one more single Davis moved on to cut one-offs for Sack and ABC. He found a home at Carl Davis' new label Dakar in 1968, when a Texas DJ flipped his first release over and started playing the B-side, "Can I Change My Mind." Showcasing Davis' lovelorn pleading to best effect, the song went all the way to number one on the R&B charts, and reached the pop Top Five as well.

Teamed with producer/arranger Willie Henderson, who'd masterminded "Can I Change My Mind," Davis capitalized on his breakthrough with a string of orchestrated hits that emphasized his new, smoother style, and helped point the way for Chicago soul into a new decade. "Is It Something You've Got" reached the R&B Top Five in 1969, and it was followed in 1970 by the sublime "Turn Back the Hands of Time." It was his second R&B number one, and also his biggest hit on the pop charts with a peak at number three; plus, the accompanying album of the same name ranks among the best soul LPs of its time, producing two more hits in the R&B Top Ten "I'll Be Right Here" and "Let Me Back In." Davis hit the R&B Top 40 with steady regularity over the next few years, including the Top Tens "Could I Forget You," "I Had It All the Time," "Without You in My Life," and "There It Is." In 1975, he scored his third number one R&B hit with "Turning Point," but left Dakar for Columbia the following year.

Davis' ballad mastery was a main selling point for Columbia, which made his backing orchestrations even lusher than before, but he also made the occasional concession to contemporary dance trends, which informed his debut Columbia hit "Give It Up (Turn It Loose)," a number-two R&B single from 1976. Further successes followed in "This I Swear" (1977), "Get On Up (Disco)" (1978), and the slinky ballad "In the Mood" (1979). Davis recorded his final album for Columbia in 1981, then switched to Highrise, where he promptly landed a Top Five R&B hit—his last, as it turned out—with "Are You Serious" in 1982. Short stints with Ocean-Front and Prelude followed before Davis settled in with Future for the latter half of the '80s. He spent the first half of the '90s on retro-soul label Ichiban, recording several albums, and then moved to Southern soul imprint Malaco in 1996 for an equally productive stay that lasted into the new millennium. Davis continued to release new albums and toured the soul-blues circuit as restlessly as ever. *—Steve Huey*

Can I Change My Mind / 1969 / Dakar ✦✦✦✦✦
This is the title of Davis' greatest hit, and one of the genuine '60s soul classics. This song broke Davis out of the pack and established him as a star. It's by far the dominant song on this album of otherwise nicely sung, expertly produced deep soul ballads and uptempo tunes. *—Ron Wynn*

Turn Back the Hands of Time / 1970 / Rhino ✦✦✦✦✦
If the only great song on Tyrone Davis' second album *Turn Back the Hands of Time* was its impeccable title track, it still would have been a noteworthy record in the history of uptown Chicago soul and early-'70s soul. Fortunately, it's the tip of the iceberg on this terrific album that ranks among the finest soul records of its era. Not every song is as silky smooth and seductive as the title track, but there are more than its fair share of strings, backing vocals, horns, and even harpsichords (showcased on "If It's Love You're After"). Instead, it's luxurious and Davis is able to deepen it with his nuanced, soulful interpretations; he's even given a chance to try a bluesy funk with "Undying Love" and does a great slow ballad with "I Keep Coming Back." What's impressive about the record is not just that Davis is able to handle everything from those slow-burners to the soul-pop, sounding convincing in each setting, but that producer Willie Henderson has crafted utterly appropriate, intoxicating, and unique productions for each song. And those songs are all very, very strong. There were other singles pulled from *Turn Back the Hands of Time* that scaled the charts—"Is It Something You've Got" and "I'll Be Right Here," both R&B Top Ten hits, plus "Let Me Back In"—but the album tracks are also magnificent, including "All the Waiting is Not in Vain," the Impressions-styled "Just Because of You," and the great, great, funky "Love Bones." There's not a weak moment here (and there shouldn't be, considering that the whole thing clocks in at under 30 minutes), just great early-'70s soul. It's a forgotten gem. *—Stephen Thomas Erlewine*

I Had It All the Time / 1972 / Dakar ✦✦✦
Tyrone Davis scored another smash R&B hit with the title track, although it wasn't a chart topper. Davis was about to exit the Dakar label and did only one more album for them before signing a big money deal with Columbia. This is prototype early '70s soul, sparsely produced and wonderfully performed. *—Ron Wynn*

It's All in the Game / 1974 / Dakar ✦✦✦
The final Dakar album before Tyrone Davis left to join Columbia. It's right in line with his others: earthy ballads, heartfelt wailers, and blues-oriented uptempo numbers. It was the end of an era, as "deep" soul, already in decline, was about to be completely swamped by the coming of disco. *—Ron Wynn*

In the Mood With Tyrone Davis / 1979 / Columbia ✦✦✦✦✦
His best overall Columbia album. Tyrone Davis surprised many observers when the title cut smashed the embargo non-Southern urban contemporary stations had on soul music and soared into the Top 10, peaking at number six. The rest of the album was a bit slick by past Davis' standards, but even the sappiest numbers were performed with Davis' customary grit and soulfulness. *—Ron Wynn*

I'll Always Love You / 1991 / Ichiban ✦✦

Something's Mighty Wrong / 1992 / Ichiban ✦✦✦
Tyrone Davis' *Something's Mighty Wrong* finds the singer in a grand showcase that vigorously updates his brand of Chicago soul. The radio-aired ballad "Running in and out of My Life" offers some of Davis' most heart-tugging vocals ever. "Big Cat" has a pumping bassline like the earlier hit "Ever Lovin' Girl," the swinging "Ain't Gonna Get It," and the charming "I'm Learning." Produced by Leo Graham, the singer and the synths are tastefully balanced in the mix, with the focus kept on Davis' soulful vocals. Along with *Call Tyrone*, this is easily one of the singer's best latter-day albums. *—Ed Hogan*

The Best of Tyrone Davis: In the Mood / Jun. 4, 1996 / Columbia ✦✦✦✦
The Best of Tyrone Davis: In The Mood offers 15 gems that center mostly on romance. The title track was Davis' biggest hit with the label. With it's boudoir-minded lyrics Davis' come-ons were forward and as he sang, "Just like ice cream and honey my love is gonna make you melt," it's almost cringe time. "Ain't Nothing I Can Do" follows the same logic and has Davis singing about a "dark, cozy room" where he's no doubt doing more than talking. During this time Davis, longtime producer Leo Graham and arranger James Mack fashioned an up to-the-minute subtle Chicago sound. The streamlined yet hooky approach gave the proper emphasis on Davis' voice on the tracks "Be With Me" and the delicate "Let's Be Closer." Davis also did uptempo offerings as well. "Give It Up (Turn It Loose)" has the title being his pragmatic solution to put an end to going-nowhere relationships. This compilation's most overt dance track, the bass heavy, "Get On Up (Disco)" is skilled, kinetic and certainly shows Davis having a good time. As his Columbia output is often underrated *The Best of Tyrone Davis: In the Mood* thankfully puts these tracks back in circulation and is a must for his fans. *—Jason Elias*

Greatest Hits / Aug. 11, 1998 / Brunswick ✦✦✦✦

Turning Back the Hands of Time: The Soul of Tyrone Davis / Oct. 13, 1998 / Diablo ✦✦✦✦✦
A great anthology of Tyrone Davis' hits on the Dakar Label, covering a period from 1968 to 1976. People mistakenly labeled Davis a blues singer; he's not. Tyrone is urban R&B seasoned with southern soul. All the tunes that put him over the top are here: the shuffling, bluesy "Can I Change My Mind," the questioning, horn-accented "Is It Something You've Got" and there's "Turn Back the Hands of Time," highlighted by some sweet punchy horns. And on, and on. Lesser known releases included the excellent "Could I Forget You," "I'll Be Right Here" and "Homewreckers." Davis' bluesy, baritone/tenor is soothing, assured, and remarkably believable on the 23 tracks. An excellent import CD by one of Americas most underappreciated soul singers. *—Andrew Hamilton*

Call Tyrone / May 18, 1999 / Malaco ✦✦✦

● **20 Greatest Hits** / Oct. 23, 2001 / Brunswick ✦✦✦✦✦
Tyrone Davis seems to have more than his share of hits compilations, both domestic through Brunswick and imported courtesy of Diablo, but the rejuvenated *20 Greatest Hits* earns the recommendation because of its digital remastering job. Davis' gritty yearning and the stylish, brassy productions of Brunswick's Willie Henderson and Carl Davis sound better than ever on his biggest and best hits, "Can I Change My Mind" (quickly followed by the nearly identical "Is It Something You've Got") and "Turn the Back Hands of Time." Though *20 Greatest Hits* doesn't feature as expansive a track listing as Diablo's *Turning Back the Hands of Time*, the crisp sound and detailed liner notes make it an easy first pick for fans of Davis' expressive uptown sound. *—John Bush*

The Best of Tyrone Davis / Jan. 15, 2002 / Rhino ✦✦✦
The blessing and the curse of Rhino's 2002 collection *The Best of Tyrone Davis* is its very completeness. It spans from his very first single for the tiny Sack records, "I Tried It Over (And Over Again)," in 1967 to his '90s recordings for Ichiban. This does mean that it's a comprehensive retrospective, tracing the story of his career, but that is a fault because his best material is from the late '60s and early '70s. Although there are certainly fans of Davis' entire career, those classic recordings are what many collectors and fans prefer to hear, and this collection would have been better if it stuck to that. As it stands, this is good for what it is, but there are other collections—collections without a preponderance of '80s and '90s cuts—which are better listens. *—Stephen Thomas Erlewine*

Bobby Day

b. Jul. 1, 1932, Fort Worth, TX, **d.** Jul. 15, 1990
Vocals / Doo Wop, Rock & Roll
An important cog in Los Angeles' doo wop community during the '50s, Bobby Day wrote three often-covered early rock classics in 1957-1958. Day was part of the Hollywood Flames, one of the area's top R&B vocal groups, and briefly part of Bob & Earl, later to hit without Day on "Harlem Shuffle." Day formed his own group, the Satellites, in 1957, cutting the original "Little Bitty Pretty One" for Class Records. A nearly identical cover by Thurston Harris beat the original out, so Day countered with the driving "Rockin' Robin" in 1958, an R&B chart-topper. Its flip, "Over and Over," was a hit in its own right, although the Dave Clark Five's 1965 revival is better remembered today. Day waxed a few more hits for Class in 1959, including "That's All I Want" and a derivative "The Bluebird, the Buzzard & the Oriole," flitting from label to label during the '60s. *—Bill Dahl*

Golden Classics / Jan. 17, 1990 / Collectables ✦✦✦✦✦
Bobby Day's 1958 hit "Rockin' Robin" is one of the most memorable and recycled oldies of them all. Day, an R&B artist who fared better on the pop charts, never repeated the success of his one big hit. *Golden Classics* collects all but one of Day's chart hits on the Class label (the minor hit "Gotta New Girl" is omitted, although its B-side is here), showing him to be a fine R&B vocalist with strong pop inclinations. "The Bluebird, the Buzzard and the Oriole" is a blatant attempt to repeat the "Rockin' Robin" formula, but Day's other recordings are more varied. England's Ace label has a lengthier and better-annotated Bobby Day anthology available as an import for only a few dollars more, but *Golden Classics* is a serviceable collection and includes most of his important cuts. *—Greg Adams*

● **Rockin Robin: The Best of Bobby Day** / Mar. 12, 2002 / Ace ✦✦✦✦✦
Is this the ultimate Bobby Day compilation? With 28 songs from the late '50s and early '60s, including half a dozen that he did as part of Bob & Earl and detailed track by track liner notes, you would think so. Even admitting that he was a fine early rock & roll singer, 28 songs by Day might be too much, though. The fact is that a good number of the singles collected here sounded similar to each other, and sometimes seemed like strained attempts to make derivative knockoffs of his best-known hits, the great "Rockin' Robin," "Over and Over," and the original version of "Little Bitty Pretty One" (which are the first

three cuts on the CD). Still, it has its interest as a document of five years or so in the career of a guy who was not so much an R&B performer adapting to trends, as many in the early Los Angeles rock scene were, as someone who made records that *were* rock & roll, not R&B in the transition to rock & roll. For standouts in the track lineup, you might want to hear Bob & Earl's original 1958 version of the ballad "Gee Whiz," which would be a Top Thirty hit in 1961 for the Innocents. There are a few other ballads throughout the set, but Day's forte was actually uptempo rock & roll, even though his likable, oh so slightly raw-edged vocals were more interesting than the (save for the three hits) often generic material. The 1962 obscurity "Oop-I-Du-Pers-Ball" has to rate as one of the more eccentric twist records of the early '60s, Day's all-out raucous vocals transcending to some degree the trivial novelty that the song actually was. Three of the songs are previously unissued alternate takes. *—Richie Unterberger*

Morris Day

b. Minneapolis, MN

Vocals, Producer / Urban, Funk, Dance-Pop

With his dynamic dancing and smooth yet gutsy, vocals, Morris Day played an essential role in the development of the Twin City dance/club sound of the 1980s. A founding member of Prince's band, the Time, in 1981, he remained with the group until 1984 when he launched his solo career. Returning for the first time in 1988, he performed and recorded with the Time from 1990 until 1991 and since 1995.

Day's involvement with Prince traces back to 1980 when his composition "Partyup," originally recorded when he was a member of the Enterprise, was covered on Prince's *Dirty Mind* album. Releasing his debut solo album, *Color of Success*, in 1985, Day reached his apex with his second solo album, *Daydreaming*, two years later. Produced by ex-Time members Terry Lewis and Jimmy Jam, the album included the chart-topping R&B tune "Fishnet." Day released his third solo album, *Guaranteed*, in 1992. Day has appeared in such films as Prince's autobio-pic, *Purple Rain*, in 1984, and *New Attitude* in 1990. *—Craig Harris*

● **The Color of Success** / 1985 / Warner Bros. ✦✦✦✦

After the temporary collapse of the Time, Morris Day went into the recording studio for his first solo excursion. While the trademarked Minneapolis pop-funk sound still remains at the forefront of each composition, the absence of the magic is extremely noticeable in the production booth. That aside, *The Color of Success* offers to fans what Day does best, funky but accessible dance-pop music in the vein of many of his Minneapolis contemporaries. While the album runs a little bit on the short side, there is no filler and it is surprisingly consistent from start to finish. Fans of Day's work with the Time will enjoy this record, but first-time listeners would be better-served checking out his earlier work first. *—Rob Theakston*

Daydreaming / 1987 / Warner Bros. ✦✦✦

The Time went down in history as one of the most exciting and influential funk bands of the 1980s, although the Minneapolis outfit was only around for about half the decade. In 1984, the Time broke up, and by 1985 Morris Day and Jesse Johnson were officially full-time solo artists. Released in late 1987, Day's second solo album, *Daydreaming*, generally falls short of the excellence of his work with the Time—and, for that matter, it isn't as consistent as his first solo effort, *The Color of Success*. Nonetheless, it's generally enjoyable, if mildly uneven; even at his second best, Day could easily smoke the competition in the 1980s. Many people tend to think of *Daydreaming* as a Jimmy Jam/Terry Lewis project but, in fact, Day's former bandmates only produced two tracks: the ballad "Love Is a Game" and the sexy gem "Fishnet" (a major hit). Everything else on this album was produced by Day himself, and that includes Minneapolis funk-pop smokers like "Are You Ready" and "Moonlight (Passionlite)" as well as the melancholy ballad "A Man's Pride." Much of the time, Day's mischievous sense of humor is a definite asset—and the fact that he is usually so humorous and playful makes the melancholia of "A Man's Pride" really stand out. Generally decent and occasionally excellent, *Daydreaming* falls short of essential but is still worth acquiring for fans of the Minneapolis sound. *—Alex Henderson*

Otis Day & the Knights

f. 1978

Group / R&B, Soul

A quarter of a century after they were brought together to perform in the John Belushi-starring film *Animal House*, Otis Day & the Knights continued to live up to their claim as "the number one party band in America." Led by effervescent vocalist/actor DeWayne Jesse, the group continued to inspire dancing and good times with their treatment of late-'50s and early-'60s R&B and rock.

Madison, WI-born Jesse has been performing since earliest memory. As a teen, he wore a mouse suit to entertain diners at a local Chuck E. Cheese restaurant. Making his film debut in Jeff Bridges' 1970 flick, *Halls of Anger*, he went on to appear in *Car Wash*, *Thank God It's Friday*, and *Where the Buffalo Roam*. He received an Image award as a "supporting character" in *The Bingo Long Traveling All Stars and Motor Kings*.

Jesse based his life-changing portrayal of the fictitious Otis Day on his brother, who played in a band, the Slayers. When *Animal House* proved to be a major commercial success, and became one of the top 50 grossing films of all time, producers Ron Kurtz and Don Polodor encouraged the band to tour. An immediate hit, Otis Day & the Knights performed more than 260 sold-out concerts the first year.

Primarily a live band, Otis Day & the Knights only recorded one album—*Shout*, produced by George Clinton and released in 1989. A concert video, *Otis!, My Man!*, had been released in 1986. In celebration of the 25th anniversary of *Animal House*, Otis Day & the Knights embarked on a 70-city tour in August 2002. *—Craig Harris*

● **Shout** / Oct. 3, 1989 / MCA ✦✦✦

Talk about a cash-in effort—this CD fits into an unusual popular recording category, the album as a response to fiction. Ruben & The Jets, Naz Nomad & The Nightmares, and the infamous Masked Marauders are occupants of the same category, albeit in different divisions. There is no Otis Day & the Knights, really—they were the "band," fronted by singer DeWayne Jesse, playing the toga party and the road house in *Animal House*, and Jesse did such a good job and got so much lingering exposure from that mega-hit film in its theatrical, television, and home video runs, that he was soon playing the college circuit as "Otis Day and the Knights." Then came this album, by DeWayne Jesse and Amelia Jesse, co-produced by television/music veteran Topper Carew. Unfortunately, *Shout* can't decide whether it wants to be a good period R&B/dance album or a contemporary funk recording. It isn't too distinctive in the latter category, although the ballad "Ice Melting" is pretty good, and the two covers from the movie, "Shout" and "Shamalama Ding Dong," aren't as effective here as they were in *Animal House*. Indeed, "Shamalama Ding Dong" ought to have been a superb track, but it is marred by the use of electric drums over a rather sweet arrangement. It's not terrible, but renting *Animal House* is more fun. *—Bruce Eder*

Dazz Band

f. 1977, Cleveland, OH

Group / Funk

The Cleveland-based Dazz Band was one of the more popular funk groups of the early '80s. Bobby Harris formed the group in the late '70s, merging two Cleveland funk bands, Bell Telefunk and Mother Braintree. After myriad lineup changes, the end result was an eight-piece band featuring Harris, Sennie "Skip" Martin III, Pierre DeMudd on horns and vocals, guitarist Eric Fearman, bassist Michael Wiley, drummer Isaac Wiley, keyboardist Kevin Frederick, and percussionist Kenny Pettus. Harris and lead songwriter/guitarist Mike Calhoun's concept for the group was "danceable jazz"; he shortened the description to "dazz" and called the group Kinsman Dazz. Under that name, the group had two small hits in the U.S. during 1978 and 1979. After Calhoun left they changed their name to the Dazz Band in 1980 and signed to Motown.

Invitation to Love, the band's first release for the record label, was released in 1980. Once the group veered away from the more melodic, pop-oriented dance music that dominated their debut and started playing a tougher, more groove-oriented funk, the Dazz Band began racking up the hits. "Let It Whip," taken from their second album *Keep It Live* (1982), reached number five and won a Grammy Award for Best Performance by an R&B Vocal Duo or Group. While they never reached those heights again, the Dazz Band had a string of six consecutive Top 100 albums that ran until 1986; during that time, they scored two other Top 100 singles, "Joystick" and "Let It All Blow." In 1985, Fearman and Frederick left the band; they were replaced by Marlon McClain and Keith Harrison, respectively. The Dazz Band switched labels to Geffen in 1986. That year they had their final charting album, *Wild and Free*. Soon after its release, the band switched to RCA. The group failed to have another hit and quietly faded away. *—Stephen Thomas Erlewine*

Invitation to Love / 1980 / Motown ✦✦✦✦

The debut album by the erstwhile Kinsman Dazz Band, debuting both their newly abbreviated name and their arrival on Motown (following a handful of singles for 20th Century), *Invitation to Love* was released in 1980 and immediately placed the Dazz Band on the R&B fast track, bathing in a spotlight they wouldn't leave for the better part of a decade. A classic combination of up- and down-tempo grooves, the Dazz Band proved themselves to be strong in multiple genres. At ease with the fiery, classic late-'70s funk sounds of "Shake It Up," which is dominated not only by a fat bass and Bobby Harris' outstanding horns, but by vocals that are very reminiscent of Earth, Wind & Fire, the group was equally at home across the sweet and sensual title track. All smooth grooves, again dominated by horns but supplemented by Skip Martin III's absolutely stunning soul vocals, "Invitation to Love" was as good a ballad as any out there. Both songs would hit the R&B charts. The Dazz Band kicked up the funk a few more notches across "Magnetized" and "Skate Lovers," while "Beyond the Horizon" closed the set with a string- and horn-driven instrumental. Although their sound would change dramatically as the 1980s unfolded, especially after the success of 1982's "Let It Whip" placed them firmly in a synthesized dance vein, *Invitation to Love* is still a wonderful introduction to the Dazz Band's early output, capturing them on the cusp of Motown soul and the furious '80s funk that would make their name. *—Amy Hanson*

Let the Music Play / 1981 / Motown ✦✦✦

Having already released two albums to little fanfare on 20th Century, under their original name Kinsman Dazz, 1980-1981 saw the band shorten their name, sign to R&B powerhouse Motown, and come back with the near-total reinvention of *Let the Music Play*. Bucking the early-'80s trend of synthesizing absolutely everything, the Dazz Band kept their music flowing around the more traditional funk trappings of exquisitely elastic basslines and brightly crafted horns. Keys were introduced only to make a sonic point—they work to their best advantage on the rambunctiously quirky "Freaky Lovin'," and the midtempo moves on the title track. "Don't Stop," meanwhile, only adds to the upbeat energy with its snappy bass-driven danceability. The rest of the set, however, is dedicated to a softer, smoother, vocally focused R&B style that is spread liberally across "What Will I Do Without You," "This Time It's Forever," and "I Believe in You." "Knock Knock," the best of the bunch, emerged as *Let the Music Play*'s sole charting single, reaching the Top 50 in August. Patchy in places, and leaning more heavily on a bland, soft style than the band needed, it's obvious that the Dazz Band were stretching their wings and finding the groove that would keep them in heavy chart rotation through the entire decade. *—Amy Hanson*

Keep It Live / 1982 / Motown ✦✦✦

This album spawned "Let It Whip" and contains a mixture of "Whip"-ish tracks and slow tantalizing ballads. "Keep It Live" and "Whip" both feature throbbing bass lines and spirited vocals. "Whip" is an unusual dance tune in that the song was successful but the dance never caught on. Lead Skip Martin III displays his romantic skills on the shuffling

"Gamble With My Love" and "Let Me Love You Until." Despite the big hit, this is not their best overall. Dazz was experiencing growing pains—they wanted to produce themselves totally, but had to defer and follow Motown's suggestions on what the finished product should sound like. —*Andrew Hamilton*

On the One / 1983 / Motown ✦✦✦
Following grandly in the style of their 1981 smash "Let It Whip," the Dazz Band laid down another excellent set of contemporary funk, shot through with a heavily synthesized dance groove—their trademark, and a winning combination. Although the advent of CDs would make a mockery of their ambition, the Dazz Band programmed the album for two very separate moods—side one, for the most part, heaves with pounding funkers, side two takes the tempo way down for a clutch of sweet ballads. Both sides, of course, have their devotees. With a Parliament-esque style that broke in waves across the opening "Party Right Here," side one is a nonstop whipping, the party sliding gleefully into "Cheek to Cheek" and, from there, the effusive, "On the One for Fun." The biggest charting hit of the three, the song seems perpetually on the verge of slipping into "Let It Whip"—which was probably the intention. That it reached number nine on the R&B charts is no great surprise. "A Love Song" slows down somewhat, but with its vibe wrapped around a jazzy horn-driven, uptempo smooth talker, it never quite immerses itself in balladic waters. That is, indeed, left to side two, where only "Nice Girls" shakes things up with a fistful of funk. —*Amy Hanson*

Joystick / 1983 / Motown ✦✦✦
From Cleveland to Cincinnati to Dayton, Ohio was famous for its funk bands in the 1970s. One of the many OH funk outfits that emerged during the decade was Cleveland's Dazz Band, which was originally known as Kinsman Dazz. Like so many Midwestern funksters, the Dazz Band had a killer horn section. But in 1983, horn bands were quickly going out of fashion and a new style of electro-funk was taking over—one that favored keyboards and drum machines over horns and showed an awareness of hip-hop production techniques. The popularity of electro-funk put a lot of 1970s bands out of business, but the Dazz Band managed to hang in there and change with the times. On 1983's *Joystick*, the Dazz Band is a lot more high-tech than it was in the late '70s, but is still quite gritty. Tracks like "Straight Out of School," "Rock With Me," and the hit single "Swoop (I'm Yours)" find the Dazz Band meeting the demands of the electro-funk market with pleasing results—anyone digging Prince, Midnight Star, and the System in 1983 could easily get into the Dazz Band as well. While other horn bands had a hard time going high-tech, the Dazz Band pulled it off. *Joystick* isn't the Dazz Band's most essential album, and it doesn't contain the group's biggest hit, "Let It Whip." But it's a solid, respectable effort from an outfit that, in 1983, was making a valiant effort to avoid sounding dated. —*Alex Henderson*

Jukebox / 1984 / Motown ✦✦✦

Hot Spot / 1985 / Motown ✦✦✦

Greatest Hits / 1986 / Motown ✦✦✦✦
What's not to like about the Dazz Band's highly combustible "Let It Whip"? Its funky drum machine rhythms and diabolical mini-Moog basslines are wicked. Reggie Andrews produced and co-wrote the sizzling groove that was number-one R&B chart for five consecutive weeks, and scaled to number-five Pop. "Joy Stick" is as potent as Viagra with its maniac, thumping beat. But, "Party Right Here," and "Keep It Live (On the K.I.L.)" are formulaic stiffs, all flash and no substance. "Swoop (I'm Yours)" has appeal, and some of the dancefloor drawing power of "Whip." Fans of Dazz Band ballads will not have much use for this CD, only two made the disk: the ultra romantic "Invitation to Love," and the melodramatic "Knock, Knock," where lead singer Skip Martin III begs like a baby. Dazz Band's honcho Bobby Harris experiments with their sound on "On the One for Fun," and "Let It All Blow," and both sound better on CD than vinyl. Each features creative fusion/funk licks, sweetened by razor-sharp horns, chant vocals and frivolous lyrics. —*Andrew Hamilton*

Wild & Free / 1986 / Geffen ✦✦

Rock the Room / 1988 / RCA ✦

• **Funkology: The Definitive Dazz Band** / Nov. 15, 1994 / Motown ✦✦✦✦
Easily the most comprehensive hits compilation for the Dazz Band, *Funkology: The Definitive Dazz Band* is a tasteful combination of not only their greatest hits from both phases of their career, but hard-to-find B-side alternate mixes and an amazing Megamix to kick off the album. Dazz delivers all of the goods you would expect from an OH funk group from that era: gorgeous production combined with well-thought-out songwriting arrangements wrapped around a slick bassline, topped off with a soulful melody. Since it is out of print, listeners would be well-served by checking out Universal's easily attainable *20th Century Masters—The Millennium Collection: The Best of the Dazz Band.* But if you can find this, by all means *Funkology* is the way to go. —*Rob Theakston*

Bill Deal & the Rhondels

b. Virginia Beach, VA

Vocals / Frat Rock, Pop-Soul, Blue-Eyed Soul, Rock & Roll, R&B

Bill Deal & the Rhondels were among the first of a cadre of big band rock outfits that began showing up in the mid- to late '60s. Working in a more accessible vein than the more progressive Blood, Sweat & Tears, Deal and his septet released five nationally charting singles in 1969 and 1970 with a soulful dance-rock sound. Deal put together the Rhondels in 1965 and they made their names and a fair living over the next few years by playing clubs in Virginia and the Carolinas. They became popular regional attractions, and by 1968 they cut their first record, an inspired cover of Maurice Williams' "May I," which had been part of their stage act for so long that they'd tired of playing it; until a chance request led them to spontaneously rework it one night on-stage, and the results were so impressive that they went in and cut it the next day for the Beach label. Suddenly Bill Deal & the Rhondels were in the Top 40, scraping at number 39 with a record that was some of the most vibrant and danceable white soul music of its era. The group was an improbable candidate for this kind of success—the Rhondels looked and dressed more like a lounge act than a rock & roll band, and their sound could be decidedly MOR ("Nothing Succeeds Like Success")—but their best sides had a soulful sound and a great beat. They did better with their next single, a cover of Ray Whitley's "I've Been Hurt" that made it to number 35 nationally. "What Kind of Fool (Do You Think I Am)," another Whitley song, got to number 23; it became the peak of their national sales success. —*Bruce Eder*

The Best of Bill Deal & the Rhondels / Oct. 24, 1994 / Castle ✦✦✦✦✦
For real fans, this 22-song CD contains all but one track off of Varese's CD, plus ten more songs, among them the group's covers of the Bee Gees' "Words," the Spector-Barry-Greenwich "River Deep, Mountain High," and the Doors' "Touch Me," and the four Buddah Records sides, never before compiled anywhere. "Words" is OK, with an intense performance, though they do better with Maurice Williams' repertory—"River Deep, Mountain High" is absolutely funky, a too-brief reinterpretation, while their cover of "Touch Me" could almost pass for a lost Motown demo, with fine playing and ensemble singing that grabs the seductive side of the words like they're really meant; they might have reworked this into a disco version eight years later. Among the Buddah songs, their attempt to put a very quick tempo to Carole King's "It's Too Late" was an interesting but futile venture, which would almost be a parody if they weren't trying so hard (the synthesizer is the kiss of death here, and doesn't add anything to "Everybody's Got Somethin' to Hide"). The only drawback is that the album version of "Swingin' Tight" isn't here. The 1999 Heritage Records CD version is a re-release, with no changes, of the 1994 Sequel Records version of this title. —*Bruce Eder*

• **Vintage Rock** / Mar. 11, 1997 / Varese ✦✦✦✦✦
In the beach music scene of VA in the late 1960s, nobody could shake a dancefloor like Bill Deal and the Rhondells. A horn-powered band like Blood, Sweat & Tears or Chicago but with an eye firmly scoping out the club floor at all times, Deal and his octet knew their audience cold. And that audience liked to dance, dance, dance to their favorites and Bill and the band responded with hoof-shaking rearrangements of Tams singles and other shag-worthy material. While seldom remembered today, Deal and the band racked up five chart singles in a year's time, and those well crafted 45s ("What Kind Of Fool [Do You Think I Am]," "May I," "Swingin' Tight," "I've Been Hurt," and "Nothing Succeeds Like Success") form the core of this 15-track collection's appeal. Not even remotely hip, creative, or innovative, but as grade-A floor-moving music of the time period, this compilation is a delightful invitation to the dance. —*Cub Koda*

DeBarge

f. 1978, Grand Rapids, MI, **db.** 1989

Group / Adult Contemporary, Urban

Groomed to be the heirs to the Jackson 5 throne in the early '80s, DeBarge mirrored the Jacksons early success with a string of hits, but were unable to sustain their winning streak. Originally formed in 1978 and hailing from Grand Rapids, MI, the quintet was comprised of four brothers (Eldra, Mark, James, and Randy) and one sister (Bunny). The band signed on with the same label that the Jacksons started with, Motown, courtesy of their two older brothers, Tommy and Bobby (both of whom were members of another Motown act at the time, Switch). Led by the soft-and-sweet vocals of Eldra (or El, for short), DeBarge issued a debut album in 1981, *The DeBarges*, which showed that the group had yet to hone their hit-making style. But the quintet soon found the formula, as their sophomore effort, 1982's *All This Love*, would go on to become DeBarge's first gold-certified success, and spawn such hit singles as "I Like It," "Time Will Reveal," and the title track.

In a Special Way, from 1983, was another gold-certified smash, spawning another hit single with "Love Me in a Special Way," and landing an opening slot on a sold-out U.S. tour with Luther Vandross. For their fourth release overall, 1985's *Rhythm of the Night*, DeBarge enlisted the aid of songwriter Diane Warren plus respected producers David Foster, Richard Perry, Giorgio Moroder, and Glen Ballard, which resulted in the group's third gold album in a row; as well as the biggest hit single of their career, the uptempo title track, which nearly topped the pop singles charts and was featured in the movie *The Last Dragon* the same year. Further hit singles were plucked from the album ("Who's Holding Donna Now?" and "You Wear It Well"), but not all was well behind the scenes.

While 1986 saw the release of the group's first best-of compilation, *Greatest Hits*, it also signaled El DeBarge's exit from the group to pursue a solo career; he scored a considerable hit right off the bat with a self-titled debut before sinking into obscurity. DeBarge failed to do much better after their leader's exit, as the El-less version of the band managed to issue just one more release, 1987's *Back on Track*, before splitting up two years later (during the same time, another DeBarge brother, Chico, would also launch a recording career). Further DeBarge compilations saw the light of day subsequently, including 1997's *Ultimate Collection* and 2000's *20th Masters: The Millennium Collection.* —*Greg Prato*

The DeBarges / 1981 / Motown ✦✦✦
This is the introductory album for the DeBarge family. Their older brothers, Bobby and Tommy, had helped them land a deal with Motown through their connection playing with Switch. Although they sang tentatively on several songs and hadn't really meshed, they displayed enough potential to alert both the company and the urban contemporary/R&B audience that an interesting new group was on the scene. —*Ron Wynn*

All This Love / 1982 / Motown ✦✦✦✦
The second album from the Grand Rapids, MI, natives DeBarge featured three singles, the first of which ("Stop! Don't Tease Me") showcases El on lead; the song peaked at number 46 after a short eight weeks. The follow-up was "I Like It," a very danceable, yet laid-back number in which Randy carries the initial verse and El brings up the rear. With

impeccable penmanship and arrangement, it clocked in at number two on the R&B charts and became the group's first pop Top 40 entry. The follow-up single was the title track "All This Love." Solely led by El's convincing tenor, this composition, in its traditional arrangement, sails along like the winds of a cool summer night. The longevity of this number can be heard in every note, including a melodious acoustic guitar solo. The remaining songs fall closely behind the aforementioned numbers. *—Craig Lytle*

In a Special Way / 1983 / Motown ♦♦♦♦♦

After the release of 1982's *All This Love*, the group became one of the most popular and talented acts in music. While that effort was a likeable though uneven affair, *In A Special Way* was in short, a classic. This boasts a minimalist and artful sound and rumor has it that the horn tracks were lost during the recording. So as a result *In A Special Way* is one of the most spare and effective albums of the '80s. The first track, the synth based "Be My Lady" and the bittersweet and pragmatic "Need Somebody" both feature lead vocals from James DeBarge. Despite fact this did offer more lead spots for other DeBarge's, *In a Special Way* also marked the coming of age of the vocally gifted El DeBarge as a producer and writer. The biggest hit here, the poignant and spare "Time Will Reveal" is perfect from its beautiful arrangement, the flawless backing vocals to El DeBarge's amazing lead. His prowess also makes the potentially overdone sentiments of "Love Me in a Special Way" come off romantic and effective. The last track, "A Dream" was written and sung by Bunny DeBarge. With a great melody line, the song accurately attains a sense of longing as Bunny DeBarge's lead is particularly moving. Although R&B and rap have appropriated segments of this album in every conceivable manner, the greatness begins and ends with this album. *—Jason Elias*

Rhythm of the Night / 1985 / Motown ♦♦♦

This marked the third album by the Grand Rapids, MI, natives, and it was also an attempt by the label to increase the group's pop appeal. Of the album's four releases, two were Top Ten singles on the *Billboard* pop charts: "Rhythm of the Night" (number three) and "Who's Holding Donna Now" (number six). The former, which is featured in the Berry Gordy movie *The Last Dragon*, conveys a grande fiesta ambience with its Caribbean rhythm. The single stayed on the *Billboard* R&B charts for 23 weeks, peaking at number one. The latter is a midtempo number that stays nestled in its mellow pulse kindled by El DeBarge's inquisitive vocals. The single held the number-two spot on the charts for four consecutive weeks. While most of the album is pop-oriented, "You Wear It Well" houses a soulful beat fueled by El's expedient delivery. With its catchy hook line and its female-commending lyric, the single peaked at number seven. "The Heart Is Not so Smart" is clearly a pop tune, and it is no challenge to El's vocal talent; nonetheless, the single peaked at number 39 after 14 weeks. The beautifully written composition "Share My World" was never a release (it was also featured on the group's self-titled debut album). However, it has a soft, gentle air with much crossover appeal. It features El and Bunny DeBarge on lead. Though Bunny's vocals are plausible, El's reign supreme. Aside from the aforementioned, the other selections are marginal. *—Craig Lytle*

● **Ultimate Collection** / Mar. 25, 1997 / Motown ♦♦♦♦♦

The most in-depth collection of the group's work available, DeBarge's *Ultimate Collection* gathers 16 of the group's biggest hits from the early and mid-'80s. The compilation includes milestone singles such as "Love Me in a Special Way," "Who's Holding Donna Now?," "Who's Johnny?," and a dance remix of "Rhythm of the Night"; it would've been nice if the album also included the original version. The group's slightly less-definitive tracks reveal them to be equally adept at lively, upbeat pop like "You Wear It Well," sweet ballads such as "A Dream," and surprisingly funk- and soul-tinged turns like "Stop! Don't Tease Me" and "I Like It." Latter-day singles such as "Save the Best for Me (Best of Your Lovin')" and "Dance All Night" round out the album nicely; though they don't have the impact of the group's work with El DeBarge, including them gives *Ultimate Collection* a feeling of closure and completion. Fans who want more than a just-the-hits compilation like *20th Century Masters—The Millennium Collection* should be satisfied by this well-crafted retrospective. *—Heather Phares*

Chico DeBarge

b. 1966

Vocals, Producer / Adult Contemporary, Urban, Neo-Soul, Dance-Pop

Brother to the singing DeBarge family, Chico launched a promising solo career on Motown in the late '80s. Despite a hit single and a hit debut album, his career was sidelined by imprisonment on a drug charge. After he completed his sentence, DeBarge launched a comeback in November 1997 with the release of *Long Time No See*. *The Game* followed in 1999. *—Rick A. Bueche*

● **Chico DeBarge** / 1986 / Motown ♦♦♦♦

His best album for Motown was a fine start, but his brushes with the law and eventual imprisonment stifled his success. It includes the funky hit "Talk to Me." *—Rick A. Bueche*

Kiss Serious / 1988 / Motown ♦♦

Following his 1986 self-titled debut album, which included the Top 10 R&B/Top 21 pop hit "Talk to Me," Chico DeBarge's *Kiss Serious* was a worthy follow-up. With most tracks produced by one-time Prince & the Revolution bassist Brownmark, it's steeped in an '80s-era Minneapolis sound. The funk is poppin' on "I've Been Watching You," "Will You Be Mine," "Don't Move So Fast," and the title track second single. The gentle steppers cut "Rainy Nights," produced by Skip Drinkwater and Laythan Armor, received massive radio play as an album track before becoming a Top 18 R&B single in late 1987. *—Ed Hogan*

Long Time, No See / Nov. 18, 1997 / Kedar/Universal ♦♦♦

The Game / Oct. 26, 1999 / Motown ♦♦♦

El DeBarge

b. Jun. 4, 1964, Grand Rapids, MI

Vocals, Producer / Adult Contemporary, Urban, Dance-Pop

El DeBarge was the lead singer of the '80s R&B group DeBarge throughout their career, including the hits "All This Love," "Love Me in a Special Way," "Who's Holding Donna Now," and "Rhythm of the Night." After leaving the group in 1985, he launched his solo career in 1986 with a self-titled debut album that featured the number three hit "Who's Johnny?," featured in the film *Short Circuit*. DeBarge has recorded several albums and singles since 1985; none of his subsequent efforts have been successful, apart from his appearance on Quincy Jones' 1990 hit "The Secret Garden (Sweet Seduction Suite)." *—Stephen Thomas Erlewine*

● **El DeBarge** / 1986 / Motown ♦♦♦♦♦

His first and best solo album included "Who's Johnny" from the *Short Circuit* soundtrack. *—Rick A. Bueche*

Gemini / 1989 / Motown ♦♦♦

Despite some serious legal problems, El DeBarge emerged from the DeBarge family group as the best solo performer. This was his second album in the late '80s, and it got widespread chart and radio attention. Although it didn't generate as big a hit as anything from the prior release, there were three songs that were widely aired, and DeBarge eventually was recruited by Quincy Jones to be one of the singers on the hit "The Secret Garden," which DeBarge also co-wrote. *—Ron Wynn*

In the Storm / Mar. 17, 1992 / Warner Bros. ♦♦♦

Joey Dee & the Starliters

b. Jun. 11, 1940, Passaic, NJ

Vocals / Rock & Roll

Joey Dee led the house band at NY's Peppermint Lounge, immortalizing the joint in his 1961 charttopper "Peppermint Twist." Born Joseph DiNicola in Passaic, NJ, Dee teamed with veteran producer Henry Glover to cut "Peppermint Twist" for Roulette, and the huge hit led to a starring role in the film *Hey, Let's Twist*. Most of Dee's hits, including a supercharged revival of the Isley Brothers hit "Shout" in 1962, were firmly in the twist mode, although he took a successful stab at a softer sound that year with a Johnny Nash tune, "What Kind of Love Is This." Dee gave several future stars early breaks with the Starliters, notably the Ronettes, three-quarters of the Young Rascals, and Jimi Hendrix. Dee is still active on the oldies circuit. *—Bill Dahl*

● **Hey Let's Twist!: The Best of Joey Dee and the Starliters** / Jun. 1990 / Rhino ♦♦♦♦♦

While Dee is generally looked upon as the quaint bearer of the twist to a mass audience (clean covers of R&B tunes palatable to white audiences), the truth is that Dee had a racially integrated band (in 1961, no less) that not only delivered the goods, but put some high voltage energy into the tunes as well. Although this 18-track compilation brings together all the chart hits ("Peppermint Twist," "Shout," "Everytime," "What Kind of Love Is This," "I Lost My Baby," "Dance, Dance, Dance") from Dee & the Starliters' brief run for the gold, it omits several barn-burning covers from the second live album and opts for the edited "part one" version of "Shout" as opposed to the six-minute-plus workout that's on the *Doin' the Twist* album. That said, it's still a wonderful introduction to the music of this seldom-lauded rock & roll pioneer. *—Cub Koda*

Starbright / Sep. 28, 1999 / WestSide ♦♦♦♦

A two-disc collection of all the group's Roulette singles, A and B sides, all the subsequent Jubilee singles and the rare 1966 album, *Hitsville*. Rounding out the rarities are both sides of a single sung in German and a premium record available from Vaseline Hair Tonic, the spoken word "Joey Dee Teaches You How to Dance the Authentic Peppermint Twist," one of the more surreal exercises in rock & roll history. *—Cub Koda*

Joey Dee in Hollywood / Oct. 19, 1999 / Soundies ♦♦♦

Although credited to Joey Dee, the two original soundtrack albums that comprise *In Hollywood* (*Hey Let's Twist!* and *Two Tickets to Paris*) are various-artist affairs with contributions from Jo-Ann Campbell, Gary Crosby, Teddy Randazzo, and Dee's Starlighters backing an assortment of vocalists. Despite a few pop ballads and orchestral tracks, most of the songs are in alignment with the twist craze. Jeri Lynne Fraser's "Teenage Vamp" is a camp classic, and a few of Dee's biggest songs, such as "Roly Poly" and "Peppermint Twist, Pt. 1," are included. *In Hollywood* is full of twistin' fun and offers a few oddities for collectors, too. *—Greg Adams*

The Deele

f. 1981, Cincinnati, OH, **db.** 1993

Group / Quiet Storm, Urban

The Deele is best-known as the group that brought Babyface (b. Kenny Edmonds) and L.A. Reid (b. Mark Rooney) to prominence. Based in Indianapolis, IN, Bobby G. Summers and L.A. Reid formed the Deele in the early '80s with lead vocalist Carlos "Satin" Greene, Darnell "Dee" Bristol, Stanley Burke, and Kevin Roberson. Prior to joining the Deele Babyface had been a member of Manchild, who had a minor R&B hit with "Especially for You" in 1977.

The Deele had their first hit in late 1983, when "Body Talk" began climbing the R&B charts. Though the song only reached 77 on the pop charts, it reached number three on the R&B charts, helping the group's debut album *Street Beat* crack the top 100. Two subsequent singles from the record, "Just My Luck," and "Surrender," dented the R&B charts, but the group's second album *Material Thangz*, was a disappointment, launching only one hit R&B single with the number-14 title track.

Between the release of *Material Thangz* and 1988's *Eyes of a Stranger*, Babyface and L.A. Reid began making a name for themselves as urban producers and songwriters, with their work for Pebbles ("Girlfriend") and the Whispers ("Rock Steady") becoming hits. In the wake of Babyface and Reid's new-found success, *Eyes of a Stranger* became a hit, going gold and launching the Top 10 pop and R&B hit, "Two Occasions," as well as the number-10 R&B hit "Shoot 'Em Up Movies." Following the release of *Eyes of a Stranger*, the group went on hiatus, with Babyface and L.A. Reid continuing their successful production and songwriting work. The Deele reunited without Babyface and Reid in 1993 to release *Invitation to Love*, which failed to earn much attention. *—Stephen Thomas Erlewine & Al Campbell*

Street Beat / 1984 / Solar ♦♦♦
On the basis of the Deele's debut *Street Beat*, it would have been hard to predict that Babyface and L.A. Reid would change the course of urban R&B during the late '80s and '90s. Though the record—especially the Top 10 R&B hit "Body Talk" and its two follow-ups, "Just My Luck" and "Surrender"—is pleasant, synthesized soul and lite funk, it doesn't show many signs of innovation, and only the hit single demonstrate much songcraft. In other words, it's a good, but not extraordinary debut, by two artists who would prove themselves exceptional. *—Leo Stanley*

Material Thangz / 1985 / Solar ♦♦

Eyes of a Stranger / 1987 / Solar ♦♦♦♦
With group members Kenny "Babyface" Edmonds and Antoine "L.A." Reid's popularity increasing, and their productions skills in demand, it was inevitable that this would be the final album by the urban funk ensemble. The LP featured the very credible "Two Occasions"; as Dee gives a depiction of the song through some metaphoric verses, Babyface tenderly intercedes on the pre-hook in support of Dee's lyric. This is the only song on the album that features Babyface on lead. In spite of its superb arrangement and production, the quiet-storm classic peaked at number four after 24 healthy weeks on the charts even though it was worthy of a number-one ranking. The follow-up single, "Shoot 'Em Up Movies," has an arrangement that is reminiscent of the golden doo wop era. The creatively composed number peaked at number ten inside of 15 weeks. *—Craig Lytle*

● **Shoot 'Em Up: The Best of the Deele** / Aug. 13, 2002 / Castle ♦♦♦♦
Castle U.K.'s *Shoot 'Em Up: The Best of the Deele* trumps all previous attempts at anthologizing the R&B group led by Babyface and L.A. Reid with an extensive track selection and remastered sound. This covers all the essential singles, including hot R&B/singles-chart occupants like "Two Occasions" (number four), "Body Talk" (number three), "Shoot 'Em Up Movies" (number ten), "Material Thangz" (number 14), "Can U Dance" (number 48), and "Suspicious" (number 66). All the synthesizers and programmed beats are no more of their time than the elements that characterize any other period or movement, so it'd be completely unfair to fault this group for sounding like they came from the '80s. Admittedly, each Deele album has a good chunk of filler, so a compilation like this one is a good way to go. *—Andy Kellman*

Sam Dees

b. Birmingham, AL
Producer, Vocals / Soul
Prolific songwriter/producer/recording artist Sam Dees is mentioned in the same breath as other top soul/pop songwriters as Lamont Dozier, George Jackson, Bunny Sigler, and Jo Armstead. In 1969, the Birmingham, AL, native began cutting for Natte McCalla's Birmingham label, Lola Records, including a song originally meant for Percy Sledge, "It's All Wrong." In the early '70s, he recorded singles for Chicago-based Chess Records: "Love Starvation" b/w "Maryanna" and "Can You Be a One Woman Man" b/w "Put You Back in Your Place." In the late '70s, Dees co-wrote and co-produced half of Gladys Knight & the Pips' *Visions* LP.

Other artists who recorded songs by Dees are Atlantic Starr ("Am I Dreaming," "Send for Me"), Larry Graham ("One in a Million You"), Gladys Knight & the Pips ("Save the Overtime (For Me)"), Whitney Houston ("Lover for Life"), Loleatta Holloway ("Cry to Me"), Barbara Hall ("Drop My Heart Off at the Door"), Carl Carlton ("I Never Got Over You," "Mama's Boy," and "Free Fine and 21"), Rozetta Johnson ("Who Are You Gonna Love"), Rockie Robbins ("Hang Tough"), Tyrone Davis ("Homewreckers"), Margie Joseph ("Just as Soon as the Feeling's Over"), Dorothy Moore ("Special Occasion"), Denise LaSalle ("Keep Your Pants On"), and Anita Ward ("Spoiled By Your Love"). Forming his own Pen Pad label, Dees issued his *Secret Admirer* album in 1988. Other Dees-related releases are his own *Second to None* (1995) and *Heritage of a Black Man* (1998). *—Ed Hogan*

Second to None / 1995 / Kent ♦♦♦
Prior to Sam Dees writing hit songs for Atlantic Starr, Larry Graham ("One in a Million You"), Whitney Houston, Gladys Knight & the Pips, and others, he toiled first in a group, then solo, recording on many southern labels during the '60s and '70s. He never had any significant hits but kept extremely busy writing and producing songs for the likes of C.L. Blast, Denise LaSalle, Frederick Knight, and others. His name was a fixture on *Billboard* and Cashbox R&B surveys as a writer, and you thought he lived well, not rich by any means, but eking out a decent living as a songwriter. Not! During the height of the Northern soul explosion in England, a writer for *Black Music* and *Jazz Review* did the best interview on Dees to date. Garnering more popularity in northern England than his homeland, Dees flew there to do some shows at Northern soul clubs, take pictures, do interviews, and—for once—get the star treatment. The BMJR writer came armed with more facts about him than even Dees remembered, so the soul singer/writer/producer—knowing he couldn't BS the guy—was brutally straight when asked about his songwriting income, poignantly stating, "I've never made a dime from a song." *Second to None* features many of those early—"I've never made a dime"—songs. Many are demos that were dropped as finished products on other artists, and some were originally released by Dees. Three are from his 1975 Atlantic album, *The Show Must Go On*. Instrumentation is light but Dees' heart is heavy as he sings his words as only he can: from the guts. Included are his versions of "Cry to Me" and "Worn Out Broken Heart" (which are more known by Loleatta Holloway), "Vanishing Love," "Homewreckers," "Your Love Is Like a Boomerang," and "You've Been Doing Wrong for So Long." *—Andrew Hamilton*

● **Heritage of a Black Man** / Sep. 29, 1998 / Kent ♦♦♦
This is the second healthy compilation of Sam Dees' recordings compiled and released by Kent Records. The first ran 23 tracks, and this one has 22 killer doses of soul—look for a third from Kent, since they still haven't captured all of this Southern soul icon's recordings on CD. "Fragile, Handle With Care"; "I'm So Glad"; "Lonely for You Baby"; a lilting duet with Bettye Swann, "Just As Sure," which should have blown up; and too many more to list are available on vinyl or tape only. This is a more consistent, albeit less raw, set than Dees' previous Kent compilation; missing are the demo and unreleased tracks that made *Second to None* attractive to collectors and historians. But absolute grit isn't missing—Dees delivered that like he had a warehouse full of it. More than just a singer, he either wrote or co-wrote nearly every song. He gets introspective on "Why Must I Be in Love Alone," "I, Me, Myself," and "Why Must I Live in Chains"; pleads shamelessly on "Reconsider Baby" and "Meet Me Half Way"; and delivers the norm on "Mess on Your Hands" and "Lovers or Enemies." If you like soul with an edge, you'll love this razor-sharp collection. Dees penetrates so deep, you feel wounded after listening to these mini-dramas. Not a CD to get lifted by, more of a misery-loves-company enabler. *—Andrew Hamilton*

The Del-Vikings

f. 1955, Pittsburgh, PA, **db.** 1965
Group / Doo Wop
The story of the Dell-Vikings (or Del Vikings, or Del-Vikings) is one of the most glorious, complicated and frustrating of any successful doo wop group in music history. With two major national hits ("Come Go With Me," "Whispering Bells") to their credit—one more hit than most other successful doo wop groups ever had—they had a jump on virtually all of their competition. Just as they were ascending those heights of fame and success, however, internal fractures and some greed and misdirected ambition helped destroy any chance they had of making a lasting place for themselves at the top of their profession. They left behind two hits and a large body of very good records that weren't nearly as well known, as well as a reputation as one of the few successful integrated vocal groups of their era.

The group had its origins at the Pittsburgh Air Force Base, where five black enlisted men, Corinthian "Kripp" Johnson (first tenor), Clarence E. Quick (bass), Don Jackson (second tenor), Bernard Robertson, and Samuel Paterson, began singing together during 1955 at the camp hall. They won a talent contest on the base in early 1956, and then competed nationally in NY and Bermuda, where they placed first and second, respectively. By that time, they were starting to attract local attention, most notably from disc jockey Barry Kaye, who wanted to record the Del Vikings, as they were then known (just one "l," and no hyphen).

The origins of their name have been ascribed to various sources. Some stories say that the members had read of the Vikings in an encyclopedia and liked the sound, the "Del" being rather more mysterious. Others claim that Clarence Quick had known a basketball team called the Vikings in Brooklyn, and suggested the name.

The Del Vikings' lineup was fairly fluid due to the nature of military service, and by early 1956, Robertson and Paterson were gone, transferred to Germany. Their replacements were Norman Wright (lead tenor) and David Lerchey (baritone). Lerchey's presence in the group as its first white member was more a matter of expediency than design, as he was simply the talent that was available; it did make the group slightly more distinctive, although other integrated singing groups had already achieved considerable exposure, including the Meadowlarks ("Heaven and Paradise") and the Mariners, who had appeared nationally on Arthur Godfrey's network television show.

This second lineup was the version of the Del Vikings that Barry Kaye recorded. The resulting sessions yielded nine songs done a cappella, including early versions of Clarence E. Quick's "Come Go With Me" and Kripp Johnson's "How Can I Find True Love." The demo tapes, which contained only the most rudimentary backing, were sent around to all of the major labels, each of which passed on the chance to record the Del Vikings. Finally, the group was signed by Joe Auerbach, the owner of a small Pittsburgh-based label called Fee Bee. A new recording session yielded a fully realized version of "Come Go With Me," backed by the quintet's own band, including their resident backup men Joe Lopes (later a top recording engineer for RCA) and Gene Upshaw on sax, with the lead sung by new member Norman Wright.

The single, released late in 1956, quickly outgrew Fee Bee's ability to exploit it, and Auerbach leased it to Dot Records—that version appeared in early 1957 and began a 31-week run on the charts, reaching number four on the pop chart and number three on the R&B chart during the spring and early summer. The group was now a national phenomenon and was booked on tours across the country, as well as a featured spot in one of Alan Freed's Brooklyn Paramount shows. Their lineup had already changed again, the group acquiring its second white member, Gus Backus, who replaced Don Jackson as second tenor. Even so, military obligations sometimes prevented all of the members from participating at once in these performances.

The success of "Come Go With Me" should have positioned the group well for future success, but instead it began a process of fracturing their lineup. Fee Bee tried to maintain the momentum by releasing a single early in 1957 on which the group had sung backup, but that disappeared without a trace. They finally got their all-important second hit, "Whispering Bells" (also written by Clarence Quick), in the late summer of 1957, which reached number nine on the pop charts.

Behind the scenes, however, maneuvers were taking place that were to nullify these two huge successes. With "Come Go With Me" storming the charts, the Del Vikings were suddenly in demand from many of the same major labels that had passed on them a year earlier. What made their interest possible at all, in the view of their manager—who was also the legal representative for the air base where they were stationed—was that the group's contract with Fee Bee had a major flaw, in that some of the members were under 21 at the time it was signed. Faced with the chance to make new and major amounts of money for all concerned, in the midst of the group's chart run with "Come Go With Me," their manager signed the group to Mercury Records under a contract that specifically covered the members who had been underage in 1956.

Meanwhile, the group—or a version of it—had released "Whispering Bells" on Fee Bee and Dot. The result was that the group split into two rival outfits, one called the Dell-Vikings (the spelling of the outfit that released "Whispering Bells") on Dot Records, with Kripp Johnson and the returned Don Jackson; and the Del-Vikings, as their name was spelled, on Mercury, led by composer Clarence E. Quick and featuring Norman Wright, David Lerchey, Gus Backus, and new member William Blakely. The situation was extremely complicated: Mercury had the majority of the members who'd been on "Come Go With Me," as well as the man who had written it and the man who'd sung lead on it, but the Mercury group's members were still in the Air Force and not free to tour as they might have wanted; Dot Records had one founding member of the group in Kripp Johnson and another key singer, and they and the group they assembled were out of the Air Force and free to tour as they wished.

Further complicating the group's—or groups'—situation at the time were the demos they'd recorded for Barry Kaye. He sold these to Luniverse Records, a label whose co-owners included Dickie Goodman and George Goldner. In the midst of the chart run of Dot's "Come Go With Me," Luniverse redubbed the a cappella demo recordings with a full band and released eight of the nine songs in edited form on an LP, *Come Go With the Del-Vikings*, as well as issuing one 45 of "Over the Rainbow" and "Hey Senorita."

The Kripp Johnson-led "Whispering Bells" on Dot, recorded by the Dell-Vikings, was followed onto the charts by the Mercury Del-Vikings' "Cool Shake," a fast-paced rocker sung by Gus Backus, which didn't do as well, probably as a result of the fact that record retailers and distributors, as well as radio programmers, were starting to get confused by the presence of two groups with nearly identical names on two different labels. By the summer of 1957, Mercury and Dot were both claiming the same single pairing of "When I Come Home" and "I'm Spinning" as their own. Court action followed, with Mercury winning the rights to the group and the name the Del-Vikings and any variations of it. Yet another group lineup, with Joe Lopes filling in for David Lerchey, appeared alongside Fats Domino and the Diamonds in the movie *The Big Beat* in 1957.

The Kripp Johnson version of the group, now known as the Versatiles and featuring Don Jackson, Chuck Jackson, Arthur Budd, and Ed Everette, kept recording, but without success, and by the end of 1957, Kripp Johnson was back with the Mercury Del-Vikings. Now the "classic" Del Viking lineup was restored and the group was back to full strength, but the moment had passed, and the Del-Vikings had no further national hits.

In 1959, the Mercury contract ended, and after a few detours, the group—now a sextet including Johnson, Quick, Ritzy Lee, Billy Woodruff, Willie Green, and Douglas White—signed with ABC-Paramount. They had little success at ABC, despite having made some excellent records. By the time of their ABC contract, the group had come to sound somewhat like the Drifters, especially in terms of the arrangements they were using. By 1965, it was over for the Del-Vikings. The group experienced a revival under Clarence Quick in 1972 amid the oldies boom, and they recorded a new version of "Come Go With Me" for the New York-based Scepter label that got some notice in *Billboard* early in 1973. By 1980, Kripp Johnson had reformed his own "Dell-Vikings" (the Mercury contract having long since ended, there was no party to lay final claim to the name) with Norman Wright, Ritzy Lee, John Byas, and David Lerchey, and his and Quick's Del-Vikings hovered around each other, avoiding direct confrontation by staying out of each other's way on tours through different parts of the country, until Quick's death in 1985 and Johnson's death in 1990.

The juggling of the group membership, name, and label affiliation makes collecting the Del-Vikings (or Dell-Vikings) very complicated. The "Come Go With Me" group on Dot in the main moved over to Mercury without any major hits, as the Del Vikings, so it is a good idea to own both the Dot and Mercury stuff. But the Mercury group eventually (from late 1957 until 1959) included all of the key original members, and they eventually moved over to ABC-Paramount in 1960 or so, and MCA now owns both Dot and ABC, meaning that the collections of the group's work aren't simple to divide or arrange. MCA's *Best of the Del-Vikings* has the beginning and end of the classic group, late-1956 to mid-1957 with a jump to 1960-1963, while Mercury has the glorious middle, mid-1957 to 1959 (and both collections include "When I Come Home" and "I'm Spinning"). And Collectables has the original 1956 demos, with yet another lineup of Dell Vikings.

Whether they were spelling their name Del-Vikings, Del Vikings, or Dell-Vikings, the group left behind one of the most satisfying bodies of R&B and doo wop music this side of the Drifters. The lingering appeal of "Come Go With Me" and "Whispering Bells"—used in movies like George Lucas' *American Graffiti* and Rob Reiner's *Stand By Me*—has helped their music remain among the most accessible bodies of doo wop music well into the CD era. *—Bruce Eder*

For Collectors Only / Nov. 30, 1992 / Collectables ♦♦♦♦♦

This really isn't for collectors only—it is the only single collection of the group's stuff that shows the full range of this sadly underrated vocal group. As it is, its mere existence as a mid-priced double CD, alongside the presence of the two best-of compilations from MCA and Mercury, makes collecting the best Dell Vikings material extremely complicated. Collectables Records got access to the complete recordings that the original group made for Fee-Bee Records, which covers their history from 1956 through 1957, overlapping with the history of the Mercury version of the group. This includes the hit version of "Come Go With Me," as well as "Whispering Bells" (both of which appear on MCA's best-of in those very same versions) and their other early tracks. Collectables also got access to an extraordinary body of outtakes—a magnificent fast version of "I'm Spinning" that's completely different from the version that appears on both the MCA and Mercury best-of discs. There are distinctive outtakes of "Willette" and oddities such as the Joey Biscoe single "What Made Maggie Run," on which the group sang backup in a hurried attempt to get them out before the public again after that first hit. More important are tracks like "Uh Uh Baby," a fast jump number that shows the group at about its rockingest and nimblest, with a killer guitar solo courtesy of the late Joe Lopes. Other highlights include radiant outtakes of "Girl, Girl" and "Cold Feet" (done a cappella), little snippets of session chatter (amazing the stuff survived 40 years), and rehearsal and audition versions of the group's songs and generally the fullest account possible of the history of the Fee-Bee Records version of the group that you'll ever see. *—Bruce Eder*

The Best of the Del-Vikings: The Mercury Years / Jul. 16, 1996 / Mercury ♦♦♦

Read the title carefully, because the Del-Vikings' two great doo wop hits—"Come Go with Me" and "Whispering Bells"—were *not* recorded for Mercury, and so are not contained on this compilation. This disc has 22 sides they recorded for Mercury in 1957-1958, with a lineup that had some but not all of the members that recorded "Come Go with Me" and "Whispering Bells." (To make matters more confusing, a different Del-Vikings, led by Kripp Johnson, who had sung lead on "Whispering Bells," kept recording for a different label.) The Mercury Del-Vikings did have a Top 20 hit right out of the box, "Cool Shake" (included here), but never had a big single again. Most of this is routine doo wop that's below the standards of their Dot sides, sometimes clouded by inadvisable attempts at pop-oriented material and production. It's only of value to hard-core doo wop bugs, who will appreciate the inclusion of many tracks only available on rare EPs, singles, and compilations, as well as one previously unissued in the U.S. The intro to "The Bells," by the way, bears a close similarity to the famous wordless scats that kicked off the Marcels' classic "Blue Moon" several years later. *—Richie Unterberger*

★ **Come Go With Me: The Best of the Del-Vikings—The Dot/ABC Recordings** / Jun. 17, 1997 / Hip-O ♦♦♦♦♦

As one of the first interracial vocal groups of the rock & roll era—and the first to score a Top Ten million-selling record on their very first try—the Del-Vikings seemed poised for very big things indeed. But when "Come Go With Me" became a national hit, the greed caused the Del-Vikings to split into two separate groups. Recording at various times with almost the same name, sometimes utilizing interchangeable group members as the two groups released follow-up singles on both Dot and Mercury simultaneously (with errant tracks showing up a couple of years later on a third label, Luniverse), this put the brakes on the group's success in a most confusing manner, raising the ire of disc jockeys and radio station programmers alike. This 16-track compilation from the Hip-O subsidiary is subtitled *The Dot-ABC Recordings* and does a better than average job of cherry picking through their sides for that label. Their big hit, "Come Go With Me," kicks things off, followed by the A- and B-sides of five early Fee-Bee, Dot, and ABC-Paramount singles. Filling out the compilation are the top sides of four more ABC singles. Oddly enough, the follow-up to "Come Go With Me," a two-sided rocker ("What Made Maggie Run" and "Little Billy Boy"), isn't here, making this collection somewhat incomplete. But as a basic hits primer, this tells the story of the "original Del-Vikings" in a thoroughly digestible way. *—Cub Koda*

The Delfonics

f. 1965, Philadelphia, PA, **db.** 1974

Group / Smooth Soul, Pop-Soul, Quiet Storm, Philly Soul, Soul

The Delfonics were one of the first groups to sing in the sleek, soulful style that became popularized (thanks to producer Thom Bell) as the "Philadelphia sound." A vocal trio made up of brothers William and Wilbert Hart and high school friend Randy Cain, the Delfonics roots go back to doo wop singing at school dances in the early '60s. They were well-known in the Philly area for their supple, airtight harmonies talent that brought them to the attention of record producers, eventually landing them a contract with Cameo-Parkway. While their early records brought them little if any notice, it did bring them to the attention of producer/arranger Thom Bell who signed the band to his soon-to-be influential soul label Philly Groove. Right from the start this was a perfect match as the band released the classic "La La Means I Love You" in 1968, a song that began a string of hits lasting into the mid-'70s.

The sound that Bell created for the Delfonics was the antithesis of the soul sound that came from Stax in Memphis and Muscle Shoals in AL. He sandpapered away the grit, lightened up on the backbeat, brought in string sections, and created a smooth, airy, sound. Critics enamored of the soul singing of Wilson Pickett and Otis Redding, accused Bell and his groups of creating aural wallpaper, but the reality was that Bell and the Delfonics and were setting the stage for a different kind of groove where subtlety and nuance reigned.

The hits slowed for the Delfonics in the mid-'70s, and in 1971. Randy Cain quit the band and was replaced by Major Harris. A few more minor hits followed but Harris left the band for a solo career in 1975 effectively finishing the Delfonics. In the late '90s the group played a significant musical role in Quentin Tarantino's film *Jackie Brown*. Tarantino, a borderline obsessive fan of '70s pop culture, used "La La Means I Love You," and their best single "Didn't I (Blow Your Mind This Time)" as a way of underscoring the relationship between actors Pam Grier and Robert Forster. In the film, Forster's character is so struck by the music (and Grier), he goes out and buys the Delfonics *Greatest Hits* cassette the following day. Something I'd recommend you do too. *—John Dougan*

La La Means I Love You / 1968 / Bell ♦♦♦♦♦

Philly soul has rarely sounded as regal as it does on Buddah Records "Original Masters" reissue series. Their initial batch of releases includes the first three long-players from the Thom Bell-produced and arranged Delfonics. While *La La Means I Love You* is the trio's debut LP, they had actually been working with Bell as far back as their 1966 single "He Don't Really Love You." By the time this album was cut, Bell had begun to establish a core of key Philadelphia musicians who would later become internationally recognized as MFSB. This conglomerate further enhances the already mellifluous vocal blend of the original Delfonics, which included brothers William Hart, Wilbert Hart, and Randy Cain. The multi-task role that Bell plays in the success of the Delfonics—as well as most every other Philly-based group fortunate enough to have been guided by his discernible ears—included producing and arranging as well as co-writing over half of the original material on the album. Among them are the Top 40 hits "I'm Sorry" and "Break Your Promise," as well as the title track, which would become one of the group's signature tunes. The sublime smooth grooves seemingly inherent in these arrangements practically define the distinction between the Philly soul scene and those more established in Detroit (Motown), Memphis (Stax), or Chicago (Chess). Bell's trademark easy and languid rhythms, when married to the trio's lush vocal harmonies, add new hues to the sonic soul music palette of the late '60s and early '70s. The effectiveness of Bell's innovative arrangements is perhaps most evident on the cover tunes. Astute listeners will inevitably note the influence of another highly regarded and successful songwriting/arranging team. The inclusion of two Bacharach/David classics—"The Look of Love" and "Alfie"—gives listeners more than just a hint at where much of Bell's fresh and distinct ideas may have taken root. Additionally, the Delfonics' cover of "Hurt So Bad" should not be missed, as it bests, or at the very least updates, Little Anthony & the Imperials' more familiar version. Buddha's 2001 reissue marks this title's CD debut by mirroring the original vinyl release—even going so far as to faithfully reproduce both sides of the original LP jacket. Newly inked liner notes—as well as complete discographical and personnel information—have also been added in the six-panel foldout. Above all, the remastered sound yields the best this material has had. *—Lindsay Planer*

The Sound of Sexy Soul / 1969 / Philly Groove ✦✦✦✦

The Sound of Sexy Soul is the Delfonics' second long-player and builds upon the notable impact of their first, *La La Means I Love You*. This album provides the trio a platform for their next batch of crossover soul/pop hits, including "Somebody Loves You" and "Ready or Not Here I Come (Can't Hide From Love)." The developing Philly soul revolution which was being led by writer/musician/producer and arranger Thom Bell is increasingly evident throughout this disc. Incorporating lush tempos, potent string arrangements, as well as the Delfonics' dense vocal blend is a triumphant combination not only for Bell, but all devotees of Philadelphia's embryonic smooth-grooves movement. Evenly divided between six originals and six cover tunes, *The Sound of Sexy Soul* is perhaps the most accurate name an album of this nature could have. While the title might insinuate a collection of slow ballads, that is only a portion of the soul and pop crossover magic. There is certainly nothing leisurely about the original "You Can't Be Loving Him" or the feisty rendition of "Ain't That Peculiar," which happily suffers from an undeniable Motown groove, propelled by a familiar-sounding rhythm not too far removed from its Motor City roots. Among the other cover versions that the Delfonics reinvent for themselves on this LP are a psychedelic reading of "Scarborough Fair" and a midtempo reworking of "Going out of My Head." As with their previous album, the songwriting team of Thom Bell and William Hart scored not only the aforementioned hits—"Ready or Not Here I Come (Can't Hide From Love)" and "Somebody Loves You"—but several hidden gems, including "Everytime I See My Baby" and "My New Love." These tunes are textbook Philly soul and include trademark muted brass and string arrangements that support without impeding the trio's timeless vocal blend. In essence, they are able to delineate as well as personify the combination of influences that Bell and company drew upon in their quest to create a whole new soul music subgenre. The 2001 Buddha Records reissue marks the first time that *The Sound of Sexy Soul* has been available on CD. It boasts nearly perfect sound and a four-panel liner notes foldout which includes a historical essay from noted musicologist Bill Dahl as well as a reproduction of the original LP jacket. *—Lindsay Planer*

The Delfonics / 1970 / Bell ✦✦✦✦✦

Although self-titled, *The Delfonics* was actually the fourth long-player for the Philly soul vocalists. The album would not only be the band's entrée into the Top 100 pop album chart upon its release in 1970—peaking at number 61—it would also sport five hit singles over the course of two years. The success came with a price, however, as the album would be among the final collaborative efforts between the original trio—which consisted of brothers William Hart and Wilbert Hart, and Randy Cain—and their mentor Thom Bell. In two unrelated and evolutionary incidents, Cain would be replaced by Major Harris. While Bell—who was just beginning to receive the international acclaim so deserving of his work—would begin recording with the Spinners, Stylistics, and even established artists such as the O'Jays. All of the individual elements that helped create the distinctive "smooth grooves" sound synonymous with the Delfonics coalesce on this album with undeniable intensity. Indeed the material has arguably never been stronger—with nine of the album's ten tracks composed by either Thom Bell and/or William Hart. The performances are likewise ideally scored, incorporating string and brass sections without overpowering the vocal blend or seeming pretentious. Stylistically, the extroverted uptempo arrangement on tracks such as the psychedelic "Funny Feeling" is equally as potent as the intimate ballad "I Gave to You." Several sides on this disc are among the group's best-known works, as well as definitive entries into the distinct Philly-brand soul music scene. The leadoff track, "Didn't I (Blow Your Mind This Time)," would not only become a staple of Top 40 and R&B radio in 1970, but nearly two decades later inspired the 20-volume soul music compilation *Soul Hits of the 70s: Didn't It Blow Your Mind*. Additional crossover pop/R&B chart hits include: "Over & Over," "Trying to Make a Fool of Me," and "When You Get Right Down to It." *The Delfonics* also includes several "sleeper" tracks that would remain somewhat obscured by the overwhelming strength of the rest of the album. It was not until the disc was issued on CD by Buddha Records in 2001 that "Delfonics' Theme (How Could You)"—a timeless showcase for the unmistakable soaring falsetto of William Hart—as well as the slinky syncopation of Hart's "Think About Me" were rediscovered. Again, considering the power of the rest of the release, it is easy to see how they were relegated to becoming deep cuts. *—Lindsay Planer*

Tell Me This Is a Dream / 1972 / Philly Groove ✦✦

Some signs of decline were starting to emerge on this release, mainly because they never replaced Major Harris. The Harts can still hit the shimmering, compelling high notes, but were beginning to run out of good songs and also were sabotaged by the lack of interest displayed from the label. *—Ron Wynn*

Alive & Kicking / 1974 / Philly Groove ✦✦

This is a mediocre album by Delfonics standards, although there are a few good moments. But the magic was gone by the mid-'70s, and the Delfonics were being surpassed by their rivals, like Blue Magic and the Stylistics, who benefited from far superior songs. They kept trying, but didn't click nearly as often, nor as much as needed. *—Ron Wynn*

● **La-La Means I Love You: The Definitive Collection** / Aug. 26, 1997 / Arista ✦✦✦✦✦

Here is a lush collection of classy Delfonics tracks. The trio had a more soulful sound than the Stylistics whom Thom Bell (who produced the lion's share of these tracks) later produced. Initially flooring the world with "La, La Means I Love You," the Harts, William & Wilbert, Randy Cain, and later Major Harris churned out delightful ear candies for years. "I'm Sorry," "Break Your Promise," "Ready or Not Here I Come," and "You Got Yours I'll Get Mine," included here, were as potent as "La, La." But, it took the eloquent, French-horn embellished "Didn't I Blow Your Mind This Time," however, to put them on top again. "Somebody Loves You" is a luscious B-side featuring William's sweet falsetto and harmonies that run over. Later, less successful recordings provide the most thrills: "Over & Over," "Lying to Myself," "Think It Over," and "I Told You So" are as smooth and as creamy as whipped cream. "Hey Love," an exquisite slow jam, featuring Wilbert Hart's heavier tenor, has shown an amazing longevity for a flip side. Not quite definitive, they could have omitted the awkward "Funny Feeling," and "Loving Him"—a B-side—for "I Gave to You" and "Can You Remember." But this is still fantastic, and more than enough Delfonics for most; you'll want two copies—one for the car and one for the crib. *—Andrew Hamilton*

Forever New / Nov. 16, 1999 / Volt ✦✦✦

When Fantasy reactivated the Volt label in 1999, it recorded urban contemporary newcomer Angel Sessions, as well as older soul veterans like the Delfonics, the Dramatics, and Brenda Holloway. Although not in a class with the Delfonics' seminal recordings of the late '60s and early '70s, 1999's *Forever New* is an enjoyable outing that finds the group in good form 31 years after "La La Means I Love You" burned up the R&B charts. William Hart's distinctive voice has held up well over the years, and his performances on "I Will Remember You," "When You're Gone," and other selections, demonstrate that time has not robbed the Philadelphian of his charisma. Produced by Fred Pittman and Preston Glass, *Forever New* tends to favor a high-tech urban contemporary production style that is a departure from the lush orchestral approach Thom Bell was known for (although Bell arranged "She's The Kinda Girl"). The horns and strings are missed, and the Delfonics (whose lineup on *Forever New* consists of Hart, Major Harris, and Futures graduate Frank Washington) would have been better served by an honest-to-God band—even so, the material generally sounds organic rather than forced and unnatural. Also noteworthy is a remake of "Break Your Promise," which falls short of the excellence of the original version but is pleasing nonetheless. *Forever New* isn't essential—casual listeners would be better off with a collection of the Delfonics' late-'60s/early-'70s hits—but it's still a CD that seasoned Delfonics fans will appreciate. *—Alex Henderson*

The Dells

f. 1952, Chicago, IL, **db.** 1986

Group / Soul, Chicago Soul, Smooth Soul, Pop-Soul, Northern Soul, Doo Wop, R&B

The Dells are one of the finest and longest-lived R&B vocal groups in history, and what's most amazing is that they've done it with nearly all the same members—they haven't changed personnel since 1960. They were one of the very few doo wop outfits to successfully update their sound, finding their strongest commercial niche in the late '60s and '70s as a polished smooth soul harmony group. While their chart fortunes have certainly fluctuated over the years, they remained a viable act right up into the '90s, by which time they had long since achieved legendary status in the R&B community.

The Dells were formed in 1953 in southern suburbs of Chicago, specifically the town of Harvey, IL, where all the members attended high school together. The original lineup featured lead baritone Marvin Junior, lead tenor Johnny Funches, tenors Verne Allison and Lucius McGill, second baritone Mickey McGill, and bass Chuck Barksdale. Initially called the El-Rays, the group recorded their first single, "Darling I Know," for Chess Records subsidiary Checker that year; it flopped. Lucius McGill departed not long after, and wasn't replaced, cutting the group down to a quintet. Newly christened the Dells, they got another shot in 1955 when they signed to Vee-Jay. They had a minor R&B hit with the ballad "Dreams of Contentment" that year, but really scored big in 1956 with the doo wop classic "Oh What a Nite," which featured Funches singing lead and went Top Five on the R&B charts. Thus established, the Dells hit the road, although they found it difficult to duplicate their chart success. Tragedy nearly struck in 1958; on their way to a gig in Philadelphia, the body of the group's station wagon failed, resulting in a serious accident which lacerated Junior's larynx (slightly altering his voice thereafter) and nearly cost McGill the use of his leg. The Dells went on hiatus to recover; in the meantime, Barksdale became a temporary member of the Moonglows, where he sang alongside Marvin Gaye.

The Dells reconvened in 1960 and successfully auditioned to tour with Dinah Washington, as both her opening act and backup group. Funches, however, was tired of touring and decided to stay home with his family, which would be the last time any member left the group. He was replaced by lead/falsetto tenor Johnny Carter, a former member of the Flamingos. Working with vocal coach Kirk Stewart, the Dells perfected the more challenging art of jazz harmony singing. They toured with Washington for two years, subsequently signing with the Chess subsidiary Argo and releasing four jazz-flavored singles, all of which tanked. They returned to Vee-Jay in 1964 and began recording R&B again, though their local nightclub act centered more around jazz; 1965 brought them a Top 30 R&B hit with "Stay in My Corner," their biggest success since "Oh What a Nite." However, Vee-Jay went bankrupt in 1966, and the Dells returned to Chess for a third time, this time the Cadet subsidiary; their first two singles, "Thinking About You" and "Run for Cover," became local hits. Also in 1966, the Dells became Ray Charles' touring vocal backup, giving them an opportunity to sing in some of their biggest concert venues yet.

Cadet was where the Dells' career really started to take off. In 1967, the label assigned producer Bobby Miller and arranger Charles Stepney to handle the group, and they began to exploit the striking contrast between Junior's earthy baritone and Carter's luminous falsetto, adding lush orchestrations and plenty of horn charts. The Dells' first album under the Miller-Stepney aegis, *There Is*, was a smashing success, spawning no less than four hit singles including an expanded remake of "Stay in My Corner" that topped the R&B charts and went Top Ten pop. Suddenly the group was bigger than they'd ever been; their follow-up album, 1968's *Always Together*, spun off another four singles. 1969's *Love Is Blue* gave them another R&B number one and pop Top Ten with a remake of their '50s classic "Oh What a Nite." Miller moved on to other projects in early 1970, and Stepney became the Dells' producer on the following year's *Freedom Means*, which featured the hit ballad "The Love We Had (Stays on My Mind)." After a Dionne Warwick repertory album in 1972, Cadet hired Don Davis as the group's new producer, which paid immediate dividends in the form of the Dells' first certified million-selling single, 1973's "Give Your Baby a Standing Ovation." After a few more hits with Davis, the Dells left Cadet in favor of Mercury in 1975.

Although the group's production kept pace with the times, incorporating nods to disco, their Mercury stint wasn't as successful, and they switched labels again in 1978, jumping to ABC for a couple of albums. It seemed their career momentum had stalled, at least until 1980's *I Touched a Dream* LP, recorded for 20th Century. Produced by the Chi-Lites' Eugene Record, *I Touched a Dream* recaptured the Dells' old magic, and was greeted with enthusiastic reviews. The follow-up, *Whatever Turns You On*, wasn't quite as successful, though, and the Dells wound up spending a number of years off record, returning with a little-noticed old-style soul album in 1988's *The Second Time*. It looked as though they might be consigned to the oldies circuit until filmmaker Robert Townsend approached them to serve as consultants on his movie about a fictional vocal group, *The Five Heartbeats*. The Dells recorded a song called "The Heart Is a House for Love" for the soundtrack, which became a left-field R&B chart hit when it was released as a single in 1991. That led to a new album for Zoo in 1992, *I Salute You*, which attempted to mate the Dells' sound with urban contemporary and new jack swing production; however, it wasn't a hit, and the group returned to touring. Former lead singer Johnny Funches passed away in 1998, and Verne Allison underwent a successful triple bypass in 2000, the same year the Dells released *Reminiscing* on the revived Volt label; it was their first album of new material in eight years. *—Steve Huey*

There Is / 1968 / Chess ✦✦✦✦✦

Other than their greatest-hits compilations, this by far is the Dells' finest LP release. Bobby Miller excelled in assembling this strong package. The six-minute-plus "Stay in My Corner" remains a live show staple and R&B classic. Written by Wade Flemons, Bobby Miller, and Barrett "Money" Strong, the epic ballad shattered the belief that pop songs had to be three minutes or less to get air play; it was a remake of a shorter version by the Dells released on Vee-Jay in 1965. Miller uses the idea of the quick hook on "Wear It on Our Face," the opening rhythms explode like firecrackers on this driving, high-energy sing-along. Few realize it, but the Dells cut and released "Your Love Keeps Lifting Me Higher" before Jackie Wilson did. A good remake of "Close Your Eyes," and the enthralling "Love Is So Simple" proved the guys hadn't forsaken their doo wop roots. The beautiful "O O I Love You" began the longest run on the charts in the Dells' history; originally Cadet released it with "There Is" on the flip side, and it went to number-22 R&B and number-61 Pop. "There Is" followed with a different flip, "Show Me," and became their biggest pop recording to date, nesting at number 20. Ironically, the Dells hated "There Is" when Bobby Miller first played it for them, it had a marching beat, and they couldn't see recording it. Marvin Junior, Johnny Carter, Chuck Barksdale, Verne Allison, and Mickey McGill never sounded better then they do on these 12 tantalizing entrees. *—Andrew Hamilton*

The Dells / 1969 / Chess ✦✦✦✦✦

This features tremendous vocals and production, coupled with superb ballads and good uptempo cuts. The Dells were never better than during the late '60s when they moved to Cadet and Charles Stepney's vision was fulfilled. Although he was never fully credited, lead singer Marvin Junior stands as one of soul's great vocalists, and he showed it repeatedly on this set. Johnny Carter's floating falsetto was another major weapon expertly utilized in The Dells' soul success. *—Ron Wynn*

Love Is Blue / 1969 / Cadet ✦✦✦✦✦

Here is a fine album that included their excellent version of the title cut, some other stirring ballads, and some good uptempo tunes. The Dells were now in peak form, with Marvin Junior's booming voice and Charles Stepney's productions and good arrangements turning them into the hitmakers they never were in the doo wop days. *—Ron Wynn*

Freedom Means / 1971 / Cadet ✦✦✦

A fine early-'70s date, with the title track one of the more socio-political songs the Dells ever recorded. Both Marvin Junior and Johnny Carter were in fine form, and while this was pretty basic material, they sang it with passion and exuberance. *—Ron Wynn*

Sweet as Funk Can Be / 1972 / Cadet ✦✦✦

Although not as striking as some other Dells albums, this was still good enough. There were some first-rate ballads, a few decent uptempo tracks, and plenty of fine lead vocals as always by Marvin Junior with Johnny Carter's angelic answering falsetto coming in right on time. *—Ron Wynn*

Give Your Baby a Standing Ovation / 1973 / Cadet ✦✦✦✦

Named after their million-selling salute to women, *Give Your Baby a Standing Ovation* is a tight, nine-song creation of the legendary Don Davis. A mellow "You Don't Care" provides a good vehicle for the guys to display their blending skills; Marvin Junior's ear-popping baritone enhances the biting lyrics. They shine on "Closer," a smooth, aggressive number with a slick production; it could have been a hit, but Cadet decided to slap it on the back of "Give Your Baby a Standing Ovation." They update "The Glory of Love" in a '70s, Dells style, and do a credible job with "Ain't No Sunshine." For some reason this LP has never been easy to find. *—Andrew Hamilton*

New Beginnings / 1978 / ABC ✦✦

This was one that sounded good on paper, but didn't work out as anticipated. Al Hudson & the Soul Partners, along with George Clinton, tried to update The Dells' classic style, but instead wound up force-feeding them material that wasn't designed for their strength. They made one other album for the label, but the group's stay on ABC wasn't the most profitable. *—Ron Wynn*

I Touched a Dream / 1980 / 20th Century ✦✦✦✦✦

This is the last great Dells album, and one of the year's big surprises. The Dells were on another new label, and now were working with Carl Davis and Eugene Records (also of the Chi-Lites). The pair simply restored the Dells' strengths; each production made sure Marvin Junior's roaring leads and Johnny Carter's wavery falsetto were at the forefront. They also got them a superb ballad in the title track, a good message song in "It's All About The Paper," and other fine cuts. *—Ron Wynn*

I Salute You / 1992 / Zoo ✦✦✦

The Dells formally celebrated their 40th anniversary with this nice 10-cut session, juggling overproduced urban contemporary and new jack selections with classic, close harmony numbers that spotlighted Marvin Junior's still-impressive, swaggering baritone and Johnny Carter's always-mellow falsetto. The contemporary material wasn't horrible; even the rap insert on "Baby Don't Go Away Mad" wasn't overbearing, while the arrangements on the title track were acceptable. But it was the ballads that signaled that these were still the Dells; "Somebody's Gotta Move," "Oh My Love," and "Closer to You" had the familiar ingredients—steamy, inviting or even despairing lyrics. *—Ron Wynn*

Dreams of Contentment / Nov. 17, 1993 / Vee-Jay ✦✦✦✦✦

The Dells never made it over the hump while at Vee-Jay, despite making many impressive singles. They were a top-flight doo wop group, but they couldn't find a way to advance beyond the R&B margins. Only when they moved to Chess, changed their style, and made Marvin Junior the lead singer did they enjoy the success they deserved. Still, as this 24-track reissue shows, there wasn't anything wrong with their Vee-Jay output. They experimented on such numbers as "Lil Darlin'," "It's Not for Me to Say," and "It's Not Unusual" with jazz/pop harmonies and covers. In addition, songs like "Now I Pray" and "Pain in My Heart" are wonderfully sung and harmonized, even if they weren't huge sellers. *—Ron Wynn*

Passionate Breezes: The Best of the Dells 1975–1991 / Oct. 1995 / Mercury ✦✦✦

By the last half of the '70s, the Dells had already gone through two phases in their career, transforming themselves from an R&B vocal group into a smooth soul outfit and scoring hits in both incarnations. During the late '70s and '80s, the group continued to perform, usually in the same vein as their early-'70s hits. Even if the strength of their voices hadn't diminished, their audience had. Nevertheless, much of the material they recorded during this era was fine, as *Passionate Breezes: Best of 1975-1991* proves. It's not as compulsively listenable as the group's doo wop hits or their early-'70s material, but there is still enough first-rate music here to satisfy fans. *—Stephen Thomas Erlewine*

Bring Back the Love: Classic Dells Soul / Feb. 27, 1996 / Chess ✦✦✦✦✦

Chess' *Bring Back the Love: Classic Dells Soul* doesn't contain any of the group's big hits, but that's fine, since it offers a nice, 14-song roundup of the Dells' early recordings for Chess in the '50s. These may not be well-known, but they're uniformly strong singles, highlighted by a nice version of "The Glory of Love," "If You Really Love Your Girl (Show Her)," and "I Can't Do Enough." *—Stephen Thomas Erlewine*

Oh What a Night! The Great Ballads / Jan. 13, 1998 / MCA ✦✦✦✦✦

Oh, What a Night! The Great Ballads is a wonderful collection of 15 ballads the Dells recorded for Chess Records between 1967 and 1974. Among the songs included are the hits "Stay in My Corner," "Oh, What a Night!," "Always Together," "The Love We Had (Stays on My Mind)" and "Open Up My Heart," which is available for the first time on CD in its original long version; "Since I Fell for You" and "Soul Strollin'" also make their CD debut on this disc. Since it concentrates on ballads, *Oh, What a Night!* can't be considered a definitive retrospective, but anyone looking for a fine selection of the group's romantic material will find this the perfect choice. *—Stephen Thomas Erlewine*

★ **Anthology** / Sep. 28, 1999 / Hip-O ✦✦✦✦✦

The Dells were one of the few groups that rode the transition from doo wop to smooth soul without missing a beat and without falling off the charts. Just as remarkably, the group did so without declining much in quality, as Hip-O's definitive double-disc *Anthology* proves. Throughout these 36 tracks, the music changes, from street-corner R&B to string-drenched disco-soul, but in all their incarnations, the Dells always sound wonderful. There are a handful of minor hits missing, but all the big singles—including both the Vee-Jay and Cadet versions of "Oh, What a Nite" and "Stay in My Corner"—are here, assembled chronologically. As such, it tells an epic story of a group whose history mirrored the story of R&B vocal groups from the '50s through the '70s. The latter-day material may pale somewhat in comparison to the band's early classics, but it holds up well against other '70s soul. The final cut, the group's surprise 1991 hit "A Heart Is a House for Love"—their contribution to Robert Townsend's *The Five Heartbeats*, which was a loose tribute to the Dells themselves—illustrates that the group sounded terrific well into their third decade of performing, which is a true sign of greatness. *Anthology* is a testament to their greatness, offering solid proof that they were one of the greatest vocal R&B groups of their time. *—Stephen Thomas Erlewine*

The Very Best of the Dells / Oct. 17, 2000 / Collectables ✦✦✦✦

A fine chronological CD of the Dells' Vee-Jay recordings, from their 1955 debut "Tell the World" to 1964's immortal "Stay in My Corner"—with liner notes by Robert Prueter, the godfather of Chicago's soul scene. The original Dells recorded the bulk of these tracks with Johnny Funches; exaggerated falsetto Johnny Carter replaced Funches in 1959. Their recording debut (as the El-Rays) was 1954's "Darling I Know," which didn't make the 25 tracks—nor did a few early-'60s releases on Argo Records when they broke from Vee-Jay for a spell. Singularly, and occasionally together, tenor Verne Allison and baritone Michael McGill wrote most of the material, with blustery baritone lead Marvin Junior chipping in a few tunes as well. All the Dells wrote songs but rarely together. These are the Chicago area recordings from whence the Dells' legend spread. —*Andrew Hamilton*

The Delta Rhythm Boys

f. 1934, Langston, OK, **db.** 1987

Group / Jazz Blues, Harmony Vocal Group, R&B

This group origins date back to 1934, when they formed at Langston University in OK. They moved to Dillard University in New Orleans in 1936, and worked with Dr. Frederick Hall as both the New Orleans Quintet and Frederick Hall Quintet. Their most famous lineup included Carl Jones, Traverse Crawford, Kelsey Pharr, and Otha Lee Gaines, with accompanist/arranger Rene DeKnight. They had one big hit, a version of "Just A-Sittin' and A-Rockin'" in 1936, and an adaptation of a Duke Ellington tune by Gaines. They remained together in various aggregations until Gaines died in 1987, after which they disbanded. —*Ron Wynn*

● **Just A-Rockin' & A-Jivin': Anthology, Vol. 1 (1941–1946)** / Nov. 6, 2001 / Dee-Jay ✦✦✦✦✦

The first volume in Dee-Jay's prescient three-part anthology series featuring those kings of vocal rhythm, *Just A-Rockin' & A-Jivin'* is loaded with excellent performances. Urbane and refined or earthy and rhythmic, the Delta Rhythm Boys were quite dexterous and performed admirably with a wide variety of material: gospel updates ("Dry Bones," "Joshua Fit de Battle of Jericho"), jive novelties ("Gimme Some Skin," "No Pad to Be Had"), and their many versions of Duke Ellington standards ("Just A-Sittin' and A-Rockin'," "Do Nothin' Till You Hear From Me," "Take the 'A' Train," and "Just Squeeze Me [But Don't Tease Me]"). One of the biggest highlights comes at the end with "A One-Sided Affair," a song that finds them paired with artists as agile and sparkling as themselves, the Les Paul Trio. —*John Bush*

Jump & Jive 'Til One O'Clock: Anthology, Vol. 2 (1947–1950) / Nov. 13, 2001 / Dee Jay ✦✦✦✦

The second in a trio of German collections of the Delta Rhythm Boys' recordings of the 1940s, *Jump & Jive 'Til One O'Clock* focuses less on rarities/transcriptions and arguably trumps its predecessor. Completely opposite to the progression of the Ink Spots and Mills Brothers, the Delta Rhythm Boys grew more inventive and radical as they continued recording. The quintet just kept pushing vocal music forward during the late '40s with the same tight, swinging harmonies but increasingly experimental charts. For this chronological collection, early high points like "Dry Bones" and "My Blue Heaven" give way to slightly less traditional material that still excels. Other highlights include their versions of "One O'Clock Jump" and "Don't Ask Me Why." —*John Bush*

Radio, Gimme Some Jive: Performances 1941–1945 / Nov. 13, 2001 / Dee-Jay ✦✦✦

Radio, Gimme Some Jive is the last of three Delta Rhythm Boys collections available from the German label Dee-Jay, featuring 29 exuberant performances from one of the brightest harmony/rhythm groups of the '30s and '40s. Led by tenor Carl Jones, the quintet could harmonize like few other groups of the era, but they also proved capable of uptempo swing on the order of the Spirits of Rhythm or the Four Blazes. As the title indicates, these are transcriptions, originally recorded during the American war years for radio broadcast or movie soundtracks, plus the rare soundie (an early version of what was later known as music videos, available in nickelodeons). The sound quality isn't bad for the period, and the performances are solid, whether the group is tackling swing standards ("One O'Clock Jump," "Take the 'A' Train," "I'm Beginning to See the Light," "Just A-Sittin' and A-Rockin'," the latter their lone hit) or superficially silly harmony novelties like "Rigoletto Blues," "Snoqualomie Jo Jo," or "Texas Polka." There's also some wonderful interplay between lead and backing harmonies on many tracks, especially "Take the 'A' Train." —*John Bush*

Deodato (Eumir Deodato Almeida)

b. Jun. 21, 1942, Rio de Janeiro, Brazil

Arranger, Keyboards, Conductor / Crossover Jazz, Fusion, Disco, Dance-Pop

Despite a productive career, Deodato will always be best-known for a 1972 hit record, his catchy adaptation of "Also Sprach Zarathustra (Theme from *2001: A Space Odyssey*)." He began his career playing in a popular local rock group as a teenager. At 17 he was asked to arrange for a recording session orchestra and, despite never having written a score before, the teenager succeeded at quickly learning what was necessary. Although Deodato spent time studying engineering, he eventually decided to make a career in music due to the popularity of his writing. After working in Brazil's studios, he moved to the U.S. in 1967. Deodato wrote for the American studios and was involved in the still fertile bossa nova movement. He wrote arrangements for Astrud Gilberto, contributed three charts to Wes Montgomery's *Down Here on the Ground* and was soon working for major names in several fields including Aretha Franklin, Bette Midler, Frank Sinatra, Earth, Wind & Fire, Stanley Turrentine and Antonio Carlos Jobim among others. With the release of *Prelude* in 1973 (his first solo album and the one that included the "Theme From *2001*"), Deodato became a major name for a time. He recorded sets for CTI, MCA and Warner Bros. through 1979 although the efforts tended to be overarranged and none caught on as well as *Prelude*. Since that time, Deodato has mostly been outside of jazz, working as a producer and arranger behind the scenes, including for Kool & the Gang during 1979-1983. —*Scott Yanow*

● **Prelude** / Sep. 12, 1972-Sep. 14, 1972 / CTI ✦✦✦✦

Prior to this album, Eumir Deodato was primarily known, if at all, as a tasteful, lyrical, bossa nova-based sometime arranger for the likes of Antonio Carlos Jobim, Frank Sinatra, Wes Montgomery, etc. Enter Creed Taylor, who gave Deodato a chance to step out on his own as a pianist/leader, doing a few tunes of his own plus a healthy quota of CTI/patented jazz interpretations of classical pieces by Richard Strauss ("Also Sprach Zarathustra (*2001*)"), Debussy ("Prelude to the Afternoon of a Faun") and bowdlerized Borodin ("Baubles, Bangles and Beads"). Well, "*2001*"—a clever, uptempo Latin-groove takeoff on the opening measures of Strauss' tone poem suddenly exploded and became an improbable hit single. In its wake, *Prelude* soared to number three on the pop LP charts, and Deodato was propelled out of the arranger-for-hire business. Though overshadowed by "2001," the other tracks also hold up well today, being mostly medium-tempo, sometimes lushly-orchestrated, conga-accented affairs that provide velvety showcases for Deodato's lyrical electric piano solos. The record also made a temporary star out of John Tropea, whose electric guitar has a lot of rock & rolling zip and fire, and Hubert Laws, Stanley Clarke and Marvin Stamm each get a little solo room too. This would be the biggest hit Deodato and CTI ever had, and though short on playing time (32 minutes), it still makes enjoyable listening. —*Richard S. Ginell*

Deodato 2 / Apr. 12, 1973-May 16, 1973 / CTI ✦✦✦

It didn't take long for Eumir Deodato and Creed Taylor to figure out that it was high-energy jazz-rock and kernels of classical music, not Deodato's old lush post-bossa nova romanticism, that made *Prelude* a hit. As a result, *Deodato 2* is hotter than *Prelude*, more cranked up in its group dynamic, less reliant upon orchestrations to make its point. Of course, guitarist John Tropea is back to lend some of rock's sting to his solos, and Deodato introduces a synthesizer into his arsenal, though he uses it like one of those gimmicky so-called "synthesizer" keyboards that home organs once had. The track that hits hardest, then and now, is Deodato's own furious "Super Strut"; the ones that don't hold up as well, ironically, are the classical adaptations—Ravel's "Pavanne for a Dead Princess" and a labored attempt to turn Gershwin's "Rhapsody in Blue" into another "*2001*." Overall this one hasn't worn quite as well as *Prelude* but it still retains some of its ebullience—and the CD version contains three outtakes, of which only Deodato's dreamy 6/8-meter "Venus" has anything different to say. —*Richard S. Ginell*

Whirlwinds / 1974 / MCA ✦✦

Love Island / 1978 / Warner Bros. ✦✦

Des'ree

Group / Adult Contemporary, Urban

With her second album, 1994's *I Ain't Movin'*, soul singer Des'ree became a star. Des'ree's contemporary soul is smooth enough to fit into most urban contemporary play lists, yet it has enough grit and emotional style to attract fans of early-'70s R&B. Her first album—*Mind Adventures* (1992)—didn't attract an audience, yet her second record, 1994's *I Ain't Movin'*, was a pop and R&B smash; thanks to the Top Ten hit "You Gotta Be," the record sold over a million copies. *Supernatural* followed in 1998, and *Endangered Species* in 2000. —*Stephen Thomas Erlewine*

Mind Adventures / 1992 / Epic ✦✦✦

● **I Ain't Movin'** / 1994 / Epic/550 Music ✦✦✦✦

British soulstress Des'ree caused little more than a ripple with her 1992 debut, *Mind Adventures*, but caught fire with her sophomore effort, *I Ain't Movin'*, and the smash single "You Gotta Be." The uplifting song was a U.S. Top Five hit and best exemplified Des'ree's smooth blend of pop/R&B music and power-of-positive thinking lyrical style. Nothing else on *I Ain't Movin'* manages to endear itself quite as much, but it's hardly a washout. Des'ree possesses a pleasing vocal delivery and it serves her well on songs like the slinky, midtempo "Feel So High," the breezy "Little Child," the hypnotic groove of "Trip on Love," and the confessional title cut. Some of the lyrics are a bit half-baked and fail to achieve much depth and the production is a bit slick at times, but not enough to mar an otherwise satisfying release. —*Tom Demalon*

Supernatural / Aug. 11, 1998 / 550 Music ✦✦✦

On her third album of adult R&B, new age princess Des'ree offers up more musical self-help tips and self-esteem makeovers for the chronically lovesick and spiritually down-hearted. And while there's nothing as peacefully sublime as "You Gotta Be" (from 1994's *I Ain't Movin'*) on *Supernatural*, the listen is a soothing one. Credit Brit Des'ree herself for this; her voice—a reassuring tool that envelops everything around it—has never been better. Working her softened tones around the mostly forgettable material (many of the songs try to rewrite "You Gotta Be" by essentially sticking with the same formula of making sophisticated urban soul), she creates a melodic new age tone (complete with a cover of Bruce Springsteen's "Fire") that may not stick with you a lifetime, but it sure feels like the most tranquil place on earth for its 50 minutes. —*Michael Gallucci*

Endangered Species / May 23, 2000 / Sony International ✦✦✦

Sugar Pie DeSanto (Umpeylia Marsema Balinton)

b. Oct. 16, 1935, Brooklyn, NY

Vocals / Chicago Soul, Soul

Born Umpeylia Marsema Balinton, this artist was given her stage-name as well as her recording debut by rhythm and blues Übermensch Johnny Otis. He dubbed her "Little Miss Sugar Pie" in 1955, and not because she had a sweet tooth or liked to bake. "While we were in the studio he named me Sugar Pie," DeSanto recalled in an interview, "Because I was so little. I wore a size three shoe and I weighed about 85 pounds. I was very tiny." She's a half-pint in size, true, but in talent or voice assuredly not. Although typecast as a blues singer, she also takes care of business on the soul end of things and is a convincing jazz vocal stylist as well. That would be enough to gain most singers a reasonable slice of glory, but DeSanto also happens to be a hilarious comedienne, a show-stopping dancer and a superb and highly original songwriter whose compositions have been cut by Fontella Bass, Billy Stewart, Little Milton, Bobby McClure, Minnie Riperton, Jesse James, the Dells and the Whispers.

Otis discovered her performing at the Ellis Theater, the venue which she feels was sort of a birthing ground for her musical style. Otis dropped by one of the venue's regular talent shows only to observe DeSanto walking off with first prize. He promptly offered her a contract to come to Los Angeles to cut her first record ever. From the late 50s onward she performed regularly at R&B havens such as the Apollo in New York, the Regal in Chicago and the Howard in Washington, D.C. At the Apollo she made quite an impression on the so-called "Godfather of Soul", James Brown, leading to her becoming his opening act for two years. In 1964 DeSanto was the only female performer on a touring American Folk Blues Festival bill with a lineup that would make a blues fan soak the concert program with drool, including Willie Dixon, Sleepy John Estes, Clifton James, Sunnyland Slim, Hubert Sumlin, Lightnin' Hopkins and the second Sonny Boy Williamson, also known as Rice Miller. She has written some 100 songs and prefers to perform her own material. On a series of four excellent compact discs on the Jasman label, only two songs are not written by her. *Classic Sugar Pie*, released in 1997, was the first full-length live recording by this artist whose on-stage workout has always totally bypassed her record releases in terms of creativity and intensity. This recording reveals that advancing age isn't stopping her from continuing to expand her talent base: She branches out into country and western. *—Eugene Chadbourne*

Sugar Pie DeSanto / 1961 / Checker ♦♦♦
One of the least recognized, yet outstanding female soul singers of the early '60s, Sugar Pie DeSanto could do coy, innocent songs, tough, hard-edged blues, romantic fluff, or heartache ballads. She was hurt by being on the same label as Etta James and not getting enough quality songs, as was the case with this set. *—Ron Wynn*

Lovin' Touch / 1987 / Diving Duck ♦♦♦♦
Hopefully, Diving Duck Records will release this on CD one day. *Lovin' Touch* is 43 minutes of the vivacious, electrifying Peylia Young, aka Sugar Pie DeSanto. DeSanto was married a number of times so her surname changed frequently. She was actually more prolific as a songwriter than a singer. Broadcast Music Incorporated lists 93 compositions by Sugar Pie under various names: DeSanto, Young, Parham, etc. These 16 songs were recorded by Chess Records between 1959 and 1964, and are highly representative of Sugar Pie, who was overshadowed at Chess by the similar sounding Etta James. "Slip in Mules" and "Soulful Dress" are two tough party songs about sprucing up and going out for a night on the town; "Dress" was written by Maurice McCallister, who sang lead with the Radiants. "Baby It Ain't Right," "Jump in My Chest" and "Mama Didn't Raise No Fools" get right to the point, the rhythms on these jams are so funky they probably had to burn incense in the studio to sweeten the air. It's a shame more interest wasn't showed Sugar Pie. She had it all, looks, voice, writing skills, and was a superb entertainer. *—Andrew Hamilton*

• **Down in the Basement: The Chess Years** / 1989 / Chess ♦♦♦♦♦
This is saucy, bluesy, mid-'60s R&B with a soulful edge, the excellent collection *Down in the Basement: The Chess Years* features her 1960 Top Ten hit "I Want to Know" and a pair of duets with Etta James, "In the Basement" and "Do I Make Myself Clear." *—Bill Dahl*

Destiny's Child

f. 1990, Houston, TX
Group / Teen Pop, Urban

Destiny's Child rose to become one of the most popular female R&B groups of the late '90s, eventually rivaling even TLC in terms of blockbuster commercial success. Their accomplishments came in spite of several abrupt personnel changes, which were accompanied by heated, well-publicized feuds in the media and the courts. In fact, for a time, Destiny's Child was known for that drama just as much as their music. Once the group stabilized again, though, they emerged with even more hitmaking power than ever before.

Destiny's Child was formed in Houston, TX, in 1990, when original members Beyoncé Knowles and LaTavia Roberson were just nine years old; the two met at an audition and became friends, and Knowles' father Mathew set about developing an act based on their singing and rapping, taking their name from a passage in the *Book of Isaiah*. Beyoncé's cousin Kelendria "Kelly" Rowland joined the group in 1992, and shortly thereafter they landed an appearance on *Star Search*, where they performed a rap song. The quartet's lineup was finalized (for the time being) when LeToya Luckett joined in 1993, and they spent the next few years working their way up from the Houston club scene, eventually opening for artists like SWV, Dru Hill, and Immature. Finally, in 1997, Destiny's Child was offered a recording contract by Columbia.

The group made its recorded debut on 1997's "Killing Time," a song included on the soundtrack of the blockbuster *Men in Black*. Their self-titled debut album was released in early 1998, featuring production by Wyclef Jean and Jermaine Dupri, among others. Its lead single, the Jean-produced "No No No," was a smash hit, selling over a million copies and topping the R&B charts. The follow-up singles—"With Me" and "Get on the Bus," the latter of which was taken from the soundtrack of *Why Do Fools Fall in Love?*—didn't quite duplicate the success of "No No No," although *Destiny's Child* would eventually go platinum (after the group's later success). Destiny's Child re-entered the studio quickly, bringing in producer Kevin "She'kspere" Briggs to handle the majority of their next record. Lead single "Bills, Bills, Bills" became the group's first number-one pop hit (and second R&B number one) in the summer of 1999, and paced by its success, the accompanying album *The Writing's on the Wall* entered the charts at number six upon its release.

That was just the beginning of the group's breakout success. The second single, "Bug a Boo," didn't perform as well, but the third single, "Say My Name," was another massive hit, their biggest so far; it hit number one on both the pop and R&B charts for three weeks apiece in early 2000, and made Destiny's Child a pop-cultural phenomenon. However, at the peak of "Say My Name"'s popularity, the group splintered. In December 1999, Roberson and Luckett attempted to split with manager Mathew Knowles, charging that he kept a disproportionate share of the band's profits, attempted to exert too much control, and unfairly favored his daughter and niece. While they never intended to leave the group, relations naturally grew strained, and when the video for "Say My Name" premiered in February 2000, many fans (not to mention Roberson and Luckett) were surprised to find two new members—Michelle Williams and Farrah Franklin—joining Knowles and Rowland. Infuriated, Roberson and Luckett took legal action in March, suing both Knowles and their former bandmates for breach of partnership and fiduciary duties. A war of words followed in the press; meanwhile, the next Destiny's Child single, "Jumpin' Jumpin'," hit the Top Ten, and *The Writing's on the Wall* went on to sell a whopping eight-million copies.

The personnel-turnover drama still wasn't over; in July 2000, just five months after joining, Farrah Franklin split with the group. The official reason was that Franklin missed several promotional appearances and concert gigs, although in later interviews she spoke of too much negativity and too little control in the group environment. Now reduced to a trio, Destiny's Child was tapped to record the theme song for the film version of *Charlie's Angels*; released as a single in October, "Independent Women, Pt. 1" raced up the charts and spent an astounding 11 weeks at number one. Destiny's Child was now indisputable superstars, the biggest female R&B group on the scene, and they quickly began work on a new album to capitalize. In the meantime, toward the end of 2000, Roberson and Luckett dropped the portion of their lawsuit aimed at Rowland and Knowles in exchange for a settlement, though they continued to pursue action against Knowles' father; as part of the agreement, both sides were prohibited from ripping each other publicly.

Beyoncé Knowles had long since emerged as the group's focal point, and on the third Destiny's Child album, she assumed more control than ever before, taking a greater hand in writing the material and even producing some of the record herself. While recording sessions were going on, Rowland released the first Destiny's Child solo track; "Angel" appeared on the soundtrack of Chris Rock's *Down to Earth*. Former members Roberson and Luckett also announced the formation of a trio called, coincidentally, Angel, and Farrah Franklin set about starting a solo career.

Survivor—whose title was reportedly inspired by a DJ's crack about Destiny's Child members voting one another off the island, much like the popular CBS reality series—hit stores in the spring of 2001, and entered the charts at number one. The first two singles, "Survivor" and "Bootylicious," were predictably huge hits, with the latter becoming the group's fourth number-one pop single. A cover of Andy Gibb's "Emotion" was also successful, albeit less so, and *Survivor* sold well—over four-million copies—but not as well as its predecessor. Toward the end of the year, the group released a holiday album, *8 Days of Christmas*, and announced plans for a series of side projects, including solo albums from all three members (to be staggered over the next year and a half, so as to avoid competition). In early 2002, shortly after *This Is the Remix* was released to tide fans over, Roberson and Luckett sued the group again, claiming that some of the lyrics in "Survivor" made reference to them (in violation of the earlier lawsuit settlement). Meanwhile, the first Destiny's Child solo album was released in April; Michelle Williams' all-gospel project *Heart to Yours*, which featured a duet with gospel legend Shirley Caesar. Meanwhile, Beyoncé Knowles won a leading role opposite Mike Myers in the third Austin Powers film *Goldmember*, playing blaxploitation-style heroine Foxy Cleopatra; her first solo single, the Neptunes-produced "Work It Out," appeared on the soundtrack. *—Steve Huey*

Destiny's Child / Feb. 17, 1998 / Columbia ♦♦♦♦
Destiny's Child isn't quite just another debut album from an R&B girl-group. The quartet worked with Wyclef Jean and Jermaine Dupri among others, and their voices sound beautiful together. Still, much of the album sounds indistinguishable from all the other female groups out there. When Destiny's Child does sound different, as on the single "No, No, No (Part II)," they're more than competent. *—John Bush*

• **The Writing's on the Wall** / Jul. 27, 1999 / Columbia ♦♦♦♦
With their second album, *Writing's on the Wall*, Destiny's Child still suffers from slightly uneven songwriting, but it's nevertheless an assured step forward from the girl group. Not only are they maturing as vocalists, they are fortunate to work with such skilled, talented producers as Kevin "She'kspere" Biggs, Rodney Jerkins, Dwayne Wiggins, Chad Elliot, Daryl Simmons and Missy Elliott, who all give the quartet rich, varied music upon which to work their charm. So, even when the album fails to deliver memorable songs, it always sounds alluring, thanks to the perfect combination of vocalists and producers. *—Stephen Thomas Erlewine*

Survivor / May 1, 2001 / Columbia ♦♦♦
Nobody would have predicted that Destiny's Child would rule over the contemporary R&B scene in the beginning of the new millennium—not after "Bills, Bills, Bills" hit the top of the charts, not even after "Say My Name" became an anthem in 2000. But nobody challenged their position, so they reigned supreme in the early '00s, eventually inheriting the title of the great girl group of their era. Since they had a couple of pretty good singles, namely the aforementioned pair, most conceded them that position, particularly since they *seemed* more talented than their peers, but *Survivor*, their first album as full-fleged superstars—also their first album since most of the group disappeared due to managerial conflicts—is as contrived and calculated as a Mariah Carey record, only without the joy. This is a determined, bullheaded record, intent on proving Destiny's Child has artistic merit largely because the group survived internal strife. So, whatever pop kitsch references the title may have—and it's hard not to see it as an attempt to tap into the American public's insatiable love for CBS' brilliant reality TV show of the same name—the title is certainly heartfelt, as the members of Destiny's Child want to illustrate that they are indeed survivors. This doggedness may fit on occasion, as on "Independent Women, Pt. 1," the theme to *Charlie's Angels*, but it usually takes precedence over the music—such as on the title track, a flat-out terrible song and the worst the group has ever recorded. "Survivor" is painfully labored, stuttering over a halting melody that Beyoncé Knowles breathlessly pushes to absolutely nowhere, working it so hard that it's difficult to listen. Unfortunately, that pattern repeats itself way too often on *Survivor*, as the group undercuts its seductive mainstream R&B with repellent pandering and naked ambition. This isn't even the case where you can rely on the label and its cohorts to find the best

tunes for the radio, since the moments where Destiny's Child sounds the best are when the group is not vying for airplay. When the group swings for the bleachers, Beyoncé oversells the song, rivaling Christina Aguilera in the diva sweepstakes. There are moments where the group makes it work, but this is a truly uneven record, bouncing between appealing midtempo soul numbers and hard-sell feminist anthems, where the ambition of Beyoncé and her cohorts is too naked. You can hear them work on "Nasty Girl," as they appropriate the theme from Salt-N-Pepa's "Push It," then inexplicably borrowing "Tarzan Boy" for the chorus. You can hear them trying to take Andy Gibb's "Emotion" slow, attempting to give it emotional resonance, yet such heartfelt overtures are toppled by the arrogant "Gospel Medley," where their secular pyrotechnics sound mannered, not inspired. Each of these are intended to give Destiny's Child a different level of depth—a pancultural, knowing appropriation of pop's past, balanced by a chart-savvy cover of a pop classic, plus a showy display of prowess. Each of these steps are calculated, as is the album itself. It's a record that tries to be a bold statement of purpose, but winds up feeling forced and artificial. *—Stephen Thomas Erlewine*

This Is the Remix / Mar. 12, 2002 / Columbia ♦♦♦♦
Striking while the iron is hot, Destiny's Child presents its third full-length release in less than a year, following *Survivor* (May 2001) and *8 Days of Christmas* (October 2001). An album of remixes is a profit-taking exercise by definition, but one needs only to gaze back a few weeks from this disc's release to Jennifer Lopez's *J to the L-O! The Remixes*, which went straight in at number one, to see that the profits can be considerable. And in this case, they deserve to be. Destiny's Child ascended to superstar status in 1999-2000 behind a series of well-produced number one hits that gave them the opportunity to trumpet female self-assertion in a material world. In contrast to TLC, the more street-savvy girl group whose niche they usurped, they were a triumph of packaging over musical substance, an appropriate focus at a time when teen pop was ascendant. At first glance, *This Is the Remix* does not retreat from that stance; the singers appear on the cover applying makeup. And certainly the album is all about packaging—actually, repackaging. Typically, the word "remix" is far too modest to describe what such knob twiddlers as the Neptunes, Rockwilder, and Timbaland have undertaken. Retaining only the barest bones of the original recordings, if that, they have built wholly new musical tracks and brought in a bevy of guests, including Wyclef Jean, Da Brat, Jermaine Dupri, and Lil Bow Wow, and for the most part the results are all to the good. Fans may buy this album thinking of it as a de facto greatest-hits set, but if so they will be surprised to find that, for example, Rockwilder's take on "Bootylicious" sounds almost nothing like the version they heard on the radio. And these versions aren't only different; usually, they're better than the originals. *—William Ruhlmann*

The Detroit Emeralds

f. 1968, Little Rock, AK
Group / Soul
Abrim, Ivory, Cleophus, and Raymond Tilmon formed the Detroit Emeralds in the '60s. They were actually a Little Rock vocal group. They had some success with "Show Time" for Ric-Tic in 1968, but by 1970 were down to a trio, with Abrim and Ivory Tilmon and James Mitchell. They stayed that way for a long run on Westbound that yielded R&B hits "Do Me Right," "You Want It, You Got It," and "Baby Let Me Take You (In My Arms)" in 1971 and 1972, as well as "You're Gettin' a Little Too Smart" in 1973. They expanded the roster to a quartet in 1977, but with three new members. Abrim Tilmon was now joined by Paul Riser, Johnny Allen, and Maurice King. Their backing band from 1971 to 1973 was Chapter 8. Though many regard "Feel the Need" as their best song, it was far from a hit, although it was their last chart entry in 1977.

James Mitchell and Marvin Wills teamed to form an offshoot group, the Floaters, in 1977. Carl Johnson was Abe Tilmon's replacement in the Emeralds, with Abe Tilmon forming his own Detroit Emeralds. Each group stayed active on the oldies and cabaret circuit during the '70s and '80s. Michael Henderson, then a 13-year-old, was one of their members for a short time. *—Ron Wynn*

Do Me Right / 1971 / Westbound ♦♦♦

You Want It, You Got It / 1972 / Westbound ♦♦♦♦
The Detroit Emeralds are reminiscent of funky the Four Tops; while their lead didn't have Levi Stubbs' mesmerizing baritone, their music had a similar feel. Centered around their R&B hit "You Want It, You Got It," this LP of the same title illustrates another side of Detroit. The title track smokes from the first second to the fade. "Feel the Need in Me" is slower but as funky—no doubt their roots (Little Rock, AR) gave the guys that Southern slant that was absent from most Detroit recordings. The most charming cut for many is "Baby Let Me Take You (In My Arms)" with its sloop beat and cool strutting rhythms. A few ballads are mixed with dancers like "I Bet You Get the One You Love" for a well-rounded set. An English recording firm has reissued this LP with another Detroit Emeralds LP, *Do Me Right*. Two for the price of one. *—Andrew Hamilton*

Feel the Need / 1973 / Westbound ♦♦♦♦♦

● **Greatest Hits** / 1998 / Westbound ♦♦♦♦♦
Westbound's *Greatest Hits* collects all of the highlights from the Detroit Emeralds' '70s recordings, including the U.K. hits "Feel the Need in Me," "You Want It You Got It" and "I Think of You," making it the definitive career overview of this underrated soul group. *—Stephen Thomas Erlewine*

Do Me Right/You Want It, You Got It / Jun. 30, 1998 / Westbound ♦♦♦
The first two albums by the Detroit Emeralds—one of Detroit's finest and most unheralded vocal groups—are here burned on one CD. Thank you technology. These 22 tracks contain just the right mixture of uptown cool and Southern soul to please most everybody. Their hits "Do Me Right," "You Want It You Got It," and "Baby Let Me Take You (In My Arms)" are the cream, but "Wear This Ring (With Love)," "Feel the Need in Me," "I Bet You Get the One You Love" (also done by the Floaters), John Lennon/Paul McCartney's "And I Love Her," and others also work. *—Andrew Hamilton*

William DeVaughn

b. 1948, Washington, D.C.
Vocals / Soul, Smooth Soul
Singer/songwriter/guitarist William DeVaughn had a million-seller the first time out with his inspiring "Be Thankful for What You Got." Those who first heard the smooth track thought it was a new record from Curtis Mayfield. DeVaughn's high tenor does bear some resemblance to Mayfield's and the simple, encouraging lyrics were similar to the kind found in the catalog of the Impressions leader. "Be Thankful for What You Got" also found its way onto the playlist of some gospel radio programs. One of the lyrics: "Diamond in the back/sunroof top/digging the scene with a gangster lean" became a catchphrase and appeared in numerous rap/hip hop records of the '90s.

The Washington, D.C. native was working for the government when he paid $900 for a recording session at Philadelphia's Omega Sound Inc. (basically a "vanity record" operation). Usually the results of such efforts are anything but star-making, but Omega featured the services of MFSB's main rhythm section (guitarist Norman Harris, drummer Earl Young, bassist Ron Baker, and vibist Vince Montana). Omega vice-president Frank Fioravanti was impressed with the record and began shopping it around to various labels.

Finally issued on Wes Farrell's Roxbury imprint and produced by Frank Fioravanti and arranger John Davis, "Be Thankful for What You Got" sold nearly two-million copies, gliding up to the top of the R&B charts and number-four pop in spring 1974. The album of the same name had an almost religious tone (DeVaughn was a Jehovah's Witness) and yielded several radio-aired LP tracks: "Give the Little Man a Great Big Hand" (the third single), "We Are His Children," "Sing a Love Song," and "You Can Do It." The second single, "Blood Is Thicker Than Water," made it to number-ten R&B and number-43 pop in summer 1974. Akin to the post-heyday performances of a converted Al Green, DeVaughn preached to and admonished his audience from the stage. He lost interest in the music business not long after, though he did remake "Be Thankful for What You Got" for TEC and charted again with the Top 40 R&B hit "Figures Can't Calculate" in summer 1980 for the label. *—Ed Hogan*

Be Thankful for What You Got / 1974 / Collectables ♦♦♦
William DeVaughn, a native of Washington, D.C., beat the odds when "Be Thankful for What You Got," scaled the charts and sold a million copies. You see, DeVaughn paid for the session. All artists who signed with Omega Productions paid to record. The title track, with its cool, shuffling beat and Biblical-influenced lyrics, was the summer jam of 1974. "Diamond in the back/sunroof top/digging the scene with a gangster lean" was the buzz phrase. The rest of the songs are charming and have merit, but lack the impact and timing of the title track. *—Andrew Hamilton*

Figures Can't Calculate / 1980 / T.E.C. Tones ♦♦♦♦
After a six-year sabbatical from recording to spread the word of Jehovah, William Devaughn returns with new found strength and creativity. This completely satisfying album includes his Number-37 hit "Figures Can't Calculate," a splendid Jerry Butler-ish "Love Comes So Easy," a tender "You Send Me," an update of his monster "Be Thankful For What You Got," where he uncannily mimics Curtis Mayfield, and the disco-ish "Boogie Dan"—a quality stepper. Too bad DeVaughn never got his head right for the secular scene. The D.C. native had so much to offer. This is even better than his enjoyable debut album. *—Andrew Hamilton*

● **Be Thankful for What You Got/Figures Can't Calculate** / 1995 / Sequel ♦♦♦♦♦

Terry Dexter

b. 1978
Vocals / Urban
R&B singer/songwriter Terry Dexter was raised in Detroit, joining her first group, the vocal trio Tristar, at age nine and staying with them until she was 14. In high school, she found occasional session work, including singing backup for Simply Red. After graduating, she attended the University of Michigan for a year, but left when she was signed to a recording contract by University Music Entertainment, which released her debut album, *Terry Dexter*, through Warner Bros. in 1999. Her debut single, "Better Than Me," made the R&B charts. *—William Ruhlmann*

● **Terry Dexter** / Jul. 13, 1999 / Warner Bros. ♦♦♦
Terry Dexter is a year older than Brandy and two years older than Monica, which makes her, at 21 when her debut album was released, already at a disadvantage in competing for the young R&B diva crown. Like her better known peers, she sings songs of romantic discord and devotion over generally slow, prominent percussion tracks, providing the lead variations over repetitive choral parts. She is co-credited as a songwriter on several of the songs, including the lead-off single "Better Than Me," but that doesn't make them any more distinctive. Eight different producers contribute, including Jazze Pha and, on four of 11 tracks, Darryl "Day" Pearson, and they successfully give Dexter a contemporary R&B sound that apes much of what other singers of her ilk are wailing over. And she wails competently, but no more so than any other youthful Mariah Carey wannabe on the market. *—William Ruhlmann*

Tracey Dey

Vocals / Girl Group
One of the more talented girl group-styled solo singers of the 1960s who never got a big hit, Tracey Dey never even made the Top 50, although three of her singles got to lower chart positions. Her "I Won't Tell" is one of the top ten non-hit girl group singles of all time, with its great catchy chorus, full stomping production, surprise false ending, and assertive singing. "I Won't Tell," like several of Dey's singles, was written by Bob Crewe and Bob Gaudio, the same team responsible for penning most of the Four Seasons'

big hits. Crewe also helped write some of Dey's singles even when Gaudio wasn't involved, and certainly tried to give Dey a shot, producing discs for her on Vee-Jay, Liberty, and Amy.

Dey was certainly better than most girl group singers of the time that didn't make it, and better than some that did, with a full and mature voice. She and Crewe didn't get that one piece of outstanding material that might have set her on course for a successful career, though, and when they did (with "I Won't Tell") it didn't catch on as it should have. Much of Dey's 1960s material is available on a hard-to-find CD that also includes tracks by one-shot early-'60s singer Marcie Blane. *—Richie Unterberger*

- **Marcie Blane Together With Tracey Dey** / Missing ♦♦♦

Hard-to-find, probably unauthorized CD combines 12 tracks by Blane with 13 by the even more obscure 1960s girl-group-style vocalist Tracey Dey. Nothing else has the hooks that made "Bobby's Girl" (which is here, of course) a hit, and Blane's slight, girlish voice doesn't make the material into anything more than it is. If you're a huge 1960s girl group/girl singer fan, though, it's certainly representative of the sound of an era, with production that fairly screams 1962-1963—not quite part of the teen-idol era, but not quite as modern as Phil Spector (or even the Shirelles) either. "She'll Break the String" and "After the Laughter" are the only tunes that would even cut the ice as items on compilations of decent or half-decent overlooked girl-group recordings; the rest are pretty meaningless. Tracey Dey's half of the CD, incidentally, is considerably better, with some fairly good obscure girl group-style singles (such as "I Won't Tell"), which could tip the balance in favor of purchase if you collect this genre. *—Richie Unterberger*

Diamond Joe

Vocals / New Orleans R&B, R&B

Virtually nothing is known of this singer, whose double-sided single "Moanin' and Screamin' Pts. 1 and 2," for Minit during the early '60s, is a killer track. Joe's agonized vocal performance, almost operatic in its depth, sung in front of a surprisingly restrained female chorus and a basic piano blues with drums and bass accompaniment, should have earned him a shot at an album. *—Bruce Eder*

The Diamonds

f. 1953, Ontario, Canada, **db.** 1962

Group / Doo Wop, R&B

One of the leading cover groups of the mid-'50s, the Diamonds adapted current R&B hits into pop gold of their own. Hailing from Toronto, the Canadian quartet (consisting of Ted Kowalski, Phil Leavitt, Bill Reed and Dave Somerville) signed with Mercury in 1955 and immediately zoomed up pop playlists with covers of the Teenagers' "Why Do Fools Fall in Love," The Willows' "Church Bells May Ring," and their biggest hit of all, a sanitized version of the Gladiolas hit "Little Darlin'." Fronted by David Somerville, the quartet hit with an original, the smooth dance outing "The Stroll." After weathering major personnel changes, the Diamonds notched their last hit in 1961. Somerville remained active as a solo artist for a time, and the Diamonds often toured the oldies scene. *—Bill Dahl*

- **The Best of the Diamonds: The Mercury Years** / 1996 / Mercury ♦♦♦♦♦

Here are 22 tracks from 1956-1961, including most of their hit singles (the 1958 Top 20 entry, "Kathy-O," is oddly missing). "Little Darlin'" and "The Stroll" are quite obviously the class of the bunch, and there's a higher quantity of inferior pop-inclined covers of R&B/rock numbers than you might remember ("Why Do Fools Fall in Love," "Words of Love," "Silhouettes," "The Church Bells May Ring"). It's certainly the collection of choice, though, including a 1959 Australian single that was previously unavailable in the U.S., and the previously unreleased 1961 track "Chimes in My Heart" (written by Bill Medley of the Righteous Brothers). *—Richie Unterberger*

Bo Diddley (Ellas Otha Bates McDaniels)

b. Dec. 30, 1928, McComb, MS

Vocals, Guitar, Violin / Rock & Roll, R&B, Electric Chicago Blues

He only had a few hits in the 1950s and early '60s, but as Bo Diddley sang, "You Can't Judge a Book by Its Cover." You can't judge an artist by his chart success, either, and Diddley produced greater and more influential music than all but a handful of the best early rockers. The Bo Diddley beat—bomp, ba-bomp-bomp, bomp-bomp—is one of rock & roll's bedrock rhythms, showing up in the work of Buddy Holly, the Rolling Stones, and even pop-garage knock-offs like the Strangeloves' 1965 hit "I Want Candy." Diddley's hypnotic rhythmic attack and declamatory, boasting vocals stretched back as far as Africa for their roots, and looked as far into the future as rap. His trademark otherworldly vibrating, fuzzy guitar tone did much to expand the instrument's power and range. But even more important, Bo's bounce was fun and irresistibly rocking, with a wisecracking, jiving tone that epitomized rock & roll at its most humorously outlandish and freewheeling.

Before taking up blues and R&B, Diddley had actually studied classical violin, but shifted gears after hearing John Lee Hooker. In the early '50s, he began playing with his longtime partner, maraca player Jerome Green, to get what Bo's called "that freight train sound." Billy Boy Arnold, a fine blues harmonica player and singer in his own right, was also playing with Diddley when the guitarist got a deal with Chess in the mid-'50s (after being turned down by rival Chicago label Vee-Jay). His very first single, "Bo Diddley"/"I'm a Man" (1955), was a double-sided monster. The A-side was soaked with futuristic waves of tremolo guitar, set to an ageless nursery rhyme; the flip was a bump-and-grind, harmonica-driven shuffle, based around a devastating blues riff. But the result was not exactly blues, or even straight R&B, but a new kind of guitar-based rock & roll, soaked in the blues and R&B, but owing allegiance to neither.

Diddley was never a top seller on the order of his Chess rival Chuck Berry, but over the next half-dozen or so years, he'd produce a catalog of classics that rival Berry's in quality. "You Don't Love Me," "Diddley Daddy," "Pretty Thing," "Diddy Wah Diddy," "Who Do You Love?," "Mona," "Road Runner," "You Can't Judge a Book By Its Cover"—all are stone-cold standards of early, riff-driven rock & roll at its funkiest. Oddly enough, his only Top 20 pop hit was an atypical, absurd back-and-forth rap between him and Jerome Green, "Say Man," that came about almost by accident as the pair were fooling around in the studio. As a live performer, Diddley was galvanizing, using his trademark square guitars and distorted amplification to produce new sounds that anticipated the innovations of '60s guitarists like Jimi Hendrix. In Great Britain, he was revered as a giant on the order of Chuck Berry and Muddy Waters. The Rolling Stones in particular borrowed a lot from Bo's rhythms and attitude in their early days, although they only officially covered a couple of his tunes, "Mona" and "I'm Alright." Other British R&B groups like the Yardbirds, Animals, and Pretty Things also covered Diddley standards in their early days. Buddy Holly covered "Bo Diddley" and used a modified Bo Diddley beat on "Not Fade Away"; when the Stones gave the song the full-on Bo treatment (complete with shaking maracas), the result was their first big British hit.

The British Invasion helped increase the public's awareness of Diddley's importance, and ever since then he's been a popular live act. Sadly, though, his career as a recording artist—in commercial and artistic terms—was over by the time the Beatles and Stones hit America. He'd record with ongoing and declining frequency, but after 1963, he'd never write or record any original material on par with his early classics. Whether he'd spent his muse, or just felt he could coast on his laurels, is hard to say. But he remains a vital part of the collective rock & roll consciousness, occasionally reaching wider visibility via a 1979 tour with the Clash, a cameo role in the film *Trading Places*, a late-'80s tour with Ronnie Wood, and a 1989 television commercial for sports shoes with star athlete Bo Jackson. *—Richie Unterberger*

Bo Diddley / 1957 / Chess ♦♦♦♦♦

For anyone who wants to play rock & roll, *real* rock & roll, this is one of the few records that you really need. Along with Chuck Berry, Elvis, Little Richard, Jerry Lee Lewis, Muddy Waters, B.B. King, and a few select others, Bo Diddley was one of the founders of the form—and he did it like no other. Diddley had only one real style, that being the Bo Diddley beat: a syncopated, rhythmic drive, loaded with tremolo. There are 12 examples of it on this record, and that is about all you need. It's one of those records that, after listening to just a few cuts, will find you tapping the beats on every available surface. Diddley's guitar and vocals have a gruff feeling that recalls bluesmen such as Waters, yet he has his own style. Buttressed by drums, funky piano, and usually maracas, it's absolutely infectious. This is one of the greatest rock sounds that you're likely to hear, and it's all on this one record, too. *—Matthew Greenwald*

Have Guitar, Will Travel / 1959 / Chess ♦♦♦♦

Amazingly, Bo Diddley's third album—containing classics such as "Cops and Robbers," "Run Diddley Daddy," and "Mona (I Need You Baby)"—has only been reissued on vinyl, and even that's out of print. More than one British Invasion band learned what they needed to know about American rock & roll from the songs on this record (the Stones cut "Cops and Robbers" at their earliest recording session, and later released a killer version of "Mona," though the most interesting British version of the latter was done by an all-girl band with an attitude called the Liverbirds). This record is every bit as raunchy as Diddley's first two albums (the guitars may even be cruncheir, and the singing shows more range), and has more than enough to recommend it to collectors and fans. This is the album that began the funny cover photos on Diddley's records. *—Bruce Eder*

Bo Diddley in the Spotlight / 1960 / Chess ♦♦♦♦

As with Bo Diddley's first five albums (except *Have Guitar, Will Travel*), the most important cuts (but not all the good ones) off of this album have been included on *The Chess Box* from MCA, which doesn't mean that this record isn't a good separate issue, just somewhat redundant if you have the box. There are surprises from these 1960-vintage recordings, including the languid, Caribbean-sounding "Limber"; the soft, romantic "Love Me"; the doo wop-style "Deed and Deed I Do"; the loping "Walkin' and Talkin'"; upbeat, gospel-tinged rockers such as "Let Me In" interspersed with the hot and raunchy "Road Runner," "The Story of Bo Diddley," "Craw-Dad" (a genuine diamond in the rough), and "Signifying Blues"; and solid instrumentals like "Scuttle Bug" (really "Live My Life" with the vocals removed and Otis Spann overdubbed on piano) that make this record more than worthwhile. *—Bruce Eder*

Bo Diddley Is a Gunslinger / 1961 / Chess ♦♦♦♦

Not only does it sport one of the most striking album covers of its era (Diddley decked out in cowboy finery, about to get the drop on some unfortunate varmint with one of his fieriest guitars lying at his feet), this 1961 album contains some fine music. The title track continues the legend of you-know-who, while "Ride on Josephine" and "Cadillac" rock like hell (and Ed Sullivan must have been glad to see that Diddley finally learned "Sixteen Tons"). Two bonus cuts, "Working Man" and "Do What I Say," make this one a must. *—Bill Dahl*

Bo Diddley Is a Lover / 1961 / Checker ♦♦♦♦

There's not a bad song on this long-forgotten album; in fact, it's all good, and so little of it has been reissued that it's a crime. There are a lot of familiar moments here: Diddley slips most effectively into his "Say Man" groove on "Bo's Vacation"; plays some serious Chicago blues on "Call Me (Bo's Blues)" and makes it count; invades Chuck Berry territory by way of Howlin' Wolf on the window-rattling "Hong Kong Mississippi" (a track so riveting and funny, and so rippling in superb guitar work, it makes this album worthwhile on its own); bounces back to his signature beat on the title song, the hysterically funny autobiographical "Bo Diddley Is Loose," "Quick Draw," "Back Home," and "Not Guilty" (a song that deserves enshrinement as one of Diddley's best); and slips into a romantic groove on "You're Looking Good." Find it, buy it, and savor it. *—Bruce Eder*

Bo Diddley's a Twister / 1962 / Checker ♦♦♦

Bo Diddley & Company / 1962 / Checker ♦♦♦♦

This album is almost worth owning just for the cover photo of Bo and the Duchess, aka Norma-Jean Wofford, each with their axe. What makes it really cool, though, is the music, which is among the best of Bo's 1960s output. "Bo's a Lumberjack" is one of the most ferociously sexual and funny signature songs Bo ever cut, "(Extra, Read All About It) Ben" is a sort of sideways version of "Say Man," with a rollicking beat and very effective use of piano in the backing band, with a grim subject matter handled in a humorous manner, and "Help Out" is one of Bo's better guitar workouts, with the man getting lots of help from the Duchess. It was records like this that helped keep Bo's reputation alive in England when Americans stopped buying his stuff. "Met You on a Saturday" is an unusual slow, romantic number from Bo, very much in a late-'50s style that was probably a few years late to capture anyone's imagination. Other material, like "Diana" (a reworking of "Hey Bo Diddley") and "Little Girl" is less compelling but still solid rock & roll, as are "Gimme Gimme," "Same Old Thing," "Met You on a Saturday," "Put the Shoes on Willie" (written by Earl Hooker), and "Pretty Girl." The latter has a great chorus, and turned up in the repertories of several British Invasion bands. *—Bruce Eder*

Hey! Bo Diddley / 1962 / Chess ♦♦♦

Bo's music was beginning to slip in sales—though he remained a popular concert act—when Chess released this album in the summer of 1962. "I Can Tell," written by Samuel Smith, showed Bo trying out a slower, more seductively soulful sound, a whole four-and-a-half-minutes long—it is different, though not very distinguished. "Bo's Twist" isn't much more impressive, a fairly standard instrumental with an unusually grungy (like you were expecting Julian Bream) guitar sound, with the first prominent appearance of an organ in the backing of a Bo Diddley record; "Sad Sack" is a somewhat more successful instrumental. "Mr. Kruschev" is one of the funniest, most delightfully nonsensical pieces of topical songwriting Bo ever engaged in, writing about wanting to go into the army and go over to see the Soviet leader and get him to stop nuclear testing, to a background of "Hut, two—three four!" "You All Green" is first-rate Bo, and deserved to be anthologized somewhere. "You Can't Judge a Book By the Cover" was the one standard from the album, but other tracks deserving of better exposure include "Bo's Bounce" and "Who May Your Lover Be," which takes off from Howlin' Wolf's "Moaning at Midnight," recasting it in a Bo Diddley beat, with Bo sounding a lot like Wolf here, and "Give Me a Break (Man)," which is a very animated impromptu guitar jam. The album filler tracks include "Mama Don't Allow No Twistin'," Bo's take on "Mama Don't Like Music," a song that was old when C&W/novelty singer Smiley Burnette covered it successfully in the 1930s, "Babes in the Woods" (featuring a backing chorus mimicking the doo wop parody "Get a Job") and "Diddling," a routine Bo instrumental. *—Bruce Eder*

Surfin' With Bo Diddley / 1963 / Checker ♦♦

Bo Diddley's Beach Party / 1963 / Checker ♦♦♦♦♦

A blistering live album, especially in genuine mono (the re-channeled stereo is barely passable)—and quite simply the finest live rock & roll album of its era, cut live by Diddley and band at Myrtle Beach, SC, on July 5 and 6, 1963. From the opening track (erroneously listed as "Memphis" and credited to Chuck Berry as composer) to the final note, this is some of the loudest, raunchiest guitar-based rock & roll ever preserved. It also bears an uncanny resemblance to the sound that the Rolling Stones achieved on their own *Got Live If You Want It*, which only shows how much the Stones learned from Diddley. Highlights include "Gunslinger," "Hey Bo Diddley," "Road Runner," and "I'm All Right." The sound doesn't necessarily translate ideally to compact disc, but that shouldn't dissuade anyone. *—Bruce Eder & Cub Koda*

Two Great Guitars / 1964 / MCA ♦♦

Diddley shared this 1964 Chess album with his labelmate Chuck Berry. They duel it out on a pair of incredibly lengthy instrumentals (brilliantly titled "Chuck's Beat" and "Bo's Beat") that get tiresome long before they run their full course. Better (and briefer) are two numbers where they don't cross paths—Diddley's rendering of "When the Saints Go Marching In" and Berry's amazing country breakdown "Liverpool Drive." A couple of bonus Bo Diddley sides ("Stay Sharp" and "Stinkey") also make this digital reincarnation worth acquiring. *—Bill Dahl*

Hey, Good Lookin' / Apr. 1965 / Checker ♦♦♦

One of Bo's least known albums, mostly recorded in April of 1964 and released a year later, at the point when none of his records were selling in America. With an edgy, raunchy sound and modern record techniques (it's in stereo), Bo and band come up with a solid '60s version of his original sound. The title track is a real jewel, featuring Jerome Green on the maracas and Lafayette Leake on the piano. "Mama Keep Your Big Mouth Shut" isn't a bad soul-styled number, with Bo abandoning his standard beat in favor of a smoother, more Motown-like sound. He tries for a similar sound on "I Wonder Why (People Don't Like Me)" and "Brother Bear." In addition to the title track (which is *not* the Hank Williams tune), the Bo Diddley beat gets a workout on "La La La," "Rain Man," and "Bo Diddley's Hoot'nanny." Bo gets to have some real fun on "London Stomp," his commentary on the sudden fashionability of British rock & roll, parodying the accents and attitudes of most of the bands that he encountered on his visit to England in October of 1963. Other tracks sound like they'd have worked well as part of extended jams of the kind that Bo did on stage—"Yeah Yeah Yeah," in particular, could've come from the middle of one of Bo's 15-minute shuffle-and-chant workouts, and would've been great in such a setting, although here, as a free-standing 2:25 track it's a little weak. There is some filler here, most notably "Let's Walk A While" and "Rooster Stew," but that can be forgiven in view of the strength of the rest of the material. *—Bruce Eder*

500% More Man / 1965 / Checker ♦♦♦♦

By the end of 1965, Bo was making a conscious effort to recapture both the black listenership that had deserted him and the white audience that was buying all of those soul records. Unfortunately, neither he nor Chess knew exactly how to go about it, and the result was another good album largely unheard by the public. The title track marks Bo's return to the Muddy Waters beat that he appropriated for "I'm a Man" (and that Muddy took back in "Mannish Boy") a decade earlier, and is one of Bo's greatest '60s sides. "Greasy Spoon" mentions Muddy amid its comical description of the offerings of a particularly unclean eatery (it's amazing when you think of it—ten years recording in Chicago, and longer than that living there, and Bo was still nearly as much a country blues artist as he was when he started). "Let Me Pass" is a hot number with an infectious beat and some very funny lyrics, and Bo playing some delectable guitar. "Stop My Monkey," featuring Bo backed by the singing group the Cookies, has him again trying for a commercial soul sound in a Motown vein, and "Tonight Is Ours" is one of Bo's most heartfelt romantic numbers, with the Cookies singing their hearts out while Bo tries his hand at a song that might've fit well on either of the first two albums by the Miracles, while "Hey, Red Riding Hood" brought back the Bo Diddley beat for another go around, this time with delightfully raunchy lyrics amid crisper textures and a much finer sound than ever before. "Hey's So Mad" is pretty lackluster except for the guitar break, but "Root Hoot" should've been more widely heard than it was, being one of Bo's more infectious chant-based songs. "Corn Bread" has a neatly stinging, Slim Harpo-type lead guitar sound, and is overall an okay instrumental. And then there's "Soul Food," another great Bo Diddley rocker lost in the middle of the 1960s soul boom—Bo is so smooth, impassioned, sexy, and raw, and the Cookies sound so good backing him to one of his best instrumental tracks ever, that the fact this song was never a hit is a crime. By 1965, however, nobody in America was buying his records, even ones like this filled to bursting with good music and good humor, and even the British were beginning to lose interest in Bo's latest records. This was among Bo's last sessions with the Duchess, and the group he's using is more or less the studio equivalent of the band he's seen with in The Big TNT Show (aka That Was Rock). *—Bruce Eder*

The Originator / 1966 / Checker ♦♦♦♦

By 1966, Bo Diddley was a long way from chart success in America, and *The Originator* was to be his last official album for four years (in the interim he would appear on the two Chess "Super Blues" all-star jam albums). Strangely enough, this is also one of his best albums, mostly comprised of rare early 1960s singles ("Pills") and B-sides and filled out with some fun new recordings ("Yakky Doodle"). This record is a bit of a throwback compared with *500% More Man*, which preceded it by nearly a year, representing the Bo Diddley of the early 1960s—all of the material has the signature beat and guitar, or other virtues to recommend it, including some very high spirits. *—Bruce Eder*

The Black Gladiator / Jun. 1970 / Checker ♦♦

It was four years between the release of Bo's last album of all new cuts, *500% More Man*, and this album, during which time he'd spent time recording with Chess's top bluesmen, Muddy Waters and Howlin' Wolf. The death of Leonard Chess in October of 1969 resulted in the sale of the label to the GRT corporation, and cost the company what little artistic guidance it had. The result was *The Black Gladiator*, an attempt to reshape Bo into a funk artist, in the manner of Sly and the Family Stone. As an experiment it's understandable, and Bo tries very hard (even making another song-length sexual boast on "You, Bo Diddley," which also ends with a great guitar/organ duet between Bo and Bobby Alexis), but he finally fails to find a groove that works. Despite some good guitar here and there, this record falls into the same category as Muddy's *Electric Mud* and *After the Rain* albums and Howlin' Wolf's *New Album*, attempts to transform each into a psychedelic rocker. "Power House" is a pretty good cut, using a modified Muddy Waters-"I'm a Man"/"Mannish Boy" beat and lyrics. Much of the rest is for absolute completists only, however. *—Bruce Eder*

Another Dimension / 1971 / Chess ♦♦

By the end of 1970, most of Bo Diddley's income was derived from his concert work, primarily as an "oldies" act in rock & roll revival shows such as the Toronto concert where he shared a stage with the Plastic Ono Band. But he and Chess believed there was still a way for him to try and reach a wider, more contemporary audience. This album was the result, a valiant effort to update Bo Diddley's sound and image, somewhat in the vein of Muddy Waters' *Electric Mud* only a few years later and very slightly more successful in that quest, in the sense of yielding one lasting addition to Bo's repertory. Relevance was the key word, not only in the song selection, which includes three John Fogerty songs ("Lodi," "Bad Moon Rising," "Down on the Corner") and covers of numbers by the Band and Elton John, but a new song entitled "Pollution" that tries hard to integrate the Bo Diddley beat into a message piece—it's a good try, but nothing on this record (including "Pollution") was going to challenge Marvin Gaye's *What's Going On* for primacy or effectiveness. The record starts off well enough, with a superb, deeply soulful cover of Al Kooper's "I Love You More Than You'll Ever Know," and a decent rendition of "The Shape I'm In." But two of the Fogerty covers ("Lodi" is the only one that sort of works) are embarrassing, with the girlie chorus killing "Bad Moon Rising." And "Bad Side of the Moon" was a waste of studio time. One song from this album has remained part of Bo's concert set for decades, however—"I Said Shutup Woman," which has the most traditional sound of anything on *Another Dimension*. *—Bruce Eder*

Where It All Began / 1972 / Chess ♦♦♦

Johnny Otis and Pete Welding produced this surprisingly successful soul effort by Bo, which succeeded in reshaping his sound, not as a Sly Stewart wannabe or a lounge act covering Creedence Clearwater Revival hits. Bo at least sounds comfortable and natural doing songs like "Look At Grandma" and "Woman," and the latter is a pretty damn good song—Bo finally emerged as a soul singer in his own right, and it worked, artistically at least. "Hey Jerome" even recalled tracks like "Say Man" in a not unflattering light. Unfortunately, none of this mattered to the people who still cared about Bo Diddley—they wanted the beat and the old sound, which was present here, on "I've Had It Hard" and the extraordinary "Bo Diddley-itis," but not in the kind of quantity they craved, amid the more modern sounds; and they wanted the old songs, which he gave them in concert. And it all came so late in the day, not only in terms of Bo's identification as anything but an oldies act but the history of Chess Records (now subsumed into the GRT corporate operation, the Chess imprint having no meaning or significance), that *Where It All Began* vanished from sight leaving scarcely a trace or a ripple on the charts. *—Bruce Eder*

☆ **Bo Diddley/Go Bo Diddley** / 1986 / Chess ♦♦♦♦♦
Legendary guitarist, gifted songwriter, master of rhythm, snappy dresser—Bo Diddley is all these things and more, and this two-fer CD, which reissues Diddley's first two albums on one convenient compact disc, offers a solid introduction to this man's special brand of musical innovation. While anyone looking for a full overview of Diddley's career should obviously go elsewhere (*His Best (Chess 50th Anniversary Collection)* is a great one-stop shopping place for beginners), these 23 tunes serve up a young Bo Diddley at his raw and primal best, and confirm that right out of the box the guy didn't sound like anyone else in rock & roll. Between Diddley's hypnotic, rhythmic guitar lines; the implacable rattle of Jerome Green's maracas; the spacy echo that threatens to envelop everything around it; and the borderline surrealism of the lyrics (witness the updated "Mr. Bones" routine of "Say Man," the overpopulated family of "Say Bossman," or the supreme bad-ass-ism of "Who Do You Love"), this man's music existed in a world of its own, and while you might not want to live there, the one-hour tour offered on *Bo Diddley/Go Bo Diddley* makes it sound like a great place to take a vacation. In the interest of accuracy, this disc even includes the same take of "Dearest Darling" twice, since the tune managed to appear on both *Bo Diddley* and *Go Bo Diddley*; nice to know someone at Chess' reissue department was paying attention to the details. *—Mark Deming*

☆ **The Chess Box** / Jul. 26, 1990 / Chess ♦♦♦♦♦
Not every single track you'll ever want or need by the legendary shave-and-a-haircut rhythm R&B/rock pioneer, but a great place to begin. Two discs (45 songs) in a great big box with a nice accompanying booklet contain the groundbreaking introduction "Bo Diddley" (never again would he be referred to as Ellas McDaniel), its swaggering flipside "I'm a Man," the killer follow-ups "Diddley Daddy," "I'm Looking for a Woman," "Who Do You Love?," and "Hey Bo Diddley;" signifying street-corner humor ("Say Man"), piledriving rockers ("Road Runner," "She's Alright," "You Can't Judge a Book by Its Cover"), and numerous stunning examples of his daringly innovative guitar style. *—Bill Dahl*

Rare & Well Done / Sep. 10, 1991 / Chess ♦♦♦♦
Here are sixteen extreme rarities from the deepest recesses of the Chess vaults that date from 1955-1968. The grinding "She's Fine, She's Mine" and snarling "I'm Bad" are comparatively well known, at least to collectors; far more obscure are the previously unissued "Heart-O-Matic Love," "Cookie-Headed Diddley," and "Moon Baby." *—Bill Dahl*

Bo's Blues / 1993 / Ace ♦♦♦♦♦
This features 22 of Bo Diddley's best blues-oriented sides from the Chess catalog, including some rare stuff—the rip-roaring 1959 outing "Run Diddley Daddy," a jive-loaded "Cops and Robbers" from 1956 that features maraca shaker Jerome Green more than Diddley, and a surging "Down Home Special." If you think that everything Bo Diddley ever made has that same shave-and-a-haircut beat, this collection will set you straight! *—Bill Dahl*

The Chess Years / 1993 / Charly ♦♦♦♦♦
Bringing this box set home on the train, it started gyrating to a shave-and-a-haircut-two-bits beat on my lap... no, not really, but that would be a great TV ad for this release. Charly Records' *The Chess Years* has assembled most—though not quite all—of the music that the Originator recorded for Chess Records, which, unfortunately, means a lot of his lesser work as well—282 recordings, made between 1955 and 1974, on 12 CDs; looking at it is like staring across the Grand Canyon, except you *want* to jump into this if you have any sense. If the collection seems like overkill, that's because it is, and there's some poor material here from the late 1960s/early 1970s, when Bo was searching for a new commercial sound, although some of his later work isn't really bad—his covers of Al Kooper's "I Love You More Than You'll Ever Know" or the Band's "The Shape I'm In" from *Another Dimension* are soulful and moving, but just aren't what one buys a Bo Diddley album to hear (and we could've done without the girlie chorus on "Bad Moon Rising"). There are more than enough jewels—and jewels that are likely *never* to appear otherwise on compact disc—to attract serious rock & roll listeners, *if* you can swing the price, which is around $120. The highlights (which would be far more costly to find on vinyl today) include "Bo Meets the Monster," his catchy (and very funny) answer to "Purple People Eater"; "Here 'Tis," which became famous when covered by the Yardbirds, but only really comes to life in the hands of the Originator; the comical "Bucket," "Lazy Woman" and "Run Diddley Daddy"; the rousing, slashing "Puttentang"; the side-splittingly funny biographical song "All Together," a sort of sequel to "The Story of Bo Diddley"; the complete *Bo Diddley's Beach Party* album, and a handful of demos from the late 1960 sessions that yielded tracks for the *Bo Diddley Is a Twister* album. Additionally, the collection gives the listener a chance to see how Bo explored different variations on his sound, adapting it to doo wop, folk, and even calypso, all of which worked better than one would have expected, plus soul and funk, which didn't. The sessionography is very detailed and pretty cool, and the notes are among the better biographical accounts of Bo's life and career—oh, and there are lots of pictures of Bo and the Duchess re-created throughout the set. There are problems with the mastering, however—momentary gaps exist in one or two songs, and the sound quality in certain places, such as the live *Beach Party* material, leaves something to be desired. But at its best, and that is often (at least through the mid-'60s), this set presents one of the primal forces in rock & roll. *—Bruce Eder*

Let Me Pass . . . Plus / 1994 / See for Miles ♦♦♦
Another British import version of a vintage Checker album, with a few highly desirable bonus cuts at the end to further recommend it. Most of the CD mirrors Diddley's 1965 *500% More Man* LP (the title track obviously being a sequel to his "I'm a Man"), but the extra items include the amusing "Mama, Keep Your Big Mouth Shut" and a danceable "We're Gonna Get Married." *—Bill Dahl*

A Man Amongst Men / May 21, 1996 / Atlantic ♦♦♦
Bo Diddley's major-label '90s comeback effort *A Man Amongst Men* is overflowing with guest stars, but it rarely gels into something distinctive. The presence of such heavyweights as Keith Richards, Ron Wood, and Jimmie Vaughan actually weighs down the set, preventing Diddley from digging deep into the grooves. The band never quite rocks hard enough and no one tears off an inspired solo—*A Man Amongst Men* is pleasant, but it never approaches compelling listening. *—Stephen Thomas Erlewine*

★ **His Best (Chess 50th Anniversary Collection)** / Apr. 8, 1997 / Chess ♦♦♦♦♦
With his various hits and anthology packages all out of print and the multi-disc deluxe box set out of pocketbook reach for most casual consumers, MCA finally comes up with a 20-track compilation that hits the bullseye and makes this rock pioneer's best and most influential work available to everyone. The song list reads like a primer for '60s British R&B and '90s blues bands: "Bo Diddley," "I'm a Man," "Diddley Daddy," "Pretty Thing," "Before You Accuse Me," "Hey! Bo Diddley," "Who Do You Love," "Mona" and "Roadrunner" are the tracks that made the legend and put his sound on the map worldwide. The transfers used on this set are exemplary, the majority of them utilizing masters that have a few extra seconds (or more) appended to the fades, which will cause even hardliners to hear these old standards with fresh ears; especially revelatory are the "long versions" of "I Can Tell" and "You Can't Judge a Book By Its Cover." If the box set is too big a trigger to pull and you want all of Bo's influential sides in one package, this one should be first-stop shopping of the highest priority. *—Cub Koda*

Varetta Dillard

b. Feb. 3, 1933, Harlem, NY, **d.** Oct. 4, 1993, Brooklyn, NY
Vocals / R&B
Varetta Dillard was a wailing, shouting mama who scored a trio of hits for Savoy in the early '50s. Dillard was born crippled, but that didn't stop her from being an excellent R&B vocalist. She had a great voice and sang flamboyant, suggestive lyrics with verve and fire. Dillard won two Amateur Night contests at the Apollo and was subsequently signed by Savoy in 1951. Her first hit was "Easy, Easy Baby" in 1952, followed by "Mercy, Mr. Percy," her trademark song, in 1953, and "Johnny Has Gone," an evocative tribute to Johnny Ace, in 1955. The latter two peaked at number six on the R&B charts. Dillard switched to gospel in the '60s, joining the Tri-Odds. She died in 1993. *—Ron Wynn*

● **Got You on My Mind: The Complete Recordings 1958–1961, Vol. 1** / 1989 / Bear Family ♦♦♦♦♦
Bear Family issued a pair of CDs in 1989 presenting 51 of Varetta Dillard's songs. This disc, which contains 29 numbers, leads off with a curious novelty, "The Square Dance Rock." The other tunes are divided between earnest covers ("See See Rider Blues" and "Pennies From Heaven"), robust stompers ("Mama Don't Want (What Poppa Don't Want)") and teen laments ("Pray For Me Mother"). There's also an intriguing tribute piece, "I Miss You Jimmy (Tribute To James Dean)," prompting speculation as to whether the song was Dillard's idea or a company ploy to exploit Dean's tragic demise in 1956. Dillard makes most of these songs entertaining, and sometimes turns in a triumph. *—Ron Wynn*

The Lovin' Bird: The Complete Recordings 1958–1961, Vol.2 / 1989 / Bear Family ♦♦♦♦♦
Bear Family's second CD featuring songs by R&B vocalist Varetta Dillard empties their vaults with a mix of comical novelty tunes, hard-hitting tracks and heartache numbers. Dillard moves from the hip silliness of the title track and "Mercy Mr. Percy" to the anguished "What Can I Say" and "A Little Bitty Tear." She's also outstanding on "Scorched," "You Ain't Foolin' Nobody" and "Rules Of Love." The disc's 22 tracks offer a portrait of a fine vocalist who consistently sang with vigor and depth, regardless of a number's lyrical quality. *—Ron Wynn*

Dion (Dion DiMucci)

b. Jul. 18, 1937, New York, NY [The Bronx]
Vocals / Teen Idol, Doo Wop, Rock & Roll, Folk-Rock
Bridging the era between late-'50s rock and the British Invasion, Dion DiMucci (b. Jul. 18, 1939) was one of the top white rock singers of his time, blending the best elements of doo wop, teen idol, and R&B styles. Some revisionists have tried to cast him as a sort of early blue-eyed soul figure, although he was probably more aligned with pop-rock, at first as the lead singer of the Belmonts, and then as a solo star. Drug problems slowed him down in the mid-'60s, yet he made some surprisingly interesting progressions into blues-rock and folk-rock as the decade wore on, culminating in a successful comeback in the late '60s, although he was unable to sustain its commercial and artistic momentum for long.

When Dion began recording in the late '50s, it was as the lead singer of a group of friends that sang on Bronx street corners. Billing themselves as Dion & the Belmonts (Dion had released a previous single with the Timberlanes), their first few records were prime Italian-American doo wop; "I Wonder Why" was their biggest hit in this style. His biggest single with the Belmonts was "A Teenager in Love," which pointed the way for the slightly self-pitying, pained odes to adolescence and early adulthood that would characterize much of his solo work.

Dion went solo in 1960 (the Belmonts did some more doo wop recordings on their own), moving from doo wop to more R&B/pop-oriented tunes with great success. He handled himself with a suave, cocky ease on hits like "The Wanderer," "Runaround Sue," "Lovers Who Wander," "Ruby Baby," and "Donna the Prima Donna" cast him as either the jilted, misunderstood youngster or the macho lover, capable of handling anything that came his way (on "The Wanderer" especially).

In 1963, Dion moved from Laurie to the larger Columbia label, an association that started promisingly with a couple of big hits right off the bat, "Ruby Baby" and "Donna the Prima Donna." By the mid-'60s, his heroin habit (which he'd developed as a teenager) was getting the best of him, and he did little recording and performing for about five years. When he did make it into the studio, he was moving in some surprisingly bluesy directions; although much of it was overlooked or unissued at the time, it can be heard on the *Bronx Blues* reissue CD.

In 1968 he kicked heroin and re-emerged as a gentle folk-rocker with a number-four hit single, "Abraham, Martin and John." Dion would focus upon mature, contemporary material on his late '60s and early '70s albums, which were released to positive critical feedback, if only moderate sales. The folk phase didn't last long; in 1972 he reunited with the Belmonts, and in the mid-'70s cut a disappointing record with Phil Spector as producer. He's been recording and performing fairly often over the last two decades (sometimes singing Christian music) to indifferent commercial results. But his critical rep has risen steadily since the early '60s, with many noted contemporary musicians showering him with praise and citing his influence, such as Dave Edmunds (who produced one of his periodic comeback albums) and Lou Reed (who guested on that record). *—Richie Unterberger*

Presenting Dion & the Belmonts / 1959 / Laurie ✦✦✦
Rock & roll albums were something of a novelty, if not a rarity, in 1959—apart from Elvis' releases, few of them sold well, and most that were out there by white artists, apart from hits compilations, didn't always reflect well on the music. The debut album by the Bronx-based doo wop group holds up well, however, and is well worth hearing beyond the hits "I Wonder Why," "Where or When," "Don't Pity Me," and "A Teenager in Love." The predominant subject is girls, no surprise as the work of an R&B vocal group in 1959, but there's amazingly little feeling of repetition on these 14 cuts, partly because the producers and the group did vary the sound. There are surprisingly successful attempts at a mild country sound ("You Better Not Do That") as well as pop ("Just You") and an amazing blues ("I Got the Blues") that reveals some of the real depth behind Dion DiMucci even at this early stage of his career—he may have looked and sounded like a teen idol on some of those records, but he had a musical soul all of his own that transcended the limitations of teen pop; it also goes a long way toward explaining why he was responsible for some of the best white rock & roll to come out of NY during this period. It may not be in a league with Elvis Presley's first three albums as essential listening, but it is all well played as well as beautifully sung, showing off a prodigious array of talent from the group on down to the session players involved. *—Bruce Eder*

Runaround Sue / 1961 / Collectables ✦✦✦
Dion as a solo artist was initially a kind of hybrid performer, known for his teen idol image but trying for a harder and also a more advanced sound, as revealed on this album. The hits included here, "Runaround Sue," "The Wanderer," and "The Majestic," are so familiar that they tend to eclipse the rest of this 14 song album—all of the rest, however, is well sung, played, and arranged, ranging from basic hard rock & roll ("Kansas City") to smooth teen pop, which always keeps at least one foot up to the ankle in rock & roll (hence the electric guitar solo on "Could Somebody Take My Place Tonight"). "Little Star" has rated inclusion on several key collections, while "Lonely World" is perhaps the lost single off of this album, with a great beat, killer hooks, and a beautifully shaped performance by the singer and his backup vocalists. What's more, even the covers of familiar material such as "Dream Lover" and "In the Still of the Night" are performed in a style unique to Dion and are worth hearing and owning. The singer was still straddling the gap between teen idol and serious rock & roller, and between late-'50s doo wop and a harder early-'60s sound, although the more serious love songs and the surprisingly articulate guitar solo on "Kansas City" clearly showed that he was winning the musical battle for his own distinct sound. It wasn't a long jump from the repertory here to his distinctive covers of R&B classics like "Ruby Baby." *—Bruce Eder*

Lovers Who Wander / 1962 / The Right Stuff ✦✦✦✦
This is a better-than-average early-'60s effort. Besides the oft-anthologized singles "Lovers Who Wander," "Little Diane," "Sandy," and "(I Was) Born to Cry," it has some hot covers ("The Twist," "Stagger Lee," and "Shout") that Dion makes his own. The haunting "Lost for Sure," which Dion co-wrote, is one of his best obscure Laurie-era tracks. *—Richie Unterberger*

Dion / 1968 / The Right Stuff ✦✦✦✦✦
Featuring his Top Five comeback single "Abraham, Martin and John," this folk-rock and blues-flavored effort remains his most fully realized album. In addition to the impressive anti-war original "He Looks a Lot Like Me," it contains mature interpretations, arranged both acoustically and with strings, of songs by Fred Neil, Joni Mitchell, Leonard Cohen, Bob Dylan, and Lightnin' Hopkins (though the florid version of Jimi Hendrix's "Purple Haze" is embarrassing). [The CD reissue adds the highly sought-after non-LP B-side "Daddy Rollin'," a Dion original that ranks as his most country blues-influenced performance.] *—Richie Unterberger*

★ **24 Golden Greats** / 1983 / Arista ✦✦✦✦✦
24 Golden Greats contains all of Dion & the Belmonts' biggest hits, plus all of Dion's solo hits from the late '60s and early '70s, making it the definitive compilation of the vocalist's long, successful career. *—Stephen Thomas Erlewine*

Deja Nu / Jul. 25, 2000 / Ace ✦✦✦✦✦

● **King of the New York Streets** / Dec. 5, 2000 / Capitol ✦✦✦✦✦
Although Dion's career wasn't over when *King of the New York Streets* appeared, this three-CD package is likely to be the most thorough overview of his output to be heard in one place. "Most thorough" is not synonymous with "best music of his career," however, and while this box contains much of major significance, it really does slide downhill after the early '70s. That point is reached around the middle of the second disc, so that leaves about half of this material as average, or duller than average, stuff. In its favor, the box set has all the familiar hits from the salad days, from the Belmonts' "I Wonder Why" through "Abraham, Martin and John," as well as a number of fine cuts that are largely known only to collectors. Those include his hard-rocking 1965 cover of the obscure Bob Dylan song "Baby, I'm in the Mood for You"; the folk-rock version of Tom Paxton's "I Can't Help but Wonder Where I'm Bound" from the same era; the little-heard 1966 ABC single "My Girl the Month of May" (with the Belmonts); the bluesy B-side "Daddy Rollin'"; and the anti-drug "Your Own Backyard." The post-early-'70s tracks do have their high points, like "(I Used to Be a) Brooklyn Dodger," but they're just not remotely on the same level as what precedes them. Anyone wanting to focus on Dion's best music can get more of it, in more concentrated doses and for about the same amount of money, by purchasing several other less extensive compilations that target a specific period of his work. *—Richie Unterberger*

The Complete Dion & the Belmonts / 2001 / Collectors' Choice Music ✦✦✦
This two-CD set is pretty impressive on its face—47 songs recorded by Dion & the Belmonts during their three-year association. The problem for all but the most hardcore fans of either Dion or the Belmonts, however, is that a lot of the material is decidedly uneven, and a good deal of it isn't rock & roll by any stretch of the imagination. That doesn't mean that it isn't good—merely that anyone expecting some undiscovered rock & roll or R&B gem along the lines of another "I Wonder Why" or "A Teenager in Love" is going to be sorely disappointed, as the seldom-heard tracks here are more along the lines of "When the Red, Red Robin Comes Bob, Bob Bobbin' Along." On the other hand, Dion completists and Belmonts completists, as well as fans of vocal pop music may well love this two-CD set, which traces the evolution of their sound from 1957 across three years, from mainstream mid-'50s pop into rock & roll, and back into pop music. It fills in all of the holes left in this corner of the lead singer's career in the Dion box set, which also makes it a little disillusioning; the group was pushed very quickly and energetically into pop music by their label, Laurie Records, but that was the norm for many careers in the years 1958-1960. Completists may also appreciate the little snippets of recording sessions for "I Wonder Why" and other key early songs, as well as the presence of a half-dozen outtakes, although casual listeners may find the session fragments and back-and-forth talk to be almost as annoying as rock & roll fans will the presence of songs such as the group's rather flaccid version of "In the Still of the Night." The sound is excellent and the tape research and restoration are impeccable, and the notes are extremely thorough. *—Bruce Eder*

The Diplomats

Group / R&B, Soul

The Diplomats were a trio from Washington, D.C., whose early origins goes back to 1958 and a quintet named Tiny Tim & the Hits. Formed by William Collier, Thomas Price, Lionel Brown, Orlester Smith, and Howard "Timothy" Wilson, the group had a pair of singles on Roulette: "Wedding Bells" and "Golden Moments."

Nearly five years passed before Collier resurfaced with Samuel Culley and Ervan Waters as the Diplomats on Arock Records. The tight-harmony trio remake of "Unchained Melody" was the first single, and they got their foot halfway through the door with their second single, "Here's a Heart" (October 1963). A fourth Arock single, however, took them back to square one. On to Wand Records in 1965 for two singles that also failed to go, before a one-off on Minit Records in 1966, "Honest to Goodness." Whether for contractual reasons or simply change, the trio's next single, "Right or Wrong," (on Fat Back), was credited to the Four Puzzles (Thomas Price from the Tiny Tim & the Hitmaker's days had come onboard). A second Fat Back recording, "My Sweet Baby," was released in February 1968 and credited simply to Puzzles after Collier left.

Constantly changing names, the trio's first (of six) Dynamo singles, "Hard to Get," was credited to Sam, Erv & Tom. For the next five singles, including Herb Rooney's (L.A. Reid's father) "I Can Give You Love," they were the Diplomats again. It made no difference what they called themselves, as nothing was clicking on a national level. During their Dynamo stay, they accompanied (uncredited) Tony Drake on their singers Musicor and 3rd World Records' recordings.

In 1973, with George Kerr handling the productions, the Diplomats became the Skull Snaps who many think were a funk band. Newcomer George Bragg joined Culley and Waters for their recordings on Lloyd Price's GSF label. GSF issued four singles and a much sought-after album. Another Skull Snaps' recording on Grill Records, "Ain't That Lovin' You," is scarcer than the GSF tracks. After one last 45 ("Come Back") appeared on two labels, New Moon and Right On, they disappeared. (Or they recorded under another name and nobody has caught on yet.) *—Andrew Hamilton*

● **Here's a Heart** / Aug. 27, 1996 / Collectables ✦✦✦
This is a compilation of Diplomats recordings from 1963 to 1970 issued on Arock, Wand, Minit, and Dynamo Records; omitted are tracks from a stint with Fat Back Records as the Four Puzzles (1967), then as the Puzzles (1968) when William Collier left. Their Dynamo debut in 1968 as Sam, Erv & Tom (Price)—the remaining Diplomats—is missing as well. So are tracks cut after 1970 as the Skull Snaps (a trio comprising Samuel Culley and Ervan Waters with newbie George Bragg) on GSF Records, and "Come Back," credited to the Fantastic Puzzles (issued on New Moon and Right On Records). The endearing "Here's a Heart" was their second release and biggest recording; they liked it so much they redid it for their final Dynamo single in 1970; it originally came out on Arock Records in 1963. They never equaled its impact, sales-wise or artistically. If you only know them by "Here's a Heart," then this CD will disappoint you; only "I'm So Glad I Found You" and "So Far Away" (both sweet, lilting ballads), "Accept Me," and the gospel-ish "In My Heart" can run with it. But if you enjoy '50s doo wop/R&B, some of the more dated sounds will please your palate. The 18 tracks represent a good but hardly complete overview of the vast recordings of a group that never smelled the pop Top 40 and barely sniffed the R&B charts. *—Andrew Hamilton*

Direct Current

f. Philadelphia, PA

Group / Club/Dance, Vocal Pop, Pop, Funk, House, Soul

Philadelphia vocal group Direct Current's lineup was Deborah, Dorothy, and Denise Clement. The trio's sole charting single, "Everybody Here Must Party," was released on Philly label TEC and made it to number-83 R&B on the R&B chart in summer 1979. The album of the same name followed that year, and the trio were also heard on Instant Funk's 1982 Salsoul LP *Looks So Fine*, which included "Why Don't You Think About Me," the swaying ballad "Jumpin' to Conclusions," the NBA tribute "Slam Dunk the Funk," and the skaters/steppers favorite "Gotta Like That." Nick Martinelli (Loose Ends, Stephanie Mills, Regina Belle) and songwriter Johnny Bellmon (Wilson Pickett's "Don't Let the Green Grass Fool You") were among the group's producers. *—Ed Hogan*

● **Everybody Here Must Party** / 1979 / Hot Productions ♦♦♦

Consisting of catchy disco-funk grooves, Philadelphia trio Direct Current's 1979 debut set served as the launching pad for producer Nick Martinelli's short-lived TEC label, which gradually evolved into WMOT. The standout here is the group's self-penned title track—a chunky, churning tune boasting a wicked bassline that is ever-ready for sampling (and, in fact, seminal hip-hop DJ Lady B utilized it later that same year on "To the Beat, Y'All"). But it's not just the bass and overall groove that distinguishes the track from much standard disco fodder; it's also the unique juxtaposition of the spacious arrangement with the Clement sisters' endearing, well-crafted harmonies. The results are not only kinetically rewarding, but also vocally irresistible. Along similar lines, the contagious "Boogie Man" delivers the same rhythmic creativity to the story line of a figurative disco bandit. Though the set is only five songs long, it leaves a lasting impression for its distinctiveness from standard Salsoul and Euro-disco, which in 1979, was running a bit short on ideas. [Note: Hot Productions' CD reissue of this LP (titled *Sweet Release*) listed separate tracks for "When It's Love" and "Wrong or Right."] *—Justin M. Kantor*

The Dirty Dozen Brass Band

f. 1975, New Orleans, LA

Group / New Orleans Brass Bands, New Orleans Jazz, Funk

The Dirty Dozen Brass Band in its prime successfully mixed together R&B with the instrumentation of a New Orleans brass band. Featuring Kirk Joseph on sousaphone playing with the agility of an electric bassist, the group revitalized the brass band tradition, opening up the repertoire and inspiring some younger groups to imitate its boldness. Generally featuring five horns (two trumpets, one trombone, and two saxes) along with the sousaphone, a snare drummer, and a bass drummer, the DDBB was innovative in its own way, making fine recordings for Rounder, Columbia, and the George Wein Collection (the latter released through Concord). Guest artists have included Dr. John, Dizzy Gillespie, and Danny Barker. Unfortunately, the group became much more conventional over the years, still using R&B riffs but with a standard (and less distinctive) rhythm section. The DDBB re-emerged in 1999 with John Medeski as its producer, and many called the group's *Buck Jump* release a return to classic form. The group then returned in 2002 with yet another surprising album, *Medicated Magic*. *—Scott Yanow*

★ **My Feet Can't Fail Me Now** / 1984 / Concord Jazz ♦♦♦♦♦

The Dirty Dozen Brass Band's *My Feet Can't Fail Me Now* is a rollicking, infectious set that captures the spirit of classic New Orleans R&B and jazz because it isn't enslaved to those traditions. The group is willing to play around and have fun, adding different rock, pop, and R&B influences to their sound. The result is a wonderful, unpredictable album that is as wild and rich as New Orleans itself. *—Leo Stanley*

Live: Mardi Gras in Montreux / Jul. 1985 / Rounder ♦♦♦

Not at the same level as their debut (*My Feet Can't Fail Me Now*), this second outing by the Dirty Dozen Brass Band (taken from a couple sets performed at the 1985 Montreux Jazz Festival) is overly loose in spots and has some lightweight material that was better heard live than on record. The party music does have its strong moments, the mightly sousaphone playing of Kirk Joseph (who simulates an electric bass) pushes the group and the joy of the band is not to be denied, but "The Flintstones Meets the President" is only worth hearing once. *—Scott Yanow*

The New Orleans Album / Aug. 1989-Dec. 1989 / Columbia ♦♦♦♦

A bit of a hodge-podge, this CD features the Dirty Dozen Brass Band (comprised of two trumpets, two saxes, sometimes one trombone, the sousaphone of Kirk Joseph, snare drum and bass drum) welcoming such guests as singer Eddie Bo, guitarist-vocalist Danny Barker (showcased on "Don't You Feel My Leg"), trumpeter Dave Bartholomew (heard on "The Monkey") and rock singer Elvis Costello. However it is the R&B-ish parade band that is the main star, romping through group originals plus Cannonball Adderley's "Inside Straight" and "Kidd Jordan's Second Line." *—Scott Yanow*

Buck Jump / May 25, 1999 / Mammoth ♦♦♦♦

If you have been yearning for the original sound of the Dirty Dozen Brass Band to return, this is it. Produced by John Medeski, the ensemble returns to their roots, but with a twist. They remain the ultimate party group, but are fastened to the stage with a drummer, organist, the full complement of horns sounding funky and fresh with that deep tuba and baritone sax underpinning; there's some daring improvisation rooted in counterpoint and upper-atmospheric blasts that are a familiar signature of this progressive New Orleans dance machine. Everything on the nine-song CD is saturated with, as one of the titles suggests, "Old School" style. The solos are inspired, riffs fly left and right, and they aren't afraid to moan and wail. Horn charts are tight as can be, repeated figures give the others a platform to improvise, and occasionally a calypso beat creeps in, as on the classic "Run Joe" or the Latin-inflected "Pet the Kat." It's all in the name of fun ... upbeat, positive, and with nary a trace of excess. They're at their zenith on "Duff," the collective Dozen reaching out and hammering the upper registers of their instruments, and at their most soulful on "Inner City Blues," approaching it in a most unconventional way. Of course, this band needs to be heard live for full effect, but this recorded effort might be their best yet. Every cut is solid, and the high level of musicianship is clearly evident. Singular in their stance and sound, mature like never before, and bent on having a really good time, this Dirty Dozen CD sets the bar high in mixing jazz and joy—a hard combination to beat. *—Michael G. Nastos*

Disco Tex & the Sex-O-Lettes

Group / Disco

As evidenced by their name, Disco Tex & the Sex-O-Lettes were a dance/disco outfit and one of the genre's originals formed in the early '70s (just prior to the world being swept up in the disco craze circa *Saturday Night Fever*). Formed by Bob Crewe and Sir Monti Rock III (born Joseph Montanez, who was a teen idol/talk show regular of the '60s), the gay-oriented group scored a pair of sizable hits early on in their career, 1974's "Get Dancing" and 1975's "I Wanna Dance With Choo," as well as several full-lengths, including a self-titled release and *Manhattan Millionaire* (future dance singer Jocelyn Brown supplied backup vocals for the group for a time, as well).

The group faded from view shortly thereafter, but with a renowned interest in '70s nostalgia came the '90s nad the group's two hits found their way once more on countless dance compilations. The group was also name-checked by the Pet Shop Boys on the song "Electricity" off their 1996 release *Bilingual* with the lyric "It's the greatest show with the best effects, since Disco Tex & the Sex-O-Lettes." *—Greg Prato*

● **Get Dancin'** / 1974 / Collectables ♦♦♦♦

If one had to define Western culture in the mid-'70s in any sort of fashion, one could do worse than to pick *The Rocky Horror Picture Show* and this insane, ridiculously entertaining album. As calculated, stagy, and utterly bizarre an attempt at rocketing someone to fame as humanly possible, *Get Dancin'* sounds like what would happen if a Broadway production squad with no ideas of their own found themselves at a prime Parliament/Funkadelic show and decided to see what they could do with it. The result beggars description, thanks in large part to the putative ringmaster of the whole thing, Disco Tex, aka Monti Rock III, himself. Whether hairdresser, failed actor, or more or less or all combined, his screaming queen MC rants never fail to raise a smile—the question is whether he realized the humor was unintentional or not. The title track provides some of his most memorable moments, screaming things during the instrumental breaks like "America needs you! We need you to go dance! We need you to get together, and boogie woogie woogie woogie! RADAR LOVE IS HERE! THE STAR OF STARS! THIS IS YOUR NIGHT! THIS IS YOUR LIFE!" He only seems to appear on the album irregularly, while the Sex-O-Lettes, whoever or whatever they might be, create a fake but hysterical concert recording with functional yet unavoidably hamhanded funk/disco leading the way, with lame hooks, bad horn charts, terrible backing singers, clear ripoffs of "The Hustle," and more. It all works in spite of itself, a cliché of a cliché, so beyond seriousness, parody, or irony that the only thing to do is enjoy it without guilt. Terrible sexual innuendoes crop up everywhere, bad homages to music from the early 20th century appear, and that's just the start. A bargain-bin classic, and thousands of times more entertaining than nearly all the prog rock recorded during the decade. *—Ned Raggett*

Disco Tex & His Sex-O-Lettes / 1975 / Chelsea ♦♦♦♦

Manhattan Millionaire / 1976 / Chelsea ♦♦♦

Dixie Belles

Group / Girl Group

The Memphis-based Dixie Belles enjoyed a brief moment in the spotlight in 1963, when they scored a Top Ten pop hit with their first single, "(Down At) Papa Joe's." They had a Top 20 follow-up hit as well, with "Southtown U.S.A." Mary Hunt, Mildred Pratcher, and Shirley Thomas had previously worked as backup singers around the South, but their career really began to take off in 1963 after they met producer Bill Justis, the man behind the boards for Elvis Presley, Johnny Cash, and Jerry Lee Lewis in the 1950s. Justis even had his own measure of success with an instrumental hit, "Raunchy." Fred Foster, the president of Monument Records, signed Justis and his protégées to his label and chose for their first single the unusual "(Down At) Papa Joe's," which began with the girls laughing uncontrollably to the sound of Dixieland-styled piano and continued into an ode to an old saloon where "they serve fried-chicken and collard greens." The song proved to be quite popular, climbing to number nine on the pop charts, and even prompted a soundalike follow-up, "Southtown U.S.A.," which bounded into the Top 20.

An album produced by Bill Justis called *(Down At) Papa Joe's* (engineered by Billy Sherrill) was quickly released. Now considered a rarity, it was followed by the Dixie Belles' third single, which followed the style of their two previous hits. This one, however, didn't click and despite quite a bit of airplay, it failed to make the Top 100. The Dixie Belles were dropped from Monument and no other singles followed. The group presumably went their separate ways and it is not known if they ever regrouped to tour. *—Bryan Thomas*

(Down At) Papa Joe's / 1963 / Savage ♦♦♦♦

Combining girl group vocals with the punch of Dixieland, the Dixie Belles made an enjoyable album of sing-a-long songs that are long on enthusiasm and fun. Everything presented is similar in tempo (fast) and all vocals are sung in unison. Dixieland figures prominently in songs such as "Way Down Yonder in New Orleans" and "Bourbon Street Parade." The album includes the top ten hit "Down at Papa Joe's" and the follow up hit "Southtown U.S.A." (number 15). Not everything here is quite as enjoyable as the two hits, but even the lesser material is produced with a tight instrumental attack that fits in well with the other songs. The group sings with such enthusiasm that even a jaded cynic might enjoy what is presented here. Don't delve into this album if you like your rock & roll serious, but if you like a kind of innocent enthusiasm with a big beat, you may want to dig into this one. Interestingly, this album is produced by Bill Justis and engineered by Billy Sherrill. *—Michael Ofjord*

● **Golden Classics** / Apr. 22, 1997 / Collectables ♦♦♦♦

The Dixie Cups

f. 1963, New Orleans, LA, **db.** 1966

Group / Brill Building Pop, Girl Group

A '60s girl group, the Dixie Cups consisted of one cousin (Joan Marie Johnson) and two sisters (Barbara Ann Hawkins and Rosa Lee Hawkins). All three young ladies were from New Orleans, as was producer and singer Joe Jones, who discovered the talented threesome and took them to New York.

The trio was almost known as the Meltones—or worse, Little Miss & the Muffets—but the name Dixie Cups was settled on by 1964. That was the year the girls recorded the well-remembered song "Chapel of Love" on the Red Bird Records label. The number was written by Phil Spector, Ellie Greenwich, and Jeff Barry, and intended to be released by the Ronettes, Darlene Love, or the Crystals. That one single was enough to carry the group into music history. It became the Dixie Cups' biggest success, a million-seller, and a worldwide hit. A few other hits followed through 1964 and into 1965, like "You Should Have Seen the Way He Looked at Me," "Little Bell," "Iko Iko," and "People Say." A year later, Red Bird Records was out of the picture. The trio moved to ABC-Paramount, but there were no more hits, and 1966 saw the end of the Dixie Cups. There had been other singles, like "Gee the Moon Is Shining Bright" and "Girls Can Tell," but there weren't enough fans to back the releases.

In 1974, Rosa Lee and her sister Barbara Ann left NY behind to return to New Orleans and found work as models for awhile. When the sisters began to sing and tour again, their cousin Joan Marie declined to join in, so her spot was filled by Dale Mickle. *—Charlotte Dillon*

• **The Very Best of the Dixie Cups: Chapel of Love** / Feb. 2, 1999 / Collectables ✦✦✦✦✦

Collectables doesn't have the best reputation in collectors' circles, as many of their early releases were rather shoddy and poor sounding. However, 1999's *The Very Best of the Dixie Cups: Chapel of Love* is not only an excellent compilation—with outstanding sound and informative, well-designed liner notes—it's probably the best single-disc Dixie Cups compilation available. Containing both sides of all five of the group's charting singles alongside other worthy tunes and two previously unreleased bonus tracks (a negligible alternate take of the minor hit "People Say" and an outstanding a cappella version of the spooky classic "Iko Iko" that shows off the girls' New Orleans roots to their best advantage), the album is thorough without getting bogged down in arcane. All but three tracks are in stereo, a great improvement over the sometimes-muddy mono mixes found on many budget compilations, and *Chapel of Love: The Very Best of the Dixie Cups* should be useful both for devoted fans and casual listeners who want to own the classic title track. *—Stewart Mason*

The Complete Red Bird Recordings / Aug. 13, 2002 / Varese ✦✦✦✦✦

Only three years before the release of this CD, another comprehensive Dixie Cups anthology, *Chapel of Love: The Very Best of the Dixie Cups*, had appeared on the Collectables label. This has a very slight edge, however, as in addition to including everything from that prior compilation, it adds two more tracks: the fair midtempo pop/rocker "Wrong Direction," previously only available on the 1979 import compilation *Teen Anguish, Vol. 1*, and a less notable mono single version of "Gee the Moon Is Shining Bright." In any case, it's a very good collection, containing the A-sides and B-sides of half a dozen 1964-1965 singles they did for Red Bird, rounded off with less essential odds and ends (including an alternate version of "People Say" and an a cappella alternate version of "Iko Iko"). The Dixie Cups are usually remembered only for "Chapel of Love" and perhaps "Iko Iko," but as this disc demonstrates, there were a good number of solid girl group sides on their other Red Bird recordings. Many of them were written by the estimable Brill Building hitmaking team of Jeff Barry and Ellie Greenwich, and some are quite good despite almost total obscurity (such as "Little Bell" and "Another Boy Like Mine"); a few other tracks have a strong New Orleans R&B influence. It's one of the better single-artist girl group anthologies, and makes one regret that such a likable, melodic act was unable to record longer for Red Bird, where the group teamed with such a suitable production and songwriting supporting cast. *—Richie Unterberger*

Dr. Buzzard's Original Savannah Band

f. 1974, New York, NY, **db.** 1979

Group / Disco

Dr. Buzzard's Original Savannah Band was one of the most original musical ensembles of the disco era. They were formed in the Bronx in 1974 by Stony Browder Jr. (b. 1949), his brother August Darnell (born Thomas Browder, 1951), singer Cory Daye (b. 1952), Andy Hernandez (b. 1950), and Mickey Sevilla (b. 1953). The concept of the group was the re-creation of a '30s dance band... à la Cab Calloway, with witty lyrics and a disco beat. All of this was in evidence on their debut album, *Dr. Buzzard's Original Savannah Band*, released in 1976. It produced the dancefloor hit "Cherchez La Femme" and went gold. A follow-up album, *Dr. Buzzard's Original Savannah Band Meets King Penett*, was less successful. After the release of a third album, *James Monroe HS Presents Dr. Buzzard's Original Savannah Band Meets King Penett*, the group fragmented, with Darnell and Hernandez going off to form Kid Creole & the Coconuts. Browder reorganized and issued a Dr. Buzzard's Savannah Band (dropping the "original") album titled *Calling All Beatniks!* in 1984. *—William Ruhlmann*

Dr. Buzzard's Original Savannah Band / 1976 / RCA ✦✦✦✦✦

Dr. Buzzard introduced a big band sheen to '70s dance music with the hit "Cherchez La Femme" and the rest of this charmingly neo-retro album. *—William Ruhlmann*

Dr. Buzzard's Original Savannah Band Goes to Washington / 1979 / Elektra ✦✦✦

Dr. Buzzard's Original Savannah Band Goes to Washington recaptures the New York disco nostalgia of the band's landmark 1976 debut while excluding most of the experimentation which bogged down their admirable follow-up, *Dr. Buzzard's Original Savannah Band Meets King Penett.* Although RCA reshuffled the songs from the first two albums and reissued them under the deceptive title *The Very Best of Dr. Buzzard's Original Savannah Band*, no overview of the group is truly complete without acknowledging what would be their final album before Cory Daye went solo and August Darnell and "Sugar Coated" Andy Hernandez formed Kid Creole & the Coconuts. In many ways, *Dr. Buzzard's Original Savannah Band Goes to Washington* serves as a bridge between the band and their subsequent careers. The pan-cultural beats and worldly wisdom of Kid Creole can be heard in songs like "Once There Was a Colored Girl..." and "Italiano," while the retro dance energy of "Call Me" was revisited by Daye on her solo debut, *Cory and Me*. As always, Daye's friendly vocals and exuberant personality take center stage before a supporting chorus of bandmates, and Darnell's clever travelogues are buoyed by a genre-blending mix of tropical melodies, danceable tempos, and dramatically orchestrated pop hooks. There is no surefire classic like their breakthrough hit "Cherchez La Femme," but... *Goes to Washington* provides enough pleasant surprises to delight Dr. Buzzard and Kid Creole fans who may have overlooked this unique curio from the disco era. *—Vince Ripol*

• **The Very Best of Dr. Buzzard's Original Savannah Band** / Jul. 2, 1996 / RCA ✦✦✦✦✦

The Very Best of Dr. Buzzard's Original Savannah Band compiles the highlights from the group's first two albums, which featured the kitschy, big band-influenced disco group at the height of their powers. All of the group's hits—"I'll Play the Fool," "Whispering/ Cherchez La Femme/Se Si Bon," "Sour and Sweet/Lemon in the Honey"—are included on the collection, as well as a number of first-rate album tracks, making it not only the perfect place to start, but also the only Dr. Buzzard album any fan needs to own. *—Stephen Thomas Erlewine*

Dr. John (Malcolm John Rebennack Jr.)

b. Nov. 21, 1940, New Orleans, LA

Piano, Vocals, Keyboards, Guitar / New Orleans R&B, Rock & Roll, Piano Blues

Although he didn't become widely known until the 1970s, Dr. John had been active in the music industry since the late '50s, when the teenager was still known as Mac Rebennack. A formidable boogie and blues pianist with a lovable growl of a voice, his most enduring achievements have fused New Orleans R&B, rock, and Mardi Gras craziness to come up with his own brand of "voodoo" music. He's also quite accomplished and enjoyable when sticking to purely traditional forms of blues and R&B. On record, he veers between the two approaches, making for an inconsistent and frequently frustrating legacy that often makes the listener feel as if the "Night Tripper" (as he's nicknamed himself) has been underachieving. In the late '50s, Rebennack gained prominence in the New Orleans R&B scene as a session keyboardist and guitarist, contributing to records by Professor Longhair, Frankie Ford, and Joe Tex. He also did some overlooked singles of his own, and by the 1960s had expanded into production and arranging. After a gun accident damaged his hand in the early '60s, he gave up the guitar to concentrate on keyboards exclusively.

Skirting trouble with the law and drugs, he left the increasingly unwelcome environs of New Orleans in the mid-'60s for Los Angeles, where he found session work with the help of fellow New Orleans expatriate Harold Battiste. Rebennack renamed himself Dr. John, the Night Tripper when he recorded his first album, *Gris-Gris*. According to legend, this was hurriedly cut with leftover studio time from a Sonny & Cher session, but it never sounded hastily conceived. In fact, its mix of New Orleans R&B with voodoo sounds and a tinge of psychedelia was downright enthralling, and may have resulted in his greatest album. He began building an underground following with both his music and his eccentric stage presence, which found him conducting ceremonial-type events in full Mardi Gras costume. Dr. John was nothing if not eclectic, and his next few albums were granted mixed critical receptions because of their unevenness and occasional excess. They certainly had their share of admirable moments, though, and Eric Clapton and Mick Jagger helped out on *The Sun, Moon & Herbs* in 1971. The following year's *Gumbo*, produced by Jerry Wexler, proved Dr. John was a master of traditional New Orleans R&B styles, in the mold of one of his heroes, Professor Longhair. In 1973, he got his sole big hit, "In the Right Place," which was produced by Allen Toussaint, with backing by the Meters. In the same year, he also recorded with Mike Bloomfield and John Hammond Jr. for the *Triumvirate* album.

The rest of the decade, unfortunately, was pretty much a waste musically. Dr. John could always count on returning to traditional styles for a good critical reception, and he did so constantly in the 1980s. There were solo piano albums, sessions with Chris Barber and Jimmy Witherspoon, and *In a Sentimental Mood* (1989), a record of pop standards. These didn't sell all that well, though. A more important problem was that he's capable of much more than recastings of old styles and material. In fact, by this time he was usually bringing in the bacon not through his own music, but via vocals for numerous commercial jingles. It continued pretty much in the same vein throughout the 1990s: New Orleans supersessions for the *Bluesiana* albums, another outing with Chris Barber, an album of New Orleans standards, and *another* album of pop standards. In 1994, *Television* did at least offer some original material. At this point he began to rely more upon cover versions for the bulk of his recorded work, though his interpretive skills will always ensure that these are more interesting than most such efforts. His autobiography, *Under a Hoodoo Moon*, was published by St. Martin's Press in 1994, and in 1998 he resurfaced with *Anutha Zone*, which featured collaborations with latter-day performers including Spiritualized, Paul Weller, Supergrass, and Ocean Colour Scene. *Duke Elegant* followed in early 2000. *—Richie Unterberger*

Gris-Gris / 1968 / Collectors' Choice Music ✦✦✦✦✦

The most exploratory and psychedelic outing of Dr. John's career, a one-of-a-kind fusion of New Orleans Mardi Gras R&B and voodoo mysticism. Great rasping, bluesy vocals, soulful backup singers, and eerie melodies on flute, sax, and clarinet, as well as odd Middle Eastern-like chanting and mandolin runs. It's got the setting of a strange religious ritual, but the mood is far more joyous than solemn. *—Richie Unterberger*

Babylon / 1969 / Wounded Bird ✦✦✦

Dr. John's ambition remained undiminished on his second solo album, *Babylon*, released shortly after the groundbreaking voodoo-psychedelia-New Orleans R&B fusion of his debut, *Gris-Gris.* The results, however, were not nearly as consistent or impressive. Coolly received by critics, the album nonetheless is deserving of attention, though it pales a bit in comparison with *Gris-Gris.* The production is sparser and more reliant on female backup vocals than his debut. Dr. John remains intent on fusing voodoo and R&B, but the mood is oddly bleak and despairing, in comparison with the wild Mardi Gras-gone-amok tone of his first LP. The hushed, damned atmosphere and after-hours R&B sound a bit like Van Morrison on a bummer trip at times, as peculiar as that might seem. "The Patriotic Flag-Waiver" (sic), in keeping with the mood of the late '60s, damns social ills and hypocrisy of all sorts. An FM underground radio favorite at the time, its ambitious structure remains admirable, though its musical imperfections haven't worn well. To a degree, you could say the same about the album as a whole. But it has enough of an eerie fascination to merit investigation. *—Richie Unterberger*

Remedies / 1970 / Wounded Bird ♦♦♦

The Sun, Moon & Herbs / Sep. 1971 / Wounded Bird ♦♦♦

Originally intended as a triple album, *The Sun, Moon & Herbs* was chopped up, whittled down and re-assembled into this single-disc release, and while Dr. John never liked this version much, perhaps this single disc is testament to the "less is more" theory. The seven cuts are all quite lengthy and the spells Dr. John and his consorts weave are dark and swampy. "Black John the Conqueror" comes from old Cajun folklore which the good Dr. has modernized and given a beat. The swampy "Craney Crow" is the younger sibling of his earlier "Walk on Guilded Splinters" and has a similar effect on the listener. "Pots on Fiyo (Fils Gumbo)" combines Latin American rhythms with lots of Cajun chants and spells. The vocals are nearly incomprehensible and actually serve as another instrument in the mix. "Zu Zu Mamou" is so thick that you can almost cut the music with a knife. Here, the atmosphere takes on a whole other meaning altogether. *The Sun, Moon & Herbs* is best listened to on a hot, muggy night with the sound of thunder rumbling off in the distance like jungle drums. Dr. John was definitely on to something here, but just what is left up to the listener. *—James Chrispell*

Dr. John's Gumbo / Apr. 1972 / Atco ♦♦♦♦♦

Dr. John's Gumbo bridged the gap between post-hippie rock and early rock & roll, blues and R&B, offering a selection of classic New Orleans R&B, including "Tipitina" and "Junko Partner," updated with a gritty, funky beat. There aren't as many psychedelic flourishes as there were on his first two albums, but the ones that are present enhance his sweeping vision of American roots music. And that sly fusion of styles makes *Dr. John's Gumbo* one of Dr. John's finest albums. *—Stephen Thomas Erlewine*

In the Right Place / Mar. 1973 / Atco ♦♦♦♦♦

Dr. John finally struck paydirt here and was certainly *In the Right Place.* With the hit single "Right Place Wrong Time" bounding up the charts, this fine collection saw many unaware listeners being initiated into New Orleans style rock. Also including Allen Toussaint's "Life" and a funky little number entitled "Traveling Mood," which shows off the good doctor's fine piano styling, and with able help from the Meters as backup group, *In the Right Place* is still a fine collection to own. *—James Chrispell*

Desitively Bonnaroo / Apr. 1974 / Label M ♦♦♦

When you latch on to a hit formula, don't mess with it, and that is just what the doctor ordered with *Desitively Bonnaroo.* With installment number three of Dr. John's funky New Orleans styled rock & roll, trying to strike gold again proved elusive. There wasn't the big hit single this time around to help boost sales, and the tunes were starting to sound a little too familiar. While not a carbon copy of his previous releases, *Desitively Bonnaroo* was a disappointment to his fans. Good as it was, it was the end of an era for Dr. John and his type of music. *—James Chrispell*

Hollywood Be Thy Name / 1975 / One Way ♦♦♦

In 1975 Dr. John took his well-honed New Orleans musical revue on the road and made a stop in Hollywood, with the recorded highlights released as *Hollywood Be Thy Name.* This is an enjoyable combination of live New Orleans soul and barrelhouse piano mixed with studio tracks including a reworking of his psychedelic anthem "Babylon." The live cover versions range from a soulful "Yesterday," a medley of "Its All Right With Me," "Blue Skies," and "Will the Circle Be Unbroken," plus the Roy Montrell New Orleans jump classic "Mellow Saxophone" retitled here as "I Wanna Rock." The only wrong turn taken is on the title track, which dips into a flashy Las Vegas routine complete with cheesy disco beat, that needless to say didn't suit Dr. John. *—Al Campbell*

Tango Palace / 1979 / Horizon ♦♦

Dr. John's second and final album for the Horizon jazz subsidiary of A&M Records finds him working with producers Tommy LiPuma and Hugh McCracken on a rollicking set that emphasizes his New Orleans roots while attempting to update his sound with '70s effects such as deep, plucked bass notes and occasional disco rhythms. The album leads off with "Keep That Music Simple," a somewhat caustic admonishment to musicians and the music business whose message is disregarded elsewhere on the record, as LiPuma and McCracken seek to cover all stylistic bases from funk to fusion to second line. Dr. John emerges from the production intact, but he is not quite as swampy as when heard at his best. *—William Ruhlmann*

Dr. John and His New Orleans Congregation / 1990 / Ace ♦♦♦

Ace's *Dr. John and His New Orleans Congregation* isn't a Dr. John compilation in the strictest sense of the term—in other words, if you're looking for nothing but his funky hippie gumbo, you'd better look elsewhere. This disc is actually a great collection of cuts Mac Rebennack either played on or produced during the late '50s. all of which were released on Ace Records. Only "Storm Warning" is a genuine Rebennack song; the rest are New Orleans R&B at its funkiest. Not all of the songs are classics—in fact, only a handful, such as Earl King's "Let the Good Times Roll" come close to that status—but many of them are quite entertaining, especially for hardcore New Orleans R&B fanatics, making this a nice addition to either Dr. John or serious New Orleans R&B collections. *—Stephen Thomas Erlewine*

Goin' Back to New Orleans / Jun. 23, 1992 / Warner Bros. ♦♦♦

Having cut an album of standards on his first Warner Brothers album, *In a Sentimental Mood* (1989), Dr. John turned for its follow-up to a collection of New Orleans standards. On an album he described in the liner notes as "a little history of New Orleans music," Dr. John returned to his hometown and set up shop at local Ultrasonic Studios, inviting in such local musicians as Pete Fountain, Al Hirt, and the Neville Brothers and addressing the music and styles of such local legends as Jelly Roll Morton, Huey "Piano" Smith, Fats Domino, James Booker, and Professor Longhair. The geography may have been circumscribed, but the stylistic range was extensive, from jazz and blues to folk and rock. And it was all played with festive conviction—Dr. John is the perfect archivist for the music, being one of its primary popularizers, yet he had never addressed it quite as directly as he did here. *—William Ruhlmann*

Mos' Scocious: Anthology / Oct. 19, 1993 / Rhino ♦♦♦♦♦

Over his 35 years of recording, Mac "Dr. John" Rebennack has worn many hats, from '50s greasy rock & roller to psychedelic '70s weirdo to keeper of the New Orleans music flame. All of these modes, plus more, are excellently served up on this two-disc anthology. From the early New Orleans sides featuring Rebennack's blistering guitar work ("Storm Warning" and "Morgus the Magnificent") to the fabled '70s sides as the Night Tripper to his present-day status as repository of the Crescent City's noble musical tradition, this is the one you want to have for the collection. *—Cub Koda*

Television / Mar. 29, 1994 / GRP ♦♦

Dr. John's debut for GRP doesn't deviate from any release he's made for several other labels. It's still his chunky, humorous take on New Orleans funk; these are his songs, visions and performances, and there's none of the elevator material or laidback, detached fare that's a customary GRP byproduct. Such songs as "Witchy Red," "Spaceship Relationship" and the title selection are a delicate mix of seemingly outrageous but actually quite sharp commentary and excellent musical performances from Dr. John on keyboards, Hugh McCracken on guitar, and several other veterans, among them the great Red Tyler on tenor sax. While not quite as fiery as his classic sessions for Atlantic, if anyone can bring the funk to a company that's famous for avoiding it, it's Dr. John. *—Ron Wynn*

Cut Me While I'm Hot: The Sixties Sessions / 1995 / Magnum ♦♦♦

The liner notes for this 19-song compilation are brief, but at least have the honesty to admit that "the precise details of the circumstances surrounding these recordings may be lost forever." It speculates that the first half of the outtake-sounding program was cut in New Orleans during the first half of the 1960s, while the latter part dates from L.A. sessions from 1965-1967. It actually sounds like much of this postdates the mid-'60s, with a feeling not unlike his early-'70s work. Most of the titles are self-penned, and there are also a few Professor Longhair covers. The material isn't really up to the level of his better early records, and the earlier tracks boast muffled audio (though fidelity is listenable throughout). At the same time, if you like vintage Dr. John, this is not much worse than the official stuff, the jiving throaty vocals, humorous songwriting, and distinctive keyboard playing all in place. It's low on outstanding compositions, but isn't bad at all, meaning there's no need to rush out and buy it, but also that committed fans won't mind having it around. *—Richie Unterberger*

Afterglow / Feb. 7, 1995-Feb. 9, 1995 / Blue Thumb ♦♦♦

Producer and GRP Records president Tommy LiPuma, a longtime associate of Dr. John's, revived his old Blue Thumb label as an imprint of GRP/MCA with this album, which served as something of a sequel to the last Dr. John/Tommy LiPuma collaboration, *In a Sentimental Mood.* On that earlier album, the two had covered pop standards. Here, they again turned to evergreens by the likes of Irving Berlin and Duke Ellington. But if *Sentimental Mood* was stylistically linked to the '20s and '30s, *Afterglow* was more a recreation of the late '40s and early '50s, with its big-band arrangements and the inclusion of jump blues numbers like Louis Jordan's "I Know What I've Got." Such songs allowed Dr. John plenty of room to play his trademark New Orleans piano solos, and, in the second half of the record, some of the Doctor's own compositions were snuck in among the classics without disturbing the mood. Of course, the dominant sound remained Dr. John's gravel-and-honey voice, an even more appropriate instrument for these bluesier standards than it was for the *Sentimental* ones. *—William Ruhlmann*

● **The Very Best of Dr. John** / Apr. 25, 1995 / Rhino ♦♦♦♦♦

Dr. John has recorded many great albums, but it's difficult to argue with such a perfect distillation of his catchy, grooving, slapdash pop work as this Rhino set. Coming out of the R&B studio subculture of New Orleans, the former Mac Rebennack possessed songwriting smarts and reams of recording expertise, each of which had reached their peak by the early '70s. Focused squarely on that prime era, 1970 through 1974, the collection begins with his only Top Ten hit, 1973's irrepressibly fatalistic "Right Place, Wrong Time." Two others come from his best album (1973's *In the Right Place*), the jaunty "Such a Night" and "Qualified." 1972's *Dr. John's Gumbo* also rates three tracks: the New Orleans classics "Iko Iko" and "Tipitina," plus "Junko Partner." The compilers were also wise to choose three songs from *Gris-Gris,* his unjustly neglected psychedelic debut, including "Mama Roux" and "I Walk on Guilded Splinters" (but unfortunately, not the glorious "Gris-Gris Gumbo Ya Ya"). A version of Jimmy Liggins' jump-blues classic "Honeydripper," from 1981's *Dr. John Plays Mac Rebennack,* spotlights his sparkling boogie-woogie piano, and the set closes with a pair of standards from his latter-day Warner Bros. years (one of which is the unofficial Mardi Gras theme "Goin' Back to New Orleans"). Whether it's for a first listen or the perfect road-trip disc, *The Very Best of Dr. John* has all of the New Orleans master's best recordings in one spot. *—John Bush*

Anutha Zone / Aug. 11, 1998 / Virgin ♦♦♦♦
Dr. John has spent so much time turning out perfectly enjoyable but interchangeable records that it may be easy to forget the spooky voodoo vibes of his earliest, arguably best, records. He may have forgotten it himself, too, but there was a whole generation of British musicians, from Modfather Paul Weller to Spaceman Jason Pierce to the teenaged punks in Supergrass, who remembered the haunted vibe lurking in *Gumbo* and *Gris-Gris*. Citing his name in interviews, covering his songs and enlisting him as a session musician (Mr. Rebennack played on Spiritualized's acclaimed 1997 album, *Ladies and Gentlemen, We Are Floating in Space*), they created a buzz around Dr. John and were more than willing to play on *Anutha Zone*, hopefully generating some sales for him in return. As should be expected from any project that is a marketer's dream, the collaborations occasionally seem awkward, but what is surprising is how often it works. Pierce helps Rebennack conjure the psychedelic R&B of his earlier albums, while Weller and Supergrass help keep things cooking; furthermore, members of Primal Scream and Portishead help make "Sweet Home New Orleans" a titanic workout. The Brits aren't as funky as the classic New Orleans musicians, but they are willing to push Dr. John into his best work in years. *Anutha Zone* isn't a perfect album by any means, but it's Rebennack's most ambitious and rewarding album in many a year. —*Stephen Thomas Erlewine*

Medical School: The Early Sessions of Mac "Dr. John" Rebennack / Jun. 22, 1999 / Music Club ♦♦♦♦
Dr. John's early work as a producer, sessionman, and songwriter for Ace Records is legendary, not only among fans of Mac Rebennack but among devotees of New Orleans R&B. Unfortunately, there was no easy way to hear this material until Music Club's 1999 release, *Medical School: The Early Sessions of Mac "Dr. John" Rebennack*. Clocking in at 18 tracks, the disc isn't complete, but it is definitive—all the best-known cuts are here, along with a generous selection of little-known gems. To anyone but scholars and aficionados, most of the names on the compilation will not be familiar (the Ends, Al Reed, Ronnie & the Delinquents, Sugar Boy Crawford, Bobby Hebb, among others), and many of these cuts have never been well-circulated, or even released, but that's what makes the compilation so special. Not only are these lost classics from Dr. John, but these are lost gems from the prime period of New Orleans R&B. And this is not hyperbole—listening to *Medical School*, it's hard not to escape the feeling that almost every song is a hit you've never heard or have forgotten about. The instrumentals are not weak, the novelties (such as "Morgus the Magnificent") are fun, and cuts like "It Ain't No Use," "Bad Neighborhood," "You Don't Leave Me No Choice," and "Keeps Dragging Me On" are simply fantastic, sounding for all the world like classics, not throwaways. And that's the reason why *Medical School* isn't simply a necessary addition to Dr. John's catalog—it's an essential addition to any New Orleans R&B library. —*Stephen Thomas Erlewine*

Creole Moon / Oct. 9, 2001 / Blue Note ♦♦♦
Between his various standards albums of the '90s and the heavily collaborational *Anutha Zone* from 1998, by the end of the millennium it'd been nearly a decade since Dr. John's last record of straight-ahead New Orleans R&B. *Creole Moon* rectifies that situation nicely—it's "a personal interpretation of New Orleans" (as he says in the liner notes), and these 14 vignettes of New Orleans life are soaked in Crescent City soul. *Creole Moon* is also a return to the sound of his classic mid-'70s records (*Dr. John's Gumbo, In the Right Place*), right from the spidery electric piano and testifying backup vocals on the opener "You Swore." Most of his band, the Lower 9-11 Musician Vocaleers, have been playing with him for close to 20 years, and provide solid accompaniment. Dr. John also invites some friends along, including David "Fathead" Newman, slide guitarist Sonny Landreth, fiddler Michael Doucet, and a tight horn section led by Fred Wesley. And there's few better than Wesley to knock out a tough James Brown groove, as he and the band do on "Food for Thot" while Dr. John vamps over the top. Most of the other songs are little more than those loose grooves, and the booklet's constant references to African-derived rhythms (or an included Creole dictionary, aka "Gumbo-izms") may be too much for most listeners, but *Creole Moon* shows Dr. John doing what he's done best for nearly 30 years. —*John Bush*

Bill Doggett

b. Feb. 16, 1916, Philadelphia, PA, **d.** Nov. 13, 1996, New York, NY
Organ (Hammond), Piano / Soul-Jazz, Swing, R&B
Although he was early on known as a fine swing-based pianist, Bill Doggett found his greatest fame in the 1950s as an R&B-ish organist, particularly after recording his big hit "Honky Tonk" in 1956. He led his own big band in 1938, which accompanied Lucky Millinder for a year. After stints with Jimmy Mundy's short-lived orchestra (1939) and back with Millinder (1940-1942), Doggett arranged for the Ink Spots (1942-1944) and recorded with Johnny Otis and Illinois Jacquet (1945-1947). He replaced Wild Bill Davis with Louis Jordan's Tympany Five (1948-1951) and, following Davis' example, took up the organ. After recording with Eddie "Lockjaw" Davis and Ella Fitzgerald, Doggett led his own groups, recording frequently for King throughout the 1950s. He was heard in more jazz-oriented settings in the 1970s on sessions for the Black & Blue label and recorded for After Hours in 1991. —*Scott Yanow*

Everybody Dance to the Honky Tonk / 1956 / King ♦♦♦♦♦
This hugely influential jazz-laced R&B quartet plays their classic two-part instrumentals and several more groovers, with guitarist Billy Butler and saxist Clifford Scott incendiary throughout the album. —*Bill Dahl*

Dance Awhile With Doggett / 1958 / King ♦♦♦♦♦

● **Leaps N' Bounds** / 1991 / Charly ♦♦♦♦♦
Nineteen tracks from the 1950s, including both parts of the massive hit "Honky Tonk." The packaging could be a little more coherent, and the grooves may sometimes get a little too similar for some. But it's solid instrumental organ-sax-guitar jump blues on the verge of turning into rock & roll, with occasional standouts like "Big Boy" supplying evidence that Doggett wasn't solely a one-song wonder. —*Richie Unterberger*

Fats Domino (Antoine Domino)

b. Feb. 26, 1928, New Orleans, LA
Vocals, Piano, Songwriter / New Orleans R&B, Rock & Roll, R&B, Piano Blues
The most popular exponent of the classic New Orleans R&B sound, Fats Domino sold more records than any other black rock & roll star of the 1950s. His relaxed, lolling boogie woogie piano style and easygoing, warm vocals anchored a long series of national hits from the mid-'50s to the early '60s. Through it all, his basic approach rarely changed. He may not have been one of early rock's most charismatic, innovative, or threatening figures, but he was certainly one of its most consistent.

Domino's first single, "The Fat Man" (1949), is one of the dozens of tracks that have been consistently singled out as a candidate for the first rock & roll record. As far as Fats was concerned, he was just playing what he'd already been doing in New Orleans for years, and would continue to play and sing in pretty much the same fashion even after his music was dubbed "rock & roll."

The record made number two on the R&B charts, and sold a million copies. Just as important, it established a vital partnership between Fats and Imperial A&R man Dave Bartholomew. Bartholomew, himself a trumpeter, would produce Domino's big hits, co-writing many of them with Fats. He would also usually employ New Orleans session greats like Alvin Tyler on sax and Earl Palmer on drums—musicians who were vital in establishing New Orleans R&B as a distinct entity, playing on many other local recordings as well (including hits made in New Orleans by GA native Little Richard).

Domino didn't cross over into the pop charts in a big way until 1955, when "Ain't That a Shame" made the Top Ten. Pat Boone's cover of the song stole some of Fats' thunder, going all the way to number one (Boone was also bowdlerizing Little Richard's early singles for pop hits during this time). Domino's long-range prospects weren't damaged, however; between 1955 and 1963, he racked up an astonishing 35 Top 40 singles. "Blueberry Hill" (1956) was probably his best (and best-remembered) single; "Walking to New Orleans," "Whole Lotta Loving," "I'm Walking," "Blue Monday," and "I'm in Love Again" were also huge successes.

After Fats left Imperial for ABC-Paramount in 1963, he would only enter the Top 40 one more time. The surprise was not that Fats fell out of fashion, but that he'd maintained his popularity so long while the essentials of his style remained unchanged. This was during an era, remember, when most of rock's biggest stars had their careers derailed by death or scandal, or were made to soften up their sound for mainstream consumption. Although an active performer in the ensuing decades, his career as an important artist was essentially over in the mid-'60s. He did stir up a bit of attention in 1968 when he covered the Beatles' "Lady Madonna" single, which had been an obvious homage to Fats' style. —*Richie Unterberger*

Here Stands Fats Domino / 1958 / Imperial ♦♦♦
As with most of Imperial Records' LP releases on Fats Domino, this one reached across a lot of time for its dozen tracks, although the centerpiece was the hit "I'm Walkin'" in its first LP appearance. Also aboard was the latter's B-side, "I'm in the Mood for Love," but a lot of the rest dated from Domino's first Imperial sessions in December of 1949, making this something of an oldies album, or at least an excursion backward to a time and a sound from a decade earlier. Among the best of those cuts were the surprisingly elegant ballad "Hideaway Blues," with its supple piano trills, and the pounding rocker "She's My Baby," which had been two sides of a single at the outset of the '50s; also of note are the slow blues "Brand New Baby," highlighted by Ernest McLean's understated lead guitar and some supremely subtle sax work, and the jaunty "Little Bee," a charmingly raunchy and suggestive number from his second Imperial session in January of 1950. —*Bruce Eder*

Fats Is Back / 1968 / Bullseye Blues ♦♦♦
Like many of the early legends of rock & roll, Fats Domino didn't command a lot of attention in the late '60s. Not only had the British Invasion pushed Fats, Chuck, Little Richard, and their contemporaries off the charts, but post-1965 developments like psychedelia and folk-rock made straightforward rock & roll and rolling New Orleans R&B sound a little old-fashioned. In other words, it was time for the first generation to stage a comeback. Producer Richard Perry never neglects the essentials of Fats' music—he retains the easygoing charm and endearing shuffles, just updating it slightly. In retrospect, *Fats Is Back* feels like Perry's blueprint for Ringo Starr's star-studded extravaganzas of the mid-'70s—he selects an impeccable set of songs, nearly all covers but not just relying on obvious selections, assembles a first-rate cast of musicians, and then puts on a show. After all, this is an album that begins with a roll call of Domino's greatest hits and then ends with "One More Song for You"—it's intended to be spectacular and it comes damn close to being one. Part of the reason *Fats Is Back* works is that it's designed to entertain but never oversells itself—sort of like the man himself, actually. Fats delivers tailor-made new songs, Barbara George's "I Know," a remake of his classic "I'm Ready," and two Beatles covers (McCartney's Fats tribute "Lady Madonna" and "Lovely Rita") with equal gusto. Years on from its initial release, *Fats Is Back* still sounds like a sly, endearing update of the classic Domino sound. It may not match his classic Imperial recordings, yet it will no doubt please anyone wishing to dig a little deeper. —*Stephen Thomas Erlewine*

☆ **My Blue Heaven: The Best of Fats Domino** / Jul. 30, 1990 / EMI ♦♦♦♦♦
For the budget-minded fan, this 20-track single-disc compilation of Fats Domino's Imperial smashes will serve nicely. Not much of his early pre-rock stuff—"The Fat Man" and "Please Don't Leave Me" are all that are here—but there's plenty of his hit-laden output from 1955 on—"Ain't It a Shame," "Blue Monday," "I'm in Love Again," "Blueberry Hill," "I'm Ready," among others. One small but substantial difference between this set and the larger packages: It uses non-sped-up masters of his mid-'50s material (some of his hits

from this era were mastered slightly faster than true pitch). Even if they're not historically correct, these versions actually sound better. *—Bill Dahl*

☆ **They Call Me the Fat Man: The Legendary Imperial Recordings** / Oct. 22, 1991 / EMI ✦✦✦✦✦

If you can't quite finance the Bear Family box, this four-disc compilation is the next best thing; an even 100 of the best Imperial sides, including a great many from 1958 on that turn up in crystal-clear stereo (as they also do on the Bear Family package). All the hits are aboard, along with a nice cross section of the important non-hits. The saxes (usually including Herb Hardesty and sometimes Lee Allen) roar with typical Crescent City power, Fats rolls the ivories, and magic happens—over and over again! Another nice booklet with plenty of photos (but a less detailed discography without sideman credits). *—Bill Dahl*

Out of New Orleans / 1993 / Bear Family ✦✦✦✦✦

An amazing piece of work—a massive eight-disc boxed set that contains every one of Fats Domino's 1949-1962 Imperial waxings. That's a tremendous load of one artist, but the legacy of Domino and his partner Dave Bartholomew is so consistently innovative and infectious that it never grows tiresome for a second. From the clarion call of "The Fat Man," Domino's 1949 debut, to the storming "Dance with Mr. Domino" in 1962, he typified everything charming about Crescent City R&B, his Creole patois and boogie-based piano a non-threatening vehicle for the rise of rock & roll. A thick, photo-filled book accompanies the disc, and there's an exhaustive discography that makes sense of Domino's many visits to Cosimo Matassa's studios. If you care about Fats Domino, this is the package to purchase! *—Bill Dahl*

The Fat Man: 25 Classic Performances / Aug. 20, 1996 / Capitol ✦✦✦✦

Ostensibly replacing the compact disc *My Blue Heaven* as the definitive single-disc collection of Fats Domino's biggest hit singles, *Fat Man: 25 Classic Performances* features most of Fats Domino's biggest hits, but it inexplicably neglects such hits as "Walking to New Orleans," "Be My Guest" and "I'm Gonna Be a Wheel Someday." The only justification for the omission of so many hits is that the intent of the collection is to portray Fats Domino as the R&B heavyweight that he undoubtedly is, but seldom receives credit for being. Nevertheless, *Fat Man* masquerades as a greatest hits collection, billing itself as "25 Classic Performances," which leads you to believe that it is simply another hits collection. As an R&B compilation, *Fat Man* is strong—and, like any proper R&B collection, it presents the singles at the speed they were recorded at, not the sped-up versions that became hits—but because it lacks these hits, *My Blue Heaven* remains a preferable collection and introduction to Fats. *—Stephen Thomas Erlewine*

Rock and Rollin' With Fats Domino/Million Sellers By Fats / Jul. 28, 1998 / Collectables ✦✦✦✦

Rock and Rollin'/This Is Fats / Jul. 28, 1998 / Collectables ✦✦✦✦

☆ **Legends of the 20th Century** / Nov. 2, 1999 / Capitol ✦✦✦✦✦

Released as part of Capitol/EMI's *Legends of the 20th Century* series, this single-disc collection is an excellent summary of Fats Domino's legendary singles. Technically, it doesn't have all the hits—it's missing such gold singles as "Bo Weevil," "It's You I Love," and "Wait and See"—but it has every classic: "The Fat Man," "Ain't It a Shame," "I'm In Love Again," "My Blue Heaven," "Blueberry Hill," "Blue Monday," "I'm Walkin'," "Whole Lotta Loving," "I'm Ready," "I Want to Walk You Home," "I'm Gonna Be a Wheel Some Day," "Be My Guest," "Walking to New Orleans," "My Girl Josephine," and "Let the Four Winds Blow," among others. Yes, it's essentially the same as many of the other greatest hits collection, but it's done well, sounds good, and, at 25 tracks, is quite generous, making it an ideal choice for most listeners. *—Stephen Thomas Erlewine*

★ **Fats Domino Jukebox: 20 Greatest Hits the Way You Originally Heard Them** / Mar. 12, 2002 / Capitol ✦✦✦✦✦

Released in conjunction in 2002 with the four-disc box set *Walking to New Orleans*, as well as three other titles in EMI/Capitol's *Crescent City Soul* series, *The Fats Domino Jukebox: 20 Greatest Hits the Way You Originally Heard Them* becomes the definitive single-disc Fats collection on the market nearly by default—it's remastered, it's the one in print, and it has a flawless selection of songs. It's not markedly better than, say, the '90s' definitive Fats compilation, *My Blue Heaven*, since it has essentially the same track selection and even if the tapes were restored to their originally running speed, the difference is not enough for most ears to notice, but it's still a great collection of some of the greatest music of its time, and it summarizes Domino's peaks excellently. So, if you don't already have a Fats Domino collection, this surely is the one to get (despite the really ugly art). *—Stephen Thomas Erlewine*

☆ **Walking to New Orleans** / Mar. 12, 2002 / Imperial/Capitol ✦✦✦✦✦

Of all the early rock & rollers, Fats Domino gets a short shrift. Too easygoing for rockers, too popular for New Orleans R&B devotees, he fell into a middle ground—a middle ground that was extremely popular at the time, but didn't give him the proper respect within hipster history, probably because his music is just so damn enjoyable. Few musicians have made good music sound so easy, so effortless as Fats, and that's best appreciated in an exhaustive compilation, such as EMI's 2002 box set *Walking to New Orleans*, because the sheer scope of Fats' accomplishment becomes stunning only at this scale. Sure, it's easy to appreciate the brilliance of Domino on a hits collection, even one as generous as a 20-track collection like *My Blue Heaven*, but the true scope of his accomplishments becomes clear on a set like this, since there's not a bad cut among these 100 tracks. Yes, some are greater than others, usually the hits, but the momentum never sags because the quality of the material is so strong. Of course, much of this was already heard on the great, seminal box set, 1991's *They Call Me the Fat Man*, and this collection follows the very flow, the very sequence, of that set to a tee; even the Imperial-aping artwork on the CDs and Jeff Hannusch's liner notes are replicated. There are a few song substitutions along the way, usually skewing toward R&B instead of rock & roll, but the ten or so songs that are different don't affect the overall feel of the box, which remains one of the greatest, most listenable box sets in rock & roll. The biggest difference is in the sound (remastered and bettered, but not so much so that most listeners will notice), the packaging (no longer boxed jewel cases; it's now the easy-to-wear book), and the artwork (based on the beautiful promotional photo of the original, but now uglified with an off-kilter, cartoony illustration), all attempts to modernize the set. These differences are so minimal that anyone who already has *They Call Me the Fat Man* need not bother with this set, but anyone who missed that should pick up this slightly inferior set since the music is so fresh and good, it transcends any flaws with the packaging. *—Stephen Thomas Erlewine*

Don & Dewey

f. 1957, Pasadena, CA

Group / R&B

Wailing in tandem like twin Little Richards, Don & Dewey cut numerous blistering rockers for Specialty from 1957 to 1959 without registering a single hit, only to see other acts revive their songs to much greater acclaim. Don Harris (b. 1938) and Dewey Terry (b. 1938) were born and raised in Pasadena, CA, joining a group called the Squires and recording for Vita before branching off on their own. Their Specialty output included the savage rockers "Jungle Hop," "Koko Joe" (written by Sonny Bono), and "Justine," the latter pair later covered by the Righteous Brothers. Don & Dewey's Specialty discography also includes the original "I'm Leavin' It Up to You," a hit for Dale & Grace; "Big Boy Pete," ditto for the Olympics; and "Farmer John," the Premiers' only smash. Don laid down his guitar for a violin during the '60s and, billed as "Sugarcane" Harris, sawed his rocked-out fiddle beside John Mayall and Frank Zappa. *—Bill Dahl*

● **Jungle Hop** / 1991 / Specialty ✦✦✦✦✦

Man, is this stuff great! So, why don't you already have this in your collection? Perhaps you haven't heard of it yet, or perhaps you've just heard *of* Don & Dewey, a pair of high school friends who started performing as a duo after playing in the Squires together, recording many sides for Specialty Records in the late '50s. They never had hits on their own, but they wrote and recorded songs that others brought to the charts, including the Sonny Bono-penned "Koko Joe" and the originals "Big Boy Pete," "Jungle Hop" and the perennial garage rock classic, "Farmer John." That alone suggest that they were first-rate songwriters, but their talent runs deep—these may be the stand-outs, but their other singles and the songs not issued until this 1991 collection are uniformly excellent. And that's just one side of the group. Just as importantly, they were dynamite musicians, rocking hard (Dewey Terry played a *mean* guitar, and Don "Sugarcane" Harris wasn't a slouch himself on the instrument, though his violin talents weren't fully appreciated here) supported by the Specialty house band (the same that played on Little Richard records) and singing delirious tag-team vocals that make this sound insanely alive with life. There's not a bad track here, and even if they didn't have hits and are still a cult item, they left behind a hell of a legacy, as evidenced by this necessary disc. *—Stephen Thomas Erlewine*

Don & Juan

f. 1962

Group / Doo Wop

Don & Juan, born Claude Johnson and Roland Trone, scored one big hit in 1962, entitled "What's Your Name." The single has become a doo wop classic, but its smooth ballad style also hints at the beginning of the emergence of soul.

Johnson and Trone got their start in a Brooklyn band called the Genies. In 1959, they released an uptempo single, entitled "Who's That Knocking," on Shad Records. The song reached number 71 on the U.S. charts. They were unable to reproduce that success and were dropped from the label. Johnson and Trone continued to perform sporadically while working as painters on Long Island, and were rediscovered by an agent named Peter Paul, who arranged for them to sign with Big Top Records. They changed the name of their duo to Don & Juan and recorded "What's Your Name," which eventually peaked at number seven on the charts. Only one other single, "Magic Wand," charted, though the band continued to record until 1967. Trone died in 1983 and Johnson later revived the act with another former member of the Genies, Alexander Faison, who stepped in as the new Juan. *—Stacia Proefrock*

● **What's Your Name** / Apr. 24, 1995 / Collectables ✦✦✦✦

A nice 14-track collection of this obscure one-hit wonder duo from the early '60s. Apartment painters Claude Johnson and Roland Trone—Don and Juan respectively—contributed one hit to the history of rock & roll, "What's Your Name," a track that skirts the fine line between old '50s doo wop and the emerging proto-soul style waiting in the wings. The duo never found another hit, but tracks like "Chicken Necks," "Two Fools Are We," and "Magic Wand" are equally fine examples of their sound. A minor collection by these one-hit wonders, but great fun anyway. *—Cub Koda*

Lee Dorsey

b. Dec. 24, 1924, New Orleans, LA, **d.** Dec. 1, 1986, New Orleans, LA

Vocals / New Orleans R&B, R&B, Soul

Lee Dorsey epitomized the loose, easygoing charm of New Orleans R&B perhaps more than any other artist of the '60s. Working with legendary Crescent City producer/writer Allen Toussaint, Dorsey typically offered good-time party tunes with a playful sense of humor and a loping, funky backbeat. Even if he's remembered chiefly for the signature hit "Working in a Coalmine," it was a remarkably consistent and winning combination for the vast majority of his recording career.

Dorsey was born in New Orleans on December 24, 1924 (although some sources list 1926), and moved to Portland, OR, at age ten. After serving in the Navy during WWII, Dorsey returned to Portland and became a successful light heavyweight boxer, fighting under the name "Kid Chocolate." He retired from boxing in 1955 and returned to his birthplace, where he eventually opened a successful auto-body shop. He pursued a singing career by night, and wound up recording singles for several different labels, most of which made little noise (although "Lottie Mo" sold respectably). In 1961, he signed with Bobby Robinson's Fury label, where he entered the studio with producer Allen Toussaint for the first time. Dorsey's nonsense ditty "Ya Ya"—reportedly inspired by a children's rhyme—became his first national hit that year, reaching the pop Top Ten and hitting number one on the R&B charts. Despite its popularity, following it up turned out to be difficult, and with a large family to support, Dorsey returned to his auto repair business after a few more singles flopped.

Still, Allen Toussaint loved Dorsey's voice, and kept him in mind for future sessions. Toussaint's hunch paid off in 1965 when, signed to the Amy label, Dorsey turned "Ride Your Pony" into a Top Ten R&B hit. The accompanying album of the same name sold respectably as well, and Dorsey began cutting a multitude of Toussaint compositions, often with the legendary New Orleans funk ensemble the Meters as his studio backing band. *The New Lee Dorsey* was released later in 1966, and supplied Dorsey's best-known song, the irresistible "Working in a Coalmine" (which he co-wrote with Toussaint). With its clanking sound effects and Dorsey's comic exclamations, "Working in the Coal-Mine" became his second Top Ten pop hit and signature song, and Dorsey toured internationally with the Meters backing him up. A few follow-ups, particularly "Holy Cow" and "Everything I Do Gohn Be Funky (From Now On)," met with some success, but Dorsey was once again hard pressed to duplicate his big hit, and once again left music for the practical concern of running his business. 1970's *Yes We Can* (on Polydor) was his last album for some time, with the title track becoming his last chart single.

After guesting on the Southside Johnny & the Asbury Jukes cut "How Come You Treat Me So Bad?," Dorsey attempted a comeback in 1977 with the ABC album *Night People*, which wasn't a commercial success despite mostly positive reviews. Still, it was enough to land him supporting slots on tours by the likes of James Brown, Jerry Lee Lewis, and even the Clash, whose 1980 tour was his last major concert jaunt. In the meantime, other artists mined his back catalog for covers: "Working in the Coal-Mine" was redone by robotic new wavers Devo and country duo the Judds; "Ya Ya" by Ike & Tina Turner, John Lennon, and Buckwheat Zydeco; "Everything I Do Gohn Be Funky (From Now On)" by jazzman Lou Donaldson; and "Yes We Can" by the Pointer Sisters (under the new title "Yes We Can Can"). Dorsey continued to perform sporadically, as opportunities presented themselves, until he contracted emphysema; he died in New Orleans on December 1, 1986. *—Steve Huey*

The New Lee Dorsey / 1966 / Sundazed ♦♦♦♦

Here is some good New Orleans R&B, soul, and novelty pop, particularly "Working In the Coal Mine" and "Holy Cow." This was perhaps Dorsey's best mid-'60s album, and offers prototype '60s production and arrangements. *—Ron Wynn*

Ride Your Pony / 1966 / Sundazed ♦♦♦♦

Holy Cow!: The Best of Lee Dorsey / 1985 / Arista ♦♦♦♦♦

This is a nice single-disc anthology featuring the best-known cuts and biggest pop hits of New Orleans R&B and soul singer Lee Dorsey, one of the Crescent City's best comic/novelty artists and a fine traditional R&B vocalist as well. The title track, "Working in a Coal Mine," and "Ride Your Pony" are superb songs that use the second line rhythm and boast outstanding arrangements, clever lyrics, and great vocals. *—Ron Wynn*

Soul Mine / 1993 / Charly ♦♦♦

Charly's 1993 compilation *Soul Mine* has a great cover shot of Lee Dorsey pointing a pistol into the camera, no liner notes, and all the usual suspects: "Ya Ya," "Do-Re-Mi," "Great Googa Mooga," "Ride Your Pony," "Get out of My Life Woman," "Confusion," "Working in the Coal Mine," "Holy Cow," "My Old Car," and "Everything I Do Gohn Be Funky (From Now On)." It also has the relatively latter-day single "Sneakin' Sally Through the Alley," plus a couple of good rarities: "Love Lots of Lovin'," "Go Go Girl," "Give It Up," "Night People," "Soul Mine," "Freedom for the Stallion." The lesser-known songs are all good—during his heyday, Dorsey was never bad—but it's not necessarily enough to make this worth seeking out for anyone but completists. Still, the disc overall is good enough to satisfy the curious and the casual fan if they happen to find it at a good price. *—Stephen Thomas Erlewine*

★ **Wheelin' and Dealin': The Definitive Collection** / Aug. 26, 1997 / Arista ♦♦♦♦♦

Wheelin' and Dealin': The Definitive Collection pretty much lives up to its title, presenting 20 choice selections from one of the greatest figures of New Orleans R&B. All of his big singles are here—"Ya Ya," "Do-Re-Mi," "Ride Your Pony," "Get Out of My Life Woman," "Working in a Coal Mine," "Holy Cow," "Everything I Do Gohn Be Funky (From Now On)"—along with lots of great lesser-known singles like "Confusion," "Can You Hear Me," and "My Old Car." There are some really good songs missing, both from his prime Bell recordings and such latter-day singles as "Sneaking Sally Through the Alley," but that's primarily because everything Dorsey cut was consistently enjoyable; even when the quality of the material dipped, the band and Dorsey remained appealing. So, even if there's a handful of songs that could have been here, it's impossible to argue with what is, since it does result in a wonderful, endlessly listenable collection. *—Stephen Thomas Erlewine*

The EP Collection / Mar. 21, 2000 / See for Miles ♦♦♦♦♦

See for Miles' series *The EP Collection* is always fascinating, since it not only provides collectors with a nifty compilation of pop artifacts, but it also provides a chance-taking, unpredictable singles collection. Such is the case with Lee Dorsey's *The EP Collection*. There's not a bad track to be found on this dynamite 26-track collection that boasts three original British EPs, two French EPs, and six A-sides from "Ya Ya" to "Sneakin' Sally Through the Alley." The very fact that there aren't any weak moments is a testament to just how damn good Lee Dorsey was. It wasn't just that he was backed by stellar musicians under the direction of Allen Toussaint—it was that he was a supremely gifted vocalist with a sly turn of phrase. He could make throwaway songs sound substantial, and he brought unexpected twists to stronger numbers. These talents are readily apparent on any Dorsey collection, but this is one of the very finest, ranking just beneath the slightly tighter Arista compilation, *Wheelin' and Dealin'*. The truth of the matter is this—Lee Dorsey sounds terrific in any context and the singles sound great in any sequence, so even if you buy this for the handful of tracks that you don't have, you'll be satisfied. And if you get this as your first Lee Dorsey album, you're bound to be converted. *—Stephen Thomas Erlewine*

Working in a Coalmine: The Very Best of Lee Dorsey / Apr. 24, 2001 / Music Club ♦♦♦♦

Music Club's *Working in a Coalmine: The Very Best of Lee Dorsey* contains a few songs that don't normally make it on Dorsey collections, from both his Bell recordings and late-'60s/early-'70s funky Allen Toussaint-produced recordings. "Hoodlum Joe," "Messed Around (And Fell in Love)," "People Sure Act Funny," "Can I Be the One?," and "If She Won't" all don't regularly make it on Dorsey collections, which means this is something more for collectors than the neophyte who the title suggests this is aimed at. On that level, it's a neat item to pick up, even if does contain the usual suspects that any Dorsey fan has many times over. If it's viewed as an introduction, however, it falls short—for that, get *Wheelin' and Dealin'* first, then move to this to fill in some holes later. *—Stephen Thomas Erlewine*

Double Exposure

f. Philadelphia, PA, **db.** 1980

Group / Disco, Soul, Urban

Philadelphians Leonard Davis, Joe Harris, Chuck Whittington, and Jimmy Williams were Double Exposure, one of the more prominent groups on the mighty disco label Salsoul. The quartet was one of the most soul-steeped on the roster. This had more than a little to do with their background as a soul group called United Image, which got together in 1966 and recorded a single for Stax in the early '70s ("African Bump" b/w "Hit Man"); and, being from Philadelphia, the group couldn't help but soak up the sounds laid out by the likes of Harold Melvin & the Blue Notes, the Stylistics, the Spinners, and the Intruders. Despite the thick soul leanings of Double Exposure's sound, they failed to light up the U.S. charts. However, they did fare much better in clubs and enjoyed more success in England.

In 1976, *Ten Percent* was released, featuring a pair of major club hits with the title track and "My Love Is Free." Both songs were remixed by Walter Gibbons, who maximized the dancefloor appeal; his ten-minute mix of "Ten Percent" was initially issued to DJs and caught fire so fast that it was eventually released to the public. Contrary to common belief, it wasn't the first 12-inch remix single, but it was one of the most popular of the format's early days. The album also included a rather controversial song called "Everyman," which called for people to take care of their own needs (in the song, a down-and-out person asks for change and gets a scolding instead). With the addition of a couple ballads and a cover of Holland-Dozier-Holland's "Baby I Need Your Loving," *Ten Percent* is one of Salsoul's best single-artist LPs.

Four Play (1978) and *Locker Room* (1979) followed, and both were also released on Salsoul. Neither built on nor continued the strengths evident in the debut, but *Locker Room*'s "I Got the Hots for Ya" became another club favorite. By the end of 1980, the group was no more; in 1999, Charly issued *The Best of Double Exposure*, which ties up Double Exposure's brightest moments. *—Andy Kellman*

Ten Percent / 1976 / Salsoul ♦♦♦♦♦

Black radio has often shied away from what it considers "club records," and that was exactly what happened in the late '70s with soul/disco quartet Double Exposure. Although a major hit in dance clubs, the single "Ten Percent" didn't receive nearly as much black radio airplay as it should have. But make no mistake: this unmistakably Philly-sounding album (reissued on CD in 1993) is very mindful of disco's soul roots. Dancefloor treasures like "My Love Is Free," the Norman Harris-produced title song and an inspired cover of the Four Tops' "Baby, I Need Your Loving" make Exposure's debt to groups like the Intruders, the Spinners and Harold Melvin & the Blue Notes evident, as do the slow jams "Pick Me" and "Just Can't Say Hello." This is music that's exciting both on and off the dancefloor. *—Alex Henderson*

Four Play / 1978 / Salsoul ♦♦♦

● **The Best of Double Exposure** / Jul. 1, 1999 / Charly ♦♦♦♦♦

If obtaining "Ten Percent," "Everyman," and "My Love Is Free" through a various-artists Salsoul compilation or two doesn't give you enough Double Exposure, there's always Charly's *The Best of Double Exposure*. The group's filler-prone albums don't offer enough buried gems to make investment in those a recommendable action, so it would be best to go for this single disc. Beyond the opening trio of songs, which respectively hit number one, number one, and number four on the disco singles chart, it's easy to be struck with the thought that Double Exposure shot its wad early on. But plenty of disco groups released consistently fine material without ever tasting the type of chart success enjoyed by this group; it's only comparing the lack of popularity of later songs (such as "Fallin' in Love With You," "I Got the Hots for You," and "Handy Man") to the big hits that makes what followed seem lackluster. This group thrived on group harmonies and tough rhythms and took a page from Philly soul with its sense of sophistication. One aspect that made the group different from most disco acts was its forthright lyrics, best exemplified in "Everyman." *—Andy Kellman*

Carl Douglas

b. Jamaica

Vocals / Disco

The one-hit wonder behind the disco novelty smash "Kung Fu Fighting," Carl Douglas was also the first Jamaican-born artist to score a number-one single in the U.S. Douglas was raised in both CA and Jamaica, and eventually moved to England to study sound engineering. In 1964, he formed a group called the Big Stampede, which released a couple of U.K. singles; two years later, he formed the Explosions while living in Spain. Upon returning to England, Douglas teamed up with a band called Gonzales, which quickly led to his becoming a session vocalist for Pye Records.

In 1972, Douglas worked with Indian-born producer Biddu on the soundtrack to the Richard Roundtree film *Embassy*; so, two years later, when Biddu was searching for a vocalist to record the Larry Weiss composition "I Want to Give You My Everything," he contacted Douglas. Needing a quick B-side, Biddu set a melody to some lyrics Douglas had written about the kung fu craze sweeping pop culture courtesy of Bruce Lee's *Enter the Dragon* and David Carradine's TV series *Kung Fu*. "Kung Fu Fighting" was recorded in just ten minutes and elevated to the A-side of the single at Pye's insistence. The song topped the charts first in the U.K., then the U.S. and several other countries, selling over nine-million copies worldwide.

Pye quickly cobbled together an LP featuring a few novelty tracks and some straight-up soul/disco tunes, releasing it as *Kung Fu Fighting and Other Great Love Songs*. The follow-up single, "Dance the Kung Fu," flopped in America, pegging Douglas as strictly a novelty act, but it made the Top 20 in Britain, and "Run Back" reached the U.K. Top 30 in 1977. Douglas went on to release two more albums, *Love, Peace and Happiness* in 1979 and *Keep Pleasing Me* in 1983; the title track of the former was a U.K. Top 30 hit. Douglas eventually moved to Hamburg, Germany, where he owns a profitable production company that supplies music for films and advertisements. *—Steve Huey*

Kung Fu Fighting and Other Great Love Songs / 1974 / 20th Century ♦♦♦
When your big hit is a novelty item, you run the risk of becoming the proverbial one-hit wonder—and Carl Douglas was exactly that. In 1974, the Jamaican singer enjoyed a major hit with the campy but fun "Kung Fu Fighting," which set out to exploit the popularity of Asian martial arts films like *Enter the Dragon*. Unfortunately for Douglas, the tune that sent his name to the top of the R&B and pop charts proved limiting—and the stations that also played the lesser known but equally campy "Dance the Kung Fu" didn't do him any favor (obviously, the song only reinforced the belief he couldn't do anything but novelty items). The media and the public refused to take Douglas seriously, which is why his 1974 LP *Kung Fu Fighting and Other Great Love Songs* isn't as well known as the "Kung Fu Fighting" single—a lot of people who bought the single assumed that the LP was a collection of novelties and decided to pass. But in fact, most of the tracks *aren't* novelty items. While "Kung Fu Fighting," "Dance the Kung Fu" and "Witchfinder General" fall into the novelty category, the other songs have more romantic lyrics and are competent, if unremarkable, examples of Northern soul-pop. Had "I Don't Care What People Say," "Never Had This Dream Before" or "I Want to Give You My Everything" been recorded by Al Wilson, Johnny Bristol, Willie Hutch or Johnnie Taylor in 1974, critics would have at least acknowledged them as decent. But whenever Douglas' name came up, people laughed and say, "Oh, yeah, the Kung Fu guy." This album had been out of print for a long time when, in 1995, Hot Productions offered eight of its nine songs on the 16-track CD *Kung Fu Fighting: The Best of Carl Douglas*. *—Alex Henderson*

● **The Soul of the Kung Fu Fighter** / May 11, 1999 / Sequel ♦♦♦♦
The tragedy of Carl Douglas' career is that he was actually a good singer, capable of being more than a novelty act. Nobody really cares, though, because he was the guy that sang "Kung Fu Fighting," a delightfully silly artifact of the '70s, combining disco and kung fu films in an absurdly catchy, unforgettable way. Saddled with such an indelible novelty hit, Douglas' skills faded into the background, particularly since he recorded his fair share of songs that either were kitschy (the talk-box heavy "Too Hot to Handle") or were direct rip-offs of "Kung Fu Fighting" ("Dance the Kung Fu," "Green Tangerines and Wild Evergreens" which has the *exact same melody* as the hit). These and much, much more (including a contemporary remix of the hit, which was a British hit itself and the reason why this Castle collection was assembled for U.K. release) are included on the 22-track *The Soul of the Kung Fu Fighter*, which is likely more than anybody really needs from Carl Douglas, though it is easily the most comprehensive and best collection assembled on the artist yet. Due to that range, it does illustrate that Douglas could have done more than novelties, given the right material and right producer—not much more, perhaps, but he was good journeyman vocalist and when he's given solid genre material like "When You Got Love," the results are indeed pleasant. There's not that many great songs here, however, so this hardly counts as a testament to a great forgotten talent. Nevertheless, Douglas was not without talent, and his pleasant voice makes these period disco, pop-soul and dance productions enjoyable, even if they never transcend their generic origins and are often bogged down by their own novelty. *—Stephen Thomas Erlewine*

Carol Douglas

b. Apr. 4, 1948, Brooklyn, NY
Vocals / Disco, Club/Dance
There's more to Carol Douglas than what meets the eye. On the surface she seems like your typical one-hit wonder disco star, but dig deeper and you'll find a beautiful diva with show business in her blood. Douglas was born April 4, 1948, in Brooklyn, NY. Her mother, Minnie Newsome, sang in some of the many jazz clubs in the Apollo theater area—she was the inspiration for Cab Calloway's "Minnie the Moocher"—and the late, great R&B singer Sam Cooke was a cousin. "Doctor's Orders" remains Douglas' biggest hit to date: it charted at number-11 pop in February 1975 and established her as a beautiful ambassador of disco.

Douglas' show business career began in her teens via TV commercials and small film and TV roles. She appeared in the off-Broadway play *Moon on a Rainbow* with James Earl Jones and Cicely Tyson. In the early '70s, she sang with the regrouped Chantels ("Maybe") before beginning a solo career in 1974. Her big hit came almost immediately—"Doctor's Orders" had been a U.K. hit for Sunny Leslie. Midland International Records plucked it from her debut album; the song came courtesy of songwriters Roger Cook, Roger Greenaway, and Geoff Stephens. Producer Ed O'Laughlin worked with Douglas on her first four albums.

Unfortunately, the follow-ups didn't fare as well. "A Hurricane Is Coming Tonight" ran out of gas at number-81 pop in 1975. "Burnin'," which many consider her best record, did well in clubs and discos but didn't chart as well as "Hurricane"; critically acclaimed, it was nominated for a Grammy in 1978. She sang "You Make Me Feel the Music" for the motion picture *Haunted* in 1977. Douglas doesn't appear in *Saturday Night Fever* but her name does: it's displayed on the marquee outside the famous disco 2001 Odyssey. Douglas spent the rest of the '70s and '80s re-recording popular songs like "Dancing Queen," "Night Fever," and "My Simple Heart." She also recorded some good songs ("Who, What, When, Where, Why" and "I Got the Answer") that went unnoticed by all but diehard fans. In the early '80s, "You're Not So Hot" received a few spins but failed to chart.

Douglas continues to record and perform. She sang several of her hits at the Annual Martin Luther King Summer Concert Series in Brooklyn in the summer of 1997; she sang at Beatstock '97; and in January 1998, she performed in the *Saturday Night Fever* 20th anniversary reunion. *—Andrew Hamilton*

The Carol Douglas Album / 1975 / RCA ♦♦♦
Although the material on Douglas' initial outing may seem somewhat routine these days, it's actually quite notable considering it preceded the actual fruition of disco. The perennial "Doctor's Orders" alone would make this a classic, but the quality is far from limited to that track. Earthy dance gems like "A Friend in Need" and "Baby Don't Let This Good Love Die" are a nice cross between the late-'60s sound of Detroit soul and late-'70s dance-floor soul. Meanwhile, the mellow "Take Me (Make Me Lose Control)" and "I Fell in Love With Love" show a calmer side, while still keeping the groove alive. Douglas has a sophisticated, understated approach that is fully soulful without any dramatic gestures, and she brings a rich vibe to each tune. The only drawback is the presence of somewhat formulaic melodies and lyrics at some points—an aspect usually overcome by the classy arrangements. On a few tunes, the singer lacks a certain warmth, perhaps because she's trying to play it a little too cool. Overall, *The Carol Douglas Album* is an impressive pre-disco effort which helped pave the way for many subsequent albums by dance-driven R&B acts. [Unidisc's CD release of the album also includes an extended version of "Doctor's Orders," as well as the singer's '80s cover of The Three Degrees' "My Simple Heart."] *—Justin Kantor*

Midnight Love Affair / 1976 / RCA ♦♦
Carol Douglas' soft, reedy vocals haven't impressed everyone, but she could sing disco floaters à la "Midnight Love Affair," as well as anyone with her cute sexy voice. Her vocal shortcomings, however, become painfully obvious on uptempo numbers. She just didn't have the power of a Gloria Gaynor or a Donna Summer to deliver on "Headline News" and similar disco boogies. Douglas was more at-home singing European-style disco (side one) than the rougher, more demanding U.S. disco (side two). *—Andrew Hamilton*

Full Bloom / 1977 / Grunt ♦♦♦
Considering Douglas and producer Ed O'Laughlin were early path-setters for disco, it's surprising to find her covering ABBA's "Dancing Queen" here, rather than offering more original dance material. Not straying far at all from the Swedish supergroup's version, Douglas' reading is passable, if not particularly inspiring. Furthermore, her cover of "Light My Fire" falls somewhere in the land of banality. But fortunately, the remainder of material far outweighs the aforementioned in merit. Most consistent are the ballad selections, ranging from the plush groove of "We Do It," to the soft melody and subtly poetic lyrics of "I Got You on My Mind" to "We're Gonna Make It," with traces of Philadelphia soul stylings. Of the uptempo fare, the strongest is "Who, What, Where, When, Why," later recorded by Dionne Warwick on her 1979 *Dionne* album. So, subtract the unnecessary covers, and you have a 75 percent satisfactory album, worth a place in the collections of Douglas fans and aficionados of '70s soul balladry. *—Justin Kantor*

Burnin' / 1978 / Unidisc ♦♦♦♦♦
Douglas' strongest full-length effort, *Burnin'*, was released at the height of the disco craze in 1978. Coincidentally, of all her works, the selection here is the most obviously influenced by the genre in its arrangements. The strongest moments are the two opening cuts, also released as singles: "Fell in Love for the First Time Today," an easygoing, melodic foot-stomper, and the title track, a steady, funky swayer that showcases a bolder shade of Douglas' voice. These two cuts are the perfect match of artist, material, and production and surpass in merit many of the artist's prior single releases. Also notable is the breezy, midtempo "So You Win Again" and the groovy "Let You Come Into My Life." An essential for any Douglas fan. *—Justin Kantor*

Come into My Life / 1979 / Midsong ♦♦♦

● **Doctor's Orders: The Best of Carol Douglas** / Feb. 1, 1995 / Hot Productions ♦♦♦♦
Though a browse through *Billboard* chart books might suggest Carol Douglas was a one-hit wonder, the story is not that short. Besides her Top Ten R&B and Top 15 pop 1974 single "Doctor's Orders," Douglas subsequently scored a number of successful dance singles, including 1976's "Midnight Love Affair" and 1979's "I've Got the Answer." This collection contains all of her '70s essentials for Midland/RCA, as well as two of her '80s recordings for Next Plateau. Highlights include the subtly sassy "Who, What, When, Where, Why," later recorded by Dionne Warwick; "My Simple Heart," a simple yet catchy club number with a funkier edge than most of Douglas's material; and the classic "Midnight Love Affair"—its quiet passion and fervor atop an irresistible but not overbearing beat is timeless. She doesn't have the dynamic pipes of Donna Summer or Martha Wash, but Douglas adapts her sultry pipes effortlessly to each setting and in the process gives a refreshingly different slant to the phrase "dance diva." *—Justin Kantor*

Don Downing

b. Texas
Vocals / Soul
Though singer Don Downing's lone charting single was the Memphis soul-tinged "Lonely Days, Lonely Nights," which charted at number-65 R&B in summer 1973, he's a longtime favorite of dance music devotees for "Doctor Boogie." The pumping brassy number was

a huge hit in disco clubs and found its way onto the play list of major market radio stations in Chicago and elsewhere in 1978. Downing is the brother of singer Al Downing who had a double-sided *Billboard*-charting hit on Chess Records with "I'll Be Holding On." From TX, Downing's perennial dance favorite was written by Gary Knight and Gene Allan, produced by Tony Bongiovi and guitarist Lance Quinn, had a dazzling arrangement by David Vanderpitte that boasted cooing background vocals, punctuating horns, and swirling strings, and co-engineered by Bob Clearmountain. The *Doctor Boogie* album featured some top NY session musicians: drummers Jimmy Young and Alan Schwartzberg, bassists Bob Babbitt and Wilbur Bascomb, guitarist Jeff Miranov, pianist Pat Rebillot, and percussionist Jimmy Maelan.

The *Doctor Boogie* LP cover is vintage '70s with Downing and two of the three lovelies draped around him sporting huge Afros amid a dark and silvery disco club background with multi-colored star-bursting floodlights. Another Downing favorite, "Dreamworld," was arranged by Meco Monardo (had a platinum single as Meco with a cover of the *Star Wars* theme, Gloria Gaynor's "Never Can Say Goodbye" and "Casanova Brown" from her *Experience* LP; Carol Douglas' "Doctor's Orders"). It was released on RS International through NY based distributor HOB Records. The 1998 Collectables CD *Very Best of Don Downing: Dream World* is basically a CD reissue of the *Doctor Boogie* LP. *—Ed Hogan*

Doctor Boogie / 1979 / Roadshow ♦♦♦

• **The Very Best of Don Downing: Dream World** / Jan. 5, 1998 / Collectables ♦♦♦
Don Downing had several hit singles during the disco era, but they never crossed over into the mainstream—they remained underground club hits, and that's the reason why there wasn't a collection of his material until 1998, when Collectables released *The Very Best of Don Downing: Dream World*. All of Downing's hits, most notably "Dream World," "Dr. Boogie," "Lonely Days, Lonely Nights" and "Love Doctor," are included on this eight-track collection, many in their original 12-inch format. "Dream World" is a forgotten gem, but the rest of the collection is fairly standard disco—the kind of music that will interest cultists and collectors, but will be of little interest to anyone with just a passing interest in the genre. *—Stephen Thomas Erlewine*

Will Downing

b. New York, NY
Vocals / Club/Dance, Urban
Brooklyn vocalist and composer Will Downing has hovered on the cusp of stardom since the late '80s, occasionally making some arresting album cuts but never the major hit or string of records he needs to establish himself. Downing sang in Arthur Baker's "Wally Jump Junior" group, and then employed Baker as his producer when he signed with Island. He did session work in the early and mid-'80s, singing on dates with Darryl Payne, Marc Sadane, Warp 9, and Jennifer Holiday. Downing's 1988 debut, *Will Downing*, included a revised version of John Coltrane's "A Love Supreme." Downing recorded and produced a duet with British soul songstress Mica Paris in 1989, remaking "Where Is the Love." His second release, *Come Together as One*, was in more of an Urban Contemporary mode, but his third one took a jazz-oriented turn. 1991's *A Dream Fulfilled* included an ambitious version of War's "The World Is a Ghetto." He has been a favorite of audiences in England, but has not yet clicked with American R&B or Urban Contemporary fans, releasing *Pleasures of the Night* in 1998 and *All the Man You Need* two years later. *—Ron Wynn*

A Dream Fulfilled / 1991 / Island ♦♦♦♦♦

Love's the Place to Be / Aug. 3, 1993 / Mercury ♦♦♦
Following his semi-successful stint with Island, Will Downing moved to Mercury records and recorded *Love's the Place to Be*. The album spawned a few minor R&B hits—"There's No Living Without You," "Do You Still Love Me," "Break Up to Make Up," and "Nothing Has Ever Felt Like This"—though none of them hit the pop charts. Nonetheless, these songs were all some of Downing's best work—even if he didn't write the songs—showcasing his vocal prowess. While the album-opening title track began the album with an energetic spark, Downing also sang quite a few low-key ballads on *Love's the Place to Be*, including "Do You Still Love Me" and "Nothing Has Felt Like This"—the latter a duet with Rachelle Ferrell. *—Jason Birchmeier*

Invitation Only / Oct. 28, 1997 / Mercury ♦♦♦
Invitation Only is another typically tasteful and accomplished set of smooth jazz and urban R&B from Will Downing, who has recorded a diverse set of musicians—including Gerald Albright, Norman Brown, Kirk Whalum, Jonathan Butler and the Yellowjackets—in support. The album is divided between standards, quiet storm R&B and new contemporary R&B. While there are still a few slow spots on the record, where the style takes precedent over the material, *Invitation Only* once again confirms that Will Downing has such a rich, deep talent that he should be a much bigger star than he is. *—Leo Stanley*

All the Man You Need / Jul. 18, 2000 / Motown ♦♦♦
All the Man You Need was hailed as Will Downing's return to R&B music. Though after a listen, there isn't a huge difference between this album and his R&B/smooth jazz-oriented recordings of the mid- to late '90s; which isn't a bad thing. Though the beats may hit a little harder and there's more adherence to R&B ballad song structure, the focus is still on Downing's warm baritone vocals, soothing production, and good songs. The singer makes fine use of a soaring sample from Noel Pointer's cover of Stevie Wonder's "Superwoman" on the breezy "Share My World." Other highlights are "Real Soon," the Downing/Chante Moore duet "When You Need Me," the snappy, ultra jazzy "Tired Melody," a string-laced cover of Bill Withers' "Grandma's Hands," and the smooth, skirting title track. Fans of Will Downing and adult-oriented R&B music will be thoroughly pleased. *—Ed Hogan*

• **Greatest Love Songs** / Jan. 15, 2002 / Hip-O ♦♦♦♦♦
Greatest Love Songs compiles many of smooth vocalist Will Downing's best and most passionate songs, beginning with his self-titled album (1988) and reaching all the way to his later work with Motown, *All the Man You Need* (2000). It's a nicely balanced compilation, featuring a few songs from each of Downing's albums, including some of his R&B hits such as "Free," "I Try," and "I Go Crazy." Since most of Downing's albums can be quite spotty, it's convenient to have a distillation of his work such as this, even if it focuses mostly on his more seductive and gentle songs. As an added bonus, Downing includes brief observations on each of the songs in the liner notes. *—Jason Birchmeier*

Lamont Dozier

b. Jun. 16, 1941, Detroit, MI
Producer, Songwriter, Vocals / Motown, Soul, Quiet Storm, Urban, Funk
Singer/songwriter/producer Lamont Dozier was part of the legendary Motown production team of Holland-Dozier-Holland. A galvanizing force in the '60s pop and R&B chart-dominance of the Detroit-based independent record label, the trio later formed Invictus and Hot Wax Records, and enjoyed gold-record-laced success with the Chairmen of the Board, Freda Payne, 100 Proof (Aged in Soul), the Honey Cone, and 8th Day.

Born June 16, 1941, in Detroit, Dozier was a part of the Motor City's late-'50s vibrant vocal scene, singing with the Romeos and the Voice Masters. Signing with then-fledgling local songwriter and producer Berry Gordy, Dozier's first single, "Let's Talk It Over," was issued in 1960 on Gordy's sister's label, Anna Records, and was credited to his nom de plume, Lamont Anthony. He also worked with Gordy on Motown singles for Marv Johnson. Two other singles followed. Then in 1963, he was teamed with singer/songwriter Eddie Holland for a single release. Eddie Holland had a Motown hit with the Jackie Wilson-sound-alike single "Jamie" in early 1962. The following year, Dozier, Eddie Holland, and his brother Brian began writing together. Beginning with the Supremes' number-one R&B smash "Where Did Our Love Go," the HDH writing/arranging/production trio enjoyed a phenomenal five-year run at the top of the R&B and pop charts, selling millions of records for Motown. Another Motown act, the Four Tops, had a certain affinity for HDH's songs, scoring number-one R&B and pop hits such as "I Can't Help Myself (Sugar Pie, Honey Bunch)" and "Reach Out I'll Be There."

Amid lawsuits, royalty disputes, and creative differences, HDH left Motown in 1967, setting up Invictus and Hot Wax Records. Dozier restarted his solo artist recording career on Invictus with the midtempo ballad "Why Can't We Be Lovers," which went to number-six R&B. The follow-up single, "New Breed Kinda Woman"—a duet with Eddie Holland—peaked at number-61 R&B in 1973. That same year, the HDH team splintered and Dozier signed with ABC Records as a solo artist. His debut ABC LP, *Out Here on My Own*, yielded the hit ballad, "Trying to Hold on to My Woman" and the upbeat "Fish Ain't Bitin'," with its Richard Nixon reference ("tricky dick trying to be slick"). His next album, *Black Bach*, included the singles "Let Me Start Tonite," "All Cried Out," "Put out the Fire," "Rose," and "Thank You for the Dream." Around this time, Dozier produced and wrote most of the tunes for the self-titled debut album of actor Lawrence Hilton-Jacobs. Despite becoming a collectible in later years because of its high quality, *Lawrence Hilton-Jacobs* wasn't a sales success. Switching to Warner Bros. Records in 1976, Dozier's next LP was *Right There*. The LP was full of smooth-as-molasses groovers: "Groovin' on a Natural High," "With a Little Bit of Mending (We Could Be as Good as New)," "Joy," "Ain't Never Loved Nobody (Like I Love You)," "Wild Frame of Mind," and "Good Eye." The LP briefly charted when it was released. His next WB album, 1977's *Peddlin' Music on the Side*, also charted briefly. The 12-inch version of "Going Back to My Roots" is a collectible and the tune was later a 1981 disco hit for the group Odyssey. The 1979 dance-oriented album *Bittersweet* was produced by Motown alumni Frank Wilson (Eddie Kendricks, the Supremes).

Although Dozier was having a hard time cracking the charts, a single he produced for the group Zingara titled "Love's Calling" (with James Ingram on lead vocal) hit number-29 R&B in late 1980. By 1981, the multi-talented musician was signed to ARC (American Recording Company). The album *Working on You* was issued in the spring of that year. Tracks included the energetic, brassy "Cool Me Out," the bubbly "Nobody Told Me," the smooth title track, and the top-notch ballads "Too Little Too Long" and "Why (Ain't My Love Enough)." His next LP, *Lamont*, was created by former Motown executives Mike Roshkind and Mike Lushka. One single, the jubilant "Shout It Out," peaked at number 61 in early 1982.

Holland-Dozier-Holland were inducted in the Rock and Roll Hall of Fame in 1990. The following year, Dozier's *Inside Seduction* was released by Atlantic and was co-produced by Phil Collins. Previously, Collins had collaborated with Dozier on the 1988 number one pop single "Two Hearts." The two dueted on "The Quiet's Too Loud." Dozier's songs have appeared on a host of releases, including Eric Clapton's *August* album and Nicole Renee's 1998 Atlantic debut. In 1997, Dozier appeared at the 1997 Celtic Harmony Festival in Ireland. *Goin' Back to My Roots* was issued three years later. *—Ed Hogan*

Out Here on My Own / 1973 / ABC ♦♦♦
Here are some strong '70s R&B from the great songwriter Lamont Dozier. It was one of the better combinations of socio-political commentary and urgent soul vocals done in the period. The title cut, as well as the single "Fish Ain't Bitin'" and "Out Here on My Own," were sizable hits. *—Ron Wynn*

Black Bach / 1974 / ABC ♦♦
A well-sung but uneven album from legendary songwriter Lamont Dozier. Dozier didn't get his momentum going as a solo act until the next album. This was his introductory vehicle, and it served to let him work out the kinks. Everything except the lyrics was first-rate; his vocals, the production, and the arrangements worked, and Dozier sounded convincing on the uptempo tunes and compelling on the ballads. *—Ron Wynn*

Right There / 1976 / Warner Bros. ♦♦♦
Lamont Dozier enlisted Grade A L.A. musicians, including fellow Motown alumnus, bassist James Jamerson, for his 1976 Warner Bros. debut, *Right There*—an engaging set of soul and pop music. The first single, the smooth ballad "Can't Get Off Until the Feeling Stops," was in the vein of his earlier hit, "Let Me Start Tonite." Dozier vocally milks the smooth-as-molasses groovers: "Groovin' on a Natural High," "With a Little Bit of Mending (We Could Be as Good as New)," "Joy," "Ain't Never Loved Nobody (Like I Love You)," "Wild Frame of Mind," and "Good Eye." The singer/songwriter/producer reworks

the Four Tops' "It's the Same Old Song," giving it a restrained, classical sheen through the use of a prominent string section. *Right There* runs a very close second to being Dozier's best, and most consistent LP, but that distinction belongs to *Working On You.* —*Ed Hogan*

Peddlin' Music on the Side / 1977 / Warner Bros. ✦✦✦✦
For his second Warner Bros. LP, *Peddlin' Music on the Side*, Motown veteran Lamont Dozier turns the production reigns over to Stewart Levine (the Crusaders, Minnie Riperton's *Adventures in Paradise*, Hugh Masekela). Pianist Joe Sample & bassist Wilton Felder of The Crusaders are on hand to make stellar contributions, giving Dozier his most jazz flavored album. As usual with a Lamont Dozier album, you have the top musicians, singers, arrangers, and engineering staff involved. The propulsive album opener, "Sight for Sore Eyes," opens with a striking string and horn arrangement. For the chugging, low key "What Am I Gonna Do 'bout You (Girl)" Dozier slyly caresses the lyric in a manner that suggests that he thinks that "his bad girl is good." "Break the Ice" bops along on thumping bass and soft conga. The inspiring "Tear Down the Walls" has lyrics that admonish: "there's no hope unless we change within/ let protect our let's be friends/ peace on earth and harmony/ it could be a reality/ it's up to you and me/ tear down the walls." The Afro-centric disco hit "Going Back to My Roots" was co-arranged by Hugh Masekela and has a message that most can relate to: "zipping up my boots/ going back to my roots/ to the place of my birth/ back down to earth/ ain't talkin' 'bout no roots in the land/ talkin' 'bout the roots in the man." The 12-inch version of "Going Back to My Roots" is a collectible and the song was a 1981 disco hit for RCA Records group Odyssey ("Native New Yorker"). The heart-tugging, dramatically arranged "Family" paints a picture of the family under attack. The warm-toned ballad "Peddlin' Music on the Side" lists the travails of trying to make it in the music business. This album stands as one of Lamont Dozier's finest works. —*Ed Hogan*

Bittersweet / 1979 / Warner Bros. ✦✦✦
The illustrious singer turned songsmith cranks out eight post-Motown and Hotwax/ Invictus tracks sounding like a bad cross between Levi Stubbs and Junior Walker—lacking the dynamics and authority of Stubbs and the charisma and urgency of Walker, plus he doesn't have Junior's big tenor sax to bail him out. The overall production is the only thing that keeps this album from being a straight ho hummer. He executes songs in every tempo but fails to lock it in the pocket on any, really. The best moments occur on "True Love Is Bittersweet," a lighthearted romance; "Tough Act to Follow," a midtempo number with interesting lyrics and a good vocal performance from Dozier; and "I Got It All With You," a sweet urban ballad. And "Boogie Business" and "We're Just Here To Feel Good" have dancefloor potential. —*Andrew Hamilton*

Lamont / 1981 / M&M ✦✦✦
It's amazing that one of Lamont Dozier's most satisfying LPs appeared on the miniscule, short-lived M&M Records. No, there's nothing as pointedly woeful as "Fish Ain't Bitin'," as compelling as "Why Can't We Be Lovers," or as gripping as "Trying to Hold on to My Woman," but on his previous albums, the pickings got slim once you got past those songs. Not so here; there's enough to keep you listening through all nine selections, with the standouts being "You Oughta Be in Pictures," the pulsating "The Pressure Is On," and the toe-tapping, handclapping "Shout About It." —*Andrew Hamilton*

Working on You / 1981 / Sony ✦✦✦
Motown alumnus Lamont Dozier's most consistent and thoroughly charming album was his 1981 Columbia LP *Working on You.* The prolific singer/songwriter/producer wrote every song and performed all the lead and background vocals on the album. His only release for the label, *Working on You* spawned the perennial U.K. Northern soul/beach music favorite "Cool Me Out." Standout tracks are the longing-filled "Why (Ain't My Love Enough)," the shimmering, fluttering "(You Got Me) Wired Up," the lilting and optimistic "Starting Over (We've Made the Necessary Changes)," the warm and earnest title track, and the reggae-flavored "Chained (To Your Love)." The outstanding backing band includes the fresh keyboard work of John Barnes and Tony Palter. Amazing none of the singles ("Cool Me Out," "Too Little Too Long") or the album itself charted upon its original spring 1981 release. Pristinely recorded, *Working on You* cries out for a CD reissue with full liner notes. Until then good music lovers can enjoy the vinyl reissue of *Working on You* issued by Sony Music Entertainment during spring 2000. —*Ed Hogan*

Bigger Than Life / 1983 / Demon-Megaphone ✦✦✦✦
Put this one near the top of the heap of Lamont Dozier's solo releases. He brought a bag of gimmicks to the studio to complement some top-shelf songs. "Roundtrip Ticket" is a romantic beauty, sweet and melodic with a catchy hook; the title track bounces smoothly along, accented by techno voices; and he changes his modus operandi on "Love Wars," a fast, funky ditty punctuated by slapping bass licks. "Right Where I Wanna Be" and "Second Wind" are above-average ballads. The Hall of Fame songwriter pays homage to Jesus on "Hero of My Heart," concluding an album of strong, well-produced tunes that unfortunately fell by the wayside. —*Andrew Hamilton*

Inside Seduction / 1991 / Atlantic ✦✦✦

The ABC Years and Lost Sessions / 2000 / Expansion ✦✦✦
Lamont Dozier's *The ABC Years and Lost Sessions* culls select tracks from his two ABC albums, *Out Here on My Own* (1973) and *Black Bach* (1974). Both LPs were produced by McKinley Jackson who co-wrote Dozier's biggest hits. It could also serve as somewhat of a greatest-hits set for the Motown alumnus. It includes his highest charting singles, the deliciously melodramatic ballad "Trying to Hold on to My Woman," the cheerful "Fish Ain't Bitin'" with its President Nixon/Watergate reference ("Tricky Dick trying to be slick"), and the tender ballad "Let Me Start Tonite," which is laced with picking banjos and hickory-flavored harmonica. If you're familiar with the original albums, Lamont Dozier's *The ABC Years and Lost Sessions* will serve to make you long for full album reissues on *Out Here on My Own* and *Black Bach.* An unreleased Dozier track from the '70s was used as the basis of Omar's "Outside" on his 1995 RCA CD *For Pleasure.* —*Ed Hogan*

● **The Best of Lamont Dozier** / Dec. 5, 2000 / Castle ✦✦✦✦
Lamont Dozier compilations are breaking out all over. But this one is a little different. "Going Back to My Roots" is a churning zinger and rare slab of social consciousness from Dozier; Odyssey ("Native New Yorker") redid it. You also can't go wrong with "Fish Ain't Bitin'," "Trying to Hold on to My Woman," "Out Here on My Own," and a remake of the Four Tops' "It's the Same Old Song," which he co-wrote. Three selections from his obscure M&M album *Lamont*, makes this disc unique. Yes, only three—"You Ought to Be in Pictures," "I Ain't Playing," and the triumphal "Shout About It"—but that's more than you'll find on any other CD to date. Dozier's earthy vocals are real as day-old collard greens but you never felt he took his singing career seriously. He produced these top-shelf recordings with the comfort of a fat bank account and songwriting royalties pouring in like water; think what he could have done if he was hungry. —*Andrew Hamilton*

The Dramatics

f. 1962, Detroit, MI, **db.** 1983
Group / Smooth Soul, Quiet Storm, Soul

Before assuming the name the Dramatics, the vocal sextet comprised of Rob Davis, Ron Banks, Larry Reed, Robert Ellington, Larry "Squirrel" Demps and Elbert Wilkins initially released two singles as the Dynamics on the Wingate imprint that saw no chart action. The group became a quintet upon Ellington's exit, and also changed their name to the Dramatics. They migrated to the Sport label and in 1967 released their first single to hit the charts, "All Because of You," which peaked at number 42 on the R&B charts. However, in spite of the exposure and limited record sales, some group members became discouraged, which facilitated a major personnel change. William "Wee Gee" Howard replaced lead singer Reed, and Willie Ford of the Capitols replaced bass Rob Davis. Also during this time, the Dramatics had signed with producer Don Davis' productions company.

Even though the group managed to stay together, the ensuing years were unproductive for chart action and sales. Between 1967 and 1971, the Dramatics made very little noise on the national scene. By the end of 1971, Davis summoned the group to the studio to record producer/songwriter Tony Hester's "Watcha See Is Watcha Get." The single was the Dramatics' first major national hit, peaking at number three on the R&B charts, and sustaining chart action for 15 weeks. That single was followed by the R&B Top Ten single "Get Up and Get Down."

The following year the Dramatics released "In the Rain," which was also penned by Hester. The single torpedoed its way to the number-one spot on the R&B charts, maintaining that position for four consecutive weeks; the single also peaked at number five on the pop charts. Ironically, in spite of the national attention the group was receiving, another personnel shuffle was simmering.

Larry "L.J." Reynolds, who had been a member of Chocolate Syrup and was pursuing a solo career during this time, met Dramatics member Banks at the Apollo following a performance by the group. It just so happened that Howard was absent that night. Reynolds auditioned for Banks backstage; it was not too long afterwards that Reynolds, who was also signed to Don Davis' production company, began to occasionally sit in with the Dramatics during Howard's absences.

In 1973, Howard's decision to leave the group opened the door for Reynolds' entrance; Reynolds' vocal presence and permanent entry into the group was manifested with the release of the R&B Top Ten single "Hey You! Get Off My Mountain." And while Reynolds was replacing Howard, Lenny Mayes was replacing Wilkens, which spelled out identity problems for the remainder of the group. Wilkens formed his own version of the Dramatics and began touring. During this time and pending legal procedures, the name of the group was changed to Ron Banks & the Dramatics.

The Dramatics' success continued with mainly R&B Top 20 hits during the heyday of disco, cracking the R&B Top Ten just once more with "Welcome Back Home" in 1980. In 1981, Reynolds went solo; the group disband after Banks went solo in 1983. The group managed to stay active, reuniting to record new material every three or four years since the early '80s. —*Craig Lytle*

Whatcha See Is Whatcha Get / 1971 / Stax ✦✦✦✦
The Dramatics had been around in one form or another for nine years before the members got to release their first LP, and the result was a pair of breakthrough hits over the spring and summer of 1971, beginning with the title track, a Top Ten single that boasted not only extraordinary singing from bass to falsetto, but a soaring, punchy horn arrangement and some of the best fuzztone guitar heard on a hit record since the Rolling Stones' "Satisfaction." The Afro-Cuban-flavored "Get up and Get Down" followed it into the R&B Top 20, and the *Whatcha See Is Whatcha Get* album followed them both. It was the third hit off of the album, "In the Rain," a delicate ballad that was issued separately as a single in early 1972, topping the R&B charts and reaching number five on the pop charts, that solidified the group's reputation and elevated them to the front rank of '70s soul acts. The album showcased the group equally well doing uptempo dance numbers ("Mary Don't Cha Wanna") and ballads ("Thank You for Your Love," "Fall in Love, Lady Love"), melding very attractive vocals to arrangements that instantly grabbed the listener, all of it pulled together by songwriter/producer Tony Hester. Even the lesser material, such as "Gimme Some (Good Soul Music)"—on which Hester knew that one minute and 34 seconds was all that was needed to make its point—were so attractive and rousing that they easily carried their portion of the album, whose short running time was its only flaw. All of the members, from Willie Ford's powerful bass to Ron Banks' airy falsetto, were presented to best advantage, but none more so than William "Wee Gee" Howard's lead vocals; ironically, this would be Howard's only completed album with the group, and their only album for two years to come because of the accompanying personnel problems. Still, it's a match for any soul album of its era. [In 2002, ZYX Records of Germany issued a new CD edition of

Whatcha See Is Whatcha Get with its original cover art re-created and re-mastered in 24-bit digital audio, which is so crisp that it has to be heard to be believed.] *—Bruce Eder*

A Dramatic Experience / 1973 / Stax ♦♦♦♦
A Dramatic Experience (1973) seems to split the difference between a concept album dealing with the evils of drugs and polished, well-arranged ballads and dance tracks. Quiet as it was kept, this album has two different lineups and as William Howard and Elbert Wilkins departed, L.J. Reynolds and Lenny Mayes replaced them. The majority of the concept side of *A Dramatic Experience* is marred by a heavy hand. "The Devil Is Dope" has lead singer William "Wee Gee" Howard's David Ruffin-derived vocals coming this close to parody. The slightly humorous "Jim, What's Wrong With Him?" does attain the eerie nature of drug abuse and has powerful production values. "Beware of the Man (With the Candy in His Hand)" has its odd monster/pusher sentiment only redeemed by Tony Hester's great and innovative production. The non-concept tracks work best here. "Now You've Got My Loving You" has a pitch-perfect falsetto vocal from Ron Banks and particularly strong harmony from the group. The romantic and melodic "Beautiful People" has lead vocals and from Banks, the newly arrived Reynolds, and great group chemistry. Songs featuring the Howard-era group, the rock-based "Stand Up and Clap Your Hands" and "Hum a Song (From Your Heart)" close the effort. *A Dramatic Experience* isn't ranked as a great concept effort, but the romantic ballads make this a necessity to lovers of '70s R&B. *—Jason Elias*

Dramatically Yours / 1973 / Stax ♦♦♦♦♦
This is one of their finest albums. The Dramatics had solidified their sound and personnel in the early '70s. L.J. Reynolds was now doing the leads, with Ron Banks' feathery falsetto and Willie Ford's booming baritone perfectly positioned at the top and bottom of the arrangements, and Reynolds and Lenny Mayes right in the center. Although they didn't generate much crossover success, they were on the R&B charts regularly with singles pulled from the album. *—Ron Wynn*

The Dells Vs. The Dramatics / 1974 / Cadet ♦♦♦
A fine set from both parties. The Dells and Dramatics were quite similar in their style, except that the Dells' signature soul sound came from the interaction of two, rather than three great singers. Each group took some songs on its own, and they also teamed on the single "Love Is Missing From Our Lives," the only song that proved a hit. The overall results were outstanding, although the album didn't do as well as anticipated. *—Ron Wynn*

Drama V / 1975 / ABC ♦♦♦♦
Settled into their own groove, the Dramatics were burning on all cylinders. Their group harmonies were as solid as ever, and they demonstrated their vocal versatility by rotating lead on most of the tracks, including the bass of Willie Ford. This album featured two singles, the first being the sanguine Top Ten R&B hit "You're Fooling You." The follow-up was "Dramatic Theme/Treat Me Like a Man," fueled by a full orchestra and a midtempo groove. Ford's commanding bass opens the lyric, followed by other group members. "Just Shopping, Not Buying Anything" was never a release, but it's worthy of any radio. The song is introduced with a Latin-spiced guitar augmented by a spellbinding music arrangement in which Banks and L.J. Reynolds tenderly embrace the lyric. The Dramatics keep the vocal creativity flowing throughout the album, preventing monotony. *—Craig Lytle*

The Dramatic Jackpot / 1975 / ABC ♦♦♦
A satisfying Dramatic collection that includes their revised, campy version of "Me and Mrs. Jones" that remains a staple of their live shows. Astrology was riding high in the mid-'70s and "I'm Going by the Stars in Your Eyes" provided fodder for astrological discussions as the guys' poo poohed the differences in personality traits associated with the signs. A good balance of fast and slow tunes help make this a winner, "Good Things Don't Come Easy" and "Never Let You Go" are two frantic dancers that chug along faster than a speeding locomotive. While "Trying to Get Over Losing You" succeeds in treating losing your lover in a positive, uplifting way. The guys must have been loaded with material to keep this one off a 45. Likewise for the aching, painful "I Cried All the Way Home," one of Tony Hester's best compositions, and easily the best ballad on the album. *Jackpot* has been reissued on CD and at a good price. *—Andrew Hamilton*

● **The Best of the Dramatics** / 1976 / Stax ♦♦♦♦♦
In the 1960s, Stax Records was best known for raw Southern soul that rejected the type of sleekness and pop sensibilities favored by the Northern soulsters at Motown. But by the early '70s, Memphis soul was losing its popularity, and Stax's A&R department started to emphasize northern and so-called "uptown" soul in order to stay competitive. One of Stax/Volt's biggest sellers was the Dramatics, a Detroit group that, like the Temptations at Motown and the O'Jays in the Gamble & Huff camp, effectively combined gritty soul belting with a sleek production style. Thanks to major hits ranging from the delightfully funky "Whatcha See Is Whatcha Get" to slow jams and ballads like "Hey You! Get Off My Mountain," "Toast to the Fool" and the melancholy "In the Rain," the Dramatics were on quite a roll in the early- to mid-'70s. All of those gems are included on the hour-long CD, *The Best of the Dramatics*, which offers a fine overview of the quintet's Stax/Volt years. Many Dramatics albums are worth owning, but if a listener were allowed to own only one Dramatics CD, this would be it. *—Alex Henderson*

Joy Ride / 1976 / ABC ♦♦♦
Joy Ride featured three singles, the first being the dance track "Finger Fever." Ron Banks and L.J. Reynolds co-lead this gritty number with its multi-directional arrangement. The single peaked at number 23 on the R&B charts. The second release was the classic "Be My Girl." Simultaneously released with Michael Henderson's version, the Detroit quintet is in superior form on this soulful number. In addition to being the author of the song, Henderson also produced the Dramatics' version, which peaked at number three on the R&B charts. The final release was the grieving ballad "I Can't Get Over." Reynolds gives a breathtaking performance with his explosive baritone. This single also made the *Billboard* R&B Top Ten at number nine. While side one is more dance-oriented with moderately paced compositions, side two is more ballad-seasoned with mellow numbers. The group's sleek lead and background vocals remain consistent on every track, and not having any obvious album fillers is also a plus. *—Craig Lytle*

Shake It Well / 1977 / ABC ♦♦♦
Shake It Well spawned two Top 20 hits on the R&B charts, the first being the gritty title track, led by Larry "Squirrel" Demps' innovative vocal delivery. The follow-up single, "Ocean of Thoughts of Dreams," an exquisitely mellow track, is inarguably the most enticing and comforting number on this excellent collection. With a sweet guitar introduction building next to a splendid string accompaniment, the tenor of Lenny Mayes takes center stage with precision. L.J. Reynolds displays his ever-impressive talent on the midtempo number "(I Like) Makin' You So Happy" and the slightly faster-paced "That Heaven Kind of Feeling." Reynolds is able to stretch his baritone to the level of a tenor, and instantaneously ignites with a surge of vocal energy. Ron Banks' falsetto on the midtempo "Spaced Out Over You" improves on a melody that is as enjoyable as the lead and background vocals. All selections showcase creative background arrangements. *—Craig Lytle*

Do What You Wanna Do / 1978 / ABC ♦♦♦

10 1/2 / 1980 / MCA ♦♦♦♦♦
A celebratory album that marked their being together for over a decade, this was one of the group's best MCA/ABC albums, even though it didn't generate enormous success. "Welcome Back Home" and "Be With the One That You Love" were superbly performed and produced, while Reynolds' swaggering, soaring lead on "It Ain't Raining in Nobody's House But Mine" ranked among his best efforts. *—Ron Wynn*

New Dimensions / 1982 / Capitol ♦♦♦

Somewhere in Time / 1986 / Fantasy ♦♦♦

Positive State of Mind / 1989 / Volt ♦♦♦
After a lengthy absence, the Dramatics regrouped in 1989. The new personnel included longtime veterans Ron Banks, L.J. Reynolds, William Howard, Willie Ford, and Lenny Mayes. This was a well-produced, expertly sung soul work with a few urban contemporary production trappings, mostly drum tracks and synthesized backbeats. Sadly, the group found out that six years on the urban contemporary landscape was more like 60; they didn't get much response except from old fans happy they were back. *—Ron Wynn*

Stone Cold / 1990 / Volt ♦♦♦

Be My Girl: Their Greatest Love Songs / Jan. 27, 1998 / Hip-O ♦♦♦♦
During the 1970s, the Dramatics were one of the smoothest purveyors of romantic ballads, and this 16-track collection brings together some of their best moments in that genre. Highlights include "In the Rain," "Fall in Love, Lady Love," "The Stars in Your Eyes," "Door to Your Heart," "Do What You Want to Do," "Ocean of Thoughts and Dreams" and "You're the Best Thing in My Life." The Dramatics are hard to beat for romantic ambience, and this collection brings together some of their very best work. *—Cub Koda*

Shake It Well: The Best of the Dramatics 1974–1980 / Oct. 20, 1998 / MCA ♦♦♦
This is a nice collection of this Detroit-based group's best records for the Cadet and ABC-MCA labels between 1974-1980. Besides the title track (a number-five R&B hit that crossed over to the pop charts), highlights include "I Can't Get Over You," "Be My Girl," "You're Foolin' You," "Love Is Missing From Our Lives," "Don't Make Me No Promises" and the pop crossover smash "Do What You Want, Be What You Are." Although their earlier sides for Wingate, Sport and Volt aren't on here (thus leaving off their biggest hit, "Whatcha See Is Whatcha Get"), this is still a nice collection of tunes by one of the '70s' most prolific and dependable R&B acts. *—Cub Koda*

Say the Word: Their Greatest Love Songs, Vol. 2 / Jan. 26, 1999 / Hip-O ♦♦♦♦
A second helping of Dramatic love ballads. Omissions from the first volume are included, yet the excellent "I Cried All the Way Home" remains a no-show, I would have preferred it to "Yo' Love (Can Only Bring Me Happiness)," "Me Myself & I" or "Call Me." "Love Birds" would have been a nice inclusion too, but oh well. It's nice to see "She's a Rainmaker" getting some recognition, the excellent Tony Hester composition languished on *Dramatic 1V*, it's as teary as "In the Rain," and just as painful. Original lead William "Wee Gee" Howard leads "Thank You for Your Love," an exquisite floating ballad where he humbly gives praise to the women in his life. The backing harmonies weave in and out, complemented by a tasty string section. The Dells are featured with them on "I'm in Love," a lovely number that features Ron Banks' delightful falsetto. Their version of "Love Is Here," originally done by the Futures, is a treat. A good remake though not as tight as the original, it never escaped their *10 1/2* LP. "Toast to the Fool" and "My Ship Won't Sail Without You" are winners, but the title track, "Say the Word," is overblown and too slick. Most of these cuts were album tracks, a long version of "Stop Your Weeping" and "Toast" are the only real hits. *—Andrew Hamilton*

If You Come Back to Me / Nov. 16, 1999 / Volt ♦♦♦
Having recorded some of their most essential work for Stax/Volt in the early '70s, the Dramatics were an obvious choice when Fantasy reactivated Volt in 1999. Although 1999's *If You Come Back to Me* isn't in a class with the Motor City soulsters' classic '70s output for Stax/Volt and ABC, it's a respectable outing that finds the voices of Ron Banks (the only remaining original member), L.J. Reynolds, Willie Ford, Wenzell Kelly, and Lenny Mayes, continuing to hold up nicely. No, there isn't another "Whatcha See Is Whatcha Get" or another "In the Rain," but diehard fans of the veteran group will be glad to hear how good they sound on such romantic ballads as "Hello Love" (which features Angel Sessions, one of the younger artists Volt signed in 1999), "Maddy," and "If You Come Back to Me." The most intriguing track, however, is an unlikely recording of the 16th Century British folk song "Scarborough Fair," which the Dramatics successfully give

an R&B/pop makeover. Coincidentally, they weren't the only R&B artists to record "Scarborough Fair" in 1999—Samantha Siva, a very promising urban contemporary singer who grew up in Manchester, England but currently lives in NY, gives the classic her own unique and personal interpretation on her second album, *Identity*. While Siva's interpretation is more hypnotic and subtle, the Dramatics' version finds Reynolds doing some gritty, gospel-influenced belting that somehow manages to bring the African-American church to the English countryside. But, as satisfying as it is, *If You Come Back to Me* won't go down in history as one of the Dramatics' essential albums—for casual listeners, *The Best of the Dramatics* (Fantasy's 16-song collection of their early '70s hits) would be a much better purchase. Even so, this CD demonstrated that they were still capable of delivering a meaningful album as they prepared to enter the 21st century. *—Alex Henderson*

Ultimate Collection / Sep. 19, 2000 / Hip-O ♦♦♦♦
Spanning their biggest singles from the '70s and '80s, the Dramatics' *Ultimate Collection* includes staples like "In the Rain," "Whatcha See Is Whatcha Get," and "Be My Girl." "You're Fooling You," "Welcome Back Home," "I'm Going By the Stars in Your Eyes," and "Me and Mrs. Jones" are some of the other notable tracks from this retrospective, which covers the group's years with Stax, ABC, and Volt. Though it doesn't go into as much depth as some previous Dramatics collections, *Ultimate Collection* does a good job of presenting highlights from the majority of the group's career. *—Heather Phares*

Dream Machine

Group / Funk, Soul
When Norman Whitfield left Motown his association with the Temptations ended as well. He started Whitfield Records, brought the Undisputed Truth along, and to many, produced them as eccentric versions of the Tempts. All good things come to an end, however, and soon the label went under. Whitfield still had the producing bug so in 1980 he created Dream Machine, a self-contained band including a pair of ex-members of the Undisputed Truth (Taka Boom and Joe Harris). Dream Machine consisted of Taka Boom (aka Yvonne Stevens, Chaka Khan's sister), Joe Harris, Melvin Stewart, Lloyd Williams, Trey Stone, James McKinney, Ron Artis, and Pete Carr. Their first single "Shakedown" was an item in clubs, but the frenzy didn't translate to record sales. Their first and only album was self-titled and released on RCA in 1981, but was widely ignored despite bass-heavy funkers like "Dream Machine" and "Living Too High." RCA had a short fuse and an eye on the bottom line, and dropped Dream Machine before a second LP appeared. *—Andrew Hamilton*

- **Dream Machine** / 1981 / RCA ♦♦♦

Dream

f. 2000, Los Angeles, CA
Group / Teen Pop, Urban, Dance-Pop
The sexy pop group Dream is made up of four talented singers: Diana Ortiz, Holly Blake, Melissa Schuman, and Ashley Poole. The foursome, all from California, came together when a production company in Los Angeles held an audition to form a girl band.

The new group was quickly signed by Puff Daddy to his Bad Boy label. Dream made big waves in the music world in 2000 with the release of "He Loves U Not." The chart-making single kept the radio airwaves hot for weeks and drew lots of attention toward the young singing team. The girls toured through the U.S. and into Canada with hot groups like *NSYNC. When they had a break from live performance, the quartet went back into the studio to work on their debut album, 2001's *It Was All a Dream*. Midway through recording a follow-up to the smash *It Was All A Dream* in spring 2002, Melissa Schuman left Dream to pursue a career in acting. *—Charlotte Dillon*

- **It Was All a Dream** / Jan. 23, 2001 / Bad Boy ♦♦♦

As Puff Daddy's entry into the teen-pop sweepstakes, Dream can't help but feel a little contrived—that's what they are, after all. Still, there's a weird sense of calculation on the album, from the tinted cover shot of the girls wearing Puff's clothing line to the sketches that pepper the album to the deliberately sexy grooves that anchor the album. These girls are singing material that is in the teen pop formula, yet it's tarted up just a little bit too much—it's closer to the sexiness of All Saints and TLC than the teasing of Britney and Christina. Nevertheless, it is true that Puff can afford first-rate songwriters and producers, and much of the record (particularly the single "He Loves U Not") sounds good, even if it runs on a bit too long, starting to drift toward the end. Also, there's the basic problem that Dream isn't particularly charismatic—their voices are serviceable, and, embedded in this professional production, the record can sound alluring, but they never really wind up establishing identities of their own. Not that they're really supposed to—part of teen pop's appeal is that its knowingly generic, but what separates the good from the great is personality, which is lacking on the otherwise adequate *It Was All a Dream*. *—Stephen Thomas Erlewine*

The Dreamers

Group / Doo Wop, Girl Group, Pop-Soul
The Dreamers were one of the relatively few all-female doo wop groups in the mid-'50s, recording several singles on which they backed noted R&B singer Richard Berry. They did just one single under their own name, "Do Not Forget"/"Since You've Been Gone," which came out on Flip in 1957. They also recorded a 1954 single billed as the Dreamers Featuring Richard Berry, and also did a couple of singles for Class as the Rollettes. They were more pop-influenced than most doo wop groups of the time, but sang effectively on their now-obscure singles with Berry.

Their name was changed to the Blossoms when they were signed to Capitol Records in 1957. The Blossoms recorded singles for several labels, but are most known as one of the most prominent session backup-vocal groups of the early '60s. Darlene Love, the most famous member of the Blossoms, actually did not join the group until 1963, and was not a member of the Dreamers. The Dreamers' Flip single, as well as a couple of the Rollettes' tracks and some odds and ends related to Berry and the Dreamers' '50s careers, were packaged on the Dreamers' *They Sing Like Angels* compilation for Ace in 2001. *—Richie Unterberger*

- **They Sing Like Angels** / Dec. 13, 2001 / Ace ♦♦♦

Although this 20-track CD is billed to the Dreamers, it's stretching it some to call it a legitimate Dreamers disc. Only two of the songs are billed solely to the Dreamers. Two others are billed to "the Dreamers featuring Richard Berry," on which Berry actually takes lead vocals; a couple of others are billed to Richard Berry & the Pharaohs with Gloria Jones (who was a member of the Dreamers); three are billed to the Rollettes, the name the Dreamers used when recording a couple of singles for Class; a couple of others are billed just to Richard Berry & the Pharaohs, which might, possibly, include Jenell Hawkins, who recorded with the Dreamers at one point, among the backup vocalists. Then there's a side, "The Mess Around," bearing the unwieldy billing of Jenell Hawkins with Richard Berry & the Lockettes, and an instrumental by Googie Rene & His Wham Bams which was on the flip side of one of the Rollettes' singles. Six of the other tracks are billed to Richard Berry and the Dreamers, and one billed just to Richard Berry. It's enough to make your head whirl, figuring out all the connections, and unless you're a dedicated fan, you will probably have to read the liner notes several times over for all of this to click. Of course, it's primarily dedicated fans who will be picking this up, and after all's said and done, it might be of more interest to Richard Berry fans than to anyone else, since he's the featured singer on no less than 13 of the 20 songs. Judged in that light, it's fair mid-'50s R&B, with more of a pop-doo wop cast than the raunchy proto-rock and humorous novelty songs for which Berry's more known. Only his "Have Love Will Travel" (from 1959) really stands out, though the more rollicking numbers (like "Daddy Daddy" and "Jelly Roll") are decent, and it's fun to hear him do "Besame Mucho." When the Dreamers sing on their own, they manage fair but run-of-the-mill doo wop. *—Richie Unterberger*

The Dreamlovers

f. 1956, Philadelphia, PA
Group / Doo Wop, R&B
The Dreamlovers were an early-'60s Philadelphia-based R&B quintet formed in 1956. The group—Don Hogan (lead), James Dunn (bass), his brother Clifton Dunn (baritone), and tenors Tommy Ricks and Cleveland Hammock—were originally known by several other names, including the Romancers (for a demo tape sent to the Cameo/Parkway label) and the Midnighters (for a 1958 jump tune called "The Twist," backing a new personality named Ernest Evans, later renamed Chubby Checker). In addition, they recorded for V-Tone briefly before signing with Heritage Records. Their biggest hit on their own was 1961's uplifting "When We Get Married," a reverent homage in vocal harmony harkening back to doo wop's heyday. The recording featured a full sound of harmony by the group and a strong lead by Hogan over melodic vibraphone instrumentation.

They returned to the charts on a smaller scale the next year with "If I Should Lose You," a ballad for George Goldner's End Records, and then managed to record quite a few delicious samples of East Coast R&B groove and vocal harmony, including a slow doo wop-styled ballad ("I'm Thru With You") and an infectious uptempo dance number ("Anna Belle Lee"). As they continued recording, their vocal style seemed to change with the times, always sounding ahead of their time. "When We Get Married" was later revived by the Intruders in 1970. *—Bryan Thomas*

The Best of the Dreamlovers, Vol. 2 / 1990 / Collectables ♦♦♦♦♦
Listening to this lively, seductive, gorgeous collection, one has to ask at some point, was doo wop music ever really as pretty as this CD makes it out to be? There are about a million ways one could spend 30 minutes that wouldn't be as pleasant, enlightening, or fun as listening to the dozen songs featured here. The collection opens with its most uncharacteristic track, the majestic, rhythm-guitar driven "You Gave Me Somebody to Love," which possesses a grandeur not in evidence elsewhere until "Doin' Things Together With You," which sounds about a decade ahead of its time as a modern soul ballad of the kind that the Delfonics might've cut around 1969. Most of the rest fits into a more conventional early-'60s East Coast R&B vocal groove. "I'm Thru With You" and "Anna Belle Lee" are beautiful rockers, the former a slow doo wop-style ballad and the latter an infectious uptempo dance number—"Amazons and Coyotees" is even more compelling, a quick-tempo piece jaw-dropping in its passion. "For the First Time" isn't far behind, a gorgeously sung account of a first love that manages to be romantic but not treacly—the guitar player strumming beneath the singing and behind the drummer deserved some sort of award. The sound is decent, though a remastering will probably be in order at some point, and there are no liner notes, release dates, composer credits, or other information. *—Bruce Eder*

- **The Best of the Dreamlovers: The Heritage Years Plus...** / Oct. 24, 1994 / Castle ♦♦♦♦♦

The Best of the Dreamlovers: The Heritage Years Plus... features the Dreamlovers' Heritage sides from around 1961 and later releases on Swan and other labels. The Philly crooners are money for two bar bets—almost sure winners each: What group sang behind Chubby Checker on "The Twist"? And who originally recorded "When We Get Married"? "The Dreamlovers" is the answer to both questions. They employed swooning harmonies on slowies mostly written by member Don Hogan, but they also recorded plenty of outside material by the likes of Jerry Ross, Joe Renzetti, Kenny Gamble, and others. The group that most inspired the Intruders glistens on "I'm Thru With You," a dose of sweet doo wop sugar, the ultra romantic "When We Get Married," and uptempo numbers like "Amazons and Coyotes," "Pretty Little Girl," and "Zoom Zoom Zoom," which are as riveting as any early R&B/rock & roll you'll find anywhere. A quintet with five good voices, the Dreamlovers utilized them all, albeit mostly in the background. A high tenor floats behind the lead, the bass has an uncontainable bubbling persona, and with another tenor and a baritone they create delicious harmonies behind Hogan's leads. Very similar to the Heartbeats (later Shep & the Limelites), only the Dreamlovers loved singing beaters as much as they did sentimental ballads. *—Andrew Hamilton*

Patti Drew

b. Dec. 24, 1944, Charleston, SC

Vocals / Brown-Eyed Soul, Pop-Soul, Pop

Singer Patti Drew had the first hit version of "Workin' on a Groovy Thing," later a 1969 Top 20 R&B/pop hit for the 5th Dimension. She began her singing career as the lead singer of the Drew-vels, which included her sisters Lorraine and Erma and bass vocalist Carlton Black. Born December 29, 1944, in Charleston, SC, Drew grew up in Nashville, TN, and later moved with her family to the Chicago suburb of Evanston. During her teens, she attended Evanston High and sang with her mother and sisters in church. Her mother was a domestic worker whose employer, Maury Lathowers, was the regional promoter for Los Angeles, CA-based Capitol Records. She invited Lathowers to come to her church to hear her daughters sing and, impressed, he invited them to his home for an audition and got the group a deal with Capitol.

Their debut single, "Tell Him" was a huge local hit around the Chicago area and charted number-90 R&B in early 1964. The Drew-vels broke up later that year, and in 1966, Drew signed to Peter Wright's Quill label. The following year, Drew signed a solo deal with Capitol. Her first single, a re-recording of "Tell Him," hit number 22 on the R&B charts in fall 1967. A Capitol LP, *Tell Him*, was also issued. One year later, her recording of the Neil Sedaka/Roger Atkins song "Workin' on a Groovy Thing" made it to number-34 R&B. A *Workin' on a Groovy Thing* LP was issued along with two more Capitol LPs, *I've Been Here All the Time* (1969) and *Wild Is Love* (January 1970). Drew's other singles were "Hundreds of Guys," "Keep on Movin'," and "My Lover's Prayer."

In 1971, she left the music business. She resurfaced with a release on Carl Davis and E. Rodney Jones' Innovation Records in 1975. During the '80s, she reunited with Carlton Black in the group Front Line and performed around the Evanston area. Most of her Capitol singles can be found on the Collectables 1994 CD *Tell Him: Golden Classics Edition*. *—Ed Hogan*

I've Been Here All the Time / 1969 / Capitol ♦♦♦

Tall, striking Patti Drew's sensuous alto is always a pleasure to listen to even when the material and arrangements are lacking. This LP consists of two minor hits, "I've Been Here All the Time" and "Hard to Handle"; the many remakes include "Fever," "Save the Last Dance For Me," "I Who Have Nothing," "Midnight Confessions," and "What the World Needs Now Is Love." Manager/producer Peter Wright was obviously priming the Charleston, SC, native for the lucrative Vegas/Reno/Tahoe casino clubs, as the album lacks an edge and disappointed her fan base. *—Andrew Hamilton*

● **Tell Him: Golden Classics Edition** / Feb. 15, 1994 / Collectables ♦♦♦♦♦

Although it suffers from minimal packaging and adequete sound, Collectables' *Tell Him: Golden Classics Edition* remains the best Patti Drew collection available, because it has all the original versions of her Hi singles. Granted, there aren't many Drew compilations on the market, but anyone looking for a collection will be reasonably satisfied with this disc. *—Stephen Thomas Erlewine*

The Drifters

f. May 1953, New York, NY

Group / Doo Wop, R&B, Soul

The history of rhythm-and-blues is filled with vocal groups whose names—the Orioles, the Cadillacs, the Crows, the Flamingos, the Moonglows, the Coasters, the Penguins—are held in reverence by fanatics and devotees. The Drifters are part of an even more exclusive fraternity, as a group that managed to carve out a place for themselves in the R&B firmament and also define that music, not only at its inception as a national chart phenomenon in the early '50s but also in the decade that followed. Their place in history is as complex as their role in it, by virtue of the fact that there are two distinct phases to their music and the continuity of their membership, and their extraordinary longevity—only the Platters could claim as great a span of years as an active recording unit, though the latter group, due to major differences in the way they were organized, were far more stable in their membership and output. The Drifters can also claim a unique place in popular music history, as a major R&B group founded at the instigation of a record-label chief.

Their story began in early 1953, when Clyde McPhatter, the soaring high-tenor lead singer in the Dominoes, a vocal quintet formed by Billy Ward three years earlier, quit that group. The Dominoes were playing a scheduled gig at the NY club Birdland, one of their first performances without McPhatter, when one of the audience members present asked after the singer backstage. That fan was Ahmet Ertegun, a onetime record collector who had started Atlantic Records in the late '40s; as soon as he learned of McPhatter's having left the Dominoes, he contacted the singer and signed him to Atlantic.

It was Ertegun who gave McPhatter the impetus, as part of his contract, to start a group of his own, which came to be called the Drifters. The origins of the name and credit for thinking of it are obscure, although no one at Atlantic liked "the Drifters" at first, thinking it sounded too country & western—the explanation sometimes offered by those present was that the members simply drifted in from other groups.

The main source for McPhatter's backing singers was the ranks of former members of the Mount Lebanon Singers, the gospel group with which McPhatter had sung in the '40s. He went through several attempts at assembling a group that would be acceptable to Ertegun and producer Jerry Wexler, going through as many as a dozen friends and acquaintances, a handful of whom actually made it to formal recording sessions. The initial, unsuccessful lineup, featuring William Anderson, David Baughn, David Baldwin (the brother of author James Baldwin), and James Johnson, recorded four songs on June 28, 1953, of which only "Lucille," a McPhatter-authored song, was ever released. In August, a second Drifters lineup was put together, with Gerhart Thrasher, Andrew Thrasher, two very experienced gospel singers on tenor and baritone, respectively, bass singer Willie Ferbee, and Walter Adams on the guitar.

From the beginning, the group was unusual among R&B vocal ensembles in that a guitarist was part of their core lineup and the electric guitar central to their arrangements; Jimmy Oliver, who would soon take that spot as his own, also proved to be an important songwriter for the Drifters, especially for tenor Gerhart Thrasher. The new edition of the group cut five numbers on August 9, 1953, one of which was "Money Honey," written by arranger/pianist Jesse Stone. Released within a few weeks, it hit the number-one spot on the R&B chart by mid-fall of that year, and it was occasionally cited in later years as the first rock & roll record, and it later entered the repertory of Elvis Presley and dozens of lesser talents. The group's career was made after that, at least as long as McPhatter was singing lead with them.

This success didn't stop the regular lineup changes that would characterize the Drifters' history. By the time the Drifters were enjoying their breakthrough hit, a reconstituted lineup, with bass Bill Pinkney and guitarist Jimmy Oliver joining Gerhart Thrasher and Andrew Thrasher, cut their first session. This was the lineup that lasted for the year that followed and cut "Such a Night," a number two R&B hit, at that session, and a second R&B chart-topper, "Honey Love," in early 1954. By that time, the charts and radio play, along with audience sensibilities, had opened up and "Honey Love" also made number 21 on the pop charts late that spring. Not for the last time, it seemed as though the Drifters were headed for big things together, but a key member had developed other ideas by the fall of 1954.

Although he'd been assured of a considerable amount of musical control, McPhatter found that Ertegun and Wexler were, as the producers, always trying to push the group into directions of their own choosing. McPhatter didn't begrudge them their efforts at finding new sounds that might sell records to white as well as black audiences, but he didn't feel like participating. His goal was to cross over to pop audiences as a balladeer. He saw himself as having the potential to become another Nat King Cole, or perhaps a black answer to Frank Sinatra or Perry Como. By October of 1954, he had parted company with the group in favor of a solo career that would make him a success for the rest of the 1950s.

Rather than see the group in which they'd invested 18 months of their time go out of existence, Ertegun and Wexler were still interested in recording the Drifters, but that group's internal circumstances were vastly different once McPhatter was gone. McPhatter had organized the Drifters under the auspices of his own business entity, Drifters Incorporated, so that he would have a share of its earnings, something that he'd been denied in the Dominoes; his own willingness to share those earnings with the other members has never been broached or questioned. He was half-owner of the group with his manager, George Treadwell, a former jazz musician who had masterminded the solo career of his first wife, Sarah Vaughan; when McPhatter left the group, rather than making a provision for the other members and his eventual successor to get his share, he sold out his interest in Drifters Incorporated to Treadwell.

This basically doomed the group to a permanent revolving-door lineup. From that day forward, all of the members of the Drifters were salaried employees, earning as little as 100 dollars a week even into the early '60s and getting no share of royalties from record sales, or benefit from the concert fees they commanded, or any claim to the use of the name "the Drifters" if they left, no matter how successful the group became through their efforts. It thus became impossible for the group to hold onto anyone with serious talent or aspirations for a long-term career in music. This made the Drifters, for those present after McPhatter's exit, little more inviting than his own tenure with the Dominoes, and he later regretted making the decision, recognizing not only what he had cheated himself out of by not hanging onto his share of the ownership but also what he had done to his fellow musicians.

The immediate problem facing all concerned in 1954, however, was finding a replacement for McPhatter, and some would argue that they never did. David Baughn, who had sung with a very early version of the Drifters, came in as a temporary replacement, singing at one recording session and serving as lead vocalist for six months' worth of live engagements (which was how the group generated most of its income). Baughn's singing was good enough, but the group sounded like an imitation of the McPhatter-era Drifters, and Atlantic declined to release any of these sides at the time, possibly due to their potential to interfere with McPhatter's solo releases, which were selling well. The label didn't know whether to shoot for an entirely new sound or to try to find a replacement who sounded like the former lead singer who, by 1956, was a major R&B star in his own right. Additionally, Baughn soon demonstrated an erratic personality, sufficiently unnerving to force Treadwell to recruit a second lead vocalist in Bobby Hendricks, who had previously sung with the Five Crowns and the Swallows. Attempts were made to record this lineup, and even bass singer Bill Pinkney was cut doing a lead vocal, but none of it was considered acceptable.

The lineup itself began to shift as Baughn quit, but the group soldiered on, drawing good crowds at their shows based on the quality of their earlier recordings. In 1955, however, they auditioned a young man who approached the group after a show in Cleveland. Johnny Moore had been a member of a group called the Hornets, who had done a little bit of recording without making any more than a local reputation for themselves. He sounded enough like McPhatter, however, with his pleasing high tenor and was offered a spot in the Drifters the next day. Moore would prove to be a mainstay of the group in two different decades.

The Drifters resumed recording in September of 1955, with Nesuhi Ertegun and songwriter Jerry Leiber producing and with Moore singing lead. The result was a number-one R&B chart single, "Adorable," which went a long way toward establishing their post-McPhatter reputation. This proved to be one of the very few major chart records they would enjoy during this era, however—the Drifters were still absent from the top of the pop charts, where the real money and huge sales figures lay. Their records during the late '50s were overlooked by most young white listeners, despite the presence of future rock & roll standards such as "Ruby Baby" in their output.

Dion would enjoy a much bigger hit with the latter song in the early '60s, but it was an important recording for the Drifters, marking their introduction to the talents of songwriters Jerry Leiber & Mike Stoller, who would later take over the job of producing the group. The group's lineup was also stabilized for the first time in over a year. The original Drifters now entered their "silver age" behind Moore's cool high tenor, ably supported by the bass singing (and occasional lead spot) from Bill Pinkney and Bobby Hendricks' tenor. "I Gotta Get Myself a Woman," written by Jesse Stone and cut during the summer of 1956, brought the group a number-11 R&B hit and the group's fortunes once again seemed to be on a consistent upswing.

As it turned out, the black record-buying public wasn't prepared to fully accept a new Drifters without McPhatter—black audiences practically worshipped the singer, who commanded a passionate loyalty that anticipated the future success of Sam Cooke. Additionally, the music was changing—white teenagers were now a much bigger part of the market than they had been in 1953-1954, and Atlantic set its sights on that potentially much richer vein of listeners.

The end of 1956 saw the release of the first album by group, entitled *Clyde McPhatter & the Drifters.* Late 1956 was also the point when the consequences of the Drifters' business organization caught up with the group. Their recent hits had led to more bookings than at any time since 1954, which was good for Treadwell and his partners, but difficult for the members, who were still working on straight salary and, by Bill Pinkney's estimation, very low salaries.

By late 1958, Treadwell was about to find himself without a group and faced with upcoming engagements to fulfill at the Apollo Theater in New York. He spotted his way out of this impasse at the Apollo, way down on a bill on May 30, 1958, on which the about-to-be-fired Drifters were headlining. The Five Crowns, or the Crowns, as they were then known, had been a fixture in Harlem for most of the 1950s, predating the Drifters without ever making a mark as a recording act, and enjoying precious little reputation as performers. Treadwell approached their manager, Lover Patterson, explaining that he was dumping the existing Drifters and needed a new group to fulfill their performing obligations. Patterson agreed and the group followed suit, and all of the individual members' contracts, except for that of one of the group's two baritones, were sold to Treadwell. The new Drifters lineup consisted of Charlie Thomas as lead, baritone Benjamin Earl Nelson, later known as Ben E. King, baritone Doc Green (who had held the Crowns together), and Elsbeary Hobbs singing bass. They did as they were required under the agreement and for ten months worked in the shadow of the old group, playing live gigs characterized by the awkwardness of performing the old songs as though they were their own, to mostly black audiences who knew that these weren't the Drifters. Atlantic still hoped to profit from the group, however, and a second Drifters LP, *Rockin' & Driftin',* was released in late 1958, comprised entirely of single tracks recorded by the 1955-1958 lineup.

The group still had a recording contract with Atlantic Records and, despite the fact that the old Drifters' recent releases had done little business, the label decided to try once more with the new lineup and get a record out. On March 6, 1959, they went into the studio to cut four songs with Leiber & Stoller producing. Charlie Thomas was supposed to sing lead but he developed mick-fright in the studio, and so Nelson was deputized for "There Goes My Baby," which he had co-written, "Hey Senorita," and "Oh My Love." "There Goes My Baby," co-written by Nelson and orchestrated by Stan Applebaum, was as much a landmark in the history of R&B and soul as "Money Honey" had been six years earlier. At the time, nobody present was sure of what they had because it sounded so chaotic, strange, and complicated—no one had ever used a string section, much less one recorded as prominently as this one was, on an R&B record, and no R&B record up until that time had ever dared sound so complex, overlaying Latin percussion, violins, and a fiercely passionate performance by the singer. It not only didn't sound anything like the old Drifters, but it didn't sound like anything else that had ever been heard on a commercial recording before. "There Goes My Baby" peaked at number two, their biggest hit to date on the pop charts and their biggest seller up to that time, winning over both R&B and pop audiences and transforming the group and its image.

The post-1959 Drifters (which also included guitarist Billy Davis) are usually thought of as "the Ben E. King Drifters," but the reality is that he was gone from the group as a member by the end of that same year. King's first successor was Johnny Williams, who exited suddenly in late 1960, but the Drifters quickly found a replacement in Rudy Lewis. An ex-member of the Clara Ward Singers, Lewis was the singer on "Some Kind of Wonderful," "Up on the Roof" (a Top Five hit), "Please Stay," "What to Do," and "On Broadway" (a Top Ten hit), among numerous other classic tracks by the group. Lewis, tragically, wasn't the longest lasting of the group's lead vocalists but his tenure with the group, following King's, arguably constituted the second half of a second golden age in their history. Whoever was involved on a particular record, the group was once again at a peak of influence in those years.

The Drifters continued recording for Atlantic with a succession of producers until 1972. By that time, the company itself was part of a huge corporate conglomerate, far removed from its origins—Led Zeppelin, Yes, and Emerson, Lake & Palmer were the stars of the Atlantic roster then, and scarcely anyone at the company except Ertegun and Wexler likely even remembered who the Drifters were or how they'd started. Moore still sang lead, but there were no more hits after the mid-'60s. They tried altering their sound to mainstream adult pop, cutting old-style standards in an effort to capture older listeners. As the hits faded away and the bookings dried up, the group broke up yet again—in the end, Moore was the only recognizable Drifter and he did most of the singing on the records as well.

The 1970s saw a proliferation of acts trading on the Drifters name as the rock & roll revival suddenly made the group's classic repertory profitable again. Founding member Bill Pinkney led a group sometimes called "the Original Drifters" while Charlie Thomas led another version and Moore kept the fully authorized group under the auspices of Treadwell's widow, aye. *—Bruce Eder*

Clyde McPhatter & the Drifters / 1956 / Atlantic ♦♦♦♦

The Drifters' debut album didn't appear until 1956, more than a year after Clyde McPhatter had left the group that he founded. Thus, this LP was actually an oldies release from the date of its first appearance, and even more so when it was repackaged in 1958 (a time when McPhatter's solo career was running as hot as a pistol) with new notes. With McPhatter's high tenor voice featured as the lead on every song (basso Bill Pinkney occasionally stepped forward as well), this release and its title made perfect commercial sense on either date. For fans of the singer or the group, or anyone who wasn't around to buy the singles assembled here when they first came out, this was an awesome collection. Numbers like "Money Honey" became the basic language of rock & roll as surely as anything ever written by Chuck Berry, and soaring soul ballads like "Warm Your Heart" and "Lucille" (a rare McPhatter song copyright) are good to hear in any era. On hot "jump" numbers like "What'cha Gonna Do?," McPhatter uncannily anticipates the sound upon which Jackie Wilson would build his career in the second half of the 1950s. In short, this is an album that just didn't stop rocking. Helping along in the endeavor were saxman Sam "The Man" Taylor and guitarist Jimmy Oliver (who shines with some particularly hard-edged playing on "Warm Your Heart." The original LP has since been supplanted by several CD reissues that are very carefully mastered, but it had a pretty cool cover and, in the 1958 reissue, some of the most extensive jacket notes seen on an LP outside the jazz or classical fields up to that point (focusing, of course, on McPhatter's career). *—Bruce Eder*

Rockin' & Driftin' / 1958 / Atlantic ♦♦♦

The second LP by the Drifters was, almost as much as its predecessor *Clyde McPhatter & the Drifters,* a catch-up effort comprised of three years of recordings by a group whose membership was in a constant state of flux. The lead singers were Johnny Moore, Bobby Hendricks, Gerhart Thrasher, or David Baughn, McPhatter's successors from 1955 through 1958. This collection lacks the mystique of the first album, partly because none of these singers approached McPhatter's name recognition, and also because the records themselves simply weren't as good. (This isn't meant to put them down—it's difficult to imagine a body of 20-plus songs that could match the Drifters' output from 1953-1954.) Additionally, these were all very different vocalists. Johnny Moore was as close as any of them to his predecessor's style and he lacked McPhatter's sheer power, although he had excellent intonation and on occasion sounded remarkably like Jackie Wilson (nowhere more than on "It Was a Tear"). However, his ballads lacked the almost otherworldly quality that imbued McPhatter's work, and his tenure with the group, as represented here, was a far more conventional period without much commercial success. "On Moonlight Bay" is the album's nadir, an abortive attempt to turn the pop standard into a doo wop-style number. By contrast, "Adorable," dating from 1955, anticipated Sam Cooke's attempt to meld soul balladry with mainstream pop by a good three years—indeed, it even calls to mind Cooke's "I Love You for Sentimental Reasons" in its opening and chorus. There are also signs of an attempt to transform the Drifters into an outfit similar to their Atco labelmates the Coasters, doing highly animated novelty songs like "Yodee Yakee." There is one classic rock & roll number here, "Ruby Baby," which didn't sell much at the time but, along with another track off this record, "Drip Drop," became a huge hit for Dion early in the following decade. There's also a gorgeous ballad in "I Know" and a trio of killer R&B dance numbers in "Fools Fall in Love," "Hypnotized," and "I Got to Get Myself a Woman" (the latter featuring Bill Pinkney), but a lot of the rest is good but relatively unexceptional R&B. The LP is worth hearing just for Sam "The Man" Taylor's sax solo on "Drip Drop." As reflected by this album, the Drifters were in a constant state of commercial and artistic turmoil during the years represented by these recordings, which ultimately led to their breakup in 1959. *—Bruce Eder*

Save the Last Dance for Me / Feb. 1962 / Atlantic ♦♦♦♦

The first LP appearance by the Ben E. King-era Drifters, as was usually the case with this group, took place more than a year after King himself had left the group, replaced by Rudy Lewis whose voice is featured on most of the tracks here. This album is more unified than its predecessor, which is understandable as it appeared in the wake of a succession of hits utilizing the same core group and the same style of production, mixing strings into an R&B sound and creating something new and attractive that crossed over very easily to pop listeners. "When My Little Girl Is Smiling," "Room Full of Tears," and the title track exemplify the sound, but the finest cut here might be "Nobody but Me." A Doc Pomus/Mort Shuman-authored B-side to the title cut, "Nobody but Me" should have been a hit in its own right. Actually, as with prior releases by the group, the album is comprised of single A- and B-sides, including "Please Stay," "Jackpot," and "Mexican Divorce." The album also provides a likely explanation for the non-release of the excellent "She Never Talked to Me That Way": its similarity (especially in the chorus) to another Pomus/Shuman number on this album, "Somebody New Dancing With You," which was cut earlier and probably precluded the release of "She Never Talked to Me That Way" on a single at the time. *—Bruce Eder*

Up on the Roof: The Best of the Drifters / Feb. 1963 / Atlantic ♦♦♦

The first best-of Drifters collection in the group's complicated ten-year existence, this 14-song LP was also a strange compilation, drawing together Clyde McPhatter-era chart singles like "Ruby Baby," Ben E. King-sung classics like "There Goes My Baby" and "This Magic Moment," and Rudy Lewis-era masterpieces such as "Up on the Roof." It also freely mixes in odd but worthy sides like the hard R&B piece "What to Do" (never an actual hit) among the chart-busters. At the time of its release, this compilation provided a decent cross-section of some recent and classic singles by the two versions of the group. It's superior to the subsequent *Golden Hits* collection as an introduction to the Drifters' history, but has been supplanted by many subsequent LP and CD reissues. *—Bruce Eder*

Under the Boardwalk / 1964 / Atlantic ♦♦♦♦

Under the Boardwalk appeared very quickly after the *Our Biggest Hits* compilation, which was then deleted. The two LPs originally had the same cover jackets and one difference to the music inside—the "Under the Boardwalk" single replaced "Drip Drop" on the *Under the Boardwalk* LP. With the music on this album, the Drifters began a new era in their history under tragic circumstances, given the sudden and still mysterious death early in 1964 of Rudy Lewis, who had been the group's lead singer since 1960. Lewis was succeeded by Johnny Moore, who had rejoined as lead tenor in 1963 and had previously been Clyde McPhatter's successor in the old Drifters in 1955. This album mixes songs cut when Lewis was still with the group, but on which Moore sang lead, along with some of Lewis' last successes such as "Up on the Roof" and "On Broadway." It's a superb example of pop-oriented soul, with two excellent singers given equally fine material to work with. Much of the music was made under the direction of producer Bert Berns, who was to guide the Drifters to their very last period of major recording success. This album, the last of the Drifters' LPs to resonate with huge hits, is also considered a classic for the very cool cover image on its second version, a multicolored overlay depicting the five-man Drifters lineup led by Johnny Moore, complete with guitarist Billy Davis, who was a key (if understated) component in the group's sound. *—Bruce Eder*

The Good Life With the Drifters / Feb. 1965 / Atlantic ✦✦
During the Drifters' 19 years on Atlantic Records, nine LPs of their music were released, but in all of that time and among that array of 12-inch platters, this was the only one that was recorded as an actual album, as opposed to having been assembled from singles and B-sides. And the irony is that it is really a Drifters album in name only—it's credited to the group, and the four singing members are shown on the front cover, but Johnny Moore is the main focus throughout and the rest of the group is pushed so far into the background that they're scarcely audible. *The Good Life* was produced by Tom Dowd with the goal of creating a soft pop album, similar to the kind of supper club music that Sam Cooke delved into and that Sammy Davis Jr. was making. Johnny Moore was up to the task but the choice of material was less than inspiring—his intonation is beautiful, and the nuances of his singing embrace the songs and their melodies, but he also sounds unchallenged and, indeed, almost bored doing songs like "Tonight," "On the Street Where You Live," and "What Kind of Fool Am I." What makes this record doubly frustrating is that, with Dowd producing, the elegant orchestrations have a magnificent sound technically, but it is just not a Drifters record or representative of what they or Johnny Moore were about. On the other hand, for all of its flaws, it is an interesting attempt at an unofficial Johnny Moore solo record, and he does reveal himself as at least having had the potential to be another Sam Cooke, although on "Temptation," the old Nacio Herb Brown/Arthur Freed chestnut and the most awkward track here (Moore's voice having been dubbed onto a backing track originally recorded with Ben E. King in 1959), he sounds more like he's trying to imitate Howard Keel. As a result of its unusual origins, this is the least desirable Drifters album among their classic Atlantic long-players, although fans of Johnny Moore will find it a choice addendum to their classic sides, and it is relatively easy to find among their non-"best-of" albums. In its defense, it did make it to number 103 on the charts, probably on the strength of the recent hit "Saturday Night at the Movies" having been stuck onto it (which completely broke up the underlying sound and concept of the sessions and the LP anyway). *—Bruce Eder*

I'll Take You Where the Music's Playing / 1965 / Atlantic ✦✦✦
Atlantic Records expected a big return on this LP featuring material by the Brill Building elite: Jeff Barry, Ellie Greenwich, Bert Russell, Gerry Goffin, Carole King, Kenny Young, Artie Resnick, Doc Pomus, Mort Shuman, and others, but failed to come close to its forecast. The Drifters—Johnny Moore, Charles Thomas, Eugene Pearson, John Terry, and guitarist Billy Davis—perform the light pop/rock tunes to perfection, but none became major hits: "I've Got Sand in My Shoe" (number 33 on the pop charts) and "At the Club" (charting at number 43) were the biggest. "Follow Me" (adulated by Northern soul fans because of its rigid four-on-the-floor cadence and tenor wails on the fade) didn't bust the Top 50; likewise, for "Far From the Maddening Crowd" and "Come Over to My Place." The songs, although written by the same composers who served the Drifters—"On Broadway," "Up on the Roof," and "This Magic Moment"—lack the charm and luster of those monsters. *—Andrew Hamilton*

Live at Harvard University / 1986 / New Rose ✦✦✦
This live album is a vital document for serious fans of the Drifters, containing a complete (or near-complete) concert from December 1972 by a lineup that could claim reasonable authenticity. Charlie Thomas, Elsbeary Hobbs, and Doc Green had all been members of the group in its 1960s incarnation along with guitarist Abdul Samaad (previously known as Billy Davis). The one new member, Bobby Ruffin, was a good first tenor—one pauses, however, when Charlie Thomas announces "Honey Love" as a song that "we recorded with the late, great Clyde McPhatter." The Drifters cut the song with McPhatter, true enough, but Thomas and the others were so far from the lineup of the group at that time that he should have gagged on the sentence. The performance is spirited, however, and there is some superb harmonizing here. Time was when Charlie Thomas lost out on his chance to be the lead singer of the Drifters because of mike-fright in the studio, but on stage he had far fewer problems, as demonstrated here. The raps by Thomas extend some songs, such as "Save the Last Dance for Me," to extreme lengths, and depart from the songs altogether at times, though the sing-along on the latter ends up being fun to hear. Basically, the group was trying to form a compromise between its core repertory and late-'60s/early-'70s soul, with Samaad's nimble guitar playing—alternating rhythm and lead in front of a small backing band—providing a solid base on which to build. The versions of "This Magic Moment," "True Love True Love," "Lonely Winds," "White Christmas," and "The Bells of St. Mary's" receive elegant performances that are faithful to the originals, while "Money Honey" more than does justice to the 1953 classic, with a brief blues break by Samaad that genuinely adds some new facets to the piece. "Under the Boardwalk" and "On Broadway" both get delightful, soaring performances, and "There Goes My Baby" isn't far behind, except that it does seem a little ragged (despite their best vocal efforts) as a finale—though one can't imagine what other song (except perhaps "Money Honey") could possibly have been their finale. The tape itself is a pretty fair professional job that evidently was privately owned and licensed to New Rose; the sound is better than good, but the "notes" are rather pathetic in both depth and accuracy. *—Bruce Eder*

☆ **All-Time Greatest Hits & More: 1959–1965** / 1988 / Atlantic ✦✦✦✦✦
If Rhino's *Very Best of the Drifters* is a fine R&B snack, then *All-Time Greatest Hits & More: 1959-1965* is a three-course gourmet meal with dessert built on the same ingredients. Forget about the higher price and the fact that 40 songs might seem to be more Drifters than most casual listeners would want—*All-Time Greatest Hits & More: 1959-1965* is a towering and magnificent collection of some of the best popular R&B ever done this side of Sam Cooke. And, as with Sam Cooke, the beautiful part of the Drifters' work during this period is that any look beyond and behind their hits reveals a lot more songs that were every bit as good as those hits. There's not even a slightly weak track anywhere on *All-Time Greatest Hits & More*, which contains the biggest hits Ben E. King, Rudy Lewis, and Johnny Moore sang for the group. "There Goes My Baby," "This Magic Moment," "Save the Last Dance for Me," "Sweets for My Sweet," "I Count the Tears," "Some Kind of Wonderful," "Up on the Roof," "On Broadway," and "Under the Boardwalk" are all here, mastered in surprisingly good sound for the late '80s. There's a lot more than that, however—the producers have also included killer B-sides (such as "Let the Music Play") that hadn't been in print since the mid-'60s, and they've dug even deeper to throw in finished tracks that were left in the vaults until the '70s. The notes by Colin Escott are an added bonus, displaying his usual command for historical detail. *—Bruce Eder*

☆ **Let the Boogie-Woogie Roll: Greatest Hits 1953–1958** / 1988 / Atlantic ✦✦✦✦✦
This is a repackaged and re-sequenced version of the similarly titled 1988 Atlantic double CD, containing the 40 songs recorded by the early Drifters in their Clyde McPhatter, David Baughan, and Johnny Moore eras—and it's as fine a body of rhythm & blues-cum-rock & roll as you'll ever find. The work runs from the ethereal, soulful balladry ("Gone") to bluesy laments ("Don't Dog Me") and distinctive reinterpretations of classic songs ("White Christmas," "The Bells of St. Mary's") to out and out rock & roll ("Money Honey," "Let the Boogie Woogie Roll," "Bip Bam") with lots of classic moments and songs. Certainly Clyde McPhatter never cut better music than the 20 tracks he did with the Drifters, all laid out on disc one. Their string of hits was unbroken by the arrival of Johnny Moore, so the second disc in this set is as enjoyable as the first. The improvement to this set over the original includes a bigger typeface for the notes, and the altered sequencing, which puts everything in order of recording, not release, thus, presenting the way the group evolved, step by step and song by song. The sound, in addition to showing off the group's extraordinary vocal prowess, also highlights the playing of guitarist Mickey Baker and saxman Sam "The Man" Taylor. *—Bruce Eder*

★ **The Very Best of the Drifters** / Apr. 20, 1993 / Rhino ✦✦✦✦✦
This mid-priced 16-song collection is the successor to the old Atlantic Records *Drifters Golden Hits*, covering the group's very best songs from "There Goes My Baby" in 1959 on up through 1964 in a more comprehensive way. Very pleasingly remastered and handy on its own terms, *The Very Best of the Drifters* also provides just a taste of what the post-1958 group had to offer, even in terms of singles. No one will dislike anything about it, but those who have heard even part of the two-CD package *All-Time Greatest Hits & More* will recognize *The Very Best of the Drifters* as nothing but a superficial sampler of what the Ben E. King/Rudy Lewis/Johnny Moore version of the group left behind. *The Very Best of the Drifters* is a great place to start, but the leap from this material to the rest of the Drifters' best is such a short one that, unless time or budgetary limitations dictate otherwise, it can be bypassed in favor of Atlantic's double-disc *All-Time Greatest Hits & More*. *—Bruce Eder*

Rockin' & Driftin': The Drifters Box / 1996 / Rhino ✦✦✦✦✦
This triple-disc 79-song compilation looks pretty impressive, and in some ways it is, representing most of the best work of each incarnation of the Drifters from 1953 through 1976. There's a lot of classic music here, including all of the big hits and many interesting (even musically glorious) flops and B-sides, but the limitations of three CDs make this less than ideal. Atlantic had already released a pair of two-CD sets, *Let the Boogie Woogie Roll: Greatest Hits 1953-1958* and *All-Time Greatest Hits & More: 1959-1965*, eight years earlier, each of which covers those major periods in question far more generously than does this box—although it must be conceded that the sound on the cuts included on *Rockin' & Driftin'* is improved over those late-'80s digital transfers, good as they seemed at the time. Additionally, almost concurrent with this release from Rhino Records in America, Sequel Records in England issued its Drifters *Anthology* series, assembling the group's complete Atlantic Records output on seven separate CDs, organized somewhat awkwardly at times but also including a number of outtakes, so serious fans may want to opt for that group of discs. This set, had it gone to four CDs, could have been truly comprehensive, covering all of those bases by grabbing some of the best of those genuinely beautiful outtakes, such as "In the Park"—as it is, the only unreleased cut here is the group's version of "Only in America"—and oddities like the achingly soulful "She Never Talked to Me That Way," plus all of the official live recordings that they left behind from the mid-'60s. At three CDs, it's a little squeezed, especially as the producers devote some space and attention on concurrent solo hits by Clyde McPhatter and Ben E. King. *—Bruce Eder*

Clyde McPhatter & the Drifters/Rockin' & Driftin' / Jul. 28, 1998 / Collectables ✦✦✦✦

Up on the Roof/Under the Boardwalk / Jul. 28, 1998 / Collectables ✦✦✦✦

Save the Last Dance for Me/The Good Life With the Drifters / Jun. 20, 2000 / Collectables ✦✦✦✦

Dru Hill

f. 1995, Baltimore, MD

Group / Club/Dance, Urban, Hip-Hop

High-school friends Jazz, Sisqó, Nokio and Woody formed Dru Hill in 1995—named in honor of their Baltimore neighborhood, Druid Hill Park. The rappers performed at the music-industry convention Impact '96 and were signed by Island not long after. By late

1996, Dru Hill had released its self-titled debut album, produced by Keith Sweat, Stanley Brown and Tim "Dawg" Patterson. The single "Tell Me"—culled from the soundtrack to the film *Eddie*—became a Top Five R&B hit and later went gold; *Enter the Dru* followed in 1998. *—John Bush*

● **Dru Hill** / Nov. 19, 1996 / Island ♦♦♦♦
Rich harmonies and sleek R&B production with an abundance of vocal acrobatics are all key elements of Dru Hill's eponymous debut. Immediate comparisons to Jodeci and Boyz II Men come to mind, but what makes Dru Hill stand out from the pack is the rawness of Keith Sweat's productions. Other songs on here are of noteworthy interest only to die-hard Dru Hill fanatics, but it was the monster "Tell Me" that effectively put Dru Hill near the head of R&B's class of 1996—a year that featured stellar releases by Aaliyah, Jay-Z, and several others at the peak of their games. An impressive debut and a razor-sharp clue of the great things to come. *—Rob Theakston*

Enter the Dru / Oct. 27, 1998 / Island ♦♦♦
The best of the late-'90s R&B crooning quartets ups the musical ante on their sophomore album, lacing the silky-smooth grooves with splashes of street-tough shouts that are meant to antagonize as much as they are to seduce. And for a good deal of *Enter the Dru*, the formula works. There's a gutsy edge to the songs here (especially the hard-knocking "How Deep Is Your Love") that make onetime peers like Boyz II Men sound like the soulless R&B robots they are. Even when they get all warm and cozy with Babyface on the potentially mushy "These Are the Times" (in spite the absurdity of the straight-faced line "Tear you up in little pieces/Swallow you like Reese's Pieces"), Dru Hill slice into the section of '90s soul music that crosses bedroom come-ons with classic street savvy (and nervy beats) without sounding at all whipped. *—Michael Gallucci*

Dru World Order / Nov. 26, 2002 / Def Soul ♦♦♦
After Sisqó's solo debut pushed two big hits ("Thong Song," "Incomplete") to the top of the charts, it appeared Dru Hill was going to have to recruit a replacement for its best-known name. When the group finally returned in 2002, though, it not only welcomed Sisqó back to the fold but added a member (Skola) to make the group a quintet. The third album, *Dru World Order*, proves the group possesses as much talent as any of their contemporaries in the R&B world. First of all, it's largely self-contained; Nokio produced over half the album, and much of the songwriting was kept in-house as well. And with the gospel fervor of new addition Skola, Dru Hill sounds stronger and smoother than it has in the past. The single "I Should Be..." is solid, if a little in the line of standard material for them, but "On Me" (featuring N.O.R.E.) and "Old Love" are two of the most inspired songs they've ever recorded. The songwriting tends to similar themes, as do the songs themselves, but having the most polished harmonies on the R&B block makes Dru Hill capable of smoothing over any of the rough spots on *Dru World Order*. *—John Bush*

The Du Droppers

f. 1952, **db.** 1955
Group / R&B
New York's Du Droppers managed to score two Top Five hits during their short run: "I Wanna Know" (number-three R&B) and "I Found Out (What You Do When You Go Round There)" (number-three pop). The original members were Caleb Ginyard—aka "J.C." or sometimes "Junior"—on lead, brothers Willie Ray and Harvey Ray on tenor and baritone, respectively, and Eddie Hashow on bass (who was soon replaced by Bob Kornegay). They began as a gospel group in 1952; each member had been in previous gospel groups (including the Royal Harmony Singers, the Dixie-Aires, the Jubilaires, and the Southwest Jubilee Group). The Du Droppers began performing R&B vocal-group songs and soon auditioned for record producer Bobby Robinson and DJ Joel Turnero, both owners of the Harlem-based label and record shop Red Robin.

Their first record, "Can't Do Sixty No More," released by the group in December 1952, was an "answer" record to the massively popular Dominoes hit, "Sixty Minute Man." It earned the group instant popularity and airplay, but Red Robin let the Du Droppers slip through their fingers; soon the group was recording for RCA Victor, one of the major labels looking to break out in the fast growing field of R&B. In mid-March of 1953, their next single, "I Wanna Know," made a huge impact and climbed to number three.

In June 1953, the Du Droppers released the follow-up to their RCA smash, and "I Found Out (What You Do When You Go Round There)" climbed to number three on the pop charts. Soon they were embarking on a late-summer tour of one-nighters through the South with the Joe Morris Blues Cavalcade. Subsequent singles, however, failed to generate much new interest in the group. In November, RCA paired the group with pop music singer Sunny Gale for a (now highly collectable) single, "Mama's Gone Goodbye." In 1954, the Du Droppers began recording for a new RCA subsidiary, Groove Records, which was meant to be strictly for R&B acts signed to the major label. Unfortunately, they failed to improve upon their track record and subsequent Groove singles saw them slipping from the charts.

In early 1955, Groove attempted to persuade Ravens' vocalist Joe Van Loan to join the group and help shake things up, but he was already under a personal service contract with Herald Records; while this was being sorted out, Charlie Hughes was brought in to sing lead on recordings only, though he wasn't allowed to perform with the group. Groove released another single and an EP, but the Du Droppers were unraveling even as it happened. In August, the label issued one last single, but soon thereafter, Junior Ginyard re-treated back to gospel music, joining the Golden Gate Quartet, so the others decided to call it a day. *—Bryan Thomas*

● **Can't Do Sixty No More** / 1987 / Dr. Horse ♦♦♦♦♦

The Dubs

f. 1957, New York, NY [Harlem]
Group / Doo Wop, R&B
Best remembered for their enduring Top 40 doo wop classic "Could This Be Magic," the Dubs developed during the early '50s out of two short-lived vocal acts: the Five Wings and the Scale-Tones. The Harlem-based Five Wings had recorded a few singles for King Records, though three of the Five Wings then quit the group (including lead Jackie Rue, who went on to form Jackie & the Starlites of "Valerie" fame). That prompted second tenor Billy Carlisle and bass Tommy Grate to join up with Kenny "Butch" Hamilton (formerly of the R&B group the Sonics) and later, backing vocalist Bill Nelson. Soon after their initial November 1955 session, Carlisle's cousin Richard Blandon joined the group. In February 1956, they released the single "Walk Along."

The Five Wings soon met up with another Harlem-based group, the Scale-Tones, who had just recorded their first and only single for Joe Davis' Jay Dee label. After some prompting by Richard Blandon (who wanted to sing lead), a new group emerged from the two. This lineup featured Richard Blandon (lead) and Billy Carlisle (second tenor), plus former Scale-Tones Cleveland Still (first tenor), Jake Miller (baritone), and Thomas Gardner (bass). The Blandon-led group signed to ABC Paramount late in 1956 and issued their first single in November. The Five Wings' manager, Hiram Johnson (brother of famed musician and bandleader Buddy Johnson), later decided to form his own label, Johnson Records, and in early 1957, the Marvels changed their name to the Dubs.

Their first single under this moniker—the Blandon-penned "Don't Ask Me to Be Lonely"—was released in March. Radio jumped on the single immediately and Johnson soon found himself with a hit. Next up was Blandon's "Could This Be Magic," and by the first week of November, the Dubs had their second national pop Top 40 song of the year. The Dubs continued to tour extensively; however, subsequent singles from the group failed to connect. In November 1958, after the group's "Chapel of Dreams" was released to little reaction, the Dubs decided to call it a day. In July 1959, some eight months after its initial release, "Chapel of Dreams" was reissued. The single quickly jumped into the Top 100 on August 24, rising to number 74 after six weeks. The Dubs, thinking they were being given a second chance, came together again, replacing Still with Cordell Brown, and re-signed with ABC Paramount, the same label they were with three years before as the Marvels.

Though all five of their second-wave ABC singles were fine recordings, their two-year run—from November 1959 to November 1961—yielded no chart results. By the '70s, the Dubs were still clinging to life, but their popular chart successes were clearly behind them. All total, the Dubs (at least the groups featuring lead vocalist Richard Blandon) recorded for ten record labels, from the '50s through the mid-'70s, but never enjoyed much in the way of success or made any headway outside doo wop circles. *—Bryan Thomas*

● **The Best of the Dubs** / Nov. 25, 1991 / Collectables ♦♦♦
Their big hit "Could This Be Magic" is merely the tip of the iceberg on this 14-track collection of the group's best songs. This set brings together sides recorded in the group's heyday with Richard Blandon's unmistakable lead voice driving the tracks. A classic slab of New York doo wop harmony. *—Cub Koda*

The Unavailable 24 / 1993 / Juke Box Treasures ♦♦♦
Richard Blandon and the Dubs are best known to vocal group harmony fans for their hit record of "Could This Be Magic." These later efforts, recorded under a variety of circumstances and varying in recording quality, capture much of what made Blandon and the group so special. *—Cub Koda*

The Duettes

Group / Girl Group, Soul
The Duettes—Barbara Livsey (aka Barbara Bates) and Mary Francis Hayes—were two Chicago teens that recorded for the George Leaner family of labels. Duettes recordings appeared on M-Pac, One-derful, and Mar-V-Lus Records, with Otha "Otis" Hayes, Andre Williams, Verlie Rice, Monk Higgins, and others supplying the material. Despite magnetism and solid sounds they never enjoyed a chart record, or even a regional breakout. Their recording career began with "Mister Steel" in 1963, followed by "Move on Down the Line" and "I'm Gonna Love You" in 1964—all on M-Pac. Leaner switched them to the One-derful label for "Lonely Days," with "Please Forgive Me," riding shotgun; a final single, "Sugar Daddy," dropped on Mar-V-Lus Records in 1965. "Lonely Days" appeared a second time on Lost Nite Records in 1965 but didn't do any better than the previous attempt. No more Duettes recordings were released, though Barbara Livsey-Bates surfaced in 1970 as Barbara & the Uniques. *—Andrew Hamilton*

The Dukays

f. 1960, **db.** 1965
Group / R&B, Soul
The Dukays' bright future dimmed only when record-company shenanigans did them in; their 1961 smash "The Duke of Earl" was credited solely to their lead singer, Eugene Dixon (aka Gene Chandler), who left the group after it was re-released on another label. One of the most popular groups on Chicago's South Side (the Englewood neighborhood), the Dukays consisted of Dixon, Shirley Jones (tenor/soprano), James Lowe (second tenor), Earl Edwards (baritone), and Ben Broyles, the unforgettable bass on "Duke of Earl." Songwriter Bernice Williams befriended the Englewood sensations and became their main songwriter when they soon signed with Nat Records. The group's first single, "The Girl Is a Devil," sold locally and did a little business outside of Chicago in 1961. They were showstoppers live: everything about them was exciting, especially Shirley Jones (Dixon's cousin), who stepped and blew notes right along with the fellows, almost a funky edition of the Platters. In December of 1961, Nat released their third single, "The Duke of Earl" b/w "Kissin' in the Kitchen," and all hell broke loose. By the following month, a deal was consummated with Vee-Jay Records, who re-released "Duke of Earl" and credited it to Gene Chandler (he adopted the surname from actor Jeff Chandler and people always shortened his first name anyway). The Dukays felt slighted, abused, and mistreated. Vee-Jay didn't re-record the song, but simply slapped their label on new pressings on the Nat acetate.

As appeasement, Vee-Jay signed the group to a separate deal and reissued their second single "Nite Owl." Charles Davis (aka Nolan Chance) replaced Chandler and Margaret "Cookie" Stone took over for Shirley Jones, who quit. Vee-Jay issued three singles by the Dukays, two in 1962 and one in 1963, but none of them clicked. They appeared uncredited on a few of Chandler's solos, before he switched to Constellation Records, the label that made him an R&B icon.

Nearly two years passed before the Dukays surfaced in November 1964 on the Jerry-O label with "The Jerk." The new group featured Claude McRae (lead), Richard Dixon, Earl Edwards, and James Lowe. In 1965, Jerry-O, owned by Jerry J. Murray, issued the final Dukays single, "Mellow-Fezneckey" b/w "Sho-Nuf M.F." (a scandalous title for the times); neither did much business and they disbanded. Nolan Chance recorded solo for Constellation and other labels, while Chandler carved a stellar solo career. *—Andrew Hamilton*

Doris Duke

b. Sandersville, GA

Vocals / Soul

Hailing from a strong gospel heritage, Doris Duke was a native of Sandersville, GA. During the '60s, she found work as a background vocalist in New York City before cutting her only major hit, "To the Other Woman (I'm the Other Woman)," in 1970 for the Canyon label. It was a Top Ten R&B hit that year, and prompted a full album, *I'm a Loser.* She also recorded a full-length (titled *Woman*) for Scepter in 1975. *—Bill Dahl*

● **I'm a Loser** / 1970 / Contempo ♦♦♦♦♦

I'm a Loser is the standout recording from Southern soul singer Doris Duke; problem is, it's nearly impossible to find. Originally released on the Canyon label in 1970, *I'm a Loser* found only intermittent life on small domestic and Japanese labels. For fans of the gritty soul style of early Millie Jackson and Denise LaSalle recordings, this title is worth searching for. The 12 medium-tempo tracks were mostly penned by fellow Southern singer Gary "U.S." Bonds and producer Jerry Williams Jr. and are executed nicely by a crack Capricorn Studio band. There's nothing here on the level of Aretha Franklin's contemporary triumphs for Atlantic either in the quality of the vocals or material, but Duke's own gospel-imbued voice, with its slightly hoarse and urgent tone, finds its own niche. The lean, Stax-inspired numbers also are very decent and even contain Duke's big hit "To the Other Woman (I'm the Other Woman)." The fate of the love weary is the main subject matter here and all its attendant drama is not only captured well by Duke's pleading vocal delivery, but it is unobtrusively underscored by the minimal and tasteful string arrangements. *I'm a Loser* may be a somewhat obscure title, but it is one that would fit into any good soul collection. *—Stephen Cook*

Woman / 1975 / Scepter ♦♦

A pretty bland set from Southern soul singer Doris Duke, who scored with "To the Other Woman (I'm the Other Woman)." The only winner here is a remake of Holland/Dozier/Holland's contradictory "Love Is Here and Now You're Gone," made popular by the Supremes. If you play this LP once, there's no need to play it again; you didn't miss anything the first time, and it doesn't get any better the second time around. *—Andrew Hamilton*

Deep Soul Queens / Oct. 1992 / Charly ♦♦♦

Two of the least recognized early-'70s soul singers, Doris Duke and Sandra Phillips never had any really big hits, but they did record for a few years. Much of their music and a good deal of the 24 songs included here are mediocre by Southern soul standards. Doris Duke has an awkward, heavy alto voice which doesn't always enunciate clearly and far too often sounds out of place with fast rhythms. She does best when performing heartfelt cheating ballads, such as the classic "To the Other Woman (I'm the Other Woman)" and the midtempo "He's Gone," which expresses the pathos known as the blues. Sandra Phillips is no more melodic a singer than Duke, but she has a lighter voice which seems to be more adaptable to these crudely produced tracks. She does fine versions of Dee Dee Warwick's "She Didn't Know (She Kept on Talking)" and Duke's "To the Other Woman (I'm the Other Woman)." *—Bill Carpenter*

Champion Jack Dupree

b. Jul. 23, 1909, New Orleans, LA, **d.** Jan. 21, 1992, Hanover, Germany

Vocals, Piano, Drums / Piano Blues, New Orleans Blues, Chicago Blues, Acoustic Chicago Blues, R&B

A formidable contender in the ring before he shifted his focus to pounding the piano instead, Champion Jack Dupree often injected his lyrics with a rowdy sense of downhome humor. But there was nothing lighthearted about his rock-solid way with a boogie; when he shouted "Shake Baby Shake," the entire room had no choice but to acquiesce. He spent his formative years in New Orleans, then lived in Chicago, Detroit and Indianapolis while boxing during the mid-'30s. He first recorded in 1940, for OKeh and Columbia, exhibiting a strong New Orleans tinge despite the Chicago surroundings. After a stretch in the Navy during World War II (he was a Japanese POW for two years), Dupree cut records for Continental, Joe Davis, Alert, Apollo, and Red Robin, often in the company of Brownie McGhee.

King Records corralled Dupree in 1953 and held onto him through 1955 (the year he enjoyed his only R&B chart hit, the relaxed "Walking the Blues"). After a year on RCA's Groove and Vik subsidiaries, he made a masterpiece LP for Atlantic (1958's *Blues From the Gutter*) but left for Europe in 1959, continuing to record prolifically for Storyville, British Decca and many other firms. Dupree returned to New Orleans in 1990 and recorded three albums of new material before his death in 1992. Jack Dupree was a champ to the very end. *—Bill Dahl*

★ **Blues From the Gutter** / 1958 / Atco ♦♦♦♦♦

The 1958 masterwork album of Dupree's long and prolific career. Cut in NY (in stereo!) with a blasting band that included saxist Pete Brown and guitarist Larry Dale, the Jerry Wexler-produced Atlantic collection provides eloquent testimony to Dupree's eternal place in the New Orleans blues and barrelhouse firmament. There's some decidedly down-in-the-alley subject matter—"Can't Kick The Habit," "T.B. Blues," a revival of "Junker's Blues"—along with the stomping "Nasty Boogie" and treatments of the ancient themes "Stack-O-Lee" and "Frankie & Johnny." *—Bill Dahl*

The Duprees

f. 1962, Jersey City, NJ, **db.** 1970

Group / Doo Wop

One of the final Italian doo wop groups to make a wave in the early '60s, the Duprees were in some senses not a rock & roll act at all. They relied on updates of pre-rock pop standards for most of their material, dressed up in classy big band arrangements. Their NJ street-corner roots were still audible in their doo wop harmonies, giving their treatments of moldy oldies enough of a contemporary flavor to compete in the rock and pop marketplace. They were very good at what they did, and in 1962-1963, they were very successful: "You Belong to Me" (previously recorded by Jo Stafford, Patti Page, Dean Martin, *and* Joni James) made the Top Ten, and "My Own True Love" (from the soundtrack of *Gone With the Wind*), "Have You Heard," and "Why Don't You Believe Me" were also Top 40 hits. The Duprees were already retro when they were at their peak, and were washed out by the British Invasion, although they continued to record throughout the late '60s, sometimes in a Jay & the Americans/Vogues style. *—Richie Unterberger*

● **Their Complete Coed Masters** / Mar. 19, 1996 / Ace ♦♦♦♦♦

If you're interested enough in the Duprees to invest in an album, you may as well cough up a few extra bucks for this import 31-song single-disc collection, which offered 13 more tracks than the domestic best-of on Rhino. It has everything they cut for Coed between 1962 and 1964, as well as a single that lead singer Joey Vann released in 1965 (rumored to have used the Duprees as backing vocalists). Their Coed output was very consistent, so fans of the group will find the additional material not present on the Rhino CD well worth acquiring. *—Richie Unterberger*

● **All-Time Greatest Hits** / Jun. 25, 2002 / Varese Vintage ♦♦♦♦♦

This 18-track compilation is missing a few songs that are on other Duprees anthologies, such as Ace's 31-track *Their Complete Coed Masters*, and even Rhino's 18-song *The Best of the Duprees.* Where this has a possible edge on the competition is the inclusion of three late-'60s songs from Heritage singles, where the other comps include only 1962-1964 Coed recordings. That's a small edge, since those late-'60s cuts are just average harmonized AM pop with a modernized doo wop tinge. If you're not fussy about having the complete Duprees Coed catalog, the other tracks on the CD cover that era—which is the bread 'n' butter of the group's discography—satisfactorily, including the big hits "You Belong to Me," "My Own True Love," and "Have You Heard," as well as numerous lower-charting and non-charting sides from singles. It's a reasonable overview of one of the more talented Italian-American vocal groups from the tail end of the doo wop era, tilting closer to adult pop music than rock, but done with good taste and fine harmonies. *—Richie Unterberger*

Jermaine Dupri

b. Sep. 23, 1973, Atlanta, GA

Producer, Mixing, Executive Producer / Pop-Rap, Urban, Hip-Hop

Beginning with breakout success in 1992 upon the discovery of teenage rappers Kris Kross, Jermaine Dupri became one of the most consistent and all-persuasive producers of the 1990s, producing practically the entire careers of many artists on his label, So So Def Recordings (including platinum entries like Xscape and Da Brat as well as Kris Kross). In addition, Dupri provided a steady hand to many of the most high-profile R&B albums of the decade, such as TLC's *CrazySexyCool* (ten times platinum) and Mariah Carey's *Daydream* (eight times platinum).

His promising musical career began before he was even ten years old. His father, Atlanta manager Michael Mauldin, had coordinated a Diana Ross show in 1982; to the delight of concert-goers, Dupri managed to get on stage and dance along with Ross. He began performing around the country, appearing with Herbie Hancock and Cameo before he opened the New York Fresh Festival, with Run-D.M.C., Whodini and Grandmaster Flash. Dupri's production career began in 1987, when at the age of 14 he produced and secured a record contract for the trio Silk Tymes Leather. Two years later, he formed So So Def Productions in Atlanta; by 1991 Dupri had found his first platinum act.

After seeing the pint-size rap duo Kris Kross performing in a local mall, he signed them and prepared their debut album. *Totally Krossed Out* spent two weeks at number one, and quickly sold four-million copies. The pair's lack of staying power was somewhat obvious, and Dupri kept working, producing tracks on TLC's first two albums, which sold over 15 million copies between the two of them.

During 1993-1994, Dupri debuted two of his new So So Def acts, Xscape and Da Brat. Both debut albums hit platinum, thanks in large part to Dupri, and by the end of 1994, he had become one of the most respected R&B producers in the business. He worked with superstar Mariah Carey and old-school rap acts like Run-D.M.C. and Whodini. Dupri's next major success came in 1997, when he took over the production for a sophomore album by a suave teenage R&B singer named Usher. The album, *My Way,* became one of the biggest of the year, selling over two-million copies in its first three months of release. Taking a page from the book of fellow super producer Sean "Puffy" Combs (who debuted a solo project in mid-1997), Dupri returned to performing in early 1998 with a single, "The Party Continues." After collaborating with Snoop Doggy Dogg, fellow Atlanta residents Outkast, Slick Rick, Nas and Master P, he released his debut solo album (as JD), *Life in 1492,* in July 1998. *—John Bush*

● **Jermaine Dupri Presents: Life in 1472** / Jul. 21, 1998 / So So Def ♦♦♦♦

Long before he released his first solo album, Jermaine Dupri established himself as a hip-hop hitmaker to be reckoned with. He sent Kris Kross, Da Brat and Xscape to the top of the charts, provided hit remixes for the likes of Dru Hill and ran the So So Def label—all before he decided to launch a career with *Jermaine Dupri Presents: Life in 1472* in 1998. Like many producers, Dupri has surrounded himself with an all-star cast of guest performers, all to make the spotlight a little less harsh. As it turns out, he needn't worry about his own skills—he's a fine rapper, putting such peers as Puff Daddy to shame—but all the other rappers and singers help make *Life in 1472* feel like a real party. It's one of the few star-studded records to actually work, precisely because JD is such a talented producer—he crafts slamming tracks with real bass grooves and catchy hooks. *Life in 1472* drags a little in the middle, like almost any party, but the vibes are good throughout, and it creates some nice memories, which is enough to make it a top-notch debut. *—Stephen Thomas Erlewine*

Instructions / Oct. 2, 2001 / Sony ♦♦♦

For his second solo album, Atlanta producer/entrepreneur Jermaine Dupri goes out of his way to yet again show you just how much of a self-described "baller" he is. This mentality partly informs this album's title, *Instructions*, with JD telling you what it's like at the top and how you'll never get there. As you can probably imagine, there's little modesty here and JD could care less—he seems to revel in his own vanity. Even if you wanted to, you'd have a hard time arguing with him: His So So Def label delivered popular albums and artists throughout the '90s—Kris Kross, Jagged Edge, Usher, Da Brat, Lil' Bow Wow—and he hires a star-studded roster of big-money guests for this album. Unfortunately, despite his big reputation and even bigger bank account, JD doesn't live up to his own hype on *Instructions*. His rhymes flow well but are overflowing with clichés and constant boasting. He's better at co-opting rhymes than coming up with his own. Moreover, it also doesn't help that he produces nearly the entire album—he's certainly no Dr. Dre. And you can't help but wonder who's coming up with the beats, JD or co-producer Bryan-Michael Cox. Like JD himself, *Instructions* seems to rely more on its surface gloss than its substance. The album isn't a total disappointment, though. There are some highlights, mostly courtesy of the guests, some of the more noteworthy moments being "Ballin' Out of Control" with Nate Dogg, "Welcome to Atlanta" with Ludacris, and "Money, Hoes & Power" with UGK. *—Jason Birchmeier*

Dyke & the Blazers

f. 1964, **db.** 1971

Group / Pop-Soul, Funk, Soul, Deep Funk

Dyke & the Blazers were one of the first acts—possibly the first notable act—to play funk other than James Brown. Indeed, they often sounded like a sort of junior version of Brown & the J.B.'s, playing songs in which the rhythms and riffs mattered more than the tune. Similarly, vocalist Dyke Christian sang-grunted words that mattered more for the feeling and rhythm than the content. Their best-known track, "Funky Broadway," was covered for a bigger hit by Wilson Pickett, though Dyke & the Blazers got a few more R&B hits before Dyke was shot to death in 1971.

Arlester "Dyke" Christian was born in Buffalo, NY, in 1943, and by the mid-'60s was singing and playing bass with the O'Jays backing band, the Blazers. Dyke and some of the other Blazers were stranded in Phoenix when the O'Jays' couldn't afford to bring them back to Buffalo, and the Blazers based themselves in Phoenix, having no means to travel elsewhere. Their "Funky Broadway" was released on the Phoenix indie Artco in late 1966, and picked up for distribution by the L.A.-based Original Sound label. It became a sizable R&B hit (and a small pop one), and may have been the first record to use the word "funky" in the title.

As with James Brown, Dyke & the Blazers' records sold far better, and charted much better, with the R&B audience than the pop one, which were for the most part unaware of the band. In the late 1960s and early 1970s, Dyke and the band issued a series of gut-bucket funk singles with scratchy guitar riffs, greasy organ, hoarse vocals, and jazzy horns—all traits that James Brown and his band had developed, admittedly. But Dyke did the style well (right down to issuing several two-part singles), although not with a great deal of variety. For some of his sessions, Dyke recorded in Los Angeles with musicians who would later play in the Watts 103rd Street Band (guitarist Al McKay would later be in Earth, Wind, & Fire). According to Original Sound producer Art Laboe, most of the singles came from 15-20-minute jams that were edited down to a length that could fit on the 45 RPM format.

Dyke & the Blazers had Top Ten R&B singles with "We Got More Soul" and "Let a Woman Be a Woman—Let a Man Be a Man" in 1969, and smaller sellers with "Uhh," "You Are My Sunshine," and "Runaway People." Dyke Christian, sadly, was fatally shot on the street in Phoenix on March 13, 1971. *—Richie Unterberger*

Funky Broadway / 1967 / Original Sound ♦♦♦♦

The late Dyke (Arlester Christian) was from Buffalo yet, after once backing the O'Jays in Phoenix, the band either became stranded or decided to stay there. It was the luckiest break they ever had, since they met someone who knew someone, which resulted in the recording and release of "Funky Broadway," a rough, funky, bass heavy dance tune written by Christian that rocketed up the charts. "Funky Broadway" scored again when Wilson Pickett recorded it; his version had better musicians, but Dyke's rawer, amateurish original, had more gut appeal. "Uhh Parts 1 & 2" is just as simplistic, but proves that lightning rarely strikes twice in the same place, and the rest of the songs are all in the same rut. Dyke featured a showman but not a singer, and rarely played ballads. *—Andrew Hamilton*

• **So Sharp!** / 1983 / Kent ♦♦♦♦♦

The best Dyke & the Blazers collection has 24 tracks, including all the key singles: "Funky Broadway," "Uhh," "Runaway People," "We Got More Soul," "Let a Woman Be a Woman—Let a Man Be a Man," "Funky Walk," "Funky Bull" (like James Brown, Dyke was not a man averse to milking an idea with a series of similar song titles). What's more, the disc includes parts one and two of the multi-sided singles "Funky Broadway," "Funky Walk," "Funky Bull," and "Uhh." Not much development of style or ideas over the four years or so encompassed by this anthology, but that's not the main point of funk dance music. "Runaway People" does look forward to the more sophisticated urban funk of the early 1970s with its addition of strings—reminiscent, ironically, of the production eventually adapted by Dyke's old buddies the O'Jays. Note that *So Sharp!* was originally issued by Kent on LP in 1983, but the CD version has extra tracks. *—Richie Unterberger*

Funky Broadway: The Very Best of Dyke & the Blazers / Mar. 23, 1999 / Collectables ♦♦♦♦♦

At first glance, Collectables' *Funky Broadway: The Very Best of Dyke & the Blazers* appears to be inferior to Kent's *So Sharp!*, featuring only 18 tracks as opposed to 24. But look closer: Kent separates the group's multi-part singles into separate tracks, while Collectables runs them together. The only real difference between the two is that *So Sharp!* features an alternate, two-part version of "Uhh" in addition to the edited single version, while *Funky Broadway* has only the edit; otherwise, the track selections are identical. Either way, you get an hour's worth of some of the hardest, earthiest funk the late '60s produced. Dyke & the Blazers weren't innovators, but they were among the earliest—and best—to pick up on James Brown's early funk sound. Their grooves were loose, choppy, and improvisational, and pretty much defined the word "stanky." Dyke's singing voice could charitably be described as a bleat, so it's no wonder he spent more time chanting, shouting, and riding the groove than trying to carry a tune. Put it all together, and Dyke & the Blazers' brand of funk was not a pretty thing—which, of course, is what made them great. Their original version of "Funky Broadway" makes Wilson Pickett's hit cover sound like it rolled off the Motown assembly line. Aside from the ten-minute narrative "The Wrong House," most of these songs are short and to the point, working a groove for the length of a 45-rpm record. Whatever their limitations, though, Dyke & the Blazers' work still holds up extremely well, and funk fans shouldn't hesitate to embrace these early standard-bearers. *—Steve Huey*

The Dynamic Superiors

Group / Soul

This Washington, D.C., quintet signed with Motown in the early '70s and found limited success on the soul charts. Though not as vocally dynamic as the Temptations or the Four Tops, they were excellent showmen with energetic and inventive choreography. They were also unique in that they sported a gay lead singer—who often did his shows in drag. *—Rick A. Bueche*

The Dynamic Superiors / 1975 / Motown ♦♦♦♦

The Dynamic Superiors plus Nicolas Ashford & Valerie Simpson equals some stupendous sounds. The two groups brought out the best in each other. No doubt the late Sylvester, who surfaced later, copied lead singer Tony Washington's phrasings. "Shoe Shoe Shine" is one of the best Ashford/Simpson songs; it also turned out to be the D.C. natives' most popular record, with the exciting "Leave It Alone" a close second. A second lead with a good tenor provided a good foil for Washington's cloud-high vocals on most selections. This is a must for vocal-group fanatics. *—Andrew Hamilton*

Pure Pleasure / 1975 / Motown ♦♦♦

Pure Pleasure picks up where *The Dynamic Superiors* left off. There's nothing quite as charming as "Shoe Shoe Shine," but it's a more even record overall. Ashford & Simpson obviously wrote "Nobody's Gonna Change Me," for openly gay lead Tony Washington. Its meaningful lyrics, great singing, catchy hook, and excellent production should have propelled it to the top of the charts. "Hit & Run Lover" has a slinky, lilting groove. Music lovers should demand a best-of CD. *—Andrew Hamilton*

You Name It / 1976 / Motown ♦♦

There's not an Ashford/Simpson production or song to be found, and not a memorable song in the lot. None of these sides are as strong as the weakest tunes on the group's first two albums. A sparse seven tunes make up the whole of *You Name It*. For diehard Dynamic Superior fans or collectors only. *—Andrew Hamilton*

• **Give and Take** / 1977 / Motown ♦♦♦♦

Though it lacked the hit singles of their early work, the disco-oriented *Give and Take* was the best work the Dynamic Superiors ever did for Motown. *—Rick A. Bueche*

The Dynamics

Group / Pop-Soul, Motown, Doo Wop, R&B, Soul

Isaac "Zeke" Harris, George White, Fred Baker, and Samuel Stevenson were the Dynamics. (Zerben R. Hicks also sang with them but left shortly after their first album release.) All Detroit natives, the group was managed by Ted White, who was married to the Queen of Soul, Aretha Franklin.Their first Cotillion release, the metaphoric "Ice Cream Song," did quite well on R&B charts. Following the lead of Atlantic recording Aretha in the South, White took the Dynamics to Memphis to record, which is why "Ice Cream Song" sounds like something the Mad Lads would have recorded at Stax. The Dynamics, however, were more versatile than the Mad Lads, and the material was better too. They had three lead voices, one being an outstanding falsetto. Chips Moman and Tommy Cogbill produced their early sides; the rhythm section consisted of Memphis stalwarts Reggie Young (guitar), Bobby Emmons (organ), Bobby Wood (piano), Mick Leach (bass), and Gene Chrisman (drums). They recorded two albums: *First Landing* on Cotillion and *What a Shame* on Black Gold. *—Andrew Hamilton*

• **First Landing** / 1969 / Cotillion ♦♦♦♦

First Landing is a superb debut album by one of Detroit's most under-appreciated groups. The Dynamics cut these tracks in Memphis, TN, giving the album a deep soul sound. "The Ice Cream Song," written by former member Zerben R. Hicks, raced up the R&B charts and remains their most popular recording. A killer version of the Motown classic "Since I Lost You," punctuates these soulful selections; the gorgeous Ronnie Shannon ballad "What Would I Do" is impeccably done. *—Andrew Hamilton*

What a Shame / 1973 / Black Gold ♦♦♦

Managed by Ted White, Aretha Franklin's husband (at the time), the Dynamics released a slew of singles and two albums but never achieved any sustained chart action; they're visually unknown to most, even to those who know their recordings. "What a Shame," the title track, is arguably their best single, a sweet falsetto sings the woeful tale in a mournful voice usually associated with wakes and funerals. Like everything else on the album, it was written and produced by the now-deceased Ronnie Shannon, an eccentric songwriter from Detroit who gained fame writing hits like "Baby, I Love You" for Aretha. "Woe Is Me" paves the same mournful path, as does "You'll Never Find a Man Like Me." Shannon speeds it up on "Shucks I Love You," a happy-in-love tune carried by an airy falsetto lead. Brass is prominent on "Funky Key," a groove daddy that probably worked better live; the lead is rough, countering the melodic and smooth backing vocals. The Dynamics had at least three lead singers and used them all. "Count Your Chips" is a slow beauty, typical of sounds emanating from Philly, yet it failed to sell despite a sugary lead vocal. Other notables include "Voyage Thru the Mind" and "Let Me Be Your Friend." *—Andrew Hamilton*

Dynasty

Group / Urban, Dance-Pop

The creation of producer/label-head Dick Griffey and Leon Sylvers, this Los Angeles band did light funk and clever dance/pop numbers in the late '70s and '80s. Bassist Kevin Spencer and vocalists Nidra Beard and Linda Carriere comprised the group. They got off to a fast start with the single "I Don't Want to Be a Freak (But I Can't Help Myself)" from their 1979 LP *Your Piece of the Rock*. The next single, "I've Just Begun to Love," was their lone Top Ten R&B hit, peaking at number six in 1980. They continued recording for Solar through the '80s, but never registered any other major records. Leon Sylvers joined them in 1981, but his presence didn't rectify the situation. They remained on Solar until 1988. *—Ron Wynn*

Your Piece of the Rock / 1979 / Solar ✦✦

Produced by Leon F. Sylvers III, Dynasty's debut LP *Your Piece of the Rock* sported the almost eight-minutes long disco smash "I Don't Wanna Be a Freak (But I Can't Help Myself)," which went to number 36 on the R&B charts in the fall of 1979. The title track, "Satisfied," and "Still a Thrill" were also dancefloor favorites.The midtempo ballad "Dial My Number" hearkens back to the producer/group leader's work with his family, the Sylvers. *Your Piece of the Rock* was reissued as a 1999 CD, and some of the album's tracks can be found on *Greatest Hits* and the 1994 Sequel CD *The Best of Dynasty*. *—Ed Hogan*

Adventures in the Land of Music / 1980 / Solar ✦✦✦✦

By 1980, it was obvious that Dick Griffey's Solar Records had as distinctive and recognizable a sound as Motown and Stax in the 1960s or Philadelphia International in the 1970s. Put on just about any late-'70s or early- to mid-'80s recording by the Whispers, Shalamar, Midnight Star, or Dynasty, and it only takes a few notes to realize that you're listening to a Solar recording. Dynasty wasn't as big as the Whispers or Shalamar, but the Los Angeles-based vocal group did enjoy a few hits and made some valuable contributions to the Solar catalog. *Adventures in the Land of Music*, which came out on vinyl in 1980 and was reissued on CD by the Canadian Unidisc label in 2001, is Dynasty's second album—and it is arguably the group's most essential. *Adventures* contains the Angelinos' biggest hit, "I've Just Begun to Love You," as well as the equally danceable single "Do Me Right," but the singles aren't the only things that make this album produced by Leon Sylvers III worth owning—*Adventures* also contains a lot of memorable album tracks, which range from dance-oriented numbers like "Ice Breaker," "Day and Night," and "Groove Patrol" to the soul ballad "Take Another Look at Love." Dynasty is best remembered for uptempo dance and disco-funk material, but "Take Another Look at Love" demonstrates that the group was quite capable of handling romantic soul ballads. Because Dynasty favored a lot of male/female vocal interaction and was so Solar-sounding, the group was often compared to another part-male, part-female group, Shalamar. But Dynasty had an appealing identity of its own, and that identity serves the quartet well on this excellent sophomore effort. *—Alex Henderson*

● **Greatest Hits** / Apr. 15, 1994 / Unidisc ✦✦✦✦✦

Ronnie Dyson

b. Jun. 5, 1950, Washington, D.C., **d.** Nov. 11, 1990, Philadelphia, PA

Vocals / Soul

Washington, D.C. vocalist Ronnie Dyson enjoyed both stage and R&B success. He was the lead actor in the Broadway production of the musical *Hair*, and his initial hit was a song from the off-Broadway musical *Salvation*. "(If You Let Me Make Love to You Then) Why Can't I Touch You" was both Top Ten R&B and pop in 1970, and "I Don't Wanna Cry" was also Top Ten R&B that same year. Dyson kept recording for Columbia until 1978, scoring one more hit in 1976 with a very different type of song, "The More You Do It (The More I Like It Done to Me)," a marked departure from the vulnerable, anguished numbers that had characterized his approach in the past. He moved to Cotillion in the '80s, but didn't have much success there. Dyson also was in the film *Putney Swope*. His final recording was "See the Clown" in 1990. He died that year of a heart attack. *—Ron Wynn*

(If You Let Me Make Love to You Then) Why Can't I Touch You? / 1970 / Columbia ✦✦✦✦

One Man Band / 1973 / Columbia ✦✦✦✦

The finest album of Ronnie's career, Philly stalwart Thom Bell's productions dominate the LP and are the best thing that ever happened to the NY-raised actor/singer. Ronnie's full-throated, youthful tenor and Bell's lush arrangements are quite compatible. The worthy repeat plays include the following nuggets: "I Think I'll Tell Her," "Point of No Return," "I Just Don't Want to Be Lonely," and Barry Mann's "When You Get Right Down to It." Columbia placed a good chunk of promo money on "One Man Band (Plays All Alone)," an adventurous song, but it lacked the directness and earthiness of the aforementioned songs. Bill Jackson and Stan Vincent also contributed their producing skills. *—Andrew Hamilton*

The More You Do It / 1976 / Columbia ✦✦✦

New Yorker Ronnie Dyson trekked to the Windy City to work with Chuck Jackson and Marvin Yancy for this album. Jackson and Yancy were hot, their tunes and productions had Natalie Cole eating high on the hog, and Dyson's management wanted them to work some magic with their guy. The eight cuts consist of originals—including "You and Me," the only hit "More You Do It," and "Close to You"—along with remakes of the Bee Gees' "Jive Talkin'," Major Harris' "Love Won't Let Me Wait," and Leon Russell's "Song for You." While nothing earth shattering, this is a good album that merited a second. *—Andrew Hamilton*

Love in All Flavors / 1977 / Columbia ✦✦✦

Though never classified as such, Ronnie Dyson had a cabaret voice—classy but not too stiff with an underlying permeating quality appreciated by R&B and pop fans alike. But other than a few hits, he never got his just dues and will be remembered for "(If You Let Me Make Love to You Then) Why Can't I Touch You" and little else. *Love in All Flavors* was Dyson's next-to-last album for Columbia Records. Like a previous effort, Chuck Jackson and Marvin Yancy produced it in Chicago. This is a fine set, but with no hits to push it it dropped from sight without fanfare. The best of the nine includes updates of "Sara Smile" and "I Want to Be Where You Are," the bouncy "Don't Be Afraid," and "Ain't Nothing Wrong." *—Andrew Hamilton*

● **His All Time Golden Classics** / 1995 / Collectables ✦✦✦✦

Collectables Records are correct this time; these 23 selections will satisfy the late Ronnie Dyson's most fanatic fan. The collection includes his career-breaking hit "(If You Let Me Make Love to You Then) Why Can't I Touch You?," as well as a slew of charters and remakes: "I Think I'll Tell Her," "When You Get Right Down to It," and remakes of "Band of Gold," "Fever," "Bridge Over Trouble Water," "Just Don't Want to Be Lonely," "Something," and "I Don't Wanna Cry." Fans of Dyson's more soulful selections will enjoy "The More You Do It (The More I Like It)," "Point of No Return," and "She's Gone" (not the Hall & Oates song). If you took a blindfold test listening to Dyson music, knowing nothing about the artist, you'd have a tough time guessing whether the singer is male or female, especially on ballads. *—Andrew Hamilton*

E

Sheila E.

b. Dec. 12, 1959, San Francisco, CA

Percussion, Drums, Vocals / Urban, Dance-Pop

Before she became a solo artist in 1984, drummer Sheila E. played with Azteca, the Latin jazz-fusion band led by her father, percussionist Pete Escovedo; she also played on two of his solo albums recorded for Fantasy Records. Prince discovered Sheila E. around 1983 and had her sing on "Erotic City," the B-side to his number one 1984 single, "Let's Go Crazy." Prince also helped her secure a record contract with Warner Bros.; she released her debut album, *Sheila E. in the Glamorous Life*, in 1984. Written by Prince, the title track hit the U.S. Top Ten and her second single, "The Belle of St. Mark," charted in both the American and British Top 40. The following year she released *Sheila E. in Romance 1600*, which featured the number 11 hit "A Love Bizarre." Her self-titled album was released in 1987, yet it didn't have the commercial impact of her two previous records. Sheila E. joined Prince's band for the 1987 *Sign O' the Times* tour and is featured prominently in the resulting film documentary of the same name. Four years later, she returned with her fourth album, *Sex Cymbal*. Despite it's heavy dance beats and vivacious compositions, *Sex Cymbal* failed to chart. After her brief stint ringleading the band on Magic Johnson's late-night show, *The Magic Hour*, Sheila E. returned to recording and released *The Writes of Passage* in fall 2000. *—Stephen Thomas Erlewine*

● **The Glamorous Life** / 1984 / Warner Bros. ✦✦✦✦✦

When Sheila Escovedo started going by Sheila E. and soared to the top of the R&B charts with 1984's "The Glamorous Life," those who didn't know anything about her background assumed that she was just another Vanity or another Apollonia—in other words, a sexploitive Prince disciple who was entertaining but had limited ability as a vocalist. It's true that the singer/drummer/percussionist doesn't have a great voice, but anyone who was hip to her work with Azteca, Pete Escovedo (her father), and George Duke knew that she was an excellent musician. As a drummer/percussionist, Escovedo has major chops—and even though she doesn't have a mind-blowing vocal range, she has no problem getting her points across on her debut solo album, *The Glamorous Life*. Produced by Prince, this is one of the best albums that came out of the Purple One's Minneapolis funk-rock empire in the 1980s. The hit title song is a classic, and the same goes for the quirky, new wave-ish "Oliver's House," the Latin-tinged "The Belle of St. Mark," and the funky instrumental "Shortberry Strawcake." Although Prince's stamp is all over this LP, Escovedo did most of the writing herself. *The Glamorous Life* isn't the only excellent album that Escovedo provided in the 1980s, but it's definitely the most essential. *—Alex Henderson*

Romance 1600 / 1985 / Paisley Park ✦✦✦✦

In 1985, a 25-year-old Sheila Escovedo, aka Sheila E., followed up her debut solo album, *The Glamorous Life*, with the equally Prince-influenced *Romance 1600*. The album cover found Escovedo and her band members sporting the attire of 17th century Europe, and the musicians were given such names as Dame Kelly, Benentino the Wizard, the Earl of Grey, and Sir Stephan. But once you get past the aristocratic imagery, *Romance 1600* isn't much different from *The Glamorous Life*. Although Escovedo did most of the writing and producing herself, Prince's influence is strong throughout the album—"Bedtime Story," "Sister Fate," and other selections all have that distinctive Minneapolis vibe. The only track that Prince co-wrote and co-produced with Escovedo is the funk gem "A Love Bizarre," which became a major hit and finds the two of them performing a vocal duet. As a vocalist, Escovedo never had Prince's range, but like Madonna and Janet Jackson, she demonstrates that singing can be meaningful even if the artist doesn't have the world's biggest voice. Although *The Glamorous Life* remains Escovedo's most essential album of the 1980s, *Romance 1600* is a respectable follow-up and is also highly recommended to fans of Minneapolis funk-rock. *—Alex Henderson*

Sheila E. / 1987 / Paisley Park ✦✦✦

Sex Cymbal / 1991 / Warner Bros. ✦✦✦

Seven years after Sheila E. burst upon the scene with her Top Ten single "The Glamorous Life," the talented percussionist's fourth release, *Sex Cymbal*, reflects the sound of successful, late-'80s artists like Janet Jackson and Paula Abdul. It's a solid mix of pop/R&B ballads like the pretty (if unspectacular) "Loverboy" and more dance-oriented tracks. The title track is a slinky come-on and Sheila E. leads her band through a horn-laden version of "Lady Marmalade." The musicianship is not-surprisingly strong and there are a couple cool instrumental jams. *Sex Cymbal* is a sure-footed, groove-oriented album, but it lacks anything as memorable as her earlier hits. *—Tom Demalon*

The Writes of Passage / Oct. 10, 2000 / Concord Jazz ✦✦✦

Everyone out there surely remembers Sheila E. from her mid-'80s heyday as one of Prince's protégées, when songs like "The Glamorous Life" and "A Love Bizarre" (produced by the enigmatic pop star) helped launch the young singer/percussionist to brief but memorable stardom. Though she delighted millions recording and touring with Prince, Sheila Escovedo's real fans know there's a jazzier side of the story: She began her career as a teenager playing with George Duke and has been a top touring percussionist with numerous jazz and pop notables. Recorded with her longtime performing band, the E Train, Sheila's Concord Records debut, *Writes of Passage*—her first effort as a leader in nine years—combines funk-inflected smooth jazz, 1970s-influenced fusion, gospel, and, as is her family tradition, an exciting Latin influence. She takes a lead vocal on only one song, the gentle and inspirational "N Perfect Time," and only lets loose a few times on percussion solos (most notably at the end of the easy-swaying exotica of "Rituals," featuring Ray Obiedo's rolling guitar lines and Eric Leeds' mix of punchy sax improv and sassy flute). Her wild fills on the Yellowjackets-influenced closer "Virtuosity" help spur her bandmates onto some zesty playing themselves. The rest of the time, she blends happily into her formidable ensemble, switching off drum- and percussion-anchoring duties with her brother, Peter Michael Escovedo, as Leeds, Obiedo, and keyboardist Renato Neto trade moments in the spotlight. Often those moments draw together impressively, as at the end of "Paragon," where Obiedo's screeching electric guitar bounces off the sax melody while Neto bubbles under on harmony. The title track is the one obvious middle-of-the-road smooth jazz cut, with melodic pleasantries showing off Leeds' pretty side. *—Jonathan Widran*

Heaven / Aug. 28, 2001 / Concord Jazz ✦✦✦

Sheila E. has been one of music's top drummers and percussionists since her debut in Prince's band. Alongside her legendary father, Pete Escovedo, and as a solo performer, she continues to enjoy commercial as well as artistic success on such recordings as her year 2000 release on the Concord Vista label, titled *Writes of Passage*. This time around, the highly talented musician has followed up with *Heaven*. Created with a little help from her friends, including George Duke, Gerald Albright, and many more, Sheila E. adds her vocal, percussion, drum, producing, composing, and arranging skills and other cool tools to yet another jazz style. She's cool, yet beautifully orchestrated, but most of all, she has opened her musical treasure trove and delivered some new grooves, R&B-inflected vocals, smooth gospel, and funky jazz. The 12 compositions include seven either written or co-written by Sheila E., with a memorable percussion solo and miniMoog solos by Sheila E. and Byron Williams, respectively, on "Trust Me," and smooth jazz solos from saxophone master Gerald Albright and guitarist Paul Jackson Jr. on the title track. "Bahia" is a Brazilian jazz composition with breezy vocals from Lynn Mabry and Sheila E., and is quite beautiful. Saxophonist Eddie M. closes the program with a beautiful, poignant smooth gospel song titled "Revelation." *Heaven* does not feature many of Sheila E.'s fiery, trademark Latin percussion jam sessions that she plays with the Escovedo family, but certainly delivers an assortment of musical styles—R&B, smooth jazz, smooth gospel, Brazilian jazz, and funk—and is remarkably different from anything she has done. *—Paula Edelstein*

The Earls

f. 1957, New York, NY [The Bronx]

Group / Doo Wop

Among the more revered white doo wop groups, the Earls began as the High Hatters. They formed in 1957 at the Tecumseh Social Club in the Bronx. Lead vocalist Larry Figueiredo changed his name to "Larry Chance"; he was joined by Bob Del Din, Eddie Harder, Larry Palumbo, and Jack Wray. They started recording for Rome in 1961. They scored their lone hit in 1963 with "Remember Then" for Old Town. It barely cracked the R&B Top 30 (number 29), but they continued until 1970, when they disbanded. The Earls gave it another try in 1975 with Chance on board again, this time singing with Ronnie Calabreese and Tony Olbert. *—Ron Wynn*

Remember When?: All the Early and Rare Sides / 1991 / Emor ✦✦✦✦

This disc is probably not where the casual listener should start with the Earls—one might do better with Collectables records' *Remember Then!* But as a second Earls CD, or for collectors and completists, and general doo wop enthusiasts, this 31-song compilation, covering the years 1961-1968, is a great value, and it shows how long the group remained artistically viable, advancing their sound with the times into white soul. The producers have raided the vaults to give a much better and fuller impression of the Earls' actual history and their potential which, sadly, was unrealized. The officially released material goes back to the group's first success, with their uptempo rendition of "Life Is but a Dream" on the Rome records label—not only with its original B-side "It's You" (which was removed shortly after release) but the replacement flip side, "Without You." That's where things start to get really interesting, with a brace of unissued Rome Records singles and extended versions of other numbers that were only issued in cut form; additionally, we get two early outtakes of "Remember When"—which subsequently evolved into their signature tune, "Remember Then"—one running most of a minute longer than the other, though neither is as effective as the hit version; the longer version includes some interesting and entertaining vamps, however, along with material that was better off being jettisoned. The previously unissued slow version of "My Heart's Desire" is a gorgeous take on this ballad; a medium-tempo version, just as pretty but completely different in tone and texture, is also included, along with the original fast version, which offers yet another, totally different, hard-rocking take on the song, complete with chugging rhythm guitars. One of the more interesting discoveries that one can make on this CD is precisely how unlike other doo wop groups the Earls were—perhaps owing to the fact that they started late and their history ran up against the British Invasion and other mid-'60s phenomena, they made much more (and more effective) use of a full-band backing than most of their contemporaries. They could do the Harptones-influenced slow harmony R&B, but also hard-rocking versions of songs like "Dreams Come True" (which also appears here in its finished, more playful rendition). Along with this array of outtakes and unedited masters, the disc includes a pair of Larry Chance solo numbers that are a little more pop-oriented in their arrangements but still eminently enjoyable teen pop/rock, and one true oddity, "(The Story Of) The In-Between Years," a two-sided single by James MacArthur on which the Earls performed—it's a pure period piece with the actor (best remembered for his work on *Hawaii Five-O*) reciting around the group's singing, which is excellent; the whole thing plays like an audio version of the plots of the kind of teen movies that were in vogue around 1962-1963. Much more effective musically are "If I Could Do It Once Again" and "Daddy's Home," a pair of more recent, nostalgia-oriented songs credited to "Jimmy Cee with the Earls." Even better than those are "It's Been a Long Time Coming" and "In My Lonely, Lonely Room," outstanding examples of white soul, with Larry Chance sounding a lot like Ben E. King, from the group's brief 1968 stint on ABC records. The annotation is very thorough and the sound is generally excellent, but this disc can also be difficult to find; much of what's here also appears on the German-imported Dee Jay label's *Rome Records And Beyond* compilation. *—Bruce Eder*

● **Remember Then!** / Sep. 28, 1999 / Collectables ♦♦♦♦

This is an expanded and remastered successor to Collectables' much older Earls collections. If the three additional songs aren't enough to justify the purchase, the improved sound will be. The title track is the most recognizable of their songs, but there's a lot else here to recommend owning this CD—"Never" is, if anything, an even more impressive song with an extraordinary performance by Larry Chance and an achingly beautiful chorus. The only thing missing that might've been nice to hear is "It's You," the original B-side of their debut single. The range of songs includes everything from classics of the theater ("Ol' Man River") to reprises of 1950s standards ("I Believe") to group compositions that showcase their most radiant ensemble work. *—Bruce Eder*

Earth, Wind & Fire

f. 1969, Chicago, IL

Group / Funk, Soul, Smooth Soul, Urban, Disco, Blaxploitation, Quiet Storm, Psychedelic Soul

Earth, Wind & Fire was one of the most musically accomplished, critically acclaimed, and commercially popular funk bands of the '70s. Conceived by drummer, bandleader, songwriter, kalimba player, and occasional vocalist Maurice White, EWF's all-encompassing musical vision used funk as its foundation, but also incorporated jazz, smooth soul, gospel, pop, rock & roll, psychedelia, blues, folk, African music, and, later on, disco. Lead singer Philip Bailey gave EWF an extra dimension with his talent for crooning sentimental ballads in addition to funk workouts; behind him, the band could harmonize like a smooth Motown group, work a simmering groove like the J.B.'s, or improvise like a jazz fusion outfit. Plus, their stage shows were often just as elaborate and dynamic as George Clinton's P-Funk empire. More than just versatility for its own sake, EWF's eclecticism was part of a broader concept informed by a cosmic, mystical spirituality and an uplifting positivity the likes of which hadn't been seen since the early days of Sly & the Family Stone. Tying it all together was the accomplished songwriting of Maurice White, whose intricate, unpredictable arrangements and firm grasp of hooks and structure made EWF one of the tightest bands in funk when they wanted to be. Not everything they tried worked, but at their best, Earth, Wind & Fire seemingly took all that came before them and wrapped it up into one dizzying, spectacular package.

Maurice White founded Earth, Wind & Fire in Chicago in 1969. He had previously honed his chops as a session drummer for Chess Records, where he played on songs by the likes of Fontella Bass, Billy Stewart, and Etta James, among others. In 1967, he'd replaced Red Holt in the popular jazz group the Ramsey Lewis Trio, where he was introduced to the kalimba, an African thumb piano he would use extensively in future projects. In 1969, he left Lewis' group to form a songwriting partnership with keyboardist Don Whitehead and singer Wade Flemons. This quickly evolved into a band dubbed the Salty Peppers, which signed with Capitol and scored a regional hit with "La La Time." When a follow-up flopped, White decided to move to Los Angeles, and took most of the band with him; he also renamed them Earth, Wind & Fire, after the three elements in his astrological charts.

By the time White convinced his brother, bassist Verdine White, to join him on the West Coast in 1970, the lineup also consisted of Whitehead, Flemons, female singer Sherry Scott, guitarist Michael Beal, tenor saxophonist Chet Washington, trombonist Alex Thomas, and percussionist Yackov Ben Israel. This aggregate signed a new deal with Warner Brothers and issued their self-titled debut album in late 1970. Many critics found it intriguing and ambitious, much like the 1971 follow-up *The Need of Love*, but neither attracted much commercial attention, despite a growing following on college campuses and a high-profile gig performing the soundtrack to Melvin Van Peebles' groundbreaking black independent film *Sweet Sweetback's Baadasssss Song*.

Dissatisfied with the results, White dismantled the first version of EWF in 1972, retaining only brother Verdine. He built a new lineup with female vocalist Jessica Cleaves, flute/sax player Ronnie Laws, guitarist Roland Bautista, keyboardist Larry Dunn, and percussionist Ralph Johnson; the most important new addition, however, was singer Philip Bailey, recruited from a Denver R&B band called Friends & Love. After seeing the group open for John Sebastian in New York, Clive Davis signed them to CBS, where they debuted in 1972 with *Last Days and Time*. Further personnel changes ensued; Laws and Bautista were all gone by year's end, replaced by reedman Andrew Woolfolk and guitarists Al McKay and Johnny Graham. It was then that EWF truly began to hit their stride. 1973's *Head to the Sky* (Cleaves' last album with the group) significantly broadened their cult following, and the 1974 follow-up *Open Our Eyes* was their first genuine hit. It marked their first collaboration with producer, arranger, and sometime songwriting collaborator Charles Stepney, who helped streamline their sound for wider acceptance; it also featured another White brother, Fred, brought in as a second drummer. The single "Mighty Mighty" became EWF's first Top Ten hit on the R&B charts, although pop radio shied away from its black-pride subtext, and the minor hit "Kalimba Story" brought Maurice White's infatuation with African sounds to the airwaves. *Open Our Eyes* went gold, setting the stage for the band's blockbuster breakthrough.

In 1975, EWF completed work on another movie soundtrack, this time to a music-biz drama called *That's the Way of the World*. Not optimistic about the film's commercial prospects, the group rushed out their soundtrack album of the same name (unlike *Sweet Sweetback*, they composed all the music themselves) in advance. The film flopped, but the album took off—its lead single, the love-and-encouragement anthem "Shining Star," shot to the top of both the R&B and pop charts, making Earth, Wind & Fire mainstream stars; it later won a Grammy for Best R&B Vocal Performance by a Group. The album also hit number one on both the pop and R&B charts, and went double platinum; its title track went Top Five on the R&B side, and it also contained Bailey's signature ballad in the album cut "Reasons." White used the new income to develop EWF's live show into a lavish, effects-filled extravaganza, which eventually grew to include stunts designed by magician Doug Henning. The band was also augmented by a regular horn section, the Phoenix Horns, headed by saxophonist Don Myrick. Their emerging concert experience was chronicled later that year on the double-LP set *Gratitude*, which became their second straight number one album and featured one side of new studio tracks. Of those, "Sing a Song" reached the pop Top Ten and the R&B Top Five, and the ballad "Can't Hide Love" and the title track were also successful.

Sadly, during the 1976 sessions for EWF's next studio album *Spirit*, Charles Stepney died suddenly of a heart attack. Maurice White took over the arranging chores, but the Stepney-produced "Getaway" managed to top the R&B charts posthumously. *Spirit* naturally performed well on the charts, topping out at number two. In the meantime, Maurice White was taking a hand in producing other acts; in addition to working with his old boss Ramsey Lewis, he helped kickstart the careers of the Emotions and Deniece Williams. 1977's *All 'N All* was another strong effort that charted at number three and spawned the R&B smashes "Fantasy" and the chart-topping "Serpentine Fire"; meanwhile, the Emotions topped the pop charts with the White-helmed smash "Best of My Love." The following year, White founded his own label, ARC, and EWF appeared in the mostly disastrous film version of *Sgt. Pepper's Lonely Hearts Club Band*, turning in a fine cover of the Beatles' "Got to Get You Into My Life" that became their first Top Ten pop hit since "Sing a Song." Released before year's end, *The Best of Earth, Wind & Fire, Vol. 1* produced another Top Ten hit (and R&B number one) in the newly recorded "September."

1979's *I Am* contained EWF's most explicit nod to disco, a smash collaboration with the Emotions called "Boogie Wonderland" that climbed into the Top Ten. The ballad "After the Love Has Gone" did even better, falling one spot short of the top. Although *I Am* became EWF's sixth straight multi-platinum album, there were signs that the group's explosion of creativity over the past few years was beginning to wane. 1980's *Faces* broke that string, after which guitarist McKay departed. While 1981's *Raise* brought them a Top Five hit and R&B chart-topper in "Let's Groove," an overall decline in consistency was becoming apparent. By the time EWF issued its next album, 1983's *Powerlight*, ARC had folded, and the Phoenix Horns had been cut loose to save money. After the lackluster *Electric Universe* appeared at the end of the year, White disbanded the group to simply take a break. In the meantime, Verdine White became a producer and video director, while Philip Bailey embarked on a solo career and scored a pop smash with the Phil Collins duet "Easy Lover." Collins also made frequent use of the Phoenix Horns on his '80s records, both solo and with Genesis.

Bailey reunited with the White brothers, plus Andrew Woolfolk, Ralph Johnson, and new guitarist Sheldon Reynolds, in 1987 for the album *Touch the World*. It was surprisingly successful, producing two R&B smashes in "Thinking of You" and the number one "System of Survival." 1990's *Heritage* was a forced attempt to contemporize the group's sound, with guest appearances from Sly Stone and MC Hammer; its failure led to the end of the group's relationship with Columbia. They returned on Reprise with the more traditional-sounding *Millennium* in 1993, but were dropped when the record failed to recapture their commercial standing, despite a Grammy nomination for "Sunday Morning"; tragedy struck that year when onetime horn leader Don Myrick was murdered in Los Angeles. Bailey and the White brothers returned once again in 1997 on the small Pyramid label with *In the Name of Love*. *—Steve Huey*

Earth, Wind and Fire / 1970 / Warner Bros. ♦♦♦♦♦

The debut for the nine-member Earth, Wind & Fire was as assured as that of any rock band from the '60s and early '70s. Already fluent with the close harmonies of the classiest soul groups, the deep funk of James Brown, and the progressive social concerns and multiple vocal features of Sly & the Family Stone, the group added (courtesy of auteur Maurice White) a set of freewheeling arrangements, heavy on the horns, that made *Earth, Wind and Fire* one of their finest albums—the artistic equal of their later hits, if not on the same level commercially. Unlike the work of most early funk bands, the songwriting was as strong and focused as the musicianship; the record boasts a set of unerringly positive compositions, reflecting the influence of the civil-rights movement with nearly every song urging love, community, and knowledge as alternatives to the increasing hopelessness plaguing American society. The stop-start opener "Help Somebody," the deep funk extravaganza "Moment of Truth," and the sweet ballad "Love Is Life" were unified in their pursuit of positivity, while even the potentially incendiary title "Fan the Fire" was revealed in a peaceful context: "The flame of love is about to die/Somebody fan the fire."

And the instrumental closer "Bad Tune" is hardly a cast-off; the furious kalimba work of Maurice White and wordless backing vocals combine to create an excellent piece of impressionist funk. *—John Bush*

The Need of Love / 1971 / Warner Bros. ♦♦♦
The ambitions of Earth, Wind & Fire only increased after their stellar debut, and the group brought an abstract sense of composition to their sophomore record, *The End of Love*. The opener, a ten-minute piece named "Energy," is proof enough, with several extended passages inspired by everything from free jazz as well as in-the-pocket funk like Kool & the Gang. The next song up, "Beauty" is also positive and intriguing, though in an overly similar groove as "Fan the Fire" from the first album. The closer, a cover of Donny Hathaway's gloriously funky "Everything Is Everything," does justice to the original (and that's saying a lot). Compared to the debut, *The End of Love* lacked a sense of exuberance as well as a passel of solid songs and performances. *—John Bush*

Last Days and Time / 1972 / Columbia ♦♦♦
Earth, Wind & Fire were nothing if not ambitious, and by the time of their third album they had forged an individual sound by absorbing nearly everything that had gone before them in the previous ten years. It was as if they were trying to encapsulate every eclectic foray pursued by Motown, from catchy, rhythmic pop to churning funk, and even from Stevie Wonder singing borrowed folk songs like "Blowin' in the Wind" (here, Bailey did "Where Have All the Flowers Gone") to the schmaltzy, string-filled pop that spelled legitimacy to Motown. Not only that, they wanted to incorporate Sly & the Family Stone's horn-filled, gutbucket R&B and some of the fusion style of Weather Report. On *Last Days and Time*, they succeeded in pulling all that into their orbit, but they hadn't yet managed one crucial thing: They hadn't learned to write hits. That would come next. *—William Ruhlmann*

Head to the Sky / May 1973 / Columbia ♦♦♦
As phenomenally popular as Earth, Wind & Fire was from the mid-'70s to the early 1980s, it's easy to forget that the band was hardly an overnight success. With *Head to the Sky*—EWF's fourth album overall, second with Philip Bailey and second for Columbia—Maurice White's very spiritual and ambitious brand of soul and funk was starting to pay off commercially. The Latin-influenced "Evil" became the soulsters' biggest hit up to that point, and material ranging from the hauntingly pretty title song (which boasts one of Bailey's finest performances ever) to the jazz-fusion gem "Zanzibar" is just as rewarding. The lineup White unveiled with *Last Days and Time* was working out beautifully; Bailey was clearly proving to be a major asset. Also worth noting is the presence of singer Jessica Cleaves, who left after this album and, several years later, resurfaced in George Clinton's eccentric female group the Brides of Funkenstein. EWF still had what was basically a cult following, but that was beginning to change with *Head to the Sky*. And when EWF took off commercially in 1974 and 1975, many new converts went back and saw for themselves just how excellent an album *Head to the Sky* was. *—Alex Henderson*

Another Time / 1974 / Warner Bros. ♦♦♦
Once Earth, Wind & Fire became the top black music band in the world, Warner Bros. realized the mistake they had made in not giving Maurice White complete creative freedom. They rushed out this anthology featuring the group's early music, hoping to piggyback off their huge Columbia hits. These songs are certainly worth hearing again, but few people who hadn't originally purchased the Warner Bros. tracks were enticed to get them. *—Ron Wynn*

Open Our Eyes / Mar. 1974 / Columbia/Legacy ♦♦♦
Finally, after almost half a decade of serious dues-paying, Earth, Wind & Fire took off commercially with its fifth album, *Open Our Eyes*. EWF had been delivering great albums since 1971, but it wasn't until 1974 that the public proved genuinely receptive to Maurice White's mystical and unorthodox take on soul and funk. No longer would EWF enjoy only a small cult following. Thanks to treasures like "Kalimba Song," the gritty funk smoker "Mighty Mighty," and the unforgettable "Devotion," *Open Our Eyes* became EWF's first gold album and went to the top of the R&B charts. It's also interesting to note that with this album, singer Jessica Cleaves was gone, resulting in the first time EWF had an all-male lineup. The 2001 CD reissue adds four previously unreleased bonus tracks, one of them a "Walkin' in N'awlins" mix of "Fair But So Uncool," though the other three songs did not appear on the original album in an alternate form. *—Alex Henderson*

That's the Way of the World / Mar. 1975 / Columbia/Legacy ♦♦♦♦♦
Earth, Wind & Fire has delivered more than its share of excellent albums, but if a person could own only one EWF release, the logical choice would be *That's the Way of the World*, which was the band's best album as well as its best-selling. *Open Our Eyes* had been a major hit and sold over half a million units, but it was *World* that established the members of EWF as major-league, multi-platinum superstars. Fueled by gems ranging from the sweaty funk of "Shining Star" and "Yearnin', Learnin'" to the gorgeous ballad "Reasons" and the unforgettable title song, EWF's sixth album sold at least five million units. And some of the tracks that weren't major hits, such as the exuberant "Happy Feelings" and the gospel-influenced "See the Light," are equally powerful. There are no dull moments on *World*, one of the strongest albums of the 1970s and EWF's crowning achievement. The 1999 CD reissue has five previously unreleased "sketches" from late 1974, including much briefer instrumental run-throughs of "Shining Star" and "That's the Way of the World," the first take alternate vocal of "All About Love," an alternate of "Happy Feelin'," and the jazz-oriented jam "Caribou Chaser" (the only one of the five not to be represented in a different version on the proper album). *—Alex Henderson*

Gratitude / Dec. 1975 / Columbia/Legacy ♦♦♦♦♦
With *That's the Way of the World* having made Earth, Wind & Fire one of the best-selling soul bands of the 1970s, Maurice White & Co. had no problem filling large arenas. As dynamic as EWF was on-stage, it's a shame that there isn't more documentation of the band's live show. Only one live EWF album was released by a major label in America, the superb *Gratitude*. First a two-LP set and later reissued on CD, *Gratitude* brilliantly captures the excitement EWF generated on-stage at its creative peak. Neither hardcore EWF devotees nor more casual listeners should deprive themselves of the joys of the live versions of "Shining Star" and "Yearnin', Learnin'." Maurice White is magnificent throughout, and Philip Bailey truly soars on extended versions of "Reasons" (which boasts a memorable alto sax solo by guest Don Myrick) and "Devotion." The album also introduced some excellent new studio songs, including the haunting "Can't Hide Love" and the uplifting "Sing a Song." One could nitpick and wish for live versions of "Evil," "Keep Your Head to the Sky," and "Kalimba Song," but the bottom line is that *Gratitude* is one of EWF's finest accomplishments. *—Alex Henderson*

Spirit / Sep. 1976 / Columbia/Legacy ♦♦♦♦♦
With *That's the Way of the World* having enjoyed multi-platinum success, Earth, Wind & Fire had a lot to live up to when the time came for another studio project. And the soul powerhouse didn't let anyone down (either commercially or creatively) on the outstanding *Spirit*, which boasted hits ranging from the optimistic "On Your Face" and the passionate funk classic "Getaway" to the poetic ballad "Imagination." Philip Bailey is as charismatic as ever on "Imagination" and the gorgeous title song. Maurice White's message and vision (an interesting blend of Afro-American Christianity and Eastern philosophy) was as positive and uplifting as ever, and as always, EWF expressed this positivity without being Pollyanna-ish or corny. And even if one didn't take EWF's calls for unity, hard work, self-respect, and faith in God to heart, they had no problem with their solid grooves. The 2001 CD reissue adds five previously unreleased bonus tracks, including an alternate mix of "Saturday Nite," an "Angels Mix" of "Imagination," "Departure (The Traveler)," and two songs that did not appear on the original album in an alternate form. *—Alex Henderson*

All 'N All / Nov. 1977 / Columbia/Legacy ♦♦♦♦
Earth, Wind & Fire's artistic and commercial winning streak continued with its ninth album, *All 'N All*, the diverse jewel that gave us major hits like "Serpentine Fire" and the dreamy "Fantasy." Whether the visionary soul men are tearing into the hardest of funk on "Jupiter" or the most sentimental of ballads on "I'll Write a Song for You" (which boasts one of Philip Bailey's many soaring, five-star performances), *All 'N All* was a highly rewarding addition to EWF's catalogue. Because EWF had such a clean-cut image and fared so well among pop audiences, some may have forgotten just how sweaty its funk could be. But "Jupiter"—like "Mighty, Mighty," "Shining Star," and "Getaway"—underscores the fact that EWF delivered some of the most intense and gutsy funk of the 1970s. [The 1999 CD reissue adds three bonus tracks: "Would You Mind" (a demo version of "Love's Holiday"), the "original Hollywood mix" of "Runnin'," and a live version of "Brazilian Rhyme," recorded live in 1980.] *—Alex Henderson*

☆ **The Best of Earth, Wind & Fire, Vol. 1** / Nov. 1978 / Columbia/Legacy ♦♦♦♦♦
When it was originally released in 1978, *The Best of Earth, Wind & Fire, Vol. 1* was a succinct, ten-track collection of the group's best and biggest singles up to that point. There was one brand-new song, the excellent "September," which soon became a hit in its own right, plus the non-LP Beatles cover "Got to Get You Into My Life," which was recorded for the *Sgt. Pepper's Lonely Hearts Club Band* film, makes its first appearance on an EWF album here. EWF's commercial prime hadn't yet ended when this collection appeared; thus, it's missing several crucial latter-day hits, including the slinky funk of "Serpentine Fire," the ballad "After the Love Has Gone," and the disco smashes "Let's Groove" and "Boogie Wonderland." But even if it's an incomplete hits collection, *The Best of Earth, Wind & Fire, Vol. 1* still ranks as a strong encapsulation of EWF the funk innovators. The singles gathered here constitute some of the richest, most sophisticated music the funk movement ever produced; when the absolute cream of the group's catalog is heard in such a concentrated fashion, the effect is dazzling. That's why *The Best of Earth, Wind & Fire, Vol. 1* was remastered and reissued along with the rest of EWF's catalog, even though it's been supplanted by more extensive single-disc (*Greatest Hits*), double-disc (*The Essential Earth, Wind & Fire*), and triple-disc (*The Eternal Dance*) anthologies. The 1998 release, *Greatest Hits* now stands as the definitive single-disc EWF overview, but for the budget-minded and the disco-phobic, this still makes for an excellent listen. *—Steve Huey*

I Am / Jun. 1979 / Columbia ♦♦♦
Disco was at the height of its popularity in 1979, when Earth, Wind & Fire responded with its most disco-influenced single ever, the glossy and infectious "Boogie Wonderland." Up to that point, EWF had pretty much ignored disco, and when the band finally acknowledged the style, the soulsters weren't about to inundate listeners with it. "Boogie Wonderland" (which features the Emotions, a female group for whom Maurice White had been producing major hits) isn't representative of *I Am* on the whole. From the hit ballad "After the Love Has Gone" to the exuberant "Let My Feelings Flow," *I Am* isn't a radical departure from its predecessor, *All 'N All*. Though not in a class with *That's the Way of the World, Spirit*, or *All 'N All, I Am* is a rewarding album that has a lot going for it. *—Alex Henderson*

Faces / Oct. 1980 / Columbia ♦♦♦
Although they were catching more flak from critics for an alleged obsession with socio-political commentary and quasi-mystical references, R&B audiences hadn't yet tired of Earth, Wind & Fire. While this album admittedly had less memorable material and was more dependent on what had become production clichés and stock devices, it still landed plenty of hits on the charts. But it was becoming clear to even the most devoted fans that songs like "In the Stone" and "Let Me Talk" weren't their finest hour. *—Ron Wynn*

Raise! / Oct. 1981 / Columbia ♦♦
The end was near for Earth, Wind And Fire. This wasn't quite the disaster it was made out to be at the time, but it was their least distinguished overall album since the early

days on Warner Bros., with the exception of their participation in the disastrous *Sgt. Pepper's Lonely Hearts Club Band* film soundtrack in 1978. "Let's Groove" was just a recycled midtempo tune from the mid '70s, and everything else sounded desultory and uninspired. It was no surprise that after two more albums White and company decided to take some time away from the scene. —*William Ruhlmann*

Powerlight / Feb. 1983 / Columbia ✦✦✦✦
Many groups lose the steam that propelled them to the top; Earth, Wind & Fire, contemporary sound and all, were still blazing when this album was released. "Fall in Love With Me" was the first single. With its festive rhythm and sauntering vocals, it became a number-four hit on the *Billboard* R&B charts and a number-17 pop hit. The percolating single "Side By Side" was the second release. The precise horns, sensuous female backing vocals, and Maurice White's animated vocal make this an entertaining piece. Though it should have fared better, it settled in at number 15 on the R&B charts. The final release was "Spread Your Love." The sonically aggressive special effects are contrasted with a soothing chanting chorus. The single peaked at 57. All three of the above feature Maurice White on lead. Throughout the entire album, White's unifying message is fueled by the aggressive rhythms and relaxing melodies. —*Craig Lytle*

Electric Universe / Nov. 1983 / Columbia ✦✦
Commercially, Earth, Wind & Fire was slipping in 1983. Though a decent album, *Powerlight* wasn't the type of big seller EWF was used to. Maurice White responded with a change of direction that proved to be both a commercial and artistic fiasco. Working with very in-demand (and very formula-oriented) studio figures like Martin Page and David Foster, EWF went for a much slicker and more high-tech approach on the weak and disappointing *Electric Universe*. White saw that synthesizers and drum machines were playing more and more of a role in both R&B and pop, and wanted to acknowledge technology's impact on music with this album. But EWF usually ends up sounding insincere and even sterile. The type of synth-funk that worked so well for the System doesn't work for EWF. A few of the songs are interesting (including "Electric Kingdom" and the single "Magnetic"), but they don't prevent *Electric Universe* from being EWF's weakest album ever. When this release flopped, EWF's members temporarily went their separate ways, with Philip Bailey and Maurice White concentrating on solo careers. —*Alex Henderson*

Touch the World / Oct. 1987 / Columbia ✦✦✦
Four years passed between 1983's embarrassing *Electric Universe* and their reunion album, *Touch the World*. Before the album's release, there was excitement as well as skepticism among Earth, Wind & Fire fans. Was EWF still capable of delivering a great album? And even if it was, how well would the album do in an R&B market that was radically different than that of the 1970s? As it turned out, a lot of the old magic was still there, and Maurice White and Philip Bailey proved that they could still be a powerful combination. From "Evil Roy" (which describes an urban youth's life of crime) to the major hit "System of Survival," *Touch the World* proved that EWF was still quite capable of excellence. Though White doesn't shy away from technology, he uses it in an organic fashion and remains faithful to the outfit's rich history. Despite "System of Survival"'s success, the album wasn't the huge commercial hit it deserved to be, but it wasn't a bomb either. —*Alex Henderson*

The Best of Earth, Wind & Fire, Vol. 2 / 1988 / Columbia/Legacy ✦✦✦✦✦
The second collection covering hit singles from the '70s top funk and soul band, Earth, Wind & Fire. This anthology has recently been supplanted by a box set covering virtually all of their big Columbia singles and some early Warners material. If you enjoyed their disco and late '70s cuts more than the early tracks, this anthology is worth getting. The 2000 CD reissue has two bonus tracks: the moderate 1973 hit "Keep Your Head to the Sky" and "I'll Write a Song for You," from the 1977 album *All 'n All*. —*Ron Wynn & Richie Unterberger*

Heritage / Jan. 1990 / Columbia ✦✦
After making an exciting comeback with the impressive *Touch the World*, Earth, Wind & Fire disappointed us bitterly with *Heritage*, which, next to *Electric Universe*, is the band's weakest and most forgettable album. *Heritage* suffers from the same problem as *Universe*—Maurice White obviously wanted to keep EWF sounding contemporary and up to date, but he ended up with something forced and unnatural. Bringing MC Hammer and the Boyz on board for guest spots and incorporating a heavy dose of hip-hop and urban contemporary elements, EWF goes out of its way to appeal to younger listeners and fails to be true to itself. The high-tech album usually ends up sounding stiff and insincere, like the result of a market meeting rather than artistic inspiration. Even an appearance by Sly Stone doesn't help. This is a release that only completists and avid collectors should spend their money on. —*Alex Henderson*

The Eternal Dance / Sep. 8, 1992 / Columbia/Legacy ✦✦✦✦✦
Covering three discs and including all the hits, as well as a healthy selection of rarities, *The Eternal Dance* is not designed for the casual listener; only hardcore fans will remain enthralled through the numerous rarities. Most listeners will be content with the two greatest hits collections, but this comprehensive box set remains essential for hardcore Earth, Wind & Fire fans. —*Stephen Thomas Erlewine*

Millennium / Sep. 14, 1993 / Reprise ✦✦
Since the mid-'80s, Earth, Wind & Fire's output had been erratic and quite uneven. One never knew whether the veteran soul/funk band would come out with something as impressive as *Touch the World* or something as embarrassing as *Heritage*. After many years with Columbia, EWF switched to Warner Bros.—ironically, a label that gave Maurice White and friends the boot back in 1972—with *Millennium*. While *Heritage* found EWF bending over backwards to appeal to urban contemporary tastes, sounding unnatural and even silly in the process, *Millennium* is a more honest and organic recording. Though hardly in a class with *That's The Way of the World* or *Spirit*—or for that matter, *Touch the World—Millennium* is a decent offering that finds the crew being true to itself. Much of the material, especially "Sunday Morning," "Chicago (Chi-Town) Blues" and "Honor the Magic," is fairly memorable. Unfortunately, the urban contemporary audience wasn't receptive to EWF's honesty. As influential as EWF had been, and as often as it had been sampled in hip-hop, the group was treated like it was expendable. —*Alex Henderson*

In the Name of Love / Jul. 22, 1997 / Rhino ✦✦✦✦
Earth, Wind & Fire's return to Warner Bros. with 1993's *Millennium* proved to be short-lived—the album failed to meet the company's expectations commercially. Four years later, EWF ended up on the independent, Miami-based Pyramid label with the surprisingly retro *In the Name of Love*. More personnel changes had taken place, but thankfully, Maurice and Verdine White and Philip Bailey were still on board for what was EWF's most live-sounding, least high-tech offering since 1983's *Powerlight*. (However, EWF had been touring without Maurice since 1994). Live horns and real instruments abound, and everything from the ballads "Cruising," "When Love Goes Wrong" and "Right Time" to the punchy funk ditty "Rock It" sounds like it could have been recorded in the 1970s. One very pleasant surprise is a remake of "Love of Life," which the pre-Bailey EWF embraced on its self-titled debut album of 1971. Bailey's son, Sir James Bailey, raps on the sociopolitical "Revolution," but on the whole, this excellent CD is unapologetically retro. —*Alex Henderson*

★ **Greatest Hits** / Nov. 17, 1998 / Columbia/Legacy ✦✦✦✦✦
Columbia's 1998 collection of Earth, Wind & Fire's *Greatest Hits* in many ways stands as the group's definitive compilation. Even though there have been more extensive overviews of the group's work, such as the triple-disc set *The Eternal Dance*, this is the first collection to contain all of the group's biggest hits on one disc. All but one ("Love Music") of the ten songs from 1978's *The Best of Earth, Wind & Fire* are included, while six of the ten songs from *The Best Of, Vol. 2* are featured; the remaining two cuts on the 17-track collection are the minor early single "Kalimba Story" and the album cut "Gratitude." These are fine additions to the album, but the true meat of the collection lies in the hits—"Shining Star," "That's the Way of the World," "Sing a Song," "Getaway," "Got to Get You Into My Life," "September," "Boogie Wonderland," "After the Love Has Gone," "Let's Groove," and so many others. They might not be presented in chronological order (the only flaw in this otherwise flawless collection), but it's a sheer delight to have all of the hits on one terrifically entertaining and valuable disc. —*Stephen Thomas Erlewine*

The Essential Earth, Wind & Fire / Jul. 23, 2002 / Columbia/Legacy ✦✦✦✦✦
Columbia/Legacy's double-disc set *The Essential Earth, Wind & Fire* lives up to its title by offering 34 tracks of the groundbreaking funk band at their peak. All of the hits, whether they're R&B or tunes that crossed over to the pop charts, are here, along with important album tracks that capture the range and depth of EWF. Since this focuses on their peak of the '70s and early '80s, there's very little here that doesn't qualify as "essential," which makes it a better bet than their box set. The single-disc *Greatest Hits* remains the choice for the casual and the curious listener due to its concise concentration of classics, but anybody who wants a thorough retrospective should choose this. —*Stephen Thomas Erlewine*

The Ebonys

f. 1967, Camden, NJ, **db.** 1976
Group / Philly Soul, Funk, Soul
Another '70s soul group whose commercial track record doesn't do its music justice, the Ebonys made gripping, dramatic ballads that no soul fan undervalues. On the Philadelphia International label during an era when they routinely cranked out transcendent, genre-smashing hits, this New Jersey vocal group started in 1968. Jenny Holmes, David Beasley, James Tuten, and Clarence Vaughn formed the lineup, and Leon Huff discovered them. They scored their first hit with "You're the Reason Why," a number-ten R&B single in 1971. Their greatest song, "It's Forever," appeared in 1973; it only reached number 14. That was their last hit; their other Philadelphia International singles were often nicely done, but commercial flops. —*Ron Wynn*

The Ebonys / 1973 / Philadelphia International ✦✦✦
Even though their vocal ability was as good as many, if not supreme, this Camden, NJ-based vocal quartet did not threaten the chart action of any of their competitors; however, this album is home to the group's most popular single, "It's Forever." With its serene intro, the foursome harmonize their way to the verse where the lead vocals, both baritone and falsetto, bring enhancing deliveries to an already outstanding track. The single peaked at number 14 on the R&B charts after 13 weeks. The second single was "I Believe." Originally a pop hit for Frankie Laine in 1953, the Ebonys' version retains some of that pop texture. However, the group's vocal explosiveness leaves a lasting R&B impression. After 13 weeks, the song reached number 34 on the charts. "Life in the Country" was the third single—a moderately paced ballad reminiscent of early Stylistics, who were also emerging around the same time this album was released. While this album is balanced with moderate grooves, the aforementioned ballads and the unreleased "I'll Try" stand out. The production work of Kenny Gamble & Leon Huff and their colleagues is outstanding. —*Craig Lytle*

Sing About Life / 1976 / Buddah ✦✦✦
The Ebonys' second LP (the first was on Philadelphia International) doesn't have the highs of the Gamble & Huff production, but it doesn't have the lows, namely "Sexy Ways" and "Hook Up and Get Down," either. Their only Buddah hit "Makin' Love Ain't No Fun," charted at number 83 in 1976 but didn't make this party for some inexplicable reason. The label did, however, include that song's successor, "Neighborhood Gossip," which made some club noise but didn't chart. There's some heavy soul wailing on "If You're in

Need," and "Mr. Me, Mrs. You," which producer Tony Camillo did again with Creme D'Cocoa; Jennifer Holmes, who co-leads it here, did the same on the Creme D'Cocoa version, a group whose lineup included Holmes and three former Ambassadors ("I Really Love You"). The other Ebonys were David Beasley, James Tuten, and Clarence Vaughn. Also contained here is a torchy rendition of Average White Band's "A Love of Your Own." *—Andrew Hamilton*

- **Golden Philly Classics** / 1995 / Collectables ♦♦♦♦

Ecstasy, Passion & Pain

f. 1973, New York, NY

Group / Pop, Disco, Funk

Disco group Ecstasy, Passion & Pain boasted the vibrant, supple lead vocals of Barbara Roy and dance classics produced by Philly soul arranger/songwriter Bobby Martin. Besides singer/guitarist/songwriter Roy (she wrote their hits, "I Wouldn't Give You Up" and "Ask Me"), the group lineup included drummer Althea "Cookie" Smith, bassist Joseph Williams, guitarist Jimmy Clark, percussionists Carl Jordan and later Alan Tizer, organist Billy Gardner, and keyboardist Ronnie Foster, who later became a popular contemporary jazz artist and top session player in the '80s and '90s. Though they were an actual band, Martin used MFSB and the background vocals of the Sweethearts of Sigma on their hits.

Born Barbara Gaskins in Kingston, NC, Roy first recorded with her niece Brenda Gaskins as Barbara and Brenda ("Let's Get Together" on Avanti, "That's When You've Got Soul" on Heidi, and "If I'm Hurt You'll Feel the Pain"). Her niece retired from the music business and Barbara Roy began playing guitar for Inez and Charlie Foxx ("Mockingbird") and on various recording sessions in New York. In 1973, Ecstasy, Passion & Pain was formed and shortly afterwards, through manager Phil Braxton, the group had a recording contract. Getting a deal with Roulette Records, Ecstasy, Passion & Pain recorded a stream of hits in the mid-'70s: "I Wouldn't Give You Up," "Good Things Don't Last Forever" (written by Bunny Sigler, Norman Harris, and Allan Felder), the chugging "Ask Me" (written by lead singer Roy with an intro that recalls First Choice's "Armed and Extremely Dangerous"), the jubilant "One Beautiful Day," "Touch and Go" (another Sigler/Harris/ Felder song), and "Passion." Four years later, the group resurfaced on the lead singer's own Roy B label with the 12-inch single "If You Want Me," a dance club hit. In 1986, Barbara Roy was a solo act on RCA Records, charting number-83 R&B with "Gotta See You Tonight" in the fall of that year. She was later heard on the 1989 Paul Simpson/ Togetherness LP *We Are the Ones* for Simp-House/Cooltempo. *—Ed Hogan*

Ecstasy, Passion & Pain / Feb. 16, 1999 / Koch International ♦♦♦

Ecstasy, Passion & Pain is a more fitting description of lead singer Barbara Roy's voice than the group as a whole. Roy's tough, gritty vocals might seem better suited to the earthy recordings of labels such as Stax or Hi, but she fits right in with Bobby Martin's Philly soul settings on the R&B hits "Ask Me," "I Wouldn't Give You Up," and "Good Things Don't Last Forever," the last of which was co-written by Bunny Sigler and Norman Harris. The input of such Philly soul veterans elevates the best of Roy's compositions to the level of second-tier Gamble & Huff imitations, although those legendary producers never worked with a talent like Roy when they applied their Midas touch to female groups like the Three Degrees and the Jones Girls. Unfortunately, Martin's orchestrated impersonations are not as successful on the group's ballads, partly because Roy's commanding presence is less effective on slower, more restrained material. Ironically, the most enjoyable song, the swirling "I'll Do Anything for You," was relegated to the B-side of a later single, although it could easily become a hit for any shrewd girl group who rediscovers it. The CD reissue includes the group's later singles "One Beautiful Day" and "Touch and Go," thus helping to counter the inconsistency of the original debut release. Despite admirable contributions from other group members and outside sources, Roy is definitely the main reason to check out *Ecstasy, Passion & Pain*, which remains the best documentation of her abilities as a singer and songwriter. *—Vince Ripol*

- **Good Things: The Roulette Recordings 1973–77** / Mar. 2, 1999 / WestSide ♦♦♦♦

Good Things is a double-disc set including every track released by Ecstasy, Passion & Pain plus nearly an entire disc's worth of unreleased material by the mid-'70s soul act. *—Keith Farley*

Eden's Crush

f. Los Angeles, CA

Group / Club/Dance, Dance-Pop, Urban

Los Angeles based female teen pop quintet Eden's Crush was formed after its members auditioned for the reality series *Popstars*, broadcasted by the WB Network. The vocal act's debut album, also titled *Popstars*, was released by London-Sire Records in 2001, produced by David Foster and Matthew Gerrard, and featured a Spanish version of "1000 Words," plus a cover of Sheila E.'s "Glamorous Life." Eden's Crush became the first female group to debut at number one on the sales chart with their first single, "Get Over Yourself." *—Drago Bonacich*

- **Popstars** / May 1, 2001 / Sire ♦♦♦

The members of Eden's Crush were designed to play the role of disposable pop stars, a prefabricated collection of attractive female entertainers who would star on the WB's TV show *Popstars*, while promoting a record of the same name. This they can do, and they do it reasonably well—they sing, dance, and display some charisma and talent. But—and maybe this shouldn't come as a surprise—it sounds like a television show, not pop music. A pretty good approximation of pop music at times, whether it's on ballads like "Love This Way" or standard-issue dance-pop like "What's Good 4 the Goose" or "Get Over Yourself," but the girls either don't have or aren't allowed to display charisma as strong as Britney or Christina, or even 3LW. This hardly means it's a terrible album, but it's hardly a memorable one; it, like the show, will be best remembered as an artifact from the teen-tastic early years of the new millennium. *—Stephen Thomas Erlewine*

Kevon Edmonds

Indianapolis, IN

Vocals / Contemporary R&B, Urban

Not only is Kevon Edmonds the brother of producer/songwriter/singer Kenneth "Babyface" Edmonds, he was also a member of the vocal group After 7, who had two back-to-back number one R&B/Top Ten pop gold singles with "Ready or Not" and "Can't Stop" as well as several R&B/pop hits during the '90s.

The Indianapolis, IN, native started the group After 7 with brother Melvin Edmonds and Indiana University classmate Keith Mitchell. After graduation, the trio worked nine-to-five jobs. Meanwhile, L.A. Reid and Babyface had signed a production deal with Virgin Records and were scouting around for acts to produce. After they chose to work with their relatives, there was a period where the singing trio wasn't sure of the producers' intent, as they waited for L.A. and Babyface to finish other projects. But once things started rolling, they really started rolling.

The first single from After 7's debut self-titled album was "Heat of the Moment," which hit number-five R&B in summer 1989. "Ready or Not" parked at number-one R&B for two weeks in early 1990. "Can't Stop" with Edmonds on lead went to number-one R&B, number-six pop in summer 1990. *After 7* followed with two certified gold albums: *Takin' My Time* (1992) and *Reflections* (1995).

The group went on hiatus just about the time Babyface was looking for real singers to join him in a fictitious group called Milestone for *Soul Food*, a film he was co-producing. He recruited Kevon, Melvin, and siblings K-Ci & JoJo from Jodeci. The result was 1997's stirring ballad and instant hit "I Care About You," which the group also performed in the movie. In fall 1999, Edmonds' solo debut *24-7* was issued on BMG. *—Ed Hogan*

- **24-7** / Oct. 26, 1999 / RCA ♦♦♦

Kevon Edmonds' solo debut *24-7* proves that he can make it on his own, apart from After 7, even if it isn't a full-fledged knockout. Like his brother Babyface, Edmonds has an appealingly sophisticated spin on contemporary urban soul, never pushing the music too hard and keeping everything smooth and suave. This elegant approach carries him through stretches where the material isn't really distinguished, but fortunately, there aren't too many weak moments on the album. At times, the music can seem a little samey, but at its best—the opening trilogy of "Never Love You," "Love Will Be Waiting," and "24/7," plus the Babyface duet "A Girl Like You"—*24/7* showcases Edmonds as a sweetly ingratiating urban crooner. *—Stephen Thomas Erlewine*

The Edsels

f. 1959, Campbell, OH, **db.** 1961

Group / Doo Wop

A brief encounter with fame came for the Edsels when they recorded the doo wop masterpiece "Rama Lama Ding Dong." Originally released in 1959, the single became a hit some three years after its intial release, thanks to the efforts of diligent record collectors and disc jockeys.

Taking their name from Ford's legendary failed automobile, the Edsels formed in in the tiny mill town of Campbell, OH, in the late '50s. The group consisted of lead vocalist George Jones Jr., James Reynolds, Marshall Sewell, Harry Greene, and Larry Greene. The group auditioned for a local Ohio music publisher in 1958. Through the publisher, the group landed a record deal with the small Dub Records. The Edsels' first single was a song Jones had written, "Rama Lama Ding Dong." The first pressings on Dub Records were mislabelled "Lama Rama Ding Dong."

"Rama Lama Ding Dong" became a local hit, but made no impact nationally. In 1961, disc jockeys began playing the song again because it sounded similar to the Marcels' current hit, "Blue Moon." Within a few months, the single was re-released on Twin Records—this time with the correct song title—and it quickly scaled the pop charts, peaking at number 21. Ironically, the group had broken up by the time "Rama Lama Ding Dong" became a hit in 1961. *—Stephen Thomas Erlewine & Cub Koda*

- **Rama Lama Ding Dong** / 1992 / Relic ♦♦♦♦♦

This is a complete 19-track collection of the group's best sides, including the title track, one of the great nonsense doo wop sides of all time. *—Cub Koda*

Dennis Edwards

b. Feb. 3, 1943, Birmingham, AL

Vocals / Quiet Storm, Motown, Urban, Soul

Once a Temptation, always a Temptation might be the motto for explosive vocalist Dennis Edwards, who's joined, left, and rejoined the group three times. Edwards was born in Birmingham, but his family moved to Detroit when he was seven. As a high school student, Edwards sang with the Crowns of Joy gospel group, then formed a soul-jazz band called Dennis Edwards & the Firebirds, inspired by organist Richard "Groove" Holmes. Motown bass legend James Jamerson heard Edwards singing one night and suggested he audition. They needed a lead singer quickly for the Contours, and his feature on "It's So Hard Being Alone" was Edwards' entry into the company. A song he recorded for Soulsville, "I Didn't Have To (But I Did)," got moderate reaction, but Edwards was soon enlisted to replace David Ruffin as lead singer of the Temptations in 1968. He spent the next nine years in that role, his gritty leads fueling such songs as "Cloud Nine," "I Can't Get Next to You," "Ball of Confusion," and "Psychedelic Shack," as well as the groundbreaking singles "Papa Was a Rolling Stone" and "Masterpiece."

He left for the first time in 1977, returned in 1979, and left again in 1983. A year later he made one of the great duets of the decade, "Don't Look Any Further," with Siedah Garrett. It didn't make it to the top of the R&B charts, but there weren't many numbers that better combined sensuality, vocal assertiveness, excellent production, and a superb arrangement. The follow-up, "(You're My) Aphrodisiac," was a Top 20 R&B single, but things then cooled considerably. "Coolin' Out" was Edwards' final hit, peaking at number 23, but he returned to the Temptations in 1987. Edwards briefly teamed with ex-Temptations David Ruffin and Eddie Kendricks in the trio Ruffin/Kendricks/Edwards, but nothing was ever released. *—Ron Wynn*

Don't Look Any Further / 1984 / Motown ✦✦✦✦
Don't Look Any Further is the first released solo album from Dennis Edwards, the sometime Temptations lead vocalist. Edwards first made a solo recording in 1977, but had nothing to show for it but an unreleased album. He returned stronger than ever, but then again left in the middle of the sessions for *Back to Basics*. For *Don't Look Any Further*, Edwards teamed with producer Dennis Lambert, who was behind the boards for 1983's Temptations effort *Surface Thrills*. This effort skillfully merged the loveman persona reminiscent of Teddy Pendergrass with the confident early-'80s Al Jarreau-style pop. With Edwards in great voice and spirits, *Don't Look Any Further* is a thoroughly enjoyable listen. The big hit here, the reggae-tinged title track, was supposed to be a duet with Chaka Khan. Siedah Garrett, who did the demo, appears instead and displays great chemistry with Edwards. The slow-burning "(You're My) Aphrodisiac" soon has Edwards screaming the paint off the walls. What's remarkable about *Don't Look Any Further* is how is continues to succeed in light of potentially album-stalling premises and sometime so-so production. The breakdancing-ready style of "Shake Hands (Come Out Dancing)" suits Edwards' bluster quite well. The album's biggest surprise, the sweet ballad "Just Like You" has Edwards singing with surprising emotion. *Don't Look Any Further* presents Edwards as a potent solo act and displays the depth and subtlety inherent in his best work. *—Jason Elias*

Coolin' Out / 1985 / Motown ✦✦

● **The Essential Collection** / Sep. 24, 2002 / Spectrum ✦✦✦✦
Since Dennis Edwards recorded only two albums for Motown, this Spectrum anthology of his mid-'80s work for the label has to dig pretty deep to find songs worthy of the title. There are only three, really: his charming hit duet of "Don't Look Any Further" with Siedah Garrett, and the follow-ups "(You're My) Aphrodisiac" and "Coolin' Out." Also included are a passel of intriguing album tracks, including the period "Shake Hands (Come Out Dancing)" and a cover of "Try a Little Tenderness." *—John Bush*

Tommy Edwards

b. Feb. 17, 1922, Virginia, **d.** Oct. 22, 1969, Henrico County, VA
Vocals / R&B
Vocalist, pianist, and composer Tommy Edwards began performing in Richmond when he was nine. He made his first impact in R&B circles in 1946, writing "That Chick's too Young to Fry." He began recording for Top in 1949 and had his first hit in 1951 with "All Over Again" for MGM, a song that made it to number ten on the R&B charts. Nearly seven years later, a song that Edwards originally recorded in 1951 became his biggest hit and an R&B and pop staple. "It's All in the Game" was issued on MGM in a slightly different version. The 1958 edition topped both R&B and pop charts. Edwards later had another hit with a reworked song he had released in 1952, as "Please Mr. Sun" reached number-18 R&B and number-11 pop as the follow-up single. His last chart tune was "My Melancholy Baby" in 1959. *—Ron Wynn*

● **Complete Hits of Tommy Edwards** / Apr. 16, 1995 / Eric ✦✦✦✦✦
Here are twenty of Tommy Edwards' best, including both versions of "It's All in the Game," a song he first placed on the charts in 1951 (number 18), and with a new arrangement, it went all the way to number one in 1958. The 1958 hit was amazing considering Edwards was a '40s crooner. His engaging tenor justifies every track, including Gene Pitney's "Blue Heartaches." *—Andrew Hamilton*

The Best of Tommy Edwards / 1997 / PGD Special Markets ✦✦✦
A budget-priced CD of Tommy Edwards hits featuring ten of the velvet crooner's memorable easy listening recordings, including "It's All in the Game." Edwards cracked the pop Top 20 twice with the Charles Dawes/Carl Sigman composition, once in 1951 at number 18 and again in 1958 when he aced *Billboard* with an updated arrangement. *—Andrew Hamilton*

Willie Egan

Piano / Boogie-Woogie, Piano Blues, Rock & Roll
Known by true aficionados for the handful of great boogie rockers that he cut for the Louisiana-based Mambo and Vita imprints during the mid-'50s, pianist Willie Egan should have enjoyed a considerably larger share of fame than he did.

Born on the bayou outside of Shreveport, Egan was lucky to escape his rustic existence for Los Angeles at the age of nine. Piano swiftly became his passion, as he listened to and learned from the recordings of Amos Milburn, Hadda Brooks, and Camille Howard. A 1954 single for John R. Fullbright's Elko label preceded a series of 1955-1956 gems for Larry Mead's Mambo and Vita labels, notably "Wow Wow," "What a Shame," "Come On," "She's Gone Away, But," and "Wear Your Black Dress." Egan's surname was frequently misspelled on these platters as Eggins or Egans. After a stint as one of Marvin Phillips' several duet partners (billed as Marvin & Johnny), Egan largely hung it up (a 1983 European tour got him back in the studio for one fresh album, anyway). *—Bill Dahl*

● **Come On** / 1993 / Relic ✦✦✦✦✦
The R&B boogie pianist waxed some rip-roaring rockers for the tiny Los Angeles-based Vita and Mambo logos during the mid-'50s. Fourteen of his best are collected here for a long-overdue airing. This guy deserved a lot more respect than he got, judging from the jumping Louisiana-tinged "Wow Wow," "Come On," and "She's Gone Away, But..." Also aboard: 11 more obscure goodies from the same labels' vaults, notably four tracks by Harmonica Slim (including "Drop Anchor") and Big Boy Groves' lament "You Can't Beat the Horses." *—Bill Dahl*

The Egyptian Lover (Greg Broussard)

Producer, Vocals / Electro, Old School Rap, Club/Dance, West Coast Rap, Urban
One of the most innovative producers of the old-school/electro era, Egyptian Lover's Greg Broussard recorded a parade of singles during the mid-'80s that proved influential for decades. Influenced himself by Kraftwerk/hip-hop soundclashes like Afrika Bambaataa's "Planet Rock" and Man Parrish's "Hip-Hop Be Bop (Don't Stop)," as well as the extroverted black-lover soul of Prince and Zapp, Broussard began recording from his Los Angeles base in 1983. One year later, he emerged with the breakdancing anthem "Egypt, Egypt," released on the Freak Beat label. Similar to excellent tracks being produced all over America—from Detroit (Cybotron) to New York (Mantronix)—"Egypt, Egypt" and successors "What Is a DJ If He Can't Scratch," "And My Beat Goes Boom," and "Computer Love (Sweet Dreams)" spent much time in DJ crates during the '80s and '90s. Broussard also released several LPs during the mid-'80s, including 1984's *On the Nile* (practically a greatest-hits compilation), 1986's *One Track Mind*, and 1988's *Filthy*; the first two appeared on his own Egyptian Empire label. After several years away from music, he returned in 1994 with *Back From the Tomb* and the following year's *Pyramix*. *—John Bush*

● **On the Nile** / 1984 / Egyptian Empire ✦✦✦✦✦
Before Ice-T, N.W.A., and the late Eazy-E made Los Angeles famous (or infamous) for gangsta rap in the late '80s, the city's rap community was best known for a high-tech, futuristic approach that owed a lot to Afrika Bambaataa's 1982 classic, "Planet Rock." In the early to mid-'80s, L.A.-based electro-hoppers like the Egyptian Lover, the World Class Wreckin' Cru (the group that Dr. Dre belonged to before N.W.A.), the Arabian Prince, and Uncle Jam's Army didn't get much respect from East Coast hip-hoppers, who insisted that their music wasn't gritty enough. But those artists did enjoy a cult following in Southern California. Besides, the Egyptian Lover never claimed to be a hardcore rapper; *On the Nile*, his debut album of 1984, doesn't pretend to be a Run-D.M.C., L.L. Cool J, or Fat Boys release any more than Grover Washington Jr. claimed to be a jazz purist. The closest this LP comes to an East Coast hip-hop vibe is the single "What Is a DJ If He Can't Scratch"; all of the other tracks offer a synthesizer-driven blend of rap, dance music, and electro-funk. Though "Planet Rock" is a strong influence on this release, it is hardly the Egyptian Lover's only influence—his sound also owes a debt to Germany's seminal Kraftwerk (whose innovations greatly influenced "Planet Rock"), Prince, Man Parrish, and Giorgio Moroder, as well as Middle Eastern and North African music. The Egyptian Lover never had great rapping skills, but he was definitely an original and imaginative producer/writer—and his risk-taking spirit serves him well on definitive, high-tech tunes like "Egypt Egypt," "My House (On the Nile)," and "Girls." *On the Nile* isn't the only Egyptian Lover LP that is worth owning, but most fans insist that it is his most essential and consistent album—and they're absolutely right. *—Alex Henderson*

One Track Mind / 1986 / Egyptian Empire ✦✦✦
When the Egyptian Lover's second album, *One Track Mind*, came out in 1986, gangsta rap had yet to become huge. Ice-T's *Rhyme Pays* and N.W.A's *N.W.A. & the Posse*—two landmarks in West Coast gangsta rap—didn't come out until 1987, and East Coast hip-hoppers still associated Southern California with the electro-hop style that the Egyptian Lover is best known for. Anyone who expects to find hardcore rap on *One Track Mind* is bound to be disappointed; this LP isn't for rap purists. But those who appreciated his first album, *On the Nile*, will find this to be a respectable, if imperfect, sophomore effort. Egyptian's influences remain the same; the quirky rapper/producer still combines his appreciation of Afrika Bambaataa's "Planet Rock," Prince, Man Parrish, and Kraftwerk with elements of North African music and Egyptian imagery. It's a strange mixture—Egyptian inhabits a place in which rap, Prince's Minneapolis sound, European synth pop, and North African music come together. But it's a mixture that works well on infectious electro-hop jams like "Livin' on the Nile," the single "Freak-A-Holic," and "A Stranger Place (The Alezby Inn)," which bears a bit of a resemblance to Prince's "Erotic City." As the title *One Track Mind* indicates, the Egyptian Lover shares Prince's love of all things erotic. But this LP is never X-rated; the lyrics are suggestive rather than explicit, which is why some of the tunes on *One Track Mind* had urban radio potential. Egyptian, however, was never a superstar, although he did enjoy an enthusiastic cult following. While *One Track Mind* isn't as essential as *On the Nile*, it's a likable release that fans of the electro-hop sound will enjoy. *—Alex Henderson*

Filthy / 1988 / Priority ✦✦✦

Eighth Day

f. 1966, Detroit, MI
Group / Soul, Smooth Soul, Pop-Soul
Many of the groups Lamont Dozier and Eddie & Brian Holland (HDH) signed to their family of labels (Invictus, Hot Wax, Music Merchant) in the late '60s were super-grouped or piecemealed together. When the labels went under, the groups followed suit, and understandably so; they had no ties, and often weren't even friends. The songs published by Gold Forever Music aren't often performed live because the entities ceased to exist a day after the company folded. Hits like "Want Ads," "Give Me Just a Little More Time," "Somebody's Been Sleeping in My Bed," "Westbound #9," and many more, including "She's Not Just Another Woman," by Eighth Day, or was it by them?

The Fall of 1970 found 100 Proof assailing the charts with "Somebody's Been Sleeping in My Bed," led by Steve Mancha (nee Clyde Wilson). It was their second release, they debuted with "Too Many Cooks Spoil the Soup," an R&B hit, but "Somebody's Been Sleeping" climbed to number-eight Pop and sold a million copies. Hotwax released an LP to roll with the single. Everybody knew "She's Not Just Another Woman" was a hit, some jocks were already playing it off the album. Not wanting to interrupt the flow of 100 Proof's hit, HDH decided to release the R&B jump, led by Mancha, under the name Eighth Day on Invictus. As expected it ascended the charts and became a major hit, but there was no Eighth Day. Not yet. As the next Eighth Day single "You Got To Crawl Before You Walk" climbed the charts, HDH assembled a group with Melvin Davis, a solo artist on Invictus, Antonio "Tony" Newsome, Lyman Woodard, Larry Hutchison, Ron Bykowski, and three females. Their other singles never equaled the first, which they didn't sing anyway.

Davis disliked the sterile atmosphere at Invictus/Hotwax, "There was no place to jam or exchange ideas." He also wanted to create more, and disliked the assembly-line approach of HDH. Davis remains in Detroit. A prolific songwriter, Davis wrote "I Don't Wanna Lose You" (Johnnie Taylor) and "Love Bug Got a Bear Hug." Bykowski later gigged and recorded with Parliament/Funkadelic. *—Andrew Hamilton*

Eighth Day / Jul. 1971 / Invictus ♦♦♦♦

The Eighth Day's membership remains a mystery. Were the members interchangeable with 100 Proof (Aged in Soul)? Three of these tracks are on 100 Proofs' debut album: "I've Come to Save You," "Too Many Cooks," and "She's Not Just Another Woman"—the same identical tracks and vocals. A Melvin Davis solo release, "I'm Worried," also appears here. "She's Not Just Another Woman," with its passionate singing and jerky beat, assaulted the charts; their next release, "You Got to Crawl Before You Walk," features a thick funky groove. A good album with a few outstanding tracks and no weak ones. *—Andrew Hamilton*

I Gotta Get Home (Can't Let My Baby Get Lonely) / Jan. 1973 / Invictus ♦♦♦♦

While not as arresting as their debut LP, this is still a keeper, if you can find a copy. It contains "Good Book," a solo release by Melvin Davis (who obviously was a member—why else would Invictus stick his single releases on the Eighth Day's albums?). The title track's a good Holland Dozier production, driven by a shuffling, soul-drenched rhythm. Two gospel songs are also featured: "Faith Is the Answer" (written by Davis) and "Heaven Is There to Guide Us" (also recorded by the Glass House). [A compilation CD of the Eighth Day's best efforts is available on Fantasy Records.] *—Andrew Hamilton*

● **And on the Eighth Day . . . God Created Soul: The Invictus Sessions** / 1999 / Sequel ♦♦♦♦♦

The Eighth Day was a studio-based congregation on Invictus Records, the post-Motown label from Holland-Dozier-Holland. There wasn't an official group and the musicians and singers in the Eighth Day were featured on other Invictus/Hot Wax groups—most notably 100 Proof (Aged in Soul)—but sweating over the details of who did what and who was where misses the point of the Invictus sound: The sound and the songs took prominence over group membership, and why not? The team at Invictus was tremendous, creating big, wall-of-sound productions that were nevertheless nimble, stylish and lush: a perfect expansion of the Motown aesthetic for the post-psychedelic smooth soul era. The first Eighth Day record is among their greatest efforts and it's here in its entirety on *And on the Eighth Day . . . God Created Soul: The Invictus Sessions*, along with their second album, *I Gotta Get Home (Can't Let My Baby Get Lonely)*, making this a complete overview of their career. That alone is enough to make this essential for serious collectors, but if your tastes run toward the group's irresistible hits—"She's Not Just Another Woman," "You've Got to Crawl (Before You Walk)," "Too Many Cooks (Spoil the Soup)"—you may be better off with sticking with a hits collection, since the second Eighth Day album is a misguided affair into jam-oriented funk-soul that loses the plot quickly. There are some good moments, to be sure, but it lacks the panoramic, technicolor sweep of that first album and its hits and is more of a curiosity than a legitimate cult item. That first album, though, is one of the best of its kind and it's heard here in all its glory—and the music is so good, it doesn't really matter who performed it, since the overall sound is the key. *—Stephen Thomas Erlewine*

Eighties Ladies

Group / Disco, Urban, Funk

Under the direction of Roy Ayers, the Eighties Ladies released one album, *Ladies of the '80s*, in 1980. The group was a quintet of vocalists featuring Sylvia Striplin, Marva Hicks, Susan Beaubian, Vivian Prince, and Denie Corbett. *Ladies of the '80s*, released on Ayers' Uno Melodic imprint, failed to do much sales-wise, but two cuts off the fine album, "Turned on to You" and "I Knew That Love," fared well in clubs and continue to be favorites of those into the rare groove scene. Striplin had some solo success with Ayers around the same time; Hicks became involved with Broadway, sang backup for Stevie Wonder for a stretch, and released a solo album in 1991. *—Andy Kellman*

● **Ladies of the '80s** / 1980 / Charly ♦♦♦♦

On their first—and last—album, *Ladies of the '80s*, the disco/soul group Eighties Ladies displays the style and vocal prowess that also served its members well in other parts of their career: Marva Hicks went on to a solo career of some note, and Sylvia Striplin also performed with Aquarian Dream. Most significantly, perhaps, the album was written and produced by Roy Ayers, whose smooth but slightly edgy style elevates the project into something more interesting than just a would-be supergroup. *Ladies of the '80s* rings in the new decade with a set of funky disco and urban songs, including the title track, which is a feminist rallying cry along the lines of Sister Sledge's "We Are Family," and groove-based tracks like "It's Easy to Move" and "I Knew That Love." Ayers' arrangements and productions really stand out on the instrumental version of "Ladies of the '80s" and "Turned on to You," which mixes lightly strummed guitars, brass, Latin-tinged percussion, and the Ladies' voices into a soft, sleekly sexy album-closer. Ayers fans as well as aficionados of late-'70s/early-'80s funk and disco will find a lot to like about this stylish, if slightly obscure, release. *—Heather Phares*

The El Dorados

f. 1954, Chicago, IL, **db.** 1958

Group / Doo Wop, R&B

One of the leading R&B vocal groups on Vee-Jay, the El Dorados had a relatively short career with their first lineup, during which they scored a massive crossover hit, 1955's "At My Front Door" (number 17 on the pop charts and number-one R&B, where it remained for 18 weeks). They managed only one other charting record, 1956's "I'll Be Forever Loving You," before their initial breakup in 1959. Subsequent lineups and name changes (and alterations) brought no further success, but they continued performing well into the '80s. The original group featured five members—Pirkle Lee Moses Jr. (lead), Louis Bradley (tenor), Jewel Jones (second tenor and baritone), James Maddox (baritone and bass), and Robert Glasper (bass)—when they formed in the Englewood section of Chicago's South Side in 1952 while still attending Englewood High School. They were calling themselves the Five Stars. In 1954, just after graduation, Moses and Glasper took advantage of the Air Force's 90-day active duty program, but while Moses returned, Glasper remained with the Air Force. By then, Arthur Bassett (tenor) had temporarily replaced Moses, and Richard Nickens came in for Glasper. The Five Stars were now six, and a name change was inevitable. They were about to become the Cardinals when the craze for naming your group after a popular car model hit, and since they couldn't call themselves the Cadillacs, the settled for Cadillac's luxurious two-door model, the El Dorado, for inspiration.

The El Dorados came to the attention of local Chicago WWCA disc jockey Al Benson, who arranged for the group to audition at a contest hosted by Vee-Jay Records at the Park City Skating Rink. Amateur groups were challenged to compete against Vee-Jay's Spaniels. The El Dorados rose to the challenge, winning the contest and a recording contract with the label. The El Dorados' first single, a bluesy ballad called "My Loving Baby," was issued in September 1954, and was a popular regional seller. Their next effort had the group backing up Hazel McCollum on "Annie's Answer," which was Vee-Jay's contribution to the ongoing "Annie" saga begun by Hank Ballard & the Midnighters. During the third week of September 1955, Vee-Jay released the group's "At My Front Door," which stormed the *Billboard* R&B charts. By the end of the year it had climbed to number 17 on the pop charts and number-one R&B, where it remained for 18 weeks. Their follow-up, "I'll Be Forever Lovin' You" (originally recorded by the Rip Chords but never released), was issued during the second week of December. It was a rocker that exuded jazz, pop, and R&B overtones, but although it made it to number-eight R&B in February 1956, it never charted on the pop lists. A few additional singles performed well in certain U.S. cities, but didn't measure up to their prior hit status. Their next single, "Tears on My Pillow" (a different song from Little Anthony & the Imperials' hit record), was the last by all of the original El Dorados; soon after its release, the group and Moses separated over a disagreement about new management.

Moses soon joined another Vee-Jay act, the Kool Gents, who had been left without a singer when their frontman, Dee Clark, departed for a solo career. John McCall (tenor), Douglas Brown (second tenor), Teddy Long (second tenor and baritone), and Johnny Carter (bass) of the Kool Gents joined with Moses, to become the New El Dorados. They released two singles in 1958 for Vee-Jay, but neither sold. During this same time, the remaining El Dorados—Jones, Bradley, and Maddox—joined up with new lead singer Marvin Smith. Smith had moved with his family to the West Side of Chicago in the late '40s, where he attended Crane High and sang on street corners and in church choirs, before joining the group as their new lead vocalist. To avoid legal problems with Vee-Jay, the group's name was changed to Those Four El Dorados for 1958's "A Lonely Boy." Marvin Smith went on to join the Artistics on OKeh and Brunswick Records as the lead for such R&B charters as "I'm Gonna Miss You" and "Girl I Need You." Johnny Carter, meanwhile, tried to keep the name alive by forming yet another new New El Dorados in late 1959, with John McCall, Danny Edwards, and Eugene Huff. This group lasted until 1965. Carter tried again in 1971, hooking up with Huff, Spence Goulsby Jr., and Lee Toussaint on lead for two sides on Paula. *—Bryan Thomas*

● **At My Front Door . . . Crazy Little Mama: The Very Best of the El Dorados** / Oct. 17, 2000 / Collectables ♦♦♦♦♦

A 25-track collection of the Eldorados' Vee-Jay recordings spanning from 1954 to 1958; the southside Chicagoans recorded until 1971, so this isn't a complete overview, but it does contain the tracks from their hottest period. It's titled after their biggest hit, "At My Door (Crazy Little Mama)," which aced the R&B chart and was a number-17 pop hit; the rocker is considered one of the best of its genre of all times. This is '50s Chi-town doo wop at its finest. Featured is their bluesy debut led by the late Pirkle Lee Moses, "My Loving Baby"; their second release, "Annie's Answer," a response to "Work With Me Annie" and "Annie Had a Baby"; and others as good as "At My Front Door" that didn't achieve its success. Collectables omitted the B-side of "Lights Are Low" ("Oh What a Girl"), their final Vee-Jay single, but that's a micro-matter. Robert Pruter's liner notes enhances the music and makes this truly a collectible. *—Andrew Hamilton*

Donnie Elbert

b. May 25, 1936, New Orleans, LA, **d.** Jan. 26, 1989, Philadelphia, PA

Vocals / Soul, Smooth Soul, R&B

Both a multi-instrumentalist and good vocalist, Donnie Elbert sang with the Vibraharps from 1955 to 1957. He then recorded for DeLuxe and scored a Top 20 R&B hit with "What Can I Do." Elbert went 13 years before getting another hit, "Can't Get Over Losing You," for Rare Bullet in 1970. He had a string of singles, mostly for All Platinum, in the early '70s, the best being "Where Did Our Love Go" in 1971. It peaked at number six on the R&B charts (number-15 pop) and was his lone Top Ten single. Elbert landed another song in the R&B Top 20 in 1972, a cover of the Four Tops' "I Can't Help Myself (Sugar Pie, Honey Bunch)" for Avco. He returned to All Platinum from 1972 from 1977. Elbert became A&R director for Polygram's Canadian division in the mid-'80s. *—Ron Wynn*

Have I Sinned? / 1971 / Deluxe ♦♦♦♦

If Donnie Elbert had never recorded another track, these glorious songs (recorded in the late '50s) would have permanently engraved his stratospheric falsetto in the hearts of R&B and soul fans. *Have I Sinned?* includes the indescribably delicious Top 20 hit "What Can I Do," and the equally incredible "Have I Sinned," "When You're Near Me," and "My Confession of Love." The Newbeats' lead singer, who many dismissed as a novelty act hitting only with bubblegum songs, sang in a similar range and tone as Elbert; but Donnie sang about love, holding nothing back as he demonstrates on these 12 gut-wrenching performances. *—Andrew Hamilton*

Where Did Our Love Go / 1971 / All Platinum ♦♦♦♦

Released on the heels on Elbert's number-15 pop hit remake of "Where Did Our Love Go," popularized by the Supremes, this ten-song album contains updates of some of Donnie's most acclaimed recordings, including mind-blowing falsetto showcases: "What Can I Do" (if you never heard this song, make an effort to do so), "If I Can't Have You," and "That's

If You Love Me," with the new and improved renditions being as formidable as the originals. If you can't find his Deluxe album, this may be easier to acquire, but it won't quench your musical thirst for Elbert; buying his *Golden Classics* CD on Collectables Records will help that problem, and you don't have to go on an expedition to cop. *—Andrew Hamilton*

- **The Greatest Hits of Donnie Elbert** / Nov. 5, 1996 / Collectables ✦✦✦✦

There's really only one hit by Donnie Elbert on this Collectables set, his glorious, caressing 1957 ballad "What Can I Do." Since this *Greatest Hits of Donnie Elbert* only includes his work from the '50s and '60s, none of his All Platinum hits are represented. Instead, it's his complete work for DeLuxe during 1957-1958, both sides of eight singles, plus three early-'60s sides for Vee-Jay and four for Gateway from the mid-'60s. The arrangements are strictly period pop-soul, with modestly squawking saxes and a few swinging vocal choruses. The songs aren't much better, but Elbert shines in almost any setting; "Tell Me So" is a great follow-up to his hit that didn't make the charts, while his Vee-Jay A-sides "Will You Ever Be Mine" and "Half as Old" are great performances as well. Despite the presence of so many hits on the other volume, this one gets the nod since it's only a single disc and Elbert's crystal falsetto sounds better backed by music with a hint of doo wop than the slightly mushy arrangements on his '70s material. *—John Bush*

R&B Maverick / 1997 / Sequel ✦✦✦✦

Maverick isn't the word often used to describe the ineffably sweet master falsetto Donnie Elbert, but his records certainly belonged to a category of artist rarely found, even in soul circles. The Sequel disc *R&B Maverick* collects over two dozen of Elbert's '70s sides for the All Platinum label, with which he hit the R&B charts fairly regularly from 1970 to 1977. Elbert's two big hits, both of which reached the pop Top 40, were covers of Motown chestnuts, the first a strolling version of the Supremes' "Where Did Our Love Go" and the second a driving midtempo run through the Four Tops' "I Can't Help Myself (Sugar Pie, Honey Bunch)." (Unfortunately, though, "I Can't Help Myself (Sugar Pie, Honey Bunch)" was recorded during a brief interlude at Avco and isn't available here.) Elbert was hardly an oldies act, even during the '70s; he wrote much of his own material, and it ranks as his best here: "Can't Get Over Losing You," his moderate hit from 1970, plus "If I Can't Have You," and "Will You Ever Be Mine." Two discs of Donnie Elbert may be too much for the casual listener, but Sequel also bulked up what would've been a short two-disc program with three interesting additions: Lonnie Youngblood's "Reaching for a Dream," Shirley & Company's "Cry Cry Cry," and "Mr. Peanut Goes to Washington," an amusing update of the hilarious '50s chestnut "Peanut" delivered by the original's lead vocalist, Little Joe Cook. *—John Bush*

The Elegants

f. 1957, Staten Island, NY

Group / R&B, Doo Wop

This New York doo wop group earned notoriety for their masterpiece "Little Star" in 1958, which topped both R&B and pop charts. They were a white ensemble led by Vito Picone with Arthur Venosa, Frank Tardogono, Carmen Romano, and James Mochella. All had been in other groups before uniting as the Elegants. They continued recording for Hull, United Artists, Limelight, Photo, IPG, and Laurie through the '50s,'60s and into the '70s, but never had another hit, despite cutting a number of solid ballads. There were two other editions in the mid-'60s, Vito Piccone with the Elegants and Vito & the Elegants. *—Ron Wynn*

- **Little Star: The Best of the Elegants** / Nov. 25, 1991 / Collectables ✦✦✦✦✦

One of the better white doo wop groups from Staten Island, although they didn't have many hits. All the members had worked in other bands before they came together in 1957. They did have one huge smash, the chart-topping "Little Star," which was both an R&B and pop hit and seemed to get their career as a group off to a bang. Unfortunately, it would be their only major record through the late '50s and early and mid-'60s. These are still nicely sung, with the emphasis on romantic wailers and tearjerkers. *—Ron Wynn*

The Elgins

f. 1962, Detroit, MI, **db.** 1967

Group / Motown

Of all the groups calling themselves the Elgins—there was an L.A.-based doo wop group and another group of Elgins who recorded for Congress, while Ritha Mae and the Temptations even used the name for awhile—this Detroit-based quartet proved to be the most memorable, scoring two minor R&B hits in 1966 with their Motown debut "Darling Baby" (pop number 72/R&B number four) and "Heaven Must Have Sent You" (pop number 50/R&B number nine, also a major R&B hit for Bonnie Pointer in 1979). Both songs were written and produced by the powerful Holland-Dozier-Holland triumvirate.

The group's story begins in 1962 with a vocal trio calling themselves the Downbeats. Johnny Dawson, Cleo "Duke" Miller, and Robert Fleming had occasionally accompanied Marv Johnson—including their uncredited backing on "Once Upon a Time"—prior to Johnson's hits for United Artists Records. The Downbeats also cut tracks for the Lupine family of labels before signing to the Tamla label. Their releases for the Motown family imprint were sporadic, however.

In 1966, lead vocalist Sandra Mallett (aka Sandra Edwards)—one of the finest vocalists in the Motown Records stable—joined Dawson, Miller, and Fleming. Four years earlier, in 1962, Mallett had recorded "It's Going to Be Hard Times" b/w "Camel Walk" for Tamla as Sandra Mallett and the Vandellas. Motown was all set to issue the quartet's debut for their VIP label, "Darling Baby," a Holland-Dozier-Holland production credited to the Downbeats. The song had been adapted from Lamont Dozier's solo release, "Dearest One" (Melody Records, June 1962). However, before Motown shipped the "Darling Baby" single, they slapped new labels on the 45s with the group's new name: the Elgins. Berry Gordy—who reportedly insisted they change their name—wanted to use the name now that the original Temptations—Otis Williams, Paul Williams (no relation to Otis), Al Bryant, Melvin Franklin, and Eddie Kendricks—were no longer using the name once they signed to Motown's Miracle subsidiary.

VIP failed to promote the single outside the greater Detroit area, but it still managed to score a slot on the national R&B charts (number four) and charted at number 72 on the pop charts. Eight months later, the Elgins issued "Heaven Must Have Sent You," which charted Top Ten R&B briefly at number nine and number 50 on the pop charts. They followed up with a full album, *Darling Baby*, and another single, "I Understand My Man," but chart success eluded them and they disbanded shortly afterwards in 1967.

In 1971, Motown re-released "Heaven Must Have Sent You" in 1971. In the late '80s, a new group of Elgins was formed by British-born mogul/producer Ian Levine, who had previously worked with the re-formed Miracles and Contours (to name two). Johnny Dawson was the only original Elgin in the lineup. Sandra Mallett—now going by Sandra Edwards—was replaced by Yvonne Vernee-Allen. The other members were Jimmy Charles and Norman McLean. This newly configured lineup recorded a remake of "Heaven Must Have Sent You," which had been a major hit for Pointer when she covered it only a few years prior. Levine also recorded a solo effort by Edwards. *—Bryan Thomas*

Darling Baby / 1966 / VIP ✦✦✦✦

The Elgins resulted as a merger between the Downbeats and Sandra Mallett; both acts recorded singles on Tamla prior to becoming the Elgins. Johnny Dawson, Cleo "Duke" Miller, and Robert Fleming recorded "Your Baby's Back" as the Downbeats, which is not included on this set. Sandra recorded "It's Gonna Be Hard Times," backed by the Vandellas and released in 1962, which is included. Their first Motown release, "Darling Baby," was initially labeled as the Downbeats, but the company quickly corrected the error by slapping Elgin stickers over the misprinted labels. By this time, Sandra's last name had changed to Edwards. *Darling Baby* displays the Elgins' versatility. Half the LP is good classic Motown, while the other half is average Southern soul. A male singer handles the deep soul tracks, which have all the ambience of recordings produced in Memphis or Muscle Shoals. The classic Motown tracks, however, glisten like precious stones. "Darling Baby" is one of Holland, Dozier, & Holland's most charming creations; its soulful, slinky doo wop beat provides the backdrop for some crafty crooning by the fellas and a soulful lead by Sandra. Sandra's solo release "It's Going to Be Hard Times" is a sentimental declaration that borders on blues; "I Understand My Man" has a similar production and is probably a leftover solo track. The rollicking "Heaven Must Have Sent You" is one the finest examples of Motown, and still sounds fresh after more than 30 years. More of that classic sound would have made this a super album. *—Andrew Hamilton*

Take the Train / 1990 / Motorcity ✦✦✦

- **The Best of the Elgins** / Sep. 17, 1996 / Motorcity ✦✦✦✦✦

The Elgins are famous for two minor hits that should have achieved greater success: "Darling Baby" and "Heaven Must Have Sent You," both written and produced by Rock Hall of Famers Holland, Dozier & Holland. For the unaware, this is not a collection of their Motown recordings; these sides were waxed in the late '80s by Britisher Ian Levine. Give Levine credit for capturing the essence of the Elgins' sound, something he didn't do when he recorded the Miracles and the Contours, to name two. Johnny Dawson is the only original on board; the revamped Elgins are Jimmy Charles, Norman McLean, and Yvonne Vernee-Allen, who replaced Sandra Mallet (Edwards). The songs are some of Levine's best, especially "Souvenirs of Love," a groovy mover that Yvonne Vernee-Allen tears up, sounding a little like Betty Lavette. A nice remake of "Heaven Must Have Sent You" almost rivals the original. No remake of "Darling Baby," though; Levine recorded it with Sandra Edwards, the original lead on the song. *—Andrew Hamilton*

Yvonne Elliman

b. Dec. 29, 1951, Honolulu, HI

Vocals / Pop/Rock, Soft Rock, Disco

Yvonne Elliman had a brief moment in the spotlight during the middle of the '70s, yet she appeared on many of the decade's biggest hits as a backing singer. While she was in high school in Hawai'i, Elliman sang in a group called We Folk. She moved to London in 1969 and began singing at the Pheasantry folk club, located on Kings Road in Chelsea. It was here that songwriters Andrew Lloyd Webber and Tim Rice discovered her. The duo offered her the role of Mary Magdalene in their new rock opera, *Jesus Christ Superstar*; the role brought her instant fame. Elliman played the Magdalene character in the film version of *Superstar*, for which she won a Golden Globe award; it also gave her a hit with "I Don't Know How to Love Him." The hit single became the title of her debut album, which was released in 1972. Pete Townshend helped Elliman prepare her second album, 1973's *Food of Love*. During this time, she appeared in the American production of *Jesus Christ Superstar* on Broadway, where she met Bill Oakes, the president of RSO Records; the two married soon afterward. Oakes introduced her to Eric Clapton, inviting her to sing backup vocals on "I Shot the Sheriff." Elliman became part of the guitarist's band afterward; she stayed with him for five years.

She joined RSO's roster in 1975, releasing the Steve Cropper-produced *Rising Sun*. Barry Gibb and Robin Gibb wrote the title song for Elliman's next album, 1976's *Love Me*; the song became a U.K. hit, paving the way for her greatest chart success, the *Saturday Night Fever* soundtrack. The Bee Gees wrote several songs on the soundtrack specifically for Elliman, including the number one single "If I Can't Have You." She never followed through on the song's success—she released two more albums before becoming solely a session musician. *—Stephen Thomas Erlewine*

Rising Sun / 1975 / RSO ✦✦✦✦✦

Six years after Steve Cropper co-created *The Detroit-Memphis Experiment* with Mitch Ryder, he helped coordinate *Rising Sun* for Yvonne Elliman. Though it yielded no hits, coming in the five year period between her first and second Top 30 adventures, it is a very musical and multifaceted recording. Elliman contributes two titles, "Steady As You Go" and the sublime "Who's Gonna Save The World?," where she sounds like Jackie DeShannon, a real departure for the Yvonne Elliman people knew from *Jesus Christ*

Superstar. She covers Rick Danko of the Band, a wonderful rendition of "Small Town Talk," adventurous music which was more hip than the adult contemporary packaging would lead one to believe. The piano-heavy remake of the Eagles' "Best of My Love" would seem like a Johnny Mathis move, "let's put familiar tunes on an album to sell it," but this is Steve Cropper at the helm, and like Doris Troy performing "Lyin' Eyes," it has its own majesty separate from the familiarity of the Eagles. The singer also draws from two of Barry Manilow's songwriting sources, taking David Pomeranz' "If You Walked Away" and giving it a performance which deserved to top the adult contemporary charts as her cover of Barbara Lewis' "Hello Stranger" would two years later, and issuing Will Jennings and Richard Kerr's "Somewhere in the Night," doing so almost simultaneous with Kim Carnes' version (they shared some of the same players, Lee Sklar and Mentor Williams to name two), both women beating Barry Manilow and Helen Reddy to the punch (Reddy hit with it in 1979, Manilow in 1976). But maybe the real find on this album is Todd Rundgren's "Sweeter Memories"; with Rundgren, Moogy Klingman, and Ralph Schuckett, it's Booker T. meets Utopia, sounding nothing like either, but a blend that creates an as yet undiscovered classic. There are so many potential pop hits on *Rising Sun*, classy material and top-notch players, it is truly an enigma that it wasn't a monster. Simply amazing work. *—Joe Viglione*

Night Flight / 1978 / RSO ♦♦♦♦

Night Flight is a gorgeous album containing Yvonne Elliman's only number-one hit, "If I Can't Have You," written by the three Bee Gees brothers, from the film *Saturday Night Fever.* It is a pop masterpiece, the only track on the album produced by Freddie Perren. Perren gives the song a big production, which sounds like the Bee Gees's work with Albhy Galuten and Karl Richardson, and the hardworking singer from Honolulu gets a much deserved chart topper to help spread her gospel. She opens the album with Neil Sedaka's "Baby Don't Let It Mess Your Mind," featuring a slow tempo more laid-back than the composer's version, and simply delightful. She covers "Prince of Fools," a song co-written by Nickey Barclay from the group Fanny, Stephen Bishop's moody "Sailing Ships," her distinctive and powerful voice gliding over Robert Appere's shimmering production work, and Mentor Williams' "I'll Be Around," not the much covered Spinners' hit but a nice ballad co-written by the famous producer and Jack Conrad. There's a taste of reggae with "Lady of the Silver Spoon," and a truly elegant adult contemporary number, "Down the Backstairs of My Life." As Grace Slick left the sexual ambiguity in "Sally Go 'Round the Roses," so too does Elliman on this rendition, and good for her. These were the disco days, and it is so subtle it no doubt went over the heads of casual listeners. The back cover has Elliman in a long flowing dress with her hair wild in the wind, it's beautiful imagery with a red background on an album which might have got lost because of all the attention paid to the *Saturday Night Fever* soundtrack. There are major names galore here, Kiki Dee, James Newton-Howard, Dee Murray, and Davey Johnstone from the Rocket Records/ Elton John camp; guitarists Lowell George, Steve Hunter and Steve Cropper, keyboardist Eric Carmen, and many more included. Elliman albums always enjoy marquee players, and her talent truly deserved the support. With Alice Cooper manager Shep Gordon onboard as executive producer, and the number-one hit, it is amazing Elliman didn't give Linda Ronstadt, Helen Reddy, and Barry Manilow more chart competition. Her five hits were always welcome on '70s pop radio, but they only hinted at the depth of her full-length recordings, music worthy of more notice. *—Joe Viglione*

The Very Best of Yvonne Elliman / 1995 / Taragon ♦♦♦♦♦

Here are ten of Yvonne Elliman's best, sized just right for casual fans of the exotic songbird whose beauty rivals her singing ability. With the exception of "Hello Stranger," an inferior yet competent rendition of Barbara Lewis' classic, most of the songs owe more to pop/rock than R&B/soul; this is a good thing because the former is Elliman's element. She's absolutely stunning on "Everything's Alright" and makes the Who's "I Can't Explain" palatable for non-rockers. The Bee Gees pushed the right buttons with Elliman, as is evident on "Love Me" and "If I Can't Have You." The soft, flowing "Hello Stranger" blends well here among Elliman's more strident efforts. *—Andrew Hamilton*

● **The Best of Yvonne Elliman** / Apr. 22, 1997 / Polydor ♦♦♦♦♦

The Best of Yvonne Elliman is the first comprehensive collection ever assembled on the '70s pop/disco diva. Elliman first came to attention as Mary Magdalene in the London production of *Jesus Christ Superstar* (from which "I Don't Know How to Love Him" and "Everything's Alright" is included), but she shot to fame as part of the Eric Clapton Band, which eventually led to her placement on the *Saturday Night Fever* soundtrack. *Saturday Night Fever* launched her biggest hit, "If I Can't Have You," which branded her as a one-hit wonder. *The Best of Yvonne Elliman* doesn't really disprove that—there's a lot of filler here, even if it culls 16 highlights from her entire career—but it does demonstrate that she possessed a pleasant, professional voice and did make several enjoyable pop/disco records, which happened to be her singles. Which, of course, makes *The Best of Yvonne Elliman* not only a terrific introduction, but also all you need to know. *—Stephen Thomas Erlewine*

Missy Elliott

b. 1971, Portsmouth, VA

Vocals, Producer / Alternative Rap, Urban, Hip-Hop

No female rap artist paralleled the success of Missy Elliott, neither during her reign nor before, and none was more deserving. Unlike most of urban music's female superstars, Missy writes her own songs as well as performs them, and her creative wit in on a par with her stylish demeanor. In addition to her talent and showmanship, though, she established herself as a genuine hitmaker alongside her longtime producer, Timbaland. She intitially scored hits for others, namely Aaliyah ("One in a Million," "If Your Girl Only Knew") and to a lesser extent 702 ("Steelo"), before moving on to score a dazzling run for herself. Her debut album, *Supa Dupa Fly* (1997), spawned a number of hits such as "The Rain" that were more trend-setting than they were chart-topping. The chart-toppers, of course, came soon after: "She's a Bitch" and "Hot Boyz" (1999); "Get Ur Freak On" and "One Minute Man" (2001); and "Work It" (2002). In each of these, Missy proved that, with both dignity and joviality, women could be sexual as well as forceful. As a result, she defied every stereotype imaginable without forsaking her heterogeneous fanbase.

Born in Portsmouth, VA, in 1971 as Melissa Elliott, Missy's professional music career began when Jodeci member/producer DeVante Swing signed her and her group, Sista, to his Swing Mob record label. Unfortunately, Swing Mob Records fell through and along with it the plans for Sista's debut album. Determined to move forward, Missy turned to longtime aquaintance Timbaland, who happened to be producing some tracks for Aaliyah's *One in a Million* (1996) album. It proved to be a key move for Missy, as the album racked up enormous sales. Soon record execs were knocking on her door. Missy began working with a number of artists as either a songwriter or a vocalist/rapper before finally signing herself a deal with Elektra in 1996. A year later *Supa Dupa Fly* hit the streets and soon after went platinum thanks to "The Rain." Besides the sales numbers, the album also proved critically successful, impressing nearly everyone who heard it. It had not only radio-ready singles ("Sock It 2 Me," "Beep Me 911," "Hit 'Em Wit da Hee") but also an astounding array of album tracks that showcases just how multi-talented Missy indeed was, singing on some, rapping on others.

In 1999, she returned with her much-awaited follow-up album, *Da Real World*, an even more ambitious album that featured two mammoth hits—"She's a Bitch" and "Hot Boyz"—along with an array of often daring collaborations with such unlikely candidates as Eminem. Around this same time, she began appearing in TV ads for the Gap and Sprite, proving that not only was she a musical talent but also an important icon for the era. The cycle repeated itself in 2001 when she released *Miss E... So Addictive*, again powered by two huge hits: "Get Ur Freak On" and "One Minute Man." Her remarkable popularity continued a year later with her next album, *Under Construction*, and its lead-off single, "Work It." *—Jason Birchmeier*

● **Supa Dupa Fly** / Jul. 15, 1997 / Goldmind/Elektra ♦♦♦♦♦

Missy Elliott's debut record as a performer is a magnificent success. Her idiosyncratic rapping is a perfect match with producer Timbaland's distinctive style, and a whole host of guest performers, including Busta Rhymes and Da Brat, come by to lend their talents. For once, this is not mere hip-hop braggadocio; Elliott is an extremely prolific songwriter who is also graced with a good R&B voice and a completely unique vision. Witness the way she pairs an Ann Peebles sample with a pot-haze rap in "The Rain (Supa Dupa Fly)." With the exception of the horrifically stupid "Pass da Blunt" (which uses a modified version of the chorus to Musical Youth's "Pass the Dutchie" with disastrous results), the songs are uniformly compelling. One of the reasons for this is the fact that Elliott and Timbaland, either through an odd choice of words or a gutsy production move, are constantly courting disaster. The fact that a major train wreck does not occur is absolutely thrilling. Such is the uniqueness of Elliott's music, and this record is highly recommended to hip-hop fans, both devoted and casual. *—Daniel Gioffre*

Da Real World / Jun. 22, 1999 / Goldmind/Elektra ♦♦♦♦

It's really not that difficult to hurdle the sophomore blues provided you're an excellent songwriter and performer, that you have the same, equally excellent producer behind the scenes who contributed to the first album, and most importantly, that you haven't tampered with the hit-making formula from the first. Thankfully, *Da Real World* is clearly a Missy Elliott album in most respects, with Timbaland's previously trademarked, futuristic-breakbeat production smarts laced throughout. The churchgoing Elliott has often remarked that she wishes she didn't need profanity to get attention, and the album accordingly includes satirical nods to other clichéd notions of hip-hop—the single "She's a Bitch" is the best example, wherein Elliott reappropriates the insult to refer to strong females. She also takes on the cartoonish Eminem for "Bus a Rhyme," a track that turns out to be one of the best on the album. Da Brat and Aaliyah make repeat appearances, and Redman and OutKast's Big Boi also contribute to this excellent follow-up. *—Keith Farley*

Miss E ... So Addictive / May 15, 2001 / Goldmind/Elektra ♦♦♦♦♦

Sounding more assured of her various strengths than at any time since her startling debut, Missy "Misdemeanor" Elliott broke in several directions for 2001's *Miss E... So Addictive.* At the same time, she's a sexed-up rapper demanding respect from men, a loved-up club diva leading the charge of rappers into the brave new world of dance culture, and a sensitive female spreading syrup over a few great ballads. It's a tribute to her incredible songwriting skills and Timbaland's continuing production excellence that she can have it any way she wants it and still come away with a full-length that hangs together brilliantly. She definitely starts out hardcore, with a pair of self-explanatory titles ("Dog in Heat," "One Minute Man") featuring Elliott cooling down on a trio of rappers (Redman, Method Man, Ludacris) and definitely getting the best of them. By "Get Ur Freak On," the lead single, she's changed angles and become a new-millennium diva straddling the worlds of hip-hop and commercial dance with bumping club tracks like "Scream a.k.a. Itch" and "4 My People." But before listeners can reconcile Elliott the club kid, special guest Ginuwine takes the album into love-ballad territory with "Take Away," a half-step ballad with an irresistible plucked-string production from Timbaland. Though *Miss E... So Addictive* is undeniably Elliott's affair, Timbaland's production really stretches out and pulls the album together. He's less reliant on his oft-copied trademarks, and more willing to experiment with left-field samples and seemingly odd bridges that always work despite the audio high-wire act. Though it fails to come up with anything to top her big singles hit, "The Rain (Supa Dupa Fly)," *Miss E... So Addictive* is her best album so far. *—John Bush*

Under Construction / Nov. 12, 2002 / Elektra ♦♦♦♦♦

The fact that Missy Elliott still considers her work to be "under construction" should, justifiably, send everyone else in the rap world scurrying back to the drawing board. No other commercial rapper sounded more in command of her production and flow than Elliott during 2002, and it's no surprise that *Under Construction* ranks as one of the best rap LPs of the year (granted, it came against relatively weak competition). While Timbaland's stark digital soul girds these tracks, Missy herself continues her artistic progression, trying to push hip-hop forward with an almost pleading intro and neatly emphasizing her differences from other rappers by writing tracks for nearly every facet of the female side of relationships. The hit single "Work It" turns the tables on male rappers, taking charge of the sex game, matching their lewdest, rudest rhymes, and also featuring the most notorious backmasked vocal of the year. Elliott more than keeps up with a dirty-minded Method Man as well on "Bring the Pain," strikes back at haters on the self-explanatory "Gossip Folks," and produced her own duet with Beyoncé Knowles, "Nothing Out There for Me," a track that finds her trying to lure Knowles out to a party (using her best Timbaland impression) over the wishes of the diva's home-bound man. She also recognizes the constantly changing aspects of sexuality, admitting how dependent she is on a man during "Play That Beat" but ruminating on the curious power of the female persuasion on "P***ycat." Elliott goes on a refreshing old-school tear with "Back in the Day," featuring Jay-Z having more fun than he's had in a while and Missy crooning, "What happened to those good old days, when hip-hop was so much fun/those parties in the summer y'all, and no one came through with a gun." The disc closes with the TLC duet "Can You Hear Me," a tribute to Aaliyah and Lisa "Left Eye" Lopes. Missy Elliott obviously understands how important hip-hop can be when rappers concentrate on the music instead of the violent lifestyle; fortunately, her talents are just as strong than her vision. *—John Bush*

Pee Wee Ellis (Alfred Ellis)

Sax (Tenor) / Funk, R&B, Soul

Pee Wee Ellis played on many of James Brown's greatest hits in the '60s and '70s, and also served for a time as his band director. He recorded one album (1992's *Blues Mission*) for Gramavision, then several for the Minor label. He plays several saxophones, but is most noted for his baritone and alto work. He's also done many sessions. *—Ron Wynn*

● **Blues Mission** / May 1992 / Gramavision ✦✦✦✦✦

Longtime James Brown arranger and band member Pee Wee Ellis took the spotlight on this set of hot instrumentals, blues-based uptempo numbers, and inspired covers. Ellis' tenor sax solos are strong, exuberant, and tight. His band members include guitarist Jean-Paul Bourelly in a more restrained role than usual, while Tyrone Jefferson provides the trombone fills and effects much as Fred Wesley did in The J.B.'s. The group pays homage to Ellis' past with the stinging "Cold Sweat Mother Popcorn," rivaling the original Brown orchestra in their execution, funk, and energy. *—Ron Wynn*

What You Like / 1997 / Minor Music ✦✦✦

Leading the German NDR Big Band, saxophonist Pee Wee Ellis turns in a competent, occasionally stilted collection of soul-jazz and classic funk. The production and the playing is a bit too mannered for the music to actually catch fire, but there are moments—such as Fred Wesley's cameo on "Tune with a View" or Van Morrison's vocal spotlight on "I Will Be There"—that make the disc a worthwhile listen. *—Stephen Thomas Erlewine*

Live and Funky / Jun. 11, 2002 / Instinct ✦✦✦✦

Saxophonist Pee Wee Ellis may not be a household name, but his name is spoken with reverence by other funk musicians and fans of vintage soul. A former music director for James Brown (and co-composer of such soul classics as "Cold Sweat" and "Say It Loud—I'm Black and I'm Proud"), he collaborated with Brown and fellow J.B.'s Fred Wesley, Bootsy Collins, Maceo Parker, and others to establish the parameters of modern funk. This live album finds him reunited with several of his old compadres as well as singer Fred Ross for an unabashed revival of that sound, including a number of James Brown tunes ("Pass the Peas," "I Got the Feeling," "Cold Sweat," "I Got You [I Feel Good]"). There are a couple of missteps: The cover of Bill Withers' emotionally damp "Grandma's Hands" was utterly unnecessary, and it's not at all clear why Ellis chose to take "I Got You (I Feel Good)" at half the normal tempo. But overall, this album is lots of good, sweaty, greasy, funky fun. Recommended. *—Rick Anderson*

Shirley Ellis

b. 1941, New York, NY [The Bronx]

Vocals / Pop-Soul, Soul

New York vocalist and composer Shirley Ellis was in the Metronomes before earning fame as co-composer and performer of some enjoyable soul novelty tunes in the mid-'60s. These included the Top Ten R&B hits "The Nitty Gritty" and "The Name Game." "The Name Game" was co-written with her manager and husband Lincoln Chase, and peaked at number-four R&B and number-three pop in 1965. She and Chase also collaborated on the follow-up, "The Clapping Song (Clap Pat Clap Slap)," which reached number-16 R&B, but also represented the end of the creative line for the trend. Ellis landed one final moderately successful, more conventional soul tune two years later, "Soul Time." All except "Soul Time" were recorded for Congress; she had moved to Columbia by 1967, when "Soul Time" was issued. *—Ron Wynn*

Shirley Ellis in Action / 1964 / Congress ✦✦✦

The Name Game / 1965 / Congress ✦✦✦

Television stars weren't the only entertainers who got typecast; for every Jerry Mathers (*Leave It to Beaver*), Gary Colman (*Different Strokes*), and Mr. Ed (*Mr. Ed*), the recording industry produced characters like Tiny Tim, Chubby Checker, and Shirley Ellis. Ellis started out singing soul, but after a debut LP on Congress went unnoticed, she came up with the gimmick on this sophomore album with hubby/manager Lincoln Chase of turning nursery rhymes and jump-rope sayings into popular songs. Make no mistake about it, "The Name Game" was a popular item, everybody sung the lyrics using their own nouns and pronouns in the rhyming scheme. "The Nitty Gritty" was less of a novelty, hit too. Give her producer credit, though; the many remakes are all unique—"Bring It on Home to Me" has a strange arrangement owing little to Sam Cooke's original, "Shy One," a pop-ish ballad, is the most serious offering, well maybe "Stardust" too—but most of these tunes, while well-executed, lack substance. *—Andrew Hamilton*

● **The Complete Congress Recordings** / May 15, 2001 / Connoisseur Collection ✦✦✦✦

Shirley Ellis was a much better singer than her material would indicate, and though she recorded a lot of songs slanted toward the charts, *The Complete Congress Recordings* offers quite a bit to fans of '60s pop-soul. All boasting bright, bouncy arrangements and some clapping polyrhythms, her surprising string of hits—"The Nitty Gritty," "(That's) What the Nitty Gritty Is," "The Clapping Song (Clap Pat Clap Slap)," "The Name Game," and "The Puzzle Song (A Puzzle in Song)"—are all featured, along with her surprisingly strong versions of R&B standards like "Kansas City" "C.C. Rider," and even "Stagger Lee." Also included is one of the most charmingly titled songs in the history of popular music: "Ever See a Diver Kiss His Wife (While the Bubbles Bounce About Above the Water)?" *—John Bush*

Terry Ellis

b. 1966, Texas

Vocals / New Jack Swing, Urban, Hip-Hop

Terry Ellis began her musical career in 1990 as a member of For You, along with Dawn Robinson, Cindy Herron, and Maxine Jones. The group later changed its name from For You to En Vogue and recorded a parade of R&B hits.

By the mid-'90s, the members of En Vogue took a three-year break from recording, which gave Ellis a chance to record an album of her own, 1995's *Southern Gal*, released on Elektra. Two of the singles became hits: "Wherever You Are" and "What Did I Do to You." Dawn Robinson, who also went solo, didn't come back, but Ellis and the other two En Vogue members rejoined forces in 1997 to complete another album, *EV3*. *—Charlotte Dillon*

● **Southern Gal** / Nov. 28, 1995 / East West ✦✦✦✦✦

En Vogue member Terry Ellis' solo debut, *Southern Gal*, is quite similar to the records of her band. Produced by Denzil Foster and Thomas McElroy, who helmed both of the En Vogue albums, *Southern Gal* is a smooth, commercial-oriented of hip-hop-informed, contemporary R&B with pop leanings. Ellis' voice is in fine form and the songs sound immaculate, with all the parts intertwining in a graceful, subtle manner. However, the album is far from compelling. Even with all the production detail and Ellis' strong performance, the album sinks from its lack of high quality songs. *—Stephen Thomas Erlewine*

John Ellison

b. Aug. 11, 1941, Montgomery, WV

Vocals / Soul, R&B

The sky-high level of soulful intensity John Ellison brought to his lead vocals with the Soul Brothers Six came straight from the church. No surprise there, since he grew up in a religious household. But the way Ellison harnessed that sanctified passion on the group's secular sides was anything but common.

Leaving the coal mines of West Virginia for a more musically opportune Rochester, New York at age 18, Ellison sang soul and styled hair before hooking up with four brothers named Armstrong (Sam, Charles, Harry, and Moses) and bassist Vonell Benjamin. The Soul Brothers Six were a completely self-contained unit—they played their own instruments in addition to singing. Their first 45s on Fine (1965's "Move Girl") and Lyndell ("Don't Neglect Your Baby" the following year) veritably dripped gospel-soaked inspiration but went nowhere.

The sextet decided to relocate to Philadelphia. On the way there, Ellison wrote the magnificent "Some Kind of Wonderful," the song that put the group on the map. Atlantic Records issued the irresistible soul workout in 1967, and it slipped onto the pop charts (becoming their only hit). Deserving encores on Atlantic didn't recapture the 45's success, and the original lineup broke up in 1969. Ellison assembled another band by the same name and soldiered on at Phil L.A. of Soul Records during 1972-1973. Meanwhile, Grand Funk Railroad's graceless cover of "Some Kind of Wonderful" proved a gigantic pop smash in 1974.

The John Ellison story might have ended there (he's mostly been ensconced in Canada since then). But not too long ago, After Hours Records bosses Marty Duda and Gregory Townson happened upon the long-lost legend sitting in at a Rochester ginmill with bluesman Joe Beard. The upshot was a 1993 solo Ellison disc, *Welcome Back*, that reintroduced the singer to the American market. Two tracks, including a remade "Some Kind of Wonderful," even reunited the singer with the Armstrong brothers. Pretty wonderful, eh? *—Bill Dahl*

Welcome Back / 1993 / After Hours/Ichiban ✦✦✦

John Ellison was once a member of the Soul Brothers Six, a fine group who didn't score many hits, but made one unforgettable number, the anthemic "Some Kind of Wonderful." Ellison's gritty, crisp voice doesn't sound any softer or less soulful in the 1990s than it did in the 1960s. This includes a good, if not quite transcendent, remake of "Some Kind of Wonderful," and also contains some heartfelt ballads, a quasi-country number in "You Ain't Ready" and a couple of decent midtempo and dance-flavored tunes. The production, sensibility and mood are vintage 1960s, which will limit its appeal and possibilities. But it's good to hear John Ellison again, even if his disc is more a nod to the past than a beacon to the future. *—Ron Wynn*

● **The Very Best of John Ellison and the Soul Brothers Six** / 1995 / Forevermore ✦✦✦✦✦

Well, not quite all their best: this gospel-rooted R&B group enjoyed one real hit in 1967 for Atlantic, the glorious "Some Kind of Wonderful." Alas, a recent remake of the tune, albeit a nice one, graces this 20-track collection. The best stuff is the chronologically earliest—a previously unissued 1966 outing "(You're Gonna) Be By Yourself" and obscure mid-'60s 45s "Move Girl" and "Don't Neglect Your Baby" that soar to the heavens with rich sanctified harmonies. Ten 1972-1973 Soul Brothers Six items for Phil L.A. of Soul are also aboard, as are five items from Ellison's recent comeback disc for After Hours. *—Bill Dahl*

Lorraine Ellison

b. 1943, Philadelphia, PA, **d.** Aug. 17, 1985

Vocals / Soul, Ballads, Vocal Pop

Lorraine Ellison is best known for her hit ballad "Stay With Me" and her cover of Jerry Butler's "I Dig You Baby." She originally recorded "Just a Little Bit Harder," later covered by Janis Joplin. She's also a favorite with U.K. Northern soul devotees. Born in 1943 in Philadelphia, PA, the deep soul vocalist first recorded with the gospel groups the Ellison Singers (who recorded for Sharp/Savoy in 1962) and the Golden Chords (who recorded for CBS in 1963). By 1964, she began recording R&B music, and her first hit was the 1965 R&B hit "I Dig You Baby" (later made into a pop smash by Jerry Butler).

One year later, she released her signature song—the intense, symphonic-drenched ballad "Stay With Me," written and produced by Jerry Ragovoy and issued by the Warner label. It hit number 11 on the R&B charts in the fall of 1966. Some of her other singles were "Heart Be Still," "Don't Let It Go to Your Head," "Try," and "I've Got My Baby Back." Songs that she wrote with her manager Sam Bell (of Garrett Mimms & the Enchanters) were recorded by Mimms and Howard Tate. Ellison's Warner LPs include *Heart and Soul* (1966), *Stay With Me* (1969), and *Lorraine Ellison* (1974) and the compilation *The Best of Philadelphia's Queen* (1976). Lorraine Ellison died on August 17, 1985. *—Ed Hogan*

Stay With Me / 1969 / Line ✦✦✦✦✦

Stay With Me was produced by Jerry Ragovoy and includes title track, covered by Terry Reid; "Try (Just a Little Bit Harder)," covered by Janis Joplin; "You Don't Know Nothing About Love," covered by Irma Thomas. Few soul albums have ever matched the intensity of this one. *—Christine Ohlman*

● **Stay With Me: The Best of Lorraine Ellison** / 1995 / Ichiban/Soul Classics ✦✦✦✦✦

Here is the definitive compilation: 23 songs from 1966-1973, including three non-LP singles, three unreleased cuts from an aborted 1970 session at Muscle Shoals, her only two charting singles ("Stay With Me" and "Heart Be Still"), and even an Al Kooper song from an obscure 1970 soundtrack. These are among the foremost examples of the collision of soul, gospel, and pop, with the accent on the soul and gospel. The first half of the program, consisting of 1966-1970 sides produced by Jerry Ragavoy (who also wrote most of those songs), have the edge over the early-'70s sessions. But Ellison's vocals are hard to fault anywhere. Includes the orignal version of "Try (Just a Little Bit Harder)," covered by Janis Joplin. *—Richie Unterberger*

The Emotions

f. 1968, Chicago, IL, **db.** 1986

Group / Smooth Soul, Quiet Storm, Soul, Disco

A trio of sisters with a strong gospel base, the Emotions (based in Chicago) was one of the leading female R&B acts of the '70s. Lead singer Sheila Hutchinson and her sisters Wanda and Jeanette were only teenagers when they crashed the soul charts in 1969 with the engaging "So I Can Love You," but they sang gospel as children and enjoyed secular fame locally before signing with Memphis-based Volt and working with producers Isaac Hayes and David Porter. When Stax folded in 1975, the group hooked up with Maurice White of Earth, Wind & Fire, an association that led to the number-one pop/R&B hit "Best of My Love" in 1977.

Two years after *Best of My Love*, Maurice White and the Emotions (now featuring younger sister Pam Hutchinson) collaborated on "Boogie Wonderland," which was both a number-two R&B and number-six pop hit. They issued three more albums on White's ARC label from 1979 to 1981, but were unable to duplicate their earlier success. They moved to the Red label for the 1984 LP *Sincerely*, which included the single "All Things Come in Time." They issued three other singles from the album, but none made much impact, though each one charted. They then signed with Motown, but issued only one album, *If I Only Knew*. Sheila Hutchinson was a featured vocalist on Garry Glenn's "Feels Good to Feel Good" in 1987. Pam and Jeanette Hutchinson did background vocals on Helen Baylor's gospel song "There's No Greater Love" in 1990. Wanda Hutchinson and Jeanette sang on Earth, Wind & Fire's *Heritage* in 1990. *—Bill Dahl and Ron Wynn*

So I Can Love You / 1970 / Stax ✦✦✦

The Hutchinson sisters were an excellent gospel act billed as the Heavenly Sunbeams before they turned to secular material. This was their soul debut, and the title track was produced by Isaac Hayes and penned by Sheila Hutchinson. It was a nice bit of gospel-tinged soul, and was an indicator that the sisters weren't going to have any trouble turning to more earthly concerns. *—Ron Wynn*

Untouched / 1972 / Volt ✦✦✦

Jeanette Hutchinson was replaced by fellow Chicagoan Theresa Davis for the group's second album. But there was little change in the kind of sweet gospel-soul the trio sang—perhaps it was a shade poppier than the first LP, but barely. Includes the small hit "Show Me How," and "Blind Alley," which was sampled in 1988 for Big Daddy Kane's 1988 hit "Ain't No Half-Steppin'," and then again by Mariah Carey on her hit "Dream Lover." [*Untouched* and the Emotions debut LP (*So I Can Love You*) were combined onto one CD on a 1996 reissue.] *—Richie Unterberger*

Flowers / 1976 / Columbia ✦✦✦

The Hutchinson sisters' first charting album since 1969, 1976's *Flowers* found the Emotions out of the Volt enclave and under the wing of Earth, Wind & Fire's Maurice White. Revamping their classic girl group soul sounds to incorporate the more eclectic nuances of White's production, the resultant brassed-up disco proved to be on target and their Kalimba debut cruised straight into the Top Five in August. With fellow Earth, Wind & Fire members Verdine and Fred White adding their unmistakable chops to the sound, the Emotions ultimately emerged with an absolutely stunning brew that kept their powerful vocal harmonies well spotlighted, while adding more than a little funk to the sound. Leading with the one-two punch of the hit singles "I Don't Wanna Lose Your Love" and "Flowers," the combination brought the marriage of their styles fully to bear as the former sizzled with Verdine's classic, elastic bass and the latter smoothed the mood with the girls' sweet R&B vocals. With those two songs revealing *Flowers*' intentions, the rest of the set spools out in similar fashion, as the punchy funk of "We Go Through Changes" is tempered by the quiet "Me for You," while the lighthearted pathos of "No Plans for Tomorrow" falls deliciously in the middle. And, although the Emotions wouldn't sweep the top spot until their massive "Best of My Love" the following year, *Flowers* nevertheless remains an important and, even more significantly, eminently pleasant precursor to that groove. *—Amy Hanson*

Rejoice / 1977 / Columbia ✦✦✦✦

This album featured two singles, and both rendered Top Ten action. The first was the rapidly paced R&B number one "Best of My Love." This spirited cut is seasoned with a fierce arrangement, in particular the horns, and incomparable vocals. In addition, it claimed the number-one position on the pop charts for five straight weeks. The second single, "Don't Ask My Neighbor," came on a mellower note. This album, the second under the tutelage and production of Maurice White of Earth, Wind & Fire, could have continued with several more chart-successful releases. The radiance the Emotions impart is heartwarming and uplifting. Their gospel roots bring a welcome spiritual feel to this album, which is a superb effort. *—Craig Lytle*

Sunbeam / 1978 / Columbia ✦✦✦

The Emotions' third album for Columbia, *Sunbeam* was also their third recording under the direction of producer Maurice White. As White's signature can be detected throughout most of the compositions, he is humble enough to give room for the Emotions to flourish vocally. This album featured the Top Ten hit "Smile." The aggressively paced number, from the simmering verses to the spellbinding change-up, bounces with effervescence. Uptempo as well, "Whole Lot of Shakin'" only managed to show at 44. "Walking the Line" has a hypnotizing rhythm and an even more magnetic melody. The cooing texture of the trio's cohesive vocals gel with each note. This album is titled after the name three were known by as young girls with their father, the Hutchinson Sunbeams. *—Craig Lytle*

Sunshine / 1978 / Stax ✦✦✦

The Emotions never really established themselves at Stax like they should have. Yet their Stax sides are more pleasing to many than their later, more successful recordings on Columbia Records under the auspices of Maurice White. *Sunshine* has some excellent cuts, and some that don't quite fit the Chicagoans' style. If Stax hadn't been close to folding, "Shouting Out Love" would have raced up the charts; this sweetie has everything, a good beat, a great hook, and sensational vocals from the Emotions on a song equally suitable for the Staple Singers. Then you have songs like "Runnin' Back (And Forth)," contributed by Eddie Floyd and Bonny "Mack" Rice, that should have been cut by someone else. Lambert and Potter's "Put a Little Love Away" departs from the Emotions' sound and is overbearingly pop. Group member Sheila Hutchinson contributed three of the better songs here: "Baby I'm Through," "I Really Miss You," and "I Wanna Come Back." And let's not forget the perennial Christmas favorite "What Do the Lonely Do at Christmas." *—Andrew Hamilton*

Come into Our World / 1979 / Columbia ✦✦✦

Queens of disco and light R&B, the Emotions are now best remembered for their 1977 hit "Best of My Love." But history has cruelly made one-hit wonders of a group who played their career out over two decades and seldom disappointed the listener. 1979's *Come Into Our World*, their sixth album to enter the R&B charts, appeared just six months after they were on the top with "Boogie Wonderland," their collaboration with Earth, Wind & Fire. It was a provocative invitation. Still produced by that band's Maurice White (who first worked with them as the Sunbeams in the 1960s and snapped them up in the wake of the Stax label's demise), and backed at various times by further members of Earth, Wind & Fire (Verdine White's bass is unmistakable), the Emotions were churning out uptempo, feel-good dance classics like there was no tomorrow. White co-wrote three songs, including the LP's only hit, "What's the Name of Your Love?," which combines snappy horns with breathless lyrics and is peppered throughout with very Moroder-esque Euro-disco overtones. It is the strongest, if most predictable, track on the album, but a close runner-up emerges in "I Should Be Dancing." Elsewhere, "Layed Back" sports an elastic bass and brass, while a sweet little ballad percolates through "On & On." Indeed, while there is nothing staggeringly remarkable about any of the songs, the album is so absolutely dominated by good feelings and high spirits, by bright arrangements and light harmonies, that it's impossible not to join in the fun. *—Amy Hanson*

New Affair / 1981 / Columbia ✦✦✦

This was the Emotions' final album for Maurice White's ARC label, and it wasn't among their more memorable outings. Their collective arrangements and harmonies were still solid, but the passion and energy that had marked their best singles was missing, while the production was routine and the arrangements lifeless and uninspired. They got a couple of moderate R&B chart hits out of it, but weren't the sparkling, vibrant ensemble they had been in the mid-'70s. *—Ron Wynn*

Sincerely / 1984 / Red Label ✦✦✦

The Emotions regrouped on a new label in the mid-'80s and seemed about to recapture their past glory. This album was their most exuberantly sung and tightly produced since the late '70s, but unfortunately times had changed, and their brand of Southern, gospel-inflected "deep" soul no longer packed much punch above the Mason-Dixon line. They were able to get three singles on the charts, but none were big hits. *—Ron Wynn*

● **Best of My Love: The Best of the Emotions** / Mar. 12, 1996 / Columbia/Legacy ✦✦✦✦✦

This 16-track, 69-minute disc surveys the Emotions' five-year, five-album stay on Columbia Records (and the custom label ARC), which was the group's most successful period, featuring the gold number one hit "Best of My Love" and the gold Top Ten hit "Boogie Wonderland" (on which the Emotions backed their mentors, Earth, Wind & Fire), both of which are heard here, along with four other songs that saw action on the pop charts. Surprisingly, the Emotions' five singles that only made the R&B charts are excluded in favor of album tracks. Unlike their earlier period at Stax, at Columbia the Emotions essentially were an adjunct to EWF and its leader, Maurice White, and since EWF featured tenor and falsetto vocals, the similarity was often heightened, especially on "Boogie Wonderland." Nevertheless, the sisters sang well over the horns and disco rhythms that characterized the pop/R&B music of the period. *—William Ruhlmann*

So I Can Love You/Untouched / Mar. 19, 1996 / Stax ✦✦✦✦✦

Love Songs / Apr. 6, 1999 / Columbia/Legacy ✦✦✦✦
A fine companion piece to the earlier *Best of My Love: The Best of the Emotions*, this 13-track compilation focuses on the trio's most affecting songs of love, not only of the romantic variety but the spiritual as well. The majority of the songs are drawn from the group's mid-'70s efforts *Flowers* and *Rejoice*; the former, produced by Maurice White and the great Charles Stepney, remains the Emotions' most personal and accomplished work, a gorgeously arranged set that showcases both their solo and harmony vocals to beautifully ethereal effect. *—Jason Ankeny*

En Vogue

f. Jul. 18, 1988
Group / New Jack Swing, Club/Dance, Urban
The female vocal quartet En Vogue was conceived and put together by the production team of Denzil Foster and Thomas McElroy, both former members of Club Nouveau. Foster and McElroy wanted a vocal group who could exude sultriness and intelligence in addition to vocal proficiency, and as producers, they wanted material that would fuse R&B and girl group traditions with hip-hop and new jack swing rhythms. The two held auditions and settled on a membership of former Miss Black California Cindy Herron, Maxine Jones, Dawn Robinson, and Terry Ellis. The new group performed two songs on Foster and McElroy's *FM2* album, and the producers crafted an image of them as stylish, sophisticated, and sexy.

Originally called For You, the women switched to the more elegant Vogue, and then En Vogue after learning of another group with a very similar name. En Vogue's debut album, *Born to Sing*, appeared in 1990 and launched the pop crossover smash "Hold On," which peaked at number two and helped the album go platinum. The group attracted comparisons to the Supremes, even though group members shared lead vocals and intentionally designated no particular singer the "star." In between albums, Herron appeared in the film *Juice*. When En Vogue returned in 1992 with *Funky Divas*, critical and commercial response was overwhelming. The album's wide array of styles, from pop, rock, and R&B to rap, rock, and reggae, were lauded in print; the first three singles—"My Lovin' (You're Never Gonna Get It)," "Giving Him Something He Can Feel" (both covers of songs written by Curtis Mayfield), and "Free Your Mind" (which borrowed a chorus line from George Clinton)—reached the Top Ten, and the album went multiplatinum. En Vogue was in the Top Ten again in 1993, backing Salt-N-Pepa on their hit "Whatta Man."

As En Vogue was recording its third album, Dawn Robinson left the group. Before they released the record, "Don't Let Go (Love)," a song the group contributed to the *Set It Off* soundtrack, became a number two single in early 1997. Six months later, the band released their third album, *EV3*. The group's first compilation, *The Best of En Vogue*, was released in the summer of 1999. *—Steve Huey*

Born to Sing / 1990 / Atlantic ✦✦✦✦
The '80s produced countless "three girl and a drum machine"-type acts, but 1990 produced the trendsetting quartet En Vogue (courtesy of producers Thomas McElroy and Denzil Foster), who, with their individual vocal skills, sophisticated sense of fashion, sultry videos, and smart singles, went on to become one of the decade's most successful and influential acts. The album that started it all was *Born to Sing*, which scored two pop hits and two more R&B hits. First and foremost is "Hold On," a cool, shuffling, timeless hip-hop R&B track which peaked at number two on the pop charts and showcased the girls' effortless harmonies. "Lies," which alternated lead vocalists (and featured a rap courtesy of Debbie T.), managed to crack the Top 40 while proving that all members of the quartet were equally adept at handling lead vocals. The biting "You Don't Have to Worry" and the sensual "Don't Go" both scored high on the R&B charts without becoming pop hits. Other highlights include the funky new jill swing track "Strange" and their one-minute version of "Boogie Woogie Bugle Boy" (which should have been a full-length recording). There are a couple of duds, including "Part of Me," "Just Can't Stay Away," and the CD bonus track, "Waitin' on You," but overall this album is a winner, and was just a preview of the massive success they would achieve with 1992's *Funky Divas*. *—Jose F. Promis*

Remix to Sing / 1991 / East West ✦✦✦
Combining classic and robust girl group harmonies with elements of high-tech funk and hip-hop, En Vogue has been one of the most distinctive and appealing R&B acts of the 1990s. One can make all kinds of comparisons—the Shirelles, Martha & the Vandellas, Honey Cone, First Choice—but there's no denying that En Vogue has a richly appealing sound all its own. The Oakland quartet had taken the R&B world by storm in 1991, when East West sought to cash in on the success of its debut album, *Born to Sing*, with this generally enjoyable, though not essential, collection of remixes. While all of the songs themselves are superb, the remixes (done by house music heroes Frankie Knuckles and Steve "Silk" Hurley and hip-hop producer Marley Marl, among others) range from inspired to pedestrian. "Strange" and "You Don't Have to Worry" take on a whole new life in a house setting, whereas Marl's remix of "Hold On" is a disappointment, relying on one tired hip-hop cliché after another. Interestingly, East West classifies this CD (which is primarily for hardcore fans) as an EP, although it's about as long as a vinyl LP. *—Alex Henderson*

Funky Divas / Sep. 1, 1992 / East West ✦✦✦✦
The 1990s was a time when hip-hop infused with R&B became pop music, and at the forefront of this movement was En Vogue. Their most commercially and critically successful album, *Funky Divas*, stands as one of the best pop/R&B albums to emerge from that time, incorporating soul, hip-hop, pop, dance, and rock to create one of the era's most diverse, dazzling, and exciting pieces of work. The album, which is basically free of filler, scored no less than five hit singles, three of which became Top Ten pop hits. Additionally, several other album tracks became dance hits and received considerable airplay as well. These include the unstoppable "My Lovin' (You're Never Gonna Get It)," which combined perfect harmonies, street sass, and 1990s female assertion to create one of the biggest hits of 1992, as well as a catch phrase which became ubiquitous in popular culture. Other hits include their sophisticated, shimmering Top Ten remake of "Giving Him Something He Can Feel," a ghetto love fable initially popularized by Aretha Franklin, the doo wop good-feelin' "Give It Up Turn It Loose," the jazzy "Love Don't Love You," and the hard rock smash "Free Your Mind." The last was a hit which, following the summer of the Los Angeles riots, struck a chord with national audiences by coaxing people to let down their guards about racism and prejudice. Other highlights include the great opener "This Is Your Life," the hip-hop tracks "Hip Hop Lover" and "It Ain't Over Till the Fat Lady Sings," the house track "What Is Love," the sexy, Middle Eastern-influenced "Desire," and their wonderful, should-have-been-a-hit version of Curtis Mayfield's "Hooked on Your Love." Combining sass, elegance, and class with amazing vocals and perfect production, this delightful set stands as one of the 1990s definitive pop albums. *—Jose F. Promis*

Runaway Love / Sep. 21, 1993 / East West ✦✦
Runaway Love was a stopgap EP released after the major success of *Funky Divas*. Apart from the great title track, there is little in this collection of filler and remixes of interest to anyone but dedicated fans. *—Stephen Thomas Erlewine*

EV3 / Jun. 17, 1997 / East West ✦✦✦
The sound of En Vogue isn't greatly affected by the departure of Dawn Robinson for their third album, *EV3*, since the group's harmonies remain remarkably supple and soulful. Instead, the band is hurt by its selection of producers and songwriters. En Vogue decided to work with Denzil Foster and Thomas McElroy only occasionally on *EV3*, choosing to hire such professional songwriters and producers as Babyface, David Foster, Diane Warren and Ivan Matias, who arranged their hit single "Don't Let Go (Love)." At times, these pairings work: Babyface's "Whatever" is funkier than his previous work, and Matias brings a gospel-drenched sensibility to his songs. In the cases of Warren and Foster, they reshape En Vogue as an adult contemporary band, sapping the group of any of their energy or style. Still, there are enough strong moments scattered throughout the album to make it worth the wait. *—Leo Stanley*

Best of En Vogue / Jun. 1, 1999 / Elektra ✦✦✦✦✦
En Vogue did make some fine albums, but they always shone on singles. As a matter of fact, the best of their hits—"My Lovin' (You're Never Gonna Get It)," "Whatta Man," "Runaway Love," "Free Your Mind," "Hold On," "Don't Let Go (Love)"—were among the very best singles of the '90s, regardless of genre. That's why *The Best of En Vogue* is such a welcome addition to their catalog. Serious and casual fans alike will find this 14-track collection a captivating listen, since there's a certain intoxicating thrill in hearing each great single flow into the next. It can be argued that the high quality of the material makes this En Vogue's best record, but at the very least, *The Best of En Vogue* is a dynamite, definitive compilation. *—Stephen Thomas Erlewine*

Masterpiece Theatre / May 23, 2000 / East West ✦✦✦✦
Whether it was caused by Dawn Robinson's absence or the questionable manipulations of their production team, En Vogue's first release as a trio, *EV3*, was a disappointment. *Masterpiece Theatre*, their second album since Robinson's departure, shows the group in much finer form. The silky-smooth harmonies are still there, combined with forceful solos and sassy and intelligent lyrics. "Love U Crazay" and "Those Dogs" both explore the liabilities of love in an aggressively funny way, set to famous classical music melodies, while still keeping funky R&B flavors. More traditional love songs pepper the rest of the album, but throughout, *Masterpiece Theatre* manages to accomplish what few albums do—being clever and classy at the same time. *—Stacia Proefrock*

● **The Very Best of En Vogue** / Aug. 21, 2001 / Rhino ✦✦✦✦✦
En Vogue may not have been as visionary as TLC, but they were still one of the best female urban groups of the '90s, which is why their *Very Best* collection works so well. Album by album, they delivered terrific singles, from the swaggering "My Lovin' (You're Never Gonna Get It)" and "Free Your Mind" to the yearning "Don't Let Go (Love)" and "Hold On," plus such wonderful duets as "Whatta Man," where they team with Salt-N-Pepa to deliver a songs so sexy it hurts (but, as John Mellencamp says, it hurts so good). All these are here on this 16-track collection, along with several other singles that didn't climb as high on the charts, plus album tracks, and, well, filler, like a remix of "Hold On." This collection gets the nod over 1999's *Best of En Vogue* because it has a sharper selection of songs that really make a good case for their gifts. It may have benefited from fewer songs, since it would be a better listen if it was nothing but their ten best songs, but it still offers the best encapsulation of their talents imaginable. *—Stephen Thomas Erlewine*

Enchanette

Group / Urban, Hip-Hop
Often favoring a hip-hop-influenced style of R&B, Enchanette is a Detroit-based vocalist who came to the attention of hit producer/songwriter Michael J. Powell in the 1990s. The singer, who was born Enchanette James in the Motor City on April 9, 1978, first met Powell in 1996. That year, Powell assembled a female vocal group called the City Girls and decided to hire Enchanette (who was 18 at the time) as a member. The City Girls, who were modeled after female urban contemporary groups like TLC and Brownstone, recorded a song titled "Let's Ride" for the D-Town label. But the City Girls didn't last very long, and when the group broke up, Powell encouraged Enchanette to pursue a solo career. The singer (who has a degree in English and communications from the University of Detroit, Mercy) signed

with Volt as a soloist artist in 1999 when Powell produced her debut album, *Can You Feel Me?* The CD was released by Volt/Fantasy in June of 2000. *—Alex Henderson*

- **Can You Feel Me?** / Jun. 6, 2000 / Volt ✦✦✦

When Fantasy reactivated the Volt label in 1999, it signed veteran soulsters like the Dramatics, the Delfonics and Brenda Holloway as well as younger urban contemporary artists such as Angel Sessions and Enchanette. One hears a lot of potential on Enchanette's debut solo album, *Can You Feel Me?*, which was produced by Michael J. Powell. Known for his work with well known R&B goddesses like Anita Baker, Gladys Knight, Regina Belle and Aretha Franklin, Powell has a long résumé. Even though his work can be formulaic and contrived, the guy has produced some classics-Baker's *Rapture* (1986) immediately comes to mind. *Can You Feel Me?* doesn't have the makings of a classic, but it's decent and satisfying, if less than fantastic. The material on this CD (most of which Powell co-wrote) ranges from romantic slow jams to more hip-hop-ish medium-tempo grooves—nothing distinctive or groundbreaking is heard, although Enchanette shows herself to be a talented singer who has chops as well as charisma. The Detroit native has an impressive vocal range, and her memorable interpretation of Carole King's "It's Too late" lets us know that she's capable of depth. Evaluating this CD, listeners should bear in mind that even Mary J. Blige didn't have an earth-shattering debut; her first album, *What's The 411?*, was competent but unremarkable, although she became more and more exciting as the 1990s progressed. And listening to *Can You Feel Me?*, one hopes that Enchanette can also make the transition from decent to excellent. Enjoyable but not a gem, *Can You Feel Me?* indicates that Enchanette is well worth keeping an eye on. *—Alex Henderson*

Enchantment

f. 1967, Detroit, MI
Group / Soul

Their music is soulful, smooth, romantic and melodious. Their lyrics are warm, affectionate, loving and understanding. And they present a sound that is distinctively their own, conveying stories of reality and fantasy, with the ultimate message being love. The golden sound of Enchantment was formed in 1967 at Pershing High School in Detroit. Two years later, the multi-talented group, which consists of Emanuel "E.J." Johnson, Joe Thomas, Dave Banks, Ed "Mickey" Clanton and Bobby Green, obtained their first recording contract, in addition to $500, by winning first place in a talent contest sponsored by a local radio station (WCHB).

In 1970, Enchantment joined forces with Artists International, a talent development agency for up-and-coming artists (founded by renowned manager Dick Scott). While with Artists International, Enchantment really began to perfect their craft, concentrating on-stage presence, choreography, and expanding their theatrical talents by performing in numerous musical plays around the city. Enchantment became acquainted with their producer-to-be, Michael Stokes, in 1973 while performing at a local nightclub (Stage One). Through this union, they recorded a movie score on Polydor Records in 1974 entitled *Deliver Us From Evil*, which was released in 1975.

By 1976, Enchantment had signed with the Roadshow label and recorded their self-entitled debut album. The first single to ride the charts for the fledgling group was "Come on and Ride." Later that year, the charismatic showmen received national acclaim with the release of their second single, "Gloria." Written and arranged by dynamic lead singer E.J. Johnson, "Gloria" became a smash, and was one of the most popular songs of 1976-1977. They followed it up with another smash hit, "Sunshine," from the same album.

The self-contained group entered the studio in the fall of 1977, and recorded their second album, *Once Upon a Dream*. Their third consecutive number one single, "It's You That I Need," reigned for a solid four weeks. It was followed by "If You're Ready (Here It Comes)," also a Top Ten single. Enchantment continued their hit-making ways with a string of soul-stirring hits: "Where Do We Go From Here," "Forever More," "Moment of Weakness," "Enchanted Lady," and many others, influencing such artists as After 7, Johnny Gill, and Warren G, to name a few.

Since 1976, the sound of Enchantment has had an everlasting affect on all who have had the pleasure of listening to their great music, and contrary to rumors, the group has never disbanded. Enchantment's longevity is attributed to their vitality and the dedication they have for their craft. The group continues to impressively demonstrate their quality golden sound at concerts and events around the country. *—Craig Lytle*

Enchantment / 1976 / United Artists ✦✦✦✦

After ten years of developing their style, sound and image, the Detroit quintet Enchantment was well prepared for the release of their self-titled debut album. Polished with superb background vocals arranged by Emanuel "E.J." Johnson, the LP is seasoned with string and horn arrangements. With disco controlling the charts, it was only appropriate that the first release be an uptempo number to fit that format. "Come on and Ride" surges forward with a locomotive rhythm while E.J. Johnson's soulful lead tenor exerts pure vocal power. The second single from the album, "Gloria," provided a platform for Johnson to extend his soaring tenor right from the song's inception, and as the melody builds so does his delivery. The compassionate single topped the charts after a healthy 24 weeks, and also reached number 25 on the pop charts. The third single was "Sunshine," which utilizes the lead vocals of Joe Thomas as well as Johnson. As Thomas introduces the lyric of each verse with his mild, inquisitive vocals, Johnson's thundering tone sends the listener reeling. The album was written and arranged, in its entirety, by E.J. Johnson and Michael Stokes. Songs like the romantic "My Rose" (led by Thomas and Johnson) and the funky, upbeat "Dance to the Music" (led by Dave Banks) were never singles, but they still receive airplay in their respective radio formats. With the exception of the two aforementioned songs and "Sunshine," Johnson showcases his lead vocal talent on all the other outstanding numbers with his dynamic range. *—Craig Lytle*

Once Upon a Dream / 1977 / Roadshow ✦✦✦

With Enchantment still riding high on the strength of their self-titled debut album, *Once Upon a Dream* spawned some soul classics, including the number one single "It's You that I Need." With a percussive introduction complemented by a mesmerizing string and horn ensemble, Joe Thomas' falsetto cries out a mournful lyric just shy of a whisper, which slowly transcends to urgent appeals. The song's vamp entails each member of the group; Mickey Clanton carries the bottom with his agile bass while other members exchange lyrics, and E.J. Johnson takes the song home with his improvising, roaring tenor. The second single was "If You're Ready (Here It Comes)," featuring a plucking bassline layered on a funky rhythm track. Led by E.J. Johnson's uncompromising vocals, the song also showcases an impressive, percussive interlude. With the exception of "It's You That I Need," every other number here is led by Johnson's overwhelming tenor—including "Trying to Get Over (With You)," "Angel in My Life," and the masterpiece, "Silly Love Song." The former and latter of the three songs were both penned by Johnson, whose creative nature is reflected in his lyrics and his superior vocal articulation on all the other tracks. Defying the odds against it due to disco, this album was certified gold by RIAA. *—Craig Lytle*

Journey to the Land Of . . . Enchantment / 1978 / Roadshow ✦✦✦

Soft Lights, Sweet Music / 1980 / Roadshow/RCA ✦✦✦

As with most of Enchantment's album, this one too was battling the transition that the music industry was making from disco to the electronic age of music in the '80s. Nonetheless, the Detroit-based showmen maintained their dedication to a wholesome repertoire of music, and this album, their fourth, is no exception. Turning their attention toward more uptempo and midtempo grooves, Enchantment does not forfeit their loyalty to that golden vocal sound that has made their music everlasting. The title track, "Soft Lights, Sweet Music," is a dance number blazing with admirable background vocal exchanges that are varnished with E.J. Johnson's skilled vocal delivery that transcends to a merciful ad lib. "I Believe in You" is somewhat of a duet; it features Dave Banks on lead through most of the song, and Johnson, who seductively carries the vocal interlude, augments the end of each verse with his rich tenor.

"I Can't Fake It" is reminiscent of two other group's that originated in Detroit: the Temptations and the Miracles. Showcasing Joe Thomas on lead, "I Can't Fake It" has all the workings of a Motown classic with a curvaceous background vocal arrangement, compliments of Johnson. Thomas' lead is also featured on "Moment of Weakness." A soft and easy-flowing number that graced the *Billboard* R&B charts for eight weeks and peaking at number 47. "You and Me," written and led by Johnson's nurturing tenor, this composition is in a class of its own. Maintaining the beautiful arrangement and mesmerizing tone in spite of the creative 3/4 rhythm arrangement. *—Craig Lytle*

Enchanted Lady / 1982 / Columbia ✦✦✦

After four releases under the Roadshow imprint, via United Artists and RCA, Enchantment was signed to Columbia by veteran record executive Larkin Arnold. In spite of music-industry trends, the Detroit quintet maintained their sound with one voluptuous string and horn arrangement after another. Popular for their romantic love songs, Enchantment kicked off this project with "I Know Your Hot Spot," a mid-rhythm number with a relentless groove and a creative arrangement that allows some impressive lead-vocal exchanges. "Toe Jammin'" boogies right along with a James Brown-fashion bridge, and features each member interjecting their uncanny vocal ability on lead. The love songs on this album have an irresistible appeal. While seasoned with lucid background vocals, which jell in their exemplary arrangement, Emanuel "E.J." Johnson's impeccable tenor radiates through each lyric of "Enchanted Lady" and "I Can't Forget You." The former is a sweet and gentle love song that blossoms with a testimonial lead by Johnson. The latter is a tear-jerking number, both musically and lyrically, incorporating exquisite harmonies. Johnson's delivery echoes with grief and heartache, and at the same time maintains that prudent command of vocality. Joe Thomas takes center stage on the serene arrangement of "Adora," blending his natural voice with his falsetto. These three compositions, in spite of the fact that the album as a whole was not promoted by Columbia, rank as R&B classics and quiet storm jewels. *—Craig Lytle*

Utopia / 1983 / Columbia ✦✦✦

Golden Classics Featuring "Gloria" / Sep. 12, 1991 / Collectables ✦✦✦✦

Golden Classics is a fitting title for a group with a sound as golden as Enchantment's. That ambience can be attributed to the golden sound of lead singer Emanuel "E.J." Johnson, who was responsible for the vocal arrangements on these and the all the other Enchantment recordings. Johnson's vocal versatility is demonstrated on songs like "Come on and Ride" and "If You're Ready (Here It Comes)." While delivering an abrasive tone in one breath, he comes back in a smooth lyric the next. These selections are taken from the vocal quintet's first two albums titled *Enchantment* and *Once Upon a Dream*, respectively. (Songs from the group's other four albums are omitted, as they had different label affiliation). Moreover, these selections were originally recorded under the Roadshow/United Artists family, which was sold to Capitol-EMI. Between the two albums, there were four R&B Top Five singles. Unreleased songs like "Silly Love Song," "My Rose" and "Trying to Get Over (With You)" have emerged as radio regulars, and all were written by the incomparable Johnson. This compilation is one of Collectables' top selling units and would be a great addition to any collection. *—Craig Lytle*

- **If You're Ready: The Best of Enchantment** / Aug. 20, 1996 / EMI ✦✦✦✦✦

Enchantment were one of the very last "sweet soul" groups of the '70s to reach fruition and chart success. Not slick enough to be dubbed "urban contemporary," they offered a polished take on the early '70s soul of Motown (especially the Temptations and Marvin Gaye) and Philly (the O'Jays, particularly on the more uptempo numbers). Indeed, by the time of their first hits in 1976, the disco boom was already making them sound a bit like an anachronism. This has 14 cuts from 1976-1979, including the hits "Gloria," "If You're Ready," "It's You That I Need," and "Sunshine," as well as a bunch of LP tracks. *—Richie Unterberger*

The Energetics

Group / Disco, Funk, Soul

The Energetics were a nondescript, self-contained band of varying members of the mid-'70s and early '80s whose claim to fame was one album and two singles on Atlantic Records, all produced by Eddie and Brian Holland. Primary members were Melvin Franklin, Roscoe Mills, Joey Lites, Herbert Johnson, and John Borders; their first known recording, "Me and My Girl" b/w "If at First," came out on Top Top Records in 1975. It did so poorly that they didn't record again until the Holland brothers took them into the studio to record the *Come Down to Earth* album in 1978. The riff-laden LP has a few good spots, but lacked the Holland brothers' Midas touch. Both singles, "Living By the Strength of Your Love" and "Come Down to Earth," flopped. They resurfaced under a new name spelling, the Energettics (which was probably a typo), on Cobra Records with "You Make Me Nothing" b/w "Rainy Days and Mornings." It died upon release like the previous three singles, and the band hasn't surfaced since. *—Andrew Hamilton*

- **Come Down to Earth** / 1978 / Atlantic ✦✦✦

Eddie and Brian Holland's production on the Energetics represents one of the famous duo's better post-Motown/Invictus/Hotwax productions. Except for "Let's Say Goodbye to Goodbye," a sweet falsetto ballad that mimics Eddie Holland's vocal style, the material is upbeat, including unrelenting stompers like "Beat the Heat," "Come Down to Earth," "Ain't Nothing Wrong in Going to a Disco," and the catchy "She Ain't Fancy but She's Good." *—Andrew Hamilton*

Barbara Jean English

Vocals / Soul

Barbara Jean English was a member of the popular New Jersey girl group the Clickettes and recorded many pop-soul sides with them in the late '50s and '60s. She returned in the '70s to record two albums of lushly produced soul with a concentration on sensual ballads. After a brief hiatus, she re-teamed with the Clickettes in the '90s to tour the oldies circuit. *— Wade Kergan*

- **Barbara Jean English** / 1993 / Collectables ✦✦✦

These eight songs all sound curiously cold and lifeless. Curious, because George Kerr produced the album and wrote many of the songs—the same George Kerr that produced Linda Jones' "Hypnotized" and the O'Jays' "Look Over Your Shoulder," both gripping soul classics. Unfortunately, his résumé isn't of much help here. *—Andrew Hamilton*

The Equals

f. 1965, North London, England

Group / Psychedelic Pop, Bubblegum, Funk

An energetic East London combo, the Equals balanced maximum R&B with plenty of pop, plus a few nods to vocalist Eddy Grant's West Indian background. Grant, born in British Guyana, moved to England with his family at the age of 12, and settled in a council estate named Hornsey Rise in northeast London. Four years later, he formed the Equals with schoolmates Lincoln Gordon (guitar), his twin brother Dervin Gordon (originally the vocalist), Pat Lloyd (guitar, then bass), and drummer John Hall. The band began gigging around London, amazing audiences with their apparently limitless energy and a distinct style fusing pop, blues, and R&B plus elements of ska and bluebeat.

By 1965, the Equals began doing dates in Europe as well, and released their first single on President Records. Though "Hold Me Closer" didn't perform on the charts, DJs began playing the flip side and by 1967 "Baby, Come Back" had hit the top of the charts in Germany and the Netherlands. One year later, the single hit number one in Britain as well, and brushed the charts in America. Subsequent singles lacked the immediate punch of "Baby, Come Back," however, and the Equals landed only two more Top Ten hits: "Viva Bobby Joe" and "Black Skin Blue Eyed Boys," the latter an apt message track from one of the few racially mixed bands of the era.

Grant left the Equals for a solo career in 1971, and though the band never charted again, they remained a popular live act, especially on the continent. Drummer Ronald Telemacque and guitarists Dave Martin and Frankie Hepburn were later added to the lineup. *—John Bush*

- **First Among Equals: The Greatest Hits** / 1995 / ICE ✦✦✦✦✦

This two-CD, 40-song compilation is not so much a greatest hits as a lengthy retrospective. In any case, the designation "greatest hits" is pushing it in the U.S., where only "Baby Come Back" (included here, of course) made the Top 40. Forty songs might seem like too much, but actually it should be your first choice, because of both its consistent quality and the consideration that it's more available, and no more expensive, than whatever other Equals compilations you might find (which will invariably be imports). Much of this is good-time romantic rock-soul-ska, occasionally lifting or varying some well-known soul and rock riffs, sometimes with a touch of British mod rock (as on "I Can See, But You Don't Know" and "Fire"). Political and racial concerns occasionally make themselves known (as on "Police on My Back," covered by the Clash, and the British hit "Black Skin Blue Eyed Boys"); even more occasionally, there is a spacy lyricism ("Give Love a Try," "Reincarnation," "Let's Go to the Moon"). Interesting, accomplished (if sometimes too similar-sounding) stuff from Eddy Grant's formative years, though it's marred by the almost total absence of details about the Equals' career in the liner notes. *—Richie Unterberger*

Unequalled/Explosion / 1996 / Repertoire ✦✦✦✦✦

Eramus Hall

Group / Soul, Funk

Eramus Hall was an obscure funk/soul group that recorded two rare albums released on Westbound in the early '80s. Despite the misleading name, Eramus Hall was indeed a group and not a solo artist—the group took its name from a historical building located in Chicago. They recorded their debut album (*Your Love Is My Desire*) in late 1978 but Westbound, their Detroit-based label, didn't release it until 1980. Hardly any copies of the minimally pressed album made it outside of Detroit, so several soul fans and insiders wondered whether or not it actually existed. *Go Head*, the group's second and final album, was released on Capitol in 1984. Like its predecessor, it failed to make much of an impression. As the years carried on, interest in the band's debut, specifically the title cut and "Just Me 'n' You," picked up. The U.K.-based Ace label reissued the album on vinyl—and then later on CD—in the late '90s. *—Andy Kellman*

- **Your Love Is My Desire** / 1980 / Westbound ✦✦✦

Until it was issued on CD by Ace in 1999, the existence of Eramus Hall's *Your Love Is My Desire* was debated. Recorded in late 1978 by the soul/funk group—the artwork and the artist name lead one to believe this a solo work, but Eramus Hall took its name from a historical building in Chicago—the Westbound label was unable to release it until 1980. "Release" is putting it loosely, as the small pressing hardly allowed for any copies to reach anywhere outside of Westbound's base in Detroit. Prior to and since the Ace reissue, *Your Love Is My Desire* has been proclaimed a masterpiece by several noted record hounds, which is another debatable issue. The LP is undeniably uneven, with something of a personality crisis that seems torn between smooth soul of its own character and a hand-me-down funk style that, while written and played with skill, falls flapjack flat when compared to inspirations like Slave and Funkadelic. While several groups during this period were able to combine styles on their albums, the effect here is that of two very different records being switched on the listener on a track-to-track basis. Despite its major flaws, fans of smooth late-'70s soul will love to have this album for "Your Love Is My Desire" and "Just Me 'n' You," two beautiful numbers with impeccable arrangements and soaring voices. *—Andy Kellman*

The Escorts

f. 1972, NJ, **db.** 1974

Group / R&B, Soul

The Escorts—Reginald Haynes, Lawrence Franklin, Robert Arrington, William Dugger, Stephen Carter, Frank Heard, and Marion Murphy—with assistance from producer/writer/singer George Kerr, literally tried to sing their way out of Rahway State Prison (NJ). All seven were serving time for various felonies and somehow hooked up with Kerr who was allowed to bring recording equipment into the slammer, which accounts for the less than sterling quality of their tracks; Kerr recorded the Escorts in prison then sweetened the tracks on the outside.

The project lasted from 1973 to 1974 and resulted in five singles, the first, "All We Need Is Another Chance, Pts. 1 & 2," written by Kerr, was tailored for them. The Alithia Records release reminds you of Kerr's productions on the Whatnauts, but not nearly as sharp, though the Escorts multi-man (seven singers) lineup provided for a full harmony sound. The record saw airtime in Jersey, New York, Philly, Virginia, Maryland, and a few other locales, mostly along the East Coast, but it never really broke. But just recording and having record releases gave the Escorts tons of hope.

Kerr chose the remake route for singles two and three. "Look Over Your Shoulder" b/w "By the Time I Get to Phoenix" didn't cut the mustard; Kerr had already cut a far superior version of the A-side on the O'Jays for Bell Records a few years earlier. The Escorts closed out 1973 with two more Kerr productions previously done by the O'Jays: "I'll Be Sweeter Tomorrow" b/w "I'm So Glad I Found You"; once again, the originals reigned supreme.

Kerr, who sung with the Serenaders, usually managed at least one R&B Top 20 hit with everybody he produced, but never could get the Escorts that high on the charts. Prior to working with them, he enjoyed success with the Moments, Linda Jones, the Whatnauts, Barbara English, and others. Alithia issued one more single the summer of 1974 entitled "Lets Make Love at Home" (arguably one of their finest), but the results were the same—a lot of promise, but it charted low and royalties never materialized. An album, *3 Down 4 to Go*, dropped in 1973 and Collectables Records released a CD *All We Need Is Another Chance* in 1994; subsequent CDs', *The Best of the Escorts* (Sequel) and *Prisoners of Soul* (Priority Records) are fine efforts. Some of the Escorts best (unreleased as singles) songs are on these compilations and the digitally remastered compact disks are far superior to the original vinyl releases.

Franklin and Arrington resurrected the Escorts in 1981 for an unsuccessful two-single run. With new Escorts—George Byles, James Green, Frank Harris, and Grover Troutman—they cut "Love Is Like a Dream" b/w "Make Me Over Lord" and "Heart of Gold" b/w "Sing a Happy Song" on Knockout Records. Reginald "Reggie" Haynes, the Escorts' original lead singer, embarked on a solo career that fizzled quick; his "Get Ready to Move" b/w "I'll Be Sweeter Than Yesterday" on Escort Records bombed in 1986. *—Andrew Hamilton*

All We Need (Is Another Chance) / 1973 / Collectables ✦✦✦

Recorded at Rahway State Prison in the '70s, this is the Escorts' weakest recording. Features an overblown rendition of the Miracles' "Ooh, Baby Baby" that's two minutes too long, and interviewing bites with their producer George Kerr interspersed before various cuts. Kerr redoes three songs with the Escorts that he previously did with the O'Jays, but weak versions of "I'll Be Sweeter Tomorrow," "Look Over Your Shoulder," and "I'm So Glad I Found You" are no matches for the Eddie LeVert-led originals. The best track, "All We Need Is Another Chance," finds them repenting for their wrongs and pleading for a second chance. *—Andrew Hamilton*

3 Down 4 to Go / 1973 / Collectables ✦✦✦

The Escorts were inmates at Rahway State Prison in New Jersey when George Kerr produced this album (originally released in 1973). The title refers to how prisoners count time—three down (years served), four to go. A sugary falsetto, similar to Billy Garnett of the Whatnauts (but not as striking), handles the leads along with a rough tenor. "Let's Make Love (At Home Sometime)" is a slow pleader with smooth choral harmony. Remakes of Smokey Robinson & the Miracles' "We've Come Too Far to End It Now," the Delfonics' "La La Means I Love You," and the Flamingos' "I Only Have Eyes for You" will not make you discard the originals. Two tracks, "Brother" and "Corruption (Man's Self Destruction)," deal with social problems, Temptations style. Kerr cut the vocals at Rahway State Prison, so the quality isn't all that great, but harmony lovers will overlook the flaws. *—Andrew Hamilton*

Prisoners of Soul / Aug. 19, 1997 / Sequel ♦♦♦♦
Recording entities have jumped on tracks by the Escorts, reissuing them under various prison-related names, including this import from Sequel Records—*Prisoners of Love*. All the titles are apropos; the Escorts called New Jersey's Rahway State Prison home when producer George Kerr undertook the project of recording them for Alithia Records. The sound is similar to what Kerr was concurrently doing with the Whatnauts; the uptempo tunes spoke of social problems, and the original and new renditions of ballads were sweet enough to syrup a stack of pancakes. The falsetto-led ballads and the uptempo tracks are the most soulful; the ballads led by the light, unemotional tenor—he signs 'em straight with no vocal runs or inflections for dramatics, and this will please lovers of light soul/pop, but will disappoint fans who like a little more emotional evolvement. *—Andrew Hamilton*

• **The Greatest Hits** / Oct. 22, 2002 / Empire Musicwerks ♦♦♦♦
A much better compilation than could be expected for these forgotten soul captives, *The Greatest Hits* collects 20 tracks of smooth, sweet soul by Rahway State's finest. Each of their four R&B hits of the '70s are present—"Look Over Your Shoulder," "Disrespect Can Wreck," "I'll Be Sweeter Tomorrow," and "Let's Make Love (At Home Sometime)"—plus a pair of interesting commentary songs ("All We Need Is Another Chance," "Corruption"), and a few OK period covers ("Little Green Apples," "By the Time I Get to Phoenix"). The final track includes an interview with members of the Escorts. *—John Bush*

Coke Escovedo (Thomas Escovedo)

b. Apr. 30, 1941, Los Angeles, CA, **d.** Jul. 13, 1986, Montebello, CA
Timbales, Percussion / Latin Jazz, Latin Soul
Born April 30, 1941 in Los Angeles to a musical family that includes Pete Escovedo, Alejandro Escovedo and Sheila Escovedo, percussionist Coke Escovedo first rose to prominence in the 1969 as a member of Santana. His playing can be heard on the third Santana album, which included the hit "Everybody's Everything" and "No One to Depend On," which he co-wrote. Escovedo and his brother Pete Escovedo left Santana to form their own Latin rock hybrid, Azteca, which recorded two albums, a self titled debut in 1972 and *Pyramid of the Moon* in 1973, both for Columbia.

Always in demand, Coke toured with Stevie Wonder before releasing his first solo effort in 1975, simply titled *Coke*. Featuring a sophisticated fusion of jazz, soul, and Latin elements, the album did well enough to lead to a second date as leader in 1976, the more pop oriented *Comin' at Ya*. A final release as a leader in 1977, "Disco Fantasy," proved critically and commercially disappointing and signaled the last time Escovedo would helm his own project. This nevertheless did not signal the end of his career, as busy as ever, Coke toured with Santana again and joined Herbie Hancock for his 1979 release *Feets Don't Fail Me Now* and became a member of his touring band. The '80s saw him record and tour with his niece and Prince collaborator, Sheila Escovedo. Coke Escovedo died at the age of 45 on July 13, 1986. *—Wade Kergan*

• **Coke** / 1975 / Mercury ♦♦♦♦
The late percussionist Thomas "Coke" Escovedo came from a very musical family—he was the brother of Pete Escovedo and the uncle of Sheila Escovedo, who started going by Sheila E. after joining forces with Prince in the 1980s. Although not as well known as those relatives, Coke Escovedo had an impressive track record that included working with Santana and founding the band Azteca. In the 1970s, Escovedo recorded three little known solo albums for Mercury, the first of which was 1975's *Coke*. The music is soul/funk with occasional jazz and Latin overtones—not as ambitious as Santana or Azteca, but generally rewarding nonetheless. Escovedo wasn't a lead singer, which means that on *Coke*, Linda and Calvin Tillery provide the lead vocals. Linda has her share of inspired moments, and she really lets loose on the funky "Easy Come, Easy Go" as well as Smokey Robinson's "Love Letters" and a stunning remake of Santana's "No One to Depend On" (which Escovedo co-wrote). Calvin's contributions aren't as memorable as Linda's—his performance on Leon Ware's "If I Ever Lose This Heaven" is pleasant, although it falls short of the excellence of the Average White Band's better known version. But more often than not, *Coke* is excellent—and it's also the most essential of Escovedo's three solo albums. *—Alex Henderson*

Comin' at Ya / 1976 / Mercury ♦♦♦
Inevitably, many artists will be plagued by the dreaded sophomore curse—they will impress you with a very promising debut album only to disappoint you with their second album. That was the case with *Comin' At Ya*, Coke Escovedo's follow-up to his generally excellent debut album, *Coke*. Released in 1976, *Comin' At Ya* isn't a bad album—it's generally decent, if uneven. But after a debut as strong as *Coke*, one couldn't help being disappointed by an album that was merely decent. While Linda and Calvin Tillery were the lead vocalists on *Coke*, Errol Knowles provides the lead vocals this time—and his performances are likable but not fantastic on soul/pop material that ranges from the funky "Runaway" to Carlos Santana's "Everything Is Coming Our Way." Jazz great Joe Henderson (tenor sax) is featured on three covers—Ernesto Lecuona's "The Breeze and I," Johnny Bristol's "I Wouldn't Change a Thing" and José Feliciano's "Stay With Me"—while guitarist Gabor Szabo is heard on the Latin-influenced "Vida." But the presence of those well respected musicians doesn't erase the fact that this LP, although competent, is the least essential of Escovedo's three solo albums. *—Alex Henderson*

Disco Fantasy / 1977 / Mercury ♦♦♦♦
Creatively, Coke Escovedo bounced back with his third album, *Disco Fantasy*. This LP wasn't the commercial breakthrough that Escovedo was hoping for—like *Coke* in 1975 and *Comin' At Ya* in 1976, *Disco Fantasy* didn't sell. But from a creative standpoint, the LP is a success. This time, Escovedo is obviously intent on providing a danceable funk/disco party album, and the Bay Area percussionist does exactly that thanks to infectious numbers like "Won't You Gimme the Funk," "Hot Soul Single" and "Trash Man." Those who are into irony should appreciate "Doesn't Anybody Want to Hear a Love Song," which finds singer Linda Tillery (who provides all of the lead vocals) complaining about the shortage of love songs in disco-crazed 1977—the thing is that this very funky track is hardly a love song, and *Disco Fantasy* is far from an album of romantic ballads. There are a few slow jams on this record, including the pleasing Northern soul item "Something Special." But most of the time, *Disco Fantasy* takes dead aim at the dancefloor and does so with exhilarating results. *—Alex Henderson*

ESG

f. 1978, New York, NY [South Bronx]
Group / Old School Rap, Electro, Club/Dance
An art-funk ensemble from the South Bronx, ESG was formed by sisters Renee, Valerie, and Marie Scroggins, all of whom handle vocals and percussion, and friend Leroy Glover (bass). ESG's music is centered around the sisters' complex polyrhythms, with atmosphere supplied by bass and pop-flavored guitar. During their first incarnation, the group signed with 99 Records and issued a debut self-titled EP in 1981 that featured three live and three studio songs, the latter produced by the legendary Martin Hannett (Joy Division, etc.). *ESG Says Dance to the Beat of the Moody* EP, from 1982, continued in a similar vein, as did their first full-length album, 1983's *Come Away With ESG*. ESG disbanded shortly thereafter, but unexpectedly re-formed in the early '90s, heralding their comeback with a self-titled 1991 compilation of previously released material.

The group's work had become popular among hip-hop artists searching for samples, with such acts as TLC, the Wu-Tang Clan, the Beastie Boys, Big Daddy Kane, and indie rockers Unrest all making use of ESG beats; the group addressed this issue on the 1992 12-inch EP *Sample Credits Don't Pay Our Bills*. *ESG Live!* appeared in 1995, featuring both old and new material. The group continued to record during the late '90s, and even added Scroggins' daughters Chistelle and Nicole. The major retrospective *A South Bronx Story* appeared on Universal Sound in 2000. *—Steve Huey*

• **A South Bronx Story** / May 8, 2000 / Universal Sound ♦♦♦♦♦
With their limited resources, the Scroggins sisters put the boogie down in the Boogie Down Bronx. Major kudos to Universal Sound for compiling ESG's best works for *A South Bronx Story*, a crucial document of sparse, old school funk. Until 2000, the group's scant material had been nearly impossible to find. The most legendary inclusion is the Martin Hannett-produced 7-inch EP that was originally released on Factory (later released as a 12-inch in the U.S. by 99 with live tracks backing it). This release featured their trademark "Moody," which ended up being listed as a Top 50 classic by nearly all of New York's dance clubs; it was also immortalized on a volume of Tommy Boy's excellent *Perfect Beats* series, lodged between Liquid Liquid and Strafe. Like the remainder of their recorded output, it featured the three "R"s: rhythm, rhythm, and more rhythm. Also on the debut EP was their most sampled "UFO"; the nauseous siren trills at the beginning found sped-up use in at least half a dozen rap tracks in the late '80s and early '90s. Big Daddy Kane and LL Cool J used it, and the Bomb Squad slyly swiped it for Public Enemy's "Night of the Living Baseheads." But arguably their best moment was "Dance" with its jumpy Motown rhythm, post-punk bass, and narrative/old school vocals. It sounds like a wild mix of the Supremes and *Metal Box*-era Public Image Limited. Deborah's bass, though not as musicianly, captures the spirit of PIL's Jah Wobble copping Motown session bassist James Jamerson. It's that sort of sprited, unconscious hybrid that made ESG so unique. After all, they played the opening night of Manchester's Factory club and the closing night of Larry Levan's Paradise Garage. *—Andy Kellman*

Esquerita (Eskew Reeder, Jr.)

b. New Orleans, LA, **d.** Oct. 23, 1986, Harlem, NY
Vocals, Piano / Rock & Roll
With a six-inch pompadour, brocaded shirts, rhinestone shades, and a rhythmic, belligerent style of piano playing, Esquerita was the original Little Richard, years before Mr. Penniman tutti-frutti'd his way to stardom. Working around the Dallas-New Orleans circuit in the early '50s, Esquerita's shot at the big time came when Capitol Records decided they needed their own version of Little Richard, after signing their answer to Elvis, Gene Vincent. The resulting recordings, though smartly produced, stand as some of the most untamed and unabashed sides ever issued by a major label. Long revered by rock & roll fans the world over, they make Little Richard's Specialty sides look highly disciplined by comparison. Though Esquerita continued to record in a tamer style through the '60s, his Capitol sides stand as a monument to the potential of rock & rolls lunatic power and the off-kilter genius of Esquerita. *—Cub Koda*

Capitol Collectors Series / 1990 / Capitol ♦♦♦♦♦
The Esquerita volume of the *Capitol Collectors Series* reissued a whopping 28 sides by the rock & roll wildman, recorded over 1958-1959. These constituted his complete output for the label, not to mention the most unhinged recordings of his career. When this CD was originally released in 1990, ten of the songs had never before seen release in the U.S., appearing only on a double-LP set released in France. As such, it's the definitive look at Esquerita's recording career, and a necessary purchase for anyone interested in what made early rock & roll seem so dangerous. There's never much doubt as to what Esquerita is *really* singing about on songs like "Gettin' Plenty of Lovin'" or "Hey Miss Lucy," and the wild voodoo-jungle sound of "Esquerita and the Voola" must have sounded like Satan himself was about to storm out of the speakers. Esquerita fans hold that his screaming, howling, piano-pounding antics trump even those of his admirer, Little Richard, but that's debatable. Where Little Richard can kick a song into overdrive with a lung-bursting screech, Esquerita is more apt to slip into a hoarse growl—it's sleazy, to be sure, but

doesn't have quite the same impact. Still, that's only a relative judgment—this stuff is crazier than at least 95 percent of its competition. *Capitol Collectors Series* went out of print, but fortunately Collectables gave its music a straight-up reissue under the new title *Rockin' the Joint*. —*Steve Huey*

Vintage Voola / 1997 / Norton ♦♦♦

Originally issued as a vinyl album, this compact disc reissue adds some new tracks and wild, eye-boggling color photos to the original package. The seven original demo acetates Esquerita cut in Dallas at Sellers' Recording in 1958 are still aboard, sounding raw and wonderful as ever, fleshed out with his contribution to Paul Peek's lone NRC single, "Sweet Skinny Jenny" and "The Rock-A-Round," which he helped co-author. Added to this is Esquerita's late-'60s original version of "Dew Drop Inn" (later recorded by Little Richard) and a Little Richard interview where he waxes effusive about the artist who influenced him so greatly. Although a bit short in the running time department, this nonetheless is the perfect companion piece to any solid collection of his Capitol sides from 1958. —*Cub Koda*

• **Rockin' the Joint** / 1998 / Collectables ♦♦♦♦♦

Rockin' the Joint is a reissue of the 1990 *Capitol Collectors Series* anthology with a new name and different cover, but otherwise the two are the same. Since many of the discs in the *Capitol Collectors Series* have been deleted, Collectables has given a few of them facelifts and another crack at the marketplace. Esquerita, the R&B pianist who profoundly influenced Little Richard, is at the top of his game on these recordings from the late '50s. He somehow managed to convince the Jordanaires to drop by the studio and lay down some vocal tracks on their way to the funeral of Elvis Presley's mother, and they appear on "I Live the Life I Love" and "This Thing Called Love." The 28 tracks on this collection constitute Esquerita's complete Capitol recordings, and they are a vital addition to the collection of any enthusiast of '50s rock & roll or R&B. —*Greg Adams*

The Esquires

f. 1957, Milwaukee, WI

Group / Chicago Soul, Soul, R&B, Vocal Pop

The Esquires were a vocal group from Milwaukee, WI, formed in 1957 at the height of the R&B vocal boom. Gilbert Moorer, his brother Alvis, and sister Betty were children of a musical family—their father had sung in a gospel group called the Friendly Five, while their mother played piano. Gilbert, Alvis, and Betty Moorer were in high school when they formed the Esquires in 1957.

During the Esquires' early years in Milwaukee, they saw many people pass through their lineup. Some key members joined and remained, including Sam Pace in 1961 and, four years later, Shawn Taylor. During this same period, however, Betty Moorer departed the group. By 1966, the Esquires—Gilbert Moorer, Alvis Moorer, Sam Pace, and Shawn Taylor—felt ready to try for a record deal and the chance at a national career. The group moved to Chicago, where they first tried without success to interest Curtis Mayfield—then trying to run the Windy C and Mayfield labels—in giving them a chance to record.

Several more approaches to other producers finally led them to Bill "Bunky" Sheppard, who owned a small Chicago label called Constellation, which had recorded Gene Chandler and Nolan Chance, among others. Sheppard not only liked the Gilbert Moorer song "Get on Up," that they had recorded as a demo, but liked the group. His interest resulted in a hook-up with a new voice, in the person of Millard Edwards, a bass singer already in the Constellation stable.

It was Sheppard's intention to record the Esquires on Constellation, on their own single and backing Edwards on one of his records, but the failure of the latter single, coupled with the collapse of Constellation late in 1966 made for some changes. The first was a shift to the Bunky label, which Sheppard salvaged out of the wreckage of Constellation, and the second was the addition of Millard Edwards to their lineup.

The Esquires debut single, "Get on Up," finally appeared on the Bunky label, distributed nationally by New York-based Scepter Records. "Get on Up" was a huge success, soaring to number three on the R&B charts and number 11 as a pop single. Suddenly, the Esquires, who'd spent 10 years preparing for this moment, were one of the hotter R&B vocal groups of 1967. "Get on Up" completed the transition of the Esquires from a local to a national act. They played venues that included the Regal Theater in Chicago and the Apollo in New York. In the process, they also lost Shawn Taylor, whom Sheppard regarded as unreliable for his late arrival to some shows. In October of 1967, the Esquires issued a follow-up recording, "And Get Away" (also written by Gilbert Moorer), which charted at number 22 and number 9, pop and R&B, respectively. With this second hit under their belts, the group's debut (and only) LP followed as a matter of course, cut for Bunky Records. March of 1968 saw the group's third single, "You Say," get to number 41 on the R&B charts, and three months later, "Why Can't I Stop" charted at number 48 (R&B).

At the end of 1968, following the release of their fifth single, the Esquires left Bunky Records and signed directly with Scepter, which placed the group on its Wand imprint. Their next two singles, "You've Got the Power" and "I Don't Know," reached numbers 29 and 37 on the R&B charts, respectively.

They left Scepter after one year and were back with Bunky Sheppard beginning in 1969, before jumping briefly to Capitol in 1970 for one single ("Reach Out"). More lineup changes took place that year, as Millard Edwards left and Shawn Taylor returned to the Esquires. The group made another run up the charts on Lamar Records with "Girls in the City," which got to number 18 in 1971. The Esquires were absent from the charts for the next five years, but they continued performing. In 1976, they recut their biggest hit as "Get on Up '76," which managed to chart, closing out their recording career. For the next two decades, the Esquires were exclusively a performing act, based in Milwaukee where they started out, with new members periodically coming in to work alongside Gilbert and Alvis Moorer.

In 1992, the group's two biggest hits, "Get on Up" and "And Get Away," appeared on Capricorn Records' *The Scepter Records Story*. In 1998, England's WestSide label released the CD *Get on Up and Get Away*, a comprehensive retrospective containing most of their singles (including all of the hits) from various labels, and highlights from the album of that name. —*Bruce Eder*

Get on Up / 1967 / Collectables ♦♦♦♦

This CD reissue of the Esquires' classic debut LP will have you wondering why big-time success eluded the harmony-laden foursome. The often-changing lineup consisted at this point of Gilbert Moorer, Alvis Moorer, Shawn Taylor, and Millard Edwards. Edwards, who sang with the Sheppards, was from Chicago, while the other three were Milwaukee natives. Everyone is familiar with "Get on Up," a monster, and its knockoff follow-up, "And Get Away"; however, not many know of the excellent slow and midtempo numbers that B-sided their faster A-sides. Gilbert, Shawn, and Millard shared the leads (Sam Pace later replaced Shawn). Gilbert's soaring falsetto and Millard's deep bottom made all their songs interesting. If you can find the import on London's WestSide label, *Get on Up... And Get Way With the Esquires*, then go for it—it has 23 cuts, compared to the twelve on this one. —*Andrew Hamilton*

• **Get on Up... And Get Away With the Esquires** / Aug. 11, 1998 / WestSide ♦♦♦♦♦

Sweet captivating sounds from the Esquires of Milwaukee, WI. This glorious import CD contains 23 tracks of essentials, with the only obvious omission being "Girls in the City," recorded on Lamar Records. Everyone's familiar with "Get on Up," but it's the B-sides and obscure A-sides that make you exhale. Underappreciated and under-promoted gems—"Woman," "The Feeling Is Gone," "Why Can't I Stop," "No Doubt About It," "Listen to Me" and "Everybody's Laughing"—are strong. The main ingredient is Gilbert Moorer's unbelievably high, honey-sweet falsetto, but they also had an able tenor, baritone and deep voiced Millard Edwards' booming bottom, which often counterpointed Moorer's high tones. It includes chart entries "Get on Up," "And Get Away," the exciting "You Got the Power" and "You Say." —*Andrew Hamilton*

The Essex

f. 1962, Camp LeJeune, NC, **db.** 1964

Group / Girl Group, R&B

Fondly recalled for their 1963 chart-topper "Easier Said Than Done," R&B vocal quintet the Essex was formed in 1961 by Walter Vickers and Rodney Taylor, a pair of U.S. Marines stationed in Japan; upon returning stateside to Camp LeJeune, NC, the duo recruited fellow leathernecks Anita Humes, Billie Hill and Rudolph Johnson and recorded a demo tape which earned them a contract with the Roulette label. Highlighted by Humes' distinctively sassy lead vocal, "Easier Said Than Done" reached the top of the American pop charts in July of 1963, although the Essex found promoting the single trying as they were forced to coordinate their live appearances around their Marine duties. Johnson's subsequent shipment to a military base in Okinawa, Japan, further complicated matters, but the group's follow-up "A Walkin' Miracle" nevertheless reached the number-12 spot; when the Essex's third single "She's Got Everything" stalled, however, their chart run was over, and after a handful of little-noticed records like "Curfew Lover," they disbanded. Humes later pursued a solo career. —*Jason Ankeny*

Easier Said Than Done / 1963 / Roulette ♦♦♦♦♦

A Walkin' Miracle / 1963 / Roulette ♦♦♦

Pleasant family-like harmonies were the Essex's trademark, though the members were only family in the sense that they all were Marine Corpsmen. This contains their second biggest hit "A Walkin' Miracle" and its less than successful follow-up, "She's Got Everything." The Essex's unique blend was fun to listen to but with military obligations, singing took a back seat, despite scoring a million seller with "Easier Said Than Done." Other pleasantries include "Curfew Lover," "What I Don't Know Won't Hurt Me," and a remake of Frankie Lymon & the Teenagers' "Why Do Fools Fall in Love." —*Andrew Hamilton*

• **Easier Said Than Done/A Walkin' Miracle** / Jun. 8, 1999 / Collectables ♦♦♦♦♦

The Essex's lead singer Anita Humes sounded and looked like Florence Ballad (Supremes). She must have been a huge fan of early Motown, because many of these selections mimic the sound. Humes and the rest of the group—Walter Vickers, Rodney Taylor, Rudy Johnson, and Billie Hill—were active Marine Corps members when the bubblegum-ish "Easier Said Than Done" zoomed to number one on July 6, 1963. Collectables combined their two most successful albums on this CD. *Walkin' Miracle*, which was similar to *Easier*... shot to number 12, their only other chart record was "She's Got Everything" (included), but don't let that put you off. Their two big hits were aberrations, they had a much more soulful persona as they prove on "I Love Her," and "Every Night," which sounds like Smokey Robinson's productions on Mary Wells with the Lovetones accompanying. "Whenever I Need My Baby" showcases the fellas' pleasant harmony. They weren't the Moonglows, but were smooth, crooners who blended in unison. Contains some good ballads, exquisitely done by Humes including "All in My Mind" and upbeat numbers like Frankie Lymon & the Teenagers' "Why Do Fools Fall in Love." Listening to Humes you wonder why Berry Gordy didn't give her a call for the Supremes gig when Florence got the pink slip. —*Andrew Hamilton*

Gloria Estefan (Gloria Fajardo)

b. Sep. 1, 1957, Havana, Cuba

Vocals / Club/Dance, Adult Contemporary, Latin Pop, Dance-Pop, Tropical

As one of the biggest new stars to emerge during the mid-'80s, singer Gloria Estefan predated the coming Latin pop explosion by a decade, scoring a series of propulsive dance hits rooted in the rhythms of her native Cuba before shifting her focus to softer, more ballad-oriented fare. Born Gloria Fajardo in Havana on September 1, 1957, she was raised primarily in Miami, FL, after her father, a bodyguard in the employ of Cuban president Fulgencio Batista, was forced to flee the island following the 1959 coup helmed by Fidel Castro. In the fall of 1975, Fajardo and her cousin Merci Murciano auditioned for the Miami Latin Boys, a local wedding band headed by keyboardist Emilio Estefan. With their addition, the group was rechristened Miami Sound Machine and four years later,

Fajardo and Estefan were wed. As Miami Sound Machine began composing their own original material, their fusion of pop, disco, and salsa earned a devoted local following, and in 1979 the group issued their first Spanish-language LP on CBS International. Despite a growing Hispanic fan base, they did not cross over to non-Latin audiences until "Dr. Beat" topped European dance charts in 1984.

With 1985's *Primitive Love*, Miami Sound Machine recorded their first English-language effort, scoring three Top Ten pop hits in the U.S. alone with the infectious "Conga," "Bad Boy," and "Words Get in the Way." For 1988's triple-platinum *Let It Loose*, the group was billed as Gloria Estefan & Miami Sound Machine, reeling off four Top Ten hits—"Rhythm Is Gonna Get You," "Can't Stay Away From You," the chart-topping "Anything for You," and "1-2-3." 1989's *Cuts Both Ways* was credited to Estefan alone and generated her second number-one hit, "Don't Wanna Lose You"; however, while touring in support of the album, on March 20, 1990, her bus was struck by a tractor-trailer. She suffered a broken vertebrae that required extensive surgery and kept her off the road for over a year. Emilio Estefan and the couple's son were injured in the crash as well, but all three recovered. Estefan resurfaced in 1991 with *Into the Light*, again topping the charts with "Coming Out of the Dark," a single inspired by her near-fatal accident; two more cuts from the album, "Can't Forget You" and "Live for Loving You," secured her foothold on the adult contemporary charts.

With 1993's *Mi Tierra*, Estefan returned to her roots, recording her first Spanish-language record in close to a decade and earning a Grammy Award for Best Tropical Latin Album; on the follow-up, 1994's covers collection *Hold Me, Thrill Me, Kiss Me*, she also recalled her dance-pop origins with a rendition of the Vicki Sue Robinson disco classic "Turn the Beat Around." Another all-Spanish effort, *Abriendo Puertas*, earned the Grammy as well, while *Destiny* featured "Reach," named the official theme of the 1996 Summer Olympics. As Latin pop made new commercial headway thanks to the efforts of acts like Ricky Martin and Enrique Iglesias, Estefan reigned as the most successful crossover artist in Latin music history, with international record sales close to the 50 million mark. In 1999, she also made her feature film debut alongside Meryl Streep in *Music of the Heart*, recording the film's title song as a duet with *NSYNC and scoring both a massive pop hit and an Oscar nomination in the process. A new Spanish-language album, *Alma Caribeña*, followed in the spring of 2000. Several months later, Estefan was awarded a Grammy for Best Music Video for "No Me Dehes De Querer at the first annual Latin Grammy Awards. Her husband, Emilio, won for Producer of the Year. *—Jason Ankeny*

Eyes of Innocence / 1984 / Epic ✦✦
Gloria Estefan has a nice voice and does an interesting live show, but her albums are about as rigidly produced and routinely performed as anyone's this side of Julio Iglesias. This has some light Afro-Latin influences, but otherwise is generic pop. *—Ron Wynn*

Primitive Love / 1986 / Epic ✦✦✦
Gloria Estefan occasionally gets an above-average song, and her live show sometimes includes an Afro-Latin spot where she returns to her roots. Neither was the case on this mid-'80s set, which is certainly well produced, engineered, and arranged. If you're a fan, you enjoyed it. Otherwise, it was tough sledding. *—Ron Wynn*

Let It Loose / 1988 / Epic ✦✦✦✦✦
The group was still billed as "Gloria Estefan & Miami Sound Machine" on this album, which showed the singer and her bandleader husband, Emilio, retaining the jazzy, Latino flavor of their earlier music while moving determinedly into the pop mainstream and incidentally positioning Gloria as a superstar. Such goals were reached by a record that sold two million copies, went Top Ten, and produced the hits "Rhythm Is Gonna Get You," "Betcha Say That," "Can't Stay Away from You," "Anything for You," and "1-2-3." *—William Ruhlmann*

Cuts Both Ways / Jul. 1989 / Epic ✦✦✦
Dispensing with the "Miami Sound Machine" name, Estefan continued to successfully to mix Latin-tinged dance numbers with strong ballads on this million-selling Top Ten solo album, which included "Don't Wanna Lose You," "Get on Your Feet," and "Here We Are." *—William Ruhlmann*

Into the Light / Dec. 2, 1991 / Epic ✦✦✦
With this successful album, Estefan demonstrated that she had recovered from her serious accident of 1990. The album contains the telling hit "Coming Out of the Dark" but showed her moving even farther toward the middle of the road and sacrificing her younger fans in the process—most of the singles from this album performed better on the Adult Contemporary charts than on the Hot 100. *—William Ruhlmann*

● **Greatest Hits** / Oct. 6, 1992 / Epic ✦✦✦✦
In 1985, she started off as the lead singer of Miami Sound Machine. By 1987, after scoring four big hits from their first major U.S. album, they became Gloria Estefan & Miami Sound Machine, and by 1989, after even bigger success, it was simply Gloria Estefan. This greatest-hits collection covers the years 1985 to 1992, featuring most of the pop confections that propelled her to the top of the charts and to international stardom. Among the hits included are her three number ones: "Anything for You," "Coming Out of the Dark," and "Don't Wanna Lose You," as well as other Top Ten hits including "Conga," "Words Get in the Way," "Rhythm Is Gonna Get You," "Can't Stay Away From You," "Here We Are," and the single mix of "1-2-3." There are a few glaring omissions, however. "Bad Boy," her second Top Ten hit, was left off, and that is unfortunate because the hit version was a remix of the original album version and is extremely difficult to find on CD. Other omissions include "Dr. Beat," "Falling in Love (Uh-Oh)," "Oye Mi Canto," "Live for Loving You," and "Can't Forget You." To round off the set are four new recordings, including the album's first single "Always Tomorrow," the Jon Secada-penned "I See Your Smile," the irresistible Latin-flavored dance track "Go Away," and the semi-tepid holiday tune "Christmas Through Your Eyes." This is a good collection from a great artist that could have been a great collection had they included all the hits. *—Jose Promis*

Mi Tierra / Jun. 22, 1993 / Epic ✦✦✦✦

Hold Me, Thrill Me, Kiss Me / Oct. 18, 1994 / Epic ✦✦✦
This is a stretch for Estefan, but it's a genuinely worthy one, even if it sometimes strays too far from her Latin roots. This album of classic covers includes brilliant pop hits ("How Can I Be Sure," "Turn the Beat Around"), moments of genuine pathos ("Traces," "It's Too Late"), and some pure dreck ("You've Made Me So Very Happy"). While the record enhances Estefan's reputation as a savvy, sophisticated pop singer, it also lays bare her limitations, confirming that she's more stylist than soulstress. *—Eddie Huffman*

Destiny / Jun. 1996 / Epic ✦✦✦
With *Destiny*, Gloria Estefan ties together the Cuban and Latinbeat influences she had been exploring on her Spanish albums with the adult contemporary pop that dominated her early '90s records. It's a stylish concept and, for the most part, Estefan pulls it off. Like most of her albums, *Destiny* suffers from uneven material and a creeping sense of sameness between the songs, but Estefan's voice keeps getting stronger with age, which helps her rescue the weaker material on the record. And the best moments of *Destiny*—including the Olympic anthem "Reach," "I'm Not Giving You Up," and "Higher," among others—rank with her finest work. *—Stephen Thomas Erlewine*

Gloria! / Jun. 2, 1998 / Epic ✦✦✦✦
After spending some time exploring her Cuban roots and traditional pop, Gloria Estefan returns to straight-up dance-pop with the infectious *Gloria!* With its percolating disco beats and sunny melodies, the record recalls her glory days of the late '80s, but there is a stronger Latin rhythmic underpinning which gives the music depth. Some of the songs themselves are slight, but most of them rank among her best uptempo and ballads, especially since her singing is better than ever. In fact, *Gloria!* proves that some dance-pop divas can get better—and more adventurous—with age. *—Stephen Thomas Erlewine*

Alma Caribeña / May 23, 2000 / Epic ✦✦✦
Alma Caribeña (Caribbean soul), Gloria Estefan's third Spanish-language album, is another assured, varied effort in the tradition of its predecessors, *Mi Tierra* (1993) and *Abriendo Puertas* (1995), both of which were popular successes. The album is a virtual tour of the Caribbean islands, not only presenting styles from the singer's native Cuba but also from other Latin American countries. Much of the record has a traditional feel with acoustic instruments prominent, but that doesn't prevent a wide range of rhythms and musical approaches from being used. Salsa, son, murga, bolero, bachata, and Afro-Cuban styles are mixed, sometimes several in one song. Estefan sings with assurance and is joined for one song each by Latin music forbears Celia Cruz and José Feliciano. Though the album is intensely rhythmic, there is little for the singer's dance audience until the end when a remix of the first single, "No Me Dejes De Querer (Don't Stop Loving Me)," provides the requisite dancefloor entry. *— William Ruhlmann*

Greatest Hits, Vol. 2 / Feb. 6, 2001 / Epic ✦✦✦✦
Gloria Estefan's second volume of greatest hits seems more progressive than her first, considering the techno-leaning sounds of her 1990s hits that dominate this set as compared to the more straight-ahead pop from her 1980s hits. This collection assembles nearly all of her Hot 100 hits since her last *Greatest Hits* album (only "Don't Let This Moment End" is missing). Most of the songs are included in their original album versions, save for a couple which may be of interest to the collector. "If We Were Lovers," one of her loveliest and classiest ballads, was originally on the *Mi Tierra* album in its Spanish-language form, titled "Con Los Anos Que Me Quedan." The English version of the song had never been available on any of her albums until now. Also making its first appearance on a Gloria Estefan album is her duet with *NSYNC, "Music of My Heart." "You'll Be Mine (Party Time)" and "I'm Not Giving You Up" are featured in remixed forms which had previously only been available as singles. The real treat, however, are the three new songs, which rank among the singer's best, especially "You Can't Walk Away From Love," a dramatic, sweeping, Middle Eastern-tinged ballad. Also included is an updated remix of her first U.S. hit, "Conga." All in all, this is a fine greatest-hits album, almost superior to her first, with classy ballads, great pop songs, and high-energy dance numbers. *—Jose Promis*

Toni Estes

b. Tulsa, OK

Vocals / Southern Rap, Urban, Contemporary R&B

R&B singer/songwriter Toni Estes, a native of Tulsa, OK, grew up in a home filled with music, honing her vocal skills around the house and in church. She began appearing in TV commercials when she was six, and by her teens was opening for Natalie Cole and Gladys Knight. After high school graduation, Estes knew she wanted to be a professional singer. Through a friend, Estes met producer Jon Jon (who had worked with Babyface), and she trekked to Los Angeles to began recording demos. Though signed to a major label at the age of 17, she got a release from her contract (citing "politics") and began looking for a new recording deal. Desmarie Guyton, whom Estes had met at her former label, passed a tape to Mark Brown of Priority Records, which led to a contract and the release of her album debut, *Two * Eleven*, in 2000. *—Ed Hogan*

● **Two * Eleven** / Sep. 26, 2000 / Priority ✦✦✦
Hot songwriters are given recording deals for numerous reasons; their songs are proven sellers and giving them a record deal somehow may imbue the songwriter to give the label's artists some kind of "first look" preference to their songs. Sometimes these releases are embarrassing affairs. Such is not the case with singer/songwriter Toni Estes, whose résumé lists Whitney Houston's million-seller "It's Not Right, but It's OK," Laurnea's "Can't Let Go," and "Hot" from the *Next Friday* soundtrack. There are the necessary hip-hop slammers ("Independent Woman" produced by Teddy Riley), but it's on the more mellow material that the Tulsa, OK, native shines. Definitely a student of the old skool, such tender ballads as "I Adore," "Let Me Know," "She's Already," and "Stupid (I Believe)" bespeak a talent that'll be around long after the hottie tottie "girlies" of the moment are long forgotten. "Still Your Son" echoes Michael Jackson's "Billie Jean" in both chorus and theme. *—Ed Hogan*

E.U.

f. 1970, Washington, D.C.
Group / Go-Go, Funk
E.U., originally known as Experience Unlimited, is one of D.C.'s original go-go bands, but they never scored a pop hit until 1988, when "Da Butt" became a dance sensation, thanks to Spike Lee's *School Daze* movie. While they didn't record many great albums—1989's *Livin' Large*, which was riding on the success of "Da Butt," came the closest—each of their records has something that would appeal to hardcore funk fans. But E.U.'s strength was never captured on vinyl—it was their energetic, groove-oriented live shows that earned them a large following in the '80s, not their records. *—Stephen Thomas Erlewine*

- **E.U. Live: Two Places at the Same Time** / 1986 / Island ✦✦✦

This album was released just as go-go appeared on its way to a national breakthrough, and listening in retrospect, it's easy to understand some of the optimism. Essentially a pair of side-long extended jams (with a short studio piece, "The Theme From Escape From Del Go-Go," tacked on for good measure), it does a more than adequate job of capturing the percussive power generated by one of the best-ever go-go bands in its prime. That neither performance was recorded in front of a hollering hometown crowd in D.C. is the only real drawback, but with producer E.T. Thorngren at the board, the great sound quality is an acceptable tradeoff. "N.Y. Comes to Boogie," recorded at New York's New Music Seminar, is the better of the two long cuts. It's a seamless, 20-minute workout that folds in bits of everything from "Dance to the Drummer's Beat" to "La Di Da Di," showing off the ten-man band's musical versatility, and proving that go-go's swinging, steamrolling beats could absorb just about any music (a lesson hip-hop would later take much, much further). "Sho Nuff Bumpin'," despite the presence of some imported Washington fans, isn't quite as memorable, but unbeatably charismatic vocalist Greg "Sugar Bear" Elliot and dynamic drummer William "Juju" House could make much lesser material than this great. Though not an unqualified go-go masterpiece on the order of Trouble Funk's *Live*, *Two Places at the Same Time* makes a nice substitute. *—Dan LeRoy*

Go Ju Ju Go / 1987 / E. Unlimited ✦✦✦

Livin' Large / 1989 / Virgin ✦✦✦

Go-go is a musical form some have figured to be chart-resistant, thanks to its propensity for extended jams as heavy on percussion as melody. But with the smash 1988 single "Da Butt," E.U. proved that go-go could cross over, and this follow-up album was crafted to drive that point home. Overseen by the usual committee of producers (including Marcus Miller), the keyboard-laden *Livin' Large* is just about as studio slick as go-go can get and still keep its infectious swing. The biggest flaw is glaring: the drumming of William "Juju" House, the band's funky heartbeat, has mostly been replaced by unpleasantly clean mechanical grooves. That this unfortunate situation doesn't doom the album is in large part thanks to vocalist Gregory "Sugar Bear" Elliot, whose charisma and nasal "ows" can't help but generate smiles. There are also some pretty decent tunes inside the dressed-up arrangements; the remake of the Isley Brothers' "Shake Your Thang," featuring Salt-N-Pepa, was a deserving hit, and a redone "Da Butt," while slightly inferior to the original, still packs a rump-shaking wallop. Even the slow jamming "Taste of Your Love" and "Don't Turn Around," while having little to do with go-go, are surprisingly nice. After this effort failed to herald a commercial breakthrough, go-go largely went back to Washington, D.C., and went about its business, but *Livin' Large* was a brave and, for the most part, successful attempt to widen the genre's reach. *—Dan LeRoy*

Cold Kickin' It / 1990 / Virgin ✦✦

Adriana Evans

b. San Francisco, CA
Vocals / Contemporary R&B, Urban
Alternative R&B singer Adriana Evans was born and raised in San Francisco; her mother, Mary Stallings, was herself a gifted vocalist who sang with Count Basie and Dizzy Gillespie and issued a series of fine solo records. At 18, Evans relocated to Los Angeles, befriending aspiring rapper Dred Scott and collaborating on his 1994 album *Breakin' Combs*. Her own self-titled debut followed on RCA in 1997. *—Jason Ankeny*

- **Adriana Evans** / Apr. 15, 1997 / RCA ✦✦✦

Despite some jazz and hip-hop touches here and there, Adriana Evans' promising debut album leaves no doubt that her primary inspiration is the sleek "uptown" soul music of the 1970s. Indeed, smooth yet earthy gems like "Heaven," "Looking for Your Love" and "Love Is All Around" sound like they could have been recorded 20 years earlier by the Emotions, Minnie Riperton or Jean Carn. Evans, an expressive and charismatic singer, is the daughter of jazz belter Mary Stallings, and her exposure to jazz has left is mark. The seductive "Reality," in fact, isn't unlike something jazz vibist turned soul and funk singer Roy Ayers would have done in the late '70s. But make no mistake: Evans is an R&B artist first and foremost. In contrast to the homogenized nature of so much of the urban contemporary music recorded in 1997, this CD sounds consistently organic and heartfelt. *—Alex Henderson*

Faith Evans

Jun. 10, 1973
Vocals / Urban, Hip-Hop
In spite of the fact that Faith Evans carved out a recording career in her own right, her name will forever remain linked in the minds of many to her late husband the Notorious B.I.G. Evans was an active session singer and songwriter before signing her own solo deal and marrying Biggie, and while she never matched the level of his stardom, she continued to come into her own as a vocalist in the years after his untimely death.

Faith Evans was born on June 10, 1973, and grew up in Newark, NJ, where she began singing in church at the mere age of two. A high school honor student, she sang in her school's musical productions before winning a full scholarship to Fordham University. After just one year, though, she left college to put her jazz and classical training to use in the field of contemporary R&B. It didn't take her long to find work and over the next few years, she sang backup and wrote songs for artists like Hi-Five, Mary J. Blige, Pebbles, Al B. Sure!, Usher, Tony Thompson, and Christopher Williams. Thanks to her work on Blige's 1994 sophomore effort, *My Life*, Evans met producer/impresario Sean "Puffy" Combs, who signed her to his Bad Boy label. In 1995, Evans released her debut album, *Faith*, which went platinum on the strength of the hit R&B singles "You Used to Love Me" and "Soon As I Get Home." The same year, she met fellow Bad Boy artist the Notorious B.I.G. (some accounts say at a photo shoot, others a phone conversation) and married him after a courtship of just nine days; shortly thereafter, she guested on a remix of his smash single "One More Chance."

Over the next couple of years, Evans continued her behind-the-scenes work, performing and writing for records by the likes of Color Me Badd and LSG. She and Biggie also had a son, Christopher Wallace Jr., in late 1996; however, by that point, their marriage had already become strained. Biggie had publicly taken up with rapper Lil' Kim and rumors had been spreading about an Evans liaison with Biggie's rival 2Pac (alluded to on 2Pac's venomous "Hit Me Off"). The couple had unofficially separated when Biggie was shot and killed in March 1997. A grief-stricken Evans was prominently featured on the Puff Daddy tribute single "I'll Be Missing You," which with its cribbed Police hook zoomed to the top of the charts and became one of the year's biggest hits.

Evans' sophomore effort *Keep the Faith* followed in 1998 and it spun off several R&B hits over the next year, including "Love Like This," "All Night Long," and the Babyface-produced R&B number one "Never Gonna Let You Go." In the meantime, she worked with Aaron Hall, Tevin Campbell, and DMX, among others, and also made high-profile guest appearances on two 1999 hits, Whitney Houston's "Heartbreak Hotel" and Eric Benet's "Georgy Porgy." She began dating and eventually married record executive Todd Russaw, who took an active role in helping manage her career. In 2001, Evans released her third album, *Faithfully*, a more uptempo record that received her strongest reviews to date; it also produced hit singles in "You Gets No Love" and "I Love You," and her duet with Carl Thomas on "Can't Believe" was nominated for a Grammy. *—Steve Huey*

Faith / 1995 / Bad Boy ✦✦✦

Faith Evans had written songs for a variety of new jack and hip-hop artists (including Mary J. Blige, Al Be Sure!, Pebbles, and Christopher Williams) before releasing her first album, *Faith*. The record proves that she is as powerful in the spotlight as she is behind the scenes. Evans builds on a basic, hip-hop-influenced funk, alternating between simmering grooves and sultry ballads. *Faith* does have a couple of dull spots, but the album is a first-class debut. *—Stephen Thomas Erlewine*

Keep the Faith / Oct. 27, 1998 / Bad Boy ✦✦✦✦

Faith Evans' second album *Keep the Faith* was met with quite a bit of anticipation. The album was released three years after her acclaimed, soulful, and raw debut *Faith*, and in that time she had witnessed the murder of her husband the Notorious B.I.G., which led to the biggest hit of her career (and one of the biggest of the 1990s), the tribute "I'll Be Missing You" (in collaboration with Puff Daddy). *Keep the Faith* proved to be a success, and she happily avoided the curse of the sophomore slump. The album scored two Top Ten singles with the irresistible dance/R&B cut "Love Like This" and its follow-up, the equally intoxicating "All Night Long." Aside from those two dance numbers, the rest of the album falls somewhere between heavy ballads and midtempo grooves. Ms. Evans shines when she sings fast or midtempo songs, such as the slick "Life Will Pass You By," but the ballads weigh too heavily on this otherwise fine album. Some of the ballads stand tall, such as the gorgeous "My First Love" and the inspiration-tinged "Keep the Faith," while others are about as entertaining and inspired as tree sap ("Anything You Need" and the yawn-inducing interludes). Unfortunately, these ballads are all lumped together on this album, to the point where they almost blend into one long drip of molasses. However, the classy Ms. Evans possesses a beautiful voice, is a gifted songwriter, and happily steers clear of the tacky clichés that burden so much contemporary R&B. So despite the heavy reliance on ballads, this is actually a fine album, and is without a doubt a highlight of 1990s soul-pop music. Other notable tunes include the beautiful "Never Gonna Let You Go," which could be classified as the last great Babyface hit song of the 1990s (that song, incidentally, topped the R&B charts and hit the Top 20 on the pop charts), and the Diane Warren-penned "Lately I," which never became the hit it should have been. *—Jose Promis*

- **Faithfully** / Nov. 6, 2001 / Bad Boy ✦✦✦✦✦

Given Faith Evans' somewhat spotty track record and Puff Daddy/P. Diddy's slippage since his name change, it might have made some sense to greet Evans' third album, *Faithfully*, with a bit of skepticism. As it turns out, such doubts were unwarranted, since this is her grittiest, funkiest, best record to date. There are so many collaborators on each track and so many producers—usually around five songwriters for each track (but if a song is sampled, as many as 14 writers are credited)—that it seems a minor miracle that it holds together at all, but *Faithfully* gels better than any previous Faith Evans record, in large part because so much of it is devoted to hard-edged, funky dance numbers, whether it's hip-hop-influenced cuts like "Alone in This World" or the wonderful neo-disco "Back to Love." This switch from her previous album, which emphasized ballads and midtempo grooves, gives the album more character, since the dance numbers mix well with the sultrier numbers and they both work equally well. If the album is hurt by anything, it's its length—like most modern hip-hop-related albums, it runs too long—but it is rich with vibrant songs, lively production, and Evans' best singing to date on what ultimately is not just her best album, but another excellent female urban R&B album in a year overflowing with them. *—Stephen Thomas Erlewine*

Betty Everett

b. Nov. 23, 1939, Greenwood, MS, **d.** Aug. 17, 2001, Beloit, WI
Vocals, Piano / Pop-Soul, Soul
Betty Everett sang gospel growing up in Greenwood, MS, before relocating to Chicago and moving into secular music. She began recording for Cobra in 1958, then joined

Vee-Jay in the early '60s and started to land hit records. Her original version of "You're No Good," though sung with fire and verve, didn't make much impact until it was turned into a number-one pop hit by Linda Ronstadt in 1975. Her next single, "The Shoop Shoop Song (It's in His Kiss)," was her first major release, peaking at number-six pop in 1964. Her next success was the duet "Let it Be Me" with Jerry Butler, a soul version of the Everly Brothers tune that reached number-five R&B that same year. Everett's finest song as a solo act was 1969's "There'll Come a Time," which reached number two on the R&B charts and also cracked the pop Top 30 at number 26. Everett was now on Uni, where she remained until 1970. She continued recording for Fantasy until 1974 and made one other record for United Artists in 1978. A comeback performance for the 2000 PBS special *Doo Wop 51* was her last public appearance; she died at her Wisconsin home in August 2001. *—Ron Wynn*

There'll Come a Time / 1969 / Varese Sarabande ✦✦✦✦✦
Everett made her best records for Vee-Jay in the mid-'60s, but this album, originally released on Uni in 1969, isn't far behind in merit. Featuring her number two R&B single (and Top 40 pop hit) "There'll Come a Time," this has much more of a sweet soul flavor than her Vee-Jay sides, at times blending the trademarks of her brassy native Chicago scene with a Philadelphia influence. It's far from too sweet, though, with strong material, punchy arrangements, and Everett's always dependably energetic and warm vocals. It also contains the R&B hit "I Can't Say No to You." The CD reissue adds three valuable 1969-1970 singles that were previously unavailable on album, including the Top 20 R&B hit "It's Been a Long Time," arranged by Donny Hathaway and written by Kenny Gamble, Leon Huff, and Jerry Butler. *—Richie Unterberger*

● **The Shoop Shoop Song** / Nov. 22, 1993 / Vee-Jay ✦✦✦✦✦
Though sometimes classified as a girl group singer because of the Top Ten success of "The Shoop Shoop Song," Betty Everett's main thrust was much more in the R&B/soul vein. This excellent 25-track anthology of her 1963-1965 material shows her facility with various soul, R&B, and pop styles. She had three other minor hits—the original hit version of "You're No Good," the energetic Goffin/King pop/rocker "I Can't Hear You," and Van McCoy's soulful "Gettin' Mighty Crowded"—all of which are featured here. But most of the other material is equally enjoyable, including other early efforts by McCoy, Valerie Simpson, and Nick Ashford, and even P.F. Sloan (whose "Can I Get to Know You" is presented in a much earthier, slower version here than the Turtles' rendition several years later). This CD doesn't include her hit duets with fellow Chicago soulster Jerry Butler, but is a consistently enjoyable retrospective of an underrated singer who straddled the soul and pop worlds. *—Richie Unterberger*

The Fantasy Years / Oct. 3, 1995 / Fantasy ✦✦✦
For the first half of the 1970s, Everett recorded updated soul-pop for the Fantasy label with mixed but generally positive results. This 18-track compilation features cuts from two mid-'70s LPs, as well as various singles from the early '70s, including the R&B hits "I Got to Tell You," "Ain't Nothing Gonna Change Me," and "Sweet Dan." Not nearly as pop-oriented as her more famous mid-'60s recordings, this finds Everett in fine, expressive voice, but somewhat at the mercy of the quality of the material, which is variable. The selections from the 1975 *Happy Endings* album are kind of anonymous, but much of the rest is good, gutsy '70s soul. Johnny "Guitar" Watson helps out on a few numbers, as co-producer, guitarist, and occasional songwriter, and a couple were cut in Memphis with the Hi Rhythm Section. *—Richie Unterberger*

● **The Shoop Shoop Song (It's in His Kiss)** / Jun. 20, 2000 / Collectables ✦✦✦✦✦
These are Betty Everett recordings, minus the duets with Jerry Butler, from 1963 to 1966—the Vee-Jay years. A thorough overview for the period covered, but not a definitive collection of Everett's career because it doesn't include earlier tracks (she began recording in 1961), or later recordings on ABC, Uni ("There Come a Time"), Fantasy, Soundstage, United Artists, or 20th Century Fox Records. But if you want her solo Vee-Jay Records' story, this is it, includes the substantial hits "The Shoop Shoop Song" and "You're No Good"; Van McCoy's unsung "Getting Mighty Crowded"; as well as three early Valerie Simpson/Nicholas Ashford/Joshie Armstead compositions, "Too Hot to Hold," "The Real Thing," and "The Shoe Won't Fit." *—Andrew Hamilton*

The Exciters

f. 1961, Jamaica, NY
Group / Girl Group, Brill Building Pop
Despite the presence of lone male Herb Rooney, the Exciters made some of the best girl group records of the early '60s. Led by vibrant-voiced Brenda Reid, the originally all-female quartet came from Jamaica, NY, as the Masterettes. After signing on with saxist Al Sears as their manager, they switched their name to the Exciters and cut "Tell Him" in 1962 for United Artists. Produced by Jerry Leiber and Mike Stoller, the brilliant uptown soul effort proved a major smash. Reid's roaring pipes were expertly spotlighted on the follow-ups "He's Got the Power," "Get Him," and their original reading of "Do-Wah-Diddy," immortalized later that year by Manfred Mann. The group later appeared on Roulette, Band, Shout, and RCA. Reid and Rooney were married for a time, and Reid now performs with her children backing her. *—Bill Dahl*

Black Beauty / 1971 / Today ✦✦✦
Herb Rooney and Brenda Reid were the only constants throughout the Exciters' extensive career. Many thought they were all girls, but Herb was always there, if not vocally, in spirit as the deal-maker and shot-caller. Rooney arranged, produced, and wrote most of the material on this album. There are some good songs, but the Exciters, seeking an identity and a commercial edge, meandered all over the place, mixing Southern wailers like "Leaving Him Tomorrow," with "Stay Right Here This Morning," a Motown-ish rehash. A good ballad featuring Brenda's strong vocals and an uptempo jam are decent, but nothing reeks of a hit. *—Andrew Hamilton*

Heaven Is Where You Are / 1976 / 20th Century ✦✦

● **Tell Him** / 1995 / Collectables ✦✦✦✦✦
A reissue of a reissue, this 1995 Collectables package is the same as EMI's 1991 *Legendary Masters* entry on this New York vocal group from the early 1960s. Hits like the title track, "He's Got the Power" and the original version of "Do-Wah-Diddy" are class-A New York rock & roll all the way, and lead singer Brenda Reid's chops are as exciting, always making the material more interesting than it sometimes is. Very interesting are the inclusion of the longer unedited versions of "Tell Him" and "He's Got the Power," both remixed here in true stereo. Though not *technically* a girl group (they featured a male bass singer in the lineup), the Exciters were one of the best working in the genre. *—Cub Koda*

The Best of the Exciters: Reaching for the Best / Aug. 8, 1995 / Record Shack ✦✦
These tracks represent some of Britisher Ian Levine's earliest recordings. The Exciters, anchored by Herb Rooney and Brenda Reid (parents of Arista Records' President, Antonia L.A. Reid), performs 12 lackluster tracks. "Reaching for the Best" was a lightweight hit in England in 1975; there's also a seven-minute disco mix that dropped in 1988—pick your poison. Levine wanted Northern soul and Rooney wanted a more contemporary sound. They collaborated on "Reaching for the Best," but fought tooth and nail about everything else. It climbed as high as number 31 on British Top 50 selling 60,000 units. While those are paltry figures in the States, in Britain, the tally was substantial. "You're Gonna Make Me Love You," originally by Sandi Sheldon, got jacked in the mix and flopped. Rooney wrote "Suffering" and a couple others, but the overall production wasn't competitive. *—Andrew Hamilton*

Executive Suite

f. Philadelphia, PA
Group / Philly Soul, Disco, Soul
Executive Suite was the Philly group that Daryl Hall contributed vocals to on their first single ("Christine," for Jubilee Records) in 1970. The members were Vincent Unto, Henry Tuten, William Tyler, and Charles Conyers. Their next release, a smooth, Philly ballad named "I'm a Winner Now" from 1972, remains the jewel of their career. Babylon Records picked it up for national distribution in 1973, but the move didn't help much as the record never expanded beyond the Philly/New York area. A 1974 release, "When the Fuel Runs Out," embraced disco, Philly style, and achieved some club notoriety.

Two more singles "Your Love Is Paradise" and "You Believed in Me," suffered from indifferent promotion. Polydor released an LP, *Executive Suite 1*, in 1974 that contains the North Bay singles, produced at Sigma Sound Studios by an assortment of Philly's finest: Norman Harris, Phil Hurtt, Bunny Sigler, and the Harris Machine. They released one final single "Hey Pearl" on United Artists but the results didn't change. Unto and Tyler previously sang with the Millionaires on Castle Records; Tyler also sang with the Jewels, and Conyer with the Lovenotes. *—Andrew Hamilton*

● **Executive Suite 1** / 1974 / Polydor ✦✦✦
A Philadelphia quartet with deep Philly roots, the members were part of various recording entities before Executive Suite. When the Philly sound took off, old friends Bunny Sigler, Norman Harris, and Phil Hurtt decided to give them a shot. The seven tracks come from their four singles on Babylon Records, two of which are part two's, so there are really only five songs. The album is essential listening because of the lovely "I'm a Winner Now" and "Your Love Is Paradise"; they got some run with the disco-ish "When the Fuel Runs Out," but more serious efforts like "You Believed in Me" defined Executive Suite's sound. *—Andrew Hamilton*

Experience Unlimited

Group / Funk, Jazz-Funk
Experience Unlimited was the original full name of the Washington, D.C., band that later shortened its name to E.U. and became one of the city's definitive go-go artists. Before their commercial success in the latter half of the '80s, however, Experience Unlimited was a more spiritual, jam-oriented outfit that took their name from Jimi Hendrix's *Are You Experienced?*; they evolved into a jazzy, funky groove band that took some of their cues from Earth, Wind & Fire. Signed to the Black Fire label—along with the similar-sounding D.C. act Oneness of Juju—Experience Unlimited released their debut album, *Free Yourself*, in 1977. They went on to issue the 12-inch single "Knock Him Out Sugar Ray" in 1980, plus a low-profile LP, *Just the Way You Like It*, on Inner City in 1981. As E.U., of course, they went on to score the biggest hit of D.C.'s largely localized go-go movement, "Da Butt." *—Steve Huey*

● **Free Yourself** / 1977 / Blackfire ✦✦✦
Funking along in the jazz/R&B footsteps of such groups as Oneness of Juju and Earth, Wind & Fire, this is stone party music. They're at their best on their long, ornate instrumentals. The ensemble vocals on the other pieces can get a little precious, and when they go political it's tough to believe. But taken simply as a nasty groove in search of an ass to move, this is a funky good time and a vacuous 40 minutes you owe yourself. *—Rob Ferrier*

Exposé

f. 1984, Miami, FL
Group / Club/Dance, Adult Contemporary, Urban, Dance-Pop, Freestyle, House
In the long-standing tradition of prefabricated pop acts, the Miami-based trio Exposé was the creation of producer/songwriter Lewis A. Martineé. Martineé brought together Ann Curless, Jeanette Jurado, and Gioia Bruno, supplying them with a batch of songs penned by himself and the result was a slew of pop, dance, and R&B charting singles. Injecting it all with a bit of Latin flavoring, Martineé and Exposé scored big with their first outing, simply titled *Exposure*. Released in 1986, the album reeled off a string of hits, including the pop Top Tens "Come Go With Me," "Point of No Return," and "Let Me Be the One," and a number one with the ballad "Seasons Change." The album itself sold over two-million

copies and reached the Top 20. Martineé did little to tamper with the formula on the follow-up release, *What You Don't Know*, aside from giving it a slightly more pop feel and enlisting outside songwriters for a couple tracks (one of which, Diane Warren's "Your Baby Never Looked Good in Blue," became another Top Ten hit). While not as successful as the debut, *What You Don't Know* still managed to notch four hit singles and achieve gold-selling status. Bruno left the trio in 1992 due to health reasons and was replaced by Kelly Moneymaker for a self-titled release later that same year. By now, the formula had worn thin and only "I'll Never Get Over You Getting Over Me" managed to click at radio, leaving the album to fail to even go gold. Their output since has been limited to greatest-hits compilations. *—Tom Demalon*

Exposure / 1986 / Arista ✦✦✦✦✦

Exposé's debut album, *Exposure*, set the stage for one of the hottest female groups of the '80s, with no less than four Top Ten singles, one of which soared all the way to number one. The album was a massive dancefloor sensation, and Exposé was the biggest group in their genre (and one of the biggest of the rock era), which also included acts like Sweet Sensation and the Cover Girls. "Come Go With Me" and "Point of No Return" were massive club hits as well as Top Five pop hits, and typify late-'80s freestyle/pop and Miami-based dance music. Note, however, that the version of "Point of No Return" on this album is different than the hit single—this version had been released to clubs in 1985 (as was "Exposed to Love"), and featured a different lead singer. The single remix of "Point of No Return," with Jeanette Jurado's vocal, can be found on their 1995 *Greatest Hits* album. Also on *Exposure* is the aggressive, soulful Top Ten hit "Let Me Be the One," which featured strong lead vocals from Gioia Bruno, although the single version was considerably beefed up from the version found here. Bruno also lends her powerhouse vocals to the dramatic ballad "December," and exemplifies how this trio differed from the rest—all three members were talented and effective lead singers, and were just as adept tackling club tunes, R&B songs, and pop ballads. (Ann Curless takes the lead on the club hit "Exposed to Love," among others.) Finally, this set includes their most famous ballad, "Seasons Change," a number one smash from early 1988 which further showcased the group's versatility. This album typifies the essence of '80s pop/dance music, and no accurate '80s collection would be complete without these hits from Exposé, one of the biggest acts of their time. *—Jose F. Promis*

What You Don't Know / 1989 / Arista ✦✦✦✦✦

Producer Lewis Martineé fashioned Exposé with a poppier sound on their sophomore set. The sturdy dance grooves are still there, but they're not as steeped in the nightclubs as those on *Exposure*. A healthy variety of strong selections are included. Among the best are the spunky title track (a Top Ten pop hit), replete with snazzy horns, a colorful guitar solo, and a fiery lead vocal by Gioia; "Stop, Listen, Look & Think," a subtler uptempo number with an understated yet memorable lead by Ann Curless; and the sultry, summertime slow-groove "When I Looked at Him" (also a Top Ten hit), on which Jeanette Jurado's laid-back performance brings to mind Belinda Carlisle. Perhaps the strongest cut, though, is the defiant ballad "Didn't It Hurt to Hurt Me." Gioia's assured, powerful delivery here makes the perfect match for the soulful melodies and honest, straightforward lyrics. (Sadly, a vocal cyst would force her to depart the group in 1991, but she would return to singing in 1997 fronting the rock band Wet.) A solid set essential for any fan of '80s pop/dance. *—Justin M. Kantor*

Exposé / Nov. 3, 1992 / Arista ✦✦✦✦

Exposé had a hard time fitting into the radio trends of the moment with their third album, which came three and a half years after *What You Don't Know*. The Latin-spiced dance/club sounds that made such an impact on pop radio in the latter half of the '80s had been replaced by grunge and alternative rock, and the "girl group" concept had fizzled. Despite this, the trio managed a Top Ten hit with the Diane Warren-penned ballad "I'll Never Get Over You," a somewhat formulaic AC number. Arista tried to capitalize on this success by releasing two other Wilson Phillips-esque soft rock numbers, "As Long as I Can Dream" and "In Walked Love." This wasn't to much avail, and the cream of the crop was never tasted. Surefire dance numbers like the house-driven "I Think I'm in Trouble," the nostalgic "Angel" and "Give Me All Your Love," a return to the group's freestyle roots, were sorely overlooked. Though the powerful voice of Gioia is missed here (she left the group in 1991), replacement Kelly Moneymaker brings added depth to the group's harmony, and Ann Curless shows her flexibility as a lead singer for the first time. Another first is the use of producers besides Lewis Martineé, which results in a more varied sound that is a bit scattered at times, but ultimately disproves the notion of Exposé as studio puppets. *—Justin M. Kantor*

● **Greatest Hits** / 1995 / Arista ✦✦✦✦✦

F

Facts of Life

Group / Deep Soul, Soul, Disco

Millie Jackson credits friends Keith Williams and Chuck Carter with teaching her how to sing at the outset of her music career. She met Jean Davis (Tyrone Davis' sister) on the road; Jean was opening for Tyrone and they became friends. When lack of time prevented Jackson from producing individual records on Williams, Carter, and Davis, she assembled them into a group called Facts of Life. They were similar to the Soul Children, but less dynamic than the Memphis group. Jackson produced them independently, but couldn't cut a deal with a major label and was about to give up when her producer, Brad Shapiro, offered Facts of Life a contract with his Kayvette label.

Their first single was Homer Banks' and Carl Hampton's "Caught in the Middle," which did OK on Southern stations but never mainstreamed. However, the second release, a remake of the country hit "Sometimes," soared to number 31 on the pop chart in the spring of 1977. Kayvette hurried an album out, Millie was hot at the time, and had little time for the project. George Jackson and Raymond Moore contributed two songs, and they tried another country standard "Looks Like We Made It." Poor packaging, including typos, misspelled words, and a bad picture hurt the album's appeal. Despite the problems though, RCA Records plucked it for mass distribution.

A second LP, *A Matter of Time*, spawned no hits. Overloaded, Millie Jackson concentrated more on her career, and other than mass mailings, little promotion took place. Williams, Carter, and Davis separated and never surfaced again. *—Andrew Hamilton*

• **Sometimes** / 1978 / RCA ♦♦♦

The protégés of Millie Jackson, Facts of Life were two men and one woman who came across like the Soul Children on barbiturates. A remake of "Sometimes" was more country than soul, but the lyrics and straightforward vocals hit home, and it became the pinnacle of their short career. Their first release, "Caught in the Act," got some airplay in the South but never broke anywhere else, and Frederick Knight's "Uphill Peace of Mind" stalled. If you like deep soul with a country flavor, this isn't bad, but their lineup forces comparisons to the Soul Children, and given a choice, the latter is preferred. *—Andrew Hamilton*

A Matter of Time / 1978 / Kayvette ♦♦♦

The Facts of Life's final LP traveled the same road as their first, except it didn't produce any hits. The Facts of Life are invariably compared to the Soul Children, but whereas the Soul Children sung Southern and deep soul, the Facts specialized in saucing up country and R&B covers, which they do here on "He Ain't Your Baby" and "I'm Way Ahead of You." Their first LP was a rush job, but they had more time with this one, working in "This Ain't No Time to Sleep Apart" and Aretha Franklin's "Dr. Feelgood," as well as "We Can't Hide It Anymore," a flop for Sylvia Robinson and Chuck Jackson. A remake of Johnny Taylor's "Did He Make Love to You?" is marred by an unconvincing, scripted rap between Jean Davis and one of the male singers. *—Andrew Hamilton*

The Falcons

f. 1956, Detroit, MI, **db.** 1963

Group / Soul

Often credited as having cut the first true soul record in 1959 with "You're So Fine," a host of '60s soul stars called themselves Falcons at one time or another, including founder Eddie Floyd, Wilson Pickett, Bonny "Mack" Rice, and 100 Proof Aged in Soul's Joe Stubbs. Originally an integrated R&B group headed by Floyd, the Falcons debuted on Mercury in 1955. Under the production aegis of Robert West, the Falcons' sound became more gospel-based as time passed, and with Stubbs as lead, the seminal "You're So Fine" was a major hit in 1959. Pickett screamed the gospel-fired ballad "I Found a Love" to national prominence on West's LuPine label in 1962, backed by guitarist Robert Ward's Ohio Untouchables. When Pickett went solo shortly thereafter, the members went their separate ways. West recruited another group, the Fabulous Playboys, who took over the Falcons name, but with little success. *—Bill Dahl*

You're So Fine / 1986 / Relic ♦♦♦♦

The Falcons started as a racially mixed group; Eddie Floyd was the nephew of Bob West, the owner of Lupine and Flick Records. West routinely farmed their singles out to United Artists Records for national distribution. After the exit of the two Caucasians, Bob Manardo and Tom Shetler, one got drafted, and the other joined the Army, the group continued with Joe Stubbs, Willie Schoefield, Bonny "Mack" Rice, Lance Finnie and Eddie Floyd. Rice previously recorded with the Five Scalders, and later scored as a songwriter with "Mustang Sally" and "Respect Yourself." You couldn't call the Falcons R&B until Joe Stubbs joined, adding his rough tenor leads. "You're So Fine," led by Stubbs (Levi Stubbs' brother), had a bouncy, shuffle beat; a plucky guitar played a prominent role, also. It became their biggest-selling single charting at number-six R&B and placing number-17 pop. A copy-cat follow-up, "Just for Your Love," stalled at number-26 R&B. They only released two or three singles a year during their peak. Some of their better numbers were never released as singles. One such track, "Girl of My Dreams," features a righteous lead from Stubbs and perky unison backing blends. Many of the songs were recorded prior to Stubbs joining, and all are pre-Wilson Pickett, who took Stubbs' place when Joe left. The pre-Stubbs material sounds like a different group, they were straight '50s pop and had no edge. Supposedly, "Goddess of Love," a slow, Johnny Mathis-type ballad, is led by Eddie Floyd. Like other Floyd leads from this era, he sounded nothing like he did years later at Stax Records. In fact, you'll think it was one of the white members. As there is no resemblance to the guy who later scored with southern-fried soul confessions like "Knock on Wood" at all. *You're So Fine* is a mixture of the two different styles. *—Andrew Hamilton*

• **I Found a Love** / 1986 / Relic ♦♦♦♦

Part two of the Falcons' story includes tracks by a young Wilson Pickett. It also omits some tracks by Pickett like "Pow! You're in Love," so the selections could have been better. Pickett was 19 years old when he recorded the soulful "I Found a Love," and while it's been remade by heavyweights like Johnny Taylor, none can touch the original. Despite its majesty it only went to number-75 pop; however, it cracked the R&B Top Ten at number six. Pickett also showed early brilliance on "Take This Love I Got." No knock to Joe Stubbs, but with Pickett on lead the Falcons were magic. It was Stubbs who led their most successful recording "You're So Fine" (number-17 pop, number-two R&B). The Falcons used many leads, including Bonny "Mack" Rice ("Good Fellas"), Stubbs ("You Know I Must Love You," among others), Carlis Monroe ("Lonely Nights," "Has It Happened to You") and Eddie Floyd. The helping is decent—16 sides cut the old way, and most were mundane—but when label owner Robert West got it right, the results were breathtaking. *—Andrew Hamilton*

The Family

f. Minneapolis, MN, **db.** 1984

Group / Urban

When the Time broke up in 1984, its ex-members had no problem keeping busy. Morris Day pursued a solo career, while Jesse Johnson formed Jesse Johnson's Revue and produced albums for singer Ta Mara and her band the Seen. And three other Time graduates—singer/keyboardist St. Paul Peterson, drummer Jellybean Johnson, and percussionist Jerome Benton—assembled a short-lived band called the Family (which shouldn't be confused with a gospel act of the same name). When they hired lead singer Susannah Melvoin (the daughter of jazz pianist Mike Melvoin and the twin sister of Wendy Melvoin of Revolution and Wendy & Lisa fame) and saxophonist Eric Leeds in 1984, the Family's five-person lineup was in place. The band quickly signed with Prince's Paisley Park label, and its self-titled debut album came out the following year. Although the Family had an intriguing single in "The Screams of Passion," its very Minneapolis-sounding album wasn't the major hit that the Time's three albums had been. In 1985, the Family broke up without ever recording a second album. *—Alex Henderson*

• **The Family** / 1985 / Paisley Park ♦♦♦

As huge as Prince's Minneapolis sound was in 1985, one would have expected a band boasting three ex-members of the Time to hit big. But the urban contemporary and pop markets can be incredibly fickle, and this self-titled debut album by the Family wasn't the blockbuster some folks predicted it would be. Not surprisingly, this release is about as Minneapolis-sounding as it gets, and the heavy Prince/Time influence is undeniable. *The Family* isn't among the true classics that came from Minneapolis in the 1980s; it isn't in a class with Prince's *Purple Rain*, the Time's *Ice Cream Castles*, or Sheila E.'s *The Glamorous Life*, but it's competent and generally decent. Produced by David Z, this LP ranges from the sweaty funk of "High Fashion" and "Mutiny" to moodier items like "Desire" and the single "The Screams of Passion." Also noteworthy is the band's interesting version of Prince's "Nothing Compares 2 U." After the Family's breakup, this LP went out of print. And by the end of the 1980s, it was becoming increasingly difficult to find. *—Alex Henderson*

The Family Stand

Group / Club/Dance, Acid Jazz, Urban, Soul

The Family Stand consists of Dallas, TX, native Sandra St. Victor, Jeffrey Smith, and Peter Lord, a native New Yorker. Lord and Smith originally answered to Evon Jeffries & the Stand, and recorded under that name two years prior to becoming the Family Stand. Though they have three albums to their credit, their biggest fame has come from "Promise of a New Day," a tune co-written with Paula Abdul and sung by the former Los Angeles Lakers dancer. Jacci McGhee, replaced St. Victor on *Connected*, their latest CD, released in 1998.

St. Victor left to solo, coming out with *Mack Diva Saves the World* on Warner Brothers Records. The members have played with the top names in rock; Smith, as a saxophone player. Lord, a vocalist and keyboardist, earned a degree in musical composition from Howard University and played with bands from the D.C. area. Returning to New York,

Lord teamed with Smith and produced and wrote for Miki Howard, the Mac Band, Donna Allen, Good Fellas, Will Downing, Corey Glover, and Ali to name a short list. St. Victor attended the University of Kansas and studied classical music. Moving to New York, she became in demand as a vocalist on the road and in the studio working with Freddie Jackson, Roy Ayers, Chaka Khan, Nile Rodgers, Kashif, Glenn Jones, and others.

The Family Stand's first LP *Chain*, produced the single "Ghetto Heaven," a favorite in discos, none of the Atlantic LP's other songs' "Sweet Liberation," "In Summer I Fall," "Chain," or "Twisted," broke out. A second LP *Moon in Scorpio*, appeared on East West Records but had too much rock and not enough soul for urban listeners and failed to register; they didn't release another CD until 1998, the much ballyhooed *Connected*, on Elektra/Asylum Records. The album loses the tripping acid sound and delves heavily into the brand of soul that made the '70s musically exciting. When it didn't sell, Elektra released them at their insistence. During the six years between albums, Lord & Smith added McGhee and concentrated on writing and producing. Don't be surprised if the Family Stand rises again, it's hard to keep a good, talented group down. *—Andrew Hamilton*

Chain / 1990 / Atlantic ♦♦♦

Chain consists of ten tracks traveling in different directions. The much ballyhooed "Ghetto Heaven" attempts to capture the power of Marvin Gaye and Curtis Mayfield in social significancy but has the impact of a mosquitoe. It gets better with "Only" which has a mock reggae beat that bottoms an infectious melody; "In Summer I Fall" is a sweet beat ballad with a warm lead from Sandra St. Victor. "Oversaxed" displays V. Jeffrey Smith smooth sax skills. "The Last Temptation" owes as much to gospel as it does soul, and exemplifies the diversity of this LP. The title track "Chain," is melodic in a muddy way, the muffled sound gives the shuffling rhythm an eerie effect. Third member Peter Lord contributes vocals and his immense keyboard skills to a project that doesn't equal the sum of the individuals involved. *—Andrew Hamilton*

• **Moon in Scorpio** / 1991 / East West ♦♦♦♦

The Family Stand's small but loyal following argued that *Moon In Scorpio* was simply too ambitious and too creative for urban contemporary radio, and they're right. Much of the material was too rock-minded for R&B stations, and even the CD's less guitar-heavy offerings (such as "The Education of Jamie," "Plantation Radio" and the Prince-like "Quiet Desperation") didn't make the playlists of stations that were only interested in finding the next Guy clone or yet another Teddy Riley wannabe. "Plantation Radio," in fact, lambasts urban radio's frustrating conservatism. But while *Moon In Scorpio* wasn't a huge commercial hit, its meaty blend of R&B and rock was a creative triumph. One can hear a variety of soul and rock influences on this album—not only Prince and Sly & the Family Stone, but also, Ike & Tina Turner and Mother's Finest. In fact, Sandra St. Victor's gritty vocals bear a definite resemblance to MF singer Joyce Kennedy, while Peter Lord's singing has a Prince-like quality. Although such comparisons are well and good, it's important to stress that the Family Stand is a fine band in its own right. *Moon In Scorpio* is an underexposed gem that's well worth searching for. *—Alex Henderson*

Connected / Feb. 24, 1998 / East West ♦♦♦

Years after attempting to take the urban R&B world by storm, the Family Stand returned in 1998 with *Connected*. Peter Lord and Jeffrey Smith have added a new vocalist, Jacci McGhee, who fits right into the group's retro-soul. The band excels at classy soul and funk, sounding like a hybrid of Sly Stone, Prince, Marvin Gaye and Stevie Wonder. When they try to push their limits a bit too far, they collapse under their own ambition, be it lyrical or musical, but at its best, *Connected* is well-constructed contemporary soul that shows more craft and heart than many efforts in a similar vein. *—Stephen Thomas Erlewine*

The Fantastic Four

f. 1965, Detroit, MI

Group / Pop-Soul, Disco, Funk

Detroit R&B and soul group the Fantastic Four formed in 1965. "Sweet" James Epps, Ralph and Joseph Pruitt, and Wallace Childs were the original members. Childs and Ralph Pruitt later departed, and were replaced by Cleveland Horne and Ernest Newsome. Their first single on Ric-Tic, "The Whole World Is a Stage," was their lone huge hit, peaking at number 6 on the R&B charts in 1967. The next release, "You Gave Me Something (And Everything's Alright)," reached number 12 that same year. Motown eventually purchased Ric-Tic, and they had another Top 20 R&B hit with "I Love You Madly," which came out in 1968 and was also issued on Soul.

The Fantastic Four enjoyed renewed appeal during the disco era with some singles on Westbound that were moderately successful, among them "Alvin Stone (The Birth & Death of a Gangster)" and "I Got to Have Your Love." Dennis Coffey produced "B.Y.O.F. (Bring Your Own Funk)" in 1979, but didn't have much luck with it. The Fantastic Four have remained active, and released "Working on a Building of Love" in 1990 for Britian's Motorcity label. In 2000, however, the Fantastic Four lost one of its long-time members, Cleveland Horne when he suffered a heart attack and died on April 13, 2000. *—Ron Wynn*

• **Best of the Fantastic Four** / 1969 / Motown ♦♦♦♦

An overdue compilation of the Fantastic Four's Ric-Tic Record releases; strangely, only one Motown release is included, that being "I Love You Madly." Motown acquired Golden World/Ric-Tic Records, making the Fantastic Four Motown artists. The group had a changing lineup, but the personnel on most of these cuts was lead James Epps, Ralph Pruitt, Joseph Pruitt, and Wallace Childs; Ernie Newsome sang with them on their Westbound sides, and possibly on some Motown recordings. All the songs that made them chitlin circuit favorites are included: "The Whole World Is a Stage," "You Gave Me Something (And Everything Is Alright)," and "To Share Your Love." "Just the Lonely" is interesting because it's so similar to "Just Another Lonely Night" by the Temptations. "Man in Love" was a new direction for the fellas; it has a nice jazzy break and some soothing vocal blends. Hopefully, one day Motown will compile a CD that will include all their Motown sides along with the Ric-Tic cuts. *—Andrew Hamilton*

Alvin Stone (The Birth and Death of a Gangster) / 1975 / Westbound ♦♦♦♦

The Fantastic Four were Detroit nightclub legends who never made the big time, members came and went, with lead singer James Epps the only constant. *Alvin Stone (The Birth and Death of a Gangster)* remains the brightest star of a lackluster career. The cover depicts the front page of a newspaper with a headline announcing the death of Alvin Stone. The title track chronicles and glorifies the life of fictional gangster Alvin Stone; it has good lyrics worthy of a gangsta-rap update, a throbbing beat, and a great vocal from Epps. Three churning ballads, some of the group's best ever, also make this LP essential: "Words" speaks of the power of words as weapons—good creative stuff; "Let This Moment Last Forever" displays the group at their best, singing about love on a number loaded with sentiment; the tempo of "My Love Won't Stop at Nothing" changes from slow to fast, climaxing at the end. Only six songs, but each is a powerhouse. *—Andrew Hamilton*

Night People / 1976 / Westbound ♦♦

Alvin Stone (The Birth and Death of a Gangster)/Night People / May 22, 2001 / Westbound ♦♦♦

The Fantastic Johnny C. (Johnny Corley)

b. Apr. 28, 1943, Greenwood, SC

Vocals / Pop-Soul, Soul

The Fantastic Johnny C. was born Johnny Corley on April 28, 1943, in Greenwood, SC. He joined the armed services at an early age, leaving Brewer High in Greenwood before graduating to enlist. When his military duty ended, he moved to Norristown, PA, a small city 18 miles from Philadelphia, and found work as a heavy-equipment operator while becoming increasingly unable to resist the temptation to sing professionally. R&B producer Jesse James attended the same church as Corley and quickly spotted his talent. James made a career out of transforming gospel singers into secular performers; he discovered Cliff "the Horse" Nobles a short time later at the same church. James became Corley's manager and wrote songs for him—one of them, "Boogaloo Down Broadway," convinced Corley to give pop music a serious try. "Broadway" became a big hit, hitting number five on the R&B charts and number seven on the pop charts. The follow-up, "Got What You Need," didn't surpass or equal "Broadway," but it did chart, while "Hitch It to the Horse" bounced onto the R&B charts, and even crept into the pop Top 40, in 1968.

His stage name came about when some acquaintances of both James and Corley stated almost in unison, "That's fantastic—what are you going to call him?" after hearing "Boogaloo Down Broadway." Hearing their response, James first came up with the Fantastic Johnny Corley before shortening it to the Fantastic Johnny C. His first gig was at the Uptown Theater in Philadelphia, sharing a bill with Sam & Dave, the Vibrations, and Joe Simon. Phil La of Soul released his only album, *Boogaloo Down Broadway*, a mini-masterpiece of gritty soul containing the deep soul cuts "Warm and Tender Love," "Shout Bamalama," and many dance tunes: "Cool Broadway," "Barefootin'," "The Bounce," and "Land of a Thousand Dances." Corley continued to sing in church while recording secular music. When he scored his first hit, he stated that his goal was to be the "number one soul brother," and, while he failed to achieve that lofty title, he did land among the stars for brief period courtesy of his explosive recordings. *—Andrew Hamilton*

• **Boogaloo Down Broadway** / 1968 / Phil-L.A.S. ♦♦♦♦♦

Hot on the heels of his "Boogaloo Down Broadway" single, this album was not a burningly original statement, and didn't contain anything else on the order of "Boogaloo Down Broadway," but was an enjoyable mix of soul covers and originals penned by producer Jesse James. The arrangements cook really well in a lean funk-soul groove; "Cool Broadway," admittedly a knockoff of the "Boogaloo Down Broadway" vibe, has a fractured rhythm anticipating the innovations of the Meters a couple of years later. "Got What You Need" was a small soul hit, and "Baby I Need You" was a capable deep soul-type ballad. [The CD reissue adds two bonus tracks: "Hitch It to the Horse," a minor hit in 1968, and "Look What Love Can Make You Do," awhich is basically the same track as "Boogaloo Down Broadway" with different lyrics.] *—Richie Unterberger*

Fantasy

Group / Club/Dance, Euro-Dance, Disco

Fantasy was a group comprised of two females and two males, assembled and produced by Tony Valor. Their biggest single "You're Too Late" charted disco for five weeks in 1981. It was taken from the *Fantasy* album on Pavillion Records, the first of two albums—the second being 1982's *Sex & Material Possessions*. Vocally they were weak, more pop than soul, with too much reliance on a light-voiced female vocalist. Unlike New York and Philly disco, Fantasy was a flyweight, the sound didn't have the devastating beats that American clubbers like, but was more classy, hustle-styled disco. Hot Productions remembers them with repackaged compilations of their Pavillion recordings: *The Best of Fantasy* in 1990, and two more in the mid-'90s, *He's Number One* and *You're Too Late*. *—Andrew Hamilton*

Fantasy / 1981 / Pavillion ♦♦♦

Not to be confused with the rock group Fantasy, this Fantasy was among the numerous R&B/disco/funk groups to be heavily influenced by Chic. Fantasy had a Chic-like image—two women (Tamm E. Hunt, Carolyn Edwards) and two men (Ken Robertson, Rufus Jackson) wearing very upscale disco attire—and this self-titled LP even employs Chic alumnae Luci Martin and Norma Jean Wright as background vocalists. But despite all that, it would be wrong to think of Fantasy as Chic clones. True, the Chic influence is impossible to miss on "Love Explosion" and the single "You're Too Late." But a more Shalamar-influenced approach prevails on "(Hey Who's Gotta) Funky Song," and the harmonies on "Read Between the Lines" are closer to the Emotions than Chic. Meanwhile, the sentimental "Now That I Have Everything" successfully blends disco, doo wop, and Afro-Caribbean music. Not a gem but definitely pleasing, *Fantasy* is far from the work of knee-Chic clones—even though Chic's influence is among the useful tools in the group's arsenal. *—Alex Henderson*

Sex and Material Possessions / 1982 / Pavillion ♦♦♦

• **The Best of Fantasy: You're Too Late** / Jun. 27, 1990 / Hot Productions ♦♦♦
Tony Valor produced, arranged, and wrote (most of) the tracks. The quartet consists of two ladies and two men with one of the females delivering most of the leads in a light, airy vocal style that seldom ranges up or down. Valor saddles them with a light pop-ish sound that may please music lightweights, but not a heavyweight. Some decent tracks include "You're Too Late," "Move Into the Groove," "I Just Want to Get Your Lovin'," and "He's Number One." *—Andrew Hamilton*

Dionne Farris

Vocals / Urban

Dionne Farris came to the attention of the music world with her vocal contributions to Arrested Development's breakthrough hit single "Tennessee," plus other tracks on the group's 1992 debut. Farris started singing in high school, performing in her school's choir in Bordentown, NJ, and starring in a production of *Annie*. From there, she sang on Manhattan's club circuit, both solo and with a female vocal group called Onyx, but grew frustrated in her late teens. She moved to Atlanta to live with her father in 1990 and started dating drummer Rasha Don, an early member of Arrested Development. The group was looking for a female singer, and while joining a band didn't fit Farris' plans, she had nothing better to do. Farris was never really an official member of Arrested Development, characterizing herself more as part of its extended family.

After "Tennessee" broke, Farris got enough media attention to cause personal conflicts with bandleader Speech, and she split from the group in 1993. Chrysalis, Arrested Development's record company, was willing to offer her a solo deal, but Farris took a gamble and rejected it, hoping for more artistic control than Chrysalis wanted to give her. She contacted former members of funk-rock band Follow For Now, David Harris and Milton Davis, and she and guitarist Harris began to collaborate on material. Her demo made its way to Sony Music, and her solo debut, *Wild Seed—Wild Flower*, was released in the summer of 1994, spawning the hit single "I Know." *—Steve Huey*

• **Wild Seed—Wild Flower** / 1995 / Columbia ♦♦♦♦♦
Following a successful stint with Arrested Development, including lending her vocals to their smash "Tennessee," Dionne Farris enlisted members of the band Follow For Now for her 1994 debut. Although *Wild Seed—Wild Flower* only managed to spawn one hit, the percolating, infectious "I Know" was a monster, dominating the airwaves and lodging inside the Top Ten for months. It's hardly the only noteworthy track on this consistently engaging debut which blends funk, rock, pop, and folk. The insightful, soul-searching, and often self-empowering message of the lyrics is given added credence by the supple, soulful vocals of Farris and the musicianship doesn't let her down. Highlights include the sample-laden "Stop to Think" (with musical assistance from Lenny Kravitz), the uplifting "Passion," the heartfelt, introspective "Food for Thought," and the potent "Don't Ever Touch Me (Again)." Intelligent and winning, *Wild Seed—Wild Flower*'s charms run much deeper than "I Know," making for a striking initial effort. *—Tom Demalon*

The Fascinations

db. 1969

Group / Girl Group, Uptown Soul, Pop-Soul

The Fascinations were a girl group with a dazzling family tree, a distinctive sound, and a hook-up with one of the great artist-producers of the 1960s—yet, in one of the great mysteries of the soul music boom of the mid-decade, they never made it in America, but sold lots of records in England.

Detroit in the late '50s was a city seething with musical activity—Robert West's LuPine label, Berry Gordy's embryonic Motown, and the immensely successful Vee-Jay label were just the tip of a pop culture iceberg. One of the groups trying to get a foothold on success in those days was an all-girl outfit called the Sabre-ettes, who were in the market for some new members. Two co-founders, Shirley Walker and Martha Reeves, were doing the auditions, and they brought gospel singers Joanne and Bernadine Boswell into the lineup, which quickly expanded by one more slot with the addition of Fern Bledsoe. The resulting quintet was rechristened the Fascinations. Martha Reeves left the group in 1960 for her own path to stardom, and the Fascinations were permanently a quartet. Two years later, they made the acquaintance of Fred Cash and Sam Gooden, two members of the Impressions. They, in turn, introduced the Fascinations to Curtis Mayfield, who got the group signed to ABC-Paramount, where they released a trio of singles (written and/or produced by Mayfield) over the next year that failed to sell in significant numbers.

ABC-Paramount lost interest in the Fascinations, but Mayfield never did—his success in 1966 with the Windy C label enabled him to start the Mayfield label, and to sign the Fascinations. The group's first Mayfield release, "Say It Isn't So," only got to number 47 on the R&B charts, but their second, "Girls Are out to Get You," did crack the lower reaches of the pop charts, while ascending to number 13 as an R&B hit. It also became the group's first release in England, on EMI's Stateside label (ironically, also the company's outlet for Motown). The quartet never scored very high in America, despite a switch to ballads, with which they were far more comfortable—it seemed as though they were never there with the right song at the right time. By 1969, they'd decided to call it quits as far as recording, and their history on vinyl came to an end.

The irony was that, in England, their records continued to sell. "Girls Are out to Get You" became immensely popular in British dance clubs, and was reissued by the Sue Records label, for which it sold steadily. In 1971, the song charted in the U.K. when it was reissued yet again, this time on the Mojo imprint of British Polydor—the number 32 placement, with heavy airplay, even led to a reunion and a British tour by the quartet—it was a brief, welcomed moment in the spotlight, before thousands of adoring fans from one corner of the globe, even if it wasn't their corner, and made the nine or ten years of work seem sweeter. Unfortunately, Mojo's efforts to coax similar sales out of their other Mayfield releases came to nothing, and the members soon returned to their post-career activities. The Fascinations weren't much more than an odd footnote in the history of Detroit-based R&B, in terms of their sales impact and their early history as Martha Reeves' first group. They never recorded steadily or successfully enough to justify an album release during the time they were together, but they turned in some delightful and intensely passionate (and playful, in the case of "Girls Are out to Get You") soul performances. They deserved (and, for a moment in England, got) the kind of recognition and treatment that seemed to come easily to a lot of Motown-signed girl groups of the period. *—Bruce Eder*

• **Out to Get'cha** / May 6, 1997 / Sequel ♦♦♦♦♦
Where to begin? For starters, this is an almost perfect collection of the Fascinations' work, containing all of their released work for Mayfield Records plus a couple of outtakes—the only thing that might've been better would have been to get the rights to the ABC-Paramount sides, as well. As it is, we're presented with the extraordinarily upbeat, infectiously memorable and beautifully sung work of a one great group that Berry Gordy and Motown never got a crack at. Each song is like a new piece of buried treasure unearthed, an ear-stunning chorus here, a lung-bursting lead vocal there, and hard, precise arrangements with thick, muscular horn sounds and razor textures on the guitars, courtesy of Mayfield's production ("Trusting in You" alone is worth the price of the CD, just for the texture of the voices and the backing band that Mayfield and company achieve). "Girls Are out to Get You" is a known quantity, catchy and exciting, but the ballads, such as "I'm So Lucky" and "Such a Fool" have an elegant beauty all of their own-Bernadine Boswell is the most prominent singer here, a magnificently expressive soul singer whose gospel roots are revealed in her every sustained note and passionate inflection. Boswell's performance on "I Can't Stay Away From You," a combination of spoken introduction and exit, and a slow, agonizingly soulful middle, is the stuff that Grammy nominations are made of in charting records (alas . . . .) "Say It Isn't So," which is as close as Mayfield or the Fascinations ever got to imitating Motown, appears in two completely different takes, of which the second is more clearly enunciated but the first sings in a juggernaut group sound. The 13 Fascinations sides are augmented by the presence of ten tracks cut by the Mayfield Singers, a generic ensemble associated with the label, left in varying states of completion—they're just icing, however, on an extraordinary musical cake. *—Bruce Eder*

Fat Larry's Band

f. 1977, Philadelphia, PA, **db.** 1987

Group / Disco, Funk

This was an entertaining Philadelphia funk band, fronted by drummer "Fat" Larry James. Fat Larry's Band never scored any major hits, but their singles for Stax, Fantasy, and Omni were prototype late-'70s and '80s East Coast jazz-tinged funk. Trumpeter and flute player Arthur Capehart, trombonist and alto saxophonist Jimmy Lee, saxophonist Doug Jones, keyboardist Erskine Williams, guitarist Ted Cohen, bassist Larry LaBes, and percussionist Darryl Grant completed the lineup. Their best song aesthetically was "Act Like You Know," a 1982 tune with a surging bassline and simple but catchy lyric refrain. James also played with the Delphonics and Blue Magic and managed the group Slick. A good performer and charismatic personality, James died very prematurely in 1987 at age 38. *—Ron Wynn*

• **Greatest Hits** / 1995 / Fantasy ♦♦♦♦

Fatback Band

f. 1970, **db.** 1985

Group / Funk, Disco

A seminal funk ensemble, the Fatback Band made many great singles through the '70s and early '80s, ranging from humorous novelty tunes to energetic dance vehicles and even occasional political/message tracks. The original lineup featured drummer Bill Curtis, trumpeter George Williams, guitarist Johnny King, bassist Johnny Flippin, saxophonist Earl Shelton, and flute player George Adam. Synthesizer player Gerry Thomas, saxophonist Fred Demerey, and guitarist George Victory were integral parts of the group during their peak years. They began recording for Perception in the early '70s, and had moderate luck with "Street Dance" in 1973. They moved to Event in 1974, and while funk audiences loved such songs as "Wicki-Wacky" and "(Are You Ready) Do the Bus Stop," they didn't generate much sales action. Their first sizable hit was "Spanish Hustle" in 1976, which reached number 12 on the R&B charts.

They shortened their name to Fatback in 1977, and landed their first Top Ten R&B hit with "I Like Girls" in 1978. Their 1979 single "King Tim III (Personality Jock)" is widely considered the first rap single in many circles. But their biggest year was 1980. They scored two Top Ten R&B hits with "Gotta Get My Hands on Some (Money)" and "Backstrokin'," their finest tune. Fatback kept going through the mid-'80s, landing one more Top 20 hit with "Take It Any Way You Can Want It" in 1981. They were backed by the female vocal trio Wild Sugar in 1981-1982, and Evelyn Thomas also provided the lead vocal for "Spread Love" in 1985, their last song for Spring. Fatback also recorded a pair of LPs for Cotillion in 1984 and 1985. *—Ron Wynn*

Let's Do It Again / 1972 / Perception ♦♦♦

People Music / 1973 / Deep Beats ♦♦♦♦
Following up on its first successful R&B single, "Street Dance," the Fatback Band released 1973's *People Music* (their second album on the Perception label). While it doesn't include any hits or even near misses, it does have a nice mix of the group's signature, in-the-pocket funk-jazz jams. Combining the horn-driven soul of Stax with the tight groove of the J.B.'s (James Brown's early-'70s band), the band works through nine mostly solid tracks. The influence of the J.B.'s is readily heard on the fast-paced "Fatbackin'" and "Kiba," while premonitions of the coming disco era are evident on bumpin' cuts like "Nija Walk" and "Soul March." Supplying contrast to these instrumentals, the band indulges in a few vocal cuts with various band members taking the mike; although the after-hours jazz and flutes cut "To Be With You" includes a regrettable vocal turn by bassist Johnny Flippin, guitarist Johnny King's pleading and vulnerable performance on "Baby Doll" does comes off nicely. And rounding out the group's impressive roster are other original

members like tenor saxophonist George Adams, trumpeter George Williams, and drummer Bill Curtis. *People Music* is an enjoyable disc, but newcomers might want to check out one of the band's greatest hits packages first. *—Stephen Cook*

Keep on Steppin' / 1974 / Southbound ♦♦

The Fatback Band didn't enjoy as much chart success with this mid-'70s LP as most others from this period. There weren't any classic novelty tunes or great dance or message tracks; it was simply a functional album with decent horn charts, competent vocals and an occasionally interesting bassline or horn solo. It's among their least remembered and celebrated albums. *—Ron Wynn*

Yum Yum / 1975 / Southbound ♦♦

Fatback's first album outing of 1975 has pleasant grooves to spare but lacks the consistent material or cohesive feel that would make it a memorable album. The highlight is the title track, a relentless groove built on a thick bass line that features the band trading lively double entendres about how "hungry" they are. The ballad "Feed Me With Your Love" tackles similar lyrical territory, but uses a silky midtempo groove layered with plenty of keyboards to powerful effect. Sadly, much of the other material is too thin to sustain the album. Songs like "Put the Funk on You" and "Boogie With the Fatback" have got a similar party-hearty style and benefit from an engaging live-in-the-studio feel, but lack the strong hooks and clever arrangement that characterize "Yum Yum." The album is also saddled with weak tracks like "Trompin'" and "Let the Drums Speak," songs that trudge along through endlessly repeated chants as they run their central riff into the ground. While *Yum Yum* shows the promise that would later be realized on albums like *Fired Up 'N' Kickin'*, it is too unfocused and tentative to please anyone except Fatback's most devoted fans. Since the hit title track can easily be tracked down on compilations, funk fanatics should think twice before getting this album. *—Donald A. Guarisco*

Raising Hell / 1975 / Southbound ♦♦♦

Fatback's second album of 1975 is a serious improvement over *Yum Yum*: the arrangements are tighter, the hooks are stronger, and the grooves keep the listener riveted from start to finish. It downplays the live feel of previous albums like *Keep on Steppin'* in favor of a more carefully arranged feel that highlights the tasty keyboard and synthesizer work of Gerry Thomas. *Raising Hell* also produced two major hits for the group: "(Are You Ready) Do the Bus Stop" capitalizes on the dance craze of the title with a steady bass-driven groove that works in layers of keyboards, guitars, and horns to keep things interesting, and "Spanish Hustle" is a propulsive dance jam that alternates synthesizer flights of fancy with intense Latin percussion breaks guaranteed to make the listeners shake their hips. The album tracks that back up these singles don't make their presence felt as strongly, but none ever descend to the level of filler: "Groovy Kind of Day" alternates smooth harmony vocals with jazzy electric-piano riffs to create a smooth midtempo track and the group's cover of the Four Tops' classic "I Can't Help Myself" is cleverly re-arranged to fit Fatback's dancefloor format. The result is a fine collection of funky dance music that helped Fatback solidify their reputation as one of New York's foremost disco groups. It remains just as listenable and is worth a spin for disco and funk fans alike. *—Donald A. Guarisco*

Night Fever / 1976 / Southbound ♦♦

This 1976 release from Fatback is an odd proposition: While nothing on it is unlistenable, it is also lacks any memorable moments. The problems begin with the title track: While it bounds out of the gate with a forceful, funky energy, it also recycles riffs and structural ideas from their previous big hit, "Spanish Hustle." The rest of *Night Fever* plays out in a similarly uninspired fashion—it has plenty of energy but lacks the quality songs and carefully constructed arrangements necessary to create a worthwhile dance music album. The result is an album that tries hard but ends up chasing its own tail. A lot of the tracks drive potentially exciting riffs into the ground because they lack an effective arrangement ("The Joint [You and Me]"), while other songs feature the group repeating a chant *ad infinitum* while the band performs an uninspired vamp in the background ("Disco Crazy" and "No More Room on the Dance Floor"). There is also an uninspired cover of the Four Seasons' hit "December 1963 (Oh What a Night)," which fails to add any new ideas to the sound or style of this song. The one track that manages to stand out is "If That's the Way You Want It": While this ballad is as minimalist in style as most of the other tracks here, it benefits from a solid arrangement, atmospheric synthesizer backing, and a truly lovely group-harmony hook. Unfortunately, this bright spot can't make up for the overwhelmingly lackluster quality of *Night Fever*. Even hardcore Fatback fans may want to think twice before picking this album up. *—Donald A. Guarisco*

NYCNYUSA / 1977 / Southbound ♦♦

Man With the Band / 1978 / Southbound ♦♦

Man With the Band finds Fatback stylistically treading water: While they are moving closer to the distinctive blend of funk and disco they would perfect on albums like *Fired Up 'N' Kickin'* and *XII*, the tracks presented here lack the focus and distinctive hooks that made those albums work. The result is an album that grooves along without ever picking up a lot of steam. The epic title track that kicks off the album represents these problems: While it contains some hypnotic moments where the band's energy merges seamlessly with the song's handful of hooks, it ends up dragging because these magical moments are interspersed with too much aimless jamming. Other tracks are reasonably energetic throughout but lack the distinctive riffs or creative arrangements that would make them notable ("Master Booty" and "Funk Backin'"). There are also a couple of throwaways, the most notable one being "Zodiac Man," which tosses out some silly astrology-inspired lyrics over a repetitive, lightweight groove. Despite these problems, there are some moments that manage to gel in a memorable way: "Mile High" blends high harmony vocals and spacy synthesizer lines to create an engagingly jazzy dance tune and "Midnight Freak" carefully molds its relentless groove into a tight arrangement that makes it a strong midtempo jam with a memorably sultry atmosphere. In the end, *Man With the Band* has enough strong moments to make it a worthwhile purchase for disco fanatics but isn't consistent enough to keep the casual listener interested. *—Donald A. Guarisco*

Fired Up 'N' Kickin' / 1978 / Southbound ♦♦♦

Brite Lites, Big City / 1979 / Southbound ♦♦♦

While it doesn't overflow with high points like *Fired Up 'N' Kickin'*, *Brite Lites, Big City* remains a solid album's worth of funky disco. The hooks aren't as instantly catchy as the ones that propelled past hits like "Spanish Hustle" or "I Like Girls," but songs like "Freak the Freak the Funk (Rock)" sport nice big grooves that will keep the listener's toes tapping. The album's big highlights are "Big City," a tribute to New York driven by a surprisingly jazzy horn riff, and "Let Me Do It to You," a percolating funk showcase that cleverly pits male and female vocal sections against each other as it doubles its thumping bass line with the chant mentioned in the title. "Wild Dreams" is another highlight, an interesting tune that contrasts mellow female harmonies against an insistent beat churned out by the rhythm section. Some of the tunes get a bit repetitive at times, most notably "Hesitation" and its reliance on an endlessly-reiterated chant, but the band's performance is strong enough throughout the album to overshadow these moments of weakness. The result is an album that isn't strong enough to win over people who aren't already fans, but will definitely satisfy fans of the Fatback sound. *—Donald A. Guarisco*

XII / 1979 / Southbound ♦♦♦

Fatback maintained the same high standard of quality to produce another impressive slab of funk-tinged disco. *XII* is notable to hip-hop historians for the track "King Tim III (Personality Jock)," a song often tagged as the first rap song (it was released as a single shortly before the more popular "Rapper's Delight" by the Sugarhill Gang). "King Tim" remains a killer blast of hip-hop, seamlessly mixing a slick old-school rap into the band's intensely funky blend of organ, energetic horn blasts, and a relentless walking bassline. However, this isn't all there is to *XII*: The album's other tracks present a consistent mix of funky grit and disco slickness. Standout tracks include "Gimme That Sweet, Sweet Lovin'," which layers a Bee Gees-style falsetto vocal with an addictive midtempo groove anchored by a synthesizer bass, and "Disco Bass," which blends a catchy chant-along chorus with the serpentine hook mentioned in the title. *XII* is also notable for the high quality of its sound, which filters the energy of their sound through a carefully crafted soundscape that brings out all the details of their sound: a good example is how the huge drum sounds that propel "You're My Candy Sweet" seem to leap out of the speakers. The only track that tends toward the filler that has marred past Fatback albums is "Disco Queen," but even it is redeemed by its punchy horn arrangement and some catchy background vocals. All in all, *XII* is one of Fatback's finest albums and a treat for anyone who likes their disco music especially funky. *—Donald A. Guarisco*

Hot Box / 1980 / Southbound ♦♦♦

In 1980, the carefully studio-crafted combination of funk and disco Fatback had been developing on their last few albums paid off with *Hot Box*, an album that spawned some serious R&B chart hits. The big hit from this long-player was "Gotta Get My Hands on Some (Money)," a song driven by a rock-solid synthesizer bassline and a freewheeling, Parliament-like rap about the singer's need to score some cash to keep his head above water. It further spices up its funky stew with an array of vocal-harmony hooks and squiggly, ear-catching synthesizer flourishes to create one of Fatback's finest hits. The album's other notable success was "Backstrokin'," a tune that layered plenty of saucy double entendres over a combination of elongated synthesizer lines and staccato horns. Sadly, the rest of the album never quite captures the infectious yet carefully controlled energy of these hits: The title track works hard but never builds up the head of steam that would make it come to life and "Come and Get the Love" sports a lovely group harmony hook but suffers from humdrum lyrics that lack a fresh take on its very traditional subject. The song that gets closest to the arresting quality of the singles is "Love Spell," which triumphs over its uninteresting rap-styled lead vocal thanks to a doubled group vocal/synthesizer hook that digs deep into the listener's consciousness and takes hold. Overall, *Hot Box* is a solid listen for Fatback fans but those interested in the album's hits would probably be better off picking up a copy of *The Fattest of Fatback*. *—Donald A. Guarisco*

14 Karat / 1980 / Southbound ♦♦♦

Gigolo / 1981 / Southbound ♦♦♦

Tasty Jam / 1981 / Southbound ♦♦♦

By 1981, large-scale R&B bands like Fatback were being pushed to the sidelines by smaller groups whose primarily electronic sounds excluded traditional soul music frills like horn sections. Fatback was obviously paying attention because *Tasty Jam* pares down the group's sound to push synthesizers to the forefront. The resulting fusion of old-fashioned grooves and up-to-date electronics resulted in the group's strongest, most consistent album since *XII*. *Tasty Jam* simply presents six slices of dense, rhythmic electronic funk. It lacks the catchy pop elements of past Fatback outings, but compensates with tight arrangements and arresting rhythms: "Take It Any Way You Want It" is built on a pulsating, polyrhythmic bed of electric piano and synthesizer hooks and "Keep Your Fingers Out the Jams" pits the effectively harmonized chant of the title against a rolling synthesizer bassline guaranteed to induce some hip shaking. "High Steppin' Lady" is another strong track that hooks in listeners with the intriguing contrast between its Latin-flavored percussion and its bubbly, percolating synthesizer lines. The album drags a bit in places, most notably the repetitive grooves of "Kool Whip," but none of the songs ever truly wear out their welcome and the group's compelling mastery of their groove makes up for these occasional shortcomings. In the end, *Tasty Jam* lacks the standout singles that would give it crossover appeal but remains a solid listen for fans of electronic-oriented dance music. *—Donald A. Guarisco*

On the Floor With Fatback / 1982 / Southbound ♦♦♦

Is This the Future? / 1983 / Southbound ♦♦♦

Fatback was always well aware of where the future lay. Keeping their eyes and their funk firmly on the pulse of R&B, Fatback (aka Fatback Band) took their audiences on a two-decade journey of perpetual evolution, wrapping their roots in psychedelic R&B, pop, soul, disco, and on into hip-hop, as that genre was formulated as well. By 1983, the musical pulse was firmly in the hands of the new wave—both in soul and pop. Michael Jackson, Prince, and Cameo ruled the R&B roost, while a thousand bubblegum wannabes beat at the door behind them. Fatback absorbed all this excitement, and once again proved that they could match anyone. *Is This the Future?* is eminently danceable, light funk infused with synthesizers and '80s bass to create a vital brew. Fatback recorded one of the first rap records in 1979, and they repeat the form here. This time, Gerry Bledsoe takes the mike, with a DJ rap through the title track which gives the band a Top 50 R&B hit. "Spread Love," meanwhile, was a strong, effusive slab of danceable pop—and, alongside "The Girl Is Fine (So Fine)" and "Up Against the Wall," really kept the pace flowing. In fact, only "Funky Aerobics (Body Movement)" really lets the side down, a weak presentation of not very well-placed sexual innuendo, and little more than wasted space. On the whole, *Is This the Future* succeeds. It's not the driving funk of earlier renown—in places, it's not even really that funky, and was never intended to be so. It is, however, extremely entertaining, infused with bright energy and further evidence of just what remarkable chameleons Fatback were—changing with the musical tide while keeping their essence intact. *—Amy Hanson*

● **The Fattest of Fatback** / Mar. 18, 1997 / Rhino ♦♦♦♦♦

Those who fail to understand funk often complain about its use of repetition, but funk enthusiasts will tell you that repetition (as James Brown showed us) is something to be savored. A first-class party band, Fatback knew quite well that the secret to effective funk is finding a killer groove and working it to death. That's exactly what happens much of the time on *The Fattest of Fatback*, a 1997 CD that spans 1975-1983 and boasts many of the New York band's essential hits. From "I Like Girls" and "Gotta Get My Hands on Some (Money)" to "Backstrokin'" and "The Girl Is Fine (So Fine)," this CD shows us how exciting Fatback could be when it found the right groove. With 1979's "King Tim III," Fatback became one of the first R&B acts to acknowledge rap, and the pessimistic sociopolitical number "Is This the Future?" was among 1983's most vital and compelling rap singles. Though Fatback was best known for funk, "Can't You See" and "Angel" demonstrate that the band was quite capable of delivering excellent soul ballads. For those checking out Fatback for the first time, *The Fattest of Fatback* is definitely the best starting point. *—Alex Henderson*

Funky / 2002 / Southbound ♦♦♦♦♦

That Fatback Band were enormously influential to the advent of modern hip-hop is an undisputed fact. But it's important, too, to remember how vital the group was to the 1970s funk scene—laying down reverberatingly heavy grooves without antics, combining a tough New York back story with surprising calypso breaks just for fun, and unerringly bringing feet to the dancefloor with unsurpassed energy and finesse. It's odd, and sad really, that listeners would have to be reminded of this via an outstanding U.K. import. With 11 tracks highlighting the best of Fatback Band's 1974-1979-era output, leaning heavily on mid-decade nuggets, there is not one moment to sit back and take a breather. From the brass that kicks off 1974's "Mr Bass Man," which remains one of the most overlooked funk jams to ever hit the streets, to the calypso backbeat that makes "Wicky Wacky" irrepressible and the rolling bass and hooky guitars that drive "Happy," there is not one ounce of wasted space. Also of note is the incredibly textured "(Hey) I Feel Real Good," which just vibrates—a crash of harmonies, horns, deep beats, and rock riffs that would feel out of control in anyone else's hands. While the band enjoyed a massive singles-chart run in the U.S., it's interesting that only two of those hits are included here, but the album is better in the long run because of it. Rather than a chronological rehashing of what everyone else liked, *Funky* focuses on those stellar moments that allowed Fatback to take their place in the upper echelon of funk. And even thought the majority of the songs fell by the wayside, it's refreshing to see them all on *Funky*, splashed across a flawless set. This is absolutely crucial listening. *—Amy Hanson*

Mellow / 2002 / Southbound ♦♦♦

Fatback Band showcase their more down-tempo, relaxed side on *Mellow*. Replacing many of their heavy-backbeat drum breaks with smooth mid-'80s R&B drum-machine presets, the group does a brilliant job covering such classics as "At Last" and the Chi-Lites' standard "Oh Girl," but the standout track is the 1983 politically charged rap "Is This the Future." While not an essential release by any means, it's a worthwhile purchase for any longtime fans looking to fill the gaps in their collection. *—Rob Theakston*

F.A.T.E.

f. 1997

Group / Contemporary R&B, Urban

F.A.T.E. (a name derived from the phrase "for all that's endured") is an R&B vocal group made up of Tiffany ("Tiff") Chisolm, Shaunesa ("Shy") Walker, and Patricia ("Precious") McKelvin. Chisolm and Walker met in high school in Jersey City, New Jersey and encountered the Harlem-based McKelvin when they auditioned for a group of which she was already a member. They formed F.A.T.E. in 1997 and hooked up with managers Valerie Hicks and Alegna Harris, who managed to get a demo to an employee at the Flavor Unit production company, where it was heard by Queen Latifah's partner Shakim Compere, who signed F.A.T.E. to their GhettoWorks label, which had a distribution deal with Warner Bros. Records. The group's first recording, "Just Because," appeared on the soundtrack to *Deep Blue Sea* and on the compilation *The Takeover*, and was released as their first single. Their debut album, *For All That's Endured*, was released in April 2000. *—William Ruhlmann*

● **For All That's Endured** / Apr. 18, 2000 / Warner Bros. ♦♦♦

When "Fallin'," the lead-off track on F.A.T.E.'s debut album *For All That's Endured* is quickly overlaid by rapper Rowdy Rahz talking about his ability to "sex" some woman, you might suppose that the disc is going to be more of a hip-hop effort than it really turns out to be. This trio of teenage singers from the New York-New Jersey area is, of course, just a mouthpiece for various songwriting/production teams, and the overall style is the kind of slavishly rhythmic ballads with call-and-response vocals currently popular in R&B. The lyrics explore the physical contours of teen romance, notably the conflicting desire expressed in the first single, "Just Because," and "If I Tell You Yes," as well as its material aspect in such songs as "Soon as You Get Paid" and "I Don't Need Your Money." But the singers seem unusually concerned with hitting their notes, which makes this a more satisfying vocal effort than most. And the arrangements are at least as concerned with melody as rhythm so that there are real tunes here. Such qualities are in danger of being tagged "old school," and yet these tracks are as current as any. As a result, *For All That's Endured* is a cut above the run-of-the-mill release; no more than that, to be sure, but that's still a small pleasure. *—William Ruhlmann*

The Fi-Tones

Group / Doo Wop

Originally a Brooklyn-based street corner vocal group calling themselves the Cavaliers Quartet, the Fi-Tones first changed their name to the Fi-Tones Quintette after the core group—Cecil Holmes, Marlowe (aka "Lowe") Murray, and Ron Anderson (bass)—added Gene Redd (lead vocals) and Lloyd Davis (lead vocals) to their lineup.

Their first recordings, in 1954, were for Tommy Robinson's Harlem-based independent Atlas Records and were played by Alan Freed and Tommy "Dr. Jive" Smalls in the New York area thoughout the fall and early winter of 1955. Of these, "Foolish Dreams" fared best, scoring first place in a WNJR (Newark, NJ) listener's poll of favorite vocal groups. They later appeared on "Dr. Jive's Rhythm & Blues Easter Review" at the Apollo Theater in Harlem.

By mid-summer 1956, the group's "I Belong to You" was climbing the national charts and landed in the Top Ten in Kansas City. They continued to perform live, but by the end of 1957, the sales had dipped. Atlas issued their last single, and in 1958, the Fi-Tones were off the label. They next recorded for Hy Weiss' Old Town label. Lloyd Davis left and was replaced by Reggie Barnes, but this lineup disbanded after the single failed to chart and were gone by late 1958. *—Bryan Thomas*

Foolish Dreams / Feb. 15, 1996 / Relic ♦♦♦♦

● **The Complete Recordings** / Dec. 5, 2000 / Preserved ♦♦♦♦

Lee Fields

Vocals / Funk, Retro-Soul, Deep Funk Revival

Lee Fields initially made his name among diehard funk fans with a series of hard-hitting singles recorded for various small labels during the '70s. Everything about Fields—his look, his vocals, the grooves on his records—was so indebted to James Brown that he earned the nickname "Little J.B." Fields never hit it big, but his rough-and-tumble singles went on to become popular collectors' items. After a lengthy hiatus, Fields returned in the '90s as a soul-blues belter playing to female-heavy audiences on the Southern circuit. Thanks to sample-obsessed hip-hoppers and British rare-groove aficionados, interest in obscure vintage funk reached a peak in the late '90s, and Fields was fortunate enough to have remained active when new recordings in the style became a viable proposition. Energized by his return to raw, heavy, James Brown-style funk, Fields emerged as the leading light of the so-called deep funk movement with a series of recordings that often equaled, and sometimes outdid, his early work.

Fields released his first single on the Bedford label in 1969, "Bewildered" b/w "Tell Her I Love Her." After the 1973 one-off "Gonna Make Love" on London, Fields caught on at Norfolk Sound; 1973 also saw the release of one of his most enduringly popular 45s, "Let's Talk It Over" b/w "She's a Love Maker" (though it wasn't a big seller at the time). Another prized item was 1975's "Everybody Gonna Give Their Thing Away to Somebody (Sometime)" b/w "East Coast Rapper," issued on SoundPlus. Fields spent most of the latter half of the '70s cutting sides for Angle 3, including perhaps his most sought-after single of all, "The Bull Is Coming" b/w "Funky Screw" (credited to Lee Fields & the Devil's Personal Band, which only heightened its surface appeal). His last single with Angle 3 came in 1981, by which time he'd finally released a full-length album, *Let's Talk It Over*; naturally, it also went on to become a rare and pricey collector's item.

Fields was quiet for most of the '80s, but mounted a comeback in the early '90s, signing with the modern-day incarnation of the Mississippi-based Ace label. Debuting in 1992 with *Enough Is Enough*, Fields plied his trade on the Southern soul and blues circuit, wearing the glitzy costumes of old and crooning love songs and come-ons to largely female audiences who'd never lost their taste for his style of music. Fields also played keyboards and synthesizers on his Ace albums, which included 1995's *Coming to Tear the Roof Down* and 1996's *Dreaming Big Time*; he switched to Avanti in 1998 for *It's Hard to Go Back After Loving You*.

By that time, Fields had already hooked up with the New York-based Desco Records, a trailblazing label devoted to releasing new material designed to appeal to old-school funk collectors. Fields guested on one track on the debut album by the label's house band the Soul Providers, 1997's *Gimmie the Paw*. He subsequently began performing live with the Soul Providers at Desco's showcase gigs in New York, and released several limited-edition 45-rpm singles. In 1999, he became the first Desco artist to release a full-length album, the smoking *Let's Get a Groove On*. Its strict adherence to organic, classic-style James Brown funk—with no synthesizers or drum machines—won admiring reviews and helped put Desco on the map with a hip underground audience that previously never would have paid attention to new Fields material. Desco subsequently broke apart into two labels, Daptone and Soul Fire, and when the dust settled Fields recorded for both of them. He issued two 7-inch singles on Daptone over 2001-2002 ("Give Me a Chance" and

"Shot Down") and then released his next full album, *Problems*, on Soul Fire in late 2002. *Problems* again won high praise from the funk community. *—Steve Huey*

- **Let's Get a Groove On** / May 15, 1999 / Desco ♦♦♦♦♦

Lee Fields spent most of the '90s on the Ace label, recording soul-blues albums whose funkiness was often dampened by cheap-sounding, partly synthesized backing tracks. Judging by his performance on his Desco Records debut full-length *Let's Get a Groove On*, Fields' move to the pioneering old-school funk-revival label freed him to do the kind of gritty, authentic funk album he'd been itching to record for quite some time. Laying out his principle of "rough ... nasty ... genuine" funk in a spoken intro, Fields positively smokes through the whole record, capturing all the fire of late-'60s James Brown (whom he strongly and unashamedly resembles, vocally) with the help of the Desco house band, the Soul Providers, who lay down a richly organic set of guitar-and-organ-dominated funk backings. *Let's Get a Groove On* is blatantly derivative of its influences, but the simple act of returning wholeheartedly to those influences—in a musical climate which has assimilated and moved away from them—could in itself be considered an innovation. Regardless, it's a stunning performance from Fields and the record that fulfills Desco's promise—quite possibly one of 1999's best, and definitely one of its most overlooked. *—Steve Huey*

Problems / Oct. 1, 2002 / Soul Fire ♦♦♦♦

After the terrific retro-funk label Desco split into the Soul Fire and Dap-Tone camps, flagship artist Lee Fields recorded for both but issued his next full-length on the former, which preferred a distinctly lower-fidelity grit to its product. That recording approach informs *Problems*, Fields' second album of unadulterated James Brown worship aimed at the burgeoning deep-funk revival scene, though it isn't as scratchy-sounding as much of Soul Fire's output. Initially, *Problems* might be a bit of a letdown after the blazing funk firestorm that was *Let's Get a Groove On*. It's just as raw and organic, to be sure, but lacks a certain immediacy in comparison. The Soul Fire house band is a crackerjack unit, grooving with a trippier vibe than Fields' previous outing—more guitar effects, electric piano, flute, and African-flavored percussion. While the music is terrific on its own terms, it sometimes seems a little laid-back and slow-paced for Fields' irresistible James Brown Disciple Number One act, and as a result *Problems* doesn't feel like the super-bad statement of purpose that its predecessor was. Plus, with just over half an hour's running time, it's disappointing that two of the ten tracks are band-only. But given time, Fields' infectious enthusiasm and the quality musicianship behind him are too winning to end up really dissatisfying. And there are plenty of great moments for Fields fans: Fields confessing his dirty past on "You Made a New Man Out of Me"; the humorous, age-old advice on women dispensed on "Rapping With Lee"; the funked-up ballad "Honey Dove"; the percolating midtempo grooves of "The Right Thing" and the philosophical title track. Even if *Problems* winds up a cut below *Let's Get a Groove On*, it shows that Fields is still a vital and dynamic funk force to be reckoned with. *—Steve Huey*

The Fiestas

f. 1958, Newark, NJ

Group / Doo Wop, R&B

The Fiestas' career spanned nearly 20 years, and they came along at a time when soul music was gaining prominence in the vocal group scene. Their biggest hit was 1959's "So Fine," which reached number three on the R&B charts before crossing over to number 11 on the Hot 100. The Fiestas—lead vocalist Tommy Bullock, Eddie Morris, Sam Ingalis, and Preston Lane—were originally from Newark, NJ. They were signed to Old Town by owner Hy Weiss in 1959 after he heard the group singing "So Fine" in the bathroom next to his office (which was run out of the cloak room of the Triboro Theatre on 125th Street and Third Avenue in Harlem). The single shot onto the charts immediately.

Weiss followed suit with the group's next single, "Last Night I Dreamed," which failed to connect. He continued trying, however, issuing soulful R&B sides that were similar to what artists like Sam Cooke and Jackie Wilson had been doing. Of these, favorites include "You Could Be My Girlfriend," a cover of Arthur Alexander's "Anna," and its flipside, "Think Smart," which is now a much-coveted Northern soul rarity. A ballad from 1962, "Broken Heart," scored number 18 on the R&B charts, but failed to chart on the pop lists.

The Fiestas eventually moved over to Strand (a New York label that started as a full-priced label but soon began specializing in budget issues) and then to Vigor, recorded through the '60s and into the mid-'70s, but never again enjoyed any hits. *—Bryan Thomas*

- **The Very Best of the Fiestas: So Fine** / Jan. 25, 2000 / Collectables ♦♦♦♦

The most complete retrospective of the group available, *The Very Best of the Fiestas: So Fine* collects 25 of their recordings for Old Town, including the hit "So Fine" and the less-successful but solid follow-ups "You Could Be My Girlfriend," "Anna," and "Think Smart." In between are ballads like "Our Anniversary" and "The Hobo's Prayer"; uptempo numbers such as "Good News," "Mr. Dillion, Mr. Dillion," and "I Feel Good All Over"; as well as more straightforward R&B-inflected songs like "Dollar Bill." While 25 songs from a somewhat lesser-known group like the Fiestas may seem like overkill, the quality of all of their material is consistent enough to not only satisfy doo wop diehards, but also win over fans of the Coasters, Chubby Checker, and other prominent acts who mine similar artistic territory. *—Heather Phares*

The 5th Dimension

f. 1966, Los Angeles, CA

Group / Sunshine Pop, Pop-Soul, Pop

The Fifth Dimension's unique sound lay somewhere between smooth, elegant soul and straightforward, adult-oriented pop, often with a distinct flower-power vibe. Although they appealed more to mainstream listeners than to a hip, hardcore R&B audience, they had a definite ear for contemporary trends; their selection of material helped kickstart the notable songwriting careers of Jimmy Webb and Laura Nyro, and their biggest hit was a medley from the hippie musical *Hair*, "Aquarius/Let the Sunshine In." The group's soaring, seamless harmonies were given appropriately sweeping, orchestrated period production by Bones Howe, which often placed their records closer to California-style sunshine pop. That's actually part of the reason why the best singles from the Fifth Dimension's heyday of the late '60s and early '70s still evoke their era with uncanny precision.

The Fifth Dimension began life in Los Angeles in 1965 as the Versatiles. Lamonte McLemore, Ron Townson, and Billy Davis Jr. all grew up in St. Louis, and moved to Los Angeles independently of one another; each was trained in a different area—jazz, opera, and gospel/R&B, respectively. Marilyn McCoo was the first female singer to join, and she was soon augmented by Florence LaRue; both were ex-beauty pageant winners who'd attended college in the L.A. area. Their demo tape was rejected by Motown, but after a one-off single for Bronco, they caught the attention of singer Johnny Rivers, who'd just set up his own label, Soul City. Rivers signed the group in 1966 on the condition that they update their name and image, and thus the Fifth Dimension was born. Their first Soul City single, "I'll Be Lovin' You Forever," was a flop, but a cover of the Mamas & the Papas' "Go Where You Wanna Go" climbed into the Top 20.

Budding young songwriter Jimmy Webb ("Macarthur Park," "By the Time I Get to Phoenix," etc.) supplied the Fifth Dimension with their breakthrough hit, 1967's "Up, Up and Away." An ode to the pleasures of flying in a beautiful balloon, the song became the group's first Top Ten hit, peaking at number seven, and went on to sweep the Grammy Awards, taking home five total (including Record of the Year and Song of the Year). Its success pushed the Fifth Dimension's first album, also titled *Up, Up and Away*, to gold sales status. The group stuck with Webb for its second album, *The Magic Garden*, which featured only one non-Webb composition; it produced a couple of minor hits in "Paper Cup" and "Carpet Man," but nothing on the level of "Up, Up and Away." Their third LP was thus more diverse, featuring several compositions by another up-and-coming songwriter, Laura Nyro. The title cut, Nyro's "Stoned Soul Picnic," went all the way to number three in the spring of 1968, selling over a million copies and putting Nyro on the map. The Nyro-penned follow-up single, "Sweet Blindness," also reached the Top 20.

The Fifth Dimension's success peaked in 1969 when the group caught a Broadway production of *Hair*, and immediately decided to cut a medley of two songs from the show. "Aquarius/Let the Sunshine In" was a monster hit and grew to become one of the era's defining pop records; it spent six weeks at number one, sold a whopping three-million copies, and won the group their second Record of the Year Grammy. Accompanying LP *The Age of Aquarius* went gold and nearly hit number one, and their Nyro-penned follow-up single, "Wedding Bell Blues," followed its predecessor to number one as well. The song was something of a mirror of real life; Billy Davis and Marilyn McCoo were married that year, and Florence LaRue also married group manager Marc Gordon.

Johnny Rivers sold Soul City to the Bell label in 1970, and the first Fifth Dimension LP on Bell was that year's *Portrait*, which spawned several minor hits and the Top Five smash "One Less Bell to Answer," a Burt Bacharach composition. In 1970, a controversial performance at the White House took place; although the group sang "The Declaration," a socially conscious critique, the simple act of appearing before President Nixon further alienated the Fifth Dimension from the black wing of their fan base, at a time when their releases had already begun to peak higher on the pop charts than on the R&B side. Indeed, their Bell recordings moved farther into soft pop and away from R&B and the gently trippy vibes of their late-'60s material. Their album sales began to taper off, and their vocal arrangements now tended to spotlight soloists rather than unified harmonies.

McCoo emerged as a focal point, singing lead on the 1972 Top Ten hits "(Last Night) I Didn't Get to Sleep at All" and "If I Could Reach You." They proved to be the group's last major successes; another Bacharach tune, 1973's "Living Together, Growing Together," barely made the Top 40, and the following year's *Soul & Inspiration* LP marked the end of their relationship with producer Bones Howe. 1975's *Earthbound* was another full-length collaboration with Jimmy Webb, and much like *The Magic Garden*, its thematic unity failed to produce a significant hit single. It was also the last album by the original lineup; McCoo and Davis left the group to form a duo, and scored a big hit in 1976 with "You Don't Have to Be a Star."

The remaining trio carried on with new members, and nearly had a hit in 1976 with the LaRue-sung "Love Hangover"; unfortunately, Motown issued Diana Ross' own version shortly after the Fifth Dimension's hit the charts, and hers proved far more popular. Strangely enough, the Fifth Dimension signed with Motown not long after, releasing two albums in 1978. Townson briefly left the group to try a solo career, but soon returned, as the group resigned themselves to the nostalgia circuit; meanwhile, McCoo served a stint as the host of *Solid Gold*. Phyllis Battle joined in the mid-'80s, and the original quintet reunited in 1990 for a tour. In 1995, the quintet of LaRue, Townson, McLemore, Battle, and Greg Walker recorded a new album, *In the House*, for Click Records. In 1998, Willie Williams replaced Townson, who passed away in 2001 due to kidney failure. Battle departed in 2002, to be replaced by Van Jewel. *—Steve Huey*

Up, Up and Away / May 1967 / Buddha ♦♦♦

This is the first album release from the often maligned though talented and singular group the 5th Dimension. Released in 1967, this set was the first with Jimmy Webb, who contributed to one track and arranged and conducted the whole effort. The most well-known song remains one of the finer songs of the decade. "Up, Up and Away" matched the group's gorgeous harmonies with a great and ethereal yet full-bodied production. Their cover of the Mamas & the Papas' "Go Where You Want to Go" is such a carbon copy, Billy Davis Jr. probably wore one of John Phillips' big hats for the session. Despite that groundbreaking song, *Up, Up and Away* is mostly the group finding their sound with mixed results. The cover of "Poor Side of Town" is pointless and the Motown-inspired "I'll Be Loving You Forever" comes off forced and as phony as a sack of three dollar bills. *Up, Up and Away* is certainly commendable for the style forged here but even better work was ahead for the group. [The 2001 reissue came with bonus tracks.] *—Jason Elias*

The Magic Garden / Dec. 1967 / Buddha ♦♦♦

This record did contain the small hits "Paper Cup" and "Carpet Man," but the group, or more likely arranger/conductor Jim Webb, was probably shooting for something a bit higher than the Top 40. Aside from a misfired cover of the Beatles' "Ticket to Ride," Webb wrote everything on this album, which—with between-track segues, lyrics expounding dreams and possibility, and dense orchestral settings—seemed to be aiming for a song cycle of sorts. It's not *Pet Sounds*, however, or even Van Dyke Parks' *Song Cycle*. It's over-ambitious MOR pop-soul with mild psychedelic colors, and a bit ludicrous, though not unattractive due to the typically conscientious harmonies. "Orange Air" is probably the group's best shot at pseudo-psychedelia; "The Girls' Song," on much firmer MOR territory, was done much better by Jackie DeShannon; and "The Worst That Could Happen," Webb at his most disagreeably sentimental, was covered for a huge hit by the Brooklyn Bridge about a year later. A recent biography of cult singer/songwriter Nick Drake, by the way, revealed that this album, along with such estimable underground classics as Love's *Forever Changes* and Van Morrison's *Astral Weeks*, was a special favorite of his because of its combination of rock and orchestration. That means it might suddenly become a lot harder to find in the dollar bins, although many of those copies will probably find their way right back there after Drake fans play it once or twice. [The album was also reissued by Soul City under the title *The Worst That Could Happen*.] *—Richie Unterberger*

Stoned Soul Picnic / Aug. 1968 / Buddha ♦♦♦

One of the 5th Dimension's finest all-around albums, *Stoned Soul Picnic* is not only home to the title tracks, but also to the hits "Sweet Blindness" and "California Soul." All three of these songs provide excellent examples of the band's sunny and buoyant appeal. Although the singers' awesome vocal gifts deserve all the credit they get, it's also important to realize the immense contributions from producer Bones Howe and vocal arranger Bob Alcivar. The group was far more than a black version of the Mamas & the Papas. There are also some excellent album cuts here, such as Jeff Companor's "It'll Never Be the Same Again," where Ron Townson's exquisite soul pipes get off an amazing solo around an excellent Motown-driven arrangement. If you're going to pick up one 5th Dimension album (aside from a greatest hits package), you'd be hard-pressed to find a better one than this. *—Matthew Greenwald*

The Age of Aquarius / May 1969 / Buddha ♦♦♦♦

The Age of Aquarius, the 5th Dimension's fourth album, was the group's commercial peak. They had already topped the charts with their medley of two songs from the Broadway musical *Hair*, "The Age of Aquarius" and "Let the Sunshine In (The Flesh Failures)," a platinum single that would earn them Grammy Awards for Record of the Year and Best Contemporary Vocal Performance, Group, when they released this album. It turned out that was only the tip of the iceberg: They returned to number one with another platinum single, "Wedding Bell Blues," penned by Laura Nyro, who had given them "Stoned Soul Picnic" the year before. And the album also spawned Top 40 hits in Nyro's "Blowing Away" and Neil Sedaka's "Workin' on a Groovy Thing." The 5th Dimension were the successors to the L.A. vocal group mantle passed on by the Mamas & the Papas (they even inherited the studio band of Hal Blaine, Joe Osborn, and Larry Knechtel). They smoothed out and commercialized everything they sang, and their work had a sheen and a zest that sometimes contrasted with the original tone of the material. On Broadway, the *Hair* songs seemed full of hippie rebellion; here, they seemed enthusiastic and optimistic. In a conflicted time, the 5th Dimension thrived on their ability to equivocate, and this album was their triumph—just listen to them harmonize on "Sunshine of Your Love"! *—William Ruhlmann*

Portrait / Apr. 1970 / Buddha ♦♦♦♦

Along with *Stoned Soul Picnic*, this may very well be the 5th Dimension's finest album. Home to one of their finest singles ever—the Bacharach/David "One Less Bell to Answer," on which Marilyn McCoo gives the vocal performance of her career—the record also contains the surprisingly funky and rocking "Puppet Man." Some great covers also include Dave Mason's "Feelin' Alright," Jimmy Webb's gorgeous "This Is Your Life," and Laura Nyro's anthemic "Save the Country." This vibe is echoed by the album's centerpiece, a medley of "A Change Is Gonna Come" and "People Gotta Be Free" preceded by "The Declaration." It's an ambitious suite, yet one that works well; it provides a great marriage between the group's pop leanings and the counterculture of the late '60s. Progressive, yet still encapsulating, which is the 5th Dimension's sunny appeal, *Portrait* is a minor masterpiece. Famed expressionist artist Leroy Neiman's appropriate cover and liner paintings are literally icing on the cake. *—Matthew Greenwald*

The July 5th Album / Jul. 1970 / Soul City ♦♦

By 1969, the 5th Dimension were peaking in popularity and artistic success. Fresh on the heels of *The Age of Aquarius*, *The July 5th Album* is a compilation of B-sides and album cuts from their previous albums, no doubt intended to eke out some mileage from the back catalog while the gettings were good. And while the album does have a "warmed over" leftovers air to it, there are some standouts. As funny as it first seems to hear the 5th Dimension's light-as-air California pop-soul sound applied to the Cream classic "Sunshine of Your Love," it's really a vibrant, richly sung cover. The best tunes on the album are those where the R&B grit level is turned up a few notches, whether it's the Wall of Sound arrangement of "It'll Never Be the Same Again" or the more groovy Memphis soulish "Don'tcha Hear Me Callin' to Ya." If anything, their soulfulness is more apparent on this compilation than their popular A-side hits might suggest. By its nature, *The July 5th Album* is a scattered, inconsistent affair. Yet, with arrangers like Jimmy Webb, Bones Howe, Bob Alcivar, and Johnny Rivers at the helm, plus notable studio pros like Hal Blaine on the backing tracks, the level of professionalism keeps the low points (such as the cloying "Those Were the Days") from being too shallow. And it's nice to hear the 5th Dimension's multi-layered harmonies applied to classics like "Let It Be Me" and Johnny Rivers' "Poor Side of Town." Still, it's hard to justify this album for anyone but completists. None of the best-known hits are here, and even hardcore fans are likely to scoop up the other tracks on the original albums. *—Jim Esch*

The 5th Dimension/Live! / Oct. 1971 / Bell ♦♦♦

Reflections / Oct. 1971 / Bell ♦♦♦

Reflections was the 5th Dimension's second album for Bell Records. While not a greatest-hits album, this compiles some of the better tracks from their Soul City albums. The melodic and haunting "It'll Never Be the Same Again" has Billy Davis Jr. turning in a brilliant, dramatic performance. The group's work with Jimmy Webb is limited here to the sad and whimsical "Carpet Man." Despite their normally high level of work, *Reflections* does have a fair amount of clinkers. The group's covers of an oddly peppy take on "Sunshine of Your Love" and draggy "Ticket to Ride" are as bad as they got. Narrowly escaping being lame, the cover of "Those Were the Days" benefits from Davis Jr. not changing his soulful inflection one iota. Ashford & Simpson's great, though never a hit, "California Soul" is also included in this collection. *Reflections* is one of those albums that even fans might have missed on the shelves. This isn't a perfect or even comprehensive greatest-hits set, but fans will probably like to have it anyway. *—Jason Elias*

● **Greatest Hits on Earth** / Sep. 1972 / Arista ♦♦♦♦♦

Until Rhino issued its anthology, this was the best hits package for the 5th Dimension, a group that in its peak was among the best at doing lighthearted pop with a soulful foundation. Certainly, they weren't a hardcore R&B or earthy singing group, but they did put some punch into songs that were really kind of silly otherwise, like "Wedding Bell Blues." *—Ron Wynn*

Up, Up and Away: The Definitive Collection / May 20, 1997 / Arista ♦♦♦♦♦

The subtitle on this anthology is correct: This is truly the definitive collection of the 5th Dimension's music, including all the hits and most of the album cuts that anyone could want. The 20-bit digital mastering provides a crisp, bright audio experience, and the joyous harmonies bring back the positive side of the late-'60s/early-'70s era in which the songs were recorded. The megahits are all here: Jimmy Webb's "Up, Up and Away," Laura Nyro's "Stoned Soul Picnic" and "Wedding Bell Blues," the Bacharach/David opus "One Less Bell to Answer," the beautiful "(Last Night) I Didn't Get to Sleep at All" and the Grammy-winning number one smash from the spring of 1969, "Aquarius/Let the Sunshine In" from *Hair*. There are not-quite-Top Ten hits like "Sweet Blindness," "Go Where You Wanna Go," "California Soul," "Workin' on a Groovy Thing," "Blowing Away," "Save the Country," and "Love's Lines, Angles and Rhymes." What a run this quintet had on the pop charts from 1967 to 1972. This two-disc set successfully makes the case for the 5th Dimension to be remembered among the finest purveyors of pop song vocal harmony in the rock era. Baby Boomers will delight at the memories this collection conjures up and will find surprises they may have forgotten or never known: "Paper Cup," "Carpet Man," "Puppet Man," "Light Sings," and the group's medley of "The Declaration/A Change Is Gonna Come/People Gotta Be Free." Listening to *Up, Up & Away: The Definitive Collection* is a great antidote for the blues, lifting the listener up with a smile and reminding those who may have forgotten that there once was a time when it seemed that music really could bring us all together. *—Jim Newsom*

The Master Hits: The 5th Dimension / Jul. 27, 1999 / Arista ♦♦♦♦

Arista celebrated its 30th anniversary by releasing *The Heritage Series*, spotlighting the most popular artists on the label. The Fifth Dimension installment in *The Heritage Series* is pretty much a straight hits collection—the first such assembled on the pop-soul group. While they were at Arista, the Fifth Dimension had such hits as "Up, Up and Away," "Go Where You Wanna Go," "Stoned Soul Picnic," "Aquarius/Let the Sunshine In," and "Wedding Bell Blues." All those songs are here, along with some highlights from their albums, providing a nice retrospective of their time with Arista. *—Stephen Thomas Erlewine*

Fine Young Cannibals

f. 1984, Birmingham, England

Group / College Rock, Blue-Eyed Soul, Pop/Rock

When the Beat (known as the English Beat in the U.S. only) split in 1983, it came as a surprise to guitarist Dave Cox and bassist David Steele. The first time they realized that the group's vocalists, Ranking Roger and Dave Wakeling, had gone off to form a group without them was when their accountant phoned to finalize the divorce. While the defectors had formed General Public, Cox and Steele set about creating something new of their own. Apart from not wanting to repeat the mistakes the Beat made, and a vague notion of adding both jazz and soul to the Beat's ska roots (they also decided to feature a strong vocalist), there was no real master plan. They found Roland Gift singing with a barroom R&B band named the Bones, looking like Sidney Poitier but sounding like Otis Redding. He was their man. Gift had spent his teenage years in youth theater, until the advent of punk made music his main passion. As punk gave way to the two-tone ska, which gave rise to groups like Madness and, ultimately, the Beat, Gift took up saxophone and singing in a local band. Keeping live work down to just the occasional one-off date, the Fine Young Cannibals signed to London Records in early 1985. Resisting the record company's attempts to team them up with a producer, the Fine Young Cannibals released a demo version of "Johnny Come Home" as their first single. Its instant success allowed them to team up with a compatible producer, Robin Millar, for the first Fine Young Cannibals album. Five years later, a second album emerged, *The Raw & the Cooked*. The single "She Drives Me Crazy" was a worldwide number-one hit. Since then, the Fine Young Cannibals have remained elusive. *—Ed Nimmervoll*

Fine Young Cannibals / Dec. 1985 / IRS ♦♦♦♦

When Dave Wakeling and Ranking Roger split from the rest of the English Beat to form General Public, Andy Cox and Dave Steele originally advertised on MTV for a new lead singer for the Beat. When that didn't pan out (although it did work for Wall of Voodoo), Cox and Steele hooked up with the unique and soulful singer Roland Gift and formed the Fine Young Cannibals. Though the trio first hit the mass U.S. consciousness with 1989's electronic dance-pop *The Raw & the Cooked*, their 1985 debut was a soul-jazz pop charmer that's more low key but every bit as entertaining. Along the lines of early Everything But the Girl (the two groups share a producer, Robin Millar) with a heavier Motown influence, the songs on *Fine Young Cannibals* are uniformly strong. The singles "Johnny Come Home" (a plea to a runaway that sounds like the Beat's ska stripped down to its tense and obsessive essentials) and "Blue" (one of the more oblique and successful anti-Margaret Thatcher tracks of its era) are terrific, but album tracks like the casually devastating "Funny How Love Is" and the manic "Like a Stranger" (which incongruously ends with a female chorus shrieking "You've been too long in an institution!" repeatedly while Gift tries out his Otis Redding impression) are even better. The album's highlight, though, is a reworking of "Suspicious Minds" (with scarifying backing vocals by Jimmy Somerville) that, while it doesn't replace Elvis' version, certainly takes the song into an interesting new direction. Although often overlooked, especially in the U.S., in the wake of their massively successful follow-up, *Fine Young Cannibals* is a powerful and satisfying debut. The U.S. CD adds two extended remixes of "Johnny Come Home" and "Suspicious Minds." *—Stewart Mason*

● **The Raw & the Cooked** / Feb. 20, 1989 / IRS ✦✦✦✦✦
One of the most exciting albums released during a decade of artifice and extravagance, in a mere ten songs and 35 minutes the Fine Young Cannibals created a masterpiece. Admittedly the trio had some help—backing singers, guest musicians (including former Squeeze pianoman Jools Holland and Talking Head's Jerry Harrison)—but that doesn't take away the band's own accomplishment. Remaining true to the FYC's vision of tying past and present musical styles together into artful new pop packages, *The Raw & the Cooked* features a shopping list of genres. Mod, funk, Motown, British beat, R&B, punk, rock, and even disco are embedded within the songs, while the rhythms, many synthetically created, are equally diverse. In less delicate hands this would be nothing more than an everything including the kitchen sink motley mess, but FYC manage this mix with subtlety and élan. Two-thirds of the record were released as U.K. singles, all were hits, and each one proudly boasted a distinctly different blend of styles. "Good Thing," for example, was the trio's tribute to the legendary all-night Northern soul parties of the '60s, but is much more than a mere meld of mod and Motown. It's actually built round a slinky R&B riff, fueled by a boogie-woogie piano, and slammed home with a cracking beat. "I'm Not the Man I Used to Be" is a torrid torch song, but fired by a futuristic jungle beat and an almost housey production. Then, of course, there's "She Drives Me Crazy," which features the most unique, and instantly identifiable, beat/riff combination of the decade. Even the four tracks that didn't make the singles cut could have, if MCA had the audacity to keep releasing them. "Tell Me What" perfectly re-creates the *Tamla* sound, with only the synth giving it a modern touch, but on the rest FYC delve deeper into funk, disco, soul, and lovingly coax them into the modern era. Every one of *Raw*'s tracks simmers with creativity, as the hooks, sharp melodies, and irrepressible beats are caressed by nuanced arrangements and sparkling production. Never has music's past, present, and future been more exceptionally combined. *—Jo-Ann Greene*

The Raw & the Remix / Dec. 1990 / IRS ✦✦
Coming up on two years since the release of *The Raw & The Cooked*, and with no new album in sight, IRS Records put together various 12-inch remix versions of songs from the 1989 album and released this 59-minute collection. There are extended, alternate versions of such hits as "She Drives Me Crazy," "Good Thing," and "Don't Look Back." Off the dancefloor, none of this improves on the originals. *—William Ruhlmann*

Finest / Nov. 26, 1996 / MCA ✦✦✦✦✦
Fine Young Cannibals only released two albums, so it's slightly unusual that they even have a greatest hits collection like *Fine Young Cannibals Finest*. After all, a dedicated fan will have both records, and casual fans will only want the singles on *The Raw and the Cooked*, thereby eliminating the audience for the collection. Despite these misgivings, *Finest* does its job well, featuring 12 of their biggest hits and best-known songs ("She Drives Me Crazy," "Johnny Come Home," "Good Thing," "Suspicious Minds," "Don't Look Back"), plus two unreleased cuts ("The Flame" and "Since You've Been Gone") to entice collectors. If you want the highlights, *Finest* is fine, but most fans will want to stick with the two original albums. *—Stephen Thomas Erlewine*

Fingers Inc.

f. 1985, Chicago, IL, **db.** 1988
Group / House, Club/Dance, Acid House
The top early Chicago house group and the first outlet for the production genius of Larry Heard, Fingers Inc. was formed in 1985 by Heard with vocalists Robert Owens and Ron Wilson. Though the group often took a sideline to Heard's solo jaunts as Mr. Fingers, at their best they rivalled Ten City with expressive club gems like "You're Mine," "It's Over" and "A Love of My Own." The group also spawned the first (and some say best) house LP, 1988's *Another Side*. That album was basically the end of Fingers Inc., though; Heard produced singles by Owens and Wilson, but then moved on to a solo career by the end of the decade. *—John Bush*

● **Another Side** / 1988 / Indigo Music/Jack Trax ✦✦✦✦✦
The only LP from Fingers Inc. was the first full-length in the genre and an unabashed house classic. Obviously, it's chocked with uptempo singles perfectly primed for easy-steppers on the dancefloor ("Bye Bye," "Music Take Me Up," "Distant Planet"), and vocalist Robert Owens' gospel flavor and strong voice is a special treat. What makes *Another Side* more than just a statistic, however, is Heard's surprising adeptness at sustaining interest over the course of a full album. His flare for melancholy had been previously hinted at only by the Detroit techno producers, and it resulted in the rare mainstream house LP that succeeded on several levels. *—John Bush*

Fireflies

f. 1957, Philadelphia, PA
Group / R&B
The Fireflies' career spanned eight single releases on five labels from 1958 to 1967. They formed in Philadelphia in 1957 and went through several lineup changes, but the actual membership is a mystery. Ritchie Adams (born Richard Ziegler) sang lead but wasn't an original member; it's believed he sang lead on their biggest hit, their second single "You Were Mine" (Ribbon 1959), which followed "The Crawl," which they debuted with in 1958 on Roulette. A guy known only by his last name, Granahan, supposedly sang background vocals. The romantic "You Were Mine" barely missed the pop Top 20, a height the Fireflies never scaled again. It spawned an answer record by the Paulette Sisters, entitled "I Was Yours," and was redone by Wayne Thomas.

Ribbon (a New York label owned by Alan Kallman) followed with "I Can't Say Goodbye" the same year, but without the same success. It bombed and so did "Marianne," released on Canadian American Records in 1960, which competed with a final Ribbon release "My Girl." It's a good bet that Adams left to pursue a solo singing career and answer a songwriting calling before the Fireflies dropped their first single on Taurus Records in 1962. The first Taurus release was a play on the Fireflies big hit called "You Were Mine for Awhile," which promptly flopped. So did "Blacksmith Blues" on Hamilton; likewise for three more Taurus platters.

After the Fireflies, Adams cut solo singles on Beltone, Congress, Imperial, and other labels, and wrote many of them, something he didn't do with the Fireflies, but never charted with any significant impact. He made up for it, however, with his songwriting. Adams has written nearly 375 songs and scored two mammoth hits, "Tossin' and Turnin'" and much later with "After the Lovin'." He wrote songs for the Banana Splits and the Archies, and also sang lead on "Love Is Living in You," the only Archies' single that doesn't feature Ron Dante. *—Andrew Hamilton*

● **You Were Mine** / 1961 / Taurus Universal ✦✦✦

First Choice

f. 1971, Philadelphia, PA, **db.** 1984
Group / Disco, Philly Soul, Smooth Soul, Soul
The '70s Philly disco vocal group First Choice's first big breakthrough was the infectious "Armed and Extremely Dangerous" (with its urgent "calling all cars!" intro), a Top 20 R&B/Top 30 pop hit in 1973. New attention was brought to the female trio when Mary J. Blige did a faithful cover of their dance classic "Let No Man Put Asunder" in 1999. Lead singer Rochelle Fleming, Joyce Jones, and Chester, PA, native Annette Guest were originally known as the Debonettes and performed around Philadelphia. Radio DJ Georgie Woods introduced them to Philly soul guitarist/songwriter/producer Norman Harris, who produced the debut single "This Is the House Where Loved Died," which received airplay in Philly and other markets but failed to chart nationally. Their next single, the Harris-produced "Armed and Extremely Dangerous," was their first big hit, going to number-11 R&B in early 1973 for Stan Watson's Philly Groove label, which was distributed by Bell Records. It was also a Top 20 U.K. hit. The *Armed and Extremely Dangerous* album was released in fall 1973.

For the bulk of their records, First Choice was backed by the tight rhythm section of guitarist Harris, bassist Ron Baker, and drummer Earl Young who were part of MFSB, the house band for Gamble & Huff's Philadelphia International Records. The next single, "The Player, Part 1," was their highest-charting R&B single, hitting number seven R&B in summer 1974, though the group enjoyed many high-charting hits on *Billboard*'s disco charts. *The Player* LP was issued in fall 1974. Switching to Warner Bros., they charted with "Gotta Get Away (From You Baby)" in spring 1976 and "Let Him Go" in fall 1976, and they released an LP, *So Let Us Entertain You*.

Around 1977, Joyce Jones left the group and was replaced by Ursula Herring. The following year, Norman Harris formed Gold Mind Records, which was distributed by dance label pioneer Salsoul Records and co-founded Baker-Harris-Young Productions with his bandmates. First Choice signed with Gold Mind and their first release for the label, the ultra-catchy "Doctor Love," went to number-23 R&B in summer 1977. *Delusions* followed in fall 1997. Generally regarded as the trio's best LP, it featured lyrically rich dance tunes as well as luscious ballads and gave Philadelphia native Fleming her best showcase, displaying one of the most distinctive lead vocalists in soul/dance/pop music. Fleming's vocals are also one of the most sampled, heard on countless dance records from around the world. Their next Gold Mind LP, *Hold Your Houses*, was released in March 1979, with the title track becoming a disco classic. That same year, Debbie Martin replaced Ursula Herring. Around 1983, Salsoul ceased operations to focus on the emerging home video market by starting their First Choice Video division, and the following year, the trio split.

In 1987, Fleming reformed a version of First Choice with her cousin Laconya Fleming and Lawrence Cottel, who recorded a single for Prelude Records, "Love Itch." In the '90s, Rochelle Fleming continued to record in the U.S. and Europe. *—Ed Hogan*

Armed and Extremely Dangerous / 1973 / Philly Groove ✦✦✦
Other than the title cut, a remake, and a Motown wannabe, there's nothing of substance here. The wannabe "This Is the House Where Love Died," their debut single was popular in their hometown of Philly; they sound just like Martha & the Vandellas on the midtempo Motown-ish track. Their second single, "Armed and Extremely Dangerous," was explosive—its tough storyline and pulverizing hook should have placed it higher on the charts, but it stalled at number-11 R&B and number-28 pop. A remake of "Love and Happiness" works, but "Smarty Pants" and "Newsey Neighbors" are bubblegum-ish attempts at commercialism that failed to crack the R&B Top 20. *—Andrew Hamilton*

The Player / 1974 / Philly Groove ✦✦✦
First Choice's sophomore release won't curl your toes. "The Player" stabs at toughness like "Armed and Extremely Dangerous," but the chorale chorus saps its intensity. There's a vocal *and* instrumental version of "Guilty," but the song is derivative disco and the double dose is unnecessary and annoying. The songs by Norman Harris, Allan Felder, Bunny Sigler, and others are uninspiring. Producer Norman Harris took advantage of his shoestring budget by using them (strings) on every track whether needed or not. *—Andrew Hamilton*

Delusions / 1977 / Gold Mind ✦✦
Interesting arrangements and memorable hooks makes this reissue a better overall affair than their Philly Groove albums. Originally released on Gold Mind in 1977, new member

Ursula Herring joins Rochelle Fleming and Annette Guest on this fanciful disco excursion. Clubbers like "Doctor Love" and "Indian Giver," and infectious midtempo numbers like "Let No Man Put Asunder" and "Gamble on Love" get the feet moving. The judicious use of strings, especially on their thumping, sensual remake of Stevie Wonder's "Love Having You Around," one of their better sides, is most effective. *—Andrew Hamilton*

Hold Your Horses / 1983 / Charly ♦♦

A super three-song medley: "Let Me Down Easy," "Good Morning Midnight," and "Great Expectations" runs for more than 16 minutes and kicks off the Philly trio's second album for Gold Mind Records. A funky off-kilter bass provides a deadly groove on "Love Thang," a commercial multistyled piece; however, formulaic cookie cutters like "Double Cross" and "Hold Your Horses" are strictly disco. Not a bad offering, and not as golden as their previous Gold Mind album, but definitely worthwhile. First Choice's roots are gospel, yet they recorded rump shakers almost exclusively, some good, some not; sadly, the list of ballads they recorded is extensive. *—Andrew Hamilton*

● **Greatest Hits** / Nov. 26, 1996 / Salsoul ♦♦♦♦♦

One of the many first-class R&B groups that came out of Philadelphia in the 1970s, First Choice had no problem making the transition from Philly soul to Philly disco/soul. If the Three Degrees were the city's version of the Supremes, First Choice was closer in spirit to Martha & the Vandellas. This rewarding two-set shows that the soul-to-disco transition was a pretty smooth one for the exuberant divas and illustrates the impact Philly's prolific scene had on disco's development. Indeed, syncopated gems like "Armed and Extremely Dangerous" and "Smarty Pants" preceded the disco era by a few years, and helped pave the way for its creation. Meanwhile, such captivating disco-era hits as "Doctor Love," "Indian Giver" and "Hold Your Horses" prove that First Choice never forgot its soul and gospel roots. For fans of the Philly sound, *First Choice's Greatest Hits* is essential listening. *—Alex Henderson*

The Five Blind Boys of Alabama

f. 1937, Talladega, AL

Group / Traditional Gospel, Southern Gospel, Black Gospel

Evolving out of the Happyland Jubilee Singers, this traditional black gospel quartet was formed in 1937 at the Talladega Institute for the Deaf and Blind in Alabama. By the '40s they became "The Blind Boys" and recorded for Specialty, Vee-Jay, Savoy, Elektra, and other labels. Their first hit was "I Can See Everybody's Mother but Mine" in 1949. The current lineup is: Joe Watson, Jimmy Carter, Sam & Bobby Butler, Curtis Foster, Johnny Fields, and Clarence Fountain. They appeared on Broadway in *The Gospel at Colonus*, but gained much more fame during the late '90s and early '00s while recording for Peter Gabriel's Real World label a series of albums beginning with the collaboration-heavy *Spirit of the Century*. The group also appeared on Gabriel's 2002 album *Up*. *—Bil Carpenter*

★ **The Sermon** / 1993 / Specialty ♦♦♦♦♦

A treasure trove of previously unreleased material, this brings together 25 new tracks, all recorded between 1953 and 1957. Only two songs, "Heaven on My Mind" and "I'm Going Through," were ever released in any form, but the quality of the material is certainly as high as any of their early sides. Here's one of gospel's greatest groups, singing their hearts out in their absolute prime. *—Cub Koda*

Hallelujah: A Collection of Their Finest / May 18, 1999 / Music Club ♦♦♦♦

This 15-track collection brings together both live and studio recordings made for the HOB label. Both of the famous leads with the group—Clarence Fountain and Louis Dicks—are featured on tracks like "Something's Got a Hold on Me," "When I Come to the End of My Journey," "Too Close to Heaven," "Lord's Been Good to Me" and "I Got Jesus on My Mind," their two magnificent voices trading off on "Alone and Motherless," "Running for My Life," and the perennial favorite "I Saw the Light." The live tracks on here literally sweat with emotion and fervor. A nice set. *—Cub Koda*

Spirit of the Century / Apr. 24, 2001 / Real World ♦♦♦♦♦

From start to finish this album defies categorical classification. It employs the best of R&B, Afro-beat, folk, and blues while remaining true to the Blind Boys' gospel roots. And with a tasteful selection of material by Tom Waits, Mick Jagger & Keith Richards, and Ben Harper, in addition to their usual array of traditional gospel hymns and folk tunes, it will appeal to generations of listeners. Though varied in its stylings, the album works as a whole due to the high-quality production, arrangements, and musicianship throughout. The traditional "No More," in a slow and soulful arrangement, starts off with a plaintive slide guitar sampling of "Amazing Grace" and sits comfortably beside "Run for a Long Time," which features George Scott rapping over a percussive, groove-filled (à la Danny Thompson on double bass) and harmony-laden reworking of this classic. And the Stones' "Just Wanna See His Face," which is given a jubilee-like treatment that rivals the original, follows up a somber "Motherless Child" with grace and acuity. Other guests include Charlie Musselwhite on harmonica, John Hammond on guitar and Dobro, and David Lindley on oud and electric slide. *—Travis Drageset*

Higher Ground / Aug. 27, 2002 / Real World ♦♦♦

Higher Ground, the Five Blind Boys of Alabama's second album for Real World, is even more of a crossover effort than 1997's *Spirit of the Century*. It sports a classics-heavy track listing, including great choices of inspirational material from R&B legends Stevie Wonder ("Higher Ground"), Curtis Mayfield ("People Get Ready"), Aretha Franklin ("Spirit in the Dark"), Prince ("The Cross"), Jimmy Cliff ("Many Rivers to Cross"), and George Clinton ("You and Your Folks"). Another inspired choice is the backing band, sacred-steel guitarist Robert Randolph & the Family Band, which provides a rock-solid rhythm, yet also lends the feeling necessary to frame the vocals. Leads Clarence Fountain and George Scott, who've been performing together for over 50 years, direct the ensemble with gospel fire; Fountain's original, "Stand By Me," is a rollicking jubilee number done with all the energy of his mid-'50s performances. Elsewhere, Randolph contributes some great licks to "I May Not Can Se," another group original, and Ben Harper stops by to deliver a piercing high tenor on "People Get Ready." Admittedly, the Five Blind Boys aren't able to add much to often-heard classics like "Higher Ground" or "Many Rivers to Cross," and even their performance of the gospel standard "Wade in the Water" is quite wooden. *—John Bush*

The Five Crowns

f. 1951, New York, NY, **db.** 1959

Group / Doo Wop, R&B

You won't find the Five Crowns mentioned in most music reference books, even those devoted specifically to 1950s rock & roll. Many fans of R&B vocal groups, however, regard them as the definitive Harlem vocal group, and a few simply declare them the greatest vocal group that ever lived. Although the Five Crowns under their own name never made any impression on the national charts, they regularly charted locally in New York and were stars in Harlem. Their later 1950s incarnation, featuring original member Doc Green, James "Poppa" Clark, Elsbeary Hobbs, Benjamin Nelson (aka Ben E. King), and Charles Thomas, became the post-1958 Drifters, responsible for "There Goes My Baby" and the core of the group that later recorded "Up on the Roof," "Under the Boardwalk," and "On Broadway."

The Five Crowns were founded in the early 1950s on 115th Street in Harlem, and originally consisted of Wilbur "Younkie" Paul, Dock Green, and James "Poppa" Clark, John "Sonny Boy" Clark, and Claudie "Nicky" Clark. James Clark and Wilbur Paul alternated as lead singer, while Doc Green sang the baritone and bass parts. Their manager, Lover Patterson, also handled the Cadillacs, another New York-based vocal group that would make a considerable national splash of their own.

The group was signed to a contract with Rainbow Records in the summer of 1952, and released their first single, "A Star"/"You're My Inspiration," in September of 1952—"You're My Inspiration" rose to number nine locally on the Cashbox charts, and lingered there right into December of that year. Their second single, "Who Can Be True"/"$19.50 Bus," vanished without leaving much of a trace late in 1952, and their third, "Keep It a Secret"/"Why Don't You Believe Me?," issued in early 1953, didn't do much better, although "Why Don't You Believe Me?" became one of their most fondly remembered songs. Those two were intrinsically rare records, even in Harlem, the former released only on 78 rpm and the latter on a red vinyl 45, and are highly prized by collectors. Their next single, "Alone Again"/"I Don't Have to Hunt No More," also failed to sell in any serious quantity.

That record marked the end of their contract with Rainbow Records, and the group next turned up on the New York-based Old Town label, where they debuted with "You Could Be My Love"/"Good Luck Darling," followed by "Lullaby of the Bells." By this time, the group had lost cohesion, and Paul and Green worked with the Duvals on the side (two of their songs, "You Came to Me" and "Ooh Wee Baby," were issued as a Five Crowns record in early 1955).

In 1955, Doc Green revived the Five Crowns with a new lineup and a new contract with Gee Records, where they released one single. They ceased working after one more single for the Transworld label. The group was next heard from under the name the Crowns, with the lineup of Green, Clark, Hobbs, Nelson (aka Ben E. King), and Thomas.

Fortune finally smiled on the Crowns in late 1958 at an appearance at the Apollo Theater in Harlem, where they were spotted by manager George Treadwell, who had a serious problem at the time. Treadwell was the manager of the legendary R&B group the Drifters who, since 1954, had amassed an enviable record of national hits and a major name for themselves. The Drifters in late 1958 had included Bobby Hendricks (who, according to some sources, passed through one version of the Five Crowns), Gerhart Thrasher, Charlie Hughes, and Bill Pinkney. This lineup had collapsed amid infighting between each other and Treadwell. Treadwell had a major contractual obligation coming up, an appearance by the Drifters at the Apollo Theater. He heard the Crowns and offered them the chance, then and there, to become the new Drifters. They reported to Atlantic Records the following day to see how things worked in a real studio, and the following day the Five Crowns-turned-Drifters recorded "There Goes My Baby," which became the number-one single in the country.

The Five Crowns' history is scattered among the Rainbow, Old Town, Riviera, and Transworld labels, and only the Rainbow material (including the Younkie Paul/Doc Green Duvals "You Came to Me"/"Ooh Wee Baby") has been reissued in a comprehensive way. *—Bruce Eder*

● **Rainbow Sessions** / Oct. 28, 1994 / Relic ♦♦♦♦♦

The 14 songs recorded between 1952 and 1955 for Rainbow Records, showed off the daunting stylistic range of this quintet. "A Star" is a glorious piece of soaring R&B, but the real surprise is "Good Luck Darling," a jump number with a romping piano that shows off a side of the group often overlooked in favor of their elegant harmonizing. "You're My Inspiration" is perhaps the group's high point in the harmony category. They also show off their bluesier side on numbers like "$19.50 Bus," which—for reasons that likely will never be fully understood—was released but never promoted. "Ooh Wee Baby," which was Wilbur Paul and Doc Green singing with the Duvals but originally credited to the Five Crowns, is the best rock & roll song here, a midtempo dance number with a solid beat, tasteful sax, and unpretentious harmonies—it is closer in spirit to the later Drifters' sound than many of the early Five Crowns numbers. The Duvals/Five Crowns "You Came to Me" is the song that really defines the group, despite the fact that two-fifths of the group weren't on it—those achingly beautiful falsetto lead vocals and the elegant backing are what the best doo wop is about. "Man From the Moon," one of four numbers here that didn't see the light of day until the mid-'80s, is also a wonderfully smooth piece of commercial R&B. "I Don't Have to Hunt No More" is almost a throwback to the best of 1950s pop, but the sax solo in the middle is a killer. "At the Fair" is almost worth the price of the disc by itself, an outtake that shows off the group's harmony, jump, and blues sides all at once. The sound quality fluctuates, but overall it's fairly consistent, and anyone who regards themselves as a serious Drifters or general R&B fan should own this disc, if only to hear what some future Drifters were doing around the time the Drifters were just getting together and recording for the first time. *—Bruce Eder*

The Five Discs

f. 1958, Brooklyn, NY

Group / Doo Wop, R&B

Like many street-corner vocal groups who came from Brooklyn's Bed-Stuy section in the early '50s, the Five Discs had limited chart success. In 1954, lead vocalist Mario DeAndrade and Andy Jackson (bass)—both formerly of the Love Notes—joined up with Joe Barsalona (baritone), Paul Albano (first tenor), Tony Basile (second tenor), and Joe Brocco to form a new group, calling themselves the Flames. On Valentine's Day 1956, the Flames appeared on their first show with the local acts the Royaltones and the Paragons, but it wasn't until 1957 that they would cut their first demo. A songwriter named Billy Martin eventually heard the demo and recommended they re-cut it. He played their new version for Gene Schwartz, who later offered them a contract for the Emge label. At the suggestion of Albano's sister, they changed their name from the Flames to the Five Discs. In early 1958, the group recorded "I Remember" for a third time. The single on Emge was debuted on WMGM and ultimately climbed up to number 28 on the New York charts and number two in Boston.

Soon afterwards, Schwartz launched his Laurie Records, scoring an immediate hit with Dion & the Belmonts' "I Wonder Why." Because he was busy with its promotion, the Five Discs single failed to get promoted. Eager to move on, the Five Discs signed with Dwain Records and cut two sides. Due to a poor mixing job, however, the group was forced to redo the songs again. Unfortunately, neither version received any airplay. By 1960, the Five Discs signed with a new label, Yale Records, and released several singles, none of which connected them with a larger audience. By 1961, another label became interested in the group: Andy Leonetti's Tap Records, releasing a single on the Calo subsidiary. It, too, failed to sell. Soon after, the Five Discs recorded a single for Cheer Records. This single, "Never Let You Go," won Murray the K's Record of the Night and Record of the Week contests on WINS in New York City. In 1963, with Herb Kessler now acting as their manager, the Five Discs signed with Kapp Records and recorded three tracks. Once again, with a new label and new manager, came a name change, this time to the Boyfriends. *—Bryan Thomas*

- **Best of the 5 Discs** / EMGE ✦✦✦

The Five Du-Tones

Group / Soul

The Five Du-Tones originally recorded "Shake a Tail Feather" in 1963, but reaped few benefits from being the first to do so. It was their biggest record, but only reached number 51 on the pop charts and number 28 on the R&B charts. Ike & Tina Turner cut a version, as did James & Bobby Purify, whose "Tail Feather" fared better than the Five Du-Tones', going to number 25 on the pop charts and number 15 on the R&B charts in 1967 (four years after the original). It even showed up in the film *Hairspray* in 1988.

The explosive quintet members were Willie Guest, Frank McCurrey, LeRoy Joyce, James West, and Andrew Butler. They formed at Patrick Henry High School in St. Louis, MO, in 1957. St Louis was a hotbed of music talent; significant artists such as Ike & Tina Turner, Luther Ingram, Mel & Tim, Fontella Bass, and others developed in the City on the River. From 1963 to 1966, the Du-Tones recorded nine singles on George Leaner's One-derful Records. The first, "Please Change Your Mind" b/w "The Flea," sunk without a trace, as did the second, "Come Back Baby" b/w "Dry Your Eyes." However, their final release in 1963 got them working on the chitlin circuit; "Shake a Tail Feather" b/w the hilarious "Divorce Court" exploded over R&B stations across the country, and was extremely large in Chicago. The sales and chart positions didn't justify the airplay it received—it should have made the R&B Top Ten and cracked the pop Top 40.

The follow-up to "Tail Feather" was "The Gouster" backed with "Monkey See Monkey Do." The B-side was better and got some airplay, but neither side built on the momentum of its predecessor. Single number five discarded the dance craze altogether but to no avail; "Nobody But (My Baby)" b/w "That's How I Love You" did nothing. So it was back to the dance crazes, with "The Cool Bird" and "The Chicken Astronaut" being their final single for 1964; despite an incessant beat, however, "Bird" was ignored by disc jockeys. The Du-Tones' sister group, the Duettes, recorded "Bird" the same year on Mar-V-Lus, a subsidiary of One-derful; both versions flopped. One-derful dropped two more of the Du-Tones' singles in 1965: "Sweet Lips" and "The Woodbine Twine." Their most popular recording next to "Tail Feather," "Woodbine Twine" received only sporadic play, but is sought after as a collectable. The last Five Du-Tones single, "Mountain of Love"/"Outside the Record Hop," dropped in 1966; they disbanded in 1967. Leaner folded his group of labels, which included Mar-V-Lus and M-Pac Records, in 1968. *—Andrew Hamilton*

- **Shake a Tailfeather** / 1979 / P-Vine ✦✦✦✦

Japan's P-Vine Records has done what no company in the States ever did: compile and release an album by the Five Du-Tones. It's a curious assembly, though. The group cut eight singles for Chicago's One-derful Records, but this collection omits four: their debut, "Come Back Baby," "Monkey See, Monkey Do," "The Cool Bird," and "Mountain of Love." The collection does include the original "Shake a Tail Feather," which didn't chart as high as its remakes but was their biggest record. The Du-Tones were exciting live, and just as energetic in the studio. "Divorce Court" is a rollicking R&B number that hits like a dumpster of bricks. The non-charting singles "The Woodbine Twine," "That's How I Love You," and "Let Me Love You" are other standouts. "Don't Let Go," "The Flea," "My World," and "Soul" never appeared on singles, raising the possibility of other unreleased Five Du-Tones tracks lying around somewhere. *—Andrew Hamilton*

The Five Keys

f. 1949, Newport News, VA

Group / East Coast Blues, Doo Wop, R&B

The Five Keys are generally regarded by aficionados of 1950s R&B vocal group harmony as one of the finest groups to ever record in this genre. They are best-known for their Capitol recordings of "Wisdom of a Fool," "Close Your Eyes," "Ling Ting Tong," and "Out of Sight, Out of Mind." But in collectors' circles their earlier recordings for Aladdin such as "My Saddest Hour," "Glory of Love," and "Red Sails in the Sunset" are even more highly revered and sought after.

The group originally consisted of two sets of brothers: Rudy and Bernie West and Raphael and Ripley Ingram, all hailing from Newport News, VA. The West and Ingram brothers initially took on the name the Sentimental Four and soon decided to show off their talents by entering a local amateur program at the Jefferson Theater. After winning three consecutive weeks of amateur contests at the Jefferson, they were invited to perform at the prestigious Apollo Theater in New York City, where they also won. This led to subsequent engagements at the Royal and Howard Theaters.

As the group established their reputation along the Eastern Seaboard, they were noticed by Eddie Mesner, owner of the California-based Aladdin Records, who signed them to a recording contract. About this time, Raphael went into the army and was replaced by Maryland Pierce (formerly of the Avalons). Also added was another singer, Dickie Smith, and a sixth man, piano player Joe Jones. Reflecting the personnel changes, their name was changed from the Sentimental Four to the Five Keys. The Keys toured both the East and West Coasts and their Aladdin songs were recorded in New York and Los Angeles.

In 1953, both Rudy and Dickie entered the army and were replaced by Ramon Loper and Ulysses Hicks. By mid-1954, the Keys' contract with Aladdin was expiring and their last Aladdin release, "Deep in My Heart," was reviewed in June of that year. In July of 1954, the Five Keys found themselves in the RCA studios, where they recorded four tracks. Two remained unreleased, and "Lawdy Miss Mary" backed with "I'll Follow You" was issued in August 1954 on RCA's subsidiary Groove label. The Keys' manager, Saul Richfield, must have been working very hard for his group at this time, for on August 29, 1954, Capitol announced that they had signed the Five Keys. Now recording for Capitol, the Five Keys released "Ling Ting Tong," with Pierce on lead. The record was successful enough to eventually land them a spot of *The Ed Sullivan Show*. When Hicks died suddenly in 1954, and before Rudy returned home from the service, the lead tenor position was filled temporarily by Dickie Smith's cousin, Willie Winfield of the Harptones.

But by 1955, Rudy West was back and the Five Keys were in the right place at the right time to be recorded using Capitol's advanced audio production techniques. With Rudy on lead, and backed by the Howard Biggs Orchestra, they recorded "Out of Sight, Out of Mind" and "Wisdom of a Fool." Another great Capitol release, "Close Your Eyes," featured Maryland Pierce on lead, echoed hauntingly by Rudy's high-floating tenor. Tired of touring, Rudy retired from the group in 1958. In 1959, with the addition of Dickie Threat in Rudy's spot, they recorded several sides for the King label, the most notable being "Dream On" and "One Great Love." Perhaps it was because the record market was changing, or maybe the Keys weren't quite the same without Rudy, but they could not sustain the success they had achieved at Capitol. *—Jim Dunn & Nikki Gustafson*

Capitol Collectors Series / 1989 / Capitol ✦✦✦

Worthwhile companion volume to *The Aladdin Years*, containing all of their Top 100 singles—"Ling Ting Tong," "Wisdom of a Fool," "Let There Be You," and "Out of Sight, Out of Mind"—as well as lesser-known tracks like "I Wish I'd Never Learned to Read" and "My Pigeon's Gone." *—Stephen Thomas Erlewine*

- **The Aladdin Years** / 1991 / EMI America ✦✦✦✦✦

This early '50s doo wop has a highly polished, easy-on-the-ears sheen. Heavy on the ballads, it also has a few uptempo items. *—Bill Dahl*

Dream On / 1991 / Charly ✦✦✦✦

Strictly speaking, this 24-song collection misses the best-known Five Keys material, instead covering their history with King Records, where they signed after their stays with Aladdin and Capitol Records, and after the departure of original lead singer Rudy West. Thomas Threat is singing lead, backed by Bernie West, Ripley Ingram, Maryland Pierce, and Dickie Smith. But musically, this is an extraordinarily powerful body of work, an hour of stirring and stunningly beautiful vocal R&B, passionate, jaunty, and representative of the best of what this music had to offer before the arrival of Motown co-opted the sound and took it into new directions. The songs were cut between August of 1959 and March of 1960, and feature the group once again as a pure R&B vocal harmony ensemble, without any of the pop-style embellishments of their Capitol sides. The material is, in many ways, a throwback to their early sides, with soulful ballads dominating. At various times, they sound like the Platters or the Coasters, and even Bo Diddley's influence shows up on "Will You." Both the title tune and "Too Late" show Thomas Threat sounding more than a little like Jackie Wilson or Clyde McPhatter in their respective primes. Even the novelty tunes here work—"Dancing Senorita" is presented with such infectious good spirits that it is impossible not to like. The only pity is that the session records don't reveal the names of the backup band members, who were also quite good here. *—Bruce Eder*

Golden Classics / 1993 / Collectables ✦✦✦✦✦

The Newport News, VA, crooners deliver 20 of their classiest, including their big novelty hit "Ling Ting Tong" and the original, enchanting version of Chuck Willis' "Close Your Eyes." Three excellent lead singers—Rudy West, Maryland Pierce, and Dickie Smith—kept their sound fresh. Among the selections are many R&B interpretations of standards including "She's the Most," "Dream," and "My Pigeon's Gone." *—Andrew Hamilton*

Best of the Capitol and the Aladdin Years / Nov. 28, 2000 / Collectables ✦✦✦✦✦

This two-CD set packages the Aladdin and Capitol tracks of the warblers from Newport News, VA. The 45 tracks released from 1951 to 1958 encompass all their hits and misses. The songs are not in chronological order, which is a real bummer; instead, they're compiled according to popularity. "Ling Ting Tong" (Capitol, September 1954), their must successful recording (number five on the R&B chart and number-28 pop) is the first track, while their first single, "With a Broken Heart" (Aladdin, April 1951), doesn't appear until the 21st track. The collection features their original rendition of Chuck Willis' "Close Your Eyes" and the Ink Spots-ish "The Verdict," along with "Out of Sight, Out of Mind," "Let There Be You," "I Wish I'd Never Learned to Read," and many more. Some later recordings on King and other small labels are not included. *—Andrew Hamilton*

The "5" Royales

f. 1952, Winston-Salem, NC, **db.** 1965

Group / R&B

The "5" Royales were a relatively unheralded, but significant, link between early R&B and early soul in their combination of doo wop, jump blues, and gospel styles. Their commercial success was relatively modest—they had seven Top Ten R&B hits in the 1950s, most recorded in the span of little over a year between late 1952 and late 1953. A few of their singles would prove extremely popular in cover versions by other artists, though—James Brown and Aretha Franklin tore it up with "Think," Ray Charles covered "Tell the Truth," and the Shirelles (and later the Mamas & the Papas) had pop success with "Dedicated to the One I Love." Almost all of their material was written by guitarist Lowman Pauling, who influenced Steve Cropper with his biting and bluesy guitar lines, which at their most ferocious almost sound like a precursor to blues-rock.

Pauling's guitar is pretty muted on their early sides, though, which sometimes walk the line between gospel and R&B. The gospel elements aren't surprising, given that the Royales were originally known as the Royal Sons Quintet when they formed in Winston-Salem, NC. In fact, they were still known as the Royal Sons Quintet when they began recording for Apollo in the early '50s, although they had six members. They would change their name to the "5" Royales in 1952, although they would, confusingly, remain a six-man outfit for a while; the quotes around the 5 in their billing were designed to alleviate some of the confusion. The Apollo singles "Baby Don't Do It" and "Help Me Somebody" made number one on the R&B charts in 1953, and they had a few other hits for Apollo before being lured away to King Records in 1954.

Although the group would remain on King for the rest of the 1950s, they would only enter the R&B Top Ten two more times, with "Think" and "Tears of Joy" (both in 1957). Their later sides, however, are their best, as Pauling became much more assertive on the guitar, dashing off some piercing and fluid solos. Some of these solos are among the heaviest and wildest in '50s rock, on both relatively well-known cuts like "Think," and virtually unknown numbers like "The Slummer the Slum." Greil Marcus once wrote something to the effect that a young Eric Clapton would have once paid to hold Pauling's coat. They remained primarily a harmony vocal group, though, and if their late-'50s sides are considerably more modernized than their early Apollo hits, they're still a lot closer to doo wop than soul.

Even when their records weren't selling, the "5" Royales were a popular touring band. Their constant activity at King Records, in all likelihood, had some influence on the young James Brown, then starting his career on the same label; one of Brown's first big R&B hits was a frenetic cover of "Think." They couldn't sustain themselves without more hits, though. After leaving King and recording some more sides in the early '60s, they finally broke up by 1965. *—Richie Unterberger*

Dedicated to You / 1957 / King ✦✦✦✦✦

This may be the great lost R&B record of the 1950s. The "5" Royales were a fine singing group long before this release, but on these sides recorded between 1955 and 1957, guitarist Lowman Pauling cuts loose with the most fiery guitar fills this side of Ike Turner. From the opening shout of "Think" to the closing notes of "Thirty Second Lover," Dedicated to You is a guitar *tour de force*. The album's crowning moment comes on "Say It," where Clarence Paul's pleading vocal is answered with Pauling's bluesy replies. Other highlights include Bill Doggett's gospel-tinged organ on "Someone Made You For Me," several fine sax solos ("Don't Be Ashamed," "Right Around the Corner") and the straightforward rocker "Messin' Up." An overlooked classic. *—J.P. Ollio*

Sing "Baby Don't Do It" / Dec. 1987 / Relic ✦✦✦✦✦

Sing "Laundromat Blues" / Dec. 1987 / Relic ✦✦✦

★ **Monkey Hips and Rice: The "5" Royales Anthology** / Mar. 8, 1994 / Rhino ✦✦✦✦✦

The "5" Royales are legendary, primarily in the sense that their legend grew over the years, as the status of what they achieved began to be realized. Like many trailblazing groups, the "5" Royales made music that wasn't fully appreciated at the time and is pigeonholed into the influential but not heard category. This makes their list of accomplishments seem academic—they pushed through gospel and doo wop, incorporating jump and urban blues and, eventually, rock & roll, paving the way toward the soul of the '60s. Led by guitarist/songwriter Lowman Pauling, the group was remarkably versatile, stretching the accepted limits of what a vocal group could do, particularly because Pauling's guitar and earthy, soulful songwriting ignored boundaries and let the group follow suit. Listen to "Think," their second best-known song ("Dedicated to the One I Love" ranks as their first, with covers by the Shirelles and the Mamas & the Papas). Later covered by James Brown in a rampaging, unhinged fashion, this has the basic stuttering, stop-start rhythm of that version, surrounded by gospel-influenced harmonies and great bluesy guitar—touching on nearly everything the group fused together to create their own sound, one that uncannily suggested the sound of soul in the '60s. This approach gelled a little later in their career, toward the end of the '50s, during the recordings chronicled on the second disc of *Monkey Hips and Rice*, Rhino's impeccable career-spanning 1994 collection. On the first disc, the group is still quite innovative, even if the seams show, as the group blends together harmony groups, gospel, blues and R&B in a lively fashion. They take off toward the end of the first disc, stretching through the second disc, with a stretch of invigorating music that is among the greatest R&B ever recorded. Perhaps two discs may seem like a lot for those that haven't heard the "5" Royales before, but this is not just the most comprehensive set of "5" Royales material yet assembled, it's also the best, illustrating not just their importance, but making that history lesson fun. *—Stephen Thomas Erlewine*

● **Apollo Sessions** / Sep. 1, 1995 / Collectables ✦✦✦✦✦

Although not the career-long survey of the Rhino anthology, this 23-song, 62-minute collection covers the "5" Royales' very best years, spent with Apollo Records from 1951 until 1955, first as the Royals ("Give Me One More Chance") and then as a quintet under their more familiar name. Their sound here is vocally very smooth yet passionate, but the instrumental backings are exuberant and raunchy, the kind of combination that made acts like this such a threat to the established popular music of the era. The mix of jump blues with accomplished gospel-influenced harmony singing (best represented on the delightful "What's That" or "All Righty," or, most startling of all, "Baby Take All of Me," with its abandoned wailing in the background) helped make their music some of the most expressive and satisfying of the period. Their way with a chorus and a phrase made the Royales one of the top R&B acts of their era, although it wasn't until much later that they made the jump to pop stardom. Unfortunately, during the period represented here, they were one of those R&B acts whose radio play exceeded their record sales (at least, as reported by Apollo, one reason they jumped to King Records). From 1951 until 1955, they helped provide the soundtrack against which mainstream rock & roll was born and took root with the public. On that basis alone, this material is worth hearing and owning; it was the soil in which rock & roll sprouted, the stream in which other acts' commercial hits were spawned and nurtured. They later had their share of successes, but this is their real sound, raw, sweet and elegant all at the same time. *—Bruce Eder*

All Righty!: Apollo Recordings / Mar. 3, 1999 / WestSide ✦✦✦✦

All Righty! is the first complete collection of the "5" Royales' recordings for Apollo Records from 1951 to 1955, including even their gospel sides (recorded as the Royal Sons Quintet). *—John Bush*

Take Me With You Baby / Mar. 14, 2000 / Purple Pyramid ✦✦✦✦

A nice collection of the group's latter-day material originally waxed for the Memphis House of Blues imprint. Some of these sides were later issued on Vee-Jay and ABC/Paramount, but the Memphis stamp of Willie Mitchell's early work is all over these tracks. Highlights include the previously unissued "Show Me," "I Got to Know," "She Did Me Wrong," and a nice stab at James Brown's "Please Please Please." Usually, latter-day sides are a load of diminished returns, but these tracks are every bit as enjoyable as their more famous counterparts. Well worth adding to the shopping cart. *—Cub Koda*

The Five Satins

f. 1956, New Haven, CT, **db.** 1961

Group / Doo Wop

The Five Satins are best-known for the doo wop classic "In the Still of the Night," a song that was popular enough to make the group one of the most famous doo wop outfits, although they never had another hit of the same magnitude.

The origins of the Five Satins lie in the Scarlets, a New Haven, Connecticut, doo wop group led by Fred Parris. The Scarlets formed in 1953, while Parris was still in high school. The group had a local hit with "Dear One" the following year. In 1954, Parris formed the Five Satins with vocalists Al Denby, Ed Martin and Jim Freeman. Within the next year, Parris had the group record "In the Still of the Night," a song he had recently written, in the basement of a local church. The first single the group released was "In the Still of the Night." The single was released on Standard Records in the spring of 1956. By the end of the year, it had been leased to Ember and it became a huge hit, peaking at number three on the R&B charts and number 25 on the pop charts.

By the time "In the Still of the Night" scaled the charts, Parris had been drafted into the army. He was stationed in Japan when the song became a hit, and he was still stationed in Japan when the group recorded the follow-up single, "To the Aisle." For that single, Bill Baker handled the lead vocals. "To the Aisle" became a Top Ten R&B hit in the summer of 1957. Parris returned from the army in 1958. Upon his return, he reorganized the group, adding Richie Freeman, Sylvester Hopkins, West Forbes, and Lou Peeples. This incarnation of the group had a minor hit in the fall of 1959 with "Shadows."

In 1960, "In Still of the Night" re-entered the pop charts thanks to its exposure on Art Laboe's first *Oldies but Goodies* compilation. The repeated success of the single sparked another minor hit for the band in 1960, a cover of the standard "I'll Be Seeing You." During the remainder of the '60s and early '70s, Parris led various incarnations of the Five Satins through oldies revues in America and Europe; they also recorded occasionally during this time. In 1974, the group signed a contract with Kirsner Records and released a single, "Two Different Worlds." Two years later, they briefly changed their name to Black Satin and released a single called "Everybody Stand Up and Clap Your Hands (For the Entertainer)," which became a Top 50 R&B hit.

Shortly afterward, the group reverted to the Five Satins name. In 1982, the Five Satins had their last hit with a doo wop medley entitled "Memories of Days Gone By." The single, which was released on Elektra Records, peaked at number 71 on the pop charts. For the remainder of the '80s and the '90s, Fred Parris led various lineups of the Five Satins and the group performed regularly at oldies shows in America and Europe. *—Stephen Thomas Erlewine*

The Five Satins Sing Their Greatest Hits / 1982 / Collectables ✦✦✦✦✦

The Five Satins Sing Their Greatest Hits may not have the fanciest packaging, and the sound is merely adequate, but it remains a hell of a good Five Satins collection, containing a robust 24 tracks. That means it doesn't just have "In the Still of the Night," it has a wealth of other singles that prove that the group was one of the finest doo wop outfits. Perhaps it could have been presented with a little more care, but it's still a terrific overview. *—Stephen Thomas Erlewine*

● **In the Still of the Night** / 1990 / Relic ✦✦✦✦✦

Everything you need from this sumptuous and smoochy late-night doo wop quintet is here. The title cut is a work of art worth listening to over and over. *—John Floyd*

Five Special

f. 1978, Detroit, MI, **db.** 1981

Group / Soul, Urban

This Detroit vocal group included lead singer Bryan Banks, the brother of the Dramatics' Ron Banks. They got off to a fast start in 1979, as their Elektra single "Why Leave Us Alone" made it to number nine on the R&B charts. It was their lone big hit; two other singles scrapped the R&B Top 30, and they soon disbanded. Greg Finley, Steve Harris, Steve Boyd, and Mike Petillo were the other members. *—Ron Wynn*

● **Five Special** / 1979 / Elektra ♦♦♦

This is the first of only two albums the group recorded. While most of the songs are attractively arranged and written with buoyant melodies, they seem to deviate from that joyous feeling initially conveyed. On some of the tracks, Bryan Banks' lead vocals are inconsistent, with the exceptions being "Why Leave Us Alone" and "You're Something Special." The former did crack the R&B Top Ten, with its disco rhythm track. The latter is the most adoring number on the album. The arrangement complements the lyric, which comes across as tender and sincere as ever. *—Craig Lytle*

Special Edition / 1980 / Elektra ♦♦♦

Ron Banks (of the Dramatics) produced Five Special, a five-man group featuring his younger brother Bryan. The two groups are vastly different; Five Special is more laid-back and jazzy than the Dramatics. Bryan sings in a light, wafer-thin falsetto that's pretty to hear but lacks bite and fire. *Special Edition* is like a Chinese meal; you enjoy it while it's playing, but it fails to satisfy, and you're starving for sounds again in an hour. That said, "Jam," "Heaven You Are to Me," "Do Something Special for Your Lady," and "Why Not Be Mine for a While" are all arresting concoctions, good late-night music that would have been more compelling with Ron Banks on lead. The group's deep bass singer and expressive tenor are excellent and should have been featured more. *—Andrew Hamilton*

The Five Stairsteps

f. 1965, Chicago, IL, **db.** 1976

Group / Chicago Soul, Soul, Pop-Soul, Uptown Soul

The Five Stairsteps were "The First Family of Soul." A title bestowed upon the Chicago-based teenaged group in part because of their astounding five-year run of hits, which included the 1970 million-selling single "O-o-h Child." "The First Family..." title was later adapted by the Jackson 5.

The children of Clarence Sr. and Betty Burke, the Five Stairsteps were formed in 1958 as a five-member brother and sister teenaged vocal group. The group got its name, "the Five Stairsteps," when "Momma Stairsteps" as Betty Burke was affectionately called, noticed that her kids looked like stair steps when stood next to each other according to age. Most of the members, Clarence Jr., Aloha, James, Dennis, and Kenneth attended Harlan High School. Clarence Jr., the eldest son, was the group's lead singer, choreographed dance routines, was the principal songwriter, and played guitar. Contralto Aloha also attended Harlan High where she played trumpet in the school's concert orchestra. First tenor James sang lead on the group's Top 40 R&B hit "Ooh Baby Baby"; he also played guitar and was a skilled line artist who won three scholarships to the Art Institute of Chicago and won an Artist of the Year Award from the Chicago Board of Education. Second tenor Kenneth was a talented bass player.

Clarence Sr., a detective for the Chicago Police Department, played bass, oversaw the group's material, and was their manager. He backed the group on bass guitar and co-wrote songs with Clarence Jr. and Gregory Fowler. After winning first prize in a talent contest at the legendary Regal Theater, the Five Stairsteps were deluged with recording contract offers. Neighbor and family friend Fred Cash of the Impressions introduced the group to Curtis Mayfield.

Signing with Mayfield's Windy City label, distributed by Philadelphia-based Cameo Parkway Records, their first single was the Burke-written ballad "You Waited Too Long" b/w the upbeat "Don't Waste Your Time," a Mayfield song. A double-sided hit in Chicago, the A-side charted number-16 R&B on *Billboard*'s charts in the spring of 1966. More hits followed: the soft, lilting "World of Fantasy" b/w "Playgirl's Love," the "blue light in the basement" ballad "Come Back" b/w "You Don't Love Me," and the slinky, exotic "Danger! She's a Stranger" b/w "Behind Curtains"—most of the singles were on the LP *The Five Stairsteps*.

About the end of 1967, Cameo-Parkway folded and Windy C switched to Art Kass' NY-based Buddah Records through former Cameo-Parkway executive Neil Bogart who joined the new label as co-president. Bogart would late be president of Casablanca Records. The group's second album, *Family Portrait*, whose cover was a collection of Burke family photos, was recorded and produced in Chicago by Clarence Jr. With the addition of their three-year-old brother, the group became the Five Stairsteps & Cubie. *Family Portrait* yielded two hit singles, "Something's Missing" b/w "Tell Me Who," a cover of Jimmy Charles & the Revelletts' 1960 R&B/pop hit "A Million to One" b/w "Tell Me Who," and "The Shadow of Your Love" b/w "Bad News."

Switching to Mayfield's Curtom Records, they continued to chart with "Don't Change Your Love" b/w "New Dance Craze," "Baby Make Me Feel So Good," "Madame Mary," and the midtempo groover "We Must Be in Love." The group often toured with the Impressions. Signing with Buddah Records, the group was once again known as the Five Stairsteps. In the spring of 1970, the group released their sole certified million-seller and biggest pop hit, "O-o-h Child" (written by Stan Vincent), which hit number-14 R&B and number-eight pop. The flip side, a cover of John Lennon & Paul McCartney's "Dear Prudence," charted number 49 R&B.

The following year, the group resurfaced as the Stairsteps with two charting Buddah singles: "Didn't It Look So Easy" and "I Love You-Stop." The group appeared in the 1970 movie *Soul to Soul*, a documentary of a benefit concert filmed at New York's Yankee Stadium and on the NY-produced nationally syndicated show *Soul*. During the early '70s, sister Aloha married and both she and Cubie left the group. Kenneth played bass on records and tours of Billy Preston, who later introduced the Stairsteps to the Beatles and the group signed with George Harrison's Dark Horse label distributed by A&M Records. *2nd Resurrection* was issued in February 1976, produced by Billy Preston, Robert Margouleff, and the Stairsteps. "From Us to You," written by Clarence Jr. and Kenneth Burke, was the group's biggest hit since "O-o-h Child," peaking at number-ten R&B in early 1976 (b/w "Time").

Kenneth Burke became Keni Burke, a top session bassist, co-writing with Allan Felder the inspiring "Risin' to the Top," which was on his 1982 RCA LP *Changes* and later was the source of numerous rap/hip-hop hits including Mary J. Blige's "Love No Limit" and Doug E. Fresh's "Keep Risin' to the Top." He also carved out an impressive career as a producer. He can be heard on Bill Withers' *Greatest Hits*, *Lose Control* by Silk, *People Get Ready: The Curtis Mayfield Story*, *Best of My Love: The Best of the Emotions Keep It Comin'* by Keith Sweat, *Radio Raffi* by Raffi, Ecstasy's *Dance: The Best of Narada Michael Walden*, *Steppin' Out* by George Howard, *Happy Love* by Natalie Cole, D.J. Rogers (*Love Music & Life*, RCA 1977), *Billy Preston*, the 1999 Music Club CD, *Classic Philadelphia Years*, and the Jones Girls' *Keep It Comin'* and his 1998 Expansion/ Sony/3MW CD *Nothin' but Love*. The Stairsteps evolved into the Invisible Man's Band and their Mango single "All Night Thing" hit number nine R&B in spring 1980. *—Ed Hogan*

The Five Stairsteps / 1967 / Windy ♦♦♦♦♦

A sparkling debut by the offspring of Clarence Burke and Mama Stairstep. The Stairsteps are four brothers and one sister, all between the ages of 13 and 17: Clarence Jr., Aloha, James, Dennis, and Kenneth Burke. Curtis Mayfield produced the set and highlighted their unique and arresting bloodline harmonies. Clarence was only 16 when he cut "Come Back," but he sings (or cries) it like he has experienced the agonizing pain of losing someone dear first-hand. "World of Fantasy" (written by Clarence Jr.) finds the teenager crooning about a world where he's never alone, a world of true make-believe—some pretty surreal lyrics for a high schooler. Only on "Playgirls Love" is their whimsical kid side evident. Clarence Jr. wrote most of the material; Curtis Mayfield contributed "Behind Curtains" and "Don't Waste Your Time," an enjoyable, energetic romp about romance. The flip side, "You Waited Too Long," was a far more serious tale of love that was applicable to all ages; the crying ballad, along with others, should have established the group as heavy hitters, but it was only a modest hit for the Burke children. Brother James cries as good as Clarence on the group's rendition of "Ooh Baby Baby." In all, ten slices of magic from the First Family of Soul. *—Andrew Hamilton*

Our Family Portrait / 1967 / Buddah ♦♦♦

This fine album by the Five Stairsteps would have been better if they hadn't included everybody in their family on the project. The original five Burke siblings display their classic harmonies and crying leads on a well-rounded selection of songs. "Something's Missing," "Bad News," "Find Me," and "You Make Me So Mad" are all excellent tales of unrequited young love. Sister Aloha co-leads Hal David & Burt Bacharach's "The Look of Love" with brother Clarence Jr. and does a beautiful job; the backing harmonies boomerang around the leads and embellish the exquisite song. A good remake of Jimmy Charles' "A Million to One" rounds up the good stuff. Now for the mediocre: "Momma and Poppa Stairsteps" (Betty Burke and Clarence Sr.) each lead a song. Clarence Sr. does an archaic version of "I Remember You" (the old classic from the '40s) in classic '40s style. This is not what buyers and fans of the Stairsteps expected to find on a contemporary album. Betty Burke harkens back to the '40s also, with an easy listening rendition of "Windows of the World." The two would have been better off doing an album together, sans their children. The Burke parents both possessed quality voices; they just sang in an old style. Cubie's "New Dance Craze" is a joke; having a four- or five-year-old babbling over a bubblegum musical track does not a song make. *—Andrew Hamilton*

Love's Happening / 1968 / Curtom ♦♦♦

Producer Curtis Mayfield gives the revamped Five Stairsteps a bouncy, younger sound on their sophomore release. Member Clarence Burke Jr. composed most of the songs on their first album; this time, Mayfield has the biggest say. Clarence sounded like he was crying on the first LP; on this release, Mayfield has eliminated most of the pain in his voice. Three Impression remakes get a half-hearted treatment by the Stairsteps. However, they excel on Mayfield's "Stay Close to Me" and the gorgeous, floating, testimonial "Baby Make Me Feel So Good." The backing vocals on "Baby" are unique to the Stairsteps; the chorus is sung in staccato blips with voices bouncing around the lead like pinballs. Unlike the remakes, these Mayfield compositions seemed tailored for the group. A common misconception with this LP is that Cubie played a major role—he didn't. Cubie was only four or five years old when they waxed this; that's Cubie babbling on "New Dance Craze." *—Andrew Hamilton*

The Stairsteps / 1970 / Buddah ♦♦♦

Because of "O-o-h Child," a million-seller, this is probably the Five Stairsteps' best-selling album, but it's definitely not their most satisfying. The group attempted to expand their fan base by including a couple of Lennon & McCartney selections and appearing like a '70s psychedelic gang on the album cover. One of the songs is entitled "Vice the Lights"—I have no idea what that means. Side two is more melodic than side one, but except for "O-o-h Child" and "Who Do You Belong To," the slowies don't compare to their earlier whiners. The album's nine songs adds up to only 26 minutes of music; the whole shebang fits on one side of a blank 60-minute cassette with room to spare. *—Andrew Hamilton*

Step by Step by Step / 1970 / Buddah ♦♦

Scraped into *Billboard*'s Top 200 Albums at number 199 early in 1971, a disappointing showing considering this 14-track LP features the cream of the siblings Curtom recordings and their biggest hit, "O-o-h Child." Collectable Records updated this album on CD, *The Five Stairsteps Greatest Hits*, but used the cover of the Stairsteps' (then the Five Stairsteps) first Curtom LP instead of the *Step by Step by Step* cover. Ones you'll never tire of include the winners: "You Waited Too Long," "World of Fantasy," "Come Back," and "Baby Make Me Feel Good," a floater with intricate backing harmonies that seemingly only family can accomplish. *—Andrew Hamilton*

Comeback: The Best of the Five Stairsteps / Aug. 19, 1996 / Sequel ♦♦♦♦

Comeback: The Best of the Five Stairsteps contains all of the group's major R&B hits, from "You Waited Too Long" and "World of Fantasy" to "O-o-h Child." For some listeners, there may be a little bit too much material here, especially since their lesser-known singles weren't quite as good as the hits, but this remains the definitive overview of the group's career. *—Stephen Thomas Erlewine*

- **The First Family of Soul: The Best of the Five Stairsteps** / Nov. 6, 2001 / Buddha ✦✦✦✦✦

Though fans of the Jackson 5 or the Staple Singers would love arguing the claim of the title, the Five Stairsteps recorded some solid Windy City soul during the late '60s and early '70s, just a small step below the level of the Chi-Lites or the Impressions (whose Curtis Mayfield signed the group to his Windy C label and produced much of their material). Since their only well-known hit, "O-o-h Child," was also one of their last, it's appropriately relegated to the end of this collection, though neophytes may find it a difficult chore waiting 16 tracks to get to it. Easing the way are a pair of early Mayfield gems—"You Waited Too Long" and "Danger! She's a Stranger"—both superb examples of yearning, baroque soul. "Playgirl's Love" would've been a perfect fit on an Impressions LP, while a cover of Smokey Robinson & the Miracles' "Ooh Baby Baby" proved a splendid choice of material. Though hit-seekers may prefer the *Greatest Hits* or *Encore Collection* sets, fans of the breezy Chicago sound or smooth supper-club soul will find much on this Buddha compilation to love. *—John Bush*

5 Star

f. 1983, England

Group / Urban, Disco, Soul

This family quintet from Britain featured lead vocalist Deniece, plus Stedman, Doris, Lorraine, and Delroy Pearson. Their RCA debut single, "All Fall Down," reached 16 on the R&B charts, while "Let Me Be the One" started a string of Top Ten hits. It was their biggest, reaching number two; "Love Take Over" and "Can't Wait Another Minute" were the others. They also landed "If I Say Yes" and "Are You Man Enough" in the Top 20. They released a comeback LP in 1994, and continued recording into the new millennium. *—Ron Wynn*

Luxury of Life / 1985 / RCA ✦✦

The best album from the British family group 5 Star. It had an innocence, genuine interaction, and intensity that came both from good production and the finest songs they ever received. They scored two chart singles, got good response in both America and England, and seemed on their way. *—Ron Wynn*

- **Silk & Steel** / 1986 / RCA ✦✦✦

A good entry from the British brother and sister act 5 Star. It wasn't as consistently well done as its predecessor, but the production was just as polished and the arrangements evenly divided between cutesy dance-pop and harder soul. They solidifed the base they had with the American R&B audience and also made a successful international tour. *—Ron Wynn*

Roberta Flack

b. Feb. 10, 1939, Asheville, NC

Vocals, Piano / Soul, Soft Rock, Smooth Soul, Quiet Storm, Urban

Classy, urbane, reserved, smooth, and sophisticated—all of these terms have been used to describe the music of Roberta Flack, particularly her string of romantic, light-jazz ballad hits in the 1970s, which continue to enjoy popularity on MOR-oriented adult contemporary stations. Flack was the daughter of a church organist and started playing piano early enough to get a music scholarship and eventual degree from Howard University. After a period of student teaching, Flack was discovered singing at a club by jazz musician Les McCann and signed to Atlantic. Her first two albums were well-received but produced no hit singles; however, that all changed when a version of Ewan MacColl's "The First Time Ever I Saw Your Face," from her first LP, was included in the soundtrack of *Play Misty for Me*. The single zoomed to number one in 1972 and remained there for six weeks, becoming that year's biggest hit.

Flack followed it with the first of several duets with Howard classmate Donny Hathaway, "Where Is the Love." "Killing Me Softly With His Song" became Flack's second number one hit (five weeks) in 1973, and after topping the charts again in 1974 with "Feel Like Makin' Love," Flack took a break from performing to concentrate on recording and charitable causes. She charted several more times over the next few years, but a major blow struck in 1979 when Hathaway committed suicide. Devastated, Flack was forced to find another partner and eventually did in Peabo Bryson, with whom she toured in 1980. The two recorded together in 1983, scoring a hit duet with "Tonight, I Celebrate My Love." Flack spent the remainder of the '80s touring and performing, often with orchestras, and also several times with Miles Davis. She returned to the Top Ten once more in 1991 with "Set the Night to Music," a duet with Maxi Priest. *—Steve Huey*

First Take / Jun. 20, 1969 / Atlantic ✦✦✦✦✦

Roberta Flack's debut album, titled *First Take* in true underachiever fashion, introduced a singer who'd assimilated the powerful interpretive talents of Nina Simone and Sarah Vaughan, the earthy power of Aretha Franklin, and the crystal purity and emotional resonance of folksingers like Judy Collins. Indeed, the album often sounded more like vocal jazz or folk than soul, beginning with the credits: a core quartet of Flack on piano, John Pizzarelli on guitar, Ron Carter on bass, and Ray Lucas on drums, as fine a lineup as any pop singer could hope to recruit. With only one exception—the bluesy, grooving opener "Compared to What," during which Flack proves her chops as a soul belter—she concentrates on readings of soft, meditative material. A pair of folk covers, "The First Time Ever I Saw Your Face" and "Hey, That's No Way to Say Goodbye," are heart-wrenching standouts; the first even became a surprise hit two years later, when its appearance in the Clint Eastwood film *Play Misty for Me* pushed it to the top of the pop charts and earned Flack her first Grammy award for Record of the Year. Her arrangement of the traditional "I Told Jesus" has a simmering power, while "Ballad of the Sad Young Men" summons a stately sense of melancholy. Flack also included two songs from her college friend and future duet partner, Donny Hathaway, including a tender examination of the classic May-December romance titled "Our Ages or Our Hearts." The string arrangements of William Fischer wisely keep to the background, lending an added emotional weight to all of Flack's pronouncements. No soul artist had ever recorded a record like this, making *First Take* one of the most fascinating soul debuts of the era. *—John Bush*

Chapter Two / Aug. 1970 / Atlantic ✦✦✦✦

A great album and the release that made Roberta Flack a major soul and R&B artist in the early '70s. She had a soft, compelling, alluring voice, and was able to convincingly switch gears and also convey anger, regret, hurt, or despair. Those who thought Flack was a one-hit wonder, or didn't think she could make the transition from doing mostly jazz to other styles, were convinced otherwise. *—Ron Wynn*

Quiet Fire / Nov. 1971 / Atlantic ✦✦✦✦✦

Quiet Fire proves to be an apt title, as Flack's MOR-informed jazz and gospel vocals simmer just below the surface on the eight sides here. Forgoing the full-throttled delivery of, say, Aretha Franklin, Flack translates the pathos of gospel expression into measured intensity and sighing, elongated phrases. There's even a bit of Carole King's ashen tone in Flack's voice, as manifested on songs like "Let Them Talk," Van McCoy's "Sweet Bitter Love," and a meditative reworking of King's "Will You Still Love Me Tomorrow." The album's other high-profile cover, "Bridge Over Troubled Waters," features the ideal setting for Flack's airy pipes with a tasteful backdrop of strings and a chorus featuring soul songstress Cissy Houston (Whitney's mom). Switching from this hushed sanctity, Flack digs into some groove-heavy Southern soul on "Go Up Moses," "Sunday and Sister Jones," and an amazing version of the Bee Gees hit "To Love Somebody" (this perennial number has been done by everyone from Rita Marley to Hank Williams Jr.). Flack finally completes the modern triumvirate of Southern music, adding the country tones of Jimmy Webb's "See You Then" to the *Quiet Fire*'s stock of gospel and soul. And thanks to top players like guitarist Hugh McCracken, organist Richard Tee, bassist Chuck Rainey, and drummer Bernard Purdie, the varied mix all comes off sounding seamless. One of Flack's best. *—Stephen Cook*

Roberta Flack & Donny Hathaway / Apr. 1972 / Atlantic ✦✦✦✦

Here is a duet classic, and perhaps the most popular album Roberta Flack made. Their single "Where Is the Love" dominated urban contemporary radio for almost the entire year, while "You've Got a Friend" was just as influential and was later covered by numerous artists (of course they didn't write it, but a lot of folks thought they did). It did so well that Flack eventually did other duet material and also became very close to Hathaway. *—Ron Wynn*

Killing Me Softly / Aug. 1973 / Atlantic ✦✦✦✦✦

The title track was another smash for Roberta Flack, and the album continued in the same tradition as *Chapter Two* and *A Quiet Fire*. She made simmering ballads, declarative message songs, and better-than-average uptempo numbers, and at the time was among the top-selling female vocalists in any style. *—Ron Wynn*

Feel Like Makin' Love / Mar. 1975 / Atlantic ✦✦✦

Capping off a string of early-'70s hits with this album's title track, Roberta Flack would soon take a sabbatical from the spotlight in 1975. And while she would return to the stage and studio, Flack never quite hit the heights of this and the handful of other MOR soul releases from the first half of the decade. Her Carole King-meets-Gladys Knight sound is particularly impressive on highlights like "Mr. Magic" and "Feelin' That Glow." Helping out with the stellar backing are such luminaries as vocalist Patti Austin, drummer Alphonse Mouzon, keyboardist Bob James, and guitarist Hugh McCracken. Maybe not as fine an album as 1971's *Quiet Fire, Feel Like Making Love* will still please the singer's dedicated fans. *—Stephen Cook*

Blue Lights in the Basement / Dec. 1977 / Atlantic ✦✦✦

This is a soulful setting with the intoxicating "The Closer I Get to You" duet with Hathaway, "This Time I'll Be Sweeter." Background vocals by Deniece Williams, etc. Ahmet Ertegun produced. *—Bil Carpenter*

Born to Love / Jul. 1983 / Capitol ✦✦✦

This features a duet set with Peabo Bryson on which they sing mood songs like "Tonight, I Celebrate My Love" and "You're Lookin' Like Love to Me." *—Bil Carpenter*

- **Softly With These Songs: The Best of Roberta Flack** / Jun. 22, 1993 / Atlantic ✦✦✦✦✦

Roberta Flack was blessed with one of the loveliest, most soothing voices in the music industry. In the 1970s, she not only appealed to pop and R&B audiences, but also fit in with the era's more serious, sensitive singer/songwriters. She scored some of the decade's biggest hits with classics such as "The First Time Ever I Saw Your Face," "Killing Me Softly With His Song," and "Feel Like Making Love," as well as her legendary duets with Donny Hathaway, all which have gone on to become standards in the pop pantheon. This single-disc set attempts at collecting her best and most successful recordings from the 1970s to the 1990s, when she enjoyed the success of another Top Ten hit with Diane Warren's "Set the Night to Music" (with Maxi Priest). However, this ambitious collection, even with such stellar material, proves a little frustrating due to the omission of several key tracks from Flack's catalog, among those "Jesse," "If I Ever See You Again," "You've Got a Friend," and several others. It does, however, manage to incorporate other Flack collectibles, including her soundtrack hit "Making Love," her hit with Peabo Bryson, "Tonight I Celebrate My Love," her lovely, breezy, chart-topping 1988 R&B hit "Oasis," and a sleek 1990s house track, "Uh-Uh Ooh-Ooh Look Out (Here It Comes)." This ambitious yet frustrating collection not only highlights Flack's long, illustrious career, but also brings to attention the fact that a multi-disc retrospective on this legendary singer would be a most welcome addition to her catalog. *—Jose F. Promis*

Flaming Ember

f. 1967, Detroit, MI, **db.** 1972

Group / Blue-Eyed Soul, Soul

A blue-eyed Detroit soul group that enjoyed a short time in the spotlight during 1970-1971, they were initally known as the Flaming Embers. The band included guitarist Joe

Sladich, pianist Bill Ellis, bassist Jim Bugnel, and drummer Jerry Plunk. They first recorded for Ric-Tic in 1968, then moved to Hot Wax and dropped the "s." The songs "Mind, Body and Soul," "Westbound #9," and "I'm Not My Brother's Keeper" each made the pop Top 40 and R&B Top 20. But "Stop the World and Let Me Off" flopped, despite being released on both Hot Wax and Radio Active Gold. The group later changed its name to Mind, Body and Soul and became a fixture on the Detroit bar scene through the late '70s. *—Ron Wynn*

Westbound #9 / 1970 / Hot Wax ♦♦♦

Flaming Ember's name rarely comes up in blue-eye soul discussions, neither Hot Wax nor Ric-Tic before them—where they cut six singles—never marketed them as such. Many who bought their records simply didn't know or don't care, they liked the heavy soul sound and never gave much thought to their ethnicity. Yet, they were more successful then most of the known blue-eye soul artists and *Westbound #9* proves that. Their first Hot Wax recording, "Mind, Body and Soul made noise wherever it was played. The sweet ballad with the rough edge introduced the Detroiters to the world. (The Ric-Tic singles were poorly promoted and only received scant air play in the Motor City area.) Another excellent slow single, "Shades of Green" didn't do as well but it gave further credence to their singing prowess. The explosive *Westbound #9* became their biggest seller, the lead singer proved he could wail with the best and was a vocalist to reckon with. Excellent versions of "Going in Circles," and "Spinning Wheel" fit in well with originals like "The Empty Crowded Room," "Why Don't You Stay," "Heart On (Loving You)" "Flashbacks and Reruns" and others. *—Andrew Hamilton*

Sunshine / 1971 / Hot Wax ♦♦♦

The blue-eyed soul band's third Hot Wax LP continues the soulful grooves paved on two previous long-players. A longstanding Detroit club band, it was widely believed they first cut on Ric-Tic Records, but they actually debuted on Jack and Devora Brown's Fortune setup. Leader Jerry Plunk wrote some tracks, with others handled by Hot Wax's electric producing and writing corp. The themes fluctuate from message songs like "I'm Not My Brother's Keeper" to stark love missions like "1200 Miles From Heaven." Additional takes "Sunshine," the acid blues, more than seven minutes long, bonging "Ember's Groove," and "Stop the World and (Let Me Off)" make this a winning package. *—Andrew Hamilton*

● **The Best of Flaming Ember** / 1992 / Fantasy ♦♦♦♦♦

Sequel/Castle later released an extensive Flaming Ember set, containing virtually all of the blue-eyed soul band's recorded work, but that's for the serious listener. This is for those that don't need to dig as deep, as well as those that want a compilation with the exhilerating single cut of "Westbound Number 9," the group's best song. Pared down to just singles and assorted album tracks, the group's psychedelic album-rock flourishes are left behind, but that merely reveals what a fine group this was—varied, soulful, melodic and grittier than you'd expect. *—Stephen Thomas Erlewine*

The Flamingos

f. 1952, Chicago, IL

Group / Doo Wop

Both prolific and seminal in their influence and impact, the Flamingos may have been the greatest harmonizing vocal ensemble ever, and were certainly among the premier units of the doo wop/R&B era. Cousins Jake and Zeke Carey moved to Chicago from Baltimore in 1950. They met Paul Wilson and Johnny Carter at the Church of God and Saints of Christ Congregation, a black Jewish church. They began singing in the choir, and the foursome met Earl Lewis (not the Channels' lead vocalist) through one of the members' sisters, who was his girlfriend at the time. They originally called themselves the Swallows, but had to change names when they found out that a Baltimore group already had the name. Carter suggested El Flamingos, which was changed to the Five Flamingos, and later the Flamingos.

Ralph Leon of the King Booking Agency eventually became their manager. Sollie McElroy replaced Lewis as their lead singer in the early '50s, with Lewis joining the Five Echoes. They recorded with Chance in 1953, and "If I Can't Have You" attracted some attention and did well in the Midwest and on the East Coast. "That's My Desire" and "Golden Teardrops" were marvelously sung numbers, particularly "Golden Teardrops," with its sweeping harmonies on top and bottom framing McElroy's wondrous lead. But none of their great Chance recordings generated enough national attention to make the R&B charts, nor did the three numbers they recorded for Parrot.

McElroy departed and was replaced by Nate Nelson. They enjoyed their first chart success with Checker in the late '50s, scoring a Top Ten R&B hit with "I'll Be Home" in 1956. They temporarily disbanded in 1956 and regrouped in 1957 with Nelson, Jake Carey, Paul Wilson, and Tommy Hunt as the lineup, and the group now a quartet. Zeke Carey returned in 1958, and they signed with End late that year. "I Only Have Eyes for You" in 1959 was their biggest hit, peaking at number-three R&B and number-11 pop. It was a cover of a song that had been a huge hit for Eddy Duchin in 1934, and was the start of a productive period that saw the Flamingos issue four albums for End and get two more R&B Top 30 singles, one the Sam Cooke composition "Nobody Loves Me Like You" in 1960. Hunt left in 1961, and the group returned briefly to Checker in 1964. They later recorded for Phillips, Julman, and Polydor, but couldn't regain their former standing. They remained among the genre's most beloved groups, and anthologies of their material on Chance and Checker have been reissued. In 1993, *The Flamingos Meet the Moonglows* was reissued by Vee-Jay. *—Ron Wynn*

Flamingo Favorites / 1960 / Collectables ♦♦♦

One of the group's End albums, *Flamingo Favorites* is a nice blend of standards, a few stray rockers, and the ballads that were this group's meat. Highlights include "Besame Mucho," "Dream Girl," and the Coasters-like turn on "Crazy, Crazy, Crazy." *—Cub Koda*

Requestfully Yours / 1960 / Collectables ♦♦♦♦

Along with a wealth of other doo wop groups that emerged during the early '50s, the Flamingos used their considerable gospel vocal chops to strike pop gold. While maybe not as successful as, say, the Platters were, the Flamingos still had an equal share of talent, as their late-'50s and early-'60s records on the End label attest. In addition to a huge hit cover of "I Only Have Eyes for You," the Flamingos also cut solid long-players like *Requestfully Yours* during this time. Featuring the group's second smash, a version of Sam Cooke's "Nobody Loves Me Like You," the album also includes stunning renditions of "In the Still of the Night," "When I Fall in Love," and "Tenderly." Rounding out the set, there are the fine crooners cut "Beside You" and singer Tommy Johnson's impressionistic "You, Me and the Sea." Complementing their tasty harmony work, Johnson and his cohorts (Zeke Carey, Tommy Hunt, and Nate Nelson) all take lead vocal turns and provide some of the instrumental backing as well. Containing a seamless mix of doo wop, big band pop, and innovative harmonies that would prefigure soul vocal outfits like the Delphonics, these 12 sides make for a fine introduction to the Flamingos' prime recordings. *—Stephen Cook*

★ **The Best of the Flamingos** / May 1990 / Rhino ♦♦♦♦♦

The Best of the Flamingos is an 18-track collection that compiles all of the Flamingos' biggest hits and best songs. *The Doo Bop She Bop* ignores the group's latter-day soul hits and concentrates solely on their doo wop material, which makes for a stronger, more cohesive collection. "I Only Have Eyes for You" is the acknowledged classic, while "I'll Be Home" and "A Kiss From Your Lips" were hits in their own right, but the compilation proves that the Flamingos were one of the greatest doo wop groups with its lesser-known numbers like "The Vow" and "The Ladder of Love." *—Stephen Thomas Erlewine*

For Collectors Only / Feb. 21, 1992 / Collectables ♦♦♦♦♦

The title on this two-CD set is more than a little unfair—in fact, it's downright inaccurate. *For Collectors Only* is one of the more impressive collections of material by this celebrated R&B vocal group, consisting entirely of songs cut for George Goldner's Gone Records, which was their most successful commercial period and arguably represents the group's best years. The 42 songs here include three tracks ("I'll Be Home," "A Kiss From Your Lips," "Lovers Never Say Goodbye") which are either previously unissued outtakes or previously unreleased altogether, and they're icing on the cake. This collection's real virtue is its assembly of the previously issued numbers; the highlights are, of course, the group's treatment of ballad standards such as "I Only Have Eyes for You," "My Foolish Heart," and "Love Walked In," but this set also includes unusual parts of their repertory, like the riveting, fast-paced Gone Records version of "Jump Children" (to which they were seen miming brilliantly, in a stunning performance clip, in the 1959 movie *Go Johnny Go*). Its presence, along with the outtakes, makes this double disc preferable to Rhino's *The Best of the Flamingos*, and essential listening for anyone who owns MCA's compilation of the group's Chess recordings. The annotation is especially frustrating, however—it consists of a reprinted interview with two of the group's original members discussing their days with Chance Records, which considerably pre-dates any of the songs here. The sound is acceptable if unexceptional, and has been outstripped by the audio quality on WestSide's 1998 two-LP-on-one-CD reissues of the Flamingos' albums. *—Bruce Eder*

The Flamingos Meet the Moonglows on the Dusty Road of Hits / 1993 / Vee-Jay ♦♦♦

The Flamingos and Moonglows were among doo wop's finest and longest-running ensembles. These groups defined the idiom's virtues: beautiful, impassioned harmonies, breathtaking lead vocals, and often unforgettable storytelling abilities. This 25-track reissue, matching the groups with either the King Kolax or Red Holloway Orchestras, contains numerous incredible selections. The Flamingos' "Golden Teardrops" and "Jump Children" are doo wop standards, as are The Moonglows' "Secret Love" and "Just a Lonely Christmas." Sound quality fluctuates due to a lack in some cases of master tapes, but nothing diminishes the vocal excellence displayed on every cut. *—Ron Wynn*

I Only Have Eyes for You: The Best of the "End" Years / Oct. 24, 1994 / Sequel ♦♦♦♦

In between their first recordings for the small imprint Chance and several mid-'60s dates for the likes of Philips, Checker, and Polydor, the Flamingos hit it big with the End label from 1958-1961. Four albums and several singles produced their biggest hits, "I Only Have Eyes for You" and the Sam Cooke-penned "Nobody Loves Me Like You," as well as several low-profile standouts like "Lovers Never Say Goodbye" and "At Night." Sequel has collected these and many other solid cuts from the group's End heyday, giving Rhino's equally excellent roundup some serious competition (although the Rhino disc has a bit of advantage with its two Chance stunners, "Golden Teardrops" and "That's My Desire"). Still, this is certainly a worthwhile collection. *—Stephen Cook*

Complete Chess Masters Plus / May 20, 1997 / Chess ♦♦♦♦♦

The Flamingos didn't have many hits while they were at Checker, but those two singles—"I'll Be Home" and "A Kiss From Your Lips"—were terrific, sketching out the lush sound they would later blossom on "I Only Have Eyes for You." *Complete Chess Masters Plus* contains all 18 songs, including two previously unreleased tracks, the group recorded for Checker and Chess. Although it's not a definitive career overview, it's an essential item for collectors of doo wop and vocal R&B, since it's lovingly packaged and contains numerous gems, including "The Vow" and "Dream of a Lifetime." *—Stephen Thomas Erlewine*

Flamingo Serenade/Flamingo Favorites / Jun. 23, 1998 / WestSide ♦♦♦♦♦

Requestfully Yours/The Sound of the Flamingos / Jun. 23, 1998 / WestSide ♦♦♦♦

The Flares

f. 1959

Group / R&B, Doo Wop

Known for their 1961 uptempo dance doo wop hit "Foot Stompin' Pt. 1," the Flares were related to, but not exactly the same as, the 1950s Los Angeles doo wop group the Flairs. The lineup changes undergone by both the Flairs and the Flares are difficult to track and digest, but basically the Flairs were formed by teenagers in L.A. in the early '50s and founded by future the Coasters member Cornell Gunter. Managed by Buck Ram (whose most famous clients were the Platters), the Flairs recorded for Modern, ABC-Paramount, and Antler. By 1960, just two of the original Flairs—Tommy Miller and George Hollis—were left, the quartet had expanded to a quintet, and female singer Beverly Harris was a member. At that point, they were recording for Felsted and changed their name to the Flares.

"Foot Stompin' Pt. 1," boasting infectious interaction between the lead harmonizers, the bass singer, and rhythms that were indeed created by foot stomps, got to number 25 in late 1961. The Flares never followed that up with another hit, though they recorded more than a half-dozen subsequent singles over the next couple of years or so, occasionally under the name the Peppers. Many of these sides were too-similar variations on the early soul-dance craze vibe that had fueled "Foot Stompin' Pt. 1," sometimes featuring lead female vocals. It's hard to keep up with the exact personnel shuffles of the lineup during the early '60s, but Aaron Collins (who wrote much of the Flares' material, including "Foot Stompin' Pt. 1") and Willie Davis were certainly involved in singing on their recordings and shared lead vocals on "Foot Stompin' Pt. 1," though they weren't always identified as members in publicity materials. Even more confusingly, several female singers recorded and performed with the group (who were pictured in press shots as a quintet with four guys and one girl), and the Flares that toured were not always the same as the Flares that recorded in the studio. At any rate, not many were paying attention to such matters by the time they disbanded around 1964. *—Richie Unterberger*

● **Foot Stompin'** / May 7, 2002 / Ace ♦♦♦♦♦

Like many a one-hit early rock & roll vocal group, the Flares never came up with anything else to match their sole smash ("Foot Stomping Pt. 1") creatively or commercially. So this 26-track collection of 1960-1963 material will be of interest almost solely to serious doo wop collectors, assembling most of the songs from the singles they did for the Felsted and Press labels (including the Press single they did under the name the Peppers), adding a few tracks from their 1961 album and three previously unreleased cuts. The Flares were good singers and their records had solid R&B/rock & roll backing with shades of soul, blues, and jazz, but they came up against the limitations so common to many second-division groups of the era: their material wasn't that special and also stuck to a formula too often. In the Flares' case, that formula was uptempo early soul records wedded to a type of dance, whether it was "Hand Clappin'," "Doing the Hully Gully," "Shimmy and Stomp," "The Monkey Walk," or covers of "The Stroll" and "Pony Time." Occasionally they broke away from that pattern, though not with astounding results, as on the contrived two-part novelty "Rock and Roll Heaven" or several cuts that find a female vocalist taking the lead part. Some of the later cuts edge toward a more modern sound akin to early Motown sides by groups like the Contours, though the songs and production weren't as good. The liner notes gamely make sense of the group's complicated and confusing evolution from the '50s doo wop act the Flairs into the related but different early-'60s aggregation of the Flares. *—Richie Unterberger*

The Fleetwoods

f. 1958, Olympia, WA, **db.** 1963

Group / Doo Wop, Pop

Although the Fleetwoods' sound was smooth, without many of the rougher edges of doo wop groups, they were one of the few white vocal groups of the late '50s and early '60s to enjoy success not only on the pop charts, but also the R&B charts. The Fleetwoods' forte was ballads—beginning with their 1959 debut single, "Come Softly to Me," the group racked up a number of hits over the next three years, and nearly all of them were ballads. The group broke up in 1963, but their songs—particularly "Come Softly to Me"—became pop-rock classics of the pre-British Invasion era.

Gretchen Christopher, Barbara Ellis, and Gary Troxell formed the Fleetwoods while attending high school in Olympia, WA. Originally, the group consisted only of Christopher and Ellis, but the duo soon asked Troxell to accompany them on trumpet. Shortly after his arrival in the group, Troxell abandoned the trumpet and concentrated on singing once the other two members heard a portion of a song he had written. Following some contributions from Christopher and Ellis, the group had written "Come Softly to Me." They began performing the song at various events around Olympia, eventually gaining the attention of Bob Reisdorff, who ran the Seattle-based label, Dolphin Records.

Dolphin released "Come Softly to Me" early in 1959 and the song became an instant hit, climbing to number one on the pop charts and number five on the R&B charts; it also reached the Top Ten in U.K. The Fleetwoods weren't able to immediately produce a follow-up single as successful as their debut, but their third single, "Mr. Blue," was a number-one pop and Top Five R&B hit in the U.S. in late 1959. By the time of its release, Dolphin had changed its name to Dolton. For the next three years, the Fleetwoods had a string of minor pop hits. The group wasn't able to consistently place singles in the upper regions of the charts partially because Troxell was drafted into the navy at the height of the group's popularity at the end of 1959. Troxell was replaced by Vic Dana, who would later have a string of his own hit singles in the early '60s.

The Fleetwoods last Top Ten single arrived in the spring of 1961, when "Tragedy" climbed the U.S. charts. The group disbanded two years later, after releasing their final single, a cover of Jesse Belvin's "Goodnight My Love." Over the next three decades, the Fleetwoods reunited occasionally to perform concerts and oldies revues. In 1973, the group recorded an album with producer Jerry Dennon, but the resulting recordings were unsuccessful. In 1990, the Fleetwoods—featuring Christopher, Troxell, and instead of Ellis a singer called Cheryl Huggins—played a tour on the American oldies circuit after Rhino released the compact disc collection, *The Best of the Fleetwoods. —Stephen Thomas Erlewine*

The Very Best of the Fleetwoods / 1975 / United Artists ♦♦♦♦♦

Though the Fleetwoods (named after an Olympia, WA telephone exchange) generally don't receive a lot of critical acclaim, their best recordings are rather unique in presentation and mood. On this 1975 LP, which contains all but one ("Lovers By Night, Strangers By Day") of their nine Top 40 hits, the listener is treated to their soft, gentle style of doo wop that has a strong undertone of melancholy. The equal blend of the male and female voices as showcased, especially in "Come Softly to Me," gives a resonance that most soft-rock hits lack, and the spare folk-style instrumentation is mixed in such a way that it blends with the voices but never overpowers them. In other words, what normally might come across as mere lightweight pop takes on more power than one might think. Also, the loneliness that pervades much of the lyrics and music gives the material added style. Though later stars such as Gene Pitney and Roy Orbison brought more melodrama to their songs of solitude, the roots of their music lie—at least in part—in the Fleetwoods' style. A modern-day counterpart to the Fleetwoods might be the lovelorn confessions of Chris Isaak. Though this recording contains only ten songs, it is still a fine introduction to the essence of the Fleetwoods' style of late-'50s doo wop. *—Michael Ofjord*

The Best of the Fleetwoods / May 1990 / Rhino ♦♦♦♦

Rhino's *Best of the Fleetwoods* contains all of their hits ("Come Softly to Me," "Mr. Blue," and 16 other songs) on a smartly assembled collection. *—Stephen Thomas Erlewine*

● **Come Softly to Me: The Very Best of the Fleetwoods** / Aug. 10, 1993 / EMI ♦♦♦♦

While the single-disc collection *Come Softly to Me—The Very Best of the Fleetwoods* is a treasure for devoted fans, featuring alternate takes, radio commercials, a comprehensive discography, fine liner notes, and unreleased tracks. Casual listeners will find all of this material extraneous; they will find everything they need on Rhino's collection. *—Stephen Thomas Erlewine*

The Flirtations

Group / Pop-Soul, Soul

The Flirtations were one of the more active all-girl R&B groups of the mid- to late '60s, though they had to go pretty far from home to find their most lasting success. The group had started life as a quartet called the Gypsies, consisting of three sisters, Betty Pearce, Shirley Pearce, and Earnestine Pearce, and Viola Billups, who worked for three years under that name. They changed their name to the Flirtations in 1965—some sources say that Betty Pearce left the lineup at this time, while others indicate that she remained with the group until 1967—and they were signed to Josie Records that year. Their one release on the label, "Change My Darkness Into Light" b/w "Natural Born Lover," co-produced by J.J. Jackson and Sidney Barnes, was released in 1966, and they got one more single out on the Festival label.

In 1967, by which time the Flirtations were a trio, the group had gone to England, where they found a fresh start as both a performing and recording act. American soul was going over in a serious way at the time in the U.K., and the group came to the attention of Decca Records producer Wayne Bickerton, who signed the trio up. With Bickerton choosing their material (as well as writing some of it) and managing their recording sessions, the Flirtations made their British recording debut with "How Can You Tell Me" b/w "Someone Out There" in 1967 on the Parrot label. The group was shifted to the Deram Records label the following year and released a classic piece of late-'60s soul in "Nothing But a Heartache." The single proved a success in America as well as England, riding the charts in *Cashbox* magazine for many weeks in 1969 and getting up to number 31. The group's fortunes remained high for most of the next decade, and they built up an especially fervent following in England; like other girl-soul groups such as the Fascinations, the Flirtations discovered that they were treated far more special on the far side of the Atlantic from where they were born.

The group left Deram after 1972 and signed with Polydor, where they saw more success with their cover of Marvin Gaye's "Little Darling." Viola Billups left the Flirtations in 1974 to pursue a solo career and was replaced by Loretta Noble. The group was still performing during the 1980s and beyond, and saw a new single, "Read About It," issued on the Passion label in 1986. The group has continued to perform intermittently in some form in the years since, and was included on Rhino's *Beg Scream & Shout! The Big Ol' Box of '60s Soul.* Viola Billups and Earnestine Pearce performed together in public during March of 2001 in England, on the occasion of their former producer Sidney Barnes' first concert tour of the U.K., joining their one-time mentor from the 1960s on-stage. Like Barnes, and like the Fascinations, the Flirtations have been idolized for years by Britain's enthusiasts on the Northern soul scene. *—Bruce Eder*

● **Love Makes the World Go Round** / 1975 / RCA ♦♦♦

Floaters

f. 1976, Detroit, MI

Group / Quiet Storm, Soul

A short-lived spinoff group formed by onetime Detroit Emeralds members James Mitchell and Marvin Willis, the Floaters scored a number-one R&B and number-two pop hit with their debut "Float On" for ABC. It was neither a lyrical nor vocal triumph, but still was among the biggest selling R&B singles of 1977. Lead singer Charles Clark, along with Larry Cunningham, Paul and Ralph Mitchell, and Jonathan Murray weren't able to sustain whatever magic they generated with "Float On." The next two singles were actually superior performances to the hit. "You Don't Have to Say You Love Me" and "I Just Want to Be With You" demonstrated that Clark could be an effective ballad singer, but neither could move beyond moderate R&B chart status. *—Ron Wynn*

Floaters / 1977 / ABC ♦♦♦

This Detroit quartet's debut album spawned the mega-smash hit "Float On." With its humble production and inflexible arrangement, the foursome was able to distinctly convey each individual's vocal talent. The urban ballad stayed on the *Billboard* R&B charts for 20 weeks, claiming number one for six of those weeks. It labored on the pop charts at number two for two straight weeks. The follow-up single, "You Don't Have to Say You Love Me," is a mellow number. It is slightly pop-oriented with some doo wop seasoning. It peaked at number 28 after only seven weeks. This album has some pop, doo wop and soul numbers, but none of them have the same texture of the hit single "Float On". *—Craig Lytle*

● **Float On** / 1977 / MCA ♦♦♦♦♦

"I Am So Glad I Took My Time," released on Fee Records, was their debut single, but the Detroit quartet struck gold with their second release (actually, the Floaters were actually a quintet; Ralph Mitchell missed the "Float On" session and the album's photo shoot for some unexplained reason, though he was present for the other tracks). "Float On" was 11 minutes and 46 seconds of pure magic; the tune echoed the group's name, for it just floated on a bed of rhythm and harmony as the guys introduced themselves and gave their astrological signs. The other Floaters are Paul Mitchell, Jonathan Murray, Charles Clark, and Ralph Cunningham. Disk jockeys loved "Float On," they could pair it with Issac Hayes' "By the Time I Get to Phoenix," make a munchie run, and be back before Ike sings "she'll be rising." "Float On" aced *Billboard*'s R&B chart and Great Britain's pop chart. Nothing else as magical appears on this LP. They followed with "You Don't Have to Say You Love Me," which surprisingly charted despite Charles Clark's whiny, uninteresting falsetto lead. *—Andrew Hamilton*

Magic / Aug. 1978 / ABC ✦✦✦
The Floaters went down in history as one of the one-hit wonders of '70s soul. Although their 1977 single "Float On" was a smash—the ballad soared to number one on *Billboard*'s R&B singles chart and number two on its pop chart—none of their subsequent singles were major hits. *Magic*, the Detroit vocal quintet's second LP, didn't contain any major singles; nonetheless, it is a generally pleasant, if less than exceptional, sophomore effort. To their credit, the Floaters don't inundate listeners with weak imitations of "Float On." That type of thing was quite common in the late '70s—an artist would enjoy a smash hit and their label would urge him/her to record a carbon copy. But nothing on *Magic* sounds like a carbon copy of "Float On." Even though "Magic (We Thank You)" is somewhat similar to that 1977 smash, the mellow, airy offering has a personality of its own. The Floaters sound like they are making an honest effort to move ahead on tracks that range from the perky "I Dedicate My Love to You" to the reggae-influenced "Anything That Keeps You Satisfied." Romantic ballads were the Floaters' strong point, and the LP's best tracks are the smooth ballads "Let's Try Love (One More Time)" and "The Time Is Now"—both of which are easily identifiable as Detroit soul. In the '70s, Detroit had its own brand of Northern soul (as did Philadelphia and Chicago), and the Floaters were as Detroit-sounding as the Dramatics, the Temptations, or the Four Tops. But unlike those Motor City vocal groups, the Floaters never provided an LP that was superb from start to finish. However, they did have their moments, and *Magic* isn't a bad record—it just isn't the gem that the Floaters needed in 1978. *—Alex Henderson*

Float Into the Future / 1979 / MCA ✦✦✦
In 1979, the Floaters were desperately in need of another hit single. *Magic*, their sophomore album of 1978, had been a commercial disappointment—and they hoped that their third album, *Float Into the Future*, would do better. For this 1979 LP, the Floaters recruited producer/songwriter Gene McDaniels, who was known for (among other things) writing Roberta Flack's early-'70s smash, "Feel Like Makin' Love." McDaniels had a track record but, unfortunately, he didn't give the Floaters the big hit they were hoping for. Although not a bad album, *Into the Future* is uneven and inconsistent. There are a few standout tracks, including the funky "Brand New Lite" and the romantic soul ballad "The Best of Our Love" (which features a likable but little-known female vocalist named Afreeka Trees). But overall, *Float Into the Future* is unremarkable. "Go Down to the Disco" and "Levitation" are average funk-dance numbers, and in 1979 the Floaters needed material that was more than just average—they needed an album full of exceptional, first-rate songs. But *Float Into the Future* does not fit that description, and this LP received very little attention. In fact, it's safe to say that most of the people who bought the "Float On" single in 1977 ignored *Float Into the Future*, which went out of print only a few years after it was released. In 1979, the Floaters were hoping that *Float Into the Future* would prevent them from being one-hit wonders but, regrettably, that's exactly what they turned out to be. *—Alex Henderson*

Eddie Floyd

b. Jun. 25, 1935, Montgomery, AL
Vocals / Soul, Memphis Soul, Deep Soul
Soul singer/songwriter Eddie Floyd scored one of the defining hits of the Memphis soul sound with "Knock on Wood," a number-one R&B smash that typified the Stax house style at its grittiest. Floyd was born in Montgomery, AL, in 1935, but grew up in Detroit, where his uncle Robert West owned a couple of record labels, including Lupine. In 1955, Floyd co-founded the seminal proto-soul group the Falcons, who eventually scored a major R&B hit with "You're So Fine" in 1959 (with Joe Stubbs, later of the Contours and 100 Proof Aged in Soul, as lead singer). After Stubbs' departure, Floyd spent a brief period as the Falcons' lead singer, until Wilson Pickett joined up. Now recording for West's Lupine imprint, the Falcons and Pickett cut their second undisputed classic, the gospel-inflected ballad "I Found a Love," in 1962. Pickett subsequently went solo, and the Falcons broke up in 1963.

Floyd recorded a few solo sides for Lupine, and moved to Washington, D.C., for a time to work with his DJ friend, Al Bell; the two founded a label and production company, Safice, co-writing songs and releasing Floyd's recordings. When Bell accepted a job as promotions director at Stax, Floyd followed him to Memphis, where he signed on with Stax as a staff writer and producer. He worked chiefly with Carla Thomas and William Bell at first, and often wrote in tandem with house guitarist Steve Cropper. In early 1966, their composition "634-5789 (Soulsville, USA)" became a number-one R&B hit for Wilson Pickett; around the same time, Floyd released his first single for Stax, "Things Get Better," which failed to chart. That summer, Floyd cut "Knock on Wood," another song he'd written with Cropper; initially intended for Otis Redding, the tune wasn't big with Stax management because it was strongly based on the chord changes of Wilson Pickett's "In the Midnight Hour." However, distributor Atlantic smelled a hit, and released the song nationally; their instincts proved correct, as "Knock on Wood" became Stax's third number-one R&B hit by the end of the year (strangely, it barely made the Top 30 on the pop charts). Floyd followed his instant soul classic with several more Top 40 R&B hits over the next four years, including "Raise Your Hand," "Love Is a Doggone Good Thing," "On a Saturday Night," "I've Never Found a Girl (To Love Me Like You Do)" (his second biggest hit), and a cover of Sam Cooke's "Bring It on Home to Me."

In spite of diminishing commercial returns, Floyd stayed with Stax as a performer and writer right up to the label's bankruptcy in 1975. He spent two years with the Southern soul/blues label Malaco, recording the album *Experience* in 1977; while it was regionally popular, the Southern soul sound had long since fallen out of commercial favor. A brief stint at Mercury failed to remake Floyd for the disco age, and after recording with British mod revivalists Secret Affair, he largely drifted away from the studio. Floyd attempted a comeback on Ichiban with 1988's *Flashback* album; the following year, he performed at President Bush's inaugural ball, and went on to tour with the Blues Brothers Band. In 1998, Floyd made a guest appearance in *Blues Brothers 2000*, and also performed "634-5789" with Pickett and Jonny Lang. Meanwhile, countless artists have covered "Knock on Wood," most prominently a disco version by Amii Stewart that topped the pop charts in 1979. *—Steve Huey*

Knock on Wood / 1967 / Stax ✦✦✦✦
In contrast to the 1970s—when artists ranging from Curtis Mayfield to Parliament/Funkadelic were praised for their albums—singles defined soul music in the 1960s. It has often been pointed out that many Stax and Motown albums of the '60s had their share of filler—nonetheless, others were full of gems that should have been released as singles. Reissued on CD in 1991, *Knock on Wood* is one of Eddie Floyd's best albums. The soul shouter successfully embraced sleeker Northern soul on other projects, but here he sticks to the type of raw, hard-edged Memphis soul that Stax was first known for. From the unforgettable title song (a number-one R&B hit) to covers of J.J. Jackson's "But It's Alright," Jerry Butler's "I Stand Accused," and Wilson Pickett's "634-5789," this CD beautifully illustrates the splendor of down-home Southern R&B. *—Alex Henderson*

Looking Back / 1968 / Ember-TKO Magnum ✦✦✦✦
Eight sides (the credits list seven, but it's eight—the slow ballad "When You're In Love" was left off the label) cut by Eddie Floyd for his uncle Robert West's LuPine Records, in between the breakup of his group the Falcons and his eventual jump to Stax Records (paired with seven sides by the Primettes aka the Supremes). These sides didn't sell at all, but they do show that Floyd had everything that he needed, in terms of style and voice, for stardom as early as 1962, when they were cut. The numbers bridge the gap between doo wop-type R&B and his subsequent, more soulful and mature sound at Stax, with some killer tracks, Floyd's own "Bye Bye Baby," "Never Get Enough of Your Love," and "I'll Never Find Another Girl Like You," plus one cool shouter, "The Whip"; his singing and the emotions he calls up are nearly enough to bring the listener's heart to their throat. Much of what is here is a little too busy, having been cut too close to the doo wop era, but the ingredients for success are all here. Additionally, these sides kept Floyd in contact with West, who eventually went into partnership with Al Bell, before Bell joined Stax Records and brought Floyd with him to the new label, where he finally got the sound and the break he needed. *—Bruce Eder*

Never Found a Girl / 1968 / Stax ✦✦✦
The title track was one of Floyd's biggest hits, while the other songs were fairly standard Southern soul, not particularly outstanding by Stax standards but well sung and performed. *—Ron Wynn*

Rare Stamps / 1969 / Stax ✦✦✦✦✦
A pair of remarkable soul hits, "Knock on Wood" and "I've Never Found a Girl," enabled Eddie Floyd to attain national success in 1968. But the longtime singer and composer, whose roots dated back to the Detroit group the Falcons in the late '50s, was a steady, if not spectacular, performer for many years before and after those two songs. Several of Floyd's finest pieces are compiled on the 25-track CD *Rare Stamps*, including a wonderful testimonial to Otis Redding, "Big Bird." There are also two super duets with Mavis Staples, "Never Let You Go" and "Ain't That Good," which rank with anything that the label issued. *—Ron Wynn*

You've Got to Have Eddie / 1969 / Stax ✦✦✦
Although he wasn't getting massive hits, Eddie Floyd continued to make solid Southern soul material in the late '60s. This album did have three moderately successful singles, but more importantly, every track features effective wailing leads and country/blues arrangements. An excellent example of the Stax sound. *—Ron Wynn*

California Girl / 1970 / Stax ✦✦✦
Eddie Floyd got the '70s under way in fine form with this release. The title track and two other singles, including a good version of "My Girl," made their way into the charts, and Floyd got good mileage out of the album, even though there were danger signs ahead for the Stax label. *—Ron Wynn*

Down to Earth / 1971 / Stax ✦✦
This was another consistent release for Eddie Floyd, although it met with less success than most of his other releases. Only one single charted, and it didn't stay there long. But Floyd still sang with hard-edged drive and conviction, and he had the reliable Stax studio pros and producers giving it the necessary support. *—Ron Wynn*

Baby Lay Your Head Down / 1973 / Stax ✦✦
Floyd was never one of Stax's greatest talents, and this 1973 album, like so much product from the label during this time, suffered from a certain facelessness in both the songs and production. The reggae-tinged title track (cut in Jamaica) was a mild R&B hit and was about the best song on an album that featured sweeter (in the negative sense) arrangements than Stax was known for on several tracks; "Check Me Out" does have some nice melodic turns. The album was reissued in its entirety on *Soul Street*, a CD that also contains everything from Floyd's following album (also called *Soul Street*). *—Richie Unterberger*

Soul Street / 1974 / Stax ✦✦✦
Floyd's seventh and last album for Stax contained a tiny R&B hit in the title track. The record employed the Con Funk Shun rhythm section that would soon rise to soul stardom

on their own. But there wasn't much special about the tunes, which revealed some influences from the sounds of Philadelphia and Hi Records, both of which were then peaking in popularity. The CD reissue pairs the album and its predecessor, *Baby, Lay Your Head Down (Gently on My Bed)*, onto one disc, although it's sequenced so that the earlier LP plays first. *—Richie Unterberger*

Experience / 1977 / Malaco ✦✦
Eddie Floyd resurfaced in the late '70s on the Jackson-based label that many felt would become the new Stax in the '70s and '80s. It didn't, but that's another story. This album did moderately well on a regional level, and a nice Floyd duet with Dorothy Moore even reached the middle of the R&B charts. But by the late '70s, soul was no longer palatable as a national sound. *—Ron Wynn*

● **Chronicle: Greatest Hits** / 1979 / Stax ✦✦✦✦✦
Like Otis Redding, Sam & Dave, Wilson Pickett, and Rufus Thomas, Eddie Floyd was among the artists who epitomized tough, rugged Southern soul in the 1960s. The Alabama native wasn't oblivious to what soulsters were doing up north—in fact, he successfully embraced Northern-style soul on some of his albums. But because "Knock on Wood," Floyd's biggest hit, was such a definitive example of Memphis soul, he will forever be identified with Stax records and Southern R&B. Quite appropriately, this 48-minute best-of CD opens with "Knock on Wood," which soared to number one on *Billboard*'s R&B singles chart in 1966 and received a disco-soul makeover from singer Amii Stewart in 1978. But not everything on *Chronicle: Greatest Hits* is as overtly Southern as "Knock on Wood." Spanning 1966-1974, this is a diverse CD—one that ranges from very Memphis-sounding gems like "Soul Street," "Love Is a Doggone Good Thing," and "Raise Your Hand" to sleeker, more Northern-influenced treasures such as "I've Never Found a Girl" (a number-two R&B hit) and "California Girl." One of the most interesting tracks is a remake of the Temptations' "My Girl," which started out as Motown soul but gets a very Stax-sounding makeover from Floyd. The singer/producer was quite capable of performing Detroit soul, but when he covers a song that Smokey Robinson co-wrote for the Temptations, he is in a Memphis state of mind. Technically, *Chronicle: Greatest Hits* is a misleading title for this 16-song CD because not all of these recordings were hits. But all of them are excellent, and *Chronicle: Greatest Hits* is a fine starting point if you are exploring Floyd's work for the first time. *—Alex Henderson*

California Girl/Down to Earth / Oct. 1995 / Stax ✦✦✦

Force M.D.'s

f. 1983, Staten Island, NY
Group / Quiet Storm, New Jack Swing, Urban
Although not as well-known as other New York hip-hop acts of the early '80s, Staten Island's Force M.D.'s was a vital crew in the early history of street hip-hop and one of the first vocal groups to fuse doo wop-influenced harmonies with hip-hop beats. Originally a street troupe known as the LD's, the group sang and danced on Greenwich Village street corners and the Staten Island ferry. Its members included brothers "Stevie D." and Antoine "T.C.D." Lundy, their uncle Jesse Lee Daniels, and friends Trisco Pearson and Charles "Mercury" Nelson. The group hooked up with DJ Dr. Rock, and billing themselves as Dr. Rock & the MC's, began playing in local hip-hop venues. However, by the time the group signed to Tommy Boy in 1984 as the Force M.D.'s (M.D. standing for "musical diversity"), they had evolved into a more straightforward R&B vocal group, distinguished mostly by their street attitude. The M.D.'s had a string of R&B hits through the '80s, but their only pop hit was the Top Ten Jimmy Jam/Terry Lewis-penned ballad "Tender Love," which was featured in the movie *Krush Groove*. 1987 produced the group's first R&B number one, "Love Is a House," but their popular appeal began to ebb the following year. Mercury and Trisco left in 1990 and were replaced by Rodney "Khalil" Lundy and Shawn Waters. The group released the album *Get Ready* in 1994 as several members worked with other artists as producers. Though Nelson, Lundy and DJ Dr. Rock each died an early death (Nelson of a heart attack, Lundy of Lou Gehrig's disease), the group returned in 1998 and signed to a contract thanks to fellow Staten Island-natives Wu-Tang Clan. *—Steve Huey*

Love Letters / 1984 / Tommy Boy ✦✦✦
The debut album from this quintet offered a mix of R&B, hip-hop, dance and an excellent vocal presentation. "Let Me Love You" and "Forgive Me Girl" were two of the four singles released from this album. Both singles peaked at number 49 after ten weeks on the *Billboard* R&B charts. The latter is an uptempo track with a hip-hop backbeat featuring the whistling falsetto of the late Antoine Lundy. But the big hit off this album was "Tears," a doo wop-flavored ballad also featuring Lundy, but with a more apologetic tone. The single peaked at number nine after a 21-week run. This album set the stage for the success that the group would later enjoy. *—Craig Lytle*

Chillin' / 1986 / Tommy Boy ✦✦✦✦✦
This is a mid-'80s album featuring the Long Island hip-hop/doo wop group the Force M.D.'s. They predated the current hot trend featuring singing groups blending classic R&B and soul harmonies with hip-hop productions. While their sound now seems dated, it was quite revolutionary in its time. This album had three chart hits, and the group was then at its peak. *—Ron Wynn*

Touch and Go / 1987 / Tommy Boy ✦✦✦
The title track was a Top 10 R&B hit, and the Force M.D.'s were at their best on this album. The leads, harmonies, songs, production, and arrangements never sounded better, and they certainly paved the way for the many new jack swing vocal groups of the '90s. *—Ron Wynn*

Step to Me / Sep. 4, 1990 / Tommy Boy ✦✦✦

For Lovers and Others: Force M.D.'s Greatest Hits / Feb. 18, 1992 / Tommy Boy ✦✦✦✦
This is a solid collection of captivating love songs, featuring singles taken from the quartet's previous albums. However, of the 12 selections presented, four never charted, the most notable being "Sweet Dreams." Groomed around the smooth-sailing falsetto of the late Antoine "T.C.D." Lundy, the single is augmented by the group's faintly audible background vocals. With this album's debut, the label seized the opportunity to release "Your Love Drives Me Crazy"; previously appearing on the quartet's gold-selling album *Touch and Go*, Antoine Lundy humbly steps into the intro with a juvenile vocal expression, which does not discredit his delivery. As the melody develops, Lundy's voice graciously amplifies with maturity and emotion. The featured single on this compilation release, "Your Love Drives Me Crazy" peaked at 78 after only six weeks on the *Billboard* R&B charts. This is a classic R&B cut among many. *—Craig Lytle*

● **Let Me Love You: The Greatest Hits** / Mar. 20, 2001 / Tommy Boy ✦✦✦✦
The Force M.D.'s predated the explosion of new jack swing in the late '80s, but they definitely helped lay the groundwork, fusing R&B vocal harmonies with street-level hip-hop beats. Their most popular material, however, tended to concentrate more on the urban R&B end of that spectrum, as displayed on *Let Me Love You: The Greatest Hits*. The collection gathers a generous 17 cuts, making it the definitive overview of the group's achievements. *—Steve Huey*

Frankie Ford

b. Aug. 4, 1939, Gretna, LA
Vocals / New Orleans R&B, Rock & Roll
It's ironic that some of the greatest New Orleans R&B of the 1950s was sung by a white man. Although he could have passed for a teen idol, Frankie Ford sang with as much grit as anyone of any color in the Crescent City. He recorded some fine singles for the Ace label in the late '50s, particularly the pounding "Sea Cruise," which made the Top 20 in 1959 and remains one of the hits most identified with the classic New Orleans R&B sound. "Sea Cruise" actually began life as a Huey "Piano" Smith song with Bobby Marchan on vocals, but producer Johnny Vincent had the inspired idea of dubbing Ford's singing on top of Smith's backing track. "Sea Cruise," with its bleating foghorn and irresistible piano groove, was an impossible act to follow, and Ford never approached the Top 20 again. But he cut several more gutsy sides for Ace that featured top New Orleans players like Huey Smith and saxophonist Red Tyler; one of the best, "Roberta," was covered by the Animals in the mid-'60s. A few of his singles found him following ill-advised swing jazz and teen idol directions, and he faded from view in the 1960s, although he made a cameo appearance in the film version of Alan Freed's life. *—Richie Unterberger*

New Orleans Dynamo / 1984 / Ace ✦✦✦
Recorded in 1984 in London, this is a surprisingly decent effort that emulates the sound of New Orleans R&B-rock circa 1960 with reasonable accuracy. Ford's voice sounds pretty much unchanged as he goes through a set heavy on remakes of old New Orleans tunes, like "A Certain Girl," "Sick and Tired," Huey Smith's "Don't You Know Yockomo," "Lipstick Traces (On a Cigarette)," and "Bony Moronie." The album is now available as part of Ace's CD reissue *Cruisin' With Frankie Ford*, which also includes 14 songs done by the singer for Imperial from 1960-1962. *—Richie Unterberger*

Ooh-Wee Baby!: The Best of Frankie Ford / 1998 / WestSide ✦✦✦✦✦
Frankie Ford's one big hit, "Sea Cruise," may rank him as a one-hit wonder, but his tenure at Ace produced other material in the fine Crescent City tradition, loaded with Ford's exuberant vocals and great playing from the New Orleans 1950s A-team of session stalwarts. The collection opens with take one of Ford's great hit, different enough but really great, a true hit in the making. Both sides of his first Ace single ("Cheatin' Woman" b/w "Last One to Cry") follows that in fine fashion, and of course, the issued version of his big hit is here too. The majority of Ford's later recordings find him trying for Sinatra respectability via the Bobby Darin route, but tunes like the undubbed take of "Hour of Need," "Watchdog" and "Morgus the Magnificent" (with a young Mac Rebennack on lead guitar) are fine rocking and soulful additions to complete the big picture on this 27-track collection. *—Cub Koda*

Sea Cruise: The Very Best of Frankie Ford / Jun. 16, 1998 / Music Club ✦✦✦✦
Frankie Ford's one big hit, "Sea Cruise," is one of the truly great one-shot marvels of rock & roll history, all noise and groove and a big invitation to the party. But Ford also knew how to sell a song and the efforts of his recorded legacy at Ace Records is slimmed down to essentials on this 18-track very-best-of collection. Both sides of his debut single ("Cheatin' Woman" and "Last One to Cry") are aboard, along with Ford's later recordings, where the move into nightclub respectability all but quenches the rock & roll fire out of his music. This budget package features nine less tunes than the more deluxe WestSide package and duplicates everything there. But the transfers are crisp and clear and if you still want the bare bones essentials, this also makes a recommended purchase. *—Cub Koda*

Cruisin' With Frankie Ford / Nov. 24, 1998 / Ace ✦✦✦
This has both sides of all six singles Ford did for Imperial from 1960-1962 and a couple of unissued tracks from the same era, as well as his 1984 Ace recording *New Orleans Dynamo*. The main attraction is the Imperial material, which was very hard to find before this reissue. Ford's association with Imperial wasn't very fruitful commercially, producing just a couple of small hits in covers of Joe Jones' "You Talk Too Much" and Boyd Bennett's "Seventeen." This batch lacks anything on the order of "Sea Cruise," but it's still pretty solid vintage New Orleans R&B, produced by Dave Bartholomew. Some of the cuts are sweetened up with strings and backup female singers, but it's mostly on the earthy side; when he slows the pace down on "Dedicated to Fats" and "One Hour," he can sound uncannily like Fats Domino. *New Orleans Dynamo* is well above average for a 1980s effort by a 1950s rocker; nothing new here (in fact, many of its songs are covers of old New Orleans classics), but Ford and the London musicians execute the Crescent City R&B sound convincingly. *—Richie Unterberger*

● **Let's Take a Sea Cruise** / Aug. 24, 1999 / Ace ✦✦✦✦✦
This fine collection of 18 vintage sides, including "Sea Cruise" and "Roberta," establishes Ford's claim as one of the first of the great white R&B singers. Most of this is first-rate

New Orleans R&B with a swinging bounce, enhanced by Ford's cool and cocky vocals, although a few tracks are lame excursions into trad jazz or teen idol fare. For now it's the definitive Ford anthology, but there's room for improvement: Documentation for when the tracks were originally released is nonexistent, and much of the music was obviously dubbed from vinyl records, not from master tapes. *—Richie Unterberger*

Jesse Fortune

b. Feb. 28, 1930, Macon, MS

Vocals / Electric Chicago Blues

Chicago vocalist Jesse Fortune's voice is as large as his discography is small. A mere handful of 45s headed by his 1963 classic "Too Many Cooks" and a 1993 album on Delmark constitute his entire catalog.

Fortune grew up in Hattiesburg, MS, influenced by the pleading blues vocals of B.B. King. He arrived in Chicago in 1952 and started singing professionally with guitarist Little Monroe. He also worked with Otis Rush and Buddy Guy before the prodigious Willie Dixon officially discovered him. In April of 1963, Fortune waxed four sides for USA Records under Dixon's supervision, including the Dixon-penned minor-key rhumba "Too Many Cooks" (his sidemen at the session included Guy, Big Walter Horton on harp, and pianist Lafayette Leake). Robert Cray revived the tune for his 1980 debut album on Tomato, *Who's Been Talkin'*.

Dissatisfied with the monetary return on his date, Fortune shied away from recording (he made his living as a barber) until young guitarist Dave Specter began working the club circuit with the powerful singer. The upshot was *Fortune Tellin' Man*, the singer's debut disc for Delmark, with swinging support from Specter and his band, the Bluebirds. *—Bill Dahl*

- **Fortune Tellin' Man** / 1993 / Delmark ✦✦✦✦✦

Team one of the criminally overlooked blues vocalists inhabiting Chicago's WestSide with a tight young combo sporting a decidedly retro approach and you get this fine album, veteran singer Jesse Fortune's debut set. Guitarist Dave Specter and his band, the Bluebirds admirably back the big-voiced Fortune as he recuts his Willie Dixon-penned USA label classic "Too Many Cooks," and shouts some lesser-known B.B. King gems and a few new items. Definitely a case of better late than never! *—Bill Dahl*

The Foundations

f. 1967, England, **db.** 1970

Group / Pop-Soul, Soul

The Foundations are a surprisingly obscure late-'60s outfit, considering that they managed to reach the top of both the British and American charts more than once in the space of a year and had a solid three years of recordings. At the time of their debut in mid-1967, they were hailed as being among the most authentic makers of soul music ever to emerge from England—the best practitioners of the Motown sound to be found on the far side of the Atlantic—and were also accepted in jazz circles as well. "Baby Now That I've Found You," "Build Me Up Buttercup," and "In the Bad, Bad Old Days" were the biggest hits for this multi-racial octet, made up of Londoners and West Indians.

The Foundations were formed in January 1967 in the basement of a local coffee bar in Bayswater, gathered together through advertisements in *Melody Maker*. Lead singer Clem Curtis was a former boxer from Trinidad, while lead guitarist Alan Warner had been making his living in the printing trade in London while waiting for music to pay off. Flutist/saxman Pat Burke hailed from Jamaica, tenor saxman Mike Elliott had played with Colin Hicks (brother of Tommy Steele) in his band the Cabin Boys, as well as in several jazz bands, and trombonist Eric Allan Dale was another jazz veteran. Tony Gomez (keyboards), Peter Macbeth (bass), and Tim Harris (drums) rounded out the lineup. They selected a name Foundations based on their surroundings, a rehearsal space in the basement of a building.

They were spotted by record dealer Barry Class, who was impressed enough with what he heard to become their manager. He arranged a meeting with Pye Records producer/songwriter Tony Macaulay. He'd written a song with his partner John Macleod called "Baby Now That I've Found You," which seemed to suit the Foundations. The resulting single, issued in the summer of 1967, got no reaction from the public or on the airwaves until it got picked up by the BBC's newly founded Radio 1. By November, the single held the number-one spot on the British charts. Meanwhile, their debut single got to number 11 on the American charts in the hands of MCA's Uni label, and it was equally well-received in the rest of the world, selling something more than three-and-a-half million copies. Suddenly, the Foundations were a British phenomenon and had a worldwide following. They were hailed for being the first British band to come up with an authentic soul sound, and the fact that they were first multi-racial band to top the British charts only made their success that much more impressive. What's more, the group had the goods to back up the press' accolades. Their performances revealed a seasoned, well-rehearsed, exciting stage presence and a bold, hard soul sound that most British bands managed to imitate only in the palest manner, if at all.

Unfortunately, a follow-up single, "Back on My Feet Again," didn't crack the British Top Ten, despite very heavy airplay and promotion, and barely made the U.S. Top 50. Its relative failure led to the beginnings of a split between the group and Macaulay, as both songwriter and producer, exacerbated by the latter's decision—as their producer—not to permit the group to record any of their own songs, even as B-sides. Additionally, they felt that Macaulay reined in their "real" sound, making them seem more pop-oriented than they were. These disagreements occurred at just about the same time that the group itself began experiencing internal fractures. Curtis was persuaded to pursue a solo career, ironically right after he'd recorded perhaps the best track he ever cut with the group, a killer rendition of "It's All Right." Additionally, saxman Elliott quit as well and was never replaced. Curtis was succeeded by Colin Young, a good singer in his own right who fit in perfectly with the group's sound, and the reconstituted group hit once more in early 1969 with "Build Me Up Buttercup," written by Macaulay with Mike D'Abo, which reached number two in England and number one in America. "In the Bad, Bad Old Days (Before You Loved Me)" was yet another hit, reaching the U.K. Top Ten and the U.S. Top 30.

The band's success finally faltered when Macaulay exited Pye Records. With his departure, the group were cut off from the composer who'd written all of their hits. Additionally, the sounds of soul were changing faster than the group could assimilate it all—they tried for a funkier, James Brown-type sound on their last recordings together in 1970 but failed to attract any attention. *—Bruce Eder*

Baby Now That You've Found Me / May 11, 1999 / Sequel ✦✦✦✦✦

The proof of a reputation is in the listening, and this double CD just oozes proof in its 41 songs, 23 of them off of *From the Foundations* and *Digging the Foundations*. At their worst, the Foundations sound like early Rare Earth (or maybe Three Dog Night) on a really good day, and most of this collection is a lot better than that: smooth, slightly poppy but eminently danceable soul, stuff that Berry Gordy and company and their fans lived for—*and* it's beautifully remastered and very carefully put together to make the most of the CD format. Ironically, the hits are among the least interesting of the songs here, although they'll sell the set. Two of the bonus tracks, "I Need Your Love" and "Something for My Baby" by the New Foundations (Colin Young with new backup), are lost treasures that ought to have filled the international airwaves in 1976, when they were cut. And the utterly infectious "Where the Fire Burns," recorded by the original band in 1970, is a lost funk-instrumental jewel, with soaring horns and thick, twangy rhythm guitars. An astonishing, glorious collection, only missing cuts off the live second album, *Rocking the Foundations*, which is due for a separate reissue. *—Bruce Eder*

- **The Very Best of the Foundations** / Jun. 25, 2002 / Sanctuary ✦✦✦✦✦

British '60s octet the Foundations, whose claim to fame was their ability to re-create the sound of Motown, were really two-hit wonders in the U.S., those two hits being "Baby Now That I've Found You" and "Build Me Up Buttercup." The casual listener may be forgiven for thinking these songs, perpetually familiar due to oldies radio and the occasional soundtrack placement, were performed by a Motown act such as the Four Tops. Because the group recorded for the Pye Records label, which licensed their recordings to the Decca subsidiary Uni in the U.S., and all of those imprints have long-since been retired (at least, in their '60s identities), there is no major label to keep a hits collection continually in print. But Britain's Sanctuary Group had access to their catalog in 2002, and this compilation is issued by Sanctuary with U.S. distribution through BMG. It is not as good a selection as, for example, 1995's *The Very Best of the Foundations* on Taragon, which features a stereo alternate of the otherwise monophonic "Baby Now That I've Found You." But as of 2002, it was probably the most readily available Foundations album in the U.S. All seven of the group's U.S. and/or U.K. singles chart entries are included, along with another seven album tracks, giving a good sense of the band's sound, and Colin Escott's liner notes concisely tell their story. *—William Ruhlmann*

The Four Blazes

f. Chicago, IL

Group / Harmony Vocal Group, R&B, Vocal Jazz

Holy blazes! How many Blazes were there? This influential vocal group recorded as the Four Blazes, the Three Blazes, the Five Blazes, and even the just plain Blazes on a bad counting day in the studio. The group was founded in 1940 as the Four Blazes by drummer Paul Lindsley "Jelly" Holt, already a veteran of sizzling string groups such as the Five Rhythm Rocketeers. The other charter Blazes, previously known under the nasty band moniker of the Four Dusty Demons, were Jimmy Bennett and William "Shorty" Hill, who between them covered guitar, tipple, ukulele, and mandolin, with Prentice Butler on bass. All sang and did impressions as well. In 1941, swing stalwart Floyd McDaniel switched from acoustic to electric guitar and replaced Bennett, considerably changing the sound of the group in the process. A further addition was made in 1945 in the form of Pittsburgh pianist Ernie Harper. Legendary Chicago bandleader Duke Groner was the Blazes' bass player at some point between 1943 and 1946.

By this time, it seemed prudent to change the name to the Five Blazes, but this caused confusion, since a Los Angeles-based group called itself the Four Blazes at the time. The group even recorded a number, entitled "Chicago Blues," as if intentionally obscuring those who track down missing groups by looking for locational clues in song titles. The Chicago group's recording career actually didn't begin until 1947, with Aristocrat. As the Five Blazes, the group was only the second act to cut sides for what would become an important Chicago independent label, eventually to be transformed into the Chess blues kingdom. Three years later, it was back to the Four Blazes, with Ernie Harper going out in 1950. (He died around the same time.) At the end of 1951, a bassist named Tommy Braden pulled into town with saxophonist J.T. Brown's band. Braden's singing and songwriting would be central to the Blazes' sound for the remainder of the group's existence. His 1952 ditty "Mary Jo" hit the top on the R&B charts. Recordings made in this period utilized the talents of session reed player Eddie Chamblee, who pitched in on both clarinet and tenor sax. Although when he overdubbed himself on "Perfect Woman," the result was so imperfect that even a heavy dose of reverb couldn't fix it.

The group continued recording until nearly the mid-'50s, but the final recording sessions indicate more lineup changes. An organist named Gordon Fairholt is suspected of having played piano on some tracks, but has yet to be completely proven as the culprit. In 1953, there were newspaper advertisements for the Five Blazes, suggesting further incendiary growth. The fire was stoked further by the presence of sax giant Red Holloway on the last sessions and not Chamblee, as sometimes listed in discographies. This session produced the classic "Did You Ever See a Monkey Play a Fiddle," once again written by Braden, who left soon thereafter to form his own Tommy Braden Quintet. The Four Blazes went on with another vocalist, though Braden still seemed interested in the studio projects and was back in the fold for the last session in 1955. The group broke up the same year. Tommy Braden died in 1957, Jelly Holt carried on singing with the Four Whims (retiring in the early '60s), while Floyd McDaniel (1915-1995) continued on the scene, including years with the Ink Spots. Chicago blues fans noticed he was still around in the '80s and he made at least one CD after his rediscovery. *—Eugene Chadbourne*

- **Mary Jo** / Feb. 10, 1998 / Delmark ♦♦♦

Considering the nostalgic significance now given to even the most obscure R&B acts of the '40s and '50s, it's surprising that the Four Blazes remain virtually unknown to modern listeners. Suave, danceable, and impeccably played, many of the songs on *Mary Jo* are on par with the best records of the day, and the stunning sound quality belies their early-'50s recording date. Lead singer Tommy Braden sounds like a tonier Wynonie Harris, able to perform racy R&B material and sympathetic ballads equally well. The only real argument that can be leveled against the group is that they rarely stray from the sensible bop of the title track, but since their sound owes as much to the Ink Spots as the Dominoes, this only makes sense, and the exotic cadence of "All Night Long" and the later cuts, with their snapping, T-Bone Walker-style lead guitar, manage to break the mold. *—Jim Smith*

The Four Coins

f. Canonsburg, PA

Group / Rock & Roll, R&B, Harmony Vocal Group

Hailing from Canonsburg, PA, the doo wop quartet Four Coins scored a few moderate-sized hits during the mid- to late '50s. Their biggest hit was 1957's "Shangri La" (which barely missed the Top Ten, hitting number 11 on the charts) while such other songs as "My One Sin," "One Love, One Heart," and "Heartache Street" proved to be standouts from their repertoire. But "Shangri La" remains their best-known song, as it has been covered by several other artists over the years, including composer Robert Maxwell as a Top 40 instrumental hit in 1964, Vic Dana scored a Top 40 hit with it in 1964, and lesser-known versions by the Lettermen and Al Capps appeared in 1969 and 1973, respectively. Jackie Gleason later used his melody of "Shangri La" for the theme of his Reginald Van Gleason III character on his hit TV series in the early '60s. *—Greg Prato*

- **In Shangri-La** / Apr. 24, 1995 / Collectables ♦♦♦♦♦

In Shangri-La is a reissue of the 1958 album *The Four Coins in Shangri-La* with the addition of some bonus tracks, which together account for all of the group's Top 30 hits. "Shangri-La" was the group's biggest recording, a soaring example of group harmony that is better-remembered and more widely covered than its number-11 chart placement would suggest. Much of the repertoire that follows is similar to the Four Freshmen-influenced "Shangri-La," but the Four Coins go in directions the Four Freshmen did not, like the mild rock & roll of "Ting-a-Ling Telephone" and the cover of Charlie & Ray's R&B hit "I Love You Madly." *In Shangri-La* is not a complete greatest-hits collection, but it is an excellent and reasonably generous anthology of their Epic recordings from the 1950s. *—Greg Adams*

The Four Fellows

f. 1955, New York, NY

Group / Doo Wop

The Four Fellows will always be remembered for "Soldier Boy," a definitive mid-'50s hit. Jim McGowan (lead), Dave Jones (tenor), Teddy Williams (baritone), and Larry Banks (bass) originally formed in Brooklyn, NY, calling themselves the Schemers, which they changed to the Four Fellows after landing an early TV appearance.

In 1954, they recorded one single for Derby Records, but it failed to gain an audience. They soon signed with Phil Rose's newly formed Glory Records and recorded a handful of singles, including "Grow Along With Me," which featured a lead vocal by Betty McLaurin. In the late spring of 1955, the Four Fellows recorded "Soldier Boy," which earned them a spot on the bill of Tommy Smalls' Dr. Jive's R&B Revue at the Apollo Theater in June of that year, performing alongside Harvey Fuqua's Moonglows, Gene & Eunice, the Nutmegs, Bo Diddley, and Buddy Johnson & His Orchestra with Ella Johnson and Nolan Lewis. Meanwhile, "Soldier Boy" was covered by many popular artists, including Sunny Gale and Edyie Gorme.

The group successfully toured the South and Midwest and ended the year by performing at the big Christmas Revue at the Brooklyn Paramount Theater. They were less successful with their releases, however, and didn't hit again (after several attempts) until August of 1956, when the uptempo "I Sit in My Window" was released. Additional singles faltered. In 1957, the Four Fellows added Toni Banks (formerly of Three Guys & a Doll) as a lead vocalist and recorded a final single for Glory, but it failed to generate enough sales or airplay to merit keeping the band on their roster and except for the occasional backup singing job—including working with folk-blues artist Josh White—the Four Fellows career came to an end before the dawn of the '60s. *—Bryan Thomas*

- **The Best of the Four Fellows** / Relic ♦♦♦♦

The Four Mints

f. Columbus, OH

Group / Smooth Soul

Columbus, OH, natives' Ben "Pete" Caldwell, James Brown, Donald Russell, and Jimmy Harmon were the Four Mints, a band who recorded for Bill Moss' Capsoul Records. The label's roster also included Johnson, Hawkins, Tatum & Durr ("You Can't Blame Me"), Cool Blues (a duo featuring John Prim and Bill Gilbert), Marion Black ("Go on Fool"), Elijah & the Ebonites ("Sock It To 'Em Soul Brother"), and Ronnie Taylor ("Without Love"). The group's first single "You're My Desire" got limited play in some minor markets. Caldwell, the lead singer, wrote both sides of the midtempo wailer (later included on a handful of compilation albums, including *Dynamite Soul Harmony*, and a northern soul favorite).

The second release was their finest moment, the floater "Row My Boat," led by Caldwell and written by Dean Francis. It was a favorite of young groups and bedroom-mirror singers, and always brought ovations when performed by locals at talent shows. "Row My Boat," hit the R&B charts, and was their biggest record. The success of "Row My Boat" prompted their only LP, *Gently Down Your Stream*, in 1973. (Bill Moss reissued the LP on CD in 1995.) The success of "Row My Boat" took the Four Mints gigging to the Washington, D.C., area, Kentucky, Indiana, and Michigan. A third and final release, "Can't Get Strung Out" (released in 1973), never got started; disenchanted, the fellows disbanded. *—Andrew Hamilton*

- **Gently Down Your Stream** / 1995 / Capsoul ♦♦♦

Originally released in 1973, this set of both strong and weak numbers gets a rebirth on CD. The title comes from a line in "Row Your Boat," their most popular recording, a would-be hit that was loved everywhere it got played; but this complex, gentle floater with the breathtaking hook never got the saturated amount of play needed for serious chart action. "You're My Desire" is a harmony workout and Northern soul favorite. The good stuff includes two compositions by Dana Middleton and Jeffrey Smith—"Why Did I Go" and "Do You Really Love Me"—as well as Erwin Cochran's "Can't Get Strung Out." *—Andrew Hamilton*

The Four Tops

f. 1956, Detroit, MI

Group / Motown, Soul, Pop-Soul

The Four Tops' story is one of longevity and togetherness: These Motown legends teamed up in high school and spent over four decades without a single personnel change. In between, they became one of the top-tier acts on a label with no shortage of talent, ranking with the Temptations and the Supremes as Motown's most consistent hitmakers. Where many other R&B vocal groups spotlighted a tenor-range lead singer, the Four Tops were fronted by deep-voiced Levi Stubbs, who never cut a solo record outside of the group. Stubbs had all the grit of a pleading, wailing, gospel-trained soul belter, but at the same time, the Tops' creamy harmonies were smooth enough for Motown's radio-friendly pop-soul productions. From 1964-1967, the Four Tops recorded some of the Holland-Dozier-Holland team's greatest compositions, including "Reach Out, I'll Be There," "I Can't Help Myself (Sugarpie, Honeybunch)," "Standing in the Shadows of Love," "Bernadette," and "Baby I Need Your Loving." The group's fortunes took a downturn when their chief source of material left the label, but they enjoyed a renaissance in the early '70s, which saw them switching to the ABC/Dunhill imprint. Regardless of commercial fortunes, they kept on performing and touring, scoring the occasional comeback hit.

The Four Tops began life in 1953 (some accounts say 1954), when all of the members were attending Detroit-area high schools. Levi Stubbs and Abdul "Duke" Fakir went to Pershing, and met Northern students Renaldo "Obie" Benson and Lawrence Payton at a friend's birthday party, where the quartet first sang together. Sensing an immediate chemistry, they began rehearsing together and dubbed themselves the Four Aims. Payton's cousin Roquel Davis, a budding songwriter who sometimes sang with the group during their early days, helped them get an audition with Chess Records in 1956. Although Chess was more interested in Davis, who went on to become Berry Gordy's songwriting partner, they also signed the Four Aims, who became the Four Tops to avoid confusion with the Ames Brothers. The Four Tops' lone Chess single, "Kiss Me Baby," was an unequivocal flop, and the group moved on to similarly brief stints at Red Top and Riverside. They signed with Columbia in 1960 and were steered in a more upscale supper-club direction, singing jazz and pop standards. This too failed to break them, although they did tour with Billy Eckstine during this period.

In 1963, the Four Tops signed with longtime friend Berry Gordy's new label, specifically the jazz-oriented Workshop subsidiary. They completed a debut LP, to be called *Breaking Through*, but Gordy scrapped it and switched their style back to R&B, placing them on Motown with the Holland-Dozier-Holland songwriting team. After a full decade in existence, the Four Tops finally notched their first hit in 1964 with "Baby I Need Your Loving," which just missed the pop Top Ten. Early 1965 brought the follow-up ballad hit "Ask the Lonely," and from then on there was no stopping them. "I Can't Help Myself (Sugarpie, Honeybunch)" went all the way to number one that spring, and the follow-up "It's the Same Old Song" reached the Top Five. The hits continued into 1966, with "Something About You" "Shake Me, Wake Me (When It's Over)," and "Loving You Is Sweeter Than Ever" all coming in succession. The fall of 1966 brought the group's masterpiece in the form of the virtual soul symphony "Reach Out, I'll Be There"; not only did it become their second number-one pop hit, it also wound up ranking as the creative peak of the group's career and one of Motown's finest singles ever. During this period, the Tops also earned a reputation as one of Motown's best live acts, having previously honed their performances for years before hitting the big time.

The Four Tops kicked off 1967 with the dramatic Top Ten smash "Standing in the Shadows of Love," which was followed by the Top Five "Bernadette." "Seven Rooms of Gloom" and "You Keep Running Away" reached the Top 20, but toward the end of the year, the Holland-Dozier-Holland left Motown over a financial dispute, which didn't bode well for the Four Tops' impressive hit streak. Their next two hits, 1968's "Walk Away Renee" and "If I Were a Carpenter," were both covers of well-known recent songs (by the Left Banke and Tim Hardin, respectively), and while both made the Top 20, they heralded a rough couple of years where top-drawer material was in short supply. They enjoyed a resurgence in 1970 under producer Frank Wilson, who helmed a hit cover of the Tommy Edwards pop standard "It's All in the Game" and a ballad co-written by Smokey Robinson, "Still Water (Love)." The Tops also recorded with the post-Diana Ross Supremes, scoring a duet hit with a cover of "River Deep—Mountain High" in 1971.

When Motown moved its headquarters to Los Angeles in 1972, the Four Tops parted ways with the company, choosing to remain in their hometown of Detroit. They signed with ABC/Dunhill and were teamed with producers/songwriters Dennis Lambert and Brian Potter, who did their best to re-create the group's trademark Motown sound. The immediate result was "Keeper of the Castle," the Four Tops' first Top Ten hit in several years. They followed it in early 1973 with "Ain't No Woman (Like the One I've Got)," a gold-selling smash that proved to be their final Top Five pop hit. That year they also recorded the theme song to the film *Shaft in Africa*, "Are You Man Enough." Several more R&B chart hits followed over the next few years, with the last being 1976's "Catfish"; after a final ABC album in 1978, the Tops largely disappeared from sight before resurfacing on Casablanca in 1981. Incredibly, their first single, "When She Was My Girl," went all the way to number one on the R&B charts, just missing the pop Top Ten. The accompanying album *Tonight!* became their last to hit the Top 40.

The Four Tops rejoined Motown in 1983, the year of the company's 25th anniversary, and toured extensively with the Temptations. They also recorded a couple albums of new material which failed to sell well, and wound up leaving Motown amidst confusion over proper musical direction. Meanwhile, Levi Stubbs provided the voice for Audrey the man-eating plant in the film version of *Little Shop of Horrors*. The Four Tops next caught on with Arista, where in 1988 they scored their last Top 40 pop hit, the aptly titled "Indestructible." The Four Tops were inducted into the Rock and Roll Hall of Fame in 1990, and continued to tour the oldies circuit. In 1997, Lawrence Payton passed away due to cancer of the liver, which proved to be the only thing that could break up the Four Tops. After some consideration, the remaining members hired Theo Peoples to take Payton's place on tour. *—Steve Huey*

The Four Tops / Oct. 1964 / Motown ✦✦✦✦
You'd be hard pressed to find two better singles on a debut album than "Ask the Lonely" and "Baby I Need Your Loving." These were the cornerstones of The Four Tops' first LP, and besides netting them one Top Ten and Top 20 pop single each, as well as a Top Ten and Top 20 R&B single, it established Levi Stubbs' resounding voice as another unforgettable one at Motown. Even the tunes that didn't do so well, like "Left With a Broken Heart" or "Without the One You Love (Life's Not Worth While)," were marvelously sung. It was a debut to remember. *—Ron Wynn*

The Four Tops' Second Album / Nov. 13, 1965 / Motown ✦✦✦✦
The Four Tops followed their fine debut album with an even more magnificent second effort. They landed their first number-one pop and R&B hit with "I Can't Help Myself (Sugar Pie, Honey Bunch)." There was also "Something About You," a great uptempo shouter that seemed a disappointment at number 19 (number-nine R&B), but didn't lack vocal authority or production genius. The album also contained "It's the Same Old Song," a tidy little number that reached number five (number-two R&B) and had one of the greatest lyric hooks and titles ever. *—Ron Wynn*

On Top / Jul. 1966 / Motown ✦✦✦
Beginning with *On Top*, Motown started constructing their Four Tops LPs from singles and a few similar-sounding album tracks, along with plenty of crossover material (usually attempts at MOR covers or light supper-club standards). The first four songs display the Four Tops at the peak of their power; opening with the swinging "I Got a Feeling," the quartet paused only briefly with a ballad ("Brenda") before delivering their two biggest and best hits of the time, "Loving You Is Sweeter Than Ever" and "Shake Me, Wake Me (When It's Over)." Hoping older listeners might be lured in by crossover versions of a few current hits, Motown devoted the last half to some seriously misguided covers: "Matchmaker," "Quiet Nights of Quiet Stars," "In the Still of the Night," and a rather stiff version of the Beatles' "Michelle." Though it reached the pop Top 40, doubtless most teenagers never even bothered flipping this one over, and the crossover material hasn't aged well. *—John Bush*

The Four Tops Live / Nov. 1966 / Motown ✦✦✦
One of the few live albums that really conveys the flavor of the group without sacrificing performance quality. The Four Tops' stage shows have always been among the most participatory and enjoyable of any R&B or soul group, and that was clearly the case on this release. *—Ron Wynn*

On Broadway / Mar. 1967 / Motown ✦✦✦
Produced by Frank Wilson, with vocal arrangements by Lawrence Payton, this LP was too drastic a step to take, deviating too far from what the public expected of the Four Tops. Wilson did not attempt to incorporate the Four Tops' winning formula into these songs. The only listenable track is an endearing rendition of "Make Someone Happy"; Levi is allowed to emote a little on the fade. It's a mystery how this one escaped; Motown usually left experiments like this high and dry. *—Andrew Hamilton*

Reach Out / Jul. 1967 / Motown ✦✦✦✦
Though it's one of the best Four Tops records of the '60s, *Reach Out* still feels weighted down by a few vain attempts at adult pop crossover. It certainly starts out right, with the glorious "Reach Out, I'll Be There," the group's second pop/R&B chart-topper. After a faithful cover of the Left Banke's "Walk Away Renee," though, listeners are forced to sit through trite versions of "If I Were a Carpenter," "Last Train to Clarksville," and "I'm a Believer" to get to real highlights like the dramatic, impassioned "Standing in the Shadows of Love" and "Bernadette." There is room for a great lesser single ("I'll Turn to Stone"), but the flip side finds the Four Tops taking on "Cherish," which could've worked well but didn't. *Reach Out* still did better than any other original LP by the group, almost breaking the Top Ten. *—John Bush*

Greatest Hits / Aug. 1967 / Motown ✦✦✦✦✦

Yesterday's Dreams / Aug. 1968 / Motown ✦✦✦
On *Yesterday's Dreams*, the Four Tops began looking back. Their songwriting and production mainstays, Holland-Dozier-Holland, had recently left the company in a royalties dispute and the LP included just one last song from the collective, "I'm in a Different World." Unfortunately, it was the biggest hit here, and nothing else compared to "Reach Out, I'll Be There" or "Standing in the Shadows of Love." Still, songs and productions from Ivory Joe Hunter (the title track, "We've Got a Strong Love [On Our Side]") and Ashford & Simpson ("Can't Seem to Get You Out of My Mind") filled the gaps with no discernible loss in quality. Even the unavoidable covers are treated very well; Hunter and Frank Wilson altered "By the Time I Get to Phoenix," "Sunny," and even "Daydream Believer" to sound more natural next to a *real* Motown song like "Remember When." If it never hit the chart heights of 1967's *Reach Out*, *Yesterday's Dreams* still proved more of a solid listen. *—John Bush*

The Four Tops Now! / May 1969 / Motown ✦✦✦
This wasn't among their biggest hit albums, but was a well-produced, nicely sung set anyhow. They were one of Motown's most versatile ensembles, and their albums tended to be all over the stylistic board, some ballads, some show tunes, some jazzy pop. That was the case with this one as well, with only one single making it to the middle of the R&B charts. *—Ron Wynn*

Soul Spin / Nov. 1969 / Motown ✦✦✦
For *Soul Spin*, producer Frank Wilson stirred nearly everything into the pot, directing the Four Tops to darker, topical material like the paternity case "Barbara's Boy" and "Lost in a Pool of Red," but also including two Burt Bacharach covers and Motown's take on the Mamas & the Papas' "California Dreamin'." Elsewhere, the Beatles cover "Got to Get You Into My Life" has a dated chart but a tearing Levi Stubbs lead to save it, and "Light My Fire" is a startling success, with a slow-burn feel and great group vocals on the chorus. These are only curiosities, though, perfect for hardcore Motown fans listeners interested in digging deeper. *—John Bush*

Still Waters Run Deep / Mar. 1970 / Motown ✦✦✦
In early 1970, the group was assigned to Norman Whitfield disciple Frank Wilson for production, and he managed to breathe some life into their stagnating career. They earned a pair of Top Forty hits with "Still Water (Love)" and a remake of Tommy Edwards' "It's All in the Game." *—John Lowe*

Changing Times / Sep. 1970 / Motown ✦✦✦
The Four Tops entered the '70s still among the dominant vocal ensembles. This release included a superb performance by Levi Stubbs and company on the title track, and many other equally well-sung numbers. Motown wasn't dominating the pop world anymore, but the Four Tops were one of the groups that were still doing a solid job with in the early '70s. *—Ron Wynn*

Nature Planned It / Apr. 1972 / Motown ✦✦✦✦
Positive proof that Motown was capable of putting out a good Four Tops LP without the aid of Holland-Dozier-Holland. Levi Stubbs' warm, emotive baritone takes Ashford & Simpson's "I am Your Man" to the river and back. "It's the Way Nature Planned It" is one of the group's top songs, with an engaging lead and Abdul Fakir, Lawrence Payton and Renaldo Benson's smooth harmonies. The medley "Hey Man—We Got to Get You a Woman" garnered quite a few spins when released, the song has a happy optimistic feel that went over well. "I'll Never Change" and "I Can't Quit Your Love" are both sung by Stubbs near the top of his register, adding even more fuel to the already dynamic arrangement. The public liked this one as it rose to number 50 on *Billboard*'s Top 200 Album Chart, a decent showing for an LP that didn't have a Top Ten single. *—Andrew Hamilton*

Keeper of the Castle / Dec. 1972 / Motown ✦✦✦
The Four Tops finally left Motown in the early '70s, signing first with ABC/Dunhill. This was their debut for the label, and it was a moderate success. They did much more pop-oriented material than they ever did for Motown, and the title track was the first of several hits they would enjoy while on ABC. *—Ron Wynn*

Main Street People / 1973 / ABC/Dunhill ✦✦✦
One of the first major defections from Motown, the Four Tops signed to ABC/Dunhill and immediately hit with the 1973 album *Keeper of the Castle* and its biggest single, "Ain't No Woman (Like the One I Got)." The follow-up, *Main Street People*, was produced by Steve Barri, Dennis Lambert, and Brian Potter. Although they all had a heavy pop resumé, they gave the Four Tops a strong L.A. pop/R&B sound that wasn't far from what Motown was doing at the time. Recorded at ABC Recording Studios with a cadre of session players, including Wilton Felder on bass and drummer Paul Humphrey, this was one of the finest of all of the group's ABC endeavors. The best track, the poignant, midtempo "I Just Can't Get You out of My Mind" is in the mold of the Spinners' "I'll Be Around," featuring a couple of choice bellows from lead singer Levi Stubbs. The warm and melodic "Am I My Brother's Keeper" displays the group's trademark left-of-center harmonies as well as the skill of the backing band. *Main Street People* loses steam however, during side two, as barren lyrics and uninspired arrangements make it less than essential. The title track, however, is a flawless mix of R&B and pop with a good arrangement and more smooth vocal riffs from the group. *Main Street People* may seem like sacrilege to some R&B fans, but it's actually better thought out than some of the groups 1968-1972 work with Motown. *—Jason Elias*

Live & In Concert / 1974 / ABC/Dunhill ✦✦✦
As live recordings go, this one isn't half bad. The Four Tops perform a mixture of past and present hits to a full orchestra aided by a crack sound system. Selections like "Midnight Flower," "Keeper of the Castle," and "Ain't No Woman (Like The One I've Got)" rival the studio recordings, and Levi Stubbs' soliloquy on "I Am Your Man" will have you rolling. *—Andrew Hamilton*

Meeting of the Minds / 1974 / ABC/Dunhill ✦✦✦
Meeting of the Minds, the proper studio follow-up to 1973's *Main Street People*, wasn't a big seller either. The production failed to capitalize on the group's chemistry, offering songs that were formulaic and stale. The hokey "One Chain Don't Make No Prison" starts off promisingly, with a searing guitar riff, but then a weak set of lyrics tests Levi Stubbs' credibility. "Midnight Flower," with a faint Oriental motif, has Stubbs unabashedly singing of having the hots for a prostitute. Since the Tops' pop/R&B sound was beginning to run out of gas, they also tried other ideas. "The Well Is Dry" is reminiscent of the group's dramatic work with Holland-Dozier-Holland, but a perfunctory arrangement makes it sound artificial. Unlike many efforts, this featured other group members getting a lead vocal. The best of the lot is "Tell Me You Love Me (Love Sounds)." The song features Lawrence Payton, whose voice is lighter than Stubbs', but had his exact phrasing. The

track, complete with a cooing woman and a breezy L.A. pop/R&B arrangement, is fun to listen to. *Meeting of the Minds* seemed to be an extension of *Keeper of the Castle*, but the group sounded a little tired and the production seemed too listless. Despite a few good tracks, this didn't blaze any new trails for the group. *—Jason Elias*

☆ **Anthology** / Jul. 1974 / Motown ♦♦♦♦♦
A bountiful three-record collection later issued on two CDs, the Four Tops' *Anthology* presented, in chronological order, every notable song from the group's tenure at Motown, from their 1964 breakout hit "Baby I Need Your Loving" all the way to 1972's "A Simple Game." (The compact disc also tacked on two songs from the '80s: "I Just Can't Walk Away" and "Don't Tell Me That It's Over.") Over the course of six sides, *Anthology* tells the group's story with every one of their three dozen hits of the '60s and early '70s, leaving just enough room for low-level hits or solid album tracks ("Just Seven Numbers (Can Straighten Out My Life)," "Can't Seem to Get You Out of My Mind," and a nice version of the Supremes' "Reflections") as well as some pop cover curios ("Climb Ev'ry Mountain," "A Place in the Sun," the surprising hit "If I Were a Carpenter," a beautifully wistful "Everybody's Talking," and a melody of "Hey Man" and Todd Rundgren's "We Gotta Get You a Woman"). It boasted far more attention to detail than the usual hits compilation and the sound was good for the time, though it became less crucial for Four Tops obsessives when Motown finally released the long-awaited box set *Fourever* in 2001. *—John Bush*

Catfish / 1976 / ABC ♦♦♦
"Catfish" is one of the Four Tops' most entrancing numbers, a tale about a disco queen from New Orleans who dances up a storm. It may have been a little risqué for radio stations, with the line "makes my nature rise" being the point of contention. A percolating organ introduces the song, punctuated by a string of "well wells" from the Tops before Levi Stubbs' type-A baritone enters the foray and mesmerizes you. Unfortunately, the rest of the album fails to come close to the title track. Only "Look at My Baby" has anything that resembles charm. The rest is strictly second-rate songwriter-workshop stuff. *—Andrew Hamilton*

The Show Must Go On / 1977 / ABC ♦♦♦
Produced by group member Lawrence Payton, the Four Tops' *The Show Must Go On* was the follow-up to their *Catfish* album, which included the Top Seven R&B/pop-charting title track single. The first single, "The Show Must Go On," an energetic ode to the age-old showbiz ethic, was a disco hit and managed to chart R&B in late 1977. The LP's standout tracks, though, came courtesy of fellow Detroiter Ronnie McNeir. The two-tempoed "I Can't Live Without You" is a grand showcase for Levi Stubbs' plaintive vocals. The gospel-ish/chunky, clavinet-laced "You'll Never Find a Better Man" did much to bolster the group's well-liked, regular-guy appeal. In later years, McNeir became the group's touring musical director and appeared on the group's 1995 Motown album *Christmas Here With You*. Other highlights are the message-oriented cuts "See the Real Me," "Love Is a Joy," and the baritone-led ballad "Candy." *—Ed Hogan*

At the Top / 1978 / ABC ♦♦♦
At The Top is a quality Four Tops album, produced by Norman Harris at Sigma Sound in Philadelphia; the songs, productions, and singing deserved a better fate. Future Temptation Ron Tyson co-wrote five songs: the minor hit "H.E.L.P.," and the beautiful, harmony-filled "Seclusion," "Put It on the News," "This House," and "Just in Time," an excellent ballad. Many found this production formalized, but those listeners miss the essence. The disjointed, jerky, soulful "When Your Dreams Take Wings and Fly" is anything but a formula song, and Levi Stubbs' emotional singing on "Seclusion" is the real deal. This was the Tops' last LP for ABC, which may account for the lightweight promotion. *—Andrew Hamilton*

One More Mountain / 1982 / Casablanca ♦♦

Back Where I Belong / Oct. 1983 / Motown ♦♦♦
Back Where I Belong marks the Four Tops' return to Motown after stints with ABC and Casablanca Records. The foursome also united with the hit songwriting and production team of Holland-Dozier-Holland on some cuts. The slow, meandering "I Just Can't Walk Away," not one of HDH's best, died upon release, while the much better, shuffling, percolating "Make Yourself Right at Home" suffered from a total lack of promotion. "Hang," a duet with the Temptations, had a good message and sparkling, creative vocals, but got stuck as the B-side of the debut single; few, if any, DJs flipped it over. The duet with Lady Soul Aretha Franklin "What Have We Got to Lose" pales in comparison to earlier duets by the two super acts. Overall, the Four Tops are more mellow and subdued here than in the past. *—Andrew Hamilton*

Magic / 1985 / Motown ♦♦
The Four Tops returned to Motown in the mid-'80s, although things didn't work out for them in the end. This was the most successful of three albums they cut during their second stay, with two songs doing moderately well, and "Sexy Ways" becoming one of their last chart hits. A duet with Phyllis Hyman also got substantial urban contemporary airplay. *—Ron Wynn*

Indestructible / 1988 / Arista ♦♦♦
This is one of the later Four Tops albums, although the group's classic sound remained intact. Levi Stubbs' booming voice still resounded on a set of mostly routine tracks. They did get a little attention from the single "Loco in Acapulco," which was featured in the soundtrack of the film *Buster*. *—Ron Wynn*

Until You Love Someone: More of the Best (1965–1970) / Feb. 16, 1993 / Rhino ♦♦♦♦
This compilation gathers 18 non-hit album tracks from eight LPs that the Four Tops cut for Motown between 1965 and 1970 (some of which appeared on B-sides). A major soul group they might have been, but the Tops' pinnacle was actually quite brief, and that's reflected in this collection. No less than two-thirds of the songs date from 1965 and 1966, six from 1965's *Second Album* alone. Not so coincidentally, all but one of those cuts were written by the legendary Holland-Dozier-Holland songwriting team. The production is faultless, the songs very characteristically HDH, and Levi Stubbs' lead vocals are unfailingly gritty and pleasurable. Yet none of these have the unforgettable hooks of their hit singles of the period like "Reach Out, I'll Be There" and "I Can't Help Myself." As enjoyable as the formula is, the uniformity of the sound limits this disc's appeal to serious Motown and soul collectors. Curiosities among the non-HDH cuts include little-known tunes by Smokey Robinson and Stevie Wonder, and a non-hit single from 1969, "What Is a Man." *—Richie Unterberger*

Keepers of the Castle: Their Best 1972–1978 / Jul. 29, 1997 / MCA ♦♦♦♦
When the Four Tops moved from Motown to Dunhill in the early '70s, they encountered the dilemma faced by most '60s soul giants, from Motown or elsewhere: how to update their sound while maintaining some degree of personality. Commercially at least, things got off to a smashing start with "Keeper of the Castle," "Ain't No Woman (Like the One I Got)," and "Are You Man Enough?" (all included here). Yet it was evident that the Four Tops, removed from the magic of '60s Motown, would be trend followers rather than pacesetters. Most of this 14-song compilation shows them as a competent but rather generic '70s soul vocal group, adding Philly soul and funk elements to their sound without asserting much of an identity. Even "Are You Man Enough?," as good as it is, is something of a son-of-"Back Stabbers"; "Ain't No Woman," similarly, could be easily mistaken for a Spinners cut by the unschooled. Save the occasional standout like "Love Music," not much else here measures up to the early Dunhill hits, though if you want one post-early-'70s Four Tops compilation, this is probably the best. *—Richie Unterberger*

★ **The Ultimate Collection** / Oct. 7, 1997 / Motown ♦♦♦♦♦
The Ultimate Collection series was a rare success from Motown, one of the first of the label's many compilation series to do justice to some of the finest performers, arrangers, and musicians of the soul era. Nearly every artist with an entry was given the luxury treatment, with a disc-filling running time, excellent compilation decisions, and a pleasing design scheme that reflected the artists in their prime. The Four Tops' entry is arguably the best in the series, since the 25 tracks prove the perfect length to summarize the group's decade at Motown. From 1963 to 1972, the group reached the R&B charts 28 times, and all but a very few are presented here (among the missing are three decidedly unnecessary covers: "MacArthur Park," "If I Were a Carpenter," and "River Deep—Mountain High"). Though the tracks aren't presented chronologically, thoughtful sequencing makes for an even better listen; *The Ultimate Collection* opens with "Reach Out (I'll Be There)," perhaps the ultimate pop single of the '60s, and flows smoothly through the best of their 1964-1967 prime: "Baby I Need Your Loving," "I Can't Help Myself (Sugar Pie, Honey Bunch)," "It's the Same Old Song," "Bernadette," and "Standing in the Shadows of Love." And though the hits began to dry up after the Holland-Dozier-Holland machine departed Motown in 1968, the Four Tops' later years are represented well with "It's All in the Game," "Still Water (Love)," "(It's the Way) Nature Planned It," and the driving non-album hit "A Simple Game." Unless you're the type of fan who needs the box set (2001's *Fourever*), this is all the Four Tops-on-Motown you really need to hear. *—John Bush*

Best of the ABC Years 1972-1977 / Jan. 18, 1999 / Music Club ♦♦♦
A 14-track release of the Four Tops ABC Records tracks that includes some and omits some songs that were on an earlier compilation. Look for the Four Tops ABC sides to be released in various combinations, like their Motown sides, to the point of pain. Contains the essentials "Catfish," "Are You Man Enough," "Keeper of the Castle," "Midnight Flower," and "One Chain Don't Make No Prison." And includes some album cuts that may be unfamiliar to many: "Strung Out For Your Love," "Am I My Brother's Keeper," and "Tell Me You Love Me." A medley, taken from their *Live* LP on ABC, is also included. *—Andrew Hamilton*

Lost and Found: Breaking Through / Sep. 28, 1999 / Motown ♦♦♦
The Four Tops' early years as a jazz-vocal group are generally glossed over in capsule histories. Long before they signed to Motown—nearly a full decade as a matter of fact—they had been one of the popular Detroit jazz-vocal groups, earning the admiration of such luminaries as Smokey Robinson and Billy Eckstine, whom the group supported. After some persuasion, the group signed with Motown on the condition that they could record jazz. Over the course of a year, they cut nearly two albums' worth of material, which boiled down to one album, *Breaking Through*. Berry Gordy pulled the record at the last minute, believing that it would have been a commercial failure. Gordy's fears were not unfounded—indeed, had the album that comprises *Breaking Through (1963-1964)* been put out in 1964, it likely wouldn't have found much of an audience. Still, *Breaking Through* is a strong record, firmly within its tradition and working well on those terms. The Four Tops may not sound as distinctive singing jazz as they did with pop-soul, but they are convincing, as are the Motown house band. Neither of them take many chances, however. The songs are primarily standards, plus four new songs that feel like standards, all given good generic arrangements. This may sound like a dismissal, but it isn't; it's hard to do this kind of music right, but the group most certainly does. And it's not just one member that shines; everyone gets to take a lead, and the results are uniformly strong. Even so, *Breaking Through* appeals primarily to hardcore fans of the group, plus a handful of straight-ahead vocal-jazz aficionados. Reminiscent of a cross between Eckstine and the Four Freshmen, it's good stuff, but it's essentially a curiosity. *—Stephen Thomas Erlewine*

On Top/Reach Out / 2001 / Motown ♦♦♦

Yesterday's Dreams/Soul Spin / 2001 / Motown ♦♦♦

Fourever / Sep. 25, 2001 / Hip-O ♦♦♦♦♦
The last of the major Motown groups to receive proper box set treatment, the Four Tops in a sense got the best of the bunch, since this tells a ripping history while providing a cornucopia of rarities. The latter part of that statement is what prevents the set from being

a true must-have for those who just want a comprehensive history, because there are too many major songs present in alternate mixes or versions that are slightly different than the hits that brought the group its deserved fame and fortune. Not that any of these are bad—it's just that it presents the group's history through a slightly skewed prism, enough to prevent it from being thoroughly comprehensive. Still, it's an accurate history and a wholly engaging one, largely because the Four Tops had a fairly extensive pre-history before joining Motown, and they continued to have hits after leaving Motown, thereby giving the box a real narrative thrust—especially because the late-'50s recordings that dominate the first half of the first disc are as gritty and powerful as their mid-'70s recordings were smooth, stylish, and sexy. Like many comprehensive four-disc box sets, it spends too much time in the post-hit era. Sure, the Four Tops continued to chart until the early '80s, but this extends into the early '90s, meaning that the record just sort of peters out to a less-than-satisfying conclusion. Nevertheless, that's a minor quibble, because the box does tell the story very effectively and is filled with great music, great sound, and solid liner notes, especially notable for its rare pictures. For the hardcore fans who have been waiting a long time for a Four Tops set, such loving presentation and abundance of alternate takes and mixes makes it worth the wait. *—Stephen Thomas Erlewine*

Inez & Charlie Foxx

f. 1962, Greensboro, NC, **db.** 1968

Group / R&B, Soul

This brother/sister duo from Greensboro made a little noise on the soul scene in the '60s. They signed with Juggy Murray Jones' Symbol label in 1962. Their biggest hit was "Mockingbird," in 1963, which was a number-two R&B and number-seven pop smash. Their vocal tradeoffs and arrangement were primarily responsible for its appeal, though Foxx could do some sizzling numbers on her own. They continued with "Ask Me" and "Hurt by Love," then switched to Musicor. Their final moderate hit was "(1-2-3-4-5-6-7) Count the Days" in 1967 for Dynamo, which reached number 17 on the R&B charts. Inez Foxx had a solid LP on her own for Volt in 1969, *At Memphis*. But her solo songs for the label didn't generate much interest in the early and mid-'70s. James Taylor and Carly Simon later did a cover of "Mockingbird." *—Ron Wynn*

Come By Here / 1965 / Dynamo ♦♦♦

The sibling duo's third album was more consistent than the two previous Juggy Murray Jones productions. While there isn't a "Mockingbird," there are many solid soul cuts, including the gospel-ish "Come By Here," a remake of "I Stand Accused" (a soul classic), and a sparkling rendition of "I Love You a Thousand Times," a tune Inez co-wrote which was a hit for the Sonny Turner-led Platters. *—Andrew Hamilton*

Inez & Charles Foxx / 1965 / Sue ♦♦♦

Inez & Charles Foxx's second album features both sides of their smash single "Mockingbird" b/w "Jaybirds"; the pair of tunes was also on their debut album on Symbol (a subsidiary of Sue Records). But it's not a problem; the mix makes the package stronger. It features "Ask Me" from 1963, the sister/brother duo's final of four singles from that prolific year, and subsequent singles: "Hurt By Love," (later ripped-off by the New Beats as "Bread & Butter"), "La De Da I Love You," "I Fancy You," and "My Mommy Told Me." For the unacquainted, Inez & Charles Foxx were like Ike & Tina Turner, with Charlie playing more of a role vocally than Ike, and Inez, while sassy and soulful, not as dynamic as Tina. *—Andrew Hamilton*

At Memphis / 1972 / Volt ♦♦

The Inez Foxx of "Mockingbird" fame is missing in action. None of the sides approaches the magnitude of that number-7 pop hit for Foxx in September 1963. Foxx's version of Mitty Collier's soulful "I Had a Talk With My Man" is simply a less compelling rehash. Inez does better on Jeanette "Baby" Washington's "The Time," injecting new life into the timeless ballad. "You Don't Want My Love (All You Want Is My Loving)" is a good match for Foxx's light voice; it has a similar groove to Johnnie Taylor's "Just Keep on Loving Me." The last track, "Mousa Muse," is not a song, but a short interview of Inez about recording in Memphis for the first time by an interviewer named Mousa. Not what it could have been, Stax failed to deliver on this one. *—Andrew Hamilton*

● **Mockingbird: The Best of Charlie & Inez Foxx** / 1986 / Collectables ♦♦♦♦

This covers the period (probably about 1963-1966, although dates are not given for all the tracks in the liner notes) in which Inez & Charles Foxx were on Symbol Records, a subsidiary of Sue. The original hit version of "Mockingbird" leads off the 14-song disc, and it's simply a great early pop-soul song with irresistible vocal sparring between the sister and brother. Of course, nothing else on the CD matches that classic, although "Hurt By Love" was a moderate hit for them in 1964 on both sides of the Atlantic. This is average pop-soul of the era, albeit more R&B-oriented than many records in the genre. Sometimes they sounded like Ike & Tina Turner (who were themselves pretty spotty on record during the period). At other times, they tried to mimic the Supremes ("La De Dah I Love You"), or just tried to rework the "Mockingbird" sound, with predictably lesser results. Any compilation worthy of the name *The Best of Charlie & Inez Foxx* needs to incorporate some of their 1966-1968 material for Musicor, which is collected on the Charly anthology *Count the Days*. It also needs to have better packaging than it gets on the no-frills sleeve that Collectables gave this release. *—Richie Unterberger*

Count the Days / Oct. 17, 1995 / Charly ♦♦♦

With 20 songs from 1966-1968, this summarizes the duo's stint with Musicor/Dynamo, in which they offered fair but on the whole unremarkable New York soul. As was true of much of their prior material with Sue, their format often recalls that of Ike & Tina Turner. The production is better and more varied than their Sue sides, but the material and delivery aren't as strong as the Turners were at their best. Note that the version of "Mockingbird" which leads off the disc is not the original 1963 hit, but an inferior 1968 remake. This compilation has been superseded in value by the 2001 Kent CD anthology, *The Dynamo Duo*, which has four more tracks from this same era, although *Count the Days* does have one song not present on *The Dynamo Duo*, "I Got It." *—Richie Unterberger*

The Dynamo Duo / Mar. 13, 2001 / Kent ♦♦♦

Dynamo was the name of the Musicor subsidiary for which Inez & Charlie Foxx did most of their late-'60s recordings, and this collects a couple dozen tracks the duo cut for Musicor/Dynamo from 1966-1969. Their Dynamo output was more consistent than what they had recorded for Sue, thanks in part to input from producer Luther Dixon, who was married to Inez Foxx at the time. However, there was no outstanding single on the order of "Mockingbird" during their time with the label, and the pair still often sounded like a lesser, more pop-oriented version of Ike & Tina Turner. This is respectable but somewhat middling New York soul with, as was true of much of the city's 1960s soul output, a slicker sheen to the production than soul product from most other regions. On "I Love You 1,000 Times," they seem to be trying to mimic 1963-1964 Motown, and although they don't do so badly, that's a strategy doomed to failure. The comparison to the Turners bobs higher above the surface in the bluesy and sultry "I Stand Accused"/"Guilty" medley, one of the disc's highlights. A lowlight, however, is the outrageous 1968 medley of "Vaya Con Dios"/"Fellows in Vietnam," in which the traditional song turns into a rap about the Vietnam War. Just as you're getting all set for a protest or at least moving commentary, it builds into a plea for us to encourage American soldiers to get out of their foxholes and "kill another enemy to set us free, and to keep us free"—not the sort of sentiment that could be heartily endorsed for a conflict that took so many needless lives, a disproportionate amount of whom (on the U.S. side) were African-Americans. This CD is preferable to a prior compilation of the Foxx's Musicor/Dynamo work, *Count the Days*, as this has four more tracks, including a 1969 Inez Foxx solo effort, "You Shouldn't Have Set My Soul on Fire." Be cautioned that the version of "Mockingbird" is not the original 1963 hit single, but a 1968 remake with strings. *—Richie Unterberger*

Foxy

Group / Disco

Foxy was Ish Ledesma (lead vocals), Arnold Pasiero (bass), Richie Puente Jr. (percussion), Charlie Murchiano (keyboards), and Joe Galdo (drums). They worked as the house band for Henry Stone's T.K. Records after KC & the Sunshine Band, and supplemented their income by gigging. It was at a club in Maryland that the idea for "Get Off," a number-one R&B hit, first struck. The boys worked the number up back in Miami at T.K.'s studio, adding female vocals for the chorus. The subsequent release, "Rrrrrrock," did little, and they disbanded after recording three LPs in three years: *Get Off*, *Hot Numbers*, and *Party Boys*. Since then, two CDs have dropped: *Get Off: The Best of Foxy* in 1995, and *Get Off: Hot Numbers* in 1998. Ledesma's next venture was the band Oxo ("Whirly Girl") and then a solo album before delving full-time into producing other artists. *—Andrew Hamilton*

Foxy / 1976 / Dash ♦♦♦

Many people think that 1978's *Get Off* was Foxy's debut album, which is understandable because the title song was the Latino band's big commercial breakthrough. But in fact, Foxy's first album came in 1976, when it provided this self-titled LP for the T.K.-distributed Dash label. While *Foxy* didn't contain any major pop/Top 40 radio hits, it enjoyed a fair amount of club exposure. Those who know Foxy for "Get Off" or "Hot Number" might be surprised to hear that the band wasn't nearly as funky or as in-your-face in 1976; catchy, if unremarkable, tunes like "Let's Love," "You Make Me Hot," and the club hit "Get Off Your Aahh and Dance" favor a lush, glossy, much softer approach that is best described as Euro-disco with Latin overtones. One of *Foxy*'s less European-sounding tracks is "Baby, I'm Leaving," which combines disco with the sort of Latin soul sound that artists like El Chicano, Tierra, José Feliciano, and Malo were known for in the 1970s. Not a gem but generally decent, *Foxy* isn't among the band's essential releases but is worth hearing if you're a hardcore disco collector. *—Alex Henderson*

Get Off / 1978 / TK ♦♦♦♦♦

With its second album, *Get Off*, Foxy gave itself quite a makeover. The Latin influences (Afro-Cuban as well as Brazilian) remained, and Foxy's forte was still disco. But while the combo's self-titled debut album of 1976 favored lush, glossy Euro-disco with Latin overtones, *Get Off* is a tougher, much funkier record that found Foxy getting away from the European sound. The softness of 1976's *Foxy* was gone, and a more aggressive band emerged. Both commercially and creatively, it was a change for the better. The decadent, in your face title song became a major hit, and Foxy is equally confident on memorable tracks like the passionate "You" and the playful "Tena's Song." While *Foxy* was merely pleasant, *Get Off* is downright inspired. Of course, many pop/Top 40 listeners had no idea that *Get Off* was a change of direction for Ish Ledesma and his allies—*Foxy* was strictly a club record, and many of the people who heard *Get Off*'s smash title song on the radio in 1978 were hearing the band for the first time. So they didn't know that Foxy had sounded any other way. A major step forward for Foxy, *Get Off* is its most consistent and essential album. *—Alex Henderson*

Hot Numbers / 1979 / TK ♦♦♦♦

When a band enjoys a major hit, there is often the temptation to follow it up with something similar. Foxy did that in the late '70s, following up the 1978 smash "Get Off" with a similar disco-funk single titled "Hot Number" (which became Foxy's second and last major hit). "Hot Number" isn't an outright clone of "Get Off," although the two are undeniably similar. There were no other major singles on the *Hot Numbers* LP, which is regrettable because the rest of the album is rewarding more often than not. "Headhunter," "Devil Boogie," and the optimistic "Chicapbon, Chicapbon" are infectious disco-funk items, while "Nobody Will Ever Take Me Away From You" is a sentimental Latin soul ballad that should please anyone who spent a lot of time listening to José Feliciano or El Chicano in the 1970s. Meanwhile, "Lady of the Streets" almost sounds like a combination of reggae and Steely

Dan—not the sort of thing one expected from Foxy, but enjoyable. If *Get Off* is Foxy's most essential album, *Hot Numbers* runs a close second. *—Alex Henderson*

Live / 1980 / Dash ♦♦♦

The vast majority of disco artists who emerged in the 1970s never recorded live albums. For every Donna Summer, Sylvester, or Cerrone who provided a live album, there were countless others who didn't. Another exception was Foxy, whose live album of 1980 received very little attention. This enjoyable, if less than essential, LP finds Foxy performing its two major hits ("Get Off" and "Hot Number") as well as material from 1980's *Party Boys* (including the title song, "Girls," "Please," "She's So Cool," and the single "RRRRRock") and four new songs that aren't on any of its studio albums: "Sex Symbol," "Ba Ba Cool," "Banshee," and "Gimme What Ya Got." All the new tunes combine funk with rock and new wave, and they indicate that, in 1980, Foxy didn't want to be thought of as strictly a disco band. The sad thing is that if Foxy hadn't thrown in the towel and broken up in 1981, it might have been scoring hits again by 1983 or 1984; after all, the 1980s were full of artists who managed to be relevant to both dance music and rock (Duran Duran and Frankie Goes to Hollywood, among many others). While this LP is enjoyable, it's far from definitive. Some of Foxy's best songs aren't performed (including "Headhunter," "Tena's Song," and "Chicapbon, Chicapbon") and, as pleasing as the new rock-influenced material is, Foxy would have been better off saving it for a studio album. All things considered, this out of print LP can only be recommended to Foxy's hardcore fans. *—Alex Henderson*

Party Boys / 1980 / TK ♦♦♦

In 1980, a lot of disco artists were feeling nervous. Rumor had it that disco was dying, and they feared a trip to the unemployment line. But the rumors of disco's demise were, as the saying goes, greatly exaggerated. Disco never died; it simply changed its name to dance-pop in the 1980s and evolved into such styles as deep house, Hi-NRG, and Latin freestyle. Some people would blame Foxy's early-'80s breakup on disco's so-called "demise," arguing that there was simply little or no demand for disco after 1979. But that's nonsense—inadequate promotion was really the thing that killed Foxy. With the right marketing and promotion, 1980's *Party Boys* would have done well. Unfortunately, only Foxy's most hardcore fans bought this LP, which is a very good party album even if it isn't quite in a class with *Get Off.* "Girls," "I Can't Stand the Heat," and the single "RRRRRock" are solid disco-funk smokers, and some of the tunes even have a rock edge (including "Let's Be Bad Tonight," "She's So Cool," and "Fantazy"). "Sambame" has a strong Brazilian flavor, while "Pensando en Ti" is a tender Latin-pop ballad that finds lead vocalist Ish Ledesma singing in Spanish. But *Party Boys* didn't sell, and it turned out to be Foxy's last studio album. *—Alex Henderson*

- **Get Off: The Best of Foxy** / 1995 / Hot ♦♦♦♦♦
- **Get Off/Hot Numbers** / Jul. 28, 1998 / Collectables ♦♦♦♦♦

Carol Fran

b. Oct. 23, 1933, Lafayette, LA

Vocals, Piano / Soul-Blues, Soul

Soul-blues diva Carol Fran was born October 23, 1933, in Lafayette, LA. After beginning her career as a teen singing jump blues with the Don Conway Orchestra, she eventually landed in New Orleans, marrying saxophonist Bob François. Abbreviating her married name to simply Fran, she became a constant presence on the Bourbon Street club circuit before mounting an extended tour of Mexico. In 1957, she cut her first sides for the R&B label Excello, scoring a regional smash with her debut single "Emmitt Lee." Though she recorded extensively for Excello, only three more singles were released during Fran's abbreviated tenure with the label and she soon signed on as a featured vocalist with blues legend Guitar Slim. She continued touring with the group in the wake of Slim's 1959 death, appearing alongside various substitutes, including Nappy Brown, Lee Dorsey, and Joe Tex.

In 1962, Fran signed to Lyric and released a pair of singles, including a swamp pop rendition of "The Great Pretender"; she spent two more years on the road before catching on with the Jubilee subsidiary Port for a 1964 cover of the Orioles' classic "Crying in the Chapel." The single was then reissued on the Josie label, but was lost in the shuffle when Elvis Presley scored with his own reading of the song soon after.

Undaunted, Fran remained with Port for a series of smoldering soul sides spotlighting her crystalline vocals to magnificent effect. While the follow-up "You Can't Stop Me" featured a Sammy Lowe arrangement, her third effort for the label, the lovely "A World Without You," was penned by Bobby Darin. Sadly, both failed to make any commercial headway; however, and after one more single for Port, "Any Day Love Walks In," Fran returned to touring. She did not re-enter the studio until 1967, signing to Roulette for a cover of Brook Benton's "So Close." Despite cutting a surplus of material during her Roulette stay, the sessions remained in the can—embittered by her label experiences and stung by years of ill-informed financial dealings, she returned to Louisiana and spent over a decade confining her activities to small clubs. In 1982, Fran was reunited with Clarence Hollimon, a noted studio guitarist she briefly dated a quarter century earlier; the couple eventually married and relocated to Texas, appearing live together and in 1992 signing to Black Top to issue the album *Soul Sensation. See There!* followed two years later, and after a long studio hiatus, Fran and Hollimon resurfaced on JSP with the aptly titled 2000 release *It's About Time. —Jason Ankeny*

Soul Sensation / 1992 / Black Top ♦♦♦♦

The new sweethearts of the blues' debut for Black Top is an uncommonly varied affair, the pair performing blues, jazz, and every stylistic stripe in between. Hollimon's red-hot licks are seldom short of amazing (his instrumental showcase "Gristle" is a stunner), and Fran's full-throated vocals shine on everything from a Gulf Coast-styled "My Happiness" and a reprise of Mitty Collier's emotionally charged "I Had a Talk With My Man" to the lounge-slanted "Anytime, Anyplace, Anywhere" and the rousing sanctified closer "This Little Light." *—Bill Dahl*

- **See There!** / 1994 / Black Top ♦♦♦♦♦

The duo's Black Top encore was a slightly more focused effort than their debut. They still exhibit considerable versatility on a highly infectious dance number, "Door Poppin'," and the Louisiana-rooted "Daddy, Daddy, Daddy," and soulful remakes of Tyrone Davis's "Are You Serious" and Gladys Knight & the Pips' earthy "I Don't Want to Do Wrong," but there's a more satisfying context overall. The album was waxed in New Orleans and Texas with two entirely different bands, lending laudable variety to the selections. *—Bill Dahl*

Aretha Franklin

b. Mar. 25, 1942, Memphis, TN

Vocals, Piano / Soul, Deep Soul, Southern Soul, Quiet Storm, Urban, Black Gospel

Aretha Franklin is one of the giants of soul music, and indeed of American pop as a whole. More than any other performer, she epitomized soul at its most gospel-charged. Her astonishing run of late-'60s hits with Atlantic Records—"Respect," "I Never Loved a Man," "Chain of Fools," "Baby I Love You," "I Say a Little Prayer," "Think," "The House That Jack Built," and several others—earned her the title "Lady Soul," which she has worn uncontested ever since. Yet as much of an international institution as she's become, much of her work—outside of her recordings for Atlantic in the late '60s and early '70s—is erratic and only fitfully inspired, making discretion a necessity when collecting her records.

Franklin's roots in gospel ran extremely deep. With her sisters Carolyn and Erma (both of whom would also have recording careers), she sang at the Detroit church of her father, Reverend C.L. Franklin, while growing up in the 1950s. In fact, she made her first recordings as a gospel artist at the age of 14. It has also been reported that Motown was interested in signing Aretha back in the days when it was a tiny start-up. Ultimately, however, Franklin ended up with Columbia, to which she was signed by the renowned talent scout John Hammond.

Franklin would record for Columbia constantly throughout the first half of the '60s, notching occasional R&B hits (and one Top 40 single, "Rock-a-bye Your Baby With a Dixie Melody"), but never truly breaking out as a star. The Columbia period continues to generate considerable controversy among critics, many of whom feel that Aretha's true aspirations were being blunted by pop-oriented material and production. In fact there's a reasonable amount of fine items to be found on the Columbia sides, including the occasional song ("Lee Cross," "Soulville") where she belts out soul with real gusto. It's undeniably true, though, that her work at Columbia was considerably tamer than what was to follow, and suffered in general from a lack of direction and an apparent emphasis on trying to develop her as an all-around entertainer, rather than as an R&B/soul singer.

When Franklin left Columbia for Atlantic, producer Jerry Wexler was determined to bring out her most soulful, fiery traits. As part of that plan, he had her record her first single, "I Never Loved a Man (The Way I Love You)," at Muscle Shoals in Alabama with esteemed Southern R&B musicians. In fact, that was to be her only session actually at Muscle Shoals, but much of the remainder of her '60s work would be recorded with the Muscle Shoals Sound Rhythm Section, although the sessions would actually take place in New York City. The combination was one of those magic instances of musical alchemy in pop: the backup musicians provided a much grittier, soulful, and R&B-based accompaniment for Aretha's voice, which soared with a passion and intensity suggesting a spirit that had been allowed to fly loose for the first time.

In the late '60s, Franklin became one of the biggest international recording stars in all of pop. Many also saw Franklin as a symbol of black America itself, reflecting the increased confidence and pride of African-Americans in the decade of the civil rights movements and other triumphs for the black community. The chart statistics are impressive in and of themselves: ten Top Ten hits in a roughly 18-month span between early 1967 and late 1968, for instance, and a steady stream of solid mid- to large-size hits for the next five years after that. Her Atlantic albums were also huge sellers, and far more consistent artistically than those of most soul stars of the era. Franklin was able to maintain creative momentum, in part, because of her eclectic choice of material, which encompassed first-class originals and gospel, blues, pop, and rock covers, from the Beatles and Simon & Garfunkel to Sam Cooke and the Drifters. She was also a fine, forceful, and somewhat underrated keyboardist.

Franklin's commercial and artistic success was unabated in the early '70s, during which she landed more huge hits with "Spanish Harlem," "Bridge Over Troubled Water," and "Day Dreaming." She also produced two of her most respected, and earthiest, album releases with *Live at Fillmore West* and *Amazing Grace.* The latter, a 1972 double LP, was a reinvestigation of her gospel roots, recorded with Rev. James Cleveland & the Southern California Community Choir. Remarkably, it made the Top Ten, counting as one of the greatest gospel-pop crossover smashes of all time.

Franklin had a few more hits over the next few years—"Angel" and the Stevie Wonder cover "Until You Come Back to Me"—being the most notable—but generally her artistic inspiration seemed to be tapering off, and her focus drifting toward more pop-oriented material. Her Atlantic contract ended at the end of the 1970s, and since then she's managed to get intermittent hits—"Who's Zooming Who" and "Jump to It" are among the most famous—without remaining anything like the superstar she was at her peak. Many of her successes were duets, or crafted with the assistance of newer, glossier-minded contemporaries such as Luther Vandross. There was also another return to gospel in 1987 with *One Lord, One Faith, One Baptism.*

Critically, as is the case with many '60s rock legends, there have been mixed responses to her later work. Some view it as little more than a magnificent voice wasted on mediocre material and production. Others seem to grasp for any excuse they can to praise her whenever there seems to be some kind of resurgence of her soul leanings. Most would agree that her post-mid-'70s recordings are fairly inconsequential when judged against her prime Atlantic era. The blame is often laid at the hands of unsuitable material, but it should also be remembered that—like Elvis Presley and Ray Charles—Franklin never thought of herself as confined to one genre. She always loved to sing straight pop songs, even if her early Atlantic records gave one the impression that her true home was earthy soul music. If for some reason she returned to straight soul shouting in the future, it's doubtful that the phase would last for more than an album or two. In the meantime, despite her lukewarm recent sales record, she's an institution, assured of the ability to draw live audiences and immense respect for the rest of her lifetime, regardless of whether there are any more triumphs on record in store. *—Richie Unterberger*

☆ **I Never Loved a Man the Way I Love You** / Mar. 10, 1967 / Rhino ✦✦✦✦✦
While the inclusion of "Respect"—one of the truly seminal singles in pop history—is in and of itself sufficient to earn *I Never Loved a Man the Way I Love You* classic status, Aretha's Atlantic label debut is an indisputable masterpiece from start to finish. Much of the credit is due producer Jerry Wexler, who finally unleashed the soulful intensity so long kept under wraps during her Columbia tenure; assembling a crack Muscle Shoals backing band along with an abundance of impeccable material, Wexler creates the ideal setting to allow Aretha to ascend to the throne of Queen of Soul, and she responds with the strongest performances of her career. While the brilliant title track remains the album's other best-known song, each cut on *I Never Loved a Man* is touched by greatness; covers of Ray Charles' "Drown in My Own Tears" and Sam Cooke's "Good Times" and "A Change Is Gonna Come" are on par with the original recordings, while Aretha's own contributions—"Don't Let Me Lose This Dream," "Baby Baby Baby," "Save Me" and "Dr. Feelgood (Love Is a Serious Business)"—are perfectly at home in such lofty company. A soul landmark. *—Jason Ankeny*

Aretha Arrives / Aug. 4, 1967 / Rhino ✦✦✦
Recorded in 1967 after the first flush of back-to-back successes with "Respect" and "I Never Loved a Man," this captures Aretha Franklin in peak form. Lady Soul provides her own piano accompaniment on the majority of tracks here, and the core band is the same one that provided the fire on her previous album. The tunes are an eclectic batch, and while "Baby, I Love You" was the hit of the album, Franklin turns in strong versions of "Satisfaction," "You Are My Sunshine," "Night Life," "Ain't Nobody (Gonna Turn Me Around)," and a quirky cover of "96 Tears" for good measure. An essential addition to her discography. *—Cub Koda*

☆ **Lady Soul** / Jan. 22, 1968 / Rhino ✦✦✦✦✦
Appearing after a blockbuster debut and a sophomore set that was rather disappointing (in comparison), 1968's *Lady Soul* proved Aretha Franklin, the pop sensation, was no fluke. Her performances were more impassioned than on her debut, and the material just as strong, an inspired blend of covers and originals from the best songwriters in soul and pop music. The opener, "Chain of Fools," became the biggest hit, driven by a chorus of cascading echoes by Franklin and her bedrock backing vocalists, the Sweet Inspirations, plus the unforgettable, earthy guitar work of guest Joe South. The album's showpiece, though, was "(You Make Me Feel Like) A Natural Woman," a song written expressly for her by Brill Building pop stalwarts Gerry Goffin & Carole King, based on a title coined by producer Jerry Wexler. One of the landmark performances in pop music, the song floats serenely through the verses until, swept up by Ralph Burns' stirring string arrangement again and again, Franklin opens up on the choruses with one of the most transcendent vocals of her career. And just as she'd previously transformed a soul classic (Otis Redding's "Respect") into a signature piece of her own, Franklin courageously reimagined songs by heavyweights James Brown, Ray Charles, and the Impressions. Brown's "Money Won't Change You" is smooth and kinetic, her testifying constantly reinforced by interjections from the Sweet Inspirations. Curtis Mayfield's "People Get Ready," a 1965 civil-rights anthem and a hit for the Impressions, is taken at a slower pace than the original; after a quiet verse, Franklin lets loose amidst a magisterial brass arrangement by Arif Mardin. Powered by three hit singles (each nested in the upper reaches of the pop Top Ten), *Lady Soul* became Aretha Franklin's second gold LP and remained on the charts for over a year. *—John Bush*

Aretha Now / Jun. 14, 1968 / Rhino ✦✦✦✦✦
Though a bit short on running time at ten songs, this still caught Franklin at the peak of her early form. "Think," "I Say a Little Prayer," "See Saw," and "I Can't See Myself Leaving You" were all big hits. Her choice of cover material included some of her most R&B-drenched early Atlantic cuts, like "Night Time Is the Right Time," "You Send Me," and "I Take What I Want." *—Richie Unterberger*

Aretha in Paris / 1968 / Rhino ✦✦✦
Atlantic's Jerry Wexler once said that this concert album was an embarrassment to him, criticizing the inferior band (actually, the musicians that usually accompanied her live in the late '60s). Composed of her first few big singles and cuts from her first three albums, it doesn't match the classic studio versions and could be considered her least essential '60s Atlantic LP. That's not to say, though, that it doesn't sound pretty good, with fine if basic readings of a lot of her most popular late-'60s material, although the horns fall distressingly out of tune at a key point in the instrumental break of "Chain of Fools." *—Richie Unterberger*

Soul '69 / 1969 / Rhino ✦✦✦✦✦
This is one of her most overlooked '60s albums, on which she presented some of her jazziest material, despite the title. None of these cuts were significant hits, and none were Aretha originals; she displayed her characteristically eclectic taste in the choice of cover material, handling compositions by Percy Mayfield, Sam Cooke, Smokey Robinson, and, at the most pop-oriented end of her spectrum, John Hartford's "Gentle on My Mind" and Bob Lind's "Elusive Butterfly." Her vocals are consistently passionate and first-rate, though, as is the musicianship; besides contributions from the Muscle Shoals Rhythm Section, session players include respected jazzmen Kenny Burrell, Ron Carter, Grady Tate, David Newman, and Joe Zawinul. *—Richie Unterberger*

Spirit in the Dark / 1970 / Rhino ✦✦✦✦✦
Spirit in the Dark was one of Aretha Franklin's more overlooked albums from her Atlantic prime, despite the inclusion of a couple hit singles (the title track and "Don't Play That Song"). The disc includes five of her own compositions (the most she ever recorded for a single album) and her usual eclectic choice of cover material. On this record, the covers ranged from B.B. King and Dr. John to Jimmy Reed and Goffin/King's "Oh Not My Baby." The album also benefits from great backup players: Both the Muscle Shoals Rhythm Section and the Dixie Flyers contributed to the sessions, and Duane Allman lends his guitar to a couple of tracks. Though it doesn't rank with her very best Atlantic LPs, it's an exuberant and remarkably consistent effort. The 1993 CD reissue has detailed liner notes on the songs and sessions by David Nathan. *—Richie Unterberger*

Sweet Bitter Love / 1970 / Columbia ✦✦
Here is some uneven, but superbly sung, light pop, overproduced R&B, and soul from Aretha Franklin's days on Columbia. The label has been steadily recycling Franklin material, and while much of it deserves a second listen, there are some better anthologies than this one. The title track, however, is an excellent number, and there are some others that are equally solid. *—Ron Wynn*

This Girl's in Love With You / Jan. 15, 1970 / Rhino ✦✦✦
The title song (a cover of Herb Alpert's "This Guy's in Love With You") might lead you to believe this is one of Aretha's more pop-oriented albums, but in fact, this is the only song of the sort on this solid and fairly earthy effort. Besides the hit singles "Call Me" and "Share Your Love With Me," it also includes her most well-known Beatle covers ("Eleanor Rigby" and "Let It Be"), and her interesting version of "The Weight," a Top 20 single featuring slide guitar by Duane Allman. *—Richie Unterberger*

Aretha Live at Fillmore West / 1971 / Rhino ✦✦✦
Aretha Franklin's 1971 album *Live at Fillmore West* was as seminal a soul breakthrough as Albert King's visit had been for blues. It finally cemented her status beyond soul audiences as both a recording and live attraction, and it matched her with a phenomenal rhythm section in King Curtis & the Kingpens. Franklin adroitly mixed pop, rock, and soul material throughout the three nights, including Stephen Stills' "Love the One You're With," and Bread's "Make It With You," and the Beatles' "Eleanor Rigby," as well as tried and true favorites "Respect," "Don't Play That Song," and "Spirit in the Dark," which brought Ray Charles out of the audience for a spirited duet. There's more than enough here to make this absolutely essential. *—Ron Wynn*

Young, Gifted & Black / 1971 / Rhino ✦✦✦✦✦
It's nearly impossible to single out any of Aretha Franklin's early '70s albums for Atlantic as being her best, particularly given the breadth of her output during this era. In terms of albums rather than singles, it's probably her strongest era, and if you count live albums like *Amazing Grace*, choosing a standout or a favorite record isn't any easier. Yet of this stunning era, *Young, Gifted & Black* certainly ranks highly among her studio efforts, with many arguing that it may be her greatest. And with songs like "Rock Steady," that may be a valid argument. But there's much more here than just a few highlights. If you really want to go song by song, you'd be hard-pressed to find any throwaways here—this is quite honestly an album that merits play from beginning to end. You have upbeat songs like the aforementioned "Rock Steady" that will get you up out of your seat moving and grooving, yet then you also have a number of more introspective songs that slow down the tempo and are more likely to relax than rouse. And if that wide spectrum of mood isn't enough reason to celebrate this album, you get some unlikely songs like a take on "The Long and Winding Road." Plus, you also have to keep in mind that Franklin was in her prime here, not only in terms of voice but also in terms of confidence—you can just feel her exuding her status as the best of the best. Furthermore, her ensemble of musicians competes with any that she had worked with on previous albums. So even if this isn't *the* greatest Aretha album of the early '70s, it's certainly a contender, the sort of album with which you can't go wrong. *—Jason Birchmeier*

Amazing Grace / 1972 / Atlantic ✦✦✦✦✦
Aretha Franklin disproved the notion that once you leave the church, you can't go back. She returned in triumph on this 1972 double album, making what might be her greatest release ever in any style. Her voice was chilling, making it seem as if God and the angels were conducting a service alongside Franklin, Rev. James Cleveland, the Southern California Community Choir, and everyone else in attendance. Her versions of "How I Got Over" and "You've Got a Friend" are legendary. *—Ron Wynn*

Hey Now Hey (The Other Side of the Sky) / 1973 / Rhino ✦✦✦
Hey Now Hey (The Other Side of the Sky) was just about Franklin's last gasp before succumbing to disco. This odd album, with its cheesy, junky artwork, contains some gems—notable are a poignant cover of Bernstein's "Somewhere," and a sparkling "Moody's Mood," and the beautiful Carolyn Franklin composition "Angel." *—George Bedard*

Let Me in Your Life / 1974 / Rhino ✦✦✦
This is a nice, if at times overbearing, mid-'70s Franklin set. She was still singing with the stunning delivery, amazing timing, and majestic soul that highlighted her late-'60s releases. Her version of "Until You Come Back to Me (That's What I'm Gonna Do)" is the only one that might be superior to Stevie Wonder's great original, while "I'm In Love" and the title cut are prime Franklin. *—Ron Wynn*

With Everything I Feel in Me / 1974 / Atlantic ✦✦✦
This respectable but not earth-shattering release was part of the gradual decline of Franklin's artistic and commercial achievements at Atlantic. The leadoff track, "Without Love," was a Top Ten R&B hit, and the title track, written by Franklin, was Top 20 R&B. There were a couple of familiar but completely rearranged Burt Bacharach tunes and a contribution from Stevie Wonder. Franklin was in good voice, and the studio band was accomplished, but this was all a far cry from the standard Franklin had set in the late '60s. It was also a far cry from the sales she enjoyed then: This was her first new album since her 1967 breakthrough to peak below the Top 30. *—William Ruhlmann*

You / 1975 / Atlantic ✦✦
Here is the first album that represented signs of stagnation. Aretha Franklin had issued two excellent albums in 1974, but in 1975 just didn't get enough quality songs to flesh out *You*. While she still put everything into them, often salvaging dismal lyrics and awkward production, Franklin only equaled past glories on the song "It Only Happens (When I Look At You)." Otherwise, it was a case of wonderful vocals but little else. *—Ron Wynn*

Sparkle / 1976 / Rhino ✦✦✦✦
Aretha Franklin's career was in a down period in the mid-'70s when she collaborated with Curtis Mayfield to sing his compositions for the film *Sparkle*. The film proved a non-event, but for Franklin it marked a return to glory. Once again she was the Queen of Soul, doing the chilling, spectacular leaps, cries, whoops, and shouts that defined secularized gospel in the late '60s. The title cut was a sizable hit, while "Giving Him Something He Can Feel" became an anthem. Mayfield's lyrics and production shouldn't be overlooked; he added just the right amount of background trappings, and the Kitty Haywood Singers provided Franklin's best continuing backgrounds since the Sweet Inspirations. *—Ron Wynn*

Aretha Sings the Blues / 1980 / Columbia ✦✦
Although not a blues singer in the strictest sense, Aretha Franklin's glorious voice could never make anything dull, especially not blues classics. These songs didn't attract a lot of attention when they came out in the '60s, with a couple of exceptions. Since Columbia issued all these anthologies, there has been a great debate raging as to whether or not it was a marketing failure or a production failure preventing Franklin from achieving more success at the label. The question won't be answered by this release. *—Ron Wynn*

Aretha / Oct. 25, 1980 / Arista ✦✦✦
This is her first album with Arista after ending a 13-year, largely successful stint with Atlantic Records. By as early as 1973, Franklin's album turnout became spotty as late-'70s entries, *Sweet Passion* and *La Diva* came and went quickly. For *Aretha*, Arista label president Clive Davis drummed out a certain amount of fanfare for this initial effort, and for the most part it was deserved. *Aretha* attempts to pull out all of the stops, which is suitable for a major artist coming to a new label. The best moments here reestablish Franklin as a phenomenal singer, not just an icon. The brilliantly sung "United Together" and autumnal "Come to Me" have both Franklin and producer Chuck Jackson seeming like they'd recorded together for years. What undoes *Aretha* is a few overproduced tracks of dubious distinction. The too busy cover of the Doobie Brothers "What a Fool Believes" fails Franklin, skimming past the song's lyrical. Her gospel-fueled childhood recollection "School Days" and a discofied cover of "I Can't Turn You Loose" are both ingratiating and potentially nerve racking. This effort was meant to reestablish Franklin, and it was more popular than most of her late-'70s Atlantic albums, but this could have been better. *—Jason Elias*

Love All the Hurt Away / 1981 / Arista ✦✦
Aretha Franklin's post-Atlantic material has the same problems as the Columbia cuts. There are too many songs in which the wondrous Franklin voice was simply inserted into otherwise routine situations, with singles issued to take advantage of her hard-earned credibility and reputation. The title cut was a nice duet between Franklin and George Benson, and there were some other decent songs, but this was overall a disappointment. *—Ron Wynn*

Jump to It / 1982 / Arista ✦✦✦
Aretha Franklin scored some hits with this early-'80s album and managed to make concessions to urban contemporary tastes without totally distorting her classic soul sound. While it's certainly not in the class of past recordings, the title cut gave Franklin her first number-one hit of the '80s, and "Love Me Right" was a decent follow-up. *—Ron Wynn*

Get It Right / 1983 / Arista ✦✦✦
Luther Vandross scored a popular success with *Jump to It*, but this follow-up is less impressive and proved less successful. Vandross wrote most of the material, including the number-one R&B title track and the R&B Top Ten hit "Every Girl (Wants My Guy)," although he also has Franklin tackle the Temptations hit "I Wish It Would Rain," in a painfully overwrought production. With this record, what had seemed to be an artist/producer marriage made in heaven hit the rocks. *— William Ruhlmann*

Never Grow Old / 1984 / Chess ✦✦✦
Actually credited to "Reverend C.L. Franklin and Aretha Franklin," this album was recorded live—very live—in church. The Reverend Franklin takes most of the leads on traditional gospel songs, with keyboard accompaniment, shouting and singing, although his daughter also has a couple of spotlights. The music is moving, and the audience is moved: one or two of them scream uncontrollably. *— William Ruhlmann*

★ **30 Greatest Hits** / 1985 / Atlantic ✦✦✦✦✦
30 Greatest Hits zeroes in on Aretha Franklin's prime recording period for Atlantic, from her breakout in 1967 with "I Never Loved a Man (The Way I Love You)" through the end of 1974, during which the Queen of Soul truly reigned over the charts—she averaged over one pop hit every two months. This two-disc set delivers all of her classics ("Respect," "Do Right Woman, Do Right Man," "(You Make Me Feel Like) A Natural Woman," "Chain of Fools," "Think," "Spanish Harlem," "Rock Steady"), plus much more excellent material for those who won't recognize much more than the songs (and there are quite a few) that have entered the cultural consciousness ("I Say a Little Prayer," "The Weight," "Spirit in the Dark," "Day Dreaming"). It's a great foundation to any collection that has yet to be equaled by a pair of Rhino sets, the two-volume *Very Best of Aretha Franklin* from 1994 and *Aretha's Best* from 2001. *—John Bush*

Who's Zoomin' Who? / 1985 / Arista ✦✦✦
After nearly a two-year hiatus from the charts, the Queen of Soul returned in style with three *Billboard* R&B Top Ten singles, including the number one smash hit "Freeway of Love." With its festive rhythm arrangement and electric sax solo by Clarence Clemons, Aretha Franklin injects her lively vocals. It held the number-one spot for five straight weeks. The title track, "Who's Zoomin' Who," has a more soulful bounce, including Franklin's delivery. Its sputtering bassline and chiming keyboards are augmented by Franklin's soulful delivery; her improvising ad libs are laudable to say the least. The single peaked at number two for four consecutive weeks. She had another Top Ten hit with "Another Night," a midtempo number with a light rock feel. It was a number-nine hit. Her duet with Eurythmics, "Sisters Are Doin' It for Themselves," faltered at number 66. This album has a slight pop texture. Narada Michael Walden is credited with the majority of the production on this sound outing. *—Craig Lytle*

Aretha / Nov. 15, 1986 / Arista ✦✦
Don't be confused by the generic title; this is a new Aretha Franklin album from 1986 and a moderately succesful one, notable for containing five R&B hits, four of which also made the pop charts: "Jumpin' Jack Flash" (produced by Keith Richards and featured in the Whoopi Goldberg movie of the same title), "Jimmy Lee" (number-two R&B), "I Knew You Were Waiting (For Me)" (a duet with George Michael that went number-one pop), "Rock-A-Lott," and "If You Need My Love Tonight" (a duet with Larry Graham). [*Aretha* is also available in an import release.] *— William Ruhlmann*

One Lord, One Faith, One Baptism / 1987 / Arista ✦✦✦
Although nowhere as anthemic as *Amazing Grace* (what could be?), this was still much better than most contemporary gospel. There were socio-political speeches by Jesse Jackson and Carl Franklin for those who wanted earthly concerns addressed alongside spiritual ones, but the real impact came from Franklin's rousing voice and the contributions of such guest stars as Mavis Staples and Aretha's sisters Erma and Carolyn. If she hadn't issued *Amazing Grace* or *Aretha Gospel* as a teen, this set might have gotten better notices and more critical respect. Instead, it was virtually dismissed, and it deserves better than that. *—Ron Wynn*

Through the Storm / 1989 / Arista ✦✦✦
Having scored in the recent past with producer Narada Michael Walden and some star duets, Franklin and Arista turned out another album with the same approach but less successful results. The title duet with Elton John went Top 20, but its follow-up, "It Isn't, It Wasn't, It Ain't Never Gonna Be" was an embarrassing failure for both Franklin and the previously pop-perfect Whitney Houston. The rest was even less distinguished, including a song with the Four Tops and Kenny G and a remake of the old hit "Think." *— William Ruhlmann*

☆ **Queen of Soul: The Atlantic Recordings** / 1992 / Rhino ✦✦✦✦✦
Queen of Soul: The Atlantic Recordings is an 86-track, four-disc box set that covers Aretha Franklin's Atlantic career, spanning from 1967's "I Never Loved a Man (The Way I Love You)" to 1976's "Something He Can Feel." Over the course of the set, all of Aretha's best-known songs, including all of her Top Ten pop and R&B singles, are included. For fans that only know the singles, the set is primarily notable for the wealth of album tracks and forgotten singles that are included, which nearly equal the hits in terms of quality. Stopping just short of her move to disco, *The Queen of Soul* just misses being a totally comprehensive collection, but it remains definitive—it may miss some of her later hits, but every one of her greatest tracks is on the box. *The Queen of Soul* is one the cornerstones of any soul collection. *—Stephen Thomas Erlewine*

Greatest Hits (1980–1994) / Feb. 22, 1994 / Arista ✦✦✦
This compilation collects the Queen of Soul's biggest hits from 1980-1994, after she left her legendary tenure with Atlantic and moved on to Arista. The material collected here is not quite as essential as her Atlantic recordings—instead, the focus seems to weigh heavily toward middle-of-the-road, adult contemporary soul pop, which continued to translate into chart success, albeit a little more sporadic. This album includes her '80s smashes "Freeway of Love," "Jump to It," "Who's Zoomin' Who," "Another Night," and "Jimmy Lee," as well as her chart-topping 1987 duet with George Michael, "I Knew You Were Waiting (For Me)," and her adult contemporary hit duet with Michael McDonald, "Everchanging Times." Also included is the soulful "Doctor's Orders" with ace crooner Luther Vandross, and "United Together," the greatest song Whitney Houston never recorded. This collection is not free of annoying omissions, among those are her essential duet with Eurythmics, "Sisters Are Doin' It for Themselves"; her hit duet with Elton John, "Through the Storm"; and her hit remake of the Rolling Stones' "Jumpin' Jack Flash." That song, however, is included as a bonus track on select pressings of the album. A few new tracks are thrown in, including the Babyface-penned, assembly-line ballad "Willing to Forgive," which became her first American Top 40 hit in five years, and her version of the Clivelles & Cole club anthem "A Deeper Love," which went on to top the dance charts. The album closes with two live tracks, one being "You Make Me Feel (Like a Natural Woman)" with Bonnie Raitt and Gloria Estefan, and the fantastically soulful "I Dreamed a Dream." Not a bad collection by any means, but some of the material is a little spotty, and it could have been quite better had they included all the hits. *—Jose F. Promis*

The Very Best of Aretha Franklin, Vol. 1 / Mar. 22, 1994 / Rhino ✦✦✦✦✦
30 Greatest Hits is still the preferred essential document for the Atlantic years, but this is certainly an excellent 16-track primer of her most popular late-'60s tracks. Most of them are also on *30 Greatest Hits*. But if you've got a particular yen for Aretha's early Atlantic period (which was also her very best), you'll find all the biggest smashes from that era here, including "Respect," "Chain of Fools," "Think," "The House That Jack Built," "Baby I Love You," "I Never Loved a Man," and so forth. *—Richie Unterberger*

The Very Best of Aretha Franklin, Vol. 2 / Mar. 22, 1994 / Rhino ✦✦✦✦✦
Covering 1970-1976, this isn't quite as top-notch as *The Very Best of, Vol. 1*. And, like *Very Best of, Vol. 1*, much of this is also found on the more comprehensive *30 Greatest Hits* (although some of it is not). Still, it contains the prime stuff from the first half of the '70s,

including "Spanish Harlem," "Don't Play That Song," "Bridge Over Troubled Water," and "Until You Come Back to Me," along with less-traveled items like "Oh Me Oh My" and "Brand New Me." *—Richie Unterberger*

Lady Soul/Aretha Now / Feb. 14, 1995 / Mobile Fidelity ✦✦✦✦✦

The Delta Meets Detroit: Aretha's Blues / Jan. 13, 1998 / Rhino ✦✦✦

The Delta Meets Detroit: Aretha's Blues is one of the few non-hits compilations that makes sense. Selecting 16 tracks from her Atlantic recordings, the disc spotlights Aretha at her bluesiest—there are no hits here, but there's also no shortage of remarkable songs here, as "Today I Sing the Blues," "Night Life," "Night Time Is the Right Time," "Good to Me As I Am to You," "Going Down Slow," "Drown in My Own Tears," and "Dr. Feelgood (Love Is a Serious Business)" rank among her grittiest performances. If you're only familiar with the hits, this is an excellent way to dig deeper into her catalog, and if you already have this material on their original albums, *The Delta Meets Detroit* actually offers some revelations you may not have expected. *—Stephen Thomas Erlewine*

A Rose Is Still a Rose / Mar. 10, 1998 / Arista ✦✦✦✦

For much of the '90s, Aretha Franklin acted as if she couldn't even care about appealing to a younger audience. She rarely recorded, and when she did, it was usually slick adult contemporary material. That's what makes the fresh *A Rose Is Still a Rose* such a surprise. Although it certainly has its share of predictably glossy ballads fit for adult radio (usually produced by Narada Michael Walden or Michael Powell), the most notable element of the album is that Franklin collaborates with a fresh talent, all of whom are either prominent rap figures or at least fluent in hip-hop. That's not to say that *A Rose Is Still a Rose* is a rap album—it simply illustrates that the album sounds contemporary, which is the last thing most observers would have expected from Aretha in 1997. That in itself is heartening, but that doesn't necessarily mean everything works. Lauryn Hill's "A Rose Is Still a Rose" is a perfect match, lyrically and musically, but it only shows how shallow Puff Daddy's writing really is on "Never Leave You Again." Still, Dallas Austin's "I'll Dip," Jermaine Dupri's "Here We Go Again" and "Every Lil' Bit Hurts," and Daryl Simmons' "In the Morning" and "In Case You Forgot" all work, and Franklin's original "The Woman" is arguably her most soulful performance in years. These make the awkward moments forgivable because they find Aretha sounding vital, which is something that had not happened throughout most of the '90s. *—Stephen Thomas Erlewine*

Amazing Grace: The Complete Recordings / May 4, 1999 / Rhino ✦✦✦✦✦

Among Aretha aficionados, *Amazing Grace* has long been considered one of her high-water marks, since it captured her glorious return to her gospel roots in front of a live audience. The original 1972 album contained just 14 tracks, culled from two live performances with the Southern California Community Choir, Ken Lupper, and the Rev. James Cleveland at the New Temple Missionary Baptist Church in Los Angeles. Fans have long wished for the release of the two complete concerts—which is exactly what Rhino's *Amazing Grace: The Complete Recordings* gives them. Over the course of two discs and 29 tracks, every performance Franklin gave that January, along with comments from Cleveland and solo tracks from Lupper and the Choir, is unfurled, and if anything, the music is even more impressive when heard complete and unedited. Of course, the nature of this set makes it of interest primarily to dedicated fans, but they'll likely be delighted by the entire package. *—Stephen Thomas Erlewine*

Aretha's Best / May 15, 2001 / Rhino ✦✦✦✦✦

Rhino's *Aretha's Best* is notable for attempting to squeeze highlights of every era of Aretha's career onto one disc. Unfortunately, the compilers threw logic and chronology out the window, preferring to vacillate between classic Atlantic recordings and very good latter-day Arista recordings. There are certainly some great performances missing, but this pretty much hits the majority of the big numbers, from "Respect" to "Freeway of Love." Unfortunately though, it does this within the course of three songs, which gives the compilation no grounding whatsoever. But if you're looking for just the basics—just the basic hits without any rhyme or reason to the presentation—this will suit your needs. The compilation would have been close to essential, however, if it had just made some sense. *—Stephen Thomas Erlewine*

The Queen in Waiting: The Columbia Years 1960–1965 / Sep. 24, 2002 / Columbia/Legacy ✦✦✦

Franklin's Columbia years are hard to summarize in compilations, even fairly extensive ones such as this two-CD set, which includes six previously unreleased tracks and one previously unavailable alternate take among its 40 songs. In part that's because she explored several different styles during this era without really finding a home in any of them, in part that's because the quality of the recordings themselves were so erratic, and in part it's because Sony keeps putting out compilations that duplicate each other to a fair extent. About half the songs on this anthology, for instance, also appear on the most comprehensive previous Franklin/Columbia retrospective, *Jazz to Soul.* On its own merits, this is a fair summation of some of her more notable Columbia recordings, slightly more pop-oriented in its track selection than *Jazz to Soul*, and at least including something new in the handful of unissued numbers. David Ritz's informative liner notes make a case for viewing the Columbia years as ones with numerous artistic successes. But the fact remains that the mixture of lush pop, Billie Holiday-style jazz-blues, Dinah Washington/Nancy Wilson-style jazz-pop crossover, early Dionne Warwick-style light soul-pop ("Cry Like a Baby" is actually a quite good cut of that sort), and hints of gospel is unfocused, if often promising. And it's not nearly as good or expressive as the soul she'd delve into at Atlantic after leaving Columbia. Her accompanists sometimes deserve their share of blame as well; the drums of "Nobody Knows the Way I Feel This Morning" almost totally lose the rhythm at one point, and the harmonica player on "Evil Gal Blues" sounds like she or he had just been dragged in off the street. There's not much soul music here, in the accepted stylistic sense, other than the two best tracks, "Soulville" and "Lee Cross," which are the ones that point most convincingly to her future triumph as the Queen of Soul. The previously unreleased items (all on disc one) are as variable as the rest of the set, ranging from the satisfyingly bluesy cover of Ray Charles' "Hard Times (No One Knows Better Than I)" (with some fine Franklin piano) and the respectable jazz/R&B/gospel of "Please Answer Me" to trifling Bobby Scott-produced orchestrated pop ballads and an unremarkable alternate take of "Bill Bailey, Won't You Please Come Home." *—Richie Unterberger*

Carolyn Franklin

b. 1945, Memphis, TN, **d.** Apr. 25, 1988, Bloomfield Hills, MI

Vocals / Soul, R&B

Aretha Franklin's youngest sister, Carolyn Franklin wrote some moderately successful songs for both herself and her other sister Erma. "Without Love," "Baby Baby Baby," "I Was Made for You," and "Sing It Again-Say It Again" are among the various Carolyn Franklin compositions. She was one of Aretha's background vocalists five years, and also recorded as a solo artist for RCA. Her most successful release was "It's True I Gonna Miss You," which reached number 23 on the R&B charts in 1969. She died of cancer in 1988. *—Ron Wynn*

- **Chain Reaction** / 1970 / RCA ✦✦✦

Carolyn Franklin, the late sister of Aretha, is known best for the gripping ballads "Ain't No Way" and "Angel," both of which she wrote for big sis. Carolyn was the baby of the Franklin siblings. *Chain Reaction* consists of mostly remakes. On the Moments' "Not on the Outside," she mimics the original, but gives it female flavor. Same for the Masqueraders' soulful proclamation, "I Ain't Got to Love Nobody Else, I Got You." Yes, that's the correct title. She deserves brownie points for redoing a Masqueraders' song, a neglected soul group who was outstanding. They aren't covered much because few singers can do justice to their originals. For some reason, Carolyn didn't write any of the songs. Surprising, because, besides the remakes, the rest of the LP is cluttered with ordinary attempts at commercialism like "Chain Reaction," and "Shattered Pride." *—Andrew Hamilton*

Erma Franklin

b. Mar. 13, 1938, Shelby, MS, **d.** Sep. 7, 2002, Detroit, MI

Vocals / Chicago Soul, Pop-Soul, R&B, Soul

Erma Franklin's musical accomplishments will forever be overshadowed by those of her younger sister Aretha, especially since she recorded very sporadically through the '60s. As a singer in her own right, Franklin is best known for recording the original version of "Piece of My Heart," which of course became one of Janis Joplin's signature tunes in a much different arrangement. Franklin was born March 13, 1938 in Shelby, MS, and moved with her family to Memphis, Buffalo (where she made her singing debut in her father's church at age five), and finally Detroit. She sang with sisters Aretha and Carolyn in their church choir, and during high school performed with a vocal group called the Cleo-Patrettes, which won a state talent contest and recorded for the small Detroit label JVB. The Cleo-Patrettes broke up after high school, and Franklin toured with her father's gospel group for two years; she subsequently had chances to record for Chess and to join Motown's early roster, but wound up following her father's wishes that she attend college before trying a singing career.

Franklin successfully auditioned for Epic in 1961, and moved to New York to record. Aretha was on the parent label Columbia at the time, and Erma had much the same problem as her sister, namely that pure R&B wasn't the label's area of expertise, and they simply didn't know how to handle her. Franklin's debut album, *Her Name Is Erma*, appeared in 1962, and featured jazz and pop standards as well as R&B tunes; one of several commercially ignored singles, "Abracadabra," was written by Van McCoy, later of "The Hustle" fame. Frustrated with Epic's choice of directions for her, Franklin waited out her contract while spending 1961-1966 on the road as a featured vocalist in New Orleans R&B legend Lloyd Price's show.

When Aretha's career suddenly took off at Atlantic, Franklin signed with producer/songwriter Bert Berns' Shout Records in 1967. "Piece of My Heart," a song Berns had co-written with Jerry Ragovoy, became Franklin's first Top Ten R&B hit later that year; unfortunately, before Franklin could begin work on a proper LP, Berns died suddenly of a heart attack, throwing the company into chaos. In the meantime, Franklin backed her sister on many Atlantic recordings, and toured the U.S. and Europe behind "Piece of My Heart." She signed with Brunswick in 1969 and scored a minor R&B hit with "Gotta Find Me a Lover (24 Hours a Day)," also releasing her second LP *Soul Sister.* But once again, Franklin found herself with a label that didn't know what to do with her; after Brunswick nixed a proposed session with Aretha in the producer's chair, Franklin waited out her contract and moved back to Detroit in 1972 to work at a PR firm. She performed with Aretha off and on through the '80s and '90s, and eventually took an upper-level job at the Boysville children's charity. Franklin's original recording of "Piece of My Heart" enjoyed an early-'90s revival in Europe, where it was featured in a jeans commercial. Franklin passed away on September 7, 2002 after a battle with cancer. *—Steve Huey*

- **Golden Classics** / 1993 / Collectables ✦✦✦✦✦

As the liner notes to this compilation are nothing more than a reprint of some old LP sleeve notes with nothing in the way of dates or recording info, there's no way to confirm when these tracks were recorded or who wrote them. That's an inexcusable shame, but it certainly is the best (if not the only) Erma Franklin CD compilation to appear. The original version of "Piece of My Heart" is here, and is the only song that will be familiar (and usually in the Janis Joplin cover version, at that) to most listeners. Most of the rest, however, is quality overlooked soul with a slight uptown feel, not all that much like her famous sister Aretha's work. At a guess the tracks seem to originate from a multi-year time span covering the early to late '60s; "Don't Catch the Dog's Bone" is first-rate blues-soul, while "Open Up Your Soul" *does* recall the kind of material Aretha Franklin cut in 1967. Other cuts obviously date from a slightly earlier period with their pop-soul arrangements (such as "Abracadabra"), though these are decent too. The covers of R&B standards ("Pledging My Love") and supper club-ish material ("Detour Ahead") are unremarkable, but fortunately they're in the minority on this anthology. Now if someone could take the essence of this disc and give the package the annotation and design it deserves, Franklin's legacy would be much better served. *—Richie Unterberger*

Brunswick's Super Soul Sisters / Oct. 27, 1998 / Diablo ✦✦✦✦

Kirk Franklin

Producer, Vocals, Piano / Contemporary Gospel, Black Gospel, Urban

Since his debut, 1993's *Kirk Franklin & the Family*, Kirk Franklin has been one of the brightest stars in contemporary gospel music. The album spent 100 weeks on the gospel charts (some of those on top), crossed over to the R&B charts, and became the first gospel debut album to go platinum. His second album, *Kirk Franklin & the Family Christmas*, became the genre's first Christmas album to make it to number one, and his 1996 album *Whatcha Lookin' 4* went gold as soon as it was distributed. With such phenomenal success, it is small wonder that some have hailed him "the Garth Brooks of Gospel." Still, despite all the adulation and brouhaha, Franklin remains a humble, devout Christian, eschewing the title "entertainer" in favor of labeling himself as just a "church boy."

Franklin's road to the top, though quick, was far from smooth. Abandoned by his mother and never having known his father, Franklin was reared by his Aunt Gertrude, a deeply religious woman who raised him as a strict Baptist. When he was four, she paid for his piano lessons by collecting aluminum cans. The lessons were money well-spent, for Franklin was a natural musician who could sight read and play by ear with equal facility. At age 11, he was leading the Mt. Rose Baptist Church adult choir near Dallas. Despite, or because of his church background, Franklin began rebelling in his teens and getting into trouble until one of his friends was accidentally shot and killed at age 15. Realizing that he had chosen a bad road, Franklin returned to the fold and began composing songs, recording and conducting. Since 1991, he has been backed up by his 17-member choir, the Family, a group comprising friends and associates from his younger days (interestingly, one member of the Family, Jon Drummond, made it to the semi-finals heat of the 100-meter sprint at the 1996 Olympics). Support from his pastor, his wife Tammy, whom he married in early 1996, and the two children they brought to the marriage help keep Franklin close to his religious core, and he returned in 1998 with *The Nu Nation Project*. *—Sandra Brennan*

• **Kirk Franklin & the Family** / Jun. 29, 1993 / Sparrow ✦✦✦✦✦

Kirk Franklin & the Family's eponymous debut album is a stunningly assured blend of old-fashioned gospel, contemporary soul and hip-hop. Franklin remains, in his words, a "church boy," but he doesn't hesitate to embrace the conventions and styles of contemporary R&B, which results in some inspired, unexpected fusions. It is truly a record that updates, recontextualizes and redefines what contemporary gospel can mean in the '90s. *—Rodney Batdorf*

Whatcha Lookin' 4 / 1995 / Gospo Centric ✦✦✦

Although it isn't quite as consistent as his debut, *Whatcha Lookin' 4* remains exceptional urban gospel, exhibiting passion, soul and grit. *—Rodney Batdorf*

The Nu Nation Project / Sep. 22, 1998 / Interscope ✦✦✦✦

Kirk Franklin designed *The Nu Nation Project* as a revitalization of contemporary gospel, a way to bring it to an audience accustomed to the slick, funky innovations of hip-hop and rap. It's an ambitious project and one that's not too far removed from his earlier records, simply because it finds him adding R&B production techniques and the occasional grandiose flourish, such as the cameos from R. Kelly, Mary J. Blige and Bono on the admittedly stirring "Lean on Me." Occasionally, the album feels as if Franklin is pushing a bit too hard for the mainstream audience and all that entails (namely, superstardom for himself), but the end result is every bit as engaging as his previous records, thereby confirming his status as one of true visionaries in '90s contemporary gospel. *—Rodney Batdorf*

The Rebirth of Kirk Franklin / Feb. 19, 2002 / Gospocentric ✦✦✦✦

This project is as close as it gets to having a true, bona fide masterpiece. The artistic genius of Kirk Franklin weaves through each of the 17 songs included on this gem. The title of this project, *The Rebirth of Kirk Franklin*, says it all. Musically speaking, he has been born again. The project effectively mixes live tracks recorded in Houston, TX, in early 2001, with some stellar studio tracks. Many naysayers have unjustly criticized Franklin for departing the successful formula of this self-titled debut project, which included the mega-hit "Why We Sing." Well, in that regards, he has returned to the traditional/contemporary-flavored mix of his early work, only with a more progressive feel. Franklin has never been noted or recognized for his singing ability, a fact that he readily recognizes, sticking ever closely to his spoken-word rap. He relies on his talented background vocalist, along with the all-star list of special guests, to take care of the vocal chores. Featured throughout are such artists as Donnie McClurkin, Crystal Lewis, Jackie Velazquez, Shirley Caesar, Richard Smallwood, the late Willie Neal Johnson, Yolanda Adams, and Bishop T.D. Jakes, among others, with the latter joining Franklin on the track "911." There is also a hidden bonus track entitled "J Train," featuring Franklin and DC Talk's Tobymac. The true brilliance of Kirk Franklin shines again. *—Tim A. Smith*

John Fred

b. May 8, 1941, Baton Rouge, LA

Vocals / Blue-Eyed Soul

Remembered only for his fluke 1968 number-one hit "Judy in Disguise," John Fred actually made quite a few records in the '60s. Though he was from Louisiana, Fred's vocals strongly recall Eric Burdon at times and Georgie Fame at others. A capable songwriter ("Judy in Disguise" was an original), he also cut several fine, deep Southern soul ballads that distinguish him as one of the best American white R&B singers. *—Richie Unterberger*

34.40 of John Fred / 1967 / Paula ✦✦✦

Best of John Fred & the Playboys / 1984 / Sugarcane ✦✦✦

This is decent 12-song overview of Fred's best '60s recordings, with a late '50s track thrown in. It was made redundant by the far more thorough *History* CD, which includes every one of these songs among its 26 cuts. *—Richie Unterberger*

History of John Fred & the Playboys / 1991 / Paula ✦✦✦✦

This features eclectic 26-song assortment of pop/rock/soul/R&B. Highlights are his 1964 cover of John Lee Hooker's "Boogie Chillen," which stands up to the best early British R&B; the odd, moody "Agnes English" and "Sun City," which shows a strong Animals influence, and of course "Judy in Disguise." A 1958 track that he cut as a teenager recalls a frat-rock Frankie Ford with its low-wattage emulation of the New Orleans sound. Unfortunately there are little in the way of liner notes here, but the grooves prove Fred to be a versatile stylist with much greater depth than the usual one-shot. *—Richie Unterberger*

• **With Glasses: The Very Best of John Fred & His Playboy Band** / Mar. 13, 2001 / West-Side ✦✦✦✦

Free Life

Group / Soul, Pop-Soul

Philip Bailey of '70s supergroup Earth, Wind & Fire produced the singing group Free Life, who charted with the Epic single "Wish You Were Here." The Bailey-written ballad peaked at number 91 on the R&B charts in early 1979. The single and the album *Free Life* had EWF influences. Though there was another single from *Free Life*, "Stomp and Shout," and a non-LP single, "Dance Fantasy," none charted. Group member Carl Carlwell later became a member of the '90s group 101 North ("So Easy"), who recorded a couple of albums with producer George Duke: *101 North* (1987) and *Forever Yours* (1991) for Capitol. Also, he was the brother of Minneapolis singer Sue Ann Carwell ("Let Me Let You Rock Me"). *—Ed Hogan*

• **Free Life** / 1978 / Epic ✦✦✦

When Earth, Wind & Fire was in its prime in the late '70s, you could have spent hours talking about all of the artists who were being influenced by the soul/funk superband. Artists who had no connection to EWF were claiming Maurice White & Co. as a major influence, and its influence was impossible to miss on albums by Deniece Williams, the Emotions, Pockets and others who were part of the EWF family. An obscure nine-member soul/funk outfit, Free Life brings a very EWF-influenced sound to this self-titled debut album—and that isn't surprising considering that the LP was co-produced by EWF's Philip Bailey (who also helped with the arranging and wrote or co-wrote several of the songs). Despite Bailey's presence, the little known *Free Life* isn't a great album—a competent album, but not a great one. Even though EWF-minded tunes like "I Confess" and "Wish You Were Here" are likable enough, it's clear that Bailey was saving his best writing for EWF. This is an LP that simmers without ever burning or exploding. *—Alex Henderson*

Free Movement

f. 1970, Los Angeles, CA

Group / Pop-Soul, Soul

The six-member group Free Movement hit in 1971 with "I've Found Someone of My Own," a Top Five pop/Top 20 R&B hit on Decca Records. The group's sound was similar to the 5th Dimension. Godoy Colbert (the Pilgrim Travelers, the Pharoahs), Josephine Brown (the Five Bells of Joy), Cheryl Conley, Jennifer Gates, and brothers Adrian and Claude Jefferson met in Los Angeles and began recording demos. Decca issued the single "I've Found Someone of My Own," which made it to number-20 R&B and number-five pop on *Billboard*'s charts in the spring of 1971.

By then, the group had signed to Columbia Records. *I've Found Someone of My Own* was the title of their Columbia LP, released in January 1972. "The Harder I Try (The Bluer I Get)" b/w "Comin' Home" was the follow-up single peaking at number-49 R&B, number-50 pop in early 1972. Another single was a cover of Stephen Stills' "Love the One You're With." The group never charted after the second single. *—Ed Hogan*

I've Found Someone of My Own / Jan. 1972 / Columbia ✦✦✦✦

• **Golden Classics** / Nov. 5, 1996 / Collectables ✦✦✦✦

Freedom

f. 1975

Group / Funk, Soul, Southern Soul, Deep Funk

It was 1975 in Jackson, MS, when lead guitarist, Caleb Tyrone Armstrong, a student at Wingfield high school, and Ray Smith (bass), a student at Jackson State College, formed Freedom. The other members were Joe Leslie (lead singer and bongos), David Thigpen (sax), Victor Mason (drums), Larry Addison (keyboards & vocals), Adolph Adams (sax and vocals), and Robert Black (trumpet).

Armstrong started musically in his father's gospel group, Seven Star, with his brother, Leroy, who wasn't a part of Freedom. He switched to secular music in his teens and debuted with "Can't You See That I'm in Love" on Freedom Records; limited resources kept it local. They signed with Malaco Records in 1979. Their first single was "Dance and Sing Along" b/w "Set You Free," from the album *Farther Than Imagination*, which, like subsequent albums, consisted of group-written material.

Their second Malaco single became a virtual pot of gold, earning its writers Armstrong and Smith royalties that continue to check in. "Get Up and Dance" b/w "Summer Memory" was popular in the South, New York, and New Jersey. Freedom toured throughout the South with the top funk bands: the Bar-Kays, Con Funk Shun, Cameo, SOS Band, Graham Central Station, and Lakeside. Malaco didn't break the bank promoting the single or the album and both failed to register nationally, but the tune didn't escape Grandmaster Flash & the Furious Five's ears.

Renamed "Freedom" the revised "Get Up and Dance" scored a number-19 R&B hit for Grandmaster Flash & the Furious Five and Sugar Hill Records. The new version listed seven names as songwriters, but not the creators' names—Armstrong and Smith or the publishing companies. Malaco sued Sugar Hill for copyright infringement and received a big settlement for all the pertinent parties. Malaco and Thompson & Weakley Publishing shared the publishing income, and Armstrong and Smith got credit and songwriting royalties. KRS-One redid the same song as "You Must Learn." KRS-One's version credited Armstrong and Smith along with Lawrence Parker, alias KRS-One (Knowledge Reigns Supreme Over Nearly Everyone). SWV later cut it as "Anything" with Armstrong & Smith sharing writers' credit with Brian Morgan. Chris Rock used it regularly on his television show; it was featured in the soundtracks: *Above the Rim* and *New Jack City*, and has been sampled by others, but few remember the original.

A second LP, *Free*, dropped in 1980 and included the songs "Funny Way," "Freedom Funk It Up," "Time to Get It On" and "Come on and Dance." Nothing scored until 1981 when "At the Party" b/w "I Give You Love," received a little love. The year saw the release of album number three—*Changes of Time*, which featured the single, and "Stacked Back," "School Teacher," and "I Give You Love." Later in 1981, tragedy struck when lead singer Joe Leslie was killed; the group slowly disbanded.

Jesse Thompson recruited a new Freedom, but the public who knew the originals didn't fall for or appreciate the ruse. The occurrence confuses discographers who always lump the new group with the old group. This was easy to do; they both recorded for Malaco. Tyrone Armstrong became an engineer at Chrysler and became involved in running MTL (Music Technology Lab) recording studios with his brother Leroy. He also wrote many songs for his church, Christ the King. He continued to play gigs at the Delta Blues Festival, the McCoomb Blues Festival, and other events. Ray Smith worked with Armstrong in the studio and remained active in music. David Thigpen played sax in church, occasionally hanging out at MTL. Larry Addison stayed in music and was a staff songwriter for Malaco as well as assisting at MTL. *—Andrew Hamilton*

● **Farther Than Imagination** / 1979 / Malaco ✦✦✦
Freedom's debut album contains hot dance tracks and smoldering ballads. A prominent bass groove dominates the uptempo tracks "Dance and Sing Along" and "Get Up and Dance." As singers and players, Freedom's sweet harmonies prevail on "Summer Memory," "Wake Up Your Mind," "Know You Better," and "You've Just Got to Be the One." "Get Up and Dance" was later redone by Grandmaster Flash & the Furious Five as "Freedom," by KRS-One as "You Must Learn," and by SWV as "Anything." *—Andrew Hamilton*

Are You Available / 1984 / Malaco ✦✦
Here is Southern funk, urban contemporary, and a little hip-hop flavoring featuring Freedom, a group that Malaco had little success with in breaking out beyond the Deep South, though they tried for many years. The album had some decent uptempo numbers and a few good ballads, but still couldn't break the regional embargo. *—Ron Wynn*

Bobby Freeman

b. Jun. 13, 1940, San Francisco, CA
Vocals, Songwriter / Pop-Soul, Northern Soul, R&B
Bobby Freeman's energetic vocals punctuated two R&B dance hits in the late '50s and mid-'60s. The San Francisco performer started the Romancers as a 14 year old and later formed the West Coast Vocaleers, whose sound was much more pop-oriented than the Harlem group of the same name. Freeman's single "Do You Want to Dance" just missed topping the R&B charts in 1958, staying at number two for two weeks (number-five pop). It was one of three hits he enjoyed that year on Josie, although "Betty Lou Got a New Pair of Shoes" and "Need Your Love" only reached numbers 20 and 29, respectively. "C'Mon and Swim" parlayed the 1964 dance craze into his second Top Ten R&B hit, reaching number five. But the follow-up went to the water once too often, as "S-W-I-M" fizzled at number 56. Both were for Autumn. It was also Freeman's final visit to the R&B charts. *—Ron Wynn*

Do You Wanna Dance / 1958 / Collectables ✦✦✦
The title track is one of the great pieces of '50s R&B/rock and roll and was Freeman's moment of glory. The rest of the album is decent, occasionally above-average pop and light R&B, sung in an energetic fashion but not exactly spectacular stuff. It is fun, however, and if you can find the album, it's well worth getting. *—Ron Wynn*

C'mon and S-W-I-M / 1964 / Autumn ✦✦✦
Bobby Freeman's only album for the Autumn label was, as expected, based around his huge "C'mon and Swim" hit. Part one of that song leads off side one; part two of the song leads off side two; and the small hit follow-up single "S-W-I-M" ends the LP. In between swim tunes, most of this is energetic covers of popular numbers like "Ya Ya," "Money," and "Walkin' the Dog," along with party soul dance swingers (sometimes with live-in-the-studio party noise) in the same vein, written or co-written by producer Sylvester Stewart (aka Sly Stone). This is decent hard-charging mid-'60s soul, with more of a rock influence than most such soul recordings. What keeps this from making that leap from fun to meaningful is that old nuisance that hinders so many albums, from then and from any time: a shortage of high-quality original material. The more serious side of Freeman & Stone does come through on two decent Sly Stewart originals, "I'll Never Fall in Love Again" (not the same as the famous Bacharach/David composition) and "That Little Old Heartbreaker Me," both of which are solid midtempo pop-soul laments. All 12 of the LP's songs are on the Ace CD retrospective of Freeman's Autumn work, also called *C'mon and S-W-I-M*, which adds 13 bonus cuts from non-LP singles and previously unissued outtakes and alternates. *—Richie Unterberger*

● **Best of Bobby Freeman** / 1992 / Sequel ✦✦✦✦✦
It's a shame that most listeners only know Bobby Freeman's "Do You Wanna Dance" in the Beach Boys' or Cliff Richard's cover versions, which is lively enough but still a white-bread workout compared to the 1958 original. This 20-song collection, covering "Do You Wanna Dance" on Josie-Jubilee, up through his last hit, the Sylvester (Sly) Stewart co-authored "C'mon and Swim," does a lot to restore Freeman's name to the consciousness, and not just through shouters like "Do You Wanna Dance" and "Betty Lou Got a New Pair of Shoes." He acquits himself well on ballads like "Need Your Love" and standards like "Ebb Tide." The collection, mostly made up of the dance numbers that Freeman made his specialty, also includes one previously unissued cut, the doo wop style "Follow the Rainbow," and the notes provide a detailed account of the confusing state of Freeman's recording history (at one point, he seems to have been working for two labels simultaneously). The sound is somewhat uneven, a bit tinny on certain cuts, while others, especially on the later tracks, are above average, giving a good account of his solid backing band on those cuts. *—Bruce Eder*

C'mon and S-W-I-M / Jun. 26, 2000 / Ace ✦✦✦✦
Although this has the same title as Freeman's only Autumn album, 1964's *C'mon and S-W-I-M*, this is in fact a retrospective of Freeman's entire stint with the label. In addition to all twelve songs from the original *C'mon and S-W-I-M* LP, it has five non-LP cuts from 1963-1965 singles, and seven previously unissued outtakes and alternates. At the very least, it's enjoyable uptempo party soul. At its most ambitious, there are fusions of rock and soul elements—hard slicing guitars, unusual and crafty melodic lines—that point to the directions explored, in much deeper and more effective fashion, by Sly Stone a few years later. That should not come as a great surprise, given that Sly Stone, then known as Sylvester Stewart, produced this material, in which he was also involved as arranger and frequent songwriter. In fact, "I'll Never Fall in Love Again" (heard here in both its LP version and faster single version) would be done on Sly & the Family Stone's *Dance to the Music* album, although Larry Graham and not Sly Stone would do lead vocals. More impressive than the energetic dance outings with live-in-the-studio-sounding party noise are Stone/Stewart's pop-soul-rock compositions, including "I'll Never Fall in Love Again"; "That Little Old Heartbreaker Me"; "Friends," with its James Brown-like horns and Latin rhythms; and the idiosyncratically, melodically twisting "Cross My Heart." (The last of these only appeared on 45 originally.) The outtakes and alternates, incidentally, are pretty worthwhile, and not just footnotes, particularly as they include a few Sly Stone-penned tunes. Of those, "Swing Me" is a pretty good Motown approximation, while "Honest" gets into some more personal, melancholy writing that certainly anticipates some of Stone's work a few years down the line. Not a brilliant disc, but a good one that has more historical importance in the rock and soul lineage than has been recognized. *—Richie Unterberger*

Fresh

f. 1975, **db.** 1979
Group / Funk Metal, Soul
Influenced by Sly & the Family Stone and Rare Earth, Fresh was an obscure, little-known 1970s band that combined soul and funk with rock. The interracial outfit, which shouldn't be confused with either the 1990s hip-hop engineer or other bands that have called themselves Fresh, didn't get very far commercially—quite possibly, its three LPs were too funky for rock stations and too rock-influenced for R&B stations. Fresh was formed in 1975, when its original six-person lineup consisted of lead singer Bill Pratt, lead guitarist Paul Marshall, rhythm guitarist Elaine Mayo, keyboardist David Kaffinetti, bassist Milo Martin, and drummer Fred Allen. In 1976, the band signed with MCA, which released its debut album, *Get Fresh*, the following year. It was also in 1977 that Fresh was an opening act for Rufus & Chaka Khan; Fresh received generally favorable responses from Rufus fans, but regrettably, that didn't translate into record sales.

Get Fresh bombed commercially, and the band parted company with MCA. In 1978, Fresh resurfaced on Motown's Prodigal label with its sophomore effort, *Feelin' Fresh*, and unveiled a new seven-person lineup. Most of the original members were still on board, although a saxophonist, George Englund, had been added—and Kaffinetti had been replaced by keyboardist Frank Savino. After *Feelin' Fresh*, Mayo left the band. Neither *Feelin' Fresh* nor Fresh's third album, *Omniverse* (which Prodigal/Motown released in late 1978) received much attention—and in 1979, the band broke up. All three of Fresh's albums were out of print by the 1980s and are unlikely to ever be reissued on CD. *—Alex Henderson*

● **Get Fresh** / 1977 / MCA ✦✦✦✦
In 1977, Fresh seemingly had reason for optimism. The rock-minded soul/funk band had a contract with MCA and was an opening act for Rufus & Chaka Khan, who were huge at the time. Plus, its debut LP, *Get Fresh*, is excellent. So why did this album bomb commercially? Inadequate promotion probably had a lot to do with it, and it's quite possible that smokers like "Ain't Got No Money," "Lookout," "In the Morning," and "Sweet Music" were simply too black for rock stations and too rockin' for R&B stations. Of course, Rufus & Chaka Khan, LaBelle, George Clinton, Graham Central Station, the Isley Brothers, and Rick James all had rock influences in the 1970s—and none of them were obscure. So it's also quite possible that Fresh would have been big with the right marketing. At any rate, this LP should have done a lot better. From the uptempo material to passionate ballads like "She Was a Lady" and "I'm Ready to Love You," *Get Fresh* is the band's most essential album. *—Alex Henderson*

Feelin' Fresh / 1978 / Prodigal ✦✦✦
Fresh moved from MCA to Motown's Prodigal label with its second album, *Feelin' Fresh*, which falls short of the excellence of its first album, *Get Fresh*, but is decent and enjoyable. Ironically, this 1978 LP opens with the Gavin Christopher song "Just How Does It Feel," which asks a well-known singer how it feels to have become a superstar; it's ironic because Fresh never enjoyed that type of exposure. *Get Fresh* received very little attention, and *Feelin' Fresh* didn't do any better. Like its predecessor, this record seemed to be too rockin' for black stations and too funky for rock stations. But for those who hold both soul-funk and rock in high regard, *Feelin' Fresh* is easy to enjoy. Anyone who has spent hours and hours listening to Sly & the Family Stone or Rare Earth should have no problem getting into sweaty tracks like "Preparation," "Whatever Happened to Rock and Roll," and "Let Yourself Go." These songs aren't in a class with Stone or Rare Earth's best work, but they do remind us that a strong appreciation of rock can be a healthy thing for a

soul-funk band. Even though *Feelin' Fresh* isn't Fresh's most essential album, it didn't deserve to be ignored. *—Alex Henderson*

Omniverse / 1978 / Prodigal ♦♦♦

Fresh hoped that its third album, *Omniverse*, would be its commercial breakthrough. But like Fresh's two previous albums, *Omniverse* was ignored by both soul-funk and rock audiences, and that's regrettable because this LP is generally decent and sometimes excellent. When *Omniverse* came out in late 1978, disco was huge, but Fresh refused to jump on the disco bandwagon. Its roots were in the classic soul-funk-rock of Sly & the Family Stone and Rare Earth, and the band sticks to its creative guns on original material as well as on likable covers of Larry Williams' "Bony Maronie" and Sam & Dave's "Hold on, I'm Coming." To fully appreciate this album, you need to be someone who treasures both R&B and rock. The basslines are unapologetically funky, while the electric guitars rock without hesitation. But Fresh's creativity continued to go unrewarded, and its third album turned out to be its last. *—Alex Henderson*

The Friends of Distinction

f. 1968, Los Angeles, CA, **db.** 1973

Group / Sunshine Pop, Pop-Soul, Quiet Storm, Soul, Psychedelic Soul

Founded by Harry Elston and Floyd Butler, the Friends of Distinction also comprised Jessica Cleaves and Barbara Jean Love (plus Charlene Gibson, who replaced Love during her pregnancy). Elston and Butler's involvement in music entailed several groups, including the Hi-Fi's, Ray Charles' backing band. When the group disbanded in 1966, Elston and Butler recruited Cleaves and Love for a new band; initially, Elston came up with the name Distinctive Friends, but Love suggested reversing the words to Friends of Distinction. After polishing up their act for a few six months during 1968, the group hit the local tour circuit in Los Angeles. With well-developed talent and the support of a well-known manager, former football great Jim Brown, the group signed with RCA Records. In 1969, the group released their first single "Grazing in the Grass." Originally recorded by famed trumpeter Hugh Masekela (Elston wrote the lyrics to Masekela's trumpet lead), the song became a smash hit. It graced the R&B charts for 17 weeks, peaking at number five. Four months later, the second release, "Going in Circles," surpassed its predecessor. It climbed its way to number three after a prosperous 19 weeks.

Three more singles charted for the group—"Love or Let Me Be Lonely," "Time Waits for No One" and "I Need You"—though none were as rewarding as the group's first two hits. The group encountered some personnel changes following the two smash hits. Jessica Cleaves and Barbara Love both departed the group. Cleaves joined up with other R&B acts (Earth, Wind & Fire, Parliament, etc.). After the release of their fifth and final single, the decline of Friends of Distinction was on the horizon, but not by their own doing. By the mid-'70s, the group's well had run dry. With more than five years elapsed since their first release, Elston and Butler called it quits. The two parted ways and didn't speak for several years. When they finally overcame their differences however, Butler died of a heart attack—in Elston's arms. In 1996 Elston ultimately accomplished what he and Butler had agreed to do: he reformed the group with new members Patti Brooks, Van Jewel and Drake Frye. *—Craig Lytle*

Grazin' / 1969 / RCA ♦♦♦♦

Jessica Cleaves, Barbara Love, Harry Elston, and Floyd Butler were the Friends of Distinction, Southern California natives who sought to imitate the Fifth Dimension's success. They shared similar lineups—two women, two guys, each dressed differently with no overt attempts to coordinate. "Grazing in the Grass" made them known across America; lyrics were added to Hugh Masekela's clanging, cowbell-driven, African tune, and it sold in droves, as radio stations played it, people liked it, and even jazz aficionados dug it. "Going in Circles" duplicated "Grazing"'s success and has been redone by R&B greats; the falsetto lead on the fade should be time capsuled. I forgot which female leads "I Really Hope You Do," but the sweet, husky soprano never fails to jumpstart my heart; RCA mistakenly tacked it on the B-side of something. They take Eddie Floyd's "I Ain't Never Found a Girl" out the country and into the city. Lennon & McCartney's "And I Love Him" is given a soulful, erotic reading by one of the Friends of Distinction women. Cole Porter's somber "Lonesome Road" shows a desire to do jazzier selections. *—Andrew Hamilton*

Highly Distinct / 1969 / RCA ♦♦♦

It opens with "Impressions," which is not a song, but two minutes of Harry Elston, Floyd Butler, Jessica Cleaves and Barbara Love—the Friends of Distinction, tripping. *Highly Distinct* is close to their debut album but lacked the obvious hit; it's more jazzy and less R&B. They're mesmerizing on "We Got a Good Thing Going," where their four-part harmonies riding the bubbling arrangement is simply delicious. I've yet to hear a bad rendition of Neil Sedaka's lilting "Working on a Groovy Thing," and the Friends version, with their impeccable harmonies, is one of the best; it should have made their *Best Of* CD. A harmony-filled "It's Wonderful" is merely a vehicle to display their amazing blending skills, melody and lyrics buried in a sea of harmony. The Doors' rocker "Light My Fire" works well all jazzed up; it seems like a live recording but could have been manufactured in the studio. Nothing is blatantly commercial, and the uplifting "Let Yourself Go" stirred some chart action but strayed too far from mainstream to seriously compete. *—Andrew Hamilton*

• **The Best of the Friends of Distinction** / Nov. 26, 1996 / RCA ♦♦♦♦♦

It's the summer of 1969, and the whole world is joyfully singing, "Grazing in the grass is a gas, baby, can you dig it!" The Friends of Distinction's debut single was a made-for-radio pop masterpiece that captured the ebullience of that last summer of the '60s in its three minutes of harmonic exuberance. While the group never quite reached those heights again, the Friends did produce a small body of work in their brief lifetime that has held up well. The foursome's two other major hit singles, "Love or Let Me Be Lonely" and "Going in Circles" have joined "Grazing in the Grass" in the permanent rotations of most "fun and oldies" formats. Other highlights of this 20-song compilation include "Grazing's" flipside, "I Really Hope You Do," the group's reading of the Four Tops' hit "Ain't No Woman (Like the One I've Got)," David Gates' "It Don't Matter to Me," and the beautifully baritoned "Love Can Make It Easier." *—Jim Newsom*

Grazin'/Highly Distinct / Oct. 24, 2000 / One Way ♦♦♦♦

Fugi

Group / Psychedelic, Funk, Soul, Psychedelic Soul, Deep Funk

Fugi was a psychedelic soul/funk band signed to Chess subsidiary Cadet in the late '60s. Their music was influenced particularly by the acid rock side of Jimi Hendrix, and bore a resemblance to the druggy, guitar-driven soul of early Funkadelic. Their lone LP, *Mary, Don't Take Me on No Bad Trip*, was released in 1968, and the title cut later became a cult collector's item. Fugi went on to release a couple of singles in 1970, "Revelations" and "I'd Rather Be a Blind Man," before fading from view. It's known that Fugi was connected to a similar psychedelic funk-rock group on Chess called Black Merda; some accounts hold that they were one and the same, while others credit Black Merda only with production help on some of Fugi's recordings. *—Steve Huey*

• **Mary, Don't Take Me on No Bad Trip** / 1968 / Tuff City ♦♦♦♦♦

Signed by Chess, recorded, and promptly forgotten, Fugi is a great "what if" of American music. They carved a niche all their own as a sort of sinister Curtis Mayfield, albeit with the darker, druggier tones of early Funkadelic woven through their particular fantasy. The nuggets of something truly grand are here, especially in the paranoid fantasy of the title track. That song alone might be worth the price. One can only wonder what might have happened if they had gotten the attention they so richly deserved. A tragedy for sure. *—Rob Ferrier*

Lowell Fulson

b. Mar. 31, 1921, Tulsa, OK, **d.** Mar. 6, 1999

Vocals, Guitar, Leader / Soul-Blues, West Coast Blues, Texas Blues, Electric Texas Blues

Lowell Fulson has recorded every shade of blues imaginable. Polished urban blues, rustic two-guitar duets with his younger brother Martin, funk-tinged grooves that pierced the mid-'60s charts, even an unwise cover of the Beatles' "Why Don't We Do It in the Road!" Clearly, the veteran guitarist, who's been at it now for more than half a century, isn't afraid to experiment. Perhaps that's why his last couple of discs for Rounder are so vital and satisfying—and why he's been an innovator for so long.

Exposed to the western swing of Bob Wills as well as indigenous blues while growing up in Oklahoma, Fulson joined up with singer Texas Alexander for a few months in 1940, touring the Lone Star state with the veteran bluesman. Fulson was drafted in 1943. The Navy let him go in 1945; after a few months back in Oklahoma, he was off to Oakland, CA, where he made his first 78s for fledgling producer Bob Geddins. Soon enough, Fulson was fronting his own band and cutting a stack of platters for Big Town, Gilt Edge, Trilon, and Down Town (where he hit big in 1948 with "Three O'Clock Blues," later covered by B.B. King).

Swing Time records prexy Jack Lauderdale snapped up Fulson in 1948, and the hits really began to flow: the immortal "Every Day I Have the Blues" (an adaptation of Memphis Slim's "Nobody Loves Me"), "Blue Shadows," the two-sided holiday perennial "Lonesome Christmas," and a groovy midtempo instrumental "Low Society Blues" that really hammers home how tremendously important pianist Lloyd Glenn and alto saxist Earl Brown were to Fulson's maturing sound (all charted in 1950!). Fulson toured extensively from then on, his band stocked for a time with dazzling pianist Ray Charles (who later covered Lowell's "Sinner's Prayer" for Atlantic) and saxist Stanley Turrentine. After a one-off session in New Orleans in 1953 for Aladdin, Fulson inked a longterm pact with Chess in 1954. His first single for the firm was the classic "Reconsider Baby," cut in Dallas under Stan Lewis' supervision with a sax section that included David "Fathead" Newman on tenor and Leroy Cooper on baritone.

The relentless midtempo blues proved a massive hit and perennial cover item—even Elvis Presley cut it in 1960, right after he got out of the Army. But apart from "Loving You," the guitarist's subsequent Checker output failed to find widespread favor with the public. Baffling, since Fulson's crisp, concise guitar work and sturdy vocals were as effective as ever. Most of his Checker sessions were held in Chicago and L.A. (the latter his home from the turn of the '50s).

Fulson stayed with Checker into 1962, but a change of labels worked wonders when he jumped over to Los Angeles-based Kent Records. "Black Nights," from 1965, became his first smash in a decade, and "Tramp," a loping funk-injected workout co-written by Fulson and Jimmy McCracklin, did even better, restoring the guitarist to R&B stardom, gaining plenty of pop spins, and inspiring a playful Stax cover by Otis Redding and Carla Thomas only a few months later that outsold Fulson's original.

A couple of lesser follow-up hits for Kent ensued before the guitarist was reunited with Stan Lewis at Jewel Records. That's where he took a crack at that Beatles number, though most of his outings for the firm were considerably closer to the blues bone. Fulson has never been absent for long on disc; 1992's *Hold On* and its 1995 follow-up *Them Update Blues*, both for Ron Levy's Bullseye Blues logo, are among his most recent efforts and both are quite solid. Few bluesmen have managed to remain contemporary the way Lowell Fulson has for more than five decades. And fewer still will make such a massive contribution to the idiom. *—Bill Dahl*

Hung Down Head / 1954 / MCA/Chess ♦♦♦♦♦

The most indispensable collection in Fulson's vast discography. He was hitting on all burners during the mid-'50s when he was with Chess, waxing the immortal "Reconsider Baby," and swinging gems like "Check Yourself," "Do Me Right," and "Trouble, Trouble," and the supremely doomy "Tollin' Bells," here in many truncated false takes before he and the band finally jell. *—Bill Dahl*

Soul / 1966 / United ♦♦♦♦♦

Lowell Fulson was one of the early artists to blend the tough melodic sensibilities of the blues with the more accessible (but no less emotional) framework of 1960s soul, and his

1966 set, *Soul*, finds him walking both sides of the fence on these 12 songs. Of course, some of these songs were a lot more soul- (or blues-) flavored than others, and ironically Fulson would dig deeper into a soul groove on his next album, *Tramp*; perhaps using this title was a bit premature for him. For the most part, *Soul* sounds like straight-ahead blues session, through the bold horn charts on "Talking Woman" and "Change Your Ways" (among others) at once strengthen the arrangements and give it a more modern, uptown feel, while Fulson's vocals, rich without sounding heavy, certainly fit the boundaries of the soul idiom like a glove, and his guitar work is in fine fettle. Like a fine brandy, Lowell Fulson's best stuff manages to be potent and smooth at the same time, and that's just what he delivers on *Soul*. *—Mark Deming*

Tramp / 1967 / United ♦♦♦♦♦
Lowell Fulson's comfortably laid-back but groovin' soul-blues workout "Tramp" quickly became one of his biggest hits (and fared even better in a cover version by Otis Redding and Carla Thomas), and this album (released to tie in with the single's success) finds Fulson following a similar stylistic path. While most of *Tramp*'s tunes lean more heavily on traditional blues structures than the title tune, Fulson was obviously aiming for a funky ambience rather than the heavy emotional crush of the deep blues, and his clean, uncluttered guitar solos are warmer and more approachable than the typical Chicago-style axe work of the day. There's a sly playfulness to this material that's winning, and even the most down-and-out songs here display a light touch and creative intelligence that sets Fulson apart. Hardly a masterpiece, *Tramp* is still the sort of album to please fans and new admirers alike. *—Mark Deming*

Now! / 1969 / United ♦♦♦
Now! was actually comprised largely of 1967-1968 singles, filled out by three cuts which made their first appearance on this LP. It's loosey-goosey late-'60s blues-soul crossover, with a sassy attitude and adroit combinations of stinging blues guitar, strutting vocals, soulful horns, and organ, never heard better than on "I'm a Drifter." Actually, the record sounds better than much of his slightly earlier '60s Kent stuff because it's not as unduly repetitious, though it's filled out with cover versions of familiar tunes like "Funky Broadway," "Let's Go Get Stoned," and "Everyday I Have the Blues." Perhaps it wasn't cutting edge as far as late-'60s soul went, but it had some of the rawness of '50s electric blues and some of the slickness of late-'60s soul brass, and B.B. King-like horn charts, and the combination usually clicked. All of the tracks from *Now!* are on the Ace CD compilation *The Final Kent Years*, which also includes his 1978 album *Lovemaker*, a 1972 single, and three previously unissued cuts from around the time of the *Now!* sessions. *—Richie Unterberger*

I've Got the Blues / 1973 / Fuel 2000 ♦♦♦
I've Got the Blues is as simple and straightforward as its title as Lowell Fulson lays down tracks like "Teach Me," "Crying Won't Help" and "Stoned to the Bone" in his inimitable West Coast style. *—Jason Ankeny*

Lovemaker / 1978 / Big Town ♦♦♦
Lovemaker is not the most exciting Lowell Fulson album by a long shot. But it's respectable soul-blues, and not as inappropriately polished as the usual late-'70s recordings by blues veterans. Actually, Fulson was more in the straight-ahead blues bag by this time than he had been on his mid- to late-'60s soul-influenced records, including a couple of revivals of "It Hurts Me Too" (retitled "When Things Go Wrong") and "Sittin' on Top of the World" (retitled "I Am Not Worried"). The accent is on good-natured, straightforward urbane blues, the backing less passionate than Fulson's vocals, the groove sticking mostly to the midtempo, getting into mild funk here and there, particularly on the title track. All of the tracks from *Lovemaker* are on the Ace CD compilation *The Final Kent Years*, which also includes his 1968 album *Now!*, a 1972 single, and three previously unissued cuts from around the time of the *Now!* sessions. *—Richie Unterberger*

One More Blues / Mar. 11, 1984 / Evidence ♦♦♦
Fulson hasn't been as prolific over the last couple of decades as he was during the 1950s, but when he does get a chance to enter a studio, he usually emerges with some pretty impressive work. This 1984 album, first out on Black & Blue over in France, is no exception—the band is tight (Phillip Walker is rhythm guitarist), and Fulson came prepared with a sheaf of solid originals. *—Bill Dahl*

The Complete Chess Masters (50th Anniversary Collection) / Nov. 4, 1997 / MCA/Chess ♦♦♦♦♦
This is a two-CD, 45-song compilation that covers Fulson's Chess years, which spanned 1954 to 1963. Fulson didn't have a great deal of commercial success at Chess (the big exception being "Reconsider Baby," and which leads off this set), and his jazzy West Coast form of R&B/blues was considerably more polished than the electrified Delta blues for which Chess is most renowned. Most of this, in fact, was recorded not in Chicago, but in Los Angeles, where Fulson could work with combos more sympathetic to his style. You'd have to consider this Fulson's peak, however, and the two discs' worth of material is not excessive, due to the consistency of his material and vocal confidence throughout the decade. It's not without its weird moments of rawness, either, as in "Blues Rhumba," the Bo Diddley-esque guitar that opens "Please Don't Go," Willie Dixon's classic dirge moaning blues "Tollin' Bells," and the (deliberately?) out-of-tune guitar licks that open "K.C. Bound" with a bang. "Smokey Room" and "Be on Your Merry Way" were previously unreleased in the U.S.; "Father Time" and the alternate takes of "Lonely Hours" and "Check Yourself" were previously unreleased anywhere. *—Richie Unterberger*

★ **The Tramp Years** / May 16, 2000 / Ace ♦♦♦♦♦
The first of a planned series of three compilations devoted to Fulson's '60s Kent sides, this focuses on the chronological middle (and commercial peak) of his Kent output. "Tramp" itself, possibly Fulson's most well-known song (certainly to the pop and soul audience), leads off the disc, whose 24 tracks span 1966 to 1969. Much of the material shows Fulson to be one of the masters of blues-soul crossover (and one of the first to explore that sub-genre), his work the equal of somewhat more renowned artists working the field, like B.B. King, Albert King, and Little Milton. There's a loose and lean feel that sets this off—in a good way—from the beefier, more disciplined blues-soul outings recorded by Stax and some other labels. Possibly because this series is so thorough in its coverage, the material is not always top of the line; some of the outings are routine, going through the blues motions in songwriting if not performance. Still, more often than not this is a pleasure, both for Fulson's relaxed vocals and his contrasting stinging, fluid guitar licks. Half of the dozen of the tracks are previously unissued, including "It Takes Money," a song recorded right after "Tramp"; Fulson expressed annoyance in interviews that Kent withheld this from release. As another bonus for the committed collector, four songs ("I'm Sinking," "Blues Pain," "What the Heck," and "Price for Love") are presented in extended versions from their original issue. *—Richie Unterberger*

Black Nights / May 8, 2001 / Ace ♦♦♦
In the trio of Ace CDs that document Fulson's stint with Kent in the 1960s, *Black Nights* covers the first part of that era (although, confusingly, it was not the first of the reissues to be released). The 1965 release "Black Nights" itself was his big success of the period, stopping just outside the R&B Top Ten and even getting into the bottom of the pop charts. A brassy and sassy feel-good tune despite the sorrowful lyrics, it also features a guitar with a twang so unusual it verges on sounding rather like an electric sitar. It's the unquestioned highlight of a collection that documents a time at which Fulson was modernizing, but only slightly, his brand of urban blues. All of the material dates from the mid-'60s, much of it written by Fats Washington, though Fulson wrote a few of these numbers himself. It's well-constructed blues-R&B with adult lyrics and just a slight 1960s soul influence (especially in some of the horn arrangements). It sounds like it could have been recorded in the 1950s, which is not so much of a drawback as the midtempo similarity of many of the songs to each other, and the lack of many tunes on the same level as "Black Nights." The guitar still stings admirably, though. Two of the songs were previously unissued. *—Richie Unterberger*

The Final Kent Years / Feb. 19, 2002 / Ace ♦♦♦♦
The last of Ace's three compilations devoted to Fulson's Kent product basically combines his late-'60s *Now!* album with his 1978 *Lovemaker* album, adding three unissued cuts and a 1972 single. *Now!* was actually comprised largely of 1967-1968 singles, and it's this material, which takes up the first half of the CD, that holds up best. It's loosey-goosey late-'60s blues/soul crossover with a sassy attitude and adroit combinations of stinging blues guitar, strutting vocals, soulful horns, and organ, never heard better than on the opening "I'm a Drifter." Actually the *Now!* cuts sound better in this grouping than much of his slightly earlier '60s Kent stuff, because they're not as unduly repetitious, though they're filled out with cover versions of familiar tunes like "Funky Broadway," "Let's Go Get Stoned," and "Everyday I Have the Blues." Perhaps it wasn't cutting edge as far as late-'60s soul went, but it had some of the rawness of '50s electric blues and some of the slickness of late-'60s soul brass and B.B. King-like horn charts, and the combination usually clicked. *Lovemaker*, actually issued on the Big Town label (which like Kent was run by the Bihari brothers), isn't as interesting. But it's respectable soul-blues, and not as inappropriately polished as the usual late-'70s recordings by blues veterans. The 1972 single "Let's Talk It Over" (aka "Come Back Baby")/"Worried Life" is passable, as are the three previously unissued tracks (including a remake of "Blue Shadows") that date from around the time of the *Now!* LP. *—Richie Unterberger*

The Funk Brothers

f. Detroit, MI
Group / Motown
The Funk Brothers were the brilliant but anonymous studio band responsible for the instrumental backing on countless Motown records from 1959 up to the company's move to Los Angeles in 1972. Woefully underappreciated as architects of the fabled "Motown sound," the individual musicians were rarely credited on the records that relied upon their performances, which downplayed their importance to the label. Motown's sophisticated, urbane brand of R&B certainly would have been difficult to achieve without the extensive jazz training that many of the Funk Brothers brought to the table. In order to keep that sound a distinctive brand name, Motown signed most of the group to exclusive, highly restrictive contracts during their tenure, although a few peripheral members were able to moonlight on sessions for other companies from time to time. In more recent years, the Funk Brothers' legacy has begun to receive proper attention, most notably in Allen Slutsky's 1989 book *Standing in the Shadows of Motown*, which focused on bass genius James Jamerson, and the 2002 documentary film of the same name, which covered the group as a whole.

Motown head Berry Gordy Jr. first assembled a studio band in 1959, culling its members from Detroit's fertile club scene. Most of the players came from a jazz background, although some had more experience with blues or R&B, and there was a great deal of crossover among working musicians of the time. Among the early members were pianist/bandleader Joe Hunter (not to be confused with blues balladeer Ivory Joe Hunter) and the rhythm section of bassist James Jamerson and drummer William "Benny" Benjamin, who would go on to become the backbone of the Motown beat. Other regulars who came on board prior to 1962 were guitarists Robert White, Eddie Willis, and Joe Messina, alternate drummer Richard "Pistol" Allen, percussionists Jack Ashford (who handled the tambourine work) and Eddie "Bongo" Brown, and the aggressive pianist Earl Van Dyke, as well as numerous horn players. Eventually nicknamed the Funk Brothers, this aggregation would soon become an integral part of Motown's rise to prominence and its commercial dominance during the glory years of 1963-1967. By 1964, Hunter had quit as bandleader, paving the way for classically trained keyboardist Johnny Griffith to join, and for Van Dyke to become the group leader; drummer Uriel Jones also became an active member around the same time. In addition to the numerous hit singles they played on, the Funk Brothers also played quite often around the Detroit club scene.

Things began to change over 1967-1968. The Motown hit factory was forced to reinvent its sound to fit changing trends, and with producer Norman Whitfield's brand of psychedelic soul guiding the label's fortunes, guitarists Dennis Coffey and Wah Wah Watson came on board to update the Funk Brothers' sound. Moreover, the groundbreaking rhythm section of James Jamerson and Benny Benjamin was coming apart due to substance abuse problems. Benjamin passed away in 1968, and Jones took a much greater role in the aftermath of his death. Meanwhile, the massively influential Jamerson had grown unreliable; while he still performed, white bassist Bob Babbitt picked up much of his slack, and did an excellent job of replicating Jamerson's unpredictable melodicism. This core group remained together until 1972, when Gordy moved the Motown offices to Los Angeles, unceremoniously abandoning the Funk Brothers. Still, the group did get one glorious last hurrah in Marvin Gaye's 1971 masterpiece *What's Going On*, which made full use of the band's jazz training (and listed full musician credits).

Some of the Funk Brothers went on to other session and backup gigs, while others soon drifted out of the music business; regardless, most of them remained in Detroit. James Jamerson passed away in 1983, and only received wider recognition posthumously; he was finally inducted into the Rock and Roll Hall of Fame in 2000 in the sideman category. Eddie "Bongo" Brown also died in 1983; Earl Van Dyke passed on in 1992, and Robert White did the same in 1994. The surviving core members of the Funk Brothers reunited for Paul Justman's documentary *Standing in the Shadows of Motown*, which was released in 2002 to generally excellent reviews; the same year, however, Richard "Pistol" Allen and Johnny Griffith both passed away. *—Steve Huey*

• **Standing in the Shadows of Motown [Original Soundtrack]** / Sep. 24, 2002 / Hip-O ♦♦♦♦

During Paul Justman's film documentary *Standing in the Shadows of Motown*, based on Al Slutsky's book of the same name about the session musicians who played on Motown recordings in Detroit from the late '50s to the early '70s, one of the interviewees is heard to comment that once those musicians, who dubbed themselves the Funk Brothers, finished cutting a backing track, it almost didn't matter who sang over it. It is no criticism of the singers who appear on this soundtrack album, which consists mainly of the new performances of Motown hits that punctuate the film, to say that the music heard here bears that observation out. The singers have been well chosen for the songs. Me'Shell NdegéOcello, for example, offers a contemporary gloss on Smokey Robinson's "You've Really Got a Hold on Me" and channels Eddie Kendricks on the Temptations' "Cloud Nine," while Gerald LeVert makes like Levi Stubbs on the Four Tops' "Reach out I'll Be There," Joan Osborne lives up to Martha Reeves on the Vandellas' "(Love Is Like A) Heat Wave," and Bootsy Collins brings humor and outrageousness to the Contours' "Do You Love Me" and the Capitols' "Cool Jerk." But the legend on the back of the disc, "Starring the Funk Brothers on all tracks" is well put. This is a cohesive group, not just some studio professionals. The band is mixed louder and much more clearly than they were in the 1960s, when their sound was compressed, toned down behind the vocalists, and presented (at least on the AM radios on which it was most frequently heard) in mono. While the Motown sound was the product of its singers, songwriters, arrangers, and producers as well as the musicians who played the instruments, their contribution has been undervalued, and this recording demonstrates that amply. *— William Ruhlmann*

Funk, Inc.

f. 1969, Indianapolis, IN, **db.** 1976

Group / Soul-Jazz, Jazz-Funk, Funk

Highly regarded in soul-jazz circles, organ combo Funk, Inc. has specialized in a very accessible, groove-oriented blend of jazz, funk and R&B. The group was founded in Indianapolis in 1969 by organist Bobby Watley, who recruited tenor saxman Eugene Barr, guitarist Steve Weakley, drummer Jimmy Munford and conga player Cecil Hunt. In the early 1970s, the original lineup came to the attention of Bob Porter, a well respected producer who signed Funk, Inc. to Prestige and paved the way for the band to record five albums for that label. After stressing improvisation on its first three albums *Funk, Inc., Chicken Lickin'* and *Hangin' Out*, Funk, Inc. started to lose its way in the mid-'70s and turned to heavier production, more arranging and background vocals. This slicker approach led to tension within the group, and Funk, Inc. broke up in 1976. Watley continued to play live gigs on his own in the Midwest, and it wasn't until the mid-1990s that he would organize a new Funk, Inc. lineup. With Britain's acid jazz scene having focused attention on Funk, Inc.'s work, Watley organized a new lineup that included Hunt and newcomers Teddy Patterson (alto & tenor sax), Doug Swanigan (guitar) and Phil Brines (drums). Sadly, original members Munford and Barr had died. With this lineup in place and Funk, Inc. recording for Prestige once again, the band entered the studio in 1995 and recorded its first album in 21 years, *Urban Renewal*. It was also during that 1990s that Fantasy reissued some of Funk's 1970s efforts on CD. *—Alex Henderson*

• **Funk, Inc./Chicken Lickin'** / Apr. 17, 1995 / BGP ♦♦♦♦♦

In the 1990s, the popularity of acid jazz (especially in the U.K.) was great news for fans of Funk, Inc., whose 1970s Prestige dates had long been out of print. England's Ace label reissued all five of Funk's Prestige albums on CD, and in 1995, Fantasy combined the organ combo's first two albums, *Funk, Inc.* (1971) and *Chicken Lickin'* (1972), on this excellent 70-minute CD. When they first came out, both albums received their share of negative reviews from the more dogmatic jazz critics, who hated the idea of combining jazz with funk and soul. But the fact is that this material is infectious, captivating and hard-swinging. Funk, Inc. realized that jazz didn't have to be extremely intellectual to be worthwhile, and its mission (at least in the beginning) was to grab R&B fans with foot-pattin' grooves but expose them to the improvisational freedom of jazz. Soul-jazz tunes like "Bowlegs," "The Whipper" and "Sister Janie" were to the early '70s what the music of Count Basie, Jimmie Lunceford and Lionel Hampton had been during the swing era—improvisational party music that fared well among young African-American audiences. Other high points of the CD are B.B. King's "The Thrill Is Gone" and Sly Stone's "Running Away," both of which Funk really interprets instead of simply playing note-for-note covers. If you're getting into Funk, Inc. for the first time, this CD is the place to start. *—Alex Henderson*

Urban Renewal / Oct. 23, 1995-Nov. 9, 1995 / Milestone ♦♦♦♦

In 1995—21 years after Funk, Inc.'s breakup—organist and Jimmy Smith-disciple Bobby Watley decided to assemble a new edition of his gritty soul-jazz quintet. Two original members—conga player Cecil Hunt and Watley himself—were joined by saxman Teddy Patterson, guitarist Doug Swanigan and drummer Phil Brines. Watley unveiled his new Funk with *Urban Renewal*, a solid effort that, like such classics as *Chicken Lickin'* and *Hangin' Out*, effectively combines the immediacy of soul and funk with the spontaneity of jazz. Before its demise, the original Funk had deteriorated quite a bit by smothering itself with overproduction; but that's not a problem here. From the earthy, down-home blues themes of "Sneaky" and "Get Some More" to a commanding interpretation of Herbie Mann's "Memphis Underground," Renewal makes it clear that accessibility and artistic integrity aren't mutually exclusive. *—Alex Henderson*

Funkadelic

f. 1968, **db.** 1981

Group / Funk, Soul, Psychedelic, Psychedelic Soul, Hard Rock

Though it often took a back chair to its sister group Parliament, Funkadelic furthered the notions of black rock begun by Jimi Hendrix and Sly Stone, blending elements of '60s psychedelia and blues plus the deep groove of soul and funk. The band pursued album statements of social/political commentary while Parliament stayed in the funk singles format, but Funkadelic nevertheless paralleled the more commercial artist's success, especially in the late '70s when the interplay between bands moved the Funkadelic sound closer to a unified P-Funk style.

In the grand soul tradition of a backing band playing support before the star takes the stage, Funkadelic began life supporting George Clinton's doo wop group, the Parliaments. After having performed for almost ten years, the Parliaments had added a rhythm section in 1964—for tours and background work—consisting of guitarist Frankie Boyce, his brother Richard on bass, and drummer Langston Booth; two years later, the trio enlisted in the Army. By mid-1967, Clinton had recruited a new backing band, including his old friend Billy "Bass" Nelson (born January 28, 1951, Plainfield, NJ) and guitarist Eddie Hazel (born April 10, 1950, Brooklyn, NY). After several temporary replacements on drums and keyboards, the addition of rhythm guitarist Lucius "Tawl" Ross (born October 5, 1948, Wagram, NC) and drummer Ramon "Tiki" Fulwood (born May 23, 1944, Philadelphia, PA) completed the lineup.

The Parliaments recorded several hits during 1967, but trouble with the Revilot label backed Clinton into a corner. He hit upon the idea of deserting the Parliaments' name and instead recording their backing group, with the added vocal "contributions" of the former Parliaments—same band, different name. Billy Nelson suggested the title Funkadelic, to reflect the members' increased inspiration from LSD and psychedelic culture. Clinton formed the Funkadelic label in mid-1968 but then signed the group to Detroit's Westbound label several months later.

Released in 1970, Funkadelic's self-titled debut album listed only producer Clinton and the five members of Funkadelic—Hazel, Nelson, Fulwood, and Ross plus organist Mickey Atkins—but also included all the former Parliaments plus several Motown session men and Rare Earth's Ray Monette. Keyboard player Bernie Worrell also appeared on the album uncredited, even though his picture was included on the inner sleeve with the rest of the band.

Worrell (born April 19, 1944, Long Beach, NJ) was finally credited on the second Funkadelic album (1970's *Free Your Mind... and Your Ass Will Follow*). He and Clinton had known each other since the early '60s, and Worrell soon became the most crucial cog in the P-Funk machine, working on arrangements and production for most later Parliament/Funkadelic releases. His strict upbringing and classical training (at the New England Conservatory and Juilliard), as well as the boom in synthesizer technology during the early '70s, gave him the tools to create the horn arrangements and jazz fusion-inspired synth runs that later trademarked the P-Funk sound. Just after the release of their third album, *Maggot Brain*, P-Funk added yet another big contributor, Bootsy Collins. The throbbing bass line of Collins (born October 26, 1951, Cincinnati, OH) had previously been featured in James Brown's backing band, the J.B.'s (along with his brother, guitarist Phelps "Catfish" Collins). Bootsy and Catfish were playing in a Detroit band in 1972 when George Clinton saw and hired them.

The Clinton/Worrell/Collins lineup premiered on 1972's *America Eats Its Young*, but soon after its release several original members left the camp. Eddie Hazel spent a year in jail after a combination drug possession/assault conviction, Tawl Ross left the band for medical reasons relating to an overdose of LSD and speed, and Bill Nelson quit after more financial quarrels with Clinton. Funkadelic hired teenaged guitar sensation Michael Hampton as a replacement, but both Hazel and Nelson would return for several later P-Funk releases.

Funkadelic moved to Warner Bros. in 1975 and delivered its major-label debut, *Hardcore Jollies*, one year later to lackluster sales and reviews. The same year, Westbound raided its vaults and countered with *Tales of Kidd Funkadelic*. Ironically, the album did better than *Hardcore Jollies* and included an R&B Top 30 single, "Undisco Kidd." In 1977, Westbound released *The Best of the Early Years* while Funkadelic recorded what became its masterpiece (and arguably the best P-Funk release ever), 1978's *One Nation Under a Groove*.

During the most successful year in Parliament/Funkadelic history, Parliament hit the charts first with "Flash Light," P-Funk's first R&B number one. "Aqua Boogie" would hit number one as well late in the year, but Funkadelic's title track to *One Nation Under a Groove* spent six weeks at the top spot on the R&B charts during the summer. The album, which reflected a growing consistency in styles between Parliament and Funkadelic, became the first Funkadelic LP to reach platinum (the same year that Parliament's *Funkentelechy Vs. the Placebo Syndrome* did the same). In 1979, Funkadelic's "(Not Just) Knee Deep" hit number one as well, and its album (*Uncle Jam Wants You*) reached gold status.

At just the point that Funkadelic appeared to be at the top of its powers, the band began to unravel. As is sometimes the case, commercial success began to dissolve several old friendships. In 1977, original Parliaments members Fuzzy Haskins, Calvin Simon, and Grady Thomas had left the P-Funk organization to record on their own. In early 1981, they hit the R&B charts with a single called "Connections and Disconnections," recorded as Funkadelic. To confuse matters more, the original Funkadelic appeared on the charts at the same time, with the title track to *The Electric Spanking of War Babies.*

During 1980, Clinton began to be weighed down by legal difficulties arising from Polygram's acquisition of Parliament's label, Casablanca. Jettisoning both the Parliament and Funkadelic names (but not the musicians), Clinton began his solo career with 1982's *Computer Games.* He and many former Parliament/Funkadelic members continued to tour and record throughout the '80s as the P-Funk All Stars, but the decade's disdain of everything to do with the '70s resulted in critical and commercial neglect for the world's biggest funk band, especially one which in part had spawned the sound of disco. During the early '90s, the rise of funk-inspired rap (courtesy of Digital Underground, Dr. Dre, and Warren G.) and funk rock (Primus and Red Hot Chili Peppers) re-established the status of Clinton & Co., one of the most important forces in the recent history of black music. *—John Bush*

Free Your Mind . . . And Your Ass Will Follow / 1970 / Westbound ♦♦♦♦
It's one of the best titles in modern musical history, for song and for album, and as a call to arms mentally and physically the promise of funk was never so perfectly stated. If it was just a title then there'd be little more to say, but happily, *Free Your Mind* lives up to it throughout as another example of Funkadelic getting busy and taking everyone with it. The title track itself kicks things off with rumbling industrial noises and space alien sound effects, before a call-and-response chant between deep and chirpy voices brings the concept to full life. As the response voices say, "The kingdom of heaven is within!" The low and dirty groove rumbles along for ten minutes of dark fun, with Worrell turning in a great keyboard solo toward the end—listening to it, one gets the feeling that if Can were this naturally funky, they'd end up sounding like this. From there the band makes its way through a total of six songs, ranging from the good to astoundingly great. "Funky Dollar Bill" is the other standout track from the proceedings, with a great, throw-it-down chorus and rhythm and a sharp, cutting lyric that's as good to think about as it is to sing out loud. The closing "Eulogy and Light," meanwhile, predates Prince with its backwards masking and somewhat altered version of the Lord's Prayer and Psalm 23. At other points, even if the song is a little more straightforward, there's something worthwhile about it, like the random stereo panning and Hazel's insane guitar soloing on "I Wanna Know If It's Good for You," with more zoned and stoned keyboard work from Worrell to top things off. The amount of drugs going down for these sessions in particular must have been notable, but the end results make it worthy. *—Ned Raggett*

Funkadelic / 1970 / Westbound ♦♦♦♦♦
Funkadelic's self-titled 1970 debut is one of the group's best early- to mid-'70s albums. Not only is it laden with great songs—"I'll Bet You" and "I Got a Thing . . ." are obvious highlights—but it retains perhaps a greater sense of classic '60s soul and R&B than any successive George Clinton-affiliated album. Recording for the Detroit-based Westbound label, at the time Funkadelic were in the same boat as psychedelic soul groups such as the Temptations, who had just recorded their landmark *Cloud Nine* album across town at Motown, and other similar groups. Yet no group had managed to effectively balance big, gnarly rock guitars with crooning, heartfelt soul at this point in time quite like Funkadelic. Clinton's songs are essentially conventional soul songs in the spirit of Motown or Stax—steady rhythms, dense arrangements, choruses of vocals—but with a loud, overdriven, fuzzy guitar lurking high in the mix. And when Clinton's songs went into their chaotic moments of jamming, there was no mistaking the Hendrix influence. Furthermore, Clinton's half quirky, half trippy ad libs during "Mommy, What's a Funkadelic?" and "What Is Soul" can be mistaken for no one else—they're pure-cut P-Funk. Successive albums portray Funkadelic drifting further toward rock, funk, and eventually disco, especially once Bernie Worrell began playing a larger role in the group. Never again would the band be this attuned to its '60s roots, making self-titled release a revealing and unique record that's certainly not short on significance, clearly marking the crossroads between '60s soul and '70s funk. *—Jason Birchmeier*

★ **Maggot Brain** / 1971 / Westbound ♦♦♦♦♦
It starts with a crackle of feedback shooting from speaker to speaker and a voice intoning "Mother Earth is pregnant for the third time, for y'all have knocked her up" and talking about rising "above it all or drown in my own shit." This could only have been utterly bizarre back in 1971 and it's no less so 30 years on; though the Mothership was well on its way already, *Maggot Brain* really helped it take off. The instrumental title track is the key reason to listen, specifically for Eddie Hazel's lengthy, mind-melting solo. Clinton famously told Hazel to play "like your momma had just died," and the resulting evocation of melancholy and sorrow doesn't merely rival Jimi Hendrix's work but arguably bests a lot of it. Accompanied by another softer guitar figure providing gentle rhythm for the piece, the end result is simply fantastic, an emotional apocalypse of sound. *Maggot Brain* is bookended by another long number, "Wars of Armageddon," a full-on jam from the band looping in freedom chants and airport departure announcements to the freak-out. In between are a number of short pieces, finding the collective merrily cooking up some funky stew of the slow and smoky variety. There are folky blues and gospel testifying on "Can You Get to That" (one listen and a lot of Primal Scream's mid-'90s career is instantly explained) and wry but warm reflections on interracial love on "You and Your Folks, Me and My Folks," its drum hits distorted to give a weird electronic edge to the results. "Super Stupid" is a particular killer, pounding drums and snarling guitar laying down the boogie hard and hot, while "Hit It and Quit It" has a great chorus and Bernie Worrell getting in a fun keyboard solo to boot. *—Ned Raggett*

America Eats Its Young / 1972 / Westbound ♦♦♦
A double album and worth every minute of it, *America Eats Its Young* makes for a freaky, funky, and aware good time. Compared to the endless slabs of double-album dreck that came out around the same time from all sources, here Funkadelic brought life, soul, and much more to the party. With Clinton credited only for arranging and producing, here the mad cast he brought together went all out. Worrell in particular now had a new importance, credited as co-arranger with Clinton as well as handling string and horn charts on a number of songs. His surging, never-stop keyboards, meanwhile, took control from the start, with his magnificent lead break on the opening "You Hit the Nail on the Head" making for one of the best performances ever on Hammond organ. Bootsy Collins (credited as William) is also somewhere in the crowd on bass and vocals, while old favorites like Hazel and Fulwood, among many others, can be found. Perhaps to fill in the time, a few numbers from the first Parliament album *Osmium* two years before cropped up, namely "Loose Booty" and the hilariously sleazy "I Call My Baby Pussycat," here performed with a noticeably slower, dirty groove. The straightforward social call to arms appears throughout, with one song title saying it all—"If You Don't Like the Effects, Don't Produce the Cause." Other winners include the vicious title track, combining everything from mysterious, doom-laden voices and weeping wails to slow, sad music, and the concluding "Wake Up," while "Everybody Is Going to Make It This Time" is a lovely, gospel-informed ballad that heads for the skies and hearts. There are more mundane concerns as well, such as "There Was My Girl," a quirky weeper, and the weird if smoothly delivered "Miss Lucifer's Love," with more than one target in mind. *—Ned Raggett*

Cosmic Slop / 1973 / Westbound ♦♦♦♦
With a much more stripped-down version of the band, if the credits are to be believed (five regular members total, not counting any vocalists), Funkadelic continued its way through life with *Cosmic Slop.* A slightly more scattershot album than the group's other early efforts, with generally short tracks (only two break the five-minute barrier) and some go-nowhere ballads, *Cosmic Slop* still has plenty to like about it, not least because of the monstrous title track. A bitter, heartbreaking portrait of a family on the edge, made all the more haunting and sad by the sweet vocal work—imagine an even more mournful "Papa Was a Rollin' Stone"—the chorus is a killer, with the devil invited to the dance while the band collectively fires up the funk. Elsewhere, the band sounds like it's more interested in simply hitting a good groove and enjoying it, and why not? If introductory track "Nappy Dugout" relies more on duck calls and whistles than anything else to give it identity, it's still a clap-your-hands/stomp-your-feet experience, speeding up just a little toward the end. As for the band members themselves, Worrell still takes the general lead thanks to his peerless keyboard work, but the guitar team of Gary Shider and Ron Bykowski and the rhythm duo of Lampkin & Mosson aren't any slouches, either. Clinton again seems to rely on the role of ringleader more than anything else, but likely that's him behind touches like distorted vocals. Certainly it's a trip to hear the deep, spaced-out spoken word tale on "March to the Witch's Castle," a harrowing picture of vets returning from Vietnam—and then realizing that Rush ripped off that approach for a song on its *Caress of Steel* album a year or two later! *—Ned Raggett*

Standing on the Verge of Getting It On / 1974 / Westbound ♦♦♦♦
Expanding back out to a more all-over-the-place lineup—about 15 or so people this time out—Funkadelic got a bit more back on track with *Standing on the Verge.* Admittedly, George Clinton repeats a trick from *America Eats Its Young* via another re-recording of an *Osmium* track, namely leadoff cut "Red Hot Mama." However, starting as it does with a hilarious double soliloquy (with the first voice sounding like the happier brother of Sir Nose D'Voidoffunk) and coming across with a fierce new take, it's a good omen for *Standing on the Verge* as a whole. Eddie Hazel's guitar work in particular is just plain bad-ass; after his absence from *Cosmic Slop,* it's good to hear him fully back in action with Bernie Worrell, Cordell Mosson, Gary Shider, and the rest. In general, compared to the sometimes too polite *Cosmic Slop, Standing on the Verge* is a full-bodied, crazy mess in the best possible way, with heavy funk jams that still smoke today while making a lot of supposedly loud and dangerous rock sound anemic. Check out "Alice in My Fantasies" if a good example is needed—the whole thing is psychotic from the get-go, with vocals as much on the edge as the music—or the wacky, wonderful title track. There are quieter moments as well, but this time around with a little more bite to them, like the woozy slow jam of "I'll Stay," which trips out along the edges just enough while the song makes its steady way along. In an unlikely but effective turn, meanwhile, "Jimmy's Got a Little Bit of Bitch in Him" is a friendly, humorous song about a gay friend; given the rote homophobia of so much later hip-hop, it's good to hear some founding fathers have a more open-minded view. *—Ned Raggett*

Let's Take It to the Stage / Apr. 1975 / Westbound ♦♦♦♦
One of Funkadelic's goofiest releases, *Let's Take It to the Stage* also contains more P-Funk all-time greats as well, making for a grand balance of the serious and silly. Perhaps the silliest is at the end—there's not much else one can call the extended oompah/icing rink start of "Atmosphere." The title track is as much a call to arms as "Free Your Mind and Your Ass Will Follow" is, but with a more direct musical performance and a more open nod to party atmospheres (not to mention the source of one of Andrew Dice Clay's longest-running bits). The targets of the band's good-natured wrath are, in fact, other groups—"Hey, Fool and the Gang! Let's take it to the stage!" There's no mistaking the track that immediately follows makes it even more intense—"Get Off Your Ass and Jam" kicks in with one bad-ass drum roll and then scorches the damn place down, from guitar solo to the insanely funky bass from Bootsy Collins. It may only be two and a half minutes long, but it alone makes the album a classic. Hearing Collins' unmistakable tones is usually enough to get anything on the crazy tip, but "Be My Beach" just makes it all the more fun, as does the overall air of silly romance getting nuttier as it goes. "Good to Your Earhole" sets the outrageous mood just right—it's one of the band's tightest monsters of

funk, guitars sprawling all over the place even as the heavy-hitting rhythm doesn't let one second of groove get lost. Of course, there's also one totally notorious number to go with it, but "No Head No Backstage Pass" has one of the craziest rhythms on the whole album, not to mention lip-smackingly nutty lines delivered with the appropriate leer. *—Ned Raggett*

Hardcore Jollies / 1976 / Priority ♦♦♦♦

Funkadelic's major-label jump brought its version of life more into line with Parliament, though the crucial difference between the two—Funkadelic's guitars vs. Parliament's horns—remained intact. Eddie Hazel, as ever, is missed, but Gary Shider and Mike Hampton do fine work. Whoever peels off the concluding solo at the end of "Comin' Round the Mountain" deserves credit, even if it's sometimes flash for flash's sake. Similar exercises in feedback can be found on the title track and elsewhere, sometimes great, sometimes timekeeping. Still, after all, the album itself is dedicated "to the guitar players of the world," so it can't be said that Clinton & Company aren't keeping the proper focus on things. Generally things are fairly light on *Hardcore Jollies,* though a remake of earlier highlight "Cosmic Slop" retains the sharp sentiments, if not quite as strongly delivered as before (musically it's much more centered around the bass and drums, though things get duly crazed all around toward the end). Otherwise, the emphasis is on fairly clean jams and rhythms, with lower-key goofiness than before but still merrily out there. If it's not truly gone and great like *Maggot Brain* or *Let's Take It to the Stage,* it's still good listening at its best moments. "If You Got Fun, You Got Style" makes for a better chat-up dancefloor appreciation than most, while "Soul Mate" balances out obvious "want you bad" sentiments with squirrelly lead vocals that don't quite fit the subject at hand. And who could knock the use of the "there's a place in France/where the ladies wear no pants" melody in "You Scared the Lovin' Outta Me"? Pedro Bell does some of his best work ever for the cover and inside art, while the accompanying short story is hilarious. *—Ned Raggett*

Tales of Kidd Funkadelic / 1976 / Westbound ♦♦♦

Some leftover jams, songs, and funk pieces from the Funkadelic era. George Clinton was in the midst of moving Funkadelic to another label, and the Westbound folk released a bunch of vault material to get another Funkadelic album on the market. There were still some fine cuts, but the random element prevented it from being a great album because it lacked the thematic organization and vision Clinton provided for the concept LPs. *—Ron Wynn*

★ **One Nation Under a Groove** / 1978 / Priority ♦♦♦♦♦

One Nation Under a Groove was not only Funkadelic's greatest moment, it was their most popular album, bringing them an unprecedented commercial breakthrough by going platinum and spawning a number-one R&B smash in the title track. It was a landmark LP for the so-called "black rock" movement, best-typified in the statement of purpose "Who Says a Funk Band Can't Play Rock?!"; more than that, though, the whole album is full of fuzzed-out, Hendrix-style guitar licks, even when the music is clearly meant for the dancefloor. This may not have been a new concept for Funkadelic, but it's executed here with the greatest clarity and accessibility in their catalog. Furthermore, out of George Clinton's many conceptual albums (serious and otherwise), *One Nation Under a Groove* is the pinnacle of his political consciousness. It's unified by a refusal to acknowledge boundaries—social, sexual, or musical—and, by extension, the uptight society that created them. The tone is positive, not militant—this funk is about community, freedom, and independence, and you can hear it in every cut (even the bizarre, outrageously scatological "P.E. Squad"). The title cut is one of funk's greatest anthems, and "Groovallegiance" and the terrific "Cholly" both dovetail nicely with its concerns. The aforementioned "Who Says a Funk Band Can't Play Rock?!" is a seamless hybrid that perfectly encapsulates the band's musical agenda, while "Into You" is one of their few truly successful slow numbers. The original LP included a three-song bonus EP featuring the heavy riff rock of "Lunchmeataphobia," an unnecessary instrumental version of "P.E. Squad," and a live "Maggot Brain"; these tracks were appended to the CD reissue. In any form, *One Nation Under a Groove* is the best realization of Funkadelic's ambitions, and one of the best funk albums ever released. *—Steve Huey*

Uncle Jam Wants You / 1979 / Priority ♦♦♦♦♦

Almost as if Clinton and company wanted to atone for parts of *One Nation Under a Groove, Uncle Jam Wants You* takes not merely a more daring musical approach but a more forthright political stance. The cover art alone is brilliant, front and back showing Clinton in Huey P. Newton's famous Black Panther pose. The main goal is the cover subtitle's stated claim to "rescue dance music 'from the blahs,'" and "Uncle Jam" itself does a pretty funny job at doing that, starting out like a parody of patriotic recruitment ads before hitting its full, funky stride. It's still very much a disco effort, but one overtly spiking the brew even more than before with P-Funk's own particular recipe, mock drill instructors calling out dance commands and so forth. The absolute winner and most famous track, without question, is the 15-minute deep groove of "(Not Just) Knee Deep." It'd be legend alone for being the musical basis for De La Soul's astonishing breakthrough a decade later with "Me, Myself and I," but on its own it predates the mutation of disco into electro thanks to the stiff beat and Worrell's crazy keyboards. Elsewhere there are pleasant enough jams like "Field Maneuvers," kicking around some good guitar work amidst the hop-and-skip beat, and the weepy ballad "Holly Wants to Go to California," intentionally undercut by all the cheering and noise deep in the mix. It's not to say that Funkadelic hasn't left the entire world of coke spoons and pointing to the sky behind them, as "Freak of the Week" shows, which isn't entirely far off from the early Sugar Hill party/zodiac aesthetic. Then again, lines like "disco-sadistic, that one beat up and down, it just won't do" amidst the whistles and screams have their own impact. *—Ned Raggett*

Connections & Disconnections / 1981 / LAX ♦

Original Parliament members Fuzzy Haskins, Calvin Simon, and Grady Thomas left the fold for 1981's *Connections & Disconnections,* also billed as Funkadelic but in fact containing no contributions by George Clinton. Though the trio spend most of the album criticizing Clinton's shifty business practices (which may be quite valid), the only thing that comes through is how much they need his production expertise. Never quite terrible, *Connections & Disconnections* makes small claims at mediocrity on scattered tracks. [Eleven years later, the album was re-released on CD as *Who's a Funkadelic?*] *—John Bush*

The Electric Spanking of War Babies / 1981 / Priority ♦♦♦♦♦

With George Clinton, a humorous phrase could be nothing more than playful tomfoolery, or it could be a double entendre with a deep political meaning. The phrase "electric spanking of war babies" falls into the latter category—it referred to what the funk innovator saw as the U.S. government using the media to promote imperialistic wars. To Clinton, the American media functioned as a propaganda machine during wartime. But whether or not one cares to examine its hidden political messages, *Electric Spanking* is an above-average party album. *Spanking* falls short of the excellence of *One Nation Under a Groove* and *Uncle Jam Wants You* and didn't boast a major hit single, but amusing funk smokers like "Electro-Cuties" and "Funk Gets Stronger" aren't anything to sneeze at, nor is the reggae-influenced "Shockwaves." *Spanking* turned out to be the last album Clinton would produce under the name Funkadelic—when he hit the charts again in 1983, Mr. P-Funk was billing himself as a "solo artist." *—Alex Henderson*

Who's a Funkadelic? / 1981 / Rhino ♦

Who's a Funkadelic? is a 1992 CD re-release of the 1981 album recorded by original Parliament members Fuzzy Haskins, Calvin Simon, and Grady Thomas, who left the P-Funk fold in the late '70s and later recorded *Connections & Disconnections* with no help from George Clinton. Though the trio spends most of the album criticizing Clinton's shifty business practices (which may be quite valid), the only thing that comes through is how much they need his production expertise. Never quite terrible, *Connections & Disconnections* makes small claims at mediocrity on scattered tracks. *—John Bush*

★ **Music for Your Mother** / Mar. 31, 1993 / Westbound ♦♦♦♦♦

Though *Tales of Kidd Funkadelic* brought together some oddballs and rarities from Funkadelic's early- to mid-'70s existence, it wasn't until *Music for Your Mother* came out that there was a full compilation of all the band's singles from birth to the mid-decade switch to Warner Bros. And what a compilation it is: Bringing together some of the band's best material as well as some of its craziest, *Music for Your Mother* does the business for any self-respecting P-Funk clone. Given that the focus is on A- and B-sides rather than album cuts, it isn't a truly exhaustive overview—that would require the inclusion of songs like "Maggot Brain" and "Free Your Mind and Your Ass Will Follow," for a start. It's a small quibble in context, though, especially given the inclusion of a number of songs that never made it onto the original eight albums. Most notable is a curious rarity, the semi-smooth soul "I Miss My Baby" single, which was credited to U.S., with music by Funkadelic (U.S. being a group led by eventual P-Funk guitarist Gary Shider). As for the other B-sides and uncollected numbers, they're an understandably mixed but often interesting bunch, including alternate instrumental takes of "Music for Your Mother" and "I Wanna Know if It's Good to You," the unreleased "Can't Shake It Loose" single, the gospel/feedback freakout "Open Our Eyes," and the hilariously titled "Fish, Chips and Sweat." The amazing bonus to the whole collection is the exhaustive 24-page booklet, reviewing the entire early history of Funkadelic via archival photos and a slew of interviews with the surviving participants. Plenty of fun tales are told, but George Clinton didn't participate—not surprising, given the unflattering picture eventually painted of him—while the depressing fates of Eddie Hazel and Tawl Ross get deserved attention. *—Ned Raggett*

The Best of Funkadelic (1976-1981) / Sep. 27, 1994 / Charly ♦♦♦

This 1994 Charly best-of functioned sufficiently for its time, but the label ultimately trumped it by releasing *The Very Best of Funkadelic* a few years a later, a double-disc collection that features everything here plus more. Besides just having twice the material, *The Very Best of Funkadelic* also featured a version of "Maggot Brain" and the full-length version of "(Not Just) Knee Deep." In sum, it's worth the extra money. In support of *Best of Funkadelic (1976-1981)* though, the collection does live up to its name, featuring all the mandatory moments from the four latter-day Warner albums. The album's primary flaw lies in its struggle to cram as many songs on the CD as possible, resulting in a highly edited version of "(Not Just) Knee Deep" that comes nowhere near approaching the original 15-minute version in terms of power or scope. Furthermore, the album also truncates "Uncle Jam," but this may arguably be a bonus since the song isn't one of the group's better moments. Get either *The Very Best of Funkadelic* if you can find it or go for one of the *Funk Gets Stronger* best-ofs, which are available in either double-disc or single-disc formats. In fact, it might be a good idea to just go for the LPs, starting with *One Nation Under a Groove* and then *Hardcore Jollies.* Chances are that a best-of will only make you hungry for more. *—Jason Birchmeier*

Hardcore Funk Jam / Dec. 6, 1994 / Charly ♦♦♦

Since there aren't many Funkadelic best-ofs widely available, and since there are even less that live up to their function, this single-disc best-of may have to suffice. Yet *Hardcore Funk Jam* isn't an ideal collection by any means. In fact, you'd be better off purchasing *One Nation Under a Groove* and going one LP after another from there. First of all, this album only culls its selections from Funkadelic's four latter-day Warner albums. And even worse, it manages to somehow skip over "(Not Just) Knee Deep," one of the P-Funk collective's undeniable best songs ever, if not *the* best. There are a few other songs such as "Electric Spanking of War Babies," "Comin' Round the Mountain," "Cholly," and the live versions of "Cosmic Slop" and "Maggot Brain" that are also noticeably absent. Any of these songs would be better choices than questionable inclusions such as "Uncle Jam" and

"Electro-Cuties," two of Funkadelic's more awkward moments. Still, from beginning to end, *Hardcore Funk Jam* is just that, funky and filled with great jams. There are better options out there though, such as the single-disc *Best of Funkadelic (1976-1981)*, the double-disc *The Very Best of Funkadelic*, or the *Funk Gets Stronger* collections. But again, an even better idea is to just head straight for *One Nation Under a Groove*—it won't disappoint you. That way you'll be positioned to slowly make your way through their better albums one after another rather than even messing with these inadequate best-ofs. *—Jason Birchmeier*

Live: Meadowbrook, Rochester, Michigan 12th September 1971 / 1996 / Westbound ♦♦♦

Not released until 1996, this was an unusual gig for the band, who were breaking in a new rhythm section (this may have been their first show) without much or any rehearsal. You can't tell from this 77-minute disc, which offers a typically amorphous, freefloating set of black rock—which is to say, judged by most standards, it's not typical music at all. Seguing from spaced-out jams to occasional numbers with vocals by George Clinton, and throwing in imaginative improvisations by guitarist Eddie Hazel and keyboardist Bernie Worrell, it sounds something like a combination of Jimi Hendrix, James Brown, and Sun Ra. The 14-minute "Maggot Brain" verges on prog rock/psychedelia (in the good sense), with its almost mystical guitar lines; earthier pleasures are offered with cuts like "I Call My Baby Pussycat" (two versions). The fidelity is pretty good, though the vocals lack the presence of the instruments. Funkadelic is still shown to their best advantage on their studio recordings of the era, but this is certainly a fascinating find for fans, augmented by detailed liner notes about the gig by Rob Bowman. *—Richie Unterberger*

Finest / 1997 / Westbound ♦♦♦♦

Contains their Westbound singles from 1969 to 1976, including Funkadelic's first significant single "I Bet You," co-written by George Clinton while under contract to Motown for five fruitless years. Motown never released it or any other Parliament song. Billy Butler's rendition of "I Bet You" preceded Funkadelic's stoner version. Guitars dominate every track, either as lead instruments or as electric wallpaper; Bernie Worrell's keyboard and synthesizer skills glue everything together. The erotic "I Wanna Know if It's Good for You" messes with your head for ten funky minutes. Worrell plays a multitude of keyboards on the musically happy "A Joyous Process." They emulate the Temptations on "You Can't Miss What You Can't Measure" by bouncing the lead around like a hot potato. "Red Hot Mama" scorches, "Hit It and Quit It" has an orgasmic, jerky beat. In-your-face openers "Let's Take It to the Stage" and "Get Off Your Ass & Jam" have been P-Funk concert staples for more than 25 years. "Cosmic Slop" and "Undisco Kidd" display a trend toward commercialism that crystallized and paid dividends on *One Nation Under a Groove*. A live version of "Maggot Brain" featuring guitarist Michael Hampton is a bonus. *—Andrew Hamilton*

The Very Best of Funkadelic / Sep. 30, 1998 / Charly ♦♦♦♦

Finding a quality Parliament best-of to start with is simple. In fact, the most difficult part is narrowing down your choices. Conversely, finding a quality Funkadelic best-of to start with is daunting. First of all, the group split its 11-year career between two labels, Westbound and Warner Bros., which makes assembling a career-spanning best-of a problem. If you want a compilation documenting the group's early years at Westbound, you have few options, none of which are comprehensive or easy to find with the exception of Ace's *Finest*. The group's Warner Bros. years aren't much easier to find documented. There are some single-disc best-ofs that have surfaced over the years, but they're inadequate. "(Not Just) Knee Deep" itself spans the course of 15 minutes, and many of Funkadelic's better moments such as "One Nation Under a Groove" aren't short songs either, meaning you only get a small sample of songs on a 75-minute single-disc best-of. So if you really want to hear what Warner Bros.-era Funkadelic was all about, it's recommended to find something more extensive or just buy the four Warner Bros. LPs. In terms of double-disc best-ofs, there's no better choice than either *Funk Gets Stronger* or *The Very Best of Funkadelic*, which are near facsimiles. The latter includes all the group's hits from the Warner Bros. era in unedited format, while focusing its attention primarily at the flawless *Hardcore Jollies* and *One Nation Under a Groove* albums rather than the less engaging *Uncle Jam Wants You* and *Electric Spanking of War Babies*. Because the band included live versions of "Cosmic Slop" and "Maggot Brain" on its Warner Bros. albums, you luckily get those pre-Warner Bros. classics here too. But what you don't get is any Westbound material predating the four Warner Bros. albums. In other words, this isn't exactly the one-stop you might hope it is. *—Jason Birchmeier*

Gwen Fuqua

b. Detroit, MI, **d.** California

Songwriter / Motown, Soul

Gwendolyn "Gwen" Gordy-Fuqua deserves a big footnote in Motown's history. Writing songs with her boyfriend Billy Davis, who often used the name Tyran Carlo, and hooking up with Berry Gordy Jr., the songwriters became a formidable team. They wrote for the Five Stars and Marv Johnson, among others, but found their biggest success when they wrote five hits in a row for Jackie Wilson: "Reet Petite," "Lonely Teardrops," "That's Why I Love You So," "To Be Loved," and "I'll Be Satisfied."

Gwen and Billy formed Anna Records (named after Anna Gordy, a limited partner), whose artists included Joe Tex, the Voice Masters, Johnny (Bristol) & Jackey (Beavers), Lamont Anthony (Dozier), Herman Griffin, and David Ruffin. Berry started Tamla Records around the same time, but the jocks greeted his endeavor with indifference. When Berry produced "Money," by Barrett Strong, he struck a deal with Gwen and Billy for national distribution, while Tamla handled the record in Michigan. Ironically, it became Anna's biggest record.

Problems between Gwen and Billy started before Leonard Chess (who distributed Anna) dispatched Harvey Fuqua, the former Moonglow, to Detroit to help out at Anna. Davis was on the road a lot promoting Anna recordings, and his absence made Gwen's heart wander. Harvey and Gwen fell in love, and Davis left to form Checkmate Records, which Chess distributed, taking Ruffin and recording "Mr. Bus Driver" and "Action Speaks Louder Than Words." Gwen and Harvey forged on with Anna.

Even with Harvey's hookups Anna had problems staying afloat, forcing Gwen to borrow $10,000 from Berry. Still, by 1961—after 28 single releases—Anna Records was history. Harvey and Gwen started Tri-Phi and Harvey Records, taking many of Anna's artists, and adding others, including the Spinners, Shorty Long, Junior Walker & the All-Stars, the Five Quails ("Got to Get to School on Time"), and the Challengers featuring Anne Bogan ("Honey, Honey, Honey"). Slow payment from distributors sunk the labels, and by the middle of 1963, most of their artists, producers, and writers merged with Motown.

Gwen became a main cog at Motown in artist development, where artists learn all the rules of etiquette; Harvey did a variety of jobs. Motown took off like a rocket after they rid themselves of the blues artists and session musicians, and brought in the jazzier sounds of the Funk Brothers and younger artists. Plus, they had people like Smokey Robinson, Holland-Dozier-Holland, Norman Whitfield, and William Stevenson & Ivy Hunter writing and producing monster hits. Staying in the background during Motown's glory years, Gwen also worked as a fashion model. Toward the late '60s her marriage with Harvey ended and she became more involved with the label. A prolific songwriter, she wrote "Distant Lover," with Sandra Green and Marvin Gaye, and has more than 75 songs to her credit, including "Lonely Teardrops," "To Be Loved," and "You Got What It Takes." When Berry left for Southern California, most of the Gordys followed except Esther and George, who remained in Detroit. Gwen lived in a fantastic house in Beverly Hills and threw legendary, lavish parties. She was financially healthy and owned the publishing to Anita Baker's "Sweet Love." She finally succumbed to cancer on November 8, 1999, in her San Diego home. *—Andrew Hamilton*

Harvey Fuqua

b. Jul. 27, 1929, Chicago, IL

Producer, Vocals / Doo Wop, R&B

Harvey Fuqua founded the seminal doo wop group the Moonglows, was a mentor to Marvin Gaye (co-producing "Sexual Healing" and Gaye's hit duets with Tammi Terrell), helped to develop several Motown acts, and helped launch the careers of '70s soul-pop group New Birth and disco superstar Sylvester.

Born on July 27, 1929, in Louisville, KY, Harvey Fuqua (the nephew of Charlie Fuqua of the Ink Spots) started the Moonglows with lead singer and fellow Louisville native Bobby Lester, Alexander Graves, and Prentiss Barnes. Mentored by legendary rock & roll DJ Alan Freed, the group appeared with Freed on his radio show, concerts, and with him in the movies *Rock, Rock, Rock* (1956) and *Mr. Rock and Roll* (1957). Originally called the Crazy Sounds, Freed christened the group the Moonglows. The Moonglows' first releases were for Freed's Champagne label in 1953. The following year, the group signed with Art Sheridan's Chicago, IL-based Chance label, scoring a regional hit with a cover of Doris Day's "Secret Love." When Chance folded that same year, label exec Ewart Abner suggested they try to get a deal with another Chicago label, Chess Records.

Their Chess single "Sincerely" parked at number-one R&B for two weeks, number 20 on the pop charts in late 1954. The group's "blow harmony" can be heard on other Chess hits: "Most of All," "We Go Together," the double-sided hit "See Saw," a cover of Percy Mayfield's "Please Send Me Someone to Love," and "Ten Commandments of Love," credited to Harvey & the Moonglows. The group's lineup consisted of former members of the Washington, D.C., doo wop group the Marquees: Gaye, Reese Palmner, James Knowland, Chester Simmons, and Chuck Barksdale on loan from the Dells.

In 1958, Fuqua left the Moonglows and label owner Leonard Chess suggested that he join Anna Records in nearby Detroit, MI. Retaining Gaye, he gave the other three Marquees members tickets back to D.C. and traveled to Detroit. While with Anna, Fuqua recorded Lamont Anthony (aka Lamont Dozier) and Johnny Bristol, two talents who would later have huge success with Motown. In 1961, he started his own labels, Tri-Phi and Harvey Records. On their rosters were the Spinners, Junior Walker & the All Stars, and Shorty Long.

Tired of the rigors of running a small independent label with no distribution or manufacturing edge against major-label competition, Fuqua was glad when Motown founder Berry Gordy hired him to head the label's artist development department, basically a charm school for the label's artists. He was assisted by Gordy's sisters Gwen (Fuqua's wife) and Anna, Maxine Powell, and Cholly Atkins and brought the Spinners and Johnny Bristol to Motown. Fuqua co-produced several hits with Bristol, all having a sprinkling of the Moonglows' sound: Gaye and Tammi Terrell's "Ain't No Mountain High Enough," "Your Precious Love," and "If This World Were Mine," in addition to former Temptations member David Ruffin's "My Whole World Ended (The Moment You Left Me)."

Around 1971, Fuqua left Motown and signed a production deal with RCA Records. Two acts signed to Fuqua's talent agency were signed to the label: the Nitelighters and New Birth. The Moonglows reunited in 1972 with Fuqua, Lester, Graves, Doc Williams, and Chuck Lewis. They recorded an RCA LP, *The Return of the Moonglows*, and a remake of "Sincerely." Fuqua reunited with Gaye in summer 1982, collaborating on the singer's *Midnight Love* LP, which included "Sexual Healing." *—Ed Hogan*

The Futures

f. 1968, Philadelphia, PA

Group / Philly Soul, Soul

One of Philadelphia's finest groups, the Futures made good music, but Lady Luck refused to work her magic on them. Frank Washington, Kenny Crew, James King, John King, and Henry McGilberry emulated the Temptations. Amjo Records released their first single in 1970, "Breaking Up" b/w "Our Thing." Richard Wright (deceased) sang lead on the Amjo side along with other members that, with one or two exceptions, differed from the previously mentioned names. Avalanche Records reissued the Amjo single the following year. The next single, "Love Is Here," appeared on Kenny Gamble & Leon Huff's Gamble label. It was a lovely Gamble & Huff song featuring a searing falsetto, McGilberry's deep bass, and weaving harmonies that only got spot play in a few cities; the Dramatics recorded an inferior version on their *10 1/2* album.

The Futures made a terrible career move when Gamble Records ended by signing with Buddah Records and missing a golden opportunity with Philadelphia International Records. Their first Buddah release, "(That's) The Way of a Woman in Love" b/w "Grade A Woman," dropped in January 1974 to a deafening silence. The second single, "No One Could Compare" b/w "You Better Be Careful," also failed to register. As they wallowed in obscurity, the O'Jays and Harold Melvin & the Bluenotes bloomed on Philadelphia International and the Spinners and the Stylistics reaped the benefits of their productions.

Buddah released the Futures' third single, "Castles," June 1975, which continued the string of flops. They issued the Futures' first album, *Castles in the Sky*, in 1975, which didn't include the first two singles and its promotion was almost nonexistent. Barbara Mason wrote their final Buddah single, "We Got Love," prompting a poorly promoted tour with Philly's First Lady of Soul.

They reunited with Gamble & Huff in 1978 at Philadelphia International Records, but the company's glory days were over. The first release, "Party Time Man," an energetic dancer with a terrific vocal, never charted high, yet was their most successful single. Its delightful successor, "Ain't No Time for Nothing," was succeeded by three more singles, including "Mr. Bojangles." Philadelphia International released two albums by the Futures: *Past Present & the Futures* and the obscure *Greetings of Peace*.

Warped Records issued the final Futures' recordings in 1982: "Let's Get to It" b/w "Young & Tender" and "Angel in Disguise" b/w "Betcha Come Back." McGilberry joined the Temptations in 1996, replacing Ray Davies, who replaced Melvin Franklin. *—Andrew Hamilton*

Castles in the Sky / 1975 / Buddah ♦♦♦
It's a mystery why Buddah would released this album and not promote it; they didn't issue but one single from the LP. Seven of the eight songs are Reginald Turner, Victor Drayton, John Bellmon, and Jerry Akines compositions, the talented Philadelphia singers and songwriters who penned "Don't Let the Green Grass Fool You," a hit for Wilson Pickett and the Spinners. They also recorded themselves under various names including the Formations, the Corner Boys, and Frightened Majority. Barbara Mason penned the other song, a funky jam entitled "Ninety Days (In the House of Love Correction)." There are some good songs including "Super Love," "(Love Lives on A) Windy Hill," and "Don't Close the Book." "Castles," in June of 1975, was the only single issued. A good catch if you can find a copy. *—Andrew Hamilton*

Past, Present and the Futures / 1979 / Philadelphia International ♦♦♦♦
Kudos to the producers, musicians, writers, and the Futures for this effort. The record business has problems when an invigorating dancer like "Party Time Man," fails to bust the Top 40. It was a minor hit in the Philly/New York area but ignored virtually everywhere else. Felix Hernandez played it at his Rhythm Revue Dance in New York recently and had to add it to permanent rotation. The storyline is about a guy who works hard all week, then transforms into a party animal on the weekends. "Ain't No Time Fa Nothing," is an excellent dancer with a killer intro and hearty vocals. Their five-man lineup resembles the Temptations' voices, from falsetto to the uncannily low bass of Henry McGilberry, who joined the Temptations in 1996. "Deep Inside Me" features the same excellent falsetto that led to their first Gamble & Huff recording "Love Is Here" (not included here), on Gamble Records in 1972. They romance that special lady on "Sunshine and You" and "Someone Special," two warm floaters. Also included is "I Wanna Know: Is It Over," a hurtin' tune with a spoken intro and refined harmonies. *—Andrew Hamilton*

The Greetings of Peace / 1980 / Philadelphia International ♦♦♦♦
The Futures' vocal blend ranged from deafening bass to piercing falsetto, giving them a musical quilt effect. But they lacked luck, timing, and adequate promotional budgets—the ingredients necessary for hit recordings—and they never achieved much acceptance. This LP was released cloak and dagger style; many don't know it exists. There's an update of "Mr. Bojangles," a rousing "We're Gonna Make It Somehow," an exquisite remake of "Silhouettes," "Peace," and the romance specials "Feels Just Like the First Time" and "I'm So Proud of You Woman." *—Andrew Hamilton*

● **Past, Present and the Futures/Greetings of Peace** / Mar. 3, 1999 / WestSide ♦♦♦♦♦

The Fuzz

f. 1970, Washington, D.C., **db.** 1972
Group / Smooth Soul, Soul
This Washington, D.C.-based trio, who originally were called the Passionettes, got off to a strong start on Calla in 1971 with the single "I Love You for All Seasons." It was written by their lead singer, Sheila Young, who teamed with Barbara Gilliam and Val Williams. The sentimental number was their only Top 10 hit. The followup reached number 14, but the third single didn't fare as well, and the trio disbanded shortly afterward. *—Ron Wynn*

● **The Fuzz** / 1971 / Calla ♦♦♦♦
The Fuzz were three teenage females from Washington, D.C. who scored with the lovely "I Love You for All Seasons," written by lead singer Sheila Young. "Seasons'" is a sentimental ballad with a loping bass line and a soothing feel; it's sweetly innocent and captivates you every time you hear it. The strings are tastefully arranged by Joe Tate. The other songs are all about love, and the Fuzz delivers these well-crafted tales in a mature fashion that belies their ages, including an eye-wetting rendition of "Ooh, Baby, Baby." Unfortunately, none of their other releases did much. "Like an Open Door" followed "Seasons" and had the same sweet, innocent sound, but did little to further their careers. *—Andrew Hamilton*

G

Earl Gaines

b. Aug. 19, 1935, Decatur, AL

Vocals / Modern Electric Blues, Soul-Blues, Retro-Soul

Best known for his 1955 R&B chart-topper "It's Love Baby (24 Hours a Day)," recorded with Louis Brooks & the Hightoppers, Earl Gaines was born August 19, 1935, in Decatur, AL. After growing up singing in church, he headed to Nashville at the age of 16, lured by the city's booming blues scene; there he signed on with local impresario Ted Jarrett, who helped book the young singer in clubs and landed him a number of demo recording sessions. Through Jarrett, Gaines was also introduced to Brooks, who soon tapped him to become the Hightoppers' lead vocalist; his distinctive tenor helped make "It's Love Baby" a tremendous success for the Excello label, and the group recorded a series of subsequent singles for the company before Gaines went solo.

He went on to record for labels including Deluxe/King, Hanna Barbera and Sound Stage 7, but by the late 1960s he was essentially out of the music business, working as a cross-country trucker throughout the next two decades. He resurfaced during the mid-'90s thanks to the efforts of Fred James, a Nashville-based producer whose affection for the classic Excello sound also resulted in the resurrection of onetime label staples including Clifford Curry and Roscoe Shelton; for Appaloosa, Gaines issued his 1995 comeback effort *I Believe in Your Love*, and in 1997 he also joined Curry and Shelton for a joint live recording. *—Jason Ankeny*

Everything's Gonna Be Alright / Oct. 20, 1998 / Black Top ♦♦♦♦♦
Earl Gaines started his career as the singer with Louis Brooks & His High Toppers, scoring an R&B hit in 1955 with "It's Love Baby (24 Hours a Day)" for Excello. More solid sides followed for Champion, Deluxe, Hollywood, Ace and Sound Stage 7 into the late '70s before hanging up his spikes. Not unlike his Excello labelmate Roscoe Shelton, he was lured out of retirement and cut new albums in the mid-'90s for Appaloosa and Magnum before cutting this one for Black Top in 1998. Smartly produced by Fred James, who also contributes all the fine guitar work, this leans more toward the blues than soul side of Shelton's musical equation, but his gritty style is best illuminated on tracks like "Is It Good to You Baby," "Two Lovers Are Better Than One," "Every Night of the Week" and the title track. With his vocal chops still in platinum shape, Gaines makes a strong showing with this one. Highlights include "You Put a Spell on Me," "I'll Carry a Torch," "Sittin' Here Drinkin'" and the humorous "Your Butt's Too Big." A winner every note of the way. *—Cub Koda*

• **24 Hours a Day** / Feb. 9, 1999 / Black Magic ♦♦♦♦♦
A 20-track compilation of Gaines' early tracks for Champion and his entire album for HBR produced by Hoss Allen. This is R&B/soul/blues from the late '50s to mid-'60s and Gaines' honeyed tones sound every bit as fine as they do on his Excello sides. The numerous highlights include "Best of Luck Baby," "Now Do You Hear," "Don't Take My Kindness For Weakness," and "Love You So." *—Cub Koda*

Lovin' Blues: The Starday-King Years 1967–1973 / Sep. 15, 1999 / WestSide ♦♦♦♦♦
The years covered on WestSide's 1999 compilation *Lovin' Blues: The Starday-King Years 1967-1973* are not necessarily among Earl Gaines' best-known or most-celebrated sides. The singles he cut in the late '50s and early '60s, primarily for Excello, form the core of his legacy, but this music is high-grade Southern soul all the same. It's in a similar vein as the Excello recordings, but it's clear that this is post-Stax material with the punchy horns and gritty rhythm section. The first part of the compilation is devoted to the 1969 album *Lovin' Blues*, which is a tight, passionate, unheralded minor gem of soul-blues, and then the rest of the compilation is devoted to singles and unreleased tracks. Some of this material is a little generic and faceless, while others are simply serviceable covers of R&B standards like "Sixty Minute Man," but it's all listenable and its completeness is certainly a boon to collectors. But the real reason to get this compilation (once you've already absorbed the Excello recordings, that is) is that *Lovin' Blues* is a fine Southern soul-blues record, worth seeking out by aficionados. *—Stephen Thomas Erlewine*

The Gallahads

f. Seattle, WA, 1957

Group / Doo Wop, R&B

The Gallahads—led by Jimmy Pipkin—are best remembered for "Lonely Guy," an enormous smash hit in 1960. Lead vocalist Pipkin, Bobby Dixon (first tenor and lead), "Tiny" Tony Smith (second tenor), and bass man Ernie Rouse formed this vocal group in Seattle, WA, in 1952, while they were still in junior high. At first they called themselves the Echoes, but by the time they traveled to L.A. to record for Del-Fi Records and the Donna subsidiary, they were calling themselves the Gallahads. The group had only three releases on Del-Fi, but each had enormous impact.

Their first single, "Lonely Guy," was released on both the Del-Fi and Donna labels, almost simultaneously. It proved to become an enormous smash, charting between June and September of 1960 and peaking at number nine in the Top Ten. In Los Angeles, it spent ten weeks at number one on the KFWB Fabulous Forty, the number-one station in town. It also charted at number 111 on the national pop charts.

By the time of their next release, the Gallahads' lineup had changed a little bit: joining lead singer Pipkin and Ernie Rouse were fellow Seattlite Ray Robinson and L.A.-based doo wop/R&B musician/arranger/producer Charles Wright, who also worked with label-head Bob Keane as an A&R man and produced and arranged recordings by Little Caesar & the Romans and other acts. The A-side, "Be Fair," was sung in classic doo wop style and generated a bit of controversy because the story involved a blind boy ("it's no fun being blind") crossing the street with his girl friend who realizes that while his girl is "holding my hand, she's kissing my best friend." It's not clear who objected to the song, but the single hit another snag regardless. Disc jockey Alan Freed, whose radio show was broadcast on L.A.'s KDAY in 1960, failed to compensate the Gallahads for a few scheduled appearances, so they signed a complaint with AFTRA (a musician's union). Freed not only dropped the record but influenced fellow DJ Dick Clark to do the same, and it quickly fell off the charts.

Pipkin's final Gallahads single failed to earn them airplay as well and the original group soon split up. By 1962, Tiny Tony Smith had formed the Statics, an integrated R&B group with Neil Rush on sax and his teenage wife Merrilee on keyboards. Meanwhile, the Gallahads name resurfaced again in 1964 with "My Offering," this time with Billy Burns on lead vocal and a white teen band called the Counts backing them up. The Seattle-based Pipkin continued to perform with an oldies version of the Gallahads. Tiny Tony died in the mid-'80s. *—Bryan Thomas*

Kenneth Gamble

b. Aug. 11, 1943, Philadelphia, PA

Producer / Philly Soul, Pop-Soul, Smooth Soul, Disco, R&B

In tandem with his partner Leon Huff, producer and songwriter Kenny Gamble was the principal architect behind the lush and seductive Philly soul sound, one of the most popular and influential musical developments of the 1970s. Born in Philadelphia on August 11, 1943, he first teamed with Huff during the late '50s while a member of the harmony group the Romeos, a unit which also included another aspiring area musician named Thom Bell, who would become crucial to Gamble's later success. "The 81," a 1964 single by the little-known Candy & the Kisses, was the inaugural Gamble-Huff co-production, and three years later the duo scored their first Top Five pop hit with the Soul Survivors' "Expressway to Your Heart." Soon recruiting the aforementioned Bell as arranger, they subsequently scored with smashes including Archie Bell & the Drells' "I Can't Stop Dancing" and Jerry Butler's "Only the Strong Survive," gradually forging their own distinctive sound.

Gamble and Huff's success on labels including Atlantic and Chess—as well as their own Neptune and Gamble imprints—spurred them to contact Columbia in the hopes of opening a new affiliate company, one inspired by the continued success of Berry Gordy and Motown. Columbia agreed, and in 1970 the duo's Philadelphia International Records was born. Given a $75,000 advance for 15 singles, with LPs budgeted at $25,000 apiece, Gamble and Huff soon exploded into the national musical consciousness, selling some ten million records in the span of nine months thanks to monster hits including Billy Paul's "Me and Mrs. Jones," Harold Melvin & the Blue Notes' "If You Don't Know Me by Now" and the O'Jays' "Back Stabbers" and "Love Train." Their signature aesthetic—an intoxicating combination of sweeping strings, smoky horns and insistent rhythms—emerged as the definitive soul sound of the early '70s, also becoming the blueprint for the rise of disco during the latter half of the decade.

Under Gamble and Huff, Philadelphia International launched hit after hit from acts including the Intruders, MFSB, and the Three Degrees. The bottom fell out in 1975, however, when the label became embroiled in a payola scandal; charged with offering bribes in exchange for radio airplay, Gamble was fined $2500, although Huff was acquitted. Probably not coincidentally, the duo's work began to suffer at much the same time, and as the decade drew to a sound their classic Philly soul sound began to grow stale and derivative. Hits became increasingly rare, although the 1979 McFadden & Whitehead single "Ain't No Stoppin' Us Now" was a significant return to form. Throughout the disco era Philadelphia International's most consistent hitmaker was Teddy Pendergrass, but in the wake of the tragic 1982 car accident which left the singer paralyzed, the career of Gamble and Huff began to dissipate as well, and they rarely resurfaced on record in the years to follow. *—Jason Ankeny*

The Gap Band

f. 1967, Tulsa, OK

Group / Funk, Urban, Quiet Storm

The first major hit for the Gap Band was a snazzy juke toon called "Shake." Just prior to the completion of their first album, Charlie Wilson cited the song for his brothers thinking they might ridicule the lyric. His brothers loved it though, and the song was a smash number-four single on the R&B charts, elevating the group to national status.

Born and raised in Tulsa, OK, the Wilson brothers began singing and playing in their father's Pentecostal church, and it was also mandatory they practice their music lessons at home as well. They learned various instruments which primarily included the piano. As much as they despised the lessons at the time, it proved to be a value tool for all three. With Ronnie being the oldest, he established his own band by the age of 14. Charlie, a few years younger, joined a rival band a couple of years later. One night the two bands were performing across the street from one another. Ronnie stopped by to check out Charlie grooving on the organ. While there, Ronnie asked Charlie to join his band for $50 over what he was making. Though Charlie's bandmates doubled his offer, he joined his brother's band, as Ronnie gave him no choice.

At a gig not too long after the two had joined forces, the group's bass player quit and Ronnie and Charlie summoned their younger brother Robert, barely 14, to the group to play bass. For a short while, the band performed without a name. Finally they began going by the name the Greenwood, Archer & Pine Streets Band. As advertising such a name on posters became too lengthy, the group shortened the name to the G.—A.—P. Street Band. Due to a typographical error, the group was advertised as G A P Band and it stuck. They performed at various venues around the Tulsa area, which included country western joints, tennis clubs, rock clubs and whoever else called on their services. However, by the middle of the 1970s, Charlie Wilson became interested in Los Angeles and left Tulsa to explore his possibilities. A short time later, Charlie convinced his brothers to join him. The group floundered about L.A. hittin' and missin' on record deals, gigs and the like. Still maintaining their interest, the group met entertainment businessman Lonnie Simmons through their friend, singer/musician D.J. Rogers. Simmons owned a nightclub and a recording studio at the time and signed the group to his company. (He would later start-up a record label.)

The Top Five single "Shake" followed in 1979, along with "Steppin' Out" (number ten) and "I Don't Believe You Want to Get Up and Dance (Oops, Up Side Your Head)" (number four) in 1980. The latter was inspired at a concert in Pittsburgh where some kids were chanting the groove and the Gap Band picked up on it. In December of 1980, the trio dropped their first number one single with "Burn Rubber (Why You Wanna Hurt Me)" and followed it with the Top Five ballad "Yearning for Your Love" (1981). The group went on to score three more number-one songs ("Early in the Morning" and "Outstanding" in 1982 and "All of My Love" in 1989), three more number-two songs ("You Dropped a Bomb on Me" in 1982, "Beep a Freak" in 1984 and "Going in Circles" in 1986) and a horde of Top Ten hits. They also did the soundtracks for Leon Isaac Kennedy's *Penitentiary III* and Keenan Ivory Wayans' *I'm Gonna Get You Sucker.* The group was given only 24 hours notice to complete the title song.

In 1984 Ronnie Wilson became a born-again Christian and started pastoring. He joined Melba Moore and David Peaston in the touring play *Mama, I'm Sorry.* Charlie Wilson has been one of most sought-after vocalists in the music industry. He has worked with Quincy Jones, Ray Charles, Eurythmics, Snoop Dogg and scores of others. The Gap Band has recorded for various labels, including Mercury and Capitol Records. The group has remained together enduring the good with the bad. *—Craig Lytle*

Magician's Holiday / 1974 / Shelter ✦✦

The Gap Band / 1976 / Tattoo ✦✦✦

Like L.T.D., the Gap Band didn't enjoy a major commercial breakthrough until its third album. Some R&B lovers think that 1979's self-titled *The Gap Band* (which contained the hit "Shake") was the combo's first album but, in fact, the Wilson Brothers had recorded two little-known LPs before that. First, they provided *Magician's Holiday* for Shelter in 1974, and in 1977 they recorded this self-titled sophomore LP for Tattoo. This record (which shouldn't be confused with the self-titled album they recorded for Mercury in 1979) wasn't a huge seller; in fact, most of the people who know the Gap Band for "Outstanding" or "Burn Rubber on Me" have never heard it. Nonetheless, this is a competent effort even though it is uneven and falls short of the excellence of the group's subsequent work. In 1977, the Gap Band wasn't as Parliament-minded as it would become a few years later—the funk that dominates this album is actually closer to Sly & the Family Stone, Tower of Power, or Stevie Wonder (who was a major influence on lead singer Charles Wilson). This LP isn't a masterpiece, although its best songs (which include "Knuckle Head Funkin'" and "God Is Watching You") indicated that the Gap Band had a lot of potential—and in 1979, the Wilson Brothers started living up to that potential. *The Gap Band* is far from essential, but from an historic perspective, it's interesting to hear what the group sounded like before Lonnie Simmons came into the picture. *—Alex Henderson*

The Gap Band / 1977 / Mercury ✦✦✦✦

Many Gap Band fans think that 1979's *The Gap Band* was the Wilson Brothers' first album, but, in fact, it was their third. Before becoming well-known, they recorded 1974's *Magician's Holiday* for Shelter and 1977's *The Gap Band* (which shouldn't be confused with this album, although both are self-titled) for Tattoo. However, this release marked several firsts for the Gap Band—it was their first album for Mercury, their first collaboration with producer Lonnie Simmons, and the first Gap Band album that was commercially successful. The funk gems "Shake" and "Open Up Your Mind (Wide)" became the Wilson Brothers' first hit singles, earning them a sizable following. And for the first time, the Wilson Brothers provided an album that was generally excellent instead of merely competent. This LP is, without question, stronger and more consistent than the Gap Band's previous albums of 1974 and 1977. The above-mentioned hits established the Gap Band as funk heavyweights, and yet not everything on this album is hardcore funk—equally appealing are tracks that range from the hypnotic disco number "Baby Baba Boogie" and the soul ballad "You Can Count on Me" to the jazzy quiet storm item "Messin' With My Mind." Now, here's the ironic part: As strong as this album is, it isn't as essential as the Wilson Brothers' next three albums. *The Gap Band* is impressive, but 1979's *Gap Band II,* 1980's *Gap Band III,* and 1982's *Gap Band IV* are even more impressive. Nonetheless, this album was definitely a major step forward for the Gap Band—both creatively and commercially. *—Alex Henderson*

The Gap Band II / 1979 / Mercury ✦✦✦✦✦

The Gap Band II has often been described as the Wilson Brothers' second album, but truth be told, it was their fourth. However, the vast majority of fans that they acquired with 1979's *The Gap Band* never heard the little-known albums they had recorded in 1974 and 1975. So even though that 1979 breakthrough wasn't really their debut album, it was the first Gap Band album that enjoyed a great deal of attention—arguably, that self-titled album was to the Wilson Brothers what *Meet the Beatles* was to John Lennon, Paul McCartney, George Harrison, and Ringo Starr. And with the gold *The Gap Band II,* they continued to forge ahead commercially and creatively. Produced by Lonnie Simmons, this excellent album boasts five-star funk gems like "Party Lights," "Steppin' (Out)," "Who Do You Call," and the Parliament-minded hit "I Don't Believe You Want to Get Up and Dance (Oops)." George Clinton and the Ohio Players are both strong influences on the funk tracks, while Earth, Wind & Fire's influence asserts itself on the smooth quiet storm slow jam "No Hiding Place." But the Gap Band never sounds like it is going out of its way to emulate any of its influences; in fact, the Wilson Brothers are recognizable and distinctive regardless of who is influencing a particular song. Even when they make a surprising, totally unexpected detour into pop/rock/soft rock on "The Boys Are Back in Town," they're recognizable as the Gap Band. Not to be confused with the Thin Lizzy smash, this congenial tune wouldn't have been out of place on a Billy Joel, Elton John, or Chicago album. But R&B, not pop/rock, was the Gap Band's forte, and *Gap Band II* is a funk/soul album first and foremost. It is also among the Wilson Brothers' most essential releases. *—Alex Henderson*

The Gap Band III / 1980 / Mercury ✦✦✦✦✦

When *Gap Band III* came out in 1980, the Wilson Brothers were widely regarded as true heavyweights in the funk field. Many funk experts will tell you that creatively, they were right up there with the likes of Cameo, Rick James, the Isley Brothers, and the Bar-Kays in the early '80s. Over the years, *The Gap Band III* (which was the group's fifth album, not its third) has often been described as the ultimate Gap Band album—and it's hard to disagree with that assertion. Produced by Lonnie Simmons, this exceptional album boasts three of the Wilson Brothers' biggest radio hits: "Burn Rubber on Me" (a funk classic), the Parliament-minded "Humpin'," and the quiet storm slow jam "Yearning for Your Love." But *The Gap Band III* is also full of gems that weren't big radio hits, including "Gash Gash Gash" (another funk classic), the perky, Earth, Wind & Fire-ish "Are You Living" and the ballad "Nothin' Comes to Sleepers." There isn't a dull moment on *The Gap Band III,* which is excellent from start to finish and is essential listening for funk addicts. *—Alex Henderson*

Gap Band IV / 1982 / Mercury ✦✦✦✦✦

This album featured a complete line-up of uptempo, midtempo and alluring ballads. The feature releases, in order, were "Early in the Morning," "You Dropped a Bomb on Me" and "Outstanding." The first two are energized numbers seasoned around horrific basslines and Charlie Wilson's dazzling vocals. Respectively, they peaked at number one and two on the *Billboard* R&B charts. Not as aggressive, the latter is a festive number paced an unorthodox percussive beat. It claimed the number one spot on the *Billboard* R&B charts as well. There were no other official selections to grace *Billboard.* However, every song visited radio, and rightly so. The sentimental numbers "Stay With Me," "Seasons No Reason to Change" and "I Can't Get Over You" have become standard among R&B radio. The latter features a sentimental flugelhorn exhibition by Ronnie Wilson. Mellow numbers always seem to retain that timeless appeal whereas uptempo numbers fade with time. This album is different; the uptempo numbers remain inviting as well. This is a great album. *—Craig Lytle*

Gap Band V: Jammin' / 1983 / Mercury ✦✦✦

The Gap Band had given themselves some big shoes to fill in the wake of their 1982 *The Gap Band IV* LP. It had, of course, spawned "You Dropped a Bomb on Me"—one of the defining songs of the decade and indeed of the contemporary funk genre. But with aplomb and finesse, the band returned the next year with *The Gap Band V: Jammin'* and only just missed its predecessor's number-one chart position. From the opening instrumental "Where Are We Going," *The Gap Band V: Jammin'* is a slick, smooth set dominated by some archetypal Gap Band classics. "Shake a Leg" is very typically Gap Band, with a superbly circular rhythm punctuated by bright horns. And, of course, Charlie Wilson's vocals always keep it all together. "I'm Ready if You're Ready," meanwhile, utilizes handclapping to keep the flow and is a sweet R&B-flavored song. "Party Train," a number-three R&B hit, sails the rails hard, complete with sound effects as Wilson calls "all aboard." Full and textured, this song is a dark little groover, leaden without any weight at all and completed with a Motown-esque subversion deep within the mix. It's the ultimate kicker for the dancefloor. Guest vocalist Stevie Wonder is a sublime treat on the LP's closer, "Someday," a tribute to Dr. Martin Luther King Jr., that showcases the band in a role not often associated with them—socially aware. Uptempo without the over-the-top grooviness that punctuates much of the Gap Band's output, it is pure inspiration and a moving moment to be sure. *—Amy Hanson*

The Gap Band VI / 1985 / Total Experience ✦✦✦

As the Gap Band's star power rose, they continued to dominate the R&B charts, even when their material didn't necessarily earn that honor. This is certainly the case with their 1984 LP, *Gap Band VI,* which patters across a set that is surely slick, and wonderfully sophisticated at times, but ultimately lacks the punch and fire listeners had come to expect from their earlier material. Even the guest vocals of fiery Brides of Funkenstein diva Dawn Silva couldn't add a spark. With quiet storm balladeering tempering pop, the most interesting song on the album, "Video Junkie," saw the band open with a snippet from the "Dragnet" theme—the Art of Noise wouldn't electronically co-opt the song until 1987—before zeroing in on some of the decade's more lithesome electronic antics, including synth drums and flashy guitar licks. It's surprising the song didn't chart. That honor went instead to "Beep a Freak." The song has some nice funk elements, and does highlight the '80s version of the cell phone, but it's just too sluggish to ever really catch fire. Elsewhere, two short, Eastern-inflected instrumental interludes preface the closing "The Sun Don't Shine Everyday." It's an elegant song that, while occasionally sounding like the Gap Band, looked toward Bill Withers' "Ain't No Sunshine" for inspiration. It is nevertheless one of their better ballads, quietly allowing empty space to carry emotion as surely as the vocals do. With several outstanding moments, then, *Gap Band VI* surely earned its number-one spot, with the filler simply filling in as passable pop. *—Amy Hanson*

Gap Gold: The Best of the Gap Band / Mar. 1985 / Mercury ✦✦✦✦✦
These three natives of Tulsa, OK, made up one of the consummate bands of the late 1970s and the 1980s. The Gap Band's brand of funk was explosive and colorful. From their first major hit "Shake" (*Billboard* number four) to "Yearning for Your Love" (number five), which was a preamble to the group's sizzling style of romance, they left a lasting mark on the music industry. "Stay With Me" and "Season's No Reason to Change" are the only two singles here never to hit the *Billboard* R&B charts. The former is an uptempo number with a delightful melody, and the latter is mellow, sentimental song with a universal appeal. Every other selection here was Top Five or better including three number-one singles: "Burn Rubber," "Outstanding" and "Early in the Morning." On each selection, Charlie Wilson's undeviating lead vocals are exemplary. The endowed singer's technique and delivery have come to be emulated by many singers throughout the music industry. This album covers the group's albums through 1985 as the latter half of the decade brought more hits. *—Craig Lytle*

The Gap Band VII / 1986 / Total Experience ✦✦✦
With their 1985 LP, *The Gap Band VII*, reaching a still-stellar number-six R&B, the band found themselves out of the very top of the charts for the first time in the better part of a decade. Still slick and sure of their intent, the Gap Band had reached a point where their material was beginning to become stagnant. But stagnant by their standards still equaled solid-gold hits by anyone else. With odd guitar slides and heavy bass wandering through the near-synth pop of the opening "Desire," the band cleaved their way right into the heart of the mid-decade mainstream, pausing only to take their softly strained R&B ballad "Going in Circles" to number two. But, for the band, it was quickly back to business across the eminently catchy tunes "Automatic Brain" and "Ooh, What a Feeling," leaving both "L'il Red Funkin' Hood" and "Bumpin' Gum People," which features funkier vocals than listeners had heard from the band in quite some time, to round out the set with some good-old Gap Band sonics. Elsewhere, the band pulled a quiet storm trick out of their bag on "I Know We'll Make It." *Gap Band VII* isn't a bad set. But, in light of what listeners would come to love this band for, it emerged strangely disappointing, and more sadly still, ultimately lacking the group's usual snap and fire. *—Amy Hanson*

The Gap Band VIII / 1987 / Total Experience ✦✦
Their third LP for Total Experience, *The Gap Band VIII* wasn't nearly as good as the Gap Band's heyday material, but nevertheless proved that they were still a markedly popular commercial entity. With lighthearted and high-spirited songs, the band continued to incorporate eminently danceable music within a loose funk framework. Although, by the middle of the decade, the emphasis was off the funk and on to a popped-out dance ethic, still it was a winning mix that allowed the Gap Band to remain one of the funk genre's most viable 1980s acts. This LP has two high points, the effusive jam of "Big Fun" and the funky "Get Loose, Get Funky," a sparking, fiery blast which has been sorely overlooked. Mixing cunning vocals, horns, and a rhythm slow enough for smooth grooving, the song breaks in and out of time between guitar and vocals, bass and drums. Unfortunately, the rest of the album is a fast downhill slide, packed with balladic and light R&B filler. They're not bad; they just aren't anything that couldn't have been recorded, and probably better, by a dozen other bands at the time. Sacrificing style for commercialism is a sin, but *The Gap Band VIII* is probably best left behind by all but the band's most die-hard fans. There are much better ways to experience the Gap Band—such as sticking with the early material. *—Amy Hanson*

Straight from the Heart / 1988 / Total Experience ✦✦
The group's final album for the Total Experience label wasn't among their most memorable. The vocals were lifeless, the production and arrangements stagnant, and there was little energy or inspiration in the musical backdrops. It had the sound and feel of something churned out to satisfy contractual obligations, and the Band moved on to Arista and then to Capitol. *—Ron Wynn*

Round Trip / Aug. 1989 / Capitol ✦✦
Long after its popularity had declined, the Gap Band was having an impact on the African-American music scene. The end of the 1980s found the funksters being sampled frequently by hip-hoppers, and it was hard to miss their tremendous influence on the extremely popular new jack swing outfit Guy. The Gap Band itself, however, had started to go downhill both commercially and creatively in the mid-'80s. When the Wilson brothers signed with Capitol in 1989, optimists were hoping to see them return to the top, but sadly, much of the old magic was gone. *Round Trip* isn't terrible, and tunes ranging from the seductive "We Can Make It Alright" to the hard funk of "It's Our Duty" and the single "Addicted to Your Love" are fairly decent. But play this high-tech recording alongside 1979's *Gap Band II* or 1980's *Gap Band III*, and it becomes obvious that the Gapsters were long past their prime. While those classics burned and exploded, *Round Trip* merely simmers. *—Alex Henderson*

Testimony / 1994 / Rhino ✦✦✦
This album is far from the Gap Band's chart-busting albums of the '70s and '80s. The title track is an inspirational ballad. The two most notable numbers are dance-oriented: "Come Into My Life" and "I Can Make You Dance." The former is midtempo and the latter is aggressively uptempo. While Charlie Wilson's vocals are still in tact, the material is no challenge to the gifted singer. Moreover, the album lacks that bite, the roar and the excitement that's associated with a Gap Band project. "Gap's Jam" and "Based on GAP" are primarily rap efforts featuring lesser known rapper Almighty Gee. As his delivery is precise, it does little to elevate this album. No singles charted from this album. *—Craig Lytle*

The Best of the Gap Band / 1995 / Mercury ✦✦✦✦✦
A collection from the Mercury funk lineup that covers the hits from the first five Gap Band albums. Every major hit that they had is included here. What one might notice is that all of the major hits ("You Dropped a Bomb on Me," "Burn Rubber on Me," "Early in the Morning," and "I Don't Believe You Want to Get Up and Dance") all sound surprisingly similar. This may or may not be a large surprise to everyone, but the bright note about their similarity is that the basic riffs and rhythms that they all use are extremely catchy. The energy that the Gap Band exudes in the midst of producing a song is stunning, and this compilation displays that to the fullest extent. For a basic introduction to the forms of funk that the Gap Band followed, this album would certainly suit any given listener. For those who only need one Gap Band album in their collection, this one also fits the bill perfectly. For die-hard fans who already have all of the band's albums, this one would probably only really serve as a summary. *—Adam Greenberg*

Ain't Nothing But a Party / May 5, 1995 / Raging Bull ✦✦

● **Ultimate Collection** / Feb. 6, 2001 / Hip-O ✦✦✦✦✦
This 19-track collection does come very close to fulfilling its promise of delivering the *Ultimate Collection*, delivering all the group's big hits—"Shake," "Burn Rubber (Why You Wanna Hurt Me)," "I Don't Believe You Want to Get Up and Dance (Oops Up Side Your Head)," "Early in the Morning," "You Dropped a Bomb on Me"—as it stretches through all of the Gap Band's recordings for Mercury/Total. In some ways, it might stretch a little bit too far, as it extends all the way into two 1990 tracks, but as a relatively comprehensive, far-reaching retrospective of the band at its peak, this fills the bill (plus, it's topped off by nice packaging and good notes by Sean Ross). *—Stephen Thomas Erlewine*

Don Gardner & Dee Dee Ford

f. Philadelphia, PA
Group / R&B, Soul
A male-female duo, Don Gardner & Dee Dee Ford reached the charts in 1962 with "I Need Your Loving," a Top 20 hit in the mould of Ike & Tina Turner. Gardner had formed a Philadelphia group called the Sonotones in 1952, but teamed up with Ford ten years later. After the success of "I Need Your Loving," several records followed with little success. *—Jim Worbois*

Need Your Lovin' / 1962 / Collectables ✦✦✦
A good collection from Don Gardner, although his hits came in duets with Dee Dee Ford. This has above-average sound, and while much of it is period-piece material, it's done in an earnest, soulful manner. He wasn't a first-line star, especially without Dee Dee, but was a good second-line artist. *—Ron Wynn*

Don Gardner & Dee Dee Ford in Sweden / 1965 / Sue ✦✦

● **The Very Best of Don Gardner & Dee Dee Ford** / Oct. 26, 1999 / Collectables ✦✦✦✦
Singing drummer Don Gardner and vocalist/Hammond organist Dee Dee Ford were knocking them dead at Small's Paradise in Harlem when they suddenly scored big with the call-and-response rave-up "I Need Your Lovin'" in 1962. This 26-track collection rounds up all the material recorded for Bobby Robinson's Fire label, all taken from sparkling stereo masters. Robinson augmented the duo with top-flight New York R&B session players, and their rhythmic core is what drives these tracks, proto-soul drenched in gospel. Well worth picking up. *—Cub Koda*

Taana Gardner

b. Newark, NJ
Vocals / Disco, Club/Dance
Vocalist Taana Gardner was one of the leading lights of West End Records, a New York label that released some of the finest and most influential disco during the late '70s and early '80s. At a very young age, the Newark, NJ-born Gardner knew that she wanted to act and sing. Her grandmother, a former opera singer, began giving her vocal lessons at the age of five. Before she hit her teens, she was already a playwright; her work was featured at the Lincoln Center and also at the Apollo.

Despite having such an accomplished background at such an early age, it was something of a fluke that she became involved with the disco scene. Producer and songwriter Kenton Nix had a song, "Work That Body," that needed vocals. An early instrumental version of the track had been auditioned and approved by the beyond legendary Paradise Garage DJ Larry Levan, and Levan immediately introduced Nix to West End (and part Paradise Garage) owner Mel Cheren. Cheren set Nix up, but the singer who was slated to record the vocals fell ill on the day they were supposed to be laid down. Nix's brother, who worked for Gardner's father, called up the Gardner household that day—Thanksgiving Day, 1978—and invited Taana down. Taana accepted, recorded her vocals, and also gained another gig that same day when members of Dr. Buzzard's Original Savannah Band overheard her voice and asked her to sing on the record they were working on. (This record actually turned out to be *Spooks in Space* by the Aural Exciters, released on Ze).

"Work That Body," remixed by Levan, was an instant hit at the Paradise Garage, sparking a succession of West End classics helmed by Nix, sung by Gardner, and tweaked for maximum dancefloor effect by Levan. "We Can Work It Out," "When You Touch Me," "Just Be a Friend," and "Paradise Express" came later in 1979, and the massive "Heartbeat" (the basis of Ini Kamoze's ubiquitous 1995 summer hit "Here Comes the Hotstepper," not to mention a source for several rap producers throughout the years) and "No Frills" both followed in 1981.

Gardner took a step back from the limelight for several years to devote time to her children. 1985 saw the release of another Nix production, "Over You," for the YES label. She released a production of her own around the same time for Next Plateau ("You Can't Keep Coming In and Out of My Life"), and a cover of LaBelle's "What Can I Do for You?" appeared on Elegal in 1992. In 1998, she teamed up again with Nix and West End for "I'm Comin'." Four years later, West End issued the *Anthology of a Diva* compilation. Gardner has also leant her skills to several acts, including Kool & the Gang, Peabo Bryson, Edwin Starr, and Harold Melvin & the Blue Notes. —*Andy Kellman*

- **Taana Gardner** / 1979 / West End ♦♦♦

Joanne Garrett

b. Chicago, IL

Vocals / Chicago Soul, Northern Soul, Soul, R&B

As a 15-year-old student at Chicago's DuSable High School, Joanne Garrett won a recording contract with Chess Records for finishing first in a Regal Theater talent show, no small feat considering Chicago's vast talent pool. The deal produced "Stay By My Side," a huge local hit, in 1966. She followed with Dee Clark's "You Can't Come In" (March 1967) and a remake of the Heartbeats' "Thousand Miles Away" (1968), with the Dells (uncredited) providing backing vocals on the A-sides. Garrett left Chess in 1968 to record for Duo Records and another label. With Andre Williams producing, she cut "That Little Brown Letter" backed with "I've Gotta Be Loved" in 1968 on Duo; later in 1968 she cut "One Woman," arguably her most popular recording. Chess emptied their vaults and released "It's No Secret" and "Unforgettable" b/w "We Can Learn Together" in 1970, but they were strictly local.

Despite her age, Chi-town producers recorded Garrett in a Dinah Washington-esque vein, but that changed on her sole release for Don Robey's Duke/Peacock setup in Houston, TX, where she waxed Barbara Hammonds' "I'm Under Your Control" b/w "Sting Me Baby"; it was her first record in three years, but the 1973 release duplicated her previous paltry sales figures and the Duke stay was brief. A final single, "Don't Abuse Your Faithful Love" b/w "Charlie Boy (We Got to Love One Another)," credited as The Rock With Joanne Garrett, appeared on Scorpio Records; it flopped, and sadly, after a good start, Garrett rarely saw the inside of a recording studio again. Her flops became popular Northern soul items. —*Andrew Hamilton*

- **Just a Taste** / 1969 / Chess ♦♦♦

Chess omitted Garrett's first two singles but added two excellent replacements: Aretha Franklin's "Ain't No Way" and Dionne Warwick's "Walk on By." Garrett's pretty soprano soars on the Heartbeats' "Thousand Miles Away" and is spunky on "Soul Town." Local hits "It's No Secret," "Depend on Me," and "Unforgettable" are tasteful Chicago soul. An excellent album that's nearly impossible to find. —*Andrew Hamilton*

Vernon Garrett

b. Jan. 18, 1933, Omaha, NE

Vocals / Retro-Soul, Contemporary Blues, Modern Electric Blues

Though a traditional soul singer in style, song content, and vocal approach, Vernon Garrett is actually a California-based performer. He has recorded for several labels, without much commercial luck, since the late '60s. His only R&B chart singles have been for Venture and ICA, both making the Top 40 but not rising past number 33. —*Ron Wynn*

- **Caught in a Crossfire** / 1991 / Ichiban ♦♦♦

The late Gary B.B. Coleman did a fair amount of blues and R&B producing at Ichiban in the 1980s and early 1990s. One of the albums he produced for the Atlanta-based label was *Caught in the Crossfire* by Vernon Garrett, a little-known electric blues and soul singer. Coleman was definitely an appropriate man for the job—B.B. King was a big influence on Garrett, and Coleman held King in such high regard that he named himself B.B. So Coleman and Garrett had a lot of common ground on 12-bar blues numbers like "If You Can't Help Me, Baby," "Drifting Apart" and "Bottom Line" as well as soul offerings (such as Denise LaSalle's "Love Me Right"). This isn't a remarkable album, but it's competent and likable. —*Alex Henderson*

The Gaturs

Group / New Orleans R&B, Deep Funk, Funk

The Gaturs were not as well known as the Meters and not as minimalist in their take on funk, but like that group they created a distinct sound based on the party atmosphere for which New Orleans is famous. Led by veteran session musician Willie Tee, the Gaturs' jazz-inflected funk and soul only made it to a handful of singles, but did pave the way for Tee's next project—as bandleader for the festive chants of Mardi Gras Indians the Wild Magnolias. —*Wade Kergan*

- **Wasted** / 1970 / Funky Delicacies ♦♦♦

If *Wasted* ended after "Gatur Bait," the third song, it would be a soul classic. Smooth grooves—in the best sense—that never let the jazz leanings take over, the Gaturs brought a less-drum-specific take to the New Orleans funky soul sound, complete with some great tambourine-shaking. Leader/keyboardist Willie Tee had scored earlier regional hits with "Teasin' You" and it's sound-alike follow-up, "Thank You John," two of the sweetest-sounding songs in the pimping songbook. By the time of these early-'70s recordings, Tee had played behind many of New Orleans' top artists, both on record and on-stage. His voice had also deepened. However, none of that can explain the vapidness of much of *Wasted*. Juxtaposed with standouts "Booger Man" and "Cold Bear" are downright boring lite-jazz vamps with lyrics that make many latter-day adult contemporary songs seem insightful. Just when you're ready to give up completely, the Gaturs sucker you in for some more with a decent track like "Funky Funky Twist." —*Kurt Edwards*

Marvin Gaye (Marvin Pentz Gay Jr.)

b. Apr. 2, 1939, Washington, D.C., **d.** Apr. 1, 1984, Los Angeles, CA

Vocals, Keyboards, Drums / Motown, Soul, Urban, Blaxploitation, Smooth Soul, Quiet Storm, R&B

One of the most gifted, visionary, and enduring talents ever launched into orbit by the Motown hit machine, the career of Marvin Gaye blazed the trail for the continued evolution of popular black music: moving from lean, powerful R&B to stylish, sophisticated soul to finally arrive at an intensely political and personal form of artistic self-expression, his work not only redefined soul music as a creative force but also expanded its impact as an agent for social change.

Marvin Pentz Gay Jr. (in the style of his hero Sam Cooke, he added the "e" to his surname as an adult) was born April 2, 1939 in Washington, D.C. The second of three children born to Marvin Sr., an ordained minister in the House of God—a conservative Christian sect fusing elements of orthodox Judaism and Pentecostalism that imposes strict codes of conduct and observes no holidays—he began singing in church at the age of three, quickly becoming a soloist in the choir. Later taking up piano and drums, music became Gaye's escape from the nightmarish realities of his home life—throughout his childhood, his father beat him on an almost daily basis.

After graduating high school, Gaye enlisted in the U.S. Air Force; upon his discharge, he returned to Washington and began singing in a number of street-corner doo wop groups, eventually joining the Rainbows, a top local attraction. With the help of mentor Bo Diddley, the Rainbows cut "Wyatt Earp," a single for the OKeh label which brought them to the attention of singer Harvey Fuqua, who in 1958 recruited the group to become the latest edition of his backing ensemble, the Moonglows. After relocating to Chicago, the Moonglows recorded a series of singles for Chess including 1959's "Mama Loocie"; while touring the Midwest, the group performed in Detroit, where Gaye's graceful tenor and three-octave vocal range won the interest of fledgling impressario Berry Gordy Jr., who signed him to the Motown label in 1961.

While first working at Motown as a session drummer and playing on early hits by Smokey Robinson and the Miracles, he met Gordy's sister Anna, and married her in late 1961. Upon mounting a solo career, Gaye struggled to find his voice, and early singles failed; finally, his fourth effort, "Stubborn Kind of Fellow," became a minor hit in 1962, and his next two singles—the 1963 dance efforts "Hitch Hike" and "Can I Get a Witness"—both reached the Top 30. With 1963's "Pride and Joy," Gaye scored his first Top Ten smash, but often found his role as a hitmaker stifling—his desire to become a crooner of lush romantic ballads ran in direct opposition to Motown's all-important emphasis on chart success, and the ongoing battle between his artistic ambitions and the label's demands for commercial product continued throughout Gaye's long tenure with the company.

With 1964's *Together*, a collection of duets with Mary Wells, Gaye scored his first charting album; the duo also notched a number of hit singles together, including "Once Upon a Time" and "What's the Matter With You, Baby?" As a solo performer, Gaye continued to enjoy great success, scoring three superb Top Ten hits—"Ain't That Peculiar," "I'll Be Doggone," and "How Sweet It Is (To Be Loved by You)"—in 1965. In total, he scored some 39 Top 40 singles for Motown, many of which he also wrote and arranged; with Kim Weston, the second of his crucial vocal partners, he also established himself as one of the era's dominant duet singers with the stunning "It Takes Two."

However, Gaye's greatest duets were with Tammi Terrell, with whom he scored a series of massive hits penned by the team of Nickolas Ashford & Valerie Simpson, including 1967's "Ain't No Mountain High Enough" and "Your Precious Love," followed by 1968's "Ain't Nothing Like the Real Thing" and "You're All I Need to Get By." The team's success was tragically cut short in 1967 when, during a concert appearance in Virginia, Terrell collapsed into Gaye's arms on-stage, the first evidence of a brain tumor which abruptly ended her performing career and finally killed her on March 16, 1970. Her illness and eventual loss left Gaye deeply shaken, marring the chart-topping 1968 success of "I Heard It Through the Grapevine," his biggest hit and arguably the pinnacle of the Motown Sound.

At the same time, Gaye was forced to cope with a number of other personal problems, not the least of which was his crumbling marriage. He also found the material he recorded for Motown to be increasingly irrelevant in the face of the tremendous social changes sweeping the nation, and after scoring a pair of 1969 Top Ten hits with "Too Busy Thinking About My Baby" and "That's the Way Love Is," he spent the majority of 1970 in seclusion, resurfacing early the next year with the self-produced *What's Going On*, a landmark effort heralding a dramatic shift in both content and style which forever altered the face of black music. A highly percussive album which incorporated jazz and classical elements to forge a remarkably sophisticated and fluid soul sound, *What's Going On* was a conceptual masterpiece that brought Gaye's deeply held spiritual beliefs to the fore to explore issues ranging from poverty and discrimination to the environment, drug abuse and political corruption; chief among the record's concerns was the conflict in Vietnam, as Gaye structured the songs around the point of view of his brother Frankie, himself a soldier recently returned from combat.

The ambitions and complexity of *What's Going On* baffled Berry Gordy, who initially refused to release the LP; he finally relented, although he maintained that he never understood the record's full scope. Gaye was vindicated when the majestic title track reached the number-two spot in 1971, and both of the follow-ups, "Mercy Mercy Me (The Ecology)" and "Inner City Blues (Make Me Wanna Holler)," also reached the Top Ten; the album's success guaranteed Gaye continued artistic control over his work and helped loosen the reins for other Motown artists, most notably Stevie Wonder, to also take command of their own destinies. Consequently, in 1972, Gaye changed directions again, agreeing to score the blaxploitation thriller *Trouble Man*; the resulting soundtrack was a primarily instrumental effort showcasing his increasing interest in jazz, although a vocal turn on the moody, minimalist title track scored another Top Ten smash.

The long-simmering eroticism implicit in much of Gaye's work reached its boiling point with 1973's *Let's Get It On*, one of the most sexually charged albums ever recorded; a work of intense lust and longing, it became the most commercially successful effort of his career, and the title cut became his second number one hit. *Let's Get It On* also marked another significant shift in Gaye's lyrical outlook, moving him from the political arena to a deeply personal, even insular stance which continued to define his subsequent work. After teaming with Diana Ross for the 1973 duet collection *Marvin and Diana*, he returned to work on his next solo effort, *I Want You*; however, the record's completion was delayed by his 1975 divorce from Anna Gordy. The dissolution of his marriage threw Gaye into a tailspin, and he spent much of the mid-'70s in divorce court; to combat Gaye's absence from the studio, Motown released the 1977 stopgap *Live at the London Palladium*, which spawned the single "Got to Give It Up (Pt. 1)," his final number-one hit.

As a result of a 1976 court settlement, Gaye was ordered to make good on missed alimony payments by recording a new album, with the intention that all royalties earned from its sales would then be awarded to his ex-wife. The 1978 record, a two-LP set sardonically titled *Here, My Dear*, bitterly explored the couple's relationship in such intimate detail that Anna Gordy briefly considered suing Gaye for invasion of privacy. In the interim, he had remarried and begun work on another album, *Lover Man*, but scrapped the project when the lead single "Ego Tripping Out"—a telling personal commentary presented as a duet between the spiritual and sexual halves of his identity, which biographer David Ritz later dubbed the singer's "divided soul"—failed to chart. As his drug problems increased and his marriage to new wife Janis also began to fail, he relocated to Hawaii in an attempt to sort out his personal affairs.

In 1981, long-standing tax difficulties and renewed pressures from the I.R.S. forced Gaye to flee to Europe, where he began work on the ambitious *In Our Lifetime*, a deeply philosophical record which ultimately severed his long-standing relationship with Motown after he claimed the label had remixed and edited the album without his consent; additionally, Gaye stated that the finished artwork parodied his original intent, and that even the title had been changed to drop an all-important question mark. Upon signing with Columbia in 1982, he battled stories of erratic behavior and a consuming addiction to cocaine to emerge triumphant with *Midnight Love*, an assured comeback highlighted by the luminous Top Three hit "Sexual Healing." The record made Gaye a star yet again, and in 1983 he made peace with Berry Gordy by appearing on a television special celebrating Motown's silver anniversary. That same year, he also sang a soulful and idiosyncratic rendition of "The Star-Spangled Banner" at the NBA All-Star Game which instantly became one of the most controversial and legendary interpretations of the anthem ever performed; it was to be his final public appearance.

Gaye's career resurgence brought with it an increased reliance on cocaine; finally, his personal demons forced him back to the U.S., where he moved in with his parents in an attempt to regain control of his life. Tragically, the return home only exacerbated his spiral into depression; he and his father quarrelled bitterly, and Gaye threatened suicide on a number of occasions. Finally, on the afternoon of April 1, 1984—one day before his 45th birthday—Gaye was shot and killed by the Reverend Marvin Gay Sr., in the aftermath of a heated argument. In the wake of his death, Motown and Columbia teamed to issue two 1985 collections of outtakes, *Dream of a Lifetime*—a compilation of erotic funk workouts teamed with spiritual ballads—and the big-band inspired *Romantically Yours*. (*Vulnerable*, a collection of ballads which took over 12 years to complete, finally saw release in 1997.) With Gaye's death also came a critical re-evaluation of his work, which deemed *What's Going On* to be one of the landmark albums in pop history, and his 1987 induction into the Rock and Roll Hall of Fame permanently enshrined him among the pantheon of musical greats. *—Jason Ankeny*

Soulful Moods / Jun. 8, 1961 / Motown ♦♦♦

That in the years after the release of this album Marvin Gaye became one of the greatest and most influential singers in the fields of soul and R&B is hardly a matter for discussion. What kind of impression the listening public might have picked up from this, his debut recording project, is another question as it is certainly an uncharacteristic collection, starting off with a whole run of standard numbers from the great era of American songwriting, before tossing in a couple of trivial numbers from the developing Motown stable, including a Berry Gordy number that compares most unfavorably with the Irving Berlin, Cole Porter and Rodgers & Hart numbers that surround it. Fans of saloon singing may be curious to know how well Gaye fares in this difficult genre, and for the most part these are fine performances considering the versatile range of his voice and the depth of feeling he brought to most of his performances. No, this is not Gaye with a fully-developed style, and it is hardly the innovative legend of *Let's Get It On* or *What's Going On* but there is nothing he could have been embarrassed about here. The studio musicians come up with nice arrangements of the material, sometimes even with hints of the punch they would bring to his later, chart-topping material. The label re-released this project years later with a new cover subsituting the artist's face for a jukebox, an unglamorous move no doubt intended to fool a hurried buyer into thinking they are getting a greatest hits package. *—Eugene Chadbourne*

That Stubborn Kinda Fellow / Jan. 31, 1963 / Motown ♦♦♦

Here is vintage Gaye and Motown, following all the formulas that made the label the '60s' finest record company. The title track was an instant classic and is still among his finest '60s uptempo tunes. The other cuts are just as fantastic, and any doubts anyone might have had about Gaye were immediately and forever quashed with this album. *—Ron Wynn*

On-stage Recorded Live / Sep. 9, 1963 / Motown ♦♦♦

While the selections and overall production are spotty, there's nothing erratic or uneven about Gaye's vocals. This was his third Motown album and first live date, and he sounded refreshed, energetic, and triumphant. This came close to equaling his late '70s live set done in London and is among the best '60s live albums that Motown released. *—Ron Wynn*

When I'm Alone I Cry / Apr. 1, 1964 / Motown ♦♦

Hard as it may be to believe today, at the beginning of his career, Gaye was far more interested in crooning jazz standards than singing soul music, and took every opportunity to vent his jazz pipes in the studio. However much he may have wished otherwise, just about every listener agrees that he was a great soul singer, but a mediocre jazz vocalist. This album, cut at a time when he was already a rising soul star, consists of ten pop-jazz standards and is really only of interest to collectors. Certainly it's competently done, but it's supper-club fare, in which Gaye comes off as a sub-Nat King Cole rather than his own man. The CD reissue, interestingly, presents the entire album in both mono and stereo versions. *—Richie Unterberger*

Together / Apr. 15, 1964 / Motown ♦♦

The idea for the pairing of Marvin Gaye and Mary Wells came from Paul & Paula's success with "Hey Paula." The thinking was that if two unknowns could go number-one pop, then two popular male and female singers would be a lock—well, not quite. The first (and only) single release, "What's the Matter With You Baby" b/w "Once Upon a Time," was a two-sided hit but didn't ace either the pop or R&B chart. Some stations played both sides, while others spun one side over the other, depending on the DJ's preference. Unfortunately, the hit single comprised two of few originals on the album. The other tracks are mostly lighthearted pop regurgitations that fail to bring out the best of either singer. Vee-Jay Records, who turned down "Hey Paula," had second thoughts and entered the fray with duets by Jerry Butler & Betty Everett. *—Andrew Hamilton*

How Sweet It Is to Be Loved by You / Jan. 21, 1965 / Motown ♦♦♦

This is another great album; Gaye was at this time Motown's finest solo vocalist (Smokey Robinson, Eddie Kendricks, David Ruffin, and Levi Stubbs were all heading groups). His vocal on the title track was both smooth and churning, celebratory and introspective. He could do no wrong during this period, regardless of content, tempo, or arrangement. *—Ron Wynn*

A Tribute to the Great Nat King Cole / Nov. 1, 1965 / Motown ♦♦♦

A wonderful album that got buried when it was initially released. Nat King Cole was a primary influence on Marvin Gaye for Gaye's entire career, and he got a chance on this album to display his affection for sentimental, romantic fare and his skill in singing it. *—Ron Wynn*

Marvin Gaye and Kim Weston / 1966 / Motown ♦♦♦

Although they weren't as great a team as Gaye & Tammi Terrell, the Gaye/Weston duo turned out a few solid numbers. The finest was "It Takes Two," a steamy bit of uptempo soul that came close to equaling any fast duet number Gaye ever made at Motown. The rest was well done, but not quite on the same level. *—Ron Wynn*

Moods of Marvin Gaye / May 23, 1966 / Motown ♦♦♦♦

After Marvin Gaye recorded tributes to Broadway and Nat King Cole in the previous two years, Motown fans may have had their suspicions raised by an LP titled *Moods of Marvin Gaye*. Yes, there are a few supper-club standards to be found here, but Gaye moves smoothly between good-time soul and adult pop. Most important are his first two R&B number ones, "I'll Be Doggone" and "Ain't That Particular," both from 1965 and both produced by Smokey Robinson. Berry Gordy's right-hand man also helmed "Take This Heart of Mine" and "One More Heartache," another pair of big R&B scores, and just as good as the better-known hits. As for the copyrights *not* owned by Jobete, the chestnut "One for My Baby (And One More for the Road)" certainly didn't need another reading, but Gaye's take on Willie Nelson's after-hours classic "Night Life" was inspired. Marvin Gaye was improving with every record, gaining in character and strength of performance, and *Moods of Marvin Gaye* is a radically better record than its predecessors. *—John Bush*

☆ **Marvin Gaye's Greatest Hits, Vol. 2** / 1967 / Motown ♦♦♦♦♦

Other than the *Anthology* line, this was for quite a while the best single album set featuring Gaye's early and mid-'60s hits. There isn't a dud in the bunch, but both the *Super Hits* and *Anthology* line give you more cuts, while the boxed set has more variety. But this isn't by any stretch a bad release. *—Ron Wynn*

United / Aug. 29, 1967 / Motown ♦♦♦♦♦

United was the first of Marvin Gaye & Tammi Terrell's three LPs, and quite possibly the best of the lot. Harvey Fuqua and Johnny Bristol handled the productions and gave the photogenic duo a slightly harder edge than subsequent productions by Valerie Simpson and Nickolas Ashford. Three blockbusters—"Ain't No Mountain High Enough," "If I Could Build My World Around You," and "Your Precious Love"—propelled the album to number 29 on the pop charts, the highest rating of any of the duo's LPs. Plus, you had treats like "Little Ole Boy, Little Ole Girl," a remake of Loe & Joe's little-known release on Fuqua's Harvey Records in 1962. "Two Can Have a Party" grooves from start to finish and could have been the fourth hit, but Motown thought otherwise. I like the duo's rendition of "Hold Me Oh My Darling," a song Tammi first recorded on her solo album; the stuttering chorus and bass backing voice makes it unique. You won't find two better ballads than "Give a Little Love" or the often-recorded "If This World Were Mine"; written by Marvin Gaye, the starry-eyed proclamation has become an R&B standard, and rightfully so. *—Andrew Hamilton*

You're All I Need / Aug. 1968 / Motown ♦♦♦♦

You're All I Need equals the debut of Marvin Gaye & Tammi Terrell in every way except chart position and newness. It reached number-60 Pop, which was a good showing but 31 rungs lower than *United*, their debut. It includes arguably their finest recording, "You're All I Need to Get By," a testament to their singing skills and the writing/producing talents of Nickolas Ashford & Valerie Simpson—and "Ain't Nothing Like the Real Thing" is no slouch either. The urgent "Keep on Lovin' Me Honey" is the lesser of three single releases, but a quality cut just the same, thanks in part to the twang in Tammi's voice on the uptempo pleader. Johnny (Bristol) and Jackie (Beaver's) "Baby Dontcha Worry" gets an update; Johnny & Jackie first recorded the chugger on Harvey Fuqua's Tri Phi label in 1962. As on all three releases, Marvin & Tammi perform one of Tammi's solo cuts; in this case, "Come on and See Me" takes a back seat to the original. "Memory Chest," an overlooked number, is one of their most charming ballads. *—Andrew Hamilton*

In the Groove / Aug. 26, 1968 / Motown ♦♦♦
Never overly reliant on the Holland-Dozier-Holland machine, Marvin Gaye weathered their departure pretty well, turning to Norman Whitfield (for the epochal "I Heard It Through the Grapevine") as well as Ivory Joe Hunter, Ashford & Simpson, Frank Wilson, and, for two songs, his own pen. One of Gaye's other R&B hits from *In the Groove*, the impassioned "You," is in the Four Tops style (it's patterned after "Reach Out"), while "Chained" is another brilliant performance and production of a sub-standard tune. The Brill Building standard "Some Kind of Wonderful" and "There Goes My Baby" were early-'60s throwbacks in sound and feel, quite a jarring effect in context. After "I Heard It Through the Grapevine" became one of the biggest hits of 1968, Motown re-released the LP as *I Heard It Through the Grapevine*. *—John Bush*

I Heard It Through the Grapevine / 1968 / Motown ♦♦♦

M.P.G. / Apr. 30, 1969 / Motown ♦♦♦
An underrated late '60s album, this one has sometimes been overlooked because it seemed like a generic throwaway. But it included some outstanding songs. Motown wisely has included it on their list of Gaye albums that got reissued on CD. *—Ron Wynn*

Easy / Sep. 16, 1969 / Motown ♦♦♦
Not as arresting as two previous albums, it only produced one bonafide hit, "Good Lovin' Ain't Easy to Come By," while the others spawned three each. Tammi became ill before this record was completed, and Valerie Simpson had to perform many of the tracks. Simpson is a good singer but doesn't have the charm, charisma, or sexy Southern drawl with which Tammi was blessed. A remake of Terrell's solo outing "I Can't Believe You Love Me" adds nothing to the original; likewise for lackluster renditions of "California Soul," "I'm Your Puppet," and "Baby, I Need Your Loving." "The Onion Song" has to be Ashford & Simpson's silliest composition despite its positive social message. Along with the hit, the best songs here are "This Poor Heart of Mine," an uptempo number and good workout for the duo, and "Love Woke Me Up This Morning," an endearing exercise in romanticism. Fans weren't awestruck by this release, its highest rating was number 184 on *Billboard*'s pop album chart. *—Andrew Hamilton*

That's the Way Love Is / Jan. 8, 1970 / Motown ♦♦♦
The title cut was another Gaye classic, while much of the other material was equally impressive. Gaye was beginning to become disillusioned with Motown, but that hadn't affected his album output or his singing. Anyone hearing this wouldn't have suspected that Gaye was about to unleash *What's Going On*. *—Ron Wynn*

☆ **What's Going On** / May 20, 1971 / Motown ♦♦♦♦♦
What's Going On is not only Marvin Gaye's masterpiece, it's the most important and passionate record to come out of soul music, delivered by one of its finest voices, a man finally free to speak his mind and so move from R&B sex symbol to true recording artist. With *What's Going On*, Gaye meditated on what had happened to the American dream of the past—as it related to urban decay, environmental woes, military turbulence, police brutality, unemployment, and poverty. These feelings had been bubbling up between 1967 and 1970, during which he felt increasingly caged by Motown's behind-the-times hit machine and restrained from expressing himself seriously through his music. Finally, late in 1970, Gaye decided to record a song that the Four Tops' Obie Benson had brought him, "What's Going On." When Berry Gordy decided not to issue the single, deeming it uncommercial, Gaye refused to record any more material until he relented. Confirmed by its tremendous commercial success in January 1971, he recorded the rest of the album over ten days in March, and Motown released it in late May. Besides cementing Marvin Gaye as one of the most important artists in pop music, *What's Going On* was far and away the best full-length to issue from the singles-dominated Motown factory, and arguably the best soul album of all time.

Conceived as a statement from the viewpoint of a Vietnam veteran (Gaye's brother Frankie had returned from a three-year hitch in 1967), *What's Going On* isn't just the question of a baffled soldier returning home to a strange place, but a promise that listeners would be informed by what they heard (that missing question mark in the title certainly wasn't a typo). Instead of releasing listeners from their troubles, as so many of his singles had in the past, Gaye used the album to reflect on the climate of the early '70s, rife with civil unrest, drug abuse, abandoned children, and the spectre of riots in the near past. Alternately depressed and hopeful, angry and jubilant, Gaye saved the most sublime, deeply inspired performances of his career for "Mercy Mercy Me (The Ecology)," "Inner City Blues (Make Me Wanna Holler)," and "Save the Children." The songs and performances, however, furnished only half of a revolution; little could've been accomplished with the Motown sound of previous Marvin Gaye hits like "Stubborn Kind of Fellow" and "Hitch Hike" or even "I Heard It Through the Grapevine." *What's Going On*, as he conceived and produced it, was like no other record heard before it: languid, dark and jazzy, a series of relaxed grooves with a heavy bottom, filled by thick basslines along with bongos, conga, and other percussion. Fortunately, this aesthetic fit in perfectly with the style of long-time Motown sessionmen like bassist James Jamerson and guitarist Joe Messina. When the Funk Brothers were, for once, allowed the opportunity to work in relaxed, open proceedings, they produced the best work of their careers (and indeed, they recognized its importance before any of the Motown executives). Jamerson's playing on "Inner City Blues (Make Me Wanna Holler)" functions as the low-end foundation but also its melodic hook, while an improvisatory jam by Eli Fountain on alto sax furnished the album's opening flourish. (Much credit goes to Gaye himself for seizing on these often tossed-off lines as precious; indeed, he spent more time down in the Snakepit than he did in the control room.) Just as he'd hoped it would be, *What's Going On* was Marvin Gaye's masterwork, the most perfect expression of an artist's hope, anger, and concern ever recorded. *—John Bush*

Trouble Man / Dec. 8, 1972 / Motown ♦♦♦
Marvin Gaye turned to soundtracks in the early '70s, and came out with one that ranked right alongside the epic scores done by Curtis Mayfield and Isaac Hayes. The film itself was a typical '70s "blaxploitation" effort, but Gaye's vocals, seamless production, and a nice mix of uptempo funk, light ballads, and pseudo-macho camp were brilliant. *—Ron Wynn*

☆ **Let's Get It On** / Aug. 28, 1973 / Motown ♦♦♦♦♦
After brilliantly surveying the social, political, and spiritual landscape with *What's Going On*, Marvin Gaye turned to more intimate matters with *Let's Get It On*, a record unparalleled in its sheer sensuality and carnal energy. Always a sexually charged performer, Gaye's passions reach their boiling point on tracks like the magnificent title hit (a number-one smash) and "You Sure Love to Ball;" silky and shimmering, the music is seductive in the most literal sense, its fluid grooves so perfectly designed for romance as to border on parody. With each performance laced with innuendo, each lyric a come-on, and each rhythm throbbing with lust, perhaps no other record has ever achieved the kind of sheer erotic force of *Let's Get It On*, and it remains the blueprint for all of the slow jams to follow decades later—much copied, but never imitated. *—Jason Ankeny*

Live / Jun. 19, 1974 / Motown ♦♦♦
Released during Marvin Gaye's two-and-a-half-year sabbatical following the chart-topping success of *Let's Get It On*, *Live* features the erratic soul superstar moving briskly through some of his biggest hits. This brisk tempo acts as a double-edged sword, though. On the one hand, it establishes an uptempo, kinetic sense of euphoria never dulled by any lulls; however, the dizzying sense of energy also overwhelms you, never letting you relax and fully soak up the music's exuded beauty. Either way, Gaye's in top form here, delivering nothing but perennial anthems to a rabid crowd. The album-opening "Trouble Man" wields considerable weight, instantly establishing an engaging tone. From there Gaye moves toward an 11-minute medley of his '60s classics that comes across as almost a montage of nostalgia, evoking wistful memories of a more innocent and untainted Marvin. Following this medley, the album hits its fiery peak with versions of "Let's Get It On" and "What's Going On," his two biggest hits of the moment. *Live* isn't quite as essential as 1977's *Live at the London Palladium*, lacking the scope and instrumentation of that double LP. Regardless, it's still a great snapshot of Gaye at a key point in his career—the mid-'70s sabbatical from which he would never return quite the same. Thus, *Live* most interestingly functions as an artifact that revealingly alludes to Gaye's disposition during this time: elated and crowd-pleasing yet also somewhat uncomfortable and frantic. *—Jason Birchmeier*

I Want You / Mar. 16, 1976 / Motown ♦♦♦♦
Together with Leon Ware, Gaye created 1976's *I Want You*. Some of these tracks were to go on Leon Ware's Motown debut, *Musical Massage*, until Berry Gordy got a listen and decided that they'd be even better for Gaye, as the artist had not released a studio album since 1973's *Let's Get It On*. The title track to *I Want You* was the album's most successful effort, but certainly not the best. Like many of his albums, *I Want You* has Gaye's peaks not so much coming from the singles but rather the album cuts and the totality of the effort itself. Not that all of the lyrics and intentions here are crystal clear, though. In fact, Gaye does sound somnolent in spots, and it gives credence to the rumors that he did some of the tracks lying on a couch. "Come Live With Me," produced by Ware and Hal Davis, is the most focused track here. The refined and atmospheric "Feel My Love Inside" has Gaye giving a commanding upper-register vocal and has some doo wop backing vocals thrown in for good measure. To most fans, *I Want You* probably sounds unlike anything Gaye recorded. They're not wrong. In fact, this has the feel of a Leon Ware album with a more persuasive voice on top. "Since I Had You" typifies that idea as Gaye skillfully maneuvers through Ware's compelling and complicated arrangement, and he puts an accent on notes that other singers wouldn't even think to. *I Want You* is one of Gaye's best albums, and the production set a standard that few have been able to match. *—Jason Elias*

Live at the London Palladium / Mar. 15, 1977 / Motown ♦♦♦♦
A nearly 80-minute live album from 1977, *Live at the London Palladium* effectively compresses most of Marvin Gaye's numerous career highlights, making it a wonderful retrospective of the justly mythologized soul singer's accomplishments. Almost everything is here that could be: his '60s hits, his duets, the best moments from *What's Going On*, a trio of highlights each from *Let's Get It On* and *I Want You*, and even a bonus studio track, the magnificent 12-minute disco-funk epic "Got to Give It Up." Gaye performs with a sense of exuberance no doubt fueled by the large, appreciative audience. Furthermore, his rapport with the audience becomes overtly apparent, and welcome, during "Come Get to This" and "Let's Get It On"; during this pair of back-to-back odes to sex, you can feel the sultry passion in his voice as his singing drifts close to moaning and his ad libbing approaches tasteful, amorous aural lovemaking. Yet as intimate as Gaye is while singing, he's undeniably uncomfortable when talking: Just before beginning his medley of '60s hits, he stumbles over his mumbled words, confessing "I'll tell you, I don't do this so good so, you know, I might just stop and go right into the song. I'm really nuts," before halting mid-sentence rather than shamefully rambling any longer. Another revealing moment comes just before the duet medley, when Marvin speaks pensively of Tammi Terrell—after the audience applauds her name, he wistfully whispers, "Oh, she'd like that . . . for her I thank you." These subtle between-song moments prove revealing in retrospect, illustrating just how shaken Gaye is at this troubled point in his career. Listen carefully and you can sense the struggling instability that would erupt cathartically a year later with *Hear, My Dear*. In addition to being historically noteworthy, though, *Live at the London Palladium* also stands as the best and most readily available portrait of Gaye's live performances—a far different and more intimate experience than his studio releases that every fan should experience. *—Jason Birchmeier*

Here, My Dear / Dec. 15, 1978 / Motown ♦♦♦♦♦
Pre-dating the voyeuristic tendencies of reality television by 20 years, *Here, My Dear* is the sound of divorce on record—exposed in all of its tender-nerve glory for the world to consume. During the amazing success of *I Want You* and his stellar *Live at the London Palladium* album, Marvin Gaye was served with divorce papers from his then-wife Anna Gordy Gaye (sister of Motown Records founder Berry Gordy). One of the conditions of the settlement was that Gordy Gaye would receive an extensive percentage of royalties as well as a portion of the advance for his next album. Initially, Gaye was contemplating giving less than his best effort, as he wouldn't stand to receive any money, but then reconsidered at the last moment. The result is a two-disc-long confessional on the deterioration of their marriage; starting from the opening notes of the title track, Gaye viciously cuts with every lyric deeper into an explanation of why the relationship died the way it did. Gaye uses the album, right down to its packaging, to exorcise his personal demons with subtle visual digs and less-than-subtle lyrical attacks. The inner sleeve had a pseudo-board-game-like illustration entitled "Judgment," in which a man's hand passes a record to a woman's. One side of the sleeve has Gaye's music and recording equipment, while the other side of the board included jewelry and other luxurious amenities. Musically the album retains the high standards Gaye set in the early '70s, but you can hear the agonizing strain of recent events in his voice, to the point where even several vocal overdubs can't save his delivery. Stripped to its bare essence, *Here, My Dear* is no less than brilliantly unsettling and a perfect cauterization to a decade filled with personal turmoil. *—Rob Theakston*

In Our Lifetime / Jan. 15, 1981 / Motown ♦♦♦♦
This album came after the confessional and meadering double album 1978's *Here My Dear.* Although this better set does seem effortlessly conceived, it wasn't that simple. Gaye originally envisioned a "party" album and almost released one called *Love Man.* After some consideration, Gaye nixed the idea and aimed for an effort that would spotlight his religious concerns. Thankfully *In Our Lifetime* splits the difference between the two mindsets. The first single from the aborted *Love Man* shows up here. "Ego Tripping Out" works as both a parody of the "love man" with a few autobiographical flourishes as he sings, "Got a sweet tooth/ For the chick on the floor." Slowly but surely the religious matters do surface here. The buoyant "Praise," has a blithe riff inspired and or lifted from Stevie Wonder and has Gaye getting his message across without being preachy. Although no song is especially brilliant here, the level of Gaye's musical sense and his vocal prowess carries him throughout. The unfinished and non-Gaye approved, "Far Cry" has lyrics that are stream of consciousness and are barely decipherable. The mesmerizing "Love Me Now or Love Me Later" that has Gaye examining both good and evil with equal skill. The last track, the title song, has Gaye back in the party frame of mind and has great horn charts and a propulsive beat. *In Our Lifetime* is one of his finest later albums and captures him as his craft was maturing and becoming more multi-faceted. *—Jason Elias*

Midnight Love / Oct. 1982 / Columbia/Legacy ♦♦♦♦
Larkin Arnold, former CBS Records (Sony Music) senior executive VP, convinced Marvin Gaye to leave his flat in Belgium and sign with Columbia Records; the result would become the soul singer's last album before his untimely death. Of all his number-one songs, this album's first release, "Sexual Healing," became his longest running number-one single on the *Billboard* R&B charts (ten straight weeks). With the exception of the guitar, the Washington, D.C. native performed every instrument on this classic hit. Gaye concocted a pioneering percussive sound that was balladic in taste but stimulating in feel. As this project may not be an absolute erotic expression or a socially challenging plea from Gaye like on some of his previous albums, nonetheless, *Midnight Love* is a classic Marvin Gaye effort. In addition to this project thriving with Gaye's enthusiastic spirit, it has his harmonious background vocals, his stunning vocal arrangements and his creative penmanship, as he wrote all the selections. [The 2000 CD reissue on Sony/Legacy adds historical liner notes by Gaye biographer David Ritz and a bonus track, an instrumental version of "Rockin' After Midnight" (which actually does feature a bit of vocalizing by Gaye).] *—Craig Lytle*

Every Great Motown Hit of Marvin Gaye / 1983 / Motown ♦♦♦
The title is a bit of a misnomer, as you could count up on the fingers of both hands all the early hits that *aren't* on this 15-track collection. But if it's latter-day Marvin you're looking for—from "How Sweet It Is (To Be Loved By You)" through tracks like "Let's Get It On" and "Mercy Mercy Me (The Ecology)"—this set will fill the bill nicely, despite the utter lack of decent liner notes or recording date information. There's some great music here; just don't expect to fill your Marvin Gaye collection with this one disc, and you'll be just fine. [When Motown remastered and reissued the set in 2000, two tracks were added: "Ain't That Peculiar" and "I'll Be Doggone."] *—Cub Koda*

Romantically Yours / 1985 / Columbia ♦♦♦
Longtime Motown impresario and former Gaye colleague Harvey Fuqua picked and mixed the tracks that comprised this mid-'80s Gaye retrospective. As you might expect, it was a far superior package to many other Gaye sets, both in content and sound quality. There are some wonderful ballads that sat in Motown's vault for reasons only they know, and a set that should have gotten much more publicity hype than a lot of the other recycled collections. *—Ron Wynn*

Dream of a Lifetime / May 1985 / Columbia ♦♦
The commercially revitalized Gaye, who was back in the grips of psychosis and cocaine addiction, was planning a follow-up to 1982's *Midnight Love.* That, of course, was aborted when his father murdered him. *Dream of a Lifetime* is a mish-mash of tracks that range from bare-bones newer work as well as early-'70s Motown throwaways. The big hit, the percolating "Sanctified Lady," picks up where *Midnight Love* left off. Gaye originally sung another word instead of "lady"; part of it is still audible and it's still shocking, but not surprising. "Savage in the Sack" has Gaye playing on old-aged myths and having the time of his life. Despite the ready laughs, Gaye's sexual fantasies are often on the dark side here. "Masochistic Beauty" showcases a pedestrian rhythm as Gaye sings in the world's worst English accent as he says, "If you do it right, you'll get the pipe." For some it's unsettling, but it's also hilarious especially as he employs a vocoder as his lewd partner in crime. The Motown-era tracks come from various sessions from the '70s. While that fact would denote quality if not "treasures," there are few to be found here. "Life's Opera" and the title track are both heavy-handed with their overwrought sentiments. Only "It's Madness" with its patently early-'70s production style rises above the muck. Unlike many of Gaye's posthumous releases, *Dream of a Lifetime* offers a fair amount of dispensable work. *—Jason Elias*

The Marvin Gaye Collection / Sep. 1990 / Motown ♦♦♦
Marvin Gaye has more than enough great music to make a superb box set, but the haphazard *Marvin Gaye Collection* isn't it. The four discs within the set are arranged thematically: one terrific disc of hits, one good disc of duets, one largely uninteresting disc of rarities, and one wildly uneven disc of ballads. By spreading out the material this way, Motown shortchanges Gaye's musical accomplishments; there is no sense of growth or innovation. Although many of the songs are wonderful, some of the selections are puzzling—they seem to be chosen because they're arcane, not because they're significant. This very quality makes *The Marvin Gaye Collection* essential for his most devoted fans; however, most fans will find this box set disappointing. *—Stephen Thomas Erlewine*

Seek & You Shall Find: More of the Best (1963–1981) / 1993 / Rhino ♦♦♦♦♦
While it features nothing much in the way of big hits or difficult-to-find rarities, *Seek & You Shall Find: More of the Best (1963-1981)* offers a remarkably concise picture of the creative twists and turns of Marvin Gaye's career at Motown Records. Over the course of these 18 tracks, you can hear the Motown production style evolve from the brassy force of "Wherever I Lay My Hat (That's My Home)" to the subtle and sophisticated funk of "Heavy Love Affair," and Gaye's voice undergoes a similar metamorphosis as he learns the nooks and crannies of his instrument and grows from another solid soul singer into one of the most gifted and idiosyncratic artists in the history of R&B. And while the song titles may not ring many bells, every cut here is top-notch; if this is the "bubbling under" chart of Marvin Gaye's career, the relative obscurity of these songs speaks volumes about how consistently strong his music was during this period. While better-suited to devoted fans than beginners, anyone interested in hearing the great Marvin Gaye at the peak of his powers will want to give *Seek & You Shall Find: More of the Best (1963-1981)* a listen. *—Mark Deming*

The Norman Whitfield Sessions / Aug. 23, 1994 / Motown ♦♦♦
All of Gaye's recordings with producer Norman Whitfield are collected on the appropriately titled *The Norman Whitfield Sessions.* The sessions proved beneficial to both Gaye and Whitfield, as they produced the classic "I Heard It Through the Grapevine." While nothing on the set matches that seminal single, most of the music is captivating. Nevertheless, the disc will appeal mainly to the devoted Marvin Gaye collector, since most of the material is either alternate takes or outtakes. *—Stephen Thomas Erlewine*

The Master 1961–1984 / Apr. 25, 1995 / Motown ♦♦♦♦♦
The average fan is better off with *Anthology,* which covers almost all of Gaye's true classics. But for those who want the hits and then some, and have the budget and interest to go further, this four-CD box set is an excellent retrospective of his career. The 89 tracks include all the chart hits (both on his own and with Mary Wells, Kim Weston, Tammi Terrell, and Diana Ross) and many interesting B-sides, album tracks, and misses. There are also over a dozen previously unreleased cuts, most dating from the early part of his career; they don't rank among his best work, but they're almost all good and interesting. With a long essay by his biographer, David Ritz, this is the best overview of Gaye's evolution and versatility, and a much-recommended alternative to the previous Gaye box, *The Marvin Gaye Collection.* *—Richie Unterberger*

★ **Anthology** / Aug. 22, 1995 / Motown ♦♦♦♦♦
The 1995 version of *Anthology* was remastered and slightly retooled from the 1986 reissue, which was in turn updated from the original triple-LP set Motown released in 1974. That first *Anthology* featured nothing from *Let's Get It On* or afterward; the newest *Anthology* adds even more from that era while subtracting a bit from Gaye's earlier years, including a few of his numerous duets. Even so, it still stands as a near-definitive document. It's well-nigh impossible to encapsulate a career as lengthy and trailblazing as Gaye's on just one disc; *Anthology* hits all the high points of the Motown years in a more concise fashion than the collector-oriented box set *The Master,* making it the best summation of Gaye's career yet released. Kicking off with his first hit "Stubborn Kind of Fellow," disc one traces Gaye's rise to stardom as part of the Motown hit machine, featuring 20 solo cuts from the '60s as well as seven of his most important duets with Tammi Terrell, Kim Weston, and Mary Wells. Disc two covers Gaye the visionary auteur, beginning with material from his epochal *What's Going On* LP. If this disc can't reproduce the flowing, carefully calibrated moods of his albums from the period, it does touch upon every major facet of his '70s work—the urgent social commentary, the smoldering eroticism, the soul-baring confessions. It's a rich, engaging listen from top to bottom, even with around two-and-a-half hours of music. Unfortunately, *Anthology* has since gone out of print, to be replaced by the two-disc *Very Best of Marvin Gaye.* While the newer compilation has the advantage of licensing Gaye's post-Motown smash "Sexual Healing" (which is missing from *Anthology*), it unfortunately contains 13 fewer tracks, making *Anthology* the preferred alternative if you can track it down. *—Steve Huey*

Vulnerable / Mar. 25, 1997 / Motown ♦♦♦
Vulnerable is the end result of a project entitled "The Ballads that Marvin Gaye began in 1966." Gaye intended the project as a showcase for his crooning, as well as a way to pay

tribute to the pop and jazz standards he loved. It was a labor of love that took him 12 years to complete, and even after it was finished, the record wasn't released until 1997. Was it worth the wait? For dedicated fans, it certainly was, since Gaye's voice is as beautiful and soulful as ever. However, anyone who is not a dedicated fan will find *Vulnerable* intriguing but significantly flawed, especially since several of the songs seem ill-suited for Gaye's seductive vocals. Which means that even though *Vulnerable* is a nice addendum to his catalog, it's little more than a curiosity. *—Stephen Thomas Erlewine*

Midnight Love & the Sexual Healing Sessions / Nov. 10, 1998 / Columbia/Legacy ♦♦♦♦♦

After a series of business and personal upheavals as well as a couple of artistically satisfying but commercially disappointing albums, Marvin Gaye scored a final triumph with *Midnight Love* on which he embraced dancefloor rhythms derived from Rick James, horn charts that echoed Earth, Wind & Fire, and the kind of lover-man lyrics he himself had pioneered on earlier hits such as "Let's Get It On." The breakthrough track was his last major hit, "Sexual Healing," a relaxed groove tune with burbling percussion, doo wop backup vocals, and a new twist on the old romantic come-on. But the album as a whole made Gaye's case as a contemporary R&B artist. Then he was gone. This reissue compilation contains the entire *Midnight Love* album on the first disc, followed by a full, 74-minute disc of previously unreleased work tapes and alternate takes of most of the album's songs, among them four versions of "Sexual Healing." Since Gaye developed the tracks himself, playing keyboards and percussion, the alternates illuminate his creative process, but they contain no real revelations and will be of interest primarily to Gaye fans and hip-hop musicians searching for samples. Everybody else can stick with the original album. *—William Ruhlmann*

Lost and Found: Love Starved Heart [Expanded Edition] / Sep. 28, 1999 / Motown ♦♦♦♦

Originally issued as part of a 1994 box set and newly expanded here with nine additional performances, *Love Starved Heart* assembles 25 unreleased tracks recorded by Marvin Gaye between 1963 and 1971, Motown's golden era. That it took three decades for these songs to see the light of day speaks far more to the intensity of the label's assembly line production ethic than to the quality of the material itself—at their most pedestrian, these are fine performances simply lost in the shuffle, but at moments like "It's a Desperate Situation," "When I Feel the Need," and "This Love Starved Heart of Mine (It's Killing Me)," Gaye achieves the same peaks of his hits of the era, crafting performances of such sublime beauty and haunting poignance that their failure to reach the masses until now is nothing short of remarkable. Still, where classics like "I Heard It Through the Grapevine" and "Ain't That Peculiar" tend to suffer from years of oldies radio wear and tear, *Love Starved Heart* sounds positively refreshing—in their own way, these long-lost songs reaffirm the timelessness of Marvin Gaye's brilliance even more than the familiar hits on which his reputation rests. *—Jason Ankeny*

What's Going On [Deluxe Edition] / Feb. 27, 2001 / Motown ♦♦♦♦♦

If it's easy to be a little cynical about Universal/Motown's *2001 Deluxe Edition* reissue of Marvin Gaye's *What's Goin' On*, it's only because Motown endlessly reissued the album during the CD era, trumpeting each as the definitive issue (rather ironic for an album Berry Gordy didn't even want to release at the time). Still, Universal's *Deluxe Edition* series is proving to be a phenomenal collectors-oriented line, filled with lavish, detailed packaging and unpredictable turns, and *What's Goin' On* is no exception to the rule. To begin with, the remastering of the original album is excellent, the best yet, although that still isn't enough to make this worth buying for the hardcore fans who have purchased the album again and again over the years. That's what the other *disc and a half* of bonus material is for. First, there's the "original Detroit mix" of the album prepared while Gaye was out of town, filming a movie. A little bolder and sparer than the released record, with the strings noticeably relegated to the background, it's interesting, not revelatory, though its stripped-back feel is refreshing after hearing the album countless times. A rhythm-and-strings mix of "What's Going On" is tacked onto the end of the first disc, before the second disc begins with a new, previously unreleased live album that finds Gaye running through the album (minus "Mercy Mercy Me (The Ecology)") and performing a medley of '60s hits. It was his first performance in four years, and while unnecessary, it is fascinating and certainly worth the time of hardcore fans, as are the original single versions of "What's Going On," "God Is Love," and "Sad Tomorrows," plus the previously unreleased "'Head Title' aka Distant Lover." This is certainly a package for fans, but it's also the ideal fan package—beautifully made and filled with rarities that are necessary for fans, making them feel fine about buying this record again. Especially since this is so well done, it's hard to imagine Universal/Motown bettering it. *—Stephen Thomas Erlewine*

The Very Best of Marvin Gaye / Jul. 17, 2001 / Motown ♦♦♦♦♦

Frankly, there are enough different Marvin Gaye best-of compilations that are on the market, or have been on the market, that fans should be forgiven if they couldn't quite muster a great deal of enthusiasm for yet another one at the time of this release. On its own terms, this double disc is a very good survey of Gaye's most popular songs, starting with his first hit single in the early 1960s ("Stubborn Kind of Fellow") and going all the way up to "Sexual Healing," also including his big duet hits with Tammi Terrell. It's a good starting point for those who want a little more than a standard single-disc Gaye best-of, or one that spans his entire career instead of just some of it. Nevertheless, the 1995 *Anthology* release is a better deal from every standpoint, including more songs (47 to *The Very Best of*'s 34). It also has some good early hits that do not appear on *The Very Best of*, such as "One More Heartache," "Try It Baby," and "Baby Don't You Do It," not to mention his 1964 duet hit with Mary Wells, "What's the Matter With You Baby" (though it doesn't have "Sexual Healing"). Those that are willing to spend just a little more time or money on their purchase should consider alternatives, whether *Anthology* or the more comprehensive *The Master* box set. Of course, there's always a catch that might cause dedicated fans to hesitate passing this by entirely, namely two rare tracks. One's a previously unreleased stereo mix of the spiritual "His Eye Is on the Sparrow." The other, more interesting find is the previously unreleased 1972 track "Where Are We Going?," a fair but not great track in the same vein as material from the *What's Going On* album, but poppier; the song was also done by Donald Byrd on his *Black Byrd* record. *—Richie Unterberger*

Let's Get It On [Deluxe Edition] / Sep. 18, 2001 / Motown ♦♦♦♦♦

This deluxe edition is a two-disc celebration of the hedonistic R&B masterpiece *Let's Get It On*. The album is Marvin Gaye's follow-up to the groundbreaking social statement he made on *What's Going On*, which can also be thoroughly examined on the likewise expanded *What's Goin' On [2001 Deluxe Edition]*. The two-and-a-half-hour package is divided into four sections, beginning with a complete sonic resurrection of the original eight-song album, which now boasts a 24-bit digital transfer exclusive to this collection. A nine-track sessions segment follows consisting of entirely unissued materials. These exist in the form of instrumentals and undubbed and alternate versions of previously issued songs. This is continued throughout the third section, which contains demos, alternate mixes, and more, ending with a further ten alternate mixes and unissued pieces in various states of completion. These are in effect the recordings that connect such diametric and otherwise polar opposite musical sentiments as *What's Going On* with *Let's Get It On*. The sound is uniformly breathtaking. The often-jarring and always harsh and brittle sonics that previously plagued the high frequencies throughout the original disc—most specifically the tambourine and other percussion during "Distant Lover," for instance—is now organic and unprocessed. The copious bonus material sounds opulent considering it spans over five years. Any slight audio anomaly should be regarded as proof of authenticity. The laid-back strings on "Cakes," "Symphony," and "Song #3" observe a new side of Gaye's talents that rivals the likes of Barry White in terms of swinging soul arrangements. The inclusion of various works-in-progress and other related productions—such as the Miracles' ("I Love You Secretly") as well as the Originals (1968) and the Monitors' (1970) respective renditions of "Just to Keep You Satisfied"—examine the close-knit influence that Motown had among its own ranks. Accompanying the two discs—which are housed in a cardboard digi-pack—is a 24-page booklet replete with previously unpublished photos as well as essays from Gaye biographers David Ritz, Ben Edmunds, and Harry Weinger, producer and annotator of *Let's Get It On [Deluxe Edition]*. *—Lindsay Planer*

The Complete Duets / Nov. 20, 2001 / Universal ♦♦♦♦♦

Most listeners will be satisfied enough with a best-of compilation to cover the work that Gaye and Terrell did together. Those who want to hear more should make *The Complete Duets* their next and only subsequent stop. The two-CD collection includes everything from their three Motown duet albums, along with the previously unreleased "We'll Be Satisfied," an alternate take of "Ain't Nothing Like the Real Thing," and an alternate vocal of "Keep on Lovin' Me Honey." For good measure, the second half of disc two is devoted to rare solo Terrell sides. That includes four songs from 1965-1966 singles, including the non-LP B-side "Baby Don'tcha Worry," all of which were also released as duets with added Gaye vocals; it sounds like they're trying to make her a mini-Mary Wells on "Hold Me Oh My Darling." There are also nine previously unreleased Terrell solo tracks (though all of the songs were also featured, with Gaye on duet vocals, on the Gaye-Terrell LPs). It would have been good for the otherwise satisfactory liner notes to include more specific details on those unreleased Terrell items, and in all the non-hits on the package are enjoyably generic late-'60s Motown, rather than being of particularly exceptional merit. At the same time, it's of reasonably strong consistency and a useful compendium of the total known output of one of soul's top duets. *—Richie Unterberger*

Nona Gaye

Vocals / Urban

The daughter of beloved R&B/soul vocalist Marvin Gaye, Nona Gaye issued her debut release in 1992, *Love for the Future*. No one expected that she would equal her father's remarkable abilities, and she didn't. But Gaye did make a creditable and, by urban contemporary standards, soulful release and got off to a solid start. *—Ron Wynn*

● **Love for the Future** / Oct. 13, 1992 / Third Stone ♦♦

Signing with Atlantic and sporting a sexy image, Marvin Gaye's grown-up daughter, Nona Gaye, set her sights on 1992's urban contemporary market with *Love for the Future*. The inevitable question was, "Does she sound anything like her father?," and the answer is a definite "no." Nor does she need to. Gaye should, of course, be judged on her own merits and not held up to the impossibly high standards he set. Those who complained because this CD sounded nothing like *What's Going On* were being ridiculous and unfair. Gaye obviously wanted to record urban contemporary music, not soul. But even by urban contemporary standards, this is an unremarkable album. Gaye isn't a great singer by any means, and she sounds like a lukewarm Janet Jackson wannabe on both formulaic, knee-jerk synth-funk like "Fever " (which features Charles Wilson of the Gap Band) and "Natural Motion" and slower numbers such as "I'm Overjoyed" and "The Things That We All Do For Love." *Love for the Future* is an album to avoid. *—Alex Henderson*

Gloria Gaynor

b. Sep. 7, 1949, Newark, NJ

Vocals / Disco, Urban

Perhaps second only to Donna Summer, Gloria Gaynor has become one of the best-known female disco artists from the '70s due to the ongoing success of her monster 1979 hit (and subsequent "woman's anthem"), "I Will Survive." Born Gloria Fowles on September 7, 1949, in Newark, NJ, the singer (who began going by Gloria Gaynor by the early '70s), first sang as part of the obscure R&B outfit the Soul Satisfiers before being discovered by MGM Records head honcho Clive Davis (and eventual leader of the Arista label), who decided to sign the singer to his label after several auditions. Gaynor began issuing albums on a regular basis beginning in 1975 and with her 1976 release *Never Can Say Goodbye*, the singer became one of the first-ever dance artists to issue an album aimed primarily for club use (there were no breaks between the songs, as one track would automatically segue into the next), a method used to this day by DJs and certain dance artists.

Although Gaynor enjoyed a few moderate hits, it wasn't until the release of 1979's aforementioned disco gem "I Will Survive" that Gaynor racked up her first true smash hit. The song was awarded the first and only Grammy Award for Best Disco Recording in 1980 (the category was discontinued upon disco's fall from favor shortly afterward) and although Gaynor was unable to follow up "I Will Survive" with another sizable hit, the track subsequently took on a life of its own. It remains popular in dance clubs and has appeared on countless movie soundtracks and dance/disco compilations. Gaynor continues to issue albums and play shows (especially in Europe) and during the late '90s issued an autobiography (also titled *I Will Survive*), as well as appearing for a two-week run on Broadway's hit musical *Smokey Joe's Café*. *—Greg Prato*

Never Can Say Goodbye / 1975 / MGM ✦✦✦✦✦

Although 1979's "I Will Survive" is Gloria Gaynor's most famous recording, it was hardly her first. In 1975, the singer established herself as one of disco's early divas with her debut album *Never Can Say Goodbye*, which dance club DJs went wild over. With side one of this LP, Gaynor helped to popularize the art of the nonstop dance mix, a concept that was still alive and well when the 21st century arrived 25 years later. There are no breaks between songs on side one; the intoxicating opener "Honey Bee" segues into Gaynor's hit remake of "Never Can Say Goodbye" and that Clifton Davis gem (which had been recorded by the Jackson 5 and Isaac Hayes in the early '70s) segues into a stunning interpretation of the Four Tops' "Reach Out, I'll Be There." Put those three gems together and you have a nonstop 19-minute dance mix that thrilled the club DJs of 1975 to no end. Meanwhile, side two isn't as club-driven; all of the songs are under four minutes, and there are breaks between them. In other words, side two is more typical of R&B LPs from the mid-'70s. While side one was revolutionary and daring for 1975, side two favors a more conventional Northern soul approach. This isn't to say that "Real Good People," "False Alarm," and other songs on side two aren't pleasing; side two is generally solid, although side one proved to be more trend-setting. Gaynor sings with a great deal of feeling on both sides, making *Never Can Say Goodbye* an impressive and highly memorable debut. *—Alex Henderson*

Experience Gloria Gaynor / 1975 / MGM ✦✦✦

Gloria Gaynor's excellent sophomore effort *Experience Gloria Gaynor* found the influential disco diva embracing the same format she had favored on her first album, *Never Can Say Goodbye*; side one is a nonstop three-song dance mix that clocks in at almost 19 minutes, whereas on side two, there *are* breaks between songs. Not surprisingly, dance club DJs tended to favor side one, which opens with the dreamy "Casanova Brown" and keeps the momentum going with the hit "If You Want It (Do It Yourself)" and Gaynor's glossy interpretation of the standard "How High the Moon." Jazz lovers will tell you that in the 1940s and 1950s, countless bebop tunes were based on "How High the Moon"; a great song, to be sure, but one that was overdone in its day. To her credit, Gaynor breathes new life into the standard and demonstrates that it can work remarkably well in a disco-soul setting. Side two isn't nearly as danceable as side one; the tempos are generally slower, and solid Northern soul items like the melancholy "What'll I Do" and the ballad "I'm Still Yours" are clearly for listening rather than dancing. Side two ends on an impressive note with an inspired cover of the Burt Bacharach/Hal David favorite "Walk on By," which had been previously recorded by Dionne Warwick and Isaac Hayes, among others. Whether or not Gaynor is catering to dancefloors, the singer shows no signs of a sophomore slump on *Experience Gloria Gaynor*. *—Alex Henderson*

I've Got You / 1976 / Polydor ✦✦

Although not as consistently strong as *Never Can Say Goodbye* or *Experience Gloria Gaynor*, the singer's third album, *I've Got You*, is a generally decent but uneven disco-soul release that has its moments. Once again, Gaynor turns side one into a nonstop three-song dance mix while providing breaks between songs on the less club-oriented side two. Club jocks, as expected, were drawn to side one, which includes the charming "Let's Make a Deal" as well as the catchy, if unremarkable "Be Mine" and Gaynor's interpretation of the Cole Porter standard "I've Got You Under My Skin." By 1976, that standard had been recorded by numerous artists, and Gaynor deserves a lot of credit for bringing something fresh to a song that had been done so many times; in fact, "I've Got You Under My Skin" is the most memorable track on the album. Meanwhile, side two contains five Northern soul offerings that are enjoyable but not mind-blowing. *I've Got You* isn't Gaynor's finest hour, but its strengths outweigh its weaknesses. *—Alex Henderson*

Glorious / 1977 / Polydor ✦✦

Gloria Gaynor decided to switch producers with her fourth album, *Glorious*. While her first three albums were produced by the Meco Monardo/Tony Bongiovi/Jay Ellis team, *Glorious* was produced by disco ace Gregg Diamond and guitarist Joe Beck. The latter is primarily a jazz musician, but like so many jazz improvisers, Beck knows how challenging it can be trying to earn a living playing jazz; so in the 1970s, he took part in some more commercial projects. For Gaynor, working with different producers and songwriters meant some changes. Side one isn't turned into a nonstop dance mix this time, and Gaynor got away from the idea of having the dance-oriented tracks in one place and the slower material in another. Unfortunately, Diamond and Beck don't do as much for Gaynor as one would hope; *Glorious* isn't a bad album, but it's an album that never really catches on fire either. "This Side of the Pain," "Life Ain't Worth Living," and other disco-soul numbers are competent but not remarkable; except for the haunting "Most of All," none of the material is in a class with earlier gems like "Casanova Brown" and "Honey Bee." Meanwhile, Gaynor's disco version of the standard "As Time Goes By" is surprisingly stiff. While Gaynor really soared on her interpretations of "How High the Moon" and "I've Got You Under My Skin," she doesn't sound nearly as inspired on "As Time Goes By." Considering that Diamond's work with the Andrea True Connection had been excellent, one would expect him and Gaynor to be a powerful combination. But *Glorious* fails to live up to its potential and is strictly for Gaynor's most die-hard fans. *—Alex Henderson*

The Best of Gloria Gaynor / 1977 / Polydor ✦✦✦✦✦

Because Gloria Gaynor is best known for "I Will Survive," some listeners might have a hard time imagining that an album titled *The Best of Gloria Gaynor* could lack that disco-soul classic. But when this German LP came out in 1977, "I Will Survive" was still two years away, and Gaynor was best known for her work with the Meco Monardo/Tony Bongiovi/Jay Ellis team. Full of gems, this LP boasts some of the strongest tracks from Gaynor's first four albums, including "Never Can Say Goodbye" and "Honey Bee" from 1975's *Never Can Say Goodbye*; "Casanova Brown," "If You Want It (Do It Yourself)," and "How High the Moon" from 1975's *Experience Gloria Gaynor*; "Let's Make a Deal" and "I've Got You Under My Skin" from 1976's *I've Got You*; and "We Can Start All Over Again" and the haunting "Most of All" from 1977's *Glorious*. Of the four albums, *Glorious* is the least memorable; but to its credit, Polydor's German division picks two of the stronger tracks from that competent though unremarkable release. In 1977, dance club DJs didn't find this album terribly useful because Polydor favors the shorter versions of Gaynor's hits over the extended dance versions. But then, *The Best of Gloria Gaynor* wasn't aimed at club DJs, and Polydor wouldn't have been able to squeeze 12 songs onto the LP if it had gone with the longer mixes. If you needed a concise overview of Gaynor's career in 1977, *The Best of Gloria Gaynor* was a logical choice. *—Alex Henderson*

Gloria Gaynor's Park Avenue Sound / 1978 / Polydor ✦✦✦

Gloria Gaynor's fifth album was titled *Gloria Gaynor's Park Avenue Sound*, but it might as well have been titled *Gloria Gaynor's Broad Street Sound* because much of this soul-disco LP is heavily influenced by Philadelphia R&B. (Broad Street is a main thoroughfare in Philly). Two of the arrangers on *Park Avenue Sound* are Norman Harris and Ron "Have Mercy" Kersey, both of who were prominent figures on Philly's R&B scene in the 1970s, and Bobby Eli, another well known R&B musician from Philly, is employed on guitar. With such heavyweights on board, *Park Avenue Sound* should have been a gem. But the album isn't as strong as it could have been, although Philly-influenced cuts like "Kidnapped" and "This Love Affair" are decent and likable. One of the less Philly-sounding tunes on *Park Avenue Sound* is a remake of the Marvin Gaye/Tammi Terrell classic "You're All I Need to Get By," which is arguably the best thing on the album and favors the type of disco-meets-Motown approach that had worked well for Gaynor in the past. *Gloria Gaynor's Park Avenue Sound* falls short of excellent and isn't essential, but it has more ups than downs and is worth hearing if you're a die-hard fan. *—Alex Henderson*

Love Tracks / 1979 / Polydor ✦✦✦✦✦

Boasting the mega-hit "I Will Survive," Gloria Gaynor's sixth album, *Love Tracks*, was the strongest, most consistent album she had recorded since 1975's *Experience Gloria Gaynor*. "I Will Survive," one of the most famous anthems of the disco era, is the gem that made this 1979 LP a big seller, but it isn't the only song on the album that deserves to be called a gem. Gaynor is also captivating on five-star offerings that range from the funky club hit "Anybody Wanna Party?" to the smooth soul ballad "Please Be There" and a memorable remake of Little Anthony & the Imperials' "Goin' out of My Head." The album's uptempo selections didn't hurt Gaynor's standing with dance clubs, and yet *Love Tracks* is a great LP to sit down and listen to. Gaynor was well aware of disco's Northern soul roots, which is why she brings such a strong Motown flavor to "Substitute." Produced by Dino Fekaris, *Love Tracks* is among her most essential albums. *—Alex Henderson*

I Have a Right / 1979 / Spring ✦✦✦

When Dino Fekaris produced *Love Tracks* in early 1979, he helped Gloria Gaynor deliver one of the best and most successful albums of her career. And most of the time, the producer/songwriter is an asset on Gaynor's next album, *I Have a Right*. The LP gets off to a very weak and contrived start with the opener "Let Me Know (I Have a Right)," which is nothing more than a poor person's "I Will Survive." There can only be one "I Will Survive," and Gaynor and Fekaris should have known better than to offer such a pale imitation. But the rest of the material is excellent. Fekaris serves Gaynor nicely on uptempo disco-soul numbers like "Midnight Rocker" and "Don't Stop Us," as well as the slower, more 1960s-flavored Northern soul pearl "Say Somethin'." In the 1970s, Gaynor always included at least one cover on her albums, and on *I Have A Right*, the cover is the Stephen Sondheim/Leonard Bernstein classic "Tonight," which she transforms into a glossy disco barnburner. From both a disco standpoint and a Northern soul standpoint, *I Have a Right* is a welcome addition to Gaynor's catalog. *—Alex Henderson*

Stories / 1980 / Polydor ✦✦✦

Gloria Gaynor entered the 1980s with *Stories*, which marked the third time she worked with producer/songwriter Dino Fekaris. Once again, Fekaris showed a great understanding of what made Gaynor tick. Although Gaynor was among the top disco divas of the 1970s, her roots were Motown and Northern soul; and Fekaris, much to his credit, made sure that 1979's *Love Tracks*, 1979's *I Have a Right*, and 1980's *Stories* had both disco appeal and Northern soul appeal. *Stories* isn't in a class with the superb *Love Tracks* or the generally excellent *I Have a Right*, but it's solid and enjoyable, if less than spectacular. Gaynor is in good form on exuberant dance items like "Make Me Yours," "All My Life," and the Motown-minded "On a Diet of You," and she is equally pleasing on the smooth Northern soul slow jams "I Let Love Slip Right Through My Hands" and "The Luckiest

Girl in the World." *Stories* is an appropriate title for a Gaynor album because throughout her recording career she set out to provide dance records that told a story; to Gaynor, a worthwhile dance record needed more than just a beat. While *Stories* isn't among Gaynor's essential albums, it's worth hearing if you're a seasoned fan. *—Alex Henderson*

Gloria Gaynor / 1983 / Polydor ♦♦♦♦

Gaynor's first post-Polydor effort is a vibrant mélange of early-'80s R&B midtempo grooves and pop-savvy dance tunes. Largely overseen by Ollie E. Brown, the tunes range in color from the jazzy quiet storm pleaser "Mack Side" to the patriotic "America." The standout number, however, is the unique cover of the Supremes' "Stop in the Name of Love." Aided by the affluent production of Amir Bayyan (aka Kool & the Gang founder Robert "Kool" Bell), Gaynor serves up an earnest, pleading vocal. The zesty new chorus is anthemic, and the background vocal arrangements are the kind that are both radio-friendly and dancefloor-riveting. But perhaps the most surprising entry is "Even a Fool Would Let Go," originally recorded by Dionne Warwick in 1980. A slightly country-oriented ballad, it shows a more subtly soulful and gospel-tinged side of Gaynor's abilities that brings to mind Thelma Houston. On the whole, this set is more consistent than much of the singer's Polydor catalog. Originally released on Atlantic, Hot Productions issued the album on CD in 1997 with the addition of an '80s re-recording of Gaynor's signature song, "I Will Survive." This version is notable for its understated arrangement and the melodic alterations made, though many fans of the song's powerful message will find it not nearly as inciting as the original. *—Justin M. Kantor*

I Will Survive: The Anthology / Apr. 21, 1998 / Polydor ♦♦♦♦

Gloria Gaynor was one of the main disco divas, scoring a number of crossover hits, including "I Will Survive" and "Never Can Say Goodbye," in addition to pioneering extended mixes on her 12-inch singles. Instead of relying on her hit singles, all of which are compiled on *Greatest Hits*, the double-disc *I Will Survive: The Anthology* concentrates on her dancefloor classics. In other words, if you're looking for brief, catchy disco-pop, look elsewhere; this has nothing but full-length album tracks and three extended disco medleys, each running around 18 minutes—the length of one side of a 12-inch single. For some, this will be tedious listening, but any disco fanatic will find plenty of interesting material here, and for those with hardcore dance tastes, *I Will Survive* may even be preferable to *Greatest Hits*. *—Stephen Thomas Erlewine*

• **20th Century Masters—The Millennium Collection: The Best of Gloria Gaynor** / Sep. 26, 2000 / Polydor ♦♦♦♦

The Millennium Collection: The Best of Gloria Gaynor gathers highlights from her soul and disco years, including "How High the Moon," "Casanova Brown," "Let Me Know (I Have the Right)," and "I Will Survive." "This Love Affair," "(If You Want It) Do It Yourself," and "Walk on By" are some of the other highlights of this compact but entertaining compilation. Though it's not as extensive as some of the other available Gaynor collections, *The Millennium Collection* gives casual fans a taste of her powerful sound. *—Heather Phares*

Paul Gayten

b. Jan. 29, 1920, New Orleans, LA, **d.** Mar. 26, 1991, Los Angeles, CA

Piano, Vocals, Leader / New Orleans R&B, Jump Blues

Paul Gayten, a seminal figure in New Orleans R&B, led a varied career in the music business as a bandleader, producer, label owner, and one-time overseer of the West Coast operation of Chess Records. A nephew of blues-piano legend Little Brother Montgomery, Gayten once led one of the top bands of New Orleans, but he gave up the performing life in 1956 to turn his attention to production and eventually to his own California-based Pzazz label (which featured Louis Jordan, among others). Gayten wrote Larry Darnell's 1949 classic "For You My Love" and recorded a few Top Ten hits of his own for Regal and DeLuxe (1947-1950), some of them with vocalist Annie Laurie. *—Jim O'Neal*

• **Chess King of New Orleans/The Chess Years** / 1989 / MCA/Chess ♦♦♦♦♦

Here is sizzling mid-'50s New Orleans R&B from this veteran. *—Bill Dahl*

Barbara George

b. Aug. 16, 1942, New Orleans, LA

Vocals / Soul, New Orleans R&B

Barbara George's "I Know (You Don't Love Me No More)" topped the R&B charts in 1961 and has proven a popular cover item ever since. The New Orleans native had never been in the studio before she brought her extremely catchy melody to Harold Battiste's fledgling A.F.O. label. Benefiting from her pleasing, unpolished vocal and a melodic coronet solo by Melvin Lastie, the tune caught fire, vaulting high on pop playlists. Amazingly, nothing else George did ever dented the charts, although she waxed some listenable follow-ups for A.F.O. and Sue. *—Bill Dahl*

• **I Know (You Don't Love Me Anymore)** / 1962 / Collectables ♦♦♦♦♦

With her lone smash hit as the centerpiece, Barbara George's A.F.O. album from 1962 is surprisingly free of filler, almost a prerequisite in those singles-dominated times. Her follow-up hit, "Talk About Love," is also aboard, and other highlights include nice takes of "Since I Fell for You," the bouncy "Don't Ask Me No Questions," and the soulful ballad "Honest I Do." With top-notch playing from Harold Battiste and others, this is classic early-'60s New Orleans music all the way. [Later reissued as part of Collectables' *Golden Classics* series.] *—Cub Koda*

Donny Gerrard

Vocals / Contemporary R&B, Soft Rock, Adult Contemporary, Urban, Television Soundtracks

Smooth soul singer Donny Gerrard started his career as the lead singer of the Vancouver-based pop group Skylark, who recorded two albums and had a Top Ten hit with "Wildflower" in 1973 (they also launched the career of pop producer extraordinaire David Foster). After the group broke up, Gerrard embarked on a solo career, issuing his debut single "(Baby) Don't Let It Mess Your Mind" on Elton John's Rocket label in 1975. He subsequently signed with the Los Angeles-based Greedy label, where he issued his self-titled debut album in 1976. A mix of sweet, romantic ballads, disco, and jazzy flourishes, the album spawned several singles, including the 12-inch "Greedy (For Your Love)" (now a collector's item), "Stay Awhile With Me," "He's Always Somewhere Around," and "Words."

After one further single in 1977, Gerrard made a steady living as a backing vocalist for recording sessions and tours; in this capacity, he worked with some of the biggest names in popular music, including Elton John, Ray Charles, Bette Midler, Bruce Springsteen, Aaron Neville, Neil Diamond, Bob Seger, Donna Summer, Cher, Dolly Parton, Bobby Womack, and a solo John Fogerty, among many others. He also went on to appear on the soundtracks of *The Rose* and *St. Elmo's Fire*, and sang television advertising jingles for extra income. A recording of Barbara Lewis' "Baby I'm Yours" for a '90s car commercial led to a deal with WEA subsidiary Lightyear for a brand-new album; released in 1999, *The Romantic* found Gerrard working in smooth pop territory, à la Nat King Cole or Johnny Mathis. *—Steve Huey*

• **Donny Gerrard** / 1976 / Greedy ♦♦♦

Smooth sensuality delivered by Donny Gerrard's delicious light tenor on his solo debut. The jazzy tracks are courtesy of some of L.A.'s best session men, Wilton Felder, Jay Graydon, and a host of other sharp studio players. Gerrard caresses "Stay Awhile," a Van McCoy/Joe Cobb composition, drives the message home on Lennon and McCartney's "Long and Winding Road," and gets funky (for Donny) on Curtis Mayfield's infectious, pleading "You Must Believe in Me." Nine romantic offerings by the underrated balladeer who tantalized the world with "Wildflower" as a member of the British Columbia group Skylark. *—Andrew Hamilton*

The Romantic / Jan. 26, 1999 / Lightyear ♦♦♦

For lovers, ex-lovers, and the brokenhearted, *The Romantic* features mature smooth sounds eloquently done by Donny Gerrard. This is romance, sweet and bitter, on a higher plane. He emulates Nat "King" Cole on "Very Thought of You" and "I Love You for Sentimental Reasons." A re-recording of "Wildflower," a song he led as a member of Skylark, is as cloying and as passionate as the original. Candlelight renditions of Barbara Lewis' "Baby I'm Yours," "Nothing in Common," "Then You Can Tell Me Goodbye," and "Time Was" are alone worth the price of this CD. Welcome back, Donny. *—Andrew Hamilton*

Johnny Gill

b. May 22, 1966, Washington, D.C.

Vocals / New Jack Swing, Urban

Born in Washington, D.C., Johnny Gill was discovered by singer Stacy Lattisaw after singing in his family's group Wings of Faith from age five. His solo career began in 1983 with the Top 30 R&B single "Super Love." In duo with Lattisaw, he scored an R&B Top Ten hit in 1984 with "Perfect Combination." In 1988, Gill joined New Edition, replacing Bobby Brown. In 1989 he sang on two R&B hits: "Where Do We Go from Here," a number-one hit by Stacy Lattisaw, and "One Love," by George Howard. Gill finally scored as a solo singer in 1990 with the release of his album *Johnny Gill*, which sold a million copies, topped the R&B chart, and made the Top Ten in the pop chart. Following the relative failure of 1993's *Provocative*—which didn't produce any Top 10 R&B singles and only went gold—Gill reunited with New Edition in 1996. A month after New Edition released *Home Again* in September of 1996, Gill released *Let's Get the Mood Right*. *—William Ruhlmann*

Johnny Gill / 1983 / Atlantic ♦♦♦

Atlantic Records brought in the heavy artillery for Johnny Gill's first album. Producer, Freddie Perren came with a long résumé of hit productions by the Jacksons, Tavares, the Sylvers, and others. The combination flowed on paper but didn't jell in the studio—no chemistry. Perhaps this is why Atlantic titled Gill's second LP *Chemistry*. "Super Love" has a heavy, thud-beat that's derivative and mundane; ditto for "Guilty"—a song needs more than just a wicked bassline. A remake of Sam & Dave's "When Something Is Wrong With My Baby" is easily the best ballad. The others—"Thank You," "Show Her Love," "I'm Sorry," and "You"—are average and indistinguishable. "I Love Makin' Music" is the best of the uptempo numbers, but when you consider the others, that's not saying much. *—Andrew Hamilton*

Chemistry / 1985 / Atlantic ♦♦♦

Two years after Gill's disastrous self-titled debut on Atlantic that lacked "chemistry" between Gill and producer Freddie Perren, Atlantic mocks that effort by titling Gill's new release *Chemistry*. These tunes find common ground with Gill's masculine baritone, and the young crooner sounds alive again. Featured here are tasty selections like "I Can't Wait Til Tomorrow," an urban-jump with a big-band sound, and the lilting "I Found Love." Linda Creed, the writer of many classics with Thom Bell, contributes her lyrical talents to three songs, including the moving ballad "Half Crazy," a dramatic, builder that Johnny nearly goes half crazy singing. There's also "Chemistry," a beautiful midtempo floater with a slick cosmic opening. *—Andrew Hamilton*

• **Johnny Gill** / 1990 / Motown ♦♦♦♦♦

Here is Gill's long-in-coming solo breakthrough, featuring the hits "Rub You the Right Way," "My, My, My," and "Fairweather Friend." *— William Ruhlmann*

Provocative / Jun. 8, 1993 / Motown ♦♦♦

Basically, *Provocative* is a retread of *Johnny Gill*, but it's a retread done right, since Gill's voice is in prime form and the dueling production teams of Jimmy Jam & Terry Lewis and L.A. & Babyface Reid make the music smooth, stylish, and funky. *—Stephen Thomas Erlewine*

Let's Get the Mood Right / Oct. 8, 1996 / Motown ♦♦♦♦

Johnny Gill released his fifth album, *Let's Get the Mood Right*, only a few months after he participated in the New Edition reunion. In other words, it was timed to cash in on the group's massive comeback success. If he had delivered a dud, such crass commercial planning would have been in poor taste, but it's his strongest album in years, thanks to an excellent selection of songs and a stellar cast of producers, which includes Babyface, Tony Rich and Jimmy Jam & Terry Lewis. Gill shines at smooth soul like the title track, but what is remarkable about the album is how comfortable he sounds with the uptempo, albeit low-key, dance numbers. It's his best, most consistent album since *Johnny Gill.* *—Stephen Thomas Erlewine*

Favorites / Nov. 11, 1997 / Motown ✦✦✦✦✦
A marvelous compilation of Johnny Gill's Motown sides. Someone was even thoughtful enough to include "There U Go," an overlooked gem from the *Boomerang* soundtrack. Gill's lusty baritone is a flexible instrument, and he has complete control over it, never failing to conjure an emotion from listeners. He doesn't sing for himself, he sings to please others, and it shows in his phrasing and delivery. Johnny outdoes himself with an absolutely marvelous vocal on "If You're Wondering," arguably one of the best urban ballads of the '90s. Gill's vocal range amazes on the lilting, dreamy concoction that is better known in Europe. A duet with childhood friend Stacy Lattisaw, "Where Do I Go From Here," shows their vocal skills but is too predictable; it's one of those tunes you think you heard before, but Lattisaw still sounds luscious belting out the love tale. Johnny proves he can sing hip-hop by hitting the number-one spot on *Billboard*'s R&B Chart with "Rub You the Right Way," an energetic workout for the balladeer. "My, My, My" also topped the R&B chart in July 1990. Just as good is the irresistible "Wrapped My Body Tight" with its incessant beat. A great package of Gill. *—Andrew Hamilton*

● **Ultimate Collection** / Mar. 26, 2002 / Hip-O ✦✦✦✦✦
You can't be any hotter than R&B singer Johnny Gill was in the early '90s; he participated in five consecutive singles that hit number one or number two on the *Billboard* R&B charts between February 1990 and April 1991, while his self-titled label debut on Motown Records went double-platinum. Subsequent efforts were not as successful, and as of the spring of 2002, Gill had been MIA since releasing a Christmas single in 1997, but the liner notes to this collection report him to be "reportedly in the studio." Meanwhile, Hip-O's *Ultimate Collection* lives up to its title (as the imprint's other volumes in this series have) by lavishing 79-and-a-half minutes on a straightforward, chronological assemblage of the highlights of Gill's career, including work done for labels not controlled by Hip-O parent Universal, such the Stacy Lattisaw duet "Perfect Combination" that first came out on the Atlantic subsidiary Cotillion in 1984. An R&B singer's career these days is a dizzying combination of regular singles, soundtrack excerpts, and featured appearances on other people's records, but this compilation gathers up all of Gill's most popular recordings, including "I'm Still Waiting" from the movie *New Jack City,* Shanice's "Silent Prayer," and Shabba Ranks' "Slow and Sexy," the latter two guest appearances by the singer. Also included is the chart-topping New Edition song "Can You Stand the Rain," and, of course, all of Gill's own major hits, most of them written and produced by the likes of Jimmy Jam & Terry Lewis and L.A. & Babyface, are included. (There is also one worthy album-only track, "Maybe," from 1996's *Let's Get the Mood Right.*) The result outdistances a previous Gill best-of, *Favorites*, which focused only on his Motown solo hits. For the moment, this is Johnny Gill's best so far; one can only hope there will be more. *—William Ruhlmann*

Ginuwine (Elgin Baylor Lumpkin)

b. Oct. 15, 1975, Washington, D.C.
Vocals / Contemporary R&B, Hip-Hop, Club/Dance, Urban

Ginuwine was one of R&B's pre-eminent love men during the '90s heyday of hip-hop soul. Initially teamed with Timbaland, the most innovative producer of the late '90s, Ginuwine's sultry, seductive crooning earned him a substantial female following and made him a regular presence on the R&B charts, even after the futuristic production he favored was eclipsed by the more organic, retro-leaning neo-soul movement.

Ginuwine was born in Washington, D.C., on October 15, 1975, with the unlikely name of Elgin Baylor Lumpkin (after D.C.-born Basketball Hall of Famer Elgin Baylor). As a youngster, Lumpkin's interest in music was ignited by Prince and Michael Jackson, especially the latter's legendary moonwalking performance on the Motown 25th-anniversary special. At the mere age of 12, he began performing at parties and bars with the local hip-hop group the Finesse Five. He later worked as a Michael Jackson impressionist and sang with another local outfit, Physical Wonder; in the meantime, he earned a paralegal degree from a local community college, in case music didn't work out. In 1996, he adopted the name Ginuwine and was discovered by Jodeci. In New York, he met up with young producer Timbaland and cut the track "Pony," whose slow, halting groove and impassioned vocals helped Ginuwine land a deal with Sony's 550 Music imprint.

With the strikingly inventive Timbaland behind the boards, Ginuwine cut his debut album, *Ginuwine... The Bachelor,* and released it later in 1996. "Pony" became a number-one R&B smash, also reaching number six on the pop charts, and the album became an eventual double-platinum hit. It spun off several more R&B hits over the next year, including "Tell Me Do U Wanna," "I'll Do Anything/I'm Sorry," "Holler," and "Only When Ur Lonely"; it also featured a homage to one of Ginuwine's main influences in the cover of Prince's "When Doves Cry." In the wake of the album's success, demand for Timbaland's production services exploded, and Ginuwine became a bona fide sex symbol. He toured heavily in support of *The Bachelor,* and kept his name in the public eye in 1998 with his hit "Same Ol' G," which was featured on the soundtrack to Eddie Murphy's *Dr. Doolittle.* Late that year, he also made his acting debut on an episode of the CBS series *Martial Law.*

Ginuwine returned with his second album, *100% Ginuwine*, in early 1999. Again produced by Timbaland, it entered the pop charts at number five and gave rise to another significant crossover hit in "So Anxious." "What's So Different?" and "None of Ur Friends Business" were also successful on R&B radio, and there was another cover of a Ginuwine hero, this time Michael Jackson's "She's Out of My Life." *100% Ginuwine* became the singer's second straight platinum album. He followed it in the spring of 2001 with *The Life*, his first album to be helmed by producers not named Timbaland. Nonetheless, it was another success, debuting at number three on the charts and once again going platinum. Moreover, the ballad "Differences"—the second single released from the album, after "There It Is"—became Ginuwine's biggest pop hit yet, climbing to number four later that year. In 2002, Ginuwine made his feature-film debut in the gender-bending basketball comedy *Juwanna Mann*, playing (what else?) a slick R&B singer. That summer, Ginuwine returned to the Top Ten courtesy of his duet with P. Diddy on "I Need a Girl (Part Two)." Around the same time, in a somewhat bizarre incident, police captured a Minnesota man who'd been impersonating the singer for the past few years and bilking money from business contacts. *—Steve Huey*

● **Ginuwine... The Bachelor** / Oct. 8, 1996 / 550 Music/Epic ✦✦✦✦
By the time *Ginuwine... the Bachelor* was released, Ginuwine was already well on his way to becoming R&B's next big thing—thanks mainly to the ferocious word of mouth his lead single, a cover of Prince's "When Doves Cry," perpetuated. Make no mistake, this was the album that indeed started it all for the young R&B sensation, catapulting him from relative obscurity to the limelight in less time than most of his contemporaries. Led by the ferocious chart-topping opener "Pony," Ginuwine not only became a staple for commercial R&B radio, but he upped the sexual reference ante for many up-and-coming male singers such as Dru Hill, Blackstreet, and such established producers as R. Kelly. Combining the influences of funk, quiet storm, soul, and even a tad bit of electro, Ginuwine effortlessly displays not only a powerful voice, but sharp songwriting and production skills. *Ginuwine... the Bachelor* was a promising debut and only a slight notion of great things to come. *—Rob Theakston*

100% Ginuwine / Mar. 16, 1999 / 550 Music/Epic ✦✦✦✦
Ginuwine's debut album certainly sounded like little else in the modern soul front. Thanks to Timbaland's inventive production, it blended classic soul songwriting with inventive sonic textures, borrowed equally from hip-hop, trip-hop, and electro-funk. For the follow-up, Ginuwine and Timbaland decided that if it ain't broke, just spiffy it up a little bit—which means *100% Ginuwine* uses *The Bachelor* as a blueprint but goes further, boasting more inventive productions and a stronger set of songs. If nothing grabs the ear like "Pony," most of the songs slowly work their way underneath the skin, revealing themselves as either seductive ballads or ingratiating dancefloor numbers. Timbaland continues to prove that he's one of the savviest producers in modern hip-hop and soul, but Ginuwine remains the star of the show, thanks to his rich, inviting voice. *—Stephen Thomas Erlewine*

The Life / Apr. 3, 2001 / Epic ✦✦✦
On his third album, Ginuwine is even more of a practiced R&B loverman than he was on his first two releases. Big Dog Productions, Inc. and the team of Troy Oliver and Cory Rooney produce the bulk of the beats here, which, as usual, mostly range from slow to very slow tempos with such trendy touches as acoustic guitar passages. But all that just serves as a bed for Ginuwine's elastic tenor and his message to the women in his audience. The singer sounds like he's been reading women's magazines and tried to construct a persona that's as appealing as possible. "Baby," he croons in "Why Did You Go," "I'm sorry for whatever I've done and I want you to be my wife." In "Differences," he talks about how much he has improved since meeting the woman he's addressing, concluding, "I'm so responsible." Even when he's criticizing a woman, as he does in the album's first single, "There It Is," it's because she's not contributing to the relationship, while he's holding down a steady job and paying the bills. It's only in the album's eighth cut, "How Deep Is Your Love" (an original, not the Bee Gees song), that he begins to apply pressure for sex, ungallantly suggesting that if the woman doesn't come across he'll start cheating on her. "Show After the Show" is a come-on to a post-concert groupie, which seems to negate what's gone before, and "Role Play" moves on to kinky sex, but in the album-closing "Just Because," Ginuwine acknowledges the temptations of his occupation and pleads, "I'm trying to learn to be committed." It's hard to believe that anyone who's swallowed his line before is going to become skeptical now, so *The Life* looks like another winner for him. *—William Ruhlmann*

Nikki Giovanni (Yolande Cornelia Giovanni)

b. Jun. 7, 1943, Knoxville, TN
Poetry / Poetry

One of the most popular and acclaimed African-American poets of the 20th century, Nikki Giovanni came of age in the heady, militant era of the civil rights movement, and her most influential poetry was suffused with all the spirit and vitality of a new age. Giovanni was born Yolande Cornelia Giovanni in Knoxville, TN, on June 7, 1943; her family moved to Cincinnati shortly thereafter, but Giovanni returned to Knoxville to live with her grandparents in 1957. She was an early enrollee at Nashville's all-black Fisk University in 1960, but was dismissed before completing her first year; she returned to Cincinnati and worked for a few years, then returned to Fisk in 1964 to finish her B.A. While there, she served as an assistant in the writers' workshop and got involved in the university chapter of SNCC, a non-violent civil rights organization. After graduating, she moved to New York in 1968 to attend Columbia's School of Fine Arts, and published three poetry collections over 1968-1970 to considerable attention and acclaim.

In 1970, Giovanni established her own NikTom publishing company, and the following year recorded some of her most celebrated poems for the Right On label as *Truth Is on Its Way*, with gospel backing by the New York Community Choir. The record was a genuine hit, climbing all the way to number 15 on the R&B album charts. A second outing with the New York Community Choir, *Like a Ripple on a Pond*, was released on the NikTom imprint in 1973 and just missed the Top 50. Giovanni switched gears for her third musical outing, enlisting Arif Mardin to write backing music for 1975's *The Way I Feel.* Naturally, Giovanni stayed with her primary creative outlet as a poet during this time, in addition to lecturing across the country; motherhood brought a surge of poetry written for children, and Folkways issued two recordings in this vein, *The Reason I Like Chocolate* (1976) and *Cotton Candy on a Rainy Day* (1978); Folkways also put out another Giovanni recording, *Legacies*, in 1976. She continued to write and lecture through the '80s and '90s, and has served as a professor of English at Virginia Tech since the late '80s. A new recording taken from a 1997 live reading, *In Philadelphia*, was released on Collectables, which also reissued her first three albums on CD. *—Steve Huey*

- **Like a Ripple on a Pond** / 1973 / Collectables ♦♦♦♦

Nikki Giovanni's second album backed by the New York Community Choir, *Like a Ripple on a Pond*, didn't build on the success of the African-American poet's debut, but it did reach just outside the Top 50 on the black albums chart in 1973. It is just as strong as the debut, featuring Giovanni's voice up in front, while arranger and director Benny Diggs directs the powerful gospel choir behind her. The poet relates experiences both personal and of her people, but she's at her best when she speaks in the first person and describes the struggles she has gone through in a plainspoken yet warm manner—those struggles aren't far off from the struggles many others have gone through. Giovanni's ability to relate to her audience, combined with the sections where the choir is allowed to let loose, makes this album a timeless one. *—Andy Kellman*

In Philadelphia / Oct. 21, 1997 / Collectables ♦♦♦♦

In Philadelphia is a wonderful collection of 18 poems performed live in Philadelphia by Nikki Giovanni. The poetry here is graceful, passionate and thought-provoking, providing an excellent entry to Giovanni's work. *—Leo Stanley*

The Girlfriends

Group / Brill Building Pop, Girl Group

Girl group one-shot the Girlfriends was an offshoot of the famed Los Angeles session vocal group the Blossoms. Singers Gloria Jones (nee Goodson), Nanette Jackson, Fanita James and Darlene Wright first joined forces as members of Richard Berry's backing group the Dreamers; in 1957, the foursome founded the Blossoms, scoring a hit four years later with the single "Son-in-Law" but earning their greatest renown as one of the finest session units in the business. When producer Phil Spector tapped James and Wright for his group Bob B. Soxx & the Blue Jeans (renaming the latter Darlene Love in the process), the remaining duo of Jones and Jackson enlisted former Ikette Carolyn Willis to form the Girlfriends. The group's lone single, the David Gates-produced Colpix release "My One and Only Jimmy Boy," remains one of the best Spector homages of the era, but struggled to crack the Top 50 in late 1963; no follow-ups were forthcoming, although rumors exist of a sequel titled "I Don't Believe in You" (possibly recorded with an altogether different set of vocalists). In 1969, Willis returned to the charts as one-third of the soul trio the Honey Cone; she and Jones later reunited to tour oldies circuits as one of several groups calling themselves the Shirelles. *—Jason Ankeny*

The Girls

f. 1983, Minneapolis, MN, **db.** 1985

Group / Urban, Funk

Assembled by Prince associate André Cymone in Minneapolis in 1983, the Girls were an obscure, little known female trio along the lines of Vanity 6 and Apollonia 6. Vanity 6 had done well for Prince in 1982, and Cymone was hoping to direct a hit female group of his own when, in 1983, he hired singers Sheila Rankin, Germain Brooks, and Doris Rhodes and called them the Girls. With a sexy image, R-rated lyrics, and a very Prince-influenced blend of funk, rock, and pop, the Girls were extremely Minneapolis-sounding. All of them were under 20: Rhodes, the oldest of the three, was 19, while Brooks was 18, and Rankin was 17. With Cymone guiding them, the Girls signed with Columbia in 1983, and their debut album, *Girl Talk*, came out the following year. In addition to producing *Girl Talk*, Cymone wrote or co-wrote all of the material, including the single "Don't Waste My Time." Cymone had high hopes for the album, but much to his disappointment, it didn't sell. The Girls were dropped by Columbia, and in 1985 the trio broke up without ever recording a second album. *—Alex Henderson*

- **Girl Talk** / 1984 / Columbia ♦♦♦

When the Girls' *Girl Talk* came out in 1984, Prince's Minneapolis sound was huge. R&B was full of Prince and Time imitators, and many artists reasoned that an easy way to score a quick hit was to be as Minneapolis-sounding as possible. But not every Minneapolis-style recording that came out in 1984 was successful, *Girl Talk*, in fact, received very little attention. Despite the fact that Prince associate André Cymone produced this album and wrote or co-wrote all of the material, *Girl Talk* fell through the cracks. Nonetheless, this isn't a terrible record. Although the material tends to be derivative and not very original, Cymone comes up with some catchy synth-funk and new wave grooves here and there. Obviously, Cymone modeled the female trio after Vanity 6/Apollonia 6, it's impossible not to think of Vanity and Apollonia when you're listening to R-rated synth-funk ditties like "S-E-S-E-X," "Girl Talk," and the single "Don't Waste My Time" or the pop/rock/new wave numbers "Nu Boy" and "My Man." Again, *Girl Talk* won't win any awards for originality, but it has its moments. *—Alex Henderson*

The Glass House

f. 1969

Group / Soul, Smooth Soul, Pop-Soul

One of Holland-Dozier-Holland's cut-and-paste groups whose members' scattered in separate directions (as did Chairmen of the Board, the Honey Cone, Eighth Day, and 100 Proof) when the recording sessions and salaries stopped. Scherrie Payne, Pearl Jones, Tyrone Hunter, and Larry Mitchell didn't woodshed together in hallways or under streetlights; no bond existed among them prior to the Glass House project, and a major age discrepancy existed between Hunter and the other members. Hunter sang in the Romeos with Lamont Dozier & the Voice Masters, he also chipped out solo records on Anna and Chess Records.

Payne, Jones, Hunter, and Mitchell impressed Holland-Dozier-Holland individually and were placed in Glass House, a group who dressed in futuristic uniforms rather than conventional attire. The intent was to eventually break Payne and Hunter as solo acts.

"Crumbs off the Title" (September 1969), an Edith Wayne/Ronald Dunbar tune led by Scherrie Payne (Freda Payne's sister), was Invictus Records' first release by anybody; it went to number-seven R&B and number-59 pop. Laura Lee redid it on Hot Wax Records, and Dusty Springfield updated it on her *See All Her Faces* LP. Invictus took its time issuing the second Glass House single; the astrological-themed "I Can't Be You, You Can't Be Me" came out June 1970, with Payne leading again. It rode the R&B chart but avoided the pop 40 and doesn't appear on either of their two albums. "Stealing Moments From Another Woman's Life" (November 1970), led by Pearl Jones, became their second most popular recording.

Having three straight R&B chart records has some significance, but provided little solace for Glass House, who missed out on "Want Ads," a gold record for the Honey Cone. Glass House recorded the song, with Payne on lead, before Honey Cone, and those who know say the versions are twins—every female Eddie Holland produced phrased like him anyway; Glass House threw a tirade when it sold a million.

"Touch Me Jesus" (May 1971) an Angelo Bond/Lamont Dozier/Brian Holland tune bombed; the gap between it and their last recording (seven months) didn't help. Invictus issued "Look What We've Done to Love," a beautiful Ty Hunter-led ballad that shoulda, coulda, that didn't explode as expected. Holland-Dozier-Holland's "Playing Games" (January 1972) did absolutely nothing. *Inside the Glass House* dropped without fanfare late in 1971, without a picture of the group on either cover. They never hit like the Honey Cone, Freda Payne, 100 Proof, Eighth Day, Flaming Ember, Chairmen of the Board, or Laura Lee—artists under the same creative umbrella—and their foundation started crumbling. "Giving Up the Ring" (March 1972) kept the wrecking ball swinging. "VIP" (April 1972)—previously a Honey Cone B-side—was Scherrie Payne's solo; its flip, "It Ain't the World It's the People Living in It," was plucked from Glass House's debut album. Ty Hunter's solo "I Don't See Me in Your Eyes Anymore" (1972) was a new take on a Brotherly Love B-side, and the quivering falsetto's rendition of Eddie Holman's "Hey There Lonely Girl" provided a solid B-side.

"Thanks I Needed That" from the LP of the same name closed the book on Glass House. Eric Dunham was a member, but it's unclear whether he was an original replaced by Mitchell or if he joined later. Holland-Dozier-Holland switched Invictus' distribution from Capitol to CBS Records in 1973, but the fact didn't elate Glass House as they got pink slips and quietly disbanded. Scherrie Payne became a Supreme and now sings with the Former Ladies of the Supremes with Freddie Poole and Sundray Tucker, aka Cindy Scott; Ty Hunter joined the Originals replacing CP Spencer; Jones, Mitchell, and Dunham vanished from sight. *—Andrew Hamilton*

Inside the Glass House / 1971 / Invictus ♦♦♦

Eddie Holland, Lamont Dozier, and Brian Holland handpicked the members of Glass House: Scherrie Payne (Freda's sister), Ty Hunter, Pearl Jones, and Larry Mitchell. A common occurrence at Invictus/Hot Wax Records, Chairmen of the Board, Eighth Day, the Honey Cone, and 100 Proof (Aged in Soul) were formed the same way. The album starts on a mellow note with "Look What We've Done To Love," led by Hunter who sang with Dozier in the Romeos, the Voice Masters, and later took over for C. P. Spencer in the Originals. Hunter's falsetto croons the hurting lyrics about the perils of taking love for granted, the LP version flows over four minutes, the single only gave you 2:45 of the harmonious ballad. Their biggest record "Crumbs Off the Table" led by Payne has snappy lyrics and a hesitating groove; it reached number seven on the Soul Chart, but failed to crack the Top 40 stalling at number 59. Other tasty nuggets include a remake of "Hey There Lonely Girl," "Heaven Is There to Guide Us," "Touch Me Jesus," and "You Ain't Livin' Unless You're Lovin'" led by Jones. *—Andrew Hamilton*

Thanks I Needed That / 1972 / Invictus ♦♦♦

Not as charming as their debut LP. Ty Hunter, Scherrie Payne, Sylvia Smith and Larry Mitchell, all good singers, don't have much here to show their skills. Sylvia gives her all on the moving ballad "That Man I'll Never Have," and "Stealing Moments From Another Woman's Life" is alright. Scherrie Payne, (Freda's sister) does a quality version of "A House Is Not a Home." The rest sounds like rejects from Honey Cone sessions. *—Andrew Hamilton*

- **Crumbs off the Table: The Invictus Sessions** / 1999 / Sequel ♦♦♦♦♦

Of all the acts of Holland-Dozier-Holland's acts on Invictus/Hot Wax, Glass House very well might have been the grittiest, the one that recorded the hardest soul, albeit still within the hyper-detailed, big-scale Invictus/Hot Wax sound. It wasn't just that the singers were earthier—the songs and the rhythms had a grittier gait, making them an interesting variation on the label. They also had a consistent run on the label, as this 24-track collection proves. *Crumbs off the Table: The Invictus Sessions* contains the entirity of their two albums for the label—1971's *Inside the Glass House* and 1972's *Thanks I Needed That*—along with four non-album tracks. Though few songs stand out as clearly as "Crumbs off the Table," their powerhouse one-hit wonder, the tunes are all solidly crafted and delivered with style, particularly in the exquisitely detailed productions. This may be music for the serious soul collector, but they're not likely to be disappointed with what they find here. *—Stephen Thomas Erlewine*

Quinn Golden

b. Memphis, TN

Vocals, Producer, Songwriter / Retro-Soul, Memphis Soul, Soul-Blues

Soul singing, Memphis, TN native, Quinn Golden sang with the Elements of Love while still in his teens; he left to work with Canteca and the opportunity to tour with a variety of Stax artists. They warmed crowds for the Bar-Kays on the Memphis funk band's biggest event—their acclaimed Cold-Blooded Tour of the late '70s. He played the bass and sang background for Al Green for seven years, complementing Green's other vocalists, notably Margaret Foxworth, Al's former girlfriend, and a native of Cleveland, OH. He played with White Heat, from Akron, OH, who released an LP on RCA Records produced by Barry White; members of White Heat united with Bobby and Tommy DeBarge from Grand Rapids, MI, and Akron's Philip Ingram to form Switch. Golden's career highlights include working with Ike Turner, Shirley Brown, Denise LaSalle, and doing sessions with rock luminaries the stature of Bob Dylan and Ron Woods. He always wanted to solo and got the opportunity with Traction Records in Jackson, MS, waxing "I'm Serious About Your Love," in 1990. A five-tool artist, Golden writes, sings, produces, records, and performs. He records for Ecko Records and has released two sizzling CDs: *Cover You With a Kiss*, and *What's The Name of That Thang*, in 1999. *—Andrew Hamilton*

• **What's the Name of That Thang** / Sep. 14, 1999 / Ecko ✦✦✦✦
Quinn Golden's voice is a cross between Bobby Womack's and J. Blackfoot's; his rendition of Womack's "Woman Gotta Have It" is as soulful as the version by Womack. Golden is potent on shufflers, ballads, or uptempo numbers. "Peepin' in the Window" and the title tracks are peppy, upbeat sagas. The shufflers include "Woman," where Quinn brags about his lady, "Threesome," which is straight from *the Jerry Springer Show*, and "Damned If I Do, Damned If I Don't," which is a Tyrone Davis sound-alike. Also featured are two eye-wetting ballads: "The Way You Layed It on Me" and "Won't You Make Up Your Mind." You don't hear Southern soul on the radio unless you live in the South, an indictment of AM and FM radio, and a crying shame. *—Andrew Hamilton*

On Q / Mar. 12, 2002 / Ecko ✦✦✦
Quinn Golden continues his output of good old-fashioned Southern soul music for the Memphis, TN-based Ecko Records label with *On Q*. Like his previous releases for the label—*Cover You With a Kiss* (1998), *What's the Name of That Thang?* (1999), and *A Little Sumpin' Sumpin'* (2001)—*On Q* finds Golden infusing the retro-soul, primarily played by producer John Ward, with his voice, which is as precious as his last name may lead you to presume. As mentioned, Ward not only produces this album but also plays much of the music, credited for the rhythm tracks and sequencing for each of the albums songs as well as the guitar. Moreover, Ward co-writes the majority of the album's songs, along with songwriting partner Raymond Moore. Overall, *On Q* is an excellent continuation of the work Golden had begun with his previous Ecko releases. *—Jason Birchmeier*

Cuba Gooding

b. Apr. 27, 1944, New York, NY
Vocals / Urban, R&B, Soul, Contemporary Gospel
Cuba Gooding sang lead on hits by the Main Ingredient, including the gold singles "Everybody Plays the Fool" and their remake of "I Just Don't Want to Be Lonely." Gooding's agile tenor worked well on the group's pop love songs and their inspirational-themed material like "Shame on the World," "Rolling Down a Mountainside," and Brian Auger's "Happiness Is Just Around the Bend."

Gooding, born April 27, 1944, in New York City, grew up in Harlem with Tony Silvester, Luther Simmons Jr., and Donald McPherson. Silvester, Simmons, and McPherson formed the vocal group the Poets in the mid-'60s. They released singles on legendary songwriter/production team Leiber & Stoller's Red Bird label: "Merry Christmas Baby" and "I'm Stuck on You." As the Insiders, the group signed with RCA Records and their label debut was the single "I'm Better Off Without You" b/w "I'm Just a Man."

Changing their name to the Main Ingredient, they began to have hits, starting with "You've Been My Inspiration," a remake of the Curtis Mayfield & the Impressions hit "I'm So Proud," "Spinning Around (I Must Be Falling in Love)," and "Black Seeds Keep on Growing." McPherson sang lead on all the group's hits, but when he became too ill to tour, Gooding, who contributed background vocals on their records, sang lead during the Main Ingredient's live concerts. Though the group believed he would return, Donald McPherson died of leukemia on July 4, 1971. With Gooding on lead vocals, the Main Ingredient had their first million-selling single with "Everybody Plays the Fool."

In 1977, Gooding signed as a solo artist with Motown Records. Amid much anticipation and critical raves, his solo debut, *The First Cuba Gooding Album*, produced by Dennis Lambert and Brian Potter (Tavares, the Four Tops), was released in spring 1978 with only one single, "Mind Pleaser," charting number-91 R&B in spring 1978. Another Motown LP, *Love Dancer*, produced by Michael Lovesmith, was issued in spring 1979. Gooding re-teamed with Silvester and Simmons, recording the Main Ingredient LPs *Ready for Love* (RCA, fall 1980) and the Patrick Adams-produced *I Only Have Eyes for You* (RCA, late 1981). Gooding then recorded a remake of "Happiness Is Just Around the Bend" for Streetwise Records, which became a huge dance hit in late 1983. *—Ed Hogan*

• **The First Cuba Gooding Album** / 1978 / Motown ✦✦
The title suggests a long, fruitful career with Motown, but the association ended after two albums; *Love Dancer*, the second Cuba Gooding album was released in 1979. Dennis Lambert and Brian Potter had some success producing Tavares and others but came up empty this time. Only "Mind Pleaser" emerged on a 45, backed with the dreadful "Where Would I Be Without You"; it deserved better. Lambert and Potter built it around Motown's tradition—a ringing intro, a hot chorus, a lively hook, and spirited singing—but its lackluster sales were a major disappointment. Nothing else, except "All I Can Give You Is Love," is as pleasing. The ballads are mundane and familiar, and the midtempo numbers are irritating; on one tune Lambert and Potter have Gooding sounding like Mickey Mouse. No kidding. *—Andrew Hamilton*

Rosco Gordon

b. 1934, Memphis, TN, **d.** Jul. 11, 2002, New York, NY [Rego Park, Queens]
Vocals, Piano / R&B, Soul
Rosco Gordon was best known for being one of the progenitors of a slightly shambolic, loping style of piano shuffle called "Rosco's Rhythm." The basic elements of this sound were further developed after Jamaican musicians got a hold of 45s Gordon recorded in the early '50s—which were not available to Jamaicans until 1959—and created ska, which took its name for the sound of this particular shuffle as it sounded being played on an electric guitar (ska-ska-ska).

No less an authority than Chris Blackwell—he was the founder/president of Island Records who produced Bob Marley, the Wailers, and Peter Tosh, to name a few—has cited Gordon's importance to reggae and ska music and championed the sound he helped create. Gordon had originally been a member of the famed Beale Streeters, a Memphis, TN-based group that also featured the considerable talents of Johnny Ace, B.B. King, and Bobby "Blue" Bland, in the late '40s. They were scouted by none other than Ike Turner for Modern Records, who recorded the Beale Streeters' first single in 1951.

Gordon was soon recording sides for Sam Phillips and his Sun Records label. Phillips later sold the master of Gordon's own "Bootin'" to two competing labels, Chess and RPM, both of whom released it as a single. This "mix-up" did not, however, prevent the song from hitting number one on the R&B chart in 1952.

The follow-up to "Bootin'," called "No More Doggin'," was the first song to feature the now-familiar shuffle rhythm of Gordon's design, with a strong accent on the off-beat that repeated the oft-monotonous guitar phrasing. Though Gordon had recorded the song in the living room of a friend's home, in fact, the sound was fully developed and unique for its time. On July 11, 2002, Gordon died of a heart attack at his home in Queens, NY. He was 74. *—Bryan Thomas*

Just a Little Bit / Oct. 1993 / Vee-Jay ✦✦✦✦✦
Gordon's late-'50s and early-'60s Vee-Jay sessions have been treasured collector's items for years, and this new disc features 16 selections (half previously unissued in America). The revival of "No More Doggin'" was even closer to ska than the original, with Gordon smoothly angling in on the offbeat. Gordon remains a hero in Jamaica for his influence on ska and bluebeat; it's great to have these recordings available once more. *—Ron Wynn*

Memphis, Tennessee / 2000 / Stony Plain ✦✦✦
Here is one of the pioneers of the Memphis R&B movement. This man was a huge influence in Jamaica for the starting of the ska rhythms; he had a loping and relaxed style that fit right into the early propensities of early ska artists. He hasn't been popular in the states since "Just a Little Bit," his early-'60s hit, stormed the R&B charts. At this time he married and devoted himself to his wife and growing family. It was only her untimely demise from bone cancer and the growing up of his children that allowed him to get back on the road again (mostly in Europe and Canada). But here he is back in full voice, with the help of Duke Robillard and his band to re-ignite the flames that have lain dormant all these years. He either wrote or co-wrote all but one of the songs here, showing he has not sat idly by during his hiatus from recording. This is an exceptionally fine effort and kudos must go to Stony Plain for taking the time to make this available for our pleasure. *—Bob Gottlieb*

• **The Very Best of Rosco Gordon: Just a Little Bit** / Jan. 30, 2001 / Collectables ✦✦✦✦✦
Calling this compilation *The Very Best of Rosco Gordon* is a bit of a misnomer, since it only features material Gordon recorded for the Vee-Jay label, ignoring his frantic early sides for Sun and other classic material released on RPM. But if you're looking for a one-disc overview of Gordon's fine Vee-Jay recordings, you came to the right place; these 15 tunes (lucky consumers get two, yes two takes of "New Orleans, LA") all feature Gordon's trademark loping rhythms, walking basslines, percussive guitar lines, and vocals, which sound comfortably laid-back even at their most emphatic. While Gordon spent most of his career in Memphis, he certainly learned the lessons of the classic New Orleans R&B masters, and these tunes capture his own distinctive and flavorful variation on the Crescent City sound, a bit bent but still recognizable, and a significant inspiration on the nascent Jamaican music scene, who would further rework these proto-Louisiana sounds into what would become ska. Fascinating as history and a lot of fun as music, though the final and definitive Rosco Gordon collection still remains to be compiled. *—Mark Deming*

I'm Gonna Shake It / 2002 / Varese ✦✦✦✦✦
This 22-track CD doesn't have all of Rosco Gordon's Sun recordings, or, as should be more properly stated, all of the recordings he did under the auspices of Sun Records chief Sam Phillips. The 1958 B-side "Torro," for some reason, doesn't appear, and nor do some sides he cut with Phillips in the early '50s that were leased to RPM and Chess. Still, this does have seven of the eight songs that showed up on Gordon's four Sun singles, as well as no less than 15 tracks spanning 1951-1957 that lay unreleased at the time. As such, it's a bountiful survey of his Sun (or Sam Phillips-allied) output, establishing him as a second-tier but admirable talent combining blues, boogie, R&B, and a little bit of rock & roll and rockabilly. Gordon had an above-average sense of fun and humor for such a performer, qualities that help him make the somewhat average R&B material better than it would have been with many other performers, almost comically so on "Weeping Blues," with some of the most over the top bawling to be heard on any popular music recording. When he let a little rockabilly into the mix, as on "Love for You Baby," "I'm Gonna Shake It," and particularly his final Sun single, "Sally Jo," the results were most interesting, distinguishing it from much of the other R&B-blues that bled into early rock & roll during the period. It's a good anthology, but note that it's not synonymous with a Rosco Gordon best-of, not representing the numerous sides he cut for other labels, and missing his biggest hit, the 1960 number two R&B smash "Just a Little Bit." *—Richie Unterberger*

Berry Gordy Jr.

b. Nov. 28, 1929, Detroit, MI
Producer / Motown
The founder of Motown Records, Berry Gordy did what many people of his time believed could never be done: he brought black music into millions of white Americans' homes, helping both black artists and their culture gain acceptance, and opening the door for a multitude of sucessful black record executives and producers. Though the music of Motown was not as raw or edgy as other R&B labels, such as Chess and Stax, the songs that were written, produced, and released from "Hitsville USA" comprise some of the most enduring, sophisticated and popular music of our time. Influential artists such as Marvin Gaye, Stevie Wonder, Diana Ross, Michael Jackson and Smokey Robinson were all discovered and their talents fostered by Berry Gordy. Motown groups like the Four Tops, the Supremes and the Temptations are regarded as some of the best vocal groups

ever to record. Even now, years after Gordy sold the company, the reputation of excellence he forged at Motown continues to stay with the famous label.

Berry Gordy was born in Detroit in 1929, during the early years of the Depression. The seventh child of eight, his father was an enterprising man who ran a grocery store, a plastering business, and managed apartment buildings, among other things. A high school dropout, Gordy had two loves in his teens: music and boxing. Dividing his time between writing songs on the piano and training at a local Detroit gym under champion trainer Eddie Futch, Gordy fostered both talents. A fairly successful lightweight, at 19 Gordy had an epiphany concerning his future. Realizing the tough life of a boxer compared to the classier life of a musician, he devoted all his energies to songwriting.

After a stint in the army temporarily sidelined his musical ambitions, Gordy returned to Detroit and opened a record shop, his first real foray into the music business. The shop failed, but it gave Gordy an even deeper drive to be a part of the music industry. Supporting his wife and three children by working in a Detroit auto plant and songwriting at night, Gordy's compositions were soon finding their way into the hands of local artists. Through his sister Gwen, Gordy met a local manager named Al Green; when one of his new acts, Jackie Wilson, needed a song, Berry was the man who provided it. In late 1956, "Reet Petite," co-written by Gordy, sister Gwen and friend Roquel Davis, became a hit for Wilson. Several more hits followed, including "Lonely Teardrops," "To Be Loved," and "I'll Be Satisfied," all written by Gordy. The trio's hits for Wilson and Etta James ("All I Could Do Was Cry") gave them the reputation of movers and shakers in the business, and soon aspiring artists, songwriters and producers were coming to them in hopes of catching a break. When a dispute over royalties on a Jackie Wilson hit broke out between Gordy and Green, Gordy vowed not to give another song to Wilson. The resulting split left Gordy on his own.

Setting up a publishing company, Gordy met a young singer named William "Smokey" Robinson, who fronted a group called the Miracles. Gordy became their manager and together they co-wrote the hit "Got a Job." Two more hits and a distribution deal with United Artists followed, and a long creative partnership and friendship began between the two men. Bolstered by his recent success and aided by his family and friends, Gordy bought a house at 2648 West Grand Boulevard in Detroit, named it "Hitsville USA," and started his own label, Tamla. The house doubled as a recording studio, and with talented young Detroit musicians such as Smokey Robinson, Barrett Strong and Eddie Holland hanging around, it wasn't long before Tamla was turning out hits. In 1960, the first song wholly conceived and produced at Hitsville, the Gordy composition "Money (That's What I Want)," became a hit. Not long afterwards, the Miracles hit with "Way Over There" and "Shop Around," Motown and Berry Gordy were national.

With the success of the Miracles, endless numbers of young, talented artists from the area began to show up at Hitsville. Soon Marvin Gaye, the Temptations, the Supremes, the Four Tops and Stevie Wonder were all recording for Tamla and its parent label Motown. No fool to the ways of business, Gordy set up an environment of stiff competition at the label (sometimes directly, sometimes indirectly) where artists and producers were constantly trying to outdo one another and were, in the process, outdoing their own last releases. The strategy worked, and the company had hit after hit during the early '60s with songs, like "My Guy," that broke the color barrier, reaching not just the black radio stations, but going pop and succeeding among white audiences as well.

Over the next several years, Gordy drew on his automobile-production roots to create an assembly line of hits and hitmakers at Motown. The label's new motto was "the sound of young America," and writers like Holland-Dozier-Holland, Harvey Fuqua and Norman Whitfield churned out million-seller after million-seller for the Supremes, Martha & the Vandellas and the Temptations. Gordy, realizing that great presentation is key, also hired Maxine Powell to run the Motown Finishing School, a glorified charm school that made Motown artists look, talk and act like the stars they were becoming. Throughout the '60s Motown was riding high, and Gordy emerged as one of the young black elite in show business. Yet the family atmosphere for which Motown was known was beginning to crack through the years of forced competition and favoritism. It was no secret that Gordy favored Smokey Robinson and Diana Ross over many of the other artists, and in 1968, the production team of Holland-Dozier-Holland left Motown, filing a $20 million lawsuit against Gordy. In 1970, Diana Ross & the Supremes, a virtual symbol of Motown's success, broke up, ending an era.

Not long after, Gordy pulled up stakes in Detroit and relocated the multi-million dollar operation to L.A. There he concentrated on Ross' acting career, producing the Ross vehicle *Lady Sings the Blues*. Though the company had recently signed the Jackson 5, and Marvin Gaye and Stevie Wonder were entering the most successful eras of their career, in L.A. Gordy's stranglehold on the magic of Motown lessened. Ross' solo career was not as triumphant as he had hoped, and Gordy had lost much of the tight-knit family atmosphere that originally made Motown so successful. By the mid-'80s, Motown was losing millions, and in 1988 Gordy did what he never thought he could: he sold Motown to MCA for $61 million. The sale of Motown, though sad for many, was concrete proof of Gordy's success. Taking an $800 loan from his family, he turned Motown into the most successful black-owned label in history. In the process, Gordy also brought the world countless memorable songs not only through his vision for spotting talent in others, but also his own talent as a songwriter and producer. *—Steve Kurutz*

GQ

f. New York, NY

Group / Disco, Quiet Storm

A Bronx group that effectively mixed East Coast disco and Chicago soul covers in the late '70s and early '80s, GQ began as Sabu & the Survivors in 1968. Lead vocalist Emanuel Rahiem LeBlanc, Keith Crier, Herb Lane, and Paul Service were original members, but by 1980 GQ was a trio following Service's departure. They had two Top 10 R&B and Top 20 pop hits, as well as a number-one R&B single in 1979, with "Disco Nights (Rock-Freak)" also peaking at number-12 pop; the single also won GQ an American Music Award. Their remakes of the Billy Stewart classics "I Do Love You" and "Sitting in the Park" were number-five and number-nine R&B singles in 1979 and 1980, respectively, with "I Do Love You" also reaching number-20 pop. They enjoyed one other Top 30 R&B single in 1981, "Shake." All their hits were on Arista from 1979 to 1982. *—Ron Wynn*

Disco Nights / 1979 / Arista ♦♦♦

The four members of GQ—Emmanuel Rahiem LeBlanc, Keith "Sabu" Crier, Herb Lane, and Paul Service—first recorded as the Rhythm Makers for Vigor Records. Their smash "Disco Nights (Rock Freak)" was first recorded on Vigor as "Soul on Your Side"; the track is identical, but a new title and lyrics were added to cash in on the disco craze. "Disco Nights" topped the R&B charts for two weeks in 1970. LeBlanc first recorded at the tender age of 13 with a group he formed called Sons of Darkness. GQ was self-contained and wrote most of the material on this LP, except for A Taste of Honey's "Boogie Oogie Oogie" and Billy Stewart's classic "I Do Love You," which nearly went to number one also. "It's Your Love" is a beautiful, airy-sounding ballad that is uniquely arranged; the enthusiastic, positive message of "Make My Dream a Reality" will have you disco dancing to its lively beats and urgent, pleading vocals. *—Andrew Hamilton*

Two / 1980 / Arista ♦♦♦

With the success of "Disco Nights" taken from their debut album, GQ followed with another upbeat number, "Standing Ovation." Not as groovin' as its predecessor, nonetheless it manages to stand in at number 12 after 15 weeks on the *Billboard* R&B charts. The quartet followed with the re-make of a song that Billy Stewart made popular among R&B lovers, "Sitting in the Park." The patient rhythms of the track provide a humble foundation for Emmanuel Raheim LeBlanc to dislpay his appealing vocals. After 16 weeks, the single maxed out at number nine. This review cannot conclude without taking notice of "Don't Stop This Feeling." With a combination of R&B and smooth jazz, this composition maintains a steady rhythm seasoned with LeBlanc's placid articulation of each lyric and improvising guitar solo. Though this number was not a release, it has become popular on the play lists of many quiet storm formats. *—Craig Lytle*

The Best of GQ / Jun. 6, 1995 / Alex ♦♦♦♦

Known primarily for one of the most successful underground disco hits of the entire era with the award-winning "Disco Nights," *Best of G.Q.* compiles some of the finer moments of the group's career for this 1995 release. What is surprising is the number of covers that are included, rather than original material. Renditions of the Taste of Honey chart-topper "Boogie Oogie Oogie" as well as two Billy Stewart classics and an Emperor Soul cover are all included, all done tastefully well. At times the material, notably the slower songs, borderline on what was to later be deemed smooth jazz. On the whole, it's an impressive record and an intriguing look at one of disco's underground hitmakers. *—Rob Theakston*

● **GQ's Greatest Hits** / Dec. 1, 1998 / Thump ♦♦♦♦

This greatest hit's collection first appeared on Arista in 1979. The pulsating "Disco Nights (Rock Freak)" blasted all over the discos, the skip beat and snappy production proved more effective than an earlier version they cut as the Rhythm Makers entitled "Soul on Your Side." The yearning "Make My Dream a Reality" is one of GQ's best compositions, and proves disco didn't have to be mundane. Jams aside, GQ made their mark re-making Billy Stewart's two classics: "I Do Love You," and "Sitting in the Park," fine efforts, but neither could touch the originals. The tender, lamenting "Sad Girl," originally done by Emperors Soul 69 on Futura Records, and later the Intruders, didn't scorch the charts like the Stewart remakes. A good introduction to GQ. *—Andrew Hamilton*

Tribute to Marvin Gaye & Billy Stewart / Mar. 16, 1999 / ITP ♦♦♦

This is another goodie from ITP Records. GQ's lead singer and guitarist, Emanuel Rahiem LeBlanc uncannily clones the phrasings and vocal inflections of Marvin Gaye and Billy Stewart. A new song "Star in Your Eyes" sounds like an old Billy Stewart tune, but isn't, and "Time For Classics," tributes' the good ole days, the Originals ("Baby I'm For Real") assist GQ on the number. LeBlanc gives Stewart and Gaye's material masterful, readings. His voice sounds better on "I Do Love You," and "Sitting in the Park," then it did the first time he remade them years ago. One of Stewart's prettiest ballads "Strange Feeling" is closer to the original than a recent rendition by label mates, Sly, Slick & Wicked. He's as effective doing Gaye, LeBlanc's interpretations of "Let's Get It On," "Distant Lover," "What's Going On," and "If I Should Die Tonight," reeked of authenticity, and are as enjoyable as the originals. *—Andrew Hamilton*

Jaki Graham

b. Birmingham, AL

Vocals / Club/Dance, House, Euro-Dance, Disco

Midlands-based soul singer Jaki Graham established herself as one of the most popular R&B and dance artists in the U.K. with a string of hits in the '80s. Among her chart entries were Top Ten placings for "Could It Be I'm Falling in Love," "Round and Round," and "Set Me Free." Graham also made appearances on releases by other artists, lending her sensual vocals to tracks by UB40, Kim Wilde, Paul Hardcastle, and Afrika Bambaataa. Despite her star status in the U.K., Graham's success in the States has failed to crossover from the dance audience, although she has had success with club audiences, including scoring a massive hit with "Ain't Nobody." Her output beyond the '80s was neither as prolific or high-profile, with many of her albums seeing release only in Japan, where she maintains huge popularity. *—Tom Demalon*

From Now On / Sep. 19, 1989 / Orpheus ♦♦

A gifted British soul vocalist, Jaki Graham has seldom gotten the kind of songs that her great skills could turn into breakout hits. These are mostly disposable formula filler that she tries to elevate but can't, despite often stunning vocal treatments. She's a great producer away from being a star, and could certainly be a great disco diva with the right tracks. *—Ron Wynn*

● **Real Life** / Sep. 13, 1994 / Avex ♦♦♦

Including the radio-ready single "You Can Count on Me," Jaki Graham weaves a fine line between house rhythms and elements of R&B and soul on this Avex U.K. release. *—John Bush*

Larry Graham & Graham Central Station

b. Aug. 14, 1946, Beaumont, TX

Bass, Vocals, Guitar / Funk, Soul, Quiet Storm, Adult Contemporary, Club/Dance

Graham Central Station was a showcase for the revolutionary pop-and-slap bass guitar of Larry Graham, an alumnus of Sly & the Family Stone largely responsible for originating the percussive groove which typified the progressive funk sound of the 1970s. Born August 14, 1946, in Beaumont, TX, Graham was raised in Oakland, CA; by his teens he was adept not only on bass but also guitar, harmonica and drums, and at the age of 15 began performing with the Dell Graham Trio, his mother's lounge act. While attending college, he served as a supporting musician with the likes of John Lee Hooker, Jackie Wilson, Jimmy Reed and the Drifters; in 1968 he joined Sly & the Family Stone, appearing with the group during the halcyon period which gave rise to such classic albums as *Stand!* and *There's a Riot Goin' On*, as well as smash singles like "Dance to the Music" and "Everybody Is a Star," both of which prominently feature Graham's cavernous baritone in addition to his enormously influential thumping bass style.

In the wake of behind-the-scenes turmoil, Graham exited the group in late 1972; after initially agreeing to produce a band named Hot Chocolate (not the same act famed for hit singles like "Emma" and "You Sexy Thing"), he eventually joined their lineup, renaming the unit Graham Central Station. A propulsive, infectious funk ensemble, their original roster also included guitarist David "Dynamite" Vega, keyboardists Robert "Butch" Sam (formerly with Billy Preston) and Hershall "Happiness" Kennedy, percussionist Patrice "Chocolate" Banks, and drummer Willie "Wild" Sparks; the debut Graham Central album, an eponymously titled effort released in 1974, proved highly successful, launching a minor pop hit with "Can You Handle It." Another hit, "Feel the Need," emerged from *Release Yourself*, issued later that same year; the third GCS LP, 1975's *Ain't No 'Bout-A-Doubt It*, yielded the single "Your Love," a Top 40 pop hit which also topped the R&B charts. *Mirror* followed a year later.

With 1977's *Now Do U Wanta Dance*, Graham Central Station scored another R&B smash with the title track; by the release of 1978's *My Radio Sure Sounds Good to Me*, Graham's wife Tina had signed on as a vocalist, but pop crossover success remained elusive, and after *Star Walk* the following year, the group disbanded. Graham then turned solo, moving from funk to soulful ballads; his debut effort, 1980's *One in a Million You*, reached the Top 30, the title track becoming a Top Ten hit. 1981's *Just Be My Lady* yielded another hit with its own title cut, while 1982's *Sooner or Later* was also successful. However, after 1983's *Victory*, Graham's career took a downward turn, with 1985's *Fired Up* released solely in Japan. Aside from 1987's "If You Need My Love Tonight," a minor hit duet with Aretha Franklin, he was largely out of the public eye in the years to follow, instead working as a songwriter and sideman.

By the early '90s, Graham was leading Psychedelic Psoul, a nine-piece band which toured with comedian/singer Eddie Murphy; he also toured with the Crusaders. Following Sly & the Family Stone's 1993 induction into the Rock and Roll Hall of Fame, he re-formed Graham Central Station, eventually bringing into the fold former Family Stone bandmates Cynthia Robinson on trumpet and Jerry Martini on saxophone. Throughout Graham's lean years, one of his most vocal supporters remained the Artist Formerly Known as Prince, who readily acknowledged the influence of GCS not only on his music but also on his flamboyant stage show; by 1997, Graham Central Station was ensconced as the regular supporting act on the Artist's extended Jam of the Year tour, with the group also issuing a Japanese album titled *By Popular Demand*. Sessions at Minneapolis' Paisley Park Studios yielded the release of *GCS 2000* in 1998. *—Jason Ankeny*

Graham Central Station / 1973 / Warner Bros. ✦✦✦

This promising 1973 album represents bass wizard Larry Graham's first post-Sly & the Family Stone work. Much like his previous band, Graham Central Station was a multiracial unit that blended soul grooves and pop hooks to create an exuberant hybrid. However, *Graham Central Station* gives Graham's bass work a more upfront role in the sound and adds further layers of rhythms with drum machines and rhythmic-sounding keyboards like the clavinet. The result is a disc that is equal parts pop-soul ("Ain't No Fun to Me") and funk ("We Be Gettin' Down"). The blend isn't as seamless as one might hope, which means some songs are stronger on groove then they are on melody: "Tell Me What It Is" has a great groove built on a seamless mix of thumping bass and throbbing drum machine, but lacks the melodic hooks necessary to make it a truly memorable song. Another problem is that the lyrics are underdeveloped in places: "People" rails against injustice but fails to point the finger at a specific cause, and "Why?" treads on too-familiar love lament territory. Despite these problems, *Graham Central Station* remains an engaging listen thanks to fine musicianship; even when the songs are lacking in hooks, there is an abundance of cool riffs and stellar vocal harmonies that will make funk fans smile. When this musicianship is applied to the right songs, the results are pure magic: "Hair" wraps a clever lyric about tolerance around a huge groove driven by one of Graham's serpentine basslines, and "Can You Handle It?" effectively fuses a pop melody built on a sing-along chorus to a propulsive bass/keyboard groove (it also became the group's first chart hit). In short, casual listeners may want to pick up this album's highlights on a compilation, but funk lovers will find plenty to enjoy on *Graham Central Station*. *—Donald A. Guarisco*

Release Yourself / 1974 / Warner Bros. ✦✦✦✦

After a tentative but promising 1973 debut album, Graham Central Station returned the next year with a head-spinning blend of R&B styles that realized their promise in a truly impressive fashion. *Release Yourself* touches on everything from gospel music to psychedelia, as the band puts forth an impressive set of songs that strike an effective balance between accessibility and complexity. This time, keyboards carry a new level of importance: songs like "G.C.S." and "I Believe in You" flow forth on elaborate keyboard riffs layered with plenty of spacey synthesizer leads. The album's most impressive achievements are the title track, a pulse-pounding tribute to the joys of self expression that combines churchy organ riffs and stately horns over a furiously-paced bass/clavinet rhythm, and "'Tis Your Kind of Music," a psychedelic-funk masterpiece that has Patryce "Chocolate" Banks and Graham trading sultry lead vocals over an otherworldly blend of keyboard and Mellotron riffs with a fluid bassline. Another stunner is "Today," a funk-rock workout that starts with a slowly-woven tapestry of keyboard riffs before launching into a cosmic vocal section that underscores the group's choral harmonies with some fiery guitar leads. Although it lacks an overtly pop-flavored classic like "Can You Handle It?" or "Your Love," nothing on this album is less than interesting thanks to stellar arrangements and the group's obvious love for what they do—the sunny energy that propels songs like the title track and "Got to Get Through It" is positively infectious. The result is a true gem that is a treat for funk fanatics and a required listen for anyone with a serious interest in Graham Central Station. *—Donald A. Guarisco*

Ain't No 'Bout-A-Doubt It / 1975 / Warner Bros. ✦✦✦

On their third album, Graham Central Station created an album full of trademark infectious pop-soul grooves, but one that lacked the consistently strong work that defines a true classic. However, that doesn't mean that *Ain't No 'Bout-A-Doubt It* is less than listenable: in fact, it contains some of the group's finest songs. The album's all-time funk classic is the opening track "The Jam," a "Dance to the Music"-styled funk workout that intersperses a dazzling group groove with individual solos for each player. "Water" is another strong funk tune, an insistently rhythmic song that blends thump-popping basslines with backwards tape loops to create an intriguing blend of funk and psychedelia. *Ain't No 'Bout-A-Doubt It* also produced a number one R&B smash in "Your Love," which marries the group's talent for funky grooves to an old-fashioned love song with a melody that harkens back to doo wop. However, not everything on *Ain't No 'Bout-A-Doubt It* is as strong as these highlights: "It Ain't Nothing but a Warner Bros. Party" is a lightweight jam with throwaway lyrics, and the group's rote version of the Ann Peebles classic "I Can't Stand the Rain" fails to add anything memorable to the song. All in all, *Ain't No 'Bout-A-Doubt It* lacks the strong material to make it memorable, but its high points make it a worthwhile listen for funk enthusiasts. *—Donald A. Guarisco*

Mirror / 1976 / Warner Bros. ✦✦✦

The irony to this album is that the group's music is funky as always, but its lyrical content has many gospel and religious overtones. Though the title track was not a featured release, its synth-propelled rhythm and stirring vocals blend well on this moderately uptempo number. The Top 20 single "Love" is arranged in a free-flowing, mellow tempo. It peaked at number 14 on the *Billboard* R&B charts. It was followed by the juiced-up funk track "Entrow." Supported by its unwavering beat, group members take turns on vocals and musical exhibitions. While "Save Me" has an aggressive disco groove, the lyric is religious as the title reflects. "I Got a Reason" and "Forever" have similar religious messages. With Larry Graham being the writer on every song on the album, it is highly likely that he was experiencing a transformation in his personal and professional life. *—Craig Lytle*

Now Do U Wanna Dance / 1977 / Warner Bros. ✦✦✦

The fifth album from the funk aggregate generated a smash hit with the title track, "Now Do-U-Wanta Dance." Paced by Graham's rumbling bass and animated lead vocals, which features the group leader on the vocorder, the synthesized funk track stayed on the *Billboard* R&B charts for ten weeks, peaking at number ten. The influence doo wop had on the bassist is revealed on songs like "Stomped, Beat-up and Whooped" and "Happ-E-2-C-U-A-Ginn." The former, paced by a rhythm track and Gail Muldrow's vocals, has a catchy hook phrase; it was the second single from the album to hit the *Billboard* R&B charts (number 25, 11 weeks). The latter is an upbeat, joyous a cappella number groomed around a melodious arrangement, Graham's streetcorner ad libs and the group's vocal exchanges. Larry Graham's musical talents are inviting. He gives his own rendition of the Al Green classic "Love and Happiness." Maintaining that soulful appeal, Graham injects his robust riffs and his own dose of funk can be found throughout this album. Even when he tones down the funk, the relish remains ever so present. *—Craig Lytle*

My Radio Sure Sounds Good to Me / 1978 / Warner Bros. ✦✦✦✦

Benny Golson is hardly the first person one would expect to co-produce a funk/soul album. In the late '50s, the Philadelphian made a name for himself in the jazz world playing tenor sax alongside the likes of Lee Morgan and Curtis Fuller in Art Blakey's Jazz Messengers—and his name continues to be synonymous with hard bop. But there isn't a trace of bop to be found on *My Radio Sure Sounds Good to Me*, a funk/soul LP that Golson produced with Larry Graham. This record marked the first time that Graham called his band Larry Graham & Graham Central Station (as opposed to simply Graham Central Station). But despite the name change and despite Golson's presence, *Radio* is state-of-the-art GCS—gritty 1970s funk jams ("Pow," "Boogie Witcha, Baby," "It's the Engine in Me") are right at home with sentimental soul ballads ("Is It Love?") and gospel-influenced message songs ("Mr. Friend"). Golson handles most of the LP's horn and string arrangements, but his jazz background doesn't make its presence felt—not even in a subtle way. Graham hired Golson to co-produce an R&B project, and he did what he was paid to do. *My Radio Sure Sounds Good to Me* isn't GCS' most essential album, but it's a solid effort that is easily recommended to anyone with a taste for gutsy, horn-powered 1970s funk. *—Alex Henderson*

Star Walk / 1979 / Warner Bros. ✦✦✦✦

By the late '70s, Sly Stone wasn't nearly as popular or as visible as he had been in the late '60s and early '70s. But his former bassist Larry Graham was still going strong. Released in 1979, *Star Walk* was the last album that Graham would record with Graham Central Station for quite some time; in 1980, the influential singer/electric bassist officially became a full-time solo artist and soared to the top of the R&B charts with his debut solo single, "One in a Million You." And not until 1998's *GCS 2000* would Graham use the GCS name on another album. If the name GCS had to be put to rest for a long time, at least the band went out with a bang on *Star Walk*. This excellent LP, which Graham produced himself, is full of sweaty, aggressive funk treasures; anyone who appreciates gutbucket funk would have a hard time not loving "Scream," "The Entertainer," and the single "(You're A) Foxy Lady." But not everything on this record is hardcore funk. "Tonight" is a lush Northern soul ballad, and the unexpected title song finds Graham getting into a synthesizer-driven Euro-disco groove—if you didn't know better, you would think that Graham traveled to Munich, Germany, and hired Giorgio Moroder to produce the tune. *—Alex Henderson*

One in a Million You / 1980 / Warner Bros. ✦✦✦✦✦
As the leader of Graham Central Station, Larry Graham was responsible for some of the nastiest, grittiest, most gutbucket funk of the 1970s. But when he launched a solo career with 1980s *One in a Million You*, the singer/electric bassist surprised the R&B world by emphasizing ballads. And if anyone doubted that Graham's fans wanted to hear him doing a lot of romantic crooning, their fears were put to rest when this LP's sentimental title song became a major hit and Warner Bros. successfully released Graham's remake of "When We Get Married" (previously recorded by the Dreamlovers and the Intruders) as the follow-up single. This isn't to say that *One in a Million You* is devoid of uptempo material; one of the best things on the album is the very danceable and infectious "I Just Can't Stop Dancing." Nonetheless, the LP is best-known for its ballads. "I Just Can't Stop Dancing" was meant to recall "Dance to the Music," a Sly & the Family Stone smash that Graham had played on in the late '60s—although the song is equally mindful of 1960s Motown and has an appealing personality of its own. Less impressive is "I'm So Glad It's Summer Again," which is nothing more than a poor man's "Hot Fun in the Summertime." But this album's strengths by far outweigh its weaknesses, and *One in a Million You* is enthusiastically recommended to R&B lovers. *—Alex Henderson*

Just Be My Lady / 1981 / Warner Bros. ✦✦✦
Removed from his heavy funk days, Larry Graham mixes this album with ballads and midtempo numbers. The chart-topper from this album was the title track "Just Be My Lady." With his brawn sound, Graham sails through the lyric with agility and ease. With its affectionate connotation, the single became a popular wedding number; it peaked at number four on the *Billboard* R&B charts after 19 weeks. On an even more serene note, "Guess Who" was released as the follow-up single. It only fared at number 69 after a mere four weeks on the charts; however, it is still a touching number. While side one is filled with one ballad after another, side two has all moderate numbers. Some selections are shaded with Graham's doo wop and gospel influence, and all have much appeal. *—Craig Lytle*

- **The Best of Larry Graham and Graham Central Station, Vol. 1** / Apr. 1996 / Warner Bros. ✦✦✦✦✦

Although Sly Stone was the musical genius of the legendary Sly & the Family Stone, bassist Larry Graham was their heart and soul. Graham proved to be a master of the bass while with the Family Stone, singlehandedly inventing the slap and pop technique of funk bass, which is now commonplace in popular music. Following his departure from the band after the 1971 classic *There's a Riot Going On* (due to Sly's unpredictable behavior and drug abuse), Graham set out to form his own band, Graham Central Station. And soon it became apparent that the party had moved—Graham and company kept racking up the hits, while the Family Stone hit the skids. *The Best of Larry Graham and Graham Central Station* does an excellent job of collecting highlights from their 1974 debut all the way up to their softer early-'80s period. By far the best track on the compilation is the hard funk of "Hair," and a down-and-dirty number about equality not being based on appearance. Graham Central Station also had a knack for writing some infectious, uptempo numbers that, once put on your turntable, turn the room into an instant party ("It's Alright," "The Jam," and especially "Now D-U-Wanta Dance"). Also included is the group's biggest hit, the soulful ballad "One In a Million You," which skyrocketed to number one on the R&B chart and hit number nine on the pop charts in 1980. *The Best of Larry Graham and Graham Central Station Vol. 1* is essential funk. *—Greg Prato*

- **The Jam: The Larry Graham & Graham Central Station Anthology** / Oct. 2, 2001 / Rhino ✦✦✦✦✦

The Jam: The Larry Graham & Graham Central Station Anthology is an exhaustive, lovingly assembled double-disc retrospective of Graham's entire career, following his immediate post-Sly & the Family Stone recordings with Graham Central Station, through his luxurious solo quiet storm hits of the late '70s and early '80s, to his reunion with the Station in the '90s. Along the way, it hits every big hit and major jam among its 33 tracks, which culminates full circle with a live version of "I Want to Take You Higher" from 1992. Topped off by thorough, conversational liner notes by Rickey Vincent and a lot of photos, this is a terrific set for the dedicated and the serious funk/urban fan, and it will certainly give them what they're looking for—however, it's likely a bit too long and exhaustive for listeners that don't have such a deep interest in Graham. *—Stephen Thomas Erlewine*

Earl Grant

b. Jan. 20, 1933, Oklahoma City, OK, **d.** Jun. 11, 1970, Lordsburg, NM
Vocals, Keyboards / R&B, Vocal Pop
Earl Grant was a triple-threat entertainer as a pianist, organist, and vocalist. While much of his material fell into the arenas of either light pop or jazz-schmaltz, Grant scored two R&B hits in the late '50s and early '60s, the most memorable being "Sweet Sixteen Bars" in 1962. It reached number nine on the R&B charts. His prior smash "The End" was his lone pop hit, reaching number seven in 1958. Grant also was in the films "Tender Is the Night," "Imitation of Life," and "Tokyo Night." He was killed in 1970 in a car wreck at age 39. *—Ron Wynn*

In Motion / 1968 / Decca ✦✦✦
Released in 1968, *In Motion* is a typical album for soul-jazz organist and pianist Earl Grant, placing the keyboardist in front of either a small combo (eight tracks) or a Creed Taylor-style orchestra (three tracks, including a choral version of "What the World Needs Now Is Love"), with a song list taken largely from the pop hits of the day. The Burt Bacharach & Hal David songbook is raided three times, most effectively for a slinky organ version of "The Look of Love." Less effective are versions of Roger Miller's "King of the Road" and Bobbie Gentry's "Ode to Billie Joe," country-pop tunes that don't take well to Charles Bud Dant's ultra-slick middle-of-the-road production. Better are the two originals, the title track, a rollicking reworking of the standard "When the Saints Go Marchin' In," and the bossa nova-tinged ballad "Green Eyes." Earl Grant's albums, particularly late in his career, were notoriously uneven, but overall, *In Motion* does a fair job of staying to the good. *—Stewart Mason*

Earl Grant's Greatest Hits / 1979 / Decca ✦✦✦✦
This greatest-hits collection contains some of Earl Grant's most memorable recordings. Grant showcases his organ virtuosity on every cut, and throws in some skillful piano solos for good measure. His rendition of Ben E. King's "Stand By Me" stands out. Grant had every genre down pat, as he proves on Ray Charles' bluesy "Sweet Sixteen Bars." He displays a quality singing voice on the Caribbean-flavored "House of Bamboo," "I Can't Stop Loving You," "At the End of a Rainbow," and "Old Man River." Grant's organ on "Ebb Tide" is as eerily beautiful as it was years ago. Curiously, Decca omitted Grant's only pop hit (and first recording for the label), "The End." *—Andrew Hamilton*

- **Singin' & Swingin': The Best of Earl Grant** / Oct. 20, 1998 / MCA ✦✦✦✦

Grant was a multiple talent: a great singer, a swinging organist whose mastery of the Hammond B-3 was a thrill to listen to, and a songwriter who could come up with material as solid as the standards he regularly recorded for Decca in his all-too-short career. This 21-track collection brings together the cream of his stay at Decca, featuring hits like "The End," "Ebb Tide," "Misty," "Teach Me Tonight" and his own "Swingin' Gently," with the bonus track of "The End" sung in Italian thrown in to round out the package. A great song selection and superb mastering makes this a marvelous introduction to this pop-jazz artist. *—Cub Koda*

Carl Graves

b. Calgary, Alberta, Canada
Vocals, Keyboards / Blue-Eyed Soul, Soul
Carl Graves' smooth single "Baby Pick Up the Phone" was a Top 20 R&B hit in 1974. Graves who was from Calgary, Alberta, Canada, sang with the band Skylark (which also included David Foster and singer Donny Gerrard) who had a 1973 number-nine pop hit with "Wildflower." Signed as a solo artist to A&M Records and working with producer Spencer Proffer, Graves' own "Baby Pick Up the Phone" reached the R&B charts in late 1974 and was on his self-titled LP *Carl Graves*. His next charting singles were the more uptempo "Heart Be Still," from the LP of the same name, and the Ariola America single "Sad Girl." Graves can also be heard on Lee Oskar's 1997 album, *So Much in Love*. *—Ed Hogan*

Dobie Gray (Leonard Victor Ainsworth)

b. Jul. 26, 1943, Brookshire, TX
Vocals / Pop-Soul, Country-Soul, Disco, Soul, Country-Pop
Best known for his 1973 smash "Drift Away," Dobie Gray was a versatile vocalist who could handle soul, country, and pop, not to mention musical theater. Gray's origins are somewhat ill-defined; different sources alternately list his birth name as Leonard Victor Ainsworth or Laurence Darrow Brown, and his TX birthplace as Brookshire or Simonton. His likely birthdate is July 26, 1942 (though some sources list 1940). Whatever the case, Gray grew up in a family of sharecroppers, and discovered gospel music through his grandfather, a Baptist minister. He also soaked up the R&B and country music of his surroundings, and in the early '60s he moved to Los Angeles to seek his fortune.

Before adopting the name Dobie Gray, he recorded several singles under the names Leonard Ainsworth, Larry Curtis, and Larry Dennis. His seventh single, "Look at Me," became his first chart hit in 1963, but his true breakout was a 1965 recording of "The 'In' Crowd," whose Motown-style bounce distinguished it from jazzman Ramsey Lewis' celebrated version. Gray hit the Top 20 with "The 'In' Crowd" and also had some success with the follow-up, "See You at the Go-Go"; this period—spent mostly on the small, poorly distributed Cordak, Charger, and White Whale labels—was the most soul-oriented of his career. It would be some time before Gray returned to the charts; in the meantime, he pursued a concurrent acting career, eventually spending two-and-a-half years with the Los Angeles production of *Hair*. During his *Hair* years, Gray also sang with the band Pollution, which recorded two albums on Prophecy beginning in 1971.

In 1972 Gray resurfaced as a solo artist on MCA, with producer/songwriter Mentor Williams in his camp. Gray promptly scored the biggest hit of his career with the Williams-penned "Drift Away," which hit the Top Five in early 1973 and remains an oldies-radio staple today. The subsequent "Loving Arms," written by Tom Jans, grew into a much-covered repertory item, recorded by singers from the realms of rock, country, and R&B. Gray's own sound was shifting more toward country as well, and when he moved to Capricorn in 1975, he recorded in Nashville with new songwriting collaborator Troy Seals (he eventually relocated there permanently). Gray's popularity in Europe and Africa was growing steadily, and he managed to talk South African authorities into allowing him to play to integrated audiences during the apartheid era.

Gray's tenure in Nashville was marked by a commercial downturn, but his increased activity as a songwriter—mostly in a country vein—resulted in covers by the likes of Don Williams, Charley Pride, George Jones, and John Denver, among others. The disco-flavored "You Can Do It" became his final Top 40 hit in 1978, the same year he recorded the first of two LPs for Infinity. When Infinity went bankrupt, Gray concentrated exclusively on songwriting for a few years, then re-emerged on Capitol in the mid-'80s as a full-fledged country artist. He made the lower reaches of the country charts with singles like "That's One to Grow On" and "From Where I Stand," but found it impossible to break through to a wider country audience, and again faded from view after two albums. In 1997, Gray released *Diamond Cuts*, a mix of new songs and re-recorded past hits. *—Steve Huey*

Drift Away / 1973 / Decca ♦♦♦
"Drift Away" may have been the best of single of its year, but the supporting album doesn't quite meet that standard. *Drift Away*'s other tracks are pleasant enough, with Dobie Gray's mellow yet soulful voice stealing the show. The sound is laid back L.A. rock scattered with steel guitars and the occasional fiddle—an odd combination that works on the better cuts like "L.A. Lady" and "Now That I'm Without You." The fine ballads "We Had It All" and "Sweet Lovin' Woman" round out this solid if unspectacular album. *—J.P. Ollio*

● **Drift Away: His Very Best** / Jul. 23, 1996 / Razor & Tie ♦♦♦♦♦
Razor & Tie's *Drift Away: His Very Best* is the definitive Dobie Gray collection, containing all of his Top 40 pop hits and all of his charting R&B singles—"The 'In' Crowd," "Drift Away," "Loving Arms," "Find 'Em, Fool 'Em & Forget 'Em," "You Can Do It"—plus 12 other lesser-known singles and album tracks. A few of the songs may fall flat, but there are more hidden gems on the collection than you might expect; in particular, the country-soul of "There's a Honky Tonk Angel" and "Watch out for Lucy" sounds particularly good. Either way, *Drift Away* captures the full range of Gray's talent and provides an excellent summation of his career. *—Stephen Thomas Erlewine*

Out on the Floor With the In Crowd / Jul. 18, 2000 / Empire Music ♦♦♦♦♦
This is one of several Dobie Gray compilations on the market, all of which have something to recommend them, but *Out on the Floor With the In Crowd* is particularly notable for featuring all of Gray's '60s sides for Cordak, Charger, and White Whale Records in one place. That includes not only the two cuts referred to in the CD's title, but also the ethereal "No Room to Cry" and his rousing debut Cordak single, "Look at Me"; the Motown-style dance number "See You at the Go-Go"; and "In Hollywood," a semi-autobiographical song that vaguely resembles "On Broadway" in its tempo and arrangement. The White Whale sides, coming a couple of years after the Charger singles, offer smoother sounds, more elaborate production, and a looser, freer definition of soul, encompassing numbers such an early recording of Joe South's "Rose Garden," which subsequently became a hit for Lynn Anderson; the string-accompanied "Where's the Girl Gone?"; the horn-dominated, ebullient "What a Way to Go"; and the achingly beautiful and dramatic "Guess Who." The sound is excellent throughout and the notes by Chris Bolton are nicely detailed, and as a mid-priced item it's a bargain on every level. *—Bruce Eder*

● **Ultimate Collection** / Apr. 3, 2001 / Hip-O ♦♦♦♦♦
Listening to Dobie Gray's *Ultimate Collection* is like going through a musical time capsule. This collection includes his first charted single, "Look at Me," his first big hit "The 'In' Crowd" and its follow-up, "See You at the Go-Go," all which have a distinctive, mid-'60s big go-go sound. Other early songs, such as "Out on the Floor," are full of contemporary colloquialisms (such as "groovy" and "the chicks are outta sight!"). By the time the album reaches his stellar version of "Rose Garden," the music shifts into more mid-'70s adult leaning material, especially evident by his signature, much-loved anthem "Drift Away." Then there's the soul-country/rock of "The Time I Loved You Most," the lamenting ballad "Loving Arms," the total country of "Watch out for Lucy," and the disco of the "Stayin' Alive" sound-alike "You Can Do It" (his last Top 40 hit). Also included is his 1986 country hit "That's One to Grow On." This album collects all three of his U.S. Top 40 hits, as well as most of his other charted singles (unfortunately "Find 'Em, Fool 'Em, Forget 'Em" was omitted), and stands as a testament to an artist who was totally unafraid to sing what he wanted, whether it be rock & roll, soul, or country. And best of all, he always sounded as if he was having the time of his life. *—Jose Promis*

Macy Gray (Natalie McIntyre)

b. Sept. 9, 1970, Canton, OH

Vocals / Contemporary R&B, Urban, Neo-Soul, Adult Alternative Pop/Rock

Macy Gray parlayed an utterly unique voice and an outlandish sense of style into R&B stardom at the turn of the millennium, appealing to audiences of all colors in search of a fresh alternative to mainstream soul. Gray was actually born Natalie McIntyre in Canton, OH, in 1970, and grew up a shy, awkward youngster who was frequently teased about her odd-sounding voice. She studied classical piano for seven years, but also soaked up the music of soul legends like Stevie Wonder, Marvin Gaye, and Aretha Franklin, not to mention old-school hip-hop; at boarding school as a teenager, she was exposed to a variety of white rock & roll as well. She moved to Los Angeles to enroll in USC's screenwriting program, where one day she agreed to write lyrics for a musician friend's original songs. A demo session was scheduled to get the songs on tape, and when the singer failed to show up, Gray—having adopted the full name of an elderly neighbor in Canton as her creative alias—wound up singing on the recordings herself, in spite of her distaste for her own voice. One of the songs was never overdubbed with another vocal, and when the tapes started making the rounds of the local music scene, Gray's raspy growl attracted a lot of attention, much to her surprise. She was offered a job singing jazz and pop standards with a band that performed in hotels around Los Angeles, and her continued work as a demo singer created a buzz around the unlikely diva.

Gray organized an after-hours club called the We Ours, which took place in a small coffeehouse; in addition to welcoming open-mike acts, Gray and her jazz group performed there regularly. She signed with Atlantic Records, who declined to release the album she recorded for them; devastated by this rejection and the breakup of her marriage (her third child was on the way at the time), Gray retreated to Canton. However, her demo tape continued to make the rounds, and she returned to L.A. to accept a publishing deal with Zomba. This in turn helped lead to a new record contract with Epic in April 1998, and Gray spent the next year recording what was to become her debut album, *On How Life Is*. Released in the summer of 1999, *On How Life Is* won glowing reviews and word-of-mouth, but in spite of all that—plus a moderate hit single in "Do Something"—the record was slow to catch on at first. That all changed early the next year, when Gray received two Grammy nominations (for Best New Artist and Best Female R&B Vocal), and the single "I Try" started to take off on radio. "I Try" proved to be an enormous hit, and *On How Life Is* suddenly sold like hotcakes, entering the Top Ten and going triple platinum by the end of 2000. Gray scored a smaller follow-up hit with "Why Don't You Call Me," and also raised eyebrows with the album track "I've Committed Murder," in which the protagonist gets away with her crime.

Although Gray lost out her first time at the Grammys, she was nominated again the following year for Best Female Pop Vocal thanks to "I Try," and this time won (although the song lost out on Record of the Year and Song of the Year honors). In late 2000, Gray contributed two vocal tracks to Fatboy Slim's *Halfway Between the Gutter and the Stars* album; she subsequently recorded with the Black-Eyed Peas, cut a duet with rap legend Slick Rick for the *Rush Hour 2* soundtrack ("The World Is Yours"), and made her screen acting debut in the Denzel Washington police drama *Training Day*. By the time she set about readying her second album, Gray was developing a reputation for surreal public appearances and interviews, culminating in an August 2001 incident in which she was booed for apparently stumbling over the lyrics to the national anthem. Released the following month, *The Id* was a determined effort to play up the crazy side of Gray's image; it entered the charts at number 11 and quickly went gold on the strength of lead single "Sweet Baby." However, in spite of guest appearances by Erykah Badu and the Red Hot Chili Peppers' John Frusciante, among others, its sales stalled much sooner than expected. In 2002 Gray appeared as herself in the blockbuster film *Spider-Man*, and guested on Santana's new album *Shaman*. *—Steve Huey*

● **On How Life Is** / Jul. 27, 1999 / Epic ♦♦♦♦
Macy Gray is such an assured, original vocalist that it's hard to believe *On How Life Is* is her debut album. She recalls a number of other vocalists, particularly jazz singers like Billie Holiday and Nina Simone, but she is unquestionably from the post-hip-hop generation, which is evident not just from the sound of the record, but the style of her songwriting, which is adventurous and unpredictable. Thankfully, she's worked with a producer (Andrew Slater, who pulled a similar trick with Fiona Apple's debut, *Tidal*) that lets her run wild and helps her find sounds that match her ideas. That's not to say that *On How Life Is* is a perfect album—at times, Gray attempts more than she can achieve—but it's always captivating, even during its stumbles. And when it works, it soars higher than most contemporary R&B. *—Stephen Thomas Erlewine*

The Id / Sep. 18, 2001 / Epic ♦♦♦
Macy Gray's throaty, somewhat strangled growl was a large reason why listeners were captivated by her debut album. They also loved the way the classicist songwriting was wrapped in fresh, colorful grooves and an idiosyncratic personality, sexy in its bohemian funkiness. *What Life Is* became a word-of-mouth smash as much with the traditional urban R&B audience as it was with suburban college kids and NPR listeners, which left her with the freedom to do what she wanted on her second record, *The Id*. Here, Macy Gray lets her freak flag fly, almost to the detriment of everything else. Layers of overdubs are piled onto the record—endless backing vocals, bubbling drum machines, loops, glistening synths, and gurgling guitars—giving the record the appearance of a widescreen '70s soul fantasia filtered through postmodern hip-hop. Unfortunately, it's more appearance than reality, since there's not enough structure to support what the record wants to be. It often sounds good, often like a bright, contemporary take on *Riot*- and *Fresh*-era Sly Stone, but plays better in small doses. Over the course of the album, there's just too much effort in demonstrating Gray's "freakishness," culminating in the Germanic stomp of "Oblivion," and she just doesn't seem to have that much to say outside of cheerleading for "freaks" like her. So, it's an uneven second album, but there are moments that live up to the debut, such as "Sexual Revolution," "Boo" and, best of all, the Erykah Badu duet "Sweet Baby," easily the highlight of the album. There are just not enough of them to make this an entirely successful sophomore effort. *—Stephen Thomas Erlewine*

R.B. Greaves

b. Nov. 28, 1944, Georgetown, British Guyana

Vocals / Pop-Soul, Soul

R.B. Greaves has an interesting family background and history, one that's actually more significant than his R&B track record. Greaves was born on an Air Force base in what was then British Guyana and grew up on a Seminole reservation. The nephew of Sam Cooke, Greaves moved to England in 1963, and was lead singer of Sonny Childe & the TNT's. He had his moment of glory in 1969 with "Take a Letter Maria," a fine song blending soap opera narrative and soulful vocals that peaked at number-two pop and number-ten R&B. His remake of "Always Something There to Remind Me" stiffed, and he was soon off Atlantic's subsidiary label Atco. Greaves tried again in 1977, recording for the Bareback label. It didn't revive his career. *—Ron Wynn*

● **R.B. Greaves** / 1970 / Atco ♦♦♦
By far the best release of his short career, that claim doesn't say much for Greaves, because this record is as sporadic as they come. Containing the self-penned sing-along hit "Take a Letter Maria," at points Greaves shows signs of developing into a successful pop songwriter. Yet, just as the salsa-flavored horns on "... Maria" leave you smiling, Greaves' reading of Sam Cooke's "Cupid" and the Bacharach-David classic "Always Something There to Remind Me" leave the listener frustrated. It seems his voice is never as smooth as a pop singer, never as gritty as an R&B singer, and the middle ground he treads is devoid of any true feeling. Even the fact that the album was produced by Ahmet Ertegun and recorded at Muscle Shoals Sound cannot make up for the lack of emotional conviction in Greaves' voice. *—Steve Kurutz*

Al Green

b. Apr. 13, 1946, Forrest City, AR

Vocals / Soul, Pop-Soul, Smooth Soul, Memphis Soul, Contemporary Gospel

Al Green was the first great soul singer of the '70s and arguably the last great Southern soul singer. With his seductive singles for Hi Records in the early '70s, Green bridged the gap between deep soul and smooth Philadelphia soul. He incorporated elements of gospel, interjecting his performances with wild moans and wails, but his records were stylish, boasting immaculate productions that rolled along with a tight beat, sexy backing vocals, and lush strings. The distinctive Hi Records sound that the vocalist and producer Willie Mitchell developed made Al Green the most popular and influential soul singer of the early '70s, influencing not only his contemporaries, but also veterans like Marvin Gaye. Green was at the peak of his popularity when he suddenly decided to join the ministry in the mid-'70s. At first, he continued to record secular material, but by the '80s, he was concentrating solely on gospel. During the late '80s and '90s, he occasionally returned to R&B, but he remained primarily a religious performer for the rest of his career. Nevertheless, Green's classic early '70s recordings retained their power and influence throughout the decades, setting the standard for smooth soul.

Green was born in Forrest City, AR, where he formed a gospel quartet, the Green Brothers, at the age of nine. The group toured throughout the South in the mid-'50s, before the family relocated to Grand Rapids, MI. The Green Brothers continued to perform in Grand Rapids, but Al's father kicked the boy out of the group after he caught his son listening to Jackie Wilson. At the age of 16, Al formed an R&B group, Al Green & the Creations, with several of his high school friends. Two Creation members, Curtis Rogers and Palmer James, founded their own independent record company, Hot Line Music Journal, and had the group record for the label. By that time, the Creations had been renamed the Soul Mates. The group's first single, "Back Up Train," became a surprise hit, climbing to number five on the R&B charts early in 1968. The Soul Mates attempted to record another hit, but all of their subsequent singles failed to find an audience.

In 1969, Al Green met bandleader and Hi Records vice president Willie Mitchell while on tour in Midland, TX. Impressed with Green's voice, he signed the singer to Hi Records, and began collaborating with Al on his debut album. Released in early 1970, Green's debut album *Green Is Blues* showcased the signature sound he and Mitchell devised—a sinewy, sexy groove highlighted by horn punctuations and string beds that let Green showcase his remarkable falsetto. While the album didn't spawn any hit singles, it was well-received and set the stage for the breakthrough success of his second album. *Al Green Gets Next to You* (1970) launched his first hit single, "Tired of Being Alone," which began a streak of four straight gold singles. *Let's Stay Together* (1972) was his first genuine hit album, climbing to number eight on the pop charts; its title track became his first number one single. *I'm Still In Love With You*, which followed only a few months later, was an even greater success, peaking at number four and launching the hits "Look What You Done For Me" and "I'm Still In Love With You."

By the release of 1973's *Call Me*, Green was known as both a hitmaker and an artist that released consistently engaging, frequently excellent, critically-acclaimed albums. His hits continued uninterrupted through the next two years, with "Call Me," "Here I Am," and "Sha-La-La (Make Me Happy)" all becoming Top 10, gold singles. At the height of his popularity, Green's former girlfriend, Mrs. Mary Woodson, broke into his Memphis home in October 1974 and poured boiling grits on the singer as he was bathing, inflicting second-degree burns on his back, stomach and arm; after assaulting Green, she killed herself with his gun. Green interpreted the violent incident as a sign from God that he should enter the ministry. By 1976, he had bought a church in Memphis and had become an ordained pastor of the Full Gospel Tabernacle. Though he had begun to seriously pursue religion, he had not given up singing R&B and he released three other Mitchell-produced albums—*Al Green Is Love* (1975), *Full of Fire* (1976), *Have A Good Time* (1976)—after the incident. However, his albums began to sound formulaic, and his sales started to slip by the end of 1976, with disco cutting heavily into his audience.

In order to break free from his slump, Green stopped working with Willie Mitchell in 1977 and built his own studio, American Music, where he intended to produce his own records. The first album he made at American Music was *The Belle Album*, an intimate record that was critically acclaimed but failed to win a crossover audience. *Truth N' Time* (1978) failed to even generate a major R&B hit. During a concert in Cincinnati in 1979, Green fell off the stage and nearly injured himself seriously. Interpreting the accident as a sign from God, Green retired from performing secular music and devoted himself to preaching. Throughout the '80s, he released a series of gospel albums on Myrrh Records. In 1982, Green appeared in the gospel musical *Your Arms Too Short to Box With God* with Patti LaBelle. In 1985, he reunited with Willie Mitchell for *He Is the Light*, his first album for A&M Records.

Green tenatively returned to R&B in 1988 when he sang "Put a Little Love in Your Heart" with Annie Lennox for the Bill Murray comedy *Scrooged*. Four years later, he recorded his first full-fledged soul album since 1978 with the U.K.-only *Don't Look Back*. In 1995, he released *Your Heart's in Good Hands*, an urban contemporary record that represented his first secular album to be released in America since *Truth N' Time*. Though the album received positive reviews, it failed to become a hit. Al Green was inducted to the Rock and Roll Hall of Fame in 1995. *—Stephen Thomas Erlewine*

Back Up Train / 1967 / Hot Line ♦♦♦

Nearly forgotten by all but serious soul fans, *Back Up Train* is Al Green's debut. Released in 1967, when he was still billed as "Al Greene" and before he worked with producer Willie Mitchell, the record is a perfectly serviceable of slightly sweet period soul—perhaps a little generic, but never less than pleasant. Much of the record was either written or co-written by the album's producers Palmer James and Curtis Rogers, who were not just part of Hot Line Records, but in the Creations, Green's previous backing band. Though they're fine as producers, they didn't have strong material as songwriters, never producing something as limber and memorable as Green's lone songwriting credit, "Stop and Check Myself." Musically, this number, along with a few other cuts, suggest the tight, sexy sound of his seminal Hi albums, but it's nowhere near as seductive as those slow grooves, nor is it as effortless. Still, it's possible to hear its roots throughout the record. Green's voice, while not as smooth as it would be just a few years later, shows enormous talent, he's equally comfortable with ballads and funky workouts, and the production, while dated, is quite appealing in how it falls somewhere between the grit of Memphis and the sweetness of Chicago soul. *Back Up Train* is good enough that if Green hadn't gone on to greater work, this would be the kind of record soul fanatics would treasure and trade, speculating on what might have happened if Green had been given another shot. Of course, Green went on to bigger, better things, and this stands as no more than a footnote to career, but it's an interesting, enjoyable footnote all the same. *—Stephen Thomas Erlewine*

Green Is Blues / 1970 / The Right Stuff ♦♦♦

The first album linking the soul-singing greatness of Al Green with the production brilliance and expertise of Willie Mitchell. The results were mutually beneficial; Green got the great production, arrangements, and backing from the Hi Rhythm Section that often turned good songs into classics, and he sang with the conviction and talent that provided the final component in an artistically and commercially satisfying union. *—Ron Wynn*

Gets Next to You / 1971 / The Right Stuff ♦♦♦♦♦

After the shaky start of *Green Is Blues*, Al Green and producer Willie Mitchell established their classic sound with Green's second album, *Gets Next to You*. The main difference is in the rhythm section. Abandoning the gritty syncopations of deep Southern soul, the Hi Rhythm Section plays it slow and seductive, working a sultry, steady pulse that Green exploits with his remarkable voice. Alternating between Sam Cooke's croon and Otis Redding's shout, Green develops his own distinctive style, and *Gets Next to You* only touches the surface of its depth. Although the album is filled with wonderful moments, few are as astonishing as Green and Mitchell's reinterpretation of the Temptations' "I Can't Get Next to You," which turns the original inside out. *—Stephen Thomas Erlewine*

☆ **Let's Stay Together** / Feb. 1972 / The Right Stuff ♦♦♦♦♦

Prior to this album, Al Green never had a number one song. The title track, "Let's Stay Together," achieved that status and held it for nine consecutive weeks. Green's ingenuity produced one of the all-time classics, which has the bounce of a dance cut and the passion of a ballad. The dynamic soul singer's whispers, animated cries, and riffing enhance his already stirring delivery. This album was sold on the strength of the title track as there were no other selections to grace the *Billboard* charts. However, this album includes the timeless gem "How Can You Mend a Broken Heart" and lesser-known beauties like the exulting "Judy," the cookin' testimonial "I Never Found a Girl," and the soothing blues effort "It Ain't No Fun to Me." The Arkansas native and his creative partner Willie Mitchell season these selections with lucid rhythm arrangements complemented by the faint strums of a guitar and brawn, unchiding horns. *—Craig Lytle*

☆ **I'm Still in Love With You** / Dec. 1972 / The Right Stuff ♦♦♦♦♦

I'm Still in Love With You shares many surface similarities to its predecessor, *Let's Stay Together*, from Al Green and Willie Mitchell's distinctive, sexy style to the pacing and song selection. Despite those shared traits, *I'm Still in Love With You* distinguishes itself with its suave, romantic tone and its subtly ambitious choice of material. Green began exploring country music with this album, performing a startling version of Kris Kristofferson's "For the Good Times," as well as a wonderful, slow reinterpretation of Roy Orbison's "Oh Pretty Woman." And the soul numbers are more complex than they would appear—listen to how the beat falls together at the beginning of "Love and Happiness," or the sly melody of the title track. There isn't a wasted track on *I'm Still in Love With You*, and in many ways it rivals its follow-up *Call Me* as Green's masterpiece. *—Stephen Thomas Erlewine*

☆ **Call Me** / Jul. 1973 / The Right Stuff ♦♦♦♦♦

Al Green reached his creative peak with the brilliant *Call Me*, the most inventive and assured album of his career. So silky and fluid as to sound almost effortless, Green's vocals revel in the lush strings and evocative horns of Willie Mitchell's superbly intimate production, barely rising above an angelic whisper for the gossamer "Have You Been Making Out O.K."; with barely perceptible changes in mood, *Call Me* covers remarkable ground, spanning from "Stand Up"—a call to arms delivered with characteristic understatement—to renditions of Hank Williams' "I'm So Lonesome I Could Cry" and Willie Nelson's "Funny How Time Slips Away," both of them exemplary fusions of country and soul. Equally compelling are the album's three Top Ten hits—"You Ought to Be With Me," "Here I Am (Come and Take Me)," and the shimmering title cut. A classic. *—Jason Ankeny*

Livin' for You / Dec. 1973 / The Right Stuff ♦♦♦

Starting in 1971 with *Al Green Gets Next to You*, Al Green albums became necessities. *Livin' for You* is Green's sixth album, and the fourth to be certified gold. (Its predecessor, the classic *Call Me*, was still on the charts when this was released.) Each of Green's albums with Mitchell are singular, with their own distinct style, and *Livin' for You* is no exception. It takes a more relaxed approach and offers some of his best ballads; the title track is Green at his most engaging, even when he sang potentially mood-interrupting lines like, "I'm tired of your bright ideas about leaving me." "Home Again" and "So Good to Be Here" are romantic if not hypnotic, offering subtle drumming, economical keyboards, and gentle vocals. The biggest track here, the proficient and smooth "Let's Get Married" has Green being a little wishy-washy as he sings, "I didn't mean to say all the things I said/ The way I felt in my heart it came out that way." Although the originals here rank with his best, Green also did good cover work too. The often useless "Unchained Melody" shows up and benefits from Green's methodical delivery. In many ways, *Livin' for You* is the perfect, intimate album for his fans. *—Jason Elias*

Al Green Explores Your Mind / 1974 / The Right Stuff ♦♦♦♦

By the time of 1974's *Al Green Explores Your Mind*, this version of the Memphis sound was the production style for only a handful of artists. Producer Willie Mitchell used a lighter touch for his most famous artist, and it's all but crafted into the Al Green sound. Despite his skills, Green never falls into mannerism here and gives heartfelt and cogent vocals rooted in intelligence and technique. "Sha-La-La (Make Me Happy)," although lyrically slight, has the artist's charisma and Mitchell's pop chops. "Take Me to the River," with perfect backing from Hi Rhythm and a horn and string arrangement, finds Green at his most persuasive. The last track, "School Days," has Green longing for a school girlfriend and despite the potentially sappy sentiment, it works like a charm. The greatness of *Al Green Explores Your Mind* comes from a collective effort, including James Mitchell's dreamlike string arrangements and the always skilled backing vocals of Rhodes, Chalmers & Rhodes. But the biggest draw here is Green's phrasing and intimate vocals, making the record an extremely strong effort. —*Jason Elias*

★ **Al Green's Greatest Hits** / Apr. 1975 / The Right Stuff ♦♦♦♦♦
Upon its original release in 1975, *Al Green's Greatest Hits* pretty much summed up everything about Green, containing his ten biggest hits up to that point. A few years later, it was followed by a second volume, which contained hit singles that charted since the release of the first collection. In 1995, the Right Stuff reissued *Al Green's Greatest Hits*, adding five of the highlights from the second volume of greatest hits as bonus tracks. The result was a definitive single-disc compilation, featuring 15 of Green's absolute best songs, including "Tired of Being Alone," "Let's Stay Together," "I'm Still in Love With You," "Call Me," "Here I Am," "Sha-La-La (Make Me Happy)," and "L-O-V-E (Love)." The original version of *Greatest Hits* was great, but the revision made it nearly perfect. —*Stephen Thomas Erlewine*

Al Green Is Love / Oct. 1975 / The Right Stuff ♦♦♦♦
In a short time, Al Green became a premier singer in R&B and pop. With songs like "Look What You've Done for Me" and "Here I Am (Come and Take Me)," among many others, Green and producer Willie Mitchell refined the sounds of each genre. As *Al Green Explores Your Mind* was the peak of Green's insouciance, *Al Green Is Love* finds a starker reality—the majority of the tracks here are ruminative but not always coherent. The first track, the propulsive "L-O-V-E (Love)," would be even more believable if Green didn't sound so ambivalent. Other uptempo tracks, "I Gotta Be More" and "Rhymes," are edgy and dark, with great riffs from guitarist Mabon Hodges. The heart of *Al Green Is Love* is the ballads, though Green's not very happy, and those looking for heartwarming thoughts on romance won't find it here. "The Love Sermon" and, even better, "I Didn't Know" are spare, dirge-like songs that give Green great opportunities to turn in raw and emotional performances. "I Wish You Were Here" and "Could I Be the One" have producer Willie Mitchell offering suitably bleak arrangements to go with Green's airy vocals. The best track here, "There Is Love," strikes a balance between the customary production grace and the album's pervading sorrow. *Al Green Is Love* might be too depressing for some, but his fans will find Green's truthfulness appealing and some of the songs among his best. —*Jason Elias*

Full of Fire / Apr. 1976 / The Right Stuff ♦♦♦
Full of Fire is the second-to-last '70s effort that Al Green co-produced with Willie Mitchell. While much of Green's previous work (*I'm Still in Love With You, Call Me, Al Green Explores Your Mind*) spotlighted Green's skill at doing songs filled with romance and longing, on *Full of Fire* he's more concerned with his burgeoning religious nature. Although that may seem slightly boring, the album is better structured and, as a whole, comes off even better than *Al Green Is Love*. The first track, "Glory, Glory," sneaks in religion so deftly that even Willie Mitchell probably didn't even get it until the track was done. One of the few romantic tracks, the sweet and old-fashioned "Always," has him coming in soft with much charm. "I'd Fly Away" and "Soon as I Get Home" both have Green fantasizing about heaven, but they're both spacy rather than morbid. The last track, the hard-edged "Let It Shine" is enlivened by Howard Grimes' patently surprising drumming. Although Green isn't always all there on *Full of Fire*, his co-production with Mitchell and the playing of Hi Rhythm makes this an essential offering. —*Jason Elias*

Have a Good Time / Dec. 1976 / Hi ♦♦♦
Al Green was riding right along, still singing with confidence, power, and authority. Although this was kind of a transition effort, with Green beginning to head toward gospel, his vocals retained their edge and relaxed fire. Mitchell and Hi Rhythm did their usual excellent supporting job. —*Ron Wynn*

The Belle Album / Dec. 1977 / The Right Stuff ♦♦♦♦
Al Green severed his ties with longtime producer Willie Mitchell in 1977, establishing his own backup band and seizing the production reins. But he hadn't yet made the final break with soul; this was the last secular work he would make for many years, and it was brilliant, even though it didn't come close to equaling his previous commercial heights. In retrospect, many just didn't understand where he was going, while others were turned off by the blurred lyrical focus of songs like "Belle." But "I Feel Good" had as much danceable energy and soulful fire as any Green uptempo tune, and "Lovin' You" and "Dream" were sorely underrated compositions. —*Ron Wynn*

Truth N' Time / 1978 / Hi ♦♦♦
Returning to the formula of his classic Hi albums, Al Green assembled a fine collection of originals and covers for *Truth N' Time*. Although Green is in good voice, and his version of "Say a Little Prayer" is impressive, the album feels a bit like a holding pattern, simply repeating ideas that were more fruitful the first time around. Given the generally listless nature of *Truth N' Time* and the way Green sounds vaguely uninterested in the material, it's not a surprise that it was his last secular record for a very long time. —*Stephen Thomas Erlewine*

The Lord Will Make a Way / 1980 / Myrrh ♦♦♦
This 1980 album was released after Green received a wake-up call by way of tumble off a stage in Cincinnati. No doubt Green planned a straight-laced, devotional work with *The Lord Will Make a Way*, but his charisma and sex appeal was also part of the package. The title track is powerful, reverent, and sensual, with Green's voice possessing the intensity and tone of his earlier secular tracks. Like many of his best albums, this one has an immediacy that makes it a joy to listen to. Although Green's clear switch in his lyrical manner—changing she/her for love of the Lord, Jesus, and God—should be striking, the transition is seamless. The gospel standard "Pass Me Not" gets the Al Green treatment with his acoustic-guitar strums and strong call-and-response vocals. Another standard, Alex Bradford's "Too Close" has a poignant segment near the end that has Green repeatedly whispering "thank you Jesus" with his guitar sweetly strumming in the background. An original track, the pragmatic and committed "In the Holy Name of Jesus" has the poise of his Willie Mitchell productions. Green creates a relaxed atmosphere for *Lord Will Make a Way*, an excellent debut for his gospel career. —*Jason Elias*

Tokyo Live / 1981 / The Right Stuff ♦♦♦♦
This is a wonderful live set that serves as both a retrospective and a defining release showing that Green sang the same way regardless of musical and lyrical content. He did many of his greatest soul hits, performing them with the relaxed, powerful grace that made him the '70s' finest soul vocalist and the '80s' best male gospel artist. —*Ron Wynn*

Higher Plane / Feb. 1981 / Hi ♦♦♦♦
By the late '70s, Al Green had turned his concerns chiefly to gospel, releasing critically acclaimed though low-selling albums. While many were pleased that Green went full throttle with his religious devotion, 1980's *Lord Will Make a Way* found him occasionally over-cautious. That's certainly not the case here. *Higher Plane* is a heartening return to form that has Green again imbuing his music with strong measures of sensuality and humor—especially for such a buttoned-down genre. The title track has Green again strutting with characteristic charm and sets the tone of the album. A duet cover of Curtis Mayfield's "People Get Ready" has Green and Margie Joseph slowing the song down and singing the refrain "Thank the lord" enough times it has to break through. A pair of strong album tracks—the playful "By My Side" and the drama of "The Spirit Might Come—On and On"—exemplify *Higher Plane*'s skill of running the gamut of emotions without a false note. "Where Love Rules" and "His Name Is Jesus" are simply two of Green's finest songs, hitting a strong level of emotion, especially for being uptempo. Green seems more than comfortable incorporating his quirks and sound in the pure religious idiom for *Higher Plane*. That fact makes this an inspired and definitive album from an artist who has his fair share of them. —*Jason Elias*

He Is the Light / 1985 / Excelsior ♦♦♦
Al Green suffered a slight lull in his gospel career with 1984's *Trust in God*. As a response, he reunited with producer Willie Mitchell, who admittedly preferred the secular to the gospel. At this point, Green was unwavering in his faith and presents a challenge for *He Is the Light*. "Going Away" and "True Love" are great updates of the classic 1971-1976 sound with Green's dulcet, anxious vocals above an updated version of the sound that made him famous. The cover of "Be With Me Jesus" has Green in a playful mood despite the dire lyrics, and shows how Mitchell could coax vocals from Green no one else could. To Mitchell's credit, this album not only embraced Green's pop/gospel but also the newer sounds and styles Green had been working on in the '80s. The cover of the Clark Sisters' "You Brought the Sunshine" features adroit synth work and fun vocals. On the flip side, "Power," "Building Up," and "Nearer My God to Thee" are too cautious and quite boring. While *He Is the Light* finds Green in better voice than his last '70s efforts with Mitchell, it still has weak spots that prevent it from being a resounding success. —*Jason Elias*

I Get Joy / May 1989 / A&M ♦♦♦
The '80s found Al Green again connecting to pop and R&B audiences with his brand of charming and sometimes erotic gospel. After signing with the independent A&M in 1985, Green seemed to grow a little tired of straight-ahead gospel fare and satisfied his yen for pop by way of covers or songs with ambiguous meanings. *I Get Joy* follows the trend. The ballad "You're Everything to Me" could either be about God or a woman, but he does a nice high-pitched vocal on it. The resigned yet fatalistic "The End Is Near" finds Green snatching the music from the Jackson 5's "I'll Be There." The title track is a rousing old-time gospel tune with churning organs juxtaposed by synthesizers; of course, it also has Green doing some great riffs and growling, "I feel good today." The hit from the album, the new jack swing remix of "As Long as We're Together," was done by Al B. Sure. Unfortunately, the track has too much hardware and the original *Truth N' Time*-style version of the song was infinitely better. The gorgeous "Blessed" does a better job with the synths; Green sings about everything from an indifferent landlord and returned money to sweating out employment woes, making you believe every syllable. "Tryin' to Get You" would have worked alright if it wasn't for the melody, uncomfortably close to the Eagles' "Take It to Limit." *I Get Joy* isn't a great Green effort, but with some of his vocals it often comes close. —*Jason Elias*

Love Is Reality / 1992 / Word/Epic ♦♦♦
After years of refusing to sing anything but gospel, Green decided the time had finally come to fuse the godly and the secular elements of his soul. *Love Is Reality* made an overt play for the mainstream R&B market. Unfortunately, Christian dance-pop producer Tim Miner works from formulas, while Green runs on inspiration. Green sounded great, but the final result paled in comparison to the rest of his catalog. —*Brian Mansfield*

The Supreme Al Green: The Greatest Hits / 1992 / Hi ♦♦♦♦♦
Released by the British division of Hi, *Supreme Al Green: The Greatest Hits* is a terrific 18-track collection that contains almost all of Green's hits, including "Tired of Being Alone," "Call Me," "I'm Still in Love With You," "Let's Stay Together," "I Can't Get Next to You," "Love and Happiness," "Sha-La-La (Make Me Happy)," "Take Me to the River," and "How Can You Mend a Broken Heart." Although it inexplicably overlooks "Here I Am (Come and Take Me)" and contains a bit too much latter-day material for some tastes, it's

still one of the best single-disc collections yet assembled on Green, rivaling the revamped *Greatest Hits* the Right Stuff released in the mid-'90s. *—Stephen Thomas Erlewine*

Your Heart's in Good Hands / Nov. 7, 1995 / MCA ♦♦♦
Designed as Al Green's triumphant comeback to the R&B mainstream, *Your Heart's in Good Hands* is a mixed blessing. Although Green's voice is still astonishing, the album is undermined by a sterile urban R&B production that fails to capture the sensuality inherent in his music. As a result, *Your Heart's in Good Hands* is quite frustrating—you can hear Green hit new heights with his performance, but the music is constantly reined in by the lifeless production and the lackluster songs. *—Stephen Thomas Erlewine*

Anthology / Feb. 11, 1997 / Capitol ♦♦♦
Theoretically, an Al Green box set should be easy to assemble, given the overall excellence of his material, but the four-disc *Anthology* is a botched job. Instead of simply condensing the best of Green's prolific output, including all of the hits, the compilers were concerned with telling a story—literally. Three of the discs are spiked with lengthy interview segments; furthermore, most of the rarities are concert tracks, which means classics like "I Can't Get Next to You," "How Can You Mend a Broken Heart," "Love and Happiness," and "Sha-La-La (Make Me Happy)" are presented in inferior live versions. The live cuts, interviews, and rarities cut severely into the set's pacing, and they don't make *Anthology* useful for the fan that wants one, definitive collection—their appeal is solely for collectors, who already have the material elsewhere. Consequently, *Anthology* isn't useful for either the casual or dedicated fan, both of whom would be better off with the original albums and the *Greatest Hits* collection, which does contain the essence of Al Green, and most of his hits, on one disc. *—Stephen Thomas Erlewine*

More Greatest Hits / Jan. 27, 1998 / Right Stuff ♦♦♦♦
For its 1995 reissue, the Right Stuff revamped Al Green's *Greatest Hits*, adding five bonus tracks, four of which were featured on the original *Greatest Hits, Vol. 2*. As a result, when it came time to reissue *Greatest Hits, Vol. 2*, the Right Stuff decided to replace it with *More Greatest Hits*, since they would simply be replicating a good portion of their previous collection. However, *More Greatest Hits* isn't exactly the perfect supplement to *Greatest Hits*. Combining minor hits, album tracks, and rarities, the collection doesn't have the cohesiveness of its predecessor. Furthermore, tracks like "Back Up Train" (his first charting single, previously available only on the box set), the long version of "Let's Stay Together" (exclusive to this compilation), and 1968's "Guilty" are strong, but are mainly here to bait collectors, while his latter-day duets with Al B. Sure ("As Long As We're Together") and Lyle Lovett ("Funny How Time Slips Away") pale next to "Livin' for You" and "Love and Happiness," two highlights from *Vol. 2* that are curiously missing here. Even with these flaws, *More Greatest Hits* does contain more than its share of great moments—no Green collection is complete without "Take Me to the River," "For the Good Times," and "How Can You Mend a Broken Heart"—and in that sense, it acts as a nice supplement to the expanded *Greatest Hits*. Nevertheless, it doesn't act as a substitute for such classic albums as *Call Me* and *I'm Still in Love With You*, which is where anyone digging deeper into Green's catalog should start after they've exhausted *Greatest Hits*. *—Stephen Thomas Erlewine*

Hi and Mighty: The Story of Al Green (1969–1978) / Oct. 27, 1998 / Hi ♦♦♦♦♦
This 37-track CD covers Green's work from 1969 to 1978, taking tracks from all of Green's recordings of the era, in chronological order. All of the big hits are here except for 1972's "Look What You've Done for Me," and although that omission is glaring, it's the only misstep. Due to the no-frills mix of this entire project, tracks like the single version of "Let's Stay Together" and "I'm Still in Love With You" closely resemble the way they originally sounded. *Hi and Mighty: The Story of Al Green (1969-1978)* also warmly brings together tracks that usually don't show up on Green compilations, like patented album tracks "What a Wonderful Thing Love Is" and the perfect "Funny How Time Slips Away." The second disc, covering his 1974-1978 work, also earns raves for showing all aspects of Green's personas. The nervous ballads "The Love Sermon" and a single B-side "Strong as Death (Sweet as Love)" both have Green coming unhinged as his eccentricities began to reign supreme. Although this can't make any of the tracks from *Have a Good Time* sound any more useful than they are, it takes four tracks from 1977's *The Belle Album*. His first set without Willie Mitchell finds Green sounding renewed on the best tracks: "Belle" and the awe-inspiring "Loving You." Although there are no doubt more technologically savvy compilations available, *Hi and Mighty: The Story of Al Green* attains the cohesion inherent in Green's best work. *—Jason Elias*

Arista Heritage Master Hits / Jul. 27, 1999 / Arista ♦♦♦♦
Most of the entries in *Arista Heritage Master Hits* series are good compilations, but Al Green's volume is different—and it's a distinction Green fanatics will be eager to embrace. His *Arista Heritage Master Hits* is a remastered reissue of his debut album, *Back Up Train*, which was previously unavailable on CD. The record wasn't a masterpiece, yet it wasn't bad at all, showing that Green's talent was blindingly evident even at the inception of his career. This is a grittier sound than his classic Hi recordings, which doesn't always suit Green's sweet vocals, and the songs are a little spotty. Nevertheless, the album is highly enjoyable, especially for the hardcore fans that have been longing for this record to finally be available on CD. And to make a good package even nicer, the disc boasts two previously unreleased songs from the sessions: "What's It All About" and "A Lover's Hideaway." *—Stephen Thomas Erlewine*

Greatest Gospel Hits / Mar. 28, 2000 / The Right Stuff ♦♦♦
If you like Al Green's gospel material but are hesitant to check this out since there was a previous best-of Green's gospel compilation—*One in a Million*—there are a few good reasons not to be wary. Right off the bat, it should be clear that there is little duplication between *Greatest Gospel Hits* and *One in a Million*, as only two songs from the latter ("Amazing Grace" and "Where Love Rules") are on the former. Also, *Greatest Gospel Hits* has 17 tracks, whereas *One in a Million* only has ten. Plus, it definitely seems as though *Greatest Gospel Hits* has been conceived as a more accessible introduction to Green's gospel world: *One in a Million* was heavy on spiritual standards, while *Greatest Gospel Hits* leans toward gospel with a soul bent. That's evidenced by the greater presence of more contemporary material, including songs written or co-written by Green, and covers of Bill Withers' "Lean on Me" and Curtis Mayfield's "People Get Ready." The chronological span is also wider, covering 1974-1995, although the focus is largely upon his 1980s work. As for the music, there are two ways of looking at this. One is that it's going to have far more secular appeal than most gospel, since Green is an excellent soul singer in both the pop and gospel contexts and uses much the same style in gospel as he did on his classic soul sides. On the other hand, it's the 1970s soul records that are stronger, musically speaking, and which will be preferred by most casual listeners, even if his vocals on the gospel sides are equal in ability and command to those on the soul discs. It's still a decent overview, particularly for those who want a taste of Green's gospel material without getting deep into his gospel catalog. *—Richie Unterberger*

The Hi Singles: A's and B's / Aug. 15, 2000 / Hi ♦♦♦♦♦
A marvelous idea that hopefully other companies emulate, these 43 tracks feature both sides of Al Green's Hi Records singles, in sequence. The uneven number of tracks (43), suggests that a track or two might have served double duty as the flip side of more than one single. The engaging B-sides include "Wish You Were Here," "What Am I Gonna Do With Myself," "All Because," "Ride Sally Ride," "I'm Glad You're Mine," "Old Time Lovin'," "What a Wonderful Thing Love Is," and "School Days." The A-sides are familiar to everyone: "Let's Stay Together," the Beatles' remake "I Want to Hold Your Hand," and "Tired of Being Alone." Some excellent album cuts like "Have You Been Making Out Okay" didn't fit the format so there's more Green to get to complete your library of one of the all-time greats. *—Andrew Hamilton*

Take Me to the River / Sep. 12, 2000 / Capitol ♦♦♦♦♦
As this two-CD best-of draws wholly from Green's prime as a Hi artist, and, as it contains almost everything from his *Greatest Hits* collection, one might reasonably assume that it's a good investment for those looking for a greatest hits anthology that's deeper than the single-disc *Greatest Hits*. Generally that's true, but there are some shortcomings to the packaging that might give you pause. The version of "Sha-La-La (Make Me Happy)" here is a live performance, not the original studio one, and his 1975 Top 30 hit "Full of Fire" (which *is* on *Greatest Hits*) is missing. It's also too bad that no original release dates are given for specific tracks in the sleeve notes and that the cuts are only sort of sequenced chronologically. This does have almost all of his Top 40 hits and some significant songs that are not on *Greatest Hits*, particularly "Take Me to the River" itself and his cover of "How Can You Mend a Broken Heart." Still, the material present on this collection that is not on *Greatest Hits* is definitely not as essential as his big single. If you're just concerned with whether this is a good collection of major soul music, of course it is, covering virtually all of Green's major highlights and then some. *—Richie Unterberger*

Testify: The Best of the A&M Years / Sep. 25, 2001 / A&M ♦♦♦♦
After turning to his ministry full-time in the late '70s, Al Green moved from Hi Records, where he had scored most of his hits, to the religious Myrrh label. But in 1985 he moved back to a secular record company, A&M Records, signaling a renewed interest in the musical mainstream, even if he continued to record material with inspirational lyrics. *He Is the Light*, his debut A&M album, marked a reunion with his Hi producer, Willie Mitchell, and it recreated the Memphis soul sound of their previous collaborations to the point that if one didn't listen to the lyrics too closely, one would think it was one of his '70s albums. Maybe that was the problem. Black pop music had moved on since those days, and *He Is the Light* didn't reach the charts, although one of its tracks, "Going Away," won a gospel Grammy (his sixth in the genre since 1981). For 1987's *Soul Survivor*, he took a more contemporary approach, the production sounding like a Luther Vandross record on occasion, and covered pop songs like "He Ain't Heavy, He's My Brother" and "You've Got a Friend." (The latter, written by Carole King, who is Jewish, wasn't composed with Jesus in mind, of course.) The result was some chart action, including Top 40 R&B status for the Grammy-winning "Everything's Gonna Be Alright." In 1988, Green accompanied Annie Lennox on a revival of "Put a Little Love in Your Heart" for the film *Scrooged* and they made the pop Top Ten. *I Get Joy*, his third and last A&M release, mixed approaches and sold modestly, though it produced the Top 20 R&B hit and Grammy-winner "As Long as We're Together." *Testify: The Best of the A&M Years* traces this history well. Just don't buy it expecting Al Green's greatest hits. *—William Ruhlmann*

Grant Green

b. Jun. 6, 1931, St. Louis, MO, **d.** Jan. 31, 1979, New York, NY
Guitar / Hard Bop, Soul-Jazz, Jazz-Funk
Grant Green was one of the most creative exponents of Blue Note-style funk-jazz, during that music's heyday in the early '60s. Green's linear style steered clear of certain guitar conventions; he asserted that his greatest influences were horn players, and certainly his bop-ish manner of phrasing and limited use of chordal playing bears out that claim. Green's version of modern jazz was leavened with a heavy blues tinge, combining the relative harmonic intricacies of bebop with the straightforward expressivity of popular idioms.

Green played with Jimmy Forrest, Harry Edison, and Lou Donaldson in the '50s. His collaborations with Jack McDuff, Big John Patton, Gloria Willette, and Larry Young in the early '60s helped establish the popularity of the "organ trio" (organ, guitar, drums) as a performing unit. From 1961-1964, Green recorded a series of albums for Blue Note that solidified his creative reputation. His sidemen on those dates included many of that label's biggest names, including Herbie Hancock, Bobby Hutcherson, McCoy Tyner, Joe Henderson, and Elvin Jones. Green also recorded under other Blue Note leaders, such as Stanley Turrentine, Johnny Hodges, Hank Mobley, Lee Morgan, and Ike Quebec. Green retreated from the scene due to drug problems during the mid-'60s; he resumed recording in the late '60s and early '70s. For the last several years of his life, Green was essentially an R&B player. *—Chris Kelsey*

Carryin' On / Oct. 3, 1969 / Blue Note ✦✦✦
Reissued on CD as part of Blue Note's *Rare Groove* series, *Carryin' On* was Grant Green's first album for Blue Note since 1965, an absence of four years during which he recorded just two albums for other labels. Green's return was accompanied by a seismic shift in direction—*Carryin' On* was an album of commercially accessible jazz-funk with a heavy R&B influence, plus miles and miles of Fender Rhodes electric piano. It would typify Green's approach over the next few years, which later made him a hero among acid-jazz aficionados, even though it was the last thing purists wanted to hear from him. Those audiences will certainly be split over *Carryin' On*, whose entire first half is devoted to R&B covers—the Meters' "Ease Back"; Little Anthony & the Imperials' doo wop standard "Hurt So Bad"; and a tense, barely recognizable version of James Brown's "I Don't Want Nobody to Give Me Nothing." The hottest soloing comes on Green's original "Upshot," and closer "Cease the Bombing"—though it has no lyrics—has all the hallmarks of a starry-eyed save-the-world anthem, yet was later covered by Pucho & the Latin Soul Brothers. The presence of Brown-inspired funky drummer Idris Muhammad virtually guarantees a load of sample-ready breakbeats, and Green and the rest of the mostly anonymous sextet work a simmering groove over his propulsive rhythms. Green's playing features more chordal work than usual, but gets very bluesy when he does grab the spotlight. While it won't win over fans of Green's older work, *Carryin' On* is a solid addition to any acid-jazz/funk/rare-groove library, as are most of Green's albums from this period. *—Steve Huey*

Green Is Beautiful / Jan. 30, 1970 / Blue Note ✦✦✦
The second album of Grant Green's thorough jazz-funk makeover, *Green Is Beautiful* finds the guitarist growing more comfortable with harder, funkier R&B than he seemed on the softer-hued *Carryin' On.* The switch from Fender Rhodes electric piano back to the more traditional Hammond organ certainly helps give the session a little extra grit, but it doesn't return Green to the land of soul-jazz by any means. *Green Is Beautiful* is still explicitly commercial and accessible to non-jazz audiences, and (purist objections notwithstanding) that's not necessarily a bad thing. Green's take on James Brown's "Ain't It Funky Now" is one of the funkiest items in his rare-groove period; it may be chordally very simple, but the groove is tight and percolating, and Green, tenor saxophonist Claude Bartee, and trumpeter Blue Mitchell all come up with hot, exciting solos. The album also benefits from Green's discovery of composer and occasional organist Earl Neal Creque, who contributes two bright, slinky, horn-driven originals: "The Windjammer," which became one of the signature tunes of Green's late period, and "Dracula." They help give the album a more original voice, and indicate that Green was actively making himself at home in his new musical environment, not just mixing dull originals with phoned-in covers of pop and R&B hits (as he and many other '70s Blue Note artists were accused of doing). Of course, there are still pop covers present—the Beatles' "A Day in the Life" is a mellow, midtempo groove, and Bacharach's "I'll Never Fall in Love Again" doesn't stray far from the melody. Even if those aren't particularly distinctive, the remainder of *Green Is Beautiful* proves that Green's reinvention as a jazz-funk artist wasn't the misguided disaster it was initially made out to be. *—Steve Huey*

Alive! / Aug. 15, 1970 / Blue Note ✦✦✦✦

Visions / May 21, 1971 / Blue Note ✦✦✦
Grant Green's early-'70s recordings for Blue Note are continually attacked by jazz critics for being slick, overly commercial sessions that leaned closer to contemporary pop and R&B than hard bop or soul jazz. There's no denying that Green, like many of his Blue Note contemporaries, did choose a commercial path in the early '70s, but there were some virtues to these records, and *Visions* in particular. Often, these albums were distinguished by hot, funky workouts in the vein of Sly Stone or James Brown, but that's not the case here. On *Visions*, the guitarist crafted a set of appealingly melodic, lightly funky pop-jazz, concentrating on pop hits like "Does Anybody Really Know What Time It Is," "Love on a Two Way Street," "We've Only Just Begun," and "Never Can Say Goodbye." Supported by minor-league players, Green nevertheless turns in an elegant and dignified performance—after stating the melody on each song, he contributes typically graceful, memorable solos. Simply put, he sounds fresh, and his playing here is the best it has been since 1965's *His Majesty, King Funk.* Ultimately, *Visions* is a bit laid-back, and the electric piano-heavy arrangements are a little dated, but Grant Green never made a commercial pop-jazz album as appealing and satisfying as *Visions.* *—Stephen Thomas Erlewine*

The Best of Grant Green, Vol. 2 / May 21, 1971-Apr. 21, 1972 / Blue Note ✦✦✦✦✦
Grant Green signed to Blue Note for a second time in 1969. Where his first stint with the label was nearly all hard bop, the recordings from his second stay were almost all funky soul-jazz. Predictably, these are sessions that jazz purists have dismissed throughout the years, even though—when judged strictly on the level of funky, groove-oriented dance music—the music is quite strong. During the '80s and '90s, dance and hip-hop fans rediscovered Green's records from the late '70s and sampled his playing and grooves on their own records. Blue Note assembled *The Best of Grant Green, Vol. 2* to capitalize on the popularity of this acid-jazz movement. All of the material on this disc is drawn from albums—*The Final Countdown, Live At the Lighthouse, Visions*—that never received much attention in jazz circles. Nevertheless, fans of this sound will find *The Best of Grant Green, Vol. 2* to be a delight—there's a lot of wonderfully funky, dense grooves on here, and many of the songs have been out of print since their original issue. Hard bop fans will not be reconsider their negative opinion of this music based on this compilation, but acid-jazz, groove and hip-hop fans will find this disc to be an excellent addition to their Grant Green collection. *—Stephen Thomas Erlewine*

The Main Attraction / Mar. 12, 1976 / Kudu ✦✦

His Majesty, King Funk/Up With Donald Byrd / May 23, 1995 / Verve ✦✦✦
This single Verve CD reissues the complete contents of two unrelated LPs: Grant Green's *His Majesty King Funk* (great title) and *Up With Donald Byrd.* Unfortunately the music overall is not as rewarding as Green and Byrd's work of the period for Blue Note. Green is okay with a quintet that includes tenor-saxophonist Harold Vick and organist Larry Young but the material (mainly fairly simple funk riffs) is disappointing. Trumpeter Donald Byrd has a potentially strong group with both Jimmy Heath and Stanley Turrentine on tenors along with pianist Herbie Hancock and guitarist Kenny Burrell. However the three- or four-voice "Donald Byrd Singers" and the arrangements by Claus Ogerman weigh down the date. Each album watered down its music to an extent in hopes of gaining commercial success but neither really caught on. The results are interesting but somewhat forgettable. *—Scott Yanow*

● **Blue Breakbeats** / Jun. 16, 1998 / Blue Note ✦✦✦✦✦
Blue Breakbeats is an essential collection of six of the funkiest breakbeat heavy songs in Grant Green's deep Blue Note catalog. Prolifically sampled by beat thirsty hip-hop producers and stylistically influential in separating Green from Wes Montgomery's ever-looming shadow, these songs were compiled from *Green Is Beautiful, Visions, Alive!, Carryin' On*, and *The Final Come Down* by DJ Smash. While certainly nothing new here for the collector, it's a great starter piece for newcomers and those seeking out the original breaks sampled over and over on late-20th century hip-hop records. Playful grooves and classic drumbeats thump underneath some of the slickest jazz guitar work of the 1970s, while stellar instrumentation alone is worth the price of admission. With it being said that these groundbreaking Blue Note soul/jazz records are the foundation of hip-hop, these cuts are brick-by-brick testimonials. *—Nicholas Gordon*

Vernon Green & the Medallions

Vocals / Doo Wop, R&B
This mid- to late-'50s vocal group on Dootone is best known for the songs "The Letter," "Edna," and "Buick '59." The group had two distinct sides to its work, the romantic ballads that were sung straight, in almost agonizing purity, and the faster rocking numbers, which were partly tongue-in-cheek. *—Bruce Eder*

● **Golden Classics** / 1992 / Collectables ✦✦✦✦✦
All of the group's best known material is included among these dozen songs, which are cleanly mastered and given a nice, close sound. The group obviously regarded slow ballads like "The Letter" as their strong point, but "Don't Shoot" has a great beat and "Speedin'" is a pretty impressive car song, complete with car effects effectively created by a voice, and a comic ending à la the latter-day Cadillacs. The rocking "Give Me the Right" is also a solid song and may impress more than some of their close-harmony work, much as the latter was at a virtuoso level in its time. And then there's "Buick '59," one of the sexiest, lustiest, (intentionally) funniest car songs ever cut by a doo wop outfit. They also had a sense of humor with regard to their songs, following up "The Letter" with "The Telegram," which is an even better song. *—Bruce Eder*

Susaye Greene

Vocals / Urban, Contemporary R&B
Susaye Greene has stockpiled a lot of credits to her resumé without becoming a very recognizable name to the public, in part because it wasn't until 2002 that her first solo album appeared. Prior to that, she was perhaps best known for being in the Supremes for a couple of years, *long* after their hitmaking heyday, forming part of the lineup with original Supreme Mary Wilson and Scherrie Payne. She appeared on their last two albums and also recorded, wrote, arranged, and produced the *Partners* album with Payne. She also wrote Deniece Williams' hit "Free"; was in Stevie Wonder's *Wonderlové*; co-wrote, with Wonder, Michael Jackson's "I Can't Help It," from Jackson's smash *Off the Wall* album; sang with Ray Charles and Harry Belafonte; sang on jazzman Courtney Pine's "Children of the Ghetto"; managed singers, writers, producers, and actors; and worked as a book illustrator. She also managed to produce and write or co-write all but one of the songs on her debut solo work, *No Fear Here.* The record is a versatile but bland assemblage of contemporary R&B styles, with some adult contemporary, dance, and show music influences. *—Richie Unterberger*

● **No Fear Here** / Feb. 26, 2002 / Dollface ✦✦✦
Although Greene has a good number of credentials to her name, stretching back more than two decades prior to this solo debut, *No Fear Here* is a forgettable mainstream urban contemporary album. Yes, within that format, it's diverse, starting off with slightly menacing hip-hop-dipped soul in "End of Days," going into more standard adult contemporary ballads with a dancebeat tinge, getting into straight dance soul on "Letting You Go" (the song that would make one most suspect her prior experience in the Supremes), and covering "Bali H'ai" from *South Pacific.* Diverse, however, doesn't by definition mean exciting. This is unexciting, both in respect to material and to Greene's adequate voice, which only seldom demonstrates that it's capable of scaling a very high register. *—Richie Unterberger*

Greyboy Allstars

f. 1993

Group / Club/Dance, Acid Jazz, Urban
An acid jazz band that focuses more on jazz than groove-oriented dance music, the Greyboy Allstars came together in 1993 when noted rare-groove DJ Greyboy (aka Andreas Stevens) met up with Karl Denson, a saxophone player who was then touring with Lenny Kravitz. The pair collaborated on two tracks for Ubiquity Records' *Home Cookin'* compilation, and then worked on Greyboy's 1994 solo album for Ubiquity, *Freestylin'.* After forming their own label, Greyboy Records, the duo gradually amassed

members for a house band—guitarist Michael Andrews (formerly with the Origin), bassist Chris Stillwell, drummer Zak Najor and keyboard player Robert Walter. The Greyboy Allstars toured around the area and in 1995 released their debut album *West Coast Boogaloo* (with contributions from groove legend Fred Wesley). Tours throughout Europe and the States followed that year (as well as a second solo album from Greyboy himself), and the group released a concert document *Live* in April 1997. Two months later, the Greyboy Allstars released their second studio LP, *Town Called Earth*, recorded with a recent recruit, guitarist Elgin Park. Apart from Greyboy, Karl Denson and Robert Walter have each recorded solo LPs as well. —*John Bush*

Live / Apr. 8, 1997 / Relaxed ✦✦✦

It's hard to know how to categorize the San Diego-based Greyboy Allstars. They tend to get thrown in with the acid jazz crowd, but while they do play jazz, their music is influenced at least as heavily by James Brown and Curtis Mayfield; the herky-jerk drums and funky, melodic basslines all come straight out of 1960s and '70s soul. This live album documents their 1998 tour and prominently features sax player Karl Denson, particularly on the Lou Donaldson number "Hot Dog" and on Denson's own "Tenor Man." Keyboardist Robert Walter contributes the very soulful "Freshman 10," which sounds for all the world like something the J.B.'s might play while waiting for James Brown to hit the stage—guitarist Elgin Park is in particularly fine form, throwing out vintage rhythm riffs with funky precision. Everything on this disc is up to that standard—it's over an hour of good, sweaty, old-school fun. —*Rick Anderson*

● **A Town Called Earth** / Jun. 10, 1997 / Greyboy ✦✦✦✦✦

A Town Called Earth is a fresh combination of jazz, R&B, soul and funk that reminds us of the vitality of live funk in an era dominated by pre-packaged samples. Zak Najor (drums), Robert Walter (keys), Karl Denson (sax and flute) and Elgin Park (guitars and bass), embrace their musical history and cover a diverse range of styles. Denson's flute on "Blues for Celia" recalls Herbie Mann's progressive flute work of the late '60s, when he worked with a Memphis-based horn section. "The Many Moods of Erik Newson" and "A Town Called Earth" pull from Miles Davis' *Bitches Brew* work as well as alt-rockers like the Smashing Pumpkins. Some songs, like "Sportscaster," may seem pithy unless you give the tracks a careful listen, so please do. —*Ryan Randall Goble*

Billy Griffin

b. Aug. 15, 1950, Baltimore, MD

Vocals, Songwriter / Soul

Billy Griffin sang lead and co-wrote the Miracles' million-selling number-one pop hit "Love Machine," the sensual "Do It Baby," its follow-up "Don't Cha Love It," and the steppers cuts "Don't Let It End ('Til You Let It Begin)" and "Take It All." Griffin's own solo favorites are the crisp "Hold Me Tighter in the Rain," "Serious," "Believe It or Not," and the steppers cut "So Many Ways."

Born William Griffin on August 15, 1950, in Baltimore, MD, Griffin sang with such groups as Last Dynasty, grooming his flexible tenor before eventually getting his big break. When Smokey Robinson decided to concentrate on his executive duties at Motown Records and chose to spend more time with his family, a national talent search was conducted to see who could take over his lead vocal duties with the Miracles. Griffin, who bared a slight resemblance to Robinson, was chosen to sing lead with the group. The group's first post-Robinson LP, *Renaissance*, was issued in summer 1973. Freddie Perren produced the crystalline second single, "Don't Let It End ('Til You Let It Begin)." Perren also produced the group's groundbreaking LP *City of Angels* in early 1976. The Miracles signed with Columbia Records in 1977. Griffin's brother, guitarist Donald Griffin, was added to the group's lineup. Billy and Warren "Pete" Moore wrote all the songs on the group's label debut, *Love Crazy*.

In the early '80s, Griffin signed as a solo artist with Columbia. His solo debut, *Be With Me*, was produced by keyboardist John Barnes, who had played on Griffin's sides with the Miracles. The first single, "Hold Me Tighter in the Rain," received airplay in Chicago and other markets but failed to chart in the U.S. even though it was a Top 30 hit in the U.K. The follow-up single was the ginger loping ballad "2nd Day Love Story." Griffin's second LP, *Respect*, was again produced by Barnes and was a more cohesive album. The title track single charted on the R&B charts in fall 1983 and was followed by the silky "Serious" in spring 1984. Todd Cochrane produced Griffin's third Columbia album, *Systematic*, issued in 1985. It listed a cover of "If I Ever Lose This Heaven" co-written by Leon Ware and the sumptuous "Waiting to Touch." Griffin resurfaced on a 1986 Atlantic single, "Believe It or Not," produced by keyboardist Derek Nakamoto, who had worked with him on the *Be With Me* and *Respect* albums. —*Ed Hogan*

Be With Me / 1982 / CBS ✦✦✦

Former Miracles lead singer Billy Griffin collaborated with keyboardist/producer John Barnes on his first solo effort, *Be With Me*, first issued by Columbia in 1982. The two had previously worked together on several Miracles hits including the million-selling hit "Love Machine" from the fresh concept album *City of Angels*. *Be With Me* is distinguished by its underlining jazzy feel on some tracks (including a pre-stardom Gerald Albright) and the inclusion of the exuberant "Hold Me Tighter in the Rain." The track boasts spicy percussion, a buoyant synth bassline, dreamy electric piano, and some of Griffin's most emotive vocals, like "Hold Me Tighter in the Rain," a hit in the UK. *Be With Me*'s uptempo tracks are "The Beat Is Getting Stronger" (which has snatches of "Elephant Walk" and Prince's "Controversy"), and the thumping bass workout "Breaking Out." The album's closing number, "Understand," has a loping gait similar to "I Can't Help It," a Stevie Wonder song covered both by Michael Jackson on his *Off the Wall* album and Grover Washington Jr. on his *Skylarkin'* LP. Taken as a whole, *Be With Me* is pretty satisfying. The LP also works as a musical benchmark for what would later become the quiet storm genre. The second single, "2nd Day Love Story," would fit on a quiet storm/smooth jazz radio play list quite comfortably. Griffin and Barnes better realized their musical version a couple of years later on the much sought after *Respect*. —*Ed Hogan*

Respect / 1983 / Columbia ✦✦

After a run of singles and LPs with the Miracles, replacing Smokey Robinson, Billy Griffin goes solo. But after listening to this, you'll scratch your head and wonder why. Griffins' airy, light tenor sounded more manly with Pete Moore, Ron White and Bobby Rogers backing him up. After listening intently, I'm still trying to find a reason for this recording. Eight songs and not a compelling one in the bunch. The title cut and "Serious" are, at best, C minuses. And that's being as generous as Judge Eugenia Williams was to Holyfield in his controversial draw with Lennox Lewis. My expectation may be too great, but how can you co-write sizzlers like "Love Machine" for the Miracles and then sink to this level? —*Andrew Hamilton*

Systematic / 1985 / CBS ✦✦✦

Billy Griffin followed his well-received 1983 quiet storm precursors *Be With Me* ("Hold Me Tighter in the Rain") and *Respect* with *Systematic*, a decidedly more radio-friendly album. Some of his fans were disappointed that *Systematic* didn't wholly continue in the same vein as *Respect*. Still, if taken on its own merit, *Systematic* delivers and has a quiet storm contender in the form of the lush and sensuous "Waiting to Touch." Instead of being produced by John Barnes, Griffin's third solo LP was produced by keyboardist/songwriter Todd Cochran and Motown alumnus Leon Ware. Griffin, as a member of the Miracles, sang lead on such Ware co-compositions as "Give Me Just Another Day" and "Calling Out Your Name" from *Do It Baby*, the sumptuous "I Don't Need No Reason" from *Renaissance*, and "What Is a Heart Good For." Highlights are the kinetic "Systematic," which is in the same vein as "Hold Me Tighter in the Rain"; the energized "Electrified"; and the playful "Everybody Needs Somebody." Though some tracks received radio play in various markets, the LP and singles ("Systematic," "If I Ever Lose This Heaven") failed to chart. Griffin resurfaced in 1986 with an Atlantic single, "Believe It or Not," that had quiet storm touches. It was produced by Derek Nakamoto who had worked with Griffin on his *Be With Me* and *Respect* albums. —*Ed Hogan*

● **The Best of Billy Griffin** / Feb. 20, 1996 / Motorcity ✦✦✦✦

To many, Billy Griffin will always be the young light-skinned brother who replaced Smokey Robinson in the Miracles. A couple of CBS albums spawned a couple of U.K. hits that got ignored in the States; if you haven't heard them, you haven't missed much. Ian Levine takes his knocks, but these tracks represent the prolific producer at his best. Like Motown's producers did, Levine makes Griffin's airy tenor come to life. His remake of Eddie Kendricks' "Date With the Rain," has more bite than the pop-ish original. Equally as captivating "So Hung Up on You," plodding beat is the perfect vehicle for Griffin's mating lead. A bouncy beat permeates most of these tunes, and Billy rides the seesaw grooves like a cool cowboy; includes a remake of "Love Machine," that's not bad, and a succulent duet "Shoulda Been Loving You (Accept This Apology)" with an unidentified female. Levine had a special chemistry with Griffin. Includes "First In Line" the first Motorcity Records single. Eighteen enjoyable tracks. —*Andrew Hamilton*

Mary Griffin

b. New Orleans, LA

Vocals / Contemporary R&B, Urban

Mary Griffin is an urban R&B singer who released her debut album, *For the First Time*, in 1997. Griffin was born in New Orleans, the daughter of a local minister. As a child, she sang in churches with her family, and by her teens she had realized she wanted to pursue a musical career. Her style eventually developed into a gospel-inflected contemporary update of classic soul; even though she was a New Orlean native, there was very little Crescent City R&B in her style. She was discovered singing at a local club in the mid-'90s by some talent scouts and by 1997 she had signed with Curb Records. Her debut album, *For the First Time*, was released in the fall of that year. —*Stephen Thomas Erlewine*

● **For the First Time** / Oct. 14, 1997 / Curb ✦✦✦

Mary Griffin's debut album, *For the First Time*, is a well-crafted collection of urban contemporary R&B and adult contemporary pop that showcases her dynamic vocals to fine effect, even when the songwriting is less than stellar. In fact, Griffin often outshines her material—given the right songs, she could be something else—but when she has a good song, such as the sultry "Just No Other Way" or the grooving "Make It Up to You," she makes it her own and establishes that she's a singer with some real potential. —*Leo Stanley*

Groove Collective

f. 1990, New York, NY

Group / Acid Jazz, Contemporary Jazz, Club/Dance, Urban

The acid-jazz outfit Groove Collective was formed in downtown New York City in 1990 by flute player Richard Worth, DJ Smash and rapper Nappy G, all three staples of a nomadic dance club called Giant Step. In time, the trio was joined by keyboardist Itaal Shur, drummer Genji Siraisi and bassist Jonathan Maron, earning a growing cult following and eventually attracting the attention of Steely Dan vibist Bill Ware, who soon signed on along with saxophonist Jay Rodriguez, trombonist Josh Roseman, trumpeter Fabio Morgera and percussionist Chris Theberge. The Groove Collective's self-titled debut LP appeared on Reprise in 1993, followed three years later by the GRP label release *We the People*. The group resurfaced in 1998 with *Dance of the Drunken Master*. *It's All In Your Mind* was issued three years later. —*Jason Ankeny*

Groove Collective / Jun. 25, 1993-Jun. 27, 1993 / Reprise ✦✦✦

In the mid-'90s there have been many attempts to combine jazz with dance music in hopes of making creative music more accessible to younger listeners. Most of these projects have flopped due to the jazz being watered down but this effort from the ten-piece Groove Collective is one of the more successful hybirds. Not counting a pair of juvenile raps, the music is strong from the jazz standpoint and the funky rhythms are generally infectious, resulting in a set of intelligent jazz-oriented dance music. —*Scott Yanow*

Dance of the Drunken Master / May 19, 1998 / Shanachie ✦✦✦✦
With their brand of acid jazz, the Groove Collective mix the spirit of horn bands like Earth, Wind & Fire with the snap of hip-hop and the edge of hard bop. While jazz purists might wince at the gurgling rhythms, most will find it hard to keep still with the thick funk on these tracks. This is music with a sense of fun. *—Tim Sheridan*

● **Declassified** / Jul. 20, 1999 / Shanachie ✦✦✦✦✦
Groove Collective's completely uninhibited, party-based jazz-funk is inspired by Sly Stone, acid jazz, hip-hop, salsa, Stevie Wonder, drum 'n' bass, Parliament-Funkadelic, Fania—that is, anything or anyone from the late '60s on who knew how to get down. Their fourth album overall finds the congregation in a most jubilant mood, happy to simply stretch out on a series of infectious singalong jams, starting with the openers "Up All Night" (which trades honking sax solos with some great stuttered drum programming) and "Everything Is Changing" (a shuffling disco stomp). With no less than 14 pieces in the group, it's obvious that Groove Collective shouldn't have any trouble filling spaces, and truth to tell, just about every song on *Declassified* bristles with so many ideas, solos, and licks that listeners may get dizzy without a few listens under their belt. "On a Feeling," the spotlight for rapper Nappy G, isn't exactly the tightest hip-hop joint ever heard, but the sheer instrumental and musical prowess abundant all over this album makes it a joy for all to hear. *—John Bush*

It's All in Your Mind / Jan. 9, 2001 / Shanachie ✦✦✦
Nearly ten years after their formation in the early-'90s New York soul-jazz scene, Groove Collective has developed into a tightly knit orchestra of highly skilled musicians full of life and danceable spirit. *It's All in Your Mind* is a good representation of their artistic development and, as is with any progression, Groove Collective has upped the ante just enough to ensure further progress on future records. *It's All in Your Mind* experiments with jazzy and spacy elements, but never veers too far to the left or right. Though the first cut, "Time Pilot," is a slow and gentle groove that initially sounds like Hooverphonic or Portishead, the band jumps right back to their rootsy Afro-beat comforts with the second track, the Fela Kuti-esque "Ransome." They dance around in techno-influenced space on "Dance With You" and even rock out on "Skye." Though it may seem as though GC bounces around a lot, they maintain their focus beautifully, drifting seamlessly from genre to genre. As well, *It's All in Your Mind* tests the band's technical boundaries as electronics are more prevalent than on previous records. *It's All in Your Mind* illustrates an evolution of sorts for the collective from their meager hip-hop/jazz beginnings to a full-on ensemble. What's more is that the Collective plays like a jazz combo, giving each player enough room to show off his considerable individual talents. There are numerous standouts on the record, but Chucho Valdes' appearance on "Stargazer" is likely the most memorable as it elevates the record to new sonic heights. Generally, *It's All in Your Mind* is a bit more mellow than previous recordings but a wonderful record nonetheless. *—Ken Taylor*

Gwen Guthrie

b. 1950, Okemah, OK, **d.** Feb. 5, 1999, Orange, NJ
Vocals / Dance-Pop, Disco
Gwen Guthrie is best known for her number one R&B single "Ain't Nothin' Goin' on But the Rent," a popular self-written bouncer. A prolific songwriter and a good pianist, she also penned "Supernatural Thing" for Ben E. King and "This Time I'll Be Sweeter" for Martha Reeves, which was later popularized by Angela Bofill and Issac Hayes. In all, Guthrie logged approximately 50 compositions, and many thought Guthrie and songwriting partner Patrick Grant had the potential to become another Ashford & Simpson. Born in Okemah, OK, in 1950, but raised in Newark, NJ, Guthrie started singing in high school with a female quartet called the Ebonettes. (Another of its members, Brenda White King, pursued music like Guthrie and became an in-demand session singer.) Guthrie sang lead for a group (East Coast Band) formed by Larry Blackmon (later of Cameo) in New York, but got her big break when she was asked to do a background session for Aretha Franklin, the number-one R&B hit "I'm in Love," from 1974. Six months later, Guthrie signed as a staff writer with Bert Coteaux Productions and co-wrote "Love Don't Go Through No Changes," the first hit for Sister Sledge, and many others with Grant. The collaboration didn't last long, however.

Guthrie continued to write with a variety of partners, and supplied backing vocals to many recording sessions. Working with Peter Tosh in the late '70s, Guthrie befriended reggae stars Sly Dunbar and Robbie Shakespeare, who invited her to Nassau to record vocals for an album they were producing. Hearing her unique voice in the studio, Island Records founder Chris Blackwell inked her to a contract, and the Dunbar/Shakespeare project, assisted by David Conley of Surface, became her first solo release, a self-titled LP. She did score a dancefloor hit in the '80s in the U.K. with "It Should Have Been You," a ballad from the first album. Her second LP, *Portrait*, released in 1983, followed the same formula: simplistic dance tracks and trite grooves. Album number three, *Good to Go Lover*, dropped in 1986, and spawned her chart-topper "Ain't Nothin' Goin' on But the Rent," plus the torching ballad "You Touched My Life." On *Lifeline* (1988), Guthrie was more involved in the writing and production. *Hot Times* was Guthrie's final LP release, hitting the streets in 1990. Like the previous LP, she wrote nearly everything, except for a moving remake of Stephanie Mills' "Never Knew Love Like This Before." Guthrie also had two LP releases: *Just for You* (1985) and *Ticket to Ride* (1988) on Fourth & Broadway Records. Guthrie died on February 4, 1999, of uterine cancer in Orange, NJ. *—Andrew Hamilton*

Just for You / 1985 / 4th & Broadway ✦✦
Former session vocalist Gwen Guthrie made some dancefloor noise in the mid-'80s with a string of well-produced albums that usually had a couple of smash songs mixed in with generic disco and dance-pop filler. This album landed Guthrie three moderate R&B successes and even had the bonus of some light reggae elements added by way of The Sly & Robbie production team, who assisted on some cuts. *—Ron Wynn*

Good to Go Lover / 1986 / Polydor ✦✦
Gwen Guthrie landed her biggest hit album with this mid-'80s release. The song "Ain't Nothing Going On But The Rent" was a huge smash on both sides of the Atlantic, while she also did well with a Carpenters cover and another album cut. She did her strongest, most confident and consistent singing on these tracks. *—Ron Wynn*

Lifeline / 1988 / Jellybean Prod. ✦✦
Gwen Guthrie didn't have as much success when she moved to Warner Bros. as she'd enjoyed in the mid-'80s with Polydor. This album did get her one moderate hit, but overall, it didn't have either the solid grooves of past albums or any real definitive ballad. She sang as strongly as before, but was unable to really get her focus on this one. *—Ron Wynn*

● **The Ultimate Collection** / Jul. 27, 1999 / Hip-O ✦✦✦✦
Hip-O's *The Ultimate Gwen Guthrie* covers the best of her late-'80s recordings from Garage and Polydor Records, which happens to be when she had her one big hit, "Ain't Nothin' Goin' on But the Rent." Prior to that song, she had a few moderate hits for Island (highlighted by "Love in Moderation"), and after leaving Polydor, she had a couple other minor hits, but the years *The Ultimate* covers are the peak of her career, and it does a good job of rounding up the 13 best tunes (plus a dub mix of "Ain't Nothin' Goin' on But the Rent"). It may not be definitive, since it doesn't chronicle her entire years, but it does an excellent job of anthologizing the years most casual listeners will want to hear. *—Stephen Thomas Erlewine*

Guy

f. 1987
Group / New Jack Swing, Club/Dance, Urban
This seminal R&B trio was the first group to sport the new jack swing sound, essentially traditional soul vocals melded to hip-hop beats, with credit for the genre's invention going to founder, multi-instrumentalist, and superproducer Teddy Riley. Riley formed his first band, Wreckx-N-Effect, while still a teenager, with brothers Markell Riley and Brandon Mitchell; Guy followed a few years later in 1987. Its first incarnation featured vocalists Aaron Hall and Timmy Gatling. Their self-titled debut album was an instant smash, producing the R&B hits "I Like," "Groove Me," "Spend the Night," and "Teddy's Jam." Meanwhile, Riley found himself in strong demand as a songwriter and producer; in 1988, Riley produced Bobby Brown's *Don't Be Cruel*, the album that helped new jack swing cross over into the pop mainstream. Riley has also worked with Kool Moe Dee, Michael Jackson (*Dangerous*), Stevie Wonder, Keith Sweat, Jane Child, and SWV, among others. In between albums, Guy contributed songs to the soundtracks of *Do the Right Thing* and *New Jack City*.

By 1989, Guy was in turmoil; Riley's brother Brandon Mitchell was killed in a shooting, and the group became involved in an acrimonious split with manager Gene Griffin over money. 1990's *The Future* featured Hall's brother Albert Damion Hall in place of Gatling and spawned R&B hits in "Let's Chill," "Do Me Right," "D-O-G Me Out," and "Long Gone." However, by the time Riley and Guy finally started to attract media attention for their innovative and influential work, the trio had broken up. Riley concentrated on his production and songwriting career for several years before forming the band Blackstreet with vocalists Chauncey "Black" Hannibal, Dave Hollister, and Levi Little. The quartet released a self-titled debut in 1994. Aaron Hall released his solo debut, *The Truth*, in 1993; brother Damion followed in 1994 with *Straight to the Point*. Guy reunited in 1999, issuing *Guy III* early the following year. *—Steve Huey*

● **Guy** / 1988 / MCA ✦✦✦✦✦
One of the most seminal and influential releases of late '80s, Guy's self-titled debut album did more than its part to popularize new jack swing, a style that would soon become inescapable on urban contemporary radio. Teddy Riley didn't actually invent new jack swing with Guy—he'd already gotten the ball rolling on Keith Sweat's 1987 debut *Make It Last Forever*—but this album did more than any other to make it so incredibly popular in the R&B world. With their tough blend of hip-hop, R&B, and Gap Band-influenced funk, hits like "Groove Me" and "Teddy's Jam" defined new jack swing and served as the blueprint for countless new jack recordings in the late '80s and early- to mid-'90s. One shameless Guy clone after another would pop up on urban radio, the vast majority of whom weren't even a fraction as inventive as Riley's distinctive trio. For anyone with even a casual interest in new jack, this CD is absolutely essential. *—Alex Henderson*

The Future / 1990 / MCA ✦✦✦
New jack swing, a hard-edged, high-tech blend of funk, R&B, and rap/hip-hop, had been milked for all it's worth and run into the ground by Guy's numerous imitators in the late '80s and early- to mid-'90s. But in the hands of its highly influential orginators, Guy, it sounds fresh and inspired. Though not as strong as the debut album of 1988, *The Future* is one of the more appealing—and certainly more authentic—examples of "new jack swing." Lead by the ubiquitous producer/songwriter Teddy Riley, the trio brings a definite urgency to grinding, forceful funk like "Teddy's Jam 2" and "Her" and to such slow jams as "Do Me Right" and "Tease Me Tonight" (both of which recall the Gap Band à la "Outstanding"). Especially riveting is the all-rap number "Total Control," a brutally honest commentary on exploitation in the music business. It's important to absorb Guy's music and realize that it is proof, in the interest of understandable complaints about the glut of faceless "new jack swing" artists saturating the market, that it wasn't always cheap and formulaic. *—Alex Henderson*

Guy III / Jan. 25, 2000 / MCA ✦✦✦✦
More than ten years after their sophomore album—titled, ironically, *Future*—appeared to draw the curtain on urban forerunners Guy, Teddy Riley, Aaron Hall, and Damion Hall came back for their third album. In the interim, both Hall brothers released solo albums, and Riley continued his hit-making success by producing Bobby Brown, Michael Jackson, Stevie Wonder, and SWV (among others), and by appearing in yet another superstar group, Blackstreet. After Blackstreet's third album *Finally* failed to chart as high as its

predecessor, Riley and the Halls re-formed. Guy was always more than just an above-average soul group, and though Riley's production schedule slowed slightly during the late '90s, he was still one of the biggest names in contemporary R&B. *Guy III* equals the extraordinary expectations that any new material from Guy provokes, occasionally exceeding their work in the past. *—Keith Farley*

Jasmine Guy

b. Mar. 10, 1964, Boston, MA

Vocals / Urban

Jasmine Guy starred in *the Cosby Show* TV spin-off *A Different World* that ran on NBC-TV from 1987 to 1993. Her role as the snooty, heavy-Southern-accented Whitley Gilbert was one of the highlights of the show. She also had three R&B hits, "Try Me," "Another Like My Lover," and "Just Want to Hold You." Born March 10, 1964, in Boston, MA, Guy grew up in Atlanta, GA. She was a dancer with the Alvin Ailey Dance Troupe and later danced as a part of the cast of the '80s NBC-TV series *Fame*, which was based on the hit movie of the same name. Guy also appeared in numerous off-Broadway shows and in the Spike Lee movie *School Daze* with Lawrence Fishburne.

Being on a TV show that was a spin-off of a phenomenally successful, groundbreaking TV series had its benefits. Guy was afforded the opportunity to become a recording artist. Signing with Warner Bros., Guy's first single, "Try Me," was written and produced by Full Force. The ultra-sexy video of the song was heavily hyped and premiered after a segment of *A Different World*. "Try Me" made it to number-14 R&B in fall 1990. Her self-titled debut LP made it to number-38 R&B on *Billboard*'s charts in late 1990.

Guy received kudos for her steely-eyed, menacing performance in the 1989 Eddie Murphy/Richard Pryor/Redd Foxx/Della Reese/Arsenio Hall movie *Harlem Nights*. Guy also voiced a part in the 1997 animated movie *Cats Don't Dance* and toured in the late '90s in *Chicago* the Musical with Ben Vereen. *—Ed Hogan*

Jasmine Guy / Oct. 16, 1990 / Warner Bros. ✦

All too often, actors and actresses who decided to pursue careers as singers made listeners wish they had stuck with acting. One embarrassing example was Jasmine Guy, who aimed at the urban contemporary market with this generic release. Guy's thin, Paula Abdul-ish voice isn't the least bit impressive, and it certainly isn't enough to make weak, mundane tunes like "Everybody Knows My Name," "Tuff Boy" and the new jack swing-influenced "Try Me" come to life. The funk-rock song "Don't Want Money" isn't bad, but most of the CD is shamelessly formulaic. And having accomplished producers like Full Force, Mic Murphy (formerly of the System) and Timmy Gatling on board doesn't erase the fact that Guy's voice and the material simply aren't happening. This album made it clear that acting, not singing, was Guy's calling. *—Alex Henderson*

H

Hall & Oates

f. 1972, Philadelphia, PA

Group / Blue-Eyed Soul, Pop/Rock, Soft Rock, Adult Contemporary

From their first hit in 1974 through their heyday in the '80s, Daryl Hall and John Oates' smooth, catchy take on Philly soul brought them enormous commercial success—including six number-one singles and six platinum albums—yet little critical success. Hall & Oates' music was remarkably well-constructed and produced; at their best, their songs were filled with strong hooks and melodies that adhered to soul traditions without being a slave to them by incorporating elements of new wave and hard rock.

Daryl Hall began performing professionally while he was a student at Temple University. In 1966, he recorded a single with Kenny Gamble & the Romeos; the group featured Gamble, Leon Huff, and Thom Bell, who would all become the architects of Philly soul. During this time, Hall frequently appeared on sessions for Gamble & Huff. In 1967, Hall met John Oates, a fellow Temple University student. Oates was leading his own soul band at the time. The two students realized they had similar tastes and began performing together in an array of R&B and doo wop groups. By 1968, the duo had parted ways, as Oates transferred schools and Hall formed the soft rock band Gulliver; the group released one album on Elektra in the late '60s before disbanding.

After Gulliver's breakup, Hall concentrated on session work again, appearing as a backup vocalist for the Stylistics, the Delfonics, and the Intruders, among others. Oates returned to Philadelphia in 1969, and he and Hall began writing folk-oriented songs and performing together. Eventually they came to the attention of Tommy Mottola, who quickly became their manager, securing the duo a contract with Atlantic Records. On their first records—*Whole Oates* (1972), *Abandoned Luncheonette* (1973), *War Babies* (1974)—the duo were establishing their sound, working with producers like Arif Mardin and Todd Rundgren and removing much of their folk influences. At the beginning of 1974, the duo relocated from Philadelphia to New York. During this period, they only managed one hit—the number 60 "She's Gone" in the spring of 1974.

After they moved to RCA in 1975, the duo landed on its successful mixture of soul, pop, and rock, scoring a Top Ten single with "Sara Smile." The success of "Sara Smile" prompted the re-release of "She's Gone," which rocketed into the Top Ten as well. Released in the summer of 1976, *Bigger Than the Both of Us* was only moderately successful upon its release. The record took off in early 1977, when "Rich Girl" became the duo's first number-one single.

Although they had several minor hits between 1977 and 1980, the albums Hall & Oates released at the end of the decade were not as successful as their mid-'70s records. Nevertheless, they were more adventurous, incorporating more rock elements into their blue-eyed soul. The combination would finally pay off in late 1980, when the duo released the self-produced *Voices*, the album that marked the beginning of Hall & Oates' greatest commercial and artistic success. The first single from *Voices*, a cover of the Righteous Brothers' "You've Lost That Lovin' Feeling," reached number 12, yet it was the second single, "Kiss on My List" that confirmed their commercial potential by becoming the duo's second number-one single; its follow-up, "You Make My Dreams" hit number five. They quickly released *Private Eyes* in the summer of 1981; the record featured two number-one hits, "Private Eyes" and "I Can't Go for That (No Can Do)," as well as the Top Ten hit "Did It in a Minute." "I Can't Go for That (No Can Do)" also spent a week at the top of the R&B charts—a rare accomplishment for a white act. *H20* followed in 1982 and it proved more successful than their two previous albums, selling over two million copies and launching their biggest hit single, "Maneater," as well as the Top Ten hits "One on One" and "Family Man." The following year, the duo released a greatest-hits compilation, *Rock 'N Soul, Pt. 1*, that featured two new Top Ten hits—the number two "Say It Isn't So" and "Adult Education."

In April of 1984, the Recording Industry Association of America announced that Hall & Oates had surpassed the Everly Brothers as the most successful duo in rock history, earning a total of 19 gold and platinum awards. Released in October of 1984, *Big Bam Boom* expanded their number of gold and platinum awards, selling over two million copies and launching four Top 40 singles, including the number one "Out of Touch." Following their contract-fulfilling gold album *Live at the Apollo With David Ruffin & Eddie Kendrick*, Hall & Oates went on hiatus. After the lukewarm reception for Daryl Hall's 1986 solo album, *Three Hearts in the Happy Ending Machine*, the duo regrouped to release 1988's *Ooh Yeah!*, their first record for Arista. The first single, "Everything Your Heart Desires," went to number three and helped propel the album to platinum status. However, none of the album's other singles broke the Top 20, indicating that the era of chart dominance had ended. *Change of Season*, released in 1990, confirmed that fact. Although the record went gold, it only featured one Top 40 hit—the number-11 single, "So Close." The duo hasn't released an album since 1997. *—Stephen Thomas Erlewine*

Whole Oates / 1972 / Atlantic ✦✦✦

Hall & Oates' debut album was a tentative effort, with the two singers hesitantly working their way around slick but relatively undistinguished material that displayed their folk roots more than any other record they would later make. *—Stephen Thomas Erlewine*

Abandoned Luncheonette / 1973 / Atlantic ✦✦✦✦✦

Abandoned Luncheonette, Hall & Oates' second album, was the first indication of the duo's talent for sleek, soul-inflected pop/rock. It featured the single "She's Gone," which would become a big hit in 1975, when it was re-released following the success of "Sara Smile." *—Stephen Thomas Erlewine*

War Babies / 1974 / Atlantic ✦✦

After crafting the fitfully accomplished blue-eyed Philly soul-pop of *Abandoned Luncheonette*, Hall & Oates retreated to a more rock-oriented sound on *War Babies*, recorded with producer Todd Rundgren. Some of the tracks work, but the duo's performance sounds forced throughout much of the record. *—Stephen Thomas Erlewine*

Daryl Hall & John Oates / Sep. 1975 / Buddah ✦✦✦✦✦

Switching to RCA, Daryl Hall & John Oates recorded a self-titled album that fulfilled their early promise as pop-savvy blue-eyed soul craftsmen. A few of the tracks fall flat—including the reggae-tinged "Soldering" and the pompous "Ennui on the Mountain"—but much of the album is lush and catchy, featuring ballads and mid-tempo numbers that are nearly as engaging as their breakthrough single "Sara Smile." *—Stephen Thomas Erlewine*

Bigger Than the Both of Us / 1976 / RCA ✦✦

Bigger Than the Both of Us continued the gold success of its predecessor by adding a cleaner, more pop-oriented gloss to the production, as well as fine songwriting that builds on the bright pulse of "Rich Girl." *—Stephen Thomas Erlewine*

Beauty on a Back Street / 1977 / RCA ✦✦✦

Beauty on a Back Street isn't quite as accomplished as its two predecessors, yet it is more ambitious and diverse, as Hall & Oates begin to add some arena-rock conventions to their sound, particularly distorted guitars and anthemic choruses. On *War Babies* they had tried a similar attack, but on *Beauty on a Back Street*, the duo's songwriting was stronger, which meant that the instrumental approach didn't overwhelm the actual songs. *—Stephen Thomas Erlewine*

No Goodbyes / 1977 / Atlantic ✦✦

Released after the success of their first RCA album, *No Goodbyes* is a compilation of their three Atlantic albums that includes three unreleased tracks. *No Goodbyes* concisely sums up the high points of the duo's early years (in particular, the soaring single "She's Gone"), and confirms the fact that the pair were still developing their signature style. *—Stephen Thomas Erlewine*

Along the Red Ledge / Sep. 1978 / RCA ✦✦✦

Continuing the more rock-oriented approach of *Beauty on a Back Street*, *Along the Red Ledge* is more successful than its predecessor, as the duo landed on a polished melodic pop/rock style that managed to retain their Philly soul influences without drowning their voices in distorted guitar flourishes. They would refine this sound two years later on *Voices*, the record that established them as pop/rock superstars. *—Stephen Thomas Erlewine*

X-Static / 1979 / Buddah ✦✦✦

After coming up with a sleek and soulful template on *Along the Red Ledge*, Hall & Oates took a temporary detour on *X-Static*, concentrating on disco rhythms. A few tracks were successful—in particular, "Wait for Me"—but the record sounds unfocused and misguided. *—Stephen Thomas Erlewine*

Voices / 1980 / RCA ✦✦✦✦✦

This is the album that took Hall & Oates from being a successful '70s pop duo to being one of the four biggest singles acts of the '80s (the others: Michael Jackson, Prince, and Madonna). The sound is a wonderful pop pastiche, from the Beatles-esque "How Does It Feel to Be Back" to the neo-Philadelphia soul of the hits "Kiss on My List" and "You Make My Dreams." *—William Ruhlmann*

Private Eyes / 1981 / RCA ✦✦✦✦✦

Voices brought Hall & Oates into the new wave era, establishing their sleek fusion of synthesizers, Philly soul, mechanical beats, and pop hooks, but they didn't quite perfect it until *Private Eyes*. Powered by no less than three Top Ten singles, the album is filled with effortlessly catchy hooks and a handful of great songs that don't stop at the hits. Sure, "Private Eyes," "I Can't Go for That (No Can Do)," and "Did It in a Minute" all have remarkably graceful melodies, but what's unexpected is how flat-out terrific the pounding soul of "Looking for a Good Sign" is, or how deftly the arena-rock hooks of "Head Above Water" are executed. There's still a bit of filler, highlighted by John Oates' supremely silly

"Mano a Mano," but Hall & Oates never made a record quite as good as *Private Eyes* ever again. *—Stephen Thomas Erlewine*

H2O / 1982 / RCA ✦✦✦✦✦

From the Motown beat of "Maneater" to the lush ballad "One on One," Hall & Oates continue to make the top pop of the early '80s. Also contains "Family Man." *—William Ruhlmann*

Big Bam Boom / 1984 / RCA ✦✦✦

Big Bam Boom was the last blockbuster album soul-rockers Hall & Oates generated (and their last to make the Top Ten album chart). The album was percussion-heavy, and as the title suggests, bombastic. It produced four hit singles, including their last chart-topper, "Out of Touch," and the soulful Top Ten hit "Method of Modern Love." Also included is the critically acclaimed third single, "Some Things Are Better Left Unsaid," which, although not a major Top Ten smash, ranks as one of the album's finer (and darker) moments. The fourth and final single was the lightweight "Possession Obsession," which featured John Oates manning the vocals. Incidentally, the version of "Possession Obsession" issued as a single, which featured a saxophone, is not the version included here. The rest of the album features dance-rock-oriented numbers, among them "Going Through the Motions" and "Dance on Your Knees," which, unfortunately, sound somewhat dated, and the Latin-flavored "All American Girl." Also of note is the excellent and brooding "Cold Dark and Yesterday." This album, which went on to sell two million copies, marked the end of an era for one of rock music's most successful duos. *—Jose F. Promis*

Live at the Apollo / 1985 / RCA ✦✦

Ooh Yeah! / 1988 / Arista ✦✦

From 1980-1984, the *Billboard* chart could have been dubbed the Hall & Oates chart for their seemingly never ending assault of number-one singles (amazingly, they never had a number-one album). However, after *Big Bam Boom* and their live pre-sabbatical *At the Apollo*, Hall again embarked on his solo album for six/seven years and the overblown *Three Hearts* and its happy ending machine were born. When they returned on Arista in 1988, they delivered a very good album in *Ooh Yeah!* But the legendary Hall & Oates were treated as comeback artists. Pulling the rug from under their feet, critics slammed the album as the worst for a decade. A case of old news. *Ooh Yeah!* is shock horror as good as *H2O* or *Private Eyes*, but the stigma of bad apple gave it a bad name. Ironically, Oates enjoyed U.S. Top Ten success at the time thanks to a collaboration with Icehouse on "Electric Blue," and with Hall, the lead single "Everything Your Heart Desires" managed an admirable number three. The album itself is more or less standard but shows a creative touch towards the end with its trilogy: "Soul Love," "reaLove," and "Keep on Pushing Love." *—Kelvin Hayes*

Change of Season / 1990 / Arista ✦✦

Apart from the hit "So Close," *Change of Season* is largely undistinguished, relying more on sound than songcraft. Not surprisingly, it was Hall & Oates' lowest-charting album of original material since 1974's *War Babies*, even if it did go gold. *—Stephen Thomas Erlewine*

● **The Atlantic Collection** / Jan. 23, 1996 / Rhino ✦✦✦✦✦

Drawing from Hall & Oates' four Atlantic albums and adding one previously unreleased song, *The Atlantic Collection* is a definitive overview of the duo's early years. Although they only had one hit during this period—"She's Gone," which is included here in its full-length album version—their early recordings contained some of their richest, most diverse music. Much of the material is based in soul, particularly the smooth Philly soul of the early '70s, yet it also has strong folk overtones, as well as distinct pop/rock leanings. Within these 21 tracks, it is possible to hear the roots of their later hits, as well as directions they never wound up pursuing. For serious Hall & Oates fans, *The Atlantic Collection* can be a revelatory listen. *—Stephen Thomas Erlewine*

Marigold Sky / Sep. 30, 1997 / Push ✦✦✦

★ **The Very Best of Daryl Hall & John Oates** / Jan. 23, 2001 / RCA ✦✦✦✦✦

There's one thing wrong with *The Very Best of Daryl Hall & John Oates*, and it's minor—the promotional 12-inch mix of "Adult Education" is included in favor of the 7-inch version. This isn't a big deal and it doesn't mar what is the best overview of Hall & Oates' RCA years, the era when they became the biggest-selling duo in the history of rock. If the Atlantic years were more adventurous, dabbling in folk and album rock, *The Very Best of* demonstrates the virtues of consistency, since these blue-eyed soul songs rank among the very finest singles (and songs) of their time. And Hall & Oates weren't *un*adventurous, either, since they deftly blended elements of new wave, contemporary soul, and soft rock into their signature sound. Most impressively, smaller hits like "Wait for Me" and the splendid "Did It in a Minute" (easily one of the greatest songs they ever cut) more than hold their own alongside familiar items like "Sara Smile," "You Make My Dreams," "Private Eyes," and "Maneater." Hall & Oates may not have been hip, but they made addictive soul-pop that not only rocketed to the top of the charts but has stood the test of time as some of the best pop made during the early '80s. *—Stephen Thomas Erlewine*

Aaron Hall

Vocals / New Jack Swing, Urban

Former Guy vocalist Aaron Hall made his solo debut in 1993 with *The Truth*. Although quite erratic, the best songs displayed the confident, authoritative voice and range Hall had demonstrated while with Guy. After a series of soundtrack appearances, he finally released his second full-length effort *Inside of You* in 1998. *—Ron Wynn*

● **The Truth** / 1993 / Silas ✦✦✦✦✦

It was Aaron Hall's vocals that powered tracks like "My Fantasy" and "Jam" during his tenure as the lead singer of Guy. After Guy split in 1990, it was inevitable that Hall would go on to a solo career. Released in 1993, *The Truth* hit the shelves sounding dated in spots, due in part to the ever-changing style of early-'90s urban contemporary. Over the course of this debut solo album, Hall's use of the Gap Band's Charlie Wilson as a reference point does get tiring. More often than not, the production strength overshadows Hall's persona, which is barely there. Much to the dismay of many fans, Hall's 1991 big hit, "Don't Be Afraid," shows up here as a remix rather than the superior version released on the *Juice* soundtrack. That mistake makes this album less than it could have been. Truth be told, Hall's slick Romeo act was also a bust-out, as the top-notch weeper "I Miss You" has Hall giving the best performance here. "Don't Be Afraid (Sex You Down Some Mo' Version)," despite it's he-man subtitle, has Hall begging and calling himself "little ol' me." "Let's Make Love" steams it up successfully despite his showboating and breathy spoken intro. The last full track, "Until the End of Time," possesses a great melody and coasts on the good momentum of the better songs. Divorced from the new jack swing demands and crossover aims, *The Truth* is an enjoyable listen. *—Jason Elias*

Inside of You / Oct. 20, 1998 / MCA ✦✦✦

When new jack swing (urban contemporary's dominant trend of the late 1980s and early 1990s) saw its popularity fade in the mid-'90s, Aaron Hall's supporters contended that the former Guy singer had enough talent to survive. They were right—his post-Guy solo efforts weren't remarkable, and some of them were erratic and forgettable, but Hall came up with enough decent material to indicate that we should continue to keep an eye on him. No one can claim that Hall wasn't influential; his style of belting (sort of Charles Wilson of the Gap Band by way of Steve Arrington and Stevie Wonder) influenced many of the young "jeep soul" artists who were popping up left and right in the 1990s. *Inside of You* isn't all that different from Guy's slower material. If you removed the uptempo, rap-heavy new jack swing that dominated Guy's albums and were left with nothing but ballads and slow jams, you'd have something similar to *Inside of You* (minus Teddy Riley's input, of course). Hall is in lover-man mode throughout the CD, which favors slow burners and offers nothing for the dancefloor. The overall result is a disc that is slightly stronger than his previous solo efforts and is often enjoyable, even if it is rather predictable. *—Alex Henderson*

The Halos

f. New York, NY [The Bronx]

Group / Doo Wop, R&B

Bronx-based doo wop foursome The Halos enjoyed a modest hit in 1961 with the song "Nag," but they were more widely heard as a backup group working with other artists of the late 1950s and early 60s. Al Cleveland, Arthur Crier, Phil Johnson and Harold Johnson first began working together as backing vocalists for producer Morty Craft, who used them to accompany Shirley & Lee on "Let The Good Times Roll", along with a number of other sides. Under the name The Craftys (a nod to their producer), they cut their first single, "L-O-V-E," in 1960, but were billed as the Halos for their next record, "Nag," which peaked at 25 on the *Billboard* Pop charts. Several more singles followed, none of which reached the same level of chart success. However, the group continued to be busy on the studio scene, cutting several singles with singer Cammy Carol and adding doo wops and harmonies to two early Phil Spector productions, Curtis Lee's "Pretty Little Angel Eyes" and Gene Pitney's "Every Breath I Take." While the Halos would never achieve true stardom, Arthur Crier's influence as a musician certainly paid off for his family—Crier's son Sabu Crier was a member of the group GQ, and Crier's grandson Keith Sabu Crier Jr. would become a major R&B star under the stage name Keith Sweat. *—Mark Deming*

● **Nag: A Golden Classics Edition** / Sep. 1, 1995 / Collectables ✦✦✦✦

The Halos were hardly the first or last doo wop group to have been strongly influenced by the Coasters, but they certainly followed their lead closer than most, and it says a great deal about how good the Halos could be that they didn't sound embarrassing in comparison. Like the Coasters, the Halos had tight but smooth harmonies, anchored by a solid bass singer (Arthur Crier) and a tenor who had a great flair for comic narratives and vocal sound effects. However, unlike the Coasters, the Halos didn't have Jerry Leiber & Mike Stoller writing material for them, and while the singers are in fine fettle on every cut of this compilation, songs like "Nag," "Mean Old World," and "I Went to a Party" don't hold a candle to what their obvious inspirations had at their disposal. ("L-O-V-E," which parodies the old Lava soap jingle, comes a lot closer than the rest of the set manages.) *Nag: A Golden Classics Edition* shines brightest when the Halos have less gimmicky (and lyrically stronger) material to work with, such as the rapid-fire "Down the Road," the engagingly weird and echo-laden "Village of Love," and a great R&B-slanted cover of the Everly Brothers' "Bird Dog." While hardly lost classics of doo wop, the cuts on this album at least make it clear the Halos had plenty of talent, if not the best material, and fans of classic vocal group sounds will eat this up. *—Mark Deming*

Larry Hamilton

Vocals, Bass / New Orleans Blues, R&B, Southern Soul, Soul-Blues, Retro-Soul

Crescent City blues and R&B vocalist Larry Hamilton had a revelatory experience at age five when he first heard the Mardi Gras beats of Shriners bands. He took up drums, but his grandmother arranged for him to take piano lessons. He began singing at age nine and wrote his first lyrics when he was 12. By the time he was 15, he began singing professionally with David Batiste & the Gladiators. His influences include Ray Charles, Nat KingCole, Sam Cooke, Big Joe Turner and Otis Redding. Hamilton sang with the Gladiators from 1965 until the mid-'70s, but also toured with Curtis Mayfield, Bettye Swann, Jimmy Hughes, Jackie Wilson, Percy Sledge, Little Johnny Taylor, David Ruffin, Major Lance, Z.Z. Hill and Al Green. As a songwriter, Hamilton composed "Get On Your Job" for Etta James, "Feel Like Dynamite" for King Floyd, "She's Taking My Part" for Irma Thomas, and "The Feeling" for Albert King. He has also written tunes for Jean Knight, Wayne Cochran and Johnny Adams.

At a recording session in the late 1970s, Hamilton met producer/songwriter and impresario Allen Toussaint. He joined Toussaint's group and did some touring with him. The two remained close friends, and in 1996, Toussaint signed Hamilton to record for his own NYNO (New York/New Orleans) Records label. Hamilton has one album, *Larry Hamilton* (1997), out on the label. Although many of the songs on Hamilton's debut are Toussaint compositions, future recordings will likely showcase more of Hamilton's original material. *—Richard Skelly*

● **Larry Hamilton** / Apr. 8, 1997 / NYNO ♦♦♦♦
Larry Hamilton's music is R&B in its smooth incarnation, going along the path blazed by the likes of Lou Rawls; it isn't the grit-infused R&B of Bobby Evans and Terry King, or the Holmes Brothers. He has the benefit of being produced by Allen Toussaint and singing in front of the Sea-Saint House Band, a superb aggregation of New Orleans musicians. They seem to flow as one, providing exactly what is needed to highlight the lead instrument—that is, Larry Hamilton's rich, powerful voice—and let it take the spotlight. A powerful first effort on NYNO Records for Larry Hamilton. *—Bob Gottlieb*

Roy Hamilton

b. Apr. 16, 1929, Leesburg, GA, **d.** Jul. 20, 1969, New Rochelle, NY
Vocals / Ballads, R&B
An extremely influential vocalist despite having a rather short career, Roy Hamilton had both classical training and gospel experience. Hamilton studied commercial art in high school and was a heavyweight Golden Gloves boxer before starting his music career as a member of the Searchlight Singers. During the mid- and late '50s, Hamilton's dramatic, searing voice and treatments of such songs as "You'll Never Walk Alone," "If I Loved You," "Ebb Tide," and "Unchained Melody" were enormously popular. "You'll Never Walk Alone" topped the R&B charts for two months in 1954, while "Unchained Melody" topped the R&B charts for three weeks, and was his only Top Ten pop hit. Jackie Wilson and Roy Brown were among the singers whose sound was affected by Hamilton, while the Righteous Brothers did their own versions of "You'll Never Walk Alone," "Ebb Tide," and "Unchained Melody" (which later got new life via the film *Ghost*). Hamilton had to retire from 1956 to 1958 due to exhaustion. He suffered a stroke in 1969 and died at age 40. *—Ron Wynn*

Golden Classics / Nov. 25, 1991 / Collectables ♦♦♦♦♦
Golden Classics provides a succinct offering of Roy Hamilton's finest moments, showcasing his blend of dramatic, gospel-informed vibrato and classical training that would prove influential to both Sam Cooke and Jackie Wilson. His first number-one hit, "You'll Never Walk Alone," stayed on the R&B charts for five months and remained at number one for almost two full months. Other hits followed, including another number one, "Unchained Melody," which returned to the charts twice more, both times as a hit for the Righteous Brothers. The other chart hits here follow a similar formula of orchestral balladry, but the rest of the tracks here clear up any notion of Hamilton being a monochrome crooner; both "A Great Romance" and "You're Gonna Need Magic" present a vigorous and, of course, well-polished R&B singer. *—Wade Kergan*

● **Anthology** / Oct. 1995 / Collectables ♦♦♦♦♦
Anthology offers 18 selections that cover Roy Hamilton's recording career with Epic, a decade-long relationship that produced a prolific 16 albums' worth of material and spawned ten Top 20 R&B hits. Like Billy Eckstine before him, Hamilton possessed a rich baritone voice with ample vibrato, although the dramatic punch of his delivery was purely his own. He also had the versatility to switch from swinging R&B numbers like his 1958 hit "Don't Let Go," to material that cast him as a pop balladeer like "Ebb Tide" and his chart-dominating debut single, "You'll Never Walk Alone," which spent a staggering eight weeks at number one in 1954. His best songs bridge styles, none more so than "Unchained Melody," later recast as a hit for the Righteous Brothers, or the protean country R&B of "I'll Walk Alone." Most of *Anthology*, however, treads the dinner-club terrain of pop standards like "Mona Lisa," "Stormy Weather," and "Route 66," all of which Hamilton delivers with appropriate elegance, but tend to leave him with the pack rather than leading it. *—Wade Kergan*

Clay Hammond

b. Jun. 21, 1936, Roseback, TX
Vocals / Soul, Retro-Soul, R&B
Hammond may be best remembered as the author of Little Johnny Taylor's huge soul hit, "Part Time Love." He was also a decent Sam Cooke-style soul singer in his own right, however, who recorded for various labels in the 1960s. His most well-known efforts from that time are the four singles he did for Kent between 1966-1969. These mixed Southern soul, gospel, and blues styles, yet also had a somewhat lighter and poppier production aura than much Southern soul, perhaps because they were recorded in Los Angeles. All eight songs from these 45s, as well as eight others that were recorded but not released in the 1960s, appear on the Ace CD *Southern Soul Brothers*, which also includes ten tracks recorded for Kent around the same time by fellow soul vocalist Z.Z. Hill. Hammond recorded sporadic singles and albums for various labels after the 1960s, in addition to singing in the lineups of groups such as the Drifters and the Rivingtons on the oldies circuit. *—Richie Unterberger*

● **Southern Soul Brothers** / Aug. 29, 2000 / Kent ♦♦♦♦♦
Hammond has 16 of the 26 tracks on this split-artist compilation, which also includes ten songs recorded by Z.Z. Hill for the same label (Kent) during the same era (the mid- to late 1960s). Hammond's 16 cuts include both sides of all four of his 1966-1969 Kent singles, as well as four from the same period that did not surface until a 1988 LP, and four more from the same time that were previously unissued until this CD. He was a minor but a worthy Southern soul-style vocalist who sounded much like a gentler Sam Cooke, writing all of his material on this disc. On his Kent sides (he had previously recorded for other labels), he adeptly crossed soul with shades of blues and gospel, although the arrangements were not as lugubrious and brassy as much soul actually produced in the South was. Occasionally he used pop-style production to good effect, as on the 1966 single "You Brought It All on Yourself," with its swinging, slightly jazz horn lines. Interestingly, his 1968 B-side "Do Right Woman" is not the famous Chips Moman/Dan Penn song, but a different song (albeit with some similarities to the more famous one), recorded at Moman's studio, no less. The eight songs that were not released in the 1960s are good by outtakes standard. "Togetherness" has something of the ballad feel of Cooke's "A Change Is Gonna Come," while "My Sweet Baby Is Coming Home," with only an electric guitar as backup, anticipates the sound of fellow Cooke acolyte Ted Hawkins. The ten songs that follow from Hill, incidentally, are average period soul that also have some stronger blues elements than many recordings from the genre, combining a few of Hill's 1966-1969 singles with four previously unissued numbers. *—Richie Unterberger*

Herbie Hancock

b. Apr. 12, 1940, Chicago, IL
Piano, Piano (Electric), Keyboards, Synthesizer, Composer, Leader / Hard Bop, Post-Bop, Modal Music, Fusion, Jazz-Funk, Funk, Electro
Herbie Hancock will always be one of the most revered and controversial figures in jazz, just as his employer/mentor Miles Davis was when he was alive. Unlike Davis, who pressed ahead relentlessly and never looked back until near the very end, Hancock has cut a zig-zagging forward path, shuttling between almost every development in electronic and acoustic jazz and R&B over the last third of the 20th century and into the 21st century. Though grounded in Bill Evans and able to absorb blues, funk, gospel, and even modern classical influences, Hancock's piano and keyboard voices are entirely his own, with their own urbane harmonic and complex, earthy rhythmic signatures, and young pianists constantly cop his licks.

Having studied engineering and professing to love gadgets and buttons, Hancock was perfectly suited for the electronic age; he was one of the earliest champions of the Rhodes electric piano and Hohner clavinet, and would field an ever-growing collection of synthesizers and computers on his electric dates. Yet his love for the grand piano never waned, and despite his peripatetic activities all around the musical map, his piano style continues to evolve into tougher, ever-more-complex forms. He is as much at home trading riffs with a smoking funk band as he is communing with a world-class post-bop rhythm section, and that drives purists on both sides of the fence up the wall. *—Richard S. Ginell*

Fat Albert Rotunda / Oct. 3, 1969+Dec. 8, 1969 / Warner Bros. ♦♦♦♦♦
Centered around some soundtrack music that Hancock wrote for Bill Cosby's *Fat Albert* cartoon show, this was Herbie's first full-fledged venture into jazz-funk—and his last until *Head Hunters*—making it a prophetic release. At the same time, it was far different in sound from his later funk ventures, concentrating on a romping, late-'60s-vintage, R&B-oriented sound with frequent horn riffs and great rhythmic comping and complex solos from Hancock's Fender-Rhodes electric piano. The syllables of the titles alone—"Wiggle Waggle," "Fat Mama," "Oh! Oh! Here He Comes"—have a rhythm and feeling that tell you exactly how this music saunters and swaggers along—just like the jolly cartoon character. But there is more to this record than fatback funk. There is the haunting, harmonically sophisticated "Tell Me a Bedtime Story" (which ought to become a jazz standard), and the similarly relaxed "Jessica." The sextet on hand is a star-studded bunch, with Joe Henderson in funky and free moods on tenor sax, Johnny Coles on trumpet, Garnett Brown on trombone, Buster Williams on bass, and Tootie Heath on drums. Only Williams would remain in the electric Hancock Sextet to come. Also trumpeter Joe Newman, saxophonist Joe Farrell, guitarist Eric Gale, and drummer Bernard Purdie make guest appearances on two tracks. An engaging, friendly record, it is now available on CD as part of *Mwandishi: The Complete Warner Bros. Recordings*. *—Richard S. Ginell*

★ **Head Hunters** / 1973 / Columbia/Legacy ♦♦♦♦♦
Head Hunters was a pivotal point in Herbie Hancock's career, bringing him into the vanguard of jazz fusion. Hancock had pushed avant-garde boundaries on his own albums and with Miles Davis, but he had never devoted himself to the groove as he did on *Head Hunters*. Drawing heavily from Sly Stone, Curtis Mayfield, and James Brown, Hancock developed deeply funky, even gritty, rhythms over which he soloed on electric synthesizers, bringing the instrument to the forefront in jazz. It had all of the sensibilities of jazz, particularly in the way it wound off into long improvisations, but its rhythms were firmly planted in funk, soul, and R&B, giving it a mass appeal that made it the biggest-selling jazz album of all time (a record which was later broken). Jazz purists, of course, decried the experiments at the time, but *Head Hunters* still sounds fresh and vital two decades after its initial release, and its genre-bending proved vastly influential on not only jazz, but funk, soul, and hip-hop. *—Stephen Thomas Erlewine*

Thrust / Aug. 26, 1974 / Columbia/Legacy ♦♦♦♦
The follow-up to the breakthrough *Head Hunters* album was virtually as good as its wildly successful predecessor: an earthy, funky, yet often harmonically and rhythmically sophisticated *tour de force*. There is only one change in the Headhunters lineup—swapping drummer Harvey Mason for Mike Clark—and the switch results in grooves that are even more complex. Hancock continues to reach into the rapidly changing high-tech world for new sounds, most notably the metallic sheen of the then-new ARP string synthesizer which was already becoming a staple item on pop and jazz-rock records. Again, there are only four long tracks, three of which ("Palm Grease," "Actual Proof," "Spank-A-Lee") concentrate on the funk, with plenty of Hancock's wah-wah clavinet, synthesizer textures and effects, and electric piano ruminations that still venture beyond the outer limits of post-bop. The change-of-pace is one of Hancock's loveliest electric pieces, "Butterfly," a match for any tune he's written before or since, with shimmering synth textures and Bennie Maupin soaring on soprano (Hancock would re-record it 20 years later on *Dis Is Da Drum*, but this is the one to hear). This supertight jazz-funk quintet album still sounds invigorating a quarter of a century later. *—Richard S. Ginell*

Man-Child / Jan. 1976 / CBS ♦♦♦
Perhaps the funkiest album of Herbie Hancock's early- to mid-'70s jazz/funk/fusion era, *Man-Child* starts off with the unforgettable "Hang Up Your Hang Ups," and the beat just keeps coming until the album's end. "Sun Touch" and "Bubbles" are slower, but funky nonetheless. Hancock is the star on his arsenal of keyboards, but guitarist Wah Wah Watson's presence is what puts a new sheen on this recording, distinguishing it from its predecessors, *Head Hunters* and *Thrust*. Others among the all-star cast of soloists and accompanists include Wayne Shorter on soprano sax, Stevie Wonder on chromatic harmonica, and long-time Hancock cohort Bennie Maupin on an arsenal of woodwinds. *—Jim Newsom*

Secrets / Jun. 1976 / Columbia ♦♦♦
Having long since established his funk credentials, Hancock continues the direction of *Head Hunters* and its U.S. successors here, welding himself to the groove on electric keyboards while Bennie Maupin again shines sardonic beams of light on a variety of reeds. In "Doin' It," the most successful track, Hancock makes a more overt bid for the dance floor, for the tune is basically one long irresistible groove with a very commercial-sounding bridge. Again Hancock chooses to re-compose one of his standards; "Cantelope (sic) Island" is almost unrecognizable, converted into a sauntering, swaggering thing. A streamlining process has set in—the drumming has been simplified, some of the old high-voltage drive has been muted—yet there are still enough enjoyable, intelligently musical things happening here to hold a Hancock admirer's attention. *—Richard S. Ginell*

Sunlight / 1977 / Columbia ♦♦♦

Feets, Don't Fail Me Now / 1979 / Columbia ♦

Monster / 1980 / Columbia ♦♦

Mr. Hands / 1980 / Columbia ♦♦♦♦
Hancock's lackluster string of electric albums around this period was enhanced by this one shining exception: an incorrigibly eclectic record that flits freely all over the spectrum. Using several different rhythm sections, Herbie Hancock is much more the imaginative hands-on player than at any time since the prime Headhunters period, overdubbing lots of parts from his ever-growing collection of keyboards. He has regained a good deal of his ability to ride in the groove. "Calypso" finds him playing synthesized steel drums and interacting with customary complexity and ebullience with V.S.O.P. mates Tony Williams and Ron Carter. Disco rears its head, but inventively this time on "Just Around the Corner," and in league with Jaco Pastorius' vibrating, interlacing bass, Hancock gets off some good, updated jazz-funk on "Spiraling Prism" and "4 AM." There is even a reunion of the original Headhunters on a rhythmically tangled remake of "Shiftless Shuffle"; drummer Harvey Mason sounds like a rhythm machine gone bonkers. Easily the outstanding track—and one of Hancock's most haunting meditations—is "Textures," where he plays all of the instruments himself. This would be the last outcropping of electronic delicacy from Hancock for some time, and it was mostly—and unjustly—overlooked when it came out. *—Richard S. Ginell*

Magic Windows / 1981 / Columbia ♦♦♦

Lite Me Up / 1982 / Columbia ♦♦

Future Shock / 1983 / Columbia/Legacy ♦♦♦
Herbie Hancock completely overhauled his sound and conquered MTV with his most radical step forward since the sextet days. He brought in Bill Laswell of Material as producer, along with Grand Mixer D.ST on turntables—and the immediate result was "Rockit," which makes quite a post-industrial metallic racket. Frankly, the whole record is an enigma; for all of its dehumanized, mechanized textures and rigid rhythms, it has a vitality and sense of humor that make it difficult to turn off. Moreover, Herbie can't help but inject a subversive funk element when he comps along to the techno beat—and yes, some real, honest-to-goodness jazz licks on a grand piano show up in the middle of "Auto Drive." *—Richard S. Ginell*

Sound-System / 1984 / Columbia/Legacy ♦♦♦

Perfect Machine / Oct. 1988 / Columbia ♦♦♦

The Best of Herbie Hancock: The Hits / Feb. 8, 2000 / Columbia/Legacy ♦♦♦♦♦
This CD is a collection of Herbie Hancock's best-known work from his fusion years, beginning with two tracks from the seminal *Head Hunters*: the 15-minute psychedelic soul opus "Chameleon," and the African remake of "Watermelon Man." It then traces his explorations of funk with tracks like "You Better Bet Your Love" and "Ready or Not," and his early-'80s breakout from a growing commercial/funk rut with the explosive techno-pop hit "Rockit." *The Best of Herbie Hancock: The Hits* also presents a rather compelling look at one artist's explorations into fusion, a period of jazz often overlooked and denounced by purists. In doing this it showcases how Hancock's roots as a Blue Note musician were still present, even if the long solos were on a synthesizer instead of a piano. More importantly, it's a good example of just how much traditional jazz played a part in influencing funk, hip-hop, and even electronic music. While a retrospective is never quite as compelling as the original albums, it still serves as an exceptional introduction Hancock's work in the '70s and early '80s. *—Curtis Zimmermann*

Future 2 Future / Sep. 25, 2001 / Transparent Music ♦♦♦♦
One of Herbie Hancock's greatest attributes is his ability to take a contemporary form of music and add his own unique perspective through his recordings. *Future 2 Future* is no exception to the rule. Teaming with Bill Laswell, Hancock recruits some of the most forward-thinking musicians in music for *Future 2 Future*. The contributions of electronic music pioneer Carl Craig, vocal diva Chaka Khan, drum 'n' bass producer A Guy Called Gerald, as well as jazz legends Jack DeJohnette and Wayne Shorter make the album feel like a cross between modern electronica and world music. While a lineup with such immense talent promises the delivery of a powerhouse record, the finished product only delivers the goods moderately. Several pieces produced for the album were almost completed before Hancock contributed keyboards. This production method leaves the record lacking the spontaneity and continuity that grace several of his early electronic-based records and tenure with the Headhunters, to the point of relegating Hancock to the status of session musician on some songs and leaving the listener to wonder what *Future 2 Future* could have been if a greater sense of creative collaboration/improvisation between Hancock and this all-star cast would have ensued. While this record is most definitely not an album for jazz purists, those with an ear for modern electronic music will find *Future 2 Future* an enjoyable exercise in watching one of the greats in jazz music redefine himself with the times once again. *—Rob Theakston*

Harlem River Drive

f. 1970, New York, NY [East Harlem]
Group / Latin Rock, Jazz-Funk
Eddie Palmieri's supergroup Harlem River Drive was the first group to really merge black and Latin styles and musicians, resulting in a free-form brew of salsa, funk, soul, jazz, and fusion. Though it was led by pianist Palmieri, the group also included excellent players from both the Latin community (his brother Charlie, Victor Venegas, Andy Gonzales) and the black world (Bernard "Pretty" Purdie, Ronnie Cuber). Named as an ironic reference to the New York City street which allowed predominantly suburban drivers to bypass East Harlem entirely on their way to lower Manhattan, Harlem River Drive released their groundbreaking debut album in 1970 on Roulette, including Latin and underground club hits like the title track and "Seeds of Life." Unfortunately, *Harlem River Drive* was their only album, though the group did appear co-billed on Eddie Palmieri's two-part 1972 release, *Live at Sing Sing, Vols. 1-2*. *—John Bush*

★ **Harlem River Drive** / 1971 / Roulette ♦♦♦♦♦
The reason this record is "legendary" is because it marks the first recorded performances of Eddie and Charlie Palmieri in the United States after their relocation from Cuba (1970). The reason it should be a near mythical recording (it has never been available in the U.S. on CD, and was long out of print on LP before CDs made the scene), is for its musical quality and innovation. The Palmieris formed a band of themselves, a couple of Latinos that included Andy Gonzales, jazz-funk great—even then—Bernard Purdy, and some white guys and taught them how to play a music that was equal parts Cuban mambo, American soul via Stax/Volt, blues, Funkadelic-style rock, pop-jazz, and harmonic and instrumental arrangements every bit as sophisticated as Burt Bacharach's or Henry Mancini's or even Stan Kenton's. One can hear in "Harlem River Drive (Theme)" and "Idle Hands" a sound akin to War's on *World Is a Ghetto*. Guess where War got it? "If (We Had Peace)" was even a model for Lee Oskar's "City, Country, City." And as much as War modeled their later sound on this one record, as great as they were, they never reached this peak artistically. But there's so much here: the amazing vocals (Jimmy Noonan was in this band), the multi-dimensional percussion section, the tight, brass-heavy horn section, and the spaced-out guitar and keyboard work (give a listen to "Broken Home") where vocal lines trade with a soprano saxophone and a guitar as snaky keyboards create their own mystical effect. One can bet that Chick Corea heard in Eddie's piano playing a stylistic possibility for Return to Forever's *Light As a Feather* and *Romantic Warrior* albums. The band seems endless, as if there are dozens of musicians playing seamlessly together live—dig the percussion styling of Manny Oquendo on the cowbell and conga and the choral work of Marilyn Hirscher and Allan Taylor behind Noonan. *Harlem River Drive* is a classic because after 30-plus years, it still sounds as if listeners are the ones catching up to it. It's worth every dime you pay for it, so special order it today. *—Thom Jurek*

The Harptones

f. 1953, New York, NY
Group / Doo Wop, R&B
Despite not landing on the R&B or pop charts during their entire careers, the Harptones were a superb doo wop ensemble. They initially emerged from a 1953 union of members of the Harps and Skylarks. Willie Winfield and his brothers Jimmy and Clyde first teamed with Bill Galloway and Johnny Bronson as the Harps. When Galloway sought a pianist for the Harps, he found Raoul Cita in the Skylarks. Eventually a new group with Winfield and Galloway plus former Skylarks Cita, Curtis Cherebin, and Bill Dempsey became the new Harps. Unlike most doo wop and R&B units, the Harptones (who took that name in 1953 after Bruce Records executives Morty Craft and Monte Bruce informed them there was already a group on Savoy called Little David Baughn & the Harps) were more jazz-oriented in their harmonies and arrangements, thanks to Cita. But they weren't so sophisticated that they lacked earthiness or grit, thanks to Winfield. "I Want a Sunday Kind of Love" featured Winfield's silky vocals and the group's magnificent harmonies. It was a big regional success, but never got national attention. That was the story for virtually every Harptones single.

Though they were popular enough to be included in the historic 1955 Rock and Roll Ball at St. Nicholas Arena in New York alongside the Drifters, Clovers, Fats Domino, Moonglows, and Big Joe Turner, they never scored a national hit. They recorded for Essex, Old Town, Rama, Tip Top, Gee, Warwick, Coed, Cub, Comp, and Raven, among others, besides Bruce. The Harptones cut an LP, *Love Needs the Harptones*, for Ambient Sound in 1981. They continued playing clubs and oldies shows into the '90s. *—Ron Wynn*

● **The Complete Recordings** / 2000 / Preserved ♦♦♦♦♦
The title of this 18-song collection is a little misleading, as it only contains the songs that the group did for the Bruce Record Co., but that's really good enough, as far as it goes—those sides, released between 1953 and 1955 (including both the 45 rpm version of "Sunday Kind of Love" and its slightly slower, more luxuriant 78 rpm version), are the foundation of the harmony vocal group's legacy. The sound, remastered by Walter DeVenne (of Relic records fame), is excellent, bringing out every nuance of the achingly beautiful harmony singing on ballads like "Sunday Kind of Love" and "I'll Never Tell" and the full, thumping impact of rockers like "High Flying Baby" and "Mambo Boogie," and mixing

the two attributes—the soaring harmonies and the beat of their rhythm section (augmented with some beautifully understated electric guitar)—on an exquisitely slow-paced version of Ivory Joe Hunter's "I Almost Lost My Mind" and Raoul Cita's "It Was Just for Laughs." The sound is astonishingly good, and the annotation by Donn Fileti gives the best account yet written of the group's early history. *—Bruce Eder*

Very Best of the Harptones: Life Is But a Dream / Jan. 25, 2000 / Collectables ♦♦♦
A more apt title for this CD would be "The Very Best of the Harptones and Friends." Among the 18 tracks are two done with Peggy Farmer and two with Ruth McFadden. Farmer and McFadden have one tune in common with the Harptones, "Dreamin's No Good." All the other selections, except "You're Going to Need Me Somebody" and "You Know You're Doing Me Wrong," have two takes. For instance, you get take one and take 20 of "On a Sunday Afternoon." This is mellow East Coast doo wop with a modern harmony feel. Not comprehensive or a complete overview by any means, but special because of the alternate takes and the collaborations with Farmer and McFadden. *—Andrew Hamilton*

Betty Harris

b. 1941, Orlando, FL
Vocals / Deep Soul, R&B, Soul, New Orleans R&B
Betty Harris was born in Orlando, FL, in 1941, and was bitten early by the singing bug. At 19, she got the opportunity to cut her first single, "Taking Care of Business" backed with "Yesterday's Kisses," for Douglas Records in 1960. The record didn't do much saleswise, but it did gain her a bit of notoriety, and she began touring with Big Maybelle. While with Maybelle, she caught the ears of some fat cats at Jubilee Records and was offered a recording contract. Her very first Jubilee release, "Cry to Me," entered *Billboard*'s pop Top 40 in 1963 and became the biggest seller of her career. Originally recorded by Solomon Burke, producer Bert Berns slowed the pace and created a deep soul classic in the process. (The Rolling Stones covered the song on their *Out of Our Heads* album, and they based their version on Betty's rendition, not Solomon's.)

Jubilee followed with "Kiss Me," which managed to scrape into *Billboard*'s Top 100 for a few weeks. Subsequent Jubilee recordings failed to chart—even her soulful "Mo Jo Hannah" was a no-show. In 1965, she switched to Sansu Records, and under the tutelage of Allen Toussaint had her next high chart entry two years later with the touching ballad, "Nearer to You." Two previous Sansu recordings failed to chart and nothing after "Nearer" did either. Even a duet with Lee Dorsey, "Love Lots of Lovin'"/"Take Care of Our Love," went unnoticed, as did her remake of Dorsey's "Ride Your Pony." Four years with Sansu failed to meet the expectations of Harris or the label heads, so she moved to her final label, SSS Int'l, in 1969, who released, "There's a Break in the Road"/"All I Want Is You." The deal with SSS Int'l materialized when her old label, Jubilee, re-released "Cry to Me" in 1969, and it charted again on *Billboard*'s R&B charts. When Harris' work on SSS Int'l also failed to impress record buyers, she called it quits and got out of the business.

Charly Records has released a CD of Betty Harris sides, *In the Saddle*, mostly consisting of her Sansu recordings. WestSide Records has done Charly one better by releasing a complete collection of Betty Harris sides called *Soul Perfection Plus*. Today Betty Harris drives a big rig truck for a living. *—Andrew Hamilton*

● **Soul Perfection Plus** / Nov. 24, 1998 / WestSide ♦♦♦♦♦
Subtitled "complete Jubilee, Sansu, SSS International masters, 1963-1969," this is a thorough retrospective of the minor but quality soul singer's 1960s work. The Jubilee sides, all from 1963 and 1964, are decent New York pop-soul, several of them written by top NYC songwriter-producer Bert Berns, and most of them produced by Jerry Leiber & Mike Stoller. "Cry to Me" (also done by Solomon Burke, and covered by the Rolling Stones) was the only hit from this batch, but if you like the style you'll like what's here; "His Kiss," for instance, sounds a lot like the songs Burke was doing at the same time. From 1965 to 1969 Harris recorded under the direction of the great New Orleans producer and songwriter Allen Toussaint, who wrote every last one of the 20 Harris sides on this disc that were cut during the collaboration. The presence of an ace producer-songwriter is often what's needed to make a good, but not great, vocalist like Harris into something special. While the Toussaint material here is satisfying New Orleans soul, it didn't get Harris over the hump commercially (although "Nearer to You" was an R&B hit), or endure as top-line classic soul. The tracks certainly cover a lot of territory, from the good commercial pop-soul of "What a Sad Feeling" and arching soul balladry of "Can't Last Much Longer" to numbers whose arrangements recall the New Orleans bounce of Lee Dorsey (who duets with Harris on a couple of songs). Some of the later tracks move into the kind of funk associated with the Meters, not a surprise as musicians from the Meters are supposed to have supplied the rhythm section for at least some of these sides. *—Richie Unterberger*

Don "Sugarcane" Harris

b. Jun. 18, 1938, Pasadena, CA, **d.** Dec. 1, 1999, Los Angeles, CA
Vocals, Violin, Songwriter, Piano / R&B, Blues-Rock, Funk, Album Rock
Beginning his career as the guitar-playing half of the 1950s rock duo, Don & Dewey, Don "Sugarcane" Harris, put down the guitar and picked up the violin after the lack of success for Don & Dewey (oddly enough the group's songs became hits for other artists such as the Righteous Brothers and the Premiers). Classically trained as a violinist, Harris' skill at improvisation began attracting attention from the rock world and soon he was appearing on records by John Lee Hooker, Frank Zappa and Johnny Otis. In 1970 Harris joined forces with British blues musician John Mayall when the latter was forming his first all American backing band. In addition to joining the backing bands of Mayall, Zappa and others, Harris also recorded a series of albums for labels such as Epic and Polydor. After a lengthy battle with pulmonary disease, on December 1, 1999 he was found dead in his Los Angeles apartment at the age of 61. *—Steve Kurutz*

Sugarcane / Jan. 1970 / Epic ♦♦♦
The best thing about this album is the front cover, which is about as out-and-out bizarre as the opening sequence of cult director Sam Fuller's classic film *The Naked Kiss*. The association with Frank Zappa made audiences expect something bizarre and shocking from electric violinist Don "Sugarcane" Harris; this cover photograph and the underground comics by Rick Griffin on the back cover created a tie-in with the psychedelic culture and again promoted a sense of weirdness that is basically just not there in this collection of fairly standard rhythm & blues tracks produced and arranged by Los Angeles soul scene ubermensch Johnny Otis. He had a long connection with Harris, and they were sympathetic partners, so it is not like this is some sort of production mismatch. What it is really is material that was cooked up prior to or with no connection to the newly developing stage personality of Harris, meaning the electric violin is not emphasized all that much and musically the connection with Zappa is nothing more than the vital lifeline to the California roots blues scene. While this demands a great deal of respect, these tracks are the sort of performances Otis and his henchmen could whip up without breaking a sweat while someone else prepares their dinner. While any of the tracks would work fine on a jukebox in some dive, only a few, such as the marvelously greasy "Funk and Wagner," rise to the level demanded by the serious album listener. The material is all written by either Harris or Otis in various songwriting collaborations and combinations. *—Eugene Chadbourne*

Major Harris

b. Feb. 9, 1947, Richmond, VA
Vocals, Guitar / Northern Soul, Philly Soul, Smooth Soul, Urban
After years of trying, Major Harris finally scored a big hit with the romantic, sensual "Love Won't Let Me Wait" in the summer of 1975. The ballad, with sexy backing vocals supplied by session singer Barbara Ingram, made its mark at number five on the pop charts while topping the R&B chart. He was born into a musical family on February 9, 1947, in Richmond, VA, as Major Harris III. His grandparents worked in vaudeville, his father was a professional guitarist, and his mom led the church choirs. His brother is Joe Jefferson, a Philadelphia songwriter who's responsible for many of the Spinners hits like "Mighty Love," "Love Don't Love Nobody," and "One of a Kind Love Affair." His cousin is longtime Philly stalwart Norman Harris, a guitarist, producer, songwriter, and former record company owner.

Harris paid major dues: he sang with the Charmers, was briefly a member of Frankie Lymon's Teenagers, recorded with the Jarmels, issued solo singles on Laurie and OKeh Records, and later sang with Nat Turner's Rebellion on Philly Grove Records. None of his previous efforts brought him fame or success. He recorded with the Jarmels after they hit with "A Little Bit of Soap." Harris' first big break came when he joined the Delfonics, replacing Randy Cain; his first tour of duty with them ended in 1974 when he went solo. While with the group his mellow tenor was featured on quite a few recordings as a foil to lead William "Pookie" Harris' soulful falsetto, as is evident on "Think It Over Baby," "Lying to Myself," and "I Told You So."

Having left the Delfonics, he passed a solo audition for W.M.O.T. (We Men of Talent) productions and was signed as a solo act. An album was produced and released on Atlantic Records. The first release, "Each Day I Wake Up," was credited as being by the Major Harris Boogie Blues Band. When Atlantic later sprung "Love Won't Let Me Wait" on the public, the seductive ballad achieved a million in sales and became the high mark of Harris' career. It was recorded in a darkened Sigma Sound Studio with only a small light at Harris' lyric stand: Barbara Ingram, Carla Benton, and Yvette Benson supplied the backing vocals. MFSB played on the tracks with that distinctive, prevalent guitar supplied by Bobby Eli, who also produced the session and wrote the song with Gwendolyn Woolfolk (under her pen name of Vinnie Barrett). Subsequent ballads by Harris fared well on the charts for a while, but when the hits dried up Harris went back to the Delfonics.

As a solo act he was featured on an excellent live recording with Blue Magic and Margie Joseph, which showed that he was an even better entertainer than recording artist. He has also toured with one of the two groups called the Delfonics; his version features original members William Hart and Randy Cain. (The other group includes William Hart's brother, Wilbert (an original member), and two new guys.) *—Andrew Hamilton*

● **My Way** / 1975 / Atlantic ♦♦♦♦♦
My Way contains Major Harris' number-one R&B hit "Love Won't Let Me Wait," a smooth exercise in romantic eroticism, and its bouncy successor, "Loving You Is Mellow." The disc features a smooth, aching remake of Blue Magic's "Sideshow," co-written by guitarist Bobby Eli, as were the two previously mentioned singles, "Sweet Tomorrow," and "Just a Thing That I Do." "Each Morning I Wake Up" and "After Loving You" are the best of three compositions by Melvin and Mervin Steals, aka Mystro & Lyric, best known for scribing the Spinners' "Could It Be I'm Falling in Love." The title track is Harris' Philly soul rendition of Frank Sinatra's "My Way," which really doesn't stray that far from the original. *—Andrew Hamilton*

Jealousy / 1976 / Atlantic ♦♦♦
Major Harris' soulful, smokey voice exudes emotion on "I Got Over Love," "Jealousy," and a remake of Blue Magic's "Talking to Myself." Four of the eight songs are courtesy of Joe Jefferson and Charles "Charlie Boy" Simmons; there's two by Bobby Eli and Vinnie Barrett (nee Gwendolyn Woolfolk), an Eli/Collins song, and "Ruby Lee," by Ron Baker and Norman Harris. Jefferson is Major's brother, and Harris his cousin—a family affair. *—Andrew Hamilton*

The Best of Now and Then / Apr. 15, 1994 / Hot Productions ♦♦♦♦

Norman Harris

d. 1986, Philadelphia, PA
Producer, Arranger, Guitar / Philly Soul, Disco, Soul
Guitarist/producer/arranger/songwriter Norman Harris can be heard on countless Philly soul sessions of the '60s, '70s, and '80s. He was a founding member of MFSB, the rhythm/strings/horns aggregation that was the house band for Gamble & Huff's Philadelphia International label. As one third of the production trio of Baker-Harris-Young, he

produced hits on First Choice, Eddie Holman, the Salsoul Orchestra, and Love Committee for Salsoul Records, as well as Atlantic Records acts the Trammps. He also had hits with Gloria Gaynor ("Honey Bee"), the Delfonics ("La La Means I Love You," "Didn't I Blow Your Mind"), Jerry Butler ("Hey Western Union Man," "Only the Strong Survive"), Wilson Pickett ("Engine Number 9," "Don't Let the Green Grass Fool You"), Joe Simon ("Drowning in the Sea of Love," "Power of Love"), and the Spinners ("I'll Be Around," "Could It Be I'm Falling in Love"), among many others. Beside fellow MFSB members drummer Earl Young and bassist Ron Baker, Harris' frequent songwriting partners were Allan Felder and Bunny Sigler. He came up with his unique string and horn arrangements by composing the parts on his guitar.

Harris and Baker first teamed up late in the '50s, and began playing in Philly-area clubs. When they got calls for recording sessions in the '60s, the duo began working with drummer Karl Chambers. Later adding drummer Young, the trio began to build up a considerable reputation as a tight rhythm section. After playing on so many hits, they decided to form a record label and music-publishing firm called Golden Fleece, and worked out a deal with Sigma Sound Studios owner Joe Tarsia. Vocal trio First Choice was introduced to Harris by WDAS DJ Jimmy Bishop, and began recording for the Philly Groove label distributed by Bell Records. The hits began to come: "Armed and Extremely Dangerous," "Smarty Parts," "The Player," and "Newsy Neighbors." When Harris started his own Salsoul-distributed Gold Mind label in 1979, he signed the group. Harris also became a recording artist, recording as the Harris Machine and one self-titled 1979 Salsoul LP as a part of Baker-Harris-Young. *—Ed Hogan*

● **The Harris Machine/Here to Create Music** / Oct. 26, 1999 / WestSide ♦♦♦♦

Peppermint Harris (Harrison D. Nelson Jr.)

b. Jul. 17, 1925, Texarkana, TX, **d.** Mar. 19, 1999, Elizabeth, NJ

Vocals, Guitar / Jump Blues, West Coast Blues, Modern Electric Texas Blues

The contemporary blues boom resuscitated the career of many a veteran blues artist who had been silent for ages. Take guitarist Peppermint Harris, who in 1951 topped the R&B charts with his classic booze ode "I Got Loaded." Nobody expected a new Peppermint Harris CD in 1995, but Home Cooking producer Roy C. Ames coaxed one out of old Pep for Collectables nonetheless. *Texas on My Mind* may not be as enthralling as Harris' early-'50s output, but it was nice to have him back in circulation.

By the time he was in his early 20s, Harrison Nelson Jr. was lucky enough to have found a mentor and friend on the Houston blues front: Lightnin' Hopkins took an interest in the young man's musical development. When Harris was deemed ready, Lightnin' accompanied him to Houston's Gold Star Records. Nothing came of that jaunt, but Harris eventually recorded his debut 78 for the company in 1948 (as Peppermint Nelson). Bob Shad's Sittin' in With label was the vehicle that supplied Harris' early work to the masses—especially his first major hit, "Raining in My Heart," in 1950. These weren't exactly formal sessions—legend has it one took place in a Houston bordello! Nor was Shad too cognizant of Pep's surname—when he couldn't recall it, he simply renamed our man Harris.

Harris moved over to Eddie Mesner's Aladdin Records in 1951, cutting far tighter sides for the firm in Los Angeles (often with the ubiquitous Maxwell Davis serving as bandleader and saxist). After "I Got Loaded" lit up the charts in 1951, Harris indulged in one booze ode after another: "Have Another Drink and Talk to Me," "Right Back on It," "Three Sheets in the Wind." But try as they might, the bottle let Harris down as a lyrical launching pad after that.

He drifted from Money and Cash to RCA's short-lived subsidiary "X" and Don Robey's Duke logo (where he allegedly penned "As the Years Go Passing By" for Fenton Robinson) after that, but it wasn't until a long-lasting association with Stan Lewis' Shreveport, LA-based Jewel Records commenced in 1965 that Harris landed for longer than a solitary single. Later, Harris worked various day jobs around Houston, including one at a record pressing plant, before moving to Sacramento, CA, and then to New Jersey to be with his daughter. *—Bill Dahl*

Peppermint Harris / 1962 / Time ♦♦♦

Sittin' in With / 1979 / Mainstream ♦♦♦♦

Here are fifteen well-chosen 1950-1951 masters from Bob Shad's Sittin' in With label by Houston bluesman Peppermint Harris, including his hit "Rainin' in My Heart." Rowdy little bands behind the powerful singer sometimes included Goree Carter on guitar. *—Bill Dahl*

● **I Got Loaded** / 1987 / Route 66 ♦♦♦♦♦

Harris hit his full stride after signing with Aladdin Records in 1951 and moving his recording base to Los Angeles. Under saxist Maxwell Davis' direction, Harris waxed his smash "I Got Loaded" and a few more potent rounds after that ("Three Sheets in the Wind," "Have Another Drink and Talk to Me"). Unfortunately not yet available on CD, these sides comprise Pep's chief claim to fame. *—Bill Dahl*

Being Black Twice / 1991 / Collectables ♦♦♦

This is a curious collection of late-'50s and early-'60s recorded titles with unissued mid-'70s sides to pad things out. Oddly enough, Pep sounds the same despite the intervening years; his pleasing baritone rumbles through a set of his originals and standards like "Cherry Red" and "Key to the Highway." Collections of Harris' best are not exactly plentiful, but this one isn't the place to start; seek out his Aladdin sides instead. *—Cub Koda*

Texas on My Mind / Dec. 1995 / Collectables ♦♦♦

From the late '40s through the early '60s Peppermint Harris recorded for a variety of labels to moderate success. Although he had a few records in the '70s, he was basically retired until 1994, when he recorded *Texas on My Mind* at the age of 72. Although the songs on the album are quite good (most of the numbers are originals), Harris' abilities have dwindled; with his limited voice and guitar skills, he simply doesn't have the power to captivate an audience. *—Thom Owens*

Penthouse in the Ghetto / Oct. 21, 1997 / M.I.L. Multimedia ♦♦♦

Penthouse in the Ghetto features 20 tracks from Texas bluesman Peppermint Harris, including some of his famed "blues drinking songs." *—Steve Huey*

Thurston Harris

b. Jul. 11, 1931, Indianapolis, IN, **d.** Apr. 14, 1990, Pomona, CA

Vocals, Saxophone / Rock & Roll, R&B

Thurston Harris recorded with the Lamplighters, one of the many groups on the early R&B scene in South Central Los Angeles, in the early '50s. The group later evolved into the Tenderfoots, then the Sharps, and it was under this last name they were credited to when they backed up Harris on his most famous hit, 1957's "Little Bitty Pretty One" (number-two R&B and number-six pop) for Aladdin. In 1957, while signed as a solo artist to Aladdin, Harris recorded a cover of Bobby Day's classic novelty number, with a solid band featuring the ubiquitous Earl Palmer on drums and his friends in the Sharps doing background vocals. The single propelled Harris immediately to the front-ranks of the R&B scene. In 1958, Harris scored a Top 20 R&B hit with "Do What You Did," but he failed to have any chart success afterwards. In 1990, Thurston Harris died of a heart attack in Pomona, CA, at age 58. "Little Bitty Pretty One" has gone on to become one of the best-loved oldies of the late '50s. *—Bryan Thomas*

● **Little Bitty Pretty One** / 1984 / EMI America ♦♦♦♦♦

Thurston Harris / 1987 / Aladdin ♦♦♦

Wynonie Harris

b. Aug. 24, 1915, Omaha, NE, **d.** Jun. 14, 1969, Los Angeles, CA

Vocals, Drums, Leader / Jump Blues, R&B

No blues shouter embodied the rollicking good times that he sang of quite like raucous shouter Wynonie Harris. "Mr. Blues," as he was not-so-humbly known, joyously related risque tales of sex, booze, and endless parties in his trademark raspy voice over some of the jumpingest horn-powered combos of the postwar era.

Those wanton ways eventually caught up with Harris, but not before he scored a raft of R&B smashes from 1946 to 1952. Harris was already a seasoned dancer, drummer, and singer when he left Omaha for L.A. in 1940 (his main influences being Big Joe Turner and Jimmy Rushing). He found plenty of work singing and appearing as an emcee on Central Avenue, the bustling nightlife strip of the black community there. Wynonie Harris' reputation was spreading fast—he was appearing in Chicago at the Rhumboogie Club in 1944 when bandleader Lucky Millinder hired him as his band's new singer. With Millinder's orchestra in brassy support, Harris made his debut on shellac by boisterously delivering "Who Threw the Whiskey in the Well" that same year for Decca. By the time it hit in mid-1945, Harris was long gone from Millinder's organization and back in L.A.

The shouter debuted on wax under his own name in July of 1945 at an L.A. date for Philo with backing from drummer Johnny Otis, saxist Teddy Edwards, and trumpeter Howard McGhee. A month later, he signed on with Apollo Records, an association that provided him with two huge hits in 1946: "Wynonie's Blues" (with saxist Illinois Jacquet's combo) and "Playful Baby." Harris' own waxings were squarely in the emerging jump blues style then sweeping the West Coast. After scattered dates for Hamp-Tone, Bullet, and Aladdin (where he dueled it out with his idol Big Joe on a two-sided "Battle of the Blues"), Harris joined the star-studded roster of Cincinnati's King Records in 1947. There his sales really soared.

Few records made a stronger seismic impact than Harris' 1948 chart-topper "Good Rockin' Tonight." Ironically, Harris shooed away its composer, Roy Brown, when he first tried to hand it to the singer; only when Brown's original version took off did Wynonie cover the romping number. With Hal "Cornbread" Singer on wailing tenor sax and a rocking, socking backbeat, the record provided an easily followed blueprint for the imminent rise of rock & roll a few years later (and gave Elvis Presley something to place on the A-side of his second Sun single).

After that, Harris was rarely absent from the R&B charts for the next four years, his offerings growing more boldly suggestive all the time. "Grandma Plays the Numbers," "All She Wants to Do Is Rock," "I Want My Fanny Brown," "Sittin' on It All the Time," "I Like My Baby's Pudding," "Good Morning Judge," "Bloodshot Eyes" (a country tune that was first released on "King" by Hank Penny), and "Lovin' Machine" were only a portion of the ribald hits Harris scored into 1952 (13 in all)—and then his personal hit parade stopped dead. It certainly wasn't Harris' fault—his King output rocked as hard as ever under Henry Glover's supervision—but changing tastes among fickle consumers that accelerated Wynonie Harris' sobering fall from favor.

Sides for Atco in 1956, King in 1957, and Roulette in 1960 only hinted at the raunchy glory of a short few years earlier. The touring slowed accordingly. In 1963, his chaffeur-driven Cadillacs and lavish New York home a distant memory, Harris moved back to L.A., scraping up low-paying local gigs whenever he could. Chess gave him a three-song session in 1964, but sat on the promising results. Throat cancer silenced him for good in 1969, ending the life of a bigger-than-life R&B pioneer whose ego matched his tremendous talent. *—Bill Dahl*

☆ **Good Rocking Tonight** / 1990 / King ♦♦♦♦♦

This is an equally splendid compilation of the raspy shouter's King label output from the British Charly logo. Contains 20 sides, including a few essentials that Rhino didn't bother with: a roaring "Rock Mr. Blues" that grants Harris vocal group backing; the lascivious rocker "I Want My Fanny Brown" and "Lollipop Mama," and a celebratory "Mr. Blues Is Coming to Town." Harris and King always used inexorably swinging bands—saxists include Red Prysock, David Van Dyke (who duel it out on the amazing "Quiet Whiskey"), Big John Greer, Hal Singer, and Tom Archia. *—Bill Dahl*

★ **Bloodshot Eyes: The Best of Wynonie Harris** / 1993 / Rhino ♦♦♦♦♦

Rhino's 1994 collection *Bloodshot Eyes: The Best of Wynonie Harris* chronicles his hits for King records, beginning in 1947 with the seminal "Good Rockin' Tonight" and concluding in 1954 with "Git to Gittin' Baby." Lots of hits come between those two songs, but there were a lot of recordings that appeared before and after those songs, so why choose

Bloodshot Eyes over other compilations? Because it offers the best of his best work, concentrating on the cream of his recordings for King, when he was at his peak. This is hard-driving, relentless jump blues/R&B, propelled by the powerhouse vocals of Harris along with his joyously rampaging band. Truth be told, Harris rarely departed from this formula, but the cuts showcased on this collection capture him at his best, not just in terms of performance, but in terms of material. There are more comprehensive collections on the market—collections that span his entire career, collections that narrowly focus on a few years—but this is the ideal collection that contains the best from his peak, with no fat whatsoever. Essential music for any serious R&B, blues or rock & roll collection. *—Stephen Thomas Erlewine*

Women, Whiskey & Fish Tails / 1993 / Ace ♦♦♦♦
Ace's *Women, Whiskey & Fish Tails* spotlights some of the famous blues-shouter's latter-day work (1952-1957) for independent R&B label King. Now joined by Ace's '50s-centric Harris survey, *Lovin' Machine*, this 21-track disc takes the somewhat more obscure path through the catalog, substituting the still-electric likes of "Greyhound" and "Drinkin' Sherry Wine" for chart hit "Bloodshot Eyes" and the classic alcoholism narrative "Drinkin' Blues." Far from just an artist in repose, though, Harris is in top form for most of it, especially on the gospel-infused "The Deacon Don't Like It" and collection standout "Shake That Thing." The Ace titles are best left to listeners looking for a second roundup, while newcomers probably will want to first check out survey discs on Rhino or the chronologically minded Classics label for more of Harris' essential early hits and sides ("Good Rockin' Tonight"). *—Stephen Cook*

Wilbert Harrison

b. Jan. 5, 1929, Charlotte, NC, **d.** Oct. 26, 1994, Spencer, NC
Vocals, Guitar, Piano / Rock & Roll, R&B, Soul
Perceived by casual oldies fans as a two-hit wonder (his 1959 chart-topper "Kansas City" and a heartwarming "Let's Work Together" a full decade later), Wilbert Harrison actually left behind a varied body of work that blended an intriguing mélange of musical idioms into something quite distinctive. Country and gospel strains filtered into Wilbert Harrison's consciousness as a youth in North Carolina. When he got out of the Navy in Miami around 1950, he began performing in a calypso-based style. Miami entrepreneur Henry Stone signed Harrison to his Rockin' logo in 1953; his debut single, "This Woman of Mine," utilized the very same melody as his later reading of "Kansas City" (the first rendition of the Jerry Leiber-Mike Stoller composition by pianist Little Willie Littlefield came out in 1952, doubtless making an impression). Its flip, a country-tinged "Letter Edged in Black," exhibited Harrison's eclectic mindset.

After moving to Newark, NJ, Harrison wandered by the headquarters of Savoy Records one fortuitous day and was snapped up by producer Fred Mendelsohn. Harrison recorded several sessions for Savoy, beginning with a catchy cover of Terry Fell's country tune "Don't Drop It." Top New York sessioneers—arranger Leroy Kirkland, saxist Buddy Lucas and guitarists Mickey Baker and Kenny Burrell—backed Harrison on his 1954-1956 Savoy output, but hits weren't forthcoming.

That changed instantly when Harrison waxed his driving "Kansas City" for Harlem entrepreneur Bobby Robinson in 1959. With a barbed-wire guitar solo by Wild Jimmy Spruill igniting Harrison's no-frills piano and clenched vocal, "Kansas City" paced both the R&B and pop charts soon after its issue on Fury Records (not bad for a $40 session). Only one minor problem: Harrison was still technically under contract to Savoy (though label head Herman Lubinsky had literally run him out of his office some years earlier!), leading to all sorts of legal wrangles that finally went Robinson's way. Momentum for any Fury follow-ups had been fatally blunted in the interim, despite fine attempts with "Cheatin' Baby," the sequel "Goodbye Kansas City," and the original "Let's Stick Together." Harrison bounced from Neptune to Doc to Constellation to Port to Vest with little in the way of tangible rewards before unexpectedly making a comeback in 1969 with his infectious "Let's Work Together" for Juggy Murray's Sue imprint. The two-part single proved a popular cover item—Canned Heat revived it shortly thereafter, and Bryan Ferry chimed in with his treatment later on. Alas, it was an isolated happenstance—apart from "My Heart Is Yours," a bottom-end chart entry on SSS International in 1971, no more hits were in Wilbert's future. But Harrison soldiered on, sometimes as a one-man band, for years to come. *—Bill Dahl*

Let's Work Together / 1969 / Sue ♦♦♦
A quickie album, *Let's Work Together* was supervised by Juggy Murray to cash in on the unexpected success of Harrison's big hit, but it's not a bad effort all the same. Harrison brings his unique vocal delivery to oldies such as "Blue Monday," "Stagger Lee," "Louie Louie," and "Stand by Me," imparting his own personal stamp to each. *—Bill Dahl*

Small Labels / 1986 / Krazy Kat ♦♦♦♦
This is a vinyl survey of Harrison's forays away from the famous indie diskeries, both before and after he hit with "Kansas City." Weirdly, his 1953 effort "This Woman of Mine" uses the same melody as "Kansas City," some six years prior to his hitting big with it. Harrison was liable to try anything to land a hit—he brands himself a "Calypso Man," tries a hillbilly tack on "Letter Edged in Black," and offers a salute to the 1964 "New York World's Fair"—all in that distinctive slurred voice of his. *—Bill Dahl*

Listen to My Song / 1987 / Savoy ♦♦♦♦
Harrison's first label association of any endurance commenced when he signed with Herman Lubinsky's Savoy logo in 1954 for a two-year stretch. Top New York sessioneers like guitarists Mickey Baker and Kenny Burrell and saxists Buddy Lucas and Budd Johnson help out on these 16 Savoy tracks (still unavailable on CD). He liked that C&W; Terry Fell's "Don't Drop It" is a tremendously catchy hillbilly tune given an R&B flavor by the young singer. *—Bill Dahl*

Kansas City / 1992 / Collectables ♦♦♦♦
Finally, paydirt! Harrison smashed the charts in 1959 with his massive hit "Kansas City" for Bobby Robinson's Fury logo. Here we have 22 fine sides from the Fury hookup, some in stereo and many with Wild Jimmy Spruill on lead guitar. "Cheatin' Baby," "C.C. Rider," "1960," and the inevitable sequel "Goodbye Kansas City" are prime examples of Harrison's slightly off-kilter approach to his craft, while this infectious "Let's Stick Together" developed into the more worldly "Let's Work Together" toward the end of the decade. *—Bill Dahl*

● **Kansas City: His Legendary Golden Classics** / Jun. 17, 1994 / Collectables ♦♦♦♦
After his pop smash "Kansas City," Wilbert Harrison never recorded a single to match it, the only close call being his other chart hit, the pleasantly grooving "Let's Work Together." Those songs lead off this Collectables set (the second appears in its full two-part version), followed by a parade of Harrison's versions of R&B hits of the '50s and '60s, among them "C.C. Rider," "Stand by Me," "Blue Monday," and "Stagger Lee." These weren't just tossoffs, though. Harrison's performances were more interesting than the usual R&B crossovers of the day; he possessed the pacing of an urbane blues vocalist like Jimmy Rushing but his delivery and pitch were oddly reminiscent of honky tonk singers (check out his especially strong version of the Lenny Welch hit "Since I Fell for You"). "Kansas City" and "Let's Work Together" are his only true classics, but Wilbert Harrison recorded some other solid material during his time with Bobby Robinson's Fury label. *—John Bush*

Dan Hartman

b. Dec. 8, 1950, Harrisburg, PA, **d.** Mar. 22, 1994, Westport, CT
Vocals, Keyboards, Guitar, Bass / Blue-Eyed Soul, Soft Rock, Adult Contemporary, Pop/Rock, Disco, Urban
During the '70s, Dan Hartman was a member of the Edgar Winter Group, as well as being in Johnny Winter's band for a time. Hartman was also a session musician that supported artists as diverse as Ian Hunter, Stevie Wonder, Todd Rundgren, and Ronnie Montrose. After releasing one undistinguished solo pop/rock album in 1976, he hit the big time with the fine disco album, *Instant Replay*. Its follow-up, *Relight My Fire*, wasn't as successful and Hartman retreated to the studio, producing .38 Special, the Average White Band, and James Brown; he was behind the board for Brown's comeback hit, "Living in America," in 1986. Hartman had one more hit in 1985 with the pop-soul "I Can Dream About You." Again, his follow-ups weren't successful and he returned to producing. He was preparing a new album at the time of his death in March of 1994. *—Stephen Thomas Erlewine*

Images / 1976 / Blue Sky ♦♦♦
Dan Hartman's *Images* came before his solo success with "Instant Replay" and "I Can Dream About You," and for the most part it is a pleasant set of recordings. "My Love" is hardly the Paul McCartney, Lionel Ritchie, or Petula Clark tune; it is John Wilcox from Todd Rundgren's Utopia and bassist John Siegler working with Hartman to give the world a luscious pop tune that should have charted as the songs by the above-referenced artists did using this same theme. This is slick, dense, complex pop music with lots of guest stars. Ronnie Montrose adds his guitar to the driving "The Party's in the Back Room," while Randy Brecker guests on "Can't Stand in the Way of Love." Hartman plays the kalimba on "Love It Too Much," an island tune with more than a touch of reggae, but keeping to the pop which this artist embraced so fully. "If Only I Were Stronger," resplendent in Tom Strohman flutes and heavy keyboards, is a blue-eyed Sound of Philadelphia song. The Harrisburg native had a good grasp of the sounds around him, and *Images* takes many journeys, from this Ambrosia-meets-Harold Melvin & the Blue Notes number to "High Sign and "Telephone," two songs which vaguely resemble Billy Squier's material with his band Piper. Squier's "Telephone Relation" is poppier than Dan Hartman's "On the Telephone"—and Squier was playing his tune in the Sidewinders years before. "High Sign," which also features Ronnie Montrose, borrows from Piper's "Who's Your Boyfriend," and you know these artists were on the same circuit—it's fun seeing the similar themes show up on two albums from the same time period. "Can't Stand in the Way of Love" is more slick R&B which would have suited a latter-day Chairman of the Board or Spinners very well. Rick Derringer plays acoustic lead and rhythm guitars on "Thank You for the Good Times," while Edgar Winter co-writes the first track, "Hear My Song," almost a sequel to their hit "Free Ride." It's a very mainstream album from a very mainstream artist. The "Cat Scratch Fever" riff of "The Party's in the Backroom" beat Ted Nugent by a year on this 1976 outing—and *Images* remains a worthy testament to the many sides of the late, multi-talented recording artist. *—Joe Viglione*

Instant Replay / 1978 / Blue Sky ♦♦♦

Relight My Fire / 1979 / Blue Sky ♦♦

I Can Dream About You / 1984 / MCA ♦♦♦♦
One of Dan Hartman's most essential solo albums came in 1984, when the late singer/composer signed with MCA and produced *I Can Dream About You* with Jimmy Iovine. This is primarily a pop/rock album, but it's a pop/rock album with a fair amount of urban contemporary/dance-pop appeal. Though Hartman was a member of a major '70s rock act, the Edgar Winter Group, he also had strong R&B and disco credentials—1979's "Instant Replay" and 1980's "Relight My Fire" both received a lot of airplay on R&B stations. And this excellent album finds Hartman showing his enthusiasm for R&B on pop/rock gems that range from the hit title song and the anthemic "We Are the Young" to the Motown-tinged "Name of the Game" and the new wave-ish "Electricity," which he co-wrote with LaBelle graduate Nona Hendryx. Most of the songs, however, were written by Hartman and partner Charlie Midnight, who proves to be as valuable to Hartman as Iovine—a studio heavyweight who is known for his work with everyone from Bruce Springsteen to Stevie Nicks. Hartman, Midnight, and Iovine all do their part to make *I Can Dream About You* the focused, consistently rewarding album that it is. *—Alex Henderson*

● **Keep the Fire Burnin'** / 1994 / Chaos/Columbia ♦♦♦
This collection of hits and unreleased material by Dan Hartman, the late multi-instrumentalist, producer and songwriter, is only so-so. The hits include the huge

dancefloor single "Instant Replay" and a bad remix of the excellent "I Can Dream About You." Also included are Hartman's versions of "Free Ride," written by Hartman as a member of the Edgar Winter Group, and "Living in America," James Brown's huge comeback hit, also written by Hartman. Dan Hartman deserves a better retrospective. *—Tim Griggs*

Clarence "Fuzzy" Haskins

b. Jun. 8, 1941, Elkhorn, WV
Guitar, Vocals / Funk, Soul
An oustanding guitarist, Fuzzy Haskins was part of the original Funkadelics backing band that accompanied George Clinton and his Parliaments. Clinton subsequently changed the name to Parliament, then folded Funkadelic into Parliament and began using both lineups interchangeably. Haskins went on to play with numerous Clinton groups, and released two albums for Westbound, 1976's *A Whole Nother Thang* and 1978's *Radio Active*. An Ace compilation from 2001 reissued both albums on one CD. *—Ron Wynn*

A Whole Nother Thang / 1976 / Westbound ♦♦♦♦

● **A Whole Nother Radio Active Thang** / Aug. 7, 2001 / Ace ♦♦♦♦♦

Roger Hatcher

b. 1946, Birmingham, AL
Producer, Songwriter / Deep Soul, Soul, R&B
Roger Hatcher's biggest claim to fame is being a cousin to Edwin Starr (Charles Hatcher). Unfortunately, Hatcher's success hasn't come close to Edwin's. A prolific songwriter, Roger has written more than 1,000 songs. His two biggest successes were an album cut by the Dramatics of his "I Dedicate My Life to You," and Clarence Carter's rendition of "I Got Caught," a deep soul classic.

Born in Birmingham, AL, in 1946, he moved to Detroit in 1964 and signed with Dotty's Records. Two singles were released: "Get a Hold of Yourself" and "Party Over Yonder." The flop of both singles sent him traveling to Nashville, where he secured a contract with Excello Records recording "I Dedicate My Song to You," released in 1968. Hatcher moved on and connected with Don Davis, who had previously recorded Hatcher's "Girl Come on Home" on Major Lance for Volt Records. Davis remade "I Dedicate My Love to You" into "I Dedicate My Life to You," and Stax released it on its Volt label in 1972.

Hatcher cut "Caught Making Love" on his own Black Soul label in 1973. He shopped it to all the majors to no avail, so he pressed up some more copies and sold them himself, at which time Mickey Eichner of Columbia Records picked it up and released it in 1974. Hatcher's version was risqué, to say the least, particularly for the mid-'70s. Halfway through Hatcher's record was a recording of Virginia Davis having an orgasm. Many stations banned the record, killing its chance for wider exposure. Carter heard it, added a rap, took out the woman's voice, and got a release on ABC Records in 1975. The song became a deep soul hit. *—Andrew Hamilton*

● **Roger Hatcher Collection** / 1998 / Expansion ♦♦♦♦♦
The rareness of the material makes this an essential catch for serious soul collectors. Casual and front running fans, however, will have little interest in this obscure soul singer—and prolific songwriter, with over 1,000 titles registered with BMI to his credit. Roger Hatcher's most significant compositions: "Caught Making Love," an R&B hit for Clarence Carter, and "I Dedicate My Life to You," done by the Dramatics' on *Dramatically Yours*, represent his finest efforts. Here you get an earful of Roger's earthier versions of both songs. Hatcher's a crying singer, blessed with a natural whine, that enthrals many and fuels his cult following. His "Sweetest Girl in the World," found support amongst Northern soul fans, and others like "Stormy Love Affair," "All My Love Belongs to You," and "I Cried Like a Baby," illustrates vulnerable heartfelt soul. And you'll marvel at his painfully soulful remake of Vernon Harrell's "That's When I'll Stop Loving You" (originally by Linda Jones), and one of the few songs that Roger didn't write. This import is the only legitimate compilation of Roger Hatcher's recordings available; a bad quality bootleg of dubious origins circulated among collectors for years, but this is much better. *—Andrew Hamilton*

Donny Hathaway

b. Oct. 1, 1945, Chicago, IL, **d.** Jan. 13, 1979, New York, NY
Vocals, Keyboards, Piano / Soul, Smooth Soul, Chicago Soul
Donny Hathaway was one of the brightest new voices in soul music at the dawn of the '70s, possessed of a smooth, gospel-inflected romantic croon that was also at home on fiery protest material. Hathaway achieved his greatest commercial success as Roberta Flack's duet partner of choice, but sadly he's equally remembered for the tragic circumstances of his death—an apparent suicide at age 33. Donny Hathaway was born October 1, 1945, in Chicago, but moved to St. Louis when he was very young, and began singing in church with his grandmother at the scant age of three. He began playing piano at a young age, and by high school, he was impressive enough to win a full-ride fine arts scholarship to Howard University to study music in 1964.

While in college, he performed with a cocktail jazz outfit called the Ric Powell Trio, and wound up leaving school after three years to pursue job opportunities he was already being offered in the record industry. Hathaway first worked behind the scenes as a producer, arranger, songwriter, and session pianist/keyboardist. He supported the likes of Aretha Franklin, Jerry Butler, and the Staple Singers, among many others, and joined the Mayfield Singers, a studio backing group that supported Curtis Mayfield's Impressions. Hathaway soon became a house producer at Mayfield's Curtom label, and in 1969 cut his first single, a duet with June Conquest called "I Thank You Baby." From there he signed with Atco as a solo artist, and released his debut single, the inner-city lament "The Ghetto, Pt. 1," toward the end of the year. While it failed to reach the Top 20 on the R&B charts, "The Ghetto" still ranks as a classic soul message track, and has been sampled by numerous hip-hop artists. "The Ghetto" set the stage for Hathaway's acclaimed debut LP, *Everything Is Everything*, which was released in early 1970. In 1971, he released his eponymous second album and recorded a duet with former Howard classmate Roberta Flack, covering James Taylor's "You've Got a Friend." It was a significant hit, reaching the Top Ten on the R&B charts, and sparked a full album of duets, *Roberta Flack & Donny Hathaway*, which was released in 1972. The soft, romantic ballad "Where Is the Love?" topped the R&B charts, went Top Five on the pop side, and won a Grammy, and the accompanying album went gold.

Also in 1972, Hathaway branched out into soundtrack work, recording the theme song for the TV series *Maude* and scoring the film *Come Back Charleston Blue*. However, in the midst of his blossoming success, he was also battling severe bouts of depression, which occasionally required him to be hospitalized. His mood swings also affected his partnership with Flack, which began to crumble in 1973. Hathaway released one more album that year, the ambitious *Extension of a Man*, and then retreated from the spotlight; over the next few years, he performed only in small clubs. In 1977, Hathaway patched things up with Flack and temporarily left the hospital to record another duet, "The Closer I Get to You," for her *Blue Lights in the Basement* album. The song was a smash, becoming the pair's second R&B number one in 1978, and also climbing to number two on the pop charts. Sessions for a second album of duets were underway when, on January 13, 1979, Hathaway was found dead on the sidewalk below the 15th-floor window of his room in New York's Essex House. The glass had been neatly removed from the window, and there were no signs of struggle, leading investigators to rule Hathaway's death a suicide; his friends were mystified, considering that his career had just started to pick up again, and Flack was devastated. *Roberta Flack Featuring Donny Hathaway* was released in 1980, and both of the completed duets—"Back Together Again" and "You Are My Heaven"—became posthumous hits. In 1990, Hathaway's daughter Lalah launched a solo career. *—Steve Huey*

● **Everything Is Everything** / Jul. 1, 1970 / Atlantic ♦♦♦♦♦
Already a respected arranger and pianist who'd contributed to dozens of records (by artists ranging from the Impressions to Carla Thomas to Woody Herman), with this debut LP Donny Hathaway revealed yet another facet of his genius—his smoky, pleading voice, one of the best to ever grace a soul record. *Everything Is Everything* sounded like nothing before it, based in smooth uptown soul but boasting a set of excellent, open-ended arrangements gained from Hathaway's background in classical and gospel music; before going to Howard University in 1964, his knowledge of popular music was practically nonexistent. After gaining a contract with Atco through King Curtis, Hathaway wrote and recorded during 1969 and 1970 with friends including drummer Ric Powell and guitarist Phil Upchurch, both of whom lent a grooving feel to the album that Hathaway may not have been able to summon on his own (check out Upchurch's unforgettable bassline on the opener, "Voices Inside (Everything Is Everything)"). All of the musical brilliance on display, though, is merely the framework for Hathaway's rich, emotive voice, testifying to the power of love and religion with few, if any, concessions to pop music. Like none other, he gets to the raw, churchy emotion underlying Ray Charles' "I Believe to My Soul" and Nina Simone's "To Be Young, Gifted and Black," the former with a call-and-response horn chart and his own glorious vocal, the latter with his own organ lines. "Thank You Master (For My Soul)" brings the Stax horns onto sanctified ground, while Hathaway praises God and sneaks in an excellent piano solo. *Everything Is Everything* was one of the first soul records to comment directly on an unstable period; "Tryin' Times" speaks to the importance of peace and community with an earthy groove, while the most familiar track here, a swinging jam known as "The Ghetto," places listeners right in the middle of urban America. Donny Hathaway's debut introduced a brilliant talent into the world of soul, one who promised to take R&B farther than it had been taken since Ray Charles debuted on Atlantic. *—John Bush*

Donny Hathaway / Apr. 2, 1971 / Atlantic ♦♦♦
With just one exception, Donny Hathaway's second full-length is a covers album, featuring one of the most most pop-averse artists in soul music surprisingly offering interpretations of contemporary hit material like "A Song for You," "He Ain't Heavy, He's My Brother," "Magnificent Sanctuary Band," and (most effectively) "Put Your Hand in the Hand," a laid-back yet rolling, gospel-choir version of the song he was born to sing. In striking contrast to his debut, *Donny Hathaway* is a very dark record, and it opens on a particularly low note, with "Giving Up" (a 1964 R&B hit for Gladys Knight & the Pips). Most of Hathaway's performances are slow, piano-led laments, powerfully delivered but with little melodic sway to convert listeners. It's no coincidence then, that the only uptempo song, "Magnificent Sanctuary Band," is the standout. "Little Girl" is a nice piece of gospel testifying with great male harmonizing on the chorus, and "He Ain't Heavy, He's My Brother" is a solid rendering of a song usually drenched in pathos. Still, whereas *Everything Is Everything* saw him leading the choir up in the front of church, *Donny Hathaway* sounds like the lament of a man alone in the sanctuary after services are finished. *—John Bush*

Live / 1972 / Atlantic ♦♦♦♦♦
Donny Hathaway's 1972 *Live* album is one of the most glorious of his career, an uncomplicated, energetic set with a heavy focus on audience response as well as the potent jazz chops of his group. The results of shows recorded at the Troubadour in Hollywood and the Bitter End in New York, the record begins with Hathaway's version of the instant soul classic "What's Going On," Marvin Gaye's original not even a year old when Hathaway recorded this version. His *own* classic "The Ghetto" follows in short order, but stretches out past ten minutes with revelatory solos from Hathaway on electric piano. "Voices Inside (Everything Is Everything)" is another epic (14-minute) jam, with plenty of room for solos and some of the most sizzling bass work ever heard on record by Willie Weeks. Any new Donny Hathaway record worth its salt also has to include a radical cover, and *Live* obliges nicely with his deft, loping version of John Lennon's "Jealous Guy." The audience is as much a participant as the band here, immediately taking over with staccato handclaps to introduce "The Ghetto" and basically taking over the chorus on "You've Got

a Friend." They also contribute some of the most frenzied screaming heard in response any Chicago soul singer of the time (excepting only Jackie Wilson and Gene Chandler, of course). Hardly the obligatory live workout of most early-'70s concert LPs, *Live* solidified Hathaway's importance at the forefront of soul music. *—John Bush*

Extension of a Man / Jun. 18, 1973 / Rhino ✦✦✦✦
Ranging from inner-city soul to orchestral grandeur to a bluesy ballad to easy-listening pleasantries, *Extension of a Man* was Donny Hathaway's most ambitious LP, the justly titled capstone to his phenomenal career. Coming, however, from one of soul music's most widely talented figures, this wasn't exactly a surprise; both of his previous studio full-lengths, *Everything Is Everything* and *Donny Hathaway*, treated soul as merely a starting point to express his multitude of ideas concerning music and arrangement, song and performance. On *Extension of a Man*, the ambition began *and* peaked with the opener, a six-minute orchestral piece titled "I Love the Lord; He Heard My Cry, Pts. 1-2." Arranged and orchestrated for 45 musicians by Hathaway himself, it applied the buoyant optimism of Gershwin's *Rhapsody in Blue* to a religious context, and segued smoothly into the transcendent "Someday We'll All Be Free," one of Hathaway's most beloved songs. The next two pieces, "Flying Easy" and "Valdez in the Country," were also Hathaway originals, first recorded during the late '60s as part of Chess studio groups; the first is a piece of pop-soul fluff lifted up by his superb reading, the second a smooth jazz-fusion jam with Hathaway illustrating on electric piano his excellent improv capabilities. "Love, Love, Love" and "Come Little Children" were the charting singles, the former a sublime love song heavily influenced by Marvin Gaye's *What's Going On*. Unfortunately, these disparate pieces, brilliant as they are, don't coalesce into a single work as well as on his masterpiece *Everything Is Everything*, but Hathaway never stops impressing with his conceptions of arrangement and performance. Crippled by depression, he would never release another solo album during the last five years of his life, though among the projects he'd hoped to record was the four-part concerto *Life*, to be performed by the Boston Pops Symphony Orchestra with him in the conductor's chair, and the score of an epic biblical film. *—John Bush*

The Best of Donny Hathaway / 1978 / Atlantic ✦✦✦✦

A Donny Hathaway Collection / Apr. 12, 1990 / Atlantic ✦✦✦✦✦
Unfortunately, Atlantic's *A Donny Hathaway Collection*, one of the few career retrospectives available (and basically the only one in print), isn't quite definitive; it presents a version of Hathaway's career inordinately focused on his commercially successful duets with Roberta Flack and his slowest, most dirge-like solo recordings. A few of his best uptempo tracks are represented ("The Ghetto," his live cover of "What's Going On"), but not before haunted material like "I Love You More Than You'll Ever Know" and "Giving Up." Admittedly, his duets with Flack are among the best recordings of his career, ranging from the depressed ("Where Is the Love") to the atmospheric ("The Closer I Get to You") to the downright driving ("Back Together Again"). But *A Donny Hathaway Collection* neglects far too much material from his two greatest solo albums, 1970's *Everything Is Everything* and 1973's *Extension of Man*, to be considered the perfect first choice. It may simply be a matter of embellishing the myth of the tortured artist, but this doesn't present both sides of the Hathaway legend. *—John Bush*

Lalah Hathaway

b. Chicago, IL
Vocals / Urban
The daughter of the great Donny Hathaway, Lalah Hathaway made a good impression with her debut recording *Lalah Hathaway* in 1990. She not only displayed poise, confidence, and good technique, but was also versatile enough to do more than just light urban contemporary ballads. Her stage shows included jazz, pre-rock pop, and even gospel, and Hathaway later appeared on Black Entertainment Television doing jazz and fusion. *—Ron Wynn*

• **Lalah Hathaway** / 1990 / Virgin ✦✦✦✦
When Lalah Hathaway's self-titled debut album came out in 1990, there was reason to believe that she might evolve into one of the top female R&B singers of the 1990s. Donny Hathaway's daughter certainly had a lot going for her—not only a big range, but also plenty of charisma, passion and charm to go with it. The material on this CD ranges from excellent to routine, depending on who's writing and/or producing a particular song. Hathaway doesn't always have fantastic material to work with, but when she does, the results are quite memorable. The producers/songwriters who really do Hathaway justice include Angela Winbush on "Baby, Don't Cry" and "I Gotta Move On" and Andre Fisher on "Smile" and "Somethin'." While those selections come across as personal, Hathaway slips into a routine, less-than-memorable urban contemporary grind thanks to Chuckii Booker on "Sentimental" and Craig T. Cooper on "Obvious" and "U-Godit Gowin On." Again, not everything on the album is a gem. But when Hathaway had strong material to work with, it was clear that she had a lot of potential. *—Alex Henderson*

A Moment / 1994 / Virgin ✦✦✦
Lalah Hathaway should have become as big a name in 1990s R&B as the equally talented and equally Chaka Khan-influenced Mary J. Blige, but regrettably, the singer never became as visible as she should have been. Donny Hathaway's daughter didn't record often enough (four years passed between her first album and her sophomore effort *A Moment*), and unlike Blige, she never provided a consistently excellent album. Like *Lalah Hathaway*, *A Moment* is a mixed bag ranging from the strong to the decent to the routine (depending on who's producing and/or writing a particular song). Hathaway is well served by Sami McKinney on "Do You Suppose" and the melancholy "Better as a Memory" and by Martyn Ware on a likable remake of Sly & the Family Stone's "Family Affair." Chuckii Booker's work on Hathaway's first album was ho-hum, but this time, he comes through for her with the angrily funky "Bad By Myself." Unfortunately, "ho-hum" describes the contributions of Brian Alexander Morgan on "Let Me Love You" and Keith Ware on "Lean On Me" (which Hathaway co-wrote) and "Separate Ways." Overall, this is a slightly weaker effort than Hathaway's debut. One hoped that eventually, she would live up to her promise and deliver a truly outstanding album, one that would become a huge name in R&B. *—Alex Henderson*

Edwin Hawkins

b. Aug. 1943, Oakland, CA
Vocals, Keyboards, Leader, Arranger / Traditional Gospel, Contemporary Gospel, Black Gospel
A trailblazing force behind the evolution of the contemporary gospel sound, Edwin Hawkins remains best known for his 1969 classic "Oh Happy Day," one of the biggest gospel hits of all time and a major pop radio smash as well. Born in Oakland, CA, in 1943, he began singing in his church youth choir while still a toddler, and by age five was playing piano; just two years later, he assumed full-time piano accompaniment duties for the family gospel group, making their recorded debut in 1957. A decade later, Hawkins and Betty Watson co-founded the Northern California State Youth Choir, drawing on the finest soloists from throughout the Bay Area to build the 50-member ensemble, which soon entered the studio to cut the 1968 LP *Let Us Go into the House of the Lord*, its modern, R&B-influenced production pointing the way to a new era in gospel recording.

Among the highlights of *Let Us Go into the House of the Lord* was the track "Oh Happy Day," which unexpectedly found a home on underground FM playlists across San Francisco; the single soon began earning airplay on mainstream R&B and pop outlets across the country, and in the spring of 1969 it reached the U.S. Top Five on the on its way to selling an astounding seven million copies and taking home a Grammy award. At this time the choir was rechristened the Edwin Hawkins Singers, although the featured voice on "Oh Happy Day" belonged to singer Dorothy Combs Morrison, who soon exited in pursuit of a solo career. Her loss proved devastating to Hawkins' long-term commercial fortunes, although in 1970 the ensemble did make a return appearance on the pop charts in support of Melanie on her hit "Lay Down (Candle in the Wind)."

Still, Hawkins remained a critical favorite, and in 1972 the Singers won a second Grammy for *Every Man Wants to Be Free*. Recording prolifically throughout the remainder of the decade, in 1980 they won a third Grammy for *Wonderful*; a fourth, for *If You Love Me*, followed three years later. In 1982, Hawkins also founded the Edwin Hawkins Music and Arts Seminar, an annual week-long convention that offers workshops exploring all facets of the gospel industry and culminating each year with a live performance by the assembled mass choir. Although Hawkins recorded less and less frequently in the years to follow, he continued touring regularly, including a series of 1995 dates with the Swedish choir Svart Pa Vitt. *—Jason Ankeny*

Oh Happy Day / 1969 / Pair ✦✦✦✦✦

The Best of the Edwin Hawkins Singers / Jun. 3, 1997 / Capitol ✦✦✦✦✦
The Best of the Edwin Hawkins Singers is a solid overview of the soulful gospel group's late-'60s/early-'70s heyday, featuring not only the hit "Oh Happy Day," but also great album cuts like "Jubilation" and inspired covers of such hits as "Lean on Me." *—Stephen Thomas Erlewine*

• **Oh Happy Day!: The Best of the Edwin Hawkins Singers** / Aug. 7, 2001 / Buddha ✦✦✦✦✦
One of the few Edwin Hawkins compilations to escape the bounds of the LP medium, Buddha's *Oh Happy Day!: The Best of the Edwin Hawkins Singers* offers 15 tracks from one of the most uplifting artists of the late '60s and '70s. Beginning with the title track of their debut LP, *Let Us Go Into the House of the Lord*, the disc includes the full version of the surprise pop hit "Oh Happy Day," along with several of Hawkins' own excellent compositions, among them "I Shall Be Free," "Precious Memories," and "Late in the Evening." The Edwin Hawkins Singers did some intriguing covers as well, and two of the best are included here: the Five Stairsteps' "O-o-h Child" and Bob Dylan's "Blowin' in the Wind" (the latter is nearly seven minutes of testifying bliss). *—John Bush*

Roy Hawkins

Vocals, Piano / West Coast Blues, Piano Blues, R&B
Not only was Roy Hawkins dogged by bad luck during his career (at the height of his popularity, the pianist lost the use of an arm in a car wreck), he couldn't even cash in after the fact. When B.B. King blasted up the charts in 1970 with Roy Hawkins' classic "The Thrill Is Gone," the tune was mistakenly credited to the wrong composers on early pressings.

Little is known of Hawkins' early days. Producer Bob Geddins discovered Hawkins playing in an Oakland, CA, nightspot and supervised his first 78s for Cavatone and Downtown in 1948. Modern Records picked up the rights to several Downtown masters before signing Hawkins to a contract in 1949. Two major R&B hits resulted: 1950's "Why Do Things Happen to Me" and "The Thrill Is Gone" the following year. Hawkins recorded for the Bihari brothers' Modern and RPM imprints into 1954. After that, a handful of 45s for Rhythm and Kent were all that was heard of the Bay Area pianist on vinyl. He's rumored to have died in 1973. *—Bill Dahl*

Highway 59 / 1984 / Ace ✦✦✦✦
Early-'50s rarities from the vaults of the Bihari brothers' Modern label, with a good amount of unissued masters recommending this 16-song LP (no CD equivalent yet). Hawkins' cool California blues piano blends well with the tasty little combos Modern provided; of special interest are the title cut and "Would You," a pair of 1952 gems that feature T-Bone Walker's incomparable guitar work. *—Bill Dahl*

• **The Thrill Is Gone** / Aug. 29, 2000 / Ace ✦✦✦✦✦
Here are 24 of Hawkins' 1949-1952 Modern sides, mostly taken from singles that came out during those years. Even by the standards of the Modern roster, Hawkins is a fairly forgotten figure—although he was, according to the liner notes, briefly the label's biggest

moneymaker. As with all of Modern's early-'50s recordings, this has a dependable urban, slightly jazzy West Coast groove, very accomplished and not as variable as one might like over the course of a couple dozen numbers. Hawkins was a good piano player and a sufficient easygoing, slightly foggy-textured vocalist, capable of both rapid jump shuffles and morose ballads. "Gloom and Misery All Around" and "I Don't Know Just What to Do" were entirely typical sentiments of his slower tunes. His band featured an excellent underrated guitarist, Ulysses James, whose burning tone shines when it's given a little space to strut, as on "Wine Drinkin' Woman." His Modern output was most notable for the self-pitying ballad "Why Do Everything Happen to Me," a number three hit later covered by B.B. King and James Brown, and, more memorably, the original version of "The Thrill Is Gone," which became B.B. King's biggest hit a couple of decades later. The original renditions of both are on this CD, and the gloomy "The Thrill Is Gone," far more piano-based and small band-scaled in its arrangement than King's classic cover, in particular outclasses anything else in Hawkins' discography. Otherwise, Hawkins is not among the first West Coast blues stars of the era, or even among the first such artists on the Modern roster, one should hear, though if you've a jones for that style, this reliably delivers the goods. *—Richie Unterberger*

Screamin' Jay Hawkins

b. Jul. 18, 1929, Cleveland, OH, **d.** Feb. 12, 2000, Paris, France

Vocals, Piano / Rock & Roll, R&B

Screamin' Jay Hawkins was the most outrageous performer extant during rock's dawn. Prone to emerging out of coffins on-stage, a flaming skull named Henry his constant companion, Screamin' Jay was an insanely theatrical Figure long before it was even remotely acceptable. Hawkins' life story is almost as bizarre as his on-stage shtick. Originally inspired by the booming baritone of Paul Robeson, Hawkins was unable to break through as an opera singer. His boxing prowess was every bit as lethal as his vocal cords; many of his most hilarious tales revolve around Jay beating the hell out of a musical rival!

Hawkins caught his first musical break in 1951 as pianist/valet to veteran jazz guitarist Tiny Grimes. He debuted on wax for Gotham the following year with "Why Did You Waste My Time," backed by Grimes & His Rockin' Highlanders (they donned kilts and tam o' shanters on-stage). Singles for Timely ("Baptize Me in Wine") and Mercury's Wing subsidiary (1955's otherworldly "[She Put the] Wamee [On Me]," a harbinger of things to come) preceded Hawkins' immortal 1956 rendering of "I Put a Spell on You" for Columbia's OKeh imprint.

Hawkins originally envisioned the tune as a refined ballad. After he and his NY session aces (notably guitarist Mickey Baker and saxist Sam "The Man" Taylor) had imbibed to the point of no return, Hawkins screamed, grunted, and gurgled his way through the tune with utter drunken abandon. A resultant success despite the protests of uptight suits-in-power, "I Put a Spell on You" became Screamin' Jay's biggest seller ("Little Demon," its rocking flip, is a minor classic itself). Hawkins cut several amazing 1957-1958 follow-ups in the same crazed vein—"Hong Kong," a surreal "Yellow Coat," the Jerry Leiber/Mike Stoller-penned "Alligator Wine"—but none of them clicked the way "Spell" had. Deejay Alan Freed convinced Screamin' Jay that popping out of a coffin might be a show-stopping gimmick by handing him a $300 bonus (long after Freed's demise, Screamin' Jay Hawkins was still benefiting from his crass brainstorm).

Hawkins' next truly inspired waxing came in 1969 when he was contracted to Phillips Records (where he made two albums). His gross "Constipation Blues" wouldn't garner much airplay, but remained an integral part of his legacy for quite awhile. The cinema was a beneficiary of Screamin' Jay's larger-than-life persona in later years. His featured roles in *Mystery Train* and *A Rage in Harlem* made Hawkins a familiar visage to youngsters who never even heard "I Put a Spell on You." He died February 12, 2000, following surgery to treat an aneurysm; Hawkins was 70. *—Bill Dahl*

I Put a Spell on You / 1957 / Collectables ♦♦♦

I Put a Spell on You is Screamin' Jay's landmark Epic album from the '50s. His wild-ass reinventions of old, staid standards like "I Love Paris," "Deep Purple," and "You Made Me Love You (I Didn't Want To Do It)" must be heard to be believed, but for surrealism at its best, check out "Take Me Back to My Boots and Saddle" and a dead straight reading of "Swing Low, Sweet Chariot" in the middle of all of it. The perfect opening shot from this one-of-a-kind artist. *—Cub Koda*

What That Is! / 1969 / Phillips ♦♦♦

Screamin' Jay Hawkins never made an album that wasn't wildly uneven in performance quality, songs, production, arrangements, and musicianship. This one is no less erratic; sometimes Hawkins' inspired lunacy makes its mark, and other times it falls woefully short. But it's fun hearing him keep trying. *—Ron Wynn*

A Night at Forbidden City / 196 / Sounds of Hawaii ♦♦♦

A characteristically weird, all-over-the-place album on an offbeat label by Screamin' Jay Hawkins. He's the type of artist much better in small doses than over a full album. Despite his congenial, humorous style, Hawkins isn't a great R&B or blues vocalist, and tries to compensate through comic effects, gimmick vocals, and unusual songs. Those couldn't help him on this album, which just doesn't have enough good songs to keep it interesting. *—Ron Wynn*

Screamin' Jay Hawkins / 1970 / Phillips ♦♦♦

Here is an entertaining, if at times almost unbearable, workout by Screamin' Jay Hawkins. At this point, Hawkins' voice still had its power and bizarre edges, and he could sometimes overcome weak tracks by simply hollering or yelling or being wild. Other times, the songs can't be saved by his comic routines. *—Ron Wynn*

Frenzy / 1982 / Edsel ♦♦♦♦

Screamin' Jay Hawkins was a truly demented R&B shouter, as evidenced by the classic "I Put a Spell on You." It wasn't long before his camp schtick overshadowed his musical abilities, but for a brief while he had a certain warped genius. Most of these tracks were recorded for OKeh, and the 14-track compilation *Frenzy* contains most of the best of these recordings. Nothing ever quite touched "I Put a Spell on You," but the songs that came the closest are here. *Frenzy* may not be a comprehensive collection, but for anyone who wants more of the sound that made "I Put a Spell on You" a hit, this will suffice. *—Stephen Thomas Erlewine*

● **Voodoo Jive: The Best of Screamin' Jay Hawkins** / Feb. 1990 / Rhino ♦♦♦♦♦

Screamin' Jay Hawkins—genius or lunatic? An investigation of Hawkins' body of work suggests these two options were hardly mutually exclusive in his case, and while he certainly tended to favor material that indulged his fondness for the vocal freak-out, the man also possessed a solid baritone voice and knew just what to do with it. (A careful examination of his music reveals that Screamin' Jay could sing "straight" and do it quite well if the occasion called for it—he simply wasn't asked to do so very often.) At his best, Hawkins was a musical eccentric in the great tradition of Spike Jones, Captain Beefheart, and Prince, determined to follow his own unique path, consequences be damned. Sadly, most of Hawkins' albums were wildly uneven, but *Voodoo Jive: The Best of Screamin' Jay Hawkins* filters out the duds to serve up 17 perverse gems from his work on a handful of labels; along with his biggest hit, the once-scandalous "I Put a Spell on You," you get such wonders of modern recording as "Alligator Wine" and "Feast of the Mau Mau," his singular interpretations of "I Love Paris" and "You Made Me Love You (I Didn't Want to Do It)," and the definitive music statement on the inability to void, "Constipation Blues" (which actually charted in Japan, proving this theme truly spans cultural boundaries). If you're only going to own one Screamin' Jay Hawkins disc, *Voodoo Jive* is definitely the one to get, though we accept no responsibility for the reaction of your neighbors if you play "(She Put The) Wamee (On Me)" at three in the morning. *—Mark Deming*

Cow Fingers & Mosquito Pie / 1991 / Epic ♦♦♦♦♦

This is a magically weird 19-song collection of the bizarre shouter's mid-'50s OKeh/Epic output, when he was at the height of his strange and terrifying vocal powers. In addition to the prerequisite "I Put a Spell on You" and the surreal rockers "Yellow Coat," "Hong Kong," "Alligator Wine," and "Little Demon," there's the amusing "There's Something Wrong With You," a previously unissued "You Ain't Foolin' Me," and a deranged takeoff on the cowboy ditty "Take Me Back to My Boots and Saddle" (and what Jay does to the formerly stately "I Love Paris" and "Orange Colored Sky" is truly indescribable!). *—Bill Dahl*

Spellbound! 1955–74 / 1991 / Bear Family ♦♦♦

Bear Family's *Spellbound! 1955-74* is a double-disc set that captures highlights from Screamin' Jay Hawkins' recordings for Wing, Decca, Phillips, and RCA. It's not quite the bargain it seems. Half of the 48 tracks were already issued on two Phillips albums, which were combined on one Edsel CD. Furthermore, most of these songs date from the '60s, with only a handful coming from Hawkins' '50s peak. Strangely, of those songs, not one of them is the original "I Put a Spell on You," which makes this hardly the definitive overview that it should be. Instead of focusing on the best of Screamin' Jay Hawkins' best material, it has the campy, silly stuff from the '60s, which will try the patience of anyone outside devoted fans—and those devoted fans will prefer more complete compilations than this strangely scattershot effort from Bear Family. There are some good moments here, but overall, it has to rank as a disappointment. *—Stephen Thomas Erlewine*

Portrait of a Man / Feb. 14, 1995 / Edsel ♦♦♦

Portrait of a Man is a collection of rarities and obscurities from a man whose very career was filled with arcania. Of course, it contains the original version of "I Put a Spell on You," but what Screamin' Jay Hawkins collection doesn't? The main point of the disc is rarities that aren't anywhere else, whether it's a remake of "I Put a Spell on You" or his freak English hit "Heart Attack and Vine." There are more interesting things here than the average Screamin' album, which is both good ("Mountain Jive") and bad ("Armpit No. 6"). Either way, it's one of the handful of Hawkins compilations that aren't strict hits collections but are worth hearing. *—Stephen Thomas Erlewine*

Best of the Bizarre Sessions: 1990–1994 / Jul. 11, 2000 / Manifesto ♦♦♦

Essential Recordings / Aug. 8, 2000 / Golden ♦♦♦

Ted Hawkins

b. Oct. 28, 1936, Biloxi, MS, **d.** Jan. 1, 1995, Los Angeles, CA

Vocals, Guitar / Modern Acoustic Blues, Contemporary Blues, Soul-Blues, Singer/Songwriter

Overseas, he was a genuine hero, performing to thousands. But on his L.A. hometurf, sand-blown Venice Beach served as Ted Hawkins' makeshift stage. He'd deliver his magnificent mélange of soul, blues, folk, gospel, and a touch of country all by his lonesome, with only an acoustic guitar for company. Passersby would pause to marvel at Hawkins' melismatic vocals, dropping a few coins or a greenback into his tip jar on the way by. That was the way Ted Hawkins kept body and soul together until 1994, when DGC/Geffen Records issued *The Next Hundred Years*, his breakthrough album. Suddenly, Hawkins was poised on the precipice of stardom. And then, just after Christmas that same year, in a bout of cruel irony, he died of a stroke.

After growing up in Mississippi, Hawkins moved to L.A. in 1966 and cut his debut 45, the soul-steeped "Baby"/"Whole Lot of Women," for Money Records. He also recorded some material in 1971, which appeared on Rounder in 1982 (as *Watch Your Step*). The album gained a five-star review from *Rolling Stone*, and Hawkins recorded another album, *Happy Hour*, in 1986. He moved to England later that year and became a well-known presence performing around Europe and even Japan. After returning to America in the early '90s, DGC ever so briefly propelled him into the major leagues. *Love You Most of All: More Songs From Venice Beach* was issued posthumously in 1998. *—Bill Dahl*

Watch Your Step / 1982 / Rounder ♦♦♦

Guitarist/vocalist Ted Hawkins was an instant sensation when this session was originally released in 1982. At a time when slick, heavily produced urban contemporary material was establishing its domination on the R&B scene, Hawkins' hard-edged, rough, cutting voice, plus his crisp acoustic guitar accompaniment and country-blues roots, seemed both dated and extremely fresh. This 15-track CD includes four numbers with Hawkins backed by Phillip Walker and his band, and others ranging from the humorous "Who Got My Natural Comb?" to the poignant "If You Love Me" and two versions of the title track. He also teamed with his wife Elizabeth on "Don't Lose Your Cool" and "I Gave It All I Had" for moving duets. *—Ron Wynn*

Happy Hour / 1986 / Rounder ✦✦✦✦✦
Guitarist/vocalist Ted Hawkins' second Rounder record enhanced his reputation. *Happy Hour* features Hawkins' memorable compositions, plus a wonderful version of Curtis Mayfield's "Gypsy Woman." Hawkins' vocals were even more gritty and striking, as was his acoustic guitar backing and chording. He teamed with his wife Elizabeth on "Don't Make Me Explain It," "My Last Goodbye," and "California Song," and with guitarist Night Train Clemons on "Gypsy Woman" and "You Pushed My Head Away." Hawkins blended soul and urban blues stylings with country and rural blues inflections and rhythms, making another first-rate release. *—Ron Wynn*

The Next Hundred Years / Mar. 29, 1994 / Geffen ✦✦✦
The former L.A. street musician's major label breakthrough was in a great many ways a far weaker outing than what came before, largely due to a plodding band unwisely inserted behind Hawkins that tends to distract rather than enhance his impassioned vocals and rich acoustic guitar strumming. Mostly originals ("There Stands the Glass" returns, as does "Ladder of Success") that would have sounded so much better in an intimate solo context. *—Bill Dahl*

The Kershaw Sessions: Live at the BBC / 1995 / Varese Sarabande ✦✦✦
The material on *The Kershaw Sessions: Live at the BBC* was recorded for disc jockey Andy Kershaw's BBC radio show between 1986 and 1989. It captures Ted Hawkins in an intimate, unvarnished setting that strips his music down to its purest essentials, making it an intriguing listen for fans who want more of Hawkins' bare-bones street-troubadour sound. Only a little over half the songs are Hawkins compositions; the high percentage of covers and the minimalist production give *The Kershaw Sessions* a vibe similar to *Songs From Venice Beach*. This is the way many British listeners were introduced to Hawkins' music, and it makes an excellent listen for American devotees as well. *—Steve Huey*

Songs From Venice Beach / Oct. 1995 / Evidence ✦✦✦✦
Blending every form of roots music imaginable into his own singular soulful stew, the incomparable Ted Hawkins stuck mostly to R&B covers on this splendid 1985 solo outing—songs by Sam Cooke (his idol), Jerry Butler, Bobby "Blue" Bland, the Temptations, and Garnet Mimms receive gorgeous readings by the acoustic guitarist. But even though he only contributed one original, the touching "Ladder of Success," to the set, Hawkins wasn't content to remain in one genre—his commanding revival of Webb Pierce's hillbilly weeper "There Stands the Glass" ranks with the disc's very best moments (of which there are many). *—Bill Dahl*

The Final Tour / Jan. 13, 1998 / Evidence ✦✦✦✦✦
Ted Hawkins' story is one of the most interesting—and tragic—in the history of R&B. Who'd have thought that a 50-something street singer who performed 1960s-type soul in Venice Beach, CA, would have signed with Geffen's DGC label after decades of obscurity? That's exactly what happened, but tragically, a 58-year-old Hawkins died from a diabetes-related stroke just when things were really looking up for him. Recorded live at three 1994 concerts and released in 1998, *The Final Tour* shows how great Hawkins was sounding during the last months of his life. Nothing slick or elaborate happens on this album—it's just the charismatic Hawkins and his acoustic guitar, drawing on Sam Cooke's influence but always sounding like his own man. Those familiar with Hawkins' Rounder output will be familiar with heartfelt originals like "Bad Dog," "Bring It on Home, Daddy" and "Revenge of Scorpio," all of which demonstrate that he was as superb a composer as he was a singer. Hawkins is equally captivating on interpretations of Brook Benton's "I Got What I Wanted" and "All I Have to Offer You Is Me," a hit for country great Charley Pride that easily lends itself to Hawkins' brand of acoustic R&B. Soul lovers who haven't experienced the joys of Hawkins' music should make a point of obtaining this magnificent album. *—Alex Henderson*

● **The Ted Hawkins Story: Suffer No More** / Jan. 13, 1998 / Rhino ✦✦✦✦✦
Taken individually, Hawkins' albums didn't measure up to his critical reputation, due to uneven material, occasionally inappropriate production, and overreliance upon covers. More than most best-ofs, this 20-song compilation is a revelation of sorts. By focusing on his best moments, it's much easier to make a convincing case for Hawkins as a major, if erratic, roots-music performer who sounded like a coarsened, acoustic-oriented Sam Cooke. The set goes all the way back to both sides of his rare (and good) 1966 soul single on the Money label and highlights the best originals from the '70s and '80s sessions released on Rounder, wisely selecting sparsely from his cover-dominated albums of the mid-'80s. The songs from his major-label finale *The Next Hundred Years* can veer toward production slickness, but there's a pleasing bonus in three acoustic, previously unreleased cuts from the early 1990s. It's an intelligently selected, well-rounded disc, presenting several sides of this idiosyncratic artist: composer, folky interpreter of material by Sam Cooke and Brook Benton, and country-tinged soul artist. *—Richie Unterberger*

Love You Most of All: More Songs From Venice Beach / Sep. 29, 1998 / Evidence ✦✦✦
Ted Hawkins always resisted being called a blues singer, and a look at his repertoire shows why. While Hawkins' strong but weather-beaten voice could communicate sorrow and heartbreak as few others could, he could also summon up a joyous fire that's a wonder to behold, and he could work this magic with practically any song he chose to perform, from Sam Cooke's "Bring It on Home to Me" to John Denver's "Take Me Home, Country Roads." Both of those songs appear on *Love You Most of All: More Songs From Venice Beach*, which (as the title suggests) features 13 songs from the same 1985 bare-bones guitar and voice sessions that produced Hawkins' *Songs From Venice Beach*, and, like the earlier album, it consists primarily of tunes Hawkins sang while busking for change along the Venice, CA, boardwalk. "Take Me Home, Country Roads" features a striking, hypnotic coda, in which Hawkins chants "so glad I'm a country boy/so glad I'm a country boy" until he's taken Denver's song to a soulful place no one (except possibly Toots Hibbert) could have imagined it going, and Hawkins manages a similar alchemy with such chestnuts as "Green Green Grass of Home," "Your Cheatin' Heart," and even "North to Alaska," as well as more likely Sam Cooke and Otis Redding covers. On this disc's best moments, Hawkins stands beside Arthur Alexander as one of the great unacknowledged links between country and R&B. Unfortunately, the best of the material from these sessions was used on the first album, and the five originals recorded in 1990 that close out the album simply aren't on a par with such Hawkins compositions as "Strange Conversation," "Sorry You're Sick," or "The Good and the Bad." But he never sound less than committed on any of the 18 tunes of *Love You Most of All*, and anyone who has encountered the heart-tugging power of Ted Hawkins voice knows he never gave a bad performance in front of a microphone—and this disc preserves more than a few great ones. *—Mark Deming*

The Unstoppable Ted Hawkins / Feb. 27, 2001 / Catfish ✦✦✦
Ted Hawkins had been accepted more warmly in England in the late '80s than he had been in his native America. To his countrymen, he was a has-been soul singer, ex-junkie, and ex-con who'd never made it and was now a busker on the Venice Beach boardwalk. What America wouldn't get until his major label debut in 1994 was something the Brits seemed to grasp instinctively—Ted Hawkins was one of the great soul singers, a very decent writer, but an interpreter of other peoples' material blessed with a perfect insight to bring things to life. And he proves that here, on what was meant to be just a soundboard cassette recording. From Sam Cooke to Brook Benton, even the maudlin "Please Come to Boston" takes on a magic and depth in his voice, while something as innocuous of "Zip Pe Dee Doo Dah" positively brims over with spirit. His guitar work was never more than rudimentary, strumming an open chord, his left hand gloved to protect it, but it did the perfect job of framing that magnificent voice, which, as this album shows, was best heard live, where he could open up and let his dramatic tendencies take over without ever going overboard. His own writing coexists well with the better-known work, "Bring It on Home Daddy" a good juxtaposition to "Your Cheating Heart." But genre never mattered—it was about whether the song worked, be it something as wonderful as his take on Otis Redding's "Dock of the Bay" or John Denver's "Country Roads," his set closer. Saying it's all good can cheapen things. But in the case of Ted Hawkins, it really *was* all good. *—Chris Nickson*

Tramaine Hawkins

b. Oct. 11, 1957, San Francisco, CA
Vocals / Contemporary Gospel, Black Gospel, Urban
Born Tramaine Davis in San Francisco and raised in Berkeley, Tramaine Hawkins is the granddaughter of Bishop E.E. Cleveland, one of the founders of the Church of God in Christ Church, the largest black Pentecostal organization in the U.S. She got her start as a teenager in 1968 performing with the Edwin Hawkins Singers during the home-made recording session that produced the crossover smash "Oh Happy Day," the biggest-selling gospel single to date. In the early '70s, she married Walter Hawkins, Edwin's brother, who went on to lead the Berkeley Love Center Church of God in Christ Church. There she sang lead soprano with her husband's Love Center Choir and appeared on the *Love Alive* album, a recorded Sunday session featuring her husband's sermon, Edwin on piano, and Hawkins on lead vocals. It and its follow-up, *Love Alive II*, were both best-sellers.

Hawkins began her solo recording career in the mid-'80s. As a solo artist, she drew from a variety of genres, and her albums demonstrate that she is as much at home shouting traditional tunes as she is belting out the blues, crooning silky-smooth soul numbers, or even doing hard-driving urban funk. Her tendency to utilize popular music has caused controversy amongst conservatives and even caused others to question her faith, but a close listen to her music demonstrates that even though her music has crossed over, her faith and good intentions are rock-solid. *—Sandra Brennan*

● **The Search Is Over** / 1983 / A&M ✦✦✦✦✦
Although Tramaine insisted that she never deserted the church, it was hard to tell the difference between most of this album's songs and standard secular urban contemporary material. They were sung with the same vigor and fire that Tramaine Hawkins brought to her gospel tunes, but only someone with a truly generous definition of gospel would equate *The Search Is Over* with religious or spiritual material. *—Ron Wynn*

Live / 1990 / Sparrow ✦✦✦✦✦

Still Tramaine / Aug. 14, 2001 / Gospo Centric ✦✦✦
This release is the first from landmark contemporary gospel artist Tramaine Hawkins since the mid-'90s. The long lapse of time between projects has done nothing to diminish Hawkins' power-packed, yet distinguished voice. *Still Tramaine* effectively infuses a nice mixture of traditional and contemporary gospel material. Hawkins is once again united with the Love Center Choir, who serve as backing vocalists on the tracks "I'll Wear a Crown," "On & On," "It's Your Power," and "Simple Song." The dance house rhythms filtering through the remixed track "By His Strength" are reminiscent of her landmark '80s crossover dance smash, "Fall Down (Spirit of Love)." One of the highlights of this splendid piece of musical artwork is the track "It's Your Power." The song features a hot vocal duet between Hawkins and album co-producer Walter Hawkins. *—Tim Smith*

Isaac Hayes

b. Aug. 20, 1942, Covington, TN

Vocals, Keyboards, Piano, Saxophone, Arranger, Songwriter / Soul, Funk, Blaxploitation, Disco

Few figures exerted greater influence over the music of the 1960s and 1970s than Isaac Hayes; after laying the groundwork for the Memphis soul sound through his work with Stax-Volt Records, Hayes began a highly successful solo career which predated not only the disco movement but also the evolution of rap. Hayes was born on August 20, 1942, in Covington, TN; his parents died during his infancy, and he was raised by his grandparents. After making his public debut singing in church at the age of five, he taught himself piano, organ and saxophone before moving to Memphis to perform on the city's club circuit in a series of short-lived groups like Sir Isaac & the Doo-Dads, the Teen Tones, and Sir Calvin & His Swinging Cats. In 1962, he began his recording career, cutting sides for a variety of local labels.

Two years later, Hayes began playing sax with the Mar-Keys, which resulted in the beginning of his long association with Stax Records. After playing on several sessions for Otis Redding, Hayes was tapped to play keyboards in the Stax house band, and eventually established a partnership with songwriter David Porter. Under the name the Soul Children, the Hayes-Porter duo composed some 200 songs, reeling off a string of hits for Stax luminaries like Sam & Dave (the brilliant "When Something Is Wrong With My Baby," "Soul Man," and "Hold on, I'm Comin'"), Carla Thomas ("B-A-B-Y,") and Johnnie Taylor ("I Got to Love Somebody's Baby," "I Had a Dream").

In 1967, Hayes issued his debut solo LP *Presenting Isaac Hayes*, a loose, jazz-flavored effort recorded in the early-morning hours following a raucous Stax party. With the release of 1969's landmark *Hot Buttered Soul*, he made his commercial breakthrough; the record's adventuresome structure (comprising four lengthy songs), ornate arrangements, and sensual grooves—combined with the imposing figure cut by his shaven head, omnipresent sunglasses, and fondness for gold jewelry—made Hayes one of the most distinctive figures in music. After a pair of 1970 releases, *The Isaac Hayes Movement* and *To Be Continued*, he reached his commercial zenith in 1971 with the release of *Shaft*, the score from the Gordon Parks film of the same name. Not only did the album win Hayes an Academy Award for Best Score (the first African-American composer to garner such an honor), but the single "Theme From 'Shaft,'" a masterful blend of prime funk and pre-rap monologues, became a number-one hit.

After 1971's superb *Black Moses* and 1973's *Joy*, Hayes composed two 1974 soundtracks, *Tough Guys* and *Truck Turner* (in which he also starred). By 1975, relations with Stax had disintegrated following a battle over royalties, and soon he severed his ties with the label to form his own Hot Buttered Soul imprint. Although both 1975's *Chocolate Chip* and 1976's *Groove-A-Thon* went gold, his records of the period attracted considerably less attention than prior efforts; combined with poor management and business associations, Hayes had no choice but to file for bankruptcy in 1976.

After the 1977 double-LP *A Man and a Woman*, recorded with Dionne Warwick, Hayes began a comeback on the strength of the hit singles "Zeke the Freak," "Don't Let Go" and "Do You Wanna Make Love." Following the success of his 1979 collection of duets with Millie Jackson titled *Royal Rappin's*, he issued a pair of solo records, 1980's *And Once Again* and 1981's *Lifetime Thing* before retiring from music for five years. After returning in 1986 with the LP *U Turn* and the Top Ten R&B hit "Ike's Rap," Hayes surfaced two years later with *Love Attack* before again dropping out of music to focus on acting.

In 1995, fully enshrined as one of the forefathers of hip-hop and newly converted to Scientology, Hayes emerged with two concurrent releases, the vocal *Branded* and instrumental *Raw and Refined*. Under the official name Nene Katey Ocansey I, he also served as a member of the royal family of the African nation of Ghana while continuing simultaneous careers as an actor, composer, and humanitarian. In 1997, Hayes provided the voice of what was slated to be a one-time character on the animated series *South Park*—Jerome "Chef" McElroy, the main characters' favorite school cafeteria worker. Hayes was an instant hit, and Chef became a regular character on the show, lending advice and, oftentimes, breaking into songs that gently sent up Hayes' image as one of R&B's ultimate love men.

South Park made Hayes more visible than ever and cemented his status as an icon with a whole new generation. He contributed the infamous "Chocolate Salty Balls" to the *South Park* tie-in album *Chef Aid*, and naturally appeared in the film *South Park: Bigger, Longer, Uncut*. In 2000, Hayes revisited his biggest triumph of the past by appearing in the remake of *Shaft* starring Samuel L. Jackson. The following year, he supported Alicia Keys as a musician and arranger on her acclaimed debut *Songs in A Minor*. *—Jason Ankeny*

Presenting Isaac Hayes / 1967 / Stax ♦♦♦

Here are Isaac Hayes' earliest single efforts, and he hadn't yet perfected his lengthy raps and symphonic soul formula. These were rather the same type of songs he and David Porter turned into classics for many other Stax artists. They were mostly short gospel and country tinged soul ballads, vamps, and uptempo numbers. Hayes sang them well, his domineering baritone revealing itself as a potent weapon. While none of them did that well, the album revealed the enormous potential Hayes would begin to fulfill with his next album. *—Ron Wynn*

☆ **Hot Buttered Soul** / 1969 / Stax ♦♦♦♦♦

Released at the tail end of the '60s, *Hot Buttered Soul* set the precedent for how soul would evolve in the early '70s, simultaneously establishing Isaac Hayes and the Bar-Kays as major forces within black music. Though not quite as definitive as *Black Moses* or as well-known as *Shaft, Hot Buttered Soul* remains an undeniably seminal record; it stretched its songs far beyond the traditional three-to-four-minute industry norm, featured long instrumental stretches where the Bar-Kays stole the spotlight, and it introduced a new, iconic persona for soul with Hayes' tough yet sensual image. With the release of this album, Motown suddenly seemed manufactured and James Brown a bit too theatrical. Surprising many, the album features only four songs. The first, "Walk on By," is an epic 12-minute moment of true perfection, its trademark string-laden intro just dripping with syrupy sentiment, and the thumping midtempo drum beat and accompanying bassline instilling a complementary sense of nasty funk to the song; if that isn't enough to make it an amazing song, Hayes' almost painful performance brings yet more feeling to the song, with the guitar's heavy vibrato and the female background singers taking the song to even further heights. The following three songs aren't quite as stunning but are still no doubt impressive: "Hyperbolicsyllabicsequedalymistic" trades in sappy sentiment for straight-ahead funk, highlighted by a stomping piano halfway through the song; "One Woman" is the least epic moment, clocking in at only five minutes, but stands as a straightforward, well-executed love ballad; and finally, there's the infamous 18-minute "By the Time I Get to Phoenix" and its lengthy monologue which slowly eases you toward the climactic, almost-orchestral finale, a beautiful way to end one of soul's timeless, landmark albums, the album that transformed Hayes into a lifelong icon. *—Jason Birchmeier*

The Isaac Hayes Movement / 1970 / Stax ♦♦♦♦♦

His second huge hit album and a great follow-up to the superb *Hot Buttered Soul*. Those critics who thought there was no way Hayes could repeat that triumph got fooled. He included a brilliant remake of Jerry Butler's "I Stand Accused" and also did a 12-minute version of the Beatles' "Something," complete with a wailing violin solo from jazz-rocker John Blair. This album showed that Hayes was going to be around for a long time and perform just as consistently on his own as he did teaming with Porter. *—Ron Wynn*

. . . To Be Continued / 1970 / Stax ♦♦♦♦

Released in late 1970 on the heals of two chart-topping albums, *Hot Buttered Soul* (1969) and *The Isaac Hayes Movement* (also 1970), Isaac Hayes and the Bar-Kays retain their Successful approach on those landmark albums for *. . . To Be Continued*, another number-one album. Again, the album features four songs that span far beyond traditional radio-friendly length, featuring important mood-establishing instrumental segments just as emotive and striking as Hayes' crooning. Nothing here is quite as perfect as "Walk on By," and the album feels a bit churned out, but *. . . To Be Continued* no doubt has its share of highlights, the most notable being "You've Lost That Lovin' Feelin'." The album's most epic moment opens with light strings and horns, vamping poetically for several minutes before Hayes even utters a breath; then, once the singer delivers the song's orchestral chorus, the album hits its sentimental peak—Hayes elevating a common standard to heavenly heights once again. Elsewhere, "Our Day Will Come" features a nice concluding instrumental segment driven by a proto-hip-hop beat that proves just how ahead of his time Hayes was during his early-'70s cycle of Enterprise albums. It's tempting to slight this album when holding it up against Hayes' best albums from this same era, but a comparison such as this is unfair. Even if Ike isn't doing anything here that he didn't do on his two preceding albums—*Hot Buttered Soul, The Isaac Hayes Movement*—and isn't quite as daring as he is on his two successive albums—*Black Moses, Shaft— . . . To Be Continued* still topples any Hayes album that came after 1971. It didn't top the R&B album chart for 11 weeks on accident—this is quintessential early-'70s Isaac Hayes, and that alone makes it a classic soul album. *—Jason Birchmeier*

Black Moses / 1971 / Stax ♦♦♦

For many, this is Ike's finest overall effort, and despite the ego trippin' title—*Black Moses*—the music backs the brag. Hayes' low register is mesmerizing on 14 refurbished R&B and pop songs. Every track is carefully crafted and well-spaced. "Ike Raps" enhances and bands them all together. The key is balance, while there's nothing as mournful as "By the Time I Get to Phoenix," soulful as "I Stand Accused," or bad as "Do Your Thing," every cut is a close second. "Going in Circles," "Man's Temptation," "Need to Belong to Someone," "Never Can Say Goodbye," and the rest are done with maturity and reverence by the self-acclaimed One. *—Andrew Hamilton*

Shaft / 1971 / Stax ♦♦♦♦♦

Of the many wonderful blaxpoitation soundtracks to emerge during the early '70s, *Shaft* certainly deserves mention as not only one of the most lasting but also one of the most successful. Isaac Hayes was undoubtedly one of the era's most accomplished soul artists, having helped elevate Stax to its esteemed status; therefore, his being chosen to score such a high-profile major-studio film shouldn't seem like a surprise. And with "Theme From Shaft," he delivered an anthem just as ambitious and revered as the film itself, a song that has only grown more treasured over the years, after having been an enormously popular hit at the time of its release. Besides this song, though, there aren't too many more radio-targeted moments here. "Soulsville" operates effectively as the sort of down-tempo ballad Hayes was most known for, just as the almost 20-minute "Do Your Thing" showcased just how impressive the Bar-Kays had become, stretching the song to unseen limits with their inventive, funky jamming. For the most part, though, this double-LP features nothing but cinematic moments of instrumentation, composed and produced by Hayes while being performed by the Bar-Kays—some down-tempo, others quite jazzy, nothing too funky, though. Even if it's not quite as enjoyable as Curtis Mayfield's *Superfly* due to its emphasis on instrumentals, *Shaft* still remains a powerful record; one of Hayes' pinnacle moments for sure. *—Jason Birchmeier*

Live at the Sahara Tahoe / 1973 / Stax ♦♦

You could expect Hayes to be in his element at a resort venue—lounge soul was his forte, and this double album offers almost two hours of it. Ike demonstrates his versatility by getting "Shaft" out of the way right off the bat and alternating between originals and covers of a wide range of tunes, including "Light My Fire," "Never Can Say Goodbye," "Rock Me Baby," "Stormy Monday Blues," "Feelin' Alright," and "It's Too Late" (yes, the Carole King song). Often these are linked together, of course, by Hayes' brotherly raps; for Bill Withers' "Ain't No Sunshine," he tests the limits, stretching the tune just past the ten-minute mark. The set has a funky lounge lizard charm, but it's too much to bear at once, except for the most devoted of fans. *—Richie Unterberger*

Joy / Dec. 1973 / Stax ♦♦♦♦
With seven massive number-one records trailing in his wake, Isaac Hayes donned his stylin', funky gold-chain link vest once again and capped 1973 with *Joy*, a set which might have proven the lucky-streak breaker—it missed the top spot by one place—but still waded into gold-record waters with ease. "Joy" itself, of course, was the album's crowning glory, a gargantuan 15-minute piece which essentially devoured side one of the album (the accompanying "I Love You That's All" is merely an afterthought). Heady, smoky, ubiquitous—an instrumental and vocal foray into the land of good grooves—it was sexy and sassy, with strings and innuendo stripped bare and smoothly built to lead anyone within earshot toward a classic climax. The song continued to impact via sampled revitalization from as far afield as TLC, Massive Attack, Eric B. & Rakim, and Big Daddy Kane. But don't forget that *Joy* is an entire album, with Hayes continuing his silky vocal assault across a further three slow, simmering songs. The best, and perhaps most interesting, is the closing "I'm Gonna Make It (Without You)." Markedly un-steamy, the song finds Hayes trading in his come-ons, choosing instead to open up and lay himself down in the wake of a broken romance. It's *Joy*'s most touching moment, equally on par with the opener. Indeed, with those two glorious bookends, this album becomes a must-have for any '70s soul aficionado. *—Amy Hanson*

Tough Guys / Mar. 1974 / Enterprise ♦♦
This 1974 soundtrack sounds pretty much like what you would expect—period funk, mostly instrumental. It's much more effective as background to screen action than home listening, where it sounds like backing tracks in search of vocals, or incidental grooves that need much more flesh on their bones. It's been combined with another 1974 Hayes soundtrack, *Truck Turner*, on the double CD reissue *Double Feature*. *—Richie Unterberger*

Truck Turner / Jul. 1974 / Enterprise ♦♦♦
This soundtrack was considerably lengthier and more varied than the one Hayes had released earlier in 1974 (*Tough Guys*), including Holiday Inn funk, a lugubrious vocal ("You're in My Arms Again"), and some jazz and blues riffs peppering the instrumental grooves. While the length ensured more variety, though, it also makes it a challenge to sit through the hour-plus program when you don't have images to fit the music. It's been combined with *Truck Turner* on the double-CD reissue *Double Feature*. *—Richie Unterberger*

Chocolate Chip / 1975 / Stax ♦♦♦
A fine mid-'70s album on which Isaac Hayes adapted to the disco era. His productions were already ideal for dancefloors, and he now updated his charts to include some stomping segments with horns and layered beats, while maintaining his soulful vocals on both uptempo tunes and ballads. This album got two Top 20 hits for Hayes and was his last really big hit album in the '70s. *—Ron Wynn*

Disco Connection / 1976 / ABC ♦♦
Appearing under the aegis of Isaac Hayes Movement, 1975's instrumental *Disco Connection* was sandwiched in between the mightily successful *Chocolate Chip* and the tongue-in-cheeky *Groove-A-Thon*, outstanding albums which defined Hayes' mid-'70s sound. Disco Connection, however, foundered in comparison, but still proved a hit with the fans, easily slipping into the Top 20 early in 1976. Focusing on groovy brass and blistering guitars, the album is best represented by the title track, which is an uptempo disco jam punctuated by Charles Pitts' mighty picking and sweeping strings. "Disco Shuffle," meanwhile, slows the pace but repeats the beats, again augmented by some fierce guitar. Elsewhere, and especially on "Aruba" and "St. Thomas Square," the set slides effortlessly into Hayes' unmistakably classic instrumental arrangements, which are so definitive and derivative of that era. *Disco Connection* remains largely forgotten, though, as Hayes' style slipped in and out of fashion. This LP in particular was perhaps a little too easy on the ear with its light sounds and the lack of a blockbuster hit. But while it's true that there are far finer ways to experience Hayes in all his glory, *Disco Connection* remains a slick reminder of the finesse which drove the simple arrangements of guitar, strings, and brass to such sweeping ends. *—Amy Hanson*

Groove-A-Thon / 1976 / ABC ♦♦
The title track employs "Shaft"-like guitar licks, but the similarity ends there: It's a lame attempt at disco done in by Ike's lazy singing and irritatingly banal lyrics. But it's the LP's only sore point. Ike returns to his roots on "Your Loving Is Much Too Strong," a slow, romantic ballad that he and his girls, Hot Buttered Soul Unlimited, make you feel. "Rock Me Easy Baby," a slinky, syncopated shuffle, has more groove appeal than the vaunted "Groove-A-Thon," mainly because Ike constructs it for maximum soul appeal by running it for more than eight exquisite minutes. The uptempo happy-in-love ditty "We've Got a Whole Lot of Love" showcases HBS' sterling voices. Ike shows a different side on the soft, longing "Wish You Were Here," whose horn arrangements and backing vocals are simultaneously enticing and titillating. After a weak opening, the album settles into a comfortable groove, ending splendidly with "Make a Little Love to Me." *—Andrew Hamilton*

Juicy Fruit / 1976 / ABC ♦♦♦
This is the follow-up to his successful 1975 album *Chocolate Chip*. But what was so enduring and skilled on that effort doesn't show up here. By 1973, Hayes' hitmaking skill became streaky. On this effort, he seems to be in a holding pattern. Hayes doesn't make any significant strides forward and fails to expound on the melodic richness of *Chocolate Chip*. This starts off with the title track. "Juicy Fruit (Disco Freak)" is just one of those songs that had to happen. The song has no shame and features a two-minute intro of Hayes and his bandmembers at a "disco," whopping it up with some loud woman. Although this is the unquestionable nadir, with lyrics like "They say disco music is here to stay/And it will never go away," Hayes' trademark arranging skills bailed him out. By this time, Hayes' fans could tell one of his lackluster efforts from miles away. This is one. The ballad "Let's Don't Ever Blow Our Thing" clocking in at 6:08 is probably too long-winded for even his biggest fans. Being one of the more talented and underrated artists, Hayes was going to get one or two prime moments. The album's best track is the haunting "Lady of the Night." The song has Hayes perplexed and falling in love with a prostitute as he sings, "How many johns have come and gone/I wonder but I really don't want to know." That track is about as interesting as Hayes was going to get here. This album was oddly reminiscent of his mid-'70s disappointments *Tough Guys* and *Truck Turner*. Hayes sounds a little distracted throughout, and without any big hits, this album quickly came and went. *—Jason Elias*

New Horizon / 1977 / Polydor ♦♦♦
After 1975's classic *Chocolate Chip* and a strong production job for the Masqueraders album *Everybody Wanna Live On*, Hayes' subsequent work with ABC was often poorly executed and conceived, save for the one or two tracks that properly displayed his melodic genius. With his last ABC effort being a live album with Dionne Warwick that just didn't sell, some changes had to be made. This is the first effort for Polydor and it turned out to be successful partnership. With a new label, Hayes also began to record at Master Sound in Georgia rather than his studio in Memphis, Hot Buttered Soul. Both the label and locale switch seemed to freshen up his musical approach. This album didn't start off on the best footing though. Hayes' ghastly discofied cover of "Stranger in Paradise" shows little trace of his arranging skills or song picking abilities. The other dance tracks are markedly better. "Moonlight Lovin' (Ménage à Trois)" has him doing Barry White one better by bringing an extra woman into the mix. With its playful rhythm and sweeping changes, he sang gleefully about the "the rendezvous of me and you and you" and said *ménage à trois* enough times his until his "dates" thought it was their idea. On *New Horizons* Hayes turns in two of his best ballads. The meditative "Don't Take Your Love Away" has him going for more subtle surroundings in a style that suffered the most on his post *Chocolate Chip* work. On "It's Heaven to Me" he displays a winning vulnerability, and it is easily one of the prettiest songs he's ever recorded. Although some of the best tracks on *New Horizon* are available on compilations, the entire album is worth seeking out. *—Jason Elias*

For the Sake of Love / 1978 / Polydor ♦♦♦
Two of Ike's best disco takes—"Zeke the Freak," with its ultra-funky bassline, and the ear-buzzing "Shaft II"—act as adrenaline for the slower tracks here; also upbeat is the inspiring "If We Ever Needed Love." The rest of the songs are slow, romantic items, with Ike's traditional raps inserted in just the right spots. He tacks a rap onto the beginning of Billy Joel's "Just the Way You Are," slows it to a rush-hour crawl, and drains it for every drop of emotion he can; he uses the same technique on "Believe in Me" and the best performance—a slow, heartfelt rendition of James Taylor's "Don't Let Me Be Lonely Tonight." This is the best album from Ike in some time. *—Andrew Hamilton*

Hotbed / 1978 / Stax ♦♦
Isaac Hayes didn't equal his past production, compositional, or performance greatness on this release, although much of the material was good. It just lacked the magic that had become almost routine with his '70s efforts. There were no magnificently narrated, drawn-out tales of romantic woe or any memorable arrangements. Instead, this was a routine, if well-done, session. *—Ron Wynn*

Don't Let Go / 1979 / Polydor ♦♦♦
Isaac Hayes' 1977-1982 stint on Polydor had him often doing strong work that differed from both his efforts at Enterprise and ABC. By the late '70s, Hayes had refined and updated his sound and stopped recording in Memphis. Although this album's predecessor, *New Horizon*, wasn't a big seller, it certainly helped him adapt to the changing musical landscape. In turn, *Don't Let Go* has Hayes even more confident and comfortable with his new sound. The title track has Roy Hamilton's jaunty classic all but unrecognizable with Hayes' propulsive and expert disco take. With pushy horns, cooing background girls, and his subdued vocal, he effortlessly attained disco's sense of fun. The song's insouciance seemed to rub off on the rest of this album. "What Does It Take" has Hayes steaming it up with help from a high-pitched bassline and a subtle buzzing guitar. On the best ballad here, the teasing "Few More Kisses to Go," Hayes plays the pathway to adulthood as waits for his "precious moment," singing "girl's gonna be a full-grown woman, before this night is through." The best tracks on this album have Hayes' infallible sense of melody, but there are a few duds. His disco version of "Fever" comes off a little desperate and pointless. The last track, "Someone Who Will Take the Place of You," is a good angry ballad, but clocking in at ten-and-a-half minutes, it's a little too much of a good thing. *Don't Let Go* is Hayes' most successful effort for Polydor. *—Jason Elias*

And Once Again / 1980 / Polydor ♦♦♦
Hayes' late-'70s to early-'80s work with Polydor often gets forgotten, but even at its most mediocre, he changed with the times and it no doubt outstripped his last efforts for ABC. The success of 1978's *Don't Let Go* seemed to make the proceedings of this album more relaxed and confident. The ballads typify *And Once Again* more than anything else. Throughout most of the slow tracks here Hayes seems to be trying to attain a more thoughtful approach and seems to be reminiscent of his *Black Moses* era. His cover of "It's All in the Game" is slowed down a little bit and he gives a surprisingly impassioned vocal and an updated and deft arrangement. The entertaining "Ike's Rap VIII" has a glorious string arrangement and flows into a good cover of Angie Bofill's 1978 classic "This Time I'll Be Sweeter." Another ballad, "Wherever You Are" has an atmospheric and haunting melody that made up for the wobbly lyrics. The dance tracks here aren't great. Both "I Ain't Never" and "Love Has Been Good to Us" had rhythms and production values that were on the way out by the time this hit the shelves. Hayes seemed to give his best dance material for a production job with Linda Clifford. This effort didn't have an especially long chart run and was a chart disappointment in contrast to *Don't Let Go*. Although

there is nothing groundbreaking here, the sound arrangements and Hayes' vocals make this more than worthwhile. *—Jason Elias*

The Best of Isaac Hayes, Vol. 1 / 1986 / Stax ✦✦✦✦✦
A decent attempt to present some of Isaac Hayes' past hits on an anthology. But as one of R&B and soul's first concept and album artists, it's impossible to appreciate his contributions out of sequence. His early- and mid-'70s albums helped change the course of contemporary black music production approaches, and that can't be understood by listening to condensed versions of hit singles, or even just by hearing the singles themselves removed from the album context. *—Ron Wynn*

The Best of Isaac Hayes, Vol. 2 / 1986 / Stax ✦✦✦✦✦
These two compilations dutifully boil down Isaac Hayes' sometimes long-winded albums to their essential parts—in other words, they're both singles collections, highlighted by '70s landmarks such as "Theme From 'Shaft'" and "By the Time I Get to Phoenix." Fanatics may want to investigate *Hot Buttered Soul* and *Black Moses*. *—John Floyd*

U-Turn / 1986 / Columbia ✦✦
Long, long past his stellar 1970s heyday, by the mid-'80s Isaac Hayes was foundering. He was certainly still the master of his style, but, thrust out of his era and trying to bridge the gap by updating his sound, much of his 1980s output proved to be a deal-breaker for his fans. *U-Turn* hit the racks in 1986 and, from the absence of charting singles, apparently stayed there. Leaving behind the funky grooves of yesteryear but promoting their sweet soul undercurrents to the very fore, Hayes contemporized his sound on the perky opener "If You Want My Lovin', Do Me Right." The title was comforting, but the synth pop sonics must have been a shock to die-hard fans. There are some excellent turns, most notably his wrenching cover of the Freddie King classic "Hey Girl," which itself follows the latest installment in Hayes' "Ike's Rap" series of messages. This time, upset by the rampant drug use building during the decade, Hayes imbibed "Ike's Rap VIII" with a strong anti-crack message. Also of note is Hayes' take on the Four Seasons' "Can't Take My Eyes off You," which emerges as a quiet ballad orchestrated à la the Isaac Hayes Experience. At the end of the day, however, and despite the precious nuggets to be found on the album, there are far better ways to sample Isaac Hayes' delicacies than *U-Turn*—which leads, of course, to the inescapable truth that this isn't Hayes' best period—period. *—Amy Hanson*

• **Greatest Hit Singles** / Jun. 11, 1991 / Stax ✦✦✦✦✦
The best-available Isaac Hayes compilation, *Greatest Hit Singles* bypasses a couple of his later disco hits, but the result is a more unified sound that helps illustrate why Hayes was so important to the development of '70s soul. Of course, a major part of his legacy consists of the epic-length suites that helped usher R&B into the album age, and that facet of his work is necessarily underrepresented here. But as a concise, easily digestible introduction to Hayes' work, *Greatest Hit Singles* is indispensable. Hayes may have been a master of mood and flow when he crafted his albums, but his innovative, slow-building style also lent itself to indulgence. *Greatest Hit Singles* presents just what the title suggests—the single versions of these songs, which prune away Hayes' excesses and boil his core sound down to the bare essentials. Even if this doesn't capture the full scope of his talents, it still gives a sense of Hayes' genius as an arranger and the groundwork he laid for the R&B love-man archetype. There's only one of his trademark "raps" here, on "By the Time I Get to Phoenix," which is slimmed down to seven minutes. Everything else clocks in under five, which usually involves heavy editing. Oddly, for one of the most accomplished soul songwriters of the '60s, Hayes' solo hits tended to be covers; only four of the 12 tracks here are Hayes originals, and two of those were movie themes. His vision as a solo artist lay more in the elaborate presentation and, often, reimagination of his repertoire. If you want to experience the full-length versions, see Stax's two volumes of *The Best of Isaac Hayes*, or buy the original albums. But for a more concentrated dose of Hayes at his best, *Greatest Hit Singles* is hard to beat. *—Steve Huey*

Double Feature: Truck Turner/Tough Guys / 1993 / Stax ✦✦✦✦

Branded / May 23, 1995 / Pointblank ✦✦✦
Isaac Hayes launched a comeback in the spring of 1995 by releasing two records, *Branded* and *Raw and Refined*. *Branded* was a vocal album, while *Raw and Refined* was comprised of instrumental jams. Neither of them were a departure from the music Hayes made in the '70s—*Branded* was filled with laid-back, lush soul and *Raw and Refined* was a deep, dirty funk workout—but they were effective reminders of Hayes' influence on '90s soul. *—Stephen Thomas Erlewine*

Raw and Refined / May 23, 1995 / Pointblank ✦✦✦

The Best of Isaac Hayes: The Polydor Years / Feb. 6, 1996 / Polydor ✦✦✦✦✦
Isaac Hayes' stint with Polydor in the late '70s isn't always looked at as being one of his better eras. In fact, it's not looked upon highly at all by many of his fans. It's important to keep in mind, though, that Hayes had already seen enormous success and had released a sizable amount of legendary albums by the time the late '70s came around. In this respect, you really can't expect his later work to be on par with his classic early-'70s era with Stax—no one could one-up albums like *Shaft* and *Black Moses*. Plus, the late '70s wasn't a kind era for any early-'70s soul icons as disco and funk moved black music from behind closed doors and into the clubs. Hayes had learned this the hard way during his short-lived mid-'70s run with ABC Records where he struggled to even chart, not to mention score a big hit. So when you really look at things from a wider view, sure, Hayes' Polydor years—which began with *New Horizon* (1977) and ended with *Lifetime Thing* (1981)—weren't on par with his Stax years, but they were still successful nonetheless. Hayes became more of a singles artist than an album artist as he had been with Stax. Because of this, it's perhaps best to seek out a best-of such as *The Polydor Years* rather than bother with his individual albums. This album collects 12 of his best moments from the era such as the somewhat notorious "Moonlight Lovin' (Ménage à Trois)" and other disco-flavored songs like "Zeke the Freak" that may have not stormed up the charts but did fill the dancefloor on occasion. This collection provides the insight for fans about a difficult period in Hayes' career where he struggled to age gracefully and adjust to the jarring force of disco. It shows that contrary to popular belief, Hayes did find success during this era, even if it was only sporadic. *—Jason Birchmeier*

Ultimate Collection / Apr. 11, 2000 / Hip-O ✦✦✦✦
Since the majority of Hayes' most memorable work was during the '70s, this collection nabs 13 of its 16 tracks from that decade. The two later cuts that close the disc—especially the meandering "Ike's Rap" from 1986—are disposable. More problematic though is the surreptitious editing of Hayes' longer material like "Never Can Say Goodbye," "Walk on By," and "Joy" (although interestingly, not the nine-minute "Hyperbol"), which are all severely shortened from their original versions. Unfortunately that essential information is nowhere to be found on the outside sleeve or liner notes. That said, the meat of those extended songs is still represented in the edits, and Hayes' trademarked slow-burn soul/funk permeates the bulk of this collection. The decision to eliminate most of his soundtrack work—save for two tracks from *Shaft*—was a smart one, and except for the cliché disco of "Don't Let Go" and the upbeat rubber band groove of "Out of the Ghetto," the album sticks primarily to Hayes' unhurried funk. Not as good as it could have been even with the single disc restrictions, the *Ultimate Isaac Hayes* is a reasonable place to start exploring, but falls short of providing a well-rounded look at the legendary musician. *—Hal Horowitz*

Leon Haywood

b. 1941, Houston, TX

Keyboards, Organ / Brown-Eyed Soul, Pop-Soul, Northern Soul, Beach, Disco, Soul
Soul/funk journeyman Leon Haywood periodically dented the charts in the 1970s with hits that tapped into the grooves and musical hooks of the day's trends. An accomplished songwriter and arranger, Haywood never pretended to be an innovator, and his hits are cheerful derivations of '70s midtempo funk and romantic ballads, usually embellished by smooth string charts. His best material recalled the late-'60s/early-'70s Motown sound; on the slower material in particular, his vocals bore a resemblance to those of Marvin Gaye. Haywood's roots extend way further back than the '70s; he toured and recorded with R&B saxophonist Big Jay McNeely's band (which also backed Sam Cooke on the road) in the early '60s. In the mid-'60s, he had his first chart entry with "She's with Her Other Love," on Imperial. In 1967 he had a solid R&B hit (and small pop one) with "It's Got to Be Mellow," whose commercial soul sound betrayed his Motown influence.

He didn't come into his own as a solo artist until the mid-'70s, when he had big R&B hits with "Strokin'," "Come and Get Yourself Some," and "Keep It in the Family." His biggest single, "I Want'A Do Something Freaky to You" (with orgasmic female gasps and moans that made it pretty clear what "freaky" really meant), crossed over to the Top 20 pop listings. The disco-ish "Don't Push It Don't Force It" was his biggest splash, making number-two R&B in 1980. After the mid-'80s, he eased out of the record business into business ventures; in the 1990s, he produced blues albums by Jimmy McCracklin and others on his own EveJim label. *—Richie Unterberger*

Soul Cargo / 1966 / Fat Fish ✦✦✦

Come and Get Yourself Some / 1975 / 20th Century ✦✦✦✦
Released in 1975, *Come and Get Yourself Some* boasts one of Leon Haywood's biggest hits: the sexy, alluring "I Want'A Do Something Freaky to You," which L.A. gangsta rappers Dr. Dre and Snoop Doggy Dogg sampled on their 1993 smash "Nuthin' but a G Thang." A teen-age hip-hopper of 1993 might not have known the name Leon Haywood—who is someone the hip-hopper's Baby Boomer parents were more likely to be familiar with—but he/she no doubt knew Haywood's unforgettable melody from the Dre/Snoop single. Back in 1975, "Freaky" made *Come and Get Yourself Some* one of Haywood's best selling albums. "Freaky" and the title track were the album's biggest hits, although the rest of the material is also well worth hearing. Smooth, laid-back Northern soul items like "Consider the Source" and "This Feeling's Rated Extra" appealed to Haywood's diehard fans, many of whom he had won over with his 1967 hit "It's Got to Be Mellow." But a tougher, less sleek approach prevails on "Who You Been Giving It Up To," which recalls the Isley Brothers' "It's Your Thing." Unfortunately, *Come and Get Yourself Some* has been out of print since the '80s, and it had yet to be reissued on CD when the 21st century arrived. But the album is recommended to fans of 1970s soul, if they're able to track down a copy. *—Alex Henderson*

Leon Haywood Naturally / 1980 / 20th Century ✦✦✦✦
Leon Haywood is known for 1975's "I Want'A Do Something Freaky to You" and his 1967 hit "It's Got to Be Mellow," and the soul man wasn't doing badly in 1980, when he enjoyed a number-two R&B hit with the funky "Don't Push It, Don't Force It" and followed it up with the equally funky, equally infectious "If You're Lookin' for a Night of Fun." Both of those hits are included on *Naturally*, one of Haywood's strongest albums. Those who acquired the vinyl LP for its singles also found a lot to admire about the songs that weren't played on the radio, which range from the gritty "That's What Time It Is" (a James Ingram song) to the insistent rap gem "Lover's Rap." Haywood doesn't do any singing at all on "Lover's Rap"—he raps all the way through the tune, which was unusual for an R&B artist back in 1980. At the time, many R&B singers considered hip-hop a passing fad and doubted that it would last more than a few years; little did they know that it would be going strong 20 years later. Haywood's rapping on "Lover's Rap" indicates that he had been paying close attention to early hip-hoppers like Kurtis Blow and the Sugarhill Gang, and he deserves credit for acknowledging hip-hop at a time when many other R&B vocalists refused to take it seriously. However, "Lover's Rap" is the only tune on *Naturally* that has anything to do with hip-hop. This is a soul/funk LP first and foremost, and it's a record that Haywood should be proud of. *—Alex Henderson*

• **The Best of Leon Haywood** / May 21, 1996 / Mercury ✦✦✦✦✦
This 19-song collection on Mercury focused on his '70s output, including the hits "I Want'A Do Something Freaky to You," "Don't Push It Don't Force It," "Come and Get Yourself Some," "Keep It in the Family," and other small singles. It also has his 1967 soul hit for Decca, "It's Got to Be Mellow." *—Richie Unterberger*

Eddie Hazel

b. Apr. 10, 1950, Brooklyn, NY, **d.** Dec. 23, 1992, Plainfield, NJ
Guitar / Funk, Psychedelic, Hard Rock, Heavy Metal
Somewhat of a mythical figure, original Funkadelic guitarist Eddie Hazel pioneered an innovative funk-metal sound in the early '70s, best exemplified on his mammoth classic instrumental jam "Maggot Brain." His mythological reputation arises from his brief, mysterious era of productivity, a shadowy three-album cycle capped by *Maggot Brain* that came to a close as Hazel's drug problems began to trouble him. Even though Hazel's notable accomplishments are few—reserved mostly to the first three Funkadelic albums, a 1977 solo album, and legendary live performances—these accomplishments were highly influential. At the time, Hazel seemed a clear successor to the deceased Jimi Hendrix, one of the few black guitar players merging an acid rock approach with an R&B aesthetic. Furthermore, Hazel took things a step further, integrating a heavy dose of funk into his fiery guitar work as well, setting the precedent for successive Parliament/Funkadelic guitarists as well as later generations of funk-metal guitarists.

Though born in Brooklyn on April 10, 1950, Hazel grew up outside the city in Plainfield, NJ. As a youth, he spent most of his time playing the guitar. He met Billy "Bass" Nelson when he was only 12, and the two instantly began playing together, teaching each other to sing and play guitar. Once they met up with yet another local youth, drummer Harvey McGee, they began jamming together as a trio, trying to learn all the early-'60s Motown hits. In 1967, another much more established Plainfield group, the Parliaments, wanted to mount a tour. The George Clinton-led band needed a backing band, though, and when they went back on tour in September 1967, Nelson and Hazel were anchoring the rhythm section. In Philadelphia during a show at the Uptown Theater, Hazel met Tiki Fulwood, who was the Uptown's house drummer. The two instantly became close friends, going out partying after the show together. By the time they left Philadelphia, the Nelson/Hazel/Fulwood rhythm section was finally in place, a tight squad that spawned Funkadelic.

The band was essentially just a continuation of the Parliaments. With group member Calvin Simon gone off to the war, and with Hazel and Fulwood now in the group, the Parliaments abandoned their uniforms, donned extravagant costumes or street clothes, and began playing increasingly rock-influenced music driven by Hazel's dirty fuzz tone and Hendrix-influenced acid rock approach. The change to Funkadelic then became official with the introduction of Tawl Ross on rhythm guitar and Bernie Worrell on keyboards, resulting in a series of three landmark albums: the group's self-titled debut (1970), *Free Your Mind... and Your Ass Will Follow* (1970), and *Maggot Brain* (1971). The latter ended up being one of the group's more essential albums, primarily because of Hazel's guitar playing. In particular, the title track has become his legacy, an epic instrumental piece fashioned as an emotive eulogy that has become a perennial staple of the group's live shows over the decades.

Unfortunately, following Hazel's most promising moment and greatest accomplishment to date, his career began descending quickly. Clinton became frustrated with Hazel's and Fulwood's growing drug abuse, often cutting off their pay so that they wouldn't go spend it on illicit substances. These problems most obviously came to light on the follow-up to *Maggot Brain*, 1972's *America Eats Its Young*, where Hazel's role was minimal. The guitarist began working with fellow Detroiters the Temptations instead, contributing guitar and songwriting to *Zoom* (1973) and *Song for You* (1975). In his absence, Clinton integrated the potent duo of Gary Shider and Ron Bykowski into Funkadelic, and later Michael Hampton. Hazel returned from exile for 1974's *Standing on the Verge of Getting It On* and made strong contributions, but by the next album, *Let's Take It to the Stage*, he was again taking a secondary role to the new roster of Parliament/Funkadelic guitarists. While Hazel's role in Parliament/Funkadelic had diminished by the late '70s, the guitarist did record a solo album for Warner Brothers, 1977's *Games, Dames & Guitar Thangs*. The album featured instrumental covers of "California Dreamin'" and "I Want You (She's So Heavy)," along with a few songs written by Clinton and Bootsy Collins. The nine songs all prominently feature Hazel's lead guitar work along with a considerable amount of backing vocals courtesy of the Brides of Funkenstein. Incredibly rare and highly collectable as a vinyl-only release, the album remains one of the better P-Funk albums of the late '70s, highlighted by its guitar-heavy sound. Following this album, Hazel continued to play with Clinton in successive years, but his contributions were never major, and he slowly descended further into oblivion, eventually suffering from chronic stomach problems and ultimately dying on December 23, 1992, from internal bleeding and liver failure. In the wake of his death, two posthumous collections of unreleased material were released: *Jams From the Heart* and *Rest in P*. *—Jason Birchmeier*

• **Games, Dames & Guitar Thangs** / 1977 / Warner Bros. ✦✦✦✦
A hidden gem among the many Parliament/Funkadelic-affiliated albums released during the mid- to late '70s, Eddie Hazel's only official solo album may not sport any perennial classics and may be a bit short on content, yet it became incredibly revered in subsequent years following its quiet release. Part of this album's magnetic allure to P-Funk fans no doubt arises from its rare status as a considerable collector's item capable of fetching substantial prices. There's more to the album than rarity, though. Hazel never really garnered the acclaim he deserved as a pioneering funk-metal guitarist during his time, and this album showcases just how stunning his guitar abilities really were. Each of the six full-length songs on the brief album feature Hazel laying down fiery guitar solos over loose song structures while the rest of his bandmates hold the song together and the Brides of Funkenstein handle a majority of the vocals. The two epic covers of "California Dreamin'" and "I Want You (She's So Heavy)"—clocking in at six-and-a-half and nine-and-a-half minutes, respectively—demonstrate this perhaps better than anything else on the album, as the band spends more time jamming than concerning themselves with staying true to the originals. The other songs here are rather traditional late-'70s Parliament/Funkadelic songs written by George Clinton and Bootsy Collins that emphasize yet more of Hazel's manic lead guitar. Though this album doesn't exactly boast great songwriting or stand as a landmark album in the sense of *Mothership Connection*, it does feature some amazing guitar work on Hazel's part, clearly a vehicle for his soloing. And that in itself makes it great and worth hearing, particularly since the pioneering guitarist seemed to disappear into near oblivion after the *Maggot Brain* album, leaving fans with little recorded output to appreciate after his untimely demise. *—Jason Birchmeier*

Jams From the Heart [EP] / 1994 / JDC ✦✦✦

Rest in P / Apr. 18, 2000 / P-Vine ✦✦✦✦
Like *Jams From the Heart*, *Rest in P* isn't a full-length LP but rather a compilation of vault recordings dug up to satisfy P-Funk fans' insatiable hunger for Eddie Hazel material. A Japanese import, *Rest in P* actually manages to eclipse the brief four-song *Jams of the Heart* by featuring that material under different song titles as well as additional material. Standout moments include the three epic jams: "Juicy Fingers" (14 minutes), "We Three" (12 minutes), and "No, It's Not!" (nine-and-a-half minutes). These songs showcase exactly why Hazel became so revered among later generations of P-Funk aficionados—his '70s studio work, with the exception of "Maggot Brain" and "Free Your Mind... And Your Ass Will Follow," only hints at his Hendrix-like soloing ability. Note that this collection is primarily instrumental studio brainstorming and was never intended for release. Hazel's 1977 solo album, *Games, Dames & Guitar Thangs*, is recommended first, since it features a more polished sound actually intended for mass release, along with songs to actually accompany the jamming; unfortunately, that album is near impossible to find. Either way, this is still a fine collection of Hazel's unreleased studio work from the late '70s that will provide ample insight to this man's ongoing legacy as an under appreciated funk-metal guitarist. *—Jason Birchmeier*

Roy Head

b. Jan. 9, 1943, Three Rivers, TX
Vocals / Pop-Soul, Blue-Eyed Soul, Traditional Country, Rock & Roll
Actually a country and rock vocalist rather than an R&B star, Roy Head nevertheless cut one of the great pieces of uptempo soul in the mid-'60s. "Treat Her Right" on Back Beat made it to number two on the R&B charts and number-two pop, and the fact that Head was white was soft-pedaled in R&B circles while the song made its way up the charts. That performance alone was enough to qualify Head as one of the finest blue-eyed soul singers of the 1960s. But in fact, Roy was one of the most versatile stylists of the era, capable of hard R&B/rock tunes, mournful, soul-tinged country, and straight R&B and blues covers.

The Texan singer is remembered as a one-shot artist, but he actually cut many records (some under the auspices of noted producer Huey Meaux) throughout the 1960s on a confusing variety of labels. A few of these were tiny hits in the wake of "Treat Her Right," only a couple ("Just a Little Bit" and "Apple of My Eye") sneaking into the Top 40. Quite a few of his records were dynamic, sleek hybrids (in varying degrees) of soul, rock, and country, all featuring Head's cocky, confident vocals. In the 1970s, after several years without success in the rock or R&B fields, Head returned to country, and landed quite a few chart hits in the arena between 1974 and 1985. *—Ron Wynn & Richie Unterberger*

Treat Me Right / 1965 / Bear Family ✦✦✦✦✦
Read the title carefully; it's not "Treat Her Right," the title of Head's 1965 megasmash, but *Treat Me Right*, an entirely different song. Yes indeed, this is an exploitation release of material Head cut for a different label than the one that issued "Treat Her Right," repackaged after the hit to capitalize on its unexpected success. The final punchline is that, as exploitative as this LP is, it's quite good. The ten songs—mostly revved-up R&B, with a bit of country-soul thrown in—are solid evidence of Head's stature as one of the finest white soul singers of the '60s. The small combo R&B arrangements are spare and tight, investing even overdone standards like "Money" with excitement. Long out of print, it still shows up in the used bins from time to time and is worth picking up. *—Richie Unterberger*

Dismal Prisoner / 1972 / T.M.T. ✦✦✦
While ignored commercially, this was a very respectable piece of swamp-pop that showed Head capable of convincingly updating his white R&B sound into the early '70s. Produced by Steve Cropper, it falls somewhere between the vibe of Van Morrison's early-'70s albums and Tony Joe White; indeed, Head covers Morrison's "You Got the Power" and White's "Dismal Prisoner 0613" (on which White himself guests on guitar). Whether getting into horn rock, quasi-funk, or white soul, Head's vocals are consistently fine and assured, complemented by suitably rootsy Southern rock/R&B arrangements. *—Richie Unterberger*

Slip Away: His Best Recordings / Aug. 5, 1993 / Collectables ✦✦✦

• **Treat Her Right: The Best of Roy Head** / Aug. 29, 1995 / Varese ✦✦✦✦✦
This is a long overdue anthology of Head's best sides, mostly recorded for the Back Beat label in the mid-'60s. Besides "Treat Her Right," it has all five of his other singles that dented the charts at the time. These aren't necessarily the highlights of these 18 tracks; "Pain" is country-soul moan at its best (although it's a thinly veiled rewrite of Lonnie Mack's "Why"), "To Make a Big Man Cry" is his best foray into country-pop from the period, and "You're (Almost) Tuff" is one of his toughest rockers, with a sound that almost verges on Texas garage. This collection is the most solid evidence of Head's superb talents, which were never rewarded with the consistent material or national recognition he deserved. *—Richie Unterberger*

Texas Soul and Country Man: The Crazy Cajun Recordings / Jul. 27, 1999 / Edsel ✦✦✦✦
It's good to see that music lovers worldwide are finally recognizing Roy Head. The Texas wailer got busy on soul radio in the '60s with the ladies' favorite "Treat Her Right,"

included here. Head wriggled more than Presley and could out-sing Conway Twitty without the flashy, theatrical props of showmen like Wayne Cochran. This is pure, uncompromising, gutbucket soul with many standouts including "I Can't Stand It," Johnny Ace's "Pledging My Love," "Don't Want to Make It Too Funky," and "Get Out of My Life Woman," a cuttin' rendition of Lee Dorsey's classic. This 15-song import showcases Head at his down-to-earth best and includes some country cuts, but there's no big style change between Head's soul songs and his country songs; he meshes both genres well. *—Andrew Hamilton*

The Headhunters

f. 1973

Group / Crossover Jazz, Fusion, Soul-Jazz, Worldbeat, Jazz-Funk, Funk

The Headhunters represented a major turning point for Herbie Hancock, whose approach to fusion became slicker and more commercial (though not without substance or integrity) with the formation of this popular band in 1973. Before that, the chameleonic pianist/keyboardist had been leading a daring unit called the Sextant, which fused jazz, R&B and rock with world music and took more than its share of chances. But regrettably, the Sextant's three albums for Warner Bros. were modest sellers at best, so in 1973, he disbanded the Sextant and formed the Headhunters. Employing saxman/clarinetist Bennie Maupin (a holdover from the Sextant), bassist Paul Jackson Jr., drummer Harvey Mason and percussionist Bill Summers, Hancock made a point of being more accessible when he unveiled the Headhunters with his 1973 Columbia date *Head Hunters*. Fusing jazz with funk and rock, the album sold over a million copies and attracted many R&B and rock fans. In fact, *Head Hunters* even outsold Miles Davis' popular *Bitches Brew*. Defined by the catchy "Chameleon" (which was interpreted by jazz singer Eddie Jefferson in 1976 and sampled by various rappers in the 1980s and 1990s) and a funky remake of his 1962 boogaloo "Watermelon Man," *Head Hunters* set the tone for subsequent Columbia projects with the Headhunters, including *Thrust* (1974), *Man-Child* (1975), *Secrets* (1976) and *Sunlight* (1977).

By the end of the decade, the Headhunters were no more, and Hancock was turning his attention to everything from outright R&B to standards and acoustic post-bop. In the 1990s, Sony's Legacy label reissued most of the Headhunters' work on CD, and in 1998 the group reunited to record *Return of the Headhunters!* *—Alex Henderson*

● **Survival of the Fittest** / 1976 / Arista ♦♦♦♦♦

In 1975, Herbie Hancock's group the Headhunters, which brought him immense success at the time, released their first solo album. Produced by Hancock, but without his participation, the lineup features the *Thrust* group of Mike Clark on drums, Paul Jackson on bass, Bill Summers on percussion and Bennie Maupin on various reeds, plus new guitarist DeWayne "Blackbird" McKnight, who toured with Hancock and was on the *Man-Child* and *Flood* albums. They added a few guests: three further percussionists (Zak Diouf, Baba Duru and Harvey Mason—the latter was the first Headhunters drummer) and flute player Joyce Jackson. While the thought of a Hancock-less Headhunters might puzzle some listeners, the group did extremely well without him—in fact, *Survival of the Fittest* may be the ultimate space-funk album. The interplay between all musicians is tighter than tight, especially in the rhythm section of Jackson-Clark-Summers, who can effortlessly make everything groove and move. The first track, "God Make Me Funky," marks Jackson's debut as a lead vocalist—a role he unfortunately wouldn't reprise too often. While his singing is a bit off-key, his vocals owe much to the blues tradition and carry great urgency and authenticity. At the end of the song, his voice is quite reminiscent of Ray Charles. The track starts off as a funky R&B number (the beginning bears close resemblance to their earlier "Palm Grease"), with background vocals being provided by the Pointer Sisters; it then turns into a fast chase with an intense, frantic Bennie Maupin solo which borders on the atonal. "Mugic" starts off like the funk version of "Watermelon Man" and turns out to be a showcase for Bill Summers' various percussion instruments. "Here and Now" starts aimlessly, develops into a lopey groove and gains speed as Maupin delivers another excellent solo, accompanied by ethereal guitar sounds. "Daffy's Dance" is in a similar vein, though it's rhythmically more consistent and has a rather funny melody. "Rima" is extremely spacy—McKnight's guitar serves as a substitute for keyboards and produces lots of freaky sounds; Joyce Jackson's echoey alto flute provides a good counterpart for Maupin's bass clarinet; Summers adds atmospheric percussion, and the groove is very subdued. The last track, "If You've Got It, You'll Get It," returns to a funk/R&B mode, featuring a catchy bass riff and a sing-along chant, though this time McKnight steps into the solo spotlight. *Survival of the Fittest* is consistently interesting and features lots of great performances by excellent musicians—and it never forgets to groove. Unfortunately, the album is out of print and was only issued on CD in Japan. *—Chris Genzel*

Return of the Headhunters! / Jul. 21, 1998 / Verve Forecast ♦♦♦

After a two-decade-long hiatus, Herbie Hancock's Headhunters returned to action in 1998 with their funk groove pretty much intact, allowing for some technological and stylistic updating. The core of the band—the too-long-neglected Bennie Maupin (saxes, bass clarinet), Paul Jackson (bass), Bill Summers (percussion), and the group's second drummer Mike Clark—still has the complex funk telepathic interplay down pat, though occasionally the rhythms are simplified for contemporary audiences. Hancock himself only appears on four tracks, where he tries to comp and stomp out on latter-day digital instruments (alas, he doesn't quite generate the same superfunky feeling that he once could on analog clavinets, Fender-Rhodes pianos and ARP synths). Billy Childs fills the keyboard chair in more genteel fashion on the other six tracks, with occasional help from Patrice Rushen, Mark Goodman and Darrell Smith. The main hangup here is that the revived Headhunters didn't come up with much memorable material, the strongest tracks being the back-to-1974 retro workout "Funk Hunter," and the rhythmically tricky "Kwanzaa," and "Watch Your Back," which features the obligatory rap honoring elder statesmen of music (strange how reverential the nominally rebellious younger set often can be). *—Richard S. Ginell*

The Heartbeats

f. 1955, Jamaica, NY, **db.** 1958

Group / Doo Wop, R&B

Lead singer James "Shep" Sheppard co-wrote a series of velvety doo wop ballads for the Heartbeats during the mid-'50s; one entry, "A Thousand Miles Away," was a huge R&B seller in 1956. The Queens, NY, quintet began their string of street-corner classics with "Crazy for You" and "Darling How Long," culminating with "A Thousand Miles Away." The Heartbeats recorded for Hull, Rama, Roulette, Gee, and Guyden before packing it in. In 1961 the lead singer formed a new trio, Shep & the Limelites, and scored on the charts with a heartwarming sequel to his first hit, "Daddy's Home," for Hull. "Our Anniversary" also sold well for the trio the next year, but they broke up soon thereafter. Sheppard was found dead in his auto on the Long Island Expressway in 1970. *—Bill Dahl*

● **The Best of the Heartbeats** / Apr. 1990 / Rhino ♦♦♦♦♦

Here's a one-stop shopper that really rings the bell. This 20-track set not only brings all of the cool tracks by the Heartbeats together (their biggie was "A Thousand Miles Away"); it also ropes in the later hits by Shep & the Limelites, who followed the storyline with subsequent efforts like "Daddy's Home" and "Our Anniversary." The song selection is primo, the sound is stellar, and the notes from doo wop mavens Phil Groia and Donn Fileti are exhaustive and informative. Vocal group compilations don't get much better than this. *—Cub Koda*

For Collectors Only / Feb. 21, 1992 / Collectables ♦♦♦♦♦

This features all of the Heartbeats and Shep & the Limelights' best recordings—two groups with slightly different lineups and one strong constant: James Sheppard on lead vocals. The 40 tracks make this collection definitive, but some may balk at paying for two discs worth of material. Sheppard's smooth tenor was obviously a source of inspiration for George "Smitty" Smith, the Manhattans' original lead singer, who sang with a similar ache in his tenor. There are many timeless pieces here, most written by Sheppard, to warm your heart, including "A Thousand Miles Away," "Down on My Knees," "500 Miles to Go," "Three Steps From the Altar," "Our Anniversary," "Daddy's Home," and "What Did Daddy Do." A slow-song specialist, Sheppard did many uptempo tunes with both the Heartbeats and the Limelights, making this a varied collection. *—Andrew Hamilton*

Daddy's Home / Jun. 18, 1996 / Remember ♦♦♦♦

Here is a nice 20-track collection of the two groups both led by James "Shep" Sheppard. "Daddy's Home" was the answer song by Shep & the Limelites to the Heartbeats' "A Thousand Miles Away," and some of the follow-ups that continued the story sequence are aboard here. Sheppard was one of the smoothest of all the doo wop balladeers, and this collection is classic George Goldner (the group's producer) New York-style vocal group every note of the way. There is an extra bonus with some of the tracks being in true stereo, a rarity in doo wop records. *—Cub Koda*

The Hearts

f. New York, NY [The Bronx]

Group / R&B

The R&B vocal group the Hearts—high schoolers Louise Harris, Joyce West, Hazel Crutchfield and Forestine Barnes—was originally assembled by Bronx, NY-based Zell Sanders, an aspiring composer who recruited the girls to rehearse her songs. Accompanied by Sanders' neighbor Rex Garvin on piano, the Hearts cut the single "Lonely Nights" for the tiny Baton label, scoring one of the earliest girl group hits when the record reached the R&B Top Ten in 1955.

It looked like the group might never be heard from again when in 1963 the Hearts returned to the charts with "Dear Abby"; none of the original members remained, however—by now Sanders ran her own label, J&S Records, for which the same five vocalists (Johnnie Louise Richardson, Ethel Davis, Mary Sue Wells, Yvonne Bushnell, and Ada Ray) recorded under a variety of aliases including not only the Hearts but also the Poppies, the Z-Debs and, most famously, the Jaynetts, to whom the 1963 classic "Sally Go 'Round the Roses" was credited. Rex Garvin, meanwhile, later cut a series of underground soul classics backed by his group the Mighty Cravers. *—Jason Ankeny*

● **I Feel So Good** / 1959 / Zells ♦♦

The Hearts of Stone

Group / Soul, Motown

The Hearts of Stone popped up unexpectedly on Motown's VIP label in 1970 with the album *Stop the World: We Wanna Get Off.* Surprising, since artists like the Velvelettes, Carolyn Crawford, Barbara Randolph, the Satintones, Kim Weston, and others hadn't been honored with album releases, yet this unknown group gets one produced by Henry Cosby. The album wasn't Motown and sounds as if it would have fared better in the late '50s or early '60s than 1970. The members were John Myers, Lindsey Griffin, Floyd Lawson, and Carl Cutler.

Myers had been around, first with the Five Pennies on Savoy on "Mr. Moon" b/w "Let It Rain" (1955), "My Heart Trembles" b/w "Money" (1956), and unreleased tracks on the Herald label; the Chimes, with Freddie Scott on Arrow Records, who made "Please Call" b/w "The Letter Comes This Morning" and "Lovin' Baby" b/w "A Faded Memory" both in 1957; the Four Jokers "Written in the Stars" b/w "The Runaround" on Sue in 1958; and the Four Pennies "You Have No Time to Lose" b/w "You're a Gas With Your Trash," on Brunswick in 1964. The Five Pennies consisted of Clifford Curry, Constance Holloway, Booker T. Washington, and Herbert Myers, John's brother. The Five Pennies backed Big Miller on his 1955 Savoy release "All Is Well" b/w "Try to Understand." Herbert also sang with James in the Four Jokers.

VIP Records issued two singles by the Hearts of Stone from their album: "It's a Lonesome Road," a fast upbeat number with a gospel flavor and secular lyrics, and "If I Could Give You the World" (1971), a midtempo song with a sluggish beat that came out ten years too late. It's unclear what happened to the group after their stint with Motown, but it's believed that John Myers drifted into gospel music. *—Andrew Hamilton*

● **Stop the World: We Wanna Get Off** / 1970 / Motown ✦✦
This is a very odd Motown release. Didn't they have quality control? It's not even the Motown sound, and there isn't a memorable tune in the bunch. The singles did absolutely nothing on the charts. More deserving Motown artists like the Velvelettes and Carolyn Crawford never had an LP release on Motown, and yet, the label dropped this disaster. Henry Cosby produced *Stop The World We Wanna Get Off*, a poor effort that doesn't come close to his Stevie Wonder productions. *—Andrew Hamilton*

Heatwave

f. 1975, **db.** 1984

Group / Quiet Storm, Urban, Disco

Completely cosmopolitan with international grooves to spare, Heatwave emerged as one of the disco era's funkiest dance groups. American serviceman brothers Johnnie Wilder and his brother Keith Wilder were based in Germany when they first began performing, and upon their discharge from the Army, the duo stayed in that country. Both singers, the pair gigged in clubs and bars with an assortment of bands while still enlisted. However, they were constantly looking to expand their horizons, and in mid-year they relocated to the U.K. to link up with songwriter/keyboardist Rod Temperton. The nascent Heatwave quickly came together with the addition of Spanish bassist Mario Mantese, Czechoslovakian drummer Ernest Berger, and American guitarists Jesse Whitten and Eric Johns. With so many musical roots between them, it was only natural that they rapidly developed a sophisticated sound, an edge which Temperton would use to push Heatwave ahead of their peers.

Jamming, and ceaselessly touring the London club circuit allowed Heatwave to define and refine their music, eschewing straight disco beats for a sound that certainly contained that element, but fused it with a rich funk groove. That hard work paid off as the band signed to U.K. label GTO (Epic in the U.S.) and began formulating their first album in fall 1976. They were paired in the studio with GTO house producer/session guitarist Barry Blue, who'd had his own string of hit singles ("Dancing on a Saturday Night" and "Do You Wanna Dance" among them) in the early '70s. A pair of singles, "Ain't No Half Steppin'" and "Super Soul Sister," appeared before the end of 1976, followed by January 1977's anthemic "Boogie Nights." That single reached number two on the British pop charts (it wouldn't appear on the American radar until later that summer, when it became a Top Five hit). The group's long-awaited debut album, *Too Hot to Handle*, finally appeared in late spring 1977, giving Heatwave a number-11 hit in the U.S.—it cruised to number five on the R&B charts. The next single, the sweet soul ballad "Always and Forever," closed out the year with a number-two U.S. hit in December.

Although their star power seemed unstoppable, Heatwave were to take some hard knocks, as Johns and Temperton quit the band. Although Temperton would continue writing new songs for Heatwave, he swiftly became better-known for his songwriting for other artists, penning award-winning songs for some of funk's heaviest hitters, including Rufus and the Brothers Johnson. He also wrote for Herbie Hancock and Quincy Jones, but his most famous partnership remains the one forged with Michael Jackson, writing two songs, "Rock With Me" and "Off the Wall," for Jackson's 1979 *Off the Wall* LP. He then returned to Jackson's camp in 1982 with three songs for the *Thriller* LP, including the seminal title track.

Heatwave received another dismal blow as Roy Carter left to carve his own path as a producer, ultimately having major success with Linx in the early '80s, and just as it seemed that the band might finally put their shake-ups behind them, founder Johnnie Wilder was himself involved a terrible car crash. Although he survived the accident, he was paralyzed from the neck down. Determined to continue working with the band he'd nurtured since the very beginning, Wilder remained on board for studio work and Temperton again provided the songs. Heatwave's spotlight seemed to be waning though, as the November 1980 single "Gangsters of the Groove" proved to be their last pop hit, reaching number 21 in the U.S. Derek Bramble quit the band at the end of 1982, like Carter, for a career in production (he would go on to work with David Bowie on 1984's *Tonight* LP, and later mastermind Jaki Graham's breakthrough). J.D. Nicholas, too, decamped to fill Lionel Richie's shoes in the Commodores. At the end of a staggering series of departures, the remaining members of Heatwave essentially brought down the curtain—the band was rendered inactive, and for all intents disbanded. *—Amy Hanson*

Too Hot to Handle / 1976 / Epic ✦✦✦✦
This was the debut album from the soul/funk ensemble, and it was well received by R&B and pop fans. Their initial release was the disco anthem "Boogie Nights." From the suspenseful, interlude-like intro to the adamant vocal delivery, the single had a lasting effect on the charts. It peaked at numbers five and two on the *Billboard* R&B and pop charts, respectively. The ballad "Always and Forever" was and continues to be a ageless piece. Johnnie Wilder's vocal exhibition throughout the vamp is breathtaking. It peaked at number two on the *Billboard* R&B charts. These two releases were respectively certified platinum and gold singles. Heatwave did not waste any recording time. This album employs nothing but quality tracks. The moderately paced "Ain't No Half Steppin'" was received warmly by radio, and it remains a staple. While Rod Temperton was writing excellent songs, Johnnie Wilder's supreme vocals gave the songs their identity. *—Craig Lytle*

Central Heating / 1977 / Epic ✦✦✦✦
If you could use only one adjective to describe Heatwave's sound, it would be "smooth." The band's romantic ballads and slow jams were the epitome of smooth, and that adjective also describes many of their uptempo funk grooves. This isn't to say that Heatwave's funk lacked grit—it had plenty of grit, but even so, it was an undeniably smoother style of funk than Parliament/Funkadelic, James Brown, Tower of Power, Rick James, or the Bar-Kays. In fact, when Kool & the Gang switched to a smoother, sleeker approach in 1979 and hired J.T. Taylor as its new lead vocalist, Heatwave was a big influence. The Kool & the Gang that emerged on 1979's *Ladies' Night* is certainly a lot more Heatwave-like than the gutbucket, down-and-dirty Kool & the Gang of "Jungle Boogie" and "Hollywood Swinging." And it isn't hard to hear the parallels between Taylor and Heatwave's Johnnie Wilder. It's safe to assume that when Kool & the Gang was reinventing itself, its members had *Too Hot to Handle* and *Central Heating* in their collections. With this excellent sophomore effort, Heatwave lived up to the promise it showed on *Too Hot to Handle*. The invigorating funk smash "The Groove Line" became a disco-era anthem, and the album's other big hit, "Mind Blowing Decisions," is a quiet-storm classic. From uptempo funk grooves like "Party Poops" and "Put the Word Out" to the romantic Northern soul of "Happiness Togetherness" and "Leaving for a Dream," *Central Heating* is among Heatwave's strongest releases. *—Alex Henderson*

Hot Property / 1978 / Epic ✦✦✦✦
Heatwave's third album, *Hot Property*, marked the first time one of their records wasn't produced by Barry Blue; instead of using Blue, the band went with Phil Ramone this time out. *Hot Property* isn't quite in a class with *Too Hot to Handle* or *Central Heating*, and its main single, "Eyeballin'," isn't the disco-era anthem that "The Groove Line" became. Nonetheless, the album has a lot going for it. Once again, Heatwave are as convincing on uptempo numbers as they are on slower material. "Eyeballin'" (not to be confused with the Mass Production song), "Raise a Blaze," and "One Night Tan" are infectious examples of the type of smooth funk that Heatwave did so well, while "That's The Way We'll Always Say Goodnight" and the Stylistics-influenced "First Day of Snow" demonstrate that the band were equally appealing on romantic ballads and slow jams. To their credit, Heatwave weren't afraid to bring jazz and Latin influences to their R&B foundation: "Therm Warfare" and "Razzle Dazzle" are funk-dance numbers with jazz overtones, while the exuberant "Disco" contains hints of Brazilian music. If you already have *Too Hot to Handle* and *Central Heating* in your collection, *Hot Property* is the next Heatwave album to acquire. *—Alex Henderson*

Candles / 1981 / Epic ✦✦✦
Heatwave had come a long way from 1977's smash "Boogie Nights" by the time the decade rolled over. They still were masterfully pulling together a smooth blend of soul, funk, and disco, but numerous lineup changes over two years took their toll. At the same time, though, the ease with which they brought a more subtle texture to their music was testament to their enduring dedication. And even through vocalist Johnnie Wilder Jr. elsewhere was paralyzed in an automobile accident before recording, he was able to return to the band to cut studio vocals for *Candles*, making this album a joyous occasion. Full of smooth soul breaks and fiery funk riffs packed around a healthy helping of pure disco, *Candles* does pale somewhat in comparison to earlier singles, but nevertheless remains a strong addition to the genre—no easy feat for any album appearing after disco's true heyday. By 1980, most bands had forgotten how important a good groove was in their haste to synthesize anything not nailed down. Heatwave did not. And that is reflected across this album. From "Gangsters of Groove," which gave the band their hit, to the effusive "Jitterbuggin'" and the absolutely marvelous "Turn Around," Heatwave keeps their feet firmly in organic territory. Johnnie Wilder Jr.'s elsewhere "Goin' Crazy," meanwhile, could still turn in a slab of soft funk. *Candles* also boasts a staggering five tracks penned by former bandmate Rod Temperton, now carving out a career penning hits for Michael Jackson and Rufus, among others. The partnership he retained with his old crew certainly adds an interesting slant to their overall sound. This is a strong album, better perhaps than its predecessors given its resulting cohesion. The frenzy is gone, to be replaced by a sweet sound—a different kind of Heatwave, then; one which percolates, rather than hitting you straight on. *—Amy Hanson*

Current / 1982 / Epic ✦✦

Power Cuts / 1982 / Epic ✦✦✦
Released in 1982 as Heatwave fell into disarray, Epic's first hits compilation, *Power Cuts*, relied on the band's late-in-the-day heavy-hitters for the bulk of its content, then rounded out the sound with a heaping handful of hits from its first two albums, all but ignoring the (admittedly) less-than-stellar *Hot Property* altogether. With recent songs "Posin' 'Til Closin'," "Big Guns," "Look After Love," and "Lettin' It Loose" standing as an example of how Heatwave assimilated its earlier funk-fueled sound with the synth pop of the newer wave, it's up to the early hits to provide the blueprint of just how brilliantly U.K. disco could be done. Those examples lie in the band's two seminal smash hits, "Boogie Nights" and "The Groove Line," while several ballads, including Heatwave's 1977 smoker "Always and Forever," highlight the band's more traditional soul sound, leaving one wondering why they didn't include the absolutely stunning "Happiness Togetherness." That disappointment, though, is adequately compensated by the inclusion of the too-often-overlooked brass and disco funk of "Too Hot to Handle." With such a well-rounded set, it's up to the woefully miscast "Razzle Dazzle" to bob the aforementioned *Hot Property* above the surface. Devilishly hard to find, *Power Cuts* remains a fairly comprehensive look at Heatwave's too-often-dismissed canon, and a sure-fire bet for fans who want to sample the best of the band's last two LPs. *—Amy Hanson*

● **The Best of Heatwave: Always & Forever** / 1996 / Epic/Legacy ✦✦✦✦
Always and Forever is a masterful look at one of the funkiest disco bands ever to grace a DJ's table. This compilation, set up like most, is packed with hits in chronological order, showcasing not only a great dance set, but also the important chronicle of an underrated band. With the band's two smash singles "Boogie Nights" and "The Groove Line" kicking things off, this disc essentially traces Heatwave's history though their singles releases with a smattering of extra tunes thrown in for good measure. As a whole, the set is also

a record of the subtle changes in composition and performance that took the band from disco sensibilities to a richer and far more textured soft funk, most notably on "Gangsters of the Groove." Of course, there is some pure funk here too, and "Lettin' It Loose" is a reminder that this band did have a few other tricks up their sleeves. And, of course, since Heatwave are best remembered as a disco band, the fans won't be disappointed either. Special disco versions of "The Groove Line" and "Eyeballin'" replace regular album cuts. Rounding out the mix are "Central Heating" and "Happiness Togetherness," while the sweet soul ballad "Look After Love" closes the album as certainly as "Boogie Nights" opens it. Disco, funk, soul—Heatwave incorporate all genres with ease. And no matter how you categorize this band, there is a little groove for everyone. And while it's true that the band will never be lauded with the best of the best, they still recorded some absolutely delicious nuggets. *—Amy Hanson*

Heaven & Earth

f. 1971

Group / Quiet Storm, Urban

A vocal quartet that originally went by the name the Soul Majestics, and consisted of brothers Dwight Dukes (falsetto/lead tenor) and James Dukes (bass), Keith Steward (tenor) and Michael Brown (baritone). Under the direction of producer Clarence Johnson, they recorded four albums as Heaven & Earth: one for General Entertainment Corporation (GEC), three for Mercury (Phonogram) and one for WMOT. Brown recorded on the first album and subsequently departed the group in 1978 and was replaced by Dean Williams. Williams recorded on the second album, and he too then departed, being replaced by Greg Rose.

The group could not manage to retain a compatible fourth member, whose vocal input was essential considering he was the baritone. In 1982, Dwight Dukes departed the group and formed the trio Cashmere with McKinley Horton and Daryl Burgee, recording on Philly World Records. Later that year Steward joined the group, and shortly thereafter Heaven & Earth disbanded. Even though the Chicago-based quartet didn't shake up the charts with their releases, their recordings were absolute quality. In particular, the tracks written and produced by the songwriting/production team of Rodney G. Massey and Lawrence Hanks. Heaven & Earth is a must listen for vintage R&B lovers. *—Craig Lytle*

● **Heaven & Earth** / 1978 / Mercury ✦✦✦✦✦

Heaven & Earth's debut release on Phonogram (Mercury) featured a string of ballads, which highlighted impressive vocals, arrangements and harmonies. Dean Williams demonstrates his vocal prowess throughout the album. Beginning with "Let's Work It Out," he complements the song's vintage bass groove with his soaring baritone lead, reminiscent of Teddy Pendergrass. Dwight Dukes' vibrant falsetto shines through the romantic ballad "Distant Melody." Dukes and Williams blend their crafty vocals on the doo wop-seasoned "How Do You Think You're Gonna Find Love," which is accompanied by a splendid string and horn arrangement. The featured single, "Guess Who's Back in Town," is Heaven & Earth's longest-charting single (12 weeks) and highest charted single (R&B number 42) on *Billboard.* Williams' baritone simmers throughout the verses and choruses, and begins to get energized on the tail end of the last verse. During a time when Philippe Wynne of the Spinners was a dominant vocal force in R&B, this single is accented by the a cappella-harmonizing vamp of the group and Williams' soulful ad lib in Wynne fashion. *—Craig Lytle*

That's Love / Dec. 14, 1994 / Hot Productions ✦✦✦

This features the songs that winded down Heaven & Earth's recording career: the WMOT tracks. "Just in Time" originally appeared on TEC in 1980, but was licensed to the larger WMOT Records in 1981. "That's Love" is a haunting falsetto-led floater that's made for late-night listening; the vocalist, who has a similar sound to Damon Harris, delivers a heartfelt performance on "Just in Time," the most arresting of the nine selections. A natural tenor and a baby baritone front the majority of the tracks, all uptempo, including "I Really Love You," "He Don't Really Love You," "Kick It Out," and the infectious "You're a Blessing." "Give Love One More Chance," is one of those always-fresh beat ballads that recording companies often overlook. A minute-longer disco version of "I Really Love You" is included that's not on a previous version of this CD on Hot Productions. *—Andrew Hamilton*

Bobby Hebb

b. Jul. 26, 1938, Nashville, TN

Multi Instruments, Vocals, Guitar, Spoons, Arranger, Producer / Soul

Bobby Hebb made his stage debut on his third birthday, July 26, 1941, when tap dancer Hal Hebb introduced his little brother to show business at the Bijou Theater. Nashville establishments like The Hollywood Palm, Eva Thompson Jones Dance Studio, The Paradise Club, and the basement bar in Prentice Alley as well as the aforementioned Bijou Theater found Bobby and Hal dancing and singing tunes like "Lady B. Good," "Let's Do the Boogie Woogie," "Lay That Pistol Down Babe," and other titles that were popular at that time. Hebb's father, William, played trombone and guitar, and his mother, Ovalla, played piano and guitar.

Hal would eventually join Excello recording artists the Marigolds while Bobby, with so much musical influence and inspiration, would go on to pen hundreds upon hundreds of tunes, among them "Sunny." Georgie Fame and Cher charted with the title in England, but it was the original which reached the highest on charts in Europe and America. Covers by Frank Sinatra with Duke Ellington, Ella Fitzgerald, Stevie Wonder, Frankie Valli, Nancy Wilson, the Four Tops, Wilson Pickett, Dusty Springfield, and so many others ensured the song would reach audiences outside of those who heard and continue to hear it on Top 40 and "oldies" stations. But the song reached out beyond Top 40, climbing the country and R&B charts as well.

Hebb's influence goes far beyond "Sunny." When he joined Roy Acuff's Smokey Mountain Boys around 1952 in Nashville, he was one of the first African-American artists to perform on the *Grand Ole Opry.* Around 1958 Hebb tracked "Night Train to Memphis," a song written by Owen Bradley for Roy Acuff's Smokey Mountain Boys. After that Hebb worked with Dr. John and left Nashville for New York. Hebb eventually replaced Mickey in Sylvia Robinson's group Mickey & Sylvia, who originally hit with "Love Is Strange." The duo became Bobby & Sylvia after Mickey left for Paris. After Bobby & Sylvia, Hebb was represented by Buster Newman, the man who got 'Sunny' happening in a lot of different ways.

While other groups in 1966 like Remains and the Ronnie Spector-less Ronettes opened for the Beatles, Hebb was headlining the tour *with* the Beatles. After this, Hebb met comedian/composer Sandy Baron and the two got busy writing a Broadway show that never made it to Broadway. However, two of the songs—"A Natural Man" and a tune they were writing about Marvin Gaye, "His Song Shall Be Sung"—were picked up by Lou Rawls and released on MGM. The pair had actually rejected "A Natural Man" from their Broadway play. The original title of the song was "Natural Resource," but they doctored it up and gave it a different groove after Baron got Rawls interested in what became a huge hit for him. *—Joe Viglione*

Sunny / 1966 / Phillips ✦✦✦

Produced by Jerry Ross and arranged by Jerry Renzetti, "Sunny" emerged from a twelve-song disc released on the Phillips label, a division of Mercury records. Although Bobby Hebb is known as "the song a day man," he only composed three of the dozen titles included on this collection. The title track, of course, which was *the* song of the summer of 1966, "Yes or No or Maybe Not," and "Crazy Baby." The follow-up, "A Satisfied Mind," was also a Top 40 hit that year, but it wasn't until 1971, when Lou Rawls had a Top 20 hit with "Natural Man," did Hebb get another smash. A pity, and a definite statement about the music industry when a man as prolific and talented as Robert Von Hebb constructs and delivers pop tunes with a voice and feeling that crosses genres and ethnic boundaries. Kal Rudman himself penned the liner notes on the back of the disc (at the time he was R&B Editor of *Record World* magazine, a publication still missed by the industry). Rudman reports that "Sunny" hit number one in Detroit and the surrounding area on the R&B, pop, and country & western charts. A monster smash, with covers by Ella Fitzgerald, Frank Sinatra with Duke Ellington, *Star Trek*'s Leonard Nimoy, there is no doubt this is Hebb's signature tune, but according to Marty Balin of the Jefferson Airplane he has "a pocketful of Miracles," implying the author/singer who gave us "Sunny" has mountains of songs that the world needs to hear. The producer/arranger team of Ross/Renzetti also penned "Bread," the flip side of the first 45, and "Love Love Love" on this album. Ross & Gamble co-authored "You Don't Know What You've Got Until You Lose It," McCoy's "For You," and there's even Barry Mann & Cynthia Weil's "Good Good Lovin'." All in all, this is a very pleasant pop album that remains an important snapshot of an important artist at the peak of his powers. As Rudman notes in the liners, Hebb was hired by Roy Acuff at the age of 12 to perform at the Grand Ole Opry. Hearing this album again makes one wonder why it isn't mandatory for major labels to sign artists of Bobby Hebb's stature for a minimum of 200 albums. *—Joe Viglione*

● **Love Games** / 1970 / Epic ✦✦✦✦

Michael Henderson

b. Yazoo City, MS

Bass / Quiet Storm, Urban

Vocalist/bassist Michael Henderson has enjoyed successful careers as a player and performer. He moved from Yazoo City, MS, to Detroit in the early '60s, and was a session player. As a 13-year-old, Henderson played bass with the Fantastic Four, Detroit Emeralds, Billy Preston, and other Motown acts in 1964 and 1965. He later toured with Stevie Wonder and Aretha Franklin before joining Miles Davis. Henderson played and toured with Davis for seven years. When he met drummer/producer Norman Connors, Henderson pitched him some songs. Connors recorded "Valentine Love" on his *Saturday Night Special* LP, featuring Henderson with Jean Carne. This was his vocal debut, and it reached number ten on the R&B chart. Henderson wrote two other hits for the LP, "We Both Need Each Other" and "You Are My Starship," which peaked at number four.

Those successes landed Henderson his own Buddah deal in 1976, and in 1978 he got his first Top 10 R&B hit with "Take Me I'm Yours" for Buddah. Henderson recorded for Buddah from 1976 to 1983, earning his biggest hit in 1980 with "Wide Receiver," a number four hit. He moved to EMI in 1986. Henderson also recorded "Can't We Fall in Love Again" with Phyllis Hyman on her own LP, and sang with Bobby Womack and Johnnie Taylor, as well as producing the Dramatics. He also helped discover Cherelle, who was his next door neighbor in the late '70s. She sang background and toured with him for four years. *—Ron Wynn*

Solid / 1976 / Buddah ✦✦✦

Michael Henderson's solo debut *Solid* brought immediate recognition to the longtime backing vocalist/musician. The mesmerizing ballad "Be My Girl" was the first release, and it propelled Henderson to number 23 on the R&B charts. (He later produced the same song for the Dramatics.) Composed by Henderson, "Valentine Love" is an even more indelible ballad. The spirited, seductive sax introduction bows to a poetic narrative and a smooth rhythm in which Henderson gives a ample vocal exhibition. The single was originally featured on Norman Connors' *Slewfoot* album, with Henderson sharing lead vocal duties with Jean Carne. The injustice here is that Henderson's solo version was never a release, though it is just as good as the duet. (Connors' version peaked at number ten on the R&B charts.) The second release from this impressive debut release was the upbeat "You Haven't Made It to the Top." While it's clear Henderson has his own style, the Brothers Johnson come to mind on this number. The remainder of the album is pleasantly diverse. The Mississippi native's grooves are inviting, from blue-funk instrumentals like "Time" and the title track to the free-flowing "Let Love Enter," where he vocally strides into the lyric. Henderson interjects his jazz roots on "Treat Me Like a Man," setting an urban mood while he patiently pleads his case. The songs on this collection are truly R&B gems, and Henderson's efforts are underrated. *—Craig Lytle*

Goin' Places / 1977 / Buddah ♦♦♦♦♦
After doing plenty of R&B and jazz session work as an electric bassist (including a stint with Miles Davis), Michael Henderson started making a name for himself as a soul singer when he was featured on the Norman Connors hits "You Are My Starship," "Valentine Love" and "We Both Need Each Other." The Detroit resident went solo in 1976, and the following year, he delivered his superb sophomore effort *Goin' Places*. Henderson had become known primarily for seductive, classy, Marvin Gaye-influenced romanticism, and jazzy pearls like "At the Concert" (a duet with Roberta Flack), "Let Me Love You" and the title song didn't exactly change that. But he was also a top-notch funkster; "Whip It" and "I Can't Help It" boast some of the most wicked funk grooves of 1977. Henderson recorded several excellent albums, but *Goin' Places* (which first came out on Buddah and was reissued on CD by The Right Stuff in 1994) remains his crowning achievement as a solo artist. *—Alex Henderson*

In the Night-Time / 1978 / Buddah ♦♦♦
In the Night-Time was Michael Henderson's third album and his only gold album (although its successor, 1980's *Wide Receiver*, sold respectably). Fueling *Night-Time* impressive sales was "Take Me, I'm Yours," a charming duet with Detroit singer Rena Scott that went to number three on *Billboard*'s R&B singles chart and became his biggest hit. "Take Me, I'm Yours" certainly didn't hurt the singer/bassist's reputation as a master of smooth romantic soul; nor did sexy slow jams like "We Can Go On," "Whisper in My Ear," "Am I Special" and the title song (a number-15 R&B hit). Funk isn't a high priority on this Buddah date (which The Right Stuff reissued on CD in 1994), but what little funk it does contain is first-rate. As sophisticated and classy as Henderson was on ballads, the mostly instrumental "Happy" proves that he had no problem turning around and delivering the nastiest of funk grooves. *—Alex Henderson*

Wide Receiver / 1980 / Buddah ♦♦♦♦♦
Although Michael Henderson was best known for romantic ballads and smooth quiet storm grooves in the mid- to late 1970s, his biggest hit was the quirky funk smoker "Wide Receiver." When this 1980 gem soared to number four on the R&B singles charts and Buddah followed it up with another funk single, "Prove It" (Henderson's cynical commentary on the entertainment business), the R&B press acted like he had suddenly turned into George Clinton or Bootsy Collins. But in fact, the singer/bassist had always been capable of providing wicked funk grooves; anyone who had heard "Whip It" (not to be confused with the Devo hit) and "I Can't Help It" on 1977's *Goin' Places* or "Happy" on 1978's *In the Night-Time* could attest to that. The truth is that *Wide Receiver* isn't much different from Henderson's previous releases—hardcore funk jams take up one-third of the album at best, and romantic ballads, slow jams and quiet storm material dominate the self-produced *Wide Receiver* just as they had dominated *In the Night-Time, Solid, Goin' Places* and *Do It All*. It's just that this time, Buddah chose to give the funk tunes the most promotion; nonetheless, the quiet storm formats that favored smooth album tracks like "Reach Out for Me" and Henderson's cover of the Four Tops' "Ask The Lonely" knew that he hadn't abandoned them. Even though *Wide Receiver* contained Henderson's biggest hit, it wasn't his best selling album—that honor goes to 1978's gold *In the Night-Time*. But *Wide Receiver* sold respectably, and it was a valuable addition to his catalog. *—Alex Henderson*

● **The Best of Michael Henderson** / Oct. 25, 1994 / Sequel ♦♦♦♦♦
Definitive Michael Henderson courtesy of Britain's Sequel Records. Henderson career leaped from playing in road bands for artists like Stevie Wonder, session work, a featured vocalist on Norman Connors' albums, to stardom as a soloist. Unfortunately, his career descended even faster; surprising, since he had the ability to write and produce himself. Henderson duets with Phyllis Hyman and Jean Carne on some of these tunes, with the most spectacular being his titles cut under Norman Connors' name. The lilting, futuristic "You Are My Starship," "Valentine Love," and "Take Me I'm Yours," have adult themes and top-notch productions. His most enduring song "Be My Girl," became a big hit for the Dramatics, but I like Henderson's stark, sparse version better. As a solo act he went for a more commercial sound and the results had less appeal. "You Haven't Made It to the Top," "Wide Receiver," "Make Me Feel Better," and "(We Are Here To) Geek You Up," were formulaic attempts to reach the booming disco market. Remakes of "To Be Loved," and "Reach Out For Me," shows a flair for the past, but are only adequate. But you won't find a more absolute compilation of Michael Henderson's recordings anywhere. *—Andrew Hamilton*

Best of Michael Henderson / Apr. 18, 2000 / BMG ♦♦♦
When session bassist Michael Henderson got a chance to sing on Norman Connors' *You Are My Starship* album, everyone thought a lasting star had been unveiled. He came out solo smooth with a hypnotic "Be My Girl" that aesthetically topped his previous production on the Dramatics. He followed with a mixture of slow grooves and uptempo jams like "Take Me I'm Yours," a duet with Rena Scott, "You Haven't Made It to the Top," "In the Night-Time," and "Wide Receiver." Then, suddenly, creativity went south, but unlike migrating birds, never returned. Henderson resorted to rehashing Hal David and Burt Bacharach songs and ladling out subpar originals. The 15 songs tell an incomplete story; for example, the collection omits his update of "To Be Loved," originally by Jackie Wilson. After the tenth song, most interests will wane (some before that); this is where the exclusion of his pre-solo joints with Connors looms the largest. *—Alex Henderson*

Nona Hendryx

b. Oct. 9, 1944, Trenton, NJ
Vocals / Pop/Rock, Urban, Disco
One-third of the pop/soul act LaBelle (their big hit was "Lady Marmalade"), Nona Hendryx, by far and away, made the hippest solo records of any member of that group (the others being Patti LaBelle and Sarah Dash). After LaBelle called it quits in 1976, Hendryx released her self-titled debut record, which was an amazingly strong amalgam of soul and hard rock. It also went almost completely ignored by critics, soul fans, and even LaBelle fans, and Hendryx took her strong, clear, booming voice and did lots of session work in the late '70s and early '80s. It was here that she fell in with a hip crowd of musicians, specifically as a result of her time singing backup for the Talking Heads. This association with David Byrne led to her working with Bill Laswell, who, along with his band Material, helped Hendryx put together a second solo record entitled *Nona*. A strong album that's not as wild-eyed as her debut, *Nona* did spark greater interest in Hendryx's considerable talents, and after that, her solo career flourished to the point where she no longer needed studio work to supplement her income. Although some of her late-'80s records sound a little formulaic, Nona Hendryx is a dynamic, daring, and extremely talented performer, who, as is often the case, didn't receive the credit she's due. But unlike Patti LaBelle, who has chosen a career as the most histrionic singer in MOR soul/pop, or the relative invisibility of Sarah Dash, who sang backup for Keith Richards' Xpensive Winos, Hendryx has taken the road less traveled, and that has meant a more aesthetically rewarding and interesting career. *—John Dougan*

Nona Hendryx / 1977 / Epic ♦♦♦♦♦
Wearing skintight pants, black leather and brandishing a Bowie knife on the LP cover, Nona Hendryx announces her intentions loudly and clearly on her debut record. At the time, this record was unpromotable (hell, it would be today), mainly because the record company and radio stations didn't know what to do with a huge-voiced African-American woman who was comfortable and capable of singing hard rock as well as soul music. So, as usual, they turned their backs on the record and it disappeared almost as quickly as it was released. Which is a shame, because it's a nasty, relentless chunk of hard-edged rock and soul that was just a bit ahead of its time. Long out of print, but worth searching for. *—John Dougan*

Nona / 1983 / RCA ♦♦
After a few years doing session work, Hendryx, with help from the band Material, came up with this winner that drops the hard rock of her debut for a more Talking Heads-tinged pop/funk. Although the songwriting could be a little sharper, Hendryx's powerful voice gives the record focus and always commands your attention. Extra musical emphasis provided by Sly Dunbar, Jamaaladeen Tacuma and Nile Rodgers. *—John Dougan*

● **Skin Diver** / Jul. 1989 / Private Music ♦♦♦♦♦
A transitional album from the word go, Hendryx plays synthesizer and works with producer and former Tangerine Dream member Peter Baumann, and the result is this lush (at times too lush) pop record that sounds unlike anything else Hendryx recorded. Fans of her previous work may be taken aback by this record, but the dense, almost ambient, soundscapes she constructs and her always great singing make this a satisfying foray into uncharted territory. *—John Dougan*

You Have to Cry Sometime / 1992 / Shanachie ♦♦♦

● **Transformation: The Best of Nona Hendryx** / Jan. 12, 1999 / Razor & Tie ♦♦♦♦♦
A concise and well-assembled overview of Nona Hendryx's career, *Transformation* is the ideal opportunity to discover this unique performer—collecting 15 of her most noteworthy tracks, it includes the Grammy-nominated "Rock This House" as well as "Baby Go-Go," credited to one J. Coco (aka Prince). *—Jason Ankeny*

Clarence "Frogman" Henry

b. Mar. 19, 1937, Algiers, LA
Vocals, Trombone, Songwriter, Piano / New Orleans R&B, R&B
He could sing like a girl, and he could sing like a frog. That latter trademark croak, utilized to the max on his 1956 debut smash "Ain't Got No Home," earned good-natured Clarence Henry his nickname and jump-started a rewarding career that endures to this day around the Crescent City.

Naturally, Fats Domino and Professor Longhair were young Clarence Henry's main influences while growing up in the Big Easy. He played piano and trombone with Bobby Mitchell & the Toppers from 1952 to 1955 before catching on with saxist Eddie Smith's band. Henry improvised the basic idea behind "Ain't Got No Home" on the bandstand one morning in the wee hours; when the crowd responded favorably, he honed it into something unique. Paul Gayten (New Orleans A&R man for Chess Records) concurred, hustling Henry into Cosimo Matassa's studio in September of 1956. Local DJ Poppa Stoppa laid the "Frogman" handle on the youngster when he spun the 45 (issued on the Chess subsidiary Argo), and it stuck.

Despite some fine follow-ups—"It Won't Be Long," "I'm in Love," the inevitable sequel "I Found a Home"—Frog sank back into the marsh sales-wise until 1960, when Allen Toussaint's updated arrangement melded beautifully with a country-tinged Bobby Charles composition called "(I Don't Know Why) But I Do." Henry's rendition of the tune proved a huge pop smash in early 1961, as did a Domino-tinged "You Always Hurt the One You Love" later that year.

Frogman continued to record a variety of New Orleans-styled old standards and catchy originals for Argo (Chess assembled a Henry album that boasted what may be the worst cover art in the history of rock & roll), even recording at one point with Nashville saxist Boots Randolph and pianist Floyd Cramer. But the hits dried up for good after 1961. Henry opened 18 concerts for the Beatles across the U.S. and Canada in 1964, but his main source of income came from the Bourbon Street strip, where he played for 19 years. *—Bill Dahl*

● **Ain't Got No Home: The Best of Clarence "Frogman" Henry** / 1994 / Chess ♦♦♦♦♦
Scoring an unexpected novelty hit with the title track in 1956, Henry disappeared from the charts for four years before roaring back with two smashes in the early '60s, "(I Don't Know Why) But I Do" and "You Always Hurt the One You Love." Actually, Clarence recorded a fair number of singles for Chess' Argo subsidiary between 1956 and 1964 in the relaxed New Orleans R&B styles of his big hits. *Ain't Got No Home* includes 18 of these sides, most of which were previously unavailable on a U.S. album. Henry developed slightly over the course of his career, adding beefier horn sections that occasionally reached back to the spirit of Dixieland. Crescent City legends like saxophonist Lee Allen and pianists Allen Toussaint and Paul Gayten crop up on these sessions; when Henry traveled to Memphis for a session, he was backed by the all-star band of Bill Justis (guitar),

Boots Randolph (sax), and Floyd Cramer (piano). A bit more eccentric and unpredictable than Fats Domino, not as contemporary or inventive as, say, Lee Dorsey, Henry's vocals were consistently warm and humorous, his recordings always polished. That said, the hits remain the standouts on this collection. The rest is pleasant and fun, but don't vary much from the prototype or cause exceptional interest. A couple tracks worth noting are "I Love You, Yes I Do," an R&B ballad subsequently covered by several acts during the 1960s, and the 1964 single "Long Lost and Worried," written by a young Dr. John. The informative booklet includes a neat photo of Clarence with the Beatles, ironic considering that the British Invasion made types like Clarence an anachronism. *—Richie Unterberger*

The Hesitations

f. 1965, Cleveland, OH, **db.** 1968

Group / Soul, R&B

Cleveland vocal group the Hesitations specialized in soulful treatments of blatantly pop melodies, epitomized by their biggest R&B smash, a stirring 1968 rendering of the theme from the movie *Born Free.* Although their initial bow on the R&B charts in 1967 was titled "Soul Superman," the Hesitations were best known for items like "The Impossible Dream" and "Who Will Answer," hardly typical soul fare. Lead singer George "King" Scott died from a gunshot wound in February of 1968. *—Bill Dahl*

Soul Superman / 1967 / Kapp ♦♦♦

A solid Cleveland singing group who never were able to make it past the second level in soul circles, even though they were an energetic harmonizing unit. Their debut album got them a mild hit with the title track, but didn't do much beyond that despite the glossy leads of George Scott and some emphatic group support underneath him. *—Ron Wynn*

The New Born Free / 1968 / Kapp ♦♦♦

The Hesitations came as close as they ever would during their existence as a group with their second album. The title cut made it to number four, and they made a run of concert and television appearances. But the album itself was simply too thin material-wise, and while they managed to get a second Top 20 hit in "The Impossible Dream," all that did was type them as a remake group. *—Ron Wynn*

Where We're At / 1968 / Kapp ♦♦♦

Tragedy would strike the Hesitations in 1968, when lead singer George "King" Scott was accidentally killed by a gun owned by group member Fred Deal. They went down as one of those bands that couldn't get over the hump, even though they were fine harmonizers and Scott had been an above average lead vocalist. This album exemplified their plight; it had the necessary components for success, but just didn't click. *—Ron Wynn*

● **Let's Groove** / 2002 / Official ♦♦♦♦♦

This features Cleveland, OH's Hesitations' successful soul interpretations of pop favorites: "Born Free" and "the Impossible Dream"; Bobby & Richard Poindexter's lilting "Love Is Everywhere"; and a strong rendition of Sam Cooke's "A Change Is Gonna Come." These 23 tracks don't get the love their pre-"Born Free" tracks—considered classic four-on-the-floor Northern soul—receive. This is an injustice. The arrangements are more elaborate, the vocals more varied, and the songs classier. The pop remakes took precedent over the more traditional soul they cut during this period; but "I Wish It Could Be Me," "Overworked and Underpaid," and "Who Will Answer" are solid. A third try at pop remaking, the exhilarating "Climb Every Mountain," is also on board. Surprising, however, are the omissions of B-sides: "Nobody Knows You When You're Down and Out" and "If You Ever Need a Hand"; and both sides of "With Pen in Hand" and "A Whiter Shade of Pale," their final Kapp single. Not to mention the GWP sides where they backed Debbie Taylor. Not a complete picture, but still a wonderful CD. Arthur Blakely is a thrilling singer; his preachy Type-A tenor is countered by Leonard Veal's mellower Type-B vocalizing. *—Andrew Hamilton*

Howard Hewett

b. Oct. 1, 1955, Akron, OH

Vocals / Urban

Among the great pure vocalists of the Urban Contemporary era, Howard Hewett has seldom found material worthy of his tremendous skills. He grew up in Akron, OH, and relocated to Los Angeles. Hewett danced on *Soul Train,* and became one-third of Shalamar with Jeffrey Daniel and Jody Watley in 1979. They had several big hits before Hewett departed for a solo career in 1985. He signed with Elektra, and his second single, "I'm for Real," was a number-two R&B hit in 1986. The follow-up single, "Stay," also made the Top Ten, while "I Commit to Love" in 1987 reached number 12. Hewitt remained on Elektra through the '80s and into the '90s, earning another hit with "Strange Relationshp" in 1988, and cutting duets with Dionne Warwick and Anita Baker. He's also been busy as a writer, producer, and session vocalist. Hewett co-wrote and produced "Frustration" for LaToya Jackson in 1984, and sang on her LP *Heart Don't Lie.* He did lead vocals on LPs by Stanley Clarke and George Duke in 1984 and 1986, a duet with Stacy Lattisaw on "Ain't No Mountain High Enough," and sang with Firefox in 1986, as well as doing backgrounds on a Donna Summer release. *—Ron Wynn*

● **I Commit to Love** / 1986 / Elektra ♦♦♦♦

Howard Hewett made a smooth transition from being a member of the trio Shalamar to becoming a bona fide solo artist. His first single to hit the *Billboard* R&B charts was the romantically enchanting "I'm for Real." Too fast to be a ballad and not fast enough to be a jam, Hewett still captivated radio and his audience with this moderate number. The Ohio native glides from his lacerating tenor to his stirking falsetto highs supported by cogent backing vocals. The classic piece peaked at number two on the charts. The single "Stay" has a crossover appeal, but it never made a dent in the pop charts. It is not half as impressive as "I'm for Real." However, it did manage to show at number eight on the *Billboard* R&B charts. "I Commit to Love" falls short as well. It too is saturated with pop seasonings. Nonetheless, it tipped in at number 12 on the *Billboard* R&B charts. The final release was the inspirational selection "Say Amen," which is Hewett's personal testimony of being given a second chance after his battle with life's various vices. It has become an anthem among many. Inside ten weeks, it peaked at number 54. The shortcoming on this album is the material. As Hewett can deliver on the vocals, the songs do nothing for his talent as they lack excitement and mesmerizing melodies; the two elements commonly associated with his great voice. *—Craig Lytle*

Forever & Ever / 1988 / Elektra ♦♦♦

Howard Hewett's lack of solo success after leaving the group Shalamar was among the more frustrating stories of the late '80s. He had the vocal skills and the looks to be a major attraction, but couldn't get the consistently good material he needed. This 1988 album had three charts hits, including the superb "Once, Twice, Three Times," but just couldn't earn Hewett the star power he deserved. *—Ron Wynn*

Howard Hewett / 1990 / Elektra ♦♦♦

On this album, Howard Hewett has a string of solid ballads and midtempo numbers before bowing to some experiemental material. The first release was "Show Me." Hewett delivers a compassionate performance as he craves to make good on the lyric. For two consecuive weeks it held the number-two spot on the *Billboard* R&B charts. On a more midtempo note, the second single "If I Could Only Have That Day Back" comes across as a pop-oriented number. Nonetheless, the single is inviting; it peaked at 14. The third release "Let Me Show You How to Fall in Love" is groomed around a midtempo rhythm; it too has that crossover appeal as well. It peaked at 67 after only eight weeks on the charts. The misfortune on this album is that "When Will It Be" and "I Do" were never released. Both are moderate numbers. The former is a duet with the incomparable Anita Baker. The two gifted singers earnestly complement one another in a lyric centered around the bewildering quest for world harmony; the song is cradled in a elegant, jazzy arrangement that is contagious to any listener. Truly a great song. "I Do" slowly builds through the verse to the chorus. The change-up prior to the chorus is irresistibly engaging. As simplistic as the lyrics are, they are appealing as well. The midtempo and ballad numbers outshine the uptempo numbers. *—Craig Lytle*

Allegiance / 1992 / Elektra ♦♦♦♦

This is the follow-up to his 1990 hit *Howard Hewett.* For this, Hewett split the production duties between Tommy LiPuma, Narada Michael Walden, Barry Mann, Nick Martinelli, and himself. One would think that he would get lost in this, but the opposite becomes true. While on the surface this seems like a by-the-numbers effort, with its unearthly momentum, *Allegiance* is an oddly fascinating record. Hewett is a little intense to pull off the insouciant lover-man act as "Save Your Sex for Me" and the Prince-penned "Allegiance" proves. What Hewett is great at is melodic and hooky R&B/pop, and once *Allegiance* gets going it really doesn't stop. The best Walden productions, "Can We Try Again" and "Can't Get Over Your Love," have Hewett subtly attaining the sensuality he was begging for a few songs earlier. LiPuma places Hewett in the "sounds like a classic" pop-based direction and he gets to the point even faster. On the ballads "How Fast Forever Goes" and "Just Like a Woman," and the theatrical "Ronnie-O," Hewett gives a sense of believability and charisma with each line. This album is so charmed that the overwrought though well-intentioned inspirational number "To Thee I Pray" is enjoyable too. Unfortunately, *Allegiance* wasn't a big seller but it presents Hewett in great voice and displays his underrated range and likability. *—Jason Elias*

● **The Very Best of Howard Hewett** / Jun. 5, 2001 / Rhino ♦♦♦♦

Rhino's 2001 collection, *The Very Best of Howard Hewett,* is a terrific collection, containing a generous 16 tracks that span not only his solo hits, but "Heaven Sent You," the Stanley Clarke tune on which he sang lead, plus two songs that he sang for in Shalamar ("This Is for the Lover in You," "Somewhere There's a Love"). For most listeners, this is all the Hewett that's necessary, and by adding these unofficial Hewett recordings to the repertoire, they've made this the kind of record that's essential for most of the non-dedicated Hewett fans. *—Stephen Thomas Erlewine*

Hi Rhythm

f. Memphis, TN

Group / Southern Soul, Soul

Hi Records producer Willie Mitchell constructed his vaunted house rhythm section around three talented Hodges brothers during the late '60s: guitarist Mabon (nicknamed "Teenie"), bassist Leroy, and organist Charles. With drummer Howard Grimes (and on some of Al Green's sides, MG's trapsman Al Jackson Jr.) rounding out the lineup, this skintight Memphis quartet laid down surging, simmering grooves behind the entire Hi stable during the label's 1970s heyday: Green, Ann Peebles, Otis Clay, Syl Johnson, and Mitchell himself, to name but a few. Mitchell had patiently molded the unit since when the Hodges Brothers were in their teens (Grimes was a bit older, having worked as a sideman over at rival Stax during the early '60s).

As the succinctly named Hi Rhythm, they recorded the 1976 LP *On the Loose* and remained a cohesive unit well into the '90s, providing luxurious backing on Johnson's wonderful 1994 comeback set for Delmark, *Back in the Game.* Meanwhile, as the Hodges Brothers, they released a 1994 disc called *Perfect Gentlemen* on the tiny Velvet Recordings of America logo that also featured a fourth brother, Fred, on keys and veteran soul singer Percy Wiggins on several tracks. *—Bill Dahl*

● **On the Loose** / 1976 / Hi ♦♦

Originally released in 1976 during high times for Hi Records, this interesting album never got much exposure. The group is the basic Hi Rhythm section; the guys who backed Al Green, Syl Johnson, Don Bryant, Ann Peebles, and others in the studio. The lead vocalist on "Superstar," "Since You've Been Gone," and some other cuts sounds like Al Green on a beer binge. "I Remember You, Do You" sounds like a hit, a twist on the obvious. "Save All My Lovin'" and "You Got Me Comin'" are good Southern bar jams, while "Skinny Dippin'" is both humorous and lewd. *—Andrew Hamilton*

Hi-Tension

Group / Disco, Funk

This British funk group started as Hott Waxx in the early '70s before becoming Hi-Tension. Lead vocalist, primary songwriter, and keyboardist David Joseph, bassist Ken Joseph, guitarist Paul Phillips, percussionist Jeff Guishard, saxophonist Paul McLean, drummers David Reid and Paapa Mensah, trumpeter Guy Barker, trombonist Peter Thomas, and saxophonists Bob Sydor and Ray Alan Eko were the original lineup. Despite having an energetic, sometimes catchy sound, they never made much impact on American shores, although they were quite successful in Britain. "Hi-Tension" and "British Hustle" were big English dance hits in the late '70s. They resurfaced with an altered lineup in the mid-'80s on Streetwave. Ken Joseph, Leroy Williams, and Jeff Guishard tried to rekindle the sparks but didn't make much headway with a pair of singles in 1984 and 1985. *—Ron Wynn*

● **Hi-Tension** / 1978 / Island ✦✦✦

If you ask a British R&B expert about England's R&B scene of the 1970s, two of the names that will inevitably come up are Hot Chocolate and Hi-Tension. Hot Chocolate wasn't as big in the U.S. as it was in England, but at least American R&B fans know that band for "You Sexy Thing" and "Everyone's A Winner"—most American R&B fans have never even heard of Hi-Tension, although the funk/disco/soul band was well known in Great Britain. Released in the U.S. in 1978, this self-titled LP contains the funk singles "Hi-Tension" and "British Hustle"—both of which were major hits in England but received hardly any airplay on American stations. *Hi-Tension* isn't a masterpiece, but the uptempo funk selections (which draw on influences ranging from Kool & the Gang and Earth, Wind & Fire to Brass Construction) are generally catchy and enjoyable. Also pleasing are the LP's romantic slow jams, which include "Autumn Love" and the War-influenced "You're My Girl." This respectable, if imperfect, LP didn't sell in the U.S., but if you're discussing British R&B of the 1970s, it's an album that has to be mentioned. *—Alex Henderson*

Chuck Higgins

b. Apr. 17, 1924, Gary, IN

Vocals, Sax (Tenor) / R&B

Saxophonist Chuck Higgins earned R&B fame for his composition "Pachuko Hop," which remains a perennial favorite among Latino fans, but didn't gain enough general R&B acclaim to chart in the early '50s. Higgins also played trombone and trumpet. He moved from his native Gary to Los Angeles in 1940 as a teen. Higgins played trumpet in his high school band and later attended the Los Angeles Conservatory. While there, Higgins started a band with pianist Frank Dunn and saxophonist Johnny Parker, among others. Higgins later became the band's saxophonist and wrote "Pachuko Hop." Its furious pace, roaring sax solo, and raw sound, plus the inclusion of the term "Pachuko," which was slang for a Mexican-American dressed in baggy pants with a key chain, made the song a '50s anthem for area Latinos. The B-side, "Motorhead Baby," was later the inspiration for Frank Zappa sideman James "Motorhead" Sherwood and the heavy metal band Motörhead. Higgins played dates in Los Angeles with everyone from Charlie Parker to the Orioles and his band at one point included Johnny "Guitar" Watson. Although none of Higgins' many singles for Aladdin, Caddy, Lucky, Specialty, or Dootone ever earned national acclaim, he was an extremely popular regional attraction through the '50s and into the early '60s, when he retired from performing to become a music teacher at local high schools and a college. A comeback faltered in the mid-'70s, when Higgins tried to update his sound by going disco. He returned to honking R&B in the late '70s and toured England in the mid-'80s, while performing once more in Los Angeles clubs. *—Ron Wynn*

● **Pachuko Hop** / 1956 / Specialty ✦✦✦✦✦

Raucous R&B tenor saxist Higgins, a longtime L.A. favorite, honks and blows like a wildman on these 20 sides, dating from 1954-1956. Much of Higgins' work for the Specialty and Money logos laid unissued before this collection came out. His band included guitarist Jimmy Nolen (later a James Brown mainstay), pianist H.B. Barnum, and Chuck's brother Fred (as Daddy Cleanhead) handling vocals. *—Bill Dahl*

High Fashion

f. 1980, **db.** 1985

Group / Disco, Dance-Pop

A mixed (male/female) trio that was the brainchild of Guadeloupe-born producer Jacques Fred Petrus, who moved to Bologna with dreams of becoming the Gamble & Huff of Italy; (while that didn't occur), he did produce noted disco albums by the B.B.&Q. Band, Change, the Ritchie Family, High Fashion, and others. Petrus molded High Fashion (New Yorkers Alyson Williams, Me'lisa Morgan, and Eric McClinton) after Chic. Williams and Morgan first met in 1977 when both competed in Hal Jackson's Talented Teen International Scholarship Competition created for young women around the world 13 to 17 years old to display their intelligence and talent while networking with peers and competing for scholarships.

High Fashion debuted on Capitol Records in 1982 with *Feelin' Lucky*. It spawned one little disco hit, "Feeling Lucky Lately." A second LP, *Make Up Your Mind*, dropped in 1983; sales were embarrassing, Morgan booked, and by 1985, High Fashion disbanded. A remake of Prince's "Do Me Baby" earned Morgan a number one R&B hit in 1985 for Capitol; she notched two more Top Ten R&B singles: "Do You Still Love Me?" and "If You Can Do It: I Can Too" before moving on to Arista Records in 1987 and hitting with a duet with Kashif ("Love Changes") that reached the number-two spot (R&B). After Arista, she went with Pendulum Records.

Williams, the daughter of bandleader/trumpeter Bobby Booker, joined the Affair after High Fashion; before High Fashion, she was a sought-after session vocalist and worked on a long list of projects. A Def Jam single in 1987 began a solo career that ran out of gas in the late '90s. On Def Jam, in addition to solo work, she paired with Chuck Stanley ("Make You Mine Tonight") and Oran "Juice" Jones on "How to Love Again."

McClinton, whose masculine vocals accented High Fashion's sound, has been the least-active of the trio. He contributed backing vocals to Petrus' sessions, including the B.B.&Q. Band's *She's a Woman* LP. Jacques Fred Petrus met an untimely end: He was found weighted down in waters outside of Mexico City in 1986, the apparent victim of a mob hit. *—Andrew Hamilton*

● **Feelin' Lucky** / 1982 / Capitol ✦✦✦

Someone could easily spend hours listing the numerous artists who were, in some way, affected by Chic's distinctive sound—a list that would include everyone from Queen, ABC, and Duran Duran to Soul II Soul, Madonna, and the Sugarhill Gang. One of the many early-'80s R&B groups to be heavily influenced by Chic was the trio High Fashion, whose debut album, *Feelin' Lucky*, sounds like Chic-meets-Change with hints of Kashif. In fact, this decent, if formulaic, LP was produced by Jacques Fred Petrus and Mauro Malavasi—the same European duo that produced Change—and Kashif serves as one of the associate producers in addition to writing or co-writing three selections. Not surprisingly, one of the background singers is none other than Chic's Diva Gray. *Feelin' Lucky* is, without question, highly derivative, but it's also quite enjoyable. Cuts like "You're the Winner," "Hold On" (one of the songs that Kashif wrote), and the hit "Feelin' Lucky Lately" won't win any awards for innovation; nonetheless, the grooves are tough to resist, and you just might find yourself patting your foot while you're commenting on High Fashion's lack of originality. *—Alex Henderson*

High Inergy

f. Pasadena, CA, **db.** 1983

Group / Urban, Disco

This female quartet was discovered by Gwen Gordy Fuqua while they performed in their native Pasadena, CA, during a Bicentennial show. The group was comprised of lead singer Vernessa Mitchell, her sister Barbara Mitchell, Linda Howard, and Michelle Martin. (The Mitchell sisters were singers, Howard and Martin had dance backgrounds.) Signed by Motown in 1977, they immediately clicked on the pop and soul charts with the sultry ballad "You Can't Turn Me Off (In the Middle of Turning Me On)," which was the cornerstone of of their debut album, *Turnin' On* (1977). But after the follow-up album *Steppin' Out*, (1978), Vernessa Mitchell left the group to concentrate on gospel music and Barbara took over lead-singing chores on subsequent albums. But after struggling for several years without another major hit (or even name recognition), the group quietly disbanded in 1983. *—John Lowe*

● **Turnin' On** / 1977 / Gordy ✦✦✦✦✦

This is the first (and best) of their albums, before inferior songwriting and unsympathetic production sabotaged their promising career. The hit single, "You Can't Turn Me Off (In the Middle of Turning Me On)," is the focal point, along with some good, if not necessarily distinctive numbers to fill it out. *—John Lowe*

Steppin' Out / 1978 / Gordy ✦✦✦

Steeped in Berry Gordy's Motown tradition and touted as the next Supremes, High Inergy had already tasted the top of the charts with their 1977 debut, which spawned the number two hit single "You Can't Turn Me Off (In the Middle of Turning Me On)." Clearly, *Steppin' Out* was designed to reach even higher. Packed with smooth vocal arrangements that occasionally do resemble the artistry of the Supremes crossed with a disco-pop sound, the album flipped between dancefloor steppers and soul ballads. The formula was there for success, but luck was not on High Inergy's side. The album just cracked the Top 20. The songs themselves are good, if a bit bland. "Lovin' Fever" is sweet and, despite its disco groove, easily recalls the innocence of love in true Motown style. "You Captured My Heart," on the other hand, is a sophisticated, sultry number with excellent vocals and even better instrumentation completing the mood, as horns and guitar provide a smattering of funk. "We Are the Future," meanwhile, despite gracing the film *Almost Summer*, feels like celluloid filler, and "Fly Little Blackbird" falls by the wayside. *Steppin' Out* is a respectable album, but remains uneven across its tracks despite some really special moments. It is the sound of a band learning to find a niche. *—Amy Hanson*

Shoulda Gone Dancin' / 1979 / Gordy ✦✦

Regrouping after the effervescent Vernessa Mitchell decamped for a solo career in gospel, High Inergy, now with sister Barbara handling lead vocals, re-emerged in 1979 to take another crack at success with *Shoulda Gone Dancin'*. Unfortunately, that was not to be, as the band was unable to even come close to matching the chart successes of their earlier efforts. The LP limped to a mere number-76 R&B in May. The title track, which proved the album's sole hit, does utilize some sizzling arrangements and interesting vocal turns across an energetic beat, and would emerge the album's only real standout. The sultry beginning of "Let Yourself Go," meanwhile, which flips into disco without any warning, is interesting, but would have been better had it remained a ballad. That leaves the band to cover some of their more familiar bases across the traditional Motown trappings of "Midnight Music Man" and the closing "Too Late," a stilted blend of the Supremes and the Shangri-Las. While not a bad effort, *Shoulda Gone Dancin'* just doesn't have enough merit to render it one of the era's sparklers and, although the band would continue to record and chart into 1983, by 1979 it was already clear that their star power was well in decline. *—Amy Hanson*

Frenzy / 1979 / Gordy ✦✦

Hold On / 1981 / Motown ✦✦✦

After four albums on Gordy, Berry Gordy switched High Inergy to the Motown label. This wasn't just a cosmetic change—the Motown labels were under one umbrella but Gordy placed them with different distributors. For instance, at least two different distributors handled the various Motown labels in the Chicago area, and this was true for all locales. After hitting out-the-box with "You Can't Turn Me On," the girls from Pasadena, now trimmed from a quartet to a trio, were jonesing for a hit. So maybe a different line of distributors would curtail the steep slide into oblivion and the enormous debt they were accruing with the company. It didn't. This good album went as unnoticed as the first four and the four that followed. Like all their albums, this one had a handful of should-have-been hits, with the standouts here being a better-than-the-original remake of Bettye Swann's "Make Me Yours," the disco-ish "I Just Can't Help Myself," and the grooving "It Was You Babe," written by Angelo Bond, William Weatherspoon, and High Inergy's lead singer Barbara Mitchell. —*Andrew Hamilton*

High Inergy / 1981 / Motown ✦✦
When you think of great female R&B vocal groups that were active in the 1970s, High Inergy isn't a name that comes to mind. One thinks of Honey Cone, the Three Degrees, First Choice, the Emotions, the Pointer Sisters, or LaBelle. Under the right circumstances, however, High Inergy could have become a major force in R&B. If the ladies had been signed to Philadelphia International and worked with Gamble & Huff, Bunny Sigler, and Bobby Martin on a regular basis—or if Norman Whitfield, Quincy Jones, or the Nile Rodgers/Bernard Edwards team had been in their corner—perhaps their chops and talent would have paid off. But they didn't have the right guidance, and consequently, most of their albums were unfocused. Released in 1981, this self-titled release is generally disappointing but does have a few worthwhile tracks. The sentimental "Heaven's Just a Step Away (Every Time I Hold You)" isn't bad, and their performance of Ashford & Simpson's "Now That There's You" is enjoyable. But the LP didn't contain a strong single and has its share of inferior material, so it was added to the list of High Inergy albums that went nowhere commercially. —*Alex Henderson*

So Right / 1982 / Gordy ✦

Groove Patrol / 1983 / Gordy ✦✦

Martha High

b. Washington, D.C.
Vocals / Funk, Soul, R&B
James Brown's longest running female vocalist, Martha High (aka Martha Harvin), began her career in Washington, D.C. She attended the same high school (Roosevelt) and sang in the same church (Trinity AME Zion) as Sandra Bears, Carrie Mingo, Grace Ruffin, and Margie Clark, the Four Jewels, but didn't join until Carrie Mingo quit. From the district's northwest area, the original group woodshedded along with the Rainbows, the Marquees (Marvin Gaye), and Billy Stewart (Grace Ruffin's first cousin) in Bo Diddley's basement. Initially, Bob Lee managed them, but Diddley grabbed the reins and orchestrated their first recording deal with Chess/Checker Records.

The Four Jewels released a string of singles that were popular in the D.C./Baltimore/Virginia area on Checker, Chess, Start, and Tec Records before Harvin replaced Mingo. The move brought a stroke of luck; changing to the Jewels, they scored their biggest hit on Carole King's Dimension label. "Opportunity" sold well in many locales; with Bears on lead, the catchy ditty brought them some national attention. Its successor, "But I Do" b/w "Smokey Joe," didn't do nearly as well and the Dimension association ended.

In 1964, they landed a gig with the James Brown Revue. The Jewels, with Harvin firmly entrenched and co-leading with Bears, toured all over America on a relentless schedule of one-nighters. The revue consisted of the Jewels, James Crawford, Vicki Anderson, Baby Lloyd, and Elsie "TV Mama" Mae, a 350-pound singer who delighted crowds with a side-splitting rendition of "All of Me." Smash Records recorded the show live on the 1967 release *Presenting the James Brown Show*, which features everybody but TV Mama. When the tour hit Detroit, the girls moseyed over to Motown Records to show their stuff, feeling the hitmaking organization was what the doctor ordered, but, to their dismay, the place was closed the only day they were in town.

After a year and a half, and two 45s produced by James Brown, the Jewels disbanded but continued in the business; in fact, they never retired. Martha Harvin changed her name to Martha High and continued with Brown for more than 30 years. She sang with Brown on "Summertime," which they transformed into an ecology song, and appears on the *James Brown Original Funky Divas* LP; High recorded a self-titled solo album for Salsoul Records in 1979. She's fondly remembered by fans of the James Brown shows as the jet-black sister with glowing blond hair.

High left Brown around 1995 to tour with Maceo Parker, Brown's ex-saxophone player. Parkers' band consisted of Parker, High, Charles "Sweet Charles" Sherrell (ex-James Brown vocalist), Bruno Speight (guitar), Corey Parker (vocals), Greg Boyer (trombone), Jerome Thomas (drums), Rodney "Skeet" Curtis (bass), Ron Tooley (trumpet), and Will Boulware (organ). —*Andrew Hamilton*

● **Martha High** / 1979 / Salsoul ✦✦✦✦
Breaking from the James Brown Revue with Brown's permission, Martha High recorded this neglected LP produced by Thomas Stewart in Georgia; Stewart, along with Julian Chatman and Harold Daniels, wrote every song except High's high octane rendition of "Don't Ask My Neighbor," a crowd pleaser originally done by the Emotions, that Martha kicks up a notch. High's demanding vocals serve up generous helpings of "Showdown (On the Dance Floor)," the bawdy "He's My Ding Dong Man," "Wallflower," and "Oh This Feeling." —*Andrew Hamilton*

Jessie Hill

b. Dec. 9, 1932, New Orleans, LA, **d.** Sep. 17, 1996, New Orleans, LA
Vocals / New Orleans R&B, Southern Soul
Loose and wild, Jessie Hill cut a New Orleans party classic with his crazed "Ooh Poo Pah Doo." The two-sided single, a 1960 Allen Toussaint production on Minit, has Hill shouting the nearly unintelligible lyrics over a strong Crescent City groove, while the flip is an instrumental featuring saxist David Lastie. Hill cut several more boisterous outings with Toussaint at the helm before heading to the West Coast, where he made a disappointing album for Blue Thumb in 1970. —*Bill Dahl*

Hurts So Bad / 1982 / Capitol ✦✦✦
Hill was a good, occasionally great New Orleans vocalist, drummer, and pianist, better known for the time he spent playing with Huey "Piano" Smith than on his own. Hill did have one superb single in "Ooh Poo Pah Doo," but that wasn't on this batch of decent Southern soul and R&B tracks. There's nothing to get excited about, but they're all done with energy and conviction. —*Ron Wynn*

● **Golden Classics** / 1989 / Collectables ✦✦✦✦✦
Collectables' *Golden Classics* is the only CD collection of the classic New Orleans vocalist, Jessie Hill. These are recordings from the early '60s, produced by the incomparable Allen Toussaint, and while only "Ooh Poo Pah Doo" stands as a classic single, the rest of it is easy-rolling, highly enjoyable New Orleans R&B that makes for a fine addition to any collection. —*Stephen Thomas Erlewine*

Lauryn Hill

b. May 26, 1975
Vocals / Contemporary R&B, Alternative Rap, Urban, Hip-Hop, Neo-Soul
Call Lauryn Hill the mother of hip-hop invention; with her 1998 solo debut *The Miseducation of Lauryn Hill*, the Fugees' most vocal member not only established herself as a creative force on her own, but also broke new ground by successfully integrating rap, soul, reggae, and R&B into her own sound.

Raised in South Orange, NJ, Hill spent her youth listening her parents' multi-genre, multi-generational record collection. She began singing at an early age, and was soon snagging minor roles on television (*As the World Turns*) and in film (*Sister Act II: Back in the Habit*). Her on-again, off-again stint in the Fugees began at the age of 13, but was often interrupted by both the acting gigs and her enrollment at Columbia University. After developing a following in the tri-state area, the group's first release—the much-hyped but uneven *Blunted on Reality*—bombed, almost causing a breakup. But with the multi-platinum *The Score*, the Fugees (and especially the camera-friendly Hill) achieved international success, though some pundits took shots at their penchant for cover songs.

That criticism made *Miseducation* even more of a surprise. Hill wrote, arranged, or produced just about every track on the album, which is steeped in her old-school background, both musically (the Motown-esque sing-along of "Doo Wop (That Thing)") and lyrically (the nostalgic "Every Ghetto, Every City"). As *Miseducation* began a long reign on the charts through most of the fall and winter of 1998—initially thanks to heavy buzz and overwhelming radio support for "Doo Wop (That Thing)"—Hill became a national media icon, as magazines ranging from *Time* to *Esquire* to *Teen People* vied to put her on the cover. By the end of the year, as the album topped virtually every major music critic's best-of list, she was being credited for helping fully assimilate hip-hop into mainstream music. (Such an analysis, however, is lightweight at best: Hip-hop had been a huge force on the sales and radio fronts for most of the decade, and rappers Jay-Z, DMX, and OutKast had dropped similarly lauded LPs prior to or just after *Miseducation*'s release, adding to the genre's dominant sales for the year). The momentum finally culminated at the February 1999 Grammy awards, during which Hill took home five trophies from her 11 nominations, including Album of the Year, Best New Artist, Best Female R&B Vocal Performance, Best R&B Song, and Best R&B Album; the most ever for a woman. Shortly after, she launched a highly praised national tour with Atlanta rappers OutKast.

Hill also faced a lawsuit from two musicians who claim they were denied full credit for their work on the album. In an interesting twist, Hill's album proved to be such a commercial and critical success that it shed doubt on the Fugees' future. Their in-fighting became common knowledge, and matters were complicated when many fans interpreted *Miseducation*'s various anti-stardom rants as a public dissing of co-Fugee Wyclef Jean. She did continue shaping her solo career. The double-disc *MTV Unplugged No. 2.0* appeared in spring 2002, showcasing a deeply personal performance from Hill. —*Brian Raftery*

● **The Miseducation of Lauryn Hill** / Aug. 25, 1998 / Columbia ✦✦✦✦✦
This highly anticipated album from Lauryn Hill features a mix of soul, rap, and reggae. Hill, who gained national attention by singing in the movie *Sister Act II*, was previously a member of the hip-hop trio the Fugees, which consisted of her partners Wyclef Jean and Prakazrel "Pras" Michel. This, her first solo album, houses some hip-hop-induced soul numbers. "Ex-Factor" has a bouncing flow, an enticing change-up, and a supplicating vamp accentuated by a soothing melody. The charged rhythm of "Doo Wop (That Thing)" presses on with Hill rapping and singing from verse to chorus augmented by some juiced-up horns and a whopping bassline. "Nothing Even Matters," a duet with soul singer D'Angelo, breezes in its dulcet rhythm. Their vocals maintain that consistent pitch throughout the song as they humbly complement each other from their cries to their lyrical sighs. There is much here to savor for aficionados of rap, reggae, and hip-hop/soul music. The Fugees alumna is eloquent throughout the set with her message of love, education, peace, perseverance, understanding, and patience. While the young talent is fluent in each respective genre she embraces, the ambience she exudes with her singing has a magnetic, mesmerizing feel. A great effort by a rising star. —*Craig Lytle*

MTV Unplugged No. 2.0 / May 7, 2002 / Columbia ✦✦✦✦
Lauryn Hill's debut album, *The Miseducation of Lauryn Hill*, became a critical and commercial blockbuster, which the artist herself, always distrustful of the music business, seems to have found a disorienting experience. She has therefore waited nearly four years to make another album, and the album she has made deliberately flies in the face of the previous one and its reception. Resurrecting the MTV *Unplugged* program, she has gone before an audience with an acoustic guitar in her hands to sing a new group of songs. But that unadorned approach is only the beginning. Everything about the performance is unpolished. One suspects that she would resist even calling it a performance; "I used to be a performer," she notes at the outset. What she is after, in her life and her music, she explains, is "reality," which means everything from being willing to sing the entire set with a raspy voice because that's the state her voice is in on that day to stopping and starting, going up on the lyrics, and even breaking down in tears. The style naturally places an emphasis on the words to the songs, which reinforce Hill's unvarnished approach, attacking the music business and anyone who wants her to be what's she's not, and witheringly

criticizing institutions such as the judicial system ("Mystery of Iniquity"). The songs themselves would not require two discs to contain, but they are alternated by lengthy remarks, one spoken interlude running more than 12 minutes, in which Hill elaborates on the importance of being honest and confronting falsehood. She's usually full of herself, and she's often full of it. But that's okay. The point is the unfinished, unflinching presentation of ideas and of a person. It may not be a proper follow-up to her first album, but it is fascinating. *—William Ruhlmann*

Z.Z. Hill (Arzell Hill)

b. Sep. 30, 1935, Naples, TX, **d.** Apr. 27, 1984, Dallas, TX

Vocals / Retro-Soul, Modern Electric Blues, Soul-Blues

Texas-born singer Z.Z. Hill managed to resuscitate both his own semi-flagging career and the entire genre at large when he signed on at Malaco Records in 1980 and began growling his way through some of the most uncompromising blues to be unleashed on black radio stations in many a moon. His impressive 1982 Malaco album *Down Home Blues* remained on *Billboard*'s soul album charts for nearly two years, an extraordinary run for such a blatantly bluesy LP. His songs "Down Home Blues" and "Somebody Else Is Steppin' In" have graduated into the ranks of legitimate blues standards (and there haven't been many of those come along over the last couple of decades). His debut single, the gutsy shuffle "You Were Wrong," showed up on *Billboard*'s pop chart for a week in 1964.

With such a relatively successful showing his first time out, Hill's fine subsequent singles for the Kent logo should have been even bigger. But "I Need Someone (To Love Me)," "Happiness Is All I Need," and a raft of other deserving Kent 45s went nowhere commercially. A 1972 hookup with United Artists resulted in three albums and six R&B chart singles over the next couple of years. From there, Z.Z. moved on to Columbia, where his 1977 single "Love Is So Good When You're Stealing It" became his biggest-selling hit of all. From 1980 until 1984, when he died suddenly of a heart attack, Z.Z. bravely led a personal back-to-the-blues campaign that doubtless helped to fuel the current contemporary blues boom. It's a shame he couldn't stick around to see it blossom. *—Bill Dahl*

Brand New Z.Z. Hill / 1971 / Mankind ✦✦✦

Dues Paid in Full / 1972 / Kent ✦✦✦✦

Z.Z. Hill's second album for Kent, *Dues Paid in Full*, collects a number of singles that he recorded for the label between 1964 and 1965. Hill pretty much played in a straight Texas style during these days, turning out a series of stinging high-octane singles during those two years. Granted, there wasn't much in the way of originality, but there were strong signs of individuality, which makes *Dues Paid in Full* worth investigation for both Hill fans and anyone with a fondness for electric Texas blues. *—Thom Owens*

Let's Make a Deal / 1978 / Columbia ✦✦✦

One of the most commercial of Hill's albums, this disco-tinged release included the minor hits "This Time They Told the Truth" and "Love Is So Good When You're Stealing It." *—Richie Unterberger*

The Mark of Z.Z. Hill / 1979 / Columbia ✦✦✦

Hill's second and final Columbia LP was essentially a continuation of the first. On both, Hill sounds like a journeyman Southern soul singer embellished with period disco/mainstream R&B production, which neither added to the quality of the music nor made it unlistenable. *—Richie Unterberger*

☆ **Down Home** / 1982 / Malaco ✦✦✦✦✦

This is one of the very few classic blues albums of the 1980s. Hill revitalized the genre among African-American listeners with his "Down Home Blues," which earned instant standard status. But the entire album is tremendously consistent, with the percolating R&B workouts "Givin' It Up for Your Love" and "Right Arm for Your Love" contrasting with an intimate "Cheatin' in the Next Room" and the straight-ahead blues "Everybody Knows About My Good Thing" and "When It Rains It Pours." *—Bill Dahl*

★ **In Memorium (1935–1984)** / 1985 / Malaco ✦✦✦✦✦

Most of the highlights of Hill's glorious blues-singing stint at Malaco, although the individual albums possess more than their share of worthwhile moments that aren't here. But with hallowed titles like "Down Home Blues," "Someone Else Is Slippin' In," and "Everybody Knows About My Good Thing," this stunning collection neatly summarizes Hill's heartwarming rise to blues power. *—Bill Dahl*

The Complete Hill/UA Recordings / Mar. 19, 1996 / Capitol ✦✦✦✦

The gritty singer made three albums for United Artists (mostly under his brother Matt's supervision) from 1972 to 1975, and they were an idiomatically mixed bag. All three LPs are housed in their entirety on this two-disc set, its selections ranging from the deep soul sincerity of "I've Got to Get You Back" and "Your Love Makes Me Feel Good" and the country-soul hybrids "You're Killing Me (Slowly But Surely)" and "Country Love" to the funky Lamont Dozier-produced "I Created a Monster" and an Allen Toussaint-supervised "I Keep on Lovin' You." *—Bill Dahl*

This Time They Told the Truth: The Columbia Years / Feb. 17, 1998 / Columbia ✦✦✦✦

The best of Hill's late-'70s stay at Columbia Records, *This Time They Told the Truth* might be a bit of a shock to listeners not familiar with the period, for Hill's always smooth vocals are embellished with a very disco-fied production, not always disturbing, but definitely obtrusive in several places. The songs themselves are quite good (distilled from 1978's *Let's Make a Deal* and 1979's *The Mark of Z.Z. Hill*), including "Stop by and Love Me Sometime," "A Message to the Ladies" and the title track. *—John Bush*

Eddie Hinton

b. Jun. 15, 1944, Jacksonville, FL, **d.** Jul. 28, 1995, Birmingham, AL

Vocals, Guitar / Blue-Eyed Soul, Retro-Soul

Guitarist/vocalist Eddie Hinton is widely regarded as perhaps the premier white Southern soul artist. His dusky, gritty vocals and expert riffing and chording, as well as his songwriting abilities, have been evident since the the '70s. Hinton, a native of Tuscaloosa, AL, became a session musician after moving to Muscle Shoals. He and partner Marlin Greene wrote songs for Aretha Franklin, Dusty Springfield, and Percy Sledge before Hinton signed a solo deal with Phil Walden's Capricorn label in 1977. Hinton's debut LP, *Very Extremely Dangerous*, was a well-written and performed outing featuring the contributions of such session veterans as Roger Hawkins, Jimmy Johnson, David Hood, and Barry Beckett. Capricorn's financial demise left Hinton temporarily displaced, but he returned in 1987 with another excellently produced and sung soul set that flopped commercially, *Letters From Mississippi*. His 1990 Rounder release *Cry and Moan* continued Hinton's string of magnificent soul works that never got much mainstream attention. His last release before his death was *Very Blue Highway* in 1993. *—Ron Wynn*

● **Very Extremely Dangerous** / 1978 / Capricorn ✦✦✦✦✦

In his book *Sweet Soul Music*, Peter Guralnick described Eddie Hinton as "the last of the great white soul singers," and his debut album, 1978's *Very Extremely Dangerous*, sounds like a glorious throwback to the salad days of the Muscle Shoals, AL, R&B hit factory of the 1960s, where Wilson Pickett and Aretha Franklin cut some of their most memorable songs. Hinton had already earned an estimable reputation as a session guitarist by the time he finally got to step up to the mike as a solo artist, and *Very Extremely Dangerous* features him backed up by the always-expert Muscle Shoals Rhythm Section, and Hinton's strong and wiry guitar runs fit the group's emphatic support like a glove. (Hinton and his friends also knew how to bring a solid rock drive to these songs without losing their soulful groove in the process.) As a singer, Hinton was never afraid to step on the gas, and if his vocals are sometimes a bit over the top, they're also consumed with a raw and sweaty joy; like Wilson Pickett, Hinton is able to bring a surprising musicality to a shouting style that can express the pleasures of a hard-partying Saturday night ("Shout Bamalama") as well as the tender agony of love ("I Got the Feeling"). It was Eddie Hinton's poor fortune to cut a great blue-eyed soul album just as disco and funk had bumped deep soul off the charts, but *Very Extremely Dangerous* still stands as a fine example of latter-day soul at its most accomplished. *—Mark Deming*

Letters from Mississippi / 1987 / Zane ✦✦✦

Cry & Moan / 1990 / Bullseye Blues ✦✦✦

Very Blue Highway / Apr. 1, 1993 / Bullseye Blues ✦✦✦✦✦

The late Eddie Hinton never got his due by mass culture standards, though soul music lovers everywhere are deeply indebted to him. Over the course of only six recordings, Hinton defined the ethos of the Southern white soul singer. Many who heard his records on jukeboxes in bars and bowling alleys and never saw his photograph were shocked to discover he was, in fact, not African-American. The most important point, however, is that Hinton was a natural; he never had to cultivate his sound—he owned it from the very beginning. His second-from-last album, recorded for the Rounder subsidiary Bullseye Blues, evidences a solid, even acrobatic performance from Hinton and a band that includes bassist Owen Brown and organ hero Ron Levy. Thankfully, Hinton handled all the guitar chores himself; his round, fat, funky textures adorn his razored yet sweet vocals like a blanket. Standout tracks are the deep, horn-inflected "I Love Someone," with its Stax/Volt groove and rough and ready production. "Poor Ol' Me" moves with a punch-drunk blues vibe that collects the horn section around Hinton and pushes him deeply into the song's stop-and-start melody. But nothing matches the intensity of the swamp soul of the last three tracks: "Standin' In," "Hey Justine," and the literally stunning "Nobody But You." On all three, Hinton's voice is unadorned by production; it's almost shot from years of tobacco and whiskey and yet, even at half power, he has more raw courage, more inspiring emotion to bring it on home to the listener full-bore. He carries the band on these songs, driving them deep into the tune's rhythms and harmonies with a feral grace and unstoppable spirit that will echo hopefully for decades to come, even though the singer is gone. This is bad-assed soul music from the heart, without regard for niceties or trends. A classic. *—Thom Jurek*

Hard Luck Guy / Feb. 9, 1999 / Capricorn ✦✦✦✦✦

Cobbled together from tracks Hinton recorded at Capricorn Studios during the *Very Extremely Dangerous* sessions and with additional recording in the '90s, this is arguably Hinton's masterpiece, though he didn't live to see its release. Heavies like Spooner Oldham; keys, Dan Penn; vocals, Johnny Sandlin; drums, Donnie Fritts; Hammond B-3, and many more, weighed-in to finish the tracks after Hinton died in 1995; it may be one explanation for the absolutely contemporary and immediate feeling to the recording. "Lovin' Chain" swings with the familiarity of an Atlantic Records soul-era classic; "Three Pounds of Hongry" is a back porch country blues; "I Got My Thang Together" is good ol' Southern rock; "Here I Am" with its doo wop melody and brand of sexual bravado is a simple plea for love. The set's heartbreaker is its title track. Like that weird note Otis Redding reaches for in "I've Been Lovin' You Too Long," Hinton hits one in "Hard Luck Guy." It's difficult not to be struck by his aching sound and the song's sentiment given the singer's fate. *—Denise Sullivan*

Joe Hinton

b. Nov. 15, 1929, Evansville, IN, **d.** Aug. 13, 1968, Boston, MA

Vocals, Producer / Soul, Black Gospel, Country-Soul, R&B

Joe Hinton was a super gospel vocalist and an even finer soul singer, among the most emphatic and gripping among '60s stylists. Hinton originally was a member of the Chosen Gospel Singers and later was a lead vocalist for the Spirit of Memphis quartet before turning to soul in the mid-'60s. While none of his songs for Backbeat were ever huge hits, his releases were masterfully crafted, emotionally arresting performances. His signature song was a 1964 remake of Willie Nelson's "Funny How Time Slips Away," complete with a shattering, octave-leaping finale. It reached number 13 on the R&B charts, but deserved a much better fate. Hinton unfortunately died in Boston in 1968, and never got the wider notoriety he deserved. *—Ron Wynn*

● **Funny How Time Slips Away** / 1964 / Back Beat ✦✦✦✦

Hodges, James & Smith

f. Detroit, MI

Group / Pop-Soul, Soul

Hodges, James & Smith (HJS) was the brainstorm of producer/writer William "Mickey" Stevenson, Motown's A&R Director during their glory years. All Detroit natives, Pat Hodges, Denita James, and Jessica Smith were handpicked by Stevenson, though they each took different routes to get there. Hodges played the clarinet in a local band, then attended college and earned a B.A. in music. James studied ballet and tap dancing, while Smith had a gospel background.

Mickey Stevenson had a great vision for HJS and groomed them to play the top, plush clubs. He created a snazzy nightclub act for them that rivaled the Supremes. They played the sweet gigs throughout Europe and recorded *Incredible* on 20th Century Fox in 1973, but the only thing incredible about it was the speed it reached cutout bins at discount record stores. Although a solid album, it just didn't get a decent push. Another 20th Century album, 1975's *Power in Your Love*, disappeared so fast that most people can't recall its title. The lack of recording success though, didn't douse HJS' flame; they continued traveling, doing the plum gigs.

In 1976, they signed with London Records. *What's on Your Mind* received quite a bit of promotion and acclaim that, unfortunately, didn't transform into sales. A second London release *What Have You Done for Love*, met a similar fate. Other artists including Bobby Womack, and Sylvester used them on sessions, but after a few more years of the same the trio disbanded, never having achieved the success they and Stevenson tried so hard to obtain. *—Andrew Hamilton*

What's on Your Mind / 1976 / London ✦✦

A mildly successful girl group masterminded by Motown A&R man Mickey Stevenson, Hodges, James & Smith were groomed to rival the likes of the Supremes and the Emotions. Despite a handful of well-placed singles, though, for the most part mainstream success eluded these Detroit natives, more often than not because they just didn't have the vocal prowess and strength to carry the material. 1976's *What's on Your Mind* was the third in a string of mediocre efforts, here highlighted by the passable opener "Don't Take Away Your Love." It resonates with Motown style, while the six-plus-minute chest-beater "Since I Fell for You" adds sax, strings, and rough-and-tumble soul, ultimately culminating in quite a remarkable song. Combined with "I'm Falling in Love" in a medley for its single release, the song proved a winner, reaching number 24 on the R&B charts in July 1977. But that's just about where the high points begin and end. With the possible exception of the edgy "People Needing People," the rest of *What's on Your Mind* is given over to a dull mix of soul ballads and uptempo R&B. It's better to skip this set and go straight to the more established divas of the day. There's less cringing that way. *—Amy Hanson*

● **What Have You Done for Love** / 1978 / London ✦✦✦

During 1977, they had a few singles that nested in the nose-bleed section of the charts: "Don't Take Away Your Love," and a medley "Since I Fell for You/I'm Falling in Love," but no major busters. The highbrow, campy treatment given to some of these selections will turn off diehard R&B and soul fans. Producer William Stevenson tries to make Hodges, James, & Smith all things to all people, but the Broadway-flavored "Home Is Where Your Love Belongs" and "What Have You Done for Love" are more irritating than impressive. The ballads, however, are more than worthy of praise; HJS can sing, and they display their talent best on "Darling I Promise," "You Know Who You Are," and Earth, Wind & Fire's "You Can't Hide Love." The trio offers a good remake of Stevie Wonder's "Seems So Long," but other upbeat numbers are mundane and predictable. *—Andrew Hamilton*

Jimmy Holiday

b. Jul. 24, 1934, Sallis, MS, **d.** Feb. 15, 1987, Iowa City, IA

Songwriter, Vocals / Northern Soul, Singer/Songwriter, Soul, R&B

A distinctive singer/songwriter, Jimmy Holiday co-wrote Jackie DeShannon's "Put a Little Love in Your Heart" but also recorded several hits of his own. While recording for Everest during the mid-'60s, he scored with 1963's "How Can I Forget," a Top Ten R&B hit and a pop entry as well. After moving to the New Orleans hit factory Minit by 1966, Holiday recorded a few moderate R&B hits during 1967 and 1968, but remains best-known for penning "Put a Little Love in Your Heart," a number-four hit for Jackie DeShannon in 1969. *—Richard Pack*

● **Everybody Needs Help** / 1986 / Stateside ✦✦✦✦✦

This seventeen track Minit label compilation includes his best recordings, including the big 1966-1968 hits "Baby I Love You," "Everybody Needs Help," and "Spread Your Love." *—Richard Pack*

How Can I Forget / Aug. 27, 1996 / Collectables ✦✦✦

This collection of Jimmy Holiday's Everest recordings includes each of the 12 sides the soul singer/songwriter recorded for the label between 1963 and 1965: the original hit version of "How Can I Forget?" plus "Janet," "Poor Boy," and "I Believe in Love," among others. *—Richard Pack*

Holland-Dozier-Holland

f. Detroit, MI, **db.** 1973

Group / Motown, Soul

A Hall of Fame songwriting and production trio, this all-star lineup paired brothers Brian & Eddie Holland with Lamont Dozier. Berry Gordy put the three together in the early '60s, after it became evident that Eddie Holland wasn't going to last as a solo act. The laundry list of Holland-Dozier-Holland hits seems endless; they include "Where Did Our Love Go," "Baby Love," "Reach Out I'll Be There," "Standing in the Shadows of Love," "This Old Heart of Mine," "Nowhere to Run," "I'm a Road Runner," and many others. They produced gems for the Supremes, Junior Walker & the All Stars, the Four Tops, Martha & the Vandellas, the Isley Brothers, and the Elgins until they left in 1968.

After moving from Detroit to Los Angeles, the trio created the Hot Wax and Invictus labels. Freda Payne, the Chairman of the Board, Laura Lee, 100 Proof (Aged in Soul), and the Honey Cone were among the acts that scored hits in the early '70s. They also did outside productions for such artists as Dionne Warwick and issued their own hit single, "Why Can't We Be Lovers," in 1973. Lamont Dozier then decided to start a solo career, and the long partnership ended. Invictus remained in business until 1977, and Brian Holland produced the New York Port Authority. *—Ron Wynn*

The Picture Never Changes / 1992 / Fantasy ✦✦✦✦

Lamont Dozier and Brian & Eddie Holland made their mark as songwriters and producers. The trio's songs dominated the charts in the '60s, and all three are now members of the Rock and Roll Hall of Fame. Few know that all three began as singers. Lamont had recorded with the Romeos for Atco, then cut solo singles; Brian recorded "Shock" for a small Detroit label prior to Motown, and cut a single at Motown with Dozier; Eddie sang for United Artists and Motown before joining brother Brian and Lamont to form the blockbuster songwriting team. Most of the recordings by Holland-Dozier-Holland featured either Lamont Dozier or Brian Holland. Lamont led their most popular recording, "Why Can't We Be Lovers," a rambling, romantic number. Brian leads the compelling "Don't Leave Me Starving for Your Love," a pleader with the piano way up in the mix; "New Breed Kinda Woman" is possibly Lamont's most energetic lead, while "Super Woman, You Ain't No Ordinary Woman" follows the same road but misses the mark. "Slipping Away" is led by either Brian or Eddie and has a sleek groove. Fourteen tracks and all are interesting creations, some better than others, but no real dogs. Still, all except a few are rungs below their productions for artists like the Supremes, Four Tops, Marvin Gaye, Chairmen of the Board, etc. *—Andrew Hamilton*

● **Why Can't We Be Lovers: The Invictus Sessions** / 2000 / Castle ✦✦✦✦✦

Why Can't We Be Lovers: The Invictus Sessions spans two discs of Holland-Dozier-Holland productions for the group's label, Invictus. The trio were the driving force at the label, responsible for many of the songs and the overall feel of the label, but their own recordings weren't much like the recordings of the Eighth Day or Glass House, to name but two hitmakers on Invictus/Hot Wax. They were recorded a few laters, closer to the heyday of disco, and they reflect that genre's influence in the lush, stylish, sexy sounds. This is late-night romantic mood music, where the sound and feel is more important than the particulars of the song or performance. As such, it's best for background listening (or used as a treasure trove of samples) than intent listening, which is surprising for such a notable group of songwriters. This may mean that this 28-track collection is primarily a curiosity for serious soul collectors, but it nevertheless is a pretty interesting one. *—Stephen Thomas Erlewine*

Eddie Holland

b. Oct. 30, 1939, Detroit, MI

Songwriter, Vocals / Motown, Soul

One-third of an amazing songwriting and production trio, Eddie Holland hasn't been as successful on his own as when teamed with brother Brian Holland and Lamont Dozier. The trio wrote numerous hits for Motown acts through the '60s before departing in 1968. They formed their own label in 1970, Hot Wax/Invictus, and had success for a while with such acts as the Chairmen of the Board, Laura Lee, and the Honey Cone. Eddie Holland scored his biggest hit as a solo artist back in 1962, with "Jamie" reaching number six on the R&B charts and peaking at number-30 pop. He recorded three more songs for Motown in the mid-'60s, but none of them were hits, and he then concentrated on songwriting and production. *—Ron Wynn*

Eddie Holland / 1962 / Motown ✦✦✦

Eddie Holland's first and only Motown LP has the future Hall-of-Fame songwriter doing his best Jackie Wilson imitation. Most of the songs were co-written by brother Brian Holland, except his hit "Jamie" and the lackluster "It's Not Too Late." Written by Barrett "Money" Strong and William "Mickey" Stevenson, "Jamie" featured swirling strings, the Rayber Singers, percolating rhythms, and a sterling vocal from Holland. Ironically, the condemning "You Deserved What You Get" followed "Jamie" as a single, but was omitted from this collection. Most of the material sounds dated, even for 1962, the biggest culprits being "Take a Chance on Me," "Last Night I Had a Vision," and "It's Too Late." "If It's Love It's Alright" attempts to clone "Jamie," but failed to generate the same interest. Unfortunately, Eddie Holland's best Motown singles—"Just Ain't Enough Love," "Leaving Here," and "Candy to Me"—were released after this album, but Motown never saw fit to release another Holland album. *—Andrew Hamilton*

● **The Complete Eddie Holland** / 1997 / Marginal ✦✦✦

It took a Belgian recording company to finally release a complete collection of Eddie Holland recordings. Motown only released one album on Holland, and it didn't contain many of his better recordings; United Artists never released an album on Eddie Holland. The compilers only missed "You Deserve What You Get," the follow-up to "Jamie," but did include "Welcome Back," an unissued Motown recording, and many hard-to-find United Artists cuts. The sound quality is poor, especially on "Everybody's Going," which is virtually unplayable. However, in this case, you take the bitter with the sweet. What you have is 78 minutes and 31 tracks of a Jackie Wilson soundalike who's in the Rock Hall of Fame as one of the greatest pop songwriters in history. Three songs here didn't make Holland's first album—"Just Ain't Enough Love," "Candy to Me," and "Leaving Here"—and they're among his best, showing that he had the voice to sell a Holland-Dozier-Holland song as well as anybody. If he had chosen to, he could have been a significant recording artist, but obviously his head was elsewhere. "Brenda" is one of few compositions that Eddie wrote alone; the tender ballad was later recorded by the Four Tops. "Merry-Go-Round" was first released on Tamla, then United Artists, but despite some clever lyrics and a good reading from Holland, it flopped. Many recordings from his first LP are overblown attempts, musically and vocally, to make Holland a pop artist and may not go over well to lovers of that classic Motown sound. This collection would be much better if digitally remastered, and channeled for stereo. *—Andrew Hamilton*

Jennifer Holliday

b. Oct. 19, 1960, Houston, TX

Vocals / Quiet Storm, Musical Theater, Vocal Jazz

Texan Jennifer Holliday gained national recognition when she had the lead in the Broadway musical *Your Arm's Too Short to Box With God.* Her performance led to her star-making performance in *Dreamgirls*, an adaptation of the Supremes' saga. The show featured her show-stealing take on "And I Am Telling You I'm Not Going," which became a hit single in 1982. That led her to a career in pop music, although she never recaptured her initial success. She returned to the stage in 1985, appearing in *Sing, Mahalia, Sing*; she continued to release pop music albums while starring on Broadway. In either setting, she's a hardy, throaty, soul belter who chews on every lyric, infusing them with emotional statements. *—Bil Carpenter*

Feel My Soul / 1983 / Geffen ♦♦♦

Maurice White was the producer of choice for Jennifer Holliday's debut album. After the huge splash she'd made in the Broadway shows *Your Arm's Too Short to Box With God* and *Dreamgirls*, the entire R&B/soul and urban contemporary community was poised for her first release. It was good, but not the masterpiece many anticipated. Still, it landed her a number-two hit in "I Am Love" and another Top 30 single, and got her off to a good start in the album arena, one she's been unable to sustain. *—Ron Wynn*

Get Close to My Love / 1987 / Geffen ♦♦

A soaring, often astonishing singer while in the cast of *Dreamgirls*, Holliday never came close to sustained success simply because each album was an uneven, frustrating conglomeration of overproduced tracks and inferior tunes. The one strong number on this album, "Heart on the Line," was a masterpiece, even though it didn't make it beyond the mid-levels on the R&B chart. Her enormous potential remains unfulfilled, at least on album. *—Ron Wynn*

On & On / 1995 / Intersound ♦♦♦

● **The Best of Jennifer Holliday** / Sep. 9, 1996 / Geffen ♦♦♦♦♦

Here is long-overdue compilation celebrating the erratic recording career of Jennifer Holliday. The set includes 16 tracks, not all her best music; but enough of it to buoy the album title. Of course, the set boasts her signature tune "And I'm Telling You I'm Not Going" and "I Am Changing," both from *Dream Girls*. Her warm chart ballads "I Am Love," "Say You Love Me" and "I'm on Your Side" are here, as are her mediocre dance hits. There are a couple of previously unreleased jewels, such as the Bee Gees' "Love Me" and her Grammy-winning cover of Duke Ellington's "Come Sunday." What's strangely missing is her tender "Mr. Magic" and hard-driving rendition of the early Gladys Knight & the Pips' "Giving Up." *—Bill Carpenter*

20th Century Masters—The Millennium Collection: The Best of Jennifer Holliday / Oct. 3, 2000 / Interscope ♦♦♦♦

The Millennium Collection: The Best of Jennifer Holliday gathers highlights from the Tony Award-winning singer/actress, including "And I Am Telling You I'm Not Going" and "I Am Changing" from the original cast album of *Dreamgirls*, the musical that made her a star. "This Game of Love," "Just Let Me Wait," "No Frills Love," and "New At It" are some of the other standout tracks from this compilation, which isn't quite as comprehensive as Geffen's *The Best of Jennifer Holliday* but is nevertheless a concise, enjoyable overview of some of her definitive moments. *—Heather Phares*

Dave Hollister

Vocals / Urban, Club/Dance, Pop-Rap

Onetime R&B session vocalist Dave Hollister first appeared on the soundtrack of *Boyz N the Hood*, but got his big break as an original member of Teddy Riley's Blackstreet, performing on their 1994 debut album. He departed shortly thereafter to pursue a solo career, not only as a singer but also as a songwriter and producer. Hollister's first recorded effort as a solo act, the Erick Sermon/Redman collaboration "Weekend," was featured on the movie soundtrack *The Ride* and released as a single in 1998. His solo debut album, *Ghetto Hymns*, was issued in 1999. *Chicago '85... The Movie* followed a year later. *—Steve Huey*

● **Ghetto Hymns** / May 25, 1999 / DreamWorks ♦♦♦♦

Dave Hollister's *Ghetto Hymns* is something of a concept album about the triumphs and pitfalls of love and relationships in the inner city. Of course, that doesn't mean it's always serious or realistic, but what matters is that Hollister knows how to mix hard-hitting beats with his own smooth singing and a number of cameo raps by the likes of Erick Sermon, Redman, Jazze Pha and Too Short. The result is a record that, while it could have been trimmed a bit, will generally please fans of Hollister's former group, Blackstreet, and of other hip-hop/soul hybrid artists. *—Steve Huey*

Chicago '85 . . . The Movie / Nov. 21, 2000 / DreamWorks ♦♦♦

Chicago native Dave Hollister recalls his past situations on *Chicago '85... The Movie*. A great follow-up to his gold CD *Ghetto Hymns*, the singer/songwriter enlists top talent such as Mike City (who has worked with another Chicago native, Carl Thomas) to make his recollections crystal clear. The title actually refers to a rough period in Hollister's life when he found out that his father was actually his stepfather and in an act of rebellion began gangbanging. Chicago-based producer Steve Huff, who also had success with Avant, produced the lead single, "One Woman Man," which began quickly racing up the charts. On the solid midtempo slammer "Keep on Lovin' Me," Hollister sings about a woman he admires even when she curses him out and makes his bail. The singer almost reaches operatic vibes on the sparse "Destiny" with its swirling string arrangement. On the confessional "Doin' Wrong," Hollister gives one of his best vocal performances over a funky stop-and-go guitar/bass riff. The chugging "I Don't Want to Be a Hustler" spells it all out with Hollister apologizing to his mother because he wasn't raised that way. Amid the baby mama dramas and the thug-life odes, Dave Hollister communicates an authenticity through clearly expressed lyrics that makes *Chicago '85... The Movie* thrilling "viewing." *—Ed Hogan*

Things in the Game Done Changed / Sep. 17, 2002 / Motown ♦♦♦

Former Blackstreet member Dave Hollister has a problem all too common in R&B: finding songs half as memorable as his voice. But his third solo album—and first for Motown—makes some progress in that quest, suggesting that a little Detroit magic might have rubbed off on this Chicago hustler. Despite its title, *Things in the Game Done Changed* doesn't mark any substantial shift in Hollister's formula: He still favors repetitive tunes rooted in gospel, substituting the ebb and flow of his powerful pipes for catchy hooks and melodies. It's an approach he shares with contemporaries like Gerald LeVert—but while LeVert has made a virtue of consistency, concentrating exclusively on the bedroom, a little variety serves Hollister better. Working with a variety of producers (including Tank, a younger kindred spirit), Hollister eschews the hip-hop collaborations that marked *Ghetto Hymns*, but a few rousing soul shouters on the order of "We Gonna Make It," plus a newfound optimism, give this collection a welcome spark, and make you appreciate his ability to spin the thread of a good idea into complex emotional tapestries like "Tonight" and the anguished "Tell Me Why." There's still no hit that would give Hollister the recognition his voice deserves, but he's finally made an album as rock-solid as his singing style. *—Dan LeRoy*

Brenda Holloway

b. Jun. 21, 1946, Atascadero, CA

Vocals, Violin / Pop-Soul, Motown, Soul, Urban

One of the sexiest singers on the Motown label, Brenda Holloway was also one of its grittiest, with a strong gospel influence more typical of Southern soul than the company's usual polish. Best known for her ballad hit "Every Little Bit Hurts," Holloway also recorded (and co-wrote) the original version of "You've Made Me So Very Happy," which soon became a hit for jazz-rockers Blood, Sweat & Tears. Holloway was born in Atascadero, CA, in 1946 and grew up in the Watts section of Los Angeles; as a child, she learned violin and began singing in church with her younger sister Patrice (who later became a prominent session singer and contributed vocals to Josie & the Pussycats). After singing with the group that later became the Whispers, Holloway's first professional recording was made at age 14, backing 12-year-old Patrice on a locally released single. Brenda herself soon began cutting records on several different L.A. labels, and she and her sister also found work as session vocalists.

In 1964, Holloway performed a rendition of Mary Wells' "My Guy" at a DJ convention in Los Angeles. Motown founder Berry Gordy happened to be there, and he was so struck by the power of her vocals (not to mention her physical form) that he made Holloway his first West Coast signing, placing her on the Tamla subsidiary. Her debut single, "Every Little Bit Hurts," was an R&B smash that also reached number 12 on the pop charts, and was covered by British R&B aficionados like the Spencer Davis Group and the Small Faces; it became the title track of her first album, also released in 1964. Holloway also found fans in the Beatles, who gave her an opening slot on their 1965 American tour. She scored several more R&B hits through 1965—"I'll Always Love You" and the Smokey Robinson-penned tracks "When I'm Gone" and "Operator." However, Tamla scrapped a follow-up album, which would have been called *Hurtin' and Cryin'*, and Holloway began to feel that she was getting the short end of the stick. She frequently traveled from her home in Los Angeles to record in Detroit, and began to feel that the material she was given wasn't always up to snuff, perhaps because of her distance. She began to work more on her own writing, often in partnership with her sister, and with a bit of outside help they co-wrote "You've Made Me So Very Happy" in 1968. Holloway's version was a minor R&B hit, but Blood, Sweat & Tears turned it into a major pop hit the following year.

Holloway's second album, *The Artistry of Brenda Holloway*, was finally released in 1968, but that year she announced her retirement from the music business, citing her disillusionment with Motown and her fears of being drawn into the stereotypical hedonistic lifestyle (which conflicted with her still-deep religious convictions). She later married a minister and raised three daughters, returning to music in 1980 with the gospel album *Brand New*. Holloway's records remained popular on England's so-called "Northern soul" scene, and in 1987 she traveled to the U.K. to record several Motown-style singles for producer Ian Levine's Motorcity label. In 1995, motivated by the death of Mary Wells, she returned to live performance around the L.A. area, often in tandem with fellow soul veteran Brenton Wood. She performed in the U.K. as well, and in 1999 she signed with the revived Volt label to record *It's a Woman's World*, which took a more contemporary urban approach. *—Steve Huey*

Every Little Bit Hurts / 1964 / Motown ♦♦♦

The title track was one of Motown's grittiest singles ever, but it didn't put Brenda Holloway into the spotlight she deserved. Her sound and style were so gospel-tinged and powerful that she was out of place on a label that wanted more polished, sophisticated material. This album had some marvelous classics and stands as Holloway's finest. While Motown had many other superb soul artists, Holloway may have been one who'd have done better at Stax or any of the Southern outlets who specialized in rawer, "deep" country and gospel-tinged productions. *—Ron Wynn*

The Artistry of Brenda Holloway / 1968 / Motown ♦♦♦

● **The Very Best of Brenda Holloway** / Feb. 23, 1999 / Motown ♦♦♦♦♦

This 15-track collection gathers up the very best of Holloway's recordings for Motown. A peripheral figure in the company's history, Brenda made the trek from Los Angeles to Detroit to record, working with producers Smokey Robinson, Mickey Stevenson, Henry Cosby, Frank Wilson, and label boss Berry Gordy. Holloway's big hits "Every Little Bit

Hurts," "I'll Always Love You," and "When I'm Gone" are aboard, along with the original version of "You've Made Me So Very Happy," later appropriated by Blood, Sweat & Tears. Solid album material from the canceled Motown album *Hurtin' & Cryin'* makes up the majority of this collection, with "Hurt a Little Everyday," and "You Can Cry on My Shoulder" being two of the highlights. Two previously unreleased tracks, "You've Changed Me" and "Til Johnny Comes," round out the package. Holloway was a big-voiced gospel-style belter, and while not in the Motown front racks, this scintillating package makes a welcome addition to any soul collection. *—Cub Koda*

It's a Woman's World / Nov. 16, 1999 / Volt ✦✦✦

Soul music suffered a major loss when, in 1968, a 22-year-old Brenda Holloway decided to retire from the music industry. It wasn't until 1999, when she turned 53, that the vocalist returned to recording secular R&B in the U.S. (although she provided a gospel album in 1980 and recorded some secular R&B in England in 1987). The Volt label, which Fantasy reactivated in 1999, is synonymous with classic soul; but for the most part, you won't find a classic soul approach on this CD. *It's a Woman's World* gets off to a 1960s-like start with a remake of the Everly Brothers' "Walk Right Back," although most of the material that follows is surprisingly urban contemporary. No, Holloway isn't trying to be Mary J. Blige, Missy Elliot, or a member of Destiny's Child, but this isn't an album of Motown covers either—and high-tech, hip-hop-influenced items like "No Regrets" and "Don't Keep Runnin' (In and Out My Life)" are a lot more urban contemporary than listeners might expect from Holloway. Some of the ballads, meanwhile, have a lot of adult contemporary appeal. Produced by Preston Glass and Fred Pittman, this decent, if unremarkable, CD demonstrated that Holloway's voice had held up well over the years and that she could still be charming and charismatic. Even though *It's a Woman's World* falls short of the excellence of her classic Motown output of the 1960s, it's nice to see her recording again. *—Alex Henderson*

Greatest Hits & Rare Classics / Sep. 18, 2001 / Spectrum ✦✦✦✦✦

When first packaged, this 18-track Brenda Holloway collection was definitely definitive. It features the bulk of Holloway's Motown releases, save a few, and includes strong B-sides like "I've Got to Find It." However, *A Cellar Full of Motown* (2002) features some excellent previously unreleased Holloway tracks, glossed by a melting read of "Who You Gonna Run To," the old Temptations album track (*Gettin' Ready*), and has reduced this assemblage from best to good. But it's still the finest collection of Holloway's releases available—that is, when it's available. "Every Little Bit Hurts" maintains its melancholy grip and "You've Made Me So Very Happy" sounds like the million-seller that wasn't. She glows on four Smokey Robinson tunes as well as "A Favor for a Girl (With a Love Sick Heart)," Kay and Helen Lewis' "Where Were You," and "I'll Always Love You." The definitive Brenda Holloway collection will contain these tracks and a good scoop of those previously unreleased nuggets. *—Andrew Hamilton*

Loleatta Holloway

b. 1946, Chicago, IL

Vocals / Northern Soul, Soul, Disco, Garage/House

It may surprise some that perennial dance diva Loleatta Holloway's highest charting solo record was a soulful ballad, "Cry to Me." Still, Holloway is best known for dancefloor workouts like "Love Sensation," "Hit and Run," and "Run Away." Born in Chicago in 1946, Holloway developed her throaty, full-bodied vocal style and dramatic presentation while singing with her mother in the gospel group, the Holloway Community Singers. She later began taking acting classes. As a teenager, she joined classic gospel group the Caravans led by Albertina Walker who recorded for Savoy Records. In the early '70s, she joined the Chicago cast of the musical *Don't Bother Me I Can't Cope*. Around this time, she met her future producer, manager, and husband Floyd Smith. Smith produced a cover of Gene Chandler's 1963/1965 hit "Rainbow '71" for his Apache label. Atlanta businessman Michael Thevis, who had just started GRC (General Recording Corporation), signed Holloway to his Aware label. The small double-sided hit "Our Love" (number-43 R&B)/"Mother of Shame" (number-63 R&B) charted during the summer of 1973. The tunes were included on her debut album, *Loleatta* (1973). "Cry to Me," the title track of her second album, gave Holloway her highest charting solo single on the R&B and pop charts; written by master songwriter Sam Dees, it hit number-ten R&B in early 1975.

While with GRC, Holloway met promotion director Gus Redmond whom she would later work with at Salsoul Records. In 1976, GRC went out of business and Holloway signed with Norman Harris' Salsoul-distributed label, Gold Mind Records. Guitarist/arranger/songwriter/producer Harris was a veteran of the Philly soul scene, having been a member of MFSB, the studio band for Gamble & Huff's Philadelphia International Records. He'd joined with fellow MFSB vets bassist Ron Baker and drummer Earl Young to form Baker-Harris-Young Productions (the Trammps, First Choice, Double Exposure, Love Committee, Eddie Holman). Oddly enough (possibly the label was hedging their bets), dance-oriented Gold Mind's first release on Holloway was the Dees ballad "Worn Out Broken Heart." The catchy Harris-produced uptempo flip side "Dreamin'" reached number-72 pop and was popular in discos. Her first Gold Mind LP *Loleatta* (released March 1977) was both produced in Chicago by Floyd Smith and in Philadelphia by Baker-Harris-Young. In addition to "Worn Out Broken Heart," the album included "Hit and Run," which peaked at number-56 R&B. The two elongated alternate jam session takes of "Hit and Run" are disco classics. "Run Away," co-written by Vincent Montana Jr., was released as the Salsoul Orchestra featuring Loleatta Holloway and was Holloway's next chart single (number-89 R&B in late 1977).

After Gold Mind folded, all of their acts were transferred to Salsoul. Her first Salsoul LP, *Queen of the Night* (September 1978), yielded the disco hits "Catch Me on the Rebound," "Mama Don't, Papa Won't," and "I May Not Be There When You Want Me." The LP also spawned her second highest charting single on the R&B charts, the duet ballad "Only You" by Loleatta Holloway and Bunny Sigler, which hit number-11 R&B in late summer 1978. Her next album, *Loleatta Holloway* (September 1979), included the disco hits "All About the Papers," "That's What You Said" (another Holloway/Sigler duet), "The Greatest Performance of My Life," and the deep-soul ballad "There Must Be a Reason."

Around 1979, Holloway contributed vocals to "Relight My Fire," a massive disco hit for Dan Hartman ("Instant Replay," "I Can Dream About You"). Hartman produced what became the singer's signature tune, "Love Sensation," which caused quite a sensation on the disco charts. The song was also the title of Holloway's 1980 LP that spawned the disco hits "Dance What Cha Wanna" and "Short End of the Stick." Holloway was reunited with the Salsoul Orchestra on a track written and produced by Patrick Adams (Inner Life, Phreek), "Seconds." Though she never had a pop hit in the U.S., Holloway had a huge following in Europe and Japan. In the mid-'80s, Salsoul ceased operations and Holloway was without a recording contract. Shortly after producing a cover of Rufus & Chaka Khan's "Sweet Thing" for Holloway, Floyd Smith died in 1984. That same year, the singer signed with Streetwise Records, a label owned by producer Arthur Baker (Afrika Bambaataa and the Soul Sonic Force). The single "Crash Goes Love" b/w "Sweet Thing" peaked at number-86 R&B in late summer 1984.

Throughout the '80s and '90s, Holloway recorded for a succession of labels: DJ International, Saturday, Warlock, and Select, among others. During the '90s, audio sampling became in vogue and snippets of Holloway's vocals can been heard on numerous dance records from around the world. This practice has led to some litigation (Black Box's "Ride on Time"). Holloway's fortunes took a turn for the better when Mark Wahlberg, younger brother of New Kids on the Block's Donnie Wahlberg, sampled "Love Sensation" for his million-selling 1991 hit. "Good Vibrations" by Marky Mark and the Funky Bunch featuring Loleatta Holloway hit number-one pop during the fall of that year. The disco diva was in more demand than ever, riding the momentum of a number-one pop hit. Holloway occasionally tours and resides in Chicago. *—Ed Hogan*

Loleatta / 1973 / Aware ✦✦✦

Cry to Me / 1975 / Aware ✦✦✦

Loleatta / Mar. 1977 / Goldmine ✦✦✦✦

Originally issued in March 1977, *Loleatta* was the singer's debut release for Philly soul guitarist Norman Harris' Gold Mind label distributed by NY-based Salsoul Records. It was both produced in Chicago by her husband Floyd Smith and in Philadelphia through Baker-Harris-Young Productions. The LP boasted Holloway's highest-charting R&B single, the Sam Dees ballad "Worn Out Broken Heart," and the dance classics "Hit and Run" and "Dreamin'." The former has two extended alternate "jam session" takes that are found on the original 12-inch pressings baring the Gold Mind logo. One of the takes is on *Original Salsoul Classics: The 20th Anniversary* and is sometimes found on CD reissues of the LP. Another passion-soaked ballad, "What Now," a Curtis Mayfield song, received radio play as an album track. The upbeat "We're Getting Stronger (The Longer We Stay)" has a smokin' rhythm break. A Satoshi Tomiie remix of "Dreamin'" issued by Salsoul/The Right Stuff/EMI topped *Billboard*'s Hot Dance Music/Club Play chart on December 9, 2000. *—Ed Hogan*

Greatest Hits / Jul. 23, 1996 / Capitol ✦✦✦✦✦

During the disco era of the mid- to late '70s, no female vocalist sang with more passion and authority than Loleatta Holloway. Her roots were Northern soul, and when she took dance clubs by storm with the classics heard on this 1996 compilation, the Chicago native never forgot disco's debt to soul and gospel. "Runaway," "Catch Me on the Rebound," "Hit and Run" and other exuberant hits (many recorded in Philadelphia) aren't Euro-disco à la the Silver Convention, Cerrone or Love & Kisses, but are distinctly American gems showing how powerful it could be when Philly soul gave way to Philly disco/soul. "Love Sensation" influenced '90s rap singles ranging from Marky Mark's "Good Vibrations" to Biscuit's "My Music." Though fast tempos dominate the superb collection of Salsoul and Gold Mind material, "Worn Out Broken Heart" and Curtis Mayfield's "What Now" illustrate her excellence with ballads. For anyone with even a casual interest in disco, this superb CD is essential listening. *—Alex Henderson*

● **Runaway: The Best of Loleatta Holloway** / Jul. 1, 1999 / Charly ✦✦✦✦✦

Charly's *Runaway: The Best of Loleatta Holloway* overlaps Capitol's *Greatest Hits* with just over half its selections and, like that compilation that was released just a year prior in the U.S., it concentrates on her '70s work as a disco diva for the revered Salsoul label. The differences between this U.K. release and *Greatest Hits* has more to do with what caught on in the respective countries than anything else. Both compilations do justice to Holloway's discography, but this one is slightly better in its track selection. For instance, this disc rectifies the major gaffe of *Greatest Hits*' exclusion of "Dreamin'," a single that hit number three on the *Billboard* club chart in the U.S. Apart from that, both discs include the most significant moments of this era of Holloway's career. Regardless of how the discs stack up next to each other, you'll get over an hour of exemplary '70s dance music either way. *—Andy Kellman*

Queen of the Night: The Ultimate Club Collection / Jan. 23, 2001 / Capitol ✦✦✦✦

Like Gloria Gaynor and Linda Clifford, Loleatta Holloway was one of the dance divas you turned to in the late '70s and early '80s if you liked your disco drenched with soul. In Holloway's hands, disco was a logical extension of Northern soul; it merely added another floor to the house that big-voiced goddesses like Aretha Franklin, Etta James, Gladys Knight, Irma Thomas, and Martha Reeves had built. Thankfully, Holloway's influence didn't end with the 1970s. *Queen of the Night: The Ultimate Club Collection* reminds us how much she influenced house music, hip-house, and dance-pop in the 1980s and '90s. This CD is, for the most part, a collection of remixes. The Right Stuff provides Tom Molton's famous 1980 mix of "Love Sensation" (which has been sampled to death) and the original 1979 version of the classic Dan Hartman/Holloway duet "Vertigo/Relight My Fire," but other late-'70s and early-'80s gems (including the 1976 hit "Dreamin'") are given high-tech house or hip-house makeovers. On this disc, Morales D'Master's 2000 remix of Black Box's 1990 smash "Ride on Time" (which sampled "Love Sensation") is right at home with DJ Johnny Vicious' 1994 club hit "Stand Up" (which was based on "Dreamin'") and Junior Vasquez's Holloway-minded single "Gotta Be #1" (a club hit in 1992). *Queen of the Night: The Ultimate Club Collection* isn't meant to be a greatest-hits package—those who need an introduction to Loleatta Holloway would be much better off starting out with *Runaway: The Best of Loleatta Holloway.* This club-oriented CD, in fact, is probably too esoteric for anyone who has only a casual interest in Holloway's work. But for serious club hounds, *Queen of the Night: The Ultimate Club Collection* is an interesting release that shows us just how long lasting the singer's influence has been. *—AlexHenderson*

The Hollywood Flames

f. 1949, Los Angeles, CA, **db.** 1967

Group / Doo Wop, R&B

This was a long-lasting Los Angeles doo wop aggregation with a very fluid personnel roster. Bobby Day was one of the group's founders in 1950, and they recorded prolifically for Hollywood, Specialty, Lucky, Swingtime, Money, and other firms before cutting their one major hit, the rocking "Buzz Buzz Buzz," in 1957 for Ebb Records. Earl Nelson, who was later half of Bob & Earl, sang lead on the tune, and some of their subsequent Ebb 45s were rocking novelties. Day went on to solo success with "Rockin' Robin," and the group managed one more chart item, "Gee," for Chess in 1961 with Donald Height as lead. *—Bill Dahl*

● **The Hollywood Flames** / Aug. 3, 1992 / Specialty ✦✦✦✦✦

Though not in a class with the Moonglows, the Five Satins, or the Platters, the Hollywood Flames were a solid doo wop group that should have been much better known. The only song on this CD that was a major hit is the infectious "Buzz Buzz Buzz." Otherwise, listeners are treated to excellent material that fell through the cracks, which ranges from invigorating uptempo songs like "Strollin' on the Beach," "A Little Bird," and "Crazy" to such engaging ballads as "Give Me Back My Heart," "A Star Fell," and "My Confession." While "Frankenstein's Den" shows that the Flames could be as much fun as the Coasters, the atypical and previously unreleased "This Heart of Mine" is as brooding as something Bobby "Blue" Bland would do. For doo wop aficionados who only know the Flames for "Buzz Buzz Buzz," this collection demonstrates that they had many other inspired moments. *—Alex Henderson*

The Hollywood Flames & Friends: 1950–1965 / 2000 / Vintage ✦✦✦

During a 15-year career, this Los Angeles-based doo wop/R&B group recorded under at least seven names for at least 19 different recording companies. The group's lineup changes make the Temptations' members' departures (over a much longer time frame) seem minor. Vintage Records did a yeoman job assembling these 27 tracks from the many nooks and crannies they had to investigate. Like the early O'Jays in northeast Ohio, the Hollywood Flames were similarly large in southern California; most of their records made the play lists of area R&B stations, but few—save "Buzz, Buzz, Buzz" (their biggest hit), "Elizabeth" (about the actress Elizabeth Taylor), "Believe in Me" (a masterful ballad), and a few others—received any accolades outside their home haven. This album includes sides they recorded as the Turks and the Jets, but excludes tracks they did under names like the Satellites (who cut the original rendition of "Little Bitty Pretty One"). Original member Robert Byrd and later member Earl Nelson also recorded as Bob & Earl. A treat for collectors is the inclusion of both sides of their first single "Please Tell Me Now" and "Young Girl," issued when they were the Flames. *—Andrew Hamilton*

Eddie Holman

b. Jun. 3, 1946, Norfolk, VA

Vocals / Pop-Soul, Philly Soul, Soul

Eddie Holman's 1970 number two smash "Hey There Lonely Girl," with its creamy falsetto vocals and lush Philly soul arrangement, is one of the most well-remembered one-shot soul hits. Actually, Holman had been recording since the early '60s, scoring some minor hits with "This Can't Be True" (1965) and "Am I a Loser (From the Start)" (1966). In 1969, he hooked up with Philadelphia producer Peter DeAngelis, best known for his work with teen idols Fabian and Frankie Avalon. His arrangements for Holman, however, rivaled Gamble & Huff's in quality, yielding some other minor R&B hits in 1969 and 1970 with "I Love You," "Don't Stop Now," and "Cathy Called," as well as an album in 1970. Most identified with his rich falsetto, Holman actually sang in a much more traditional vocal range on much of his material, some of which was written by him or his wife, Sheila. He largely vanished from sight after 1970, though he recorded for several labels in the '70s. *—Richie Unterberger*

● **I Love You** / 1970 / Varese Sarabande ✦✦✦✦

Here is first-class romantic soul, featuring Holman's swooping vocals and lush Philly string and backup vocal arrangements. Includes "Hey There Lonely Girl" and his other minor R&B hits from the same period. [The CD reissue adds three non-LP cuts from 1969 and 1970 singles.] *—Richie Unterberger*

A Night to Remember / 1977 / Salsoul ✦✦✦✦

One of those LPs where you wish you had been at the session cause it sounds like one helluva party. Eddie Holman applies his stratospheric falsetto to eight jams aimed at the disco club scene. He's backed by a full complement of Philly's finest musicians and a star-studded backing crew that includes Phil Hurtt, Ron Tyson, Bruce Gray, Carl Helm, and Barbara Ingram. Contains the hit "This Will Be a Night to Remember," written by Ron Tyson & Ron Baker, which remains one of Holman's most electrifying moments. Tyson who sung with the Ethics, Love Committee, and has enjoyed a long tenure with the Temptations co-wrote the LP's three other treats "You Make My Life Complete," "Immune to Love," and "Time Will Tell." Originally released on Salsoul Records in 1977, and produced by Norman Harris, Baker & Earl Young. *—Andrew Hamilton*

Eddie's My Name: A Collection of Rare 60s Soul / 1993 / Goldmine ✦✦✦

Unfortunately there are no original dates or label information whatsoever in the liner notes, but one can surmise that this is a collection of early Holman sides, all predating his "Hey There Lonely Girl" smash. Probably these date mostly or entirely from the mid-'60s, as the twenty tracks include his 1965-1966 R&B hits "This Can't Be True" and "Am I a Loser," and do not duplicate anything from the *I Love You* compilation of his early ABC sides. Holman was a journeyman Philadelphia soul singer in his early days, but a good one. He stood out somewhat from the pack, due both to his extraordinary falsetto and his reliance upon original material (writing or co-writing most of the tunes here). These performances are not as lushly produced as the ones he did under Peter DeAngelis at ABC, but are fairly solid. While some of the songs are derivative of doo wop (like "Don't Stop Now," which he would remake at ABC) and Motown, he also had an occasional flair for dramatic and unpredictable chord and key changes, as heard on "This Can't Be True." The version of "Am I a Loser" here is the original, not the ABC remake; likewise, "I Surrender" is described on the track listing as the "original demo," and is not the ABC version. *—Richie Unterberger*

The Holmes Brothers

f. 1980, New York, NY

Group / Retro-Soul, Soul-Blues, Modern Electric Blues

The Holmes Brothers' unique synthesis of gospel-inflected blues harmonies, accompanied by good drumming and rhythm-based guitar playing, gives them a down-home rural feeling that no other touring blues group can duplicate.

Brothers Sherman and Wendell Holmes, along with drummer Popsy Dixon (the falsetto voice), are the group's core members, although they occasionally tour with extra musicians. All three harmonize well together. Although people like Bo Diddley and especially Jimmy Reed were early influences on Wendell & Sherman, gospel music also played an important role in their respective upbringings.

Although they'd been performing in Harlem for years, the Holmes Brothers—originally from Christchurch, VA—took their time becoming international blues touring stars. Thanks to a fair deal at Rounder Records, the group has released three recordings for that label, beginning with a 1989 release, *In the Spirit.* When this album made waves and got them off and running on the festival and club circuit around the U.S. and Europe, they followed it up two years later with *Where It's At* (1991), *Soul Street* (1993) and *Promised Land* (1996). The group's career has been aided by the interest of people like Peter Gabriel, who recruited them for his WOMAD (world music) Festivals in England and who also recorded them in a gospel context on the album *Jubilation,* for his Real World subsidiary of Virgin Records in 1992. Joan Osborne was also a supporter of the group. Early in her career Osborne befriended the Holmes Brothers and eventually took them on tour as her backing band when she opened for Bob Dylan in 1997. She produced the group's first release on Alligator Records *Speaking in Tongues* in 2001. *—Richard Skelly & Al Campbell*

In the Spirit / 1990 / Rounder ✦✦✦✦✦

The Holmes Brothers' voices are too potent, their harmonies too smashing and their love of vintage sounds too immense for them to be content with producer-dominated, softer urban contemporary sounds. This set included some riveting gospel tunes like "None But the Righteous" and "Up Above My Head," plus a credible (if a little lengthy) version of "When Something Is Wrong With My Baby" and the tighter, hard-hitting tunes "Please Don't Hurt Me," "Ask Me No Questions" and "The Final Round." If straight-ahead, rousing shared leads and booming harmonies interest you, the Holmes Brothers do it the way they used to throughout the South in the '60s and '70s. *—Ron Wynn*

Where It's At / 1991 / Rounder ✦✦✦✦

Their second release contained 11 more wonderful tunes that easily moved from surging R&B to rousing blues with an occasional venture into gospel or country. They covered "Drown in My Own Tears" and "High Heel Sneakers" and had the requisite qualities for each one down pat, as well as "Never Let Me Go," "The Love You Save" and "I Saw The Light." But their own numbers, like "I've Been a Loser" and the title track, were even better, displaying a contemporary sensibility and classic style and sound. *—Ron Wynn*

Jubilation / 1992 / Real World ✦✦✦

Jubilation is a revealing, wonderful collection of the Holmes Brothers' distinctive soul. The brothers tie together a seemingly disconnected array of styles—everything from straightforward blues, R&B, and gospel to worldbeat and country—and come up with a cohesive whole. Even when the group delves into soukous or works with a Chinese flutist, it manages to retain the pure qualities of American blues and R&B. *—Thom Owens*

Soul Street / 1993 / Rounder ✦✦✦✦✦

This album continued the Holmes Brothers' tradition of doing tremendous covers ("You're Gonna Make Me Cry," "Down In Virginia" and "Fannie Mae"), authentic originals ("I Won't Hurt You Anymore," "Dashboard Bar") and adding gospel ("Walk in the Light") and honky-tonk ("There Goes My Everything") into their blend. There's little to criticize about the Holmes Brothers; their sound, vocals and harmonies aren't laid-back or restrained, and everything they sing is done with exuberance and integrity. It may not be commercially viable, but it's musically sound. *—Ron Wynn*

Promised Land / Apr. 1996-Jun. 1996 / Rounder ✦✦✦✦

The Holmes Brothers have honed their blend of rock, blues, gospel and soul to perfection on this, their fifth release. Whether it's Popsy Dixon's stunning interpretation of Tom Waits' "Train Song," the soul stirring harmonies on the gospel standard "I Surrender All," or an original, gritty guitar workout like "Start Stoppin'," there is simply not a bad song on this album. The Holmes Brothers continue to defy all classifications, except one: damn good music. *—Steve McMullen*

Speaking in Tongues / Jan. 30, 2001 / Alligator ✦✦✦✦✦

The sixth album by New York's Holmes Brothers is another all-spirituals set—though not in the traditional sense of the word. Produced by pop singer Joan Osborne (before she was a superstar, Osborne woodshedded with the Brothers and developed a fine rootsy singing style of her own), who was there in the Manhattan trenches with the band, this set goes a long, long way to capturing raw, excruciating grooves. With the a trio of singers as soulful as any group Memphis or Motown ever produced, the Holmes Brothers take it to the gut each and every time. This set opens with Ben Harper's "Homeless Child," and let's just say after the deep, grease-fire funk the vocalizing creates, Harper should never play it again. This song now *belongs* to the Holmes Brothers. Sherman Holmes' groove on his "Speaking in Tongues" borrows a piece of a Rick James bassline and builds an entire gospel-funk number on top of it. This might not be the song you'd hear in church, but you should—you might actually go. With a six-voice chorus kicking the refrain through every single barrier between spirituality and carnality, weight is lent to the notion that this Jesus that Sherman sings of is a flesh-and-blood Jesus, inspiring devotion and reverence in the everyday world. Osborne is able to accomplish what no other producer who has worked with this band has been able to do: She leaves their sound alone. Its rough edges, knotty corners, and rough-hewn grace are all displayed without reservation or apology. This is the band's barroom sound enhanced with a trio of female voices who, if anything, make it more raucous, more slippery, and somehow nastier, even though this is sanctified music. It's body music that seeks to transcend the body. Thank God it hasn't yet. Their Memphis soul-styled reading of Sister Rosetta Tharpe's "Can't No Grave Hold My Body Down" is revelatory. Taking her already deep blues and chunking it up with Wendell's wah-wahed guitar, and with Rob Arthur doubling on rhythm loops and funky organ, the thing threatens to lift right off the ground. Only the Precious Three anchor the tune's body to its heart and keep it earthbound. And besides the Holmes originals, another definitive reading of Harper's "I Want to Be Ready," and Bob Dylan's "Man of Peace," their radical reworking of Gamble & Huff's classic disco-gospel tune "Love Train" is confounding in its essentialism. It takes the harmony of the original tune and uses it to drop the melody out; it's replaced with a different shuffling rhythm and a Curtis Mayfield-styled chorus. With the Holmes Brothers, the song becomes an anthem of a different kind. Only Wendell, Sherman, and Popsy Dixon could take secular material and redeem it without stretching the truth. If anything, they inject truth directly into the meaning of a song that merely implies it. And they do so with such openness and beauty, without judgment or musical one-upmanship, that their courteous grace is apparent everywhere. This is the finest of the Holmes Brothers' recordings to make the street. It will be too bad if critics fault them for using Osborne as a producer, when she was uniquely qualified to bring their vision to the public. She's done a fine job, and one can only hope some of her fans will take notice of the greatest soul/gospel/blues/funk group on the planet. Awesome. *—Thom Jurek*

• **Righteous! The Essential Collection** / Jul. 16, 2002 / Rounder ✦✦✦✦✦

Andy Breslau described the Holmes Brothers' music as "gospel-infused doo wop funk," which pretty much captures the spirit and synthesis of their style. Combining old R&B, soul, and gospel, brothers Sherman and Wendell Holmes along with Popsy Dixon create a rich sound filled with lovely harmony. The intensity of the group's studio performances evokes a live feel, offering an inkling of what their performances at Lynch's in Manhattan must have sounded like during the '80s. *Righteous!* collects almost 75 minutes of material from the group's four Rounder albums, beginning with *In the Spirit* in 1990 and ending with *Promised Land* in 1996. The album kicks off with a bit of electric blues topped with a healthy dose of soul on "Got Myself Together," a song that jumps out of the gate at a gallop and holds to a steady gait for five minutes. Gospel-drenched pieces like "Promised Land," complete with electric guitar, will have non-believers singing along, while classics like "There Goes My Everything" combine classic soul with a touch of country. One also wouldn't want to miss the Holmes Brothers' takes on Tom Waits' "Train Song" and the Beatles' "And I Love Her." Breslau's liner notes, which travel back to the Holmes Brothers' residency at Lynch's, are both edifying and fun to read. While all of the albums the Holmes Brothers recorded for Rounder are worthy efforts, *Righteous!* offers a solid introduction to anyone who has missed out on their wonderful music. *—Ronnie D. Lankford Jr.*

Redd Holt (Isaac Holt)

b. May 16, 1932, Rosedale, MS

Drums / Pop-Soul, Soul-Jazz, Soul, Funk

Born May 16, 1932, jazz drummer Redd Holt first came to prominence in 1956 as part of the Ramsey Lewis Trio, with whom he recorded popular instrumentals for the next nine years, including the 1965 pop-jazz hits "Hang on Sloopy" and "The In Crowd." Shortly after this commercial success, Holt and bassist Eldee Young left Lewis' group to record for Brunswick as the Young-Holt Trio with pianist Don Walker. After minor success with the soul novelty of "Wack Wack," Young & Holt restructured their group once again, this time emerging with the moniker (Young-Holt Unlimited) that yielded them their biggest hit, "Soulful Strut." Holt started his own group in the '70s, Redd Holt Unlimited, that continued with the soul-jazz style of his previous groups. In the early '80s he played with Ramsey Lewis again briefly before concentrating on touring and performing as a leader. *—Wade Kergan*

Look Out! Look Out! / Dec. 1961 / Argo ✦✦✦

Isaac, Isaac, Isaac / 1974 / Paula ✦✦✦

• **The Other Side of the Moon** / 1975 / Paula ✦✦✦✦

This 1975 slab by drummer Redd Holt was his second outing after the disintegration of the Young-Holt Unlimited rhythm team. Tighter and more adventurous than *Isaac, Isaac, Isaac*, its predecessor, Holt goes for the heart of rhythm here, letting it flower over the top of all the other arrangements. As a way of signifying this, he opens the set with a short but deeply funky and soulful rendition of Bob Marley's "I Shot the Sheriff." With less than two-and-a-half minutes of clock time, it's get out and go or nothing and Holt makes his tom-toms pop like snares, keeping only the slamming guitaristry of Randy Ford on top with him. Elsewhere, as on "Gimme Some Mo," Holt intertwines with keyboardist Eugene Curry to allow bassist Jose Holmes to cut the groove fast and deep, popping it all over the sonic spectrum like Bootsy Collins but with more finesse. One of the album's standouts is the spaced-out jazz-funk of the title track, with Curry's B-3 offering huge chords that are vamped on by Holt, who carries the beat into the stratosphere and is responded to by some truly inspired single-string playing from Ford. The phase shifters on the drums are a bit annoying and date the track and the album, but it's a small complaint with music that's this hot. There's also a bit of smooth Latin groove on "Tica Chita" and a killer cover of Billy Preston's "Nothing From Nothing" that showcases Curry's many keyboard skills, with Holmes playing like he was the bass player in Sly Stone's band. This is a solid little album, wrapped up jelly tight, that embodies the best of easy-grooving funky soul from the mid-'70s and, with the exception of its extraneous sound effects, has aged extremely well. *—Thom Jurek*

Honey & the Bees

f. 1965, Philadelphia, PA, **db.** 1973

Group / Soul

A minor but talented Philadelphia female soul quartet, Honey & the Bees made some relatively little-known records for the Arctic and Josie labels in the late '60s and early '70s with the aid of musicians that played on classic 1970s Gamble & Huff productions. These included Leon Huff himself on piano, and Ron Baker, Earl Young, Bobby Eli, and Norman Harris in the rhythm section; Harris and Thom Bell were among those who contributed to the songwriting. Honey & the Bees spent years on the club circuit, opening for bigger soul acts in Philadelphia and throughout the East Coast before disbanding in 1973. Group member Gwen Oliver married Fred Wesley of the J.B.'s, whom she met when Honey & the Bees opened for James Brown in 1971. *—Richie Unterberger*

Dynamite / 1999 / Jamie ✦✦✦

This disc has 14 of their Arctic sides (four previously unreleased), nine of which are from 1966-1969 singles. Lamentably, the liner notes do not include any dates or original release information. Although Honey & the Bees were more competent than distinctive as vocalists, the material and arrangements amount to some pretty decent Philadelphia soul from a time when the genre was starting to coalesce around the Gamble-Huff-Bell sound. What's here is not as slick or commercially successful as the Gamble-Huff-Bell blockbusters of the early and mid-'70s, which is fine, as it has an airiness that often escaped such blockbusters. The Gamble-Huff-Bell comparisons, however, are not gratuitous: Huff himself plays piano on some of the cuts, and the rhythm section includes Ron Baker, Earl Young, Bobby Eli, and Norman Harris, all of whom were present on many Philly soul smashes in later years. Honey & the Bees were versatile performers who could handle styles and songs ranging from emotional, melodic ballads ("Make You Mine") and midtempo dance tunes ("Why Do You Hurt the One Who Loves You") to harder, funkier outings betraying the influence of more progressive soul trends ("Love Addict," "Music (Makes You Want to Dance," "Baby, Do That Thing"). Fred Wesley of the J.B.s, who married group member Gwen Oliver, wrote the liner notes. *—Richie Unterberger*

• **Come Get It: The Complete Josie Recordings 1970–1971** / May 2, 2000 / WestSide ✦✦✦✦

Honey Cone

f. 1969, Los Angeles, CA, **db.** 1972

Group / Soul, Smooth Soul, Pop-Soul

Edna Wright, Carolyn Willis, and Shellie Clark comprised the vocal trio Honey Cone, which only stayed together for four years but was still one of the best female soul groups of the early '70s. Although Honey Cone (which lead singer Wright formed in 1969) was based in Los Angeles, their recordings were Northern-style soul—specifically, Detroit soul. Martha & the Vandellas and the Marvelettes—two of the female vocal groups that epitomized Motown Records' sound in the '60s—were among Honey Cone's main influences, and the group (which favored a blend of sweetness and grit) worked closely with three producer/songwriters who used to work at Motown: Brian Holland, Lamont Dozier, and Eddie Holland. However, Honey Cone's members had been in the music industry before they joined forces with the famous Holland-Dozier-Holland team. Willis (born 1946, Los Angeles, CA) had been with Bob B. Soxx & the Blue Jeans, who were known for '60s hits like "Why Do Lovers Break Each Other's Heart?" and "Not Too Young to Get Married." Clark (born in 1943, Brooklyn, NY) was an ex-member of the Ikettes, (Ike & Tina Turner's female backup singers), while Wright (born 1944, Los Angeles, CA) had been with the Blossoms. In fact, Wright's older sister is singer/actress Darlene Love, who was a member of Bob B. Soxx & the Blue Jeans as well as the Blossoms (in addition to doing a lot of recording by herself). Wright also recorded as a solo artist in the '60s; her Champion single "A Touch of Venus" (recorded under the pseudonym Sandy Wynns) was a small regional hit in southern California. And like so many of the soul singers who were active in the '60s and '70s, Wright wasn't without gospel credentials. She had a Christian upbringing and sang gospel with the Church of God in Christ Singers, but ended up making secular R&B her primary focus.

Wright, Clark, and Willis had only been together a few months when, in 1969, the group caught the attention of Eddie Holland (who came up with the name Honey Cone). The prolific Holland-Dozier-Holland team (which wrote countless mega-hits for Motown artists) had recently left Motown and started their own Detroit-based soul label Hot Wax/Invictus, and Honey Cone became the company's first signing. Honey Cone's first release, a 1969 single titled "While You're Out Looking for Sugar," was also Hot Wax's first release. The very Motown-sounding tune was not a major hit; it reached number-26 on *Billboard*'s R&B singles chart and number 62 on the magazine's pop singles chart. But for a small upstart label, that single was a decent start.

Honey Cone's next single, "Girls, It Ain't Easy," was equally Motown-sounding and *did* become a major hit, reaching number eight on *Billboard*'s R&B singles chart. After that, Honey Cone enjoyed their biggest hits of all. Released in late 1970, the infectious "Want Ads" (which Taylor Dayne covered in 1988) got off to a slow start and the song had been out four months before it even charted in either *Billboard* or *Cash Box* (*Billboard*'s main competitor at the time). But when "Wants Ads" finally took off, it *really* took off and soared to number one on *Billboard*'s R&B and pop singles charts. In 1971, Honey Cone had another number-one R&B hit with "Stick Up," which was also a number-11 pop hit. And a few more major hits followed in 1972, including the ballad "The Day I Found Myself" and the Latin-influenced "One Monkey Don't Stop No Show" (a number-five R&B single and a number-15 pop hit).

But as big as Honey Cone was from 1969-1972, it didn't fare nearly as well in 1973; none of the three Honey Cone singles that Hot Wax put out in 1973 ("If I Can't Fly," "The Truth Will Come Out," and "Ace in the Hole") were big hits. Sadly, Hot Wax/Invictus found itself experiencing a serious cash flow problem in 1973, despite having put out big sellers by Honey Cone as well as Freda Payne, 100 Percent (Aged in Soul), Laura Lee, and the Chairmen of the Board. The problem wasn't that Hot Wax/Invictus' releases lacked commercial appeal; the problem, allegedly, was that the company was not getting paid by its independent distributors. In 1973, Honey Cone broke up, and Hot Wax/Invictus went out of business the following year. Wright went on to record by herself, providing the solo LP *Oops! Here I Go Again* for RCA in 1976. All five of the LPs that Honey Cone recorded for Hot Wax—*Honey Cone* in 1969, *Take Me With You* in 1970, *Sweet Replies* and *Soul Tapestry* in 1971, and *Love, Peace & Soul* in 1972—went out of print when the label folded. However, all of Honey Cone's major hits are included on a 14-song *Greatest Hits* CD that Fantasy assembled in 1990. And the comprehensive *Soulful Sugar*, which Castle put out in 2001, boasts no less than 45 tracks. *—Alex Henderson*

Take Me With You / 1971 / Hot Wax ♦♦♦

Sweet Replies / 1971 / Hot Wax ♦♦♦♦

Sweet Replies is Honey Cone's second Hot Wax LP. The million-seller "Want Ads" propels this twelve-song assortment, with help from the R&B hits "Take Me With You" and the beautiful piano-driven declaration "The Day I Found Myself." Edna Wright, Shellie Clark, and Carolyn Willis both sang and looked good. Classy photos on the front, back, and inside covers of the three wearing stylish hot pants outfits didn't hurt sales. *—Andrew Hamilton*

Love, Peace & Soul / 1972 / Hot Wax ♦♦♦

Do yourself a favor if you come across this album: play side one once, then take a pin and drag it across the grooves; this way you'll never make the mistake of playing it again. Three beautiful R&B classics—"Ooh Baby Baby," "Stay in My Corner" and Smokey Robinson's endearing "Who's Loving You"—are disrespected big time. The arrangements are poor and the vocals are uninspired, but don't blame L.A. natives Edna Wright, Shellie Clark, and Carolyn Willis (the Honey Cone)—these charts would have dampened James Brown's fire. "Sittin' on a Time Bomb (Waitin' for the Hurt to Come)" climbed the charts and made a respectable showing; it's the Honey Cone's style, it's what they're about. The piano-driven "Ace in the Hole" is the LP's other gem; this should have rocketed up the charts, but it did little, probably because Hot Wax was in the process of dissolving and the promotion was little or nil. *—Andrew Hamilton*

● **Greatest Hits** / 1990 / Fantasy ♦♦♦♦♦

One of the finest girl groups of the early '70s, Honey Cone was often compared to Martha & the Vandellas for a number of reasons. The fact that the label they recorded for, Hot Wax/Invictus, was owned by former Motown producers/songwriters Holland-Dozier-Holland made it an obvious comparison. And also, the robust nature of Honey Cone's harmonies certainly bring the Vandellas to mind. On "Want Ads," "Stick Up," "One Monkey Don't Stop No Show," and other hits included on this superb CD, the singers effectively combine sweetness and grit—pop sleekness and gospel-influenced soulfulness. To be sure, Honey Cone could pack quite a punch emotionally and harmonically. But as much potential as Honey Cone had, its success was short-lived—and the singers were gone from the charts by 1974. With its albums long out of print, *Greatest Hits* can serve as a fine introduction to Honey Cone's soul/pop legacy. *—Alex Henderson*

● **Soulful Sugar: The Complete Hot Wax Recordings** / Jan. 1, 2002 / Castle ♦♦♦♦♦

Honey Cone, the girl group with the sweet name and the bumblebee persona, didn't masquerade as biker babe wannabes like the Angels, come off as fly foxes like the Ikettes, or fight their battles with tears either. They tell it like it is on "While You're Out Looking for Sugar (Somebody's Gonna Take Your Honey and Be Gone)," "One Monkey Don't Stop No Show," "Stick Up," "Want Ads," and others written by a consortium of General Johnson, Angelo Bond, and Gregg Perry, with some Edith Wayne/Ronald Dunbar and HDH tracks in the mix. This complete account of Honey Cone's Hot Wax recordings features the excellent "Ace in the Hole" twice—the long album version with the funky, bubbling break and the single edit. Instead of wailing at an imminent breakup, Honey Cone gets philosophical (e.g., "Sitting on a Time Bomb (Waiting on the Hurt to Come)," "The Day I Found Myself," "It's Better to Have Love and Lost," and "Girls It Ain't Easy"). They show vulnerability behind a strong façade on "Take Me With You" and cloying versions of "Ooo Baby Baby" and "Stay in My Corner." With 45 tracks, this gargantuan collection has enough soulful honey to fill a bee hive. *—Andrew Hamilton*

The Honeydrippers

f. 1984

Group / Rock & Roll, Roots Rock

The Honeydrippers were a post-Led Zeppelin side project for singer Robert Plant, allowing him to indulge his sincere love for vintage R&B. Though best known for the all-star aggregate that waxed the group's only recording in 1984, Plant actually formed the Honeydrippers in 1981 as a way to return to his pre-Zeppelin roots in American blues and R&B; the group took its name from blues pianist Roosevelt Sykes' nickname. The original lineup featured guitarists Robbie Blunt and Andy Sylvester, saxophonist Keith Evans, saxophonist/harmonica player Ricky Cool, bassist Jim Hickman, and drummer Kevin O'Neil. However, when Plant began collaborating with Blunt on original material, he deemed it more suited to his goals as a solo artist, and he accordingly formed a hard rock backing unit, putting the Honeydrippers on the back burner.

After his second solo album, Plant revived the Honeydrippers, this time with an impressive roster of studio guests including guitarists Jimmy Page, Jeff Beck, and Nile Rodgers, keyboardist Paul Shaffer, bassist Wayne Pedziwiatr, and drummer Dave Weckl. Together they recorded the five-song EP *The Honeydrippers, Vol. 1*, which was released in 1984 and featured Plant's takes on '50s and '60s R&B numbers. The first single, a cover of Phil Phillips' "Sea of Love," was a smash, peaking at number three on the American charts—one spot better, in fact, than Led Zeppelin's highest-charting single "Whole Lotta Love." The follow-up "Rockin' at Midnight," a Roy Brown jump blues tune, was also fairly successful. Stray Cats guitarist Brian Setzer joined the Honeydrippers' concert lineup, and performed with the group on *Saturday Night Live*. After touring with the Honeydrippers in 1985, Plant resumed his solo career; there has never been a Honeydrippers, Vol. 2. *—Steve Huey*

● **The Honeydrippers, Vol. 1** / 1984 / Es Paranza ♦♦♦♦♦

This five-song EP features Robert Plant singing such oldies as the hit remake of "Sea of Love," with a backup that includes Nile Rodgers, Jeff Beck, and Jimmy Page. *—William Ruhlmann*

Sonny Hopson

D.J. / Soul, Radio Shows

Sonny Hopson was a popular soul DJ on Philadelphia radio in the 1960s. He was also involved in managing and producing artists (including the Fantastic Johnny C., Charles Earland, the Emanons, the Cooperettes, Ann Robinson, George Freeman, and Herb Ward), hosting TV shows, and owning local clubs. An excerpt (or possibly excerpts) from his 1969 radio show was issued on CD by Philly Archives in 1969, featuring his slithery, speedy announcements in front, in back, and over soul tunes of the period, interspersed with commercials and news bulletins. *—Richie Unterberger*

● **The Mighty Burner** / 1999 / Philly Archives ♦♦

This is an hour-long excerpt from one of Hopson's 1969 radio shows (or, perhaps, from several of his shows), originally broadcast on Philadelphia's WHAT-AM. This is much more of a time capsule than something you'd want to play over and over. Motormouthed Hopson interjects talk and slogans between, and often over, a bunch of soul discs from the period. It would have been nice if the slim liner notes had identified the cuts Hopson span, since they're not really big hits by any means. One can pick out Charles Wright's "Express Yourself" (apparently number one on the station the week this was broadcast) and songs by James Brown, the Isley Brothers, the Delfonics, and the Intruders. But who does the odd soul version of "By the Time I Get to Phoenix" is left to anyone's guess (not Isaac Hayes). The commercials for clothing stores and the like are no less hyperactive than Hopson's raps, and after throwing in news bulletins like then-President Richard Nixon's trip to Thailand, one does get a feel for how this music sounded when it was broadcast back in the day, especially if one was too young to hear these programs (or unborn) at the time. Some of the cuts are only partially broadcast, there are voiceovers on others, and the fidelity is harsh and a little muddled, as AM radio was. *—Richie Unterberger*

Hot Chocolate

f. 1970, Brixton, London, England

Group / Funk, Soul

An interracial English funk and soul group, Hot Chocolate scored a pair of huge hits in the '70s but were otherwise more enthusiastic than skilled. Lead singer Errol Brown, guitarist Harvey Hinsley, keyboardist Larry Ferguson, bassist Tony Wilson, drummer Tony Connor, and conga player Patrick Olive were the original lineup. They recorded for Big Tree from 1975 to 1978, scoring a Top Ten R&B and pop hit with "You Sexy Thing" in 1975, which also was a gold single. They repeated the trick in 1978 with "Every 1's a Winner," once more earning a gold single in the process. No other Hot Chocolate song ever made it beyond number 40 on the R&B chart, and their albums never packed much commercial punch either. Wilson departed in 1975, and Olive switched to bass in his place. *—Ron Wynn*

Cicero Park / 1974 / Big Tree ♦♦

Hot Chocolate's albums tended to be mildly uneven—typically, a Hot Chocolate LP would have its share of five-star gems as well as some filler. That is definitely the case with *Cicero Park*, the British soulsters' debut album of 1974. Not everything on this vinyl LP is great, but more often than not, *Cicero Park* is quite promising. The more impressive tracks range from the somber title song and the Curtis Mayfield-influenced "Could Have Been Born in the Ghetto" to the funky, infectious "Disco Queen" and an interesting remake of the Stories' "Brother Louie" (which tackles the subject of interracial romance and finds a half black, half white couple being confronted with racism). "Emma" is a real treasure, although a depressing one. Combining Brit-rock and soul, this tear-jerker is sung from the perspective of a man whose sweetheart, an aspiring actress, ends up committing suicide. *Cicero Park* received very little attention in the U.S., although the Brits who bought the record agreed that Hot Chocolate had a lot of potential. *—Alex Henderson*

Hot Chocolate / 1975 / Big Tree ♦♦♦♦

When Hot Chocolate's first album, *Cicero Park*, came out in 1974, the majority of American soul fans didn't even know that it existed. But the band received more attention in the U.S. the following year, when this self-titled sophomore effort was released and the playful "You Sexy Thing" became a major hit. Many of the Americans who heard "You Sexy Thing" on either soul or pop/Top 40 radio bought the single but passed on the *Hot Chocolate* LP, and that's regrettable because the Brits' second album has a lot going for it. *Hot Chocolate* isn't perfect-this LP isn't devoid of filler, but the material is solid more often than not. Except for "You Sexy Thing," the album's best tracks are its message songs. Thoughtful, reflective offerings like "A Child's Prayer," "The Street" and "Dollar Sign" explore the socio-political territory that Marvin Gaye, Curtis Mayfield and Donny Hathaway had been exploring, except that Hot Chocolate brings a British perspective to the table.

On "Amazing Skin Song," lead vocalist Errol Brown sings from the perspective of a black man who is in love with a white woman and refuses to let racism on the part of either blacks or whites keep him from being with her. Those who heard "You Sexy Thing" on the radio thought of Hot Chocolate as a lighthearted group, but most of the time, this is a very serious-minded album. *—Alex Henderson*

Man to Man / 1976 / Big Tree ♦♦♦

Although Hot Chocolate's self-titled second album contained the playful, lighthearted smash "You Sexy Thing," much of the record was serious-minded and message-oriented. But with its third LP, *Man to Man*, the British band decided to provide more of a party album. Most of this 1976 release isn't socio-political, and infectious funk grooves like "Heaven Is in the Back Seat of My Cadillac," "Sugar Daddy" and "You Could've Been a Lady" are clearly aimed at the dancefloor. Not that everything on *Man to Man* is an uptempo party jam; the title song is a poignant ballad, while the relaxed, slightly David Bowie-ish "Seventeen Years of Age" is a thoughtful description of how a teen-age girl makes the transition from adolescence to womanhood. The latter points to the fact that while the distinctive Hot Chocolate was primarily a soul/funk band, it knew how to use rock and pop influences to its creative advantage. Unfortunately, this decent to excellent LP wasn't a big seller in the U.S., where Hot Chocolate was definitely underrated. *—Alex Henderson*

Every 1's a Winner / 1978 / EMI ♦♦♦

Hot Chocolate enjoyed an enthusiastic following in England, but in the U.S., the British band didn't receive nearly as much exposure as it should have. Regrettably, Hot Chocolate only had two major hits in the U.S.: "You Sexy Thing" in 1975 and "Every 1's A Winner" in 1978. That rock-influenced soul gem is the opener on the group's fourth album, which is also titled *Every 1's a Winner*. Although none of the other songs on this LP were big hits in the U.S., most of them are quite solid-and that includes the moving ballad "Sometimes It Hurts to Be a Friend" as well as the message song "Love Is the Answer One More Time" and the moody Euro-disco number "Put Your Love in Me." This is a soul/funk album first and foremost, but it's a soul/funk album that isn't afraid to draw on British pop-rock influences like David Bowie and Elton John. Nor was Hot Chocolate afraid to incorporate Afro-Caribbean influences-"Confetti Day," for example, could be described as an interesting marriage of reggae, Bowie and Stax/Volt. While *Every 1's a Winner* falls short of perfect, it hits its mark more often than not and makes one wish that Hot Chocolate had acquired a larger following on the American side of the Atlantic Ocean. *—Alex Henderson*

Going Through the Motions / 1979 / Rak ♦♦♦

Some people think of Hot Chocolate as a Euro-disco band, but most of its recordings can't be lumped in with the Euro-disco of the Silver Convention, Cerrone, Giorgio Moroder, the Munich Machine or Love & Kisses. Hot Chocolate was primarily a soul/funk band, although the Londoners didn't hesitate to incorporate elements of pop-rock (David Bowie was an influence) and Afro-Caribbean music. Released in 1979, *Going Through the Motions* was a departure for Hot Chocolate in that it found the band making a conscious effort to appeal to Euro-disco audiences. Hot Chocolate's previous albums might have had the occasional Euro-disco item, but this time, the Euro-disco style is dominant. Moroder-style synthesizers are prominent, and tunes like "Dance (Get Down to It)," "I Just Love What You're Doing"—and "Mindless Boogie" are obviously club-minded. Thankfully, most of the material has heart. "Dance (Get Down to It)" is rather stiff and mechanical, but Hot Chocolate's soulful, gritty inclinations prevail on "Night Ride," "Mindless Boogie" and "I Just Love What You're Doing"—all of which are rewarding. "Mindless Boogie," in fact, is brilliant, not to mention very ironic. Back in the late '70s, the death-to-disco crowd frequently described disco as "mindless boogie"—and it wasn't a compliment. On the surface, "Mindless Boogie" might seem like a typically escapist Euro-disco number, but the gem actually has a socio-political message. Mentioning events like the nuclear arms race and the Jonestown Massacre, "Mindless Boogie" concludes that because the world is such a mess, music is the drug that people use as an escape. *Going Through the Motions* isn't without its shortcomings, but all things considered, it's an LP that the British soulsters can be proud of. *—Alex Henderson*

● **Every 1's a Winner: The Very Best of Hot Chocolate** / 1987 / Capitol ♦♦♦♦

Hot Chocolate may never be included on the roster of heavy-hitting funk bands, but they were certainly a valuable part of the U.K.'s contribution to the genre. Able to bounce around and blend styles which ranged from funk-lite to pure pop and disco, Hot Chocolate gave the U.K. and then the States a string of chart hits and club favorites throughout the 1970s and into the '80s. Hot Chocolate's reign in England began in 1969 with their cover of John Lennon's "Give Peace a Chance," and continued on with some of the early '70s most stylish soul/funk compositions. However, they didn't register in the U.S. until 1974's "Emma" gave them their first Stateside hit. Heavy on post-1975 material, this compilation is a nice summary of the band's U.S. career, but doesn't pay sufficient tribute to the truly great band they were beforehand. From the pure pop-funk of "You Sexy Thing," which gave the band their first Top Five pop hit in the U.S., and early favorites "So You Win Again" and the gospel-tinged ballad "I'll Put You Together Again," to the latter-day classic "Are You Getting Enough Happiness," *Every 1's A Winner* doesn't miss a beat. Where the disc is better, then, is across the excellent pre-1975 tracks. The sinisterly impassioned and politically charged "Brother Louie" is probably one of the best songs the band recorded. Also of note is 1970's outstanding "Love Is Life," one of several songs which authors Errol Brown and Tony Wilson originally envisioned giving to Herman's Hermits. Using this compilation as a yardstick, Hot Chocolate would seem to defy any real categorization, a portrait which is grossly unfair. Anybody searching for a true representation, then, would be better served seeking out a European collection, where the emphasis is on the entire career. *—Amy Hanson*

Hot Chocolate

f. 1971, Cleveland, OH, **db.** 1973

Group / Funk, Deep Funk, Soul

During the '70s, a pair of different bands used the Hot Chocolate moniker: one was based in the U.K. (scoring a massive worldwide disco hit with "You Sexy Thing"), while the other was lesser-known and hailed from the U.S. (Cleveland, OH, to be exact). Consisting of members Lou Ragland (vocals, guitar), George Pickett (bass), and Tony Roberson (drums), Hot Chocolate built a regional following by playing live shows, but only managed to issue a pair of singles (1970's "We Had True Love" b/w "Good for the Gander" and 1973's "Since You Said You'd Be Mine," the latter of which was credited solely to Ragland) and a seven-track self-titled debut album from 1971. When the trio found out that another band shared their name, they decided to rename themselves Seven Miles High. Although Hot Chocolate's debut sank without a trace upon its initial release, it has become a cult classic within record-collecting circles and for funk fans. *—Greg Prato*

● **Hot Chocolate** / 1971 / Soul Brother ♦♦

Hot Chocolate, originally released in 1971 on Coco Records, was recorded by a trio comprised of Tony Roberson (drums), George Pickett (bass), and lead singer/guitarist Lou Ragland. Ragland recorded a handful of singles for various recording entities in Cleveland and also served as Saru Records' A&R director and main producer prior to former O'Jays' Bobby Massey assuming the duties. If you like elaborate productions, you'll find this collection crude and garage-esque, but to many the sparse instrumentation gives it charm and flavor. This is pure heart: raw funk-soul done on a mini-budget, reminiscent of New Orleans funkmeisters the Meters. The selections feature funkers and dancefloor items like "Ain't That a Groove" and "What You Want to Do"; the instrumental "Messin' With Sly" with the band vamping to "Sing a Simple Song"; and the two wailers "We Had True Love" and "What Should I Do," the latter which Ragland released in 1974 on SMH Records as a solo venture. Ballads are Ragland's forte; his rendition of "Never Let Me Go" on Way Out Records (1964) is still to be cherished. The cover depicts the trio hot tubbing in a cup of hot chocolate with Ragland and Pickett holding their guitars. An original copy on Coco (only 500 were pressed) is worth plenty in collectors' circles. *—Andrew Hamilton*

Cissy Houston (Emily Drinkard)

b. 1932, Newark, NJ

Vocals / Soul, Urban, Black Gospel

A soul singer who is known primarily as Whitney Houston's mother rather than for her own considerable talents, Cissy Houston was born Emily Drinkard and began her career as a member of her family's gospel group, the Drinkards. In the early '60s, she joined forces with a floating group of singers known simply as the Group (including at various points Doris Troy and Dee Dee Warwick) to provide backup vocals on numerous soul, pop, and rock sessions. They contributed to many Atlantic sessions in particular, and Atlantic executive Jerry Wexler signed the act to the label in 1967. Named the Sweet Inspirations, they recorded some excellent gospel-flavored soul in the late '60s, managing a few hits (as well as continuing to back up other artists, most notably Aretha Franklin) before Houston left to go solo at the end of 1969.

She recorded an impressive album for Commonwealth United in 1970, *Presenting Cissy Houston*, which yielded a couple of small R&B/pop hits: "I'll Be There" and "Be My Baby." Much in the manner of the Sweet Inspirations, although the material consisted of fairly well-worn soul, rock, and pop tunes, the state-of-the-art arrangements and gospel-ish vocals made them sound fresh. Her contract was sold to Janus Records later in the year, and while she issued a few singles there until the middle of the '70s, she never received the support and promotion she deserved. A case in point was her little-known original version of "Midnight Train to Georgia," taken to the top of the charts about a year later by Gladys Knight & the Pips. Houston recorded several albums for Private Stock beginning in the late '70s, as well as continuing her regular work on sessions and commercial jingles. She recorded a duet with daughter Whitney ("I Know Him So Well") in 1987, and cut a duet album with veteran soul singer Chuck Jackson in 1992. *—Richie Unterberger*

Warning—Danger / 1979 / Columbia ♦♦♦♦♦

Throughout the history of R&B, there have been major talents who made great secular recordings but ultimately gave up secular music because they felt that gospel was their calling. Whitney Houston's mother Cissy Houston is such an artist. Although Cissy Houston provided some of the finest recordings of the Disco Era, she eventually decided that being a disco diva wasn't her calling and became a full-time gospel artist. Houston's approach to disco wasn't a Euro-disco approach à la Cerrone, the Silver Convention, Love & Kisses, the Munich Machine or early Donna Summer—rather, *Warning—Danger* is an LP that emphasizes disco's Northern soul and gospel roots. Like Gloria Gaynor, Loleatta Holloway and Linda Clifford, Houston is a gritty, big-voiced belter who made sure that her late-'70s disco recordings had maximum soul appeal. When she passionately tears into "Think It Over" (a dance club favorite), "Somebody Should Have Told Me" and the title song, Houston sounds like she's well aware of disco's Motown and Philadelphia International heritage. Produced by Michael Zager (of "Let's All Chant" fame), *Warning—Danger* is essential listening for those who like their disco/soul with a lot of grit. *—Alex Henderson*

● **Midnight Train to Georgia: The Janus Years** / Apr. 25, 1995 / Ichiban/Soul Classics ♦♦♦♦♦

This is a fine 21-track compilation of almost everything she recorded between 1970 and 1975, including most of her 1970 album *Presenting Cissy Houston*, ten songs that were previously available only on singles, and a couple that were previously unreleased in the U.S. Highlights include excellent interpretations of two Bacharach-David classics ("I Just Don't Know What to Do with Myself," "This Empty Place") and Tim Hardin's "Hang on to a Dream," as well as the original version of "Midnight Train to Georgia." *—Richie Unterberger*

Thelma Houston

b. May 7, 1943, Leland, MS

Vocals / Quiet Storm, Club/Dance, Motown, Urban, Disco, Soul

Singer Thelma Houston is best known for her number one pop classic disco cover of "Don't Leave This Way." Originally a hit for Harold Melvin & the Blue Notes featuring Teddy Pendergrass, the Gamble & Huff/Cary Gilbert song soars through the gospel music-honed vocals of the Leland, MS, native. Houston's energetic performance takes the song in the same way that Aretha Franklin takes "Repect"—with no disrespect to either artist.

The singer came from humble beginnings. Her mother picked cotton to support Houston and her three sisters. During her youth, the family relocated to Long Beach, CA. As an adult, Houston graduated from high school, got married, had two children, and was later divorced. She got a job in the health care field. Staying active in music, she became a member of the Art Reynolds Singers, singing lead on their popular single cover of "Glory Glory Hallelujah," on Capitol. Fifth Dimension manager Marc Gordon was impressed by her vocal skills and helped to get her a recording deal with Dunhill Records. In 1969, renowned songwriter Jimmy Webb produced her debut LP *Wildflower.* One single, a cover of Laura Nyro's "Save the Country," charted in early 1970.

During 1971, Houston signed with Motown, with her label debut *Thelma Houston* being issued on the MoWest imprint. Over the next few years, the singer issued numerous singles that failed to be hits, though one Motown single, the catchy "You've Been Doing Wrong for So Long," lingered in the lower half of the R&B charts. She can be seen in the classic *Billy Dee Williams/James Earl Jones* Negro League baseball movie, *The Bingo Long Traveling All Stars and Motor Kings*, produced by Motown and released through Universal Pictures. Houston's background vocals are woven throughout Jermaine Jackson's 1976 gold LP, *My Name Is Jermaine.*

Finally, synchronicity in Houston's favor came in a big way in the form of the release of the 1976 LP *Any Way You Like It*, produced by Hal Davis (Diana Ross' "Love Hangover") and issued on Motown's Tamla imprint. Davis had heard the Blue Notes' version at a party while he was in the process of recording tracks for the album. First taking off in disco and on both disco-oriented and soul music radio stations, "Don't Leave This Way," went to number-one R&B in February 1977 and number-one pop in April 1977 (*Billboard*). It can be found on Rhino's *Disco Box, Billboard Top Hits: 1975-1979, Disco Nights, Vol. 9: Motown Dance, 70s Disco Ball Party Pack*, and *The Disco Years, Vol. 1: Turn the Beat Around.* A 12-inch version is on *Pure Disco [Polygram]* and *Essential 12": The 70s.* Her other hits include "If It's the Last Thing I Do," "I'm Here Again," "Saturday Night, Sunday Morning," and the RCA single "If You Feel It." A pre-mega stardom Jimmy Jam & Terry Lewis produced the smooth, percolating Top 20 R&B dance track, "You Used to Hold Me So Tight," from her 1984 MCA album, *Qualifying Heat.* She duets with the Winans on a cover of Bill Withers' "Lean on Me," the title track of the same named 1989 Morgan Freeman movie. She does backing vocals on guitarist Scott Henderson's 1997 Atlantic CD, *Tore Down House.*

Thelma Houston appeared on cable channel VH1's *100 Greatest Dance Songs* during October 2000. *—Ed Hogan*

Sunshower / 1969 / Dunhill ✦✦✦✦✦

Any Way You Like It / 1977 / Motown ✦✦✦✦✦

With quality production from the mid-'70s, it includes great dance tracks. *—Rick A. Bueche*

Thelma & Jerry / 1977 / Motown ✦✦✦

The best of two albums Thelma Houston & Jerry Butler made during Houston's '70s stay at Motown. The pair were slick, smooth, and soulful, with Houston reigning in her gospel excesses and Butler finding a way to mesh his mellow style with her heated delivery. *—Ron Wynn*

The Devil in Me / 1978 / Gordy ✦✦✦

An excellent album of light disco on "I'm Here Again." Versatile ballads ("I Can't Go on Living Without Your Love") and a sassy tune ("Triflin") are also included. *—Bil Carpenter*

Ready to Roll / 1978 / Motown ✦✦

Motown released one more Thelma Houston album after this one; then Ms. "Don't Leave Me This Way" jumped to RCA Records. *Ready to Roll* has live and dead spots. The uptempo "Saturday Night, Sunday Morning," the only 45 release, is a fast, funky disco number with potential that somehow had chart phobia. "Midnight Mona," a sassy upbeat number, lacked exploitation; Motown also neglected "Can't We Try," a pleasant shuffler, and two classy ballads, "I Wanna Start My Life All Over Again" and "Am I Expecting Too Much." *—Andrew Hamilton*

Ride to the Rainbow / 1979 / Motown ✦✦✦

Whoever decides to put out a multi-disc Thelma Houston package should include a few of these babies. While some selections like "Saturday Night, Sunday Morning" (which, oddly, was also on *Ready to Roll* [issued prior to this LP]) are a bit formulaic, Houston's fiery vocals never are. "I Want to Go Back There Again," "Imaginary Paradise," and Stevie Wonder and Syreeta Wright's "Just a Little Piece of You" got lost on this poor-selling album. Motown tries to duplicate Thelma's successful remake of Harold Melvin & the Blue Notes' "Don't Leave Me This Way" with the Miracles' "Love Machine"; it didn't make much noise in the States, but was so popular in Japan they renamed this album after it. *—Andrew Hamilton*

I've Got the Music in Me / 1981 / Sheffield Lab ✦✦✦

An interesting, if uneven, release. Thelma Houston teamed with the band Pressure Cooker in the early '80s, doing a fusion/instrumental pop/R&B/soul work for Sheffield Labs. That affiliation ensured that it would be brilliantly engineered, and it sounded spectacular, especially for an early '80s release. Unfortunately, much of the musical output didn't match the mastering brilliance, despite an energetic effort from Houston. But her voice was too much for what was basically a warm-up caliber backing group. It would have been great to hear Houston doing these songs supported by the Tower of Power. *—Ron Wynn*

Throw You Down / 1990 / Reprise ✦✦

Thelma Houston raised a few eyebrows in 1990 when this album was released. She still had a soulful, galvanizing voice, and she was equally good at fitting into pop, dance, or R&B contexts. While the album itself wasn't a great effort and was strictly aimed at the crossover market, thanks to producer Richard Perry, the single "Out of My Hands" was one of Houston's best songs and among the better unpublicized gems of 1990. *—Ron Wynn*

● **The Best of Thelma Houston** / 1991 / Motown ✦✦✦✦✦

Motown's *The Best of Thelma Houston* covers her late-'70s/early-'80s output for the label, including her hit cover of "Don't Leave Me This Way." A few other covers, including "Jumpin' Jack Flash" and "Me and Bobby McGee," hint at Houston's range as an interpreter; originals like "If It's the Last Thing I Do," "I Want to Go Back There Again," and "Stealin' in the Name of the Lord" show her finesse with lush ballads, quintessential Motown, and gospel-inflected pop, respectively. Along with "Don't Leave Me This Way," tracks such as "Saturday Night, Sunday Morning," "Love Machine," and "I'm Here Again" reflect Houston's sophisticated but fiery take on disco. While the Spectrum collection has a slightly grittier edge to it, this compilation does a fine job of showing the breadth and depth of her Motown work. *—Heather Phares*

Whitney Houston

b. Aug. 9, 1963, Newark, NJ

Vocals / Urban, Dance-Pop, Club/Dance, Adult Contemporary

Whitney Houston is inarguably one of the of the biggest female pop stars of all time. Her accomplishments as a hitmaker are extraordinary; just to scratch the surface, she became the first artist ever to have seven consecutive singles hit number one, and her 1993 Dolly Parton cover "I Will Always Love You" became nothing less than the biggest hit single in rock history. Houston was able to handle big adult contemporary ballads, effervescent, stylish dance-pop, and slick urban contemporary soul with equal dexterity; the result was an across-the-board appeal that was matched by scant few artists of her era, and helped her become one of the first black artists to find success on MTV in Michael Jackson's wake.

Like many of the original soul singers, Houston was trained in gospel before moving into secular music; over time, she developed a virtuosic singing style given over to swooping, flashy melodic embellishments. The shadow of Houston's prodigious technique still looms large over nearly every pop diva and smooth urban soul singer—male or female—in her wake, and spawned a legion of imitators (despite some critics' complaints about over-singing). Always more of a singles artist, Houston largely shied away from albums during the '90s, releasing the bulk of her most popular material on the soundtracks of films in which she appeared. By the end of the decade, she'd gone several years without a true blockbuster, yet her status as an icon was hardly diminished.

Whitney Elizabeth Houston was born in Newark, NJ, on August 9, 1963; her mother was gospel/R&B singer Cissy Houston, and her cousin was Dionne Warwick. By age 11, Houston was performing as a soloist in the junior gospel choir at her Baptist church; as a teenager, she began accompanying her mother in concert (as well as on the 1978 album *Think It Over*), and went on to back artists like Lou Rawls and Chaka Khan. Houston also pursued modeling and acting, appearing on the sitcoms *Gimme a Break* and *Silver Spoons.* Somewhat bizarrely, Houston's first recording as a featured vocalist was with Bill Laswell's experimental jazz-funk ensemble Material; their 1982 album *One Down* placed Houston alongside such unlikely avant-gardists as Archie Shepp and Fred Frith. The following year, Arista president Clive Davis heard Houston singing at a nightclub and offered her a record contract. Her first single appearance was a duet with Teddy Pendergrass, "Hold Me," which missed the Top 40 in 1984.

Houston's debut album *Whitney Houston* was released in March 1985. Its first single, "Someone for Me," was a flop, but the second try, "You Give Good Love," became Houston's first hit, topping the R&B charts and hitting number-three pop. Houston's next three singles—the Grammy-winning romantic ballad "Saving All My Love for You," the brightly danceable "How Will I Know," and the inspirational "The Greatest Love of All"—all topped the pop charts, and a year to the month after its release, *Whitney Houston* hit number one on the album charts. It eventually sold over 13-million copies, making it the best-selling debut ever by a female artist. Houston cemented her superstar status on her next album, *Whitney*; despite the unimaginative title, it became the first album by a female artist to debut at number one, and sold over nine-million copies. Its first four singles—"I Wanna Dance With Somebody (Who Loves Me)" (another Grammy winner), "Didn't We Almost Have It All," "So Emotional," and "Where Do Broken Hearts Go"—all hit number one, an amazing, record-setting run of seven straight (broken by "Love Will Save the Day"). In late 1988, Houston scored a Top Five hit with the non-LP single "One Moment in Time," recorded for an Olympics-themed compilation album.

Houston returned with her third album, *I'm Your Baby Tonight*, in 1990; a more urban-sounding, R&B-oriented record, it immediately spun off two number-one hits in the title track and "All the Man That I Need." But the quality of the material was generally viewed as, overall, much weaker than her previous efforts, and following those two hits, sales of the album tapered off quickly, halting around four-million copies. Nevertheless, Houston remained so popular that she could even take a recording of "The Star Spangled Banner" (performed at the Super Bowl) into the pop Top 20—though, of course, the Gulf War had something to do with that. In retrospect, the erratic quality of *I'm Your Baby Tonight* seemed to signal Houston's declining interest in making fully fleshed-out albums. Instead, she began to focus on an acting career, which she hadn't pursued since her teenage years; she also married singer Bobby Brown in the summer of 1992. Her first feature film, a romance with Kevin Costner called *The Bodyguard*, was released in late 1992; it performed well at the box office, helped by an ad campaign which seemingly centered around the climactic key change in Houston's soundtrack recording of the Dolly Parton-penned "I Will Always Love You." In fact, the ad campaign undoubtedly helped "I Will Always Love You" become the biggest single in pop music history. It set new records for sales (nearly five-million copies) and weeks at number one (14), although those were later broken by Elton John's "Candle in the Wind 1997" and Mariah Carey and Boyz II Men's "One Sweet Day," respectively. Meanwhile, the soundtrack eventually sold an astounding 16-million copies, and also won a Grammy for Album of the Year.

Once Houston had stopped raking in awards and touring the world, she prepared her next theatrical release, the female ensemble drama *Waiting to Exhale*. A few months before its release at the end of 1995, it was announced that she and Brown had split up; however, they called off the split just a couple months later, and rumors about their tempestuous relationship filled the tabloids for years to come. *Waiting to Exhale* was released toward the end of the year, and the first single from the soundtrack, "Exhale (Shoop Shoop)," topped the charts; the album sold over seven-million copies. For her next project, Houston decided to return to her gospel roots; the soundtrack to the 1996 film *The Preacher's Wife*, which naturally featured Houston in the title role, was loaded with traditional and contemporary gospel songs, plus guest appearances by Houston's mother, Shirley Caesar, and the Georgia Mass Choir. Houston also began making headlines for what appeared to be increasing unreliability, cancelling several TV and concert appearances due to illness.

In 1998, Houston finally issued a new, full-length album, *My Love Is Your Love*, her first in eight years. Houston worked with pop/smooth soul mainstays like Babyface and David Foster, but also recruited hip-hop stars like Missy Elliott, Wyclef Jean, Lauryn Hill, and Q-Tip. The album sold even fewer copies than *I'm Your Baby Tonight*, but it received Houston's most enthusiastic reviews in quite some time. Moreover, it produced one of her biggest R&B chart hits (seven weeks at number one) in the trio number "Heartbreak Hotel," done with Faith Evans and Kelly Price. She also duetted with Mariah Carey on "When You Believe," a song from the animated film *The Prince of Egypt*. Unfortunately, Houston was also back in the tabloids in early 2000; she was arrested in Hawaii when airline authorities reportedly found marijuana in her luggage (the charges were later dismissed). Speculation about Houston's personal life only grew when she was dropped from the Academy Awards telecast that March, officially because of a sore throat, but reputedly due to poor rehearsals and a generally out-of-it air. Later in the year, Arista released the two-disc compilation *Greatest Hits*, which actually featured one disc of hits and one of remixes; it also included new duets with Enrique Iglesias, George Michael, and Deborah Cox. It was also announced that Houston had signed a new deal with Arista worth 100-million dollars, requiring six albums from the singer. In late 2001, Arista released another compilation, the love-song-themed *Love, Whitney*. *—Steve Huey*

● **Whitney Houston** / 1985 / Arista ♦♦♦♦♦

The legend of Whitney Houston began with this self-titled album. It marked her shift away from the experimental songs she did with the group Material and a move into heavily produced, very slick urban contemporary and adult pop. Although Houston had learned her craft working in New York nightclubs and singing in a Baptist church in Newark, she was steered into radio-friendly ballads that emphasized style over substance. The album did yield an unprecedented string of number-one hits, but "Saving All My Love for You" and "How Will I Know" created an impression of an incredibly talented vocalist using only a minimum of her skills. It also contained one of her few legitimate soul workouts in "The Greatest Love of All." *—Ron Wynn*

Whitney / 1987 / Arista ♦♦♦♦

Whitney Houston became an international star with this album. It sold more than ten million copies around the world, yielded a string of number-one hit singles across the board like "I Wanna Dance With Somebody (Who Loves Me)," "Didn't We Almost Have It All," and "Love Will Save the Day," and established Houston as the era's top female star. She later went on to more than solidify that status, with other hit albums and a budding film career. While this is a far cry from soul, it's the ultimate in polished, super-produced urban contemporary material. *—Ron Wynn*

I'm Your Baby Tonight / 1990 / Arista ♦♦

While Houston's voice always provides some interesting listening, this is somewhat of a disappointing release, with very few memorable songs. While she attempts to make a larger foray into dance music, she fails to make the crossover impact of artists such as Mariah Carey and Taylor Dayne. The two high points she does reach on this album come in the form of ballads—the uplifting tale of another's love being enough to provide happiness in "All the Man That I Need" and the powerful verses surrounding a love lost through one's own devices in "Miracle." *—Ashley S. Battel*

My Love Is Your Love / Nov. 17, 1998 / Arista ♦♦♦♦

For all intents and purposes, Whitney Houston retired from being a full-fledged recording artist after her third album, 1990s *I'm Your Baby Tonight*, choosing to be a Streisand-like celebrity who cultivated a career through movies, soundtrack contributions, and social appearances. She may have been content to continue in that direction for many years if Arista president Clive Davis didn't push her into recording *My Love Is Your Love*, her first album in eight years, which easily ranks among her best. Never before has Houston tried so many different sounds or tried so hard to be hip. It's one thing to work with Babyface, the standard-bearer of smooth soul in the '90s, but it's quite another to hire Wyclef Jean, Lauryn Hill, Missy Elliott, and Q-Tip—all cutting-edge artists (albeit on the accessible side of the cutting edge), the kind who never would have been associated with Houston in the late '80s. The gambit works. There is still a fair share of David Foster-produced adult contemporary ballads, but the true news is on the uptempo and midtempo dance numbers. In fact, the songs that feel the stiffest are the big production numbers; tellingly, they're the songs that are the most reminiscent of old-school Houston. That's not to say she can no longer belt out ballads convincingly—in fact, the best ballads are where she restrains herself, delivering them with considerable nuance. Houston has never been quite so subtle before, nor has she ever shown this desire to branch out musically. That alone would be reason enough to rank *My Love Is Your Love* among her more interesting albums, but the fact that it works more often than not pushes it into the top rank of her recorded work. *—Stephen Thomas Erlewine*

The Greatest Hits / Apr. 18, 2000 / Arista ♦♦♦♦

Although *The Greatest Hits* is a double-disc package, only the first disc actually contains original versions of Houston's hit singles; the second disc, *The Greatest Remixes*, collects remixes new and old for hardcore fans. Of course, it would be impossible to fit all of Houston's 20-plus chart singles onto one disc, but that format still could have produced a fantastic and near-definitive collection. That is, if Arista hadn't made the ridiculous choice not to include four number-one hits: "How Will I Know," "So Emotional," "I Wanna Dance With Somebody (Who Loves Me)," and "I'm Your Baby Tonight." Granted, those songs are all present on *The Greatest Remixes*, but anyone wanting the original versions will have to purchase the *three* different albums they appeared on. That said, the compilation does do fans a few favors; there are three new tracks, including one duet apiece with Deborah Cox and Enrique Iglesias, and two hits make their first appearance on a Houston album: "One Moment in Time" (the 1988 Olympic theme) and "If You Say My Eyes Are Beautiful," a 1986 duet with Jermaine Jackson. Houston's Top 20 hit recording of "The Star-Spangled Banner," performed at Super Bowl XXV during the Gulf War, is tacked onto the remix disc as well. The *Greatest Hits* disc amply reinforces what a fine singles artist Houston has been for the entirety of her career. Overall, though, it's a frustrating package marred by record company greed—not only because of the glaring and intentional omissions, but also because casual fans won't appreciate paying double the money for a remix disc they probably aren't interested in owning. *—Steve Huey*

Just Whitney / Dec. 10, 2002 / Arista ♦♦♦

The four-year wait between 2002's *Just Whitney* and her previous album, 1998's *My Love Is Your Love*, was half that between that record and *its* predecessor, 1990's *I'm Your Baby Tonight*, but it felt twice the length, since Whitney Houston's career nose-dived during those four years. She retreated from the spotlight and as she cancelled concerts, scrapped albums, and pulled out of public appearances, rumors swirled that she and husband Bobby Brown were dangerously addicted to drugs. Following a disastrous performance at the September 2001 Michael Jackson tribute concert, where she looked as if she had already wasted away, the chattering reached a fever pitch and she needed to restore her reputation—hence the title of *Just Whitney*, an assertion that she's returning to her basics. But that's not the half of it. As her trainwreck interview with Diane Sawyer on *PrimeTime Live* the week prior to *Just Whitney*'s release proved, she's arrogantly defensive about her "bad habits" and is "Unashamed" of "the life that [she] leads," as she sings on the eighth song on this odd, disarmingly brief (under 40 minutes) self-styled comeback album. Just listen to the first single, the roundly ignored "Whatchulookinat" (produced by husband Brown, who Whitney thanks for being the best producer in the world, although he only helmed this track on the album), where she plays the victim, claiming that the gossip-mongers "messing with my reputation/ain't you got no education... don't even have a clue about what I'm facin'," coming across as if she had something to hide. It's a sentiment that runs throughout the album—phrases like "you don't know what I'm goin' through" and "you criticize my actions/even though you don't stand in my shoes" pop up regularly—and undermines an album that's otherwise a not-bad set of contemporary soul. Certainly, Whitney is in better voice than rival diva Mariah Carey (whose near simultaneously released *Charmbracelet* found her voice in tatters) and she's fortunate enough to have Babyface for four productions, three of which are among the highlights of the album. Though Missy Elliott produces a track here, this is nowhere near as concerned with hip production as *My Love* was and who can blame her? When a career is on the rocks, it's best to play it safe. And that's what *Just Whitney* is: a measured attempt to salvage a career that's on the verge of destruction. Does it work? Well, musically, it's not bad, though few songs are memorable. It would be a good standard-issue Whitney album if it wasn't for her disarming, defensive attempt to defuse every rumor hurled in her direction. Even an otherwise innocuous duet with Brown is presented like it's the two of them against the world, nearly celebrating the fact that Bobby's voice is very strained these days. Worst of all, there seems to be nobody to check Whitney and prevent her from indulging in bad ideas. After all, surely somebody in the Houston camp should have realized that at this crucial time in her career, as she admits drug "habits," that covering "You Light Up My Life" might not be the smartest move to make right now. *—Stephen Thomas Erlewine*

Adina Howard

b. Grand Rapids, MI

Vocals / Club/Dance, Urban

Grand Rapids, MI, native Adina Howard became a national sensation with the funky R&B of her 1995 debut album, *Do You Wanna Ride*, and its single, "Freak Like Me." Her sophomore effort, *Welcome to Fantasy Island*, appeared in 1997. *—Stephen Thomas Erlewine*

● **Do You Wanna Ride?** / 1995 / East West ♦♦♦

Do You Wanna Ride is the lackluster debut release from Michigan native Adina Howard. Although the album includes the somewhat catchy 1995 hit single "Freak Like Me," there's not much more to recommend the album. The main problem with *Do You Wanna Ride* is more work was put into the production than into the songwriting. The employment of several producers for various songs doesn't mask Adina Howard's inability to move beyond the basic R&B bump-and-grind clichés of "Freak Like Me," and her limited vocal range doesn't allow her to soar above the mediocre material. Judging from the album's cover photograph, it's obvious Adina Howard relies too much on a sexy image instead of true talent. Listeners weren't fooled; "Freak Like Me" was the only hit from the album. *—William Cooper*

Welcome to Fantasy Island / Jul. 29, 1997 / East West ♦♦♦

While it lacks a standout single along the lines of "Freak Like Me," Adina Howard's second album *Welcome to Fantasy Island* is a more consistent record than its predecessor,

Do You Wanna Ride, boasting a better selection of songs and grooves. Howard still isn't much of a vocalist—her idea of being seductive is panting heavily, and she doesn't have much power for the soulful numbers—but she does have considerable sexual charisma, which is enough to make funky workouts like "(Freak) And U Know It" infectious. There's plenty of mediocre material scattered throughout *Welcome to Fantasy Island*, but it's ideal makeout music for the young urban professional. *—Leo Stanley*

Miki Howard

b. Chicago, IL

Vocals / Quiet Storm, Urban, Vocal Jazz

Miki Howard was born into music. She grew up in the church where both of her parents were gospel singers. Her mother was also a member of the gospel group the Caravans, and was acquainted with various entertainers. As a child, Howard's mother would take her to the homes of various stars such as Aretha Franklin and Mavis Staples.

While still in elementary school, Howard moved to Los Angeles with her mom. At the age of 15, she performed in a teen pageant. After the show, she met Side Effect member Augie Johnson, who happened to be in the audience and began working with Howard creatively. After a period of time, Howard became a Side Effect member upon the departure of Sylvia St. James. Howard's tenure with Side Effect lasted a few years. During this time, she also had two children by Johnson. In addition to singing with Side Effect, she did background vocals for Wayne Henderson, Roy Ayers, Stanley Turrentine and others. After leaving Side Effect, Howard signed a deal with Atlantic Records. Her first hit for Atlantic was the *Billboard* R&B Top Ten single "Come Share My Love." She followed that with the remake of Glenn Miller's 1940 hit "Imagination." Her success continued with two more Top Ten singles, "Baby Be Mine" and "That's What Love Is." The latter was a duet with Gerald LeVert, and was the result of the creative union Howard formed with Marc Gordon and LeVert. Howard and LeVert later became romantically involved, and that romance spawned one of Howard's biggest hits, "Love Under New Management." The song was written during their brief love affair, but was released after their romance had dissolved.

In 1990, Howard signed a deal with the now-defunct Giant Records, which facilitated the release of her number-one smash hit "Ain't Nobody Like You." Howard's lifeline at Giant was cut short due to an altercation her husband had at the label. She also made an appearance as Billie Holiday in a club scene in the Spike Lee movie *Malcom X.* Howard continued issue albums throughout the '90s, however her success wasn't recognized like prior occasions. Her roster includes: *Femme Fatale* (1992), *Shining Through* (1993), *Live Plus* (1996), and *Can't Count Me Out* (1997). *Three Wishes* marked her new millennium debut with Peak in early 2001. *—Craig Lytle*

Come Share My Love / 1987 / Atlantic ✦✦

Former gospel singer and Side Effect member Miki Howard made a fine debut in 1986 with this album. Her version of "Imagination" showed that she could sing jazzy pop, while she also got a huge R&B and urban contemporary hit from the late-blooming title cut. *—Ron Wynn*

Love Confessions / 1988 / Atlantic ✦✦✦

With this, Miki Howard continued building on the good rapport and reputation established with her solid debut album. She got more hits with the song "Crazy" and a fine duet with Gerald LeVert, and also did extensive touring, demonstrating that her excellent vocals weren't merely the result of studio manipulations. *—Ron Wynn*

● **Miki Howard** / 1989 / Atlantic ✦✦✦✦

Since making her debut as a solo artists in 1986 with the smash single "Come Share My Love," Miki Howard no doubt had her eyes set on attaining that number one song. This album proves to be the facilitator of that quest. There were four featured singles on this set. The first release, the uptempo dance cut "Ain't Nuthin' in the World," grooved its way up the *Billboard* R&B charts to number one. The Chicago native stayed in the Top Three with "Love Under New Management" and "Until You Come Back to Me (That's What I'm Gonna Do)." The former is testimonial expression from the soul songstress while the latter is a re-make of the Aretha Franklin classic. Respectively, they peaked at number two and three. The fourth release was the pleading, midtempo number "Come Back to Me." Cresting at 53 on the charts, it too is an excellent selection. An honorable mention goes to "I'll Be Your Shoulder." A duet with one of the consummate soulman of the day, Gerald LeVert. This is a superb effort by Miki Howard. *—Craig Lytle*

Femme Fatale / Sep. 15, 1992 / Giant ✦✦✦

Howard's big voice is in good form here, and much of the material—provided by such people as Kenny Gamble & Leon Huff, David Foster, and Billie Holiday—suits her. The very best of the songs ("Ain't Nobody Like You," "Release Me") are also among the very best she's recorded. Still, there's a sameness running through the grooves that becomes a bit oppressive by record's end. It's a varied effort with some good tunes buried. *—Michael Gallucci*

● **The Very Best of Miki Howard** / Jul. 3, 2001 / Rhino ✦✦✦✦

Rhino's 2001 retrospective *The Very Best of Miki Howard* is a generous, near-definitive overview of Howard's biggest R&B hits from the '80s. She didn't have many crossover hits, but she did have numerous entries on the R&B charts, all of which are here, including a duet with Gerald LeVert, "That's What Love Is." Although this is a little lengthy for listeners with abbreviated attention spans, it does summarize Howard's peak very well, and is as comprehensive a Howard retrospective as could be hoped for. *—Stephen Thomas Erlewine*

Al Hudson

b. Detroit, MI

Producer / Urban, Disco, Quiet Storm, Soul

Detroit vocalist Al Hudson has led various funk and soul aggregations since the late '70s. Although he never landed anything remotely close to a big hit, with the group Soul Partners, consistently recorded through the '70s and into the early '80s. Hudson & the Soul Partners signed with ABC in the mid-'70s and made their debut with the LP *Especially for You.* They became One Way in 1979. The group remained on ABC until the early '80s, then switched to Capitol. Hudson produced an LP for Bert Robinson, but his own solo LP wasn't released. *—Ron Wynn*

Especially for You / 1977 / ABC ✦✦

This self-contained Detroit group's debut for ABC Records has some good moments but is not as pleasing as later efforts. "I Got a Notion, You Got the Motion" is the obvious pick, but it only stands out because the other tracks are lacking, especially the two with the word "Disco" in their titles. Remakes of "Feelings" and "When Something Is Wrong With My Baby" displays potential that didn't ignite until they became One Way and started recording for MCA Records. *—Andrew Hamilton*

● **Cherish** / 1977 / ABC ✦✦✦

This is a good offering from one of the most exciting live acts to emerge from Detroit's overflowing music scene. Al Hudson & the Soul Partners are not a traditional vocal group lineup, though they sound like one. The personnel are Al Hudson (lead vocals), Kevin McCord (lead vocals & bass guitar), Cortez Harris (vocals & guitar), Jack Hall (piano), and Theodore Dudley Jr. (drums). This eight-song collection is stuffed with ballads. Al Hudson sings in a gospel-inspired tenor that's more commonly heard on recordings produced below the Mason-Dixon line. Kevin McCord has one of the coolest falsettos in soul music; it's similar to the false voice of the late William Powell (O'Jays). The title track is an epic ballad that reveals Hudson's roots; "Tripped, Slipped, Stumbled and Fell" is a classic '60s love song that features Hudson, McCord, and Harris on vocals. The material could be stronger; still, it's well executed by these Detroiters. *—Andrew Hamilton*

Spreading Love / 1978 / ABC ✦✦✦

At least two minutes pass before you hear vocals on "Spread Love"; there's a long, unnecessary intro created for the disco era. Al Hudson leads a masterful rendition of the O'Jays' "You and I," sounding as dramatic but not nearly as powerful as Eddie LeVert. "Small Talk" is a good indication of what was coming in the future when the group evolved into the funky disco sounds of *One Way*; though not riveting, its disco ambience, percolating bass, chanting lyrics, and hand-clapping keeps you interested. Kevin McCord (who also plays bass) give you chills when he sings "Lost Inside of You" in one of the coolest falsettos ever recorded. A live studio feel flavors "How Do You Do," which sounds like the stuff Kool & the Gang recorded before James (J.T.) Taylor joined. A solid outing from the self-contained Detroit natives. *—Andrew Hamilton*

Happy Feet / 1979 / ABC ✦✦✦

Al Hudson's Detroit-based group changed their name on several occasions. Originally called Al Hudson & the Soul Partners, the Motor City residents went by Al Hudson & the Partners for awhile before changing their name to One Way Featuring Al Hudson in 1979. And in the 1980s, they dropped "Featuring Al Hudson" from their name and simply became One Way. Released in 1979, *Happy Feet* was their last album as Al Hudson & the Partners, in fact, this LP was still on the R&B charts when they started calling themselves One Way Featuring Al Hudson. A generally decent soul/funk/disco outing, *Happy Feet* ranges from snappy dance numbers like "Rock," "In the Basement," and the single "You Can Do It" to romantic ballads and slow jams such as "I Don't Want You to Leave Me" and Peabo Bryson's "Another Love Song." The singer who stands out the most on this album is, without question, Alicia Myers; a passionate, big-voiced goddess who went solo in the early '80s, and is best known for her 1981 hit "I Want to Thank You." Arguably, Myers was the best vocalist that Hudson's outfit ever had, which is ironic when you consider that One Way had some of their biggest hits after her departure. *Happy Feet* isn't the group's best or most essential album, but it's enjoyable nonetheless, and Myers' participation makes it worth the price of admission. *—Alex Henderson*

Hues Corporation

f. 1969, Los Angeles, CA, **db.** 1977

Group / Disco, Philly Soul

A Los Angeles vocal trio, the Hues Corporation enjoyed two big hits in the mid-'70s, notably "Rock the Boat" in 1974 for RCA. While it was lightweight, mainly pop work, it did take the Hues Corporation to number two on the R&B charts and get them their lone pop chart topper. The next single, "Rockin' Soul," peaked at number six on the R&B charts and number 18 on the pop charts. They had their final R&B hit the next year with "Love Corporation," which reached number 15, but it was evident that the audience was losing interest in their material. "I Caught Your Act" was the last release in 1977. H. Ann Kelley, Flemming Williams, and Bernard "St. Clair Lee" Henderson were the original lineup. Tom Brown replaced Williams in the wake of "Rock the Boats'" success. He was then replaced by Karl Russell in 1975. *—Ron Wynn*

Freedom for the Stallion / 1973 / RCA ✦✦

Although this band is perhaps best remembered for laying the groundwork for some of the earliest disco with "Rock the Boat," their genesis is much more in tune with the soul sounds of the late '60s than the all-out disco-ball '70s. But it wasn't until this RCA debut that Hues Corporation was on the receiving end of mainstream recognition. The songs across this LP are sweet, smooth numbers that capture the trio's vocal harmonies within their boundaries. But that's certainly not to say these songs are bland—just more "of an era." From the gospel-tinged "The Salvation Lady (1-3-5)," which does pack some horns, to the sweet ballad "Bound on a Reason," Hues Corporation produces some decent material. "Live a Lie," meanwhile, is an overly dramatic down-tempo song that hovers somewhere between an off-Broadway ballad and modern hymn. But, of course, the band stretched their legs to deviate from form to record what has become an iconographic song. "Rock the Boat" was *Freedom for the Stallion*'s odd track out, and remained largely forgotten until its release as a single in 1974. Packed with an energy that begged to be danced to and a construction that highlighted the strings, horns, and guitars that would fire 100 disco hits after it, "Rock the Boat" rampaged its way up both the pop and R&B charts, taking the top two spots, respectively. It was a huge success—and helped to kick-start the next musical wave. *—Amy Hanson*

Love Corporation / 1975 / RCA ✦✦✦

I Caught Your Act / 1977 / Warner Bros. ✦

Rock the Boat: Golden Classics / Mar. 16, 1993 / RCA ✦✦✦✦

Rock the Boat: Golden Classics may not have many songs as great as "Rock the Boat" (although it's nice to hear Allen Toussaint's "Freedom for the Stallion") but it summarizes the Hues Corporation's recordings well. It's frothy pop-soul and disco, with pleasing grooves—sometimes the grooves get a little repetitive, but nothing is outright bad here, either. Not really something to seek out, but not bad, all the same. *—Stephen Thomas Erlewine*

● **The Very Best of the Hues Corporation** / Aug. 25, 1998 / Camden ✦✦✦✦✦

Leon Huff

b. Apr. 8, 1942, Camden, NJ

Producer, Keyboards, Composer, Songwriter, Piano / Philly Soul, Soul, Smooth Soul

Session pianist Leon Huff became half of a seminal R&B songwriting and production team when he teamed with Kenny Gamble in 1965. Huff played on sessions for Phil Spector, the Ronettes, and Carole King in New York City before moving to Philadelphia. He formed the Locomotions, and did sessions for Cameo and Swan. Huff performed on the song "The 81," which was co-written by Kenny Gamble, who was at the session seeing the tune being recorded by Candy & the Kisses. Huff earned his first hit as a composer writing "Mixed-Up Shook-Up Girl" for Patty & the Emblems in 1964. He joined the Romeos the next year, then teamed with Gamble to form Gamble Records. They subsequently co-wrote and co-produced songs for the Soul Survivors, the O'Jays, and others before forming Philadelphia International Records in the early '70s.

Their use of strings, the sophisticated yet soulful sound, and careful mix of socially conscious and romantic tunes provided hits for the O'Jays, Harold Melvin & the Blue Notes, Teddy Pendergrass, MFSB, the Intruders, and others. Huff also wrote hits on his own for the Ebonys, People's Choice, Carolyn Crawford, and Bunny Sigler. He issued two singles as a solo artist on Philadelphia International in 1980 and 1981, with "I Ain't Jivin', I'm Jammin" getting some moderate recognition. A mystery remains as to why the label collapsed in the '80s. *—Ron Wynn*

● **Here to Create Music** / 1980 / Philadelphia International ✦✦✦

As half of the legendary Gamble & Huff team and a co-owner of Philadelphia International Records, Leon Huff was among the top soul producer/songwriters of the 1970s. Huff was 37 when, in 1980, he surprised the R&B world by recording his only solo album, *Here to Create Music.* This largely instrumental effort, which was out of print for many years before finally being reissued on CD in 1999, is surprising in a number of respects. First, Huff's partner Kenny Gamble has nothing to do with it—Huff does all of the writing and producing himself. Second, *Here To Create Music* didn't go out of its way to appeal to black radio; much of it has a loose, casual, informal quality. The CD's weakest offering is "Your Body Won't Move If You Can't Feel the Groove," a generic, clichéd disco opener that wastes the talents of Teddy Pendergrass, Eddie LeVert and other Philly International artists of 1980. But after that, things improve considerably. Huff, who is heard on organ and keyboards, keeps listeners guessing by hitting them with everything from the haunting "No Greater Love" (which sounds like the type of instrumental that War's Lee Oskar was providing on his solo albums) to the gritty blues number "Low Down, Hard Time Blues" and the catchy, Jimmy Smith-like soul-jazz tune "Tasty." *Here to Create Music* falls short of essential, but it's a decent, generally sincere outing that isn't without historic significance. *—Alex Henderson*

Terry Huff

b. North Carolina

Vocals / Quiet Storm, Soul, R&B

Terry Huff is an obscure Washington, D.C.-based singer whose biggest hit was the ache-filled "The Lonely One," a substantial hit along the East Coast. Terry was born in North Carolina and raised in Maryland foster homes; he started singing in church at an early age before graduating to school talent shows. At the shows he would sing songs by Little Richard and the Everly Brothers with his brother Andy.

Terry Huff moved to Washington, D.C., in 1959, where the Huff brothers sang on street corners and porches. In 1962, they auditioned their newly formed group for Van McCoy, who rejected them. Luck struck in 1963 when a restaurant owner sponsored their trip to New York for a recording session. As Andy & the Marglows, they recorded "Just One Look" for Liberty Records, who released it two weeks before the hit version by Doris Troy. Troy's version won that battle, as the Marglows never received any exposure. The follow-up, "I'll Get By," generated few sales despite several publicity appearances in the area. Shortly after the second flop and being dropped by Liberty, Andy & the Marglows were history.

In the mid-'60s, the Huff brothers tried again to interest several producers, including Van McCoy; they were again rejected. Terry Huff finished his education and became a member of Washington, D.C.'s police force. By 1973 the music bug hit the Huff brothers again; Terry also befriended Al Johnson (the Unifics). Terry Huff quit the police force in 1974 and joined Act 1, a group who had recorded for Spring Records. The group left Spring for Mainstream Records, re-formed with Huff, and changed their name to Special Delivery. Terry Huff, George Barker, Chester Fortune, and Reginald Ross auditioned for Van McCoy with a painful ballad written by Huff titled "I Destroyed Your Love." The song quickly became a staple on quiet storm radio stations and remained on the low end of the R&B charts. Before Mainstream could record a follow-up, the group disbanded over musical, business, and personal differences. Terry Huff recorded and produced "The Lonely One" with help from Al Johnson. Johnson and Huff's two brothers (Andy and Jimmy) did the backing vocals. For commercial reasons, Mainstream released it as being by Special Delivery featuring Terry Huff. The song's success caused a demand for an LP, which Huff and Johnson rushed to New York to record. The album fizzled and soon Terry Huff was back where he started: in D.C., looking for a deal. Special Delivery surfaced again, recording sporadically on small labels; they released an LP titled *Living on the Run*, but they faded from the scene without fanfare after disappointing sales. *—Andrew Hamilton*

● **The Lonely One** / 1976 / Mainstream ✦✦✦✦

R&B groups from the D.C./Baltimore area were unique in that they would create elaborate vocal arrangements to complement the lead; they didn't just ooh and ah in the background. "I Destroyed Your Love (Pts. 1 & 2)" is a prime example of the trend—lead singer Terry Huff's shrill falsetto cries and whines as Reginald Ross, George Parker and Chester Fortune, singing in ringing three-part harmonies, add some sparkling choruses to the drama; a tenor emerges from the threesome and provides some needed relief from Huff's soprano high pleadings. Only Terry is pictured on the album's cover; Special Delivery was an ever-changing ensemble of singers. Andy Huff and Jimmy Huff (Terry's brothers) are the backing voices on "The Lonely One." A charmer from the first note, Terry sounds real hurt, the type of hurt that lasts for years. All of the songs centered on Terry's real-life problem: a knock-down, drag-out divorce. He missed the family pet so much he wrote a sentimental ballad about the mutt entitled "Poochie"; seems his ex got to keep the dog. This is not a happy album; the songs are some of the saddest imaginable, all filled with self-condemnation. These songs provided a needed release for Terry, who wrote everything except "When You're Lonely"—another "I'm gonna jump" tune. I hate to think what Terry might have done if he had not found an outlet by writing and recording this album. *—Andrew Hamilton*

Grayson Hugh

b. Connecticut

Vocals, Piano / Urban

This Connecticut vocalist excited soul fans for a brief period in 1988 with his LP *Blind to Reason*, which was about as close to being gritty, gospel-tinged material as anyone was cutting at that time. The single "Talk It Over" made the pop Top 20, but the next single, "Bring It All Back," fizzled. Hugh was shortly off the scene. *—Ron Wynn*

● **Blind to Reason** / 1988 / RCA ✦✦✦✦

Blue-eyed, Southern soul singing Grayson Hugh deviates from his strident tenor that sounds above his natural range a couple of times on this album, but not nearly enough to keep so many of the tracks from sounding similar. But the real thorn is the material: it's good, sure, but hardly above average. Name brand musicians and vocalists accompany Hugh, but nothing jumps out at you. While "Talk It Over" and "Hard Life" are credible wringers, the rest are average moaners. *—Andrew Hamilton*

Road to Freedom / 1992 / MCA ✦✦✦

When Nile Edwards and Bernard Edwards were leading Chic in the late '70s and early '80s, the producers' main focus was disco funk. But after Chic's breakup, they went their separate ways, became increasingly diverse, and produced their share of rock-oriented projects. The fact that Edwards had both rock and R&B credentials made him the ideal producer for Grayson Hugh's *Road to Freedom.* Released in 1992—three years before Edwards' untimely death—this generally appealing, if slightly uneven, CD has one foot in roots rock and Americana and the other in '60s-style soul. Fans of Bruce Springsteen, John Cougar Mellencamp, and Tom Petty should have no problem getting into earthy originals like "Lost Avenue" and "Soul Cat Girl," but at the same time, *Road to Freedom* also has a lot of soul appeal—Otis Redding, Ike & Tina Turner, and Sam Cooke are all prominent influences. When this CD came out, one reviewer compared Hugh's phrasing to that of the Isley Brothers' Ronald Isley—which isn't a bad comparison because Cooke was a major influence on Isley. And even if Isley isn't a direct influence on this album, there is no denying that Isley and Hugh have a mutual influence in Cooke. But whoever Hugh is compared to, he's a talented artist in his own right. And while *Road to Freedom* falls short of perfect, it is generally rewarding and is arguably the singer/songwriter's best release. *—Alex Henderson*

Freddie Hughes

Vocals / Soul, Urban, R&B

Freddie Hughes had the distinction of being one of the last successful artists on Vee-Jay Records before the label collapsed in the mid-'60s. In 1965, he charted a pair of Top 20 R&B singles with "Oo Wee Baby, I Love You" and "You Can't Take It Away." He moved on to Scepter Records' Wand imprint and scored another hit with "Send My Baby Back," co-written, produced, and arranged by Lonnie Hewitt, which got to number 20 on the R&B charts and number 94 pop, sufficient to get him a chance to do a complete album for the label. He left Wand Records in 1969 to sign with Brunswick Records. *—Bruce Eder*

Baby Boy / 1970 / Brunswick ✦✦✦

Features Hughes' massive soul hit "Ooo Wee Baby I Love You" and its follow-up, "Baby Boy," where he boastfully sings, "They call me baby boy, the product of a new generation." A Eddie Holland sound-alike, the rest of the album is competent but bogged with remakes: "Son of Hickory Holler's Tramp," "Georgia on My Mind," "People," and "San Francisco Is a Lonely Town." To his credit, Fred Henry Hughes balances the remakes with six original compositions, including the two hits. While competent, the updates have the effect of parking lot speed bumps; Hughes had much to offer and so many remakes weren't necessary on his debut album. *—Andrew Hamilton*

● **Fred Hughes & His Groups** / Oct. 2000 / Veltone ✦✦✦✦

Fred Hughes' multi-faceted recording career is revealed via 11 solo sides and 14 others featuring Hughes fronting groups from the Markeets' 1957 release on Melatone Records ("Teardrops") to "God Bless Our Love Pt. 1 & 2," recorded as the Fabulous Ballads on Bay

View Records. The discourse includes "I Hope I Never Fall in Love" by the Cymbals, the Four Rivers' "I Confess," four selections from his stint with the Music City Soul Brothers, and "We Got to Keep On" by Casanova Two. Solo tracks include "Send My Baby Back," "My Baby Came Back," and "Where's My Baby," These 25 tracks represent a mere sampling of Hughes' solo and group endeavors as many of the groups' B-sides and A-sides were omitted, as well as some of Hughes' biggest solo hits, such as "Ooo Wee Baby I Love You" and "Baby Boy." *—Andrew Hamilton*

Jimmy Hughes

b. Florence, AL

Vocals, Bass / Northern Soul, Country-Soul, Soul

Jimmy Hughes established producer Rick Hall's fledgling Fame studio as an R&B mecca with his 1964 blues ballad "Steal Away." The ex-gospel singer hooked up with Hall in 1962 but it wasn't until the explosive "Steal Away" was issued on the Fame label that his career took off. With an intense, crying vocal style that was perfect for deep soul ballads, Hughes scored with the pleading "Why Not Tonight" in 1967, although the untypically uptempo "Neighbor, Neighbor" proved another giant hit. Hughes broke away from Hall and recorded an album for Volt before retiring from performing in the mid-'70s. *—Bill Dahl*

Steal Away / 1964 / Vee-Jay ✦✦✦

A classic pleading Rick Hall-produced ballad leads off this impressive debut album by the Alabama singer. It is available only on vinyl. *—Bill Dahl*

● **Why Not Tonight** / 1967 / Atco ✦✦✦✦✦

It's criminal that this Muscle Shoals soul classic isn't on CD—it includes aching, atmospheric lovelorn ballads and the ominous pounding hit, "Neighbor, Neighbor." *—Bill Dahl*

Something Special / 1969 / Volt ✦✦✦

Tommy Hunt

b. Jun. 18, 1933, Pittsburgh, PA

Vocals / R&B, Soul, Rock & Roll

Pittsburgh-born vocalist Tommy Hunt's recording career began at age 20, when he cut singles with his first group, the Five Echoes, in 1953. It was five years later, however, that he made his greatest mark on popular music, rock & roll, and R&B, as a member of the Flamingos from 1958 thru 1961. Those years coincided with the group's being signed to End Records, and the release of their biggest, most identifiable hit, "I Only Have Eyes For You"—Hunt's dramatic background singing, coupled with the restrained piano backing, made it one of the transcendant documents of '50s R&B. He can also be seen singing lead in a killer jump-blues performance in the juke-box movie classic *Go, Johnny, Go*, as the group (back to a five-piece) mimes to their End recording of "Jump Children."

Hunt left the Flamingos in 1962 and signed as a solo artist with Florence Greenberg's Scepter Records in New York. Greenberg reportedly wasn't impressed with Hunt as a singer or an individual, but Luther Dixon, the company's chief of A&R and general music director, loved Hunt's voice, providing him with "Human," which became a No. 5 R&B hit in late 1961. Hunt continued with the label for another three years, until 1964, cutting a complete album (*I Just Don't Know What to Do With Myself*) in late 1962. His version of the title track was never a single, but it predated the more famous hit by Dusty Springfield by nearly two years. In late 1963, following the departure of Dixon from Scepter, Ed Townsend became the company's music director, and one of his very first productions was Tommy Hunt's recording of Townsend's "I Am a Witness," which featured Bernard Purdie on drums and Mickey Baker on guitar, with Hunt's vocals backed up by the Shirelles, Dee Dee Warwick, and the Sweet Inspirations. The single was Hunt's last chart entry for the label, reaching number 71. Hunt left Scepter in 1964, and later moved to the Dynamo label, for which he charted a single in 1967. He later moved to Europe, and continued to perform in Germany and other Central European countries in the 1990s. Hunt's only album, for Scepter has never been reissued, but tracks from it, as well as his hit singles from the label and several other sides, turned up on Capricorn's 1992 *Scepter Records Story* double-CD set. *—Bruce Eder*

Human / 1961 / Collectables ✦✦✦✦✦

A Sign of the Times / 1976 / Spark ✦✦

This release is a sorry attempt to update Tommy Hunt, the ex-Flamingo who relocated to Amsterdam. The weak production kills it, not to mention the limp Northern soul efforts. Only a remake of Kris Kristofferson's "Help Me Make It Through the Night" is worthy of repeated listens. Even the ballads and midtempo romancers like "A Miracle Like You," "Loving You Is," and "Sunshine Girl," fail to register any emotional impact. A remake of the Jackson 5's "Never Can Say Goodbye" is as dry as an overcooked pork chop. *—Andrew Hamilton*

● **The Biggest Man** / May 20, 1997 / Kent ✦✦✦✦✦

This 29-song compilation of Hunt's 1961-1968 recordings for the Scepter and Dynamo labels features, as the liner notes declare, "80% of Tommy Hunt's U.S. solo recordings." Most of the CD is taken from Hunt's 1961-1964 singles for Scepter (including the original version of Bacharach-David's "I Just Don't Know What to Do With Myself" and his biggest hit, 1961's "Human") and outtakes from the period that showed up in the '80s and '90s on assorted Kent compilations. There are also less impressive tracks from his stay at Luther Dixon's Dynamo label in 1967-1968. The notable but odd New York 1960s soul offered here has its virtues, but nonetheless, it is not immediately arresting—not enough to garner more than a cult following. Hunt, like fellow Scepter artists Dionne Warwick, Chuck Jackson, and Maxine Brown, benefited from the label's patented "uptown" brand of soul, with its sumptuous string arrangements, choral backup vocals, and theatrical pop songwriting. Yet Hunt lagged behind everyone else in that list regarding his commercial impact and, ultimately, the quality of his work. He had a deep voice which was a tad overwrought, but not as dramatically overwrought (and therefore appropriate for the Scepter/Wand production mill) as that of his rival Chuck Jackson. With the singular exception of Bacharach-David's "I Just Don't Know What to Do With Myself," he was not gifted with material as outstanding as the best of what Warwick, Jackson, and Brown received. However, for the listener who both digs the Scepter sound and is willing to settle for less brilliance than could be found with those other singers, this is a recommended disc, if only for the commendably typical and pleasing Scepter production and arrangements, complemented by Hunt's competent delivery. There are some nice surprises along the way, like the dramatically arching "This and Only This," one of the finest overlooked Leiber-Stoller compositions, and "It's All a Bad Dream," with its unusual fish-tank sound effects. *—Richie Unterberger*

Ivory Joe Hunter

b. Oct. 10, 1914, Kirbyville, TX, **d.** Nov. 8, 1974, Memphis, TN

Vocals, Piano, Songwriter / West Coast Blues, Piano Blues, R&B

Bespectacled and velvet-smooth in the vocal department, pianist Ivory Joe Hunter appeared too much mild-mannered to be a rock & roller. But when the rebellious music first crashed the American consciousness in the mid-'50s, there was Ivory Joe, deftly delivering his blues ballad "Since I Met You Baby" right alongside the wildest pioneers of the era.

Hunter was already a grizzled R&B vet by that time who had first heard his voice on a 1933 Library of Congress cylinder recording made in Texas (where he grew up). An accomplished tunesmith, he played around the Gulf Coast region, hosting his own radio program for a time in Beaumont before migrating to California in 1942. It was a wise move since Hunter—whose real name was Ivory Joe, incidentally (perhaps his folks were psychic!)—found plenty of work pounding out blues and ballads in wartime California. He started his own label, Ivory Records, to press up his "Blues at Sunrise" (with Johnny Moore's Three Blazers backing him), and it became a national hit when leased to Leon Rene's Exclusive imprint in 1945. Another Hunter enterprise, Pacific Records, hosted a major hit in 1948 when the pianist's "Pretty Mama Blues" topped the R&B charts for three weeks.

At whatever logo Hunter paused from the mid-'40s through the late '50s, his platters sold like hotcakes. For Cincinnati-based King in 1948-1949, he hit with "Don't Fall in Love With Me," "What Did You Do to Me," "Waiting in Vain," and "Guess Who." At MGM, then new to the record biz, he cut his immortal "I Almost Lost My Mind" (another R&B chart-topper in 1950), "I Need You So" (later covered by Elvis), and "It's a Sin." Signing with Atlantic in 1954, he hit big with "Since I Met You Baby" in 1956 and the two-sided smash "Empty Arms"/"Love's a Hurting Game" in 1957.

Hunter's fondness for country music reared its head in 1958. Upon switching to Dot Records, he scored his last pop hit with a cover of Bill Anderson's "City Lights." Hunter's Dot encores went nowhere; neither did typically mellow outings for Vee-Jay, Smash, Capitol, and Veep. Epic went so far as to recruit a simmering Memphis band (including organist Isaac Hayes, trumpeter Gene "Bowlegs" Miller, and saxist Charles Chalmers) for an LP titled *The Return of Ivory Joe Hunter* that hoped to revitalize his career, but it wasn't meant to be. The album's cover photo—a closeup of Hunter's grinning face with a cigarette dangling from his lips—seems grimly ironic in the face of his death from lung cancer only a few years later. *—Bill Dahl*

16 of His Greatest Hits / 1958 / King ✦✦✦

Other than ruining his 1949 smash "Guess Who" entirely with hideous stereo overdubs, King has done pretty well by the pianist on this collection of his postwar output for the Cincinnati firm. Hunter was primarily in a sentimental blues ballad bag back then, some of his hits displaying a tinge of country influence. Sound quality is okay if not superlative. *—Bill Dahl*

The Return of Ivory Joe Hunter / 1971 / Epic ✦✦✦

Commendable attempt to update Ivory Joe Hunter's sound for early-'70s consumption, with an all-star Memphis aggregation that included Isaac Hayes on organ, saxist Charlie Chalmers, and a sax section lifted from the Hi studios. The ploy worked reasonably well, producing updated remakes of Hunter's hits and tasty versions of Don Covay's "I'm Coming Down With the Blues" and Chuck Willis' "What Am I Living For." *—Bill Dahl*

● **Since I Met You Baby: The Best of Ivory Joe Hunter** / Oct. 19, 1994 / Razor & Tie ✦✦✦✦✦

The definitive pop compilation of the urbane postwar crooner and oldest rock & roller, *Since I Met You Baby: The Best of Ivory Joe Hunter* compiles 25 of his sides for MGM and Atlantic from 1949 to 1958. Best of all are his two big hits, "I Almost Lost My Mind" and "Since I Met You Baby," as sheepish and love-struck a pair of pop performances as have ever been heard. Much of the rest is at a similarly high level, including his several R&B hits from the late '50s—"It May Sound Silly," "A Tear Fell," "Love Is a Hurting Game," "Empty Arms," and "Yes I Want You"—when he was equally comfortable in supper clubs, urban blues joints, or the rock & roll package shows that criss-crossed the nation. A few uptempo songs like "Rockin' Chair Boogie" and "Shooty Booty" prove he could rollick with the youngsters as well. *—John Bush*

Ivory Joe Hunter/Sings the Old and the New / Jul. 27, 1999 / Collectables ✦✦✦✦

Don't let the 28 tracks fool you: Collectables doesn't attempt a thorough overview of Ivory Joe Hunter's five-decade recording career, which spanned from the '30s to the '70s. These 28 tracks chronicle the Texas-born purveyor of West Coast blues' '50s stint with Atlantic Records. For some artists it can be done, but trying to cover Hunter's output in less than 30 songs is as impossible as covering a king-size mattress with a twin-size sheet. Hunter preceded dinosaurs like Frank Sinatra, Nat King Cole, the Andrews Sisters, Vic Damone, and the Isley Brothers. This disc features Hunter's two late-'50s Atlantic albums, the period of "Since I Lost My Baby (I Almost Lost My Mind)," the hit that made Hunter the oldest performer on the rock circuit. He matches that velvety offering with other smoothies. Ivory Joe Hunter was a stylish blues crooner who influenced countless singers with his low-key approach. *—Andrew Hamilton*

Howard Huntsberry

Vocals / Urban

Howard Huntsberry scored only a few times as a solo singer, but he did turn in some excellent performances while the lead vocalist of Klique, an '80s trio that also included his sister Deborah Hunter and Isaac Suthers. Their finest number was a cover of Jackie Wilson's "Stop Doggin' Me Around" in 1983. Huntsberry's rendition was so similar to Wilson's that he was tapped to play the soul star in 1987's *La Bamba*. Klique recorded for MCA from 1981 to 1985, getting one other Top 20 hit with "A Woman, a Lover, a Friend" in 1985. *—Ron Wynn*

● **Portrait of a Singer** / Dec. 26, 1994 / Oglio ♦♦♦♦

Willie Hutch (Willie McKinley Hutchison)

b. 1946, Los Angeles, CA

Vocals, Guitar / Blaxploitation, Soul, Urban, Quiet Storm

A versatile figure during Motown's "golden years," Willie Hutch penned hits for other artists, as well as issuing albums on his own. Born Willie McKinley Hutchinson in 1946 in Los Angeles, CA, Hutch was raised in Dallas, TX, where he began signing as a teenager (as a member of an outfit called the Ambassadors). It was also during his teenaged years that Hutch began penning his own songs, and in 1964 issued a debut solo single, "Love Has Put Me Down." Soon after, his songwriting talents attracted the attention of the soon-to-be renowned '60s pop-soul outfit the 5th Dimension, for whom Hutch penned several tracks, as well as earning a co-production credit for the group's 1967 debut full-length *Up, Up and Away*. In 1970, producer Hal Davis asked Hutch to help finish off a song he desperately needed completed for the Jackson 5, "I'll Be There." Hutch delivered; the band recorded Hutch's version the next day, as it eventually became one of the 5's biggest early hits, and led to Motown head honcho Berry Gordy hiring Hutch to act as a songwriter/producer for other Motown artists on a regular basis.

Hutch then produced albums for Michael Jackson and Smokey Robinson during the early '70s, during which time Hutch penned the soundtrack to the 1973 blaxploitation flick *The Mack* on his own. The soundtrack is often considered to be one of the era's finest, as it spawned such funk-soul classics as the title track, "Brother's Gonna Work It Out," and "Slick." Hutch continued to issue solo releases for Motown, including such titles as *Fully Exposed* (1973), *Foxy Brown* (1975), *The Mark of the Beast* (1975), *Concert in Blues* (1976), and *Color Her Sunshine* (1976), among others. After briefly relocating to the Whitfield record company for a few releases, Hutch returned back to Motown where he issued further solo albums and worked with others; including a duet between the Four Tops and Aretha Franklin (1983's "What Have We Got to Lose"), Sammy Davis Jr.'s "Hello Detroit" (1984), in addition to a soundtrack album for the 1985 movie *The Last Dragon*. Hutch sporadically issued further solo sets in the '90s (1994's *From the Heart* and 1996's *The Mack Is Back*), before returning six years later with 2002's *Sexalicious*. *—Greg Prato*

The Mack / 1973 / Motown ♦♦♦♦♦

When an act called Sisters Love were offered a cameo in the blaxploitation film *The Mack*, their manager suggested that Willie Hutch do the soundtrack. It became to be one of the great '70s film scores, including a pair of classic funk tunes, "Brothers Gonna Work It Out" and the title cut. The results proved to be another soundtrack that far surpassed the quality of its film. *—Ron Wynn*

Foxy Brown / 1975 / Motown ♦♦♦

Willie Hutch is a multi-talented performer who never achieved fame or stardom. Despite some good moments, the sales here failed to meet or exceed the numbers of his previous soundtrack, *The Mack*. "Chase" borrows heavily from "Shaft," maybe too much. Hutch is full of fire on "The Theme of Foxy Brown," his distinctive tenor wringing the most from each note. "Give Me Some of That Good Old Love" had a foot-tapping groove, tough backing vocals from Maxine Williard, Julie Tilman, and Carol Willis, and all the elements of a hit record. Unfortunately, Motown only released "Foxy Brown" as a single, and nothing else. The vamping "Out There" and "Foxy Lady" are nasty and contagious. "You Sure Know How to Love Your Man" copies a bit of "Love Machine"'s bassline; it's Willie and the girls' most spirited performance, with Hutch showing that Wilson Pickett isn't the only person who can intersperse soulful screams between lyrics. The melodic "Ain't That (Mellow Mellow)" sounds like another single, but Motown wasn't hearing it; they were too busy concentrating on his *Love Power* LP, which also flopped. *—Andrew Hamilton*

Ode to My Lady / 1975 / Motown ♦♦♦

The gritty sound of Willie Hutch had an unmistakable silkiness, and this album brings out that distinctiveness. This album featured two singles. "Love Power" was the first release. With its progressive string and horn arrangement, Hutch, with his Sam Cooke phrasing, croons his way through this earnest number. It peaked at number eight on the *Billboard* R&B charts after 20 weeks. The second single was the comparable "Party Down." With the lyrical content shifting to the dancefloor, Hutch's energy does not swagger. The groove on this number has some of that Ohio Players spirit. The single peaked at 19 after 15 weeks. The soulful deliveries that Hutch convey are uplifting. This album has a consistent mixture of selections, including the soul singer's rendition of the classic "The Way We Were." The title track is a midtempo instrumental. *—Craig Lytle*

Color Her Sunshine / 1976 / VIP ♦♦♦

Making a Game out of Love / 1985 / Motown ♦♦♦

From the Heart / 1994 / GGIT ♦♦♦

In the 1990s, soul veterans like Willie Hutch have two choices: they can either stick with the type of soul music they've always done, or they can go high-tech and aim for success in the urban contemporary arena. The latter approach isn't necessarily bad—as long as the artist is true to himself/herself. And Hutch generally sounds sincere on the urban-oriented *From the Heart*. Hutch's voice had held up well over the years, and his charisma is advantageous on "Love You With a Feeling," "She's a Super Lover" and other smooth cuts that aren't unlike something Freddie Jackson would do. On "So Excited," Hutch transforms the Pointer Sisters' mega-hit into a relaxed slow jam. Though not on a par with his classic '70s recordings, this is an enjoyable effort that Hutch's more devoted fans should be aware of. Unfortunately, the obscure CD received very little attention, and in fact, many fans of '70s soul had no idea that he was still recording. *—Alex Henderson*

● **The Very Best of Willie Hutch** / Aug. 25, 1998 / Motown ♦♦♦♦♦

One of the unsung heroes of 1970s soul, Willie Hutch was never the big name he deserved to be. The smooth singer/composer had a few major and moderate hits, but commercially, he didn't make it to the level of Marvin Gaye, Ronald Isley, and Curtis Mayfield (all of whom he inspires comparisons to). Released in late 1998, *The Very Best of Willie Hutch* spans 1972-1982 and reminds us how engaging a singer he was in his heyday. Hutch could get funky when he wanted to, and he does so with splendid results on "Get Ready for the Get Down" (a number-24 R&B hit), "Brothers Gonna Work It Out," and the theme from the 1973 blaxploitation film *Foxy Brown*. But for the most part, Hutch made his mark as a romantic crooner. It is Hutch's smooth, romantic side that prevails on "Sunshine Lady," "I Choose You," "What You Gonna Do After the Party," and his inspired makeover of Barbra Streisand's "The Way We Were." Appropriately, the CD opens with Hutch's biggest hit: the perky, feel-good anthem "Love Power," which went to number nine on the R&B singles charts. Full of gems that were recorded during Hutch's peak years, this CD is essential listening for lovers of 1970s soul. *—Alex Henderson*

Leroy Hutson

b. Jun. 4, 1945, Newark, NJ

Vocals, Piano / Chicago Soul, Quiet Storm, Blaxploitation, Soul

One of the most underrated soul producers of the '70s, multi-talented producer/singer/songwriter/instrumentalist Leroy Hutson began his career in various vocal groups around his hometown of Newark, NJ, in the '60s, but saw his early success as a co-writer for Howard University roommate Donny Hathaway's 1970 hit single "The Ghetto." Hutson would later replace Curtis Mayfield in 1971 as the lead singer in the Impressions and stayed with them until 1973, when he followed in Mayfield's footsteps and launched his own solo career. His smooth, imaginative productions set the bar very high for everyone at the label (including its owner) to follow suit. Although his lyrics were not as politically fueled as Mayfield's, Hutson's love-inspired songs were responsible for a string of mid-'70s classics which he and Curtom are best known for.

While he would enjoy the commercial success during a string of albums in the mid- to late '70s, he also lent his production and songwriting skills to several labelmates, including the Natural Four. After the closing of Curtom Records in 1980, Hutson's career diminished into obscurity with the exception of 1982's jazz-funk-tinged *Paradise*. However, he has maintained a strong cult following among soul collectors to this day, and in 2000 Sequel Records had the good sense to reissue not only the original albums on CD but a two-disc anthology spanning the greatest hits of his career. *—Rob Theakston*

Love Oh Love / 1973 / Charly ♦♦♦

After working as a writer and producer for such soul music stalwarts as Donny Hathaway and a stint replacing Curtis Mayfield as the lead vocalist in the Impressions, Leroy Hutson embarked on a solo career with 1973's *Love Oh Love*. The album combines the kind of smooth soul music that Hutson performed with the Impressions with more ambitious and conceptual outings in the vein of Marvin Gaye and Stevie Wonder. When Hutson sticks to love songs, *Love Oh Love* is magical: "So in Love With You" combines a honey-sweet romantic vocal from Hutson with a spine-tingling string arrangement to create an elegant and heartfelt ballad, while the title track raises its tale of lost love to an uptempo level with jazzy horns and a percolating rhythm arrangement. "As Long as There's Love Around" is another effective romantic track that layers Hutson's velvety vocals over a complex instrumental track that combines gentle strings and brash horns with an insistently grooving bassline. The progressive-minded tracks are less satisfying: "Time Brings on a Change" is a political commentary song whose use of a Martin Luther King Jr. sample is a little too gimmicky for its own good, and "Getting It On" is a funk instrumental that fails to work any memorable hooks into its pleasant groove. Despite these problems, nothing on the album is less than listenable and everything flows together nicely to create a cohesive (if somewhat short) album. In short, *Love Oh Love* is one of the most consistent albums in the Leroy Hutson catalog and a good introduction to his silky soul style. *—Donald A. Guarisco*

The Man! / 1974 / Curtom ♦♦

After a promising start with the smooth soul of *Love Oh Love*, Leroy Hutson set out to establish himself as a multi-hyphenate soul artist in the vein of Stevie Wonder on *The Man!* Indeed, the cover of the album promotes him as a "writer/producer/artist/superstar." While the resulting album leaves no doubts as to his technical skill as a writer and producer, *The Man!* shows that Hutson was better as a craftsman than an artist, and that he lacked the top-shelf material to be a superstar. Although the album benefits from tight arrangements and slick production, the material never quite lives up to its sense of ambition; "Can't Say Enough About Mom" is a family values tune that suffers from dull, obvious lyrics and an overblown arrangement, while "Gotta Move Gotta Groove" is a tale of musician life that lacks the specific insights and clever lyricism that would help it rise above the norm. The album also suffers from padding despite its short length, the worst example being "Dudley Doright," a grating novelty tune that wrecks its potentially funky groove with silly horse-snort sound effects. Despite this dearth of fully-realized material, *The Man!* has its moments: "Ella Weez" is a likable slice of uptempo pop soul built on a catchy call-and-response vocal hook, and "The Ghetto '74" is Hutson's smooth update of a mostly-instrumental hit he wrote for Donny Hathaway. However, moments like these are the exception instead of the rule, and *The Man!* ends up being too uninspired and generic to live up to its title. *—Donald A. Guarisco*

Hutson / Jul. 1975 / Curtom ♦♦♦
Released on Curtom Records in 1975, *Hutson* illuminates the fickleness and unpredictable nature of the music business. Leroy Hutson seemed to have it all going for him; he replaced Curtis Mayfield in the Impressions, then branched out solo, was a friend of Donny Hathaway (who also worked for Mayfield at the time), and was given *carte blanche* to produced hits—with the help of others—for himself. The biorhythms must have been out of whack, because it never really happened for the talented guy. This is a fine effort with bouncy tunes, stirring ballads, and crack productions—yet the masses never heard it. Best bets: All. But special mention to "Lucky Fellow," "All Because of You," and "So Much Love." *—Andrew Hamilton*

Hutson II / 1976 / Curtom ♦♦♦
Every Leroy Hutson album features a sweeping, make-you-feel-good opening tune; this time "Love the Feeling" warms you for a collage of soulful ballads, midtempo romps, and steppers. The best of the lot is "I Do, I Do (Want to Make Love to You)," a sensuous booty call reminiscent of Peabo Bryson. Jonesing for a hit, some of the cuts come off cookie-cutter, but Hutson's singing shines throughout. "Blackberry Jam" and "Sofunktiscation" are formulaic but pleasing funkers. *—Andrew Hamilton*

Closer to the Source / 1978 / Charly ♦♦♦
After a series of albums where he handled much the production and writing as a one-man show, Leroy Hutson teamed up with a number of collaborators (including Linda Clifford producer Gil Askey) to record 1978's *Closer to the Source*. The result is an unambitious but slick album of pop-soul. The big problem with this album is that its music is too derivative too often to make a strong case for Hutson's gifts as a performer: The jazzy melody of "They've Got Love" sounds almost identical to Stevie Wonder's late-'60s string of orchestrated pop-soul hits and the Marvin Gaye-inspired "Where Did Love Go" has a lovely, string-sweetened arrangement but quotes "What's Going On" a little too closely for its own good. Another problematic cut in this area is the title track, which closely imitates the light, jazzy sound that was bringing Earth, Wind & Fire hit after hit around this time. Although the outside writers and production help aid the album's consistency, the best cuts on *Closer to the Source* are the ones either written or co-written by Hutson himself: "Get to This (You'll Get to Me)" builds a strong melody on the tension between an ethereal melody and percolating, horn-spiced groove, and "Heaven Right Here on Earth" is the kind of silky slow jam that Hutson always excelled at. In the end, *Closer to the Source* is a solid album that will please Hutson's cult of fans but will probably seem a little too derivative to other soul music enthusiasts. *—Donald A. Guarisco*

Unforgettable / 1979 / Charly ♦♦

Paradise / 1982 / Elektra ♦♦
Leroy Hutson's 1982 Elektra album has an almost jazzy feel to it, due in part to a prominent electric piano on most tracks and the sparseness: no big horn sections or strings. Most of the cuts are laid-back, perfect for chilling out. The cornerstone track is his luscious cover of fellow Chicagoans Omni's "You Make It Happen." The dance track could serve as a sampling precursor as it includes a section of the Whispers' "In the Raw" and the guitar riff from Zapp's "More Bounce to the Ounce." Other highlights are the midtempo sax-laced title track, "Nice and Easy," the funky dance jam "Nobody but You," and the upbeat, uplifting "Stay at It" with backing vocals by Carl Carlton. *—Ed Hogan*

● **Lucky Fellow: The Curtom Anthology 1972–79** / Nov. 14, 2000 / Sequel ♦♦♦♦
A generous helping of Leroy Hutson's tracks from his Curtom Records days, courtesy of England's Sequel Records. This contains everything: the descriptive singer's biggest single "So in Love With You," "Love Oh Love," the title track, and good stretched-out numbers like "All Because of You," "Unforgettable," and "(You Put the Funk) In My Life." And there are enough ballads to satisfy most listening palates. The only significant omission from the 23 tracks is his rendition of "The Ghetto," the gritty cut he co-wrote with Donny Hathaway that broke Hathaway on soul radio; Hutson does a nice version of the influential groove that's been imitated by so many. *—Andrew Hamilton*

Phyllis Hyman

b. Jul. 6, 1941, Philadelphia, PA, **d.** Jun. 30, 1995, New York, NY
Vocals / Quiet Storm, Urban, Vocal Jazz, Disco
Phyllis Hyman began her career as a silky voiced, jazz-influenced singer and gradually moved into slick, heavily produced urban contemporary ballads and light dance numbers. Hyman won a scholarship to music school and then began her professional career with the group New Direction in 1971. When they disbanded after a national tour, Hyman joined the Miami ensemble All the People. She also worked there with another local group, the Hondo Beat, and appeared in the film *Lenny*. That was followed by a two-year stint heading Phyllis Hyman & the P/H Factor, before relocating to New York.

Hyman did background vocals on Jon Lucien's *Premonition* LP and built her reputation performing in New York clubs. Norman Connors made her his featured vocalist in the mid-'70s, and she was highlighted on a cover of the Stylistics' "Betcha By Golly Wow," which appeared on Connors' *You Are My Starship* LP. Hyman also sang with Pharaoh Sanders & the Fatback Band while cutting two singles as a lead artist. Buddah released *Phyllis Hyman* in 1977, but she really began making an impression when she was signed by Arista the next year. The songs "Somewhere in My Lifetime" and "You Know How to Love Me" both made the R&B Top 20. Hyman got her lone Top Ten hit in 1981 with "Can't We Fall in Love Again," but her albums did consistently well through the '80s. The production teams of James Mtume/Reggie Lucas and Narada Michael Walden/Thom Bell gave her material that showcased her skill with sophisticated ballads.

Hyman had more success when she left Arista for Philadelphia International in 1986, with the single "Living All Alone" putting her back in the R&B Top 20. She also sang on fusion and light jazz dates by Joe Sample, Ronnie Foster, and Grover Washington Jr., a more conventional jazz session for McCoy Tyner, and a pop date with the Four Tops. Tragically, Hyman took her own life on June 30, 1995; *Forever With You* was issued posthumously. *—Ron Wynn*

Phyllis Hyman / 1977 / Buddah ♦♦♦
This 1977 set is the debut from one of music's most emotional and loved singers. Her career got a jump-start from her work on Norman Connors's 1976 album *You Are My Starship*, where Hyman gave a melancholy and skilled reading of the Stylistics' hit "Betcha By Golly Wow." That album set the standard for Hyman's career and features classy, mellow R&B sound made by players with esteemed jazz/R&B players. But among her late-'70s and early-'80s output, *Phyllis Hyman* is curiously one of her most forgotten efforts, though it included many songs she would be later be identified with. Skip Scarborough's "No One Can Love You More" is indicative of her plentiful sensual charm and her rich vocal timbre. Although Hyman's vocal prowess is well known, this set also shows that she was gifted with an uncommon maturity. Hyman was only in her mid-'20s when this was recorded. That self-possession made her glide through the majority of the material here. Thom Bell and Linda Creed's "I Don't Want to Lose You" (originally recorded by the Spinners) has Hyman's version even more of a tearjerker. From singing the chorus in the intro, to doing a Sarah Vaughan-like scat in the middle, the song was hers. The debut also displays her skill, the blessing and curse of making half-baked material interesting. On "Beautiful Man of Mine" and Hubert Eaves' "Children of the World," her vocals are undoubtedly the best thing about the tracks. *Phyllis Hyman* veers from instant melodic classics to unformed ideas, a mix that prevents it from being essential. *—Jason Elias*

Somewhere in My Lifetime / 1979 / Arista ♦♦♦
Somewhere in My Lifetime, Phyllis Hyman's second album (but her first for Arista), is similar to many of her efforts: a great singer, but too many so-so songs. The album starts off with a cover of Exile's disco/pop hit, "Kiss You All Over"; despite her best attempts, the horrible lyrics and the song's origins make this a waste of precious studio time. The lachrymose title-track ballad, produced by Barry Manilow and Ron Dante, finds Hyman's voice poorly recorded and placed into a schmaltzy arrangement. Still, the album features quite a few of the songs she came to be identified with: "The Answer Is You," "Gonna Make Changes," and Gary Glenn's "Be Careful (How You Treat My Love)," all skillfully produced by then-husband Larry Alexander and Skip Scarborough. The song "Be Careful" followed the Norman Connors example of providing Hyman with a sympathetic arrangement, then getting the best take possible. After all of the botched crossover attempts and so-so dance moves, *Somewhere in My Lifetime* ended on a good note. "Here's That Rainy Day" has her accompanied only by a piano, and she turns in an affecting performance, neither self-pitying nor melodramatic. Although this effort had a few career-threatening detours, Hyman's charisma and some solid songs make this a solid effort. *—Jason Elias*

You Know How to Love Me / 1979 / Arista ♦♦♦♦
You Know How to Love Me was Phyllis Hyman's most successful album and was carefully tailored to become the artist's crossover breakthrough, with prolific producer/songwriters James Mtume and Reggie Lucas on board. The end result is a carefully constructed blend of contemporary disco-styled songs and ballads, some better than others, and the more routine tracks are always rescued by Hyman stellar pipes. The album never truly realized its full potential, but does include the song that would become one of Hyman's signature tunes, "You Know How to Love Me." The song was never a blockbuster hit, but has grown into a classic, covered by artists such as Lisa Stansfield and Robin S. Other highlights include the excellent quiet storm of "Some Way," which allows Hyman's husky voice to shine; the somber, sublime piano ballad "But I Love You"; and the jazzy saxophone ballad "Complete Me." *You Know How to Love Me* is as close as Hyman truly came to becoming a commercial force and is an important and essential chapter in this star's musical legacy. The album was re-released in 2002, boasting excellent liner notes by biographer David Nathan, rare photos, and a bonus track, "You're the One," recorded in 1977, which blends in perfectly with the rest of the disc. This is the case of an album that was not a blockbuster upon initial release, but, like a great overlooked film, has grown into a classic whose importance will only increase with the passing of time. *—Jose F. Promis*

Can't We Fall in Love Again / 1981 / Arista ♦♦

Goddess of Love / 1983 / Arista ♦♦♦

Living All Alone / 1987 / Philadelphia International ♦♦♦♦
Coming off a successful though problematic tenure with Arista, Phyllis Hyman signed with Philadelphia International shortly after the label switched from CBS to Capitol. Like Shirley Jones' 1986 album *Always in the Mood*, *Living All Alone* typified the synth-based but still melodic mid- to late-'80s Philly sound. The producers and writers gave her an album's worth of instant-classic singer's songs. The album's first single, the bittersweet "You Just Don't Know," typified the powerful and classy proceedings. "First Time Together" also follows the same style. While Hyman's vocals are top-notch here, fans listening to *Living All Alone* can't help but be struck by the sense of melancholy apparent in the sessions. That's not true of the title track, an oddly sensual song that has her trademark fire, as she does some great vocalizations and screams, and seems to live the lyrics. The poignant Thom Bell & Linda Creed gem "Old Friend" quickly became a fan favorite. Although most of *Living All Alone* is emotionally draining, it's one of Hyman's finest efforts. *—Jason Elias*

Under Her Spell: Phyllis Hyman's Greatest Hits / 1989 / Arista ♦♦♦♦♦
Phyllis Hyman's soft, sultry, suggestive voice was featured on several pop/jazz and fusion hits during the 1970s and '80s. Hyman had the mellow, relaxed tone that struck a chord with the emerging urban contemporary, and fusion audience. The ten tracks on this collection include the big hits "You Know How to Love Me," "Somewhere in My Lifetime," her cover of the Stylistics' "Betcha by Golly Wow" and the title track, plus others that weren't commercially prominent, but were equally indicative of her direction during that

period. These include "Can't We Fall in Love Again" with Michael Henderson and "Gonna Make Changes." These songs remain her most successful and most memorable as a solo artist. *—Ron Wynn*

Prime of My Life / 1991 / Philadelphia International ♦♦♦♦

Listening to Phyllis Hyman's 1991 emotional *tour de force Prime of My Life* is at once a happy and sad experience. Happy because it finds Hyman at a moment when she was not tortured by her inner demons and tragic because it provides an undeniable glimpse into Hyman's tortured soul and the pending suicide which would materialize four years later. *Prime of My Life* granted the sophisticated lady her first R&B chart-topper with the saucy "Don't Wanna Change the World," which incorporates elements of new jack swing, hip-hop, and early-'90s house, and even features a rare, sexy rap by the songstress herself. The album opens with the jazzy quiet storm hit "When You Get Right Down to It" and features several shimmering, gorgeous ballads, most notably the timeless audience favorite "Meet Me on the Moon," one of the high points of Hyman's catalog, period. Other gems include the light, bittersweet closer "Whatever Happened to Our Love," "I Can't Take It Anymore," which is a sad tune pitted against a happy beat, and the self-assured yet ultimately tragic "Prime of My Life." One of the true highlights, however, is the over-seven-minutes-in-length "Living in Confusion," which Hyman belts with unmistakable integrity, growling out the bewildered lyrics with overflowing conviction, and provides more than a glimpse into what was really going on in the singer's life. Hyman could take an average song and tear through it like a tiger, which is what made her music so appealing. This album is a true gem and proves that the husky-voiced Hyman was a timeless song stylist in a class all her own. [The Japanese version of the album includes a bonus track, "Hottest Love Around."] *—Jose F. Promis*

I Refuse to Be Lonely / Nov. 21, 1995 / Volcano ♦♦♦♦

Loving You, Losing You: The Classic Balladry of Phyllis Hyman / Mar. 26, 1996 / EMI ♦♦♦

Hyman was a singer of tremendous gift and skill. Since her suicide in 1995, she has been the recipient of many compilations, but few seem to capture her essence. Unfortunately, *Loving You, Losing You: The Classic Balladry of Phyllis Hyman* also misses the mark, ignoring a huge portion of her work and only covering the years 1977 to 1981. That's fine if you think she was washed up by the time of the first Reagan administration, but of course, she wasn't. But of course this being Phyliis Hyman, some great songs are included here. "The Answer Is You," "Gonna Make Changes," and "I Don't Want to Lose You" are still quiet storm staples. Like most compilations, this also has to offer some things not found on other sets. The haunting "Sounds Like a Love Song," her previously unreleased version of a song originally done by the Whispers in 1976, is technically raw, but worth hearing. A few songs show up in alternate takes, though "Be Careful (How You Treat My Love)" in particular can't compete with the perfection of the original. Like many other compilations, the omissions are glaring. "Some Way," from 1979 isn't here. Other absent songs include her phenomenal work with McCoy Tyner on the tracks "Love Surrounds Us Everywhere" and "In Search of My Heart" from his 1982 set *Looking Out.* Since this compilation covers Hyman's balladry, "Loving You, Losing You" shouldn't be here. Not only is it a dance track, Engelbert Humperdinck did a better job with it. *The Classic Balladry of Phyllis Hyman* is a good way to get acquainted with the artist, but fans may not be so moved. *—Jason Elias*

Forever With You / Jul. 28, 1998 / Philadelphia International ♦♦♦♦

Issued three years after Phyllis Hyman's death, *Forever With You* collects 12 unreleased songs recorded between 1985-1995, during her tenure with Philadelphia International. Not a single track on this set sounds like filler—the whole album is comprised of well-produced, elegant, and sophisticated songs, running a gamut of musical styles, and further showcases the loss that the music world suffered with Hyman's tragic passing. The album opens with the upbeat, Latin-tinged title track, and then heads into quiet storm territory with "Funny How Love Goes" (a duet with newcomer Damon), "Come Right or Not at All," "The Strength of a Woman," and her faithful cover of the Stylistics' "Hurry Up This Way Again." The album veers into left gear with the energetic house track "How Long," which works incredibly well and, had things gone differently, could have opened up a whole different market for Hyman. "Someone to Love," the greatest torch song Barbra Streisand never recorded, is a definite album highlight, and brings to mind the music of classic Hollywood films of the 1940s. Hyman tackles hip-hop lite with "Tell Me What You're Gonna Do," provides a socially conscious quiet storm ballad with "The Kids," and vamps coyly on the sexy "Set a Little Trap," another album highlight. This set closes with the shuffling, hip-hop-laced "No One but You" and the soaring ballad "Souvenirs." *Forever With You*, which also includes several songs co-written by Hyman, is a must for any fan, and sounds like an actual, cohesive set, as opposed to a compilation of rarities and unreleased material. As always, however, the star is Hyman's tortured, elegant, and ferocious voice, and the unparalleled conviction that she injects into each song. Another four-star set from the great, regal Sophisticated Lady. *—Jose F. Promis*

● **Master Hits: Phyllis Hyman** / Jul. 27, 1999 / Arista ♦♦♦♦

Arista celebrated its 30th anniversary by releasing *The Heritage Series*, spotlighting the most popular artists on the label. The Phyllis Hyman installment in *The Heritage Series* is pretty much a straight hits collection, featuring highlights from her stint at the label. While she was at Arista, she achieved the peak of her popularity with such hits as "Betcha By Golly Wow," "Somewhere in My Lifetime," "Kiss You All Over," "Complete Me," and "Just Another Face in the Crowd." All those songs are here, along with some highlights from her albums, providing a nice retrospective of her time with Arista. *—Stephen Thomas Erlewine*

I

Iceberg Slim (Robert Beck)

b. Aug. 4, 1918, Chicago, IL, **d.** Apr. 28, 1992

Speech/Speaker/Speaking Part, Rap, Vocals / Blaxploitation, Social Commentary, Stories

Best known as an author of gritty tales of street life and hustling, Iceberg Slim (Robert Beck) sold over six-million copies of his books, the most popular being *Pimp: The Story of My Life.* Since many authors before him had seen fit to record and release spoken word albums, Slim followed suit in 1976 with *Reflections* which found him reciting his lurid vignettes over suitably funky backing from the Red Holloway Quartet. The street-tough pimp persona projected by Slim proved highly influential to hip-hop, especially two artists who paid tribute to him through their own names, Ice-T and Ice Cube. Slim passed away in 1992 at the age of 73. *—Wade Kergan*

● **Reflections** / 1976 / Infinite Zero ✦✦✦✦✦

With his polished delivery and smooth, almost soothing voice, Iceberg Slim could have been one of any number of beatnik poets, delivering elaborate monologues over smooth background music on 1976's *Reflections.* The difference is Iceberg Slim (nee Robert Beck) was a pimp, and his stories are scathingly explicit, and, more often than not, extraordinarily compelling. The language can get graphic; this is not an album for the squeamish. For those who aren't easily offended, though, this album will be spellbinding. Slim's skills as a storyteller cannot be overstated; even at his crudest, he still spins riveting yarns. "The Fall" is virtually autobiographical, depicting his last days as a pimp and what sent him on a downfall to prison, leavened with scabrous humor. "Broadway Sam" is a mean, hilarious story of another pimp who has the tables turned on him in prison. The second half of the record, though, is more poignant, as Slim remembers a lost love on "Durealla" and comes to terms with his relationship with his late mother on "Mama Debt." Throughout the record, Slim is backed by jazzy music courtesy of the Red Holloway Quartet, which enhances the stories without overshadowing them. Many years later, of course, Slim would serve as the inspiration for gangsta rappers like Ice-T (who named himself after Slim) and Schoolly D. Too many of Slim's followers, though, lack the mixture of street smarts and the intellectual and emotional depth shown here. For anyone interested in the roots of modern urban culture, *Reflections* is a must-hear. *—Victor W. Valdivia*

The Ides of March

f. Chicago, IL

Group / Blue-Eyed Soul, Pop/Rock, Hard Rock, Psychedelic

Chicago's Ides of March burst onto the national scene in 1970 with the million-selling single "Vehicle," a tune that bore more than a passing resemblance to the then mega-selling Blood, Sweat & Tears. But the band's pedigree went back further than BS&T's, and with a much different origin. Formed in the mid-'60s in the Windy City, founding member Jim Peterik put the original Ides together as a teen band, strong on original material and British pop harmonies. Soon the band was recording for London's Parrot Records subsidiary, releasing five singles between 1966 and 1967, including the local hit "You Wouldn't Listen." By the late 1960s, however, Peterik had reconfigured the band to include a full horn section, and a new sound and style for the band was born. Ever the crafty commercial songwriter, Peterik fashioned a new single, "Vehicle," to showcase this sound, which mirrored the success of horn rock bands like Chase and Blood, Sweat & Tears. The record was a huge hit, spawning the soundalike follow-up "Superman."

The other chart hit for the group (and a complete about-face from the horn-dominated sound of "Vehicle") was the wistful "L.A. Goodbye." Personnel problems and a label shift to RCA-Victor spelled the end of the band as Peterik eased into the 1980s in the role of producer/songwriter, penning several hits for the likes of .38 Special and others. The group re-formed in 1993 to record an album of new material and recuts of their hits going all the way back to "You Wouldn't Listen," and Peterik remains quite active both as a tunesmith and producer. *—Cub Koda*

● **Vehicle** / 1970 / Warner Bros. ✦✦✦✦

The band's first album (they had done five singles for Parrot when they were a Chicago teen band) finds them following the structure of their hit single with much of the music mirroring the then-fashionable horn rock sounds of Blood, Sweat & Tears and fellow Windy City jazz rockers Chase. *—Cub Koda*

Common Bond / 1971 / Warner Bros. ✦✦✦

By the time the Ides came to record their second album for Warner Bros. in 1971, the heavy horn rock cadences had given way to a softer, more acoustic sound. The big hit from this album was "L.A. Goodbye," their last chart record of any consequence. *—Cub Koda*

World Woven / 1972 / RCA ✦✦✦

A label change from Warner Brothers to RCA Victor in 1972 didn't bring the band back to the charts, but much fine music resulted in this very laidback collection of songs. *—Cub Koda*

Midnight Oil / 1973 / RCA ✦✦

The final album (until their reunion album in 1993) from the band finds them desperately in search of a hit while still trying to reinvent themselves as an acoustic-dominated, laidback kind of organization. Poco's Rusty Young guests on both metal-bodied dobro and steel guitar. *—Cub Koda*

Ideology / 1992 / I.O.M. ✦✦✦✦

It was almost 20 years since their last record together when the Ides of March re-formed to cut this one, a collection of recuts of their classic hits from the 1960s ("You Wouldn't Listen") and '70s ("Vehicle," "Aire of Good Feeling," "Bald Medusa," "L.A. Goodbye," and "Hot Water") and seven new tunes recorded expressly for this collection. Jim Peterik was the original heart and soul of the band, singing, writing, playing guitar and producing, later going on to write hits for .38 Special and others. This disc finds him front and center, laying it down with an enthusiasm befitting a 20-year-old out to hustle his first record deal. With strong new material in the form of "Rebel Girl," "I'd Love Her Anyway," "Cry of the Wild Heart," "Reflection of Desire," "Love Don't Choose," "You, You, You," and the anthemic "Spirit of Chicago," this album charts new ground as well. Seldom do reunion albums muster this much energy and commitment from its members, but this one does in a big way. *—Cub Koda*

Age Before Beauty / 1997 / IOM ✦✦✦

Seldom can bands reform, even with all the original members intact, and play and sing with even a smidgen of the power they once possessed. But the Ides of March have done exactly that with this marvelous five-song mini-LP/EP/CD of all new material. With leader/lead singer/guitarist/songwriter/band visionary Jim Peterik at the helm, the Ides come back with a contemporary sound that recasts their horn-heavy style in a new and most attractive light. "Friendly Stranger (Vehicle Overture)" takes their biggest hit and totally revamps it with an instrumental movie soundtrack feel that's both familiar and new. The title track is a strong rocker that recalls the salad days of the band from a 20/20-hindsight perspective, while "Roller Coaster" is an uptempo summer tune with solid harmonies and loads of jangly guitar. "Moon out of Phase" spotlights Peterik's more atmospheric side of his songwriting talents and shows up twice, in both vocal and an equally strong instrumental mix versions. An impressive comeback disc. *—Cub Koda*

● **Ideology** / Mar. 28, 2000 / Sundazed ✦✦✦✦✦

This collection of 1965-1968 material, taken from rare regional singles along with a couple of previously unreleased tracks, is far removed from the Ides of March's horn-rock era (as heard on their 1970 hit "Vehicle"), both chronologically and stylistically. When they started, the Ides were a Chicago teen band, recording mostly original songs heavily influenced by folk-rock and the British Invasion, although a few of these cuts do use brass. In general that's good news (and preferable to the horn-rock of their later career), but the harmony-heavy pop/rock of this early work isn't too exciting. In common with several other groups from the Chicago and Midwest areas, the group favored a rather clean-cut, Americanized take on British Invasion bands like the Beatles and the Hollies, though the folk-rock of the Byrds is heard in the guitar arrangements especially. The local Chicago hits "You Wouldn't Listen" (which made number 42 nationally) and "Roller Coaster" are here, but to be tough about it, there's not enough light and shade here to put the Ides on the level of good British Invasion bands, or even of good British Invasion-influenced bands from the same region, such as the New Colony Six. More to the point, there's too much light and not enough shade; although the harmonies are fairly impressive and the execution polished, the material is too often sunnily bland. The great exception to that is the riveting, raw folk-rocker "I'll Keep Searching," buried on a B-side, which has great bittersweet melodic hooks, melancholy harmonies, and dramatic stop-start tempos. The disc includes two 1965 songs that they recorded as the Shondels on a super-rare self-released 45, as well as the previously unreleased originals "One and One Does Not Make Three" and "I'll Take You Back." The latter of these, an uncommonly moody tune, is actually a highlight of the collection. *—Richie Unterberger*

The Ikettes

f. 1960, **db.** 1973

Group / Soul

Ike Turner formed the Ikettes to replace the Artettes as the backing group for the Ike & Tina Turner Revue. Despite their beginnings, the Ikettes became successful artists in their own right; in fact, they actually had more significant hits in the early and mid-'60s than Ike & Tina, charting with "I'm Blue (The Gong, Gong Song)" in 1961, "The Camel Walk" in 1964, and "Peaches and Cream" and "I'm So Thankful" in 1965. Unheralded, they were arguably one of the ten top R&B female groups of all time. Ike never paid them much, which caused their lineup to change frequently, and they never received royalties. When

"Peaches and Cream" exploded, Ike sent a different set of Ikettes on the road and kept the ones who recorded the song on tour with his revue.

The Ikettes began recording in 1960 when lead Delores Johnson (aka Flora Williams), Eloise Hester, and Joshie Armstead accompanied Tina Turner on her first recording, "A Fool in Love." They cut "I'm Blue" the following year and Tina returned the favor by wailing behind the Ikettes on the song "Salt N' Pepa" (revived years later for the group of the same name as the mega hit "Shoop"). Ike produced the record and leased it to Atco Records who issued three more unsuccessful Ikette's singles in 1962. The following year, Ike switched them to his Teena label for two singles: "Crazy in Love" (credited as Robbie Montgomery & the Ikettes) and "Prisoner in Love." "Here's Your Heart" popped out on Innis in 1964 but failed to go national; nor did a Phi-Dan single in 1965.

A six-record stint from 1964 through 1966 on Modern Records saw a new lineup of Robbie Montgomery (ex-Artette), Vanetta Fields, and Jessie Smith. Armstead, the first of the originals to leave, went solo and sang with groups before hooking up with a pre-Motown Nickolas Ashford & Valerie Simpson to form the formidable songwriting/production team of Ashford/Simpson/Armstead. The Ikettes scored three hits on Modern: "The Camel Walk," "Peaches and Cream," and "I'm So Thankful." Ultra funky remakes of "Sally Go Round the Roses" and "Da Doo Ron, Ron" didn't go as well; neither did "He's Gonna Be Fine, Fine, Fine," though it sounded like a precursor to the stuff Betty Davis did later.

After their run on Modern, Fields, Montgomery, and Smith left Ike Turner, renamed themselves the Mirettes, and recorded for Mirwood Records during 1966-1967. A stint with Revue proved luckier; their first two singles, a sexy "In the Midnight Hour" and "Take Me For a Little While," made impressions. A third single "First Love" stiffed as did a single on Minit Records in 1968 entitled "Help Wanted." Delores Johnson, the Ikette's original lead singer, also sang with the Mirettes, lending credence to discographers who lump their recording output with the Ikettes. Innis, attempting to earn some money from its unreleased material, issued "So Blue Over You" b/w "So Fine" credited to Ike & Tina Turner & the Ikettes in 1968.

Pompeii and Liberty Records issued singles credited to the Ikettes in 1969 and 1970 respectively, but only a remake of Sly & the Family Stone's "I Want to Take You Higher" got much notice. A shift to Uni Records was more fruitful for the Mirettes, the songs weren't big hits but they are all keepers. Zea Records dropped the raunchy "Ain't My Stuff Good Enough" in 1970. It was followed by two more singles credited to the Ikettes on United Artists, including a remake of "Camel Walk" in 1971 and "Two Timin', Double Dealin'" in 1973, the last known single either by the Ikettes or the Mirettes. The end came when the Ikettes left the Revue; managed by Tina's sister Alline, they tried to book a 60-day tour as the Mariettes formerly the Ikettes, but Ike nailed that shut legally (restraining order) and physically (had people stop them from going on-stage) and they disbanded in frustration. *—Andrew Hamilton*

The Ikettes (G)Old & New / 1974 / United Artists ✦✦✦✦
With more push, the Ikettes would be mentioned with the greatest female vocal groups. Their lineup changed constantly, but talent always replaced talent, and they never lost their assertive, attacking sound. "Peaches & Cream," an explosive slab of pop/soul, is aggressive and gritty. "Camel Walk" has a rolling beat and exudes soul; its chorus includes a sexy, funky count from one to 11. The easy, rhythmic "I'm So Thankful" reigns as their most relaxed hit, it's similar to the Supremes' "Where Did Our Love Go." Two Supremes remakes, "Someday We'll Be Together" and "Come See About Me," get a soul/funk infusion. Billy Preston's "Will It Go Round In Circles" and the Doobie Brothers' "Listen to the Music"—high energy rockers—spotlight the Ikettes' powerful voices. "I'm Blue," a soul shaker that features Tina Turner wailing in the background, is definitive Ikettes. The Sweet Inspirations redid "Blue" on Atlantic Records, and Salt N' Pepa used key elements from it on "Shoop." Out of print, and unfortunately, to date, a good compilation CD of Ikettes recordings has not surfaced. *—Andrew Hamilton*

● **Fine, Fine, Fine** / Jun. 7, 1996 / Kent ✦✦✦✦
For some unexplainable reason Kent Records omitted "I'm Blue" which Salt N' Pepa rearranged into "Shoop." *Fine, Fine, Fine* was first released in 1965, reissued in 1987, and re-reissued on CD by Ace Records in the late '90s. Most of the Ikettes' funky, infectious singles are here, including "Camel Walk," "He Is (Fine, Fine, Fine") and "Peaches 'n' Cream." Their soulful Supremes imitation "I'm So Thankful," written by Marc Gordon and Frank Wilson, display a modest side of Ike Turner's hand-picked mini-skirted, rump-shakin' divas. They slathered soul sauce all over the Jaynettes' eerie "Sally Go Round the Roses," and the soulful, lamenting "How Come Nobody Loves Me" is a crusher. For the price, the 15 cuts—boosted to 24 for the Ace version—are a bargain. *—Andrew Hamilton*

Imagination

f. 1981, London, England, **db.** 1995
Group / Urban, Club/Dance
Imagination was a trio from the U.K. that put a synthesized and often clubby spin on soul groups from the '70s. In fact, a couple of '70s groups have direct ties to Imagination; Lee John and Ashley Ingram spent time during that decade playing supportive roles in the Delfonics and Chairmen of the Board, prior to Imagination's formation. Along with drummer Errol Kennedy, vocalist John and bassist Ingram formed the group in 1981. By the end of that year, they already had their first album released and a minor hit in the form of that album's title track, "Body Talk."

The group's second album, 1982's *In the Heat of the Night*, was their most successful, spawning a trio of U.S. R&B chart hits in the form of "Just an Illusion" (number 27), "Magic and Lights" (number 52), and "Changes" (number 46). Those singles were even more popular in their home country, with the first pair reaching the top five. The remix collection *Night Dubbing* appeared the following year, as did the group's third proper album, *Scandalous*. The group's success fizzled until their mid-'90s breakup (at the time, Lee John was the only remaining original member), though 1984's "This Means War" was able to put a dent in the U.S. R&B chart. John remained active in the entertainment industry, hosting U.K. television programs and continuing his recording career as a solo artist and collaborator. Since the group's split, several compilations have been released; Music Club's *The Very Best of Imagination* is the best place to start. *—Andy Kellman*

Body Talk / 1981 / R&B ✦✦✦✦
Imagination's *Body Talk* was a magnificent breakout for both the group and the group's producers and co-songwriters, Tony Swain and Steve Jolley (both of whom would team to produce Spandau Ballet and Bananarama). Not only was *Body Talk* one of the best debut albums of 1981, it continues to stand as one of the best pop-oriented R&B albums of the decade it was released. Even if it suffered a drastic dropoff in quality after the first three songs, it remained an exceptional record; that opening 18-minute stretch is as close to perfection as a record gets. On the first two tracks, Jolley and Swain prove to be masters of the slow and simple, two characteristics that provide an ideal backdrop for the group. While most albums released during the time opened with one or two upbeat numbers to grab the listener's attention, *Body Talk* begins with two tracks that flow like lava. They're just as hot, too; "Body Talk"'s erotic simmer is based on an insistent, unchanging rhythm that is decorated by occasional piano vamps, keyboard trickles, swelling synth notes, and three soft voices. "So Good So Right" picks up the pace ever so slightly and is even more hypnotizing. As repetitive as it is, it needs its seven minutes to unwind and unleash its spell. The third song, "Burnin' Up"—a favorite of Warehouse DJ Frankie Knuckles—was several years ahead of its time and had an immense influence on Chicago house music, most particularly songs like Marshall Jefferson's "Move Your Body." A dance track through and through, its open spaces, loose feel, and fluid piano runs are more fitting for dancefloor tiles than the rumpled bedsheets caused by the opening pair of songs. A dip from here on out can only be expected, but it's hardly a steep decline; both the clubby, echo-filled "Flashback" and the moody "In and out of Love" sustain this lean album's excellence. *—Andy Kellman*

In the Heat of the Night / 1982 / R&B ✦✦✦✦
Imagination's most substantial moments lie in this seamless sophomore effort. The formula is close to that of 1981's *Body Talk*. Lee John's angelic and serene falsetto surrounded by Ashley Ingram's voluptuous tenor vocals and darkly textured keyboard riffs and Errol Kennedy's steady, subtle, funky backbeat. Yet the tempo is varied a bit more with the onset of three ballads and some slightly more aggressive uptempo tracks. Four singles were released to success in the U.K., with three crossing over to U.S. shores: the groovy, underground dance number "Changes" (R&B number 46) with a contagious chorus and nabbing percussion breakdown pattern used throughout the tune; the equally insidious "Just an Illusion" (R&B number 27); the moody title track; and "Music and Lights" (R&B number 52). In addition to these treats, the elegant slow-groover "All Night Loving" and the disco-influenced "Heart Soul," a softly splashy early house effort (check the colorful keyboard solo) that segues into "Music and Lights" are particularly notable. Interestingly, Kennedy stopped his involvement with writing on this set, but John and Ingram continued these duties, along with producers Tony Swain and Steve Jolley. *—Justin Kantor*

New Dimension / 1984 / Elektra ✦

Like It Is / 1989 / RCA ✦✦✦✦
As a generally rewarding, remix-oriented collection spotlighting some of Imagination's triumphs, *Like It Is* succeeds on a number of levels. Club-oriented versions of "Changes," "Burning Up," "L.T.O. (Love's Taking Over)," the aforementioned "Just an Illusion" and other sleek tracks are highly recommended for die-hard fans. This collection functions easily as a "best-of" and an introductory overview of Imagination's career up to 1989. The style of house music known as deep house (which makes vocal personality the focal point instead of production, and draws heavily on late-'70s soul/disco) is a strong influence on many of these remixes. Thankfully, Imagination's more uptempo songs often lend themselves to that approach quite nicely. *—Alex Henderson*

● **The Very Best of Imagination** / Oct. 16, 2000 / Music Club ✦✦✦✦✦
This *Very Best of Imagination*, released in 2000 by the U.K.'s Music Club, is the best introduction to the clubby R&B group's work. Not to be confused with the 1998 release of the same title from BR, which is two-thirds the same selection-wise, this holds a slight edge over the several other Imagination anthologies with a smarter crop of inclusions. Like most of the other Imagination anthologies, this one concentrates on material from the group's first three albums, when they were at their peak both artistically and commercially. There are no glaring omissions, and all seven minutes of "So Good, So Right" are rightfully included, so this one gets the nod. *—Andy Kellman*

Imajin

Group / Contemporary R&B, Urban
Although it's easy to dismiss the contemporary R&B quartet Imajin as simply a "boy band" (just check out their debut album's cover), there's more than meets the eye to this group. In addition to writing and arranging most of their songs, the members even play the instruments on a few of them. Formed in the late '90s (drawing inspiration by such past outfits as Jackson 5, New Edition, Hi-Five, Immature, and Mint Condition), the group consists of members Jamal Hampton, Talib Kareem, Olamide Faison, and John Fitch, all of who were still in their teens at the time. Producer Bert Price lent a hand in assembling the band and guiding them, resulting in a recording contract with the Jive label shortly thereafter. Their self-titled debut album was released in 1999, which was produced by Ron "Amen-Ra" Lawrence and Deric "D-Dot" Angelettie (both of which are associates of Mr. Puff Daddy). *—Greg Prato*

● **Imajin** / 1999 / Jive ✦✦✦
The teenage R&B foursome known as Imajin have loads of talent between them, writing and arranging most of the tracks on their debut album and playing on quite a few of them. Though producers Ron "Amen-Ra" Lawrence and Deric "D-Dot" Angelettie (both are heavy Puff Daddy associates) put a sheen over the entire album, the individual talents

in the group do shine on this assortment of R&B and light hip-hop songs. Though tracks like "Shorty (You Keep Playin' With My Mind" and "You're the Bomb" probably won't make much of an impression on listeners over the age of 20, Imajin make urban R&B much more enjoyable than any in the Backstreet Boys/*NSYNC ilk. *—John Bush*

Immature

f. 1990, Los Angeles, CA

Group / Pop-Rap, Club/Dance, Urban, Hip-Hop, New Jack Swing

Pre-teenage R&B sensations in the early '90s, Immature was formed in Los Angeles by producer/mentor Chris Stokes around barely ten-year-olds Marques "Batman" Houston, Jerome "Romeo" Jones and Kelton "LDB" Kessee. The trio recorded their debut album *On Our Worst Behavior* for Virgin in 1992 and scored a modest R&B hit with "Tear It Up" (from the animated film *Bebe's Kids*). After moving to MCA for 1994's *Playtyme Is Over*, Immature scored with the pop hits "Never Lie" and "Constantly," pushing the album into gold territory. The trio then appeared in the Kid 'N Play film *House Party 3*. The third album *We Got It* also did well, though no single cracked the Top 40; "Feel the Funk," from the movie *Dangerous Minds*, came the closest, at number 46. For their fourth LP *The Journey*, Immature flirted with changing their name—the obvious choice was Mature—but decided to focus the change in direction on the music. *The Journey* did well on the R&B charts, but failed to translate to a pop success.The new millennium, however, saw the release of a greatest hits package, issued in February 2001. *—John Bush*

Playtyme Is Over / 1994 / MCA ✦

Enjoying a largely teenage and preteen following, Immature moved from Virgin to MCA with its sophomore effort, *Playtyme Is Over*. The label switch didn't mean a change in focus—the group (whose members were 11 or 12 at the time) still offered an abundance of hip-hop-influenced, medium-tempo new jack R&B grooves. And the same comparisons were being made; if you believed the hype, Immature was to the 1990s what Frankie Lymon & the Teenagers were to the 1950s, the Jackson 5 was to the 1970s and New Edition was to the 1980s. But those groups had the chops and excellent songs to back up their hype; none of the tunes on *Playtyme Is Over* are memorable, let alone excellent. Cuts like "Walk You Home" and "Never Lie" have a generic, cookie-cutter quality, and they sound like the product of a marketing meeting rather than artistic inspiration. When Lymon, Michael Jackson and Bobby Brown were teenagers and sang about adolescent love, the sincerity jumped right out at you—put on Lymon's "Why Do Fools Fall in Love," New Edition's "Mr. Telephone Man" or the Jackson 5's "I Want You Back," and you find yourself thinking about what a bittersweet time adolescence could be. Put on *Playtyme is Over*, and all you're thinking about is how contrived and formulaic Immature sounds. *—Alex Henderson*

We Got It / Dec. 1995 / MCA ✦✦✦

● **The Journey** / Sep. 23, 1997 / MCA ✦✦✦✦

When Immature debuted in 1992 with *On Our Worst Behavior*, there were those who compared the preteen urban contemporary trio to the Jackson 5 and early New Edition. The problem with that comparison was that the members of those groups were better singers and had far superior material to work with. By the time *The Journey* came out in 1997, the members of Immature were 15 and had improved somewhat. Lead vocalist Marques "Batman" Houston hadn't turned into a great singer by any means, but some of the material on this CD is decent, including the Keith Sweat produced "Extra Extra," the moody, flamenco-influenced "Tamika" and the haunting "24/7," which was produced by Marc Gordon of LeVert fame. *The Journey* also has its share of throwaways, and on the whole, the album isn't all that memorable. It's best to pass. *—Alex Henderson*

Impact

Group / Philly Soul, Disco, Soul

Members of the group later known as Impact burst onto the recording scene with the name the Young Tempts on the Isley Brothers' T- Neck label. The first single, "I've Been Good to You" b/w "Too Busy Thinking About My Baby," ripped the Temptations' earlier versions, and both tracks appeared on the *Gettin' Ready* album with Eddie Kendricks on lead. Impact's falsetto Otis Robert Harris Jr. sounded like a fuller Kendricks, but he lacked Kendricks' edge. Objecting to the name, Motown filed an injunction and had the record recalled; T-Neck renamed the act the Young Vandals and pressed more copies with the new moniker. After two more singles for T-Neck during 1970, the Baltimore natives disbanded when Otis Harris landed a gig with the Temptations, the group he admired so, later in 1970. (He changed his name to Damon since, as he said "the group already had an Otis"). What he thought was a lifetime gig, however, turned into a four-year stint for Damon. Dejected, but not for long, he re-formed the Young Vandals and renamed them Impact. The quartet consisted of the same members: Damon Harris, John Quinton Simms, Charles Timmons, and Donald Tighman (who's related to Sonny Til of the Orioles and whose real name was Earlington Tighman).

They signed with a Philadelphia production company who secured a masters' deal with Atco Records. An album titled *Impact* dropped first, followed by the single "Happy Man," a popular 1976 disco cut. Impact put as much work in their backing vocals as the lead, something peculiar with D.C./Baltimore-area groups; the background voices competed with the lead for attention, making the songs more exciting. In addition to Harris' buttery falsetto, Impact had a David Ruffin-ish tenor and both were a joy to hear.

The same procedure was followed with "Love Attack" and "One Last Memory." While the singles and the album had a winning sound, sales figures were less than projected and the Atco association terminated. They surfaced on Fantasy in 1977 with a new album, *The Pac Is Back*. Fantasy released two singles—"Rainy Days" and "Smile Awhile"—but with only minimal chart action and scant sales, they proved to be Impact's final releases. Harris later went solo and cut a couple of critically acclaimed albums that didn't do much. He later disappeared from the scene, moved to Reno, NV, to finish college, and still lives there. The whereabouts of the other members are unknown, but it's believed all live in the Baltimore/D.C. area. *—Andrew Hamilton*

● **Impact** / 1976 / Atco ✦✦✦✦

This is the group that features the falsetto Damon Harris. As a member of the Temptations from 1971-1975, Harris' airy yet earthy falsetto powered such classics including "Papa Was a Rolling Stone" and the drug epic "Hurry Tomorrow." After his stint with the group, Harris rejoined his childhood group. The production here is reminiscent of his then-W.M.O.T. labelmates Blue Magic, and is produced by Bobby Eli. Impact finds Harris' vocals getting warmer gives his fans a chance to hear him in a fresher context. This group also had a raspy vocalist reminiscent of David Ruffin, who provided a good juxtaposition to Harris. The first track and single, "Happy Man," is prime, rough-edged Philly disco and shows great chemistry between the group. While they no doubt had the goods, Impact is unfortunately a victim of a Philly lyrical mill that was running itself in the ground by the time this was released. But there are still gems here. Eli and Vinnie Barnett's "Man and Woman" is a classic sounding ballad with another fulfilling vocal from Harris as well as great harmony from the rest of the group. The last track, the bittersweet and midtempo "It Only Happens in the Movies," is reminiscent of *Mighty Love*-era Spinners and certainly was strong enough to be released as a single. Impact displays the vocal gifts of Harris as well as the Philly sound and both facts make this a must for fans. *—Jason Elias*

The Impalas

f. 1958, Brooklyn, NY, **db.** 1961

Group / Doo Wop

The Impalas were a racially integrated vocal group from Brooklyn who are best remembered for their 1959 hit "Sorry (I Ran All the Way Home)," which scored them their only Top 20 hit (number-two pop, number-14 R&B). Forming in 1958, the group—Joe "Speedo" Frazier (the only black singer), Richard Wagner, Lenny Renda, and Tony Carlucci—were signed to the Cub label, a subsidiary label of MGM that also issued high-quality stereo recordings by the Five Satins, the Harptones, the Stereos, the Velours, and the Wanderers, to name a few. In August of 1959, Cub issued an album, *Sorry (I Ran All the Way Home)* which featured other recordings the Impalas made for the label. Unfortunately, no further hits ever came, and they disbanded in 1961. *—Bryan Thomas*

● **Sorry (I Ran All the Way Home)** / 1960 / Cub ✦✦✦✦✦

The Impalas' highly collectible 1960 Cub LP *Sorry (I Ran All the Way Home)* contains the vocal group's two hits: the smash title track and the minor hit "Oh, What a Fool." Lead singer Joe Frazier frequently wanders out of key, but the lightweight material is fun and doesn't invite serious criticism. "Sorry (I Ran All the Way Home)" is by far the group's most substantial pairing of song and performance and can be heard on oldies anthologies such as Eric Records' *Hard to Find 45s on CD, Vol. 1*. Fans who simply can't get enough of the Impalas will probably be cured of their condition with the acquisition of this disc. *—Greg Adams*

The Imperial Wonders

f. Cleveland, OH

Group / Smooth Soul, Soul, Pop-Soul

Talented and flashy, the Imperial Wonders was Cleveland, OH's answer to the Temptations, mimicking the Motor City giants with Lester "Jelly" McKenzie's Eddie Kendricks-ish falsetto, Avon Wells, deep Melvin Franklin-esque bass, and Leo Green's rough Paul Williams-ish baritone. A quintet like the Tempts, the other members were Al Boyd, a former Rotation, and Walter Channey. They hit their stride in the early '70s recording a string of singles, changing labels on virtually every release.

A short-lived local label, Daywood Records owned by Bob Davis & Melvin Wood, released their debut recording in 1969; the bouncy "Just a Dream," had that lilting quality that make records magic, but Daywood had neither the expertise nor the funds to do anything with the record. Their next and arguably most popular recording came out on Black Prince Records located in Tennessee; "Trying to Get to You," displayed McKenzie's oil-slick falsetto; the tune was similar musically to "Just a Dream," but accented with a spoken part by Wells; the flip was just as good, a remake of the standard "When I Fall in Love," featured Wells on lead, sounding identical to the Temptations' Melvin Franklin. It was a big hit on R&B radio in Cleveland and probably picked up some plays in other localities as well, but not nearly enough for the guys to realize any monies for their effort. With former O'Jay Bobby Massey producing, the guys waxed a side for Musicor Records that even went unnoticed in Cleveland. Two last shots on Cleveland's Solid Foundation Records, produced again by Massey, produced one minor hit in Cleveland "Turned Around Over You."

After the Imperial Wonders disbanded, Green and Boyd sang with Truth; Lester McKenzie wrote songs for many Cleveland acts including the tender "Son-In-Law" for the Elements, who also recorded as Moving Violation for Atco Records. McKenzie died in the mid-'90s, and Green moved to Atlanta, GA; Wells and Channey are believed to be on the West Coast, along with Al Boyd. Boyd got a position as a staff writer for Motown where he penned such notables as "Shakey Ground," a hit for the Temptations and Phoebe Snow. *—Andrew Hamilton*

● **Time Machine** / 2001 / DYOB ✦✦✦

Originally from Cleveland, OH, the Imperial Wonders lit up their hometown in the early '70s with hot local tokes like "Trying to Get to You," "Just a Dream," and "Turned Around Over You." After a single on Musicor Records in 1973, the entertainers took a 28-year hiatus before dropping *Time Machine*, their first LP, with a revamped lineup consisting of originals Al Boyd and Avaughn Wells along with E.J. Welch, Russell Watts, and Darol King. The group's patented, unison "bong bong" harmonic fills are missing, but their imperial-quality soul and transcendental aura of romance are represented on every cut. These are singers born to express themselves musically. There are no scraps—these are eight prime soul filets worthy of serving to royalty. Addiction comes fast on the opening track, "DNA," with its sly reference to O.J. Simpson and its infectious romping rhythm;

the lead switches between the tenor, falsetto, and baritone, with Wells' Melvin Franklin-quality bass trolling the bottom like an ocean predator. Dangerous listening on a bar stool—you might bounce right off grooving to it. The level remains high as a giraffe on "Tales From the Grip," a haunting son of a gun with horror movie ambience and tightly strung vocals around a compelling lead. You'll think the Dramatics stopped by when "Time Machine," written by Boyd and Larry Hancock, unrolls. Wells mimics Willie Ford on the intro and the lead enchants with a beguiling vocal reminiscent of Lenny Mayes, only stronger, on the smoldering slow jam. They bounce the lead lines around on "Sweet Delight" and "Just Leave," a free-flowing Delfonic-ish ballad that showcases their strong voices. "You're Good in Bed" is a turn-off-the-lights and lets-get-it-on song. A passionate lead, impeccable backing vocals, sensuous lyrics, tantalizing music, and a vamp that brings back memories of New Birth's "Been Such a Long Time" set this one out. Two more hotties, "Spiritual Love" and "In the Bedroom," wrap up the Imperial Wonders' first LP with a bang. Al Boyd co-authored the Temptations' "Shakey Ground" and wrote or co-wrote every song on *Time Machine*. *—Andrew Hamilton*

The Impressions

f. 1958, Chicago, IL, **db.** 1983

Group / Soul, Chicago Soul, Uptown Soul, Pop-Soul, Northern Soul

The quintessential Chicago soul group, the Impressions' place in R&B history would be secure if they'd done nothing but launch the careers of soul legends Jerry Butler and Curtis Mayfield. But far more than that, the Impressions recorded some of the most distinctive vocal-group R&B of the '60s under Mayfield's guidance. Their style was marked by airy, feather-light harmonies and Mayfield's influentially sparse guitar work, plus, at times, understated Latin rhythms. If their sound was sweet and lilting, it remained richly soulful thanks to the group's firm grounding in gospel tradition; they popularized the three-part vocal trade-offs common in gospel but rare in R&B at the time, and recorded their fair share of songs with spiritual themes, both subtle and overt. Furthermore, Mayfield's interest in the civil rights movement led to some of the first socially conscious R&B songs ever recorded, and his messages grew more explicit as the '60s wore on, culminating in the streak of brilliance that was his early-'70s solo work. The Impressions carried on without Mayfield, but only matched their earlier achievements in isolated instances, and finally disbanded in the early '80s.

The Impressions were formed in Chicago in 1957 as a doo wop group called the Roosters, a group of Chattanooga, TN, transplants that included vocalists Sam Gooden and brothers Richard and Arthur Brooks. Lead singer Jerry Butler joined up and soon brought in his friend Curtis Mayfield as guitarist; the two had previously sung together in a church choir and a couple of local gospel groups as youths. Renamed the Impressions by their manager, the group scored a major hit in 1958 with the classic ballad "For Your Precious Love," which hit the pop Top 20 and the R&B Top Five. Butler's gospel-inflected lead vocal was a departure from the norm, and the fact that the single billed him in front of the rest of the group foreshadowed his quick exit for a solo career, after just one more single ("Come Back My Love"). With new vocalist Fred Cash in tow, Mayfield took over the lead tenor role, eventually becoming the group's chief composer as well. First, though, he hit the road as guitarist and musical director for Butler's backing band, and also co-wrote some of Butler's earliest singles, including the R&B number one "He Will Break Your Heart" in late 1960.

Mayfield's success as a songwriter encouraged him to form his own publishing company. With the money he earned by working with Butler, he reconvened the Impressions and brought them to New York to record for ABC-Paramount in 1961. Their first single, the Latin-inflected "Gypsy Woman," was a number-two R&B smash, also reaching the pop Top 20. Several follow-ups failed to duplicate its chart success, and the Brooks brothers left the group in 1962; now down to a trio, the Impressions returned to Chicago and began recording with arranger Johnny Pate, whose horn and string embellishments added a bit more heft to their sound. They struck gold in 1963 with "It's All Right," whose gospel-style lead-swapping helped make it not only their first R&B number one, but their biggest pop hit as well, with a peak of number four. The same year, they issued their eponymous first LP, which many critics still consider one of their finest. In 1964, the hit single "Keep on Pushing" was released, the first of Mayfield's numerous black pride anthems (though at this stage, his sentiments were much less explicit than they would later become). The album of the same name also featured a marching-beat cover of the gospel standard "Amen," inspired by the song's inclusion in the Sidney Poitier film *Lilies of the Field*. Gospel also informed what became perhaps the best-known Impressions hit, 1965's "People Get Ready"; if its lyrics weren't overtly political, Mayfield's intent was clear, as the song became an anthem of transcendence for the civil rights movement and an oft-covered soul standard.

The mid-'60s saw Mayfield trying to keep pace with the Motown hit factory by incorporating elements of its style into his own writing. The group recorded prolifically in 1965, but their commercial fortunes dropped off over the next couple of years. When the Impressions returned to the upper reaches of the R&B charts, it was with 1968's "We're a Winner," the most straightforward celebration of black pride Mayfield had yet composed. That summer, the group left ABC to record for Mayfield's newly formed Curtom imprint, which allowed them greater freedom in terms of the lyrical content Mayfield wanted to pursue. More aggressive message tracks like "This Is My Country," "Choice of Colors," and "Check Out Your Mind" followed over the next couple of years, as did some of the group's most consistent albums, particularly *The Young Mods' Forgotten Story* (1969). *Check Out Your Mind*; from 1970, was Mayfield's final album with the Impressions, but the group remained on Curtom after his departure, and he continued to write and produce some of their material.

Mayfield was replaced on lead vocals by Leroy Hutson, who debuted on LP with 1972's *Times Have Changed*. At this point, the Impressions were still overshadowed by their ex-leader, who was riding high with brilliant works like *Superfly*. But Mayfield's solo momentum cooled down a bit, and after Hutson departed in 1973, new singers Ralph Johnson and Reggie Torian joined Cash and Gooden for the R&B chart-topper "Finally Got Myself Together (I'm a Changed Man)," cut with ex-Motown producer Ed Townsend in 1974. Townsend continued to work with the group for the next couple of years with some success, but in 1976 Johnson left to join the unsuccessful Mystique. Around that point, the Impressions parted ways with Curtom; Nate Evans replaced Johnson, and the group recorded for Cotillion and 20th Century/Chi-Sound with little chart success. Evans eventually departed, leaving the group a trio again. They recorded their final album, *Fan the Fire*, in 1981; Gooden and Cash occasionally reunited with Mayfield and sometimes Butler for touring commitments. Mayfield was paralyzed in a heartbreaking stage accident in 1990, when a lighting scaffold toppled over on him; he passed away in 1999. *—Steve Huey*

The Impressions / Oct. 1963 / Paramount ✦✦✦✦✦

The first Impressions LP was one of the finest debuts of any '60s soul act, though it excelled in part because it featured a backlog of chart singles (five had charted previously, and "It's All Right" became the sixth after it was quickly added to the original program). Curtis Mayfield wrote all but two of the songs, stretching back to 1961's "Gypsy Woman" (which he'd actually written at the age of 14) but mostly including strong 1962-1963 material like the hit "Little Young Lover," "Grow Closer Together," "I'm the One Who Loves You," and "Minstrel and Queen." "It's All Right" was easily the best song here, accented by the group's sublime harmonies, arranger Johnny Pate's swinging horn section, and Mayfield's precise guitar work. The group also showed an unsurprising reverence for classic doo wop, beautifully remaking "Never Let Me Go," a Top Ten R&B hit for Johnny Ace in 1954. Even the closer, a tossed-off novelty called "Twist and Limbo," is an excellent performance and a genuinely fun song. Mayfield's disarmingly brilliant songs were really the only necessary element toward making *The Impressions* a strong LP, but the mesmerizing vocals and sympathetic arrangements made for a classic work of Chicago soul. *—John Bush*

The Never Ending Impressions / 1964 / Paramount ✦✦✦

The Never Ending Impressions, the first record to boast the full collaborative power of Johnny Pate and Curtis Mayfield, pushed the idea of the trio as a supper-club act, with covers of "Satin Doll," "September Song," and "Lemon Tree" among the questionable—if not misguided—covers. The group's immense talents prevent any of these versions from being complete failures, but they sound much more assured on Mayfield originals like the ballad "I'm So Proud," a Top 20 hit on both the R&B and pop charts. Scattered among the adult pop chestnuts are a few good songs, including the uptempo "Sister Love" and a pair of great overlooked Chicago soul nuggets: "Girl You Don't Know Me" and "A Woman Who Loves Me." *—John Bush*

Keep on Pushing / 1964 / Paramount ✦✦✦✦

Already a celebrated songwriter by the time of the third Impressions album, Curtis Mayfield introduced a political element to his material with the Top Ten hit "Keep on Pushing." An anthem of the burgeoning civil-rights movement (the 1964 Civil Rights Act was signed several weeks after its release), "Keep on Pushing" cemented his blend of gospel optimism with a relentless spirit of self-improvement. Though it was the only message song present, the album featured all the hallmarks of an Impressions set: impeccably smooth harmonies, the dynamic horn charts of Johnny Pate, and many more of Mayfield's irresistible songs (each with a clever spin on the usual love lyric as well as a strong sense of melody). "Talking About My Baby," the album's other big hit, was an adoring love song driven by a simple chorus and delivered by soul music's greatest harmonists. The simple ballad "I've Been Trying" was one of the most delicate and powerful the group had ever delivered, and the gospel march "Amen" became a Top Ten pop hit in early 1965 after its use in the Sidney Poitier film *Lilies of the Field* (for which Poitier became the first African-American to receive an Academy award). *Keep on Pushing* was the Impressions' first Top Ten album hit, and an excellent introduction for pop audiences just waking up to the inspirational power of soul music's finest group. *—John Bush*

People Get Ready / 1965 / Paramount ✦✦✦✦

As with the previous year's *Keep on Pushing*, *People Get Ready* featured another big Curtis Mayfield hit, one that made as strong an impact on the civil-rights movement as on the charts. One of the most beautiful songs of the '60s, "People Get Ready" set the oft-used "gospel train" as its theme, with Mayfield speaking of faith for the present and deliverance in the future, while Sam Gooden and Fred Cash contributed beautiful harmony vocals (and a few lines of their own). That career touchstone aside, the rest of the material on the LP wasn't as strong as *Keep on Pushing* or the Impressions' marvelous debut. The two winners were "Woman's Got Soul" and "You Must Believe Me," both in a similar brassy, uptown mode as expected from the Chicago soul kingpins. A few of the songs were hauled out from as long as three years ago, like Mayfield's own version of "Can't Work No Longer," a Billy Butler hit he'd produced (also in 1965). The exceptional harmonies and arrangements were still in place, but for a few songs it was clear that Mayfield had tired of concocting novelties that looked back to the age of doo wop. *—John Bush*

One by One / 1965 / Paramount ✦✦✦✦

The Impressions continued a great run of hit singles and fine albums with this outstanding release, one of three that were issued on ABC in 1965. The structure by now was both fixed and marvelous; songs revolved around Mayfield's leads, superb production and arrangements, guitar licks and riffs anchoring the backdrop, and Fred Cash and Sam Gooden interacting with Mayfield on the choruses, bridges, and turnarounds. *—Ron Wynn*

Ridin' High / 1966 / Paramount ✦✦✦

The Impressions were certainly dominating the charts and making wonderful albums in the '60s, and this one didn't break the string. They would depart from ABC in two years, but at this point there were no concerns, even though they didn't match the previous years' glittering array of hits. But their singing was no less emphatic or compelling, nor had Mayfield's writing, productions, or arrangements slipped. *—Ron Wynn*

The Fabulous Impressions / 1967 / Paramount ♦♦♦
Although *The Fabulous Impressions* was a solid enough soul record on its own merits, it's not one of the more notable entries in the Impressions' catalog. There aren't any big hits, although a couple cuts, "You Always Hurt Me" and "I Can't Stay Away From You," were modest R&B charters. At times it seemed that Mayfield was trying to follow in Motown's footsteps, as on "You Always Hurt Me" (which isn't far removed from Smokey Robinson workouts like "The Tears of a Clown") and "You Ought to Be in Heaven" (which has a saxophone that sounds like a dead ringer for Junior Walker). Mayfield doesn't always take the lead part, which to be honest will signify that it's not going to be one of the stronger tracks. "It's All Over" is the Impressions' version of a song that had already been a hit for Walter Jackson, and the cover of Gene McDaniels' "One Hundred Pounds of Clay" (the only selection not written by Mayfield) is filler. The above comments might lead you to believe this album is worse than it actually is; it's dependable, enjoyable, quality soul, with "Isle of Sirens" recalling earlier efforts like "Gypsy Woman," and "She Don't Love Me" offering a chunkier and tougher approach than their typical heartfelt optimism. It's been reissued, together with 1968's *We're a Winner*, on an Ace CD that combines both albums onto one disc. *—Richie Unterberger*

We're a Winner / 1968 / Paramount ♦♦♦♦♦
While the title track was one of Mayfield's classic civil rights-conscious anthems, most of this album was actually dedicated to standard romantic themes. This wasn't necessarily a drawback; almost every cut was a quality Mayfield original, and the harmonies and vocal interplay among the group were outstanding. "Nothing Can Stop Me," which had been a hit in 1965 for Gene Chandler, was an uptempo highlight, and "Little Brown Boy" showed more of the African-American pride that had been explored in "We're a Winner," albeit in a more tender ballad mode. The closing cover of "Up Up and Away" is misplaced, but overall this is one of the better Impressions albums to pick up if you want more than what's found on the greatest-hits collections, with excellent production and Johnny Pate arrangements throughout. It's been reissued, together with 1967's *Fabulous Impressions*, on an Ace CD that combines both albums onto one disc. *—Richie Unterberger*

This Is My Country / 1968 / Charly ♦♦♦♦♦
Despite a few indications to the contrary, the Impressions' first record for Curtis Mayfield's new label, Curtom, didn't make for a large leap from their most recent work at ABC (1968's *We're a Winner*). The cover photo was radical enough, featuring the trio standing in front of a decrepit building (which shifted the meaning of the title from pride to accusation). Most of the arrangements were tight late-'60s soul rather than '50s doo wop, and the group spent less time harmonizing than before. Still, there were only two message tracks: the title track, which stood up for blacks' place in America, and an impassioned plea for education titled "They Don't Know." For the most part, Curtis Mayfield continued to investigate the vagaries of love and relationships, with the bombastic hit "Fool for You" leading the way. "Stay Close to Me" is a bright, bouncy track, more Motown than Chicago soul but as tight and joyous as some of the Impressions' other great material. The chugging ballad "Love's Happening" is another solid performance, while "I'm Loving Nothing" is utter heartbreak. Two of the minor songs featured writing co-credits from Donny Hathaway, then recording for Curtom with the Mayfield Singers. *—John Bush*

The Versatile Impressions / 1969 / ABC ♦♦
As the title suggests, *The Versatile Impressions* was constructed (by the group's former label ABC-Paramount) to display the Impressions at work in various musical idioms. And as was the case with many soul albums of this sort in the 1960s, it found them tackling show tunes, pop-jazz-numbers, and Lennon-McCartney covers that weren't nearly as satisfying as their straight soul outings. There are a couple of fair soul cuts here, "Sermonette" and "Don't Cry My Love" (a small anti-war hit single, co-written by Mayfield and jazz singer Oscar Brown Jr.). "Yesterday" and "Fool on a Hill" are good songs, but not as sung by the Impressions; "Oo You're a Livin' Doll" and "This is the Life" are embarrassing cabaret-style swingers; "The Look of Love" isn't half-bad; and "East of Java" and "Just Before Sunrise," both done for the *East of Java* soundtrack, are intriguing curiosities. All ten of the songs, along with five unreleased ones cut at the same sessions, are included on the Kent *ABC Rarities* compilation, a recommended alternative to the original LP. *—Richie Unterberger*

The Young Mods' Forgotten Story / 1969 / Curtom ♦♦♦♦♦
The title read like a concept album (and the opener seemed to introduce a larger idea at work), but *The Young Mods' Forgotten Story* hung together only as the usual (read: brilliant) late-'60s LP from the Impressions: a few solid songs with a social or inspirational viewpoint and the rest featuring Curtis Mayfield's continuing exploration of love in all its forms. Two of the message songs were among the best of the group's history; "Choice of Colors" tenderly investigated black feelings about race, while the party song "Mighty Mighty (Spade & Whitey)" gave blacks and whites a rare chance to celebrate empowerment together. Mayfield's romantic songs ranged farther than usual, from the innocent, delicate "The Girl I Find" (complete with turtledove cries) to a deconstruction of the end of a long affair ("Seven Years") to the overbearing "Jealous Man," all with great arrangements provided by veteran Johnny Pate and newcomer Donny Hathaway. (Hathaway's addition didn't alter the Impressions' sound significantly, though his harmonic expertise and affinity for the church do find their way into a couple of tracks.) Only one song, "Wherever You Leadeth Me," found the group treading water (it could just as easily have appeared five years earlier). The rest was intriguing late-'60s soul from one of the best acts in the business. *—John Bush*

Check Out Your Mind! / 1970 / Curtom ♦♦♦♦
Just before he departed the Impressions for a solo career, Curtis Mayfield performed on one last album with the group. *Check out Your Mind!* saw Mayfield departing with class, driven by big, brassy nuggets of psychedelic soul like "Check out Your Mind," "You're Really Something, Sadie," and "(Baby) Turn on to Me." Despite the raised consciousness of the title, *Check Out Your Mind!* also featured quite a few fine examples of traditional sweet soul, like the hit "Can't You See" (which hearkened back to the group's early days), "You'll Always Be Mine," and "Only You." Mayfield wasn't quite the workhorse he seemed to be; though *Check Out Your Mind!* was released around the same time as his solo debut, a few of the songs here weren't *really* new: He'd originally written both "Madame Mary" and "We Must Be in Love" for the Five Stairsteps, while "Do You Want to Win?" takes elements from both "You're Really Something Sadie" and "(Baby) Turn on Me." Still, there was much more great material than average, and the trio ended with style an eight-year reign as one of the most talented, intelligent, and successful of all soul groups. *—John Bush*

Times Have Changed / 1972 / Curtom ♦♦♦
The first Impressions album without the presence of Curtis Mayfield suffers from his absence, even though he again wrote and produced for the record. The first track, Mayfield's "Stop the War," was the most strident Impressions song yet, a long piece with an emotive vocal from Fred Cash and several abstract passages (including the chant "Hell no, we won't go/Stop the war! stop the war!"). New addition Leroy Hutson quickly proved he had the talent to step into Mayfield's shoes, sweetly singing (with just a hint of resignation) on the title track and arranging the Impressions' cover—admittedly, rather faithful—of Marvin Gaye's "Inner City Blues (Make Me Wanna Holler)." Mayfield's songs, six of the eight heard on the LP, aren't as strong as he was noted for; perhaps, since he'd recorded three original solo albums in the previous two years, even his formidable talents were stretching thin. Still, subpar Curtis Mayfield songs possessed a special power, and the smooth "Potent Love" featured a classic Johnny Pate arrangement plus the heavenly falsetto of Leroy Hutson to do it justice. The lone Hutson original, "This Love's for Real," was a pleasant but unremarkable attempt to write a classic Impressions love song. *—John Bush*

Finally Got Myself Together / 1974 / Curtom ♦♦♦

Loving Power / 1976 / RSO ♦♦

It's About Time / 1976 / Cotillion ♦♦♦
The Impressions were one of the great groups of the '60s who had to deal with the familiar woes of facing the next decade. After Curtis Mayfield's early-'70s departure, the group became a grinding wheel having to deal with diminishing sales, exits, and lack of direction. Mid-'70s efforts *First Impressions* and *Loving Power* both had slack production values that eroded their fan base. In contrast, the skill of *It's About Time* is a complete surprise. For this effort, baritone Nate Evans replaces 1973-1976 lead singer Ralph Johnson. Evans, who has a more earthy and mellifluous tone, worked well with members Sam Gooden, Fred Cash, and Reggie Torian. "In the Palm of My Hands" and "You'll Never Find" are potent though anonymous tracks. After a while *It's About Time* does start to kick in. "Same Old Heartaches," written by Mervin and Melvin Steals is a smooth and melodic track with a great vocal from Evans. The hooky ballad "I Need You" has Torian giving a nice understated solo with help from Evans on the bridge. The smoldering and drama-filled "I'm a Fool for Love" has Evans desperately trying to "break-a-loose" from a bad woman. The majority of *It's About Time* has a confident L.A./R&B sound produced by McKinley Jackson and features string and horn arrangements by Gene Page, Gil Askey, and H.B. Barnum. *It's About Time* doesn't sound like an Impressions album, but the production and the tracks makes this surprisingly good and better than most of their post-Mayfield work. *—Jason Elias*

The Complete Vee-Jay Recordings / Nov. 22, 1993 / Vee-Jay ♦♦♦♦♦
The Impressions' early music has taken a back seat to what they did after Jerry Butler departed and Mayfield began doing the lead vocals, writing, producing, and arranging. This excellent 18-track disc helps put the early years into focus, with Butler showcased on seven cuts and Mayfield on eight. The Impressions weren't a bad five-member harmony unit; they just were not a great one in an era when you had to be fantastic simply to break out of the pack. These are mostly nice love songs, and they aren't lyrically different from thousands of similar tracks, but they did deserve a better fate than to be dropped from the Vee-Jay label in 1959. *—Ron Wynn*

The Impressions/The Never Ending Impressions / Oct. 1995 / Kent ♦♦♦♦♦

Keep on Pushing/People Get Ready / Mar. 19, 1996 / Kent ♦♦♦♦♦

This Is My Country/The Young Mods' Forgotten Story / Apr. 24, 1996 / Sequel ♦♦♦♦♦

Further Impressions / Jul. 1996 / Hip-O ♦♦♦♦
Featuring a selection of 14 songs making their compact disc debut, *Further Impressions: More Soulful Classics* fills in the gaps left by the single-disc MCA *Greatest Hits* collection and the more comprehensive double-disc anthology. Only four R&B hits are present, but the remaining ten songs are all first-rate album tracks that are nearly equal in quality. *Further Impressions* doesn't overlap at all with MCA's two previous Impressions sets, so it is a necessary addition to any fan's CD library. *—Stephen Thomas Erlewine*

Check Out Your Mind!/Times Have Changed / Dec. 17, 1996 / Sequel ♦♦♦

Preacher Man/Finally Got Myself Together / 1997 / Sequel ♦♦♦
Sequel Records combines the Impressions' 1973 non-charting album, *Preacher Man* and *Finally Got Myself Together*, which reached rung 174 on *Billboard*'s Pop 200 Albums chart the following year on one CD providing for an interesting contrast in production styles. *Preacher Man*, the more adventurous (lyrically) of the two, is message laden. And with the exception of Gene Chandler and James Thompson's musing "Color Us All Grey (I'm Lost)," Richard Tufo's productions rule. Ed Townsend produced *Finally Got Myself Together*, a solid soul harmony album featuring "(I'm a Changed Man) Finally Got Myself Together," "If It's in You to Do Wrong" and "We Go Back a Ways," a smooth red-light ballad. The Impressions, who sought an identity from the time Curtis Mayfield departed

until they disbanded, is comprised of Reggie Torian, Ralph Johnson, Fred Cash and Sam Gooden on these tracks. *—Andrew Hamilton*

★ **The Very Best of the Impressions** / Feb. 4, 1997 / Rhino ♦♦♦♦♦
A wise buy for those curious about the kings of Chicago soul, *The Very Best of the Impressions* is a tad brief, but it hits on all cylinders for most of its running time. Beginning with the early hits "Gypsy Woman" and "It's All Right," this chronological 16-track collection compiles the best from the Impressions' growing social consciousness ("People Get Ready," "Keep on Pushing," "Amen"), then charts the later Curtis Mayfield days with "We're a Winner," "This Is My Country," "Choice of Colors," and "Check Out Your Mind." As sometimes happens on a Rhino set, however, the compilers were overly reliant on the pop charts: many superior songs from their early and middle years—"I'm So Proud" and "Mighty Mighty (Spade and Whitey)," to name only two—are sacrificed for three post-Curtis Mayfield songs, when only one, "Finally Got Myself Together (I'm a Changed Man)," was really necessary. Still, even if the title isn't 100 percent accurate (*Greatest Hits* would've been the right choice), *The Very Best of the Impressions* is the most succinct set of Impressions material available. *—John Bush*

One by One/Ridin' High / Jun. 23, 1998 / Kent ♦♦♦

Fabulous Impressions/We're a Winner / Sep. 29, 1998 / Kent ♦♦♦♦♦

The ABC Rarities / Jun. 8, 1999 / Kent ♦♦♦
This is a 26 song compilation of non-LP singles, rarities that only showed up on obscure reissues and various-artists collections, and material (both released and unreleased) from their sessions for their late-'60s *The Versatile Impressions* album. As a listen it's a little uneven, due in large part to the over-preponderance of standards from *Versatile*. None of this is on level with the best '60s recordings by Mayfield & the Impressions. Much of it, though, is the fairly solid sort of stuff that fans who care enough about the act to go beyond greatest-hits compilations will like to have. Actually, some of these were not terribly obscure; "Never Could You Be" was a small R&B hit in the mid-'60s, and "We're Rolling On (Pts. 1 & 2)" was a small pop entry in 1968, as was the 1968 antiwar ballad "Don't Cry My Love" (written by Mayfield with jazz singer Oscar Brown Jr.). Oddities from the *Versatile* LP include the two lushly orchestrated songs they did for the *East of Java* soundtrack. However, much of the *Versatile* period is unsuitably pop in both material and production for the Impressions, although "Sermonette" and the previously unreleased "Devil in Your Soul" eschew that approach for some pretty gutsy, bluesy soul. *—Richie Unterberger*

Indelible Impressions: The Curtom Anthology 1968–1976 / Jun. 20, 2000 / Sequel ♦♦♦♦
Already an exemplar of the self-contained soul group (songwriting, production, and performance), the Impressions grabbed the reins of executive power by 1968, moving from ABC/Paramount to their own Curtom label with the justly liberating *This Is My Country* LP. And though linchpin Curtis Mayfield left for a solo career just two years later, the Impressions continued putting out strong material for several years afterward—thanks in part to Mayfield's continued involvement on the songwriting and production side, as well as solid replacements (Leroy Hutson, Ralph Johnson, Reggie Torian) and the exquisite harmonies of Sam Gooden and Fred Cash. *Indelible Impressions: The Curtom Anthology 1968-1976*, Sequel's two-disc package of the latter-day Impressions, begins by closing out the Mayfield era with forceful statements of purpose like "This Is My Country," "Mighty Mighty (Spade and Whitey)," and "Check Out Your Mind," balanced with several tender ballads ("Choice of Colors," "Soulful Love"). (Sequel even tosses a bone to fans of the band's early days by adding invigorating remakes of four early-'60s hits: "Gypsy Woman," "Keep on Pushing," "I'm So Proud," and "I've Been Trying.") The second disc begins with the brief period when Leroy Hutson served as lead vocalist, then picks its way carefully through the last three years of the group's Curtom years with the late masterpiece "Finally Got Myself Together (I'm a Changed Man)." It's one of the next best purchases after *The Very Best of the Impressions*, and a perfect summarization of the high points (and there are many) on some scattershot LPs by one of the finest soul groups of all time. *—John Bush*

Ultimate Collection / Oct. 16, 2001 / Hip-O ♦♦♦♦♦
This is an *Ultimate Collection* for the Impressions, not Curtis Mayfield, which are two separate things, no matter how closely intertwined their histories are. This begins with "For Your Precious Love," when Jerry Butler was the lead singer, and ends with two tracks that he neither wrote nor sang, giving a good basic history of the band's career from 1958 to 1975. Not every great Impressions song is here, but nearly ever song here is great (the quality does dip a bit toward the end); this certainly delivers a good summary of—and even introduction to—the group, which was one of the greatest of its time, regardless of genre. That said, it won't give you everything you need—but it certainly will get your love started. *—Stephen Thomas Erlewine*

Incognito

f. 1979, London, England
Group / Jazz-Funk, Acid Jazz, Funk, House, Club/Dance
An acid jazz project with surprisingly deep roots in the 1970s jazz/funk/fusion world, Incognito was originally formed by Jean-Paul Maunick (aka Bluey) and Paul "Tubbs" Williams. Both were leaders of the late-'70s disco-funk group Light of the World, who scored several moderate British hits, including a cover of "I Shot the Sheriff." Just after the release of Light of the World's third LP (*Check Us Out*), Maunick and Williams shifted the lineup slightly and renamed the conglomeration Incognito.

Incognito debuted with the single "Parisienne Girl" and released the 1981 LP *Jazz Funk*, but were inactive during the rest of the 1980s. Maunick continued to write material for his group, even while working with Maxi Priest and others. (Williams later moved to Finland.) By the beginning of the 1990s, DJ legend and early Incognito fan Gilles Peterson had founded the Talkin' Loud label and he made Incognito one of his first signings. The 1991 single "Always There" (with vocals by Jocelyn Brown) became a Top Ten hit as part of Britain's booming acid jazz scene, prompting the release of Incognito's second album overall, *Inside Life*. It was largely a studio affair, with Maunick and engineer Simon Cotsworth directing a large cast with many of the best musicians in Britain's fertile groove community.

With 1992's *Tribes, Vibes and Scribes*, Maunick added a more established vocalist, the American Maysa Leak. A cover of Stevie Wonder's "Don't You Worry 'Bout a Thing" became another Incognito hit, and the album ascended Britain's pop charts even as it rose on America's contemporary jazz charts. The third album, *Positivity*, became the group's biggest album success, with much attention across Europe as well as Britain. Leak unsuccessfully attempted a solo career with Blue Note, leading to the temporary vocal replacement Pamela Anderson (not the *Baywatch* pinup) on 1995's *100° and Rising*. Leak returned, though, appearing on the following year's *Beneath the Surface*. Incognito later expanded its discography with 1996's *Remixed*, 1998's *Tokyo Live*, and 1999's *No Time Like the Future*. *—John Bush*

Tribes, Vibes and Scribes / 1992 / Verve ♦♦♦♦
This England-based dance and funk, but mostly jazz, band brings nothing but energy to this project. The production is sleek, and the arrangements are precise. Maysa Leak reaches her higher notes without abandoning the fullness of her unwavering lower range. Half of the songs on this album utilize her vocals, while the others are instrumentals. The instrumental tracks feature bebop-influenced solos, in particular "L'Arc en Ciel de Miles," which is an admirable tribute to the late famous jazz trumpeter. However, each song's solo is just as riveting as the next. The one constant on this album is the steady strum of bassist Randy Hope-Taylor. Contrary to the group's name, their music is anything but incognito—it's excellent and as conspicuous as ever. *—Craig Lytle*

Positivity / 1994 / Talkin' Loud ♦♦♦♦
This is an excellent collection of jazz and fusion numbers featuring the wholesome, peerless vocals of Maysa Leak and group newcomer Mark Anthoni. With gritty, urban rhythms and painstaking arrangements, Leak's radiant vocals ring with invitation. The lyrical content is upright and substantive. All the songs have an aggressive backbeat regardless of their tempo, providing an unobstructed platform for these artistic musicians to express their chic brand of music. Group leader Jean-Paul "Bluey" Maunick's vision of intertwine various genres of music (bebop, soul, classical, dance, etc.) into one incomparable sound is exemplary. *—Craig Lytle*

100° and Rising / Jun. 6, 1995 / Talkin' Loud ♦♦♦
On *100 Degrees and Rising*, the pioneering acid house outfit Incognito turn in another first-rate record, featuring their trademark mixture of jazz, soul, and funk. There's not much to distinguish *100 Degrees* from their previous handful of records, but the band is smooth, accomplished and deep, finding new variations on their trademark sound. *—Stephen Thomas Erlewine*

Beneath the Surface / 1996 / Talkin' Loud/Verve Forecast ♦♦♦
Beneath the Surface finds original lead singer Maysa Leak returning to the Incognito fold. Coincidentally or not, the record finds the group moving deeply into smooth, laid-back, jazzy soul. It's a seductive sound and the group executes it well, even though there ironically isn't that much substance beneath the surface. *—Leo Stanley*

Remixed / Jul. 15, 1996 / Talkin' Loud/Verve Forecast ♦♦♦
Remixed features a number of the group's tracks for Talkin' Loud/Verve remixed by stars like Pete Rock and Roger Sanchez. Some of these 12 songs have previously been released, but the bulk of the disc have never been easily available—most are promotional-only remixes. Frequently these versions, including a steaming "Always There," actually improve on the original take, offering deeper, more textured grooves. In fact, it is arguably the finest, most consistent Incognito album available. *—Leo Stanley*

● **Best of Incognito** / Apr. 25, 2000 / Blue Thumb ♦♦♦♦♦
The greatest hits of Jean-Paul "Bluey" Maunick's dream band are compiled on this Blue Thumb release. *The Best of Incognito* features the acid jazz and funk that kicked off the funk jazz scene in the United Kingdom and chronicles their biggest hits. Included is the hot dance groove "Everyday" from the album *100° and Rising* and the killer cover "Don't You Worry About a Thing" by Stevie Wonder from *Tribes, Vibes and Scribes*. Selections from seven of Incognito's great CDs and a bonus track featured on the Japanese version of *No Time Like the Future* make up this choice set for dancing, grooving, or just relaxing. *—Paula Edelstein*

The Incredibles

f. 1963, Los Angeles, CA
Group / Soul
A mid-'60s Los Angeles soul group that issued a pair of singles on the Audio Artists label, neither of which made much impression. Cal Waymon, Carl Gilbert, Jean Smith, and Alda Denise Edwards were the group members. Waymon, Gilbert, and Smith met at Jefferson High School, while Edwards had been in the Vi-Dels. *—Ron Wynn*

● **Heart & Soul** / 1969 / Collectables ♦♦♦
Some good easy R&B from the Incredibles, a trio from Los Angeles consisting of two males and a female. Led by Cal Waymon, the Incredibles specialized in crying ballads, even when the message was positive. On their biggest record, "Heart & Soul," the overall feel was one of sadness and despair; when they sing Sam Cooke's hit "For Sentimental Reasons," it sounds more like wishful thinking than actually being in love and being loved in return. The titles all depict rejection and heartache: "Standing Here Crying," "Crying Heart" (which has a midtempo beat), "Lost Without You," "Stop the Raindrops," and on and on. "I Found a Love" is the most uplifting tune on the album—at least on this track, the singer finds a new love after being dumped. Although sad, most of the tunes

work well. "I'll Make It Easy," for example is a lovely ballad where Cal pleads with his woman to return home, because if she does he'll make it easy; the touching refrain rivals "Heart & Soul" for the honor of their most popular recording, and upon release it crept into the Top 20 rotations on many R&B stations across America. A 1998 CD reissue compiled the tracks from the original LP, on Audio Arts Records, with five bonus tracks. *—Andrew Hamilton*

Indeep

f. New York, NY

Group / Disco, Dance-Pop

Hailing from New York, the dance-disco outfit Indeep scored a massive hit in 1983 with "Last Night a DJ Saved My Life." Led by songwriter Michael Cleveland, the band issued a full-length album under the same title shortly thereafter, but with the disco movement almost extinct by this time (and with the emergence of such styles as rap), Indeep subsequently had a tough time following up their smash and were delegated to "one-hit wonder" status. The act continued recording into the mid-'80s, and issued a few quickly forgotten albums: *When Boys Talk*, *Buffalo Bill*, and *The Record Keeps Spinning*. But the group's lone hit has become a dancefloor classic over the years, and 1991 saw the release of the 23-track best-of set, *The Collection*. *—Greg Prato*

Last Night a DJ Saved My Life / 1983 / Sound of New York ♦♦♦

One of the more quirky and humorous dance-funk-urban contemporary groups of the early to mid-'80s was Indeep, which soared to the top of 1983's R&B singles charts with the clever "Last Night a DJ Saved My Life." Indeep was definitely original—though the group was heavily influenced by Chic, its lyrics were a lot more humorous. And Indeep had its own way of incorporating hip-hop elements. Those who acquired this debut album because of its hit title song found the rest of the material to be equally fun, including the goofy "Buffalo Bill" and the pointed yet amusing "When Boys Talk" (which was also a hit and has a good laugh at the expense of men who brag about their sexual conquests). Most of the songs are originals, although Indeep concludes the LP with an infectious cover of James Brown's "There It Is." Unfortunately for Indeep, the urban contemporary market can be extremely fickle—and the group was unable to maintain the popularity that it enjoyed in 1983. Nonetheless, *Last Night a DJ Saved My Life* is a very fun and memorable footnote in the long history of R&B. *—Alex Henderson*

● **The Collection** / Sep. 24, 1991 / Unidisc ♦♦♦

Each Indeep album is avoidable for the percentage of filler, so *Collection*, released on Unidisc in 1991, is all you need—unless you're a DJ desperate to expose some buried album cut that no one else paid attention to. This has everything you'd expect and more, including the number-two club single "Last Night a DJ Saved My Life," "When Boys Talk" (number-16 club), "The Record Keeps Spinning" (number-32 club), and "Buffalo Bill" (number-81 black singles). Apart from the chart hits, there's nothing too memorable, and most of those cuts are either hampered by cloning attempts (the sub-Prince of "You Got to Rock It," for instance) or the kind of tacky saxophone soloing heard in too much mid-'80s pop. Still, there's no mistaking the fact that "Last Night a DJ Saved My Life" is an essential '80s dance track and should be obtained in some form. You might be better off hunting it down on a various-artists compilation. *—Andy Kellman*

The Independents

f. 1971, **db.** 1975

Group / Smooth Soul, Soul

Among the more interesting male/female vocal groups, the Independents made some outstanding singles in the early '70s. Chuck Jackson, Marvin Yancy, Maurice Jackson, Helen Curry, and Eric Thomas specialized in almost melodramatic, overwrought, but perfectly performed love songs. Their first single for Wand, "Just as Long as You Need Me," set the stage in 1972, reaching number eight on the R&B charts. They topped those charts in 1973 with "Leaving Me," while "Baby I've Been Missing You" made it to number four. They never had any song attract much pop support, but soul fans loved the lyrical scenarios and group interplay. Their last hit was "Let This Be a Lesson to You" in 1974, another R&B Top Ten hit. Jackson and Yancy went on to attain success as a production/songwriting team, scoring hits with Ronnie Dyson and Natalie Cole. *—Ron Wynn*

The First Time We Met / 1972 / Wand ♦♦♦♦

A stellar debut from Chicago's the Independents, a quartet that featured activist Jesse Jackson's younger brothers: Chuck on lead vocals, and Maurice; the other members were Marvin Yancy, who wrote and produced the tunes with Chuck, and lone female member Helen Curry who blended with the guys and added some eye candy for the fellows (she was fine). They were at their best on southern drawl—slow, meandering ballads with hitches in the rhythms. Four of their finest, "First Time We Met," "Leaving Me" (a million seller), "Just As Long As You Need Me" (a duet featuring Chuck and Marvin), and "Baby I've Been Missing You," stand out like diamonds among coals when compared to the other selections. Picking their A-sides was a piece of cake as they waxed either hits or garbage (a term Berry Gordy Jr. used for songs that didn't get enough votes by his quality control panel to get released as singles). *—Andrew Hamilton*

Discs of Gold / 1974 / Wand ♦♦♦

Here is a good history of Independents recordings. Calling them *Discs of Gold*, however, is a stretch; most of these cuts didn't go gold. The members were Chuck Jackson (younger brother of civil rights activist Jesse Jackson), Maurice Jackson, Eric Thomas, and sole female Helen Curry. Chuck handles the leads in a smooth baritone, sometimes adding a meandering slow rap to some of the songs, while the group harmonizes like a mini-choir. "Understated" best describes this LP; neither Chuck nor the group ever break loose and let it all hang. Wilson Pickett would have been screaming all over these tracks. *—Andrew Hamilton*

● **Golden Classics** / Nov. 25, 1991 / Collectables ♦♦♦♦♦

The Independents were a fine early and mid-'70s soul ensemble whose roster included songwriter/vocalist Chuck Jackson. Jackson and Marvin Yancy co-wrote most of their tracks, and they had some nice romantic and ballad hits in 1973 and 1974, topping the R&B charts with "Leaving Me." This Chuck Jackson was not related to the great shouter who recorded for Wand/Scepter. He later teamed with Yancy to crank out hits for Natalie Cole and Ronnie Dyson, while Yancy and Cole at one time were married. *—Ron Wynn*

James Ingram

b. Feb. 16, 1956, Akron, OH

Vocals, Keyboards / Quiet Storm, Adult Contemporary, Urban

James Ingram began performing with the band Revelation Funk in the early '70s, moving from Akron, OH, to Los Angeles in 1973. During the '70s, Ingram supported Ray Charles on the road with backup vocals and piano, played keyboards behind the Coasters on Dick Clark's oldies revues, and was Leon Haywood's musical director. After hearing a demo of him singing "Just Once," Quincy Jones asked Ingram to perform on his new album. Released in 1980 on *The Dude*, the number-17 "Just Once" was Ingram's first success, resulting in three Grammy nominations—Best New Artist, Best Pop Male Vocal, and Best R&B Vocal—winning in the two latter categories. Throughout the '80s, Ingram had steady popular success singing duets, but all of his solo albums failed to make a dent in the charts; in 1990 he scored his first solo hit, "I Don't Have the Heart." *—Stephen Thomas Erlewine*

Never Felt So Good / 1988 / Qwest ♦♦♦

James Ingram became a major artist in the '80s on the strength of his work with Quincy Jones and his duets with Patti Austin. He got plenty of urban contemporary airplay and exposure with this mid-'80s album, his last for Jones' Qwest label. It reinforced both the appeal of the urban production style (polished charts, great productions) and its problems (overly slick vocals and thematic sameness in the performances). *—Ron Wynn*

The Greatest Hits: Power of Great Music / Sep. 24, 1991 / Qwest ♦♦♦♦

James Ingram racked up a number of adult contemporary-styled R&B pop hits in the 1980s, many of them duets, and the bulk of those hits are collected on this 12-track 1991 compilation. His music may at times seem somewhat melodramatic, registering on the pop spectrum somewhere between Michael Bolton and Billy Ocean, but nonetheless exemplifies top-notch 1980s adult contemporary pop production at its zenith. This set includes his two hit duets with Patti Austin, those being "How Do You Keep the Music Playing" and their timeless chart-topper "Baby Come to Me." Also included is his monster duet with Linda Ronstadt, "Somewhere Out There," and his hit duet with Michael McDonald, the funky "Yah Mo B There" (definitely one of Ingram's coolest songs). A few rarities make an appearance, including "Where Did My Heart Go?" from the film *City Slickers*, and the BET theme "Remember the Dream." To round out the collection are his solo hits, among them the Grammy-winning "Just Once," "One Hundred Ways," and his only solo chart-topper, "I Don't Have the Heart." Buyer beware, however, because a more "extensive" hits collection, *Forever More*, was issued in 1999, with newly recorded (and inferior) versions of "Just Once," "One Hundred Ways," and "I Don't Have the Heart." *—Jose Promis*

● **Forever More (Love Songs, Hits & Duets)** / Apr. 13, 1999 / Private Music ♦♦♦♦

James Ingram never became a superstar, but he racked up a respectable number of adult contemporary and urban soul hits during the '80s and early '90s, many of which were duets. *Forever More: Best of James Ingram* collects 14 highlights from his career, including the hits "Just Once," "One Hundred Ways," "Baby, Come to Me," "Yah Mo B There," "Somewhere Out There" and "I Don't Have the Heart." The remaining songs may not be as recognizable as the singles, but they're in the same vein and should please the casual fans that were lured in by the well-known hits. *—Stephen Thomas Erlewine*

Luther Ingram

b. Nov. 30, 1944, Jackson, TN

Vocals / Soul, Smooth Soul, Southern Soul, Country-Soul

This Jackson, TN, Southern soul singer was one of the top artists at Stax during the early '70s. Hooking up with producer Johnny Baylor's tiny KoKo label, Ingram appeared regularly on the R&B charts after Baylor brought his firm into the Stax fold in 1969. Ingram's intimate vocal approach was well suited to ballads, and his 1970 hit revival of "Ain't That Loving You (For More Reasons than One)" set the stage for his R&B chart-topping classic "(If Loving You Is Wrong) I Don't Want to Be Right" two years later. Long after Stax had folded, Ingram was still releasing hit singles—clear into 1987. *—Bill Dahl*

I've Been Here All the Time / 1972 / Koko ♦♦♦

Luther Ingram established himself as a comer on the Southern soul scene with his debut album for Koko. He moved from Jackson, Tennessee to New York, but then Stax contacted him, and he eventually began recording for Koko. Booming, energetic, and unsophisticated wailing was his stock-in-trade, plus a country/blues influence. *—Ron Wynn*

If Loving You Is Wrong (I Don't Want to Be Right) / 1972 / Koko ♦♦♦♦♦

Luther Ingram earned his biggest R&B and pop hit with the title track, one of the last hurrahs for gospel-tinged and country-flavored confessional soul. The song would later become a country hit for Barbara Mandrell. Ingram landed one other Top Ten R&B single with "I'll Be Your Shelter (In Time of Storm)," and the album contained some other earnest soul ballads that weren't hits in "I Can't Stop" and "Help Me Love." Ingram never again enjoyed similar crossover heights, and the tide was turning against deep soul in both pop and R&B camps. *—Ron Wynn*

Do You Love Somebody / 1977 / Koko ♦♦♦

Luther Ingram / 1986 / Profile ♦♦♦♦♦

Luther Ingram made a brief return to the R&B charts with this 1986 LP issued on a predominantly dance-oriented label, which mixed his classic soul voice with urban contemporary production. It wasn't an early new jack swing number, as there were no hip-hop or rap elements, but it did contain drum machine tracks and synthesizer-dominated arrangements. Otherwise, Ingram was still singing heartache ballads, doing confessional country-soul and sounding raw and urgent on "Baby Don't Go Too Far" and "Don't Turn Around." The album also contained an interesting, although flawed, remake of Bob Dylan's "Gotta Serve Somebody." *—Ron Wynn*

● **Greatest Hits** / Apr. 1996 / The Right Stuff ♦♦♦♦♦

Managed and produced by the late and notorious Johnny Baylor, the guy many accused of causing Stax's demise, Luther Ingram had a rich, soulful tenor that dripped with soul. He recorded many classic deep soul sagas, hitting his pinnacle with "If Loving You Is Wrong (I Don't Want to Be Right)," a gripper that passionately justified infidelity, with a whining guitar underscoring Ingram's heartfelt testimonial to his outside woman. The soulful "Ain't That Loving You (For More Reasons Than One)" dropped before "If Loving You" and should have been Ingram's first monster. You'll have to search a bit to find a more endearing tribute from a man to his woman. The midtempo, good-time feeling "I'll Be Your Shelter," like the previous two tracks, was co-written by Homer Banks, a Southern soul songwriting fool. It did well on the charts and provided a break from the heavy ballads, which was likewise for the joyful "My Honey & Me." Other goodies include "Steal Away to the Hideaway," "Missing You" and a scrumptious remake of Sam Cooke's "You Were Made for Me." Ingram's adaptation to Stax surprised many; before Stax, he had recorded urban and Northern soul 45s for tiny companies that were little more than P.O. boxes. *—Andrew Hamilton*

The Ink Spots

f. 1938, Indianapolis, IN

Group / Vocal Pop, R&B, Harmony Vocal Group

The Ink Spots played a large role in pioneering the black vocal group-harmony genre, helping to pave the way for the doo wop explosion of the '50s. The quavering high tenor of Bill Kenny presaged hundreds of street-corner leads to come, and the sweet harmonies of Charlie Fuqua, Deek Watson, and bass Hoppy Jones (who died in 1944) backed him flawlessly. Kenny's impeccable diction and Jones' deep drawl were both prominent on the Ink Spots' first smash on Decca in 1939, the sentimental "If I Didn't Care." From then through 1951, the group was seldom absent from the pop charts, topping the lists with "We Three (My Echo, My Shadow, and Me)" (1940), "I'm Making Believe" and "Into Each Life Some Rain Must Fall" (both in 1944), and "The Gypsy" and "To Each His Own" (both in 1946).

Watson eventually split to form his own group, the Brown Dots, and appeared in numerous low-budget film musicals, while Kenny attempted a solo career, notching a solo hit in 1951 with the uplifting "It Is No Secret." Countless groups masquerading as the Ink Spots have thrived across the nation since the '50s. *—Bill Dahl*

Swing High Swing Low / 1989 / ASV/Living Era ♦♦♦

The focus of this set is on the Ink Spots' early years: it begins with their third recording session and continues through the first year of their widespread success. During what annotator Peter Gammond calls "the transitional years," they experimented with different styles, cutting everything from swing standards like "Stompin' at the Savoy" and "Christopher Columbus" to the Gershwins' "Let's Call the Whole Thing Off" and "Slap That Bass." But soon after their commercial breakthrough with "If I Didn't Care" in the spring of 1939, they adopted that record's arrangement as a formula style. There was also a personnel changeover before the hit-making period set in, with lead singer Jerry Daniels replaced by Bill Kenny. This evolution is obscured by the sequencing of the album, which goes back and forth between the earlier and later work. Nevertheless, most of the group's first batch of hits, 1939-1940, is included, though oddly their first chart-topper, "Address Unknown," is missing. *—William Ruhlmann*

★ **The Greatest Hits** / Oct. 26, 1989 / MCA ♦♦♦♦♦

Spanning just seven years, yet perfectly encapsulating the Ink Spots' entire recording career, MCA's 15-track *Greatest Hits* has everything the curious require to understand what made this quartet so influential for the thousands of R&B vocal groups to come, from the Ravens to Boyz II Men: close harmonies, sparkling romantic monologues, and the interplay of high tenor Bill Kenny and deep bass Orville "Hoppy" Jones. In residence are all of the biggest hits—"If I Didn't Care," "When the Swallows Come Back to Capistrano," "We Three (My Echo, My Shadow and Me)," "Java Jive," and "The Gypsy"—though there is one notable exclusion: the double-sided chart-topper "I'm Making Believe" b/w "Into Each Life Some Rain Must Fall," from the movie *Sweet & Lowdown*. Everything else here is pure gold. *—John Bush*

☆ **The Anthology** / Jun. 16, 1998 / MCA ♦♦♦♦♦

Two discs and almost 50 tracks of the Ink Spots, all recorded within a relatively narrow 13-year window, could be enough to overwhelm anyone not intimately interested in close-harmony vocal music, especially such a humid, narcoleptic sound as the Ink Spots tended toward. For those unhindered by the prospects of two and a half hours of gentle crooning, though, *The Anthology* earns its title and then some, sprinkling the big hits already anthologized many times over—"If I Didn't Care," "My Prayer," "We Three (My Echo, My Shadow and Me)," "Java Jive," "I Don't Want to Set the World on Fire," and "Don't Get Around Much Anymore"—among a parade of obscure yet intriguing performances. Prime among the latter are the kinetic "Your Feet's Too Big," one of their first recordings, and "That's When Your Heartaches Begin," probably more famous now as an Elvis Presley cover than an Ink Spots original. As often happened during the 1940s and '50s, the Ink Spots also recorded dozens of songs in the standards repertory, and several of those ("Who Wouldn't Love You," "Prisoner of Love," "I Cover the Waterfront," "I Get the Blues When It Rains") make for the biggest surprises on this bountiful compilation. *—John Bush*

Inner Life

f. 1979, New York, NY

Group / Club/Dance, Disco, Urban

The group Inner Life spawned a handful of amazing disco singles and three accomplished LPs that have remained as powerful as they day they were recorded. Not so much a group as a shifting unit of closely connected producers and musicians, the most significant constant of the group was the presence of Jocelyn Brown, a vocalist who can logically be referred to as the Queen of Disco. Throughout Inner Life's existence, the work of several luminaries graced the group's recordings. Patrick Adams, Leroy Burgess, Greg Carmichael, Stan Lucas, Bob Blank, Tee Scott, and Larry Levan each played significant roles in Inner Life's output.

Inner Life's breakout occurred in 1979 with "I'm Caught Up (In a One Night Love Affair)" a sad but redemptive single written in part by the venerable Patrick Adams (who put together Musique, another Jocelyn Brown group that scored with "In the Bush" and "Keep on Jumpin'"). Arranged by Adams and produced by him with help from Greg Carmichael and Debbie Hayes, the song peaked at number 22 on the U.S. R&B chart but deserved even better. The single was originally released on Carmichael's TCT imprint, but soon after its initial release, a bidding war broke out between a number of labels for the license to release it a second time. Prelude won out by paying $17,500 and helped take it to the charts with exposure that Carmichael's small label could not provide.

The group switched over to Salsoul for the remainder of their releases. A self-titled 1981 album featured a remake of Ashford & Simpson's "Ain't No Mountain High Enough," but the remix from Paradise Garage DJ Larry Levan lifted the song above the clouds. Stretching the original out to ten minutes and turning it into a mammoth, sweeping, incredibly dynamic disco song with all sorts of dazzling segments—not to mention Brown's vocal turn, one of the most impressive ever recorded, regardless of genre—Levan helped make the song an instant disco classic.

The misleadingly titled *Inner Life II* (apparently they weren't counting the brief *I'm Caught Up* as an LP), the group's third album, featured arranger/producer/guitarist Stan Lucas (Dazzle), songwriter/arranger/ vocalist/keyboardist LeRoy Burgess (Black Ivory, Logg, Convertion), bassist James Calloway (Black Ivory), and songwriter Sonny Davenport (a frequent Burgess/Calloway collaborator). Generally considered to be the finest Inner Life LP, it featured "Moment of My Life," a joyous song with an infectious skipping/hopping feel to it. The project ended shortly after that, with all the involved parties continuing their careers and often working together again in various capacities. Brown continued to rack up credit after credit, releasing solo material and guesting on records made by several admirers. *—Andy Kellman*

I'm Caught Up (In a One Night Love Affair) / 1979 / Prelude ♦♦♦♦

This isn't an album that houses the joyous hop of "Moment of My Life," and it doesn't contain the towering triumph of "Ain't No Mountain High Enough" either, but Inner Life's *I'm Caught Up (In a One Night Love Affair)* is an immensely enjoyable full-length—one of the Prelude label's finer moments despite its low profile. Save for the assistance of Patrick Adams and Debbie Hayes on the sad title track, everything is produced with the sensitive touch of Greg Carmichael. The album is rife with sweet, upbeat dancefloor material, including "You Got Me Dancing," "You Don't Have Dancing on Your Mind," and the particularly excellent "I Want to Give You Me." What truly makes this album—beyond the stellar production, slick arrangements, and crafty session work—are the vocals of Jocelyn Brown, who turns in typically lively and forceful singing throughout. It's safe to say that the greatness of "I'm Caught Up" is overlooked due to the preeminence of Inner Life's other classic singles, but it's probably one of the finest "proper" songs of the disco era. Admittedly, at only five songs that clock in at just over half an hour, the album is a bit thin in terms of length. When Unidisc released the album on compact disc, they added the radio edits of "I Want to Give You Me" and "I'm Caught Up." *—Andy Kellman*

Inner Life / 1981 / Salsoul ♦♦♦

Inner Life was essentially the versatile Jocelyn Brown on lead vocals (she could do slow jams as well as disco), plus a contingent of studio musicians. On this release, the ballad "It's Wonderful" builds to a frenzy but never climaxes. "You Got to Pay Girl," a minor hit, has a magnificently arranged musical interlude featuring a tinkling piano, a boastful foghorn, and clapping hands. She gives Ashford & Simpson's "Ain't No Mountain High Enough" feeling and elasticity; aided by La Rita Gaskins, Carol Sylvan, Connie Harvey, and Dennis Collins, Jocelyn transforms the classic into a testifying revival while a zany synthesizer colors the pulsating rhythms. "(Knock Out) Let's Go Another Round" is exciting and tasty. The Salsoul label used electronic drums and synthesizers better than most, making them funky and essential. *—Andrew Hamilton*

● **Inner Life II** / Oct. 1982 / Salsoul ♦♦♦♦

Inner Life II was the NY-based studio group's best album. Produced by guitarist/songwriter Stan Lucas, it yielded some of the group's most enduring material. It's also a real treat for Jocelyn Brown fans, as she does lead vocals on all of the cuts Leroy Burgess co-wrote, and she sang and played keyboards on the uplifting "Moment of My Life," which tells of spiritual redemption. Brown *really* went to "cherch" on that one. The tight rhythm section of Burgess, bassist James Calloway, and drummer Sonny Davenport is featured on the track. It became an instant dance classic, receiving airplay on R&B and college stations. Its follow-up was the playful "I Like It Like That." The album version sounds different from the single and 12-inch versions—like it was a different take, though it could just sound that way because of the clever mixing skills of Shep Pettibone. The ballad "Feel What I'm Feeling" almost rivals "Make It Last Forever"—not the Keith Sweat hit—from *Inner Life* in its sheer sensuality. The four-on-the-floor jam "Got to Find Me Somebody" is a rousing album closer. *—Ed Hogan*

Instant Funk

f. 1978, Trenton, NJ, **db.** 1985

Group / Funk, Disco, Urban

Instant Funk burst on the '70s disco scene with the million-selling single "I Got My Mind Made Up (You Can Get It Girl)" and the gold album *Instant Funk*. Based in Trenton, NJ, the band started out with the core lineup of bassist Raymond Earl, drummer Scotty Miller, and guitarist Kim Miller. It later expanded to include keyboardist Dennis Richardson, lead singer James Carmichael, horn players Larry Davis, Eric Huff, and Johnny Onderlinde, and percussionist Charles Williams. In the mid-'60s, Earl met Scotty Miller in grade school and formed the duo the Music Machine.

In 1968, they began backing local vocal group the TNJs, appearing at local dances and venues building up a good reputation. Around 1971, the group's manager, Jackie Ellis, christened them Instant Funk because they could come up with funky grooves instantaneously. Philly soul producer Bunny Sigler was invited by Ellis to see Instant Funk and the TNJs perform. Sometime during the show, Sigler was called on-stage to perform. He was impressed that the band knew "Sunshine," a song he co-wrote with Phil Hurtt that was made popular by the O'Jays. As a result, Instant Funk began backing Sigler, the Manhattans, and various other R&B acts. As a staff songwriter/producer at Gamble & Huff's Philadelphia International Records, Sigler began using Instant Funk on his sessions along with the TNJs. They backed Sigler on three of his PIR albums: *That's How Long I'll Be Loving You*, *Keep Smilin'*, and *My Music*.

Instant Funk released a single on PIR's TSOP imprint, "Float Like a Butterfly," and an album, *Get Down With the Philly Jump*, issued in November 1976, whose title track and "It Ain't Reggae (But It Sho Is Funky)" were popular in disco clubs. In 1977, MFSB guitarist Norman Harris started his own label, Gold Mind Records, distributed by NY-based Salsoul Records. Sigler signed on as a recording artist, and his single "Let Me Party With You" hit the R&B Top Ten. Instant Funk signed with Gold Mind, but by the time their single "I Got My Mind Made Up" was released, the label had folded and all of its acts were transferred to Salsoul.

The million-selling "I Got My Mind Made Up (You Can Get It Girl)" (remixed by Larry Levan) parked at number one R&B for three weeks, and reached number 20 on the pop charts. Their second album, 1979's *Instant Funk*, went gold and hit number-one R&B. Other Salsoul LPs that feature Instant Funk are Loleatta Holloway's *Queen of the Night* and *Loleatta*; Double Exposure's *Locker Room*; and the Salsoul Orchestra's *How High*. On Curtis Mayfield's Curtom Records, Sigler and the band appear on Barbara Mason & Bunny Sigler's *Locked in This Position*, Mystique's self-titled debut, and Mayfield's own *Heartbeat*. When the Cayre brothers, owners of Salsoul, decided to fold the label in 1984, Instant Funk was without a record deal; they toured for a few years before disbanding. *—Ed Hogan*

Get Down With the Philly Jump / Nov. 1976 / TSOP ✦✦✦

When Instant Funk's debut album, *Get Down With the Philly Jump*, came out in 1976, those who heard the LP agreed that the Philadelphians had a very recognizable and distinctive sound. Instant Funk had one foot in the sophisticated Philly soul/disco sound and the other in the gritty, down-and-dirty funk of pre-J.T. Taylor Kool & the Gang—put those things together, and you have a group that was certainly unique and risk-taking. Although Bunny Sigler produced *Get Down With the Philly Jump* at Philly's famous Sigma Sound Studios, this LP isn't as strong as Instant Funk's subsequent releases would be. The album is uneven, and it doesn't contain a blockbuster hit like "I Got My Mind Made Up." Nonetheless, the material is generally decent; one can hear Instant Funk's potential on infectious tracks like "I Know Where You're Coming From," "Hup Two, Hup Two (Get in Line, Say Get in Line)" and "Philly Jump." In 1976, the best was yet to come for Instant Funk, but *Get Down With the Philly Jump* indicated that the Philadelphians had a lot of possibilities. *—Alex Henderson*

Instant Funk / Jan. 1979 / Charly ✦✦✦✦

Instant Funk, the nine-piece funk unit discovered by Bunny Sigler, created a stir in 1979 when Salsoul released the single "I Got My Mind Made Up (You Can Get It Girl)." Swirling, screaming horns announce the chorus; hand claps, tambourines and a maniacal rhythm guitar battle the heavy bottom; and a woman delivers erotic lines for added impact. Salsoul followed the number-20 pop and number-one R&B (for three weeks) hit with "Crying," a race horse whose relentless beat only subsides near the fade; Carmichael's vocal is passionate, almost deranged. "Never Let Me Go Away," a rare Instant Funk ballad, was so overblown the melody got buried. Spooky voices and haunted-house sounds wallpaper "Dark Vader"'s comic-book lyrics and funky hooks. Rolling horns pump "I'll Be Doggone" (not the Marvin Gaye hit), a cooker that rolls for seven minutes. Four of the eight tracks are killers; a pretty good average for a disco/funk group. *—Andrew Hamilton*

Witch Doctor / Nov. 1979 / Salsoul ✦✦✦✦

When Instant Funk moved from Philadelphia International's TSOP label to Salsoul, all of the pieces fell into place for the band—both commercially and creatively. While its first album, *Get Down With the Philly Jump*, was decent but uneven, its second and third albums were generally excellent. For Instant Funk, switching labels didn't mean switching producers—the Philadelphians worked with Bunny Sigler at TSOP and continued to work with him at Salsoul. Sigler was the ideal producer for Instant Funk because he really understood what the band was going for: an unorthodox blend of Philly soul/disco and the type of hardcore funk that other cities were better known for. Sigler is a major asset on *Witch Doctor*, which was Instant Funk's second album for Salsoul and its third album overall. From the sweaty funk of "Bodyshine" (a major hit), "Slap, Slap Lickedy Lap," and "Witch Doctor" to the smooth ballad "I Had a Dream," Sigler does right by Instant Funk on this solid effort. *—Alex Henderson*

The Funk Is On / 1981 / Salsoul ✦✦✦

On their third Salsoul album, *The Funk Is On*, Philly soul band Instant Funk shows an acute pop music sensibility. But funk fans need not worry, this album lives up to its title; the band still funks. The title track single, written by Brass Construction's Randy Muller, is pure, unadulterated funk. The same could be said for the gritty "You Want My Love." The second single, "Everybody," has a serious bounce groove along the lines of Zapp's "More Bounce to the Ounce" or Vaughn Mason's "Bounce, Skate, Rock, Roll." The Larry Levan 12-inch extended remix clocked in at 8:47 and features Jack Faith's dynamic arrangement and James Carmichael's arousing guttural groans towards the track's climax. The funny, plucky "Funk-n-Roll" has yodels. The snappy "It's Cool" is a skater's favorite and shows off some deft guitar and bass. The third single was the sweet, simmering ballad "What Can I Do for You" that should have given the band its first hit ballad. Producer Bunny Sigler shows the band's lighter side on the melodic, swing jazz-flavored "Can You See Where I'm Coming From" and the upbeat "You're Not Getting Older." *The Funk Is On* (reissued on CD in the spring of 1999 by U.K. label Charly) gives Instant Funk fans what they want and a little bit more. *—Ed Hogan*

Looks So Fine / Mar. 1982 / Salsoul ✦✦

Instant Funk V / 1983 / Salsoul ✦✦✦

Reduced to a quintet by 1983, Instant Funk was then comprised of Scotty Miller (drums, background vocals), Kim Miller (guitar, background vocals), Raymond Earl (bass, background vocals), Dennis Richardson (keyboards, background vocals), and James Carmichael (lead vocals); five additional rhythm players, a five-piece horn section, and additional backing vocalists augment the band. Tom Moulton mixed two bouncers: "No Stoppin' That Rockin'," a groovy techno funk piece, and "Who Took Away the Funk," a low groove with P-Funk-style vocals. "Smack Dab in the Middle" is a tender ballad with a winsome, heartfelt chorus. A remake of "A Hard Day's Night" features punchy horns, choppy rhythms, rock guitar, and energetic vocals. While OK, this is a nonessential album. *—Andrew Hamilton*

Kinky / Sep. 1983 / Salsoul ✦✦

Greatest Hits / Jul. 23, 1996 / Salsoul ✦✦✦

From Sister Sledge to Blue Magic to Teddy Pendergrass, the soulsters who came out of Philadelphia in the 1970s were known for their sophistication and sleekness. Philly was full of soul and disco stars who could handle funk, but bands specializing in hardcore funk (such as Cameo, the Gap Band and Parliament/Funkadelic) seemed to come from other cities. The unique thing about Instant Funk was that they had one foot in the Philly sound and another in the down-and-dirty funk of other locations. "Witch Doctor," "Bodyshine," "Why Don't You Think About Me" and other infectious classics on this 1996 CD are the work of a band that had Philly's trademark sophistication, but was also well aware of what Rick James and Cameo were up to. "Who Took Away the Funk" is clearly inspired by George Clinton's P-Funk, while "Crying" (written by Philly's prolific Bunny Sigler) has a very O'Jays-ish appeal. And 1979's "I Got My Mind Made Up" (IF's biggest hit) is the perfect blend of funk and disco. Most of IF's Salsoul albums of the late 1970s and early '80s are worth hearing, but for a starting point, *Greatest Hits* would be the best choice. *—Alex Henderson*

● **The Best of Instant Funk** / Jul. 1, 1999 / Charly ✦✦✦✦

The Best of Instant Funk is a far better Instant Funk compilation than the 1996 issue *Greatest Hits* on Capitol, which was essentially a fleshed-out version of *Instant Funk*, the mother album of "I Got My Mind Made Up (You Can Get It Girl)," the group's only real hit. At 13 tracks, this spinner contains three more cuts than the Capital CD and the jams cover a wider time frame. The band always suffers from indifferent mixes; no doubt their waxings sounded like dragon slayers in the studio, but that essence didn't transfer well (of many tunes) to vinyl but does come to life in CD format. Stylewise, Instant Funk was too funky for pure disco-ites, too eclectic for urban radio tuners, and didn't place enough emphasis on the dominant one beat to interest hardcore funk fans. The baker's dozen include the pulsating, pumping nine-minute and 49-second 12-inch mix of "I've Got My Mind Up," "Slap, Slap Lickedy Lap," "Wide World of Sports," and "Slam Dunk the Funk." *—Andrew Hamilton*

The Intrigues

f. 1968

Group / Philly Soul, Soul

The Intrigues were a slick trio that served up funky Philly soul during the early '70s. Their biggest hit in 1969 on the Yew label, "In a Moment," was slickly arranged and produced by Bobby Martin and Thom Bell, although its flip, "Scotchman Rock," was a rocking throwback to simpler times. The Intrigues' lush 1971 hit on Yew, "The Language of Love," was co-produced by Van McCoy. After an extended absence from the R&B charts, the trio reemerged from the shadows in 1985 with "Fly Girl." *—Bill Dahl*

● **In a Moment** / 1970 / Collectables ✦✦✦✦✦

This features slickly produced Philly R&B from the late '60s and early '70s featuring smooth harmonies and crisp arrangements. *—Bill Dahl*

The Intruders

f. 1960, Philadelphia, PA, **db.** 1975

Group / Pop-Soul, Philly Soul, Rock & Roll, R&B, Soul

As the first group to score hits with the songwriting/production team of Kenny Gamble & Leon Huff, the Intruders played a major role in the rise of Philadelphia soul, but are sometimes lost in the shuffle amid better-known acts like the O'Jays or Harold Melvin & the Blue Notes. The Intruders were originally formed as a doo wop group in 1960, and sang around Philadelphia for several years. Lead singer Sam "Little Sonny" Brown, Eugene "Bird" Daughtry, Phil Terry, and Robert "Big Sonny" Edwards signed with Gamble & Huff's fledgling Gamble label in 1966. They scored a Top 20 R&B hit that year with "(We'll Be) United," and followed it up a year later with "Together," as well as their first album *The Intruders Are Together*. 1968, though, was the Intruders' breakthrough year: "Cowboys to Girls," a template for what would become Philly soul's trademark sound, topped the R&B charts and climbed to number six on the pop side, giving the group their biggest hit. The follow-up "(Love Is Like A) Baseball Game" was their only other Top 40 pop hit, and the accompanying LP *Cowboys to Girls* wound up their most popular.

Gamble & Huff's success with the Intruders helped convince Columbia to grant them the money to launch Philadelphia International, which became the most successful soul label of the early '70s. The Intruders, meanwhile, were undergoing some internal turmoil; when they resurfaced on the 1970 Gamble LP *When We Get Married*, lead singer "Little Sonny" Brown had been replaced by nightclub singer Bobby Starr (b. Robert Ferguson). The title cut, a Dreamlovers cover, was a hit on the R&B charts, as was the follow-up "(Win, Place or Show) She's a Winner." Starr's tenure with the group was short-lived; Brown returned for the 1973 LP *Save the Children*, which spawned the Intruders' last two big hits, "I'll Always Love My Mama" and "I Wanna Know Your Name." For the 1974 follow-up *Energy of Love*, the Intruders were switched from the Gamble imprint to the Philly International subsidiary TSOP; however, it was less successful than the quartet's previous releases, and they disbanded in 1975. Eugene Daughtry formed a new lineup in 1984 (without any other original members); they recorded an album titled *Who Do You Love?* for the UK imprint Streetwave before disbanding once again. Daughtry passed away in 1994 after a bout with cancer, while Brown unfortunately committed suicide following years of drug and alcohol problems. Bobby Starr, meanwhile, continues to lead another version of the group that features no other original Intruders. *—Steve Huey*

The Intruders Are Together / 1967 / Gamble ♦♦♦
The Intruders Are Together is the first Gamble LP by Sam "Little Sonny" Brown, Phil Terry, Eugene "Bird" Daughtry and Robert "Big Sonny" Edwards. They had previously recorded on a small Philadelphia label, where Kenny Gamble (this LP's producer) had also cut a single. Good luck trying to find this rare bird, you'll have better luck hitting the lotto. And that's a shame because many of these cuts can't be found on later cassettes and CDs. Songs with the quality of the intriguingly beautiful "A Devil With an Angel Smile," the aching "Baby I'm So Lonely" and the sad "A Book for the Brokenhearted," can't be found on their otherwise superb double CD on Collectable Records. The bouncy, spirited "A Love That's Real," with its bong-bongs was the Philly natives' first bona fide R&B hit. With its romantic lyrics, "United" served as the wedding song for many in the late '60s and early '70s; the harmonies of Phil, Bird and Big Sonny never got the credit deserved, but their blends were superb and beautifully done, and are especially spine tingling on the shuffling "Together." Some record company should combine this with their *Cowboy to Girls* LP, the combination would make one helluva CD. *—Andrew Hamilton*

Cowboys to Girls / 1968 / Gamble ♦♦♦♦
The Intruders cracked the pop charts with the title cut, which is still their best-known song. It topped the R&B hit list and made it to number six on the pop side. The rest of the album wasn't quite that strong, but it did have two more wonderful ballads, and was their biggest LP overall. *—Ron Wynn*

When We Get Married / 1970 / Gamble ♦♦♦
If you see a copy of this album, swoop it up because one day it'll be a collector item. The lead singer for the Intruders on this is not Sam "Little Sonny" Brown, but Bobby Starr, an unheralded Philadelphia lounge singer. This is the only Intruders recording that didn't feature Little Sonny's rough, dragging, seemingly flat, yet charming tenor. Starr mimics Brown to perfection; his voice is much smoother, but the tone and phrasings are identical. Titled after the Intruders' remake of the Dreamlovers' "When We Get Married," this is a commendable 11-song set. "This Is My Love Song" charted R&B, but you won't find it on the Intruders double CD *Cowboys to Girls*. A pleasing rendition of "Brand New Me," originally waxed by Dusty Springfield, adds a pleasant touch. "I Didn't Know" has Starr and the guys expending a little energy. Little Sonny returned on subsequent Intruders LPs and Bobby Starr returned from whence he came, never to surface again. *—Andrew Hamilton*

Save the Children / 1973 / Philadelphia International ♦♦♦
No argument—this is the best Intruders album, other than their greatest-hits compilations, ever released. Little Sonny (Sam Brown) returns to join his buddies, Phil Terry, Eugene "Bird" Daughtry, and Robert "Big Sonny" Edwards, after an unexplained hiatus. "Save the Children" is a socially significant floater where the guys' voices ride the waves of MFSB's fantastic sound. Gamble & Huff spotlight the return of Little Sonny on "I Wanna Know Your Name"; the song employs a convincing rap by the singer. It also became a popular remake, as versions by the Force M.D.'s and Wallace & Scotty (of the Whispers) have since been waxed. "To Be Happy Is the Real Thing" and "Hang on in There" are two upbeat, positive-thinking songs that make you feel better about yourself. The Philadelphians reveal their doo wop roots by doing a credible rendition of Lee Andrews & the Hearts' "Teardrops." The cream is the spirited, tear-inducing "I Always Love My Mama," the best mama song ever. The Intruders rap about their teen years during the break before the song builds to a frantic end. A mellow rendition of Paul Simon's "Mother and Child Reunion" shows the group's versatility. *—Andrew Hamilton*

Energy of Love / 1974 / TSOP ♦♦♦
This is the Intruders' last known recording, their final collaboration with Gamble & Huff, or anyone else for that matter. "Energy of Love" is a positive midtempo statement about finding the power of love, which didn't attract many buyers despite its message of goodwill. "How Can a Nice Girl Like You" made a little noise as a single with its reverse psychology lyrics, Little Sonny's charming, dragging tenor, and the Intruders' glowing harmonies. The Philly natives sparkle on four remakes: Marvin Gaye's "Jan," William DeVaughn's "Be Thankful for What You Got," Mary Wells' "What's Easy for Two Is So Hard for One," and Paul Simons "Rainy Days and Mondays"; they do justice to all, sounding especially frisky on DeVaughn's hit. "Plain Old Fashion Girl," co-written by Cary Gilbert, slams big city babes and gives props to old-fashioned country gals. Little Sonny shows his MOR skills on "Lonely, Lonely." The inspiring but mellow "Everybody Is a Star" grooves like "Be Thankful for What You Got," probably because John Davis produced both numbers. "Be on Time" is the only bummer; it must have been recorded for some type of community project, as it's a five-minute lecture about the virtues of being prompt for work, functions, dates, etc. *—Andrew Hamilton*

Philly Golden Classics / 1995 / Collectables ♦♦♦♦♦
This features all the great Intruders tracks uncut and digitally remastered; 112-plus minutes divvyed among 30 tracks. These light, peppy sounds are so arresting they play more quickly than their times. Diehards will lament the omissions of "I'm Girl Scoutin'," "Devil With an Angel's Smile," "Lollipop," "Give Her a Transplant," "Old Love," and some strong B-sides, but this is good and all that the Intruders' big fans will ever need. Little Sonny (Sam Brown) displays snake-charming ability via a sandpapery tenor, and Eugene Daughtery, Phil Terry, and Robert Edwards provide some of soul's most enjoyable harmonies. Check the pings in "A Love That's Real." *—Andrew Hamilton*

● **The Best of the Intruders: Cowboys to Girls** / Oct. 31, 1995 / Epic/Legacy ♦♦♦♦♦
The prototype for Gamble & Huff's classic Philly soul groups of the early '70s, the Intruders didn't spend much time in the pop Top 40—especially compared to heavy-hitters like the O'Jays or Harold Melvin & the Blue Notes—but their smooth performances and Gamble & Huff's strong arrangements usually triumphed over the occasional novelty-ridden nature of their songs. The title track, "Cowboys to Girls," isn't a novelty by any means; it's one of the paragons of soul music, a delicious blend of subtle strings, punchy brass, and crystal harmonies from the group, with Sam "Little Sonny" Brown's strong lead keeping it all together. The follow-up (and their only other Top 40 hit), "(Love Is Like A) Baseball Game," *was* a novelty, but a good one, as were the R&B hits "A Love That's Real" and "(Win, Place or Show) She's a Winner." At 20 tracks, *Cowboys to Girls: The Best of the Intruders* has room for all the Intruders' hits, including a few engaging latter-day entries like 1969's "Sad Girl" and 1970's "When We Get Married" (the latter during Bobby Starr's brief tenure at the head of the group). *—John Bush*

Philly Soul Rarities, Vol. 1 / Apr. 22, 1997 / Collectables ♦♦♦
These are Ben-Lee Productions, a company started in 1962 by Frank Bendinelli and writer/arranger Leroy Lovett in Philadelphia. The Intruders get top billing on this various artist's album for marketing purposes, but they only do two songs: the bouncy "I've Got Love for You" and "You're My One and Only Baby," a Leon Huff composition. Both are good early recordings of the group who hit high gear a few years later on Gamble Records. The most interesting aspect of this CD is the names of people who went on to greater things with Philadelphia International Records like the previously mentioned Intruders, Leon Huff, and Phil Hurtt (co-writer of "I'll Be Around"). Hurtt co-wrote two songs for the Masters with Andrew Smith: "Pretty One" and "Heresay." Cindy & the Cousins do two 16 magazine-type girl group songs: "What Are You Doin' to Me" and "I've Got News for You." Cindy is Cindy Scott (nee Sundray Tucker). Timmy Carr's featured on four songs, two as Timmy & the Empires and two as Timmy & the Persianettes. Carr's strident tenor shines on all four; unfortunately, he never did get that elusive hit record. *—Andrew Hamilton*

The Invisible Man's Band

Group / Dance-Pop
The Invisible Man's Band was made up of the Burke brothers (Clarence Jr., Dennis, James, and Keni), all former members of the Five Stairsteps, best known for their 1970 million seller "O-o-h Child." The Burkes' highest-charting single under this moniker was the chugging dance single "All Night Thing," which was issued on Island Records' Mango imprint and hit number nine R&B on *Billboard*'s charts in spring 1980.Their lone LP, *The Invisible Man's Band*, was issued in summer 1980. Other charting singles were "Really Wanna See You," released on Neil Bogart's Boardwalk Records (with whom the group had worked with during their Five Stairsteps days), and "Sunday Afternoon" on Move 'n' Groove. *—Ed Hogan*

● **The Invisible Man's Band** / 1980 / Mango ♦♦♦

Big Dee Irwin

b. 1939, New York, NY, **d.** Aug. 27, 1995, Las Vegas, NV
Vocals / Soul, Brill Building Pop
Big Dee Irwin first came to prominence in the Pastels, a group that sang doo wop during the 1950s. The New York City native, whose real name was Defosca Erwin (sometimes spelled Difosco Ervin), joined forces with three other young men to form the group in 1954 when all were stationed at a U.S. Air Force base in Greenland. Lead singer Irwin joined a talent competition held for servicemen, along with baritone Jimmy Willingham, first tenor Richard Travis, and second tenor Tony Thomas. When all four singers received orders that took them to Washington, D.C., Irwin & the Pastels began to entertain at nightspots that catered to servicemen, as well as at functions hosted by the USO. In 1957, after receiving a warm and encouraging response for their performance in an annual Air Force competition called Tops in Blue that was staged on the grounds of Mitchell Air Force Base in New York, Irwin and the others set out to land a recording contract. That summer they almost landed a deal with Central Records. Some sources say that Irwin and the Pastels actually did snag a long-term contract, but the group never made a record for the label. Instead, the Pastels landed on the doorstep of Hull Records. The four singers belted out "Been So Long," which Irwin had penned. With a few changes and some fine-tuning of the arrangement, the song was put out late in 1957 by Mascot, a division of Hull. "My One and Only Dream" landed on the flip side.

Irwin received his military discharge papers the following year. By that time, his fellow group members also had been released from duty, and "Been So Long" was doing extremely well on the charts. It reached the Top Five in R&B and crossed over to pop, where it landed at number 24. Irwin and the others embarked on a tour of the southern states of the U.S., including stops in Florida and Louisiana. By then, Chess Records had reissued the record on the Argo label. Irwin led the group through a succession of live shows around the country. Several were staged at the Apollo Theater in Harlem, where they shared the stage with the Deltones, Little Willie John, and others. At the Uptown Theater in Philly, they were part of the Georgie Woods Show' along with Chuck Berry, the Chantels, Little Joe & the Thrillers, among others. They also appeared in the lineup for concerts staged by rock & roll showman Alan Freed across the U.S., alongside such acts as Buddy Holly & the Crickets, Jerry Lee Lewis, Screamin' Jay Hawkins, the Diamonds, and Frankie Lymon. Irwin sang lead on the Pastels' next record, "You Don't Love Me Anymore," which was issued in 1958, as well as "So Far Away" six months later. Irwin and the Pastels returned to the Apollo for a week's worth of gigs that same year, the first on Halloween night.

When the Pastels fell apart the following year, Irwin remained in New York City to try for a solo career. Things started to click for him in 1963 when he recorded "Swinging on a Star" and headed to the U.K. for an extended tour. The refurbished Bing Crosby hit from 19 years earlier also featured vocals from Little Eva. She again joined the heavyset singer on "Happy Being Fat." Irwin continued to record as a solo artist for the remainder of the decade. In addition, he penned numbers for Isaac Hayes, Ray Charles, Bobby Womack, and the Hollies, who included his "What Kind of Boy" on their first full-length release. By the mid-'70s, he had reinvented himself as DiFosco and was recording disco for Roxbury. Heart failure claimed his life in 1995. *—Linda Seida*

● **Another Night With Big Dee Irwin** / May 5, 1998 / WestSide ✦✦✦✦

R&B baritone singer Big Dee Irwin came up thru the ranks, first as a member of the Pastels on Chess' Argo label, then with a spate of tunes under his own name while writing tunes for others in the Brill Building during the early 1960s. His tenure at Don Kirshner's Dimension Records is what's principally chronicled here, with 25 tracks going back to his pre-Dimension cuts for Hull, along with later ones for Roulette rounding out the package. His big hit "Swinging on a Star" is here, along with his Christmas duets with Little Eva ("The Christmas Song," "I Wish You a Merry Christmas") and equally strong material in the inclusion of "Another Night With the Boys," "Skeeter," "Soul Waltzing," "You're My Inspiration," the novelties "Happy Being Fat," "Everybody's Got a Dance But Me," and "Heigh Ho." Finishing out this package are some previously unissued Roulette tracks from the early 1960s including "The Mouse" and "Discotheque," showing Ervin's ability to keep up with the times while still turning out top-notch material. All in all, a great overview on a talented artist often overlooked. *—Cub Koda*

The Isley Brothers

f. 1954, Cincinnati, OH

Group / R&B, Frat Rock, Soul, Psychedelic Soul, Funk, Quiet Storm, Urban

First formed in the early '50s, the Isley Brothers enjoyed one of the longest, most influential, and most diverse careers in the pantheon of popular music—over the course of nearly a half century of performing, the group's distinguished history spanned not only two generations of Isley siblings but also massive cultural shifts which heralded their music's transformation from gritty R&B to Motown soul to blistering funk. The first generation of Isley siblings was born and raised in Cincinnati, OH, where they were encouraged to begin a singing career by their father, himself a professional vocalist, and their mother, a church pianist who provided musical accompaniment at their early performances. Initially a gospel quartet, the group was comprised of Ronald, Rudolph, O'Kelly and Vernon Isley; after Vernon's 1955 death in a bicycling accident, tenor Ronald was tapped as the remaining trio's lead vocalist.

In 1957, the brothers went to New York City to record a string of failed doo wop singles; while performing a spirited reading of the song "Lonely Teardrops" in Washington, D.C. two years later, they interjected the line "You know you make me want to shout," which inspired frenzied audience feedback. An RCA executive in the audience saw the concert, and when he signed the Isleys soon after, he instructed that their first single be constructed around their crowd-pleasing catch-phrase; while the call-and-response classic "Shout" failed to reach the pop Top 40 on its initial release, it eventually became a frequently-covered classic.

Still, success eluded the Isleys, and only after they left RCA in 1962 did they again have another hit, this time with their seminal cover of the Topnotes' "Twist and Shout." Like so many of the brothers' early R&B records, "Twist and Shout" earned greater commercial success when later rendered by a white group—in this case, the Beatles; other acts who notched hits by closely following the Isleys' blueprint were the Yardbirds ("Respectable," also covered by the Outsiders), the Human Beinz ("Nobody But Me"), and Lulu ("Shout"). During a 1964 tour, they recruited a young guitarist named Jimmy James to play in their backing band; James—who later shot to fame under his given name, Jimi Hendrix—made his first recordings with the Isleys, including the single "Testify," issued on the brothers' own T-Neck label. They signed to the Motown subsidiary Tamla in 1965, where they joined forces with the famed Holland-Dozier-Holland writing and production team. Their first single, the shimmering "This Old Heart of Mine (Is Weak for You)," was their finest moment yet, and barely missed the pop Top Ten.

"This Old Heart of Mine" was their only hit on Motown, however, and when the song hit number three in Britain in 1967, the Isleys relocated to England in order to sustain their flagging career; after years of writing their own material, they felt straitjacketed by the Motown assembly-line production formula, and by the time they returned stateside in 1969, they had exited Tamla to resuscitate the T-Bone label. Their next release, the muscular and funky "It's Your Thing," hit number two on the U.S. charts in 1969, and became their most successful record. That year, the Isleys also welcomed a number of new members as younger brothers Ernie and Marvin, brother-in-law Chris Jasper and family friend Everett Collins became the trio's new backing unit. Spearheaded by Ernie's hard-edged guitar leads, the group began incorporating more and more rock material into its repertoire as the 1970s dawned, and scored hits with covers of Stephen Stills' "Love the One You're With," Eric Burdon & War's "Spill the Wine" and Bob Dylan's "Lay Lady Lay."

In 1973, the Isleys scored a massive hit with their rock-funk fusion cover of their own earlier single "Who's That Lady," retitled "That Lady (Pt. 1);" the album *3 + 3* also proved highly successful, as did 1975's *The Heat Is On*, which spawned the smash "Fight the Power (Pt. 1)." As the decade wore on, the group again altered its sound to fit into the booming disco market; while their success on pop radio ran dry, they frequently topped the R&B charts with singles like 1977's "The Pride," 1978's "Take Me to the Next Phase (Pt. 1)," 1979's "I Wanna Be With You (Pt. 1)," and 1980's "Don't Say Goodnight." While the Isleys' popularity continued into the 1980s, Ernie and Marvin, along with Chris Jasper, defected in 1984 to form their own group, Isley, Jasper, Isley; a year later, they topped the R&B charts with "Caravan of Love."

On March 31, 1986, O'Kelly died of a heart attack; Rudolph soon left to join the ministry, but the group reunited in 1990. Although the individual members continued with solo work and side projects, the Isley Brothers forged on in one form or another throughout the decade; in 1996, now consisting of Ronald, Marvin and Ernie, they released the album *Mission to Please*. Ronald and Ernie hooked up several years later for *Eternal* (2001), a brand new selection of R&B cuts featuring collaborative efforts with Jill Scott, Jimmy Jam & Terry Lewis, and Raphael Saadiq. On that particular release, Ronald also introduced the alter-ego Mr. Biggs. *—Jason Ankeny*

Twist & Shout! / 1962 / Sundazed ✦✦✦

On this album, The Isleys tried to mine the "Twist & Shout" groove for all it was worth. Produced by Bert Berns, over half the material was written or co-written by "Russell"; the same Russell who co-wrote "Twist and Shout," it was a pseudonym for Berns himself. Not that this was always necessarily a bad thing; "Twist and Shout" was a stone classic, and many of the other tunes do their best to emulate its groove with Latin rhythms and The Isleys' frayed, gospelish vocals. Some of the tracks, though, do little more than rework the basic riff, and even the ones that aren't blatant rewrites don't measure up to the hit. The ballad "Time After Time" is a nice change of pace, and the brothers are never less than energetic and entertaining, but this is really not that strong as a whole. The CD reissue on Sundazed includes three bonus tracks: the previously unreleased (and unremarkable) "Crazy Love" and the cool singles "Twistin' With Linda" and "Nobody But Me," which are easily available on Rhino's *Story* compilation. *—Richie Unterberger*

Take Some Time out for the Isley Brothers / 1964 / T-Neck ✦✦✦

The Isley Brothers were slowly getting their act together in the mid-'60s. The vocal teamwork and harmonies had sharpened, and they began to move more in the direction of funk and rock as well as soul. This album didn't break them out, but was one of their better foundation efforts. *—Ron Wynn*

This Old Heart of Mine / 1966 / Motown ✦✦✦✦

A powerful set by the Isley Brothers, who tasted success with "Shout" and "Twist & Shout" before joining Motown. Brian Holland and Lamont Dozier produced the lion's share of tracks, and wrote most of them with the aid of Eddie Holland. An infectious "This Old Heart of Mine" took off—its throbbing beat, memorable melody and inspired vocals are as irresistible now as they were in 1966. The urgent "Take Some Time Out for Love," with its wailing vocals, made a little R&B noise; a creation of Robert Gordy and Thomas Kemp, it's one of two tracks not handled by Holland-Dozier-Holland. The other is the insightful, biblically titled "Seek and You Shall Find," done magnificently by Ron Isley, who sings the positive lyrics with understated fire. "I Guess I'll Always Love You" is a midtempo gem sung by Ron in his natural register, as he does all these songs; the sweet falsetto he used almost exclusively in the '80s and '90s is nowhere to be found. Isley versions of "Nowhere to Run," "Stop in the Name of Love," "Baby Don't You Do It" and "I Hear a Symphony" are comparable to, if not better than, the originals. *—Andrew Hamilton*

Soul on the Rocks / 1967 / Motown ✦✦✦

The group's final Motown album yielded one good song and hit, but otherwise was a summation of everything that went wrong while they were there. They never got the in-house support or push they needed, and by now were disillusioned and going through the motions. That was probably suitable, for most of what they sang here was routine anyhow. *—Ron Wynn*

The Brothers: Isley / 1969 / T-Neck ✦✦✦✦

The late '60s and early '70s remain a favorite period in the Isley Brothers evolution. Ronald sung hard, and brothers O'Kelly & Rudolph supplied church-inspired backing whoops to his lead. The tunes had catchy titles and creative, rhyming lyrics. This recording is loaded with that rocking, "It's Your Thing" style. "The Blacker the Berry the Sweeter Juice" isn't about fruit but speaks of the desirability of dark-complexioned women. "I Turned You On" has a grinding, churning rhythm; "sock it to me" was a catch phrase at the time and the Isleys included the popular phrase prominently in the song. "Feels Like the World" is a slow morbid statement about one's condition, while "Was It Good to You" is fast, fluid and asks the universal lover's question. A good period for the trio, Ron sung close to his natural register, which will please those who dislike the softer falsetto voice he fell in love with later. *—Andrew Hamilton*

It's Our Thing / 1969 / T-Neck ✦✦✦✦✦

A very important album for the Isley Brothers, 1969's *It's Our Thing* found Ronald, O'Kelly and Rudolph reviving their T-Neck label and marked the beginning of their association with Buddah (where they would remain until moving T-Neck to Epic/CBS in 1973). Creatively, this excellent LP put the siblings in the driver's seat—they did all of the producing and songwriting themselves—and they enjoyed the type of artistic freedom that they could only dream about when they were with Tamla/Motown from 1965-1968. At Tamla/Motown, Berry Gordy's team of producers and songwriters called the shots, but at T-Neck/Buddah, the Isleys' own vision was allowed to flourish. And that creative freedom made *It's Our Thing* a commercial triumph as well as an artistic one. The funky title track soared to number two on the R&B charts, and equally invigorating gems like "Give the Women What They Want" and "I Know Who You Been Socking It To" also went down in history as soul classics. Nor are tough, gritty album tracks like "He's Got Your Love" and "I Must Be Losing My Touch" anything to complain about. *It's Our Thing* made it clear that Tamla/Motown's loss was Buddah's gain. *—Alex Henderson*

Live at Yankee Stadium / 1969 / T-Neck ♦♦♦

Hot off the sales of their rocking, bouncing "It's Your Thing" and a slew of R&B hits like "I Turned You On," the Isley Brothers performed in concert at Yankee Stadium. They brought along some T-Neck Records underlings, such as Judy Clay and the Sweet Cherries, along with Brooklyn Bridge and the Five Stairsteps. All of the acts except the Five Stairsteps came out well on vinyl. The Stairsteps did "Don't Change Your Love," one of their weakest singles, and seemed to experience mike problems. Chirping an Isleys composition, "Love Is What You Make It," the Sweet Cherries were three foxy devils who sang like birds. The ladies were pictured in hot sequined mini-dresses on the album's cover. Judy White (Josh White's daughter) did a rousing version of her T-Neck release "Somebody's Been Messin' With My Thang," sounding sassy and sexy; Judy could belt 'em with the best of them. Blue-eyed soul singers Brooklyn Bridge, fronted by Johnny Maestro, got the crowd clapping with a spirited medley of Curtis Mayfield songs. The Isleys did a handful of their recent T-Neck sides, including "It's Your Thing" and "I Know Who You Been Socking It To"; no mike problems for them—their funky brand of soul comes through loud and clear. *—Andrew Hamilton*

Get Into Something / 1970 / T-Neck ♦♦♦

Another T-Neck release to receive reissue through Sony's Legacy division in the late '90s, *Get Into Something* boasts six Top 30 R&B chart hits. The first side serves up horn-inflected party jams, including the rousing title track and "Freedom," the latter of which sums up the record's overall uplifting theme of independence. The record isn't without its missteps—the sexist lyrics of "Take Inventory" are highly questionable: "Don't be so loyal and don't be so true/'cause if you are boy, they'll run over you." "Bless" is an obvious re-write of "It's Your Thing"; the Isleys would have been better off leaving that classic alone. A trio of ballads are offered up on the flip, including "I Got to Find Me One." A song of devotion, it pleads for "one girl who believes in me and wants to marry me." Call me crazy, but wouldn't marriage render the taking of inventory an impossibility? Though not revolutionary or trailblazing, *Get Into Something* is every bit an excellent and vibrant funk/soul record. *—Andy Kellman*

In the Beginning / 1970 / T-Neck ♦♦♦

These are the first offerings from the Isley's T-Neck record label, which many consider special because Jimi Hendrix played lead guitar. However, these tracks bombed as singles. "Testify" is noisy and congested, too much is going on. Hendrix's guitar is prominent, and identifies him as conclusively as an DNA sample. The Isley's imitate popular singers Stevie Wonder, Ray Charles and James Brown on "Testify," but the imitations are weak and sound like clones of each other. "Move Over and Let Me Dance" has some of "Testifys' " problems but works a little better, it has a danceable groove and a much better hook. The only soft selection is "The Last Girl," which has an airy sound, and features a rare laid-back vocal from Ron Isley during this phase of his career. Hendrix fans will love this, but fans of the Isley's later stuff will not be impressed. *—Andrew Hamilton*

Givin' It Back / 1971 / T-Neck ♦♦♦♦

Givin' It Back is as much a time capsule as an album. Not that it can't be enjoyed on its own absolute musical terms by someone just off a boat who wasn't even around in 1971, but to really appreciate how daring it was and how delightful it is, that side of its history should be known. Those who are old enough should recall the time whence it came, an era in which hatred and disunity over the Vietnam War, civil rights, school desegregation, the environment, and a multitude of other issues were threatening what seemed, potentially, like the beginning of a new civil war, this one not between states but between factions and ethnic and racial groups in 1,000 individual neighborhoods. The opening cut of *Givin' It Back*, "Ohio/Machine Gun," is a slap-in-your-face reminder of just how angry the times and the people were. The track evokes instant memories of the campus bloodshed of 1970, not just at Kent State but also the often-forgotten killings a few days later at Jackson State University in Mississippi, where the victims of a fusillade of sheriff's deputies' bullets were black students. More than that, the track itself is also a reminder of the divisions that existed on the left; to listen to pundits on the right, the anti-war and civil rights movements, along with the counterculture, were all part of one vast, organized, calculated left-wing conspiracy. The truth is that there was nearly as big a split, culturally and politically, between young blacks and young whites on the left and on college campuses as there was anywhere else in the population. Blacks reacting to years of oppression had little use for mostly middle-class white college students, however sympathetic many of them purported to be to their situation, while well-meaning white students and activists couldn't begin to know what privation of the kind experienced by blacks and Hispanics in most American towns and cities was. In music, too, there was a lot of division; blacks usually didn't resonate to the top artists in the white world and, in particular, were oblivious to (and even resentful of) the adoration accorded Jimi Hendrix by the white community. So, when the Isley Brothers—whose appeal among black audiences was unimpeachable—opened *Givin' It Back* with a conflation of Neil Young's "Ohio" and Jimi Hendrix's "Machine Gun," they were speaking to anger and bloodshed in the streets, but they were also performing an act of outreach that was about as radical as any they could have committed on record in 1971. That they incorporated a prayer into their reformulation of the two songs, amid Ernie Isley's and Chester Woodard's guitar pyrotechnics, turned it into one of the most powerful and personal musical statements of its era, and it's worth the price of the album just for the one cut. *Givin' It Back* is filled with virtues of that kind, however; it was the first Isley Brothers album to rely entirely on outside material, but the group's reworkings of songs by James Taylor ("Fire and Rain") and Stephen Stills ("Love the One You're With") show no lack of originality. They're unafraid to take the song apart and rebuild it from the ground up, smoothing Bob Dylan's "Lay Lady Lay" into a sensual soul ballad, turning the James Taylor number into a sweaty, earnest shouter, and transforming War's "Spill the Wine" into an extended workout for voices, electric guitars (several layers deep), flute, and percussion. The album was also an early showcase for Bill Withers, whose funky blues "Cold Bologna" is covered by the group with the composer—who was about to emerge as a major star in his own right—on guitar. And the closer, "Love the One You're With," is sent soaring to heights that the Stephen Stills original could only gaze up at. *Givin' It Back* is often held at arm's length by soul listeners, who don't regard it as central to what the Isley Brothers or their music are about; on the contrary, the group is so successful at remaking all of the songs here their own in style and approach and sending careful messages (alas, largely lost with the passage of time) in their selection as well as their content, that it really represents a lot of what the Isley Brothers and soul music were about in 1971, and it's still great listening. Reissued in 1997 by Sony with new notes, and worth every cent of its list price. *—Bruce Eder*

Brother, Brother, Brother / 1972 / T-Neck ♦♦♦♦

With 1972's *Brother, Brother, Brother*, younger brothers Ernie and Marvin, along with in-law relative Chris Jasper, began to play major roles in the groups' sound. This also marked their first attempt to Isleyize classics made famous by others. Their rendition of Carole King's "It's Too Late" rivals the original, Ron Isley sings the tender ballad in a softer voice then he used on previous recordings. An update of Jackie Shannon's "Put a Little Love in Your Heart" is an uplifter. They didn't completely alienate fans of their harsher sound, the rocking, humorous "Pop That Thang" and "Lay Away" are fine examples of R&B/Rock. "Pop That Thang" has a sloopy beat and biting lyrics, while "Lay Away" takes off on the popular buying option before the advent of the credit card. The Isleys were big Carole King fans, in addition to "It's Too Late," they perform two other King songs, "Brother, Brother" and "Keep on Walkin'." The latter is coupled with "Sweet Season." Their own "Work to Do" is a stone rocker that has been recorded by many, including the Average White Band, who scored big with the cooker 30 years after its release, it remains one of the Isley Brothers' most requested songs. *—Andrew Hamilton*

☆ **3 + 3** / 1973 / T-Neck ♦♦♦♦♦

Recorded in 1973, *3 + 3* was a major turning point for the Isley Brothers. With this album, the Isleys moved their T-Neck label from Buddah to Epic/CBS (which became Epic/Sony in the early '90s), and it was at Epic that they unveiled their new lineup. Lead singer Ronald Isley and his siblings O'Kelly and Rudolph remained, but the Isleys became a sextet instead of a trio when cousin Chris Jasper and younger brothers Ernie and Marvin were added. This new lineup was called 3 + 3, and the addition of Jasper on keyboards, Ernie on guitar, and Marvin on bass added exciting new elements to the Isleys' sound. One of finest R&B bassists of the 1970s, the ever-so-funky Marvin is in a class with heavy-weights like Larry Graham and Louis Johnson—and Ernie is a stunning guitarist who is heavily influenced by Jimi Hendrix but has a distinctive style of his own. The Isleys had always been lovers of rock, but with the addition of Ernie, their sound became even more overtly rock-influenced. Nonetheless, the rock and pop elements didn't alienate R&B audiences, which ate this album up. The single "That Lady" (which is based on an Impressions-like gem they had recorded in 1964) was a major hit, and the Isleys are equally captivating on soul interpretations of Seals & Crofts' "Summer Breeze," James Taylor's "Don't Let Me Be Lonely Tonight," and the Doobie Brothers' "Listen to the Music." With this superb album, the Isley Brothers sounded better than ever—and they gained a lot of new fans without sacrificing the old ones. *—Alex Henderson*

The Isleys Live / 1973 / Rhino ♦♦♦♦♦

The Isleys Live is one of the finest funk/soul live albums ever recorded. The first eight tracks come from club gigs in 1971 and 1972, while the last three are from a 1969 show at Yankee Stadium. The group's biggest and most identifiable hit, "It's Your Thing," is featured twice, each version extremely inspired. But the most interesting thing about *The Isleys Live* is the inclusion of several cover songs, such as Carole King's "It's Too Late," Neil Young's "Ohio," Bob Dylan's "Lay Lady Lay," and Stephen Stills' "Love the One You're With." The covers aren't straight-ahead rock readings, either; the Isleys inject their own funk 'n' soul into them, making the songs their own. The album is also a showcase for the talents of the woefully underrated guitarist Ernie Isley, who simply wails on a cover of Jimi Hendrix's "Machine Gun," and plays fantastically throughout. *The Isleys Live* received the makeover treatment in 1996 by Rhino Records, who remastered the whole disc and lengthened it with several extra selections not included on the original. *—Greg Prato*

Live It Up / 1974 / T-Neck ♦♦♦♦

One of the many classic albums the Ohio natives recorded. This set features two uptempo numbers: the title track "Live It Up" and "Midnight Sky." The former is a soulful funk track paced by a humpin' bassline, robust background vocals, and Ernie Isley's electrifying guitar solos. It checked in at number four on the *Billboard* R&B charts. The latter is a smoother dance number in which Ronald Isley's vocals go from a cool, calm delivery to a resolute clamor. It peaked at number eight. Both have lengthy vamps, ideal for parties. As for the romance, "Hello It's Me" and "Brown Eyed Girl" are two gems. "Hello It's Me" is the classic ballad. Ronald Isley's melodic intro is mesmerizing as he finesses the lyric "Hello," which sets the tone for this beautiful number. His artistic interpretation of the lyric is demonstrated without blemish. This song was formerly recorded by Todd Rundgren who also wrote it. "Brown Eyed Girl" is a midtempo number that's seasoned with a folk-like guitar and the rich vocals of Ronald Isley. Neither single was ever a release, but today both are radio regulars. *—Craig Lytle*

The Heat Is On / 1975 / T-Neck ♦♦♦♦♦

The *The Heat Is On*, from 1975, was the third album that the Isley Brothers recorded with their 3 + 3 lineup, and by that time, the lineup had really perfected its attractive soul/rock sound. The Isleys were providing great R&B long before keyboardist Chris Jasper, bassist Marvin Isley, and the distinctive guitarist Ernie Isley came on board in 1973; nonetheless, the newcomers added a lot to the group and helped it provide some of its best recordings. Marvin's basslines are as funky as it gets, and the Jimi Hendrix-influenced Ernie is a killer guitarist; he would have been perfect for Deep Purple, Blue Öyster Cult, or Judas Priest if the Isley Brothers hadn't kept him busy in the 1970s. One of the 3 + 3 gems that no Isleys fans should be without is *The Heat Is On*, which is best known for the sweaty funk classic "Fight the Power" and the sexy quiet storm slow jam "For the Love of You." Lead vocalist Ronald Isley is as convincing on the funk scorchers as he is on caressing ballads like "Make Me Say It Again Girl" and "Sensuality." Meanwhile, "Hope You Feel Better Love" is brilliant because it contrasts those two sides of the *3 + 3* lineup—the verses are sweetly melodic, but the chorus is forceful and explosive. Superb from start to finish, *The Heat Is On* is among the Isleys' most essential albums. *—Alex Henderson*

Harvest for the World / 1976 / T-Neck ✦✦✦✦
The Isley Brothers came with love, funk and the too seldom mentioned socially conscious songs; this album is titled after one of those social gems. However, "Who Loves You Better," with its disco flair, was the album's first release. Ronald Isley's aggressive delivery blends nicely with Ernie Isley's tantalizing guitar solos. It was a top three single on the *Billboard* R&B charts. The title track is a *tour de force*. Preceded by a mellow intro in which Ronald Isley's earnest plea rings with urgency, the timeless lyric and festive rhythm make "Harvest for the World" a welcomed anthem for all the people of the world. It cracked the *Billboard* R&B top ten at number nine. Ronald Isley changes his tone on some of these compositions by adding a roughness to his still smooth tenor, like on the relentless jams "People of Today" and "You Wanna Stay Down." Then there are those priceless ballads like "Let Me Know" and "Let Me Down Easy"; Ronald Isley sweetly caresses the lyric with compassion and agility. Neither of these two selections were releases but remain staples on R&B radio. *—Craig Lytle*

Go for Your Guns / 1977 / T-Neck ✦✦✦✦
Every ten years the Isley Brothers reinvented themselves and managed to snatch enough consumer dollars and generate enough chart action to remain contemporary. *Go for Your Guns* was a further attempt by the Isleys to broaden their fan base; earlier in the decade they redid many rock standards to expand from the R&B base they were mired in. The Isleys shoot for the moon, never make it, but always land among the stars. This seven-song set got played to death on urban radio. "Living in the Life" rocks so hard it makes cheap speakers pop; "Go for Your Guns" is an instrumental jam featuring the second generation Isley brothers: Ernie, Marvin, and Chris Jasper (Rudolph Isley's brother-in-law). The lovely, mystical "Voyage to Atlantis" is a staple of their live concerts, its opening strains acknowledged by deafening, enthusiastic applause. Like many Isley tunes, the loping, midtempo love tale "Footsteps in the Dark" has been sampled silly; "Pride" is a steady beater with uplifting words for the downtrodden. Nothing dull, no filler. *—Andrew Hamilton*

Showdown / 1978 / T-Neck ✦✦✦✦
The Isley Brothers' 3 + 3 lineup only lasted about ten years, which isn't that long when you consider that the group was formed in 1954 (19 years before the 3 + 3 lineup was unveiled) and was still touring in the late '90s. By 1980, you were hearing more and more complaints about how formulaic the 3 + 3 lineup had become, but when *Showdown* came out in 1978, the lineup hadn't lost any of its freshness. *Showdown*, in fact, is generally excellent. The Isleys bring a great deal of passion to funk/rock scorchers like "Rockin' With Fire," "Love Fever," and the number-one hit "Take Me to the Next Phase," and they are equally appealing on the smooth, caressing slow jam "Groove With You" (another major hit). Meanwhile, the slow-burning "Ain't Givin' Up No Love" is one of the most bluesy things that the 3 + 3 sextet recorded. 1977's *Go for Your Guns*, the album that preceded *Showdown*, was an incredibly tough act to follow. But even if *Showdown* isn't quite in a class with that treasure, it comes impressively close. *—Alex Henderson*

Winner Takes All / 1979 / T-Neck ✦✦✦
This was originally released as a two-album set, which reflected how popular the group was during this period of time. It features some rather lengthy but entertaining pieces. Ronald Isley's silky tenor remains untarnished throughout the album. "I Wanna Be with You" made its claim on the *Billboard* R&B charts, peaking at number one. "Winner Takes All" and "It's a Disco Night" followed in that order and only managed a 38 and 27 showing on the charts, respectively. Decent songs they are, but not as explosive as some of the Isley Brothers previously released uptempo numbers. As danceable as they, they come closer to good-listening songs. However, there are three solid ballads: "Let's Fall in Love," "How Lucky I Am" and "You're the Key to My Heart." Not one ever made a chart appearance, but all three remain popular to radio. *—Craig Lytle*

Go All the Way / 1980 / T-Neck ✦✦✦
Although regarded as the beginning of their decline, this 1980 album did get the Isley Brothers three more chart hits. But they were so locked into their uptempo dance/R&B, ballad, rock guitar solo format that each LP became more and more predictable. The internal difficulties that finally tore the group apart were also surfacing with this album. *—Ron Wynn*

Grand Slam / 1981 / T-Neck ✦✦✦
Despite getting three more hits, including one Top Ten R&B song, the bloom was definitely off the Isley Brothers' rose. Stagnation and internal bickering were taking their toll, and the innocent, energetic air that sparked their '70s albums was gone. It had been replaced by a calculating, indifferent attitude that clearly affected their music. *—Ron Wynn*

Between the Sheets / 1983 / T-Neck ✦✦✦
Compared to their past material, this album lacks the consistent mix of sultry ballads and funky dance numbers. There are really only two Isley Brothers' classics on this project: "Choosey Lover" and the title song "Between the Sheets." The former has a romantic flow and the latter is just shy of midtempo but not a bona fide ballad. When one thinks of a quiet thundering storm, this song's bassline comes to mind. As soothing as it is, it also has that trembling affect. It fell short of number one peaking at three on the *Billboard* R&B charts. "Choosey Lover" has that charismatic appeal. After scores and scores of recording sessions, Ronald Isley's vocals maintain that zeal. It was becoming obvious that the group continuity was fading. Not so much from dissension within the group, but more so from dwindling interest in the music industry among group members, this was the group's last album as 3 + 3. Marvin and Ernie Isley and their brother-in-law Chris Jasper would release an album the following year as Isley/Jasper/Isley. *—Craig Lytle*

Smooth Sailin' / 1987 / Warner Bros. ✦✦✦
This was the first album the Isley Brothers made after O'Kelly suffered a heart attack and died in 1986. It's both poignant and painful, because Ronnie demonstrates the vocal presence and soulful character that always made his ballads so vital. Angela Winbush, who later became Ronnie Isley's wife, served as background vocalist, co-composer, and producer. *—Ron Wynn*

Spend the Night / 1989 / Warner Bros. ✦✦✦
They were down to a duo by the time this record was released. O'Kelly Isley had died of a heart attack a couple of years earlier. Ronnie Isley was the featured vocalist, and he still had a soaring, dynamic sound. Angela Winbush, whom he later married and who also served as manager, worked closely on the album, but the magic was clearly gone. At times, listening to this album was a chore for any longtime Isley Brothers follower. *—Ron Wynn*

Shout!: The Complete Victor Sessions / 1991 / RCA ✦✦✦✦
The Isley Brothers' year-long stay (1959-1960) on the RCA Victor label has long had the reputation for uneven results, as well as being something of a mystery to all but hardcore fans, mostly owing to the fact that the majority of it was barely available until well into the CD era. Beyond "Shout" and "Respectable," none of what they released for the label ever made an impact, and both of those songs are much better known in recordings by other acts, including Joey Dee & the Starliters and the Outsiders. The group more properly should have been on the company's Vik Records subsidiary, which was more oriented toward R&B, rather than working under the aegis of producers Hugo Peretti and Luigi Creatore at Victor, who evidently saw the trio as a potential crossover pop act in the same manner that they would later treat Sam Cooke. As this CD demonstrates, the fit was an awkward one at times, the trio trying to transform pure pop like "I'm Gonna Knock on Your Door" into R&B, attempting (without success) to overcome the presence of a pop string section on "Not One Minute More," stumbling through "St. Louis Blues," and wasting a lot of good effort on "Gypsy Love Song." Still, the good moments outnumber the bad—"Tell Me Who," "When the Saints Go Marching In," "Ring-A-Ling-A-Ling (Let the Wedding Bells Ring)," "That Lucky Old Sun," and even "Rock Around the Clock" show them in excellent form, if not exactly breaking new ground. What's more, there are some genuine musical delights buried among these 19 tracks, in the form of Irving Berlin's "How Deep Is the Ocean," which is given a beat and arrangement very close to that of "Respectable," and "Without a Song," which is made to sound a lot like Jackie Wilson's "Lonely Teardrops." This was the second RCA CD devoted to the Isley Brothers and is preferable to its 1991 predecessor simply based on its improved sound quality, and for the presence of two very different versions of "Respectable," both the fine album rendition and the more raucous and passionate single version. Serious fans, however, might want to spring for the Bear Family CD of the very same material, containing as it does more thorough session information. *—Bruce Eder*

Tracks of Life / 1991 / Warner Bros. ✦✦✦
After spending the late '80s as a duo consisting of Ronald and Rudy Isley, the Isley Brothers become a trio again with Rudy's departure and the return of siblings Ernie and Marvin. Though not on a par with such classic '70s albums as *Go for Your Guns*, *The Heat Is On* and *Showdown*, *Tracks of Life* is a solid and respectable collection that benefits greatly from Angela Winbush's contributions to the songwriting. Ron sounds genuinely inspired on everything from the driving synth-funk of "Get My Licks In" and "No Axe to Grind" to sexy ballads and slow jams like "Bedroom Eyes," "Sensitive Lover" and "Lost in Your Love." With its subtle references to bondage, "Whatever Turns You On" is tastefully kinky. To be sure, the CD has its flaws—Ron and Winbush's producing could have been less high-tech, and it's disappointing that a guitarist as magnificent as Ernie has so little room. But on the whole, the album makes it clear that in the '90s, the Isleys could still captivate. *—Alex Henderson*

Greatest Hits & Rare Classics / Feb. 1991 / Motown ✦✦✦✦✦
Although the Isleys recorded some good stuff for Motown in the late '60s, it's generally true that the label's attempts to fit them into the standard Motown production line inhibited their creativity and individuality. This 22-track retrospective of their Motown days is dominated by material from in-house songwriters like Eddie Holland, Smokey Robinson, and Ivory Joe Hunter and doesn't rank among the Isleys' best work, though it's respectable enough. The best tracks—the Top Ten hit "This Old Heart of Mine," "Behind a Painted Smile," and "Take Some Time out for Love"—are available on the Rhino best-of, but Isleys fans will find this a worthwhile summary of their brief Motown stay. Includes the original versions of two of their biggest hits cut for other labels, "Twist and Shout" and "It's Your Thing." *—Richie Unterberger*

The Complete UA Sessions / Mar. 26, 1991 / EMI America ✦✦✦✦
United Artists Records was one of about a half-dozen labels that the Isley Brothers were signed to during their first seven years, and all 20 tracks that they left behind (four of them previously unissued) appear on this CD. That makes this disc especially valuable, as only a single United Artists track made it onto Sony's three-CD retrospective on the group, and also very frustrating, as it is out of print as of 2002. In contrast to their RCA Victor sides, some of which tended toward pop, the group's United Artists records were

solidly ensconced in soul music—loud, raw, pounding, exuberant, yet often melodic and always memorable, and rousing from front to back, without a clinker in the bunch. Their music here initially evolved directly out of their Wand Records hits "Twist and Shout" and "Twistin' With Linda," but quickly moved beyond the somewhat predictable (though delightful) "Surf and Shout." Jimi Hendrix joined the Isley Brothers' backing group as lead guitarist during their stay at United Artists, but even before his arrival, there was good, solid punchy guitar to be heard on jaunty, rocking numbers like "Stagger Lee." Juxtaposed with the latter is the gloriously lyrical ballad "You'll Never Leave Him," showing off a soft harmony side to the trio's singing that was frequently overlooked in favor of their dance numbers; they also add more variety to the singing on Hank Ballard's "Let's Go, Let's Go, Let's Go" than most listeners thought the song was capable of containing, and with a gorgeous sax solo in the middle to boot. Their versions of "Long Tall Sally" and "Do the Twist" showed more vocal embellishment than either song was usually given, and surrounding those covers are beautiful originals like "My Little Girl" (which also shows up in a faster-tempo alternate take), offering the purest soaring harmonies and a beat that borrows very creatively from "Stand by Me," and shattering, pounding, gospel-tinged ballads like "Lord Open Up Her Eyes." The latter dates from January 14, 1964, the one United Artists session to include Hendrix in the band, and assuming that it is him playing, his contributions are much less flashy than one would expect; he's out there a tiny bit on a pair of previously unissued instrumentals, "The Basement" and "Conch," but otherwise plays in only a slightly more animated manner than most of his contemporaries. The sound is good if not exceptional, and the annotation offers the most extensive career-wide history of the group available on any anthology of their work. There's also a very handy discography that goes far beyond the boundaries of their United Artists releases. *—Bruce Eder*

★ **The Isley Brothers Story, Vol. 1: Rockin' Soul (1959–68)** / Apr. 2, 1991 / Rhino ✦✦✦✦✦
When Sony/Legacy decided to reassert control of the Isley Brothers' catalog, it sent Rhino's excellent two-volume set *The Isley Brothers Story* out of print. Unfortunately, thus far, Legacy hasn't done nearly as good a job re-compiling the Isleys' catalog in any coherent fashion, meaning that if you can track down the Rhino anthologies somehow, you'll be much better off. *The Isley Brothers Story, Vol. 1: Rockin' Soul* is a single-disc overview of their R&B material (20 tracks in all) prior to their metamorphosis into a self-contained funk band. In reality, 1959-1968 were uneven years for the Isleys, who leaped from style to style and label to label, cutting records of variable quality. But their best moments could be positively transcendent, and the neat trick of *Vol. 1* is that it makes the group sound as though they could do no wrong, no matter what they tried. Spinning through gospel-drenched call-and-response tunes, twist-craze dance records, smoother Chicago-style soul, and even a stint on Motown, the collection holds together surprisingly well, thanks to the group's own frenzied energy. Ronald Isley's unhinged leads, and the chemistry he and his brothers share, will make you wonder why the Isleys aren't mentioned as early architects of soul music more often. That's especially true on the call-and-response insanity of cuts like "Shout" and "Testify," where the group works itself up into a raucous frenzy of screams, cries, and wails, all taken at a mind-blowingly manic pace. But their chemistry enlivens everything here, even the smoother and more produced Motown material; in fact, that helps make "This Old Heart of Mine (Is Weak for You)" one of the label's all-time greatest moments. Interesting trivia: "Who's That Lady" was later transformed into the funk smash "That Lady," and "Testify" marks one of the earliest recordings by a young Jimi Hendrix. *—Steve Huey*

★ **The Isley Brothers Story, Vol. 2: The T-Neck Years (1969–85)** / Apr. 2, 1991 / Rhino ✦✦✦✦✦
When Sony/Legacy decided to reassert control of the Isley Brothers' catalog, it sent Rhino's excellent two-volume set *The Isley Brothers Story* out of print. Unfortunately, thus far, Legacy hasn't done nearly as good a job re-compiling the Isleys' catalog in any coherent fashion, meaning that if you can track down the Rhino anthologies somehow, you'll be much better off. *The Isley Brothers Story, Vol. 2: The T-Neck Years* is a double-disc look at the group's transformation from a vocal R&B group into a self-contained, instrumentally proficient funk band—simply by adding more family members. After landing a comeback hit with 1969's "It's Your Thing," the core trio of Isleys added younger brothers Ernie (guitar) and Marvin (bass), plus cousin Chris Jasper on keyboards. Together they crafted a loose, jam-friendly brand of funk that could be sweet and smooth or swirling and trippy, loaded with group vocals, Hendrix-style guitar, and bubbling synths. There's a little bit of jazz in the chord progressions, and a whole lot of rock feeling in the grooves, which have been heavily sampled over the years by hip-hoppers. Early in this phase, the group underlined its debt to rock by covering pop and rock tunes, represented here by "Love the One You're With," "Spill the Wine," and "Summer Breeze" (no "Lay Lady Lay," however). As time progressed, the Isleys made a few concessions to the discotheque, but never radically altered their blueprint. By the time the collection winds up with the Isley/Jasper/Isley spinoff group's 1985 R&B smash "Caravan of Love," it's clear that the Isleys' seemingly endless adaptability was no mere fluke—at their best, they had a genuine feel for just about any new trend that contemporary R&B could throw at them. *—Steve Huey*

Mission to Please / 1996 / Island ✦✦✦✦
On their second album of the '90s, the Isley Brothers capitalize on the smooth love ballads epitomized by crooners like Babyface, Keith Sweat, and R. Kelly. Since all three of those artists were influenced by the Isleys' classic '70s records, they were willing to come on board to produce and co-write *Mission to Please*. The new blood reinvigorates the Isleys and the album is one of their strongest efforts of the latter part of their career. *Mission to Please* is devoted to the group's sensual side—it's all ballads, no funk. And that's not a bad thing at all. Ronald still has a smoldering, seductive voice and Ernie is such a gifted, sympathetic guitarist that he can pull magic out of pedestrian material. Thankfully, he doesn't need to prove the truth in that statement on *Mission to Please*. The majority of the songs on the album are first-rate contemporary '90s R&B and those that aren't quite as strong make for pleasing filler. As a result, *Mission to Please* is a testament to the talents of not only the Isley Brothers, but also their far-reaching influence—they are fortunate to have given inspiration to such gifted songwriters and musicians as Babyface, R. Kelly, and Keith Sweat. *—Stephen Thomas Erlewine*

It's Your Thing: The Story of the Isley Brothers / Aug. 24, 1999 / Epic/Legacy ✦✦✦✦✦
Divided into two volumes and spanning three discs, Rhino's 1991 compilation *The Isley Brothers Story* was the definitive retrospective of the groundbreaking R&B outfit, containing all of the hits plus key album tracks. Epic/Legacy's similarly titled *It's Your Thing: The Story of the Isley Brothers* attempts to best that record by offering a three-disc box set, filled with all the hits, plus an abundance of rarities. As a matter of fact, in order to differentiate this box from the previous retrospective, the compilers leaned a little too heavily on rarities, putting on alternate takes, live cuts, and outtakes with abandon, sequencing them between the hits and album tracks (at times, this even results in songs repeated back to back, as when "Shout" is followed by a live performance of the same song). All this is worthy material and will certainly be of interest to collectors. On the other hand, they weigh down the collection somewhat for less dedicated listeners. They hardly ruin the set, which is quite useful for anyone that wants a comprehensive hits and highlights collection, but compared to the earlier Rhino set, it isn't as engaging or exciting a listen. Ironically, by trying to outdo *The Isley Brothers Story* as a historical piece, it undercuts the band slightly—on the Rhino set, the Isleys always seem as if they're bursting vitality. That same music still sounds extraordinary here, but the context is somewhat a little too studied to replicate that same sense of dynamism. It's still a worthy set, but *It's Your Thing* nevertheless remains in the shadow of *The Isley Brothers Story*. *—Stephen Thomas Erlewine*

Shake It Up, Baby: Shout, Twist and Shout / Mar. 21, 2000 / Varese ✦✦✦✦
If you've been collecting Isley Brothers compilations over the years, you might not be enthused at the prospect of getting "Shout," "Twist and Shout," "Nobody But Me," "Respectable," and "Twistin' With Linda" for the second or third time. Indeed, 12 of these 16 cuts show up on Sundazed's reissue of the *Twist and Shout* album. That consideration aside, this is a good compilation of their early years, spanning the late 1950s to the early 1960s, and focusing mostly on the sides they cut for Wand. In fact, it's all from Wand, except for the key early RCA sides "Shout" and "Respectable"; there's nothing from their UA or T-Neck sessions. Overall, this collection represents the Isleys at their most untamed and gospel-R&B-informed, though it's definitely rock & roll, with a pop appeal added by New York production and outside songwriters like Bert Berns. As for the sides you might not have yet on CD if you're an Isley Brothers fan, the two to look out for are their nice cover of "Make It Easy on Yourself" (which wasn't released until it showed up on an Ace import in 1990) and the upbeat, so-so 1964 single "I'm Laughing to Keep From Crying." *—Richie Unterberger*

The Ultimate Isley Brothers / Oct. 17, 2000 / Epic/Legacy ✦✦✦✦✦
The Isley Brothers have had such a long and varied career that trying to sum up their highlights in a best-of package is bound to fall short of the mark. That hasn't, of course, kept people from trying to do so, in both single-disc and multi-disc sets. Every song on this 17-song, single-disc anthology was a hit. Yet it's so chronologically unbalanced, and so debatably chosen, as to be nothing more than a trek though some of their most commercially successful releases, entirely omitting many of their finest songs and severely short-changing their vital (and extensive) pre-1970 output. The pre-"It's Your Thing" era is represented by just two tracks, "Twist and Shout" and "Shout," omitting not just bona fide hits like "This Old Heart of Mine," but great cuts like "Nobody But Me" and "Testify." As a survey of their 1970s and early-'80s hits this does a more reasonable job. But still, few would agree that their cover of Seals & Crofts' "Summer Breeze," for instance, is among their best 17 songs, even if it did make number ten on the R&B listings in 1973. One good thing this collection *does* manage to do is include their cool 1971 cover of "Spill the Wine," which somehow did not make it onto the three-CD 1999 box set, *It's Your Thing: The Story of the Isley Brothers*. Other than "Spill the Wine," every song here appears on that box set, which is a recommended alternative if you can cough up a little more dough. Or better yet, try to find Rhino's two-volume, three-CD *Story* series, which not only has better selection and packaging than the Epic/Legacy collections, but sensibly divides the pre-"It's Your Thing" era and the post-"It's Your Thing" era into separate installments. *—Richie Unterberger*

Eternal / Aug. 7, 2001 / DreamWorks ✦✦✦
Within seconds of listening to "Move Your Body," the opener to *Eternal*, the latest by the Isley Brothers, audiences will easily agree—the forefathers of *boudoir faire* still have it. Forty years in the business have not chiseled away at the talented brothers: Ronald Isley's falsetto is unwavering and remains inimitable in 2001, when the R&B market is saturated. Ernie Isley soars on guitar—"Ernie's Jam" showcases the brother playing soulful and tasty solos, à la "Jimi Hendrix"—adding further sexiness to this already sensual disc. Cheaters are blatantly busted on the slithering "Contagious," where the rogue-lover is caught in the act. The words coming from the jilted are so vivid and painful. Ronald specifically describes walking toward the bedroom, hearing his lover crying out someone else's name. Ouch. While it's all about sex and pleasing a lover on the arousing "Just Like This," the disc is not just skin on skin. The album poignantly explores commitment on such romantic slow jams as "You're All I Need," "Settle Down," and the title track. An impressive roster of collaborators—writers, performers, and producers—grace *Eternal* and they span old-school and modern R&B players such as R. Kelly, Jimmy Jam, Terry Lewis, and Jill Scott. There is nothing groundbreaking on this recording, however, the longtime

R&B legends prove they're still very much worth their salt and can keep up very well with the Joneses. Indeed, the Isley Brothers are eternal. *—Liana Jonas*

Isley/Jasper/Isley

f. 1984, **db.** 1987

Group / Urban

A spin-off from the Isley Brothers, bassist Marvin Isley, drummer/guitarist Ernie Isley, and their keyboardist cousin Chris Jasper worked in the Isley Brothers 3 + 3 band from 1969 until 1984. They signed with Columbia as a separate entity at that time, and had substantial success with their debut LP *Broadway's Closer to Sunset Boulevard.* Their 1985 release *Caravan of Love* included their only R&B chart-topping single in the title cut, which had a three-week reign at number one. They scored three other Top 20 singles in 1986 and 1987, "Insatiable Woman," "8th Wonder of the World," and "Givin' You Back the Love." *—Ron Wynn*

Broadway's Closer to Sunset Blvd. / 1985 / CBS ✦✦

Isley/Jasper/Isley's debut release boasted the Top 14 R&B smash "Look the Other Way," as well as two stepper favorites: the "Between the Sheets"-like ballad "Serve You Right" and the samba-tinged "I Can't Get Over Losing You." Keyboardist Chris Jasper's fluid dexterity is displayed on the pulsating "Sex Drive" and light pop sensibilities on the shimmering "Love's Gonna Last Forever." *—Ed Hogan*

● **Caravan of Love** / 1985 / Epic ✦✦✦✦✦

The splinter group of Ernie and Marvin Isley, plus their cousin Chris Jasper, departed from the Isley Brothers 3 + 3 conglomerate in 1984, and for a while seemed ready to enjoy their own success. The album's title track topped the R&B charts and was an international smash; it was later covered by the Housemartins. But the trio began to suffer its own personality and direction conflicts and wouldn't survive them. *—Ron Wynn*

Different Drummer / 1987 / Epic ✦✦✦

The final album of three issued by the second generation of Isleys was a disappointment, and was marred by the personality problems and artistic differences that caused the original 3 + 3 group to disband. The singing was perfunctory, the production and arrangements routine, and they got little mileage from any of the material. *—Ron Wynn*

Ernie Isley

b. Mar. 7, 1952, Cincinnati, OH

Vocals, Drums, Guitar / Funk, Pop/Rock, Urban, Soul

Guitarist/drummer/singer/songwriter Ernie Isley infused the Isley Brothers with a Jimi Hendrix-like virtuosity that took the veteran R&B group into a more rockin' direction, earning 11 gold and five platinum albums. Later as a member of Isley/Jasper/Isley, he sang lead on the R&B hit "Look the Other Way" and scored a number-one R&B hit with "Caravan of Love." Born March 7, 1952, in Cincinnati, OH, Ernie grew up watching his older brothers Ronald, Rudolph, and O'Kelly have such hits as "Shout," "Twist and Shout," and "This Old Heart of Mine." Around this time, he and his brothers moved to New Jersey. After hearing José Feliciano's 1968 classic, "Light My Fire," he picked up the guitar. Completing music studies at C.W. Post College in Long Island, NY, Ernie joined the Isley Brothers. He made his debut on their *3 + 3* LP issued in summer 1973. That was the beginning of a string of hit albums that spanned 13 years.

In 1984, the group split and Chris Jasper and the younger Isleys, Ernie and Marvin, formed the trio Isley/Jasper/Isley. They got a custom deal with CBS Associated Labels with their first release, the self-produced *Broadway's Closer to Sunset Boulevard.* It yielded the number-14 R&B hit "Look the Other Way." The title track of their next LP, *Caravan of Love*, parked in the number-one R&B spot for three weeks.

The final Isley/Jasper/Isley album was *Different Drummer.* Soon afterward, the group disbanded. Ernie recorded a 1990 Elektra LP, *High Wire,* that was a fine display of amazing guitar skills. In the late '90s, he reunited with Ronald Isley and they began touring as the Isley Brothers, performing a memorable outdoor concert televised on *The Oprah Winfrey Show.* They also scored a platinum-plus-selling album with *Mission to Please.* *—Ed Hogan*

● **High Wire** / 1990 / Elektra ✦✦✦✦✦

An astonishingly diverse solo debut by the Isleys' axeman, *High Wire* is full of screaming guitars, tight riffs, ear-tugging melodies, and evocative vocals. *—John Floyd*

J

Jackie & the Starlites

f. 1960, **db.** 1963

Group / Doo Wop, R&B

Jackie and the Starlites were another one-hit wonder doo wop group—"Valerie," cut for Bobby Robinson's Fury label in 1960, being their one hit; it was cut at the tail end of the doo wop era and, indeed, may have been among the first songs in that style to appeal as an "oldie" in style. It barely brushed the national charts, but it was embraced by the community of doo wop singers as a standard.

Jackie La Rue originally started singing with an outfit called the Five Wings in the early 1950s, and cut a pair of singles with the group for King Records in 1955 before breaking up that year. Two of their members went on to form the Dubs, but La Rue wasn't heard from again in music until 1960, when the Starlites coalesced, consisting of Jackie Rue, as he was then known, Alton Thomas, John Felix, and Billy Montgomery. Rue was the star of the show as a superb acting singer, whose feigned weeping was apparently utterly convincing to onlookers and listeners. Their records following their successful debut were a mix of soul and upbeat ballads that failed to capture the imagination in the manner of "Valerie." By 1963, Fury Records was bankrupt, although the group managed to move on to Mascot Records in 1962 before disbanding sometime in the mid-'60s. Jackie Rue died of a drug overdose sometime in the late '60s or early '70s. *—Bruce Eder*

Jackie & the Starlites Meet the Bopchords: Golden Classics / Apr. 19, 1990 / Collectables ✦✦✦✦

Jackie & the Starlites specialize in wild and unique doo wop. The songs are for the most part doo wop numbers, but the voice seems like it is being beamed in from Mars. Lead vocalist Jackie Rue doesn't so much sing a song as he acts it out using the broadest strokes imaginable. Like the Jerry Lewis of doo wop, he is overflowing with personality. Sometimes it gets in the way of the music, but mostly he brings it to life and blows any doo wop clichés away with the sheer insanity of his voice. On the slow weepers he breaks down into sobs; their big hit, "Valerie," finds him on his knees begging and moaning for the return of his girl; on "Aint'cha Ever Coming Home" he's in such pain that he has to stretch his words out into completely unintelligible nonsense. On the uptempo tracks like "Seven Day Fool," he sings with an ear-to-ear grin like he doesn't have a care in the world. The 16 tracks here represent all you will ever need by this group, a mixed bag of slow and fast tunes, of course including "Valerie." After you finish laughing and crying your way through the best of Jackie & the Starlites, Collectables for some reason tacks on six tracks by the rather more mundane doo wop group the Bopchords. They pale in comparison to Jackie & the Starlites; most doo wop groups do. Fans of the genre need this CD. *—Tim Sendra*

● **Valerie** / 1991 / Relic ✦✦✦✦✦

This is one of the better doo wop collections one can buy, despite its coming out very late in the history of the form. Maybe the biggest surprise here is "I'm Comin' Home," and a track that anticipates the Rolling Stones' show-stopped "I'm Alright" with echoes of Smokey Robinson & the Miracles' "Way Over There," with a wailing, vocal cord-ripping performance by Rue. A lot of this stuff holds up well, even if Rue's weeping act gets a little predictable at times. "Don't Be Afraid," "Valerie," "Seven Day Fool," "I'm Coming Home," and a half-dozen others put this collection over the top, and one nice bonus amid the singing is the surprisingly dexterous guitar backing on a lot of the material here. Proper master tapes seem to have been used, and some of this stuff appears here in stereo for the first time ever. *—Bruce Eder*

The Jacks

f. Los Angeles, CA

Group / Doo Wop, R&B

The Los Angeles-based Jacks were so good at covering popular hits of the day that their versions were often equal to (if not better than) the original versions. They were versatile in R&B, jump tunes, ballads, calypso songs, and recorded some of the greatest early rock & roll songs ever, including "Stranded in the Jungle." Mostly, though, the Jacks are remembered for recording under two names simultaneously: as the Jacks (for Modern) and the Cadets (for RPM). Each group had its own hits and each with a slightly different sound and musical direction.

The Jacks/Cadets began as a gospel group during the late '40s in Los Angeles, under the guidance of former Dixie Hummingbirds baritone Lloyd McCraw. In 1954, McCraw joined up with first tenor Austin "Ted" Taylor, lead and second tenor Aaron Collins (brother of Betty and Rosie Collins, who recorded as the Teen Queens), tenor Willie Davis, and Will "Dub" Jones (lead and bass), who possessed a stratospheric falsetto. The band on most of the group's sessions was led by tenor saxophonist Maxwell Davis.

It was Modern's Joe Bihari who came up with the idea of having one group with a split personality, envisioning the Jacks as a ballad harmony group utilizing the writing talents of Aaron Collins and the Cadets as an uptempo and novelty song quintet who mostly covered other acts' material. As a rule, either Dub Jones or Aaron Collins sang lead on the Cadets recordings, while Davis fronted the Jacks.

In late 1954, the quintet—as the Cadets—recorded a version of Nappy Brown's "Don't Be Angry" and a calypso-flavored cover of "Rolling Stone," which outsold the original by Excello's Marigolds. By the summer of 1955, the Cadets had released "Annie Met Henry," a single that fell in line with the whole "Annie" craze created in the aftermath of Hank Ballard & the Midnighters' big hit "Work With Me Annie," which had been released some 16 months earlier and was still going strong. The Cadets' next Modern release was "Do You Wanna Rock," an exciting uptempo revision of the Drifters' big R&B hit (number two) "Whatcha Gonna Do." It was the Cadets' next single, the buoyant "How Soon," that scored the regional airplay and sales. By February 1956, the Cadets had moved on to new cover material, including Elvis Presley's "Heartbreak Hotel" and the Willows' "Church Bells May Ring." The Jacks' "Why Don't You Write Me?" hit the R&B charts on August 6th, and jumped up to number-three R&B by September; it even managed to cross over to the pop charts to reach number 82, charting before the Cadets charted with their outlandish cover of "Stranded in the Jungle." When the ballad side began to break big in the pop field, Bihari immediately bumped the B-side and a second pressing was hastily issued with a ballad on the flip side, "My Darling."

The instant that Bihari heard the Jay Hawks' "Stranded in the Jungle," a rough and ragged original that had been waxed first, then heard the version done by his own act, the Cadets, while in the studio, he knew that his group's was far superior. He quickly pressed up copies and got them to radio stations in strong regional markets across the country and into stores in those areas, before the Jay Hawks even had a chance to make a move themselves. Released in June of 1956, the song shot up the charts, to number-four R&B/number-15 pop. What would prove to be singer Prentice Moreland's only Cadets/Jacks recording session provided the group with a catch phrase of their own; he delivered the line "Great googly-moogly, let me outta here," on "Stranded in the Jungle."

Subsequent Jacks/Cadets sides from 1956 failed to generate interest or sales for Modern, however. The Jacks tried again with a few original ballads and eventually hit with "Love Bandit," their last record of 1956, which was cut from the same cloth as "Stranded in the Jungle." The Jacks never again achieved the measure of success that "Stranded" had achieved. In February 1957, Modern issued *Rockin' and Reelin'*, the Cadets' first LP, one of the very first R&B group LPs, which collected most of their previously released A- and B-sides. In March, eight months after their last release and 22 months after the release of their only hit, RPM put out the Jacks' *Jumpin' With the Jacks* LP, which contained ten sides of which three ("You Belong to Me," "Do You Wanna Rock," and "Wiggie Waggie Woo") were released on singles by the Cadets. By this time, Bihari and Modern had given up on the Jacks part of the equation and from that point on, the group was exclusively known as the Cadets. Their last RPM single was "Ring Chimes," issued in December 1957. *—Bryan Thomas*

Jumpin' With the Jacks / 1956 / RPM ✦✦✦

These jumping Jacks were also those rockin' and reelin' Cadets, and vice versa: a comparison of the cover of this to the cover of *Those Rockin' and Reelin' Cadets* proves that, change of matching suits aside, it's obviously the same group. Whether the Jacks covering the Feathers' "Why Don't You Write Me" came before they were split into the Cadets to cover the Jayhawks' "Stranded in the Jungle" is somewhat lost to history; they *did* become both groups before they ever had a chance to record under their real name, however. Once success came with both records, however, the general pattern was that all the smooth ballad material would be issued as the Jacks, with all the uptempo sides issued under the Cadets banner. This was the game plan followed on the Jacks' singles, but their lone album for Crown is liberally peppered with uptempo jump material ("Oo Wee Baby," "Let's Make Up," the wild "Do You Wanna Rock") far better suited to, well, a group like the Cadets. But the ballads are nonetheless just as fine, with "You Belong to Me" and "Dream a Little Longer" being particular highlights. They may have led a somewhat Jekyll-and-Hyde existence on record, but they sure could sing, whoever they were marketed as. *—Cub Koda*

The Jackson 5

f. 1966, Gary, IN

Group / Motown, Soul, Pop-Soul, Disco, Urban

The Jackson 5 were one of the biggest phenomenons in pop music during the early '70s, and the last great group to come out of the Motown hitmaking machine, before Marvin Gaye and Stevie Wonder shifted the label's focus to more individual visions. The Jackson 5's infectious brand of funky pop-soul was a definite departure from the typically smooth, elegant Motown sound, as befitting the group's youth and the dawn of a new decade. That youth, coupled with the merchandising juggernaut that sprang up behind them, inevitably got them tagged a bubblegum group. But they were far more talented musically than that label would suggest, especially lead singer Michael, and their material, while sunny and upbeat, didn't pander to its audience. Solo careers and overexposure gradually weakened the Jackson 5, but their best music still holds up surprisingly well as some of the most vibrant mainstream pop/R&B of its era.

Originally, the Jackson 5 were composed of brothers Jackie (born Sigmund Jackson, May 4, 1951), Tito (guitar, born Toriano Jackson, October 15, 1953), Jermaine (bass, lead vocals, born December 11, 1954), Marlon (born March 12, 1957), and Michael (lead vocals, born August 29, 1958). By all accounts, the Jackson family's upbringing in Gary, IN, was strict; their mother Katherine was a devout Jehovah's Witness, and their father Joe was a stern, temperamental disciplinarian. Allowed few outside interests, the boys gravitated to music, which was in their blood—prior to his job as a crane operator for a steel company, Joe had played guitar in an R&B group called the Falcons (not the same group that launched Wilson Pickett's career). One night, Joe discovered that Jackie, Tito, and Jermaine had been playing his treasured old guitar without permission; though initially furious, he quickly discovered that his sons had genuine talent, and began to conceive of a family singing group that might eventually get them out of their tough working-class life in Gary. The eldest three sons began performing around the area together in 1962, teamed with two cousins (Johnny Jackson and Ronnie Rancifer), who were replaced by Marlon and five-year-old Michael. Supervised by Joe, who became their manager and began working only part-time, the group practiced and rehearsed often, and improved as dancers, singers, and instrumentalists at a rapid rate. In particular, Michael proved himself a dynamic performer, soon replacing Jermaine as the featured lead vocalist, and establishing himself as a nimble dancer able to mimic talents like James Brown. At first, the group was known as Ripples & Waves Plus Michael, then the Jackson Brothers, and finally the Jackson 5.

In 1966, the Jackson 5 won an important local talent competition with a Michael-led rendition of the Temptations' "My Girl." Their father, who had been chauffeuring them to out-of-state performances, also booked their first paid professional gigs that year. In 1967 the group won an amateur talent competition at Harlem's legendary Apollo Theater, where they earned an influential fan in Gladys Knight (probably the first person to recommend the group to Motown). At the end of the year, the Jackson 5 made their first studio recordings for the small Gary-based Steeltown label, and their single "Big Boy" became something of a local hit. Championed again to Motown by Bobby Taylor, a member of the Vancouvers who'd seen the group in Chicago, and Diana Ross, the Jackson 5 finally got a chance to audition for the label in the summer of 1968. Desperately needing new blood, an impressed Berry Gordy signed the group and flew them out to his new headquarters in Los Angeles, where he and his assistants groomed them to be the label's next breakout stars. Having lost his famed Holland-Dozier-Holland songwriting team, Gordy formed a new partnership with Freddie Perren, Fonce Mizell, and Deke Richards dubbed the Corporation, which set about crafting material for the group.

In August 1969, shortly before Michael turned 11, the Jackson 5 opened for Diana Ross at the L.A. Forum, and in December, they issued their debut album, *Diana Ross Presents the Jackson 5*. In January 1970, the Jackson 5 released their first single, "I Want You Back," a Corporation composition that had originally been intended for Gladys Knight. It was an instant smash, hitting number one on both the pop and R&B charts. So did their next two singles, "ABC" and "The Love You Save" (both from their second album *ABC*), which solidified the group's so-called bubblegum-soul sound and certified them as pop sensations. *Third Album* was released before year's end, spawning the hit ballad "I'll Be There," which not only proved that the group (and lead singer Michael) were more mature and versatile than their bright, bouncy initial singles let on, but also made them the first group in pop history to have their first four singles hit number one. It also became the best-selling single in Motown history, spending a stellar five weeks at number one. And it had still been less than a year since the group's national debut.

A virtual Jackson 5 cottage industry sprang up in the wake of their success, producing everything from dolls to a cartoon show on—what else?—the ABC network (during the summer of 1971). Younger and younger listeners were brought into the fold, adding to an already broad appeal that transcended color lines, and the record label that once billed itself as "the Sound of Young America" could once again lay legitimate claim to the title. Meanwhile, following their four straight number ones, the Jackson 5 opened 1971 with a pair of number two hits, "Mama's Pearl" and the ballad "Never Can Say Goodbye"; "Maybe Tomorrow" was their first single not to make the pop Top Ten, though it still reached the R&B Top Five. That year, Motown executives began grooming Michael and Jermaine for solo careers that would run concurrently with the Jackson 5. Michael was the first to debut on his own (toward the end of 1971), and was an instant success; his first two singles, "Got to Be There" and "Rockin' Robin," both made the Top Five, and later in 1972 he scored his first pop number one with "Ben." Jermaine debuted at the end of 1972, and his first single "Daddy's Home" reached the Top Ten, though the follow-ups didn't sustain the momentum as well as Michael.

In the meantime, the fantastically hyped Jackson 5 craze was beginning to cool down. Their prolific LP release schedule slowed a bit, and while their singles continued to perform reliably well on the R&B charts, they were no longer a surefire bet for the pop Top Ten. After a relatively lengthy drought, the Jackson 5 scored what would be their last major smash for Motown, the 1974 number-two hit "Dancing Machine," a nod to the emerging sound of disco (it also topped the R&B charts). The group's frustrations with Motown had been building—not only did the label seem less interested in their career, but they still refused to allow the Jacksons to write or choose their own material, or play their own instruments on their records. Finally, in early 1976, they left Motown to sign with Epic. When the legal battles finally ended, Motown won a breach-of-contract settlement and retained rights to the Jackson 5 name, forcing the group to become the Jacksons. They also lost Jermaine, whose marriage to Berry Gordy's daughter Hazel made it extremely impractical for him to join his brothers. He was replaced by younger brother Randy (born Steven Randall Jackson, October 29, 1961), who had been appearing (unofficially) with the group as a percussionist for some time.

The Jacksons' first few records on Epic were somewhat erratic affairs produced by Philly soul legends Gamble & Huff. However, the group truly assumed control over their music and hit full stride on 1978's *Destiny*, which most regard as the strongest studio LP the Jacksons recorded together in any incarnation. *Destiny* was self-produced and largely self-written, and its success helped encourage Michael to return to solo work. In 1979 the brilliant *Off the Wall* made him a star in his own right, signifying his arrival as a mature adult artist, but he remained with his brothers for the time being, helping them record a Grammy-nominated follow-up to *Destiny* in 1980's *Triumph*. The staggering success of Michael's next solo album, *Thriller*, signaled the beginning of the end for the Jacksons, but not quite yet; Jermaine re-joined the group for 1984's *Victory*, the only album to feature all six brothers. The single "State of Shock," which featured guest vocalist Mick Jagger, hit number three that year, and the group's ensuing tour was a blockbuster success, despite expensive (for the time) ticket prices. Michael and Marlon both left the Jacksons, the latter trying out an unsuccessful solo career; Randy, Tito, and Jackie appeared as the Jacksons on the soundtrack of *Burglar*, and subsequently became highly regarded session musicians. The Jacksons reconvened in 1989 for the album *2300 Jackson Street*, which featured every Jackson sibling save LaToya on the title cut. However, it wasn't as successful as hoped, and to date there have been no further reunions on record. In 1997, the Jackson 5 were inducted into the Rock and Roll Hall of Fame. *—Steve Huey*

Diana Ross Presents the Jackson 5 / 1969 / Motown ✦✦✦✦✦
This Gary, IN, family ensemble exploded onto the national scene with immediate and long-lasting impact in 1970. This album's combination of youthful exuberance and innocence, coupled with Motown production magic, yielded quick results, as "I Want You Back" topped both R&B and pop charts. Michael Jackson, the nine-year-old lead singer, became a national darling. Once they hit the big time, there was controversy over whether Diana Ross actually discovered them, but there was no question that Motown had unveiled another superstar act. *—Ron Wynn*

ABC / Apr. 1970 / Motown ✦✦✦✦✦
This is a fabulous album, arguably their best on Motown. While the debut album established the group's sound, this one cemented it and also made it clear that Michael was going to be a huge star for a long time. His blend of gentility, soul, and innocence sparkled on the title cut and throughout the album, while the songs, production, arrangement, and musical support were superb. *—Ron Wynn*

Third Album / Aug. 1970 / Motown ✦✦✦
The Jackson 5 solidified the audience they enjoyed with their first two albums by turning in a consistently produced and occasionally exciting third record. It included the fine ballad "I'll Be There" and another hit in "Mama's Pearl"; the group hadn't yet become hardened by Motown manipulation or troubled by internal dissension. Michael Jackson was still widely beloved and seen as the 1970s' Frankie Lymon, and this LP became their third Top Ten album in a row. *—Ron Wynn*

The Jackson 5 Christmas Album / Oct. 1970 / Motown ✦✦✦✦✦
Here is one of the greatest holiday albums ever. But Michael and company carry off the seasonal bit well, and their versions of these dusty hymns and carols could even charm Scrooge. *—Ron Wynn*

Maybe Tomorrow / 1971 / Motown ✦✦✦
This is another fine album, with Michael Jackson displaying surprising conviction and earnestness on the title track. The group was rolling along with a strong mix of novelty/dance hits, ballads, and soul covers, scoring massive pop success and turning up all over the airwaves. *—Ron Wynn*

Lookin' Through the Windows / 1972 / Motown ✦✦✦
The Jackson 5 were still an engaging, delightful family unit when this album was released. They hadn't yet lost their innocent qualities and were also continuing to get first-rate material, production, and arrangements. They were three years away from the bitter fights that marred their exit from Motown, and Michael hadn't yet become a huge solo act. *—Ron Wynn*

Get It Together / 1973 / Motown ✦✦
Although they were still getting hits, there were some problems creeping into the Jackson 5's Motown albums. The main one was that the company was no longer in the forefront of black music production, and their '60s-style efforts were sounding dated. Only Michael Jackson's individual brilliance and the group's polished performances salvaged much of this material, and they soon openly expressed their disapproval. *—Ron Wynn*

Skywriter / 1973 / Motown ✦✦
The Jackson 5 slipped a bit with this album, although they still had two pop and R&B hits. But it wasn't anywhere near as dominant or popular an album as their earlier ones and wound up being one of their final three releases for Motown. They later did some recording with Stevie Wonder, Michael cut some solo material, and everyone except Jermaine headed for Columbia. *—Ron Wynn*

Dancing Machine / 1974 / Motown ✦✦✦✦
For a brief time, it seemed as if the magic was back between Motown and the Jackson 5. The title track was their best uptempo hit since "ABC," and put them back on top of the R&B charts for the first time in three years. It just missed topping the pop charts as well, peaking at number two. They even got a second chart hit from the album, and it restored their position within the pop and R&B communities. *—Ron Wynn*

Moving Violation / 1975 / Motown ✦✦

The Jacksons / 1976 / Epic ✦✦✦
After the commercial reprieve of the innovative "Dancing Machine" single (and album of the same name), the Jackson 5's successful five-year relationship with Motown and Berry Gordy ended. Their last Motown effort, *Moving Violation*, had barely made a dent. After an acrimonious split, brother Jermaine Jackson stayed at Motown, and Gordy fought and won, keeping the Jackson 5 moniker. *The Jacksons* isn't only their Epic label debut, it's the first album to feature youngest brother Randy Jackson. To ensure chart success, the group was teamed with Philadelphia producers Kenneth Gamble & Leon Huff, as well as their staff of writers and players. Despite the promise, *The Jacksons* is hampered by

derivative tracks and a lack of knowing what to do with the group, particularly lead singer, Michael Jackson. The big hit here, the jerky "Enjoy Yourself," perfectly captured Michael Jackson's late adolescence, with his newfound vocal tics and inflections. "Show You the Way to Go" best captures the Philly sound, with a pretty melody and a great vocal from Michael, but it's a weak lyric. The Dexter Wansel-written and -produced "Keep on Dancing" matches a substandard discofied track to Michael Jackson's singular vocals. The last track, the graceful "Blues Away" marks the writing debut of the group and is a great match between artists and producers. For the most part, *The Jacksons* gives the guys by-the-numbers Philly tracks that could have been easily done by Lou Rawls. Despite the best songs, *The Jacksons* misses more than it hits. *—Jason Elias*

Joyful Jukebox Music / 1976 / Motown ♦♦♦
Although *Joyful Jukebox Music* was released after the Jackson 5 had left Motown for Epic Records, missed the charts, and produced no hit singles, it's not half-bad. Motown has famous archives, recording its artists extensively and only releasing a portion of the results. Here, as would not be true on Epic, the focus is firmly on Michael Jackson (who gets a "featuring" title credit) and he effectively handles everything from dance pop to ersatz '30s schmaltz. This isn't one of The Jackson 5's most memorable collections, but it is better than you would have expected under the circumstances. *—William Ruhlmann*

☆ **Anthology** / Jun. 15, 1976 / Motown ♦♦♦♦♦
The Jackson 5's volume in Motown's *Anthology* series was a three-LP extravaganza boasting 33 of the quintet's greatest hits, plus room to collect a few solo hits (mostly from Michael). There's no need to argue with most of the inclusions here, while the long running time also permits a few gorgeous album tracks ("Don't Know Why I Love You," "Corner of the Sky"), and a few rare songs like "Teenage Symphony" and a version of the Supremes' "I Hear a Symphony" (credited to Michael but also featuring the other Jacksons). When it was re-released as two compact discs in 1986, *Anthology* featured 40 tracks, including a raft of solo hits from Michael, Jermaine, and even Jackie Jackson ("Love Don't Want to Leave"). In 2000, a radically revamped version of the original replaced both of these versions. *—John Bush*

Goin' Places / 1977 / Epic ♦♦♦
The Jacksons' move to Epic regenerated their enthusiasm and spirit for several years. The Gamble & Huff team brought them fresh material and new production ideas, as well as better tracks and arrangements than they'd gotten in quite a while on Motown. This album got them R&B and pop hits and kept the family act in the spotlight for a little while longer. *—Ron Wynn*

Destiny / 1978 / Epic ♦♦♦♦♦
The Jacksons are finally turned loose to write and produce themselves, and the result is their best (non-hits collection) ever. The dance tracks still sound fresh; "Blame It on the Boogie," "Shake Your Body (Down to the Ground)"; and the ballads are heartfelt and smooth. This album is a dry run for Michael Jackson's adult solo career. *—William Ruhlmann*

Triumph / 1980 / Epic ♦♦♦♦♦
This album's predecessor *Destiny* was a high-selling album that featured the guys maturing and delving into self-production. In 1980, Michael Jackson's classic *Off the Wall* was still selling. This album has the group fleshing out their sound and songwriting abilities even more. The anthemic "Can't You Feel It" has enough hubris and undeniable craft to get this polished work started. But as *Triumph* plays, what's striking is that the songs don't immediately leap out at you but they all land on their feet. The blissful and funky "Lovely One," with its effortless, punchy horns, has Michael Jackson with his quirky vocals and charisma. At it's best, this is a collaborative effort, not just super-hot Michael Jackson talking his brothers out for a spin. The Jackie Jackson-penned "Your Ways" creates the right mix of paranoia and uncertainty that meshed well with Michael Jackson's high-pitched and haunted lead. That certainly mixes well with *Triumph*'s best song, "Heartbreak Hotel." The track is an early instance of Michael Jackson's patented love as horror, kisses as doom ethos. The song's creepy aura and sound effects maximize the effect. The only ballad, "Time Waits for No One" has Michael Jackson getting weepy on the delicate and well-arranged track. The masterful "Walk Right Now" and "Give It Up" are two great examples of the group's chops in the studio and their grasp of the L.A. pop/funk sound. *Triumph* is a gorgeous effort and remains an absolute necessity for any comprehensive collection. *—Jason Elias*

The Jacksons Live / 1981 / Epic ♦♦
It's not one of their better albums from a material standpoint, but it contained some energetic performances and was one of the last times Michael worked with the family unit. This was mainly sold in England, and disappeared from print very shortly after it was issued. *—Ron Wynn*

Victory / 1984 / Epic ♦♦♦
Victory has the distinctions of being the only Jacksons album to feature all six brothers and the last Jacksons album to feature Michael Jackson. In the four years that had passed since the last Jacksons studio album, *Triumph*, Michael had become the biggest pop star in the world because of 1982's *Thriller*. He had little excuse other than family ties to work with his brothers again, but he agreed to a final album and tour. So, here one has the ludicrous situation of an album in which Marlon Jackson has as prominent a role as Michael Jackson. That's how it sounded to listeners in 1984, anyway, and they weren't fooled—"State of Shock," on which Michael shared vocals with Mick Jagger, was a gold Top Ten hit, and "Torture," which teamed Michael with Jermaine, made the Top 40, while the album went platinum. But the tracks by other group members went virtually ignored. In retrospect, *Victory* is a competent album of slick contemporary R&B, occasionally goosed toward greatness by the appearance of one of pop music's most identifiable voices. Which is the same thing you can say about nearly the entire Jackson 5/Jacksons catalog. *—William Ruhlmann*

2300 Jackson Street / 1989 / Epic ♦♦♦
This was the final gathering of the entire Jackson family, and it turned out to have both historical significance and some musical value. The team of L.A. Reid and Babyface, then emerging as major producers, spearheaded the track "Nothin' Compares to U," and the title track was a nice autobiographical/family outing song. *—Ron Wynn*

Soulsation! / Jun. 27, 1995 / Motown ♦♦♦♦♦
Motown finally tops *Anthology*'s 33-track, three-LP compilation with this 82-track, four-and-a-half-hour, four-CD/cassette box set 19 years after its release. The Jackson 5 were long overdue for box set treatment, and this one is well done. All the hits by the group as well as those by Michael and Jermaine Jackson are here (that is, from 1969-1975, the J5's tenure at Motown), along with a representative sampling of album cuts. The J5's albums were afterthoughts to their singles, but some of these songs are nevertheless interesting, whether the group is covering Sly & the Family Stone or Jackson Browne. An entire disc is given over to previously unreleased or rare tracks from the Motown vaults. Taken together, it may be more than all but the most die-hard fan wants to hear, which may be why Motown rushed out yet another single-disc hits collection, *The Ultimate Collection*, a couple of months later. But if you want the Jackson 5 on Motown, a big chunk of it is here. *—William Ruhlmann*

★ **The Ultimate Collection** / Aug. 15, 1995 / Motown ♦♦♦♦♦
The first single-disc Jackson 5 collection to take full advantage of the compact-disc medium, *The Ultimate Collection* is certainly the ultimate for any but the most hardcore fans. Ranging from 1969's "I Want You Back" to 1975's "I Am Love, Pts. 1-2," these 21 tracks include each of the group's hits, among them "ABC," "The Love You Save," "I'll Be There," "Never Can Say Goodbye," "Maybe Tomorrow," "Lookin' Through the Windows," "Get It Together," and "Dancing Machine." And unlike previous hits collections (barring only the multi-disc *Anthology*), there's plenty of space for more material: a few solo hits from Michael ("Got to Be There," "Rockin' Robin," "Just a Little Bit of You") and Jermaine ("Daddy's Home"), plus a pair of previously unreleased tracks ("It's Your Thing," a slowed-down Isleys cover, and "The Life of the Party"). Despite a few classic albums, the Jackson 5 were singles artists first and foremost, and their two-minute blasts of rhythm and energy are best-heard on a compilation. The best of that lot is this one. *—John Bush*

Pre-History: The Lost Steeltown Recordings / Jun. 4, 1996 / Brunswick ♦♦♦
It sounds like Steeltown cut these 14 unpolished, pre-Motown Jackson 5 tracks in a garage, but that's the charm of this CD. Remakes of popular R&B songs rule this roost, and a couple originals had potential. Two tracks came out on a 45 credited to Ripples & Waves plus Michael. On "Let Me Carry Your Schoolbooks," shoddy production killed any possibilities it had; the vocals are practically knocked out by the horrible mix. "I Never Had a Girl," the best original ballad, features some serious crooning from Michael, Jackie, Tito, Jermaine, and Marlon. The "Monologue" and "Jam Session, Pt. 1 & 2" capture the youngsters in the studio unaware the tape was rolling. Motown liked the shuffling "You've Changed" so much they redid it and included it on the Jacksons' debut album. You'll enjoy their adolescent remakes of "My Girl," "Tracks of My Tears," "Under the Boardwalk," and "Saturday Night at the Movies." *—Andrew Hamilton*

Anthology / Oct. 24, 2000 / Motown ♦♦♦♦♦
Newly remastered and recompiled for 2000, this version of the Jackson 5's *Anthology* takes the place of the original double-CD set, which was first issued on LP back in 1976. The main difference is that where the first *Anthology* featured some of Michael and Jermaine's earliest solo hits, this one is devoted exclusively to Jackson 5 material, with a little more detail added to the pictures of their early pop-soul years and their later, disco-influenced work. All of the group's charting singles are here, as well as important B-sides and album tracks, including several songs that have never previously appeared on CD. Later hits like "Dancing Machine" and "Hum Along and Dance" are also presented in their full-length LP versions. *—Steve Huey*

Dancing Machine/Moving Violation / Aug. 7, 2001 / Motown ♦♦♦
Although *Dancing Machine* contained a few more choice pre-disco leanings, such as "She's a Rhythm Child" and "Life of the Party," the emphasis began to shift to album (read: longer) tracks rather than singles. That certainly isn't to imply that the hits had dried up. In fact, it was the persistent success of "Dancing Machine" from *Get It Together* that determined the direction of the album. The centerpiece of *Dancing Machine* is the opening track—a seven-plus minute epic titled "I Am Love." The stunning use of counterpoint and a mélange of pop music styles—ranging from soul ballad to album rock—are a tribute to the enormous flexibility of the Jackson 5. The album was so skewed toward a pop music audience that it failed to chart on the R&B charts, although it reached a most respectable number 16 on the *Billboard* album chart. *Moving Violations* is a more assured return to what was happening in popular soul music and the burgeoning disco scene of the mid- to late '70s. In fact, with only a few exceptions—most notably "All I Do Is Think of You" and "Breezy"—the tracks on this final Jackson 5 album were created specifically for the dancefloor. This in turn heralded the return of the quintet to the R&B album charts. Although this would be the final long-player credited to the Jackson Five, the band would continue as a quintet with youngest brother Randy Jackson replacing Jermaine on their next chapter as simply the Jacksons. As with all five in this series of the remastered Jackson 5 two-fer discs, there are a few pertinent "bonus tracks" on this disc—both of which are circa *Moving Violation*. "Through Thick and Thin" first appeared on the *Joyful Jukebox Music* compilation. "Forever Came Today"—originally by Diana Ross & the Supremes—is indeed a rarity, as the last half of the track is a dance-friendly instrumental and was originally issued on Motown's *Disc-O-Tech #3* various-artist long-player. *—Lindsay Planer*

Diana Ross Presents the Jackson 5/ABC / Aug. 7, 2001 / Motown ♦♦♦♦
Now that the entire Jackson 5 Motown Records catalog has been renovated, each single disc contains two long-players, as well as chronologically applicable bonus tracks. This CD contains their debut album, *Diana Ross Presents the Jackson 5*; the follow-up disc, *ABC*; as well as "Oh, I've Been Blessed," a track from the quintet's earliest-known recording sessions for Motown. In terms of sheer performance talent, the Jackson 5 are unquestionably among the best. The sibling-tight harmonies as well as youthful soul and funk exuberance sent these albums not only to the top of the R&B, but also the pop album charts in 1969 and 1970, respectively. It is not hard to understand why. Musically, both albums are propelled by the same exceedingly funky grooves previously sported by the likes of James Brown and Sly & the Family Stone—an obvious influence, as their cover of "Stand" is among the highlights of the debut long-player. The same can be said of the George Clinton-penned "I Bet You," which arguably eclipses the Funkadelic version featured on their eponymously titled release. Their pursuit of fresh soul sounds also inevitably led to the sophisticated arrangements of Philly soul mavericks Thomas Bell & William Hart, who provide "Can You Remember" on *Diana Ross Presents the Jackson 5*, as well as "La La (Means I Love You)" on *ABC*. The Corporation—a self-contained Motown contingent of writers, producers, and musicians—provide material from within. Their contributions include "I Want You Back" from the first album, as well as "The Love You Save" and the title track from "ABC," each of which were crossover chart-toppers on the pop as well as R&B surveys. This two-fer disc boasts 24-bit remastered sound as well as a 16-page liner-notes booklet complete with a historical essay, previously unpublished photos, and pertinent discographical information. *—Lindsay Planer*

Looking Through the Windows/Goin' Back to Indiana / Aug. 7, 2001 / Motown ♦♦♦
This single disc contains the CD debut of *Goin' Back to Indiana*—the Jackson 5's hour-long television variety special—as well as their subsequent studio album, *Lookin' Through the Windows*. Either could qualify as unique by any standard, however, together they provide transition—chronologically as well as creatively—to the next and decidedly more independent phase of the Jackson 5. Although many of the visual gags are lost in the medium, this soundtrack to the hour-long ABC network special *Goin' Back to Indiana* remains at the very least a time capsule. The show provided the context for some stellar live performances from the quartet's homecoming concert in Gary, IN. "The Day Basketball Was Saved" is a memorable fantasy sketch featuring a dream team consisting of Bill Russell, Elvin Hayes, Elgin Baylor, and Ben Davison going up against the Jackson 5. Musically, the nucleus of the album is the May 29, 1971, Gary homecoming concert. Highlights include a cover of Dave Mason's "Feelin' Alright" as well as a maniacally funky reading of the title track. Also from this performance is "Who's Lovin' You," one of the two bonus tracks on the disc. Although the Corporation—a handpicked quartet of Motown producers, arrangers, and musicians whose prime directive was to oversee the Jackson 5—had more or less disbanded, there was enough excess material to develop the album. Ironically, tracks such as "Don't Let Your Baby Catch You" and "If I Have to Move a Mountain" are among the best non-hits from the Corporation. Likewise, the album gathers some memorable cover versions as well. Chief among them are brilliant readings of Jackson Browne's "Doctor My Eyes," the Nickolas Ashford & Valerie Simpson composition "Ain't Nothing Like the Real Thing," and "Little Bitty Pretty One," which was chosen as a single. The final bonus track is "Love Song," a non-LP B-side. *—Lindsay Planer*

Skywriter/Get It Together / Aug. 7, 2001 / Motown ♦♦♦
This double-play CD contains the *Skywriter* and *Get It Together* albums as well as a trio of recordings made, but not issued, circa the Jackson 5's intermediate and increasingly independent years at Motown. While the days of immediate and successive chart-topping albums and singles had subsided, emerging was a band whose wisdom came from its members' pursuit of their unifying passion for music. Regardless of the lack of hit power on either of these albums, there is a notable maturity in the selections. Likewise, these long-players were not laden with cover songs. This allows the Jackson 5 room to explore material that would accentuate group participation, such as "Boogie Man." This should not suggest an abandonment of the quintet's unique style and approach. "Corner of the Sky"—from the Broadway play *Pippin'*—and the clavinet-driven "Uppermost" contain the same funky bubblegum stride with which they would ultimately become synonymous. Remnants of the musical machine known as the Corporation—which consisted of Motown founder Berry Gordy along with Deke Richards, Freddie Perren, and Fonce Mizell—surfaced throughout *Skywriter*. Although "You Made Me What I Am" bears the quartet's full credentials, Richards, Perren, and Mizell continued providing material for the band. The Jackson 5's next effort, *Get It Together*, doesn't hang together quite as cohesively as its predecessor. However, it does contain the proverbial "light at the end of the tunnel" as the final track: "Dancing Machine" would take the brothers head-on into disco. The song would resurface as the title track of their next long-player. *—Lindsay Planer*

Third Album/Maybe Tomorrow / Aug. 7, 2001 / Motown ♦♦
Less than three months following the release of *ABC* came the Jackson 5's aptly titled follow-up, *Third Album*. This two-fer CD also includes their subsequent long-player, *Maybe Tomorrow*, as well as bonus tracks consisting of the mono versions of the "Sugar Daddy" b/w "I'm So Happy" 45 rpm. As with their predecessors, these albums contain a diverse mixture of R&B, funk, and soul styles, all the while remaining vibrant, fresh, young, and most definitely pop. Although still formulaic in approach, the Corporation—consisting of Motown founder Berry Gordy along with Deke Richards, Freddie Perren, and Fonce Mizell—was able to garner significant success by blending a few well-placed cover songs, such as "Bridge Over Troubled Waters" and "16 Candles," with continued contributions from Philly soul stylists Thom Bell & William Hart on "Ready or Not (Here I Come)." As the Jackson 5 phenomenon continued, however, the Corporation became increasingly dependant upon their own skills and formidable credentials. Not only were all four singles—two from each album—written and produced by the team, they also provided the majority of the material for *Maybe Tomorrow*. Tracks such as "I'll Be There," "Goin' Back to Indiana," "Mama's Pearl," and "Sugar Daddy" would become well-known performance staples and fan favorites. The secondary layer of material is equally matched for the high-energy soul antics of Michael's imposing talent. That is not to dismiss the formidable contributions of the other brothers, especially on "It's Great to Be Here" and "My Little Baby." Their increased role as support and co-lead were forging new boundaries. Following the seasonally maneuvered *Jackson 5 Greatest Hits* disc in November 1971, the Corporation disbanded. The bonus tracks include their final contributions—"Sugar Daddy" b/w "I'm So Happy"—the latter of which was issued as a non-LP 45 rpm B-side. This disc incorporates 24-bit remastered sound, and the 16-page liner-notes booklet includes a historical essay, previously unpublished photos, and pertinent discographical information. *—Lindsay Planer*

Chuck Jackson

b. Jun. 22, 1937, Latta, SC
Vocals / R&B, Soul, Pop-Soul, Uptown Soul, Northern Soul
He's relatively forgotten today, and his brand of uptown soul is dismissed by the relatively vocal clique of critics who prefer their soul deep and down-home. But Chuck Jackson was a regular visitor to the R&B charts (and an occasional one to the pop listings) in the early '60s with such early pop-soul concoctions as "I Don't Want to Cry," "Any Day Now," and "Tell Him I'm Not Home." His records were very much of a piece with New York pop/rock-soul production, with cheeky brass, sweeping strings, and female backup vocalists. Those production trills make his work sound dated to some listeners, and his hoarse, emotional vocals weren't as subtle or commanding as peers like Ben E. King or Wilson Pickett. On its own terms, though, his best work is quite good, whether you prefer pop to soul or vice versa.

Jackson sang with one of the best doo wop groups, the Del-Vikings, for a while in the late '50s (although he doesn't appear on their hit singles). Spotted by Scepter Records while performing with Jackie Wilson's Revue, he started recording for the label in 1961. As was the case with labelmates Dionne Warwick and the Shirelles, Jackson's early-'60s arrangements blended pop, R&B, and New York-session professionalism. Like Warwick, Jackson was one of the first singers to successfully record Bacharach-David material; one of his best singles, "I Keep Forgettin'" (1962), was written and produced by Leiber-Stoller. Jackson had some success with some duets with Maxine Brown in the mid-'60s, but he left Wand in 1967 for Motown, at the urging of Smokey Robinson. Jackson was (perhaps understandably) lost in the shuffle during his four years at Motown, and he's barely been heard from since, although he remains a favorite on England's "Northern soul" scene. *—Richie Unterberger*

Encore! / 1963 / Wand ♦♦♦
Here are some wonderful soul ballads and good uptempo tunes, although nothing attracted much chart attention. Jackson simply couldn't get the same exposure for much of his material as Solomon Burke, Wilson Pickett, and others dominating the soul charts, although he was in their class vocally. *—Ron Wynn*

Chuck Jackson on Tour / 1964 / Wand ♦♦♦
Chuck Jackson's singles were outstanding, but he was even more electrifying live. This set features his exciting, robust vocals done before adoring, encouraging audiences whose cries and responses pushed him to even more spectacular performances. *—Ron Wynn*

Mr. Everything / 1965 / Wand ♦♦♦
Here are some shuddering, majestic soul vocals from Chuck Jackson, delivered with fierce conviction and energy. Although Jackson could be overly dramatic, there was no exaggerating the authority and power he brought to ballads, and he deserves much more attention than he's received. *—Ron Wynn*

A Tribute to Rhythm and Blues / 1966 / Wand ♦♦♦♦♦
The first of two fantastic albums featuring Chuck Jackson's smashing, soaring vocals doing definitive treatments on R&B classics. Although never a "concept" or album artist, Jackson came closest on both volumes to doing a unified project, rather than just having singles slapped together on an album. *—Ron Wynn*

A Tribute to Rhythm and Blues, Vol. 2 / 1966 / Wand ♦♦♦♦♦
This is the second volume in the series containing memorable expositions by Chuck Jackson of R&B gems. He never sang with more distinction, intensity, or energy than on these two volumes, and the second one is slightly superior to its predecessor. *—Ron Wynn*

Hold on We're Coming / 1967 / Scepter ♦♦
The second and final collaboration between Chuck Jackson and Maxine Brown isn't as good as their 1965 LP, relying much more heavily on predictable cover versions of pop, soul, and R&B tunes. One highlight is "Let's Go Get Stoned," recorded (but not released) before Ray Charles' more famous hit version. [All of the songs from the record are included on Soul Classics' *Something You Got* CD reissue.] *—Richie Unterberger*

Chuck Jackson Arrives! / 1968 / Motown ♦♦♦
Chuck Jackson's failure at Motown had little to do with the material, and everything to do with the choices for singles and lackluster promotion. "(You Can't Let the Boy Overpower) The Man in You" did nothing for either the Miracles or Jackson; it was the only single released from this set of 12 above-average tracks. Better choices for singles were the heart-rending ballad "Who You Gonna Run To," the grooving "We'll Find a Way," the explosive "Ain't No Sun Since You've Been Gone," "Lonely, Lonely Man Am I," or "Your Wonderful Love." Jackson's baritone is as robust as it was on his Wand recordings, where he enjoyed his greatest success. *—Andrew Hamilton*

Goin' Back to Chuck Jackson / 1969 / Motown ♦♦♦
Yet another nice Chuck Jackson album that didn't generate anywhere near the reaction it merited. Jackson was prevented in the '60s from being in the spotlight by a glut of great

performers, and also because he landed most of his hits in the early '60s and wasn't really in the mainstream at the peak of soul's commercial onslaught. —*Ron Wynn*

Teardrops Keep Fallin' on My Heart / 1970 / VIP ♦♦♦
Berry Gordy switched Chuck Jackson to the VIP label for his final LP for the Motown family. It didn't help sales, as this album of ballads and midtempo love sagas sold as poorly as two previous efforts. Many of Jackson's Motown tracks were remakes; the first two albums were loaded with them, but there are only two here. "The Thrill Is Gone" and "Rainy Night in Georgia" are both done in Chuck's distinctive baritone; they're nice, but they have nothing on the originals. "Baby I'll Get It," backed by "The Day My World Stood Still," flopped, as did its lumbering successor "Let Somebody Love Me," an odd choice for a single since its flip "Two Feet From Happiness" had more juice. Chuck's last two singles were Smokey Robinson productions, "Pet Names" and "Who You Gonna Run To"; both stiffed, and neither are on this collection. The latter, originally done by the Temptations, appeared on Jackson's Motown debut *Chuck Jackson Arrives*. A good CD compilation of Chuck's Motown sides is way overdue. —*Andrew Hamilton*

The Great Recordings: The Best of Chuck Jackson / 1995 / Tomato ♦♦♦♦♦
This 46-song, double-CD compilation of Wand-era recordings is the most extensive Jackson retrospective, though it doesn't include every last worthwhile track. It does contain his most important songs, as well as a few of his duets with Maxine Brown, but the programming leaves something to be desired, inserting some half-baked instrumentals, live cuts, and Elvis Presley covers among the prime stuff. —*Richie Unterberger*

Something You Got / Jun. 1996 / Ichiban/Soul Classics ♦♦♦♦♦
All 20 of the duet tracks that Jackson recorded with Maxine Brown for the Wand label between 1965 and 1967, comprising the entirety of their two albums for the company. It's reasonable pop/soul, but not nearly as memorable as the best male-female soul duets of the era (like the ones by Marvin Gaye and various Motown partners, or by Otis Redding and Carla Thomas). Highlights are the early compositions by the Jo Armstead-Nick Ashford-Valerie Simpson team, including a version of "Let's Go Get Stoned" that was recorded (though not released) before Ray Charles' more famous hit rendition. —*Richie Unterberger*

★ **The Very Best of Chuck Jackson 1961–1967** / Jun. 17, 1997 / Varese ♦♦♦♦♦
Varese's *The Very Best of Chuck Jackson* is a 16-track retrospective of his classic Wand recordings, featuring all of his biggest hits ("I Don't Want to Cry," "I Wake Up Crying," "Any Day Now," "Tell Him I'm Not Home," and the Maxine Brown duet "Something You Got") and several fine, lesser-known singles. Jackson's work was remarkably consistent, and there are many fine songs that didn't make the cut, but *The Very Best of Chuck Jackson* is the best single-disc overview of his greatest music yet assembled. —*Stephen Thomas Erlewine*

Smooth, Smooth Jackson / Jan. 27, 1998 / Sequel ♦♦♦♦
An import compilation of Chuck Jackson's All Platinum sides recorded in the '70s. Many are unaware Jackson recorded on the label that spawned the Moments, the Whatnauts, Sylvia, and Shirley Goodman before transforming into rap city with Sugar Hill Records. He only mustered two tiny hits: "Needing You, Wanting You" and "I've Got the Need," both written by Al Goodman, Harry Ray, & Walter Morris. The former features the Moments crooning delicately behind Jackson's smooth baritone; the latter is a duet with Sylvia Robinson that sounds like Al Goodman singing and not Jackson. The good stuff here includes "Cover Up or Get Ready," which is about as risqué as Jackson gets; he tells his lady "I've had a hard day but if you keep lying there like that you're gonna pay." "True Believer" and "Keep Ringing My Bell" are solid, as are Jackson's updates of his own "I Don't Want to Cry" and "Any Day Now." He transforms chart busters—"And I Am Telling You," "It's Not Unusual," and "After the Loving"—into his personal toys. A worthy collection by an R&B legend. —*Andrew Hamilton*

I'll Never Get Over You / Dec. 1, 1998 / Varese ♦♦♦♦
Chuck Jackson's resonant baritone hardly gets untracked on this Charles Wallert production. Wallert's so laid-back on these 14 songs that the sound is closer to easy listening than soul. The only song he claims is an aching rendition of "Walk Away From Love," the David Ruffin hit (the beautiful female voices deserve bonuses), and two duets: "If I Let Myself Go" and "What Goes Around Comes Around." The title track is a rather mundane, lightweight track, and Wallert's "Reaching' for the Stars" is even flimsier. An older, mellower Jackson represents here; the stud who hit with "I Don't Wanna Cry" and "Any Day Now" is missing in action. —*Andrew Hamilton*

Deon Jackson

b. Jan. 26, 1946, Ann Arbor, MI
Vocals / Pop-Soul, Soul
Still in his teens when he began recording, Deon Jackson's 1966 smash "Love Makes the World Go Round" was an engaging piece of soft Detroit soul. The Ann Arbor, MI, product caught the ear of Detroit producer Ollie McLaughlin, who began recording him for his Carla label in 1962. Jackson's first couple of singles ended up on Atlantic with little commercial feedback, but when he cut "Love Makes the World Go Round" for Carla in 1965, he was an overnight sensation. Nothing else Jackson did equaled its success, although "Love Takes a Long Time Growing" and "Ooh Baby" were solid-selling encores. Jackson's lilting vocal style has served him well over the last 15 years as a lounge entertainer in surburban Chicago. —*Bill Dahl*

Love Makes the World Go Round / 1966 / Atco ♦♦♦
The light, whimsical "Love Makes the World Go Round" was like a breath of fresh air, it soared to number-11 pop in March of 1966 prompting this LP. Jackson sung in a light, fluttery tenor and would slide in and out of falsetto for emphasis. This 12-song collection is loaded with young, adult love songs that are enhanced by Deon's vocal phrasings. His remake of Len Barry's "1-2-3" is done at a lazier pace then the original, Jackson's sounds smooth and buttery and use's his flutter to great effect on the bubblegum classic. Roger Miller's humorous, snappy "King of the Road" is another original injected with new blood. The song is a perfect vehicle for Deon's style, and was probably more to his liking than some other selections here including the title track which he supposedly hated. The song was not about romance, but was written by Deon about the civil rights riots of the '60s; Jackson felt the world needed more love. A tight cohesive production by Ollie McLaughlin. —*Andrew Hamilton*

His Greatest Recordings / 1984 / Solid Smoke ♦♦♦♦♦
A marvelous compilation of Deon Jackson's recordings. Labeled by many a one-hit wonder, he actually enjoyed a handful of R&B hits that didn't cross as big as "Love Makes the World Go Round." There's not one weak cut, though one may make a case for "Come Back Home," which isn't so much weak as it's awkward; the upbeat tune is a cross between the Newbeats ("Bread & Butter"), and Marvin Gaye's "Ain't That Peculiar." The rest are heartwarmers. His second biggest recording "Ooh Baby" is not the Smokey Robinson song, but Deon emulates him on this and many other cuts; the song's a smoldering beauty that makes you tingle when Deon slides into the chorus, singing—"oooh, oooh baby, I can't do without you," in a quivering falsetto. Four of the tracks were previously unissued, and listening to the bouncy, joyful "Still Remember the Feeling," you'll scratch your head wondering why such an obvious hit got shelved. The tunes include ballads, midtempo numbers, and a couple of straight R&B drivers like "You Said You Love Me," where he sounds like his namesake Chuck Jackson. —*Andrew Hamilton*

● **Golden Classics** / Jun. 22, 1994 / Collectables ♦♦♦♦♦

Freddie Jackson

b. Oct. 2, 1956, Harlem, New York City, NY
Vocals / Urban
To urban contemporary listeners, Freddie Jackson was one of the biggest stars of the latter half of the '80s, dominating the R&B charts seemingly at will. Jackson's forte was sophisticated, romantic soul ballads aimed at adult audiences, but he was also capable of tackling urban contemporary dance fare and even the occasional jazz tune. Yet unlike many of his peers—Luther Vandross, Anita Baker, Peabo Bryson, etc.—Jackson never managed to cross over to the pop charts, where none of his R&B smashes even breached the Top Ten. As new trends like hip-hop altered the urban contemporary landscape, Jackson gradually faded from view during the '90s.

Freddie Jackson was born October 2, 1956 in Harlem, and like so many soul stars, he was trained as a gospel singer from an early age, singing at the White Rock Baptist Church. There he met Paul Laurence, who would later become his producer and songwriting partner. After completing school, Jackson joined Laurence's group LJE (Laurence-Jones Ensemble) and played the New York club scene. During the early '80s, Jackson moved to the West Coast and sang lead with the R&B band Mystic Merlin, but soon returned to New York to work with Laurence at the Hush Productions company. He sang on demo recordings of Laurence's compositions, and also served as a backup singer for Melba Moore after she caught his nightclub act.

In 1985 Jackson landed a record deal with Capitol and issued his debut album, *Rock Me Tonight*. The Laurence-penned title track stormed the R&B charts, spending a whopping six weeks at number one, and made Jackson an instant sensation on urban contemporary radio. "You Are My Lady" gave him a second straight R&B chart-topper, and also proved to be his highest-charting single on the pop side, peaking at number 13. With "He'll Never Love You (Like I Do)" and "Love Is Just a Touch Away" also hitting the R&B Top Ten, *Rock Me Tonight* topped the R&B album charts and went platinum. Jackson wasted no time issuing a follow-up set; *Just Like the First Time* appeared in 1986 on the heels of a number-one R&B duet with Melba Moore, "A Little Bit More" (from her album *A Lot of Love*). Another platinum seller, *Just Like the First Time* continued Jackson's incredible dominance of the R&B singles charts; "Tasty Love," "Have You Ever Loved Somebody," and "Jam Tonight" all hit number one, while "I Don't Want to Lose Your Love" went to number two.

The pace of Jackson's success slowed to less superhuman levels with the 1988 release of *Don't Let Love Slip Away*, which nonetheless featured another R&B chart-topper in "Hey Lover," plus further hits in "Nice and Slow" and "Crazy (For Me)." The title track of 1990's *Do Me Again* duplicated that feat, and "Main Course" just missed, topping out at number two. Even so, Jackson's early placings in the lower reaches of the pop Top 40 had long since disappeared, and some critics charged that his albums were growing too similar to one another. Perhaps it was a lack of distinctiveness in his material that hurt Jackson's chances for a pop breakthrough; whatever the case, 1992's *Time for Love* failed to duplicate the crossover success Luther Vandross was belatedly enjoying, despite a hit cover of the soul classic "Me and Mrs. Jones."

Seeking a new beginning, Jackson parted ways with Capitol in late 1993, and signed with RCA. His label debut *Here It Is* appeared the following year, with diminished commercial returns—in part because his straightforwardly romantic ballad style was increasingly out of step with the sexually explicit new breed of R&B crooner. Following a Christmas album, Jackson split with RCA and recorded *Private Party* for the much smaller Street Life imprint in 1995. Several years of silence ensued, until Orpheus issued *Life After 30* in late 1999; the equally low-key release *Live in Concert* followed in 2000. —*Steve Huey*

Rock Me Tonight / 1985 / Capitol ♦♦♦♦♦
Here on his debut album, Freddie Jackson enjoyed admirable chart success with each of the four singles. The initial single, "Rock Me Tonight," awas a very rhythmic ballad with an easy-flowing chorus enhanced by some nostalgic lyrics. It hit the *Billboard* R&B charts in April 1985, and stayed afloat for 26 weeks. The song peaked at the number-one position, and held it for six straight weeks. Jackson came right back with "You Are My Lady," a romantic and ideal wedding song whose simplicity and substance assisted in its migration to the top spot on the charts, where it had a run of two straight weeks.

The third and fourth singles were the dance-oriented "He'll Never Love You (Like I Do)" and the picturesque "Love Is Just a Touch Away." While the beat is aggressive on the former, Jackson's debonair approach to the lyric keeps the song under control. Jackson gently caresses the lyric with his soothing tenor on the latter. Respectively, the songs peaked at numbers eight and nine after 17 and 14 weeks on the charts. The New York native even undertakes the jazz standard "Good Morning Heartache" with a mellow but fiery passion. Jackson's utilization of his vocal skills with much vibrato, which became a signature of his, was very well received. *—Craig Lytle*

Just Like the First Time / 1986 / Capitol ✦✦✦
Jackson does not lose any momentum with this album. As with his initial project (*Rock Me Tonight*), he is in excellent company with four Top Ten songs. The initial release, "Tasty Love," has that standard Jackson rhythm arrangement, the melody and his vocality remain inviting to the listener. This sumptuous single seduced the *Billboard* R&B charts for 26 weeks, claiming the number-one spot for four consecutive weeks. "Have You Have Ever Loved Somebody" is a gracefully flowing midtempo ballad, in spite of its intermittent cadence in the verse. Jackson's passionate vocal execution is an irresistible magnet to the listener. This single held the number-one spot on the charts for two weeks inside 18 weeks. Slightly slower than the aforementioned, "I Don't Want to Lose Your Love" also has a intermittent cadence supported by an appealing hook line. It became a number-two single after only 16 weeks. Jackson switches gears and ignites of the album with the chart-buster "Jam Tonight." With a bouncy groove, an irresistible rhythm and lyrics inciting dancefloor craze, Jackson cruises through this finger-snapping groove. Before bowing after 15 weeks, the single claimed the number one spot on the charts. There are no album fillers here, only quality songs. *—Craig Lytle*

Don't Let Love Slip Away / 1988 / Razor & Tie ✦✦✦

Do Me Again / Oct. 29, 1990 / Razor & Tie ✦✦✦
This album accents Jackson's strengths; no one sings with more conviction, earnestness and passion on love ballads, as he demonstrates repeatedly during such songs as "Love Me Down," "Do Me Again," "All Over You" (CD bonus cut) and "I'll Be Waiting For You." He has yet to record a captivating uptempo tune, but "I Can't Take It" came close. It's doubtful as to whether Jackson can overtake Vandross in the 1990s, but hopefully RCA will at least put him in the hunt. *—Ron Wynn*

Time for Love / Aug. 3, 1992 / Capitol ✦✦✦
Freddie Jackson ended his five-album stay at Capitol ended with *Time for Love*, a satisfying effort that isn't much different from his previous Capitol releases. The New Yorker obviously knew what his strengths were—smooth soul/urban contemporary music and romantic ballads—and once again, the singer succeeds by zeroing in on them. The standout track is a poignant cover of the Gamble & Huff classic "Me and Mrs. Jones" (recorded by Billy Paul in 1971 and subsequently by the Dramatics), and Jackson also brings plenty of honest emotion to such slick yet gritty tunes as "I Could Use a Little Love Right Now," "Trouble" and "Can We Try." Though it falls short of the excellence of *Rock Me Tonight* and *Just Like the First Time*, this CD was a welcome addition to his catalog. *—Alex Henderson*

Here It Is / Jan. 1994 / RCA ✦✦✦
After several years of R&B success but no crossover hits, vocalist Freddie Jackson left Capitol for RCA late in 1993. His RCA debut has several excellent performances, but unfortunately, there's no single standout cut. There are brilliantly sung numbers, ("Come Home II U," "I Love," "My Family") but there's no track that can stand alongside "Rock Me Tonight," "Nice and Slow" or any of a half-dozen other past Jackson hits. Jackson merits pop attention more than many others with a much larger profile. *—Ron Wynn*

● **The Greatest Hits of Freddie Jackson** / Jan. 25, 1994 / Capitol ✦✦✦✦✦
During his five-album stay at Capitol, Freddie Jackson repeatedly showed himself to be a soul man of unusual merit. Ranging from outstanding to decent, all five of his Capitol albums are worth owning. But if a listener is allotted only one Jackson CD, *The Greatest Hits of Freddie Jackson* is the logical choice. From "Rock Me Tonight," "Nice & Slow" and "Tasty Love" to "I Could Use a Little Love (Right Now)" and "Jam Tonight," all of the essential Jackson material is included. The CD does a fine job of summarizing Jackson's accomplishments at Capitol and proves that his extremely devoted following is well deserved. *—Alex Henderson*

For Old Times Sake: The Freddie Jackson Story / Aug. 20, 1996 / EMI ✦✦✦✦
Although there's a fair amount of duplication between this and *Greatest Hits*, it's not exactly a greatest hits collection, divided as it is between high-charting singles and album tracks. It's perhaps more oriented toward his lover-man outings than *Greatest Hits*, which remains the first choice if you only want one Freddie Jackson disc. *—Richie Unterberger*

Anthology / Jun. 2, 1998 / Capitol ✦✦✦✦
Sliding over notes like satin sheets, you couldn't turn on a black radio station in the '80s without hearing Freddie Jackson's velvet vocals. From 1985 to 1992, the crooner racked up 17 Top Ten hits, making him one of the decade's biggest R&B stars. *Freddie Jackson Anthology* chronicles Jackson's sexy soul singing on two CDs that display his talent for conveying heartfelt emotions. With classics such as "Rock Me Tonight," "You Are My Lady," and "Love Me Down," this collection stylishly showcases the best of '80s R&B. *—Rosalind Cummings-Yeates*

George Jackson

b. 1936, Greenville, MS

Songwriter, Guitar / Memphis Soul, Soul-Blues, R&B, Soul

Songwriter George Jackson wrote or co-wrote hits for Clarence Carter (the gold single "Too Weak to Fight"), Wilson Pickett ("A Man and a Half"), Bob Seger ("Old Time Rock and Roll," "Trying to Live My Life Without You") Z.Z. Hill ("Down Home Blues"), and the Osmonds (the million-selling "One Bad Apple" and "Double Lovin'"), among others. He also several recorded Southern soul-flavored singles, charting with "That's How Much You Mean to Me" and "Aretha, Sing One for Me."

Born in 1936 in Greenville, MS, Jackson started recording for Ike Turner's Prann label in 1963 after introducing himself to Turner when the entertainer played a concert in Greenville. The single "Nobody Wants to Cha Cha With Me" was recorded at Cosimo Matassa's New Orleans studio. After traveling to Memphis, Jackson was turned down by Stax Records, but while there he met Louis Williams and they started a vocal group called the Ovations. Recording for Goldwax Records, their single "It's So Wonderful to Be in Love" made it to number 22 on the R&B chart in 1965. While with Goldwax, Jackson wrote for label-mates James Carr and Spencer Wiggens. The Ovations broke up and Jackson got a solo deal with Decca Records under the pseudonym Bart Jackson, releasing "Wonderful Dream" in 1968.

At the suggestion of producer Billy Sherrill, Jackson journeyed to Muscle Shoals, AL, to work at producer Rick Hall's Fame Recording Studio, where he became a staff songwriter and wrote hits for Clarence Carter and Candi Staton. MGM Records act the Osmonds visited the hit factory and Jackson submitted a song he had originally written for the Jackson 5. "One Bad Apple" hit number one on the pop charts in early 1971, and stayed there for five weeks. Because of the success, Jackson was allowed to record some singles for MGM. During the mid-'80s, Jackson joined Malaco Records as a staff songwriter penning hits for Johnnie Taylor, Bobby "Blue" Bland, Benny Latimore, Denise LaSalle, and Z.Z. Hill. Jackson's own album *Heart to Heart Collect* was released by Hep Me Records in 1991. *—Ed Hogan*

● **Beggin' Ain't for Me** / 1998 / Black & Tan ✦✦✦
Revered soul songwriter George Jackson's songs didn't have the same snap, crackle, and pop when he recorded them himself—they always came off better when sung by other singers. Jackson's low voice wasn't the best vehicle to sell the hearty Southern soul dramas he wrote so prolifically; it was better suited for uptempo blues, the material that comprises the lion's share of *Beggin' Ain't for Me.* He wrote eight of the ten songs, but the most lively numbers are Elmore James' "Shake Your Moneymaker" and "Kitchen Sink Boogie" (credited to a trio of writers) with its strong lead guitar play. Jackson's no spring chicken, but "Ella May" sounds as if a much older man is singing; the lyrics don't get much more complex than, "Ella May what you got cookin' today." "Looking to Steal Somebody" is so deliberate that you have time to insert alternate lyrics before Jackson sings the ones he wrote. Jackson helps his cause by blowing a fiery harp on many selections. If you're looking for an album of jumping blues, this is top shelf, but those expecting to hear Jackson the writer of "I'm Just a Prisoner," "Cheatin' in the Next Room," and "Find 'Em, Fool 'Em, Forget 'Em" will still be looking after this CD is done playing. *—Andrew Hamilton*

Sweet Down Home Delta Blues / Amblin' ✦✦✦
George Jackson's lone album *Sweet Down Home Delta Blues* is a straight-ahead collection of Delta blues. Considering that he's a house writer for Malaco Records, where he specialized in merging contemporary blues with soul, that comes as a little bit of a surprise. Unfortunately, he doesn't do the Delta as well as he does soul-blues, and *Sweet Down Home Delta Blues* suffers from predictability and perfunctory performances. Occasionally, the music comes to life, either through inspired playing or a solid song, but that only serves to remind the listeners of what this could have been. *—Thom Owens*

J.J. Jackson (Jerome Louis Jackson)

b. Apr. 8, 1941, Brooklyn, NY

Vocals, Percussion / Pop-Soul, Soul, Disco

One of the most interesting obscure figures of '60s soul, Jackson scored a mammoth R&B hit in 1966 with one of the most infectious dance smashes of the decade, "But It's Alright." The New Yorker had worked as an arranger for Jack McDuff and Jimmy Witherspoon before his manager arranged for Jackson to come to England in 1966. Though "But It's Alright," with its classic stuttering guitar riff and sharp horn charts, sounded as authentic as any Stax/Volt single, it was actually recorded in the U.K. with British session musicians. Jackson—a mammoth, nearly 300-pound man who also played organ—was a grainy, good-natured belter in the mold of Otis Redding. A talented songwriter who penned much of his own material, he wrote the A-side of one of the Pretty Things' best mid-'60s R&B/raunch singles ("Come See Me").

Jackson never matched the success of "But It's Alright," but cut some singles which are highly valued by English Northern soul connoisseurs. His hard-to-find 1969 and 1970 albums found him exploring, in the manner of most other soul stars of the time, increased social consciousness in his songwriting and increasingly sophisticated horn and string arrangements. He later surfaced as a Los Angeles disc jockey, leading to a cameo appearance in the film *Car Wash* that has been sampled by numerous rappers. *—Richie Unterberger*

● **The Great J.J. Jackson** / 1966 / See for Miles ✦✦✦✦✦
J.J. Jackson's 1966 album *The Great J.J. Jackson* was recorded in England with British producer Miki Dallon. Includes "But It's Alright," his version of "Come See Me" (actually recorded after the Pretty Things' rendition), and the effervescent, boastful "I Dig Girls." Much more solid than the average '60s soul album, it shows Jackson as a fine songwriter and infectiously throaty vocalist on a mixture of uptempo ravers and deep soul ballads. Somewhat similar to Otis Redding, but more pop-oriented, which is not necessarily a bad thing when you can make it work as well as J.J. does. *—Richie Unterberger*

Janet Jackson

b. May 16, 1966, Gary, IN

Vocals / Urban, Dance-Pop, Club/Dance, Adult Contemporary

Few celebrity siblings can emerge from the shadows of their already famous relations to become superstars in their own right and with their own distinct personalities. That's exactly what Janet Jackson did in becoming one of the biggest female pop and R&B stars of the '80s and '90s. Since her breakthrough in 1986 with the album *Control*, Jackson's career as a hitmaker has been a model of consistency, rivaling Madonna and Whitney

Houston in terms of pop-chart success over the long haul. A big part of the reason was that Jackson kept her level of quality control very high; her singles were always expertly crafted, with indelible pop hooks and state-of-the-art production that kept up with contemporary trends in urban R&B. Once established, her broad-based appeal never really dipped all that much; she was able to avoid significant career missteps, musical and otherwise, and successfully shifted her image from a strong, independent young woman to a sexy, mature adult. With a string of multi-platinum albums under her belt, she showed no signs of slowing down in the new millennium.

Janet Damita Jo Jackson was born May 16, 1966, in Gary, IN. She was the youngest of nine children in the Jackson family, and her older brothers had already begun performing together as the Jackson 5 by the time she was born. Bitten by the performing bug at a young age, she first appeared on-stage with the Jackson 5 at age seven, and began a sitcom acting career at the age of ten in 1977, when producer Norman Lear selected her to join the cast of *Good Times.* She remained there until 1979, and subsequently appeared on *Diff'rent Strokes* (1981-1982) and *A New Kind of Family.* In 1982, pushed by her father into trying a singing career, Jackson released her self-titled first album on A&M; a couple of singles scraped the lower reaches of the charts, but on the whole, it made very little noise. She was cast in the musical series *Fame* in 1983; the following year, she issued her second album, *Dream Street*, which sold even more poorly than its predecessor. Upon turning 18, Jackson rebelled against her parents' close supervision, eloping with a member of another musical family, singer James DeBarge. However, the relationship quickly hit the rocks and Jackson wound up moving back into her parents' home and having the marriage annulled.

Jackson took some time to rethink her musical career and her father hired her a new manager, John McClain, who isolated his young charge to train her as a dancer (and make her lose weight). McClain hooked Jackson up with producers/writers Jimmy Jam & Terry Lewis, whom she'd seen perform as members of the Minneapolis funk outfit the Time. Jackson collaborated with Jam & Lewis on most of the tracks for her next album, *Control*, which presented her as a confident, tough-minded young woman (with a soft side and a sense of humor) taking charge of her life for the first time. In support of Jackson's new persona, Jam & Lewis crafted a set of polished, computerized backing tracks with slamming beats that owed more to hard, hip-hop-tinged funk and urban R&B than Janet's older brother Michael's music. *Control* became an out-of-the-box hit, and eventually spun off six singles, the first five of which—"What Have You Done for Me Lately," the catch phrase-inspiring "Nasty," the number-one "When I Think of You," the title track, and the ballad "Let's Wait Awhile"—hit the Top Five on the pop charts. Jackson was hailed as a role model for young women and *Control* eventually sold over five-million copies, establishing Jackson as not just a star, but her own woman. It also made Jam & Lewis a monstrously in-demand production team.

For the hotly anticipated follow-up, John McClain wanted to push Jackson toward more overtly sexual territory, to which she objected strenuously. Instead, she began collaborating with Jam & Lewis on more socially conscious material, which formed the backbone of 1989's *Rhythm Nation 1814* (the "1814" purportedly stood for either the letters "R" and "N" or the year "The Star-Spangled Banner" was written). Actually, save for the title track, most of the record's singles were bright and romantically themed; four of them—"Miss You Much," "Escapade," "Black Cat," and "Love Will Never Do (Without You)"—hit number one, and three more—"Rhythm Nation," "Alright," and "Come Back to Me"—reached the Top Five, making Jackson the first artist ever to produce seven Top Five hits off of one album (something not even her brother Michael had accomplished). Aside from a greater use of outside samples, *Rhythm Nation*'s sound largely resembled that of *Control*, but was just as well-crafted, and listeners embraced it enthusiastically, buying over six-million copies. Jackson undertook her first real tour (she'd appeared at high schools around the country in 1982) in support of the album and it was predictably a smashing success. In 1991, Jackson capitalized on her success by jumping from A&M to Virgin for a reported $32 million, and also secretly married choreographer and longtime boyfriend René Elizondo.

Once on Virgin, Jackson set about revamping her sound and image. Her 1992 duet with Luther Vandross from the *Mo' Money* soundtrack, "The Best Things in Life Are Free," was a major R&B hit, also reaching the pop Top Ten. The following year, she also resumed her acting career, co-starring in acclaimed director (and former junior high classmate) John Singleton's *Poetic Justice*, along with rapper Tupac Shakur. But neither really hinted at the sexy, seductive, fully adult persona she unveiled with 1993's *janet.*, her Virgin debut. Jackson trumpeted her new image with a notorious Rolling Stone cover photo, in which her topless form was covered by a pair of hands belonging to an unseen "friend." Musically, Jam & Lewis set aside the synthesized funk of their first two albums with Jackson in favor of warm, inviting, gently undulating grooves. The album's lead single, the slinky "That's the Way Love Goes," became Jackson's biggest hit ever, spending eight weeks at number one. It was followed by a predictably long parade of Top Ten hits—"If," the number-one ballad "Again," "Because of You," "Any Time, Any Place," "You Want This." *janet.*'s debut showing at number one made it her third straight chart-topping album, and it went on to sell nearly seven-million copies.

In 1995, Janet and Michael teamed up for the single "Scream," which was supported by an elaborate, award-winning, space-age video that, upon completion, ranked as the most expensive music video ever made. The single debuted at number five on the pop charts, but gradually slid down from there. In 1996, A&M issued a retrospective of her years at the label, *Design of a Decade 1986-1996*; it featured the Virgin hit "That's the Way Love Goes" and a few new tracks, one of which, "Runaway," became a Top Five hit. Jackson also signed a new contract with Virgin for a reported $80 million. Yet while working on her next album, Jackson reportedly suffered an emotional breakdown, or at least a severe bout with depression; she later raised eyebrows when she talked in several interviews about the cleansing value of coffee enemas as part of her treatment. Her next album, *The Velvet Rope*, appeared in 1997, and was touted as her most personal and intimate work to date. *The Velvet Rope* sought to combine the sensuality of *janet.* with the more socially conscious parts of *Rhythm Nation*, mixing songs about issues like domestic abuse, AIDS, and homophobia with her most sexually explicit songs ever. Critical opinion on the album was divided; some applauded her ambition, while others found the record too bloated. The lead American single "Together Again," an elegy for AIDS victims, was a number-one hit; also popular on the radio was "Got 'Til It's Gone," which featured rapper Q-Tip and a sample of Joni Mitchell over a reggae beat. "I Get Lonely," featuring Blackstreet, was another big hit; but on the whole, *The Velvet Rope* didn't prove to be the blockbuster singles bonanza that its predecessors were, which was probably why its sales stalled at around three-million copies.

Jackson toured the world again, and stayed on the charts in 1999 with the Top Five Busta Rhymes duet "What's It Gonna Be?!"; her appearance in the video remade her as a glitzy, artificially costumed, single-name diva. In 2000, she appeared in the Eddie Murphy comedy *Nutty Professor II: The Klumps*, and her soundtrack contribution, "Doesn't Really Matter," became a number-one single. Unfortunately, Jackson's marriage to Elizondo had become strained and the couple divorced in 2000, sparking a court battle over her musical income. Jackson returned with a new album, *All for You*, in 2001, which largely continued the sensual tone of *Janet.* and *The Velvet Rope*; it debuted at number one, selling over 600,000 copies in its first week alone. The title track was issued as the album's first single and quickly topped the charts, followed by another sizable hit in "Someone to Call My Lover." *—Steve Huey*

Janet Jackson / 1982 / A&M ✦✦

On her eponymous debut album, Janet Jackson demonstrated no distinctive musical personality of her own, which wasn't surprising considering that she was in her teens. If her producers had concocted a sharper set of songs and more interesting beats, *Janet Jackson* might have been a pleasant set of sunny dance-pop, but as it stands, only "Young Love" stands out among the undistinguished, sub-disco thumpers and drippy ballads. *—Stephen Thomas Erlewine*

Dream Street / 1984 / A&M ✦✦

A listen to Janet Jackson's *Dream Street* brings to mind remembrances of the then-teenaged singer's appearances on *American Bandstand*, shyly answering questions from host Dick Clark, as well as her short stint as a regular on the syndicated series *Fame.* The first single, "Don't Stand Another Chance," was a family affair, produced by brother Marlon Jackson with vocal ad-libs by Michael Jackson. It was a Top Ten R&B hit during the summer of 1984. The extended 12-inch mix rocks, showcasing outstanding synth work by John Barnes. Other standouts are the smeary Minneapolis funk cut "Pretty Boy" produced by Jesse Johnson, and both "Hold Back the Tears" and "If It Takes All Night" are prime examples of pleasing '80s pop. *—Ed Hogan*

Control / 1986 / A&M ✦✦✦✦✦

Jimmy Jam & Terry Lewis tailored their contemporary dance-pop to the emerging personality of Janet Jackson, who attempted to take control of her life on this record. In the course of that attempt, she came across as an aggressive, independent woman, notably on "What Have You Done for Me Lately." But the album was primarily a production showcase; it may have been tailored to Jackson's persona, but the real artists were Jam & Lewis. *—William Ruhlmann*

Rhythm Nation 1814 / 1989 / A&M ✦✦✦✦✦

After shocking the R&B world with 1986's *Control*—a gutsy, risk-taking triumph that was a radical departure from her first two albums—Michael and Jermaine Jackson's younger sister reached an even higher artistic plateau with the conceptual *Rhythm Nation 1814.* Once again, she enlists the help of Time graduates Jimmy Jam & Terry Lewis (one of the more soulful production/songwriting teams of 1980s and '90s R&B) with wildly successful results. In 1989, protest songs were common in rap, but rare in R&B—Jackson, following rap's lead, dares to address social and political topics on "The Knowledge," the disturbing "State of the World," and the poignant ballad "Living in a World" (which decries the reality of children being exposed to violence). Jackson's voice is wafer-thin, and she doesn't have much of a range—but she definitely has lots of soul and spirit and uses it to maximum advantage on those gems as well as non-political pieces ranging from the Prince-influenced funk/pop of "Miss You Much" and "Alright" to the caressing, silky ballads "Someday Is Tonight," "Alone," and "Come Back to Me" to the pop/rock smoker "Black Cat." For those purchasing their first Janet Jackson release, *Rhythm Nation* would be an even wiser investment than *Control*—and that's saying a lot. *—Alex Henderson*

janet. / May 18, 1993 / Virgin ✦✦✦

After *Control* and *Rhythm Nation 1814*, Janet Jackson had quite a lot to live up to. Anyone who expected Jackson to top *Rhythm Nation*—her crowning achievement and an incredibly tough act to follow—was being unrealistic. But with *janet.*, she delivered a respectable offering that, although not as strong as either *Control* or *Nation*, has many strong points. As before, Jackson is joined by the prolific Jimmy Jam & Terry Lewis team, and their input is valuable on everything from the angry "This Time" and the hypnotic "That's the Way Love Goes" to the '60s-flavored "What'll I Do" and the sociopolitical "The New Agenda" (which features Public Enemy leader Chuck D.). But perhaps the CD's most exciting track is "Funky Big Band," which samples jazz legend Lionel Hampton's 1938 big band classic "I'm In the Mood for Swing" with thrilling results. There are a few throwaways (including the lightweight ballad "Again"), but despite its shortcomings, *janet.* is a welcome addition to her catalog. *—Alex Henderson*

★ **Design of a Decade: 1986/1996** / Oct. 10, 1995 / A&M ✦✦✦✦✦

Design of a Decade: 1986/1996 is a misleading title. The bulk of Janet Jackson's greatest hits collection concentrates on *Control* and *Rhythm Nation 1814*, simply by contractual necessity. That is far from a fatal flaw. The hits from those two albums were state-of-the-art dance-pop productions at the time of their release, filled with bottomless beats and memorable, catchy hooks. None of the songs have lost any of their impact, from the funk of "Miss You Much" and "What Have You Done for Me Lately" to the ballads "Let's Wait Awhile" and "Come Back to Me." In addition to all 13 Top 40 hits from *Control* and *Rhythm Nation*—all but one went into the Top Five—*Design of a Decade* includes the biggest and best hit from *janet.*, the sultry "That's the Way Love Goes," and two new songs, "Runaway" and "Twenty Foreplay." It's a credit to Janet Jackson that the two new numbers feel like genuine hits, not tacked-on filler, and help make the album a compulsively listenable greatest hits collection. *—Stephen Thomas Erlewine*

The Velvet Rope / Oct. 7, 1997 / Virgin ♦♦♦
Where *janet.*, Ms. Jackson's third blockbuster album, implied sexuality with its teasing cover and seductive grooves, its sequel, *The Velvet Rope*, is sexually explicit, offering tales of bondage, body piercing, and bisexuality. Not that you'd necessarily know that from listening to *The Velvet Rope*, since the album sags with endless interludes, murmured vocals, and subdued urban grooves. Working with her mainstays Jimmy Jam & Terry Lewis, Jackson essentially reworks the hushed atmosphere of *janet.*, neglecting to put a new sonic spin on the material—for an album that wants to push the limits, it sounds surprisingly tame. Similarly, Jackson's attempts to broaden her sexual horizons frequently sound forced, whether it's the references to piercing or her recasting of Rod Stewart's "Tonight's the Night" as a lesbian anthem. Furthermore, the album is simply too long, which means the best moments sink into the murk. And that's unfortunate, because there are good moments on *The Velvet Rope*, but at its running time of 70-plus minutes and 22 tracks, it's hard to work up the patience to find them. *—Stephen Thomas Erlewine*

All for You / Apr. 24, 2001 / Virgin ♦♦♦♦
The Velvet Rope was a fairly bold move on Janet Jackson's part, as she got seriously sexy—too serious, actually, since it had a fairly bitter tone, underscored by hints of perversity. Four years later, marked by one hidden marriage revealed through a divorce, Janet returned with *All for You*, an album that is as about sex as much as *The Velvet Rope*, yet there's a key difference—it feels sexy, not pornographic. With her trusty collaborators Jimmy Jam & Terry Lewis in tow, she's created a record that's luxurious and sensual, spreading leisurely over its 70 minutes, luring you in even when you know better. And there are certainly moments that make you wish you knew better. For one, it's plotted like *The Velvet Rope*, filled with skits and deliberately recalling the record with its obsession with flesh and how it builds on '70s soul and soft rock. This time around, instead of Joni Mitchell, she appropriates America's "Ventura Highway" for "Someone to Call My Lover," one of the record's best cuts, and "interpolates" Carly Simon's "You're So Vain" on "Son of a Gun," with Simon singing and... well, I guess you could call it rapping... right along. The twist is, this is an anti-music industry song and a particularly foul-mouthed entry on the album, sitting comfortably alongside another industry song, the slow groove "Truth." And that fills out the three main themes of the album—divorce, industry, and sex—with a little bit of love on the side. These keep things humming throughout this overly sultry, overlong album, which intrigues with its very texture even as it lulls at its length. After all, there's a lot to be said for texture, and *All for You* is alluring, easily enveloping the listener. Though it's hardly as explicit as *The Velvet Rope*, apart from a section where she proclaims "I just want to suck you, taste you, ride you, feel you, make you come—come inside of me" (mind you, this album does *not* have a parental advisory sticker), this is her sexiest-sounding record, thanks to Jam & Lewis' silky groove and her breathy delivery, two things that make the record palatable throughout too many spoken interludes and songs that just don't quite click. Even if there is a fair share of filler, this is hardly as strained as *The Velvet Rope* (though in many respects, it's every bit as self-conscious), and there's an ease to its construction, topped off by such songs as "All for You" and "Doesn't Really Matter" that maintain Janet, Jam, & Lewis' reputation as the leading lights of contemporary urban soul. It'd be nicer if the album was leaner, concentrating on just the great songs, but indulgence is what this record encourages. Janet sprawls out throughout the album, indulging her whims, desires, and fantasies, but—fortunately for us—her indulgences are alluring in their self-absorption. Of course, it helps to have Jam & Lewis on your side to articulate your indulgence. *—Stephen Thomas Erlewine*

Jermaine Jackson

b. Dec. 11, 1954, Gary, IN

Vocals, Bass / Quiet Storm, Urban, Disco, Dance-Pop

The lone Jackson family member to stay with Motown while the other brothers split for CBS/Epic (he was then married to Berry Gordy's daughter Hazel), Jermaine enjoyed a artistically diffident career during the '70s at Motown, surfacing with an occasional hit like a remake of "Daddy's Home" (1972) and "Let's Be Young Tonight" (1975). Jermaine got a badly needed shot in the arm from Stevie Wonder, who wrote and produced "Let's Get Serious," a Top Ten pop and soul dance hit that came around the time of brother Michael's pop ascendancy. After scoring a Top 20 pop hit in 1982 with the infectious "Let Me Tickle Your Fancy," Jermaine left Motown in 1983 for Arista Records, where he scored a pair of hits in 1984 with "Do What You Do" and the scintillating dance number "Dynamite."

Subsequently, he re-joined the Jacksons in time for their ill-fated *Victory* tour in 1984. Jackson has recorded sporadically since, though he generated controversy in 1991 when "Word to the Badd," a thinly veiled attack on his brother Michael, was leaked out to urban music stations. *—John Lowe*

Jermaine / 1972 / Motown ♦♦♦
One listen to *Jermaine* and it's clear whose voice was responsible for the jumpy energy of the Jackson 5—one hint: it wasn't the afroed Jackson on the cover of this album. It's not so much that Jermaine Jackson can't sing, but rather the flowery, overly-orchestrated production by the Corporation drowns the songs in a sea of schmaltzy strings and poor arrangements, taking away all their movement (or as with "I Only Have Eyes for You," their mystery). One gets the feeling that with material like "Homeward Bound" and "Daddy's Home," Berry Gordy was trying to turn Jackson into a middle-of-the-road pop singer, but Gordy would've been better off harnessing Jackson's natural inclination toward uptempo dance material rather than sentimental ballads. *—Steve Kurutz*

Come into My Life / 1973 / Motown ♦♦♦
Jermaine Jackson has never gotten his props. During the Jackson 5 days, Michael's high-pitched and fantastically precocious, soulful vocals were anchored by Jermaine's throaty, raspy tenor that somehow conveyed a kind of world-weariness from this teenager. Take a look at just one single. The sweet, candy soul of "The Love You Save" was balanced by the aching, testifying of Jermaine's lead on the radio-aired B-side "I Found That Girl." Let's not forget Jermaine's solo successes. His 1973 million-selling remake of Shep & the Limelights' "Daddy's Home" remains a classic. Another release from around the same time, the LP *Come Into My Life*, was one of the best Motown albums from that era. The opening track, "Sittin' on the Edge of My Mind," is a steppers' classic. The LP's only charting single was "You're in Good Hands Now" with the B-side, a sweet cover of the Bobby Taylor & the Vancouvers hit, "Does Your Mama Know About Me," made it to number 35 on the R&B charts and number 73 on pop in *Billboard* during the fall of 1973. In the same vein is the gentle, appreciative ballad, "I Need You More Now Than Ever." Other standout tracks are the funky, electric piano/wah-wah guitar-laced title track, the midtempo "If You Don't Love Me," the wise, snappy "The Bigger You Love the Harder You Fall," and the heart-tugging "So in Love," which has vocals by an unaccredited Jackson 5. In the summer of 1973, *Come Into My Life* hit number 30 on R&B and number 152 on the pop charts. *—Ed Hogan*

My Name Is Jermaine / 1976 / Motown ♦♦
My Name Is Jermaine was Jermaine Jackson's first Motown album released after his brothers, the rest of the Jackson 5, had left the label for CBS Records. As pointed out in the top-rated 1992 ABC-TV miniseries *The Jacksons: The American Dream*, Jermaine felt loyalty towards the man, Berry Gordy, and the label, Motown, that had catapulted him and his family into superstardom. The first single was the classic disco single "Let's Be Young Tonight," co-written and produced by Michael Lovesmith. Labelmate Thelma Houston's vocals are interwoven throughout the LP's tracks. The Lovesmith-produced "Faithful" is one of the best vocal showcases for Jermaine and features a sizzling duet break between him and Houston. Even though Jermaine is pictured with a bass on the cover, there were no musician's credits on the original record album. So it's a mystery as to who's responsible for the outstanding, hyperkinetic bass playing on the tight cuts "Look Past My Life" and "Tonight"'s flip side "Bass Odyssey." Kenneth Lupper infuses gospel-tinged piano and organ on the sly, slow "Who's That Lady." The LP's last two tracks find Jackson at his most romantic on the record. Both the shimmering, string-filled "Stay With Me" and tender "I Just Want to Thank You" have an airy, classical romanticism, while the sax-led slow jam "My Touch of Madness" written by Michael Lovesmith received radio play as an album track and can be heard on some movie soundtracks. "Let's Be Young Tonight," is on the 1991 Motown CD *Greatest Hits & Rare Classics*. *—Ed Hogan*

Let's Get Serious / 1979 / Motown ♦♦♦♦♦
The best of his Motown albums features Stevie Wonder's brilliant songs and production. For once Jermaine sounded inspired, and that feeling is sustained throughtout. One of the high points in his career, and the effort was worth it. *—John Lowe*

I Like Your Style / 1981 / Motown ♦♦♦

Let Me Tickle Your Fancy / 1982 / Motown ♦♦♦
One of the best albums Jermaine Jackson ever made, and certainly his best at *Motown*. The title cut was a Top 10 R&B hit and Top 20 pop smash and got Jackson some significant publicity. It also was his final album at Motown, as he switched to Arista after participating in the *Victory* tour and album the next year. *—Ron Wynn*

Don't Take It Personal / 1989 / Arista ♦♦♦
Jermaine Jackson made his mark on this album with the number-one single "Don't Take It Personal." With a percussive rhythm and the coolness of Jermaine's consoling intonation, this moderate number propelled its way to the top of the *Billboard* R&B charts. One of only two songs to reach number one for the Gary, IN, native. (The other was "Let's Get Serious.") "Two Ships (In the Night)" and "I'd Like to Get to Know You" are also midtempo numbers which peaked at 21 and 27, respectively. The former, written and produced by David Conley & David Townsend of Surface, is a dulcet composition with a steady flow complemented by trembling shades of a trombone. The latter has mellow urban groove in which Jackson releases a soulful plea. It was written by Bernard Jackson, also of Surface. While "Make It Easy on Love," a duet with Miki Howard, has a sweet melody, the chorus is too busy and intense. The former Jackson 5 displays a soulful aggression on "So Right." Other excellent takes include "Rise to the Occasion," a duet with La La, and "Next to You." *—Craig Lytle*

Greatest Hits & Rare Classics / 1991 / Motown ♦♦♦♦♦
No thanks in part to the legacy (musical and not) of his siblings, Jermaine Jackson's skills as a songwriter, producer, and musician have been largely ignored by commercial audiences. His production work with several Motown groups (such as DeBarge and Switch) in the late '70s/early '80s helped to keep the label as an R&B powerhouse when the output of more well-known superstars was faltering to produce powerhouse hits the way they once did. Jermaine was also a mildly successful artist in his own right. This compilation covers a great deal of Jermaine Jackson's career as a solo artist at Motown, from his first hit (a cover of Shep & the Limelights' hit "Daddy's Home") to his last hits prior to leaving Motown for Arista—they're all included. There's also the inclusion of some lesser-known material, most notably a collaboration with the legendary Mizell Brothers. Bonus points like this only help to solidify an already extremely thorough compilation on the prime years of an extremely accomplished but overlooked artist. *—Rob Theakston*

You Said / 1992 / La Face ♦♦♦

● **Ultimate Collection** / Jun. 26, 2001 / Hip-O ♦♦♦♦♦
Jermaine Jackson is one of the finer R&B/pop singers of his generation, but due to siblings like Michael and Janet, his attributes are often overlooked. Hip-O's 2001 release *Ultimate Collection* seems to rectify that situation. While Jackson's talents are genuine this set also shows that he can be a spotty artist. The earliest tracks here, the Jackson 5's anachronistic

and slightly charming "I Found That Girl," "That's the Way Love Goes," and his cover of "Daddy's Home" display a singer with skill yet no true persona. As Jackson's voice continued to change and became strongly reminiscent of Marvin Gaye, the work became more enjoyable. His solo Motown tenure didn't yield any major hits until the early '80s. *Ultimate Collection* offers the big Motown hits like "Let's Get Serious" and "You Like Me Don't You." The great "Let Me Tickle Your Fancy" is arguably the best of the bunch. Unlike many compilations, *Ultimate Collection* offers tracks from two different labels, Motown and Arista. During the Arista years Jackson came into his own with synth pop of "Dynamite" and the top-notch ballad "Do What You Do." This set also includes the almost forgotten-though-skilled "I Think It's Love" and his 1989 hit "Don't Take It Personal." Despite the inclusions, *Ultimate Collection* could have been more eccentric and better. Jackson essentials like "Words Into Action," his duet with Whitney Houston ("If You Say My Eyes Are Beautiful"), and even the controversial version of "Word to the Badd" didn't make it here. This set is strong however and does invite even a casual fan to pick up a few more of his albums. *—Jason Elias*

LaToya Jackson

b. May 29, 1956, Gary, IN

Vocals / Urban, Disco, Dance-Pop

Perhaps the least-talented sibling in the Jackson family, LaToya has nonetheless generated lots of controversy, although it's been outside the music arena. She sang background vocals for the Jackson 5, before going solo in 1979. None of her singles during the '80s for Polydor, Larc, Private I or Palass were anything other than very slight hits, though "Bet'cha Gonna Need My Lovin'" and "Heart Don't Lie" each were R&B Top 30. During the '90s, Jackson wrote a controversial book accusing her father of incest, and has also hosted an infomercial plugging psychic phenomena. Jackson went to Nashville in early 1994 to cut a country LP. *—Ron Wynn*

LaToya Jackson / 1980 / Polydor ✦✦✦

Boosted heavily by the presence of renowned players like Ray Parker Jr., Patrice Rushen, Stevie Wonder and Emilio Castillo, LaToya Jackson became the fifth family member to record solo with this generally satisfying 1980 LP. She does best with uptempo numbers, with the straightforward romp "If You Feel the Funk" and the peppy "Save Your Love" serving as highlights. "If You Feel the Funk" is a well-chosen opener, with its enticing vocal arrangement, sturdy rhythm patterns and a memorable guitar solo from Parker seeping into the brain instantly; "Save Your Love" picks up the pace a little but is more concentrated melodically. Another primer is "Nighttime Lover," a softly seductive, simultaneously kinetic number produced by brother Michael. Otherwise, there aren't any other equally strong moments, though the snappy "Are You Ready," co-written and also recorded by Billy Ocean, is fairly impressionable. Vocally, Jackson doesn't have a lot of weight, but she has an obvious enthusiasm for the songs that comes through consistently. That factor, along with the strong cast of musicians and some memorable tunes, makes this an overall enjoyable set. The filler material is worth skipping past to soak in the finer moments. *—Justin Kantor*

My Special Love / 1981 / Polydor ✦✦

Heart Don't Lie / 1984 / Epic ✦✦✦

Despite a very mild public response to her first two albums, Jackson showed no signs of giving up, moving to Private I and recording this album of youthful, highly danceable material. Whereas most of the instrumentation on the earlier albums was live and authentic, drum programming and overdubs entered the picture in a big way here—but not to the total exclusion of the real thing. The title track, which became the most successful entry, is the most gimmicky. Even with cameos from Howard Hewett and Musical Youth, it's a bit too produced to offer any real substance. More believable and alluring are the sprightly, soulful "Bet'cha Gonna Need My Lovin'" and "Think Twice," the latter featuring a surprisingly colorful trumpet solo. Amir Bayyan's production gets a bit repetitive on occasion, resulting in a few sound-alike tunes, and Jackson's presence isn't as distinguishable as on previous output. But a handful of guilty pleasures here that are, if not much else, very catchy, making this a wise investment for anyone curious about the music of the Jackson family "outcast." *—Justin Kantor*

Imagination / 1986 / Private I ✦✦

La Toya / 1988 / Teldec/BMG ✦✦✦

After leaving her father's production company in 1986, Jackson released this set of producer-driven R&B and dance tracks in 1988. The production team of Full Force has always been capable of surrounding limited vocalists with the right machinery: clever background riffs, samples and special voice effects that can stray the listener from a singer's lack of interpretation and even a weak song. Their contributions, "You Blew" and "Such a Wicked Love," are clever jams which position Jackson as a street-hip artist. Even with the gimmicks, the overall sound is ultimately somewhat vacuous. Meanwhile, the Steve Harvey-produced "Does It Really Matter" is a genuine, insinuating club/house cut, and the Stock, Aitken & Waterman track, "Just Say No," is an easily digested anti-drug anthem that brings out the best of Jackson. *—Justin Kantor*

No Relations / 1991 / Pump ✦✦✦

Bad Girl / Aug. 1, 1995 / Tko Magnum Midline ✦✦

Michael Jackson

b. Aug. 29, 1958, Gary, IN

Vocals / Pop/Rock, Club/Dance, Dance-Pop, Motown, Soul, Funk, Urban, New Jack Swing

Michael Jackson was unquestionably the biggest pop star of the '80s, and certainly one of the most popular recording artists of all time. In his prime, Jackson was an unstoppable juggernaut, possessed of all the tools to dominate the charts seemingly at will: an instantly identifiable voice, eye-popping dance moves, stunning musical versatility, and loads of sheer star power. His 1982 blockbuster *Thriller* became the biggest-selling album of all time (probably his best-known accomplishment), and he was the first black artist to find stardom on MTV, breaking down innumerable boundaries both for his race and for music video as an art form. Yet as Jackson's career began, very gradually, to descend from the dizzying heights of his peak years, most of the media's attention focused on his increasingly bizarre eccentricities; he was often depicted as an arrested man-child, completely sheltered from adult reality by a life spent in show business. The snickering turned to scandal in 1993, when Jackson was accused of molesting a 13-year-old boy; although he categorically denied the charges, his out-of-court settlement failed to restore his tarnished image. He never quite escaped the stigma of those allegations, and while he continued to sell records at superstar-like levels, he didn't release them with enough frequency (or, many critics thought, inspiration) to once again become better known for his music than his private life. Whether as a pop icon or a tabloid caricature, Jackson always remained bigger than life.

Michael Joseph Jackson was born August 29, 1958, in Gary, IN. The fifth son of steelworker Joe Jackson, Michael displayed a talent for music and dance from an extremely young age. His childhood was strictly regimented; from the start, he was to an extent sheltered from the outside world by his mother's Jehovah's Witness faith, and his father was by all accounts an often ill-tempered disciplinarian. Joe began to organize a family musical group around his three eldest sons in 1962, and Michael joined them the following year, quickly establishing himself as a dynamic stage performer. His dead-on mastery of James Brown's dance moves and soulful, mature-beyond-his-years vocals made him a natural focal point, especially given his incredibly young age. Dubbed the Jackson 5, the group signed to Motown in 1968 and issued their debut single in early 1970, when Michael was just 11 years old. "I Want You Back," "ABC," "The Love You Save," and "I'll Be There" all hit number one that year, making the Jackson 5 the first group in pop history to have their first four singles top the charts. Motown began priming Michael for a solo career in 1971, and his first single "Got to Be There" was issued toward the end of the year; it hit the Top Five, as did the follow-up, a cover of Bobby Day's "Rockin' Robin." Later in 1972, Jackson had his first number-one solo single, "Ben," the title song from a children's thriller about a young boy who befriends Ben, the highly intelligent leader of a gang of homicidal rats. Given the subject matter, the song was surprisingly sincere and sentimental, and even earned an Oscar nomination. However, the momentum of Jackson's solo career (much like that of the Jackson 5) soon stalled. He released his fourth and final album on Motown in 1975, and the following year, he and his brothers (save Jermaine) signed to Epic and became the Jacksons.

In 1977, Jackson landed a starring role alongside Diana Ross in the all-black film musical *The Wiz*, a retelling of *The Wizard of Oz*; here he met producer/composer Quincy Jones for the first time. Encouraged by the success of the Jacksons' self-produced, mostly self-written 1978 album *Destiny*, Jackson elected to resume his solo career when his management contract with his father expired shortly thereafter. With Jones producing, Jackson recorded his first solo album as an adult, *Off the Wall*. An immaculately crafted set of funky disco-pop, smooth soul, and lush, sentimental pop ballads, *Off the Wall* made Jackson a star all over again. It produced four Top Ten singles, including the number-one hits "Don't Stop 'Til You Get Enough" and "Rock With You," and went platinum (it went on to sell over seven-million copies); even so, Jackson remained loyal to his brothers and stayed with the group.

No group could have contained Jackson's rapidly rising star for long; however, there was still no sign (if there ever could be) that his next album would become the biggest in history. Released in 1982, the Quincy Jones-produced *Thriller* refined the strengths of *Off the Wall*; the dance and rock tracks were more driving, the pop tunes and ballads softer and more soulful, and all of it was recognizably Michael. Jackson brought in Paul McCartney for a duet, guitarist Eddie Van Halen for a jaw-dropping solo, and Vincent Price for a creepy recitation. It was no surprise that *Thriller* was a hit; what was a surprise was its staying power. Jackson's duet with McCartney, "The Girl Is Mine," was a natural single choice, and it peaked at number two; then "Billie Jean" and the Van Halen track "Beat It" both hit number one, for seven and three weeks, respectively. Those latter two songs, as well as the future Top Five title track, had one important feature in common: Jackson supported them with elaborately conceived video clips that revolutionized the way music videos were made. Jackson treated them as song-length movies with structured narratives: "Billie Jean" set the song's tale of a paternity suit in a nightmarish dream world where Jackson was a solitary, sometimes invisible presence; the anti-gang-violence "Beat It" became an homage to *West Side Story*; and the ten-minute-plus clip for "Thriller" (routinely selected as the best video of all time) featured Jackson leading a dance troupe of rotting zombies, with loads of horror-film makeup and effects. Having never really accepted black artists in the past, MTV played the clips to death, garnering massive publicity for Jackson and droves of viewers for the fledgling cable network. Jackson sealed his own phenomenon by debuting his signature "moonwalk" dance step at the end of 1983 on Motown's televised 25th anniversary special; though he didn't invent the moonwalk (as he himself was quick to point out), it became as much of a Jackson signature as his vocal hiccups or single white-sequined glove.

Showing no signs of slowing down, *Thriller* just kept spinning off singles, including "Wanna Be Startin' Somethin'," the airy ballad "Human Nature," and "P.Y.T. (Pretty Young Thing)"; in all, seven of its nine tracks wound up in the Top Ten, obliterating conventional ideas of how many singles could be released from an album before it ran its course. *Thriller* stayed on the charts for over two years, spent 37 non-consecutive weeks at number one, and became the best-selling album of all time; it went on to sell 25-million copies in the U.S. alone, and around another 20 million overseas. Naturally, Jackson won a slew of awards, including a record eight Grammys in one night, and snagged the largest endorsement deal ever when he became a spokesman for Pepsi (he would later be burned in an accident while filming a commercial). At the end of 1983, Jackson was again on top of the singles charts, this time as part of a second duet with McCartney, "Say Say Say." In 1984, Jackson re-joined his brothers one last time for the album *Victory*, whose supporting tour was one of the biggest (and priciest) of the year. The following year, he and Lionel Richie co-wrote the anthemic "We Are the World" for the all-star famine-relief effort USA for Africa; it became one of the fastest-selling singles ever.

Even at this early stage, wild rumors about Jackson's private life were swirling. His shyness and reluctance to grant interviews (ironically, due in part to his concerns about being misrepresented) only encouraged more speculation. Some pointed to his soft-spoken, still girlish voice as evidence that he'd undergone hormone treatments to preserve the high, flexible range of his youth; stories were told about Jackson sleeping in a hyperbaric chamber to slow the aging process, and purchasing the skeleton of John Merrick, the Elephant Man (Jackson did view the bones in the London Hospital, but did not buy them). Jackson bought a large ranch in California which he dubbed Neverland, and filled it with amusement park rides and animals (including the notorious pet chimpanzee Bubbles), which only fueled the public's perception of him as a somewhat bizarre eccentric obsessed with recapturing his childhood. He also underwent cosmetic surgery several times, which led to accusations from the black community that his gradually lightening skin tone was the result of an intentional effort to become whiter; a few years later, Jackson revealed that he had a disorder called vitiligo, in which pigment disappears from the skin, leaving large white blotches and making direct sunlight dangerous. One of the rumors that was definitely true was that Jackson owned the rights to the Beatles' catalog; in 1985, he acquired ATV Publishing, the firm that controlled all the Lennon-McCartney copyrights (among others), which wound up costing him his friendship with McCartney.

During his long layoff between records, Jackson indulged his interest in film and video by working with George Lucas and Francis Ford Coppola on the 3-D short film *Captain Eo*. The special-effects extravaganza was shown at the enormous wide-screen IMAX theaters in Disney's amusement parks for 12 years, beginning in 1986. Finally, Jackson re-entered the studio with Quincy Jones to begin the near-impossible task of crafting a follow-up to *Thriller*. *Bad* was released to enormous public anticipation in 1987, and was accompanied by equally enormous publicity. It debuted at number one, and the first single "I Just Can't Stop Loving You," with vocal accompaniment by Siedah Garrett, also shot up the charts to number one. Like *Thriller*, *Bad* continued to spin off singles for well over a year after its release, and became the first album ever to produce five number-one hits; the others were "Bad," "The Way You Make Me Feel," "Man in the Mirror," and "Dirty Diana." Jackson supported the album with a lengthy world tour that featured a typically spectacular, elaborate stage show; it became the highest-grossing tour of all time. Although Jackson's success was still staggering, there were faint undercurrents of disappointment, partly because of the unparalleled phenomenon of *Thriller* (*Bad* "only" sold eight-million copies), and partly because the album itself didn't seem quite as exuberant or uniformly consistent when compared to its predecessors.

Jackson took another long hiatus between albums, giving the media little to focus on besides his numerous eccentricities; by this time, the British tabloids delighted in calling him "Wacko Jacko," a name he detested. When Jackson returned in with a new album in late 1991, he'd come up with a different moniker: "the King of Pop." *Dangerous* found Jackson ending his collaboration with Quincy Jones in an effort to update his sound; accordingly, many of the tracks were helmed by the groundbreaking new jack swing producer Teddy Riley. As expected, the album debuted at number one, and its lead single "Black or White" shot to the top as well. Jackson courted controversy with the song's video, however; after the song itself ended, there was a long dance sequence in which Jackson shouted, grabbed his crotch, and smashed car windows in a bizarre display that seemed at odds with the song's harmonious message. With the video given a high-profile, prime-time network premiere, Jackson was criticized for the inappropriate violence and the message it might send to his younger fans. However, Jackson would not be the biggest story in popular music for long. In early 1992, Nirvana's *Nevermind* symbolically knocked *Dangerous* out of the number-one spot; after the alternative rock revolution, the pop charts would never be quite the same. Jackson scored several more hits off the album, including the Top Tens "Remember the Time" and "In the Closet," but the aggressive "Jam" and the saccharine "Heal the World" both performed disappointingly.

Jackson had long preferred the company of children over other adults, and befriended quite a few, inviting them to stay at his Neverland Ranch and enjoy the massive playground he'd assembled over the years. In 1993, Jackson was accused of molesting a 13-year-old boy who'd become a frequent guest at Neverland. Predictably, there was a tabloid feeding frenzy, and a mainstream media circus as well. In the court of public opinion, the charges seemed all too plausible: Jackson was near-universally perceived as a weirdo, and here was a handy explanation for his heretofore asexual persona and distaste for adult companions. Additionally, Jackson entered rehab for a short time, seeking treatment for an addiction to pain killers. Investigations were unsuccessful in turning up any other boys who echoed the allegations, and Jackson counter-sued his accusers for attempting extortion; however, in spite of the fact that no criminal charges were ever filed against Jackson, he settled the boy's family's suit out of court in early 1995, paying an estimated 18-20 million dollars. Many felt the settlement was tantamount to an admission of guilt, and when Jackson married Lisa Marie Presley in 1994, the move was perceived as a desperate ploy to rehabilitate his image; the marriage broke up just 19 months later, seemingly lending credence to the charge.

In 1995, Jackson attempted to put the focus back on his music by preparing *HIStory: Past, Present and Future, Book I*, a two-CD set featuring one disc of new material and one of his greatest hits. The album debuted at number one, but the format backfired on Jackson: his fans already owned the hits, and the new album simply wasn't strong enough to offset the added cost of the extra disc for many more casual listeners. There were some encouraging signs—the lead single "Scream," a duet with sister Janet, debuted at number five, setting a new American chart record that was broken when the follow-up "You Are Not Alone" became the first single ever to enter the *Billboard* Hot 100 at number one. But on the whole, *HIStory* was something of a disappointment. Additionally, Jackson collapsed during rehearsals for an awards show later that year, and had to be rushed to the hospital; what was more, the Eagles' *Their Greatest Hits 1971-1975* was threatening to catch *Thriller*'s American sales record (it eventually did, and the two continued to run neck and neck). There were signs that Jackson was grasping at his self-proclaimed King of Pop status; the cover of *HIStory* depicted an enormous statue of Jackson, and he performed at the 1996 BRIT Awards dressed as a Messiah, with children and a rabbi surrounding him worshipfully (Pulp lead singer Jarvis Cocker stormed the stage to protest Jackson's hubris during the middle of the song). The 1997 remix album *Blood on the Dance Floor* failed to even go platinum, although remix albums historically don't perform nearly as well as new material.

In late 1996, Jackson remarried to nurse Debbie Rowe; over the next two years, the couple had two children, son Prince Michael Jackson Jr. and daughter Paris Michael Katherine Jackson. However, Jackson and Rowe divorced in late 1999. In 2001, Jackson was inducted into the Rock and Roll Hall of Fame, and later held a massive concert at Madison Square Garden celebrating the 30th anniversary of his first solo record. Among many other celebrity guests, the show featured the first on-stage reunion of the Jacksons since the *Victory* tour. In the wake of September 11, Jackson put together an all-star charity benefit single, "What More Can I Give." His new album, *Invincible*, was released late in the year, marking the first time he'd issued a collection of entirely new material since *Dangerous*; it found him working heavily with urban soul production wizard Rodney Jerkins. *Invincible* debuted at number one and quickly went double-platinum; however, its initial singles, "You Rock My World" and "Butterflies," had rather disappointing showings on the charts, with the latter not even reaching the Top Ten. To compound matters, the expensive "What More Can I Give" single and video were cancelled by Sony when executive producer Marc Schaffel was revealed to work in pornography. Jackson's camp tried to distance the singer from Schaffel, and the various corporations that were attached to it (McDonalds, Sony) claimed they had minimal involvement if any with the song.

Sony and Jackson began a press war in the summer of 2002, starting with Jackson's claims that the label asked for $200 million to pay them back for marketing costs. Although they had spent $55 million on his disappointing comeback, Sony released a statement saying that no such request had ever been made. Jackson stewed for a few weeks before launching a press attack on Sony Music chairman Tommy Mottola, calling him "devilish" and making claims that he used racist language and held down black artists. Many Sony artists, including Mariah Carey and Ricky Martin, defended Mottola, but Jackson and his family maintained that racism ended their professional relationship. From that point, Jackson's career took an extreme turn towards the bizarre, starting with MTV's annual Video Awards. When Britney Spears presented him with a birthday cake, an offhand remark about being the artist of the millennium inspired a rambling Jackson to accept a meaningless trophy (which everyone presenting on-stage received) as an actual Artist of the Millennium award. Next came accusations from a promotional company over his promises of a tour and several appearances that he then cancelled. Jackson arrived in court late, gave a drowsy testimony, and inspired gasps when he removed a surgical mask to reveal his nose had caved in from a botched cosmetic surgery. Only days later, German fans were horrified when Jackson came to the balcony of his hotel suite and briefly dangled a squirming baby over the edge with one arm. Although he apologized the next day, claiming he had gotten caught up in the moment, this only did more to cement the King of Pop's public image as an out-of-control millionaire. *—Steve Huey*

Got to Be There / Jan. 1972 / Motown ♦♦♦

Ben / Aug. 1972 / Motown ♦♦♦

Michael Jackson stunned everyone by scoring a huge hit with a song about a rat on this 1972 release. He was just beginning to make his way outside the family unit, and the single actually did better on the pop side than on the R&B charts, topping the pop list but peaking at number five on the R&B survey. The remainder of the album was good to above-average pop, establishing for any doubters that Jackson was going to succeed, indeed thrive, on his own. *—Ron Wynn*

Music and Me / Apr. 1973 / Motown ♦♦♦

This was Michael Jackson's least successful album during his solo run at Motown. The songs were undistinguished, Jackson sounded tentative and uninterested vocally, and the production and arrangements were routine at best, sometimes inferior. There's little wonder that Jackson at this point began to openly express his desires to expand his horizons and try a fresher, more contemporary approach. *—Ron Wynn*

Forever, Michael / Jan. 1975 / Motown ♦♦♦

Michael Jackson's fourth and final new studio album for Motown came nearly two years after its predecessor, *Music and Me*. It was a more mature effort for the 16-year-old singer, but lacked the contemporary dance style that had given Jackson and his brothers a career rebirth with "Dancing Machine" the year before. The album did spawn two minor chart singles, "We're Almost There" and "Just a Little Bit of You" (both produced by Brian Holland of the Holland-Dozier-Holland production team), and a third track, "One Day in Your Life," would chart as a reissue six years later. But though Jackson sang appealingly, the arrangements were noticeably similar to many older Motown charts, and there was little here to hint that, four years hence, on his next solo album, *Off The Wall*, Jackson would emerge as a major star. *— William Ruhlmann*

☆ **Off the Wall** / 1979 / Epic ♦♦♦♦♦

Michael Jackson had recorded solo prior to the release of *Off the Wall* in 1979, but this was his breakthrough, the album that established him as an artist of astonishing talent and a bright star in his own right. This was a visionary album, a record that found a way to break disco wide open into a new world where the beat was undeniable, but not the primary focus—it was part of a colorful tapestry of lush ballads and strings, smooth soul and pop, soft rock, and alluring funk. Its roots hearken back to the Jacksons' huge mid-'70s hit "Dancing Machine," but this is an enormously fresh record, one that remains vibrant and giddily exciting years after its release. This is certainly due to Jackson's emergence as a blindingly gifted vocalist, equally skilled with overwrought ballads as "She's Out of My Life" as driving dancefloor shakers as "Working Day and Night" and "Get on the Floor," where his asides are as gripping as his delivery on the verses. It's also due to the brilliant songwriting, an intoxicating blend of strong melodies, rhythmic hooks, and indelible construction. Most of all, its success is due to the sound constructed by Jackson and producer Quincy Jones, a dazzling array of disco beats, funk guitars, clean mainstream pop, and unashamed (and therefore affecting) schmaltz that is utterly thrilling in its utter joy. This is highly professional, highly crafted music, and its details are evident, but the overall effect is nothing but pure pleasure. Jackson and Jones expanded this approach on the blockbuster *Thriller*, often with equally stunning results, but they never bettered it. *—Stephen Thomas Erlewine*

The Best of Michael Jackson / 1981 / Motown ♦♦♦
Michael Jackson's greatest hits, 1971-1975, emphasize his waif-like charm and youth (he was 13 when the first of these songs appeared) in ballads such as "Got to Be There," "Ben" (even if it is a love song to a rat), and "I Wanna Be Where You Are." The upbeat cover of "Rockin' Robin" is equally appealing. *—William Ruhlmann*

One Day in Your Life / Mar. 1981 / Motown ♦♦♦
Although Michael Jackson had long since moved on to Epic, Motown got a quick cash boost in the early '80s by issuing some tracks cut in 1975. The title song even came close to making the R&B Top 40 and reached the middle of the pop charts. Jackson was so hot at that point that anything with his name on it would sell something. But it's hardly first-class material, and it truly paled beside the material that Quincy Jones was producing at that point. *—Ron Wynn*

★ **Thriller** / 1982 / Epic ♦♦♦♦♦
Off the Wall was a massive success, spawning four Top Ten hits (two of them number ones), but nothing could have prepared Michael Jackson for *Thriller*. Nobody could have prepared anybody for the success of *Thriller*, since the magnitude of its success was simply unimaginable—an album that sold 40-million copies in its initial chart run, with *seven* of its nine tracks reaching the Top Ten (for the record, the terrific "Baby Be Mine" and the pretty good ballad "The Lady in My Life" are not like the others). This was a record that had something for everybody, building on the basic blueprint of *Off the Wall* by adding harder funk, hard rock, softer ballads, and smoother soul—expanding the approach to have something for every audience. That alone would have given the album a good shot at a huge audience, but it also arrived precisely when MTV was reaching its ascendancy, and Jackson helped the network by being not just its first superstar, but first black star as much as the network helped him. This all would have made it a success (and its success, in turn, served as a new standard for success), but it stayed on the charts, turning out singles, for nearly two years because it was really, really good. True, it wasn't as tight as *Off the Wall*—and the ridiculous, late-night house-of-horrors title track is the prime culprit, arriving in the middle of the record and sucking out its momentum—but those one or two cuts don't detract from a phenomenal set of music. It's calculated, to be sure, but the chutzpah of those calculations (before this, nobody would even have thought to bring in metal virtuoso Eddie Van Halen to play on a disco cut) is outdone by their success. This is where a song as gentle and lovely as "Human Nature" coexists comfortably with the tough, scared "Beat It," the sweet schmaltz of the Paul McCartney duet "The Girl Is Mine," and the frizzy funk of "P.Y.T. (Pretty Young Thing)." And, although this is an undeniably fun record, the paranoia is already creeping in, manifesting itself in the record's two best songs: "Billie Jean," where a woman claims Michael is the father of her child, and the delirious "Wanna Be Startin' Something," the freshest funk on the album, but the most claustrophobic, scariest track Jackson ever recorded. These give the record its anchor and are part of the reason why the record is more than just a phenomenon. The other reason, of course, is that much of this is just simply great music. *—Stephen Thomas Erlewine*

Anthology / 1986 / Motown ♦♦♦♦♦
When a teenage Michael Jackson was known primarily for his membership in the Jackson 5, rock critics tended to dismiss him as bubblegum. But even at his most waifish, the pre-*Thriller*, pre-Quincy Jones Jackson could be soulful. Spanning 1971-1975, this two-CD set shows how inviting some of Jackson's early solo recordings were. Major hits like "Ben" (his oddly poignant ode to a rat), "I Wanna Be Where You Are," and "Got to Be There" are included, along with noteworthy album tracks like Bill Withers' "Ain't No Sunshine" and the standard "All the Things You Are." Anyone who doubted that he was a serious R&B/pop singer should have examined Jackson's moving version of the Philly soul classic "People Make the World Go Round" (which is heard with different lyrics than on the Stylistics' much better-known version). The package also contains a handful of Jackson 5 hits, including "Never Can Say Goodbye" and the infectious "Dancing Machine." To be sure, Jackson's solo albums of the early to mid-'70s had their share of filler, something this package isn't devoid of either. But thankfully, *Anthology* has a lot more pluses than minuses. For an introductory overview of Jackson's early accomplishments on his own, *Anthology* is the most logical choice. *—Alex Henderson*

Bad / 1987 / Epic ♦♦♦♦♦
The downside to a success like *Thriller* is that it's nearly impossible to follow, but Michael Jackson approached *Bad* much the same way he approached *Thriller*—take the basic formula of the predecessor, expand it slightly, and move it outward. This meant that he moved deeper into hard rock, deeper into schmaltzy adult contemporary, deeper into hard dance—essentially taking each portion of *Thriller* to an extreme, while increasing the quotient of immaculate studiocraft. He wound up with a sleeker, slicker *Thriller*, which isn't a bad thing, but it's not a rousing success, either. For one thing, the material just isn't as good. Look at the singles: only three can stand alongside album tracks from its predecessor ("Bad," "The Way You Make Me Feel," "I Just Can't Stop Loving You"), another is simply OK ("Smooth Criminal"), with the other two showcasing Jackson at his worst (the saccharine "Man in the Mirror," the misogynistic "Dirty Diana"). Then, there are the album tracks themselves, something that virtually didn't exist on *Thriller* but bog down *Bad* not just because they're bad, but because they reveal that Jackson's state of the art is not hip. And they constitute a near-fatal dead spot on the record—songs three through six, from "Speed Demon" to "Another Part of Me," a sequence that's utterly faceless, lacking memorable hooks and melodies, even when Stevie Wonder steps in for "Just Good Friends," relying on nothing but studiocraft. Part of the joy of *Off the Wall* and *Thriller* was that craft was enhanced with tremendous songs, performances, and fresh, vivacious beats. For this dreadful stretch, everything is mechanical, and while the album rebounds with songs that prove mechanical can be tolerable if delivered with hooks and panache, it still makes *Bad* feel like an artifact of its time instead a piece of music that transcends it. And if that wasn't evident proof that Jackson was losing touch, consider this—the best song on the album is "Leave Me Alone" (why are all of his best songs paranoid anthems?), a tune tacked on to the end of the CD and never released as a single, apart from a weirdly claustrophobic video that, not coincidentally, was the best video from the album. *—Stephen Thomas Erlewine*

Dangerous / 1992 / Epic ♦♦♦
Despite the success of *Bad*, it was hard not to view it as a bit of a letdown, since it presented a cleaner, colder, calculated version of *Thriller*—something that delivered what it should on the surface, but wound up offering less in the long run. So, it was time for a change-up, something even a superstar as huge as Michael Jackson realized, so he left Quincy Jones behind, hired Guy mastermind Teddy Riley as the main producer, and worked with a variety of other producers, arrangers, and writers, most notably Bruce Swedien and Bill Bottrell. The end result of this is a much sharper, harder, riskier album than *Bad*, one that has its eyes on the street, even if its heart gets middle-class soft on "Heal the World." The shift in direction and change of collaborators has liberated Jackson, and he's written a set of songs that is considerably stronger than *Bad*, often approaching the consistency of *Off the Wall* and *Thriller*. If it is hardly as effervescent or joyous as either of those records, chalk it up to his suffocating stardom, which results in a set of songs without much real emotional center, either in their substance or performance. But, there's a lot to be said for professional craftsmanship at its peak, and *Dangerous* has plenty of that, not just on such fine singles as "In the Closet," "Remember the Time," or the blistering "Jam," but on album tracks like "Why You Wanna Trip on Me." No, it's not perfect—it has a terrible cover, a couple of slow spots, and suffers from CD-era ailments of the early '90s, such as its overly long running time and its deadening Q Sound production, which sounds like somebody forgot to take the Surround Sound button off. Even so, *Dangerous* captures Jackson at a near-peak, delivering an album that would have ruled the pop charts surely and smoothly if it had arrived just a year earlier. But it didn't—it arrived along with grunge, which changed the rules of the game nearly as much as *Thriller* itself. Consequently, it's the rare multi-platinum, number-one album that qualifies as a nearly forgotten, underappreciated record. *—Stephen Thomas Erlewine*

Anthology: The Best of Michael Jackson / Mar. 21, 1995 / Motown ♦♦♦♦
Motown's 1995 anthology of young Michael Jackson's musical output prior to his ground-breaking era that began with *Off the Wall* is nothing short of definitive, collecting all of his charted U.S. Motown hits, including "Got to Be There," "Rockin' Robin," "I Wanna Be Where You Are," "With a Child's Heart," "We're Almost There," "Just a Little Bit of You," and his first solo chart-topper, "Ben." There are also five Jackson 5 singles, including "I'll Be There" and his incredibly soulful take on "Never Can Say Goodbye." The collection even includes "Farewell My Summer Love," which, although recorded in his youth, became a minor Top 40 hit in the spring of 1984. In his youth, Michael Jackson was impassioned, heartfelt, and soulful way beyond his young years and, had he never hit his electrifying stride that followed these releases, he would still have left quite a legacy of music, as is demonstrated by this first-rate collection. Those seeking a comprehensive anthology of Jackson's early work need look no further—all the classics are here. Incidentally, a previous issue of this anthology was issued by Motown in 1986—this one bests it with four additional tracks, those being "Greatest Show on Earth," "We've Got a Good Thing Going," "Make Tonight All Mine," and "Cinderella Stay Awhile." *—Jose F. Promis*

HIStory: Past, Present and Future, Book I / Jun. 20, 1995 / Epic ♦♦♦
Michael Jackson's double-disc *HIStory: Past, Present, and Future, Book I* is a monumental achievement of ego. Titled *HIStory Begins*, the first disc is a collection of his post-Motown hits, featuring some of the greatest music in pop history including "Billie Jean," "Don't Stop Til Ya Get Enough," "Beat It," and "Rock With You." It leaves some hits out—including the number ones "Say Say Say" and "Dirty Diana"—yet it's filled with enough prime material to be thoroughly intoxicating. That can't be said for the second disc, called *HIStory Continues* and consisting entirely of new material—which also happen to be the first songs he released since being accused of child molestation. *HIStory Continues* is easily the most personal album Jackson has recorded. References to the scandal permeate almost every song, creating a thick atmosphere of paranoia. If Jackson's music had been the equal of *Thriller* or *Bad*, the nervous, vindicative lyrics wouldn't have been quite as overbearing. However, *HIStory Continues* reiterates musical ideas Jackson has been exploring since *Bad*. Jackson certainly tries to stay contemporary, yet he has a tendency to smooth out all of his rougher musical edges with show-biz schmaltz. Occasionally, Jackson produces some well-crafted pop that ranks with his best material: R. Kelly's "You Are Not Alone" is seductive, "Scream" improves on the slamming beats of his earlier single "Jam," and "Stranger in Moscow" is one of his most haunting ballads. Nevertheless, *HIStory Continues* stands as his weakest album since the mid-'70s. *—Stephen Thomas Erlewine*

Blood on the Dance Floor: History in the Mix / May 20, 1997 / Epic ♦♦
Despite its heavy promotion, *HIStory* was a considerable sales disappointment, largely because it buried an album of new material with a greatest hits collection, causing the former to be overlooked. Although the new album was unfocused, it had its moments, which may be why Michael Jackson refused to let *HIStory* die. He remixed eight of its songs for *Blood on the Dance Floor: History in the Mix*, and then saddled that record with five new songs, which means that he repeated the same mistake by burying the new songs yet again. This time, however, it wasn't such a loss, since all the songs on *Blood on the Dance Floor* are embarassingly weak, sounding tired, predictable and, well, bloodless. The title track, a bleak reworking of "Jam" and "Scream," is indicative of the weakness of the album, but it only touches on how sad the whole affair is. It would be one thing if Jackson wasn't

relevant to the late '90s and ignored all contemporary innovations, since he could then make good music on his own terms. However, he flaunts his ignorance aggressively, as if sheer willpower will return him to the charts, making it all the more apparent that he can no longer craft a good melody or beat. And for one of the greatest musicians of the late '70s and early '80s, that's quite a depressing state of affairs. *—Stephen Thomas Erlewine*

Invincible / Oct. 31, 2001 / Epic ♦♦♦
Let's get the clichéd bad joke out of the way to begin with: At the time Michael Jackson released *Invincible* in the fall of 2001, he hardly seemed "invincible"—it was more wishful thinking than anything else, since he hadn't really had a genuine hit in ten years, and even that paled in comparison to his total domination of the '80s. That lack of commercial success, combined with a fading reputation as a trailblazer, a truly ugly public scandal, and swirling rumors about his diminishing finances, along with a huge wait between albums (by teaming his *Dangerous* follow-up with a hits collection, it wound up being overlooked, despite a gaudy publicity push), resulted in Jackson being deep down in the hole, needing to surge back out with a record that not only proved his talents, but his staying power. So, faced with a make-or-break record, what does Jackson do to save his career? What he's done since *Dangerous*, take a turn toward the street and craft a hard-driving, hard-polished urban soul album, heavy on the dance numbers and sweetened by lugubrious ballads. It's a proven formula for commercial success, but it not only doesn't push his music forward, it makes his reach seem rather timid when compared to the wildly rich, all-encompassing musical vision of *Thriller* and *Bad*. Here, he's reined in by a desire to prove himself, so he keeps his focus sharp and narrow, essentially creating a sparkly, post-hip-hop update of *Off the Wall*. It's not as good as that sounds, because the infectious joy and layered craft of that masterpiece has been replaced with a dogged, near-maniacal desire to craft something hip enough for the clubs and melodic enough for mainstream radio, thereby confirming his self-proclaimed status as the King of Pop (a really terrible title, btw). Since he is exceptionally talented and smart enough to surround himself with first-rate collaborators, this does pay off on occasion, even when it feels a little too calculated or when it feels a little padded. Ultimately, the record runs too long, losing steam halfway through, as it turns to a series of rants about "Privacy" or a deadly stretch of uncomfortably treacly, sub-"Man in the Mirror" songs about "The Lost Children," or when he says that he can't change the world by himself on "Cry." Fortunately, Jackson was clever enough to front-load this record, loading the first seven songs with really good, edgy dance numbers—even the opening "Unbreakable" isn't sunk by the creepy resurrection of Biggie Smalls—and lovely ballads, highlighted by "Break of Dawn" and "Butterflies" with its Bacharach-styled horns. Even if these are too self-conscious and a little mechanical (which they are), they still have a spark and sound better than anything Jackson has done since *Dangerous*. That's not enough to make *Invincible* the comeback Jackson needed—he really would have had to have an album that sounded free instead of constrained for that to work—but it does offer a reminder that he can really craft good pop. If only he was fueled, not constrained, by his obsessions, this could have been really interesting. *—Stephen Thomas Erlewine*

Millie Jackson

b. Jul. 15, 1944, Thompson, GA
Vocals / Soul, Retro-Soul, Southern Soul, Urban, Deep Soul, Quiet Storm, Disco
Millie Jackson's first taste of singing in front of an audience occurred one night at the famed nightclub Smalls Paradise. Sitting in the audience with friends, Jackson heckled the lady on-stage and, when dared to do better, she stepped up to belt Ben E. King's "Don't Play It No More." Jackson was hired for another gig within two weeks, but didn't get paid. A gentleman by the name of Tony Rice took her to a venue in Hoboken, NJ, a couple of weeks later and then on to Brooklyn, NY, to perform for a nominal fee.

Born in Thompson, GA, Jackson lived with her grandmother prior to moving to Newark, NJ, to live with her father in 1958. She grew up influenced by the sounds of Otis Redding, Sam Cooke, and later, the O'Jays. Her first single to chart was 1971's deceptively titled "A Child of God (It's Hard to Believe)," which many thought was a gospel track. Due to its heated lyrical content, the single was canceled, but still managed to peak at number 22 on the R&B charts. In the spring of 1972, Jackson had her first R&B Top Ten single with "Ask Me What You Want." She kept busy performing in nightclubs and enjoyed her second consecutive Top Ten single with "My Man, a Sweet Man" in August of 1972; it peaked at number seven. (Ironically, the song was not one of Jackson's favorites.) A year later, Jackson, whose vocal texture is similar to one of her idols, Gladys Knight, had her third Top Ten single with the moderately paced "Hurts So Good," which peaked at number three on the R&B charts and made the pop Top 40. The single bore the title of her album and was also featured on the movie soundtrack for *Cleopatra Jones*. Jackson produced the album with Brad Shapiro. However, she was only given credit for the album concept. In Jackson's own words, "…that's when they (label owners) met the real Millie Jackson." Thereafter, she was given credit for her efforts.

In January of 1975, Jackson released the album that would introduce what would later become her trademark rap style of racy, raunchy language; her audience loved it. The album was *Caught Up* and the featured release was "If Loving You Is Wrong I Don't Want to Be Right," for which she received two Grammy nominations. Jackson openly admits that she never had singing lessons and never thought she could sing. Consequently, she began to talk (or what was commonly known at the time as rap) on her songs in a blunt, candid manner to make up for the shortcoming and had her fourth Top Ten single with country singer Merle Haggard's "If You're Not Back in Love by Monday" (*Billboard* country charts number two). Jackson's version peaked at number five on the R&B charts. Over the next ten years, Jackson had numerous Top 100 singles for Spring Records. In 1986, she signed with Jive and released her fifth and sixth Top Ten singles in "Hot! Wild! Unrestricted! Crazy Love" and "Love Is a Dangerous Game, both respectively peaking at number nine and six on the R&B charts. In addition to her impressive music career, Jackson wrote the play *Young Man, Older Woman*; the play toured for four years. Her attention, though, has turned to the broadcast booth as a radio program host on the afternoon radio show in Dallas, TX. According to *Billboard*, Jackson is one of the top R&B acts to ever record or step onto a stage and is still giving her fans what they want as a radio host and a performer. *—Craig Lytle*

Millie Jackson / 1972 / Southbound ♦♦♦♦♦
Millie Jackson's debut is one of the freshest albums of her career, her style remarkably mature and the sound an infectious blend of '60s soul influences (from Motown to Stax to early Philly soul). Jackson's just as tough and aggressively honest here as she would be on her breakout, 1974's *Caught Up*, and songs like "I Ain't Giving Up" and "I Miss You Baby" are of the same high caliber. She injects the perfect measure of anger and genuine confusion into the hypocrisy fable "A Child of God (It's Hard to Believe)" (her first R&B hit), and has no trouble switching gears for the affectionate "My Man, a Sweet Man," with a driving bassline and handclaps making direct connections to the classic Motown sound. The biggest hit here was another love song, the swinging "Ask Me What You Want," her second R&B Top Ten entry. Even though it never came together quite like *Caught Up*, Millie Jackson's first LP introduced a major talent to the R&B world. *—John Bush*

It Hurts So Good / 1973 / Southbound ♦♦♦
Before hitting her stride with 1974's *Caught Up*, Millie Jackson delivered this tasty disc of uptown Southern soul. Both Stax raw and Philly International slick, *It Hurts So Good* percolates with smoky horns, snaking guitar lines, electric piano, strings, and bluesy funk grooves. In addition to her usually provocative take on relationships (both in the home and at the dark end of the street), Jackson—via Curtis Mayfield—delivers the affecting ghetto laments "I Cry," "Hypocrisy," and "Two-Faced World." And while some of the charts are a bit lacking, Jackson is solid throughout, especially on slow-burners like "Good to the Very Last Drop." A fine early offering from the diva of salacious sass. *—Stephen Cook*

I Got to Try It One Time / Mar. 1974 / Southbound ♦♦♦
The follow-up to *Caught Up* came hot on its heels (the same year, in fact), offering a few more songs from the same mold—Jackson's tough performances of songs charting the vagaries of modern love. There wasn't much of a concept at work here, despite a set of situation songs that would've fit well, including "One Night Stand," "How Do You Feel the Morning After," and best of all, a pair of classic Don Covay compositions ("Watch the One Who Brings You the News" and "A Letter Full of Tears"). Producer Brad Shapiro went for more of a blaxploitation feel on this record, which fit in well with the dominant emotion (mistrust) as well as Jackson's raw delivery. Other highlights include the outré "My Love Is So Fly" and her self-penned "I Got to Try It One Time," which became an R&B hit. *—John Bush*

Caught Up / 1974 / Southbound ♦♦♦♦♦
Taking the drama of a love triangle to logical extremes, Millie Jackson's *Caught Up* turns the pitfalls of tainted love into the basis for a concept album (the seeds for soul music's explicit treatment of the topic having been planted by James Carr's "Dark End of the Street"). While the "other woman's" view is taken up initially on cuts like the R&B hit "If Loving You Is Wrong I Don't Want to Be Right," the wife's plight is covered on the second half of the disc with revealing titles like "It's All Over but the Shouting." Jackson also delivers some of her patented racy commentary on the appropriately named "The Rap," while showing equal vigor in the album's wealth of fine vocal performances, including an impressive cover of Bobby Womack's "I'm Through Trying to Prove My Love to You." *Caught Up*'s standout track, though, is the version of Bobby Goldsboro's "Summer" that closes the record. Seemingly out of sync with the overriding concept, the song touches upon a girl's loss of innocence to an older man. One soon realizes, though, that beyond sexual awakening, Jackson is really emphasizing the point of no return: After the epiphany, one is sent hurdling toward the power struggles and politics of adult relations, including, potentially, the moral crossroads of infidelity. Luckily, as soon as your mind overloads from pop semiotics, the in-the-pocket grooves supplied by the Muscle Shoals Swampers provides the needed salve. Jackson shows both brains and soul on this fine release, creating what might be the only concept album one can dance and drink to. *—Stephen Cook*

Still Caught Up / 1975 / Southbound ♦♦♦♦
Still Caught Up returned listeners to the torrid backbiting and constant recriminations of Millie Jackson's blockbuster *Caught Up*, and though it didn't compare favorably, it was easily good enough to make it better than her average full-length. Though not live, it has a stagey sound, with frequent monologues, nice testifying backup vocals, an odd break-out of audience applause, and the kind of loose-limbed horn section heard during Elvis' Las Vegas appearances. Jackson sounds resigned at the beginning ("Making the Best of a Bad Situation"), but by the end side one, she's getting just as unhinged as on *Caught Up* ("The Memory of a Wife") and talking just as tough ("Tell Her It's Over"). It must have grown difficult to select appropriate material for another record of this kind, but she closes it out in style with Mac Davis' "I Still Love You (You Still Love Me)." *—John Bush*

Feelin' Bitchy / 1977 / Southbound ♦♦♦♦
Soul fans who don't have a taste for off-color humor have often argued that Millie Jackson should stay away from the racy stuff. They insist that a soulstress as talented as Jackson doesn't need to be raunchy, claiming that her sexually explicit diatribes are an unnecessary distraction. But here's the thing: Those diatribes are genuinely funny—at times, she's downright hilarious. Jackson would still be a great singer even without the R-rated and X-rated monologues, but those monologues are a nice bonus. Not without its share of raunchy humor, this 1977 LP is unlikely to get Dr. Laura's stamp of approval any time soon. But those who don't mind off-color humor will find *Feelin' Bitchy* to be a first-rate soul album. Jackson provides some hilarious diatribes on "You Created a Monster" and the bluesy "All the Way Lover" (which lambastes women who prefer soap operas over their husbands), and she fares equally well on less explicit material like Hot's "Angel in Your Arms" and Merle Haggard's "If You're Not Back in Love By Monday" (which was a number-two country hit for Haggard and a number-five R&B hit for Jackson). While Hot's original version of "Angel in Your Arms" was slick R&B/pop and crossed over to adult

contemporary audiences, Jackson's gritty remake is hardcore soul. From the explicit to the not so explicit, *Feelin' Bitchy* is among Jackson's finest albums. *—Alex Henderson*

Lovingly Yours / 1977 / Southbound ✦✦

Live and Uncensored / 1979 / Southbound ✦✦✦✦
Hilariously racy monologues were a hallmark of Millie Jackson's concerts as the title of *Live and Uncensored* implies. Beyond the foul-mouthed high jinks on this 1979 release, though, Jackson created witty narratives that covered everything from sexual foibles to soap operas and in the process dressed down both sexes; hypocritically coy women are directed to "Give It Up," while in "The Rap" and "Be a Sweetheart," bumbling and sexually rabid men get roundly manipulated. Miss Jackson turns TV critic on "The Soaps" to blast the inanity of daytime television and on "Logs and Thangs" offers up some well worn yet sophisticated sexual innuendo. And, yes, there is music here as well. Jackson delivers fine examples of her Bobby Womack/Stax inspired brand of soul on "If Loving You Is Wrong (I Don't Want to Be Right)," "Just When I Needed You Most" and "What Am I Waiting For" and prefigures hip-hop diva Mary J. Blige with her slightly hoarse yet honeyed vocal delivery on "I Still Love You (You Still Love Me)"—replete with some fine breakbeats. Womack gets his due as Jackson's medley of Rod Stewart's "Do Ya Think I'm Sexy" and Womack's own "Put Something Down on It" reveals the Brit's debt to the great soul writer/producer. Aside from a few forgettable moments like a classical music parody and some weak disco, *Live and Uncensored* is a strong document of Millie Jackson in her element. *—Stephen Cook*

Royal Rappin's / 1979 / Southbound ✦✦
Royal Rappin's certainly looks great on paper—it's the pairing of two of music's most loquacious and sexually geared acts, Millie Jackson and Isaac Hayes—but despite all its potential, the album doesn't impress quite like it could have. A few years earlier, Hayes recorded a live double album with Dionne Warwick and the sparks were more than genuine. With Jackson and the declining Muscle Shoals sound though, it seems more like a terrible blind date that can't end soon enough. Part of the problem is that Hayes doesn't have any production duties and is basically dropped into a Millie Jackson album. There are a few good moments, however. "Sweet Music, Soft Lights and You" manages to capture a groove that complements their styles. Still, the pointless covers and underdone originals sink this like a stone. The slightly perked-up "You Needed Me" is weird and the disco-fied "Feels Like the First Time" is surreal. Although Hayes and Jackson's legend of gab preceded them, the chatter here is forced and annoying, especially on "If I Had My Way" and "If You Had Your Way." Unfortunately, *Royal Rappin's* captures the worst of two great soul artists. *—Jason Elias*

For Men Only / 1980 / Polydor ✦✦✦
One of Millie's best, Jackson gives fans tough raps, raunchiness, and scathing dialogue that threads the songs together. Millie's love for country ballads shows on "I Wish That I Could Hurt That Way Again." The appeal heightens on deep soul ballads, and *For Men Only* is loaded: Check out her rendition of Benny Latimore's gritty "Ain't No Coming Back," the earthy "That Don't Turn Me On," "Despair," "This Is Where I Came In," and "A Fool's Affair." Polydor originally released this LP in 1980, but give Ichiban Records kudos for updating this classic to CD. *—Andrew Hamilton*

I Had to Say It / 1980 / Polydor ✦✦✦
Over the years, Millie Jackson has often been compared to Etta James and Denise LaSalle—and both are valid comparisons. Another frequent comparison is Gladys Knight, who was a major influence on Jackson. But while Knight and Jackson have a similar vocal texture, you would never hear Knight delivering the type of sexually explicit monologues that Jackson became known for in the 1970s. Knight would never be as in your face as Jackson, whose wild sense of humor serves her well on *I Had to Say It*. This 1980 LP gets off to a hilarious and irreverent start with the title song, a rap number that finds Jackson attacking everyone from welfare queens to black men who refuse to date black women. Influenced by early rappers like the Sugarhill Gang and the Sequence, "I Had to Say It" sounds quite dated today but was bold for 1980—back then, most R&B singers were afraid to tackle hip-hop. However, the title song isn't representative of the album on the whole; soul singing is Jackson's primary focus, and the vocalist is in good form on gritty soul offerings like "Somebody's Love Died Here Last Night," "Fancy This," and a remake of the Dobie Gray hit "Lovin' Arms." Jackson gets into more of a disco/pop groove on "Ladies First," but this is a soul album first and foremost. Although *I Had to Say It* isn't among Jackson's essential releases, it's a solid, respectable outing that her hardcore fans will appreciate. *—Alex Henderson*

Live and Outrageous (Rated XXX) / 1982 / Spring ✦✦
Millie Jackson's sequel to *Live and Uncensored*, the aptly titled *Live and Outrageous*, falls short of its predecessor's high standard as below par songs and monologues predominate. On "I Had To Say," Jackson's usual sharp wit goes soft as she embarrassingly ridicules old-school rap for an ill-perceived debt it owes to her own "rappin'" style—turning ugly with a mumbling Kurtis Blow impersonation. She falters musically too by replacing the assured, stax soul groove of *Uncensored* and her earlier *Caught Up* with thin disco arrangements and bloated covers; blasé versions of Rod Stewart's "Passion" and Kenny Loggins "This Is It" fittingly bookend the album. There are a few bright spots here, though; the keenly paced, barroom betrayal narrative "Lovers and Girlfriends" and the Gladys Knight inspired "Still." Regardless, one should stick with *Live and Uncensored* to hear Jackson at her best and leave *Live and Outrageous* for the die-hard fan. *—Stephen Cook*

Imitation of Love / 1986 / Jive/Novus ✦✦✦
Although still sassy and vulgar, Millie Jackson had passed her peak as the queen of innuendo and sexual posturing by the time she switched labels to Jive. But this album was her most successful in many years, including a pair of Top Ten R&B hits and several others that charted, including the new title cut. *—Ron Wynn*

The Tide Is Turning / 1988 / Jive/Novus ✦✦
This is a decent album, even though it lacked Millie Jackson's customary fire and soulfulness. Things got tougher for Jackson and all artists with any connections to past eras in the late '80s. Jackson tried to update her sound and retain her vocal character, and was mostly successful in the effort. But it wasn't reflected in sales of the album or any of its singles. *—Ron Wynn*

Back to the Shit / 1989 / Jive/Novus ✦✦✦

● **The Very Best of Millie Jackson** / Sep. 27, 1994 / Jive ✦✦✦✦✦
After spending over a decade with Spring Records, Millie Jackson signed with the Jive label and *The Very Best of Millie Jackson* collects songs recorded for them in the late '80s and '90s. The set includes her two Top Ten hits, "Hot! Wild! Unrestricted! Crazy Love" and "Love Is a Dangerous Game," as well as "Younger Man, Older Woman," which the singer later spun off as a successful musical. And while the selections here do represent some of the best songs of the second half of her career, Jackson has always thrived as an album artist where she can develop complex themes and moods, including her own running commentary via the spoken rap interludes she made famous. Those interludes are missing here, which takes away from the Millie Jackson experience but allows listeners to approach her simply as a singer, revealing her to be a great one at that. *—Wade Kergan*

Totally Unrestricted: The Millie Jackson Anthology / Nov. 11, 1997 / Rhino ✦✦✦✦✦
It would seem that a double-disc Millie Jackson anthology would be definitive, all that anyone would need from the notoriously raunchy soul-singer. That's not necessarily the case with *Totally Unrestricted: The Millie Jackson Anthology*. Over the course of two discs, *Totally Unrestricted* compiles highlights from her recordings for Spring Records. Jackson was with the label from 1971 to 1983. During those years she had a number of Top 40 R&B hits—including the Top Ten singles "Ask Me What You Want," "My Man, a Sweet Man," "Hurts So Good" and "If You're Not Back in Love By Monday"—and the majority of those tracks are featured on this extensive retrospective. By featuring the cream of her '70s and early '80s recordings, *Totally Unrestricted* certainly offers a good portrait of the peak of her career, but that doesn't mean the collection is flawless. For one thing, it's too long for casual fans. Two discs and 36 tracks is a lot of material, and much of Jackson's music is simply too similar for the set to be consistently compelling. Furthermore, the double-disc length might have made sense if it also encompassed her rare '60s recordings and her infamous X-rated late-'80s records for Jive, since that would have conveyed the full scope of her career. Instead, the set draws a portrait—one that some might call a little too detailed—of a specific, albeit successful, portion of her career. By doing so, it is far away the best Millie Jackson collection on the market, but most casual fans will prefer to hear this material on a single disc. *—Stephen Thomas Erlewine*

● **Caught Up/Still Caught Up** / Jan. 12, 1999 / Hip-O ✦✦✦✦✦
Hip-O made a natural choice for this repackaging of two Millie Jackson LPs: her love-triangle classic *Caught Up* from 1974, and its follow-up, *Still Caught Up*, from 1975. Sounding better than they ever have, this pair of albums chart the course of one of the most disastrous affairs in musical history. The first features sides from each perspective, with Jackson brazenly discussing her affair with her lover's wife (on "All I Want Is a Fighting Chance") and later, taking the wife's part, giving up all hope of getting her husband back ("I'm Through Trying to Prove My Love to You"). The production is lush and the playing, by a crack team of Southern soul names, is crisp and effective. While *Still Caught Up* can't help but suffer an energy loss, it's a surprisingly strong record, featuring an unbelievable closer, "I Still Love You (You Still Love Me)," featuring Jackson being dragged away to an institution screaming (she even reprised the act for her stage show). In total, *Caught Up/Still Caught Up* is basically the equal of any solid Millie Jackson compilation, with highlights scattered all over the disc: "(If Loving You Is Wrong) I Don't Want to Be Right," "It's All Over but the Shouting," "Making the Best of a Bad Situation," "Leftovers," and "I'm Tired of Hiding." *—John Bush*

Between the Sheets / Oct. 12, 1999 / 7-N Music ✦✦✦✦✦
Between the Sheets is one of the finest Millie Jackson collections ever assembled, largely because it avoids the kitsch of her salacious soul and finds her playing it straight, more or less. The compilation concentrates on her late-'70s and early-'80s material, balancing hits with lesser-known singles and album tracks. What all the material has in common is that it's smooth soul and quiet storm, something Jackson isn't exactly known for. However, this 16-track compilation offers proof that Millie Jackson is a fine soul singer who doesn't need her bawdy schtick to make an impression—and, as such, it's of interest not only to fans, but to doubting Thomases as well. *—Stephen Thomas Erlewine*

Sex and Soul / Nov. 7, 2000 / 7-N ✦✦✦✦
Between the Sheets captured Millie Jackson at her most straightforward and romantic; its sequel, *Sex and Soul*, concentrates on Jackson's other side—the bawdy, explicit soul that made her reputation, complete with raunchy spoken raps (in the original, pre-hip-hop sense of the term). All of the tracks have been remastered, and most date from Jackson's late-'70s/early-'80s stint on Spring Records, though the compilers have also licensed the full 11-minute version of her breakthrough hit, "(If Loving You Is Wrong) I Don't Want to Be Right." This stuff may seem a little kitschy at times, but it's never less than entertaining, and it's a good introduction to the best-known aspect of Jackson's career (even if it's missing much from her '70s prime). *—Steve Huey*

Rebbie Jackson

b. May 29, 1950, Gary, IN
Vocals / Soundtracks, Urban, Adult Contemporary
Singer Rebbie Jackson was awarded a gold single her first time out with "Centipede," a song written and produced by her brother, Michael Jackson. She can also be heard on "Forever Young" from *Free Willy 2: Adventure Home*, a 1995 Sony Music movie

soundtrack. Rebbie Jackson, like her siblings Janet, LaToya, and Randy, was out of the public eye when her brothers stormed the music world as the Jackson 5. Born Maureen Jackson in Gary, IN, in 1950, Rebbie was taught clarinet and piano by her mother. It wasn't until 1976, after the Jackson 5 had left Motown and signed with CBS, that Rebbie began a professional singing career, becoming a cabaret singer and background vocalist. She was credited on LPs by the Emotions, Betty Wright, and others during the '70s and '80s, and on Brand Nubian's 1998 CD *Foundation*. She also appeared on the Jacksons' short-lived 1976 variety show.

After her brother Michael's success with the mega-selling *Thriller*, he was given the chance to write and produce. His first project was Rebbie's first single "Centipede," which hit number-four R&B in fall 1984. The *Centipede* LP, released in October 1984, featured tracks produced by former Crusaders member Wayne Henderson. Her next album *Reaction* was issued October 1986 and included tracks produced by David "Pic" Conley and David Townsend of the group Surface, plus Rebbie's brother Tito Jackson. The title track single hit number 16 on the R&B charts in summer 1986. The follow-up was "You Send the Rain Away," a duet ballad with Cheap Trick lead singer Robin Zander that made it to number-50 R&B in late 1986. Another fine duet ballad, "Tonight I'm Yours" with Isaac Hayes, received substantial airplay as an album track but curiously was never released as a single.

R U Tuff Enuff was the title of her third Columbia album, issued in February 1988, featuring one single ("Plaything") that reached the R&B Top Ten. Her popularity with devotees of Britain's rare groove scene prompted the release of *The Rebbie Jackson Collection* by Expansion in 1996. After a hiatus from show business in which she moved to Virginia, Rebbie signed with Michael Jackson's MJJ label in the late '90s. Her label debut *Yours Faithfully* was released in March 1998. *—Ed Hogan*

● **Centipede** / 1984 / Columbia ♦♦♦
Although the Jacksons are R&B's most famous family, being a Jackson never guaranteed longevity. Take Rebbie Jackson, for example. In the 1980s, the sister of Michael, Janet, Tito, Randy, LaToya, Marlon, Jermaine, and Jackie Jackson had her 15 minutes of fame, but despite being very well connected, she never headlined Madison Square Garden. None of her albums had the impact of Janet's *Control*, let alone Michael's *Thriller*. But she did enjoy a lot of publicity in 1984, when Columbia released her debut album, *Centipede*. Written and produced by Michael, the alluring title song became a major hit and is a jewel of a single. But the other tracks aren't fantastic—pleasant, but not fantastic. As Rebbie's critics were quick to point out in 1984, she doesn't have a great voice—nor does Janet, for that matter, and despite her limitations as a singer, Janet has delivered some truly stunning albums. But while Janet had Jimmy Jam & Terry Lewis to help her excel on classics like *Control* and *Rhythm Nation 1814*, Rebbie doesn't get that sort of encouragement on *Centipede*. Most of the tracks were produced by Wayne Henderson, who has an impressive track record but doesn't enable her to go that extra mile. Henderson sees to it that she is pleasant on "Open Up My Love" and a remake of Smokey Robinson's "A Fork in the Road," but while this LP simmers, it rarely burns. One track that is especially revealing is Rebbie's version of Prince's "I Feel for You," which Chaka Khan also covered in 1984. While Khan's interpretation is stunning, Rebbie's is merely decent. And that is true of the album on the whole—*Centipede* is a decent record, but except for the title song, it isn't a great one. *—Alex Henderson*

Reaction / 1986 / Columbia ♦♦♦
With a better selection of songs and tighter production than its predecessor, *Centipede*, Jackson's sophomore set was the strongest of her '80s output. The breezy midtempo number "Always Wanting Something," the groovy dance cut "Ticket to Love" and "You Send the Rain Away," a sunny duet with Robin Zander of Cheap Trick, are all fine moments. The title track, an annoying rhetoric of synthesizer and vocal effects, and the dry "If You Don't Call (You Don't Care)" are wastes of time. But otherwise, this is an enjoyable effort. *—Justin M. Kantor*

R U Tuff Enuff / 1988 / Columbia ♦♦

Yours Faithfully / Mar. 3, 1998 / MJJ/Work ♦♦♦
After ten years of inactivity, Rebbie Jackson returned to recording in 1998 with *Yours Faithfully*. She received a major boost from her brother Michael, who signed her to his MJJ subsidiary and sang and co-produced "Fly Away," one of the highlights on the album. Rebbie has never had a terrific voice, but she has surrounded herself with talented producers who help make *Yours Faithfully* one of the strongest albums in her catalog. Only a handful of songs—such as the seductive title track, the house-flavored "Once in a Lifetime Love" and the cover of the Spinners' "I Don't Want to Lose You"—really take root, but the filler is well-produced and pleasant, making the record a surprisingly enjoyable comeback effort. *—Stephen Thomas Erlewine*

Walter Jackson

b. Mar. 19, 1938, Pensacola, FL, **d.** Jun. 20, 1983, Chicago, IL
Vocals / Chicago Soul, Northern Soul, R&B, Soul
Walter Jackson was '60s Chicago soul at its sweetest and, occasionally, most mainstream. In the mid-'60s, he had a brace of solid R&B hits—"Suddenly I'm All Alone," "It's an Uphill Climb (To the Bottom)," "Speak Her Name," "Welcome Home," "A Corner in the Sun"—without ever rising higher than the lower reaches of the Top 100. Recording for the OKeh stable, which was home to the top Chi-town soul talent, he benefited for a time from the production services of local masters Carl Davis and Curtis Mayfield, who handled the Impressions, Major Lance, Gene Chandler, and others. His sides employed similar punchy brass and strings, but in a smoother, more urbane fashion; Jackson was also comfortable with occasional outings into pure supper-club pop with nary a trace of R&B. Jackson had already recorded for Columbia (and unsuccessfully auditioned for Motown) when OKeh A&R director Davis saw him at a Detroit piano bar in 1962. Stricken with polio as a young boy, Jackson had never let his disability get in the way of his musical ambitions, performing on crutches. Impressed with his commanding voice, Carl Davis thought of Walter as a Nat King Cole type of singer, and procured material for Jackson from Mayfield, Van McCoy, Chip Taylor, and other top-notch songwriters.

Despite the obvious pop crossover potential of Jackson's recordings, he remained obscure to white listeners. During the latter part of his stay with OKeh, he was reassigned from Davis' stable to producer Ted Cooper. Jackson had a few hits with Cooper, but there was little success after the late '60s, although he recorded for a few more labels before dying of a cerebral hemorrhage in 1983. *—Richie Unterberger*

Welcome Home / 1965 / OKeh ♦♦♦
The title track was another in a string of majestic singles Walter Jackson made for OKeh, while the other songs were good, sometimes subpar material that Jackson's stirring vocals frequently turned into triumphs. Unfortunately, all of Jackson's OKeh material has long since disappeared and is hardly a candidate to be reissued. *—Ron Wynn*

Speak Her Name / 1967 / OKeh ♦♦♦
Walter Jackson had a resonant, impressive voice and was a superb ballad singer. He was at his soulful peak in the '60s, when he was cutting classy singles for the OKeh label that never got noticed outside the soul world, but were major party hits within it. This was one of his finest works, even though much of the material is repetitive; his treatments made everything viable. *—Ron Wynn*

Feeling Good / 1976 / Chi-Sound ♦♦♦
As a vocalist, Walter Jackson experienced success in the '60s with hits like 1965's "Welcome Home" and 1967's "My Ship Is Coming In." Those songs typify the powerful and dramatic Chicago sound, a perfect match for his precise diction and haunted baritone. Jackson's career was hampered due to his affliction with polio and unjustified commercial woes, and *Welcome Home* marked his mid-'70s return to the music scene. It certainly starts off strong enough, with a cover of Stevie Wonder's "Too Shy to Say." While Wonder's version was subdued if not somnolent, Jackson turns it into great drama. Jackson's update of his own "Welcome Home" though, finds the song not improved by an updated, hackneyed arrangement. The album's best tracks, "Love Is Even Lovelier" and "I Got It Bad Feeling Good," are customary gems from writers Pam Sawyer & Leon Ware. With flawless and nuanced arrangements, the songs are a clear indication where this effort could have gone, but didn't—to shore up Jackson's hit potential, *Welcome Home* was overloaded with cover material. Of course, the worst offender is the always awful "Feelings," a song that has stopped many an album in its tracks. Jackson's take on Elton John's "Someone Saved My Life Tonight" fares better. *Welcome Home*, produced by Carl Davis and arranged by Riley Hampton, finds them way off their game and too often not providing the proper backing for Jackson's superior vocals. *—Jason Elias*

● **The Best of Walter Jackson: Welcome Home—The OKeh Years** / Jun. 4, 1996 / Epic/Legacy ♦♦♦♦♦
Fifteen tracks from his artistic and commercial peak (1964-1967), including his slew of R&B chart hits, highlights from LPs, and a flop single version of "My Ship Is Comin' In." Commercial pop/soul with elaborate production, reaching deeply enough into the gloss on occasion to rate as a vague precursor to the quiet storm music of subsequent decades. *—Richie Unterberger*

Jade

Vocals / Adult Contemporary, Urban, Dance-Pop, Club/Dance
Tonya Kelly grew up in Chicago listening to jazz vocalists such as Sarah Vaughan and Nat Cole. Joi Marshall is also from the Windy City, but her parents raised her on Motown, especially Diana Ross. The third member of Jade, Di Reed, grew up in Houston singing gospel anywhere she could. This '90s R&B trio from diverse backgrounds hit big with their first three singles: "I Wanna Love You," "Don't Walk Away" and "One Woman." Their gold debut album *JADE to the Max* sparked a lengthy tour and spots on *The Tonight Show*, *Arsenio* and the U.K.'s *Top of the Pops*. For their second album, Kelly, Marshall and Reed co-wrote five of the songs and produced the a cappella intro and closing piece. *Mind, Body & Song* was released in 1994. *—John Bush*

JADE to the Max / 1992 / Warner Bros. ♦♦♦
Jade is another in a long line of interchangeable R&B girl groups that manage to find success without a trace of individuality. Although the members of Jade possess enough vocal talent to carry a tune, rarely do groups of this ilk manage to send a song soaring to the upper reaches of the pop charts through depth and personality. Instead, an abundance of hooks and radio-friendly production are enough to make a song a hit. "Don't Walk Away," Jade's smash hit single from its 1992 debut album *JADE to the Max*, is so infectious and irresistible, it could have been sung by almost anyone. The true mastermind behind Jade's debut release is Vassal Benford, who has written and/or produced for a myriad of performers (Toni Braxton, Sheena Easton, Surface, New Edition, Chante Moore, Atlantic Starr). His songwriting and production skills help make *JADE to the Max* more than just a run-of-the-mill R&B release. Fortunately, the members of Jade (Tonya Kelly, Joi Marshall, and Di Reed) make up for the lack of personality with talent and enthusiasm. The aforementioned "Don't Walk Away" is just one of the smash hits from *JADE to the Max*; the Janet Jackson sound-alike "I Wanna Love You" and the ballad "One Woman" also received airplay, and Jade also offers a capable cover of the Emotions' "Blessed." Despite a number of hits and an abundance of good material, *JADE to the Max* is very much a producer's creation. "Don't Walk Away" may be a familiar tune heard on the radio years after its success, but would anyone remember who performed it? Coming from an era full of similar-sounding, more successful vocal groups like En Vogue and SWV, there's a slim chance Jade will be remembered by name. Throughout rock history, many acts became successful despite providing little to no input into production or songwriting. Some (like Whitney Houston) have managed to maintain successful careers while employing songwriters and producers by the dozens, while others (like Stevie Wonder) demanded control over their own music, becoming more successful in the process.

Although Jade attempted the latter route, co-writing several tunes on its sophomore release *Mind, Body & Song* (1994) and helping out with production, the album was not a big seller, and Jade has not been heard from since. *—William Cooper*

- **Mind, Body & Song** / 1994 / Giant ✦✦✦

Jade's sophomore album, *Mind, Body & Song*, balances assembly-line R&B slow jams with funky, futuristic, and sexy midtempo cuts. Had they upped the emphasis on the latter, the album would have been more solid and the trio's future could have been brighter. Regardless, this set was released during the early- to mid-'90s American R&B onslaught, when vocal groups were literally a dime a dozen. Jade were lumped with the SWVs and Xscapes of the era, although these gals exhibited class and sophistication similar to En Vogue. The first couple of songs on this set rank as absolutely average, with lyrics rarely reaching beyond banal good lovin'-type themes. However, by the set's first single, "5-4-3-2 (Yo Time Is Up)," the focus shifts to sexy, cool, and funky midtempo cuts. This track sounds almost futuristic, and was probably quite a bit ahead of its time, which explains its lowly peak on the American pop and R&B charts. The second single, the R&B disco cut "Every Day of the Week," proved to be a long lasting sleeper hit, and was definitely the album's most infectious and sassy cut, and one of the 1990s better dance hits. Other highlights include the almost neo-soul "Everything," the steamy "Do You Want Me," the jazzy, new-jill swing of "Bangin'," and the funky, low down jams "There's Not a Man" and "It's On." Despite an average beginning, this sexy and classy album turns out to be rather intoxicating, and a couple of tracks, namely "5-4-3-2," didn't deserve the lack of attention they received. *—Jose F. Promis*

Jagged Edge

f. Atlanta, GA

Group / Urban, Contemporary R&B

This rough-but-smooth male vocal quartet Jagged Edge formed in Atlanta, consisting of identical twin brothers Brandon "Case Dinero" Casey and Brian "Brasco" Casey, who had moved from their native Hartford, CT; Kyle Norman (aka "Quick"), whom they'd met through church activities; and Richard Wingo (aka "Wingo Dollar"), a late addition to the group suggested by Xscape's Kandi Burress, who took their demo to superproducer Jermaine Dupri. Jagged Edge signed to Dupri's So So Def label and in the summer of 1997 released their debut single, "The Way That You Talk," featuring appearances by Dupri and Da Brat; it reached the Top 40 of the R&B chart and was also a pop chart entry.

Late in 1997, Jagged Edge released their first album, *A Jagged Era*, which went gold and spawned the Top 20 R&B, Top 40 pop hit "Gotta Be." Their next single, "He Can't Love U," appeared in the fall of 1998 and reached the Top Five of the R&B chart and the Top 20 of the pop chart, going gold in the process. It prefaced the group's second album, *J.E. Heartbreak*, which topped the R&B chart and hit the Top Ten of the pop chart, selling over two-million copies and spawning the number-one R&B hits "Let's Get Married" (also Top 20 pop) and "Promise" (also Top Ten pop). By the time of the release of Jagged Edge's third album, *Jagged Little Thrill*, in late June 2001, its lead-off single, "Where the Party At" (featuring Nelly), was nearing the R&B Top Ten and was in the pop Top 40. *—John Bush & William Ruhlmann*

- **A Jagged Era** / Oct. 14, 1997 / So So Def ✦✦✦✦

A Bone Thugs-N-Harmony with more polish to their harmonies and fewer rough edges image-wise, Jagged Edge perform well on their debut album, getting into the groove on singles "The Way That You Talk" and "Gotta Be," each of which is impeccably produced by Jermaine Dupri. There are a few songs which don't work at all on *A Jagged Era*, but for the most part, the quartet sounds interesting. *—John Bush*

J.E. Heartbreak / Jan. 18, 2000 / So So Def ✦✦✦

So So Def wisely held back the release of Jagged Edge's second album, *J.E. Heartbreak*, originally scheduled for the fall of 1999, into early 2000, by which time advance single "He Can't Love U" had become a major hit, thus setting the album up to best the gold-selling success of their debut album, *A Jagged Edge*. That said, the group's slavish obeisance to current R&B conventions continued to be its aesthetic stumbling block. As producer/writer Jermaine Dupri's answer to Boyz II Men, Jagged Edge turned out another set full of slow jams indistinguishable from what was already all over urban radio. Their one attempt at something actually edgy came with "Girl Is Mine," but it was marred by one of those drop-out-laden clean edits of what was no doubt a vulgarity-laced rap by Ja Rule (Why even bother to bring in a rapper if you are only going to cut his rap to ribbons?). Mostly, the group was much more tasteful, with twin brothers Brian and Brandon Casey contributing lyrics of romantic devotion culminating with "Let's Get Married." It could only be hoped that, having made their commercial breakthrough, Jagged Edge would aim for an artistic breakthrough next time. *—William Ruhlmann*

Jagged Little Thrill / Jun. 26, 2001 / So So Def ✦✦✦✦

Jagged Edge broke through from modest commercial success to star status with their second album, *J.E. Heartbreak*, which threw off three major hits and sold in the millions. The task for the follow-up, of course, is to keep the momentum going. The group and producer Jermaine Dupri deliberately previewed the album with a midtempo dance track, "Where the Party At," featuring rapper Nelly, which was bulleting up the charts when the album was released. It effectively countered the group's image, based on its massive hit "Let's Get Married," as a ballad-heavy, domestically minded outfit, the sort of people not much interested in finding out where the party is at. But the album reaffirms that image, with only a few exceptions. All of Jagged Edge's lyrics are written by twin brothers Brandon and Brian Casey, despite the inclusion of guest rappers on four tracks. (As on the previous album, the more edgy raps have had their vulgarities clipped; wouldn't it have made more sense to ask the rappers to curb their language upfront?) And the Casey brothers are very concerned with promoting responsible behavior among their male peers. Dupri has pushed their more prescriptive sentiments to the end of the album (while making sure the few midtempo and uptempo tracks are near the start), but it is these songs that really define Jagged Edge's viewpoint. On "This Goes Out," the Caseys proclaim tolerance for dodgy actions taken to make ends meet and support children, but they draw the line on "Respect," which preaches against domestic violence. Then, on "Hero of Household," they make clear that it's the man who's supposed to wear the pants in the family: "There's gotta be a leader, and that's me." Such sentiments may not please the women otherwise attracted by the group's call for "Responsibility." *—William Ruhlmann*

Jaheim (Jaheim Hoagland)

b. New Brunswick, NJ

Vocals / Urban, Contemporary R&B

Jaheim Hoagland, the new hip-hop balladeer on the block, hails from New Brunswick, NJ, where he grew up in the 176 Memorial Parkway Homes public-housing project. Misfortune hit early: his father died in 1981, when he was only two years old. Coming from a musical family helped him overcome the tragedy and the many pitfalls of his environment. His grandfather, Victor Hoagland, sung with many top groups, including the Drifters, and their family reunions were big songfests. Singing at family reunions and local talent shows preceded a successful tryout at the Apollo Theater's notoriously tough talent show. The smooth crooner who sounded like a hybrid of Teddy Pendergrass and Luther Vandross won the contest three times when he was 15.

Two years later, he experienced more tragedy when his Mom died. But Hoagland kept the faith and became a sensation in New Jersey at talent shows. He made a tape which led to a deal with Divine Mill Records (a division of Warner Brothers) four years later. Hoagland received good reactions from two singles: "Could It Be" and "Lil Nigga Ain't Mine," on *BET* and other video shows. Appearing with Hoagland on his first album was an all-star crew of RL (from Next), Blackstreet, and Darren and Cliff Lightly. The multi-talented singer also raps, models, and acts and has appeared in Source and other hip-hop publications. Prior to getting his own deal, he worked with Mag supplying backing vocals on the rappers' *Hustlaz Heaven* CD. His second album, *Still Ghetto*, was released at the tail end of 2002. *—Andrew Hamilton*

Ghetto Love / Feb. 13, 2001 / Warner Bros. ✦✦✦

On his debut album *Ghetto Love*, soulful crooner Jaheim runs the gamut of a wide variety of R&B styles, showcasing himself as a multi-faceted artist. Despite the ghetto posturing, one listen to the album reveals the baritone-voiced singer to have more in common with the likes of Will Downing or even a more street version of Luther Vandross, with song styles reminiscent of Keith Sweat, especially with his ample use of female vocalists. The album is something of a musical journey. It begins with mid- to uptempo material, from the '70s sounding "Let It Go" (complete with a horn section) to the album's smoldering first single, "Could It Be," arguably one of the best R&B songs in years. Other breezy tunes follow, such as "Happiness," the jeep-flavored "Lil Nigga Ain't Mine" (almost comically tacking an obviously sensitive issue), "Finders Keepers," and "Just In Case," which resonates as a perfect summer jam. The album is unfortunately weighted down by some unremarkable material, but thankfully is salvaged at its close, when Jaheim sings more traditional fare, allowing his gorgeous voice to truly shine. Most memorable among these tunes are "Love Is Still Here," which, unfortunately, is more of an interlude than anything else; "Ready, Willing & Able"; and the church-organ lullaby "For Moms." As a final and remarkable note, Jaheim never stoops to use foul language. The music is just as effective the way it is, without the need to degenerate itself with obscenities. Despite some dull moments, this is a first-rate debut from a very promising artist. *—Jose Promis*

- **Still Ghetto** / Nov. 5, 2002 / Warner Bros. ✦✦✦✦

Jaheim's considerable vocal talents only increased during the recording of his second album, and a stronger set of songs made *Still Ghetto* a definite improvement over the debut. As before, it all begins with his voice: a deep, throaty croon that makes him sound at least ten years older than he actually is (basically, about as old as the soul samples dotted over the record) and marks him as one of the few R&B artists active who can summon the spirit of a Teddy Pendergrass. Better yet, Jaheim takes the lover-man persona to another level, devoting more songs here to relationships than love itself; one of the best is "Put That Woman First," his remake of the Stax nugget William Bell's "I Forgot to Be Your Lover," a great performance that's a natural fit with his persona. The single "Fabulous" is simply beautiful, balancing a back-in-the-day feel with self-esteem issues and riding out with a chorus of children's voices. For "Everywhere I Am," Jaheim recorded a postcard to his mother, who died before he gained fame; it's another testament to his power as an artist that *Still Ghetto* never descends into maudlin sentiments. Just like his soul forefathers, everything about Jaheim is honest and heartfelt. *—John Bush*

Jai (Jason Rowe)

b. Yeovil, England

Vocals / Alternative Dance, Urban

Self-described as "a mod for the hip-hop generation," Jai grew up in the same British village as PJ Harvey and played in a trio whose other two members later formed her first backing band. Born Jason Rowe in Yeovil, England, he was inspired by a variety of musical sources both modern (Kraftwerk, Massive Attack, Public Enemy) and classic (Marvin Gaye, Burt Bacharach). Rowe began playing with a pop band, but when his mates left him to play with PJ Harvey, he moved to London and met up with guitarist/producer Joel Bogen while at a club. The duo began working together, combining Jai's aching falsetto with Bogen's arranging skills, inherited from rock & roll sources as well as traditional pop, soul and jazz. After assembling a three-track demo tape—including a version of Gershwin's "Summertime"—Jai signed to the small British label M&G and released his debut single "Don't Give Me Away" in January 1997. The single did well in England as well as the continent, and several impressive live shows (with a full band) enhanced Jai's image as a cocktail pop singer for the 1990s. He signed to RCA, and released his debut album *Heaven* late in 1997. *—John Bush*

● **Heaven** / Oct. 28, 1997 / RCA ✦✦✦✦
Jai's debut album, *Heaven*, is a stylish amalgam of jazzy sophisti-pop, Motown, swinging '60s rock, trip-hop and contemporary soul. While the songwriting in *Heaven* is uneven, Jai's voice is consistently thrilling, soaring to new soulful heights. That voice—along with songs that show how powerful his updated blue-eyed soul can be, like "I Believe" and "Don't Give Me Away"—is what makes *Heaven* such a promising and successful debut. *—Stephen Thomas Erlewine*

James Jamerson

b. Jan. 29, 1936, Charleston, NC, **d.** Aug. 2, 1983, Los Angeles, CA
Bass / Motown, Soul, Pop-Soul, Funk
Legendary Motown bassist James Jamerson single-handedly revolutionized R&B/pop bass playing. Throughout the entire classic Motown catalog (and some non-Motown sides), Jamerson shaped a new inventive style of bass playing and brought what had been regarded by some as a "minor" instrument to the forefront through the use of the electric Fender bass, powered by his musical genius and amazing dexterity.

James Lee Jamerson Jr. was born on January 29, 1936, in Charleston, NC. His father worked in shipyards and his mother was a domestic worker. When his parents divorced, Jamerson divided his time between his grandmother who played piano, an aunt who sang in the church choir, and practicing piano at his cousin's house. He began developing his innate musical talents while incessantly listening to gospel, jazz, and blues stations. After a bicycle accident, he spent a year in a wheelchair. Forced to wear high-topped shoes in order to walk, the incident left Jamerson with a slight limp and a gnawing self-consciousness that would haunt him for his entire life. In 1953, Jamerson's mother moved to Detroit to find work. A year later, she sent for her son. At Northwestern High, Jamerson picked up an upright bass that was lying on the floor in the music room and "found" his instrument. Never a solitary play-the-scales-millions-of-times type of musician, the budding young bassist honed his skills at jam sessions, in the high school jazz band, and by playing with some of Detroit's top jazz musicians.

After graduation, he began playing with Washboard Willie & the Supersuds of Rhythm. In 1958, Johnnie Mae Matthews, owner of Northern Records, heard Jamerson at a Supersuds club gig and asked him to play on sessions for the label. His unique style came to the attention of other Detroit-area labels, and the 22-year-old Jamerson began cutting sides for Fortune, Tri-Phi, Anna Records, and others. Some musicians invited Jamerson to a session at a small basement studio in a converted house at 2648 West Grand Boulevard, which eventually became the recording base of Motown.

The enigmatic bassist found his musical soulmates in pianist Earl Van Dyke, drummer Benny Benjamin, guitarists Robert White and Joe Messina, and the rest of the Funk Brothers (as the Motown studio band came to be known). In 1961, Jamerson switched to the newly created electric Fender Precision bass. The move made his bass lines stand out more on records. Though Motown wasn't too keen about Jamerson and the rest of the Funk Brothers recording for other labels, the Detroit music community and several music entrepreneurs, local and otherwise, took advantage of the situation, offering the band more money, leading to the Funk Brothers being heard on a lot of "backdoor sessions." The band can be heard on several hits for the local Golden World and Ric-Tic label owned by Twenty Grand Club owner Ed Wingate and on several hits for producer Carl Davis and Jackie Wilson in nearby Chicago.

In 1969 things began to change. Jamerson lost one of his closest friends, Motown drummer Benny Benjamin, to heroin addiction. Because of high demand, Motown hired other bassists in an effort to keep up with the ever-expanding recording schedules; Jamerson couldn't be in two places at once. The label's music became more dependent on written musical arrangements and less on the Funk Brothers' "off the cuff" interplay. It was hard for Jamerson to adjust to the seemingly more rigid way of doing things.

Despite being a no-show at record dates, his alcoholism, and the opinion of some Motown staffers, Berry Gordy refused to fire Jamerson. The loyalty paid off, as Marvin Gaye enlisted Jamerson to play on his 1971 multi-platinum *What's Going On*. In 1973, Motown moved to Los Angeles and Jamerson followed. The following year, the bassist's work schedule seemed to be his busiest ever as he toured with Gaye, Joan Baez, and Maria Muldaur, and recorded jingles, movie scores, TV themes (*Starsky and Hutch*), and, of course, million-selling records: Al Wilson's "Show and Tell," the Hues Corporation's "Rock the Boat," the Sylvers' "Boogie Fever," Rhythm Heritage's "Theme From S.W.A.T.," and Marilyn McCoo & Billy Davis Jr.'s "You Don't Have to Be a Star (To Be in My Show)." But things began to sour for Jamerson as chronic alcoholism, emotional problems, and medication-related mishaps plagued the bassist, leading to his eventual exclusion from the A-list of first-call session players. Much of the last years of Jamerson's life was spent in and out of hospitals and mental institutions. Just four months after the May 1983 NBC-TV broadcast of *Motown 25: Yesterday, Today and Tomorrow*, Jamerson died from complications due to cirrhosis of the liver, heart failure, and pneumonia on August 2, 1983, at the University of Southern California County Hospital. *—Ed Hogan*

Etta James (Etta James Hawkins)

b. Jan. 25, 1938, Los Angeles, CA
Vocals / R&B, Soul, Soul-Blues
Few R&B singers have endured tragic travails on the monumental level that Etta James has and remain on earth to talk about it. The lady's no shrinking violet; her autobiography, *Rage to Survive*, describes her past (including numerous drug addictions) in sordid detail. But her personal problems have seldom affected her singing. James has hung in there from the age of R&B and doo wop in the mid-'50s through soul's late-'60s heyday and right up to today (where her 1994 disc *Mystery Lady* paid loving jazz-based tribute to one of her idols, Billie Holiday). Etta James' voice has deepened over the years, coarsened more than a little, but still conveys remarkable passion and pain.

Jamesetta Hawkins was a child gospel prodigy, singing in her Los Angeles Baptist church choir (and over the radio) when she was only five years old under the tutelage of Professor James Earle Hines. She moved to San Francisco in 1950, soon teaming with two other girls to form a singing group. When she was 14, bandleader Johnny Otis gave the trio an audition. He particularly dug their answer song to Hank Ballard & the Midnighters' "Work With Me Annie." Against her mother's wishes, the young singer embarked for L.A. to record "Roll With Me Henry" with the Otis band and vocalist Richard Berry in 1954 for Modern Records. Otis inverted her first name to devise her stage handle and dubbed her vocal group the Peaches (also Etta's nickname). "Roll With Me Henry," renamed "The Wallflower" when some radio programmers objected to the original title's connotations, topped the R&B charts in 1955.

The Peaches dropped from the tree shortly thereafter, but Etta James kept on singing for Modern throughout much of the decade (often under the supervision of saxist Maxwell Davis). "Good Rockin' Daddy" also did quite well for her later in 1955, but deserving follow-ups such as "W-O-M-A-N" and "Tough Lover" (the latter a torrid rocker cut in New Orleans with Lee Allen on sax) failed to catch on. James landed at Chicago's Chess Records in 1960, signing with their Argo subsidiary. Immediately, her recording career kicked into high gear; not only did a pair of duets with her then-boyfriend (Moonglows lead singer Harvey Fuqua) chart, her own sides (beginning with the tortured ballad "All I Could Do Was Cry") chased each other up the R&B lists as well. Leonard Chess viewed James as a classy ballad singer with pop crossover potential, backing her with lush violin orchestrations for 1961's luscious "At Last" and "Trust in Me." But James' rougher side wasn't forsaken—the gospel-charged "Something's Got a Hold on Me" in 1962, a kinetic 1964 live LP (*Etta James Rocks the House*) cut at Nashville's New Era Club and a blues-soaked 1966 duet with childhood pal Sugar Pie De Santo, "In the Basement," ensured that.

Although Chess hosted its own killer house band, James traveled to Rick Hall's Fame studios in Muscle Shoals in 1967 and emerged with one of her all-time classics. "Tell Mama" was a searing slice of upbeat Southern soul that contrasted markedly with another standout from the same sessions, the spine-chilling ballad "I'd Rather Go Blind." Despite the death of Leonard Chess, Etta James remained at the label into 1975, experimenting toward the end with a more rock-based approach.

There were some mighty lean years, both personally and professionally, for Miss Peaches. But she got back on track recording-wise in 1988 with a set for Island, *Seven Year Itch*, that reaffirmed her Southern soul mastery. Her last few albums have been a varied lot—1990's *Sticking to My Guns* was contemporary in the extreme; 1992's Jerry Wexler-produced *The Right Time* for Elektra was slickly soulful, and her most recent outings have explored jazz directions. In 1998, she also issued a holiday album, *Etta James Christmas*. She was inducted into the Blues Hall of Fame in 2001.

In concert, Etta James is a sassy, no-holds-barred performer whose suggestive stage antics sometimes border on the obscene. She's paid her dues many times over as an R&B and soul pioneer; long may she continue to shock the uninitiated. *—Bill Dahl*

★ **At Last!** / 1961 / MCA/Chess ✦✦✦✦✦
After spending a few years in limbo after scoring her first R&B hits "Dance With Me, Henry" and "Good Rockin' Daddy," Etta James returned to the spotlight in 1961 with her first Chess release, *At Last*. James made both the R&B and pop charts with the album's title cut, "All I Could Do Was Cry," and "Trust in Me." What makes *At Last* a great album is not only the solid hits it contains, but also the strong variety of material throughout. James expertly handles jazz standards like "Stormy Weather" and "A Sunday Kind of Love," as well as Willie Dixon's blues classic "I Just Want to Make Love to You." James demonstrates her keen facility on the title track in particular, as she easily moves from powerful blues shouting to more subtle, airy phrasing; her Ruth Brown-inspired, bad-girl growl only adds to the intensity. James would go on to even greater success with later hits like "Tell Mama," but on *At Last* one hears the singer at her peak in a swinging and varied program of blues, R&B, and jazz standards. *—Stephen Cook*

The Second Time Around / 1961 / MCA/Chess ✦✦✦✦
Etta James' second album isn't what you pull off the shelf when you want to hear her belt some soul. Like her debut, it found Chess presenting her as more or less a pop singer, using orchestration arranged and conducted by Riley Hampton, and mostly tackling popular standards of the '40s. If you're not a purist, this approach won't bother you in the least; James sings with gusto, proving that she could more than hold her own in this idiom as well. R&B isn't entirely neglected either, with the rousing "Seven Day Fool" (co-written by Berry Gordy Jr.) a standout; "Don't Cry Baby" and "Fool That I Am" were R&B hits that made a mild impression on the pop charts as well. *—Richie Unterberger*

☆ **Etta James Rocks the House** / 1964 / MCA/Chess ✦✦✦✦✦
This is simply one of the greatest live blues albums ever captured on tape. Cut in 1963 at the New Era Club in Nashville, the set finds Etta James in stellar shape as she forcefully delivers her own "Something's Got a Hold on Me" and "Seven Day Fool" interspersed with a diet of sizzling covers ("What'd I Say," "Sweet Little Angel," "Money," "Ooh Poo Pah Doo"). The CD incarnation adds three more great titles, including an impassioned reprise of her "All I Could Do Is Cry." Guitarist David T. Walker is outstanding whenever he solos. *—Bill Dahl*

Call My Name / 1966 / Cadet ✦✦✦✦
Etta James' 1966 LP *Call My Name* is dynamite Chicago soul, with the vaunted Chess house band in uplifting support. Among the many standouts are "I'm So Glad (I Found Love in You)," "It Must Be Your Love," and "Don't Pick Me for Your Fool." *—Bill Dahl*

Tell Mama / 1968 / MCA/Chess ✦✦✦✦✦
Leonard Chess dispatched Etta James to Muscle Shoals in 1967, and the move paid off with one of her best and most soul-searing Cadet albums. Produced by Rick Hall, the resultant album boasted a relentlessly driving title cut, the moving soul ballad "I'd Rather Go Blind," and sizzling covers of Otis Redding's "Security" and Jimmy Hughes' "Don't Lose Your Good Thing," and a pair of fine Don Covay copyrights. The skin-tight session aces at Fame Studios really did themselves proud behind Miss Peaches. *—Bill Dahl*

Come a Little Closer / 1974 / Chess ✦✦✦
James was fighting serious substance-abuse problems when this record was recorded, commuting to the sessions from a rehab center. It was a triumph simply to complete the

record at all. But although James' life may have been in rough shape outside of the studio, she delivered a fairly strong set that fused forceful '70s soul arrangements with some rock (Randy Newman and John Kay both contribute compositions), jazz, and New Orleans R&B. Some of the material's routine, but there are some very strong cuts here, like a rousing "Sookie Sookie," and "Out on the Street Again," with its slightly sinister funk groove. "Feeling Uneasy," in fact, counts as one of the unsung highlights of her career, with a wrenching, near-wordless scat-moan vocal over a suitably languorous, melancholy blues-jazz arrangement. The CD reissue adds a couple of interesting bonus tracks: the 1975 single "Lovin' Arms," a good rootsy ballad, and a single edit of one of the tracks from the album, "Out on the Street Again." *—Richie Unterberger*

Deep in the Night / 1978 / Bullseye Blues ♦♦♦♦
Originally released on Warners Bros. to scant acclaim in 1978, this Jerry Wexler-produced masterpiece finds James in astounding voice with a batch of great material to apply her massive interpretive powers to. The band, including the cream of the late-'70s Los Angeles session hot-shots (Cornell Dupree, Jeff Porcaro, Chuck Rainey, Plas Johnson, Jim Horn), lays it down soulful and simple and the result is a modern-day R&B classic. Highlights abound throughout, but special attention must be turned to James' takes on "Only Women Bleed" and the Eagles' "Take It to the Limit." *—Cub Koda*

Etta Is Betta Than Evah / 1978 / Chess ♦♦♦♦
Returning to the uptempo groove of her classic LP *Tell Mama*, this release finds James backed by another tight rhythm section and as sassy as ever. Tracks like "Woman (Shake Your Booty)" and "Only a Fool" (a remake of the Bobby "Blue" Bland classic "I Pity the Fool") show that the famous soul belter has lost none of the strength of her voice. And, if anyone dare question, just listen to James' version of Randy Newman's "Leave Your Hat On," a ballsy track that exemplifies everything great about Etta. Out of print, this album is worth the hunt. *—Steve Kurutz*

R&B Dynamite / 1987 / Flair ♦♦♦♦♦
The singer in her precocious formative years, headed by her 1955 R&B smash "Roll With Me Henry" (aka "The Wallflower"). James' follow-ups included the driving "Good Rockin' Daddy," a bluesy "W-O-M-A-N," and the New Orleans raveup "Tough Lover," which found her backed by the gang at Cosimo's (notably saxman Lee Allen). Even though her tenure at Modern Records only produced a handful of hits, these 22 cuts are delightful artifacts of the belter's earliest days. The CD was reissued, with identical (though slightly resequenced) tracks and liner notes, as *Hickory Dickory Dock* on Ace 680. *—Bill Dahl*

How Strong Is a Woman: The Island Sessions / Mar. 9, 1993 / 4th & Broadway ♦♦♦

☆ **The Essential Etta James** / Jun. 8, 1993 / MCA/Chess ♦♦♦♦♦
Here are 44 tracks summarizing the long and brilliant Chess tenure of Miss Peaches, opening with her 1960 smash "All I Could Do Was Cry," and encompassing her torchy, fully orchestrated ballads "At Last," "My Dearest Darling," and "Trust in Me," and continuing on through her 1962 gospel rocker "Something's Got a Hold on Me," the Chicago soul standouts "I Prefer You" and "842-3089," and her 1967 Muscle Shoals-cut smash "Tell Mama." A few of the '70s sides that conclude the two-disc set seem makeweight when compared to what preceded them, but most of the essentials are aboard. *—Bill Dahl*

★ **Her Best** / 1997 / Chess ♦♦♦♦♦
While several best-ofs from Etta's Chess period have been available over the years—with the two-disc, 44-track *Essential Etta James* at the top of the list in giving the big picture—this 20-track collection sweats *that* bigger picture down to bare essentials. For those wishing to finally sample Etta's classic period at Chess without opening the wallet for box set-anthology expense, this single-disc retrospective will fill the bill quite nicely. Featuring 20 of the tracks that appear on the double-disc *Essential* anthology without anything literally essential left off, this scintillating little disc now officially becomes the one-stop, first-time purchase in connecting with the emotional greatness inherent in Etta's siren song. There's plenty more after this to discover, but *this* is absolutely where you start. *—Cub Koda*

☆ **The Chess Box** / Jun. 27, 2000 / Chess ♦♦♦♦♦
Etta James is one of the towering figures of the blues, the foremost female blues vocalist of the second half of the 20th century, and the foundation of her legacy is her recordings for Chess Records in the '60s. Despite her reputation and enduring popularity, Etta didn't receive a box set retrospective between 1988 and 1990, the time when Chess was honoring such heavyweights as Chuck Berry, Muddy Waters, Howlin' Wolf, Bo Diddley, and Willie Dixon with multi-disc retrospectives. They eased away from box sets during the '90s, only issuing a comprehensive double-disc Little Walter set early in the decade, but they finally returned to the sets in 2000 with a long-overdue *Chess Box* for Etta James. Like before, when they assembled terrific sets on Berry and Waters, they got it right. Collectors may find a favorite side missing, but the great majority of her best work for Argo, Cadet, and Chess is here. Although there are a handful of unreleased tracks, the point behind this set is to provide a thorough overview of the most pivotal years in James' career, and on that level, it succeeds tremendously. Like many career-spanning sets, it does dip slightly in quality on the last disc, but not enough to make this anything less than an essential addition to a thorough blues library, since even on the lesser material, she sounds terrific. As a matter of fact, it's rather astonishing how strong all these recordings are, from her terrific vocals to the songs themselves. It's a shame it didn't come out with the first round of *Chess Box*es, but it was worth the wait. *—Stephen Thomas Erlewine*

Tell Mama: The Complete Muscle Shoals Sessions / Apr. 24, 2001 / MCA/Chess ♦♦♦♦♦
As the title suggests, this is the definitive edition of Etta James' *Tell Mama* long-player. For this single-disc release the original album is augmented with five previously unissued tracks—documented during James' four Muscle Shoals sessions circa 1967-1968. The question of why a rural Alabama town became a conduit for some of the most memorable and instantly identifiable grooves may still be up for debate. The evidence exists in droves and *Tell Mama* could certainly be considered exhibit A. These sessions feature the same impact that would redirect several first ladies of soul. Notable among them are Dusty Springfield's *Dusty in Memphis*, Aretha Franklin's *I Never Loved a Man (The Way I Love You)* and to somewhat lesser acclaim, Jackie DeShannon's *Jackie. Tell Mama* showcases some of the unique and admittedly darker qualities of what might best be described as R&B noir. "I'd Rather Go Blind," "Steal Away," "I'm Gonna Take What He's Got" all exemplify the essence of the blues—making the best of a bad situation. The flipside of the sombre subject matter is the satisfying conviction in the music—which is where the remastering becomes particularly noticeable. No longer does the brass section sound alternately muffled or harsh as it has on previous releases. Likewise, the churning Hammond B-3 organ swells with rich textures. Perhaps the most sonically evident improvements are the subtle ones, such as the supple fretwork on "Sweet Dreams," "I'd Rather Go Blind," and the jazzy percussive shuffle of "The Same Rope"—which provided blue-eyed soul maven Van Morrison with the inspiration for the groove featured on his own "Sweet Dreams." *—Lindsay Planer*

Jesse James (James McClelland)

b. Oct. 3, 1943, El Dorado, AR
Vocals / Deep Soul, Soul, Urban
Deep soul singer Jesse James was born in 1943 in El Dorado, AR, with the handle James McClelland. He moved to the Bay Area while still a child, and came up during the early '60s singing in nightclubs (where his name was changed by an MC who couldn't pronounce his given name). He recorded a few singles for the area labels Shirley and Hit (several with guitar work from Sly Stone), then made the big time when he switched to 20th Century. "Believe in Me Baby, Pt. 1" was a modest pop and R&B hit during 1967, and his self-titled debut LP followed the next year. His biggest hit, 1970's "Don't Nobody Want to Get Married, Pt. 2," reached the R&B Top 20 for the ZEA label, and he continued recording during the '70s and '80s for T.T.E.D. and Gunsmoke. The latter was the label of record for full-lengths like 1988's *I Can Do Bad by Myself* and 1993's *Operator Please Put Me Through*. *—John Bush*

● **Jesse James** / 1968 / 20th Century-Fox ♦♦♦
The author of this self-titled album remains a mystery to some because of confusion with the Jessie James who produced "The Horse" and "Boogaloo Down Broadway," on Cliff Nobles & Co., and the Fantastic Johnny C, respectively. Jesse James' thin, unexpressive voice causes you to lose interest after a few tracks. None of these songs were hits, but some are respectable despite the vocal limitations. Namely, "If You're Lonely Take My Hand," written by Johnny Heartsman, who had a hand in many of these songs; Heartsman later became a recording artist himself for Alligator Records. Also, "Thank You Darlin'," written by Sugar Pie DeSanto, Jesse Mason and Jesse James, and "Facts of Life 68," a song with potential that was only promoted in a few markets. Jesse's most popular recording, "Believe in Me Baby, Pts. 1-2," credits DeSanto, Shena DeMell and Jesse Anderson as songwriters; the tune features the ambience of a nightclub and party atmosphere, with James trying to convince some young lady to believe in him enough to work the streets, and take care of him—pretty heavy stuff for the '60s. This rare slab of vinyl has long been out of print, a recent CD release, however, gives a better picture of the mysterious Jesse James. *—Andrew Hamilton*

Versatility / 1998 / Gunsmoke ♦♦
For an obscure American soul singer who can't even be classified as a one-hit wonder, this is a very optimistic import of his most significant recordings. 20th Century released an album by James in 1968, and an import, *Looking Back*, dropped in 1990. Many of the tracks from those two LPs can be found here. His thin voice makes many of the tracks sound similar; James is easier to take in small doses, a track here, a track there. However, a blind squirrel finds a nut sometimes and some of the tracks are brilliant. On "I Never Meant to Love Her," even James' limited range couldn't screw up this smoldering deep soul ballad. Doo wop influences are evident on "I Call on You." Jesse excelled on midtempo numbers and *Versatility* has some choice ones: "I Don't Want It to End," "If You Want a Love Affair" and "You Ought to Be Here With Me." He duets with a female named Synethia on "You Were Doing Bad When I Met You," an answer song to "I Can Do Bad By Myself." Parts one and two of "Believe in Me Baby" are enjoyable, the song sounding like it was recorded in a small neighborhood bar with James holding court, singing and rapping to a girl about the merits of being his lady. Despite the good stuff, it's hard to recommend this to anyone except aficionados, collectors, relatives, and close friends of James. *—Andrew Hamilton*

Jimmy James (Michael James)

b. Sep. 13, 1940
Vocals / Northern Soul, Soul, Dance-Pop, Disco
Beat R&B vocalist Jimmy James was born Michael James on September 13, 1940, and grew up in Jamaica. He started performing American soul music in the late '50s. As a solo artist he notched two number-one records in Jamaica as Jimmy James on Tip Top Records: "Bewildered and Blue," and "Come to Me Softly" (the latter reached number 70 in States). After the two solo smashes, one of Jamaica's most popular bands, the Vagabonds, approached him; they needed a lead singer and Jimmy was hot. James agreed to work with the band, and Jimmy James & the Vagabonds formed in 1960. They found steady work at the Marquee Club in London, where the British clamored to hear their bag of American soul music. The Northern soul boom was still seeding, and American soul singers rarely came to England, so Jimmy James & the Vagabonds filled a void. The Vagabonds were Rupert Balgobin (drums), Phillip Chen (rhythm guitar), Coleson Chen (bass), Wallace Wilson (lead guitar), Carl Noel (organ), Carl Griffiths & Fred Fredericks

(sax), and the focal point, next to Jimmy, Count Prince Miller, a crowd-pleaser who got the audience involved in the show.

In London, they got their first contract with Pye Records, but released only a series of unpopular singles. Sales didn't start moving until they recorded a live album at the Marquee Club that did well and another entitled *The New Religion*. Of the singles, only their 1968 cover of Neil Diamond's "Red Red Wine" resembled a hit. The Vagabonds called it quits in 1970, gave up the name, and disbanded. Jimmy owned the name and recruited new Vagabonds: a four-piece all-white band consisted of Chris Garfield (guitar), Alan Wood (bass), Russell Courtney (drums), and Alan Kirk (keyboards). They were good, but nowhere near as exciting live as the originals, and they didn't have anyone as charismatic as Count Prince Miller, who scored a solo reggae hit in 1971 with "Mule Train."

Jimmy James and his new Vagabonds scored a minor hit "A Man Like Me," produced by Biddu on Lanita Records. A few recordings for Trojan Records resulted before they reunited with Pye and Biddu. After scoring with the Biddu-produced "Help Yourself," the band spent the '70s gigging. A handful of singles during the '80s did little, and in the '90s James reunited for a few gigs with Winston Curtis and Count Prince Miller. *—Andrew Hamilton*

The New Religion / 1966 / Piccadilly ✦✦✦
With a healthy handful of singles behind them, and already ripping up the live circuit in London, it was no surprise when Jimmy James & the Vagabonds snapped heads with their 1966 debut, *The New Religion*, rounding out earlier releases with further forays into classic American-styled R&B. Bands with similar tastes were a dime a dozen in the States. But in England, where James' influences were flavored with Brit-influenced R&B (albeit an R&B-peppered with James' Jamaican roots), they had the stage to themselves. Earlier recordings "Hi Diddley Dee Dum Dum (It's a Good Good Feeling)" and the sweet, slower-tempoed "Come to Me Softly," which scored the band their belated first U.S. hit in 1968, are highly stylized and emphatic examples of just how smooth this band could be. Rounding up the Vagabonds' early singles output is the percussive, but slightly lackluster, "This Heart of Mine," which just doesn't match the sparkle of the rest of this set. There, James & the Vagabonds proved equally competent at covers, handling versions of the era's heaviest hitters with enthusiastic aplomb. James smoothes and softens his vocals on the Temptations' "It's Growing," giving the string arrangements a run for their money, while the Tony Clarke classic "Ain't Love Good (Ain't Love Proud)" is live and rollicking. Although the band's real depth would come in the following years, and while many regard them as a better live act than studio band, Jimmy James & the Vagabonds' debut was a slick slab of hybridized R&B that wowed the Crown's country. *—Amy Hanson*

Open Up Your Soul / 1968 / Pye ✦✦✦
Revolving around a remake of the tepid Neil Diamond ballad "Red Red Wine," Jimmy James & the Vagabonds' second album (third if you count their 1967 live side on the *London Swings: Live at the Marquee Club* LP) found James slipping slightly from his vibrant former style. With the Vagabonds now comprising a revolving roster of faceless musicians, the group suffered at times from a lack of dynamic style, although James' sensational vocals always stamped the songs with his unmistakable soulfulness. "Red Red Wine" is the album's launching point, James blueprinting the later reggae versions (Tony Tribe, UB40) without actually putting it to a reggae beat himself. Also outstanding is his treatment of the Beatles' "Good Day Sunshine." Taking the upbeat, punchy *Revolver* track firmly in hand, James grooves it down; inserting soul where pop was once the principle mood and spinning dirty guitar and vocals over a sweet backing chorus, he transforms a once-weak song into another dimension entirely. Elsewhere, too, James returns to his old self across his take on the Dells' "Wear It on Our Face," focusing on the snappy tempo and vocal arrangements, while the Box Tops' "Cry Like a Baby" emerges a soaring pop classic. By 1968, James had clearly found his market niche. But, although it was a nifty place that allowed him to ply his soul without needing to break new ground, it lacked much of the spark that earlier efforts had afforded. Similarly, the studio material still couldn't compare to James' live staples. Aside from these petty snafus, however, *Open Up Your Soul* remains a hefty set, a nice amalgam of British and American style all mashed up into a smooth soul groove. *—Amy Hanson*

You Dont Stand a Chance If You Can't Dance / 1975 / Pye ✦✦✦
Teaming up with disco producer Biddu brought Jimmy James & the Vagabonds a dramatic update in sound during their mid-'70s re-emergence. Although James is still well in possession of his undeniably warm voice and still master of the bright brass punches that informed his '60s-era material, 1975's *You Don't Stand a Chance If You Can't Dance* LP is a strobe-lit night to the smooth daylight sonics of 1966's *The New Religion*. From the James Brown patter than drives the title track, here split into two parts to open and close the album (and, oddly, also cross-marketed on Biddu's own 1975 effort, *Blue Eyed Soul*), to the funk fury of "Let's Have Fun," it's obvious that James has been completely revitalized. James' style also proves to be a perfect match for Biddu's lushly styled arrangements—a collusion that is absolutely perfect on the rootsy blues guitar and string-laden "Come Lay Some Lovin' on Me." Elsewhere, the smooth ballads "Suspicious Love" and "I Know You Don't Love Me but You Got Me Anyway" allow James to flex his classic smooth soul delivery. Another track, the somewhat forgettable "I Am Somebody," even managed to crack the U.S. Top 100 in 1976, although James' own adopted country cold-shouldered him out of its charts completely. There's often some trepidation surrounding the return of veteran performers as they cross from one genre to another—returning to the spotlight after the musical climate has evolved. And it's probably true that James' die-hard '60s-era fans weren't necessarily thrilled with the sonic shift. However, what James accomplished in terms of breadth and depth is fantastic. *—Amy Hanson*

I'll Go Where Your Music Takes Me / 1976 / Pye ✦✦
For anybody coming to Jimmy James recalling his 1960s prime, or even drawn into orbit by the previous year's phenomenal *You Don't Stand a Chance If You Can't Dance*, *I'll Go Where Your Music Takes Me* would not, in fact, take them anywhere they might have expected to go. Following quickly on the heels of its predecessor, and again pairing James with producer Biddu, it emerged a lackluster and surprisingly disappointing set, one that disco-ed up the energy a hundredfold but left James' superb soul sensibility hopelessly stranded in the background, somewhere between the paint-by-numbers jingles and the rote rhythms and strings that dominate almost every track. Commercially, it was a successful recipe. The AOR-inflected title track gave James a U.K. number 23 in 1976, his first hit in eight years, while the snappy funk spatter of "Now Is the Time" soared even higher, hitting the Top Five on the strength of a bouncy beat and a semi-celestial roller-disco backing chorus. How shocking, then, to turn to its six-minute LP counterpart and discover that those comforting chorales and soaring strings were actually the sandwich around a mid-song revolutionary rant that verges on the incendiary. It's an odd juxtaposition, and results in the best track on the album. The lurching "Stay With Me" also packs a funky edge, but too much of the album relies on the now almost formulaic dance sound that Biddu himself had been working for over a year—indeed, he would also record both "Disco Fever" and "I'll Go Where Your Music Takes Me" with diva Tina Charles, effectively relegating James to just another worker in the producer's disco hit factory. *—Amy Hanson*

● **I'll Go Where Your Music Takes Me: The Best of Jimmy James** / Feb. 1, 1995 / Hot Productions ✦✦✦✦
I'll Go Where Your Music Takes Me: The Best of Jimmy James collects sides recorded during the '70s, after the disbanding of James' original backing group, the Vagabonds. Aiming to do what his acclaimed '60s tracks were unable to gain and score a U.K. radio hit, James began recording in a light, disco-pop style. And while the change upset many fans of the grittier soul that James previously sang, it did accomplish the goal of putting him on the charts with the title cut. So those looking to hear serious pleadings of the heart and commentary on social ills are advised to look elsewhere, as tracks like "If You Think That This Funk Is Junk Your Drunk" and "Do the Funky Conga" are destined for the dancefloor. *—Wade Kergan*

Vagabond King: The Sixties Sides / Aug. 19, 1997 / Sequel ✦✦✦✦
Collecting the best of Jimmy James & the Vagabonds' first two studio albums for Pye, plus a handful of singles cut for the label (some initially appeared on the Piccadilly subsidiary), *Vagabond King: The Sixties Sides* is the only Jimmy James album the non-collector will ever need. Spanning just three years, from 1966 to 1968, *Vagabond King* covers all of James' bases, from the his earliest Motown-informed "Hi Diddley Dee Dum Dum (It's a Good Feeling)" label debut, to the mid-period grace of "No Good to Cry," his fabulous, horn-drenched reinvention of the Beatles' long-suffering "Good Day Sunshine," and onto "Better by Far," whose 1970 issue marked the end of James' '60s soul sound. From there, it's just an easy step back to fill in the holes across 24 more tracks which pull in further favorites "Come to Me Softly" and "I Wanna Be (Your Everything)." With the tracks shuffled with no regard for chronology, it's easy to ignore the change in raw energy that occurred between the band's 1966 debut and their 1968-era ending dénouement. But that's OK because it's James' voice that always cuts through the rough, giving a hybridized and often unique British/Jamaican/American soul treatment to a collection of heavy-hitting R&B covers. And, although connoisseurs argue that James & the Vagabonds sounded best in front of a raw club audience, this slick set still proves that, for a time and without a string of hit singles, James was on top of the world, doing exactly what he wanted in a country that did nothing but embrace him. It just doesn't get much better than that, and *Vagabond King* is an accurate sonic reflection of that. *—Amy Hanson*

Where Your Music Takes Me / May 11, 1999 / Sequel ✦✦✦✦
In 1998, the chunky *Where Your Music Takes Me* provided a nifty stopgap collection of Jimmy James, with various incarnations of Vagabonds classics spanning the Biddu-produced, 1970s Pye-era recordings. From his classic funk-fueled "You Don't Stand a Chance (If You Can't Dance)," to "I'll Go Where Your Music Takes Me," and on to the later hits, "Now Is the Time" and the ubiquitous "Disco Fever," James covers all of his uptempo bases. But the album also collects some of his softer R&B sides, too. These are highlighted across the wonderful "I Am Somebody," "Suspicious Love," and "I Know You Don't Love Me, but You Got Me Anyway," all pulled from James' 1975 *You Don't Stand a Chance If You Can't Dance* LP. Although it's James' '60s material that is most frequently lauded, this compilation reminds listeners that his mid-'70s collaboration with Biddu represents a body of exquisitely rendered work. The melding of James' sophisticated vocals and Biddu's never-less-than-ambitiously orchestrated production may never have attained the critical/commercial highs of the American-made sounds of the era, but that is the downfall of marketing as opposed to music. *Where Your Music Takes Me* is British '70s soul at its finest. *—Amy Hanson*

Rick James (James Johnson)

b. Feb. 1, 1948, Buffalo, NY
Vocals, Keyboards, Guitar, Bass / Quiet Storm, Urban, Funk
In the late '70s, when the fortunes of Motown Records seemed to be flagging, Rick James came along and rescued the company, providing funky hits that updated the label's style and saw it through into the mid-'80s. Actually, James had been with Motown earlier, though nothing had come of it. After growing up in Buffalo and running away to join the Naval Reserves, he ran away from the Navy to Toronto, where he was in a band with future Buffalo Springfield members Neil Young and Bruce Palmer, and with Goldy McJohn, later of Steppenwolf. As the Mynah Birds, they signed to Motown and recorded, though no record was ever released.

James had a journeyman's career playing bass in various groups before signing again to Motown as an artist, songwriter, and producer. His first single, "You and I" (May 1978), topped the R&B charts and reached the pop Top 40. "Mary Jane" (September 1978) was another hit. Both were on James' debut album, *Come and Get It!* (June 1978), which went gold. Subsequent efforts were not as successful, though *Bustin' Out of L Seven* (January 1979) featured the R&B hit "Bustin' Out" (April 1979). James returned to form with the number-one R&B hit "Give It to Me Baby" (March 1981), featured on the million-selling *Street Songs* (April 1981), which also featured the hit "Super Freak."

James turned his production attention to resuscitating the career of the Temptations, recently returned to Motown, and "Standing on the Top" (April 1982), credited to the Temptations Featuring Rick James, was an R&B Top Ten. (He also produced recordings by Teena Marie and the Mary Jane Girls.) James' follow-up to *Street Songs* was the gold-selling *Throwin' Down* (May 1982), which featured the hit "Dance Wit' Me." The title song of *Cold Blooded* (August 1983) became James' third R&B number one, and the album also featured his hit duet with Smokey Robinson, "Ebony Eyes." James' greatest hits album *Reflections* (August 1984) featured the new track "17" (June 1984), which also became a hit. *Glow* (April 1985) contained Top Ten R&B singles in the title track and "Can't Stop," which was featured in the summer movie blockbuster *Beverly Hills Cop. The Flag* (June 1986) featured the hit "Sweet and Sexy Thing" (May 1986).

James left Motown for the Reprise division of Warner Bros. Records as of the album *Wonderful* (July 1988), which featured his number-one R&B hit "Loosey's Rap," on which he was accompanied by rapper Roxanne Shante. Nevertheless, his "punk funk" didn't seem to rest comfortably with the trend toward rap/hip-hop. In 1989, James charted briefly with a medley of the Drifters hits "This Magic Moment" and "Dance With Me." In 1990, MC Hammer scored a massive hit with "U Can't Touch This," which consisted of his rap over the instrumental track of "Super Freak." That should have made for a career rebirth, but James was plagued by drug and legal problems that frequently kept him in court and in jail rather than in the recording studio. He returned to recording in 1997 with *Urban Rhapsody*, which features collaborations with, among others, Snoop Dogg and Bobby Womack. *—William Ruhlmann*

Come Get It! / 1978 / Motown ♦♦♦♦

After returning to the U.S. from London, where he fronted the blues band Main Line, Rick James cut one album with White Cane before he turned to his own solo venture. By 1977, he'd begun working with the Stone City Band, emerging at the end of the year with an album's worth of delicious funk-rock fusion. Released in spring 1978, *Come Get It!* was a triumphant debut, truly the sum of all that had gone before, at the same time as unleashing the rudiments of what would become not only his trademark sound, but also his mantra, his manifesto—his self proclaimed punk-funk. Packed with intricate songs that are full of effusive energy, *Come Get It!* is marvelously hybridized funk, so tightly structured that, although they have the outward feel of funk's freewheeling jam, they never once cross the line into an uncontrolled frenzy. This is best demonstrated across the monumental, eight-plus minute, "You and I." With enough funk bubbling under the surface to supplant the outward disco sonics of the groove, but brought back to earth via James' vocal interpolations, "You and I" became James' first R&B chart hit, effortlessly slamming into the top spot. "Mary Jane," meanwhile, was James' homage to marijuana—honoring the love affair through slang, it dipped into the Top Five in fall 1978. More importantly, though, it also offered up a remarkable preview of his subsequent vocal development. With nods to Earth, Wind & Fire on "Sexy Lady," Motown sonics on "Dream Maker," the passionate "Hollywood," and the classic club leanings of "Be My Lady," it's obvious that James was still very much in the throes of transition, still anticipating his future onslaught of hits and superstardom. Many of the songs here have a tendency toward the disco ethics that were inescapable in 1978, and have been faulted as such; nevertheless, what James achieved on this LP was remarkably fresh, and would prove vitally important to funk as it grew older during the next decade. *—Amy Hanson*

Bustin' Out of L Seven / 1979 / Motown ♦♦♦♦

Rick James' second album, *Bustin' Out of L Seven*, maintained his status among R&B fans, almost topping the LP chart and spawning hits in the title track, "High on Your Love Suite," and "Fool on the Street," though none of them matched the popularity of the debut album's "You and I" or "Mary Jane." James managed an effective amalgam of recent R&B big-band styles, from Sly & the Family Stone to Earth, Wind & Fire and Funkadelic, overlaying the result with his jeeringly rendered sex-and-drugs philosophy. What was missing this time was a real pop crossover—if *Come Get It!* had suggested he could have the pop success of Earth, Wind & Fire, *Bustin' out of L Seven* threatened that his work would find as restricted an audience as Funkadelic, and without the critical cachet. *— William Ruhlmann*

Fire It Up / 1979 / Gordy ♦♦♦

Rick James' third album in 18 months may have spread the funk a little thin (or saturated the market), since *Fire It Up* was not as effective as his first two efforts. The usual mix of rock and R&B had some disco added, which dulled the music's edge and made it more formulaic. At the same time, James' single entendre come-ons, notably the album's biggest single, "Love Gun," were beginning to sound less provocative than just smutty. James had all the weapons for success in his arsenal, but he hadn't yet figured out a unified plan of attack, and *Fire It Up* was a holding action. *— William Ruhlmann*

Garden of Love / 1980 / Motown ♦♦♦

Without a doubt, *Garden of Love* was Rick James' most underrated release. The album went gold and was far from a flop, but Motown wanted double or triple platinum, and anything less was disappointing. And when funk fans reminisce, *Garden* isn't one of the albums they mention. A departure from the type of hard and rowdy funk that defined *Come Get It!*, *Bustin' Out of L Seven* and *Fire It Up*, *Garden* boasted only one major hit ("Big Time") and was surprisingly laid-back by James' standards. The album contains more ballads than usual, and Rick uses subtlety to his artistic advantage on songs ranging from the clever "Mary Go Round" to the haunting "Summer Love." Unfortunately, some mistook subtlety for wimpiness. But make no mistake: the songs are first-rate, though they lack the type of immediacy he was known for. Those who overlooked *Garden* need to give it a closer listen. *—Alex Henderson*

Street Songs / 1981 / Motown ♦♦♦♦♦

Disappointed because *Garden of Love* wasn't as well received as it should have been, Rick James made a triumphant return to defiant, in-your-face funk with the triple-platinum *Street Songs*. This was not only his best-selling album ever, it was also his best period, and certainly the most exciting album released in 1981. The gloves came all the way off this time, and James is as loud and proud as ever on such arresting hits as "Super Freak," "Give It to Me, Baby" and "Ghetto Life." Ballads aren't a high priority, but those he does offer (including his stunning duet with Teena Marie, "Fire and Desire") are first-rate. One song that's questionable (to say the least) is the inflammatory "Mr. Policeman," a commentary on police misconduct that condemns law enforcement in general instead of simply indicting those who abuse their authority. But then, the thing that makes this hot-headed diatribe extreme is what makes the album on the whole so arresting—honest, gut-level emotion. James simply follows what's in his gut and lets it rip. Even the world's most casual funksters shouldn't be without this pearl of an album. *—Alex Henderson*

Throwin' Down / 1982 / Gordy ♦♦♦♦

Rick James fans generally agree that 1981's *Street Songs* is his finest album—in fact, *Street Songs* is essential listening for anyone with even a casual interest in hardcore funk. Unfortunately, James tried to recycle the album's formula on many of his subsequent albums, and, by the mid-'80s, he had become a very predictable and redundant caricature of himself. But in 1982, James was still exciting. That year's *Throwin' Down*, the album that followed *Street Songs*, falls short of essential, but is still rewarding. Many of the songs are excellent, including the cynical "Money Talks" and the major hits "Standing on the Top" (which features the Temptations) and "Dance Wit' Me." Not surprisingly, hardcore funk dominates the record, although *Throwin' Down* contains a few pleasing soul ballads as well. "Happy," a duet with Teena Marie, and "Teardrops" point to the fact that James can be a very expressive ballad singer even though he is best known for his uptempo material. This album does sound like recycled *Street Songs* at times, but in 1982, James had yet to run the formula into the ground. All things considered, *Throwin' Down* was an enjoyable, if imperfect and slightly uneven, addition to the funkster's catalog. *—Alex Henderson*

Cold Blooded / 1983 / Motown ♦♦

The last gasp for Rick James, at one time the king of '80s punk-funk. He was close to the end by the time this came out, but got some fresh life from a surprising source. A ballad between James and Smokey Robinson, possibly the two least compatible male vocalists around, proved a big hit and regenerated James as a single artist for a few more years. But the remainder of the album marked his continual deterioration as a producer, arranger, songwriter, and performer. *—Ron Wynn*

Glow / 1985 / Gordy ♦♦♦♦

By the mid-'80s, Rick James' funk had become a very tired cliché. Hits like 1984's "17" found an artist who had been so exciting only a few years earlier sounding increasingly formulaic and predictable. But he got out of his artistic rut in a major way with the excellent *Glow*. In interviews, James had expressed a desire to record an all-out rock album, and while *Glow* doesn't fit that description, he does incorporate rock and pop elements with splendid results on everything from the new wave-ish "Can't Stop" to the sweaty "Rock and Roll Control." But make no mistake: This is an R&B album first and foremost, and seductive numbers like "Moonchild" and the title song would be worthy of Kashif or Luther Vandross. Regrettably, James' risk-taking didn't pay off, and *Glow* was far from a major hit. Next to *Garden of Love*, *Glow* may be the most underrated album of Rick James' career. *—Alex Henderson*

The Flag / 1986 / Motown ♦♦

Wonderful / 1988 / Reprise ♦♦

Bustin' Out: The Very Best of Rick James / May 17, 1994 / Motown ♦♦♦♦♦

In the late 1970s and early '80s, Rick James did more than anyone to challenge George Clinton's place on the funk throne. Eventually, his music would turn into a very tired cliché, but at his creative peak, James was among the most exciting and vital artists funk had to offer. Summarizing his Motown output from 1978-1986 and offering four new tracks from 1994 as well, this two-CD anthology reminds us just how great he once was, but it provides evidence of his artistic decline as well. Though some of the songs are mediocre, most are outstanding. Even the most casual funk fans owe it to themselves to savor such rowdy classics as "Super Freak," "You and I," "Love Gun," "Give It to Me, Baby" and "Ghetto Life." James was equally superb when it came to soul ballads—and anyone who thinks otherwise should give a serious listen to "Fire and Desire" (a stunning duet with Teena Marie), "Dream Maker," and "Ebony Eyes" (which features Smokey Robinson). Sadly, "Cold Blooded" and "17" illustrate how formulaic James' funk often sounded by the mid-'80s. Meanwhile, some of the new material (including an enjoyable remake of Norman Connors' "You Are My Starship") indicated that he had the potential make a comeback with the right guidance. Boasting many more pluses than minuses, this set is the best place for novices to start. *—Alex Henderson*

● **Ultimate Collection** / Mar. 25, 1997 / Motown ♦♦♦♦♦

Motown's *Ultimate Collection* line has been a massive success in putting together definitive single-disc compilations of their greatest artists, and the Rick James installment is no exception. Because this one includes some lengthier workouts, it isn't quite as complete as most of the series, but it does provide an essential look at James in his influential prime, leaving very little of his sex-and-drugs ethos to the imagination. Spanning the years 1978-1983, these 13 tracks paint an effective picture of James' groundbreaking fusion of funk, rock, and new wave, which basically constituted hardcore funk's last hurrah as the disco age wound down and the urban contemporary genre began to take shape. Unlike most of the other volumes, this *Ultimate Collection* isn't arranged chronologically; instead, it kicks off with James' three number-one R&B hits: "Cold Blooded," "Give It to Me Baby," and "You and I." From there the collection branches out into a generous selection from his best album, *Street Songs* (five in all), including his signature tune "Super Freak"; the R&B Top Tens "Mary Jane," "Dance Wit' Me," and "Bustin' Out"; and duets with Smokey Robinson ("Ebony Eyes") and protégée Teena Marie ("Fire and Desire"). It's true that later hits like "17," "Can't Stop," "Glow," "Sweet and Sexy Thing," and "Loosey's Rap" are missing. But frankly, James was past his creative prime when he recorded them, and they're not missed compared to what's here. With Stevie Wonder in a sudden creative downturn, this material almost single-handedly kept Motown Records on the charts as the '70s became the '80s, and it certainly paved the way for the hedonistic computer funk that made Prince a superstar in the '80s. A superb introduction. *—Steve Huey*

Urban Rapsody / Oct. 14, 1997 / Private I ✦✦✦

Rick James spent most of the '90s either fighting the law or incarcerated, which naturally hurt his career. But what was more damaging to his musical reputation was the fact that he had spent the latter half of the '80s in creative limbo, producing only a handful of worthy tracks. *Urban Rapsody* was the 1997 comeback effort that was supposed to restore his personal and professional reputations, and to a certain extent, it does just that. The media blitz that accompanied its release did forcefully bring him back into the spotlight, and his collaborations with Snoop Doggy Dogg and Rappin' 4-Tay brought him to a younger audience, while his collaborations with Bobby Womack and Charlie Wilson retained his older following. However, *Urban Rapsody* doesn't really offer anything new—it's the same collection of smooth ballads and freaky urban funk that he's been peddling since the late '70s. The lack of variety is a bit of a disappointment, but that disappointment is tempered by the fact that much of the album is well-crafted and performed, illustrating that James has not entirely lost it. While the lack of variety prevents *Urban Rapsody* from being a totally triumphant comeback, the cuts that do work help make the record his best album in over a decade. *—Leo Stanley*

Jamiroquai

f. 1992, London, England

Group / Alternative Dance, Adult Alternative Pop/Rock, Club/Dance, Acid Jazz, Urban, Trip-Hop, Alternative Pop/Rock

Although some choose to pass off Jamiroquai as a Stevie Wonder-clone, the band has amassed a steady stream of hits in its native U.K. and has experienced chart success in just about every other area of the world with an irresistible blend of house rhythms and '70s-era soul/funk. The band has gone though several lineup changes during their career, but through it all their leader has remained singer/songwriter Jason Kay (aka J.K.). Born on December 30, 1969, in Stretford, Manchester, Kay's mother, Karen, was a jazz singer who regularly performed at nightclubs, and in the '70s had her own TV show. After leaving home at the age of 15, Kay found himself homeless and in trouble with the law (by committing petty crimes to get by). After a near-death experience (where he was attacked and stabbed) and being arrested for a crime he did not commit, Kay decided to return home, where he chose to pursue a legitimate career over crime: music. Kay didn't have a band to back up his compositions, but he quickly came up with his future project's name, Jamiroquai, a name that combined the name of a Native American tribe (the Iroquois) along with the music-based work, jam.

Kay's home demos caught the attention of the record label Acid Jazz, which issued Jamiroquai's debut single "When You Gonna Learn?" in late 1992. With Kay enlisting the help of others (Jamiroquai's best-known lineup included drummer Derrick McKenzie, keyboard player Toby Smith, bassist Stuart Zender, and vibraphonist Wallis Buchanan), the single was a success and was soon followed by a long-term and lucrative recording contract with Sony. Jamiroquai's full-length debut, *Emergency on Planet Earth*, followed in 1993 and became a major hit in their native England (peaking at number one on the charts), spawning such Top Ten hit singles as "Too Young to Die" and "Blow Your Mind." The band's second release, *The Return of the Space Cowboy* in 1995, managed to steer Jamiroquai clear of the sophomore jinx that affects so many up-and-coming bands by outselling its predecessor in Europe and was a sizeable hit in Japan, as well.

With most of the world dancing to Jamiroquai's beat, America was next in line for the band's third effort, 1996's *Traveling Without Moving*. The album spawned the worldwide hit "Virtual Insanity," for which an award-winning video was filmed and helped the album achieve platinum status in the States by the year's end (as well as a highlighted performance at the 1997 MTV Video Music Awards). Despite achieving breakthrough success, bassist Zender opted to leave the group during sessions for its follow-up, which resulted in Kay scraping almost an entire album's worth of new tracks in order to start from scratch with a new bassist (the slot would eventually go to newcomer Nick Fyffe). During the downtime, Jamiroquai contributed a brand-new track, "Deeper Underground," to the soundtrack for the 1998 movie *Godzilla*.

But the long wait between albums seemed to kill Jamiroquai's momentum in the U.S., where a fourth release overall, 1999's *Synkronized*, was largely ignored (yet back home and across the globe, it was another major commercial success). Subsequently, it appeared as though the majority of Jamiroquai's U.S. media attention focused on non-music related events, such as the band turning down a million-dollar offer to play at a concert on New Year's Eve 1999, and when Kay was accused of assaulting a tabloid photographer (with the charges later being dropped). It didn't take Jamiroquai as long the next time around to issue another album, with *A Funk Odyssey* hitting the racks two years later in 2001. *—Greg Prato*

Emergency on Planet Earth / Aug. 10, 1993 / Columbia ✦✦✦✦

Jamiroquai made a large initial splash in 1993 with *Emergency on Planet Earth*, a psychedelic mélange of tight funky rhythms, acid rock intimations, and '70s soul melodies. Frontman Jay Kay introduces himself with an environmentally oriented manifesto inside the sleeve, and his lyrics smack of idealist save the planet revolution. But this revolution would be held on the dancefloor if the band's impressive rhythm section had anything to say about it. Horns, string arrangements, and a didgeridoo provide full texture on most of the album's tunes, and the socially aware party vibe raged into the U.K.'s number-one album slot. For a debut, *Emergency* shows quite a range of diversity, from the uptempo jazzy instrumental "Music of the Mind" to the stop-start funk of "Whatever It Is, I Just Can't Stop." *—Troy Carpenter*

• **The Return of the Space Cowboy** / 1995 / Work ✦✦✦✦✦

Jamiroquai's sophomore record had all the slinky grooves and great musicianship of the debut, but it also offered a better set of songs and more ambitious musical themes. As with *Emergency on Planet Earth*, Jason Kay's dead-on impression of Stevie Wonder and Sly Stone drives the group's blend of acid jazz and funky R&B. "Space Cowboy" and "Light Years" were hits all over the world, and made the band stars in Europe and Japan, while substantial clubplay earned them a degree of recognition for American audiences. But Jamiroquai refused to be known as simply a party band; the group takes on social issues such as homelessness and Native Americans' rights. *—John Bush*

Travelling Without Moving / Sep. 9, 1996 / Work ✦✦✦✦

Travelling Without Moving deepens the acid jazz and '70s soul fusions of *Return of the Space Cowboy*, yet it doesn't have the uniform consistency of its predecessor. Nevertheless, Jamiroquai's fusions sound more fully realized with each outing, which makes its patchy songwriting forgivable. *—Stephen Thomas Erlewine*

Synkronized / Jun. 8, 1999 / Work ✦✦✦✦

Three years after their breakout *Travelling Without Moving*, Jamiroquai returned with another album that charts Jay Kay's continuing fascination with club-bound music of the 1970s—from disco to jazz-funk to rare groove to later Motown—but also shows signs of maturity. Produced by Kay with Al Stone, who also collaborated on *Travelling Without Moving*, the album includes several tracks (like the single "Canned Heat") that work infectious acid jazz grooves, and Kay's hipster vocals give out feel-good vibes through a set of ambiguously good-time lyrics. Though other tracks show a bit of an electronica update to the affairs, each still spotlights how strong and tight the band is. It may not be a leap ahead in sound, but *Synkronized* is another solid Jamiroquai record. *—John Bush*

A Funk Odyssey / Sep. 11, 2001 / Epic ✦✦✦

After the jarring reception of 1999's *Synkronized*, Jamiroquai constructed *A Funk Odyssey*, something more polished and slick inside the band's own brand of funky disco-rock. Jason Kay and keyboardist/songwriter Toby Smith perfected a maturation that was left keyed in *Travelling Without Moving* but left open-ended on *Synkronized* for a wide scope of musical delight. *A Funk Odyssey* taps into various illustrious grooves of the Latin world, classic rock, and mainstream club culture, and Jamiroquai is tight and eager to make everyone shake their groove thing in their own light. The first single, "Little L," beams with Kajagoogoo-like synths while warping into a funk-driven hue of orchestral whirlpools, but Jamiroquai allows the band's extroverted and unattached personality to shine on the worldbeat-tinged "Corner of the Earth." Kay strips aside all disco humor and grandeur for something personally inviting, something that's heartfelt too. *A Funk Odyssey* sparks classic enthusiasm, and it feels good. Dance music is not just a design, it's something far more tangible, and Jamiroquai surely captures a fierce desire to make it more emotional on the band's own level. *—MacKenzie Wilson*

The Jarmels

f. 1959, Richmond, VA

Group / Soul, R&B, Doo Wop

The Jarmels were one of those one-hit wonder groups, responsible for a number-12 single in 1961 entitled "A Little Bit of Soap." If none of their other five singles did remotely as well, that song has lingered in the public consciousness, partly with help from periodic new hit versions by the Exciters in the mid-'60s and Showaddywaddy in England during the 1980s.

The Jarmels came from Richmond, VA, where the five members had all begun singing together in church and school. Nathaniel Ruff (b. 1939), Ray Smith (b. 1941), Paul Burnett (b. 1942), Earl Christian (b. 1940), and Tom Eldridge (b. 1941) may have come from Virginia, but the name of the group they formed in the late '50s came from a street in Harlem. Their manager was Jim Gribble, who also managed the Mystics and the Passions, and brought the Jarmels to Laurie Records in New York in 1961. They were a rather unusual addition to the Laurie roster, for most of the company's artists were white, and sounded more pop than R&B-influenced. The Jarmels combined pop and R&B influences, most notably the sound of the post-1958 Drifters.

Their first single, "Little Lonely One," was a hit in New York but never charted nationally. Their second record, "A Little Bit of Soap," written by future Neil Diamond/Van Morrison manager Bert Berns, (who also produced the Drifters), got to number 12 in America in the summer of 1961 during a six-week run on the charts. This was the Jarmels' first and last chart success, none of their four subsequent singles charting at all. They recorded their last single, "Come on Girl," in 1963, and the group soldiered on for a while into the mid-'60s with numerous personnel changes—their later membership included Major Harris, who subsequently became part of the Delfonics. *—Bruce Eder*

• **The Mystics Meet the Jarmels** / 1990 / Ace ✦✦✦✦✦

The Jarmels only ever released 12 songs on six singles, but this compilation has 14, two previously unreleased numbers ("Why Am I a Fool for You," "You Don't Believe a Word I Say") having surfaced during the preparation of this disc. The sound fairly glitters throughout, the original session tapes having been found, which also allows for the first stereo release of everything here except "A Little Bit of Soap" and the two new discoveries. The sound here is pretty diverse, ranging from catchy soul ("A Little Bit of Soap") and rousing dance pieces ("She Loves to Dance") to ethereal ballads ("Keep Your Mind on Me"), although the Drifters' influence is pretty strong, especially on songs like "One By One" and their debut, "Little Lonely One." Some of this material, such as "Why Am I a Fool for You," may be considered doo wop, but most of their records were more sophisticated than that, and not quite that pop-oriented. *—Bruce Eder*

Chris Jasper

b. Dec. 30, 1951, Cincinnati, OH

Vocals, Keyboards / Urban, Funk, Quiet Storm, Soul

Any serious list of highly influential keyboardists in the soul/pop/funk field would have to include the Isley Brothers' Chris Jasper. He can be heard laying down adept acoustic piano, organ, funky clavinet, and Moog/Arp synthesizer lines on such seminal '70s hits as "Who's That Lady," "Fight the Power," "For the Love of You," and "Who Loves You Better."

At an early age, Jasper began tickling the ivories. At age eight, his mother encouraged him to take piano lessons after she heard him play Motown tunes by ear. After high school, he went to study to study at Julliard. The Isley Brothers and Jasper grew up on the same block in their native Cincinnati. In 1969, the Isleys got a manufacturing and distribution deal with Epic Records, and the *It's Your Thing* album was the first release. Jasper came aboard the following year as principal songwriter/keyboardist. The new expanded group's premier project was the *Givin' It Back* album, which featured a smoking version of Stephen Stills' "Love the One You're With." The winning combination worked for the next 13 years. During this time, Jasper had an opportunity to work with synthesizer pioneer Malcolm Cecil. In 1984, the Isley Brothers split and Jasper and the younger Isleys, Ernie and Marvin, formed Isley/Jasper/Isley with their first release, *Broadway's Closer to Sunset Blvd.* The next album, *Caravan of Love*, featured the number-one title hit. The final Isley/Jasper/Isley album was *Different Drummer*, and after the group disbanded, Jasper formed Gold City Records distributed by CBS.

Superbad—not the James Brown standard—was the title of and the first single from Jasper's first solo album, topping the urban charts. The next album, *Time Bomb*, included the hit ballad "The First Time." He also had success with singer Liz Hogue, who charted with "Dream Lover" from the *Vicious & Fresh* album and Chaka Khan's "Make It Last" from her *C.K.* album. Taking Gold City independent, Jasper released *Praise the Eternal*, a sparking collection of contemporary gospel music and a self-titled debut by contemporary gospel trio Out Front. *Deep Inside* marked Jasper's return to R&B/pop music, a collection that includes the best of the old and the new. Against sheen '90s FM digital synth patches, you hear classic talk box-generated vocoder lines and squishy Moog bass. There's a strong Marvin Gaye influence and, in homage, Jasper updates "What's Going On." *—Ed Hogan*

Superbad / 1987 / Epic ✦✦✦

After having a number-one R&B hit with "Caravan Of Love," as a member of Isley/Jasper/Isley, singer/songwriter/keyboardist/producer and former Isley Brothers member Chris Jasper wisely chose another message song, the chugging "Superbad," for his solo debut on his own Gold City label. Its praise of education, self-determination, and all-around positive moxie enticed record buyers to give Jasper a Top Three R&B hit single his first time out. Its follow-up, the pop/rockish "One Time Love," made it to the R&B Top 12. The steppers love the sparse, midnight-mellow "Like I Do," while the earnest ballad, "Giving My All," garnered radio play as an LP track, and the gospel song, "The Son of Man," was a precursor for Jasper's foray into gospel, *Praise the Eternal. —Ed Hogan*

Time Bomb / 1989 / Gold City ✦✦✦

For his second solo LP, *Time Bomb*, Chris Jasper pretty much stuck to the winning sound he used as a member of the Isley Brothers and Isley/Jasper/Isley. The crystalline charmer "The First Time" was the first single, charting on the R&B charts. The midtempo tribute groover, "Margie," slides along on innocent romantic leanings. The funk was hitting harder on *Time Bomb*, his second self-produced release, than on his solo debut "Superbad." Keyboardist Jasper makes use of the robotic-sounding vocoder synthesizer, à la Roger Troutman, on slammin' workouts "It's Working," "In Yo' Face," and the playful "Hit On You." *Time Bomb* is a nice mid-development glance of Jasper's evolving solo sound that didn't come to fruition until *Deep Inside. —Ed Hogan*

● **Praise the Eternal** / 1992 / Gold City ✦✦✦✦

Former Isley Brothers member Chris Jasper's gospel debut *Praise the Eternal* could be described as sparkling, contemporary gospel with quiet storm overtones. Earnest vocals enliven the gentle album openers "Thank You Jesus" and "Praise the Eternal." The singer puts a new spin on remakes of his own "The Son of Man," from *Superbad*, and the Isley/Jasper/Isley number-one R&B hit "Caravan of Love" from *Caravan of Love.* Jasper's one-man band approach makes this inspiring CD even more endearing. *—Ed Hogan*

Deep Inside / Sep. 1, 1995 / Gold City ✦✦✦

Chris Jasper returned to his R&B/soul/funk roots on *Deep Inside* after making his gospel music debut on *Praise the Eternal.* The singer/songwriter/keyboardist again performed all of the music and most of the vocals on this pleasant CD that stands as the best of his solo efforts. Highlights include the buoyant ballad "Deep Inside," the gentle "Cling to Me," the floating, fidelity-filled "There for You," "Forever," the thumpin' Motown-flavored "Nobody but My Baby," and a respectful remake of Marvin Gaye's "What's Going On." Some of the grooves are similar to "Between the Sheets," a classic slow jam Jasper co-wrote and performed as a member of the Isley Brothers, but without its lyrical steamy sexual overtones. *—Ed Hogan*

Jay & the Techniques

f. Allentown, PA

Group / Soul, R&B

A Philadelphia group whose sound and songs were more pop than soul, Jay & the Techniques earned some points for the playful, joyous "Apples, Peaches, Pumpkin Pie," which was their lone Top Ten R&B and pop hit in 1967 on Smash. They got points in some circles for being an integrated group; lead vocalist Jay Proctor, Karl Landis, Ronnie Goosly, John Walsh, George Lloyd, Chuck Crowl, and Dante Dancho were in the lineup. They kept plugging away until the late '70s, but never had another hit, although their song "Baby Make Your Own Sweet Music" was quite popular in England. *—Ron Wynn*

● **The Best of Jay and the Techniques** / 1995 / Mercury ✦✦✦✦✦

This 20-song collection focuses mostly on their late '60s peak, including all of the hit singles—"Apples, Peaches, Pumpkin Pie," "Keep the Ball Rollin'," and the much smaller chart items "Strawberry Shortcake," "Baby Make Your Own Sweet Music," "The Singles Game," and "Change Your Mind." Philadelphia soul at its peppiest and poppiest, it's pleasant listening, but the somewhat formulaic and repetitious feel means that most listeners will be satisfied by the two big hits. And bigger fans probably won't be thrilled by the inclusion of three songs from the mid-'70s and a cut from 1993. *—Richie Unterberger*

The Jaynetts

f. 1963, New York, NY [The Bronx]

Group / Girl Group, Pop, Pop-Soul

The Jaynetts, from The Bronx, NY, recorded one of the more discussed recordings of all time, the mystical-sounding "Sally Go 'Round the Roses," which shot to number two on the pop charts in 1963. Though publicity photos showed three women as the Jaynetts, five were actually in the studio on the "Sally" recording session: Johnnie Louise Richardson (formerly of Johnnie & Joe), Ethel Davis, Mary Sue Wells, Yvonne Bushnell, and Ada Ray. Zell Sanders co-wrote the song with Lona Stevens, who later married producer Abner Spector. Spector, oddly enough, was a Chicago producer who later created blues recordings by the likes of Willie Dixon, Muddy Waters, Compton & Batteau, and blue-eyed soul singer Wayne Cochran. Around the time of "Sally Go 'Round the Roses," he had worked with the Corsairs and the Tune Weavers.

Spector had worked with Zell Sanders before on a record by the Hearts entitled "Dear Abby," which received some airplay but never charted. Sanders had previously recorded the Hearts, beginning in 1953 when the group members were Hazel Crutchfield, Louise Harris, Joyce West, and at various times, Betty Harris and Baby Washington. The Hearts on "Dear Abby," however, were the same young women who sang on "Sally Go 'Round the Roses." Obviously, some previous members got upset at Zell using their name so Tuff labeled subsequent recordings the Jaynetts.

Johnnie Louise Richardson remembered Abner Spector (he died of a stroke on October 25, 1988) as an electronics nut. Spector sequestered the girls in the studio on a Friday and didn't allow them to leave until the following week when the recording was completed. Anybody who came in the studio during the enduring week of recording got on the track. Buddy Miles and Artie Butler are remembered as playing on the session. It's rumored Spector had about 20 voices on "Sally," and that the session cost more than $60,000 (unlikely since that was an unheard-of amount of money to spend on a single in 1963). The song itself has a hypnotic feel, a crazy organ part, nursery rhyme-sounding lyrics, a wall of voices, and an undeniable funky beat. All kinds of theories have been tossed around about the song's meaning. Some say it's a religious experience, about a mental breakdown, about a closeted lesbian, etc.... all garbage. The song is simply a skip-rope rhyme said by girls when they jumped rope; some lyrics were added that fit the music and you had a song. With "Sally" it's not the words, it's that incessant beat, screaming organ, and the fading in and out that drives the tune. Follow-ups to "Sally Go 'Round the Roses" like "Snowman, Snowman," "Sweet Potato Nose," and "Keep an Eye on Her" did nothing. Tuff gave up on the girls, but they continued recording on Zell Sanders' J&S label, recording more non-charters: "Chicken, Chicken Crane or Crow," "Who Stole the Cookie From the Cookie Jar," and "Winky Dink." *—Andrew Hamilton*

● **Sally Go 'Round the Roses** / 1963 / Tuff ✦✦✦✦✦

A rare album that sells for at least a C-note if you can find a copy. The haunting title track, its successor "Keep an Eye on Her," and "Dear Abby" are the centerpieces. "Abby," credited to the Hearts, is a strange but effective innocent teen number that got it share of spins; the Hearts seek the advice of columnist Dear Abby and threaten to go outside and eat worms if their hearts aren't soothed. The Jaynetts sang on the Hearts' recordings and vice versa. Producer Abner Spector used whoever to achieve that sound, and singers like Baby Washington constantly dropped by. Also decent are "Seesaw," "One Track Mind," "Pick Up My Marbles," and "Archie's Melody." There's also a popular instrumental of "Sally"; Spector hated wasting good cuts as B-sides so he used instrumentals and captioned them: "Sing Along Without the Jaynetts" or "Sing Along Without the Hearts," a very popular concept back in the day. *—Andrew Hamilton*

The J.B.'s

f. 1964

Group / Funk, Deep Funk, Soul, Soul-Jazz

The J.B.'s were the legendary supporting cast of musicians behind James Brown, earning a well-deserved reputation as the tightest, best-drilled instrumental ensemble in all of funk. The name J.B.'s is most often associated with three hornmen in particular—saxophonists Maceo Parker and Alfred "Pee Wee" Ellis, and trombonist Fred Wesley, all of whom originally joined Brown's backing band at various points during the '60s. As a recording entity unto themselves, however, the J.B.'s enjoyed a distinctly defined heyday from 1970-1975, under the musical directorship of Wesley (though Brown, naturally, remained a strong presence). The J.B.'s were billed under a variety of alternate names on their own singles and albums—Fred Wesley & the J.B.'s, Maceo & the Macks, Fred & the New J.B.'s, the James Brown Soul Train, the Last Word, the First Family, and more. The core group of personnel, despite some turnover on the periphery, remained fairly steady from 1971 on, at least until Brown's creative downturn precipitated several important defections.

The first official version of the J.B.'s was formed in 1970, after the notoriously demanding Brown's regular band (excepting organist/vocalist Bobby Byrd) walked out on him. Caught in a pinch, Brown recruited a Cincinnati-based R&B band called the Pacemakers, who'd already toured behind Brown favorite Hank Ballard. Brothers Phelps "Catfish" Collins (guitar) and William "Bootsy" Collins (bass) anchored the lineup, as well as the first J.B.'s single, 1970's "The Grunt." The Collins brothers, of course, would play a crucial role in Brown's transition to heavy, groove-centered funk. One by one, some of Brown's previous band members returned to the fold, including Fred Wesley, who accepted Brown's offer to become musical director of the J.B.'s in December 1970. However, the lineup splintered with the departure of the Collins brothers just a few months later, leaving Wesley with only guitarist Hearlon "Cheese" Martin, drummer John "Jabo" Starks, and tenor saxman St. Clair Pinckney. This nucleus was quickly fleshed out with bassist Fred Thomas and saxophonist Jimmy Parker (who'd never played alto prior to joining the band); soon, there was also a trumpet section, usually featuring Jerone "Jasaan" Sanford, Russell Crimes, and Isiah "Ike" Oakley.

Brown began to release recordings by the newly constituted J.B.'s on his own People label with some frequency beginning in 1971, and the group scored a couple of Top 40 R&B hits with "Pass the Peas" and "Gimme Some More." By 1972, previous Brown guitarist Jimmy Nolen had returned alongside Cheese Martin, and conga player Johnny Griggs was back in tow as well. That year saw the release of the first J.B.'s full-length, *Food for Thought.* Wesley was still the band's only real soloist, so in early 1973, Brown convinced legendary alto man Maceo Parker to rejoin. His first record back with the group was "Doing It to Death," a long jam with guest vocals from Brown that topped the R&B charts in edited form; it was also the title track of their second album, and the first single credited to Fred Wesley & the J.B.'s, affirming that Wesley was still without question the leader. Still, the J.B.'s also began to cut sides under the name Maceo & the Macks, including the Top 20 R&B hit "Soul Power '74" and the 1974 album *Us!!* Meanwhile, under their original name, the Wesley-led J.B.'s released another successful LP that year in *Damn Right I Am Somebody,* which spun off three Top 40 R&B hits in "Same Beat," "If You Don't Get It the First Time, Back Up and Try It Again, Party," and the title track. The follow-up album *Breakin' Bread,* issued later that year, was credited to Fred & the New J.B.'s, even though the band's personnel remained essentially the same (although John Morgan was easing into Starks' slot as the regular drummer).

By late 1974, however, Brown's commercial momentum was beginning to slow, and that carried over to the J.B.'s as well. The First Family single "Control (People Go Where We Send You)," which featured Brown, Lyn Collins, and other vocalists, failed to perform up to expectations. By the time of 1975's *Hustle With Speed* album, band morale was low, and Wesley was growing frustrated with Brown's sudden loss of direction. On the Fourth of July, Wesley quit the group to join up with George Clinton, and Maceo Parker soon followed. Bassist Thomas, drummers Starks (who'd joined B.B. King's band) and Morgan, guitarist Martin, and saxophonist Jimmy Parker all drifted away, leaving Jimmy Nolen and Russell Crimes the only consistent members left on the final J.B.'s single, 1976's "Everybody Wanna Get Funky One More Time." Polydor subsequently shut down Brown's People imprint, effectively ending the myriad side projects he'd managed during the first half of the decade. He continued to tour with differing versions of the J.B.'s, including a late-'70s outfit dubbed the J.B.'s International, but for all intents and purposes, the true J.B.'s no longer existed.

Periodic J.B.'s reunions ensued in the years to come; Wesley, Parker, and Alfred Ellis (who actually only played on a couple of J.B.'s sessions) toured Europe with Bobby Byrd in 1988, and cut a reunion album, *Pee Wee, Fred and Maceo,* the following year. They continued to tour and record together off and on during the '90s under the name the JB Horns. A more extensive J.B.'s reunion took place in 2002 on the album *Bring the Funk on Down,* which also included Bootsy Collins, Bobby Byrd, and Jabo Starks, among others. *—Steve Huey*

Food for Thought / 1972 / People ✦✦✦

Doing It to Death / 1973 / People ✦✦✦✦✦
This is an extended live "funkafizing" including a ten-minute version of the number-one R&B hit "Doing It to Death." Written, produced, and arranged by James Brown. *—Rob Bowman*

Breakin' Bread / 1974 / People ✦✦✦
Here is the last of the Fred Wesley and the J.B.'s albums. "Breakin' Bread" and "Makin' Love" charted R&B. The funk is still much in evidence, although some new twists and turns manifest themselves on the "rapped" title cut. (Credited to Fred Wesley & the New J.B.'s.) *—Rob Bowman*

Damn Right I Am Somebody / 1974 / People ✦✦✦
This is more of the same sparse, cutting-edge funk, including a Top 40 R&B hit in the title cut. (Credited to Fred Wesley & the J.B.'s.) *—Rob Bowman*

Hustle With Speed / 1975 / People ✦✦✦
The J.B.'s grab at a piece of the disco market that made Van McCoy a solo star with this production. It's excellent throughout despite James Brown's subdued arrangements on some songs. "(It's Not the Express) It's the JB's Monaurail," usually a six-minute song, rambles for over eight. Fred Wesley's funky trombone peppers "All Aboard the Soul Funky Train" (an update of "Night Train"). "Transmograpfication" is similar to jazz trumpeter Eddie Henderson's crossover attempts on his *Sunburst* and *Realization* albums. "Thank You for Letting Me Be Myself and You Be Yours" is better than the title, with a Dyke and the Blazers-type vocal that sets it right. *—Andrew Hamilton*

Pee Wee, Fred and Maceo / 1990 / Gramavision ✦✦✦
Recorded in 1989 and released in 1990, this CD is among the various projects that has come from James Brown's former sidemen. *Pee Wee, Fred & Maceo* reunites three of the Godfather's top horn players—alto saxophonist Maceo Parker, tenor saxophonist Pee Wee Ellis and trombonist Fred Wesley—for a program of instrumental funk, soul-jazz and R&B vocals. Brown was notoriously hard on his sidemen; in fact, he was famous (or infamous) for docking their pay if they hit wrong notes. So you can be sure that musicians who stayed with Brown as long as these guys had major chops, and one would naturally greet this album with high expectations. But while *Pee Wee, Fred & Maceo* is decent, it isn't as strong as it could have been. Although instrumentals like "Mother's Kitchen," "Everywhere Is Out of Town" and "Sweet and Tangy" are catchy and likable, this album isn't the gem that Parker, Ellis & Wesley were quite capable of providing. Nonetheless, it deserved more radio airplay than it received. Urban contemporary radio ignored the CD, and only the Godfather's most diehard fans bought it. *—Alex Henderson*

● **Funky Good Time: The Anthology** / Feb. 28, 1995 / Polydor ✦✦✦✦✦
The J.B.'s recorded under various billings in the early '70s, including the J.B.'s, Fred Wesley & the J.B.'s, Maceo & the Macks, the First Family, the Last Word, and others. This double CD gathers 30 of the prime tracks by all of the above configurations from the first half of the '70s, including all nine of their chart hits and quite a few rare singles and long versions. Often, James Brown himself chips in with incidental vocals (though this is mostly instrumental) and keyboards. The two-and-a-half hour program can start to sound monotonous if taken all at once, but it's prime, often riveting funk, jammed with lockstep grooves that vary between basic R&B vamps and imaginative, almost jazzy improvisation. *—Richie Unterberger*

Pass the Peas: The Best of the J.B.'s / Jun. 13, 2000 / Polydor ✦✦✦✦
Pass the Peas: The Best of the J.B.s collects all of the R&B chart hits from James Brown's backing group, including "Gimme Some More," "Damn Right I Am Somebody," and "The Grunt." "Hot Pants Road," "Doing It to Death," "Givin' Up Food for Funk," and "(It's Not the Express) It's the J.B.'s Monaurail, Pts. 1 & 2" are some of the other highlights of this collection, which features Brown on keyboards and backing vocals on many of the songs. *—Heather Phares*

Bring the Funk on Down / Feb. 12, 2002 / Instinct ✦✦✦✦
No fan of classic funk (or of the "rare groove" school of dance music) will be able to look at this album without starting to drool—the period-piece cover art; the Jimmy Walker hats and bell-bottoms; and the presence of such magic names as Fred Wesley, Pee Wee Ellis, Bobby Byrd, and Clyde Stubblefield (not to mention the insanely funky bassist Bootsy Collins, who is better known as a charter member of Parliament/Funkadelic but is also a J.B.'s alumnus)—all of it will lead the perceptive groovehound to anticipate an hour or so of irresistibly booty-shaking funk. And that's exactly what you get: no frills, no synthesizers, basically no acknowledgement of change in the pop music world. From the greasy "Do the Doo" to the CD bonus track, "Mistakes and All," which ends the program, *Bring the Funk on Down* delivers almost nothing but hardcore, horn-heavy old-school funk (with a couple of brief and uninspiring excursions into ballad territory, another James Brown tradition). Highlights include the slowly simmering title track and the archetypal "Born to Groove," but the album is really pretty consistent. The only downside is the absence of Maceo Parker, who plays only on the final track. Highly recommended. *—Rick Anderson*

Wyclef Jean

b. Oct. 17, 1972, Croix-des-Bouquets, Haiti

Producer, Vocals, Guitar / Contemporary R&B, East Coast Rap, Alternative Rap, Urban, Hip-Hop

Lead Fugees rapper and sometime guitarist Wyclef Jean was the first member of his group to embark on a solo career, and he proved even more ambitious and eclectic on his own. As the Fugees hung in limbo, Wyclef also became hip-hop's unofficial multicultural conscience; a seemingly omnipresent activist, he assembled or participated in numerous high-profile charity benefit shows for a variety of causes, including aid for his native Haiti. The utopian one-world sensibility that fueled Wyclef's political consciousness also informed his recordings, which fused hip-hop with as many different styles of music as he could get his hands on (though, given his Caribbean roots, reggae was a particular favorite). In addition to his niche as hip-hop's foremost global citizen, Clef was also a noted producer and remixer who worked with an impressive array of pop, R&B, and hip-hop talent, including Whitney Houston, Santana, and Destiny's Child, among many others.

The son of a minister, Nelust Wyclef Jean was born in Croix-des-Bouquets, Haiti, on October 17, 1972. When he was nine, his family moved to the Marlborough projects in Brooklyn, NY; by his teenage years, Jean had moved to New Jersey, taken up the guitar, and begun studying jazz through his high school's music department. In 1987, he also joined a rap group with his cousin Prakazrel Michel (aka Pras) and Michel's high-school classmate Lauryn Hill. Initially calling themselves the Tranzlator Crew, they evolved into the Fugees, a name taken from slang for Haitian refugees. The trio signed with Ruffhouse Records in 1993 and released their debut album, *Blunted on Reality,* the following year; it attracted little notice, thanks to an inappropriate hardcore stance that the group wore like an ill-fitting suit. But the Fugees hit their stride on the follow-up *The Score,* ignoring popular trends and crafting an eclectic, bohemian masterpiece that sounded like nothing else on the hip-hop landscape in 1996. Thanks to hit singles like "Fu-Gee-La" and "Killing Me Softly," *The Score* became a chart-topping phenomenon; in fact, with sales of over six-million copies, it still ranks as one of the biggest-selling rap albums of all time.

Wyclef Jean was the first Fugee to declare plans for a solo project, setting to work soon after the group completed its supporting tours. Released in the summer of 1997, *The Carnival* (full title: *Wyclef Jean Presents the Carnival Featuring the Refugee All-Stars*) was even more musically ambitious than *The Score.* Its roster of guests included not only the remainder of the Fugees, but also Jean's siblings (who performed together in the duo Melky Sedeck), Cuban legend Celia Cruz, New Orleans funk mainstays the Neville Brothers, and Bob Marley's female backing vocalists the I Threes. The breadth of his ambition was further in evidence on the album's two hit singles; "We Trying to Stay Alive" recast the Bee Gees' signature disco tune as a ghetto empowerment anthem, and the Grammy-nominated "Gone Till November" was recorded with part of the New York Philharmonic Orchestra. Those two songs helped push *The Carnival* into a Top 20, triple-platinum showing, and most reviews were naturally quite positive.

In the wake of *The Carnival,* Wyclef stepped up his outside work for other artists; over the next few years, he collaborated as a producer, songwriter, and/or remixer with a typically diverse list of artists: Destiny's Child ("No No No"), Sublime, Simply Red, Whitney Houston (the title track of her *My Love Is Your Love* album), dancehall reggae star Bounty Killer, Cypress Hill, Michael Jackson, Eric Benet, Mya, Santana ("Maria Maria"), Tevin Campbell, the Black Eyed Peas, Kimberly Scott, Sinéad O'Connor, Mick Jagger, and Canibus. Clef also served as Canibus' manager for a short time in 1998; prior to their split, a report surfaced that Wyclef had pulled a gun on *Blaze* editor Jesse Washington over a negative Canibus review the magazine was slated to run (Wyclef vehemently denied the accusation, and no charges were filed).

By the time Wyclef began work on his second solo album, rumors were flying about tension between individual Fugees, and despite their denials, the fact that no follow-up to *The Score* was in sight seemed to lend credence to all the speculation. Although Wyclef had previously announced he would put off his sophomore effort until after the next Fugees album, he was well into the project by early 2000, giving an early release the anti-police brutality track "Diallo" (with guest vocals from Senegalese superstar Youssou N' Dour) via the Internet. The full album, titled *The Ecleftic: 2 Sides II a Book*, was released toward the end of the summer and entered the charts at number nine. Besides N'Dour, guests this time around included Mary J. Blige (on the Grammy-nominated duet "911"), Earth, Wind & Fire, Kenny Rogers, and even wrestling star the Rock ("It Doesn't Matter"); Clef also threw in a left-field cover of Pink Floyd's "Wish You Were Here." This time around, some critics suggested that Wyclef's sprawling ambitions were growing messy, but the record went platinum nonetheless. Shortly after its release, he also started up his own record label, Yclef.

With no Fugees reunion in sight, Wyclef began preparing his third solo album, *Masquerade*, in 2001; he also appeared in the Jamaican gangster flick *Shottas*, and, sadly, suffered the death of his father in a home accident. *Masquerade* was released in the summer of 2002, and in addition to the usual worldbeat fusions, it found Wyclef reworking songs by Bob Dylan and Frankie Valli, and featured guest shots from Tom Jones and Israeli violinist Miri Ben-Ari. *Masquerade* entered the charts at number six, proving that Wyclef's freewheeling approach still held quite a bit of appeal. *—Steve Huey*

● **Presents the Carnival Featuring the Refugee All Stars** / Jun. 24, 1997 / Columbia ♦♦♦♦
The Score was one of those rare hip-hop albums that came out of nowhere and rewrote the rules. In the aftermath of its success, many pundits predicted that rap would move away from gangsta and toward a richer, more varied existence. Given such heady praise, perhaps it was reasonable that Wyclef Jean, the guitarist and male rapper for the Fugees, decided to follow *The Score* with a solo project. However, *Presents the Carnival* comes across like Jean presenting his case that he is the *true* genius in the Fugees. And he's partially right. He has the ambition and drive common to many great artists, but he lacks the skills to fulfill his vision. Of course, the very fact that he has an original vision makes Jean one of the more compelling figures of late-'90s hip-hop. Not content to rely solely on hip-hop, Jean adds all manners of influences to his music. You can hear reggae, soul, disco, Caribbean rhythms, worldbeat, and opera scattered throughout *The Carnival*, giving the record the riotous atmosphere of its title. Even so, Jean occaisonally tries too hard, forcing disparate genres to mix and spending more time on production than songwriting. But even with all its faults, *The Carnival* delivers great thrills when operating at full strength, demonstrating that Jean is at least half a genius. *—Leo Stanley*

The Ecleftic: 2 Sides II a Book / Jul. 25, 2000 / Columbia ♦♦♦♦

Masquerade / Jun. 18, 2002 / Columbia ♦♦♦
Wyclef Jean prides himself on having a vision, which he does. Few of his peers are as determined to appeal to as broad an audience as a possible, dabbling in everything from ragga to sugary pop, tying it all together as a self-conscious "big statement." His ambition has been clear since *The Score*, if not the Fugees' debut, and with each of his post-Fugees solo projects, he's worked with the same basic template—a lot of pop, a lot of hip-hop, reggae, and worldbeat touches, lots of social consciousness, a little does of party anthems, all produced with enough gloss and melody to reach a wide audience, yet with enough NPR sensibility to bring in the serious-minded progressives, no matter their age. If anything, he perhaps tipped a little bit too close to the pop last time around, letting Kenny Rogers in for a new version of "The Gambler," so the first part of his third album, *Masquerade*, feels like a bit of an over-correction, as he toughens up the beats, brings in the hard(er) rappers, and aims to the street. Then, after the point has been made, it settles into a Marleyesque reggae groove, before easing into pop for awhile, then winding up back in Marley territory with "War No More." Throughout it all, Jean's musical skill is impressive and most of this long, 20-track album is quite pleasurable, but his skills as a recordmaker waver on occasion. The primary problem is that Wyclef wants to be everything to all people, so he'll hit too hard on the hip-hop, then back *way* up and invite Tom Jones into the studio for a new, not very good, version of "What's New, Pussycat," while re-writing Frankie Valli ("Oh What a Night") and Dylan ("Knocking on Heaven's Door," which now contains shout-outs "to Biggie Smalls and Tupac... to my people in the twin towers") with equal abandon. He pushes too hard on sermonizing, no matter if it's pompous pleas to the ghettos or heartfelt laments (a spoken tribute to his recently passed father, "War No More," a "Redemption Song"-styled protest song with the unforgettable line, "this looks like a scene from the movie *Star Wars*"), which off-sets the lighter tracks. Instead of sounding generous and open-hearted, it's a bit muddled and confusing, especially when taken all at once—but when isolated in parts, or heard in passing, it's an enjoyable record. *—Stephen Thomas Erlewine*

The Jelly Beans

f. 1962, Jersey City, NJ, **db.** 1965
Group / Brill Building Pop, Girl Group, R&B, Soul
The Jelly Beans were a mixed voice quintet (later a quartet) comprised of one man (Charles Thomas) and four women (Alma Brewer, Diane Taylor, Elyse Herbert, Maxine Herbert) who got together while attending high school in Jersey City, NJ. That was where their manager discovered them in 1963, and he brought them to the attention of songwriters Jerry Leiber and Mike Stoller, who were starting up a record label, Red Bird, in association with End/Gone Records founder George Goldner.

The group was put into the hands of songwriters Jeff Barry & Ellie Greenwich, then near the peak of their output together, who gave them "I Wanna Love Him So Bad." The third single issued by Red Bird, it reached number ten on the *Billboard* charts. The Jelly Beans' second single, "Baby Be Mine," didn't reach the Top 50, however, and although the Jelly Beans left behind enough songs for an album, none was forthcoming. By 1964, Red Bird had bigger acts to worry about, including the Shangri-Las and the Dixie Cups, and the group was gone from the label by the end of that year. A final single release on Eskee failed to chart, and the Jelly Beans had broken up by 1965. *—Bruce Eder*

● **The Jelly Beans and Friends** / Aug. 27, 1996 / Collectables ♦♦♦♦♦
This CD gets the highest possible rating, not so much because of the Jelly Beans' stuff—though it is good—but everything else on it. There are only ten Jelly Beans songs present on this cornucopia of girl group and East Coast soul classics and obscurities, the other eight comprising work of acts associated with the Leiber-Stoller-Red Bird orbit, plus a few unrelated tracks that just seem to fit. The Jelly Beans' songs include a good selection of girl group standards, among them "The Kind of Boy You Can't Forget," "Chapel of Love," and "Do Wah Diddy." The arrangements and the presence of a male singer in Charles Thomas gives some of the repertoire ("Ain't Love a Funny Thing," etc.) more of a doo wop feel than most girl group material, but some of the singing also displays the rudiments of mid-'60s soul. "Baby Be Mine" might have made a great Phil Spector-style track in the manner of the Crystals' "Uptown" or "He's a Rebel," if the producers had pushed the echo chamber effects a bit more, and might have had a better shot at becoming a hit, too. Other songs, such as "Whisper Sweet Things," have them sounding a lot more like the early Supremes. The rest of this CD is made up of recordings by various contemporaries of the Jelly Beans, some closer than others—Ellie Greenwich was "The Butterflies," a sort of adjunct to her efforts with Jeff Barry as "The Raindrops," her minor hit "Goodnight Baby" is here, but the real treat is her version of "I Wonder," which is very nicely sung, and has the rudiments of Spector-style production—almost like a Spector demo—but is also paced more leisurely, and with somewhat different emphasis, than the rendition by the Crystals that ultimately defined the song; but it can be considered the songwriter's interpretation of the piece. Bessie Banks' version of "Go Now," cut for Red Bird's predecessor label Tiger, may be the most obscure American original of a British Invasion hit that there is, never having been a hit; she's infinitely more soulful and moving than Denny Laine, the horns add a dimension of majesty to the song, and by itself this cut is worth the price of this CD. Evie Sands' original version of "I Can't Let Go" (later a hit for the Hollies) is in the same category of lost treasure, and could have been an early Supremes number. More early mid-'60s girl group/soul includes the Charmettes ("Stop the Wedding") and the Ad Libs' "The Boy from New York City" and "He Ain't No Angel." Also present is "Rebel Without a Cause" by the Bunnies, a genuinely obscure girl group. *—Bruce Eder*

Rodney Jerkins

b. New Jersey
Producer / Urban, Hip-Hop, Club/Dance
Prolific producer Rodney Jerkins' credits include hits by Mary J. Blige, Whitney Houston, Brandy, Monica, Joe, Kenneth "Babyface" Edmonds, Jennifer Lopez's number-one single "If You Had My Love," Tatyana Ali, Britney Spears, Will Smith, Toni Braxton, and Blackstreet, among many others. What's even more amazing is that Jerkins amassed this enviable resumé in just a few years.

Born the youngest son of a minister and choir director mother in a small town in New Jersey, Jerkins began taking classical music lessons on the piano as a small child and combining that with the gospel music that he heard in church. As he grew, he added R&B and jazz to his repertoire. He worked obsessively on music, recording rap demos for local talent. By his teens, he wanted to become a record producer and began making demos, one of which caught the attention of Teddy Riley. His first professional writing and producing job came in 1994 for an artist named Casserine, and at 15, he wrote and produced his own gospel rap album, *On the Move*, with his brother Fred Jerkins III.

In 1997, Jerkins co-wrote, arranged, and produced five songs for Mary J. Blige's four million-selling *Share My World* album, including the hit single "I Can Love You." He was named one of the hottest R&B producers in the country, and during 1999, he started his own label, Darkchild Records. The first two artists to be signed were So Plush and Rhona Bennet. *—Ed Hogan*

The Jesters

f. 1956, Harlem, New York City, NY
Group / Doo Wop, R&B
The Jesters are best known for their soaring falsetto-driven minor hit "So Strange" and for their cover versions of the Chantels' "The Plea" and the Diablos' 1954 classic "The Wind" (which had established Nolan Strong's place as an R&B legend). Like many acts before them, they exemplified the New York City vocal group sound of the mid-'50s. They were particularly influential on mostly white, early-'60s vocal groups like the Excellents and the Imaginations.

The Jesters formed in 1956, when Lennie McKay (lead), James Smith (aka "Jimmy") (second tenor), Leo Vincent (baritone), and Noel Grant (bass) were still attending Cooper Junior High School in Harlem, located on 120th Street. Meanwhile, 17-year-old Adam Jackson was attending Samuel Gompers High School in the Bronx and was singing in a quintet called the Continentals. His group managed to land a TV performance later that year singing the Flamingos' "I'll Be Home." In early 1957, Jackson joined up with the Jesters. Jackson and McKay soon began sharing the lead vocal duties (Jackson's falsetto was often the highlight to McKay's lead) and both were songwriters, but it is generally considered that McKay was the group's leader.

The group performed at the Apollo amateur night contest and after winning first prize three times, they were spotted and signed by Winley Records owner Paul Winley. The Jesters' first single was "So Strange," a drowsy doo wop song which became a local New York favorite. Their next single was a classic rhythm ballad that is often considered the epitome of mid-'50s New York doo wop: "Please Let Me Love You." Once again, McKay took the lead tenor and Jackson the falsetto. By that time, the Jesters had begun touring the chitlin' circuit. When they returned to the Apollo for shows alongside labelmates the Paragons and a stellar group of R&B stars—Ben E. King, Ruth Brown, Jimmy Jones, the Olympics, and Dante & the Evergreens—they were consummate pros. Their third single for Winley was a solid remake of the Chantels' ballad "The Plea," which climbed up the charts to number 74 pop in March 1958.

In June 1958, the Jesters dropped their fourth and final single for Winley with the original lineup, this one another two-sided classic, "Now That You're Gone," but the group was splintering by then: McKay and Grant left and Vincent had been drafted. To replace them, Jackson and Smith brought in baritone Melvin Lewis (the Climbers) along with his brother Donald Lewis on bass. By May 1960, this new Jesters quartet had its first single, a revision of the Diablos' 1954 classic "The Wind." It was an excellent version and, like the original version, this one featured the group chanting the words "blow wind" in harmony behind Adam Jackson's ethereal tenor lead and smooth-as-silk talking bridge. Their last two singles were not of the caliber of their earlier 45s and never charted. They never really ever broke up, working occasional gigs throughout the ensuing decades. *—Bryan Thomas*

● **The Best of the Jesters** / 1969 / Collectables ✦✦✦✦✦

The Jewels

f. 1961, Washington, D.C., **db.** 1968

Group / Pop-Soul, Girl Group, Soul

Famed for their classic 1964 single "Opportunity," R&B girl group the Jewels was formed in Washington, D.C., in 1961 by vocalists Sandra Bears, Grace Ruffin, Margie Clark and Carrie Mingo. Originally dubbed the Impalas, the fledgling quartet was soon befriended by Bo Diddley, who recorded their Checker label debut "I Need You So Much"; the record went nowhere though, and in 1962 new manager/producer Bob Lee changed their name to the Four Jewels. After issuing "Loaded With Goodies" for the local Start label, the group landed at Chess for the single "That's What They Put Erasers on Pencils For," followed by a stint as backing vocalists for singer Billy Stewart, Ruffin's first cousin. Martha Harvin replaced Mingo on subsequent outings for Dynamite, Federal and King, including several sessions produced by James Brown.

In 1964, the Jewels signed to Dimension, where the superb "Opportunity" reached number 64 on the pop charts that December. The follow-up, "But I Do," became a minor hit in mid-1965, but when Dimension folded soon after, the group toured with James Brown before dissolving three years later. In 1985, the original lineup of Bears, Ruffin, Clark and Mingo reunited, re-recording their classic hits for the album *Loaded With Goodies*. *—Jason Ankeny*

The Jive Five

f. 1959, Brooklyn, NY

Group / Doo Wop, R&B, Soul

Best known for the number-one R&B hit "My True Story," the Jive Five were one of the few vocal groups to survive the transistion from the '50s to the '60s. In the process, they helped move the music itself forward, providing a key link between doo wop and '60s soul.

Formed in Brooklyn, NY, the group originally consisted of Eugene Pitt (lead), Jerome Hanna (tenor), Richard Harris (tenor), Billy Prophet (baritone), and Norman Johnson (bass). The Jive Five's first hit, "My True Story," was their biggest, peaking at number one on the R&B charts and number three on the pop charts in the summer of 1961. None of the band's subsequent singles—including the minor R&B hit, 1962's "These Golden Rings"—were as popular, but the group managed to keep performing and recording. Under the direction of Eugene Pitt and Norman Johnson, the Jive Five refashioned themselves as a soul band in 1964, forming a new lineup with Casey Spencer (tenor), Webster Harris (tenor), and Beatrice Best (baritone). This new incarnation of the band signed to United Artists Records. The group only had one hit on UA, 1965's "I'm a Happy Man." In 1966, the Jive Five left United Artists and signed with Musicor, where they had the 1968 R&B hit "Sugar (Don't Take Away My Candy)." They changed labels again in 1970, signing with Decca. That same year, they changed their name to the Jyve Fyve, in order to appear more contemporary. The Jyve Fyve had only one minor R&B hit, 1970's "I Want You to Be My Baby."

The group continued to perform and record for a variety of small labels during the '70s, but they never had another hit. Throughout the '70s and '80s, the only constant member was Eugene Pitt. In 1975, Pitt changed the name of the group to Ebony, Ivory, & the Jades, but this new incarnation failed to gain much attention. In 1982, Pitt changed the name of the group back to the Jive Five and the band recorded two albums for the indie label, Ambient Sound. For the rest of the '80s and the '90s, the Jive Five were regulars on the oldies circuit. *—Stephen Thomas Erlewine*

Our True Story / 1983 / Ace ✦✦✦✦✦

An import first released in 1983 and still in print, *Our True Story* covers the Jive Five's prolific two-year (1961 to 1963) stint on Beltone Records. Beltone issued seven singles by the deacons of New York doo wop during this stretch, including the everlasting "My True Story," "What Time Is It," "Hully Gully Callin' Time," and "These Golden Rings." The gems here are the not-as-familiar ballads where lead singer Eugene Pitt's trumpeting tenor always manages a heartfelt appearance. The 18 songs include two unreleased Beltone sides, "Hurry Back" and "You Know What I Would Do." *—Andrew Hamilton*

● **The Jive Five** / 1989 / United Artists ✦✦✦✦✦

A superb 20-track collection, it features the Jive Five's finest material, recorded in the early '60s for Lescay/Belton; songs include "Rain," "My True Story," "No Not Again," "What Time Is It?," and "Hurry Back." *—AMG*

Greatest Hits / Apr. 18, 1990 / Collectables ✦✦✦

The Complete United Artists Recordings: I'm a Happy Man / Oct. 20, 1992 / Capitol ✦✦✦✦

For decades, doo wop obsessives have been singing the praises of the Jive Five (and in particular, their lead vocalist, the extraordinary Eugene Pitt) on the basis of their early sides for Beltone Records, including "My True Story" and "What Time Is It." But the Jive Five had a much longer, active life than the average doo wop act (they also got started a bit later; "My True Story" broke them nationwide in 1961, close to the end of the classic doo wop era), and this collection of the group's sides for United Artists Records (recorded between 1964 to 1966) documents Pitt and company as they evolved from a '50s-style harmony group into a soul vocal combo in the manner of the Temptations or the Four Tops. While the first couple of cuts (such as "United") sound like traditional doo wop, later tunes such as "Please Baby Please (Come Back to Me)" and "Falling Tears" combine brassy, horn-fueled arrangements with rhythmic group harmonies. At the disc's end, "You" and "You Promised Me Great Things" find the backing vocalists moving into a more unified approach, as Pitt's passionate lead vocals become the focal point of the group. If the material sometimes seems to be walking a fine line between two musical worlds, Pitt and the Jive Five never sound less than splendid, and these recordings prove this was one of the few vocal groups of the era who were able to grow and change without losing their personality (and their gifts) in the shuffle. Not just for doo wop fanatics. *—Mark Deming*

Jodeci

f. 1990, Tiny Grove, NC

Group / Club/Dance, Urban

If Boyz II Men are portrayed as a clean-cut, wholesome R&B vocal group, then Jodeci's wild, sexual, bad-boy image represents the other side of the coin. Made up of two sets of brothers, the group's name is a consolidation of three members' aliases: "JoJo" Hailey, Donald "DeVante Swing" DeGrate, and Cedric "K-Ci" Hailey; the group also includes Dalvin DeGrate. Natives of Charlotte, NC, all four members toured the South as young boys singing gospel music, even recording albums; both families belonged to the Pentecostal church, and the DeGrates' father was a minister. The boys were able to hear each other's gospel songs played on the radio, and eventually were introduced through girlfriends as teenagers. However, when they did meet, K-Ci was with a girl Dalvin had been dating, and a fight nearly broke out. The Hailey brothers and DeVante started hanging out together, partying and talking about making R&B records together, coming up with the name Jodeci at this time.

At age 16, DeVante ran away to Minneapolis to get a job in Prince's organization, but was refused. He returned to Charlotte, where he wrote a song and recorded JoJo singing it. The two planned on going to New York to shop the demo around by themselves, but both K-Ci and Dalvin decided to tag along at the last minute. By the time they got to New York, they had demo recordings of 29 songs, which they brought to the offices of Uptown Entertainment. They were almost rejected, but rapper Heavy D overheard the tape and talked Uptown president Andre Harrell into hearing the group. Harrell was impressed, and just like that, Jodeci signed a recording contract. In 1991, they recorded *Forever My Lady*, which featured the gold single "Come and Talk to Me" and went on to sell over three-million copies. A minor feud resulted over the band's follow-up album, *Diary of a Mad Band*; Jodeci, unhappy with their treatment by Uptown, flirted with the idea of leaving for Dr. Dre's Death Row Records, which resulted in almost zero promotion for their new album. It didn't matter much, as *Diary* went platinum.

The group's troubles got worse in 1993; DeVante and K-Ci were involved in an incident with a woman K-Ci met at a club and brought back to DeVante's apartment. The woman filed charges against the two, saying that K-Ci had threatened her and fondled her breast, while DeVante pointed a gun at her. Both pleaded guilty, but that wasn't all; shortly afterwards, DeVante's house was robbed of over 160,000 dollars in jewelry and clothes as the singer was held with guns in his mouth and at the back of his head.

Jodeci's third album, *The Show, the After Party, the Hotel*, was released in the summer of 1995. DeVante also was afforded the opportunity to work with Al Green, one of his idols, writing and producing the song "Could This Be the Love." *—Steve Huey*

Forever My Lady / May 28, 1991 / Uptown/MCA ✦✦✦

A pair of brother acts combined forces to form Jodeci, a singing group with one foot in the future and the other squarely in the past. Dalvin and DeVante Swing DeGrate teamed with JoJo and K-Ci Hailey for a debut album that mixed vintage soul singing with New Jack production and bravado. But it wasn't the hip-hop-flavored songs that earned them popularity; instead, urban contemporary audiences embraced the love tunes "Come and Talk to Me" and the title track, signaling the beginnings of a move away from new jack swing that's become a full-fledged retreat. *—Ron Wynn*

● **Diary of a Mad Band** / 1993 / Uptown/MCA ✦✦✦✦

Jodeci juggles new jack swing and vintage soul on their second album, and wind up with a jarring, mismatched release. The disc's love songs, particularly "Cry for You," "What About Us," and "My Heart Belongs to You," are tender, passionately sung, sincere expressions of romance and love. But they diminish these with a string of innuendo-laden come-on numbers, complete with explicit language, tired raps and samples, and the kind of sentiments and appeals better suited to a *Penthouse Forum* entry than an album. *—Ron Wynn*

The Show, The After Party, The Hotel / Jul. 18, 1995 / Uptown/MCA ✦✦✦

Although their songs imply otherwise, the Hailey brothers had extensive careers in gospel before turning to secular music. The wails, shouts, and yells that accompany most of their hits reaffirm that tradition, and it's clearly audible often on their latest Uptown entry. Again they employ a running storyline/theme through the disc, this time incorporating audio vignettes about life on- and off-stage during a concert that are interspersed through the disc and help pad things out through what is a poorly edited and sequenced CD. Unlike many other urban and R&B groups, Jodeci doesn't really produce its material with singles in mind; there's not really one song here that works as a separate entity, even though several stations are playing edited cuts. Ironically, their refusal to emphasize radio hits, which in most cases would be deemed a sage creative ploy, frequently works against Jodeci. They let ballads drone on, uptempo tunes end awkwardly, and extend sections until they lose their impact. However Jodeci's earnestness and enthusiasm often helps them overcome clichéd lyrics and melodramatic vocals, and there are enough good moments sprinkled throughout this disc to make it worthwhile for most urban contemporary listeners. —*Ron Wynn*

Joe Public

f. 1990

Group / Urban, New Jack Swing

Another new jack swing ensemble to file alongside Bell Biv DeVoe and Guy, Joe Public's self-titled debut in 1992 got them off to a good start among urban contemporary audiences. Their only other album, *Easy Come, Easy Go*, followed two years later. —*Ron Wynn*

● **Joe Public** / Jan. 28, 1992 / Columbia ✦✦✦✦

Plenty of hip-hop and new jack influence here (the credits list six different James Brown samples), but despite the generic name, Joe Public is a honest-to-goodness funk band, which lifts the group's debut above producer-created funk constructs. While the members of Joe Public are capable rappers, as the hit "Live and Learn" indicates, their real strength is their singing; three members contribute lead vocals at some point —*Brian Mansfield*

Joe (Joe Thomas)

b. Columbus, GA

Vocals, Producer, Guitar, Mixing / Adult Contemporary, Urban

An accomplished vocalist of smooth and sultry R&B productions with occcasional hip-hop beats, Joe's extensive background in gospel music has allowed him to produce his albums as well as sing on them. A native of Georgia, Joe later moved to Opelika, AL; since he was the son of *two* preachers, he spent much time in church singing, playing guitar and even directing the choir. Influenced early on by gospel stars like the Winans, Commissioned and Vanessa Bell Armstrong, Joe grew to love soul legends Stevie Wonder and Marvin Gaye plus contemporary stars Bobby Brown and Keith Sweat.

Joe graduated from high school and continued to sing and write music while working at occasional temporary jobs. Finally, he traveled to New Jersey hoping to make connections in the music industry. While working at a gospel record store and continuing his music education through a local church, he met producer Vincent Herbert and recorded a three-song demo tape. He signed to Polygram and in 1993 released his album debut, *Everything*. Joe also appeared on the soundtrack to *Don't Be a Menace to South Central While Drinking Your Juice in the Hood*, and moved to Jive/RCA for his second album, 1997's *All That I Am*. The single "Don't Wanna Be a Player" hit the Top 40, thanks to its exposure on the soundtrack of *Booty Call*. While *All That I Am* went platinum, Joe remixed a duet by Tina Turner and Barry White, "Never in Your Dreams"; he also produced and wrote for debut albums by Ideal and Deja Groove.

In 1999, Joe appeared on Mariah Carey's "Thank God I Found You" single (from *Rainbow*), and caught yet another break from a soundtrack appearance, this time with "I Wanna Know" from *The Wood*. Released as a single in the fall, "I Wanna Know" languished in the lower reaches of the charts until suddenly catching fire in early 2000; the single reached the R&B Top Five in March, setting the stage for Joe's next album, *My Name Is Joe*. —*John Bush*

All That I Am / Aug. 26, 1997 / Jive ✦✦✦✦

Joe's second album *All That I Am* is an entertaining collection of contemporary soul that alternates between smooth ballads and hip-hop-inflected dance-pop. At his best, Joe can make this music irresistible; at his worst, he merely makes it entertaining. There are a few slow spots on the record, but at its best, *All That I Am* is first-class urban soul. —*Leo Stanley*

● **My Name Is Joe** / Apr. 18, 2000 / Jive ✦✦✦✦

Joe is hardly an appropriate name for a lover man—it seems more like a moniker for a custodian than a Casanova—but that's exactly what Joe is. He's an old-fashioned romantic soul crooner in the vein of Al Green, Marvin Gaye, D'Angelo, and, well, Gregory Abbott. He's not as ambitious as D'Angelo is, but that doesn't really matter, since he delivers the goods on his third album, *My Name Is Joe*. Joe never oversings or oversells a song, he just lays back and sweetly sings. There may not be much variety or many remarkable songs on the record—"Get Crunk Tonight" stands out with its stuttering, fade-in-fade-out intro and its stylishly funky beat—but that doesn't matter because this is essentially a mood record, and that mood is love. And it's not a bad romantic mood-setter, either, since Joe is an appealing vocalist, the production is lush without being syrupy, and the songs are all fairly strong, even if only a handful are exceptional ("Somebody Gotta Be on Top," "Treat Her Like a Lady," "Get Crunk Tonight," the *NSYNC duet "I Believe in You"). And, really, that's enough, since anyone that gets hooked by a single from *My Name Is Joe* just wants an assurance that the album will deliver more of the same—and it does. —*Stephen Thomas Erlewine*

Better Days / Dec. 11, 2001 / Jive ✦✦✦

Better Days comes less than a year after Joe's popular breakthrough with "Stutter," the collaboration he did with Mystikal that turned more than a few rap listeners onto his style of urban soul. It's a sparse and succinct album, no doubt rushed to capitalize on the success of "Stutter" and the holiday season as well. To begin with, only two songs feature guests, and one of those songs, "Let's Stay Home Tonight," is a rather straightforward remix for the rap audience featuring Petey Pablo. The other collaboration, "Ghetto Child," is a bit more ambitious, featuring Shaggy and the Boys Choir of Harlem. Elsewhere, the emphasis is on Joe. There isn't a roll call of big-name producers here (though the Neptunes do make a showing), so Joe is left to carry much of the album's weight. He proves more than capable of the challenge on songs like the lead single, "Let's Stay Home Tonight," but too often these songs recycle the same songwriting techniques and find Joe revisiting the same motifs over and over. In sum, this plays like a pop album—a few obvious standout singles and lots of repetitive filler. However, if you're looking for a few quality singles rather than a consistent album, you should find this to be an engaging album, even if its rushed and ultimately thin on original ideas. —*Jason Birchmeier*

Mable John

b. Nov. 3, 1930, Bastrop, LA

Vocals / Soul, CCM, R&B

Mable John was the first female artist signed by Berry Gordy Jr. to the Tamla label, which preceded Motown by more than two years, and one of the few artists to record for the top two labels for '60s soul, Motown and Stax. John's three singles releases were part of an unsuccessful blues fling for the company; besides Mable John, Gordy released blues sides by Sammy Ward, Luther Allison, Amos Milburn, Earl King, Arthur Adams, and many others.

The eldest of nine siblings (one of which was legendary R&B artist Little Willie John, of "Fever" and "Talk to Me" fame), Mable John was born in Bastrop, LA. Her parents moved to Arkansas when she was a kid, then later to Detroit to find employment in the bustling auto industry. After graduating from Pershing High School in Detroit, John began working for Berry Gordy's mother Bertha, who ran a small insurance company. She met Gordy in 1956, started recording for him in 1959, and had her first release "Who Wouldn't Love a Man Like This" on Tamla in 1961, a solid blues item that went nowhere. Her next release, in June of 1961, "No Love" had potential, but Motown simply couldn't sell blues. Her final release "Action Speaks Louder Than Words" dropped during the latter part of 1961.

By 1962, blues at Motown became history, and Mable John was dropped from the roster. (The Supremes, who sang backing vocals on some of John's sessions, became superstars a few years after her departure.) John then moved to Ray Charles' Raelettes, performing with them before and after her stint with Stax Records. Her Stax experience began in 1966 and ended in 1968, during which time she waxed the deep soul classic "Your Good Thing Is About to End," her most successful record. Stax released six other singles by her: "You're Taking Up Another Man's Place," "Bigger and Better," "I'm a Big Girl Now," "Don't Hit Me No More," "Able Mable," and "Running Out." One album, entitled *Stay out of the Kitchen*, would have been definitive if it had included "Don't Hit Me No More."

After leaving Stax in 1968 and rejoining the Raelettes for a brief time, John retired from secular music and devoted herself exclusively to Christianity. In the mid-'70s she managed the Autographs, who had a deal with RCA (unfortunately, the label didn't release any records by them under Mable's watch). In 1994, the Rhythm & Blues Foundation inducted Mable John into their Hall of Fame. It was a just honor for the underrated, blues singer who made excellent records but never had the luck or timing to push her over the top. —*Andrew Hamilton*

● **Stay Out of the Kitchen** / 1993 / Stax ✦✦✦✦✦

If you're a fan and/or collector of deep Southern soul music from the '60s, you would have encountered in your listening some grade-A sides from one Mable John, most notably the politically incorrect "Don't Hit Me No More." A R&B veteran who did time as one of the Raelettes, her tenure at Stax Records was short, producing little in the way of substantial hits. But what Mable left behind in the vaults ends up shining like triple platinum here, 25 tracks of the best Southern soul you'll ever pop into the CD player. Even with Stax stars Steve Cropper, Al Jackson, Booker T., Isaac Hayes and David Porter all aboard, the real star of the proceedings is Ms. Mable, and better examples of the real thing are very hard to come by. —*Cub Koda*

Ernie Johnson

b. Winnsboro, LA

Bass / Retro-Soul, Contemporary Blues, Soul-Blues

Ernie Johnson continues in the soul-blues singing path forged by artists like Bobby "Blue" Bland, Z.Z. Hill, Little Milton and R.L. Griffin. Born in Winnsboro, LA, Johnson didn't begin singing professionally until after moving to Dallas. His vocal influences included Nat King Cole, Dee Clark, Clyde McPhatter, Jackie Wilson, and especially Bobby "Blue" Bland; he recalled that hearing Bland sing "Further on Up the Road" was a revelatory experience. Johnson had a chance to open for Miss Lavelle White and Guitar James in Mexia, TX, and stole the show. At that point, he quit his day job with the Dallas parks department and formed a band, the Soul Blenders. He recorded his first single, "Lovin You" b/w "Cold Cold Heart," for Fats Washington's Movin' Records in 1968.

Johnson recorded other singles before his first album for Ronn Records, *Just in Time*. Johnson has played the blues festivals in San Francisco and Monterey, and his first compact disc, *It's Party Time*, was released on the Louisiana-based Paula Records label in 1993. Johnson financed and produced the album himself, and wrote all the songs except for his rendition of Otis Redding's "Dreams to Remember." In 1995, Malaco Records released another album, *In the Mood*; *Hot and Steamy* followed three years later. Although he doesn't tour that widely, Johnson does get around on the blues festival circuit. —*Richard Skelly*

● **It's Party Time** / 1993 / Paula ✦✦✦✦

Although he doesn't show much imagination anywhere on the disc, Ernie Johnson's second album *It's Party Time* is a fine collection of contemporary soul-blues. Most of the record is devoted to originals, which are solid numbers in the classic Chicago and Stax traditions, even if they're not particularly memorable. They do give Johnson an opportunity to spill his guts out vocally, and he proves to be a good vocalist in the tradition of Bobby "Blue" Bland, Little Milton and Z.Z. Hill, even if he doesn't quite reach their heights. He is good enough, however, to make *It's Party Time* an enjoyable record for fans of that style. —*Thom Owens*

In the Mood / Oct. 3, 1995 / Waldoxy ✦✦✦

General Johnson (Norman Johnson)

b. May 23, 1943, Norfolk, VA

Vocals / Beach, Pop-Soul, Dance-Pop

Leader of the Chairmen of the Board and a top R&B songwriter/producer as well, General Johnson has enjoyed a long career stretching from his debut during the mid-'50s glory days of R&B to his status as an end-of-the-century beach music icon. Born and raised in the seaside city of Norfolk, VA, Johnson began singing in church with his father at the age of six, and made his recording debut at 12 when his group the Humdingers recorded a few unreleased sides for Atlantic. Several years later, after a change of name to the Showmen, Johnson and the group moved to the New Orleans' hit factory Minit for the 1961 rock & roll anthem "It Will Stand." The single charted both in 1961 and 1964, but the Showmen only recorded a dozen sides for Minit and Swan before breaking up in 1968.

General Johnson briefly attempted a solo career, but wound up in Detroit attached to the fledgling Invictus label helmed by Motown hitmakers Holland-Dozier-Holland. With Danny Woods (from the Showmen), Harrison Kennedy, and Eddie Curtis, Johnson formed Chairmen of the Board. Their first single, "Give Me Just a Little More Time," became a big pop hit in 1970, closely followed by "(You've Got Me) Dangling on a String" and "Everything's Tuesday." Johnson wrote another of the group's moderate hits, "Pay to the Piper," and several of his songs became hits for other artists: "Patches" made the Top Ten for Clarence Carter (Jerry Reed also recorded a country hit), and fellow Invictus act Honey Cone hit the charts with his "Want Ads," "Stick Up," and "One Monkey Don't Stop No Show."

The Chairmen of the Board slipped from the charts during the mid-'70s, and while General Johnson and Danny Woods stuck together for a time (as the Chairmen), Johnson finally earned his solo career in 1979. His self-titled album for Arista was a minor hit, translating soul into the contemporary sounds of disco. Johnson reunited with Woods early in the '80s, and the pair toured the Southeast beach music circuit to much success. The early '90s brought another album, *What Goes Around Comes Around*, also recorded with Woods. *—John Bush*

- **General Johnson** / 1979 / Arista ✦✦✦

What Goes Around Comes Around / 1993 / Surfside ✦✦✦

By 1993, General Johnson's stuttering, edgy voice hadn't lost as much edge, range or shape as might be expected. The Chairmen of the Board were a trio, and Johnson divided lead duties with Danny Woods, while their supporting arrangements and backing included the obligatory drum machines, synthesizers and new jack trappings of the urban contemporary sound. This collection reaffirmed Johnson's characteristic whimsical/ironic life views. They weren't settling for oldies glory, but the group didn't quite make the transition to sleek, quasi-sophisticated 1990s territory. *—Ron Wynn*

Janice Marie Johnson

Vocals, Guitar, Bass, Songwriter / Disco, Urban

Singer/bassist/guitarist/songwriter Janice Marie Johnson, as a founding member of A Taste of Honey, sang lead on the million-selling hits "Boogie Oogie Oogie" and a cover of Kyu Sakamoto's "Sukiyaki." The Los Angeles native, whose father was a musician, started playing music as a small child. Growing up, Johnson sang in L.A.-area jazz clubs, opening for Miles Davis, among others. While attending college she began playing bass. In about 1971, Johnson met keyboardist Percy Kimble while auditioning for a vacation cruise gig with Princess Cruises lines, and the two started a band using the title of one of their favorite songs, "A Taste of Honey," as the band's moniker. Adding guitarist Hazel Payne and drummer Donald Johnson, the group signed to Capitol Records. Shortly afterwards, the single "Boogie Oogie Oogie" topped *Billboard*'s charts at number-one R&B/pop for three weeks in fall 1978.

A Taste of Honey was a favorite in Japan long before signing with Capitol, having traveled there to play military bases and entering the Yamaha Song Festival. One of Johnson's favorite records was Kyu Sakamoto's "Sukiyaki." After hearing Linda Ronstadt's version of Smokey's "Oo Baby Baby," Johnson decided that the group (now Johnson and Hazel Payne) should do a remake of a classic song. "Sukiyaki" went to number-one R&B, number-three pop in spring 1981.

After Payne quit A Taste of Honey, Johnson released a solo Capitol LP, *One Taste of Honey*. Johnson says label president Jim Mazza was a strong supporter of her solo debut that was created in part to honor her record contract obligations. Unfortunately, by the time the LP was released, Mazza was no longer with Capitol. One charting single, the softly, "Sukiyaki"-ish "Love Me Tonite" made it to number-67 R&B in summer 1984 and became a post-release favorite. *—Ed Hogan*

- **One Taste of Honey** / 1984 / Capitol ✦✦✦✦

After A Taste of Honey's breakup in the early '80s, lead singer Janice Marie Johnson decided to pursue a solo career. She didn't get very far as a solo artist in the 1980s, which is regrettable because her first solo project, *One Taste of Honey*, is generally excellent. Those who expected this LP be a carbon copy of Honey's soul/disco were in for a major surprise—determined to move forward, Johnson often favors a harder style of urban contemporary/funk with a slight rock edge. The singer/bassist maintains some of the sweetness she was known for, but her solo material is definitely more hard-edged than anything she did with Honey. In fact, Johnson really tears it up on uptempo gems like "Last Chance Romeo," "Beverly Hills," and "Baby Sister." The Asian-tinged ballad "Love Me Tonight" (which was released as a single and became a minor hit) recalls Honey's famous remake of Japanese singer Kyu Sakamoto's 1963 hit "Sukiyaki," but for the most part, *One Taste of Honey* is the work of an artist who was refusing to live in the past. Unfortunately, corporate politics at Capitol prevented the LP from being the mega-hit it deserved to be—and Johnson was dropped by the label. *—Alex Henderson*

Jesse Johnson

b. May 29, 1960, Rock Island, IL

Guitar / Urban, Dance-Pop, Funk, Hard Rock

Illinois-born funk/soul guitarist Jesse Johnson began playing guitar when he was 15, honing his chops in local rock bands throughout his teens and early twenties. On a friend's recommendation, he moved to Minneapolis, MN, where he became the lead guitarist and a primary songwriter for the city's extraordinary funk-rock group, the Time. After writing "Jungle Love," the group's most memorable and highest-charting single, Johnson signed a solo deal with A&M in 1984 and released *Jesse Johnson's Revue* the following year. *Shockadelica* and *Every Shade of Love* followed, building on the inventive, elaborate sound he forged with the Time. By 1990 the group reformed and issued *Pandemonium*, which once again showcased his songwriting and guitar skills. The highlights of his solo albums were collected on 2000's *Ultimate Collection*. *—Heather Phares*

Jesse Johnson's Revue / 1985 / A&M ✦✦✦

In 1984, the breakup of the Time came as a major disappointment to funk lovers—after all, Morris Day and company had provided some of the most exciting funk of the early '80s. Like Day, Jesse Johnson wasted no time launching a solo career; he signed with A&M as a solo artist in 1984, and his first solo effort, *Jesse Johnson's Revue*, came out the following year. Anyone who was expecting the singer/guitarist to get away from the Minneapolis sound and try something different was in for a letdown; all of the material is quite derivative of Prince and the Time. A pop/rock classic, "I Want My Girl" is easily the best thing on the album. But most of the material, although decent, isn't earth-shattering—Johnson spends much of his time recycling the keyboard funk of Prince and the Time. That isn't to imply that *Jesse Johnson's Revue* isn't enjoyable; rock-influenced rock tracks like "She Won't Let Go" and "Can You Help Me" are infectious, if formulaic and less imaginative than Johnson's work with the Time. Johnson was, in 1985, capable of a lot more—and you were in for a letdown if you expected this album to be as ambitious as Prince's *1999*. But while *Jesse Johnson's Revue* isn't a masterpiece, it's a record that's easily to like if you're a die-hard fan of Minneapolis funk-rock. *—Alex Henderson*

Shockadelica / 1986 / A&M ✦✦✦✦

Including a ten-piece band and a duet with Sly Stone on "Crazay," this is mostly light funk and dance music that ends with bare acoustic guitar on "Black in America." *—Bil Carpenter*

Every Shade of Love / 1988 / A&M ✦✦✦

- **Ultimate Collection** / Jun. 13, 2000 / Hip-O ✦✦✦✦✦

Jesse Johnson's *Ultimate Collection* gathers the highlights from his three currently out-of-print albums—*Jesse Johnson's Revue*, *Shockadelica*, and *Every Shade of Love*—in addition to hard-to-find B-sides. Hits such as "Love Struck," "Can You Help Me," "Be Your Man," and "Crazay," and more obscure songs like "Free World," "Fool's Paradise," and "Fast Girls," provide a well-rounded look at Johnson's unique blend of soul, funk, and rock. The new, previously unreleased "Vibe" adds another layer of depth to the album. *—Heather Phares*

Marv Johnson

b. Oct. 15, 1938, Detroit, MI, **d.** May 16, 1993, Columbia, SC

Vocals / Northern Soul, Motown, R&B, Soul

Best remembered for a handful of hits including the Top Ten smashes "You Got What It Takes" and "I Love The Way You Love," Marv Johnson was also a seminal figure in the early history of Motown Records. Marvin Earl Johnson was born in Detroit, MI, in 1938, and was raised in a musical environment that mixed the gospel music of the Baptist church with the jump-jazz of Louis Jordan & His Tympany Five. By the time he was in high school he had joined a local singing group, playing carnivals and fairs. In 1958, he cut his first sides, "My Baby-O" and "Once Upon a Time;" the single failed to sell, but the recording session resulted in a meeting with songwriter and would-be record producer Berry Gordy.

After Johnson played his original song "Come to Me" for Gordy and his future wife Raynoma, the couple chose Johnson as the first artist for their fledgling record label, Tamla. Because the new label didn't have distribution outside of Detroit, "Come to Me" (credited to Gordy and Johnson) was released nationally by United Artists, and rose to number six on the R&B charts and number 30 on the pop charts. Gordy soon lost direct control of his first discovery after United Artists signed Johnson directly, but continued as the singer's manager. Johnson also toured with Motown acts such as the Miracles in addition to appearing on Alan Freed's rock & roll revues and media venues such as *American Bandstand*, and joined early package tours and stage revues where he shared bills with his idols Sam Cooke and Jackie Wilson.

Johnson's second single fared poorly, but his third, 1959's "You've Got What It Takes," exploded onto the charts, becoming a Top Ten hit and earning a gold record. The 1960 follow-up "I Love the Way You Love" also landed in the Top Ten; among his subsequent singles, "You've Got To Move Two Mountains" was a more pop-flavored effort that reached the Top 20, while "Happy Days" got to number seven on the R&B charts late in 1960. "Merry-Go-Round," issued in early 1961, was Johnson's last chart success.

In 1965, with the British invasion in full swing, Johnson's contract was dropped by United Artists; he finally came "home" to Motown, joining the Gordy label, but never enjoyed another American hit, although he earned a British gold record with "I'll Pick a Rose for My Rose" for Tamla in 1968. He later worked in a front-office job for Motown, and also wrote songs for Tyrone Davis and Johnnie Taylor. Johnson's recording career ended in the late 1960s, but he never stopped performing, and remained active on-stage until his death in 1993. *—Bruce Eder*

Marvelous Marv Johnson / 1960 / United Artists ✦✦✦✦✦

Although he was one of the early artists who helped Motown become a pop and soul empire during the 1960s, Marv Johnson made better records while recording for United Artists in the late '50s and early '60s. This is one of several compilations chronicling his cuts prior to the Motown days. Although Berry Gordy produced a number of these, the ones that clicked weren't as clever, elaborate, or pop-oriented as Motown's finest cuts. Johnson had a soulful, flexible voice and is among the transitional artists who deserve more attention for their role in Motown's emergence. *—Ron Wynn*

More Marv Johnson / 1961 / United Artists ✦✦✦

Even many R&B and soul fans have overlooked the greatness of Marv Johnson, whose smooth, exuberant, and sometimes poignant style helped turn some weepy numbers into triumphant outings. He sounded uniformly great throughout this early '60s album, doing everything from light pop to anguished soul and singing with strength, conviction, and intensity. Unfortunately, with the exception of some greatest hits anthologies, there's very little Marv Johnson on today's market except on the collector's circuit. *—Ron Wynn*

I Believe / 1966 / United Artists ♦♦♦

A wonderful, sorely overlooked late-'50s and '60s soul singer, Marv Johnson had the misfortune to have early hits on Tamla, then a tiny label and not the giant wing of Motown it would become by the mid-'60s. He was a dynamic, aggressive vocalist who excelled at heartache ballads, and, as these songs repeatedly show, was among the finest of his era in building and pacing a song, delivering a lyric, and wrenching emotion out of whatever he was singing. *—Ron Wynn*

I'll Pick a Rose for My Rose / 1969 / Motown ♦♦♦♦

Issued in the U.K. by Motown on the heels of Johnson's late-'60s hit "I'll Pick a Rose for My Rose," a number-one record in England. The record never did much in the States, nor did any of Johnson's releases on Motown's Gordy label. The company never issued this album in the States, and, for the most part, treated Johnson like an unwanted stepchild. Johnson's success came prior to his joining Motown; though he recorded in the company's studios, Berry Gordy Jr. leased his singles to United Artists Records. It's apparent why U.K. soul freaks fell for these, since most have that four-on-the-four beat (Motown-style) that they loved dancing to in clubs. "I'll Pick a Rose for My Rose," "I Miss You Baby," "So Glad You Chose Me," and remakes of "Sleep" and "Bad Girl" are solid. Another favorite is "Why Do You Want to Let Me Go," which did well in the U.K., also; Johnson really cranks it up on the chorus, and what a great chorus it is. He also does the Miracles' overlooked "Everybody Got to Pay Some Dues," singing it as if it was meant for him–maybe it was. All are genuine Motown originals waxed in the Snake Pit at 2648 West Grand Blvd. A great pickup if you can find a copy. *—Andrew Hamilton*

• **You Got What It Takes: The Best of Marv Johnson** / Aug. 11, 1992 / EMI America ♦♦♦♦♦

This is a 24 song collection, remastered from original session tapes (several tracks in stereo for the first time), including all of the hits and every key single in Johnson's American output except for the first Kudo single. The best songs could pass for Motown releases of the early 1960s, and even the most overproduced numbers have a soulful, moody power. Excellent sound and superb notes. *—Bruce Eder*

The Very Best of the Motorcity Recordings / Feb. 20, 1996 / Hot Productions ♦♦♦

This contains 18 Marv Johnson tracks originally produced by Britisher Ian Levine for Motor City and Nightmare Records. It features remakes of two tracks he recorded for Motown: "Come to Me" and "I'll Pick a Rose for My Rose." He does an admirable job on Curtis Mayfield's "Nothing Can Stop Me," also recorded by Gene Chandler and Major Lance. Includes an interesting rendition of the Miracles' "Whole Lot of Shakin' in My Heart," but excludes his equally infectious duet with Velvelettes lead singer Carolyn Gill on "Ain't Nothing Like the Real Thing," and Nightmare single number 105 "Run Like a Rabbit." This is pure Marv and not a bad job, featuring the single "By Hook or Crook," "Can't Take Another Day," "Paper Kisses," and more. *—Andrew Hamilton*

Marvelous Marv Johnson/More Marv Johnson / Aug. 14, 2001 / Collectables ♦♦♦♦

Ruby Johnson

b. Apr. 19, 1936, Elizabeth City, NC

Vocals / Soul

A tremendous Southern soul vocalist whose ability to convincingly sing heartache ballads ranks with any active performer, Ruby Johnson never got a breakout single during the soul era. The Memphis vocalist began recording for V-Tone in 1960 and signed with Volt in the mid-'60s. But she did less than a dozen songs between 1962 and 1967, also recording for Nebs in Washington, D.C. Isaac Hayes and David Porter produced her songs, and they were backed by the Mar-Key Horns and Booker T. and The MG's. But none of the Volt tunes were hits, and later Johnson sessions at various studios were never issued. She left the business in 1974. Fantasy issued a definitive Ruby Johnson collection in 1993, *I'll Run Your Hurt Away*. It contained 20 outstanding singles, 14 of them previously unreleased. *—Ron Wynn*

• **I'll Run Your Hurt Away** / 1993 / Stax ♦♦♦♦♦

Between 1966 and 1967, singer Ruby Johnson cut more than two dozen R&B sides for Stax/Volt; for whatever reason, the label released only three singles before dropping Johnson from its roster. Twenty of those songs comprise *I'll Run Your Hurt Away*, a collection of should-have-been hits from this powerful voice. While Johnson recorded a few pop standards like Aretha Franklin's "Won't Be Long" and Ben E. King's "Don't Play That Song (You Lied)," the majority of her songs were composed by Stax in-house musicians and writers. All told, there's not a weak song here; Johnson is a great soul singer who deserved far better. *—Jason Ankeny*

Syl Johnson

b. 1938, Centerville, TN

Guitar, Bass / Memphis Soul, Northern Soul, Soul, Contemporary Blues

A rollicking vocalist and gifted harmonica player, Syl Johnson has forged a career in both blues and soul. The brother of bassist Mac Thompson and guitarist/vocalist Jimmy Johnson, Syl Johnson sang and played with blues artists Magic Sam, Billy Boy Arnold, and Junior Wells in the '50s before recording with Jimmy Reed for Vee-Jay in 1959. He made his solo debut that same year with Federal. Johnson toured with Howlin' Wolf from late 1959 until 1962, when Willie Mitchell signed him to Hi Records. Johnson recorded for both Twinight and Hi in the late '60s and early '70s, clicking with the dance/novelty cut "Come on Sock It to Me" and crackling message track "Is It Because I'm Black?" He had his biggest hit with "Take Me to the River" in 1975, reaching number seven on the R&B charts. Johnson later recorded for Shama and Boardwalk. He reappeared on a collaboration with his brother Jimmy in the summer of 2002, humorously titled *Two Johnsons Are Better Than One*. *—Ron Wynn*

Dresses Too Short / 1968 / Twinight ♦♦♦

Johnson's debut album was a decent but derivative mix of cheery, uptempo Southern soul, somewhat in the mold of Joe Tex (in fact, one of the cuts, "I'll Take Those Skinny Legs," is an obvious takeoff of Tex's hit "Skinny Legs and All"). "Ode to Soul Man" also shows that Johnson was listening to a lot of James Brown at this point. "Come on Sock It to Me," his first hit, is highlighted by some fluid bluesy guitar runs that serve to help elevate the material a bit from the crowded late-'60s Southern soul pack. The album was reissued in conjunction with his second album, the more mature *Is It Because I'm Black?*, on a single disc by Kent in 1997. *—Richie Unterberger*

Is It Because I'm Black? / 1970 / Charly ♦♦♦♦♦

Johnson's first album (*Dresses Too Short*) was fairly innocuous good-time soul, but he'd obviously been doing some thinking about the world around him in the interim between it and his second release. *Is It Because I'm Black* is characterized by socially conscious songwriting, especially in the seven-and-a-half-minute title track, an elongated, serious statement of black pride with a sad funk-blues groove. It wouldn't be fair to call Johnson a bandwagon jumper; this was before Sly Stone's *There's a Riot* and Marvin Gaye's *What's Going On* had made realistic ghetto songs chic, and it was a fairly gutsy move for a minor soul singer such as Syl to put such material to the forefront. While nothing else here matches that lost mini-classic, there are some good cuts along similar lines in which Johnson pleads for tolerance and justice, including covers of jazzman Oscar Brown's "Black Balloons," and Joe South's "Walk a Mile in My Shoes," and, less successfully, the Beatles' "Come Together." The album was reissued in conjunction with 1968's *Dresses Too Short* on a single disc by Kent in 1997. *—Richie Unterberger*

• **Total Explosion** / 1976 / Hi ♦♦♦♦♦

During his eight-year stint with Hi Records, Johnson was in the shadows of both Al Green and Ann Peebles. His albums never flew off the shelves but he could be trusted to release two or three good singles a year. By 1975, Johnson's partnership with Hi Records started to yield even more success. As this album's predecessors had Johnson vacillating between being a romantic and a wretch, *Total Explosion* explores his unrepentant side with good results. "I Only Have Love for You" is a classic Memphis shuffle and finds Johnson all but boasting about his lack of financial savvy, as he sings, "All I got to give is me." With all of the ill will and venom spewed on *Total Explosion*, the innocent "Star Bright, Star Lite" just still doesn't ring true. Johnson comes back to his senses on "Steppin' Out." The dramatic, hard-edged track is all anger and domestic unrest as he sings, "Excuse me, excuse me while I get dressed"; you get the feeling he won't be back anytime soon. The album's biggest single was Johnson's slowed-down take on Green's "Take Me to the River." Although the religious/sexual imagery is lost in the translation, Johnson does a good job with it. The best track, the brilliantly arranged "Watch What You Do to Me" has Johnson playing the role of cuckold, and as he sings "I carry my piece, everywhere I go," it certainly made him more a menace than romantic balladeer. *Total Explosion* was Johnson's most successful album at Hi Records and was one of the best in the label's catalog. *—Jason Elias*

Uptown Shakedown / 1979 / Hi ♦♦♦

Back in the Game / 1994 / Delmark ♦♦♦

In 1993, a 57-year-old Syl Johnson made a long overdue return to the studio with Back in the Game, his first album since the early '80s. Various rappers (including the Geto Boys, Hammer and the Wu-Tang Clan) had been sampling Johnson's classic 1960s and '70s recordings, and learning that younger artists had thought enough of his work to sample it was one of the main things that inspired the singer to start recording again. "Inspired" is definitely a word that describes Johnson's performances on this CD, which unites him with the legendary Hi Rhythm Section of the 1970s. Joined by drummer Howard "Bulldog" Grimes and the Hodges brothers (guitarist Mabon, bassist Leroy and organist/pianist Charles), Johnson delivers one of the strongest albums of his career. The Chicago-based singer emphasizes the type of down-home soul he had favored at Hi, and he is as passionate as ever on "Dipped in the Water" (which features his daughter Syleena Thompson), "I Will Rise Again" and "Ghetto Woman." Another high point of the album is a sweaty remake of Al Green's "Take Me to the River," which Johnson had first recorded in 1975. Although the Chicagoan moves into 12-bar blues territory on "All of Your Love" and Roosevelt Sykes' "Driving Wheel," it must be stressed that the majority of songs on this album are soul rather than blues. This is an R&B album first and foremost–and a fine one at that. *—Alex Henderson*

Back for a Taste of Your Love/Diamond in the Rough / Nov. 20, 1995 / Hi ♦♦♦♦

Total Explosion/Uptown Shakedown / Nov. 20, 1995 / Hi ♦♦♦

The Best of Syl Johnson: The Hi Records Years / Jul. 23, 1996 / Capitol ♦♦♦♦♦

The Mississippi-born Syl Johnson first broke on the scene in the late '60s and early '70s, and had a few hits including, "Is It Because I'm Black" and "Concrete Reservation." He signed with Hi Records in 1971, and enjoyed a nine-year stint with the label, from which this set grabs 22 tracks. Without a flat-out amazing voice like label-mate Al Green, Johnson's skill was his impeccable timing and shrill delivery. Musically speaking, to some Johnson may not have been the recipient of the magical aspect of the Hi sound, but a few tracks here prove that isn't the case. Textbook Memphis shuffles like "Stuck in Chicago," "Music to My Ears" and the sweet "I Want to Take You Home (To See Mama)" all have the type of awe-inspiring, quirky production values for which Willie Mitchell is famous. Johnson's cast of personas were less convincing; early on, he either vacillated between being a vaguely Al Green-styled crooner to a rough-and-ready blues-influenced act. No surprise Johnson took to the former and prospered commercially and vocally. The playful and sneaky "Back for a Taste of Your Love" and "Feelin' Frisky" both present him a little shady, and that's when he's most believable. *The Best of Syl Johnson: The Hi Records Years* also takes five tracks from his 1975 classic *Total Explosion*. The songs—including Johnson's slowed-down take on Al Green's "Take Me to the River and

"Watch What You Do to Me"—have Johnson settling on more rough-hewed style with great, tough backing from the Hi Rhythm Section. Even those somewhat familiar with Johnson's work will be surprised by all of the ground covered here. *The Best of Syl Johnson: The Hi Records Years* is an illuminating look at one of R&B's most underrated talents. —*Jason Elias*

• **Twilight & Twinight (Masters Collection)** / Aug. 27, 1996 / Collectables ✦✦✦✦✦
Syl Johnson has enjoyed a long recording career, first on King Records then for Peter Wright's Chi-town setups and stints with Hi, Delmark, and other labels. The Wright sessions, featured here, represent Johnson's finest and best-known tracks, many of which became substantial R&B hits. The Hi tracks are smoother and more majestic, but for raw soul, grits, guts, and conviction, these are the tracks that collectors and aficionados covet. Johnson combined uptown soul with urban blues and stayed on the R&B charts with aggressive numbers like "Come on Sock It to Me," "Different Strokes" (the era's buzz phrase), and "Dresses Too Short." "Concrete Reservation" is a sociopolitical song about the large, brick public housing projects in inner cities that many viewed as confining, without barriers, as the original Indian reservations. He plays the race card as adroitly as a bull walking through a china shop on "Is It Because I'm Black"; the message doesn't have to be explained on this one, Johnson slaps you in the face with it, heavy stuff for the '60s. "I'll Take Those Skinny Legs" is a takeoff of Joe Tex's "Skinny Legs and All," and you must check his gritty version of "Get Ready," which Johnson gives new implications. There are some good love songs too: "Together, Forever" by bass player Bernard Reed, Joshie Armstead's "I Feel an Urge," and the braggadocio "I Can Take Care of Business." —*Andrew Hamilton*

Dresses Too Short/Is It Because I'm Black? / Sep. 23, 1997 / Kent ✦✦✦✦✦

The Hi Masters / Sep. 15, 1998 / Hi ✦✦✦
Isolated, these Hi recordings are fine, but compared to Syl's Twinight tracks they're missing something. Willie Mitchell transformed Johnson from an attitudinal soul man who wailed about social issues and miniskirted babes, to a predictable singer who does everything at the top of his register. Uptempo tracks: "Back For a Taste of Your Love," "I'm Yours," and "Take Me to a River," are well done, but too orchestrated for purists. "We Did It," "I Hear the Love Chimes," and "Wind Blow Her Back to Me," while better bets, are still far from being time capsule material. Johnson's fans will find these 15-tracks a good overview of his Hi Records era, but will discover a different, mellower singer this time around. —*Andrew Hamilton*

Talkin' About Chicago / Jul. 27, 1999 / Delmark ✦✦✦
Johnson's second CD for Delmark has the soul sender writing or co-writing 12 of these 14 songs. They continue in the Memphis Stax tradition Johnson is known for, and he also throws in a couple of Chicago style blues. Good backup comes from pianist/organist Charles Hodges, electric bassist Orlando Wright and drummer Wayne Stewart. Occasional horn and vocal complement, and the second guitar of producer Pete Nathan on four tracks juice up the proceedings even further. Singing in a style pioneered by Bobby "Blue" Bland, Johnson funks it up quite a bit. His "Come on With It," "Diff'rent Strokes" and "I'm Back Into You" groove solidly, the latter tune in the same pocket as his immortal hit "Take Me to the River." Johnson whips out the harmonica for Magic Sam's "All Night Long" and the potent title track, his tune "Surrounded" is a hit, talking about being an escaped convict of love, stating he's "happy to be on house arrest." Harder funk on the backup vocal and horn inspired "Sweet Dynamite" and the smaller groove for "Cheryl" defines the core of Johnson's good time sound. "Woo-Wee!" is more straight blues, while "Trade Secret" sends a message—fight and then make up, works every time! Johnson seems to be having a great time leading this group, it's his enthusiasm that is more infectious than the actual music being made. He's also not a bad lead guitarist, perhaps a future recording will showcase this facet of his talent more extensively. Fans surely will enjoy this recording from an underappreciated figure of the '60s-'70s soul revival. Newcomers will discover one of the Stax-men who survived. —*Michael G. Nastos*

Two Johnsons Are Better Than One / Oct. 9, 2001 / Evangeline ✦✦✦
Look beyond the jokey title on the first record co-billed to brothers Syl and Jimmy Johnson—concentrate on the music, which happens to be an easy, effortless fusion of Jimmy's modern Chicago blues and Syl's bluesy soul. Both brothers let the other breathe, giving them space to stretch out instrumentally, as well as deliver easy, soulful vocals. They smartly rely on their own material throughout most of the album, both new and old (a nice revival of Syl's classic "Is It Because I'm Black," for instance). The production, like many contemporary blues albums, relies on cleanliness and precision instead of grit, which is too bad, but that ultimately doesn't distract too much from the performances, which are warm, friendly, and engaging, filled with brotherly love. —*Stephen Thomas Erlewine*

Wallace Johnson

b. 1937, Louisiana
Vocals / Modern Electric Blues, New Orleans R&B, Soul-Blues
Vocalist Wallace Johnson last sang around New Orleans clubs more than 20 years ago, but it wasn't until the mid-'90s that his singing was recorded and made available to a larger public outside of New Orleans, thanks to New Orleans-based producer Allen Toussaint. Best described as a soul-blues singer, Johnson recorded a 1996 album, *Whoever's Thrilling You*, that was the debut for Toussaint's NYNO (New York/New Orleans) label. Born on a plantation in 1937, Johnson got married and joined the Army at age 17. He first performed in public during his term in the Army in the mid-'50s, and after singing around Thibodaux, LA, in the early '60s, he recorded four singles for AFO Records in 1962, a label Harold Battiste, Toussaint, Dr. John and other New Orleans-based musicians founded. With a growing family and a wife, Johnson reached a crossroads of sorts, and decided to put his singing career on the back burner for a number of years (though he did record eight more singles between 1965 and 1972 at Toussaint's home studios).

Between 1972 and 1992, Johnson put show business aside, working as a longshoreman and running a music club, Mr. J's, in Thibodaux for a number of years. After being urged to go back on-stage and sing by both his fiancée and his bassist Alonzo Johnson (Rockin' Dopsie), he sang in public once again in 1993 at the New Orleans French Quarter Festival. Johnson began making regular appearances in Crescent City clubs and in late 1995, returned to Toussaint's studios to record his first full-length album. Toussaint wrote nine of the album's twelve songs specifically with Johnson in mind. On the album, Johnson sings songs with a wide variety of tempos. His gospel-influenced, soul-drenched vocals are unique, powerful and moving. —*Richard Skelly*

• **Whoever's Thrilling You** / May 7, 1996 / NYNO ✦✦✦

The Jones Girls

f. Detroit, MI
Group / Philly Soul, Disco, Urban
Valerie, Shirley, and Brenda Jones spent more than ten years in the music business before they tasted success of their own. During that time, however, their voices graced the records and stage performances of dozens of established stars, including Diana Ross and Betty Everett.

The daughters of Detroit-based gospel singer Mary Francis Jones, Valerie, Shirley, and Brenda Jones spent years singing on other artists' recording sessions in Detroit and later in Los Angeles. The trio first tried making their own records for the tiny Fortune label in Detroit during the 1960s, with no success. They moved to Hot Wax-Invictus, the company formed by Holland-Dozier-Holland, during the later part of the decade, but sales of those records weren't much more encouraging.

It was during this period that session work came to dominate their activities—the Jones Girls were in heavy demand to sing on other artists' singles. In 1973, they were signed to the Curtom Records subsidiary imprint Gemigo, a label that was originally organized as an outlet for Leroy Hutson's activities as a producer and arranger. "If You Don't Love Me No More," their debut single, wasn't especially popular, but it led to a follow-up record, "Will You Be There," that proved extremey important. The single never sold but its arranger, Gil Askey, who was working for Diana Ross, recommended the Jones Girls as backup singers for her on tour for a series of engagements that lasted two years and brought them some valuable exposure. Ironically enough, Curtom was sitting on an entire LP cut by the trio that never got released. One of the songs off of the album, "Hey Lucinda," was issued as a single, but it did less good for the Jones Girls than it did for Betty Everett, who later recorded her vocals over their backing track for her version of the song, which did chart.

Their performances with Diana Ross opened up many doors, however, including a contract with Philadelphia International Records at the end of the 1970s. The trio cut four LPs in their three years with the label, enjoying a string of hits around them including "You Gonna Make Me Love Somebody Else," "Better Things To Do," "Nights Over Egypt" and "I Just Love the Man." They later left Philadelphia International for an offer from RCA, but their sales at the new label were poor. The trio never recaptured the moment they had at the end of the 1970s and the beginning of the 1980s. Shirley Jones, who was the first of the trio to record singly, with an entire album for Philadelphia International, has continued to carve out a separate career. —*Bruce Eder*

The Jones Girls / 1979 / Philadelphia International ✦✦✦
The Jones Girls' self-titled debut for Gamble & Huff's Philadelphia International Records yielded the thumpin' million-selling number "You Gonna Make Me Love Somebody Else." The album also boasts several popular radio-aired tracks: the snappy, jazz-flavored "This Feelings Killing Me," the sweet "We're a Melody," the second single "I'm at Your Mercy," and the sweet, shimmering "Who Can I Run To?" The last, the flip side of their gold single, was a 1995 gold hit cover for Xscape, "Off the Hook." In 1998, *The Jones Girls* was reissued as half of a two-fer with *At Peace With Woman.* —*Ed Hogan*

At Peace With Woman / 1980 / Philadelphia International ✦✦✦✦
Because the Jones Girls were a female trio that recorded for Kenny Gamble & Leon Huff's Philadelphia International label in the late 1970s and early 1980s, they were inevitably compared to the Three Degrees. And, to be sure, the Three Degrees influenced them along the way, but the Jones Girls were also heavily influenced by the Emotions. The bottom line is that they were an appealing R&B group in their own right, and their blend of sweetness and grit was the epitome of Northern soul. Recorded at Philly's legendary Sigma Sound in 1980, *At Peace With Woman* was their second album for Philadelphia International and boasts some of the sisters' best work. The playful "I Just Love the Man" and the perky "Dance Turned Into a Romance," both written by Gamble & Huff, were major hits—and the Jones Girls are equally impressive on album tracks that range from the nostalgic "Back in the Day" to an inspired cover of the Stylistics' "Children of the Night." Although the trio didn't record a lot of message songs at Philadelphia International, the title song is a philosophical gem that addresses the battle of the sexes and asserts that serious social problems will continue to plague the world unless men and women learn to get along better. Produced by Gamble & Huff, Dexter Wansel, and other Philadelphians, *At Peace With Woman* is among the Jones Girls' most essential albums. —*Alex Henderson*

Get as Much Love as You Can / 1982 / Philadelphia International ✦✦✦

Keep It Coming / 1984 / Philadelphia International ✦✦✦
By the time Philadelphia International released *Keep It Comin'* in 1984, the Jones Girls had switched to RCA; this LP consists of material they recorded before their departure from Kenny Gamble & Leon Huff's label. So *Keep It Comin'* was an LP of leftovers, but they're enjoyable leftovers. Most of the material sounds like it was recorded around 1982, when R&B was becoming more keyboards-minded but wasn't as high tech as it would become in 1983 and 1984. Produced and written by Gamble & Huff, "Better Things to Do"

is pure Philly soul. But the songs that were produced by Kenneth M. Burke or McKinley Jackson tend to be closer to the sort of things that Kashif and his associates were providing for Evelyn "Champagne" King in the early '80s; soul music was evolving into urban contemporary, and tunes like "Won't Let You Take It Back" and "You Can't Have My Love" find the Jones Girls changing with the times. *Keep It Comin'* isn't essential and isn't in a class with 1979's *The Jones Girls* or 1980's *At Peace With Woman*, but it's a solid, pleasing collection that the group's hardcore fans will appreciate. *—Alex Henderson*

Coming Back / Sep. 29, 1992 / ARP ✦✦✦
Coming Back was the long-awaited sixth album of the Jones Girls under the U.K. production of Errol Henry, Stephen Carmichael, Wayne Lawes, and Jazzie B. "When a Woman's in Love," co-written by Shirley Jones and Keni Burke, is a beautiful ballad accompanied with some soulful sax by Patrick Claher, while "Tell Me Why" showcases the girls' sweet vocals. Solid productions by Errol Henry are "Getting on With My Own Life," highlighted with trumpet solos from Kevin Robinson; the uptempo dancer "You Threw Your Love Away"; and the groovy "All I Want." This quality set with some brilliant songs, excellent productions, and fine vocals is a great comeback. *—Jos Veestraeten*

Get as Much Love as You Can/Keep It Coming / Oct. 13, 1998 / WestSide ✦✦✦

The Jones Girls/At Peace With Woman / Oct. 13, 1998 / Philadelphia International ✦✦✦✦

● **The Best of the Jones Girls** / Jul. 18, 2000 / Capitol ✦✦✦✦✦
The Best of the Jones Girls culls tracks from the trio's sides for Gamble & Huff's Philadelphia International. While you'll find their better-known sides like their million-seller "You Gonna Make Me Love Somebody Else," the exotic Dexter Wansel-produced "Nights Over Egypt," and their original version of "Who Can Run To" (later a 1995 gold hit for Xscape), there are also little-known gems and radio-aired album tracks: an exquisite harmonized version of the Stylistics classic "Children of the Night," the chugging "(I Found) That Man of Mine," the languid "Love Don't Ever Say Goodbye," and the blues-tinged "Why You Wanna Do That to Me." Keni Burke produces the slamming "Keep It Comin'" and the airy "Ah, Ah, Ah, Ah." For good measure, group member Shirley Jones' number-one R&B/Bunny Sigler-produced hit, "Do You Get Enough Love," is included. *—Ed Hogan*

Donell Jones

Vocals, Songwriter, Producer / Contemporary R&B, Urban
Beginning with his 1996 album *My Heart*, singer/songwriter/producer Donell Jones recorded a jazzy and soulful style of urban pop for La Face Records and scored a few modest singles in the process. His first two singles—"In the Hood" and "Knocks Me Off My Feet"—established his reputation within the cluttered urban market. In particular, the latter song, originally a Stevie Wonder song from *Songs in the Key of Life* (1976), became a substantial hit for Jones, climbing to the upper reaches of the *Billboard* R&B chart and driving the album up the charts as well. In addition to his own music, he also wrote songs for other urban artists such as Usher ("Think of You") and 702 ("Get It Together") among others.

Born the son of a gospel singer, Jones submersed himself in music at a young age. Later, when he began to fall victim to the tempations of Chicago's Southside, where he grew up. At one point, after involving himself with gang culture, he decided to dedicate himself to music rather than the streets. He met Edward "Eddie F" Ferrell (former Heavy D & the Boyz member turned Untouchables Entertainment president), and the two formed a partnership with La Face. Following the success of Usher's "Think of You" in 1994 (number-eight R&B), a song which Jones wrote, La Face executives L.A. Reid and Babyface gave the blossoming artist the go-ahead to begin work on his solo debut. Executive produced by Ferrell, Reid, and Babyface, *My Heart* peaked at number 30 on *Billboard*'s R&B chart in 1996, propelled primarily by the success of "Knocks Me Off My Feet" as well as two other singles: "In the Hood" and "You Should Know."

When Jones returned three years later in 1999 with his second album, *Where I Wanna Be*, he had become known as an accomplished songwriter. He penned songs for 702 ("Get It Together," 1997) and Drea ("Not Gonna Letcha," 1998) and was well regarded within the industry as a result. Unsurprisingly then, Jones attained impressive success with *Where I Wanna Be* and its singles: "U Know What's Up" and "Shorty (Got Her Eyes on Me)." Shortly after the album's release, Jones contributed a song to the *Shaft* soundtrack ("Do What I Gotta Do") and to Guru's *Streetsoul* album ("Hustlin' Daze," which he also contributed vocals to). Following some time off in 2001, Jones returned in 2002 with his third album, *Life Goes On*. *—Jason Birchmeier*

● **My Heart** / 1996 / Laface ✦✦✦✦
After working briefly for La Face Records as a songwriter (most notably Usher's "Think of You," a Top Ten R&B hit in 1994), L.A. Reid and Babyface gave Donell Jones the go-ahead to craft a solo debut. The resulting album, *My Heart*, introduced Jones to the masses with the help of "Knocks Me Off My Feet," his lovely cover of a classic Stevie Wonder ballad. Not only does Jones write the songs and sing them on his debut album; he also produces the album and programs both the drums and keyboards. Thus, comparisons to Wonder are somewhat inevitable, especially because Jones sings with a similarly soothing tone of voice. His later albums show him growing as an artist, but here you see Jones first blossoming. In addition to "Knocks Me Off My Feet," *My Heart* also features "In the Hood," Jones' smooth ode to street culture that appears here in two versions. *—Jason Birchmeier*

Where I Wanna Be / Jun. 15, 1999 / La Face ✦✦✦✦
Donell Jones first gained attention as a songwriter and producer for such smooth urban soul groups as Usher, Silk, Brownstone, and 702, which led Babyface to sign the singer/songwriter to LaFace. His debut album was a solid R&B hit, sketching out a jazzy, soulful variation on Babyface's smooth urban-pop, which he fills in with his second album, *Where I Wanna Be*. On the surface of things, Jones may sound similar to a lot of his peers, but there's a greater sense of musical sophistication in his music. There are light touches of jazz, suave electric pianos, and an easy seductiveness to the entire production. *Where I Wanna Be* is actually a savvy update of early-'80s quiet storm—it's a little sexier and a little sleeker, but the spirit is more reminiscent of that era than the late '90s (with the noticeable exception of Jones' tendency to oversell his vocals slightly). At times, the album relies more on style than substance, but it's crafted well, so the slips into filler aren't painful at all. Actually, the very fact that the infrequent bits of filler are enjoyable is a testament to Jones' talents as a performer and record-maker—he knows how to deliver the weaker moments with elegance. And those moments don't arrive all that often on *Where I Wanna Be*. For much of the album, Jones hits the right tone—balancing mood, song, and performance quite alluringly. It gets him and the listener where they wanna be. *—Stephen Thomas Erlewine*

Life Goes On / Jun. 4, 2002 / La Face ✦✦✦✦
Donell Jones doesn't get as much credit as he deserves. Sure, he's had hits, as a solo artist and as a songwriter and producer, but his records never seem to break out to a wider audience, which is too bad, since they're consistently satisfying. *Life Goes On*, his third platter, keeps that streak going. The quiet storm streak that characterized its predecessor, *Where I Wanna Be*, has been toned down somewhat, and he's relying more on contemporary R&B sounds and production, but the end result is the same—a seduction record that is smooth, but also romantic. Perhaps it plays a little too much like low-lights mood music, with a few songs blending together, but that's hardly a fault, since the mood is sustained alluringly from start to finish (apart from "Freakin' U," a deliberate attempt to get an uptempo change of pace in place—it works, but it interrupts the flow a little). Jones may not be as flashy as some of his modern soul peers—he's not a neo-soul artist, he's thoroughly modern, yet he never falls into the trap of putting his singing in front of the music, letting the mood take center stage—but that's what makes his records work, and what makes *Life Goes On* another fine addition to his catalog. [Note: As the sticker says on the cover, *Life Goes On* is a CD that "is protected against unauthorized copying. It is designed to play only on home audio CD players; it will not play on computers, some DVD players, or other devices." This statement is true—I slapped the CD into my computer as I was writing, not realizing the disclaimer; my system froze up, and I nearly lost my work. So, be careful out there.] *—Stephen Thomas Erlewine*

Doris Jones

b. 1948, South Carolina
Vocals / Urban, Disco, Dance-Pop
Doris Jones, an American-born soul singer, is better known in Europe than in the U.S. Born in South Carolina in 1948, she moved to New York 11 years later and started singing in the Merick Baptist Church Choir.

At 20 she formed a group called Sex, Love & Life with her sister Lumishia and a friend; the threesome played places like the Galaxy, the Jupiter, and the Boston Globe. In 1972, as the Electric Ladies, Jones and two other girls recorded "King Kong" on Mainstream Records. The record stiffed in the States and Britain. Her next project was a band, Gallery, that toured the States. After that experience, Jones regrouped with her sister and a friend named Karen and formed Black Stash. They recorded "Mighty Love Man" for Opal Productions, produced by the Exciters' Herb Rooney. Her break arrived when a Britisher, Ian Levine, came to the States searching for artists to record. He had already cut the Exciters, a group that featured Brenda Reid (L.A. Reid's mother), but was looking for more. Levine discovered Jones through Rooney and cut some tracks on her in a New Jersey studio that were released in England—"He's So Irreplaceable," and "Stranded in the Wilderness." Levine recorded Jones often and the results can be heard on CD: *The Best of Doris Jones: No Way Out*, on Hot Productions. *—Andrew Hamilton*

● **The Best of Doris Jones: No Way Out** / Sep. 19, 1995 / Hot Productions ✦✦✦✦✦
This pleasant collection contains all of the tracks (sans a brief reprise) from soulful singer Doris Jones' 1978 AVI LP *Suddenly I'm Alive*, as well as two single-only releases from 1976. Ian Levine's signature, Motown-inspired disco production gleams on tracks like the anthemic "No Way Out," the ten-minute-plus opus "Suddenly I'm Alive," and the soothing "Time on My Hands"—all lifted from the aforementioned album. However, it's a frenetic hodgepodge of vibrant strings and horns, kinetic guitar licks and percussion, and grabbing lyrics that make up the collection's most innovative, standout track, "Stranded in the Wilderness." Jones' sincere interpretation and clear diction provide the perfect counterpoint to the tune's frantic arrangement. All in all, *No Way Out* is a fine collection for lovers of disco and Northern soul alike. While Levine's other productions of the same era for artists such as Evelyn Thomas, Barbara Pennington, and L.J. Johnson sometimes overlap heavily, Jones' understated approach insures that she stands apart from the pack. *—Justin M. Kantor*

Glenn Jones

b. Jacksonville, FL
Vocals / Urban, Inspirational
While he's never been as commanding an R&B/urban vocalist as he was in his gospel days, Glenn Jones has nevertheless managed a successful switch from spiritual to secular material. Norman Connors helped Jones make the move in 1980, featuring him on a song for his LP *Take It to the Limit*. Jones later toured with Connors, and also sang on *Mr. C.* He signed with RCA in 1983, and issued a mini-album, which garnered a Top 30 R&B single in "I Am Somebody." The next LP, *Finesse*, was produced by Leon Sylvers and gave Jones his first genuine smash, the number three R&B hit "Show Me." Jones' duet with Dionne Warwick was the theme song for the 1984 television series *Finder of Lost Loves*. He also sang "Talk Me into It," which was featured in the film *Youngblood*.

Jones left RCA for Jive in 1987, and enjoyed another big hit with "We've Only Just Begun (The Romance Is Not Over)," which reached number-two R&B in 1987. He recorded for Jive until 1992, moving to Atlantic for *Here I Go Again*; *Here I Am* followed two years later, with *It's Time* appearing in 1998. *—Ron Wynn*

Take It From Me / 1986 / RCA ✦✦
Glenn Jones departed RCA after this album, which did moderately well but didn't succeed in breaking him in the urban contemporary market. The single "Stay" was a mild hit, but overall Jones was still building his reputaton after being a prime gospel singer. He demonstrated the resounding presence and soulful mannerisms that eventually made him a hit artist in spots, but this was more an evolutionary release than a finished product. *—Ron Wynn*

Glenn Jones / 1987 / Jive/Novus ✦✦

All for You / 1990 / Jive/Novus ✦✦✦✦
Singer Glenn Jones' best '90s-era album was *All For You.* His vocals confidently float over the percolating "Stay" (not the same named song written by LaLa and recorded earlier by Jones). The number-six R&B Billboard hit was produced by Bobby Khomeni and Mark Stevens. Hitmaker Teddy Riley produces the midtempo beatbox ballad "Let's Try Again," which offers Jones' most intimate song on the CD. Timmy Allen Freddie Jackson (Backstreet Boys) produces the upbeat "Let Me Be the One You're With," the slow-jam duet "That's the Way Love Should Be," and the mellow album title track. The Wayne Braithwaite-produced "No Additional Love" could easily fit on a smooth jazz radio play list. [The U.S. CD reissue boasts an extended version of "Stay." The Japanese import CD of *All for You* lists the bonus track "Living in the Limelight."] *—Ed Hogan*

Here I Go Again / 1992 / Atlantic ✦✦✦

Here I Am / 1994 / Atlantic ✦✦✦

● **Greatest Hits: Giving Myself to You** / Apr. 7, 1998 / Razor & Tie ✦✦✦✦✦
Razor & Tie's *Greatest Hits: Giving Myself to You* is the definitive retrospective of Glenn Jones' '80s recordings, featuring 14 songs including his Top Ten R&B hits "Show Me," "We've Only Just Begun (The Romance Is Not Over)," "Stay (1990)," "Here I Go Again" and "I've Been Searchin' (Nobody Like You)." *—Stephen Thomas Erlewine*

Everybody Loves a Winner/Finesse / Dec. 12, 2000 / WestSide ✦✦✦✦
For any fans of male soul from the '80s, Glenn Jones should be included in the list of underrated vocalists. His pure, gospel-rooted approach is remarkable for its juxtaposition of sensitivity and grit. Whether he's delivering widely octave-spanning ballads such as "Show Me" or electronic dance grooves like "Finesse," he gives his all to each song and makes it a successful story. This CD release of his first two solo albums for RCA may surprise fans primarily familiar with later slow-jam hits like "We've Only Just Begun (The Romance Is Not Over)" and "Here I Go Again," as the bulk of the content here lies in R&B-driven club workouts. Certainly, some of the cuts get a bit repetitive and aren't melodically or lyrically challenging enough for Jones' able pipes, but there are some worthy moments, too. Highlights of the uptempo selections include "Love Intensity"; the sprightly "Meet Me Half Way There"; and "Keep on Doin'," a duet with wife Genobia Jeter. Concerning the ballads, all four here exemplify the singer's genuine vocal power, from the simplicity of "Thank You for the Love" to the sultriness of "Everlasting Love." Though non-fans of dance-driven R&B may be unimpressed by much of the production and material here, this reissue deserves a spot in the collection of any serious fan of top-notch soul vocalists. *—Justin Kantor*

Gloria Jones

b. Sep. 12, 1938, Long View, TX
Vocals / Pop-Soul, Northern Soul, Soul
When the name of Gloria Jones comes up in rocktalk, it's usually as a trivia question. Firstly, in the mid-'60s she recorded the original version of "Tainted Love," which was covered by Soft Cell for a huge international hit in 1982. She was also the girlfriend of British glam rocker Marc Bolan, in addition to singing and playing keyboards in his T. Rex band. Her considerable talent as as a soul singer gets lost in the shuffle, especially because few of her recordings are currently available.

Jones earns a spot in rock history on the merits of "Tainted Love" alone. This propulsive mid-'60s soul stomper, wholly dissimilar to Soft Cell's wimpy synth-pop cover, is one of the great '60s hits that never was. "Heartbeat" was another throbbing near-miss, recorded with, oddly enough, producer Ed Cobb, who was more renowned for his work with garage-pop groups like the Standells and the Chocolate Watch Band. Both "Heartbeat" and "Tainted Love" were written by Cobb as well, although Jones was not without songwriting talent, co-writing Marvin Gaye and Diana Ross' 1974 hit duet, "My Mistake." Jones never had more than regional success, and (like several other minor American soul singers) moved to Great Britain, where the cultish devotion of Northern soul fans ensured regular work.

In 1974, Jones joined T. Rex (which by that time was fading rapidly) as a keyboardist and backing vocalist. Becoming romantically involved with the singer, she also helped sway him into a more soul/dance-oriented direction. Bolan in turn helped her out on her solo album *Vixen*, playing guitar and writing songs. After having a child, their time together came to a tragic end when Bolan was killed in a car accident in 1977, with Jones at the wheel. *—Richie Unterberger*

● **Come Go With Me** / 1966 / Uptown ✦✦✦
Competent but unexceptional commercial mid-'60s soul with a strong, brassy Motown flavor. Jones was clearly a powerhouse singer but wasn't getting the material her talents deserved. "Heartbeat," by far the best track on the album, was reissued in better company in Rhino's *Soul Shots* series. *—Richie Unterberger*

Grace Jones

b. May 19, 1952, Kingston, Jamaica
Vocals / Club/Dance, Disco, Dance-Pop
Grace Jones was one of the more unforgettable characters to emerge from New York City's hedonistic Studio 54 disco scene during the late '70s. Born May 19, 1952, in Kingston, Jamaica, Jones studied theater at Syracuse University before launching a career as a model. Jones' statuesque and flamboyant look proved to be a hit in the New York City nightclub scene, which led to a recording contract with Island Records in 1977. While such disco-based albums as 1977's *Portfolio*, 1978's *Fame*, and 1979's *Muse* failed to break the singer commercially, Jones soon amassed a substantial following amongst gay men with her sexually charged live show, leading to her title at the time of "Queen of the Gay Discos."

But with the dawn of the '80s came a massive anti-disco movement across the U.S., leading to Jones focusing on more new wave and experimental-based work resulting in two of her best-known and strongest releases—1980's *Warm Leatherette* and 1981's *Nightclubbing*—both produced by the noted reggae team of Sly & Robbie (the latter release spawned one of Jones' biggest hits, "Pull Up to the Bumper," as well as covers of Iggy Pop's "Nightclubbing" and the Police's "Demolition Man"). It was also around this time that Jones changed her look to suit the times by replacing her S&M look of the '70s with a detached, androgynous image. Jones' sixth solo release overall, *Living My Life*, followed in 1982, while the singer took a break from recording to focus on film work and landed roles in such movies as *Conan the Destroyer* and the James Bond flick *A View to a Kill* (Jones' romantic life also provided tabloid fodder at the time when she was linked with *Rocky IV* star Dolph Lundgren).

Jones eventually returned back to her recording career, enlisting super-producer Trevor Horn (Frankie Goes to Hollywood) to oversee 1985's *Slave to the Rhythm*, which turned out to be a somewhat autobiographical work (the same year, a ten-track compilation was issued as well, *Island Life*). Jones' penchant for working with big-name producers continued on 1986's *Inside Story*; with production chores handled by Chic's Nile Rodgers, the album spawned one of Jones' last successful singles, "I'm Not Perfect (But I'm Perfect for You)." After 1989's *Bulletproof Heart*, Jones seemed to turn her back on her recording career (although 1993 saw the release of a new single, "Sex Drive"), as she again focused primarily on movies, including a role in Eddie Murphy's hit 1992 comedy *Boomerang.* The double-disc set *Private Life: The Compass Point Sessions* (a collection of 26 tracks that Jones recorded with Sly & Robbie during their early '80s union) was released in 1998, which was followed up four years later with *Island Life, Vol. 2.* *—Greg Prato*

Portfolio / 1977 / Island ✦✦
Disco-mix king Tom Moulton produced these tracks at Sigma Sound in Philadelphia using the same musicians Kenny Gamble & Leon Huff held-hostage for their sessions. The results are quite different—while polished, these tracks don't jump at you. It's really a producer's album. Moulton probably had these tracks completed long before he knew who was going to sing them. Give Grace Jones credit though—she gives credence to old fuddies like "Send in the Clowns," "La Vie en Rose" is lilting, and "I Need a Man," displays a vulnerable Jones. *—Andrew Hamilton*

Muse / 1979 / Island ✦✦✦
A fine dance and club album, Grace Jones was still essentially a disco act when she recorded this album at the end of the '70s. The campy tendencies and flat vocals were subordinated to the array of cross-rhythms, textures, and production devices buttressing the tracks. Jones did some outstanding numbers during this era, but seldom utilized her voice beyond either a decorative or supporting role. She wasn't (and still isn't) a soulful or great singer, but future albums would demonstrate that she could do more things than mouth lines and insert herself into rhythm tracks. *—Ron Wynn*

Warm Leatherette / 1980 / Island ✦✦✦✦✦
Grace Jones teamed with the great reggae production duo of Sly Dunbar & Robbie Shakespeare on this 1980 album, and made the transition from straight dance and club act into quasi-pop star with reggae and urban contemporary leanings. The single "Private Number" was one of her best, and the overall album had more energy and production gloss than previous LPs that had been aimed completely at the club market. It helped that Jones seemed enthused about the session and really put herself into the songs. *—Ron Wynn*

● **Nightclubbing** / 1981 / Island ✦✦✦✦✦
By all means a phenomenal pop album that hit number nine on the black albums chart and crossed over to penetrate the pop charts at number 32, *Nightclubbing* saw Grace Jones working once again with reggae kings Sly Dunbar & Robbie Shakespeare twisting the knobs. *Nightclubbing* also continues Jones' tradition of picking excellent songs to reinterpret. This time out, the Police's "Demolition Man," Bill Withers' "Use Me," and Iggy Pop's "Nightclubbing" receive radical reinterpretations; "Nightclubbing" is glacial in both tempo and lack of warmth, while both "Use Me" and "Demolition Man" fit perfectly into Jones' lyrical scheme. Speaking of a lyrical scheme, "Pull Up to the Bumper" (number-five black singles, number-two club play) is so riddled with naughty double entendres—or is it just about parallel parking?—that it renders Musique's "In the Bush" as daring as Paul Anka's "Puppy Love." Drive it in between *what,* Grace? It's not just lyrics that make the song stick out; jingling spirals of rhythm guitar and a simplistic, squelching, midtempo rhythm make the song effective, even without considering Jones' presence. Sly & Robbie provide ideal backdrops for Jones yet again, casting a brisk but not bristly sheen over buoyant structures. Never before and never since has a precisely chipped block of ore been so seductive. *—Andy Kellman*

Living My Life / 1982 / Island ✦✦✦
Grace Jones essentially retired from music after this album and became a film actress for three years. The album followed her definitive *Nightclubbing* and was a commercial disappointment, although it had some nice material and excellent production and arrangements. But she often sounded distant and detached, and not even the great support could totally overcome Jones' less than enthusiastic performances. *—Ron Wynn*

Island Life / 1985 / Island ✦✦✦
A veil compilation album of Jones' Island sides from an assortment of albums, instead of calling this, "The Best of Grace Jones," Island dubbed it *Island Life.* But it doesn't matter

what name they used—many of these cuts are the typical '70s European disco mush that doesn't have enough seasoning for American music appetites. *—Andrew Hamilton*

Slave to the Rhythm / 1985 / ZTT/Island ♦♦♦♦♦
An audio biography of Grace Jones, produced by Trevor Horn, it's a sonic treat along the lines of Yes's *90125* or Frankie Goes to Hollywood's first album (both produced by Horn). The music ranges from slick R&B runaway grooves to striking audio montages, interrupted occasionally by conversation about Jones' life. Serious ear candy. *—Scott Bultman*

Inside Story / 1986 / EMI ♦♦
Chic's Nile Rodgers produced this Grace Jones album as part of a new deal she signed in the late '80s with Manhattan. Unfortunately, she didn't remain on the label very long, even though this was among her better LPs and included a fine single in "(I'm Not Perfect) But I'm Perfect For You." There were rumors that Jones and Rodgers didn't get along, and perhaps they didn't, but the album wound up being one of her most commercially viable. *—Ron Wynn*

Private Life: The Compass Point Sessions / Jun. 16, 1998 / Island ♦♦♦♦
For anyone but diehard fans, *Private Life: The Compass Point Sessions* will simply be too much Grace Jones in one place. Comprised entirely of recordings she made at Compass Point Studios during the early '80s, the double-disc set features 26 tracks, including two unreleased cuts and four previously unreleased mixes of hit songs. These are unquestionably Jones' best material, mainly because she was supported by a top-notch studio band and produced by Sly Dunbar & Robbie Shakespeare. Given that talent, it's hard to go wrong, but Jones' arch, detached persona hasn't aged well. Several of these cuts work well, several seem hampered by Jones, but there's no denying that any serious fans of her work will find this necessary. Less-dedicated listeners, however, are advised to sample with *Nightclubbing*, which is the best album to be culled from these sessions. It's much more palatable for casual listeners. *—Stephen Thomas Erlewine*

Jimmy "Handyman" Jones

b. Jun. 2, 1937, Birmingham, AL
Piano, Vocals / Northern Soul, Soul, Pop-Soul
Best known for his 1960 R&B smash "Handy Man," Jimmy Jones sang in a smooth yet soulful falsetto modeled on the likes of Clyde McPhatter and Sam Cooke. Born in Birmingham, AL, Jones moved to New York with his family and began his entertainment career as a tap dancer. In 1954, he joined his first doo wop group, the Berliners, who soon changed their name to the Sparks of Rhythm. Jones recorded a few sides with them in 1955, then left to form his own group, the Savoys. They recorded for Savoy in 1956, then jumped to Rama and changed their name to the Pretenders (after the Platters song). The Pretenders cut sides for several labels over the next few years, a few under the name the Jones Boys, before disbanding in 1959. Tired of serving as a group leader, Jones embarked on a solo career with the MGM-owned Cub label later that year. Teamed with writer/producer Otis Blackwell, Jones recorded a song he'd written back in his Sparks of Rhythm days called "Handy Man." By early 1960, "Handy Man" had rocketed into the Top Five on both the pop and R&B charts.

Jones followed "Handy Man" with another Top Ten hit, "Good Timin'," later that year. That proved to be the full extent of his major commercial success, although he kept recording through most of the '60s. He remained with Cub until 1962, scraping the lower reaches of the charts with "That's When I Cried" and "I Told You So." He recorded for Ro-Jac and Vee-Jay over the next two years, and his work gradually took on a New York-style uptown soul flavor. From 1965-1967, he cut sides for Roulette, Parkway, and Bell, none of which restored his commercial standing despite some fine performances. "Handy Man," however, remained an enduring favorite, as Del Shannon and James Taylor each found significant chart success with their own versions. In 2002, thanks to Jones' continued popularity on Britain's Northern soul circuit, Castle/Sanctuary issued a double-disc anthology titled *Good Timin': The Anthology*. *—Steve Huey*

Good Timin' / 1960 / MGM ♦♦♦

• **Good Timin': The Anthology** / 2002 / Castle / Sanctuary ♦♦♦♦

Linda Jones

b. Jan. 14, 1944, Newark, NJ, **d.** Mar. 14, 1972, Harlem, New York City, NY
Vocals / Pop-Soul, Soul
A word in support of an artist who will probably be passed over by 999 listeners out of 1000. Her biggest hit, the tastefully restrained "Hypnotized," came on the Loma subsidiary of Warner Brothers in 1967, but her later recordings for Turbo were probably the most gloriously histrionic soul records of all time. She started at a climax and worked up from there, transforming a ballad like "Let It Be Me" with her towering fury. It was pure gospel—and then some. Jones was already ill with diabetes when she cut those records, and she died in 1972 after collapsing backstage at the Apollo. *—Colin Escott*

Your Precious Love / 1988 / Turbo ♦♦♦♦
If Sequel Records had included "That's When I'll Stop Loving You," this collection would be through the roof. It's still a fine assembly of Linda Jones' songs, with most of her classic readings: "I Do" and "Not on the Outside," first done by the Moments, and Jerry Butler & the Impressions' "For Your Precious Love" with her spoken intro. She also does solid remakes of "Dancing in the Street," and "Doggin' Me Around." The original material is no joke either. "Stay With Me Forever," is a pleading love letter that Jones' litters with exclamation points. She has the blues on "Things I've Been Through," and you would too, if you'd been "slapped, kicked, and laugh at." "Hypnotized," the ultimate swept-for-you-baby song, is Linda at her emotional best. Though she sung hard, and dramatized every note, the ears never tires of Linda's big beautiful voice. *—Andrew Hamilton*

• **Hypnotized: 20 Golden Classics** / Mar. 21, 1994 / Collectables ♦♦♦♦♦
Linda Jones was a dynamic, sorely neglected late-'60s and early-'70s soul vocalist. There was no mild reaction to Jones' theatrical style; you were either amazed or appalled. She didn't deliver lyrics, she smashed and screamed them. This collection covers her bombastic hits, including the classic title track, "I'll Be Sweeter Tomorrow," "For Your Precious Love" and several others. Any vocalist picked by Gladys Knight and Patti LaBelle as one of their favorites merits closer examination. Unfortunately, her premature death in the early-'70s prevented Jones from gaining much exposure, as did the fact that she recorded for a host of small independents. *—Ron Wynn*

Never Mind the Quality . . . Feel the Soul: Live in Ohio 1970 / Oct. 21, 1997 / Sequel ♦♦♦
Only six songs are here, but six from Linda Jones are like ten from someone else. It was recorded during one of Linda's performances in Ohio in the early '70s. It's obviously a bootleg taping made by a concert patron, which Sequel thankfully remastered and released. Jones died a few years later, and this is her only live recording known to exist. Her interpretations of two Falcon tunes and Jerry Butler's "For Your Precious Love" makes this a must-buy, not to mention the dramatic "That's When I'll Stop Loving You," where Linda recites a laundry list of events that would have to occur before she left her man; but then, everything Linda sings becomes a drama. Linda had a unique way of phrasing that distanced her from the also-rans. She was truly amazing and left us much too quick. *—Andrew Hamilton*

Oran "Juice" Jones

b. 1959, Houston, TX
Vocals / Urban, Dance-Pop
Oran "Juice" Jones seemed on his way to stardom when the tough-talking single "The Rain" became a hit in 1986. Though born in Houston, Jones grew up in Harlem and was one of the first signees to the Def Jam subsidiary label OBR, which was to be devoted to vintage soul and R&B acts. Jones was actually a good "sweet" soul singer, but that facet was obscured by his façade as a gangsta. His best single was a duet with Alyson Williams, "How to Love Again." After "The Rain" topped the R&B charts in 1986, Jones was unable to land any more hits with follow-up singles. *—Ron Wynn*

• **Juice** / 1986 / Def Jam ♦♦♦♦
"The Rain" blew up, a phat tale of a guy who caught his girl cheating, sung in a sweet falsetto and accented with an Iceberg Slim-inspired rap. This Vincent Bell & Russell Simmons production broke new ground and distinguished itself from the norm. The ballads are creamy concoctions, and Juice sings them like a bird; "You Can't Hide From Love," "Your Song," and Smokey Robinson's "Here We Go Again" are quiet storm staples. No filler tracks in the bunch; every song seems babied and crafted. *—Andrew Hamilton*

G.T.O.: Gangsters Takin' Over / 1987 / Def Jam ♦♦♦
G.T.O. picks up where *Juice* left off, featuring background singers the Shades of Black. "Cold Spending My $ Money" sounds as potent as "The Rain." "U Bring Out the Best in Me" features strong bass vocals, a delightful counterpart to Juice's crystal-shattering falsetto."Not on the Outside," the Moments' first recording, gets a needed update. "Rock the Night Away" is smooth, and the humorous "We Were Friends" tells it like it is. Everything and then some is on *G.T.O.*, including a winning duet with Alyson Williams. *—Andrew Hamilton*

To Be Immortal / 1989 / Def Jam ♦♦♦

Quincy Jones

b. Mar. 14, 1933, Chicago, IL
Producer, Arranger, Composer, Leader, Trumpet, Piano, Vocals / Big Band, Swing, Bop, Traditional Pop, Jazz-Pop, Crossover Jazz, Urban
In a musical career that has spanned six decades, Quincy Jones has earned his reputation as a renaissance man of American music. Jones has distinguished himself as a bandleader, a solo artist, a sideman, a songwriter, a producer, an arranger, a film composer, and a record label executive; outside of music, he's also written books, produced major motion pictures, and helped create television series. And a quick look at a few of the artists Jones has worked with suggests the remarkable diversity of his career—Miles Davis, Frank Sinatra, Count Basie, Lesley Gore, Michael Jackson, Peggy Lee, Ray Charles, Paul Simon, and Aretha Franklin.

Quincy Jones was born in Chicago, IL, on March 14, 1933. When he was still a youngster, his family moved to Seattle, WA, and he soon developed an interest in music. In his early teens, Jones began learning the trumpet, and started singing with a local gospel group. By the time he graduated from high school in 1950, Jones had displayed enough promise to win a scholarship to a Boston-based music school, Schillinger House (which later became known as the Berklee School of Music). After a year at Schillinger, Jones relocated to New York City, where he found work as an arranger, writing charts for Count Basie, Cannonball Adderley, Tommy Dorsey, and Dinah Washington, among others. In 1953, Jones scored his first big break as a performer; he was added to the brass section of Lionel Hampton's orchestra, where he found himself playing alongside jazz legends Art Farmer and Clifford Brown. Three years later, Dizzy Gillespie tapped Jones to play in his band, and later in 1956, when Gillespie was invited to put together a big band of outstanding international musicians, Diz chose Quincy to lead the ensemble. Jones also released his first album under his own name that year, a set for ABC-Paramount appropriately entitled *This Is How I Feel About Jazz*.

In 1957, Jones moved to Paris in order to study with Nadia Boulanger, an expatriate American composer with a stellar track record educating composers and bandleaders. During his sojourn in France, Jones took a job with the French record label Barclay, where he produced and arranged sessions for Jacques Brel and Charles Aznavour, as well as travelling American artists, including Billy Eckstine and Sarah Vaughan. Jones' work for Barclay impressed the management at Mercury Records, a American label affiliated with the French imprint, and in 1961, he was named a vice-president for Mercury, the first time an African-American had been hired as an upper-level executive by a major U.S. recording company. Jones scored one of his first major pop successes when he produced and arranged "It's My Party" for teenage vocalist Lesley Gore, which marked his first significant step away from jazz into the larger world of popular music. (Jones also freelanced for other labels on the side, including arranging a number of memorable Atlantic sides for Ray Charles.) In 1963, Jones began exploring what would become a fruitful medium for him when he composed his first film score for Sidney Lumet's controversial drama *The Pawnbroker*; he would go on to write music for 33 feature films, including *In Cold Blood, In the Heat of the Night, Bob & Carol & Ted & Alice*, and *The Getaway*. In 1964, Jones' work with Count Basie led him to arrange and conduct sessions for Frank Sinatra's album *It Might as Well Be Swing*, recorded in collaboration with Basie and his orchestra; he also worked with Sinatra and Basie again as an arranger for the award-winning *Sinatra at the Sands* set, and would produce and arrange one of Sinatra's last albums, *L.A. Is My Lady*, in 1984.

While Jones maintained a busy schedule as a composer, producer and arranger through the 1960s, he also re-emerged as a recording artist in 1969 with the album *Walking in Space*, which found Jones recasting his big band influences within the framework of the budding fusion movement and the influences of contemporary rock, pop and R&B sounds. The album was a commercial and critical success, and kickstarted Jones' career as a recording artist. At the same time, he began working more closely with contemporary pop artists, producing sessions for Aretha Franklin and arranging strings for Paul Simon's *There Goes Rhymin' Simon*, and while Jones continued to work with jazz artists, many hard-and-fast jazz fans began to accuse Jones of turning his back on the genre, though Jones always contended his greatest allegiance was to African-American musical culture rather than any specific style. (Jones did, however, make one major jazz gesture in 1991, when he persuaded Miles Davis to revisit the classic Gil Evans arrangements from *Miles Ahead, Sketches of Spain*, and *Porgy and Bess* for that year's Montreux Jazz Festival; Jones coordinated the concert and led the orchestra, and it proved to be one of the last major events for the ailing Davis, who passed on a few months later.) In 1974, Jones suffered a life-threatening brain aneurysm, and while he made a full recovery, he also made a decision to cut back on his schedule to spend more time with his family. While Jones may have had fewer projects on his plate in the late '70s and early '80s, they tended to be higher profile from this point on; he produced major chart hits for the Brothers Johnson, Rufus & Chaka Khan, and his own albums grew into all-star productions in which Jones orchestrated top players and singers in elaborate pop-R&B confections on sets like *Body Heat, Sounds... And Stuff Like That!!* and *The Dude*. Jones' biggest mainstream success, however, came with his work with Michael Jackson; Jones produced his breakout solo album *Off the Wall* in 1979, and in 1982 they teamed up again for *Thriller*, which went on to become the biggest selling album of all time. Jones was also on hand for *Thriller*'s follow-up, 1987s *Bad*, the celebrated USA for Africa session which produced the benefit single "We Are the World" (written by Jackson and Lionel Richie), and he produced a rare album in which Jackson narrated the story of the film *E.T.: The Extra-Terrestrial*.

Having risen to the heights of the recording industry, in 1985 Jones moved from scoring films to producing them; his first screen project was the screen adaptation of Alice Walker's novel *The Color Purple*, which was directed by Steven Spielberg and starred Whoopi Goldberg. In 1991, he began moving into television production with the situation comedy *The Fresh Prince of Bel Air*, which gave Will Smith his first starring role. Jones' production company also launched several other successful shows, including *In the House* and *Mad TV*. He also produced a massive concert to help commemorate the 1993 inauguration of president Bill Clinton, and at the 1995 Academy Awards won the Jean Hersholt Humanitarian Award, a prize that doubtless found its place beside Quincy's 26 Grammy Awards. *—Mark Deming*

The Pawnbroker / May 1964 / Mercury ✦✦✦✦
This soundtrack to Sidney Lumet's 1964 film *The Pawnbroker* might not rate with such other Quincy Jones celluloid efforts as *In the Heat of the Night*, but its fine mix of jazz, bossa nova, soul, and vocals still makes it one of his best. Bookended by two vocal takes of the main title theme (one by Marc Allen and one from Sarah Vaughan), the bulk here shows off Jones' deft touch with mixing disparate elements into a coherent and swinging whole ("Harlem Drive," "The Naked Truth"). There's also plenty of noir-ish moodiness and even some dialogue by the star, Rod Steiger. And with trombonist J.J. Johnson and trumpeter Freddie Hubbard chiming in as well, the mix maintains its sophisticated air throughout. Now part of a two-fer that includes Jones' soundtrack to *A Deadly Affair, The Pawnbroker* is a must for both Jones fans and film music buffs. *—Stephen Cook*

Big Band Bossa Nova / 1964 / Mercury ✦✦✦
A by-product of the bossa nova fad that followed the success of "Desafinado" (and preceded the famous recording *Getz/Gilberto*), this LP finds Quincy Jones utilizing and exploiting bossa nova rhythms in his arrangements for a big band. It is a little odd that the personnel is not given on the LP, for it includes flugelhornist Clark Terry, altoist Phil Woods, pianist Lalo Schifrin, guitarist Jim Hall and (on "Soul Bossa Nova") the remarkable Rahsaan Roland Kirk. However, since the selections are all quite brief, and some of the charts are a bit cheesy and inappropriate for the gentle rhythms, this out-of-print LP (although pleasant enough) is of lesser interest. *—Scott Yanow*

☆ **Walking in Space** / Jun. 1969 / A&M ✦✦✦✦✦
The protean Quincy Jones returned to the recording studio as a leader after a long stretch in Hollywood with this triumphantly contemporary big band album. He re-established himself firmly with his big band jazz base while casting a keen eye on the pop scene and the world of electric instruments (even Ray Brown is caught playing superb electric bass here). The diplomat also unveils his uncanny ability to attract some of the biggest names in jazz as sidemen (Freddie Hubbard, Rahsaan Roland Kirk, Hubert Laws, J.J. Johnson, Kai Winding, etc.), a quality that will be put to use again and again in the following decades. For jazz buffs, the long, dramatic title track from the then-raging musical *Hair* is the highlight; Hubbard positively sizzles on muted trumpet, and the brash Kirk blasts through the grooving rhythm section under heavy reverb. You also get Jones' classic, swaggering arrangement of Benny Golson's "Killer Joe"—practically the definitive version—and a rendition of Edwin Hawkins' freak hit "Oh Happy Day" that bursts with wit and sheer joy. This is one of the great peaks of Creed Taylor's A&M period, and it still sounds spectacular today. *—Richard S. Ginell*

I Heard That! / Jun. 1969-1976 / A&M ✦✦
This two-LP set was supposed to contain a monumental suite tracing the evolution of black music but since Jones needed more time to work on it (it has yet to emerge!), he put out this stopgap set. One LP contains new material, the other is a retrospective of his previous A&M albums. The first LP is dominated by the generic soul vocals of a Quincy Jones-sponsored creation known as the Wattsline, which is largely saddled with routine soul material after a brief, promisingly funky start ("I Heard That!!"). Of the instrumentals, "Midnight Soul Patrol" doesn't quite make it despite the presence of heavyweight funksters like George Duke, Stanley Clarke, Billy Cobham and Alphonso Johnson, but "Brown Soft Shoe" again has Toots Thielemans delivering some classy cameo harmonica. The "greatest hits" disc astutely pulls eight key tracks from all six of Q's earlier A&Ms (though "Gula Matari" and "Walking in Space" are heavily edited)—and frankly, they blow his 1976 music away. *—Richard S. Ginell*

Gula Matari / Mar. 25, 1970-May 1, 1970 / A&M ✦✦✦✦✦
With his second and last album under the Creed Taylor aegis, the complexities of Quincy Jones' catholic, evolving tastes start to reveal themselves. We hear signs of his gradual gravitation toward pop right off the bat with the churchy R&B cover of Paul Simon's mega-hit "Bridge Over Troubled Water," dominated by Valerie Simpson's florid soul vocal and a gospel choir. His roots fixation surfaces in the spell-like African groove of the title track, a dramatic tone poem that ebbs and flows masterfully over its 13-minute length. From this point on, it's all jazz; the roaring big band comes back with a vengeance in "Walkin'," where Milt Jackson, Herbie Hancock, Hubert Laws, and other jazzers take fine solo turns, and things really get rocking on Nat Adderley's "Hummin'." Major Holley is a riot with his grumble-scat routine on bass. The whole record sounds like they must have had a ball recording it. *—Richard S. Ginell*

Dollars / 1971 / Reprise ✦✦✦
This soundtrack features a number of songs composed and conducted by Quincy Jones for the film *Dollars*. Jones works with well-known vocalists Little Richard and Roberta Flack, which may interest some listeners. But, ultimately, it's Jones' compositions that carry the most weight on this soundtrack and surely the reason to give this soundtrack a listen. It's not worth going out of your way to get, though. Jones released a lot of phenomenal music in his time, and though this is impressive, it's one of his less interesting projects. It'll be best enjoyed by fanatics and completists. *—Jason Birchmeier*

Smackwater Jack / 1971 / A&M ✦✦✦✦✦
This is where a lot of serious jazz purists get off the train but for the rest of us, this is an exciting journey into Quincy Jones territory where labels are meaningless. Though Q takes us deep into Hollywood and TV with his themes to *Ironside, The Anderson Tapes* and the first *Bill Cosby Show* (with humorous vocals from the Cos' himself), his jazz base remains intact in these fascinating charts, and stellar friends like Freddie Hubbard, Milt Jackson, Toots Thielemans, and Jim Hall are left alone to shine. The centerpiece, "Guitar Blues Odyssey: From Roots to Fruits" is the first of many attempts by Q to summarize musical evolution in one fell swoop. Moreover, this ambitious collage actually works—and it's great fun to hear Thielemans, Hall, Eric Gale and Joe Beck try to mimic guitarists from Robert Johnson to Wes Montgomery to Jimi Hendrix. One can't be quite as enthusiastic about Q's rather weak-kneed vocals on two tracks, but that's about the only stumble in this hugely enjoyable project *—Richard S. Ginell*

You've Got It Bad, Girl / Oct. 1973 / A&M ✦✦✦
With a predictable combination of movie/TV themes, dreary covers of Top 40 ballads, some jazz and a few striking moments, this is a maddeningly uneven follow-up to *Smackwater Jack*. A magically spooky saunter through the Lovin' Spoonful's "Summer in the City" leads it off, but the record becomes bogged down in easy-listening strings and "soulful" vocals, despite the presence of ace soloists like Phil Woods, Hubert Laws and George Duke. Things do become more exuberant as Stevie Wonder punctuates his "Superstition" on harmonica, and a fussed-over big-band rendition of Dizzy's "Manteca" delivers sporadic kicks. But Q mostly marks time before going completely off the reservation on his next outing. *—Richard S. Ginell*

Body Heat / 1974 / A&M ✦✦✦✦
At the time, this was a breathtaking leap for Quincy Jones, right into the very heart of mainstream commercial soul—and it turned out to be very lucrative, rising to number six on the pop album charts. Jazz per se has been left far behind but the same musical sensibility, the same brilliant production skills, and the same knack for what will appeal to a wider audience are still at work, and the result is a surprisingly pleasing album. Amazingly Q still draws a constellation of jazz stars into his studio bands (Herbie Hancock, Frank Rosolino, Hubert Laws, Jerome Richardson, Grady Tate, Bob James), plus soul names like Billy Preston, Bernard Purdie and the soon-to-be-ubiquitous guitarist Wah Wah Watson. The emphasis, though, is first on the honeyed soul vocals from a variety of newcomers, and second on the funky grooves laced with the buzz of now-prized analogue synthesizers and wah-wah guitars. There is one reminder of Q's big-band days, a busy electronic retrofitting of his classic chart of Benny Golson's "Along Came Betty," where one can hear Laws blow at some length. Otherwise, to paraphrase Q himself, if you check your jazz boots at the door, you might enjoy this. *—Richard S. Ginell*

Mellow Madness / 1975 / A&M ✦✦
Released not long after Quincy Jones was operated upon for a life-threatening brain aneurysm, the music community was glad to have this album around (you can almost sense Q's own relief as he holds his forehead on the cover). Basically, though, it continues the polished, percolating soul direction that Q initiated with *Body Heat*, alienating purists

but entertaining R&B audiences that rushed to buy it. The album is given its commercial edge by two new Jones discoveries, George Johnson (guitar, vocals) and Louis Johnson (bass), who would leap to fame the following year on their own as the Brothers Johnson. One attraction for jazz listeners is Toots Thielemans' "Bluesette," in which the Belgian virtuoso does a nice guitar/whistle cameo and Frank Rosolino blows some fine trombone, but the track is not helped by the overdubbed soul voices. *—Richard S. Ginell*

Roots / 1977 / A&M ✦✦✦

Quincy Jones has been threatening to write a long tone poem sketching the history of black music for decades now, and he has yet to do it. This project, rushed out in the wake of the 1977 TV mini-series *Roots*, is about as close as he has come. A brief (28 minutes), immaculately-produced and segued suite, *Roots* quickly traces a timeline from Africa to the Civil War, incorporating ancient and modern African influences (with Letta Mbulu as the featured vocalist), a sea shanty, field hollers and fiddle tunes, snippets of dialogue from *Roots* actor Lou Gossett, and some Hollywood-style movie cues. Only a fraction of this music was used in the mini-series; oddly, the most familiar piece of music, the often-repeated "Roots Mural Theme," is not by Q but by film composer Gerald Fried, who wrote most of the TV score. Though some prominent jazzers (Shelly Manne, Victor Feldman, Ernie Watts, Lee Ritenour, Richard Tee, etc.) turn up in the orchestra, there is not a trace of jazz to be heard. This is a timely souvenir of a cultural phenomenon, but merely a curiosity for jazz fans. *—Richard S. Ginell*

Sounds . . . And Stuff Like That!! / 1978 / A&M ✦✦✦

With ears dead-set on the trends of the moment but still drawing now and then on his jazz past, Quincy Jones came up with another classy-sounding pop album loaded with his ever-growing circle of musician friends. Disco was king in 1978 and Q bows low with the ebullient dance hit "Stuff Like That"—which is several cuts above the norm for that genre—along with a healthy quota of elegantly produced soul ballads. Yet amidst the pop stuff, Q still manages to do something fresh and memorable within the jazz sphere with a gorgeous chart of Herbie Hancock's "Tell Me a Bedtime Story." Hancock himself sits in impeccably on electric piano and violinist Harry Lookofsky painstakingly overdubs one of Herbie's transcribed solos on 15 violins. Despite the cast of hundreds that is now de rigueur for Q, the record does not sound overproduced due to the silken engineering and careful deployment of forces. *—Richard S. Ginell*

The Dude / 1980-1981 / A&M ✦✦✦

Now running his own Qwest label and a thousand other things, Quincy Jones still owed one more album to A&M—and he gave them a blockbuster, one that reached number ten, yielded three hit pop singles and made a star out of soul balladeer James Ingram. "Ai No Corrida," and the leadoff track, is the Quincy Jones hit method par excellence—great pacing, superb sound, a catchy tune, a hot Ernie Watts tenor sax solo and you can dance to it, too. Stevie Wonder's irresistible synthesizer hooks lift his "Betcha Wouldn't Hurt Me," and Q and omnipresent composer Rod Temperton are far-seeing enough on the title track to anticipate the rise of rap. But where does all of this pop wizardry, soon to assume mythic dimensions on Michael Jackson's *Thriller*, leave the jazz listener? Yes, Quincy has thought of you too, however briefly, on Ivan Lins' wistful "Velas," where perennial house jazzer Toots Thielemans eloquently returns, taping his part in Belgium. Obviously, though, the main purpose here is to make hit pop singles, and *The Dude* does a pretty good job of that. *—Richard S. Ginell*

Back on the Block / 1989 / Qwest ✦✦✦✦

Having let eight years pass since his last A&M album, Quincy Jones made his debut on his own label with his most extravagant, most star-studded, most brilliantly sequenced pop album to date—which could have only been assembled by the man who put together "We Are the World." Jones was one of the first establishment musicians to embrace rap, and one of the first to link rap with his jazz heritage; it's hard not to be moved by the likes of Miles Davis, Dizzy Gillespie, James Moody, Ella Fitzgerald, Joe Zawinul, Sarah Vaughan, and George Benson electronically appearing on "Birdland" and trading brief licks with the likes of Kool Moe Dee and Big Daddy Kane on "Jazz Corner of the World." Later, jazz buffs would vilify Jones for not taking fuller advantage of this one-time constellation of jazz stars, but at the time, it seemed like a marvelous dialogue between the old and the new. Of course, as he well knew, celebrating jazz history is not the surest route to a blockbuster hit record, so there are plenty of radio-friendly urban pop productions here, with Herbie Hancock and George Duke on keyboards, and Siedah Garrett and 12-year-old Tevin Campbell on vocals. Despite the presence of an enthused Ray Charles, Chaka Khan, and the Brothers Johnson, the overly busy techno remake of "I'll Be Good to You" doesn't cut the Johnsons' original—nor does "Tomorrow." Ultimately the most popular track would be the most tedious for the jazz listener, "The Secret Garden," with a parade of smooth soul balladeers producing make-out music at length. Yet *Back on the Block* remains a strikingly durable piece of entertainment, and in hindsight, a poignant signpost of the changing of the guard. *—Richard S. Ginell*

Q's Jook Joint / Nov. 1994-1995 / Qwest ✦✦

The multi-talented Quincy Jones has excelled at idiomatic combinations in his albums since the '60s, when his mix-and-match soundtracks for television and films alerted everyone he'd switched from a pure jazz mode to a populist trend. *Q's Juke Joint* blends the latest in hip-hop flavored productions with sleek urban ballads, vintage standards and derivative pieces; everything's superbly crafted, though few songs are as exciting in their performance or daring in their conception as such past Jones epics like *Gula Matari* or the score from *Roots*. Still, you can't fault Jones for his choice of musical collaborators; everyone from newcomer Tamia to longtime stars like Ray Charles, rappers, instrumentalists, male and female vocalists, percussionists and toasters. The CD really conveys the seamless quality one gets from attending a juke joint, though it lacks the dirt-floor grit or blues fervor of traditional Southern and chitlin' circuit hangouts. But no one's more knowledgeable about the spectrum of African-American music, nor better able to communicate it via disc than Quincy Jones. *—Ron Wynn*

Greatest Hits / 1996 / A&M ✦✦✦✦

Greatest Hits contains a selection of Quincy Jones' greatest pop hits of his work for A&M, including tracks from hit albums like *The Dude*, *Body Heat*, and *Smackwater Jack*. For jazz purists, this isn't a worthwhile purchase, but for fans of R&B hits like "Just Once," "Is It Love That We're Missin'," "Ai No Corrida (I-No-Ko-ree-da)" and "Stuff Like That," it's a definitive retrospective. *—Thom Owens*

In the Heat of the Night/They Call Me Mr. Tibbs / Feb. 24, 1998 / Beyond ✦✦✦

Two scores with a tone of righteous fury woven throughout. While there are differences in the approach to the two scores, Quincy Jones did manage to provide a unifying style—no mean feat, considering that the intent behind *In the Heat of the Night* was to get a Southern, blues-inflected atmosphere to support the angry, anti-racist approach of the picture, while *They Call Me Mister Tibbs* had a more open, urban attitude from its San Francisco setting. The music throughout has an edge (the lighter music in the second score is generally source music), with some interesting musical experiments going on (Jones, as one example, used cimbalom to reflect Tibbs' feelings in *They Call Me Mister Tibbs*). The Ryko CD release includes an enhanced CD portion with film material. The sound throughout the disc is excellent, although the cues from *In the Heat of the Night* show their age, and the dialogue excerpts sound very rough. [The 2002 release by Beyond includes the same 35 tracks as the 1998 Rykodisc release but features different packaging.] *—Steven McDonald*

Q: The Musical Biography of Quincy Jones / Oct. 16, 2001 / Rhino ✦✦✦✦

Although Rhino's four-disc box set, *Q: The Musical Biography of Quincy Jones*, was released to coincide with Quincy Jones' autobiography, and that's what gives the set the title, the set would have an appropriate moniker even if Jones hadn't put his life story to paper. That's because this box set really does tell his story, partially because its four discs are divided so cleanly. The first is Jumpin' in the Woodshed, devoted to Quincy Jones the jazzman, featuring sessions that he led and mostly sessions where he was a sideman. The second is Gone Hollywood, meaning that it contains selections of his work for motion pictures and television, including his productions for other artists (Ray Charles' "In the Heat of the Night," Diana Ross and Michael Jackson's "Ease on Down the Road") and songs he cut that later were popularized in movies ("Soul Bossa Nova," otherwise known as the theme to *Austin Powers*). The third is Hit Man, which is devoted to his productions and arrangements for other artists, including Michael Jackson, Frank Sinatra, George Benson, James Ingram, the Brothers Johnson, and Paul Simon. Finally, there's "The Dude Throws Down," consisting entirely of selections from his star-studded collaborations of the late '80s and '90s. That final volume may accurately represent the final chapter of his career, but apart from the great urban ballad "One Hundred Ways," it's pretty dull, illustrating why these meticulous studio concoctions of Jones are misconceived; but the other discs are pretty terrific, not just capturing the essence of his work in each style, but drawing connections where you might not think connections exist—especially on Hit Man, as Lesley Gore's girl group "You Don't Own Me" rubs shoulders with the Brothers Johnson's "Stomp!," and it's possible to hear Quincy's work on both. This may not be a set that you'd put on a whole lot, even if the first three discs work expertly as collections spotlighting Jones' various strengths, but this set couldn't have told Quincy Jones' story better, and it's worthy of being called a musical biography. *—Stephen Thomas Erlewine*

● **Ultimate Collection** / Apr. 16, 2002 / Hip-O ✦✦✦✦✦

In 1974, Quincy Jones, who already had a wide range of musical credits behind him, opted to enter the R&B mainstream by hiring vocalists and overseeing recordings in a commercial vein released under his name. The first of them was *Body Heat*, which went gold, and Jones followed with a series of records including 1981's million-selling *The Dude* and the 1990 Album of the Year Grammy-winner *Back on the Block*. Meanwhile, he switched record labels, leaving A&M for his own Warner-distributed Qwest in the early '80s. That has tended to make the assembly of a comprehensive best-of difficult, but Universal's Hip-O reissue division specializes in licensing material from other labels to construct its *Ultimate Collection* releases, and this one borrows seven out of 18 tracks from Qwest to add to Jones' A&M hits, making it the definitive one-disc compilation of Jones' pop/R&B recordings of 1974-1999. Jones himself participated in the selection, which does not strictly follow chart rankings, since a couple of R&B Top 20 hits ("I Don't Go for That" and "Slow Jams") are missing, while a few non-chart items are included. To get more songs in, the singles edits have been used in many cases. But all the major hits are here. The chronological sequencing allows an appreciation of how Jones' approach changed over the years. The '70s stuff, which holds up surprisingly well, is tasty R&B, much of it groove-oriented, uptempo music. By the late '80s, however, there are a lot of big, bland ballads that showcase superstar vocalists (Ray Charles, Barry White, etc.) and sound self-important. Like his protégé, Michael Jackson, who went from the rocking "Billie Jean" to the messianic "Man in the Mirror" in the same period, Jones seems to have begun believing his press clippings, and his work suffered accordingly. *—William Ruhlmann*

Sharon Jones

b. 1958, Augusta, GA

Vocals / Neo-Soul, Contemporary R&B, Deep Funk Revival

Although singer Sharon Jones first began attracting attention during the late '90s, her smoky, soulful voice and blistering grooves harked back three decades earlier to the heyday of funk, evoking the music of James Brown protégées like Marva Whitney and Lynn Collins with uncanny precision; not surprising, given that the veteran Jones was well into her 40s by the time she began earning wide recognition. Born in 1956 in Brown's own hometown of Augusta, GA, Jones spent her childhood shuttling between the South and New York City, where she attended school. She honed her talents singing in the church choir, and from the age of 14 onward played the organ at Queens' Universal Church of God each Sunday, a tradition she continued even after her recording career took off years later.

For years a sought-after session vocalist who headlined a number of dance records under the alias Miss Lafaye, Jones finally garnered notice from the dusties crowd upon signing to New York retro-funk label Desco, issuing a series of underground funk favorites including "Damn It's Hot," "Switchblade," "The Landlord," "You Better Think Twice" and a version of the J.B.'s "I Got the Feelin'." After Desco dissolved in 2001, Jones christened the new Daptone label with the single "Got a Thing on My Mind"; backed by the company's house band, the Dap-Kings—bassist/bandleader Bosco "Bass" Mann, drummer Homer "Funky-Foot" Jenkins, guitarist Binky Griptite, conga player Bugaloo Velez, trumpeter Anda "Goodfoot" Watkins, organist Earl Maxton, tenor saxophonist Otis Youngblood, and baritone saxophonist Jack Zapata—she released her full-length debut, *Dap-Dappin' With Sharon Jones & the Dap-Kings*, in the spring of 2002. *—Jason Ankeny*

● **Dap Dippin' With Sharon Jones & the Dap-Kings** / 2002 / Daptone ✦✦✦✦

It's hard to believe that Sharon Jones' debut LP is a product of the year 2002, for several reasons. Given the excellent singles she recorded for Desco beginning in the late '90s, it seems like she would have gotten the opportunity for a full-length sooner; plus, her brand of raw, heavy, hard-driving funk is such a throwback to the '70s, and she pulls it off so well, that you wonder how she could have escaped that decade without at least a few rare, classic 45s (in the vein of labelmate Lee Fields). It's *not* hard to believe she once made her living as a prison guard, based on the tough-as-nails, no-nonsense performances she belts out on *Dap Dippin' With Sharon Jones & the Dap-Kings*, the first full-length release on Desco's descendant, Daptone. Backed by the Daptone house band (a conglomeration of studio pros with connections reaching back to the Desco orbit), Jones delivers a storming set of tunes that would have sounded perfectly at home on the *James Brown's Original Funky Divas* compilation. The style and quality are pretty consistent all the way through, but it's hard not to single out the nearly unrecognizable cover of Janet Jackson's "What Have You Done for Me Lately," which is transformed into a churning blast of funk full of biting guitars (and nary a synth or drum machine in sight). Other highlights include the chunky leadoff track, "Got a Thing on My Mind," the would-be dance-craze "The Dap Dip," the slow-burning "Make It Good to Me," and the trials-and-tribulations tale "Ain't It Hard." Plus, label head Gabriel Roth throws in his usual "authentic" trappings—the fake live introduction running down Jones' "hits," the intentionally dated copy on the back cover—that make the whole package even more fun. All in all, a terrific debut. *—Steve Huey*

Shirley Jones

b. Detroit, MI

Vocals / Urban, Inspirational

Singer Shirley Jones of the Philly soul vocal group the Jones Girls was born into a singing family. The Detroit native's mother, Mary Francis Jones, was one of RCA Records' first gospel artists. Jones and her middle sister Brenda sang with their mother and were later joined by younger sister Valerie.

During their teenage years, the sisters turned to secular music. Hooking up with manager Dick Scott, they began opening for acts such as fellow Detroiters the Four Tops, Little Richard, and others who would play in Detroit. Becoming the Jones Girls, the group secured recording deals with Paramount Records, then Curtis Mayfield's Curtom Records. In 1976, they began to tour as background singers for Diana Ross, who gave them a brief interlude where they would sing "If I Ever Lose This Heaven," a song popularized by Quincy Jones. Kenneth Gamble of Philadelphia International Records and singer Patti LaBelle were in the audience during a Philadelphia performance, and after the show, Ross introduced them to the Jones Girls; the group signed with Philadelphia International in early 1979.

Their first Philadelphia International album, *The Jones Girls*, included the R&B/soul Top 20 hit "You Gonna Make Me Love Somebody Else," which has been rapped over numerous times. (A single from the album, "Who Can I Run To," was a hit cover for Xscape in 1995.) The group can be heard doing background vocals on various records throughout the Philadelphia International catalog as well as on releases by Leon Haywood, Michael Pedicin Jr., and others. Other Jones Girls albums on Philadelphia International were *At Peace With Woman* and *Get as Much Love as You Can*.

The group left Philadelphia International for RCA Records and released one LP: *On Target*. In 1984, Philadelphia International released an album of the group's unreleased tracks called *Keep It Comin'*. Soon after, the Jones Girls disbanded; Brenda got married and Valerie went to college. Gamble, hearing about the breakup, called Shirley to see if she was interested in becoming a solo act. Soon, she was back at Philadelphia Records working on her solo debut album. While working on a track with Dexter Wansel, Shirley convinced Bunny Sigler to let her record "Do You Get Enough Love," which was intended for the O'Jays. The song featured Sigler on piano, bass, and background vocals; former Instant Funk hornman Larry Davis on guitar; and drum programming and arranger Jack Faith on flute and horn. It went to number one on the R&B charts for two weeks in August 1986. An album called *Always in the Mood* was issued and included several follow-ups, including Wansel's "Last Night I Need Somebody" and Sigler's bossa nova-ish "Breaking Up." Around the time the album was made, Jones met and married Harold Hubbard of the Harlem Globetrotters. *—Ed Hogan*

● **Always in the Mood** / Jul. 1986 / Philadelphia International ✦✦✦

After the Jones Girls broke up, Kenneth Gamble (their former producer at Philadelphia Intl.) invited lead singer Shirley Jones back to the fold for her solo debut. Though it hasn't worn its mid-'80s vintage very well, *Always in the Mood* was a solid collection of performances that pushed one song, "Do You Get Enough Love," into the top spot on the R&B charts. Boasting the songwriting/production talents of Gamble & Huff, Bunny Sigler, Dexter Wansel, and Instant Funk's Larry Davis, the album sounded at least as good as the last few Jones Girls full-lengths, and Jones didn't sound as though she missed her sisters. Highlights include the uptempo dance track "We Can Work It Out," the classic Philly groove of the title track, and a couple of solid ballads including "Do You Get Enough Love" and "Last Night I Needed Somebody." *—John Bush*

Louis Jordan

b. Jul. 8, 1908, Brinkley, AR, **d.** Feb. 4, 1975, Los Angeles, CA

Vocals, Sax (Alto), Leader / East Coast Blues, Jump Blues, Swing, Urban Blues

Effervescent saxophonist Louis Jordan was one of the chief architects and prime progenitors of the R&B idiom. His pioneering use of jumping shuffle rhythms in a small combo context was copied far and wide during the 1940s. Jordan's sensational hit-laden run with Decca Records contained a raft of seminal performances, featuring inevitably infectious backing by his band, the Tympany Five, and Jordan's own searing alto sax and street corner jive-loaded sense of humor. Jordan was one of the first black entertainers to sell appreciably in the pop sector; his Decca duet mates included Bing Crosby, Louis Armstrong, and Ella Fitzgerald.

The son of a musician, Jordan spent time as a youth with the Rabbit Foot Minstrels and majored in music later on at Arkansas Baptist College. After moving with his family to Philadelphia in 1932, Jordan hooked up with pianist Clarence Williams. He joined the orchestra of drummer Chick Webb in 1936 and remained there until 1938. Having polished up his singing abilities with Webb's outfit, Jordan was ready to strike out on his own. The saxist's first 78 for Decca in 1938, "Honey in the Bee Ball," billed his combo as the Elks Rendezvous Band (after the Harlem nightspot that he frequently played at). From 1939 on, though, Jordan fronted the Tympany Five, a sturdy little aggregation often expanding over quintet status that featured some well-known musicians over the years: pianists Wild Bill Davis and Bill Doggett, guitarists Carl Hogan and Bill Jennings, bassist Dallas Bartley, and drummer Chris Columbus all passed through the ranks.

From 1942 to 1951, Jordan scored an astonishing 57 R&B chart hits (all on Decca), beginning with the humorous blues "I'm Gonna Leave You on the Outskirts of Town" and finishing with "Weak Minded Blues." In between, he drew up what amounted to an easily followed blueprint for the development of R&B (and for that matter, rock & roll—the accessibly swinging shuffles of Bill Haley & the Comets were directly descended from Jordan; Haley often pointed to his Decca labelmate as profoundly influencing his approach). "G.I. Jive," "Caldonia," "Buzz Me," "Choo Choo Ch' Boogie," "Ain't That Just like a Woman," "Ain't Nobody Here but Us Chickens," "Boogie Woogie Blue Plate," "Beans and Cornbread," "Saturday Night Fish Fry," and "Blue Light Boogie"—every one of those classics topped the R&B lists, and there were plenty more that did precisely the same thing. Black audiences coast-to-coast were breathlessly jitterbugging to Jordan's jumping jive (and one suspects, more than a few whites kicked up their heels to those same platters as well).

The saxist was particularly popular during World War II. He recorded prolifically for the Armed Forces Radio Service and the V-Disc program. Jordan's massive popularity also translated onto the silver screen—he filmed a series of wonderful short musicals during the late '40s that were decidedly short on plot but long on visual versions of his hits (*Caldonia*, *Reet Petite & Gone*, *Look Out Sister*, and *Beware*, along with countless soundies) that give us an enlightening peek at just what made him such a beloved entertainer. Jordan also cameoed in a big-budget Hollywood wartime musical, *Follow the Boys*. A brief attempt at fronting a big band in 1951 proved an ill-fated venture, but it didn't dim his ebullience. In 1952, tongue firmly planted in cheek, he offered himself as a candidate for the highest office in the land on the amusing Decca outing "Jordan for President."

Even though his singles were still eminently solid, they weren't selling like they used to by 1954. So after an incredible run of more than a decade-and-a-half, Jordan moved over to the Mesner brothers' Los Angeles-based Aladdin logo at the start of the year. Alas, time had passed the great pioneer by—"Dad Gum Ya Hide Boy," "Messy Bessy," "If I Had Any Sense," and the rest of his Aladdin output sounds great in retrospect, but it wasn't what young R&B fans were searching for at the time. In 1955, he switched to RCA's short-lived "X" imprint, where he tried to remain up-to-date by issuing "Rock 'N' Roll Call."

A blistering Quincy Jones-arranged date for Mercury in 1956 deftly updated Jordan's classics for the rock & roll crowd, with hellfire renditions of "Let the Good Times Roll," "Salt Pork, West Virginia," and "Beware" benefiting from the blasting lead guitar of Mickey Baker and Sam "The Man" Taylor's muscular tenor sax. There was even time to indulge in a little torrid jazz at Mercury; "The JAMF," from a 1957 LP called *Man, We're Wailin'*, was a sizzling indication of what a fine saxist Jordan was.

Ray Charles had long cited Jordan as a primary influence (he lovingly covered Jordan's "Don't Let the Sun Catch You Crying" and "Early in the Morning"), and paid him back by signing Jordan to the Genius' Tangerine label. Once again, the fickle public largely ignored his worthwhile 1962-64 offerings. Lounge gigs still offered the saxman a steady income, though, and he adjusted his on-stage playlist accordingly. A 1973 album for the French Black & Blue logo found Jordan covering Mac Davis' "I Believe in Music" (can't get much loungier than that!). A heart attack silenced this visionary in 1975, but not before he acted as the bridge between the big-band era and the rise of R&B.

His profile continues to rise posthumously, in large part due to the recent acclaimed Broadway musical *Five Guys Named Moe*, based on Jordan's bubbly, romping repertoire and charismatic persona. *—Bill Dahl*

★ **The Best of Louis Jordan** / 1977 / MCA ✦✦✦✦✦

This is a best-of CD collection that actually lives up to its name. Virtually all of Louis Jordan's hits, which musically bridged the gap between small-group swing, R&B, and rock & roll, are on this single CD, including "Choo Choo Ch'Boogie," "Let the Good Times Roll," "Ain't Nobody Here But Us Chickens," "Saturday Night Fish Fry," "Caldonia," "Five Guys Named Moe," and "Don't Let the Sun Catch You Crying." Serious collectors will want to explore a more complete series, particularly the one put out by Classics, but for a single acquisition, this is the Louis Jordan set to get. Jordan's very likable and good-humored vocals and his hot alto, as well as the playing of the Tympany Five, belong in everyone's music collection. *—Scott Yanow*

☆ **Let the Good Times Roll: The Complete Decca Recordings 1938–54** / 1992 / Bear Family ✦✦✦✦✦
The price of this multi-disc import box set is indeed a hefty one, but it contains every track the pioneering saxman waxed for Decca—the multitude of hits that inexorably influenced the future of R&B and eventually rock & roll. Bear Family's attention to detail in its presentation is always immaculate, and the sound quality follows suit. —*Bill Dahl*

☆ **Let the Good Times Roll: Anthology 1938–1953** / Feb. 23, 1999 / MCA ✦✦✦✦✦
Overlooking Bear Family's comprehensive nine-disc box, this double-CD set is the best reissue ever on Louis Jordan, and the first truly comprehensive domestic release on Jordan's work to feature state-of-the-art sound. There are holes—only a relative handful of the tracks that Jordan & the Tympany Five recorded in 1939 and 1940 are included, although those that are here represent most of the best of them—but not huge ones, and every major Jordan track from 15 years of work is present. The quality of the digital transfers is as alluring than the selection, the mastering so clean, that it sounds 20 years newer than one could ever expect any of it to, based on their actual ages. The 1941 vintage "Pan Pan" and "Saxa-Woogie" place the band practically in the listener's lap, with solos on clarinet, tenor sax, etc., that have smooth, rippling textures and barely a trace of the noise one should expect from early '40s tracks bumped to digital—and the fidelity of these, and "Boogie Woogie Came to Town," "Rusty Dusty Blues," etc., all run circles around any earlier reissues. Similarly, the drums, high-hat, trumpet, sax and ensemble singing on "Five Guys Named Moe" are crisp enough to pass for modern re-records, except they're not. Indeed, until you get to "Ration Blues," from 1943, there aren't many overt hints of the compression inherent masters of this vintage, and that's the exception—"G.I. Jive" and "Caldonia," cut one and two years later, have the kind of sound textures one more expects out of audiophile releases. Disc two opens with "Ain't That Just Like a Woman," a perfect blueprint in style and execution (check out Carl Hogan's guitar intro) for the sound that Chuck Berry popularized ten years later. Of the later material, only "Run Joe" sounds a little less distinct than the rest. "Life Is So Peculiar" features Louis Armstrong, as vocalist with Jordan, in a beguilingly funny duet from 1951. By that time, Jordan's formula for success was past its prime, and he and Decca records were looking for new approaches—"Teardrops from My Eyes" wasn't it, adding an obtrusive organ played by Wild Bill Davis to the mix. The later incarnation of Jordan's band on these tracks is a more restrained and sophisticated big-band unit, without much of the wild jump-blues feel of the '40s Tympany Five—a 19-year-old Oliver Nelson can be heard on alto sax, incidentally—but occasionally they capture the feel of the old band, as on "Fat Sam from Birmingham." This version of the band and the way they're recorded are still superior to the incarnations of Jordan's group that turn up on his later recordings for Aladdin and Mercury. —*Bruce Eder*

Montell Jordan

b. Los Angeles, CA
Vocals / Urban, Pop-Rap, Contemporary R&B
Montell Jordan began singing in his hometown of Los Angeles in talent shows, church choirs, and later nightclubs. After graduating from Pepperdine University, he spent seven years looking for a record deal, finally getting an opportunity through Paul Stewart, the president of PMP Records. Jordan and Stewart flew to New York, where Jordan sang for Russell Simmons and was promptly signed to a contract. For his first album, Jordan heavily sampled B.B. King tracks (the first to do so), and took his lyrical inspiration from the more positive side of life in his native South Central L.A. in an attempt to balance the negative pictures coming out of most SoCal gangsta rap. Jordan was rewarded with a massive number-one smash in the party anthem "This Is How We Do It," which sold over one million copies; *More to Tell* followed in 1996. Although it didn't match the success of *This Is How We Do It*, it was nevertheless a hit. In the spring of 1998, Jordan released his third album, *Let's Ride*; *Get It On . . . Tonite* followed a year later. —*Steve Huey*

● **This Is How We Do It** / 1995 / PMP/RAL ✦✦✦✦
Montell Jordan was blessed with a strong set of producers for his debut album, *This Is How We Do It*. Working with material that is essentially sub-par, the production team turns in a seamless performances, creating hooks and melodies from the deep bass and beats. Jordan's skills as a rapper are fine—he does nothing particularly noteworthy, yet he certainly does not ruin the tracks. It was just the sort of competent R&B that hits the chart, and it did hit the charts, becoming a number one R&B album. —*Stephen Thomas Erlewine*

More to Tell / Aug. 27, 1996 / Def Jam ✦✦✦
Montell Jordan's second album *More to Tell* unfortunately doesn't quite live up to the promise of its title, despite a handful of excellent tracks. Jordan hasn't backed away from the hip-hop soul that brought *This Is How We Do It* to the top of the charts, and he delivers it as well as he did his first time around, but he just doesn't have as many strong songs as he did the last time out. "Falling" is an entrancing ballad and "Bounce Ta This" is a good uptempo cut, yet they aren't enough to maintain interest over the course of the entire album. —*Leo Stanley*

Let's Ride / Mar. 31, 1998 / Def Jam ✦✦✦
When a debut single is as strong as Montell Jordan's "This Is How We Do It," it's hard to ever match or exceed the single's reputation—or at least, the perception that the single was the peak of the artist's career. As his third album, *Let's Ride*, proves, he has more to offer than just "This Is How We Do It," but it's still hard to shake that song from your head while listening to the album. The main problem is that, despite his sultry voice, Jordan has yet to establish a clear identity for himself and his material tends to have even less character. There are moments on *Let's Ride* that are quite enjoyable—after all, Jordan has a knack for classy, seductive contemporary grooves—but it never adds up to much of anything. Few of the songs make a lasting impression outside the title track, and the album essentially follows the same formula as his first two records, but with diminishing returns. There are enough good grooves to make it interesting to fans, but *Let's Ride* suggests that Jordan will have to learn a few new tricks soon if he wants to keep cruising. —*Leo Stanley*

Get It On . . . Tonite / Oct. 26, 1999 / Def Jam ✦✦✦
Montell Jordan's fourth album *Get It On . . . Tonite* is a mixed bag of intelligently written songs and overbearing clichés. Jordan established himself in the mid-'90s as a surprisingly consistent R&B star with several successful albums, each featuring at least one major hit single. He also established himself as a top-notch songwriter, especially after penning Deborah Cox's unforgettable monster smash "Nobody's Supposed to Be Here." Those reasons make it all the more frustrating when, on his fourth album, Jordan relies so heavily on R&B lover-man clichés, with tired "between the sheets" lyrics such as "your body layin' next to mine," "scream and moan," and "kisses down below" permeating way too much of his music ("Can't Get Enough" is beyond tacky). The album, which is divided into two halves (the first being "for those who like it fast," the second being "for those who need it slow"), does include several great tracks, including the irresistible lead-off single "Get It On . . . Tonite" (the single version featured LL Cool J, while the album version is just Jordan), the wonderful story song "Once Upon a Time" (which is also included as a surprisingly well-pronounced Spanish-language bonus track), the fun and funky disco party jam "Come Home," and the Latin/Asian influenced "Maybe She Will." Jordan also employs plenty of female vocalists (à la Luther Vandross) to incredibly pleasing results, and there's no denying his talent in crafting a catchy pop song. If Jordan would lay off the clichés, and concentrate on well-written songs like "Once Upon a Time" then the sky is the limit, but his overbearing reliance on tired lothario lyrics is frustrating for those listeners who are well aware of his potential. As a final note, Jordan includes an adequate cover of Phil Collins' 1984 hit "Against All Odds." —*Jose F. Promis*

Montell Jordan / Feb. 26, 2002 / Def Soul ✦✦✦✦

Margie Joseph

b. 1950, Pascagoula, MS
Vocals / Urban, Soul
A talented journeywoman soul singer who had ten modest-to-tiny R&B hits in the '70s, Joseph's style was often compared to Aretha Franklin's, though frankly the similarity is not overwhelming. Perhaps a midpoint between Franklin and Roberta Flack would be more appropriate; Joseph had a much softer delivery than Franklin, and lacked Franklin's gospel-ish firepower. After a few recordings for Volt in the late '60s and early '70s (including the small R&B hits "Your Sweet Loving" and "Stop! In the Name of Love"), Joseph moved to Atlantic in 1972, where she recorded for the next few years under the supervision of Arif Mardin. During this period, she had modest success with easygoing soul-pop singles, reaching the R&B Top Ten with a cover of Wings' "My Love."

Moving around to different studios and producers (including Lamont Dozier) over the course of the rest of the '70s, she made the R&B Top 20 with "What's Come Over Me" (a duet with Blue Magic) and "Hear the Words, Feel the Feeling," but never really established a strong identity, though her material was pleasant enough. She recorded through the late '80s and remained an active performer; the dance-flavored "Ready for the Night" was a small R&B hit in 1984. —*Richie Unterberger*

Margie Joseph Makes a New Impression / 1971 / Volt ✦✦✦✦
This is Margie Joseph's most successful and aesthetically pleasing album. It was written and produced by Fred Briggs (aka Coldwater Stone) and Daryl Carter and is a mixture of Stax and city slick R&B sounds; "Punish Me," "Sweeter Tomorrow," and "Temptation's About to Take Your Love" are prime examples. A remake lifts this LP above the average mark; Briggs and Carter transform the Supremes' "Stop! In the Name of Love" into an awesome deep soul classic. Beginning with a monologue titled "Women Talk," Joseph talks to her soon-to-be-gone man about his carousing before preceding into a lengthy Isaac Hayes-type arrangement that composers Holland, Dozier & Holland probably never envisioned. Margie's version is compelling and gripping. This album's number-67 chart position suggests it must have caught on with quite a few record buyers. —*Andrew Hamilton*

Phase II / 1972 / Volt ✦✦✦

Margie Joseph / 1973 / Atlantic ✦✦✦
Margie Joseph was never a huge name in soul—she never became as famous as Aretha Franklin, Gladys Knight, Chaka Khan, or Tina Turner. But she is a talented, charming singer with a recognizable delivery; although greatly influenced by Franklin, Joseph has a softer, more girlish delivery. Unfortunately, she has rarely enjoyed the sort of promotion she deserves—not at Stax, not at Atlantic. Joseph moved from Stax to Atlantic in 1972, recording this self-titled LP the following year. Produced by Arif Mardin, *Margie Joseph* offers an enjoyable mix of Northern and Southern soul styles. Much of the album is devoted to covers, and the songs that Joseph embraces range from Ellington Jordan's "I'd Rather Go Blind" and Al Green's "Let's Stay Together" to Brook Benton's "I'll Take Care of You." Joseph also picks a Dolly Parton song, putting a soul spin on "Touch Your Woman." Some people might be surprised to learn that Joseph recorded a tune by a country star, but then, a lot of country was very pop-minded in the early '70s. And besides, Parton is very much a crossover artist, not a hardcore honky-tonker à la Kitty Wells. This decent, if imperfect, LP has been out of print since the 1970s, but it's worth obtaining if you can track down a copy. —*Alex Henderson*

Sweet Surrender / 1974 / Atlantic ✦✦✦
After a three-year hiatus Margie Joseph surfaced on Atlantic Records smoother and more homogenized than she was at Stax Records. Her vocal style is similar to ex-labelmate Carla Thomas' without the nasal sound. "Come Lay Some Lovin' on Me" is a sweet soul strutter song in Joseph's most enticing voice. What man could resist her request? Remakes of Wings' "My Love," and Breads' "Baby I'm-A-Want You," are stunners. Joseph never oversings, or become hysterical. "Sweet Surrender" rivals the starkness of her Stax sides vocally but the trappings are fancier. The songs are good, but like at Stax, the

promotion for Margie's product wasn't the best. Quality songs like "(Strange) I Still Love You," written by Jerry Butler, Norman Harris, and Mikki Farrow, had flava but Atlantic failed to deliver. *—Andrew Hamilton*

Margie / 1975 / Atlantic ♦♦♦

In 1975, Margie Joseph enjoyed one of her greatest triumphs when she teamed up with Blue Magic for a spectacular remake of the Philadelphia soul ballad "What's Come Over Me." That hit, which Blue Magic originally recorded in 1974, was included on the group's third LP, *13 Blue Magic Lane*, but it wasn't included on Joseph's own 1975 LP, *Margie.* Unfortunately for Joseph, the success of the "What's Come Over Me" remake did little to help this modest-selling album—some R&B experts felt that Atlantic really blew it by not including that gem on *Margie.* But while *Margie* didn't do nearly as well as it should have, it's solid and pleasing. With Arif Mardin serving as producer/arranger, Joseph generally has strong material to work with—and that includes a few Carole King tunes ("Believe in Humanity" and "After All This Time"), as well as Bill Withers' bluesy "The Same Love That Made Me Laugh." Equally respectable are two songs that Joseph co-wrote with Mardin: the funky "Sign of the Times" and the lush "Stay Still" (which has so much quiet storm appeal that it was an obvious choice when saxman Ronnie Laws recorded his *Fever* album in 1976). Although *Margie* falls short of perfect, it is one of the singer's more consistent Atlantic dates and deserved a lot more attention than it received. *—Alex Henderson*

Hear the Words, Feel the Feeling / 1976 / Cotillion ♦♦♦

Joseph, an often-underrated singer, first reached success on Volt Records. At the time of this release she was best known for her time with Atlantic Records. Her early- to mid-'70s efforts were produced by Arif Mardin in a style identified with Aretha Franklin's productions of the time. *Hear the Words, Feel the Feeling* represents a label switch and a more definitive direction, courtesy of famed producer/writer Lamont Dozier. Those expecting a Motown-styled update of the girl group blithe attitude won't find it here. What is here is Joseph asserting her own pragmatic personality, doing rawer vocals and having great chemistry with producer Dozier. *Hear the Words, Feel the Feeling* often takes an almost too realistic look at relationships and the lack thereof. All of this is made better by Dozier's strong and confident production. The taunting "Didn't I Tell You" and "Why'd You Lie" mine the same problematic love terrain, with the production polish only matched by Joseph's emotive and pointed vocals. The album's best track, "Prophecy," has Joseph and Dozier again examining bleak interiors. The brilliantly arranged track has great subtle horn arrangement and impeccable rhythm guitar. *Hear the Words, Feel the Feeling* also has a fair amount of ballads. "All Cried Out" and "Feeling My Way" are hooky and idiosyncratic, as Joseph gives emotive and cogent performances. This album is prime and classy R&B/pop and features such esteemed players as Ray Parker Jr. and Lee Ritenour, as well as arrangers McKinley Jackson and David Blumberg. But the star is Joseph, and she does great work here. *—Jason Elias*

● **The Atlantic Sessions: The Best of Margie Joseph** / 1994 / Ichiban/Soul Classics ♦♦♦♦♦

Here are all eleven of her R&B chart singles from 1972 through 1984, as well as three album tracks from her early Atlantic days. Decent if unremarkable '70s soul with a sweet pop flavor. *—Richie Unterberger*

Margie Joseph Makes a New Impression/Phase II / Oct. 26, 1999 / Stax ♦♦♦♦♦

Juicy

f. North Carolina

Group / Urban

Juicy was the brother and sister duo of Jerry and Katreese Barnes who had a Top 20 R&B hit with "Sugar Free." After having releases on Arista—*Love's a Merry-Go-Round* (early 1983)—and Atlantic—*Beat Street Strut* from the movie *Beat Street* (summer 1984)—they signed with CBS-distributed Private I Records. After the singles—"Bad Boy," It Takes Two—Juicy finally hit the big time with "Sugar Free." "Sugar Free" sounded a lot like Mtume's number-one R&B gold single "Juicy Fruit." It all added up to sweet success for the Barnes', as "Sugar Free" went to number-13 R&B in early 1986. The duo had one other charting single, "Nobody but You, which hit number-59 R&B in spring of 1986 on the CBS associated label. Juicy had two charting LPs, *Juicy* (spring 1983) on Arista and *It Takes Two* (spring 1986) on Private I. *—Ed Hogan*

Juicy / 1983 / Arista ♦♦♦

● **It Takes Two** / 1986 / Private I ♦♦♦

Jerry and Katreese Barnes' second album as Juicy has a handful of spectacular songs that exemplify the heavily synthesized mid-'80s R&B sound. Though "Sugar Free," a not-so-distant descendent of Mtume's "Juicy Fruit," was the only one to put a truly significant dent on the chart, the album is rather solid from front to back. Each of the eight songs is directed at a "you," with Katreese's vocal turns coming out ahead of her brother's. Eumir Deodato's sensitive production is bright and pliable, full of echoe machine beats, zipping synthesizers, and all sorts of sparkly effects. *It Takes Two* only falters during those brief moments that are interrupted by heavy rock guitars. *—Andy Kellman*

Don Julian & the Meadowlarks

f. 1953, db. 1998

Group / Doo Wop, R&B

Don Julian & the Meadowlarks' biggest hits were the L.A.-area hit "Please (Say You Love Me)" and "The Jerk" for John Dolphin's Money label, which came not only with dance steps of its own, but Julian's encouraging lyrical instructions. Unlike many teenagers, Julian grew up in a non-musical family, and didn't sing in the church choir or have any formal vocal training to speak of. He was a high-school track star, and it was during school that he met up with the first group of Meadowlark singers: Randolph Jones (later a member of both the Penguins and the Coasters), Earl Jones, Ronald Barrett, and Billy Pruett. The group's lineup changed numerous times over the years, however, with Julian being the only constant member. Around 1952, the foursome formed a vocal group, originally calling themselves the Soulinaires, but they later decided that the name was too "church-sounding" and changed it to the Meadowlarks, this at a time when many of the popular vocal groups of the day had "bird" names.

Cornel Gunter of the Flairs (and later one of the Coasters) introduced the group to Modern Records' Bihari brothers in 1957, who subsequently released two singles on their RPM subsidiary. Despite the fact that Maxwell Davis, Modern's legendary producer, was working with the group and writing all of their vocal arrangements, Julian felt the label wasn't promoting them and he began looking for a new label.

After auditioning for Dootone label owner "Dootsie" Williams, the Meadowlarks earned a recording contract; Julian also ended up working for Dootone as a shipping clerk and learned even more about the record business. In early 1954, the success of Don Julian & the Meadowlarks' first single "Heaven and Paradise"—while the group was still in high school—changed their lives forever. The song became a hit with R&B fans and the burgeoning Mexican-American audience. In all, the Meadowlarks issued five more Dootone singles before Julian and the group left the label in 1957. They moved over to DJ Art Laboe's Original Sound label briefly; their first single, "Please (Say You Love Me)" did well locally. Julian also recorded "Slauson Shuffle" for DJ Rudy Harvey's Dynamite label before eventually ending up with a Central Avenue legend named John Dolphin, a local mini-mogul who had nearly every facet of the record business covered.

Dolphin operated a group of record stores—each was named Dolphin's of Hollywood (despite the fact that the main store, and the first to use the name, was actually located on East Vernon Ave., near the corner of Central Avenue). Dolphin also owned his own radio station, KRKD, which broadcast late-night programs from the store's shop window, and he ran several small "black" record labels, a few with appropriately inspired names revealing Dolphin's penchant for making money above all else: Cash, Money, Lucky, and Recorded in Hollywood Records (which they weren't!).

Three months after leaving Dynamite, Julian's single "The Jerk" was released on Money. It was the first to be credited to the Larks (not to be confused with other groups who also used the name, including Eugene Mumford's Larks). By now, the Larks' new lineup featured Ted Walters (who had been friends with Julian since the two graduated from high school), Charlie Morris and Julian. They continued touring and recording; Money also released an album by the group. Julian continued to stay with the label through the '60s and into the early '70s. Don Julian went on to cut albums for several additional labels, including Amazon and Magnum, and for his own label, called (appropriately enough) Jerk Records. He and the Larks also recorded the soundtrack to the 1973 blaxploitation film *Shorty the Pimp*, but the movie was never released and the soundtrack foundered as well (it was finally issued in the '90s). He passed away in 1998. *—Bryan Thomas*

Savage! Super Soul Soundtrack / 1973 / Money ♦♦♦♦

Savage! Super Soul Soundtrack finds Don Julian abandoning his doo wop roots with the Larks to construct a score for this limited-run cult blaxploitation release. While one could easily assume he was emulating the career moves of several other successful R&B producers (Isaac Hayes, Curtis Mayfield, and Willie Hutch had already started to make a name for themselves scoring blaxploitation films), Julian was taking a more traditional approach to scoring than his colleagues. *Savage!* most definitely finds its strength in small segues and incidentals, rather than properly arranged songs. However, this should not deter you from listening by any means. There's an art in gaining maximum impact from a minimal amount of instruments and timbres, and Julian does it effortlessly. *—Rob Theakston*

Golden Classics / Apr. 20, 1990 / Collectables ♦♦♦♦♦

This 12-track reissue of this West Coast vocal group's best sides for the Dootone label is a mixed blessing. You don't get much for your dough with this cheesy budget reissue: a black and white publicity photo on the front cover, and no liner notes, publishing or recording information—all typical of early cheap Collectables packaging. To compound matters, some of the masters are pulled from scratchy records with no audio cleanup applied, actually distorting a bit on some of the selections. But the music and the performances are top-notch doo wop with that decided West Coast edge that outweighs all audio concerns and lack of proper documentation. Bottom line: If you're a fan of this kind of sound, it's still worth picking up. *—Cub Koda*

Shorty the Pimp / Oct. 27, 1998 / Southbound ♦♦♦

Shorty the Pimp was to have been a blaxploitation movie around 1973, but was never released due to various problems; supposedly, only one rough cut of the movie now exists, rumored to be in the hands of director Quentin Tarantino. This is the soundtrack album that would have accompanied the project, performed by journeyman Los Angeles soul band Don Julian & the Larks. The soundtrack was canceled along with the film, though most of this made it onto official releases (usually on the Money label). Released or not, this is damn rare stuff, and aside from its appeal for blaxploitation collectors, it's pretty respectable early-'70s soul-funk on its own merits. Although this is heavily derivative of *Superfly*-era Curtis Mayfield (there's even a parody called "Super Slick") and "Papa Was a Rolling Stone"-era Temptations in its marriage of accomplished harmonies, intricate guitar and horn arrangements, and street-smart lyrics, it's well executed. On "Brother What It Is," they get into some Rahsaan Roland Kirk-like flute and jazzy grooves, while "Just Tryin' to Make It, Pts. 1 & 2" is a slow-burn instrumental reminiscent of Booker T. & the MG's doing "Summertime"; "I Love You" is a beautiful minor-key soul ballad with a cha cha feel. There are also covers of chart hits by Marvin Gaye, Stevie Wonder, Curtis Mayfield, the Staple Singers, and the like, since Don Julian & the Larks were to have played a lounge band in the movie itself. Some of these are superfluous, but some are more enjoyable than you'd expect; the version of "The Look of Love," for instance, is smooth and spooky. *—Richie Unterberger*

● **The Jerk: The Money Recordings** / Apr. 23, 2002 / Kent ♦♦♦♦♦

Although this compilation is billed to Don Julian & the Larks, in fact 21 of the 26 tracks are credited to the Larks, the group who had the Top Ten 1964 hit "The Jerk" and for whom Julian sang and wrote most of the material. For reasons not explained in the liner notes, two of the cuts are solely billed to Don Julian; two to the Meadowlarks, with whom he had recorded prior to the Larks; and one to Don Julian & the Meadowlarks. Logistical confusion aside, the important thing to know is that all of these recordings were done for the Money label between 1964 and 1967, all feature Julian, and usually they were credited as the work of the Larks. "The Jerk" is a great early soul dance hit, but even if you're head over heels in love with that cut, you might not often be in the mood to hear no less than seven other songs based around the dance called the jerk, as there are on this anthology. Even when the Larks aren't singing about the jerk specifically, they're often doing similar cheerful soul based around a dance, like "Can You Do the Duck" and "The Skate." Within the narrow thematic confines of that approach, the Larks offered pretty solid upbeat soul with a substantial Motown influence, not always specifically derivative of "The Jerk" itself (even when those words prominently featured in the lyrics). Occasionally Julian and his cohorts did step outside the format for anachronistic doo wop-like numbers, some sounding like they might have been outtakes from Julian's previous projects, recorded before 1964. Julian's solo single "What Chance Has a Man" saw him getting into lush soul with strings, and a couple of the later cuts are fair Temptations approximations. And, to cap things off, there's a previously unissued alternate take of the song that is all most people will hear of the Larks, "The Jerk." *—Richie Unterberger*

Junie (Walter Morrison)

Keyboards, Producer, Vocals / Funk

Once described by none other than George Clinton as "the most phenomenal musician on the planet," Walter "Junie" Morrison recorded several albums of his own but made his mark assembling some of the biggest funk extravaganzas of the 1970s and '80s, from the Ohio Players' first number-one R&B hit ("The Funky Worm") to Funkadelic's *One Nation Under a Groove* to Clinton's own *Computer Games*. A multi-instrumentalist, vocalist, songwriter, producer, and arranger, Morrison came from Dayton, OH, and debuted with hometown heroes the Ohio Players on 1971's *Pain* LP. He also appeared on 1973's *Ecstacy* and constructed their 1974 hit "The Funky Worm" (virtually by himself), then gained his own contract with Westbound. Within two years, he'd released three albums: 1975's *When We Do* and *Freeze* were followed by *Suzie Super Groupie* in 1976. Morrison joined the P-Funk machine shortly after, appearing on most of the conglomeration's work from 1978 until 1981. He also recorded LPs for Columbia (1980's *Bread Alone*) and Island (1984's *Evacuate Your Seats*), and was a frequent contributor to Clinton's solo releases and those by the P-Funk All Stars. *—John Bush*

When We Do / 1975 / Westbound ♦♦♦

Freeze / 1975 / Westbound ♦♦♦

Suzie Super Groupie / 1976 / Westbound ♦♦♦

While the out-of-print *The Westbound Years* collection is the best way to hear Junie's mid-'70s work for the Detroit label, this 1976 album offers something of a viable alternative (alas, it has long been deleted, too). Manning most of the instruments himself (beyond solo work, he also worked with the Ohio Players and P-Funk), Junie concocts an enjoyable mix informed by Sly Stone, the Philadelphia International label, and Parliament. He finds his own ground here, though, somewhere between the harder funk of the day and the soul-symphonic work of Gamble & Huff. The only problem is that Junie's not quite up to the task in the vocal department; had the mike work been doled out to others, this might qualify as one of the unsung gems of '70s soul. *—Stephen Cook*

● **The Westbound Years** / 1994 / Westbound ♦♦♦

After leaving the Ohio Players—upon singing to Mercury—and prior to joining Funkadelic for *One Nation Under a Groove*, Junie Morrison recorded a trilogy of albums for Westbound, Funkadelic's original label. A talented arranger, songwriter, singer, and keyboard player, Junie handled everything but the horn and string arrangements on his records—those were done under the supervision of Johnny Trudell and David Van De Pitte (with help from the Detroit Symphony Orchestra string section). This set is compiled from the *When We Do*, *Freeze*, and *Suzie Super Groupie* albums, and also includes the added unreleased track "Junie's Ultimate Departure." In encountering the tunes after so many years, it is amazing to hear the similarities between Junie and Sly Stone—the musicality and tight arrangements, the underlying backbeat funk underlying the in-your-face rhythms, and the place of texture in the melodic construction of any tune. Just check out "Walt's Third Trip" or "Johnny Carson Samba" for examples. His psychedelic chops were plentiful too, as evidenced by the title track of *When We Do*. Lenny Kravitz ripped off this cat's bag wholesale on his album. "Cookies Will Get You" is something Frank Zappa might have written had he any concept of the funk. In all, with the exception of a couple of stinker ballads here that are included only to show Junie's "diversity" (and he couldn't write a ballad for shit), this is a stellar comp. Fans of P-Funk and Sly as well as Rick James' punk funk will be right at home here in the court of the sophisticated but nasty funk. *—Thom Jurek*

Junior

b. London, England

Vocals / Dance-Pop, Urban, Funk

Singer/songwriter Junior sparked the British R&B/pop invasion of the '80s with his classic "Mama Used to Say." Though Sade, Loose Ends, Soul II Soul, and Billy Ocean had more hits, it's worth noting that Junior was a pioneer when he created and presented British-based R&B/pop music to audiences outside the U.K. some ten years earlier. Many of his sides can be found on the 1995 Mercury CD *The Best of Junior*.

Born in London, Junior Giscombe grew up listening to his older brothers' and sisters' record collection, which included the doo wop of the Moonglows, the Dells, early Motown, Otis Redding, and the reggae music of Toots & the Maytals and Bob Marley. Though as a teenager he sang lead in a local band, music more or less remained a hobby until he chose a full-time music career after college in the mid-'70s. His inspiration was Philly soul writers Thom Bell & Linda Creed, Gene McFadden, and John Whitehead. A British independent label released his single, "Hot Up & Heated," but it was Polygram's subsidiary Phonogram that gave him his first major-label opportunity. The label was rewarded when the infectious "Mama Used to Say" became a major American hit in 1982, parked at number-two R&B for two-weeks and number-30 pop. His follow-up to "Mama Used to Say" was the number-eight R&B smash "Too Late" and both were on his *Ji* album. His second album, 1983's *Inside Looking Out*, included "Communication Breakdown" and the popular ballad "Baby I Want You Back."

In 1986, Junior teamed with renowned producer Arif Mardin for *Acquired Taste*, which spawned the singles "Somebody," "Oh Louise" (Top 20 R&B), "Look What You've Done for Me," and the phat, funky "Tonight." One of his tracks, "Unison," appeared on the soundtrack for *About Last Night* and was a huge dance hit. That same year, Junior wrote and recorded "Do You Want My Love" for the multi-platinum soundtrack from the blockbuster Eddie Murphy movie *Beverly Hills Cop*. In 1987, Junior had his biggest European hit, "Another Step," a duet with Kim Wilde and just the first of a string of performances with Wilde. Towards the end of 1987, Junior completed work on his fourth and final album for Polygram, *Sophisticated Street*. The LP yielded the hit "Yes If You Want Me." After a period of self-evaluation, Junior began working with producer Alan Glass, Soul II Soul's Simon Law, Robbie Taylor, and Greg Smith for his 1991 MCA debut album *Stand Strong*. Though it wasn't a commercial success, the album's standout tracks were the title track, the jazzy "Morning Will Come," the gritty "You Can't Have What You Can't Get," and the steppers/boppers favorite, "Stop Fanning the Fire." *—Ed Hogan*

● **Ji** / 1982 / Mercury ♦♦♦♦

Ever since the rise of the Beatles in the early 1960s, England has had no problem giving the United States a serious run for its money in the rock & roll department. There is no getting around the fact that if you excluded British artists from your rock collection, it would be considerably poorer. R&B, however, has always been dominated by the U.S. and probably always will be. But that doesn't mean that England's contributions to R&B haven't been impressive-Hot Chocolate, Lisa Stansfield, Soul II Soul, the Chimes, the Brand New Heavies and Loose Ends are among the Brits who have provided excellent R&B over the years. Another major R&B talent from the U.K. is the charismatic Junior, who showed considerably promise on his debut album of 1982, *Ji*. That year, those who grooved to the singer's inspiring hit "Mama Used to Say" felt that he was destined to become a huge name in R&B-and that single wasn't the only reason for their optimism. The soulster is also quite promising on tracks that range from the melancholy "Too Late" (another single) to the funky "Let Me Know." But regrettably, Junior only had a few hits in the U.S. and didn't become as well known in North America as was in England. Some of the albums that followed *Ji* are also strong; nonetheless, *Ji* remains his most essential release. *—Alex Henderson*

Acquired Taste / 1986 / Mercury ♦♦

The specter of instant success has hounded vocalist Junior Giscombe ever since his debut single "Mama Used to Say" turned him into an immediate sensation on both sides of the Atlantic in the early '80s. He's never been able to duplicate that song, although he's made some serviceable albums, including this mid-'80s release. There were some nice songs; Stevie Wonder appeared on "Do You Really Want My Love," and Dexter Wansel toned down the fusion excesses and provided him with some decent material. But Giscombe remains locked into the "one-hit wonder" syndrome, and will probably have to have a huge album rather than merely successful ones to escape it. *—Ron Wynn*

Sophisticated Street / 1988 / London ♦♦

A nice late-'80s set of urban contemporary tracks with a light dance/pop tinge from Britain's Junior Giscombe. He only got one mild chart hit from it, but Giscombe continued plugging away throughout the '80s, seeking to get another big record and remove the stigma of "fluke" hanging over him. The problem wasn't so much that he lacked talent, but that he never issued a definitive or even significant album that would have demonstrated staying power beyond "Mama Used to Say." Unfortunately, this didn't prove to be the album. *—Ron Wynn*

Stand Strong / 1990 / MCA ♦♦

Junior Giscombe continued into the '90s seeking the elusive substantial album that would finally solidify his credentials. Once more, he failed to achieve it, even though, as usual, his second MCA album had some fine material. But it was both uneven and out-of-the-mainstream in terms of either urban contemporary, dance, or pop material. The title song got some brief airplay, but otherwise the album became another miss in a career that's become a litany of frustration. *—Ron Wynn*

The Best of Junior / 1995 / Mercury ♦♦♦♦

You won't get buyer's remorse after shelling out the coinage for these compelling sounds. This 15-track best-of include 12-inch and 7-inch mixes of Junior's best-known recordings along with some tasty appetizers that are just as contagious. If you can get just one Junior CD, get this one. *—Andrew Hamilton*

K

K-Ci & JoJo

f. 1997

Group / Urban, Hip-Hop, Contemporary R&B

K-Ci & JoJo, a solo project for one of the two brother teams which make up Jodeci, specifically Cedric "K-Ci" and Joel "JoJo" Hailey, followed up their group success with a 1997 album, *Love Always*. Emphasizing lush R&B ballads a bit more than on Jodeci records, the Haileys debuted as K-Ci & JoJo in mid-1996 on 2Pac's single "How Do U Want It," which spent two weeks at number one on the pop charts and sold over two-million copies. Their first solo single was "How Could You," and "You Bring Me Up" hit the Top 40 in August 1997, just before the release of K-Ci & JoJo's debut album, *Love Always*. *It's Real* followed two years later and *X* was released in late 2000. *—John Bush*

● **Love Always** / Jun. 17, 1997 / MCA ♦♦♦

After becoming two of the best-known R&B singers of the 1990s as half of Jodeci, brothers K-Ci & JoJo Hailey formed a cohesive duo for *Love Always*. A definite surprise to Jodeci fans, the CD contains few traces of new jack swing and lacks the type of suggestive, R-rated lyrics the foursome had become known for. It was clear that the great soul music of the 1970s was very much on K-Ci & JoJo's minds when they made this album, an unpretentious collection of ballads and slow jams that isn't mind-blowing, but is definitely above average. In contrast to the homogenized nature of so much '90s R&B, things are refreshingly organic on such cuts as "Now and Forever," "Still Waiting" and "Baby Come Back." And an impressive cover of L.T.D.'s 1976 hit "Love Ballad" may very well be the best thing the Hailey brothers have ever done—inside or outside of Jodeci. *—Alex Henderson*

It's Real / Jun. 22, 1999 / MCA ♦♦♦

K-Ci & JoJo's first album *Love Always* established the Jodeci refugees as fine R&B vocalists, blending classic soul traditions with contemporary urban production and technique. Blessed with strong sales and good reviews, *Love Always* became a hit, setting up high expectations for the duo's second album, *It's Real*. For those expecting a flat-out masterpiece, *It's Real* will disappoint, primarily because it doesn't so much as expand on past glories as it simply replicates them. Since they're good singers with generally good material, this isn't a problem, even if it makes it all seem a little too pat and predictable. Occasionally, the Hailey brothers decide to rely a little bit too much on their impressive vocal technique, taking off on soaring glissandos that ultimately distract as much as they impress. That, combined with the stylistic similarity of the material, makes *It's Real* bog down a little bit, but the very best moments—"Makin' Me Say Goodbye," "I Wanna Get to Know You," "How Long Must I Cry," "Hello Darlin'," among others—are contemporary urban romantic soul at its finest, which is reason enough to hear the disc. *—Stephen Thomas Erlewine*

X / Dec. 5, 2000 / MCA ♦♦♦

X is the Roman numeral for ten, and this late-2000 release is titled *X* because it marks Cedric "K-Ci" Hailey and Joel "JoJo" Hailey's tenth anniversary in the recording business—first as two-thirds of the trio Jodeci, then as the duo K-Ci & JoJo. *X*, the duo's third album, isn't a radical departure from its two previous albums; like 1997's *Love Always* and 1999's double-platinum *It's Real*, this CD emphasizes romantic material and combines a high-tech urban contemporary production style with an appreciation of classic soul. K-Ci & Jo-Jo were never a carbon copy of Jodeci, and *X* won't be mistaken for *Diary of a Mad Band*. Though *X* contains a few hip-hop-minded, uptempo selections (including "Game Face" and "Thug N U Thug N Me"), romantic ballads and slow jams are dominant. A few of the tunes are retro-soul gems—especially "Wanna Do You Right" and the Bobby Womack-influenced "I Can't Find the Words"—although most of the time, *X* is merely decent urban contemporary. One thing that's never in doubt is the Hailey Brothers' skills as vocalists; while a lot of urban contemporary artists get over on image alone, K-Ci & JoJo really do have impressive vocal ranges. *X* isn't a masterpiece, but unlike all of the urban artists who have nothing more than image and attitude going for them, the Hailey siblings bring some genuine talent to this generally pleasant, if predictable, CD. *—Alex Henderson*

Ernie K-Doe (Ernest Kador Jr.)

b. Feb. 22, 1936, New Orleans, LA, **d.** Jul. 5, 2001, New Orleans, LA

Vocals, Songwriter / New Orleans R&B, R&B

Ernie K-Doe scored one of the biggest hits (possibly *the* biggest) in the history of New Orleans R&B with "Mother-in-Law," a humorous lament that struck a chord with listeners of all stripes on its way to the top of both the pop and R&B charts in 1961. The song proved to be K-Doe's only major success, despite several more minor hits that were equally infectious, yet he remained one of New Orleans' most inimitable personalities. Born Ernest Kador Jr. in New Orleans in 1936, he began singing at age seven in the Baptist church where his father served as minister. During his teen years, Kador performed with local gospel groups like the Golden Chain Jubilee Singers and the Zion Travelers, when he was influenced chiefly by the Five Blind Boys of Mississippi. He entered and won talent competitions and became more interested in secular R&B and blues, and at 17, he moved to Chicago with his mother and began performing at local clubs. Thanks to connections he made there, he got the chance to sing with the Flamingos and Moonglows, as well as the Four Blazes, a gig that earned him his first recording session in late 1953 for United.

Kador returned to New Orleans in 1954 and honed his flamboyant stage act at numerous local hangouts (including the famed Dew Drop Inn), both solo and as part of the vocal group the Blue Diamonds. The Blue Diamonds cut a couple of sides for Savoy in 1954, and the following year, Kador (still billed under his real name) recorded his first solo single, "Do Baby Do," for Specialty. In 1957, he recorded a few more sides for Ember, as both Ernie Kado and Ernie K-Doe. Finally, in 1959, he caught on with the newly formed Minit label and hooked up with producer/songwriter/pianist/arranger/future legend Allen Toussaint. His first Minit single, "Make You Love Me," flopped, but the follow-up "Hello My Lover" was a substantial regional hit, selling nearly 100,000 copies. K-Doe struck gold with 1961's "Mother-in-Law," a Toussaint-penned tune on which K-Doe traded choruses with bass vocalist Benny Spellman. That, coupled with the playful cynicism of the lyrics, made for a rollicking good time in the best New Orleans R&B tradition, and K-Doe was rewarded with a number-one record on both the pop and R&B charts. He toured the country and landed a few more follow-up hits—"Te-Ta-Te-Ta-Ta," "I Cried My Last Tear," "A Certain Girl" (later covered by the Yardbirds), "Popeye Joe"—but none approached the phenomenon of "Mother-in-Law," and were more popular on the R&B side.

Minit soon went under, and K-Doe followed Toussaint to the Instant label, but two 1964 singles failed to revive K-Doe's chart fortunes, partly because the early prime of New Orleans R&B was fading as Motown gained prominence. Over the remainder of the '60s, K-Doe recorded for Peacock and Duke, landing two very minor R&B chart entries in 1967 with "Later for Tomorrow" and "Until the Real Thing Comes Along" on the latter label. However, he had a difficult time adapting his loose, playful style to the R&B trends of the day. He reunited with Toussaint for a brief period in the early '70s, to no avail, and drifted into a long period of alcoholism. Fortunately, K-Doe was able to reclaim some of his popularity around New Orleans when he began hosting a radio program in 1982, earning an audience with his wild antics and blatant self-promotion. In 1994, K-Doe opened his own club, the Mother-in-Law Lounge, in New Orleans, and frequently performed there in the years to come, occasionally returning to the studio as well. He was inducted into the city's Music Hall of Fame in 1995 and generally acknowledged for his contributions up until his death from kidney and liver failure on July 5, 2001. *—Steve Huey*

Burn! K-Doe, Burn! / 1989 / Charly ♦♦♦♦♦

The Building Is Shakin' & The Walls Are Tremblin' / Apr. 20, 1999 / Aim ♦♦♦

Produced by Milton Battiste in the mid-'90s, this baker's dozen of cuts (really 12 songs; tracks 12 and 13 are the same title) attests to the fact that Ernie K-Doe was about more than just his million-seller "Mother-in-Law." The songs are R&B, blues, contemporary soul, and reggae ("Only 11 Roses.") Highlights include a duet with Lisa Lee on "When Something Is Wrong With My Baby," a remake of Jimmy Reed's "Baby What You Want Me to Do," parts one and two of "Your Wish Is My Command," and two uptempo numbers ensconced in R&B: "A Certain Girl" and "Hello My Lover." *—Andrew Hamilton*

● **Absolutely the Best** / Oct. 30, 2001 / Fuel 2000 ♦♦♦♦♦

You can't think of Ernie K-Doe without thinking of "Mother-in-Law," his 1961 chart-topper and the only pop hit on his resumé. As the 18-track collection *Absolutely the Best* proves so well, though, K-Doe recorded many great sides, a few of which beat even the glorious "Mother-In-Law." The disc covers his early-'60s sides for the Minit and Duke logos very well, scooping up pleasant chart entries like "Te-Ta-Te-Ta-Ta" and "Popeye Joe." Fortunately, the compilers also recognized that as a lark, fans would want to hear "Get out of My House," a quasi-cover of "Mother-in-Law" featuring the same deep bass vocals repeating the title as Benny Spellman had provided for the big hit. Those unfamiliar with K-Doe's career will undoubtedly get knocked out by "A Certain Girl" and "'Tain't It the Truth," two classics of New Orleans R&B with the same laid-back, sheepish finesse that made "Mother-in-Law" such a hit. *—John Bush*

A Real Mother-in-Law for Ya: The Allen Toussaint Sessions 1959–63 / Jun. 26, 2002 / WestSide ♦♦♦♦♦

Since his big hit was "Mother-in-Law," a funny song that could easily be perceived as a novelty, Ernie K-Doe is often dismissed when it comes to the top rank of New Orleans R&B singers. That's an inaccurate assessment, as WestSide's delightful 2002 compilation *A Real Mother-in-Law for Ya* proves. Part of the reason, of course, is that these are the Toussaint sessions, and Allen Toussaint is the king of late-'50s and -'60s New Orleans R&B, not only writing classics like "Mother-in-Law," but producing sessions that had precisely the right combination of rolling rhythms, horns, mellow funk, pianos, and warm vocals from the friendly, skilled Ernie K-Doe. He didn't have as rich a selection of material as, say, Fats Domino or Lee Dorsey, but he was at the top tier of the second tier, as this compulsively listenable 29-track collection proves. This is nearly all top-shelf material—from hits like "A Certain Girl" and "I've Cried My Last Tear" (the A and B, respectively, of one of the greatest R&B singles of the early '60s), to lesser-known material like Toussaint's "Hello My Lover" or the rollicking "Wanted $10,000 Reward." After hearing this collection, it's hard not to think of Ernie K-Doe as one of the great New Orleans R&B artists of his time, and it's hard to imagine a serious New Orleans collection without this disc. *—Stephen Thomas Erlewine*

François K (François Kevorkian)

b. Jan. 10, 1954, Rodez, France

DJ, Producer / Disco, Garage/House, Club/Dance, House

Only Frankie Knuckles can lay claim to straddling a longer span of time in the thick of dance music than François Kevorkian. And though his name is no more than vaguely familiar to many dance fans, Kevorkian's influence is immense. Beginning with his production work for the crucial disco label Prelude during the late '70s and extending through an immense quantity of remixes and productions for legions of pop bands during the following decade, few producers did more to mechanize and refine the disco template into music clearly recognizable as house. After moving from his native France to New York City in the mid-'70s, Kevorkian learned the art of mixing from the era's most influential DJs (Walter Gibbons, Jellybean, Larry Levan). He began producing early reel-to-reel cut-ups, patterned on dub techniques, which pushed bouts of much-needed experimentalism into disco. He then brought the dance treatment to scores of alternative bands and pop stars who needed it during the 1980s and '90s. Unfortunately, Kevorkian never spent as much time on his own productions, releasing very few singles though he helmed his own imprint, Wave Records.

Born in Rodez, France in the mid-'50s, Kevorkian grew up in the suburbs of Paris, playing drums in several bands while studying biochemical engineering and pharmacy in college. After deciding to chuck in his studies, he moved to New York and began playing with any pick-up bands he could find. His first important work in the club-scene came when Kevorkian took a part-time gig at the club Galaxy 21 providing live fill-in drums for the DJ, Walter Gibbons. Though the club later closed, Kevorkian moved on to another named Experiment Four and became friends with its resident, Jellybean Benitez.

Kevorkian soon began producing his own tracks after he learned that Benitez owned a four-track reel-to-reel machine. Hoping to warp tracks for maximum dancefloor consumption, Kevorkian recorded dub-inspired cut-and-paste megamixes with splice and edit techniques, even adding special effects gained from movies and other sources. (One of his first productions, a version of "Happy Song and Dance" by Rare Earth, was a New York club staple for years afterward.) In mid-1977, he started DJ-ing at a club known as New York, New York—the premiere disco spot after Studio 54. While working there, Kevorkian met DJ legend Larry Levan and the two became fast friends. After Kevorkian was tapped for an A&R position at the disco label Prelude, he began working at the label's studios with Levan, creating mixes for the West End and Salsoul imprints as well as Prelude. Kevorkian's mix for Musique's 1978 single "Push Push (In the Bush)" went gold—despite an obvious lack of chart action—and his productions for another Prelude act, D Train, resulted in additional club hits like "You're the One for Me," "Music" and "Keep On."

A talent for studio mixing and his requisite dancefloor credentials made François Kevorkian one of the most in-demand producers during the 1980s. An increased momentum during the decade for general dance music pushed labels to request special nightclub versions of pop songs for the dance crowd, and Kevorkian obliged hundreds of times, for such groups as Yaz, the Smiths, Depeche Mode, Diana Ross, Adam Ant, U2, Kraftwerk, Matthew Sweet, the Pet Shop Boys, Thomas Dolby, Ashford & Simpson and Erasure, among many others. In 1987, he founded Axis Studios as well, which provided a home for recording by Madonna, C+C Music Factory, Mariah Carey and Deee-Lite.

Given his busy studio schedule, it's no wonder Kevorkian neglected his DJ-ing during most of the '80s. He returned to form in 1990, and travelled to Japan with Larry Levan for several high-profile gigs. Kevorkian became a label-owner as well in the '90s; his Wave imprint provided a home for several of his own productions, including 1997's pioneering *FK-EP*. The best document of his DJ-ing skills, *Essential Mix*, appeared in 2000. *—John Bush*

● **Essential Mix** / May 2, 2000 / London ✦✦✦✦✦

Essential Mix, François Kevorkian's two-disc meditation on the New York City dance scene over the preceding quarter-century, is appropriately expansive and all-embracing. The evident pan-global vibes and emphasis on funk and fusion will strike a chord for those who've been exposed to his sets at Body & Soul, the seminal NYC clubnight organized by himself, Joe Claussell, and Danny Krivit. As such, we hear tribal-funk tracks from Kyoto Jazz Massive ("Nacer do Sol"), Bob Holroyd ("African Drug"), Jephte Guillaume ("La-Kou-A"), Jazzanova ("Caravelle"), Billy Cobham ("Storm"), and Akwaaba ("Just Pillau"), as well as the funk side of the breakbeat spectrum with James Brown ("There Was a Time"), Tower of Power ("Squib Cakes"), Earth, Wind & Fire ("In the Stone"), D Train ("Keep On"), and George Benson ("Song for My Brother"). Sprinkled among these are more eclectic dancefloor favorites—left-field dance tracks ("Home Computer" by Kraftwerk, "Throw" by Carl Craig's Paperclip People project), two tracks by NYC hip-hop legends (A Tribe Called Quest, De La Soul), and a trio of Chicago house nuggets (Adonis' "No Way Back," Lil' Louis' "Jazzmen," Virgo's "Free Yourself"). These aren't necessarily the best dance tracks to make it big in New York between the mid-'70s and the end of the century, but Kevorkian's steady hand and supreme knowledge makes it one of the best dance compendiums ever assembled. *—John Bush*

Choice: A Collection of Classics / Jun. 4, 2002 / Azuli ✦✦✦

London's Azuli label followed Frankie Knuckles' contribution to the *Choice: A Collection of Classics* series in 2002 with another fine double-disc set of varied obscurities and bona fide classics selected by dance music luminary François K. François assembles a fun jumble of tunes (unencumbered by boundaries) that spans chronologically from the early '70s through the early '90s and sequences it with finesse. The subtitle of the series is a little misleading—not all of these tracks are classics. Though the average consumer might be a little miffed about the fact that this set isn't packed solid with instant jaw-droppers, a steady quality that serves the flow is kept throughout. Chicago house gets a fair representation with Frankie Knuckles' lewd Jamie Principle vocal number "Baby Wants to Ride," Lil' Louis' "Do U Love Me," and Fingers Inc's "Never No More Lonely" leading the way. Shalamar's opening "Right in the Socket" and Sylvester's "Over and Over" highlight the disco herd. Floor-friendly cuts from jazz figures (Donald Byrd's "Love Has Come Around," Deodato's "Super Strut") and R&B greats (Teddy Pendergrass' "Only You," Rene & Angela's "I Love You More") also play a prominent role. The packaging doesn't explicitly state the fact that each song appears in full—a fact that no doubt appeals to dance aficionados who'd love to have some of these songs in their full glory, with great sound to boot. Though it's a compilation and not a mix, the track-to-track flow is natural and makes it all function as an enjoyable listen from beginning to end. *—Andy Kellman*

Kai

f. 1992, San Francisco, CA

Group / Urban

The vocal quintet Kai formed in 1992 when A.C. Lorenzo recruited Andrew Gapuz and Leo Chan for a San Francisco-area benefit concert, then continued working with the pair. They added Errol Viray and Lorenzo's cousin Andrey Silva in 1995, and signed to the local HB Records soon after. Kai's debut single "Say You'll Stay" did well on regional radio, leading them to be signed by Geffen in 1997. Kai's self-titled debut album was released in June 1998. *—John Bush*

● **Kai** / Jun. 16, 1998 / Geffen ✦✦✦

On their eponymous debut album, Kai illustrates that they are gifted vocalists but this isn't necessarily the best judge of material. Like many of their post-Boyz II Men contemporaries, the quintet can deliver ballads in smooth, seductive tones with slight gospel overtones, plus they can do mildly funky dance-pop. They have the skills, but they don't always have the songs to sound convincing. When they do, such as on "Say You'll Stay," the results are quite engaging, but when they don't, there's not quite enough personality to make the mediocre material acceptable. Nevertheless, the group shows potential on *Kai* and that's enough to make the album a good debut. *—Stephen Thomas Erlewine*

Kain

Speech/Speaker/Speaking Part, Rap, Vocals / Poetry, Blaxploitation, Soul

Gylan Kain was a founding member of the seminal poetry/rap group the Last Poets, often cited as a primary influence on hip-hop and popular culture as a whole. Kain's introduction to performance came in 1964 when he was selected to participate in a theater group for troubled New York youths organized by actor Lou Gossett Jr. Four years later he would join the stage with poets David Nelson and Charles Davis (later known as Abiodun Oyewole) for the inaugural performance of the yet-to-be-named Last Poets. Easily the most fiery and confrontational member of the original group, Kain stayed with the ever-growing poetic and percussion collective until 1969, at which point he left the sometimes fracturous group. Some of his work from this period appeared on the Last Poets' 1970 soundtrack release *Right On!*, and in 1971 he released a scathing solo album, *The Blue Guerrilla*. He remains active in the arts: writing plays (*Epitaph to a Coagulated Trinity*), collaborating with multimedia artist and theorist Z'ev, and performing both solo and with his group in Europe, the Baby Kain Band. *—Wade Kergan*

● **The Blue Guerrilla** / 1971 / Collectables ✦✦✦✦✦

This solo album by Gylan Kain, one of the original Last Poets—before the group recorded for Douglas Records—is a study in angry poetics, performance art, and killer presentation. Recorded and issued in the early '70s, *The Blue Guerrilla* is a freestyle set before such a thing was even a dream. Kain's one pissed-off cat, raging not only against the usual necessary concerns, but also against the stereotypes in his own community. Free jazz-funk grooves on guitars, electric violins, a slew of drums, and ghostly keyboards accompany his gorgeous and disturbing ranting that is far from pointless. From the opening ritual scarification of "I Ain't Black," with it's free jazz approach and over-the-top screaming, to the poignant indictment of "Harlem Preacher," to "Black Satin Amazon" and "Constipated Monkey," Kain is a hipster without a country, a street poet without an audience, an activist without sympathy. And rather than succumb and stylize his thang to get his message across, he becomes angrier, slyer, slicker, less forgiving, and more insightful. Music is placed here not as accompaniment, but as a framework for Kain to place his poetry in a context of the African-American oral tradition and the Living Theatre. And he gives no quarter. This man makes the Last Poets he left behind sound like schoolboys trying to sound pissed off. Kain would make Gil Scott-Heron run away for fear of being exposed as the effete he became before he turned into an out-and-out drug addict. There aren't any other records like this; this is the sound of the apocalypse, one that Amiri Baraka predicted and celebrated. Sit down, listen all the way though if you can; wake up. There's a riot goin' on. *—Thom Jurek*

Karma

f. 1974, Los Angeles, CA, **db.** 1977

Group / Funk, Quiet Storm, Fusion, Soul, Meditation

Sounding like a cross between Earth, Wind & Fire and the Crusaders, Karma was an interesting but underexposed 1970s soul/funk band that sometimes detoured into jazz-fusion and quiet storm music. Karma, formed in Los Angeles in 1974, wasn't a full-time project for its members, who included saxophonist Ernie Watts, trombonist George Bohanon, trumpeter Oscar Brashear, keyboardist Reggie Andrews, bassist Curtis Robertson Jr. and drummer Josef Blocker. Many of Karma's members, who shared vocal duties, had been keeping busy on the L.A. studio scene and had solid credentials in both R&B and jazz. Karma recorded two albums for Horizion/A&M, 1976's *Celebration* and 1977's *For Everybody*, before calling it quits in 1977. *—Alex Henderson*

● **Celebration** / 1976 / A&M/Horizon ✦✦✦✦

Karma members were not only among the unsung heroes of 1970s soul and funk; they were also capable of playing solid jazz-fusion. With such talent on board as saxman Ernie

Watts, trumpeter Oscar Brashear, and trombonist George Bohanon, the L.A.-based outfit should have hit it big with *Celebration*, their first of two albums. But the LP, which was recorded in 1974 and 1976, failed to take off commercially. That may stem from the fact that while *Celebration* is a fine album, it lacked the powerhouse single necessary for the band to grab the attention of soul radio. Essentially, this is a collection of great album tracks, which range from the Earth, Wind & Fire-inflected funk song "Karma" to the bluesy "Well" and the uplifting Brazilian jazz-pop number "Kwanzaa." Karma's members really put their jazz chops to work on the 20-minute "Suite Syreeta," which gives the horn players plenty of room to stretch out. Regrettably, *Celebration* and its successor, *For Everybody*, have long been out of print, and it's unlikely that they'll ever be reissued on CD. So, if you come across either LP somewhere, grab it immediately. *—Alex Henderson*

For Everybody / Apr. 1978 / A&M ♦♦♦
With their second album, *For Everybody*, Karma added new member, vocalist Michael Greene, without altering their sound; the L.A. outfit still resembled a cross between Earth, Wind & Fire and the Crusaders. This time, however, Karma offered several gems that might have been hits if they had been released as singles and promoted aggressively. Such gems include sweaty funk songs like "For Everybody (Feel the Whooga)," "Now That's Bionic," and "Spotty Funk." However, this release also has its share of strong album tracks that didn't have much black radio appeal, including the ethereal "All Love Needs" and the jazz-funk instrumental "Abundance." This LP deserved to do well commercially, but unfortunately, it didn't sell and was Karma's final album. *—Alex Henderson*

Kay-Gee's

f. Jersey City, NJ
Group / Disco, Funk, Deep Funk
A funk outfit formed in Jersey City, NJ, Kay-Gee's had some valuable mentors in Kool & the Gang—specifically Ronald Bell, who was happy to serve as producer, arranger, and sometimes songwriter for his younger brother Kevin's band. In addition to Kevin Bell on guitar and several other instruments, Kay-Gee's featured saxophonist Peter Duarte, brass player Ray Wright, woodwind player Dennis White, keyboardist Kevin Lassiter, bassist Michael Cheek, drummer Callie Cheek, and percussionist Wilson Beckett. Signed to Kool & the Gang's own Gang imprint, Kay-Gee's issued their debut album *Keep on Bumpin' & Masterplan* in 1974. With Ronald Bell penning the majority of the material, Kay-Gee's' sound was highly similar to the hard, tight grooves of early Kool & the Gang; singles like "You've Got to Keep on Bumpin'," "Who's the Man? (With the Master Plan)" (yes, the source of that ubiquitous hip-hop sample), and "Get Down" gave them an enduring reputation among hardcore funk connoisseurs.

Burn Me Up followed in 1975, producing the single "Hustle Wit' Every Muscle," which became the theme song for the TV series *Party*. By the time of 1976's *Find a Friend*, Ronald Bell's involvement with the group had begun to decrease, resulting in a flirtation with disco on cuts like "Find a Friend" and "Waiting at the Bus Stop." Their final album, 1978's *Kilowatt*, was a full-fledged disco-funk extravaganza released on New York's De-Lite label, and featured several popular club singles, including "Cheek to Cheek" and "Tango Hustle." However, they disbanded not long afterward. *—Steve Huey*

Keep on Bumpin' & Masterplan / 1974 / Gang ♦♦♦♦♦
The debut LP from Kay-Gee's proved that the band led by Kevin Bell (brother to Kool & the Gang's Ronald) had all the deep, driving grooves, kinetic energy, and street-corner vibes of funk's master outfit. Produced by Ronald Bell and Kool & the Gang, *Keep on Bumpin' & Masterplan* featured a pair of strong lead tracks and plenty more strong material, like "Hustle Wit Every Muscle" (used as the theme song to the television show *Party*). The Kay-Gee's' horn section was equal to Kool & the Gang's, and if they lacked a few of the awesome hooks that propelled Ronald Bell's group into the R&B charts on a regular basis, alto/soprano Pete Duarte was a superior soloist and female vocal trio Something Sweet filled in the gaps on the great jam "Let's Boogie" and "Wondering." Kay-Gee's were also better at locking into great grooves, while Kool & the Gang spent too much time mixing up their style. True, a Kool & the Gang singles collection would blow Kay-Gee's' out of the water, but even they never recorded an album as good as *Keep on Bumpin' & Masterplan*. *—John Bush*

Kilowatt / 1978 / Unidisc ♦♦♦

• **Greatest Hits** / 1993 / Unidisc ♦♦♦♦♦
Though the funk collective Kay-Gee's recorded more great work than would fit on one disc, Unidisc's *Greatest Hits* does an excellent job of distilling four albums' worth of material on one lengthy compilation. Opening in the right place, with the hits run-through "Kay-Gee's Theme Song," the disc moves on to capture five tracks from their dynamic debut ("You've Got to Keep on Bumpin'," "Master Plan," "Get Down," "Let's Boogie," and "Hustle Wit' Every Muscle"), each of them perfect choices for any old-school funk anthology worth its weight. By 1976, though, Kay-Gee's were exploring different avenues, resulting in album concepts like *Find a Friend* (the title track and the moderate R&B hit "Waiting at the Bus Stop" appear) and, later, disco music (here courtesy of an extended version of "Kilowatt"). *—John Bush*

Essential Dancefloor Artists, Vol. 5 / Oct. 25, 1994 / Deep Beats ♦♦♦♦

KC & the Sunshine Band

f. 1973, Miami, FL
Group / Disco, Dance-Pop
The Bee Gees may have been the undisputed disco kings of the late '70s, but KC & the Sunshine Band weren't far behind. From the mid- to late '70s, the multi-member and racially integrated group led by bandleaders Harry Wayne "KC" Casey and Richard Finch racked up some of the era's biggest and instantly recognizable dance hits. Casey and Finch first met in 1972 while both were employed by TK Records in Miami, FL, where among other chores, Casey served as a personal secretary and booking agent for artist Timmy Thomas. KC & the Sunshine Band officially formed in 1973, but a debut single, "Blow Your Whistle," sunk from sight upon release. But it was another Casey/Finch original, "Rock Your Baby," that R&B artist George McCrae scored a hit with in 1974 as KC & the Sunshine Band began issuing further albums and singles, quickly scoring big hits on their own.

The group then began an impressive run of disco hits: 1977's "Shake Shake Shake (Shake Your Booty)," "I'm Your Boogieman," "Keep It Comin' Love," "Boogie Shoes" (the latter included on the monster-selling soundtrack to the hit John Travolta disco movie, *Saturday Night Fever*), 1979's "Do You Wanna Go Party," and 1980's "Please Don't Go." Despite earning nine Grammy nominations (receiving three awards) and selling millions of records, KC & the Sunshine Band weren't susceptible to the backlash that disco bands felt by the dawn of the '80s, eventually leading to dwindling sales and the group's split by the early '80s (although KC scored a moderate solo hit in 1983 with "Give It Up"). Come the '90s, an appreciation of everything '70s swept across the U.S., which led to a renewed interest bands from the era, prompting KC & the Sunshine Band to re-form for concert performances. That decade saw the release of countless KC "hits" collections and even an episode of VH1's popular *Behind the Music* series that studied the group's ups and downs. *—Greg Prato*

Do It Good / 1974 / TK ♦♦♦
Over the years, there have been many American artists who became well-known in England before becoming well-known in their own country. A perfect example is KC & the Sunshine Band, whose first album, *Do It Good*, was a major hit in Great Britain but only a minor hit in the United States. It wasn't until the 1975 smashes "Get Down Tonight" and "That's the Way (I Like It)" that KC & the Sunshine Band enjoyed a major commercial breakthrough in their own country; in England, they hit big in 1973 with "Sound Your Funky Horn." This LP contains all of the exuberant singles that put them on the map in the U.K., including "Sound Your Funky Horn," "Blow Your Whistle," "I'm a Pushover," and "Queen of Clubs" (which made it to number 25 on *Billboard*'s R&B singles chart but was a Top Ten hit in England). You won't hear a lot of sociopolitical commentary on *Do It Good*, although R&B message songs were still quite popular when this album was recorded in 1973 and 1974. Unlike Stevie Wonder, Curtis Mayfield, and Marvin Gaye, KC & the Sunshine Band was never about trying to save the world—this promising debut made it clear that their forte was pure, unapologetic, escapist party music. *Do It Good* isn't quite as essential as subsequent efforts like 1975's *KC & the Sunshine Band* or 1976's *Part 3*, but the record is exciting more often than not and is easily recommended to disco and funk enthusiasts. *—Alex Henderson*

The Sound of Sunshine / 1975 / TK ♦♦♦
Many Americans think that 1975's *KC & the Sunshine Band* was the disco/funk/soul outfit's first album. After all, it was that self-titled release that boasted the hits "Get Down Tonight" and "That's The Way (I Like It)," both of which soared to number one on *Billboard*'s R&B and pop singles charts and made Harry Wayne Casey, aka KC, a superstar in the United States. But, in fact, *KC & the Sunshine Band* was their third album. Before that, they provided two LPs that were better known in England than they were in the U.S.: 1974's *Do It Good* (their debut album) and 1975's instrumental *The Sound of Sunshine*. KC doesn't sing at all on this LP, which he produced and arranged with partner Richard Finch. But even without KC's distinctive vocals, his band is easily recognizable on exuberant offerings like "Sunshine City," "S.O.S.," and "Funky '75" (which is an instrumental version of the 1973 single "Sound Your Funky Horn"). Other noteworthy tracks include the single "Shotgun Shuffle" (which made it to number 25 on *Billboard*'s R&B singles chart) and a remake of the George McCrae smash "Rock Your Baby" (which KC and Finch wrote for that one-hit wonder in 1974). *The Sound of Sunshine* isn't among KC & the Sunshine Band's essential releases, but it's a decent record that's worth hearing if you're a serious disco-funk collector. *—Alex Henderson*

KC and the Sunshine Band / 1975 / TK ♦♦♦♦♦
This self-titled effort wasn't the Florida band's first album (they'd recorded an underrated album in 1973 titled *Do It Good*), but it was the first KC collection to soar to the top of the charts. Fueled by such addictive funk hits as "That's the Way (I Like It)" and "Get Down Tonight," the album established KC as one of the top stars of the disco era. But while KC was labeled a disco artist, the truth is that many of these slick yet gritty songs have more in common with the Ohio Players than the Silver Convention or Donna Summer. When Rhino reissued this album on CD in 1995 as *KC & The Sunshine Band . . . And More*, the company generously included several early KC smokers (including "I'm a Pushover") from *Do It Good* as bonus tracks. The invigorating material proves that even before the outfit hit big, its distinctive sound had been established. *—Alex Henderson*

Part 3 / 1976 / TK ♦♦♦♦♦
Arguably KC & The Sunshine Band's best album and certainly one of its most successful, *Part 3* will always be closely identified with the disco era. But for all the disco appeal that infectious gems like "Shake Your Booty," "I Like to Do It," "Baby I Love You" and "Wrap Your Arms Around Me" have, they also illustrate that this was very much a funk band. In fact, when the Floridians toured with the Ohio Players in 1976, it seemed a logical combination. Perhaps the most overtly disco-sounding hit on this album was "Keep It Coming Love," a fine example of KC at his most charismatic. In 1995, Rhino reissued *Part 3* on CD as *Part 3 . . . And More*, adding some of KC's early-'80s solo work as bonus tracks. The songs demonstrate that while KC's popularity had faded, his unapologetic funkiness definitely hadn't. *—Alex Henderson*

Who Do Ya Love / 1978 / TK ♦♦♦
Both commercially and creatively, *Who Do Ya Love* was a step down for KC & the Sunshine Band. This 1978 LP followed 1976's *Part 3*, a superb album boasting four gems that reached the Top Five on *Billboard*'s R&B and pop singles chart: "(Shake, Shake, Shake) Shake Your Booty," "I'm Your Boogie Man," "Keep It Comin' Love," and "I Like to Do It." But the biggest hit on *Who Do Ya Love*, a remake of the Four Tops' "It's the Same Old Song," only reached

number 30 on *Billboard*'s R&B singles chart. And other singles from this LP didn't fare that well; "Do You Feel All Right" went no higher than number-62 R&B/number-63 pop, and the title song struggled to make it to number-88 R&B/ number-68 pop. So is *Who Do Ya Love* really such a bad album? No, it's actually a decent, if unremarkable, collection of disco-funk and disco-soul, some of which incorporates Latin or Caribbean elements. But when you have been cranking out five-star albums, an LP that is merely decent is going to seem disappointing. And when you have had several number-one hits, you aren't going to feel triumphant when your Four Tops cover peaks at number 30 on *Billboard*'s R&B singles chart. Again, *Who Do Ya Love* isn't a bad album, but after *KC & the Sunshine Band* in 1975 and *Part 3* in 1976, one expected a lot more from the South Florida outfit. *—Alex Henderson*

Do You Wanna Go Party / 1979 / TK ✦✦✦
After burning up the pop and R&B charts in 1975, 1976, and 1977, KC & the Sunshine Band were disappointed when 1978's decent, if unremarkable, *Who Do Ya Love* failed to provide any major hits. But 1979 turned out to be a better year for the South Florida disco/funk/soul band, who returned to the top of the singles charts that year. Released in 1979, *Do You Wanna Go Party* boasts two major singles: the infectious title track song (a number-eight R&B hit) and the ballad "Please Don't Go," which soared to number one on *Billboard*'s pop singles chart. Other noteworthy tracks on this good to excellent LP include the Latin-tinged "Hooked on Your Love," the Motown-drenched "Ooh, I Like It," and a cover of Frederick Knight's "I Betcha Didn't Know That." Meanwhile, "Que Pasa" is catchy even if it does sound like KC is trying to recycle "Wrap Your Arms Around Me" or "That's the Way (I Like It)." *Do You Wanna Go Party* isn't quite in a class with 1975's *KC & the Sunshine Band* or 1976's *Part 3*, but the album is impressive more often than not and is a definite improvement over *Who Do Ya Love*. *—Alex Henderson*

• **The Best of KC & the Sunshine Band** / Jun. 1990 / Rhino ✦✦✦✦✦
From 1974-1979, KC & the Sunshine Band were one of the most popular R&B/pop acts and writers of the era. *The Best of KC & the Sunshine Band* covers the high points of the band's production team of keyboardist/vocalist Harry Wayne "KC" Casey and quirky bassist Richard Finch. The earliest tracks, "Queen of Clubs" and "Sound Your Funky Horn," are good but not great glossy, heavily produced R&B. The list of hits here is impressive whether looking from a straight-up R&B standpoint or early R&B-based disco. "Get Down Tonight" and "That's the Way (I Like It)," in fact, are the perfect examples of what happened in dance-based music. Tracks from the band's best album, *Part 3*, rightfully get a lot of slots here. Essential offerings like "I'm Your Boogie Man," "Wrap Your Arms Around Me," "I Like to Do It," and "(Shake, Shake, Shake) Shake Your Booty" display the band as a tireless polyrhythmic machine. The brilliant "Keep It Comin' Love" arguably bests them all. This best-of also includes later tracks, including the raucous and flashy "Do You Wanna Go Party" and the sweeping ballad "Please Don't Go." Although this best-of is more thorough than most, fans might notice a few omissions. "I Get Lifted" and their so-bad-it's-good cover of the Four Tops' classic "It's the Same Old Song" didn't make the cut. *The Best of KC & the Sunshine Band* is an excellent overview and proves that the band was indeed closer to R&B than they ever were to disco. *—Jason Elias*

25th Anniversary Edition / Jul. 20, 1999 / Rhino ✦✦✦
In 1999, Rhino celebrated the 25th anniversary of KC & the Sunshine Band's formation with this two-CD anthology. But technically, 1999 was their 26th anniversary—the soul/funk/disco band was formed in 1973, not 1974. For the casual listener and the budget-minded, a better and more concise choice would be Rhino's 1990 CD *The Best of KC & the Sunshine Band*, which summarizes their contributions with 16 tracks. But if your interest in KC goes beyond casual, *25th Anniversary Collection* isn't a bad release to have. The set contains all of the essential '70s hits offered on *The Best of KC & the Sunshine Band*, including "Get Down Tonight," "(Shake, Shake, Shake) Shake Your Booty," "That's the Way (I Like It)," "I'm Your Boogie Man," and "Keep It Comin' Love," as well as "Wrap Your Arms Around Me," "I Like To Do It," and the ballad "Please Don't Go." But *25th Anniversary Collection* also has its share of material that is enjoyable though less than essential—you need to be a seasoned, die-hard KC fanatic to fully appreciate the Spanish-language version of "Please Don't Go" (titled "Por Favor, No Te Vayas"), Tom Moulton's 1994 remix of "Get Down Tonight," or KC and Teri DeSario's 1980 cover of Martha & the Vandellas' "Dancin' in the Streets." And if you're that much of a collector, you'll appreciate Brian Chin's comprehensive, informative liner notes—the writer has no problem articulating why KC's music was so popular in the '70s and why his classic grooves excited many hip-hop, dance-pop and house enthusiasts in the '90s. Rock critics might have dismissed KC in the '70s, but time has made it clear that KC's admirers—not the critics who gave him scathing reviews—were the smart ones. *—Alex Henderson*

VH-1 Behind the Music: The KC & the Sunshine Band Collection / Aug. 21, 2001 / Rhino ✦✦✦✦
KC & the Sunshine Band's *VH-1 Behind the Music* is essentially a greatest-hits collection containing all of their biggest singles, including "Get Down Tonight," "That's the Way (I Like It)," "(Shake, Shake, Shake) Shake Your Booty," "Boogie Shoes," "I'm Your Boogie Man," and "Please Don't Go." There are a lot of other songs outside of these tunes, and there may be a song or two missing (most regrettably KC's solo smash "Give It Up," but this is a band collection, not a solo disc), but this still will satisfy almost any casual fan. *—Stephen Thomas Erlewine*

Kelis

Vocals / Contemporary R&B, Alternative Rap, Urban, Hip-Hop
Harlem-bred hip-hop chanteuse Kelis is a strong woman. This singer/songwriter has the fire of Alanis Morissette, the sassiness of Queen Latifah, and a poise all her own. The daughter of a jazz musician and minister father, Kelis was encouraged to discover music by her mother. Whether it was singing with the Harlem Boys Choir, taking violin lessons, or worshipping the talents of her musician father, Kelis was practically destined to make music. She left home at 16 to pursue her own goals, and four years later Kelis had a deal with Virgin. In mid-1999, Kelis was beatboxing alongside rap troublemaker Ol' Dirty Bastard on his cut "Got Your Money" and her signature technicolor spiraled afro sparked critics' interests. Her brooding vocals blend sensible R&B additives, and the hip-hop layers are funky. Kelis captured feminist desires on her debut *Kaleidoscope*, released in December 1999. *—MacKenzie Wilson*

• **Kaleidoscope** / Dec. 7, 1999 / Virgin ✦✦✦✦
This release showcases the development of a great talent. The album's flaws stem from steps taken backward toward what one could call "mainstream" R&B. It's when Kelis and her production team create tracks that best fit her voice and uniqueness that the end results are outstanding. Although comparisons to Neneh Cherry are inevitable, she does carve out a niche for herself, armed with undeniable talent. *Kaleidoscope* starts out strongly enough with standouts such as "Caught out There," "Get Along With You," and "In the Morning." Sadly enough, the focus seems to lose its footing midway and from there on out, the remaining songs run from average to good. As an artist who could become, with the proper guidance, a prominent figure for years to come, Kelis is one not to dismiss. *—Jaime Ikeda*

Wanderland / 2001 / Virgin ✦✦
Kelis' second full-length is a testimonial against the treacly fugue of her vaguely experimental hip-hop contemporaries, but it's short of her debut's grand accusatory glare and fresh psychedelia. Cue the flickers of U.K. psychedelia, Tina Turner big-earring fem-rock, and soulless, even workmanlike, duets with harmless MCs named Pusha T. If Kelis was hoping for Macy Gray-level success, particularly with outspoken admiration for British acts like Basement Jaxx or Muse, she resorts to high-strung, low-result collaborations with No Doubt ("Perfect Day") and some guy from Korn ("Easy Come, Easy Go"), effectively sidelining the Neptunes' production talents and patching together a scatterbrained world of empty beats and limp rhymes that never quite cover up her premature absence of ideas. *—Dean Carlson*

Paul Kelly

b. Jun. 19, 1940, Miami, FL
Vocals / Soul, Southern Soul, Country-Soul, Contemporary Blues
Miami soul singer/composer Paul Kelly was a consistent '70s R&B artist whose songs distinguished the repertoire of many Southern soul singers. After recording for Buddy Killen's Dial label in 1965, Kelly debuted on the R&B charts with "Stealing in the Name of the Lord" in 1970 for Happy Tiger Records. Killen produced some of Kelly's subsequent output for Warners Brothers in Nashville, including the grinding "Don't Burn Me" in 1973. Kelly's compositions graced a number of albums, including the 1991 Holmes Brothers encore album for Rounder, *Where It's At*. *—Bill Dahl*

Stand on the Positive Side / 1977 / Warner Bros. ✦✦✦
Paul Kelly's singing has a folksy, dirt-floor quality that purists admire. Like liver, however, he's not for everybody. Warner Brothers tries to mainstream the Miami-born singer on the awful Joe Tex rip "The Fat Lady That Bumped Me Down," and on "Feather in the Wind," a bad choice for Kelly despite the fact that he co-wrote it. The best tracks are "God Can," a strong gospel number, the sensual "Bathin' in Love Waters," "Feeling Good All Over," and "To the Bone Get It On." *—Andrew Hamilton*

• **The Best of Paul Kelly: Songs From the South** / Sep. 9, 1996 / Happy Tiger ✦✦✦✦✦
Miami native Paul Kelly is a man who had the right sound for the wrong era. He's surely one of Southern soul music's finest exponents, but he fettered about with no-can-do little independent labels for a dozen years before hitching up with Warner Brothers in 1971. The popularity of Southern soul music climaxed in 1968 when Otis Redding's "(Sitting on) The Dock of the Bay" spent four weeks atop the pop charts, and it was downhill from there. Kelly didn't have a chance. His own records flopped, so he hoped others could make them hits. When his buddy Sam Moore (Sam & Dave) turned down his "Stealin' in the Name of the Lord," Kelly decided to record it after all. Recorded at Muscle Shoals and released by the Happy Tiger label in 1970, the rocker critiqued ministers who pimped their congregations. After initial resistance from the church community, it peaked at number-14 R&B and remains Kelly's best-selling record. Warner Brothers then bought out Kelly's contract and captured his masters too. Those songs, and others he'd record until his four-album Warner run closed in 1977, are included on this twenty-song collection. Most tracks were produced by Buddy Killen, the white soul man who put Joe Tex on the map and later worked with country balladeer T.G. Sheppard. The results carry a light country-blues aroma, often punctuated with a little R&B. Kelly doesn't have the grit of Otis Redding nor the fluidity of Sam Cooke, but what he does own is a lot of feeling and a way of phrasing which sounds more like storytelling than singing. This gift is best exhibited on the gentle "Poor But Proud" and rockers such as "Come By Here," "I'm Into Something I Can't Shake Loose" and "Hooked, Hogtailed & Collared." Two of the nicest ballads are the previously unreleased "Love For Sale," about a man confusing the comfort of a prostitute with love, and the adultery tale "Stealin' Love on the Side." Since Kelly was never a big record seller and it's unlikely that this set will break any sales records, it's commendable that Warner Archives is releasing this material simply because it's quality music and because there are still some Paul Kelly fans out there. *—Bill Carpenter*

R. Kelly

Producer, Vocals, Keyboards / Urban, New Jack Swing, Hip-Hop, Pop-Rap
Urban R&B producer/vocalist/multi-instrumentalist/songwriter R. Kelly and his supporting band Public Announcement began recording in 1992 at the tail end of the new jack swing era, yet he was able to keep much of its sound alive while remaining commercially successful. While he created a smooth, professional mixture of hip-hop beats, soul-man crooning, and funk, the most distinctive element of Kelly's music is its

explicit carnality. He was able to make songs like "Sex Me," "Bump n' Grind," "Your Body's Callin'," and "Feelin' on Yo Booty" into hits because his production was seductive enough to sell such blatant come-ons. As his crossover success broadened, Kelly also developed a flair for pop balladry that helped cement his status as one of the biggest-selling male artists of the '90s.

Kelly & Public Announcement released their debut album, *Born Into the 90's*, at the beginning of 1992. It was an instant R&B smash, while earning a fair amount of pop airplay; "Honey Love" and "Slow Dance (Hey Mr. DJ)" were number-one R&B hits, while "Dedicated" was his biggest pop hit at number 31. *12 Play*, released in the fall of 1993, established Kelly as an R&B superstar, eventually selling over five-million copies. The first single, "Sex Me, Pts. I & II," went gold, and the second, "Bump n' Grind," hit number one on both the pop and R&B charts in 1994; it stayed on top of the R&B charts for an astonishing 12 weeks, while logging four weeks at number one on the pop charts. The follow-up, "Your Body's Callin'," was another gold single, peaking at number 13 pop. Also in 1994, he produced *Age Ain't Nothing but a Number*, the hit debut album for then-15-year-old Detroit R&B singer Aaliyah. Late in the year, it was revealed that Kelly and Aaliyah had wed in August and gotten an annulment shortly thereafter. The news sparked a small storm of controversy in the media, yet it didn't hurt the careers of either singer. Kelly next wrote and co-produced "You Are Not Alone," the second single from Michael Jackson's *HIStory* album, which was released in the summer of 1995. Later that year, Kelly released a self-titled album which became his first to top the pop charts. *R. Kelly* sold four-million copies and produced three platinum singles—"You Remind Me of Something," "Down Low (Nobody Has to Know)," and "I Can't Sleep Baby (If I)"—all of which hit number-one R&B and reached the pop Top Ten.

Kelly truly consolidated his crossover success with the 1996 single "I Believe I Can Fly," which he recorded for the Michael Jordan movie *Space Jam*. Transcending Kelly's prior sexed-up image, the song reached number two on the pop charts and won Grammy Awards for Best Male R&B Vocal Performance, Best R&B Song, and Best Song Written Specifically for a Motion Picture or for Television. Kelly remained in the public eye in 1997 with another Top Ten soundtrack tune, *Batman & Robin*'s "Gotham City." The ambitious two-disc *R.* followed in 1998, and even though it downplayed the explicit loverman routine that had made him a star, it became Kelly's biggest-selling album yet, going platinum seven times over. Its first single, a duet with Celine Dion titled "I'm Your Angel," became Kelly's second number-one pop hit with a six-week run on top. Even though subsequent singles "When a Woman's Fed Up" and "If I Could Turn Back the Hands of Time" were more successful on the R&B charts, Kelly was well on his way to landing more Top 40 hits in the '90s than any other male solo artist, and notched another with his guest appearance on Puff Daddy's R&B chart-topper "Satisfy You." Moving his blockbuster success into a new decade, Kelly returned in 2000 with *TP-2.Com*, which spent three weeks at number one on the album charts and scaled back the ambition of *R.* to return to familiar lyrical themes. He scored two more R&B number ones with "I Wish" and "Fiesta" (the latter featuring guest Jay-Z), and had further hits with "Feelin' on Yo Booty" and "The World's Greatest," the latter from the soundtrack of the Will Smith film *Ali*.

In the wake of "Fiesta," Kelly and Jay-Z teamed up to record an entire album together. *The Best of Both Worlds* was heavily hyped and even more heavily bootlegged, but problems of a much more serious nature arose in February 2002, when the *Chicago Sun-Times* reported that it had been given a videotape showing Kelly having sex with a 14-year-old girl. When the scandal broke, other reports surfaced that Kelly had settled a civil suit in 1998 involving a sexual relationship with a then-underage girl, and that he was in the process of settling another suit brought by an Epic Records intern making similar allegations. Copies of the tape in question were sold as bootlegs and on the Internet, and while there was some question as to whether the man was really Kelly, and whether the girl really was underage, Kelly's past history seemed to lend credence to the charge. Some radio stations dropped him from their play lists, and anti-Kelly protests were staged in Chicago. Meanwhile, *The Best of Both Worlds* entered the charts at number two, but sold disappointingly; some blamed the scandal, others the extensive pre-release bootlegging, although the generally unfavorable reviews suggested that the record's overall quality might also have been to blame.

Following the initial sex-tape scandal, Kelly was dogged by numerous civil suits, including one from a girl who alleged that during her relationship with Kelly (which occurred while she was underage), she had become pregnant and gotten an abortion at the singer's urging. A variety of other sex videos purporting to feature Kelly appeared as bootlegs, and a onetime Kelly protégée, a singer called Sparkle, stepped forward to identify the girl on the original tape as her then-14-year-old niece. In June, Chicago police officially charged Kelly with 21 counts of child pornography-related offenses, all related to the original tape. Kelly pleaded not guilty and released a new song, "Heaven, I Need a Hug," which got extensive airplay for a brief period. Meanwhile, work on his next album, *Loveland*, stalled amid more heavy bootlegging. Kelly eventually scrapped some of the most pirated tracks, recorded some new songs, and reassembled the album as *Chocolate Factory* (which was slated to include a bonus disc with some of the deleted material). Released in advance of the album, lead single "Ignition" shot to number one on the R&B charts in late 2002. *Chocolate Factory* itself was released in early 2003. *—Stephen Thomas Erlewine & Steve Huey*

Born into the 90's / Jan. 14, 1992 / Jive ✦✦✦
One of the last popular new jack groups, this East Coast unit had some smash singles in 1992 doing both conventional R&B/soul and hip-hop/new jack tracks. They did both originals and covers, had an enthusiastic attitude, were well produced, and stayed on the urban contemporary outlets throughout the year. *—Ron Wynn*

● **12 Play** / Nov. 9, 1993 / Jive ✦✦✦✦✦
New jack swing may have been on its way out as a primary R&B sound, but R. Kelly didn't lose any points by employing it here. Kelly skillfully mixes '70s-style funk beats, '90s hip-hop production and his own raps, as well as those of Deandre Boykins and Carey Kelly. Sometimes things come perilously close to sounding corny and dated, but he manages to bring things off successfully. Kelly is a competent vocalist, but a master at striking and maintaining a heated mood, keeping a light touch no matter how explicit the language gets and giving this album distinction even as it mines territory that's essentially played out. *—Ron Wynn*

R. Kelly / Nov. 14, 1995 / Jive ✦✦✦✦✦
With the salacious *12 Play*, R. Kelly established himself as one of the top R&B hitmakers of the mid-'90s, rivalled only by Babyface and Dr. Dre for overall consistency. *12 Play* was marred by occasionally slight tunes which were obscured by the explicit sexuality of the lyrics. *R. Kelly* isn't hampered by those flaws, although it isn't a perfect record by any means. Throughout the album, Kelly relies on melody and grooves instead of overtly carnal imagery. But that doesn't mean he has cleaned up—Kelly remains a sly, seductive crooner, and his sexiness is more effective when it is suggestive. Nevertheless, his lyrics and music are never subtle—even on the ballads which dominate this album—which can make *R. Kelly* tiresome if taken as a whole. Taken as individual songs, the album works better than anything he has recorded to date. *—Stephen Thomas Erlewine*

R. / Sep. 29, 1998 / Jive ✦✦✦
At the beginning of the '90s, R. Kelly was seen as a lewd, lascivious soulman. By the end of the decade, he had stripped those adjectives away and was seen as a contemporary equivalent of Marvin Gaye, thanks to the enormous success of "I Believe I Can Fly." Appropriately, *R.*, the double-disc album that followed "I Believe I Can Fly"'s parent album, finds Kelly trying to live up to that legacy. He may be talented, but he has neither the vision or the depth to match such classic soulmen as Al Green, Stevie Wonder, Prince or Michael Jackson, all artists he emulates on *R.* Kelly's main strength is fusing contemporary material together into a slick, palatable, radio-ready record. Nobody else could have Jay-Z and Celine Dion on their album, and he's about the only one who could make it work, since he can work sensuous grooves as well as he can deliver a soaring ballad. To some, this may sound like nothing more than calculation—a big part of the reason why he doesn't instantly enter the hall of greats—because it's easy to see how he pieces it all together. When he's on, however, such calculation doesn't really matter, since it all flows, but such incidents only occur through about 40 percent of *R.* That's a major problem, considering the sheer length of the album. Clocking in at 29 long tracks, it takes real effort to sit through the record from beginning to end, especially since Kelly begins to repeat himself. If it was pruned a bit, the album would arguably be his best record. As it stands, *R.* is an admirable effort, one that is among his better records even with all of its faults. *—Stephen Thomas Erlewine*

TP-2.Com / Nov. 7, 2000 / Jive ✦✦✦✦
For R. Kelly's follow-up to his epic double-disc *R* from 1998, the crooning ladies man scales back his artistic ambitions with *TP-2.Com*, an album harking back to his *12 Play* album from 1993. It's not so surprising that Kelly attempts to write a sequel to *12 Play*, a breakthrough album stacked with radio-friendly singles, rather than the overreaching scope of *R.* a disappointing album diluted by self-consciousness. This album's 19 songs may seem interchangeable at times in both lyrical and production terms, but Kelly manages to write some great songs that cut through the clutter. In particular, "I Wish" and the accompanying alternate version both stand out here as songs that break away from his usual romantic odes to sensuality. As he proves on nearly every song here, Kelly knows how to take proven formulas and funnel them through his own stylistic aesthetic, which usually means slowing down the tempo, laying on lush choruses of strings and background vocals, taming down the lyrics for radio, and catering his pitch primarily to wistful female listeners. *TP-2.Com* finds Kelly at his best as a pop artist, as he disregards the need to be "artistic" as he did on *R.* instead just focusing on giving the people precisely what they want: a consistent batch of well-crafted R&B odes to romance and sensuality, perfectly formatted for radio with plenty of hooks and the popular contemporary themes. *—Jason Birchmeier*

The Best of Both Worlds / Mar. 26, 2002 / Universal ✦✦

Eddie Kendricks

b. Dec. 17, 1939, Birmingham, AL, **d.** Oct. 5, 1992, Birmingham, AL
Vocals / Motown, Soul, Urban, Disco
Known for both his years with the Temptations and his major solo hits of the 1970s, Eddie Kendricks was among the many soul legends who did his part to put Motown Records on the map. The expressive vocalist (who often sang in a falsetto) grew up in Birmingham, AL, but it was Motown's original home of Detroit that made him a star. Kendricks was still living in Alabama in the late '50s, when he formed the Primes with Kell Osborne and Temptation-to-be Paul Williams. After moving from Alabama to Detroit, the Primes caught the attention of a Motor City group known as the Distants (whose members included Tempations-to-be Otis Williams, Elbridge Bryant and Melvin Franklin). The Primes broke up after being together only a few years, and the Temptations (originally known as the Elgins) were formed when, in 1961, members of the Primes and the Distants came together. With a lineup that included former Primes Kendricks and Paul Williams and former Distants Otis Williams (who was unrelated to Paul), Melvin Franklin and Elbridge Bryant, the Temptations signed with the little known Motown subsidiary Miracle. The Temptations (who went through many personnel changes over the years) didn't become successful right away, but by the mid-'60s, they had become huge thanks to such smashes as "The Way You Do The Things You Do" and "My Girl."

The Temptations enjoyed one mega-hit after another in the mid- to late 1960s, and they were still tremendously popular when Kendricks left to pursue a solo a career in 1971 (the year he sang lead on their hit "Just My Imagination"). Many Temptations fans questioned the wisdom of Kendricks leaving such a successful group, but Kendricks proved to be quite viable as a solo act thanks to early 1970s singles like "Keep on Truckin'" (a number-one R&B hit) and "Boogie Down" (which went to number two on the soul charts). Other noteworthy solo hits followed, including "Shoeshine Boy," "Get The Cream Off the Top" and "Happy" in 1975 and "He's a Friend" in 1976. Most of his solo albums came out on Motown, although Kendricks recorded *Something More* for "Arista" in 1979 and *Love Keys* for Atlantic in 1981. By that time, Kendricks' popularity had decreased considerably. The singer wasn't heard from that much in the 1980s, but he did participate in the Artists United Against Apartheid's *Sun City* project in 1985 and recorded with another former Temptation, David Ruffin, as a duo for RCA in 1988.

Sadly, the 1990s would see the premature deaths of no less than three former members of the Temptations. First, Ruffin died of a cocaine overdose in 1991, followed by the deaths of Kendricks in 1992 and Melvin Franklin (from a brain seizure) in 1995. (Tragedy was nothing new to Temptations members, for Paul Williams had committed suicide back in 1973). Kendricks was only 51 when he died of lung cancer in his native Birmingham on October 5, 1992. *—Alex Henderson*

All by Myself / 1971 / Motown ✦✦✦
Aptly titled but a lukewarm debut from Eddie Kendricks, the ex-Temptations tenor. While better than his last two releases for Hitsville U.S.A., they're weak compared to goodies like *Eddie Kendricks, Boogie Down!* and *My People . . . Hold On.* Kendricks' first single "It's So Hard To Say Goodbye" is as vanilla as the cream, a very ordinary beat-ballad; its flip "This Use to Be the Home of Johnnie Mae" is overblown and mundane. The LP has two good points: "I Did It All For You" a sweet ballad with an understated beat, and "Can I," Kendricks' signature ballad, a dreamy tune has been recorded by many, including David Peaston. *—Andrew Hamilton*

● **My People . . . Hold On** / 1972 / Motown ✦✦✦✦✦
Albums like this are why best-of and greatest-hits compilations aren't end-alls. One can find lots of good material that for a multitude of reasons never got released as singles, or if it did, went unnoticed as the flips of A-sides. The title track "My People Hold On" is one of Motown's most adventurous recordings with Eddie Kendricks; everything from African drums, a strong social message, and unorthodox backing chants makes the track a winner. Kendricks switches from his natural tenor to falsetto as easily as shifting gears in a Corvette, and no, you won't find it on *The Ultimate Collection.* Club favorite "Girl You Need a Change of Mind" features some wicked rhythms and urgent singing by Kendricks, while "If You Let Me" remains one of Eddie's best vocals; originally recorded by Jimmy Ruffin, Kendricks makes it his and his alone. The seductive slowies "Date With the Rain," "Day by Day," and "Just Memories" are aided by Eddie's sweet, innocent falsetto. *—Andrew Hamilton*

Eddie Kendricks / 1973 / Motown ✦✦✦
Though not worthy of lost-classic status like *My People . . . Hold On,* this self-titled effort is one of Kendricks' best of the early '70s. "Each Day I Cry a Little" is a painful ballad made even more gut-wrenching by the singer's strained vocals, and "Keep on Truckin'" is a great uptempo soul romp that can be heard on any classic-soul station of note. This is worth picking up if you can find it. *—Steve Kurutz*

Boogie Down! / 1974 / Motown ✦✦✦✦
Kendricks left the Temptations after seven years of constant success. As a solo act it took him a while to sustain momentum. Efforts like *All by Myself* and *People . . . Hold On* where unjustly ignored during the time of their release. Kendricks experienced a commercial breakthrough with his 1973 self-titled classic. *Boogie Down!* is his fifth solo album and shows that Kendricks had attained a mature and tasteful musical niche independent of his former group. Despite the title, *Boogie Down!* is an equal mix of dance and ballad material. Following the lead of Kendricks' number-one single, "Keep on Truckin'," producers Frank Wilson and Leonard Caston again found more like-minded tracks for Kendricks to do his trademark solo era perfunctory dance steps to. Songs like "The Thin Man" and "Son of a Sagittarius" are no doubt fatuous exercises, but not enough to be career threatening. The title track is about as monotonous as so-called early disco got and lyrics like "Let my love flood your Watergate" aren't exactly poetry. This effort is special due in part to Kendricks' treatment on the ballads. During this time, he could do anything he wanted with his voice and gained confidence as a solo act. The poignant "Honey Brown" and the affecting "You Are the Melody of My Life" display his skill at simply living the lyrics. "Girl of My Dreams" succeeds despite the shamefully overwrought '50s-style pop arrangement. Even as Kendricks sings "Oh my word" on the track, he doesn't even sound like a stooge. *Boogie Down!* cut for cut is Kendricks' strongest album. *—Jason Elias*

For You / 1974 / Motown ✦✦✦
This album was released in late 1974 and was the follow up to Kendricks' successful album *Boogie Down!* Even as talented as Kendricks could be, the line between him being inspiring and boring was remarkably fine. *For You* often finds him doing a batch of songs that simply paled in comparison to some of his stronger early-'70s work. Many songs here have good ideas but are barren lyrically speaking and often Kendricks sounds like he's on automatic pilot. The rich, musical backing of "One Tear" can't withstand the odd premise of Kendricks getting worked up over one non-falling metaphoric tear. "Shoeshine Boy" with its juvenile arrangement has Kendricks being the kid's biggest fan. As Kendricks piles on the platitudes he finally sings "Shoeshine boy/Working so hard in the noonday sun/Teasing the girls and having lots of fun." It's beyond silly. Kendricks did do good work here. "Deep and Quiet Love" is an ethereal ballad with unbelievable changes, heartfelt lyrics, and flawless and rich vocal. On that song in particular, Kendricks hit all of his spots and seemed to love the song himself. The song's repeated phrase "for you" is where this album got its title. No doubt *For You* producers Frank Wilson and Leonard Caston could come up with a few more ballad gems, but for some reason cover material was included here. "If" and "Time in a Bottle" were both songs that were pretty much summed up by the original artists and Kendricks sounded uncomfortable doing both of them. *For You* is one of Kendricks' lost album efforts and the good moments make this well worth seeking out. *—Jason Elias*

The Hit Man / 1975 / Motown ✦✦✦
The Hit Man didn't live up to its title; in fact, it sold so poorly that Motown shipped Eddie to Philadelphia to record his next two albums under the auspices of Norman Harris & His Harris Machine. Kathy Wakefield co-wrote most of the tracks with either Leonard Caston or Frank Wilson. One she didn't write, "Skipping Work Today," is the best song on the album; Eddie croons the daydream about calling off from work in a soft airy falsetto that's simply delicious. "Get the Cream off the Top" is veiled eroticism, written by Eddie & Brian Holland; it's not one of their best, but managed to chart R&B. Wakefield's best song, "Happy," also charted, but would have been a B-side or remained an album cut on Eddie's earlier and stronger albums. The rest of the songs are C-minuses. There's no need for Motown to reissue this one, since its three best tracks are available on other CDs. *—Andrew Hamilton*

At His Best / 1978 / Motown ✦✦✦
While Eddie Kendrick (or Kendricks) never made as much impact on his own as he did with the Temptations, he still made some fine singles as a solo artist on Motown. These are included on this anthology, and while three or four great tunes usually aren't enough to merit an anthology, Motown has issued them by artists who had even fewer. "Keep on Truckin'" was a disco/soul classic, and "Boogie Down" and "He's a Friend" are also outstanding. Kendricks is sorely missed by R&B and soul fans. *—Ron Wynn*

Something More / 1979 / Arista ✦✦

Love Keys / 1981 / Atlantic ✦✦

Motown Superstars Series, Vol. 19 / 1981 / Motown ✦✦✦
While better than the brief *At His Best*, this doesn't compare to the later *Ultimate Collection.* It's more on par with *One by One*, a two-CD package built around the solo releases of Eddie Kendricks, David Ruffin, Dennis Edwards and Paul Williams; so if you have that you really don't need to purchase this. Nothing new, or revealing, just the Eddie we all know and love. A jitterbugging "Keep on Truckin'" and the incessant beat of "Boogie Down" validate the CD. The beautiful "Skipping Work Today," will delight those who never heard the melodic ballad about cutting work; it's one of Kendricks finest efforts. A dark and moody "Intimate Friends" is haunting and charming; its slinky smooth groove and Kendricks' falsetto caress the touching lyrics for a winning combination. It's a shame Motown never released a live album on Eddie so people could hear the response when he sang "Intimate" and the sad, mysterious "Tell Her Love Has Felt the Need" live. Eddie was at his best on ballads, and midtempo numbers, though his biggest hits were maniac dancers. *—Andrew Hamilton*

I've Got My Eyes on You / 1983 / Ms. Dixie ✦✦✦
With the S.O.S. Band supplying the music, Eddie Kendricks' 1983 record ranks better than his last two LPs at Motown, and tops anything he waxed for Arista. "I've Got My Eyes on You" is a girl-watching tune accented with wolf whistles, male and female backing vocals, and dog barks. Known for ballads "When I'm Close to You" ranks among his best, Kendricks' weakened voice lacks power but possesses an abundance of charm. Kendricks updates "Born to Love You," a tune he first recorded with the Temptations. The newer rendition is as arresting, with the quintet, Splendor, replacing the Temptations. "Reason" has a funky reggae beat that pounds for more than four pleasurable minutes. He duets with an unidentified female on "The Very Thought of You," a sweeping ballad featuring Reather Bryant's crying, muted trumpet. "I'll Never Find Another Like You" is uptempo and pushed by a scratching guitar, thumping bass and vocals from Sheila Tyson, Sonia Rossman and Monica Green. Doc Samuels plays a plodding bass on "Long Conversation," which mixes R&B and reggae influences. A commercial failure, but the producers have no reason to hang their heads—this is good Kendricks. *—Andrew Hamilton*

● **The Ultimate Collection** / Sep. 22, 1998 / Motown ✦✦✦✦✦
When you think of R&B's great falsettos, Eddie Kendricks is a name that comes up along with Philip Bailey, Curtis Mayfield, Blue Magic's Ted Mills and the Stylistics' Russell Thompkins Jr. Most of the solo albums that Kendricks recorded for Motown in the 1970s are worth owning, but if you're on a tight budget and want to stick to his more essential solo recordings, *The Ultimate Collection* would be the most logical purchase. Released in 1998, this generous disc contains 16 songs that he recorded after leaving the Temptations. Many of them are essential gems, including "Boogie Down," "Keep On Truckin'," "Get the Cream Off the Top" and "Shoeshine Boy." The late singer could be quite charismatic, and he brings plenty of charm to the ballad "Skipping Work Today" and the title song of *He's a Friend* (which finds Kendricks expressing his Christian beliefs without preaching and/or getting in your face). Though not all of the selections are gems (some are merely decent), this is by far the best Kendricks collection available on CD. *—Alex Henderson*

20th Century Masters—The Millennium Collection: The Best of Eddie Kendricks / Oct. 10, 2000 / Motown ✦✦✦✦
Recommended for easily satisfied casual fans only, die-hard Eddie Kendricks janissaries won't find much satisfaction with this scanty run-down of Kendricks' solo career, which found the ex-Temptation constantly on the R&B charts and no stranger to pop chart success. Sadly, his two biggest pop darts ("Keep on Truckin'" and "Boogie Down") are not the lengthy album tracks but the short radio edits. Just when "Keep on Truckin'" starts kicking you're rollin' into "Boogie Down," which turns out to be a shortie too. Miraculously, his disco thumper "Girl You Need a Change of Mind" runs its full 7:33. A saving point is the inclusion of both title tracks from his overlooked albums done in Philadelphia under Norman Harris; you usually get "He's a Friend of Mine" in compilations but almost never "Going Up in Smoke." The beautiful "Tell Her Love Has Felt the Need" is a majestically executed weeper. "Can I," the ballad most identified with Kendricks (other than "Just My Imagination"), didn't make the cut—another bummer. *—Andrew Hamilton*

Joyce Kennedy

b. 1948, Anguilla, MS
Vocals / Chicago Soul, Soul, Album Rock, Adult Contemporary
Joyce "Baby Jean" Kennedy was born in Anguilla, MS, in 1948, and raised in Chicago. It's unclear how Andre Williams became her early mentor, but he produced nearly all her

early sides on Ran Dee, Fontana, and Blue Rock Records. She notched a local hit with "Darling I Still Love You," which was co-written by Williams. Released in 1963, it received little airplay anywhere else. A second release on Ran Dee, "Can't Take a Chance," also failed to perform. Kennedy then appeared on Fontana Records with "Paddle My Own Canoe." With Williams still at the helm, she released "I'm a Good Girl." The boisterous single became her second local hit, but once again, went nowhere outside of Cook County. A second Blue Rock release, "My Hi Fi Albums and Me," flopped as well, but is sought after by some collectors and is found on some Northern soul compilations.

Though the recordings ended, she still performed all over the Chicago area. She met singer Glenn Murdock, an ex-Vondells member, and the soulful duet embarked on tours across the country. After marrying, the two formed Mother's Finest in 1975, presumptively billed as the first black rock band. They had a steady stream of album releases, all critically acclaimed, but only scrounged a couple of small hits. A nonentity for black audiences, the band's fondest fans were white, and after disbanding in 1984, Kennedy signed with A&M. During 1984-1985, she enjoyed a string of hit singles, led by the Top 40 "The Last Time I Made Love" (a duet with Jeffrey Osborne), but also including "Stronger than Before," "Lookin' for Trouble," and "Hold On (For Love's Sake)." *—Andrew Hamilton*

- **Lookin' for Trouble** / Sep. 8, 1984 / A&M ♦♦♦

Former Mother's Finest lead singer Joyce Kennedy made her A&M solo debut with *Lookin' for Trouble.* The Chicago native left behind her hard rock/funk leanings but her powerhouse vocals were still in place. Produced mostly by Leon F. Sylvers III, her sound still leans toward funk, but its mixed in with such pop stylings as the Carole Bayer Sager/Burt Bacharach ballad, "Stronger Than Before." The song was covered by Chaka Khan around the same time on her *I Feel For You* LP. The highest charting single from the LP was the Kennedy/Jeffrey Osborne ballad, "The Last Time I Made Love," written by Barry Mann & Cynthia Weil. It remains the singer strongest bid for Top 40 Pop success, making it to number-two R&B/number-40 pop on *Billboard's* charts in summer 1984. It's on Osborne's *Ultimate Collection. Lookin' For Trouble* went to number-17 R&B/number-79 pop in fall 1984. *—Ed Hogan*

Chris Kenner

b. Dec. 25, 1929, Kenner, LA, **d.** Jan. 25, 1976, New Orleans, LA

Vocals / New Orleans R&B, R&B

Chris Kenner wrote a number of enduring New Orleans R&B classics, although subsequent cover versions eclipsed all but "I Like It Like That," his Grammy-nominated greatest hit in 1961. Kenner co-wrote "Sick and Tired" with Fats Domino and charted with it in 1957 on Imperial, but Domino's version blew it out of the water. Signing with Joe Babashak's Instant label, Kenner's "I Like It Like That," "Land of 1000 Dances," and "Something You Got" sported Allen Toussaint's rolling piano behind Kenner's raw vocals. *—Bill Dahl*

Land of a Thousand Dances / 1966 / Atlantic ♦♦♦♦♦

Featuring slashing soul by the writer of the title cut, this is one of the great forgotten albums. *—David Szatmary*

- **I Like It Like That: Golden Classics** / 1987 / Collectables ♦♦♦♦♦

Chris Kenner had two timeless singles in "I Like It Like That, Pt. 1" and "Land of 1000 Dances." The former was a big hit for Kenner, the latter was better-known through Wilson Pickett's cover and both became rock & roll standards. They are highlights on Collectables' *I Like It Like That: Golden Classics,* which contains the great majority of his Instant recordings from the early '60s, but they are by no means the only great songs here. Kenner's body of work was remarkably consistent, and while this collection could be presented a little bit better, the music couldn't be any more enjoyable. This is fine New Orelans R&B. *—Stephen Thomas Erlewine*

Alicia Keys

Vocals, Piano / Contemporary R&B, Neo-Soul, Urban

Her official website says she possesses an "old soul," and the hard facts seem to back up the implied claim of wisdom and experience that transcend Alicia Keys' youth. Barely in her twenties, Keys is responsible for an extremely hot debut, *Songs in A Minor.* The release, which she wrote and produced for Clive Davis' J Records, blends diverse influences, including R&B, hip-hop, classical, and jazz. The day the album went on the market, it sold more than 50,000 copies. Label executives confidently predicted similarly favorable numbers for the first week's tally.

Around the time that *Songs in A minor* was released, Keys was popping up everywhere, including an Associated Press story. Where had she been before then? Her entire life, it seems, had been an accelerated learning experience, preparing her for a career in music. A Manhattan native, her musical gifts became apparent when she was five years old. As a choir major enrolled in Manhattan's Professional Performance Arts School, she further developed her vocal talents with extra help from a teacher. By the time she was 16, Keys graduated and entered Columbia University. Music beckoned, however, and she quickly left Columbia behind.

Keys was writing songs when she was 14, with seven years of piano lessons under her belt by that time. In later years, she appeared on movie soundtracks, including *Shaft* and *Men in Black.* In 1998, she signed a deal with Arista Records when the company triumphed in a bidding war over other labels. When Davis left the company for J Records in 1999, Keys went along. Davis promoted the careers of such artists as Carlos Santana and Whitney Houston, and part of his launch strategy for Keys was to secure exposure on BET and MTV, as well as on *The Oprah Winfrey Show. —Linda Seida*

- **Songs in A Minor** / Jun. 5, 2001 / J Records ♦♦♦♦

Alicia Keys' debut album, *Songs in A Minor,* made a significant impact upon its release in the summer of 2001, catapulting the young singer/songwriter to the front of the neo-soul pack. Critics and audiences were captivated by a 19-year-old singer whose taste and influences ran back further than her years, encompassing everything from Prince to smooth '70s soul, even a little Billie Holiday. In retrospect, it was the *idea* of Alicia Keys that was as attractive as the record, since soul fans were hungering for a singer/songwriter who seemed part of the tradition without being as spacy as Macy Gray or as hippie mystic as Erykah Badu while being more reliable than Lauryn Hill. Keys was all that, and she had style to spare—elegant, sexy style accentuated by how she never oversang, giving the music a richer feel. It was rich enough to compensate for some thinness in the writing—though it was a big hit, "Fallin'" doesn't have much body to it—which is a testament to Keys' skills as a musician. And, the fact is, even though there are some slips in the writing, there aren't many, and the whole thing remains a startling assured, successful debut that deserved its immediate acclaim and is already aging nicely. *—Stephen Thomas Erlewine*

Chaka Khan (Yvette Marie Stevens)

b. Mar. 23, 1953, Great Lakes, IL

Vocals / Funk, Club/Dance, Urban, Quiet Storm, Soul

Best known for her superb 1984 cover of Prince's "I Feel for You," R&B singer Chaka Khan enjoyed solo success as well as popularity as a member of the group Rufus. Born Yvette Marie Stevens in Great Lakes, IL, on March 23, 1953, she was raised on Chicago's South Side, and at the age of 11 formed her first group, the Crystalettes. While still in high school, she joined the Afro-Arts Theater, a group which toured with Motown great Mary Wells; a few years later, she adopted the African name Chaka Khan while working on the Black Panthers' breakfast program. After quitting high school in 1969, Khan joined the group Lyfe, soon exiting to join another dance band, the Babysitters; neither was on the fast track to success, but her fortunes changed when she teamed with ex-American Breed member Kevin Murphy and Andre Fisher to form Rufus.

Debuting in 1973 with a self-titled effort on the ABC label, Rufus was among the pre-eminent funk groups of the decade; distinguished by Khan's dynamic vocals, the group earned half a dozen gold or platinum albums before she went solo in 1978. Produced by Arif Mardin, *Chaka* proved to be a significant hit on the strength of the single "I'm Every Woman" (a hit over a decade later for Whitney Houston); however, Khan's success was somewhat tempered by her public rivalry with the remaining members of Rufus, to whom she was still contractually bound for two more LPs. (Their differences were eventually resolved in a 1982 concert at New York's Savoy Theater, issued as *Live—Stompin' at the Savoy.*) As a solo artist, Khan recorded backing vocals for Ry Cooder's 1979 effort *Bop Till You Drop,* then cut her sophomore album, 1980's *Naughty*; it was not a hit, however, nor was its follow-up, *What Cha' Gonna Do for Me.*

In 1982, Khan recorded *Echoes of an Era,* a collection of jazz standards featuring performances from Freddie Hubbard, Joe Henderson, Stanley Clarke, Chick Corea and Lenny White. Her pop career was on shaky ground when she released 1984's *I Feel for You,* a platinum-seller launched by its title cut, a Grammy-winning, rap-inspired rendition (featuring memorable cameos from Melle Mel and Stevie Wonder) of a fairly obscure Prince album track. Still, while subsequent LPs like 1986's *Destiny* and 1988's *C.K.* kept Khan riding high on the R&B charts, her standing in pop's mainstream again began to wane, and at the end of the 1980s, she relocated to Europe. In 1990, she won another Grammy for "I'll Be Good to You," a duet with Ray Charles. *Come 2 My House* appeared in 1998. *—Jason Ankeny*

Chaka / 1979 / Warner Bros. ♦♦♦

Still very much an integral part of Rufus, Chaka Khan set the charts on fire with her debut solo release. The first single was the R&B chart-topper "I'm Every Woman," an Ashford & Simpson track with Khan lighting up the lyric with her tantalizing vocals. "Life Is a Dance," the second release, doesn't quite compare to its predecessor, but it still made the R&B Top 40. The sentimental ballad "Roll Me Through the Rushes" is poetically engaging, and despite never being released as a single, it became a mainstay of radio. Although Khan had much credibility from her association with Rufus, this album demonstrated that the dynamic vocalist could hold her own ground alone. The production work of acclaimed producer Arif Mardin must also be commended. *—Craig Lytle*

Naughty / 1980 / Warner Bros. ♦♦♦

By the early '80s Chaka Khan and producer Arif Mardin had a great working relationship that was responsible for her hit solo debut, 1979's *Chaka.* Despite having the hit single "I'm Every Woman," *Chaka* was often a stilted and unfocused affair. *Naughty* presents the two in a more centered working relationship. The big hit here, "Papillon (aka Hot Butterfly)," projects an effortlessness that didn't come as easy during Khan's concurrent run with Rufus. The tough, Latinized rock/funk of "Too Much Love" has one of Khan's most visceral performances. For *Naughty* Khan also does one of the better versions of Aaron Schroeder and Jerry Ragovoy's "Move Me No Mountain" that's made even better by Anthony Jackson's steady bass and Steve Ferrone's tough drumming. Despite the high points, other songs like "What You Did," "Our Love's in Danger," and even Ashford & Simpson's "Clouds" come off underdone. Recorded at Atlantic Studios in New York, most of *Naughty* represents Khan in a holding pattern, without much material to accommodate her widening range. That being said, *Naughty* is only a few songs away from being a bona fide classic. *—Jason Elias*

What Cha' Gonna Do for Me / 1981 / Warner Bros. ♦♦♦♦

As a vocalist, Khan is the one of the very few who often doesn't need great material to prosper. Thankfully on *What Cha' Gonna Do for Me,* that isn't the case. Teaming again with Arif Mardin, slowly but surely the two began to craft an even more successful and innovative sound. This effort not only bests the work before it, but it is Mardin's most fulfilling production since 1974's *Average White Band.* The cover of "We Can Work It Out" gets a brash and funky Stevie Wonder-style arrangement, with Gregory Phillinganes doing great synth work. The biggest hit here is the melodic title track and has Khan's patented mix of sexiness and intelligent phrasing. The best song here, "I Know You, I Live You," displays the brilliant bass and drum team of Anthony Jackson and Steve Ferrone whose innovation all but rendered Rufus obsolete. Their pounding yet refined sound is also on "We've Got Each Other," a hooky and propulsive duet with Khan's brother Mark Stevens. The ambitious and much loved "And the Melody Still Lingers On (Nights in Tunisia)" had Mardin and Khan creating pithy lyrics that paid homage to '40s jazz legends as well as all other subsequent musical geniuses. The track features a clavitar solo from Herbie Hancock, Dizzy Gillespie, and an "excerpted" solo break from Charlie Parker. Throughout *What Cha' Gonna Do for Me*, Mardin seems to get amazing vocals from Khan and has he certainly had fun playing with her voice. *What Cha' Gonna Do for Me* is arguably the best effort of their partnership. *—Jason Elias*

Chaka Khan / 1982 / Warner Bros. ✦✦✦✦✦
This is an excellent album from Chaka Khan, mixing tingling uptempo tunes with her characteristic soaring, glorious vocals. "Got to Be There" reached number five on the R&B charts, but it actually wasn't the album's high point. That was the marvelous "Be Bop Medley," which later led hardcore jazz purist Betty Carter to proclaim Khan the one female singer working outside the jazz arena with legitimate improvising credentials. *—Ron Wynn*

Echoes of an Era / May 1982 / Elektra ✦✦✦✦
In 1982, soul goddess Chaka Khan did the unexpected when she recorded this excellent, straight-ahead jazz LP. Regrettably, the album was released under the name Echoes of an Era instead of under Khan's own name—so it wasn't nearly the big seller it probably would have been if Elektra had fully exploited Khan's connection with the project. But while *Echoes of an Era* was the victim of questionable marketing, it was a creative triumph. Joined by Joe Henderson on tenor sax, Freddie Hubbard on trumpet and flugelhorn, Chick Corea on acoustic piano, Stanley Clarke on upright bass, and Lenny White on drums, Khan demonstrates that she is quite capable of handling hard bop and straight-ahead jazz. Corea, Clarke, and White had all been members of the fusion powerhouse of the 1970s Return to Forever, but make no mistake—*Echoes of an Era* is very much an acoustic bop date. With White producing and Corea handling the arrangements, the singer swings aggressively and really soars on Thelonious Monk's "I Mean You" and Duke Ellington's "Take the A Train" as well as on "Spring Can Really Hang You Up the Most," "All of Me," and "I Love You Porgy." In fact, Khan's jazz singing is so strong that one cannot help but wonder what would have happened if jazz had been her dominant direction instead of R&B. *—Alex Henderson*

I Feel for You / 1984 / Warner Bros. ✦✦✦✦✦
When Chaka Khan recorded her fifth solo album, *I Feel for You*, in 1984, she knew that R&B had changed a lot since the 1970s. Horn-powered funk bands, strings-laden Philadelphia soul, and orchestral disco were out of vogue, and the urban contemporary audiences of 1984 were into a more high-tech, heavily electronic style of R&B. Many artists who had been huge in the 1970s found that they no longer appealed to black radio programmers, who had abandoned them and turned their attention to electro-funksters and Prince disciples. But Chaka Khan had no problem keeping up with the times; *I Feel for You* made it clear that she could easily be relevant to the urban contemporary scene of 1984. No one would mistake *I Feel for You* for a Rufus project from 1975—it's way too high-tech—and yet, everything on the album is unmistakably Chaka Khan. That is true of uptempo items like "Love Is Alive" (an interesting remake of Gary Wright's 1976 hit) and "La Flamme," as well as the ballad "Through the Fire," which was a big hit on urban radio but crossed over to adult contemporary stations in a major way. "This Is My Night" (which was written and produced by the System) also became an urban radio hit, but the album is best known for Khan's unlikely remake of Prince's "I Feel for You." When Prince first recorded "I Feel for You" in 1979, it wasn't a hit; Khan's version, however, soared to number one on *Billboard*'s R&B singles chart. Khan had a very different take on the song than Prince; while his original version was subtle and restrained, Khan went for exuberance and added a strong hip-hop flavor. Excellent from start to finish, this album went down in history as both a creative and a commercial success. *—Alex Henderson*

Destiny / 1986 / Warner Bros. ✦✦✦
Most of the solo albums that Chaka Khan provided in the 1980s are excellent. From, 1986 *Destiny* falls short of perfect, although the LP is impressive more often than not. Many people were surprised to hear how rock-minded much of *Destiny* is, but then, Khan's former band Rufus had major rock leanings in the beginning: 1973's *Rufus* and 1974's *Rags to Rufus* underscored Khan and Rufus' appreciation of Ike & Tina Turner's soul/rock and were hardly the work of R&B purists. Nor is *Destiny*; while some of the material is straight R&B (including "Tight Fit" and the exuberant single "Love of a Lifetime"), Khan successfully combines R&B and rock elements on "My Destiny" and "Who's It Gonna Be" (which Janice Marie Johnson of A Taste of Honey fame had recorded on a little-known solo album in 1984). And some of the tunes are really more pop/rock than R&B, including "Watching the World," "The Other Side of the World," and "So Close." As much as *Destiny* has going for it, the LP isn't without its shortcomings. "Who's It Gonna Be" would have been better off without the fake applause that producers Arif and Joe Mardin pointlessly added, and the post-bop jazz offering "Coltrane Dreams" (which features saxman Sam Rivers) is too brief for its own good. Rivers, a major talent, doesn't get a chance to stretch out, and the piece ends up sounding undeveloped, which is quite frustrating because Khan can be a great jazz singer when she puts her mind to it. But while *Destiny* isn't perfect, the album has many more plusses than minuses and is easily recommended to both R&B and pop/rock enthusiasts. *—Alex Henderson*

C.K. / 1988 / Warner Bros. ✦✦✦✦
A first-class release, despite the fact that it didn't pack the normal commercial punch. But it had excellent production, many outstanding selections, and uniformly dazzling, booming, triumphant vocals from Khan. She speaks with disdain about the record business, and it's probably due to the relative failure of great records like this to break out and really enjoy the success they merit that's disillusioned her. *—Ron Wynn*

The Woman I Am / Apr. 14, 1992 / Warner Bros. ✦✦✦

• **Epiphany: The Best of Chaka Khan, Vol. 1** / Nov. 12, 1996 / Warner Bros. ✦✦✦✦✦
Chaka Khan's career is a rich one. As part of Rufus, she brought the funk home through the 1970s, across a staggering nine albums recorded with the band. She then repeated her success across a stronger solo career that spanned three decades. *Epiphany* is a chunky compilation that showcases the full range of Khan's work, embracing ballads, deep funkers, and jazzy groovers. Kicking off the proceedings is the blissful "Ain't Nobody"—probably the song most closely associated with Khan—and one of the last things she recorded with Rufus. It originally appeared on 1983's live *Stompin' at the Savoy*, and Khan's Rufus-era output is completed here with another *Savoy* track, the Stevie Wonder-penned "Tell Me Something Good." But there are other gems too, from chart-toppers to less-remembered nuggets. Khan's treatment of Prince's "I Feel for You," which features guest musicians Melle Mel and Stevie Wonder, is still a treat. Ashford & Simpson gifted "I'm Every Woman" to Khan, and gave her a number-one hit upon its initial release; "The End of a Love Affair," meanwhile, takes its cue from Ella Fitzgerald—to whom the song is dedicated, and which allows Khan to utilize her voice in an entirely different way. There's more versatility in the funky jazz of "And the Melody Still Lingers On (A Night in Tunisia)" and, while the brash "Papillon (aka Hot Butterfly)" is a weak link, this is still a wonderful compilation, packed with a fair representation of Khan's far-reaching canon. The perfect armchair companion. *—Amy Hanson*

Come 2 My House / Jul. 21, 1998 / NPG ✦✦✦

Kid Creole & the Coconuts

f. 1980, New York, NY

Group / Disco, Novelty, Latin Dance, New Wave, Calypso

Thomas August Darnell Browder (aka August Darnell) was born in Montreal on August 12, 1950, the son of a French Canadian mother and a Dominican father, but was raised in the New York City borough of the Bronx. In 1965, he formed the In-Laws with his half-brother, Stony Browder Jr. He earned a master's degree in English and became an English teacher, but in 1974 again joined his half-brother as bass guitarist, singer, and lyricist in Dr. Buzzard's Original "Savannah" Band, a group that mixed disco with big band and Latin styles. In 1976, Dr. Buzzard achieved a gold-selling album with its self-titled debut release, which featured the Top 40 hit "Whispering/Cherchez La Femme/Se Si Bon," but its subsequent recordings were less successful.

Darnell began to write and produce for other acts, co-composing Machine's 1979 chart entry "There But for the Grace of God Go I" and working with James Chance among others. In 1980, he became a staff producer at ZE Records and created the persona of Kid Creole (the name adapted from the Elvis Presley film *King Creole*) with a backup group, the Coconuts, consisting of three female singers led by his wife Adriana ("Addy") Kaegi, and a band containing vibraphone player "Sugar-Coated" Andy Hernandez (aka Coati Mundi), also from Dr. Buzzard. Kid Creole was a deliberately comic figure, a Latinized Cab Calloway type in a zoot suit and broad-brimmed hat who sang songs like "Mister Softee" that found him decrying his impotence while being berated by the Coconuts. *Off the Coast of Me*, the first Kid Creole & the Coconuts album, was released in August 1980 by Island Records subsidiary Antilles through a distribution deal with ZE. It earned good reviews for its clever lyrics and mixture of musical styles, but did not sell.

ZE made a deal with Sire Records (in turn part of Warner Bros. Records), and Sire released the second Kid Creole & the Coconuts album, *Fresh Fruit in Foreign Places*, in June 1981. It reached the charts briefly, and Coati Mundi's dance single, "Me No Pop I," was a Top 40 hit in the U.K. *Fresh Fruit* was a concept album that found the Kid Creole character embarking on an *Odyssey*-like search for a character named Mimi, and it was given a stage production at the New York Public Theater. Darnell continued the story with his third album, which was released in the U.K. under the title *Tropical Gangsters* in May 1982. The band toured Britain for the first time to promote the album, and they broke big: The LP hit number three and three singles, "I'm a Wonderful Thing, Baby," "Stool Pigeon," and "Annie, I'm Not Your Daddy," made the Top Ten, with "Dear Addy" reaching the Top 40. In the U.S., where the album was retitled *Wise Guy*, the band remained cult favorites, though the album charted and "I'm a Wonderful Thing, Baby" made the R&B singles charts. In 1983, Darnell produced side projects for the Coconuts (*Don't Steal My Coconuts*) and Coati Mundi (*The Former Twelve Year Old Genius*) before releasing the fourth Kid Creole album *Doppelganger*, which completed the Mimi cycle. The album got into the charts in the U.K., where the single "There's Something Wrong in Paradise" made the Top 40, but it did not chart at home and was a commercial disappointment after the breakthrough represented by *Tropical Gangsters' Wise Guy*.

Nevertheless, Kid Creole & the Coconuts remained a compelling live act with an imaginative visual style, which led to film and television opportunities. They appeared in the film *Against All Odds* in 1984 and continued to be tapped for movie projects in subsequent years, either for appearances or music: *New York Stories* (1989), *The Forbidden Dance* (1990), *Identity Crisis* (1990), *Only You* (1992), *Car 54, Where Are You?* (1994). They also made a TV film, *Something Wrong in Paradise*, based on the Mimi cycle and broadcast on Granada TV in the U.K. in December 1984.

Darnell broke up with his wife in 1985, and the original band split, with the Coconuts forming a group called Boomerang, while Andy Hernandez appeared in the Madonna film *Who's That Girl?* (1987). Darnell pressed on, appearing at the Montreux Jazz Festival and releasing the fifth Kid Creole & the Coconuts album, *In Praise of Older Women & Other Crimes*, which did not chart. Neither did the sixth album, *I, Too, Have Seen the Woods* (1987). The group joined Barry Manilow on "Hey Mambo," a song on his *Swing Street* album that made the singles charts. Darnell then took time off to write *In a Pig's Valise*, an Off-Broadway show that ran for 12 weeks. Kid Creole & the Coconuts, now featuring former Dr. Buzzard singer Cory Daye, resurfaced in 1990 on Columbia Records, issuing a seventh album, *Private Waters in the Great Divide*, which featured "The Sex of It," a song written by Prince that made the British Top 40 and the American R&B charts. It was followed a year later by *You Shoulda Told Me You Were. . . .*

Kid Creole & the Coconuts spent the 1990s touring internationally and releasing albums primarily outside the U.S. *To Travel Sideways* and *Kiss Me Before the Light*

Changes both appeared initially in Japan, though they found stateside release on a small label in 1995. *The Conquest of You* was released in Germany in 1997. (An American release on Fuel 2000 was scheduled for 1999, but did not occur.) In the U.S., the group appeared in Atlantic City and Las Vegas. Kid Creole starred in the British musical *Oh! What a Night*, which ran in the West End from August to October 1999. *—William Ruhlmann*

Off the Coast of Me / Aug. 1980 / Antilles ♦♦♦♦
Mixing disco, Caribbean music, and strains of big-band jazz, Kid Creole engages in a self-deprecating dialogue with his backup singers, The Coconuts, who dismiss him as "Mister Softee" and plead, "Can You Get Me Into Studio 54?" on this hilarious debut album. *—William Ruhlmann*

Fresh Fruit in Foreign Places / Jun. 1981 / ZE ♦♦♦♦

Wise Guy / Jun. 1982 / Sire ♦♦♦
The ongoing adventures of Kid Creole continue on this bouncy collection that produced three British Top Ten hits, including "Annie, I'm Not Your Daddy" and "I'm a Wonderful Thing, Baby." *—William Ruhlmann*

Doppelganger / 1983 / ZE ♦♦♦

In Praise of Older Women & Other Crimes / 1985 / Sire ♦♦

I, Too, Have Seen the Woods / 1987 / Sire ♦♦

Private Waters in the Great Divide / Mar. 1990 / Columbia ♦♦♦

● **Kid Creole Redux** / Mar. 17, 1992 / Sire ♦♦♦♦♦
This 1992 compilation released on Sire stands as the best introduction to Kid Creole & the Coconuts, a thrilling group that exemplified New York City's diverse cultural mix during the '80s. *Kid Creole Redux* reaches back to early ZE and Island singles like 1980's "He's Not Such a Bad Boy," 1981's "Going Places," and 1982's "I'm a Wonderful Thing, Baby," and it also includes cuts from the mid-'80s that saw the group reach its highest level of popularity ("My Male Curiosity," "Endicott"). Nobody knew exactly what Kid Creole & the Coconuts were—that was part of the their charm. If there's one thing this group *wasn't*, it was a novelty. Whatever they *were*, they cranked out some humorous, rhythmic, vibrant pop music that has had no problem translating to the present. *—Andy Kellman*

Kina

b. Detroit, MI
Vocals / Contemporary R&B, Urban
Former Brownstone member Kina's first solo outing, "Girl in the Gutter," burst on the scene in the summer of 2000 to critical kudos and lots of music-video airplay. Kina's rock/pop style has been compared to Tina Turner, Macy Gray, Dionne Farris, Alanis Morissette, Des'ree, one-time LaBelle member Nona Hendryx, and Rufus & Chaka Khan. The video for her single "Girl From the Gutter" was quickly added to the play lists of music-oriented cable channels MTV, VH1, and The Box.

Born Kina Cosper on January 25 in Detroit, MI, she lists Lenny Kravitz, Smokey Robinson, the Rolling Stones, and Aretha Franklin among her influences. In 1995, Kina joined Brownstone who were signed to Michael Jackson's Epic Records-distributed label, MJJ Music. The group enjoyed its biggest success with the million-selling Grammy-nominated single, "If You Love Me," and the *Billboard* hit "Grapevine." They also won the coveted spot as the opening act for Boyz II Men's 1995 U.S. tour.

During November 1997, Kina amicably parted ways with Brownstone to follow her own artistic vision. A former manager introduced her to singer/songwriter/producer London Jones (*House Party 2* soundtrack and on his own MCA LP, *For You*). The duo clicked creatively and began working on her solo debut. In the interim, Kina got a record deal with Dreamworks Records distributed through Universal Music. After catching her performance at the Mint Club in L.A., manager Benny Medina came on board as her manager. Her debut CD, *Kina*, was issued on July 18, 2000. The sultry singer co-executive produced her album with industry vet Lenny Waronker.

Anger was the spark that fueled Kina writing "Girl From the Gutter" with Jones; it definitely has an "I'm gonna show you!" theme running through the lyrics that tells the tale of a rising underdog. Other highlights are "I Love You," "Have a Cry," "Loser," and her self-produced "Hurt So Bad." Around the time of the release of *Kina*, the singer had a scheduled appearance on *The Tonight Show With Jay Leno*. *—Ed Hogan*

● **Kina** / Jul. 18, 2000 / DreamWorks ♦♦♦
Kina was formerly a member of the trio Brownstone who released the single "If You Love Me." Her self-titled solo debut draws comparisons to such pop/rock vocals as Dionne Farris and Tina Turner, but the singer/songwriter/producer has more than enough talent to make her own mark. "Girl From the Gutter" was an immediate add on the video play lists of MTV, VH1, and The Box. Its angry underdog theme of "I'm mad and I'm not going to take it anymore" has blistering lyrics. Kina cools down on such on lovely ballads as the country-ish "Have a Cry," the airy "Still Here," and the acoustic guitar laced "Give and Take." The string laced/power chord pumper "I Love You" is reminiscent of '80s era Prince ("Raspberry Beret" and production on The Family). The joyous self-love ode "Me" is both inspiring and fortifying. This self-titled release is a Grade A debut from this adventurous singer/songwriter. *—Ed Hogan*

King Curtis (Curtis Ousley)

b. Feb. 7, 1934, Fort Worth, TX, **d.** Aug. 14, 1971, New York, NY
Sax (Tenor) / Soul-Jazz, Southern Soul, Instrumental Rock, R&B, East Coast Blues
King Curtis was the last of the great R&B tenor sax giants. He came to prominence in the mid-'50s as a session musician in New York, recording, at one time or another, for most East Coast R&B labels. A long association with Atlantic/Atco began in 1958, especially on recordings by the Coasters. He recorded singles for many small labels in the '50s—his own Atco sessions (1958-1959), then Prestige/New Jazz and Prestige/TruSound for jazz and R&B albums (1960-1961). Curtis also had a number-one R&B single with "Soul Twist" on Enjoy Records (1962). He was signed by Capitol (1963-1964), where he cut mostly singles, including "Soul Serenade." Returning to Atlantic in 1965, he remained there for the rest of his life. He had solid R&B single success with "Memphis Soul Stew" and "Ode to Billie Joe" (1967). Beginning in 1967, Curtis started to take a more active studio role at Atlantic, leading and contracting sessions for other artists, producing with Jerry Wexler, and later on his own. He also became the leader of Aretha Franklin's backing unit, the Kingpins. He compiled several albums of singles during this period. All aspects of his career were in full swing at the time he was murdered in 1971. *—Bob Porter*

Have Tenor Sax, Will Blow / 1959 / Atco ♦♦♦
This is one fun dance record, right from the opening bars of "Midnight Ramble," a piece that sounds like a cross-breeding of "Bo Diddley," with both the sax and the lead guitar having fun with the central riff, and "Yakety Sax." Not everything here is as delightful, hypnotically frenetic as that Curtis Ousley semi-original, but most of the album is done with an infectious sense of humor, and even the predictable numbers here, like "Linda," with its tango tempo, is eminently listenable, if not exactly breaking any new horizons in R&B. Other tracks, like "Jaywalk" and "Lil Brother," are slightly more adventurous; and the band has a lot of fun with "Peter Gunn." The final two numbers, "Birth of the Blues" and "Chili," don't quite fit in with the rest of the record, both utilizing orchestral accompaniment in lieu of the band. *—Bruce Eder*

Country Soul / 1962 / Capitol ♦♦
This album of country standards was intended to be King Curtis' answer to Ray Charles' *Modern Sounds in Country and Western Music*. It never sold remotely as well as Charles' album, primarily because of Curtis' more perfunctory singing and some unwise choices of music to cover—"Night Train To Memphis," "Raunchy" (which *is* an instrumental), and "I'm Movin' On" work as R&B instrumentals, with the latter benefiting from some sizzling interplay between the guitars, the trumpets, and Curtis' sax. But "High Noon" and "Home on the Range" are a lot less convincing, conceptually as well as in execution. There are a few surprises, however, such as a version of "Your Cheatin' Heart" that tries desperately to transform itself into "Stand By Me." *—Bruce Eder*

Soul Twist and Other Golden Classics / 1962 / Collectables ♦♦♦♦♦
Here's an interesting set of singles featuring the great tenor saxophonist recording for various Bobby Robinson imprints. His big hit "Soul Twist" (this is the stereo remix, lacking a bit in bite from the original 45) is the centerpiece, but Curtis also sits in with Les Cooper on "Wiggle Wobble" (again the stereo mix, but sounding just fine), and tracks with Choker Campbell, Noble Watts, Curley Hammer, and Willis Jackson demonstrate what an adaptable musical giant the man truly was. Transfers vary from track to track, and again, like most early Collectables packages, there are no liner notes to speak of, but the music will have you dancing across the room. *—Cub Koda*

Soul Serenade / 1964 / Capitol ♦♦♦♦♦
Curtis' second Capitol album is a triumph on every level. The tragedy is that, apart from the hit title track, almost nothing off of this superb album was heard by the public—most of the singles he was doing were very different from this material. The album featured Curtis' covers of songs like the Bill Doggett co-authored "Honky Tonk," and Chuck Berry's "Memphis," the hottest, most soulful version of the Champs' old hit "Tequila" ever recorded, and Herbie Hancock's "Watermelon Man," as well as a re-recording of his hit "Soul Twist," and a version of his "Night Train," a big hit for Jimmy Forrest. Maybe the biggest surprise here is the cover of the blues standard "Hide Away," written by Curtis' old friend Freddie King. Sharing the spotlight with Curtis' sax throughout this record is Cornell Dupree on lead guitar, adding just the right accompaniment variously as a lead and rhythm instrument—the two make the oft-heard cover of "Hide Away" by John Mayall and Eric Clapton sound like a poor demo. There's not a wrong or wasted note. *—Bruce Eder*

Plays Hits Made by Sam Cooke / Mar. 9, 1965+Mar. 11, 1965 / Capitol ♦♦♦♦
This is about the only Sam Cooke tribute record—other than individual songs cut by Otis Redding—that one could imagine Cooke himself not only would have approved of fully, but might have enjoyed himself, had it been recorded under other circumstances. One could even visualize him dancing to the versions of "Shake," which does have a few echoes of "Night Train" in it, or "Twistin' the Night Away" or "Good Times." Curtis had known and worked with Cooke, and the singer's shooting death late in 1964 affected the saxophonist deeply, as it did millions of people. This album was the result, a dozen covers that blow away most any other Sam Cooke tribute album (including the still highly collectible Supremes' *We Remember Sam Cooke*). *—Bruce Eder*

Live at Small's Paradise / 1966 / Atco ♦♦♦
There's very little in the way of audience ambience or other interaction on this recording, done at a club in Harlem, but it does have all of the other expected virtues of a concert recording. The tension of a live performance runs throughout its ten songs, which include the most soulful rendition of "Blowin' in the Wind" this side of Sam Cooke's version, and a King Curtis vocal on "Road Runner." Not as important a document as *Live at Fillmore West*, which came considerably later in Curtis' career, but not to be ignored, either. *—Bruce Eder*

Instant Groove / Apr. 1, 1968-Apr. 23, 1969 / Atco ♦♦♦

Blues at Montreux / 1971 / Collectables ♦♦♦
This live set from the 1971 Montreux Jazz Festival was co-led by tenor saxophonist King Curtis (who tragically would be killed three months later) and veteran blues pianist/vocalist Champion Jack Dupree. With guitarist Cornell Dupree (in excellent form), bassist Jerry Jemmott and drummer Oliver Jackson laying down the foundation, Curtis and Dupree find a great deal of common musical ground. Dupree has quite a few witty vocals (particularly the near-classic "Junker's Blues") while taking choruses of irregular length that keep his sidemen continually guessing. Curtis' distinctive tenor is also heard from, making one truly regret that this was his final recording. *—Scott Yanow*

Live at Fillmore West / Feb. 5, 1971-Feb. 7, 1971 / Koch International ♦♦♦♦♦
Recorded in front of an enthusiastic audience and released just one week before Curtis' murder in 1971, *Live at Fillmore West* is a brilliant confirmation of the saxophonist's place in popular music. Backed up by Atlantic's top session men, as well as Billy Preston and the Memphis Horns, Curtis rips through some of the biggest hits of the day, transforming them into showcases for his soulful playing and the group's outstanding rhythmic interplay. Beautiful renditions of "A Whiter Shade of Pale" and "I Stand Accused" are highlights, but it's full-throttle rockers like "Changes" and "Memphis Soul Stew" that comprise the heart of the album. Curtis occasionally gets lost in the mix, but it doesn't matter; with so much great music going on, you probably won't notice. *—Jim Smith*

Blow Man, Blow! / 1993 / Bear Family ♦♦♦♦♦
71 songs spread among three CDs, covering King Curtis' tenure at Capitol from 1962 until 1965. This wasn't the most productive period in Curtis' career, but it was his first chance to make records on more than a piecemeal basis under his own name; the result is a dazzling array of sounds and songs. Hidden among the country covers and abortive early sides on disc one is a lot of gold, most notably "Slow Drag" and the previously unreleased "New Dance," which features some killer guitar; the early unissued material is superb, including the Curtis original "Frisky," a slow version of "Alexander's Ragtime Band," the beguiling "Sukiyaki," and a gorgeous bossa nova called "Amorosa." (Many of these tracks feature guitarist Cornell Dupree, who was to figure in Curtis' most successful records for Capitol.) Disc two is where things start to cook: from "More Soul" on through to the previously unreleased "Hung Over," there's not a note of filler on the disc, which encompasses all of the *Soul Serenade* album as well as a brace of unreleased songs and some very fine singles, including a dazzling cover of the Acker Bilk standard "Stranger on the Shore," and a soulful recomposition of Jackie Gleason's "Melancholy Serenade." Disc three comprises material ranging from reinterpretations of pop standards like "Moon River" and "The Girl From Ipanema" through a dozen covers of Sam Cooke songs, all worthwhile. *—Bruce Eder*

● **Instant Soul: The Legendary King Curtis** / Oct. 19, 1994 / Razor & Tie ♦♦♦♦♦
A nice overview of Curtis' solo career, *Instant Soul: The Legendary King Curtis* begins with the breakthrough success of "Soul Twist" and "Soul Serenade," then moves through his later recordings for Atlantic. It's interesting to hear Curtis in both the Memphis and Muscle Shoals settings and how he adapts his horn to different grooves along the way. A solid collection of this artist's best, although points get shaved off for the inclusion of a later recut version of "Wiggle Wobble," rather than the original by Les Cooper on which Curtis blew so magnificently. *—Cub Koda*

Soul Meeting / Dec. 7, 1994 / Prestige ♦♦♦♦♦
King Curtis, an influential and greatly in-demand R&B tenorman, made relatively few jazz dates in his career. This CD has two of the best, complete albums originally called *The New Scene of King Curtis* and *Soul Meeting*; the former is also available as a separate CD but should be skipped in favor of this one. Curtis teams up with the passionate cornetist Nat Adderley, pianist Wynton Kelly, either Paul Chambers or Sam Jones on bass and Oliver Jackson or Belton Evans on drums. The music is blues-based bop, with seven basic Curtis originals and four standards. Highly recommended, this set serves as proof that King Curtis could have been a viable jazz player. *—Scott Yanow*

Piping Hot: The Complete Enjoy Sessions / Sep. 5, 1995 / Relic ♦♦♦♦
King Curtis never officially "joined" Bobby Robinson's Enjoy label. Rather, he came aboard only provisionally, willing to cut a couple of sides and see if they hit, and once they did, he would sign. Robinson ran the session for "Soul Twist" and got Curtis to feature the guitar, the organ, and the piano alternating with his sax—the record became Curtis' first hit, and an album followed, but Curtis never signed to Enjoy, choosing to go with Capitol Records instead in May 1962. The 15 songs here were all that came of his early 1962 association with Robinson, bold numbers mostly featuring very prominent guitar (played by Billy Butler and Joe Richardson) and organ (by Ernie Hayes)—check out "What'd I Say, Pts. 1 and 2"—and even a harmonica solo by the King himself on "Harmonica Twist," along with the expected sax breaks. Robinson's big discovery was that Curtis blew all the way through his previous records, rather than using his band for contrast. The sound is excellent, and the notes, though a little sketchy, tell us a lot about how these records, among Curtis' best (certainly superior to the country & western venture Capitol threw him into) were made. *—Bruce Eder*

Hot Sax, Cool Licks / 2000 / Ace ♦♦♦
Here's a complete summary of Curtis' sessions as a soloist for Atlantic in the late '50s. It includes not only the tracks he cut under his own name for both the 45 and long-playing formats, but also five previously unissued songs, and three hits he played on as a session man (the Coasters' "Yakety Yak" and "That Is Rock & Roll," and Chuck Willis' "What Am I Living For?"). Curtis' playing on these is very good, cementing his standing as perhaps the finest rock saxophonist of the time. It also shows more versatility than he was able to convey with the famous trademark stuttering style that was heard on solos such as the one he played for the Coasters' "Yakety Yak." What keeps this from being that great a CD, though, is the failing common to many instrumental rock collections: The songs are not terribly strong *or* varied. Many of these are pretty basic R&B-rock crossover workouts (sometimes with a calypso beat), though they do benefit from support by noted sidemen, including guitarists Jimmy Spruill, Mickey Baker, and Al Casey; drummer Panama Francis; and tenor saxophonist Noble Watts. The 1958 single "Castle Rock" is the best track, with a jazzy beat, hot Casey solos, and drum solos on the order of Cozy Cole's "Topsy II." Curtis does get a chance to stretch into relatively straight jazz occasionally (as on the previously unissued "Splankin'"). The 1958 single "You Made Me Love You (I Didn't Want to Do It)" makes its first appearance on a reissue here, though as a jazz ballad with female vocals that seem to be backgrounds missing a lead, it's one of his worst records. [This U.K. import is not available for sale in North America.] *—Richie Unterberger*

King Floyd

b. Feb. 13, 1945, New Orleans, LA
Vocals / Funk, Soul
New Orleans vocalist King Floyd had some big soul hits in the early '70s, including the chart-topping "Groove Me," which also landed him his only pop hit, peaking at number six. Floyd began singing at age 11 and debuted professionally in 1961. He spent much of 1961 and all of 1962 in the Army, getting discharged in 1963. He moved to New York and stayed until he relocated to Los Angeles in 1964. He began recording for Original Sound in 1965, then went back to his hometown in 1969. After "Groove Me," Floyd showed that he was no fluke, with "Baby Let Me Kiss You" reaching number-five R&B. "Got to Have Your Lovin" didn't fare as well, but "Woman Don't Go Astray" returned him to chart prominence, reaching number three. Floyd kept recording for Chimneyville through 1976, getting one more mild hit that year with "Body English." *—Ron Wynn*

King Floyd / 1971 / Cotillion ♦♦♦

● **Choice Cuts** / Jun. 17, 1994 / Waldoxy ♦♦♦♦
When Malaco released this "best-of" collection on its Waldoxy label in 1994, it had been 17 years since King Floyd's departure from the company. After all that time, Floyd was still among the first names that came up during a discussion of Malaco's history. Recording Floyd was certainly among Malaco's finest accomplishments, and *Choice Cuts* offers considerable evidence of that fact. This 15-song CD, which spans 1970-1977, contains all of Floyd's major hits, including "Baby, Let Me Kiss You," "Woman, Don't Go Astray" and his signature song, "Groove Me." Equally strong is Floyd's cover of Otis Redding's "Hard to Handle," which had been a major hit for Patti Drew in 1968 and received the rock & roll treatment from the Black Crowes in 1990. Those gems are the epitome of deep-fried Southern soul—raw, tough and unapologetically gritty. But while Southern R&B was what Floyd did best, 1976 found the singer experimenting with disco and funk elements on the sleek, danceable "Body Language." The catchy number became a dancefloor hit, but ultimately, Floyd would be best remembered for his contributions to Southern soul. For those who've never experienced the pleasures of King Floyd, *Choice Cuts* would be the best starting point. *—Alex Henderson*

Ben E. King (Benjamin Earl Nelson)

b. Sep. 23, 1938, Henderson, NC
Vocals / Soul, Pop-Soul, Brill Building Pop
From the groundbreaking orchestrated productions of the Drifters to his own solo hits, Ben E. King was the definition of R&B elegance. King's plaintive baritone had all the passion of gospel, but the settings in which it was displayed were tailored more for his honey smooth phrasing and crisp enunciation, proving for perhaps the first time that R&B could be sophisticated and accessible to straight pop audiences. King's approach influenced countless smooth soul singers in his wake and his records were key forerunners of the Motown sound.

King was born Benjamin Earl Nelson in Henderson, NC, in 1938, and sang with his church choir before the family moved to Harlem in 1947. In junior high, he began performing with a street corner doo wop group called the Four B's, which won second place in an Apollo Theater talent contest. While still in high school, he was offered a chance to join the Moonglows, but was simply too young and inexperienced to stick. He subsequently worked at his father's restaurant as a singing waiter, which led to an invitation to become the baritone singer in a doo wop outfit called the Five Crowns in 1958. The Five Crowns performed several gigs at the Apollo Theater along with the Drifters, whose career had begun to flounder in the years since original lead singer Clyde McPhatter departed. Drifters manager George Treadwell, dissatisfied with the group members' unreliability and lack of success, fired them all in the summer of 1958 and hired the Five Crowns to assume the name of the Drifters (which he owned).

The new Drifters toured for about a year, playing to often hostile audiences who knew they were a completely different group. In early 1959, they went into the studio with producers Jerry Leiber & Mike Stoller to cut their first records. A song Nelson (still performing under his given name) co-wrote called "There Goes My Baby" became his first lead vocal and the lush backing arrangement made highly unorthodox (in fact, virtually unheard-of) use of a string section. "There Goes My Baby" became a massive hit, laying the groundwork for virtually every smooth/uptown soul production that followed. Over the next two years, Nelson sang lead on several other Drifters classics, including "Dance With Me," "This Magic Moment," "Save the Last Dance for Me," and "I Count the Tears."

In 1960, Nelson approached Treadwell about a salary increase and a fairer share of the group's royalties. Treadwell rebuffed him and Nelson quit the group, at this point assuming the more memorable stage name Ben E. King in preparation for a solo career. Remaining on Atlantic, King scored his first solo hit with the stylish, Latin-tinged ballad "Spanish Harlem," a Jerry Leiber/Phil Spector composition that hit the Top Ten in early 1961. The follow-up, "Stand By Me," a heartfelt ode to friendship and devotion co-written by King, became his signature song and an enduring R&B classic; it was also his biggest hit, topping the R&B charts and reaching the pop Top Five. King scored a few more chart singles through 1963, including velvety smooth pop-soul productions like "Amor," "Don't Play That Song (You Lied)," and the Italian tune "I (Who Have Nothing)." In the post-British Invasion years, King had a rough go of it on the pop charts but continued to score R&B hits. In 1967, the Southern-fried "What Is Soul?" was one of his last singles for Atco; seeking to revive his commercial fortunes, King departed in 1969.

A 1970 album on Maxwell, *Rough Edges*, failed to generate much attention, and King was forced to make a living touring the oldies circuit. In 1975, Atlantic president Ahmet Ertegun caught King's act in a Miami lounge and invited him to re-sign with the label. King scored an unlikely comeback smash with the disco track "Supernatural Thing, part 1," which returned him to the top of the R&B charts in 1975 and also reached the pop Top Five. While he was unable to duplicate that single's success, King recorded several more albums for Atlantic up through 1981, and also collaborated with the Average White Band in 1977 on the album *Benny and Us*. After leaving Atlantic a second time, King toured in a version of the Drifters beginning in 1982. In 1986, "Stand By Me" was prominently featured in the Rob Reiner film of the same name; re-released as a single, it climbed into the Top Ten all over again. In its wake, King returned to solo recording, issuing a new album every few years all the way up through the '90s. He also guested on recordings by Heaven 17 and Mark Knopfler, among others.

King's 1999 album *Shades of Blue* (on Half Note Records) found him branching out into jazz territory, performing with a big band and guests like Milt Jackson and David "Fathead" Newman. *—Steve Huey*

Ben E. King Sings for Soulful Lovers / 1962 / Atco ✦✦✦
Atco's *Ben E. King Sings for Soulful Lovers* was an attempt to cross King over into the territory of Tony Bennett, Vic Damone, and Andy Williams to generate lucrative gigs in the Catskills, Las Vegas, and other premier supper clubs. The original dozen, which consists of King's renditions of pop and easy listening tracks, i.e., "Moon River," "It's All in the Game," "What a Difference a Day Makes," are all here. Sequel not only reissued this 1962 Ben E. King album in CD format, but also pumped it up with additional tracks—some of King's most memorable recordings—as an added incentive to buy. The nine additions include the ex-Drifter's chart slayers: "Stand By Me," "Don't Play That Song," and "I Who Have Nothing." *—Alex Henderson*

Seven Letters / 1965 / Atco ✦✦✦
The original notes to the *Seven Letters* album indicate that it is the most diverse album of material that Ben E. King had ever recorded, and they're right. The range of material here, cut over a period of more than two years, included some impassioned soul music—"River of Tears," "I'm Standing By," "It's All Over," "In the Middle of the Night," and the title track—as well as some very personal pop ("Jamaica") and novelty ("Si Senor") tunes, and towering performances throughout. The requisite string-laden orchestral backings are present, courtesy of producers Leiber & Stoller, Jerry Wexler, Ahmet Ertegun, and the various arrangers, but there are also some nicely stripped down, more basic soul numbers. Interestingly, "Jamaica" was written by King in the wake of his 1961 tour of the island (soon to be island-nation), an event that helped spark a boom in local ska and reggae performers who were inspired by the presence of American soul stars like King on tour—the song practically chronicles the spawning of the seed that led to the ska and reggae booms (which Atlantic would grab a piece of, not only by signing Byron Lee and securing a distribution agreement with him for the Cayman Islands, but also through Eric Clapton's efforts on Bob Marley's behalf less than a decade later). The album has not a single weak spot, and boasts some strong contributions by several outside songwriters including Carole King and Gerry Goffin, whose gorgeous "Down Home" provided the vehicle for King's best singing on the entire record. Not that it did much for him at the time of its release—it had no weak spots, but also no major hits (even "I'm Standing By" was a failed follow-up to "Stand By Me," and this was the last of four Ben E. King albums issued by Atlantic in the United States. Like two of its predecessors, it disappeared without reaching any but King's hardcore audience, thus making it a choice collector's item. It lacked the hook of a massive hit single like a "Stand By Me" or a "Spanish Harlem" for a wider audience to grab onto. [Listeners are also advised to see *Anthology Four: Seven Letters*.] *—Bruce Eder*

Rough Edges / 1970 / Maxwell ✦✦✦
Count your blessings if you find a copy of this rare bird. This Ben E. King LP on Larry Maxwell's Maxwell label interrupted a string of Atco releases. Limited sales made it a one-off and King began another string of albums for the Atco family on Atlantic Records. The Bob Crewe production finds the ex-Drifters lead singing with fervor on songs the likes of which he never sniffed at while recording for Atco. Actually a hodgepodge, lighter efforts like "Little Green Apples," the much-recorded "She Lets Her Hair Down," and the emoting "Lay Lady Lay" buffer King's straight-up renditions of the Beatles' "Come Together" and Wilson Pickett's "In the Midnight Hour." But there's no attempt to re-create his popular solo or Drifters recordings; that coupled with a weak promotional effort made *Rough Edges* an early entry in the cutout bins. Scarcity, however, has made the price of a copy in mint condition worth significantly more. *—Andrew Hamilton*

Supernatural / 1975 / Atlantic ✦✦✦
In 1975, Ben E. King was attempting to blend in with the smooth soul and disco trends of the mid-'70s. Thanks to the smash hit "Supernatural Thing, part 1," he was surprisingly successful at making himself sound contemporary. While the material is uneven, the sound of the record is appealing, meaning that it was a respectable comeback. *—Thom Owens*

Benny and Us / 1977 / Sequel ✦✦✦
Benny and Us resulted from a chance meeting in Miami between Ben E. King and the Average White Band, who were vacationing there just when King was starting work on a new album. The finished album yielded two hit singles and became King's best-selling LP, rising to number 33. The sound is soulful and funky, very bright and passionate—the upbeat, relentlessly catchy "Get It Up for Love" and the soaring, horn and string driven "A Star in the Ghetto" made respectable showings on the R&B charts, and a good portion of the rest ("The Message," "What Is Soul") is pretty powerful stuff as well. "Imagine" is so busy and so self-consciously earnest that it's difficult to enjoy, but King is so good in the moments when he is on target, that it's hard to skip this track, even if it is the weakest number here. The radiant "Keepin' It to Myself" and the poignant cover of Donny Hathaway's "Someday We'll All Be Free," by contrast, are among King's very best records. *Benny and Us* was a good enough record that it nearly led to a joint tour (as opposed to some joint appearances, which actually happened) between King and the Average White Band—one can only marvel at what those shows must have sounded like, and lament that fact that no live album was cut. It also marked King's last major appearance on the charts for Atlantic. To date, however, it's only available as an import from Sequel Records. That reissue, apart from excellent sound, also includes alternate edits of "Fool for You Anyway," "The Message," and, especially, "Star in the Ghetto," including the 12-inch single version of the latter—all are worth hearing. *—Bruce Eder*

Best of Ben E. King / Jan. 12, 1993 / Curb ✦✦
Best of Ben E. King is a ten-track budget-priced collection that features some of his biggest hits (sometimes in re-recorded versions), including "Stand By Me," "This Magic Moment," "There Goes My Baby" and "Save the Last Dance for Me," along with some lesser-known items. Although this isn't a bad budget-priced disc, there are better collections available, offering more songs and better sound for not much more money. *—Stephen Thomas Erlewine*

Anthology / Apr. 20, 1993 / Rhino ✦✦✦✦✦
This two-disc, 50-song box set thoroughly documents the recordings that Ben E. King cut for Atlantic. Starting as the lead voice of the Drifters on such hits as "There Goes My Baby" and "Save the Last Dance for Me," King went on to a successful solo career with a string of singles that matched his smooth, sexy baritone with tastefully arranged string sections and Latin rhythms. All of those early hits—"Stand by Me" and "Spanish Harlem" were the biggest—are included here, along with non-hit 45s by the likes of Leiber & Stoller, Doc Pomus, Mort Shuman, Phil Spector, and Goffin & King that were nearly equal in worth. As the '60s progressed, King moved toward a more mainstream, heavier soul sound and less distinctive material, culminating in his parting from Atlantic in 1969. He returned to the label in the mid-'70s for a string of mainstream R&B successes. This compilation includes 16 non-LP singles from the '60s, which together with the hits constitute the definitive overview of this influential soul singer's work. *—Richie Unterberger*

● **The Very Best of Ben E. King** / Feb. 3, 1998 / Rhino ✦✦✦✦✦
The Very Best of Ben E. King is an excellent 16-track collection that features his biggest hits from 1959-1975, including hits he had with the Drifters in addition to his solo smashes. Among the featured songs are "There Goes My Baby," "Dance With Me," "This Magic Moment," "Save the Last Dance for Me," "Spanish Harlem," "Stand By Me," "Amor," "Don't Play That Song (You Lied)," "How Can I Forget," "I (Who Have Nothing)" and "Supernatural Thing, part 1." All of his best-known songs are available on this concise, affordable disc, which makes for an ideal introduction to this legendary R&B/soul vocalist. *—Stephen Thomas Erlewine*

Shades of Blue / Aug. 10, 1999 / Half Note ✦✦✦
Ben E. King is best known for his R&B recordings, so *Shades of Blue* is a return to his roots. He is accompanied by a band led by trumpeter Tim Ouimette that includes a single guest appearance apiece by tenor saxophonist David "Fathead" Newman and vibraphonist Milt Jackson. The orchestra is very much in the Count Basie groove, King adds a lot of soul to the lyrics without improvising much, and the music swings in a pleasing fashion. Among the selections that King interprets are "Just for a Thrill," "Hallelujah I Love Her So," "Stairway to the Stars," and "Baby Won't You Please Come Home." Nothing too surprising occurs, but the results are easy to enjoy. This is a happy set of mostly familiar material. *—Scott Yanow*

Bobby King & Terry Evans

f. Nov. 4, 1943, South Carolina, **db.** Chicago, IL
Group / Quiet Storm, Smooth Soul, Adult Contemporary, Soul
The duo of soul singers Bobby King & Terry Evans first teamed on the Los Angeles club circuit of the early '70s; both also enjoyed prolific session careers, and in 1974 lent their distinctive harmonies to Ry Cooder's *Paradise and Lunch*, the first in a series of collaborations with the acclaimed guitarist. Sessions with artists including Boz Scaggs, John Fogerty, and Bob Dylan followed and in 1988, King and Evans cut their first headlining effort, *Live and Let Live!*; *Rhythm, Blues, Soul & Grooves* followed two years later. *—Jason Ankeny*

● **Live and Let Live!** / 1988 / Rounder ✦✦✦✦✦
While much contemporary R&B and soul offers more production than quality, the duo of Bobby King & Terry Evans demonstrated on this 1988 set that they could bring 1960s passion to a 1980s recording session. The duo's shared leads, rousing singing and inspiring qualities turned such numbers as "Seeing is Believing," "Saturday Night" and the title track into exciting, smashing treatments. Although their version of "Dark End of the Street" may run a bit long at seven minutes plus, they don't do anything to ruin that number's legacy of memorable renditions. *—Ron Wynn*

Rhythm, Blues, Soul & Grooves / 1990 / Rounder ✦✦✦
The duo of Bobby King & Terry Evans followed their well-received 1988 duet session with a solid second outing, this time taking over the production chores as well as performing. The ten tracks included anguished love tunes, uptempo dance cuts and moving ballads, with the accent on their own material as they split writing duties and penned nine of the cuts. With Evans' huge, resonant bass voice often booming and soaring, King's striKing falsetto tenor contrasted it with vigor. Sadly, this sound had little chance for getting any exposure at urban contemporary radio, but those who love great singing should savor it. *—Ron Wynn*

Earl King (Earl Johnson)

b. Feb. 7, 1934, New Orleans, LA
Vocals, Guitar / New Orleans R&B, New Orleans Blues, R&B, Funk
Unilaterally respected around his Crescent City homebase as both a performer and a songwriter, guitarist Earl King has been a prime New Orleans R&B force for more than four decades—and he shows no signs of slowing down. Born Earl Johnson, the youngster considered the platters of Texas guitarists T-Bone Walker and Clarence "Gatemouth" Brown almost as fascinating as the live performances of local luminaries Smiley Lewis and Tuts Washington. King met his major influence and mentor, Guitar Slim, at the Club

Tiajuana, one of King's favorite haunts (along with the Dew Drop, of course), the two becoming fast friends. Still billed as Earl Johnson, the guitarist debuted on wax in 1953 on Savoy with "Have You Gone Crazy" (with pal Huey "Piano" Smith making the first of many memorable supporting appearances on his platters).

Johnson became Earl King upon signing with Specialty the next year (label head Art Rupe intended to name him King Earl, but the typesetter reversed the names!). "A Mother's Love," Earl's first Specialty offering, was an especially accurate Guitar Slim homage produced by Johnny Vincent, who would soon launch his own label, Ace Records, with King one of his principal artists. King's first Ace single, the seminal two-chord south Louisiana blues "Those Lonely, Lonely Nights," proved a national R&B hit (despite a soundalike cover by Johnny "Guitar" Watson). Smith's rolling piano undoubtedly helped make the track a hit.

King remained with Ace through the rest of the decade, waxing an unbroken string of great New Orleans R&B sides with the unparalleled house band at Cosimo's studio. But he moved over to Imperial to work with producer Dave Bartholomew in 1960, cutting the classic "Come On" (also known as "Let The Good Times Roll") and 1961's humorous "Trick Bag" and managing a second chart item in 1962 with "Always a First Time." King wrote standout tunes for Fats Domino, Professor Longhair, and Lee Dorsey during the '60s. Although a potential 1963 pact with Motown was scuttled at the last instant, King admirably rode out the rough spots during the late '60s and '70s. When he signed with Black Top, his performing career was rejuvenated; 1990's *Sexual Telepathy* and *Hard River to Cross* three years later were both superlative albums. *—Bill Dahl*

● **Earl's Pearls** / May 5, 1998 / WestSide ✦✦✦✦✦
This top-notch collection brings together 25 tracks from King's 1955-1960 tenure with Ace Records in Jackson, MS. Classic '50s New Orleans music doesn't come much finer than this, and Earl's contributions to the genre are plentiful on this disc, starting with his big hit, the original "Those Lonely, Lonely Nights." A real treat is hearing Huey "Piano" Smith soloing with complete abandon on tracks like "Nobody Cares," "Little Girl," "I'll Take You Back Home" and "Baby You Can Get Your Gun." Earl's guitar playing is equally fine and his Guitar Slim-derived style is well to the fore on "My Love Is Strong" and "I'm Packing Up." Although King's discography encompasses many labels and sessions, this is a great place to start absorbing this Crescent City genius. *—Cub Koda*

Evelyn "Champagne" King

b. Jul. 1, 1960, New York, NY [The Bronx]
Vocals / Quiet Storm, Disco, Club/Dance, House, Soul

Singer Evelyn "Champagne" King first came to fame with the million-selling '70s disco smashes "Shame" and "I Don't Know If It's Right." Born July 1, 1960, in the Bronx, NY, she had a showbiz lineage. Her uncle was actor/singer/dancer Avon Long, who first played Sportin' Life in the play *Porgy and Bess* and later starred in the '70s play *Bubblin' Brown Sugar.* Her father, Erik King, was a singer and often augmented groups that appeared at New York's Apollo Theater. By her teens, King had relocated to Philadelphia with her mother, and began singing in several groups. To make ends meet, King and her mother became cleaning women. For a teenager, King's voice was quite mature; many at first thought she was a grown woman.

While working one night at Philadelphia International Records' recording base, producer T. Life overheard some tantalizing vocals coming from a washroom. There he discovered 16-year-old Evelyn King and her mother. Signing the singer to a production deal and a contract with RCA, Life's first single with Evelyn "Champagne" King was "Dancin', Dancin', Dancin'." Her debut LP *Smooth Talk* was released August 1977. But it was a song written by John Fitch and Reuben Cross called "Shame," that gave her career-launching success. The extended mix began gaining radio play and eventually the Top Ten on the R&B and pop charts by spring 1978. The follow-up, "I Don't Know If It's Right" also went gold, peaking at number-seven R&B, number-23 pop in fall 1978. *Smooth Talk* went gold, and she made two more LPs with T. Life: *Music Box* and *Call on Me.*

After teaming with a new producer, Kashif, King recorded two number-one R&B hits during the early '80s, "I'm in Love" and "Love Come Down." Several of her LPs also placed high on the charts, including 1980's *Call on Me,* the following year's *I'm in Love,* and 1982's *Get Loose.* She signed to EMI-Manhattan in 1988, and was teamed with Leon F. Sylvers III for *Flirt,* which included the tender ballad "Kisses Don't Lie." On *The Girl Next Door,* the singer worked with house producer Marshall Jefferson.

In 1990, King recorded the album *I'll Keep a Light On* for the British label Expansion, whose featured musicians were Larry Graham, Jeff Lorber, and Paul Jackson Jr. Many of the singer's classic sides are on *Love Come Down: The Best of Evelyn "Champagne" King.* *—Ed Hogan*

Smooth Talk / 1977 / RCA ✦✦✦✦
With a healthy array of simple yet funky soul/disco romps, King's debut outing is a fine catch for '70s R&B connoisseurs. Grooves like the savvy title track, with its undulating drum fills and serene and stylish vocal arrangement; the assertive "We're Going to a Party"; and the quietly melodic, pondering "I Don't Know If It's Right" (R&B number seven, Pop number 23), showcase the singer's power and poise finely against solid arrangements. And then there's the perennial dancefloor classic "Shame" (R&B and Pop number seven), a bustling romp with an unforgettable transitional bridge and catchy chorus. Several forgettable numbers do surface, in the form of the bland, repetitive "Dancin', Dancin', Dancin' " and the unconvincing heavy funk stance of "Til I Come off the Road." But on the whole, *Smooth Talk* proves itself a fun, satisfying listen for the body—if not a genius piece of soul. *—Justin M. Kantor*

Music Box / 1979 / RCA ✦✦✦
Producer T. Life enlisted a few different players on King's sophomore set. The resulting flavor is a bit jazzier than 1977's *Smooth Talk,* but also more formulaic and predictable. The fun, funky grooves are replaced here by thinner dance concoctions; and furthermore, the songs themselves aren't as substantial, lyrically or melodically. King does her best to shine over the humdrum, which she does most successfully on the two-part hustler "Steppin' Out" and catchy titletrack. Both of these numbers are rhythmically enticing, offering more variety than the predominating safe outings (the washy "Out There," very repetitive "Make Up Your Mind"). She also tries her hand at a pair of slow-grooves—via a typical soul ballad, "Let's Start All Over Again," and the subdued, percussive "I Think My Heart Is Telling." The latter is remarkable for its restraint, and actually allows a nice forum for King to show her softer side. The jewels are few and considerably far between. Basically, the singer got caught up in what was probably RCA's attempt to fashion her into the somewhat mellowed-out, commercial disco trends of 1979. But in the end, *Music Box* proved much less commercially successful than its predecessor. For listeners who simply appreciate King's passionate vocals, the set is worth sifting through; but for those looking for classic King grooves à la "Love Come Down" and "Shame," *Music Box* is better passed on. *—Justin M. Kantor*

Call on Me / 1980 / RCA ✦✦
King's strong, deep-voiced stylings and sensitive edge are the saving graces on her first album of the '80s. Despite overall sturdy production, many of the melodies simply linger on and on and the arrangements don't have much chance to take off. Besides the sassy "Let's Get Funky Tonight" and the warm, understated "Just a Little Bit of Love," there aren't any particularly memorable moments. The title track is a stale midtempo romp with an embarrassing guest vocal by producer T. Life; "Bedroom Eyes" is accordingly sleepy; and "Talk Don't Hurt Nobody" has a decent lyrical theme, but lacks the musical energy needed to get the lyric across. Whereas the previous year's *Music Box* relied on formulaic disco tracks, *Call on Me* tries to establish King in a funkier vein. But the material itself is so arid that the album quickly becomes musically ineffective. *—Justin M. Kantor*

I'm in Love / 1981 / RCA ✦✦✦✦
After working with producer T. Life on her first three albums (1977's *Smooth Talk,* 1979's *Music Box* and 1980's *Call on Me*), Evelyn "Champagne" King changed producers for her fourth album, *I'm in Love*—a generally excellent release that found the singer being commercially and creatively revitalized. Half of the songs were produced by Kashif associate Morrie Brown (with Kashif and Lawrence Jones serving as associate producers), while the other half were produced by Willie Lester and Rodney Brown. Either way, *I'm in Love* is King's most rewarding and commercially successful effort since *Smooth Talk,* and she is undeniably inspired on gems that range from the funky title song (a major hit that Kashif wrote) and the assertive "If You Want My Lovin'" to the ballads "Don't Hide Our Love" and "The Best Is Yet to Come." An interesting tidbit: with *I'm in Love,* King temporarily dropped the "Champagne" from her name and simply went by Evelyn King—however, she went back to calling herself Evelyn "Champagne" King with 1983's *Face to Face.* If you only have a few King albums in your collection, *I'm In Love* should be among them. *—Alex Henderson*

Get Loose / 1982 / RCA ✦✦✦✦
Hot off the heels of her successful comeback album, *I'm in Love,* King was in her commercial prime when *Get Loose* hit stores in 1982. One of the earliest R&B/funk female vocalists to use the music video medium (for 1981's "I'm in Love"), she was frequently on airwaves in the early '80s with songs found here like "Love Come Down" and "Betcha She Don't Love You." The romantic lyrics and celestial keyboard layerings against a steady funk beat on "Love Come Down" were expertly layed down by Kashif, who would become a prominent R&B producer and artist in his own right. His stamp is also on many of the album's other cuts, though Morrie Brown is the album's actual producer. "Betcha" is another unique number—a down-paced dancefloor ditty with a rock-friendly chorus and vocal arrangement. Meanwhile the title track is a colorful uptempo number that hearkens back slightly to 1977's "Shame." Equally appealing are the refined "Back to Love" and "I'm Just Warmin' Up," the album's soothing closer. King sounds fresh and stylish throughout, making *Get Loose* one of her strongest efforts. *—Justin M. Kantor*

Face to Face / 1983 / RCA ✦✦

So Romantic / 1984 / RCA ✦✦✦✦
On the heels of 1983's artistically and commercially disappointing *Face to Face,* King served up a much more consistent follow-up with this album. From the onset of the set's vivacious opener, "Show Me (Don't Tell Me)"—with a lyrical context notably similar to 1983's "Action," *So Romantic* allows King plenty of room to showcase her flair for dance music without overcrowding her with excessive electronic gimmicks. It does an impressive job of melding dancefloor beats with rock guitars and keyboards—a vein in which the singer is very at home. Whether it be the intelligently produced "Just for the Night," boasting an understated echo-chamber effect that is concentrated in the background; the straightforward and soulful "Give Me One Reason" (one of the set's most melodic tunes, along with the emotive "Till Midnight"); or the nocturnal rocker "I'm So Romantic," the overall sound is very solid with an adept mixture of live instrumentation and synthesizers. With King's bold vocals atop them, the songs on *So Romantic* make it one of her strongest '80s albums. *—Justin M. Kantor*

A Long Time Coming (A Change Is Gonna Come) / 1985 / RCA ✦✦

Flirt / Feb. 1988 / EMI America ✦✦

The Girl Next Door / Sep. 1989 / EMI America ✦✦✦✦
King's second set for EMI boasted a noteworthy selection of snagging urban/hip-hop jams and mellow house grooves that ultimately suffered from almost zilch promotion and got lost in the hoopla of the change of decades. Catchy gems like the title track and the pulsating "Magnet" are radio-friendly in their hooks and production, and would've made strong singles. Indeed, the two singles released, "Day to Day" and "Do Right," have their strengths. The down-low funk and no-mess lyrics of "Do Right" are simply irresistible; and the quietly groovin' "Day to Day" exudes a peaceful musical vibe thoroughly enhanced by King's deep and husky vocal. But perhaps at least one more obvious single

choice would've boosted sales of *The Girl Next Door* and prevented its follow-up album (*I'll Keep a Light On*) from being shelved. Besides the aforementioned uptempo selections, the set's ballads and midtempo cuts are equally commendable. The plush, breezy "Cross Your Mind" is King's strongest slow-jam to date: not over-belted—just cool and understated, yet quite emotive. And her remake of the Isley Brothers' "Footsteps in the Dark" invokes reflections of Lalah Hathaway. It all adds up to one of her best albums. *—Justin M. Kantor*

Love Come Down: The Best of Evelyn "Champagne" King / Mar. 1993 / RCA ♦♦♦♦
Before the term "disco diva" was universally adopted, Evelyn "Champagne" King was hailed as dance music's reigning female vocalist. King was a sensation in disco's heyday, and she survived the backlash and prospered during the genre's evolution into dance music. She enjoyed a string of hits into the mid-'80s and was able to excel on rhythm-dominated material and sentimental ballads. This 15-track anthology includes her finest uptempo cuts ("Shame," "I'm In Love," and "Love Come Down," all done at the original hit length), plus underrated numbers such as "Don't Hide Our Love" and "Give Me One Reason." Those who remember King's hits will savor this collection, while others who missed her prime period will hear why she was so dominant. *—Ron Wynn*

● **Greatest Hits** / Feb. 20, 2001 / RCA ♦♦♦♦
Although its track listing is fairly similar to 1993's *Love Come Down* compilation (cutting a few numbers but featuring three more total), *Greatest Hits* gets the nod as the Evelyn "Champagne" King" collection of choice, since it features the original seven-inch single versions, plus several rare, extended 12-inch mixes. Covering King's career from 1978's breakout hit "Shame" through 1986, *Greatest Hits* is as comprehensive a retrospective of her work as is ever likely to be released, capturing all the reasons she was a popular and important disco and R&B singer. *—Steve Huey*

Fern Kinney

b. Jackson, MS
Vocals / Urban
Perhaps the prototype one-hit wonder, Jackson, MS, vocalist Fern Kinney was in the Poppies along with Dorothy Moore before she signed with Atlantic. Kinney moved to Malaco in the late '70s, and her cover of King Floyd's "Groove Me" made it into the R&B Top 30, though neither of the LPs *Groove Me* or *Fern* sustained her initial momentum. Kinney did land a number-one hit in England in 1980, "Together We Are Beautiful." *—Ron Wynn*

● **Groove Me** / 1980 / Malaco ♦♦

Kinsman Dazz

f. 1976, Cleveland, OH
Group / Funk
The roots of Kinsman Dazz lie in Cleveland, OH, where they formed in 1976. "Kinsman" is taken from both the street and the name of the lounge where they worked as the house band—the Kinsman Grill, located on the corner of East 128th and Kinsman Rd. "Dazz" sounds like "Jazz," which they liked to play, and which also was the buzz word of a hit by Brick, entitled "Dusic." Loosely, they were the mergers of two groups: Bell Telephunk and Mother Braintree. Loosely, of course, because from 1976 to 1978, when their self-titled debut LP dropped, the band had gone through nearly 30 lineup changes. Neither Telephunk nor Braintree ever recorded, though the latter toured with Edwin Starr for over a year as his road band. Larry Ross, the leader of Mother Braintree, was never a part of Kinsman Dazz, or the later Dazz Band. The brothers Wiley, Michael and Issac, were members though, and another ex-Braintree member, Pierre Demudd, joined when they signed with Motown, but was not with them when they recorded for 20th Century. Despite what you may have read elsewhere, neither was Sennie "Skip" Martin III ("Let It Whip"), a San Francisco native. He didn't join until they signed with Motown. Martin was plucked from Mighty Generation, a group from Youngstown, OH, who had gigged all the way to San Jose, CA, where Martin joined them. When they returned to Youngstown, Skip came along and met the members of Kinsman Dazz when they came there to play a gig.

Bobby Harris served as the group's defacto leader, while Earth, Wind & Fire's Philip Bailey acted as Kinsman Dazz's mentor; he co-wrote songs, arranged, sung backing vocals and produced the two 20th Century LPs. The lineup of Kinsman Dazz was ever-changing—even as their first LP hit the streets, the revolving door swung back and forth. By the time Dazz came out, guitarist/songwriter Michael Calhoun had vanished. He later surfaced on a couple of obscure 45s, released on tiny labels in his native Cleveland, OH, before disappearing. *—Andrew Hamilton*

● **Kinsman Dazz** / 1978 / 20th Century ♦♦♦
Earth, Wind & Fire's Philip Bailey produced both of the Kinsman Dazz LPs, which is why "Catchin' Up on Love" (written by Bobby Harris), sounds like Earth, Wind & Fire sideways, and backwards. Singing lead on the melodic midtempo floater was Wayne Preston, it was an immediate success, a scintillating guitar solo by Michael Calhoun, was like a cherry topping to the excellent production. The whole album had a vibrant, new feel about it; lead vocals were switched around on "I Searched Around," with Kenny Pettus handling lead vocals on a smooth, sumptuous ditty written by Calhoun. "Dancin' Free" was fast, juiced by a funky synthesizer, and punchy horns poking in and out the beat. A delightful first album, though skimpy, only six selections. *—Andrew Hamilton*

Dazz / 1979 / 20th Century ♦♦♦
Similar to their debut, *Dazz* started with a disco-flavored dancer, this time "Saturday Night (At the Disco)" getting the honor. "Dazzberry Jam" reunited the Clevelanders with their jazz roots and their days as Bell Telephunk, holding it down at Sonny Jones' Kinsman Grill Lounge. (Earth, Wind & Fire's guitarist Ralph Johnson co-wrote the infectious groove with Bobby Harris.) Producer Philip Bailey couldn't help tossing in some Earth, Wind & Fire vibes and grooves. Bailey's influence is loud and clear on "Forget About Lovin' You," lead singer, Wayne Preston imitates Bailey's powerful falsetto in tone, if not power. Bailey, however, adds punch by duplicating Preston lines, giving the lead more punch. The only ballad, "Stand in Your Way," is also the only song not written by a group member. "In My Life" and "Makin' Music" are two standout, uptempo numbers. Nine songs, three more than 20th Century tacked on their debut, makes this more fulfilling than the first, but not by much. Whether Kinsman Dazz or Dazz, they seldom recorded weak tracks, and their singles were usually two-sided goodies. *—Andrew Hamilton*

Mike James Kirkland

b. Yazoo City, MS
Vocals / Smooth Soul, Funk, Soul
Originally from Yazoo City, MS, Mike James Kirkland grew up singing doo wop and gospel. Eventually settling in California, Kirkland and his brother started a record label, Bryan Records, to release the love songs and socially conscious soul music that Kirkland had been writing. The two albums they released, *Hang on in There* in 1972 and it's follow up, *Doin' It Right*, both echoed the style and sentiments of other artists determined to comment on social issues relevant to the African-American community, soul heavies like Marvin Gaye, Curtis Mayfield, and Stevie Wonder. The reputation of both albums slowly spread over the ensuing years, finally resulting in reissues in the '90s by archival label Luv N' Haight. *—Wade Kergan*

● **Hang on in There** / Oct. 22, 1996 / Luv N' Haight ♦♦♦♦
Singer Mike James Kirkland recorded an impressive pair of albums for MCA during the 1970s but lack of interest on the label's part led to their eventual obscurity. That is until fans of ultra-rare rare groove caught wind of the sounds of *Doin' It Right* and *Hang on in There*, both of which began to change hands for astronomical prices amongst collectors. The latter drew obvious comparisons to *What's Going On*, Marvin Gaye's classic 1971 meditation on an ailing society. The first side of Kirkland's *Hang on in There* reads like an alternate version, exploring many of the same themes. "What Have We Done?" he asks on the album opener over an excellent conga and flute-spiced funk groove, a track followed by the equally pained "Where is the Soul of Man?" Both are eclipsed however, by the eight-minutes-plus title track. The album's undeniable centerpiece, "Hang on in There" is a lyrical *tour de force* over a slow-burning groove. Though arrangement touches are as lush as a film score, the underlying rhythms are rooted in urban funk: bells, backing singers and syrupy strings meshing perfectly with guitar scratch and percolating bass. Unfortunately, Kirkland drops the concept for the album's second half, turning his attention to the mysteries of love and throwing the album off balance. He would have been better off integrating the two sides or voicing the greater concerns of side one over a full-length album. Regardless, at least half of this material is the product of an underrated artist at the peak of his compositional powers. Making this disc even more desirable is a trio of tracks culled from 45s amongst them "The Prophet": a scorcher that finds the singer riding a vibrant, horn-seasoned funk rhythm that's the toughest thing on hand. *—Nathan Bush*

Doin' It Right / Jan. 12, 1999 / Luv N' Haight ♦♦♦♦
Luv N' Haight, the rare groove branch of San Francisco's Ubiquity label, followed-up the reissue of Mike James Kirkland's *Hang On in There* with *Doin' It Right*, another soul/funk treasure previously on the verge of slipping into musical darkness. According to Ubiquity, before their re-release, collectors looking for these albums could encounter price tags as high as 500 dollars. While the unconverted may wonder what the fuss is all about, the strongest material on these sets reveals an artist more than capable of matching the work of his contemporaries. Unfortunately, MCA, Kirkland's record label at the time, failed to get behind the releases and they faded from view. While the singer divided the A- and B-sides of *Hang on in There* between sobering reality themes and a batch of love songs, *Doin' It Right* focuses exclusively on the pained trials and tribulations of the heart. Once again, Kirkland's voice is set against a series of sophisticated arrangements that, at their best, avoid dipping into overly sentimental schmaltz. There are a few exceptions. The title track, an unfocused "I want you back" plea that unfolds over eight-plus minutes, begins as an unconvincing, soap-opera style drama. On a version of "O Me, O My (I'm a Fool for You Baby)," Kirkland drifts over a bed of guitar and strings for a series of verses that attempt too forcefully to tug at the heartstrings. More impressive is the singer's take on Carole King's "It's Too Late," a song whose sentiments translate easily into a soul setting. Also of note are the Kirkland originals that open and close the set: Songs like "Got to Do It Right," "Love Insurance," and "The Only Change" find the session players falling back on more reliable funk elements for more impressive results. *—Nathan Bush*

The Kittens

f. Chicago, IL
Group / Chicago Soul, Northern Soul, Soul
Like a lot of Chicago soul vocal groups, the Kittens are popular among Northern soul devotees. Another trait that they share with revered groups of that genre is that they became more popular later than when they were together and recording, during which they never had any nationally charting records. The Kittens emerged from Chicago's West Side, forming around Farragut High school student Bernice Wills and Marshall High students Thelma Mack and her cousin Laurel Ross. Arranger/producer Johnny Pate signed the group to ABC-Paramount in 1964, as newly appointed Midwest A&R director for the label, a position created specifically for him. As the arranger for the Impressions, he and the label created a Chicago branch around 14th & Michigan to tap into the vibrant Chicago soul scene of the '60s. Their ABC Paramount singles include "I Got to Know Him" and "Lookie Lookie." Around 1968, they began recording for Chess, with "Ain't No More Room," "Hey Operator," and "I've Got to Get Over You." Their other releases were "I Need Your Love Tonight" on the Don-El label and "Foolish Little Girl" on Grant. *—Ed Hogan*

Kleeer

f. 1972, New York, NY

Group / Funk, Urban, Disco, Club/Dance

Kleeer was a New York-based disco/funk group headed by drummer, arranger, songwriter, and vocalist Woody Cunningham. The group—fleshed out by vocalist/percussionist Paul Crutchfield, guitarist Richard Lee, and bassist Norman Durham—formed in 1972 as the backing group for the Choice 4. Two years later, they broke off on their own and changed their name to the Jam Band. For a brief period, the Jam Band backed up Disco Tex & the Sex-O-Lettes for touring purposes and even appeared with the group on the TV program *The Midnight Special*.

Another change came in 1975, when the Jam Band changed names again to Pipeline. The switch reflected the quartet's decision to become a hard rock band. A number of major labels balked on signing the group, but Columbia picked them up and released a single ("Gypsy Rider") that didn't fare well commercially. Pipeline was confronted with the bizarre opportunity to become the Universal Robot Band in 1976. Patrick Adams and Greg Carmichael, underground disco legends with skills in all departments of record-making, had released a single under that name—but there really was no proper band. Pipeline decided to become the Universal Robot Band and recorded and toured under that name until 1978. The quartet's desire to become self-sufficient again resulted in their defection.

Re-named Kleeer, Cunningham, Crutchfield, Lee, and Durham became a funk band with dancefloor leanings. The first song they cut as Kleeer, "Keeep Your Body Workin'," was liked by Atlantic enough to be included on a compilation. The response from DJs was overwhelmingly positive and resulted in a recording contract. (Ironically, Atlantic had rejected the group when they were Pipeline.) Between 1979 and 1985, the group released seven albums for the label and frequented the R&B charts with a series of minor hits. Three songs cracked the Top 40—1979's "Tonight's the Night (Good Time)" (number 33), 1980's "Winners" (number 23), and 1981's "Get Tough" (number 15). Nine others entered the R&B chart. Despite never becoming major players in the U.S., they were able to cultivate a rabid cult following in the U.K.

Kleeer disappeeered after the 1985 album *Seeekret*; Atlantic capped off the group's prolific run the following year with *Kleeer Winners: The Best of Kleeer*. The group reappeared briefly in the '90s; most members remained active session musicians long after the group's dissolution, and Cunningham went on to record into the 2000s as a solo artist. Kleeer's recordings have long since become a source for several rap hits, including 2Pac's "California Love," and DJ Quik's "Tonight." *—Andy Kellman*

● **The Very Best of Kleeer** / Apr. 7, 1998 / Rhino ✦✦✦✦✦

The Very Best of Kleer is an excellent 13-track collection that is, in many ways, the definitive overview of the funk band's career. All of the group's R&B hits—"Keep Your Body Workin'," "Tonight's the Night (Good Time)," "Winners," "Open Your Mind," "Get Tough," "Running Back to You," "Taste the Music," "De Ting Continues," "She Said She Loves Me," "Next Time It's for Real," "Intimate Connection," "Take Your Heart Away"—are here, usually presented in their full-length album versions instead of the edited single versions. While this might make this a little too lengthy for some casual fans who just want singles—after all, it runs over 77 minutes—it's hard to imagine a more comprehensive collection than this. *—Stephen Thomas Erlewine*

Klique

Group / Dance-Pop, Urban

The obscure early-'80s R&B outfit Klique consisted of members Howard Huntsberry, Debbie Hunter, and Isaac Suthers. Specializing in soul/funk tracks that were custom-made for the dancefloor, the trio issued three releases during its career—1981's *It's Winning Time*, 1983's *Try It Out* (which included one of Klique's best-known tracks, "I Can't Shake This Feeling"), and 1985's *Love Cycles*. The group enjoyed a lone Top Ten hit with a cover of Jackie Wilson's "Stop Doggin' Me Around," which has subsequently been issued on several best of the '80s compilations (*Billboard Hot R&B Hits 1983*, *R&B Crossover Oldies, Vol. 1*, etc.). *—Greg Prato*

● **It's Winning Time** / 1981 / MCA ✦✦✦

In the '80s, Klique was best known for covering Jackie Wilson songs, even though Wilson covers only accounted for a small fraction of their output. The problem (if you consider it a problem) started in 1983, when the trio's version of "Stop Doggin' Me Around" soared to the top of the R&B singles charts. Then, in 1985, Klique had another hit with a remake of Wilson's "A Woman, a Lover, a Friend." So whenever Klique's name was mentioned, many R&B fans would respond, "Oh yes, the '80s group that does Jackie Wilson covers." The fact that Howard Huntsberry, who was one-third of Klique's original lineup, had a very Wilson-ish voice didn't help. But Klique wasn't an oldies group, and the original Huntsberry/Isaac Suthers/Deborah Hunter lineup had yet to record any Wilson covers when their debut album *It's Winning Time* came out in 1981. Instead, those who heard this LP admired Klique for sleek dance/funk numbers like "Love's Dance" and the title song or for smooth, romantic soul ballads such as "Better Times," "You Brought My Love to Life," and "Middle of a Slow Dance." As solid as this album is, it wasn't a huge seller. If *It's Winning Time* had gone multi-platinum—and if "Stop Doggin' Me Around" hadn't been Klique's first major chartbuster—perhaps the group could have avoided being stereotyped as the '80s group that did Jackie Wilson covers. At any rate, Klique showed a lot of promise on this impressive, if underexposed, debut. *—Alex Henderson*

Klymaxx

f. 1979, Los Angeles, CA

Group / Urban, Quiet Storm, Dance-Pop, Disco

This was an all-female band formed in 1979 by producer/drummer Bernadette Cooper, guitarist Cheryl Cooley and keyboard player Lynn Malsby. The original lead vocalists were Lorena Porter Shelby and Joyce "Fenderella" Irby, who later left for a solo career. In 1990, the group became a trio, with Shelby, guitarist Cheryl Cooley, and keyboardist Robbin Grider. "I Miss You" was a major hit for the band in 1985. *—Steve Huey*

Girls Will Be Girls / 1981 / Solar ✦✦✦

The R&B/funk/urban contemporary women's ensemble Klymaxx began their careers in the early '80s with this debut album on Solar. It was a historic occasion on many levels. This marked the beginning of the Jam/Lewis production combine, as Klymaxx was the first band they wrote songs for and produced. It also marked drummer Bernadette Cooper's entry into the arena as a bandleader, making them one of the rare African-American women's groups that was as much an instrumental as vocal unit. In fact, they got more attention for the fact that everyone except Loreana Porter played an instrument than for their harmonies, which were, to put it mildly, routine. Porter had a strong voice, but used it more to punctuate songs and shout than to interpret lyrics. *—Ron Wynn*

● **Never Underestimate the Power of a Woman** / 1982 / Solar ✦✦✦✦

This was Klymaxx's second and final Solar album, and they got even louder and more assertive and confrontational than on their debut. The title track was a clever outing, although it got a little too cute in spots. But "Meeting in the Ladies Room" was a huge hit, and the group seemed on its way as a viable alternative to standard women's vocal groups. None of them were exactly great instrumentalists, but they got mileage out of being guitarists, keyboardists, and drummers as well as singers. *—Ron Wynn*

Meeting in the Ladies Room / 1984 / Constellation ✦✦

Klymaxx enjoyed their biggest success on their debut album for MCA. It got them their biggest hit with "The Men All Pause," the kind of song that they only hinted at doing before and should have continued updating long afterward. This was the last go-round for the original band, and everyone seemed inspired and energetic. It had an air of brashness and uncertainty, one they unfortunately weren't able to maintain. *—Ron Wynn*

Klymaxx / 1986 / Constellation ✦✦

Maxx Is Back / May 15, 1990 / MCA ✦✦

The Knight Brothers

f. Washington, D.C.

Group / Chicago Soul, Soul, Pop-Soul, R&B

Richard Dunbar and James Leon Diggs comprised the Knight Brothers, a duo that recorded one of soul's most wrenching singles, "Temptation 'Bout to Get Me." Both were natives of Washington, D.C.; Diggs was born in 1937 and Dunbar on May 31, 1939. Both sang with the Starfires on two late-'50s Decca singles, while Diggs also sang with the Carltons for the Chess subsidiary Argo in 1964 and 1965. Argo released the Carltons' final release in 1965, just as the Knight Brothers' second release, "I Owe Her My Life," was released. It bombed, but the Carltons' single, "I'm a Man," did slightly better.

Chess signed the Knight Brothers and the Carltons out of their New York City office. Diggs wrote both sides of their 1965 single, "Temptation 'Bout to Get Me," produced by Billy Davis. It inched to number 12 on the R&B charts, but only number 70 on the pop charts. Chess' sales department should have been ashamed for not getting the record into the pop Top 40. It was the duo's biggest seller, as they never entered the R&B Top 20 again. A follow-up single, 1966's "The Hand of Faith," did nothing. Nor did a final Checker single, "That'll Get It," and the duo lived off the laurels of one hit. The duo switched to Mercury for two singles produced by Jerry Butler's Fountain Productions. Diggs' "You're My Love" dropped without any fanfare in the fall of 1967; the association ended with "Tried So Hard to Please Her." The single flopped like the others and no more releases ever surfaced. Dunbar later sang with a revised Orioles group. *—Andrew Hamilton*

Boobie Knight

Vocals / Deep Funk, Funk, Psychedelic Soul

Funk bandleader Boobie Knight specialized in a heavy, psychedelic-tinged, guitar-centered brand of groove, something along the lines of the proverbial stoned soul picnic. Dubbing his first outfit the Soulciety, Knight landed a deal with RCA and recorded the album *Soul Ain't No New Thing* in 1972; it included jam-oriented tracks like "King of the Real Good Guys," "Power to the People," and the title cut. Moving over to Brunswick, Knight reorganized the band and renamed it the Universal Lady, taking on Al Johnson as lead vocalist. 1974's *Boobie Knight & the Universal Lady* expanded on the trippy vibes of the debut, with key cuts including "Earth Creature" and the oft-compiled "The Lovomaniacs." Knight's two albums are now considered collector's items among die-hard funk aficionados. *—Steve Huey*

Frederick Knight

b. Aug. 15, 1944, Birmingham, AL

Vocals / Soul, Southern Soul

Frederick Knight's catchy "I've Been Lonely for So Long" was a sizable R&B hit on Stax in 1972, and he wrote and produced Anita Ward's across-the-board smash "Ring My Bell" in 1979. Knight cut his own "I've Been Lonely for So Long" in Birmingham, AL, with a seasoned Southern soul crew behind him, and hit again in 1975 with "I Betcha Didn't Know That." *—Bill Dahl*

● **I've Been Lonely for So Long** / 1973 / Stax ✦✦✦✦✦

Gladys Knight

b. May 28, 1944, Atlanta, GA

Vocals / Soul, Pop-Soul, Motown, Urban, Smooth Soul, Quiet Storm

One of the great soul singers, Gladys Knight was a performer from her childhood years, forming the Pips with her brother Merald and a couple cousins. They made the Top Ten in 1961 with the heavily doo wop-influenced "Every Beat of My Heart," and recorded some fine, nowadays overlooked, pop-soul sides for the Fury and Maxx labels in the early and mid-'60s, sometimes under the direction of songwriter Van McCoy. A couple singles from this period, "Letter Full of Tears" and "Giving Up," made the Top 40, but Knight didn't hit her commercial stride until she moved to Motown in 1966. Steeped in the gospel tradition, like so many soul singers, Knight & the Pips developed into one of Motown's most dependable acts, although they never quite scaled the commercial or artistic heights of fellow stars on the label like the Supremes, Marvin Gaye, and the Temptations. With Norman Whitfield providing the production and much of the songwriting, the Pips fit into the mainstream of Motown's machine well, scoring big hits with some rabble-rousers (like "Friendship Train" and the original version of "I Heard It Through the Grapevine"), mainstream midtempo soul ("It Should Have Been Me" and "The End of Our Road"), and smooth ballads like "If I Were Your Woman."

In 1973, Knight had her biggest Motown hit with "Neither One of Us," which made number two; shortly afterwards, she and the Pips left Motown for Buddah. The group members were briefly superstars in 1973-1974, reeling off the smashes "Midnight Train to Georgia" (their only number one), "I've Got to Use My Imagination," and "Best Thing That Ever Happened to Me." This ranked as some of their best material, but Knight soon moved toward an easy listening, adult contemporary direction, one that she's maintained to this day. Now performing separately from the Pips (who have retired), her days as a high-charting star ended after the mid-'70s, although she remains fairly popular, and maintained an active recording career into the new millennium. *—Richie Unterberger*

Letter Full of Tears / 1961 / Collectables ✦✦✦

A good anthology of early tracks by Gladys Knight & the Pips, these were recorded for the Fury label in the early '60s. They were far from a polished act at the time, and didn't get the caliber of material or production they'd receive later at Motown. But the potential was shown on several tracks, notably the title cut, which the group did when Knight was only 12 years old. They later made another version of the song for Motown. This has better sound than some earlier Collectables titles. *—Ron Wynn*

Everybody Needs Love / 1967 / Motown ✦✦✦

A decent debut album that didn't quite establish a musical idenity for the group, despite the inclusion of the classic "I Heard it Through the Grapevine" and the wonderful, definitive version of the title track. (Mary Wells' little-known original ranks a close second.) The big drawback, however, is a bowdlerized (i.e., censored) version of "Take Me in Your Arms and Love Me." The editing not only severely damages the song's "story structure" (Berry Gordy had a firm belief that a song should tell a story), it undermines the erotic awareness Knight brings to the material. Thankfully, the restored version is found on *Anthology*. *—John Lowe*

Feelin' Bluesy / 1968 / Motown ✦✦✦

By then Knight & the Pips seemed to be locked in a "cutting contest" with several other Motown acts (Marvin Gaye, the Temptations, Edwin Starr, even Jimmy Ruffin) as they were covering differing versions of songs producer/writer Norman Whitfield has in his catalog. The best track here is a stunning rendition of Kim Weston's "It Should Have Been Me," given a glossy pop veneer that effectively contrasted Knight's grittiness. It was said that the group cut a series of tracks in a much rawer R&B idiom with writer/producer Ivy Joe Hunter early on their tenure, but save for a few album cuts, many of them were shelved and are still in Motown's vaults to this day. *—John Lowe*

Silk & Soul / 1968 / Motown ✦✦✦

An album of remakes by Gladys & the Pips still managed to chart (number 136) on *Billboard*'s Pop Album Chart. Only one track escaped as a single, "I Wish It Would Rain"; while beautifully done, it lacked the hurt of the Temptations' original. Renditions of "You're My Everything" and "Tracks of My Tears" work much better. Fans will enjoy the group's soulful renditions of pop hits like "The Look of Love" and "Theme From Valley of the Dolls." An update of Brenda Holloway's "Every Little Bit Hurts" is a keeper; Gladys seems to identify with the lyrics, enhancing the performance. Motown compiled and released *Silk & Soul* to capitalize on the group's slew of hits. It charted lower than normal for a Pips release because it lacked an original hit single to propel it higher, but this is still some fine listening. *—Andrew Hamilton*

Nitty Gritty / 1969 / Motown ✦✦✦

Though Gladys Knight questioned the wisdom of singing on with Motown in the mid-'60s, their tenure transformed them into consistant hitmakers. One of the reasons was their association with writer/producer Norman Whitfield, whose grittier, funkier style proved to be a key to Motown's counterattack to the rawer soul sounds that emerged in the latter part of the decade. A tough, funky reworking of Shirley Ellis' "The Nitty Gritty" and the social-consciousness classic "Friendship Train" gave them a pair of Top 20 pop hits in 1969, and they anchor this sturdy collection of fine soul and R&B tracks. *—John Lowe*

All in a Knight's Work / 1970 / Soul ✦✦✦

A curious release, since most of the tracks appeared on previous albums and Motown had just released a greatest-hits LP on them, which is essentially what this is. They resurrected their pre-Motown hits "Letter Full of Tears" and "Giving Up," tunes they had remade on earlier Motown albums. Remakes of "Fever," "Glory of Love," and Aretha's "Dr. Feelgood" are pleasing renditions. They even included "I Heard It Through the Grapevine," the stomping "End of Our Road," and the guitar-enhanced, lilting "Everybody Needs Love." No singles were released, so it went unnoticed, failing to even chart. *—Andrew Hamilton*

If I Were Your Woman / 1971 / Motown ✦✦✦

Two of Gladys Knight & the Pips' most dramatic recordings, "If I Were Your Woman" and "I Don't Want to Do Wrong," provided the juice to send this LP all the way to number 35 on *Billboard*'s album chart. The former has evolved into an R&B classic, with remakes too numerous to mention, the most famous by Stephanie Mills. "Signed Gladys" is reminiscent of "A Letter from Tina," an old Sue Record side by Ike & Tina Turner. Also included are two poles-apart remakes: the Fifth Dimension's "One Less Bell to Answer," done magnificently by the group; and an excursion into funk on Sly Stone's "Thank You (Falettinme Be Mice Elf Again)." The rest consists of average material upgraded by the recording skills of Gladys and her guys. *—Andrew Hamilton*

Standing Ovation / 1971 / Motown ✦✦

A precusor of the direction they'd later take at Buddah when glossy pop ballads supplanted the raucous soul shouting that was characteristic of their early Motown work. Aside from the minor pop hit "Make Me the Woman You Want to Come Home To," there is a stunning interpetation of Kris Kristofferson's "Help Me Make It Through the Night" that stands out as definitive. But aside from that, there wasn't anything else that was up to that standard. *—John Lowe*

All I Need Is Time / 1973 / Motown ✦✦✦✦✦

Gladys Knight & the Pips were together for almost 40 years. They started performing together in 1952 (when Knight was only eight years old), and it wasn't until 1990 that a 46-year-old Knight finally became a full-time solo artist and the Pips retired from music. Only seven of the group's 38 years were spent at Motown, but they were seven incredibly important years. They did some of their most essential work at the label, which they signed with in 1966 and left in 1973. That year, Buddah made them an offer they couldn't refuse, and a very aggressive promotional campaign on their part made 1973's *Imagination* (their first Buddah album) a blockbuster hit. That was also the year in which Motown released *All I Need Is Time*, which was recorded not long before their departure from the label. This LP wasn't the mega-hit that *Imagination* was, but even so, it is generally excellent. Knight has a lot of first-rate material to work with, and she is as impressive on romantic ballads and slow jams ("I'll Be Here When You Get Home," "Oh! What a Love I Have Found," "All I Need Is Time") as she is on uptempo gems, which include the Staple Singers' "Heavy Makes You Happy" and a superb cover of Sly & the Family Stone's "Thank You (Falettinme Be Mice Elf Again)." Meanwhile, there are hints of Philadelphia soul on "The Only Time You Love Me Is When You're Losing Me," which shows us what Knight & the Pips might have sounded like in the 1970s if they had recorded for Philadelphia International instead of Motown and Buddah. A fine album that should have done a lot better, *All I Need Is Time* is well worth obtaining if you're a fan of the group's 1970s output. *—Alex Henderson*

It Hurt Me So Bad / 1973 / Trip ✦✦✦

Pre-Motown Gladys Knight & the Pips, repackaged and released to capitalize on their Motown success, this features the Pips dominating the mike on the last four tracks. Gladys sings the teary title track like an old pro, even though she wasn't even old enough to buy beer at the time. "A Love Like Mine," with its mock marching beat, displays the Pips' harmonies flowing above the rhythm and Gladys' tough vocal knifing through. On the slow "Darling," the Pips are in the foreground, and one shares the lead with Gladys. "Come See About Me" is not the Supremes song, but the message is the same; it's a slow floater, with Supremes-like backing vocals and the Pips nowhere to be found. "Queen of Tears" is a good beat ballad that Gladys, again, sings with a conviction that belies her age. The Pips take over the last four tunes. On "Linda," they sing the lead lines in three-part harmony over a bouncy, finger-snapping beat. "To Whom It May Concern" starts slowly, with the lead lines sung in unison and a mournful falsetto riding above to kick the blend up a notch. One of the Pips leads "Bless the One," with that wailing falsetto reappearing to provide backing flavor. "Walking in Circles" finds the Pips singing the lead lines in unison over a choppy beat. This doesn't compare to their later recordings, but it's good to hear the Pips front and center. *—Andrew Hamilton*

Neither One of Us / 1973 / Motown ✦✦✦

Although they left Motown (actually Soul) shortly after they cut this album, Gladys Knight & the Pips were at their performing peak during the early '70s. This magnificent title track featured stunning vocals by Knight and equally effective backing vocals from the Pips, and had several other outstanding songs on it. Why Motown never pushed them as much as they could have mystified many at the time, and while Knight & the Pips didn't surpass their Motown material at other labels, they created enough outstanding songs to justify their decision to leave. *—Ron Wynn*

Imagination / Oct. 1973 / Pair ✦✦✦✦✦

The first album cut by Gladys Knight & the Pips for Buddah Records was a watershed in their history. Co-produced by the group and Tony Camillo, *Imagination* embodied all of what Gladys Knight & the Pips had learned in their previous six years at Motown, watching the way their records were made, combined with the maturity of the sound that they'd achieved in that time, and virtually complete freedom to choose their repertory—a factor that they were mature and sophisticated to exploit to the fullest. The result was four hit songs, including the chart-topping "Midnight Train to Georgia" (originally written as "Midnight Plane to Houston") and one of the biggest selling albums in their history—*Imagination* was sophisticated soul at its best, Knight belting out numbers with great forcefulness and passion while the group provided delicate backup. Among the surprising non-hits is the radiantly sung "Perfect Love" and a beautiful harmonized cover of "I Can See Clearly Now," featuring the Pips singing lead. Reissued on CD by BMG Special Products in 1997 with full annotation, and worth tracking down in any format. *—Bruce Eder*

Anthology / 1974 / Motown ✦✦✦✦✦

Atlanta family-group Gladys Knight & the Pips had performed together for 14 years before signing with Motown in 1966. Earlier recordings for Huntom (the master recordings were later sold to Vee-Jay), Fury, and Maxx had generated five chart hits, including the Top Ten R&B smashes "Every Beat of My Heart" and "Letter Full of Tears," but it was on the Motown subsidiary Soul that Gladys Knight and company hit their stride. This compilation more than adequately covers this period of the Pips' career. Working primarily with producer Norman Whitfield from 1967 through 1969, the group created such Motor City classics as "Everybody Needs Love," "I Heard It Through the Grapevine," "The End of Our Road," and "Friendship Train." From 1970 through 1973 the Pips worked with a variety of Motown producers, concentrating on ballads. Although they were perhaps a little less consistent, there was no shortage of hits, the most notable being 1970's "If I Were

Your Woman" and 1973's "Neither One of Us (Wants to Be the First to Say Goodbye)." The updated double-CD version of *Anthology*, featuring digitally remastered sound, replaces about a dozen songs with different ones, though this 40-track collection still contains all of the essential hits and adds lengthy liner notes. Be aware that the three early-'60s hits that lead off the volume (on both versions of *Anthology*) are Motown re-recordings, not the originals. *—Rob Bowman*

Claudine [Original Soundtrack] / 1974 / Buddah ✦✦✦

I Feel a Song / 1974 / Buddah ✦✦✦

Both commercially and artistically, switching from Motown to Buddah in the mid-'70s proved to be a very wise move for Gladys Knight & the Pips. *Imagination* and *Claudine* were gem-laden smashes, and their winning streak continued with their third Buddah date *I Feel a Song*. The dramatic "I Feel a Song (In My Heart)" and an unlikely remake of Barbara Streisand's "The Way We Were" became major hits, as did the soaring ballad "Love Finds Its Own Way." Knight's monologue on "The Way We Were" is most ironic—reflecting on the nostalgia that seems to be human nature, she noted that 1974 would someday become "the good old days." And when disco era-nostalgia took hold in the 1990s, post-baby boomers seemed to be expressing a belief that the 1970s were a simpler, less stressful time. Equally appealing are the gritty numbers "Better You Go Your Way" (written by Bill Withers) and "Don't Burn Down the Bridge." If one notices that "Seconds" sounds like something Dionne Warwick would have done early in her career, it's no coincidence—Burt Bacharach (who also co-wrote many of Warwick's early hits) co-wrote the song. Thanks to Capitol-EMI's R&B-oriented reissue label The Right Stuff, *I Feel a Song* was finally heard on CD in 1997. *—Alex Henderson*

In the Beginning / 1974 / Bell ✦✦✦✦

You could say that *In the Beginning* is a reissue of a reissue. In 1968, Bell set out to cash in on the popularity of Gladys Knight & the Pips' Motown smashes by assembling *Tastiest Hits*, a collection of their pre-Motown work. *Tastiest Hits* went out of print after a few years, but in 1974, Bell reissued the collection as *In the Beginning*. Although the cover was different, Bell provided the same 11 songs in the same order and kept the liner notes that radio man Enoch Gregory had provided in 1968. *In the Beginning* was sold as a budget LP; the record went for around $2-3 in 1974, and that wasn't a bad deal because most the selections are excellent. "Every Beat of My Heart," "Operator," "Giving Up," "Lovers Always Forgive," and "Letter Full of Tears" are all essential examples of Gladys Knight & the Pips' pre-Motown period. In fact, their version of Johnny Otis' "Every Beat of My Heart" was their first major hit. And even the songs that fall short of essential are highly appealing. In 1974, *In the Beginning* was a very affordable and attractive way to get acquainted with the work that Gladys Knight & the Pips did before Berry Gordy came into the picture. *—Alex Henderson*

Knight Time / 1974 / Soul ✦✦✦

In 1974, Gladys Knight & the Pips were no longer signed to Motown. The group had moved to Buddah, where they were enjoying their share of major hits. You can be sure that Berry Gordy wished that Motown, not Buddah, had put out "Midnight Train to Georgia" and "Best Thing That Ever Happened to Me." But Motown still had some material in the can; released in 1974, *Knight Time* contains material that the group recorded before its departure from the label (probably around 1972-1973). The LP didn't do as well as the albums that Buddah was coming out with; it wasn't nearly as successful as 1973's *Imagination*, 1974's *Claudine*, or 1974's *I Feel a Song*. Nonetheless, *Knight Time* has a lot going for it. Knight has solid material to work with, including songs that were written or co-written by the likes of Johnny Bristol ("Somebody Stole the Sunshine," "Billy, Come on Back as Quick as You Can"), Jim Weatherly ("Between Her Goodbye and My Hello"), and Pam Sawyer ("How Can You Say That Ain't Love," "Master of My Mind"). Unfortunately, the label didn't promote the LP aggressively—since Knight was among its former artists, Motown decided to throw the album against the wall and see if it would stick. And as a result, the only people who bought this album were the artist's most hardcore fans. *Knight Time* falls short of essential, but it's a pleasing record that didn't deserve to be ignored. *—Alex Henderson*

2nd Anniversary / 1975 / Buddah ✦✦✦✦

This album spawned two *Billboard* R&B Top Ten singles with "Money" and "Part Time Love." The former is a midtempo cut with a polished texture but contrasted by Gladys Knight's ardent vocals. The latter is a rather short but sweet-tempered ballad. Both peaked at number four with the latter surviving three weeks longer on the charts at 14. "Street Brother" is a blues number featuring an impressive Bubba Knight on lead vocals. The rendition of the Roberta Flack classic "Feel Like Makin' Love" has an urban, blues ambience complemented by the cohesive touch of the Pips. Eugene McDaniels, who produced much of the album, also wrote this vintage number. The songs shine with eloquence and are seasoned with an inviting Southern aura. *—Craig Lytle*

A Little Knight Music / 1975 / Soul ✦✦✦

It's a familiar pattern: An artist leaves one label, enjoys success at another label, and inspires the previous label to try cashing in with some previously unreleased material. When Gladys Knight & the Pips left Motown for Buddah in 1973, Motown still had some unreleased material in the can. So when the group's Buddah smashes were burning up the charts in 1975, Motown tried to cash in with *A Little Knight Music*, a collection of previously unreleased material that was recorded in early '70s. The LP, which Motown released on its Soul subsidiary, wasn't a hit—*A Little Knight Music* didn't get much promotion, and the only people who bought the uneven LP were Knight's most obsessive fans. As you might suspect, *A Little Knight Music* is far from a collection of masterpieces. Nonetheless, most of the material is decent. There are some pleasant Pam Sawyer/Gloria Jones songs (including "Don't Tell Me I'm Crazy" and "No One Could Love You More"), and covers of the Beatles' "Come Together," Jackie DeShannon's "Put a Little Love in Your Heart," and the Archies' "Sugar Sugar" aren't bad either. Those who think of "Sugar Sugar" as pure bubblegum will be surprised to hear how well the tune works as funky Detroit soul. The LP's only previously released track is the Johnny Bristol-produced "Can You Give Me Love With a Guarantee," originally available on the *Standing Ovation* album of 1971. Overall, *A Little Knight Music* isn't a bad record—it just isn't a great one. And with a singer of Knight's caliber, one hopes for excellence instead of an album that is merely competent. Far from one of Knight's essential releases, *A Little Knight Music* is strictly for hardcore collectors. *—Alex Henderson*

Pipe Dreams / 1976 / Buddah ✦✦✦

Some singers have branched out and become equally famous for their acting, but Gladys Knight isn't one of them. In 1976, she had a leading role in the film *Pipe Dreams* (which also starred Barry Hankerson, her husband at the time). The film was a commercial flop, and even though Knight continued to command a loyal, devoted following as a singer, she never became huge as an actress. Because the film received so little attention, it isn't surprising that the soundtrack album didn't fare much better commercially. This LP, which was reissued on CD in 1999, had a fine single in the melancholy ballad "So Sad the Song," but most of the other material is merely decent—and that is true of the funky "Alaskan Pipeline" and the perky "Find a Way," as well as the jazz-minded "Pot of Jazz." Knight and her Pips didn't record a lot of jazz-influenced material, and the tune was an interesting departure for them. Overall, this isn't a bad album—it just isn't a great one. Far from essential, *Pipe Dreams* is only recommended to Knight's most hardcore fans. *—Alex Henderson*

Still Together / 1977 / Buddah ✦✦✦

When producer/songwriter Van McCoy worked with Gladys Knight & the Pips, he usually did well by the group. It was McCoy who wrote "Giving Up" and "Lovers Always Forgive," two of their best pre-Motown singles of the early 1960s—and he also proved to be an asset to Gladys Knight & the Pips when he co-produced their 1977 LP, *Still Together*. To his credit, he knew how to change with the times. His roots were doo wop and early soul, but by the mid-'70s, people associated him with disco thanks to the 1975 smash "The Hustle." So when McCoy was hired to produce *Still Together*, Knight didn't have to worry about sounding retro. But at the same time, no one would mistake this album for McCoy's club-oriented *Disco Baby*. Even though he gave the single "Baby Don't Change Your Mind" a certain amount of disco gloss, this is a soul LP first and foremost. Five of the eight songs on *Still Together* were co-produced (with Charles Kipps), arranged, and written or co-written by McCoy, including "Baby Don't Change Your Mind," the ballad "Walk Softly," and the sentimental "Home Is Where the Heart Is." A few of the selections are excellent, and the rest are at least decent. *Still Together* isn't among Knight's essential albums, but it's an enjoyable, if mildly uneven, effort that has more plusses than minuses. *—Alex Henderson*

The One and Only / 1978 / Buddah ✦✦✦

In 1978, Gladys Knight & the Pips recorded one album as a group in addition to doing some recording separately. That year, Knight provided her first solo album, *Miss Gladys Knight*, for Buddah/Arista, while the Pips recorded *Callin'* (their second album without her) for Casablanca. And together, they recorded *The One and Only*, which didn't go down in history as one of their all-time classics but is a generally pleasant, if unspectacular, soul-pop outing. This LP finds the quartet working with various producers, including Michael Masser, Richie Wise, Tony Camillo, and the Van McCoy/Charles Kipps team. The album's best-known offering is the disco-flavored single "It's a Better Than Good Time," which Knight also recorded as a solo artist in 1978. Other decent tracks range from the vibrant "Come Back and Finish What You Started" (written by McCoy/Kipps) to the ballad "What If I Should Ever Need You" and the exuberant, gospel-minded "Saved By the Grace of Your Love." Nothing on *The One and Only* is in a class with "Midnight Train to Georgia" or "I Feel a Song (In My Heart)," but none of the material is bad either. Although not essential and not recommended to casual listeners, *The One and Only* is worth hearing if you're among Gladys Knight & the Pips' die-hard fans. *—Alex Henderson*

Miss Gladys Knight / 1978 / Buddah ✦✦✦

The year 1978 saw the release of no less than three new albums by Gladys Knight and/or the Pips. Together, they recorded *The One and Only* for Buddah—and the albums they recorded separately were the Pips' *Callin'* on Casablanca and Knight's *Miss Gladys Knight* on Buddah. This vinyl LP was Knight's very first solo album; not until 1990 did she become a full-time solo artist and part company with the Pips for good. Produced by Gary Klein or Tony Macaulay, *Miss Gladys Knight* usually finds the singer walking a fine line between R&B and adult contemporary. "It's a Better Than Good Time," which she also recorded with the Pips for *The One and Only*, is an appealing, string-laden soul-disco item that would have been perfect for Loleatta Holloway, Linda Clifford, Thelma Houston, or Gloria Gaynor. But that danceable song isn't representative of the record on the whole. This is primarily an album of ballads, and tracks like "I'm Still Caught Up With You" and "We Don't Make Each Other Laugh Anymore" have one foot in R&B and the other in adult contemporary. Although pleasant and decent, *Miss Gladys Knight* isn't a masterpiece and isn't among her essential recordings. This album is only recommended to collectors, who should be aware of the fact that in 1994, Castle reissued *Miss Gladys Knight* and *The One and Only* back to back on a single CD. *—Alex Henderson*

Gladys Knight / 1979 / Columbia ✦✦✦

Some Gladys Knight fans think that she didn't record as a solo artist until the early 1990s. But in fact, her first solo albums came in the late '70s, when she provided 1978's *Miss Gladys Knight* for Buddah and 1979's *Gladys Knight* for Columbia. Neither album was a huge seller; only her most die-hard fans bought the LPs. The singer's second, and self-titled, solo album isn't remarkable, but is a generally decent effort that ranges from R&B/adult contemporary ballads ("You Loved Away the Pain," "I Just Want to Be With You,"

"My World") to uptempo soul-disco offerings like "You Bring Out the Best in Me" and "You Don't Have to Say I Love You," both of which would appeal to a Loleatta Holloway or Thelma Houston fan. Meanwhile, the vibrant, Earth, Wind & Fire-ish "It's the Same Old Song" isn't unlike something that EWF leader Maurice White would have produced for the Emotions in the late '70s, and Knight's version of Leiber & Stoller's "I (Who Have Nothing)" recalls her dramatic 1964 hit "Giving Up." This LP, which she produced with Jack Gold, isn't recommended to casual listeners, who would be much better off with an anthology of her classic Motown and Buddah recordings with the Pips. But it's a likable record that is worth hearing if you're among Knight's hardcore fans. —*Alex Henderson*

About Love / 1980 / Columbia ✦✦✦✦✦
In 1977, 1978, and 1979, Gladys Knight & the Pips put a lot of effort into recording separately. Minus Knight, the Pips recorded two LPs as a trio (1977's *At Last the Pips* and 1978's *Callin'*, both on Casablanca), while Knight provided her first two solo albums (1978's *Miss Gladys Knight* on Buddah/Arista and 1979's *Gladys Knight* on Columbia). But by 1980, the group itself was their top priority again. The R&B department at Columbia had very high hopes for this album, and they weren't disappointed. Both creatively and commercially, *About Love* was Gladys Knight & the Pips' most successful album since 1974's *I Feel a Song*. The people they can thank for the album's excellence are the husband and wife team of Nick Ashford & Valerie Simpson, who wrote and produced all of the material. The ballad "Landlord" soared to number three on *Billboard*'s R&B singles charts, and the uptempo dance items "Bourgie, Bourgie" (originally recorded by Ashford & Simpson as an instrumental) and "Taste of Bitter Love" also became hits. Meanwhile, *About Love* also contains its share of gems that weren't released as singles, including the dramatic "Add It Up" and the smooth "Friendly Persuasion." This impressively consistent LP indicated that Gladys Knight & the Pips still had a lot of life left in them as a group, and sure enough, they stayed together for another ten years before parting company for good in 1990. —*Alex Henderson*

Visions / 1983 / Columbia ✦✦✦
Leon Sylvers produced one of the finest uptempo hits Gladys Knight & the Pips ever made in "Save the Overtime for Me." It was the kind of jubilant, celebratory, rousing performance that had marked their best Motown singles, and it put some fresh life into what had become a stagnant group. The rest of this album wasn't that good, but it hardly mattered. They got a follow-up number-five single, another chart hit with a third release, and were back in the game. —*Ron Wynn*

Life / 1985 / Collectables ✦✦✦
The final album on Columbia for Gladys Knight & the Pips did reasonably well, getting them three chart hits, but it didn't include any of the anthemic R&B or pop crossover songs they had been landing in the '80s. It was a well-produced effort, and Knight sang with her usual vigor, spirit, and intensity, but nothing seemed to click on the level that Knight & the Pips expected. —*Ron Wynn*

All Our Love / 1988 / MCA ✦✦✦
All Our Love marked the end of an era, for this 1988 release was Gladys Knight's final album with the Pips—in 1990, she officially became a full-time solo artist and the Pips retired from music. No one can say that they didn't have a long run; Knight was only eight when the group was formed in 1952, and she was 46 when it finally broke up after 38 years. Nor can anyone say that Gladys Knight & the Pips' final album together was commercially unsuccessful—thanks to major hits like "Love Overboard" and "Lovin' on Next to Nothin'," *All Our Love* went gold. In various interviews, Knight was quoted as saying that she was surprised the album did so well; she really didn't think she would ever see the top of the charts again. But then, MCA gave *All Our Love* a very aggressive promotional push and made sure that it was relevant to 1988s urban contemporary scene, hiring such producers as Reggie and Vincent Calloway, Nick Martinelli, and Sam Dees. Tracks like "Complete Recovery," "Thief in Paradise," and the above mentioned singles are pure urban contemporary—synthesizers and drum machines are prominent, and no one's going to mistake *All Our Love* for a retro soul effort. Nonetheless, the group usually manages to be true to itself; most of the time, *All Our Love* sounds fairly organic rather than forced or contrived. Sometimes excellent and sometimes merely decent, the album falls short of essential. But because it was Knight's final album with the Pips, it has historic value—and it was a pleasing, respectable way for the group to end its very long run. —*Alex Henderson*

Every Beat of My Heart / 1989 / Prime Cuts ✦✦✦
The best collection of Knight's pre-Motown sides, including both of their big early-'60s hits (the title track and "Letter Full of Tears"), but concentrating more heavily on their mid-'60s sessions. These were overseen by Van McCoy, who supplied the group with several of his own compositions as well. McCoy was one of the most melodically ambitious pop/soul composers of the era, and his songs on this compilation—"Either Way I Lose," "Why Don't You Love Me," "Lovers Always Forgive"—are achingly beautiful and rife with unexpected key changes. His "Stop and Get a Hold of Myself," on the other hand, is a more conventional (but equally first-rate) uptempo soul stomper. If there's any criticism of these sides, it's that Knight and the group don't establish a strong identity, handling doo wop-like ballads, girl group-tinged pop, McCoy's idiosyncratic songs, and more modern pop-soul with chameleon-like skill. In the end, that doesn't detract from the strength of this CD, which is a collection of fine early to mid-'60s pop/soul. The major flaw is the inexplicable omission of the McCoy composition "Giving Up," a Top 40 hit for the group in 1964. —*Richie Unterberger*

Soul Survivors: The Best of Gladys Knight & the Pips 1973–1988 / Oct. 1990 / Rhino ✦✦✦✦✦
Soul Survivors—The Best of Gladys Knight & the Pips picks up where the Motown anthology left off, containing the most important singles that Gladys Knight & the Pips recorded for Buddah, Columbia, and MCA from the early '70s until the late '80s. The Buddah tracks, highlighted by the Jim Weatherly-written "Midnight Train to Georgia" and "Best Thing That Ever Happened to Me," contain some of Knight's most impassioned vocal performances. —*Rob Bowman*

The One and Only . . . /The First Solo Album / 1995 / Sequel ✦✦

2nd Anniversary/Pipe Dreams / Jun. 20, 1995 / Sequel ✦✦✦

Imagination/I Feel a Song / Jun. 20, 1995 / Sequel ✦✦✦✦

Blue Lights in the Basement / Apr. 1996 / RCA ✦✦✦
Knight's stint for the Buddah label in the mid-'70s found her commercial success at its peak, landing hits like "Midnight Train to Georgia," "Best Thing That Ever Happened to Me," "Part Time Love," and "The Way We Were" (all included here). But this 17-track survey of 1973-1978 material is not nearly as artistically satisfying as her Motown and Vee-Jay recordings, finding her and the Pips easing into a middle-of-the-road sound that helped pave the way for mellow urban contemporary music. What's more, this compilation is not truly representative of the era, omitting the huge hit "I've Got to Use My Imagination," presumably because it's too uptempo to find a place on an anthology geared toward the quiet storm audience. —*Richie Unterberger*

The Ultimate Collection / Oct. 7, 1997 / Motown ✦✦✦✦✦
The Ultimate Collection nearly lives up to its billing, featuring 22 tracks on a single disc. Among the featured cuts are all of Gladys Knight & the Pips' Top Ten pop hits for Soul Records, including "Everybody Needs Love," "I Heard It Through the Grapevine," "The End of Our Road," "It Should Have Been Me," "The Nitty Gritty," "Friendship Train," "I Don't Want to Do Wrong," "If I Were Your Woman," and "Neither One of Us (Wants to Be the First to Say Goodbye)." For most casual fans, those who just want the hits, this will be the definitive collection of Knight's early career. —*Stephen Thomas Erlewine*

● **Essential Collection** / Sep. 28, 1999 / Hip-O ✦✦✦✦✦
There have been many Gladys Knight & the Pips collections over the years, yet few have drawn from all periods of their career. Hip-O's 1999 compilation *Essential Collection* does, beginning with their first hit for Vee-Jay, "Every Beat of My Heart," and ending with their last R&B number one, 1987's "Love Overboard." It doesn't feature every hit they ever had, but it does provide a good chronology of their career by featuring their biggest hits: "I Heard It Through the Grapevine," "If I Were Your Woman," "Neither One of Us (Wants to Be the First to Say Goodbye)," "Daddy Could Swear, I Declare," "Midnight Train to Georgia," "I've Got to Use My Imagination," "The Best Thing That Ever Happened to Me," "On and On," "Save the Overtime (For Me)," "Hero (Wind Beneath My Wings)." Anyone looking for a single disc covering the entire career of Gladys Knight & the Pips should turn here. —*Stephen Thomas Erlewine*

Jean Knight

b. Jun. 26, 1943, New Orleans, LA
Vocals / Funk, Soul
Soul singer Jean Knight's only big hit was a monster—the sassy funk classic "Mr. Big Stuff," one of the largest-selling singles ever released by the legendary Stax label. A native of New Orleans, Knight was born in 1943 and made her first recordings for producer Huey P. Meaux's Jet Stream and Tribe labels during the mid- to late '60s (many of her sides were later collected on WestSide's *Blue Soul Belles, Vol. 2*). Her success largely confined to the immediate area, Knight was working as a baker when she went to Malaco Studios in Jackson, MS, for a session with veteran producer Wardell Quezergue in 1970. The key track, a spirited putdown of male arrogance called "Mr. Big Stuff," was shopped to Stax Records, who passed on it at first. However, after King Floyd's "Groove Me" (another Malaco recording) went gold, Stax reconsidered and released "Mr. Big Stuff" in 1971. It was an enormous hit, spending five weeks at number one on the R&B charts and falling one slot short of the same position on the pop side. Despite a strong accompanying album of the same name and some similarly gritty follow-up singles (which included "You Think You're Hot Stuff" and "Carry On"), Knight couldn't manage to duplicate the success of "Mr. Big Stuff," and quickly faded from the soul scene.

In 1981, Knight scored a minor hit with a version of "You Got the Papers (But I Got the Man)," and charted with one of the more successful covers of the Rockin' Sidney zydeco smash "My Toot Toot" in 1985; "My Toot Toot" also served as the title track for a full-length LP on Mirage. Knight returned once again in the late '90s, cutting an album for Ichiban in 1997 called *Shaki De Boo-Tee*. She followed it two years later with the Formaldehyde release *Queen*. —*Steve Huey*

● **Mr. Big Stuff** / 1971 / Stax ✦✦✦✦✦
Jean Knight could do no wrong in 1971, when the strutting "Mr. Big Stuff" was climbing the pop and R&B charts, well on its way to becoming one of the most familiar chart hits of all time. Her debut album, with its no-brainer title, featured a lot of good material on it, not all of it in the same vein as her hit. Producer/arranger Wardell Quezergue (he also appeared on keyboards) handled the record well, with a band consisting of Malaco hands like guitarist Jerry Puckett and drummer James Stroud. Knight shows an admirable range on these songs, stretching out on the heartbroken ballads "A Little Bit of Something (Is Better Than All of Nothing)" and "Why I Keep Living These Memories" (each with a heavy church feel). "You City Slicker" was much too much of a "Mr. Big Stuff" sound-alike, but "Take Him (You Can Have My Man)" would've been a worthy follow-up to her only Top Ten hit. The CD reissue by Fantasy added a few of her later singles, including the charting "You Think You're Hot Stuff" and the fine "Carry On." —*John Bush*

My Toot Toot / 1985 / Mirage ✦✦✦
New Orleans vocalist Jean Knight, who enjoyed a soul smash in the 1960s with "Mr. Big Stuff," scored a novelty winner in the 1980s with her version of what was the nation's most covered song in 1985, "My Toot Toot." There were Cajun, soul, country, blues, and

pop versions, and labels were battling each other over the variations and licensing rights. Unfortunately, neither Knight's slightly soulful/humorous edition, nor the resulting album, which had a couple of good ballads, generated much attention beyond the curiosity stage. —*Ron Wynn*

The Very Best of Me / Dec. 9, 1997 / Aim ✦✦✦
Not the hits collection listeners may think it is, Jean Knight's *The Very Best of Me* is instead one of her late-period works for the Aim label. Opening with a workmanlike version of her lone hit, "Mr. Big Stuff," she later reprises another of her hits, "My Toot Toot," and turns in solid versions of a few Southern soul standards: "Precious, Precious," "Make Me Yours," and "Rocking Chair." Though she often treads familiar ground, Knight is in good voice for this 11-track set and the production is surprisingly solid as well. —*John Bush*

Blue Soul Belles, Vol. 2 / Feb. 8, 2000 / WestSide ✦✦✦
WestSide Records' second volume of the *Blue Soul Belles* series pairs Jean Knight and Barbara Lynn, a statuesque singer/guitarist from New Orleans, on 33 songs culled from Jet Stream and Tribe Records with Knight performing 19 numbers and Lynn 14. Both singers have that one big hit in common: Knight's "Mr. Big Stuff," not included but referenced on "(T'Aint It) The Truth"; ironically, Lynn's biggest hit, "You'll Lose a Good Thing," is included, but by Knight, not Lynn. Each also enjoyed a handful of smaller regional and local hits. Lynn, an accomplished songwriter, wrote much of what she sang, including three soulful uptempo jams for the feet: "Club a Go-Go," "Movin' on a Groove," and "Disco Music." But it's the Southern/bayou blues numbers that make Lynn special (i.e., the aching "Until Then I'll Suffer"). And she sings plenty of those on this 33-song smorgasbord. Knight's song choices will please the most demanding Southern soul fan. She comes hard and real on "A Tear," "Please, Please, Please," and other tough selections like "Doggin' Me Around." The disc is more representative of Lynn's hits (though none of her Jamie sides are included) than Knight's; Knight's Stax recordings are not included and her take of "You Left the Water Running" is disappointing compared to others. But overall this is a fine collection of feminine Southern soul from two of its most persistent purveyors. —*Andrew Hamilton*

Marie Knight

b. Jun. 1, 1925, Brooklyn, NY
Vocals / Soul, Pop-Soul, Black Gospel, R&B, Torch Songs
Versatile singer Marie Knight recorded gospel with the Millionaires, also cutting some nice pop-soul in the early '60s, and some jump-blues and doo wop-flavored R&B. If she's known to rock fans at all, it's because Manfred Mann covered her 1961 single "Come Tomorrow" for a big U.K., and small U.S., hit in 1965. —*Richie Unterberger*

• **The Story Of . . .** / Marginal ✦✦✦✦✦
Like all compilations on the Marginal label, this is both admirable in its length (28 songs) and quality, and frustrating in its minimal packaging (nothing save for songwriting credits and a couple of photos). The total lack of dates and supplementary information makes it difficult to accurately review for us poor sods who remain totally unfamiliar with a performer who, after all, had no hits and is not mentioned in reference books. That's a shame, because on the evidence of the music Knight was an impressive, powerful soul singer deserving of wider recognition. An educated guess, however, would put the material in the late-'50s to mid-'60s time frame. There are some straight gospel sides (possibly recorded with the Millinaires?) and some rather routine '50s R&B-styled numbers, but Knight is at her best on the more elaborate early soul cuts, which sometimes have a adult pop, torch song bounce. "Come Tomorrow," covered by Manfred Mann in 1965, is an obvious highlight, and not that similar to the cover version, with a soaring string-laden production. "A Little Too Lonely" sounds a lot like, and stands up very well to, the Bacharach-David songs recorded by Dionne Warwick at the beginning of her career. The dramatic "I Don't Want to Walk Alone" has an absolutely commanding vocal performance the equal of (or better than) many a cult soul singer. A very interesting, if stylistically diffuse, collection, recommended to soul collectors who think they've run out of things to discover. —*Richie Unterberger*

Robert Knight

b. Apr. 24, 1945, Franklin, TN
Vocals / Soul
Robert Knight made one of the greatest uptempo romantic tunes of the late '60s, the majestic "Everlasting Love" in 1967. Although it is now an acknowledged classic, the song only reached number 14 on the R&B charts, and actually did better on the pop side (number 13). Knight, a Franklin, TN-native, sang with the Paramounts before joining Dot in 1960. He never repeated his success. —*Ron Wynn*

• **Everlasting Love/Love on a Mountain Top** / Jul. 25, 2002 / Beat Goes On ✦✦✦

Frankie Knuckles

b. Jan. 18, 1955, New York, NY [South Bronx]
DJ, Producer / House, Club/Dance, Acid House, Urban
The man many call the godfather of house, Frankie Knuckles began DJ-ing in New York in the early '70s while still a teenager, years before the disco boom which proved to be the first flowering of modern dance music. Ten years later he was in Chicago, putting together megamixes of old disco hits with new drum-machine percussion for an appreciative audience at crucial clubs like the Music Box and the Warehouse. Another decade on from those first formative steps for house music, Knuckles was back in his New York home, working as a producer and remixer for the biggest pop stars in the business. His career spans more time than any dance producer and without him, the landscape would be immeasurably different.

Born in the Bronx in 1955, Knuckles listened to a lot of jazz as a child, thanks to his sister's record collection. He studied commercial art and costume design before taking his first job as a DJ in 1971. Several years later, he hooked up with childhood friend Larry Levan and the two began working at Nicky Siano's New York club, the Gallery. Levan later moved to the Continental Baths, and Knuckles worked at another club for several months before rejoining Levan. Again, Levan left—this time to set up his own club, the Soho Place—and Knuckles continued on until the Continental Baths was closed. A group of entrepreneurs initially approached Levan about becoming the DJ at a club they were starting in Chicago; instead of abandoning the interest in his own club, he declined but suggested his friend Frankie Knuckles.

Knuckles moved to Chicago in 1977 and began DJ-ing at the Warehouse, spinning Salsoul and Philadelphia Int'l records in front of a crowd unused to the New York DJ-ing style, which included beat-mixing and the addition of percussion fills (from a separate turntable) to spruce up the sound of traditional soul. In 1983, Knuckles opened his own club, the Power Plant. While Ron Hardy was entrancing a largely gay, uptown crowd at the Music Box, Knuckles introduced the sound to many of the Southside producers who made waves during the 1980s: Marshall Jefferson, Larry Heard, Adonis, Steve "Silk" Hurley and at least half a dozen others.

After more than 15 years spinning vinyl, Frankie Knuckles began recording as well, debuting with several singles released on the seminal Trax Records. Such efforts as "Your Love," "Baby Wants to Ride," "You Got the Love" and "Angel" (most credited to Knuckles though vocalist Jamie Principle undoubtedly exercised some influence) were among the best tracks released in the Chicago house explosion of the mid-'80s. Knuckles also recorded for Danica ("Let the Music Use You") and worked with younger producers like Marshall Jefferson as well as future Fingers, Inc. vocalist Robert Owens. Just as Chicago house began spreading worldwide during 1986-1987 though, Knuckles returned to New York. He formed Def Mix Productions with David Morales (one of the other major names in house music) and began working on house treatments for the biggest pop stars of the 1980s and '90s, including Michael Jackson, Diana Ross, Chaka Khan, Inner City and En Vogue.

Despite the popularity of house in the international arena, the godfather of the music waited several years before the major labels came calling for something other than a remix. Finally, Virgin signed him to an artist contract in 1991 and released his debut album *Beyond the Mix*. The singles "The Whistle Song," "Rainfalls" and "Workout" moved up the dance charts, though the album failed to connect with pop or R&B fans. Knuckles continued to produce singles and remix tracks, while his second album *Welcome to the Real World* was released in 1995. —*John Bush*

Beyond the Mix / 1991 / Virgin ✦✦✦
Any serious fan of house music knows the name Frankie Knuckles. Like Marshall Jefferson, he commands the type of respect in the genre that Grandmaster Flash enjoyed in hip-hop. When Knuckles signed with Virgin, the enthusiasm was high among house aficionados; but in fact, his Virgin debut, *Beyond the Mix*, isn't the all-out dancefloor extravaganza many were predicting it would be. The CD definitely has its strong points—including Lisa Michaels' seductive vocals on "Sacrifice" and the haunting "Rain Falls" and Shelton Becton's gutsy performances on "It's Hard Sometime" and the gospel-influenced "Soon I Will Be Done." At its best, *Beyond the Mix* is far superior to most of the songs heard on urban contemporary radio in 1991. But "Godfather" and "Party in My House" are routine hip-house numbers that are virtually indistinguishable from countless other fusions of rap and house recorded in the early '90s. —*Alex Henderson*

Welcome to the Real World / 1995 / Virgin ✦✦
As on his major-label debut, producer Frankie Knuckles uses many different dance concepts to vary the attack on his second album for Virgin, including the singles "Whadda U Want (From Me)" and the number one dance hit "Too Many Fish." —*John Bush*

Best of Frankie Knuckles / 1999 / Mirakkle ✦✦✦✦✦
The best (and only) collection of Knuckles' diverse productions during the '80s, *Best of Frankie Knuckles* includes "Your Love," "Baby Wants to Ride," "Let the Music Use You," "You've Got the Love," and "Waiting on My Angel," among others. —*John Bush*

★ **The Godfather of House Music: Trax Classics** / 2000 / Crown ✦✦✦✦✦
This compilation should be available everywhere, but unfortunately it's available hardly anywhere. Issued in Japan in 2000, *The Godfather of House Music: Trax Classics* collects a dozen productions from Frankie Knuckles, the only being who can truly lay claim to the title of the disc. These selections come from his time on Trax and center on his monumental work with Jamie Principle ("Your Love," "Waiting on My Angel," "Baby Wants to Ride," "It's a Cold World," "Bad Boy"), while offering a smattering of other Trax gems like "Children of the Night," "Boom Boom," and "Move Your Body." If you should ever see a copy, grab it; solid anthologies of early Chicago house are hard to come by. —*Andy Kellman*

Choice: A Collection of Classics / Nov. 14, 2000 / Azuli ✦✦✦
Spreading his fingers over the history of electronic dance music, from the '70s to the '90s, Frankie Knuckles mixed a solid collection of tracks, definitely focused more on contemporary house but also stretching back to the heyday of disco and jazz-funk. Knuckles ably sprinkles George Duke's "I Want You for Myself," Candido's Latin classic "Thousand Finger Man," Billy Ocean's "Nights (Feel Like Getting Down)," even a song from ex-Time singer Alexander O'Neal. While the first disc concentrates more on the old school of dance, the second captures the house scene of the early '90s with tracks from Soul II Soul ("Back to Life"), Lisa Stansfield ("Set Your Loving Free"), Jestofunk ("I'm Gonna Love You"), and Donell Rush ("Symphony"). —*John Bush*

The Kodaks

f. 1957, Newark, NJ, **db.** 1958
Group / Doo Wop, R&B
In a different, fairer reality, the Kodaks might be remembered at least as rivals to Frankie Lymon & the Teenagers. True, they never performed in any movies and only made one national television appearance, and they never wrote a song like "Why Do Fools Fall In Love"—but they had the sound, and the beat, and a lead singer with a voice as powerful

as Lymon's. Formed in Newark, NJ, during the mid- and late '50s, the Kodaks' sound was driven by Pearl McKinnon's powerful lead vocals, and as a mixed male/female singing group, they stood out from the pack. They cut four singles, none of which made the national charts, but all of which are prized by collectors and enthusiasts.

The Kodaks were originally a quartet: Jimmy Patrick (lead, first tenor), William Franklin (second tenor), Larry Davis (baritone), and William Miller (bass). They were good, but they sounded a lot like every other singing group coming out of Newark's Central Ward in the middle of the 1950s. Enter Pearl McKinnon, a 15-year-old friend of Jimmy Patrick's sister, who sang with Marian Patrick and William Miller's future wife Jean in a trio of their own at school. Her voice had a slightly, deeper, richer tone than most teenage girls, but also a fresh innocence and clear articulation that one more often associated with preteen boys—the resemblance to Frankie Lymon's singing was unmistakable, and joining the male quartet, she made them unique.

The group auditioned for Harlem-based impresario Bobby Robinson. He had, until the end of 1957, recorded Louie Lymon & the Teenchords, and heard in the Kodaks a sound uncannily similar to that of Louie's more successful brother Frankie and his group, the Teenagers. He signed the group (changing the spelling of their name on record labels to the Kodoks, to avoid a lawsuit from Eastman Kodak), releasing their first single, "Teenager's Dream" b/w "Little Boy and Girl," on his own Fury label in late 1957. That record got heavy local airplay in Newark, New York, and other nearby cities, even though it never made the national charts. With rehearsals and some polishing of their sound, they issued as second single, "Oh Gee, Oh Gosh" b/w "Make Believe World," in the spring of 1958, that made the local charts in Newark (number eight on the local *Cashbox* chart) and other East Coast cities, and saw sales in the Midwest as well. The A-side, in particular, was popular with many local deejays, and even the legendary Alan Freed played it heavily on his show.

The result of all of this was lots of East Coast gigs for the quintet, including shows at the Apollo Theater alongside the likes of Jerry Butler, the Coasters, and Lee Andrews & the Hearts, and an appearance on Dick Clark's *American Bandstand*. Not everybody was happy with the nature of their success, or the sound the group was cultivating—by the summer of 1958, Davis and Franklin, tired of emulating the music of Frankie Lymon & the Teenagers, quit the group, to be replaced by Richard "Pumpy" Dixon and Harold "Curly" Jenkins. Ironically, in the estimation of many (including Pearl McKinnon), their arrival, as veteran performers, only improved the group, strengthening their sound and making their stage choreography more exciting. The group released two more singles, "My Baby and Me" b/w "Kingless Castle," and "Runaround Baby" b/w "Guardian Angel," but neither sold as well as their predecessors.

The group dissolved when Jimmy Patrick exited to join the Monotones, and Pearl McKinnon got married. William Miller tried to keep the ball rolling, forming the "Kadaks" with his wife Jean and Harold Jenkins, and a new member, Renaldo Gamble, but they faded after two failed singles. McKinnon returned to the business less than a year later, leading Pearl & the Deltars. They issued two singles, including a recut version of "Teenager's Dream," but never had more than a local success. She later appeared in the 1970s in an outfit known as 2nd Verse, but seemed to find a part of her true destiny later still, fronting a re-formed version of the Teenagers, taking Frankie Lymon's role as lead singer. *—Bruce Eder*

● **Oh Gee Oh Gosh** / 1992 / Relic ✦✦✦

"Little Boy and Little Girl" sounds uncannily like Frankie Lymon and company's "I'm Not a Juvenile Delinquent," and "Oh Gee, Oh Gosh" sounds a lot like "Why Do Fools Fall in Love"—you get the picture. And given their role as would-be successors to Lymon and his group, none of this is a surprise, but it is also great fun, and Pearl McKinnon is a wonder to hear, sounding more like Frankie Lymon than the man himself did after 1957. The group also wasn't bad when they stepped away from the sound of the more famous group into a groove more their own, as on the exquisite slow tune "Kingless Castle" (written by Pearl McKinnon). The production is very clean, the sources and the mastering are crisp, and the whole CD was put together with a lot of love. Bonuses include a faster, more stripped-down alternate take of "Little Boy and Girl," and a faster, more upbeat version of "Oh Gee, Oh Gosh," as well as both sides of the only single released by Pearl & the Deltars, which is closer to straight urban rock & roll than to doo wop music. *—Bruce Eder*

Kon Kan

f. Canada

Group / Club/Dance, Hi-NRG, Urban

The '80s dance duo Kon Kan included members Barry Harris (vocals, keys, guitar) and Kevin Wynne (vocals). The group took their name from the phrase "Can Con" (short for "Canadian Content"), which is the name of a rule that enforces Canadian radio station to play at least 30 percent music from musicians from Canada. It was Kon Kan's sophomore album, *Move to Move*, which spawned a number-15 hit with the single "I Beg Your Pardon," which included a few lines from a previous song, Lynn Anderson's "Rose Garden." Harris and Wynne followed it up with a few more singles, including "Harry Houdini" and "Puss N' Boots/These Boots (Are Made for Walkin')," the latter of which featured samples from both Led Zeppelin's "The Immigrant Song" and Nancy Sinatra's "These Boots Are Made for Walking."

Wynne left Kon Kan shortly thereafter, but Harris retained the Kon Kan name and carried on, issuing such further albums as 1990's *Syntonic* and 1993's *Vida!* Harris then turned his attention to producing other dance outfits, including singer Kim Esty (who sang backup on Kon Kan's "I Beg, Your Pardon"), Top Kat, Outta Control, Thunderpuss 2000, and Killer Bunnies. Harris also released his own solo singles in the late '90s, including "Funk Like Dat" and "Why'd Ya Let Her." *—Greg Prato*

● **Move to Move** / 1989 / Atlantic ✦✦✦

The Canadian duo Kon Kan (musician Barry Harris and vocalist Kevin Wynne) scored an out-of-nowhere smash in 1989 with the quirky single "I Beg Your Pardon." Incorporating a repetitive drum beat, a catchy keyboard line, Wynne's droll vocal delivery (somewhat similar to New Order's Bernard Sumner) and the ingenious sampling of Lynn Anderson's hit "I Never Promised You a Rose Garden," "I Beg Your Pardon" became a dancefloor staple and eventually crossed over to the pop charts where it hit the Top 20. Kon Kan followed the single's success with the album *Move to Move*. "I Beg Your Pardon," included here in two versions, is still engaging dance-pop fluff; although released in 1989, the song could have easily been a hit in 1999. The rest of *Move to Move* goes down just as easy, even though the lightweight dance pop doesn't quite scale the heights of "Pardon." "Puss and Boots," which includes snippets from songs by Led Zeppelin and Nancy Sinatra, comes pretty close, however; it also became Kon Kan's only other chart single (at number 58.) *Move to Move* is harmless, disposable fun. Kevin Wynne eventually disappeared from the music scene; Barry Harris kept the Kon Kan name for the 1990 flop *Syntonic*, eventually forming the short-lived dance outfit Outta Control and the prolific remix team Thunderpuss 2000. *—William Cooper*

Kool & the Gang

f. 1964, Jersey City, NJ

Group / Funk, Urban, Soul

Formed as a jazz ensemble in the mid-'60s, Kool & the Gang became one of the most inspired and influential funk units during the '70s, and one of the most popular R&B groups of the '80s after their breakout hit "Celebration" in 1979. Just as funky as James Brown or Parliament (and sampled almost as frequently), Kool & the Gang relied on their jazz backgrounds and long friendship to form a tightly knit group with the interplay and improvisation of a jazz outfit, plus the energy and spark of a band with equal ties to soul, R&B and funk.

Robert "Kool" Bell and his brother Ronald (or Khalis Bayyan) grew up in Jersey City, NJ, and picked up the music bug from their father. A professional boxer, he was also a serious jazz lover and a close friend of Thelonious Monk. With Robert on bass and Ronald picking up an array of horns, the duo formed the Jazziacs in 1964 with several neighborhood friends: trombone player Clifford Adams, guitarists Charles Smith and Woody Sparrow, trumpeter Robert "Spike" Mickens, alto saxophonist Dennis Thomas, keyboard player Ricky West and drummer Funky George Brown (all of whom, except Mickens and West, still remained in the group more than 30 years later).

The growing earthiness of soul inspired the Jazziacs to temper their jazz sensibilites with rhythms more akin to R&B, and the newly renamed Soul Town Band began playing clubs in Greenwich Village. After a mix-up with a club owner resulted in the group being billed Kool & the Flames, they moderated the title to Kool & the Gang and found a leg up with the tiny De Lite Records. Three singles from their self-titled debut album hit the pop charts, and although the position wasn't incredibly high, Kool & the Gang became a quick success on the R&B charts. Always a staple of their appeal, the group's live act was documented on two 1971 LPs, *Live at the Sex Machine* and *Live at P.J.'s*, including left-field covers of "Walk on By" and "Wichita Lineman" (as well as the not so unusual "I Want to Take You Higher").

Studio albums followed in 1972 and 1973, but it was with Kool & the Gang's sixth LP, *Wild and Peaceful*, that they hit the big time. "Funky Stuff" became their first Top 40 hit at the end of 1973. Then both "Jungle Boogie" and "Hollywood Swinging" reached the pop Top Ten. During the next four years, however, Kool & the Gang could only manage an occasional Top 40 hit ("Higher Plane," "Spirit of the Boogie"), and though they did win a Grammy award for "Open Sesame" (from the *Saturday Night Fever* soundtrack), the rise of disco—a movement centered around producers and vocalists, in direct contrast to the group's focus on instrumentalists—had appeared to end their popularity.

Then, in 1979, the group added two new vocalists, Earl Toon Jr. and, more importantly, James "J.T." Taylor, a former Jersey nightclub singer. Kool & the Gang also began working with jazz fusion arranger Eumir Deodato, who produced their records from 1979 to 1982. The first such album, *Ladies Night*, was their biggest hit yet, the first of three consecutive platinum albums, with the Top Ten singles "Too Hot" and the title track. *Celebrate!*, released in 1980, spawned Kool & the Gang's only number-one hit, "Celebration," an anthem favored by innumerable wedding receptions since. With Deodato, the group produced several more hits, including the singles "Take My Heart (You Can Have It If You Want It)," "Get Down on It" and "Big Fun," and the albums *Something Special* in 1981 and *As One* a year later. After Deodato left the fold in late 1982, Kool & the Gang proved their success wasn't solely due to him; they had two immense hits during 1984-1985 ("Joanna" and "Cherish"), as well as two more Top Tens, "Misled" and "Fresh." The group's string of seven gold or platinum records continued until 1986's *Forever*, after which James "J.T." Taylor amicably left the group for a solo career.

Although Taylor did reasonably well with his solo recordings (many of which were produced by Ronald Bell), Kool & the Gang quickly sank without him. They replaced Taylor with three vocalists, Sennie "Skip" Martin III (formerly of the Dazz Band), Odeen Mays and Gary Brown, but failed to chart their albums *Sweat* (1989) and *Unite* (1993). Taylor finally returned to the group in 1995 for the release of a new album, *State of Affairs*. *—John Bush*

Kool and the Gang / 1969 / De Lite ✦✦✦

Kool & the Gang's funky debut was an unexpected hit, with a first single (self-titled) climbing both the pop and R&B charts. Subsequent singles—"The Gang's Back Again," "Let the Music Take Your Mind," and "Funky Man,"—followed the first into the charts, and there were plenty of other standout tracks: "Raw Hamburger," "Chocolate Buttermilk," and "Kool's Back Again." Though barely over a half an hour long, *Kool and the Gang* is a blast of a record containing strong elements that would become the band's trademarks: smooth melodies, suave rhythms, and brassy horns. This is one of Kool & the Gang's jazzier albums and a strong debut worth checking out, though less accessible than any of their later pop recordings. *—JT Griffith*

Live at the Sex Machine / Feb. 1971 / De Lite ✦✦✦✦

In addition to having a great title, this 1971 release is one of the best of the group's early efforts. Combining the raw groove of James Brown with the melodic talents and jazz influence of hornmen Ronald Bell, Robert Mickens and Dennis Thomas, the band gives a solid workout to songs such as "Pneumonia," "Who's Gonna Take the Weight" and the Sly Stone hit "I Want to Take You Higher." *—Steve Kurutz*

Live at P.J.'s / Oct. 1971 / De Lite ♦♦♦♦♦

Live at P.J.'s, the third Kool & the Gang record (and second live album in a row), betters the previous *Live at the Sex Machine* with a committed set balancing funky workouts ("Ronnie's Groove") with more exploratory soul-jazz ("Sombrero Sam"), and occasionally trying both on the same track ("N.T."). A night-after-night schedule of concerts all over the country had given Kool & the Gang the chops to become one of the best bands of the '70s, but it also enabled them to construct tight, interesting sets (this release would've undoubtedly sounded even *better* had the original compilers trusted the artists themselves and reissued the show in the correct running order). The opener is a version of "N.T." (short for no title), oddly slower than it was heard on record, though the relaxed tempo allowed plenty of room for solos and stretching out. At this point, Kool & the Gang had more in common with soul-jazz units like the Crusaders than a funk band, giving nearly every member a chance to shine, but especially Dennis Thomas on flute (he has some great vocalizing on "Sombrero Sam"), Khalis Bayyan on tenor and soprano sax, and Robert "Spike" Mickens on trumpet. The only misstep is a pair of covers originally heard on Isaac Hayes'... *To Be Continued*, the first a regal version of "Ike's Mood" that suddenly descends into MOR soul via a misguided attempt at "You've Lost That Lovin' Feeling." Mercury's CD reissue added a great bonus track, "The Penguin." *—John Bush*

Music Is the Message / Jul. 1972 / De Lite ♦♦♦

Kool & the Gang's fourth album—but only their second studio record—was just as strong and joyous as its live predecessors, though it featured a few more vocals and emphasized strong musicianship over hard grooves. (Of course, the band always did pretty well at both.) The title track and "Love the Life You Live" were two more great party jams to add to their repertoire, despite the growing similarity of Robert "Kool" Bell's basslines. The two-part "Electric Frog" was a squelchy instrumental spotlighting an Arp synthesizer and some great ensemble playing on the chorus, while the band reserved a great feature for trumpeter Robert "Spike" Mickens on "Blowin' With the Wind." "Love the Life You Live" was the most fully realized early Kool & the Gang jam, and the one that most looks forward to their parade of hits to come ("Funky Stuff," "Hollywood Swinging"). Ending the album with a smile (if not style) was "Funky Granny," a lightweight but hilarious sequel to their 1970 hit "Funky Man." *—John Bush*

Good Times / Nov. 1972 / De Lite ♦♦♦

Good Times was a bit spotty compared to *Music Is the Message*, compromising Kool & the Gang's legendary funk instincts for a variety of digressions that don't turn out the way they should. There's much more good than bad though, beginning with the title track, a school's-out jam just in time for summer. "Making Merry Music" is in a similar mold and just as good, while the group leaps into wild, unhinged, horn-driven funk for "Rated X" and "Country Junky." The songs that make it less interesting are the maudlin ballad "Wild Is Love," a salute by music director and tenor Khalis Bayyan to one of his influences with "I Remember John W. Coltrane," and the meandering "North, South, East, West." The closer, "Father, Father," is a solid attempt at recording social-message soul along the lines of Curtis Mayfield, but for much of the time, *Good Times* sacrifices the group's hallmarks (deep-pocket grooves and fast, intricate ensemble playing) on the altar of artistic experimentation. *—John Bush*

Wild and Peaceful / Sep. 1973 / De Lite ♦♦♦♦♦

Prior to James "J.T." Taylor adding pop flavor vocals, which help garner a handful of top-selling albums, this was Kool & the Gang's most successful album, spawning three bona fide R&B hits. Produced by Robert Bell, and featuring Donal Boyce's incredulous vocals, these songs have held up well. The fast, chugging "Jungle Boogie" was a club favorite, while "Funky Stuff," with its "whoa whoa whoa" hook, was slower and spacier than "Jungle Boogie." The band formerly known as the Jazziacs got their first R&B number one with "Hollywood Swinging," a slightly faster than midtempo song with whistles, festive ambience and lead vocals by keyboardist Ricky West. All three hits were inspired by Manu Dibango's "Soul Makossa," and were recorded in one night at a studio in midtown Manhattan. The title cut flash backs to their prerecording jazz days, when they dazzled New Jerseyites with their playing skills. *—Andrew Hamilton*

Spirit of the Boogie / 1975 / De Lite ♦♦♦♦♦

Discussing Kool & the Gang in the early '70s, James Brown enthused, "They're the second-baddest out there... They make such bad records that you got to be careful when you play a new tape on the way home from the record store. Their groove is so strong you could wreck." And that really says it all. Kool & the Gang were funk's kings in 1975, and *Spirit of the Boogie* was the finest album they ever recorded—the staggering climax of their development thus far. The record-buying public thought so too—the album gave the band their first Top Five R&B hit. *Spirit of the Boogie* may have been first and foremost a funk masterpiece, but it was also so much more. From the African art on the foldout sleeve to the spiritual and musical purity of many of the songs, this album not only bound the band's reverence for their roots to a blistering, street-smart funk, but also demonstrated a keen awareness of their own role in their musical odyssey. "Ancestral Ceremony" pays homage by quoting from Kool's earlier songs, while "Jungle Jazz" tracks back to the original pounding jams that imbibed 1973's "Jungle Boogie." The title track, meanwhile, is quintessential Kool & the Gang—fiery funk which is kept in check by rhythm and chant. It gave the band a springtime number one on the R&B charts—their third. This is a phenomenal set, a superlative album. And because the grooves are so strong, it's easy to forgive weak moments—most especially the mawkish "Sunshine and Love." Kool & the Gang were outstanding during this period, before they caught the disco bug. *Spirit of the Boogie* remains a proud achievement. *—Amy Hanson*

Love & Understanding / 1976 / De Lite ♦♦♦

Following on the heels of their 1975 smash *Spirit of the Boogie*, Kool & the Gang hit the road to tour the album and record new material. One tumultuous show, at London's Rainbow Theatre, became the core of *Love and Understanding*. Three live tracks, "Hollywood Swinging," "Summer Madness," and a dreamily mellow "Universal Sound," are all excellent reminders of just how good this band could sound when they found the vibe and had the funk firmly in hand. But as good as this stuff is, there are ominous glimmers among the goods, of musical moves the band were contemplating—heard most markedly in the bland "Sugar" and "Do It Right Now." For, despite the sureness with which they were creating driving funk, they were also struggling with the oncoming disco explosion. That push-pull was duly reflected in the album. The studio tracks are the most uneven. At their best, they are dominated by the opening title track and its near-instrumental twin shadow "Come Together," which closes. Both songs are horn heavy, an insistent call for unity, love, and peace. The rest of the album is sandwiched between this jazzy cacophony but, despite the rocky moments, *Love and Understanding* remains a remarkable album, recorded at a time when the band was still reveling in the grip of pure funk, uncorrupted by the mainstream. *—Amy Hanson*

The Force / 1977 / De Lite ♦♦

The Force is no such thing, it's a mundane set where the group from Jersey never achieves what they were trying to obtain. It comes after their first run of hits and before their celebrated era which included super hits like "Celebration," "Too Hot," and others. You won't find any chart busters here "Slick Superchick" failed miserably, and rightfully so, it's a bad example of disco/funk with an undistinguish lead vocal. They try to emulate Earth, Wind & Fire on the embarrassing "Mighty, Mighty High." "Just Be True"—not the Curtis Mayfield classic—is a boring ballad, and the title track attempts to connect fusion with funk. While the musicianship is excellent, there's not a memorable song in the bunch. *—Andrew Hamilton*

Ladies' Night / 1979 / De Lite ♦♦

Kool & the Gang closed out the 1970s by edging the door shut on their classic sound. *Ladies' Night* marked the band's initial shift from their dirty funk to a more mainstream pop—a lighter groove that primed clubbers for dance-'til-you-drop style partying. With the Brazilian fusion musician Eumir Deodato stepping into the production helm with a shared vision of "keep[ing] it simple and basic and clean," Kool & the Gang added a hot new spark to their sound, best illustrated across the title track, which topped the R&B charts for nearly a month. This ideal was also furthered on the downtempo soul of "Too Hot." The former was a jangly, spangly slab of pure dance that quickly became a club favorite, the latter a 180 degree shift that focused instead on vocalist James Taylor's rich timbre, a ballad of lost love where his vocals are smoother than even the sax solo. With the rest of the record falling into step behind these two giants, *Ladies' Night* kicked off Kool & the Gang's new musical era and, even though it certainly distanced some of their more funk-minded fans, it picked up a faithful army who'd keep the band in the charts for nearly a decade to come. *—Amy Hanson*

Celebrate! / 1980 / De Lite ♦♦♦

Although disco was well dead by the end of the 1970s, Kool & the Gang nevertheless unleashed a chart-topping, dance-club rattling monster that proved there was still life on the Excess Express. *Celebrate*, released in fall 1980, further gelled the exquisite relationship between the band and Brazilian fusion guru Deodato and, with equal nods to fusion, funk, and, yes, disco, the album gave the band a massive hit. Reaching into the Top Ten on both the R&B and pop charts, it furthered the comeback commenced with *Ladies Night*. But it was *Celebrate*'s first baby, the unstoppable "Celebration," that provided the band a comeback of unparalleled heights. Ronald Bell predicted that the song would "be an international anthem," and he was proved right. Not only did it slam to the top of the U.S. charts, it was quickly adopted as a symbol of freedom—first to welcome home the hostages released from Iran, then to laud Democrat Walter Mondale's presidential nomination. The downside was that this one song not only grossly overshadowed the album, but also set an unreachable standard for the rest of the set, which lost steam in its wake. Although "Jones Vs. Jones" crept into the charts, it was the thumping bass and drums on "Love Festival" and the disco ghosts of "Night People" which emerged as club favorites in the early part of the decade. And *Celebrate* itself marked the end of an era for Kool & the Gang, as the band would slip even farther from their funk roots and adopted dance grooves into the realms of smooth soul. But what a way to go! *—Amy Hanson*

Something Special / 1981 / De Lite ♦♦♦♦

With their long track record, Kool & the Gang have always offered dance-provoking rhythms and *Something Special* fits that bill, too. Featuring the number-one single "Take My Heart (You Can Have It if You Want It)," James "J.T." Taylor approaches the song in a cool, mesmerizing tone, closing out the vamp in his falsetto with a burst of energy while the background vocals chant the sub-title throughout the chorus. Not known to lead a song in falsetto, J.T. further utilizes this talent on the motivated rhythms of the nocturnal scenario of "Steppin' Out." It maintained a steady stride, rising to the number-ten spot on the charts. The third single from the album was "Get Down on It." As the title indicates, this is a gritty funk track that worked its way up the charts to claim the number-three position, selling more than 500,000 copies. Although there were no more charted singles from this album, the entire collection is deserving of recognition. On a slower note, "Pass It On" and "No Show" received regional airplay. The former encourages people to spread love to all children, and the latter is a sorrowful account of a man left standing in the rain, waiting for the love that never showed. Both singles have similar rhythm arrangements. As for inspirational songs, "Stand Up and Sing" is a moderately paced single with lyrics that are uplifting. *—Craig Lytle*

As One / 1982 / De Lite ♦♦♦
During their eight-year reign as one of the premier R&B/funk bands, Kool & the Gang featuring James "J.T." Taylor on lead, had one Top Ten hit after another and quite a few number-one hits. This album did not spawn any number-one singles, but it did house two festive Top Ten numbers in "Big Fun" and "Let's Go Dancin' (Ooh La, La, La)." The former has a rapid groovin' bassline accentuated by some jittering horns. The latter is Carribean-flavored single ideal for a popular party/cook-out dance called the electric slide. Respectively, they peaked at six and seven on the *Billboard* R&B charts. Though it appears that the lyric to the title song depicts a relationship between a man and woman, it is actually speaking of the band as an unit. The nine-piece outfit also pays homage to the great bandleader Cab Calloway with the rhythmic number "Hi De Hi, Hi De Ho." Aside from the two released singles, this album does not have that constant spark like some of their more accomplished efforts. *—Craig Lytle*

In the Heart / 1983 / De Lite ♦♦
By the time 1983's *In the Heart* hit the streets, Kool & the Gang had left the fast lanes of funk for the smoother ride of the adult-oriented R&B expressway. Nevertheless, their grasp of 1980s soul sonics ensured that the band continued to top the charts with a verve and style that left their early influences firmly behind. With Ronald Bell temporarily stepping off the stage to shoulder the production, the band entered yet another fruitful era. With the monster hit "Joanna" setting the pace, Kool & the Gang powered their way through a set that seemed light to some, but still had enough force to push *In the Heart* into gold disc territory. Best heard across the aforementioned number-one hit and, also, on the urgent, but still smooth "Tonight," the band also excelled on "September Love," a sleepy ballad that holds forth with a tender touch. Elsewhere, Kool & the Gang filled in the gaps with their now-trademarked synthesized brand of smooth R&B standards and, despite its own successes, *In the Heart* would ultimately be remembered as the beginning of the downward spiral upon which the band would glide for most of the decade. *—Amy Hanson*

Emergency / 1984 / De Lite ♦♦♦
This album marked the end of Kool & the Gang's 15-year association with De-Lite Records. Impressively, the group charted each of those 15 years including ten number-one singles. *Emergency* continued that tradition, and was responsible for two of those number-one singles. The first release, "Misled," with its crackin' bassline led the charge; it peaked at number three on the *Billboard* R&B charts. "Fresh," an invigorating dance single with melodic verses and accented chorus chants followed and surpassed "Misled," claiming the top spot. Mostly known for their funk and dance songs, the nine-piece band hit on a more tranquil note with "Cherish." With its adult contemporary appeal, the tender-flowing single eased its way to the top of the charts. All three of the aforementioned singles were also *Billboard* Pop Top-Ten singles. The final chapter in the group's De-Lite Records catalog was the release of the title track, "Emergency," a rock-flavored single which crested at number seven on the *Billboard* R&B charts. *—Craig Lytle*

Forever / 1986 / De Lite ♦♦♦
Kool & the Gang's penultimate album, and vocalist James "J.T." Taylor's last with the band before he left for a solo career, 1986's *Forever* marked the group's final Top Ten hit. And, while it was still a slick slab of competent R&B, *Forever* was a far cry from the driving funk grooves of Kool's earlier material. Having been fully in the grasp of the mainstream since the beginning of the decade, Kool & the Gang popped a further three songs into the Top 20 in late 1986/early 1987. Both "Victory" and "Stone Love" are sharp, synthesized pop, while "Holiday," though heavy on lyrical clichés, is graced by a wonderful bassline—sorely missed from much of the band's latter-day repertoire. The title track, meanwhile, emerges as an elegant ballad by 1980s standards, while elsewhere the band combines both elements across "Peace Maker" and the melancholy "Broadway," which hides power ballad rock guitars deep in the mix. Long past their classic funk prime, Kool & the Gang were also fast teetering on the precipice of wearing out their pop welcome as well. Despite some rocky moments, best forgotten, *Forever* remains a competent last hurrah for Taylor, and indeed for the band itself. *—Amy Hanson*

Everything's Kool & the Gang: Greatest Hits & More / Jul. 25, 1988 / Mercury ♦♦♦♦♦
Kool & the Gang's long run as a recreated pop act in the '80s formally ended with this release of this late-'80s anthology. It contained all the smooth pop winners sung by J.T. Taylor, who had already made his exit. It demonstrated how smooth, slick, yet also engaging a lead singer he'd been, and how the efforts of such producers as Deodato had successfully turned Kool & the Gang into superstars by erasing the funk beats, making the arrangements mellow and subdued, and also providing catchy, hook-filled songs like "Celebration" and "Ladies Night." *—Ron Wynn*

The Best of Kool & the Gang 1969–1976 / May 18, 1993 / Mercury ♦♦♦♦♦
Although Kool & the Gang became pop superstars in the 1980s on the strength of J.T. Taylor's silky voice and several catchy arrangements, R&B fans regard their true glory days as the 1970s. The New Jersey-based ensemble patented a jazz-tinged funk approach keyed by Robert "Kool" Bell's basslines, red-hot horn lines, chunky keyboards and guitar riffs, and functional vocals. Although they seldom ventured beyond the R&B charts during this era, their music had far more bite than their later pop hits. These 16 cuts pay homage to Kool & the Gang's funk roots, and should be a revelation to those who only know them as the light ensemble behind J.T. Taylor. *—Ron Wynn*

Celebration: The Best of Kool & the Gang (1979–87) / 1994 / Mercury ♦♦♦♦♦
This collection showcases the second and more successful phase of the career of Kool & the Gang. The tracks on this release date from 1979 through 1987. Coincidentally, lead singer James "J.T." Taylor joined the group in 1979 and had a hand in writing most of the 17 tracks on this collection. Even though early hits such as "Jungle Boogie" and "Hollywood Swinging" are not included, *Celebration* is an excellent album filled with recordings that are indeed greatest hits. *—Tim Griggs*

State of Affairs / Feb. 27, 1996 / Curb ♦

● **The Very Best of Kool & the Gang** / Mar. 30, 1999 / Mercury ♦♦♦♦♦
Spanning the band's early-'70s genesis as an unhinged funk congregation and their later resurgence with urbane R&B balladry and synth-inflected disco, *The Very Best of Kool & the Gang* may not be a unified collection, but it is the first to offer every hit that's expected—as well as a few that aren't—from the band's long career. The emphasis is definitely on their peak as a pop group, from 1979 to 1986, with pride of place going to the hits "Celebration," "Get Down on It," "Ladies Night," "Too Hot," "Misled," and "Joanna." Fans of the funk get only three tracks ("Funky Stuff," "Hollywood Swinging," and "Jungle Boogie," all from 1973's *Wild and Peaceful*), which won't cause anyone to sell their copies of *The Best of Kool & the Gang 1969-1976*, but does give pop fans a glimpse of their mid-'70s greatness. All in all, this lengthy collection doesn't transition well from hit to hit, but then again, chronological order would've forced legions of pop fans to forward through the funk material to get to their favorites. *—John Bush*

The Kool Gents

Group / Doo Wop, R&B, Chicago Soul
One of the most interesting groups to emerge from Chicago in the '50s was the Kool Gents. An early incarnation called the Golden Tones had a couple of releases on two fly-by-night labels. The original members consisted of Cicero Blake, James Harper, Howard McClain, Teddy Long, and John Carter. Delecta "Dee" Clark, John McCall, and Doug Brown replaced Harper, McClain & Blake. McCall, not Clark originally sung lead until Vee-Jay's A&R man Calvin Carter recommended that Clark sing lead. Long served as the groups' main songwriter. Clark, from Arkansas, had previously recorded "Hambone" with the Red Saunders Orchestra, as a member of the Hambone Kids.

They renamed themselves after DJ Herb "Kool Gent" Kent who introduced them to Calvin Carter and Vee-Jay Records. Their first release "This Is the Night" b/w "Do Ya Do" sold locally in 1956. A second release "I Just Can't Help Myself" b/w "You Know" did fine in Chicago also, but fail to make any inroads outside the city. The Kool Gents didn't burn up the charts, but they sounded good, so Calvin Carter and Ewart Abner decided to spoof the Democratic National Convention by releasing "The Convention" as the Delegates a.k.a. the Kool Gents. It received a tremendous amount of airplay which unfortunately didn't transform into a tremendous amount of sales. A second Delegate single, "Mother's Son" b/w Teddy Long's "I'm Gonna Be Glad" didn't even excite Chicagoans.

In 1957 Dee Clark, with Calvin Carter's OK, decided to go solo, and the Kool Gents and the Delegates recording activity ended. Some members of labelmates, the El Dorados ("At My Front Door") left leaving only lead Pirkle Lee Moses, so Calvin crowned the Kool Gents the New El Dorados and they backed Moses for two fruitless years.

John Carter resurrected the Kool Gents and they gigged until 1965 but never had any other recordings released. Dee Clark recorded several successful singles including "Rain Drops" (number-two Pop), "Just Keep It Up," "Your Friends," "Nobody But You," and "Hey Little Girl." Dee recorded for many labels before suffering a fatal heart attack in Atlanta, GA, in 1990, at the age of 52. Cicero Blake, an original member of the Golden Tones, also went solo, but never received the chart popularity of Clark, though he's enjoyed a long career. Blake recorded some marvelous records including "You Got Me Walking," "Sad Feelings," and "Love Is Like a Boomerang" on a variety of labels. Solid Smoke Records released *His Best Recordings—Dee Clark & the Kool Gents & the Delegates*, in 1984, but omitted "The Convention" from the compilation. *—Andrew Hamilton*

Kyper (Randall S. Kiper)

b. Baton Rouge, LA
Producer / Party Rap, Pop-Rap, Electro, Club/Dance, Dance-Pop
Kyper was born Randall S. Kiper in Baton Rouge, LA, in the early '70s. His self-written "Tic Tac Toe" amazingly went to number-14 pop in September 1990. Equally as astounding, the pop smash did nothing on the R&B charts. The song was a pop-disco-rap mix dominated by electronic drums and was popular in clubs. Kyper wrote all his songs and has more than 30 singles cataloged and indexed by BMI. He remained active in the music business but never charted again. Kyper borrowed heavily from Midnight Star, and "Tic Tac Toe" ripped off the guitar riff from Yes' "Owner of a Lonely Heart."

Kyper's parents say he starting hamming at an early age, singing and dancing for family and friends in Baton Rouge. His parents were educators and demanded that he graduate from college with distinction. He postponed college when one of his demos got him signed to Atlantic Records, who gave him a shot at stardom. Atlantic released two albums before discontinuing the association. Tip Top Records released a third LP. This was followed by a 12-inch single on Ace Records titled "Do You Wanna Ride." His last release was a compilation of his earlier recordings titled *Dangerous Dance, Vol. 1*, released in 1998. A sequel, *Dangerous Dance, Vol. 2*, appeared in 1999. *—Andrew Hamilton*

● **Tic-Tac-Toe** / 1990 / Atlantic ♦♦♦
In 1990, Kyper made a noteworthy contribution to "techno-rap" or "electro-hop," a style that had peaked in popularity about five years earlier. Dominated by synthesizers, this futuristic approach had its roots in the music of Kraftwerk and Giorgio Moroder, as well as Afrika Bambaataa's seminal 1982 hit "Planet Rock." The entirely electronic *Tic Tac Toe* isn't unlike the Egyptian Lover and the World Class Wreckin' Cru's mid-'80s recordings, and not surprisingly, Kyper appealed to dance clubs rather than hardcore hip-hoppers. Though jams like "Satisfaction," "Work It" and "Dangerous" are catchy enough, the song that stands out the most is the sobering "What Is This World Comin' To," which takes a look at the problems of the world and makes us wish Kyper did more political songs. Had Kyper made variety a higher priority, this CD might have been great instead of merely decent. *—Alex Henderson*

L

LaBelle

f. 1962, **db.** 1976

Group / Disco, Funk, Soul

The female trio responsible for the proto-disco funk classic "Lady Marmalade," LaBelle's outlandish space-age costumes and brash incorporation of rock & roll were a far cry from their early days as a typical '60s girl group, not to mention the later solo career of front-woman Patti LaBelle. While Patti naturally seems like the focal point in hindsight, the group was also blessed with a talented and prolific songwriter in Nona Hendryx, who followed an idiosyncratic muse into her own mercurial solo career, which often bordered on the avant-garde.

The group's first incarnation was that of a quartet. Friends Patricia Holt and Cindy Birdsong had been singing together in a Philadelphia group called the Ordettes, and in 1962 they teamed up with Wynona "Nona" Hendryx and Sarah Dash, both members of a rival outfit called the Del Capris. At the suggestion of producer Bobby Martin, Holt changed her last name to LaBelle to match with the group's official name the BlueBelles. Strangely enough, Patti LaBelle & the BlueBelles may not have even performed on their first hit; a group called the Starlets cut a single called "I Sold My Heart to the Junkman," which was released with the name the Blue-Belles on the label. Some accounts hold that the Starlets actually backed LaBelle, or that her vocal was overlaid, while others suggest that the lead voice wasn't LaBelle's at all. Whatever the case, "I Sold My Heart to the Junkman" became a Top 20 R&B and pop hit in 1962, and the BlueBelles started touring the R&B circuit behind it. Their next hit came in 1963 with the dramatic ballad "Down the Aisle," another R&B Top 20, and they hit the Top 40 again in 1964 with renditions of Rodgers & Hammerstein's "You'll Never Walk Alone" and the Irish standard "Danny Boy," solidifying their penchant for sentimental, classic-style pop.

In 1965, the BlueBelles signed with major label Atlantic, and had some success with a version of "Somewhere Over the Rainbow," which remained in Patti LaBelle's concert repertoire for decades. Despite cutting an early version of "Groovy Kind of Love" (later a number-one hit for the Mindbenders, not to mention Phil Collins), though, the BlueBelles' tenure wasn't as commercially productive as hoped. Cindy Birdsong left in 1967 to replace Florence Ballard in the Supremes, permanently reducing the group to a trio. With no real hits forthcoming, Atlantic wound up dropping them in 1969. In search of a makeover, they hired former British television producer Vicki Wickham (the music series *Ready, Steady, Go!*) as their new manager and producer in 1970. Wickham remade the group for the '70s, shortening their name to LaBelle and pushing them into a more contemporary fusion of R&B and rock; plus, the advent of glam rock suggested a new direction for their stage act, and the trio donned outrageous, space-themed costumes replete with glitter, silver, and/or feathers. LaBelle opened for the Who on an American tour and sang backup on singer/songwriter Laura Nyro's acclaimed R&B-themed album *Gonna Take a Miracle* in 1971.

Signing with Warner Brothers, the revamped LaBelle made their debut in 1971 with an eponymous album that featured soul treatments of rock and pop material by the likes of Nyro, the Rolling Stones, Kenny Rogers, and Carole King. The follow-up, 1972's *Moon Shadow*, featured the Cat Stevens-penned title track and the Who's "Won't Get Fooled Again," and also included more material written by Nona Hendryx. Neither album was all that commercially successful, and they left Warner to record one album for RCA, 1973's *Pressure Cookin'*, where Hendryx's writing constituted the vast majority of the record. In 1974, LaBelle signed with Epic, and the label sent them to New Orleans to record with famed producer Allen Toussaint. The result, *Nightbirds*, featured the deeply funky single "Lady Marmalade," an ode to a New Orleans prostitute with the indelible French chorus "voulez-vous coucher avec moi ce soir?" ("you want to go to bed with me tonight?"). Penned by Bob Crewe and Kenny Nolan, "Lady Marmalade" shot to number one on both the pop and R&B charts in early 1975, sending *Nightbirds* into the Top Ten and making it LaBelle's first gold album.

"Lady Marmalade" proved to be a tough act to follow. Despite four more charting R&B singles over the next two years, nothing duplicated the phenomenon of LaBelle's first major hit. *Phoenix*, from 1975, and 1976's *Chameleon* were relative commercial disappointments, even though they featured some of the group's finest vocal performances, plus increasingly ambitious and sophisticated writing by Hendryx. In fact, Hendryx's vision was pulling her away from the rest of LaBelle, and by the end of 1976, the group had disbanded to pursue solo careers. Hendryx immediately began recording in a funk-rock hybrid, and in the early '80s drifted into downtown New York's avant-garde scene, where she worked often with Bill Laswell; her solo records were sometimes accessible and frequently challenging. Patti LaBelle, of course, went on to a hugely successful and long-lived career as an R&B hitmaker with adult contemporary appeal, scoring hits like "New Attitude" and the number one Michael McDonald duet "On My Own." As for Sarah Dash, she made several solo albums that failed to attract much attention, but found her way into the Rolling Stones' sphere by the late '80s, working as a backup singer on both solo and group projects. *—Steve Huey*

LaBelle / 1971 / Warner Bros. ♦♦♦

Released in 1971, this self-titled LP was the first album that Patti LaBelle, Nona Hendryx, and Sarah Dash recorded under the name LaBelle. Never again would they use the name Patti LaBelle & the BlueBelles, and that's just as well; since the group had a new sound and a new image, it made sense to have a new name. And make no mistake: LaBelle was determined to forge ahead in 1971. While pop considerations were a high priority for Patti LaBelle & the BlueBelles, soul considerations define *LaBelle*: a tough, gritty, gospel-drenched effort along the lines of Aretha Franklin, Ike & Tina Turner, and Etta James. Produced by Vicki Wickham (the group's manager) and Kit Lambert, this decent, if uneven, LP isn't in a class with subsequent gems like 1974's *Nightbirds* and 1975's *Phoenix*. Nonetheless, LaBelle's performances are generally enjoyable, and the group brings plenty of passion and sincerity to original material as well as covers of Laura Nyro's "Time and Love," Carole King's "You've Got a Friend," and the Rolling Stones' "Wild Horses." In 1971, the best was yet to come for LaBelle, both creatively and commercially. But despite its imperfections, this LP made it clear that the trio had great potential. *—Alex Henderson*

Moon Shadow / 1972 / Warner Bros. ♦♦♦

These days, very few A&R people at major labels have the patience to really develop an artist; if an album doesn't sell, the artist will most likely be dropped. A lot of smaller independents are still willing to stick around for several albums if they believe in the artist, but because major labels have such high overhead, their A&R people often believe that sticking with an artist through several modest sellers is a luxury they cannot afford. And that's a tragedy because a lot of potential goes unrealized; imagine how much poorer 1970s R&B would have been if Earth, Wind & Fire, L.T.D., the O'Jays, the Gap Band, or Funkadelic had called it quits because their first album wasn't a million seller. Those artists needed time to develop, as did LaBelle. It took LaBelle (as opposed to Patti LaBelle & the BlueBelles) several albums to make the transition from decent to remarkable, and the trio was hardly an overnight sensation. What was true of 1971's *LaBelle* is also true of 1972's *Moon Shadow*; this LP isn't as conceptually brilliant as *Nightbirds*, *Phoenix*, and *Chameleon* would be, but it's a solid, heartfelt effort that is never short on guts. Whether the threesome is embracing songs by Nona Hendryx and Sarah Dash or giving the Who's "Won't Get Fooled Again" and Cat Stevens' "Moon Shadow" sweaty soul makeovers, this gospel-drenched LP is about as gritty as it gets. *—Alex Henderson*

Pressure Cookin' / 1973 / RCA ♦♦♦

Nightbirds / 1974 / Epic ♦♦♦♦♦

The finest of LaBelle's original albums, *Nightbirds* was recorded in New Orleans with funkmeister Allen Toussaint handling the production chores and, one assumes, members of the Meters taking care of the session work. Worth the price of admission for the Bob Crewe-written "Lady Marmalade" alone, the album veers between the strutting New Orleans, horn-laden singles and more mainstream pop material. *—Rob Bowman*

Phoenix / 1975 / Epic ♦♦♦

Chameleon / 1976 / Epic ♦♦♦

While Patti LaBelle was the vocal force behind the group bearing her name, Nona Hendryx was providing the material for which Patti would use to deliver her energetic sound. Of the eight numbers presented, Hendryx is credited with six. "Get You Somebody New" stayed on the *Billboard* R&B charts for nine weeks, peaking at number 50. "Isn't It a Shame" only managed to peak at a disappointing number 18 after 15 weeks on the charts. The drama, compassion and delivery easily justify it's worthiness as a number-one song. However, it remains a popular composition. While LaBelle's image was costumatic, to say the least, songs like the psychedelic "Get You Somebody New" fit the trio's extravagant look. Whereas numbers like the sensusous "Come Into My Life," the breathtaking "Isn't It a Shame" and the Gospel-propelled title track "Chameleon." bring on a stark contrast, but a welcomed one. On every level of creativity, LaBelle, the group, are as diverse as these selections. *—Craig Lytle*

Lady Marmalade: The Best of Patti and LaBelle / Feb. 28, 1995 / Epic/Legacy ♦♦♦♦

The concept behind *Lady Marmalade: The Best of Patti and LaBelle* is to draw eight tracks apiece from LaBelle's chart heyday as a group and the first five years (1977-1982) of Patti LaBelle's solo career, which she spent with Epic. Is it a worthwhile summation? That depends on what you're looking for. The LaBelle tracks constitute a serviceable overview, featuring their four chart hits ("Lady Marmalade," the R&B Top Ten "What Can I Do for You?," "Get You Somebody New," and "Isn't It a Shame"); actually, the more extensive *Something Silver* compilation doesn't have them all. Plus, there are four songs written or co-written by Nona Hendryx, an important component of their repertoire. All that's missing, really, are the group's early rock covers, many of which are collected on *Something Silver.* The Patti LaBelle solo tracks date from a part of her career that isn't usually spotlighted on other compilations, and constitute some of the funkiest material she recorded. However, the selections here are missing a few minor R&B chart hits; the similarly skimpy 1982 compilation *The Best of Patti LaBelle*—also eight tracks—includes all of them. That flaw aside, it's most likely the LaBelle group material you're after, and so far this is the best place to get it. In fact, other than "Lady Marmalade," it's pretty much the only place, other than the original, mostly out-of-print albums. *—Steve Huey*

• **Something Silver** / Feb. 11, 1997 / Warner Bros. ✦✦✦✦✦
With 1974's "Lady Marmalade," LaBelle placed itself in a spotlight that would last until Patti LaBelle left the group for a solo career some two years later. A darling of New York's Apollo Theater, the group never compromised, delivering its fiery, passionate R&B exactly as its members wanted to. Leaving behind the cookie-cutter big hair and lookalike dresses of its BlueBelles era, LaBelle took the stage after dropping out of sight to reinvent itself, and emerged as a group of glamorously modern individuals—three strong styles that melded into a universal whole of staggering proportion. This compilation rounds up the group's best songs and includes many of its covers, alongside original material. The members of LaBelle were masters of interpretation, blessed with the uncanny ability to completely co-opt a song—to turn it into something of their own without disturbing the integrity of the original and, in most cases, elevate it to heights previously unimagined. Through the use of classic R&B, funk, and dance beats that foreshadowed the disco movement, LaBelle turned its audience's attention to something vitally fresh and unique. This collection opens with LaBelle's reinvention of Gil Scott-Heron's Black Power manifesto "The Revolution Will Not Be Televised," which bleeds out of a revolutionarily balladic version of Thunderclap Newman's "Something in the Air." Coincidentally, that band's producer, Pete Townshend, then gets in on the act, as LaBelle gives "Won't Get Fooled Again" the classic girl group treatment—both bratty (in a good way) and strong. Cat Stevens' "Moonshadow" also becomes an entirely different song, slowed down and harmonized. Treatments of the Rolling Stones' "Wild Horses" and folksinger Laura Nyro's "Time and Love" are also included. The band's own songs, meanwhile, round out this chunky set with the classics "If I Can't Have You," "Shades of Difference," and "Touch Me All Over." The eternal "Lady Marmalade" winds the whole thing down with what remains, for many people, LaBelle's defining moment. An anthem for everybody, it stood apart by serving as a signpost for future generations. After all, without LaBelle to pave the way, would TLC, Destiny's Child, or the striking images of *Moulin Rouge* exist nearly 30 years later? *—Amy Hanson*

Patti LaBelle (Patricia Holt)

b. May 24, 1944, Philadelphia, PA

Vocals / Quiet Storm, Urban, Soul

Soul diva Patti LaBelle enjoyed one of the longest-lived careers in contemporary music, notching hits in a variety of sounds ranging from girl group pop to space-age funk to lush ballads. Born Patricia Holt in Philadelphia on May 24, 1944, she grew up singing in a local Baptist choir, and in 1960 teamed with friend Cindy Birdsong to form a group called the Ordettes. A year later, following the additions of vocalists Nona Hendryx and Sarah Dash, the group was rechristened the BlueBelles; with producer Bobby Martin at helm, they scored a Top 20 pop and R&B hit in 1962 with the single "I Sold My Heart to the Junkman," subsequently hitting the charts in 1964 with renditions of "Danny Boy" and "You'll Never Walk Alone."

In 1965, the quartet—now known as Patti LaBelle and the BlueBelles—signed to Atlantic, where they earned a minor hit with their version of the standard "Somewhere Over the Rainbow." The group's Atlantic tenure was largely disappointing, however, and in 1967 Birdsong replaced Florence Ballard in the Supremes. The remaining trio toured the so-called "chitlin' circuit" for the remainder of the decade before signing on with British manager Vicki Wickham in 1970; Wickham renamed the group simply LaBelle and pushed their music in a more funky, rock-oriented direction, and in the wake of their self-titled 1971 Warner Bros. debut they even toured with the Who. (The trio also collaborated with Laura Nyro on her superb R&B-influenced album *Gonna Take a Miracle*.)

By 1973, LaBelle had gone glam, taking the stage in wildly theatrical, futuristic costumes; a year later they became the first African-American act ever to appear at New York's Metropolitan Opera House, a landmark performance which also introduced their lone chart-topping single, the Allen Toussaint-produced classic "Lady Marmalade." However, after two more albums—1975's *Phoenix* and the following year's *Chameleon*—LaBelle disbanded, and its namesake mounted a solo career, issuing her eponymous debut in 1977. In addition to subsequent releases including 1979's *It's Alright with Me* and 1980's *Released*, LaBelle also turned to acting, co-starring in a 1982 Broadway revival of *Your Arm's to Short to Box With God*.

Upon signing with the Philadephia International label, LaBelle scored a number-one R&B hit with "If You Only Knew," from 1983's *I'm in Love Again*. Two years later, she reached the pop Top 20 with her *Beverly Hills Cop* soundtrack contribution "New Attitude." Her subsequent MCA debut, 1986's *The Winner in You*, went platinum on the strength of the Burt Bacharach-penned "On My Own," a duet with Michael McDonald, while the follow-up, 1989's *Be Yourself*, featured a pair of cuts written by Prince. 1991's *Burnin'* earned a Grammy for Best Female R&B Performance. LaBelle recorded less and less frequently in the years to follow, however, in 1995 publishing her autobiography *Don't Block the Blessings: Revelations of a Lifetime*. She returned five years later to release *When A Woman Loves*. *—Jason Ankeny*

Sweethearts of the Apollo / 1963 / Collectables ✦✦✦
This is more or less a straight-up reissue of the group's original Newtown album. Dubbed-on applause and all, it's a nice mix of predominately live performances (recorded in real stereo, no less) taken from both the Apollo and Philadelphia's Uptown theaters. Patti's in fine voice, her prodigious pipes pitched a bit higher but more than capable of scraping the upper registers of heaven on "Down the Aisle," "Danny Boy," and tearjerkers like "My Bridal Gown." While revisionist historians have claimed that their original hit was actually by another group called the Starlets, you'd never know it by the rendition aboard here: it sure sounds like Patti and the gals every note of the way. An interesting historical artifact of an R&B survivor. *—Cub Koda*

Over the Rainbow / 1966 / Atlantic ✦✦✦
Patti LaBelle & the BlueBelles had only moderate success at Atlantic records. It was a good run, but lowly pop entries and a few R&B hits was as good as it got. The label was far more successful with Aretha Franklin, who signed a couple of years after Patti LaBelle & the BlueBelles. Atlantic made the same mistake with the the BlueBelles that Columbia did with Aretha: too sophisticated. Instead of energizing the BlueBelles' innate, raw soul, Atlantic softened their earthy expressions with strings, brass, fancy arrangements, and too many pop songs; hence this album, which features Patti LaBelle & the Bluebelles' stirring rendition of "Over the Rainbow" and many similarities, e.g., "More," "People," "Ebb Tide," and "Try to Remember." Only Bob Finiz's "Patti's Prayer" deviates. Good, but hardly the cutting-edge sounds they later unleashed as LaBelle, minus Cindy Birdsong. *—Andrew Hamilton*

Dreamer / 1967 / Atlantic ✦✦✦✦
This heartfelt collection of soulful girl group singing is one of Patti LaBelle & the BlueBelles' best efforts before the quartet downsized into the avant-garde trio LaBelle. The quality songs and singing, along with the slick (often too-polished) arrangements and orchestrations, put it over the top. Legendary Southern soul writers Spooner Oldham and Dan Penn wrote the title track, "Dreamer"; Curtis Mayfield composed the wet-eyed "I'm Still Waiting"; Trade Martin chipped in on "Take Me for a Little While"; and Hall-of-Famers Burt Bacharach & Hal David put together "Always Something to Remind Me." Not a dog on the disc. Originally released in 1965, *Dreamer* also features unforgettables like "That's How Heartaches Are Made," "One More Phone Call," and the forgotten wedding song "Down the Aisle." *—Andrew Hamilton*

Greatest Hits / 1971 / Trip ✦✦✦

Patti LaBelle / 1977 / Epic ✦✦✦
Patti LaBelle's solo debut for Epic closed the book on a 15-year collaboration with Nona Hendryx and Sarah Dash. She mixed light pop and soul covers on this outing, turning in earnestly sung renditions of "You Are My Friend" and the Skyliners' "Since I Don't Have You," but also doing curious material like "Dan Swift Me" and "You Can't Judge a Book by the Cover." LaBelle was still finding her niche and hadn't yet become comfortable or established her now commonplace tendencies, such as the drawn-out lyric emphasis and the embellishments and lengthy holding of notes. *—Ron Wynn*

Tasty / 1978 / Epic ✦✦✦✦✦
In the late '70s, anyone who expected Patti LaBelle's solo albums to sound a lot like her work with the trio LaBelle was bound to be disappointed. From the minute she went solo, it was obvious that she was determined to forge ahead, and that her solo recordings weren't going to sound anything like her work with Nona Hendryx and Sarah Dash. No one is going to mistake *Tasty*, Patti LaBelle's second solo effort, for *Nightbirds*, *Phoenix*, or *Chameleon*. All of the things that the LaBelle trio was known for—cosmic lyrics, socio-political observations, and an aggressive rock edge—are missing from this 1978 LP. Compared to *Phoenix* or *Chameleon*, this record seems safer and less dangerous. But then, *Tasty* wasn't supposed to sound like *Phoenix* or *Chameleon*; so comparing LaBelle the solo artist and LaBelle the group is comparing apples and oranges. *Tasty* may not be as daring or as cutting-edge as *Nightbirds*, but it's a solid, heartfelt soul-pop outing. The Philadelphian is passionate and inspired on material that ranges from the salsa-influenced "Teach Me Tonight (Me Gusta Tu Baile)" and the exuberant "Eyes in the Back of My Head" to the gospel-drenched ballad "Quiet Time." LaBelle also provides a few covers, all of which are interesting. The Drifters' "Save the Last Dance for Me" is transformed into an uptempo Latin-flavored disco-soul workout, while LaBelle's cover of Boz Scaggs' "You Make It So Hard (To Say No)" is much more R&B and a lot less pop than the original version. As a solo artist, Patti LaBelle has had her ups and downs; *Tasty* is, without question, one of her finest solo efforts. *—Alex Henderson*

It's Alright With Me / 1979 / Epic ✦✦✦
In 1979, two years after LaBelle's breakup, the trio's fans were hoping that Patti LaBelle, Nona Hendryx, and Sarah Dash would someday get back together. But it was not to be; all three of them were pursuing solo careers, although Patti LaBelle was the only one who became a major superstar as a solo artist. Produced by Skip Scarborough in 1979, *It's Alright With Me* was Patti LaBelle's third solo album. This vinyl LP came at a time when disco was huge, but LaBelle doesn't provide a lot of dance grooves here. Though *It's Alright With Me* contains a few uptempo selections (including "Deliver the Funk" and the exuberant "Music Is My Way of Life"), romantic ballads and slow jams are dominant. Overall, the material is pleasant but not remarkable; this is true of the uptempo items as well as ballads like "Come What May," "My Best Was Good Enough," and "Love and Learn." This isn't a bad record, although it isn't one of LaBelle's essential albums either. Not recommended to casual listeners, *It's Alright With Me* is strictly for the singer's more devoted fans. *—Alex Henderson*

The Best of Patti LaBelle / 1982 / Epic ✦✦✦✦
Many of these songs appear on other Patti LaBelle solo compilations, but this hits package covering the singer's 1977-1982 Epic sides stands out for its inclusion of the huge LaBelle hit "Lady Marmalade." The 1974, Allen Touissant-produced classic was arguably LaBelle, Nona Hendryx, and Sarah Dash's finest hour and a wonder to behold from the funk and early-disco confluence of the mid-'70s. Appropriately, this blockbuster kicks the album off, fitting in well with disco and Philly soul tracks like "Joy to Have Your Love" and "It's All Right With Me." Switching gears, LaBelle slows things down with the gospel-imbued ballads "You Are My Friend" and "I Don't Go Shopping." And save for the overlong and limp disco manifesto "Music Is My Way of Life," the record holds up quite well over the course of its nine songs. While this skimpy offering will certainly appeal to fans in need of just an overview of LaBelle's Epic period, those looking for more thorough

compilations should check out Sony's *Love Songs* or even the greatest-hits package of her later MCA sides. *—Stephen Cook*

Pressure Cookin' / 1982 / RCA ♦♦♦
LaBelle switched from Warner Bros. to RCA with 1973's *Pressure Cookin'*, which was the trio's only album for the label. After that, the Philadelphians would sign with Epic, join forces with New Orleans dynamo Allen Toussaint, and soar to the top of the charts with *Nightbirds* and the number-one hit "Lady Marmalade." Of course, "Lady Marmalade" wasn't the first time that Patti LaBelle, Nona Hendryx, and Sarah Dash had enjoyed a major hit; they had their share of hits when they comprised three-fourths of Patti LaBelle & the BlueBelles in the 1960s. But as the trio LaBelle, they struggled in the early '70s. Produced by LaBelle's manager Vicki Wickham, *Pressure Cookin'* wasn't the commercial breakthrough the divas were hoping for and isn't as strong as LaBelle's three Epic albums would be. But it's generally likable, and Hendryx's writing is impressive on tracks that range from the ballads "Can I Speak to You Before You Go to Hollywood" and "Last Dance" to the sociopolitical title song. Also memorable is a medley of John Keen's "Something in the Air" and Gil Scott-Heron's "The Revolution Will Not Be Televised." Although *Pressure Cookin'* isn't among LaBelle's essential releases, it's well worth hearing if you're a seasoned LaBelle fan. *—Alex Henderson*

I'm in Love Again / 1983 / Philadelphia International ♦♦♦
Patti LaBelle had been a fixture on the scene since her 1960s group, the BlueBelles. The early 1970s found her fronting the influential and futuristic R&B-pop trio LaBelle. Her solo career couldn't seem to get traction despite quiet-storm staples like "You Are My Friend" and "Little Girls." In 1981 LaBelle signed with Philadelphia International. At this time, Philadelphia International's hit-making roster was down to two artists, LaBelle and The O'Jays. The best songs here attain the label's classic mature and lush sound. The title track, written by Bunny Sigler & James Sigler, boasts a beautiful arrangement and emotive yet measured vocal from LaBelle. The other ballads here were also on that level. The bittersweet "Love, Need and Want You" has her vamps near the fade particularly appealing. "If You Only Knew," written by Cynthia Biggs, Kenny Gamble, and Dexter Wansel has LaBelle subdued through most of the track until she could no longer contain herself. But as the slow songs ranked with the best of 1980s Philadelphia International, the dance tracks are what diminished this album. The derivative "Body Language" and the frenetic "I'll Never Give Up" display that even LaBelle at full throttle couldn't enliven the label's waning dance acumen. The country-tinged "Love Bankrupt" and "When Am I Gonna Find True Love" have her sounding too distracted to make more out of them. *I'm in Love Again* has LaBelle getting strong production and good songs, but too much filler prevented this from being better. *—Jason Elias*

Winner in You / 1986 / MCA ♦♦♦
Patti LaBelle enjoyed the biggest hit of her solo career when she switched labels from Philadelphia International to MCA. None of her albums had consistently clicked since she'd gone solo in 1977, but LaBelle's 1986 MCA debut topped the pop album charts, anchored by the huge hit "On My Own." The duet with Michael McDonald dominated both the pop and R&B scenes, staying atop the R&B charts for four weeks and giving LaBelle her first number-one pop single as a solo artist. She even earned a second Top 40 hit with "Oh, People," even though there was another fine single on the LP, "Kiss Away the Pain," that was ignored. Still, this album gave LaBelle the elusive solo stardom she'd sought since 1977. *—Ron Wynn*

Be Yourself / 1989 / MCA ♦♦♦
Patti LaBelle's 1989 album, *Be Yourself*, boasts a bevy of the day's brightest songwriters and producers, including the ubiquitous Diane Warren, who penned the album's lead single, "If You Asked Me To," which several years later became a massive hit for Celine Dion. Despite LaBelle's masterful, tear-inducing performance, the real gems on this set are two tunes written and produced by Prince: "Yo Mister," the set's second single (and a Top Ten R&B hit amazingly omitted from her 1996 *Greatest Hits* album), and "Love 89," which was co-written by Sheena Easton. These two songs find LaBelle at her funkiest—they each have unstoppable beats, and despite the late-'80s production, still manage to sound fresh and undated, which is not entirely the case with the Full Force production "I Got It Like That." Other standouts include the funky title track, the melodic, Narada Michael Walden-produced "Still in Love," and the ballad "I Can't Complain." Most of the album's other ballads are toward the end, with the Bacharach-Sager-penned "Need a Little Faith" rising above the others. Despite a couple of unmemorable moments, *Be Yourself* doesn't disappoint by any means and is definitely worth having if only for the forgotten gems "Yo Mister" and "Love 89," which rank as some of Prince's better songs as well. *—Jose F. Promis*

This Christmas / 1990 / MCA ♦♦♦

Burnin' / 1991 / MCA ♦♦♦
This was more a presentation and entertainment spectacle than a memorable production. Patti LaBelle greeted special guests, had a reunion with former cohorts Sarah Dash and Nona Hendryx, and put her usual flourishes and energy into several cuts that lacked enough distinction to benefit from her fierce treatments. Although the album eventually went gold, it was an aesthetic disappointment. Not only were there few hits, but there weren't even any good singles. "Somebody Loves You Baby (You Know Who It Is)" at least had a demonstrative LaBelle lead, while "Temptation" and "When You've Been Blessed (It Feels Like Heaven)" had decent production touches and frenetic vocals. *—Ron Wynn*

Gems / 1994 / MCA ♦♦♦
Patti LaBelle's ballad-heavy 1994 album, *Gems*, doesn't necessarily rank as one of the singer's crowning achievements, but as the title (and cliché) implies, this set certainly offers more than a few gems to unearth. *Gems* also features a couple of prolific productions courtesy of Jimmy Jam & Terry Lewis (on the set's uptempo first single, "The Right Kinda Lover") and new jack swing maestro Teddy Riley (on LaBelle's mellow yet hypnotic cover of DeBarge's "All This Love"). The true standout, however, is "Stay in My Corner." That song, with its gospel undertones, features LaBelle wailing as only she can, holding out her famous long notes and delivering a truly mesmerizing performance. The song is so good, in fact, that any self-respecting LaBelle fan would have to own this set if only for that number. Other highlights include another gospel-infused tune, the ballad "If I Didn't Have You," the smooth "Time Will Tell," and the album finale, "Come as You Are." As a final note, this album also contains some truly stellar background vocals. *—Jose F. Promis*

Over the Rainbow: The Atlantic Years / Aug. 23, 1994 / Ichiban/Soul Classics ♦♦♦♦♦
The BlueBelles' stint with Atlantic in the '60s was not a great commercial success, yielding only a couple minor R&B hits ("I'm Still Waiting" and "Take Me for a Little While," both included here), but that wasn't due to any shortcomings on the records themselves, either in performance or material. Patti and the group recorded fine sides in pop-soul, Motown, Aretha Franklin, and early Philly soul styles, making full use of their powerful gospel-derived lead vocals and harmonies. This 22-track anthology features most of the singles (many previously non-LP) and some key album tracks that they recorded for Atlantic between 1965 and 1969, using top-notch writers like Carole Bayer, Pam Sawyer, Lori Burton, Bert Berns, Jeff Barry, Bacharach-David, Lorraine Ellison, Spooner Oldham, Dan Penn, and Curtis Mayfield (who produced some of the later sides), as well as the BlueBelles' own Nona Hendryx and Sarah Dash. Highlights include the original version of "Groovy Kind of Love" (a big hit for the Mindbenders), the Supremes-like "Tender Words," the dramatic "All or Nothing," and the moody Oldham-Penn ballad "Dreamer." *—Richie Unterberger*

● **Greatest Hits [MCA]** / 1996 / MCA ♦♦♦♦♦
The first Patti LaBelle compilation to span her work from the '60s to the '90s. It's weighted heavily toward her pop-R&B material from the '80s and '90s, with hits like "New Attitude," "On My Own," and "Feels Like Another One." It does lead off with the version of "Over the Rainbow" that she recorded with the BlueBelles in the '60s, and also has four LaBelle cuts, including the chart-topping "Lady Marmalade." *—Richie Unterberger*

You Are My Friend: The Ballads / Feb. 11, 1997 / Epic/Legacy ♦♦♦
You Are My Friend: The Ballads collects 13 ballads Patti LaBelle and LaBelle recorded during the '70s, including "You Turn Me On," "Find the Love," "Quiet Time," "Isn't It a Shame," and "Come What May." Although the album sounds as if it is a greatest-hits compilation, very few of these songs were hits, yet that doesn't detract from the disc's worth. It's designed for Patti LaBelle fans who want to dig a little deeper into her catalog without purchasing the actual albums, and they'll find several songs to cherish, even though the song selection is slightly uneven. *—Leo Stanley*

Flame / Jun. 24, 1997 / MCA ♦♦♦

The Best of the Early Years / Feb. 9, 1999 / Hip-O ♦♦♦♦
This album chronicles the recordings of Patti LaBelle and the BlueBelles from before their creation as a group—the BlueBelles' biggest hit, "I Sold My Heart To The Junkman," was actually recorded by a different group, and they were then assembled to promote it—to their departure from the small Philadelphia label for which they recorded in the mid-'60s. They scored a handful of minor hits with covers that were surprising for an R&B girl group, such as "You'll Never Walk Alone" and "Danny Boy," but their approach was similar to the gospel-influenced rhythmic sound of Motown, and lead singer Patti LaBelle was already showing off the pipes that would make her a major star in succeeding decades. It's hard to imagine how this material could have been handled better: the tracks are well-annotated, and Robert Pruter's liner notes tell the group's story concisely, yet completely. Tracks originally used on an artificially constructed "live" album have had the bogus audience sounds stripped off them for a more accurate sound. The material may be juvenilia and, at 37 minutes, there may not be much of it, but this is a textbook case of how to do a reissue. *— William Ruhlmann*

Lafayette Afro Rock Band

f. 1970, Long Island, NY, **db.** 1978
Group / Afro-Beat, Funk
Though little known in their native U.S., the Parisian-based Lafayette Afro Rock Band was among the premier funk outfits of the 1970s, later becoming a seemingly endless source of samples and breaks for artists from Public Enemy to Janet Jackson. The group was formed on Long Island, NY, as the Bobby Boy Congress; deciding America was already overloaded with funk acts, in 1971 they relocated to France, but when frontman Bobby Boy returned stateside the remaining members—guitarist Larry Jones, bassist Lafayette Hudson, keyboardist Frank Abel, horn players Ronnie James Buttacavoli and Arthur Young, drummer Ernest "Donny" Donable and percussionists Keno Speller and Arthur Young—renamed themselves Ice and became the house session band at producer Pierre Jaubert's Parisound studio. Regularly performing live in Paris' Barbesse district—an area made up primarily of African immigrants—Ice's driving funk became increasingly influenced by African rhythms and textures, and in the wake of their 1973 debut LP *Each Man Makes His Own Destiny*, Jaubert changed the group's name to the Lafayette Afro Rock Band.

Guitarist Michael McEwan replaced Jones in time to record 1974's *Soul Makossa* (issued in the U.S. as *Movin' & Groovin'*), highlighted by the oft-covered and much-sampled "Hihache"; the follow-up, *Malik*, featured the cut "Darkest Night," its desolate saxophone intro later sampled for use by Public Enemy for the *It Takes a Nation of Millions to Hold Us Back* track "Show 'Em Whatcha Got" in addition to providing the foundation for Wreckx 'N' Effect's "Rump Shaker" and Tuff Crew's "Nut." Also in 1975, the Lafayette Afro Rock Band backed jazz pianist Mal Waldron on his unreleased *Candy Girl* album; the year following, they collaborated with expatriate bluesman Sunnyland Slim on his album *Depression Blues*. With 1976's *Frisco Disco*, the group reverted to the Ice moniker; concurrently, working under the alias Captain Dax, they scored a novelty hit in

Japan with the single "Dr. Beezar, Soul Frankenstein." *Afro Agban* followed in 1978, while as Crispy and Co., the band resurfaced that same year with *Funky Flavored* before returning to America and disbanding. *—Jason Ankeny*

• **Darkest Light: The Best of the Lafayette Afro Rock Band** / Oct. 4, 1999 / Strut ✦✦✦✦✦
The name may not be familiar, but the Lafayette Afro Rock Band's grooves certainly are. A veritable sampler's paradise, snippets of their hip-hugger-tight funk have served as the bedrock of innumerable rap records, most notably Public Enemy's "Show 'Em Whatcha Got." *Darkest Light* assembles 15 tracks from the group's mid-'70s heyday, revealing a deep, versatile unit truly justified in adopting such an international name—their music indeed embraces both Afrobeat and Western psychedelia in equal measure, complete with hard-edged guitar riffs, incendiary sax breaks, and blistering rhythms. Although the title track inspired Public Enemy, "Hihache" also features a much-sampled drum intro and the relentless "Conga" later resurfaced on a volume of the *Ultimate Breaks and Beats* series. But to break this music down to its base elements is to do the greater whole a grave disservice—*Darkest Light* merits discussion alongside any of the great documents of classic funk. *—Jason Ankeny*

The Ultimate Collection / Jun. 12, 2001 / New Power Soul ✦✦✦✦✦
A perfect, economical place to familiarize yourself with the seldom-heard yet universally celebrated brilliance of the Lafayette Afro Rock Band. Since these guys weren't as ubiquitous in the States during their mid-'70s reign, they never got the attention or acclaim that other bands like Funkadelic received. The truth, though, is that they could set the house on fire with their funk and could rival nearly any band out there at the time in terms of straight-up jamming. Of course, the band's emphasis on jamming rather than crafting accessible pop-style songs made them somewhat of a cult phenomenon since they never received the attention they deserved. So, as a result, you probably won't find many of their albums in stores; in fact, you probably won't find any. Most of their original LPs are nearly extinct, and they've never seen much of their catalog get reissued. That's what makes *Ultimate Collection* such a gem. It compiles all the band's greatest moments onto one disc, making it more than clear just how phenomenal this band was. The fact that it shares almost the identical track listing as the previously released *Darkest Light* best-of makes choosing between the two rather trivial, so don't sweat about that—you can't go wrong with either. *—Jason Birchmeier*

Lakeside

f. 1969, Dayton, OH
Group / Quiet Storm, Funk, Disco, Soul
In 1969, Dayton, OH, native Stephen Shockley formed the Young Underground after exiting the Monterreys. Vocalist Mark Woods, who was a member of the local band the Nomads, joined up with Shockley to form a more mature-sounding Young Underground. The group initially had a record deal with Curtom Records as a result of winning a talent contest in Chicago. However, Curtom folded shortly thereafter. While in Chicago the group renamed itself Lakeside Express, after the Lakeside Express Newspaper in Chicago.

In 1974, the emerging Lakeside Express and another group by the name of Liquid Funk, which featured Dallas native Fred Alexander Jr. on drums, arrived in Los Angeles around the same time. For the next couple of years the bands performed at events around the greater L.A. area, occasionally crossing paths. The members of Liquid Funk returned to Dallas, but Alexander remained in L.A. Lakeside, who by now had dropped the Express from their name, was seeking additional personnel to solidify their band. After two auditions, Alexander was welcomed into the group.

Lakeside inked a deal with Motown, but found no success. Consequently, they released a ballad on ABC Records, but that label went under. The good fortune they were seeking turned out to be at Dick Griffey's Solar Records. The group signed a deal with Griffey, and released their first Top Ten hit on Solar Records, "It's All the Way Live," which peaked at number four on the *Billboard* R&B charts.

Lakeside released a host of songs that scaled the R&B charts, but didn't threaten the position of any other artists. However, in 1980 they went storming up the charts again with their smash number-one single, "Fantastic Voyage," which was produced by the self-contained band. They followed the success of "Fantastic Voyage" with another Top Ten R&B single, a remake of the Paul McCartney and John Lennon classic "I Want to Hold Your Hand." The group continued their success with the *Billboard* Top Ten singles "Raid," "Outrageous," and a string of R&B party songs and ballads. *—Craig Lytle*

Lakeside Express / 1977 / ABC ✦✦

Shot of Love / 1978 / Capitol ✦✦✦
Shot of Love has often been called Lakeside's debut album, but in fact, it was Lakeside's second. In 1977, Lakeside came out with an album that didn't go very far, and it was *Shot of Love* that made the band well known. Fueling the success of this album (which first came out on Solar and was reissued on CD by The Right Stuff in 1997) was the gutsy funk smoker "It's All the Way Live," and almost as strong are the infectious title song and the classy soul ballads "Given in to Love" and "Visions of My Mind." But as much as *Shot* has going for it, the album on the whole isn't outstanding—enjoyable certainly, but not outstanding. A product of Ohio's rich funk scene, Lakeside was so live-oriented that it seemed to hold back a bit in the studio. (It's absolutely insane that Solar never released a double live Lakeside set.) *Shot of Love* was the first Lakeside release to boast one of its famous thematic covers—this one depicted the funksters as Robin Hood-type archers, whereas on future recordings, they'd be everything from pirates (*Fantastic Voyage*) to jockeys (*Keep on Moving Straight Ahead*) to genies (*Your Wish Is My Command*). *—Alex Henderson*

Rough Riders / 1979 / Solar ✦✦✦
The second album from the nine-piece outfit did not have the smash hit like its predecessor *Shot of Love*, but it still has its bright spots. Though the group has multiple lead vocalists, the baritone of Mark Woods is commendable. The featured releases were "Pull My Strings" and "From 9:00 Until." The former is an aggressively paced funk number. However, it does not retain that vibrant feeling for which the group is known. It peaked on the *Billboard* R&B charts at number 31. The latter is also aggressive, but has a festive atmosphere more in line with the septet's let's-get-this-party-started image. Though it's easily a Top Ten cut, it only managed to peak at number 44. "If You Like Our Music" is a classic Lakeside number but was never released. This project also features two beautiful ballads in "I Can't Get You Out of My Head" and "I'll Never Leave You," and the moderate number "All in My Mind." *—Craig Lytle*

Fantastic Voyage / 1980 / Solar ✦✦✦
Lakeside had one of R&B's most exciting live shows of the late '70s and early- to mid-'80s, but in the studio, the Dayton, OH, band generally didn't go that extra mile. Most of Lakeside's Solar albums were generally decent and had a few gems, but a consistently excellent studio album was something Lakeside never achieved. The closest Lakeside came to a great studio session was *Fantastic Voyage*, arguably the band's best album. Some of the songs are superb, including the sweaty title track (a major hit), the intoxicating "Your Love Is on the One" and the unapologetically romantic "I Love Everything You Do." Though best known for hard funk, that and "Say Yes" point to the fact that Lakeside also delivered some memorable soul ballads. Other material falls under the heading of "good but not great"—a phrase that applied to so much of Lakeside's work. The liner notes that came with the 1996 reissue of *Fantastic Voyage* incorrectly state that this was Lakeside's third album, but it was actually the fourth. *—Alex Henderson*

Keep on Moving Straight Ahead / 1981 / Solar ✦✦

Your Wish Is My Command / 1982 / Solar ✦✦✦
Kool & the Gang may have labeled themselves as the original genies of funk on *Open Sesame*, but Lakeside did a fine job of wresting away that crown across 1981's *Your Wish Is My Command*. Their third album to reach the R&B Top Ten, *Your Wish Is My Command* found Lakeside in fine fettle, returning to a stronger form after the relative disappointment of *Keep on Moving Straight Ahead*. And, although this set was packed with soft grooves that belied the heaviest funk of their early material, Lakeside nevertheless kept a smooth flow. Portrayed on the cover as be-turbaned genies with magic glitter, Lakeside triumphed immediately with the title track. A delirious blend of beat and bass, "Your Wish Is My Command not only conjured up vivid visuals, it was perfect for the dancefloor—and not only because there is just a ghost of their "Fantastic Voyage" hovering in the background. Elsewhere, both "Magic Moments" and "The Urban Man" recreate that same vibe, with the latter adding a fierce guitar solo to the bridge. "There's Something About That Woman," meanwhile, emerged the freshest flower of the bunch, and Lakeside was rewarded with a Top 30 hit. Oddly, the only other song on *Your Wish Is My Command* to enter the chart was a ballad—a style one didn't usually turn to Lakeside for. Their soulful rendering of the Beatles' "I Want to Hold Your Hand" reached number five early in 1982, and while it seemed an odd choice of cover, the band rose wonderfully to the occasion. Predictable and uneven in places, there are still some fine moments on *Your Wish Is My Command*. And, although it cannot touch the best of Lakeside's mid-'70s output, there is still room to groove. *—Amy Hanson*

Untouchables / 1983 / Solar ✦✦
A solid mid-'80s album featuring the Ohio funk band Lakeside at its prime. They did superb groove and uptempo tunes, made acceptable change of pace ballads, and never tried to be something they weren't, like a political or cause group. They were a bit smoother than their role models the Ohio Players and Slave, but still had a tougher sound than most of their other labelmates at Solar. *—Ron Wynn*

Outrageous / 1984 / Solar ✦✦✦
There is no denying that Lakeside are masterful purveyors of pleasant grooves and light electronic trickery. They were masters, too, of creating a party atmosphere. The trouble with that, however, is that what was novel in 1979-1980 was by the middle of the decade routinely commonplace, and Lakeside, who'd earlier taken the marvelous "Fantastic Voyage" to the top of the charts, now found themselves running with the pack. *Outrageous* continued the band's tradition of thematic covers, this time sending the group down the Nile à la Indiana Jones in a quest for the perfect groove. Indeed, even the inner sleeve furthered the joke with a printed map where "Outrageous" marked the spot with a decisive X. This is because as good as this entire set is, "Outrageous" is by far the standout. Reaching number seven on the R&B charts in spring 1984, the song is typically Lakeside, with a strong bassline and intricately layered construction; even better, it's included on the LP in its glorious 12-inch version. But the group was whipping out in other directions as well—especially across the very Euro-discoed "Make My Day," which is replete with Giorgio Moroder-isms throughout. The rest of *Outrageous* flawlessly falls into place from there, from the more traditional funk stylings of "Restrictions" and on to several ballads, most notably "Baby, I'm Lonely" and the lighter pap of "Something About You," which is a successful combination of both styles. While this cannot be counted among Lakeside's best-ever efforts, *Outrageous* is still a cohesive slab of smooth, tight rhythms and entertaining melody. *—Amy Hanson*

Party Patrol / 1986 / Solar ✦✦
Lakeside found that almost no funk fans were around in the early '90s, certainly not enough to keep them dominating the charts. This was among their lowest-selling albums ever, and it never got much airplay or exposure. Funk, especially '70s and '80s funk, was at its nadir, and they also didn't have a particularly good crop of songs. The production and arrangements were decent, and their collective vocals were competent, but there was no spark or energy in the performances and no standout single to pull that might have saved the album. *—Ron Wynn*

The Best of Lakeside / 1989 / Solar ✦✦✦✦✦
A decent collection of Lakeside's hits, although like most funk groups, some of the more entertaining cuts weren't necessarily the singles. This gives a truncated view of

what made them a hit act, but doesn't fully convey their scope; outstanding bassist Marvin Craig's best licks aren't on display, and their relationship to other great Midwest funk groups like the Ohio Players and Slave doesn't come across on an anthology. *—Ron Wynn*

- **Galactic Grooves: The Best of Lakeside** / Nov. 3, 1998 / Capitol ♦♦♦♦♦

Many urban contemporary acts of the 1980s and 1990s were so enslaved by studio technology that they had a hard time delivering the goods on-stage. With Lakeside, it was just the opposite—the Ohio funksters were ferocious live, but they never recorded a studio album that was as consistently exciting as their live show. Typically, a Lakeside album would contain a few gems and a lot of songs that were merely decent. Since Solar never put out a live Lakeside album (although Lakeside did have a few live performances on a double album by the Solar Galaxy of Stars), the best Lakeside purchase a casual listener could make would be *Galactic Grooves: The Best of Lakeside*. Released in 1998, this 17-song CD spans 1978-1987 and boasts all of Lakeside's essential hits, including "It's All the Way Live," "Fantastic Voyage," "Raid," "Something About That Woman," "Pull My Strings" and "Your Love Is on the One." Although Lakeside was best known for hard, aggressive funk, the Dayton natives could also be quite convincing on ballads. "Say Yes," "Given Into Love" and an unforgettable interpretation of the Beatles' "I Want to Hold Your Hand" serve as appealing examples of the band's romantic side. While that Lennon/McCartney classic was originally uptempo, Lakeside successfully transforms it into a slow ballad. It would be great if The Right Stuff unearthed a live Lakeside recording from the late '70s or early '80s and put it out on CD, but since that's unlikely to happen, *Galactic Grooves* is the best place to turn for a lesson in Introductory Lakeside 101. *—Alex Henderson*

George Lamond (George Garcia)

b. Feb. 25, 1967, Washington, D.C.

Vocals / Freestyle, Dance-Pop, House, Club/Dance

Dance-pop singer George Lamond was born George Garcia in Washington, D.C., on February 25, 1967. He first earned notice singing backup for his cousin Joey Kid, with the two later teaming as Loose Touch; as a solo act, Lamond was tapped by producers Chris Barbosa and Mark Ligget to record "Bad of the Heart" for their Ligosa label, and its success on club playlists earned the singer a deal with major label Columbia. An LP, also titled *Bad of the Heart*, yielded two additional freestyle hits, "Without You" and "Look Into My Eyes," although a 1992 follow-up, *In My Life*, was less successful. *It's Always You* followed in 1995, and four years later Lamond resurfaced with *Entrega*. *—Jason Ankeny*

Bad of the Heart / 1988 / Columbia ♦♦

An occasionally interesting, well-produced, but mostly generic dance/pop album from George Lamond, who sounded more appealing and less faceless when he worked with his cousin in the New York club band Loose Touch. The title track was a good single, but there was neither enough thematic variety nor consistent performances to build from it. *—Ron Wynn*

- **The Hits and More** / Jul. 27, 1999 / Robbins ♦♦♦♦

Hits and More balances his three of his five charting hits—"Bad of the Heart," "Look into My Eyes," "Where Does that Leave"—with a selection of newer material, highlighted by "More than Words Can Say." Since it's missing a number of singles, including his Brenda K. Starr duet "No Matter What," it can hardly be seen as definitive (a better, more thorough compilation wouldn't have focused so heavily on newer material), yet it's not a bad sampler. *—Stephen Thomas Erlewine*

Lamya

b. Oman

Vocals / Contemporary R&B, Urban

Born in the country of Oman, Lamya was raised in Kenya and then educated in England and Egypt. Singing before she could talk, Lamya (pronounced "lamb-ya") was a classically trained opera singer and vocalist. After watching an interview with Madonna from New York City, Lamya ran away to New York to pursue her musical career. After going from dance club to dance club and asking to sing, she caught her first break in New York City in 1991. Singing lead vocals on "Break 4 Love" by DJ Vaughn Mason, the song led to her singing lead vocals for Soul II Soul. From there, Lamya joined Duran Duran on tour and also performed with David Bowie and James Brown.

In 2002, Lamya released her debut album, *Learning From Falling*. Singing, producing, and composing all of her own songs, the five-octave singer used poems written since age 11 as lyrical content. Lamya has been compared to Björk and Kate Bush in her style and vocal abilities. She has also appeared on *The Tonight Show*. *—Jason MacNeil*

- **Learning From Falling** / Jul. 30, 2002 / J-Records ♦♦♦

For *Learning From Falling*, erstwhile background vocalist Lamya finally got a starring turn for herself, though her diverse heritage, songwriting skills, and the production expertise of Nellee Hooper (Soul II Soul, Björk, All Saints) fail to produce a solid record. Few would expect anything other than perfection from a vocalist with such an impressive resumé, but Lamya also has the presence and personality of a soloist; though she often sounds similar to a lot of other female singer/songwriters of the late '90s, her songwriting is unique and impressive, while the production (most of it by Hooper) ranges from alternative dance to orchestral pop and even mainstream rock. After a regal performance on the opener ("Empires") and a solid single ("Black Mona Lisa"), though, Lamya gets caught up by too much similar material; many songs on *Learning From Falling* have that vaguely edgy, vaguely happy, vaguely cutesy sound often heard piping from the speakers at Wal-Mart, and soon it becomes clear she's making the same vocal choices on song after song. There are a few promising tracks here, but as soon as she (and, more importantly, her executive producers) begin focusing on what can make her sound unique instead of bankable, she'll be able to get some great, consistent work done. *—John Bush*

Major Lance

b. Apr. 4, 1941, Chicago, IL, **d.** Sep. 3, 1994, Decatur, GA

Vocals / Chicago Soul, Uptown Soul, Pop-Soul, Northern Soul, Soul

Blessed with a warm, sweet voice, Major Lance was one of the leading figures of Chicago soul during the '60s and the top-selling artist for OKeh Records during the decade. Lance not only had a lovely voice, but his material was excellent. During the height of his success, the majority of his songs were written by Curtis Mayfield and produced by Carl Davis, and the pair developed a smooth, Latin-flavored sound that was punctuated by brass and layered with vocal harmonies, usually from the Impressions. It was urban, uptown soul and while it was considerably less gritty than its Southern counterpart, its breezy rhythms and joyous melodies made songs like "The Monkey Time" and "Um, Um, Um, Um, Um, Um" some of the most popular good-time R&B of its era. Major Lance's career declined significantly after he parted ways with Mayfield and Davis in the late '60s, but his classic OKeh recordings remain some of the best-loved soul music of the decade.

Born in Winterville, MS, Major Lance moved to Chicago as a child, where he was initially raised on the West Side of the city, before he moved near the north. While studying at Wells High School—where Curtis Mayfield and Jerry Butler also attended—Lance began boxing, but his attention soon turned to music and he formed the Floats with Otis Leavill. Although the Floats never released any records, his dancing earned him a spot on a local *American Bandstand* styled program hosted by DJ Jim Lounsbury. The DJ helped Lance secure a one-shot single for Mercury Records in 1959, and the singer recorded "I Got a Girl," which was written and produced by Mayfield. The single disappeared and Lance spent the next three years working odd jobs.

In 1962, Lance was signed to the revived OKeh Records, based on his connections with Otis Leavill and, especially, Curtis Mayfield, who signed with the Impressions to ABC Records and having hits with his own group. Later that year, Lance recorded his first single, "Delilah," for the label. Like most of the Major's material, the song was written by Mayfield who, along with OKeh president Carl Davis and arranger Johnny Pate, developed a distinctive, Latin-tinged sound for the record, filled with sliding trombones and a light-stepping rhythms in order to distinguish Chicago soul from its counterparts in the South, New York, Detroit and California. Though "Delilah" wasn't a hit, Lance's second single, "The Monkey Time," was a monster. Released in the summer of 1963, "The Monkey Time" reached number two on the R&B charts and number-eight pop, establishing not only Lance as a singer but the revitalized OKeh Records as a pop music force. "Hey Little Girl" was a Top 15 pop and R&B hit later that year, followed by the Top Ten "Um, Um, Um, Um, Um, Um" early in 1964.

"The Monkey Time" and "Um, Um, Um, Um, Um, Um" proved to be the height of Lance's popularity. Over the next year and a half, he continued to turn out a series of Mayfield-written and Davis-produced singles, nearly all of which reached the R&B Top 40, but only a handful—"The Matador" (which Mayfield didn't write), "Rhythm," "Come See"— were pop hits. Following the summer 1965 release of the Top 20 R&B hit "Ain't It a Shame," Pate departed for ABC Records and Mayfield began concentrating on his group, but Lance and Davis continued to mine the same Chicago sound, using guitarist Gerald Sim as a songwriter and co-producer. After releasing a few singles, including the R&B hit "Too Hot to Hold" and the Van McCoy-written "Everybody Loves a Good Time," Davis left OKeh Records due to arguments with his superiors at Epic Records and Lance was sent to work with Billy Sherrill in Nashville. Out of these sessions, "It's the Beat" became Lance's only Top 40 hit. Since the teaming with Sherrill wasn't working out, Lance worked with a number of producers during 1966 and 1967, with only "Without a Doubt" scraping the R&B charts in 1968. He left OKeh shortly after that single, moving to Daka Records the following year, where he had the Top 40 R&B hit "Follow the Leader." Within a year, he moved to Mayfield's Curtom label, which resulted in his last two Top 40 R&B hits—the number 13 "Stay Away From Me (I Love You too Much)" and "Must Be Love Coming Down."

Lance left Curtom later in 1971 and he moved through a variety of labels, including Volt and Columbia, over the next several years without much success. In 1972, he relocated to England, where Northern soul—a phenomenon of dance clubs playing rare, underappreciated and just plain obscure American soul and R&B records—was in full force. For the next two years, Lance was a staple on the Northern soul circuit, eventually returning to Atlanta in 1974. He signed with Playboy and released a disco version of "Um, Um, Um, Um, Um, Um" that became a minor hit, which was followed by a pair of minor hits in 1975. Shortly afterward, his career entered a downward spiral, and in 1978 he hit rock bottom when he was convicted of selling cocaine. Lance spent the next four years in prison. Upon his release, he began playing the Beach Music circuit on the Carolina coast, but a 1987 heart attack prevented him from launching a full-scale comeback. In 1994, Lance gave a final, triumphant performance at the Chicago Blues Festival, which turned out to be his last. He died of heart failure on September 3, 1994, at the age of 55, leaving behind a recorded legacy that stands among the best midwestern soul of the '60s. *—Stephen Thomas Erlewine*

Monkey Time / 1963 / Edsel ♦♦♦♦♦

For a while this 16-song best-of was the best Major Lance compilation available, but the double CD *The Best of Major Lance* includes all of this and much more. It's a good distillation of his best work, though, including all of his biggest hits. *—Richie Unterberger*

Um, Um, Um, Um, Um, Um / 1964 / OKeh ♦♦♦♦♦

Sales didn't reflect it, but this is probably Curtis Mayfield's best production, and Lance's best album: every track is a winner. "Um, Um, Um, Um, Um, Um," "Hey Little Girl" and "The Monkey Time" were major busters for Major Lance; all had a mock cha cha beat. The unheralded tracks are just as good: Lance's "Gypsy Woman" is as haunting as the Impressions' original; "Think Nothing About It" is endearing and marvelously simplistic, one of Mayfield's best compositions (Gene Chandler recorded it later). If OKeh had released "That's What Mama Say" as a single, it would have done some damage (both the Impressions and Walter Jackson recorded the tender mama-done-told-me song, and although Jackson's version scored an R&B hit, it lacks the bite of Lance's version). "You'll Want Me Back" is serene and beautiful; it was also done by the Impressions, but Lance's rendition stirs the pot. Lance had a more dynamic voice than Mayfield, his childhood friend—it was heavier and had more teeth than Mayfield's light tenor—yet Mayfield had more around skills and became far more successful. The Impressions sing background on most of the tracks, and you can hear the rainbowing of voices with Lance's cutting through and dominating like a dictator. Take "Little Young Lover," a good song by the Impressions, but a candidate for hitsville when Lance does it. He does an excellent job on "It's All Right," "I'm the One Who Loves You" and "Gotta Right to Cry"; the latter sounds like a group recording with Lance leading, and the Impressions—Mayfield (first tenor), Fred Cash (baritone) and Sam Gooden (tenor)—trying to win a harmony contest. One listen to this LP, and you'll be a Major Lance (and Curtis Mayfield) fan for life. *—Andrew Hamilton*

- **Everybody Loves a Good Time!: The Best of Major Lance** / Feb. 28, 1995 / Epic/Legacy ✦✦✦✦✦

This is a delightful 40-song, double-CD compilation of Lance's best work for OKeh between 1962 and 1967, including all of the chart singles, quite a few misses and B-sides, five previously unreleased cuts, and some Curtis Mayfield songs from his debut LP. The later tracks, recorded after producer Carl Davis and songwriter Mayfield had moved on to other projects, suffer in comparison with Lance's 1963–1965 output, as he tried to keep abreast of contemporary soul trends, especially Motown. For many listeners, a briefer best-of Lance compilation will suffice. But for soul fans, this is prime stuff, dominated by the classic Latin-influenced Chicago soul sound of the Davis-produced tracks. *—Richie Unterberger*

The Very Best of Major Lance / Sep. 5, 2000 / Epic/Legacy ✦✦✦✦✦

This 16-song, single-disc compilation concentrates on Lance's most well-known hits, including all of his highest-charting 45s: "Um, Um, Um, Um, Um, Um," "Hey Little Girl," "The Monkey Time," "Rhythm," and "The Matador." It's excellent Chicago '60s soul, but all of the cuts are also found on Epic/Legacy's 40-song, two-CD anthology *Everybody Loves a Good Time! The Best of Major Lance*. That compilation has a good number of decent non-hit tracks from the era (such as "Sweet Music") and remains the preferred alternative unless you're on a strict budget, or the type of listener who finds it hard to hear more than a single disc's worth of an artist that you like but don't love. That's not to say the selection for this best-of isn't good, with 11 of the 16 songs coming from the pen of Curtis Mayfield. *—Richie Unterberger*

Mickey Lee Lane

Vocals, Songwriter, Arranger / Rock & Roll, Blue-Eyed Soul, Northern Soul, Brill Building Pop

Perhaps best known for his mid-'60s single "Hey Sah-Lo-Ney," a soul-pop-dance tune that was covered by mid-'60s British mod band the Action, Mickey Lee Lane entered the business as a songwriter in the Brill Building, doing a single for Brunswick with his sister Shonnie in 1958. He floated around as a member of the Bell Notes, a touring pianist with Neil Sedaka, and a songwriter, placing "My Little Woman" with a fading Bill Haley.

Lane wasn't making much headway, but he kept plugging away and eventually got to put out some singles on Swan in the mid-'60s. These were odd but cool items that somehow sounded both like cynical pastiches of American pop/rock trends and inventive, rather off-the-wall dance tunes. One of these, "Shaggy Dog," sneaked inside the Top 40 in late 1964. "The Zoo," "Hey Sah-Lo-Ney," and "The Senior Class" were pretty hep tunes along the same lines. Lane could also capably offer more pop-oriented tracks, such as "Little Girl (I Was Wrong)," with its mix of Jan & Dean, the Four Seasons, and Gary Lewis, or the melodramatic "She Cried to Me," which was something like the Shangri-Las as sung from a male point of view. *—Richie Unterberger*

- **Rockin' On . . . And Beyond** / 1997 / Rollercoaster ✦✦✦

This is an interesting yet flawed overview of the career of the odd and periodically compelling career of Mickey Lee Lane, one of the more curious figures of the periphery of the 1960s Brill Building scene. Not that Lane was in the heart of the Brill Building tradition, just that he was in that milieu, scuffling to get songs recorded, experimenting with studio production, and making some records of his own. Much of this 33-song CD is devoted to his best and most well-known ("well-known" being a highly relative term here) work for Swan in the mid-'60s. The highlights are certainly the soul-rock dance novelties "The Senior Class," "Shaggy Dog," "The Zoo," and "Hey Sah-Lo-Ney," which are in some senses crass attempts to capitalize on hit formulas of the day, yet performed with a cheerful sense of outrageousness and committed earthy fun. "She Cried to Me," "Little Girl (I Was Wrong)," and "She Don't Want To" are certainly lighter and more superficial pop tunes, yet catchy and enjoyable despite themselves. There's also his cover of "Tutti Frutti," which was rated by Little Richard biographer Charles White as the best version other than Little Richard's, although really it doesn't sound as exciting as that might lead you to expect. Interspersed with the 1960s material (and some flotsam from the late '50s), however, are all manner of jams and bits of pieces (several less than a minute long) from unreleased recordings, sometimes serving as unnecessary link tracks, and not all that inspired. What's more, some of the CD's songs are obviously from the late '50s and '60s, yet given the date of 1997 on the track listings. One could assume that this means they are unreleased or have been slightly altered from their original demo form with additional overdubbed parts. Yet even after reading the extensive liner notes several times over, for many of the songs it's unclear where many of the songs were retrieved from, what year they were recorded, and whether they were subjected to remixes or overdubs. For that matter, the odd bluesy folk-rocker "Something to Live On," with really eerie reverbed harmonica, is identified as a 1959 recording on the track listings, yet discussed as a late-'60s cut in the liner notes themselves, so who's to say if there aren't more such mistakes? This patchwork assembly job makes the music more difficult to appreciate and, most important, to listen to in one sitting, and if you're motivated enough to seek out a Mickey Lee Lane CD in the first place, you'll probably agree that he deserves better. Of course, he and his brother assembled the anthology themselves, so it's not as though a wrong-headed record label is accountable. *—Richie Unterberger*

Lanier & Co.

f. 1968, Jackson, TN

Group / Soul

The pride of Jackson, TN, began in 1968 as the Jacksonians. The members were Farris Lanier Jr., lead singer (born in 1949), his brother Fenoye, drummer (born in 1952), Sam Frazier (tenor sax), Lee Freeman (guitar), Mark Brown (trumpet and background vocals) and Joseph McKinney (keyboards and background vocals). Farris Lanier Sr. managed them and named them the Jacksonians.

Work was easy to find and they backed the likes of Eddie Floyd and others from the outset. A guitar player, Billy Moten got the band noticed by someone at MGM Records. The label was trying to make some inroads in the R&B field by financing small soul labels in various cities. One label MGM assisted was Cleveland, OH's Wayout Records. Reportedly MGM advanced the label principals 80,000 dollars to produce records. The label sent the Jacksonians to Cleveland to record but Wayout paired them with Fred Towles, a soulful singer, for one release "Hook It to the Mule" credited as Fred Towles & the Jacksonians; the flip, an instrumental of the A-side, was all Jacksonians. Wayout had the Sensations under contract, and signed Jesse Fisher, the Soul Notes, Bobby Wade and others to their roster. Unfortunately for the Jacksonsonians and Towles most of the money went toward the Sensations, and "Hook It to the Mule" failed to hook listeners or sell many copies. Nothing was happening in Cleveland, so the band went back to Jackson to record for Sounds of Memphis Records (another MGM project). For their SOM and subsequent recordings Marlon Lanier, alto sax & background vocals (born Feb. 3, 1955) joined. SOM released "California Dreaming" b/w "Sparkle Eyes" to a deafening silence around 1971. Other recordings remain unreleased and for the next 11 years the band played behind many of the South's major recording artists.

Another recording opportunity came in 1982 via the Los Angeles-based LARC Records, no longer the Jacksonians, they were now Lanier & Co. The association produced three singles and an album. The first single, Philip Mitchell's "After I Cry Tonight" (1982), got the most airplay, it featured a stirring lead from Faris, the group's focal point. LARC dropped an album produced by Gene "Bowlegs" Miller, and issued two more singles: "I Just Got to Have You" b/w "Come on out Let's Party" (1983) and "Fallin' in Love Again" b/w "Share Your Love With Me" (1983). An appearance on *American Bandstand* was a highlight; a scheduled shot on *Soul Train*, however, never materialized. The singles stiffed and LARC soon dissolved. According to Marlon, LARC wanted to advance the band a tour bus, money, and other extras, but they declined the label's generosity. They had heard the horror stories of groups held as virtual slaves by recording companies and management companies because of generous advances that they never seemed able to pay back and wanted no part of that scenario.

Lanier & Co. made one last go of it on Willie Mitchell's Waylo Records. Waylo issued an album *Dancing in the Night* and two 12-inch singles: "Dancing in the Night" and "I Don't Know What to Do About You," in 1987. They also cut "Let's Go for It" a duet featuring Faris and Stephanie Beard. The group now consisted of singer Stephanie Beard, Arvill Wiley, Marvin Hill, Van Beard, and the Lanier brothers. While neither disk flew, they kept trooping until 1991 when Faris became ill and couldn't sing or tour anymore. Losing the heart of the group caused them to disband. The other members hooked up with other artists and situations. The only Lanier to continue with music is Fenoye who currently drums behind Denise LaSalle. *—Andrew Hamilton*

- **Lanier & Co.** / 1983 / Larc ✦✦✦

Lanier & Co (aka the Jacksonians) accompanied and received label credit with Fred Towles on "Hook It to the Mule" on Cleveland, OH's Wayout Records. Based in Jackson, MS, the self-contained band featured Farris Lanier Jr. on lead vocals. Produced by Gene "Bowlegs" Miller in Memphis, TN, this self titled album is a hot plate of southern inspired soul with gritty remakes of Joe Simon's "Drowning in the Sea of Love" and Marvin & Tammi's "If I Could Build My Whole World Around You," featuring Toni Green swapping lead lines with Farris. The singles: Prince Mitchell's swaying "After I Cry Tonight," the floating "Just Got to Have You" and "Fallin' in Love Again," are good, meaty sounds that never got the needed push. *—Andrew Hamilton*

Dancing in the Night / Aug. 1, 1988 / Waylo ✦✦✦

The Larks

f. 1938, Durham, NC, **db.** 1955

Group / Black Gospel, Harmony Vocal Group, Doo Wop

Not to be confused with Don Julian's Larks, his post-Meadowlarks trio (whose huge R&B hit in 1965 was "The Jerk"), or the Philadelphia-based soul group called the Larks, this group of Larks dates back to the early days of vocal music, with roots in gospel music, and featured the immense talents of Eugene Mumford. The Larks' story actually begins in Durham, NC, in the late '30s, when original core members: Thurmon Ruth, Allen Bunn, Junius Parker, Jimmy Gorham, and Melvin Coldten—a powerful gospel collective already sharing membership with the Selah-Jubilee Singers, the Southern Harmonaires, and the Jubilators—began recording for Decca Records, between 1939 through 1944.

In the mid-'40s, the Larks met Eugene Mumford, who had been singing with the Four Interns. They attempted to bring Mumford into the Selah Singers but before they could, Mumford was charged with attempted rape of a white woman and convicted (it proved to be a crime he did not commit). Nevertheless, he was sentenced to a lengthy prison sentence. Mumford ended up serving a few years on a chain gang in North Carolina, until 1949, when he was released with a full pardon from the governor of North Carolina. He quickly joined Thurmon Ruth's new group, the Jubilators, moving to New York in the fall of 1950. The group consisted of Ruth, Allen Bunn, David McNeil, and Pee Wee Barnes.

They began recording under various names: they were the Jubilators when they recorded for Regal, the Selah Singers for Jubilee, the Four Barons for Savoy and the

Southern Harmonaires for Apollo Records. Bess Berman, head of Apollo Records, was desperate to make it in the field of newer R&B sound of the then-current bird group trend (the Orioles, the Cardinals and the Ravens et al), Berman changed their name to the "Five Larks," later shortened on their first release to the Larks.

Success eluded them for their first few releases, until they covered a swing-era standard, "My Reverie," which had been a number-one hit for Larry Clinton with vocal by Bea Wain. The Larks' version proved to be a solid seller on the East Coast. A follow-up, the Allen Bunn-led "Eyesight to the Blind," was a Midwest hit, made the national R&B charts and led to various TV appearances including *Spotlight on Harlem*, *The Chesterfield Show*, and *Arthur Godfrey's Talent Scouts*, a hit show that was in fact a mainstream American version of *Amateur Night at the Apollo*. The next single, the jump blues "Little Side Car," sold in sufficient numbers, enough to place it on the Top Ten R&B charts that fall. (It was advertised by Apollo as being by "Bobby Smith and the Larks!)

In January of 1952, Allen Bunn recorded a solo outing for Apollo. Meanwhile, the Larks continued to record singles for the label, but weren't earning enough on their one-nighters to continue as performers, and struggled to place new songs on the charts; so, the Larks went their separate ways in 1952.

In February of 1954, Bess Berman of Apollo resurrected the Larks—with only Eugene Mumford sticking around from the original lineup—as a mainstream pop music group, competing with acts like the Crew Cuts, the Hilltoppers, the Ames Brothers, and the Four Lads, etc. The reconstituted group—Mumford, Orville Brooks from the Golden Gate Quartet, and David Bowers and Isaiah Bing from the King Odom Four—recorded six singles for Apollo's new subsidiary Lloyds Records, and performed at the New York Festival of Music and Drama held in the Savoy Ballroom in Harlem. However, success eluded them; the second Larks disbanded in 1955.

Eugene Mumford first went to the Serenaders (who record for Hy Weiss' Old Town), then joined David McNeil in Billy Ward & the Dominoes (he replaced Jackie Wilson). The Dominoes scored two smash hits with Mumford on lead, "Stardust" (1957) and "Deep Purple" (1957). Mumford tried a secular solo career which never took off and was reported to be singing with an Ink Spots group in the 1970s before he passed away. Raymond Barnes became a R&B session musician and is still alive, as is David McNeil. Allen Bunn continued with the Wheels, (whose "My Heart's Desire" on the Premium label was a big hit—he later became part of the successful R&B duo Tarheel Slim & Little Annie). *—Bryan Thomas*

My Reverie / 1996 / Relic ✦✦✦✦✦
There were two groups of Larks with hit records, almost a decade and one whole coast apart. This collection concerns itself with the original East Coast Larks who recorded for Apollo and Lloyds in the 1950s, rather than the L.A. group that had a hit with "The Jerk." The Apollo Larks were a tight, strong singing group who really could harmonize, as exhibited on tracks like "I Live True to You," "Stolen Love," "Let's Say a Prayer," and the title track. Most revealing, however, is their doo wop stab at Sonny Boy Williamson's blues classic "Eyesight to the Blind." As the first of two volumes, this shines the light on a band who deserve a much wider listening audience. *—Cub Koda*

● **Up With the Larks: The Uptempo Apollo Recordings 1951–1955** / Jun. 8, 1999 / WestSide ✦✦✦✦✦
This is a comprehensive collection by the early '50s' Larks, considered one of the top doo wop groups of all time. WestSide Records didn't leave any significant tracks off this compilation of songs recorded during the two-year span the group was together. (They were issued, however, over a five-year period from 1950 to 1955 by Apollo and Lloyd Records.) Embraced are their Apollo debut, "Coffee, Cigarettes and Tears," and "Hopefully Yours," a sweet ballad that was back-sided with a song that member Eugene Mumford wrote, "When I Leave These Prison Walls," while incarcerated for two years in a North Carolina prison; he was pardoned in 1949 by the governor. Also on the project is "My Reverie," a classic ballad that demonstrates their advanced ballad skills; two takes of "Eyesight to the Blind," which made the national R&B chart; and the humorous "I Ain't Fattening Frogs for Snakes." *—Andrew Hamilton*

The Best of the Larks / Jul. 25, 2000 / Jamie/Guyden ✦✦✦
Here is a comprehensive collection by the early-'50s' Larks, who are considered one of the top doo wop groups of all time. WestSide Records didn't leave any significant tracks off this compilation of songs recorded during the two-year span the group was together. (They were issued, however, over a five-year period, from 1950 to 1955, by Apollo and Lloyd Records.) Embraced are their Apollo debut, "Coffee, Cigarettes and Tears," and "Hopefully Yours," a sweet ballad that was back-sided by member Eugene Mumford's "When I Leave These Prison Walls," written while he was incarcerated in a North Carolina prison for allegedly raping a white woman; he was pardoned in 1949 by the governor. Also on the project is "My Reverie," a classic ballad that demonstrates their advanced ballad skills; two takes of "Eyesight to the Blind," which made the national R&B chart; and the humorous "I Ain't Fattening Frogs for Snakes." *—Andrew Hamilton*

Amel Larrieux

b. Greenwich Village, NY
Vocals, Songwriter / Contemporary R&B
R&B singer-songwriter Amel Larrieux grew up in New York's Greenwich Village; her mother, Brenda Dixon Gottschild, is a dance critic and professor, and she was raised in an artistic environment. She formed Groove Theory, a duo with former Mantronix member Bryce Wilson (aka Bryce Luvah), which signed to Epic Records and scored a gold-selling Top Ten pop and R&B hit in October 1995 with "Tell Me," followed by the *Groove Theory* album, which hit the Top 20 of the R&B charts. In 1996, Larrieux was a vocalist on the self-titled album by Sweetback, an instrumental group made up of former members of Sade's backup band, which reached the charts. Larrieux released her debut solo single, "Get Up," in November 1999, and it reached the R&B charts. Her debut solo album, *Infinite Possibilities*, was released by Epic/550 Music in February 2000. *—William Ruhlmann*

● **Infinite Possibilities** / Feb. 15, 2000 / 550 Music/Epic ✦✦✦
Groove Theory may no longer be in existence, but Amel Larrieux, the acts' classy jazz-trained vocalist, is gratefully still in effect. Teaming up with husband Laru Larrieux, who co-produced and wrote most of the songs with Amel, the silky-voiced chanteuse draws from jazz, hip-hop, gospel, and flashes of Middle Eastern influences while never wavering from a laid-back, sensuous path. All the while, she calls to mind female jazz greats and contemporary soul eclectics from Billy Holiday to Les Nubians. More concerned with love and spirituality, Amel segues effortlessly from the love themes of "Make Me Whole" and "Even If," to the introspective "I N I" and "Searchin' for My Soul," with the jazzy lead single "Get Up" setting the course. "Infinite Possibilities" is definitely the kind of music for which candle-lit dinners were made. As far as Larrieux's future is concerned, the possibilities are indeed, infinite. *—Derrick Mathis*

Denise LaSalle (Denise Craig)

b. Jul. 16, 1939, LeFlore County, MS
Vocals, Songwriter / Northern Soul, Soul-Blues, Urban, Black Gospel
Unlike so many other blues vocalists who just re-interpret material given to them by songwriters, Denise LaSalle is a seriously talented songwriter. Although her soul blues style has strong urban contemporary overtones at times, it's best to think of LaSalle as a modern-day Bessie Smith, because that's really what she is. She writes funny songs full of sassy attitude and it's an attitude she carries with her on-stage. Off-stage, LaSalle accommodates all autograph seekers and gladly obliges journalists and radio DJs.

The Jackson, TN-based LaSalle was raised in Belzoni, MS, (also home to Joe Willie "Pinetop" Perkins some years earlier) but she got started singing in local churches around LeFlore County. She was born July 16, 1939, as Denise Craig. Growing up, she listened to the Grand Ole Opry radio broadcasts and then in Belzoni, lived across the street from a juke joint. LaSalle's early influences, from the jukeboxes around Belzoni and over the radio, included Ruth Brown, Dinah Washington, and LaVern Baker. LaSalle moved north to Chicago when she was in her early twenties and would attend shows at the Regal Theatre, always returning home to write songs. She got to know blues musicians and began giving her songs to them, until one day a Chess Records executive stopped by at Mixer's Lounge, where LaSalle was working as a bar maid. He listened to one of her songs and took it down to Chess Records, and the company later signed her as a vocalist, but never recorded her. Two years later, LaSalle recorded and produced her own record with the help of Billy "The Kid" Emerson, the Chess executive who'd originally shown an interest in her. After the record made some waves on local radio, Chess stepped in and purchased the master and took it to Europe. Meanwhile, LaSalle continued writing songs and sitting in with blues musicians around the Chicago clubs.

LaSalle's first big hit came about in 1971 when her "Trapped By a Thing Called Love" broke on the radio in Chicago and then Detroit. That record was for the Westbound label and then she signed with ABC Records in 1975, cutting three albums in three years until the label was sold to MCA. After MCA dropped her because of the label's "difficulty in promoting black acts" at that time, she continued performing as much as she could in Chicago and Memphis. In 1980, a Malaco executive called to ask her to write a song for Z.Z. Hill. A positive relationship with the company was quickly developed, which resulted in LaSalle recording 11 discs for the label, including *Lady in the Street* (1983), *Right Place, Right Time* (1984), *Love Talkin'* (1985), *Hittin' Where It Hurts* (1989), *Still Trapped* (1990), *Still Bad* (1994), and *Smokin' in Bed* (1997). While her Malaco sides are probably her most important recordings, other than the original of her early '70s hit "Trapped," she still releases excellent gospel crossover material, including *This Real Woman* (2000) and *There's No Separation* (2001) on Ordena Records *—Richard Skelly & Al Campbell*

Trapped By a Thing Called Love / 1972 / Westbound ✦✦✦✦✦
Kicking off her Westbound stay with a gem, Denise LaSalle gave the world a new take on Southern soul with this late-nite entrée of Stax-y grooves and tales of love on the rocks. *Trapped By a Thing Called Love* and her two other Westbound LPs (*On the Loose* and *Here I Am Again*) set the pace for other Dixie divas like Millie Jackson and Betty Wright, thanks to the finely gauged originals and heavy dose of swagger they contained. The symphonic soul charts of both Gene "Bowlegs" Miller and Hi Records arranger Willie Mitchell (Al Green, O.V. Wright) are on display, too, and the fare ranges from a few choice covers (Barbara Lynn's "You'll Miss a Good Thing") to now-canonized R&B sides like the LaSalle-penned title track. Once available on vinyl and as a two-fer disc that also included *On the Loose*, *Trapped By a Thing Called Love* is lost in the vaults once again and awaiting a re-release makeover befitting its classic status. *—Stephen Cook*

● **On the Loose** / 1973 / Westbound ✦✦✦✦✦
This follow-up to LaSalle's breakthrough album, *Trapped By a Thing Called Love*, carries on with another solid round of Southern-fried blues and soul. Atop arranger Bowlegs Miller's groove-centric charts, LaSalle particularly shines on her own "Man Size Job," Bill Withers' "Lean on Me," and the Civil Rights anthem "There Ain't Enough Hate Around (To Make Me Turn Around)." Mostly, though, LaSalle evokes early influences like Ruth Brown and such contemporaries as Millie Jackson and Betty Wright while plying her gospel-infused, blues-grit way through fine cheatin' songs like "Breaking up Somebody's Home" and "Your Man & Your Best Friend." But, lest one thinks it's all about codependency and dissipation, she rebounds on the album closer, "I'm Over You," confidently stepping out on her own amidst a stunning backdrop of funky smooth strings. With a whole lot of blues and soul—plus a dash of country for good measure—LaSalle delivers a gem from her early-'70s stay at the Westbound label. *—Stephen Cook*

Here I Am Again / 1975 / Westbound ✦✦✦✦✦
Nearly eclipsing her fine *On the Loose* release from a few years before, Denise LaSalle cut this follow-up in 1974, once again utilizing James "Bowlegs" Miller's top-notch charts and the backing of the Memphis Horns and Muscle Shoals. The third and last of her

Westbound albums, *Here I Am Again* also features several fine songs from LaSalle's pen, many of which show her very original take on the Southern soul sounds of Memphis' Stax and Hi records; Miller complements this bluesy base with sage doses of electric piano and strings on the ballads and plenty of in-the-pocket organ, horn, and guitar work for the funkier cuts. LaSalle, of course, displays both power and suppleness throughout, whether bouncing atop a cool-breeze groove ("Stay With Me Awhile"), digging into a bit of shuffle-bump salaciousness ("I Wanna Do What's on Your Mind"), or hitting the vocal heights on a rootsy ballad ("Don't Nobody Live Her")—even the Barry White sound-alike, "Here I Am Again," finds its own legs under her guidance. Another fine album from LaSalle's stellar yet brief stay at Westbound. *—Stephen Cook*

Second Breath / 1976 / ABC ✦✦✦

The Bitch Is Bad / 1977 / ABC ✦✦✦

Like fellow Southern soul diva Millie Jackson, Denise LaSalle can often transform inane material into something worthwhile. On *The Bitch Is Bad*, she makes it easy to overlook the plodding disco arrangement for "Move Your Body" or overwrought synth squiggles on "A Love Magician" with solidly soulful vocal performances. Even a cheap imitation of Marvin Gaye's "Let's Get It On"—titled "Fool Me Good" here—survives thanks to her smoldering delivery. The predominantly lightweight arrangements, though, ultimately diffuse the impact of LaSalle's voice. It's not that the songs are a wash, or that LaSalle should be excluded from musical exploration; it's more that we don't get to hear her at her best, as on the 1972 Stax-inspired *On the Loose* or the recent return-to-form outings for the Malaco label. Whether it was the ABC Records' skewed career-reviving strategy or her own lapse in taste (remember Jackson's disastrous *Just a Lil' Bit Country*?), LaSalle's attempt to jump on the disco/light soul bandwagon in the late '70s didn't work. A consolation, though, certainly must be the *The Bitch Is Bad*'s over-the-top album cover—clad in a black silk night dress, LaSalle stands poolside atop a fake lionskin rug whilst being fondled by a bathing stud. It's a must for any kitsch album cover collection, but the music within unfortunately does not make this indulgent tableau icing on the cake, or represent the best LaSalle can offer. *—Stephen Cook*

Unwrapped / 1979 / MCA ✦✦✦

This is classy, sassy soul from Denise LaSalle, who peaked with "Trapped By a Thing Called Love." The Memphis Horns embellish the rhythm section and give the recording a warm sound. Denise testifies on the Newcomers' "Too Little In Common to Be Lovers," taking you straight to Soulsville, USA. Side two has only two selections: Rod Stewart's "Do Ya Think I'm Sexy" and the scrumptious 14-minute, 52-second medley of Bettye Swann's "Make Me Yours," Jackie Moore's "Precious, Precious," and LaSalle's "Trapped By a Thing Called Love." *—Andrew Hamilton*

Right Place, Right Time / 1984 / Malaco ✦✦✦

The title cut came close to getting Denise LaSalle a little attention beyond the standard Southern boundaries. The rest of the album is her familiar litany of terse, crusty dialogues, country and blues-tinged wailers, and hard-hitting soul tunes. At times, LaSalle and others of her generation seem like illogical warriors, fighting to keep alive a sound that's long since faded as a viable commercial proposition. But as long as she keeps making records and putting her heart and soul into them, they deserve a listen by fans of the genre. *—Ron Wynn*

Love Talkin' / 1985 / Malaco ✦✦✦

As with all her Malaco albums, Denise LaSalle mixes things up nicely, going from hard-hitting, trash-talking tunes to heartfelt ballads, bluesy numbers, and country/soul wailers. She's had a string of regionally successful releases since joining Malaco in the '80s, but has never been able to break the embargo on Southern soul. She's been around too long to change at this point, and really shouldn't anyway. Her albums are reliable and enjoyable, even if they're a throwback. *—Ron Wynn*

Lady in the Street / 1986 / Malaco ✦✦✦

The title track was among LaSalle's best Malaco tunes, a stomping, urgently sung, sassy bit that walked the line between confrontation, invitation, and remorse. The other tunes weren't quite as inspired, but were equally well performed. Few performers have ever staked out an area and remained loyal to it like LaSalle, who's been doing country/blues soul since the early '70s and seldom strayed from the path, despite numerous trends and changes on the black music scene. Some would call that suicidal; others would say it's commendable. *—Ron Wynn*

Hittin' Where It Hurts / 1989 / Malaco ✦✦✦✦

When high-tech urban contemporary sounds became R&B's norm in the 1980s, the small, Jackson, MS-based Malaco Records continued to specialize in traditional, southern-style soul music. One of Malaco's best sellers has been Denise LaSalle, a big-voiced soul shouter with a gospel-influenced delivery along the lines of Millie Jackson, Betty Wright and Laura Lee. One of LaSalle's strongest Malaco releases, *Hittin' Where It Hurts* was recorded in 1988, but often sounds like it could have been recorded in 1967. LaSalle sounds as inspired as ever on such gritty, horn-laden fare as "If You Can't Do Me Right," "Eee Tee" and the bluesy "Caught in Your Own Mess," all of which recall the splendor of Stax Records. Many soul veterans have gone unrecorded in the 1980s and '90s, but thankfully, LaSalle isn't one of them. *—Alex Henderson*

Still Trapped / 1990 / Malaco ✦✦✦✦

Still Trapped found Denise LaSalle entering the 1990s without having changed her approach very much since the '70s. Rejecting slick, technology-driven urban contemporary music, the gritty singer continued to excel by pretty much sticking with the type of Southern-style soul and blues Stax Records was recording 20 and 25 years earlier. LaSalle had long since disappeared from black radio playlists, but still commanded a loyal following (especially in the Deep South). A welcome addition to her catalog, *Still Trapped* is state-of-the-art LaSalle—earthy, humorous and sassy as hell. From an inspired cover of Al Green's "Love and Happiness" to such hard-edged LaSalle originals as "Chain Letter," "Drop That Zero" and "Wild Thing (All Night Long)," this CD makes listeners grateful that LaSalle has remained true to herself. *—Alex Henderson*

On the Loose/Trapped By a Thing Called Love / 1992 / Westbound ✦✦✦✦✦

Still Bad / Dec. 6, 1994 / Malaco ✦✦✦✦

Still Bad demonstrated that at 54, Denise LaSalle was still very much on top of her game. As its title indicates, the veteran soul and blues singer hadn't mellowed with age—those who love to hear LaSalle taking a sassy, in-your-face approach won't be disappointed by trash-talking numbers like "1-900-GET-SOME," "Right Side of the Wrong Bed" or "The Bitch Is Bad." But true to form, LaSalle has no problem turning around and showing a more sensitive side of herself on "Child of the Ghetto," an inspiring, poignant ballad describing a poor woman's determination to improve her life. LaSalle's Malaco output of the 1980s and 1990s was quite consistent, and with *Still Bad*, the singer once again excels by sticking with what she does best. *—Alex Henderson*

Smokin' in Bed / Mar. 4, 1997 / Malaco ✦✦✦✦

Another hot one from the first lady of raunchy Southern soul. Bright, sparkling Southern horns accent many cuts, including "Juke Joint Woman," an uptempo saga about a barfly. The blues never sounded better than on "Blues Party Tonight," which features B.B. King-inspired guitar licks on top of a laid-back groove, or "Dirty Old Woman," a dated-sounding jump number. At times her sexual tales sound contrived, but she excels on the Southern-fried ballads and midtempo smokers that dominate the latter half of the album—"Goin' Through Changes," "Never Been Touched Like This," and "Why Am I Missing You" are pure LaSalle. *—Andrew Hamilton*

Emanual Laskey

Vocals / Soul, Smooth Soul, Urban

Little is known about Emanual Laskey, a jet black complected, rail-thin Detroit soul singer. His discography lists 12 singles and no albums. Producer Don Davis wrote and produced Laskey's first four singles, the best of his disappointing career. This was before Davis worked with Steve Mancha, Darrell Banks, the Dramatics, Johnnie Taylor, and others. Nothing like those singers, Laskey was similar to Deon Jackson and Jimmy Ruffin; his light, engaging first tenor fluttered with little effort and hinted of falsetto.

Thelma Records, owned by Thelma Coleman-Gordy, Berry Gordy's Jr.'s first wife, issued Laskey's first two releases. "The Monkey" from 1963 got played in Michigan and surrounding States; a trumpet solo on the break made it different, but its flip, "Welfare Cheese," written by Davis, Richard Street, Thelma Coleman, and Emanuel Laskey was more popular. It also graced the flip of his second Thelma release, "Crazy," which had potential, but the label's limited resources couldn't do the catchy ditty justice. Laskey's next single was on NPG Records out of Pittsburgh, PA, and is arguably his best ever. Dismayed with Thelma's lack of clout, Davis and Laskey decided to test the waters. "I Need Somebody," is a sweet, floating, lamenting, midtempo number. It entered the R&B top 20 formats in many cities but never spread across the country. Laskey's fourth and last recording with Don Davis producing appeared on Detroit's Wild Deuce label; "Lucky to Be Loved by You," was as catchy as the previous three but failed to break out, and Davis never worked with Laskey again.

Laskey returned to Thelma, who welcomed him back with open arms. His fifth release, "Don't Lead Me on Baby," and its flip side were co-written by Hazel Joy Coleman, Berry Gordy and Thelma Coleman—Gordy's daughter, who later married Jermaine Jackson. The single went nowhere despite a lilting uptempo beat. Neither did two more Thelma singles in 1965: Don Juan Mancha's "I'm a Peace Loving Man," and "I've Got to Run for My Life." In 1968, Laskey recorded "Just the Way (I Want It to Be)," on the Music Now label. It stiffed, but Laskey secured a deal with Westbound Records for Mike Hanks to produce. It resulted in two 1969 single releases with "A Letter From Vietnam" serving as the flip to both "More Love (Where This Came From)" and "Never My Love," but nobody at Westbound was pushing Laskey's product. Laskey cut a two-parter, "Remember Me Always," in 1973 on Stag Records that few heard. Ditto for his final release in 1980 on Dennis Talley's DT Records, "I'd Rather Leave on My Feet." You won't find an Emanuel Laskey compilation CD, if you don't have the original 45s you're pretty much out-of-luck. He still calls Detroit home, doesn't record anymore, but occasionally performs at festivals and other occasions. *—Andrew Hamilton*

The Last Poets

f. May 16, 1969, New York, NY [Harlem]

Group / Political Rap, Poetry

With their politically-charged raps, taut rhythms and dedication to raising African-American consciousness, the Last Poets almost single-handedly laid the groundwork for the emergence of hip-hop. The group arose out of the prison experiences of Jalal Mansur Nuriddin, a U.S. Army paratrooper who chose jail as an alternative to fighting in Vietnam; while incarcerated, he converted to Islam, learned to "spiel" (an early form of rapping), and befriended fellow inmates Umar Bin Hassan and Abiodun Oyewole.

Upon the trio's release from prison, they returned to the impoverished ghettos of Harlem, where they joined the East Wind poetry workshop and began performing their fusion of spiels and musical backing on neighborhood street corners. On May 16, 1969—Malcolm X's birthday—they officially formed the Last Poets, adopting the name from the work of South African Little Willie Copaseely, who declared the era to be the last age of poets before the complete takeover of guns. After a performance on a local televison program, the group was signed by jazz producer Alan Douglas, who helmed their eye-opening eponymous debut LP in 1970. A collection condemning both white oppression ("White Man's Got a God Complex") and black stasis ("Niggas Are Scared of Revolution"), *The Last Poets* reached the U.S. Top Ten album charts, but before the group could mount a tour, Oyewole was sentenced to 14 years in prison after being found guilty of robbery, and was replaced by percussionist Nilajah.

After the 1971 follow-up *This Is Madness* (which landed them on President Richard Nixon's Counter-Intelligence Programming lists), Hassan joined a Southern-based religious sect; Jalal recruited former jazz drummer Suliaman El Hadi for 1972's *Chastisement*, which incorporated jazz-funk structures to create a sound the group dubbed "jazzoetry." Following the 1973 Jalal solo concept album *Hustler's Convention* (recorded under the alias Lightnin' Rod), the Last Poets issued 1974's *At Last*, a foray into free-form jazz; after its release, Nilajah exited, and with the exception of 1977's *Delights of the Garden*, the group kept a conspicuously low profile for the remainder of the decade.

By the 1980s, however, the proliferation of rap—and the form's acknowledged debt to the Last Poets—made their early records sought-after collectors' items; finally, in 1984 the group resurfaced with the LP *Oh, My People*, followed in 1988 by *Freedom Express*. Another layoff ensued, during which time Omar Bin Hassan issued a solo LP, 1993's *Be Bop or Be Dead* and Jalal mentored the British acid jazz unit Galliano. In 1995, two splinter groups simultaneously reclaimed the Last Poets name; while Jalal and Suliaman El Hadi teamed for the single "Scatterrap," Hassan and Abiodun Oyewole issued the LP *Holy Terror*. —*Jason Ankeny*

★ **The Last Poets** / 1970 / Metrotone ♦♦♦♦♦
Brutally honest and beautifully truthful, the Last Poets' eponymous 1970 debut would become one of proto-funk's most seminal sets. The album itself soared to the top of the R&B charts and reached respectably into the pop charts as well—an astonishing feat for such a politically-charged LP. The album's rise was made especially bittersweet as vocalist Abiodun Oyewole was sent to prison for robbery. Pulling out the primal vocal essences that would later lie just in the background of any great funk song, and bringing them straight to the front, the Last Poets layered street poetry and manifesto over sparse instrumentation and tribal beats. But, in so doing, they created a unique landscape that reflected a pure passion for sound, for words, for the revolution of education. It was a formula to which rap would later owe an enormous debt. From beginning to end, it would be easy to label this album simply spoken word. But it is testament to the brilliance of the Last Poets that it also becomes so much more. This is perhaps best heard in the outstanding opener "Run, Nigger." As Oyewole laid his poetry across spare percussion, the stage was set for a vocal subtext which allowed poetry to become song as voices became instruments. This opener set the tone for the rest of the album, as the Last Poets utilized the same construction with subtle variations across other gems: "Niggers Are Scared of Revolution," "New York, New York," and "When the Revolution Comes." At no time does *The Last Poets* falter or fail to please. And perhaps, more importantly, it will always be as vital, alive, and fresh as it was the day it was recorded. —*Amy Hanson*

This Is Madness / 1971 / Get Back ♦♦♦♦♦
Here is a legendary set featuring a group of extremely controversial street poets. The Last Poets used offensive language brilliantly, talked in graphic detail about America's social and racial failures, and helped expose a wider audience to the sentiments of the '70s black nationalists. They were the forerunners of today's Afrocentric rappers, and also showed the way to a jazz/rap union now being explored on both sides of the Atlantic. This has been reissued on CD. —*Ron Wynn*

At Last / 1974 / Blue Thumb ♦♦♦
It was the combination of poetry with almost-frighteningly intense rhythm tracks, mostly done on hand drums, that helped create the Last Poets' reputation for being way ahead of the curve on the entire development of what would come to be called rap music. This album has the feel of an earlier, less-developed session, and the 1976 release date most likely indicates the interest certain record labels might have had in locating any and all projects by these musicians while their fire was blazing so hot. This sounds much more like the typical jazz and poetry project, meaning it is kind of bad—and that word is not used as a hipster might. The poets fall into the same kind of cadences that just about every poet performing with a jazz group has, which include a strained voice in order to be heard above the racket, a rushed sense of pacing trying to fit the words in somewhere between the arco bass doodles and honking sax, and an overall cadence that rises and falls as mechanically as one of Bob Dylan's most disembodied performances. That the Poets have something significant to say and that they come up with amusing and even inspiring rhymes from time to time is a given, but there are much better examples of their recorded art. If this was truly recorded three years after the brilliant *This Is Madness*, it reveals the group's focus going fuzzy on them. —*Eugene Chadbourne*

Retro Fit / 1992 / Ced ♦♦♦♦

Holy Terror / 1994 / Rykodisc ♦♦♦
With *Holy Terror*, the Last Poets lay their claim to be the originators of hip-hop. Containing some of the Poets' most trenchant political and social lyrics, *Holy Terror* shows the Last Poets, Umar Bin Hassan and Abiodun Oyewole, still as fiery and sharp as ever. "Homesick" and "Pelourinho" are descriptions of slavery that are as vivid and riveting as any movie. "Black Rage" paints a portrait of urban hell that will chill any listener to the bone. The album is also superbly produced, with a funk sound that supports the lyrics while never overshadowing them. Credit is due to seminal producer Bill Laswell, who, armed with a first-class band made up of P-Funk alumni George Clinton, Bootsy Collins, and Bernie Worrell, along with Grandmaster Melle Mel, constructs dense, intricate grooves that are simultaneously modern and traditional. For both fans of the classic Last Poets albums and newcomers interested in one of the missing links between classic funk and modern hip-hop, *Holy Terror* is worth a listen. —*Victor W. Valdivia*

The Legend: The Best of the Last Poets / Mar. 19, 1996 / M.I.L. Multimedia ♦♦♦♦♦
The Legend: The Best of the Last Poets is a 35-track, two-disc overview of the group's career. The first covers "The Beginnings," while the second's focus is "The Real Rap Masters." —*Jason Ankeny*

Time Has Come / Apr. 15, 1997 / Mercury ♦♦♦♦
Picking up where *Holy Terror* and Omar Bin Hassan's solo album *Be Bop or Be Dead* left off, *The Time Has Come* is a scalding blend of avant-jazz, bebop and hip-hop, highlighted by cameos from Chuck D. and Pharoah Sanders. These two guests may be impressive, but they don't steal the show—they merely demonstrate that the Last Poets are too diverse and way too smart to be pigeonholed into one particular category. Occasionally, the record may be a bit unfocused, and its relentless barrage of avant-poetry may be headache-inducing to some, but few records are as politically powerful and articulate as this. —*Leo Stanley*

Chastisment/Freedom Express / Sep. 30, 1997 / M.I.L. Multimedia ♦♦♦
Some 16 years separated the releases of *Chastisement* and *Freedom Express*, both found on this two-fer; the former, from 1972, is by far the stronger of the two—recorded with former jazz drummer Suliaman El Hadi, it added jazz and funk to the group's fix to forge a new sound which they dubbed "jazzoetry." 1988's *Freedom Express* was the re-formed group's second comeback LP, and although it lacks the potency of their earlier work, it's still worth hearing. —*Jason Ankeny*

Latimore

b. Sep. 7, 1939, Charleston, TN
Vocals, Keyboards / Soul-Blues, Contemporary Blues, Soul
Deep-voiced Latimore's sultry mid-'70s output for Miami's Glades label was a steamy marriage of soul and blues. Initially billed as Benny Latimore, the Tennessean began recording for Miami mogul Henry Stone in 1965, and his late-'60s Dade singles are solid deep soul. Dropping his first name on Glades, Latimore finally found stardom in 1973 with a jazzy reading of T-Bone Walker's "Stormy Monday." He topped the soul lists in 1974 with the anguished "Let's Straighten It Out," a simmering soul/blues hybrid, and encored with the incendiary "Keep the Home Fires Burnin'" the next year. Most of Latimore's Glades sides were produced in Miami by Steve "Every Day I Have to Cry" Alaimo, and when he wasn't cutting his own hits, Latimore acted as a house pianist for parent TK Records. Latimore moved to Malaco during the '80s, his appeal undiminished. —*Bill Dahl*

More, More, More / 1974 / Glades ♦♦♦
Benny Latimore's tough-talking Southern soul began to make some inroads in the mid-'70s with this LP, which included his only number-one R&B hit, "Let's Straighten It Out." The singer, composer and keyboardist made no-nonsense, unsophisticated confessional soul and heartache ballads, plus an occasional uptempo number; at the time, he was making tunes with minimal production that put his coarse leads at the center. They were recorded for the Miami-based Glades label, and usually were regional rather than national hits. "Let's Straighten It Out" proved an exception. —*Ron Wynn*

Singing in the Key of Love / 1982 / Malaco ♦♦
Benny Latimore has done the same thing as Denise LaSalle, joining Malaco in the late '70s and remaining faithful to its brand of Southern soul and country/blues staples while never attempting to make his productions and arrangements more contemporary. That was the case on this album, which had a few nice tracks but also sometimes got bogged down in pretension. Latimore hasn't yet duplicated the energy or the wit that made his early-'70s Glades albums some of the decade's best Southern soul efforts. —*Ron Wynn*

Good Time Man / 1985 / Malaco ♦♦♦♦♦
Benny Latimore's Malaco albums have been conservatively produced, geared toward Southern tastes and moderately successful on a regional basis. That's the case with this album, which didn't land national hits but was a generally good effort. Latimore's voice isn't as commanding as it was during his 1970s run, but he can still sing in a menacing fashion, deliver convincing heartache ballads, sound vulnerable or express tenderness and concern. Unfortunately, the lack of a great single and the decidedly non-urban contemporary sound doomed this to the fate of most Malaco LPs—little exposure above the Mason-Dixon line and little radio airplay. —*Ron Wynn*

Every Way But Wrong / 1988 / Malaco ♦♦♦
A good, if at times repetitive, album by Latimore, one of his better releases on Malaco. After he'd been on the label a while, the producers began to improve the kind of songs he was given, vary the production and arrangements more, and coax stronger, more impressive leads and vocal treatments from Latimore. They still couldn't match the quality of the Glades releases, but were coming closer. —*Ron Wynn*

I'll Do Anything for You / 1988 / Malaco ♦♦
Another satisfactory album on Malaco for Latimore, who hasn't yet hit his stride on the label. His singing was soulful, but not as effective or hard-hitting as on other numbers. The production and arrangements were good, but there wasn't the energy or swaggering air that marked Latimore's best releases. His tenure at Malaco has been a successful one, but the definitive, exciting records he cut in Florida during the early '70s remain the high point of Benny Latimore's career. —*Ron Wynn*

Slow Down / 1989 / Malaco ♦♦♦♦♦
This was Latimore's best Malaco release, and arguably his finest record in the '80s. It had both moving ballads and fine uptempo tunes, and his usually resourceful, deep soul vocals were stronger and more confident and animated. The song "One Man, One Woman, One Love" was the type of simple yet engaging number that the Malaco tunesmiths didn't deliver consistently enough for their acts in the late '80s. It was also the kind of song that had a vintage sound but a contemporary outlook. —*Ron Wynn*

● **Straighten It Out: The Best of Latimore** / Sep. 19, 1995 / Rhino ♦♦♦♦♦
All of Latimore's greatest hits are included on this 17-track collection *Straighten It Out: The Best of Latimore*, making the album the best overview of the seductive '70s soul balladeer's career. —*Stephen Thomas Erlewine*

Kenny Lattimore

b. Washington, D.C.
Vocals / Urban, Contemporary R&B
After a false start with the late-'80s vocal group Maniquin, Kenny Lattimore became a minor urban R&B star in his own right in 1996, when his eponymous debut album

generated two hit singles. Lattimore was born and raised in Washington, D.C., where he grew up in a musical family. Before he reached his teens, he was winning talent shows at his junior high school. Throughout high school he performed music, from classical to R&B. Despite his love for music, he decided to pursue architecture and city planning when he enrolled at Howard University. Even though he wasn't majoring in music, he hadn't given it up as a hobby, and he joined the vocal group Maniquin. In 1987, the group signed with Epic, and, two years later, they released their debut album. The record failed to become a hit, and the group sweated it out on the grueling chitlin' circuit down South. After a year of touring, Lattimore left Maniquin in 1990.

He had decided that he would continue to pursue music, and began writing songs and collaborating with a number of artists. His songs were recorded by Glenn Jones and Jon Lucien, and he began working with Dem Twinzz, singing on the group's demos. The tapes attracted the interest of major labels, but Lattimore wanted to be a solo artist, not part of a group, so he moved to New York City in 1993.

After struggling for a few months in Manhattan, Lattimore recorded a demo of songs he co-wrote; it was produced by J. Dibbs. The demo led him to a record contract with Columbia. His debut album featured production by Kenneth and Keith Crouch, Kipper Jones, Oji Pierce, Herb Middleton, Barry Eastmond, Jimmy Abney, and Dave Hall. Lattimore did also do some preliminary production work on the album, and wrote or co-wrote six of the 12 songs. *Kenny Lattimore* was released in 1996 and it was a steady seller over the next year, going gold and spawning the Top 40 R&B hit "Never Too Busy." *From the Soul of Man* followed in 1998, offering even more original songs as well as a few covers, including a surprisingly sensual version of "While My Guitar Gently Weeps." Times had changed by the time *Weekend* arrived in 2001, and the slick R&B and soft approach of the record hit a sour note with fans. The album made little impression. so Lattimore decided to try something different the next time around. Teaming with Chante Moore, he recorded an album of duets entitled *Things That Lovers Do*. Offering new versions of songs from Keith Sweat, Marvin Gaye, Lionel Richie, and many others, the record only featured two original songs. *—Stephen Thomas Erlewine*

Kenny Lattimore / 1996 / Columbia ✦✦✦
Despite an inconsistent collection of songs, Kenny Lattimore's eponymous debut album is a promising record, showcasing his smooth voice to fine effect. His singing and the slick production makes the weaker numbers enjoyable, but when he's given a good song—such as the singles "Just What It Takes" and "Never Too Busy"—the depth of Lattimore's talent becomes apparent. *—Leo Stanley*

From the Soul of Man / Oct. 20, 1998 / Columbia ✦✦✦
Despite its lumbering length and some slick, late-'90s R&B formalities, Kenny Lattimore's second album is a real treat. Combining smooth grooves with an even silkier voice, Lattimore shifts from bedroom operator to new jack king with an ease that seems neither forced nor affected on *From the Soul of Man*. The R&B stew is made even heartier by a couple of inspired covers, even if they're not totally successful in their execution (who knew that "While My Guitar Gently Weeps" could be so sexy?). When the album tosses in basic contemporary soul ingredients—songs that are more finely chiseled than actually tuneful, occasional robotic singing, glossy production that's hiding something—it flows into mind-numbing conventionality. But when Lattimore gently soaks in the material (nearly all of it penned by him), *From the Soul of Man* is truly a spirited affair. *—Michael Gallucci*

Weekend / Oct. 9, 2001 / Arista ✦✦
Just because Kenny Lattimore's *Weekend* was executive produced by über-producer Antonio "L.A." Reid does not guarantee a hit factory. Sure, the music on this R&B affair is comparable to anything else out there in the genre (think Jagged Edge, but not as soulful or infectious). However, calling this album "comparable" is generous. *Weekend*, with its bland arrangements, cookie-cutter R&B sound, and lyrical vacuity, is a yawn. Hookin' up, the inability to breathe without "the one," and other hackneyed themes abound on this banal album. There isn't enough groove or vibrato, shirt-clutching vocals to keep listeners from growing bored, and fast. Find something else to do this weekend. *—Liana Jonas*

Stacy Lattisaw

b. Nov. 25, 1966, Washington, D.C.
Vocals / Quiet Storm, Urban
When she was a teenager in the early '80s, urban soul singer Stacy Lattisaw had a string of Top 40 R&B hits, with three songs—"Let Me Be Your Angel," "Love on a Two Way Street," "Miracles"—crossing over to the pop mainstream. Lattisaw recorded her first album for Cotillion Records at the age of 12 in 1979, under the direction of producer Van McCoy. However it wasn't until she hooked up with Narada Michael Walden, a former drummer with the Mahavishnu Orchestra who was just beginning a career as a producer, that she became a star. Under Walden's direction, she had five hit albums between 1981 and 1986. She continued recording into the late '80s, signing to Motown in 1986, but her audience slowly disappeared. By the early '90s, she decided to retire from a music career and concentrate on raising her family. *—Stephen Thomas Erlewine*

Young & in Love / 1979 / Cotillion ✦✦
A far cry from the soulful ballads that would later make her a favorite in R&B circles, Lattisaw's debut album consists of remakes of '60s and '70s pop hits and a few pleasant, if forgettable, disco entries. Recorded when she was only 12, *Young and in Love* showcases a warm, sweet voice surprisingly mature for its age. Her subtlety and youthful emotion work to great effect on serene numbers like "Love Is Here Beside Us" and the title track (both disco and ballad versions are included); and her delivery of Petula Clark's classic, "Downtown," is as enjoyable as the original. On several cuts, Lattisaw has a few intonation problems here and there. But the bulk of the performances is consistent, making it an essential item for any loyal fan. *—Justin Kantor*

● **Let Me Be Your Angel** / 1980 / Atlantic ✦✦✦
Stacy Lattisaw was only 13 when, in 1980, she made her commercial breakthrough with her second album, *Let Me Be Your Angel*. Not surprisingly, the fact that she was just barely an adolescent got a lot of press; the black teen magazines that had given the Jackson 5 and the Sylvers so much coverage were quick to run articles on Lattisaw. But *Let Me Be Your Angel* isn't a bubblegum record, and Lattisaw doesn't go out of her way to be cutesy. If anything, she sounds like a younger version of Deniece Williams or Rose Royce's Gwen Dickey—girlish, certainly, but substantial and not without grit. Although Lattisaw had some developing to do in 1980, this is a fairly promising sophomore effort. Narada Michael Walden, who produced the LP and wrote or co-wrote all of the songs, doesn't treat *Let Me Be Your Angel* like a teen record. More often than not, he gives Lattisaw solid material to work with, and that includes infectious dance-funk items like "Jump to the Beat," "Don't You Want to Feel It (For Yourself)," and the hit "Dynamite!" as well as sentimental soul-pop ballads such as "My Love" and the title track. *Let Me Be Your Angel* isn't perfect; again, Lattisaw still had some growing and developing to do back in 1980. But it's a respectable offering that has more plusses than minuses, and those who gave the LP a serious listen realized that Lattisaw wasn't a mere novelty. *—Alex Henderson*

With You / 1981 / Atlantic ✦✦✦
The Washington, D.C., native found success on her third album with the classic "Love on a Two Way Street." Released by the Moments 11 years prior (number one, five weeks), Lattisaw's maturing vocals introduce her to an older audience. Her effortless deliveries are commendable on this solid production. Her version held the number two position on the *Billboard* R&B charts for four consecutive weeks. The second single was the midtempo "It Was So Easy." Lattisaw's vocals are supreme on this relaxing number. The single peaked at number 61. The third single was the more upbeat "Feel My Love Tonight." Here too Lattisaw's vocals ring with precsion. With rap on the rise, the young vocalist ventures into the untamed territory of rap. While her enunication is articulate, the texture is painted with a juvenile sound. The titlle track is a mellow, soft number allowing Lattisaw to expand her vocality. This album was also a platform for some of Narada Michael Walden's earlier production work. *—Craig Lytle*

Perfect Combination / Feb. 1984 / Cotillion ✦✦✦

What You Need / Oct. 17, 1989 / Motown ✦✦
Though Stacy Lattisaw first came to fame with the 1980 Top Ten R&B/Top 21 pop ballad "Let Me Be Your Angel," she does mostly uptempo material on her Top 16 R&B LP *What You Need*. The standouts are the pumpin', sensual "Dance for You," "You Touched the Woman in Me," "R U Man Enuff," and "Guilty (Lock Me Up)." The title-track single broke the R&B Top 30 in the fall of 1989. Ironically, it would be a ballad duet with frequent singing partner Johnny Gill that would prove to be the album's biggest single. "Where Do We Go From Here" parked at number one R&B while curiously crossing over to the pop charts in late 1989. The followup was another ballad, "I Don't Have the Heart." "Where Do We Go From Here" is on Johnny Gill's *Ultimate Collection*. *—Ed Hogan*

● **The Very Best of Stacy Lattisaw** / Apr. 7, 1998 / Rhino ✦✦✦✦✦
The Very Best of Stacy Lattisaw is a comprehensive 16-track collection that contains all of her big R&B hits between 1979 and 1989. Since the disc draws from both her recordings for Altantic/Cotillion and Motown, it contains everything from "Dynamite!," "Let Me Be Your Angel" and "Love on a Two Way Street" to "Nail It to the Wall" and "Every Drop of Your Love." While her chart-topping duet with Johnny Gill, "Where Do We Go From Here," is missing, the collection remains the definitive summation of her career. *—Stephen Thomas Erlewine*

Paul Laurence

b. 1962, New York, NY
Keyboards / Urban, Quiet Storm
Songwriter/producer/keyboardist Paul Laurence had seven number-one R&B hits, working with Stephanie Mills, Meli'sa Morgan, Evelyn King, and Freddie Jackson. Laurence and Jackson attended school and church together at Harlem's White Rock Baptist Church, which is where the duo met in the '70s. By the '80s, both Laurence and Jackson were working for manager Beau Higgins' Hush Productions. By fall 1982, Jackson had signed as a Hush artist and began recording his debut album. Laurence wrote a swaying ballad, "Rock Me Tonight (For Old Times Sake)," especially for Jackson and played keyboards and programmed drums on the track. Higgins then got Jackson a record deal with Capitol Records, the same label Melba Moore was signed To. "Rock Me Tonight (For Old Times Sake)" became an instant smash, staying at number-one R&B for six weeks during summer 1985.

With Jackson, Laurence co-wrote "Tasty Love," which held the number-one R&B position for four weeks in late 1986. A week earlier Jackson was in the number-one R&B spot on a duet with Melba Moore, "A Little Bit More." Melba Moore then hired Jackson as a background vocalist. "Jam Tonight" jumped to number-one R&B in summer 1987 and became a steppers classic. Laurence produced a cover of Prince's "Do Me Baby" for fellow Hush signee and Capitol recording artist Meli'sa Morgan. The ballad parked at number one R&B for three weeks in early 1986. For Stephanie Mills, Laurence produced and co-wrote with Timmy Allen the chugging "(You're Putting) A Rush on Me," giving the singer her third number-one R&B hit in fall 1987. Laurence had several hits with Brooklyn singer/Capitol recording artist Lillo Thomas: "(You're A) Good Girl," "Your Love's Got a Hold on Me," "(Can't Take Half) All of You" (a duet with Melba Moore), "Settle Down," "Sexy Girl" (Laurence/Timmy Allen), "I'm in Love," and "Wanna Make Love (All Night Long)."

With all of this success, Laurence was afforded the opportunity to become a recording artist. Signing with Capitol, Laurence's debut LP, the critically acclaimed *Haven't You Heard*, was released in late 1985. The first single, "She's Not a Sleaze," featured Freddie Jackson and Lillo Thomas and charted number-50 R&B in late 1985. Other singles for Laurence were "You Hooked Me," "Strung Out," "Make My Baby Happy," and "I Ain't Wit It." *—Ed Hogan*

● **Haven't You Heard** / 1985 / Capitol ✦✦✦✦
After producing hits for Freddie Jackson, Lillo Thomas and Melba Moore, Paul Laurence assembled an impressive debut album which, unfortunately, never caught on. The first

release, "She's Not a Sleaze," showcases Laurence and labelmates Jackson and Thomas. Moderately paced around a seductive rhythm arrangement, the single peaked at number 50 on the *Billboard* R&B charts after nine weeks. Laurence followed with the pop-seasoned ballad "You Hooked Me" and socially charged "Strung Out." The latter barely cracked the Top Ten at number 48, his highest-charting single. In spite of excellent production and appealing songs in which the vocals are audible, this album was never able to the turn the corner. *—Craig Lytle*

Underexposed / 1988 / Capitol ♦♦♦

Betty Lavette (Betty Haskin)

b. Jan. 26, 1946, Muskegon, MI

Vocals / Northern Soul, Urban, Soul

A perennial cult favorite in northern soul circles, singer Betty Lavette was born in Muskegon, MI, on January 29, 1946; raised primarily across the state in Detroit, at 16 she cut her first sides for the local Lupine label, with a test pressing of the disc making its way to Atlantic Records. After signing with Atlantic, she scored an R&B Top Ten hit out of the box with her debut single "My Man—He's a Loving Man," only to fail to reach the same commercial heights again. After one more Atlantic release, 1963's "You'll Never Change," Lavette moved back to Lupine for her third record, "Witchcraft in the Air"; after a stint as a featured vocalist with the Don Gardner & Dee Dee Ford Revue, she recorded the long-unreleased "One Thin Dime" for Scepter before resurfacing on Calla with the 1965 lost classic "Let Me Down Easy," her only other record to crack the R&B Top 20. Two more Calla efforts—the fine "Only Your Love Can Save Me" and "I'm Just a Fool for You"—preceded a shift to Big Wheel, where after just one single, "I'm Holding On," Lavette again moved along, this time to the Karen imprint for "Hey Love."

Following stays at Silver Fox ("He Made a Woman Out of Me," "Do Your Duty"), SSS International ("Take Another Piece of My Heart") and her own TCA imprint ("Never My Love"), Lavette returned to Atlantic, signing to their Atco division for 1972's Neil Young cover "Heart of Gold." An LP, *Child of the 70s*, was also recorded at Muscle Shoals Studios, but Atco opted against its release after the failure of the single "Your Turn to Cry." After joining the touring company of the Broadway musical *Bubbling Brown Sugar*, Lavette briefly signed to West End for a disco effort, 1978's "Doin' the Best I Can"; she did not record again until 1982, landing at Motown and rechristening herself "Bettye." However, despite a heavy promotional push neither the LP *Tell Me a Lie* nor the single "Right in the Middle (Of Falling in Love)" proved her long-awaited chart breakthrough, and outside of a handful of recordings for Motor City during the 1990s, she focused primarily on live appearances in the years to follow. *—Jason Ankeny*

- **Tell Me a Lie** / 1980 / Motown ♦♦♦♦♦

Bettye LaVette deserved better. Although recorded in Nashville, this one-shot album's groove is more like Muscle Shoals. But it doesn't sound dated, either, as producer Steve Buckingham exercises taste and sensitivity in coming up with excellent tracks that effectively showcase LaVette's style. Although this album is out of print, the excellent, sadly neglected single "Right in the Middle (Of Falling in Love)" can fortunately be found on a pair of Motown collections, and are thus worth seeking out. *—John Lowe*

- **Bluesoul Belles** / Jun. 22, 1999 / WestSide ♦♦♦♦

The stellar *Bluesoul Belles* spotlights Betty Lavette and Carol Fran, two of the more criminally underrated singers from soul music's mid-'60s golden era. Unearthing two dozen tracks from the Calla, Port, and Roulette vaults, many of them previously unreleased alternate takes, the set offers a persuasive argument that, while never earning the critical respect or commercial kudos of their contemporaries, both women deserve consideration alongside the greats of the period. Lavette's opening "Let Me Down Easy," a staple of the Northern soul scene and the countless anthologies it's yielded, is far and away the most recognizable cut here—the song is her masterpiece, a blisteringly poignant requiem for romance gone bad distinguished by its unique, tango-like rhythm and sweeping string arrangement. The remaining seven tracks don't reach the same peaks, but from the Motown-inspired stomp of "What I Don't Know (Won't Hurt Me)" to the gospel-inflected "Cry Me a River," Lavette's versatility and raw power ring through loud and clear. Although Lavette receives top billing, Fran's contributions comprise fully two-thirds of the disc; best known for her latter-day blues efforts with guitarist husband Clarence Hollimon, the aching beauty of her mid-'60s soul sides is revelatory. Though rooted in the blues, her crystalline vocals were nevertheless ideally suited to the uptown style and sophistication of her Port dates; the chart failure of these recordings is baffling, and in particular the remarkable "Any Day Love Walks In" merits the label of lost classic. *—Jason Ankeny*

Debra Laws

b. Houston, TX

Vocals / Quiet Storm, Urban

As the sister of noted R&B and jazz notables Hubert Laws, Eloise Laws, and Ronnie Laws (of '70s powerhouse Earth, Wind & Fire), Debra Laws was a part of a very musical family. As a vocalist she has performed and collaborated with a veritable who's who of jazz, funk, and R&B segments of the recording industry. As a soloist she debuted on Elektra Records with *Very Special* in 1981 which was produced by her brothers Ronnie and Hubert Laws. Even though the title track to *Very Special* received a massive amount of airplay (and surprisingly continued to do so) the record didn't lead to as successful of a solo career as Elcktra had hoped, and it was her first and only solo record with them. Her career as a vocalist continued through the '80s and '90s, leading to a handful of performances on world-class concert halls and at some of the most internationally renowned jazz festivals. Equally impressive are her numerous credits with truly class acts of jazz and R&B including Melvin Robinson, Larry Dunn, Fred White, Garnett Brown, Michael Martin, Snooky Young, Larry Williams, Maurice Spears, Alan Rubin, Bobby Vega, Harvey Mason, and Patrick Kelly. In addition to her musical life, she has also worked as an actor on Broadway and on a series of other stage and television productions including appearances on daytime television's *General Hospital*. *—Nate Cavalieri*

- **Very Special** / 1981 / Spy ♦♦

Eloise Laws

b. 1949, Houston, TX

Vocals / Urban, Jazz-Pop, Vocal Jazz

Eloise Laws holds the distinction of being the least famous Laws sibling. Household-name stardom hasn't happened for the chic, sexy, warbler. Laws was born in 1949, in Houston, TX. Brother Hubert (the renowned flutist), is older, while sax-playing brother Ronnie and singing sister Debra are both younger. Eloise Laws has experienced everything in music except a hit record. Hubert's many jazz albums and CDs sell worldwide; he's considered a virtuoso on the flute. Ronnie has had many best-selling works, and Debra scored with "Very Special," a popular selection on quiet storm formats.

Laws began recording for Holland-Dozier-Holland's Music Merchant label and had a couple of releases in 1972-1973: "Tighten Him Up" and "Love Factory"—neither charted. When the famous songwriting team folded Music Merchant, they signed Laws to their Invictus label. They released a few singles and her first LP, *Ain't It Good Feeling Good* (which Japan's P-Vine Records has reissued on CD). "Put a Little Love Into It (When You Do It)," a sultry single, sparked but created no fires. Due to mismanagement, Invictus folded and Laws jumped to ABC Records and recorded the obscure, self-titled *Eloise*, released in 1977. Limited promotion caused the album to sink without a trace; even a single penned by Linda Creed, "1,000 Laughs," failed to ignite her career. Her Liberty record album, again self-titled, *Eloise Laws*, is even more obscure than the ABC release.

When Marilyn McCoo left the 5th Dimension, their manager, Marc Gordon, chose Laws to replace her. He saw her sing at the Playboy Club in Lake Geneva and instantly pegged her for the group. Gordon had auditioned more than 200 wannabes. Reluctantly she accepted, mainly because of problems with her manager, and the migraines associated with keeping an eight-piece touring group together. Joining the 5th was a way out; now all she had to worry about was singing. The stint lasted three weeks. Laws did one performance with the 5th—the Johnny Carson show—and quit the next day, to the dismay of all involved. Laws felt she just didn't mesh with the members. After the 5th fiasco, Laws kept busy vocalizing on Hubert's and Ronnie's albums, and sets by Lee Oskar and Ahmad Jamal. She did duets with Harry Belafonte ("So Close") on his *Play Me* release. AEMI records in Japan released *Aurex Jazz Festival—Fusion Super Jam* in 1998. On this album, Laws is the vocalist of a star-studded ensemble, including brother Hubert, Dave Liebman (sax), Leon "Ndugu" Chancler (drums), Larry Coryell (guitar), Richard Tee (keyboards), Eric Gale (guitar), and Tony Dumas (bass). Laws also appeared in the touring play, *It Ain't Nothing but the Blues*, as a vocalist. A quote attributed to Laws best describes her career: "Star? I don't wanna be a star—a star falls." In fall 2000, she resurfaced with the release *The Key*. *—Andrew Hamilton*

- **Love Factory: The Invictus Sessions** / 1999 / Sequel ♦♦♦

Le Klass

f. Augusta, GA

Group / Urban, Funk, Hip-Hop

Although Le Klass came out of Augusta, GA, the urban contemporary unit sounded like it could have been from Minneapolis and reflected leader Nelson Curry's interest in the Minneapolis/St. Paul School of Funk-Rock. Curry, who formed the band in the 1980s, loved pop and rock as much as he loved soul and funk—and he clearly admired the way Minneapolis acts like Prince, the Time and Jesse Johnson combined all of those styles. Interestingly, Curry also claimed the Beach Boys as an influence, saying that he "admired the way they carried their harmonies." But there was no discernible Beach Boys influence in the recordings of Le Klass, which also consisted of Rod Nickerson (guitars, bass), Wayne Bowman (keyboards, background vocals), Allen Curry (keyboards) and Derrick Thomas (drums, percussion). Playing around Augusta, Le Klass acquired a small local following. In fact, one Augusta resident who told Curry he felt Le Klass had a lot of potential was none other than Soul Godfather James Brown.

In the late 1980s, Le Klass came to the attention of the L.A.-based producer Jay Warsinske, who in 1990, put out its debut album, *School of Cool* on his AVC label. The catchy "That's What Love Can Do" was released as a single, but regrettably, neither the album nor the single took off. After that, Le Klass continued to play club dates in and around Augusta without ever becoming well-known nationally. *—Alex Henderson*

- **School of Cool** / 1989 / Bellmark ♦♦♦♦

The Minneapolis School of Funk-Rock-Pop—which gave us Prince, the Time and Ta Mara & the Seen, among others—provided some of the most exciting music of the 1980s. But sadly, most of the Prince clones plaguing that decade hadn't even a fraction of those artists' inventiveness or passion. One band, however, that used Prince and the Time's influence to its artistic advantage was Augusta, GA's obscure Le Klass—which makes its love of the Minneapolis Sound obvious on *School of Cool* without becoming clones or slavish imitators. When lead singer/composer Nelson Curry tears into such addictive, simmering funk as "That's What Love Can Do" and "She Can't Let Go" and the heartfelt R&B/pop balladry of "Don't Say Goodbye," "Jan" and the remorseful "Just Friends," he comes across as very much his own man. Unfortunately, this album—one of the first releases for West Coast producer James Warsinske's AVC/Solid Entertainment—didn't receive nearly the attention it deserved. *—Alex Henderson*

Otis Leavill

b. Feb. 8, 1943, Dewey Rose, GA, **d.** Jul. 17, 2002

Producer / Chicago Soul, R&B, Soul

Friendly, talented Otis Leavill Cobb was born February 8, 1943, in Dewey Rose, GA. The Cobb family moved to Chicago two years later and settled in the Londale area on the West Side. Leavill has four brothers and two sisters; a sister and a brother have expired. His father pastored the First Church of Deliverance on South Wabash, one of the first to broadcast on the radio, and formed the Cobb Singers, with Otis a member. Leavill's childhood chum, Major Lance lived in the Cabrini Green Projects near Curtis Mayfield and Jerry Butler. They slept over at each other houses and acted more like brothers than buddies. As teenagers the two pals participated in amateur boxing at St. Albees, Leavill always fought in a division five pounds heavier than Lance. At 5' 5" Leavill was short and stocky; Lance was taller and slimmer at 5' 8". They formed the Floats with two females: Barbara Tyson, and another that no one remembers. After eight months the Floats ended, they never released a record but recorded a demo that's floating around Chi-town. Always industrious, he worked at a grocery store, and Lance a drugstore in the Cabrini Green area. Leavill graduated from Crane High School, and attended Crane Junior College, and Chicago Junior College.

The Impressions recorded first, then Lance, and finally Leavill. His first record "Ride Sally Ride," dropped on Mercury's Limelight subsidiary, though Otis says he waxed it for St. Lawrence Records who evidently leased the master. His next release "Gotta Right to Cry," a Mayfield song came out on Lucky Records; Lance had already waxed and released the tune in 1963 for OKeh Records. His third release "Let Her Love Me," in 1966, gave his career the boost it needed reaching number 31 on *Billboard's* R&B chart; the lilting Mayfield ballad, with the Impressions singing in the background became Blue Rock Records first national hit. Dick Clark Caravan of Stars provided Leavill his first touring opportunity. Initially, he went along to accompany Major Lance, but with disk jockeys spinning "Let Her Love Me," Clark gave Leavill a paid slot on the Caravan to sing two songs.

Prior to that first hit he befriended record producer Carl Davis who worked at OKeh Records. At OKeh he was Davis' right-hand man, helping to schedule artists, getting musicians and backing singers to the studio, etc. Leavill could spot talent, he discovered the Chi-Lites, Tyrone Davis, Bohannon, and Manchild from Indianapolis, IN, whose members included Kenneth "Babyface" Edmonds. Leavill and Davis passed on Yvette Stevens, a fast, hot-blooded sixteen-year-old singer, and her younger sister, Yvonne, they thought Yvette in particular would be a major distraction; in spite of her young age, older men hovered around the vivacious full-throated curvy teen like flies on raw fish. Yvette became Chaka Khan, and Yvonne, Taka Boom. He raves about the Vibrations' ability to sing the "money songs" as he called standards, the tunes that got you cushy gigs in Las Vegas. Yet, it never really happened for the Californian natives like everyone predicted, their OKeh recordings' "Pick Me," "Misty," "Love in Them There Hills," and others were only modest sellers.

Blue Rock Records was Leavill's next stop. There he cut some memorable sides, including Billy Butlers' "To Be or Not to Be," and "Let Me Live." When Davis formed the Dakar label, he appointed Otis as Vice President and gave him shares in the company. Leavill also recorded for Dakar where he enjoyed his biggest hit: Eugene Record's "I Love You," a song that sounded like Otis imitating Record—the Chi-Lites' lead singer; it climbed to number-ten R&B but never threatened the Pop Top 40, stalling number 64. Another Record composition "Love Uprising" nearly repeated the success of "I Love You," checking in at number-19 R&B and number-72 Pop. Another single "There's Nothing Better Than Loving You" scraped into the lower rungs of the R&B chart. Despite some success, Dakar never released an album by Leavill. Willie Henderson produced Leavill's recordings at Dakar; and Record and Barbara Acklin, who were close but never married, did the backing vocals.

After Dakar's demise Carl Davis went to Brunswick Records, Leavill followed and had a few releases including "Can't Stop Loving You," which sells for $40 bucks to collectors, but never equaled the success he had at Dakar. His releases after that were sporadic. "Right Back in Love" came out on Columbia Records, but after a few more droppings, Leavill's recording career ended. A songwriter also, B.M.I. lists 41 songs by Leavill. He wrote "There's Goes The Lover" (Gene Chandler), "Sweet Music" for Major Lance, produced sides for Tyrone Davis, and supervised Major Lance's Motown album *Now Arriving.* More prominent behind the scenes than out front, his memories of music are all good. Divorced (from Minnie Cobb), his daughter Misti graduated from Miliken University in Decatur, IL. In 1999 he toured the European clubs with the Dells. Unknown to many, he and Carl Davis coached football at Hyde Park High for seven years. Never one to sit back and wait, Leavill also owned the 76 Car Wash and Gas Station at Washington and Pulaski and moonlighted as a policeman in a West Chicago 'burb. He formed OK Records in 2000 after a long hiatus from the record business. Sadly, Otis Leavill passed July 17, 2002, of a heart attack, he was 65. Till the end , he had lost none of the drive, hustle or energy that first won him respect as an amateur boxer at St. Albees. *—Andrew Hamilton*

Lee & the Leopards

Group / Motown, Soul

A good early Motown single was "Come Into My Palace" by Lee & the Leopards. The Gordy Records single featured a hokey '50s bass intro and inspired wailing. Lee was Lee Henry Moore, and the Leopards, well, there was Prentiss Anderson and unknowns. Moore, Brian Holland, and William Stevenson composed the April 1962 release that the Supremes redid as a ballad; the Leopards' was an uptempo novelty. Motown canned the Supremes' version for more than 25 years; Brenda, with sister, Patrice Holloway, waxed a duet version. Ironically, both sides of Lee & the Leopards' Gordy single, the flip was "Trying to Make It," was leased to Laurie Records in 1963, quite odd for Motown to do this, it usually happened the other way around. They cut a Lee Moore tune on Fortune Records in 1964 entitled "Don't Press Your Luck," undersided by "What About Me." Fortune couldn't put the mighty Nolan Strong & the Diablos over the top, so you know Lee & the Leopards didn't have anything coming from the financially strapped label. KZ Records issued a tune or two and they possibly drop one-off singles on other small labels. *—Andrew Hamilton*

Curtis Lee

b. Oct. 28, 1941, Yuma, AZ

Vocals / Brill Building Pop, Pop, Teen Idol

Curtis Lee occupies the era of rock & roll in between the death of Buddy Holly and the arrival of the Beatles—a period usually thought of as "lost years," because, apart from the Beach Boys, few of the artists involved lingered long on the charts or left an obvious legacy into the next era. Neither did Lee, but two of his songs, "Pretty Little Angel Eyes" and "Under the Moon of Love," evoke vivid associations with that innocent, romantic era.

Lee hailed from Arizona, and cut three songs for small labels while he was still in his teens. He was heard by Ray Peterson ("Tell Laura I Love Her"), who'd just started a label of his own, Dunes, and invited to cut a demo if he came to New York. By the time he made it to New York in late 1960, he'd started writing songs in partnership with a friend, Tommy Boyce, who later one half of the Boyce & Hart songwriting-producing-singing duo. Lee's first two singles, "Special Love" and "Pledge of Love," were passionate but otherwise unexceptional performances that understandly failed to chart, but for his third record, Dunes agreed to cut a Lee-Boyce original called "Pretty Little Angel Eyes." Phil Spector, who had previously produced a hit for Peterson ("Corinna, Corinna"), ran the session, and laid the orchestra and, especially, the chorus on very heavily, the latter deliberately working in a late-'50s doo wop style. The resulting record made the Top Ten, and Lee's biggest hit.

Lee and Boyce next turned in the jaunty "Under the Moon of Love," which used less of a doo wop style, in favor of a thick sax sound and a soaring girl chorus, and made the charts in late 1961. Unfortunately, this was to be Lee's last recording success. Lee never charted another record, and he left the music business. "Pretty Little Angel Eyes" is a fixture on oldies stations, however, with its distinctive sound, and both it and "Under the Moon of Love" are considered prime representatives of Phil Spector's early sound. *—Bruce Eder*

● **Pretty Little Angel Eyes** / Jun. 25, 1996 / Collectables ♦♦♦

The two most well-known songs here, the title track and "Under the Moon of Love," are so heavily anthologized that it's difficult to imagine that any fan doesn't already own them. On the other hand, there's more where that came from, as this 17-track collection demonstrates, all soaring romantic doo wop-style rock & roll. Lee's falsetto serves him well on "Gee How I Wish You Were Here," "Beverly Jean," and most of the rest, most of which is solid midtempo pop-rock without a lot to distinguish it. "Pledge of Love" is a tear-stained weeper that seems to owe quite a bit of its sound to "Tell Laura I Love Her"; "Beverly Jean" is another in a long line of songs that use the names of girls from other songs ("Peggy Sue," "Mary Lou") as incidental hooks; "Then I'll Know" sounds like a partly successful attempt to give Lee a Del Shannon-type sound (à la "You Didn't Talk About Me"); "Wobble" is a silly dance tune; and "Pickin' Up the Pieces of My Heart" was an attempt at emulating Ricky Nelson's sound. There are no real surprises here except perhaps the sound quality, which is exceptionally good, even on an alternate take of "Under the Moon of Love." *—Bruce Eder*

Jackie Lee (Earl Nelson)

Vocals / Soul, R&B

L.A. R&B legend Jackie Lee's career was intrinsically connected to two other L.A. vocalists in particular, Bobby Byrd (aka Bobby Day) and Bobby Relf, but his biggest solo success was recorded without help from either one. During the early to mid-'60s, he recorded solo R&B tracks under a various names, including Jay Dee, Earl Cosby, Chip Nelson, and finally, as Jackie Lee. It was under this name that Nelson scored his biggest solo hit with the popular R&B dance number "The Duck," waxed in 1965 for Mirwood Records.

Lee started out as a member of numerous West Coast doo wop and R&B groups, appearing under his real name (Earl Nelson), beginning with the Bobby Byrd's Hollywood Flames (that's Nelson singing lead on "Buzz, Buzz, Buzz," in fact, the group's number-18 pop hit for Ebb Records in 1958). After Bobby Byrd left (he was replaced by Bobby Relf) to continue to record solo hits Class Records—including "That's All I Want" and "The Bluebird, the Buzzard, and the Oriole," in 1959—Nelson's Flames/Satellites continued recording for both Class and Ebb until 1959.

By 1960, however, Nelson & the Hollywood Flames weren't quite ready to be extinguished, eventually signing with Atlantic's Atco subsidiary before ending up on Edsel Records. At this point, Nelson and Bobby Day both ventured off to form a duo called Bob & Earl. Day left the duo before they produced any hits, however, and Nelson soon reconfigured the act with a second "Bob," former Flame Bobby Relf. (Relf had been quite busy recording under a whole roster of identities, waxing singles as a solo artist under the names Bobby Garrett and as Bobby Valentino). Relf & Earl Nelson's lone Bob & Earl hit, "Harlem Shuffle," was a minor-key rumbler featuring a young Barry White on piano. The duo's vocal interplay presaged the talented Stax Records duo Sam & Dave, while the lyrics provided the listener with instructional R&B dance moves for a dance which was also called the Harlem Shuffle. Reportedly produced by Fred Smith—a talented R&B producer and songwriter, who had previously written hits with partner Cliff Goldsmith and produced both Little Caesar & the Romans ("Those Oldies but Goodies [Reminds Me of You]") and the Olympics ("Hully Gully," "Western Movies"), among others—and arranged by White, "Harlem Shuffle" was originally released in the U.S. on the Marc label (Marc 144), one of the several L.A.-based labels for which Bob & Earl recorded in 1964. The song climbed into the lower rungs of the U.S. Top 40 (number-36 *Cashbox*/number-44 *Billboard*) before slipping off the charts.

In 1965, Nelson teamed up with White and Fred Smith for a single called "The Duck," which was issued by Nelson under the name Jackie Lee (Jackie was Earl's wife's name and Lee his own middle name). The "Duck" single—spinning off on an orbit of its own due to the success of then-popular dance hits—was such a huge hit that Jackie Lee and company quickly recorded a full-length, cash-in album for Mirwood which featured a whole slew of related "Duck" ditties and covers of popular dance-related titles, plus a new version of "Harlem Shuffle" and a remake of "Hully Gully."

Meanwhile, Bob & Earl's "Harlem Shuffle" had gone on to achieve its biggest success when it was re-released as a single, in 1969, where it became a Top Ten U.K. hit (number-seven pop). Since its 1963 debut on the Marc logo, "Harlem Shuffle" has attracted high-profile cover versions by everyone from the Righteous Brothers, Edgar Winter, platinum-coiffed Georgia rocker Wayne Cochran, to the Rolling Stones, who revived it in 1986 for their Dirty Work LP. Nelson (aka Jackie Lee) continued to have a thriving career in music but failed to have any hits after "The Duck." *—Bryan Thomas*

- **The Duck** / 1966 / Goldmine ✦✦

A straight party-dance album released on the heels of "The Duck," a major player on R&B stations. Lee, nee Earl Nelson, sung with the Holly Flames, and he was also half of Bob & Earl who hit with "Harlem Shuffle," updated here by Lee. The dance groove never stops as he invites you to "Hully Gully," "Do the Temptation Walk," "Shotgun and the Duck," and "Bounce." The vocalist is red-hot, singing all 12 jams with conviction and fire. *—Andrew Hamilton*

Julia Lee

b. Oct. 31, 1902, Boonville, MO, **d.** Dec. 8, 1958, San Diego, CA

Vocals, Piano / Jump Blues, Swing

A popular entertainer who recorded frequently for Capitol during 1944-1950, Julia Lee's double entendre songs and rocking piano made her a major attraction in Kansas City. She played piano and sang in her brother George E. Lee's Orchestra during 1920-1934, recording with him in 1927 and 1929 (including "If I Could Be With You One Hour Tonight") and cutting two titles of her own in 1929 ("He's Tall, He's Dark and He's Handsome" and "Won't You Come Over to My House"). Lee worked regularly as a single in Kansas City after her brother's band broke up. In 1944, she started recording for Capitol and among her sidemen on some sessions were Jay McShann, Vic Dickenson, Benny Carter, Red Norvo, and Red Nichols, along with many local players. After 1952, Julia Lee only recorded four further songs, but she was active up until her death in 1958. *—Scott Yanow*

- **Julia Lee and Her Boy Friends** / Aug. 23, 1946-Jul. 9, 1952 / Pausa ✦✦✦✦✦

This 1983 LP from the obsolete Pausa label has a dozen of Julia Lee's better Capitol recordings, all but one from 1946-1949. Lee, a fine pianist, tended to sing fairly obvious but cute double entendre lyrics. Falling between swing-oriented jazz, blues, and R&B, the recordings on this set feature such interesting players and sidemen as trombonist Vic Dickenson, altoist Benny Carter, Dave Cavanaugh on tenor, and guitarist Jim "Daddy" Walker, among many others. Highlights include "King Size Papa," "Crazy World," "Snatch and Grab It," and "I Was Wrong" (which has a spot for cornetist Red Nichols). Some, but not all, of this music has since been reissued on CD in samplers. *—Scott Yanow*

Laura Lee

b. Mar. 9, 1945, Detroit, MI

Vocals / Soul, Southern Soul, Country-Soul

A tough '60s soul singer with a salty sense of humor (aimed mostly at the men in her life), Laura Lee recorded at Rick Hall's FAME studio in Muscle Shoals for the Chess label, and later for Hot Wax. In songs like "Wanted: Lover, No Experience Necessary," "A Man with Some Backbone," and the anthemic "Women's Love Rights," the female experience was brazenly discussed, debated, kicked around, and, finally, celebrated. Her music laid the groundwork for artists like Millie Jackson and Denise LaSalle to expand this proud, sexy, brash-talking corner of "women's" soul music. Lee had a country-soul, romantic side as well, as shown on her splended version of the Penn-Oldham classsic "Uptight Good Man." Lee is a fine, versatile, saucy singer whose work deserves more attention. *—Christine Ohlman*

The Best of Laura Lee / 1972 / Hot Wax ✦✦✦

Laura Lee was a soulful voice in the women's rights movement. Three cause-championing songs are on this best-of collection: "Woman's Love Rights," "Love & Liberty," and the humorous (to women) "Rip Off," where Laura flees with all the home's possessions while her man is at work, even taking the phone out of the wall so he can't make any calls. Lee's version of "Crumbs Off the Table" is sung to a slightly different arrangement than the Glass House's version. Nobody came up with more creative titles for songs than Invictus/Hot Wax Records; "If You Can Beat Me Rockin' (You Can Have My Chair)" proves that statement. Three excellent redone standards are tastefully executed by Lee: "Guess Who I Saw Today" rivals Nancy Wilson's; her rendition of "At Last" can compete with anybody's; and "Since I Fell For You" is delivered with the reverence it deserves. *—Andrew Hamilton*

Two Sides of Laura Lee / 1972 / Hot Wax ✦✦✦

Husky-voiced Laura Lee's first album for Hot Wax Records sizzles and soothes. She adds a new element to "Every Little Bit Hurts," turning the waltz-tempo whiner into a deep soul extravaganza. Her heartfelt versions of two standards, "At Last" and "Guess Who I Saw Today," makes them accessible to soul listeners who normally wouldn't give them the time of day. "Rip Off" is just what the title infers; Laura's doing a sneak number on her man by having a U-Haul parked in the driveway to remove every item in the house. The sexual implications in "If You Can Beat Me Rocking (You Can Have My Chair)" should be obvious to all. "When a Man Loves a Woman" is delivered here from a woman's point of view; Laura tags on a nice rap about men and some motherly advice at the beginning of the Percy Sledge classic. *—Andrew Hamilton*

That's How It Is: The Chess Years / 1990 / Chess ✦✦✦✦✦

- **Greatest Hits** / Jul. 1, 1991 / Fantasy ✦✦✦✦✦

Like the music of Honey Cone, Freda Payne, 100 Proof (Aged in Soul) and the Chairmen of the Board, Laura Lee's *Greatest Hits* underscores the fact that the demise of Holland/Dozier/Holland's Hot Wax label in 1974 wasn't due to a lack of strong material. Essentially, distribution problems killed the company, where former gospel singer turned brassy soul shouter Lee recorded some of her best work. The big-voiced Lee was best known for humorous yet biting songs encouraging women to demand respectful treatment in relationships—a theme that makes for powerful listening on such classics as "Wedlock Is a Padlock," "Crumbs Off the Table" and her best-known hits "Rip Off" and "Women's Love Rights." Lee's Hot Wax output has all of the trademarks of a Holland-Dozier-Holland project—tough, gospel-influenced belting is combined with a sleek production style. In fact, Lee's heartfelt singing is no less gritty than Carla Thomas' work at Stax; the main difference lies in the approach to production. But as talented as she was, Lee faded into obscurity after Hot Wax's demise. *—Alex Henderson*

Leiber & Stoller

Group / Brill Building Pop, Rock & Roll, R&B

A complete biography of the lives of Jerry Leiber & Mike Stoller and their contribution to rock & roll could easily take up an entire book. Very simply, Leiber & Stoller are two of the most important songwriters of the early days of rock & roll. Although they had penned songs for R&B artists such as Jimmy Witherspoon, Floyd Dixon, and Charles Brown in the early '50s, Leiber & Stoller more or less exploded onto the rock scene in 1953 by writing "Hound Dog" for Big Mama Thornton (later to be covered by Elvis). From that point on, the duo composed and produced a string of hits that include some of the most instantly recognizable songs in rock history. They were also pushing the art of rock songwriting (and record production) into, at the time, uncharted territory. As is noted by critic Greg Shaw in the *Rolling Stone Illustrated History of Rock and Roll*: "They were the true architects of pop/rock .... Their signal achievement was the marriage of rhythm & blues in its most primal form to the pop tradition."

Few songwriters of this era had the Midas touch as did Leiber & Stoller. A partial list of their credits include "Riot in Cell Block #9" (1953), "Love Me" (1956), "Charlie Brown" (1959), "Stand by Me" (1961), "On Broadway" (1963), and numerous songs for Elvis, including songs for the films *Jailhouse Rock* and *King Creole*. Along with wedding R&B with the pop tradition, Leiber & Stoller also introduced string arrangements to R&B records (the Drifters featuring Ben E. King's "There Goes My Baby"), and by doing so created the foundation for a new era of soul music production that would come on the heels of the fading doo wop style. Among the many artists and writers they influenced, few were more important than Phil Spector, who cut his teeth learning production techniques from them while they painstakingly assembled the great early Drifters tracks.

In 1964, Leiber & Stoller started their own record label, Red Bird, devoted to girl groups. Wisely, they also hired the talented songwriting duo of Ellie Greenwich & Jeff Barry, who were at their peak powers, composing some of the most lasting songs of the albeit brief heyday of girl group music, including the Shangri-Las' "Leader of the Pack" and the Dixie Cups' "Chapel of Love." Leiber & Stoller, however, became disinterested in the business side of Red Bird and sold the label two years later, just as the girl group sound was on the wane. So, too, were the hit-making days of Leiber & Stoller on the wane. They continued to write songs, mostly for the Coasters, but they no longer dominated the pop and R&B charts the way they once did. Still, they survived, taking on the august role of rock & roll elder statesmen, eventually landing a spot in the Rock and Roll Hall of Fame in 1987. Later, their songs were the basis of a successful Broadway musical entitled *Smokey Joe's Cafe*, which revived interest in their great body of work, and also brought the music of Jerry Leiber & Mike Stoller to a whole new audience. Not bad for a couple of guys who, in the words of Mike Stoller, never wanted to write rock & roll songs, just good R&B. *—John Dougan*

The Leiber-Stoller Big Band / Jul. 15, 1960 / Atlantic ✦✦✦✦

- **Leiber & Stoller Present the Spark Records Story** / Aug. 14, 2001 / Ace ✦✦✦✦

Before becoming fully established as national hit songwriters and producers with the Coasters, Elvis Presley, and others in the late '50s, Jerry Leiber & Mike Stoller were two of the five partners in Los Angeles R&B indie label Spark. This collects 30 of the mid-'50s sides issued by the company, many of which were written and produced by Leiber & Stoller. In fact, this comprises the majority of Spark's output; it put out only 22 singles in all. Only three of these songs will be well-known: the Robins' classic comic R&B/rock numbers "Riot in Cell Block #9" and "Smokey Joe's Cafe," and Willy & Ruth's "Love Me," the original version of a song covered with considerable success by Presley in 1956. Just because the rest is damned obscure, however, doesn't mean it isn't worth checking out. Indeed, although Leiber & Stoller's talents had yet to blossom, this is a couple cuts above the norm for a mid-'50s R&B compilation. That's mostly because there's so much more humorous verve on this stuff than there was on much R&B and early rock that was immediately forgotten. The half-dozen cuts by the Robins (who, of course, evolved into the Coasters) are still the highlights, but there are exuberant jump blues and R&B novelties by the likes of the Honey Bears, Big Boy Groves & Band, and the Sly Fox (a raw bluesy cat by Spark's standards, or anyone's standards). Some routine ballads and straight R&B tunes are interwoven as well, but this is still recommended to both fans of Leiber & Stoller, and to R&B specialists looking for something that offers pleasure as well as scholarly insight. Blues harmonica player Garland the Great's "Strike a Match" was previously unreleased, and marks the first-ever appearance of this Leiber & Stoller composition. *—Richie Unterberger*

Leo's Sunship

Group / Urban

Don't let the extraterrestrial name fool you, Leo's Sunship played funky soul music and would have been around much longer if tragedy hadn't struck. The band revolved around singers Kenny Stover, Johnny Simon, and Allen Few; all were born under the astrological sign of Leo, thus the name. Stover is the brother of Elgie Stover who contributed to some Marvin Gaye songs and "The Bells" by the Originals; the Stovers are cousins of Harvey Fuqua (Moonglows and later Motown's Artist and Repertoire Director). Kenny is from Cleveland, OH, and grew up in the Hough area on 66th and Belvedere. He moved to Detroit with big brother Elgie and both did odd jobs for Harvey and Motown. When the company moved to Los Angeles, the Stovers followed and Kenny landed a staff songwriting job, as did Elgie. He met Johnny Simon and the two, along with Barbara Thompson and Doria Glass, toured as backing singers for Marvin Gaye; that's Simon and Stover you hear on Gaye's *Hear My Dear* album. Simon migrated from Atlanta, GA, to L.A. to tour with Stevie Wonder. He was an original member of the Wallace Brothers who, as high school teens, made some crude but charming records for Sims Records and other labels. After the Wallace Brothers disbanded, Simon toiled with the Naturals, who cut singles on Quadran,

Calla, and Shout Records. After the Naturals, he relocated to Los Angeles, befriended Stover, and landed a gig backing Marvin Gaye on tour.

An exciting showman with a vocal range from falsetto to a tough as nails, Marvin Gaye-ish tenor, Simon sought the spotlight and was eager to get involved with another group. The two met Few, about whom little is known, and formed Leo's Sunship. In 1977, Leo's Sunship had recorded four songs for a proposed album when Simon took ill; he never recovered and died of cancer in his early thirties. Lyons Records eventually finished and released *We Need Each Other* with nine songs, but four of the nine were simply alternate mixes of "Give Me the Sunshine," "I'm Back for More," "Get Down People," and "Madam Butterfly," with "Leo's Sunship" the only non-repeating track. "Give Me Sunshine" was a minor hit, but with the heart and soul of the group gone, they disbanded. Stover joined Finished Touch in 1978. *—Andrew Hamilton*

● **We Need Each Other** / 1978 / Expansion ♦♦♦♦

Ketty Lester (Revoyda Frierson)

b. Aug. 16, 1934, Hope, AR

Vocals / Pop-Soul, Traditional Pop

Singer Ketty Lester has a career that spans music, TV, film, and stage. Her cover of Dick Haynes' 1945 hit "Love Letters" went to number-five pop and number-two R&B on *Billboard*'s charts in the spring of 1962. The tune was originally the title theme from the 1945 Jennifer Jones movie.

Ketty Lester was born Revoyda Frierson on August 16, 1934, in Hope, AR. She was one of 15 children born into a farmer's family. After winning a scholarship in 1955, she moved to California and attended San Francisco City College, majoring in nursing. Lester sang in church and the school choir, and performed in summer stock theater. She also appeared as a contestant on the classic '50s game show *You Bet Your Life*. Meeting country singer/comedienne Dorothy Shay at the Purple Onion club (Where Shay was performing), Lester was introduced to producers Ed Cobb and Lincoln Mayorga. Herb Newman's Era Records released the resulting single, "I'm a Fool for You" b/w "Love Letters." DJs and listeners preferred the sparse, steamy B-side, making it a Top Five pop hit. The follow-up single, a cover of George Gershwin's "But Not for Me" from the musical *Girl Crazy*, peaked at number-41 pop during summer 1962.

Ketty Lester was issued that same year. It featured two singles, "You Can't Lie to a Liar" and a cover of Woody Guthrie's "This Land Is Your Land." Another Era single was "Fallin Angel" b/w "Lullaby for Lovers." She also recorded the upbeat "West Coast" b/w the ballad "I'll Be Looking Back" for Capitol, "I Said Goodbye to My Love" b/w "Queen for a Day" for Everest, and "Measure of a Man" b/w "Cracker Box Livin'," "Show Me" b/w "Since I Fell for You," and the LP *Same* for the Pete label.

Lester recorded for RCA (*Soul of Me*, *Where Is Love*, the singles "Better World," "Roses Grow With Thorns," "You Go Your Way," "Some Things Are Better Unsaid," "The Luck of Ginger Coff") and for Tower (*When a Woman Loves a Man*, "Love Me Just a Little Bit"). She also recorded a Christian album, *I Saw Him*, for Mega Records.

Originally offered the lead role in *Julia*, starring Diahann Carroll, Lester appeared in the films *Just for Fun*, *Up Tight*, *Uptown Saturday Night*, *The Terminal Man*, *Street Knight*, *House Party 3*, and *Blacula*, and the TV movies *Louis Armstrong: Chicago Style* and *Percy and Thunder*. She also guest-starred on TV series like *Sanford and Son*, *Laugh-In*, *Quantum Leap*, *Hill Street Blues*, *Love American Style*, *The FBI*, *Harry O* (the 1975 episode with Maureen McCormick), *That Girl*, *Marcus Welby*, and *Lou Grant*. She became a regular on *Little House on the Prairie* (as Hester Sue Terhune) and the soap operas *Days of Our Lives* (as Helen Grant) and *Rituals*. The singer won an Off-Broadway Theater Award for her performance in a revival of *A Cabin in the Sky*. *Lester* also had a recurring role as Vivica A. Fox's grandmother on the 1998 sitcom *Getting Personal*. *—Ed Hogan*

● **Love Letters** / Sep. 28, 1999 / Era ♦♦♦♦

Larry Levan (Lawrence Philpot)

b. Jun. 21, 1954, Brooklyn, NY, **d.** Nov. 8, 1992, New York, NY

DJ, Producer / Garage/House, Club/Dance, Disco, House

Neglected by many because of his early death and lack of recording, Larry Levan is one of the seminal names in dance music, a legendary inspiration during the 1970s and '80s. Influenced by David Mancuso's seminal Loft parties, which presaged disco by more than five years, Levan took his cue and transferred those communal vibes to clubland with one of the most famed nightspots ever, the Paradise Garage. For more than ten years, Levan's garage style was a wildly eclectic mix including any tracks (or parts of tracks) that would make people dance, including Motown and Philly soul, Afro-Cuban and Italian disco to new wave, punk and classic hard rock. He influenced hordes of hardcore club-goers and a wave of DJs ranging from Tony Humphries to Paul Oakenfold. More than anyone, Levan set the tone for New York disco in the 1970s and garage/house music during the '80s. By the '90s, mainstream New York dance swung to a diverse cast of dance artists, who had in common the one thing that united the records on Levan's decks: they were all soulful.

Levan began his first DJ residency while still a teenager, at a New York club called the Gallery in 1971. Both there and at his next club, the Continental Baths, Levan worked with (and profoundly influenced) the future godfather of house, Frankie Knuckles. After setting up the Soho Place midway through the decade, Levan joined the Paradise Garage in 1977 and began changing the face of dance music. Unlike other disco clubs around the city (including the notoriously hip, but musically flat Studio 54), the Paradise Garage featured a nightclub built on music, with attendees who were preferential about the music they danced to—not who they were seen by. Levan and engineer Richard Long supervised construction of what has been called the best sound system ever produced, and spent hours before opening each night to make sure that acoustics, speaker placement and atmosphere were perfect. To give club-goers the ultimate dance experienece, Levan used an assortment of subtle tricks; during the night, he would even upgrade the quality of his musical selections and turntable needles until music, mixer and dancers hit their peak simultaneously. (The Paradise Garage's sound system was so good in fact that it was later bought by the London super-club Ministry of Sound, carefully disassembled, shipped overseas and installed in a new space.)

By the beginning of the 1980s, disco's flame had been extinguished by a glut of sub-par recordings and rabid anti-disco movements. Levan continued playing to an increasingly underground (though still ecstatic) audience. He also began working on studio production as well, recording remixes and special dance versions of pop songs for labels like Salsoul, Prelude and West End as well as the occasional major label. Though many of his 12-inch productions were obscurities of the highest order (except in the crates of privileged DJs), tracks by the Peech Boys, Jimmy Castor Bunch, First Choice, Loleatta Holloway and Skyy became certifiable dance classics. By the mid-'80s, the sound of New York/Chicago house music had begun to infiltrate England.

In an ironic twist, however, the man who did much to pave the way for dance music wasn't around during its rebirth. By September 1987, the Paradise Garage had closed its doors. Though Levan's name appeared on several remixes and productions during the late '80s and early '90s, he spent only a fraction of his time in the studio compared to during his heyday. Levan returned to the DJ-ing booth on a 1992 trip to Japan with François Kevorkian, though he died as a result of AIDS complications later in the year. *—John Bush*

Paradise Garage / Dec. 5, 1995 / Salsoul ♦♦♦♦♦

Paradise Garage includes seven actual Levan post-productions from the vaults of Salsoul Records—previously released as the LP *Larry Levan's Greatest Hits, Vol. 2*. Each runs over six minutes, and the selections ("I Got My Mind Made Up" by Instant Funk, "Double Cross" by First Choice and an epic 13-minute mix of "Make It Last Forever" by Inner Life featuring Jocelyn Brown) include ones many clubbers would expect to hear on an average night at the Paradise Garage. It's a great look at one of the seminal names in dance music history, and one of the only albums of its type available. *—John Bush*

Larry Levan's Paradise Garage / Mar. 18, 2000 / West End ♦♦♦♦♦

This powerful compilation highlights the remixing skills of legendary DJ Larry Levan, who popularized the songs included on this album during his stint at New York's famous Paradise Garage disco. The songs, all released between 1979 and 1982, also often feature Levan contributing to the writing and production (he even moonlighted as a member of the NYC Peech Boys, whose classic "Don't Make Me Wait" is featured here). As one might expect, the remixes are expansive in length: The shortest runs six and a half minutes and the lengthiest tops out at around ten minutes. Despite their epic nature, these songs never become dull, thanks to Levan's ability to put a record's strongest, most hypnotic rhythms and hooks front and center in the remix, while also adding plenty of sound effects and mixing touches that provide interesting twists and turns to the dance-friendly material. A good example is Ednah Holt's "Serious, Sirius Space Party," which incorporates all sorts of spacy synthesizer effects and some surprising hard rock guitar solos into its midtempo groove to keep things interesting. Another song full of surprises is the aforementioned "Don't Make Me Wait," which is thickly layered with percussive touches, keyboard riffs, and whooshing sound effects that dart in and out of the mix to startling effect. However, the four Taana Gardner tracks may be the most impressive included here; the best of these is "Heartbeat," a sultry underground classic that turns an unusually slow-paced dance beat into the backbone of a hypnotic love song whose heat is raised by Gardner's seductive vocals. The package is topped off by an informative set of liner notes charting the genesis of each remix and also including interviews with the writer and producers involved in these songs. All in all, this compilation works both as an introduction to Levan's remixing skills and as a fine set of dance songs illustrating the underground disco scene at its finest. *—Donald A. Guarisco*

★ **Live at the Paradise Garage** / Sep. 5, 2000 / Strut/West End ♦♦♦♦♦

Larry Levan is one of the few legendary figures in contemporary dance music, a DJ and remixer whose reliance on audiophile-level sound, in both the clubs he played and the records he selected, set a standard that, according to many witnesses, has never been equalled. In the years after his death in 1992, dance fans were forced to content themselves with his remix work, which admittedly, made for some great post-productions. Despite the lack of material, his legend has persisted primarily as a DJ, and primarily for his residency at one of the most revered clubs in the history of dance, the Paradise Garage. And in late 2000, more than 20 years after it was recorded, a relic from another era appeared on the British rare groove label Strut Records. High expectations notwithstanding, Levan comes through with a stunning, invigorating 80-minute set of disco movers and sweet Philly soul, the performances almost as uplifting and the bass almost as chunky as they must've sounded at the original SoHo nightspot. Though it's virtually untouched by Levan's notorious genre-bending (the Clash's "Should I Stay or Should I Go" was a Garage favorite), *Live at the Paradise Garage* is one of the best, and best-sounding, documents of the disco era ever produced. And it's a rare latter-day disco fan who will have heard many of these tracks before; though many of the artists are familiar (the Supremes, Cher, Shalamar, the Chi-Lites, Ashford & Simpson), Levan selected songs with great productions or the right tone to reflect his moods. Though the spotlight is clearly on Levan's mixing, a few highlights do appear, including "Angel in My Pocket" by Change, "By the Way You Dance (I Never Knew It Was You)" by Bunny Sigler, and "Get on the Funk Train" by Giorgio Moroder's Munich Machine. Clearly a labor of love (as well as an invaluable musical and historical document) from the people at Strut, *Live at the Paradise Garage* includes a complete history of both the club and Levan himself, as well as dozens of photos and reminiscences from inheritors like François Kevorkian, Danny Tenaglia, Joe Claussell, and Danny Krivit included in its 36-page book. *—John Bush*

LeVert

f. 1984, Ohio

Group / Quiet Storm, Urban, Retro-Soul

The son of O'Jays founder Eddie LeVert, R&B vocalist Gerald LeVert launched his own recording career in the mid-'80s as the leader of the group LeVert. Rounding out the group was another one of Eddie LeVert's sons, Sean, in addition to member Marc Gordon, as the trio issued such popular recordings as 1985's *I Get Hot*, 1986's *Bloodline* (which spawned the number one hit single "Pop Pop Pop Goes My Mind"), 1987's *The Big Throwdown*, and 1988's *Just Coolin'*, as the latter two releases earned gold certification.

By the '90s, Gerald began to split his time between LeVert and a burgeoning solo career (including a collaboration with his father, titled *Father and Son*), as LeVert released such further hit albums as 1990's *Rope a Dope Style*, 1993's *For Real Tho'*, and 1997's *Whole Scenario*. 2001 saw the release of a 14-track compilation of LeVert's hits, *The Best of LeVert*, on Rhino Records. *—Greg Prato*

I Get Hot / 1985 / Tempre ✦✦✦
The first LP from LeVert—consisting of Ed LeVert's (O'Jays) two sons, Gerald and Sean, and friend Marc Gordon—sparked a debate in Cleveland. Particularly controversial was the single "I'm Still," a heart-stopping ballad sung in classic O'Jays' style. Nobody believed Gerald was singing lead (everyone thought it was Ed) and that Tempre Records was trying to pull a fast one, but it was indeed Gerald—proof that the apple doesn't fall far from the tree. The song did well on the R&B charts and established the band as serious crooners. Unfortunately, nothing else comes close to "I'm Still"; mundane ballads like "I Want Too" and formulaic bootie shakers such as "Dancing With You," "Jam" and "All in the Way You Dance" are easily forgettable. Even the title track lacks something. This album is essential only for "I'm Still," written by Gerald and Eddie LeVert—a song you won't find on any LeVert compilation LP. *—Andrew Hamilton*

Bloodline / 1986 / Atlantic ✦✦✦
When Eddie LeVert's two sons, Gerald and Sean, teamed with Marc Gordon to form their own trio, everyone in the R&B community expected great things. They didn't get off to a good start when they recorded for the tiny Tempre label, but once they moved to Atlantic, LeVert began building their image and reputation. They earned a number-one R&B hit with "(Pop, Pop, Pop, Pop) Goes My Mind" and followed it with a Top 20 single in "Let's Go Out Tonight." Gerald's delivery, tone and approach mirrored his father's; their harmonies and production were contemporary, yet also reflected The O'Jays' influence. *—Ron Wynn*

● **The Big Throwdown** / 1987 / Atlantic ✦✦✦✦✦
LeVert's second album started a run of hits that extended into the 1990s. They earned their first pop hit and second number-one R&B single with "Casanova," while "My Forever Love" was a solid follow-up and excellent ballad. Gerald LeVert proved his mettle as a lead singer; although not as explosive as his father, he had a similar gift for communicating a lyric, and he teamed nicely with brother Sean and Marc Gordon on ballads. LeVert's singles weren't as anthemic as The O'Jays', but they were established hitmakers on the urban contemporary scene. *—Ron Wynn*

Just Coolin' / Oct. 1988 / Atlantic ✦✦✦✦✦
LeVert scored with both uptempo and ballad cuts on their third Atlantic album. The single "Pull Over" clicked with dance audiences and was aided by a video that neatly played off the lyrical hook. The title track was also an urban contemporary radio hit and successful single, although the overall record didn't match the level of its predecessor, despite eventually going gold. In fact, the first signs of creative stagnation that would really surface on their next release were evident on such songs as "Take Your Time" and "Join in the Fun." *—Ron Wynn*

Rope a Dope Style / 1990 / Atlantic ✦✦✦
LeVert still sounded energetic and appealing on such cuts as "Nobody Does It Better" and "Hey Girl." Gerald LeVert will never have the same command or dramatic presence as his dad, but he's developed into a sincere, effective vocalist. But when the raps begin on the title cut or "Nobody Does It Better," not only do they mar the song's pace, they split the listener's focus and change the mood. It doesn't help that neither rap was exciting, either lyrically or performance-wise. *—Ron Wynn*

For Real Tho' / 1993 / Atlantic ✦✦✦

Whole Scenario / Mar. 11, 1997 / Atlantic ✦✦

● **The Best of LeVert** / Mar. 20, 2001 / Rhino ✦✦✦✦✦
The Best of LeVert highlights the exciting trio's blazing career. Not a complete overview but the best thing going until something more substantial comes along. Features the group's four R&B number-one singles: "(Pop, Pop, Pop) Goes My Mind," "Casanova," "Addicted to You," and "Just Coolin'," featuring Heavy D. Their stunning debut, "I'm Still" (Tempre Records), is missing—maybe licensing was an issue, but its addition would have solidified this set. The exclusion of other singles, notably "Join in the Fun," "Sweet Sensation," "Pose," and "Fascination" keeps this enjoyable collection from being definitive. *—Andrew Hamilton*

Gerald LeVert

b. Jul. 13, 1966, Cleveland, OH
Producer, Vocals / Urban, Retro-Soul

A contemporary soul singer whose smooth, yet robust vocals bring energy and emotion to even his most serene recordings, Gerald LeVert grew up in the shadows of his father, Eddie LeVert Sr. of the O'Jays. As a child, his father's status in the music industry nurtured and helped prepare Gerald for his prosperous music career as a writer, arranger, producer and performer. As Gerald was entering his adulthood, he, good friend Marc Gordon and his brother Sean formed the trio LeVert. They recorded their first single, entitled "I'm Still," on the independent Tempre label. Even though Gerald was still maturing as a vocalist, his powerful, stirring delivery on the single is worthy of praise. Peaking on the *Billboard* R&B charts at number 70, it survived for eight weeks.

Nonetheless, that single set up a deal with Atlantic Records the following year, and it could not have been a better move. Initially, Gerald recorded with the group, scoring five number-one singles, seven Top Ten singles and four Top 20 singles on the *Billboard* R&B charts, including the Reggie & Vincent Calloway-written and produced number-one single "Casanova," which also peaked at number four on the *Billboard* pop charts. He also managed to make room for a duet with labelmate Miki Howard, recording the number four single "That's What Love Is."

In 1991, Gerald released his solo debut album, entitled *Private Line*. The title track spawned his first number one single as a solo artist on the *Billboard* R&B charts. The following year, Gerald came back with a duet with his father and scored another number one single with "Baby Hold on to Me" and the number three single "School Me," reminiscent of Babyface's "Whip Appeal." However, in the midst of all his success, Gerald's only major pop appeal remained the "Casanova" single.

Pop producer David Foster presented a pop tune to Gerald, and "I Swear" became a number one and Top 20 hit on the pop and R&B charts, respectively. Subsequently, Gerald returned to Foster's stable to record "I'd Give Anything," also produced by Foster. Formerly a number-four country hit for Boy Howdy under the title "She'd Give Anything," Gerald's version managed a pop Top 30 hit. Intended for crossover appeal, the single was actually a bigger hit on the R&B charts, peaking at number four and reinforcing Gerald's major following among R&B music lovers.

In addition to his impressive string of hits, the Cleveland, OH, native has rendered his services as songwriter, vocalist and producer to many artists, such as the O'Jays, Barry White, Stephanie Mills, Troop, Teddy Pendergrass, the Winans, Patti LaBelle, Rude Boys, and on and on. In 1997, Gerald added another dimension to his prosperous career; he joined forces with R&B vocalists Keith Sweat and Johnny Gill under the acronym LSG, spawning the hit single "My Body." As a solo act, he released *Love & Consequences* the year following, returning in 1999 with *G*. *—Craig Lytle*

● **Private Line** / 1991 / East West ✦✦✦✦✦
The debut solo release from the Ohio native, which features a nice mixture of songs, spawned four charted singles. The vocal energy Gerald LeVert brings to his songs is revealed in each lyric. The first release was "Private Line." With a locomotive rhythm track and a churnin' horn arrangement, "Private Line" is complemented with a catchy hook line. It became a favorite among many, claiming the number-one spot on the *Billboard* R&B charts. The second release was the pop-oriented single "Baby Hold on to Me." This duet, with his father Eddie Levert Sr., is a splendidly arranged ballad in which father and son immerse themselves in the lyrics. Like its predecessor, it claimed the number-one spot and number 37 on the R&B and pop charts, respectively. The third single was "School Me." With its teacher-student lyrics, the gifted vocalist stays near the top of the charts with this single as well; it peaked at number three after 19 weeks. Gerald's knack for laying down lead and background vocals is demonstrated on this number. As explosive as his baritone is, Gerald is able to inject a smoothness to his delivery; that trait is admirable. The fourth single, "Can You Handle It," has Gerald combining wholesome vocals with contemporary rhythms. It too seized a Top Ten spot at number nine. Every track on this album is as appealing as the next. Gerald's vocals are in superb form. *—Craig Lytle*

Groove On / 1995 / East West ✦✦✦
Gerald LeVert's emotive baritone excels on *Groove On*. The LeVert feel is evident on every side. Productions, arrangements and songs are by Gerald LeVert and Edwin Nicholas, save for a couple, the most notable being "I'd Give Anything" by David Foster. "Answering Service" stands out with its opening monologue; "Have Mercy" illustrates Gerald's powerful begging style of delivery to perfection. A more even collection than his debut, *Private Line*. *—Andrew Hamilton*

Father and Son / Oct. 1995 / East West ✦✦✦✦✦
Father and Son is the first full-length collaboration between Gerald and Eddie LeVert, two singers who have sustained their popularity throughout the changing climate of soul and R&B for over two decades. Appropriately, the album falls into the middle ground between the heart-stopping, smooth soul of Eddie's group, The O'Jays, and the slicker, funkier LeVert, which featured Gerald. Largely produced by Gerald and his long-time associate Edwin "Tony" Nicholas—with Eddie and Dwain Mitchell handling some of the funkiest numbers—*Father and Son* showcases both of the vocalists to fine effect. Half of the album is devoted to sweeping ballads, like the single "Already Missing You" and "Don't Make Me Beg." The other half is full of funk workouts, including a smouldering cover of The O'Jays' "You Got Your Hooks in Me" featuring Walter Williams, the singer of the original, on lead. What holds *Father and Son* is the love and respect between Gerald and Eddie LeVert, which is evident by the way the two singers play off of each other. Most duos compete for the spotlight. Here, each vocalist lets the other shine. *—Stephen Thomas Erlewine*

Love & Consequences / Jul. 21, 1998 / East West ✦✦✦✦
On *Love & Consequences*, Gerald LeVert makes a few overtures to hip-hop, but he remains, in his heart, a sensitive lover-man—which is both a good and bad thing. LeVert is a powerful, soulful vocalist who can deliver love ballads as well as any of his contemporaries, but he doesn't always exhibit much musical imagination. "No Sense" may have cameos from rappers Lazy Bone and Ken Dawg, and "That's the Way I Feel About You" is a duet with Mary J. Blige, but they only illustrate that LeVert is from the old school and doesn't really have the desire to bring his music into the present. Which means, of course, that *Love & Consequences* isn't much different than any other LeVert album from the '90s—it has a slight modern sheen, but it's a quiet storm album at its heart. It doesn't offer any surprises, but LeVert is a professional—and that means there are enough solid songs here to make it enjoyable, but not quite enough to make the entire album memorable. *—Stephen Thomas Erlewine*

G / Sep. 21, 1999 / Elektra ✦✦✦

Gerald's World / Sep. 18, 2001 / Elektra ✦✦✦
LeVert has the smooth, sweet-talkin' lover-man thing down so well by now that he can practically sing an entire album without breaking a sweat or even thinking twice about what he's saying. And, on *Gerald's World*, he's as smooth and as sweet-talkin' as ever. But

there's something automatic about it all, a sense of security with the persona and legend he's built over the years. LeVert still may have a bedroom voice, but more often than not here, he seems about ready to call it a night. Which doesn't make *Gerald's World* an awful album, just an uninspired one. There are moments where his sweet tenor overrides the lackluster sentiment and sound, just as there are times where he plays straight into the arms of lovers everywhere. There's no doubt that this was conceived as a bedroom album—not one track breaks from the measured bump 'n' grind (he even gets all sentimentally squishy on "Made to Love Ya"). In other words, another Gerald LeVert album—nothing less, nothing more. —*Michael Gallucci*

The G Spot / Sep. 24, 2002 / Elektra ♦♦♦
This modern R&B stalwart has always offered the perfect blend of dreamy old-school soul textures; jangly, guitar-driven atmospheres; and slick, modern funk grooves. And oh, that voice—mellow and sexy, seductive to the core. The best "come to beddy bye" tone since Barry White, and so steeped in that era. The vibe on "Too Much Room" artfully merges all of those things and sounds like a modern twist on the O'Jays (where his dad, Eddie LeVert, still holds court), but he gets a little ambitious with the sometimes-annoying scowl/screech of guest artist Mystical. "Since You Ain't Around" is all bedroom-eyes fun, his vocals almost a plea. "Wilding Me Out" has a sparse production (mostly just Fender Rhodes and a rhythm track) that allows for one of the clearest vocal tracks on the recording. LeVert will hopefully educate some of his fans to the art of jazz with the inclusion of Roy Ayers' vibes on "Oh What a Night." LeVert's scatting duet with Ayers is a highlight. —*Jonathan Widran*

Barbara Lewis

b. Feb. 9, 1943, South Lyon, MI
Vocals / Soul, Pop-Soul, Uptown Soul
Pop-soul doesn't get much better than Barbara Lewis, whose seductive, emotive croon took "Hello Stranger" to number three in 1963. The Michigan native had been writing songs since the age of nine, and began recording as a teenager with producer Ollie McLaughlin, who'd also had a hand in the careers of Del Shannon, the Capitols, and Deon Jackson. Lewis wrote all of the songs on her debut LP (including "Hello Stranger"), and confidently handled harmony soul numbers (some with backing by the Dells) and more pop-savvy tunes, some of which, like "Hello Stranger," were driven by an organ and a bossa nova-like beat. Follow-ups to "Hello Stranger" didn't sell nearly as well (although one of her singles, "Someday We're Gonna Love Again," was covered by the Searchers for a British Invasion hit). In the mid-'60s, she began doing some recordings in New York City, with assistance from producers like Bert Berns and Jerry Wexler, that employed more orchestral arrangements and pop-conscious material. The approach clicked, both commercially and artistically: "Baby I'm Yours" and "Make Me Your Baby" were both big hits, and both among the best mid-'60s girl group style productions.

Lewis cut an album in the late '60s for Stax (on the Enterprise subsidiary) that, as one would expect, gave her sound a grittier approach, without compromising the smooth and poppy elements integral to the singer's appeal. It passed mostly unnoticed, though, and Lewis withdrew from the music business after a few other singles. The "beach music" scene of the Carolinas remains a bastion of appreciation for Lewis' records, which continue to enjoy popularity and airplay there decades after their original release. —*Richie Unterberger*

Many Grooves of Barbara Lewis / 1969 / Stax ♦♦♦
Although this late-'60s album isn't nearly as well known as her poppier mid-'60s hits, this is excellent sweet soul that avoids slickness. Still working with producer Ollie McLaughlin, Lewis recorded this set of strong soul-pop in Chicago. The slightly updated, gutsier tone of the arrangements did nothing to obscure her characteristically smooth and assured delivery. [The CD reissue adds three bonus tracks from singles.] —*Richie Unterberger*

★ **Hello Stranger: The Best of Barbara Lewis** / Jul. 19, 1994 / Rhino ♦♦♦♦♦
Some soul singers run hot, some run cool. Barbara Lewis ran cool, and thrillingly so. She was classy and sophisticated, even in the early to mid-'60s, a time where smooth pop-soul was the standard. Her voice was as soft as silk, and Atlantic gave her productions to match, resulting in an alluring body of work that still sounds seductive, yet comforting, years after their relief. During the mid-'60s, she hit the R&B charts steadily, crossing over to the pop charts with the number-three "Hello Stranger," plus the Top 15 "Baby, I'm Yours," and "Make Me Your Baby." Those three, along with the bulk of her R&B hits, are all on Rhino's excellent compilation, *Hello Stranger: The Best of Barbara Lewis.* Since her work was so consistently good, there are inevitably some fan favorites missing, but everything here is excellent, representing her at her very best—and that means it's among the very best pop-soul of its time (or ever, for that matter). —*Stephen Thomas Erlewine*

Bobby Lewis

b. Feb. 16, 1927, Hodgerville, KY
Vocals / R&B
Bobby Lewis is one of those talented performers whose recognition is confined to a single monster hit, "Tossin' and Turnin'." Released in early 1961, the single rode the charts to 23 weeks, eventually hitting the number one spot on both the pop and R&B charts. Lewis had other hits, including a Top Ten follow-up with "One Track Mind," and had been working for years before that, yet the one song came to be his signature.

Bobby Lewis was raised in an orphanage, and ran away from his foster home at age 14. He worked carnivals, and eventually joined the Leo Hines Orchestra in Indianapolis as a singer. He worked small clubs and theaters during the 1950s, and cut "Mumbles Blues" for the Spotlight label early in that decade, passed through the Mercury Records roster, and briefly hooked up with Nat Tarnopol, who also managed Jackie Wilson.

In late 1960, while appearing at the Apollo Theater in New York, Lewis stopped at the offices of Beltone Records, a small independent outfit in Manhattan, and was prevailed upon to record a song written by another artist on the Apollo bill, Ritchie Adams, called "Tossin' and Turnin'." The single was issued at the end of 1960, and lightning struck in 1961—sales of the record were so strong that for the only time in its history, Beltone issued an accompanying album by Lewis. None of his subsequent records sold remotely as well as the three-million copies of "Tossin' and Turnin'," and by the end of 1962, Lewis seemed to have run out his string; in 1963, Beltone itself went belly-up. Lewis later had limited success ("Stark Raving Mad") on ABC-Paramount, and was soon after consigned to rock & roll history, somewhat unfairly, as a one-hit wonder. —*Bruce Eder*

● **Tossin' and Turnin'** / 1992 / Relic ♦♦♦
Bobby Lewis had somewhat more to offer than the title track of this 17-song collection—a raw and honest "Lonely Teardrops," and the soulful "Oh Yes, I Love You," the powerful "Nothing But the Blues," and the upbeat "One Track Mind" are only a couple of highlights of this disc. The mastering is clean and the notes are exceptionally well detailed. —*Bruce Eder*

Jimmy Lewis

b. Apr. 11, 1918, Nashville, TN
Producer, Vocals / Soul, Retro-Soul, Country-Soul
A reasonably interesting second-division soul singer, Jimmy Lewis released almost a dozen singles in the 1960s, including a duet with Ray Charles near the end of the decade ("If It Wasn't for Bad Luck"), and wrote and arranged every track on Charles' 1969 album *Doing His Thing*; Lewis has also worked with Charles in the 1990s. He recorded for Charles' Tangerine label and wrote material for minor soul stars like Bobby Womack, Ted Taylor, and Z.Z. Hill. He continued to write for Hill during Z.Z.'s most commercially successful period at Malaco Records, and produced one of Malaco's more popular singers, Latimore.

The most widely known of Lewis' own recordings is the 1974 album *Totally Involved*, if for no other reason than its reissue on CD in the late '90s. It's respectable Southern-styled soul (although Lewis has been based in Los Angeles for his whole career), grittier than the norm at a time when the entire genre was sliding into slickness. Still, you can hear why Lewis didn't become a star; he was at the top of the journeyman level, but didn't have a style that truly stood out, either in terms of his vocal delivery (which sometimes recalled, but did not match, Sam Cooke) or material. The best representation of his legacy is the CD *Still Wanna Be Black*, which has the entire *Totally Involved* album and twelve unissued songs from the same era. —*Richie Unterberger*

Totally Involved / 1974 / Hotlanta ♦♦♦
A couple of comeback albums appeared in the '80s and '90s, but this was basically Lewis' only chance to show what he could do at the height of his powers. It was a pleasant, unremarkable record that seemed a bit more like a catalog of styles than an original vision. "It Ain't What's on the Woman" is a good Stax-styled slice of gospel-soul (with lengthy spoken parts); "Is That Any Way to Treat a Lady" hints at a Philly soul groove; "That Won't Stop Me From Loving You" has a smidgen of Norman Whitfield's early-'70s Temptations productions; and so forth. It's not necessarily an insult to point out Lewis' derivations. He's a competent singer and songwriter who projects a good-natured compassion, and if you specialize in early-'70s pop-soul, this isn't a bad thing to have. Go for the 1997 CD reissue *Still Wanna Be Black*, though, which has everything on the album, and adds 12 unreleased songs from the same period. —*Richie Unterberger*

Golden Classics / 1993 / Collectables ♦♦♦♦

● **Still Wanna Be Black** / Nov. 18, 1997 / Kent ♦♦♦♦♦
The core of this 20-song CD reissue is Lewis' 1974 album, *Totally Involved*; Ace has essentially more than doubled the length of that record by adding 12 unreleased tracks from the same era. The unreleased bonus tracks are at least up to the standard of *Totally Involved*, and perhaps a tad better in their slightly earthier blends of pop and roots soul. He gets into some bluesy down-home soul on "I Intend to Take Your Place," and delivers a good statement of black pride, somewhat along the lines of a deep-soul Curtis Mayfield, on "Still Wanna Be Black." —*Richie Unterberger*

Linda Lewis

b. London, England
Vocals, Guitar / Urban, Northern Soul, Blue-Eyed Soul, Singer/Songwriter, Soft Rock
Born in London, Linda Lewis made her stage debut as a child, performing alongside her mother and father in the clubs near her East End home. In 1961, again encouraged by her parents, Lewis landed a bit part in the swinging film *A Taste of Honey*; another small role found her playing a star struck fan in the Beatles' 1965 film *Help.*

Acting, however, was never her first ambition. Rapidly building a reputation as a singer, she performed alongside bluesman John Lee Hooker and R&B band Herbie Goins & the Nighttimers. Signing to Polydor in 1967, the youthful Lewis cut her first single, "You Turned my Bitter into Sweet"; soon after, she joined the soul-rock outfit Ferris Wheel, alongside Diana Ferris, Bernie Holland (later of Jody Grind) and Dennis Elliot, who would go on to both If and Foreigner. A live favorite in the U.K., Lewis and Ferris Wheel also found moderate success overseas, as they undertook a succession of European tours. Working with producer Ian Samwell, Ferris Wheel cut two albums, *Can't Break the Habit* in 1967, and a self titled effort in 1970, together with a handful of singles, including "I Can't Break the Habit," "Let it be Me," "The Na Na Song" and "Can't Stop Now." Ferris Wheel disbanded in 1970.

In 1971, Lewis signed a solo deal with Warners/Reprise, having been introduced to the label by her boyfriend (and now label-mate) Jim Cregan of Family. She also launched a career as a session vocalist. Over the next few years, her powerful (not to mention idiosyncratic) range could be heard on hit albums by Al Kooper, Cat Stevens, David Bowie (she appears on 1973's *Aladdin Sane* LP), among others.

Lewis' own debut album *Say No More*—again produced by Samwell—was released in 1971, along with several singles, including "We Can Win" and "Old Smokey." Two years later, she followed up with *Lark*, well-produced by Cregan, and released on Reprise's newly launched Raft subsidiary. *Lark* proved to be an early, shining moment, taking

Lewis into the U.K. charts with "Rock-a-Doodle-Doo" in June 1973, where the song peaked at number 15 and marked Lewis' debut on the British chart show *Top of the Pops*. She also visited America as part of Cat Stevens' massive tour that year. Lewis' final Reprise album, in 1974, *Fathoms Deep*, was followed by the compilation *Heart Strings*, an excellent collection that remained unsurpassed until 2002 brought the CD collection *Reach For The Truth: The Best Of The Reprise Years*.

Moving to Bell, the punningly titled "Cordon Blues" single appeared in 1974, before Lewis was transferred to the sibling Arista label in 1975, releasing her triumphant *Not a Little Girl Anymore* LP, featuring contributions from Lowell George, Allen Toussaint and the Tower of Power horn section, among others. A new single covering Betty Everett's 1964 U.S. R&B Top Ten hit "The Shoop Shoop Song (It's in his Kiss)" appeared alongside; now retitled simply "It's In his Kiss." Lewis took her version to number six on the U.K. charts. The song made a splash Stateside as well, giving the singer her only U.S. hit in July 1975.

Further singles "Baby I'm Yours" and "Winter Wonderland" followed in 1976. While 1977 brought the critically acclaimed *Woman Overboard* album, together with further 45s "Man in the Moon," "Come Back and Finish What you Started" and "Bonfire." Lewis also maintained a high profile on the session circuit, appearing alongside Rick Wakeman, Chris Spedding, Steve Harley and Rod Stewart—husband Cregan, of course, was currently a member of the latter's band, and had himself also worked alongside Harley. As the 1970s drew to a close, it may have appeared that Lewis' own career was beginning to wind down. Rather then let things slip away, however, the singer signed to Ariola and released a knockout of an album, the Mike Batt-produced *Hacienda View* in 1979, as well as spinning out a string of singles, including "109 Jamaica Highway" and "I'd Be Surprisingly Good for You." *A Tear and a Smile*, debuted in 1983 and was well received.

With well over a decade of non-stop touring, performing and recording behind her, Lewis went to ground not long after, spending some time in Los Angeles—another ten years would elapse before she returned, with December 1995's *Second Nature* LP. A massive smash in Japan, the album rocketed to the top of that country's charts and it's success sparked a string of sell out gigs that were recorded and compiled on the 1996 live album *On The Stage—Live in Japan* (released, with one extra track, as *Born Performer* in Japan). An EP, *What's All this About*, followed in 1996; 1998's *Whatever* and 1999's *Kiss of Life* consolidated her comeback. *—Amy Hanson*

Say No More / 1971 / Reprise ✦✦✦

When even her first "best-of" collection (1974's *Heart Strings*) ignores one of the three albums at its disposal, you know there's something oddly amiss about the record in question. And elsewhere, too, Linda Lewis' first solo album is rarely afforded more than a second glance, as a clearly inexperienced vocalist steps out beneath the tutelage of two comparative giants—producer Ian Samwell and guitarist Jim Cregan—but no firm ideas of exactly how she wants to present the songs she's written. Look behind the often tentative performances, and the often unsympathetic production, however, and *Say No More* really doesn't deserve its obscurity. At least some of the credit has to go to a dynamite band arrayed behind her—guitarist Chris Spedding, Pentangle drummer Terry Cox, and King Crimson alumni Ian McDonald all make notable contributions to the landscape. But Lewis, too, has her moments. Balanced between the love songs that lined Lewis up alongside a host of other early-decade singer/songwriters, and the more personal observations of people and places that would quickly see her step to the front of the line, *Say No More*'s greatest strength is its refusal to allow its naiveté to hinder Lewis' performance. "Hampstead Way" and "Peter's Garden" are both lovely ruminations, while "Funky Kitchen" overcomes the disadvantages of a frankly dreadful title (and chorus) to illustrate her refusal to be tied to one sound. It would be another year or so before *Lark*, her second album, truly led Lewis out of the shadows. But the best of *Say No More* at least sent her on her way. *—Amy Hanson*

Lark / 1972 / Reprise ✦✦✦✦

The best of Linda Lewis' early-'70s output, *Lark* was cut before she broke into public gaze via her cameo performance on David Bowie's *Aladdin Sane*, and thus provided a point of reference for anyone induced to find out more about her. Built, again, around her instinctive musical (and personal) partnership with guitarist Jim Cregan, *Lark* is nevertheless light years ahead of her debut album, showcasing Lewis alongside a hard-hitting rhythm section that would, just a year or so later, be providing similar duties for John Cale, bassist Pat Donaldson, and drummer Gerry Conway. Only the absence of *Say No More* guitarist Chris Spedding spoils the party, but Cregan is equal to the task. The biggest difference between this album and its predecessor is in the presentation of Lewis' voice. No longer a wild weapon that can soar from childlike lilt to screaming dog whistle without a moment's notice, she channels her range to the emotions it demands, an economy most noticeable on the folky "It's the Frame," which finds her accompanied by her own guitar alone. Produced by Cregan and Lewis, *Lark* also finds space for some dramatic experimentation—opening and closing the album, the gentle "Spring Song" and the poetic "Little Indians" find her working against a landscape of Emile Latimer's dramatic percussion (and muted guitars), with the latter recorded live at Croydon's legendary Fairfield Hall, in front of an audience that is clearly spellbound by the event. Also of note is the keys-heavy title track, a studio *tour de force*, conjuring up atmospheres as free and easy as Lewis' vocal gymnastics. The end result is an album that, even today, defines Lewis at her dramatic best—and sounds as fresh to modern ears as it did to Bowie fans back then. *—Amy Hanson*

Fathoms Deep / 1973 / Reprise ✦✦✦

Perhaps the biggest surprise about the best-known of Linda Lewis' Reprise label albums is that it doesn't feature the best known of her Reprise-era songs. Though the single "Rock a Doodle Do" hit the U.K. Top 20 even as *Fathoms Deep* commenced its own rise, the hit was excluded from the main attraction—and sensibly so. Even among Lewis' staunchest supporters, the slinky, squeaky single was seen as a novelty. Helmed by a virtual supergroup featuring the likes of R&B masters Bobby Tench, Max Middleton, folkie Danny Thompson, and rocker Philip Chen, alongside the inevitable Jim Cregan, *Fathoms Deep* is a true singer/songwriter's album, tasteful and tight, but punctuated with variety enough to ensure that it never sinks into repetitive, whiny balladeering. Even when Lewis' taste for introspection does bubble to the surface, there is always something on hand to keep the heart pumping—the celeste that haunts "Lullabye," for example, or the almost radical synths that rise to race "Wise Eyes" around the block. Indeed, if *Fathoms Deep* has one major failing, it's that the dexterity of the musicians (Lewis' own guitar and keyboard playing included) and the ambition of the arrangements occasionally overwhelm the still slight and occasionally freakish nature of her vocal style. Again, there's a reason why "Rock a Doodle Do" wasn't included, and it's a shame to spoil the party by letting elements of it gatecrash. Thankfully, however, there's enough else on display to allow you to ignore them. *—Amy Hanson*

Heart Strings / 1974 / Reprise ✦✦✦

Although it has since been superseded by 2002's U.K. *Reach for the Truth* anthology, 1974's *Heart Strings* remains a worthy, if patchy, introduction to Linda Lewis' early-'70s catalog. Drawing, for the most part, from her second and third Reprise label albums, but leaving her debut completely untouched, *Heart Strings* also scoops up three single-only tracks, "Safe and Sound," "Sideway Shuffle," and the June 1973 U.K. hit "Rock a Doodle Do." Released following Lewis' departure to Arista, but prior to her Top 20 re-emergence with "It's in His Kiss," *Heart Strings*' primary objective was to illustrate the sheer dynamism of Lewis' style. As a songwriter, Lewis possessed a youthful elegance and optimism that dovetailed perfectly with her unmistakable and effervescent vocal style, whether she was sadly balladeering in a little girl chirrup, or letting rip excitedly with octave scaling, glass-shattering shrieks. It was her utter refusal to rest easy in either soul or pop sounds that made her material so special. And on *Heart Strings* that dichotomy is amplified, resulting in an album that surely packs as many moods as it has tracks. *—Amy Hanson*

Not a Little Girl Anymore / 1975 / Arista ✦✦✦

The title says it all. No matter how well-loved Linda Lewis was during her days at Reprise, still the focus of both marketing and material was on the sheer youthful glee with which she attacked every performance. Her debut at Arista, however, was built around her determination that, at last, she was going to be treated like an adult, a vow that proved to have been fulfilled long before you reached the sultry, resolute title track. Packing more covers than any of her earlier albums, *Not a Little Girl Anymore* nevertheless emerges as Lewis' most well-rounded and, perhaps, personal album yet. Cat Stevens' "(Remember the Days Of) The Old Schoolyard," a somewhat forced exercise in nostalgia in its writer's hands, is here imbibed with a genuine sense of emotion and regret. However, there is no time for maudlin reflection as "It's in His Kiss (Shoop Shoop Song)," a wily cover of the Betty Everett classic, simply erupts out of the song's closing notes with a rambunctious passion that suggests kissing is only the first thing on Lewis' mind. From there on, and to paraphrase one of the album's other prime cuts, Lewis rollercoasters through a succession of moods and styles, ranging from the emotive soul of Gwen Guthrie's "This Time I'll Be Sweeter" to her own (stylistically, aptly titled) "My Grandaddy Could Reggae," a reminder of the versatility that past albums occasionally allowed to overwhelm content, but which here is balanced with delicate precision. And, as you approach the end, the gentle "I Do My Best to Impress" leaves the listener with one thought. You succeeded. *—Amy Hanson*

● **The Best of Linda Lewis** / 1997 / Camden ✦✦✦✦✦

The Best of Linda Lewis contains all of her infectious, Northern soul-styled disco singles from the mid-'70s, including the U.K. hit cover of "It's In His Kiss," "Baby I'm Yours," and John Martyn's "May You Never." Though Lewis is always in good voice, the songs are somewhat uneven, especially toward the end of her career. Nevertheless, the disc stands as the definitive retrospective of her career. *—Stephen Thomas Erlewine*

● **Reach for the Truth: Best of the Reprise Years 1971–74** / Oct. 29, 2002 / Rhino ✦✦✦✦

Although one of her later albums was titled *Woman Overboard*, singer/songwriter Linda Lewis never made much of a splash on the States. Maybe she was just a little ahead of, or behind the times with her jazz/pop/soul/folk. Or more likely her squeaky little girlish voice just wasn't taken seriously enough in the pre-Cyndi Lauper era. Heavily influenced by Stevie Wonder, she released three very good albums plus the *Heartstrings* compilation during the titular years, all of which are represented in this anthology. Generously packed with 23 tracks including one previously unreleased selection (a closing acoustic demo version of "Red Light Ladies," the tune that also opens the album), rare photos, extensive liner notes and track-by-track descriptions from Lewis in the 24 page book, it's hard to imagine a more perfect single disc representation of her material from these years. Those who caught up with the singer later in her career when she gravitated to her slicker disco/pop mode (exemplified by her version of Betty Everett's "The Shoop Shoop Song") might find this more organic approach too self-conscious, but the material holds up surprisingly well nearly 30 years after it was recorded. In fact a more extensive collection that might include her less substantial work for Arista, would weaken the impact of this disc. Unlike many collections that are compiled by the artist, this delivers a near perfect overview of the period's highlights, seen through the filter of the decades. Dated slightly by the piano heavy production, the sound remains crisp with Lewis' remarkable voice and shimmering tunes commanding the spotlight. The non-chronological sequencing is particularly effective, and only the lack of individual musician credits by song keeps this from being a definitive package from this short but productive period. *—Hal Horowitz*

Ramsey Lewis

b. May 27, 1935, Chicago, IL

Keyboards, Piano / Pop-Soul, Crossover Jazz, Jazz-Pop, Soul-Jazz, Northern Soul

Ramsey Lewis has long straddled the boundary between bop-oriented jazz and pop music. Most of his recordings (particularly by the mid-'60s) were very accessible and attracted a large non-jazz audience. In 1956, he formed a trio with bassist Eldee Young and drummer Red Holt. From the start (1958), their records for Argo/Cadet were popular, although in the early days, they had a strong jazz content. In 1958, Lewis also recorded with Max Roach and Lem Winchester. On the 1965 albums *The In Crowd* and *Hang On*, Ramsey made the pianist into a major attraction and from that point, on his records became much more predictable and pop-oriented. In 1966, his trio's personnel changed with bassist Cleveland Eaton II and drummer Maurice White (later the founder of Earth, Wind & Fire) joining Lewis. In the 1970s, Lewis often played electric piano, although by later in the decade he was sticking to acoustic and hiring an additional keyboardist. He can still play melodic jazz when he wants to, but Ramsey Lewis has mostly stuck to easy listening pop music during the past 30 years. *—Scott Yanow*

The Choice! The Best of the Ramsey Lewis Trio / 1965 / Cadet ✦✦✦✦✦
Before assaulting the R&B and pop charts with "The In Crowd," the Ramsey Lewis Trio recorded exemplary swinging club jazz. This 1965 package came out in the same year that "The In Crowd" exploded and represents the Ramsey Lewis Trio's most popular recordings prior to their emergence. There's more improvising and the arrangements are intricate enough to display each member's chops. The selections revisit the trio's debut, *Ramsey Lewis & His Gentlemen of Swing* (Argo, 1956), with "Carmen." The Ramsey Lewis Trio recorded for three labels under Chess' umbrella: Argo, Cadet, and Chess. A good LP if you can find a copy; it represents their early years well. *—Andrew Hamilton*

● **The In Crowd** / May 13, 1965-May 15, 1965 / Chess ✦✦✦✦✦
This is the record that put the legendary Ramsey Lewis on the map. Lewis is known as an incredible stylist on piano, comfortably adapting almost any kind of music into his own jazz fusion vision. Film scores, pop, light classical hall fit comfortably into his music, and this album is an excellent example of his vision. But, it's not only Lewis alone. His absolutely fabulous rhythm section of Red Holt (drums) and Eldee Young on (bass/cello) frame all of Ramsey's performances with funk and grace and a superior forward momentum. Aside from the groovin' hit "The In Crowd," the album contains fantastic readings of Duke Ellington's "Come Sunday" and the "Love Theme From Spartacus." This album is one of the places where Afro- and funk-jazz started, and aside from it's historical significance, it's a stone groove. *—Matthew Greenwald*

Hang on Ramsey / Oct. 14, 1965-Oct. 17, 1965 / Cadet ✦✦✦
Considering that this album was an obvious follow-up to "The In Crowd," it is surprising that the music is not more commercial; that would happen in the near future. As it was, pianist Ramsey Lewis (assisted as usual by bassist Eldee Young and drummer Red Holt) had another big hit in "Hang on Sloopy," and the set (as with the previous one) was recorded at a club before an enthusiastic crowd. The enjoyable LP also includes a couple of Beatles tunes (their version of "A Hard Day's Night" caught on), "He's a Real Gone Guy," "Billy Boy" and "Hi-Heel Sneakers" among the highlights. This was the final full-length recording by the group before Young and Holt left to form their own band. *—Scott Yanow*

Wade in the Water / May 26, 1966-Jun. 29, 1966 / Jazz Time ✦✦✦✦✦
With Cleveland Eaton II (bass) and Maurice White (drums) replacing Eldee Young and Red Holt in the trio, Ramsey Lewis alters course just a bit from his handclapping soul-jazz idiom that was so popular at the time. The two new sidemen are relegated more to the background, and some punchy big band charts by Chicago's Richard Evans share the spotlight with Lewis' gospel/blues-drenched piano. Nevertheless, the old swinging fervor is left intact this time, as Lewis and company purvey a set of ten pop hits with a few others worked in. They even got a large-scale hit (number 19 on the pop charts) out of the old gospel tune "Wade in the Water" (the photo of the tall, pretty model doing so on the cover might have struck some as being sacrilegious). The best cut of the bunch is the hard-swinging, down-home treatment of the Stevie Wonder hit "Up Tight" that got almost as much airplay as the title track. Like "The In Crowd," this record evokes its era indelibly. *—Richard S. Ginell*

Dancing in the Street / 1968 / Cadet ✦✦✦✦
Only a little over a year old at the time of recording, this incarnation of the Ramsey Lewis Trio—Ramsey Lewis, Cleveland Eaton II and Maurice White (later of Earth Wind & Fire)—were well on their way to the pristine and symbiotic gel that would define their style. They were, however, still undergoing that process when they laid down this "live" set at San Francisco's *Basin Street West* club in July 1967. It's that somewhat formative vibe that makes this particular performance such a complete and utter joy. *Dancing in the Street* is this trio's recorded debut and, across a wide range of covers and styles, it's a captivating portrait of contemporary jazz. The title track, a cover of the Martha & the Vandellas R&B classic, is so smooth and stylish that it nearly outshines the original. "Django," meanwhile, is a delightful tribute to the Belgian gypsy musician Django Reinhardt. Lewis pays further homage to the greats across his cover of the Billy Taylor classic "Mood For Mendes." Also of note is the Ramsey Lewis Trio's rendition of the country song "You Don't Know Me." Originally a hit for Jerry Vale in 1956, it was revisited in 1960 by Lenny Welch and again in 1962 by Ray Charles, and it's from that great bluesman's version that Lewis took his cue with this wonderful jam. These three musicians are a joy to hear, and it's within their far-reaching vision, and the effortless incorporation of so many styles into contemporary jazz, that they were—and remain—among the genre's finest. *—Amy Hanson*

Maiden Voyage (And More) / 1968 / Chess ✦✦✦
This pop-oriented CD reissue brings back the highlights from pianist Ramsey Lewis' two Argo records *Maiden Voyage* and *Mother Nature's Son*. Although Lewis' trio of the time (with bassist Cleveland Eaton II and drummer Maurice White) is heard prominently, they are accompanied by strings, voices (including Minnie Riperton) and (on the last four numbers) a large orchestra. There are some good piano solos but the Charles Stepney arrangements (which are lavishly praised in the liner notes) are period pieces as is much of the material which includes selections from Lennon & McCartney, Bob Dylan, Burt Bacharach ("Do You Know the Way to San Jose") and Aretha Franklin. Even Herbie Hancock's "Maiden Voyage" and Mike Gibbs' "Sweet Rain" sound like pop tunes. One can hear the beginnings of the crossover music of the 1980s and '90s in recordings such as this one but the performances have not dated all that well. *—Scott Yanow*

Another Voyage / Sep. 1969 / Cadet ✦✦✦
Issued in September 1969, *Another Voyage* is one of the Ramsey Lewis Trio's best efforts, during its initial release making it into the R&B Top 35. With the lineup of Lewis, drummer Maurice White, and bassist Cleveland Eaton II, the LP serves as a prime example of the muscular Chicago sound while preserving the pianist's trademark elegance. In addition to such throbbing, kinetic workouts as Eddie Harris' "Bold and Black" and "If You've Got It Flaunt It, Pts. 1-2," there's a nice mid-groovin' cover of Stevie Wonder's "My Cherie Amour," Harris' contemplative "How Beautiful Is Spring," and the sumptuous "Opus V," written by Charles Stepney. Of special note is future Earth, Wind & Fire leader White's use of the kalimba on "Uhuru." The pumping "Do What You Wanna" became a post-release favorite during the late '90s and was included on the two-LP set *Inside Ramsey Lewis*. *—Ed Hogan*

The Best of Ramsey Lewis / 1970 / Cadet ✦✦✦
By the time this was released Lewis had enjoyed over a decade of commercial success. As one of the more popular jazz artists, Lewis effortlessly dabbled in soul, and his playing was always engaging even as some album ideas that were often ill advised at best. Prior to this retrospective, Cadet also released other compilation efforts including *Choice! The Best of the Ramsey Lewis Trio*. This 1970 set does a great job of collecting some of his best '60s performances and features great representations of Lewis' myriad styles. "The In Crowd," recorded live at Bohemian Caverns with Lewis' trio, was the pinnacle of his soul-filled and engaging style. Subsequent attempts at the same style, "Hang on Sloopy" and "Wade in the Water," try to recapture the magic to no avail. Lewis' best trait of this era was his ductile nature. By the late '60s, he moved on to more adventurous production values. The innovative "Jade East" has a singular sound, an elastic bass pattern, and, again the artist's work is animated and refined. Herbie Hancock's "Maiden Voyage" gets an even more dramatic production that features echoed voices and Lewis' judicious playing. Charles Stepney's "Les Fleur" from the *Maiden Voyage* album features backing vocals from Minnie Riperton. The last track here has Lewis turning Sam and Dave's "Soul Man" into hard-driving lounge jazz. Although this doesn't stand as a classic overview, *The Best of Ramsey Lewis* does feature him at his late-'60s best. *—Jason Elias*

Upendo Ni Pamoja / Jan. 1972 / CBS ✦✦✦
This marked Ramsey Lewis' third album for Columbia and the first to feature the Ramsey Lewis Trio. The most famous members had gone on to other successes. Red Holt and Eldee Young were signed to Atlantic as Young-Holt Unlimited, and of course later member Maurice White founded Earth, Wind & Fire. *Upendo Ni Pamoja* has the rhythm section of bassist Cleveland Eaton II and drummer Morris Jennings. Unlike many early-'70s sets, *Upendo Ni Pamoja* is a pretty straight-ahead date without Lewis indulging in tracks with funky overtones. Covers predominate here. The trio does a fairly true though subdued take on War's "Slippin' into Darkness" with Lewis on Fender Rhodes. Lewis' gentle playing is found throughout "People Make the World Go Round," although this version of the trio did an even better live take on the *Save the Children* soundtrack. The best cover, Michael Jackson's "Got to Be There," has Lewis playing a Steinway Concert Grand with an arrangement that spotlights the trio sound. The smooth title is one of Lewis' finest songs of the period. The problem with this is that few tracks stay with the listener. This is a cut or two away from being truly essential. *—Jason Elias*

Funky Serenity / 1973 / Columbia ✦✦✦

Sun Goddess / 1974 / Columbia ✦✦✦✦

Don't It Feel Good / 1975 / Columbia ✦✦✦

Salongo / 1976 / CBS ✦✦✦
Those shocked or even dismayed by the lack of jazz on 1975's *Don't It Feel Good* would no doubt be pleasantly surprised by this. Released in 1976 and produced by Maurice White and Charles Stepney, *Salongo* offers a more substantial look at African and Latin styles. Around this time Lewis always had the good fortune to be supported by good bands and excellent side players like Verdine White, Ernie Watts, Jorge Strunz, as well as many others. The first track, "Slick" mixes Latin flourishes with straight-ahead jazz. The only less than stellar track is "Aufu Oodu," which has Lewis getting lost in the Earth, Wind & Fire-derived production style. More convincing is the title track and it has a great bassline, tough drumming, strong horn arrangement, and, of course, smooth and quick electric piano solos from Lewis. The seductive "Brazilica" is a non-cloying experiment in Latin music, and is well known by fans of commercial '70s jazz and quiet storm. For the poignant "Nicole," Lewis plays both electric piano and acoustic with equal deftness and emotion. The last track, the methodical "Seventh Fold," was written by Stepney and has his characteristic adventurous approach and a sweeping string arrangement. *Salongo* earns most of its raves by being one of the few albums of the time to sidestep commercial considerations. The effort is also one of Lewis' best at getting his eclectic nature and is more enjoyable than the better-selling *Sun Goddess*. *—Jason Elias*

Tequila Mockingbird / 1977 / Columbia ✦✦

The Greatest Hits of Ramsey Lewis / 1987 / Chess ✦✦✦
From a rock or pop listener's perspective, this is inarguably Lewis' most essential material. This 18-song double album has all four of his Top 40 hits from 1965-1966 ("The In Crowd," "Hang on Sloopy," "A Hard Day's Night," and "Wade in the Water"), as well as various other cuts from 1961-1966 LPs and singles, dominated by covers of popular Motown, R&B, and pop songs. Its unabashed pop-friendly approach isn't going to impress serious jazzbos, but then, Lewis wasn't pretending to make serious art during this period. He aimed to stake out some pleasant jazz-R&B-pop grooves with good hooks, and—with

the help of sidemen like drummer Maurice White (later in Earth, Wind & Fire) and the rhythm section of Eldee Young and Red Holt (soon to form the similar Young-Holt Unlimited)—he succeeded. *—Richie Unterberger*

The Electric Collection / Mar. 15, 1991 / Columbia ♦♦♦
Although slick and commercial, most of the 1970s sides gathered on the 1991 CD *Electric Collection* are decent, creative and tasteful. Ramsey Lewis, who's heard on both acoustic piano and electric keyboards, sounds genuinely inspired on meaty yet accessible material ranging from jazz-funk workouts like "Come Back, Jack," and "The Messenger" to the playful "Blues for the Night Owl." If "Tequila Mockingbird" seems greatly influenced by Earth, Wind & Fire, it's because most of his sidemen on that appealing number are members of the soul/funk powerhouse. To be sure, there are a few duds here, including the dreadful, muzak-like "I'll Always Dream About You" and an unimaginative cover of EWF's "That's the Way of the World." But gratefully, throwaways don't dominate this generally enjoyable, though never outstanding, compilation. *—Alex Henderson*

In Person: 1960–1967 / Apr. 7, 1998 / GRP ♦♦♦♦♦
Ramsey Lewis' 1965 hit "The In Crowd" made him a major name in the pop world and resulted in some similar live sets that featured audience participation, singing and rhythmic handclapping. Actually, Lewis had had previous success in the pop/jazz world, and two of the five live albums that were skimmed for this 1998 two-CD set (none of the dates are reissued completely) predate "The In Crowd." Lewis is teamed with bassist Eldee Young and drummer Red Holt for the first four dates; they are replaced by bassist Cleveland Eaton II and drummer Maurice White on the last session. The music is taken from *The Ramsey Lewis Trio in Chicago, At the Bohemian Caverns, The In Crowd, Hang on Ramsey* and *Dancing in the Street*, all originally Argo or Cadet LPs. Highlights include "Ole Devil Moon," "Carmen," "My Babe," "The In Crowd," "Hang on Sloopy" and a "Black Orpheus Medley." It's a fine sampling of 1960s Ramsey Lewis. *—Scott Yanow*

Smiley Lewis (Overton Lemons)

b. Jul. 5, 1913, DeQuincey, LA, **d.** Oct. 7, 1966, New Orleans, LA
Vocals, Piano / New Orleans R&B, R&B, New Orleans Blues, Piano Blues
Dave Bartholomew has often been quoted to the effect that Smiley Lewis was a "bad luck singer," because he never sold more than 100,000 copies of his Imperial singles. In retrospect, Lewis was a lucky man in many respects—he enjoyed stellar support from New Orleans' ace sessioneers at Cosimo's, benefited from top-flight material and production (by Bartholomew), and left behind a legacy of marvelous Crescent City R&B. We're lucky he was there, that's for sure.

Born with the unwieldy handle of Overton Lemons, Lewis hit the Big Easy in his mid-teens, armed with a big, booming voice and some guitar skills. He played clubs in the French Quarter, often with pianist Tuts Washington (and sometimes billed as "Smiling" Lewis). By 1947, his following was strong enough to merit a session for DeLuxe Records, which issued his debut 78, "Here Comes Smiley." Nothing happened with that platter, but when Lewis signed with Imperial in 1950 (debuting with "Tee-Nah-Nah") things began to move.

As the New Orleans R&B sound developed rapidly during the early '50s, so did Lewis, as he rocked ever harder on "Lillie Mae," "Ain't Gonna Do It," and "Big Mamou." He scored his first national hit in 1952 with "The Bells Are Ringing," but enjoyed his biggest sales in 1955 with the exultant "I Hear You Knocking" (its immortal piano solo courtesy of Huey Smith). Here's where that alleged bad luck rears its head—pop chanteuse Gale Storm swiped his thunder for any pop crossover possibilities with her ludicrous white-washed cover of the plaintive ballad. But Storm wouldn't dare come near its roaring flip, the Joe Turnerish rocker "Bumpity Bump," or some of Smiley Lewis' other classic mid-'50s jumpers ("Down the Road," "Lost Weekend," "Real Gone Lover," "She's Got Me Hook, Line and Sinker," "Rootin' and Tootin'"). In front of the Crescent City's hottest players (saxists Lee Allen, Clarence Hall, and Herb Hardesty usually worked his dates), Lewis roared like a lion.

Strangely, Fats Domino fared better with some of Smiley Lewis' tunes than Lewis did ("Blue Monday" in particular). Similarly, Elvis Presley cleaned up the naughty "One Night" and hit big with it, but Lewis' original had already done well in 1956 (as had his melodic "Please Listen to Me"). His blistering "Shame, Shame, Shame" found its way onto the soundtrack of the steamy Hollywood potboiler *Baby Doll* in 1957 but failed to find entry to the R&B charts. After a long and at least semi-profitable run at Imperial, Lewis moved over to OKeh in 1961 for one single, stopped at Dot in 1964 just long enough to make a solitary 45 (produced by Nashville DJ Bill "Hoss" Allen) and bowed out with an Allen Toussaint-produced remake of "The Bells Are Ringing" for Loma in 1965. By then, stomach cancer was eating the once-stout singer up. He died in the autumn of 1966, all but forgotten outside his New Orleans home base.

The ensuing decades have rectified that miscarriage of justice, however. Smiley Lewis' place as one of the greatest New Orleans R&B artists of the 1950s is certainly assured. *—Bill Dahl*

★ **The Best of Smiley Lewis: I Hear You Knocking** / Nov. 3, 1992 / Capitol ♦♦♦♦♦
Smiley Lewis made several fabulous singles, had a booming, terrific voice, and received the same great backing and support that defined the city's R&B sound. But Lewis' records seldom made it outside New Orleans, even though they were frequently brilliant. This great 24-track anthology contains the four that did make it to the charts, among them the signature song "I Hear You Knocking." It shows Lewis doing first-rate novelty tracks, ballads, weepers, uptempo wailers, and blues, and making wonderful recordings. The set also includes a thorough discography and good notes and is superbly mastered. It's magnificent, exuberant R&B, and deserved a much better national fate than it enjoyed. *—Ron Wynn*

Shame, Shame, Shame / 1993 / Bear Family ♦♦♦♦♦
This is an exhaustive, multi-disc set comprising everything recorded by this New Orleans singer. With the songwriting talents of Dave Bartholomew aboard, utilizing the sound of the legendary J&M Studios, and the best Crescent City musicians available, this is truly New Orleans music at its very best. *—Cub Koda*

Jimmy Liggins

b. Oct. 14, 1922, Newby, OK, **d.** Jul. 18, 1983, Durham, NC
Vocals, Guitar / Jump Blues, R&B
Another of the jump blues specialists whose romping output can be pinpointed as a direct precursor of rock & roll, guitarist Jimmy Liggins was a far more aggressive bandleader than his older brother Joe, right down to the names of their respective combos (Joe led the polished Honeydrippers; Jimmy proudly fronted the Drops of Joy).

Inspired by the success of his brother (Jimmy toiled as Joe's chauffeur for a year), the ex-pugilist jumped into the recording field in 1947 on Art Rupe's Specialty logo. His "Tear Drop Blues" pierced the R&B Top Ten the next year, while "Careful Love" and "Don't Put Me Down" hit for him in 1949. But it's Liggins's rough-and-ready rockers—"Cadillac Boogie," "Saturday Night Boogie Woogie Man," and the loopy one-chord workout "Drunk" (his last smash in 1953)—that mark Liggins as one of rock's forefathers. His roaring sax section at Specialty was populated by first-rate reedmen such as Harold Land, Charlie "Little Jazz" Ferguson, and the omnipresent Maxwell Davis.

Liggins left Specialty in 1954, stopping off at Aladdin long enough to wax the classic-to-be "I Ain't Drunk" (much later covered by Albert Collins) before fading from the scene. *—Bill Dahl*

● **Jimmy Liggins and His Drops of Joy** / 1989 / Specialty ♦♦♦♦♦
The music of Jimmy Liggins differs greatly from his elder brother Joe's in many respects. Whereas Joe was a more schooled musician, Jimmy was harder, brasher and altogether from the rougher and cruder side of the street. This 25-track collection brings together all the notable tracks Jimmy recorded for Art Rupe's Specialty label between 1947 and 1954. The music Liggins made during his stay at the label produced several R&B hits, most notably the jump-blues perennial "Drunk" (complete with crudely overdubbed lead vocal) and the proto-rock & roll classic "Cadillac Boogie," which in turn provided the basis for Jackie Brenston's "Rocket 88." *—Cub Koda*

Rough Weather Blues, Vol. 2 / 1992 / Specialty ♦♦♦♦♦
Here are 25 more Specialty cookers, including an undubbed version of "Drunk," plenty of horn-leavened jump blues outings, and several unissued artifacts (including a rare example of the Drops of Joy getting jazzy on "Now's the Time"). *—Bill Dahl*

Joe Liggins

b. Jul. 9, 1915, Guthrie, OK, **d.** Aug. 1, 1987, Lynwood, CA
Vocals, Piano / Jump Blues, R&B
Pianist Joe Liggins and his band, the Honeydrippers, tore up the R&B charts during the late '40s and early '50s with their polished brand of polite R&B. Liggins scored massive hits with "The Honeydripper" in 1945 and "Pink Champagne" five years later, posting a great many more solid sellers in between.

Born in Oklahoma, Liggins moved to San Diego in 1932. He moved to Los Angeles in 1939 and played with various outfits, including Sammy Franklin's California Rhythm Rascals. When Franklin took an unwise pass on recording Liggins' infectious "The Honeydripper," the bespectacled pianist assembled his own band and waxed the tune for Leon Rene's Exclusive logo. The upshot: an R&B chart-topper. Nine more hits followed on Exclusive over the next three years, including the schmaltzy "Got a Right to Cry," the often-covered "Tanya" (Chicago guitarist Earl Hooker waxed a delicious version) and "Roll 'Em."

In 1950, Joe joined his brother Jimmy at Specialty Records. More hits immediately followed: "Rag Mop," the number-one R&B smash "Pink Champagne," "Little Joe's Boogie," and "Frankie Lee." During this period, the Honeydrippers prominently featured saxists Willie Jackson and James Jackson Jr. Liggins stuck around Specialty into 1954, later turning up with solitary singles on Mercury and Aladdin. But time had passed Liggins by, at least right then; later, his sophisticated approach later came back into fashion, and he led a little big band until his death. *—Bill Dahl*

★ **Joe Liggins & the Honeydrippers** / 1989 / Specialty ♦♦♦♦♦
Pianist Joe Liggins presented a fairly sophisticated brand of swinging jump blues to jitterbuggers during the early '50s, when his irresistible "Pink Champagne" scaled the R&B charts. This collection has 25 of his very best 1950-1954 Specialty sides including a tasty remake of "The Honeydripper;" "Rhythm in the Barnyard," and the syncopated "Going Back to New Orleans" (recently revived by Dr. John). *—Bill Dahl*

Lightnin' Rod (Jalal Mansur)

Vocals / Blaxploitation, Funk, Social Commentary, Old School Rap
A former member of the Last Poets, Lightnin' Rod helped pioneer the spoken-rhyme style that would one day become rap. His most renowned album, *Hustler's Convention*, told the story of an ill-fated ghetto "player" and featured backing instrumentation by an early incarnation of Kool & the Gang. *—Dan Heilman*

● **Hustler's Convention** / 1973 / Fuel 2000 ♦♦♦

Lil Suzy (Suzanne Casale)

b. Mar. 1, 1979, New York, NY [Brooklyn]
Vocals / Freestyle, Club/Dance, House
Freestyle diva Lil Suzy was born Suzanne Casale in Brooklyn on March 1, 1979. While still a toddler she was discovered performing on Manhattan Beach, and at age five appeared live at the famed disco Studio 54; in the months to follow she became a staple of the New York City club circuit. At age eight Lil Suzy appeared on the syndicated TV series *Star Search*, and in 1991 released her debut album, *Love Can't Wait*; the record's first single, "Take Me in Your Arms," became a massive club hit, and she was named *Billboard*'s Best New Dance Artist in 1992. After releasing *Back to Dance* in 1994, Lil Suzy formed Empress Records, at age 17 becoming the nation's youngest record label

president; her first release for the imprint, *Life Goes On*, appeared in 1995. *Paradise* followed two years later, with *Lil Suzy: The Megamix* appearing in 1999. *—Jason Ankeny*

- **The Greatest Hits** / Nov. 20, 2001 / Empire Musicwerks ✦✦✦✦

Lipps Inc.

f. 1979, Minneapolis, MN

Group / Disco, Dance-Pop, Club/Dance

Before hard funksters like Prince and the Time hit the national stage, before groundbreaking alternative rockers Hüsker Dü and the Replacements, Minneapolis was barely a blip on America's musical radar—that is until Lipps Inc. broke out with one of disco's most monumental singles, the number one smash "Funkytown." The brainchild of producer/songwriter Steven Greenberg, Lipps Inc. (meant to be pronounced as a pun on "lip sync") wound up as one-hit wonders, but that one hit still stands as one of disco's all-time classics; its computerized feel and lean, spare arrangement contrasted sharply with the perceived excesses of most disco music, yet its longing for escape (specifically, from Minneapolis, whose music scene was still in its infancy) fit the spirit of the era perfectly, sending it to the top of the charts for a full month in 1980.

A multi-instrumentalist, Greenberg had played in several bands and had been trying for some time to secure a production deal. He finally caught the Casablanca label's interest with a disco track called "Rock It," which became something of a hit locally. Casablanca asked Greenberg for a full album, and he gathered a cast of session players that initially included guitarists David Rivkin and Tom Riopelle, keyboardist Ivan Rafowitz, and bassist Terry Grant. Most importantly, he recruited lead vocalist Cynthia Johnson, the 1976 Miss Black Minnesota, who had been performing with an early version of the Time. Released nationally in late 1979, "Rock It" failed to catch on; the group's debut album, *Mouth Music*, was released in early 1980 and when "Funkytown" was pulled as a second single, it was an instant hit, climbing to number one just a couple months later and spending four weeks on top. In the wake of its success, "Rock It" was re-released, but flopped again. The six-song release *Pucker Up* followed, featuring a disco remake of the British pub rock group Ace's hit ballad "How Long." It didn't attract much attention, however; neither did the next Lipps Inc. full-length, *Designer Music*.

Johnson was already decreasing her involvement with the group, with Melanie Rosales picking up some of the slack; Johnson left for good in 1983. By the time Lipps Inc. threw in the towel, though, they'd begun to open things up on the Minneapolis music scene, not to mention giving valuable early experience to several future members of Prince's band the Revolution. *—Steve Huey*

- **Funkyworld: The Best of Lipps, Inc.** / 1992 / Casablanca ✦✦✦✦✦

Generally perceived as a one-hit wonder group, this compilation culls the strongest compositions from Lipps Inc.'s entire output of three releases. While one can instantly raise an eyebrow as to the validity of these songs being perceived as hits, there are some admittedly strong cuts that would appease even the stiffest of critics. Production foreshadowing both the imminent arrival of electro and Minneapolis boogie is glazed with Cynthia Johnson's consistently passionate vocals. And though the true reason for most people to pick this up is the obvious anthem ("Funkytown"), patient listening and resisting the urge to hit the eject button are rewarded with previously undisclosed riches. *—Rob Theakston*

Lisa Lisa & Cult Jam

f. 1985, **db.** 1991

Group / Club/Dance, Dance-Pop, Freestyle, Electro

Based in Brooklyn, vocalist Lisa Lisa (born Lisa Velez) and her supporting band Cult Jam (Mike Hughes and Alex "Spanador" Mosley) were one of the most consistent pop-funk/R&B groups of the mid-'80s. Hughes and Mosley were also members of Full Force, the funk group that performed and produced the majority of Lisa Lisa & Cult Jam's albums.

Lisa Lisa & Cult Jam recorded their debut single, "I Wonder If I Take You Home," soon after forming in 1985, releasing it as an independent single. The group quickly signed to Columbia Records, which re-released the single; it climbed into the R&B Top Ten and the U.K. Top 20. The group amassed a number of hit songs throughout the '80s, yet by the end of the decade their success had begun to dry up; they disbanded after 1991's *Straight Outta Hell's Kitchen*. Lisa Lisa embarked on a solo career, releasing the commercially unsuccessful *LL 77* in 1993. *—Stephen Thomas Erlewine*

Lisa Lisa & Cult Jam With Full Force / 1985 / Columbia ✦✦✦

Lisa Velez's last name was forgotten after the single "I Wonder If I Take You Home" elevated Lisa Lisa & Cult Jam into the national spotlight. Her voice had the perfect mix of uncertainty, irony and edge, while Full Force's production was state-of-the-art for the time. There was also a fine ballad on the album, "All Cried Out," presenting Lisa Lisa's vulnerable side, and is arguably still her finest performance. Lisa Lisa and company eventually earned a platinum album and were on their way. *—Ron Wynn*

- **Spanish Fly** / 1987 / Columbia ✦✦✦✦✦

Full Force was still hot as they produced a second consecutive platinum LP for Lisa Lisa & Cult Jam. This time, the group scored two number-one pop hits with "Head to Toe" and "Lost in Emotion," and even "Someone to Love Me For Me" had its moments. Lisa Lisa was an ingenue one moment and a tough, hardened survivor the next. The album peaked at number seven on the pop charts, but was also the apex of their union. Lisa Lisa was already beginning to show signs of strain, and the bottom would fall out on the next release. *—Ron Wynn*

Straight Outta Hell's Kitchen / 1991 / Columbia ✦✦✦✦

There weren't many kudos handed out for this album, even though producers Robert Clivilles and David Cole (C & C Music Factory) did half the tracks. They were then the premier honchos in dance music and were enlisted to restore the luster to Lisa Lisa & Cult Jam. But the voice that was once effective in a variety of emotional situations now seemed lethargic and unconvincing, while Full Force's production efforts on the album's second half were even more disconcerting. *—Ron Wynn*

LL 77 / 1994 / Pendulum ✦✦

Once a major disco and hip-hop diva, Lisa Lisa had been missing in action for several years when she released *LL 77*. She returned without either Full Force or UTFO, and tried to tap into the hip-mama scene with this collection of tracks that blend cautionary numbers with laments, heartache tracks and dance-pop. Her voice is neither dynamic nor memorable, but Lisa Lisa does a competent job of maintaining her energy level on such tracks as "Why Can't Lovers" and "Knockin' Down the Walls." Much of this is faceless, generic material, and it was a short comeback for Lisa Lisa. *—Ron Wynn*

- **Past, Present & Future** / May 7, 1996 / Navarre ✦✦✦✦✦

Past, Present & Future stands as the most complete compilation of Lisa Lisa & Cult Jam's hits, assembling all eight of their U.S. *Hot 100* hits, as well as three new songs and one new remix. The music still sounds fresh and innocent, bringing to mind old high school dances and romances, without sounding cliched or dated. What the album could use, however, is much more extensive liner notes and improved cover art. This album includes all of the bands hits, beginning with the early freestyle crossover jams "I Wonder If I Take You Home" and "Can You Feel The Beat" to the tragic high school romance ballad "All Cried Out," which resurfaced in the mid-'90s as a Top Ten hit for the vocal group Allure. The album's highlights, of course, are their two number-one hits "Head to Toe" and "Lost in Emotion," which established them as one of the premier hit-making acts of the mid- to late '80s. To round out the hits are "Little Jackie Wants to Be a Star," an earthy and organic cautionary tale about success and its pitfalls, and their surprise 1991 house-dance smash "Let The Beat Hit 'Em," produced by then-ultra-hot Clivilles & Cole of C & C Music Factory fame. The new tracks on this set don't quite live up to their golden-era hits, but include a fun remake of Teena Marie's "I Need Your Lovin' " and a new hip-hop remix of "I Wonder If I Take You Home." All in all, a surprisingly great album, with the hits sounding just as fun and fresh as they did when they first hit the airwaves. *—Jose Promis*

Little Anthony & the Imperials

f. 1958, Brooklyn, NY, **db.** 1975

Group / Doo Wop, R&B, Soul

Featuring the high-pitched vocals of Anthony Gourdine and a brace of solid material, Little Anthony & the Imperials had a much longer chart run than the majority of doo wop groups from the '50s. When the dust finally settled, the group clocked in with a total of ten entries in the *Hot 100* between 1958 to 1974, including "Tears on My Pillow," "Two People in the World," "Wishful Thinking," "Oh Yeah," "So Much," "Shimmy Shimmy Ko Ko Bop" (not to be confused with the similarly titled "Shimmy Shimmy Ko Ko Wop" by the El Capris), "When You Wish Upon a Star," "Goin' Out of My Head," "Better Use Your Head," and "Hurt So Bad."

Gourdine formed the group in the mid-'50s after his previous group, the Duponts, disbanded. Grabbing friends Clarence Collins, Ernest Wright, Tracy Lord and Nat Rogers, the group was originally called the Chesters, but had their name changed to the Imperials by popular New York disc jockey Alan Freed. Gourdine's vocal similarities to the popular Frankie Lymon-inspired "kiddie group" sound, coupled with a tendency to chop up syllables and overstress lyrics, made theirs a style deceptively simple yet enduring. After revamping the group in 1964 down to a quartet (Lord and Rogers left, and Sammy Strain joined), the sound changed from doo wop to a harder, more uptown R&B sound, best exemplified on hits like "I'm on the Outside Looking In." Little Anthony decided to work as a solo artist in 1975, while Collins continued the act in Las Vegas for many years. Sammy Strain went on to great success as a member of the O'Jays, and Ernest Wright joined as one of the Platters and sang with the group Europa. For many lovers of the genre Little Anthony & the Imperials are simply New York-styled doo wop at its smoothest and finest. *—Cub Koda*

We Are the Imperials Featuring Little Anthony / 1959 / End ✦✦✦

The group's debut album on the End label contains their first couple of big hits, "Two People in the World" and "Tears on My Pillow," along with album filler such as "Cha Cha Henry" and "Oh Yeah," as well as old standards like "When You Wish Upon a Star" and "Over the Rainbow." Almost worth having for the cover alone, this is one of the classics of '50s vocal-group harmony. *—Cub Koda*

Shades of the 40's / 1961 / End ✦✦✦✦

This album was a genuine surprise at the time of its release, and remains so today. An effort to send Anthony Gourdine and company down the same road toward mainstream pop music being followed by Jackie Wilson and, to a degree, Sam Cooke, the surprise is that it actually worked with Little Anthony & the Imperials. In fact, this might be the most listenable album of its kind this side of *The Supremes Sing Rodgers & Hart*. Opening with a smooth rendition of Duke Ellington's "Don't Get Around Much Anymore," Gourdine and the rest of the group show a genuine sympathy toward and understanding of the material, and the arrangements, if not exactly earth-shattering in their originality, are nicely in sync with the group and the repertory. "Undecided" could sound so ridiculously coy in the hands of almost any R&B group that it's almost a revelation here for being done "straight." Gourdine's powerful vocalizing at the end of "If You Are But a Dream" moves into Jackie Wilson territory in terms of its intensity, while "All or Nothing at All" is done in a playful, bouncy style. The group also milks "I'll Never Smile Again" for all of its pathos without ever getting near self-parody, and plunges successfully into a slow ballad mode on "A Lovely Way to Spend an Evening" (which became their final End Records single). Gourdine explores the tougher, more soulful side of his singing on numbers like "Dream." None of this is what fans of "Tears on My Pillow" would be buying as a first choice (that's their other End album), but it's all amazingly good, valid music. *—Bruce Eder*

I'm on the Outside (Looking In) / 1964 / DCP ✦✦✦

Producer Teddy Randazzo surrounds one of the '60's classiest ballads with Easy Listening retreads: "The Girl from Ipanema," "Exodus," "People," and "Funny." Updates of Burt Bacharach & Hal David's "Make It Easy on Yourself," and "Walk on By" have a more contemporary sound, and share a similar subject line with Randazzo's lamenting "I'm on the Outside Looking In." A new take on "Tears on My Pillow" provides a good blast from the past. An obvious rush job to capitalize on the success of the title song. *—Andrew Hamilton*

Goin' Out of My Head / 1965 / DCP ♦♦♦
A misery loves company set, the theme is unrequited love, and other than their many greatest hit packages, it's Little Anthony and the Imperials' best LP. Contains three aching ballads: "Goin' Out of My Head," "Hurt So Bad," and "Take Me Back." The unsung goodies include "What a Difference a Day Made," "I Miss You So," and a premium upgrade of "Who's Sorry Now." *—Andrew Hamilton*

Payin' Our Dues / 1967 / Veep ♦♦
After a successful stint with DCP Records, cutting classics like "I'm on the Outside Looking In" and "Goin' Out of My Head," Little Anthony & the Imperials experienced dog days at Veep Records. Most thought the hits would keep a-coming; after all, Teddy Randazzo, who produced them at DCP, was still in the cockpit. Not. Who knows what happened, but their Veep stint essentially killed them as major players on the recording tip. They later cut some nice Philly sounds with Thom Bell for Avco Embassy, but nothing crossed into the Top 40. *Payin' Our Dues* is the first of four Veep albums. That it may be the best of the lot is not saying much. Randazzo used too much seasoning; the tracks are too fussy, and the voices muddled—something that a CD remastering job would clear up, if someone ever decides to released their Veep work in that format. "Better Use Your Head," a sorry attempt at revving up their sound, was treated with cold indifference by DJs and record buyers—and it was the LP's lead single. "It's Not the Same" is a progeny of "Goin' Out of My Head," but is not as arresting. Other efforts—"Call Me the Joker," "Cry My Eyes Out," and "Lost Without You"—are not nearly as pristine as previous recordings. *—Andrew Hamilton*

Out of Sight, Out of Mind / 1969 / United Artists ♦♦♦
After a string of hits that made them one of the biggest doo wop and R&B groups of the late '50s and early '60s, Little Anthony & the Imperials survived most of the '60s dabbling in soul, surf harmonies, and psychedelia. Not that the Imperials cut another *Psychedelic Shack* or went on about the swells at Newport Beach, mind you; but they did combine their dreamy vocal blend with a bit of James Brown funk and some "Age of Aquarius" production touches. On the former end, Little Anthony (aka Anthony Gourdine) breaks it down here with his share of screams and "lookey here" exclamations on "Let the Sunshine In"; on the latter, Fifth Dimension end, if you will, he leads the group on smooth love pop sides like "You Bring Me Down." Dipping into the *Hair* soundtrack again, the group come up with one of the album's highlights in their rendition of "Easy to Be Hard." And while the one doo wop-era number, "The Ten Commandments of Love," seems out of place, other cuts like the "Summer's Comin' In," "I Look at You," and "The Ride" feature a fine mix of soul-pop arrangements, strong harmonies, and Gourdine's supple vocal work. Even though it's caught somewhere between the classic sound of the group's early hits ("Goin' Out of My Head") and a fully realized, "summer of love" soul offering, this title will ultimately be worthwhile for Little Anthony fans. *—Stephen Cook*

On a New Street / 1973 / Avco Embassy ♦♦♦
Avco divided this project between two producers, side A being the Thom Bell side and side B the Teddy Randazzo side. The Randazzo sides fall short of previous productions. "That's What Love Is All About" is a decent midtempo number, but had no chance of competing with the O'Jays, Temptations, Stylistics, Dramatics, and others. "Sooner or Later"'s doo wop leanings makes it sounds awfully dated. "Heartaches Never Entered My Mind" is the best of the Randazzo songs; Anthony sings with genuine emotion. "Easier Said Than Done" attempts to rekindle the magic of past Randazzo/Little Anthony & the Imperials collaborations, but falls short. The Bell sides save the LP. Anthony's reading of "I'm Falling In Love With You" is simply beautiful; the sound is typical Bell, except that he lets the Imperials croon the backing blends without any female supplement. Thom Bell & Linda Creed's "Lazy Susan" and "I Don't Have Time to Worry" reminds you of the Spinners; before the Little Anthony project came along, I'm sure these were on the Spinners to-do list. Both could have used a little less formula, but the latter does provide a vocal workout for Anthony. Blue Magic comes to mind when listening to "The Loneliest House on the Block"; a muted trumpet accents the breaks, and the song is almost as sad as "Sideshow." Anthony has a nice tone on "La, La, At the End," a quiet stormer that floats along some melodic grooves; the arrangement will have you swaying in your seat, as muted backing vocals chime briefly on the chorus, accented by a babbling trumpet and Anthony's signature lead. *—Andrew Hamilton*

● **The Best of Little Anthony & the Imperials** / Oct. 1989 / Rhino ♦♦♦♦♦
"Little" Anthony Gourdine's angst-ridden leads were ideal for tearjerkers and heartache ballads. Although this Brooklyn group began in the doo wop era, they were much more effective on soul songs, where group harmonies were low-key and Gourdine's voice was the major focus. This anthology includes "Hurt So Bad," "I'm on the Outside Looking In" and "Take Me Back," arguably their three finest hits, plus several others with equally theatrical vocals, but dissimilar chart performances. *—Ron Wynn*

The Best of Little Anthony & the Imperials / May 28, 1996 / EMI ♦♦♦
Unlike the collection of the same name on Rhino, this focuses solely on their mid- to late-'60s recordings for Veep and United Artists. That means you don't get any doo wop, but slickly arranged pop/soul that sometimes borders on easy listening, featuring string charts and Little Anthony's choked vocals (which could bring to mind an effeminate Johnny Mathis). The best and biggest of these cuts are also on the Rhino comp ("I'm on the Outside Looking In," "Goin' Out of My Head," "Hurt So Bad"), which gets the edge for its wider chronology. This is a satisfactory alternative, though, for those who prefer the Imperials' later phase, or want a more extensive sampler of their '60s stuff. *—Richie Unterberger*

We Are the Imperials/Shades of the 40's / Jun. 9, 1998 / WestSide ♦♦♦♦

Little Beaver (William Hale)

b. Aug. 15, 1945, Forrest City, AR
Guitar / Funk, Soul
Born William Hale on August 15, 1945, in Forrest City, AR, Little Beaver moved to Florida when he was a teenager. After recording for other labels, he recorded sides for the Cat label, an imprint of Henry Stone's TK Records of Hialeah, FL. His first charting singles were "Joey" and "Wish I Had a Girl Like You" b/w "Six Foot Hole." The next single, the hit "Party Down, Pt. 1," was later sampled by rap and hip-hop artists, like so much of the TK catalog. The midtempo groover was his biggest record. The *Party Down* LP featured vocals by Betty Wright and keyboards by Benny Latimore ("Let's Straighten It Out") and Timmy Thomas ("Why Can't We Live Together"). Post-"Party Down" singles were "Let the Good Times Roll" b/w "Let's Stick Together," both on the *Party Down* LP; "Little Girl Blue"; "I Can Dig It Baby" (co-written by Hale, Betty Wright, and Willie Clarke) b/w "Get Into the Party Life"; "Give a Helping Hand" b/w "Mama Forgo"; "Funkadelic Sound"; and "We Three." Other Little Beaver albums are *Little Beaver, Black Rhapsody, When Was the Last Time,* and *Beaver Fever,* which was credited to Willie "Beaver" Hale (all were released on Cat). *—Ed Hogan*

Joey / 1972 / Cat ♦♦
Willie "Little Beaver" Hale's melodic guitar ably accompanies his strident tenor on seven ho-hum songs written by Hale himself. "Joey," a slow, bluesy number, made a minor chart run and is easily the LP's most commercial offering. "I'm Losin' the Feelin'" is a crippled, shuffling beat tells of fading love, accented by Hale's tasty guitar licking away like a cat at a feeding bowl. On most tracks' Hale plays lead and rhythm via overdubbing, as exemplified on "What the Blues Is," a pleasant, jaunty roller. "Katie Pearl" is a personal account about a chick "that sure knows how to love her man"; on her death bed she (Katie Pearl) confesses to her mother to tell Little Beaver to record the song he wrote especially for her. "Two Steps From the Blues," the only selection that Hale didn't write, doesn't start cooking until it's nearly over, and unnecessary strings mar both "That's How It Is" and "Give a Helping Hand." *—Andrew Hamilton*

Black Rhapsody / 1974 / Cat ♦♦♦

● **Little Beaver** / 1974 / President ♦♦♦♦♦

Party Down / 1975 / President ♦♦♦
Everybody liked Little Beaver; he played guitar on TK sessions for Betty Wright, Latimore, Timmy Thomas, and others, so owner Henry Stone threw him a bone every now and then and let him record under his name. He never came up with enough quality material to fill an album, but that didn't stop TK Records from issuing Little Beaver LPs. *Party Down* features both sides of Little Beaver's finest recording, the jazzy "Party Down"; the melodic, lilting winner features his articulate lead guitar and sweet chord progressions. Only "Get Into the Party Life" is comparable; it too has jazzy overtones but is not as compelling. Nothing else merits any attention span; two cuts—"Let's Stick Together" and "I Can Dig It Baby"—sound ragged, incomplete, and not ready for release. *—Andrew Hamilton*

When Was the Last Time / 1976 / Cat ♦♦

Little Caesar & the Romans

f. 1961, **db.** 1962
Group / Doo Wop, R&B
Near the end of the doo wop era, this Los Angeles group made the Top Ten with the nostalgic "Those Oldies But Goodies (Reminds Me of You)," a piano-based ballad that sounded a bit like a bridge between the Five Satins and Little Anthony & the Imperials. Doo wop's days were numbered when this was a hit in 1961, and indeed the song's title would quickly become a catch-all phrase for rock records of all kinds that had left the charts several years ago.

Little Caesar & the Romans went on to record a few singles, and an LP, for Del-Fi in 1961 and 1962, some in a quaint vocal group manner heavily derivative of "Those Oldies But Goodies," others in a rougher, uptempo R&B mold akin to fellow L.A. artists the Olympics. They made the middle of the Top 100 with the dance tune "Hully Gully Again," and topped out at number 101 with "Memories of Those Oldies But Goodies," a single that was even *more* nostalgic than its prototype. The act, which performed in togas for a while, broke up in 1962, partly as a result of a silly dispute between lead vocalist Carl Barnett and David Johnson (who did the spoken bridge of "Those Oldies But Goodies") as to who was the *real* Little Caesar. *—Richie Unterberger*

● **Toga! Toga! Toga!** / Mar. 17, 1998 / Del-Fi ♦♦♦♦♦
Everything ever recorded by this one-shot group, with 20 tracks assembled from their singles, their sole album, and five previously unreleased songs. Almost everyone will be satisfied to limit their Little Caesar & the Romans collection to "Those Oldies But Goodies" (available on countless oldies compilations). But the rest is respectable R&B-flavored early rock, showing the group capable of handling both slow ballads and fast rock tunes with a raucous edge, although this is heavy on cover versions of previous hits. "Memories of Those Oldies But Goodies" is a kick for any doo wop fan, with its over-the-top abundance of references to hits from the genre's golden age, complete with a *slow* interpretation of some lines from the Cadets' classic novelty "Stranded in the Jungle." *—Richie Unterberger*

Little Eva

b. Jun. 29, 1943, Bellhaven, NC
Vocals / Brill Building Pop, Girl Group
Little Eva Narcissus Boyd was a babysitter for Carole King & Gerry Goffin when the songwriting team was inspired to write "The Loco-Motion," a song based on a dance that Eva would do around the house. Eva also got to sing on their demo, which impressed Don Kirshner enough to release it as it was. One of the greatest girl group hits, "The Loco-Motion," hit number one in 1962; the follow-up, "Keep Your Hands Off My Baby," was

also written by Goffin-King. Almost as good as her debut, it reached the Top 20, and was even covered by the Beatles on-stage in their early days (though they never recorded it in the studio).

Unfortunately, Eva was then pigeonholed as a dance-craze singer and given inferior material. She never again reached the soulful heights of her first two singles; "Let's Turkey Trot" (1963) was her only other Top 20 hit. —*Richie Unterberger*

● **The Best of Little Eva** / 1988 / Collectables ♦♦♦♦♦
Collectables' *The Best of Little Eva* features her smash "The Loco-Motion," her follow-up hits "Keep Your Hands Off My Baby" and "Let's Turkey Trot," as well as less-distinctive songs that are enjoyable but don't play to her strengths in the ways that her best-known songs do. Songs like "Where Do I Go?" and "Get Him" attempt to recast Little Eva as a more conventional girl group singer, while "Swinging on a Star" and "Old Smokey Locomotion" attempt to capitalize on her biggest hit with diminishing returns. "The Trouble With Boys," "What I Gotta Do (To Make You Jealous)," and "Makin' With the Magilla" come closest to matching the heights of her best work, but just don't have as much fun and danceability as "The Loco-Motion." *Llll-Little Eva! The Complete Dimension Recordings* is the definitive Little Eva collection, but *The Best of Little Eva* provides all of her hits and enough interesting misses to make it a worthwhile retrospective as well. —*Heather Phares*

The Loco-Motion / Feb. 27, 1996 / Rhino ♦♦♦
Some collectors will be glad to have some Little Eva available on CD domestically. At only ten cuts (and no liner notes), however, it's on the skimpy side, and "Let's Turkey Trot" is unexpectedly missing. The 15-song best-of on Murray Hill is considerably more extensive and well annotated (albeit getting harder to find). On the other hand, this Rhino comp does have seven songs not on the Murray Hill LP (including some obscure Goffin/King compositions), although some of these are covers of popular early-'60s hits. —*Richie Unterberger*

Llll-Little Eva!: The Complete Dimension Recordings / Feb. 27, 2001 / WestSide ♦♦♦♦♦
Little Eva Boyd was Gerry Goffin & Carole King's babysitter and ace demo singer. Together, the three of them came up with the mega-million-seller "The Loco-Motion" and its attendant album, one of the finest moments in Brill Building girl-group music history. Those 13 or so transcendent moments of glory are gathered together with 15 or so others culled from non-LP B-sides and later singles, making this the single best overview of her years at Dimension Records available. In addition to her biggest hit and her first album in its entirety, this also features her other chart hits "Let's Turkey Trot," "Keep Your Hands Off My Baby," "Old Smokey Locomotion" and her duets with Big Dee Irwin ("Swinging on a Star," "The Christmas Song," "I Wish You a Merry Christmas"). And just to perfectly bookend this collection—which begins with "The Loco-Motion" by Little Eva—the closing track is a rare tribute track recorded and released in the early '60s: "Little Eva" by the Loco-Motions! A nice piece of rock & roll history, Brill Building style. —*Cub Koda*

Little Richard (Richard Wayne Penniman)

b. Dec. 5, 1935, Macon, GA
Vocals, Piano / Rock & Roll, R&B, New Orleans R&B, Black Gospel
One of the original rock & roll greats, Little Richard merged the fire of gospel with New Orleans R&B, pounding the piano and wailing with gleeful abandon. While numerous other R&B greats of the early 1950s had been moving in a similar direction, none of them matched the sheer electricity of Richard's vocals. With his bullet-speed deliveries, ecstatic trills, and the overjoyed force of personality in his singing, he was crucial in upping the voltage from high-powered R&B into the similar, yet different, guise of rock & roll. Although he was only a hitmaker for a couple of years or so, his influence upon both the soul and British Invasion stars of the 1960s was vast, and his early hits remain core classics of the rock repertoire.

Heavily steeped in gospel music while growing up in Georgia, when Little Richard began recording in the early '50s he played unexceptional jump blues/R&B that owed a lot to his early inspirations Billy Wright and Roy Brown. In 1955, at Lloyd Price's suggestion, Richard sent a demo tape to Specialty Records, who were impressed enough to sign him and arrange a session for him in New Orleans. That session, however, didn't get off the ground until Richard began fooling around with a slightly obscene ditty during a break. With slightly cleaned-up lyrics, "Tutti Frutti" was the record that gave birth to Little Richard as we know him—the gleeful "woo!"s, the furious piano playing, the sax-driven, pedal-to-the-metal rhythm section. It was also his first hit, although, ridiculous as it now seems, Pat Boone's cover version outdid Richard's on the hit parade.

Pat Boone would also try to cover Richard's next hit, "Long Tall Sally," but by that time it was evident that audiences black and white much preferred the real deal. In 1956 and 1957, Richard reeled off a string of classic hits—"Long Tall Sally," "Slippin' and "Slidin'," "Jenny, Jenny," "Keep a Knockin'," "Good Golly, Miss Molly," "The Girl Can't Help It"—that remain the foundation of his fame. While Richard's inimitable mania was the key to his best records, he also owed a lot of his success to the gutsy playing of ace New Orleans session players like Lee Allen (tenor sax), Alvin Tyler (baritone sax), and especially Earl Palmer (drummer), who usually accompanied the singer in both New Orleans and Los Angeles studios. Richard's unforgettable appearances in early rock & roll movies, especially *The Girl Can't Help It*, also did a lot to spread the rock & roll gospel to the masses.

Little Richard was at the height of his commercial and artistic powers when he suddenly quit the business during an Australian tour in late 1957, enrolling in a Bible college in Alabama shortly after returning to the States. Richard had actually been feeling the call of religion for a while before his announcement, but it was nonetheless a shock to both his fans and the music industry. Specialty drew on unreleased sessions for a few more hard-rocking singles in the late '50s, but Richard virtually vanished from the public eye for a few years. When he did return to recording, it was as a gospel singer, cutting a few little-heard sacred sides for End, Mercury, and Atlantic in the early '60s.

By 1962, though, Richard had returned to rock & roll, touring Britain to an enthusiastic reception. Among the groups that supported him on those jaunts were the Rolling Stones and the Beatles, whose vocals (Paul McCartney's especially) took a lot of inspiration from Richard's. In 1964, the Beatles cut a knockout version of "Long Tall Sally," with McCartney on lead, that may have even outdone the original. It's been speculated that the success of the Beatles, and other British Invaders who idolized Richard, finally prompted the singer into making a full-scale comeback as an unapologetic rock & roller. Hooking up with Specialty once again, he had a small hit in 1964 with "Bama Lama Bama Loo." These and other sides were respectable efforts in the mold of his classic '50s sides, but tastes had changed too much for Little Richard to climb the charts again. He spent the rest of the '60s in a continual unsuccessful comeback, recording for Vee-Jay (accompanied on some sides by Jimi Hendrix, who was briefly in Richard's band), OKeh, and Modern (for whom he even tried recording in Memphis with Stax session musicians).

It was the rock & roll revival of the late '60s and early '70s, though, that really saved Richard's career, enabling him to play on the nostalgia circuit with great success (though he had a small hit, "Freedom Blues," in 1970). He had always been a flamboyant performer, brandishing a six-inch pompadour and mascara, and constant entertaining appearances on television talk shows seemed to ensure his continuing success as a living legend. Yet by the late '70s, he'd returned to the church again. Somewhat predictably, he eased back into rock and show business by the mid-'80s. Since then, he's maintained his profile with a role in *Down and Out in Beverly Hills* (the movie's soundtrack also returned him to the charts, this time with "Great Gosh A-Mighty") and guest appearances on soundtracks, compilations, and children's rock records. At this point it's safe to assume that he never will get that much-hungered-for comeback hit, but he remains one of rock & roll's most colorful icons, still capable of turning on the charm and charisma in his infrequent appearances in the limelight. —*Richie Unterberger*

Here's Little Richard / Mar. 1957 / Specialty ♦♦♦♦♦
Little Richard's debut album wasn't released until more than a year after he first broke through nationally with "Tutti Frutti" in early 1956. By the time Specialty Records got around to introducing him to LP buyers, Little Richard had already scored six Top 40 pop hits. This album didn't contain all of them, but it did contain "Tutti Frutti," "Long Tall Sally," "Slippin' and Slidin' (Peepin' and Hidin')," "Rip It Up," "Ready Teddy," "Jenny, Jenny," and "Miss Ann," all of which had made the pop charts and been in the R&B Top Ten. ("True, Fine Mama," also included, would chart as the B-side of "Ooh! My Soul" a year later.) Thus, *Here's Little Richard* was more of a compilation than just a debut album, a consistent collection containing many of Little Richard's classic recordings. It was also his highest charting and probably best-selling effort. —*William Ruhlmann*

Little Richard / 1958 / Specialty ♦♦♦♦♦
Like his debut album, *Here's Little Richard*, Little Richard's self-titled second album was, in essence, a compilation record rather than a newly recorded LP. Among its 12 selections were nine songs that had been chart singles between 1956 and 1958, including "Keep A-Knockin'" and "Good Golly, Miss Molly," which had hit the pop Top Ten, and "Lucille," which had topped the R&B charts. Other former singles were "Heeby-Jeebies," "The Girl Can't Help it," "Send Me Some Lovin'" (all three R&B Top Tens), "Ooh! My Soul" (Little Richard's final Top 40 pop hit), "All Around the World," and "Baby Face." Little Richard's spectacular two-year run of hits was over by mid-1958, with the singer having renounced rock & roll as of October 1957, but *Little Richard* gathers together a generous helping of his most remarkable work. —*William Ruhlmann*

The Fabulous Little Richard / 1959 / Specialty ♦♦♦
With Little Richard having long since given up pop music for religion, Specialty Records released as his third album a collection of tracks recorded mostly at his first session in 1955 (with a few 1956 and 1957 recordings as well). Richard handles these R&B songs well, but, with the exception of the medley "Kansas City/Hey-Hey-Hey-Hey" (later copied note for note by the Beatles), the songs and performances do not match his incendiary hits of the period. —*William Ruhlmann*

Grooviest 17 Original Hits! / 1959 / Specialty ♦♦♦♦♦
Despite its trendy title, *Grooviest 17 Original Hits!* was the most complete collection of Little Richard's hits yet released. By this point, Little Richard had re-recorded his hits for Vee-Jay, Modern, and OKeh, and Specialty seems to have wanted an album with the word "original" in the title, emphasizing that they possessed the actual hit versions. Taking the 12 tracks from 1963's *His Greatest Hits*, the company added five more tracks, among them "Ready Teddy," "Miss Ann," and "Ooh! My Soul," chart records they had skipped the first time around. "The Girl Can't Help It" still didn't appear on a Little Richard hits collection, but *Grooviest 17 Original Hits!* was the single-disc Little Richard hits collection to own for a long time to come. —*William Ruhlmann*

The Explosive Little Richard / Jan. 1967 / OKeh ♦♦♦
In 1966, OKeh Records took its turn at trying to revive the recording career of Little Richard. In the fall of that year, they put him in a studio in Hollywood with his former Specialty Records associate Larry Williams producing, and the two cut this album of rock & roll ravers, which was released in January 1967. Little Richard is as frantic as ever, notably on the lead-off track, "I Don't Want to Discuss It," later a showstopper for Delaney & Bonnie, but rock music trends were far removed from his style of rocking abandon by 1967, and this album went unnoticed. OKeh recorded Little Richard doing his hits that January and released the results several months later as *Little Richard's Greatest Hits Recorded Live*, but that was the end of this comeback. [*The Explosive Little Richard!* originally was released by OKeh Records in January 1967 as OKeh 14117. It has been reissued several times by Epic Records, most recently in 1986 as Epic 40390.] —*William Ruhlmann*

The Rill Thing / 1971 / Reprise ♦♦♦
The Rill Thing represented Little Richard's most serious attempt at a comeback since his 1950s heyday. "Freedom Blues," Richard's debut Reprise single, released in April 1970, was a mid-chart hit, his first in five years. "Greenwood Mississippi," released as a single

concurrently with the album, also charted. Richard adopted a cajun/country-rock approach (even covering "Lovesick Blues"), with a heavy beat and twangy guitar backing up his rough, forceful vocals. Despite the indulgence of the rambling ten-minute instrumental title track, the LP was a convincing update on his early work. But it did not propel Little Richard back to the top of the charts. *—William Ruhlmann*

☆ **18 Greatest Hits** / 1985 / Rhino ♦♦♦♦♦
18 Greatest Hits is the definitive single-disc collection of Little Richard's Specialty singles, especially for listeners who only want the hits. Every one of Richard's biggest hits—"Tutti Frutti," "Long Tall Sally," "Slippin' and Slidin'," "Rip It Up," "Ready Teddy," "The Girl Can't Help It," "Lucille," "Send Me Some Lovin'," "Keep A-Knockin'," "Good Golly Miss Molly"—are here, plus singles like "Heeby-Jeebies," "She's Got It," "Ooh! My Soul," "Miss Ann," "Kansas City/Hey Hey Hey," and "Bama Lama Bama Loo" that were bigger hits on the R&B charts than the pop charts. All of the singles are presented in chronological order, and the disc simply rips it up from beginning to end. It's a definitive collection. *—Stephen Thomas Erlewine*

The Specialty Sessions / 1989 / Specialty ♦♦♦♦♦
Dig it—a collection of all 73 songs that Little Richard cut for Specialty Records from 1955 through 1959, including early working versions of hits including "Long Tall Sally" and "Slippin' and Slidin'," may seem like overkill to the casual listener, but if you're thinking of buying this three-CD box, chances are you're not a casual listener. And if you're not thinking about it, then you should be. This set covers only four years in Little Richard's career, but manages to sum up virtually everything you need to know about him (his earlier sides, available on Bear Family, are an interesting appendix, but of his later stuff, only the early- and mid-'60s material, with Jimi Hendrix on guitar, hold any significance, mostly as a curiosity). Not only does the music make you want to get up and dance, but the notes—spread out on a lavishly illustrated booklet and the individual jewel boxes—tell the whole story of Specialty Records and the people behind it, including Art Rupe, Bumps Blackwell, Dave Bartholomew, and, of course, Richard Penniman himself. The session information alone could keep owners busy for a week. The sound is nothing less than breathtaking, loud and raunchy but razor sharp, and the price of this set makes it competitive with other Little Richard single-disc sets as well as more attractive than the price of boxes devoted to Elvis Presley and Chuck Berry. The only complaint—why couldn't the producers list the songs on the individual jewel boxes? *—Bruce Eder*

The Formative Years 1951–53 / Jul. 1989 / Bear Family ♦♦♦♦

★ **The Georgia Peach** / Aug. 5, 1991 / Specialty ♦♦♦♦♦
Perhaps the greatest of Little Richard's greatest hits compilations, the 25-track *Georgia Peach* features all of his biggest hits in chronological order, as well as terrific singles that never were as big as "Tutti Frutti" and "Good Golly Miss Molly." On top of the sublime song selection and sound, the liner notes by compiler Billy Vera are splendid and insightful. *—Stephen Thomas Erlewine*

Shag on Down by the Union Hall / Feb. 13, 1996 / Specialty ♦♦♦♦♦
For those who want more classic Little Richard than a greatest-hits collection but aren't devoted enough to spring for the expensive box sets, this is an excellent anthology of 24 of his best lesser-known tracks. Most of it dates from his classic era at Specialty (1955-1957), with alternate takes of a lot of his hits and some decent B-sides; there are also a few songs that he cut for the label during his 1964 comeback, including the minor hit "Bama Lama Bama Loo." *—Richie Unterberger*

The Best of the Vee Jay Years, Vol. 1 / Oct. 17, 2000 / Collectables ♦♦♦
This is the first of two volumes devoted to the recordings Little Richard made for Vee-Jay in the mid-'60s, many of which were re-recordings of his classic Specialty sides. The remakes aren't particularly interesting except for Little Richard's attempts to update them with loud drums and hysterical performances. The newer material veers toward soul rather than rock & roll, but still sounds pretty retro for its time. More noteworthy are the bizarre interpretations of "Memories Are Made of This" (a number-one hit for Dean Martin) and Hank Williams' "Why Don't You Love Me." Vol. 1 includes Little Richard's lone Vee-Jay hit, the soulful "I Don't Know What You've Got but It's Got Me." *—Greg Adams*

The Best of the Vee-Jay Years, Vol. 2 / Oct. 17, 2000 / Collectables ♦♦♦
Little Richard recorded for the Vee-Jay label in the early '60s, after his historic stint with Specialty Records and the restored rock & roll vigor that followed his sudden religious conversion. While at Vee-Jay, Richard re-recorded some of his classic mid-'50s tracks (in this case "Rip It Up," "Jenny Jenny," "The Girl Can't Help It," "Tutti Frutti," and "Good Golly Miss Molly"), trying to recapture the natural initial hysteria. While a toned-down Little Richard is still worth hearing, the record-buying public was duped into believing these Vee-Jay sides were the original Specialty versions, only to be greatly disappointed after getting the record home. While Richard's wild whoops and furious piano still come through, especially on the neglected newer material, it goes without saying that the Vee-Jay reissues should only be investigated after obtaining the Specialty sides. *—Al Campbell*

Talking 'Bout Soul / Feb. 1, 2001 / RPM ♦♦♦
In the mid-'60s, Little Richard was attempting, with little commercial success, to jump back into the rock and R&B frontlines with recordings on various labels. *Talking 'Bout Soul* collects 28 songs that he cut for Vee-Jay in 1964 and 1965, which (especially during the latter part of that span) were poorly exposed as Vee-Jay headed toward bankruptcy. Little Richard had just recently emerged from his layoff of several years from the rock & roll scene, and was still a strong and exciting vocalist; after all, he was still only in his early thirties. His problems, both as far as sales and the quality of his records, had more to due with unremarkable material and production. There was also a sense that his style just wasn't as adaptable to the soul era as that of a rough contemporary such as, say, James Brown. These sides are fair, but not often better than fair, soul-rockers that sometimes move into more contemporary R&B bags, such as the classy, agonized ballad "I Don't Know What You Got," written by Don Covay, or Alvin Tyler's New Orleans-flavored "Crossover." Little Richard wrote some reasonable if generic originals for Vee-Jay, too, but his repertoire was way too heavy on remakes of old '50s rock songs, whether his own or others like "Whole Lotta Shaking Going On" and "Money Honey." The production is tinnier than it should be, and the arrangements and playing sound more rushed than they should, too. Jimi Hendrix plays on a few of these sides, incidentally, although it's not made clear in the liner notes exactly which tracks are graced by his appearance. *—Richie Unterberger*

Little Sister

Group / Soul, Pop-Soul
The short-lived female R&B trio Little Sister was best known for its associations with Sylvester "Sly Stone" Stewart. Not only did Stone organize the trio, its principal member was his sister, Vaetta "Vet" Stewart (hence the group's name). Stewart, Mary Rand, and Elva Melton began singing together as touring backup for Sly & the Family Stone in the late '60s and providing backing vocals on several of their albums. In 1970, Stone produced a series of church-inflected soul tracks for them on his Stone Flower imprint. Two of them became Top Ten R&B hits: "You're the One, Pt. 1" and "Somebody's Watching You," the latter of which the Family Stone had previously recorded on their *Stand!* album. "You're the One" was the bigger hit, but the funky "Somebody's Watching You" had greater sonic impact: charting in early 1971, it was said to be the first significant pop hit to use programmed drums, and its percolating rhythm-bed presaged that of the Family Stone's own massive hit "Family Affair" later that year.

Lacking both management and Sly Stone's continued attention and involvement, the group disbanded shortly thereafter with no fanfare. *—Joseph McCombs*

Little Willie John

b. Nov. 15, 1937, Cullendale, AR, **d.** May 26, 1968, Walla Walla, WA
Vocals / R&B, Soul
He's never received the accolades given to the likes of Sam Cooke, Clyde McPhatter, and James Brown, but Little Willie John ranks as one of R&B's most influential performers. His muscular high timbre and enormous technical and emotional range belied his young age (his first hit came when he was 18), but his mid-'50s work for Syd Nathan's King label would play a great part in the way soul music would sound. Everyone from Cooke, McPhatter, and Brown to Jackie Wilson, B.B. King, and Al Green has acknowledged his debt to this most overlooked of rock and soul pioneers. His debut recording, a smoking version of Titus Turner's "All around the World" from 1955, set the pattern for a remarkable string of hits: "Need Your Love So Bad," "Suffering With the Blues," "Fever," "Let Them Talk," and his last, "Sleep," from 1961. His version of "Fever" was copied note for note by Peggy Lee and Elvis Presley, both of whom had bigger hits with it; John's version, however, remains definitive. His second hit, "Need Your Love So Bad," contains one of the most intimate, tear-jerking vocals ever caught on tape.

John had a volatile temper, fueled by a taste for liquor and an insecurity regarding his slight height (5' 4"). He was known to pack a gun and knife; in 1964, he stabbed a man and was sent to the Washington State penitentiary, where he died of pneumonia in 1968. James Brown recorded a tribute album to John that year, and his material has been recorded by scores of artists from the Beatles to Fleetwood Mac to the Blasters. Nevertheless, Little Willie John remains a stranger to most listeners and has never received the respect his talent deserves.

Little Willie John was one of the first artists featured in Rhino's King reissues series. *Fever* was issued late in 1993, and the single-disc, 20-track anthology included such John releases as "Need Your Love So Bad," "Suffering With the Blues," and the title cut. *—John Floyd*

Fever / 1956 / King ♦♦♦♦♦
Little Willie John was among the dominant R&B vocalists of the late '50s and early '60s, and one of those best equipped to make the transition to soul. His dramatic style, passionate delivery, and gospel/blues-tinged approach were ideal for the types of anguished, personalized songs that became the hallmark of the soul era. While "Fever" did well for John, it was a huge hit for Peggy Lee. It and everything else on the album was done in magnificent fashion by John. His albums were briefly available again during the early '70s in a Gusto/King reissue line, but have since disappeared again. *—Ron Wynn*

Talk to Me / 1959 / King ♦♦♦♦♦
The reissue of John's second King album includes the title hit, "Person to Person," and the exquisite "There Is Someone in This World for Me." *—John Floyd*

Mister Little Willie John / 1960 / King ♦♦♦♦♦
His third King long-player is one of the '50s finest albums. "You're a Sweetheart" is an R&B landmark. *—John Floyd*

Sure Things / 1961 / King ♦♦♦
Another vintage reissue, it features his gorgeous reading of Billy Eckstine's "A Cottage for Sale" and the original version of "I'm Shakin'," which the Blasters covered on their debut. *—John Floyd*

Come On and Join Little Willie John / 1962 / King ♦♦♦

Little Willie Sings All Originals / 1966 / King ♦♦♦

● **Fever: The Best of Little Willie John** / Nov. 16, 1993 / Rhino ♦♦♦♦♦
Little Willie John had a commanding delivery, remarkable projection and a charismatic sound that was both instantly recognizable and unforgettable. His magical singles are all contained on this superb 20-track anthology, arguably the best single-disc set of John material available. It includes his best-known song, "Fever" (Peggy Lee's cover version became a huge smash), plus such marvelous numbers such as "Home at Last," "Heartbreak (It's Hurtin' Me)" and "You Hurt Me." While John was a dynamic heartache wailer, he could also do excellent dance/novelty and double entendre tunes such as "Let's Rock

While the Rockin's Good" and "Leave My Kitten Alone." This anthology demonstrates why he's still held in such high regard throughout the world of R&B and soul. *—Ron Wynn*

The Very Best of Little Willie John / Oct. 9, 2001 / Collectables ✦✦✦✦
Collectables' *The Very Best of Little Willie John* gathers most of the influential R&B singer's definitive tracks, including "Fever," "Talk to Me, Talk to Me," "Leave My Kitten Alone," "All Around the World," "I'm Shakin'," and "Let Them Talk." Very nearly as good as Rhino's *Fever: The Best of Little Willie John*, this collection is a solid introduction to John's powerful voice and eclectic singles. *—Heather Phares*

The Early King Sessions / Jun. 11, 2002 / Ace ✦✦✦✦
A career-spanning best-of compilation will be a satisfactory helping of Little Willie John for most listeners. But for devoted fans of the singer, and indeed of 1950s R&B in general, this more specialized anthology is useful, gathering both sides of all 12 of his first singles, all originally issued in 1955-1957. The only really well-known songs here are the original version of "Fever," "All Around the World" (adapted by Little Milton into "Grits Ain't Groceries," his 1960s soul hit), and "Need Your Love So Bad," and they are the best tunes on this collection. John's vocals are uniformly rich and moving, but the material is just too similar to place it in the same league as recordings during the same era by, say, Ray Charles. Still, these are sides in which you can hear R&B, blues, rock & roll, and bits of pop (particularly in "Fever" and its sound-alike follow-up, "My Nerves") coming together in a form that hints at early soul, on songs that were more apt to dip into minor keys than much other R&B of the time. Hardcore completists will note that the version of "I'm Sticking With You Baby" is actually a different take that eventually showed up on an LP, and not the one from the original 45. *—Richie Unterberger*

Levi Little

b. Patterson, New Jersey
Vocals / Contemporary R&B
New Jersey-born vocalist Levi Little first attracted attention as the lead vocalist on Blackstreet's smash single "Joy;" his solo debut *Soul Connection* followed in 1998. *—Jason Ankeny*

● **Soul Connection** / Oct. 13, 1998 / Worldly Music ✦✦✦✦
Apparently, Levi Little can do it all. On his soulful debut, *Soul Connection*, this Patterson, NJ, native performed, arranged, mixed and produced all the track recordings, and also played most of the instruments. That's some major feat. Although some of the melodies are similar in sound to his urban music contemporaries Joe and Brian McKnight, Levi's contribution to the canon of soul artists is a considerable one. Smooth singing graces enticing songs like "Strong Love" and "Somebody to Love," creating silky romantic montages. Bruce Hornsby's expert keyboard work on "The Walls" completes this steady supply of timeless funk and sensual R&B, making this an overall impressive effort. *—Roxanne Blanford*

Hattie Littles

d. Jun. 2000, Detroit, MI
Vocals / Soul, Urban, Motown
Hattie Littles had one release on the Gordy label, "Your Wonderful Love," released in January 1963. It was not a hit and received little airplay, although Berry Gordy wrote and produced both sides. Her career lay dormant for several decades, until Ian Levine rediscovered her and brought her to England to record in the '80s. Some singles were released in England. Also, a compilation CD of her work with Levine, *The Very Best of Hattie Littles*, was released.

Blessed with a full, vibrant, dynamic voice, Littles started singing in her teens at churches and banquets. Her voice became the perfect vehicle for Motown's structured, cute, catchy songs cut an octave higher than the singer's normal range to give the recordings a sense of urgency. Her "big break" came while working at Lee's Sensation Lounge, which sponsored a talent show. After Littles won three times, Motown producer/songwriter Clarence Paul convinced Berry Gordy to sign her to a contract. Mary Wells, the Marvelettes, Barrett Strong, the Contours, the Miracles, and Marvin Gaye had all waxed hits at Motown, and Hattie jumped at the offer. Signed for four years, she recorded ten sides—only one of which was released (the others remained in the vaults).

Littles only performed her Gordy single once. The night before a Motown tour with Marvin Gaye and others, she sang it at Lee's, probably because Gordy was in the audience. Not once did she do it on the tour with Marvin. Her reason: she hated it! Berry's new sound wasn't her kind of music; she preferred singing blues and bluesy jazz, so instead of promoting her single on tour, she sang tunes by Bobby "Blue" Bland, B.B. King, Howling Wolf, and Nina Simone. This undoubtedly got back to Berry and may be the reason she had only one release.

After Motown, Littles experienced alcoholism, drugs, and stays at rehabilitation houses. Yet her recollections of Motown are good. She always felt good after hanging at Motown. Just being there, according to Littles, was equal to hours of anger therapy. She lived in Detroit until her death in June of 2000, when she suffered a heart attack. *—Andrew Hamilton*

● **The Very Best of Hattie Littles** / Sep. 17, 1996 / Hot Productions ✦✦✦✦
Hattie Little's voice is a powerful, charismatic instrument. This is not a ripoff, unlike some other Ian Levine Hot Productions. Hattie only had one single released on Gordy and it didn't receive much airplay. So there aren't any past Hattie hits to compare this to. Listening to this, you wonder why Berry Gordy didn't invest more in Hattie's career. Her rendition of "Come and Get These Memories" rivals Martha & the Vandellas' original. Hattie does the classic in a bluesy style. The quality of her voice is undeniable. *—Andrew Hamilton*

Logg

Group / Disco, Club/Dance, Funk
One of the several names under which the prolific LeRoy Burgess recorded, the short-lived Logg spawned a small handful of post-disco classics that fed directly into house, helping solidify Burgess' role as one of the unintentional instigators of house music. The underground dance-music legend already had a number of feathers in his cap—most notably with Black Ivory and as a valued session hand—just after the early 1981 release of "Let's Do It" as Convertion. Burgess and the remainder of the Convertion family (producer Greg Carmichael, bassist James Calloway, drummers Sonny T. Davenport and Trevor Gale, guitarist Sonny DeGraffenreid, keyboardist Fred McFarlane, percussionist Willis Long, and background vocalists Renee J.J. Burgess and Dorothy Terrell) intended to keep going as a unit, but Sam Weiss, owner of the label that released "Let's Do It" (SAM), had the copyright of the group's name and reached an impasse with Burgess on a deal for further releases.

Burgess moved the group over to Salsoul and, re-named by Carmichael as Logg, they quickly cut the phenomenal single "I Know You Will," had it mixed by the great Larry Levan, and had it out in the shops two weeks after its recording. The song did very well in clubs, and Logg quickly recorded an album's worth of material and released it as a self-titled Salsoul LP by the end of 1981. After all was said and done, almost all of the album's six songs received extensive play in the clubs. Though Logg was put to rest after the album, Burgess continued his fruitful career throughout the early 2000s. *—Andy Kellman*

● **Logg** / 1981 / Salsoul ✦✦✦✦
Logg can qualify as *the* Leroy Burgess album. The bulk of the prolific, inventive singer/songwriter/keyboardist/producer's work is found on hard to find 12-inch dance singles and long out-of-print albums. Co-produced by Burgess and Gregory Carmichael, the album is a top-notch, energetic showcase for the artist and the crack rhythm section of Burgess, bassist James Calloway, and drummer Sonny Davenport, all of whom co-wrote every track on the album. "I Know You Will," "You've Got That Something" (the first two singles), "Dancing Into the Stars," "Something Else," and "Sweet to Me" instantly became dancefloor classics. Initially issued on Salsoul (RCA) in August 1981, *Logg* was reissued on CD by U.K. label Charly Records in July 1999. The extended Larry Levan remix of "I Know You Will" can be found on *Salsoul Essentials*. As the 21st century began, Burgess was active again with numerous projects (one with Frankie Knuckles) in the states and overseas. *—Ed Hogan*

Shorty Long (Frederick Earl Long)

b. May 20, 1940, Birmingham, AL, **d.** Jun. 29, 1969, Detroit, MI
Vocals, Piano / Motown, R&B, Soul, Pop-Soul
Standing a little over five feet in height, Frederick Earl Long (aka Shorty Long) was one of the funkiest singers to record at Motown Records. Long was born on May 20, 1940, in Birmingham, AL. While growing up he learned about music from people like Alvin "Shine" Robinson and W.C. Handy. The multi-talented singer could play piano, organ, drums, guitar, trumpet, harmonica, and was probably an excellent hand clapper. In Birmingham he worked as a DJ, toured with the Ink Spots, and gigged at club called Old Stables. In 1959, Long moved to Detroit, caught the ear of Harvey Fuqua, and cut two singles for Fuqua's Tri-Phi label. "I'll Be Here," backed with "Bad Willie," came out in 1962 and went unnoticed; the follow-up, "Too Smart," released later in the year, stiffed as well. Fuqua, tired of fighting with distributors and doing all the things it takes to run a label, decided to sell his operation to Berry Gordy, and Shorty Long became a Motown artist.

His first release, "Devil With the Blue Dress On," was a slow bluesy grinder with a stinging solo guitar that accented the break. Long and William Stevenson wrote "Devil" and it had all the ingredients of a hit but, for some reason, didn't chart. (Detroiter Mitch Ryder recorded "Devil" at a frantic pace, and the energy propelled the song to the fourth position on *Billboard*'s pop chart.) His next release, "It's a Crying Shame," did nothing. Then came what should have been a million seller—Long's funky name-dropping soulful "Function at the Junction"; written by Shorty Long and Eddie Holland, the song had it all—funky beat, soulful singing, good lyrics, danceability, everything—yet, it only climbed to the number-97 position on the pop chart in 1966. His classic remake of the Big Bopper's "Chantilly Lace" received some spins but failed to impact, despite a cool spoken intro by Long and a rollicking honky tonk piano. Ironically, his next release, "Night Fo' Last," went to number 75 on *Billboard*'s Top 100, 22 slots better than "Function," and the song isn't half as good, a good effort that got lost in the mix.

Shorty Long had to wait until 1968 before he had his first bona fide hit in the music business. "Here Comes the Judge" was a popular catch phrase, partly because of Flip Wilson, but it was funnyman Pig Meat Markum who really coined the phrase years earlier. "Here Comes the Judge," a funky record (all of Shorty Long's recordings are funky), had some nifty lyrics and a percolating, bubbling beat, and zoomed all the way to number eight on the charts. An excellent LP was released, which included his hits, should-have-been hits, and some new stuff like "Don't Mess With My Weekends" and "Here Comes Fat Albert."

Oddly, "It's a Crying Shame" and "Chantilly Lace" weren't included, nor were the Tri-Phi singles. Sadly, just when Shorty's career was about to take off and his talent recognized, he died in a boating accident with friend Oscar Williams on June 29, 1969, on the Detroit River. Motown released a second LP, *The Prime of Shorty Long*, and like the first it showcased the many talents of the diminutive singer. Before his death, Motown allowed Shorty to produce himself; the only other Motown singer allowed to do this was Smokey Robinson. The late Earl Van Dyke, Motown's session pianist, says Shorty used to come in and say, "Today we ain't playing nuthin' but funk, if you don't feel funky, take a drink of this," and then he'll reach in his coat and pull out a bottle of liquor. *—Andrew Hamilton*

Here Comes the Judge / 1968 / Soul ✦✦✦✦✦
Motown Records had to release an LP by Frederick "Shorty" Long when his amusing "Here Comes the Judge" zoomed to number-eight pop in July of 1968. Shorty had been hanging around and recording at Motown since 1964, and for Tri-Phi before that. (Motown purchased Tri-Phi and all their masters, songs and artist contracts.) Shorty releases at Motown were sporadic at best. As good as this is, it would have been better if they had included his two Tri-Phi sides and his two earlier soul/Motown recordings. Still, you get the marvelous "Don't Mess With My Weekend," which Motown let die on the

album. "Weekend" had it all: thunder and lightning sound effects, witty lyrics, a bubbling beat, crack backing vocals, and Shorty's discourse about the fun he has on weekends. "Devil With the Blue Dress On" sounds better than ever; it's hard to understand why this slow-grinding beauty with the bluesy guitar didn't click. Likewise for the stomping "Function at the Junction," which froze at number 97 on the pop 100 chart in 1966. Motown released "Night Fo' Last" before "Judge," and it flopped. His Southern roots surface on the energetic remake of Titus Turner's "People Sure Act Funny." Another winner is "Here Comes Fat Albert," written by Long and Edwin Starr; the song parodies the lovable character created by comedian Bill Cosby. *—Andrew Hamilton*

The Prime of Shorty Long / 1969 / Soul ♦♦♦♦♦
Shorty Long must have feared being typecast. There's plenty of classic Long to hear, but the 45s picked to promote this album were not typical of the diminutive soul shouter. "I Had a Dream" did nothing when released, despite its socially significant lyrics. Good song and an A-1 performance by Shorty, but the follow-up to "Here Come the Judge"? The next choice, Procol Harum's "Whiter Shade of Pale," sank without a trace, though it made a good frisbee. Both were odd choices for single releases. Stronger selections like "Lily of the Valley" and the rockin' and rollin' "Baby Come on Home" got overlooked. The two Fats Domino tunes simply mimic the originals. "When You Are Available," co-written by Marvin Gaye, has the same feel as the sides Gaye produced for the Originals. Bad choices for single releases killed any chance this LP had. *—Andrew Hamilton*

● **The Essential Collection** / 2000 / Spectrum ♦♦♦♦♦
A valiant import compiled by Spectrum Records but not without flaws. Casual fans won't notice anything awry, but Shorty Long janissaries will readily spot two glaring omissions among the 18 tracks: "Chantilly Lace" and Marvin Gaye's exquisite "When You Are Available." The former is a bluesy update of Big Bopper's hit complete with a slick rap intro; the latter is Long's best ballad ever. Still, potent tracks like "Don't Mess With My Weekend," a funky groove with thunder effects and clever lyrics; the slow, grinding "Devil With the Blue Dress On"; cookout favorite "Function at the Junction"; and the painful "Another Hurt Like This" will leave lasting impressions. Includes his chart-blazing "Here Comes the Judge," the amusing "Here Comes Fat Albert," "Lillie of the Valley," and instrumental and vocal renditions of "Night Fo Last," a vinyl flop that comes to life on CD. *—Andrew Hamilton*

Loose Ends

f. 1980, London, England
Group / Club/Dance, Urban, Dance-Pop
One of the top British dance and urban contemporary trios in the early '80s, Loose Ends formed in London. They were originally called Loose End, and included Carl McIntosh, Jane Eugene, and Steve Nichol. Virgin signed them in 1981, and their debut was written by Chris and Eddie Amoo of the Real Thing. The group changed its name to Loose Ends in 1983, and signed with MCA in America in 1984. Their single "Hanging on a String (Contemplating)" topped the R&B charts in 1985, and they repeated that achievement in 1986 with "Slow Down." Their last hit was "Watching You" in 1988, which reached number two. The group shuffled its lineup in 1990 for the release of *Look How Long*, with McIntosh now joined by Linda Carriere and Sunay Suleyman. McIntosh also produced several artists, notably Caron Wheeler. *—Ron Wynn*

● **Real Chuckeeboo** / 1984 / MCA ♦♦♦♦♦
This was the final album featuring British dance/R&B vocalists Jane Eugene, Steve Nichol, and Carl McIntosh. They had been quite successful on both sides of the Atlantic in the mid-'80s and were at the time of this release not only performing but writing and producing tracks for Juliet Roberts, Phyllis Hyman, Five Star, Peter Royer, Cheryl Lynn, and Lavine Hudson. Their focus may have been divided, because this was their least attractive and interesting album of the string with the core trio. It did have a fine single in "Watching You," and "Mr. Bachelor" was a nice concept cut. But it was no surprise that they split following the album. *—Ron Wynn*

Look How Long / 1990 / MCA ♦♦♦♦
One of the better urban-soul groups one can find, Loose Ends, fronted by Carl McIntosh, concocts a rhythmic formula without the repetitious melodies. Through the utilization of technology, MacIntosh maximizes the use of sampling, synthesizers and drum programming. "Don't Be a Fool" was the debut release, peaking at number ten on the *Billboard* R&B charts. The two singles to follow, "Cheap Talk" and "Love's Got Me" peaked at 28 and 76, respectively. The former of the two addresses the issue of negative rumors in relationship, while the latter, in a more upbeat pulse, is a classic club track; the single is highlighted by a hyped bridge. There were no other releases from this collection, and that is unfortunate for songs like "I Don't Need to Love You." Written with similies and metaphors, McIntosh's hazy vocals put a stamp on this uptempo new jack swing track. The mellow cuts, such as "Hold Tight," "Love Controversy Pt.1" and the short take of "Symptoms of Love" are contemporary urban classics with their thick bass arrangements and the breezin' vocals of McIntosh and his female counterparts. The title track, "Look How Long," confronts former group members Jane Eugene and Steve Nichol's exit from the British trio. This project is a good production. *—Craig Lytle*

Jennifer Lopez

b. Jul. 24, 1970, Bronx, NY
Vocals, Executive Producer / Club/Dance, Latin Pop, Urban, Dance-Pop, Adult Contemporary
Actress/singer Jennifer Lopez was born in the Bronx, NY, on July 24, 1970; after starting out in musical theater as a child, at age 16 she made her film debut in the little-seen *My Little Girl*, but her career then stalled until she was tapped to become one of the dancing "Fly Girls" on the television sketch comedy series *In Living Color*. A recurring role on the TV drama *Second Chances* followed before Lopez was thrust into the limelight co-starring with Wesley Snipes and Woody Harrelson in the 1995 feature film *Money Train*; smaller roles in pictures including *My Family/Mi Familia*, *Jack* and *Blood and Wine* followed before she landed the title role in 1997's *Selena*, portraying the slain Tejano singer.

Co-starring opposite George Clooney in 1998's acclaimed *Out of Sight*, Lopez (the product of a Puerto Rican family) became the highest-paid Latina actress in Hollywood history; the following summer, she returned to her musical roots with her debut pop album *On the 6*, scoring a major hit with the infectious single "If You Had My Love." Lopez didn't waste time perfecting a sophomore effort, the appropriately titled *J. Lo*, which was issued in early 2001. *—Jason Ankeny*

● **On the 6** / Jun. 1, 1999 / Work ♦♦♦♦
Jennifer Lopez's debut album *On the 6* showcases the actress' sultry, versatile voice in a number of settings, including pop ballads, Latin pop, and R&B. Star producers like Sean "Puffy" Combs, Track Masters, and Emilio Estefan Jr. lend their talents to the album, making *On the 6* a perfectly polished and varied album, which features a musical blend Lopez calls "Latin soul." Smooth ballads such as "Should've Never," "Too Late," "Could This Be Love," and "No Me Ames," a duet with Latin superstar Marc Anthony, dominate the album's first half; while these songs show off the gentler side of Lopez's vocal gifts, they tend to sound too similar. It's on the R&B and Latin-tinged tracks where Lopez really shines. Along with the insistent first single "If You Had My Love," cuts like "Feelin' So Good" and "Let's Get Loud" have a fiery, soulful sound more in keeping with Lopez's public persona. *On the 6*'s second half capitalizes on this spicy, upbeat side, particularly on "Waiting for Tonight" and "Open Off My Love," which draws inspiration from rap, R&B, and Latin styles with its sparse arrangement of horns, keyboards, and beats. The tropical remix of "No Me Ames" and "Una Noche Mas," the Spanish version of "Waiting for Tonight," emphasize Lopez's distinctive heritage, which elevates *On the 6* from a star's vanity project to an individual but accessible work of pop songcraft by a widely talented performer. *—Heather Phares*

J.Lo / Jan. 23, 2001 / Epic ♦♦♦
Most snickered when Jennifer Lopez made her pop move in 1999, figuring that it was no more than a one-off vanity project. As it turns out, she was as serious about her pop career as she was about acting, and even if she didn't possess a particularly distinguished voice, she was earnest and had some good mainstream pop singles, delivered with some seriously sexy videos. *On the 6* was big enough of a success to raise expectations for its sequel, *J-Lo*, the first self-styled blockbuster of 2001. Essentially, this is the same album as *On the 6*, only a little longer with a little less focus and not as many memorable songs. This lack of winning singles becomes a drag, since at over an hour, the record meanders much longer than it should. Yet, meander isn't really the right word, because the album sets its tone from the start, with the ingratiating "Love Don't Cost a Thing." From that point on, the tinny, skittering drum machines, smooth midrange, and alluringly thin vocals remain the same from song to song, with the occasional Latin cut thrown in to vary the rhythm somewhat. Since both the production and Lopez play it cool, not hot, and there's not that many hooks, it all tends to blend together. Those that have hooks need a couple of spins before they catch hold, whether it's the aforementioned lead single "Love Don't Cost a Thing," "I'm Real," "Play," or "We Gotta Talk." Lopez's strong suit remains dance tunes, not ballads, which tend to disappear in this reserved production and mannered vocals (no more so than "Secretly," which never seems to gel). So, *J.Lo* winds up as musically a mixed bag. Its longer running time makes it a little less appealing than its predecessor, yet it has just about the same number of strong songs, all of which sounding of a piece with *On the Six*, which makes it a success on a certain level. Still, there's this certain feeling of staid complacency and ordinariness that makes *J.Lo* feel less fun than her debut. *—Stephen Thomas Erlewine*

J to tha L-O!: The Remixes / Feb. 5, 2002 / Epic ♦♦♦
Given that Jennifer Lopez's uptempo material tends to work much better than her slower recordings, there would seem some potential for an album of remixes of her dance-oriented tracks as more than just a stopgap between regular releases. But *J to tha L-O!: The Remixes* is a collection of odds and ends. Of course, as usual, the term "remix" is a misnomer; these are versions of Lopez recordings to which other elements have been added, not simply remixes of the existing tracks. The first four rhythmic, but not really dance-worthy tracks are really Lopez-plus-rapping, much of which clashes with the tone of the original songs. For example, Fat Joe's comments during "Love Don't Cost a Thing" seem to deny the point of the lyrics Lopez is singing. But by far the worst of the rap remixes is "Feelin' So Good," on which ex-flame Sean "Puffy" Combs provides typically lame remarks, most of which consist simply of the comment, "This is the remix," which he mutters over Lopez's vocal track. Thankfully, there are a few selections here that will work well on the dancefloor, starting with the Metro remix of "Walking on Sunshine." Pablo Flores' remix of "Let's Get Loud" is particularly impressive, and Hex Hector's take on "Waiting for Tonight" casts the song as a traditional Hi-NRG workout. The album concludes with a track that isn't a remix, the ballad "Alive" from Lopez's 2002 film *Enough*. Unfortunately, her vocal limitations come to the fore when she is spotlighted on such a song without a dance arrangement to support her. But such technical problems are not as big a deal as her lack of emotional involvement. Though she tries to fake it here and there, she still sounds like she's singing her grocery list instead of the song's clichéd lyrics. *—William Ruhlmann*

This Is Me . . . Then / Nov. 19, 2002 / Epic ♦♦♦♦
Don't pay attention to the title, which is absolutely nonsensical and bewildering—it suggests that *This Is Me . . . Then* is a compilation, which it isn't, and it also suggests that this has some sort of theme, which it doesn't—and concentrate on the music, which is the strongest, sultriest, best music Jennifer Lopez (who has abandoned the moniker J-Lo) has recorded for any of her three albums. This, of course, doesn't mean that it's a radical

musical departure, though there are differences here—the glitzy dance-pop has been phased out, there's a stronger urban soul vibe, particularly on the lush surfaces and sexy grooves—but it does mean that the album has a solid set of songs and a sharp production pitched directly at the mainstream of 2002, yet with nice allusions to classic soul and early-'80s pop-funk and soft rock. Since Lopez is a celebrity and a regular feature on gossip pages in the early days of the 21st century, and since she's unabashedly mainstream—her only attempts at street-cred are on the laughable lyrics to "Jenny From the Block," where she insists that success hasn't spoiled her yet and she's the same ol' Jen she's always been (if so, why the paparazzi on the back cover?)—it's easy for some listeners to dismiss her, but it's harder to make to make a pop album as easily enjoyable as this. Sure, there are some flaws—as mentioned above, "Jenny From the Block" is silly and no matter how much you love Ben Affleck, "Dear Ben" is unbearably mawkish—but all mainstream pop albums stumble through filler. What counts is the overall feel and the highlights. Here, the feel is sexy, stylish, and fun, and there are numerous highlights, all feeling effortless. And if you think that's easy to do, take a listen to a few other pop-R&B albums from late 2002 (*Stripped* and *Charmbracelet* come to mind) and hear how good this record is. *—Stephen Thomas Erlewine*

The Lost Generation

f. Chicago, IL

Group / Smooth Soul, Chicago Soul

Chicago soul vocal group the Lost Generation had their biggest hit with "The Sly, Slick and the Wicked," a mellow ballad that hit number-14 R&B and number-30 pop in the summer of 1970. The group members were lead singer/songwriter Lowrell Simon, Fred Simon, Jesse Dean, and Larry Brownlee. Brownlee had been a member of the singing group the C.O.D.'s, whose single on the local Kellimac label, "Michael (The Lover)," made it to number-five R&B in 1965. Born March 18, 1943, on Chicago's South Side, Lowrell formed a childhood friendship with Gus Redmond. As a teenager, Lowrell was a member of the LaVondells, a vocal group. Dropping the first two letters from their name to become the Vondells, the group had a local hit with "Lenore" on the Marvello label. Soon afterward, the group broke up. One of the members, Glen Murdock, teamed with local singer Joyce Kennedy to sing lead vocals for the funk/rock group Mother's Finest.

After Dean completed his stint in the Army, he joined Lowrell, Fred, and Brownlee in the Lost Generation. Childhood friend Redmond, who was now head of promotion and marketing for Brunswick Records, introduced the group to producer Carl Davis in 1969. The single "The Sly, Slick and the Wicked" was co-written by Lowrell, Brownlee, and Redmond. The hit tied for trade publication Record World's 1970 Record of the Year award with the Jackson 5's "ABC." The release also generated enough money for Brunswick to buy itself out from its owner, Decca Records.

On the flip side was "You're So Young but You're So True." The next single, "Wait a Minute," was written by the Chi-Lites' Eugene Record. The Simon-Brownlee-Redmond trio wrote "Someday" and "Talking the Teenage Language." All were included on *The Sly, Slick and the Wicked*, released in the fall of 1970. After their last chart hit, "Your Mission (If You Decide to Accept It) Pt. 1," the group disbanded. Brownlee and Simon joined Curtom act Mystique featuring Ralph Johnson, the former lead singer of the Impressions. The group charted with three Bunny Sigler-produced singles: "Is It Really You?," "What Would the World Be Without Music?," and "It Took a Woman Like You." Lowrell Simon co-wrote and co-produced the track "Keep on Playing the Music" on their self-titled debut LP. Lowrell Simon dropped his last name and signed to entertainer Liberace's AVI Records; the single "Mellow Mellow Right On" b/w "You're Playing Dirty" went to number-32 R&B in 1979. He also produced and co-wrote tracks for the Gemigo/Curtom act the Notations. One single, "Think Before You Stop," charted in 1985. Sadly, Larry Brownlee died in 1978 in Chicago. *—Ed Hogan*

The Sly, Slick and the Wicked / 1970 / Brunswick ✦✦✦✦

Heavenly harmonies on vinyl, Chicago's Lost Generation consists of two sets of brothers: Lowrell and Fred Simon, and Jesse and Leslie Dean. They never went platinum or gold but their biggest record *Sly, Slick & the Wicked* influenced hundreds of groups; a Cleveland, a Californian, and an East Coast group have all named themselves Sly, Slick & Wicked. Ironically, though it was intended as a warning to women, the song appeals more to men. Brunswick wasted the bouncy "You're So Young but You're So True," on the back of "Talking the Teenage Language" (not included). A silky smooth "Wait a Minute," with its hesitating beat, went to number 25 in the R&B chart. They do enjoyable renditions of Chairmen of the Boards' "Give Me Just a Little More Time," the Moments' "Love on a Two Way Street," and the Delfonics' "Didn't I Blow Your Mind." *—Andrew Hamilton*

● **The Sly, Slick and the Wicked/The Young, Tough and Terrible** / Oct. 18, 1999 / Edsel ✦✦✦✦

Love and Kisses

f. 1977, London, England, **db.** 1979

Group / Disco

Best-known for performing the theme song from the 1978 disco film *Thank God It's Friday*—which was probably disco's most famous movie next to *Saturday Night Fever*—Love and Kisses was the creation of producer/songwriter Alec R. Costandinos. With Love and Kisses, Costandinos tended to favor lush, glossy orchestral arrangements and extended performances; it wasn't uncommon for a Love and Kisses number to last 14 minutes or more. Because much of the material dragged on so long, radio programmers tended to shy away from Love and Kisses' LPs. However, the *Thank God It's Friday* theme (which only came out as a single and wasn't on any of Love and Kisses' albums) did enjoy a lot of radio airplay, and Love and Kisses had no problem appealing to club DJs. Love and Kisses signed with Casablanca in 1977 and the group recorded three albums for that label—1977's *Love and Kisses*, 1978's *How Much, How Much I Love You*, and 1979's *You Must Be Love*—before calling it quits in 1979. *—Alex Henderson*

● **Love and Kisses** / 1977 / Casablanca ✦✦✦

With the possible exception of the theme song from the 1978 movie *Thank God It's Friday*, Love and Kisses never enjoyed the sort of pop/Top 40 acceptance that Donna Summer, the Village People, the Silver Convention, and Chic did. Love and Kisses was, for the most part, the disco era's quintessential club act—most of its orchestral Euro-disco recordings didn't appeal to programmers at American pop/Top 40 stations, but club DJs were strong supporters of its music. Produced by Alec R. Costandinos in London in March 1977, Love and Kisses' self-titled debut LP contains only two songs: the 17-minute "Accidental Lover" on side one and the 16-minute "I've Found Love (Now That I Have Found You)" on side two. While "Accidental Lover" has a funky, sassy quality, "I've Found Love" is as dreamy and starry-eyed as it is campy and overblown. Disco's detractors, of course, hated the type of campiness that Love and Kisses often favored and saw this LP as a glaring example of disco's bloated excesses. But despite all those excesses, Love and Kisses could be fun—and this LP, although not a masterpiece, is an enjoyable artifact of its time. *—Alex Henderson*

How Much, How Much I Love You / 1978 / Casablanca ✦✦

You Must Be Love / 1979 / Casablanca ✦✦✦

After becoming too pretentious for its own good on 1978's disappointing *How Much, How Much I Love You*, *Love and Kisses* pleasantly surprised disco audiences by doing some of its best work on its third and final album *You Must Be Love*. Perhaps the fact that commercial radio was receptive to the "Thank God It's Friday" single inspired producer/songwriter Alec R. Costandinos to streamline Love and Kisses and make the group a bit more radio-friendly—none of the three songs on side one last eight minutes. Side one, in fact, contains some of the group's most memorable work, including the delightfully Euro-trashy "Ooh La La La La," the Latin-flavored "Your Middle Name Is Money" and the Gino Vannelli-ish adult contemporary ballad "Find Yourself a Dream." But Costandinos still has his excesses—side two is devoted entirely to the 16-minute title song, which is, like the title song of *How Much, How Much I Love You*, nothing more than a poor man's "I've Found Love (Now That I Have Found You)." *—Alex Henderson*

Love Unlimited

f. 1969

Group / Smooth Soul, Urban, Disco, Funk

Love Unlimited is the vocal trio who contributed cooing background vocals on Barry White's million-selling hits and sold-out concerts, as well as having their own gold single, "Walkin' in the Rain With the One I Love," and a number-one R&B smash, "I Belong to You." The trio consisted of sisters Glodean and Linda James and Diane Taylor. Glodean first met White, her future husband, through a mutual friend. She was a fan of White's before she even knew it, having bought Viola Wills' single "Lost Without the Love of My Guy," a song White co-wrote and arranged while he was an A&R director and producer with Bob Keene's Bronco Records.

White started working with the group, who hadn't done any professional singing. They rehearsed for almost a year. White wrote "Walkin' in the Rain With the One I Love" with lyrics that were inspired by conversations with Glodean. White christened the group Love Unlimited. A friend of White's, Larry Nunes, took the record to Russ Regan, who was the head of the Uni label owned by MCA. "Walkin' in the Rain With the One I Love," with White "phoning" in his part, went gold, peaking at number-six R&B, number-14 pop on *Billboard*'s charts. Love Unlimited's *From a Girl's Point of View We Give You*... album became a million-seller. Soon after, Regan left Uni for 20th Century Records. Without Regan, White's relationship with Uni soured.

With his relationship with Uni in chaos and Love Unlimited contract-bound with the label, White decided he needed to work with another act. He wanted to work with a male artist. White made three song demos of himself singing and playing the piano. Nunes heard them and insisted that he re-record and release them as a recording artist. They argued for days about it. Then, Nunes somehow convinced White to do it and White signed with 20th Century Records where Regan was president. This decision led to White having a gold- and platinum-laced recording career.

White got a contractual release from Uni for Love Unlimited and they joined him at 20th Century. Their first singles for the label were "Oh Love, Well We Finally Made It" (a Top 40 R&B hit), "It May Be Winter Outside (But in My Heart It's Spring)," and "Under the Influence of Love"—all from the LP *Under the Influence Of*... issued in summer 1973. White originally recorded the latter two songs with singer Felice Taylor. While working on material for the next Love Unlimited album, Glodean James suggested that White use the piano introduction from "Lost Without the Love of My Guy" on a new song. At first resistant to the idea, White relented and re-used the piano chord progression on "I Belong to You."

The majestic ballad, arranged by Gene Page, went to number-one R&B in late 1974. It was included on the album *In Heat*, issued in fall 1974. It was Love Unlimited's most exciting album, featuring the same studio band heard on White's hits: guitarists Ray Parker Jr. (Raydio, "Ghostbusters," co-writer with White on "You See the Trouble With Me"), Wah Wah Watson, Lee Ritenour, David T. Walker, Dean Parks, and Don Peake, bassists Nathan East and Wilton Felder of the Crusaders, drummer Ed Greene, and percussionist Gary Coleman. *In Heat* included the follow-up single "Share a Little Love in Your Heart" (number-21 R&B, spring 1975), and standout tracks "Move Me No Mountain," "I Needed Love—You Were There," a long version of "I Belong to You," and "Love's Theme"—with lyrics! After White left 20th Century, Love Unlimited recorded for White's CBS-distributed label Unlimited Gold, charting most notably with the steppers' favorite "High Steppin' Hip Dressin' Fella (You Got It Together)," number-45 R&B, fall 1979, from the LP *Love Is Back*. The married couple charted as Barry White and Glodean White with "Didn't We Make It Happen Baby" and "I Want You" in 1981, and recorded a full LP, *Barry & Glodean*. After eight Barry White albums, four Love Unlimited albums, four Love Unlimited Orchestra albums, constant touring, and dealing with the rigors of the music industry, White decided to take a break.

Returning to recording, White had his biggest success since his '70s heyday with the platinum single "Practice What You Preach" and the multi-platinum album *Icon Is Love* on A&M. Glodean White's background vocals can be heard on Barry White's 1999 Private Music/Windham Hill/BMG album *Staying Power.* Love Unlimited can be heard on the soundtrack of the 20th Century Fox movie *The Together Brothers*, originally released on 20th Century Records during the summer of 1974 and reissued on CD in June 1999, and 1997's *Best of Love Unlimited*, both from PGD/Polygram Pop. *—Ed Hogan*

From a Girl's Point of View We Give You . . . / 1972 / Varese Sarabande ✦✦✦✦✦

From a Girl's Point of View We Give You . . . is a cohesive album-length meditation on the highs and lows of love, delivered by a satiny girl group trio pillowed in one of the warmest production surroundings yet heard on a pop album—courtesy of one Barry White. White and Love Unlimited had spent a year working up their material, and it shows: the nine songs hang together like few soul albums of the time. Opening with a subdued monologue by Glodean James, the album does take awhile to get to the best track and biggest hit; the last one here, "Walkin' in the Rain With the One I Love," became White's first big hit, complete with ambient rain noise and a tender telephone call between White and James (who were later to marry). "I'll Be Yours Forever More" and "If This World Were Mine" (the latter a beautiful Marvin Gaye cover) are what the Supremes would've sounded like if they'd had the material, the producers, the freedom, and the ambition to record a concept album in the late '60s. Barry White's arrangements are reminiscent of the mid-'60s Holland-Dozier-Holland sound, but with all the icy edges melted off and the driving drumwork coaxed into a midtempo crawl. The only flaw to *From a Girl's Point of View We Give You . . .* is that the other songs can't carry a candle to the three or four best selections—though competently performed and seductively arranged, much of this concept record simply floats by. *—John Bush*

Love Unlimited / 1972 / UNI ✦✦✦

Under the Influence Of . . . / 1973 / 20th Century ✦✦✦✦

If there was ever to be a poster child of the disco movement, Barry White would be a top pick. Across his own solo career and through his Love Unlimited Orchestra and Love Unlimited side projects, he dominated the early days of this feel-good genre. And Love Unlimited felt best of all. White worked with vocalists Diane Taylor, Glodean James, and Glodean's sister, Linda James, for nearly a year before their 1972 debut album, a disappointing set that nevertheless yielded one of the signature hits of the age, "Walking in the Rain With the One I Love." It was that ethereal beauty that the trio hoped to re-create with the autumn 1973 release of *Under the Influence Of. . . .* They succeeded, with room to spare. The album opens with the soaring strings of the Love Unlimited Orchestra's instrumental "Love's Theme," a stupendous mood-setter that was released on that band's album nearly simultaneously and became a number-one hit in December. However, here the piece was merely intended to set the scene for all that was to follow. From the effusive "Oh Love, Well We Finally Made It" and the tender ballad "Lovin' You, That's All I'm After" to the Motown-ish strains of "It May Be Winter Outside (But in My Heart It's Spring)" (which gave the trio another Top 50 hit), Love Unlimited served up a nonstop diet of heartfelt, if not always heart-stopping, music. A sweetly tempting byproduct of its era, *Under the Influence Of . . .* doesn't walk away with top honors, and White was always best on his own material. Love Unlimited's variations on his trademark waka-waka guitar and lush strings are never less than fascinating, however, and the poignancy of the nostalgia train continues to churn. *—Amy Hanson*

In Heat / 1974 / 20th Century ✦✦✦✦✦

Love Unlimited's best LP was *In Heat.* All of the right elements came together for the group and their mentor/producer, Barry White, who co-wrote most of the songs and did some arranging. The cornerstone of the album is the elegant ballad "I Belong to You." Arranged by Gene Page, the trio's biggest hit went to number-one R&B and number-27 pop on *Billboard*'s charts in late 1974. The album version is longer than what's commonly heard on the radio. The luscious follow-up, "Share a Little Love in Your Heart," made it to number-21 R&B in spring 1975. The album brimmed with appetizing standout tracks: "Move Me No Mountain," "I Needed Love—You Were There," and a lyric-laced version of the perennial favorite "Love's Theme." Several tracks from *In Heat* are on 1997's *Best of Love Unlimited.* *—Ed Hogan*

He's All I've Got / 1977 / Priority ✦✦✦

Produced by Barry White, *He's All I've Got* is one of the trio's most consistent albums. The urgent, telegraphing, guitar-laced sound of the LP's sole charting single, "I Did It for Love," is a stylistic nod to "You Keep Me Hangin' On." Even more of White's Motown influences come to the forefront on the lively "He's Mine (No You Can't Have Him," which recalls the Supremes with its steady '60s pop marching beat. The *He's All I've Got* LP is a perfect companion to the group's excellent *In Heat* album. Two of its tracks, the heart-tugging, string-covered slow jam "I Guess I'm Just Another Girl in Love" and the cooing ballad "He's All I've Got," are on 1997's *Best of Love Unlimited.* *—Ed Hogan*

● **The Best of Love Unlimited** / May 20, 1997 / Polygram ✦✦✦✦✦

Spanning the years 1972-1980, *The Best of Love Unlimited* is a generous 17-track overview of the female trio's career, with the vast majority of the songs produced and written (or co-written) by their mentor, Barry White. Naturally, their two big hits are present: the gold-selling R&B Top Ten hit "Walkin' in the Rain (With the One I Love)" and the R&B number one "I Belong to You." But with White at the controls, Love Unlimited managed a number of other fine moments, usually with a sound that wasn't too dissimilar from White's own records. They weren't necessarily carbon copies—a classic female soul group sound pops up now and again, as with the Motown-style bounce of "It May Be Winter Outside (But in My Heart, It's Spring)." There's also an endearing, disco-fied dance track in "High Steppin', Hip Dressin' Fella (You Got It Together)." But even those bear White's instantly recognizable touch as an arranger, and his fingerprints are all over excellent minor hits like "Under the Influence of Love," "Oh Love, Well We Finally Made It," "I Needed Love—You Were There," "Move Me No Mountain," "I'm So Glad That I'm a Woman," and the ballad "Share a Little Love in Your Heart." Die-hard White fans would do well to pick this up, and it's appealing enough to play outside of that base, too. *—Steve Huey*

Love Unlimited Orchestra

f. 1974, San Pedro, CA, **db.** 1983

Group / Instrumental Pop, Urban, Disco

The longtime support unit for R&B love man Barry White, the 40-piece Love Unlimited Orchestra's lush, string-laden sound helped set the stage for the emergence of disco. The ensemble was originally formed by White to back his female protégées Love Unlimited beginning with their 1972 debut LP; the orchestra soon began supporting White himself as well, and in 1974 they issued their first LP *Rhapsody in White*, scoring a hit with the single "Love Theme." Two other albums, *Together Brothers* and *White Gold*, appeared later that same year, and in 1975 the Love Unlimited Orchestra returned with *Music Maestro Please.* Around the time of the release of 1976's *Sweet Summer Suite*, the orchestra welcomed to its ranks a new member, saxophonist Kenny Gorelick, who under the name Kenny G later went on to considerable success as a solo act.

After recording the theme to Dino de Laurentiis' big-budget 1977 remake of *King Kong*, the Love Unlimited Orchestra recorded *My Musical Bouquet* a year later; *Just a Little Bit Different* followed in 1979, and in 1981 the group yielded two more LPs, *Let 'Em Dance* and *Welcome Aboard.* 1983's *Rise* was the final new Love Unlimited Orchestra LP, although they continued backing White in the studio and on-stage. *—Jason Ankeny*

Rhapsody in White / 1974 / 20th Century ✦✦✦✦

The press may have dubbed Barry White "the walrus of love," but he was certainly the guru of something for many star-crossed lovers across his Love Unlimited Orchestra output. While White rocketed up the charts with his solo "I'm Gonna Love You Just a Little Bit More" in 1973, it was that same year's smash single "Love's Theme" that shot Love Unlimited Orchestra right up alongside him. Mostly instrumental, all orchestral, and packed with "that" tchka tchka guitar and full-fledged disco sound well before the genre reached maturity, *Rhapsody in White* set the stage and showcased the sounds that would shortly inspire a generation of producers, arrangers, and performers to start a million mirror balls spinning the world over. This album, in all its admitted smarminess, is a triumph. From the opening bars of "Barry's Theme," *Rhapsody in White* unleashes a groove which really keeps it all mellow. And even though we have to listen through three tracks to first hear White's trademarked vocal come-on on "Midnight and You" it's well worth the wait. He gets a little more vocal on side two, across "Don't Take It All Away" and again at the beginning of "Baby Blues," which has shag rug in front of a fireplace written all over its arrangement. But the masterful finale, of course, is "Love's Theme." The song's lush strings and smooth wah-wah guitars not only typified a genre, they also became an aural catchphrase for an entire generation of clubbers. And because this is, underneath it all, a Barry White album, the teaser for the nightcap is delicious. *—Amy Hanson*

Together Brothers / 1974 / 20th Century ✦✦✦

White Gold / 1974 / 20th Century ✦

Even though the Love Unlimited Orchestra was originally assembled to provide instrumentation for Barry White's Love Unlimited side project, the band was a heavy chart hitter for four years. White Gold is the band's third 1974 release and, though it cannot eclipse their debut, *Rhapsody in White*, still it would take them through the beginning of 1976. White pulls out the tried-and-true formula across this album, which is loaded with the expected orchestral numbers—heavy on the strings, of course, and interspersed with White's own vocal nuggets. The problem is, however, how many times can this really play out? *Rhapsody in White* remains the quintessential Unlimited sound and everything after that is just cream cheese filler. But if that's what the masses want. . . . "Satin Soul" was the only track to flip off the album and onto the singles chart, and it is relatively sweet, but the real gem in this album comes one track later. "Always Thinking of You," penned by Ray Parker Jr., is a much stronger song. It's rich, full of life, and has a great groove. One other track worth spinning is the horn-driven and funkified "You Make Me Feel Like This (When You Touch Me)." The rest of the album, unfortunately, is a throw-away. But still it cannot be denied; at the end of the party, no matter how good or bad, Love Unlimited Orchestra provided a sound that was integral to the decade and a service to purveyors of shag carpets and crackling fireplaces everywhere. *—Amy Hanson*

Music Maestro Please / Dec. 1975 / 20th Century ✦✦

Barry White arranged, produced, and co-wrote all of the songs for this December 1975 release from his Love Unlimited Orchestra. The final result of *Music Maestro Please* is the one of their most realized albums, next to *My Musical Bouquet.* "Makin' Believe That It's You" sweeps you along with enveloping strings and a double-time beat. Snapping guitars push the somewhat funky "Wanna Stay." Other highlights are the playful "It's Only What I Feel" and the slinky "Midnight Groove." The soaring "Bring It on Up" and the smooth midtempo "Forever in Love" can also be found on *The Best of the Love Unlimited Orchestra.* *—Ed Hogan*

● **The Best of the Love Unlimited Orchestra** / 1995 / Mercury ✦✦✦✦✦

The Best of the Love Unlimited Orchestra collects 15 tracks by Barry White's groundbreaking instrumental support outfit. Their sound as assembled by White—thick layers of sweet strings, pulsing beats, chunky wah-wah guitars, plus tinkling piano and gently swelling horns—played a huge role in creating the blueprint for disco, not to mention countless porn soundtracks. In addition to backing White and his female protégées Love Unlimited, the Love Unlimited Orchestra also made their own recordings, naturally with White at the helm. Although they recorded up to 1983, their commercial heyday lasted from 1974-1977, when they charted regularly on the pop, R&B, and disco/club listings.

They even scored a number one pop hit right out of the box with 1974's "Love's Theme," a watershed record in the history of disco. That's here, of course, plus the Orchestra's other chart hits: "Satin Soul," "Rhapsody in White," "Forever in Love," "My Sweet Summer Suite," "Bring It on Up," and their theme from the 1977 remake of *King Kong*. It's superbly evocative mood music, pretty much the instrumental equivalent of Barry White's trademark love-man come-ons. Anyone enamored of White's sound, or curious about the evolution of disco, would do well to pick this up. *—Steve Huey*

Darlene Love (Darlene Wright)

b. Jul. 26, 1938, Los Angeles, CA

Vocals / Girl Group, R&B

Amazingly, Darlene Love, a superb vocalist, hasn't had much of a track record as a solo singer, at least not in terms of hits. Love was a founding member of the Blossoms in 1957. They did several sessions and were resident singers on the television show *Shindig*. Love sang lead vocals on "He's a Rebel," which was credited to the Crystals, and "Zip-a-Dee-Doo-Dah," which was issued as Bob B. Soxx & the Bluejeans. She cut six singles for Spector's Phillies label, with "Wait Till My Bobby Gets Back Home" the most successful.

Love became busy as an actress, but reunited with Spector for the 1977 single "Lord, If You're a Woman." Love appeared in all four *Lethal Weapon* films, and was also in the Royal Shakespeare Company's co-production of Stephen King's *Carrie*. Her 1990 LP, *Paint Another Picture*, failed to chart in America. Love later toured as a background vocalist with Cher. She appeared briefly on the soap opera *Another World* in 1993. *—Ron Wynn*

Masters / 1981 / Phil Spector International ♦♦♦

For a few years this collection of Spector-produced Darlene Love sides was one of the most coveted albums of rare Spector material. It was easier to obtain in the 1990s, however, on ABKCO's *Best of* CD. *—Richie Unterberger*

● **The Best of Darlene Love** / Sep. 22, 1992 / ABKCO ♦♦♦♦♦

Darlene Love possesses one of the most distinctive and powerful voices in pop music. For years she was a backup singer for big stars like Elvis and Sam Cooke, but when she hooked up with Phil Spector she became star in her own right. Although she never was as big as the Ronettes or the Crystals, she recorded a whole boatload of classic songs. These 15 tracks are all produced by Phil Spector and feature his innovative Wall of Sound production style. Love began her time with Spector singing uncredited lead vocals on the Crystals' hit "He's Not a Rebel." That song and another Crystals song she sang, "He's Sure the Boy I Love," are classic girl group tracks. The lugubrious and glorious update of "Zip-a-Dee-Doo-Dah" (cut with Bobby Sheen as Bob B. Soxx & the Blue Jeans) is a truly wonderful work of art. The other classic Bob B. Soxx tracks she recorded are here as well: "Why Do Lovers Break Each Other's Hearts" and "Not Too Young to Get Married." Along with the hits on this set, there are many tracks that are less-known but just as great: the slow and dramatic "My Heart Beat a Little Faster," the uptempo heartbreaker "Run Run Runaway," and "Long Way to Be Happy," a brilliant track featuring one of Love's best vocals that was recorded in 1965 near the end of Spector's amazing run. Every track on this disc is worthy of a spot in the girl group hall of fame, if not the Rock and Roll Hall of Fame. The set also contains a couple of rarities—the original version of "Chapel of Love" that Spector unwisely left on the shelf. Co-writers and frequent Spector collaborators Jeff Barry & Ellie Greenwich took the song to the Dixie Cups and they had a huge hit with it. Love's version is much slower and far more sultry than the Dixie Cups' teenybop version—it most likely was too adult-sounding to be a hit. Even more exciting is the inclusion of 1975's "Lord, if You're a Woman." This powerful track was recorded during Spector's ill-fated mid-'70s comeback and should have been a hit. Love sounds strong as ever, cutting loose like she never would have ten years earlier, and Spector still had magic up his sleeve. Sadly, it was not to be and Love went back to backup work and the oldies circuit. She left behind an incredible body of work, however, and the best truly is here. If you like girl groups, good-time oldies, soul music, female vocals, dance music, or just good old pop music, you need to get this disc. There is a world of love and magic waiting for you. Now bring on volume two! *—Tim Sendra*

Mary Love

b. Jul. 27, 1943, Sacramento, CA

Vocals / Pop-Soul, Urban, Soul, Contemporary Gospel

There were many soul singers like Mary Love in the 1960s—very talented, competent performers who were nonetheless pushed to the back of the pack because they lacked exceptional material, or enough personality to truly distinguish them from a crowded field. After doing some session work as a teenager in Los Angeles, she got her chance to cut half a dozen singles for the Modern label in the mid-'60s. These were decent, commercial soul records, nothing more, nothing less, somewhat less pop-oriented than Motown, but not much. She managed to get hold of some material by noted writers Frank Wilson and Ashford & Simpson, but only managed one minor R&B hit for Modern, "Move a Little Closer," which made number 48 in 1966.

Love revisited the lower reaches of the R&B Top 50 with "The Hurt Is Just Beginning" for Roulette in 1968; mysteriously, she only issued one more 45 for the label, and that didn't come out until 1971. Over the next decade she barely recorded at all. When she re-emerged as Mary Love Comer in the mid-'80s, she sang updated soul with a Christian-centered message. England's Northern soul market ensured a tiny market for her (as it does for many other obscure soul singers), and it was in England that a CD reissue of her work appeared in the mid-'90s. *—Richie Unterberger*

● **Then & Now** / 1994 / Kent ♦♦♦

Mary Love's only career retrospective mixes ten of her mid-'60s Modern sides with 11 more contemporary recordings from the 1980s and 1990s. This is poor strategy; it's the '60s sides that almost everyone wants to hear. The 1965-1967 tracks are fair commercial period soul that will probably excite only those who want to build an extremely thorough soul collection; an obscure, stately Ashford & Simpson ballad, "Baby I'll Come," is the standout. The more recent numbers are generic urban contemporary dance tunes with Christian message lyrics that border on the pushy, as heartfelt as they may be. What's worse is that the old material is alternated with the new, rather than sequenced chronologically, a decision that will probably annoy even those who want to hear everything. The new material desperately wants you to praise the Almighty; you will, however, end up thanking God not for eternal life, but for programmable CD players. *—Richie Unterberger*

Preston Love

b. Apr. 26, 1921, Omaha, NE

Sax (Alto) / Soul, Funk

Preston Love's career has intersected, albeit quietly, with almost every aspect of popular music in the 20th century. Born April 26, 1921, in Omaha, NE, Love began playing the saxophone at 15 and by 22 he was sitting on the bandstand as a member of the Count Basie Orchestra. During the late '40s and '50s he toured the Corn Belt playing in territory bands with Nat Towles and Lloyd Hunter and eventually lead his own groups recording for Federal. He worked with Johnny Otis, who wrote and produced one of the few dates with Love as a leader, the funky R&B party of 1969's *Preston Love's Omaha Bar-B-Q*. During the early '60s he moved to California where he worked with Ray Charles and eventually became the West Coast house bandleader for Motown. Touring the U.S. and Europe quite frequently, the '90s saw Love also add lecturer and author to his already impressive resumé. *—Wade Kergan*

● **Preston Love's Omaha Bar-B-Q** / 1969 / Ace ♦♦♦♦

Saxophonist Preston Love was far more associated with the early sounds of West Coast R&B in the 1940s and 1950s than he was with modern soul-funk. However, he, like numerous other R&B vets, actually did make some recordings in a much more modern style that have been relatively ignored. By the time this CD came out in 2001 early funk was undergoing a renaissance among collectors, spurring the reissue of Love's rare 1969 LP. Helping Love out on this collection of instrumental soul-funk tunes were the legendary Johnny Otis on piano and vibraphone, Clifford Soloman on tenor sax, and, on one of his earliest recordings, legendary guitarist (and son of Johnny Otis) Shuggie Otis, just 14 years of age when this was made. It's a good, though not great, set of instrumentals that bubble along nicely, with both grit and jazzy accents. Shuggie Otis' bluesy playing is already stinging and imaginative at this point, sometimes with a slightly distorted wah-wah edge that gives the R&B-based jams a late-'60s feel, and, in fact, he and his father co-wrote most of the material. On "Cream Dream," the sounds take on a slightly psychedelic hue, with the combination of underwater bubbling noises and way-in-the-background flute by Love. It's a nice record, though quite brief at just 28 minutes. *—Richie Unterberger*

The Lovelites

f. 1967, Chicago, IL, **db.** 1973

Group / Chicago Soul, Soul

A '60s Chicago high-school female trio, the Lovelites scored a sizable teen angst hit with "How Can I Tell My Mom & Dad" for Uni in 1969. Though it was never directly stated in the song, its implicit theme was teen pregnancy, still regarded then as a fate worse than death in many circles. Patti Hamilton, her sister Rozena Petty, and Barbara Peterman were the original group, with Ardell McDaniel replacing Peterman in 1968. Joni Berlman replaced Petty in 1970, and Rhonda Grayson replaced McDaniel in 1971. The single did well enough for the group to start its own label, Lovelite Records, in 1970. It continued until 1973, while one single from their label made the R&B Top 40, "My Conscience," in 1971. They disbanded in 1973. *—Ron Wynn*

Michael Lovesmith

b. St. Louis, MO

Vocals / Urban, Quiet Storm

Singer/songwriter/multi-instrumentalist Michael Lovesmith (born Michael L. Smith in St. Louis, MO) was a member of the group the Smith Connection, which was comprised of him and his brothers Danny and Louis. They recorded for Motown's '60s hit songwriting/production trio Holland-Dozier-Holland's Music Merchant label, where they had a hit single with "(I've Been a Winner, I've Been a Loser) I've Been in Love" in early 1973. When H-D-H returned to Motown in the mid-'70s, they brought along Michael and his brothers, who recorded one album as Lovesmith for the label in the early '80s.

Lovesmith was signed to Motown's music publishing firm, Jobete Music, as a staff songwriter. Working with Brian & Eddie Holland, Lovesmith's songs were covered by Motown artists including the Jackson 5 ("All I Do Is Think of You" co-written by Lovesmith and Brian Holland). Lovesmith's smooth disco song "Let's Be Young Tonight" went to number-19 R&B on *Billboard*'s charts in fall 1976 for former Jackson 5 member Jermaine Jackson. The 1976 LP *My Name Is Jermaine* included two more Lovesmith songs, the thumping "Faithful," with interweaving vocals by Thelma Houston, and the luscious post-midnight sax-laced ballad "My Touch of Madness." The songwriter collaborated with Houston and David Jones on the title track to her 1977 Motown LP *Any Way You Like It*. He co-wrote with Jackson and Maureen Bailey "Go on Doin' What You Feel" for the Motown group Switch. Around the same time, Lovesmith produced an album for disco singer Patti Brooks on Neil Bogart's Casablanca Records.

By the early '80s, Lovesmith was a solo artist for Motown, releasing the LPs *I Can Make It Happen* (1983), *Diamond in the Raw* (1984), and *Rhymes of Passion* (1985). Lovesmith wrote songs for and produced the 1995 Motown self-titled debut of Mind, Heart & Soul and the sensuous female vocal group Harem. He co-wrote two songs with Barry White, "Whatever We Had We Had" and "Don't You Want to Know," for White's 1994 multi-platinum album *The Icon Is Love*. Others who have recorded Lovesmith's songs are Aretha Franklin ("Better Friends Than Lovers"), Gladys Knight & the Pips ("Don't Make Me Run Away"), and Bobby Brown ("You Ain't Been Loved Right"). Lovesmith also co-wrote and co-produced several songs with Motown Records founder Berry Gordy for Smokey Robinson's *Intimate* album, issued in fall 1999 on Motown. *—Ed Hogan*

I Can Make It Happen / 1983 / Motown ♦♦♦

Composer/producer Michael turned vocalist on this mid-'80s debut for Motown. After amassing a string of credits for numbers he did for everyone from The Isley Brothers to Aretha Franklin, this was a minor disappointment. While Lovesmith proved a good singer, especially on ballads, and the album was expertly produced, it was more slick than soulful, containing more than its share of self-satisfied, smug arrangements. But it at least got Lovesmith's solo career off to a decent start. *—Ron Wynn*

● **Diamond in the Raw** / 1984 / Motown ♦♦♦♦♦

His best-known album has a heavy emphasis on rhythm—a trademark of Lovesmith's. *—Rick A. Bueche*

LSG

f. 1996

Group / Urban, Contemporary R&B

LSG is Gerald LeVert, Keith Sweat and Johnny Gill, a trio of urban R&B stars who have collected 30 number-one R&B hits and album sales of more than thirty million between themselves. The superstar side project began when Sweat called LeVert and told him about his idea of recording an album with old friend Johnny Gill. Enlisting a roster of producers and co-stars worthy of their own lofty status, LSG worked with Sean "Puffy" Combs and Jermaine Dupri plus rappers LL Cool J, Busta Rhymes and MC Lyte for their debut album, 1997's *Levert.Sweat.Gill.* Led by the Top Five single "My Body," the album easily went platinum. *—John Bush*

● **Levert.Sweat.Gill** / Nov. 11, 1997 / East West ♦♦♦♦

Gerald LeVert, Keith Sweat, Johnny Gill—three vocalists who have sustained successful careers in urban R&B. They've hit the top of the charts, but they never quite became superstars. They were never washouts, either—they stuck around for years, continually racking up hits without drawing attention themselves. In short, they're R&B journeymen—you can always rely on them to deliver the goods. And that's what makes their supergroup LSG's first album—called *LeVert, Sweat, Gill*, funnily enough—so enjoyable: These guys know how to pick a good song and deliver it memorably. There are a few weak cuts scattered throughout the album, but they're so well-crafted, they're easy to enjoy. But the true moments to treasure occur when everything falls into place—when they have a strong melody and lush production, LSG's voices blend in thrilling harmony and produce some truly affecting smooth R&B. And while its roots are certainly in old-fashioned, lover-man R&B, there's a distinct new flavor to the music, thanks to contributions from such producers as Sean "Puffy" Combs and Jermaine Dupri. That helps make LSG's first album a satisfying debut indeed. *—Leo Stanley*

L.T.D.

f. 1968, Greensboro, NC, **db.** 1981

Group / Urban, Funk

Long-running funk outfit L.T.D.—Love, Togetherness & Devotion—was formed in Greensboro, NC, in 1968 by keyboardist Jimmie "J.D." Davis and bassist Abraham "Onion" Miller, both former backing musicians for the great Sam & Dave. Upon relocating to New York City, the twosome recruited guitarist Johnny T. McGhee, horn player Carle Vickers, saxophonists Arthur "Lorenzo" Carnegie, Toby Wynn and Abraham Miller, and trombonist Jake Riley Jr. Vocalist/drummer Jeffrey Osborne also signed on before the group settled in Los Angeles, where Osborne's brother, keyboardist Billy Osborne joined the lineup as well.

L.T.D. signed with the A&M label to issue their 1974 debut *Love, Togetherness & Devotion.* On their third LP, 1976's *Love to the World*, the group scored their first Top 20 pop hit, "Love Ballad." The follow-up, 1977's *Something to Love*, included the Top Five smash "(Every Time I Turn Around) Back in Love Again," and four years later L.T.D. returned to the Top 40 once again with "Shine On." However, Osborne then exited to pursue a solo career, and despite the additions of vocalists Leslie Wilson and Andre Ray, the band's commercial fortunes dimmed. In the wake of 1981's *Love Magic*, L.T.D. disbanded, but during the early '90s McGhee reformed the group, with 1999's *Marry You* featuring vocalists Greg Henneghan, Nakeisha Turner and Ronnie Henson, bassist Terry Gamble, keyboardist Ryan Cooper, drummer Jay Nichols and percussionist Mamadi Nyasuma. *—Jason Ankeny*

Love, Togetherness & Devotion / 1974 / A&M ♦♦♦

Major labels aren't always big on artist development—if your first album isn't a hit, you can expect to be dropped. But back in the 1960s and 1970s, they were more patient. If a major label seriously believed in an act, they were, in many cases, willing to give it several albums to develop. Take L.T.D., for example. Although L.T.D. evolved into one of the finest, most successful soul/funk outfits of the late '70s, it was hardly an overnight sensation—in fact, the band didn't enjoy a major commercial breakthrough until its third album, *Love to the World*, came out in 1976. And if A&M had been impatient, it would have missed out. Released in 1974, L.T.D.'s debut album, *Love, Togetherness & Devotion*, was hardly a major hit. This LP received very little attention, and it isn't in a class with gems like *Love to the World*, 1977's *Something to Love*, and 1978's *Togetherness.* Overall, the material is decent but not great. In 1974, L.T.D. had a recognizable sound and a charismatic, expressive lead vocalist in Jeffrey Osborne, but it still had some growing and developing to do. And thankfully, A&M was willing to stick around long enough for L.T.D. to make the transition from good to excellent. Although *Love, Togetherness & Devotion* is far from L.T.D.'s best or most essential album, it is interesting to listen to if you're a serious R&B historian. *—Alex Henderson*

Gittin' Down / 1975 / A&M ♦♦♦

L.T.D.'s second album, *Gittin' Down*, was the calm before the storm. In 1976, the band exploded commercially with its third album, *Love to the World*, and the smash hit "Love Ballad." But when Jeffrey Osborne and friends recorded this LP in 1974, they were still struggling. Like L.T.D.'s first album, *Love, Togetherness & Devotion*, this sophomore release was a commercial flop. Nonetheless, A&M saw L.T.D.'s potential, and even though *Gittin' Down* isn't fantastic, it's generally decent (if uneven). In 1974, some of the pieces were in place for L.T.D.—Osborne was an impressive lead singer (although he only handles about half of *Gittin' Down*'s lead vocals), and the band is as comfortable with tough, gritty funk ("Eldorado Joe," "Don't Lose Your Cool") as it is with ballads ("Tryin' to Find a Way"). L.T.D. had an appealing, recognizable sound in 1974; what it needed was material that was excellent instead of merely decent—and that didn't come until 1976. *Gittin' Down* isn't among L.T.D.'s essential releases; there is no reason why a casual listener would choose this album over classics like *Love to the World, Something to Love*, and *Togetherness.* Nonetheless, hardcore collectors and R&B historians will find the record interesting despite its imperfections. *—Alex Henderson*

Love to the World / 1976 / A&M ♦♦♦

The Mizell Brothers (Larry & Fonce) put L.T.D. on the right track, after the self-contained unit had stagnated on two subpar albums. Jeffrey Osborne sang lead, and the Mizells spotlighted the North Carolinian's powerful tenor. This album spawned the endearing, sentimental "Love Ballad," a majestic piece that Osborne crushes. L.T.D.'s Southern roots emerge on "Let the Music Keep Playing," a Southern-dipped tearjerker. The jazzy, joyous title track, "Love to the World," has a powerful message and gets a reprise as "Love to the World Prayer." Seven well-crafted tunes that never embarrass or make you want to skip to the next, originally released in 1976. *—Andrew Hamilton*

● **Something to Love** / 1977 / A&M ♦♦♦♦

Producer Bobby Martin once said of L.T.D. that "they play well, they write well, their vocals are moving, and they have a special energy." He couldn't have been more correct. What they'd begun with their delicious mix of classic funk and heart-wrenching soul on 1976's breakthrough *Love to the World* LP, they furthered just a year later on *Something to Love.* Their sonic dexterity was well-appreciated, as the album shot to number one on the charts. L.T.D. again included a little something for everyone across this fantastic, elastic set. The opening "Age of the Showdown" is an eclectic and completely cohesive mix of funky bass and intricate guitar loops, dance rhythms and pop ethic, married to Jeffrey Osborne's remarkable vocals, which themselves swing from blistering funk inflections to bluesy call outs and on to sweet R&B breaks without missing a beat. Elsewhere, the chart-topping "(Every Time I Turn Around) Back in Love Again" is a sweet slab of funk given a run for its money by "Material Things," which revolves around Johnny T. McGhee's outstanding basslines, while "We Party Hearty" weighs in with vibrant horns. And, of course, *Something to Love* wouldn't be worth its salt without a gorgeous Osborne ballad, captured here on "(Won't Cha) Stay With Me." The album stumbles only on "You Come First at Last" and "Make Someone Smile, Today!," as organist Billy Osborne steps behind the mike to handle the vocals. He's got a good voice, to be sure, but when slivered next to his brother Jeffrey, it's quickly apparent why he's the lead vocalist here. And despite that one glitch, this is still an outstanding effort and smooth blend, no matter how you cut it. *Something to Love* would mark some of L.T.D.'s last great funk material as they began to swing slowly into the waters of mellow R&B. *—Amy Hanson*

Togetherness / 1978 / A&M ♦♦♦♦

Togetherness is one of L.T.D.'s strongest albums, boasting the hit singles "Holding On (When Love Is Gone)" and "We Both Deserve Each Other's Love," as well as such solid album cuts as "Concentrate on You." There's a couple of bland moments on the record, but song-for-song it is among the group's finest records and contains some wonderful vocals from Jeffrey Osborne. *—Leo Stanley*

Devotion / 1979 / A&M ♦♦♦

Uptempo rump shakers outnumber L.T.D.'s crushing ballads on this adequate but unessential release; the killer tracks can be found on various greatest hits compilations. The fast jams are bass-heavy, flyweight funk pieces. "One on One" is upbeat and gritty, while "Stand Up L.T.D." is a rousing, opening-type signature song that competes with the infectious "Dance 'N' Sing 'N'" for the LP's best groove. The few ballads are supreme, creamy concoctions done majestically by Osborne: "Share" and "Stranger" couldn't have been executed better. *—Andrew Hamilton*

Shine On / 1980 / A&M ♦♦♦

Since the group's first national hit "Love Ballad," Jeffrey Osborne had been the featured vocalist for L.T.D. However, this recording would be his last one with the group before pursuing a solo career. This album spawned two upstanding singles—"Where Did We Go Wrong" and "Shine On"—the fomer being a rhythmic ballad enhanced by some stylish background vocals, leaving Jeffrey Osborne substantial space to demonstrate his commanding vocal ability. In spite of having all the right ingredients to attain that number-one status, the single peaked at number seven after 20 weeks on the *Billboard* R&B charts. It would be the group's last single to crack the Top Ten. The latter composition is arranged with noticeable crossover appeal augmented by Osborne's crooning vocals; the single peaked at 19 before fizzling out after 18 weeks. *—Craig Lytle*

Love Magic / 1981 / A&M ♦♦♦

For You / 1983 / Hot Productions ♦♦♦

● **Greatest Hits** / Jun. 18, 1996 / A&M ♦♦♦♦♦

All of L.T.D.'s biggest singles—including "Never Get Enough of Your Love," "Share My Love," "Holding On (When Love Is Gone)," "Where Did We Go Wrong," "Kickin' Back," "Love Ballad," and "(Every Time I Turn Around) Back in Love Again"—are included on this single-disc collection, making it the definitve retrospective of the late '70s smooth soul band. *—Stephen Thomas Erlewine*

20th Century Masters—The Millennium Collection: The Best of L.T.D. / Sep. 26, 2000 / A&M ✦✦✦✦
The Millennium Collection: The Best of L.T.D. gathers 12 of the California soul/funk outfit's biggest hits, including "We Party Hearty," "Love Ballad," and "(Every Time I Turn Around) Back in Love Again." "Where Did We Go Wrong," "Shine On," and "We Both Deserve Each Other's Love" are some of the other highlights of this collection, which isn't quite as extensive as A&M's *Greatest Hits*, but still provides an entertaining dose of funk from one of the West Coast's finest acts. *—Heather Phares*

LTG Exchange

Group / Disco, Funk
LTG Exchange was an early disco group based in New York City, with a sound that incorporated bits of funk, soul, salsa, and jazz. Their most successful year was 1974, when they charted with the cult disco classics "Corazon" and "Waterbed, Pt. 1." Several more singles followed through 1976, including "Keep on Trying," "My Love Does It Good to Me," "Money Mad," and "Huddle." Some of the group's work was reissued on CD during the '90s. *—Steve Huey*

Essential Dancefloor Artists, Vol. 7 / May 30, 1995 / Deep Beats ✦✦✦✦
The seventh volume in Deep Beats' *Essential Dancefloor Artists* series is reserved for LTG Exchange, a short-lived band who crossed disco with funk and soul. The band only released one album and had very little chart success during its mid-'70s existence, so its fan base is largely occupied by rare groove fanatics and people from the group's home of New Jersey. "Waterbed" (later covered by Herbie Mann) and "Keep on Trying" are the most significant cuts here, and the remainder is accomplished if unexceptional disco/funk. Two years after the release of this disc, Collectables issued the same exact content with a different title and cheaper artwork in the States. *—Andy Kellman*

● **The Very Best of LTG Exchange: Waterbed** / Jan. 5, 1998 / Collectables ✦✦✦✦
The Very Best of LTG Exchange: Waterbed compiles the highlights from the group's brief career, featuring the East Coast disco favorites "Corazon" and "Waterbed," plus nine other tracks. There's nothing quite as memorable as the singles, but the remainder of the disc is highly entertaining, making it a worthwhile exploration for disco/'70s soul fanatics. *—Stephen Thomas Erlewine*

Carrie Lucas

b. Los Angeles, CA
Vocals / Disco, Urban
A Los Angeles vocalist, Carrie Lucas' light, feathery voice made several Solar singles in the '80s. Lucas was the girlfriend of Solar head Dick Griffey, but also was a background vocalist for the Whispers prior to signing with the company. She was never able to land any breakout hits while with Solar or Constellation, the closest being a number-20 R&B record in 1985, a cover of Barbara Lewis' "Hello Stranger." It matched her with her old group the Whispers. *—Ron Wynn*

Simply Carrie / 1977 / Soul Train ✦✦✦
Lucas' impressionable debut album (and the rest of her catalog) finally saw well-deserved CD release at the turn of the 21st century. The set doesn't stray too far from other R&B output in 1977, but it does feature excellent musicianship on the arranging, vocal, and instrumental frontiers. Benefiting from the helping hands of Jerry Peters, "Tender" is a lushly orchestrated, beautifully delivered romancer, while Greg Phillinganes interjects lots of spunk and pep into the bustling number "I Gotta Get Away from Your Love," co-written by the arranger with Lucas. An ideal merger of a disco bassline with R&B guitar licks, keyboard layerings, and backing vocals, it uses subtle elements of Earth, Wind & Fire's sound. A few numbers are more on the generic side, mainly "I'll Close Love's Door" and the over-produced ballad "Me for You." The melodies here just don't cut it, and Lucas' vocals lack a certain inspiration present in most of the material on *Simply Carrie*. But the freshness of the remaining material—including the very memorable disco classic "I Gotta Keep Dancin'," graced by the voices of the Walter & Scotty of the Whispers—showcases an understatedly soulful vocalist with fulfilling repertoire. The only drawback to the CD release is that some of the quality of the original master appears to have been lost over the years. This aspect is most notable on a couple of tracks toward the end of the album and isn't a major detraction otherwise. *—Justin Kantor*

Street Corner Symphony / 1978 / RCA ✦✦
The subtle siren's sophomore set is a semi-successful attempt to blend '70s funk-disco rhythms with '60s-inspired vocal and horn arrangements. Lucas is at her best on the snazzy, jazz-tinged "The Depths of My Soul," wherein she blends her trademark sultriness with a little more gut. The closing lullaby, "Reflections," is also quite pleasant. Focusing too much on big arrangements and production, a bulk of the set loses sight of keeping its main attraction upfront. The dance number "The Edge of Night" and the title track, which fuses hooks from '50s and '60s pop hits (sung by Lucas & the Whispers, whom she backed prior to her own recordings) over a disco bridge, are prime examples of this problem. Even with a unique lounge feeling, the ballad "Simpler Days" suffers from over-polished production which doesn't fully complement Lucas and Dick Griffey's duet. A few worthy moments here, but definitely not the prime of the singer's work. The CD release includes 12-inch versions of the album's two singles. *—Justin Kantor*

Carrie Lucas in Danceland / 1979 / Solar ✦✦✦✦
Though this effort is undesirably brief—only six cuts long, it is a highlight of Lucas' output. Opening with the midtempo groover "Danceland" followed by the melancholy ballad "Sometimes a Love Goes Wrong," the core of the set is actually bona fide disco with an impressive amount of live instrumentation. The perennial dancefloor favorite "Dance With You" is the surefire standout, offering an irresistible concoction of funky guitars, swinging strings, a groovy organ, and one of Lucas' best vocal performances. With labelmates Lakeside performing the song's primary refrains, not to mention female support from Shelly Clark and Jody Watley (also a labelmate at the time), it is undoubtedly one of disco's shining moments. "Sometimes a Love Goes Wrong" is runner-up in quality—its melodic simplicity and endearing arrangement are classic. *—Justin Kantor*

● **Portrait of Carrie** / 1980 / Solar ✦✦✦✦
Perhaps her most characteristically varied outing, Carrie Lucas' fourth album ranges in tone from the jovial light funk of "Career Girl" to the serene ballad "Just a Memory" (a duet with her frequent musical friends the Whispers) to the chipper "It's Not What You Got (It's How You Use It)." It is clear throughout that solid production doesn't hurt in spicing up Lucas' vocals, which are consistently understated. Simultaneously, her lack of theatrics set her apart from the flock of '70s and '80s female R&B divas and contribute an unmistakable uniqueness to the arrangements. The fact that Lucas regularly served co-writing duties also gives her a distinction in the pack; and she is equally at home in dance and ballad settings. Besides the previously mentioned tracks, "Keep Smilin'," a remix of 1977's "I Gotta Keep Dancin'," is particularly notable: a great hook and clever production make it disco heaven. *Portrait of Carrie* is a close second to the vocalist's follow-up, *Still in Love*. *—Justin Kantor*

Still in Love / 1982 / Solar ✦✦✦✦
A fine blend of sweet and simple ballads and softly textured dance grooves, Lucas' fifth set is her strongest collection. The oft-sampled, hard-to-resist groove of "Show Me You're Coming From" turned out to be one of her highest charting singles (R&B number 23); and it's a wonder that nothing else here had that sort of impact. "Rockin' for Your Love" layers midnight keyboard stylings and swell guitar riffs over a slightly abstract drum groove given royal treatment by Lucas' delayed attacks and soothing tone. Produced by Nicholas Caldwell of the Whispers, the tune carries the signature Solar sound while remaining clearly distinctive. Other highlights include the comforting slow jam "Sweet Love"; "Is It a Dream," a 1970s-inspired midtempo number benefiting from crystal-clear male background harmonies; and the kinetic funk number "Men." An essential for any Lucas fan or student of early-'80s R&B. *—Justin Kantor*

Greatest Hits / May 1, 1995 / Unidisc ✦✦✦✦
The unaccredited compilation producer of this set did a fine job of assimilating Lucas' singles—and a few album cuts—in a flowing, mostly chronological sequence. The singer's strongest entries are generally the upbeat, driving dance tracks, which comprise the first two-thirds of the disc. Gems like the disco-driven "I Gotta Keep Dancin'" and "Dance With You" and the funky R&B groove "Show Me Where You're Coming From" are classic in their rhythm arrangements and still sound fresh today. Lucas' light and feathery vocals won't knock listeners out but contribute an earnest sweetness to the songs that make them what they are. On the ballad side, her subtle rendering of Barbara Lewis' 1963 hit "Hello Stranger" (R&B chart number one, pop number three) shines through. Loyal to its original, just as Lewis used popular male group of the time the Dells for backing harmonies, Lucas' soulful labelmates the Whispers add texture to her version. "Sometimes a Love Goes Wrong" and "What's the Question" are also melodic slow grooves, but they don't sit in the memory quite as easily. One of the strongest points of this set, however, is that all songs included are the full-length versions rather than common choppy edits used for hits collections. In the process, a few singles are left out; but nearly all the essentials are here, making *Greatest Hits* a fine Lucas showcase. *—Justin Kantor*

Lucy Pearl

f. 1999
Group / Neo-Soul, Contemporary R&B, Hip-Hop
Hip-hop/urban soul supergroup Lucy Pearl was formed in the summer of 1999 as the brainchild of Tony! Toni! Toné! multi-instrumentalist and vocalist Raphael Saadiq (formerly known as Raphael Wiggins), who left the band he co-founded with his brother D'Wayne in 1998. Saadiq first contacted DJ Ali Shaheed Muhammad of A Tribe Called Quest, which had disbanded after their 1998 LP *The Love Movement*, and then ex-En Vogue member Dawn Robinson, who had originally departed that group for a solo career in 1997 but jumped at the chance to work with Saadiq and Muhammad. Relying a great deal on live instrumentation in addition to samples and turntable work (Muhammad even plays bass and guitar), Lucy Pearl issued its self-titled debut album in the spring of 2000. *—Steve Huey*

● **Lucy Pearl** / May 23, 2000 / Beyond ✦✦✦
For many years, there has been a glut of slick, soulless R&B and hip-hop where talent is obscured by the canned packaging. Members of three bands who broke from that stale scene—En Vogue, Tony! Toni! Toné!, and A Tribe Called Quest—have formed the alter ego Lucy Pearl. With rock star makeovers gracing the cover and good press, you'd expect some crossbred, innovative results. But the new hip-hop, soul, rock, and R&B adventures are buried in the last third of the album. Until then, Dawn Robinson's rock hard vocals, Raphael Saadiq's melodic and guitar talents, and Ali Shaheed Muhammad's knack for intricate beats seem lost in a gloss of overproduction, forgettable lyrics, and cookie-cutter melodies, despite some trippy jazz beats and the witty "I Can't Stand Your Mother." The groove finally gets hot with the Chic-inspired "Don't Mess With My Man" and blasts into the scathing music biz attack "Hollywood"—is this the real Lucy Pearl? Drawing samples from Albert Collins and Notorious B.I.G., the trio mixes up a super-loose feel, acoustic guitars, old-school machine beats, and guest raps from Snoop Dogg and Q-Tip. The inventive, witty "Lucy Pearl Tells" looks back on college and growing up in the '80s, even calling up the Alabama A&M Marching Band covering the first Lucy Pearl single "Dance Tonight." *—Theresa E. LaVeck*

Joe Lutcher

b. Lake Charles, LA

Sax (Alto), Vocals / Jump Blues, New Orleans R&B, R&B

Alto saxophonist and vocalist Joe Lutcher had R&B hits in the late '40s with "Shuffle Woogie" (for Capitol in 1948), "The Rockin' Boogie" (for Specialty in 1948), and "Mardi Gras" (for Modern in 1949). While he was a competent vocalist, his true forte was the sax. His repertoire mixed instrumentals with vocal numbers, employing an approach that generally fell within the Los Angeles jump blues-R&B style of the late '40s and early '50s, although he often added New Orleans accents and sometimes went into a straighter big-band jazz mode. He's not nearly as well known, though, as his sister Nellie Lutcher, who was a more successful hitmaker as a vocalist.

Lutcher was born in Lake Charles, LA, moving to Los Angeles in the early '40s, following his sister (who had moved there in the mid-'30s). He played sax with the Nat King Cole Trio for a time before forming his own band and signing to Specialty in 1947. After some success with both Specialty and Capitol (where Nellie Lutcher recorded), he joined Modern in 1949. Modern encouraged him to add New Orleans spice to his recordings, and one of those tracks, "Mardi Gras," was an R&B Top 20 hit, preceding the more famous version of the song by Professor Longhair.

Lutcher did some subsequent records for Peacock, London, and Masters Music, but left R&B for gospel music, forming the gospel label Jordan Records. It's been written that he was influential in advising Little Richard to leave rock & roll for religious studies in the late '50s. *—Richie Unterberger*

• **Jumpin' at the Mardi Gras** / May 2, 2000 / Ace ♦♦♦

This is quite a comprehensive collection (25 tracks) for a relatively minor early R&B performer. However, it shouldn't be considered a best-of as it only covers his stint with Modern in the late '40s and early '50s, not including any of his Capitol and Specialty material, and thus omitting the R&B hits "Shuffle Woogie" and "The Rockin' Boogie" (although "Mardi Gras" *is* here). In fact, only nine of the numbers (both sides of four 1949-1950 singles, plus a song that didn't come out until a 1983 Ace compilation) were previously released; the remaining two-thirds are previously unissued outtakes and alternates. Like many of the musicians recording in L.A. in the late '40s (including many of the ones doing Modern sessions), Lutcher was at the pivot in the transition between jazz, jump blues, and R&B that was vital to the birth of rock & roll. As such pioneering saxophonists go, Lutcher was a little more traditional than most, at times sounding like a link between older New Orleans jazz and R&B. On other sides, such as the 1949 single "Ojai," he's closer to the big band mood of Dizzy Gillespie or even Benny Goodman than he is to R&B and pre-rock & roll. What history will most remember his Modern stint for, however, are the cuts with a Mardi Gras influence (particularly in the rhythms), which stand as some of the first tracks ever recorded to bear an identifiably New Orleans R&B stamp. "Mardi Gras" itself, which was done before Professor Longhair's more famous version, is certainly the most galvanizing of those. Otherwise the disc is an energetic but somewhat samey-sounding hybrid of jump R&B, jazz, and the occasional New Orleans flavor, encompassing vocals (including two songs with an unidentified female vocalist) and instrumentals. *—Richie Unterberger*

Nellie Lutcher

b. Oct. 15, 1915, Lake Charles, LA

Piano, Vocals / Jump Blues, Swing, R&B

Nellie Lutcher, a good pianist, had a few vocal hits in the late '40s that gave a permanent momentum to her career. She started playing in public early on. When Lutcher was 14, she played piano behind Ma Rainey at a local booking and the following year she toured with Clarence Hart's band in Louisiana and Texas; her father was on bass. Lutcher worked as a single in obscurity from 1935-1947, moving to Los Angeles when she was 23. Her young son told her about a benefit radio program to be broadcast from Hollywood High and at the last second she was able to get booked to close the show. She performed "The One I Love Belongs to Somebody Else," it was heard by A&R scout Dave Dexter and she was quickly signed to Capitol Records.

Her first two sessions (from 1947) resulted in her two biggest hits: "Hurry on Down" and "He's a Real Gone Guy," both of which have remained signature tunes for Lutcher through the decades. Also popular was "Fine Brown Frame." Lutcher's swing-styled piano worked well with her eccentric scatting and exaggerated pronunciation of words. However no other hits resulted and in 1952 she was dropped by Capitol. There were isolated recordings for Epic (1952-53), Liberty (1956) and Imperial but the singer-pianist made very few records after 1957, working instead at the local Musicians Union and gigging locally. Nellie Lutcher continued working on a part-time basis into the '90s, still most famous for her recordings of 1947. *—Scott Yanow*

• **The Best of Nellie Lutcher** / Oct. 31, 1995 / Capitol ♦♦♦♦♦

Nellie Lutcher was at the peak of her fame during her period with Capitol (1947-1951). A fine swing-based pianist, Lutcher was best-known for her unique vocal style which included witty asides that often sounded spontaneous. This well-conceived CD has 18 of her recordings from 1947 and one apiece from 1949-1951. Highlights include "Hurry on Down," "The One I Love Belongs to Somebody Else," "He's a Real Gone Guy," "Chi-Chi-Chi Chicago," "The Song Is Ended," "Fine Brown Frame" and two previously unissued numbers. With sympathetic and swinging backing from various guitarists (including Ulysses Livingstone and Irving Ashby), bassists and drummers, the spotlight is on Nellie Lutcher throughout. This highly recommended disc is easily her definitive CD. *—Scott Yanow*

Frankie Lymon & the Teenagers

b. Sep. 30, 1942, Harlem, NY, **d.** Feb. 28, 1968, Harlem, New York City, NY

Vocals / Doo Wop, R&B

Frankie Lymon (1942-1968) & the Teenagers were a New York doo wop group consisting of Joe Negroni, Herman Santiago, Jimmy Merchant, and Sherman Garnes but centered around the extraordinary talents of their lead singer, 13-year-old Frankie Lymon. Lymon was credited with their first big hit, "Why Do Fools Fall in Love" (In the early '90s, a federal judge ruled after a lengthy trial that Lymon hadn't written "Why Do Fools Fall in Love"—another member of the Teenagers had). His wise-beyond-his-years vocal and performing abilities not only made the Teenagers a group several notches above the competition but made Lymon the first black teenage pop star.

Though only together for a brief 18-month period, Lymon & the Teenagers exerted an enormous influence, spawning several "kid" vocal groups and providing initial inspiration to Berry Gordy to model his entire Motown production approach around Lymon's original vocal style. Inexplicably, the group split into two factions at the height of their success, and neither had a hit again. Lymon died from a drug overdose at age 26. Diana Ross, Smokey Robinson, Len Barry, and his principal protégé, Michael Jackson (whose early recordings with the Jackson 5 are virtual re-creations of the early Lymon sound, merely updated) all show the influence of Frankie Lymon & the Teenagers's groundbreaking work. *—Cub Koda*

The Teenagers Featuring Frankie Lymon / 1956 / Gee ♦♦♦

At the London Palladium / 1958 / Collectables ♦♦♦

An interesting live date featuring one of the truly tragic stories in American popular music annals. Frankie Lymon & the Teenagers capsulized what rock & roll was all about in the days before it became a corporate industry. Label head George Goldner was already producing Lymon as a single act when they toured London in 1957 and performed the concerts on this album. It's clear that they were far from a focused, cohesive operation by this time. This has been out of print for many years, although it was briefly back in circulation in England during the '70s. *—Ron Wynn*

The Complete Recordings / Jul. 15, 1994 / Bear Family ♦♦♦

This five-CD set contains more Frankie Lymon & the Teenagers than any casual fan has likely ever thought of listening to, much less owning. Only one of its five CDs is less than satisfying, yet only a portion of this collection contains music that is actually important to the history of rock & roll. The first disc contains everything that Lymon & the Teenagers recorded together for official release. By the second disc, we're already into the Teenagers' recordings without Lymon, as well as live performances by Lymon & the Teenagers from *The Ed Sullivan Show* and various Alan Freed concert events. The final three discs are made up entirely of Lymon's solo sides from 1957 through 1968. From the 20 or so familiar early songs, one hears them "progress" to the later numbers, where their vocalizing became more sophisticated and subtle, but less cohesive. Disc three opens the Frankie Lymon solo material, and with all due respect to his memory, it's a disaster. His early solo sides, from 1957 through early 1958, tried to appeal strictly to pop listeners, with results that had no beat or any other serious appeal. Disc four finds him back on track, featuring 30 entertaining and engaging rock & roll songs that show Lymon in extraordinarily good voice. Disc five continues with Lymon's recordings for Columbia in 1964 to his final records in 1968. The sad and surprising part is that a lot of it isn't bad at all. Lymon's voice matured into a fairly nondescript instrument, but he could still put a good song over, as many of these later tracks show. *—Bruce Eder*

Essential Recordings 1955–1961 / May 6, 1997 / Sequel ♦♦♦♦

This two-CD compilation stands midway between Rhino's perfectly good Teenagers collection and Bear Family's monster box of every extant note of music that Lymon and company ever left behind. It's mid-priced, which is an advantage, and it has very detailed notes that explain the origins of a number of songs whose histories haven't always been clear, but it may be more Frankie Lymon than most of us need. But it is fun—the first 14 songs on disc one include the entire *Teenagers* album, a staple of rock & roll collections (and the Roulette catalog) for decades, an album that Larry Lazell's notes remind us made it to number 19 on the charts, a major sales success for a 1950s rock & roll album. The first 23 songs of 32 on disc one are the quintet's complete recordings together, in the order in which they were done—they reveal a thriving enterprise, a vocal group that could do relatively little wrong within the context of their era, most of their material solid romantic doo wop-style vocal rock. The new remasterings reveal more detail than Rhino's late-'80s work, and have a brighter sound, but they're not quite ideal, revealing some flaws (especially harshness) in the surviving masters ("Share") that detract from the listening experience. The tracks dating from after that first album, such as "Together" and "You," show the group and their management searching for a more sophisticated, romantic sound, with greater emphasis on Lymon's singing and the rest of the quintet pushed increasingly into the background—and their final track together, Cole Porter's "Begin the Beguine," had Lymon singing as part of the quintet, rather than as lead. The rest of the collection is a bit more problematic, interspersing most of Lymon's solo work with the eight recordings left behind by the Teenagers, working with a succession of post-Lymon successors. These are pretty lively tracks, although they lack a defined and attractive vocal personality like Lymon's out in front. It might have been more sensible to devote the remainder of disc one to the Teenagers and pile Lymon's material all together on disc two, because the Lymon material is stylistically more unified, even as it declines from an initial high ("Goody Goody")—it's obvious listening to this material that Lymon's managers were trying to advance his career toward a harder rock & roll sound, covering numbers like "Jailhouse Rock" and "Silhouettes," but as he grew older his voice lost its distinctiveness. The material is pleasant and well-produced, but not terribly exciting and simply not interesting. Lazell's notes are informative, and the booklet re-creates various period trade ads for the group's releases. Still, most fans will likely opt for the Rhino CD, although this release does make the Bear Family and Collectables collections less desirable. *—Bruce Eder*

★ **The Very Best of Frankie Lymon & the Teenagers** / Oct. 6, 1998 / Rhino ♦♦♦♦♦

Although finally getting their due in the last few years of the 20th century, Frankie Lymon & the Teenagers have nonetheless been the subjects of several best-of packages, even including multi-album and CD box sets on Bear Family and Murray Hill. This 16-track very-best-of comes almost ten years after Rhino's release of an excellent 20-track best-of, and like that single-disc collection, all the big hits are here: "Why Do Fools Fall in Love," "ABC's of Love," "I Want You to Be My Girl," "I Promise to Remember," "I'm Not a Juvenile Delinquent," and later sides like "Goody Goody" and his last solo hit, "Little Bitty Pretty One." In fact, this new reissue even appropriates most of Bob Hyde's excellent notes from the 1989 package, trackwise only differing in the leaving off of later tracks like "Thumb Thumb," "Portable on My Shoulder," "Creation of Love" and the Teenagers' rocking "Love Is a Clown." The perfect entry-level compilation for digging this groundbreaking vocal group. *—Cub Koda*

Louie Lymon & the Teenchords

Vocals / Doo Wop, R&B

Though he has always been remembered primarily as Frankie Lymon's brother, Louie Lymon attained some notoriety on his own. He was 12 when he began singing with some neighborhood friends in Harlem. Rossilio Rocca, Lyndon Harold, and David Little were the other members of the Teen Chords. The Teen Chords earned an audition with Bobby Robinson by pirating vocalist Ralph Vaughan from backstage at the Apollo, where he was waiting to audition for his brother Frankie's group. They went to Robinson's record shop and sang. Robinson eventually launched the Fury label with The Teenchords single "I'm So Happy/Lydia." The song was a huge East Coast hit, and The Teenchords were soon touring with such major acts as Jerry Butler and the Impressions, Jessie Belvin, and Mickey & Sylvia.

They issued two more singles on Fury. They later recorded for End, and appeared in the film *Jamboree*. But by 1960, they disbanded. Louie Lymon then recorded with the Townsmen, and did some unsuccessful duets with his brother at the Apollo. He started a new version of the Teenchords in 1971 with Ralph Ramos, Louis Vasquez, Velmont Miller, and Frank San Pietro. Lymon tried with another edition of the Teenchords in 1983, and they recorded a version of the Teenagers' "I Want You to Be My Girl" in 1984 for Starlight. They cut "Dance Girl" for the same label in 1985. This lineup included John O'Keefe, Mike Nicoletti, Thomas Camuti, and Andre Gains, along with Lymon. Lymon subsequently left and co-wrote a book about his experiences that was never published. *—Ron Wynn*

• **I'm So Happy** / 1992 / Relic ♦♦♦♦♦

Right off master tapes, this CD collects their complete output for Bobby Robinson's Fury label, 1956-1958. It features the title track, "Honey Honey," "Lydia," "I'm Not Too Young to Fall in Love," and "Your Last Chance." Classic examples of the mid-'50s "kiddie group" sound. *—Cub Koda*

Barbara Lynn (Barbara Lynn Ozen)

b. Jan. 16, 1942, Beaumont, TX

Vocals, Guitar / New Orleans R&B, Soul, Modern Electric Blues, R&B

Singer/guitarist Barbara Lynn was a rare commodity during her heyday. Not only was she a female instrumentalist (one of the very first to hit the charts), but she also played left-handed—quite well at that—and even wrote some of her own material. Lynn's music often straddled the line between blues and Southern R&B, and since much of her early work—including the number-one R&B hit "You'll Lose a Good Thing"—was recorded in New Orleans, it bore the sonic imprint of the Crescent City. Lynn was born Barbara Lynn Ozen in Beaumont, TX, on January 16, 1942; she played the piano as a child before switching to guitar, inspired by Elvis Presley. In junior high, Lynn formed her own band, Bobbie Lynn & the Idols; at this point, her musical role models veered between bluesmen (Guitar Slim, Jimmy Reed) and female pop singers (Brenda Lee, Connie Francis). After winning a few talent shows and playing some teen dances, the still-underage Lynn started working the local clubs and juke joints, risking getting kicked out of school if she had been discovered. Singer Joe Barry caught her live act and recommended her to his friend, producer/impresario Huey P. Meaux, aka the Crazy Cajun.

With her parents' consent, Meaux brought Lynn to New Orleans to record at the legendary Cosimo's studio. Lynn cut a few singles for the Jamie label with the understanding that if none hit, she was to attend college instead of pursuing music right off the bat. In 1962, her self-penned ballad "You'll Lose a Good Thing" became a national hit, reaching the pop Top Ten and climbing all the way to number one on the R&B charts. Her first album (of the same name) was also released that year, featuring ten of her originals among its 12 tracks. Lynn continued to record for Jamie up through 1965, producing follow-up R&B hits like "You're Gonna Need Me" and "Oh Baby (We Got a Good Thing Goin')," the latter of which was recorded by the Rolling Stones in 1965.

In 1966, Lynn switched over to Meaux's Tribe label and cut "You Left the Water Running," which became something of an R&B standard and was covered by the likes of Otis Redding. In 1967, she signed with Atlantic and had another R&B hit with "This Is the Thanks I Get" early the following year; she also issued another album, *Here Is Barbara Lynn*, in 1968. Lynn scored one last hit for Atlantic in 1972's "(Until Then) I'll Suffer," but by this point, she had several children to worry about raising; dissatisfied with her promotion anyway, she wound up effectively retiring from the music business for most of the '70s and '80s, though she did play the occasional low-key tour.

Lynn returned to music in the mid-'80s, touring Japan for the first time in 1984; she later cut a live album there, called *You Don't Have to Go*, which was eventually issued in the States by Ichiban. Lynn had managed to retain a cult following among connoisseurs of American soul and blues in several different pockets of the world, and toured internationally during the early '90s. In 1994, Bullseye Blues issued her first full-fledged studio album in over two decades, *So Good*; *Until Then I'll Suffer* followed in 1996. Lynn later caught on with the respected blues label Antone's, and in 2000 she cut *Hot Night Tonight*, which featured a couple of raps by her son Bachelor Wise. *—Steve Huey*

You'll Lose a Good Thing / 1962 / Jamie ♦♦♦♦♦

Barbara Lynn Ozen's smoky voice and fine guitar playing was one of the better blends of soul vocals and blues embellishment. Huey P. Meaux produced this early-'60s record, which featured the classic title track. Other Lynn numbers, like "I'll Suffer," were equally outstanding; Lynn was sometimes tough and confrontational, and tender, inviting or anguished at other times. Meaux didn't clutter the works with unnecessary firepower; his arrangements and charts were just enough to augment Lynn's sturdy vocals. Lynn also wrote ten of the 12 songs. *—Ron Wynn*

Here Is / 1968 / Atlantic ♦♦♦

The Best of Barbara Lynn: The Atlantic Years / Nov. 22, 1994 / Ichiban/Soul Classics ♦♦♦

This 20-track collection gathers most of Lynn's output for Atlantic between 1968 and 1973, including most of her 1968 *Here Is Barbara Lynn* album and several non-LP singles. Commercially, Lynn's stay at Atlantic was not fruitful, yielding only a couple moderate R&B hits, the self-penned "This Is the Thanks I Get" and "Until Then, I'll Suffer" (both included). Artistically, this is fairly solid period soul, but a bit faceless. It seems as though Atlantic tried to fit Lynn into current soul trends; many of the 1968 tracks are quite derivative of Motown, and many of the later sides take a Memphis/Muscle Shoals approach. Those are fine influences, of course, but Lynn's strengths were her original songwriting and bluesy Southern phrasing. The most outstanding tracks are from her first Atlantic single, "This Is the Thanks I Get" and "Ring Telephone Ring," when much of her original relaxed Texas/New Orleans R&B style was still in evidence. The version of "You'll Lose a Good Thing" here, incidentally, is a remake, not the original 1962 hit. *—Richie Unterberger*

• **You'll Lose a Good Thing** / 1997 / Bear Family ♦♦♦♦♦

This is a single-disc, 28-track compilation of her best early sides from 1962-1965, including a half-dozen previously unreleased cuts. Although the material is a bit uneven, it's worthy, idiosyncratic stuff with a bluesier, swampier feel than most any other soul being made during the time. New Orleans-styled horns, bluesy organ, and some gutsy guitar licks usually decorate the arrangements, while Lynn puts the tunes across with an assured reserve. The prize obscurity here is the original version of "Oh Baby (We Got a Good Thing Goin')" (which Lynn wrote), covered by the Rolling Stones in 1965, though it must be said that the Stones' more assertive, guitar-driven version outclasses Lynn's less forceful presentation. The documentation is unusually incomplete by Bear Family standards—there's no indication, for instance, of when the unreleased material was recorded. But at any rate, it's good overlooked soul, usually upbeat, sometimes with a downcast feel that verges on the morose, as on "Dedicate the Blues to Me" and "Ring Telephone Ring." Another oddity is "Can't Buy My Love," on which it sounds like producer Huey Meaux was trying to replicate the organ-colored polka-rock he'd just crafted for the Sir Douglas Quintet. *—Richie Unterberger*

Cheryl Lynn

b. Mar. 11, 1957, Los Angeles, CA

Vocals / Quiet Storm, Club/Dance, Urban, Disco

Perhaps the lone artist who got her start on *The Gong Show* and remained credible, Cheryl Lynn's searing, often captivating voice and great range were showcased on some marvelous dance hits in the late '70s and early '80s. She signed with Columbia in 1978, and her debut LP *Cheryl Lynn* featured the anthem "Got to Be Real," which topped the R&B charts and reached number-12 pop. The follow-up, "Star Love," was a Top 20 R&B hit, and Lynn kept things going with "Shake It Up Tonight" in 1981, another Top Ten R&B smash. She teamed brilliantly with Luther Vandross for a remake of "If This World Were Mine" in 1982, yet another Top Ten hit, and then Lynn topped the R&B charts in 1983 with "Encore." She stayed on Columbia until 1987, then moved to Manhattan, where the 1987 single "If You Were Mine" made it to number 11. She also did background vocals with Lenny Williams. *—Ron Wynn*

Cheryl Lynn / 1978 / Columbia ♦♦♦♦

Ex-*Gong Show* contestant Cheryl Lynn hit paydirt with her self-titled debut album for Columbia. "Got to Be Real," one of those unavoidable disco-era hits—thanks to its instantly memorable bassline and Lynn's alternately soaring and barely contained giddiness—is one of the few singles of its level of success (number-one black singles, number-11 club play, number-12 pop) to decrease in value with over-saturation. Thanks to that song and the multi-tiered "Star Love," *Cheryl Lynn* reached number five on the black albums chart and provided the artist with her time in the spotlight. It's easily her best full-length, full of solid album cuts that act as support for the key singles rather than attempting to match them or even duplicate them with forced hooks and bungled attempts at making a diverse listen. In fact, "You Saved My Day" is just as great as the hits and could've been bigger with the right support—nevertheless, it was a favorite of DJ Frankie Knuckles while he was at Chicago's infamous Warehouse. A strong debut that benefits from assured ease. *—Andy Kellman*

Instant Love / 1982 / Columbia ♦♦♦

Luther Vandross tried his hand with making Cheryl Lynn a star and met with no more success than previous producers when he worked with her on this album. Their duet on "If This World Were Mine" was wonderful, one of the few that came close to rivaling the definitive Marvin Gaye & Tammi Terrell original. Both it and the title cut were big hits, and it seemed Lynn was about to make the breakthrough. But the album itself didn't quite explode, and Lynn just missed reaching the next level on the urban contemporary circuit. *—Ron Wynn*

It's Gonna Be Right / 1985 / Columbia ♦♦♦

Cheryl Lynn's final album for Columbia was a fitting conclusion to a tenure that had some chart hits but never jelled the way everyone felt it would (or should). Lynn got two more good numbers from the final effort, including the Jam & Lewis number "Fidelity," but again, there weren't enough songs to make the album a big success, nor did it have a unified concept or strategy. Lynn moved on to Manhattan the next year. *—Ron Wynn*

Whatever It Takes / 1989 / Virgin ♦♦♦

Working with producer/keyboardist/songwriter Todd Cochran, singer Cheryl Lynn had a somewhat harder, edgier sound with trash can-timbre beats and less of a light poppy feel to her material, which was best characterized by the first single, "Upset." But it was the second single, the midtempo groover "Everytime I Say Goodbye, that put her back on the charts, going to number seven on *Billboard*'s R&B charts in fall 1989; it was a nod towards her Jam & Lewis-produced number one R&B hit, "Encore." The next single, the mellow "Whatever It Takes," made it to number-26 R&B—her fans were sending her a message. Another smooth number, "You're So Good for Me," was a popular radio-aired LP track that became a steppers favorite. *—Ed Hogan*

- **Got to Be Real: The Best of Cheryl Lynn** / 1996 / Columbia ✦✦✦✦

And now... here's Cheryl! Fifteen tracks performed by one of the most explosive female singers in the rock genre. A *Gong Show* discoveree, Lynn first hit with the thumping "It's Got to Be Real," a tune with a serious groove that flew up the charts. "Star Love" was just as exciting, and gave Cheryl the perfect vehicle to display her awesome multi-octave range. You can bounce and dip to "Shake It Up Tonight," a rump mover and *Soul Train* favorite. Her exciting duet with Luther Vandross, "If This World Is Mine," the old Marvin Gaye & Tammi Terrell song, is stunning, their powerful voices will blow you away. Cheryl had it going on, she scored with Jimmy Jam & Terry Lewis' strutting "Encore," a rouser with crown ambience, and a staple of her live concerts. A singer's singer, Cheryl's voice is an exciting, warm, compelling instrument. *—Andrew Hamilton*

Gloria Lynne

b. Nov. 23, 1931, New York, NY

Vocals / Pop-Soul, Northern Soul, Traditional Pop, Standards, Vocal Jazz

Gloria Lynne recorded many albums for Everest in her early days, slipped away into obscurity and then in the 1990s made a comeback. An excellent singer whose style falls between bop, 1950s middle-of-the-road pop and early soul, Lynne was always capable of putting on a colorful show. Her mother was a gospel singer and Lynne started out singing in church. She had five years of concert training and in 1951 won the legendary amateur competition at the Apollo Theatre. Lynne sang with some vocal groups, became a single and in 1958 was discovered by Raymond Scott, who at the time was a top A&R man at Everest.

During her busy period with Everest (at least ten records were cut between 1958-63), Lynne had hits in "I Wish You Love" (a song she virtually made a standard) and "I'm Glad There Is You." She recorded with both orchestras and jazz combos, becoming quite popular for a period. However, with the rise of rock and the change in the public's musical tastes, Lynne was forgotten for a time. Only a commercial record in 1975 for ABC broke the silence. But starting in the early '80s, Gloria Lynne started working regularly again, regained some of her earlier frame and in the early '90s recorded a couple of CDs for Muse; her initial Everest date has since reappeared as an Evidence CD. *—Scott Yanow*

I Wish You Love / 1964 / Collectables ✦✦✦

This LP (singer Gloria Lynne's 12th for Everest) is most notable for including her greatest hit, "I Wish You Love." All dozen songs have the word "love" in their titles. The music ranges from swinging jazz to R&B-ish ballads. The unidentified backup group is often an orchestra. Lynne sings quite well throughout, but the arrangements, which are sometimes very middle-of-the-road, vary in quality; some of the better songs are "There Is No Greater Love," "I Can't Give You Anything but Love," "Wouldn't It Be Loverly" and, surprisingly, "Be My Love." An interesting, if not essential album from a talented singer. *—Scott Yanow*

Intimate Moments / Aug. 1965 / Fontana ✦✦✦

This is a consistently engaging album recorded during a strong stretch in the career of this singer, who tends to pop in and out of the public eye. Here she has the services of a medium-sized orchestra, taped with the lush attention such a production received in the mid-'60s, before this kind of recording artistry was forever lost. As far as material goes, the songstress has lots going for her. Then up-and-coming composer Van McCoy created the title tune, which fits right into Lynne's range and gets the album off to a good start. Then she starts laying on standards from one great songwriter or writing team after another, practically going through the roof with the hilarious "Blame it on My Youth" by Oscar Levant. Only a few of the numbers drag. The versions of "Everytime We Say Goodbye" and "My Ideal" standards are good enough to compare with the recordings of the songs done by much more succesful artists. *—Eugene Chadbourne*

Soul Serenade / Aug. 1965 / Fontana ✦✦✦✦

Gloria Lynne brought her jazz/soul/blues voice to the recording studio many, many times during her career. This album comes from her most prolific period, the 1960s. The title tune, "Soul Serenade," written for Lynne by King Curtis, joins a list of 12 tunes that will be recognizable by those who were listening to jazz/pop during that period. Many on the list are covers of tunes made popular by others. Nonetheless, Lynne brought her own special interpretation and delivery to these tunes which often set her highly dramatic, right-from-the-heart version apart from the more popular one. This is the case for such pop classics as "That's My Desire" and "Teach Me Tonight." Lynne also applied her unique way to songs from the musical stage, such as "People Will Say We're in Love" and "Joey, Joey, Joey." Richard Rodgers, Oscar Hammerstein, and Frank Loesser didn't have a soul singer in mind when they penned these Broadway standards. Irving Berlin's "All Alone" gets as impassioned a reading as it has ever received. The hit track is an incredible rendering of Herbie Hancock's "Watermelon Man," where Lynne pours all of her Harlem, gospel singing heritage into the words. On this session, Lynne is backed by a set of unidentified musicians who deliver just the right sounds to fit her voice. There's liberal use of baritone sax, organ, smoking guitar, and drums, instruments which best fit Lynne's vocal style. A fine album by a singer who combined jazz, blues, and soul into a style all her own. *—Dave Nathan*

- **Golden Classics** / Mar. 12, 1990 / Collectables ✦✦✦✦✦

This is a nice batch of hits and signature songs from a vocalist who dabbles in pop, R&B, and jazz. *—Ron Wynn*

- **Starry Eyes: The Collection** / Jul. 21, 1998 / Polygram ✦✦✦✦✦

Billy Paul was obviously a big fan of Gloria Lynne; you can hear Lynne's phrasing and vocal inflections in the singer's '70s recordings. And what a singer to pattern yourself after. Lynne's creamy alto is luscious and soothing; play one of her albums at the first sign of a headache and "the voice" might cure your pain without aspirin or Tylenol. Whether singing to soft guitar strums on "Blue Afternoon," bodacious brass on "Some of These Says," or in cozy clubs as she does on two live cuts—"Somewhere in the Night" and "For You"—Lynne's calming vocals and meticulous phrasing are awesome. An album for lovers, when love is new. *—Andrew Hamilton*

M

Willie Mabon

b. Oct. 24, 1925, Hollywood, TN, **d.** Apr. 19, 1985, Paris, France

Vocals, Piano / Piano Blues, R&B, Chicago Blues

The sly, insinuating vocals and chunky piano style of Willie Mabon won the heart of many an R&B fan during the early '50s. His salty Chess waxings "I Don't Know," "I'm Mad," and "Poison Ivy" established the pianist as a genuine Chicago blues force, but he faded as an R&B hitmaker at the dawn of rock & roll. Mabon was already well-grounded in blues tradition from his Memphis upbringing when he hit Chicago in 1942. Schooled in jazz as well as blues, Mabon found the latter his ticket to stardom. His first sides were a 1949-78 for Apollo as Big Willie and some 1950 outings for Aristocrat and Chess with guitarist Earl Dranes as the Blues Rockers.

But Mabon's asking price for a night's work rose dramatically when his 1952 debut release on powerful Windy City DJ Al Benson's Parrot logo, "I Don't Know," topped the R&B charts for eight weeks after being sold to Chess. From then on, Mabon was a Chess artist, returning to the top R&B slot the next year with the ominous "I'm Mad" and cracking the Top Ten anew with the Mel London-penned "Poison Ivy" in 1954. Throughout his Chess tenure, piano and sax were consistently to the fore rather than guitar and harp, emphasizing Mabon's cool R&B approach. Mabon's original version of Willie Dixon's hoodoo-driven "The Seventh Son" bombed in 1955, as did the remainder of his fine Chess catalog.

Mabon never regained his momentum after leaving Chess. He stopped at Federal in 1957, Mad in 1960, Formal in 1962 (where he stirred up some local sales with his leering "Got to Have Some"), and USA in 1963-1964. Mabon sat out much of the late-'60s but came back strong after moving to Paris in 1972, recording and touring Europe prolifically until his death. *—Bill Dahl*

● **Seventh Son** / 1993 / Charly ✦✦✦✦✦

Since MCA hasn't gotten around to this insinuating character's splendid Chess catalog as yet, we'll have to opt for a 16-song import that encompasses his three major hits "I Don't Know," "I'm Mad" (here in alternate take form, for whatever reason), and the Mel London-penned "Poison Ivy." Mabon's urban R&B approach was something of a departure for the Delta-rooted blues prevalent at Chess at the time, but his laconic vocals on "The Seventh Son," "Knock on Wood," and "Got to Have It" made him a star (albeit briefly). *—Bill Dahl*

The Mad Lads

f. 1963, Memphis, TN, **db.** 1969

Group / Soul, R&B

One of the few vocal groups on the Stax roster during the '60s, the Mad Lads' doo wop-influenced harmonies were more akin to what you might find in Philadelphia soul acts than those of their native Memphis. Featuring the high, innocent tenor of John Gary Williams, the group were still in high school when they were signed to Stax in late 1964. In the mid-'60s, they enjoyed solid R&B hits with "Don't Have to Shop Around," "I Want Someone," and "I Want a Girl," although they never would cross over to the pop audience.

Williams and fellow Mad Lad William Brown were drafted in 1966, and their recording career was suspended while they were in the service (although they carried on live with replacements). After their discharge, Williams and Brown were told by fellow original members Julius Green and Robert Philips that they didn't want Brown in the group; Brown and Stax co-owner Jim Stewart forced them to reinstate Williams, but their subsequent efforts were more in the Stax soul/funk formula, and not as memorable as their more atypical mid-'60s singles. They did return to the R&B Top 30 in 1968 with "Whatever Hurts You." *—Richie Unterberger*

In Action / 1966 / Volt ✦✦✦

In Action includes all of the Mad Lads' first recordings, except for their debut "Sidewalk Surf." The waltz-tempo, pleading "I Want Someone" went to number-ten R&B and number 74 pop and is their biggest selling single. Lead singer John Gary Williams had a pleading, crying singing style that was unmistakably Southern. "Come Closer to Me" features some hokey bass under Williams' enthusiastic lead. The C.O.D.'s hit with "Michael the Lover," but listening to the Mad Lads' re-recording, you'd think it was written for them. Re-makes comprise 25 percent of the album. "Don't Have to Shop Around," a slow ballad, features smooth harmonies over Williams' expressive tenor, and has a quirky doo wop sound. It may be the only Southern doo wop record ever; it's also their second best-selling record, charting at number-11 R&B and number-93 pop. The most interesting track is the chugging "Nothing Can Break Through"; it features sudden stops and changes and creative harmonies. *—Andrew Hamilton*

The Mad, Mad, Mad, Lads / 1969 / Volt ✦✦✦

The opening harmony notes of "So Nice" will hook you for the rest of this sweet Southern soul collection. I rank this higher than their debut, which had two songs enter the R&B Top 20 (none of these did). These are love songs sung by the exciting, emotional lead tenor of John Gary Williams. Williams is known for his heart-stopping, dramatic slides from natural to falsetto. "By the Time I Get to Phoenix" is given a bouncy treatment, a 360-degree difference from labelmate Isaac Hayes' elongated, slower reading; some pretty strumming by a lead guitarist lays the foundation. Despite its brilliance, "Phoenix" stalled at number-28 R&B and number-84 pop. Stax gives them a slicker, less Southern sound on "Love Is Here Today and Gone Tomorrow," and it suffers from the tinkering. They stamp "Cry Baby" as their own, giving the soul standard an extraordinary treatment. "Did My Baby Call" is a Steve Mancha composition that the Lads tear up, yet it fail to chart. You'll never mistake the Mad Lads for anything but Southern dudes. Not for one minute will you think they're from Philly, New York, Detroit, Chicago or L.A. *—Andrew Hamilton*

The Best of the Mad Lads / 1984 / Stax ✦✦✦

Madder Than Ever / 1990 / Volt ✦✦

● **Don't Have to Shop Around** / Aug. 2, 1995 / Stax ✦✦✦✦✦

Here is a career-spanning disc of material recorded between the mid-'60s and early '70s, including the hits "Don't Have to Shop Around," "I Want Someone," and "I Want a Girl," as well as more modern-styled cuts from the late '60s and early '70s. Good second-division soul, although it's missing their 1968 hit "Whatever Hurts You." *—Richie Unterberger*

Their Complete Early Volt Recordings / 1997 / Volt ✦✦✦✦

Their Complete Early Volt Recordings is an excellent collection featuring all of the Mad Lads' great early singles for the Volt label. Although the collection stops short of their late-'60s hits, it's still a terrific overview of their gritty, funky mid-'60s work. *—Stephen Thomas Erlewine*

Johnny Maestro

b. May 7, 1939, New York, NY

Vocals / Soul, Doo Wop

After making a name for himself as lead singer of the Crests, vocalist Johnny Maestro formed Brooklyn Bridge in 1967 and scored a gold record the next year on Buddah with a cover of the Fifth Dimension's heartbroken "Worst That Could Happen." Brooklyn Bridge was an amalgam of Maestro, the Del Satins (the vocal group that backed Dion on many of his early-'60s solo hits), and a brassy outfit called the Rhythm Method. Brooklyn Bridge enjoyed several more hits in 1969 and 1970, and Maestro still performs on the oldies circuit. *—Bill Dahl*

● **The Greatest Hits of Johnny Maestro & the Brooklyn Bridge** / 1992 / Collectables ✦✦✦✦✦

The Best of the Rest of Johnny Maestro & the Crests / Dec. 20, 1993 / Ace ✦✦✦✦

A veritable treasure trove for the true doo wop fan, this brings together 29 rarities and a slew of unreleased material in one delightful collection. In addition to unreleased gems like "Learning 'Bout Love," "Let Me Be the One," "Let True Love Begin," and "Strange Love," there are great alternate takes of "Six Nights a Week," "Step by Step," and "The Angels Listened In." Far from being bottom-of-the-barrel leftovers, these tunes deserve a much wider hearing. *—Cub Koda*

Magic Lady

f. Detroit, MI

Group / Urban

A female trio from Detroit, Magic Lady served as background vocalists for Enchantment, Shirley Caesar, Bob Seger, Keith Barrow, and the Soul Searchers, then landed their own deal with A&M in 1978. Linda Stokes, the wife of Michael Stokes, was the brains behind their formation. They cut one LP each for A&M and Motown, with their second album being issued in 1982. Neither proved very successful. Linda Stokes, Jackie Steele, and Kimberly Ball comprised the lineup. *—Ron Wynn*

● **Magic Lady** / 1982 / Motown ✦✦✦

A nicely balanced set of soft R&B ballads and equally light uptempo fare, subtly soulful trio Magic Lady's debut will please fans of the rare groove and quiet storm formats. The melodies and arrangements are often reminiscent of the Chi-Lites, the Delfonics, and other Philly soul stalwarts, while the vocals are surprisingly understated. The penultimate moment is "I Can't Believe I Found True Love," a jazzy, tropically flavored midtempo swirl of breezy horns, sterling keys, insinuating bass and percussion, and charming vocals. Other highlights include the pleasant "Please Don't Say Goodbye" and the summery "I Need Your Lovin'." The B-side drags momentarily with several ballads that have similar intros and weak melodies. Overall, *Magic Lady*'s strong point is in the combination of professional vocal delivery, solid production, and familiar-sounding melodies. None of those individual aspects are always completely on the mark (except for "I Can't Believe I Found True Love"), but they're certainly of just as high a caliber as commercially more successful efforts of the time by peers such as Dazz Band and Con Funk Shun. *—Justin M. Kantor*

Hot 'n' Sassy / 1982 / A&M ♦♦♦
Making a rather drastic transition from the soft, understated feeling of the group's first outing, Magic Lady's sophomore effort concentrates on passable, if sometimes generic, radio funk grooves. Save for the glowing midtempo number "Give It Up" and the quiet storm treat "Hold Tight"—the latter of which appears on several U.K. rare groove compilations—the bulk of material rests in rhythmic ditties like "Sexy Body," "Shake," and "Stand Up." Presumably, the trio was trying to cash in on the impact of Vanity 6 with the album's concept and titles like "Get Off" and "Red Hot Stuff," though it's all much more subtle than the way Prince's girls were doing it. But Magic Lady is much more musical in its approach. Their voices are light and sweet in tone, but firm in diction and strong in resonance. Notably, the group members all take on instrumental roles as well. It's just unfortunate that most of the songs don't go anywhere. They stay on one or two chords throughout and don't have all that much fire in their arrangements to make up for the sameness. *—Justin M. Kantor*

The Magnificents

Group / R&B, Doo Wop
An intriguing '50s R&B/doo wop group, the Magnificents patterned itself after the softer, more stylized singing of such groups as the Hi-Lo's and Four Lads. They began as the Tams, but were changed to the Magnificents by Chicago disc jockey "The Magnificent" Montague. Johnny Keyes, Thurman "Ray" Ramsey, Fred Rakestraw, and Willie Myles were the original lineup. Barbara Arrington later came aboard, and L.C. Cook, brother of Sam Cooke, replaced Ramsey. This was the lineup that made their one great record, "Up on the Mountain," in 1956 for Vee-Jay. They had other nice singles, but none enjoyed similar impact. *—Ron Wynn*

Magnum

f. California
Group / Funk, Soul, Deep Funk
The early '70s saw the brief flowering of a movement whereby soul, funk, rock, psychedelia, and even some jazz and Latin music combined into a new subgenre. That subgenre has never really been named, but you can hear these admixtures in the music of the period by Sly & the Family Stone and Funkadelic, and to a lesser extent in records by Miles Davis, James Brown, War, Santana, Jimi Hendrix, and others. These sounds have always been well-respected, but many have been curious as to whether there were many second-tier, obscure recordings by unknown musicians following similar paths.

That question will be hard to answer until reissue labels conduct exhaustive searches. But certainly Magnum counts as a band that fits squarely in the category of obscure groups bearing traces of all the influences mentioned in the above paragraph. Little is known about them, other than that they were from California and did only original compositions on their 1974 album *Fully Loaded*. They weren't as good as Funkadelic or Sly Stone, but they were pretty good, mixing up a sort of late-psychedelic soul-rock in their elongated, oft-humorous compositions. Crucially, they also varied their approach over the course of the LP, with long groove jams that borrowed from Latin jazz fusion, goofy sex wordplay, celebratory party funk, and some doses of cosmic consciousness. Reissued on CD in 2000, any fan of the acts that this bio compares them to should find Magnum worth hearing, should they be hungry for more of the same after having exhausting the discographies of the well-known exponents of the genre. *—Richie Unterberger*

● **Fully Loaded** / 1974 / Phoenix ♦♦♦♦♦
The songwriting and innovation barometer may not be as high on this LP as it is on early-'70s discs by Sly & the Family Stone, Parliament-Funkadelic, Miles Davis, and Santana—all of whom Magnum bear slight to strong resemblance to, at one point or another. Yet it's a pretty solid effort, and a reminder of a brief time when black music effectively synthesized R&B with numerous progressive trends while remaining both optimistic and street-smart. The collision of influences makes itself known right from the opening "Evolution," with its celebratory/revolutionary lyrics, solid funk groove, James Brown-like horns, bongos, distorted hard rock guitar riffs, and intricate sailing background harmonies. The dragging beats and druggy ambience of "Your Mind" should recall Sly Stone's *There's a Riot Goin' On* period to many listeners. The wacky hallucinogenic sex sentiments of "Natural Juices" wouldn't sound too out of place in George Clinton's world, with its spaced-out narration: "some people get off on a needle ... then there is a thumb and blanket. But the ultimate pacifier is a warm, wet nipple." "Witch Doctor's Brew" and the more impressive, ten-minute "Composition Seven," by contrast, make much use of Miles Davis-ish jazz-rock fusion keyboards in their groove-oriented, jammy passages, the latter tune boosted by an irresistible Latin beat. The album was entirely overlooked in comparison to the more famous artists mining the same grooves, both when it was made and when such sounds have come back into fashion. And it absolutely demands a hearing by anyone who digs these sorts of combinations, even if the group were not as original as the giants of the genre. *—Richie Unterberger*

Skip Mahoney & the Casuals

f. Philadelphia, PA
Group / Soul
Talk about Washington/Baltimore vocal groups from the late '60s and '70s, and the name Skip Mahoney invariably pops up. Mahoney's surname, similar to Leo Gorcey's character in *The Bowery Boys*, is actually spelled Mahoaney, he dropped the "a" when the group signed with Nashboro Records. His group, the Casuals, emerged on the Washington/Baltimore scene during the same era as the Choice Four, Dynamic Superiors, Frankie & the Spindells, the Whatnauts, Terry Huff & Special Delivery, the Vandals, and the Softones. Unlike those groups, the Casuals' fame never spread regionally or nationally. The group did shows and opened for major concerts. A record deal was harder to come by, though, and every group in the area beat them to the punch.

In 1971, Mahoaney took a hiatus from the Casuals to work as the Fuzz's ("I Love You For All Seasons") road manager. He quit the gig in 1972 to write songs with James Purdie in an effort to land the Casuals a recording deal. The record deal didn't happen until 1973, nine years after Mahoaney first started singing under streetlights. "Your Funny Moods," the first single, should have been a joyous event, but the label, D.C. International, listed the group as Skip Mahoaney & the Casuals, causing a riff between Mahoaney and the other guys. Though Mahoaney's shimmering falsetto was the focal point, they never wanted any individual name out front and the group disbanded shortly afterward. After D.C. International, Mahoaney signed with Nashboro Records, who in 1976 released *Land of Love*, which spawned two local hits: "Wherever You Go" and "Bless My Soul." This is when Mahoaney became Mahoney. Nashboro exited soul music to concentrate on gospel leaving the group without a label. Unable to get a new deal, the Casuals broke up. Mahoaney did a couple of solo ventures then sang with Third Generation before drifting out of music. *—Andrew Hamilton*

● **Land of Love** / 1976 / AVI ♦♦♦
A reissue of their 1976 Nashboro album that's absolutely dreamy on CD. Skip Mahoaney & the Casuals was a well-kept secret, few outside of Washington, D.C., knew of them or their vocal prowess. They didn't light up the charts, and most of their airplay emanated from the D.C./Baltimore area; if raised outside the District and its surrounding areas, you probably never heard or saw Skip Mahoaney & the Casuals. Mahoaney sung in a sweet falsetto reminiscent of area artists like the Whatnauts, the Vandals, and Frankie Karl & the Dreams. The killer tracks include "Land of Love," "Bless My Soul," "I Love You," and "Running Away From Love." *—Andrew Hamilton*

The Main Ingredient

f. 1966, Harlem, NY
Group / Urban, Soul, Disco
The Main Ingredient toiled in obscurity for the better part of the '60s before making it big as a sweet, romantic soul outfit with a particular flair for ballads. Paced by the impassioned lead vocals of Cuba Gooding during their prime hitmaking years, the Ingredient is best remembered for their 1972 classic "Everybody Plays the Fool," but released a number of other fine singles, mostly during the first half of the '70s. The group was formed in Harlem in 1964 as a trio called the Poets, composed of lead singer Donald McPherson, Luther Simmons Jr., and Panama-born Tony Silvester. They made their first recordings for Leiber & Stoller's Red Bird label, but soon changed their name to the Insiders and signed with RCA. After a couple of singles, they changed their name once again in 1966, this time permanently to the Main Ingredient.

Nothing much happened until the Main Ingredient hooked up with producer Bert DeCoteaux, who had an excellent sense of the lush, orchestrated direction soul music would take in the early '70s. Under his direction, the Main Ingredient reached the R&B Top 30 for the first time in 1970 with "You've Been My Inspiration." Things grew steadily from there; a cover of the Impressions' "I'm So Proud" broke the Top 20, and "Spinning Around (I Must Be Falling in Love)" went Top Ten. They scored again with the McPherson-penned black power anthem "Black Seeds Keep on Growing," but tragedy struck in 1971: McPherson, who had suddenly taken ill with leukemia, passed away unexpectedly. Stunned, Silvester and Simmons regrouped with new lead singer Cuba Gooding, who'd served as a backing vocalist on some of their previous recordings and had filled in on tour during McPherson's brief illness.

The Gooding era began auspiciously enough with the million-selling smash "Everybody Plays the Fool," which hit number-two R&B and number-three pop to become the group's biggest hit ever. The accompanying album, aptly titled *Bitter Sweet*, became their first to hit the Top Ten on the R&B charts; its follow-up, 1973's *Afrodisiac*, featured several songs written or co-written by Stevie Wonder, although it didn't produce any huge successes on the singles charts. They returned to the R&B Top Ten in 1974 with "Just Don't Want to Be Lonely," which sold over a million copies and also reached the pop Top Ten, and the disco-flavored "Happiness Is Just Around the Bend," which did not. In 1975, the group recorded several songs co-written by Leon Ware, including the R&B Top Ten "Rolling Down a Mountainside." By this point, however, Silvester was harboring other ambitions; he released a solo album called *Magic Touch* that year, and left the group to form a production team with Bert DeCoteaux.

Silvester was replaced by Carl Tompkins, but the chemistry wasn't the same, and Gooding departed for a solo career on Motown in 1977, which produced two albums; Simmons, meanwhile, left music to work as a stockbroker. Gooding, Silvester, and Simmons reunited as the Main Ingredient in 1979, and cut two more albums, 1980's *Ready for Love* and 1981's *I Only Have Eyes for You* (the latter featured a minor hit in "Evening of Love"). The trio reunited for a second time in 1986, but their Zakia single "Do Me Right" flopped, and Simmons returned to his day job. He was replaced by Jerome Jackson on the 1989 Polydor album *I Just Wanna Love You*. In the wake of Aaron Neville's Top Ten revival of "Everybody Plays the Fool," Gooding resumed his solo career and issued his third album in 1993. Silvester and Simmons re-formed the Main Ingredient in 1999 with new lead singer Carlton Blount; this lineup recorded *Pure Magic* in 2001. Gooding's son is, of course, Cuba Gooding Jr., the actor best known for his Oscar-winning performance in *Jerry Maguire*. *—Steve Huey*

The Main Ingredient L.T.D. / 1970 / RCA ♦♦♦

Black Seeds / 1971 / RCA ♦♦♦
Only spawned one R&B hit, the rallying "Black Seeds Keep on Growing" an upbeat sung celebrating African-American achievements. Member Don McPherson composed it, and the optimistic "Why Can't We All Unite." "Baby Change Your Mind" deserved more attention, as did the romantic "I've Fallen For You." Not the easiest LP to find but a good catch if you can snag it at a reasonable price. *—Andrew Hamilton*

Tasteful Soul / 1971 / RCA ♦♦♦♦
Arguably, the original Main Ingredient's (Don McPherson, Tony Silvester, and Luther Simmons) best album. Thank God for microphones and amplification, for these tall handsome New Yorkers sung softly. With the right songs, however, their smooth silky harmonies made wonderful, romantic sounds. The delicious "I'm Better Off Without You" did

well in New York area. It was so nice they recorded it twice, an earlier version appeared on another label. A carefully crafted rendition of the Impressions' "I'm So Proud" found audiences across America, as did "Spinning Around" their best from this era, the floater features sweet harmonies soaring against swirling strings. For some reason the Main Ingredient's producers used excessive strings that marred their recordings. A more stark setting, spotlighting their eloquent blends was the answer. This is especially true of "Magic Shoes," an attempt at pop, that is more annoying than likeable. An update of Bread's "Make It With You" works better, the late McPherson could croon with anybody. *—Andrew Hamilton*

Bitter Sweet / 1972 / RCA ✦✦✦
Bitter Sweet introduced new Main Ingredient member Cuba Gooding with a bang. Gooding added power to Tony Silvester's and Luther Simmons' mellow vocal blends. "Everybody Plays the Fool" paid immediate dividends, going all the way to number-three pop. A flute plays a catchy intro, the lyrics are accessible to all and Gooding's dynamic lead keeps you glued. A stuttering beat makes "You've Got to Take It" interesting; it's reminiscent of "Everything's Gonna Be Alright" by the Magictones. Heavier-than-usual backing voices accent "No Tears," which finds Gooding as excitable as ever on a tune marred by over-orchestration. They do the pop favorite "Who Can I Turn To?" in traditional style, showcasing Gooding's powerful crooning. A good debut for Gooding, who surpassed late lead singer Don McPherson vocally but lacked his songwriting skills. *—Andrew Hamilton*

Afrodisiac / 1973 / RCA ✦✦✦
Mellow and marvelous best describes this collection. Song for song, this is the most soothing album ever recorded by the Main Ingredient, but it went virtually unnoticed because it lacked a big hit. Cuba Gooding never sounded as smooth; he reminds you of original lead singer Don McPherson on some cuts. Stevie Wonder songs and productions dominate the set. Cuba Gooding, Tony Silvester, and Luther Simmons' renditions of "Superwoman" and "Where Were You When I Needed You" are masterfully executed, and the productions are A-1. "Girl Blue" is a probing, harmonious, understated ballad that could work as a poem. They do justice to the Isley Brothers' "Work to Do," the only mover. These songs speak of mature love situations and not the unrequited adolescent predicaments that monopolized early-'70s R&B. *—Andrew Hamilton*

Euphrates River / 1974 / RCA ✦✦✦✦
While nothing soared as high as "Everybody Plays a Fool" from the *Bitter Sweet* LP, *Euphrates River* is tighter and has more zap than the previous year's beautiful but hitless *Afrodisiac*. They nailed Seals & Croft's "Summer Breeze"—the New Yorkers almost surpassed the Isley Brothers' soulful version. Cuba Gooding sings the upbeat and funky "California My Way" from the heart (the soul singer moved his family to L.A.—the only Main Ingredient to do so). The trio gives Stevie Wonder's "Don't You Worry About a Thing" all they can muster; this is an excellent rendition that should have done better on the charts. Their version of "Just Don't Want to Be Lonely" helped sell this LP; it was previously done by Blue Magic and Ronnie Dyson, but the Main Ingredient's version reigns supreme. Rolling, midtempo beaters make up the bulk of the tunes with "Euphrates" and "Happiness Is Just Around the Bend" as prime examples. *—Andrew Hamilton*

Golden Classics / Jan. 17, 1990 / Collectables ✦✦✦✦✦
The Main Ingredient were one of the few vocal groups able to be both classy and soulful. Cuba Gooding (father of talented film actor Cuba Gooding Jr.) had the ability to sound earnest and anguished while singing sentimental, even sappy lyrics. Their polished harmonies made them mid-'70s romantic idols, and while they weren't as emphatic as trios like the Delfonics or Moments, they still cranked out many hit albums for RCA. This anthology collects their biggest chart hits and is a soul ballad bonanza. *—Ron Wynn*

● **The All-Time Greatest Hits** / Oct. 25, 1990 / RCA ✦✦✦✦
It wasn't until 1971 that the Main Ingredient's fortunes changed; when Cuba Gooding replaced Donald McPherson, his engaging voice helped make them part of the "sweet" soul trend. Gooding's leads made "Spinning Around (I Must Be Falling in Love)" and "Everybody Plays the Fool" huge hits, as well as "Just Don't Want to Be Lonely" and "Happiness Is Just Around the Bend." These and several other hits are featured on this anthology covering their prime years on RCA. *—Ron Wynn*

A Quiet Storm / Apr. 1996 / RCA ✦✦✦✦
Be cautioned that this 20-track retrospective of material spanning the late '60s to the mid-'70s is not a best-of, although it does include some of their biggest hits ("Just Don't Want to Be Lonely," "Everybody Plays the Fool"). As the title indicates, this focuses on the mellow and romantic side of the group. As the Main Ingredient largely specialized in mellow and romantic songs, this ends up being close to something of a best-of anyway. The relentless soft-pillow ambience of the tracks can become wearisome; in this context, the easygoing "Everybody Plays the Fool" sounds more like a blitzkrieg than a "quiet storm." *—Richie Unterberger*

The Majors

f. 1961, Pennsylvania
Group / R&B
The Majors scored an R&B/pop Top 30 hit in 1962 with "A Wonderful Dream." They are remembered for their outrageous falsetto lead vocals (often criticized for them) and for being one of the many acts produced by Jerry Ragovoy, an important behind-the-scenes force behind East Coast soul music. The Majors—lead singer Ricky Cordo, Eugene Glass, Frank Troutt, Ronald Gathers, and Idella Morris—formed in 1961 in Philadelphia. Early on the group decided to highlight Cordo's exaggerated falsetto leads, which to some, sounded like they could have been sung by the group's lone female, Idella Morris, instead.

They soon came to the attention of Ragovoy, a producer who worked at Chancellor Records at the time (where Fabian and Frankie Avalon had hits). Ragavoy had already begun producing doo wop acts (often distinguished by a conspicuous gospel feel) in the Philadelphia area in 1953, when he and Herb Slotkin (owner of Tregoobs appliance store) formed Grand Records. They later issued early doo wop releases by the Castelles. Ragovoy produced the group's lone hit, "A Wonderful Dream," but they failed to hit with anything further. After working with forgotten doo wop acts like the Majors, he went on to become quite a successful songwriter, writing or co-writing several classic New York and Philadelphia soul records in the 1960s, including Garnet Mimms' "Cry Baby" (which was co-written with another excellent early-'60s songwriter/producer Bert Berns) which landed at number four in 1963.

In the mid-'60s, Ragovoy also wrote a song for jazz trombonist Kai Winding, "Time Is on My Side," covered by Irma Thomas, and a U.S. Top Ten hit for the Rolling Stones. (Like some other of Ragovoy's best songs, this one was written under the pseudonym of "Norman Meade").

Ragovoy became even more prominent in his role as a mentor for Janis Joplin, who seemed to have a yen for Ragovoy-penned material, covering (with Big Brother & the Holding Company, or as a solo singer) his "Piece of My Heart" and "Try (Just a Little Bit Harder)," which had been originally recorded by Lorraine Ellison. In most cases, Joplin's interpretation eventually became the best-known version of these Ragovoy songs. Ragovoy continued to live comfortably from the songwriter's royalties brought in by Joplin's cover versions, as well as some of his other compositions, but he wasn't too active after the 1960s. He later produced Bonnie Raitt in the 1970s. *—Bryan Thomas*

Malo

f. 1971, San Francisco, CA, **db.** 1974
Group / Latin Rock, Funk
When Latin funk and Latin rock had its brief moment in the sun during the '70s, a number of groups emerged. Most were imitation Santanas, but at least Malo could boast that it had a real Santana in the lineup. Carlos Santana's brother Jorge headed Malo, and he possessed a little of his brother's vocal sound. Unfortunately, he didn't have enough to keep Malo going more than a few years. Their debut LP for Warner Bros. reached number 14 on the pop charts, but it was all downhill from there. The single "Suavecito" peaked at number-18 pop. They got very little attention from R&B or funk fans. *—Ron Wynn*

Malo / Apr. 1972 / Warner Bros. ✦✦✦✦✦
Malo's debut album remains their best and best-known work, primarily for the inclusion of the hit single "Suavecito." That track managed to make a Chicago-like pop-soul song sound hip with its smooth integration of Latin rhythms and irresistible "la la la" chorus. However, it represented just one facet of a band who, despite some expected similarities to Santana, played some of the most exciting and exuberant fusions of rock, soul, and Latin music. The six extended tracks (all clocking in at over six minutes apiece) leaned more heavily on hot Latin jazz brass than Santana did, though Jorge Santana himself generated plenty of friction with his burning electric guitar. It's not an exaggeration to state that by the time this came out in 1972, Malo's Latin rock blend sounded fresher than Santana's, if only because they sound hungrier and less formulaic than Santana did by that point. The Santana comparisons are unavoidable, though in this case it's to Malo's credit, as they too boasted a deft balance of improvisatory instrumental passages, solid multi-layered percussive rhythms, and emotional, romantic singing in both Spanish and English. [The album has been reissued on CD as one of the discs in Rhino Handmade's *Celebracion* box set, with the addition of five bonus tracks, though those are merely edited single versions of songs on the LP.] *—Richie Unterberger*

Dos / Aug. 1972 / Warner Bros. ✦✦✦✦
Malo's second album was cut with a lineup that had been reorganized following their debut. It's a little slicker than their first LP and the material isn't as strong. It's nonetheless a strong and invigorating rock/Latin jazz fusion, boasting some really hot playing, both in the ensemble work and improvisation. The six cuts, save one, all run more than five minutes, the closing "Latin Boogaloo" approaching ten minutes in length. Often this is closer to rockified salsa music than it is to the salsified rock music of lead guitarist Jorge Santana's brother, Carlos Santana. Occasional dives into sentimentality, as on the opening part of "I'm for Real," with its floating violin and percussive tinkles, are more than compensated for by some smoking Santana leads, particularly on the hyperactive "Held." "I'm for Real" was the cut most likely to follow up on the success of their "Suavecito" single, both because it was sung in English and because it had traces of the same kind of smoochy soul. Again, it wasn't too typical of the album as a whole, which combined several tributaries of pop with imagination and high levels of musicianship. Sometimes this was stretched out with jamming much more intelligent and fully thought-out than most lengthy, instrumental-oriented rock cuts, particularly on "Latin Boogaloo." [The album has been reissued on CD as one of the discs in Rhino Handmade's *Celebracion* box set, with the addition of three bonus tracks, though those are merely edited single versions of songs on the LP.] *—Richie Unterberger*

Evolution / 1973 / Warner Bros. ✦✦✦
Evolution was Malo's third album within a year. Perhaps because of that rapid pace and another shift in supporting players around the core trio of Jorge Santana, Pablo Tellez, and Arcelio Garcia, the band was starting to sound more formulaic and anonymous. There was a heavier reliance on fusion jazz keyboards and a lower fire in Jorge Santana's guitar than there had been on the band's initial two albums. It's still competent and often pleasing Latin rock/jazz, given as ever to lengthy but taut, well-structured instrumental sections. And there was, again, a soul-slanted romantic song that seemed more pointed toward the singles market than most of their repertoire, "I Don't Know." The most Latin-oriented facets of the band came to the fore on "Merengue" and "Dance to My Mambo," as their sappiest pop leanings did on "All for You." When set against tougher, funkier items like "Street Man," the band did not seem to be maintaining their eclecticism as much as starting to lose some of their focus. [The album has been reissued on CD as one of the

discs in Rhino Handmade's *Celebracion* box set, with the addition of single edits of "I Don't Know" and "Merengue."] *—Richie Unterberger*

Ascencion / 1974 / Warner Bros. ♦♦♦

The fourth Malo album continued the drift toward pop that had begun ever since their debut, though it's still hardly a mainstream pop record. There was more material, however, that could make them seem something like a Latin rock band, hipper Chicago or Tower of Power, which is not the greatest of goal posts. New lead singer Willie Garcia, a veteran of recording who had done many records with underrated Latino Los Angeles soul-rock band Thee Midniters in the '60s, was a key pivot to their direction, although it turned out to be the only album he did with Malo. The romantic, love-will-save-the-world lyrics got heavy-handed at times, and there was less of the jazzy, multi-sectioned riffing that had typified much of their prior work. Occasionally there was a funk pop tint, particularly to the keyboards, that seemed to be emulating then-current soul sounds by Stevie Wonder, Dr. John, and Billy Preston, though this did more to make Malo's identity less distinctive than it did to get them into the charts. Plenty of Latin roots, however, came through on tracks like "Offerings," which gives much room for speedy percussion and guitar soloing, and "A La Escuela." The album has been reissued on CD as one of the discs in Rhino Handmade's *Celebracion* box set, with the addition of single edits of "Love Will Survive" and "Think About Love." *—Richie Unterberger*

● **The Best of Malo** / Feb. 11, 1992 / GNP ♦♦♦♦♦

The single-disc compilation *The Best of Malo* covers the brief recording career of a great Latin rock band. Grabbing tracks from a two-year period (which encompassed four albums), the disc sounds all of a piece, a mix of torrid salsa rockers from the band's first two albums with the soft balladry it often dipped into during its time together. The disc begins perfectly, with the smart, brassy, kinetic "Nena," boasting extended solos for Roy Murray on trombone, Jorge Santana on guitar, and Richard Kermode on keyboards. It's actually a better song than the band's only chart hit, "Suavecito," which is just as smooth a piece of summer-day Latin soul as the title indicates, though it doesn't pose much of a challenge to one of Latin rock's finest groups. Almost three-fourths of Malo's first two albums are collected here, along with about half from the last two. A pair of wise additions are the intense Latin workouts "Merengue" and "Dance to My Mambo," both from 1973's *Evolution*, as well as the deep Santana groove of "Cafe." Though Malo's debut album is still a can't-miss for fans of Latin rock, this compilation does little wrong too. *—John Bush*

Celebracion: The Warner Bros. Recordings / Aug. 31, 2001 / Rhino Handmade ♦♦♦♦

While one has to wonder whether the demand for Malo's product is wide enough to merit a four-CD box set rather than individual reissues of some or all of their albums, *Celebracion* certainly does a great job of presenting the band's legacy in total. Each of their four 1972-1974 Warner Brothers albums is included in gatefold sleeves, with a 20-page booklet that goes over the band's history with some depth, bolstered by interview quotes from several bandmembers. Two to five bonus tracks are added to each disc/album, though unfortunately these are just shorter single edits of album tracks. There's one previously unreleased cut, "Pana," but that's just an unreleased single edit of the same track of that name that appears on their debut album. Although the albums are erratic and slightly but steadily decline in quality after the debut, *Malo*, they amply illustrate the band's importance as one of the most exciting outfits to fuse rock with Latin and jazz. Certainly there are similarities with Santana, as might be expected from a band featuring Carlos Santana's brother on guitar. But Malo was more Latin-oriented and sometimes expert at constructing multi-part extended tracks with blistering interplay between hard rock guitar, Latin percussion, and jazz brass. In addition, they could sometimes summon heartfelt, sentimental soul ballads, the hit "Suavecito" being the famous one, though each album has one or two songs (albeit less impressive ones) in the same vein. They couldn't avoid a certain formulaic quality after a while, and the group drifted toward less-satisfying pop inclinations as time went on and personnel changed, but at its best, this set contains some of the finest Latino rock ever laid down. *—Richie Unterberger*

Steve Mancha (Clyde Darnell Wilson)

b. Dec. 25, 1945, Walhall, SC

Vocals, Songwriter / Urban, Deep Soul, Northern Soul, Soul

Soul singing Steve Mancha was born Clyde Darnell Wilson on Christmas, 1945 in Walhall, SC. He only lived in God's country five years before the Wilson's moved to Detroit, MI, to take advantage of the high-paying jobs opening in the city for African-Americans. By 1960, Wilson was singing around town, and befriended Melvin Davis who already was recording on Fortune Records. Clyde's first studio check came as one half of Two Friends, with Wilburt Jackson who released one single "Just Too Much To Hope For," on Harvey Fuqua's short-lived HPC label. HPC had little clout and the record flopped miserably; Marvin Gaye & Tammi Terrell redid it years later.

After HPC, Fuqua ran Tri-Phi and Harvey Records with Gwen Gordy. But when Harvey, formerly of the Moonglows, found Johnny Bristol & Jackey Beavers (Johnny & Jackey), Two Friends got placed on the back burner. With Motown emerging and Tri-Phi and Harvey suffering from diminishing returns, Harvey and Gwen merged with Motown, who got Wilson and Jackson in the deal. If Motown recorded them, either as a group or as solo artists, the tracks were never released. They wrote a few songs that never did much like "Number One In Your Heart" (the Monitors); all were either buried on albums, served as B-sides, or remain unreleased. Wilson did no better without Jackson, his best effort was "Give a Little Love," the B-side of Marvin & Tammi's "Ain't No Mountain High Enough."

Neglected, Wilson left Motown in 1965 to work with Don Davis. Davis suggested a name change, Clyde Wilson just wasn't cutting it, and for the rest of his secular recording career he was Steve Mancha. The first Davis' production "Did My Baby Call" b/w "Whirlpool," dropped on Wheelsville Records in 1965. It did OK in some markets but wasn't a breakout; years later the Mad Lads did a remake on Volt Records. It was followed by three releases on Groovesville "You're Still In My Heart" b/w "She's So Good" (10/65) was the first. Mancha's solo string was interrupted by a Holidays single "I'll Love You Forever," on Golden World Records; these Holidays were actually Edwin Starr (lead), Mancha, and J. J. Barnes. It became an R&B hit, but the trio never toured as the Holidays; Davis assembled some more guys for road duty and future recordings. Mancha's next Groovesville single "I Don't Want to Lose You," was a beautiful, soulful floater that charted at number-34 R&B in 1966; the third Groovesville single "Don't Make Me a Story Teller," matched its predecessor by charting number-34 R&B in 1967, it was later recorded by the Dells. Davis switched Mancha to his Groove City label for "Hate Yourself in the Morning," released March 1968, it wasn't as successful but is just as good as the others. Another solo shot "Sweet Baby" issued on Groove Records did nothing.

A golden opportunity came via Eddie Holland, Brian Holland, & Lamont Dozier who left Motown around 1967 to start the Invictus/Hot Wax/Music Merchant labels. The Hall-of-Fame songwriters chose Mancha, Joe Stubbs, and Eddie Holiday to front 100 Proof (Aged in Soul). The hot group imploded on Hot Wax with "Too Many Cooks (Spoil The Soup)" (number 28 R&B) in 1969, but the next release "Somebody's Been Sleeping," not only set the R&B chart on fire, it went to number eight Pop. As the record simmered on the charts, Mancha hit again, this time as 8th Day with "She's Not Just Another Woman," a song he wrote that was the same track on 100 Proof's debut album. As the song exploded, HDH put a group together called 8th Day that featured Steve's friend, Melvin Davis.

100 Proof recorded many memorable recordings including "One Man's Leftovers (Is Another Man's Feast)," "Driveway," "90 Day Freeze," "I Rather Fight Than Switch," "Everything Good Is Bad," and "Don't Scratch Where It Don't Itch." By 1973, however, 100 Proof's recordings stopped, but was resurrected with new members for a couple of releases in 1977. While 100 Proof was scoring at Hot Wax, Don Davis leased Steve Mancha's old tracks to Stax Records which resulted in the *Rare Stamps*, album on Volt Records which also included recordings by J. J. Barnes; it was later released on CD with an entire Darrell Banks' album added. When HDH moved to California and Mancha didn't, his career ended. Stax had gone under, stoned by bankruptcy and payola charges, and Don Davis was steadfastly leaving the music business. He eventually did and once—and may still—owned a bank in Detroit. Mancha's first mentor, Harvey Fuqua was in California too. But for some strange reason, maybe it's a fear of earthquakes, Steve never left the Motor City.

He switched to gospel music but hasn't found the success he enjoyed with secular music, though it's obviously more spiritually fulfilling. Producer, Ian Levine unearthed Steve in 1998 and recorded "It's All Over the Grapevine," it became a Northern soul favorite but did anything in the States. Mancha's more known overseas, even the hits with 100 Proof and 8th Day didn't win him any recognition, 100 Proof wasn't a touring group, they did a few gigs, but most people never saw them; they didn't have an identity beyond their recordings. Steve did a concert in London in year 2000, with Edwin Starr and J. J. Barnes, it was Mancha's first trip across-the-pond. *—Andrew Hamilton*

● **Detroit Soulman: The Best of Steve Mancha** / 2000 / VSOP ♦♦♦♦♦

Steve Mancha's gritty recordings personify deep soul, uptown style. Don Davis didn't reap much financial success producing Mancha, but 30 some years after the fact, the recordings are finally getting the acclaimed they deserved. Mostly from outside the United States, despite hit recordings with 100 Proof (Aged in Soul) and 8th Day, Mancha is virtually unknown at home. He recorded these 20 tracks on Groovesville, Wheelsville, and Groove City—all owned by Davis—from 1968 to 1969. There are too many great performances to mention them all, but the short list includes "Did My Baby Call," "Hate Yourself in the Morning," "I Don't Want to Lose You," "Don't Make Me a Story Teller," and "Think Before You Walk Away." Every soul music collection worth its salt should have some Steve Mancha. *—Andrew Hamilton*

Manchild

f. 1972, Indianapolis, IN

Group / Disco, Funk, Soul

Manchild paid their dues in local clubs for most of the early and mid-'70s, before they were signed by the Chi-Sound label in 1977. Their funk and soul sound seemed to finally find a niche, but they couldn't pump their music through the din of the disco era, only scraping the charts with "Especially for You" that year. The label stuck with them through two LPs but by the end of the decade they were once more free agents. Out of the group's alumnus, one genuine star emerged in the guise of Kenneth Edmonds, aka Babyface, who became both a top-selling artist and massively successful producer and songwriter (chalking up hits with Gladys Knight, among numerous others) during the 1980s and 1990s. Lead singer/guitarist Reggie Griffin also carried on with a career, first as a member of West Street Mob and then forming Reggie Griffin & Technofunk, which eventually became known as Griffin (not to be confused with the industrial band of that name). Griffin has worked with Babyface and acts such as Boyz II Men, the Bee Gees, Roberta Flack, Aretha Franklin, Phyllis Hyman, the Isley Brothers, the Sugarhill Gang, and Chaka Khan. *—Bruce Eder*

Manchild 1 / 1972 / Capitol ♦♦♦

Power & Love / 1977 / ChinaTown ♦♦♦

A self-contained septet that included Kenneth Edmonds, before he was crowned with the nickname Babyface, and his close friend and collaborator Daryl Simmons. The group's sound touched on several formats. The uptempo numbers, like "Red Hot Daddy," "Power and Love," and "Funky Situation," are heavily rock-oriented. The latter has a jazzy improvisational sax solo, and is the only number that features Babyface on lead vocals. The socially conscious "We Need We" falls more in line with R&B with its appealing arrangement. The group comes full circle with its R&B sound on "Especially for You." The serene composition features an undeviating guitar solo, and was Manchild's only single to crack the *Billboard* R&B charts; it peaked at 70 inside of eight weeks, and features the lead vocals of Chuckie Bush. One other notable is the '70s classic "Takin' It to the Streets," originally recorded by the Doobie Brothers a year earlier. Flash Ferrell gives an ardent delivery supported by cohesive background vocals and a spirited sax solo by Reggie Griffin. *—Craig Lytle*

Feel the Phuff / 1977 / ChinaTown ♦♦♦♦
Kenny "Babyface" Edmonds cut his creative teeth in Manchild, a seven-piece, self-contained band from Indianapolis, IN, that recorded two albums for Carl Davis' Chi-Sound Records. "The Phuff" and "If You Don't Tell No One" are black rock songs complete with the acid guitar, written by Reginald Griffin and Kevin Farrell; unfortunately, black rock never caught on with urban radio. Early examples of Babyface's brilliance are evident on the plaintive ballads "One Tender Moment" and "Our Message." An album of many styles, with "Joy" an obvious attempt to emulate Earth, Wind & Fire. A polished set, but there are no real highs, but on the other side, no real lows either. —*Andrew Hamilton*

• **Power & Love/Feel the Phuff** / Jul. 1, 1999 / Charly ♦♦♦♦♦

David Mancuso

DJ / Club/Dance, Garage/House, Disco
The origins of disco (and clubland in general) lie in the early '70s and David Mancuso's Greenwich Village apartment, where he sponsored weekly after-hours get-togethers for much of the city's party population. The Loft's sound system was just as good as most legal clubs, and Mancuso played a wide range of music, including Latin and African, Motown, Philly soul and funk. —*John Bush*

• **The Loft** / Aug. 30, 1999 / Nuphonic ♦♦♦♦
The Loft set a standard for club-going, beginning at the dawn of the '70s as a series of invite-only parties thrown by David Mancuso at his Soho apartment. Throughout the years, weathering legal issues and several relocations, the Loft gradually became known as one of the key influences behind club culture. Mancuso provided a world-class sound system and was beyond hospitable to his guests, creating an atmosphere that—according to anyone who DJ'd or came to party at the Loft—could never be matched. *The Loft* is an impressive multimedia document compiling two discs' worth of material that figured prominently in the club's rotation while including a booklet of anecdotal history, testimonials, and several pictures. For those who only care about the music within, there's a mixed bag of disco, R&B, and house that ranges from the early '70s to the mid-'90s. Some of it is spectacular, remaining favorites of DJs decades down the road, thanks in no small part to the support received from those who spun at Mancuso's gatherings. The loopy roller-boogie of T.W. Funkmasters' "Love Money," the deliciously warped disco-funk of Ednah Holt's "Serious, Sirius Space Party," the horn-spiked Afro-dazzle of Manu Dibango's "Soul Makossa" (its surprising success was the direct result of Mancuso's support), and the still-quaking Chicago house of Fingers Inc.'s "Mystery of Love" (in instrumental form here) highlight the package. Most significantly, the 12-minute version of Loose Joints' "Is It All Over My Face" makes its first appearance. A Loft-birthed classic, this version features lead vocals from producer Arthur Russell and differs significantly compared to its female-led counterpart. The remainder is a bit spotty, perhaps for the fact that some of the weaker material could only come to life on Mancuso's hi-end system. —*Andy Kellman*

The Loft, Vol. 2 / Oct. 10, 2000 / Nuphonic ♦♦♦
Like its predecessor, the packaging of the second volume of *The Loft* ably demonstrates that receiving an invitation to one of David Mancuso's loft parties was the equivalent of winning a golden ticket within the New York dance scene. The fellowship was like no other, the sound system was like no other, the range of music played was like no other, ad infinitum. Celebrating nearly 30 years of Mancuso's parties—held at five different locations between 1970 and 1998—*The Loft, Vol. 2* spreads 20 tracks across two discs that no doubt sounded great on those standard-setting sound systems provided by Mancuso (the echoes placed on Sandee's voice for "Notice Me," for instance, must have sounded absolutely maddening). As historical artifacts, the two volumes of *The Loft* are equally crucial. But when it comes down to it, most record buyers couldn't give a toss about such a thing—they just care about the music. In that respect, *The Loft, Vol. 2* still stands up. Much more than a dance music audiophile's wet dream, it's a great package of underground/rare/experimental/overlooked dance music that just so happens to have a story behind it. Each track is presented as it was at the parties—in full, extended glory. Not only that, but they're sequenced like one of Mancuso's parties in miniature, beginning with Fred Wesley's welcoming "House Party" and concluding with the Orb's "Little Fluffy Clouds" and Dorothy Morrison's "Rain." A handful of other highlights: D Train's uplifting old-school classic "Keep On" (funny how his amazing voice is followed by Jah Wobble's, which, to put it lightly, relies more on spirit than skill), Dinosaur L's downcast-but-propulsive "#5 (Go Bang)," Nuyorican Soul's gorgeous "The Nervous Track (Ballsy Mix)," and Eddie Kendricks' epic, multi-tiered "Girl You Need a Change of Mind." Highly recommended for historians and dance addicts alike. —*Andy Kellman*

Mandrill

f. 1968, Brooklyn, NY
Group / Funk, Fusion, Latin Rock, Soul
One of funk's most progressive outfits, Mandrill paid the price for their ambitions in commercial returns—not that they never earned a reputation or an audience, but their expansive, eclectic vision often worked better when given an album's worth of room to roam, rather than being condensed into hit singles. Mandrill's jam-heavy brand of funk was liberally infused with Latin, Caribbean, and jazz influences, plus blues, psychedelia, African music, and straight-up rock. Their freewheeling approach was a definite influence on the Parliament-Funkadelic collective (an early incarnation of which actually served as their opening act), and their grooves have been sampled by numerous hip-hop acts in modern days.

Mandrill was formed in Brooklyn in 1968 by brothers Ric Wilson (sax, vocals), Lou Wilson (trumpet, vocals), and Carlos Wilson (trombone, vocals), all of whom were born in Panama and raised in the Bedford-Stuyvesant neighborhood by musically inclined parents. Ric Wilson had already taken up a career as a cardiologist when the group officially formed; the brothers had performed together for quite some time, rehearsing at the beauty salon where their mother worked. Taking their name from the variety of West African ape (because of its distinctive, colorful face and well-developed, family-oriented social organization), Mandrill soon added keyboardist Claude "Coffee" Cave, guitarist Omar Mesa, bassist Bundie Cenas, and drummer Charlie Padro. They signed with Polydor and released their eponymous debut album in 1970, displaying the influence of the burgeoning jazz-rock and Latin-rock movements in addition to soul and funk. For the follow-up, 1972's *Mandrill Is*, Fudgie Kae Solomon replaced Cenas on bass, and the group scored their first hits with "Ape Is High" and "Git It All."

With new drummer Neftali Santiago, Mandrill scored their biggest hit with 1973's *Composite Truth*, which also produced their highest-charting single, "Fencewalk." This incarnation ranked as the classic Mandrill lineup, but didn't take long to splinter; after 1973's *Just Outside of Town* (which featured the hit "Mango Meat"), guitarist Mesa left (citing "spiritual reasons") and was replaced by Dougie Rodriguez, formerly of Santana. After the soundscape-heavy double LP *Mandrilland*, disputes over the Wilson brothers' control of the band led to the departure of every non-Wilson member save for Claude Cave.

Leaving Polydor, Mandrill cut two albums for United Artists with a session rhythm section over 1975-1976, and subsequently caught on with Arista. Their label debut, 1977's *We Are One*, proved to be their biggest hit since *Composite Truth*, spawning the club hits "Funky Monkey" and "Can You Get It"; it also marked the temporary return of Santiago on drums, the addition of another brother, Wilfredo "Wolf" Wilson, on bass, and the debut of guitarist Joaquin Jessup. Two more albums for Arista followed over the next two years (*New Worlds* and *Getting in the Mood*), and the band also handled the soundtracks for the Muhammad Ali flick *The Greatest* (1977) and the cult gang film *The Warriors* (1979). Mandrill went on to cut one more album, *Energize!*, for Montage in 1982 before disbanding. Fudgie Kae Solomon later died of a drug overdose. —*Steve Huey*

Mandrill / 1970 / Polydor ♦♦♦
Mandrill's debut isn't half the album it could've been, since the band's talented musicianship and desire to experiment were often subverted—by ambitions of pop success as well as a dry, over-serious approach to music-making. The three Wilson brothers, though masters of over a dozen instruments, still hadn't mastered the added burden of songwriting; "Warning Blues" is perfunctory (as is the vocal performance) and "Symphonic Revolution" is a bland summer-day soul song with cloying strings. The group sounds much more confident getting into a good groove and allowing room for some great playing; the band's self-titled song, "Mandrill," is the best here, featuring great solos for flute and vibraphone. Mandrill also loved playing with different musical forms: "Rollin' On" moves from an average rock song to a torrid Latin jam and climaxes with a testifying gospel session. Most ambitious of all is the five-part, 14-minute suite "Peace and Love," but the intriguing concept is negated by a few bizarre pieces, one of which sounds like a parody of a Vincent Price reading over a Santana jam. The band would soon learn that experimentation and stylistic change-ups were a means, not an end. —*John Bush*

Mandrill Is / 1972 / Polydor ♦♦♦♦
Apparently learning from the mistakes of its debut, Mandrill crafted a follow-up with fewer stylistic detours than the first record, but much more energy and greater maturity. The two singles, "Ape Is High" and "Git It All," are unhinged performances from all involved that have the sense of musical invigoration so key to a funk band—and so sorely lacking on this band's debut. "Children of the Sun" is a somber, flute-led piece, much more assured and better-conceived than anything on its first record (it also showed how well Mandrill could've done soundtracking a blaxploitation film). The guitars are much more prominent on *Mandrill Is*; in fact, both "Git It All" and "Here Today Gone Tomorrow" have passages almost reminiscent of metal's heavy riffing. The first two compositions from Claude "Coffee" Cave are big successes, "Cohelo" being a traditional Latin form and "Kofijahm" a tribal funk piece. Not everything works, however: the spoken-word piece "Universal Rhythms" is a tad over-ripe, with a raft of unpoetic, pseudo-mystical nonsense over backing from an angelic choir. —*John Bush*

Composite Truth / 1973 / Polydor ♦♦♦♦♦
Composite Truth is Mandrill's most successful album, commercially as well as artistically. Although the band's sense of freewheeling experimentation had been tempered, its gradual transition to a straight-ahead funk band was made perfect with two of the biggest hits of its career: "Hang Loose" and "Fencewalk." "Hang Loose" is all over the place (in a good way), moving from a grooving funk jam to midtempo guitar skronk and back, all part of an impassioned call to peace. "Fencewalk" also had several transitions, with a crooning chorus and an extended middle section powered by heavy brass and a screaming guitar solo. Elsewhere, Mandrill turns in a very convincing impression of a salsa band ("Hágalo"), breaks into killer loose-groove funk ("Don't Mess With People," with a splendidly undecipherable vocal), and stumbles only with the long, rasta-fied San Francisco tribute "Polk Street Carnival," featuring a bass part that would make even a student smirk. (For such a strong band, Mandrill's basslines were often uncharacteristically weak.) In the main, the songs on *Composite Truth* were catchier than on its first two albums, and the band never appeared subservient to the sense of experimentation that had troubled it before. Even if on *Composite Truth* Mandrill sounded more like other funk bands of the time, no one could argue with the fact that the results were more exciting *and* consistent. —*John Bush*

Just Outside of Town / 1973 / Polydor ♦♦♦
It lacked the delicious hooks and tight funk of *Composite Truth*, but *Just Outside of Town* was as solid and confident a piece of music-making as the band ever accomplished. The single "Mango Meat" is a tough Latin funk number with some inspired group harmonizing, and Mandrill stretched out with a pair of love songs, "Never Die" and the aptly titled "Love Song," the latter beginning with a few minutes of atmospheric bliss that boasted unrealized cinematic/soundtrack possibilities. "Fat City Strut" moves back and forth between blasts of brass-powered funk and the sweet seduction of Latin percussion

and a vibes solo. The distorted funk monster "Two Sisters of Mystery" is another classic, one that later enticed producer Gary G-Wiz to sample it for Public Enemy's "By the Time I Get to Arizona." The last two songs were very uncharacteristic for Mandrill, one a bluesy/country song with a pop gloss, the other an ambling instrumental led by an acoustic guitar and including a few out-of-place synthesizer shadings. It certainly wasn't Mandrill going out on top (for an album, or for its period at Polydor), but it certainly summed up the promise of one of funk's most courageous bands. *—John Bush*

● **The Best of Mandrill** / 1975 / Polydor ✦✦✦✦✦
Rounding up the greatest grooves from the band's first five albums, right up until it left for United Artists in 1975, *The Best of Mandrill* is a top compilation for one of the most freewheeling bands of the early '70s. Unsurprisingly for a funk group, Mandrill excelled at recording catchy, well-played material with deep grooves, though unlike many bands, all of it was tempered by an experimentalist bent and a restless desire to explore many different avenues (occasionally in the same song). The compilation opens perfectly with "Ape Is High," "Fencewalk," "Git It All," and "Hang Loose"—the band's four biggest hits, and (not a coincidence) its four greatest songs. The other seven tracks aren't always the best available: "Mango Meat" and its self-titled debut single are solid choices, but substituting a pair of album tracks ("House of Wood," "I Refuse to Smile") for the R&B hits "Positive Thing" and "The Road to Love" doesn't make much sense. Most importantly, though, *The Best of Mandrill* includes every song Mandrill's known for, in a punchy sequencing that does justice to the band's uncommon style. *—John Bush*

We Are One / 1977 / Arista ✦✦✦
In 1977 Mandrill showed signs of having listened to fusion and had more or less left the Latin rock behind. The African influences were also granted less room on their records, and if they still stuck out from the bulk of funk bands, the gap was slowly closing. *We Are One* starts with the two dance hits "Can You Get It" and "Funky Monkey," complete with inspired monkey screams. These are maybe the strongest tracks on the album, with great percussion work, fat basslines, and building horns. And ironically, in being just excellent funk numbers, they are also proof of Mandrill losing some of the creativity that made them different from most other funk bands. But if it is true that one won't find rumbling African drums or musical journeys through all African-American musical styles on this album, the rest of the songs do offer a banjo-esque guitar, a harmonica solo, and some distorted rock riffs, all uncommon in late-'70s funk. And even if some of the songs are a little tired, a tired Mandrill is more than just a another band trying to sound like Parliament. *—Lars Lovén*

Fencewalk: The Anthology / Feb. 4, 1997 / Polydor ✦✦✦✦✦
Right from the start of this two-disc collection, with the track that shares the band's name, it's clear that Mandrill had some seriously heavy funk credentials—and broad ranging ones at that. Only early Santana and War gained the same level of attention and appreciation for their exciting, invigorating Latin/funk hybrids. *Fencewalk: The Anthology* actually isn't the best of purchases for long-time fans; unlike many multi-disc CD anthologies, there aren't any rarities or previously unreleased songs available, outside of the concluding "Echoes in My Mind," which surfaced on the soundtrack to *The Warriors*. It's a reasonable enough number but not particularly special by the band's standards and not reason enough alone to pick this up. But as a more than fine overview of Mandrill's work throughout the '70s, from start to finish of those ten years, this is required listening for anyone exploring the roots of electric funk, two and a half hours of party music aiming to move minds and bodies in equal measure. The Wilson brothers and their fellow musicians had an ear for just about everything, from the sweetest of soul harmonies over lush strings to the loudest of acid rock-inspired riffs and plenty of roots-deep inspiration from salsa and Latin jazz. Claude "Coffee" Cave throughout demonstrates why he ranks up as one of the best keyboardists of his time—at his best he easily gives Bernie Worrell a well-deserved run for the money—while the interplay of drummers Charles Prado and, later, Neftali Santiago with the Wilsons on percussion is maximum groove energy on many levels. An appreciative, well-written essay on Mandrill's heyday and abilities from Pablo Guzman is very welcome, while Gary Mayo's remastering job deserves full marks for bringing out the detail of the arrangements beautifully into the digital realm. *—Ned Raggett*

The Ultimate Collection / Nov. 28, 2000 / Collectables ✦✦✦✦
Not will only will Mandrill's music make you dizzy, the price tag of this limited-edition four-CD box set will too. Be prepared to shell out more than $50 for this 38-track collection, featuring their first four Polydor albums (*Mandrill, Mandrill Is, Composite Truth,* and *Just Outside of Town*). Mandrill's music is practically unpeggable, much like the U.K.-based Osibisa; they never gave the impression they were working from any semblance of a format. The multi-racial septet led by the talented Wilson Brothers—Carlos, Lou, and Dr. Ric Wilson (a practicing cardiologist)—were classified by many as a funk band, but that's misleading: Their style included funk, soul, Latin, and fusion, all presented in convoluted arrangements. The 14-minute "Peace and Love (Amani Na Mapenzi)" suite is therapeutic, as are many of these joints. This is as good as it gets, but if you're looking for chartbusters, look elsewhere; also, each of the discs in this package are available separately at the same price. *—Andrew Hamilton*

The Manhattans

f. 1962, Jersey City, NJ
Group / Urban, Quiet Storm, Soul, Northern Soul, Doo Wop
The Manhattans were one of those classic R&B vocal groups who manage to achieve incredible career longevity by adapting their style to fit changing times. Formed in the '60s as a doo wop-influenced R&B quintet, the Manhattans reinvented themselves as sweet smooth-soul balladeers during the '70s. In doing so, they somehow overcame the death of lead singer George Smith, and with new frontman Gerald Alston became more popular than they'd ever been, landing an across-the-board number one hit in 1976 with "Kiss and Say Goodbye." Under the leadership of Winfred "Blue" Lovett (who also composed some of the group's biggest hits), the Manhattans survived as a viable chart act well into the '80s, over two decades after their formation.

The Manhattans got together not in their namesake location, but in nearby Jersey City, NJ, in 1962. The group was centered around lead singer George "Smitty" Smith and bass (and sometime lead) vocalist Winfred "Blue" Lovett; the other original members were Kenny Kelly, Richard Taylor, and Edward "Sonny" Bivins, the latter of whom sometimes co-wrote material with accomplished songwriter Lovett. In 1964, the Manhattans signed with the Newark-based Carnival label and teamed up with producer Joe Evans; they scored their first hit in early 1965 with "I Wanna Be (Your Everything)," a number-12 R&B hit that established their way with a ballad right from the beginning. It was the first of eight singles for Carnival, a string that continued up through 1967. None were huge hits, but nearly all of them reached the Top 30 on the R&B charts, and are still prized by collectors of vocal-group soul for their aching harmonies, Smith's intense leads, and lack of concession to mainstream pop audiences.

In 1969, the Manhattans signed on with Deluxe and issued several singles over the course of 1970. Unfortunately, Smith fell ill that year, and the group hired Phil Terrell as a temporary fill-in. Sadly, Smith passed away in 1971; he was replaced on lead vocals by Gerald Alston, who brought a smoother, more pop-friendly sound to the group. That quality soon became apparent when the Lovett-penned "One Life to Live" zoomed into the R&B Top Five in late 1972, giving the Manhattans their first major hit. The following year, they left Deluxe for Columbia, where their debut single "There's No Me Without You" (written by Sonny Bivins) equaled the R&B chart peak of "One Life to Live" by reaching number three. Initially working with producer Bobby Martin, the Manhattans' records now fell into line with the sweet, string-laden sound of contemporary '70s soul. The Manhattans hit the R&B Top Ten again in 1974 with "Don't Take Your Love" and 1975 with "Hurt," but their biggest success was still to come.

In early 1975, the Manhattans had recorded a Blue Lovett composition called "Kiss and Say Goodbye," which was released as a single almost a full year later. It became the second platinum single in history (after Johnnie Taylor's "Disco Lady") and their first number-one hit in the spring of 1976, not just on the R&B charts, but the pop side as well—a remarkable feat, considering that they'd never had a single peak higher than number 37 on that survey. While it proved difficult to match the crossover success of "Kiss and Say Goodbye," the Manhattans reeled off a string of Top Ten R&B hits—"I Kinda Miss You," "It Feels So Good to Be Loved So Bad," "We Never Danced to a Love Song," and "Am I Losing You"—that lasted into early 1978 and made them staples on the newly emerging quiet storm radio format. Their momentum slowed over the next couple of years, but they came back strong in 1980 with "Shining Star"—not a cover of the Earth, Wind & Fire hit, but a co-write by their new producer Leo Graham. "Shining Star" reached the Top Five on both the pop and R&B charts, went gold, and won a Grammy—overall, not a bad haul.

The Manhattans' last major hit came with 1983's "Crazy," which put them in the R&B Top Five for the final time; they bade farewell to the Top 40 in 1985 with a cover of Sam Cooke's "You Send Me." That year Richard Taylor left the group, which carried on as a quartet for a few years; Taylor passed away in December 1987. Gerald Alston signed with Motown as a solo artist in 1988, upon which point the group finally parted ways with Columbia and recorded an album for the small Valley Vue label before disbanding. Alston and Lovett reunited in 1993; with new members Troy May and David Tyson, they toured regularly into the new millennium, with the occasional recording appearing on a small label. *—Steve Huey*

With These Hands / 1970 / Deluxe ✦✦✦✦
Life after Carnival Records finds the Manhattans recording for the Deluxe label, where they cut some charmers. George "Smitty" Smith had polished his God-given, captivating, crying tenor into an instrument that ranked with the greats. *With These Hands* is the closest the Manhattans came to recording an album of standards or pop material. The album's ten songs consist of five standards and five cold-blooded originals. You can't help but feel the aching pain in "It's Gonna Take a Lot to Bring Me Back," a minor R&B hit that had major potential; the slow weeper oozes soul. "Give Him Up" displays the quintet's lovely uptempo harmony; the shuffler unfortunately got lost as a B-side. The tear jerking "If My Heart Could Speak" is a slow, tenderly sung ballad and one of their best. Winnie Lovett, Kenny Kelly, Edward Bivins and Richard Taylor provides splendid backing to Smitty's lead on "People Get Ready," "Can't Take My Eyes Off You," "Georgia on My Mind," "By the Time I Get to Phoenix" and the title track, all ably arranged by Chico O'Farrill. *—Andrew Hamilton*

There's No Me Without You / 1973 / Columbia ✦✦✦
Things changed considerably for the Manhattans in the early '70s. George "Smitty" Smith left the group and later died tragically. Gerald Alston replaced him and the group signed with Columbia. The title track of this album was their first huge hit with Columbia, and quickly showed them how much clout a smash on a major label meant. The single reached number three on the R&B charts, almost made the pop Top 40, and ensured that Alston's smoother, but equally powerful and declarative voice wouldn't have any problem fitting into their new sound. *—Ron Wynn*

It Feels So Good / 1977 / Columbia ✦✦✦
Another addition to the Manhattans' bulging cache of mellow sounds. Gerald Alston, Winnie Lovett, Edward Bivins and Kenny Kelly made a career of recording romance, heartache and make-out tunes. The popular "We Never Danced to a Love Song" fits in well with their other ballads, as does the majestic "It Just Can't Stay This Way" and "Let's Start All Over Again." They hit the charts with the somewhat contrived "I Kinda Miss You," and the title track, the eloquent "It Feels So Good to Be Loved So Bad" is classic—the harmony is tight and they add a little doo wop for good measure. You can't go wrong with any Manhattan album; they give their fans what they want, and never do they offend or alienate them by recording and releasing something out of character. *—Andrew Hamilton*

There's No Good in Goodbye / 1978 / Columbia ♦♦♦
Gerald Alston & the Manhattans—Winnie "Blue" Lovett, Edward Bivins and Kenny Kelly—are mellow as Moet on this sophisticated soul showcase. Remakes of "Then You Can Tell Me Goodbye" and "Tomorrow" sound like originals; they stamped their imprint on the two pop classics so definitively you forget about other versions. The eloquent "Am I Losing You" is an understated and heart-rending ballad. The chugger "Movin'" is the only uptempo number, while "Everybody Has a Dream is a motivational piece. Alston sings like a Baptist preacher on the Dr. Martin Luther King Jr. inspired message song. Despite Blue's depressing spoken intro, "Goodbye Is the Saddest Word" is not as depressing as the title or Blue's opening suggests—it has a buoyant midtempo beat and a happy-go-lucky feel. *—Andrew Hamilton*

Love Talk / 1979 / Columbia ♦♦♦♦
Even though this album does not feature any chart-busters, it does have an impressive blend of uptempo and midtempo numbers, along with some sensuous ballads. The only singles spawned by this album are "Here Comes the Hurt Again" and "The Way We Were/Memories." The former is a calm, easy-flowing number augmented by some whispering, yet animated background vocals. The single peaked at number 29 on the *Billboard* R&B charts inside 13 weeks. The latter is a medley rendition of two classic pop ballads. The Manhattans add an inviting, soulful twist to these nostalgic numbers, groomed with Gerald Alston's expansive vocals. It cracked the R&B charts at number 33 after 12 weeks. Any one of these vintage R&B numbers could stand alone. Uptempo tracks like the sizzling, soulful title number and the jumpin' "New York City," and ballads like "That's Not Part of the Show" and "Devil in the Dark," are exemplary. Not only does Alston give compelling deliveries, but he does it with versatility. In spite of the lackluster chart action, this is an outstanding album. *—Craig Lytle*

After Midnight / 1980 / Columbia ♦♦♦♦♦
This is the finest Manhattan album in their second incarnation. The original group with George Smith had a slightly rougher, more traditional R&B/doo-wop sound, while the soul unit featuring Gerald Alston was smoother, but no less anthemic, especially on ballads. This album didn't make it as high on the pop charts as their self-titled 1976 work, but had more consistently compelling tracks. "Shining Star" and "Girl Of My Dream" are masterful ballads. *—Ron Wynn*

Greatest Hits / 1980 / Columbia ♦♦♦♦♦
This spotlights the biggest records from the Manhattans' second phase. After George "Smitty" Smith died, eventual replacement Gerald Alston brought them a fine heartache and love ballad stylist. The move to a major label in the early '70s also helped, as Columbia provided them much more publicity muscle and promotional assistance than they ever received at Carnival and Deluxe. During the mid-'70s and early '80s, they also earned their first crossover exposure with the number-one hit "Kiss And Say Goodbye," one of the songs featured on this anthology spotlighting their soul and pop hits for Columbia. *—Ron Wynn*

Black Tie / 1981 / Columbia ♦♦♦
A good, although not classic or spectacular, early '80s Manhattan album. The group dipped a bit from its peak of 1980, in part because the company chose to issue a greatest hits album in 1980 rather than just ride out an internal situation and wait for a fresh release. They got two more chart hits out of the album, but never regained the momentum or status they enjoyed in 1980. *—Ron Wynn*

Forever by Your Side / 1983 / Columbia ♦♦
Although this was a nice album, the Manhattans were beginning to encounter problems in the mid-'80s with Columbia. The hits were drying up, and although their harmonies and Alston's soothing leads were still first-rate, they had become strictly an R&B band in appeal and weren't generating any pop attention. They tried being even smoother and more romantic than ever, softening the production and toning down the group interaction. The results were some excellent singles in "Just the Lonely Talking" and "Locked Up in Your Love," but they couldn't move the album or the group ahead. *—Ron Wynn*

Back to Basics / 1986 / Columbia ♦♦♦
The Manhattans tried to return to the soul form of past years with this mid-'80s release. It contained songs written and produced by the great Bobby Womack and less pop/crossover arrangements and influences. Gerald Alston was preparing to leave the group, but still sang with his customary warmth and style. But the person who made the most impact on this album was new co-vocalist Regina Belle. She became an urban contemporary star in the Anita Baker/Dianne Reeves quasi-jazz vein, but on this album she was singing with more soul and less polish. Belle toured with the band that year and turned a lot of heads. It didn't do as well as some past Columbia efforts, but was a worthy final project for Alston. *—Ron Wynn*

Dedicated to You: Golden Carnival Classics, Pt. 1 / Apr. 24, 1990 / Collectables ♦♦♦♦♦
The first of two superb volumes covering the Manhattans' early years on the Carnival label, the period many regard as their greatest. While they didn't come close to equaling the crossover/pop success they would enjoy with Columbia in their second incarnation, these were the pure soul works. The group featured both a glorious George "Smitty" Smith and young Blue Lovett, and their songs were produced solely with soul/R&B audiences in mind. There was little of the slick, polished orchestrations or smooth arrangements that were the hallmark of the Columbia hits. Instead, Smith's aching, soaring leads and the group's alternately mellow and frenzied harmonies were the high points. No matter what the sound quality, both this album and its counterpart are essential purchases for soul fans. *—Ron Wynn*

For You and Yours: Golden Carnival Classics, Pt. 2 / Apr. 24, 1990 / Collectables ♦♦♦♦♦
For many Manhattans fans, their earliest singles for Carnival were their greatest. These featured the wondrous George "Smitty" Smith, a young Blue Lovett, and some classic heartbreak and anguished soul singles, such as the divine "I Wanna Be (Your Everything)." These haven't been available on anthologies very often, and haven't been available anywhere since the early days of the Solid Smoke series. While Collectables' reissues sometimes leave a lot to be desired in the sound category, these songs are so good and so rare that any anthology featuring them has to get the highest recommendation, regardless of technical merit. This is the second of two volumes covering this era. *—Ron Wynn*

● **Kiss and Say Goodbye: The Best of the Manhattans** / Oct. 31, 1995 / Columbia/Legacy ♦♦♦♦♦
The Best of the Manhattans: Kiss and Say Goodbye is a terrific, 19-song overview of the Manhattans' recordings for Columbia in the '70s. All but two of the group's Top Ten R&B hits for the label are featured—there's no "We Never Danced to a Love Song" or "Crazy," but "There's No Me Without You," "Don't Take Your Love," "Hurt," "Kiss and Say Goodbye," "I Kinda Miss You," "It Feels So Good to Be Loved So Bad," "Am I Losing You" and "Shining Star" are all present—and several fine lesser-known singles and album tracks are added for good measure. Although the collection might be a bit too extensive for casual fans, it's the definitive overview of the Manhattans' time as a smooth soul group, illustrating how they helped develop the quiet storm subgenre. *—Stephen Thomas Erlewine*

Dedicated to You/For You and Yours / Nov. 20, 1995 / Kent ♦♦♦

Love Songs / Jan. 18, 2000 / Columbia/Legacy ♦♦♦
Like Sony's other *Love Songs* compilations, this one runs the risk of overlapping too much with greatest-hits discs for some consumers' tastes. Seven of the 13 tracks here are on *The Best of the Manhattans: Kiss and Say Goodbye*, which, like *Love Songs*, surveys their recordings from the 1970s and early 1980s for Columbia. Still, this collection does retrieve three R&B chart singles that eluded *The Best of the Manhattans*...: "We Never Danced to a Love Song," "Girl of My Dream," and "The Way We Were/Memories." The disc is filled out by a couple of album tracks and their 1972 single "A Million to One," which was actually on the Deluxe label. *—Richie Unterberger*

The Mar-Keys

f. 1958, Memphis, TN
Group / Memphis Soul, Instrumental Rock, Soul, Southern Soul
Despite scoring only one national hit, the 1961 instrumental smash "Last Night," the Mar-Keys remain one of the most important groups ever to emerge from the Memphis music scene. As the first house band for the legendary Stax label, they appeared on some of the greatest records in soul history, with their ranks also producing such renowned musicians as guitarist Steve Cropper and bassist Donald "Duck" Dunn. The Mar-Keys formed in 1958 and included drummer Terry Johnson, pianist Jerry Lee "Smoochie" Smith, saxophonists Don Nix and Charles Axton, and trumpeter Wayne Jackson in addition to Cropper and Dunn.

Originally dubbed the Royal Spades, in 1960 the group joined the staff at Axton's mother Estelle's Satellite label, backing artists that included Rufus Thomas and his daughter Carla. A year later, the Mar-Keys headlined the Chips Moman-penned "Last Night," which reached the number-three spot in the summer of 1961. When Satellite changed its name to Stax, the Mar-Keys remained on board, laying the foundation for the classic Memphis soul sound through with their funky, sophisticated grooves; concurrently they recorded a series of singles including "Pop-Eye Stroll," "The Morning After," and "Philly Dog," although none repeated the commercial success of "Last Night."

In 1962 Cropper and Dunn left the lineup to co-found the famed Booker T. and the MG's. Other personnel changes followed, although the Mar-Keys continued on for several more years before the name was eventually dropped. Jackson then formed another top-notch session group, the Memphis Horns, while Axton led the Packers, scoring a 1965 hit with "Hole in the Wall." Nix, meanwhile, mounted a solo career, also producing records for artists including Freddie King, Jeff Beck, and Furry Lewis. *—Jason Ankeny*

The Last Night! / 1961 / Atlantic ♦♦♦
"Last Night" was a great early-'60s instrumental rock hit, and an important one in helping to establish the basic sound of Stax soul music. It's the linchpin of the Mar-Keys' first album, and despite the single's greatness, the LP is a mediocre, filler-filled effort that typifies the low standards of the full-length rock recording at the time. These are basic sax- and organ-driven soul-rock dance instrumentals, good for dancing to in the live shows the Mar-Keys were doing, but pretty boring one after another on record. Only a few of these are group originals, the rest of the cuts including covers of jazz tunes (Cannonball Adderley's "Sack o' Woe"), popular standards ("Misty," "Ebb Tide"), classic R&B ("Sticks and Stones"), and even Paul Anka's "Diana." In 2002 the album was paired on CD with the Mar-Keys' second (and similar) LP, *Do the Pop-Eye*, also released in 1962. *—Richie Unterberger*

Do the Pop-Eye / 1962 / Atlantic ♦♦♦
The Mar-Keys' second album was much like their first, *Last Night!* (issued earlier in 1961): functional, simple early-'60s soul-rock instrumentals, prominently featuring sax and organ and easy to dance to. And like *Last Night!*, it was unimaginative and dull to listen to altogether, with the disadvantage of lacking a single as good as the classic "Last Night," though it was a little funkier in its song selection and execution. The bouncy "Pop-Eye Stroll" had been a very small hit (making number 94), and probably for that reason there were a couple of knockoffs elsewhere on the LP, "Pop-Eye Rider" and "Too Pooped to Pop-Eye." Historically this is an important record, only because three of the musicians to play in Booker T. & the MG's—Steve Cropper, Booker T. Jones, and Duck Dunn—play on it (Cropper and Jones also wrote a bit of the material). You can hear antecedents to the Booker T. & the MG's' sound on some of the better cuts, like "Straight From the Can" and "Sit Still," which has some stinging Cropper licks; Rufus Thomas wrote one of the other tracks, "'Cause I Love You." [In 2002 the album was paired on CD with the *Last Night!* album.] *—Richie Unterberger*

The Great Memphis Sound / 1966 / Atlantic ✦✦✦

Back to Back / 1967 / Atlantic ✦✦✦✦✦

Recorded live at Paris in 1967, when the Stax-Volt Revue was touring Europe. This is just about exactly what you'd expect: solid, straight-ahead live versions of the instrumental group's best-known tunes, in good sound. Booker T. & the MG's take seven of the album's ten tracks, including their hits "Green Onions" and "Hip Hug-Her"; the Mar-Keys do "Last Night" and a couple of other numbers. *—Richie Unterberger*

Mellow Jelly / 1968 / Atlantic ✦✦

Damifiknow! / 1969 / Stax ✦✦✦

For this session, the Mar-Keys were basically Booker T. & the MG's, augmented by trumpeter Wayne Jackson and tenor saxophonist Andrew Love (who would soon become the Memphis Horns). It's not quite fair to call this laid-back set easy listening, but it's certainly not much more than background listening as they wind their way through a mix of originals and covers of shopworn '60s tunes like "Mustang Sally," "Soul Man," and "Daydream." It's pleasant and executed with the expected precision, but it has to rate among the musicians' more secondary efforts, whether they're calling themselves the MG's or something else. [The album was combined with the 1971 Mar-Keys LP *Memphis Experience* onto a single-CD reissue in 1994.] *—Richie Unterberger*

Memphis Experience / 1971 / Stax ✦✦

The Mar-Keys had a history of strange personnel changes; their previous LP (1969's *Damifiknow!*) had basically been Booker T. & the MG's-plus-horn section playing under the Mar-Keys name. Yet *Memphis Experience* was even stranger, demonstrating that the Mar-Keys at this point meant nothing more to Stax than a name that could be exploited. Three of the seven cuts were Bar-Kays outtakes that were scrapped when that band underwent one of its own numerous reorganizations. The rest of the album was recorded by an assortment of Memphis musicians. The result was serviceable period instrumental soul-funk, occasionally creeping into psychedelia (especially on the nine-minute "Cloud Nine," with several minutes of weird screams and whispers). It's an oddity in the Stax discography, related to the rest of the Mar-Keys' releases in name only, and not worth paying attention to unless you're determined to track down every available Stax recording. [The album was combined with the 1969 Mar-Keys LP *Damifiknow!* onto a single-CD reissue in 1994.] *—Richie Unterberger*

● **Damifiknow!/Memphis Experience** / May 20, 1994 / Stax ✦✦✦✦

This is a two-for-one disc combining a couple strange releases, neither of which were truly the Mar-Keys. *Damifiknow!* was played by Booker T. & the MG's, supplemented by a horn section that would become the Memphis Horns; *Memphis Experience* combined Mar-Keys outtakes with instrumentals by Memphis musicians with no connection to prior Mar-Keys lineups. It's a convenient way for major Stax/soul collectors to pick up two of the group's odder records, but it's not a representative reflection of the Mar-Keys. Nor is the music especially noteworthy: *Damifiknow!* is easygoing, rather humdrum soul instrumentals that don't pack nearly the punch of the MG's at their best, while *Memphis Experience* is average wordless early '70s soul-funk with occasional psychedelic/hard rock tinges. *—Richie Unterberger*

The Marathons

Group / R&B, Doo Wop, Novelty, Frat Rock

The five singers who sang on "Peanut Butter," a popular R&B novelty tune, were really the Vibrations masquerading as the Marathons. These same guys, save for a couple of changes, had previously recorded as the Jay Hawks, charting with "Stranded in the Jungle" in 1956. "Stranded in the Jungle" was a novelty tune and probably was the first instance of "sampling"—sound bites from popular songs jumped from the lyrics like news bulletins. Don Bradley (bass), Carl Fisher (second tenor), Dave Govan (baritone), Jimmy Johnson (lead), and Richard Owens (first tenor) had a hit as the Vibrations with "The Watusi"; the dance song peaked at number 25. Multi-talented H.B. Barnum thought the group's sound was ideal for "Peanut Butter," a novelty tune he had co-written. Few imagined the tune would become as big as it did.

A lawsuit resulted when Checker Records discovered the charade. The Vibrations' members had individual contracts with Checker, and the label won the rights to market copies of "Peanut Butter" under their logo. Not to be denied, Arvee Records promptly secured the rights to the name the Marathons. Arvee released "Tight Sweater," written by a young Sonny Bono, as the follow-up. The recording failed to further the Marathons' name, as did Arvee's album release by the Marathons. Arvee rounded up some more singers to record "Peanut Butter"'s successor and the album tracks; the same group also performed as the Marathons. *—Andrew Hamilton*

The Marcels

f. Pittsburgh, PA

Group / Doo Wop, R&B

This Pittsburgh ensemble deserved a much better fate than being known primarily for a novelty-tinged cover of "Blue Moon." Baritone vocalist Richard F. Knauss teamed with Fred Johnson, Gene J. Bricker, Ron Mundy, and lead vocalist Cornelius Harp, an integrated ensemble. They named themselves after Harp's hairstyle, the marcel. The group did a string of covers as demo tapes that were sent to Colpix. The label's A&R director had them cut several oldies at RCA's New York studios in 1961, one of them being "Blue Moon." They used the bass intro arrangement from the Cadillacs' "Zoom" and the results were a huge hit. It eventually topped both the pop and R&B charts, and also was an international smash. The group eventually appeared in the film *Twist Around the Clock* with Dion and Chubby Checker. They eventually recorded an 18-cut LP for Colpix.

Alan Johnson and Walt Maddox later replaced Knauss and Gene Bricker, making them an all-black unit. The group did score another Top Ten pop single with "Heartaches," another cover of a pre-rock single. This peaked at number seven pop and number 19 R&B in 1961. They continued recording on Kyra, Queen Bee, St. Clair, Rocky, and Monogram with varying lineups, but never again equaled their past success. *—Ron Wynn*

● **The Best of the Marcels** / Apr. 1990 / Rhino ✦✦✦✦✦

Lest anyone think the Marcels were a one-song phenomenon (i.e., "Blue Moon"), this CD will be a valuable learning experience, as well as delightful listening. Drawing primarily from their singles (with three LP cuts and an unissued outtake filling out the song lineup), this is a fairly dazzling array of vocal acrobatics, much of it hung around old pop standards, among them "Summertime," "That Old Black Magic," "My Melancholy Baby," and "Over the Rainbow," as well as songs of more recent vintage. Among the discoveries to be made here is a gloriously radiant recording of an otherwise "lost" Barry Mann/Cynthia Weill number called "Find Another Fool." Cornelius Harp's lead on "Summertime" is a glorious thing to hear, while the brilliantly arranged "Heartaches"—dominated by Walt Maddox's baritone—which managed to hit number nine nationally, manages to encompass something essentially poignant about R&B and rock & roll, and elicit a laugh or two (or three) in the process. Original producer Stu Phillips, whose subsequent career involved him in everything from the Monkees to the soundtrack of *Battlestar Galactica*, did a brilliant job on these tracks, which hold up very well today, the voices always out front and in your face, and just enough rhythm section and whatever lead instrument (usually a sax) to sweeten the mix and add a little punch behind the group. If this disc has any flaw, it's that the makers didn't follow the chronological order of the recording dates, which means that the sounds of the two distinctly different lineups of the group are intermingled—but the notes also include a chart delineating precisely which lineup sang on which songs, and that's excellent compensation. The sound holds up extremely well for a CD mastered in 1990, and the only reason for not picking this up would be to grab Sequel records' *Complete Colpix Sessions* instead, which features 38 songs from the same source as these 18. *—Bruce Eder*

Summertime / 1992 / Relic ✦✦✦✦✦

Fans of this extraordinary doo wop outfit will have to own this CD, containing 24 demo tracks including "Zoom," and the number that ultimately evolved into their celebrated cover of Rodgers & Hart's "Blue Moon." Also on hand are "A Sunday Kind of Love," "Over the Rainbow," "I Could Have Danced All Night," "Spanish Harlem," "Save the Last Dance for Me," "Got a Job," "Stormy Weather," and "That Lucky Old Sun" (two different versions), among others, rounded out with a quartet of completed numbers from much later in their history. The notes are entertaining and surprisingly honest in their admission of lack of information on certain tracks and their histories. *—Bruce Eder*

The Complete Colpix Sessions / Apr. 16, 1995 / Castle ✦✦✦✦✦

A complete collection from the Marcels' most fruitful recording period—1961 to 1963 on Colpix Records—that ranges from their debut blaster, "Blue Moon," which went to number-one pop and R&B, to "Last Kiss," their final Colpix single. The 38 tracks feature some "Blue Moon" juniors and wannabes as well as some smacking good early-'60s R&B sounds. The original group does 18 tracks; the rest includes varying substitutes, but casual fans won't discern much difference. The Pittsburgh natives recorded exciting music. Many think of them as a '50s doo wop group, but their first single came out in 1961. A '50s influence, however, is quite evident in their vocal approach. While there are too many pleasing cuts to single out, some primes include: "Heartaches," a number-seven pop hit; "My Melancholy Baby"; the Moonglows' "Most of All"; "Over the Rainbow"; and "Sweet Was the Wine." *—Andrew Hamilton*

Bobby Marchan

b. Apr. 30, 1930, Youngstown, OH

Vocals / New Orleans R&B, Doo Wop, R&B

A premier female impersonator, Bobby Marchan was part of a troupe called the Powder Box Revue. Before going on his own, Marchan played with Huey "Piano" Smith and the Clowns, toured with Shirley & Lee, and led his own band, the Tick Tocks. He landed his lone number-one hit in 1960, a powerhouse version of "There's Something on Your Mind" for Fire. He continued recording for various tiny labels, and in 1966 had a Top 20 R&B single with "Shake Your Tambourine" for Cameo. *—Ron Wynn*

● **Clown Jewels: The Ace (Ms.) Masters 1956–75** / Oct. 27, 1998 / WestSide ✦✦✦✦✦

Female impersonator Bobby Marchan was the lead singer/band and show organizer for Huey "Piano" Smith & the Clowns during their heyday, singing on all of the latter's big hits (after "Rockin' Pneumonia and the Boogie Woogie Flu") and leaving a wealth of recording behind, both issued and unissued, in the Ace Records Jackson, MS vaults. This 24-track collection brings together all the best of those recordings from his beginnings at the label in 1956 to his latter day sides for them in 1975. Included are a nice collection of sides that were issued under Huey's name ("Don't You Just Know It," "Hush Your Mouth," "High Blood Pressure"), his own ("You Can't Stop Her," "Chickee Wah Wah," "Rockin' Behind the Iron Curtain") and his earliest Ace efforts as Bobby Fields (three previously unreleased versions of "Pity Poor Me," "Helping Hand" and "Little Girl of Mine"). Rounding things out are Marchan's later contemporary soul-R&B records waxed for the label in 1974, including the funky "Push the Button" and "Baby Get Your Yo Yo (Wind It Up)." An essential set of 1950s New Orleans music, cut at the right place at the right time with the right people involved. *—Cub Koda*

There's Something on Your Mind / Oct. 26, 1999 / Sphere Sound ✦✦✦✦

The exciting New Orleans R&B/blues singer revisits the spotlight with this reissue. Bobby Marchan's potent deliveries are glossed over 18 well-baked tracks, including his famous two-part songs "There's Something on My Mind," "You're Still My Baby," "The Things I Used to Do," and a previously unreleased take of "Yes It's Written All Your Face." Marchan, a female impersonator, breaks out in an extremely feminine singing and speaking voice on some tracks that sounds like the real deal. He handles uptempo tunes like "Booty Green," "What You Don't Know Won't Hurt You," and "Snoopin' and Accusin'" as skillfully as he does slow-moaners like "The Things I Used to Do" and "All in My Mind." Bobby Marchan's recordings are blue-plate specials comprised of rock & roll, R&B, blues, soul, and novelty items. *—Andrew Hamilton*

Arif Mardin

b. Mar. 15, 1932, Istanbul, Turkey

Arranger, Strings, Synthesizer, Producer / Pop/Rock, Pop-Soul, Funk

A longtime house producer and arranger with Atlantic Records, Arif Mardin assisted in the creation of many of the classic pop and jazz recordings of his era, enjoying perhaps his greatest success in collaboration with Aretha Franklin. Born in Istanbul, Turkey on March 15, 1932, he graduated from the Berklee College of Music in 1961, signing on with Atlantic a short time later. Mardin's earliest production duties focused on projects with jazz artists including Sonny Stitt, Freddie Hubbard and Eddie Harris, but his stock truly began to rise in the wake of Franklin's 1967 arrival on the label roster. In conjunction with the legendary producer Jerry Wexler and engineer Tom Dowd, Mardin set the stage for the singer's artistic and commercial breakthrough, arranging Franklin's landmark 1967 LP *I Never Loved a Man (The Way I Love You)* and its classic single "Respect"; another Franklin watershed, *Lady Soul*, followed from the same studio team a year later.

Also in 1968, Mardin produced the debut album from the great Isaac Hayes, *Presenting Isaac Hayes*; additionally, he continued a long partnership with the Rascals, overseeing perennial hits like "Good Lovin'" and "Groovin'" and earning the title of the group's unofficial fifth member. In 1969, Mardin worked on the Dusty Springfield masterpiece *Dusty in Memphis*; a year later, he moved on to produce Laura Nyro's *Christmas and the Beads of Sweat*, and also released his first solo LP, *Glass Onion*. His collaboration with Franklin continued on as well, yielding superb records like *Spirit in the Dark*, *Young Gifted and Black* and *Amazing Grace*. In 1971, Mardin shifted gears entirely to helm folkie John Prine's acclaimed self-titled debut. From there, he went on to work with new Atlantic signings like Hall & Oates, Bette Midler and Doug Sahm.

In 1974, Mardin travelled to Miami to produce the Bee Gees, who were at the time struggling to recapture their late-'60s pop success. On the orders of manager Robert Stigwood, Mardin reinvented the group's sound to capture the flavor of American R&B; while his first attempt, *Mr. Natural*, was not a success, with its 1975 follow-up *Main Course* the Bee Gees found themselves pioneering the commercial rise of disco, scoring a number-one hit with the single "Jive Talkin'." Mardin's knack for blue-eyed funk also came to the fore through his concurrent work with the Average White Band. Albums with Rod Stewart, George Benson and Carly Simon followed, and in 1980 he also began an extended partnership with Chaka Khan. Although Mardin's pace slowed in the years to follow, he continued to work with high-profile younger artists like Culture Club and Howard Jones, and also reunited with the likes of the Bee Gees and Hall & Oates. *—Jason Ankeny*

Glass Onion / Feb. 1970 / Atlantic ✦✦

Journey / Mar. 1975 / Atlantic ✦✦

Teena Marie

b. Mar. 5, 1956, Santa Monica, CA

Producer, Vocals / Disco, Dance-Pop, Urban, Funk, Pop/Rock, Quiet Storm

No white artist has sang R&B more convincingly than Teena Marie, whose big, robust vocals are so black-sounding that when she was starting out, some listeners wondered if she was a light-skinned African-American. Not to be confused with Brazilian jazz singer Tania Maria, Marie grew up in West Los Angeles in a neighborhood that was nicknamed "Venice Harlem" because of its heavy black population. The singer/songwriter/producer was in her early 20s when, around 1977, she landed a job at Motown Records. It was at Motown that she met her mentor and paramour-to-be, Rick James, who ended up doing all of the writing and producing for her debut album of 1979, *Wild And Peaceful*. That LP, which boasted her hit duet with James, "I'm Just a Sucker For Your Love," didn't show Marie's picture—so many programmers at black radio just assumed she was black. When her second album, *Lady T*, came out, much of the R&B world was shocked to see how fair-skinned she was. But to many of the black R&B fans who were eating her music up, it really didn't matter—the bottom line was she was a first-rate soul singer whose love of black culture ran deep.

By her third album, 1980's gold *Irons In The Fire*, Marie was doing most of her own writing and producing. That album boasted the major hit "I Need Your Lovin'," and Marie went gold again with her next album, *It Must Be Magic* (which included the major hit "Square Biz"). *It Must Be Magic* turned out to be her last album for Motown, with which she had a nasty legal battle. Marie got out of her contract with Motown, and the case ended up with the courts passing what is known as "The Teena Marie Law"—which states that a label cannot keep an artist under contract without putting out an album by him or her.

Switching to Epic in 1983, Marie recorded her fifth album *Robbery* and had a hit with "Fix It." In 1984, Marie recorded her sixth album, *Starchild* and had her biggest pop hit ever with "Lovergirl." Though Marie had often soared to the top of the R&B charts, "Lovergirl" marked the first time she'd done so well in the pop market. Ironically, Marie was a white singer who had enjoyed little exposure outside the R&B market prior to "Lovegirl." Three more Epic albums followed: 1986's *Emerald City*, 1988's *Naked To The World* (which contained her smash hit "Ooh La La La") and 1990's *Ivory*. Unfortunately, Marie's popularity had faded considerably by the late 1980s, and Epic dropped her. In 1994, the singer released *Passion Play* on her own Sarat label. *—Alex Henderson*

Wild and Peaceful / 1979 / Motown ✦✦✦

When Teena Marie first hit big, many listeners had no idea she was white. Her mentor and paramour Rick James has commented that when they first met, even he was shocked at how black-sounding she was. It was James who was responsible for Marie signing with Motown, and for the excellence of her debut album, *Wild and Peaceful*. Rick handles all of the producing and most of the writing, making everything from their flirtatious duet on "Sucker for Your Love" to the beautiful reflection on reincarnation "Deja Vu (I've Been Here Before)" come alive. Also quite impressive is Marie's passionate cover of Smokey Robinson's "Don't Look Back." The bottom line is that whatever Marie's skin color, this album made it abundantly clear that she was a first-class soul singer. *—Alex Henderson*

Lady T / 1980 / Motown ✦✦✦

Teena Marie's second album, *Lady T*, found her working with producer Richard Rudolph, husband of the late Minnie Riperton. Though not as strong as *Wild and Peaceful*, this decent but not essential release had many strong points and offered much evidence that she was a soul goddess to be reckoned with. The single "Behind the Groove" is a funk smoker, and "Could It Be Love" and "Aladdin's Lamb" show how charming Marie can be. Rick James' influence could still be felt, though it was clear that Marie had many impressive ideas of her own. Unlike *Wild and Peaceful*, *Lady T* showed Marie's picture on the front cover—many of the fans she'd acquired were shocked to see that she was white. *—Alex Henderson*

Irons in the Fire / 1980 / Motown ✦✦✦

With her third album, *Irons in the Fire*, Teena Marie did something that was rare for a female R&B artist—she handled all of the producing and writing herself. Marie took on a lot of responsibility, and she knew she had done the right thing when the album became both a commercial and artistic triumph. By now, it was common knowledge that Marie was white, something that didn't seem to matter much to the many black R&B fans who bought this recording. Like so much of her work, the irresistible single "I Need Your Lovin'" became a major R&B hit, but didn't do much on pop radio. Interestingly, Marie was having the same problem as Maze & Frankie Beverly in that she could have a gold album without any help from pop audiences. But then, she obviously realized that she didn't need their support in order to be legit. From the seductive "You Make Love Like Springtime" and the sweaty "First Class Love" to the moving title song, everything on this album is a gem. *—Alex Henderson*

It Must Be Magic / 1981 / Motown ✦✦✦

The last of Teena Marie's four albums for Motown, *It Be Must Magic* found the songstress continuing to do all of her own writing, producing and arranging, with magnificent results. *Irons In the Fire* proved that she didn't need the input of a big-name producer in order to deliver first-class albums, and Marie provided additional evidence of that fact on an album that gave us such gems as the playful "Square Biz" (one of her biggest hits, and an early example of an R&B artist incorporating rap), the thought-provoking "Revolution," and the gritty title song. Marie has periodically shown a strong love of jazz, which is exactly what happens on the ballad "Yes Indeed" and the sexy "Portuguese Love." *Magic* didn't do much in the pop market, but thanks to a largely black R&B following, the album went gold. *—Alex Henderson*

Starchild / 1984 / Epic ✦✦✦✦

This was the definitive album Teena Marie was never allowed to do while at Motown. She not only zoomed up the R&B charts, but even had a pop smash with "Lovergirl," and suddenly Motown executives went scrambling for cover. "Mr. Dear Mr. Gaye" was one of the better tribute songs done to Gaye, although it didn't generate the attention it deserved for Marie. The album wound up being Marie's most successful. *—Ron Wynn*

Greatest Hits / 1985 / Motown ✦✦✦

Emerald City / 1986 / Epic ✦✦

A puzzling album for Teena Marie, perhaps the most disappointing of her career. She tried a concept work, doing thematically related songs and longer, jazz-influenced ballads. Many of them were well sung; some were a bit self-indulgent, but overall, it was a nicely performed work. But it flopped, indicating that her fans preferred short, to-the-point soul tunes and hard-hitting dance or funk to more introspective, slow-to-develop pieces and socio-political commentary. *—Ron Wynn*

Naked to the World / Apr. 1988 / Epic ✦✦✦✦✦

Teena Marie's popularity had decreased by 1988, when she found herself competing with considerably less talented Prince clones, Madonna wannabees and Paula Abdul soundalikes. But she managed to have both a hit album and an artistic triumph in *Naked to the World*, which found her taking a more high-tech, contemporary-sounding (by 1988 standards) approach to production without abandoning the classic soul and funk elements that made her so appealing to begin with. Among the treasures: the unapologetically sentimental, early-'70s ballad "Ooo La La La" (which proudly proclaims its allegiance to soul music's golden era with references to Bloodstone's "Natural High" and Al Green's "Let's Stay Together"), the addictively funky "Work It" and the sassy, clever "Trick Bag." The sparks usually flew when Lady T formed a duet with Rick James, and the sweaty "Call Me (I Got Yo Number)" and the ballad "The Once and Future Dream" are no exceptions. *—Alex Henderson*

Ivory / 1990 / Epic ✦✦✦

Ivory, Lady T's last album for a major label, was an intentionally ironic title in that she's a white singer who sounds convincingly black (much to her credit), has a largely African-American following and has enjoyed little support from pop audiences. Unfortunately, Marie didn't enjoy much commercial success period with *Ivory*—a generally decent album, certainly, but one that fell short of the overall excellence of *Naked to the World* and earlier offerings like *Irons in the Fire* (1980) and *Wild and Peaceful* (her 1979 debut). Marie's use of hip-hop elements comes across as forced, clichéd and contrived on "Mr. Icecream" and "Here's Looking at You." But she has definite treasures in the infectious funk number "The Sugar Shack," the seductive "Just Us Two" and "If I Were a Bell"—a fine example of the type of heart-on-her-sleeve, '70s soul balladry she'd long since mastered. With a folk-rock appeal not unlike Edie Brickell—believe it or not—"How Can You Resist" is a major departure for her. Marie had been producing and writing her own albums since *Irons in the Fire*—a claim few other female soul divas can make—but turns to Soul II Soul founder Jazzie B with likeable, thought not breathtaking, results, on "Since Day One." *—Alex Henderson*

Greatest Hits / 1991 / Epic ♦♦♦♦
In 1991, Epic Records offered an overview of Teena Marie's eight-year, four-album tenure with the label with this 58-minute best-of CD, which boasts mostly first-rate material, but misses some high points and should have been ten to fifteen minutes longer. The more obvious choices—such as the rock-influenced "Lovergirl" (one of Lady T's few pop hits), the ballad "Dear Lover" and "Ooo La La La"—are included along with some pearls that weren't major hits like her poigant tribute to Marvin Gaye, "My Dear Mr. Gaye," and her jazz ballad "Casanova Brown." But amazingly, the collection omits 1983's "Fix It"—her first hit after leaving Motown and resurfacing on Epic. *—Alex Henderson*

● **I Need Your Lovin': The Best of Teena Marie** / May 17, 1994 / Motown ♦♦♦♦♦
Although most of the '90s found Teena Marie without a record deal, both Motown and Epic continued to profit from her legacy by putting out best-of collections. In 1994, Motown released *I Need Your Lovin': The Best of Teena Marie*, a generous, gem-laden collection that spans 1977-1981 and clocks in at 73 minutes. Essential Motown hits like "I Need Your Lovin'," "Square Biz," "Behind the Groove" and "I'm a Sucker for Your Love" are offered along with some excellent album tracks, including "Deja Vu" (a lovely ballad that was written by Rick James and reflects on reincarnation) and *Irons in the Fire's* title song. Motown also offers two previously unreleased ballads that were recorded before she had any albums or singles out: 1977's enjoyable "Don't Turn Your Back on Me" and a heartfelt cover of the Gladys Knight & the Pips hit "Every Little Bit Hurts" (which James wrote and produced for Marie in 1978). It's unfortunate that the songs remained in the can for 16 and 17 years, but better late than never. All four of the albums that Marie recorded for Motown in the late '70s and early '80s (*Wild and Peaceful, Lady T, Irons in the Fire* and *It Must Be Magic*) are well worth having. But if you're seeking an introduction to her Motown output, this 12-song CD would be the logical place to go. *—Alex Henderson*

Lovergirl: The Teena Marie Story / Feb. 11, 1997 / Epic/Legacy ♦♦♦♦♦
Lovergirl: The Teena Marie Story collects all of Marie's mid-'80s hits for Epic, including "Lovergirl," "Work It," "If I Were a Bell," "Just Us Two," "Jammin'," and "Ooo La La La." While some casual listeners will find the inclusion of 12-inch extended mixes somewhat redundent, those mixes actually give a better idea of how Marie's music was appreciated during the time, and makes *Lovergirl* a fine greatest hits compilation. *—Leo Stanley*

● **Ultimate Collection** / Feb. 1, 2000 / Hip-O ♦♦♦♦♦
It's not quite the ultimate, but it's close. A Teena Marie album that doesn't include "Deja Vu (I've Been Here Before)," "Dear Lover," "Out on a Limb," and "Fire & Desire" doesn't merit the ultimate tag. Still, there are plenty of goodies. The soulful Lady T will bring you to tears on "Young Love," "My Dear Mr. Gaye," and "Irons in the Fire"; she remains as effective on upbeat rockers like "I Need Your Lovin'," "Work It," and "Square Biz." The album also includes her biggest charting single "Lovergirl," the exotic "Portuguese Love," and her career-blossoming hit with Rick James' "I'm Just a Sucker for Your Love." *—Andrew Hamilton*

Martha & the Vandellas

f. 1963, Detroit, MI, **db.** 1972
Group / Girl Group, Motown, Soul, Pop-Soul
Along with the Supremes, Martha & the Vandellas defined the distaff side of the Motown sound in the 1960s; their biggest hits, including "Heat Wave," "Dancing in the Street," and "Nowhere to Run," remain among the most potent and enduring dance records of the era. The vocal group was led by Martha Reeves who, along with fellow Detroit natives Annette Sterling Beard, Gloria Williams, and Rosalind Ashford, founded the Del-Phis in 1960. After Reeves landed a secretarial position at the offices of Motown Records, the Del-Phis were tapped to record a one-off single for the label's Melody imprint, which they cut under the name the Vels.

The single fizzled, and Williams exited, reducing the group to a trio. After backing Marvin Gaye on the superb 1962 record "Stubborn Kind of Fellow," they were renamed Martha & the Vandellas, taking inspiration from Detroit's Van Dyke Street and Reeves' heroine Della Reese. When singer Mary Wells failed to show up for a recording date, musicians' union rules demanded that a vocalist be found to fulfill contractual obligations; as a result, Reeves was yanked from the secretarial pool and laid down what would become Martha & the Vandellas' first record, 1963's "I'll Have to Let Him Go."

The Top 30 success of the ballad "Come and Get These Memories" brought the group the attention of Motown's hit-making production team Holland-Dozier-Holland, who crafted their next smash, the galvanizing Top Five classic "Heat Wave," which perfected the mix of impassioned call-and-response vocals, pulsing rhythms, and full-bodied horns that became the trio's trademark. Following another Top Ten hit, "Quicksand," Beard retired, and was replaced by former Velvelette Betty Kelly. After singer Kim Weston turned down the Marvin Gaye/Ivy Jo Hunter/Mickey Stevenson composition "Dancing in the Street," the song was shuttled to Martha & the Vandellas; refashioned by Holland-Dozier-Holland to fit the group's formula, the anthem became their biggest hit and definitive statement, reaching number two in the summer of 1964. A year later, they returned with another smash, the savage "Nowhere to Run," followed by "I'm Ready for Love."

In 1967, Kelly exited, and was replaced by Reeves' younger sister Lois; on subsequent releases, the group was billed as Martha Reeves & the Vandellas. 1967's "Jimmy Mack" and "Honey Chile" were the last records overseen by the Holland-Dozier-Holland team before their defection from Motown, and were also the final significant Vandellas hits; in 1968, Martha Reeves fell seriously ill, and in 1969 Ashford departed, with another former Velvelette, Sandra Tilley, assuming her position. The trio continued unsuccessfully for a few more years before breaking up in the wake of a December, 1972, farewell performance at Detroit's Cobo Hall. After Motown relocated its corporate offices to Los Angeles (a move Reeves denied she was privy to), the singer, who had begun a solo career, sued to have her contract with the label annulled; in her 1994 autobiography, *Dancing in the Street*, she charged that the Vandellas' career, though highly successful in its own right, could have been even greater had Motown founder Berry Gordy Jr. given their music the same obsessive attention he afforded to Diana Ross & the Supremes.

Reeves recorded her debut solo effort, *Martha Reeves: Produced by Richard Perry*, for MCA in 1974; though a few more LPs followed, including 1976's *The Rest of My Life* and 1978's *We Meet Again*, she received little notice on her own, and eventually suffered a pair of nervous breakdowns that led to a brief period of institutionalization. Lois Reeves, meanwhile, went on to work with Al Green, while Sandra Tilley retired from music; she died in 1982 following surgery on a brain tumor. In 1989, Martha Reeves, Annette Beard, and Rosalind Ashford successfully sued Motown for back royalties, and occasionally reunited for performances in the 1990s. Reeves also continued as a solo artist, and in addition performed with a Vandellas unit consisting of Lois and a third sister, Delphine. *—Jason Ankeny*

Heat Wave / Sep. 30, 1963 / Gordy ♦♦♦
Martha & the Vandellas began making their first noise on the pop and soul charts with this 1963 album. The title song was a classic, while there were also decent remakes of such vintage tunes as "Mocking Bird" and "My Boyfriend's Back." These proved that the group was a singles rather than an album act, and that a little more effort needed to be extended toward finding more material (they even put "Danke Schoen" on this album). But no one really cared, since "Heat Wave" was such a triumph. *—Ron Wynn*

Come and Get These Memories / 1963 / Gordy ♦♦♦
Their debut album finds the Vandellas in a more lightweight and pop-oriented style than they would become known for, with some girl group and doo-wop roots still in evidence. As was often the case during this era, the best tracks were the singles: the title track (the group's first big hit), "There He Is (At My Door)," and The Shirelles-like "I'll Have to Let Him Go." Most of the material was written by Holland-Dozier-Holland, but beyond the singles, there aren't any exceptionally noteworthy cuts. *—Richie Unterberger*

Dance Party / 1965 / Gordy ♦♦♦♦♦
One of the great party albums of the 1960s, *Dance Party* was, oddly enough, the work of a Motown act that wasn't known for delivering great albums. Martha & the Vandellas had enjoyed some serious hits from 1964 onward, but hadn't quite measured up in the LP department until the release of *Dance Party* in the spring of 1965. Made up of material from singles that went back to the previous summer, the album benefited from the presence of the group's biggest single, "Dancing in the Street," its follow-up, the hypnotically pounding, driving, soaring "Wild One," and the classic "Nowhere to Run," surrounded by a trio of well-above-average B-sides and covers of such Motown dance standards as "Mickey's Monkey" and "Hitch Hike." Even the rest was hardly filler, however, with Martha Reeves turning in a gloriously impassioned performance on the ballad "There He Is (At My Door)" and the group acquitting itself beautifully on "Motoring." Each side was always good for at least two plays at any self-respecting teen party of the '60s, and it all still holds up today. *—Bruce Eder*

The Motortown Revue in Paris / Nov. 1965 / Tamla ♦♦♦♦
Berry Gordy Jr. took a select few artists across the pond in 1965 and documented the event with this live recording in Paris. The LP is a big improvement, sonically speaking, over the two previous live *Motortown Revue* releases. Session pianist Earl Van Dyke gets billing because the Motown label had received some spins in Europe; Van Dyke's records remain more popular in European countries than in the States. He starts the festivities with a pumping instrumental version of "Too Many Fish in the Sea." The Supremes, the Miracles, Martha & the Vandellas, and Stevie Wonder put on exceptional shows, each seemingly trying to best the other. Stevie in particular had a supercharged, electric quality about him this evening, and it showed on his stinging rendition of Tommy Tucker's "High Heel Sneakers," plus a mellow "Funny How Times Slip Away," where he's joined vocally by producer/writer Clarence Paul. Martha Reeves is one of the few singers who could turn "If I Had a Hammer" into a soulful number, which she did to the delight of the Parisians. The Supremes sound elegant and sure of themselves, excelling on "Somewhere." The Miracles' "Ooo Baby Baby" had the crowd spellbound, and a jumping version of "Mickey's Monkey" had them rockin'. *—Andrew Hamilton*

Greatest Hits / 1966 / Motown ♦♦♦♦♦

Watchout! / 1966 / Gordy ♦♦♦♦
It's usually presented as a given that, separated from the work of the Holland-Dozier-Holland songwriting team, Martha & the Vandellas were somewhat at sea. But H-D-H only had three songs on *Watchout!*—albeit two of which were the hits that drove the album's sales—and the group came off better than one could have hoped on the rest of the record. As a follow-up to *Dance Party, Watchout!* is usually thought of as less successful, with the H-D-H songs "Jimmy Mack" and "I'm Ready for Love" dominating. It's a little more complicated than that, however, because *Watchout!* is actually a very different kind of album, with ballads outnumbering the dance numbers. It's a chance to immerse oneself in the sensitive, reflective side of Martha & the Vandellas, and a very beautiful record, if not as exciting as its predecessor. Oh, to be sure, "Let This Day Be" isn't doing much more than filling up track space, but the rest is misplaced treasure from the Motown vaults, well worth hearing, and more than once. Holland-Dozier-Holland's "One Way Out" is similar to their earlier "Nowhere to Run" (and was later a single B-side), and the wrenchingly emotive "Keep It Up" (a forgotten Smokey Robinson number) shows off a more delicate side to the group's sound that was often overlooked. "Happiness Is Guaranteed" is the kind of anthemic ballad, with a big central melody, that one suspects was rejected for the Supremes; Martha Reeves and company do a wonderful job with it, even though it needed the more delicate lead vocal attentions of Diana Ross to have gotten heard more widely. "I'll Follow You," co-authored by ex-Moonglows leader Harvey Fuqua, is so sweet in its sensibilities beneath a driving beat that it's like listening to two songs in one (both of them very good). "Tell Me I'll Never Be Alone" is another oft-overlooked gem, and then there's the lost single off this album, "No More Tearstained Make Up," a slow, haunting, beautiful piece of female heartache set to music. *—Bruce Eder*

Martha & the Vandellas Live! / 1968 / Gordy ♦♦♦
Motown tried to pull a fast one with this recording, which has the same cover as the successful, trend-setting Temptations live album. Buyers of the Temptations' live set would surely purchase this one. Problem is, it's not nearly as good. For one, original Vandella Annette Beard had long since departed; Betty Kelly took her spot alongside Rosalind Ashford. Although Kelly resembled Beard, Ashford couldn't harmonize with her. It shows as the harmonies fail to duplicate the voices of the Andantes on their recordings; after Beard departed, the Vandellas no longer participated in studio recordings. Still, you can't deny Martha's buttery, irresistible, shrilled deliveries, or the girls' enthusiastic fills. *—Andrew Hamilton*

Ridin' High / 1968 / Gordy ♦♦♦
This represents their last gasp as a commercially viable recording act, with minor singles and the usual filler. Like their stable mates the Supremes and the Four Tops, they suffered commercially as well as artistically from the abrupt departure of the Holland-Dozier-Holland production team. Aside from "Honey Chile," their last major pop hit (staff songwriter Sylvia Moy conceived the song with Reeves in mind), there's not much to recommend that rises above conventional adequacy, though "(We've Got) Honey Love" is a decent confection and "Love Bug Leave My Heart Alone" was a modest Top 40 hit. *—John Lowe*

Sugar & Spice / 1969 / Gordy ♦♦♦
Here Motown holds a fire sale in an effort to keep the Vandellas as a viable commercial force in the pop marketplace. The closest thing resembling a hit here is "Taking My Love (And Leaving Me)," a mild soul hit that missed making the pop charts. Since the exodus of Holland-Doizer-Holland, Reeves had to struggle to get good material. And though she is struggling with not-too-distinctive material from second-tier songwriters, she does pull it off respectfully. "You're the Loser Now" is one of her better later efforts. *—John Lowe*

Natural Resources / 1970 / Gordy ♦♦♦
By this time Motown was trying to turn Reeves into a Diana Ross clone, with sometimes disastrous results (case in point: "The Hurt Is Over"). Even so, there is the curiousity item that arouses some interest, like the bluesy stroll ballad "Love, Guess Who" and the anti-Vietnam War soap opera "I Should Be Proud." Unfortunately, their inclusion in *Live Wire! The Singles 1962-1972* renders its value redundant. *—John Lowe*

Black Magic / 1972 / Gordy ♦♦♦
Martha & the Vandellas were nearing the end when this LP was issued. They reformed in 1971 with Martha's sister Lois Reeves and Sandra Tilley and made one last attempt at pop and soul glory. But while Reeves still had the old power, drive and fire, they weren't getting the inspiring songs or magnificent lyrics of their timeless 1960s hits. Instead, the best tunes, such as "Bless You," "No One There" or "Your Love Makes It Worthwhile," seemed like second-level material that would have simply filled out earlier releases. No hits resulted from this album, and Reeves would soon be a solo performer. *—Ron Wynn*

Anthology / 1974 / Motown ♦♦♦♦♦
Until the label issued the definitive two-disc set *Live Wire: The Singles 1962-1972* in 1993, this two-record set was the ultimate Martha Reeves & the Vandellas set. It's still worth hearing, as it contains all the essential hits from their early-'60s run. But the 2-CD set has better sound than the original vinyl, plus more extensive notes, discographical information and photos. *—Ron Wynn*

☆ **Live Wire! The Singles 1962–1972** / Sep. 7, 1993 / Motown ♦♦♦♦♦
This two-CD box set includes all of the top singles and many of the flip sides that Martha Reeves & the Vandellas cut for Motown. All the hits are here, of course; the collector will be especially interested in the B-sides and non-hit singles, many of which employed the songwriting talents of Motown regulars like Holland-Dozier-Holland and Mickey Stevenson. There's also the rare single (featuring Gloria Williamson on lead vocals) cut by the Vells in 1962, before Reeves took top billing and the group changed their name. Eight of these cuts have never been released on album before. Among the non-hits, there isn't anything to match "Heat Wave" or "Dancing in the Street," but Reeves' astonishingly powerful voice never falters. She was arguably Motown's most talented female singer, but the label's investment in her seemed to flag as the decade progressed. The later material lacks the distinction of her classic period, though the 1970 album track "I Should Be Proud" is a little-known (if somewhat heavy-handed) protest against the Vietnam War. *—Richie Unterberger*

Early Classics / 1996 / Spectrum ♦♦♦♦♦
One of Motown's greatest girl groups and arguably more interesting musically and aesthetically than the Supremes, Martha Reeves & the Vandellas better embodied the sound of Detroit than any other female group at the label. This German collection brings together virtually all of the top-charting singles, such as "Dancing in the Streets," I'll Have to Let Him Go" (the group's first single), "(My Love Is Like A) Heatwave," "Wild One," "Third Finger Left Hand," "Jimmy Mack," "Nowhere to Run," and "Motoring." But there are others as well, such as the torch songs "My Baby Loves Me" and "Never Leave Your Baby's Side," as well as album tracks such as "Come and Get These Memories," "Dance Party," "Hello Stranger," and "Wait Till My Bobby Gets Home." The bottom line is that this is a much more interesting compilation—single disc anyway—than Motown has ever issued in the States. Blending the charting singles—some of which charted two and three times in England—with B-sides and album tracks of overlooked treasures, this is the most well-rounded portrait of one of the true legends of Motown's glory years, and the music sounds as fresh and timeless as it did when it was issued in the 1960s and 1970s. Awesome. *—Thom Jurek*

★ **The Ultimate Collection** / Feb. 10, 1998 / Motown ♦♦♦♦♦
This volume of Motown's *Ultimate Collection* series was especially welcome, as there was no box set on Martha & the Vandellas for serious fans to go to (there was *Live Wire!*, a now-deleted two-CD compilation of single A- and B-sides, but that's not quite the same thing). This disc put the group's 25 most important tracks, all of the pop and R&B hits plus the most significant B-sides and an album track or two, together in one place. What's more, it did it in what was then state-of-the-art sound, something that few Motown CDs had ever been able to boast of. Thus, the musical content is a given and then some, and the power of Martha Reeves' lead singing and the surrounding harmonies comes through as never before. It's most gratifying on some of the harder dance numbers, such as "(Love Is Like A) Heat Wave" and "Dancing in the Street," to hear the gorgeously complex percussive mix of piano, bass, and drums (lots of drums) pounding away to their own rhythms within the overall beats of the songs—the detail is there, without sacrificing any of the raw power of the songs and the mixes. Add to that decent annotation, discography, and musician information, and this is an essential part of any soul or '60s collection and, indeed, until Motown began reissuing Martha & the Vandellas albums in 2002 in England, the only way to get a significant chunk of their music with good sound. *—Bruce Eder*

Come and Get These Memories/Heat Wave / Apr. 2002 / Motown ♦♦♦

Dance Party/Watchout! / Apr. 2002 / Motown ♦♦♦♦♦

Martika (Marta Marrero)

b. May 18, 1969, Whittier, CA
Vocals / Dance-Pop, Teen Pop, Urban, Bubblegum, Adult Contemporary
Martika appeared after teen girls like Tiffany and Debbie Gibson returned adolescent bubblegum to the pop charts. Martika was born as Marta Marrero in Whittier, CA, on May 18, 1969. Her parents were originally from Cuba; however, they left the country during a revolution. Raised in California, Martika started acting before launching a recording career, appearing in the film version of *Annie* in 1982 and on the TV series *Kids Incorporated* from 1984 to 1986. In 1988, her first single, "More Than You Know," landed on the American charts; a year later, its follow-up, "Toy Soldiers," was number one in the U.S. for two weeks. Martika's self-titled debut album was also released in 1989. On her second LP, 1991's *Martika's Kitchen*, she received songwriting assistance from Prince, to whom she was also briefly romantically linked. Martika returned to television by joining the cast of *Wiseguy*. In 1999, she recorded "The Happy Song." *—Michael Sutton*

● **Martika** / 1989 / Columbia ♦♦♦♦
Not just the Madonna wannabe she is often remembered as, Martika had songwriting skills and enough savvy to choose some of the best hooks of the '80s for her debut album. You'll find yourself singing these songs months after you've heard them. And that's a good thing. Her voice is thin and a bit limited, but she surrounds herself with producers who understand how to put a sheen on a great pop gem. The catchiest song is also the dumbest; "If You're Tarzan, I'm Jane," about a girl willing to adapt to anything her man wants her to be, is somewhat sexist, but it's such fun it's hard to not sing along. The big hit single, "Toy Soldiers," works with its childlike vocals and lyrics, creating a haunting, effective dichotomy with its subject of drug addiction. Martika even has the chutzpah to cover a Carole King song—"I Feel the Earth Move"—and actually does it justice. Producer Michael Jay—writer or co-writer of "Toy Soldiers," "If You're Tarzan, I'm Jane," "More Than You Know," "Cross My Heart," "You Got Me Into This," "It's Not What You're Doing," and "See If I Care"—shows he has the ear of an amazing pop artist à la Bernie Taupin. The melodies and productions make this album a major success, but if pop isn't your thing, you might not care that these are hooks many superstars would kill for. *—Bryan Buss*

Martika's Kitchen / 1991 / Columbia ♦♦♦

Nancy Martinez

b. Aug. 26, 1960, Quebec City, Quebec, Canada
Vocals / Dance-Pop, Latin Pop, Urban, Latin Freestyle
Best known for her Latin-flavored 1986 club hit "For Tonight," Nancy Martinez never became a major pop star in the U.S. but fared well in dance clubs in the 1980s. The big-voiced dance diva spent most of her pre-adult life in Montreal, where she studied classical piano as a child before studying acting and singing in high school. Martinez's debut album, *Lay It Down*, was released in Canada in 1983, and "Excited" became the first single from that LP. The following year, Martinez's "Sunshine Reggae" single became a major hit in Canada—its B-side was a cover of Edith Piaf's "La Vie en Rose."

In 1986, the bilingual Martinez (who is fluent in both English and French) recorded "For Tonight" for the Canadian Sizzle label—and the song came out in the U.S. when "Atlantic" picked it up. It was also in 1986 that "Atlantic" released "Martinez"'s *Not Just the Girl Next Door*, which was produced by Teneen Ali and was full of Latin-flavored dance grooves. The album enjoyed a lot of attention from club DJs, but unfortunately, Martinez didn't record any more albums for Atlantic. *—Alex Henderson*

● **Not Just the Girl Next Door** / 1986 / Atlantic ♦♦♦♦
Critics of 1980s dance-pop will tell you that most or all of it was about style over substance—that once you get past the high-tech production gloss, pretty faces, and carefully designed images, you're left with music that is soulless and disposable. The problem with such a generalization is that an artist like Nancy Martinez did, in fact, have a lot to offer when it came to talent and chops. Producer Teneen Ali gives *Not Just the Girl Next Door* a very slick, high-tech sound, but Martinez would have sounded great even without all that studio gloss. When the Canadian dance diva passionately tears into "For Tonight" (a major club hit), "Rhythm of Your Heart," "Move Out," and other Latin-influenced numbers, it's clear that she has an impressive range and isn't trying to hide behind technology. Some dance-pop artists have, indeed, tried to camouflage their lack of talent with studio gloss, but technology is only one of the various tools in Martinez's arsenal. She definitely has the chops, warmth, and charisma to make this LP special. For those who want to hear one of the best Latin freestyle-oriented albums of the 1980s, *Not Just the Girl Next Door* is highly recommended. *—Alex Henderson*

The Marvelettes

f. 1960, Inkster, MI

Group / Girl Group, Motown, Pop-Soul, Soul

Probably the most pop-oriented of Motown's major female acts, the Marvelettes didn't project as strong an identity as the Supremes, Mary Wells, or Martha Reeves, but recorded quite a few hits, including Motown's first number one single, "Please Mr. Postman" (1961). "Postman," as well as other chirpy early-'60s hits like "Playboy," "Twistin' Postman," and "Beechwood 4-5789," were the label's purest girl group efforts. Featuring two strong lead singers, Gladys Horton and Wanda Young, the Marvelettes went through five different lineups, but maintained a high standard on their recordings. After a few years, they moved from girl group sounds to uptempo and midtempo numbers that were more characteristic of Motown's production line. They received no small help from Smokey Robinson, who produced and wrote many of their singles; Holland-Dozier-Holland, Berry Gordy, Mickey Stevenson, Marvin Gaye, and Ashford & Simpson also got involved with the songwriting and production at various points.

After the mid-'60s Wanda Young assumed most of the lead vocal duties; Gladys Horton departed from the group in the late '60s. While the Marvelettes didn't cut as many monster smashes as most of their Motown peers after the early '60s, they did periodically surface with classic hits like "Too Many Fish in the Sea," "Don't Mess With Bill," and "The Hunter Gets Captured By the Game." There were also plenty of fine minor hits and misses, like 1965's "I'll Keep Holding On," which is just as memorable as the well-known Motown chart-toppers of the era. The group quietly disbanded in the early '70s after several years without a major hit. *—Richie Unterberger*

Please Mr. Postman / 1961 / Motown ✦✦

Essentially, this is nothing but a period curio—the title hit and some throwaway junk, rushed out to capitalize on the song's success on the pop charts. Still, there an occasional surprise, like Wanda Young's lead vocal (not to mention the instrumentation) on "I Want a Guy," which served as a sketch for the formula Smokey Robinson contrived in the mid-'60s when "Don't Mess With Bill" clicked on the charts. *—John Lowe*

The Marvelettes Sing / 1962 / Tamla ✦✦

This out-of-print album, the Marvelettes' second, is the least memorable of any they ever made. It was shotgunned on the market to capitalize on "Twisting Postman," their follow-up to "Please Mr. Postman," a number-one pop smash. Rehashes of other groups' hits make up the bulk of the ten tracks, including a rendition of Mary Wells' "The One Who Really Loves You" (originally issued as *The Marvelettes Smash Hits of 1962*, a very apropos title). *—Andrew Hamilton*

Playboy / 1962 / Tamla ✦✦✦

Despite being one of Motown's first big acts, the Marvelettes didn't record as many albums as the Temptations, Supremes, Miracles, Stevie Wonder or Martha & the Vandellas, but the girls from Inkster, MI, did record some unforgettable sides and some good LPs. *Playboy*, titled after their big hit, was one of the good ones, yet Motown has never reissued it. "Playboy" flew up the charts; its message was a warning to girls about players. A spirited "Beechwood 4-5789" keep the hits flowing—its teenish backing vocals and Horton's innocent lead are contagious. Smokey Robinson's first Marvelette production, "I Think I Can Change You," was a forerunner to the string of hits he later produced for them with Wanda Young on lead. "Forever," later done by Marvin Gaye, is a sentimental thriller. A hopeful "Someday, Someway"—written by Brian Holland, Lamont Dozier & Freddie Gorman (the Originals), who also wrote "Forever"—was a staple of their early stage shows. This is far more enjoyable than their *Please Mr. Postman* debut. *—Andrew Hamilton*

The Marvelous Marvelettes / 1963 / Tamla ✦✦✦

Recently restored to the Motown catalog, this set is basically minor hits ("Locking Up My Heart," "Strange I Know") and some fairly interesting contributions from a young Norman Whitfield ("Silly Boy" shows them as their least self-serious). Surprisingly, the most interesting song is the bonus track: Holland-Dozier-Holland's "Knock on My Door," which first turned up in a 1986 compilation of previously unreleased material. *—John Lowe*

On Stage / Jul. 1963 / Tamla ✦✦✦

This short eight-song set of the Marvelettes' live show pales when compared to later live efforts aided by new technology, but in 1963, when this was released, there wasn't much to compare it to. The group had trimmed to a quartet of Georgeanna Tilman, Wanda Young, Gladys Horton, and Katherine Anderson. A coupling of "Strange I Know" and "Someday, Someway" was their best effort; they sounded mature beyond their years on these sensitive ballads written by Brian Holland, Lamont Dozier, & Freddie Gorman. You can almost feel the excitement on "Twistin' Postman"—they may not have been the best female singing group at Motown, but they were definitely the most dynamic. Wanda Young-Rogers displays her falsetto on "So Long Baby," a popular number for the Inkster, MI, natives. They close with "Playboy" to applause, screams, and wolf whistles. *—Andrew Hamilton*

The Marvelettes' Greatest Hits / 1966 / Motown ✦✦✦✦✦

A good collection spotlighting one of Motown's least appreciated great female groups. The Marvelettes not only gave the label its first number-one pop hit, but strung together a good series of tunes, especially when Smokey Robinson was writing and producing them. They went from being a quintet to a quartet to a trio during their Motown years, but seldom failed to give an energetic performance. *—Ron Wynn*

The Marvelettes / 1967 / Motown ✦✦✦✦✦

Perhaps the best studio album the Marvelettes ever recorded. The spotlight was shared between Horton and Young, and one can attest to the differences in their styles (Horton was earthier, Young the more pop-oriented). In addition to their classic hit "The Hunter Gets Captured By the Game" and what is the best version of the Van McCoy warhorse "When You're Young and in Love," there are some would-be hits such as "The Day You Take One (You Have to Take the Other)" and the lovely ballad "This Night Was Made For Love." This was an artistic triumph and proof that girl groups can mature with age. *—John Lowe*

Sophisticated Soul / 1968 / Motown ✦✦✦✦✦

By this time Gladys Horton left the group and was replaced by the talented but eccentric singer/songwriter Anne Bogan. Young took control of the group and moved them more into a softer pop sound, closer to the frothy Supremes than Martha & the Vandellas. Although the material was a bit weaker, there are plenty of good songs, most notably Smokey Robinson's amusing "My Baby Must Be a Magician" and the haunting "Destination: Anywhere," in which Young performs a tremendous vocal. *—John Lowe*

In Full Bloom / 1969 / Motown ✦✦✦✦

Not as cohesive as their previous two albums, but it gives Wanda Young more emotional range, and the material provides her with an opportunity to test herself. On the album's best numbers—"That's How Heartaches Are Made," "The Truth's Outside My Door," "I Have Someone (Who Loves Me Too," and even "Sunshine Days" work because they provide the perfect springboard for Young's raucous voice. Unfortunately, a commercial decline led to the group's break-up by the end of the decade. *—John Lowe*

Return of the Marvelettes / 1970 / Motown ✦✦✦

Initially, their last studio album for the Tamla label was planned as a solo outing for lead singer Wanda Young, but Berry Gordy chose instead to market it as a Marvelettes album. Although there are a pair of great ballads in "Take Me Where You Go" and "After All," the album comes off as emotionally monotone, and not even Smokey Robinson's studio expertise can save Young from banality. *—John Lowe*

Anthology / 1975 / Motown ✦✦✦✦✦

This traces the group's Motown history, including the hits "Beechwood 4-5789," "Don't Mess with Bill," "The Hunter Gets Captured by the Game," "Please Mr. Postman," "That's How Heartaches Are Made," "Too Many Fish in the Sea," and many others. *—Rick A. Bueche*

Now! / 1990 / Motorcity ✦✦

In the '80s, Britisher Ian Levine recorded almost every ex-Motown artist living, many whose careers had been dormant for decades, so it's hard to criticize his efforts. He did admirable productions on Bobby Taylor, the Originals, the Elgins, Hattie Littles and some others, but fared worse on productions with Edwin Starr, the Satintones, the Monitors and the subjects of this review, the Marvelettes, whose early hits were pop-oriented, teen-ish sounds. Which means songs like "Beechwood 4-5789," "When You're Young and in Love," "Too Many Fish in the Sea," "My Baby Must Be a Magician" and "Don't Mess With Bill," don't come across well sung by ladies 40 and 50 years old. Levine's work would have sounded better with a crack rhythm section on the Motorcity recordings—and what happened to the hand claps? *—Andrew Hamilton*

Deliver: The Singles (1961–1971) / Sep. 7, 1993 / Motown ✦✦✦✦✦

This has 41 songs, featuring most of both the A-sides and B-sides, nine of which had never been issued on album before. The ace Motown songwriting and production stable was involved in virtually every one of these tracks, making for a surprisingly strong and consistent collection. Includes all the chart hits, as well as rarities like the Phil Spector-style single they released in 1963 as the Darnells. *—Richie Unterberger*

● **The Ultimate Collection** / Feb. 10, 1998 / Motown ✦✦✦✦✦

Motown is notorious for recycling their catalog as endless hit collections, but *The Ultimate Collection* is one of the finest series of greatest-hits CDs they have ever assembled. Each disc contains all of the major hits from an artist, plus important B-sides, album tracks, and minor hits. The Marvelettes' entry in the series is no exception to the rule, boasting all their Top Ten pop and R&B hits, not only from their early-'60s heyday but also their late-'60s comeback: "Please Mr. Postman," "Playboy," "Beechwood 4-5789," "Someday, Someway," "Strange I Know," "Don't Mess With Bill," "My Baby Must Be a Magician," "The Hunter Gets Captured By the Game," and "When You're Young and in Love." The disc also features a number of smaller hits and B-sides, resulting in a total of 25 tracks. For anyone who wants a definitive hits collection but is hesitant to invest in the double-disc *Deliver, The Ultimate Collection* is an ideal choice. *—Stephen Thomas Erlewine*

The Marvelows

f. Chicago, IL

Group / Chicago Soul, Soul, Pop-Soul, Beach, Doo Wop, R&B

The Marvelows were a Chicago soul group who scored just once, with the upbeat "I Do," a pop Top 40 hit in 1965. The group was formed in Chicago Heights, IL, when Melvin Mason met the recently relocated Paden brothers (Frank who sang bass, and Johnny who sang tenor) in the late '50s. Joined by tenor Willie (Sonny) Stephenson and Mason's wife's cousin Jesse Smith, the quintet became the Marvelows.

Smith's mother suggested that he look up a former schoolmate of hers, Johnny Pate. Pate, who had just been given the position of Midwest A&R for ABC/Paramount, secured a deal with the label and recorded four tunes for the group, the doo-wop ballad "A Friend," "My Heart," the solid midtempo "Hey Hey Baby," and "I Do." The latter song was only written as a warm-up song, something to sing to prepare their voices, but it hit number-seven R&B and number-37 pop in the spring of 1965. Around 1966, Jesse Smith left and was replaced by Andrew Thomas. The Marvelows (now the Mighty Marvelows to avoid confusion with the West Coast group the Marvellos) had their second single (and the only other one to chart) with the ballad "In the Morning" in the spring of 1968. Other Marvelows (or the Mighty Marvelows) singles are "I'm Without a Girl," "Fade Away," "Your Little Sister" "You're Breaking My Heart," and "Wait Be Cool." ABC/Paramount issued *The Mighty Marvelows* LP in 1968, but the group broke up one year later. A brief reunion in 1974 was their only other time together. *—Ed Hogan*

The Mighty Marvelows / 1968 / Paramount ♦♦♦♦
The Marvelows recorded in the wrong decade, they had a couple of hits in the late '60s, but their hearts were in the '50s. Their biggest hit "I Do," was a harmony favorite that actually did better for the J. Geils Band. They ventured deeper into the '50s with throwbacks "My Heart," "Shim Sham," "Hey, Hey Baby," and "A Friend," a humorous bass vocalist accents the selections, pumped by energetic, exaggerated backing vocals. The Marvelows achieve a more up-to-date sound on "In The Morning," a pretty swooping ballad, and the upbeat "Talking About You Baby." Look elsewhere if you prefer the typical '60s group sound, but if you like doo wop, you'll love *The Mighty Marvelows.* —*Andrew Hamilton*

• **A Golden Classics Edition** / Jun. 11, 1996 / Collectables ♦♦♦♦♦

Marvin & Johnny

f. 1953
Group / R&B, Doo Wop
One of the first notable R&B duos, Marvin & Johnny weren't so much a permanent act as Marvin Phillips (b. Oct. 23, 1931) and several partners that he would name "Johnny." Although Emory Perry was the most frequent of these, Phillips also duetted with Jesse Belvin (making number two in the R&B chart, as Jesse & Marvin, with "Dream Girl") Carl Green, and others, though Phillips called Perry "my main Johnny." Whoever was singing, Marvin & Johnny were significant, if not major, figures in the transition from West Coast jump blues to hotter sax-driven R&B sides that began to approach rock & roll; they were also forerunners of doo wop with their appealingly grainy harmonies and occasional sly sense of humor. Recording for Specialty and Modern, they had a couple of Top Ten R&B hits, "Baby Doll" (1953) and "Tick Tock"/"Cherry Pie" (1954), and also issued several other strong singles, sometimes in a sort of updated Louis Jordan style. They faded after the mid-'50s, although they would also record for Aladdin and several other small Los Angeles labels. —*Richie Unterberger*

• **Flipped Out** / Jul. 29, 1992 / Specialty ♦♦♦♦♦
Here are 25 early- to mid-'50s tracks cut for the Specialty label, some previously unissued, varying between loose uptempo grooves and ballads. "Baby Doll" was the hit, but the pounding boogie of "Wine Woogie" and the sassy duetting on "Boy Loves Girl" are other highlights of a pretty strong set of early-'50s R&B. But it doesn't have material they recorded during the same era for Modern, including their most famous single, "Tick Tock"/"Cherry Pie." —*Richie Unterberger*

Hugh Masekela

b. Apr. 4, 1939, Witbank, South Africa
Vocals, Flugelhorn, Trumpet, Leader / African Jazz, Jazz-Pop, Soul-Jazz, World Fusion
Hugh Masekela has an extensive jazz background and credentials, but has enjoyed major success as one of the earliest leaders in the world fusion mode. Masekela's vibrant trumpet and flügelhorn solos have been featured in pop, R&B, disco, Afro-pop, and jazz contexts. His style, especially on flügelhorn, is a charismatic blend of striking upper register lines, half valve effects, repetitive figures and phrases, with some note bending, slurs, and tonal colors. Though he's often simplified his playing to fit into restrictive pop formulas, Masekela's capable of outstanding ballad and bebop work.

He played with a variety of South African jazz bands before leaving the country in 1960 with his his wife at that time, Miriam Makeba. During the early '60s, Masekela recorded for MGM, Mercury, and Verve, developing his hybrid African/pop/jazz style. He even started his own record label (Chisa) and cut several albums that expanded his style and scored pop success; the single "Grazing in the Grass" topped the charts in 1968. During the 1970s, Masekela moved in a more ethnic direction, playing with Nigerian Afrobeat great Fela Kuti, working on a session with Dudu Pukwana, and others that resulted in his finest jazz/African album, *Home Is Where the Music Is.* In the '80s, he returned to South Africa and was part of Paul Simon's *Graceland* tour. Though the jazz content of his work has varied over the years, Hugh Masekela has far more material on the plus side than the negative. —*Ron Wynn*

The Emancipation of Hugh Masekela / 1966 / Chisa ♦♦♦♦
South African expatriate Hugh Masekela was the architect of an extremely interesting and viable musical form, an audacious blending of South African rhythms, swing jazz, and rock & roll. *Emancipation* is the first American effort in this area, and it's a fantastic, soul-deep affair. With a crack band including Charlie Smalls on piano and two drummers (the original Big Black on percussion), Masekela's vocals and intense trumpet have the perfect platform from which to fly. One track in particular, "She Doesn't Write," is almost a template for "Grazing in the Grass," which was a huge hit the following year. Masekela was also involved with the Jim Dickson/Byrds/Peter Fonda crowd at the time, and that influence can be felt here as well. A perfect introduction to Hugh Masekela. —*Matthew Greenwald*

The Promise of a Future / 1968 / One Way ♦♦♦

Home Is Where the Music Is / Jan. 1972 / Blue Thumb ♦♦♦♦♦
An outstanding blend of Afro-pop and jazz with strong work by Dudu Pukwana. —*Ron Wynn*

Masekela Introducing Hedzoleh Soundz / Jul. 1973 / Blue Thumb ♦♦♦

The Boy's Doin' It / 1975 / Casablanca ♦♦♦♦♦
No other work during Hugh Masekela's long and fruitful career blended all of his interests—jazz, funk, pop, Afrobeat, and R&B, plus a little Latin and a lot of disco—into such an exciting mixture as 1975's *The Boy's Doin' It,* his first record for Casablanca. Influenced by Kool & the Gang as well as the growing tendency for Latin artists (like Joe Bataan) to cross over toward contemporary dance trends (and labels), Masekela recruited a few veterans from the Ghanian highlife band Hedzoleh Soundz—with whom he'd worked with on one album before. Recorded in Lagos, Nigeria and dedicated to Fela Kuti, *The Boy's Doin' It* has six extended jams, each of which does an excellent job of playing off deep grooves against ensemble vocals and catchy hooks, with plenty of room for Masekela's own trumpet and every note polished to a fine '70s sheen. It didn't matter what type of music fan you were: pop, disco, funk, world music, and any but the most hidebound jazz purist could get into these tracks. —*John Bush*

• **The Lasting Impression of Ooga Booga** / Jun. 18, 1996 / Verve ♦♦♦♦♦
In patching together a program of Hugh Masekela's MGM recordings onto a single overstuffed CD, Verve took the original *The Americanization of Ooga Booga* album, leapfrogged over its successor, *Next Album*, and coupled it with the third MGM LP, *The Lasting Impressions of Hugh Masekela.* That made good sense since the two albums originate from the same live date at the Village Gate, recorded when the trumpeter was still in the process of making an impression in the U.S. Masekela is full of wild, sputtering, high-rolling exuberance, developing some of his familiar signature trumpet riffs, freely exploring South African rhythms, harmonic sequences, and chants, and mixing them with soul-jazz at a time when hardly anyone else would bother (the mixture of township jive and jazz works especially well on "U-Dwi"). He also ties into Brazil with a fine rendition of Jorge Ben's "Mas Que Nada" and assimilates Coltrane into his bloodstream with a tribute called "Mixolydia." In general, the *Americanization* tracks are the picks of the crop (*Impressions,* after all, had been compiled in 1968 to cash in on Masekela's surprise number one single, "Grazing in the Grass"). With the rhythm section of Larry Willis on piano, Harold Dotson on bass, and Henry Jenkins on drums, this music still holds up marvelously today. —*Richard S. Ginell*

• **Grazing in the Grass: The Best of Hugh Masekela** / Oct. 16, 2001 / Columbia ♦♦♦♦
Columbia/Legacy's 2001 collection *Grazing in the Grass: The Best of Hugh Masekela* may seem a little skimpy if judged simply by the number of tracks—a mere 14 songs. It is true that this collection does not constitute a comprehensive, label-spanning overview containing selections from all of the labels that Masekela recorded for, instead concentrating solely on recordings he made for Columbia. So, that means this isn't the last word, but it is still rather essential because it does contain the best of his recordings for Columbia and contains nice, track-by-track notes by Masekela himself. This all results in one of the best compilations on Masekela yet assembled; even if it doesn't contain every aspect of his career, it gives an excellent idea of what he's all about. —*Stephen Thomas Erlewine*

Barbara Mason

b. 1949, Philadelphia, PA
Vocals, Songwriter / Pop-Soul, Soul, Urban
An interesting minor soul performer, Mason initially focused on songwriting when she entered the music business in her teens. As a performer, though, she had a huge hit in 1965 with her self-penned "Yes, I'm Ready" (number-five pop, number-two R&B), a fetching soul-pop confection that spotlighted her high, girlish vocals. One of the first examples of the sweet, lush sound that came to be called Philly soul, she had modest success throughout the rest of the decade on the small Arctic label, reaching the pop Top 40 again in 1965 with "Sad, Sad Girl."

In the early and mid-'70s, Mason toughened her persona considerably, singing about sexual love and infidelity with a frankness that was uncommon for a female soul singer in songs like "Bed and Board," "From His Woman to You," and "Shackin' Up." Sweet soul continued to be her groove, and she continued to write some of her material. But the production, as it was throughout soul in the '70s, was more funk-oriented, and at times Mason would interrupt her singing to deliver some straight-talkin' raps about romance. Curtis Mayfield produced her on a cover of Mayfield's "Give Me Your Love," which restored her to the pop Top 40 and R&B Top Ten in 1973; "From His Woman to You" and "Shackin' Up" were also solid soul sellers in the mid-'70s. After leaving Buddah Records in 1975, she only dented the charts periodically, with "I Am Your Woman, She Is Your Wife" (1978), "Another Man" (1984), and a couple of other singles. —*Richie Unterberger*

Yes, I'm Ready / 1965 / Arctic ♦♦♦♦
Barbara Mason was very much a teenager when "Yes, I'm Ready" climbed the charts and this endearing debut LP was released. "Ready" is a captivating ballad that has been remade by many. Her first hit single, "Girls Have Feelings Too," shows the sweet innocence of youth. "Sad, Sad Girl," another self-written Mason ballad, drips with hurt as she explains how blue her world has become since she lost her fellow. Mason wrote most of her singles and has said they're based on real life experiences; she often could be seen visibly crying on-stage while delivering one of her songs. Other than the B-sides, the rest of the album consists of remakes like "Something You Got," "Moon River," and "Misty." Mason wasn't at her best redoing the material of others; the efforts seem lackluster compared to her recordings of original compositions. —*Andrew Hamilton*

Oh How It Hurts / 1968 / Arctic ♦♦♦♦
Barbara Mason's second and final LP for Arctic Records was released three years after her first. The Arctic label released 60 records before folding; 14 were Mason releases. Jimmy Bishop, a Philadelphia DJ, owned the label and included "Yes, I'm Ready" on this collection to bolster sales, since all of Mason's Arctic hits except the title track are on her debut. Incidentally, that's Kenny Gamble crooning backing vocals on "Ready"; Gamble also recorded for Arctic and wrote some sides for Mason before going on to form Gamble, Neptune, and Philadelphia International Records. Only "Oh How It Hurts" sold well from this collection, and deservedly so; the sad ballad touches the heart every time you hear it. Mason sings with pain and the lyrics hit home. The excellent "Is It Me, or Is It Her" makes this a must collection. You won't find this jewel on any other compilation to date; it's even missing from the excellent 27-track Bear Family anthology of her Arctic years. The rest of the tracks are misses and flip sides. Mason always covered songs; her first LP had six remakes but there are only a few here, the best being "You Can Depend on Me," a nifty reworking of the Miracles song. Mason has yet to receive the credit she deserves for being an innovator of the sweet Philly sound; all the other sweet Philly singers—Brenda & the Tabulations, the Delfonics, Blue Magic, the Stylistics, and others—came

after Mason. The rhythm section of MFSB played on Mason's recordings long before gaining recognition on the Philadelphia International label. *—Andrew Hamilton*

If You Knew Him Like I Do / 1970 / GNC ✦✦✦

This is a failed crossover attempt. Mason's manager Jimmy Bishop moved his protégée from his own Arctic Records to the short-lived National General Records. The resulting album didn't score many points with her fan base. Seven of the 11 songs are rehashes of pop hits including "Bridge Over Troubled Water," "There's Always Something There to Remind Me," and "Breaking up Is Hard to Do." She scored a smallish hit with a rendition of "Raindrops Keep Falling on My Head." A Bishop/Mason composition "Yes It's You" followed and flailed in obscurity as did a final single "Jean," also included here. She cut four singles for National General before the label went under. Mason then went with Buddah Records and became a sultry singing diva, discarding any pop pretense and abandoning the sweet, innocent teen of Arctic Records forever. The National General experience wasn't a total loss; the label known for movie soundtracks allowed Mason to do her first soundtrack, *The Last Cowboy*, and contribute to blaxploitation films like *Gordon's War* and *Sheba Baby*. *—Andrew Hamilton*

Give Me Your Love / 1973 / Buddah ✦✦✦

Barbara Mason becomes a woman on this Buddah release. No longer the love-struck teen who hit with "Oh How It Hurts," "Girls Have Feelings," and "Sad, Sad Girl," the new Barbara makes the rules and gives the ultimatums. She unleashes a sensuous contralto on "Bed And Board," Curtis Mayfield's "Give Me Your Love," and a rekindled "Yes I'm Ready." And is marvelous on "You Can Be With the One You Don't Love," a lamenting ballad that Barbara creams. *—Andrew Hamilton*

Another Man / 1984 / Hot Productions ✦✦✦✦

A well-done collection originally recorded in the early '80s under the charge of Butch Ingram, who plays off of both of Mason's personas, the sweet & innocent and the mature woman. The Philadelphian's remake of Smokey Robinson's "The Agony and the Ecstasy" is worth the cost of the CD alone; when Mason sings the word "agony," you feel it in your bones. "Winter Love" features a recitation before blooming into a beautiful ballad. The Mason/Ingram composition "Don't I Ever Cross Your Mind" has it all: lyrics, hooks, vocals, accompaniments—the works. She gloats for nearly eight minutes about being the outside woman on "She's Got the Papers (But I Got the Man)" and answers it with "Another Man." One worth seeking out. *—Andrew Hamilton*

● **The Very Best of Barbara Mason** / May 7, 1996 / Sequel ✦✦✦✦✦

Most of this 15-track compilation deals with her 1972-1975 stint on Buddah, ending with a few tracks from the late '70s and early '80s. Those who prefer '60s soul to '70s soul will prefer her early work, but at the time of its release this was the best CD compilation of her material available, including the hits "Give Me Your Love," "From His Woman to You," and "Shackin' Up." The version of "Yes I'm Ready" here, by the way, is not the 1965 original, but an early-'70s remake. *—Richie Unterberger*

Yes, I'm Ready / Nov. 1, 1997 / Bear Family ✦✦✦✦✦

These are Barbara's early sides for Arctic Records; it's not complete, but the rest of her Arctic stuff appears on *Oh How It Hurts*, also on Bear Family. Buy both and you should have everything she recorded at Arctic. She cut as many remakes and originals, some were standards, which suggests Arctic had hopes of crossing her over to the pop market, which never happened to any significant degree. The remakes run the gamut from Archie Bell's "Tighten Up" to Barbara Lynn's "You'll Lose a Good Thing," a perfectly suited vehicle for Mason's innocent, sweet, aching voice. *—Andrew Hamilton*

The Best of the Buddha Years / Jul. 10, 2001 / Buddha ✦✦✦

Barbara Mason's Buddha years spanned from 1971 to 1975 and represented a growth period from a wet-eyed soprano to a mature, throaty-singing, bodacious woman. While not as arresting to some as her teary breakout Arctic Records sides, these were stellar waxings by a talented singer who had a unique way of phrasing lyrics, and who never hesitated to reveal the fragility of her mental being or often-bruised heart. The 14 tracks include an update of "Yes I'm Ready," complete with monologue, the scandalous (for the times) "Shackin' Up," and a bourbon/gin special "You Can Be With the One You Don't Love" that will have you reaching for a bottle. There's a fair share of he-say, she-say dramas: "Betty Crutcher" and Lester Snell's "From His Woman to You," Norma Toney's "So He Is Yours Now," a long salty version of Billy Paul's "Me and Mrs. Jones" (revised as "Me and Mr. Jones"), and Mason's self-written dilemma, "Caught in the Middle." *—Andrew Hamilton*

The Masqueraders

Group / Memphis Soul, Soul, Pop-Soul

This Memphis-based soul group was started by Isaac Hayes, who produced several of their singles. They actually came from Texas, and consisted of Lee Hatim, Robert Wrightsil, David Sanders, Harold Thomas, and Sammie Hutchins. Their biggest hit was the beautifully sung "I Ain't Got to Love Nobody Else" in 1968 for Bell. "I'm Just an Average Guy" was also an excellent soul number, but it only made the R&B Top 30. The group failed to generate much action with subsequent releases, though one '80s single, "It's So Nice," was an underground hit. They resurfaced in 1992 in Memphis, and are still performing and recording. *—Ron Wynn*

● **Everybody Wanna Live On** / 1976 / ABC ✦✦✦✦

The Masqueraders had been around since the early '60s, releasing singles for labels such as Bell, Wand, and Chips Moman's Memphis-based AGP. In the '70s, the group released two singles for Hi Records, then this 1975 album debut. *Everybody Wanna Live On* benefited from the subtle and innovative production values of Isaac Hayes; the title track is a powerful dance number that boasts not quite didactic lyrics and Jones' patented robust vocals. Although the group excelled at midtempo material, like the hooky "Please Don't Try (To Take Me Up to the Sky)," what typified the Hayes/Masqueraders alliance was mature and thoughtful ballads. One track in particular stands out, the dream-like "(Call Me) The Traveling Man," boasting both a poignant arrangement and a perfect performance from Jones. "(My Love For You Is) Honest And True" and "Your Sweet Love Is a Blessing" also mine ballad territory, both exhibiting the group's strong harmonies and commitment. *Everybody Wanna Live On* represents the sublime pairing of the right group with a sympathetic producer, and the results are highly skilled. *—Jason Elias*

Love Anonymous / 1977 / ABC ✦✦✦

The second Masqueraders album was also produced by Issac Hayes, and released through his Hot Buttered Soul imprint. Hayes and the Masqueraders' first effort together, *Everybody Wanna Live On*, was one of the stronger group albums of the time. *Love Anonymous* catches Hayes while his arrangements began to lack surprises. That's not to say it's a bad effort; in fact, *Love Anonymous* picks up where its predecessor left off, although it's a little more labored. The melodic and hooky first track, "Modern Day Woman," has Jones offering a pithy hook, "She wanna be loved," and he manages to make it sound like a novel thought. "Love Between a Woman and a Man" has a soaring melody and "It's a Terrible Thing to Waste Your Love" has Jones playing Mr. Right by default, as he begs and croons himself into her good graces. The best ballad, "Can't Nobody Love Me Like You Do," has Hayes bringing out the texture of the group's voices with an understated and concise production. This being closer to the disco era, *Love Anonymous* has its share of dance material. While no one probably wants to hear the pabulum of "Bicentennial," "Be for Real" is a glossy, highly danceable song. The last track, "Runaway Slave," has Jones likening his relationship to servitude with the ringing chorus, "Got to be free from you free/Free from you free." Although Hayes' production hand could have been more deft, *Love Anonymous* is recommended for fans of intelligent and stylish R&B. *—Jason Elias*

The Masqueraders / 1980 / Bang ✦✦✦

The Masqueraders, all from different parts of Texas, are one of those acts that manage to give an above-average effort each and every time they visit a recording studio. The five merged from as many groups in high school and have been recording since the early '60s. This self-titled LP kicks off with a fast and frenzied "Desire"; lead singer Lee Hatim shows why he's considered one of the most underrated voices in soul music, exhorting and pumping the lyrics with genuine conviction. "Starry Love" is a dreamy ballad with an edge; the Masqueraders couldn't sound wimpy if they tried. Hatim did a double on this one by singing and playing piano on the sessions; make that a triple—he wrote or co-wrote all the songs too. The electrifying "Into Your Soul" has Hatim singing a very personal lyric to someone special while apparently tickling the ivories, the fire in his voice emerging at times like a raging bull. Members Harold Thomas, Sammy Hutchins, Robert Wrightsil, and David Sanders were missing in action on "For the Sake of Pride" as Hatim goes solo. If you like a reggae beat, then "I'll Be Your Shoulder to Cry On" has elements of the world-renowned Jamaican groove complete with clacking calypsos, hand-clapping, and island-flavored backing vocals. The only disappointment is "Rock Jam," a poor attempt to cash in on disco. James Stroud produced this LP and played drums and percussion on the tracks. A good effort that went unnoticed, like many of their recordings. *—Andrew Hamilton*

Mass Production

f. Richmond, VA, **db.** 1983

Group / Urban, Disco, Funk

Based in Richmond, Virginia, the ten-piece soul and disco group Mass Production had a series of minor R&B hits in the late '70s and early '80s. Mass Production consisted of LeCoy Bryant, Kevin Douglas, James Drumgole, Agnes "Tiny" Kelly, Larry Marshall, Gregory McCoy, Emmanuel Redding, Ricardo Williams, Samuel Williams, and Tyrone Williams. Their best-known song, "Firecracker," hit number four on the R&B charts in the late summer of 1979. The group stayed together for several more years, scoring a string of small hits, before deciding to disband in 1983. *—Stephen Thomas Erlewine*

Believe / 1977 / Cotillion ✦✦✦✦

When James Brown popularized funk in the 1960s, he elevated repetition to an art form in the R&B world. The cardinal rule became "find the perfect groove and work it to death," and the goal was musical hypnosis. Brown, of course, didn't single-handedly invent musical repetition—in India, Hindu musicians were celebrating the joys of repetition centuries before he was even born. But the Godfather did pave the way for numerous funk, disco, house, Latin freestyle, jungle, and trance artists who liked to stay on the groove. In the 1970s, the use of repetition worked wonders for everyone from Parliament/Funkadelic and the Ohio Players to Donna Summer and Cerrone—and the value of repetition certainly wasn't lost on Mass Production, whose hypnotic funk-disco continued to sound fresh on its second album, *Believe*. There are no signs of a sophomore slump on this LP; the club DJs who went wild over MP's first album were equally impressed with exuberant, ultra-danceable offerings like "Free and Happy," "People Get Up," and "I Believe in Music." The record also contains a few dreamy soul ballads, including "Keep My Heart Together" and "Being Here." But *Believe* is party album first and foremost, and it's an exciting one. *—Alex Henderson*

● **Welcome to Our World** / 1977 / Cotillion ✦✦✦✦

When Mass Production made its vinyl debut with 1976's *Welcome to Our World*, the band found itself being compared to Brass Construction, BT Express, and the Crown Heights Affair—and the fact that Mass Production rhymes with Brass Construction certainly wasn't lost on listeners. Like those other bands, Mass Production favored a horn-powered style of funk-disco that club DJs found to be extremely useful. Creatively, Production hit the ground running with this LP, which wasn't a huge radio hit but enjoyed a great deal of exposure in danceclubs. And it isn't hard to see why the Richmond outfit was a club favorite in the late 1970s; hypnotic tracks like "Wine-Flow Disco," "I Like to Dance," and "Fun in the Sun" are endlessly danceable. "Magic," in fact, predicts the house music that came out of Chicago in the 1980s. Not everything on this album is uptempo; "Just a Song" and "Galaxy" (which has a cosmic spirituality along the lines of Earth, Wind & Fire or Lonnie Liston Smith) point to the fact that Production also gave us some memorable ballads. Most of the time, however, *Welcome to Our World* takes dead aim at the dancefloor. Some of Production's subsequent albums were uneven and inconsistent, but its recording career was off to a promising start with this impressive LP. *—Alex Henderson*

Three Miles High / 1978 / Cotillion ✦✦✦

In the Purest Form / 1979 / Cotillion ✦✦✦✦
Because 1978's *Three Miles High* was uneven and inconsistent, one greeted Mass Production's next album, *In the Purest Form*, with a bit of apprehension. But creatively, the Richmond band bounced back on this generally excellent 1979 LP, which contains the number-four R&B hit "Firecracker." A funk classic that boasts a truly addictive groove, "Firecracker" became Mass Production's biggest hit and is the song that the band is best remembered for. Thankfully, the rest of the album is also quite strong. "Can't You See I'm Fired Up" and "Eyeballin'" (not to be confused with the Heatwave song, which also came out in 1979) are addictive funk-disco jams, and Agnes "Tiny" Kelly (one of the lead vocalists) has a memorable spot on the smooth soul ballad "With Pleasure." Mass Production was never famous for playing ballads; uptempo funk-disco dominated its albums. Nonetheless, all of these albums did contain at least one ballad or slow jam. For those who viewed *Three Miles High* as the work of a band that was going downhill creatively, *In the Purest Form* was a very pleasant surprise. *—Alex Henderson*

Massterpiece / 1980 / Cotillion ✦✦✦
In the '80s, Mass Production's entire Cotillion catalog went out of print, and when the year 2000 rolled around, none of its Cotillion albums of 1976-1983 had been reissued on CD. If you wanted to hear Mass Production on CD in the '90s, your best bet was Rhino's 1996 release *Firecrackers: The Best of Mass Production*. At places that still sell used vinyl, dance club DJs continue to chase after copies of the band's old LPs, some of which inspire more enthusiasm than others. *Massterpiece*, MP's fifth album, isn't among its essential recordings. This isn't a bad record, but it doesn't contain any classics either. While funk tunes like "Your Love," "Come Back Hot," and "Nature Lover" are catchy, nothing on this 1980 LP is in a class with "Firecracker," "Wine-Flow Disco," or "Free and Happy." The ballad "Please Don't Leave Me Now" is pleasant; Mass Production's ballads were usually enjoyable. But on *Massterpiece*, the funk tunes are merely adequate. Like 1978's *Three Miles High*, this LP is only recommended to completists. *—Alex Henderson*

Turn Up the Music / 1981 / Cotillion ✦✦✦

In a City Groove / 1982 / Cotillion ✦✦

Mass Production '83 / 1983 / WEA ✦✦

● **Firecrackers: The Best of Mass Production** / Oct. 15, 1996 / Rhino ✦✦✦✦✦
Firecrackers: The Best of Mass Production is a comprehensive collection of the late-'70s soul band, featuring the majority of their R&B hits, including "Welcome to Our World (Of Merry Music)," "Turn Up the Music," and the Top 10 R&B hit "Firecracker." The compilation spans from their first album in 1977 to their farewell 1983 record, hitting every peak along the way. Though the material isn't always consistent—some of the lesser-known songs have dated rather badly—*Firecrackers* remains the definitive retrospective of Mass Production. *—Stephen Thomas Erlewine*

Mastermind

Group / Funk, Soul
Comparable to Brass Construction and Mass Production but not nearly as well known, Mastermind was an obscure ten-piece funk-soul band that recorded in New York in the late '70s. Unlike the Ohio Players, Earth, Wind & Fire, Tower of Power, the Commodores and other big funk-soul bands of the '70s, Mastermind didn't have a really identifiable lead vocalist. Several of its members could contribute vocals if called upon to do so, but everyone in the band was a musician first and foremost with the overall sound of the band being more important than the vocals. Even though funk-soul was Mastermind's foundation, its very danceable and horn-driven music contained jazz overtones. In fact, jazz musicians David Sanborn, Steve Khan and Jon Faddis were employed on Mastermind's self-titled debut album, which Prelude released in 1977. Unfortunately, the LP didn't sell, and the band broke up without ever recording a second album. Mastermind's members included trumpeter/vocalist Anselm Scrubb, baritone and tenor saxophonist Mario Ford, tenor saxophonist/flutist Guy Fuertes, alto saxophonist/flutist Lenny White (not to be confused with the Return to Forever and Twennynine drummer), guitarist/ vocalist Joe Frye, keyboardist/vocalist Geoffrey Williams, bassist/ vocalist Carl Bain, drummer/ vocalist Brian Wilson (not to be confused with the Beach Boys member), percussionist/ vocalist Wendell Derrick and percussionist Juan Clouden. *—Alex Henderson*

● **Mastermind** / 1977 / Prelude ✦✦✦
When R&B went high-tech in the '80s, genuine bands became harder and harder to find. There were still plenty of groups in the '80s and '90s, although honest-to-God *bands* that had nine or ten members and boasted full horn sections became the exception instead of the rule. When Cameo and the Ohio Players downsized in the '80s, you knew that large funk bands were becoming an endangered species. But back in 1977, when Mastermind's first and only album came out on Prelude, R&B was still full of large, horn-driven bands. Listening to this enjoyable, if uneven, LP, you won't be blown away by the singing—Mastermind didn't have a great lead vocalist like Earth, Wind & Fire's Philip Bailey, L.T.D.'s Jeffrey Osborne, or the Commodores' Lionel Richie to win you over. What you *will* appreciate is the overall sound of the band and the horn-driven, jazz-influenced, very danceable funk grooves—cuts like "Mother Nature," "I Am Music," and "Hustle Bus Stop" could easily appeal to fans of Brass Construction, Mass Production, the Crown Heights Affair, or BT Express. Several jazz musicians are employed as guests, including saxman David Sanborn, trumpeter Jon Faddis, and guitarist Steve Khan. But none of them do a great deal of improvising—they're only on board to support Mastermind, whose LP wasn't a big seller and has long been out of print but is worth acquiring if, by some chance, you come across a copy somewhere. *—Alex Henderson*

Cosimo Matassa

b. Apr. 13, 1926, New Orleans, LA
Engineer / New Orleans R&B, R&B, Soul, Rock & Roll
As an engineer and proprietor of J&M Studios and Cosimo Recording Studio in New Orleans, Cosimo Matassa was crucial to the development of the New Orleans R&B, rock and soul sound of the '50s and '60s. Little Richard and Fats Domino recorded some of their greatest hits at these studios, and major instrumentalists and producers like Dr. John and Allen Toussaint got key, early experience there. Matassa is not nearly as well known as other pioneers of early rock production, like Sam Phillips of Sun Records, but in his way was almost as important. Matassa was originally in the jukebox and record retail business, starting his studio at the back of his shop in 1945. It was in the ten-by-twelve-foot J&M Studios that Fats Domino's "The Fat Man," one of the first New Orleans R&B classics and one of the first records of any sort to be retroactively classified as rock & roll, was recorded. In 1955, he moved to the larger Cosimo Recording Studio, and over the next decade the flow of New Orleans R&B continued, with records by giants like Allen Toussaint and Lee Dorsey. He moved the studio again in 1966, although this failed by the end of the '60s. Matassa was also involved in Allen Toussaint's Sea-Saint Studios, which recorded acts like Paul McCartney, Dr. John, the Neville Brothers and LaBelle in the '70s, and was still in operation in the '90s.

Matassa was not a producer and independent label entrepreneur, like Sam Phillips, but as an engineer he was skilled at microphone placement and capturing the sound of New Orleans R&B with a naturalistic feel. As explained by Dr. John in John Broven's *Rhythm and Blues in New Orleans*, "Cosimo was the type of engineer who believed in one type of scene. He would set the knobs for the session and very rarely moved anything. If the piano was mixed too low at the beginning it would stay mixed too low until the end of the session, unless the producer came and changed it. But this was how record sessions were conducted for a long time. He developed what is known as the 'Cosimo Sound' which was strong drums, heavy bass, light piano, heavy guitar and light horn sound and a strong vocal lead.

"That was the start of what eventually became known as the New Orleans Sound, with the guitar doubling the bassline, the baritone and tenor doubling the bassline, making it a real strong sound and playing around it. It got to be known as 'Cosimo's Sound' but it was the musicians' sound because they were playing the music. But it was his little mix job which got the credit, and the record companies used to say, 'Cos has got a good sound, so we'll cut a record in New Orleans.' There were so many hits coming out of New Orleans and this was why the record companies were interested in coming there." *—Richie Unterberger*

Maurice & Mac

Group / Northern Soul, Soul, R&B
Maurice & Mac emerged when Maurice McAlister and McLauren Green splintered from the Radiants in 1966. McAlister was a founding member, lead singer, and songwriter for the group; Green replaced first tenor Charles Washington before the Radiants started recording for Chess Records.

The Radiants, composed of members from the Greater Harvest Baptist Church Youth Choir (located in Chicago, IL), formed in 1960 to record some stellar but poorly promoted singles for Chess Records. On their biggest record, "Voice Was Choice" (1964), the members were McAlister, Wallace Sampson, and Leonard Caston. The Army snatched Green, and Caston, an organist at Greater Harvest, had recently returned from the service. "Voice Your Choice" went to number-51 pop and number-16 R&B, but deserved better; its successor, "Ain't No Big Thing," scraped into *Billboard*'s pop 100 at number 91, but did better on the R&B chart (number 14). Later editions of the Radiants consisted of different members and a different sound. The group was initially a quintet, then a quartet, a trio, then back to a quartet before disappearing.

The first Maurice & Mac single surfaced around 1967 or 1968 on Checker Records, a subsidiary of Chess. But "Try Me" b/w "So Much Love" went unnoticed by everyone except the parties involved with the recording. Their second release brought some acclaim, but no fame, and no fortune. "You Left the Water Running," released in 1968, and written by Dan Penn & Spooner Oldham, is one of the best Southern soul recordings, period. Yet, it never made *Billboards*' pop or R&B charts; *Cashbox*'s survey listed it for three weeks, but it never rose from the bottom rungs. Recorded at the Fame Studios in Muscles Shoals, AL, the production is so tight that the vocals and the instrumentation literally explode from the compelling, shuffling track that reaches its zenith with a gut-wrenching "Lord Have Mercy" near the end.

Chess did an awful job promoting the single and the guys were fuming. But they forged on with a third single, "Lay It on Me" b/w "What Am I Gonna Do," which few people knew about, much less purchased. The fourth and last Checker single, "Baby You're the One" b/w "Oh What a Time," duplicated the dismal showings of the first and third singles. The last-known release by Maurice & Mac surfaced on Chess Records. But the move from Checker to the parent label didn't help, as "You Can't Say I Didn't Try" b/w "Lay It On Me" failed miserably and became the final straw. They gigged sporadically but received no support from Chess Records so there were no tours. Chess is lauded for their recordings, and should be, they waxed some remarkable sides, but none of their artists enjoyed long careers, and few had album releases. Neither the Radiants nor Maurice & Mac ever had an LP release on Chess.

When Maurice & Mac disbanded, McAlister washed his hands of the music business. After a promising start with the Radiants, and writing songs for others, such as Sugar Pie DeSanto's "Soulful Dress," McAlister's songwriting efforts ended at 36 titles licensed by

BMI. Leonard Caston went on to write and produce Eddie Kendricks' two monsters, "Keep on Trucking" and "Boogie Down." Little do the rights owners of the Radiants' recordings know, but to many, the Radiants, and Maurice & Mac were all that, and a compilation CD chronicling their respective careers is long overdue. *—Andrew Hamilton*

• **Lean on Me** / 1984 / P-Vine ♦♦♦

This early compilation (1984) has 14 tracks by soul preachers Maurice & Mac, five more than the excellent *The Regal Theater Presents the Radiants* offer. The ex-Radiants recreate themselves as Southern soul vendors with dramatic, soap opera-ish songs with no hint of Chicago soul or harmony. Maurice's biting tenor contrasts Mac's roughneck delivery as they swap lines like tag team wrestlers. The platter is labeled, the Chicago Side for A, and the Muscle Shoals Sides for B and showcases "You Left the Water Running"—their sole hit—along with "What Am I Going to Do," "Lay It on Me," "Baby You're the One" (uptempo with a blasting horn arrangement), the immortal "Kick My Cat, I'll Beat Your Dog," and "Lean on Me." P-Vine doesn't offer this in CD format so if you don't have a turntable you're out of luck. *—Andrew Hamilton*

Maxwell

b. May 23, 1973, Brooklyn, NY

Vocals / Neo-Soul, Contemporary R&B, Urban

Along with fellow founders D'Angelo and Erykah Badu, Maxwell was enormously important in defining and shaping the neo-soul movement that rose to prominence over the latter half of the '90s. Drawing his greatest inspiration from the concept of the R&B auteur (looking to artists like Prince, Marvin Gaye, Stevie Wonder, etc.), Maxwell recorded some of the most ambitious R&B of his time, becoming wildly popular and often earning critical raves in the process. What was more, his recurring theme of romantic monogamy set him apart from the vast majority of his bump 'n' grind lover-man contemporaries.

Maxwell was born May 23, 1973, in Brooklyn, NY; he adopted his middle name as his stage moniker, keeping his real identity a closely guarded secret out of concern for his family's privacy. Born of Puerto Rican and black Caribbean stock, Maxwell suffered the loss of his father (in a plane crash) when he was just three years old. The experience made him a deeply religious child, and he first began singing in his Baptist church. Still, he didn't really get serious about music until age 17, when he began writing his own songs using a cheap Casio keyboard given to him by a friend. Initially influenced by early-'80s urban R&B, he progressed rapidly, and by 1991 he was performing on the New York club scene, despite ridicule from classmates who couldn't imagine the shy, awkward teenager doing anything of the sort. After making a name for himself, he signed a recording contract with Columbia in 1994.

Maxwell recorded his debut album that year, working extensively with several collaborators: songwriter Leon Ware (who'd co-written much of the material on Marvin Gaye's *I Want You* album in 1976), guitarist Wah Wah Watson (who'd also worked with Gaye), and multi-instrumentalist Stuart Matthewman (a longtime cohort of Sade). *Maxwell's Urban Hang Suite* was a romantic concept album in the vein of Gaye's greatest '70s work, with a more modern flavor courtesy of Prince's influence; inspired by a brief but intense affair, the record's giddy celebration of committed monogamy could have come off as old-fashioned as its classic influences, given the marketplace dominance of hip-hop soul at the time. Partly for those fears, it wasn't released right away, although a series of shake-ups in Columbia's management played a bigger role in the delay. It wasn't until the spring of 1996 that *Maxwell's Urban Hang Suite* finally appeared. Sales were slow to take off at first, even though Maxwell scored some airplay with "...Til the Cops Come Knockin'." The gold-selling second single "Ascension (Never Wonder)" lit the fuse, however, and *Urban Hang Suite* went platinum before a year had passed, also earning a Grammy nomination.

Now elevated to sex-symbol status, Maxwell capitalized on his breakthrough with the *Maxwell Unplugged EP*, taken from his live MTV performance. It attracted attention and acclaim outside the R&B community with the left-field cover choices "This Woman's Work" (by prog rocker Kate Bush) and "Closer" (the Nine Inch Nails hit). Additionally, the *Unplugged* version of "Whenever, Wherever, Whatever" earned him another Grammy nomination (for Best Male Pop Vocal). Anticipation for his second full-length album was high, and when *Embrya* was released in 1998, it entered the charts at number three. Reviews were more mixed this time around, with some critics charging that Maxwell's ambition had crossed the line into indulgence; still, the record duplicated its predecessor's platinum sales. In 1999, Maxwell scored his biggest hit to date with the single "Fortunate," an R. Kelly composition he recorded for the soundtrack of the film *Life*; it was a mammoth success, ranking as the number-one R&B hit of the year in *Billboard* magazine. Later that year, he also cut two songs for the soundtrack of *The Best Man.*

In August 2001, Maxwell returned with his third full-length album, *Now*, which was touted as a return to the more straightforwardly romantic atmosphere of his debut. It entered the album charts at number one and quickly launched a hit single in "Lifetime." *—Steve Huey*

• **Maxwell's Urban Hang Suite** / Feb. 27, 1996 / Columbia ♦♦♦♦♦

Maxwell's debut offers up a sophisticated and stylized take on late-'60s and early-'70 soul. Sam Cooke, Marvin Gaye, Al Green, and the like are subtly referenced over the course of these 11 tracks of wide-screen soul. Mixing sensual funk with ballad sincerity, Maxwell coolly sings through highlights like "Welcome," "...Til the Cops Come Knockin'," and "Ascension (Don't Ever Wonder)." The atmospheric, cool-breeze soundscape comes courtesy of Maxwell and Sade cohort Stuart Matthewman. More expansive and airy sounding than the deep groove and gospel sides by fellow retro-soulster D'Angelo, *Urban Hang Suite* is destined to become a classic contemporary R&B disc. *—Stephen Cook*

Maxwell Unplugged EP / Jul. 15, 1997 / Columbia ♦♦♦

The very fact that Maxwell performed on *MTV Unplugged* indicates that he is more ambitious than the average urban soulster, and that suspicion is confirmed by his covers of Kate Bush's "This Woman's Work" and Nine Inch Nails' "Closer" on the program. Both songs, as well as a selection of songs from his debut *Urban Hang Suite*, are showcased on the *Maxwell Unplugged EP*, which illustrates that he is a skilled, subtle vocalist capable of more nuance than the majority of his contemporaries. As a result, *Maxwell Unplugged*, with its soaring vocalists and sexy, sinewy rhythms, only whets the appetite for his second full-length album. *—Stephen Thomas Erlewine*

Embrya / Jun. 23, 1998 / Columbia ♦♦♦

Maxwell's ambition was one of the appealing qualities of his debut, *Urban Hang Suite*, especially since very few of his contemporaries were attempting to expand the boundaries of contemporary R&B. However, blessings can be curses, and that very ambition gets the better of Maxwell on his second album, *Embrya.* Loaded with pretentious song titles ("Gestation: Mythos," "Arroz con Pollo," "Luxury: Cococure"), the album bogs down in its own sophistication and his desire to make deep, serious music. Like Terence Trent D'Arby—whose *Neither Fish Nor Flesh* offers a frightening parallel to *Embrya*—Maxwell wants to be so much more than another soul crooner, but his gifts become obscured the more he pushes them forward. To be sure, *Embrya* is far from a wash-out. Maxwell does have a remarkable voice and he can write really good modern soul songs—it's just that he has a tendency to think that's not enough and then he over-stuffs his songs with ideas that lead nowhere. With a little more focus, *Embrya* could have been an impressive second step. As it stands, it's a bit of a sophomore stumble, albeit one with promising moments. *—Stephen Thomas Erlewine*

Now / Aug. 14, 2001 / Columbia ♦♦♦♦

Maxwell is a gifted record-maker, which isn't necessarily the same thing as a gifted songwriter. He has a nice, sweet voice, a healthy love for classic soul from Marvin to Prince, an appealing arty streak largely missing from contemporary R&B, and he can arrange his self-recorded productions quite alluringly, balancing the guitars, synths, drum machines, and horns nimbly, often coming up with fresh songs. If only his songs were as memorable as his sounds! True, *Now* is more song-centric than his previous releases, barring possibly his debut, but this is still well-crafted mood music in which the overall seductive sound matters more than what he's saying specifically. That's part of the reason why his cover of Kate Bush's "This Woman's Work" (revived here after being debuted on his *MTV Unplugged*) is so startling—it's not just that he's picked an unlikely source for a great cover, but it's the one time that he marries his sumptuous sound to a song with substance. That's not to say that *Now* is a bad record—it's hard to call anything that sounds this good a bad album—but it's held back by Maxwell's emphasis on sound over song. If he were just making mood music, that would be acceptable, but he's trying to live up to the tradition of Marvin and Prince, and while his productions often live up to that legacy, he has yet to write songs memorable enough to truly justify those comparisons. *—Stephen Thomas Erlewine*

Curtis Mayfield

b. Jun. 3, 1942, Chicago, IL, **d.** Dec. 26, 1999

Vocals, Guitar / Funk, Blaxploitation, Soul, Psychedelic Soul, Chicago Soul, Uptown Soul

Perhaps because he didn't cross over to the pop audience as heavily as Motown's stars, it may be that the scope of Curtis Mayfield's talents and contributions have yet to be fully recognized. Judged merely by his records alone, the man's legacy is enormous. As the leader of the Impressions, he recorded some of the finest soul vocal group music of the 1960s. As a solo artist in the 1970s, he helped pioneer funk and helped introduce hard-hitting urban commentary into soul music. "Gypsy Woman," "It's All Right," "People Get Ready," "Freddie's Dead," and "Superfly" are merely the most famous of his many hit records.

But Curtis Mayfield wasn't just a singer. He wrote most of his material at a time when that was not the norm for soul performers. He was among the first—if not the very first—to speak openly about African-American pride and community struggle in his compositions. As a songwriter and a producer, he was a key architect of Chicago soul, penning material and working on sessions by notable Windy City soulsters like Gene Chandler, Jerry Butler, Major Lance, and Billy Butler. In this sense, he can be compared to Smokey Robinson, who also managed to find time to write and produce many classics for other soul stars. Mayfield was also an excellent guitarist, and his rolling, Latin-influenced lines were highlights of the Impressions' recordings in the '60s. During the next decade, he would toughen up his guitar work and production, incorporating some of the best features of psychedelic rock and funk.

Mayfield began his career as an associate of Jerry Butler, with whom he formed the Impressions in the late '50s. After the Impressions had a big hit in 1958 with "For Your Precious Love," Butler, who had sung lead on the record, split to start a solo career. Mayfield, while keeping the Impressions together, continued to write for and tour with Butler before the Impressions got their first Top 20 hit in 1961, "Gypsy Woman."

Mayfield was heavily steeped in gospel music before he entered the pop arena, and gospel, as well as doo wop, influences would figure prominently in most of his '60s work. Mayfield wasn't a staunch traditionalist, however. He and the Impressions may have often worked the call-and-response gospel style, but his songs (romantic and otherwise) were often veiled or unveiled messages of black pride, reflecting the increased confidence and self-determination of the African-American community. Musically he was an innovator as well, using arrangements that employed the punchy, blaring horns and Latin-influenced rhythms that came to be trademark flourishes of Chicago soul. As the staff producer for the OKeh label, Mayfield was also instrumental in lending his talents to the work of other Chi-town soul singers who went on to national success. With Mayfield singing lead and playing guitar, the Impressions had 14 Top 40 hits in the 1960s (five made the Top 20 in 1964 alone), and released some above-average albums during that period as well.

Given Mayfield's prodigious talents, it was perhaps inevitable that he would eventually leave the Impressions to begin a solo career, as he did in 1970. His first few singles boasted a harder, more funk-driven sound; singles like "(Don't Worry) If There's a Hell

Below, We're All Gonna Go" found him confronting ghetto life with a realism that had rarely been heard on record. He really didn't hit his artistic or commercial stride as a solo artist, though, until *Superfly*, his soundtrack to a 1972 blaxploitation film. Drug deals, ghetto shootings, the death of young black men before their time: all were described in penetrating detail. Yet Mayfield's irrepressible falsetto vocals, uplifting melodies, and fabulous funk pop arrangements gave the oft-moralizing material a graceful strength that few others could have achieved. For all the glory of his past work, *Superfly* stands as his crowning achievement, not to mention a much-needed counterpoint to the sensationalistic portrayals of the film itself.

At this point Mayfield, along with Stevie Wonder and Marvin Gaye, was the foremost exponent of a new level of compelling auteurism in soul. His failure to maintain the standards of *Superfly* qualifies as one of the great disappointments in the history of black popular music. Perhaps he'd simply reached his peak after a long climb, but the rest of his '70s work didn't match the musical brilliance and lyrical subtleties of *Superfly*, although he had a few large R&B hits in a much more conventional vein, such as "Kung Fu," "So in Love," and "Only You Babe."

Mayfield had a couple of hits in the early '80s, but the decade generally found his commercial fortunes in a steady downward spiral, despite some intermittent albums. On August 14, 1990, he became paralyzed from the neck down when a lighting rig fell on top of him at a concert in Brooklyn, NY. In the mid-'90s, a couple of tribute albums consisting of Mayfield covers appeared, with contributions by such superstars as Eric Clapton, Bruce Springsteen, and Gladys Knight. Though no substitute for the man himself, these tributes served as an indication of the enormous regard in which Mayfield was still held by his peers. He died December 26, 1999 at the age of 57. *—Richie Unterberger*

☆ **Curtis** / Sep. 1970 / Rhino ✦✦✦✦✦

The first solo album by the former leader of the Impressions, *Curtis* represented a musical apotheosis for Curtis Mayfield—indeed, it was practically the "*Sgt. Pepper's*" album of '70s soul, helping with its content and its success to open the whole genre to much bigger, richer musical canvases than artists had previously worked with. All of Mayfield's years of experience of life, music, and people were pulled together into a rich, powerful, topical musical statement that reflected not only the most up-to-date soul sounds of its period, finely produced by Mayfield himself, and the immediacy of the times and their political and social concerns, but also embraced the most elegant R&B sounds out of the past. As a producer, Mayfield embraced the most progressive soul sounds of the era, stretching them out compellingly on numbers like "Move on Up," but also drew on orchestral sounds (especially harps), to achieve some striking musical timbres (check out "Wild and Free"), and wove all of these influences, plus the topical nature of the songs, into a neat, amazingly lean whole. There was only one hit single off of this record, "(Don't Worry) If There's a Hell Below, We're All Going to Go," which made number three, but the album as a whole was a single entity and really had to be heard that way. In the fall of 2000, Rhino Records reissued *Curtis* with upgraded sound and nine bonus tracks that extended its running time to over 70 minutes. All but one are demos, including "Miss Black America" and "The Making of You," but mostly consist of tracks that he completed for subsequent albums; they're fascinating to hear, representing very different, much more jagged and stripped-down sounds. The upgraded CD concludes with the single version of "(Don't Worry) If There's a Hell Below We're All Going to Go." *—Bruce Eder*

Curtis/Live! / 1971 / Rhino ✦✦✦✦✦

Curtis/Live! is, simply, one of the greatest concert albums ever cut on a soul artist, and one of the legendary live albums of all time. Cut in January of 1971 during four nights at The Bitter End (then Greenwich Village's leading music venue) in New York, the resulting double LP transcended any expectations in both its programming and execution—Mayfield performed numbers off of the *Curtis* album ("[Don't Worry] If There's a Hell Below, We're All Going to Go"), as well as exciting and urgent new versions of songs originally performed by the Impressions ("We're a Winner," "People Get Ready," "Gypsy Woman"), plus a very moving R&B version of "We've Only Just Begun." This is all beautifully stripped-down work by a quintet consisting of Mayfield (vocals, guitar), Craig McMullen (guitar), Tyrone McCullen (drums), "Master" Henry Gibson (percussion), and Joseph "Lucky" Scott (bass)—a solid, intense performance, with quietly elegant guitar playing against a rock-solid rhythm section, as Impressions hits are rethought and reconfigured in a new context, and Mayfield's early solo repertory comes to life in newer, longer live versions. [The British import from Sequel adds the complete contents of 1973's live *Curtis in Chicago*.] *—Bruce Eder*

Roots / 1971 / Rhino ✦✦✦✦✦

Curtis Mayfield's visionary album, a landmark creation every bit as compelling and as far-reaching in its musical and extra-musical goals as Marvin Gaye's contemporary *What's Goin' On*. Opening on the hit "Get Down," the album soars on some of the sweetest and most eloquent—yet driving—soul sounds heard up to that time. Mayfield's growing musical ambitions, first manifested on the *Curtis* album, and his more sophisticated political sensibilities, presented with a lot of raw power on *Curtis Live!*, are pulled together here in a new, richer studio language, embodied in extended song structures ("Underground"), idealistic yet lyrically dazzling anthems ("We Got to Have Peace," "Keep on Keeping On," and, best of all, the soaring "Beautiful Brother of Mine"), and impassioned blues ("Now You're Gone"). The music is even bolder than the material on the *Curtis* album, with Mayfield expanding his instrumental range to the level of a veritable soul orchestra; and the recording is better realized, as Mayfield, with that album and a tour behind him, shows a degree of confidence that only a handful of soul artists of this era could have mustered. Charly Records had this album out on CD in the 1980s, but Rhino's acquisition of the Curtom catalog in 1996 led to a remastered and expanded reissue in 1999 with superior sound, detailed annotation, and the addition of four bonus tracks. Apart from a slow, funky, stripped-down but eminently listenable demo of "Underground" (which reveals just how sophisticated Mayfield's conceptions—forget the finished versions—of his songs were), the latter consist of the single edits of "Get Down," "We Got to Have Peace," and "Beautiful Brother of Mine." They seem redundant after the album versions, though they don't detract at all from the extraordinary value of this mid-priced CD. *—Bruce Eder*

☆ **Superfly** / Jul. 1972 / Curtom ✦✦✦✦✦

The choice of Curtis Mayfield to score the blaxploitation film *Superfly* was an inspired one. No other artist in popular music knew so well, and expressed through his music so naturally, the shades of gray inherent in contemporary inner-city life. His debut solo album, 1970's *Curtis*, had shown in vivid colors that the '60s optimist (author of the civil-rights anthems "Keep on Pushing" and "People Get Ready") had added a layer of subtlety to his material; appearing on the same LP as the positive and issue-oriented "Move on Up" was an apocalyptic piece of brimstone funk titled "(Don't Worry) If There's a Hell Below, We're All Going to Go." For *Superfly*, Mayfield wisely avoids celebrating the wheeling-and-dealing themes present in the movie, or exploiting them, instead using each song to focus on a different aspect of what he saw as a plague on America's streets. He also steers away from explicit moralizing; through his songs, Mayfield simply tells it like it is (for the characters in the film as in real life), with any lessons learned the result of his vibrant storytelling and knack of getting inside the heads of the characters. "Freddie's Dead," one of the album's signature pieces, tells the story of one of the film's main casualties, a good-hearted yet weak-willed man caught up in the life of a pusher, and devastatingly portrays the indifference of those who witness or hear about it. "Pusherman" masterfully uses the metaphor of drug dealer as businessman, with the drug game, by extension, just another way to make a living in a tough situation, while the title track equates hustling with gambling ("The game he plays he plays for keeps / hustlin' times and ghetto streets / tryin' ta get over"). Ironically, the sound of *Superfly* positively overwhelmed its lyrical finesse. A mélange of deep, dark grooves, trademarked wah-wah guitar, and stinging brass, *Superfly* ignited an entire genre of music, the blaxploitation soundtrack, and influenced everyone from soul singers to television-music composers for decades to come. It stands alongside *Saturday Night Fever* and *Never Mind the Bollocks Here's the Sex Pistols* as one of the most vivid touchstones of '70s pop music. *—John Bush*

Curtis in Chicago / 1973 / Get Back ✦✦✦✦✦

Released just two years after the intimate club set *Curtis/Live!*, *Curtis in Chicago* consists of a different kind of show, a dream concert celebrating Curtis Mayfield's musical history and Curtom Records for which one is grateful the audio-tape machines were running properly (there was a public-television broadcast of the show, under the same name, that would be a choice video release today). Mayfield; the current Impressions; the original Impressions (including Jerry Butler), the successful mid-'60s version of the group; Gene Chandler (reworking "Duke of Earl"); and Leroy Hutson get to do their best songs, this time in a kind of big-band soul setting backed by the Curtom Rhythm Section augmented by the presence of Phil Upchurch. [A British import release from Sequel includes *Curtis/Live!* and *Curtis in Chicago*.] *—Bruce Eder*

Back to the World / May 1973 / Curtom ✦✦✦

Back to the World, the first album Curtis Mayfield recorded and released after hitting number one with the intense inner-city vignette *Superfly*, returned him to a steady balance of optimism for the future and direct social commentary regarding the problems of his people. The lead single, "Future Shock," was inspired by Alvin Toffler's 1970 book of the same name, which warned readers that industrial society was changing so radically that environmental and social problems could be endemic for decades. The track tapped into the same grooves and brass heard on *Superfly* (perhaps overly so), but said more about the world around ("We got to stop all men, from messing up the land/When won't we understand, this is our last and only chance?"). The title track was very upbeat and positive, as were the refreshing "If I Were Only a Child Again" and "Future Song (Love a Good Woman, Love a Good Man)." With no hit singles to even approach the three high performers from *Superfly*, though, *Back to the World* was a distinct disappointment; the music wasn't as powerful as fans were expecting, and though the songs were up to Mayfield's usual high standards, there were many similarities (musically and thematically) to material from each of his proper solo albums. *—John Bush*

Sweet Exorcist / 1974 / Curtom ✦✦✦

Curtis Mayfield hit a stride during the '70s that was unparalleled among R&B/soul performers from an album standpoint. He was writing, producing, arranging, and performing on great album after great album, then distributing them on his own label as well. This one included the big hit "Kung Fu," plus the title song, and once more perfectly blended rigorous message tracks and steamy love songs. *—Ron Wynn*

Got to Find a Way / 1974 / Curtom ✦✦✦

Curtis Mayfield continued his run of excellent albums in the '70s with this follow-up to the huge hit *Superfly* soundtrack. This album had more love songs than some of his earlier material, although he didn't tone down his searing attacks on American injustice and hyprocisy. His vocals continued to be alternately poignant, urgent, and accusatory, while his lyrics, production, and arrangements were once again magnificent. *—Ron Wynn*

There's No Place Like America Today / 1975 / Curtom ✦✦✦✦

The title is intended in an ironic way, as illustrated not only by the cover—a grim parody of late-'40s/early-'50s advertising imagery depicting white versus black social reality—but the grim yet utterly catchy and haunting opening number, "Billy Jack." A song about gun violence that was years ahead of its time, it's scored to an incisive horn arrangement by Richard Tufo. "When Seasons Change" is a beautifully wrought account of the miseries of urban life that contains elements of both gospel and contemporary soul. The album's one big song, "So in Love," which made number 67 on the pop charts but was a Top Ten soul hit, is only the prettiest of a string of exquisite tracks on the album, including "Blue

Monday People" and "Jesus" and the soaring finale, "Love to the People," broken up by the harder-edged "Hard Times." The album doesn't really have as clearly delineated a body of songs as Mayfield's earlier topical releases, but it's in the same league with his other work of the period and represents him near his prime as a composer. *—Bruce Eder*

Give Get Take Have / 1976 / Ichiban ♦♦♦

Less sociopolitical than previous efforts, *Give Get Take Have* offers "Mr. Welfare Man" as its sole attempt to enlighten and enhance. Mayfield was obviously experiencing the joys of new love when he cut "Only You Babe" and "This Love Is Sweet," and the tear-jerking numbers "In Your Arms Again" and "Party Night." His aching falsetto coos and purrs, but sounds weakened on this LP. Overall, the album falls short of Mayfield's former releases, but even great artists don't always achieve their usual high standards. *—Andrew Hamilton*

Never Say You Can't Survive / 1977 / Ichiban ♦♦♦

Never Say You Can't Survive was the last Curtis Mayfield album done in a pure soul vein for the next three years—its style and sound place it in a direct continuity with the rest of his output right back to 1958. The singing on love songs such as "Show Me Love," "Just Want to Be With You," and "When We're Alone" is among the most achingly lyrical and passionate of his career. The title track boasts ravishing backup singing by Kitty & the Haywoods (who also perform outstandingly on "I'm Gonna Win Your Love") and a beautiful arrangement by James Mack. The album's final track, "Sparkle" (written for Sam O'Steen's movie of the same name, starring Philip Michael Thomas, Irene Cara, and Lonette McKee), gets one of three distinct treatments that the song ever received (the others from the soundtrack and Aretha Franklin's version). *—Bruce Eder*

Do It All Night / 1978 / Curtom ♦♦♦

The last Curtis Mayfield album distributed by Warner Bros., during Curtom Records' declining years of 1977-1978, was a maddening album, a complete break in style as Mayfield moved into a pure disco vein. It was his most successful album in three years, but it alienated many longtime fans because he deliberately dumbed down his writing—he traded his core audience, who couldn't abide the album, for a slightly larger disco audience that had previously eluded him, painting himself into an artistic and career corner. The title track was indicative of the artistic nadir to which Mayfield had to descend to find where the mass audience had gone, a number without an ounce of poetry that he wouldn't have wasted his time with in the studio, much less completed or released, in years past; the beat and the arrangements rather overwhelm anything that Mayfield is saying or singing throughout this album. The closest one gets to the old Curtis Mayfield sound, which is to say, to Curtis Mayfield at all, is "In Love, In Love, In Love," a relatively subdued and soulful number which would have been a secondary track on almost any album that preceded this one, and it is practically lost here, sandwiched in between the commercial dance numbers "Keeps Me Loving You" and "You Are, You Are." Mayfield would adapt his style better to the needs of disco with *Heartbeat*, his next album. *—Bruce Eder*

Heartbeat / 1979 / RSO ♦♦

A thinking man's soul singer, whose abilities combined the lyrical passions of Marvin Gaye with the musical range of Sam Cooke, Curtis Mayfield proved singularly unsuited to the disco era, at least on his own terms. Thus, for *Heartbeat*, he put himself in the hands of other producers—Bunny Sigler and the Philadelphia team of Norman Harris & Ronnie Tyson—for the first time in his career on seven of the ten songs, and the result was a first-rate disco album that got to number 42 on the pop charts and number-17 R&B, Mayfield's best-selling album in three years. It doesn't sound too much like Mayfield's best work, but it did get him some needed airplay just at the point where he and Curtom needed all the help they could get. The beat throughout is infectious, and Mayfield's vocalizing is impeccable, a match for his best work on any of his classic albums. The pounding disco arrangements (especially "What Is My Woman For?") are showy and so different from Mayfield's own true sound, that they are bound to offend some of his listeners—this is sort of his equivalent to the Muddy Waters *Electric Mud* album, except it plays much better and Mayfield was able to perform some of this album's repertory in concert. Indeed, the beautifully lyrical ballad "Between You Baby and Me"—one of only three Mayfield-produced tracks on the album, and the first studio duet between Mayfield and Linda Clifford—led to a joint tour and a duet album for the two. [A 1999 two-fer compilation from Sequel paired *Heartbeat* with the following year's *Something to Believe In*.] *—Bruce Eder*

Something to Believe In / 1980 / Ichiban ♦♦

Something to Believe In was the result of previous album *Heartbeat*'s success, a great-selling comeback for Curtis Mayfield in his own style, fully in his control. The album's sales success was limited, but its musical triumphs were myriad—the beautiful "Something to Believe In," an extended track that is one of the most personal and ambitious records in Mayfield's whole output; the exquisite solo remakes of the Impressions hits "It's Alright" and "Never Let Me Go"; and the gorgeous ballad "Never Stop Loving Me," a sensual soul outing that provides a superb finish to the album. Strangely enough, the commercial single side "Love Me, Love Me Now" is one of the less impressive sides, on a production or composition level, among the seven tracks here. [A 1999 reissue by the British Sequel label combined *Something to Believe In* with 1979's *Heartbeat*.] *—Bruce Eder*

Honesty / 1983 / Epic ♦♦♦

Unlike Mayfield's more well-known work in the 1970s, his 1980s material is more soulful than funky. Songs like "Hey Baby (Give It All to Me)" and "Still Within Your Heart" are missing the hard-hitting urban commentary and focus instead on a romantic vibe similar to love songs by Al Green, Barry White, and Marvin Gaye. No clunkers here, but "Dirty Laundry'" is an outstanding track, and one of Mayfield's best during the decade. *Honesty* is a soft, sensual album that transports the listener back to the days of the Impressions more than those of *Superfly*. [In 2000, Boardwalk re-released this underrated album.] *—JT Griffith*

Live in Europe / Jul. 1987 / Curtom ♦♦♦

Although Curtis Mayfield's album sales had decreased significantly by the late '70s, the smooth Chicago soul veteran remained a popular live attraction well into the '80s. Audiences still longed to hear both gems from his years with the influential Impressions and his early solo hits, and he gives them exactly what they want on this album (released as both a single CD and a two-CD set). Mayfield reminds us just how great the Impressions were on heartfelt versions of such '60s classics as "Gypsy Woman" (which greatly influenced the Isley Brothers), "It's Alright" and the inspirational "People Get Ready," and is equally captivating on incisive, early-'70s sociopolitical hits like "Pusherman," "Freddie's Dead," and "If There's a Hell Below." *Live in Europe*'s main flaw isn't Mayfield's performances, but a band that, although decent, just doesn't go that extra mile or do this superb material justice. Horns, a main ingredient of many of his hits, are sorely missed—especially on "Move on Up"—and Buzz Amato's keyboards simply can't take their place. *—Alex Henderson*

Take It to the Streets / Feb. 1990 / Curtom ♦♦♦

In the 1980s and '90s, some soul veterans turned to high-tech urban-contemporary sounds in an effort to appeal to black radio. Curtis Mayfield, however, continued to deliver rewarding albums by remaining true to himself and sticking with the type of classic soul approach that put him on the map. *Take It to the Streets* falls short of the unmitigated excellence of *Superfly* or *Sweet Exorcist*, but is a respectable effort demonstrating that he could still pack a punch as a vocalist, composer, and producer. There's much to savor and admire here, including "Homeless" (which makes it clear that Mayfield hadn't lost his touch when it came to biting sociopolitical commentary), "He's a Fly Guy," the charismatic "Who Was That Lady," and an engaging remake of "On and On" (a gem he wrote for Gladys Knight & the Pips in 1973). With the re-emergence of hard-hitting "blaxploitation" (black exploitation) films in the late '80s, the gritty imagery of "I'm Gonna Get You Sucka" and the haunting "He's A Fly Guy" proved quite timely. While this material could have used some horns, Mayfield generally employs technology in a soulful way—employing "real instruments" along with keyboards and drum machines, and never letting his production sound stiff, unnatural, or forced. *—Alex Henderson*

★ **The Anthology 1961–1977** / Dec. 8, 1992 / MCA ♦♦♦♦♦

MCA's double-disc *The Anthology 1961-1977* is the definitive overview of Curtis Mayfield's career, as the only compilation to draw from both his solo work and the best of his output with the Impressions. In fact, even discounting the four Curtom tracks that spill over onto disc two, the first disc's 26 selections constitute far and away the most extensive Impressions best-of on the market. Toss in ten of the most essential Mayfield solo tracks, and the result is breathtaking in its progression from romantic soul, often informed by doo wop and gospel, to expansive, ambitiously arranged funk jams. It's also fascinating to hear Mayfield's social conscience emerging as the '60s progress, since he was among the very first R&B artists to explore political issues in his music, paving the way for countless others to do so during the '70s. If you're only interested in Mayfield's funkier solo work, Rhino's *The Very Best of Curtis Mayfield* features all but one of the solo tracks included here, plus several more. But in order to fully grasp Mayfield's impact on R&B and his talent as a singer, songwriter, musician, and producer, *The Anthology 1961-1977* is absolutely essential. *—Steve Huey*

☆ **Curtis Mayfield's Chicago Soul** / Nov. 7, 1995 / Epic/Legacy ♦♦♦♦♦

Curtis Mayfield doesn't actually sing on any of the music heard here, but it's all material produced and, in many cases, written by him during his two years working at Columbia's revived OKeh Records label as a producer. The years 1963–1965 directly preceded Mayfield's founding of his first label, Windy C, which was the predecessor to Curtom Records, and you can hear the roots of the Curtom sound throughout these sides. In one fell swoop, he developed a signature every bit as soulful as anything coming out of Motown Records, with acts like the Opals, Gene Chandler, Walter Jackson, Billy Butler & the Enchanters, and Major Lance. The roster represents a nexus in Mayfield's career, with a name or two that later ended up on Curtom and, by way of Billy Butler, brother of Mayfield's Impressions compatriot Jerry Butler, and if you close your eyes, the Opals sound a lot like the Jones Girls. The music is very smooth and elegant, including the harder sounds, which reveal even greater intricacy of construction than the creations of the Motown label during this same era. Fans of Mayfield's own music with the Impressions or from his solo career will love this CD as a valid extension of his legacy, and casual listeners will also find a great deal to embrace on this disc—one only wishes there were some full-length LPs associated with his period at OKeh. *—Bruce Eder*

People Get Ready: The Curtis Mayfield Story / Feb. 27, 1996 / Rhino ♦♦♦♦♦

Like most large box sets, this three-CD, 51-song production is too extensive for the casual fan and sacrifices consistency in an attempt to span an entire career. The focus is on Mayfield's solo work; much of the first disc is devoted to his most popular work with the Impressions, but the remainder of the compilation surveys his solo output, from 1970 to 1990. The Impressions tracks are uniformly excellent, but the Mayfield-only cuts are more problematic. The best of these—the *Superfly* highlights, of course, and early '70s singles like "(Don't Worry) If There's a Hell Below We're All Going to Go" and "Beautiful Brother of Mine"—are as good as everything he ever did. But even in the early '70s, he was erratic, and after *Superfly* (his career summit), nothing he did smacked of brilliance. Some of the post-*Superfly* stuff is OK, but considering that this period takes up half of disc two and all of disc three, it means you're in for a pretty swift downhill slide over the last half of the box. Mayfield never lost his vocal abilities, or his production skills, but after the late '70s his material was simply unimpressive, getting into pedestrian dance music and romantic urban contemporary. For a Mayfield retrospective, you're much better off with MCA's two-disc *Anthology*, which goes into the Impressions period with much greater depth, and includes the cream of his '70s solo recordings. *—Richie Unterberger*

The Very Best of Curtis Mayfield / Mar. 10, 1996 / Rhino ✦✦✦✦✦
Rhino's *The Very Best of Curtis Mayfield* is devoted to material the legendary soul man recorded after leaving the Impressions, focusing particularly on his classic songs from the early '70s. There are more comprehensive compilations on the market, namely the sublime double-disc *Anthology* and the flawed but worthwhile box *People Get Ready*, but this is the best bet for anyone wanting a concise sampler of Mayfield's groundbreaking funk-soul, since it contains all of the bare-bone essentials: "(Don't Worry) If There's a Hell Below, We're All Going to Go"; "Move on Up"; "We Got to Have Peace"; "Freddie's Dead"; "Superfly"; "Pusherman"; "Future Shock"; and "Kung Fu." Yes, Mayfield also made cohesive, frequently stunning albums during this era and his work with the Impressions was just as influential, but this disc benefits from its narrow focus, since the end result is a collection ideal for the curious and the novice, while also providing a great listen for anyone who already knows the records. *—Stephen Thomas Erlewine*

Love Is the Place/Honesty / Apr. 24, 1996 / Castle ✦✦✦

New World Order / Oct. 1, 1996 / Warner Bros. ✦✦✦
New World Order is a touching, moving comeback from Curtis Mayfield. As the first new music Mayfield has recorded since he was paralyzed in 1990, the album engenders a lot of goodwill—it's undeniably affecting to hear him sing again, especially with the knowledge that his performances had to be recorded line-by-line, due to his paralysis. The joy of hearing him sing makes the inconsistency of the album forgivable, especially since he is in good voice. Narada Michael Walden, Daryl Simmons, and Organized have all contributed productions where are sensitive but strong, which gives the album added weight. The songs are hit-and-miss, but the main strength of the record is that it illustrates that Mayfield can make music that is still vital. *—Leo Stanley*

Love, Peace, Understanding / 1997 / Sequel ✦✦✦✦
The triple-disc *Love, Peace, Understanding* box set released by Sequel Records in the U.K. compiles many of Curtis Mayfield's best-known singles along with quite a few rare demos from the early part of his solo career and some seldom-heard latter-day songs. The second disc in the set, which features the early-'70s recordings Mayfield is best remembered for—"(Don't Worry) If There's a Hell Below," "Move on Up," "Freddie's Dead," "Superfly," "So in Love," and so on—is wonderful, no doubt, but that's probably not the reason to seek out this collection. Most admirers already have these songs either on the original full-lengths or else on other, more succinct best-ofs like Rhino's single-disc *The Very Best of Curtis Mayfield* or Sequel's double-disc *Move on Up: The Singles Anthology*. If you want a true best-of featuring Mayfield's best solo work, those are the collections to own; not this one. However, there is a reason to splurge on this sprawling triple-disc set, and it's mostly because of the demos featured on disc one. Many of these 17 songs are not readily available in any format, though some would appear later in more polished versions, such as in the case of "Ghetto Child," for example, which would later appear on the *Superfly* soundtrack a few years later as "Little Child Runnin' Wild." In addition to these hard-to-find demos, the third disc on this box set is also somewhat of a curiosity, featuring songs from Mayfield's post-1975 work. Though this era of Mayfield's solo career wasn't his most accomplished by any means, characterized more by frustration and disappointment than success or brilliance, most listeners probably aren't familiar with these songs, so it's nice to have a distilled selection of latter-day work to sample rather than scour through those hard to find and often painful latter-day albums. So, in total, you get a little bit of everything on this box set: a disc of early demos, a disc of genius hits, and a disc of failed comeback attempts, all in chronological order. Plus, you get a handy booklet with helpful liner notes, explaining the story behind the demos and the latter-day comeback attempts. *—Jason Birchmeier*

Superfly: Deluxe 25th Anniversary Edition / Nov. 11, 1997 / Rhino ✦✦✦
This expanded version of the classic album adds so much material that it really needs to be reviewed separately from the original article. The first disc of the two-CD set presents the entire album as it was originally sequenced, with the addition of the single mixes of "Freddie's Dead" and "Superfly." It's disc two that's really of interest to collectors, assembling about 40 minutes of different material from the same era, all but two tracks previously unissued (and those two were not released in the U.S.). In some cases this is fairly extraneous, as in the alternate mix of "Pusherman," but there's some interesting, even gripping stuff as well. Especially good is "Ghetto Child," which served as the harder, sparser demo of the song that eventually became "Little Child Runnin' Wild," and the 1970 demo "The Underground," whose hard-hitting lyrics and heavy guitar riffs are obvious prototypes for the *Superfly* approach. The full-length take of the instrumental "Junkie Chase," as well as instrumental versions of a couple of songs that had vocals on the original album, are atmospheric if not as essential; there are also a couple of radio spots and a seven-minute 1995 interview with Mayfield about the record. The second disc is good listening, though probably not of much interest to fans who aren't curious about the music's history. It makes a great bonus if you're upgrading to CD, however, as does an accompanying booklet with detailed text about the songs. *—Richie Unterberger*

Give It Up: The Best of the Curtom Years 1970–1977 / 1998 / Empire Music ✦✦✦✦
Give It Up illustrates the sociopolitical side of Curtis Mayfield. The pulsating, horn-driven "Move on Up" has all the social significance of his early positive songs with the Impressions, and "We the People Who Are Darker Than Blue" showed the world that Mayfield was possessed of unique insight. "Back to the World" speaks of soldiers returning from Vietnam, while "Billy Jack" and "Superfly" are apt depictions of inner-city characters. This also contains motivators like "We Got to Have Peace," "Keep On Keeping On," "People Get Ready," and "Mighty, Mighty Spade and Whitey." *—Andrew Hamilton*

Heartbeat/Something to Believe In / 1999 / Sequel ✦✦✦✦

Never Say You Can't Survive/Do It All Night / 1999 / Sequel ✦✦✦

We Come in Peace/Take It to the Streets / 1999 / Sequel ✦✦✦✦✦

Gospel / Jan. 19, 1999 / Rhino ✦✦✦
This enjoyable (yet somewhat questionable) compilation gathers together many of the religious songs that Curtis Mayfield penned and performed, both with the Impressions in the '60s and as a solo artist in the '70s. As a songwriter, Mayfield was astounding. In addition to the well-known lyrics of "Amen" and "People Get Ready," there are several songs that are open to interpretation; while Mayfield may have been addressing God in "You Ought to Be in Heaven" and "When We're Alone," they work equally well as conventional love songs. The older material, performed with the Impressions, doesn't sound dated in the least. Some of the later songs, however, are prone to excesses not uncommon in '70s music (excessive overdubbing, and the obligatory string section.) One may wonder why Rhino would release this compilation of readily available material (excluding one unnecessary unreleased live track), but it is lively, enjoyable and in some cases essential music. (No Mayfield collection is complete without "People Get Ready," but newcomers will be better served in purchasing one of his many "Best-of" compilations.) *—Steve McMullen*

Curtis/Live! & Curtis in Chicago / Mar. 2, 1999 / Sequel ✦✦✦✦✦

There's No Place Like America Today/Give Get Take Have / Mar. 2, 1999 / Sequel ✦✦✦✦

Move on Up: The Singles Anthology / May 16, 2000 / Sequel ✦✦✦✦✦
Curtis Mayfield is inarguably one of the giants of soul, turning out work equally great with the Impressions and as a solo artist alike—and making great singles and albums simultaneously. There are so many great moments in his catalog that it's easy to make a good collection of highlights, which Sequel's *Move on Up: The Singles Anthology* most certainly is. That doesn't mean it's the perfect collection. At two discs and 39 tracks, it actually suffers from over-length and evenhandedness, offering a bit too much of the late-'70s work that simply isn't as good as the music from the early '70s. Nevertheless, this is a thorough overview of Curtis' Curtom singles, and for some listeners, that may be a selling point, even though MCA's 1992 *Anthology 1961-1977* provides a better overview of his peak work. *—Stephen Thomas Erlewine*

Percy Mayfield

b. Aug. 12, 1920, Minden, LA, **d.** Aug. 11, 1984, Los Angeles, CA
Vocals, Songwriter, Piano / R&B, Urban Blues, West Coast Blues, Piano Blues, Soul
A masterful songwriter whose touching blues ballad "Please Send Me Someone to Love," a multi-layered universal lament, was a number-one R&B hit in 1950, Percy Mayfield had the world by the tail until a horrific 1952 auto wreck left him facially disfigured. That didn't stop the poet laureate of the blues from writing in prolific fashion, though. As Ray Charles' favorite scribe during the '60s, he handed the Genius such gems as "Hit the Road Jack" and "At the Club."

Like so many of his postwar L.A. contemporaries, Mayfield got his musical start in Texas but moved to the coast during the war. Surmising that Jimmy Witherspoon might like to perform a tune he'd penned called "Two Years of Torture," Mayfield targeted Supreme Records as a possible buyer for his song. But the bosses at Supreme liked his own gentle reading so much that they insisted he wax it himself in 1947 with an all-star band that included saxist Maxwell Davis, guitarist Chuck Norris, and pianist Willard McDaniel.

Art Rupe's Specialty logo signed Mayfield in 1950 and he scored a solid string of R&B smashes over the next couple of years. "Please Send Me Someone to Love" and its equally potent flip "Strange Things Happening" were followed in the charts by "Lost Love," "What a Fool I Was," "Prayin' for Your Return," "Cry Baby," and "Big Question," cementing Mayfield's reputation as a blues balladeer of the highest order. Davis handled sax duties on most of Mayfield's Specialty sides as well. Mayfield's lyrics were usually as insightfully downbeat as his tempos; he was a true master at expressing his innermost feelings, laced with vulnerability and pathos (his "Life Is Suicide" and "The River's Invitation" are two prime examples).

Even though his touring was drastically curtailed after the accident, Mayfield hung in there as a Specialty artist through 1954, switching to Chess in 1955-1956 and Imperial in 1959. Charles proved thankful enough for Mayfield's songwriting genius to sign him to his Tangerine logo in 1962; over the next five years, the singer waxed a series of inexorably classy outings, many with Brother Ray's band (notably "My Jug and I" in 1964 and "Give Me Time to Explain" the next year). It's a rare veteran blues artist indeed who hasn't taken a whack at one or more Mayfield copyrights. Mayfield himself persisted into the '70s, scoring minor chart items for RCA and Atlantic while performing on a limited basis until his 1984 death. *—Bill Dahl*

My Jug and I / 1966 / Tangerine ✦✦✦✦✦
Mayfield's gentle vocal delivery and the big, brassy sound of Ray Charles' orchestra were a match made in heaven. Mayfield brought some first-class material to this party (which begs for CD reissue): "My Jug and I," "Stranger in My Own Home Town" (later covered by Elvis Presley), the untypically jumping "Give Me Time to Explain," and a handful of Specialty remakes. *—Bill Dahl*

Bought Blues / 1969 / Tangerine ✦✦✦✦
Here is another elegant, beautifully arranged collection fraught with brilliant, sometimes heartbreaking material: "Ha Ha in the Daytime," "We Both Must Cry," "My Bottle Is My Companion." *—Bill Dahl*

★ **Poet of the Blues** / 1990 / Specialty ✦✦✦✦✦
The insightful songwriting skills of this West Coaster were matched by his wry, plaintive vocal delivery (Mayfield was usually his own best interpreter). The 25 sides here date from his hit-laden 1950-1954 stay at Art Rupe's Specialty logo and include his universal lament "Please Send Me Someone to Love," and the resolutely downbeat "Strange Things Happening" and "Lost Love," and an ironic "The River's Invitation." Saxman Maxwell

Davis led the horn-powered combos providing sympathetic support behind Mayfield. *—Bill Dahl*

Percy Mayfield Live / 1992 / Winner ♦♦♦
Although the first-ever release of live Mayfield material is culled from performances between 1981 and 1983, the twilight of the singer's blues career, he remains in fine, laid-back voice throughout. The selections draw on all periods of his three decades as a songwriter, and include "Please Send Me Someone to Love," "The River's Invitation," and "Don't Start Lying to Me." Founding Paul Butterfield Blues Band pianist Mark Naftalin backs Mayfield throughout the collection; he also served as the set's producer. *—Jason Ankeny*

Memory Pain / Sep. 17, 1992 / Specialty ♦♦♦♦♦
Ranging from major hits to alternate takes and rarities, this CD illustrates the prolific nature of Percy Mayfield's Specialty Records output during the 1950s. Though not everything on *Memory Pain* is essential, the collection of early R&B and 12-bar blues is consistently satisfying. The best known song here is the number-one hit of 1950, "Please Send Me Someone to Love," and many listeners will also be familiar with such gems as "Strange Things Happening" and the title song. A singer who was flexible as well as charismatic, Mayfield is as convincing on a rare version of the mournful, jazz-tinged "Nightless Lovers" as he is on 12-bar numbers like "My Blues" and "The Big Question." The CD ends on an interesting note with a demo of "Hit the Road Jack" (which became a major hit for Ray Charles). Highly recommended. *—Alex Henderson*

Maze Featuring Frankie Beverly

f. 1976

Group / Urban, Funk

Combining a Philadelphia soul sound with a strong appreciation of Marvin Gaye, Maze Featuring Frankie Beverly was among the top R&B acts of the late '70s and '80s. The distinctive Maze and its charismatic lead singer, founder, producer, and songwriter Beverly didn't have many pop hits, but they were extremely popular among soul and urban contemporary audiences and enjoyed at least six or seven gold albums. Beverly was born Howard Beverly in Philadelphia, PA, on December 6, 1946; he started calling himself Frankie after hearing Frankie Lymon & the Teenagers (a major doo wop group) when he was only nine years old in 1956. Before that, Beverly had been singing gospel in church, and it was Lymon who made him realize that he wanted to perform secular music. That isn't to say that Beverly's appreciation of gospel ever went away; the gospel influence remained when he was in his forties and fifties, but secular R&B would be his main focus.

When Beverly was 12, he joined the Philly doo wop group the Silhouettes (who were known for their hit "Get a Job") and went on tour with them in 1959. Then, in the early '60s, he founded and led a short-lived doo wop/soul vocal group called the Blenders. After the Blenders' breakup, a 17-year-old Beverly founded another vocal group in 1963: the Butlers, who favored a Northern soul approach. The Butlers never became well-known nationally, although they did provide a few singles (including "The Sun's Message" and "She Tried to Kiss Me") and recorded for small, Philly based labels like Fairmount, Liberty Bell, and Guyden. The Butlers also recorded for Gamble Records, a small label that was named after producer/songwriter Kenny Gamble (who went on to co-own a huge R&B empire when he ran Philadelphia International Records with fellow Philadelphian Leon Huff in the '70s).

It was in 1970 that Beverly founded the band that eventually came to be known as Maze Featuring Frankie Beverly. Originally, Maze went by Raw Soul; using that name, it recorded three singles for Philly's small Gregar label in the early '70s (one of which was a cover of bluesman Taj Mahal's "Today May Not Be Your Day"). Although Beverly was born and raised in Philly, he has been quoted as saying that he never thought of himself as part of the Philly sound, and while his band does have Philly influences, it didn't fit into either the Gamble & Huff/Philadelphia International school of Philly soul or the Thom Bell/Linda Creed school (which the Delfonics, the Moments, and the Stylistics were a part of). Further, Raw Soul's sound owed as much to Marvin Gaye and the Isley Brothers as it did to any of the soulsters who came out of Philly in the '60s or '70s.

Feeling out of place in his home town, Beverly moved Raw Soul to the San Francisco Bay Area in 1971. Raw Soul had been playing the San Francisco/Oakland scene for several years when Beverly's idol, Marvin Gaye, became aware of the band. Quite impressed by Beverly's singing and songwriting, Gaye sang Raw Soul's praises to Capitol and helped them land a deal with that major label in 1976. One thing Gaye *didn't* like about Beverly's band was the name Raw Soul. The late soul giant insisted on a name change and after considering a few other names (including Karma and Charisma), Raw Soul officially became Maze Featuring Frankie Beverly in 1976. (The name Karma wouldn't have worked because an obscure, L.A.-based funk/jazz outfit called Karma was recording for A&M around 1976-1977).

Maze's self-titled debut album was released by Capitol in 1977; that album (which contains the hits "Happy Feelin's," "While I'm Alone," and "Lady of Magic") went gold and earned Maze an extremely devoted following. The band's 1977 lineup consisted of Beverly on lead vocals and rhythm guitar, Wayne Thomas on lead guitar, Sam Porter on keyboards, Ronald "Roame" Lowry and McKinley "Bug" Williams on percussion and background vocals, and Joe Provost on drums. In 1978, Provost was replaced by Ahaguna G. Sun, formerly of a little-known soul/funk group called Sunbear; subsequently, Sun was replaced by Billy "Shoes" Johnson. There were other personnel changes along the way; keyboardist Phillip Woo (formerly of Roy Ayers' band Ubiquity) joined Maze in 1980, and Ron Smith was the guitarist who replaced Thomas. But regardless of who was coming or going, Maze always reflected Beverly's vision—Beverly was to Maze what George Clinton was to Parliament/Funkadelic.

Maze's second album, *Golden Time of Day* was released in 1978 and contains the number-nine R&B hit "Workin' Together." *Golden Time of Day* went gold, as did 1979's *Inspiration* and 1980's *Joy and Pain* (the album that gave us the major hit "Southern Girl"). In the late '70s, Maze earned a reputation for having one of the best live shows in R&B and their first live album, *Live in New Orleans* (a two-LP set), came out in 1981. Another live double-LP, *Live in Los Angeles*, was released in 1986, which was the year after Maze's funky "Back in Stride" reached number one on *Billboard*'s R&B singles chart and became their biggest hit ever.

In 1989, Maze left Capitol for Warner Bros. and recorded *Silky Soul*; the title track, an ode to Marvin Gaye, was a major hit. By that time, Maze was receiving a lot of attention from the rap world—their recordings were being sampled extensively by hip-hoppers. In 1988, rapper Rob Base used the chorus of Maze's "Joy and Pain" on a single that had the same title—unfortunately, Base did so without permission and Beverly threatened legal action. Maze didn't enjoy many hits in the '90s, although their live shows continued to be well-received by a very devoted fan base. *—Alex Henderson*

Maze Featuring Frankie Beverly / 1977 / Capitol ♦♦♦♦♦
At a time when disco reigned supreme, Maze & Frankie Beverly took the R&B charts by storm with a smooth yet gritty soul/funk approach that rejected the disco beat entirely. Growing up in the soul hotbed of Philadelphia had a definite impact on Maze's distinctive sound, which owed as much to Marvin Gaye as it did to Philly soul. Classics like "While I'm Alone," "Lady of Magic," "You," and the hit "Happy Feelin's" earned Maze an intensely devoted bunch of followers, who will tell you in a minute that the charismatic Beverly is the very essence of a soul singer. Though it wasn't a single, one of the best offerings on the album is "Colorblind," a jewel expressing Beverly's frustration over the racial polarization that plagued the U.S. in 1977 and remained alive and well years later. This outstanding debut album didn't do much in the pop market, but thanks to enthusiastic support from the R&B market, it went gold. *—Alex Henderson*

Golden Time of Day / 1978 / Capitol ♦♦♦
Maze & Frankie Beverly had a lot to live up to when the time came to record a second album, and while *Golden Time of Day* isn't quite as strong as their magnificent debut, it's nonetheless an excellent soul/funk offering. Disco was still incredibly popular in 1978, but it had little impact on Maze, which continued to avoid disco's hyper tendencies and favored a comfortable, more relaxed soul groove instead. The idealistic "Workin' Together" (a call for unity) and the reflective title song were well received by black radio, and the poignant album track "Song for My Mother" never became the hit single it should have been. On pop stations, Maze still couldn't get arrested. But a lack of pop support certainly didn't prevent *Golden Time of Day* from going gold. *—Alex Henderson*

Inspiration / 1979 / Razor & Tie ♦♦♦♦♦
Arguably Maze's best album, hands down, *Inspiration* lives up to its grandiose title. Frankie Beverly's compositions are executed to perfection by the seven-piece Maze ensemble: Ahaguna G. Sun (drums), Wayne Thomas (lead guitar), Sam Porter (keyboards), McKinley Williams (vocals & percussion), Roame Lowry (vocals & congas), Robin Duhe (bass), and Frankie Beverly on rhythm guitar and lead vocals—the originals. If you're still down after listening to "Lovely Inspiration"'s positive, glowing, shimmering praise to the Supreme One, you have some serious issues. The fusion of R&B and reggae on "Feel That You're Feelin'" fueled its way up the R&B chart rungs; it remains a staple of Maze's live show. It's hard to get any better than "Call Me," on which Beverly outdoes himself during a sensitive, tear-jerking confession of a man whose woman left him for another; the parting is handled with maturity, and the lamenting lover extends an invitation for his ex to call him if it doesn't work out, or if she has a change of heart. Just as inspiring is the spirited "Timin'," a rollicking number about keeping your spirits up, because if it doesn't work out, it's not solely your fault, it's just a matter of timin'; why Capitol held back on this track is mystifying, since it has all the elements of a monster. That kick-happy beat is extended to "Welcome Home," a tune about a lover returning after discovering the grass wasn't greener on the other side of the fence. "Women Is a Wonder" is a slow tribute to women featuring some tantalizing guitar notes from Thomas; very nice, but a better bet if the supplementary vocals hadn't been buried so deep in the mix. Captivating, tinkling chimes introduce the laid-back "Ain't It Strange"; the vocal interaction between Beverly, Duhe, Williams, and Lowry are reminiscent of the Frankie Beverly & the Butlers years. An instrumental version of "Lovely Inspiration" ends the masterpiece. *—Andrew Hamilton*

Joy and Pain / 1980 / Razor & Tie ♦♦♦♦♦
With their fourth album, *Joy and Pain*, Maze & Frankie Beverly once again went gold with little or no support from pop radio. One of the band's most celebrated releases, this classic soared to the top of the R&B charts thanks to such hits as "Southern Girl" and the haunting title song (which, in 1988, rapper Rob Base would use without Beverly's permission). In interviews, Beverly expressed some disappointment over the fact that Capitol promoted Maze as strictly an R&B act and made no effort to promote *Joy and Pain* to pop audiences. And yet, Beverly wasn't about to become less R&B-oriented in order to cross over—his contention was that like Al Green and Marvin Gaye, he could reach pop radio without having to compromise. An essential album, *Joy and Pain* is the work of a band that made consistently rewarding soul and funk by sticking to its guns. *—Alex Henderson*

Live in New Orleans / 1981 / Capitol ♦♦♦♦

Maze / 1982 / Capitol ♦♦♦
Formerly known as Raw Soul, Frankie Beverly and his band took a new name when they relocated from Philadelphia to San Francisco, as well as broadening their style from mainly standard soul to a funk/soul hybrid. They signed with Capitol in the mid-'70s, and their first album under the new pact was their finest set, with Beverly's energetic lead vocals and an excellent band that included keyboardists Phillip Woo and Sam Porter, bassist Robin Duhe, and guitarist Ron Smith. They made an immediate impact with their hard-driving sound, not as strictly on the beat as the Dayton bands like the Ohio Players or Slave, but just as soulful. *—Ron Wynn*

We Are One / 1983 / Capitol ♦♦♦♦
The northern California-based octet presents an album with the supreme focus being love and understanding. The first release, "Love Is the Key," temphasizes this by the title alone.

An uplifting composition that features a tantalizing keyboard solo, it peaked at number five on the *Billboard* R&B charts. "Never Let You Down," the title track and "I Wanna Thank You" were also releases; the highest charted single of three was the compassionate "Never Let You Down," which managed to peak at number 27. The majority of the album is written and arranged in the same vein. As simplistic as these recordings are, each song still manages to offers its own unique appeal. With the exception of "Love Is the Key," none of these songs were chart-busters. Nonetheless, the album exceeded sales of 500,000, signifying how popular these songs were among Maze followers and remain to this day. *—Craig Lytle*

Can't Stop the Love / 1985 / Razor & Tie ♦♦♦

Live in Los Angeles / 1986 / Capitol ♦♦♦

Silky Soul / Sep. 1989 / Warner Bros. ♦♦♦♦

In 1989, many of the soul and funk bands that emerged in the '70s had either broken up or disappeared from the charts. But Maze Featuring Frankie Beverly was not only hanging in there—it was still selling a lot of albums. Released in 1989, *Silky Soul* was yet another big seller for Maze; it was also the band's first Warner Bros. release (after more than a decade at Capitol). On *Silky Soul*, Beverly favors a more high-tech production style than he had in the past. Maze's founder and lead singer knew that urban radio was very technology-minded, and he makes some urban contemporary moves by using more synthesizers and drum machines. Nonetheless, *Silky Soul* is state-of-the-art Maze. In fact, *Silky Soul* is an appropriate title for this CD because tracks like the funky "Love's on the Run" and the melancholy "Can't Get Over You" are essentially soul music—the production style is more urban contemporary, but Beverly's singing and writing is still that of a soul man whose musical personality was shaped by the classic R&B of the '60s and '70s. Marvin Gaye is still a prominent influence, and Beverly pays tribute to the late soul singer on the hit title song. *Silky Soul*'s title track is simply brilliant—parts of the tune allude to Gaye's "What's Going On," but without obscuring Maze's own distinctive personality. Another great track is "Mandela," which calls for the release of South African freedom fighter Nelson Mandela. In 1989, Mandela was still confined to a South African prison, but after the racist apartheid system was ended, he became South Africa's president. An excellent album, *Silky Soul* demonstrated that Maze could be relevant to 1989's urban contemporary scene without being unfaithful to its soul roots. *—Alex Henderson*

The Greatest Hits of Maze . . . Lifelines, Vol. 1 / Nov. 8, 1989 / Capitol ♦♦♦♦

When the Philadelphia band Raw Soul moved to San Francisco in the mid-'70s, they changed their name to Maze and made Frankie Beverly their lead singer. Beverly's personality and exuberance and their evolution into one of the tightest bands on the soul scene turned Maze into an institution. This collects formative hits from their years on Capitol, including "Golden Time of Day" and "Joy and Pain." It shows that they were both an enjoyable uptempo and funk band and a convincing ballad and love song ensemble. *—Ron Wynn*

Back to Basics / 1993 / Warner Bros. ♦♦

• **Anthology** / Jan. 23, 1996 / Capitol ♦♦♦♦♦

Maze has been a fan favorite since the mid-'70s; while they've received little critical notice or adulation except among soul and R&B scribes, Maze has seldom been out of the charts since making their debut on Capitol. Lead singer Frankie Beverly's roots extend back to classic doo wop and East Coast soul; although he made the transition to funk, then urban material, Beverly always had plenty of soul and passion in his vocals. Maze also blazed their own musical trail; when such competitors as Earth, Wind & Fire, the Bar-Kays, Con Funk Shun, and Slave were featuring surging horn sections and jazz-tinged arrangements with heavy basslines, Beverly and company favored rock-influenced guitar parts juxtaposed against soulful organ riffs or synthesizer riffs and just a trace of reggae and/or Latin rhythm. Beverly enjoyed several hits on Capitol, but became unsatisfied with their inability to break the group beyond the R&B/funk market. They departed Capitol in the late '80s, and resurfaced on Warner Bros., where they continued making strong, distinctive releases. *Anthology* gathers the best (at least most of the best) singles the band did for Capitol, among them classics like "Southern Girl," "Before I Let Go," the complete "Joy and Pain" and "Happy Feeling." Despite being only an 18-cut, single-disc release, there's a completeness not often available in a single CD set. British journalist David Nathan's notes are comprehensive, and nicely combine anecdotal and discographical references. While it would be good if Capitol and Warner Bros. could combine on a multi-disc set, until (or if) that happens, here's a fine tribute to one of R&B's most underrated and consistently enjoyable bands. *—Ron Wynn*

Greatest Slow Jams / Sep. 8, 1998 / Capitol ♦♦♦♦

Inspiration/Joy and Pain / Jul. 13, 1999 / Capitol ♦♦♦♦♦

Maze Featuring Frankie Beverly/Golden Time of Day / Jul. 13, 1999 / Capitol ♦♦♦♦

Music critic Jonathan Gold once compared Maze fans to Grateful Dead fans. That might seem like an odd comparison—those two bands don't sound anything alike, although both have a Bay Area connection. But then, Gold was comparing their audiences, not their music. And his analogy is a good one because Maze fans have the sort of intense, unwavering devotion that Deadheads are known for. A concert, like the Dead's concert, is more than a concert—it's almost like a secular revival meeting. Serious Maze devotees will tell you that its music is the essence of soul, and listening to this release, it isn't hard to see why they feel that way. Assembled in 1999, this two-CD set contains its first two albums: its self-titled debut album of 1977 and its sophomore effort, *Golden Time of Day* (1978). Though *Maze Featuring Frankie Beverly* is the more essential of the two, *Golden Time of Day* is also excellent. These are the albums that put Maze on the map and established Frankie Beverly as one of R&B's true heavyweights; gritty yet polished classics like "Happy Feelin's," "Lady of Magic," and "Look at California" made Maze a household word in R&B. When these two albums came out in the late 1970s, it was obvious that Maze & Frankie Beverly weren't bandwagon jumpers. Their distinctive sound—an appealing blend of Philly soul and Marvin Gaye—wasn't relevant to the disco scene. And even though this double-CD contains some infectious funk grooves ("Workin' Together," "Colorblind"), it isn't the sort of hard, gutbucket funk that Parliament/Funkadelic, Cameo, and the Bar-Kays were providing—Maze's funk was a smoother, more laid-back style. Anyone with a taste for 1970s soul should make a point of obtaining this double-CD. *—Alex Henderson*

We Are One/Can't Stop the Love / Jul. 13, 1999 / Capitol ♦♦♦♦

Toussaint McCall

Vocals, Organ / Soul, Black Gospel, Soul-Jazz, R&B

At times a stirring soul balladeer, organist/vocalist Toussaint McCall doesn't have a lengthy string of hits. But his 1967 version of "Nothing Takes the Place of You" was among that year's finest performances. It gave McCall his lone R&B hit, reaching number five. It was one of two singles he had that year for Ronn that clicked, the other being "I'll Do It For You," which made the Top 30. *—Ron Wynn*

Nothing Takes the Place of You / 1967 / Ronn ♦♦♦♦

• **Nothing Takes the Place of You: The Ronn Recordings** / Feb. 6, 2001 / Fuel 2000 ♦♦♦♦♦

Mighty Sam McClain

b. 1941, Monroe, LA

Vocals / Soul-Blues, Retro-Soul, Modern Electric Blues

Vocalist Mighty Sam McClain is a specialist in Southern soul-blues, one of the original masters from the 1960s, when the music enjoyed its peak popularity. Like so many other soul-blues vocalists, McClain began singing gospel in a choir. He left home at 13 and later hooked up with Little Melvin Underwood, working first as a valet but then as a featured vocalist in his road show. While working in Florida, he recorded Patsy Cline's hit "Sweet Dreams." After this, visits to Muscle Shoals yielded singles like "Fannie Mae" and "In the Same Old Way." He also recorded a single for Malaco and two singles for Atlantic in 1971 before falling out of the music scene for over a decade.

He returned in the mid-'80s, recording a single for Orleans Records as part of a band and appearing on *Hubert Sumlin's Blues Party* for BlackTop in 1987. McClain began to re-establish his former reputation as a great soul-blues singer, touring with Sumlin and his entourage. He finally recorded a studio album under his own name with 1992's *Give It Up to Love*, followed by 1995's *Keep on Moving* and *Sledgehammer Soul and Down Home Blues* one year later. Most of the songs on all three albums utilize a full horn section, and on top of this ride McClain's deep, powerful vocals, oftentimes in self-penned songs. Since the late '80s, McClain's career has been on the upswing again, as he's put together some great backing bands and carved a niche for himself in Europe. *—Richard Skelly*

Live in Japan / 1988 / Orleans ♦♦♦

A sophisticated bluesman in the tradition of Bobby "Blue" Bland or Joe Williams, Mighty Sam McClain had not recorded in some 13 years when he cut a demo of song called "Pray" in 1984. The demo attracted the attention of a Japanese promoter, who subsequently coordinated the Japanese tour from which this live album, recorded in Tokyo, is culled. Despite the presence of ace session guitarist Wayne Bennett, McClain's backing band is sub-standard and lifeless; few moments generate any heat. *—Jason Ankeny*

Give It up to Love / Nov. 1992 / AudioQuest ♦♦♦♦

McClain sings soul with incredible power—he knows when to pull the punches and when to cool it down. "Give It Up to Love," the title track, acknowledges his gospel roots; he performs it as a vocal prayer to God asking for wisdom, love, and strength. Bruce Katz's contributions on B-3 Hammond organ expands McClain's sound, particularly on the "Green Onions"-influenced "What You Want Me to Do." The sparsely effective arrangement on "Here I Go Falling in Love Again" brings McClain up front as he cries of being a soul stripped to the bare bones. Kevin Barry's funky bass blows while McClain declares himself as a child of God in "Child of the Mighty Mighty." *—Char Ham*

• **Papa True Love: The Amy Sessions** / Jul. 18, 2000 / Sundazed ♦♦♦♦

This compilation of the singer's prime 1960s work has both sides of his eight 1966-1968 Amy singles, as well as "Nothing but the Truth" from Bell's LP *Bell's Cellar of Soul Vol. 2* and a previously unreleased 1966 cover of Don Gibson's "A Stranger to Me." Mighty Sam was a good 1960s Southern soul singer, but not a great one; the kinds of people who collect this sort of stuff can go back and forth as to whether he was a top-of-the-second-division artist or the best of a journeyman class. Often he sounded like a somewhat bluesier Otis Redding, more apt to break into growly rasps, though not as inclined in that direction as, say, James Brown was. "Sweet Dreams (Of You)" in particular seems like a conscious emulation of the kind of success Otis Redding was having in 1965-1966 with wrenching ballads like "I've Been Loving You Too Long." He did benefit from a few Spooner Oldham-Dan Penn compositions but didn't get the sort of classic material that might have made him more than a cult favorite. All that taken into consideration, this remains a fairly solid platter of little-known soul music, the vocalist shining brightest on midtempo tunes that have him pleading a case without getting too sentimental. The production's pretty good as well, with frequent stinging blues-soul guitar licks and eerie organ of the kind made famous on Percy Sledge's "When a Man Loves a Woman." *—Richie Unterberger*

Bobby McClure

b. Apr. 21, 1942, Chicago, IL, **d.** Nov. 13, 1992, Los Angeles, CA

Vocals / Chicago Soul, Urban, Soul, R&B

Soul singer Bobby McClure was born on April 21, 1942, in Chicago, IL. By the time of his second birthday, his family had relocated to St. Louis, and by the age of nine, McClure had begun singing in church. His fine tenor voice quickly caught the attention of others, as he sang with several of the area's best-known gospel groups, including the Soul Stirrers, which Sam Cooke was singing lead with at the time. It wasn't long though until McClure tried his hand at singing other musical styles, including R&B and doo wop, honing his talents with such outfits as Bobby & the Vocals, drummer Big Daddy Jenkins' band, and singing in renowned bandleader Oliver Sain's outfit. McClure also took a pair of up-and-coming artists under his wing, Little Milton and Fontella Bass, who would both go on to successful music careers (McClure and Bass would eventually record a duet together in 1965, "Don't Mess Up a Good Thing," which was a U.S. Top 40 hit). During the '60s, McClure had relocated back to Chicago, where he worked with both Otis Clay and Little Milton, before moving to St. Louis, where he duetted with Shirley Brown and recording a few singles for the Memphis-based Hi label. Although McClure would record a few singles during the '80s, for the most part, he turned his back on music, working as a corrections officer in an Illinois penitentiary. But he couldn't stay out of music for long, as he moved to Los Angeles to play with others and record. But McClure's career was cut short on November 13, 1992, when he died at the age of 50 from a stroke following a brain aneurysm. *—Greg Prato*

- **Bobby McClure & Willie Clayton** / 1992 / Hi ✦✦✦

Marilyn McCoo

b. Sep. 30, 1943, Jersey City, NJ

Vocals / Adult Contemporary, Soft Rock, Pop, Inspirational, Soul

Vocalist Marilyn McCoo is featured on the 5th Dimension's million-selling hits "Wedding Bell Blues," "One Less Bell to Answer," and "(Last Night) I Didn't Get to Sleep at All." In the mid-'70s, McCoo and husband Billy Davis Jr. left the 5th Dimension and began performing as a duo. Landing a contract with ABC Records, they recorded their 1976 debut album, *I Hope We Get to Love in Time*, with Detroit producer Don Davis (Johnny Taylor, the Dramatics). The first single was the title track, which was a mid-chart hit. The second single, "You Don't Have to Be a Star (To Be in My Show)," went to number one on both the R&B and pop charts during January 1977. Motown great James Jamerson is featured on bass. McCoo & Davis were awarded a gold single and a gold album their first time out. The third single, "Your Love," went Top Ten R&B and Top 20 pop.

In the summer of 1977, the couple had their own variety show, *The Marilyn McCoo and Billy Davis Jr. Show*, on CBS. Their next ABC album, 1977's *The Two of Us*, was produced by Motown alumni Frank Wilson (Eddie Kendricks, New Birth) and boasted the singles "Look What You've Done to My Heart," "Wonderful," the ballad "My Reason to Be Is You," and the tender title track. Switching to Columbia Records, their *Marilyn & Billy* album was released during the fall of in 1978. One charting single, a cover of "Shine on Silvery Moon," became a favorite in disco clubs.

McCoo recorded her first solo LP for RCA Records, with the single "Heart Stop Beating in Time," written by the Bee Gees, being a small hit. Other solo albums by McCoo are *White Christmas* (1996) and *The Me Nobody Knows* (1991). During the '80s, McCoo hosted the nationally syndicated pop music show *Solid Gold* and appeared on NBC shows *Night Court* and the soap opera *Days of Our Lives*. She also took to the stage, appearing in *Dreamgirls*, *Showboat*, and *Man of La Mancha*. McCoo and Davis continue to perform around the country in concerts (some being 5th Dimension reunions) and musicals such as *It Takes Two* and *Hit With a Hot Note!: The Duke Ellington Songbook*, and celebrated their 30th wedding anniversary with a cover story in the August 9, 1999, issue of *Jet* magazine. *—Ed Hogan*

- **I Hope We Get to Love in Time** / 1976 / Razor & Tie ✦✦✦

Former Fifth Dimension members Marilyn McCoo & Billy Davis Jr. hit gold the first time out. Produced by Don Davis (Johnnie Taylor, the Dramatics), the charming million-selling single "You Don't Have to Be a Star (To Be in My Show)" went to number one on *Billboard*'s R&B and pop charts in 1976. Other highlights from their debut LP include the upbeat followup single, "Your Love," and the languid title track. The couple performed some of the songs on their CBS summer variety series. In 1999, they appeared on the cover of *Jet* magazine and on a segment of Jamie Foxx's WB sitcom. *I Hope We Get to Love in Time* was reissued as a 1996 Razor & Tie CD. *—Ed Hogan*

Marilyn & Billy / 1978 / Columbia ✦✦

You immediately notice the reversal of billing, since the duo began as Billy Davis and Marilyn McCoo; granted, the female name should have been first all along, but McCoo's solo success doubtlessly prompted the change. This disjointed album mixes MOR with Southern whoop-'em-ups. Their revival of Sam & Dave's "I Thank You," and "Carry On," a deep soul drama, don't cotton with poppy ballads like "I Thought It Took a Little Time" and the original rendition of "Saving All My Love for You," which Whitney Houston elevated to new heights years later. The bouncy "I Got the Music, You Got the Words" owes its foundation and being to LTD's "Back in Love Again." *—Andrew Hamilton*

The Me Nobody Knows / Aug. 13, 1991 / Warner Alliance ✦✦✦

The Me Nobody Knows is one of Marilyn McCoo's more ambitious albums, finding her exploring laid-back, jazzy soul, as well as Caribbean rhythms. A few of the songs fall flat, yet McCoo is in good voice and the production is appealingly polished, making this one of her better latter-day efforts. *—Rodney Batdorf*

Van McCoy

b. Jan. 6, 1944, Washington, D.C., **d.** Jul. 6, 1979, Englewood, NJ

Vocals, Songwriter, Piano, Producer / Disco, Soul

Producer/composer Van McCoy had a lengthy career in R&B, soul, and dance music, although he is best known by the general public for "The Hustle." But McCoy's experiences dated back to the '50s, when he sang with both the Marylanders and in the Starlighters with his brother. The Starlighters cut three singles for End in 1959. McCoy had his own label, Rock 'N, in 1960 and became an A&R man at Scepter/Wand from 1961 to 1964. He penned numbers for Chuck Jackson, the Shirelles, Jackie Wilson ("I Get the Sweetest Feeling"), and Ruby & the Romantics ("When You're Young and in Love"), and produced sessions by the Shirelles, Gladys Knight, and the Drifters.

McCoy also ran Vando and Share and owned Maxx during the '60s, supervising such artists as Chris Bartley and the Ad-Libs. He later created Van McCoy Productions in 1968, and formed Faith, Hope & Charity in the early '70s before becoming a solo artist and signing with Avco. "The Hustle" was a number-one R&B and pop hit in 1975, as well as a gold single. McCoy also had a Top Ten R&B hit with "Change With the Times" that same year, also on Avco. He continued on "H&L" and MCA through 1976. McCoy wrote and produced material for Gladys Knight & the Pips, Aretha Franklin, Linda Clifford, Stacy Lattisaw, Melba Moore, and Barbara Lewis before he died in 1979. *—Ron Wynn*

Disco Baby / 1975 / Avco Embassy ✦✦✦

One thing Van McCoy could never be accused of when he was alive was refusing to keep up with the times. In the '60s, he made a name for himself by writing or producing for such prominent soulsters as Jackie Wilson, the Drifters, Chuck Jackson, and Gladys Knight & the Pips. But when the disco era started in the mid-'70s, McCoy got in on the ground floor. Released in 1975, *Disco Baby* is among the albums that helped to usher in the disco era. This LP boasts McCoy's number-one hit "The Hustle," which became one of disco's anthems and is the song that he is best remembered for. For McCoy, an album like *Disco Baby* was a major departure from the type of things he had done in the '60s and early '70s: Back then, his focus was writing, producing, or arranging for vocalists. But on *Disco Baby*, vocal personality isn't the main thing: This album is primarily about the beat, the track, and the production. Except for "The Hustle"—which pop and black radio couldn't get enough of—*Disco Baby* was much more of a club record than a radio record. Club DJs, not radio programmers, were the only ones who looked beyond "The Hustle" and paid attention to the BT Express-like title song or McCoy's slick, symphonic versions of the Ohio Players' "Fire," the Temptations' "Shakey Ground," Carol Douglas' "Doctor's Orders," and other hits of 1974 and 1975. To be sure, *Disco Baby* is so club-oriented and producer-driven that its limitations become obvious outside of a club setting. But despite those limitations, *Disco Baby* is an enjoyable and groovin', if clichéd, artifact of its time. *—Alex Henderson*

The Disco Kid / 1975 / Avco Embassy ✦✦✦

Too much, too soon—those are the only words to describe Van McCoy's second 1975 effort (or third, if you count the 1972 LP that shot into the charts on the heels of his massive, monstrous, genre-defining "The Hustle" single). That said, this rushed set is another slick and highly styled combo of instrumental proto-disco swishes and balladeering. However, coming just six months after *Disco Baby* topped the charts, the songs here just end up feeling like rehashes, with the title track in particular little more than "The Hustle" in disguise. "Keep on Hustlin'," meanwhile, does just what it implies, and even the funky "Roll With the Punches" is sliced clean through with a "Hustle"-styled chorus. But at the time, moms and dads and clubbers just couldn't get enough of McCoy, and *The Disco Kid*'s Top 20 spot is testament to that. To his credit, McCoy does manage to keep the swings and balances poised with a handful of soulful ballads that focus more on his vocals than on the strings and sighs of America's hottest dance mania. Both "Words Spoken Softly at Midnight" and a cover of "I'm Gonna Love You" are tenderly wrought, proof that even though McCoy may have been cashing in (and who wouldn't), he was still interested in sincerity and was singing for his own enjoyment. *—Amy Hanson*

- **The Hustle and the Best of Van McCoy** / 1976 / H&L ✦✦✦✦✦

Originally released in 1976, these 15 tracks showcase Van McCoy's alter ego as a purveyor of perky disco, a striking contrast from the memorable soul tunes (e.g., "Sweet Bitter Love," "Giving Up," "Right on the Tip of My Tongue," "Sweetest Thing This Side of Heaven," and "When You're Young and In Love") that made him a fat cat in the '60s. A good buy for the sophisticated club dancers to slide in every now and then and test their motor skills. It contains bonus tracks that weren't on the original vinyl platter—but why shouldn't there be, since the CD costs more. *—Andrew Hamilton*

The Real McCoy / 1976 / H&L ✦✦✦

Though released only a year after his smash disco anthem, "The Hustle," the material on *The Real McCoy* doesn't quite hold up as well as the above-mentioned ubiquitous track. Awash with lush strings, horny voices and a pulsing rhythm section, the songs sound so dated you can almost feel the shag carpeting under your feet during tunes like "Jet Setting" and "Night Walk." Furthermore, with a disco version of "Theme From Star Trek" and a portrait of a rhinestoned McCoy on the album sleeve, the kitsch factor is on high during most of *The Real McCoy*. Unless you're into high camp or need a score for the '70s-themed adult movie you're shooting, it's best to avoid this album altogether and opt for the hundreds of disco compilations that invariably contain "The Hustle." *—Steve Kurutz*

My Favourite Fantasy / 1978 / MCA ✦✦

Lonely Dancer / 1979 / MCA ✦✦✦

Although most people associate Van McCoy with his production work for the likes of Gladys Knight & the Pips and the Stylistics, or for "The Hustle," the 1975 disco hit that spawned a hundred imitators, it's important to remember that McCoy created an enormous body of solo work before his early death from a heart attack in 1979. And his final album, *Lonely Dancer*, while not perhaps his best-ever work, becomes, in hindsight, a poignant sign-off from this often overlooked and underrated musician. Equally at home with pure-driven disco and sweet, soulful ballads, McCoy divides his time between the two styles across the LP—and, yes, there is a "Hustle-esque" song included here, as "the Samba" revisits his best-known stomping ground. But that song, in actuality, is one of the album's throwaways; McCoy emerges much stronger across the flashy, grungy disco of the mammoth seven-minute opus "Lonely Dancer," a song that really should have been a hit. Where *Lonely Dancer* takes its nicest turn, however, is across the tender ballads, which slow the mirror-ball ethics. They may be construed as slightly clichéd, with their overly lush strings and heartfelt backing vocals, but they also spotlight McCoy singing songs you could actually believe HE believed in. "Merry Go Round" is his best example, but McCoy repeats the process across "Decisions" and "I Wish You Well," and, with hindsight, one wonders if these songs are autobiographical goodbyes of sorts. The feeling of finality that permeates *Lonely Dancer* may merely be an imprint of circumstance, but it may not. What is clear is that Van McCoy wasn't just a one-dance man. And this set proves that he shouldn't have been treated as a one-off joke. *—Amy Hanson*

Jimmy McCracklin

b. Aug. 13, 1921, St. Louis, MO
Vocals, Piano, Leader / Soul-Blues, West Coast Blues, Contemporary Blues, Piano Blues, R&B
A full half-century from when he started out in the blues business, Jimmy McCracklin is still touring, recording, and acting like a much younger man. In fact, he vehemently disputes his commonly accepted birthdate—but since he began recording back in 1945, it seems reasonable. After moving to the West Coast in the mid-'40s, McCracklin recorded for a daunting array of tiny labels in Los Angeles and Oakland prior to touching down with Modern, Swing Time and Peacock for approximately two-year hitches. By 1954, the pianist was back with Modern logo and really coming into his own with a sax-driven sound.

After a few sessions for Irma in 1956 came McCracklin's first major hit "The Walk," a rudimentary dance number on Checker that hit the Top Ten on both the R&B and pop charts. The nomadic pianist returned to the hit parade with the tough R&B workout "Just Got to Know" in 1961 for Art-Tone. McCracklin's songwriting skills shouldn't be overlooked as an integral factor in his enduring success. He penned the funky hit "Tramp" for his old pal, guitarist Lowell Fulson. Ever the survivor, McCracklin made a string of LPs for Imperial and segued into the soul era totally painlessly. Two recent discs for Bullseye Blues prove that McCracklin still packs a knockout punch from behind his piano—no matter what his birth certificate says. *—Bill Dahl*

I Just Gotta Know / 1961 / Imperial ✦✦✦✦✦
It's always a "Shame, Shame, Shame" (to quote one of this LP's best numbers) when a 35-year-old slab of vinyl must be cited as what may be an artist's finest collection—but since no one has yet touched McCracklin's massive '60s Imperial catalog for CD reissue, here you go! Contains his definitive soul-tinged ballad "Just Got to Know," the Amos Milburn-derived jump blues "Club Savoy," and several more late-'50s rockers that Imperial acquired from various small concerns after he began to hit with regularity. *—Bill Dahl*

Twist With Jimmy McCracklin / 1961 / Crown ✦✦✦✦
Undoubtedly it was a mite difficult to twist to jump blues records from the mid-'50s, but this budget LP at least gave McCracklin's Modern catalog renewed life in the Crown catalog. Some of his best 1950s rockers: the hilarious "Couldn't Be a Dream," "You Don't Seem to Understand," "Reelin' and Rockin'," "I'm Gonna Tell Your Mother." Overdue for CD reissue!! *—Bill Dahl*

My Answer / 1966 / Imperial ✦✦✦✦✦
Conveniently enough, Imperial slapped together what amounts to a greatest-hits set here, and it long served as the best available introduction to the pianist's '60s catalog. Contains "Just Got to Know," "Every Night, Every Day," "Think," "Steppin' Up in Class," and the title item—every one of them occupying an intriguing island midway between blues and soul. *—Bill Dahl*

High on the Blues / 1971 / Stax ✦✦✦
Given that this was co-produced by Al Jackson (of Booker T. & the MG's) and Willie Mitchell (of Hi Records), and adds embellishment by the Memphis Horns, it's unsurprising that this is very much a soul-blues record. It's a workmanlike effort with an early-'70s Stax period feel, including remakes of two of his past R&B singles, "Think" and "Just Got to Know." The CD reissue adds a couple of previously unreleased bonus tracks. *—Richie Unterberger*

The Mercury Recordings / 1992 / Bear Family ✦✦✦✦
McCracklin's liaison with Mercury was relatively brief, from late 1958 to the fall of 1960, and Bear Family has only managed to locate 13 songs for this CD. But it's a rewarding chapter in the pianist's endlessly nomadic recording career, featuring his original dance tunes "Georgia Slop" and "Let's Do It (The Chicken Scratch)," a New Orleans-cut cover of Johnny Cash's "Folsom Prison Blues," and some smoothly arranged (by Clyde Otis, Brook Benton's collaborator) pop/R&B outings that suggest Mercury had big plans for McCracklin that never quite panned out. *—Bill Dahl*

● **The Walk: Jimmy McCracklin at His Best** / 1997 / Razor & Tie ✦✦✦✦✦
McCracklin has always been one of those artists whose currency always ran higher in the black blues community than it has in the subsequent years of white historical revision. But decent career retrospectives of McCracklin—who had sides issued on almost a dozen labels in as many years—on compact disc are somewhere between few and far between and non-existent. But this 20-track single-disc compilation goes a long way toward rectifying that situation. Containing his biggest hits (the title track, the original versions of "The Georgia Slop" and "Get Back"—later hits for Big Al Downing and Roy Head, respectively) along with the best of his Art-Tone and Imperial sides ("Just Got to Know" and "Every Night, Every Day," now both staples of the Chicago blues repertoire after being covered in the early '60s by Magic Sam), this makes a perfect introduction to his style as well as a powerful testament to his superb songwriting skills. *—Cub Koda*

Modern Recordings 1948–1950 / Jul. 27, 1999 / Ace ✦✦✦
Although McCracklin had already been recording for a few years, his association with Modern marked his first reasonably long tenure with an established label. This 25-track disc covers his first stay with the company, covering a half dozen singles, three songs that first showed up on the 1981 Ace album *And His Blues Blasters*, and ten demos, outtakes, and alternate takes that were previously unissued. It's solid small-combo West Coast jump blues, sometimes embellished by the tenor saxophone of Maxwell Davis. It's more interesting on the speedy, jumpy numbers, although McCracklin was competent at setting an after-hours vibe on the slower ones. The drums-piano-guitar trio, especially guitarist Robert Kelton, gets into a real frenetic groove on the 1948 instrumental "Blues Blasters' Shuffle"; "Hamburger Joint" is a silly novelty whose spoken repartee verges on sleaziness. In a more serious mood are two previously unissued McCracklin solo piano demos, "Mistreating Me" and "Bad Health Blues." *—Richie Unterberger*

George McCrae

b. Oct. 19, 1944, West Palm Beach, FL
Vocals / Disco, Soul
Along with wife Gwen McCrae, Miami-based artist George McCrae was a prime mover on the early disco front with his own R&B chart-topper "Rock Your Baby" in 1974. With disco kings Harry Casey and Richard Finch of KC & the Sunshine Band producing and writing his output on Henry Stone's T.K. label, McCrae rapidly returned with the double-sided hit "I Can't Leave You Alone"/"I Get Lifted," but fads being fickle, McCrae's fortunes slipped as the decade ensured. *—Bill Dahl*

Their Golden Classics / Aug. 5, 1993 / Collectables ✦✦✦
This is not an album of duets, since the then-married couple only sing one song together, "Winners Together or Losers Apart"; the rest is a cherry picking of individual releases on T.K. Records. This slim crop is far from comprehensive but does feature George's monster, 2-million plus seller "Rock Your Baby," the syncopated "I Get Lifted" and the robotic "Love In Motion." Gwen cranks her chart makers "Rockin' Chair," "Love Insurance" and "Damn Right I'm Good." While not the essences of either artist these 12 songs are a good sampling of both. *—Andrew Hamilton*

● **The Best of George McCrae: Rock Your Baby** / Feb. 1, 1995 / TK ✦✦✦✦

Gwen McCrae

b. Dec. 21, 1943, Pensacola, FL
Vocals / Disco, Club/Dance, Soul
Best remembered for her number-one R&B hit "Rockin' Chair" from 1975, Gwen McCrae was a gutsy Southern soul diva with a particular affinity for dance tracks. Along with her husband George ("Rock Your Baby"), Gwen was part of the Miami-based T.K. Records stable, which laid a great deal of groundwork for the disco explosion. Born Gwen Mosley in Pensacola, FL, in 1943, she grew up singing in her Pentecostal church and later discovered secular singers like Sam Cooke and Aretha Franklin. She began performing in local clubs as a teenager, also singing with local groups like the Lafayettes and the Independents. In 1963, she met a young Navy sailor named George McCrae, whom she married within a week. When George was discharged, he re-formed an earlier group he'd sung with called the Jivin' Jets, and invited Gwen to join as well. Soon, however, George and Gwen split off to form a duo—aptly dubbed George & Gwen—and moved to West Palm Beach to perform in clubs all over South Florida.

George & Gwen were discovered in 1967 by singer Betty Wright, who helped get them signed to Henry Stone's Alston label. Their debut single, "Three Hearts in a Tangle," was released in 1969; the follow-up, "Like Yesterday Our Love Is Gone," marked the first time they worked with the writing team of Clarence Reid (who would later morph into the bawdy comic Blowfly) and Willie Clarke. Both were regional hits, as was third single, "No One Left to Come Home," although none of those records broke nationally; meanwhile, the McCraes and Wright were collectively earning a reputation as stellar session vocalists. In 1970, one of Gwen's solo recordings, the Bobby "Blue" Bland cover "Lead Me On," was picked up by Columbia and became her first Top 40 hit on the R&B charts. In the wake of that breakthrough, George temporarily retired from singing to become her manager, and Alston leased her contract to Columbia; she recorded several more singles over the next few years, but without comparable chart success.

Columbia declined to renew McCrae's contract in 1973, and she was signed to a different Henry Stone label, the T.K. subsidiary Cat. She had a regional hit with "He Keeps Something Groovy Goin' On" that year, and then her second national hit with the R&B Top 20 "For Your Love" (originally recorded by Ed Townsend). However, her minor 1974 hit "It's Worth the Hurt" was overshadowed by George's across-the-board smash "Rock Your Baby," a song originally intended for Gwen that heralded disco's arrival on the pop charts. It was Gwen's turn in the spotlight the following year, when she took the sexy Reid/Clarke composition "Rockin' Chair" all the way to the top of the R&B charts, not to mention the pop Top Ten. In the wake of its success, McCrae released her first-ever album (also called *Rockin' Chair*) and scored further R&B hits with "Love Insurance" and "Cradle of Love."

By this time, the separate successes were taking their toll on the McCraes' marriage (Gwen has since alleged that her husband beat her frequently). A 1976 duet single, "Winners Together, Losers Apart," fell short of the R&B Top 40, and a full album of duets failed to assuage matters. The couple split later that year, and Gwen scored what turned out to be her last chart hit for Cat, "Damn Right It's Good." Despite a fine effort with the 1978 LP *Let's Straighten It Out*, McCrae's commercial momentum was stalled, and although 1979's "All This Love That I'm Giving" later became a favorite on Britain's Northern soul scene, it didn't attract much attention upon its release. With the T.K. label family in serious financial trouble, McCrae moved to New Jersey and signed with Atlantic in 1980, a stint that produced two albums (*Gwen McCrae* and *On My Way*) and several chart singles still prized by collectors: "Funky Sensation," "Poyson," and "Keep the Fire Burning." Feeling underpromoted, McCrae moved back to Florida, cut a one-off single for the small Black Jack label in 1984 called "Do You Know What I Mean," and retired from the music business.

McCrae was rediscovered by the British Northern soul and rare groove scenes during the '80s, and she traveled to England to record a couple of singles for Rhythm King in 1987. Pleased with her enduring popularity in the U.K., McCrae eventually recorded an entire album for the British Homegrown label in 1996, titled *Girlfriend's Boyfriend*. Upon returning to America, she signed with the revived Goldwax label, distributed by Ichiban, and recorded another album later that year, *Psychic Hot Line*. In 1998, Ichiban reissued *Girlfriend's Boyfriend* in the U.S. McCrae returned in 1999 with *Still Rockin'*, which received favorable reviews in blues and classic soul circles. *—Steve Huey*

Rockin' Chair / 1975 / Cat ♦♦♦

This album marked the long-playing debut of Gwen McCrae, a sultry voiced singer who remains popular with soul music cultists today. *Rockin' Chair* collects the material that she had been recording for the Cat label, a subsidiary of disco giant T.K. Records. Despite the fact that it was not technically conceived as an album, all the material on *Rockin' Chair* hangs together nicely: Everything here was produced by Miami soul stalwart Steve Alaimo, who strikes an effective balance between silky soul and gospel-tinged funk on all the tracks. The obvious standout is the title tune, a mid-paced invitation to romance that frames McCrae's seductive vocal with stately horns and churning, infectious percussion. The end result is downright hypnotic and it deservedly became a massive hit on both the R&B and pop charts during 1975. None of the remaining tracks are as instantly infectious as the title hit, but they all make for fine listening: "Move Me Baby" is a gently-loping funk jam built on some silky keyboard riffs, and "Your Love Is Worse Than a Cold Love" is a convincing declaration of frustrated passion that gets a gutsy, gospel-tinged treatment from McCrae. Trivia fans will also want to take note that Harry Casey of KC & the Sunshine Band lent a hand on the production of "Move Me Baby." However, the album's unsung gem is "90% Of Me Is You": This hypnotic tune is a grand showcase for McCrae's emotive skills, allowing her to unfold a tale of emotional enslavement over a sleek backing track that balances yearning strings with a moody funk groove. All in all, *Rockin' Chair* is a solid soul collection that will appeal to any fans of the 1970s soul style. *—Donald A. Guarisco*

Something So Right / 1976 / Cat ♦♦♦

Miami soul songstress Gwen McCrae never scored another huge hit after 1975's "Rockin' Chair," but she did continue to make fine soul recordings through the end of the decade. One of the best of them is 1976's *Something So Right*. While it lacks an obvious hit single, this album is a solid, soulful showcase for McCrae's vocals. Her style retains the emotional earthiness needed to truly connect with her listeners. A good example of her style arrives with her performance on the title track, the cover of a Paul Simon classic, which balances an elegant and controlled delivery on the verses with a more emotional delivery on the chorus. She also displays a brassy sense of authority on dance-oriented numbers like "Mr. Everything" and "Iron Woman." *Something So Right* further benefits from Clarence Reid and Steve Alaimo's smooth production, which keeps a solid groove rolling as it sweetens the sound with yearning string arrangements. They also apply a creative touch to the album's cover versions: for instance, the classic Little Anthony doo wop tune "Tears on My Pillow" is transformed into a elegant ballad that gives McCrae room to throw in Millie Jackson-styled spoken interjections. The downside of *Something So Right* is that it favors track-to-track consistency over the kind of songs that would connect with a larger audience; this makes it likely that this album will remain a cult item. That said, anyone with a yen for 1970s soul will find plenty to enjoy on *Something So Right*. *—Donald A. Guarisco*

Let's Straighten It Out / 1978 / Cat ♦♦

This probably isn't Gwen McCrae's best-selling album, since it doesn't contain her best-selling single, but it's definitely McCrae's most satisfying. She excels on all ends, including the upbeat and midtempo numbers and the smoldering ballads. On the robotic tip there are high scale shufflers like "Cradle of Love," "Love Insurance," the speedy dancer "Early Morning Love," and a good but predictable remake of Stevie Wonder's "Signed, Sealed, Delivered." The four other selections include three remakes of classic ballads, bested by a chilling rendition of "Let's Straightened It Out," which rivals the original by labelmate Latimore; McCrae makes you think that she's going to have a breakdown before the song ends. She handles Mel & Tim's "Starting All Over Again," adding so much soul and passion that you'd think she wrote the song. She also coughs up a good rendition of "Tonight's the Night" and concludes with the infectious "At Bedtime." If you see this one, snatch it fast; it's worth the coins. *—Andrew Hamilton*

Melody of Life / 1979 / Cat ♦♦♦

After spending years being produced by some of Miami's finest soul record producers, Gwen McCrae took the inspired step of turning over the production reins to a fellow artist, Betty Wright, on this 1979 album. It was a smart decision, because the album that resulted is tight and tuneful. *Melody of Life* starts with a bang thanks to "All the Love That I'm Givin'," which bolsters a strong and soulful vocal from McCrae with a thick synthesizer bassline and some effective background vocals on its tag. Though it wasn't a big hit at the time, this became an underground dance favorite that remains popular today. From there on, *Melody of Life* opts for simple but elegant soul backgrounds to support McCrae's always-impassioned vocals: "I Can Only Think of You" employs gentle strings and a catchy flute hook to back up its tale of yearning for an absent lover, and "The Joy" layers a sprightly horn section over an elastic bass groove to set a joyful mood for its tribute to newfound love. McCrae rises to the occasion with a set of vocals that wring all the emotion out of each lyric: The best example of this technique is "Ease the Pain," a tale of loneliness that climaxes with McCrae letting loose with a multiple-second wail at its finale. The only real drawback to *Melody of Life* is that, although it has no obvious filler tunes, it is lacking in the kind of strong and unforgettable material that would increase its appeal beyond soul music cultists. That said, *Melody of Life* remains a solid choice for any fans of '70s soul sounds. *—Donald A. Guarisco*

● **The Best of Gwen McCrae** / 1992 / Sequel ♦♦♦♦♦

Gwen McCrae recorded some fine silky soul and proto-disco for the T.K. subsidiary Cat Records. This 19-track collection has cuts from her four albums made between 1975 and 1979 and also features three duets recorded with her husband, George McCrae, in 1975. Her best album for Cat is *Rockin' Chair*, and the first six songs are taken from it. "Rocking Chair" is a funky treat matching Gwen's searching with a very funky backbeat and sounds quite similar to her hubby's smash "Rock Your Baby." "It's Worth the Hurt" is another highlight, a tough blues that shows off Gwen's rough and tumble side. The duets with George are fun and funky, an Otis & Carla for the disco era. The rest of the tracks are a little more hit and miss. "Damn Right It's Good" is a powerful stomper with more tough vocals putting men in their proper place; "Let's Straighten It Out" has a sultry, slow groove and some heart-punch vocals; but the rest of the tracks are not as direct and the compilation loses steam as the sound becomes more refined. A respite from encroaching disco blandness comes with the last track, a Betty Wright-produced rocker with some outer-space keyboards and a gritty vocal. This is a decent summation of McRae's career but a better listen would be a two-fer that holds *Rockin' Chair* and her second record, *Something So Right*. Unfortunately, West Side decided to group *Rockin' Chair* with the inferior-to-*Something So Right* third album, *Let's Straighten It Out*, leaving *The Best of Gwen McCrae* your best bet to pick up on this unheralded soul diva. *—Tim Sendra*

Gene McDaniels

b. Feb. 12, 1935, Kansas City, MO

Vocals / Soul, Pop-Soul, Pop, R&B, Jazz-Funk

Gene McDaniels had some early-'60s success with a pop-flavored R&B style. Born in Kansas City, he sang in Omaha choirs during the '40s and attended the Omaha Conservatory of Music. McDaniels led his own band in the '50s, then signed with Liberty. He had a Top Ten pop and Top 20 R&B hit in 1961 with "A Hundred Pounds of Clay," but the follow-up single, "A Tower of Strength," was his biggest. It was number five on both the R&B and pop charts, and "Point of No Return" just missed each list's Top 20. He appeared in the 1962 film *It's Trad, Dad*, which contained his song "Another Tear Falls." McDaniels continued to record for Liberty until 1965, then switched to Atlantic in the early '70s. He scored as a writer with the composition "Feel Like Making Love," a number-one pop and R&B hit for Roberta Flack in 1974. He also produced Merry Clayton and other performers. *—Ron Wynn*

A Hundred Pounds of Clay / 1961 / Liberty ♦♦♦♦

Tower of Strength / 1962 / Liberty ♦♦♦

Headless Heroes of the Apocalypse / 1971 / Atlantic ♦♦♦♦

When *Headless Heroes of the Apocalypse* was first released in 1971, so the legend goes, Spiro Agnew himself called Atlantic Records to complain about the album's incendiary lyrics. Promotional efforts dried up, and since then, the album has become one of the great rare gems of the funk era. With this first-ever CD release from Label M, it is available again in all its strange, eclectic glory. McDaniels had earned his living as a producer and songwriter for artists like Roberta Flack and Gladys Knight, and was in all honesty not much of a singer, but somehow his clumsy lyrics and dry delivery combined to carry his message across. In an unthreatening manner that hardly warranted a call from the White House, McDaniels warns that man's struggles against each other are pointless, as some dark sinister force controls us all ("Headless Heroes"), and that protest without action is futile ("no amount of dancing is going to make us free," he sings in "Freedom Death Dance"). With a dry wit he recounts an episode of everyday racist brutality in "Supermarket Blues," and finds simple carnal pleasures in the acoustic folk-flavored "Susan Jane." It all gets wrapped up in an appealing stew that draws from rock, funk, folk, soul, and even free jazz. Considering the number of times McDaniels' sinewy beats and chunky guitar riffs have been sampled over the years, it's about time a proper re-release can allow listeners to hear the whole picture. *—John Duffy*

A Hundred Pounds of Clay & Other Hits / 1992 / CEMA ♦♦♦♦♦

Although he preferred singing jazz, blues and/or R&B, Gene McDaniels enjoyed some success in the late '50s and early '60s with highly arranged, elaborately produced and orchestrated pop. McDaniels was locked into short, sometimes humorous and/or vocally exaggerated romantic dilemma vehicles. He seldom got to explore serious themes or extend himself, instead hitting the hooks and then exiting backed by strings, female vocalists and/or a bombastic instrumental background. This anthology's 25 tracks include his biggest hits, "Tower of Strength," "Chip Chip," "Point of No Return," and the title track. There are also B-sides, unreleased cuts and singles that weren't hits, but more accurately reflected McDaniels' style. *—Ron Wynn*

● **A Hundred Pounds of Clay: The Best of Gene McDaniels** / 1995 / Collectables ♦♦♦♦♦

A reissue of a reissue, this 1995 Collectables package is the same as EMI's 1991 *Legendary Masters* entry on this jazz singer turned pop artist. McDaniels' formidable pipes soar over these tracks and hits like "Point of No Return," "Tower of Strength," "Chip Chip," and the title track show him to be one class act. The production is grade-A, with lots of brass, strings and solid rhythm earmarking everything on here, making each song a minor gem. Because this is a reissue of the earlier EMI package, the liner notes and recording information are top-notch, a rarity with most Collectables packaging from this era. A hidden classic from rock & roll's supposed fallow period. *—Cub Koda*

A Hundred Pounds of Clay/Tower of Strength / Feb. 23, 1999 / BGO ♦♦♦♦

McFadden & Whitehead

f. Philadelphia, PA

Group / Philly Soul, Disco, Soul

A Philadelphia songwriting, production, and performing duo who were prominent at Philadelphia International during the '70s, Gene McFadden & John Whitehead also scored a number-one R&B hit as vocalists. Their single "Ain't No Stoppin' Us Now" was number-one R&B in 1979 and peaked at number 13 pop. The two were members of the Epsilons as teens, a band that toured with and were managed by Otis Redding until his death in 1967. They later signed with Stax and had a moderate hit in 1970 with "The

Echo." When Lloyd Parkes left, McFadden & Whitehead changed their name to Talk of the Town and began working with Gamble & Huff. Although they were being primed to record for North Bay, when Gamble & Huff discovered the duo's writing talents, they decided instead to employ them in that capacity at their label, Philadelphia International. Their first collaboration came on the Intruders' "I'll Always Love My Mama."

They later wrote and/or produced such classics as "Backstabbers" for the O'Jays, "Bad Luck" and "Wake Up Everybody" for Harold Melvin & the Blue Notes, and "Let's Groove," "Soul City Walk," "Strategy," and "Don't Let Love Get You Down" for Archie Bell & the Drells. They also worked with Carolyn Crawford and did outside projects during the '70s and '80s with Melba Moore, Gloria Gaynor, Freddie Jackson, Willie Collins, and Beau Williams. The duo cut their own album, *McFadden & Whitehead*, in 1979 and made more singles for TSOP in 1980 and Capitol in 1982. "I Heard It in a Love Song" was a Top 30 R&B hit in 1980. *—Ron Wynn*

• **McFadden & Whitehead** / 1979 / The Right Stuff ♦♦♦

After writing and producing many hits for numerous artists, the dynamic duo take the spotlight with their debut release, which featured the platinum-selling single "Ain't No Stopping Us Now." This uptempo dance number was groomed with all the right tangibles, from the rhythm arrangement to the melody to John Whitehead's testimonial lead. The rejoicing single claimed the top position on the *Billboard* R&B charts and number 13 on the pop charts. The follow-up single was "I've Been Pushed Aside." Not nearly as successful as its predecessor, it only managed to peak at number 73 after a mere seven weeks on the charts. Nonetheless, it is a soulful composition with much feeling, and it also showcases Gene McFadden on lead enhanced by Whitehead's supporting vocals. However, the unfortunate thing about this album is that any single to follow "Ain't No Stopping Us Now" would have been subpar to such an outstanding song. *—Craig Lytle*

Stick McGhee (Granville H. McGhee)

b. Mar. 23, 1917, Kingsport, TN, **d.** Aug. 15, 1961, New York, NY

Vocals, Guitar / R&B, Jump Blues

He may have not been as prolific or celebrated as his brother Brownie, but guitarist Stick McGhee cut some great boozy blues and R&B from 1947 to 1960—including the immortal "Drinkin' Wine Spo-Dee-O-Dee" (a tune that Jerry Lee Lewis, for one, picked up on early in life and has revived often since).

Young Granville McGhee earned his nickname by pushing his polio-stricken older brother Brownie through the streets of Kingsport, TN, on a cart that he propelled with a stick. McGhee was inspired to pen "Drinkin' Wine" while in Army boot camp during World War II; it was apparently a ribald military chant that the McGhees cleaned up for public consumption later on. McGhee's first recorded version of the tune for J. Mayo Williams' Harlem logo made little impression in 1947, but a rollicking 1949 remake for Atlantic (as Stick McGhee & His Buddies) proved a massive R&B hit (brother Brownie chiming in on guitar and harmony vocal). The tune has attracted countless covers over the years—everyone from Jerry Lee Lewis and Johnny Burnette to Wynonie Harris and Larry Dale has taken a sip from this particular wine flask.

After one more smash for Atlantic, 1951's "Tennessee Waltz Blues," McGhee moved along to Essex, King (where he waxed some more great booze numbers from 1953 to 1955—"Whiskey Women and Loaded Dice," "Head Happy With Wine," "Jungle Juice," "Six to Eight," "Double Crossin' Liquor"), Savoy, and Herald, where he made his last 45 in 1960 before lung cancer cut him down the following year. *—Bill Dahl*

• **New York Blues** / 1994 / Ace ♦♦♦♦♦

The British Ace label—long a prime source for quality compilations—has done Brownie's little brother proud, collecting his dozen 1953-1955 jump blues sides for the King logo, many of them detailing the effects of booze. Also aboard are four country blues-styled numbers by Ralph Willis, and four more by the pseudonymous Big Tom Collins (two of them feature Brownie McGhee's vocals, the other pair Champion Jack Dupree!). *—Bill Dahl*

Brian McKnight

b. Jun. 5, 1969, Buffalo, NY

Vocals, Producer, Arranger / Quiet Storm, Adult Contemporary, Urban, Contemporary R&B

Brian McKnight grew up in a family where music came naturally. He was a member of the church choir along with his immediate family; his grandfather was the director. With a gospel upbringing, McKnight explored other genres of music. Still in his early teens, he exercised his writing ambitions by penning instrumentals (soft jazz, easy listening). He formed a band and began performing his originals at local venues. By the age of 18, McKnight had secured a publishing deal. His calling to the national scene manifested itself when his older brother Claude and the group he was a member of, Take 6, signed a recording contract with a major label.

After sending out numerous demos to various record companies, McKnight's tape drew the interest of Mercury Records president Ed Eckstine (son of Billy Eckstine). Eckstine was so impressed with McKnight's sound that the young artist was signed to a deal within two weeks. McKnight's first release on Mercury was "The Way Love Goes," peaking at number 11 after 19 weeks on the *Billboard* R&B charts. His two follow-up singles barely cracked the *Billboard* R&B Top 60, including "Love Is," a duet with Vanessa Williams featured on *Beverly Hills 90210*. Ironically, that single peaked at number three on the *Billboard* pop charts, introducing McKnight to a crossover audience.

In addition to being a singer, McKnight is a songwriter, multi-talented musician, arranger, and producer. The success he has achieved as producer and songwriter on his own projects has facilitated his popularity as a producer and songwriter for other artists. However, the Buffalo native retained the services of hip-hop producer Sean "Puffy" Combs on the release of his 1997 CD *Anytime*, which features the club-flavored single "You Should Be Mine." A Christmas album, *Bethlehem*, followed in 1998, and a year later McKnight returned with *Back at One*. *—Craig Lytle*

Brian McKnight / Nov. 1991 / Mercury ♦♦♦

Brian McKnight's self-titled debut album is a mix of quiet storm and jazz-tinged R&B lite, with a few uptempo numbers thrown in. The album opens with the new jack swing lite of "Yours," and leads into other midtempo, early-'90s sounding R&B. Some songs, including "Stay the Night," even incorporate the electric guitar, an instrument which was virtually forgotten in pop music by the end of the decade. The album produced one major hit, the teary ballad "One Last Cry." Brian McKnight, with his brand of songwriter-driven, piano-man quiet storm, was unique among 1990s male solo singers, and unexpectedly became one of the genre's biggest (and only) stars, with each album building on the previous one's success. For that reason, perhaps, this album is less commercial and more jazz-leaning than his later discs, especially towards the album's second half. Other highlights include his silky cover of the Hall & Oats staple "I Can't Go for That" (which features the album's only rap) and the jazz nugget "Is the Feeling Gone." A great album for a rainy winter afternoon. *—Jose F. Promis*

I Remember You / 1995 / Mercury ♦♦♦

Brian McKnight has become the latest in a series of after-hours style R&B heroes, matinee idols with decent voices who parlay suggestiveness, romantic lyrics and sex appeal into sizable popularity among female fans. McKnight's strength is his coy delivery and savvy selection of material; he never does any tune that forces him to stretch the upper or lower register, nor does he experiment much with reggae, hip-hop or cutting-edge production. McKnight keeps it simple, mostly mellow and love-oriented, though the single "Keep It on the Down Low" demonstrates an effectiveness with faster numbers not previously evident. As a songwriter he's efficient, if rather straightforward; as a singer, he's more steadfast than soulful, and more predictable than unforgettable. There's not a lot to like or dislike about *I Remember You*, which may be the problem; it's so generic and reflective of everything and nothing that it doesn't do much for anyone who wants to be confronted, inspired or even mildly stimulated. It's the ideal late-night, quiet storm session, aimed at those who enjoy getting the ambience of R&B without the intensity. *—Ron Wynn*

Anytime / Sep. 23, 1997 / Mercury ♦♦♦

On his third album, *Anytime*, Brian McKnight continues with the mellow romantic urban R&B that has become his trademark, but there's a new twist. Most of the album consists of songs he has written and produced, but "You Should Be Mine," the first single pulled from *Anytime*, is produced by Puff Daddy and features a rap by Mase. On paper, the pairing seems a little crass and commercial, but it works surprisingly well, as does "Hold Me," which was co-written by Mary J. Blige and features Trackmasterz. These cuts are fresher than the rest of the album, which is stuck in early-'90s swingbeat—while that sounds good, it's also beginning to sound a little tired and predictable. He hasn't exhausted its possibilities yet—*Anytime* is as strong as its predecessor—but "You Should Be Mine" and "Hold Me" suggest that he may be better off pursuing a new, hip-hop-influenced direction. *—Stephen Thomas Erlewine*

Back at One / Sep. 21, 1999 / Motown ♦♦♦

Brian McKnight backs away ever so slightly from the streetwise rhythms Puff Daddy injected into *Anytime* with his fifth album, *Back at One*. That's not to say that the album doesn't sound contemporary or fresh—quite the opposite. McKnight has figured out a way to make his gospel-flavored contemporary urban soul sound fresh, mainly by keeping the focus on the songs. There's nothing extraneous on *Back at One*: All 13 songs are given clean presentations, and he blesses them with impassioned performances. At times, the material itself is not particularly interesting, but most albums have filler; what counts is the good stuff, and there's enough of it on *Back at One* to make it another solid effort from McKnight. *—Stephen Thomas Erlewine*

Superhero / Aug. 28, 2001 / Motown ♦♦♦

R&B crooner Brian McKnight dropped his fifth studio release, *Superhero*, in 2001. The recording essentially offers up the same romantic and sensitive midtempo R&B love songs McKnight has become famous for. However, there are some choice departures by McKnight, reflecting his adventurous side. The title track is a steady and strong (gasp!) rock song, complete with electric guitars and driven percussion; it is slightly reminiscent of a (gentler) Living Colour style. The generally soft McKnight should venture into the rock arena more often, as he wears this hat well. McKnight also plays a wailing solo on the song to boot. Nice job. Elsewhere, the bonus track, "Groovin' Tonight," is a bouncing R&B jam with flows courtesy of Nate Dogg and backing vocals by McKnight. This is fun stuff. Returning to McKnight's standard fare, "My Kind of Girl," featuring *NSYNC's Justin Timberlake, is a sweet, breezy number, centered around light acoustic guitar playing, an instrument most fans don't associate with McKnight, who is generally shown behind the keys. The winning combination of the two singers' smooth vocals adds to the song's airy appeal. While the album is not groundbreaking, it does show consistency and growth by the talented McKnight. Is it super? No. Worthy? Yes. *—Liana Jonas*

• **From There to Here: 1989–2002** / Nov. 5, 2002 / Motown ♦♦♦♦

Thirteen years is a long time in urban/R&B circles, which leaves the rangy career of Brian McKnight sounding like the work of several different artists when compiled in a package like *From There to Here: 1989-2002*. Most of his material has the sound of soulful adult contemporary, as on quite a few tracks compiled here: "One Last Cry," "Crazy Love," and "Love Is" (the latter featuring Vanessa Williams). McKnight also proved amenable to adding hip-hop beats and contemporary productions comparatively early in his career, and the collection follows this angle as well. The song selections are quite good, ably showing McKnight's technically perfect and artistically pleasing voice to good effect. What makes this a better compilation than ones on most other artists is the fact that Brian McKnight albums tended to have far too much filler to justify getting into the records on their own. One quibble, though: this would've been the perfect disc to anthologize his popular version of the Christmas chestnut "God Rest Ye Merry Gentlemen." *—John Bush*

Barbara McNair

b. Mar. 4, 1939, Racine, WA

Vocals / Motown, Soul

A glamorous actress, Barbara McNair moonlighted as a pop singer between TV and film roles during the 1960s. McNair was a classy addition to Berry Gordy's talent roster when his firm attempted to diversify its appeal. She cut a pair of albums for Motown in 1966 and 1969 squarely aimed at the MOR crowd instead of the traditional Motown R&B audience. *—Bill Dahl*

Livin' End / 1964 / Warner Bros. ♦♦♦

● **Here I Am** / 1966 / Motown ♦♦♦♦

When this was released November of 1966, Motown was hotter then the blast furnace at the local Ford plant. Having a record on one of Berry Gordy's labels was like money in the bank. It wasn't so much the artist, but the system employed at 2648 West Grand Blvd. that was credited for the success. Classy, beautiful Barbara McNair had previously recorded for Coral and Warner Brothers Records; she enjoyed active careers in television, movies and as a performer. *Here I Am*, her first Motown LP, transforms the MOR singer into a sophisticated R&B artist. McNair had released "You're Gonna Love My Baby" on Motown prior to this, but it was omitted; co-written by Barbara, it's a prized collectable and a Northern soul favorite. Three singles were released, the best being Barbara's seductive version of Smokey Robinson's "Here I Am Baby"; popularized months later by the Marvelettes, the versions are note-for-note clones. Barbara's hit the streets first, but the Marvelettes probably recorded it before her. McNair's version stiffed, yet it's her most popular Motown recording. Two other singles, "Everything Is Good" and "Steal Away Tonight," failed miserably. The LP is divided almost equally between classic Motown and MOR or easy listening selections. Songwriting heavyweights Eddie Holland, Ron Miller, Smokey Robinson, and Clarence Paul all contributed. Everything was first-class but the promotion, which failed to generate any chart action for this fine LP.*—Andrew Hamilton*

I Enjoy Being a Girl / 1966 / Warner Bros. ♦♦♦♦

Quite some production went into this effort, including three different recording sessions, each with elaborate bands. Singer Barbara McNair is heard backed by strings, an expanded small combo that boasts four loud trombones plus other horns and a rhythm section, and a rip-roaring 15-man horn section that makes "On the Other Side of the Tracks" sound like the tracks are running right through the room. Arranger and conductor Ralph Carmichael tends toward the obvious and won't stop any clocks with his instrumental game plan. But the choice of material is both tasteful and unusual, and McNair always manages to put a surprising element of adventure into her vocal interpretations. "If I Had a Hammer" may seem to be a folk song that is done to death, but it is presented here as if it rolled off the stage at a late-night New Orleans jazz jam session, coming back to life quite nicely in the process. The version of "Irma la Douce" is savory, the strings providing a nice touch of irony. McNair has the voice for difficult numbers such as "Hi-Lili, Hi Lo" and can be genuinely moving on thoughtful pieces such as "My Love Is a Wanderer" and "The Friendliest Thing." *—Eugene Chadbourne*

The Real Barbara McNair / 1969 / Motown ♦♦♦

The Racine, WI, singer's second Motown album mixes Motown originals and remakes with a couple of outside tunes—"What Now My Love" and "You Lost That Loving Feeling"—thrown in for good measure. Rehashes of Mary Wells and Brenda Holloway's "When I'm Gone," the Marvelettes' "The Hunter Gets Captured By the Game," the Miracles' "If You Can Want," and the Supremes' "I Hear a Symphony" are solid and McNair's clear enunciation makes lyric sheets unnecessary. Gems like James Dean, Stanley McMullen, and William Weatherspoon's "Just One Teardrop (From a Broken Heart)" and Frank Wilson/Dennis Lussier's "Where Would I Be Without You" are additional reasons why a CD of McNair's Motown tracks is long overdue. *—Andrew Hamilton*

Big Jay McNeely

b. Apr. 29, 1927, Watts, CA

Sax (Tenor), Saxophone / Jazz Blues, Jump Blues, West Coast Blues, Soul-Jazz, R&B

His mighty tenor sax squawking and bleating with wild-eyed abandon, Big Jay McNeely blew up a torrid R&B tornado from every conceivable position—on his knees, on his back, being wheeled down the street on an auto mechanic's "creeper" like a modern-day pied piper. As one of the titans who made tenor sax the solo instrument of choice during rock's primordial era, McNeely could peel the paper right off the walls with his sheets of squealing, honking horn riffs.

Cecil McNeely and his older brother Bob (who blew baritone sax lines with Jay in unison precision on some of Jay's hottest instrumentals) grew up in Los Angeles, where jazz reigned on Watts' bustling nightlife strip. Inspired by Illinois Jacquet and tutored by Jack McVea, McNeely struck up a friendship with Johnny Otis, co-owner of the popular Barrelhouse nitery. Ralph Bass, a friend of Otis, produced McNeely's debut date for Savoy Records in 1948 (Savoy boss Herman Lubinsky tagged the saxist Big Jay, in his eyes a more commercial name than Cecil). McNeely's raucous one-note honking on "The Deacon's Hop" gave him and Savoy an R&B chart-topper in 1949, and his follow-up, "Wild Wig," also hit big for the young saxist with the acrobatic stage presence.

From Savoy, McNeely moved to Exclusive in 1949, Imperial in 1950-1951, King's Federal subsidiary in 1952-1954 (where he cut some of his wildest waxings, including the mind-boggling "3-D"), and Vee-Jay in 1955. McNeely's live shows were the stuff that legends are made of—he electrified a sweaty throng of thousands packing L.A.'s Wrigley Field in 1949 by blowing his sax up through the stands and then from home plate to first base on his back! A fluorescently painted sax that glowed in the dark was another of his show-stopping gambits.

In 1958, McNeely cut his last hit in a considerably less frantic mode with singer Little Sonny Warner. The bluesy "There Is Something on Your Mind" was committed to tape in Seattle but came out on disc jockey Hunter Hancock's Swingin' imprint the next year. McNeely's original was a huge smash, but it was eclipsed the following year by New Orleans singer Bobby Marchan's dramatic R&B chart-topping version for Fire. Since then, it's been covered countless times, including a fine rendition by Conway Twitty!

Honking saxists had fallen from favor by the dawn of the '60s, so McNeely eventually became a mailman and joined Jehovah's Witnesses (no, that's not the name of a combo). Happily, his horn came back out of the closet during the early '80s. McNeely went on to record for his own little label and tour the country and overseas regularly. *—Bill Dahl*

Big "J" in 3-D / Aug. 26, 1952-Apr. 8, 1954 / King ♦♦♦♦

Tenor saxophonist Big Jay McNeely swings and honks his way through 12 classic Federal sides from 1952-1954. Joined by brother Robert on baritone, McNeely and his combo work a well-worn jump blues groove on gospel-imbued scorchers like "Hot Cinders" and "The Goof." Equally adept at torrid and moderate tempos, McNeely also shows off his Illinois Jacquet-inspired chops with a dizzying array of bleats, screeches, and guttural smears, even throwing in some svelte lines when appropriate. And while cuts like "Ice Water" presage the coming of rock & roll, classy swingers such as "Hardtack" offer a unique blend of R&B and jazz adorned with bongo accompaniment. And then there's "3-D," the centerpiece of the set and one of the most blistering of R&B instrumentals. Even amidst the almost pneumatic rhythm, McNeely masterfully wails above the band, not missing a beat during his irrepressible call-and-response workout with the other horn players. Whether blowing teenage brains out at L.A.'s Shrine Auditorium or with classic records like this, Big Jay McNeely always backed up the hysteria with loads of good music. *—Stephen Cook*

The Deacon Rides Again / 1952-1957 / Marconi ♦♦♦

This features hot tenor licks, sweltering vocals from Jesse Belvin, and bluesy inflections courtesy of Mercy Dee. *—Ron Wynn*

Live at Birdland: 1957 / 1957 / Collectables ♦♦♦♦

This is an amazing artifact from 1957, when live recordings like this one didn't happen very often. A Seattle engineer with a spanking-new stereo tape recorder captured the contents of this disc while McNeely and his swinging combo were working out at a Seattle nightspot called the Birdland. He gets plenty of room to peel the paper from the gin joint's walls as he wails on "Flying Home," "How High the Moon," and "Let It Roll." *—Bill Dahl*

Swingin': Golden Classics / 1958-1960 / Collectables ♦♦♦♦

This collects the gymnastic sax maniac's output for L.A. deejay Hunter Hancock's Swingin' logo during the late '50s and early '60s. Naturally, his smash "There Is Something on Your Mind" is front and center, alongside the oddly titled "Back... Shack... Track," "Psycho Serenade," and "Blue Couch Boogie." Little Sonny Warner is the vocalist on some sides. *—Bill Dahl*

● **Nervous** / 1995 / Saxophile ♦♦♦♦♦

A thorough 19-track examination of McNeely's early heyday, incorporating a live 1951 reprise of his signature "Deacon's Hop," and the King label classics "3-D," "Nervous Man Nervous," and "Texas Turkey," a handful of live 1957 efforts that include the crazed "Insect Ball," and McNeely's original hit version of the incendiary blues ballad "There Is Something on Your Mind" (with Little Sonny Warner handling the Ray Charles-influenced lead vocal). *—Bill Dahl*

Ronnie McNeir

b. 1951, Camden, AL

Vocals, Synthesizer / Urban, Disco, Pop, Soul

Ronnie McNeir conceived a highly individualistic approach to music synthesis over the course of three albums and one EP. Hyperkinetic (broken chord) jazzy synth-basslines, churchy organ, multi-note piano chords, and sinewy high and mid-range ARP solo lines weave in and out of the mix while McNeir supplied all the vocals and acoustic drums. The Camden, AL, native moved to Detroit, MI, at an early age. He taught himself piano by listening to the records of the day, including the sounds of Motown and jazz artists. As a teen, he won a talent contest and was rewarded with a single release, "Sitting in My Class," on the Deto label. In 1972, he made a trip out to California and recorded his first album, *Ronnie McNeir*, for RCA. The *Ronnie McNeir* LP was reissued around 1978 and became a perennial favorite in the U.K.

Returning to Michigan, he began doing studio work, primarily at United Sound Studio in Detroit. In 1976, McNeir recorded a nice midtempo groover, "Wendy Is Gone," for Barney Ales' Prodigal label. Prodigal was Motown's "minor league" label; meaning that if a Prodigal release did real well, the act was then transferred to Motown. "Wendy Is Gone" took off in Detroit and other key markets and landed on the lower half of *Billboard*'s soul singles chart. The album *Ronnie McNeir* (the same title as his RCA debut) was released by Prodigal. The singles "Saggitarian Affair" and "I'm Your Lover" proved popular enough for McNeir to have a guest spot on *Soul Train*. Motown signed McNeir that same year. His Motown debut, *Love's Comin' Down*, was released in August 1976. Despite favorable reviews and numerous single releases, the album didn't chart. There were tracks recorded for a second Motown album, but they were never released. Around this time, McNeir recorded two tracks with the Four Tops for their 1977 ABC album, *The Show Must Go On*. He later became the group's musical director. Also during the late '70s, McNeir began working for Detroit-based producer Don Davis' Groovesville Productions, appearing on sides by David Ruffin and Dramatics vocalist L.J. Reynolds' solo Capitol LP. McNeir also recorded as a solo artist with Groovesville, releasing a duet single with Rena Scott, "A Different Kind of Love." In 1984, a four-song EP produced by Horizon Productions, *The Ronnie McNeir Experience*, was released by Capitol.

In 1985, McNeir made it to the upper half of *Billboard*'s R&B charts as the producer/composer of "I Couldn't Believe It," a hit for former Temptations members David Ruffin and Eddie Kendricks, who recorded as Ruffin & Kendricks for RCA. The prolific songwriter, session musician, vocalist, and producer appeared on albums by Little Milton (*Age Ain't Nothin' but a Number*), Rance Allen (Stax/Fantasy), Carrie Lucas' cover of Barbara Lewis' "Hello Stranger" from *Horsin' Around* (Solar/RCA), and Bobby Womack's "Caught Up in the Middle" from his *Pieces* album. *—Ed Hogan*

- **The Very Best of Ronnie McNeir** / Sep. 17, 1996 / Hot Productions ✦✦✦✦✦

The Very Best of Ronnie McNeir is a collection of early-'90s era singles the Detroit-based singer/songwriter/keyboardist Ronnie McNeir recorded for U.K. dance producer Ian Levine's Motorcity label. Understandably, the material is for the most part dance club oriented and may leave McNeir's longtime fans longing for ballads in the vein of his "I'm Your Lover." Still, if taken on its own merit, this album is a welcomed entry to the artist's catalog. The bouncy "My Lucky Number" is in the same vein as his work on another (South Carolina) beach music favorite, Ruffin & Kendricks' "I Couldn't Believe It." Another favorite is the snappy, house-tinged "Take the First Step." The snappy, Motown-ish "I Dedicate My Love" recalls the Temptations' 1965 Top Ten R&B/Top 20 pop hit "My Baby." Other standouts are "Don't Know If This Is Goodbye," "Can't Give You Up," "Keep on Giving Me Love," and the midtempo groover "Wholeheartedly." Though the title may have his fans wishing for a set made up of some of his RCA, Prodigal, Motown, and Capitol sides, *The Very Best of Ronnie McNeir* is a must. *—Ed Hogan*

Clyde McPhatter

b. Nov. 15, 1932, Durham, NC, **d.** Jun. 13, 1972, Teaneck, NJ

Vocals / R&B

Clyde McPhatter was one of the most influential R&B singers of the '50s and early '60s. In his own time, his name and voice loomed so much larger than that of the group the Drifters, which he founded, that it took five years for them to recover from his departure. McPhatter was idolized by black audiences as few singers before or since ever were, and for almost 15 years helped define R&B and its transformation into soul. In a way, he was the most improbable of R&B stars, a gentle high tenor who, superficially at least, seemed more suited to the angelic strains of gospel music. And his name gave some potential managers and agents pause—what kind of R&B singer, forget a star, was named Clyde? And Clyde McPhatter seemed like a backwoods burlesque of a black American name. But when he sang, the doubts and the laughter all disappeared—even on his live album from the Apollo Theater, recorded during his declining years, when he describes physical lust in the hit "Ta Ta," he makes it feel urgent and real, and utterly convincing.

McPhatter was born in Durham, NC, on November 15, 1932, the fourth of six children of George and Beulah McPhatter. The family that was both musical and religious, George McPhatter preached at the Mount Calvary Baptist Church where Beulah McPhatter was the organist, and Clyde became a boy soprano in the church choir. The family moved to New Jersey in 1945 and McPhatter formed his first gospel group that year in high school. The McPhatters moved to New York City, and Clyde McPhatter joined the Mount Lebanon Singers, who were one of the most popular gospel groups on the East Coast, and sang with them in the second half of the '40s. In late 1950, McPhatter made the jump to secular music when he joined Billy Ward, a former boxer-turned-singer in the Dominoes. The group, usually known officially as Billy Ward & the Dominoes, signed with Syd Nathan's King Records label, and at the end of 1950 cut "Sixty Minute Man." That song went on to become the biggest R&B hit of 1951 and the first identifiable rock & roll record (though that phrase had not yet been coined for music) by a black group to make the jump from the R&B to the pop charts. McPhatter stayed with Billy Ward & the Dominoes for three years, racking up a very respectable array of hits, including "Have Mercy Baby," "The Bells," "I'd Be Satisfied," and "These Foolish Things Remind Me of You," and playing as many engagements as they could handle. The problem for McPhatter was that Ward dominated the group's image and its finances—McPhatter's was the lead voice, and the voice that everyone identified; Ward had his name on the front end of the billing and collected all of the profits, while McPhatter, who was sometimes referred to as "Clyde Ward" by unknowing admirers, wasn't earning enough to live on from the meager salary that Ward paid him. Finally, in early 1953, McPhatter quit.

Ahmet Ertegun, the president and co-founder of Atlantic Records, was a fan of McPhatter's singing with the Dominoes and, on learning of his availability, approached him with a contract offer—to record his own group, if he could organize it. Thus were born the Drifters, originally organized by McPhatter in partnership with his manager George Treadwell. It was as the leader of the Drifters that McPhatter's career momentum picked up considerably—beginning with "Money Honey," which became the biggest R&B hit of 1954, he saw a year of notable chart activity and burgeoning popularity, around the singles "Such a Night," "Honey Love," "White Christmas," and "Whatch Gonna Do." McPhatter received his draft notice in 1954, but was lucky enough to be posted in America, which allowed him to continue to record with the group. He had already made a decision to leave the Drifters, however. He saw himself moving in a different direction from the group, toward a solo sound that would meld pop, R&B, and rock & roll all in one, and unlike a lot of other aspirants to that sort of stardom, McPhatter had what it took to pull it off. His high tenor was equally convincing on a slow ballad or a hard rock & roll number, and he saw no reason that he couldn't do both types of song his own way. He couldn't have known it at the time, but he was opening up a path that would later be followed by the likes of Elvis Presley and Sam Cooke, among many others.

Upon his discharge in 1955, McPhatter embarked on his official solo career, still recording for Atlantic Records. McPhatter first emerged in a duet with Ruth Brown on "Love Has Joined Us Together," which made number eight on the R&B charts, and in August of that year he recorded "Seven Days," which became a number-two R&B hit in early 1956. This was the first of McPhatter's attempts at a crossover record, complete with a softer pop orchestra and chorus behind his singing, but it was undercut on the pop charts by a variety of white cover versions, most notably by Dorothy Collins and the Crew Cuts. He fared better in the spring of 1956 with "Treasure of Love," which was not only his first solo R&B chart-topper, but also managed to make number 16 on the pop charts. "Just to Hold My Hand" kept him in the Top Ten on the R&B charts and the Top 30 in pop in the spring of 1957, and "Long Lonely Nights" topped out the R&B listings while just brushing the Top 50 for pop record compilers that summer. McPhatter was a big enough star that he was essentially the focus of two LP releases on Atlantic in the same year, unheard of for a black artist in those days, when R&B albums (apart from Elvis' first RCA long-players, which were considered R&B) didn't sell in serious numbers. In 1956, Atlantic released *Clyde McPhatter & the Drifters* and followed it up with *Love Ballads* soon after—the latter revealed his and the label's strategy, with a cover depicting an audience of white teenage girls in tinted overlays, looking on toward the camera excitedly and longingly. His goal, and the hope of his label, was to follow the path opened previously by Nat King Cole had done starting from jazz, and Eddy Arnold had done from country, and cross over to pop audiences—he had aspirations of rivalling Frank Sinatra and Perry Como. McPhatter saw his biggest hit on Atlantic in 1958 with "A Lover's Question," co-authored by Brook Benton, which hit number six on the pop charts that fall while topping the R&B listings. He had three more charting singles in 1959, none of which broke the Top Ten in R&B, but saw another long-player released to his credit, entitled simply *Clyde*.

He left Atlantic that year after one last hit, "Lovey Dovey," closing out his career there with another Brook Benton song, "You Went Back on Your Word." McPhatter's contract was up, and he jumped to MGM Records, which was offering a large advance in its eagerness to grab hold of the R&B market. His relationship there lasted but a year, through four singles, of which only "Let's Try Again" matched his Atlantic hits, making the R&B Top 20. He also had some minor pop hits in "I Told Myself a Lie" and "Think Me a Kiss" in 1960. The early '60s were a tumultuous time for McPhatter, personally and musically. He jumped to Mercury Records as the new decade began, and his career seemed to pick up again with an R&B Top Ten single, "Ta Ta," which also made the pop charts. "I Never Knew" also did well, and was followed by a Top Ten pop single in 1962 with "Lover Please," written by Billy Swan. Behind the scenes, however, McPhatter was walking a tightrope of alcoholism and unreliability that was expending all of the capital that he'd built up in the music community and the black community—he was a big enough name to still rate bookings at the Apollo Theater in Harlem, but hall managers and promoters, and his own backing bands, never knew what to expect from him, even in terms of repertory between rehearsals and showtime. Additionally, music was changing around him. McPhatter had served as a musical model for a soul singers of two generations who followed him onto the charts—Ben E. King in the Drifters and solo, but also Jackie Wilson and Smokey Robinson, and they were all producing hit records in prodigious numbers between 1960 and 1965. Even his former group the Drifters, now reconstructed with an entirely new lineup and with a new sound, were enjoying massive radio play and record sales during this period around the voices of King, Rudy Lewis, and Johnny Moore. Additionally, Sam Cooke, who was of the same generation as McPhatter, and had made the same journey out of the deep south to the big city, and the cross-over from gospel to R&B and pop, was the dominant figure in soul music during the early '60s. All were good and were also reliable and professional, and there was just no room for McPhatter, who wasn't any of those things at the time.

Before leaving Mercury, McPhatter enjoyed slight success with "Deep in the Heart of Harlem," a song that seemed to emulate the soft soul sound of the Drifters of that era, and "Crying Won't Help You Now," and cut a good concert album, *Live at the Apollo*, in 1964, which featured a cross-section of his hits across his career dating back to the early '50s. He spent the next few years recording for smaller labels such as Amy Records, unable to get a hit or keep his performing career going. He must have appreciated the grim irony, that his one-time Drifters stablemate, bass singer Bill Pinkney, was leading a group of "Drifters" who sang McPhatter's repertory and had a viable concert career, especially in England. And then, in a maneuver that anticipated the career course of the latter day Drifters, McPhatter moved to England. McPhatter's Dominoes and Drifters records hadn't appeared in the U.K. at the time of their original release. In the early '60s, between the booming enthusiasm for American R&B and the release of his current solo records, and the groundwork laid by Pinkney in his performances, McPhatter achieved recognition there and found a fresh audience. He found work in British clubs for a few years, until the same personal problems caught up with him. He returned to America in the early '70s, signing with Decca Records at the time and releasing an album, *Welcome Home*. It failed to make any impact, and McPhatter himself denied having any audience or fans left, which was not the case. (Even this writer—as a neophyte R&B listener in the late '60s with a lot to learn, coming from a middle-class white neighborhood where Jimi Hendrix was the black artist most often played, and in a time when not a single one of the early Drifters' songs was available on an album—knew who Clyde McPhatter was, or who he had been.)

It was too late for McPhatter, professionally and personally, however. Years of alcoholism and depression, and a failure to deal with his problems ended with a fatal heart attack in New York in 1972. It took years for Atlantic, where he'd been signed for what were probably the six most optimistic years of his career, to begin to make his music available in the United States (though their British division made some efforts overseas). In the CD era, in addition to its own best of compilation *Deep Sea Ball*, the label has licensed different parts of his legacy to Collectables and Sequel. *—Bruce Eder*

Love Ballads / 1958 / Atlantic ✦✦✦✦

One suspects that Atlantic Records had trouble actually assembling this album, based on the differences between the content and the title. As with most of Atlantic's early LPs, *Love Ballads* was comprised of existing singles and B-sides, in this case going back to Clyde McPhatter's days with the Drifters. And it is mostly made up of softer, slower numbers, such as "Heartaches," "Come What May," "When You're Sincere," "No Love Like Her Love," and "Long Lonely Nights," that most would call ballads, but in the middle are a surprising amount of what were then known as "rhythm numbers." It's a testament to McPhatter's vocal range that he pulls it all off—his voice on "Just Hold My Hand," "You'll Be There," "When You're Sincere," "There's No Love Like Her Love," or even "Lucille" (a number salvaged from the first, nearly abortive Drifters session in the spring of 1953) has a vulnerable, fragile edge that just makes the listener want to stop in his tracks, and he seems perfectly at home surrounded by a female choir. But on "Bip Bam," he hits the words incredibly hard, sounding more like a rival to Big Joe Turner than Nat King Cole. The slower songs are the direction that McPhatter preferred, aiming at a more sophisticated R&B audience and hoping for a crossover into pop circles—considering that most of the material dates from 1956-1957, it's all surprisingly sophisticated and groundbreaking in its time. *—Bruce Eder*

Clyde McPhatter / 1959 / Atlantic ♦♦♦♦♦
McPhatter's final original album for Atlantic is a must-hear release, some of the sweetest and brightest R&B of its period, a little more balanced and unified in its sound than its predecessor with more emphasis on beat. "Lovey Dovey," "A Lover's Question," "Hot Ziggity," "Try Try Baby," and "Since You've Been Gone" (which features future superstar producer Richard Perry on trombone and Gee/End/Gone Records mainstay Bert Keyes at the piano) are catchy, jaunty rockers, while "Let Me Know" and "My Island of Dreams" are ballads in the more sweepingly romantic style that McPhatter aimed for in these years. Somewhere midway between them are "Gone" and "Everyone's Laughing," stripped-down R&B ballads with a beat, and "I Can't Stand Up Alone" is a glorious flashback to McPhatter's roots as a gospel singer. *—Bruce Eder*

Live at the Apollo / 1965 / Mercury ♦♦
Clyde McPhatter ripped some pages from Joe Turner and other early R&B luminaries, made the sound more accessible, and landed on the pop charts with an uncanny frequency. Considering when this live set took place, it's hard to quibble about the quality. An ample band backs Clyde on 14-songs but never overshadows the fluid tenor who inspired many imitators, most notably Dee Clark. A feast and a must for McPhatter fans, and a good CD for lovers of classy traditional R&B the way it used to be done. *—Andrew Hamilton*

★ **Deep Sea Ball: The Best of Clyde McPhatter** / Oct. 1, 1991 / Atlantic ♦♦♦♦♦
This is about as perfect a summary of Clyde McPhatter's solo years with Atlantic as there is to buy, in the absence of a box of his complete output for the label or a Sequel Records reissue of his Atlantic LPs. Those who are most familiar with McPhatter's singing from his days with the Drifters will be pleased by all 19 songs here, which represent a more mature voice and embody musical ambitions that carried McPhatter toward the same kind of expansive, pop-oriented R&B that Sam Cooke also started working toward (and would hit bigger with) a couple of years later. He could still rock out, as on the title track, but he also had a sense of the dramatic in his singing and used it to powerful effect on songs like "Without Love." "Treasure of Love" and "A Lover's Question" may be McPhatter's best remembered solo hits, but even the non-chart sides here, like "I Can't Stand Up Alone" (which harks back to McPhatter's roots as a gospel singer) and the big-band R&B of "I'm Lonely Tonight," are gorgeous pieces of music that demand to be heard. The only drawback is that the material isn't in chronological order, which wouldn't be a problem at all if the recording dates had been listed next to the tracks in the notes. But it sounds fine and the music is so compelling that it holds up regardless of the programming decisions. *—Bruce Eder*

The Mercury Sessions: Featuring Live & Studio Recordings / 1996 / Collectables ♦♦♦
The title is a sort of catch-all, and a misnomer, as this CD doesn't even attempt to represent a cross-section of McPhatter's work on Mercury Records—but the CD itself is golden. Eleven of the 14 tracks are taken from McPhatter's 1964 vintage *Live at the Apollo* album, and show him in surprisingly good form, backed by a band that's just a little bigger than it probably needed to have been. None of that detracts from his performances on numbers ranging across his entire career, including "A Lover's Question," "Ta Ta," "Baby Baby," "Such a Night," "Lucille," and "Just to Hold My Hand." Some of this is done in a bit too much of a big-band style, especially "Such a Night," and those arrangements—along with the presence of his more pop-oriented material (including "Second Window, Second Floor" and "What's Love to Me")—make this album less revelatory than it might otherwise have been (though even then it's hard to dislike the voice). "Lucille," by contrast, is done as a hard R&B number that rates as one of his best performances on record. And "Deep in the Heart of Harlem," his then recent single, reveals McPhatter emulating the sound of the latter-day Drifters with a song that bears a pleasing resemblance to "Under the Boardwalk" in beat, texture, and theme. One suspects that, despite the Apollo Theater setting, the intent of this album was to emulate *Sam Cooke at the Copa* by presenting McPhatter in his most mainstream, accessible manner. The R&B elements were somewhat compromised, all to little avail since it never sold in large numbers anyway, but they're still the best reason for buying this reissue. *—Bruce Eder*

★ **The Forgotten Angel** / Sep. 29, 1998 / 32 Jazz ♦♦♦♦♦
Finally, a definitive compilation of Clyde McPhatter! This two-disc collection chronicles McPhatter's hits (and some tunes that should have been hits) from the early '50s through the early '60s. It begins with over a dozen selections of Drifters material from mid-1953 to late 1954, including "Lucille" and "Money Honey." After these come classics from McPhatter's solo career (the recordings here pick up in 1955), including "Without Love (There Is Nothing)," "Lover Please," "Thirty Days," "Lovey Dovey," "I Can't Stand Up Alone," and the oldies-radio regular "A Lover's Question." With this collection, which has relatively excellent sound quality (except the few live cuts), the 32 label has done fans of early R&B vocals a great service, for McPhatter is one of the undisputed greats (Smokey Robinson and Jackie Wilson were *his* fans). *The Forgotten Angel* will stand up to a lifetime of listening. *—Joslyn Layne*

A Shot of Rhythm & Blues / Jul. 18, 2000 / Sundazed ♦♦♦
McPhatter was dropping out of sight commercially when he recorded for Amy from 1965 to 1967. This compilation of both sides of his five 1965-1967 Amy singles (augmented by four previously unreleased alternate takes) demonstrates that although his voice was still in decent shape, there was really no compelling reason to think that he should have had been worthy of attention during this period. It's middling mid-'60s soul, and although McPhatter was able to record material by some name players—such as Joe Tex, Rick Hall, Billy Sherrill, and Van McCoy—he wasn't coming across great songs. And the truth was, McPhatter's voice wasn't as well suited to 1960s soul with full-bodied production as it was to doo wop and 1950s R&B. There's nothing that objectionable about these tracks, yet nothing too memorable, either, with McPhatter and his producers trying various settings, usually slick uptown soul ones. It hasn't been too easy to hear this stuff, and this reissue thus does have its value to big McPhatter fans, with Sundazed's typical thorough liner notes and documentation. *—Richie Unterberger*

The Atlantic & Mercury Sessions / Feb. 13, 2001 / Collectables ♦♦♦
This limited-edition two-disk 40-song compilation is made up of two solo albums cut for Atlantic Records, *Love Ballads* and *Clyde*, as well as *The Mercury Sessions Live* (aka *Live at the Apollo*), which included three bonus studio tracks. Clyde McPhatter recorded for MGM in between Atlantic and Mercury, but none of those tracks are included. McPhatter fans will note that his 1962 Top Ten hit, "Lover Please" (his most successful Mercury recording and final Top 40 hit), is missing, as is "Seven Days," his first solo effort, which made the pop charts but not this collection. So this is not the be all and end all McPhatter collection, but there are some pleasant surprises for those who are only in sync with the smooth balladeer's hits, as well as two versions of his biggest solo hit, "A Lover's Question" (the original and a live rendition). There are 11 live selections and the three bonus studio cuts, "I Told Myself a Lie," "Let's Try Again," and "Twice as Nice," comprising the second disk, which was recorded at Harlem's Apollo Theater with MC Bill Murray handling the intro. The clean CD sound is mesmerizing; backed by an ample orchestra, McPhatter does solid performances of "Lucille," "Second Window, Second Floor," "Without Love (There Is Nothing)" (his favorite recording), and others. These are excellent pop/R&B recordings that should have made McPhatter an international star, popular television performer, and icon in Vegas, but it never really happened like that, as he mainly worked the chitlin' circuit. *—Andrew Hamilton*

The Medallions

Group / Doo Wop, R&B

The Los Angeles-based Medallions—who formed in early 1954—are best known for their durable double-sider "The Letter" b/w "Buick '59," one of Dootsie Williams' first doo wop singles for his DooTone label. The original Medallions formed after intense 16-year-old lead singer Vernon Green, (a native of Denver, CO)—who was strolling down an East Los Angeles street, singing out loud, caught the ear of Walter "Dootsie" Williams, owner of Dootone, who encouraged Green to come to his offices. Green didn't have a group, but he wasted no time in putting together a quartet of street kids: Andrew Blue (tenor), Randolph Bryant (baritone), and Ira Foley (bass). Green, a polio victim who walked with difficulty, began calling his group the Medallions because of his penchant for wearing medallions around his neck.

Williams booked studio time for the group, and their first single, "The Letter" (written in the style of the Diablos' popular hit "The Wind"), received extensive airplay in Los Angeles and provided regional hits for the Dootone label in New York, Philadelphia, Pittsburgh, Cincinnati, and Cleveland, though its slow movement through the independent distribution territories precluded it from charting nationally. The single also started a Medallions trend for the next few singles: they continued writing in the same vein, with two distinct sides to their work: the romantic ballads on one side were sung straight, in almost agonizing purity, while the faster rockin' numbers on the flip were partly tongue-in-cheek out-of-control automobiles.

Willy Graham later replaced Blue, and Donald Woods joined to make it a quintet. There were about a dozen Dootone singles in all with this lineup. With Bryant on lead, Dootone issued the last Medallions single in mid-1955, but the group broke up shortly after. Undaunted, Green grabbed tenors Kenneth Williams and Frank Marshall and formed the Cameos, who quickly issued a single on Dootone the same month that "Edna" was released. Dootsie Williams then paired Vernon Green with the Dootones, christening them the "new" Medallions and sent them on a Canadian tour. (Their promo photo was actually a Dootones photo with a cutout of Green's head glued to the lower left-hand corner.) Woods and the others, meanwhile, left Green to strike out on their own as the Vel-Aires for Flip. In the fall of 1955, the new Medallions—Vernon and brother Jimmy Green (tenor), Charles Gardner (tenor, formerly of the Dootones), Albert Johnson (tenor), and Otis Scott (bass)—backed Johnny Morrisette on "My Pretty Baby"). Other lineups of the Medallions may have included Albert Johnson, Billy Foster, bass singers Bubba Carter and Joe Williams, and many others. Two more singles with Morrisette followed and the group became officially known as Vernon Green & the Medallions, recording three singles for Dootsie's newly re-christened Dooto label.

The new Medallions then jumped to Art Rupe's Specialty Records in 1957 and re-formed as the Phantoms. Their masquerade gimmick—wearing hoods on-stage—was a bit transparent: Green was the only known lead singer at the time in L.A. who walked with a cane because of his polio, so everyone knew who the lead "phantom" was.

Later in 1957, Green drifted back to Dooto with yet another Medallions, this time made up of Foster, Williams, and Jimmy Green. By 1962, Vernon and Jimmy Green, along with Gardner, Johnson, and Scott, recorded for Pan World and in 1964, Jerome Evans, Ed Carter, and Jimmy and Vernon Green recorded the group's next Medallions single for Minit. Green had a car accident in the mid-'60s and shunned singing for nine years, returning to Dooto as a solo artist, this time to chance his arm at soul music, in 1973. He was backed by Evans, Maxine Green (his sister-in-law), and Doris Green. Vernon Green never regained his early momentum, but he continued to perform despite occasional bouts of bad health and the fact that he was confined to a wheelchair. *—Bryan Thomas*

● **Speedin'** / Apr. 16, 1996 / Ace ♦♦♦♦♦
The Medallions are usually remembered for inspiring the phrase "pompatous of love," which Steve Miller misheard in the recitation from their hit "The Letter." The flip of that single, "Buick '59," was a "Rocket 69" rip-off with irregular meter and a lot of horsing around that became their other well-remembered hit. The success of "Buick '59" inspired the Medallions to follow up with a slew of car songs like "Volvo '59," "Speedin'," and "Push

Button Automobile," most of which feature the group's humorous sound effects and other dramatic flourishes. Lead singer Vernon Green was also a fine balladeer, as heard on his excellent composition "Magic Mountain." *Speedin'* collects all 12 of the Medallions' Dootone and Dooto singles plus the previously unreleased "Ticket to Love." The lore surrounding "The Letter" will continue to draw curious listeners, but it's arguably the car songs that make *Speedin'* such a fun and consistent listening experience. *—Greg Adams*

Glenn Medeiros

b. Jun. 24, 1970, Hawaii

Vocals / Dance-Pop, Urban

A handsome teenage poster-boy type, Glenn Medeiros produced mostly schmaltz-style love ballads, but he also branched off into harder, funkier styles. He had a big hit in 1990 with the R&B dance tune "The Girl's Not Worth It," on which Bobby Brown lent some vocals. *—Bil Carpenter*

● **Glenn Medeiros** / 1987 / Amherst ♦♦♦

A Hawaiian-born vocalist discovered through a local radio station talent search, Glenn Medeiros made marginally interesting pop/soul/rock material, but it was of such generally light value that while he did get songs on the charts, they seldom made any impression. That was the case with much of this material, although he subsequently was able to move from Amherst to MCA. *—Ron Wynn*

Bill Medley

b. Sep. 19, 1940, Santa Ana, CA

Vocals / Blue-Eyed Soul, Adult Contemporary

Best-known as the Righteous Brother with the rich baritone, Bill Medley grew up surrounded by music: his father led a band and played saxophone, while his mother sang and played piano. Medley himself sang in his church choir as a boy, with the glee club in high school, and in the early '60s in his band the Paramours. Soon after, Medley began singing with Bobby Hatfield as the Righteous Brothers, a partnership that spawned hits like "You've Lost That Lovin' Feeling" and "Unchained Melody." When the duo parted ways in 1968, Medley pursued a solo career, scoring hits such as "Brown-Eyed Woman" and releasing albums like *Soft and Soulful, Nobody Knows*, and *A Song for You.*

Medley reunited with Hatfield in 1974, then took a five-year break from performing in 1976. However, he continued to record throughout the '80s, scoring his most notable hit with the Grammy Award-winning, number-one single "(I've Had) The Time of My Life," a duet with Jennifer Warnes taken from the soundtrack to *Dirty Dancing.* Meanwhile, the Righteous Brothers' popularity rose again thanks to the inclusion of "You've Lost That Lovin' Feeling" on the *Top Gun* soundtrack and "Unchained Melody" on the *Ghost* soundtrack; Medley and Hatfield responded by reuniting again and touring the oldies circuit, which they continued to play throughout the '90s. Medley still found time for his solo career, releasing albums such as 1996's *Christmas Memories* and the following year's *Almost Home*, while living with his family in Newport Beach. *—Heather Phares*

● **The Best of Bill Medley** / 1990 / Curb ♦♦♦♦♦

Mel & Kim

Group / Dance-Pop, Pop

English-born sisters Mel and Kim Appleby rose to prominence in the late '80s thanks to the producing team of Stock, Aitken & Waterman. In late 1986, Mel & Kim released their debut single, "Respectable." The song combined '80s dance-pop with Stock, Aitken & Waterman's trademark slick production. "Respectable" became a huge international success, helping to launch their debut album *F.L.M.* up the charts in 1987. The album produced two other singles: "F.L.M." and "Showing Out."

F.L.M. was to be the sisters' only album. In 1988, Mel was diagnosed with cancer and died of the disease early in 1990. Kim recorded a solo album in the early '90s, but it was not as successful as her work with Mel and Kim. *—Jonathan Lewis*

F.L.M. / 1987 / Atlantic ♦♦

Mel & Kim can thank their success on the team of Stock, Aitken & Waterman, who were also the producers that brought the world the likes of Kylie Minogue and Rick Astley in the late '80s. Mel & Kim were, however, the least talented of their stablemates, a fact that becomes very obvious on their debut album *F.L.M.* This is one of the more insipid examples of '80s dance-pop. The songwriting is Stock, Aitken, & Waterman's weakest, and the limited vocal ability of the Appleby sisters is very apparent. Even for writers and producers of eminently disposable pop music, the three-person team have outdone themselves on this completely forgettable album. *—Jonathan Lewis*

● **That's the Way It Is: The Best of Mel & Kim** / Jan. 8, 2002 / EMI ♦♦

Mel & Tim

f. Holly Springs, MS

Group / Chicago Soul, Soul, Pop-Soul, Disco

Chicago soul duo Mel & Tim were cousins—Mel Hardin and Tim McPherson—who actually hailed from Holly Springs, MS, and made their way to Chicago via St. Louis. They were discovered by Gene Chandler and signed to his Bamboo label in 1969, when they scored a Top Ten pop and R&B single with the good-humored classic "Backfield in Motion." The follow-up, "Good Guys Only Win in the Movies," supplied the title for their first album and hit the R&B Top 20 later that year. Mel & Tim subsequently moved to Stax, where they landed a second Top Five R&B smash with the ballad "Starting All Over Again" (also the title track of their second album). Mel & Tim performed at the late-1972 charity concert *Wattstax* and were featured in the documentary film of the same name, singing "I May Not Be What You Want." Their self-titled final album appeared in 1973, after which the cousins faded away from the music scene. *—Steve Huey*

Good Guys Only Win in the Movies / 1969 / Sundazed ♦♦♦♦♦

Mel & Tim's debut album featured both of their smashes, "Backfield in Motion" and "Good Guys Only Win in the Movies." As full-length soul records of the era go, it's a bit above average, if only because the duo wrote a high percentage of their own material. It's sweet Chicago pop/soul circa 1969-1970 at its most centrist: not too slick, not terribly earthy, and not as distinctive as the Impressions or Gene Chandler, although the sound bears general similarities. The CD reissue has five extra bonus tracks from singles that were issued around the same era. *—Richie Unterberger*

● **Starting All Over Again** / 1972 / Stax ♦♦♦♦♦

Mel & Tim were a classic Chicago soul vocal duo, recording in Muscle Shoals in the Deep South for Stax, making records that fit comfortably next to those made in Philadelphia. It may sound incongruous, but their 1972 album *Starting All Over Again*—released on CD with four bonus tracks—is a wonderful record that blends the sweet production of Philly with tight Southern rhythms and Windy City harmony. And that' s not even mentioning an impeccable set of songs, many written or co-written by Phillip Mitchell, along with sharp covers of soul classics like "Wrap It Up" and "I'm Your Puppet." The title track is a stone masterpiece—an epic tale of a couple trying to repair their love—but the rest of the album isn't far behind. In fact, it ranks as one of the finest soul albums of the early '70s. *—Stephen Thomas Erlewine*

The Mello-Kings

f. 1956, Mount Vernon, NY

Group / Doo Wop, R&B

The Mello-Kings were one-hit wonders in the doo wop world, fondly remembered for the their lone national hit, "Tonite, Tonite." They were an all-white vocal group from Mt. Vernon, a working class suburb of New York City, located in Westchester County just to the north of the Bronx. Led by Robert Scholl, aka Bob Scholl (b. Jul 14, 1938 in Mt. Vernon, NY), the other members included Robert's brother Jerry Scholl, Ed Quinn, Neil Arena, and Larry Esposito, all students from George Washington High.

By the fall of 1956, they were calling themselves the Mellotones, gaining attention in the local area and catching the ear of a black pianist named Dick Levister, who offered to become the group's manager and accompany them during live performances. It was Levister who brought them to the attention of Al Silver, who owned both the Herald and Ember labels, which had been up and running since 1952. Both New York-based labels specialized in vocal group records.

Silver, one of the pioneering R&B label owners, had by this point already recorded and released numerous hit singles by acts on both Herald and Ember, including the Nutmegs (whose 1955 R&B smash hit "Story Untold" made it to number two in the nation), the Five Satins (whose "In the Still of the Night," a smash in 1956, had been leased to Ember; they later scored a hit for the label with "To the Aisle," a Top Ten R&B hit—number-25 pop—in the summer of 1957), and the Turbans (whose "When You Dance" was the group's best charter for Herald). Silver liked what he heard and the group—with their trademark white jackets (at Levister's insistence, supposedly)—helped them forge an identity with the teenage public. For the Mellotones' first release, Silver chose a tune called "Tonite, Tonite" (Herald number 502), written by Billy Myles (who also penned "All My Love You Were Made For" with Jackie Wilson). It was released during the summer of 1957 and became an immediate regional smash hit. Unfortunately, Silver discovered too late that there was already a record out that summer on George Goldner's Gee label by a group called the Mello-Tones, (their "Rosie Lee" later climbed into the Top 24 on the pop charts). A quick name change was in order and using Levister's nickname "King," "Tonite, Tonite" (Herald number 502) was quickly re-released as by the Mello-Kings. The single was a big seller in the Northeast, again having regional ties. They made more than one TV appearance with Dick Clark on both the daily *American Bandstand* and his weekly *Saturday Night* show for ABC network.

Late in 1957, the Mello-Kings recorded their next single, "The Chapel on the Hill," which failed to earn them much additional success. Their next single, "Baby Tell Me Why Why Why" also missed. However, their next single, "Valerie," became a regional hit in the New York area on its way to becoming a classic example of doo wop despite the fact that it didn't chart nationally. At the height of their popularity, they were added to "package" tours, where they performed alongside acts like the Channels, the Dells, the Flamingos, the Spaniels, and labelmates the Five Satins. The success of "Tonite, Tonite" and to a lesser extent, "Valerie," however, earned them a slot on Herald's first compilation of hits, a full-length LP entitled *Herald the Beat*, which featured hits by the Turbans, Nutmegs, Faye Adams, and unabashedly gay vocal duo Charlie & Ray. Sales of the excellent LP helped improved the Mello-Kings' visibility on the music scene in 1958. Their label continued to issue the Mello-Kings' lone hit on all subsequent compilation albums.

The group began going through some personnel changes shortly thereafter, and despite releasing five more singles on the Herald label from 1959 to 1961 while continuing to score hits with groups like the Silhouettes "Get a Job" and Maurice Williams and the Zodiacs ("Stay,") to name two, no further hits were forthcoming for the Mello-Kings. The Mello-Kings made a final appearance during one of Richard Nader's very first revival shows in 1969; they can be heard reprising "Tonite, Tonite" on the Kama Sutra release of the live recording. They subsequently broke up. Bob Scholl died in a boating accident on August 27, 1975, in New York. *—Bryan Thomas*

Tonite, Tonite / 1960 / Relic ♦♦♦♦♦

● **Greatest Hits** / Aug. 17, 1994 / Collectables ♦♦♦♦♦

Harold Melvin & the Blue Notes

f. 1954, Philadelphia, PA

Vocals / Philly Soul, Smooth Soul, Soul, Doo Wop

Harold Melvin was one of the driving forces behind Philadelphia soul, leading his group the Blue Notes to the top of the charts during their stint on Kenny Gamble & Leon Huff's Philadelphia International label. Despite Melvin's billing out front, the Blue Notes' focal point was lead singer and onetime drummer Teddy Pendergrass, whose surging baritone graced the Blue Notes' recordings during their glory years of 1972-1975 and gave them a truly distinctive sound. Their output ranged from sweeping, extended proto-disco dance tracks to silky, smoldering ballads, all wrapped up in Gamble & Huff's lushly orchestrated production. When Pendergrass left for a solo career, Melvin & the Blue Notes' commercial fortunes largely reverted to the pre-Pendergrass days (of which there were quite a few), although they did continue to record for a time. They never really disbanded, and by the time Melvin passed away in 1997, he'd been leading the Blue Notes for over four decades.

Harold Melvin was born June 25, 1939, in Philadelphia. A self-taught pianist, he began singing doo wop as a teenager with a group called the Charlemagnes, and put together the very first edition of the Blue Notes in 1954. The original lineup was a quintet featuring Melvin as the lead singer (for a time), songwriter, arranger, and choreographer; ironically, he would mostly relinquish those duties by the time the group achieved its greatest success. The other members were co-leader Bernard Williams, Roosevelt Brodie, Jesse Gillis Jr., and Franklin Peaker. The Blue Notes cut their first single, "If You Love Me," for Josie in 1956, and turned it into a regional hit. They recorded for several other labels over the next few years, Dot chief among them, before scoring their first R&B chart hit in 1960 with "My Hero" (released on Val-Ue). Numerous personnel shifts kept the group in flux despite steady recording activity, and Bernard Williams split off to lead what he dubbed the Original Blue Notes in the mid-'60s. Melvin assembled a new version of the Blue Notes centered around lead singer John Atkins, who returned the group to the R&B charts in 1965 with the Landa single "Get Out (And Let Me Cry)." Further releases on Arctic, Checker, and Uni followed over the rest of the '60s, as well as more personnel changes. During the late '60s, the group toured often with the Cadillacs, whose young drummer Teddy Pendergrass would prove to be Melvin's greatest discovery.

Pendergrass first joined the Blue Notes' backing band, but demonstrated so much vocal talent that after John Atkins left in 1970, Melvin soon elevated him to the post of lead vocalist. This move helped them land a deal with Gamble & Huff's Philadelphia International label in 1972, just as the company was taking its place as soul music's new epicenter; Pendergrass' voice was similar to that of Dells singer Marvin Junior, whom Gamble & Huff had courted heavily. By this time, the Blue Notes consisted of Melvin, Pendergrass, bass vocalist Lawrence Brown, baritone vocalist Bernard Wilson, and tenor vocalist Lloyd Parks. With Gamble & Huff now supplying top-quality material and production, Harold Melvin & the Blue Notes would become one of the most popular groups in R&B over the next few years. Their self-titled debut mostly featured songs that had been written in anticipation of landing Marvin Junior. The first single, "I Miss You," was a hit on the R&B charts, but their second was a smash—the classic ballad "If You Don't Know Me By Now," which featured an anguished, star-making vocal turn from Pendergrass. "If You Don't Know Me By Now" went all the way to number-one R&B, and also Became their only Top Five hit on the pop side; it was later covered in 1989 for a number-one hit by Simply Red.

The Blue Notes scored again in 1973 with the string-laden dance track "The Love I Lost," credited by many observers as one of the first disco records; it was their second R&B chart-topper and Top Ten pop single. The accompanying album *Black and Blue* produced another R&B Top Ten in the follow-up "Satisfaction Guaranteed (Or Take Your Love Back)." In 1974, Lloyd Parks was replaced by Jerry Cummings, who debuted on the R&B chart-topping LP *To Be True*. "Where Are All My Friends" and "Bad Luck" continued their string of Top Ten R&B hits, and a new addition to the group, female vocalist Sharon Paige, helped bring them back to the top of the R&B charts in 1975 with the duet "Hope That We Can Be Together Soon." Another excellent album followed later that year in *Wake Up Everybody*, whose title track was another R&B number one; "Tell the World How I Feel About 'Cha Baby" also reached the R&B Top Ten, and the album cut "Don't Leave Me This Way" was later covered for a disco smash by Thelma Houston.

However, tension was building within the group. The heavily spotlighted Pendergrass was hungry for separate billing, but Melvin, still the group's chief organizing force, turned him down. In 1976, Pendergrass left the Blue Notes for a solo career that quickly made him one of R&B's top sex symbols. Sharon Paige helped fill his shoes on lead vocals, as well as new male lead David Ebo, whose sound was fairly similar to Pendergrass'. However, Pendergrass' departure also signaled the end of the Blue Notes' relationship with Philadelphia International—their next recordings were for ABC, for whom they hit the R&B Top Ten in 1977 with the title track of *Reaching for the World*. It would prove to be their last major success, however; after one more album for ABC, they moved to MCA subsidiary Source in 1979 for two LPs that failed to re-ignite their commercial momentum. Cummings and Wilson had both departed in 1977, replaced by Dwight Johnson and William Spratelly, and Paige and Ebo both left in 1980. Still, Melvin soldiered on, helming one last album of new material for Philly World in 1984's hopefully titled *Talk It Up (Tell Everybody)*. It was mildly popular in the U.K., but not enough to re-establish them. Melvin continued to tour with versions of the Blue Notes steadily into the '90s, and Sharon Paige eventually returned to the fold as well. Sadly, Melvin suffered a stroke and never fully recovered; he passed away on March 24, 1997 in his beloved hometown of Philadelphia. *—Steve Huey*

Harold Melvin & the Blue Notes / 1972 / CBS ♦♦♦♦

A fantastic debut by Harold Melvin & the Blue Notes that wasn't meant to be. Most of these songs, including "If You Don't Know Me By Now," were originally written for the Dells, but the deal fell through. Harold Melvin got the opportunity because his ex-drummer Teddy Pendergrass had a voice similar to Dells lead singer Marvin Junior. The way Pendergrass tore into these songs, nobody remotely suspected that these love dramas were written for anybody but Teddy. He sounds like he's about to lose it when he sings "I Miss You" as he pleads with his ex-love about how he has changed. The poignant "If You Don't Know Me By Now" sold a million for the Blue Notes and did even better years later for Simply Red. "Be For Real" is one of the finest recorded pieces in R&B history; it's not a song, it's a pleader where a guy admonishes his woman for looking down on people. They dusted off "Let Me Into Your World" for the Blue Notes; this one was not written for the Dells, as Gamble & Huff had recorded it a few years earlier with the O'Jays for Neptune Records. A hard-hitting package that established Harold Melvin & the Blue Notes as a force to be reckoned with. *—Andrew Hamilton*

Black & Blue / 1973 / Philadelphia International ♦♦♦♦♦

Lots of goodies on Harold Melvin & the Blue Notes' second LP under the auspices of Kenny Gamble & Leon Huff. "Satisfaction Guaranteed (Or Take Your Love Back)" is tight, as is the questioning "Is There a Place for Me." Lyricist Cary Gilbert collaborates with Gamble & Huff on "I'm Weak for You," a slow drama that Teddy and the crew tear up. The driving force here is the epic "The Love I Lost," a heart-rending tear-jerker that's a tad too long; the "I lost you, sorry I lost you" background chants get mundane toward the end, where 30 seconds of that would have been more than sufficient. The only clunker is a hokey MOR production of "Cabaret." This totally inappropriate disaster will have you skipping the track every time. *—Andrew Hamilton*

To Be True / 1975 / Philadelphia International ♦♦♦♦♦

The third album from the melodramatic vocal quintet and it features an array of R&B classics. While Teddy Pendergrass was featured on this album, he did not lead every song. The three releases were "Where Are All My Friends," "Bad Luck" and "Hope That We Can Be Together Soon." All three were *Billboard* R&B top ten winners with the latter reaching number one. "Where Are All My Friends" and "Bad Luck" mirror each other in that both are uptempo numbers that depict the misfortunes of a man. The former has a smoother vocal presentation with a mid-verse rhythm change-up. The latter has an incessant groovin' rhythm where Teddy Pendergrass cuts into the lyric with conviction with his robust delivery as he does on each selection he leads. "Hope That We Can Be Together Soon" features the velvety smooth vocals of Sharon Paige on this easy-flowing number. While Harold Melvin carries most of the vocal duties, Pendergrass steps in for a one-liner and closes out on the vamp. Whereas most ballads climax towards the end of the song, the most climatic part of this number one song is the string and horn intro. The title track "To Be True" is a sleeper. Not just for its conciliating melody, but also for the lyrical content that calls for two lovers to find time for each before all is lost. Harold Melvin's debonair vocals are featured on lead. This is one of four consecutive great albums to come from the Philadelphia vocal quintet. *—Craig Lytle*

Wake Up Everybody / 1975 / Philadelphia International ♦♦♦♦

Even though Harold Melvin & the Blue Notes were an R&B group with much soul, the message in their music was truly profound, uplifting, thought provoking, and full of love. This album featured only two singles. The title track is a plea to the world to come together and rid the society of all its ills. Written by the prolific writing team of McFadden/Whitehead/Carstarphen, it conveys a message in line with the ideology of the album's producers. The connection felt when listening to the song permeates the soul, and will momentarily produce thoughts in one to make a change. This is a very moving song. It held on to the number-one spot on the *Billboard* R&B charts for two consecutive weeks. The aggressive arrangement of "Tell the World How I Feel About 'Cha Baby" carried it to number seven on the charts. Other notables are "Keep on Lovin' You," "To Be Free to Be Who We Are," and "I'm Searching for a Love." Sharon Paige is featured on the balladic flow of the latter. "Don't Leave Me This Way" became a disco theme for Thelma Houston. This album was the final chapter of Harold Melvin & the Blue Notes featuring Theodore Pendergrass, who released a solo album the following year. *—Craig Lytle*

★ **Collectors' Item (All Their Greatest Hits!)** / 1976 / Philadelphia International ♦♦♦♦♦

There's definitely a need for a thorough career retrospective of Harold Melvin & the Blue Notes: one covering their '50s and '60s period, the hit-filled run headed by Teddy Pendergrass during the first half of the '70s, and even the group's less viable post-Pendergrass years. Of course, with the maze of record companies involved, this is a tall order. So, those wanting to check out the group should start with this collection of their prime Philadelphia International hits. Although only containing eight tracks, *Collectors Items* has most of the chart-toppers, including "If You Don't Know Me By Now," "Wake Up Everybody," and "The Love I Lost." The slick, Philly bump groove marks most of the material, showing why producers Leon Huff & Kenny Gamble, as well as arranger Thom Bell, deserve a good portion of credit for their label's success beyond having a major impact on the black music scene, the Philly Sound, like Motown and Stax before, had substantial crossover appeal as well, influencing the likes of David Bowie and Elton John. And with Pendergrass' soul-fire, gospel-drenched vocal delivery lighting up extended cuts like "Bad Luck" and "Where Are All My Friends," not to mention most of the numbers here, the smooth musical backdrops are infused with just the right amount of grit. A great collection, topped off with a fine duet featuring Pendergrass and future Blue Notes singer Sharon Paige. If you feel the need for a more thorough collection than this budget-priced release, check out Epic's 15-track *If You Don't Know Me By Now: The Best of Harold Melvin & the Blue Notes*, which covers the same mid-'70s period. *—Stephen Cook*

Reaching for the World / 1977 / ABC ♦♦♦

Harold Melvin & the Blue Notes' first album without any involvement from Teddy Pendergrass and Philadelphia International Records is better than anticipated. David Ebo sounds identical to Pendergrass and delivers some spirited leads on the skimpy eight-song LP. Ebbo excels on "Reaching For the World," an uplifting, be-what-you-wanna-be song that sounds like a Gamble & Huff production. He continues the duet trend he started with Sharon Paige with the mellow "After You Love Me Why Do You Leave Me." Some of the songs are weak; "Hostage Pt. 1 & 2," for instance, doesn't live up to its intriguing title. Overall, though, this is a good first effort and proves that the Blue Notes' sound didn't leave with Pendergrass. *—Andrew Hamilton*

The Blue Album / 1980 / Valley Vue ♦♦♦

Harold trudges on, Teddy Pendergrass-less, on a lackluster effort. The *Blue Album* only has six songs; one, "Tonight's the Night," rambles on for over eight minutes. Gene McFadden and John Whitehead contribute three of the six songs—not their best, but "Your Love Is Taking Me on a Journey" isn't half bad. Harold puts some nice touches on "I Should Be Your Lover," a Gamble & Huff song originally recorded by the O'Jays. Harold added some lyrics and monologue and gets co-writer credits on the new version. *—Andrew Hamilton*

☆ **If You Don't Know Me by Now: The Best of Harold Melvin & the Blue Notes** / Feb. 28, 1995 / Epic/Legacy ✦✦✦✦✦

Blue Notes & Ballads / Feb. 17, 1998 / Epic/Legacy ✦✦✦✦

It doesn't get much better than the Blue Notes and ballads. The only way they could have improved this was by including some of Teddy Pendergrass' solo sides, like "Come and Go With Me" or "Turn Off the Lights." These are the cream of Harold Melvin & the Blue Notes' '70s ballads on Philadelphia International Records. Two delicious selections feature Sharon Paige and Harold Melvin on leads: "I Hope That We Can Get Together Soon" and the sexy, shuffling "You Know How to Make Me Feel So Good" are to love songs what Godiva's are to chocolates. Can a song get any more real then "I Miss You"? Lloyd Parks starts the mournful drama wailing like a wounded dog; Harold delivers the coolest begging monologue ever, and Teddy sings like he's going to self-destruct before the song ends. The much-recorded "If You Don't Know Me By Know" is accompanied by gems like "I'm Weak for You," "To Be True," "Let Me Into Your World," and the motivating "To Be Free to Be Who We Are." The only glaring omission is the epic "Be For Real," one of their most memorable numbers. It's a shame this incarnation of Harold Melvin & the Blue Notes didn't stay intact longer, yet it's a blessing they hung around enough to give us priceless treasures like these. *—Andrew Hamilton*

★ **The Ultimate Blue Notes** / Aug. 21, 2001 / Epic/Legacy ✦✦✦✦✦

Actually the *Ultimate Blue Notes* with Teddy Pendergrass, this collection covers their Philadelphia International years from 1972-1975 as in-depth and representative of the band's talents as a single disc can get. Not to split too many hairs, but the vocal soul group did have a handful of good songs past this period, although none that match the majestic sweep of this material. Boasting dance beats, swirling strings, smooth crooning storytelling, and Pendergrass' booming baritone, this is some of the best as well as most representative R&B of the '70s, and this 15-track compilation is all you'll need to hear why. Practically double the amount of songs as *Collectors Item* and over twice as long, this anthology adds such often ignored gems as the almost eight-minute "Yesterday I Had the Blues" and the original version of "Don't Leave Me This Way" before Thelma Houston took it Top Ten, which itself clocks in at another six minutes. An updating of Legacy's 1995 *If You Don't Know Me By Now: The Best of Harold Melvin & the Blue Notes*, this 2001 disc features improved sound, new liner notes with full chart documentation for pop and R&B positions, slightly different track selection, all full-length album versions, and a snazzier-looking package. Sequenced for most appropriate musical flow (as opposed to chronologically), the disc mixes upbeat tracks with softer ballads for a more consistent listening experience, helped by the coherent Gamble & Huff production team. If you need one album from the legendary soul vocal group, this is certainly the one to choose. *—Hal Horowitz*

The Memphis Boys

Group / Memphis Soul, Soul, Funk, Soul-Blues

Not to be confused with the Mar-Keys, Memphis Horns, Bar-Kays, or any other ensemble, the Memphis Boys were session musicians led by guitarist Reggie Young. They were a busy group who played on over 120 hits made between the late '60s and early '70s before relocating to Nashville in 1972. Keyboardist Bobby Emmons and Bobby Wood, bassist Mike Leech, and drummer Gene Chrisman were other members. They played on recordings by Bobby Womack, Joe Tex, Elvis Presley, and later with Delbert McClinton, Smokey Robinson, and the Highwaymen. *—Ron Wynn*

● **The Memphis Boys** / 1990 / Vanguard ✦✦

The Memphis Horns

Group / Soul, Funk, Retro-Soul, Disco, Urban

Arguably the greatest soul horn section ever, the Memphis Horns were a critical part of the Stax formula during the '60s and '70s, as well as prolific contributors to numerous other sessions since the label's demise. Though today the name is identified with the duo of trumpeter Wayne Jackson and tenor saxophonist Andrew Love, the band at one time also included tenor saxophonist Ed Logan, trombonists Lewis Collins and Jack Hale, and baritone saxophonist James Mitchell. This was the lineup that recorded for RCA in the '70s, cutting LPs produced by Booker T. Jones and others. They also backed King Curtis and Aretha Franklin in the '70s. But they are best known for appearances on songs by virtually every Stax artist. The duo of Jackson and Love issued their own LP in 1992 for an independent label. *—Ron Wynn*

● **The Memphis Horns** / 1971 / Telarc ✦✦✦✦

The first chance for the Memphis Horns to step to the front of the studio, their 1970 debut album was a collection of simmering grooves and brassy horns. Though they weren't as crucial on their own as the competition (Booker T. & the MG's and the Dixie Flyers, the latter with several members featured here as well), the group really impresses on Memphis standards like Otis Redding's "I Can't Turn You Loose" and "Fa Fa Fa Fa Fa (Sad Song)," the Box Tops' "Cry Like a Baby," and a torrid one-two punch: the Sam & Dave medley "You Don't Know (Like I Know)" and "Soul Man." *—John Bush*

High on Music / 1976 / RCA ✦✦✦

Get Up and Dance / 1977 / RCA ✦✦✦

When R&B went totally high-tech around 1983-1984, horns became the exception instead of the rule for many urban contemporary artists. In the '80s and '90s, it wasn't uncommon for an R&B producer to act as a one-man (or one-woman) band; instead of using a lot of studio musicians, the producer could program all the synthesizers and drum machines himself/herself. But before that, horns were a big part of many R&B recordings, and no horn section was in greater demand in the '60s and '70s than the Memphis Horns. As busy as session work kept them in the '70s, the Memphis Horns managed to record some noteworthy albums for RCA during that decade. One of them was 1977's *Get Up and Dance*, which isn't a masterpiece but is generally decent. On this diverse collection of funk, soul, and disco, the Horns employ several guest vocalists, including Deniece Williams, D.J. Rogers, Jim Gilstrap, and Lani Groves. The LP's highlights range from the hit "Just for Your Love" (a pleasant ballad) to the Parliament-influenced "What the Funk" to the sleek disco instrumental "Memphis Nights." Parts of the album are mellow, and parts of it are quite funky. *Get Up and Dance* has been out of print for a long time, but it's worth acquiring if you happen to come across a copy somewhere. *—Alex Henderson*

Memphis Horns Band II / 1978 / RCA ✦✦✦

Numerous guest vocal appearances augment the Memphis Horns here, giving the album a wider appeal. From the jazzy pop of "Living for the Music" to Average White Band clones "Don't Change It" and "Give It to Me," the horns' bright, full, brassy sound dominates. A female vocalist delivers "Our Love Will Survive," and disco numbers "Party Line" and "New Beginning" are as delightful as anything else on an excellent album that deserves to be reissued. *—Andrew Hamilton*

Flame Out / 1992 / Lucky Seven ✦✦

The Meters

f. 1966, New Orleans, LA, **db.** 1977

Group / Funk, New Orleans R&B, Soul

The Meters defined New Orleans funk, not only on their own recordings, but also as the backing band for numerous artists, including many produced by Allen Toussaint. Where the funk of Sly Stone and James Brown was wild, careening, and determinedly urban, the Meters were down-home and earthy. Nearly all of their own recordings were instrumentals, putting the emphasis on the organic and complex rhythms. The syncopated, layered percussion intertwined with the gritty grooves of the guitar and organ, creating a distinctive sound that earned a small, devoted cult during the '70s, including musicians like Paul McCartney and Robert Palmer, both of whom used the group as a backing band for recording. Despite their reputation as an extraordinary live band, the Meters never broke into the mainstream, but their sound provided the basis for much of the funk and hip-hop of the '80s and '90s.

Throughout their career, the Meters were always led by Art Neville (keyboard, vocals), one of the leading figures of the New Orleans musical community. As a teenager in high school, he recorded the seminal "Mardi Gras Mambo" with his group, the Hawketts, for Chess Records. The exposure with the Hawketts led to solo contracts with Specialty and Instant, where he released a handful of singles that became regional hits in the early '60s. Around 1966, he formed Art Neville & the Sounds with his brothers Aaron and Charles (both vocals), guitarist Leo Nocentelli, drummer Joseph "Zigaboo" Modeliste, and bassist George Porter. The band grew out of informal jam sessions the musicians held in local New Orleans nightclubs. After spending a few months playing under the Sounds name, producer Allen Toussaint and Marshall Sehorn hired the group—without the vocalists—to be the house band for their label Sansu Enterprises.

As the house band for Sansu, the Meters played on records by Earl King, Lee Dorsey, Chris Kenner, and Betty Harris, as well as Toussaint himself. They also performed and recorded on their own, releasing danceable instrumental singles on Josie Records. "Sophisticated Cissy" and "Cissy Strut" became Top Ten R&B hits in the spring of 1969, followed by the number-11 hits "Look-Ka Py Py" and "Chicken Strut" a year later. The Meters stayed at Josie until 1972, and during that entire time they reached the R&B Top 50 consistently, usually placing within the Top 40. In 1972, the group moved to Reprise Records, yet they didn't sever their ties with Sansu, electing to keep Toussaint as their producer and Sehon as their manager. Ironically, the Meters didn't have nearly as many hit singles at Reprise, yet their profile remained remarkably high. If anything, the group became hipper, performing on records by Robert Palmer, Dr. John, LaBelle, King Biscuit Boy, and Paul McCartney. By the release of 1975's *Fire on the Bayou*, the Meters had a Top 40 hit with *Rejuvenation*'s "Hey Pocky A-Way" (1974), and they had gained a significant following among rock audience and critics. *Fire on the Bayou* received significant praise, and the group opened for the Rolling Stones on the British band's 1975 and 1976 tours.

During 1975, the Meters embarked on the Wild Tchoupitoulas project with Art's uncle and cousin George and Amos Landry, two members of the Mardi Gras ceremonial black Indian tribe, the Wild Tchoupitoulas. The Meters, the Landrys, and the Neville brothers—Aaron, Charles, Art, and Cyril—were all involved in the recording of the album, which received enthusiastic reviews upon its release in 1976. Cyril joined the Meters after the record's release. Despite all of the acclaim for *The Wild Tchoupitoulas*, its adventurous tendencies indicated that the group was feeling constrained by its signature sound. Such suspicions were confirmed the following year, when they separated from Toussaint and Sehorn, claiming they needed to take control of their artistic direction. Following the split, the Meters released *New Directions* in 1977, but shortly after its appearance, Toussaint and Sehorn claimed the rights to the group's name. Instead of fighting, the band broke up, with Art and Cyril forming the Neville Brothers with Aaron and Charles, while the remaining trio became session musicians in New Orleans. Modeliste, in particular, became a well-known professional musician, touring with the New Barbarians in 1979 and moving to L.A. during the '80s.

The Meters reunited as a touring unit in 1990 with Russell Batiste taking over the drum duties from Modeliste. Four years later, Nocentelli left the band, allegedly because he and Art disagreed whether the band should be paid for samples hip-hop groups took from their old records; he was replaced by Brian Stoltz, who had played with the Neville Brothers. The Meters continued to tour throughout the '90s. *—Stephen Thomas Erlewine*

The Meters / 1969 / Sundazed ✦✦✦

This seminal New Orleans funk group's debut album features the semi-hit "Cissy Strut" and its follow-up, "Sophisticated Sissy." This 1999 reissue also offers two previously unreleased bonus tracks, "The Look of Love" and "Soul Machine." Other highlights include "Here Comes the Meter Man," "Live Wire," and "Sehorn's Farm." *—Cub Koda*

Look-Ka Py Py / Jan. 1970 / Sundazed ✦✦✦✦

The second album by Art Neville's band continues the sound that made them New Orleans legends. In addition to the title track, there's plenty of funk aboard in songs like

like "Pungee," "9 'Til 5," "Rigor Mortis," "Funky Miracle," and "Yeah, You're Right." This 1999 reissue also features two previously unreleased bonus tracks, "Grass" and "Borro." *—Cub Koda*

Struttin' / 1970 / Sundazed ♦♦♦
As the third full-length album released by the Meters, *Struttin'* may not appear to be drastically different than its predecessors, at least not on the surface. After all, the title of the lead single "Chicken Strut" intentionally recalls their previous biggest "Cissy Strut," and it has the same basic Meters groove. And if the essential sound remains unchanged, that's because that organic, earthy funk is the Meters' signature. Other groups have tried to replicate it, but nobody ever played it better. Because of that, *Struttin* is an enjoyable record, even if it never quite feels like anything more focused than a series of jam sessions; after all, that's what it was. This time around, however, the Meters did make a conscious decision to emphasize vocals, and not just with shout-alongs on the chorus ("Chicken Strut," "Same Old Thing"), but with Art Neville's leads on covers of Ty Hunter's soulful uptown shuffle "Darling, Darling, Darling," Jimmy Webb's groovy ballad "Wichita Lineman," and Lee Dorsey's "Ride Your Pony" (the Meters provided support on the original recording). This gives the album a bit more diversity than its predecessors, which is welcome, even for devotees of the group's admittedly addictive sound. But the real difference is how the band seems willing to expand their signature sound. "Hand Clapping Song" is a spare, syncopated breakdown without an obvious through-line, while "Joog" turns the group's groove inside out. These variations are entertaining—as entertaining as the vocals—and the songs that are solidly in the Meters tradition are also fun. The results are pretty terrific, though given the fact that *Struttin'* never really pulls itself into a coherent album, it may be the kind of first-rate record only aficionados of the band will need to seek out. *—Stephen Thomas Erlewine*

Cabbage Alley / 1972 / Sundazed ♦♦♦
Leaving Josie for Reprise did change the Meters, even if the change wasn't necessarily for the better. They became slicker, jammier, and, in the conventional sense, funkier, even if the grit seemed to start to dissipate. So, even if this is just the Meters' fourth album, *Cabbage Alley* does mark a sea-change in their outlook, bringing them fully into the '70s and finding them sacrificing feel for texture, even if that's a very subtle transition. Part of the problem is that the group doesn't really have any good songs to hang their sounds on to, but, if you're looking just for sounds and groove, *Cabbage Alley* doesn't disappoint. The Meters' overall feel might have gotten a little softer than necessary, but they still are a remarkably sympathetic, supple group and it's a pleasure to hear them play. Still, there's not much here outside of hearing them play, and while that's pretty great, it's hard not to wish that there were songs, even when they delve into smooth soul like "Birds" or when the group simply jams on midtempo grooves, that stood out from the pack. [Sundazed's 2000 reissue contains two bonus tracks—both parts of "Chug Chug Chug-A-Lug (Push and Shove)."] *—Stephen Thomas Erlewine*

Rejuvenation / 1974 / Sundazed ♦♦♦♦♦
The title is a tip-off, as is the garish, blaxploitation-chic photo on the cover—*Rejuvenation*, the Meters' second album for Reprise, should be seen as a bit of a new beginning for the quintessential New Orleans funk group. It's not a clean beginning, since they were pointing in this direction on *Cabbage Alley*, but this is where their glistening, clear production, crisp performances, rock influences, and hard-edged funk coalesce into a sound distinct from their Josie recordings—not better, just different. As such, this is the definitive Reprise album from the Meters, not just because the material is stronger (which admittedly is true), but because the performances are continually inspired and the production is professional but hits at a gut level, resulting in a first-class funk album. [Sundazed's 2000 reissue contains the single versions of "People Say" and "Hey Pocky-A-Way" as bonus tracks.] *—Stephen Thomas Erlewine*

The Best of the Meters / 1975 / Virgo ♦♦♦
A good collection of this quintessential New Orleans funk group's best '70s singles for the Reprise label. Of course they did their finest cuts for Josie, but turned in some reasonably good work on Reprise in a more rock/funk direction. "Hey, Pokey-A-Way" was probably the closest Reprise cut to matching the superb Josie singles. But these are the songs that got them gigs with the Rolling Stones and work with Paul McCartney and Robert Palmer, so they did have some value. *—Ron Wynn*

Fire on the Bayou / 1975 / Sundazed ♦♦♦♦♦
The Meters' third album for Reprise, *Fire on the Bayou*, is their best record for the label for a variety of reasons, not least of which is the high quality of material throughout the record and a focus from the band that keeps the music simmering, even if it never quite reaches a boil. That's not a bad thing, because the music *is* simmering, always hot and enticing, never lukewarm or too cool. There's not anything that comes out and grabs your throat, the way that "Hey Pocky Way" does, but there never seems to be a concession to mainstream funk, which *Cabbage Alley* or *Rejuvenation* seem to achieve. This just keeps things rolling, nice and smooth. There's not anything that separates itself from its partners—something that's unfortunately true of all of the Reprise albums—but the overall feel is better than the Meters' other Reprise albums, since it has more grit and presence than its compatriots. [Sundazed's 2000 reissue contains one bonus track, a "long version" of "Running Fast."] *—Stephen Thomas Erlewine*

Trick Bag / 1976 / Sundazed ♦♦
This is, undeniably, where everything started to go pear-shaped for the Meters. Take the opening track, "Disco Is the Thing Today," a four-on-the-floor pumper that sounds nothing like the Meters and everything like BT Express. For the rest of the record the Meters and producer Allen Toussaint don't necessarily prove that sentiment true, but they do strive to sound as mainstream as possible, turning out slick ballads, frothy dance numbers, and pop-funk without spine. There are a couple of exceptions to the rule—"Mister Moon" is the one time when the glossy formula works and turns sultry, "(Doodle Loop) The World Is a Little Bit Under the Weather" nearly grooves, and their take on "Honky Tonk Women" has some real grit—but this is record is pretty much a dead end, and a pretty dispiriting one at that, best evidenced by the crushing disappointment that's their flat reading of Earl King's classic title track. *—Stephen Thomas Erlewine*

New Directions / 1977 / Sundazed ♦♦♦
The title of the Meters' final album is hopeful, and *New Directions* does indeed represent if not a new direction, at least a shift from the disco dead end of *Trick Bag*. From the second "No More Okey Doke" kicks off the record, it's clear that the Meters are gritty again, kicking out some really funky grooves—maybe not as dirty as their Josie recordings, maybe a little cleaned up, but still pretty funky. The slower numbers betray their era, but in a pleasing way, something that's also true of generic numbers like "My Name Up in Lights," which may have too much talk-box guitar, but still grooves effectively. That may not be a new direction, per se, but it is a welcome change-up after the dud *Trick Bag*. It wasn't enough to save the Meters and it's not really a lost treasure, but it's a far more dignified way to bow out. *—Stephen Thomas Erlewine*

Uptown Rulers: The Meters Live on the Queen Mary / 1992 / Rhino ♦♦♦♦

☆ **Funkify Your Life: The Meters Anthology** / Feb. 28, 1995 / Rhino ♦♦♦♦♦
Rhino's *Funkify Your Life: The Meters Anthology* was the first truly comprehensive and widely available CD retrospective of the groundbreaking New Orleans funk band's work. These two chronologically arranged discs run down virtually every important track the band recorded under its own name, finally allowing a more general audience to hear why the Meters had earned such a stellar reputation among die-hard funk collectors and sample-minded hip-hoppers. Disc one, subtitled "The Josie Years," traces the group's 1969-1971 beginnings as a Booker T. & the MG's-like outfit, cutting brief instrumentals with a similar guitar/organ/bass/drums lineup. There were important differences, though; the Meters' arrangements usually carried the melody in single-note guitar lines, which gave them a distinctive calling card, and their rhythms were notably funkier. In fact, drummer Joseph "Ziggy" Modeliste pretty much establishes himself as a monster groove machine right from the beginning; his is a dominating rhythmic presence. This is the lean, earthy Meters sound most often imitated by latter-day funk revivalists like the Soul Fire label. Group vocals and wah-wah guitars start to pop up over the second half of the disc, setting the stage for their more ambitious major-label sound, which is documented on the second disc ("The Reprise/Warner Bros. Years"). Nearly all of these tracks are vocal numbers, "songs" in the more traditional sense, but the group also opens its sound up, allowing the members to show off their individual chops as soloists. There's more flash in this music, including plenty of nimble-fingered unison passages demonstrating that the band can be as tight as they are loose. It's more proof that the Meters were the most telepathic funk ensemble this side of the J.B.'s. Those with a casual interest can safely content themselves with the fine single-disc *Very Best of the Meters*, but for devoted funk fans, *Funkify Your Life* should be considered essential listening. *—Steve Huey*

★ **The Very Best of the Meters** / Jun. 10, 1997 / Rhino ♦♦♦♦♦
In keeping with the drift of Rhino's *Very Best of* volumes, this 16-track disc provides a more concise, budget-minded retrospective for listeners who might not want a set that offers twice as much or more (in this case, Rhino's own two-disc *Funkify Your Life* anthology). That's not necessarily a criticism—funk grooves can get tiring over the course of two hours if you're not a rhythm fiend. Should you want to keep your Meters to the one-sitting level, this smartly chosen, well-annotated set is fine, including all of the cuts ("Cissy Strut," "Sophisticated Cissy," "Look-Ka Py Py," "Hey Pocky A-Way," "Fire on the Bayou") you'd expect to find on a greatest-hits set. *—Richie Unterberger*

Kickback / Feb. 2001 / Sundazed ♦♦♦
Not for one minute will you mistake this collection of unreleased recordings as a proper album. It isn't just the preponderance of covers, it's the subtle shifts in production and tone, lending a general unevenness to this record, even if it's culled just from 1975 and 1976 (meaning they're leftovers from *Fire on the Bayou* and *Trick Bag*). That doesn't mean it's a bad listen by any stretch, since even if *Kickback* is second-rate and leftover Meters, they're still an incredibly supple, engaging band that can take such bad choice of material like Neil Young's "Down By the River" and turn it into something listenable. Such cover choices as that, the Beatles' "Come Together," and Stephen Stills' "Love the One You're With" all sound intriguing, particularly to the record geek that's this album's core audience, but apart from the latter (and a fine, surprisingly hard-rocking alternate version of "Honky Tonk Women"), these kind of choices play better in theory than in actuality. The rest of the record may not have as distinctive a calling card, but they're better, finding the band laying back and doing what they do best, which is laying down a solid, irresistible groove. No, there's not much here that's essential, but it's fine second-tier stuff that will satisfy the dedicated. And, truth be told, second-tier Meters still sounds pretty good to the unconverted, too. *—Stephen Thomas Erlewine*

The Meters Anthology: The Josie Years / Mar. 27, 2001 / Repertoire ♦♦♦♦♦
This two-disc import set includes the band's three early albums for the Josie label in sequence, plus a selection of outtakes from the same fertile period. Among the surprises is a heavy cover of the Beatles' "Come Together." The relentlessly syncopated backbeats and stuttering guitar lines have a way of sneaking up on the unaware listener, too—all the way to the dancefloor. This is seminal New Orleans funk in an affordable package that serves as a better introduction than Rhino's previous retrospectives (which include material from the band's Warner Brothers disco years). *—Brian Beatty*

The Metros

Group / Soul

The Metros is one of Detroit's least-known groups to have recorded on a major label: RCA Records. Under the auspices of Joe Hunter & Jack Ashford (Pied Piper Productions) the Metros' RCA output resulted in one album and three singles, all released between 1966 to 1967. The members were Percy Williams (lead), James Buckman, Robert Suttles, and Arthur Mitchell. Gordon Dunn replaced an original Metros on a final recording. Their first single, "Sweetest One" (October 1966), was their biggest record. It features a falsetto lead that finds it difficult to stay on key and a chorus similar to "The Mix-Mix Song," by the Chi-Lites. RCA followed with "Since I Found My Baby" (March 1967); it featured a strong second tenor and has that four-on-the-floor beat that Northern soul fans love, making it a popular item among the old soul collectors. The Metros' third RCA single, "The Replacer" b/w "Let's Groove," was new material; Larry Banks co- wrote both sides, but it didn't matter as it failed miserably and ended the Metros time with RCA. A final recording, "She's Not Everybody's Girl" b/w "What's Wrong With Your Love," stayed shelved 21 years before emerging on Soul King Records in 1991. *—Andrew Hamilton*

● **Sweetest One** / 1967 / RCA ✦✦

Jack Ashford & Joe Hunter produced the Metros, a short-lived group believed to be from Detroit. Ashford was Motown's ace percussionist, but found plenty of time to produce the Hesitations, Tony Hester, Debbie Taylor, and many others. "Sweetest One" got sporadic play, but is nothing special—the falsetto is weak, the track spineless, and the lyrics ineffectual. There are a couple of memorable songs here, though. "I'll Never Forget You" was also recorded by the O'Jays (the two recordings are virtual clones, not surprising considering that Herbie Williams and Ashford arranged both). "Unlucky Sun" is injected with an upbeat arrangement and sounds a lot like "The Mix Mix Song," an early recording by the Chi-Lites. The band also scores with a strong remake of "Blue Velvet" that displays a deep, harmonious vocal blend. Nothing else here is really recommendable. *—Andrew Hamilton*

MFSB

f. 1971, Philadelphia, PA, **db.** 1981

Group / Philly Soul, Instrumental Rock, Soul, Urban

Best known for recording the hit theme to *Soul Train*, MFSB was the pre-eminent instrumental outfit of Philadelphia soul, backing numerous Kenny Gamble & Leon Huff productions while recording regularly on their own throughout the '70s. The group's name stood for Mother Father Sister Brother, and prior to their formation in 1971 as the house band at Gamble & Huff's Sigma Sound studios, some of the core personnel had been working together as early as 1968. Guitarists Norman Harris and Bobby Eli, bassist Ronnie Baker, and drummer Earl Young had an uncredited dance hit with "The Horse," the instrumental flip side of singer Cliff Nobles' "Love Is All Right." As the Horse dance craze swept Philadelphia, the group also backed singers the Fantastic Johnny C and (as the James Boys) Jesse James, while also issuing singles as the Music Makers and Family.

With the rise of the lush, orchestrated Philly soul sound at the dawn of the '70s, business was booming at Gamble & Huff's Philadelphia International, and there was plenty of session work to be had. Harris, Eli, Baker, and Young formed an important part of the label's regular studio group; other prominent musicians included guitarists Roland Chambers and James Herb Smith, bassist Larry Moore, drummers/percussionists Karl Chambers, Miguel Fuentes, Quinton Joseph, and Larry Washington, saxophonist Zach Zachary, organist/keyboardist Lenny Pakula, and vibraphonist Vince Montana, plus a rotating cast of strings, horns, and other personnel that depended on availability and were often directed by Don Renaldo. MFSB provided backing on a bevy of Philadelphia International hits, most prominently for the O'Jays and Harold Melvin & the Blue Notes, as well as other Philly soulsters like the Stylistics and the Spinners. They began cutting their own sessions in 1973, releasing a self-titled debut full of extended, sometimes jazzy soul grooves.

Later in 1973, TV host Don Cornelius approached Gamble about writing an original theme for his newly nationally syndicated dance show *Soul Train*. Gamble convened MFSB in the studio with arranger Bobby Martin and supporting vocal group the Three Degrees, and the theme song that grew out of the session proved hugely popular when it debuted on the show. Gamble pushed Cornelius to release it as a single, and when it finally appeared in early 1974 under the title "T.S.O.P." ("The Sound of Philadelphia"), it rocketed to the top of both the pop and R&B charts; it also won a Grammy for Best R&B Instrumental. The accompanying MFSB album, *Love Is the Message*, was a gold-selling Top Ten hit (and a number-one R&B album); moreover, the title track became an underground hit on the New York disco scene several years later. The group's next album, 1975's *Universal Love*, produced another R&B hit in "T.L.C. (Tender Lovin' Care)," and moved MFSB further into the emerging disco movement with tracks like "Sexy" and "Let's Go Disco."

MFSB recorded five more albums for Philadelphia International over the remainder of the '70s, becoming a full-fledged disco group when they began working heavily with arranger/producer Dexter Wansel in 1978. The previous year, they contributed a cover of the Nite-Liters' "K-Jee" to the mammoth-selling *Saturday Night Fever* soundtrack, but the late '70s brought mostly diminished commercial returns. The title track of MFSB's final album, 1980's *Mysteries of the World*, was a hit in the U.K., but with the heyday of both Philly soul and disco slipping away, the group disbanded in 1981. *—Steve Huey*

MFSB / 1973 / TSOP ✦✦✦

MFSB's debut album was more of a soul-funk mix than the kind of disco for which the band would become known with their "T.S.O.P." hit. There's less of a thumping rhythm and a greater inclination to lengthy, occasionally jazzy instrumental grooves, as on the seven-minute cover of "Freddie's Dead" that opens the set. The group also made a fair instrumental workout of Sly Stone's "Family Affair," and put the flute in the lead for much of the arrangement of "Back Stabbers." It's pretty well-crafted instrumental soul that's not quite super-slick, though your attention might eventually wander if you're not using it as dance fodder. The lush pop inclinations that would form part of the bed of their later work (both as MFSB and backing numerous Philly soul artists) come more to the fore on some other tracks, particularly the grandiose "Poinciana," though even that breaks up the soaring violins with some tasty jazz-blues piano and guitar. [The 2002 CD reissue on Epic/Legacy adds a live version of "T.S.O.P. (The Sound of Philadelphia)" (which is not, incidentally, otherwise represented on the album), with the Three Degrees on vocals, that was previously issued on the Three Degrees' 1975 album *The Three Degrees Live*.] *—Richie Unterberger*

● **Love Is the Message** / 1975 / TSOP ✦✦✦✦✦

Most prominently featuring "Love Is the Message" and "T.S.O.P.," this 1975 album by MFSB serves as a landmark LP for Philadelphia's mid-'70s soul movement. While "T.S.O.P." became a giant hit for the group at the time of its release, forever being associated with the television show *Soul Train*, "Love Is the Message" would go on to be an enormous underground hit in New York's late-'70s disco scene, championed by influential DJs such as Larry Levan (becoming an anthem at Levan's Paradise Garage). In addition, the album also features the orchestra's take on "Touch Me in the Morning," a song popularized by Diana Ross that was another proto-disco classic. The other tracks here—"Cheaper to Keep Her," "My One and Only Love," and "Bitter Sweet"—are also wonderful tracks exemplifying the group's uplifting, massive sound but aren't nearly as timeless as the three aforementioned songs. Sony's *Love Is the Message: The Best of MFSB* is still the best and most readily available showcase for this group's influential accomplishments as a proto-disco group, while this album is arguably their strongest non-compilation release and one of Kenny Gamble & Leon Huff's shining moments. *—Jason Birchmeier*

Universal Love / 1975 / TSOP ✦✦✦✦

MFSB was the legendary multicultural house band for the label Philadelphia International. Debuting as an act in 1973, the band released seminal early-disco tracks like "T.S.O.P.," "Love Is the Message," and the ballad "Something For Nothing." Although this effort didn't reach the heights of its predecessor, *Love Is the Message*, *Universal Love* has the band exhibiting even more skill as a hitmaking enterprise. As with the earlier hits, seven out of the eight tracks on *Universal Love* were arranged by Bobby Martin, who always got a classic sound out of any Philly production. The tracks "Sexy" and "T.L.C. (Tender Lovin' Care)" both effortlessly employ intonations of big band that came from the horn charts and Zach Zachary's tenor sax solos. At this point the gloss and rhythm style of the MFSB players, primarily the sound of bassist Ron Baker and drummer Earl Young, helped to initiate disco. Although they were no doubt influential, the songs "MFSB" and the hard-driving "Let's Go Disco" have an inimitable production. MFSB was no doubt known as a dance outfit, but this effort also displays its skill with ballads. The last track, the reflective "My Mood," with a vibes solo from Vince Montana, all but sums up what made this particular incarnation of the band arguably the best. Although it often doesn't make the list of Philadelphia International classics, *Universal Love* perfectly captures the grace of MFSB and the Philly sound. *—Jason Elias*

Philadelphia Freedom / 1975 / Philadelphia International ✦✦✦

Summertime / 1976 / TSOP ✦✦

The End of Phase One / 1978 / TSOP ✦✦

MFSB & Gamble Huff Orchestra / 1978 / TSOP ✦✦

Mysteries of the World / 1980 / Philadelphia International ✦✦✦

By 1980, the disco boom that had supported the rise of MFSB was on its way out the door. Their stylish sound was in need of a makeover to keep up with the times, and this was accomplished by allowing Dexter Wansel, the producer/writer behind a string of jazzy solo albums like *Life on Mars*, to take the reins. The result was the stylish and jazzy *Mysteries of the World*. While this album is as mellow as the rest of the latter-period MFSB recordings, it never forgets the group's soul music underpinnings. For example, "Manhattan Skyline" fortifies its easygoing melody with a percolating, hard thumping bassline and some well-timed blasts of horns. "Mysteries of the World" also keeps the new, softer style of MFSB from drifting into easy listening blandness by playing up the jazz underpinnings of the group's sound. For proof, look no further than the title track, which wraps an array of exploratory keyboard riffs around a busy bassline. Elsewhere, the album adds surprising little twists to keep things fresh: "Old San Juan" builds its mellow soul groove around an atypical flamenco guitar hook, and "In the Shadow" works an otherworldly synthesizer line into its bossa nova groove. The end result is an album that manages to bring a new freshness to their sound without completely severing ties with its old style. *Mysteries of the World* may be a little too soft and jazzy for funk fans accustomed to the likes of "Love Is the Message" and "T.S.O.P.," but it remains a fine album of jazz-inflected instrumentals that is likely to please anyone who likes soul music at its most elegant. *—Donald A. Guarisco*

● **Love Is the Message: The Best of MFSB** / Oct. 31, 1995 / Epic/Legacy ✦✦✦✦✦

Love Is the Message: The Best of MFSB is an extensive, 16-track career summary for Philadelphia soul's greatest instrumental outfit. Despite all the strings and horns coloring its orchestrations, MFSB managed to remain fairly funky, and along with Barry White's Love Unlimited Orchestra, the band's early work helped create the instrumental blueprint for disco. *Love Is the Message* illustrates that MFSB crossed the line between smooth instrumental soul and disco quite often, even despite the fact that it's missing quite a few of the band's most popular disco cuts—"Let's Go Disco," "Get Down With the Philly Sound," "Zip," "K-Jee," "Picnic in the Park," and "Summertime and I'm Feelin' Mellow" all earned substantial club/dance play, but are nowhere to be found here. Despite that bit of revisionist history, *Love Is the Message* does make for a fine overview of the band's more soulful outings. "T.S.O.P. (The Sound of Philadelphia)," the title track, "Sexy," "My One and Only Love," and "T.L.C. (Tender Lovin' Care)" were all among the group's most popular cuts, and they're all present, as are covers of Curtis Mayfield's "Freddie's Dead," the O'Jays' "Back Stabbers," and Elton John's "Philadelphia Freedom."

Even if *Love Is the Message* isn't quite complete, though, it does accurately summarize how MFSB defined the sound of Philly soul, and it's really all that most fans will need. —*Steve Huey*

Deep Grooves / Apr. 6, 1999 / Epic/Legacy ✦✦✦✦
While the previous *The Best of MFSB: Love Is the Message* remains the best introduction to the genre-defining sound of the Philadelphia International label's ace house band, the aptly titled *Deep Grooves* is even more of a funk primer, plunging further into the thick, bad-ass soul aesthetic that distinguished its era. Always a study in contrasts—impeccably tight yet possessed of a loose-cannon edge, elegant and sophisticated yet down-and-dirty—MFSB's music remains electrifying, boasting a timelessness that has eluded the work of many of their contemporaries; their instrumental renditions of classics like "Back Stabbers," "Family Affair," and "Freddie's Dead" expand on the funk potential of the originals, pushing the groove to cavernous new extremes. —*Jason Ankeny*

MFSB & Gamble Huff Orchestra/Mysteries of the World / May 25, 1999 / Import ✦✦✦

The MG's

Group / Memphis Soul
Minus Booker T. Jones as well as Steve Cropper, the remaining members of Booker T. & the MG's (drummer Al Jackson Jr. and bassist Donald "Duck" Dunn) recorded one album for Stax as the MG's, with replacements Carson Whitsett on keyboards and Bobby Manuel on guitar. —*John Bush*

● **The MG's** / 1973 / Stax ✦✦✦
This is the first Stax effort from the principle members of the band since 1971's *Melting Pot.* Of course, a lot transpired in the two short years. Booker T. and Steve Cropper left Stax for other opportunities in Los Angeles. Al Jackson began to do more work for rival Hi Records and became a big proponent in Al Green's career. *The MG's* features the lineup of drummer Jackson, bassist Duck Dunn, Carson Whitsett on keyboards, and guitarist Bobby Manuel. Despite the fact that this 1973 effort captures a band without half of its most influential members, the playing is top-notch. It also helps that Whitsett and Manuel all but replicate the keyboard and guitar styles of the singular sounds of Booker T. and Cropper, so the effects of their absence doesn't detract as much as one might think. The funky "Sugar Cane" has Jackson's amazing snare work and Whitsett's good B-3 work. As *The MG's* goes from song to song, it is clear that it is an enjoyable effort, due to a large part of the skills of producers Jackson and Dunn. "Black Side" is another soothing instrumental featuring great hi-hat work from Jackson. The last track, the propulsive and meditative "Frustration," has a warm Fender Rhodes and, of course, the rhythmic dynamic of Jackson and Dunn. This well-recorded album gave Dunn and Jackson a chance to work again, and since they were the one of the best rhythm sections of the '60s and '70s, it makes *The MG's* worth looking into, despite the absent members. —*Jason Elias*

Miami

Group / Disco, Funk
Songwriter Willie Clarke, more noted for his songwriting with Clarence Reid, created this self-contained band around vocalist Robert Moore; the other players were Freddie Scott (drums), Warren Thompson (guitar), Andrew Curran (guitar), Bobby Williams (organ), Willie Jackson (bass), George Perry (bass), and Clarke (percussions). Personnel changes occurred, Tony Z (Zamagni), for one instance, comped with them in the late '70s before leaving for something more musically challenging.

Amid cutting three albums, Miami served as the house band for TK Records' family of labels and played on sessions for Little Beaver, George McCrae, Gwen McCrae, and Betty Wright, among others. Their first album, *The Party Freaks,* came out in 1974 and featured catchy jams like "Party Freaks" and "I Can See Through You"; a second LP, *Notorious* (1976), spawned their popular "Kill That Roach" (a reflex-phrase in tropical cities like Miami where roaches grow big as butterflies and even fly on occasions). TK's owner, Henry Stone, fattened Miami's recording budget for the second album, enabling the employment of strings, horns, and a new member: Jesus Gonzales.

A final album, *Miami,* hooked around an update of Otis Redding's "I've Been Loving You Too Long," dropped in 1978, but it didn't go and Miami splintered. TK Records was an arm of Stone's empire that included the South's biggest record distributor—if you wanted your record distributed below the Mason-Dixon Line and east of the Mississippi River you dealt with Stone; however, bankruptcy proceedings caused TK Records to be dissolved in 1980; it re-emerged under another name but the glory days were over. Polygram U.K. released a CD of Miami's finest tracks, entitled *Hey Y'all We're Miami . . . The Party Freaks.* —*Andrew Hamilton*

The Party Freaks / 1974 / Drive ✦✦✦

Notorious / 1976 / Drive ✦✦✦

● **Hey Y'all We're Miami . . . The Party Freaks** / Aug. 24, 1999 / WestSide ✦✦✦✦

George Michael (Yorgos Kyriatou Panayioutou)

b. Jun. 25, 1963, Bushey, England
Vocals, Guitar / Dance-Pop, Adult Contemporary, Urban, Pop/Rock
Yorgos Kyriatou Panayioutou (George Michael) achieved fame in the duo Wham! in his native U.K. in 1982. Through 1986, he and his partner, Andrew Ridgeley, scored hit after hit in a variety of styles from rap to uptempo pop to slow ballads. As songwriter and lead singer, Michael gradually overshadowed the group, and by the time they split, he was ready for a massively successful solo career. This began with the 1987 album *Faith,* which featured a series of chart-topping hit singles and sold more than seven-million copies. That Michael had not achieved a similar critical success was evident from the title of his follow-up album, *Listen Without Prejudice—Vol. 1,* which, though it sold a million copies, included two Top Ten hits, and hit number two, must be considered a major commercial disappointment. After the failure of *Listen Without Prejudice,* Michael engaged in a bitter legal battle with his record company, eventually buying his way out his Columbia contract and signing with Dreamworks. In 1996, he released *Older,* its sales clearly hampered by his long hiatus away from performing. In 1998, Michael made tabloid headlines when he was arrested for lewd conduct in a men's public restroom at a park near his Beverly Hills home; following the incident, he appeared on CNN and publicly revealed his homosexuality. —*William Ruhlmann*

★ **Faith** / 1987 / Columbia ✦✦✦✦✦
A superbly crafted mainstream pop/rock masterpiece, *Faith* made George Michael an international solo star, selling over ten-million copies in the U.S. alone as of 2000. Perhaps even more impressively, it also made him the first white solo artist to hit number one on the R&B album charts. Michael had already proven the soulful power of his pipes by singing a duet with Aretha Franklin on the 1987 smash "I Knew You Were Waiting (For Me)," but he went even farther when it came to crafting his own material, using sophisticated '70s soul as an indispensable part of his foundation. Of course, it's only a part. *Faith*'s ingenuity lies in the way it straddles pop, adult contemporary, R&B, and dance music as though there were no distinctions between them. In addition to his basic repertoire of funky dance-pop and airy, shimmering ballads, Michael appropriates the Bo Diddley beat for the rockabilly-tinged title track, and proves himself a better-than-decent torch singer on the cocktail jazz of "Kissing a Fool." Michael arranged and produced the album himself, and the familiarity of many of these songs can obscure his skills in those departments—close listening reveals his knack for shifting elements in and out of the mix and adding subtle embellishments when a little emphasis or variety is needed. Though *Faith* couldn't completely shake Michael's bubblegum image in some quarters, the album's themes were decidedly adult. "I Want Your Sex" was the most notorious example, of course, but even the love songs were strikingly personal and mature, grappling with complex adult desires and scarred by past heartbreak. All of it adds up to one of the finest pop albums of the '80s, setting a high-water mark that Michael has only been able to reach in isolated moments since. —*Steve Huey*

Listen Without Prejudice, Vol. 1 / Aug. 1990 / Columbia ✦✦✦✦
Michael's follow-up to the massive success of *Faith* found him turning inward, trying to gain critical acclaim as well as sales. *Listen Without Prejudice* is not an entirely successful effort; Michael has cut back on the effortless hooks and melodies that crammed not only *Faith* but also his singles with Wham!, and his socially conscious lyrics tend to be heavy-handed. But the highlights—the light, Beatlesque harmonies of "Heal the Pain," and the plodding number one "Praying for Time," "Waiting for That Day," and the Top Ten "Freedom '90"—make a case for his talents as a pop craftsman. —*Stephen Thomas Erlewine*

Older / Apr. 1996 / DreamWorks ✦✦✦
Older is the album that many observers initially believed *Listen Without Prejudice, Vol. 1* to be—a relentlessly serious affair, George Michael's bid for artistic credibility. It's an album that makes *Listen Without Prejudice* sound like *Faith.* Michael has dispensed with the catchy, frothy dance-pop numbers that brought him fame, concentrating on stately, pretentious ballads—even "Fastlove," the album's one dance track, lacks the carefree spark of his earlier work. Although Michael's skills as a pop craftsman still shine through—several songs are well-constructed ballads that rank with his best material—his earnestness sinks the album. It is one thing to be mature and another to be boring. Too often, Michael mistakes slight melodies for mature craftsmanship and *Older* never quite recovers. When melodies do pop up, he doesn't deliver them with enough force to make an impact, and the album slowly disappears as a result. —*Stephen Thomas Erlewine*

Ladies & Gentlemen: The Best of George Michael / Nov. 10, 1998 / Columbia ✦✦✦✦✦
When George Michael was riding high on the charts, only a handful of critics acknowledged that he was a brilliant mainstream pop singer/songwriter who, at his best, rivaled his idol Elton John in crafting state-of-the-art pop songs and productions. For nearly a full decade, he was a superstar in his native U.K. and the U.S., and even when *Older* failed to win an American audience, he retained his stranglehold on the British and European charts. As a solo male hitmaker, virtually nobody could touch him between 1984 and 1994, and even when his grasp began to slip, he still made compelling music. All of this is proven by his first hits compilation, *Ladies & Gentlemen: The Best of George Michael.* Spanning two discs, 28 songs, and two distinctive halves—one "For the Heart" (ballads), one "For the Feet" (dance tunes)—the collection is a monster, as impressive for its size as it is for its achievements. To some casual listeners, the sheer scope of the collection may seem overwhelming, since it doesn't just have the hits, but also rarities, compilation tracks, lesser-known singles, and duets. Of course, that's precisely what makes it worthwhile for anyone who owns all the albums. (They'll also be interested that many of the mixes sound slightly different—as if the masters were run through the antiquated "Q Sound" process that marred Madonna's similar *Immaculate Collection.*) And some skeptics may be swayed after listening to the individual discs, which are surprisingly consistent works that reveal forgotten gems, and thereby the true depth of his talent. It is true that listening to both discs in a row is a little exhausting, but there's little question that *Ladies & Gentlemen* comes close to being definitive. —*Stephen Thomas Erlewine*

Michel'le

Vocals / Club/Dance, Urban, Dance-Pop, Hip-Hop
One of the more interesting urban contemporary vocalists of the late '80s and early '90s, the Los Angeles-based Michel'le was known for having a squeaky, high-pitched speaking voice and an aggressive, full-bodied style of singing. Some people jokingly called her the Betty Boop of urban contemporary, although the Boop comparisons had more to do with her speaking voice than her singing (which could be quite gritty at times). Michel'le, who is best-known for her smash hit "No More Lies," favored a very hip-hop-minded approach to R&B, and that isn't the least bit surprising when you take into consideration the company that she kept. The members of N.W.A.—especially Dr. Dre and the late Eric "Eazy-E" Wright—were partly responsible for the success of Michel'le, who pronounces

her name "meesh-a-lay." And her manager was music industry veteran Jerry Heller, who was also managing N.W.A. back then.

Arguably, the singer was ahead of her time. Before Mary J. Blige was exalted as the "Queen of Hip-Hop Soul"—and before the rise of Faith Evans and Lauryn Hill—Michel'le was a young neo-soulstress who had strong ties to the hip-hop world. It was in 1989 that Michel'le signed with Eazy-E's Ruthless Records, which was the home of N.W.A. as well as Dallas native the D.O.C. and the female pop-rap group J.J. Fad (of "Supersonic" fame). Ruthless was distributed by different labels, depending on the artist. N.W.A. (one of the most important and influential groups in the history of gangsta rap) went through Priority, while the D.O.C., J.J. Fad, and Michel'le were signed to Ruthless/Atlantic. Although Ruthless was primarily a rap label, Dre and Eazy wanted to branch out into urban contemporary singing; and Michel'le, although quite hip-hop-influenced, was very much an urban contemporary singer. In 1989, Dre produced Michel'le's self-titled debut album; Eazy served as executive producer, while the mixing was handled by Dre and DJ Yella (another N.W.A. agitator). But, despite the participation of all those N.W.A. members, Michel'le's album didn't sound anything at all like that group's controversial and disturbing gangsta rap; and unlike N.W.A.'s *Straight Outta Compton*, it enjoyed a great deal of exposure on urban radio. The funky "No More Lies," Michel'le's debut single, was a major hit on the same R&B stations that went out of their way to avoid *Straight Outta Compton*; it was also a big pop hit and reached the Top Ten on *Billboard*'s pop singles chart. The equally funky "Nicety," which was released as a single in 1990, was another major hit, and "Keep Watchin'" (the album's third single) also fared well.

In 1991, Michel'le became the victim of some East Coast/West Coast rivalry; that year, Bronx rapper Tim Dog (formerly of the Ultramagnetic MC's) said some insulting things about Michel'le and Dre on his angry, West Coast-bashing single "Fuck Compton." Unlike the infamous, well-publicized feud that L.A.'s Death Row Records/Suge Knight clique and New York's Puff Daddy/Bad Boy Entertainment/the Notorious B.I.G. clique had several years later, Tim Dog's war of words with the members of N.W.A. didn't turn deadly; nonetheless, Michel'le was said to be furious over the things that Tim Dog said about her on "Fuck Compton." But, as much attention as Michel'le received in 1989 and in the early '90s, her popularity didn't last long. In 1996, the southern Californian had a cameo on the Dogg Pound's single "Let's Play House," but her second album, *Hung Jury* (a Priority release), didn't come out until 1998—nine years after her self-titled debut—and it wasn't nearly the smash that Michel'le's previous album had been. *—Alex Henderson*

● **Michel'le** / 1990 / Ruthless ✦✦✦✦✦
Michel'le, the girl with the squeaky speaking voice and thunderous singing voice, stormed onto the music scene in 1989-1990 with her smash self-titled debut. The album is post new jill swing, incorporating a mix of hip-hop, dance and R&B, well before Mary J. Blige and Faith Evans perfected the genre. *Michel'le* produced several huge hits, including the unstoppable (and irresistibly clever) "No More Lies," which became a Top Ten pop hit, its follow-up "Nicety," and the R&B/dance hit "Keep Watchin'." The real gems on this set, however, are the slow jams. The smoldering "Something in My Heart" became a hit well over a year after the album's release, and other tracks, such as "Silly Love Song," "Close to Me," and "If" are just as good. Unfortunately, it took Michel'le nearly a decade to deliver the follow-up, 1998's *Hung Jury*, which completely paled in comparison to its predecessor, although she was a featured vocalist on the Dogg Pound's 1996 hit "Let's Play House." So, as it goes, powerhouse chanteuse Michel'le, who actually played a part in spearheading a musical movement for which she is entirely uncredited, will be remembered for this sole, wonderful album. A true classic, and a must for fans of hip-hop and timeless R&B. *—Jose F. Promis*

Hung Jury / Aug. 25, 1998 / Priority ✦✦✦
It took Michel'le nearly a decade to release a follow-up to her hit-laden self-titled debut, and the results on *Hung Jury* are pleasant, but never really equal her previous heights. To begin with, nothing on this album is as immediate or memorable as "No More Lies" or "Something in My Heart." The title track is catchy, but is weighted down by banal lyrics like "I like to freak seven days a week." "Crazy" comes off as a somewhat tepid update of her hit "Nicety," and some of the other tracks, such as "Wasted My Tyme" and the fun "Tonight Is," sound as though they came straight from 1989. Some songs do manage to hold their own, such as "Can I Get a Witness," the aforementioned "Tonight Is," and "Here 4 U" (the album's best track), but some fall downright flat, such as "No Where 2 Run." Although this album is not without merit, it seems as though Michel'le ran out of steam somewhere between 1990 and 1998. *—Jose F. Promis*

Mickey & Sylvia

f. 1956, **db.** 1965
Group / R&B, Rock & Roll
Although this duo is primarily remembered as a one-hit act—for "Love Is Strange," which reached number 11 in 1957—they actually recorded quite a few exciting hybrids of R&B and rock & roll in the mid- and late '50s. Playing on countless '50s sessions for various labels (especially Atlantic and OKeh), Mickey Baker was one of the greatest guitar players of early rock & roll. With his partner (and former guitar student) Sylvia Robinson, he got to stretch out a bit from his usual role, with some trailblazing, piercing, lean, and bluesy leads. Vocally, Mickey & Sylvia had an engagingly playful, occasionally sly and sassy repartee that makes up in charm what it might lack in smoke and firepower. Their recordings were inconsistent, but at their best they offered a fetching blend of blues, Bo Diddley, calypso, and doo wop.

After "Love Is Strange," whose devastating licks inspired countless guitarists, the duo notched a couple more substantial R&B hits. But although they recorded as late as 1965, they never approached the Top 20 again. Mickey Baker recorded as a solo artist and enjoyed a fairly successful career as an expatriate sessionman in France. Sylvia Robinson unexpectedly re-emerged with the number three pre-disco hit "Pillow Talk" in 1973, and co-founded the pioneering rap label Sugar Hill in the late '70s. *—Richie Unterberger*

Do It Again / 1973 / RCA Victor ✦✦✦

Love Is Strange / 1990 / Bear Family ✦✦✦
This two-CD, 60-song (!) set includes many alternate takes and a fair amount of previously unreleased material, spanning 1955 to 1964. A lot of the obscurities are in the close harmony, doo wop vein, and are disappointingly short on verbal sparring and scorching Baker guitar. Lovingly packaged, but everyone except hardcore specialists should stick with the RCA compilation. *—Richie Unterberger*

Love Is Strange & Other Hits / Mar. 1990 / RCA ✦✦✦✦✦
Unless you're a major R&B collector, it's likely you've never heard anything by this duo besides "Love Is Strange," their only major hit (and a great one). With 20 cuts from 1956-1960, this disc reissues the bulk of their most interesting work. "Love Is Strange" will remain their most memorable tune after you've heard this, but on the whole, this is way-above-average '50s R&B/rock. If you're hungering for more great solos like the ones in "Love Is Strange," you'll find some here, especially in "There Oughta Be a Law" and the instrumental "Shake It Up," although Baker's virtuosity doesn't dominate most of the songs. Some of these tunes are routine doo wop, but a little over half the material is pretty strong, ranging from the calypso-rock they're best remembered for to ballads to straight-ahead R&B shouters, with King Curtis on sax. *—Richie Unterberger*

The Willow Sessions / 1995 / Sequel ✦✦✦
Mickey & Sylvia are properly thought of as '50s rock & rollers, but they actually did a good deal of recording in the '60s, though without much notable commercial success. Most of this 19-track CD was recorded in the early '60s for their own label, Willow; only one song, "Baby You're So Fine," was a hit, making the R&B Top 30. The album doesn't have the fire of their best sides for RCA in the '50s, but it's not bad, usually purveying a groove similar to their early work, though tamer. Occasionally Mickey brandishes blues-rock chops to show that he can still cut deep with his axe, especially on "Darling (I Miss You So)" and the previously unissued instrumentals "Sylvia's Blues" and "Mickey's Blues." There are also a few curious (but fairly respectable) cuts dating from the late '60s that Sylvia recorded for the All Platinum label in a much more contemporary soul vein. *—Richie Unterberger*

● **Love Is Strange: A Golden Classics Edition** / Apr. 22, 1997 / Collectables ✦✦✦✦✦
Although the packaging and sound are a little below par, *Golden Classics Edition* contains 18 tracks from Mickey & Sylvia's prime period—not just "Love Is Strange," but a wealth of strong, lesser-known singles—making it a good overview of the underrated R&B duo. *—Stephen Thomas Erlewine*

Midnight Star

f. 1976, Frankfort, KY, **db.** 1990
Group / Dance-Pop, Disco, Urban, Quiet Storm, Club/Dance
The synth-funk unit Midnight Star scored several times on the charts during the mid-'80s, led by their double-platinum album *No Parking on the Dance Floor* in 1983. Just one of the successful acts on Solar Records (also including Shalamar, Lakeside, and the Whispers), the group was formed in 1976 at Kentucky State University by the Calloway brothers, trumpeter Reginald, and trombone player Vincent, with vocalist Belinda Lipscomb. After signing with RCA near the turn of the decade, Midnight Star recorded their first album in 1980, *The Beginning*, with a conglomeration of studio players and producers. After moving to the Solar label by 1982, the group released *Victory* and then added a full band: guitarist Melvin Gentry, bassist Kenneth Gant, drummer Bobby Lovelace, and keyboard player Bo Watson.

Though the Calloways' production skills—later used to full effect on tracks by Natalie Cole, Gladys Knight, and Teddy Pendergrass—had pushed Midnight Star into the R&B charts during 1981-1982, with singles like "Hot Spot" and "I've Been Watching You," the group was unprepared for the success of the first single from their third proper album, *No Parking on the Dance Floor*. "Freak-A-Zoid" hit number two on the R&B charts in mid-1983, and though it failed to make the pop Top 40, it pushed the LP over the platinum mark. "Operator," the first single from their next album, *Planetary Invasion*, became their highest-charting single, making number 18 on the pop charts. By 1986, *Headlines* had become Midnight Star's third album to at least sell gold, but it proved their last; both Reginald and Vincent left the group to form Calloway in 1988. (Incidentally, the Calloways had introduced future legend Babyface to Solar executives for his first job, and produced Babyface's group the Deele).

Without Reginald and Vincent Calloway to lead the way, Midnight Star fell fast and far. A 1988 self-titled album flopped miserably, and 1990's *Work It Out* proved to be their last. Calloway, meanwhile, found success with their first single, 1989's "I Wanna Be Rich," which hit number two on the pop charts. The track was their only major hit, followed by "Sir Lancelot" and the title track from their 1990 debut album *All the Way*. Calloway returned two years later with *Let's Get Smooth*, but the album proved their last. The brothers continued working, with Pieces of a Dream and Bootsy Collins, among others. *—John Bush*

The Beginning / 1980 / RCA ✦✦

Victory / 1982 / Solar ✦✦✦
Another early Midnight Star album, which came close to breaking them as a hit act. The title cut and "Hot Spot" both charted, and the Calloway brothers were close to finding the right mix of uptempo and dance/funk/novelty tracks to ballads, and also perfecting their productions, arrangements, and compositions. *—Ron Wynn*

No Parking on the Dance Floor / 1983 / Solar ✦✦✦✦✦
The greatest Midnight Star album, and a dancefloor and early-'80s R&B/funk classic. The group found its niche with the silly hit "Freak-A-Zoid," and a nice, if lightweight, change-of-pace number in "Wet My Whistle." The title track was their third chart hit from the album, and "Electricity" did well as an album cut. The Calloways found the right balance between collective vocals, dance/funk arrangements, and a light fusion and instrumental pop touch in the charts. *—Ron Wynn*

Planetary Invasion / 1984 / Solar ♦♦♦♦

This nine piece band made their mark with their sci-fi instrumentation and aggressive dance numbers. This album spawned three singles that fall into that loop with the first being "Operator." With its pugnacious rhythm and frigid keyboard hits, this dance number held the number-one spot on the *Billboard* R&B charts for five weeks. "Scientific Love" was the third single; a techno-funk track seasoned with Belinda Lipscomb's intense delivery. It was a Top 20 single at number 16. Aside from its horrific title, "Body Snatchers" is all about the dancefloor with its has embraceable All three of the aforementioned utilized the wizardry of Vincent "Zino" Calloway on the vocorder. The chart success of this album was is credited to the production work of Reggie Calloway, the nucleus of the group, who was concurrently producing and writing songs for the Deele and Klymaxx. He and his brother Zino would go on to write and produce number one hits for Natalie Cole, LeVert, Teddy Pendegrass and Glady Knight. *—Craig Lytle*

Headlines / 1986 / Solar ♦♦♦

The final hit album for Midnight Star before the Calloway brothers departed. They had reached their peak and cranked out three solid R&B hits, among them the title track, "Midas Touch," and "Engine No. 9." Everything clicked, from the production and arrangements to the hook-filled lyrics and exuberant, if at times bland, vocals. But evidently the Calloways figured they had done all they could do with Midnight Star, as they bolted once the last single dropped off the charts. *—Ron Wynn*

● **Greatest Hits** / 1987 / Solar ♦♦♦♦

A CD reissue featuring the best novelty/dance cuts and ballads from Midnight Star. They symbolized, along with Lakeside, the Whispers, and Shalamar, the Solar sound. It wasn't too earthy, yet also wasn't overly sophisticated or stiff. They lacked great singers, so they surrounded the vocalists with entertaining arrangements. It was well done, but inevitably became dreary once they began repackaging it for every act on the roster. *—Ron Wynn*

Midnight Star / 1987 / Solar ♦♦♦

The Calloway brothers had left the band by the late '80s, moving on to form their own group, Calloway. The remaining members tried to keep things going, but this session didn't have enough good uptempo/dance or ballad hits to sustain the momentum that the group had built during their previous hit albums. The vocals were decent, and for a while they got some attention based on their past track record, but in the end it simply wasn't enough. *—Ron Wynn*

Work It Out / 1990 / Solar ♦♦

Although they did get a minor hit with the single "Money Can't Buy You Love," things had degenerated for both Midnight Star and '80s funk bands in general. The hip-hop and new jack coalition had almost completely taken over at urban radio stations, and groups like Midnight Star sounded outdated and stagnant. The Calloway brothers' production expertise hadn't been replaced, and they weren't a good enough ballad band to do the kind of glossy songs that helped acts like Atlantic Starr survive. *—Ron Wynn*

● **The Anniversary Collection** / Jul. 27, 1999 / Capitol ♦♦♦♦

It may not be perfect, but *Anniversary Edition* comes pretty close to being the definitive Midnight Star hits collection. All of their biggest songs—"Freak-A-Zoid," "Wet My Whistle," "Operator," "Headlines," "Midas Touch," "Don't Rock the Boat," "Snake in the Grass"—are here, along with such lesser but important hits as "Make It Last," "I've Been Watching You" and "Hot Spot." Some dedicated fans might notice a few favorites missing, but that doesn't matter—*Anniversary Edition* is close enough to being the perfect Midnight Star collection that it will satiate both casual and hardcore fans. Even if it has two unnecessary remixes tacked onto the end. *—Stephen Thomas Erlewine*

The Mighty Hannibal (James Shaw)

Vocals, Songwriter, Producer / Soul, Funk, R&B

As obscure R&B legends go, the Mighty Hannibal remains perhaps the most interesting to grace the stage or airwaves of the 1950s and 1960s. A first cousin of maligned Clinton advisor Vernon Jordan and a flamboyant player all his life, Hannibal's music was as exciting as his life. Born James Shaw he started singing doo wop as an Atlanta teenager, and eventually released a string of moderately successful (and generally highly praised) singles for a variety of independent labels. Shaw's first group, the Overalls in 1954, included future Pips Edward Patten and Merald Knight. His first notable single as a solo performer (1958's "Big Chief Hug-Um an' Kiss-Um") was released under the name Jimmy Shaw on Concept. Other early singles of note include "My Name Is Hannibal" for Pan World, the Jack Nitzsche-penned "The Biggest Cry" (it of course featured a lush string arrangement courtesy of the writer), and the bluesy "I Need a Woman ('Cause I'm a Man)." For a time, Hannibal even recorded for his own Sharob label.

But it was his mid-'60s work that put Hannibal (as he was officially known by now) on the map. "Jerkin' the Dog" and "Fishin' Pole" showed the turban-decked one growing measurably in his singing and arranging skills. But it was the prophetic Shurfine hit "Hymn No. 5," a sobering gospel-blues about a black soldier writing home from Vietnam, that Hannibal will perhaps be best known for. Released in 1966, the tune beat the white hippie acts to the punch by at least a year in its anti-war consciousness. But by now, however, Hannibal had developed a serious heroin habit and was spending more time as a pimp than a performer, and wasted much energy trying to sound like the newly funkified James Brown and producing somewhat weaker singles.

By 1972, he had kicked heroin for good and recorded some of the best work of his career to this point. On "I'm Coming Home," Hannibal again visits the Vietnam quagmire, this time (it is now 1970) sending a young black man out of cities torn by drugs and riots into an even worse nightmare (could this be the younger brother of the vet described in "Hymn No. 5" half a decade earlier?). His anti-drug screamer "Truth Shall Set You Free" saw him (now calling himself King Hannibal) finding new direction in gospel, but it marked a low period for his songwriting. Hannibal spent most of the 1970s as a bit actor in films like *The Buddy Holly Story* and *Roots* or as a staff producer at Venture Records. He even worked as entertainment editor for a time at *Atlanta Voice* newspaper. The cult glam film *Velvet Goldmine* featured some of his music and helped jump-start his career again. *—John Duffy*

● **Hannibalism!** / Aug. 14, 2001 / Norton ♦♦♦♦♦

The first-ever CD compilation of singles from the uncompromising Mighty Hannibal features his groundbreaking anti-war hit, "Hymn No. 5," as well as minor hits like "Jerkin' the Dog" and "I Need a Woman (Cause I'm a Man)." More revealing, perhaps, is the inclusion of several early-'70s tracks that inexplicably could not find a label to release them at the time. However, the sweet and tender declaration of love "We're Gonna Make It" and the good-time party tune "Meet Me at Mary's Place" do not prepare one for the saga of "I'm Coming Home." It is now five years after "Hymn No. 5," and the soldier's younger brother is shipping out, leaving a much more chaotic America behind: Drugs and riots are destroying his home city. He has hope, though, that he will return to a better country than he left. The song is as resonant and remarkable as the similarly themed material Marvin Gaye would release the following year. The fact that this song never saw commercial release is more than a little bit telling of the indifferent music industry Hannibal was forced to contend with. Perhaps if he had the support of a label with the prestige and promotional muscle of Motown, the story would be different. Hannibal's music is classic indie soul at its best. *—John Duffy*

Amos Milburn

b. Apr. 1, 1927, Houston, TX, **d.** Jan. 3, 1980, Houston, TX

Piano, Vocals / Jump Blues, West Coast Blues, Piano Blues, R&B

Boogie piano master Amos Milburn was born in Houston, and he died there a short 52 years later. In between, he pounded out some of the most hellacious boogies of the postwar era, usually recording in Los Angeles for Aladdin Records and specializing in good-natured upbeat romps about booze and its effects (both positive and negative) that proved massive hits during the immediate pre-rock era. After signing with Aladdin in 1946, his first date included a thundering "Down the Road Apiece" that presaged the imminent rise of rock & roll.

The first of Milburn's 19 Top Ten R&B smashes came in 1948 with his party classic "Chicken Shack Boogie." With the ascent of "Bad, Bad Whiskey" to the peak of the charts in 1950, Milburn embarked on a string of similarly boozy smashes: "Thinking and Drinking," "Let Me Go Home Whiskey," "One Scotch, One Bourbon, One Beer" and "Good Good Whiskey" (his last hit in 1954). Alcoholism later brought the pianist down hard, giving these numbers a grimly ironic twist in retrospect. He left Aladdin for good in 1957, and recorded a comeback album for Motown in 1962 (even Little Stevie Wonder pitched in on harp for the sessions). Nothing could jump-start the pianist's fading career by then, though. A string of strokes limited his mobility and he eventually died in 1980. *—Bill Dahl*

Rockin' the Boogie / 1954 / Aladdin ♦♦♦♦♦

Let's Have a Party / 1957 / Score ♦♦♦♦♦

The Return of the Blues Boss / Apr. 9, 1963 / Motown ♦♦♦

Milburn's sole LP for Motown was an interesting effort that updated his saucy R&B without compromising it. No need to look for the rare original vinyl; it's been reissued in its entirety on *The Motown Sessions, 1962-1964*, which adds several previously unreleased bonus tracks. *—Richie Unterberger*

☆ **The Complete Aladdin Recordings of Amos Milburn** / 1994 / Mosaic ♦♦♦♦♦

Seven discs tracing the entire 1946-1957 Aladdin Records legacy of jump blues pioneer Amos Milburn, whose rippling boogie-based piano talent and predilection of songs about booze made him a postwar R&B superstar. One hundred forty-five tracks in all (including plenty of unissued goodies) tab this as the ultimate collection for Milburn fans. He boogied like a champ at his first L.A. date for Aladdin with a thundering "Down the Road Apiece" and rocked equally hard a decade later down in New Orleans when he was recutting "Chicken Shack Boogie" with the crew at Cosimo's. Mosaic does their usual elegant presentational job on this R&B legend, not skimping on a thing. Fabulous box set. *—Bill Dahl*

★ **The Best of Amos Milburn: Down the Road Apiece** / Jan. 11, 1994 / EMI America ♦♦♦♦♦

Pianist Amos Milburn mixed boogie-woogie with vocal energy and intensity to forge a style that was among early R&B's most exciting and appealing. Milburn's 1940s and '50s singles were sometimes fiery and sometimes silly, ranging from drinking songs and celebratory uptempo numbers to stomping instrumentals and an occasional blues or love tune. This excellent 26-track anthology contains such classic Milburn anthems as "Chicken Shack Boogie," "One Scotch, One Bourbon, One Beer," "Let's Have a Party," and "Bad, Bad Whiskey," as well as lesser-known but just as spirited romps. The mastering bolsters the sound, but doesn't deaden it, while Joseph Laredo's liner notes clearly and completely outline Milburn's musical and cultural/historical significance. *—Ron Wynn*

The Motown Sessions, 1962–1964 / Feb. 1996 / Motown ♦♦♦♦♦

Signed to Motown years after his peak as an R&B star, Milburn's association with the label turned out to be something of a non-event, producing only an obscure album and flop single. A commercial non-event, that is; Milburn's skills were still intact, resulting in some fine if somewhat uncharacteristic performances. This compilation reissues that album (*The Return of the Blues Boss*) and adds seven unreleased tracks. Milburn may still have been singing blues/R&B, but he was with Motown, which meant that a fair amount of soul-pop flavor inevitably seeped through. You can hear it in the occasional female backup vocals, swinging brass arrangements, and even a brief harmonica solo by Stevie Wonder on "Chicken Shack Boogie"; the arrangement on "I'll Make It Up to You Somehow" wouldn't have been out of place on an early Mary Wells single. The results are pleasantly surprising, updating Milburn's sound (which would have been quite anachronistic in the early 1960s) into the early soul era. The material is pretty strong, including both bluesy ballads and more uptempo numbers that don't totally smother his boogie-woogie roots. *—Richie Unterberger*

Essential Recordings / Jan. 9, 2001 / Cleopatra ♦♦♦♦
"Bad, Bad Whiskey," "Baby, Baby All the Time," "One Scotch, One Bourbon, One Beer," and "Chicken Shack Boogie," the recordings that made Amos Milburn a blues legend, are as humorous as ever and crisp as frying bacon in CD format. You'll weep with the smooth blues singer on "Bewildered" and assimilate his pain on the slow piano blues quagmire "Evening Shadows Coming Down on Me." Classic drinking music by one of the classiest blues singers ever. *—Andrew Hamilton*

Stephanie Mills

b. Mar. 22, 1957, Brooklyn, NY
Vocals / Quiet Storm, Show Tunes, Urban
Stephanie Mills first came to fame as "the little girl with the big voice" as the star of the hit Broadway play *The Wiz*, an adaptation of L. Frank Baum's classic book *The Wizard of Oz*. She had many R&B hits such as "I Have Learned to Respect the Power of Love," "I Feel Good All Over," "(You're Puttin') A Rush on Me," "Something in the Way (You Make Me Feel)," and "Home" along with one certified million-selling single, "Never Knew Love Like This Before." In addition, she also had five gold albums: *Whatcha Gonna Do... With My Lovin', Sweet Sensation, Stephanie, If I Were Your Woman,* and *Home*.

Born on March 22, 1957, in Brooklyn, NY, Mills honed her rich vocals singing gospel music at Brooklyn's Cornerstone Baptist Church as a small child. At age nine, she began appearing in the Broadway play *Maggie Flynn*. She was presented with first prize after winning "The Amateur Hour" talent contest six weeks straight at New York's famed Apollo Theater when she was nine. Mills' debut album, *Movin' in the Right Direction*, was recorded for ABC Records in 1974. A year later, she won the role of Dorothy in *The Wiz*. Her rendition of the beautiful ballad "Home" was a showstopper, mesmerizing audiences nightly for a number of years. The original cast recording of *The Wiz* was produced by Jerry Wexler and issued by Atlantic Records in spring 1975.

Singer Jermaine Jackson referred Mills to Motown head Berry Gordy, who signed her to the label. Her Motown debut was *For the First Time*, written and produced by Burt Bacharach and Hal David, issued in October 1976. She signed to 20th Century Records in 1978 and was teamed with the hit production duo of James Mtume and Reggie Lucas. Her first LP for the label, *Whatcha Gonna Do... With My Lovin'*, went gold in summer 1979 and spawned the singles "Whatcha Gonna Do With My Lovin'" and "You Can Get Over." Her next LP, *Sweet Sensation*, yielded "Sweet Sensation," "Never Knew Love Like This Before," and the radio-aired LP track "Try My Love." Next came the LP titled *Stephanie* in spring 1981, which also was a huge hit, peaking at number-three R&B and number-30 pop. The album included notable songs such as "Two Hearts"—a midtempo duet with Teddy Pendergrass—"Night Games," and the radio-aired LP cut "Don't Stop Doin' What Cha Do."

In 1981, Mills switched to Neil Bogart's Casablanca Records. Her LPs for the label included *Tantalizingly Hot, Merciless,* and *I've Got the Cure*. During 1983, she signed with MCA Records, where she released her *Stephanie Mills* album. Her next LP's title cut was the Clay McMurray/Gloria Jones/Pam Sawyer song "If I Were Your Woman," originally a 1971 smash for Gladys Knight & the Pips. Philly-based producer Nick Martinelli gave Mills her second number-one R&B hit with "I Feel Good All Over." The song held the number-one R&B spot for three weeks in spring 1987 and was included on Mills' LP *If I Were Your Woman*. Paul Laurence produced and co-wrote with Timmy Allen the chugging "(You're Putting) A Rush on Me," giving the singer her third number-one R&B hit in fall 1987. The single was followed by "Secret Lady" and her covers of "If I Were Your Woman" and "Where Is the Love." Following these hits, Mills worked with singer/songwriter/producer Angela Winbush in 1989. The collaboration resulted in another number-one R&B single, "Something in the Way You Make Me Feel." *—Ed Hogan*

Movin' in the Right Direction / 1974 / ABC ♦♦♦
Though Mills' Motown LP *For the First Time* subtly suggests it was her debut album, it was really the follow-up to this very rare set from earlier the same year. Released before her successful stint on Broadway as Dorothy in *The Wiz*, the album leaves no doubt about the singer's vocal prowess even at age 19. The musical selections are often not the most substantial compositionally, but Mills' covers of "Over the Rainbow," "Danny Boy," and "Home" (from *The Wiz*) are fine moments. "Over the Rainbow" is given a funky midtempo soul treatment, and "Home" is adapted to a light early-disco feel. Of the original numbers, standouts are the understated ballad "I Knew It Was Love" and the zesty "I Don't Want to Go Back." The former was Mills' first single and aptly showcases her distinctive pipes in an emotive setting. *Movin'* is not as memorable and classic as her breakthrough work for 20th Century, overall; but her sterling quality vocal performances and a few standouts make it a quite pleasurable listen—especially for the Mills connoisseur. *—Justin M. Kantor*

For the First Time / 1976 / Motown ♦♦♦
In 1975, an 18-year-old Stephanie Mills was well known in the theatrical world for her portrayal of Dorothy in the Broadway play *The Wiz*. But as a recording artist, Mills didn't hit big until she recorded the gold *Whatcha Gonna Do... With My Lovin'* (her third album) for 20th Century in 1979. Produced and written by the Burt Bacharach/Hal David team, *For the First Time* is the only album that Mills recorded for Motown. Contrary to what its album implies, this wasn't her first album—1974's *Movin' in the Right Direction* on ABC was Mills' debut album, and this LP was her sophomore effort. Despite the participation of Bacharach & David, *For the First Time* received little attention. The producer/composers seemed to envision the artist as another Dionne Warwick, and the result is a very pop-minded album. Mills, however, is more effective as a straight-up R&B singer. While her performances of "I See You for the First Time," "Living on Plastic," and other Bacharach/David tunes are pleasant enough, she is a lot more exciting on subsequent gems like 1979's *Whatcha Gonna Do... With My Lovin'*, 1980's *Sweet Sensation*, and 1987's *If I Were Your Woman*. This isn't a bad record, but it pales in comparison to the releases that came after it. Not recommended to casual listeners, *For the First Time* is strictly for historians and die-hard collectors. *—Alex Henderson*

Whatcha Gonna Do... With My Lovin'? / 1979 / 20th Century ♦♦♦♦♦
When Stephanie Mills enjoyed a major commercial breakthrough with her third album, *Whatcha Gonna Do... With My Lovin'?*, the singer often found herself being described as a disco diva—and it wasn't a description that she agreed with. Mills saw herself as primarily a romantic R&B traditionalist, not a disco singer. If you asked her whether she had more in common with Gladys Knight or Donna Summer, Mills would have said Gladys Knight without a moment's hesitation. Nonetheless, this superb LP (which was produced by the James Mtume/Reggie Lucas team) does contain its share of dance-oriented treasures; "Don't Stop Dancin'," "You Can Get Over," and the hit "Put Your Body in It" are disco funk classics that heated up numerous dancefloors in 1979. Mills is equally impressive on romantic ballads and slow jams like "Deeper Inside Your Love," "Starlight," "You and I," and Peabo Bryson's "Feel the Fire"—and in various interviews, she insisted that those songs were more representative of her than the album's dance-oriented material. At any rate, *Whatcha Gonna Do... With My Lovin'* remains one of Mills' strongest, most essential albums. *—Alex Henderson*

Stephanie / 1981 / 20th Century ♦♦♦
Some of Stephanie Mills' fans believe that *Stephanie* was her third album, but it was actually her fifth. *Stephanie* was her third album for 20th Century as well as her third album to reach gold, not to mention the third album that James Mtume and Reggie Lucas produced for her. And when you consider that her first two LPs—1974's *Movin' in the Right Direction* on ABC and 1975's *For the First Time* on Motown—did very little commercially, you can see why some people think that Mills launched her recording career with her commercial breakthrough of 1979, *Whatcha Gonna Do... With My Lovin'*. Although not quite as strong as that album or 1980's *Sweet Sensation*, this is a generally pleasing LP that finds her romantic side prevailing. You won't hear another "Put Your Body in It" on *Stephanie*; the singer was trying to avoid being categorized as a disco diva, and it's no coincidence that ballads and slow jams are dominant. The track "I Believe in Love Songs" almost sounds like a statement of purpose from Mills, who fared well among quiet storm audiences with sleek offerings like "Magic," "Night Games," and the major hit "Two Hearts" (a duet with Teddy Pendergrass). *Stephanie* falls short of essential, but even so, it's a nice record to have in your collection. *—Alex Henderson*

Love Has Lifted Me / 1982 / Motown ♦♦

Tantalizingly Hot / 1982 / Casablanca ♦♦♦
Somewhat more varied and enticing than its predecessor, Mills' Casablanca debut scored two Top 15 R&B hits with "Last Night" and "Keep Away Girls," in addition to the lower-charting "You Can't Run From My Love" (number 59, early 1983). *Tantalizingly Hot* once again used the production of James Mtume & Reggie Lucas on five cuts. But Ashford & Simpson and Mills herself also produced, making it more well rounded than 1981's *Stephanie*. Interestingly, though, Mtume and Lucas' cuts turn out the strongest. The aforementioned "Last Night" and "You Can't Run" are both sprightly, danceable soul tunes, with "Last Night" boosting a strong hook. The A&S-produced and co-written "I Can't Give Back the Love I Feel for You" (originally recorded by Diana Ross on her 1971 *Surrender*) employs a transition from ballad to disco-fied R&B number during the second verse. It's a semi-good idea, but the corresponding arrangement is not energetic enough to make it very effective. Meanwhile, the Mills-produced "Ole Love" is pleasant, but doesn't leave as much of an impression as the Mtume/Lucas numbers "Your Love Is Always New" and "True Love Don't Come Easy." *Tantalizingly Hot* isn't the sturdiest of Mills' work, and it certainly isn't as flooring as its title suggests; rather, it's a 50/50 deal that doesn't suffer from any totally unappealing moments. *—Justin Kantor*

Merciless / 1983 / Casablanca ♦♦♦♦
The soulful songstress is at her finest on this highly entertaining nine-song set. The funky, jazzy "My Body" brings traces of early house music to the table with its feverish vocals, keyboards, and Latin-spiced percussion, while the cool and breezy—yet lyrically straight to the point—ballad "Do You Love Him" features one of Mills' most expertly delivered performances on record. She also turns in some enticing vocal interplay with singer Peggi Blu on the clever "His Name Is Michael." Unlike later "confrontational" duets by Aretha Franklin & Whitney Houston ("It Isn't, It Wasn't, It Ain't Never Gonna Be") or Brandy & Monica ("The Boy Is Mine") dealing with two-timing boyfriends, both the lyrics and Mills and Blu's interpretation give the matter a lighthearted, humorous spin that is oh so appealing. Two other fine ballads pop up in the grabbing, the Prince-penned "How Come U Don't Call Me Anymore?" (R&B number 12; also released by Prince as B-side in 1982) and the romantic "Eternal Love" (recorded the same year by Whitney Houston on co-writer Paul Jabara's *Paul Jabara & Friends* album, also on Casablanca). "Pilot Error" (R&B number 12) and the cute "Here I Am," meanwhile, are fun dance entries. Every song on *Merciless* is solid, vocally and production-wise. Producers Gary Klein, David Wolfert, and Phil Ramone bring out the best of the songs and help bring back the vocal energy that had been missing from much of the material on Mills' two preceding albums. It's definitely her best album for Casablanca, as well as one of her best overall. *—Justin Kantor*

In My Life: Greatest Hits / 1985 / Casablanca ♦♦♦♦

Home / 1989 / MCA ♦♦♦♦
Stephanie Mills majestic voice warrants quality material and production, and this album meets those terms. The first single, if not a ballad then a quiet storm regular, was "Something in the Way You Make Me Feel." While the single is funky and sleek, Mills sultry delivery gives the track that sexy appeal. It landed at the number-one spot on the *Billboard* R&B charts. The second single was the title track, "Home." Originally featured in the hit Broadway show *The Wiz*, which Mills starred in for five years, "Home" has a warm,

intimate charm. Mills exhibits superb vocality, augmented by a dynamic arrangement and the harmonious background vocals of Take 6. The song is simply chilling. It, too, made its home the top spot on the charts. The third single was the soulfully arranged "Comfort of a Man." Mills ringing vocals carry this single to the top ten, resting at number eight. "Real Love" was the fourth single. It too has that soulful arrangement. It managed only to peak at 53. However, still a beautiful song. The CD features three bonus tracks: "Love Hasn't Been Easy on Me," "I'm More Than a Woman" and an extended version of "Something in the Way You Make Me Feel." The first two are bona fide ballads. *—Craig Lytle*

Something Real / 1992 / MCA ✦✦✦

● **The Best of Stephanie Mills** / 1995 / Mercury ✦✦✦✦✦
Stephanie Mills' best-known hits are featured on this budget collection, including "Never Knew Love Like This Before," "Whatcha Gonna Do . . . with My Lovin'," "Put Your Body in It" and "Two Hearts." *—Keith Farley*

● **The Ultimate Collection** / Feb. 23, 1999 / Hip-O ✦✦✦✦✦
From 1979 to 1993, Mills' glowing voice was a frequent resident on R&B airwaves. She delivered riveting funk-disco romps and soulful ballads with equal ease and conviction. Almost all of the highlights are found here, as well as several lesser-known earlier works. The tracks are arranged in chronological order, beginning with two songs from her obscure 1974 debut album, *Movin' in the Right Direction*, and ending with two Top Ten numbers from 1989's gold *Home*. In between is a diverse selection, ranging from the gospel-rooted "I Took My Strength from You" to the pop crossover hits "Never Knew Love Like this Before" and "Whatcha Gonna Do . . . with My Lovin'" to the Prince cover "How Come U Don't Call Me Anymore?" Notably missing are the 1981 duet with Teddy Pendergrass, "Two Hearts," and the 1982 hit "Last Night." But considering this 15-track compilation includes work from all five labels for which Mills recorded secular material, it pretty much lives up to its name. *The Ultimate Collection* is a riveting retrospective to Mills' R&B career, enhanced by David Nathan's compelling liner notes. *—Justin M. Kantor*

The Power of Love: A Ballads Collection / Feb. 1, 2000 / MCA ✦✦✦
Presented here are a dozen sizzling ballads from the mighty Stephanie Mills, one of the '90s finest female vocalists. MCA Records makes sure Ms. Dynamo's reputation carries into the millennium with this emotionally charged set which includes her roasting rendition of Peabo Bryson's "Feel the Fire" and the gospel-ish "Power of Love." While you can't quibble with the inclusions, there are some glaring omissions: namely "If I Was Your Woman," "You're Puttin' a Rush on Me," and "Something in the Way (You Make Me Feel)." Crowd pleasers which Mills still performs live, these were all recorded on MCA. The exclusion of her 20th century ballads is understandable since this is an MCA release, but to leave off the three essentials is a compilation felony. *—Andrew Hamilton*

Roy Milton

b. Jul. 31, 1907, Wynnewood, OK, **d.** Sep. 18, 1983, Los Angeles, CA
Vocals, Drums, Leader / Jump Blues, West Coast Blues, R&B, Jazz Blues
As in-the-pocket drummer of his own jump blues combo, the Solid Senders, Roy Milton was in a perfect position to drive his outfit just as hard or soft as he so desired. With his stellar sense of swing, Milton did just that; his steady backbeat on his 1946 single for Art Rupe's fledgling Juke Box imprint, "R.M. Blues," helped steer it to the uppermost reaches of the R&B charts (his assured vocal didn't hurt either).

Milton spent his early years on an Indian reservation in Oklahoma (his maternal grandmother was a Native American) before moving to Tulsa. He sang with Ernie Fields' territory band during the late '20s and began doubling on drums when the band's regular trapsman got arrested one fateful evening. In the mood to leave Fields in 1933, Milton wandered west to Los Angeles and formed the Solid Senders. 1945 was a big year for him—along with signing with Juke Box (soon to be renamed Specialty), the band filmed three soundies with singer June Richmond.

"R.M. Blues" was such a huge seller that it established Specialty as a viable concern for the long haul. Rupe knew a good thing when he saw it, recording Milton early and often through 1953. He was rewarded with 19 Top Ten R&B hits by the Solid Senders, including "Milton's Boogie," "True Blues," "Hop, Skip & Jump," "Information Blues," "Oh Babe" (a torrid cover of Louis Prima's jivey jump), and "Best Wishes." Milton's resident boogie piano specialist, Camille Howard, also sang on several Milton platters, including the 1947 hit "Thrill Me," concurrently building a solo career on Specialty.

After amassing a voluminous catalog as one of Specialty's early bedrocks, Milton moved on to Dootone, King (there he cut the delectable instrumental "Succotash"), and Warwick (where he eked out a minor R&B hit in 1961, "Red Light") with notably less commercial success. Sadly, even though he helped pioneer the postwar R&B medium, rock & roll had rendered Milton an anachronism.

The drummer remained active nonetheless, thrilling the throng at the 1970 Monterey Jazz Festival as part of Johnny Otis' all-star troupe. It's a safe bet he was swinging until the very end. *—Bill Dahl*

★ **Roy Milton & His Solid Senders** / Feb. 1978 / Specialty ✦✦✦✦✦
Certainly this is the place to go for Milton's most popular and influential material—a whopping 18 of the 25 cuts made the R&B Top Ten in the late '40s and early '50s. These include such classics as "R.M. Blues," "The Hucklebuck," and "Hop, Skip & Jump" (given a great rockabilly treatment in the 1950s by the Collins Kids). All of the tracks are prime jump blues, Milton occasionally slowing down the boogies into ballads; one number ("Thrill Me") features fellow jump blues star Camille Howard on vocals. *—Richie Unterberger*

R.M. Blues / 1985 / Specialty ✦✦✦
Specialty's *R.M. Blues* is a fine collection that features 15 highlights from Roy Milton's jumping Specialty recordings. While his time at Specialty was unquestionably the finest period of his career, and there are some timeless performances here ("R.M. Blues," "Night and Day," "Wakin' Up Baby," "Milton's Boogie," "Information Blues"), these same recordings have appeared on better, more comprehensive CD reissues which are preferable to this LP edition. *—Thom Owens*

Groovy Blues, Vol. 2 / 1992 / Specialty ✦✦✦✦✦
The rarities and unissued material begin to pop up on *Vol. 2*, making it even more of a feast for collectors. Milton's Solid Senders, featuring pianist/singer Camille Howard, guitarist Johnny Rogers, and a crew of roaring saxmen, were one of the tightest and most respected on the Coast. *—Bill Dahl*

Blowin' With Roy / 1994 / Specialty ✦✦✦✦✦
The third and presumably final entry in Specialty's exhaustive Milton reissue series is by no means a makeweight affair. Even when the Solid Senders tackled Tin Pan Alley fare like "Along the Navajo Trail," "Coquette," and "When I Grow Too Old to Dream," they swung 'em. More late-'40s/early-'50s rarities and unissued items galore. *—Bill Dahl*

Garnet Mimms

b. Nov. 16, 1933, Ashland, VA
Vocals, Piano / Deep Soul, Southern Soul, R&B, Soul
Best known for his original rendition of "Cry Baby," later a major item in Janis Joplin's repertoire, Garnet Mimms' pleading, gospel-derived intensity made him one of the earliest true soul singers. His legacy remains criminally underappreciated, since for some reason he never scored another hit on the level of "Cry Baby," but his output from the early to mid-'60s—a blend of uptown sophistication and earthy, impassioned vocals—has earned comparisons to Sam Cooke and Jackie Wilson from hardcore soul aficionados.

Mimms was actually born Garrett Mimms in Ashland, WV, on November 26, 1933. He was mostly raised in Philadelphia, and began singing in church as a boy; during his teen years, he performed with several area gospel groups, including the Evening Stars, the Harmonizing Four, and the Norfolk Four, with whom he cut his first record in 1953. Mimms subsequently served several years in the military, and upon his release, he returned to Philadelphia in 1958 and formed a doo wop quintet called the Gainors, whose ranks included Sam Bell and onetime Evening Star Howard Tate (later an acclaimed solo singer in his own right). The Gainors recorded singles for several labels over the next three years, including Red Top (later picked up by Cameo), Mercury (from 1959-1960), and Tally Ho (1961). Failing to produce a hit, Mimms left the group along with Bell and put together Garnet Mimms & the Enchanters, which were completed by Charles Boyer and Zola Pearnell. Thanks to Dick Clark's *American Bandstand* program, Philadelphia had become a haven for teen idols, and Mimms took his group to New York in 1963 in search of a more receptive scene. There they met songwriter/producer Bert Berns, who signed them to United Artists and teamed them with another songwriter/producer, Jerry Ragovoy.

Mimms quickly struck gold with the proto-soul performance of "Cry Baby," a smash hit that reached the pop Top Five and topped the R&B charts in 1963. The follow-up, a cover of Jerry Butler & the Impressions' "For Your Precious Love," hit the pop Top 40 later that year, as did the flip side, "Baby Don't You Weep." Mimms and the Enchanters parted ways in 1964; the group to record separately with a new lead vocalist, while Mimms cut solo sides for UA steadily over the next few years. Ragovoy's productions became increasingly polished, mirroring the shift in R&B spearheaded by Motown, yet Mimms' vocals retained all the fire of his gospel training, making for a combination that was fairly unique for the time. Minor hits like "It Was Easier to Hurt Her" and "I'll Take Good Care of You" (the latter Mimms' last Top 40 hit in 1966) didn't perform nearly as well commercially as their quality seemed to indicate. In 1967, United Artists moved him to their Veep subsidiary, where "My Baby" was another inexplicable flop (it, too, was later covered by Janis Joplin on *Pearl*).

Mimms subsequently followed Ragovoy to Verve, where he recorded four singles to little response; ditto for his brief stint at MGM. Mimms did make one last minor chart appearance in 1977, recording for Arista as Garnet Mimms & the Truckin' Company; the disco-funk single "What It Is" was produced by Brass Construction mastermind Randy Muller. Mimms retired from the music business permanently after becoming a born-again Christian. *—Steve Huey*

Cry Baby and 11 Other Hits / Sep. 20, 1963 / United Artists ✦✦✦✦✦
Mimms' debut album was a well-above-average effort for soul LPs of the era. Besides the title smash, it featured solid material that married Garnet's gospel feel with uptown New York soul production; "Anytime You Want Me," "Wanting You," and "Baby Don't You Weep" were some of his finest songs. It's been reissued in its entirety, along with 14 other cuts, on the British CD *Cry Baby/Warm & Soulful*; most of the songs are on the domestic compilation *The Best of Garnet Mimms*. *—Richie Unterberger*

As Long as I Have You / Dec. 1964 / United Artists ✦✦✦

I'll Take Good Care of You / Apr. 1966 / United Artists ✦✦✦

Garnet Mimms & the Enchanters / Nov. 25, 1991 / Collectables ✦✦✦
Garnet Mimms had a series of excellent R&B and soul hits from 1959 to 1964 as lead singer for the Enchanters. A onetime member of the Norfolk Four and Evening Stars, Mimms had the energetic, wailing sound and range ideal for soul. He turned in some wonderful hits for Loma, which are included in this anthology. These songs are also available on an EMI anthology. *—Ron Wynn*

● **The Best of Garnet Mimms: Cry Baby** / 1993 / Capitol ✦✦✦✦✦
Excellent compilation of this early soul singer, whose influence extended beyond his one big hit, the 1963 title track. Emerging from a gospel background and obscure doo wop groups, Mimms invested the increasingly sophisticated R&B sound of the mid-'60s with both emotion and supple pipes. He never hit the Top Ten after "Cry Baby," but rang off a string of minor hits like "Baby Don't You Weep," "For Your Precious Love," "It Was Easier to Hurt Her," and "I'll Take Good Care of You." Grittier than Motown, but not as downhome as Stax, Mimms married his vocals to the uptown production values and pop songwriting savvy of his producer, Jerry Ragovoy, to produce some of the more memorable early soul recordings. This 25-track anthology, covering his recordings for United Artists

between 1963 and 1966, is unerringly consistent. It features all of his hit singles, highlights from the three albums he released during this period, and the original versions of "My Baby" (later one of Janis Joplin's signature tunes) and "Anytime You Want Me" (covered by the Who on a B-side in 1965). *—Richie Unterberger*

Cry Baby/Warm and Soulful / 1995 / BGO ✦✦✦✦✦
This 26-track compilation of Mimms' work between 1963 and 1966 (including his entire 1963 debut LP) is roughly equal in merit to the U.S. *The Best of Garnet Mimms* compilation. Each focuses upon the singer's prime; each largely duplicates the other's track selection; and each has some songs that are not on the other. The most notable item here that isn't on the American compilation is "It Won't Hurt (Half as Much)," which was also recorded by Them in the mid-'60s. The U.S. anthology, however, rates a slight edge: it's easier to locate (in North America, that is), and has the crucial track "My Baby" (covered by Janis Joplin), which is missing from this British comp. *—Richie Unterberger*

Mint Condition

f. 1991, Minneapolis, MN
Group / New Jack Swing, Urban, Club/Dance
Formed in the early '80s in Minneapolis and St. Paul, Mint Condition began as lead singer Stokley Williams, guitarist Homer O'Dell, keyboardist Larry Waddell, keyboardist/saxophonist Jeff Allen, keyboardist/guitarist Keri Lewis, and guitarist/bassist Rick Kinchen. The six talented musicians combine a variety of influences and experiences to shape their own sound. Williams began playing classic West African instruments at the age of four, while O'Dell grew up listening to his father play blues bass and singing with him in a family group. Waddell played in a recording arts band at school and mastered keyboards by listening to jazz greats Oscar Peterson and Herbie Hancock. Exposed to his father's extensive jazz collection, Allen played keyboards and sax in local bands throughout his high school years, as Lewis was mastering keyboards, percussion, and guitar while attending school. Kinchen's first and strongest influence was his family, all of whom played instruments and encouraged his interest in music. He developed his skills as a bass player by listening to records by Stanley Clarke and Louis Johnson of the Brothers Johnson. Kinchen played in various bands in his native Chicago and performed at several productions at Kennedy-King College before moving to the Twin Cities.

The band was featured at the 1986 Minnesota Black Musician Awards program and built a strong core following for themselves in a five-state area (Minnesota, Wisconsin, Iowa, Dakota, and Nebraska) as a result of their dazzling, highly energetic live shows. Mint Condition came to the attention of Minneapolis soul producers Jimmy Jam & Terry Lewis as a result of a showcase performance in 1989. The band had steady success beginning with the hits "(Breaking My Heart) Pretty Brown Eyes" and "Forever in Your Eyes" from their debut *Meant to Be Mint*, and with "Nobody Does It Betta" and "(U Send Me) Swinging" from their second album *From the Mint Factory*; they continued with the platinum success of the single "What Kind of Man Would I Be" from their gold album *Definition of a Band*. Going into the 21st century, Mint Condition was the only high profile R&B/pop band with a major-label recording represented by their excellent *Life's Aquarium*, issued in November 1999. *—Ed Hogan*

Meant to Be Mint / 1991 / Perspective ✦✦✦
The debut album from the Minneapolis-based sextet featured the lackluster uptempo track "Are You Free," which did manage to secure the 55 position on the charts. However, this album also featured two heart-wrenching ballads: "Breakin' My Heart (Pretty Brown Eyes)" and "Forever in Your Eyes." Led by Stokley's animated tenor, the former is set in a suspenseful rhythm arrangement; the song builds momentum in the interlude, allowing Stokley to explode vocally in an emotional testimony. The single sold over 500,000 copies, pacing the charts 34 weeks and peaking at number three and number six on the *Billboard* R&B and Pop charts, respectively. "Forever in Your Eyes" offers another compassionate vocal delivery by Stokley with similar arrangements, but still maintaining its own feeling. It inched its way to the number seven spot on the R&B charts in 17 weeks. The remainder of the album is extremely energized, but does not offer anything noteworthy. *—Craig Lytle*

From the Mint Factory / Oct. 5, 1993 / Perspective ✦✦✦✦
The second release from Mint Condition follows closely on the heels of their successful debut. Principal vocalist Stokely has good presence, projects sincerity and earnestness on love songs, and reflects Stevie Wonder's influence. The backing vocals, arrangements, lyrics and production style aren't overloaded with electronics, strings or any other devices, and they balance a traditional soul sensibility with a 1990s approach. Several numbers are enjoyable, although none are overpowering or remarkable. Sometimes they move into light funk or new jack, but Mint Condition is best at sentimental, breezy love material. *—Ron Wynn*

Definition of a Band / Sep. 24, 1996 / Perspective ✦✦✦✦
Mint Condition's third album, *Definition of a Band* is the smoothest effort yet from the swingbeat group. Again, lead singer Stokley Williams steals the show with his surging, passionate vocals, which are so affecting that you often wish that the songwriting was more distinguished, along the lines of the hit single "What Kind of Man Would I Be." *—Leo Stanley*

● **The Collection: 1991–1998** / Jun. 9, 1998 / Perspective ✦✦✦✦✦
The Collection (1991-1998) contains all the highlights from the Mint Condition's first three albums, plus their contribution to the *Jason's Lyric* soundtrack, "If Trouble Were Money," and two new recordings. Since Mint Condition's albums were a little uneven, a collection of this sort is welcome, even if it arrives a little early; it offers an ideal retrospective of the group's first albums. *—Stephen Thomas Erlewine*

Life's Aquarium / Nov. 16, 1999 / Elektra ✦✦✦✦
With their fourth album and first for Elektra, Mint Condition tightens up their songwriting substantially, making *Life's Aquarium* one of their best efforts to date. The group's melodies and instrumental interplay are focused and confident, and that assurance is also apparent in the album's tone: Where past Mint Condition releases were highlighted by smooth romantic material, the high points of *Life's Aquarium* tend to be in the form of sexy lover-man come-ons. It's refreshing to hear the group broadening their range somewhat, but the album's real strength is simply the fact that Mint Condition has cut down on the aimless meandering that often cluttered their past releases, helping to make the songs more consistently memorable. *—Steve Huey*

The Miracles

f. 1955, Detroit, MI
Group / Motown, Urban, R&B, Soul
In 1972, after Smokey Robinson left the group he'd founded more than 15 years earlier to concentrate on songwriting and production for a solo career, the group changed its name back to the Miracles (it had been Smokey Robinson & the Miracles since 1966). The 20-year-old Billy Griffin was brought in to replace Robinson, and once again, the Miracles started scoring more hits, including "Do It Baby" and "Don't Cha Love It," which both reached the R&B Top Ten by the end of 1975. The Miracles experienced a big success in early 1976 with "Love Machine, Pt. 1," which reached number one on the pop charts. The multi-million selling single came from their second album without Robinson, 1975's *City of Angels*, and stayed on the charts for over six months, making it the longest-running hit the band ever had.

After one final album for Motown, *Power of Music*, the group switched to CBS and added a new member, Griffin's brother Don. Their first CBS release was *Love Crazy* (1977), which contained a single, "Spy for the Brotherhood," that was pulled off the record after complaints from the FBI. The group's last charting single, "Mean Machine," made the R&B Top 100 in 1978. Griffin then pursued a solo career, while Moore became a record producer in Detroit. In the late '80s, Bobby Rogers started the New Miracles, and in 1990 the Miracles (including Griffin and Claudette Robinson) reunited to re-record "Love Machine" for the British Motorcity label. *—Joslyn Layne*

Renaissance / Apr. 1973 / Motown ✦✦✦✦
Motown assigned a number of producers to work with the Miracles on their first LP after Smokey Robinson's departure. The resulting patching of efforts excels, as each producer brought his best to the table. Newcomer Billy Griffin joins Ron White, Bobby Rogers, and Pete Moore for some delicious vocal blends. The Marvin Gaye-produced "I Love You Secretly" is comparable to his successful Original productions, "Baby I'm For Real" and "Bells." Willie Hutch contributed two numbers, the understated "Wigs & Lashes" and the exciting "I Didn't Realize the Show Was Over"; Griffin sings the former in a lower register than the latter. The most overlooked song here has to be the Mel Larson and Jerry Marcellino production "If You're Ever in the Neighborhood"; Billy's light, aching tenor and the Miracles' heart-tugging harmonies make for some smooth listening. Sadly, the single releases didn't help propel *Renaissance* up the charts; "What Is a Heart Good For," written by Leon Ware and Arthur T-Boy Ross (Diana Ross's brother) stiffed, and the sales of "Don't Let It End (Til You Let It Begin)" were disappointing. Both, however, are excellent; Ron White co-leads on the latter and displays a subtle, quality tenor. Pam Sawyer & Leon Ware's "I Don't Need No Reason" was later recorded by, of all people, Junior Walker & the All-Stars. Smokey Robinson is credited as executive producer; exactly what that means—your guess is as good as mine. Maybe he picked the material; if so, he did a helluva job. *—Andrew Hamilton*

Do It Baby / Aug. 1974 / Motown ✦✦✦
Though not the artistic success of *Renaissance*, the Miracles' second LP fared better commercially due to the sinuous "Do It Baby," their first bona fide hit without Smokey Robinson. "Do It Baby" shocked many loyal Miracles fans; they had never recorded a song as sexually explicit as the midtempo romper. It's easy to see why Billy Griffin was chosen to replace Robinson—his tenor is naturally high like Smokey's, without ranging into falsetto. Some of the songs are too saccharine, almost bubblegum; "Up Again," for example, would have been better suited for a younger group. Willie Hutch's "I Can't Get Ready for Losing You," however, is a guitar-driven smoker that speeds along like a runaway locomotive. For some reason, "What Is a Heart Good For," from the first album, is included here too. *—Andrew Hamilton*

Don't Cha Love It / 1975 / Tamla ✦✦✦
The Miracles' third LP without Smokey Robinson's leadership was the weakest to date. Attempting to ride the same formula that propelled "Do It Baby" up the R&B charts, the syrupy *Don't Cha Love It*, produced by Freddie Perren, falls short. Perren used Christine Yarian as his primary lyricist on this collection, and her words simply fail to impact. The vocal arrangements, handled by Perren, didn't suit the Miracles' voices or style. There are always a few good spots on mediocre LPs, and this one has some; "Brokenhearted Girl—Brokenhearted Boy" and "You Are Love" are pleasant enough, but listening to the whole album non-stop will have you reaching for the Tylenol. *—Andrew Hamilton*

City of Angels / Sep. 1975 / Motown ✦✦✦✦
Concept albums became the thing to do in the '70s, and the Miracles joined the fray with *City of Angels*. Their most successful album without Smokey Robinson, it was also their most controversial. One of the tracks, "Ain't Nobody Straight in L.A.," created quite a stir when released (as the follow-up to "Love Machine") with lyrics stating that nobody was straight in Los Angeles. This didn't go over well with the brothers, to say nothing of the closing rap/conversation wherein the guys ride out to a gay bar for a night of entertainment. Of course, "Love Machine" shot up the charts like a missile all the way to number one. It became the biggest hit for the Miracles ever—even with Smokey. The title track, "City of Angels," and "Smog" are probably the two slowest songs ever recorded by an R&B group. "Smog" in particular makes a waltz seem speedy. "Waldo Roderick DeHammersmith" had an unusual title, but this sucker rocks from the first seconds to the end; the song was about a street hustler named Waldo, who went by the nickname

of Butch. At the end the Miracles warn you about the guy, chirping "Butch will get you, shoo doo, shoo waa, Butch will get you, shoo doo, shoo waa." "My Name Is Michael" was written with Michael Jackson in mind; the song is a midtempo romper about a guy (Michael) who has it all, fame and money. *—Andrew Hamilton*

The Power of Music / Sep. 1976 / Motown ✦✦
The Power of Music was the Miracles' follow-up to their hit album *City of Angels*, which included the number-one pop hit "Love Machine." While *City of Angels*, produced by Freddie Perren, was a concept album with a clear theme (a look at the seamier side of L.A. and Hollywood), *The Power of Music* was produced by groupmember Warren "Pete" Moore and seemed somewhat muddled. Though it did managed to chart number 38 on the R&B and included a few nice tracks, such as "Let the Children Play," "Love to Make Love," and the slow jam "You Need a Miracle." [The latter two are on the 2002 Polygram International CD *Essential Collection*.] *—Ed Hogan*

Love Crazy / 1977 / CBS ✦✦
The Miracles tried to be the Isleys on this one and failed miserably, quickening their exile to has-been-dom. On the album cover, five Miracles are shown: Pete Moore, Ron White, Bobby Rogers, Billy Griffin and his brother Donald; Donald is shown holding a guitar, leading me to expect some Ernie Isley-influenced solos—not! The original Miracles are dressed in outfits that are far too young for them, number one; this is not their style, number two, and number three, it's a total turn-off to their loyal legion of fans. The clothes are an issue because arguably with—and even moreso without—Smokey Robinson, the Miracles were the sharpest dressers among R&B vocal groups; their clothes were unique, stylish, tailored, colorful, and dashing. The only song on *Love Crazy* to receive any airplay was the James Bond-inspired "Spy for Brotherhood"—an odd choice, but then CBS's "single pickers" didn't have much to choose from on this turkey; at least "Spy" had a grooveable *beat*. They can't blame this on anybody, since they wrote and produced everything; it illustrates the importance of a good producer. Some groups can produce themselves and some can't. *—Andrew Hamilton*

● **Collection** / Apr. 9, 2002 / Spectrum ✦✦✦✦
While a deeper dip into the Miracles' first release (*Renaissance*) wouldn't have hurt, *The Collection* is still a fine overview of their post-Smokey Robinson recordings on Motown with Billy Griffin. The CD relies heavily on cuts from their best-selling *City of Angels* album: "Waldo Roderick DeHammersmith," "My Name Is Michael," the dreamy "Smog," the controversial "Ain't Nobody Straight in L.A.," and their number-one smash "Love Machine." Other gimmes are "Do It Baby," "What Is a Heart Good For," and the super-classy "Don't Let It End (Til You Let It Begin)." Ronnie White's seldom-used (as a lead) second tenor is refreshing and provides a good contrast to Griffin's delicate first tenor on many tracks. *—Andrew Hamilton*

The Mirettes

Group / Soul
When the 1964-1966 edition of the Ikettes—Robbie Montgomery, Vanetta Fields, and Jessie Smith—decided to leave Ike Turner's organization to record on their own, they used the name the Mirettes to record for Revue. The trio's cover of "In the Midnight Hour" just missed the Top 40 in 1968, and Revue released a similarly titled LP later that year. A few other choices for covers, "On the Good Ship Lollipop" and the Spencer Davis Group's "Keep on Running," failed to make the charts. Another LP followed, 1969's *Whirlpool*, for the UNI label. *—John Bush*

● **In the Midnight Hour** / 1968 / Revue ✦✦✦
The Ikettes, fed up with not being compensated for placing "Peaches and Cream," "I'm So Thankful" and other recordings on the charts, defected from Ike Turner's camp and began recording as the Mirettes since Turner owned the name Ikettes. The soulful, leggy ladies' rendition of "In the Midnight Hour" claimed a spot on the R&B charts, as did their passionate "Take Me for a Little While." They treat you to the funkiest version of "On the Good Ship Lollipop" ever heard. They also cover "Somewhere" and the rocker "To Love Somebody." Original songs such as "The Real Thing," "I'm a Whole New Thing," "First Love" and "Keep on Running" pad the LP. *—Andrew Hamilton*

Bobby Mitchell & the Toppers

b. Aug. 16, 1935, Algiers, LA, **d.** Mar. 17, 1989, New Orleans, LA
Vocals, Trumpet / New Orleans R&B, Rock & Roll, R&B
Bobby Mitchell & the Toppers were part of the wave of New Orleans rock & rollers who followed in the wake of Fats Domino and Lloyd Price. Although the group had limited success (their best known song, "Try Rock 'n Roll," climbed into the R&B Top 20 nationally, and "I'm Gonna Be a Wheel Someday" was a smash in numerous localities without ever charting nationally) and broke up in 1954, Mitchell remained a popular figure in New Orleans R&B for 35 years.

Bobby Mitchell (August 16, 1935-March 17, 1989) was born in Algiers, LA, the second oldest of what were eventually 17 children in a family that made its living fishing the Mississippi River. When he was ten years old, Mitchell got a job after school making deliveries for a liquor store, and it was while hanging around the store that he started singing. At age 17, he was in his first singing group, the Louisiana Groovers. By that time, Mitchell was falling firmly under the influence of R&B, most especially the sound of Roy Brown. Mitchell wrote his first original song, "One Friday Morning," a doo wop-style ballad, which he cut as a demo with help from a teacher with a tape recorder (still a relative rarity in 1952). That tape got auditioned at a local radio station, and this led to the formation of a backing group called the Toppers, consisting of Lloyd Bellaire (tenor), Joseph Butler (tenor), Willie Bridges (baritone), Frank Bocage (bass), and Gabriel Flemming (piano).

Eventually, they hooked up with producer Dave Bartholomew, and at his urging they cut some demos for Imperial Records. Released in May of 1953, their debut single, a Bellaire original, "I'm Crying," didn't sell well, although it was a beginning—Mitchell's voice was powerful and extremely expressive but quirkily uneven in the beginning, which made recording him tricky; the Toppers' singing was smooth, and the backing, by Lee Allen on tenor sax, Earl Palmer on drums, and Red Taylor on baritone sax (with Bartholomew on trumpet), was as solid as any rock & roll cut in New Orleans during that era. "I'm Crying" sold well in places like Cincinnati and Houston, but Mitchell and his group were unable to appear there to push the record any further, largely because of their ages and the fact that they were still required to attend school. Additionally, they weren't able to play any nightclubs even locally because they were underage, so they played high school dances, parties, weddings, and events at places like the American Legion Hall. Their recording career continued with more sessions resulting in classics such as "4x11 Equals 44," a rock tune built around a set of popular lottery numbers.

Mitchell had trouble juggling the requirements of a career with school, and the Toppers endured until early 1954, when they finally split up after a session that included two hot songs, the raucous "School Boy Blues," with its killer guitar intro by Justin Adams, and "Sister Lucy," the latter highlighted by an Allen solo. "Sister Lucy" ended up as the B-side of a local double-sided hit with Bellaire's "My Baby's Gone"; "Sister Lucy" pulled in white listeners, while Bellaire's song reached the black stations and clubs. The Toppers' breakup came about because of the military draft, which claimed the members as they turned 18. Mitchell's sporadic success on Imperial ended in 1958, as the label dropped most of its New Orleans acts except for Fats Domino. He signed with a succession of smaller labels in the early '60s. He still played shows in Houston and Mobile, but his records weren't selling—he was back with Imperial Records very briefly, and then returned to Rip Records, where he'd previously cut a couple of singles. Those sides for Rip and Sho-Biz were among the finest songs that Mitchell ever recorded, but were largely unheard.

A heart attack in the early '60s brought an end to his career on the road. Mitchell continued performing in New Orleans, where he remained a music celebrity for the next 29 years, performing regularly and eventually finding new recognition. Toward the end of his life, he also saw the first money from his original Imperial recordings with the release of a reissue LP, *I'm Gonna Be a Wheel Someday*. Mitchell became one of New Orleans' most visible and forthcoming '50s veterans. He passed away in 1989 after years of worsening illnesses, including diabetes, kidney failure, and two further heart attacks. *—Bruce Eder*

● **I'm Gonna Be a Wheel Someday** / Mar. 18, 1997 / Bear Family ✦✦✦✦
The only earthly reason for making this two-CD set an oversized box, as opposed to a small double jewel box, was so that the booklet could accommodate the notes and photos—but it adds nothing to the retail cost, and the booklet is pretty cool. The 47 tracks here cover Mitchell's entire recording career through 1964, on the Imperial, Sho-Biz, Ron, and Rip labels, all in surprisingly consistent sound given the age and varied sources of the recordings. The early tracks, Mitchell & the Toppers' first sessions from 1953, are a little crude, as was typical of R&B from this era—though the singing and playing overcome this inherent difficulty. By the time of their 1954 sessions, the group and their recordings are rather more sophisticated, and Mitchell's vocals are more confident as well. Disc two covers the second half of Mitchell's career with Imperial, including the classic "I'm Gonna Be a Wheel Someday." The four songs that Mitchell cut for Imperial on his brief return in 1962 show him working in an Arthur Alexander-type mode, doing slow romantic ballads extremely effectively. But the real jewels on disc two are the songs Mitchell cut with Dr. John on the Sho-Biz and Ron labels, which include a raft of dazzling, soulful rockers. If anything, these rock harder than the Imperial sides, and Mitchell sounds more comfortable, with an arrangement, backing band, and tempos more suited to his strengths as a singer, stretching out and finally finding a voice and sound completely his own. Those tracks and some unreleased numbers deserved hit status, and why they failed, apart from the modest resources of the labels they were done for, is anyone's guess. The box concludes with Mitchell's answer song to his second biggest hit, "I Don't Want to Be a Wheel No More," and his towering 1963 single "Walking in Circles"—lushly scored for a full band and chorus, Mitchell's voice in these surroundings soars to majestic new heights of soulfulness. *—Bruce Eder*

Willie Mitchell

b. Mar. 1928, Ashland, MS
Producer, Trumpet / Memphis Soul, Soul-Blues, Soul
Best-known as the man who signed Al Green to Hi Records and as the producer of Green's most popular records, Willie Mitchell had a successful recording career of his own during the mid-'60s before meeting Green. Born on March, 1928, in Ashland, MS, Mitchell was raised in Memphis, TN, and began studying music and arranging at an early age, taking up the trumpet at the age of eight and learning from pianist Ozie Horn (as well as drawing from such influences as Roy Eldridge and Harry James). After he was discharged from the Army in 1954, Mitchell moved back to Memphis, where he soon became a popular, local trumpet-playing bandleader—including Elvis Presley hiring the big band to play several private parties. By 1959, Mitchell had turned his attention to studio work and he signed on with Hi Records; he is often credited as being the creator of the oft-copied and instantly recognizable Hi sound (churning organ fills, sturdy horn arrangements, a steady 4/4 drumbeat, etc.).

Throughout the '60s, Mitchell became a popular concert attraction on U.S. college campuses and he scored several moderately successful soul/dance hit singles, issuing a steady stream of solo releases for the Hi label, including such titles as *Sunrise Serenade*, *It's Dance Time*, *It's What's Happenin'*, *Hit Sound of Willie Mitchell*, *Ooh Baby, You Turn Me On*, *Willie Mitchell Live at the Royal*, *Solid Soul*, and *On Top*. When the founder of Hi Records, Joe Cuoghi, died in 1970, Mitchell suddenly found himself in charge of the label. What could have been a turbulent transition turned out to be a smooth one: A year before Cuoghi's passing, Mitchell had signed an up-and-coming soul singer named Al Green to the label. Under the guidance of Mitchell, Green's career would soon skyrocket and he became one of the '70s top soul artists with Mitchell co-producing and engineering all of Green's albums from 1970 through 1976 (the singer's most successful period), as well as such classic Top Ten hit singles as "Tired of Being Alone," "Call Me (Come Back Home)," "I'm Still in Love With You," "Here I Am (Come and Take Me)," "Let's Stay Together," "You Ought to Be With Me," "Look at What You Done for Me," "Let's Get Married," and others.

Besides racking up the hits with Green in the '70s, Mitchell continued to issue his own solo recordings, including such further releases as *Soul Bag*, *Robbins' Nest*, *Hold It*, *Listen Dance*, *Many Moods of Willie Mitchell*, and *Willie Mitchell Live*, in addition to producing albums for Ann Peebles and Syl Johnson. Mitchell continues to sporadically issue solo albums, but still continually produces recordings for other artists, including Otis Clay, Jimmy King, Preston Shannon, and O.V. Wright, among others. The late '90s saw several Mitchell compilations crop up (1998's *Hi Masters* and 1999's *Soul Serenade: The Best of Willie Mitchell*), which continued into the early 21st century with a double-disc anthology, *Poppa Willie: The Hi Years, 1962-1974*, as well as a pair of two-for-one CD releases (*It's What's Happenin'/The Hit Sound of Willie Mitchell* and *Soul Serenade/Willie Mitchell Live*). In addition to his many musical accomplishments, Mitchell also owns and operates the Royal Recording Studio in Memphis, TN. *—Greg Prato & Bruce Eder*

It's Dance Time / 1965 / Hi ✦✦✦

It's Dance Time begins with an introductory run-through of the days popular steps, a brief warm-up for the listener. From there, Willie Mitchell delivers his usual solid set of instrumentals. While the album doesn't quite match up to Mitchell's best album, *That Driving Beat*, it does have plenty of highlights, including the swaggering "Buster Browne" and "Shake"-styled "When My Dreamboat Comes Home," complete with a lively fuzz guitar and nice drum breaks. As with most Mitchell albums, most of the songs are over in two minutes' time, quickly moving on to the next dance craze, and the tracks include many tasteful cover versions. Those on *It's Dance Time* include "Twine Time," "Fever," and a bluesy "Since I Met You Baby." *—Kurt Edwards*

It's What's Happenin' / 1966 / Hi ✦✦

On Top / 1969 / Hi ✦✦✦

The disappointment that may be present when you see "I Say a Little Prayer" or "Take Five" yet again is quickly lessened by the strong performance of Willie Mitchell's band on *On Top*. Bandleader Mitchell lets the Hodges brothers loose, and they come correct with the goods. Organist Charles Hodges particularly stands out on this record, rewarding the prominent placement of his organ with confident, soulful performances. Mabon "Teenie" Hodges would come to greater fame as his silky, sinewy guitar lines helped propel Al Green to superstardom, but his contributions to Willie Mitchell records shouldn't be overlooked. His solo on the stomping "30-60-90" is comparable to Steve Cropper's best moments, adding grit to already swaggering groove. The band's greater involvement in arranging and songwriting strengthens the album thoroughly, from Mitchell's brother James Mitchell's fiery saxophone on "Sunshine of Your Love" to the entire group getting credit for "30-60-90," making *On Top* one of Willie Mitchell's most satisfying albums. *—Kurt Edwards*

Soul Bag / 1969 / Hi ✦✦✦✦✦

Recorded and issued around Halloween in 1969, *Soul Bag* was the beginning of a shift for Willie Mitchell as a musician. His earlier records were steeped in soulful but also often turgid cover versions that barely deviated from the originals they served. His groove was much more laid-back than anything else recorded at Stax during the time. It's hard to say what motivated the change, but the Mitchell who entered the studio in September had different ideas about his own records. *Soul Bag* is an exuberant, mostly uptempo collection of covers and originals that reflects new interpretive powers by Mitchell as an arranger. On Sly Stone's "Everyday People," the Memphis rave-up groove replaces the funky singsong sound of the original. Led by Booker T.'s organ and Steve Cropper's guitar with a slew of horns as a chorus, the tune reaches the apex of slippery Southern soul very quickly and stays there. Likewise, Mitchell radically reinterpreted the theme from the television program *Hawaii Five-O*, turning it into a lounge jazzer with a deeper than blue saxophone line, while the Cropper/Eddie Floyd classic "Knock on Wood," with its rolling bassline and meat-and-potatoes saxophone line playing the lyric, offered a depth to the tune that singers would often miss. This is essential Willie Mitchell, from a period of transition that changed everything not only in the way he issued his own recordings, but in the way he produced others. *—Thom Jurek*

The Many Moods of Willie Mitchell / 1970 / Hi ✦✦✦✦

The 1970 follow-up to *Soul Bag* was for the most part a further step away from where Willie Mitchell had been for the past decade. The sound on *Many Moods* is darker, funkier, greasier, and grittier. It's almost sloppy, which gives the record an immediacy virtually nothing he recorded before or since could claim. From the slippery late-night feel of "Breaking Point," with its gorgeous guitar and organ harmonics, to the endgame of "Something Nice," which is far more sexy than nice with its intricately structured horn and guitar lines weaving in and out of one another, the effect was the same: intoxicating groove science. Other standouts include "Sack-O-Woe," "Roadhouse," and "Black Fox." On these tracks what is central is the stretching of time and space through the backbeat, letting it fall just ahead or behind the rest of the band, as horn lines, Booker T.'s organ, and Steve Cropper's guitar took their places laying out the groove and punching it up with fills and flourishes. There are two quizzical places on this album that makes one wonder if the tracks were brought in from an earlier session just to fill out side two: "White Silver Sands" and "Midnight Sun" are both drenched in that sweet, shimmering sheen that most of Mitchell's earlier records had, marring what would have been a perfect release. But it's of little consequence, since what is strong here—the vast majority of the album—is a revelation. *—Thom Jurek*

Robbin's Nest / 1970 / Hi ✦✦✦

The final solo album in a concentrated period keeps to trumpeter Willie Mitchell's standard formula. His previous release, *On Top*, found Mitchell opening up to the massive talents of his bandmembers—most of whom would back up Al Green during his groundbreaking run of the early '70s. The band's skill is evident here, with organist Charles Hodges again sounding good, but subpar material, a trademark of Mitchell's releases, stunts any chance for growth. "Tails Out" and "Wade in the Water" are highlights. *—Kurt Edwards*

Ooh Baby, You Turn Me On/Live at the Royal / 1993 / Hi ✦✦✦✦✦

This two-on-one CD ought to be part of any serious soul or dance music collection. 1967's *Ooh Baby*—also released as *Soul Serenade*—was almost entirely instrumental, with a sound recalling King Curtis at his best; the playing is hot and the beat is infectious. Mitchell and his band, including Mabon Hodges on guitar, Leroy Hodges on bass, Charles Hodges on organ, and Charlie Chalmers on tenor sax, run the gamut of covers from Little Richard's "Slippin' And Slidin'," and King Curtis' magnificent "Soul Serenade," and Otis Redding's "Respect" to James Brown's "Papa's Got a Brand New Bag," all interpersed with enjoyable originals. The companion live tracks are well played and recorded, although they aren't cut together as a continuous performance, rather fading between tracks. The songs include "Mustang Sally," "My Girl," and "Soul Serenade" (which is identical to the cut on *Ooh Baby*), and given the closeness of the sound, the perfectly clean stereo separation, and the seemingly artificial sound of the audience, one might question just how "live" all (or any) of *Live at the Royal* really is. But it is fun. *—Bruce Eder*

- **Soul Serenade: The Best of Willie Mitchell** / Oct. 5, 1999 / Capitol ✦✦✦✦✦

Willie Mitchell is best known as the producer of Al Green's classic recordings for Hi in the '70s. Along with Green, he developed the seductive, tight groove that defined a whole generation of soul music—some would call it the last great era of soul, as a matter of fact. Before his seminal work with Green, Mitchell was a solo artist in his own right. During the '60s, his group was the house band at Hi, and he turned out a series of his own singles. These recordings were closer to the hard-driving Southern soul of Stax and Muscle Shoals than to the sultry sound of Hi, and while Mitchell didn't really record any classics—the closest he came was his biggest hit single, "Soul Serenade"—he cut several enjoyable sides that would satisfy most serious soul fans. *Soul Serenade: The Best of Willie Mitchell* is the definitive retrospective of these '60s singles, a 20-track compilation containing all of his charting singles plus a number of good lesser-known numbers. It's not revelatory, and the quality of Mitchell's recordings is a little uneven, but the compilation is entertaining and useful as a historical document, along with being a nice addition to the library of any dedicated fan of '60s soul. *—Stephen Thomas Erlewine*

Poppa Willie: The Hi Years, 1962–1974 / Aug. 14, 2001 / Hi ✦✦✦✦✦

This is a two-disc, 51-song set, with one disc devoted to Mitchell originals and one to covers he made between 1962 and 1974. This is an extensive collection of trumpeter/producer Mitchell's dance-inducing, funky brand of soul music. Like fellow instrumentalists of the day—Booker T., Jr. Walker, King Curtis, and the J.B.s—Mitchell was helping to define a groove that created some of the best instrumental soul ever made. His cover of the Ousley/Dixon-penned "Soul Seranade," which rivals that of King Curtis, is here, as well as his first Hi single, "The Crowd, Pt. 1," and his first chart-topper, "20-75." The set also includes "That Driving Beat" and "Everything Is Gonna Be Alright" with vocals by Don Bryant; rarities such as the Hammond B-3-filled, midtempo "Six to Go" and the raw, slow groove "On the Other Side"; and covers as diverse as "One Mint Julep" and "Turn Back the Hands of Time." Mitchell was appointed vice president of Hi Records in 1970, when he let up on touring and performing to focus on work as a producer. Some of his finer work in that context is here as well, such as recordings of his old touring band (under the name the Hi Rhythm Section) and his last release, a cover of Herb Alpert's sultry score "Last Tango in Paris." *—Travis Drageset*

Robbin's Nest/Rarities / Sep. 11, 2001 / Hi ✦✦✦

Soul Bag/The Many Moods of Willie Mitchell / Sep. 11, 2001 / Hi ✦✦✦✦✦

It's What's Happenin'/The Hit Sound of Willie Mitchell / Nov. 27, 2001 / Hi ✦✦✦

Soul Serenade/Willie Mitchell Live / Nov. 27, 2001 / Hi ✦✦✦✦✦

Moment of Truth

f. 1976

Group / Philly Soul, Disco

Comparable to the Trammps and Double Exposure, Moment of Truth was an excellent but little known East Coast quartet that combined Philadelphia soul with Philadelphia disco. The male vocal group (which consisted of Norris Harris, Ivery "Caprice" Bell, Michael Garrison, and Billy Jones) was consistently mindful of disco's soul roots and owed a strong debt to classic Philly soulsters like the Intruders and Harold Melvin & the Blue Notes. Formed in the 1970s, Moment of Truth recorded its self-titled debut album for Salsoul in 1977. Although superb, the album was ignored by radio and wasn't a big seller by any means. However, the single "Helplessly" became a minor club hit. Moment of Truth broke up without ever recording a second album, and its album was out of print for many years. But thankfully Salsoul reissued *Moment of Truth* on CD in 1993. *—Alex Henderson*

- **Moment of Truth** / 1978 / Salsoul ✦✦✦

Some disco and soul historians argue that disco was born in Philadelphia when Jerry Butler recorded the extremely danceable and highly syncopated "One Night Affair" under Kenny Gamble & Leon Huff's direction in 1972. But whether or not disco was actually created in Philly, the city undeniably made many outstanding contributions to the genre. One of the finest albums recorded in Philly in 1977 was this self-titled album by the superb but obscure soul/disco quartet Moment of Truth. Such sleek yet gritty jewels as "So Much for Love," "Chained to Your Love" and "Helplessly" (a minor club hit) pack a strong emotional punch that brings to mind groups like Harold Melvin & the Blue Notes and the Intruders, but Truth's overall approach is much more disco-oriented and club-conscious. Clearly, the group realized that the best disco stressed vocal personality, not just beats. As little known as this album is, it came as quite a surprise when, in 1993, it was reissued after being out of print for at least 13 years. *—Alex Henderson*

The Moments

f. 1968, Hackensack, NJ, **db.** 1978

Group / Soul, Smooth Soul, Pop-Soul

One of the most consistent R&B aggregations of the '70s, the Moments enjoyed a string of major hits throughout the decade. The Hackensack, NJ, trio introduced themselves and the Stang label with "Not on the Outside" in 1968, and topped the R&B charts in 1970 with the gold-plated "Love on a Two-Way Street," produced by Sylvia Robinson (one half of Mickey & Sylvia). Other major soul smashes by the Moments included "If I Didn't Care" and "All I Have" in 1970, "Sexy Mama" in 1973, and another number-one R&B item, "Look at Me (I'm in Love)," in 1975. Members Harry Ray, Al Goodman, and William Brown changed their billing to Ray, Goodman & Brown in 1978 and topped the soul lists the next year with the slickly harmonized "Special Lady" on Polydor. The renamed trio remained potent soul hitmakers through the '80s. *—Bill Dahl*

Not on the Outside, But on the Inside, Strong! / 1968 / Stang ✦✦✦

An asterisk should be placed on the Moments' first LP release for Stang Records, as the label was seeking to capitalize on the success of "Not on the Outside." Billy Brown, Al Goodman and John Morgan are pictured on the cover as the Moments, and this trio does perform the bulk of the tunes, but the guys who sang on "Not on the Outside" and "Understanding" were a completely different group. For years, many thought Billy Brown led the song; Mark Greene, a Baltimorean, actually sang lead, accompanied by John Morgan and Richie Horsley, the original Moments. Some swear there were four members on the recording. However, when released, only three members were around, and two of them—Horsley and Greene—were fired as the song ran up the R&B chart, stopping at number 13; it reached the 57th position on the pop chart. The original Moments only did one gig, a week-long Apollo Theater engagement. John Morgan leads on "Understanding," a rather dull song, and Al Goodman fronts "Pocketful of Heartbreak"—better, but still nondescript. Billy Brown handles the rest and shines on "Sunday" and "I'm So Lost," two ballads done in Brown's innocent-sounding falsetto. Brown displays restrained emotion on the supercharged ballad "Somebody Loves You Baby," one of their most underrated recordings, which was released as the B-side of "Sunday." "I Won't Do Anything," pretty but lame, was covered by labelmate Lezlie Valentine. And what became their biggest recording wasn't released immediately. Listening to "Love on a Two Way Street" critically, it's understandable as to why Sylvia held it back and viewed it as an album cut. It sounds incomplete, with an off-key clanging guitar note played during the song becoming irritating after repeated plays. *—Andrew Hamilton*

On Top / 1969 / Stang ✦✦✦

On Top is a perfect example of the subjectivity of musical taste. Among collectors, this is considered the most valuable of all the albums recorded by the Moments on Stang Records. In my opinion, it's all right, but it's not all that, and it doesn't come close to being my favorite from the three guys who later became Ray, Goodman & Brown. An original copy of this LP starts at around $50, others by the Moments go for between $10 and $20. Two minor R&B hits, "Lucky Me," a song that Billy Brown claims to hate, and "All I Have," are the most recognizable. Both are George Kerr compositions and productions, and each features Brown's ice-melting falsetto. Also included are two singles that are different from anything the group had ever done, "I Can't Help It" and "That's How It Feels." Sylvia Robinson also recorded "I Can't Help It," and to be honest, the song suited her better. It was the A-side of "To You With Love," a lovely floating ballad sung by Harry Ray that featured the groups' patented hand claps. "That's How It Feels was a two parter wherein Brown's voice rode atop a bed of rhythms on a tune more aptly define as a love suite than a song. Neither impressed the jocks nor the buying public. A charming but sorrow filled "I Lost One Bird in the Hand" is an impressive, slow lamenter crooned by Ray. The only uptempo number, other than the herky jerky "I Can't Help It," is "Sweeter as the Days Go By," led by Brown in his natural, gospel-inspired tenor. I've listened to "The Ice Is Melting" many times but can't get down with it, or "Candy Shack," both are reserved slow jams that lack bite and substance. *—Andrew Hamilton*

A Moment With the Moments / 1970 / Stang ✦✦✦

Though it's bookended by two of the sweet soul trio's biggest hits, *A Moment With the Moments* reflects the overall weaknesses in the trio's songs, performances, and most tragically, the sound of any release associated with parent company All Platinum. Harry Ray, a newcomer to the Moments, hits all the high notes on the opener, a cover of the Ink Spots' vocal standard that hit the R&B Top Ten. "Key to My Happiness" is a great buried treasure, firmly in the Motown sound, and "Love on a Two-Way Street" is as exquisite a soul ballad as ever made it to the top of the pop charts. Still, "Lovely Way She Loves" and "So This Is Our Goodbye" are weak filler material, the group straining to get the same pleading in their voice as more popular acts like the Delfonics. The arrangements are effective, and the backing by Willie & the Mighty Magnificents is fresh and inventive, but alas, the sound is sub-standard (par for the course for All Platinum) and even a 2000 CD revamping of the album by Sequel (packaged with *The Other Side of the Moments*) can't help the weak sound. *—John Bush*

Live at the New York State Women's Prison / 1971 / Stang ✦✦✦

The Moments first live LP highlights Harry Ray, Al Goodman, and Billy Brown's crooning ability and gospel/ R&B style, but the song selection disappointed fans. Nobody, including the incarcerated women, wanted to hear remakes of "More Today Than Yesterday," "Yesterday," "Wichita Lineman," or "The Letter" over their recent string of R&B singles. They also redo the Miracles' "Here I Go Again," and the Friends of Distinction's "Going In Circles," good efforts, but their material should have dominated. Only three Moments' songs appear, all on side two, and all in embarrassing short clips: "I Do," "Sunday," and "Not on the Outside." "I Do" in particular is so short its unrecognizable, all you hear is the fade. Collectables have released this on CD coupled with *Look at Me, I'm In Love.* This probably sounds better in CD format—all Stang/All Platinum recordings do. *—Andrew Hamilton*

The Other Side of the Moments / 1971 / Stang ✦✦

The Other Side of the Moments displays the New Jersey soul trio as a supper-club act, just as a few top soul acts (the Four Tops, the Impressions, the Supremes) had flirted with during the '60s. Why the Moments were attempting to court a more traditional audience during the early '70s is a mystery. The trio doesn't have much trouble with the material, but the arrangements and recording are period curiosities; a nimble electric bass attempts to update the trad strings, but fails every time. The quick pace and intimate delivery for "In the Still of the Night" make for an album highlight, but the group's performances of "What's New?" and "Angel Eyes" sound overripe and tossed-off. This "other side" of the Moments certainly wasn't fooling any Nat King Cole fans out there, and unsurprisingly bombed with soul audiences too, making it one of the group's most uninspired works. *—John Bush*

The Best of the Moments / 1973 / Stang ✦✦

Misleading title and all, this is still a fair album. (The title has you believing it's a greatest hits compilation. It's not.) "Sexy Mama" is the only bona fide hit; "What's Your Name" got some R&B play, but the other tracks are virtual unknowns. "Where Can I Find Her" features Billy Brown on lead, and "Don't Let Her Get You Down" is second-class Spinners. A sweeter side titled "I'm Willing" showed up as a Harry Ray single; when he went solo, the romantic plea defined the Moments' lush sound. *—Andrew Hamilton*

My Thing / 1974 / Stang ✦✦✦

The smooth voices of Harry Ray, Billy Brown, and Al Goodman ring true on ten hit-and-miss sides. The misses are the filler that comprise half the ten songs; they aren't irritating or ingratiating, just bland tunes with apathetic arrangements. Every artist at All Platinum/Stang Records must have recorded "My Thing"; there are versions by Sylvia, the Whatnauts, and the Moments, at the very least. The song is all right, but did it merit the countless remakes? It flopped as a single, but the flip "Girl I'm Gonna Miss You" is much better—a sad ballad sung in clear falsetto by Billy Brown. Surprisingly, it gets omitted from the many Moments compilation CDs, though it's one compelling number. Harry Ray's reading of "Baby I'm a-Want You" is magical, his light falsetto sparkling on David Gates' classic. Complete with airport ambience, "I Gotta Find a Way" is a charmer; Harry waits and contemplates at the airport about getting his baby back as a female announcer announces flights over a loudspeaker. I like the close, syncopated harmonies on "Look What You've Done," another tasty ballad. Eight of the ten songs are ballads except for "My Thing" and the twee-sounding "Life and Breath." *—Andrew Hamilton*

Those Sexy Moments / 1974 / Stang ✦✦✦

Throughout the late '60s to the late '70s, the Moments were one of the premier and loved groups in R&B. Tracks like "Love on a Two Way Street" and "What's Your Name" may be preferred to other songs from more successful acts of the time. This 1974 album finds the group successfully changing with the times and exuding more confidence with their production and singing. That's the good news. The bad news is that the Moments were signed to a small label with one of the worst studios in the business. That fact makes most of this skilled but not sonically sound. That being said, *Those Sexy Moments* is a good mix of dance tracks and the ballads they were famous for. The breezy, "You've Come a Long Way" tells the tale of childhood through adulthood romance as Harry Ray sings the potentially unsettling "I wanted you then/but you were only five." The slow songs, "How Can I Love You" and "Look at Me" (not to be confused with their hit, "Look at Me (I'm in Love)"), both employ the guitar as sitar trick and have the groups' trademark harmonies. The best songs here are basically solo spots for Ray. The big hit here, the steamy "Sexy Mama," has him singing great lines like, "This afternoon I know you like me/By tonight you're gonna love me." The innovative and melodic "Next Time That I See You" puts the spotlight on his underrated falsetto/tenor. For a group that never seemed to make undeniable albums, this effort has enough individual songs to make this worth looking for. *—Jason Elias*

Look at Me / 1975 / Stang ✦✦✦

This spawned two hits. The lush "Look at Me (I'm in Love)," arranged by Sammy Lowe, became their second biggest seller (as the Moments), reaching number-one R&B, June of 1975 for one week; "Love on a Two-Way Street" also reached number-one R&B but held the spot for five weeks, May of 1970, and climb to number-three Pop; "Look at Me," lovely backing vocals and all, only managed a number 39 Pop showing. The carousing "Girls" sparked some confusion. Label credits listed the Moments and the Whatnauts, but few knew who the Whatnauts were, their vocals are minimal, and most assumed they were the Moments' band. Their French version of "Girls" is just as satisfying as the English version. "Dolly My Love," has an upbeat, pop-ish rhythm that hit in the U.K. but did absolutely nothing in the States. The haunting "Come Away With Me," featured an exotic harp and a flute; the lulling ballad, like "Dolly," was too drastic a change for Moments' fans to feel, and went unnoticed when released in May of 1975. *—Andrew Hamilton*

Moments With You / 1976 / Stang ✦✦✦✦✦

"Look at Me (I'm in Love)" did so well (number-one R&B) the Moments continued the soft, lush, soulful sound on *Moments With You.* Side two consists of generic fodder written by Al Goodman, Harry Ray, and keyboardist Walter Morris. But side one contains three down-tempo compositions' courtesy of Carol Bayer-Sager and friends, eloquently led by Harry Ray's whisper-falsetto. The waltz paced "With You," became a substantial seller; the hurt factor alone should have pushed "I Could Have Love You," up the charts, and "I Don't Want to Go," overwhelming harmonies will leave you breathless. Billy Brown leads the tension building "Don't Cry Out Loud" (also written by Bayer-Sager) in his strong gospel trained tenor. *—Andrew Hamilton*

Live at the Miss Black America Contest / 1978 / Stang ✦✦

Sharp / 1978 / Stang ✦✦
The Moments and Stang/All Platinum Records parted after this release. Some of the cuts sound like experiments and rejects from other sessions that had been collecting dust. "Dolly My Love" sounds like it was originally designated for someone else, as the sound is different from what Moments fans expect; it bombed in the States, but flourished in the U.K. The Spinners' "I'll Be Around" has a totally different arrangement than the original; Al Goodman's bass sweetens the chorus. Lush is the word for "I Could Have Loved You," one of Harry Ray's better leads. On "Rain in My Backyard," the Moments employ Thom Bell's technique of closing the song with a gospel-inspired, improvising lead, which Billy Brown does well. Nothing else compels you to listen too intently. "Jack-in-the-Box," like "Dolly," enjoyed some popularity in Europe. *—Andrew Hamilton*

● **The Best of the Moments: Love on a Two-Way Street** / Jul. 15, 1996 / Rhino ✦✦✦✦✦
The Moments charted regularly on the R&B charts and copped the number-three position on the pop charts with "Love on a Two-Way Street." This CD chronicles a group that underwent some changes before Billy Brown, Al Goodman, and Harry Ray meshed and made the Moments a popular R&B entity. Die-hard fans will notice two omissions: "Girl I'm Going to Miss You," a floater sung by Brown in an aching falsetto, and "Somebody Loves You Baby," the B-side of "Sunday." The inclusion of "I'm Willing" by Harry Ray (one of his solo releases) and an extended version of "Sexy Mama" softens the oversights. Incidentally, Billy Brown sings all the parts on "I Do"—the lead, the background, and the spoken parts. Essential listening; don't hesitate to add this one to your shopping cart. *—Andrew Hamilton*

Moments to Remember / Jun. 10, 1997 / Deep Beats ✦✦✦✦✦
A picture-perfect chronicle of the Moments recording career as the top dogs of Sylvia & Joe Robinson's All Platinum/Stang Records empire. Deep Beats Records strings their hits in chronological order, from "Not on the Outside" to their last significant record, the poor-selling but beautiful "I Could Have Loved You," with 11 additional cuts that will stump the group's most ardent fans, including "I May Be Right, I May Be Wrong," two Tommy Keith compositions, and some unheard cuts by New Jersey writer/producer Ray Dahrouge. Forty songs strong, this multiple CD contains "I Can't Help It" and "That's How It Feels"—two obscure (i.e., flops) but interesting singles; their Whatnauts pairing ("Girls"), and "Sho Nuff Boogie," which is essentially a lush duet featuring Harry Ray & Sylvia Robinson. This '70s sweet soul-craving buster is ample enough to fill the musical hunger of the most voracious fans of sweet, buttery soul. *—Andrew Hamilton*

Lucky Me: A Golden Classics Edition / Jul. 1, 1997 / Collectables ✦✦✦✦
Don't let the lack of known titles dissuade you from purchasing this romantic collection made for lovers. Harry Ray's sugary-falsetto and Billy Brown's sharper-tinged false voice divvies 14 songs. Brown sings *au naturel* on "Beautiful Woman" in a rousing, earth-shaking, gospel tenor. Four of these songs were small R&B hits: "Just Because He Wants to Make Love" and "Gotta Find a Way"—led by Ray—and the Brown-led "What's Your Name" and "Lucky Me." For some reason you can find "Way It Should Be," "Another Day," "Part of You," and "Meeting You" on albums the trio did as Ray, Goodman & Brown. The sweet, whispery "Patty" is the title track from an ill-fated various artist album produced by Al Goodman that served as the soundtrack for a porno movie. *—Andrew Hamilton*

Look at Me/Live at the New York State Women's Prison / Jun. 22, 1999 / Collectables ✦✦✦

A Moment With the Moments/The Other Side of the Moments / 2000 / Sequel ✦✦✦

Not on the Outside, But on the Inside, Strong!/On Top / 2000 / Sequel ✦✦✦

Jerzee Monét (Tanisha Monet Carey)

Vocals / Contemporary R&B
R&B chanteuse Jerzee Monét's path to the recording industry was an ambitious journey that started on the East Coast. Monet grew up in various towns in New Jersey, shuffled back and forth between divorced parents. It was this exposure to all sides of both culture and race that gave Monet the confidence and knowledge to use her vocal talents. She settled in Trenton, NJ, as a hair stylist for a bit, but she knew music was in her blood and she had to act on her impulses. She took a job as a chef in a Virginia restaurant and by chance, the entire Ruff Ryders roster and staff came into her workplace for dinner in 1999. DMX, their most popular artist on the tour, hit it off well with Monet and eventually the group handed her several phone numbers to contact them. The company encouraged her to keep at it, so she moved back to New Jersey and took three jobs to support her goals. A contract with Dreamworks finally came her way and she recorded her debut album with producer Tyrice Jones in 2001. The final result, titled *Love & War*, was released in the summer of 2002. *—Bradley Torreano*

● **Love & War** / Jul. 16, 2002 / DreamWorks ✦✦✦
On her debut, *Love & War*, Jerzee Monét straddles the line between an eccentric soul songstress (think Alicia Keys) and a chart-bound R&B crooner (more along the lines of Ashanti or Truth Hurts). Meanwhile, her press shots make her look like the second coming of Neneh Cherry, while her affiliation with Ruff Ryders and DMX points to a degree of artistic independence and rap attitude. In the hands of producer Tyrice Jones, however, Jerzee Monét doesn't sound distinctive enough to triumph over the bland material presented here. The single "Most High" is pleasant and positive, but far too fluffy for its own good. Monét also courts the hip-hop audience with an Eve duet, and attempts to ride the coattails of Ashanti with the Ja Rule feature on "Twisted." The latter reveals her, much like Ashanti, as a solid singer in the Mariah Carey mold, but little breaks through amongst the bland, sound-alike productions and songwriting. *—John Bush*

Monica (Monica Arnold)

b. Oct. 24, 1980, Atlanta, GA
Vocals / Club/Dance, Urban
Atlanta vocalist Monica debuted in 1995 with the platinum Top Ten singles "Don't Take It Personal (Just One of dem Days)" and "Before You Walk out of My Life." After appearing on LL Cool J's *Mr. Smith* later that year, she recorded another killer duet with Brandy on "The Boy Is Mine," which spent several weeks at the top of the singles charts during summer 1998. Her second album, also titled *The Boy Is Mine*, was released in July 1998. She scored a few more chart successes through the following spring, but a long period of silence marked time between albums. The much-delayed *All Eyez on Me* finally hit stores in the winter of 2002. *—John Bush*

Miss Thang / Oct. 1995 / Rowdy ✦✦✦
Monica had signed to Arista's Rowdy imprint several years prior to this release, so she had ample time to ensure her debut would be nothing short of successful. The album focused on hip-hop and contemporary urban cuts, including a pair R&B chart-toppers. The first is "Don't Take It Personal," also a massive pop hit, propelled by a heavy bottom bass with Monica's indelible vocals ringing as she embraces an introspective lyric. The second, "Before You Walk Out of My Life," is a bittersweet lyric with unwavering vocals. "Like This and Like That" has that pocket beat; the song's flow is dictated by Monica's vocal chorus and an animated rap by Mr. Malik. Monica gives her own rendition on several numbers; while they all are plausible, the blues number "Let's Straighten It Out" is the most engaging, as she shares vocal duties with Usher. In spite of her youthful age, Monica conveyed a surprisingly mature sound. *—Craig Lytle*

● **The Boy Is Mine** / Jul. 14, 1998 / Arista ✦✦✦✦
On her second album, *The Boy Is Mine*, Monica is given a little more room to strut her own stuff. Previously, she was an inexperienced vocalist whose raw talent was sculpted by a bevy of producers. Here, she sticks with Dallas Austin; not only does he give her songs immaculately crafted musical backdrops—both ballads and uptempo dance numbers sound irresistible—but he helps her cultivate her voice so she sounds more mature than her 17 years. That doesn't exactly camouflage the uneven material, but it does make it easy to swallow. She does have a better, more consistent batch of songs here than she did on *Miss Thang*, and the best songs—such as the Brandy duet "The Boy Is Mine" or the bouncing "Street Symphony"—are as good as mainstream urban R&B gets in 1998. *—Stephen Thomas Erlewine*

Monifah

b. Jan. 28, 196?
Vocals / Urban, Hip-Hop
R&B diva Monifah grew up in Spanish Harlem in the midst of a musical family, who encouraged her to work in several musicals while at an early age. With the experience she gained singing, Monifah signed a contract with MCA and released her self-titled album in 1995. The following year, her single "I Miss You (Come Back Home)" became an R&B hit. Her second album, *Moods... Moments*, was released on MCA's Uptown subsidiary in May 1996. The Top Ten single "Touch It" made 1998's *Mo'hogany* her biggest album hit, and two years later she followed with *Home*. *—John Bush*

Monifah / 1995 / MCA ✦✦✦

● **Moods . . . Moments** / Mar. 26, 1996 / Uptown/Universal ✦✦✦✦
Monifah's rich voice is the first thing you notice on her debut album, *Moods... Moments*, and it's the thing that keeps the album afloat through its occasional dull spots. Where most of her mid-'90s urban soul contemporaries are hell-bent on demonstrating their technical prowess, Monifah lays back and lets the music build, texturing her vocals with a variety of different shades and styles. She can be jazzy or she can be soulful, she can belt out an uptempo number or croon a love ballad—it's clear that she has the gift. And, for the most part, producer Heavy D provides her with enough first-rate songs to make sure that we not only notice the gift, but that we don't forget it once the album is through, either. Although it would be nice to hear what Monifah could contribute to the songwriting, Heavy D's songs are varied and soulful, giving her a proper showcase for her prodigous talents. *Moods... Moments* does have a handful of weak songs and could have benefitted from some trimming, but that doesn't prevent the album from being a simply stellar debut. *—Leo Stanley*

Mo'hogany / Aug. 25, 1998 / Uptown/Universal ✦✦✦
Monifah's second album, 1998's *Mo'hogany*, featured the biggest hit of her career thus far, the infectious Top Ten pop hit "Touch It," which sampled Laid Back's mid-'80s hit "White Horse." The supposedly titillating song, whose video made it come off as more campy than anything else, broadened her audience to include dancefloor fanatics and popsters, but, despite the attention, the album failed to produce another substantial hit. *Mo'hogany* does incorporate a wide spectrum of sounds and styles, including rock & roll on the awkwardly titled "Monifah's Anthem/Bad Girl" and "Why," plenty of R&B ballads (of which most are lumped together in the middle of the album, weighing it down considerably) including the album highlights "Suga Suga" and the string-enhanced "Have You Ever Been Loved," irresistible funk on the album's best track, the bouncy "What's the Deal," hip-hop/soul on "Whatcha Gonna Do," and gospel on "I'm Loving You," a track while truly allows Monifah's vocals to shine. Despite some dull moments and less-than-inspired lyrics, *Mo'hogany* winds up being a decent and relatively enjoyable album. *—Jose F. Promis*

Home / Oct. 17, 2000 / Universal ✦✦✦
Those who know Monifah from her thumping 1998 dance hit "Touch It" will be pleasantly surprised by her lush vocals on *Home*. However, those who are familiar with Monifah's impressive debut album, *Moods... Moments*, will be disappointed by *Home's* poor production and meandering lyrics. Most of the highlights on *Home* come during its quieter moments. Both "I Can Tell" and "Peaches and Cream," produced by Teddy Riley &

Tyrice Jones, offer glimpses of Monifah at her most alluring. "Too Late" is one of the few times in the album that Monifah is given a strong melody to work with and she proves that she can deliver when given the proper material. Unfortunately, the smoother songs are few and far between, separated by pointless skits and soulless dance tracks like "Rescue Me" and the cliché-ridden "NaNa." Monifah is a considerable talent that is lost among the mediocrity that surrounds her. For Monifah, quality production and strong material are a long way from *Home*. *—Jon Azpiri*

The Monitors

f. 1965, Detroit, MI, **db.** 1968

Group / Soul, Motown

A short-lived group, the Monitors had only one release on Motown from November 1965 to August 1968. The group consisted of Richard Street, Warren Harris, and Sandra and John Fagin (it's unclear whether the Fagins were siblings or a couple). Harris had attended Northwestern High School in Detroit with future Temptations Otis Williams, Melvin Franklin, and Street; he joined Williams and Franklin in the Distants, but later quit—after which, the Distants merged with the Primes and signed with Motown as the Temptations.

Street then reformed the Distants and waxed "Answer Me," on Thelma Records, as Richard Street & the Distants (a young Norman Whitfield produced both sides). He also wrote songs for the Thelma label, owned by Berry Gordy's first wife, and when the label folded he joined the Peps, a group including Joe Harris (who later sang with the Ohio Players, the Undisputed Truth, and, as a teen, Little Joe & the Moroccos). The Peps, like the Monitors, were exciting live and very visual, but couldn't translate that to recording success.

After Street formed the Monitors with Harris and the Fagins, the group debuted on VIP Records with "Say You," a coy, sweet ballad that lacked promotion. (The Temptations redid it on their *Gettin' Ready* album.) The next Monitor singles, "Greetings This Is Uncle Sam" and "Since I Lost You Girl," appeared within several months but did nothing to advance the Monitors' career. Motown iced them until April 1968 before releasing "Bring Back the Love." The label then switched the Monitors to its Soul imprint for the group's final single, "Step by Step," released in August 1968. Three months later *Greetings! We're the Monitors*, originally scheduled for release on VIP, surfaced on the Soul label. The album was kind of a disappointment as it didn't include all the B-sides from their five singles, and the material wasn't up to Motown's usual standards.

British producer Ian Levine resurrected the Monitors in the late '80s and recorded quite a few tracks with a revamped group consisting of Darrell Littlejohn (lead), Herschel Hunter, Leah Harris, and originals Harris and Maurice Fagin. (Street was unavailable, since he'd joined the Temptations in the '70s to replace Paul Williams.) These new Monitors sounded similar to the Miracles—Littlejohn is Smokey Robinson's nephew, and had recorded with cousin Keith Burston as Keith & Darrell on Tamla Records, and as the Second Generation. *—Andrew Hamilton*

● **Greetings! We're the Monitors** / 1968 / Soul ✦✦✦

A rather bland set, it's made memorable only by Richard Street's fine vocals. *—Rick A. Bueche*

Grazing in the Grass / 1990 / Motorcity ✦✦

If you have no concept of the Monitors, who recorded for Motown Records in the mid-'60s, this CD won't cause any major problems, but if you do, you might scratch your head and say "huh?" The original Monitors were led by Richard Street, and the other members were Maurice Fagin, Sandra Fagin, and Warren Harris; this new group, assembled in the late '80s, consisted of Warren Harris, Leah Harris, Maurice Fagin, Herschel Hunter, and Darrell Littlejohn (Smokey Robinson's nephew) on lead. Littlejohn is vocally like his famous uncle and not at all like Street. Hence, these Monitors come off like third-rate Miracles. With a few exceptions, the songs are weak. Ex-Motowner Sylvia Moy produced the album along with Ian Levine—the mastermind of the Motorcity projects. Subjective picks: the title track, "Cold as Ice," "Rescue My Heart," and "You Are My Destiny." *—Andrew Hamilton*

The Monotones

f. 1955, Newark, NJ, **db.** 1962

Group / Doo Wop

The Monotones recorded a spate of clever novelties in the late '50s and early '60s, the most successful of which was the enduring "Book of Love," a massive Top Ten hit in 1958. The teenaged group formed at the Baxter Terrace housing project in Newark, NJ, in 1955, when lead vocalist Charles Patrick and his brother James teamed with first tenor Warren Davis, second tenor George Malone, bass singer John Smith, baritone Warren Ryanes, and his younger brother, second bass John Ryanes. They practiced in the project's recreation hall, inspired by acts like the Heartbeats, the Spaniels, the Moonglows, and the Cadillacs. The six friends and neighbors also began singing with the New Hope Baptist Choir, along with other choir members Dionne and Dee Dee Warwick, Judy Clay, Cissy Houston, Leroy Hutson (of the Impressions), and several of the Sweet Inspirations.

By 1956, the Monotones were performing the Cadillacs' "Zoom" on *Ted Mack's Amateur Hour*, winning first prize and earning a shot on the show the following week. Though James Patrick left to join another Newark group, the Kodaks, his brother Charles began writing new material for the group, the first of which was "Book of Love." Three months later, in December of 1957, the single was released on Hull's Mascot subsidiary. By January, it was too huge for cash-poor Hull, so the group licensed it to Chess Records, who issued it on their Argo subsidiary. By the late spring, it had climbed on the pop charts, charting at number five, and the R&B charts, listing at number three.

By the summer of 1958, the Monotones were back in the studio trying their hand at other rock & roll novelties; their next single, "Tom Foolery" (with its constant stops-and-starts), fared poorly, however. A third session yielded a few new songs, including the single "The Legend of Sleepy Hollow" (which featured high-speed horse clip-clops), but these singles failed to gain the group an audience. In early 1960, the Monotones issued their first true Hull release, a strange sort of answer song to their own record, called "Reading the Book of Love" (even though it had been two years since the other "Book of Love" song was a hit). The group's last session, on February 14, 1962, produced two more titles, "Book of Dance" and "Toast to Lovers," which weren't released until they were featured on a Hull compilation LP in late 1962. By then, the Monotones had decided to call it a day. *—Bryan Thomas*

● **Who Wrote the Book of Love?** / Nov. 30, 1992 / Collectables ✦✦✦✦✦

Although universally known as one-hit wonders, ("Book of Love") the Monotones reveal on this recording that their talent extended well beyond that classic doo wop number. Writing the bulk of their own material, the New Jersey sextet specialized in uptempo novelty-type tunes, in addition to the requisite number of love ballads. One of the most notable fast numbers is "Zombi," featuring a vocal line with the singer sounding like a loon in heat. The pick-to-click cut is "What Would You Do If There Wasn't Any Rock 'n' Roll?" Sounding like an anthem, and extremely catchy, this prime cut was unfortunately left unreleased at the time, but sounds as it could have returned the Monotones to the upper ends of the charts. If you like a little history or literature with your rock & roll, check out "Ride of Paul Revere" and "The Legend of Sleepy Hollow." Of course, no late-'50s album would be complete without a few slow numbers, and the Monotones obliged with strong harmony singing on the ballads. One of the strongest is "Soft Shadows." A romantic plea for love and understanding, it ends with a three-part harmony wail that is awesome in its execution, and drives home the point that the Monotones could execute exceedingly well on slow as well as fast songs. All in all, the group showed themselves to be gifted well beyond their lone hit, and deserve a listen from serious fans of doo wop or high caliber '50s rock & roll. *—Michael Ofjord*

The Montclairs

f. 1969, **db.** 1974

Group / Smooth Soul, Northern Soul, Philly Soul, Soul

An East St. Louis soul vocal group, the Montclairs recorded some fine heartache ballads in the early '70s that deserved better fates than they got. Kevin Sanlin, Phil Perry, George McLellan, David Frye, and Clifford Williams debuted for Arch in 1969. They moved to Paula in the '70s. None of their singles ever cracked the R&B Top 30 ("Beggin' Is Hard to Do" and "Dreaming out of Season" came close), but such songs as "Prelude to a Heartbreak" and "Make Up for Lost Time" are still fondly remembered. Sanlin and Perry later recorded as a duo. *—Ron Wynn*

● **Dreaming Out of Season** / 1972 / Paula ✦✦✦✦

Make Up for Lost Time: The Paula Recordings 1971–1974 / Jun. 26, 2002 / WestSide ✦✦✦

Make Up for Lost Time brings together the Montclairs one album, *Dreaming Out of Season*, and numerous singles and outtakes recorded between 1972 and 1974 for the Paula label. Based around the lead vocal and dramatic songwriting of Phil Perry, the Montclairs were part of an early-'70s renaissance for vocal groups that saw peers like the Spinners and the Chi-Lites bring sweet soul harmony to the top of the charts. While the Montclairs never achieved commercial success on that level, they did have two top 40 singles on the *Billboard* R&B chart in 1972; the sweet falsetto-led "Dreaming Out of Season" and its follow-up, a swallow-your-pride affair—"Beggin' Is Hard to Do." The real treasure of their album, however, is the eight-minute epic, "Do I Stand a Chance?" and its hypnotic vocal patterns and lush, constantly building strings. The critical and commercial disinterest in the *Dreaming Out of Season* album ultimately led to the demise of the group, but not before they released a few more singles and began work on an unfinished follow-up album. These tracks are included here, showing that the group was capable of the occasional uptempo number like the pop-soul of "Dawn of My Life," the Bobby Patterson-penned "I Need You More Than Ever," and the funky "Hung Up on Your Love." More often the material focuses on attempts, with varying degrees of success, to create ballad hits that got them attention in the first place. The awkward metaphors of "Horse With Wings" might only be for diehard fans, but anyone hungry for a smooth soul treat will find the skillfully penned "Ease the Pain" more than satisfying and well worth the time. *— Wade Kergan*

The Moonglows

f. 1951, Cleveland, OH

Group / Doo Wop, R&B

The Moonglows were among the most important R&B groups of the 1950s, despite the fact that they only had a handful of hits among fewer than 50 recorded songs, in a history that lasted just six years, in sharp contrast to such acts as the Orioles and the Drifters, who were together across decades and recorded huge bodies of work.

Chicago-born Harvey Fuqua (born July 27, 1928) was part of a musical family virtually from birth, as the nephew of Ink Spots guitarist Charlie Fuqua, and before he was in his teens was aiming for a career of his own in music. He grew up in Louisville, KY, where he learned the piano and also began singing with his high school classmate Bobby Lester (born January 13, 1930; died October 15, 1980) at dances. They formed a professional duo in Louisville during 1949, after both finished brief periods of serving in the military, and were soon working with saxman and bandleader Ed Wiley, and it was in his group that they started singing jump and blues. Eventually a lack of earnings led them to split up, with Fuqua moving to Cleveland, where he crossed paths with an army buddy, Danny Coggins, and a neighbor of his, Prentiss Barnes (born April 12, 1925), who'd previously been a gospel singer, and formed a trio.

Fuqua brought Lester into the group, which was known as the Crazy Sounds, and they started to get work in the area around Cleveland. They were an improvisational singing group that specialized in a technique called vocalese, using their voices to replace instruments, basically in a jazz context, somewhat similar to the work of the Swingle Singers and the Manhattan Transfer. Their first break came in 1952 when they came to the attention of local disc jockey Alan Freed, who was already making a name for himself playing R&B records. They auditioned and did well enough to earn a chance to record on Freed's own Champagne Records label, changing their name to the Moonglows in the process in an effort to hook their recognition to Freed's on-air persona as "Moondog." The group enjoyed a modest local hit with a Lester composition, "I Just Can't Tell No Lie." They began performing in venues throughout the industrial Midwest and underwent their first membership change when Coggins quit for a more stable life as a gas station owner. He was replaced by Alex Walton and Alexander Graves.

Lester and Fuqua shared the lead vocal spot, sometimes even on the same song, and both of them had a keen interest in songwriting as well. The group was special not only for their mix of subtle polish and visceral excitement, but also the sheer attractiveness of the singing and the way in which their arrangements locked it all together—Lester and Fuqua were the leads and the most visible talents, but there were no weak links anywhere in the Moonglows' sound; from bass to the occasional falsetto, all of the singing was dazzling, animated, and bracing, whether on the jump numbers or the ballads; each of their finished records was the total package, distinctly voiced, gorgeously textured, and exciting. In the early fall of 1953, Freed landed the group a contract with Chance Records, a small Chicago outfit that was making a serious noise in blues and R&B, and already had the Flamingos and the Spaniels under contract. For a year, they tried to chart with ballads—including a killer version of "Secret Love" with Lester singing lead—and jump numbers but saw little success at Chance, before they were dropped.

In October of 1954, the group moved to Chess Records, and their first session was one of the most productive in the history of the label, yielding 13 songs including one of the biggest hits in Chess' history, "Sincerely"—authored by Fuqua (with Freed taking half the royalties as "co-author," a common arrangement at the time for Freed and other managers), the Moonglows' recording charted in December of that year and bumped "Earth Angel" by the Penguins out of the number-one R&B spot the following month, and later climbed to number 20 on the Hot 100 pop chart. The single rode the R&B listings for 20 weeks and sold over a quarter of a million copies, an extraordinary number for Chess in those days and all of it happening before R&B had fully crossed over to white listeners. It was numbers like this that were delighting independent executives like Phil and Leonard Chess, and giving ulcers to executives at the major labels, who saw something happening in music that they'd somehow missed over the preceding year or two and were having trouble grasping even then. In the case of "Sincerely," it was such an attractive song that it begged to be covered by other artists in other styles—thus, the Moonglows became one of the earliest R&B groups to see an original of theirs picked up by a pop act, when the white sibling vocal trio the McGuire Sisters covered "Sincerely" in a pop style and got a number one pop hit and a million-selling single out of it. The success of the Moonglows' original version was the break they'd been waiting for, and they began playing some of the best gigs of their history, as part of Freed's huge package shows alongside acts like Joe Turner, the Clovers, and Lowell Fulson. In early 1955, the group's ranks expanded with the addition of Billy Johnson, a guitarist who'd previously played with Charles Brown. During the summer of 1955, the group was part of a package tour that included Muddy Waters, Sarah Vaughan, and Nappy Brown.

Alas, they found it difficult to repeat the crossover pop success of "Sincerely"—the group did produce such worthy efforts as "Most of All" (number-five R&B), "Foolish Me," "Starlite," and "In My Diary." Then, in the middle and latter half of 1956, they succeeded anew with the ballad "We Go Together," which reached number nine on the R&B charts and attracted considerable interest from young white listeners in the bargain; and the rock & roll number "See Saw," which reached number-nine R&B and got to number 25 on the pop charts. During this period, Chess also briefly attempted to double-up on the group's approach to the airwaves and radio play lists by taking some of the sides featuring Lester and Fuqua together on lead and issuing those under the name "the Moonlighters."

The group's status in the hierarchy of rock & roll—or, at least, that corner of it under the control of Freed—was confirmed when the Moonglows were included in the jukebox movie *Rock, Rock, Rock*, working alongside Chuck Berry, the Flamingos, LaVern Baker, the Johnny Burnette Trio, and Frankie Lymon & the Teenagers. Later that same year, they also began work on what was to have been their debut LP, and early in 1957 they made another screen appearance, in *Mr. Rock and Roll*, a second jukebox feature, sandwiched in between many of the same acts as the prior movie—this was to mark the last screen appearance of the original group, however.

During 1957, in the wake of their unfinished debut album, Lester receded from the lead vocal spot, yielding it to Fuqua, who already dominated the group as a producer, songwriter, and their de facto vocal arranger. "Please Send Me Someone to Love," which got to number-five R&B and number 73 on the pop charts, featured Fuqua on lead vocals and reduced Lester to backup. The friction between Lester and Fuqua continued through most of the year, and the latter's increasing control of the group's direction also caused friction with Barnes, Graves, and Johnson, who were more or less caught in the middle between the two most identifiable voices in the group. Complicating their strained internal dynamics were the changes in public taste that had taken place since 1955—they not only couldn't decide who ought to be leading them, or agree on who should sing lead, but also on which direction their music should go in, toward the more pop-oriented sound of the Platters, who were selling large numbers of records to white audiences, or toward the harder sound that seemed to be coming out of some quarters of the black community, and seemed to be where black listeners were moving.

Torn by these multiple schisms, the Moonglows' lineup collapsed under circumstances that are still a bit murky, in terms of who decided what and who exited. In late 1957, a pair of sides were recorded featuring Fuqua and possibly Johnson, and in early 1958, a new single appeared entitled "Ten Commandments of Love," featuring Fuqua as a speaker. It reached number nine as an R&B hit and number 22 as a pop single, the group's best pop performance in two years and one of their biggest sellers, except that it wasn't credited to the Moonglows—rather, it was also credited to Harvey & the Moonglows, and precisely who was singing on it behind Fuqua is still a matter of conjecture; some sources attribute the backup to the original Moonglows, whereas others say with assurance that it was Fuqua's "new" Moonglows, actually formerly known as the Marquees, a Washington, D.C., outfit consisting of Marvin Gaye, Reese Palmer, James Knowland, and Chester Simmons. What is clear is that they accompanied Fuqua over the next year or so, credited as Harvey & the Moonglows. The group's ranks changed quickly—though he kept Gaye, who had sung lead on the group's recording of "Mama Loocie," with him—and eventually included a young Chuck Barksdale, from the Dells.

In addition to his work with the new group, Fuqua was featured on solo singles throughout 1958, including "Don't Be Afraid of Love," which he co-authored with Berry Gordy Jr. and Billy Davis, and also turned up miming in the last (and best) of the Freed showcase films, *Go Johnny Go*. Fuqua's professional association with Gordy had begun when they met, on the latter's visit to Chess to license the early sides of the Miracles; the two wrote songs together, and eventually Fuqua married Gordy's sister Gwen. He continued recording for several more years, including some legendary sides with Etta James, but increasingly concentrated on the purely creative rather than the performing side of music. After operating such independent labels as Tri-Phi (where he recorded not only his own and the later Harvey & the Moonglows stuff, but also the early Spinners, whom he discovered as the Dominoes, and with whom he sang as well), he joined Motown as the executive in charge of developing new talent, and became not only successful in that department but also as a producer and songwriter, and was collaborating successfully with Smokey Robinson in the 1990s.

Having had the group and the group name pulled out from under him, Lester went solo on the Chess label for a short time, before giving up performing for a decade. His name was well-known enough and the recordings left behind with the group were good enough, however, so that as late as 1962 Chess saw the point in releasing a single credited to "Bobby Lester & the Moonglows," consisting of "Blue Velvet" and "Penny Arcade," the A-side culled from the group's abortive late 1956 album sessions—this may have been simply Chess's way of trying to amortize everything but the kitchen sink in their operation, but it is difficult to imagine any other artist of the era, apart from Elvis Presley or Clyde McPhatter (or deceased figures such as Buddy Holly or Eddie Cochran), getting their six-year-old recordings pushed as new releases.

Johnson passed through gigs backing Jackie Wilson and Brook Benton before joining Motown Records, and passed away in the late '80s. Walton put together a new Moonglows lineup in 1964 to cover some of the group's '50s sides, but this effort didn't last long, and Graves and Barnes left the music business, and the original Moonglows were consigned to history, apart from Chess' periodic attempts to continue selling sides left in the vaults. The label also released of a pair of LPs made up of the group's single sides, *Look, It's the Moonglows* (1959) and *The Best of Bobby Lester & the Moonglows* (1962). Chess kept several vestiges of the Moonglows sound alive more profitably when they signed the Dells, and the group's sound could also be heard in the early work of the Four Tops (who had also spent time on Chess) and the Temptations at Motown.

Lester tried reviving the group name twice, at the beginning and end of the '70s, and even recut "Sincerely" the first time around. That composition remained the jewel in Fuqua's songbag—in 1990, 36 years after the Moonglows cut their version and 35 years after the McGuire Sisters' pop hit, the Forester Sisters' country rendition of "Sincerely" earned a Grammy nomination; that same year, filmmaker Martin Scorsese (who is known to take a very deep interest in the music used in his movies) used the Moonglows' version of the song in the film *Goodfellas*. Between the original and the successful covers, "Sincerely" bids fair to remain a popular song well into the 21st century. *—Bruce Eder*

Look, It's the Moonglows / 1959 / Chess ♦♦♦

On Stage / 1992 / Relic ♦♦♦

This is an offbeat release for Relic, which usually issues vintage doo wop material from the 1950s. Instead, we have an undated body of live performances featuring Bobby Lewis, probably from the 1970s. Lewis' widow provided the tape, which is his musical testament to the world. The sound is stereo and pretty modern, although it's not state-of-the-art by a long shot, a two-microphone recording that does catch the group in superb form—it's just not totally professional level, the applause cut off between numbers and the "mix," such as it is, fairly basic. The songs include "Sincerely," "Love Is a River," "Sea Saw," "When I'm With You," and "The Beating of My Heart," mostly sung in achingly beautiful fashion. It is a nice coda to the MCA remastered editions of the Moonglows' work. *—Bruce Eder*

Blue Velvet: The Ultimate Collection / Dec. 7, 1993 / Chess ♦♦♦♦♦

Few rivaled the Moonglows in musical sophistication, inventiveness or flair. They could sing gorgeous heartache ballads, rollicking uptempo rhythm tunes, creditable period-piece novelty numbers, wonderful pop covers or shattering originals. This two-disc set contains 44 outstanding numbers, with every major Moonglows anthem and several others that weren't big hits but deserved to be, such as "Penny Arcade" and "Love Is a River." This collection updates and expands the *Greatest Sides* single LP release briefly available when Sugar Hill had the Chess catalog in the 1970s. It wisely restricts material to the era when they were at their best, the 1950s, and includes an excellent booklet. *—Ron Wynn*

Moonglows Acapella / Mar. 5, 1996 / Starr Digital ♦♦♦♦♦

A stone masterpiece! Arguably one of the best vocal performances ever captured on record. Absolutely stunning! The Moonglows lay down the ten commandments of harmony, a cappella, on 16 heavenly tracks. No matter what genre of music you favor, you'll appreciate this astounding display of awesomely smooth, intricate harmony blends. You'll marvel at Prentiss Barnes' foggy bass, and Pete Graves' floating tenor—meshing with Bobby Lester's mellow second tenor, and Harvey Fuqua's smooth baritone. Every cut's a musical highlight piece, but kudos to "Most of All," "In My Diary," "When I'm With You," and "The Beating of My Heart." And special honors to the four well-done medleys: the "Lonely Medley," the "Diary Medley," the "Lovers Medley," and the "Needing You Medley." *—Andrew Hamilton*

● **Their Greatest Hits** / May 20, 1997 / MCA/Chess ♦♦♦♦♦

At 16 tracks, *Their Greatest Hits* isn't nearly as comprehensive as the two-CD *Blue Velvet*, which has 44 songs. But for someone who wants just the highlights, as opposed to just about everything, *Their Greatest Hits* is the better buy, including their most celebrated tunes ("Ten Commandments of Love," "Sincerely," "Blue Velvet"). The only selection not on *Blue Velvet* is a different take of "Over and Over Again," presented in its "fast version." It does not, however, include "Mama Loocie," which featured Marvin Gaye's first recorded lead vocal. *—Richie Unterberger*

20th Century Masters—The Millennium Collection: The Best of the Moonglows / Jul. 2, 2002 / MCA ✦✦✦✦✦
This 12-song collection is the almost the same as the 1997 anthology *Their Greatest Hits*, which has all 12 of these selections plus four additional tracks. For that reason, this slightly abridged version is slightly less preferable. Still, it does hone in on their most popular 1950s Chess recordings, including the hits "Sincerely," "Most of All," "We Go Together," "When I'm With You," "See Saw," "Please Send Me Someone to Love," and "The Ten Commandments of Love." Although the packaging is on the budget side, it's a good representation of the very best of one of the era's finest R&B/doo wop vocal groups. *—Richie Unterberger*

Bobby Moore & the Rhythm Aces

f. Montgomery, AL
Group / Soul, Pop-Soul
A Mongtomery, AL, soul group, Bobby Moore & the Rhythm Aces had a solid uptempo hit in 1967, "Searching for My Love," on Checker. Moore was a tenor saxophonist. He formed the group with lead vocalist Chico Jenkins, Larry Moore, Joe Frank, Clifford Laws, Marion Sledge, and John Baldwin Jr. in the mid-'60s, and they later signed with Checker. They were unable to sustain their early success, but had two other singles issued by Checker in 1966 and 1967. *—Ron Wynn*

● **Searching for My Love** / 1966 / Checker ✦✦✦

Chanté Moore

b. 1967
Vocals / Urban, Dance-Pop, Club/Dance
Chanté Moore, the daughter of a minister, grew up on gospel music and the innovative recordings of George Duke and Lee Ritenour, sometimes applying her lyrics to their music. Moore decided as a teenager that she wanted to become a singer after an inspirational performance in a high school rendition of *The Wiz*. In addition to her writing and singing talents, she was a successful beauty pageant contestant.

Before releasing her debut CD, *Precious*, Moore lent her talents to El DeBarge's *In the Storm*; the track "You Know What I Like" showcases Moore's vocals on the chorus. The follow-up to *Precious*, *Love Supreme*, featured the single "Old School Lovin'." Four years after *Love Supreme*, Moore released her third album, *This Moment Is Mine*. In late 2000 she released *Exposed*, featuring the production talents of Jermaine Dupri and the team of Jimmy Jam & Terry Lewis *—Craig Lytle*

Precious / 1992 / MCA ✦✦

This Moment Is Mine / May 25, 1999 / MCA ✦✦✦✦
This Moment Is Mine finds Chanté Moore at the top of her game, crafting an alluring contemporary soul album that manages to avoid most of the clichés of the genre. Not that it strays from formula, however. As a matter of fact, the 14 songs that comprise *This Moment Is Mine* unmistakably follow the pattern for urban soul, whether it's the slow grooves of the ballads or the midtempo dance cuts. The difference is delivery. Moore never shouts or engages in histrionic caterwauls—she keeps her focus on the song at hand, delivering each line as if she has lived it. That, combined with the sublime production (most of it by Jimmy Jam & Terry Lewis) and an excellent selection of songs, makes *This Moment Is Mine* a first-rate urban soul album. It may not be perfect—it does have some filler—but it's certainly more alluring than most of its peers. *—Stephen Thomas Erlewine*

● **Exposed** / Nov. 14, 2000 / MCA ✦✦✦✦
There must be something in Atlanta's water table that makes for such funky producers, singers, and performers. OutKast, Jermaine Dupri, TLC—if Philly was ground zero for soul in the '70s and New York for hip-hop in the '80s, it's safe to say that at the turn of the 21st century, Atlanta, GA, was the capitol for the burgeoning hybrid of those two genres. *Exposed*, which was executive produced by Dupri and recorded mainly in Atlanta (the exception being the Jimmy Jam & Terry Lewis-produced "Love's Still Alright," which was recorded in L.A.) makes a bid to capture some of that trademark funkiness. Moore has a great set of pipes, a mix of the throaty take charge style of Toni Braxton and the soft vulnerability of Janet Jackson, an undeniable sexiness, and a real emotional conviction that lends the songs an authenticity absent in many current releases. Still, with all that she has going for her, *Exposed* only manages to be a hit-and-miss record. When Moore hits, as in the opener "Straight Up," she makes sexy music with so many melodic twists and turns one gets happily dizzy from keeping up. But several tracks, despite being technically proficient and musically sound, don't really go anywhere, and even the Jam/Lewis track is admittedly a bit boring and antiseptic. With some grittier material, though, Moore could take a rightful place among Hotlanta's funkiest. *—Steve Kurutz*

Dorothy Moore

b. Oct. 13, 1946, Jackson, MS
Vocals / Disco, Urban, Soul-Blues, Soul
Dorothy Moore had two huge hits in 1976 for Malaco with "Misty Blue" and "Funny How Time Slips Away." "Misty Blue" was a number-two R&B and number-three pop single and a sizzling piece of heartache soul, while "Funny How Time Slips Away" wasn't as definitive a soul recasting of Willie Nelson's composition as Joe Hinton's version, but it did better on the charts, reaching number-seven R&B. Moore continued on Malaco through the '80s, landing one more Top Ten R&B hit in 1977 with "I Believe You." She signed with the reactivated Volt label in the late '80s and recorded two LPs for them. *—Ron Wynn*

Once Moore With Feeling / 1968 / Malaco ✦✦
Another good, if conservatively produced, arranged, and written, Southern soul and R&B set featuring Dorothy Moore. Her sound, sensibility, delivery, and approach are simple and down-to-earth, reflecting strong blues, gospel, and country roots, that Moore inevitably wouldn't appeal to a mass audience. Malaco tried a few things, sometimes casting her in the same territory as Denise LaSalle (hard-talking sister) and other times repeating the "Misty Blue" formula (heartache ballads). But otherwise they simply let Moore go in the studio and sing with zest, then marketed the results to a regional audience. *—Ron Wynn*

Definitely Dorothy / 1970 / Malaco ✦✦✦
Dorothy Moore had one huge crossover hit with the single "Misty Blue." That was ironically not the best or most soulful song she ever made, but it was the one that struck a chord with the pop and urban contemporary audience. Moore wisely didn't try to do anything different after it hit, and made several solid, straight soul and R&B albums for Malaco, like this one. There's nothing fancy, just animated, well-sung numbers produced and arranged in standard soul fashion. Moore's gospel-tinged vocals wouldn't have made the transition to smooth pop or urban contemporary anyhow, so she was smart not to attempt it. *—Ron Wynn*

● **Misty Blue** / May 1976 / Malaco ✦✦✦✦✦

Dorothy Moore / Jul. 1977 / Malaco ✦✦

Time Out for Me / 1988 / Volt ✦✦✦
Dorothy Moore left Malaco and tried her luck with the reactivated Volt label in the late '80s, evidently thinking that Fantasy might be able to get her more exposure outside the South. That didn't prove the case with her debut for the new Volt, partly because there wasn't the monster hit that could break the urban contemporary radio embargo against Southern product. It also had such an old-time soul quality that its appeal was limited from the start. That doesn't mean it wasn't well-sung, produced, and arranged, or that Moore didn't deserve to make the music she felt comfortable doing. It just made the whole project a long shot, and it never was able to beat the odds. *—Ron Wynn*

Winner / 1989 / Volt ✦✦
One-time gospel and later soul vocalist Dorothy Moore tried a comeback in the late '80s on the reactivated Volt label. This was her second album for them, and it was well produced, with the same heartache ballads, wailers, and uptempo soul songs she'd previously recorded for Malaco and on her previous Volt release. Unfortunately, the album sank like a stone. *—Ron Wynn*

Stay Close to Home / 1992 / Malaco ✦✦✦
This is Southern soul 1970s style. Standouts include the bouncy title track and "Blues in the Night," a rocking number with heavy horn lines. Other notable tunes include the syrupy Memphis-styled ballads such as "A Woman Without Love," "It's Rainin' on My Side of the Bed" and the poppish anthem, "Till the End of Time." *—Bil Carpenter*

More of Moore / Apr. 1996 / Malaco ✦✦✦
Dorothy Moore sounds more Southern than she ever has on this late-career Malaco Records CD. The singer, who ascended the charts with "Misty Blue" way back when, now has a voice that has aged, husky and more than capable of delivering three-hearts-in-a-tangle sagas and mistreated woman dramas. Only the horns and backing singers (both splendid) keep one from classifying the ballads as deep soul; lovers of that style will find much to like with *More Moore*. Standouts include "Why Is Leaving You So Hard to Do," "Lie to Me," and "Stop What You're Doing to Me." It's shameful this type of music is absent on mainstream radio. *—Andrew Hamilton*

Misty Blue & Other Hits / Jun. 18, 1996 / Malaco ✦✦✦
Misty Blue & Other Hits contains all of Dorothy Moore's biggest hits and best-known songs, including "I Believe You," "Let the Music Play," and the title track. *—Thom Owens*

● **Greatest Hits** / Oct. 16, 2001 / Varese Sarabande ✦✦✦✦✦

Jackie Moore

b. Jacksonville, FL
Vocals / Southern Soul
One of the relatively few artists who emerged in the early '70s to enjoy a run of success with a Southern soul-based sound, this Florida singer recorded her best material for Atlantic in Miami with noted session players like the Memphis Horns and the Dixie Flyers. Putting her earthy pop-soul to ballads and midtempo material, much of it written and crafted by producer Dave Crawford, Moore had a half-dozen R&B hits for the label; the biggest, "Precious, Precious" (1970) and "Sweet Charlie Babe" (1973), were also small pop hits.

In 1972 and 1973, she cut some tunes in Philadelphia's Sigma Sound Studios with a slicker feel, with generally successful results. There was nothing especially earth-shaking about Moore's style or material, but it was solid stuff with a grittier feel than much of the soul music in vogue at the time. After leaving Atlantic, she had one more sizable R&B hit, "Make Me Feel Like a Woman" (1975). *—Richie Unterberger*

Sweet Charlie Babe / 1973 / Atlantic ✦✦✦✦
Here are ten powerhouse tracks by Jacksonville, FL, native Jackie Moore. A good mixture of Southern and urban R&B soul from the saucy, sweet soul diva. The slinky "Precious, Precious" zoomed up the charts and became her biggest hit; it employs a similar groove that made hits out of "Trapped By a Thing Called Love" by Denise LaSalle and "Make Me Yours" by Bettye Swann. "If" is lyrically infectious, Joe Simon also recorded the Bunny Sigler & Phil Hurtt tune. The floating "Both Ends Against the Middle" delights every time it spins. She does justice to the Elgins' "Darling Baby," the rolling ballad is one of Holland-Dozier-Holland's most charming songs. Moore shows no shame singing about her man Charlie, on "Sweet Charlie Babe," an upbeat testimonial, with a message similar to the Marvelettes' "Don't Mess With Bill." She dispenses wise advice on "Clean Up Your

Own Yard." "Time" is an exquisite ballad eloquently done by Moore; however, beat ballads and deep soul sagas like "Cover Me" and "Willpower" defined Moore's style. If you can't find this slab of vinyl, these songs and more are available on the CD *Precious, Precious: The Best of Jackie Moore.* —*Andrew Hamilton*

● **Precious, Precious: The Best of Jackie Moore** / 1994 / Ichiban/Soul Classics ✦✦✦✦✦
This retrospective of her 1970-1973 Atlantic material includes all of her hits and a few of her misses. Four of the tracks have never been released on album before. —*Richie Unterberger*

Melba Moore (Melba Hill)

b. Oct. 29, 1945, New York, NY
Vocals / Quiet Storm, Soul
There were early signs that Melba Moore would become an entertainer. The most obvious motivation was her mother, Bonnie Davis, who was also a successful singer. Witnessing the success that her mother endured, Moore knew the entertainment industry would not escape her. The world of performing arts was formally introduced to her by way of dance lessons at the age of four. Moore's mother impressed upon her that "if you don't touch people's hearts, it doesn't mean anything." Her stepfather would also become an instrumental figure in the development of her early career.

All her siblings were musically inclined. Melba's interest was dance. However, her stepfather insisted that she learn the piano. Against her will, she conceded—and to her benefit. She gained much admiration for the blues and jazz pianists. Upon graduating from college, she became a music teacher, which she found very fulfilling. Nonetheless, Moore's affinity for the entertainment industry persisted.

Her stepfather, also a musician, gave her invaluable advice and guidance. He sensed his stepdaughter's irresistible urge to be in the entertainment industry, so he began to show her the ropes. The results landed Moore jobs singing jingles and background vocals. She hit it big when she joined the cast of the Broadway musical *Hair*. One day while working in the studio, a barefoot gentleman asked her if she wanted to be in the play. Moore accepted and eventually won the lead role. It was the first time in history that a black actress replaced a white actress (Diane Keaton) for the lead role on Broadway. That followed with another Broadway hit, *Purlie*, which earned her a Tony Award and rave reviews.

That success was followed by appearances in film, television, and recording ventures. In 1975, she married Charles Huggins. The two formed Hush Productions and began seeking out R&B artists that they could manage and produce. The most famous being Freddie Jackson, whose presence at Hush Production was primarily due in part to Moore. In the same year "I Am His Lady" was released on Buddah (*Billboard* number 82, six weeks); it was Moore's first single to hit the charts. It would be seven years and 12 singles later before she would claim her first Top Ten single. In 1982 the New York City native cracked the *Billboard* R&B charts at number five with the dance/club track "Love's Comin' at Ya."

Moore's next ten releases spawned four Top 20 and two Top Ten singles: "Livin' for Your Love" and "Love the One I'm With" (duet with Kashif), respectively peaked at six and five. The single to follow the latter was "A Little Bit More" (a duet with Jackson). The year was 1986, and it was Moore's first number-one song but not her last. Also released in the same year, "Falling" claimed the top spot on the charts. Thereafter, Moore released seven more singles. Two were Top 20 hits and three were Top Ten hits, including the black national anthem "Lift Every Voice and Sing" (*Billboard* number ten).

All the splendor that Moore relished in would soon come to a halt. Her husband of 15 years abruptly divorced the songstress without any prior warning. In spite of the personal and professional hardships that resulted from this unforeseen misfortune, Moore was able to rebound. In 1996 she released *Happy Together*, her first album in six years. And in 1998 she began touring the country with her one-woman autobiographical musical *Sweet Songs of the Soul*. She is honorably one of the top singers the R&B world has ever known and this can be supported by her admirable chart activity, which dates back to 1975. —*Craig Lytle*

Living to Give / 1972 / Mercury ✦✦✦

This Is It / 1976 / Buddah ✦✦✦

A Portrait of Melba / 1978 / Buddah ✦✦✦

● **Ready My Lips** / 1985 / Capitol ✦✦✦✦✦
The most versatile and underrated item in Moore's often overlooked catalog, *Read My Lips* runs the gamut from funky R&B radio numbers to quietly passionate ballads to rock-stenciled uptempo fare. Moore packs a tight-lipped, defiant punch on kinetic affairs such as "Mind Over Matter" and "Winner." Meanwhile, she's pure and sultry on the slow burn of "To Those Who Wait" and the emotional intensity of "I Can't Believe It (It's Over)." Having plenty of able assistance on hand doesn't hurt her case, either: producers Keith Diamond and Paul Laurence bring a meld of jazz, funk, pop, and soul influences to the fold, and intertwine them with remarkable consistency. This resourceful approach results in material that far surpasses earlier hits like "Love's Comin' at Ya" and "Keepin' My Lover Satisfied"; and it also turns out a surprising remake of Fleetwood Mac's "Dreams." With arrangements that are always on the dot, solid songs, and stellar vocals, *Read My Lips* is a must for every Moore fan's collection. —*Justin Kantor*

The This Is It: The Best of Melba Moore / 1995 / Razor & Tie ✦✦✦✦
This Is It: The Best of Melba Moore is an excellent overview of Moore's peak years, containing all of the hits she had in the '80s on EMI America and Capitol Records. Over the course of 18 tracks, all of her Top Ten R&B hits from the decade—"Love's Comin' at Ya," "Livin' for Your Love," "Love the One I'm With (A Lot of Love)," "A Little Bit More," "Falling," "It's Been So Long"—are featured, along with some good minor hits and album tracks. Some casual fans might find 18 tracks a bit much, but there's no question that this is the definitive summation of Moore's hitmaking years. —*Stephen Thomas Erlewine*

● **Little Bit Moore: The Magic of Melba Moore** / Jan. 28, 1997 / EMI ✦✦✦✦
A selection of 14 tracks from her 1980s albums, usually sticking to a mainstream urban contemporary vein. Includes the hits "Falling," "I'm in Love," "Underlove," "Livin' for Your Love," "A Little Bit More," and "I Can't Complain," the last two of which are duets with Freddie Jackson. —*Richie Unterberger*

Rudy Ray Moore

Vocals, Rap, Producer / Blaxploitation, Blue Humor, Standup Comedy, Sketch Comedy, R&B
If Redd Foxx was the king of the party record during the '50s and '60s, then certainly Rudy Ray Moore upped the ante during the '70s with a succession of triple-X-rated platters that were so hot most stores could only sell them under the counter, even during the height of the sexual revolution. His best routines, usually spoken in rhyme, presaged the rap revolution in music by a good 20 years, while his lone acting role, starring in *Dolemite*, remains one of the great blaxploitation movies of that decade. Among his releases were 1970's *Eat Out More Often*, 1971's *The Dirty Dozens*, and 1996's *This Ain't No White Christmas*. —*Cub Koda*

☆ **Eat Out More Often** / 1970 / Kent ✦✦✦✦✦
This is his debut album and the one that launched his career. Features "Dolemite," "Shine," and a half-dozen other titles too raunchy to mention here. —*Cub Koda*

This Pussy Belongs to Me / 1970 / Nashboro ✦✦✦✦✦
In the 1970s, Rudy Ray Moore's X-rated comedy inspired comparisons to Richard Pryor and Redd Foxx. But while Pryor and Foxx reached non-black audiences in a major way, Moore had more of a cult following and was never well known outside of the African-American community. Besides, Moore is quite unique, not to mention innovative; in fact, he has often been described as a pioneer of rap. Moore's comedy wasn't stand-up in the traditional sense—with jazz and R&B musicians playing in the background, he would recite raunchy, sexually explicit rhymes that often had to do with pimps, prostitutes, players and hustlers. One of Moore's best releases is 1972's *This Pussy Belongs to Me*; listening to X-rated classics like "Signifying Monkey," "Hurricane Annie Meets Dolemite" and "Mr. Big Dick," one can see why Too Short, Luther Campbell and the 2 Live Crew consider Moore a major influence—the material is as crude and vulgar as it is entertaining and hysterically funny. Of course, an album this raunchy isn't everyone's cup of tea. But for those who have a taste for X-rated humor, *This Pussy Belongs to Me* is a cult classic. —*Alex Henderson*

☆ **The Dirty Dozens** / 1971 / Cherry Red ✦✦✦✦✦
Here is a house party with Rudy as host and playing the dozens with every guest who crosses his path. As raunchy as it gets. —*Cub Koda*

★ **Greatest Hits** / Dec. 5, 1995 / Capitol ✦✦✦✦✦
An X-rated comedian who has used jazz and R&B accompaniment when delivering his raunchy rhymes, Rudy Ray Moore has been called the Godfather of Rap (a title that has also been used to describe sociopolitical soulster Gil Scott-Heron). Among non-black audiences, Moore was never as well known as Richard Pryor, Eddie Murphy or Redd Foxx, but he has commanded a loyal cult following in the black community and has influenced hip-hoppers ranging from the 2 Live Crew to Ice-T to Big Daddy Kane (who hired him as a guest on his 1990 recording "Big Daddy Vs. Dolemite"), not to mention Blowfly. A perfect introduction to Moore's 1970s work, this 1997 CD boasts such outrageously funny cult classics as "Dolemite," "Signifying Monkey" and "Hurricane Annie." Moore doesn't hesitate to be sexually explicit, and many of his characters were pimps, players, hustlers and prostitutes. Admittedly, Moore isn't for everyone. But those who aren't offended by the profane and the sexually explicit shouldn't miss these classic recordings, which are both historically important and incredibly entertaining. —*Alex Henderson*

21st Century Dolemite / Mar. 26, 2002 / The Right Stuff ✦✦✦
Some performers stumble into bad taste, but Rudy Ray Moore has been charging head-first into the stuff like an advancing army for over 30 years. *Eat Out More Often* (1970), the album that made Moore an underground star, was X-rated party humor that would have made Redd Foxx blanch, and Moore's first album of the millennium, the appropriately named *21st Century Dolemite*, leaves no doubt that he hasn't mellowed a bit with the passing of time. Moore revived his long-dormant career as an R&B singer, and *21st Century Dolemite* is divided between dizzying rude standup comedy and equally raunchy songs that document Moore's continuing obsession with sex. As a singer, Moore isn't going to make anyone forget Wilson Pickett or Bobby Womack, but he's not bad, and he has the good sense to talk over the notes he can't hit. As a songwriter, he's far stronger on old-school R&B styled numbers like "Willa Mae" and "Hip Shakin' Papa" than on hip-hop-influenced tracks like "Put Your Weight on It" or "ABC's"; while it's true enough that Rudy was rappin' a decade before they knew what to call it, when it comes to beats he sure ain't Timbaland. (He's also something of a borrower; "Cabbage Head" is lifted wholesale from an old folk song that the Dubliners made famous as "Seven Drunken Nights.") Moore's comedy and his lyrics both come from exactly the same place, and if the constant parade of anti-PC humor gets a bit tired after 72 minutes, you've got to give Moore credit for consistency—he knows what his fans want, and he delivers it in super-sized portions here. (He's also apparently willing to dip into the past as well; "Do You Call That a Buddy?" appears to be an overdubbed version of a tune cut back in the early '60s, while the comic bits "Two Soldiers" and "Press Conference" are retreaded from early-'70s recordings.) *21st Century Dolemite* proves Rudy Ray Moore is still dedicated to giving his fans the kind of top-quality smut they've come to expect from him, and if it's not a work of warped genius like his older stuff, he's still more imaginatively filthy than anyone else in comedy. And as Rudy would say, "I ain't lyin'!" —*Mark Deming*

Morcheeba

f. 1995, London, England
Group / Electronica, Trip-Hop, Club/Dance, Urban, Downbeat, Alternative Pop/Rock
The most groove-oriented act in the mid-'90s female-fronted electronica crowd, Morcheeba relies on the sweet, fluid vocals of Sky Edwards and a laid-back mix of fusion, funk, and

blues produced by brothers Paul and Ross Godfrey, on beats/scratches and guitar/keyboards, respectively. The trio was formed in 1995 when the Godfreys decided to go out on their own after co-producing six tracks for David Byrne's album *Feelings*. They submitted several tapes of their instrumental demos to labels around London, but received little interest in return. After hooking up with vocalist Edwards at a party, however, their music began to gel and Morcheeba signed to the China label. After the release of two EPs (*Trigger Hippie* and *Music That We Hear*), the trio issued their debut album, *Who Can You Trust?* It appeared on the American Discovery label in late 1996, and Morcheeba toured the U.S. with Live and Fiona Apple the following year. *Big Calm* followed in 1998 and *Fragments of Freedom* was released two years later. *—John Bush*

Who Can You Trust? / Sep. 24, 1996 / Indochina ✦✦✦✦
Slower, smoother and more soulful than Portishead and less pop-oriented than the Sneaker Pimps, Morcheeba has an alluringly dark sound that nevertheless remains accessible. As their debut *Who Can You Trust?* illustrates, the trio has a keen sense of how to make a pop melody seem dangerous and foreign by having it crawl out of the murk of creeping beats and ominous samples. Although the group lacks the visionary spark of Tricky and Portishead, and their songs aren't as bracing as the Sneaker Pimps, Morcheeba has a distinctive, idiosyncratic sound that makes *Who Can You Trust?* entrancing. Although the latter half of the album tends to sound a little samey, without many beats or hooks to distinguish each song, the album remains a hauntingly atmospheric—and quite terrific—debut. *—Stephen Thomas Erlewine*

● **Big Calm** / Mar. 16, 1998 / Sire ✦✦✦✦
Realizing that trip-hop was a dead end, at least as far as hipness goes, Morcheeba expanded their sonic palette on their second album, *Big Calm*. Trip-hop and dance rhythms remain, but the trio has spent more time writing songs, crafting an album where pop, lounge, film soundtracks, reggae, jazz and electronica all peacefully coexist. Consequently, *Big Calm* is a stylistic *tour de force*, evidence that Morcheeba has turned into a mature, sophisticated group with impeccable taste. Occasionally, the album can sound a little distant, as if the fusions and productions were more important than the actual songs, but the trio is so musically adept, and Sky Edwards' voice is so enchanting, that *Big Calm* becomes irresistible in its own way. *—Stephen Thomas Erlewine*

Fragments of Freedom / Aug. 1, 2000 / Sire ✦✦
Even though Morcheeba was one of the later, straggling entries in the trip-hop phenomenon, their previous albums succeed because of the interplay between Sky Edwards' sweetly sensual, airy voice and the band's correspondingly mellow grooves. Unfortunately, their third album *Fragments of Freedom* scraps most of their signature sound for half-baked experiments in R&B, acid jazz, and hip-hop. Though it's certainly understandable that the group would want to move away from the dead-and-buried trip-hop sound that defined them originally, it seems that Morcheeba are just using bands like Brand New Heavies and M People as sonic templates instead of Tricky and Portishead. The bland, overly slick production softens any impact that soulless soul songs such as "Rome Wasn't Built in a Day" and "Love Is Rare" might have had, and while Edwards may be blessed with a *soulful* voice, she's unconvincing belting out pseudo-sultry lyrics like "Is that a rocket in your pocket?" The group's misguided forays into hip-hop are even worse; Mr. Complex's guest rap on "Love Sweet Love" sounds like it was surgically grafted from another track entirely, and while Bahamadia's appearance on "Good Girl Down"'s celebration of sisterhood makes more sense, it still sounds out of place with Edwards' essentially refined, delicate style. Not every song on *Fragments of Freedom* is ill-conceived, however; the opening track, "World Looking In," ranks among their finest, and the steel drum instrumental "A Well Deserved Break" is pretty and refreshing. Despite its annoying, overpowering synth bass, "Shallow End" boasts a lilting, seductive melody that showcases Edwards' voice instead of fighting against it, and the title track is a pleasant enough piece of trip-hop pastiche. But for the most part, *Fragments of Freedom*'s contrived attempts to bring the funk to Morcheeba's sound are as fake and painful as a forced smile. *—Heather Phares*

Charango / Jul. 2, 2002 / Warner Bros. ✦✦✦✦
Fragments of Freedom was released in 2000 and not received very well. If critics and fans would have been able to gaze into a crystal ball a couple of years in the future, they would have understood. With the benefit of hindsight, consider *Fragments* the prototypically disjointed transitional record that saw Morcheeba shifting focus from trip-hop to a more well-rounded mix, as *Charango* completes the journey that may have been bumpy, but with a sweet destination. Once again, guests are brought in to augment the band's sound; Lambchop's Kurt Wagner returns to help the electronica act with meditative lead vocals that fit into the film noir soundscape that is "What New York Couples Fight About," and Pace Won adds his rhymes to two tunes—the title track, which harks back to the trip-hopping salad days of the group and sees the rapper taking the lead, and "Get Along," where he makes a more subtle contribution on a dreamy cut that sounds like something from the '70s if they had more modern equipment back then. However, the best is "Women Lose Weight," which sees Slick Rick sound completely old-school with Morcheeba's pop-soul groove letting his typically clever rhymes and dark comedy dominate the song. Though the appearances of outside musicians is a positive move overall, the remainder of the disc as done by the three members of the group stands up on its own; Skye Edwards' vocals are sultry as she makes all diva-like on lead track "Slow Down," the string-drenched melancholic "Otherwise," and the lazy, tropical "Sao Paulo," and overall her performance makes *Charango* the band's best record in some time, and for anyone not a purist, it's possibly Morcheeba's best ever. *—Brian O'Neill*

Debelah Morgan

Vocals / Contemporary R&B, Urban, Dance-Pop
The owner of a five-octave vocal range, R&B singer Debelah Morgan wrote her first song at the age of eight, soon after forming her own girl's choir and serving as their arranger. At 15, she was teaching gospel choir at the University of Arizona, that same year winning Miss Teen Black Arizona honors. Morgan then relocated to Los Angeles, taking home a silver medal in the NAACP international music competition. Pursued by a number of record companies, she eventually signed with Motown, issuing her debut album, *It's Not Over*, in 1998. *Dance With Me* followed two years later. *—Jason Ankeny*

Debelah / 1994 / Atlantic ✦✦✦
Although it isn't an amazing album—decent, but not amazing—*Debelah* demonstrated that Debelah Morgan was an R&B singer with considerable potential. Throughout the album, it's impossible to miss the fact that Morgan (who was simply going by Debelah) had an impressive voice. Morgan is blessed with a five-octave range, and if you don't understand the technical meaning of that term, suffice it to say that she has sizable chops. Whether she's unveiling new songs or belting out gospel-influenced covers of Deniece Williams' "Free" or Rick James and Teena Marie's "Fire and Desire" (a duet with singer Kenny Harper), her voice is all over the place. Williams, in fact, is one of Morgan's main influences, and Williams' influence becomes especially evident when she hits the high notes. But as talented as Morgan is, she usually doesn't have five-star material to work with. Although enjoyable, slow burners like "Take It Easy," "Mind Trippin'" and "Floating" aren't mind-blowing. If Morgan had consistently excellent songs to record, she could deliver an album that was superb instead of simply decent. *—Alex Henderson*

● **Dance With Me** / Aug. 15, 2000 / Atlantic ✦✦✦
Six years after Atlantic initially dropped her, multi-talented singer/songwriter Debelah Morgan returned with her third album, *Dance With Me*, a fresh, quick-stepping dance-oriented album. Morgan collaborated with brother Giloh on production and songwriting credits, which made the 14-track album a simple urban spin on R&B grooves and sultry hip-hop beats. She is emotionally confident and smooth in heightening her Mariah Carey-like vocal range, especially on tracks such as "I Remember" and "Think of You." A definitive musical maturation is pretty obvious from her previous material, and Morgan stays sassy with upbeat songs about adoration and the lovelorn. She isn't afraid to slow things down, and the ballad "What Would You Do" is an enjoyable look showcasing Morgan's sentimental brooding. It's a nice twist for Morgan, and her move in perfecting her angular pop-laden sound shapes nicely. *Dance With Me* is sheer, decent, and carefree in the sense that Debelah Morgan made a solid record with the idea of doing it only for herself. *—MacKenzie Wilson*

Meli'sa Morgan

b. Queens, NY
Vocals / Urban
Meli'sa Morgan's solo career got off to a great start in 1985, as her cover of Prince's "Do Me Baby" topped the R&B charts. She recorded for Capitol from 1985 to 1987, and enjoyed two more Top Ten R&B singles with "Do You Still Love Me?" and "If You Can Do It: I Can Too!" before moving to Arista. Her duet with Kashif, "Love Changes," earned her another R&B hit that year, reaching number two. Morgan moved to Pendulum in 1992; her last release was *Still in Love With You*. *—Ron Wynn*

Lady in Me / 1977 / Capitol ✦✦✦
Do Me Baby and *Good Love* earned Meli'sa Morgan a reputation as a straightforward, Chaka Khan-influenced soul/urban contemporary diva who didn't go out of her way to be trendy. But the singer went for quite a chance of direction on *The Lady in Me*, sporting a Jody Watley-ish look and going for a much more high-tech production style full of hip-hop, synth-funk and new jack swing elements. Unfortunately, the results are often unimpressive and disappointing. While the CD does contain a few memorable tracks along the lines of Morgan's '80s recordings (including "I'm Better Now" and the silky "Don't You Know"), new jack numbers like "Dancing in Love" and "Can You Give Me What I Want" are about as generic as it gets. *The Lady in Me* is an album that only Morgan's most devoted followers should acquire. *—Alex Henderson*

Do Me Baby / Mar. 20, 1987 / Capitol ✦✦✦✦✦
When Meli'sa Morgan debuted with *Do Me Baby* in 1986, many R&B singers were so obsessed with crossing over to the pop charts that they bent over backwards to dilute their music—but not Morgan. Greatly influenced by Chaka Khan but far from a clone, the big-voiced belter made it clear that she was very much an R&B singer on this highly promising CD. Sounding seasoned, confident and mature, Morgan tended to appeal to the type of adult audience that also favored Luther Vandross, Freddie Jackson and Anita Baker. Morgan had major R&B hits in "Do You Still Love Me?" and a remake of Prince's "Do Me Baby," and equally impressive are songs ranging from "Fool's Paradise" (not to be confused with the 1975 Rufus/Chaka Khan song) to the insistent "I'll Give It When I Want It." If listeners own only one Morgan CD, *Do Me Baby* is definitely the best choice. *—Alex Henderson*

Good Love / 1988 / Capitol ✦✦
Former High Fashion vocalist Meli'sa Morgan inked a solo deal with Capitol in the late '80s as the group was signing their own deal. She was soon a star and then became an obscurity. Her second album for the label was one of the hottest urban contemporary items in 1987. Morgan scored both sassy uptempo hits and a romantic duet with Kashif, "Love Changes." Her fiery, sensual vocals and even hotter looks put her on the covers of many music and fashion magazines geared toward the urban contemporary/quiet storm female audience. It didn't hurt that the album was nicely produced and arranged, well-packaged, and perfectly sequenced to vary her sound and appeal. *—Ron Wynn*

● **Do You Still Love Me?: The Best of Meli'sa Morgan** / Jun. 18, 1996 / Razor & Tie ✦✦✦✦✦
Do You Still Love Me?: The Best of Meli'sa Morgan brings together most of the hit singles and key album tracks from her mid- to late-'80s work, including "If You Can Do It: I Can Do It Too!," "Love Changes," "Do You Still Love Me?," and "Do Me Baby." For the most part,

the collection focuses on the kind of smooth urban ballads with which Morgan made her name, including "Heart Breaking Decision," "Here Comes the Night," "I'll Love No More," and "Lady in Me," although the harder-edged, new jack swing-inspired "Think It Over" and the uptempo, poppy "Can You Give Me What I Want" and "So Long, Goodbye" provide a bit of stylistic diversity. Despite some rather tinny synth sounds and dated production touches here and there, Meli'sa Morgan's work has aged pretty well, and *Do You Still Love Me?* offers a fairly comprehensive look at the peak period of her career. *—Heather Phares*

Giorgio Moroder

b. Apr. 26, 1940, Ortisei, Italy

Composer, Synthesizer, Producer / Disco, Soundtracks, Dance-Pop

One of the principal architects of the disco sound, producer and composer Giorgio Moroder was born in Ortisei, Italy, on April 26, 1940. Upon relocating to Munich, Germany, he established his own studio, Musicland, and recorded his debut single "Looky, Looky" in 1969; his first LP, *Son of My Father*, was released in early 1972. Around that time Moroder was introduced to fellow aspiring musician Pete Bellotte, with whom he formed a production partnership; in collaboration with singer Donna Summer, the duo was to become one of the most powerful forces in '70s-era dance music, their success beginning with the release of 1974's *Lady of the Night*. Summer's *Love to Love You Baby* followed in 1975; the title track, clocking in at close to 17 minutes in length, was an international smash, its shimmering sound and sensual attitude much copied in the years to follow. At their mid-'70s peak, Moroder, Bellotte, and Summer were extraordinarily prolific, releasing new albums about once every six months. Concept records like 1976's *A Love Trilogy* and *Four Seasons of Love* culminated with the release of 1977's *I Remember Yesterday*, a trip through time which climaxed with the smash "I Feel Love." With its galloping bassline and futuristic, computerized sheen, the single was among the watershed hits of the disco era, and helped propel Summer to new prominence as the reigning diva of the dancefloor.

In 1978, Moroder made his initial foray into film music, winning an Academy Award for his score to Alan Parker's *Midnight Express*. Summer's double-LP *Bad Girls* followed in 1979, becoming a massive hit and spawning such chart-topping singles as "Hot Stuff" and the title cut. After one final studio LP, 1980's *The Wanderer*, the Moroder/Bellotte/Summer team disbanded, and the disco era began drawing to a close. In the early '80s, Moroder focused primarily on films; after producing the soundtracks for pictures including *American Gigolo* and *Cat People*, he turned to 1983's *Flashdance*, earning his second Oscar for the hit "Flashdance... What a Feeling," performed by Irene Cara. In 1984, Moroder courted controversy from film purists for his contemporary electro-pop score to the restored release of Fritz Lang's silent-era masterpiece *Metropolis*. After contributing to the soundtrack of the 1986 hit *Top Gun*, he turned increasingly away from dance music to focus on rock, producing the album *Flaunt It*, the debut from the heavily hyped British flash-in-the-pan Sigue Sigue Sputnik. In the years to follow, Moroder kept a low profile on the pop charts, although he remained a fixture on film soundtracks. In the 1990s, he also turned to remixing, debuting with a reworking of Eurythmics' "Sweet Dreams (Are Made of This)" and going on to tackle material from Heaven 17 and others. *—Jason Ankeny*

Knights in White Satin / 1976 / Oasis ✦✦✦

● **From Here to Eternity** / 1977 / Casablanca ✦✦✦✦✦

From Here to Eternity is Moroder's quasi-instrumental masterpiece, a continuous mix of banging Euro-disco complete with vocoder effects and this statement on the back cover: "Only electronic keyboards were used on this recording." The metallic beats, high-energy impact, and futuristic effects prove that Moroder was ahead of his time like few artists of the 1970s (Kraftwerk included), and the free-form songwriting on tracks like "Lost Angeles," "First Hand Experience in Second Hand Love," and the title track are priceless. [The 1985 quasi-compilation *From Here to Eternity... And Back* included most of the original album plus new tracks and a remix of the single "Chase."] *—John Bush*

Midnight Express / 1978 / Atlantic ✦✦✦✦

Though there are a few queasy pop/vocal tracks, Moroder's soundtrack to *Midnight Express* earns points for an array of exploratory synthesizer pieces (including "Wheel" and "Cacaphoney") as well as its opener, "Chase." One of Moroder's biggest hits, the track bounces back and forth between melodic disco and hypnotic sequencer trance just one step removed from the likes of Tangerine Dream. *—John Bush*

E=MC2 / Jan. 1980 / Casablanca ✦✦✦✦

Giorgio Moroder wasn't the first person to play electronic dance music—Kraftwerk had a synthesizer oriented sound in the early '70s, and its electro-beats paved the way for a lot of the hip-hop, synth-pop, techno, industrial noise, house, and Hi-NRG that came in the '80s and '90s. But even though Moroder (who, like Kraftwerk's members, is German) didn't invent electronic dance music single-handedly, he was among the first people to recognize its possibilities. In 1979, Moroder showed us some of those possibilities on *E=MC2*, a programmed, entirely electronic recording he produced with Harold Faltermeyer. While Moroder's work with Donna Summer and others had favored strings and lavish orchestration, synthesizers and electronic beats defined this LP. Moroder was hardly the only producer who was using synthesizers in the late '70s, but while other disco/dance-pop albums of 1979 combined them with horns, strings, and Latin percussion, they are the very foundation of *E=MC2*. "In My Wildest Dreams," "I Wanna Rock You," and "What a Night" are average disco tunes—it's the computerized digital production that made them so fresh-sounding and risk-taking for their time. To fully appreciate how forward-thinking this album was, you have to remember that in 1979 R&B and dance-pop hadn't gone completely high-tech and were still relying on a lot of studio musicians. This is the electronic dance music that preceded the rise of techno, house, and industrial noise, and it came at a time when hip-hop was in its infancy and the rave subculture had yet to be invented. Even though the songs themselves are average, Moroder and Faltermeyer's futuristic production makes *E=MC2* a historically interesting LP that anyone who has enjoyed electronic dance rhythms needs to check out. *—Alex Henderson*

16 Early Hits / 1991 / BMG ✦✦✦

● **Best of Giorgio Moroder** / Apr. 3, 2001 / Repertoire ✦✦✦✦✦

Although he is most often remembered as the production wizard behind Donna Summer's rise to prominence, Giorgio Moroder has enjoyed a successful solo career that has covered everything from bubblegum pop to proto-electronica. This welcome compilation provides a handy thumbnail sketch of Moroder's career. It starts with the pop singles that Moroder recorded as a solo artist: They're all as sugary as can be (especially "Looky Looky," which is heavily reminiscent of early ABBA), but they also show the development of the techniques that would soon make Moroder an in-demand producer: "Underdog" ably mixes a throbbing, danceable beat with its swirling violins and glam rock guitar riffs, and "Son of My Father" makes pioneering use of the synthesizer layering techniques that Moroder would later employ on his disco classics. After these singles, *The Best of Giorgio Moroder* quickly moves into the performer's disco-era solo work: Highlights here include the percolating synth pop of "Baby Blue" and a surprisingly effective reworking of "Nights in White Satin" (dubbed "Knights in White Satin" here) that recasts the song as a sultry, string-drenched disco ballad. Moroder's soundtrack skills are shown off via the inclusion of "Chase," an eight-minute techno epic from his Oscar-winning score for *Midnight Express*. The remainder of the album covers the producer's mid-'80s to early-'90s period, which found him collaborating with performers like Phil Oakey and Donna Summer. These songs are less interesting than those in the first half of the collection, but there are still plenty of worthwhile moments to be found: "Together in Electric Dreams" is techno-pop worthy of early Duran Duran and "Lady Lady" skillfully crossbreeds rock guitar riffs and gentle synthesizers into its atmospheric power ballad sound. On the downside, *The Best of Giorgio Moroder* misses some highlights due to licensing and space issues: Notable missing tracks include the synth-dance epic "Evolution" and "Cat People," Moroder's 1982 film theme collaboration with David Bowie. Despite these oversights, *The Best of Giorgio Moroder* remains a fine and reasonably comprehensive portrait of this gifted studio maven's diverse talents. *—Donald A. Guarisco*

Wendy Moten

b. Memphis, TN

Vocals / Adult Contemporary, Urban

Born and raised in Memphis, Wendy Moten first gained experience singing in her church choir. After a performance with Michael Bolton at a benefit in New York, the R&B singer signed to EMI/ERG, released a self-titled debut album, and supported Bolton on a tour. *—John Bush*

Wendy Moten / 1992 / EMI ✦✦✦

Wendy Moten's self-titled debut album only produced a couple of minor R&B chart singles ("Step by Step" and "Come in out of the Rain"), but measured in artistic terms, the record displays a confident vocalist with a theatrical flair (and, indeed, Moten did land a starring role in the off-Broadway production *Mama I Want to Sing*). Moten is equally comfortable with urban R&B and smooth adult contemporary balladry, although her true affinity seems to be for the latter. She's missing the sort of killer singles that contemporaries like Mariah Carey rode to the top of the charts, but fans of that style may want to check this decent album out. *—Steve Huey*

● **Life's What You Make It** / Jul. 1996 / Capitol ✦✦✦✦

Moten mixes R&B ballads and pop on *Life's What You Make It*, which includes the title track (a cover of the Talk Talk hit) as well as renditions of the Rascals' "People Got to Be Free" and the Police's "When the World Is Running Down." *—Jason Ankeny*

Mother's Finest

f. Chicago, IL

Group / Hard Rock, Funk, Psychedelic Soul

Georgia funk rock band Mother's Finest might appear to be only a blip on the radar screen of rock history, but not to any of the headlining bands they've stolen shows from—or any of the audiences who saw it happen. Following in the footsteps of the racially-mixed Sly & the Family Stone, Mother's Finest blended white guitarist Moses Mo and drummer B.B. "Queen" Borden with black vocalists Joyce Kennedy and Glenn Murdock, bassist Wyzard, and keyboardist Mike, for its 1976 self-titled debut album. Tracks like "Rain" and the slightly controversial "Niggazz Can't Sing Rock & Roll" made enough of a ripple to get the band out of Georgia clubs and into regional touring. The follow-up album *Another Mother Further* lived up to its title. The opening track was a cover of the Holland-Dozier-Holland songwriting team's "Mickey's Monkey," made popular by Smokey Robinson. But the guitar riff was a blatant copy of Jimmy Page's from the Led Zeppelin song "Custard Pie," released two years earlier. Perhaps because the song was a cover, or the fact that they stole from blues legends early in their career, Led Zeppelin never sued and the track (along with others like "Piece of the Rock" and "Hard Rock Lover") helped make *Another Mother Further* the group's springboard.

For the remainder of the 1970s, Mother's Finest became the most dangerous opening act in rock, blowing away headliners like Aerosmith, Frank Marino & Mahogany Rush, and Ted Nugent. A subpar third album, 1978's *Mother Factor*, took nothing away from the band's live performances, as vocalists Murdock—and particularly the powerful Kennedy—enthralled audiences over the funk rock backline of Mo, Wizzard, Borden, and Mike. The 1979 album *Mother's Finest Live* featured not only original staples like "Watch My Stylin'" and "Give You All the Love," but also Kennedy singing a stunning cover of Jefferson Airplane's "Somebody to Love" and the musicians shining on a rearranged version of Steppenwolf's "Magic Carpet Ride." It would prove a last hurrah, for Mother's Finest didn't translate well into the 1980s and never achieved its due in the largely-white world of rock. Mo, Mike, and Borden would leave the band, the latter to go polar-opposite by joining Southern rockers Molly Hatchet, but Kennedy, Murdock and Wizzard fought on. After dabbling in dance music with several different lineups in the 1980s, the trio formed an all-African-American band in the early '90s by recruiting guitarist John Hayes and drummer Dion Derek. The angry, rocking result was the 1992 CD *Black Radio Won't Play This Record*, which proved prophetic despite being the band's best since its 1979 live album (yet white radio wouldn't play it either). It's now in the cut-out bins; ignored or forgotten—much like Mother's Finest—by all except a select few. Still active, the group's latest CD is called *Not Yer Mother's Funk—The Very Best of Mother's Finest*, and features mostly material from the first two albums. *—Bill Meredith*

Mother's Finest / 1976 / RCA ♦♦♦

Another Mother Further / 1977 / Epic ♦♦♦♦♦

Mother Factor / 1978 / Epic ♦♦♦
Mother's Finest came closest with this album to getting some deserved attention. The album stayed on the pop charts for over 20 weeks, generating a mild R&B hit, and the group did some support tours. Unfortunately, it didn't have the one breakout single they needed, or even an album cut that could become a cult winner. Instead, it ended up being a close-but-no-cigar proposition, although it did keep them viable enough to secure another contract with a new label. *—Ron Wynn*

Live / 1979 / Epic ♦♦♦♦♦
Mother's Finest tried to smash the embargo blocking black rock acts with this live record. It was the closest any album came to actually conveying the kind of nonstop excitement, spontaneity, and unpredictability of their live shows, although it also showed how vocally erratic they could be in performance. The failure of a band that had as exciting a vocalist as Joyce Kennedy and did both solid rock and fine grinding funk proved one of the '80s' more puzzling questions. It couldn't just be attributed to racism either, because Mother's Finest actually did better among white audiences than black ones. *—Ron Wynn*

Iron Age / 1982 / Atlantic ♦♦♦
Whether Mother's Finest was more rock-minded or R&B-minded on a particular album usually had a lot to do with what label the band was recording for at the time and who was in charge in the A&R department. Some A&R men wanted Mother's Finest to be an urban contemporary act and cater to black radio's tastes, but on *Iron Age*, MF was clearly going after the heavy metal/hard rock audience of the early 1980s. MF never sounded more focused and inspired than it does on this excellent LP, and forceful gems like "Rock 'n Roll 2 Nite," "U Turn Me On" and "Movin' On" indicated that MF should forget about what black radio was playing and simply concentrate on being a great metal/hard rock band (which is what it really wanted to be, anyway). Black radio, which had been a strong supporter of MF's 1978 hit "Love Changes," wasn't about to play an album this metal-oriented—and sadly, rock radio ignored it as well. With the right promotion, *Iron Age* could have made MF a big hit with the Quiet Riot/Judas Priest/Scorpions crowd, but the album was a commercial flop instead of the big commercial breakthrough that it should have been. Nonetheless, the fact remains that this out-of-print LP is among MF's most rewarding albums and is well worth hunting for if you fancy yourself a metalhead. *—Alex Henderson*

If Looks Could Kill / 1989 / Capitol ♦♦

Black Radio Won't Play This Record / 1992 / RCA ♦♦♦
Though Mother's Finest had some success in the R&B market with the 1979 hit "Love Changes," the Atlanta residents were always rockers at heart. After reuniting in the late '80s, MF aimed at the urban contemporary market with *Looks Could Kill*—a pedestrian, forgettable effort that had very little going for it. But the Led Zeppelin-influenced band more than made up for that artistic blunder with the heartfelt *Black Radio Won't Play This Record.* Taking off the gloves (both musically and lyrically) and throwing urban contemporary considerations to the wind, MF excels by doing what it does best: scorching heavy metal and hard rock with a touch of Ike & Tina Turner-ish soul. Lead singers Joyce Kennedy and Glenn Murdock are as passionate as ever, and the songwriting is first-rate. While "Like a Negro" protests racism and "Stop" warns that unsafe sex can result in AIDS, "Crack Babies" addresses the horrors of babies born to cocaine-addicted mothers. MF's small but devoted following hoped that this album (arguably its heaviest since 1981's *Iron Age*) would save the headbangers from obscurity, but sadly, it enjoyed little attention. *—Alex Henderson*

● **The Very Best of Mother's Finest: Not Yer Mother's Funk** / Apr. 22, 1997 / Razor & Tie ♦♦♦♦♦
The Very Best of Mother's Finest: Not Your Mother's Funk culls 15 highlights from the group's eight albums, including the singles "Fire," "Don't Wanna Change," "Love Changes" and "Baby Love," making it the definitive retrospective of this cult funk band. *—Stephen Thomas Erlewine*

Motherlode

f. 1969, London, Ontario, Canada
Group / Pop-Soul, Sunshine Pop
Formed in the late '60s in Ontario by saxophonist Steve Kennedy, guitarist Ken Marco, keyboard player William "Smitty" Smith, and drummer Wayne Stone, Motherlode scored with a Top 40 hit in 1969—the smooth "When I Die." Two years after the release of the album of the same title, though, the group had broken up. *—John Bush*

● **When I Die** / 1969 / Buddah ♦♦♦♦
The title track went Top 20 in the summer of 1969, and it is a smooth, soulful, slick, and beautiful pop classic. Nothing else on this decent album comes close to the majesty of the hit single, but the album has merit nonetheless. "When I Die" was written by vocalist/keyboard player/bandleader William "Smitty" Smith and tenor sax/harmonica player/vocalist Steve Kennedy. It has some of the elements that the Free Movement most likely borrowed for their "I've Found Someone of My Own," which went Top Five two years after this in 1971, both bands displaying heavy gospel influences which flavored their respective singles. In the case of Motherlode, the gospel is in the grooves of the album tracks. Although this competent album as a whole is better than the full-length disc by Alive and Kicking, which sent "Tighter, Tighter" up the charts a year later ("Tighter, Tighter" being, arguably, a better song, rose higher into the Top Ten), these "one-hit wonders" did create memorable recordings that brighten up radio years later. "Child Without Mother" is written by Kennedy, Smith, and electric guitarist Ken Marco, displaying fully the marvelous pop/gospel chops by the group, though it tends to jam out a bit much.

Producers Mort Ross and Doug Riley had something here, and they should have capitalized on it with more than just this almost filler to surround the hit recording with, although that filler is well-constructed. The brilliant Carol Kay plays bass and "Acc. Guitar" on all tracks except the cover of the Johnny Bristol tune that Junior Walker made famous, "What Does It Take (To Win Your Love)." Ken Marco's "Living Life" is another of the almost-but-not-quite tunes here. It's a surprisingly listenable album with strong musicianship, the band's sincere liner notes adding a dimension of charm missing on many discs from this era. *—Joe Viglione*

Mtume

Conga, Percussion / Urban, Disco, Jazz-Funk, Fusion, Quiet Storm
A former jazz percussionist, Mtume moved into urban contemporary and funk in the late '70s and became one of the more successful producers and performers in both styles during the '80s. The son of the great jazz saxophonist Jimmy Heath, Mtume was a conga player and percussionist who recorded and toured with Miles Davis and was featured on albums by the Heath Brothers, Sonny Rollins, Herbie Hancock, Joe Henderson, and Freddie Hubbard. He even recorded as a bandleader for Strata-East before turning to funk in the late '70s. Mtume's band included the sassy, sultry vocalist Tawatha Agee, keyboardist Phil Fields, and bassist Ray Johnson. They had a number-one R&B hit with "Juicy Fruit" for Epic in 1983 and a number two single in 1984 with "You, Me and He." They recorded for Epic until the late '80s. Agee went solo in 1987.

Their final Top Ten hit was "Breathless" in 1986. Mtume also teamed with another ex-jazz musician, Reggie Lucas, who had also been in Davis' '70s band. They produced and/or wrote for such artists as Stephanie Mills, Roberta Flack/Donny Hathaway, Phyllis Hyman, Gary Bartz, Sadane, Lou Rawls, Rena Scott, and Eddie Henderson in the late '70s. The duo worked on the LP *In Search of the Rainbow Seekers* for Epic in 1980. Mtume worked on his own as a producer with several artists, among them LeVert, Tyrone Brunson, Roy Ayers, Henderson, Tease, and Sue Ann. *—Ron Wynn*

Kiss This World Goodbye / Nov. 1978 / Epic ♦♦
This debut by percussionists Mindbender Mtume unearthed the vocal talents of Mighty T, better known as Tawatha to music lovers. T simply blows you away on two spine-tingling ballads, a rendition of "The Closer I Get to You" and "Closer to the End." Also uncovered is Mtume's funky fusion style on creative ditties like "Funky Constellation," "Just Funnin'," and "Metal Flake." A fine introduction for a creative force. *—Andrew Hamilton*

In Search of the Rainbow Seekers / 1980 / Epic ♦♦♦

You, Me and He / 1984 / Epic ♦♦♦
This was one of Mtume's late-'80s "sophisti-funk" projects, with a mix of socially conscious lyrics, love songs, and uptempo cuts, plus collective vocals and sparing production and arrangements. The title cut was a huge R&B hit, peaking at number two and even generating some crossover pop action. Mtume got two other R&B smashes, one in the Top 20, and the album proved one of his best. *—Ron Wynn*

● **Juicy Fruit** / 1985 / Epic ♦♦♦♦♦
James Mtume's band Mtume hit its commercial and creative peak in 1983, when *Juicy Fruit* was released. The infectious, mildly risqué title song—which contains the controversial lyrics "I'll be your lollipop/You can lick me everywhere"—soared to number one on *Billboard*'s R&B singles chart and ended up being sampled by quite a few hip-hoppers, including the late Notorious B.I.G., aka Biggie Smalls (who used the infectious gem on his 1994 hit "Juicy"). Some of the people who heard the "Juicy Fruit" single on the radio back in 1983 bought the single but not the album, which was a mistake because the other tracks are also excellent. In fact, many of Mtume's hardcore fans agree that *Juicy Fruit* is the band's most essential album. This LP came at a time when funk was becoming increasingly technology-minded. Horn-driven funk bands were going out of style, and funksters were using a lot more keyboards and synthesizers. *Juicy Fruit* reflects that evolution; although not totally electronic, funk/urban pearls like "Hips" and "Ready for Your Love" are very keyboard-minded. Only one horn player is employed on this release: jazz saxophonist Gary Bartz, who did his share of R&B sessions in the late '70s and early '80s but eventually returned to being a full-time jazz improviser. Throughout *Juicy Fruit*, James Mtume takes a very hands-on approach—in addition to producing the album and co-writing much of the material, he plays keyboards and provides some of the lead vocals (along with the expressive, big-voiced Tawatha Agee). *Juicy Fruit* isn't the only worthwhile album that James Mtume's band came out with in the 1980s; as a rule, his 1980s output was solid. But if you must limit yourself to one Mtume release, *Juicy Fruit* would be the best choice. *—Alex Henderson*

Native Son / 1985 / MCA ♦♦♦
Mtume participated in the soundtrack for this poorly distributed, uneven remake of the film conceived out of the landmark novel by Richard Wright, who appeared in an earlier version. Oprah Winfrey was in the cast for this edition, but her presence didn't ensure them the widespread distribution or publicity necessary to salvage it. The soundtrack was quite similar to the film—strong at times, but disjointed and ultimately disappointing. *—Ron Wynn*

Theater of the Mind / 1986 / Epic ♦♦♦
Former jazz percussionist James Mtume moved into soul and funk in the 1980s, and then changed gears again in the mid- and late '80s. This was one of an album series Mtume

called "sophisti-funk" LPs, with a denser, sparser sound than his previous works and devoid of string or horn support. Mtume managed to both get R&B chart hits like "P.O.P." and also make some biting, satirical comments about materialism and commercialism. *—Ron Wynn*

Samantha Mumba

b. Dublin, Ireland

Vocals / Urban, Dance-Pop, Teen Pop

Dublin, Ireland, is the unusual birthplace of teen sensation Samantha Mumba, whose urban style and American-accented singing makes her sound like TLC's little sister. Mumba dropped out of school when she was 17 to produce her first album, which contains musical stylings that sound like they were generated by someone much older. School itself was a great preparation for her musical career, however, because Mumba attended Dublin's Billie Barry Stage School from the time she was three to 15. That school also produced members of the British boy band Westlife and provided her with the beginnings of her education in showbiz. In 2000 she released her debut album on Polydor, *Gotta Tell You*, which featured heavy pop production and an aggressive, frank style which helped set her apart from the sea of teen stars. *—Stacia Proefrock*

● **Gotta Tell You** / Oct. 31, 2000 / Interscope ✦✦✦

Shirley Murdock

b. Toledo, OH

Vocals / Quiet Storm, Urban

Singer/songwriter Shirley Murdock is best known for the ethereal ballad "As We Lay," which was produced by Roger Troutman. Murdock started out singing gospel music in her native Toledo. Troutman hired her as a background singer for his family's group Zapp, who had several hits on Warner Brothers (or its Reprise imprint). Based on this success, Troutman began recording tracks with Murdock and lead singer Sugarfoot of the Ohio Players, among others, at his Dayton-based recording studio Troutman Sound Labs. Murdock and Troutman's first charting single was a Warner single issued as Roger (Featuring Shirley Murdock), "Girl, Cut It Out," which charted at number-79 R&B in early 1985. Murdock was signed to Elektra Records with the pumping "No More," which made it to number-24 R&B in early 1986. Then came her signature hit, "As We Lay," written by Zapp's Larry Troutman and keyboardist Billy Beck (of the Ohio Players). The tender, melancholy ballad made it to the R&B Top Ten and peaked at number-23 pop in 1986. Her LP *Shirley Murdock* went gold, also helped along by the follow-up hits "Go on Without You" and "Be Free."

She also released full-lengths in 1988 (*A Woman's Point of View*) and 1991 (*Let There Be Love*). In early 2000, Murdock toured in the inspirational/gospel play, *Be Careful What You Pray For* with Cuba Gooding and David Peaston. *—Ed Hogan*

Shirley Murdock / Mar. 1986 / Elektra ✦✦✦✦

A Woman's Point of View / 1988 / Elektra ✦✦✦

She is as good a soul shouter and confessional singer as anyone active today. *—Ron Wynn*

Let There Be Love! / 1991 / Elektra ✦✦✦

Thin-voiced, girlish female singers with very limited ranges were quite popular in the urban contemporary world of the late 1980s and early 1990s, which also had its share of big-voiced divas who flew in the face of this trend, including Vesta Williams, Meli'sa Morgan, Regina Belle and Angela Winbush. Like them, Shirley Murdock was an emotional, passionate belter who believed in wailing and letting it rip. *Let There Be Love!* was produced by Roger Troutman, the funkster and George Clinton associate who was known for his extensive use of the vocoder with his band Zapp. But there are few hints of P-Funk on this decent, ballad-oriented release. While *Let There Be Love!* isn't the soul extravaganza Murdock is quite capable of delivering, R&B/pop ballads and slow jams like "The Last Hurrah," "Say It, Mean It" and the Anita Baker-ish "Anywhere" aren't anything to be embarrassed by either. Meanwhile, Murdock increases the tempo with likable results on the house-influenced title song and the slightly jazzy "We Should Be Together." *—Alex Henderson*

● **The Very Best of Shirley Murdock** / May 15, 2001 / Rhino ✦✦✦✦

Rhino/Elektra Tradition's *The Very Best of Shirley Murdock* is an excellent 16-track retrospective of her recordings for Elektra in the late '80s. This contains seven of the nine songs on her eponymous debut (or eight of 13, if you count the remixes on the record, one of which is here [the "midnight mix" of "As We Lay"], three songs from her second album, *A Woman's Point of View*, and three from her third record, *Let There Be Love*. For good measure, "Computer Love," the Zapp song she sang on and co-wrote, is also here, along with an extended mix of "Go on Without You" from a promotional 12-inch single. All of this is tied together by classy packaging and fine notes by David Nathan, making this a fine overview of her hit-making peak. *—Stephen Thomas Erlewine*

Home / Feb. 26, 2002 / Chordant ✦✦✦

Home is the debut gospel project from noted R&B vocalist Shirley Murdock. Although this is her first all-gospel offering, performing gospel music is nothing new for Murdock, having appeared on the 1997 Grammy-nominated project by T.D. Jakes entitled *Woman Thou Art Loosed* as well as Jakes' controversial 1999 release *Sacred Love Songs*. *Home* features a number of the industry's top producers, including Derrick "D.O.A." Allen, Danny Weatherspoon, Cedric Thompson, Kevin Bond, and Sanchez Harley, along with Murdock's husband, Dale Degroat. Throughout this project, Murdock displays why she was recognized as one of R&B's top vocalists. She does a splendid job covering the powerful, message-driven ballad penned by the late Thomas Whitfield entitled "We Need a Word From the Lord." Other attention-grabbing ballads include the beautiful song of encouragement "Never Let You Down" and the inspirational "The Dream That Would Not Die." Murdock does not forsake her R&B roots, offering a number of urban-flavored, groove-filled woofer-rattlers; among those are the tracks "Somebody" as well as the regular and remixed versions of "This Is That." A very pleasing effort from this talented vocalist. *—Tim Smith*

Eddie Murphy

b. Apr. 3, 1961, Hempstead, NY

Vocals / Standup Comedy, Sketch Comedy, Urban, Dance-Pop

Like Bill Cosby and Richard Pryor before him, Eddie Murphy was the preeminent African-American comic of his era; in fact, Murphy was arguably the preeminent comic of the 1980s, period—at his peak, no other performer, regardless of race, was a bigger star or a more audacious talent. Combining Pryor's viciously acute observational gifts and love of obscenities with Cosby's undeniable mainstream appeal, Murphy quickly leaped from clubs to television to film—even finding success as a serious pop singer—on the way to establishing himself as the most wildly popular comedian since the heyday of Steve Martin.

Edward Regan Murphy was born April 3, 1961, in Hempstead, NY. By his mid-teens he was already working as a professional stand-up in Long Island clubs; by the age of 17, he was performing at Manhattan's famed Comic Strip and soon mounted a club tour of the East Coast. In 1980 his precocious talent won him a recurring gig as a featured performer on *Saturday Night Live*; at the moment, the comedy institution was suffering one of its frequent dry spells, and Murphy quickly established himself as its breakout star, graduating to full-time cast member status on the strength of memorable riffs on the Claymation hero Gumby and *Our Gang* character Buckwheat as well as creations like street pimp Velvet Jones and Mr. Robinson, a ghetto counterpart to Mr. Rogers.

In 1982, Murphy issued his debut comedy album, a self-titled live effort which drew fire for its controversial portrayal of the Asian community and misogynistic overtones as well as "Faggots," the first of many homophobic routines which ultimately resulted in a boycott call from the gay community. That same year he made his feature debut costarring with Nick Nolte in the buddy comedy *48 Hrs* the film was a major success, and at the age of just 21 Murphy was a Hollywood superstar, with a 15-million-dollar deal with Paramount Pictures as his reward.

The Delirious concert tour followed in 1983; recorded at a sold-out August performance, the LP *Eddie Murphy: Comedian* reached the Top 40 while his second feature, *Trading Places*, emerged as the year's highest-grossing film. A small role in 1984's disastrous *Best Defense* was Murphy's first misstep, but a year later he returned with *Beverly Hills Cop*, one of the most successful pictures in box-office history. Also in 1985 he teamed with producer Rick James to record *How Could It Be*, a straightforward R&B album which spawned the mammoth hit single "Party All the Time." Murphy was the hottest actor in Hollywood when he signed on for the 1986 quasi-mystical action comedy *The Golden Child*; the film was a commercial and critical bomb, and for the first time his star power was in question. While 1987's *Beverly Hills Cop II* stood as the year's biggest blockbuster and restored much of his career's luster, the aptly titled concert film *Raw* drew considerable heat for its abrasive, politically incorrect ranting. After 1988's *Coming to America* raked in the revenue, Murphy wrote, directed, and starred in 1989's *Harlem Nights*, a black gangster tale which performed miserably and took a massive critical drubbing.

Following the *Harlem Nights* debacle, he agreed to reunite in 1990 with Nick Nolte in *Another 48 Hrs*. When it too bombed, Murphy's career bottomed out; neither of his 1992 efforts, *Boomerang* and *The Distinguished Gentleman*, performed as well as his earlier hits, the 1993 LP *Love's Alright* failed to chart, and even 1994's seeming sure thing *Beverly Hills Cop III* tanked. After 1995's *Vampire in Brooklyn*, an ill-advised horror comedy, he starred in a hit remake of Jerry Lewis' *The Nutty Professor* in 1996, but in the early weeks of the following year the action-adventure fiasco *Metro* took a nosedive. *—Jason Ankeny*

Eddie Murphy / 1982 / CBS ✦✦✦

Eddie Murphy is one of those people who was obviously going to be a huge star from the very beginning. The Long Island, NY-born comedian was a nationwide sensation by the time he was 21. He exploded as the breakout star on *Saturday Night Live* during the lean early-'80s years when the show faced the daunting task of rebuilding after the classic original cast had left to pursue movie stardom, which Murphy would ultimately do as well. Despite Murphy's gifts, his first standup comedy album, 1982's *Eddie Murphy*, is uneven despite containing some classic routines. *Eddie Murphy* was recorded at The Comic Strip in New York City between April 30 and May 1, 1982. "Buckwheat" riffs on his memorable *SNL* character and expands it to sarcastically note that blacks aren't named for specific breakfast cereals. "Black Movie Theaters," "Talking Cars," and "Myths/A Little Chinese" are based on various racial stereotypes—not exactly politically correct, but very funny. "Doo-Doo/Christmas Gifts" features Murphy's musings on how fathers get shafted when they receive cheap Christmas presents. The hysterical "Drinking Fathers" is loaded with belly laughs—and a horrifying, underlying look at working-class alcoholism. The manic "Hit By a Car" is the best, most clever segment as Murphy explodes into overdrive. Comics often include novelty songs on their albums, and so does Murphy—with average results. "Boogie in Your Butt" weaves Murphy's spoken and semi-rap vocals, but the best part is the funky bassline. "Enough Is Enough" is a parody of 1979's chart-topping Barbra Streisand & Donna Summer duet "No More Tears (Enough Is Enough)," with Murphy once again recreating Buckwheat and imitating effeminate fitness guru Richard Simmons. For a perfect comedy classic, you have to jump one year ahead to 1983's *Eddie Murphy: Comedian*, but *Eddie Murphy* is a promising start. *—Bret Adams*

★ **Eddie Murphy: Comedian** / 1983 / CBS ✦✦✦✦✦

Probably the best comedy album of the 1980s, *Eddie Murphy: Comedian* showed the comic genius and grace of the already established of Eddie Murphy, who was still only 22. In a concert given in Washington, D.C., in 1983, Murphy kills the crowd with material ranging from his childhood to politics to dead-on impressions of Michael Jackson, Elvis, James Brown, Stevie Wonder, and Ricky Ricardo. On the surface, he could have appeared as just a funny, foul-mouthed kid. His raunchiness and cursing, however, only endears him to the crowd as he talks seamlessly about the progression of blacks and women and his 300-pound, mustached aunt or his shoe-throwing mother. He wonders aloud, what if Mr. T was gay, or Ralph and Norton of the *Honeymooners*? He speaks fondly of the ice cream man, and the cruel song he'd sing to the kid who didn't get any: "You don't have no ice cream, you didn't get none, because you're on the welfare, you can't afford it... and your father's an alcoholic." Murphy seems to say that the best way to confront anything in life is to laugh at it. *—Ron DePasquale*

How Could It Be / 1985 / CBS ✦✦✦

Love's Alright / Feb. 23, 1993 / Motown ✦✦
Eddie takes a break from the movies to pull together a collection of big name friends that ranges from Paul McCartney to Michael Jackson (who steals "Whatzupwitu" outright) so he can indulge himself with styles that include the Beatles, the Isleys and Stax. Musically, it's okay, with some nice-sounding material coming up, but Murphy has a very weak, thin voice that doesn't improve with any of the periodic attempts to stretch his limited range (he goes resoundingly flat). The covers of "Good Day Sunshine" and "Hey Joe" might be termed, at best, ill-advised. *—Steven McDonald*

● **Greatest Comedy Hits** / May 27, 1997 / Columbia ✦✦✦✦✦

Matt "Guitar" Murphy

b. Dec. 29, 1927, Sunflower, MS
Vocals, Guitar, Arranger / Modern Electric Blues, Soul-Blues, Retro-Soul, Electric Chicago Blues
Probably best-known for playing behind the Blues Brothers (and appearing prominently in their 1980 hit movie), Matt "Guitar" Murphy deserves enshrinement in the blues-guitar hall of fame anyway. His jazz-tinged, stunningly advanced riffing behind Memphis Slim elevated the towering pianist's 1950s output for United and Vee-Jay Records to new heights.

Guitar playing ran in the Murphy household (which moved from Mississippi to Memphis when Matt was a toddler). Matt and his brother Floyd both made a name for themselves on the early-'50s Memphis scene (that's Floyd on Little Junior Parker & the Blue Flames' 1953 Sun waxings of "Feelin' Good" and "Mystery Train"). Matt played with Howlin' Wolf as early as 1948 (Parker was also in the band at the time). Murphy added hot licks to early sides by Parker and Bobby "Blue" Bland for Modern before latching on with Memphis Slim's House Rockers in 1952. Normally, the veteran pianist eschewed guitarists altogether, but Murphy's talent was so prodigious that he made an exception. Murphy's consistently exciting guitar work graced Slim's United waxings from 1952-1954 and his 1958-1959 platters for Vee-Jay.

Another solid Memphis Slim LP for Strand in 1961 and dates with Chuck Berry, Otis Rush, Sonny Boy Williamson, Etta James, and the Vibrations at Chess preceded Murphy's memorable appearance on the 1963 American Folk Blues Festival tour of Europe. On that pioneering tour, Murphy commanded the spotlight with a thrilling "Matt's Guitar Boogie" that showcased his ultra-clean rapid-fire picking. *—Bill Dahl*

● **Way Down South** / 1990 / Discovery ✦✦✦✦✦
The dazzling guitarist has recorded very sparingly as a leader over the course of his long career, preferring the relative anonymity of sideman duties behind Memphis Slim, James Cotton, and the Blues Brothers. But he acquits himself most competently here, mixing blues, funk, R&B, and a little jazz into his sparkling fretwork. His brother Floyd Murphy, a Memphis blues guitar legend himself, is on hand for a family reunion. *—Bill Dahl*

Walter Murphy

b. 1952, New York, NY
Keyboards, Instrumental / Disco
Pianist Walter Murphy studied jazz and classical piano at the Manhattan School of Music and was an arranger for Doc Severinsen and *The Tonight Show* orchestra. He had a moment of pop stardom in 1976 with the song "A Fifth of Beethoven." It topped the pop charts and reached number ten on the R&B side. Murphy soon returned to his more familiar surroundings. *—Ron Wynn*

● **A Fifth of Beethoven** / 1976 / Private Stock ✦✦✦
Walter Murphy's "A Fifth of Beethoven" put classical disco on the map. It helped that Beethoven's symphony had a heavy percussion feel which Murphy cranked up a couple of notches with his amazing ingenuity. Other selections, while creatively different, are as good, but didn't burn a hole in the charts like "Fifth." "Suit Love Symphony," "Flight 76," "California Strutt," and "Russian Dressing," will expand your mind and quench your musical thirst at the same time. "Midnight Express" is fine European boogie, while the horn-laden "Get a Little" is a funky thing. This LP is out-of-print, but Hot Productions released a 17-song compilation of Walter Murphy's best in 1996. *—Andrew Hamilton*

Rhapsody in Blue / 1977 / Private Stock ✦✦
For those who found Barry White's various instrumental projects a little heavy-going, there was an answer. Composer and bandleader Walter Murphy steered that course and lightened that style across his various outings. Inestimable creator of one of disco's favorite dirty pleasures, 1976's "A Fifth of Beethoven," which was featured on the *Saturday Night Fever* soundtrack, Murphy rode the heels of that success the following year with *Rhapsody in Blue*. The title track is a contemporary rehash of George Gershwin's classic tune, replete with disco breaks and backing vocals peppering the iconographic musical strains—a Murphy special, which is repeated again on another Gershwin number, "It Ain't Necessarily So," this time adding a tenor sax solo. Probably better appreciated at the time than it is in retrospect, it still seems somehow base to tamper with the classics. Where Murphy seems to take himself in better hands is across his own material. "Love Eyes" is pure sugar which ebbs and flows around sweeping strings, and on his "New York City Suite," the third movement, "Fish Legs (Getdown Town)" boasts an unexpected, blistering guitar solo. However, Murphy falters when he adds vocals to "Could It Be the Music," "The Only Two People in the World," and "You Are on My Mind." One never looked to him for that; the instrumentals are just fine. With almost no relevance to the 21st century, Murphy will only be remembered for his one shining moment. And perhaps that is best—for everyone because, ultimately, this music, this flux of strings and drivel, is rooted in the distant past, in a moment that only made sense at the time. *—Amy Hanson*

Phantom of the Opera / 1978 / Private Stock ✦

The Best of Walter Murphy: A Fifth of Beethoven / Jul. 16, 1996 / Hot Productions ✦✦
You have to give credit to Walter Murphy for being enterprising enough to put the type of classical spin on disco that he did with "A Fifth of Beethoven," but unfortunately the trick was carried just a little too far. It's people like Murphy and records like "Disco Duck" that give disco a bad name and provide ammo for the haters of the often thrilling—and unsurprisingly enduring—style of dance music. *The Best of Walter Murphy: A Fifth of Beethoven* includes titles such as "Toccata and Funk," "Dance Your Face Off," and "Flight '76," which, naturally, gives the dancefloor treatment to "Flight of the Bumble Bee." The titles tell you all you need to know. Songs like these can be filed with Rick Dees' "Disco Duck" and Meco's "Star Wars Theme" under novelty. The remainder of these selections fall into ballad and fluffy pop territory. It's all lightweight goo. *—Andy Kellman*

Mickey Murray

Vocals / Soul, Southern Soul
Mickey Murray parlayed a modest impression of Otis Redding into a surprising pop-chart entry in 1967, with "Shout Bamalama" making it nearly halfway up the Top 100. Murray recorded over a dozen sides for SSS Int'l, but follow-ups like his self-penned "Lonely Room" and the hard funk of "Hit Record" failed to generate any chart action. Collectables compiled 18 of his best for 1999's *Shout Bamalama: The Very Best of Mickey Murray*. *—John Bush*

● **Shout Bamalama: The Very Best of Mickey Murray** / Feb. 2, 1999 / Collectables ✦✦✦✦✦
Mickey Murray's rendition of Otis Redding's "Shout Bamalama" was a career hit for the Southern singer. He was obviously imitating Redding, because nothing else on this 18-track CD sounds like it, and he sings in a lower, less hectic voice on the others—except for "Flat Foot Sam" and "Sticky Sue," which are as boisterous and backwoods as "Shout Bamalama." The ballads—"Lonely Room," "Pledging My Love" (a sweet remake of Johnny Ace's classic), and "Am I That Easy to Forget" (slow Southern blues)—are well-done and memorable. On "Hit Record" and "Mama Got the Wagon" you'll swear you're listening to James Brown. Two tracks, "After What I've Been Used To" and "The Pig and the Pussy Cat," harken back to memories of Stax Records and their patented horns. *—Andrew Hamilton*

Musiq (Talib Johnson)

b. Philadelphia, PA
Vocals / Contemporary R&B, Neo-Soul, Urban
Philadelphia-born Talib Johnson, aka burgeoning R&B artist Musiq (Soulchild), grew up the oldest of nine children and did not finish high school. Musiq, whose influences include James Brown, Patti LaBelle, Billie Holiday, and Sly & the Family Stone, participated in Philadelphia's open-mike scene in his early teens. The son of a die-hard '70s soul music fan, Musiq performed at Philly showcases like the Five Spot and Wilhemina's until his management team, Mama's Boys (Jerome Hipps and Michael McArthur), brought him to Def Jam Records' attention. Musiq's debut album, *Aijuswanaseing*, was recorded mostly at the Touch of Jazz studios in Philadelphia. Musiq's first single, "Just Friends (Sunny)," appeared on the soundtrack to *Nutty Professor II: The Klumps*, and two years later Musiq released his second album, the spiritual and personal *Juslisen*. *—Kerry Smith*

Aijuswanaseing / Nov. 14, 2000 / Def Soul ✦✦✦
With his 2000 debut album, *Aijuswanaseing (I Just Want to Sing)*, Musiq Soulchild is sure to make an indelible mark on the R&B soundscape. *Aijuswanaseing* is a remarkable collection of songs that successfully showcases Soulchild's vocal talent and versatility as he crisscrosses the analogous styles of R&B, soul, and rap. On the uptempo track "Girl Next Door," the singer demonstrates the smooth, rich texture of his voice. "Girl Next Door" is a romantic exchange that features the vocal prowess of Ayana of the duo Aaries. Tracks like the confident and playful "Just Friends" and the indelibly funky "My Girl" pick up the pace of the album, suggesting the possibility for future dancefloor remixes. The somber, soul-searching track "Mary Go Round" and the earnest sentiments on "Love" display Musiq's mellow, sincere side. The slow-paced wonder quality of "143" echoes a snippet of the style of fellow soul sista Erykah Badu (not a surprise since Musiq lists her high on his list of influences). There is also an apparent hint of the likes of Soulchild's idol Stevie Wonder in the rhythmic finger-snapping beat and experimental vocal riffs on "143," serving as evidence that Soulchild's voice is strong enough to stand on its own. The album is a casual yet valiant excursion that mirrors the many faces of a model swooner: a calm, cool, and collected attitude, mixed with a light sense of humor and a healthy serving of poise, swank, and sensitivity. *Aijuswanaseing* paints an aural portrait of this model combination which is best brought to life on the slyly flirtatious "Just Friends (Sunny)," which is featured on the *Nutty Professor II* soundtrack (Universal, 2000). *Aijuswanaseing* is the perfect backdrop for an intimate candlelit evening or just a casual stroll on a sunny afternoon. *—Kerry Smith*

● **Juslisen** / May 7, 2002 / Def Soul ✦✦✦✦✦
On his second album, *Juslisen*, Musiq—who has dropped the "(Soulchild)" surname—delivers on the promise of his debut, turning in a slyly assured, smoothly sexy collection of neo-soul. One of the most appealing things about Musiq is that he never oversells his songs, never indulges in hyperbolic screams or exaggerated grunts and moans. He lays back on the groove but doesn't disappear into it—he deepens it and gives it character, making this more than a supremely seductive neo-soul record. And, to be sure, it is that,

a wonderfully romantic mood album, but it's more than that because Musiq has other skills besides crooning and keeping a mood. First of all, he and his collaborators are first-class writers, sustaining interest not just through the singles, but through the album tracks. Then, he and his producers know how to deliver a sound that at once hearkens back to classic '70s soul and feels lushly contemporary. Musiq doesn't hide his love for classic soul—he's seen on the back cover digging through crates of vinyl, surrounded by eight-tracks—but the great thing about what he pulls off on *Juslisen* is that this love is absorbed, ingrained in the very music, so while it's reminiscent of Stevie Wonder or Marvin Gaye at times, it never feels like a forced attempt to follow in their footsteps. Which, of course, is why it feels like a worthy heir. *—Stephen Thomas Erlewine*

Musique

Group / Disco, Club/Dance

Out of all the projects produced, arranged, and/or overseen by Harlem disco wizard Patrick Adams (Inner Life, Cloud One, Black Ivory, Bumblebee Unlimited, etc.), none of them quite reached the mainstream popularity of Musique, thanks to their suggestive 1978 single "In the Bush." The song became a surprise hit and sparked a controversy for its lyrics, which contained a repeated refrain of "Push push in the bush." Adams never expected the song to get big enough that it would become a hot-button topic for radio programmers—several across the U.S. refused to play the song due to its most popular interpretation. A humble Adams would later express regret over the song's accessibility to young children who could hear it on the radio.

Adams formed Musique and based the group around a quartet of female singers—Jocelyn Brown, Christine Wiltshire, Angela Howell, and Gina Tharps. Not only did their debut album feature "In the Bush," but it also included "Keep on Jumpin'" (the title track), another single that caught fire on dancefloors, thanks to François K's 12-inch mix. A follow-up album, *Musique II*, followed in 1979 (Mary Seymour, Denise Edwards, and Gina Taylor replaced the original vocalists) but it was unable to build on the success of the debut. The project ended shortly after that. Brown's popularity peaked shortly after Musique with Inner Life, Adams continued doing his thing (including running Harlem's P&P label and its several subsidiaries with Peter Brown), and Wiltshire was featured on Class Action's "Weekend" (coincidentally, a cover of a song by Phreek, another Adams project). *—Andy Kellman*

● **Keep on Jumpin'** / 1978 / CBS ✦✦✦✦

This 1978 album, long a favorite of hardcore disco fanatics, provides a great showcase for the talents of producer Patrick Adams. Like most of Adams' groups, Musique was a studio creation (featuring the talents of future solo star Jocelyn Brown) designed exclusively for the discotheque. It produced two major dancefloor favorites in the title track and "In the Bush"; the former effectively contrasts a stately string-section riff against a double-time rhythm section beat, and the latter is a lusty dance epic that contrasts bouncy, keyboard-driven verses with blaring bursts of horns and a sexy, overheated performance from the vocalists. The album is rounded out by "Summer Love," a hypnotic, midtempo dance ballad built on a sultry blend of strings and keyboards, and "Summer Love Theme," an all-instrumental version of "Summer Love." On the downside, *Keep on Jumpin'* is a bit slim on melody, but the rhythms are so insistent and the arrangements are so inventive that this flaw is easy for a disco fan to overlook. All in all, casual listeners may want to track down the hits on a compilation, but *Keep on Jumpin'* remains a slick, punchy album that is recommended to anyone with an interest in the club-oriented side of disco. [Collector's Note: Fans of this album should track down the Unidisc compact disc reissue, which complements the album with an array of single edits and 12-in versions of "In the Bush" and "Keep on Jumpin'" that were remixed by legendary DJ François Kevorkian.] *—Donald A. Guarisco*

Musique II / 1979 / Prelude ✦✦✦

Musique's corps of vocalists changed completely for the group's second round. Gone were Jocelyn Brown, Christine Wiltshire, Angela Howell, and Gina Tharps—Mary Seymour, Denise Edwards, and Gina Taylor replaced them. The key returning factor was Patrick Adams, who reprises his role as producer, arranger, and mixer. Along with a stable of studio hands dubbed the PA System Rhythm Section, a double 12-inch (one song per side) was cut that doesn't quite measure up to *Keep on Jumpin'*. Nothing caught fire like "In the Bush," and nothing equals the breathless brilliance of "Keep on Jumpin'," but nothing here is weak by any stretch. François Kevorkian, still on the Prelude payroll at the time, casts his indelible remixing skills to each track, custom-fitting each one for maximum dancefloor response. Adams' writing and arranging work is in fine form. "Glide," written with Stan Lucas (Dazzle, Inner Life), and "Number One" (written by Ken Mazur) sound particularly spectacular decades after the fact. "Love Massage" is definitely a sequel of sorts to "In the Bush," taking sexual innuendo even further with lines like, "Touch me where I need you/Make me wet." When Unidisc reissued the album on CD, they added six alternate mixes, including the radio edit of "Love Massage" and Adams' previously unreleased mixes of "Love Massage," "Good and Plenty Lover," and "Number One." Kevorkian's work definitely has more oomph to it, but old disco-heads will love to hear Adams' renderings, particularly the instrumental "Raw Groove" mix of "Love Massage." *—Andy Kellman*

Mutiny

Group / Urban, Funk

George Clinton's funk empire was not without its disagreements over money and control, and drummer Jerome "Bigfoot" Brailey's Mutiny project was a direct result of just such a disagreement, as well as one of the more notable offshoots of the P-Funk axis. Brailey had come to P-Funk from gigs with the Five Stairsteps and the Chambers Brothers, joining in 1975 and playing on classic albums like *Mothership Connection* and *One Nation Under a Groove*. In 1977, he and guitarist Glen Goins abruptly left P-Funk after a dispute over money; Goins re-formed his previous group, Quazar, and invited Brailey to help out. Unfortunately, Goins passed away while the group was recording its debut album, and after it was completed and released in 1978, Brailey concentrated on his own group, Mutiny. Besides Brailey on drums and, usually, lead vocals, Mutiny also featured guitarists Lenny Holmes and Skitch Lovett, bassist Raymond "Bro" Carter, keyboardist Nat Lee, onetime P-Funk saxophonist Darryl Dixon, and hornmen Melvin El and Marvin Daniels (attempts to lure other P-Funk sidemen, especially Bernie Worrell, were unsuccessful). Mutiny's debut album, *Mutiny on the Mamaship*, was released by CBS in 1979 and featured several pointed satires of Clinton, even as the music mostly replicated his style (though it did so quite effectively). After a bit of personnel turnover, *Funk Plus the One* followed in 1980, but failed to provide a commercial breakthrough, and Mutiny found itself without a contract not long after.

Brailey formed his own J. Romeo imprint and recorded a mostly instrumental album, *Black Hat Daddy & the Silver Comb Gang*, but scrapped it in favor of *A Night Out With the Boys*, another mostly instrumental effort released in 1983. Brailey subsequently became a session drummer, working with the likes of Keith Richards, Buddy Miles, Herbie Hancock, and Buckethead. He moved back home to Richmond, VA, in 1990, and in 1993, he briefly rejoined Clinton's P-Funk All-Stars for a tour. Brailey next formed a new version of Mutiny and issued the comeback album *Aftershock 2005* in 1995 (the U.S. release was on Rykodisc). In 1999, Brailey finally released the *Black Hat Daddy* album on his own Rome Dog label. *—Steve Huey*

● **Mutiny on the Mamaship** / 1979 / CBS ✦✦✦✦

One of 1979's overlooked P-Funk goodies was *Mutiny on the Mamaship*, the debut album by George Clinton disciples Mutiny. Parliament/Funkadelic's influence is impossible to miss on this very derivative LP, which can hardly be called innovative and certainly won't win any awards for its originality. Some reviewers slammed Mutiny leader Jerome Brailey for going out of his way to emulate Parliament/Funkadelic; the thing is, he does it so darn well that you'll be patting your foot while you're commenting on the album's lack of originality. When Mutiny tears into goofy Clinton-esque numbers like "Lump," "Romeo (Hope You're Feeling Better)," and "Funk 'n' Bop," the P-Funk grooves aren't mildly infectious—they're *extremely* infectious. You might end up complaining about how Mutiny goes to such trouble to sound like Parliament/Funkadelic most of the time—and your complaints wouldn't be unwarranted—but you'll want to get up and dance while you're complaining. *—Alex Henderson*

Funk Plus the One / 1980 / CBS ✦✦✦

Mutiny continued to emulate Parliament/Funkadelic on their second album, *Funk Plus the One*; unfortunately, Jerome Brailey's band didn't do it as convincingly this time. While Mutiny's previous release, *Mutiny on the Mamaship*, was quite focused and inspired—unoriginal, but definitely inspired—the grooves aren't as memorable on *Funk Plus the One*. This isn't to say that *Funk Plus the One* is a bad album. Unremarkable cuts like "Anti-Disco" and the rock-influenced "Reality" are catchy enough. Also decent is "Semi-First Class Seat," one of the few Mutiny tunes that isn't terribly George Clinton-minded; the song finds the funksters getting into Slave/Steve Arrington/Aurra territory for a change. But while *Mutiny on the Mamaship* truly burned, this LP merely simmers. Although Mutiny had a small following, *Funk Plus the One* wasn't the big commercial breakthrough that Brailey was hoping for. Not surprisingly then, Columbia dropped the band after this uneven album. *—Alex Henderson*

Aftershock 2005 / Feb. 27, 1996 / Rykodisc ✦✦✦

Jerome "Bigfoot" Brailey's comeback project is something of a disappointment. Brailey is a disaffected Parliament/Funkadelic alumnus, and living proof that you can leave P-Funk but you can't leave it alone; Brailey's band stands solidly on the foundation that George Clinton built. That's not a criticism, by any means, just an observation—after all, what funkster doesn't stand on that same foundation? But no matter how impeccable his pedigree, Brailey's work on this album is definitely hit-and-miss. Hits include the album's opening track, an instrumental funk workout called "The Growl" that features brain-searing turntable work by DXT, and the relentless "No Choice," which kicks serious groovacious booty but features obnoxious and stupid gangbanger lyrics. (Lyrics are consistently weak on this album—"Passion is the stuff that dreams are made of," he informs us on one track. "If you want it bad enough/You just have to get real tough.") Misses include the relentlessly pedestrian "It's All Good" and the portentous but threadbare apocalypse of the title track ("Will we be alive/In 2005?"). Overall, this album is good for three or four solid entries on a party tape, but that's about it. *—Rick Anderson*

Rum Rebellion / Aug. 10, 1999 / Hells Ditch ✦✦✦

Mya

Vocals / Contemporary R&B, Urban, Hip-Hop

Mya is a dancer turned smooth urban R&B vocalist who released her eponymous debut in the spring of 1998, when she was just 18 years old. Mya was born in Washington, D.C., where she took dance classes as a child. After briefly losing interest in the art, she returned to dancing in her pre-teens, eventually joining the dance troupe T.W.A. (Tappers With Attitude). She left the group after a short while, heading to New York to study at the Dance Theater of Harlem with Savion Glover, best known as the choreographer/mastermind behind the Broadway spectacular *Bring in da Noise, Bring in da Funk*. Her passion for improvisation made her a favorite of Glover, who had her perform solo at the Kennedy Center.

Although Mya was best known as a dancer, she was also musically inclined, learning how to sing and play the violin as a child. When her father—a professional musician—learned that his daughter could sing and was serious about a musical career, he shopped around the demo tapes, eventually earning the attention of Haqq Islam, president of University Music. Impressed with Mya's audition, Islam signed her to Interscope Records.

Mya and Interscope spent the next two years working on her debut record, hiring an impressive list of collaborators, including Darryl Pearson, Babyface, Diane Warren, Raphael Brown, Wyclef Jean, Missy Elliott, and Sisqo and Moko from Dru Hill. The resulting album was a smooth urban song cycle about love and growing up; it was released in April 1998. Two years later, her more mature second album, *Fear of Flying*, which featured collaborations with Lisa "Left Eye" Lopez, Jadakiss, Wyclef Jean, and Swizz Beatz, arrived. *—Stephen Thomas Erlewine*

● **Mya** / Apr. 21, 1998 / Interscope ✦✦✦✦
Mya's eponymous debut is a smooth, sultry collection of well-crafted contemporary urban soul that is actually richer than the average urban record the late '90s. Part of its success lies with the teenage Mya, who has a voice that is at once innocent and knowing, and part of it lies with her excellent team of producers and songwriters. Executive producer A. Haqq Islam has assembled a stellar behind-the-scenes team—featuring Babyface, Diane Warren, Missy Elliott and members of Dru Hill—that has written and produced a fine set of songs that manage to sound universal and strangely confessional. That's because many of the songs on the record are loosely about a teenager becoming a woman, which is a subject Mya can convincingly sell. There are a few weak moments, to be sure, but overall it's a thoroughly promising debut. *—Stephen Thomas Erlewine*

Fear of Flying / Apr. 25, 2000 / Interscope ✦✦✦
With her follow-up to her commercially successful debut album, Mya has taken a small step towards shedding her squeaky-clean image and embracing a more mature sound. Many of the best moments on *Fear of Flying* come with the help of other artists such as Jadakiss of the Lox and Left-Eye from TLC. With producer Swizz Beatz behind the soundboard for her and rapper Jadakiss making his presence felt on "Best of Me," the single is the album's highlight. "Takin' Me Over" featuring Left-Eye shows that when pushed Mya can hold her weight among R&B heavyweights. Without the energy of collaborators in the mix, many of her solo tracks wander into predictability. The album relies too heavily on tepid ballads such as the title track and "Man of My Life." Yet songs like "Can't Believe," "For the First Time," and "Lie Detector" show an emotional depth that lacked in her debut. Mya's sophomore effort proves that she is a promising young talent, but still has yet to develop the chops necessary to rank among the best of R&B divas. *—Jon Azpiri*

Alicia Myers

b. Detroit, MI
Vocals / Urban, Dance-Pop, Quiet Storm, Funk
Vocalist Alicia Myers was a charter member of Al Hudson & the Soul Partners, which later became One Way, before she departed in the early '80s for a solo career. She earned a Top Ten hit with "You Get the Best From Me (Say, Say, Say)" in 1984, although her strongest record was the gospel/soul "I Want to Thank You" in 1982. Myers made four LPs for MCA during the '80s. *—Ron Wynn*

● **Alicia** / 1981 / MCA ✦✦✦✦✦
When Al Hudson & the Partners (later One Way) recorded their *Happy Feet* LP in 1979, the singer who stood out the most was Alicia Myers. Arguably, she was the best lead vocalist Hudson ever had, which is ironic because One Way enjoyed some of its biggest hits after her departure. In 1979, it seemed inevitable that the passionate, big-voiced Myers would pursue a solo career—and sure enough, MCA released her first solo album, *Alicia*, in 1981. With the help of Kevin McCord (who produced this LP with Al Perkins and wrote most of the material), Myers was able to make her first post-Hudson effort a classic. McCord gave the Detroit singer some infectious funk-dance numbers to work with, including "Reggae Funky Dance" (which isn't reggae at all), "Don't Stop What You're Doin'," and the sweaty "Spirit of the Boogie" (not to be confused with Kool & the Gang's 1975 hit). But most of the songs that McCord provides are ballads and slow jams, which is just as well because Myers really soars on romantic gems like "If You Play Your Cards Right," "Life, Joy and Happiness," and the hit "I Want to Thank You." The latter wasn't Myers' biggest solo hit—that honor goes to 1984's "You Get the Best From Me (Say, Say, Say)," which reached the Top Ten on *Billboard*'s R&B singles chart. But "I Want to Thank You" did enjoy extensive airplay on quiet storm formats. Between Myers' expressive, gospel-influenced belting and McCord's first-rate songwriting, *Alicia* is a consistently impressive solo debut. *—Alex Henderson*

I Fooled You This Time / 1982 / MCA ✦✦✦✦
Featuring the behind-the-scenes input of One Way, Alicia Myers' *Fooled You This Time* included the singer's most enduring hit, "I Want to Thank You" (even though her "You Get the Best From Me (Say, Say, Say)" went into the R&B Top Five). The gospel-ish dance track went to number-37 R&B in fall 1982. The sparse, string-laced ballad "Better Woman or Bigger Fool" echoes Aretha Franklin circa *Sparkle*. The mellow "I Don't Wanta Bore You" has an outstanding string arrangement. ["I Want To Thank You" is on *The Best of One Way: Featuring Al Hudson & Alicia Myers* and Rhino's *Club Classics, Vol. 3*.] *—Ed Hogan*

The Mystics

f. 1958, Brooklyn, NY
Group / Brill Building Pop, Doo Wop
Formed in Brooklyn, New York, in the late '50s, this white doo wop group, consisting of Al Contrera, Al Cracolici, Phil Cracolici, George Galfo, and Bob Ferrante, scored their one and only major national hit in 1959 with the Doc Pomus/Mort Shuman-authored "Hushabye." The beauty of that one hit song, however, coupled with the quality of their subsequent work—even though none of it ever reached a wide audience—left an impression among doo wop enthusiasts that lingered for decades, leading to a comeback in the early '80s.

The Mystics' story is practically an exemplar of the best doo wop groups, in terms of longevity and recognition in the wake of momentary (but significant) chart success. The group had its origins in the Bensonhurst section of Brooklyn, a white ethnic outer borough enclave of New York City, which also spawned such vocal groups as the Passions, the Four-Evers, and the Classics. The group originated as the Overons, a quintet that included Al Cracolici (baritone), Joe Stroble (lead), George Galfo (second tenor), and Bob Ferrante (first tenor). Their original bass left the group in 1956, and Al Contrera was brought in to replace him. The new lineup worked, and when Stroble left sometime later, Phil Cracolici joined as lead singer.

In 1958, they began looking for a new name and picked "the Mystics" after a search of the dictionary. Fate took a hand soon after when an engineer who heard their attempts at a demo record at a local studio hooked them up with manager Jim Gribble, who also represented the Passions. He signed them up immediately upon hearing their clean, radiant sound, and introduced them to Bob & Gene Schwartz, who had a label called Laurie Records. Within two months they had a contract, but the label decided to delay their debut until they had a song that the Schwartzes considered strong enough. The Mystics still didn't have a song to debut with, and in exasperation, it was suggested by Gene that the songwriting team of Doc Pomus & Mort Shuman try and come up with something similar to a then-current chart hit by the Elegants, entitled "Little Star," based on a child's nursery rhyme. The result was "Hushabye," a romantic ballad that utilized a lullaby in much the same way as "Little Star."

"Hushabye" was released in May of 1959 and spent nine weeks of that spring and summer on the charts, rising to number 20. It is one of those "perfect" records, exemplifying a musical genre—the soaring, radiant harmonies were astonishing in their purity, which was matched by the innocence of the song itself. The group attempted a follow-up in the fall of 1959 with "Don't Take the Stars," a livelier, even more ambitious number showing off gorgeous multi-layered harmonies and resplendent in an achingly catchy melody, but somehow the song missed, scraping the lower reaches of the *Billboard* charts. By that time, the group's manager and record label were bringing in other talents to augment the Mystics' sound. Another single released early in 1960, the traditional "All Through the Night" (with a young Paul Simon as second tenor), failed to find a place on the charts at all, and their next single, "The White Cliffs of Dover," featuring falsetto singing by Jay Traynor, later the original Jay of Jay & the Americans, was another non-chart record.

The group's Laurie contract ended in the early '60s, but they continued to perform locally in Brooklyn and remained viable until the later part of the 1960s. They broke up for a time until the growing nostalgia boom of the early '70s resulted in new demands for the group and their performances—Phil Cracolici, Al Cracolici, and Al Contrera continued the name with new members, and in 1981, they cut an album for Ambient Sound that was both commercially successful and critically well received. An appearance on the PBS series *Soundstage*, in an installment devoted to doo wop music during 1982, allowed them to reach a new audience. *—Bruce Eder*

The Mystics Meet the Jarmels / 1990 / Ace ✦✦✦✦✦
All surviving 16 tracks recorded by the Mystics for Laurie Records, in impeccable sound. The only drawback to the excellence of this package (which also includes 14 songs by the Laurie group the Jarmels) is the slightly sketchy notes, which don't do full justice to the group or its influence. The fidelity here is astonishing, almost like being in the studio with the singers, and it puts to shame many domestic reissues of the same period. "Hushabye" is only one of the gems here, and anyone who hasn't heard "Don't Take the Stars" should make it his or her business to hear it on this collection. Amid the expected glowing harmony ballads are a few hard-rocking jump numbers like "Goodbye Mr. Blues," featuring new member Eddie Shotz on lead vocals, which came near the end of their time at Laurie, in 1961. Among the other treasures is an originally unreleased version of Ernie Maresca's "Let Me Steal Your Heart Away," with Paul Simon on lead vocal. (British import) *—Bruce Eder*

● **16 Golden Classics** / Aug. 30, 1994 / Collectables ✦✦✦✦✦
16 Golden Classics is interesting enough for the excellent Top 20 hit "Hushabye" and early guest appearances by Paul Simon and Jay Traynor of Jay & the Americans, but this undeservedly obscure vocal quintet had a consistently enchanting sound and several very good songs. The tinkling xylophone and soft harmonies make the Mystics a real find, and the group's ability to put their stamp on well-worn material redeems even the most obvious covers ("A Sunday Kind of Love," "White Cliffs of Dover"). The Mystics' rockers aren't as strong, but they are few in number, and bonus points are awarded for "Star Crossed Lovers," the group's entry into the teen tragedy sweeps. *16 Golden Classics* compiles practically everything the group recorded for Laurie Records from 1959-1961 and is a rewarding anthology for serious enthusiasts of white doo wop. *—Greg Adams*

N

Najee

b. New York, NY

Sax (Tenor), Sax (Soprano) / Smooth Jazz, Quiet Storm, Crossover Jazz, Urban

One of the best-selling instrumentalists of the late '80s to mid-'90s, Najee has been a consistent favorite in the quiet storm and so-called "smooth jazz" markets. Often compared to Kenny G, George Howard, and Dave Koz, the New Yorker has been greatly influenced by Grover Washington Jr.—although he hasn't been nearly as adventurous. Heavily produced and quite formulaic, Najee's albums have tended to avoid improvisation and strive for commercial radio airplay above all else. Debuting in 1987 with *Najee's Theme*, Najee was an immediate hit in the new adult contemporary (NAC) market. Similiar pop/urban jazz dates like 1988's *Day By Day* and 1990's *Tokyo Blue* did nothing to jeopardize his niche on smooth jazz radio. On-stage, Najee takes some risks and stretches out more—in fact, he has been quoted as saying he'd like to record a straight-ahead jazz or hard bop album eventually. But financially, Najee has had little incentive to pursue such a project. *Morning Tenderness* was released in 1998. *—Alex Henderson*

Tokyo Blue / 1990 / EMI ✦✦✦

Best known for his dynamite soprano, Najee proved his versatility with this disc by using alto and tenor, and even throwing in some tender flute work on the mellow "My Old Friend." He is a strong improvisator, but you could classify *Tokyo Blue* as R&B just as easily as jazz due to the funk grooves (which display a similar formula as George Howard's best work). There are also strong guest appearances by several vocalists here, including Freddie Jackson on Stevie Wonder's "Superwoman." Immensely pleasurable, a fun listen from beginning to end, and recommended for those pop/jazz fans who wanna shake their groove thang. Najee was one of smooth jazz's most consistent proponents of a sub genre that came to be called rhythm and jazz. Top cuts here include "Talkin'," "Tokyo Blue," and "Stay." *—Jonathan Widran*

● **Songs from the Key of Life** / Nov. 7, 1995 / EMI ✦✦✦✦✦

Throughout his career, saxophonist Najee has generally performed crossover music that mixes R&B, jazz, and pop. This particular date is one of his strongest and most jazz-oriented, a well-conceived tribute to Stevie Wonder. Najee (heard on soprano, flute, alto, and tenor) plays instrumental versions of the music from Wonder's famous *Songs From the Key of Life* album, plus several other notable Wonder songs. Assisted by such players as keyboardists George Duke, Ronnie Foster, and Herbie Hancock; guitarist Phil Upchurch; and a top-notch horn section, Najee creates fresh renditions of 21 Stevie Wonder tunes. Highlights include "Love's in Need of Love Today," "Sir Duke," "Knocks Me off My Feet," "If It's Magic," and a medley of "All Day Sucker" and "Easy Goin' Evening." Throughout the memorable set, Najee shows that he can be a strong jazz improviser while still remaining accessible. Recommended. *—Scott Yanow*

Morning Tenderness / Nov. 3, 1998 / Polygram ✦✦✦

The Best of Najee / Nov. 17, 1998 / Blue Note ✦✦✦✦

The Best of Najee contains a selection of 11 highlights from the smooth saxophonist's late-'80s and '90s recordings for EMI/Capitol. There may be a few fan favorites missing, but Najee's career lends itself better to an anthology than most musicians, mainly because it is oriented toward songs, not performances. Consequently, this disc offers a good overview of his career, since it captures not only many of the best-known songs—"For the Love of You," "Tokyo Blue," "Can't Hide Love," "Day By Day," "Betcha Don't Know," "Najee's Theme"—it also gives a good sense of what his albums sound like. An excellent choice for the curious and casual fan. *—Stephen Thomas Erlewine*

Johnny Nash

b. Aug. 19, 1940, Houston, TX

Vocals / Pop-Soul, Soul, Reggae-Pop

Though by no means an artistic innovator on par with contemporaries such as Bob Marley or Jimmy Cliff, singer Johnny Nash nevertheless proved a pivotal force behind the mainstream acceptance of reggae with the international success of his 1972 chart-topper "I Can See Clearly Now." Born in Houston, TX, on August 19, 1940, Nash signed to ABC-Paramount to release his 1957 debut single "A Teenager Sings the Blues," scoring his first chart hit early the following year with a rendition of Doris Day's "A Very Special Love." Marketed as a rival to Johnny Mathis, he even began a film career with 1959's *Take a Giant Step* before his career flagged with a series of little-noticed singles for Warner Bros., Groove, and Argo.

Nash returned to prominence in 1965 when the ballad "Let's Move and Groove Together" reached the R&B Top Five; more importantly, the record became a major hit in Jamaica, where he traveled in 1967 on a promotional tour. During a return trip, he cut the ska-influenced single "Hold Me Tight" at Byron Lee's Federal Studios—a Top Five pop hit on both sides of the Atlantic, the record was issued on his own JAD label, which in early 1970 scored a Top 40 hit with a reggaefied rendition of Sam Cooke's "Cupid" as well. The following year Nash scored a major British hit with his reading of the Bob Marley perennial "Stir It Up"; while living in Britain, he signed to Epic, which in 1972 released his biggest hit, "I Can See Clearly Now," which sat atop the American pop charts for four weeks. Although his popularity at home again dimmed, Nash returned to the U.K. charts in 1975 with his number-one cover of the Little Anthony classic "Tears on My Pillow." *—Jason Ankeny*

Hold Me Tight / 1968 / JAD ✦✦✦

Folk Soul / 1969 / JAD ✦✦✦

The title pretty much sums up the approach Johnny Nash takes to this 1969 LP. Lightly stepping in territory that Bill Withers would explore further in just a few years time, he takes in some standard folk covers and dresses them up in his typically smooth, restrained soulful vocals. The standout track is the one that closes and opens the album, "You Got Soul." The light string accompaniment, the laid-back cool of the lyrics, and the easy shuffling rhythm make the track work best, and it also happens to be the only track actually penned by Johnny Nash. This works as a testament to the songwriting craft he would find his successes with a few years down the line. The album also throws in versions of Elvis Presley's "Love Me Tender," Harry Belafonte's "Island in the Sun," and country and folk staples like "500 Miles" and "Country Boy." His mellow, bongo-laden version of Bob Dylan's "Blowing in the Wind" is one of the few points where he allows his vocals to do their work unrestrained. A final highlight of the record is his take on Sam Cooke's "Chain Gang" where the recording sounds positively ghostly and his soft croon finds a perfect place to nest. Worth the price of the LP surely just for the holographic cover alone, the album presents Johnny Nash, not at his creative peak, but just on the verge of total freedom of expression. On it's own, it is a fine collection of soul music's softer sensibilities. *—Jon Pruett*

I Can See Clearly Now / 1972 / Epic ✦✦✦✦

Singer/songwriter/producer Johnny Nash's million-seller "I Can See Clearly Now" did more to bring the reggae music sound into the mainstream than any other single record up to that point. To be sure, there were previous reggae hits (Millie Small's "My Boy Lollipop," Desmond Dekker & the Aces's 1969 hit "Israelites"), but Nash's buoyant, breezy, optimistic classic proved to be a phenomenal record holding the number-one pop position for four weeks and going to number-one adult contemporary on *Billboard*'s charts in fall 1972. Houston,TX, native Nash had been recording in Jamaica for some years before having his biggest hit. On the *I Can See Clearly Now* album, Nash used members of Bob Marley and the Wailers and recorded several Marley songs: "Stir It Up," the follow-up single, "Comma Comma," the smooth "Guava Jelly," and the Nash/Marley co-written ballad, "You Poured Sugar on Me." The tender album track "(It Was) So Nice While It Lasted" received radio play. Other standouts are the punchy horns-flavored "Ooh Baby You've Been Good to Me" and the lullaby-ish ballad "There Are More Questions Than Answers." It's a tribute to its high quality that *I Can See Clearly Now* was in print almost three decades after its original release. *—Ed Hogan*

My Merry-Go-Round / 1973 / Epic ✦✦✦✦

After the big smash of Johnny Nash's 1972 record, *I Can See Clearly Now*, this follow-up failed to catch on in the public eye in the same manner. However, this album did allow Nash to briefly touch the R&B charts (at number 40) with "Loving You." Expectations aside, this is a fine record that showcases Johnny Nash's sweet, vocal work and some truly soulful arrangements. There is no shortage of the reggae-inflected pop that made him famous, from the fine pop take on Bob Marley's "Nice Time" to the fun timeliness of "What a Groovy Feeling." Although the big, epic arrangement of the title track (complete with light synth work and a children's choir) and the heavy, theatrical synth stabs in the middle of "You Better Stop" may reek of '70s self-importance, this is—under the denim patches and groovy terminology—a soul record. Nowhere is this more evident than on tracks like the aforementioned "You Better Stop," which rolls out like a tune straight out of the Muscle Shoals studios. Meanwhile, "Gonna Open Up My Heart Again" plays like a triumphant, life-affirming anthem. The easy soul of "Loving You" is impossible to deny, while the country/gospel/soul of "Oh Jesus, We're Trying to Get Back to You" is equally affecting. While not a perfect LP from end to end, it truly is an album of sweet, down-home soul music from an under-looked soul performer. *—Jon Pruett*

Celebrate Life / 1974 / Epic ✦✦

● **The Reggae Collection** / Sep. 21, 1993 / Epic ✦✦✦✦

Nash was the first American singer to incorporate reggae rhythms, and as such deserves a lot of credit for paving the way for the acceptance of bona fide Jamaican performers. His own pop-soul-reggae concoctions, though, were often rather watery in comparison to the real thing. This brings together 20 of the reggae-style tracks he cut between 1968 and the mid-'70s, including his hits "Hold Me Tight," "Cupid," and "Stir It Up"; the version of

"I Can See Clearly Now" is an alternate take. This leans too heavily on his 1972-1975 Epic material without enough of his late-'60s work; the small hit "You Got Soul" is missing, and the delightfully light and soaring "Hold Me Tight" towers over most everything else here. Almost half the tracks were previously unreleased or previously unavailable in the U.S. *—Richie Unterberger*

The Best of Johnny Nash / 1996 / Columbia ♦♦♦♦

The Best of Johnny Nash is a terrific collection of Johnny Nash's early-'70s pop-reggae crossover hits, highlighted by "Stir It Up" and "I Can See Clearly Now." *—Stephen Thomas Erlewine*

Syd Nathan

b. Apr. 27, 1904, Cincinnati, OH, **d.** Mar. 5, 1968, Miami Beach, FL

Producer / R&B, Jump Blues

One of the truly eccentric figures of the record industry, Syd Nathan was the founder and head of the Cincinnati-based King Records. Nathan, who founded the label as an extension to his record store, had an uncanny ability to sense the types of music that African-Americans migrating from the South wanted to hear and seized the opportunity to sign some of the best R&B and country acts of the period. Referred to as "Little Caesar" because he was short, fat, and ruled his label like a dictator, the label head constantly screamed and intimidated his artists and employees. Yet, despite his tyrannical behavior, Nathan assembled a remarkably diverse and talented roster of artists. Acts who recorded for King included Tiny Bradshaw, Cleanhead Vinson, Little Willie John, the Midnighters, the "5" Royales, Cowboy Copas, and, most famously, James Brown.

Coming to the label in the late '50s as the lead singer for the Famous Flames, Brown had a stormy relationship with Nathan during his over-ten-year stay at the label (which eventually resulted in a lawsuit that gave Brown a new contract with more autonomy). It is widely known that Nathan was against paying the 5,000-dollar recording fee required to finance Brown's classic 1962 *Live at the Apollo* LP. Though Nathan could be a stubborn man, such oversights were the exception and not the rule as King produced some of the best independent country and R&B music of the '50s and '60s. *—Steve Kurutz*

The Natural Four

f. 1967, San Francisco, CA

Group / Northern Soul, Urban, Soul

The Natural Four began their quest for stardom in Oakland, CA, in the mid-'60s, landing their first deal with a local outfit called Boola Boola Records. Initially, they had two 1969 releases on Boola Boola—"You Did This for Me" and "Why Should We Stop Now"—that did well in the San Francisco/Oakland area. ABC Records took over distribution and pushed "Why Should We Stop Now" to number-31 R&B in 1969. At this junction the group consisted of lead singer Chris James, Allen Richardson, John January, and Al Bowden.

Three more releases followed on ABC: "The Same Thing in Mind," an old Boola Boola track named "I Thought You Were Mine," and a remake of the Temptations' "Message From a Black Man." Nothing approached even the minimal success of "Why Should We Stop Now," and their relationship with ABC ended on a sour note. In 1971, they did a one-off single for Chess Records ("Give a Little Love"), after which Chris James completely overhauled the Natural Four. By 1972, Richardson, January, and Bowden were out and in came Darryl Cannady, Steve Sriplin, and Delmos Whitney. They signed with Curtis Mayfield's Curtom label and released "Things Will Be Better" in 1972; it flopped, as did their second Curtom release, "Eddie You Should Know Better" (a remake from Mayfield's *Superfly* album). The third Curtom release was the charmer "Can This Be Real," which soared to number ten on the R&B charts in 1973 and cracked the pop Top 40. Its successor, "Love That Really Counts" (1974), was too similar to "Can This Be Real" to be taken seriously: same melody, different lyrics.

Leroy Hutson, the first replacement for Curtis Mayfield in the Impressions, produced the Natural Four on Curtom for several promising releases, but four flops followed during 1975-1976: "Heaven Right Here on Earth," "Love's So Wonderful," "It's the Music," and "Free." Curtom released three LPs by the Natural Four: *The Natural Four, Heaven Right Here on Earth,* and *Nightchaser.* The Natural Four certainly deserved better; they had a crisp, smooth lead singer in Chris James, who had a tenor similar to the Spinners' Bobbie Smith but heavier and more melodious. The group had no writers of substance though, and were usually at the mercy of producers and songwriters. Still, the Natural Four voiced some of the sweetest harmony ever laid down. Sequel later compiled all three LPs on two CDs in one sweet package. *—Andrew Hamilton*

Good Vibes / 1970 / ABC ♦♦♦♦

This fine debut includes two of the three singles ("Why Should We Stop Now" and "I Thought You Were Mine") that were initially released on Willie Hoskins' Boola Boola Records. Includes fresh renditions of "Going in Circles," "Message From a Black Man," "Blue Velvet," "Hurt," and "All God's Children Got Soul." ABC omitted "You Did This for Me," the flip of their two Boola Boola singles, and their first ABC single, but this out-of-print album is still a find if you can obtain a copy. *—Andrew Hamilton*

The Natural Four / 1974 / Curtom/Buddah ♦♦♦

The Natural Four's self-titled debut release on Curtom should have introduced the group's distinguishable sound to a vast R&B audience. The album features the vintage soul number "Can This Be Real," and the socially conscious "This Is What's Happening Now," and "Love That Really Counts." The latter is almost identical to "Can This Be Real," save the lyrical content. The entire LP is consistent with the sound of its day. For whatever reasons, the acclaim due to this quartet was undelivered. The serenely composed "Can This Be Real" did peak at number ten on the *Billboard* R&B charts after 18 active weeks, and remains a mainstay on quiet storm radio. If not for the scarce availability of this LP, a host of songs from this collection would receive airplay; "Can This Be Real" is only available through several compilation albums. *—Craig Lytle*

Heaven Right Here on Earth / 1974 / Curtom ♦♦♦

● **The Best of the Natural Four** / Apr. 1, 1999 / Charly ♦♦♦♦

This compilation includes 15 of the Oakland, CA, group's better recordings on Curtom, the label where they charted nationally (pop and R&B) with the smooth, melodic "Can This Be Real?" Unfortunately, that was the extent of their real chart success; many of the others here mimic the hit's groove but never scored as big, and will be new sounds to many who resided outside the listening range of Natural Four-friendly radio stations. Unraveling and playing this disc is akin to opening a Harry and David gift box; the treats include "You Bring Out the Best in Me," "Heaven Right Here on Earth," "Try Love Again," "Get It Over With," "How Have You Been," and a rendition of Curtis Mayfield's "Eddie You Should Know Better," which Mayfield first unleashed on himself via the *Superfly* soundtrack. *—Andrew Hamilton*

Me'Shell NdegéOcello (Michelle Johnson)

b. 1969, Germany

Vocals, Bass / Contemporary R&B, Alternative Pop/Rock, Singer/Songwriter, Club/Dance, Hip-Hop

Although Me'Shell NdegéOcello scored a few hits early in her career, the singer/bassist opted to concentrate subsequently on more challenging material by exploring the politics of race and sex, among other topics. Born Michelle Johnson in 1969 and spending the first few years of her life in Germany (her father was both a military man and a jazz saxophonist), NdegéOcello and her family relocated to Virginia in the early '70s as the youngster developed an interest in music.

As a teenager, NdegéOcello began to play regularly in the clubs of Washington, D.C., but eventually settled down in New York City after a stint of studying music at Howard University. After auditioning for several local bands (one being Living Colour), NdegéOcello struck out on her own (often performing solo, with just a bass, drum machine, and keyboard), and in the early '90s became one of the first female artists signed to Madonna's Maverick label. NdegéOcello's debut release, *Plantation Lullabies,* which spawned the hit "If That's Your Boyfriend (He Wasn't Last Night)," as well as three Grammy nominations, was released in 1993. But it was a duet with John Mellencamp on a cover of Van Morrison's "Wild Night" a year later brought the singer/bassist the most acclaim, as the song became one of the year's biggest hits. NdegéOcello took an extended period before a follow-up recording was issued, but during this time, she collaborated with Chaka Khan on the track "Never Miss the Water," as well as appearing on movie soundtracks (*White Man's Burden, Money Talks*) and on such multi-artist releases as *Ain't Nuthin' But a She Thing* and *Lilith Fair, Vol. 3.* Her 1996 release of a sophomore effort, *Peace Beyond Passion,* failed to match the success of her debut. Another three-year break between albums would occur, during which time a collaboration with rapper Queen Pen surfaced called "Girlfriend." NdegéOcello's third release overall, *Bitter,* was issued in 1999.

She took another three year break and emerged with *Cookie: The Anthropological Mixtape* in June 2002. *—Greg Prato*

Plantation Lullabies / 1993 / Maverick ♦♦♦♦

Me'Shell NdegéOcello's debut album twists and turns through so many genres—R&B, pop, jazz, hip-hop—that it's hard to put a finger on just where she wants to take its 13 songs. That she also spins conventional racial and sexual identity here makes *Plantation Lullabies* an occasionally overwhelming—as well as a vibrantly sophisticated—listen. NdegéOcello defies labels throughout, tagging her slinking and crawling songs with a rubbery flow that's just as rooted in '70s funky soul as it is in '90s hip-hop culture. The best songs here—"If That's Your Boyfriend (He Wasn't Last Night)," "Dred Loc," and "Outside Your Door"—work their way into their grooves with a seamless, and almost uniform, bounce. It can be a bit derivative (for all of NdegéOcello's genre-crossing, she always seems to go back to the same musical blueprint), but most of the time it's just about as boundary-busting and as affecting as '90s R&B gets. *—Michael Gallucci*

Me'Shell NdegéOcello / 1994 / Maverick ♦♦♦

● **Peace Beyond Passion** / Jun. 25, 1996 / Maverick ♦♦♦♦♦

There are times on Me'Shell NdegéOcello's second album where the funky hybrid of R&B and alterna-pop that she laid down on her 1993 debut *Plantation Lullabies* actually seems to take on an ethereal quality. Beats and grooves float effortlessly out of the fluid rhythms, and NdegéOcello herself sings with a soothing reserve that was a little too deliberate on her previous work. And it's a better album because of it. *Peace Beyond Passion* is built around a triumvirate of songs addressing man's inhumanity toward man throughout the ages (with such heavy-handed titles as "Deuteronomy: Niggerman" and "Leviticus: Faggot"), but the real highlights of the set are a wry take on Bill Withers' "Who Is He and What Is He to You" and the ultra-smooth, slow-burning "Stay." It's new age soul that's as spiritually purifying as it is musically sophisticated. *—Michael Gallucci*

Bitter / Aug. 24, 1999 / Maverick ♦♦♦♦

Bitter is an appropriate title for Me'Shell NdegéOcello's third album. Inspired by a torturous romantic relationship, *Bitter* surges with emotions, and most of them are shaded with regret, remorse, or bitterness. Undoubtedly, the relationship was painful, but it has given NdegéOcello an artistic focus missing on her two previous albums. It provides a sorrowful, meditative emotional template that she matches with moody, slow songs that flow into each other. It's the kind of album that demands close listening, otherwise it has the tendency to fade into the background. For some listeners, concentrated listening may be a little difficult, given the bleak emotions of the music, but NdegéOcello's subtle songcraft truly reveals itself upon close inspection. And, with repeated plays, *Bitter* reveals itself as the most personal—and in many ways, most rewarding—album of her career. *—Stephen Thomas Erlewine*

Cookie: The Anthropological Mixtape / Jun. 4, 2002 / Maverick ♦♦♦♦

A few things are proven on *Cookie: The Anthropological Mixtape,* mainly that Me'Shell NdegéOcello can still play bass, and that three years between albums can be worth the wait. Both concepts were tested with her previous disc, *Bitter,* which lacked NdegéOcello's playing skills and floundered under mixed reviews and limited commercial appeal. While her fifth disc may not alleviate the latter, the former should be back around in droves. The attempts at pop songcraft heard on her earlier albums and best represented with the minor hit "If That's Your Boyfriend" seem long gone. That's not to say that *Cookie* is not catchy, just not within the parameters of traditional pop methodology, as she instead brings the funk constantly, mixing it up with a smattering of jazzy sensibilities and hip-hop. Ultimately, the disc is a mix of Afrocentrifugal explosiveness—not only from the music, but also from her powerful lyrics that make the political personal and the personal political. *—Brian O'Neill*

Jimmy Nelson

b. Apr. 17, 1928, Philadelphia, PA

Vocals / R&B, Jump Blues

Heavy-voiced Jimmy Nelson was very briefly a star in 1951, when his downbeat "T-99 Blues" topped the R&B charts for Modern Records' RPM subsidiary. Strangely, he was unable to ever return back to hitdom, despite some very worthy follow-ups. Though he was based out of Houston, Nelson did most of his early recording in California. After debuting on wax in 1948 with a single for Olliet, he cut his only smash, the aforementioned "T-99 Blues," at the Clef Club in Richmond, TX, in 1951, with backup from pianist Peter Rabbit's trio. (The exultant slow blues was covered by bandleader Tiny Bradshaw for King.)

From then on, Nelson did his studio work for RPM in L.A. with a cadre of the city's top session men: saxist Maxwell Davis, pianist Willard McDaniel, guitarist Chuck Norris, bassists Red Callender and Ted Brinson, and drummer Lee Young. For unknown reasons, the ominous "Meet Me With Your Black Dress On," "Second Hand Fool," "Sweetest Little Girl," and the rest failed to repeat for the singer. Nelson made a single for Chess in Houston in 1955 (the typically laid-back "Free and Easy Mind"), ventured next to Ray Dobard's Bay Area-based Music City diskery in 1957 to wax "The Wheel," and tried his luck with a variety of tiny Texas labels during the mid-'60s with no further success. *—Bill Dahl*

● **Jimmy "Mr. T99" Nelson** / 1981 / Ace ✦✦✦✦✦

No CD exists containing Texas shouter Nelson's early-'50s output for Modern, but Ace did assemble a nice vinyl collection of his best material that'll have to suffice (if you can find it) until they get around to issuing it digitally. *—Bill Dahl*

Rockin' and Shoutin' the Blues / Jul. 27, 1999 / Bullseye Blues ✦✦✦✦

Earthy and proud, Jimmy "T99" Nelson's blues is a sax-backed, boastful, and commanding performance. His five-decade career brings him to this Bullseye release as one of the last great blues shouters. Rich Lataille and Doug James from Roomful of Blues with "Sax" Gordon Beadle provide the horns for this legendary vocalist in the tradition of Big Joe Turner. His foundation in proto-R&B jump blues makes the master of the small ensemble swing sound ripe for renewed success. Indeed, Turner mentored Nelson personally, making Nelson a living, direct connection back to these moving, vintage sounds. *—Tom Schulte*

Marc Nelson

b. Philadelphia, PA

Vocals / Contemporary R&B, Urban

Born and raised in Philadelphia, Marc Nelson is the son of Phyllis Nelson, best-known for the dance hit "I Like You." He was one of the original members of Boyz II Men while still a student at Philadelphia's renowned High School of Performing Arts. After getting a solo deal with Capitol, Nelson found a hit with his 1991 cover of Marvin Gaye's "I Want You," and the follow-up "Count on Me" also charted. His *I Want You* album was issued in September 1991, though afterwards, Nelson concentrated on developing his craft as a songwriter. After superstar writer/producer/artist Babyface heard about his talents, Nelson found himself knee-deep in outside projects; he has written songs for Toni Braxton, Brandy, Jon B, Tyrese, Tamia, Keith Washington, Aaron Neville, and Babyface. Nelson also appeared on a duet with Beyoncé Knowles, on the movie soundtrack to *The Best Man* and released his second album (*Chocolate Mood*) in November 1999. The single "15 Minutes" became his biggest hit, denting the Top 40 at number 27. *—Ed Hogan*

● **I Want You** / Sep. 3, 1991 / Capitol ✦✦

Sounding like a poor man's Keith Sweat or a low-rent version of Johnny Gill, the obscure Marc Nelson fluctuated between new jack swing and smooth, romantic neo-soul ballads on his debut album, *I Want You.* Uptempo new jack swing numbers like "It's My World," "Treat Her Right" and "Step to Me" are generic, faceless throwaways—Bobby Brown, Guy and Keith Sweat had already done this sort of thing, and quite honestly, they did a much better job. But the ballads and slow jams tend to be slightly better. The title song (which was released as a single) is a decent remake of Marvin Gaye's 1976 smash, while "Holiday" (not to be confused with Madonna's 1983 hit) and "Summer Love" are pleasant examples of R&B mood music. What Nelson lacks is a firm identity—there's nothing to distinguish him from countless other male urban contemporary singers who made their debut in the early 1990s. *I Want You* didn't sell, and Capitol didn't give Nelson a chance to record a second album. *—Alex Henderson*

Chocolate Mood / Nov. 9, 1999 / Columbia ✦✦

Phyllis Nelson

Vocals / Club/Dance, Hi-NRG

Singer Phyllis Nelson recorded the dance classic "I Like You" on Carrere Records. It was a huge dance hit for the Philadelphia vocalist, charting number-65 R&B in late 1985. Most of her hits can be found on U.K. label Hot Productions' *The Best of Phyllis Nelson: I Like You.* Other Nelson favorites are "Move Closer" and "Don't Stop the Train," among others. Her son, Marc Nelson, was a pre-stardom member of Boyz II Men, had a 1991 number-26 R&B hit with "I Want You," and had a 1999 Columbia album, *Chocolate Mood.* *—Ed Hogan*

Move Closer / 1984 / Carrere ✦✦✦

I Like You / 1985 / Hallmark ✦✦✦

● **The Best of Phyllis Nelson: I Like You** / Aug. 8, 1995 / Hot Productions ✦✦✦✦

N.E.R.D.

Group / Alternative Rap, Hip-Hop, Neo-Soul

The Neptunes are one of the most well-known and respected production teams in the hip-hop community. Comprised of Pharrell Williams and Chad Hugo, they have helped propel the talents of a number of artists since 1997, their punctuating beats and syncopated rhythms fueling a unique sonic aesthetic. N.E.R.D., which stands for No One Ever Really Dies, is their side project, and the debut album *In Search Of...* mixed everything from hard hip-hop beats to black psychedelic pop to classic rock to new wave, bringing a beguiling new sound to the pop landscape. *—Paul Clifford*

● **In Search Of...** / Mar. 12, 2002 / Virgin ✦✦✦✦

N.E.R.D. is nothing if they're not clever, and they brilliantly constructed a backstory to accompany their debut album, *In Search Of....* As every rock critic in the Western world has said in their review of the album, they originally released the record in Europe, then decided it was crap, withdrew it, re-recorded it with a live band, and then released it worldwide. Now this story is probably true—as the first album by the band driven by the powerhouse production team the Neptunes (though these are *not* interchangeable terms, as they went to great lengths to make clear in the promo interviews), there was a lot riding on this record, so it had better be right—but it certainly helped them get valuable press, elevating this record to a near-event level. So, is *In Search Of...* worth the hoopla? Well, pretty much. Musically, it's a lively affair, breaking free of the signature Neptunes approximated-Prince beats, as they borrow heavily from classic soul, breakbeat aesthetics, and postmodern alt-culture, tying it together with live beats. It pretty much deliberately does everything that most modern rap does *not* do, and it's hard not to embrace it for that very fact. Alas, there are flaws, mainly in the raps, which are hardly as nimble as the music; actually, they're rather clumsy and embarrassing, especially since they attempt to cover "socially relevant" issues (e.g., politicians are equated with strippers). Choruses that croon that "She needs me/Because I'm the shit" are hard to stomach, no matter how supple the music is (or how ironic the delivery), but if you can ignore that, *In Search Of...* does provide genuine musical thrills. Although, be forewarned—it's easy to overrate this record simply because it deviates from the norm at a time when nobody deviates from the norm or has deviated from the norm in years. With better lyrics and a little less smirking hipsterism, it could have been the record it was intended to be, but as it stands it's still a pretty terrific listen and one of the most adventurous, intriguing hip-hop albums in a long, long time. *—Stephen Thomas Erlewine*

Frances Nero

b. Detroit, MI

Vocals / Motown, Soul, Northern Soul, Urban

Frances Nero's Motown recording "Keep on Loving Me," released March 11, 1966, is a distinction that can't be taken away. Though not a hit, it's part of Motown's glorious history and so rare it sells for around 250 dollars. Her first performance came in the seventh grade when she appeared on a showcase of WNIC radio in Asheville, NC. Her first professional appearance came while attending high school, playing area gigs with a couple of glee club girls and some members of the school band. Soon, like most groups, members started dropping, the first being the two girls. She later teamed with a guy named Bill who sang with a band called the Tams. After that stint she sang with a band at a supper club owned by a doctor in Greenville, SC.

Her break came shortly after moving to Detroit. In 1965, she entered a talent contest judged by Berry Gordy and took first prize, winning 500 dollars, a dozen red roses, and a one-year Motown recording contract. A few months later she recorded for the first and last time in a Motown recording studio, with William "Mickey" Stevenson, James Dean, and William Weatherspoon writing and producing the sides. She only recorded two sides, and Motown released the single in March of 1966. The song is well-executed, typical of Motown, with the Originals crooning background vocals. WCHB played it every half-hour in Detroit with the announcement that she had won their contest. The label also took the option to extend Nero's contract for an additional year, though months went by while nothing happened—no recording and no performing, since a Motown artist had to be granted permission to perform. When Nero demanded a release, they dropped her. (She also claims she never received any money from Motown.)

After the disappointing experience at Motown, Nero recorded two songs for Shrine Records, which Eddie Singleton and Raynoma Gordy Singleton, Berry's second wife, owned. Shrine never released the recordings, going out of business after two years of flops. She also recorded two songs with Gino Parks on the same label. Again, no release. She continued to sing until her mother's death in 1978, but then cared for ill family members until Britisher Ian Levine approached her. Levine, a Motown fanatic, had already experimented with recording obscure American soul artists with little success. Nero recorded more than a dozen tunes, and earned her first hit with "Footsteps Following Me," which charted at number 17 in the Great Britain. British disc jockeys named it "The Soul Anthem of the Nineties" in 1992. Nero also appeared on many British television shows, including *Top of the Pops* and *The Terry Wogan Show.* In 1996, Hot Productions released *The Very Best of Frances Nero* in the States, consisting of Levine sides recorded in the mid-'80s. She has also released a three-song CD entitled *Love Ride* on her AJA record label. *—Andrew Hamilton*

● **The Very Best of Frances Nero** / Sep. 17, 1996 / Hot Productions ✦✦✦

Frances Nero has the distinction of being the only ex-Motowner produced by Ian Levine to have a record that made any significant impact on a chart. Her "Footsteps Keep Following Me" charted at number 17 on *Billboard*'s U.K. chart and was number three on Radio One's play list, holding steady for nine weeks. British DJs in 1992 named it "The

Soul Anthem of the Nineties." Before this, Frances' claim to fame consisted of one obscure solo release on Motown in 1966, "Keep on Lovin' Me"; the record sold the grand total of 10,000 copies. This, unlike Levine's productions for more well-known Motown acts, is a worthy release since you have no past hits by Nero for comparison. *—Andrew Hamilton*

The Neville Brothers

f. 1977, New Orleans, LA

Group / Funk, Adult Contemporary, Soul, New Orleans R&B, R&B

Throughout their long careers as both solo performers and as members of the group that bore their family name, the Neville Brothers proudly carried the torch of their native New Orleans' rich R&B legacy. Although the four siblings—Arthur, Charles, Aaron, and Cyril—did not officially unite under the Neville Brothers aegis until 1977, all had crossed musical paths in the past, while also enjoying success with other unrelated projects: Eldest brother Art was the first to tackle a recording career, when in 1954 his high school band the Hawketts cut "Mardi Gras Mambo," a song that later became the annual carnival's unofficial anthem. Both Aaron and Charles later joined the Hawketts as well, and when Art joined the Navy in 1958, he handed Aaron the group's vocal reins.

Two years later, Aaron scored his first solo hit, "Over You"; in 1966, he notched a pop smash with the classic "Tell It Like It Is," a lush ballad showcasing his gossamer vocals. Art, meanwhile, returned from the service to begin his own solo career, and recorded a series of regional hits like "Cha Dooky Doo," "Zing Zing," and "Oo-Whee Baby." In 1967, he formed Art Neville & the Sounds, which included both Aaron and Charles as featured vocalists and quickly became a sensation on the local club circuit.

In 1968 producer Allen Toussaint hired the group as the house band for his Sansu Enterprises; minus Aaron and Charles, the Sounds evolved into a highly regarded rhythm section which backed artists as diverse as Lee Dorsey, Robert Palmer, and LaBelle before eventually finding fame on their own as the Meters. Consequently, Aaron resumed his solo career, although with only sporadic success; as a result, he also worked as a dock hand. Charles, meanwhile, relocated to New York City, where his skills as a saxophonist led to tenures with a variety of jazz units; after returning to New Orleans, he was arrested for possession of marijuana and served a three-year sentence at the Angola Prison Farm. In 1975, the Meters backed the Wild Tchoupitoulas, a group led by the Nevilles' uncle, George "Big Chief Jolly" Landry. Both Aaron and Charles were enlisted for the session, as was youngest brother Cyril; when the Meters disbanded the following year, the four brothers backed the Tchoupitoulas on tour, and in 1977 they officially banded together as the Neville Brothers. Despite their gift for intricate four-part harmonies, their self-titled 1978 debut unsuccessfully cast the vocal quartet as a disco band, and following a dismal response they were dropped by their label, Capitol.

The Nevilles spent the following three years without a contract, but after signing with A&M, fan Bette Midler helped secure the services of producer Joel Dorn for 1981's superior *Fiyo on the Bayou*, which spotlighted Aaron's angelic tenor on standards like "Mona Lisa" and "The Ten Commandments of Love" along with renditions of "Iko Iko" and "Brother John." Despite widespread critical acclaim, the album sold poorly, and again the Nevilles were cut loose from their contract. After signing to the tiny Black Top label, they issued 1984's *Neville-Ization*, an incendiary live set recorded at the Crescent City landmark Tipitina's which featured Duke Ellington's "Caravan" and Aaron's perennial "Tell It Like It Is" alongside the brothers' own "Africa" and "Fear, Hate, Envy, Jealousy."

After another concert album, 1987's *Live at Tipitina's*, the Nevilles signed with EMI and returned to the studio in 1987 with *Uptown*, which again met with commercial failure despite cameo appearances from Keith Richards, Jerry Garcia, and Carlos Santana. In 1989, they re-signed to A&M and recruited the services of famed New Orleans producer Daniel Lanois; the atmospheric *Yellow Moon*, the group's finest hour, finally earned them success on the charts, thanks in part to the anthemic single "Sister Rosa." 1990's *Brother's Keeper* fared even better, no doubt spurred by Aaron's concurrent success with Linda Ronstadt on the smash duet "Don't Know Much."

In subsequent years, Aaron reignited his solo career while also remaining with his brothers; while the Nevilles retained their cult following with LPs like 1992's *Family Groove*, 1994's *Live on Planet Earth*, and 1996's *Mitakuye Oyasin Oyasin/All My Relations*, Aaron scored a Top Ten hit in 1991 with the single "Everybody Plays the Fool," taken from the Ronstadt-produced *Warm Your Heart*. In 1993, he notched a minor hit with "Don't Take Away My Heaven" from the LP *The Grand Tour*, a year later, he found success with "I Fall to Pieces," a duet with country star Trisha Yearwood. In 1990, Charles also issued the jazz collection *Charles Neville & Diversity*.

In addition, a second generation of Nevilles also began making their mark on music; in 1988, Aaron's son Ivan, a member of Keith Richards' backing band the Xpensive Winos, released his solo debut, *If My Ancestors Could See Me Now*. The Neville Brothers legacy continued in 1999 with *Valence Street*. *—Jason Ankeny*

Fiyo on the Bayou / Apr. 1981 / A&M ✦✦✦✦✦

This is a brilliant updating of the New Orleans R&B sound to include strains of Cajun, rock, and reggae on standards ranging from "Hey Pocky Way" to "The Ten Commandments of Love" and "Sitting in Limbo." *—William Ruhlmann*

Neville-Ization / Jun. 1984 / Demon ✦✦✦

It took Black Top Records two years to put this record out after the Neville Brothers recorded it live at Tipitina's in New Orleans in September, 1982, and one reason may be that it presents a mediocre, going-through-the-motions set. At their best, the Nevilles achieve a transcendent musical mixture, and even at the level of mere professionalism they're an impressive unit, but this just isn't the live album of which they are capable.*—William Ruhlmann*

★ **Treacherous: A History of the Neville Brothers** / 1986 / Rhino ✦✦✦✦✦

At the dawn of the 21st century, the Neville Brothers may well be the greatest living institution of New Orleans R&B, but it took a long time for them to achieve such a lofty status, and the talents of Aaron, Art, Charles, and Cyril Neville had been scattered through a number of different groups (and a number of different record labels) over the space of three decades before they began to finally gain the nationwide recognition they richly deserved in the mid-'80s. *Treacherous: A History of the Neville Brothers* was the first compilation album to paint a reasonably accurate picture of the full scope of the Nevilles' accomplishment, and it still stands as the best introduction to their body of work. While it predates their acclaimed collaborations with producer Daniel Lanois on *Yellow Moon* and *Brother's Keeper*, it's a near-flawless representation of the Neville Brothers' earlier period (both as individuals and collectively), blending classic New Orleans R&B, smooth balladry, traditional second-line rhythms, potent Crescent City funk, and plenty of stops in between into a mighty and potent gumbo of joyous groove. *Treacherous* also cherry-picks the highlights from several unfortunately uneven albums, and flows more comfortably than many of the group's "real" albums. Anyone with even a passing interest in New Orleans music needs to check out the Neville Brothers, and this collection is as good a starter as anyone could hope for. *—Mark Deming*

Uptown / Mar. 1987 / EMI ✦✦

The Neville Brothers displayed their eclecticism on this lone EMI album. They played with some high class guest stars, including Branford Marsalis, Jerry Garcia, Ronnie Montrose, Carlos Santana, and Keith Richards. But despite these excellent musicians and the Nevilles' usual tight playing and exuberant collective vocals, once more, the album failed to either get them a huge hit or faithfully re-create the quality of their live shows. *—Ron Wynn*

Yellow Moon / 1989 / A&M ✦✦✦✦

The Neville Brothers made a bid for pop/rock stardom with this well-produced album for A&M, their first under a new pact with the label inked in the late '80s. It was certainly as solid as any they cut for A&M; the vocals were both nicely arranged and expertly performed, the arrangements were basically solid, and the selections were intelligently picked and sequenced. The album charted and remained there for many weeks, while the Nevilles toured and generated lots of interest. It didn't become a hit, but it did respectably and represents perhaps their finest overall pop LP. *—Ron Wynn*

Brother's Keeper / Jul. 1990 / A&M ✦✦✦

Why doesn't more R&B sound like this? Although hampered by a poor mix, *Brother's Keeper* is nevertheless a classic example of what makes the Neville Brothers so good—and so frustrating. Tracks like the booty-shaking funk of "Brother Jake" or the gospel-tinged "Steer Me Right" are full of soulful vocals and wonderful harmonies. Aaron Neville's timeless voice is displayed beautifully on "Fearless," where he is joined by Linda Ronstadt for one of the strongest tracks on the record. The Neville Brothers' ecumenical spirituality permeates every second of *Brother's Keeper*, making for a few awkward moments (like the head-scratching opener "Brother Blood," for example), but a few moments of true sublimity (as when Art Neville spits "Pro choice-no choice/We're sending our sons and daughters to their slaughter" on "Sons and Daughters"). The pop material on *Brother's Keeper*, such as Link Wray's "Fallin' Rain," works well, but other tracks, like "River of Life," seem forced. If the Neville Brothers showed a little discretion with regard to their lyrics and cut a couple tracks, they would have had a much stronger album, which in a way is as good a statement as one could make about their entire career. *—Daniel Gioffre*

Treacherous Too: A History of the Neville Brothers, Vol. 2 (1955–1987) / Feb. 1, 1991 / Rhino ✦✦✦✦✦

Okay, there's no such thing as secondhand revelation, but the Neville Brothers had more than enough stray tracks from their decades of local music-making around New Orleans to justify this second, single-disc follow-up to Rhino's first Nevilles history. There's more of an emphasis on novelty material here, but once again you can hear the roots of the Nevilles' cross-genre appeal in pop, R&B, and soul music dating back to the 1950s. Since most of these songs were recorded as singles, they have an immediate surface appeal, but repeated listenings also bring out the sounds of the tight session bands (including members of the Meters) who backed up the Nevilles. Actually, it's only the five 1980s tracks from just-OK albums like *Neville-Ization* and *Uptown* that keep this collection from classic status, not the older stuff. *—William Ruhlmann*

Live on Planet Earth / Apr. 19, 1994 / A&M ✦✦✦

Clearly, this is intended to be the definitive live document of a band that has always been defined by its live work. Clocking in at 71 minutes, the album was culled from a world tour. The rhythm section of drummer Willie Green and bassist Tony Hall keeps up a steady groove from song to song, and the Nevilles trade off lead and harmony vocals on original songs that range across their career and add everything from Bob Marley compositions to "Love the One You're With" and "Amazing Grace." They Neville-ize all comers, throwing them into the pot and coming out with a tasty gumbo. If there's anything missing, it's the small club atmosphere from which the Nevilles emerged: this is a wide-screen treatment of a music that gained impact from its intimacy but now seeks to form a global conga line. *—William Ruhlmann*

Mitakuye Oyasin Oyasin/All My Relations / May 14, 1996 / A&M ✦✦✦

The Neville Brothers have made a family affair of their first studio album in four years, writing much of the material themselves and co-producing the record with James Stroud. As a result, they are making less of an effort to secure a pop hit this time, even though they do throw in a little rap and a funky cover of Bill Withers' "Ain't No Sunshine." But part of the reason they tend to be more interesting live than on record is that, beyond being well-meaning, they haven't got much to say. Most of the songs here are homilies to brotherhood, responsibility, and environmentalism, set against tracks that evoke Brazilian music, mbaqanga, reggae, R&B, and soul and are heavy on percussion and horns. Occasionally, as on the respectable cover of the Grateful Dead's "Fire of the Mountain," with guest guitarist Bob Weir, or on Aaron Neville's typically ethereal "Saved By the Grace of Your Love," the music transcends both the message and the groove. But this is an album of small pleasures rather than the larger statement it seems intended to be. *—William Ruhlmann*

● **The Very Best of the Neville Brothers** / Jan. 14, 1997 / Rhino ✦✦✦✦✦

This 16-track compilation focusing almost exclusively on the period spanning the late '70s to the late '80s. A couple of Aaron Neville's big '60s hits ("Tell It like It Is" and "Over

You") are thrown in as well, as are a couple of cuts from the Wild Tchoupitoulas' 1976 album. Some may argue that the Nevilles' sprawling output is too difficult to condense into a single disc. On the other hand, given how often they're criticized for underachieving on record, this is a pretty suitable purchase for someone whose interest only runs deep enough for one anthology. *—Richie Unterberger*

Live at Tipitina's 1982 / Aug. 18, 1998 / Rhino ♦♦♦♦♦
This two-CD set gathers both previously released albums from the Neville Brothers' September 1982 gigs at local New Orleans hangout Tipitina's, 1984's *Neville-Ization/Live at Tipitina's* and 1987's *Nevillization II/Live at Tipitina's*, and strives to roll them into one complete, concise work. The only problem is that although the albums were recorded similarly, they were eventually released under different circumstances: the second part was augmented with studio-sweetened instruments and audience noises, and at times the overdubs are glaringly, and intrusively, obvious. Still, the first half of *Live at Tipitina's* (the original *Neville-Ization* one) remains one of the Crescent City's most representative documents—"Fever," "Tell It Like It Is" and "Fear, Hate, Envy, Jealousy" just plain sizzle—and one of the Neville Brothers' most revered volumes (as well as one of the best live albums of the '80s). Think of the sequel as an extended, if not totally successful, bonus disc. *—Michael Gallucci*

Valence Street / Feb. 16, 1999 / Columbia ♦♦♦♦
For their Columbia Records debut, the Neville Brothers returned to a classic production and songwriting style more typical of their early years than of their work of the 1980s and '90s, and they named it after the street they grew up on to signal their renewed focus on local concerns. Gone was the wet, murky sound mix of Daniel Lanois, replaced by dry aural clarity and precise instrument placement in a production by the brothers themselves. While retaining the second-line funk rhythms of New Orleans, their music hewed much more to a traditional R&B/soul sound, with little dabbling in world music. The title track, written by Charles, was even an instrumental that wouldn't have sounded out of place on a Meters album, and you could also say that about "Real Funk," co-written by Art. Though the brothers traded off vocals and Cyril turned in an excellent performance on the soulful romantic ballad "Until We Meet Again," co-written by Charles, Aaron's voice had long since become so identifiable beyond the group that his vocals on songs like "Little Piece of Heaven," the standard "If I Had a Hammer," and "Give Me a Reason," and even in occasional asides on other songs, tended to stick out the way Michael Jackson used to on Jackson's albums, rendering him, through no one's fault, a solo artist within a group and hurting the record's overall balance. *— William Ruhlmann*

Uptown Rulin': The Best of the Neville Brothers / Aug. 24, 1999 / Interscope ♦♦♦♦
The Neville Brothers had always been critic's favorites, but never more so than during their tenure at A&M Records during the late '80s and early '90s. They released their first album, *Yellow Moon*, for the label in 1989, a few years after the acclaimed Rhino compilation *Treacherous: A History of the Neville Brothers* appeared on the shelves. *Treacherous* contained selections from all the Neville Brothers—not just group recordings but side-projects and solo cuts—and helped cement their reputation among record collectors and critics, which in turn set the stage for the enthusiastic reception of *Yellow Moon*. That enthusiasm failed to wane over the next few years, as each subsequent album was greeted by critics with open arms. The problem was, each record was pretty much the same. With producer Daniel Lanois, the Nevilles attempted to create grand, mythical albums, heavy with import and meaning. Lanois didn't abandon his trademark hazy, murkily mysterious production—a style that wasn't necessarily suited for the organic Nevilles, even if it did result in some evocative sonic hybrids. Consequently, each of the A&M albums functioned best as a series of moments, even if they were designed to work as individual albums (the prototype, *Yellow Moon*, unsurprisingly standing as the lone exception to the rule). That's why *Uptown Rulin': The Best Of* is a solid addition to their catalog. By collecting highlights from the A&M albums, it offers fans a good summary of these intriguing but mixed years. It isn't on the same level as *Treacherous* or its sequel, but it's a nice addendum to fans of that groundbreaking compilation. *—Stephen Thomas Erlewine*

Aaron Neville

b. Jan. 24, 1941, New Orleans, LA
Vocals / Pop-Soul, R&B, Soul, New Orleans R&B, Adult Contemporary, Country-Soul
Although Aaron Neville is often compared to singer Sam Cooke in terms of sheer vocal refinement, he has a voice and style uniquely his own. He is well known as part of the New Orleans sound of the Neville Brothers. Yet, aside from the 1967 number-one R&B hit "Tell It Like It Is," few have heard his incredible early solo recordings. Many of the first recordings of Neville, in the early and mid-'60s, were arranged, produced, and often written by the brilliant Allen Toussaint—another talent only later being really appreciated. Most of these sides were cut for the Minit and, later, Parlo labels. Songs like "She Took You for a Ride" and "You Think You're So Smart" on Parlo are masterpieces. While his more recent work, including that with Linda Ronstadt, makes for pleasant listening, it lacks the sheer persuasion of his early songs.

Neville has re-recorded his early work often, and it is important to hear the originals. The early sides are just waiting to be heard. Neville has ventured more into other waters besides R&B. *The Grand Tour* (1993) included a remake of a George Jones song that got Neville a little country attention, and he announced plans in 1994 to do a complete country album. He was also one of several R&B artists who teamed with country stars for the *Rhythm Country and Blues* session. Neville was paired with Trisha Yearwood, and the duo also performed together in a benefit concert for the LP held in Los Angeles in April 1994. The LP made history by debuting in the Top Ten on the pop, R&B, and country charts. *—Michael Erlewine and Ron Wynn*

Tell It Like It Is / 1967 / Par-Lo ♦♦♦♦
Here are 11 of Neville's best Parlo cuts, including those mentioned above on one CD, including his biggest solo smash from 1966 and more songs in the same style. It's sublime stuff. *—Bill Dahl*

Orchid in the Storm / Dec. 1986 / Rhino ♦♦♦♦♦
Aaron Neville's wondrous singing on this poorly distributed EP was overlooked by many still unaware of his stunning falsetto. But Neville covered doo wop, soul, and even country on this project, singing with a soaring conviction and poignancy that made it a delightful, though short, set. Rhino has thankfully reissued it on CD. It's actually closer to representing Neville's real style than his recent much-hyped, overproduced pop records. *—Ron Wynn*

● **Tell It Like It Is: Golden Classics** / 1989 / Collectables ♦♦♦♦♦
Here is one of many collections covering Aaron Neville's superb early R&B and soul classics. The burly Neville, whose delicate, feathery voice stands in vivid contrast to his muscular body, made great heartache ballads, uptempo wailers, and brilliantly sung originals for tiny New Orleans labels, often not even getting widespread soul airplay. Now that's he's hot property, the domestic anthologies are coming out left and right. This one is as good as any other, although for my money the import labels have still done a better job on early Neville than the American companies. *—Ron Wynn*

Greatest Hits / 1990 / Curb ♦♦♦
Early New Orleans soul from velvet-voiced Aaron Neville, including the smooth, aching "Tell It Like It Is" and the gutsy, declarative "Over You," a shuffling R&B number. The eight other selections, especially "Jail House," "Hard Nut to Crack," and "Since You're Gone," offers an insightful overview of the golden tenor whose vocal abilities get more amazing with time. *—Andrew Hamilton*

My Greatest Gift / 1991 / Rounder ♦♦♦
The songs that made Neville famous among soul and R&B fans were done years before he became a recognized star, for tiny Southern labels. The 12 tracks on this anthology were recorded in the late '60s, when Neville's soaring falsetto, emphatic delivery and gut-wrenching treatments were locked out of the pop mainstream. Although this isn't the definitive version of "Tell It Like It Is," it's far from a throwaway. On "Love Letters," "Hercules," "Mojo Hannah," and "Where Is My Baby," Aaron Neville tackled the soul mountain and conquered it. *—Ron Wynn*

Warm Your Heart / Jun. 11, 1991 / A&M ♦♦♦
When Aaron Neville signed with A&M in the early '90s, optimists were hoping for some five-star soul gems along the lines of his classic '60s recordings. Instead, his first A&M date, *Warm Your Heart*, found the veteran New Orleans singer taking a much more pop-minded approach, with generally decent results. While Neville didn't abandon soul music, this CD made it clear that A&M was intent on making him a major hit in the pop market (which had been exposed to him in 1989 thanks to his duets with Linda Ronstadt). Though hardly in a class with such classics as "Tell It Like It Is" and "She Took You for a Ride," tracks like the haunting "That's the Way She Loves," the gritty "Angola Bound," and a remake of the Main Ingredient's "Everybody Plays the Fool" showed that Neville still had plenty of warmth and charisma. But although this is far from a bad album, it must be stressed that a collection of his '60s classics would be a much wiser investment. *—Alex Henderson*

The Grand Tour / 1993 / A&M ♦♦
Although Steve Lindsay tries a little too hard to make *The Grand Tour* appeal to everyone, Aaron Neville manages to make the album another solid addition to his latter-day catalog. Lindsay keeps the sound of the album strictly in the mainstream, piling on layers of keyboards, vocalists and drum machines which neuter any rootsy elements in the music. This is particularly unfortunate, since the selection of songs is interesting, ranging from George Jones and Chuck Berry to Bob Dylan and Leonard Cohen. Nevertheless, Neville rises to the material, not the production, giving the music an emotional core. Not every teaming works, but enough songs hit the target to make *The Grand Tour* worthwhile for dedicated fans. *—Stephen Thomas Erlewine*

Aaron Neville's Soulful Christmas / Oct. 5, 1993 / A&M ♦♦♦♦

The Tattooed Heart / 1995 / A&M ♦♦♦
Aaron Neville is an unlikely example of a '60s soul hero who managed to reinvent himself as a '90s pop star without compromising his integrity. Drawing on pop as well as the type of New Orleans soul that put him on the map, Neville proved that he could once again be quite marketable. Like *Warm Your Heart*, *The Tattooed Heart* isn't on a par with Neville's early efforts, but nonetheless has a lot going for it. Though not breathtaking, material ranging from the soul ballad "Show Some Emotion" to the earthy rock number "Down Into Muddy Water" and the reggae-influenced hit "Can't Stop My Heart from Loving You (The Rain Song)" is honest and enjoyable. Another high point of this CD is an inspired remake of Bill Withers' "Use Me." Because an urban contemporary approach didn't interest him, the "new" Neville received little support from black radio—but on pop stations, he'd become a high priority. *—Alex Henderson*

To Make Me Who I Am / Oct. 14, 1997 / A&M ♦♦♦
Thanks to a few inspired collaborations, *To Make Me Who I Am* finds Aaron Neville continuing his streak of solid contemporary R&B albums. Divided between co-written originals by Neville and covers of professional songwriters like Babyface and Diane Warren, *To Make Me Who I Am* is filled with strong material, highlighted by two duets with Linda Ronstadt ("First Time Ever I Saw Your Face," "Please Remember Me"). Longtime fans might find the polished surfaces of the album a bit too slick, but Neville's singing remains elegant and graceful, helping to push the album past its MOR leanings. *—Stephen Thomas Erlewine*

The Very Best of Aaron Neville / Jan. 11, 2000 / A&M ♦♦♦♦
In some ways, *The Very Best of Aaron Neville* is a very welcome addition to his catalog, since it's the first collection to touch on all areas of Neville's long career. However, it winds up being a bit unsatisfying, not just because it only has one cut from the Neville Brothers, but because his New Orleans R&B and down-home soul just don't fit that well with his smooth, cleanly produced latter-day work. Then again, the compilers didn't spend too

much time with the early recordings, since the collection contains only a handful of R&B nuggets (including, of course, "Tell It Like It Is," plus "Over You") before settling into the '80s and '90s albums. It's not a bad summary of those albums, actually, containing such hits as "Don't Know Much" and "Everybody Plays the Fool," plus a good cross-section of album tracks and lesser-known cuts, such as his version of "Stardust" with Rob Wasserman. As such, *The Very Best of Aaron Neville* is recommended primarily to fans of his later recordings. Listeners who prefer the early R&B work or the Neville Brothers should look to compilations of that material, since they won't be satiated by this disc. *—Stephen Thomas Erlewine*

● **Ultimate Collection** / Aug. 21, 2001 / Hip-O ♦♦♦♦♦

Although it not surprisingly shares a whopping nine tracks with 2000's *The Very Best of Aaron Neville*, 2001's *Ultimate Collection* cherry picks from a far wider range of years (1960-1997) than the A&M period which was used almost exclusively for the former anthology. As such, it's a considerably broader and ultimately a better representation of the Neville Brothers' famed muscular singer with the impossibly angelic falsetto voice. The compilation kicks off with the string-laden "To Make Me Who I Am," a sort of capsule of Neville's tough life, complete with a heartfelt spoken coda which would have made a perfect album closer, certainly better than "Tell It Like It Is," his first crossover hit from 1966. The track does make a good lead-in to "Don't Know Much," the singer's smash duet with Linda Ronstadt though. From there the disc gradually shifts moods and years, smartly bunching most of the upbeat '60s selections (including some interesting obscurities like "Why Worry," the original B-side of "Tell It Like It Is") toward the middle. The collection also rescues a pair of gorgeous R&B covers ("Pledging My Love" and "For Your Precious Love") from an obscure 1985 Joel Dorn-produced EP, as well as "The 10 Commandments of Love," included in the difficult to find Neville Brothers' 1981 release, *Fiyo on the Bayou*. It smartly plays down the rest of their music which is easily available elsewhere, but does include Aaron's dramatic rendition of Sam Cooke's "A Change Is Gonna Come," one of his most stirring performances from *Yellow Moon*. Thankfully the album doesn't get bogged down in some of the slick and sappy concoctions Neville often gravitates to. While the rather forced rock & roll of Chuck Berry's "You Never Can Tell" doesn't quite fit the predominantly languorous mood, and the track list strangely omits Neville's version of George Jones' "The Grand Tour" or Skylark's "Wildflower"—both of which remain concert staples—this is a stunning and consistently enjoyable representation of one of the most distinctive and memorable voices in American music. *—Hal Horowitz*

Humdinger / May 7, 2002 / EMI ♦♦♦

For those listeners who admire the angelic voice of the inimitable Aaron Neville, this European release should be of interest. The vocalist, who records and tours with the other Neville Brothers, has long been considered a living treasure in his hometown of New Orleans. He first gained national prominence with the single, "Over You," followed by the blockbuster "Tell It Like It Is." Now people all over the world recognize the beautiful high-tenor voice of Aaron Neville. The CD *Humdinger* contains the early work that Neville did with Allen Toussaint. The R&B star of piano and song also worked in the production end of music and collaborated with Neville on a collection of songs that showcased the golden voice of the singer. The songs were originally released as a compilation in 1986. While the lyrics may be a bit strange, there is no doubting the beauty of the voice. One may wonder what these two giants of New Orleans music were thinking with lines like: "You take a bumble bee and match him with a doorbell, and whatcha got? Humdinger." But with a voice like Aaron Neville's, the lyrics may hardly matter. *—Rose of Sharon Witmer*

Art Neville

b. Dec. 17, 1937, New Orleans, LA

Vocals, Keyboards, Piano, Organ / R&B, Soul, Funk, New Orleans R&B

As a founding member of the Meters and Neville Brothers, New Orleans vocalist and keyboardist Art Neville helped immeasurably to shape the contemporary New Orleans funk sound. Neville's first band, the Hawketts, tasted local success in 1954 with the carnival perennial "Mardi Gras Mambo" on Chess. He cut some nice solo singles for Specialty during the late '50s, notably "Cha Dooky-Doo," as well as contributing two choruses of storming piano to Jerry Byrne's 1958 classic "Lights Out." "All These Things," a gentle ballad, also did well locally in 1962 on the Instant logo. He assembled the Meters in the mid-'60s and the instrumental quartet proved the Crescent City's answer to the MG's until their 1977 breakup. That's when Art and his siblings formed the Neville Brothers, who went on to reign as the leading musical export from New Orleans. *—Bill Dahl*

● **That Old Time Rock 'n' Roll** / 1992 / Specialty ♦♦♦♦♦

Here are 20 of his earliest solo sides, from the late '50s, a few of them previously unissued. A lot of this New Orleans R&B is derivative of Fats Domino and Lloyd Price, but the harder-rocking, funkier sides point to his more individual work of later decades. "Cha Dooky-Doo," "Arabian Love Call," and a previously unreleased duet with Larry Williams on "Rockin' Pneumonia and the Boogie-Woogie Flu" are typically fun and infectious New Orleans R&B novelties; "I'm a Fool to Care" gives us a taste of his soulful ballad singing. *—Richie Unterberger*

Mardi Gras Rock & Roll / Ace ♦♦♦

Art Neville cut some of this CD's most pertinent tracks right before serving in the Navy in the late '50s and never got the chance to properly promote the records that came out on Art Rupe's Specialty label. Perennial Mardi Gras favorite "Mardi Gras Mambo," which has reportedly sold more than a million copies over the years; "Cha Dooky-Doo," a regional hit; and "What's Going On," a local favorite, are the main attractions. The rest have that same Cajun flavor, making it an essential for lovers of Big Easy music. *—Andrew Hamilton*

New Birth

f. 1963

Group / Quiet Storm, Disco, Funk, Soul

Formed by Tony Churchill and music-industry veteran Harvey Fuqua, New Birth was originally named the Nite-Liters. As the Nite-Liters, they enjoyed chart action with three R&B hits: "K-Jee," "Afro-Strut," and "Pull Together." Of the three, "K-Jee" was the most successful, peaking at number 17 during a 13-week run.

The roots of the band lie with Leslie and Melvin Wilson, who were gospel singers living in Muskegon, MI. After moving on to Detroit in the late '60s, their interest remained centered in gospel. Melvin Wilson eventually met the Nite-Liters, who at the time were backing Motown artists, and expressed the possibility that he and his brother Leslie could perform with them. As fate would have it, the two brothers became acquainted with former Marvelette Anne Bogan, who introduced them to Fuqua. He had three groups under his tutelage: Love Peace & Happiness (of which Leslie and Melvin became members), the Nite-Liters, and New Birth. All but two members of New Birth had left the group around this time, leaving just Londee Loren and Bobby Downs. The three groups toured, backed each other up, and ultimately merged into one, with New Birth the name of the new group.

Leslie, with his feisty vocals, and Melvin, with his more serene appeal, emerged as the primary lead singers. New Birth's first release was the R&B Top Ten single "I Can Understand It." Led by Leslie Wilson's intense vocals and reminiscent of Bobby Womack, the single zoomed up the charts, peaking at number four after only 12 weeks. In January of 1974 they released "It's Been a Long Time," one of their celebrated hits and another Top Ten entry. That single was followed by the classic, soulful ballad "Wildflower." During this time, the group was living in California, which presented problems; from egotism associated with the lights of Tinseltown to group-management problems, the band's best interests began to suffer. Consequently, New Birth terminated its affiliation with their founder and producer Fuqua, manager Jerry Weintraub, and RCA Records. In mid-1975 they signed with Buddah Records and immediately recorded their first and only number R&B one, "Dream Merchant." They recorded just one album for Buddah, however, before signing with Warner Bros. and later Ariola. In 1977, Leslie and Melvin Wilson left the group, and by 1979 the rest of the group had disbanded. However, in 1994, Leslie and Melvin reformed the group and began performing at venues around the nation. *—Craig Lytle*

New Birth / 1970 / RCA ♦♦♦♦

Ain't No Big Thing, But It's Growing / 1971 / RCA ♦♦♦♦

Comin' Together / 1972 / RCA ♦♦♦

Birth Day / 1973 / RCA ♦♦♦

Under the banner the New Birth, from which they would later drop "the", this was the first album from the self-contained band; they came charging out of the starting gate with the gritty track "I Can Understand It." With vocals comparable to Bobby Womack, who also penned the number for himself, Leslie Wilson stepped into the lyric with total conviction. His vibrancy is augmented by a funky backing track, primarily a rumbling bass and soulful backing vocals. The single peaked at number four on the *Billboard* R&B charts after 12 weeks. The follow-up release was "Until It's Time for You to Go." Far from its predecessor, its arrangement is geared more toward a crossover audience, as it was previously a number-40 hit for Elvis Presley in 1972. It peaked at number 21 inside of ten weeks on the R&B charts for the New Birth. Nothing else made any chart noise from this album, but that does not represent the quality of this project. "Got to Get a Knutt" has a rather racy title, and rightly so. But the song takes on different themes within its mostly musical journey, including animated remarks taken from commercial jingles, riddles and the like. In addition to the urban-flavored "Theme from Buck & the Preacher" included on this album, the group gives its own rendition of the classic "Stop, Look, Listen (To Your Heart)," which does not live up to the original by the Stylistics and is the only marginal track. *—Craig Lytle*

Comin' from All Ends / 1974 / RCA ♦♦

This New Birth album almost single-handedly brought the momentum built by their previous LPs to a screeching halt. To say this uninteresting production failed to take them to next level is a gross understatement. It's not horrible, it's just *blah*. These tracks may have been hitting in the studio, bouncing out of the big speakers, but on vinyl, at home, on a Philco Phonograph, forget it. The synthesizer-ridden "I Wash My Hands of the Whole Damn Deal" got pushed as a single but failed to bring home the bacon. "Take This Train to Freedom" attempts to jar one's social consciousness, but it's so irritating the message is missed. "Do It Again" and the title track, "Comin' from All Ends," are like most of the other tracks—they're too predictable, almost as if they were produced by a computer programmed with New Birth data. *—Andrew Hamilton*

It's Been a Long Time / 1974 / RCA Victor ♦♦♦♦

Under the guiding hand of Harvey Fuqua (former Moonglow, record label owner, and Motown producer/songwriter), the New Birth cut some of the '70s' grittiest and funkiest sides. Three male vocalists sang lead—Melvin & Leslie Wilson and Alan Frye—and were complemented by the atmospheric soprano of Londee Loren. Their rendition of Skylark's "Wildflower" put them in demand on the concert circuit; people just had to see the group responsible for transforming a good pop song into a gutbucket, yet tender, emotionally charged drama. The male vocalists outdo themselves, and Loren's skyscraping screams are delicately placed throughout. The other monster here, "It's Been Such a Long Time," captivates from the beginning with its heartbeat rhythm. The lead singing is Bobby Womack-influenced, but with a stark freshness and newness, and the interaction between the lead and the background near the refrains will have you bouncing. Other keepers are "Heaven Says" and the soul-dripping "Pains of Love," while Londee gets a chance to solo on "I'd Spend My Whole Life Loving You." New Birth hit their stride on this one. *—Andrew Hamilton*

Blind Baby / 1975 / Buddah ✦✦✦
Relaunching themselves as New Birth, dropping "The" from their name following a break with their manager, and subsequently transitioning to a new label, the band rebounded with the first of two LPs cut for Buddah in 1975. Hoping to revitalize themselves with the ascendant Nite-Liters contingent coming back to the front of the group, joining new members Ben Boxtel, Roger Voice, and James Hall, the revamp proved right on the mark as the first single from *Blind Baby*, "Dream Merchant," gave New Birth their first and only number-one R&B hit that summer. With sweet melody and subtle arrangements, "Dream Merchant" informs this album, setting the bar that the band would use in crafting a set that remains sleepy and dreamy throughout, with only a couple of exceptions. Both the title track and the closing "Epilogue" utilized sexy spoken word over quiet melody, while "Forever" emerges as another well-constructed ballad. But, as comfortable as New Birth are across these tracks, so are they across more traditional funk numbers, most notably the off-kilter "Blind Man" and brass-heavy "Granddaddy." *Blind Baby* ultimately marked the end of an era for all prior incarnations of New Birth. "Dream Merchant" marked the pinnacle of their achievement and became the trail marker for their descent. Although the band would continue to record for nearly a half decade more, they wouldn't come so close, or sound so good again. *—Amy Hanson*

Golden Classics / Oct. 17, 1989 / Collectables ✦✦✦✦✦

● **The Very Best of the New Birth: Where Soul Meets Funk** / Nov. 7, 1995 / RCA ✦✦✦✦✦
A comprehensive package of producer Harvey Fuqua's concept, New Birth Incorporated, which consisted of the Nite-Liters, Love Peace & Happiness and New Birth. The Nite-Liters' "K-Jee" was the first hit out the box, scoring before New Birth, the lively, festival sounding instrumental has enjoyed an amazing longevity. It's still popular at halftimes of football games, and on classic radio shows. Love, Peace & Happiness which featured Ann Bogan, and two Wilson Brothers, who also sang with New Birth, are represented by one number, a soul-dripped version of "I Don't Want to Do Wrong," the Gladys Knight & the Pips smash. New Birth is well represented, their deep soul rendition of "Dream Merchant" still sends shivers up and down my spine, as does "WildFlower" and the popish "It's Impossible," sung by Londee Loren. Attempts at disco are less pleasing, but on this package the songs "I Wash My Hands of the Whole Damn Deal," "Comin' from All Ends" and "Keep on Doin' It" are more palatable. *—Andrew Hamilton*

Birth Day/It's Been a Long Time / Sep. 26, 2000 / Collectables ✦✦✦

Blind Baby/Comin' from All Ends / Sep. 26, 2000 / Collectables ✦✦✦

Greatest Funk Classics / Mar. 20, 2001 / RCA ✦✦✦✦
The New Birth revue's (the Nite-Liters and Love Peace & Happiness) potential went practically unfulfilled in the grand scheme of music. Talented and equipped with soulful vocalists such as the Wilson brothers (Leslie and Melvin), Londee Loren, Alan Frey, and Anne Bogan (who not only participated on some New Birth recordings, but also with Leslie & Melvin Wilson as Love, Peace & Happiness, who recorded two RCA albums), the world should have been theirs for the taking. This compilation lives up to its name and is primarily funky. Culled from recordings by New Birth, the Nite-Liters, and Love, Peace & Happiness, these are 18 gutbucket funky soul numbers. Tracks of note: "Con-Funk-Shun," whose title was adopted by another funk band; a gritty remake (even grittier than Bobby Womack's) of "I Can Understand It"; "Theme From Buck and the Preacher"; "Granddaddy"; "I'm Back"; and "Lonely Room" from Love, Peace & Happiness' *Love Is Stronger* album. The most obvious omits are the plums: "It's Been Such a Long Time," "Wildflower," "Dream Merchant," and "It's Impossible." Even so, *Greatest Funk Classics* is a straight-up winner. *—Andrew Hamilton*

New Edition

f. 1982, Boston, MA

Group / New Jack Swing, Urban, Teen Pop, Hip-Hop

New Edition's early, Jackson 5-inspired material made them the forerunners of two generations of teen pop (most of which was geared to white audiences). As they matured and progressed, they laid much of the groundwork for the fusion of hip-hop and R&B known as new jack swing. In fact, after New Edition drifted apart, all of its members had at least some significant success outside the group as part of the new jack movement, which helped ensure that their original incarnation would be remembered for much more than the bubblegum urban soul that made their name.

New Edition was formed in the Roxbury section of Boston, MA, by Ricky Bell, Michael Bivins, and Bobby Brown, who began singing together in 1978 while still in elementary school, hoping to perform for pocket cash. They eventually recruited friend Ralph Tresvant as a fourth member, and after winning a talent show in 1980, also added Ronnie DeVoe. More talent show victories followed, including a prestigious gig at the local Strand Theater, where they performed the Jackson 5's "The Love You Save." They were discovered by writer/producer/impresario Maurice Starr, who signed the group to his small Streetwise label in hopes of launching a Jackson 5 phenomenon for the '80s. "Candy Girl," a song Starr co-wrote for the group, was released as their first single in 1983, when the members ranged in age from 13 to 15. Despite a lack of major-label interest in the group, "Candy Girl" was a smash, topping the R&B charts. Their debut album, also titled *Candy Girl*, spawned two more R&B hits in "Popcorn Love" and "Is This the End?," and MCA offered the group a deal. Starr, however, wanted the group to remain with Streetwise; New Edition summarily fired him as their manager and signed with MCA. Starr attempted to sue the group for their name, unsuccessfully claiming that "New Edition" actually referred to a whole new style of pop music he'd created. Starr, of course, would go on to strike it rich with a similar concept, assembling a quintet of white teenagers he dubbed New Kids on the Block.

New Edition, meanwhile, released their eponymous MCA debut in 1984 and scored their biggest pop hit with the Top Five smash "Cool It Now," which ended with a short rap section. The Ray Parker Jr.-penned "Mr. Telephone Man" soon became their third R&B chart-topper, and the group had reached full-fledged teen idol status. Yet they were growing up fast, as demonstrated on their next album, 1985's *All for Love*. Not only were their voices changing, but their material was becoming more adult, with harder-edged funk and more mature romantic ballads. Later that year, they also released a holiday album, *Christmas All Over the World*, and struck an endorsement deal with Coke. However, rumors of Brown's growing dissatisfaction proved true and he left for a solo career in 1986. Temporarily down to a quartet, the rest of the group recorded the covers album *Under the Blue Moon*, a set of vintage doo wop and R&B numbers from the '50s and '60s; it produced a hit revival of the Penguins' "Earth Angel."

Brown's replacement came in the form of Johnny Gill, a deep-voiced friend of the group who'd been recording as a solo artist without much luck. Gill made his debut on the 1989 album *Heart Break*, which found New Edition working with star producers Jimmy Jam & Terry Lewis. The move paid immediate dividends, as they scored several R&B hits from the album, including the number one "Can You Stand the Rain." Meanwhile, Brown had become a superstar with his second album, the new jack swing landmark *Don't Be Cruel*. Feeling vindicated by *Heart Break*, New Edition split up to work on other projects. Gill returned to his solo career, with considerably more success this time around, and Tresvant also went solo. The remainder of the group teamed as Bell Biv DeVoe and wound up having greater success than anyone save Brown; their debut album, *Poison*, was another new jack style-setter and Bivins' interest in developing new talent gave Boyz II Men their big break.

By the mid-'90s, new jack swing was giving way to new fusions of hip-hop and soul that were alternately more organic or aggressive. Although their status as innovators was secure, many of the New Edition splinter acts had a hard time keeping up and maintaining their career momentum. Thus, given their individually positive reputations, it made sense for the group to announce its triumphant reunion, with all six members participating in what was essentially an R&B supergroup. The public loved the idea; when the comeback album *Home Again* was finally released in 1996, it debuted at number one, and the first single, "Hit Me Off," was a smash, hitting number one on the R&B charts. The follow-up, "I'm Still in Love With You," was another big hit, and the group embarked on a blockbuster tour that, while popular, found relationships between some of the members fraying. After the tour, New Edition returned to their various prior projects, with the prospect of any future reunions looking dim. *—Steve Huey*

Candy Girl / 1983 / Warlock ✦✦✦✦
When Maurice Starr uncovered the talents of a Roxbury vocal group in the early '80s, he envisioned a second Jackson 5. That was the direction he took New Edition in in its early days, and this album includes such overt Jackson 5 ripoffs as "Candy Girl" and the title track. None of the toughness or street touches that emerged on their later material were evident on this slick, pop-oriented session. Ralph Tresvant, Ronald DeVoe, Michael Bivins, Ricky Bell and Bobby Brown were all aged 13 to 15 when this was released. *—Ron Wynn*

New Edition / 1984 / MCA ✦✦✦✦✦
Maurice Starr's vision peaked with this second album by New Edition. They were now thoroughly Jackson 5 clones and were reaping similar commercial dividends thanks to the teen angst cuts "Cool It Now" and "Mr. Telephone Man." They earned their first platinum album, one Top Ten hit and another Top 20 pop single (both songs topped the R&B charts) and were among the hottest acts in either pop or R&B during this stretch. *—Ron Wynn*

All for Love / 1985 / MCA ✦✦✦
New Edition's voices and focus were changing in the late '80s. They'd moved away from the kiddie-pop/soul of the early '80s and were singing harder, adult love material and cutting uptempo funk tracks, although there weren't many of those on this session. While sometimes things got a bit sappy lyrically and seemed repetitive at other times, the group compensated with their strongest harmonies and vocal performances to date. *—Ron Wynn*

Under the Blue Moon / 1986 / MCA ✦✦✦
Changes were on the horizon for New Edition. They had become enormously successful by aping the Jackson 5, but were undergoing internal trauma as original member Bobby Brown bolted amid rumors of dissatisfaction with the group's direction. This album featured their covers of 1950s and '60s standards and was among early examples of the retro trend now so prominent in urban contemporary camps. While they didn't do this type of material nearly as well as the Force M.D.'s, they at least brought fresh attention to such songs as "Earth Angel" and "Tears on My Pillow." *—Ron Wynn*

Heart Break / 1989 / MCA ✦✦✦✦
This album marked New Edition's growth and maturity due in part to the production work of Jimmy Jam & Terry Lewis, and the addition of group newcomer Johnny Gill. The first single from the much anticipated album was "If Isn't Love." With its percussive rhythm and frigid keyboard effects, Ralph Tresvant applies his rigidly smooth tenor to this midtempo dance cut. The single peaked at numbers two and seven on the *Billboard* R&B and pop charts, respectively. The second single, "You're Not My Kind of Girl," has a more grueling beat. In an uptempo style and with its appealing melody, Tresvant imparts a urgent cry on this apologetic lyric. Gill enhances the track with his amplified background vocals and lyrical sighs. The single peaked at number two on the *Billboard* R&B charts. "Can You Stand the Rain" came next. Unlike any ballad the group has ever embraced, it sailed up the charts to the number-one spot. Primarily led by Gill and Tresvant, whose vocals mutually complement one another, Ricky Bell injects his vocal plea, and Michael Bivins has a small rap part. With an aggressive rhythm, "Crucial" resembles more of a Minneapolis sound in the vein of the Time and Alexander O'Neal. That does not negate the substance of the song. It peaked at number four. The fifth single was "N.E. Heartbreak." From the staccato cadence of the verse to the reeling-style bridge to the energized vamp, the single had much to offer. It peaked at 13. Two unreleased notables are the ballads "I'm Coming Home" and "Boys to Men." This is a outstanding album overall. *—Craig Lytle*

- **Greatest Hits, Vol. 1** / Oct. 1, 1991 / MCA ✦✦✦✦✦
For anyone who missed New Edition in either its Jackson 5 imitation phase or final days as a funkier, more aggressive urban contemporary vocal group with a slight dance influence, this collection contains examples of both incarnations. Kiddie-pop hits such as "Candy Girl," "Cool It Now," and "Mr. Telephone Man" are included, along with their final hits "If It Isn't Love," "Can You Stand the Rain," and the appropriately titled "Is This the End." This anthology shows how dominant New Edition was during the 1980s and early '90s. *—Ron Wynn*

Home Again / Sep. 10, 1996 / MCA ✦✦✦✦
When Bobby Brown, Ralph Tresvant, Ricky Bell, Michael Bivins, Ronnie DeVoe and Johnny Gill entered the studio for a full-fledged New Edition reunion in 1996, reactions ranged from excitement to skepticism. Would the chemistry still be there? With Brown, Tresvant and Gill (the only one who wasn't an original member) having put so much energy into their solo careers and the other three having enjoyed success as Bell Biv DeVoe, could they make a cohesive statement as a sextet? But in fact, they did prove cohesive on *Home Again*, the first New Edition album since 1988's *Heartbreak* and Brown's first with the group since 1986's *Under the Blue Moon*. Not remarkable but certainly decent, this CD is a long way from the type of Jackson 5-influenced bubblegum soul/pop Edition was recording in the '80s. Listeners wondered whether Brown or BBD's album would have the greatest impact on this project, and the truth is that both were influential. Some of the songs bring to mind BBD's in-your-face aggression, while others benefit from Brown's charisma. A few of the songs sound contrived, but in general, *Home* makes us glad the singers decided to reunite. *—Alex Henderson*

New Edition Solo Hits / Dec. 3, 1996 / MCA ✦✦✦
A 12-track compilation of four tracks each by spin-off acts of New Edition seems like a strange way to pick up their work, to say the least. Still, if you want some hits by Bobby Brown, Bell Biv DeVoe, and Ralph Tresvant, and are for some reason uninterested in scoping out their albums or waiting for their one-artist-only greatest-hits collections, this is a succinct mini-primer of one of the most successful clans in urban contemporary music. *—Richie Unterberger*

Lost in Love: The Best of Slow Jams / Nov. 17, 1998 / MCA ✦✦✦
A mixed bag ranging from the sexy to the bubblegum, *Lost In Love* looks back on some of the ballads and slow jams that New Edition members recorded from 1984-1996. To say that members of the R&B/pop group evolved radically during that 12-year period would be an understatement. The CD gets off to a very bubblegum start on early numbers like "Lost In Love" and "With You All the Way" (both of which are way too sappy for their own good), but one hears an edgier, more mature New Edition on "Boys To Men" (which the group Boyz II Men named itself after) and "Can You Stand the Rain" (both of which Jimmy Jam & Terry Lewis produced for 1989's *Heart Break*). Some of the album's best offerings are songs New Edition members recorded apart from the group, including Bell Biv DeVoe's "When Will I See You Smile Again" and Bobby Brown's 1988 hits "Roni" and "Rock Wit'cha." One curious omission is the 1984 smash "Mr. Telephone Man," and where's Johnny Gill's "My My My"? *Lost In Love* is hardly the last word on ballads by New Edition members, and it would be a mistake to think that everything on the CD is great. Nonetheless, this is a generally enjoyable collection that contains more pluses than minuses. *—Alex Henderson*

All the Number Ones / May 9, 2000 / Hip-O ✦✦✦✦✦
An excellent idea that might be slightly disappointing in the execution, *All the Number Ones* collects 18 singles that topped *Billboard* magazine's R&B charts, all performed either by New Edition or its members in their various outside projects. That results in a terrific, endlessly playable collection of urban pop-soul and new jack swing, but it also means that several of the collective's best-known songs are left off simply because they didn't top the R&B charts. Missing in action are Bobby Brown's "Roni" and "Rock Wit'cha," Bell Biv DeVoe's "Do Me!," Johnny Gill's "Fairweather Friend," and Ralph Tresvant's "Stone Cold Gentleman" and "Do What I Gotta Do," plus a bevy of New Edition hits. In fact, it might have been an even better idea to gather the biggest hits by the various New Edition spin-offs and leave the parent group's output alone; such an approach would have erased the contrast between the early New Edition bubblegum singles that lead off this collection and the grittier, funkier new jack hits that follow. Still, at least these omissions are due to the compilation's stated intent (collecting *All the Number Ones* and nothing else), rather than a record-company marketing tactic. Even casual fans will undoubtedly miss at least a couple of the aforementioned hits, but really, what *is* here makes for a great listen and a fine introduction to one of the most influential R&B family trees of the '80s and early '90s. *—Steve Huey*

New York City

f. 1972, New York, NY

Group / Smooth Soul, Philly Soul, Soul

New York City scored the first time out with "I'm Doing Fine Now," so on the surface the group may have seemed like just a bunch of guys who got together, had a hit, and disbanded. Members John Brown and Claude Johnson had illustrious histories in music. Brown sang with the Five Satins, the Cadillacs, and filled in with the Moonglows when founder and member Harvey Fuqua called. Johnson sang with the Genies and was Don of Don & Juan. Tim McQueen (lead singer) and Eddie Schell, like Brown and Johnson, had sung in countless groups around New York City.

Before New York City, the four had recorded and gigged under the name Tri-Boro Exchange—a city bridge that links three boroughs (it was suggested by producer Wes Farrell). One single was released on Buddah Records. Farrell convinced Philly legend Thom Bell to produce some tracks for the group, including "I'm Doing Fine Now," written by Sherman Marshall and Bell—it went to number-17 pop in 1973. On the strength of the hit they started making personal appearances. Backing them on the road was the Big Apple Band, whose members included the late Bernard Edwards and Nile Rodgers, who later formed Chic. None of the follow-ups came close to repeating their initial success. "Make Me Twice the Man," written by McQueen, stalled at number 93, while "Quick, Fast, in a Hurry" peaked at number 79. Chicago's Notations remade the McQueen song, a ballad that suggested their deep doo wop roots. The Chelsea label released two albums and a handful of singles, and then it was all over for New York City. *—Andrew Hamilton*

I'm Doin' Fine Now / 1973 / Chelsea ✦✦✦

Soulful Road / 1974 / Chelsea ✦✦✦

- **I'm Doin' Fine Now** / Aug. 5, 1993 / Collectables ✦✦✦✦
This CD contains tracks from New York City's debut Chelsea Records LP. The Thom Bell productions mimic the sides he was creating for the Spinners and others. Bell uses female backing like he did with the Spinners, at times making them more prominent in the mix than the group members. New York City's lead singer Tim McQueen has an expressive voice suitable for pop and sounds comfortable with Bell's orchestrations. The group's roots, however, were heavy in doo wop, as member John Brown sang with the Five Satins. The other members were Tim McQueen, Ed Shell, and Claude Johnson. "I'm Doing Fine Now" invaded the pop Top 20, nesting at number 17. Thom Bell & Linda Creed's "Quick, Fast, in a Hurry" sounds too formulaic; its chart progress halted at number 79. McQueen wrote their third release, "Make Me Twice the Man" which fared worse at number 97; yet this was more New York City's sound than Bell Productions'. Both of the above pop flops reached higher rungs on *Billboard*'s R&B chart. "Uncle James" has to be a Spinners reject. The song has Philippe Wynne written all over it; all it's missing is a Wynne-type testifying sermon. *—Andrew Hamilton*

- **The Best of New York City: I'm Doin' Fine Now** / 1995 / Sequel ✦✦✦✦✦
Best of New York City: I'm Doin' Fine Now is the final word on this unfairly underrated band, who, despite their name and place of origin, created some of the finest Philly soul of the era. The opening number "I'm Doin' Fine Now" certainly stands as one of the great forgotten singles of the genre (and the '70s in general). Both of the band's albums—1973's *I'm Doing Fine Now* and 1974's *Soulful Road*—are included in their entirety and the liner notes give a good overview of the band's career. Although nothing really can compete with the absolute brilliance of "I'm Doin' Fine Now," New York City's material was surprisingly strong on both albums, with standouts like "Make Me Twice the Man" and "Quick, Fast, in a Hurry." This collection is absolutely essential for any fan of '70s soul. *—Chris Woodstra*

New York Port Authority

db. 1978

Group / Disco, Funk, Soul

Named after the largest bus terminal in the U.S., New York Port Authority (NYPA) was an obscure funk/soul/disco band that was active in the Big Apple in the late '70s. The six-man band signed with Holland-Dozier-Holland's Invictus label in 1977, when its members included singer/bassist Reginald A. Brown, guitarist Melvin Miller Jr., trumpeter/percussionist Rodney J. Brown, keyboardist/trombonist Stafford M. Floyd, alto saxophonist John O. Hargrove, and drummer Monwell E. Lowndes. That year, Invictus released NYPA's debut album, *Three Thousand Miles From Home*, which was produced by Brian Holland and contained the single "I Don't Want to Work Today." The LP didn't sell, and in 1978, NYPA broke up without ever recording a second album. *—Alex Henderson*

- **Three Thousand Miles From Home** / 1978 / Invictus ✦✦✦
In 1977, Brian Holland of Holland-Dozier-Holland fame produced this debut album by the New York Port Authority, a little-known funk-soul-disco band that named itself after the U.S.' largest bus terminal. The band probably reasoned that its name would be an attention-getter, at least among New Yorkers; in those days, the Port Authority and its surrounding neighborhood, Times Square, had a terrible reputation. If you mentioned Times Square to a New York police officer in 1977, you would have heard a long dissertation about all the crime, drugs, prostitution, pornography, and muggings that the area had to offer. (In the 1990s, New York Mayor Rudy Guilliani cleaned Times Square up considerably.) Less interesting than the band's name is its music. *Three Thousand Miles From Home* isn't a bad album, but it's an unremarkable and uneven one. Nonetheless, this LP has its moments. The silky "Home on a Rainy Day" is an appealing Philly soul-type offering, while the single "I Don't Want to Work Today" is a catchy working man's lament. The sweaty funk tune "I Got It" isn't bad, and the glossy "Rainbow" has a Tavares-like appeal. But the other tunes are pedestrian and forgettable. NYPA's first album (which was also its last) has been out of print since the late '70s, and it is unlikely that the record will ever be reissued on CD. *—Alex Henderson*

Booker Newberry III

b. Jan. 19, 1956, Youngstown, OH

Vocals, Keyboards / Club/Dance, Urban

Singer/keyboardist Booker Newberry III was a member of mid-'70s soul groups Sweet Thunder ("Baby I Need Your Love Today") and Impact. Born January 19, 1956, in Youngstown, OH, Newberry began his professional singing career in the group Mystic Nights around 1971. Moving to Philadelphia, PA, he became the lead singer of the band Sweet Thunder, which also included drummer John Aaron, bassist Rudell Alexander, and guitarist Charles Buie. Signing with Philly-based label WMOT Records, the group's single, "Baby I Need Your Love Today" b/w "I Don't Care What You Say," stirred interest and was picked up for distribution by Berkeley, CA-based Fantasy Records. The group recorded three LPs, *Above The Clouds* (1976), *Sweet Thunder* (1978), and *Horizons* (1979, listed the single "I Leave You Stronger," which went to number-63 R&B in late 1979).

Newberry joined another WMOT Records group, Impact, who is best known for the dance hits "Give a Broken Heart a Break" and "Rainy Days Stormy Nights." The singer signed with Neil Bogart's Casablanca Records in 1983 and his single "Love Town" was a Top 20 U.K. hit. The *Love Town* LP was issued the same year. He has also recorded for Malaco Records and Omni Records (the LP *Take a Piece of Me*). —*Ed Hogan*

● **Love Town** / 1995 / Hot ♦♦♦
A fine set of early-'80s soul, ex-Sweet Thunder vocalist Booker Newberry III's solo debut contains many of the standard synthesized dance effects one would expect, but also delivers plentiful doses of strong melody and gritty vocals. The summery title track, despite somewhat odd lyrics, is a real pleaser with Bobby Eli's contagious production and Newberry's accessible delivery, while the Nick Martinelli-headed "I Get Romantic" is on par with efforts by the likes of Shalamar and Loose Ends. The singer's husky tenor often brings to mind Teddy Pendergrass, but with a bit of a smoother edge. It's unfortunate that he didn't have the backing that contemporary Luther Vandross did, as he has just as much of a unique charisma that would have served R&B radio well. With only a single release stateside, the album remained a Europe-only release until Hot Productions' 1994 CD issue. —*Justin M. Kantor*

The Newcomers

f. 1968, **db.** 1974
Group / Soul, Memphis Soul
Between 1969 and 1974, the Newcomers made half a dozen singles for the Stax label, scoring a few minor R&B hits with "Pin the Tail on the Donkey," "Keep an Eye on Your Close Friends," and "(Too Little in Common to Be Lovers) Too Much Going to Say Goodbye." These releases were reflective of the general trends at Stax in the label's latter days in that they were long on competent emulation of prevailing soul trends, but short on basic personality. Motown and the Jackson 5 are clearly the model for some of the early singles, just as clearly as Philly soul and the O'Jays are the model for some of the later ones. Pleasantly unmemorable, nine of their tracks made their way onto a compilation CD in 1996 that also featured material by an earlier '60s Stax soul group, the Astors. —*Richie Unterberger*

Next Movement

f. 1971, Chicago, IL
Group / Urban, Soul
The Next Movement were a Chicago R&B vocal group that was formed in 1971 on the city's South Side. The lineup was Alonzo Pickens, Samuel Thomas Jr., Guy Sutton, Earl Shelby, and Carnell Haywood. They recorded a 1980 album *The Next Movement* for the local GEC label that plays like a last luscious piece of delight, appearing in the waning years of Chicago soul. The midtempo groover "Never Stop Dancing" received radio play in Chicago and other markets. With amazing string and horn arrangements by Tom Washington anchored by a tight rhythm section featuring drummer Quinton Joseph, it was quite a debut. The standouts are the two ballads "How Did We Get to This" and "Kid Stuff," as well as the zesty, sparkling "Crazy 'Bout Your Lovin'." Working with music vet Gus Redmond, the Next Movement had their only *Billboard* single, the smooth dance number "All I Do," issued on the Navarre-distributed Nuance label in 1994. The group's release on New York-based Prelude Records, "Let's Work It Out," became a club hit and a dance classic. In the '90s, the Next Movement began working with manager Winfred Hatch performing R&B/soul tunes in Vegas clubs. They also recorded sides for Al Bell's Bellmark Records and appeared on the soundtrack of *Original Gangstas*, a 1996 movie that reunited many '70s-era black action movie stars. During the '90s, Japanese label P-Vine reissued their 1980 LP on CD as *Never Stop Dancing*. "Let's Work It Out" can be found on *Star Funk, Vol. 16* and *Rare Preludes, Vol. 3*. —*Ed Hogan*

● **The Next Movement** / 1980 / GEC ♦♦♦

Maxine Nightingale

b. Nov. 2, 1952, Wembley, England
Vocals / Disco, Urban
Born in November 1952, in the west London suburb of Wembley, England, Maxine Nightingale was just 16 years old when she began singing in her school band. Enjoying the spotlight so much, she swiftly made the transition to singing in a more professional capacity, appearing in a handful of local clubs and ultimately coming to the attention of Pye Records. Signing with the label, she recorded a handful of singles, including "Do Not Push Me Baby" and 1971's "Love on Borrowed Time." While neither song became a commercial hotshot, the experience only furthered the young singer's drive to succeed in her field.

Stepping out of the clubs, Nightingale spent the early '70s in theater, exploring her vocal development through roles in the era's hottest musical stage shows, including *Jesus Christ Superstar, Hair, Godspell*, as well as the well-received London play *Savages*, before pairing with the songwriter/production team J. Vincent Edwards & Pierre Tubbs in 1975. They proved the perfect pair to showcase her outstanding vocals, and after she signed to United Artists and debuted with their "Right Back Where We Started From," she found herself with a Top Ten U.K. hit in November 1975. The song proved even more popular in the States as the disco sizzler scored Nightingale a number-two pop hit in early 1976.

Backed by an outstanding assortment of session musicians and continually partnered with songwriters who were able to best direct her voice, Nightingale's 1976 debut LP, *Right Back Where We Started From*, also proved to be a hit in the United States, although, oddly, it fell far short of expectations in England. With four singles, including the title track and fellow chartmate "Gotta Be the One," the album reached number 65 in the U.S. The following year brought the Denny Diante-produced *Night Life* album, which placed "Love Hit Me" (another U.K. hit) and a cover of the Delfonics' "Didn't I Blow Your Mind This Time" into heavy club rotation. *Lead Me On* followed in 1979, bringing her another U.S. chart appearance, this time at number five with the title single, released on Windsong. The *Bittersweet* LP followed the next year, leaving room for a fine compilation, *It's a Beautiful Thing*, to round up all the hits in 1982.

That same year also saw Nightingale reach further peaks when she paired with R&B singer Jimmy Ruffin, best known for his 1966 standard "What Becomes of the Brokenhearted," for the tender duet "Turn to Me." The song never registered on the pop charts, but in November gave Nightingale her first R&B Top 20 debut. Continuing to perform live, Nightingale's focus shifted through the 1980s and 1990s from disco and pop to sultry, smoky jazz vocals. But, always conscious of her fans, she continued to pepper her live sets with some of her finest hits. —*Amy Hanson*

● **Right Back Where We Started From** / 1976 / United Artists ♦♦♦
At age 22, the former *Jesus Christ Superstar* starlet scored a major international smash with the driving R&B ballad "Right Back Where We Started From." Pushed to greater immortality by its appearance in the Paul Newman movie *Slapshot*, the song led into Nightingale's solo debut album with a promise that the remainder of the set readily lived up to. Nightingale's infectiously smoky vocals are powerful enough even to overcome some surprisingly weak material. "Everytime I See a Butterfly" really is as mawkish as its title suggests, but Nightingale transforms it into a thing of fragile beauty regardless. She is at her strongest, however, with lyrics that naturally adapt themselves to her sensuous vocal intonation. "(I Think I Wanna) Possess You" and "You Got the Love" are both moody showcases for her dynamic range, while the number-53 hit, "You Gotta Be the One" has a infectious allure all of its own. In the long run Nightingale never truly lived up to the promise that the title track suggested, and it is ironic that, of her three charting albums, her debut was the least successful. It is her finest by far. —*Amy Hanson*

Love Hit Me / 1977 / United Artists ♦♦♦

Night Life / 1977 / United Artists ♦♦♦

It's a Beautiful Thing / 1982 / Highrise ♦♦♦

98°

f. Los Angeles, CA
Group / Urban, Teen Pop, Adult Contemporary
The sweet urban soul quartet 98° was formed in Los Angeles by four former Ohio residents: brothers Nick and Drew Lachey plus Jeff Timmons and Justin Jeffre. Timmons was trying to make it in the music industry, so he called Jeffre and Nick Lachey—both former classmates at the Cincinnati School for Creative and Performing Artists—and formed 98°; Drew Lachey soon moved to the West Coast as well.

The quartet were working a variety of odd jobs to finance their talent-show appearances, but after attracting attention by trying to crash the backstage area of a Boyz II Men show, 98° were offered a chance to sing on a local radio station. From that appearance the group met Paris d'Jon, the co-manager of Montell Jordan. He arranged demos for them, and helped the group sign to Motown. The quartet's debut single, "Invisible Man," hit number 12 on the singles charts and went gold during 1997, leading to the release of their self-titled debut album in July of that year. *98° & Rising* followed in late 1998, and a year later the group returned with the seasonal effort *This Christmas*. Their third full-length, *Revelation*, featuring the single "Give Me Just One Night (Una Noche)," was released in fall 2000. It became the most-added Top 40 single in history during its first week of release. By fall, second single "My Everything" was hot while things with the band began to simmer down. Rumors of split started to brew. By February 2002, the rumor had gone far enough. The members of 98° officially announced that the band was on hiatus. Other projects were in the works, but they were still a band. *The Collection* album and DVD followed in May. —*John Bush*

98° / Jul. 29, 1997 / Motown ♦♦♦
98°' eponymous debut album is an appealing mixture of urban soul and pop-oriented hip-hop, all targeted at teens. It may lack a set of consistently engaging songs, but the best cuts suggest that the group is capable of some dynamic contemporary soul. [*98°* debut album was reissued in the spring of 1998 with the Diane Warren composition "Was It Something I Didn't Say" added as a new track. The song was included after it received exposure in the film *Fame L.A.*] —*Leo Stanley*

● **98° & Rising** / Oct. 20, 1998 / Motown ♦♦♦
Really, 98° is a great idea for a teen-pop band: take an attractive boy band in the vein of Take That or *NSYNC and have them sing Boyz II Men crossed with the Backstreet Boys. 98° followed this formula on their eponymous debut and were more or less successful. However, they've mastered the sound on their second record, *98° & Rising*. Like any teen-pop with chart aspirations, *98° & Rising* is far from a perfect album, as it alternates sure-fire hits with filler cut from the same mold, but that should be expected. What's nice is that songs like "The Hardest Thing" and "True to Your Heart" are well-crafted radio singles, with memorable hooks and excellent production. That same production—which makes the ballads smoove and the dance-pop infectious—carries weaker moments of the record, but at the end of the day, it's the singles that make *98° & Rising* entertaining. And for many fans, that will be quite enough indeed. —*Stephen Thomas Erlewine*

Revelation / Sep. 26, 2000 / Universal Music ♦♦♦
It's hard not to feel a little sorry for 98°, since they're often overshadowed by their peers, the towering giants of male teen pop, Backstreet Boys and *NSYNC. They've had hits as big as either group, but when it came time to release *Revelation* in the fall of 2000, they didn't have the grudging critical respect of the Backstreets or the cultural cache of *NSYNC, who had dolls hitting toy stores the same month *Revelation* was unleashed. They were simply a teen pop band, capable of amiable dance-pop numbers and tuneful ballads, both of which sounded quite nice coming out of the radio. Not surprisingly, they wanted a little bit more than simply being an effective singles band; they didn't just want to hold their own with the Backstreets and *NSYNC, they wanted to escape their shadow. The title of *Revelation* (much like the title of the Sync's 2000 release *No Strings Attached*) is a tip-off to their goal: They want to provide doubters with a revelation that they can indeed deliver strong music. If *Revelation* doesn't actually hold any, well, revelations, that shouldn't be held against the band, since they do wind up turning out a perfectly acceptable mainstream dance-pop album. Apart from the infectious opening cut, "Give Me Just

One Night (Una Noche)," a song clearly influenced by Ricky Martin, and maybe "Dizzy," which adopts Cher-like vocoder tricks, they never stretch the boundaries of the music too much, preferring to just serve up straight dance-pop and sweet ballads. They lean a little heavily on the ballads, thereby aligning themselves with the Backstreet Boys' classy crooning rather than *NSYNC's charged adolescent pop. That wouldn't be a problem if the songs were just a little better constructed, so that the melodies stand out prominently on the first listen, but ultimately, the album feels a little samey. Not bad, necessarily, but a little familiar, especially since the peppier songs have stronger hooks and attitude. The preponderance of ballads weighs down the album a bit, even if some of them hold up quite well on their own, and they make *Revelations* seem like it has more filler than it actually does. Ultimately, it's a good singles album, which may not be enough to make 98° hold their own with the Backstreets or Sync, but it is enough to make for a solid teen pop album. *—Stephen Thomas Erlewine*

The Collection / May 7, 2002 / Universal ✦✦✦
98° may have been typecast alongside the Backstreet Boys and *NSYNC thanks to their dashing good looks, but their music set them apart from such highly polished pop. Constructing a style that's rooted in sultry R&B and soul grooves, 98° established themselves as a strong vocal group and *The Collection* charts the band's musical maturation since their 1997 self-titled debut. From the heart-rending "Was It Something I Didn't Say?" and "I Do (Cherish You)" to the sexy Latin party of "Give Me Just One Night (Una Noche)," *The Collection* captures the highlights. A hidden treasure featured in Disney's *Mulan*, "True to Your Heart" is one of 98°'s finest moments. The collaboration with Stevie Wonder is a sophisticated match for the group and an equal favorite among fans. "Thank God I Found You" with Mariah Carey is also an added bonus. Nick Lachey and Jessica Simpson's dramatic duet on "Where You Are" is missing and that might disappoint some fans, but most will be able to overlook such a move. *The Collection* is a solid package and loyalists who've followed them from the beginning will be pleased. *—MacKenzie Wilson*

The Nite-Liters

f. 1963, Louisville, KY
Group / Funk, Soul, Instrumental Rock
Harvey Fuqua and Tony Churchill formed the Nite-Liters in 1963 in Louisville. When the band subsequently expanded to 17 members, with a pair of vocal groups and a instrumental ensemble, they were renamed New Birth, Inc. Churchill, Austin Lander, James Baker, Robert Jackson, Leroy Taylor, and Robin Russell were the original bandmembers. Ben Boxtel, Roger Voice, and James Hall were later recruits. They had two mild instrumental hits for RCA in 1971 and 1972, with "K-Jee" making the R&B Top 20. *—Ron Wynn*

Morning, Noon & the Nite-Liters / 1975 / RCA ✦✦✦
Morning, Noon & the Nite-Liters contains their biggest hit, the infectious "K-Jee," as well as "Tanga Boo Gonk," a highly contagious piece with jangling guitars and smart horn riffs, and "Pull Together," an instrumental that starts slow and then caterpillars up. The rest features more of the band's signature Meters/Booker T. & the MG's-ish breakbeat rhythms modernized by urban horn arrangements. *—Andrew Hamilton*

● **K-Jee: Golden Classics** / 1991 / Collectables ✦✦✦✦

No Authority

Group / Teen Pop, Dance-Pop, Urban
No Authority was formed as a male vocal quartet in the early '90s in southern California, consisting of lead singer Ric Felix (aka Ricky Godinez and later billed as Ricky G), born December 2, 1980, in San Bernadino, CA; lead singer Josh Keaton, born February 8, 1979, in Pasadena, CA; singer/rapper Danny Zavatsky, born June 1, 1982, in Long Beach, CA; and singer Eric Stretch, born June 22, 1980, in Yorba Linda, CA. After they had been performing locally for a few years, their manager, Richard Walters of Smash Music, managed to get their demo tape to Jerry Greenberg and Jono Kohan of MJJ Music, Michael Jackson's custom record label at Sony Music. Greenberg and Kohan passed it on to Jackson who signed No Authority, and their debut single, "Don't Stop," was issued in October 1997, followed by the album *Keep On* in November. The recordings flopped, and No Authority regrouped.

Keaton parted company with them and was replaced by Tommy McCarthy. They left Sony and went to Maverick, Madonna's custom label at Warner Bros., issuing their second album, *No Authority*, in July of 2000. (Maverick also reissued *Keep On*.) *— William Ruhlmann*

Keep On / Nov. 4, 1997 / MJJ/Work ✦✦✦
The vocalists on this debut album are four high school-age male singers, but the album's auteur is songwriter/producer Rodney Jerkins who, with a posse of associates, contributes almost all of the material. Jerkins makes No Authority sound closer to an R&B/hip-hop act than such competitors in the boy band business as Backstreet Boys, which would be a good thing if they could pull it off. But while Jerkins and company are able to keep the backup harmonies smooth, the lead singers are mediocre and rapper Danny Zavatsky is anemic. The songs are the usual beat-driven pleadings for teenage love and understanding, but none of them stand out. The lead-off track and first single, "Don't Stop," with its opening line, "Don't stop till you get enough," is a nod to MJJ label head Michael Jackson; and the album concludes with a cover of DeBarge's 1982 hit "I Like It," which has the unfortunate effect of throwing the songs before it into the shade at the same time that it reminds you there are vocal groups who could sing rings around these teenagers. (This is a "CD Extra," containing multi-media content that can be accessed with a computer, including brief biographical information, photographs, and a rehearsal video of the song "Girlfriend.") *— William Ruhlmann*

● **No Authority** / Jul. 18, 2000 / Maverick ✦✦✦✦✦
With their first album, No Authority was slightly ahead of the curve on the boy band fad; by the time they were able to get a second album out, they had fallen well behind. The southern California vocal quartet attracted the attention of Michael Jackson's MJJ custom label and was teamed with writer/producer Rodney Jerkins for the debut *Keep On*. Jerkins gave the singers an R&B edge that already sounded dated when the album was released in November 1997, shortly after the Backstreet Boys broke through in the U.S. with "Quit Playing Games (With My Heart)." But Jerkins' production was better than No Authority's uncertain vocal performance. The album disappeared, along with one of the group members and the MJJ contract, and the still-teenaged trio that remained looked like instant has-beens. The ascension of the Backstreet Boys and *NSYNC probably saved them from careers in fast food, but the boy band field quickly began filling up. They hired a new member and signed to Madonna's Maverick label, which had them slavishly copy the Backstreet/*NSYNC sound on this, their second album. (Naming the disc after the group seemed a deliberate attempt to mark a new beginning.) Herbie Crichlow, Swedish partner of leading teen pop songwriter Max Martin and co-author of "Quit Playing Games (With My Heart)," co-wrote three tracks and produced one, and the Danish team of Cutfather and Joe (Ace of Base, Aqua) handled another four. The result was the by-now painfully familiar dance pop style of icy keyboards, programmed drums, multiple lead vocals, and swirling harmonies, all in the service of songs in which a narrator pleads with a female known only as "girl" for her affections. The group's modest vocal abilities were discreetly augmented with singers whose names were buried in the album credits, and much improvement was noticeable. By the time the album was released, "What I Wanna Do" (one of the Crichlow songs) had been in heavy rotation on Radio Disney for months, and "Can I Get Your Number," dangerously similar to the Backstreet Boys' "Everybody (Backstreet's Back)," had been out as a single for four weeks, setting up the album well. The group had opened dates for Britney Spears and was set for a Nickelodeon tour. *— William Ruhlmann*

No Question

Group / Contemporary R&B, Urban, Hip-Hop
The Philly vocal quartet No Question features Damon Core, Dante Massey, Tommy Blackwell, and Nicholas Johnson performing a spread of vocal styles, from Al Green to a raw, soulful extension of Boyz II Men. Kenny Gamble & Leon Huff brought them to the forefront with a debut CD entitled *No Question* on Philadelphia International Records, which spawned the hit "I Don't Care" and a remake of "You Make Me Feel Brand New." Though solid, the disc's sales fell short of forecasts, and the group switched labels, teaming with Chris Schwartz to become Ruff/Nation Records' first R&B group. *—Andrew Hamilton*

● **No Question** / Oct. 5, 1999 / Philadelphia International ✦✦✦
After a spooky intro, the hip-hop/crooners from the ghettos of north Philly settled into a set of ballads and midtempo numbers that gets numbing after six tracks. Fifteen tracks are too many from this group to digest at one setting even when two tracks are brief skits and not songs. "This Weekend," a high-energy party track motored by kick drums surprisingly flopped as the debut single despite its glossy potential. "Cover Me" is an erotic ballad that comes off well; a second single, "I Don't Care," features a grinding beat and the memorable line: "Swingin' with the project ladies and ghetto freaks"; they execute a splendid update of "You Make Me Feel Brand New," accompanied by a female; and "Interlude" offers some comic relief and breaks the monotony. No Question has the flavor of Dru Hill, Ginuwine, and a group they probably never heard of—Smooth Approach; Smooth Approach uses a falsetto lead on some songs while No Question employs a female singer for the effect. *—Andrew Hamilton*

Cliff Nobles

b. 1944, Mobile, AL
Vocals / Pop-Soul, Soul
Though born in Grove Hill, AL, in 1944, Cliff Nobles' family moved to Mobile when he was a terrible two-year-old. He never showed any inclination toward music until high school, when he joined the school choir and started singing lead for a popular local group called the Delroys. After school, he moved to Philadelphia, PA, to seek fame and fortune. Nobles found the competition a lot stiffer than the Mobile scene and had to support himself by living commune-style with some musical friends in Norristown, a small town 18 miles from Philadelphia. Before the move, Nobles cut three singles for Atlantic Records that went unnoticed. In Norristown, he formed Cliff Nobles & Co., which consisted of Benny Williams (bass), Bobby Tucker (lead guitar), and Tommy Soul (drums). The outfit made tapes for Jimmy Rogers (not to be confused with the country singer of the same name), who made them available to producer/writer/singer Jesse James, who resided in the community. James had already heard something in Nobles' voice when he heard him sing in a local church.

Loving their energy, James started writing songs for Nobles and the band, and secured a contract for the group with Phil La of Soul Records. The first release bombed. The second featured "Love Is All Right," backed with "The Horse." "The Horse" became a huge hit and established Nobles as a legit one-hit wonder. Ironically, "The Horse" was simply "Love Is All Right" without Nobles' vocal—Nobles isn't even featured on "The Horse." He neither sings nor plays an instrument on the track; the brass playing on the song would become famous years later as MFSB. The whole incident was an accident, the side with the vocal was supposed to be the side that was plugged, but DJs kept playing the non-vocal version. The record would have gone to number one, but another instrumental, "Grazin' in the Grass" by Hugh Masekela, was even more popular and occupied the top spot for two weeks. The week of July 29, 1968, had to be the first time in modern pop music history that two instrumentals were ranked at numbers one and two, respectively, on the charts.

Shamelessly, Phil La of Soul released two more instrumentals—"Horse Fever" and "Switch It On,"—and credited them as being by Cliff Nobles, though Nobles didn't play an instrument. A later single on Roulette actually featured Nobles' singing and nearly cracked the R&B Top 40, stalling at number 42. Phil La issued an album entitled *The*

Horse that consisted of mostly instrumentals and dance tunes like "The Mule," "The Camel Walk," and "Judge Baby I'm Back," a tune sounding like a hit that Nobles sings with a feel similar to a Berry Gordy Jr. production for the Contours. Moonshot Records released an LP one year later, in 1969, where Nobles sang three songs, the rest being instrumental. The Atlantic material remains in the vaults. Supposedly, Nobles was an excellent entertainer and a gifted dancer, but, in essence, he was the Milli Vanilli of the '60s. *—Andrew Hamilton*

● **The Horse** / 1968 / Phil-L.A.S. ♦♦♦

Pony the Horse / 1969 / Moon Shot ♦♦♦

The Notations

Group / Soul, Northern Soul

An above-average Chicago soul group who could never get a breakout hit, the Notations recorded for Twinight and Gemigo in the '70s. Both "I'm Still Here" and "It Only Hurts for a Little While" were nice heartache tunes, but were only Top 30 hits. The lineup included Clifford Curry, LaSalle Matthews, Bobby Thomas, and Jimmy Stroud. They began on Tad in the late '60s. Walter Jones replaced Stroud in 1973, then departed in 1976. Curry went on to score solo success with "She Shot a Hole in My Soul." *—Ron Wynn*

● **The Notations** / 1975 / Gemigo ♦♦♦

Nu Flavor

f. 1994, Long Beach, CA

Group / Teen Pop, Dance-Pop

R&B vocal quartet Nu Flavor formed in Long Beach, CA, in 1994 after members Frank Pangelinan (tenor/lead), Jacob Ceniceros (baritone), Anthony DaCosta (tenor), and Rico Luna (alto) met at a party. The foursome soon recorded a demo featuring a cover of Journey's smash ballad "Open Arms"; after the tape made its way to Reprise president Howie Klein, he signed Nu Flavor on the spot. Their self-titled debut album followed in 1997, launching the hits "Heaven" and "Sweet Sexy Thing"; *It's On* appeared two years later. *—Jason Ankeny*

Nu Flavor / Mar. 11, 1997 / Reprise ♦♦♦

● **It's On** / Nov. 16, 1999 / Reprise ♦♦♦

The quartet known as Nu Flavor straddles both urban R&B and Latin pop, surely two of the most popular styles of the late '90s. They're more than just a marketing director's dream, however. The group harmonizes as well as the Backstreet Boys or *NSYNC, and injects a great deal more soul into their songs. Nu Flavor's sophomore album, *It's On*, is their first album in English for the American market, and proves that the group can give the usual spate of teen-pop acts a run for their money. *—Keith Farley*

Les Nubians

f. Bordeaux, France

Group / Urban, Hip-Hop

An unconventional female duo that came out of Bordeaux, France, in the 1990s, Les Nubians offered a jazzy, sophisticated style of R&B that combined French lyrics with the influence of Sade, Soul II Soul, hip-hop, and African pop. The duo consists of sisters Helene and Celia Faussart, who were born in France to a French father and a Cameroonian mother. After living in France as children, the siblings moved with their parents to the African country of Chad in 1985, when Helene (born 1975) was ten and Celia (born 1979) was six. The sisters lived in Chad for seven years before returning to France as teenagers.

Helene and Celia had been singing most of their lives, and when they first formed Les Nubians, they were an a cappella group that specialized in covers of R&B, reggae, and African songs. Eventually, they started working with bands and performing original material. Helene and Celia absorbed a variety of music along the way, and they have expressed admiration for artists ranging from Ella Fitzgerald and Abbey Lincoln to the Fugees and African icons Miriam Makeba and Fela Kuti. Their promising debut album, *Princesses Nubiennes*, was released by Virgin worldwide in France, Switzerland, and Belgium in June 1998 before coming out on Omtown/Higher Octave in the U.S. in September of that year. *—Alex Henderson*

● **Princesses Nubiennes** / Sep. 22, 1998 / Virgin ♦♦♦♦

Fans of Zap Mama, Sade and/or Soul II Soul will probably flip for this sister duo from Bordeaux, France. Theough they tend to get billed as a hip-hop act, their music is much more complex than that: it's smooth like Sade (but much more melodically interesting), bass-heavy like Soul II Soul (but much more lyrically interesting), and Afropean like Zap Mama (but much less interesting, sorry ladies). "Demain" is a smooth-jazz groove that is more tasty than nourishing, but there's a fair amount of both textural and lyrical complexity to "Makeda." "Tabou" is actually an adapted (and, frankly, much improved) version of Sade's "Sweetest Taboo" that features some excellent French rapping. "Embrasse-Moi" is both excruciatingly sexy and highly rhythmically sophisticated. Sure, they have a mildly distressing tendency to layer everything with an ultra-smooth surface sheen, but it's forgivable; chances are good that they'll rough things up a bit as they mature. In the meantime, just give up and wallow in the succulent loveliness of tracks like "Demain" and "Les Portes du Souvenir." *—Rick Anderson*

The Nutmegs

f. 1955, New Haven, CT

Group / Doo Wop, R&B

The Nutmegs are remembered today for their enduring East Coast doo wop classic, 1955's R&B smash hit "Story Untold" (number two in the U.S.). The group continued to have regional success in the northeastern U.S., scoring a Top 20 regional hit with "Ship of Love." Nearly a decade later, the Nutmegs unwittingly became the founders of an a cappella craze that swept the East Coast between 1963 and 1966, scoring numerous Top Five regional hits with a cappella versions of previously recorded singles. "Let Me Tell You" (number five), "The Way Love Should Be" (number three), "Why Must We Go to School" (number four), "Down in Mexico" (number five), and "You're Crying" (number four) were all popular in the greater New York area, but the group was never able to gain enough national exposure to chart across the country again.

Hailing from New Haven, CT (home of the Five Satins, the Scarlets, the Chestnuts, and the Four Haven Knights), the original Nutmegs—lead Leroy Griffin, Sonny Griffin (born James, he was Leroy's brother), Dieder Cobb, and a second Leroy Griffin (yes, there were two men with the same exact name) who later became Leroy Gomez—all sang together with other members—Walter Singleterry, Bill Emery, and Gomez's brother Tommy Griffin—moving in and out of the lineup. The group performed on the street corners of New Haven, especially Webster and Dixon Streets, where Jimmy "Co Co" Tyson was asked to join the key lineup and soon they were a quintet. The Nutmegs fragmented again and some of the members left to form a group of their own, the Lyres; the Gomez brothers formed the Four Haven Knights.

Now comprised of a lineup that included Emery (lead), Singleterry (first tenor), Sonny (second tenor), Tyson (baritone), and Leroy (bass), the new Nutmegs met promoter Charlie Johnson in 1953, who fell for their sound and decided to record two of Leroy's songs, "Ship of Love" and "Playboy," for his small J&G label. The single failed to sell, however, and Johnson lacked the funds to promote it properly. By 1954, the Nutmegs revised their hierarchy and Leroy switched over to lead, with Sonny now filling in as first tenor, Tyson (second tenor), Emery (baritone), and they added yet another Leroy, Leroy McNeil, for the bass vocals. Leroy Griffin's nephew Harold (Harry James, not the musician), would often sit in and listen, little knowing the part he would come to play in the group.

Late in 1954, the quintet traveled to New York and met RCA/Groove recording artists the Du Droppers, who introduced them to Herald Records executive Al Silver. By then, the Nutmegs had recorded four more sides, including a song called "Story Untold." Three of the four would eventually become the group's first singles for Herald. In March 1955, "Story Untold" was released and leaped immediately onto the R&B charts; by July, it was number two in the nation. In August, Herald followed up with "Ship of Love," which, by October, had climbed to number-13 R&B and number-five pop in the New York area, but failed to catch on across the country. The Nutmegs' fourth single, "Key to the Kingdom," was released in June 1956. It failed to sell, however. The next single, "Comin' Home," was released in December, but by then the Nutmegs had lost their momentum. The group bravely soldiered on under a different name: the Rajahs. "Shifting Sands" (Klick 7805, released January 1958) bore the same results and slipped through the cracks, as did the group's next single, "A Dream of Love" (released on Morty Craft's Tel label in 1960). Then something quite remarkable happened.

Times Square Records, a label based in New York City, began issuing 45s by the Nutmegs culled from mid-'50s demos which featured no musical accompaniment. They were called a cappella singles. The Nutmegs quickly became the leaders of a new strain of the doo wop genre and held up the standard for others to follow. In 1963 and 1964, Times Square issued a handful of a cappella Nutmegs singles, including "Let Me Tell You," which reached number five on Times Square's 1963 Top 150 survey. "The Way Love Should Be" scored number three in July of 1963 and "Why Must We Go to School" topped out at number four in December of 1963. The new year began with more a cappella hits: "Down in Mexico" scored number five on the charts in January and "You're Crying" reached number four at the end of the year in December. Herald Records was obviously aware of what was happening with their former group, so they too got into the act, issuing a cappella versions of "Story Untold" and "Ship of Love" that year to great success. *—Bryan Thomas*

The Nutmegs' Greatest Hits / Apr. 28, 1994 / Collectables ♦♦♦

● **Greatest Hits** / Relic ♦♦♦♦♦

Nytro

Group / Funk, Quiet Storm, Soul

Influenced by the Bar-Kays and the Ohio Players, Nytro was an obscure funk/soul band that worked with producer/songwriter Norman Whitfield in the late '70s. Whitfield, who scored major hits for everyone from Edwin Starr to Rose Royce, was known for having the Midas touch back then. But he didn't have much commercial success with the horn-powered Nytro, which recorded two albums for his Whitfield label: 1977's *Nytro* and 1979's *Return to Nytropolis*. Neither of those LPs (which ranged from gritty funk to jazz-influenced quiet storm material) sold and in 1980, Nytro broke up. Nytro's lineup included lead singer Robert Justice, trumpeters Kenneth Scott and LaMorris Payne, saxophonist Chris Powell, guitarist Earnest Reed Jr., bassist Theodore Willingham, keyboardist Benjamin Wilber, and drummer Daniel Smithson. *—Alex Henderson*

● **Nytro** / 1977 / Whitfield ♦♦♦

Norman Whitfield had an impressive track record in the 1960s and 1970s. Whether he was working with the Temptations, Gladys Knight & the Pips, or Rose Royce, the producer and songwriter commanded a lot of respect during R&B's golden era. But even a heavyweight champ isn't guaranteed a victory every time; one act that turned out to be a commercial disappointment for Whitfield was Nytro, which made its vinyl debut with this self-titled LP in 1977. Whitfield, who produced the album for his own Whitfield label, had high hopes for the little known soul-funk outfit. But Nytro, whose main influences included the Bar-Kays and the Ohio Players, didn't go very far commercially. Nonetheless, this is a decent record, if an uneven one. The material falls into two categories: gritty funk smokers like "Trick Bag" (not to be confused with the Teena Marie song), "Where's the Party," and "What It Is," and relaxed, jazz-influenced quiet storm tracks. The Ohio Players' influence is especially strong on the latter; Nytro's quiet storm offerings (which include "Dreaming" and "Atmosphere") make it clear that the band was well aware of Players' gems like "Sweet Sticky Thing" and "Let's Love." Though Nytro sounds undeveloped on this LP, one hears a lot of potential—which, regrettably, went unrealized. Again, *Nytro* is a decent debut, but the band was capable of a lot more. *—Alex Henderson*

Return to Nytropolis / 1979 / Whitfield ♦♦♦

O

O'Bryan

b. 1961, Sneads Ferry, NC

Multi Instruments, Vocals / Urban, Disco, Funk

"The Gigolo" was one of the prime guilty pleasures of black dance music in the early '80s, with its castrato vocals, hokey lyrics, and clavinet squiggles. It had all the earmarks of a one-shot hit, but surprisingly O'Bryan managed to cut nine singles that made the R&B charts in the 1980s, as well as record four albums for Capitol. A multi-instrumentalist, his uptempo tracks could sound something like a more mainstream Prince, though he tread far closer to the urban contemporary mainstream on his ballad "slow jams."

O'Bryan got into the business after a friend in the choir that he sang in as a young adult in southern California married Ron Kersey, who had worked in Philadelphia with groups like the Trammps in the 1970s. Upon her recommendation, Kersey got O'Bryan into a group he was forming. That quickly fell apart, but Kersey helped the singer connect with *Soul Train* impresario Don Cornelius, who helped O'Bryan land a deal with Capitol. "The Gigolo" made number five on the R&B charts in 1982, and over the next few years he had some uptempo and ballad follow-ups. "I'm Freaky," which was reminiscent of "Gigolo," was the best of these; "Lovelite" was the most successful. He hasn't released any albums, though, since leaving Capitol in the late '80s. *—Richie Unterberger*

Be My Lover / 1984 / Capitol ✦✦

Surrender / 1987 / Capitol ✦✦

● **The Best of O'Bryan** / Apr. 16, 1996 / The Right Stuff ✦✦✦✦✦

Here are 14 songs from his four Capitol albums, including the hits "I'm Freaky," "The Gigolo," "Lovelite," and "You and I." *—Richie Unterberger*

Billy Ocean (Leslie Charles)

b. Jan. 21, 1950, Trinidad, West Indies

Vocals / Quiet Storm, Adult Contemporary, Urban, Dance-Pop

Billy Ocean was one of the first Caribbean singers to be embraced by MTV, resulting in a string of Top Ten hits during the mid-'80s. Born Leslie Charles in Trinidad on January 21, 1950, Ocean moved to England at the age of eight, and by his teenaged years, was singing regularly in London clubs. During this time, Ocean paid the bills by working at Ford Motors, but continued to pen songs and perform, as he issued an obscure debut single in 1974 under the name of Scorched Earth. But by 1975, the singer had dropped his alias and was going by Billy Ocean, resulting in a self-titled debut that spawned the singer's first hit single, "Love Really Hurts Without You," peaking on the singles chart at number two in the U.K. and number 22 in the U.S. Ocean continued to issue albums (1980's *City Limit*, 1981's *Nights (Feel Like Getting Down)*, and 1982's *Inner Feelings*) plus further singles, with "L.O.D. (Love on Delivery)" and the title track from *Nights* (the latter of which crossed over onto the U.S. R&B charts) being sizeable hits; as he also began penning songs for other artists, including a track on LaToya Jackson's 1980 self-titled debut.

But breakthrough success was just around the corner for Ocean, as he scored a massive hit single in 1984 with "Caribbean Queen," a track that shot to the top of the charts worldwide. Depending on the region, the song's title and lyrics were changed slightly, resulting in the tune being known as "African Queen" and "European Queen" in other parts of the world, while the album it was taken from, *Suddenly*, was eventually certified double platinum (a few other singles, a cover of Prince's "Loverboy" and the ballad "Suddenly," were also successful). Ocean's winning streak continued with 1986's *Love Zone* (another double-platinum hit), which spawned a pair of hit singles: "When the Going Gets Tough, The Tough Get Going" (which was used as the theme song to the movie *The Jewel of the Nile*), which peaked at number two, and the number-one "There'll Be Sad Songs (To Make You Cry)." 1988 saw Ocean score another number-one single with "Get Outta My Dreams, Get Into My Car," taken from the platinum album *Tear Down These Walls*. But afterward, the hits dried up for Ocean (although his 1989 collection, *Greatest Hits*, has been a steady seller over the years), as such further albums as *Time to Move On*, *L.I.F.E.*, and *Showdown* failed to spawn hits. *—Greg Prato*

Billy Ocean / 1975 / GTO ✦✦✦✦

Way before hook-smart pop/R&B ditties like "When the Going Gets Tough" and "Get Outta My Dreams, Get into My Car" established Billy Ocean as an '80s radio icon worldwide, the singer was belting out '60s-laden soul workouts and ballads that mainly stuck a chord with U.K. audiences. This youthful debut outing boasts a nice balance of slow and fast numbers, and finds Ocean putting an abundance of energy into each track (at times perhaps a bit over-exerted). And though his style may not be as developed as on his '80s albums, there's no lack of vigor or enthusiasm. From the earnest, Motown-privy grooves of the pleading "Love Really Hurts Without You" and subtle "Let's Put Our Emotions in Motion" to the riveting pace of the assertive "Tell Him to Move Over," the album's eleven tracks provide a thorough examination of some of the many emotions associated with love. Given, this is not an unusual context for any form of popular music; but Ocean and his co-writers' down-to-earth lyrics and the singer's remarkably sensitive delivery make it a special listen. Whether it be the shy falsetto he employs on "Let's Do It All Again" or his straightforward tenor vocal on "Eye of a Storm," there's an unmistakable personal feeling that defines what "soul" is all about. His approach may not be as raw or deep as "soul" conventionally suggests, but it's just as real. *—Justin M. Kantor*

City Limit / 1980 / GTO ✦✦✦

Though his first LP, Billy Ocean, produced a string of three top-20 hits in the U.K., nearly four years would pass before GTO finally released the soulful crooner's sophomore album. The resulting output was a package much earthier and funkier than its predecessor, evidenced by the gritty horns, snazzy bassline, and urging vocals of "What You Doing to Me" and the Latin-tinged, almost-fusion titletrack. Still, there are plenty of pretty moments with remnants of Ocean's earlier sweet-soul sound. The subtly orchestrated, lightly swaying rhythms of "Who's Gonna Rock You" and the warm harmonies and from-the-heart lyrics of "Maybe Tonight" are both innocent soul numbers, but with a little more experience than comparable tunes on the first album. Unfortunately, the latter half of the album suffers from a couple of over-arranged tunes, in the form of "Whatever Turns You On" and "Taking Chances." Both of these tunes (as well as three others on *City Limit*) would turn up in new form on 1981's *Nights*. "Whatever" and "Taking" are both solid songs, but the horns play too integral a role, and swamp the tunes so much that it all sounds a bit Muzak. But on the whole, *City Limit* is a bright album with a considerable number of memorable moments. *—Justin M. Kantor*

Nights (Feel Like Getting Down) / 1981 / Epic ✦✦✦

Billy Ocean was on his way to superstardom with this album, his first big hit release on Epic. The title song was his first R&B Top Ten record, and he got another couple of chart singles before beginning his run of R&B and pop hits. It also demonstrated his equal ability doing exuberant uptempo dance tunes and convincing, if at times oversung and vapid, ballads. Epic was later left red-faced when an act they developed moved over to Jive/RCA and went platinum. *—Ron Wynn*

Inner Feelings / 1982 / Epic ✦✦

Billy Ocean went from international superstar to falling completely off the charts in one of the most amazing rise and fall stories of the 1980s and early '90s. This was an early, introductory self-produced session for Epic, with Ocean still feeling his way around in America after having enjoyed huge success on Britain's club circuit. There were some decent ballads and uptempo dance tunes, but little to suggest that Ocean was on his way to becoming Britian's pop/dance king and an urban contemporary and pop superstar in America as well. *—Ron Wynn*

Suddenly / 1984 / Jive ✦✦✦✦

Billy Ocean vaulted into international stardom with this album in 1984. The album peaked at number nine, was on the charts for over a year and a half, and yielded three R&B hits that were all also pop smashes. Ocean would sing on the soundtrack for the film *The Jewel of the Nile*, make sellout appearances around the world, and appear regularly on television and videos. At this point he was a bigger pop star than R&B artist, as two of his three hits did better as crossover vehicles than R&B tunes. *—Ron Wynn*

Love Zone / 1986 / Jive ✦✦✦✦

Billy Ocean was riding atop the charts when he issued this album in 1986. The title track contained both a fine arrangement and Ocean's emphatic lead vocal, and was a huge hit. He topped the R&B charts twice that year with both "Love Zone" and "There'll Be Sad Songs (To Make You Cry)," each of which was also a huge pop smash, the latter topping the pop chart. This was arguably his finest album, and was certainly his most successful. *—Ron Wynn*

Tear Down These Walls / 1988 / Jive ✦✦✦

Things were beginning to slip a bit for Billy Ocean in the late '80s. While he was still a successful attraction, this album wouldn't reach the multi-platinum levels of its predecessors. Ocean's voice also lacked the resonance and authority it had on earlier dance tunes and wasn't as convincing or confident on ballads. He still landed a couple more hits, and one additional chart topper (R&B and pop) with "Get Outta My Dreams, Get Into My Car," but the decline was starting. *—Ron Wynn*

● **Greatest Hits** / Oct. 1989 / Jive ✦✦✦✦✦

Billy Ocean's *Greatest Hits* packs nearly all of the singer's charted singles that were on the Jive record label. Ocean scored an impressive run of feel-good Top 40 hits in the mid- to late '80s, including three number-one singles, those being the classic post-disco jam "Caribbean Queen," the ballad "There'll Be Sad Songs (To Make You Cry)," and the high-energy pop ditty "Get Outta My Dreams, Get Into My Car." Ocean's Top Ten hits, which all appear here, include the dance-pop of "Loverboy" and "When the Going Gets Tough, the Tough Get Going" (from *The Jewel of the Nile*), the soft ballad "Suddenly," and the soul nugget "Love Zone." The music was irresistibly pop, with some of these songs ranking as the catchiest, most radio-friendly music the '80s had to offer. The only hits not found on this set are the ballad "Love Is Forever" and Ocean's first major U.S. hit, 1976's "Love Really Hurts Without You." The funky, delightful "License to Chill," a Top 40 hit in its own right, is one of two later tracks on this set. The other is the dreadful "I Sleep Much Better (In Someone Else's Bed)." As a final note, "Loverboy," "When the Going Gets Tough," and "Caribbean Queen" are included in their edited, single versions. *—Jose F. Promis*

Time to Move On / Jun. 8, 1993 / Jive ♦♦♦

After achieving worldwide stardom in the '80s, Ocean took a three-year recording hiatus in the early '90s. This resulting comeback album found him offering strong melodies, lyrics, and vocals once again, yet on occasion also showed him falling victim to current production trends. The set's highlights are the numbers produced by Steely & Clevie, R. Kelly and Dorsey "Bob" Robinson, while the tracks done by club stalwarts Hula & K. Fingers and new-school R&B figure Timmy Allen are weak and formulaic. Throughout it all, Ocean's performances are bright and compelling, as evidenced by the vivid "Everyday Sunshine" and uplifting "Pick Up the Pieces"—both featuring well-crafted, round-style vocal arrangements. And though *Time to Move On* is primarily dance-oriented, the album contains lovely R&B/pop ballads with Ocean's signature, passion-filled delivery via "Rose" and "Everything's So Different Without You." This set isn't as consistently unforgettable as earlier works like *Love Zone* or *Nights*, but is still considerably strong. *—Justin M. Kantor*

Odyssey

f. New York, NY

Group / Disco, Quiet Storm

First formed as the Lopez Sisters (Carmen, Lillian, and Louise) in 1968, Carmen dropped out and Tony Reynolds (a Manilla native) joined to form Odyssey. After performances in New York clubs, they hit it big in 1977 with the soft disco cuts "Native New Yorker" and "Easy Come, Easy Go." Their music had a subtle Caribbean feel, and while their U.S. hits soon dried up, they had a few more hits in the U.K. before the group fell apart. *—Bil Carpenter*

● **Odyssey** / 1977 / RCA ♦♦♦

Odyssey is best remembered for its 1977 disco smash "Native New Yorker," an exuberant gem that brilliantly captures the love/hate feelings New Yorkers have for their city. But those who heard that single on the radio and acquired Odyssey's self-titled debut album in the hope of hearing a lot of similar songs received a major surprise—"Native New Yorker" isn't typical of the LP on the whole. For the most part, Odyssey favors laid-back, gentle soul-pop with a subtle Caribbean flavor and occasional hints of jazz. Naturally, some of the people who expected *Odyssey* to be one big disco party were disappointed, but those who could accept the album for what it was realized that album tracks like "Weekend Lover," "Golden Hands," and "Ever Lovin' Sam" had a lot of charm. And the New York trio deserves credit for being unorthodox; in 1977, not many R&B groups were incorporating Caribbean elements. One of Odyssey's more consistent albums, this 1977 debut isn't great for dancing (except for "Native New Yorker" of course), but is always great for listening. *—Alex Henderson*

Hollywood Party Tonight / 1978 / RCA ♦♦♦

Hollywood Party Tonight, the second album by Odyssey, found the New York trio unveiling a new lineup. Lillian and Louise Lopez remained, but Tony Reynolds had been replaced by Billy McEachern. However, Reynolds' departure didn't make much of a difference; Odyssey's soft, laid-back style of soul-pop (which had a subtle Caribbean flavor and occasional hints of jazz) was still distinctive and easily recognizable. Although not as strong or as consistent as Odyssey's self-titled debut album, *Hollywood Party Tonight* is a generally decent sophomore record. The 1978 LP, which went out of print after only a few years, didn't contain any hits; nonetheless, hardcore Odyssey fans who bought it found tracks like "Hey Bill (Last Night Was Really a Thrill)" and "Single Again" to be pleasant, if unremarkable. From a commercial standpoint, the problem with this album was a shortage of disco—people associated Odyssey with the exuberant disco smash "Native New Yorker," and *Hollywood Party Tonight* doesn't contain anything as overtly dance-oriented. Not that Odyssey was under any obligation to record disco; most of the tunes on its promising debut album were for listening rather than dancing. And the same thing can be said about this uneven sophomore effort, which isn't a masterpiece but has more ups than downs. *—Alex Henderson*

Hang Together / 1980 / RCA ♦♦♦

It would be wrong to think of Odyssey as one-hit wonders because "Native New Yorker" wasn't the trio's only hit; Odyssey also climbed the R&B charts with "Don't Tell Me, Tell Her" in 1980 and "Inside Out" in 1982. Nonetheless, Odyssey didn't have a lot of blockbusters, and the New York group wasn't nearly as big as it could have been. Nor was Odyssey as consistent as it could have been; *Hang Together*, the group's third album, has more plusses than minuses but is still uneven. The more memorable songs on this 1980 LP range from the sleek "Don't Tell Me, Tell Her" to the ballad "If You're Looking for a Way Out" and the funky, LaBelle-ish "Rooster Loose in the Barnyard." Meanwhile, the catchy "Down Boy" finds Odyssey experimenting with rock elements, which was a rarity for the New Yorkers. Overall, this is a decent record, but it isn't a great one—and the thing is that Odyssey was quite capable of being consistently excellent instead of merely adequate. Listening to *Hang Together* is a lot like seeing a student with above average intelligence bringing home a report card with B's and C's; those B's and C's are preferable to D's and F's, but they're still disappointing when you know that the kid is capable of bringing home straight A's. *—Alex Henderson*

I Got the Melody / 1981 / RCA ♦♦

Greatest Hits Remixes / Apr. 7, 1998 / Hot Productions ♦♦♦

The Very Best of Odyssey / Dec. 8, 1998 / Waxworks ♦♦♦

The cover depicts two singers, but Odyssey was mostly a trio consisting of Tony Reynolds and sisters Lillian and Louise Lopez; Bill McEachern, at some point, replaced one of the Lopez sisters. While an OK career overview, it shows the problems producers encountered trying to give them a definitive sound. "Native New Yorker," a monster record, has no relatives here; its composers, Sandy Linzer and Denny Randell, never created another song for Odyssey as good. A few ballads are exquisite, and some uptempo numbers, especially Lamont Dozier's "Going Back to My Roots," are dancefloor gems. The 16 songs encompass almost as many styles, including Caribbean and Southern soul ("Shades of Blue"). Devoted Odyssey fans' won't quibble, but casual fans and curiosity seekers will want a more engaging compilation of these talented singers' tracks. *—Andrew Hamilton*

The Ohio Players

f. 1959, Dayton, OH

Group / Funk, Soul, Pop-Soul, Urban

With their slinky, horn-powered grooves, impeccable musicianship, and eye-popping album covers, the Ohio Players were among the top funk bands of the mid-'70s. Emerging from the musical hotbed of Dayton in 1959, the group was originally dubbed the Ohio Untouchables, and initially comprised singer/guitarist Robert Ward, bassist Marshall "Rock" Jones, saxophonist/guitarist Clarence "Satch" Satchell, drummer Cornelius Johnson, and trumpeter/trombonist Ralph "Pee Wee" Middlebrooks. In late 1961, a relative of Ward's founded the Detroit-based Lupine Records, and the group traveled north to the Motor City to back the Falcons on their hit "I Found a Love"; the Ohio Untouchables soon made their headlining debut with "Love Is Amazing," but when Ward subsequently exited for a solo career, the group essentially disbanded.

At that point, the nucleus of Middlebrooks, Jones, and newly added guitarist Leroy "Sugarfoot" Bonner returned to Dayton; there they recruited saxophonist Andrew Noland and drummer Gary Webster, the latter a somewhat elusive figure whose true involvement in the group's convoluted history has never been definitively answered—some sources credit him as a founding Untouchable, others even as the band's early leader. In any case, by 1967, with the subsequent addition of singers Bobby Lee Fears and Dutch Robinson, the newly rechristened Ohio Players were signed as the house band for the New York-based Compass Records, backing singer Helena Ferguson on her lone hit, "Where Is the Party," before issuing their solo debut, "Trespassin'," which hit the R&B charts in early 1968.

Although the Players' trademark bottom-heavy, horn-driven sound was already blossoming, their follow-up, "It's a Cryin' Shame," flopped, and as Compass teetered on the brink of bankruptcy they exited the label. (Their early Compass sides were later packaged as *First Impressions*.) The Players then landed on Capitol, where 1969's "Here Today, Gone Tomorrow" was a minor hit; an LP, *Observations in Time*, soon followed, with covers of "Summertime" and "Over the Rainbow" offering a strong hint of the stylistic detours to follow. In 1970 the group disbanded, however; Fears and Robinson both mounted solo careers, while the remaining members again decamped to Dayton, eventually reforming with keyboardist Walter "Junie" Morrison, trumpeter Bruce Napier, and trombonist Marvin Pierce.

Influenced by the groundbreaking funk of Sly & the Family Stone—and with the nasal, cartoon-voiced Bonner assuming vocal duties—the new Ohio Players lineup made their debut with the single "Pain," issued on the small local label Rubber Town Sounds; it was soon picked up for distribution by the Detroit-based Westbound label, reaching the R&B Top 40 in late 1971. An LP, also titled *Pain*, appeared that same year, and was followed in 1972 by *Pleasure*, which launched the absurdist smash "Funky Worm." *Ecstacy* appeared in 1973, and after 1974's *Climax*, the Players signed to Mercury; the label change also heralded yet more lineup changes, with keyboardist Billy Beck replacing Morrison (who later signed on with Parliament) and drummer Jimmy "Diamond" Williams taking over for Webster.

At Mercury, the Ohio Players enjoyed their greatest success; not only did their sound coalesce, but they became notorious for their sexually provocative LP covers, a tradition begun during their Westbound tenure. Their 1974 Mercury debut, *Skin Tight*, was their first unequivocal classic, launching the hit title track as well as "Jive Turkey." Its follow-up, *Fire*, remains the Players' masterpiece, topping the pop charts on the strength of its bone-rattling title cut, itself a number-one hit; "I Want to Be Free," one of the band's few attempts at social commentary, was also highly successful. 1975's *Honey*—which featured perhaps the Players' most controversial and erotic cover to date—was another monster, generating the chart-topping masterpiece "Love Rollercoaster" in addition to the hits "Sweet Sticky Thing" and "Fopp."

The insistent "Who'd She Coo?" from 1976's *Contradiction*, was the Players' last number one R&B hit; "O-H-I-O," from 1977's *Angel*, was their last major hit on any chart, and as the 1970s drew to a close, the band's fortunes continued to decline. *Jass-Ay-Lay-Dee* (1979) was their final Mercury effort, and upon signing to Arista, the Players returned with *Everybody Up*, followed by a pair of dismal releases on Boardwalk, 1981's *Tenderness* and 1982's *Ouch!* After 1984's *Graduation*, four years passed prior to the release of their next effort, *Back*; no new material was forthcoming, although various lineups continued performing live well into the following decade. Founding member "Satch" Satchell died in late 1995, while "Pee Wee" Middlebrooks passed on in late 1997. *—Jason Ankeny*

Observations in Time / 1968 / Capitol ♦♦♦

In the 1960s, you didn't have to live in the Deep South to have a Southern R&B sound. Aretha Franklin lived in Detroit, but many of her 1960s recordings favored the rawness and toughness of Southern soul over the sleeker, more pop-influenced soul that was coming out of Detroit as well as Chicago and Philadelphia. And even though the Ohio Players were from Dayton, many of their early recordings sound like they could have been recorded in Memphis. Produced by Johnny Brantley in New York, *Observations in Time* is full of songs that would have been perfect for a Sam & Dave or Rufus Thomas session there is no shortage of Southern-style grit on "Street Party," "The Man That I Am" or the single "Here Today and Gone Tomorrow" (which was a minor hit). However, some of these 1968 recordings hint at the type of jazz-influenced experiments that the Players would provide at Westbound in the early 1970s. The jazz influence is strong on imaginative versions of the standards "Over the Rainbow" and "Summertime," and "Cold Cold World" is the sort of jazz/blues item that one would have expected from Lou Rawls, Jimmy Witherspoon or Bobby "Blue" Bland in the 1960s. So even though the Players offer a lot of Southern-minded R&B on *Observations in Time* (which was their only album for Capitol), they aren't afraid to branch out and try some other things. Thankfully, this album was reissued on CD in the 1990s. *—Alex Henderson*

Pain / 1971 / Westbound ♦♦♦♦

Creatively, commercially, and conceptually, *Pain* was a major step forward for the Ohio Players. This 1971 album was quite a departure from their previous work—in the late-'60s, the Midwesterners' forte had been raw, hard-edged Southern-style soul along the lines of Sam & Dave, Rufus Thomas, and Wilson Pickett. But with *Pain*, they became a lot more experimental and unveiled an interesting, distinctive brand of funk that incorporated elements of jazz and blues as well as rock. The jazz influence is especially strong on "Never Had a Dream," "Singing in the Morning," and the hit title song, while "The Reds" is a progressive blues number that draws on jazz as well as psychedelic rock. It was with *Pain*, the Players' first album for Westbound, that they unveiled their goofy Granny character, which the funksters continued to have fun with on their subsequent Westbound releases but discontinued when they moved to Mercury with 1974's *Skin Tight*. And it was with *Pain* that they became famous (some would say infamous) for their erotic LP covers. Employing S&M/bondage imagery, *Pain*'s front cover was considered shocking in 1971. Although the Velvet Underground had written songs about S&M, and the British spy thriller *The Avengers* frequently hinted at kinky sex—Diana Rigg's Emma Peel character often dressed like a dominatrix—S&M and fetishism were very taboo subjects for Middle America in 1971. And not surprisingly, some retailers refused to carry *Pain*. But the album, although not huge, was a decent seller. With *Pain*, the Ohio Players' Westbound period was off to an impressive and creative start. *—Alex Henderson*

Pleasure / 1972 / Westbound ♦♦♦♦

When the Ohio Players recorded their second Westbound album, *Pleasure*, in 1972, they weren't as big as they would be from 1974-1976. But their popularity was growing—slowly but surely—and those who were hip to the band recognized it as one of the most cutting-edge acts in the funk field. A lot of bands were providing funk in 1972, but not many of them used jazz progressions as creatively as the Players use them on "Laid It," "Walked Away From You," and *Pleasure*'s title song. Those tracks are gems, and the Players are equally captivating on the sweet soul ballad "Varee Is Love." But the best known tune on the album is the goofy "Funky Worm," which employed the Players' amusing Granny character and was, in 1972, their biggest hit to date. Long after the band's popularity faded, "Funky Worm" would live on in the 1980s and 1990s thanks to the various hip-hoppers who sampled its irresistible bassline. Like *Pain* in 1971, *Pleasure* had a kinky cover that generated some controversy—the same bald woman who brandished a bullwhip and wore dominatrix attire on the front cover of *Pain* was chained up on the cover of *Pleasure*. Some folks found the Players' kinky LP covers intriguing, while others were shocked and offended. And the Players, having struggled in the 1960s, were happy to be noticed. But ultimately, it is the quality of the music—not the bondage-minded cover—that makes *Pleasure* a funk classic. *—Alex Henderson*

Ecstacy / 1973 / Westbound ♦♦♦

Throughout the 1970s, the Ohio Players were famous (or infamous) for their erotic album covers. But there are major differences between the covers of Mercury albums like *Skin Tight*, *Fire*, *Honey*, and *Contradiction* and the covers of such Westbound releases as *Pleasure* and *Pain*. At Mercury, the Players' album covers favored softcore erotica à la *Playboy* or *Penthouse*, whereas the covers of their Westbound LPs were more bizarre and offered kinky bondage/S&M imagery. Those covers came under attack from different parts of the political spectrum; some of the more radical feminists accused the Players of objectifying women, while Republicans and Christian fundamentalists accused them of promoting moral decline. And the Players were laughing all the way to the bank—at least from 1974 on. When their third Westbound album, *Ecstasy*, came out in 1973, they were still a year away from signing with Mercury and becoming really huge. But they did have a small cult following, which found that *Ecstasy* fell short of the excellence of *Pain* and *Pleasure*. Nonetheless, the material is respectable and generally decent. Serious Players fans will find sweaty funk items like "Spinning," "Black Cat," and the title song to be enjoyable even though they aren't among the band's essential recordings. While *Ecstasy* isn't recommended to casual listeners, it isn't a bad album to have in your collection if you fancy yourself a hardcore Players addict. *—Alex Henderson*

Climax / 1974 / Westbound ♦♦♦

By the time Westbound released *Climax* in 1974, the Ohio Players had left the Detroit-based label and signed with Mercury, where they would soon explode commercially with the superb *Skin Tight*. But Westbound still had enough material in the can to put together a few more Players LPs, including *Climax* and the 1975 release *Rattlesnake*. This collection contains a few songs that had already come out on previous Players albums—"Players Balling" first appeared on 1971's *Pain*, while "Sleep Talk" and the instrumental "Food Stamps, Y'all" had been heard on 1973's *Ecstasy*. But most of the tunes were previously unreleased, including the title song (a soul-jazz instrumental) and covers of "Proud Mary" and Marvin Gaye's "What's Going On." Except for "Players Balling," this collection is unremarkable—generally competent, but not remarkable or mind-blowing. *Climax* is enjoyable and interesting if you're a serious Ohio Players collector, although more casual listeners would do well to skip this album and spend their money on *Fire*, *Skin Tight*, or *Honey* instead. *—Alex Henderson*

Skin Tight / 1974 / Mercury ♦♦♦♦♦

Skin Tight was a major turning point for the Ohio Players, who had enjoyed several hits on black radio (including "Pain," "Funky Worm," "Varee Is Love" and "I Wanna Hear from You"), but hadn't been huge. Switching from Westbound to Mercury, the Dayton funksters became exactly that—huge—and went from enjoying a cult following to being one of the most celebrated funk bands of the 1970s. With *Skin Tight*, the band's erotic album covers went from employing bizarre S&M/bondage imagery to being more *Playboy*-ish, and its music became less abstract (but remained quite risk-taking and unpredictable). The title song and "Jive Turkey" are down and dirty funk classics, and the jazz-influenced "Heaven Must Be like This" illustrates the fact that the Players could also be captivatingly romantic. *—Alex Henderson*

Fire / 1975 / Mercury ♦♦♦♦♦

After greatly increasing its visibility with *Skin Tight*, the Ohio Players became even more visible with *Fire*—an unpredictable masterpiece that boasted such explosive horn-driven funk jewels as "Smoke" and the wildly addictive title song. The Players were always best known for their hard-edged funk, but in fact, there was much more to their legacy. "I Want to Be Free," the almost innocent "Together" and the remorseful "It's All Over" demonstrate that their ballads and slower material could be first-rate soul treasures. The influence of gospel imagery and the black church experience had asserted itself on *Skin Tight*'s "Is Anybody Gonna Be Saved," and does so once again on the intense "What the Hell" and the hit "Runnin' from the Devil." Without question, *Fire* was one of the Ohio Players' greatest triumphs—both commercially and artistically. *—Alex Henderson*

Greatest Hits / 1975 / Westbound ♦♦♦♦

You can be sure that when the Ohio Players' Mercury releases were burning up the R&B charts from 1974-1976, Westbound really regretted losing the band to another label. So in the mid-'70s, Westbound tried to cash in on the Players' popularity by putting out previously unreleased material that it had in the can and by assembling a *Greatest Hits* collection. Released in 1975, this vinyl LP doesn't contain any of the Players' big Mercury hits—you won't find "Love Rollercoaster," "Fire," "Skin Tight," "I Want to Be Free," or "Heaven Must Be Like This" on *Greatest Hits*. What you will find are some of the best recordings that they made for Westbound from 1971-1973, including "Pain" and "I Wanna Hear From You" from *Pain* and "Pleasure," "Funky Worm," "Walt's First Trip," and "Varee Is Love" from *Pleasure*. Less essential but still enjoyable are the title songs of *Ecstasy* and *Climax*. Sometimes excellent and sometimes merely decent, *Greatest Hits* points to the fact that the Players' Westbound period should not be overlooked. *—Alex Henderson*

Honey / 1975 / Mercury ♦♦♦♦♦

Honey may have had the most controversial LP cover of 1975. Its erotic cover, which depicted a nude model covered in honey, was protested by feminists when it was alleged that the model had become stuck to the floor during the photo shoot. Some retailers, in fact, refused to carry it. All the controversy certainly didn't hurt the album commercially. In 1975, the Ohio Players were one of R&B's most successful acts, and were inescapable for anyone who listened to black radio at the time. The album kept the band's commercial momentum going thanks to such hard-driving funk as "Love Rollercoaster" (a song that was sampled to death by rappers in the 1980s and '90s and covered by the Red Hot Chili Peppers in 1996), "Fopp," and the playfully jazz-influenced hit "Sweet Sticky Thing." While the Players' outstanding contributions to funk would continue to have an enormous impact long after the band's popularity faded, it's important to stress that only about half of *Honey* falls into the funk category. In fact, lead singer Sugarfoot's moving performance on the remorseful "Alone" makes one wish that the Players' ballads were discussed more often. *—Alex Henderson*

Rattlesnake / 1975 / Westbound ♦♦♦

When the Ohio Players' Mercury smashes were burning up the charts in the mid-'70s, Westbound no doubt regretted letting the funksters get away and wished that it had been the label that released "Fire," "Love Rollercoaster," and "I Want to Be Free." But since Westbound no longer had the Players under contract, it tried to cash in on their popularity by putting out material that it had in the can. Released in 1975 but recorded from 1972-1973—when the Players were still signed to Westbound—*Rattlesnake* is a collection that only a hardcore Players fan would find of interest. Not that the material is bad; most of it is decent, if less than remarkable. Though *Rattlesnake* contains a few songs that had already come out on 1972's *Pleasure* or 1973's *Ecstacy* (including the funky "Spinning," the infectious "Laid It," and the sentimental ballad "Varee Is Love"), its main focus is previously unreleased material. And the material that Westbound pulls from its vaults ranges from the funky title song and the disco-ish instrumental "Hollywood Hump" (which would have been at home on a KC & the Sunshine Band album) to the jazz instrumental "Gone Forever." Meanwhile, "Rooster Poot" is a mildly amusing funk tune that features the Players' Granny character, which they retired for good after signing with Mercury. Although far from essential and not recommended to casual listeners, *Rattlesnake* is an interesting listen if you're a seasoned collector. *—Alex Henderson*

Contradiction / 1976 / Mercury ♦♦♦♦

Upon the release of this album, the Ohio Players were at the pinnacle of their long music careers, which date back to the late '50s. This album produced the number one *Billboard* R&B single "Who'd She Coo." The rhythm arrangement and jazzy horn arrangement are complemented by a titillating guitar, colorful vocals, and a suggestive lyric. While the title is "Who'd She Coo," the chant is actually "oochie coo" but was modified due to its racy content. The ballad "My Life," with its rolling rhythm and frigid background vocals, shines with Leroy Bonner's agile baritone. Still on a somber note, "Bi-Centennial" sends a social message to the masses, and the title track is a direct reflection of life. Some of these compositions stray from course with instrumental interludes, but that can be understood considering that the group was initially assembled as an instrumental band. "Who'd She Coo" was the funk ensemble's last number one hit, but they would return to the Top Ten on their album *Angel* with "O-H-I-O." Though there were competitive groups emerging, internal strife facilitated the demise of this pioneering funk band. *—Craig Lytle*

★ **Gold** / 1976 / Mercury ♦♦♦♦♦
When it gets right down to it, the Ohio Players' albums were as memorable for their risqué album covers as they were for their music. Sure, there were some seriously funky individual tracks, but the Players couldn't keep the momentum up throughout the course of an entire album. And that's why *Gold* is such a useful collection, even in light of more comprehensive latter-day collections. *Gold* has the good stuff and absolutely no filler. From the scorching "Fire" and the wild "Love Rollercoaster" to the sly "Jive Turkey" and "Who'd She Coo?," nearly every one of the group's finest songs is present and accounted for on *Gold*. Naturally, there are some omissions—"Funky Worm" really should have been on the collection, especially since it was their first number-one R&B hit—but this album should satisfy most listeners who just want the hits. If you want to dig a little deeper into their catalog without sampling their albums, try *Funk on Fire: The Mercury Anthology*, but otherwise, stick with the *Gold* and you'll reap its rewards. *—Leo Stanley*

Angel / 1977 / Mercury ♦♦♦
There are three elements that can always be found on the Ohio Players' albums that were released during their heyday: funky tracks, hyped ballads and sexually suggestive album covers. This LP is no different, featuring three releases in "Body Vibes," "O-H-I-O" and "Merry Go Round." The first and last peaked at 19 and 77, respectively on the *Billboard* R&B charts. The second of the three is an uptempo cut, in which the song's title is the only lyric; it is repeated in a whispery chant in the verse and the word itself is sung throughout the chorus. This formula proved successful as the single cracked the Top Ten at number nine inside of 18 weeks. It was also the last Top Ten single for the Dayton, OH, funk aggregate. "Angel," the title track, and "Can You Still Love Me" were not released, but are classic Ohio Players compositions. "Angel" is a midtempo number honed with dancing rhythms and piercing horns that Leroy "Sugarfoot" Bonner shrouds with his trademark baritone, complemented by superb background vocals. Bonner maintains that same vocal appeal on "Can You Still Love Me," leaving room for falsetto-flavored background vocals that are creatively arranged. *—Craig Lytle*

Mr. Mean / 1977 / Mercury ♦
From "Pain" to "Heaven Must Be Like This" and "Sweet Sticky Thing," the Ohio Players often fared well when they incorporated elements of jazz. Jazz influences were especially strong when they recorded *Mr. Mean*, a soundtrack album that contains its share of instrumentals and received a variety of reactions from fans. More subtle than other Players projects, this R&B/jazz effort didn't emphasize the type of hard, aggressive funk they were best known for. To be sure, *Mr. Mean* had its detractors, who saw it as too laid-back. But while it's far from one of the Players' best albums, songs ranging from the clever title song to "The Big Score" and "Fight Me, Chase Me" aren't bad. And to their credit, the Players were experimenting and taking chances—some of which pay off, and some of which don't. *—Alex Henderson*

Jass-Ay-Lay-Dee / 1978 / Mercury ♦♦
After taking a break from aggressive, sweaty funk on *Mr. Mean*, the Ohio Players made an artistically successful return to it with the neglected *Jass-Ay-Lay-Dee*. By 1978, their popularity had decreased considerably, and funk fans were much more interested in what newer arrivals like Cameo, Bootsy Collins, Slave and Rick James were up to. But the Players still had some life left in them, and energetic offerings like "Dance (If Ya Wanta)," "Sleepwalkin'" and the single "Funk-O-Knots" aren't anything to be ashamed of. This album may not be in a class with *Skin Tight*, *Fire*, or *Honey*, but it's certainly decent. *Jass-Ay-Lay-Dee* turned out to be the Players' last album for Mercury—after that, they moved to Arista and recorded one more worthwhile album, 1979's *Everybody Up*. And when the early 1980s rolled around, a downsized version of the Players would end up on Boardwalk and record the worst albums of their career. *—Alex Henderson*

The Ohio Players / 1978 / Pickwick ♦♦♦
This self-titled budget LP from 1978 could be described as a partial reissue of 1968's *Observations in Time*, which was the Ohio Players' only album for Capitol. "Partial" is the operative word; *The Ohio Players* contains nine of the 11 songs that were on *Observations in Time*. But for some reason—possibly licensing restrictions—"Street Party" and "The Man That I Am" (both of which owe an obvious debt to the Memphis soul of Stax Records) are missing. Everything else offered on *Observations in Time* is offered on this LP, and that includes the minor hit "Here Today and Gone Tomorrow" as well as the Players' interesting, jazz-influenced versions of George Gershwin's "Summertime" and Harold Arlen's "Over the Rainbow." Back in the late '70s, no one went broke acquiring *The Ohio Players*, which sold for as little as $2 in some mom-and-pop record stores. At that price, listeners didn't expect miracles—although it would have been nice if Pickwick had reissued *Observations in Time* in its entirety. *—Alex Henderson*

Everybody Up / 1979 / Arista ♦♦♦
The Ohio Players' stay at Mercury ended with 1978's *Jass-Ay-Lay-Dee*, and the funksters switched to Arista with their next album, 1979's *Everybody Up*. By 1979, the Players were past their prime—both creatively and commercially. Hoping to regain their popularity, they decided to try something different—and that meant bringing a lot of disco gloss to their funk. On catchy, if unremarkable, cuts like "Make Me Feel," "Say It," and the title song, the Players favor a slick disco-funk approach along the lines of Earth, Wind & Fire's "Boogie Wonderland" or Kool & the Gang's "Ladies' Night." The only tune on the LP that is truly weak is "Don't Say Goodbye," which goes for the sort of bluesy ambience that characterized "Alone" but misses the mark badly and ends up sounding lethargic. For the most part, however, *Everybody Up* isn't a bad album—uneven and less than remarkable, but not bad. Although hardly in a class with *Fire*, *Skin Tight*, or *Honey*, this vinyl LP has its moments—and it is certainly superior to the two weak albums that the Players recorded for Boardwalk in the early '80s. Nonetheless, *Everybody Up* received very little attention. *—Alex Henderson*

Tenderness / 1981 / Boardwalk ♦♦♦
After being on nearly a two-year hiatus, the veteran R&B/funk aggregate signed with the now-defunct Boardwalk Records after being with Mercury for seven years and a brief stay with Arista. Hoping to jumpstart their once prosperous status, the Ohio Players recorded two Otis Redding classics: "Try a Little Tenderness" and "Sittin' on the Dock of Bay." Reduced to a quartet on this recording, they lay their patented style on the former. Beginning as a soulful ballad, the track kicks into high gear with Leroy "Sugar" Bonner's trademark baritone complemented by horns and a groovin' bassline. The single only managed to reach the number-40 position on the *Billboard* R&B charts after ten weeks, but it was truly deserving of a better outing. "Sittin' on the Dock of Bay" was never released. The Ohio Players did not present anything new on this single; this is probably more a tribute to Redding. There are also two other featured singles that were promoted by the label: "Sometimes I Cry" and "Skinny." The former is a slow, drifting song with a twist of country & western that is unlike any other Ohio Players recording; the single never charted. The latter, the title track, is a funky composition driven by Bonner's scratch baritone and a delayed, groovin' bassline; it posted a number-46 rating after ten weeks. *—Craig Lytle*

Ouch! / 1982 / Boardwalk ♦♦
In the early 1980s, hardcore fans of the Ohio Players would have loved to see the funksters come out with a truly great album and return to the top of the charts. But that didn't happen—there wouldn't be another *Fire* or *Skin Tight* for the Players, and it was obvious that the band was past their prime. The second of two little-known albums that the Midwesterners recorded for Boardwalk in 1981, *Ouch!* was a slight improvement over its forgettable predecessor *Tenderness*, but it's disappointing nonetheless. Thist LP was produced by Richard "Dimples" Fields, a talented vocalist/songwriter/producer, to be sure, but *Ouch!* is hardly his finest hour and isn't among the Players' more memorable releases. While the Players had done most of their own writing in the 1970s, almost all of the writing on *Ouch!* was done by Fields and Belinda Wilson. For all of its flaws, this album has its moments. The Players' cover of Charles Wright's "Do Your Thing" isn't bad, and some of the more likable tunes that Fields and Wilson contribute include the Motown-ish "My Baby Gets the Best of My Love," the romantic ballad "Devoted," and the Philadelphia International-ish "The Star of the Party." All things considered, however, *Ouch!* is an LP that only completists and die-hard collectors would be interested in. *—Alex Henderson*

Back / 1988 / Track Record ♦♦

Funk on Fire: The Mercury Anthology / Jun. 6, 1995 / Mercury ♦♦♦♦♦
One hour, 54 minutes and 12 seconds of innovative funk on two discs is nothing to sneeze at, particularly when the tracks are prime Ohio Players cuts. Mercury adroitly chronicles their chart-blazing career with full-length, unedited versions of winners and album treats. From the bluesy, strutting "Jive Turkey" to "More Than Love," the group displays their superb musicianship and ingenuity on 28 slabs of funk and soul. The guys proved they can slow-jam with anyone on "Together" and the super-lush "Honey." The Ohio Players were affectionally known as Sugarfoot, Billy, Pee Wee, Merv, Diamond, Jones, and Satch, all of whom contributed collectively in the writing and production of all the songs. Everyone is familiar with the hits, and most of their fans already have them; it's unsung pearls like "Good Luck Charm," and the convenience of having these smokin' grooves in one sweet package, that makes *Funk on Fire* a must. *—Andrew Hamilton*

Lonely Street / Jul. 14, 1995 / Prime Cuts ♦
Released in 1995 by a Canadian label called Retro Music, *Lonely Street* is a budget CD that contains ten songs the Ohio Players recorded for Capitol and the small Compass label in 1968. "Summertime," "Bad Bargain," "Over the Rainbow," "Stop Lying to Yourself," and "Here Today and Gone Tomorrow" are from the Capitol album *Observations in Time*, while "You Don't Mean It," "Tell Me Why," and "It's a Crying Shame" are among the recordings that came out on Compass. *Lonely Street* doesn't get a low rating because of the songs themselves, which fall short of essential but are pleasing and worth hearing if you're a serious Ohio Players collector—this CD gets low marks because of its poor sound quality. With the proper digital remastering, these recordings would have sounded good on CD. But Retro Music didn't remaster the recordings like it should have, and as a result, *Lonely Street* has its share of pops, ticks, and so on, and ends up sounding like an old, worn out LP. In fact, these recordings sounded much better on vinyl than they do on this disappointing CD. Ohio Players fans who want to hear this early material would do well to pass on *Lonely Street* and look elsewhere. *—Alex Henderson*

Ol' School / 1997 / Castle ♦♦♦
A live set from the Players that's okay but nothing to shout about. The CD is enhanced, which means you can slide it into the CD drive of your computer and view different images of the group on your monitor. Some of the songs roll on too long, like "Fire," over 11 minutes—yawn. "Pain," from their Westbound recording days, is a pleasant surprise, but they only give you a minute and 39 seconds of the classic. "Sweet Sticky Thang" comes off better live than the studio version, but "Love Rollercoaster" sounds as silly as ever. A track entitled "MegaMix" brings up the rear and is a total waste of time; it's merely a four-minute medley of the CD tracks. *—Andrew Hamilton*

Orgasm: The Very Best of the Westbound Years / Jun. 30, 1998 / Southbound ♦♦♦♦♦
The majority of music fans are familiar with the legendary Ohio Players through such mid- to late-'70s pop-funk hits as "Love Rollercoaster," "Fire," and "Fopp." What many

don't realize is that the band had been around since the '60s, and released a trilogy of hard funk records from 1972-1973 on the Westbound label—*Pain, Pleasure*, and *Ecstasy*—that were easily comparable to the early-'70s classics by their rival Westbound labelmates, Funkadelic. And since the albums have been out-of-print for some time, the European import *Orgasm: The Very Best of the Westbound Years* is a solid collection of tracks from this era. Included is the 1972 novelty hit "Funky Worm," as well as all the sizzling title tracks from the three albums. A pair of songs from outside the trilogy is added, "Climax" (one of the collection's best tracks) and a cover of Marvin Gaye's "What's Going On," both from 1974. A previously unissued track, "Ain't That Lovin' You (For More Reasons Than One)," is tacked on the end, making *Orgasm* an excellent anthology of the Ohio Players' early years, before they achieved mass mainstream success. *—Greg Prato*

The O'Jays

f. 1958, Canton, OH

Group / Soul, Philly Soul, Pop-Soul, Quiet Storm, Urban

The O'Jays were one of Philadelphia soul's most popular and long-lived outfits, rivaled only by the Spinners as soul's greatest vocal group of the '70s. In their prime, the O'Jays' recordings epitomized the Philly soul sound; smooth, rich harmonies backed by elaborate arrangements, lush strings, and a touch of contemporary funk. They worked extensively with the legendary production/songwriting team of Kenny Gamble and Leon Huff, becoming the flagship artist of the duo's Philadelphia International label. The O'Jays were equally at home singing sweet love ballads or up-tempo dance tunes, the latter of which were often mouthpieces for Gamble & Huff's social concerns. Although the O'Jays couldn't sustain their widespread popularity in the post-disco age, they continued to record steadily all the way up to the present day, modifying their production to keep up with the times.

The O'Jays were formed in 1958 in Canton, OH, where all five original members—Eddie LeVert, Walter Williams, William Powell, Bill Isles, and Bobby Massey—attended McKinley High School. Inspired to start a singing group after seeing a performance by Frankie Lymon & the Teenagers, they first called themselves the Triumphs, then switched to the Mascots in 1960. The Mascots made their recording debut in 1961 with the single "Miracles," issued on the Cincinnati-based King label. It earned them a fan in the influential Cleveland DJ Eddie O'Jay, who gave them some airplay and career advice; in turn, the group renamed themselves the O'Jays in 1963, after having recorded for Apollo Records with producer Don Davis. Under their new name, the O'Jays signed with Imperial and hooked up with producer H.B. Barnum, who would helm their first charting single, 1963's "Lonely Drifter," plus several more singles that followed. Isles left the group in 1965 and was not replaced, leaving them a quartet; late in the year, they released their first-ever album, *Comin' Through*. In 1967, the O'Jays left Imperial for Bell, where they landed their first Top Ten single on the R&B charts, "I'll Be Sweeter Tomorrow (Than I Was Today)." Discouraged by the difficulty of following that success, the group considered throwing in the towel until they met Gamble & Huff—then working as a production team for the Neptune label—in 1968. Gamble & Huff took an interest in the group, and they recorded several successful R&B singles together; however, Neptune folded in 1971, leaving the O'Jays in limbo, and Massey decided to exit the group.

Fortunately, Gamble & Huff formed their own label, Philadelphia International, and made the O'Jays—now a trio—one of their first signings. The O'Jays' label debut, *Back Stabbers*, released in 1972, became a classic landmark of Philly soul, and finally made the group stars; the paranoid title track hit the pop Top Five, and the utopian "Love Train" went all the way to number one (both singles topped the R&B charts). It was the beginning of a remarkable run that produced nearly 30 chart singles over the course of the '70s, plus a series of best-selling albums and a bevy of number-one hits on the R&B charts. The O'Jays followed up their breakthrough with another classic LP, *Ship Ahoy*, in 1973; it featured the number-one R&B hit "For the Love of Money," a funky protest number that still ranks as one of their signature songs, as well as the ten-minute title track, an ambitious suite recounting the ocean journeys of African slaves. *Survival* was another hit in 1975, spinning off the hits "Let Me Make Love to You" and the R&B number one "Give the People What They Want." *Family Reunion* found the group making concessions to the emerging disco sound, which got them their third Top Five pop hit in "I Love Music, Pt. 1."

Unfortunately, William Powell was diagnosed with cancer that year, and although he continued to record with the group for a time (appearing on 1976's *Message in Our Music*), he was forced to retire from live performing, and passed away on May 26, 1977. Powell's replacement was Sammy Strain, a 12-year veteran of Little Anthony & the Imperials. The O'Jays regrouped on the albums *Travelin' at the Speed of Thought* (1977) and *So Full of Love* (1978), the latter of which produced their final Top Five pop hit, "Use Ta Be My Girl." *Identify Yourself* (1979) began to show signs of wear and tear in the group's successful formula, and often consciously attempted to follow disco trends. Although it sold respectably, it marked the beginning of a decline in the O'Jays' commercial fortunes. Undaunted by the increasingly diminished returns of their early-'80s LPs, the group kept plugging away, and never completely disappeared from the R&B charts. They finally left Philadelphia International and signed with EMI for 1987's *Let Me Touch You*, which melded their classic sound with up-to-date urban-R&B production. Powered by the Gamble & Huff-penned R&B number-one "Lovin' You," as well as the increased visibility of Eddie LeVert's sons Gerald and Sean (two-thirds of the hit urban group LeVert), the album gave their career a much-needed shot in the arm. 1989's *Serious* supplied another big R&B hit in "Have You Had Your Love Today?"; with Nathaniel Best replacing Sammy Strain, 1991's *Emotionally Yours* and 1993's *Heartbreaker* also placed very well on the R&B charts. The O'Jays' comeback didn't really extend to the pop side, and didn't attract the sort of critical praise earned by their '70s classics; as the new jack swing craze subsided, so did the group's recording activity, though they remained consistent draws on the live circuit. In 1997, now with Eric Grant joining LeVert and Williams, they returned with *Love You to Tears*. A recording layoff followed, during which the group signed with MCA; they debuted for the label with *For the Love...*, which was released in 2001. *—Steve Huey*

Comin' Through / 1965 / Imperial ✦✦✦

The O'Jays were a fledgling five-member outfit when they issued their debut album in 1965. They generated a little attention with the dance/novelty tune "Do the Wiggle," and also issued a pair of good ballads in "Lonely Drifter" and "Lipstick Traces." None of these songs were as masterfully produced or arranged as the epic Gamble & Huff material, but it did reveal the potential they had for R&B stardom. This album has been out of print for years, although some of the songs have surfaced on anthologies. *—Ron Wynn*

Back on Top / 1968 / Bell ✦✦✦

The album cover deceptively depicts five O'Jays when actually only four members—Eddie LeVert, Walter Williams, William Powell and Bobby Massey—sing on these tracks; Bill Isle, the fifth member, quit in the late '60s, and the cover was shot in the mid-'60s, when the group recorded for Imperial Records. George Kerr produced most of these tracks, with some productions from the Poindexter brothers; the recordings were originally released on Bell Records. "I'll Be Sweeter Tomorrow," a gorgeous ballad, became their highest chart entry to date. The follow-up, "Look Over Your Shoulder," nearly duplicated its predecessor's success; both were indicators of good things to come. The B-sides of the aforementioned, "I Dig Your Act" and "I'm So Glad I Found You," were both quality uptempo grooves, and all four sides were led by Eddie LeVert. Walter Williams handled the lead on their third 45 for Bell Records, "The Choice," an energetic message about finding yourself. It did poorly, and its flip, "Going, Going, Gone," had more in common with the first two releases but was not nearly as compelling. The fourth single, "I Miss You," didn't receive much play, even in the Cantonian's adopted hometown of Cleveland. The slow, meandering ballad just didn't have enough of the right stuff. The flip, "Now That I Found You," featured LeVert and Williams alternating leads on the same song for the first time. Two more singles were released by Bell: "Don't You Know a True Love When You See It," which was a drastic change in their style, and "Four for the Price of One," released in 1973 to capitalize on their success at Philadelphia International Records. Bell slapped "Look Over Your Shoulder" onto the flip of the remake of Larry Williams and Johnny "Guitar" Watson's "Two for the Price of One." Walter Williams' best lead, "Just Another Guy," tenderly sung in his mercurial baritone, never appeared on a 45. This is an O'Jays fanatics' must-have; the only disappointment is that neither Kerr nor the Poindexter brothers saw fit to feature the late William Powell's chilling falsetto. *—Andrew Hamilton*

The O'Jays in Philadelphia / 1969 / Epic/Legacy ✦✦✦✦✦

Contrary to what its title suggests, *The O'Jays in Philadelphia* isn't a live album. Rather, the title of this studio date refers to the beginning of their association with Philly's R&B scene and producers/songwriters Kenny Gamble & Leon Huff. What they didn't know in 1969 was just how long and fruitful that association would end up being. This album wasn't the major hit that *Back Stabbers* would be, but not for lack of strong material. From "One Night Affair" to "Let Me in Your World," this superb album is quintessential Philly soul. While Eddie LeVert's gospel-influenced belting is as gritty as anything that came from Stax Records, the production is as notably sleek. A few years later, Gamble & Huff would produce a longer, heavily syncopated version of "Affair" for Jerry Butler that some soul historians exalt as the first disco single. The main problem with the CD configuration of this classic is its skimpiness—Legacy could have easily added at least another half hour of material. *—Alex Henderson*

☆ **Back Stabbers** / 1972 / Epic/Legacy ✦✦✦✦✦

Although you could lean toward *Ship Ahoy*, it would be hard to argue with the general assessment that *Back Stabbers* is the O'Jays' greatest album. Certainly, no other single in 1973 was as transcendent and definitive as "Love Train," without question their greatest track. "Back Stabbers" isn't far behind it; the message, harmonies, Eddie LeVert's lead, and the group's refrains are all testimonies to soul's glory, and Gamble & Huff were in peak form. There were other good songs on the record, like "Listen to the Clock on the Wall" and "Shiftless, Shady, Jealous Kind of People," and three other hit singles, "992 Arguments," "Time to Get Down," and "Sunshine," but they were completely blown away by "Love Train" and "Back Stabbers." [Originally released in August 1972 as Philadelphia International 31712, *Back Stabbers* was reissued on March 12, 1996, as Epic Associated/Legacy 661J13, as part of Legacy's *Rhythm & Soul* Series, with liner notes by David Ritz.] *—Ron Wynn & William Ruhlmann*

Ship Ahoy / 1973 / Philadelphia International ✦✦✦✦✦

The "other" O'Jays album masterpiece, *Ship Ahoy* combined shattering message tracks and stunning love songs in a fashion matched only by Curtis Mayfield's finest material. From the album cover showing a slave ship to the memorable title song and incredible "For the Love of Money," Gamble & Huff addressed every social ill from envy to racism and greed. Eddie LeVert's leads were consistently magnificent, as were the harmonies, production and arrangements. "Put Your Hands Together" and "You Got Your Hooks in Me" would be good album cuts, but on *Ship Ahoy* they were merely icing on the cake. *—Ron Wynn*

Survival / 1975 / Epic/Legacy ✦✦✦✦

The O'Jays followed the spectacular *Backstabbers* and *Ship Ahoy* with the good, but not on the same level, *Survival*. It was unrealistic to expect masterpieces every time out, and the LP included many strong ballads and good message tracks. But while it may not have been as epic in its performances and compositions, it was certainly the other albums' equal in sales strength. The group had two number one R&B hits in 1975, "Give the People What They Want" and "I Love Music (Pt. 1)." In addition, the title track made the charts as the B-side to "Let Me Make Love To You," another rousing ballad. *—Ron Wynn*

Family Reunion / 1975 / Philadelphia International ✦✦✦

In the 1970s, Philadelphia International Records could seemingly do no wrong where the O'Jays were concerned. The Cleveland trio recorded one gem after another under Gamble & Huff's direction, and *Family Reunion* was no exception. Nothing on this CD has the angry bite of "Back Stabbers," "Don't Call Me Brother" or "Rich Get Richer," and the mood is upbeat and optimistic on everything from the uplifting "Unity" to the ballad "Stairway to Heaven" (not to be confused with the Led Zeppelin song) to the escapist party anthem "Livin' for the Weekend." With the intoxicating"I Love Music," the O'Jays stressed the soul side of disco and provided one of the most appealing hits of the disco era. From start to finish, *Family Reunion* was a valuable addition to a catalogue that already had its share of treasures. *—Alex Henderson*

Message in Our Music / 1976 / The Right Stuff ♦♦♦
The O'Jays' vocals are stellar throughout this lively eight-song collection. Political and social lyrics weigh heavy but don't overburden this set. "Darlin' Darlin' Baby" is a killer midtempo love romp with equally effective leads by Eddie LeVert and Walter Williams. "Paradise" was overlooked, with Walter Williams doing his falsetto "doo dah"s on the breaks and the trio spitting out Gamble & Huff's lyrics at breakneck speed. "Make a Joyful Noise" finds Eddie wailing like a Baptist preacher on a song that's more gospel than R&B; the title track is a typical message song made extraordinary by a great production and sensational vocals. The harmonies on "I Swear I Love No One But You" will blow you away. Another good slice of soul from the Canton, OH, natives. *—Andrew Hamilton*

☆ **Collectors' Items** / 1977 / Philadelphia International ♦♦♦♦♦
Collectors' Items is an O'Jays compilation with a narrow range (basically 1972-1976), a contradictory title, and odd sequencing, but a parade of huge hits that make up for any of its other faults. Using two LPs (or one CD, in its digital incarnation) to collect songs from only six albums, the set has plenty of room to anthologize all of the smooth Philly soul trio's biggest singles from the early- to mid-'70s: "Love Train," "Back Stabbers," "I Love Music," "Give the People What They Want," "Livin' for the Weekend." Even though all of the songs that *had* to be here *are* here, a few bizarre choices make this less than the definitive compilation of their time: why take "Sunshine" from 1972's *Back Stabbers*, but not the far superior "Time to Get Down" or "992 Arguments" (or both)? Why use "Darlin' Darlin' Baby (Sweet Tender Love)" from 1976's *Message in Our Music*, but not the gorgeous title track? These few questionable decisions aside, *Collectors' Items* delivers exactly what fans expect, and there *is* actually one item for the collectors: a previously unreleased cover of "Wildflower," a recent hit for the Canadian group Skylark as well as the New Birth. *—John Bush*

Travelin' at the Speed of Thought / 1977 / Philadelphia International ♦♦♦
This album from the Cleveland, OH-based trio continues to primarily convey a profound social message of the album's key producers and label owners Kenny Gamble & Leon Huff. Gamble in particular was the lyrical force that kept the O'Jays' (and labelmates') songs seasoned with a conscious meaning that has come to transcend time. On this set, the only number to chart was the charged "Work on Me." While Walt Williams is as smooth as always, Eddie LeVert interjects his invigorating vocal delivery with feet-stomping ad libs. The single slipped into the *Billboard* R&B charts' Top Ten at number seven, staying afloat for 17 weeks. The threesome stay consistent with their previous Gamble & Huff releases by intertwining gospel rhythms, R&B melodies, sermonic lyrics and breathtaking vocal exhibitions. Most of the tracks here represent the upbeat groove the group is known for. The O'Jays mellow-out with "Feelings" and "Let's Spend Some Time Together." The former is a re-make of the classic pop standard. The common listener would not recognize Williams' falsetto introduction or Eddie LeVert's toned-down, somber approach to the lyric. However, as the song builds, Eddie's trademark style begans to surface. The latter is another atypical O'Jays number. Williams breezes through this doo wop-flavored number; a style for which they are not known. Both are beautiful numbers and too little heard from. *—Craig Lytle*

So Full of Love / 1978 / The Right Stuff ♦♦♦
None of the albums the O'Jays recorded for Philadelphia International in the 1970s were weak or disappointing, although some were stronger than others. *So Full of Love* isn't quite essential, and isn't in a class with *Back Stabbers*, *Ship Ahoy* or *Family Reunion*. But the platinum album does have a lot going for it, including the major hit "Use Ta Be My Girl," and the heartfelt ballads "Cry Together" and "Brandy," and the captivating "This Time Baby," which would become a hit for soul/disco diva Jackie Moore in 1979. A funk treasure that should have been a major hit was the intense "Strokety Stroke." Once again, the O'Jays worked with Philly's best—not only Gamble & Huff, but also Thom Bell & Bunny Sigler. *Love* was a departure from their previous Philly International offerings in that it contained no social or political commentary whatsoever—with the disco era in full swing, Eddie LeVert felt that the market for R&B message songs had dried up. *—Alex Henderson*

Identify Yourself / 1979 / Philadelphia International ♦♦♦
Compared to their other Philadelphia International releases, *Identify Yourself* is weak. Of the eight sides, Kenny Gamble & Leon Huff produced only four, while Thom Bell contributed one. The other three are from the O'Jays' camp. "Forever Mine" scored on the R&B charts. The rest of the LP, however, save for the title cut and "Get Out and Party," is unmemorable. "Sing a Happy Song" is catchy, but it's also irritating. *—Andrew Hamilton*

The Year 2000 / 1980 / Philadelphia International ♦♦
Futuristically titled, *The Year 2000* may arguably be the O'Jays' least compelling Philadelphia International LP. Only Bunny Sigler's sensuous, grinding "Once Is Not Enough" has that oomph, and it went unnoticed on this hitless collection. Sigler always delivered the goods for the O'Jays composing some of the Canton natives' most soulful songs—"You and I," "Sunshine," and "You Got Your Hooks in Me," to name a few. The seven other songs (some from the O'Jays camp) would have been thumbed down by Motown's quality control department and banished to the vaults forever. *—Andrew Hamilton*

My Favorite Person / 1982 / Philly ♦♦♦
Even average O'Jays releases have outstanding tracks, and *My Favorite Person* is a prime example. Its single releases didn't make much of a splash, so the LP went unnoticed, as compared to some of their other Philadelphia International offerings. "I Just Want to Satisfy You" didn't ignite the charts when dropped as the first single from the album, though it was a nice lilting number with a lazy light-baritone lead by Walter Williams. But selections like "Your Body's Here With Me (But Your Mind Is on the Other Side of Town")—a devastating soul-to-the-bone ballad that scored well on R&B stations but was ignored by pop radio—are definitive O'Jays. The same is true of the almost-as-good "Your True Heart (A Shining Star)"; a piano is raised in the mix and provides a good counter to Eddie LeVert's outstanding lead. Cleveland native Cecil Womack (Bobby Womack's brother and former Valentino) contributed as a songwriter and musician. *—Andrew Hamilton*

When Will I See You Again / 1983 / Philadelphia International ♦♦♦
The O'Jays didn't have any big crossover hits or R&B chart-toppers with this album, but it was still a fine effort. The production and arrangements were outstanding, the harmonies and leads nicely done, and there were several fine songs. It produced some R&B chart singles, although nothing proved a smash. If anything, it was proof that sometimes no matter what the artists and producers do, it just doesn't succeed to the extent that it should or they hoped. *—Ron Wynn*

Greatest Hits / 1984 / Philadelphia International ♦♦♦♦♦

Love & More / 1984 / Philadelphia International ♦♦♦
This is a nice mid-'80s album, although the O'Jays weren't scoring the huge hits that often anymore. But they had matured, were still singing wonderful adult ballads, doing an occasionally exuberant uptempo tune, and regularly selling out mid-sized arenas and black community engagements. Eddie LeVert's throaty vocals and their close harmonies remained engaging and impressive; their material was just a bit below its peak levels of the '70s. *—Ron Wynn*

Let Me Touch You / 1987 / EMI America ♦♦♦
The O'Jays made tight three-member harmonies and alternating leads from Eddie LeVert, Walter Williams, and Sammy Strain a successful formula throughout the '80s, and this album included a superb ballad, "Lovin' You." It was an R&B chart topper, one of two Top Ten singles from the album, and continued a good run for the group on Philadelphia International. *—Ron Wynn*

Reflections in Gold (1973–82) / 1988 / Charly ♦♦♦♦♦
A crafty culling of handpicked O'Jays tracks from their successful Philadelphia International recording years. The appealing selections include the sermonizing "Don't Call Me Brother," an epic dramatization that points fingers at the criminal element in our communities. "You and Me" and "Your Body's Here With Me (But Your Mind Is on the Other Side of Town)") are superlative ballads, two keepers. Most groups would die for one or two good slow jams a career; the O'Jays have had enough to stretch across Rhode Island. The moving "Ship Ahoy" is one of many tunes on *Reflections in Gold* taken from *Ship Ahoy*, arguably the O'Jays' best album. Nothing romps better then "Now That We Found Love," a popular cut that charted for Third World. The emotional "Help (Somebody Please)" is not as familiar as other tracks, but it's a gripper from the pronounced opening bass beats. This is a good pickup even if you have more complete O'Jays CDs, because many of these excellent songs were omitted. *—Andrew Hamilton*

Serious / Mar. 1989 / EMI America ♦♦♦
After a long and artistically triumphant association with Kenny Gamble & Leon Huff that lasted from 1969's *The O'Jays in Philadelphia* to 1987's *Let Me Love You*, the O'Jays broke their ties to the legendary Philly producers/songwriters, left Philadelphia International Records and opted for a more high-tech "urban contemporary" approach with *Serious*. Obviously well aware of what younger R&B units like Guy, LeVert (lead singer Eddie LeVert's young sons and relatives) and Today were up to, the veteran soulsters incorporated new jack swing and hip-hop elements and made it clear they were intent on changing with the times. But thankfully, the gritty, gospel-influenced belting that made the O'Jays so dynamic to begin with remained. Though *Serious* (whose producers include members of the O'Jays and LeVert, Terry Stubbs and Dennis Lambert) isn't in a class with gems like *Back Stabbers* or *Family Reunion*, there's a lot to admire here—including the vulnerable "Out of My Mind," the silky "Never Been Better" and the earthy ballad "Serious Hold on Me." The engaging "Pot Can't Call the Kettle Black" speaks volumes about the O'Jays' outlook —urging fellow baby boomers who criticize their kids' hip-hop to let them be themselves and remember when they were young. *—Alex Henderson*

Emotionally Yours / Jan. 21, 1991 / EMI America ♦♦♦
With *Emotionally Yours*, the O'Jays clearly had the same goals that defined *Serious*—to appeal to the urban-contemporary market, yet remain true to their soul music roots. And for the most part, this approach succeeds. The production (which is handled by two of the O'Jays plus Terry Stubbs, Narada Michael Walden, among others) is decidedly high-tech, and elements of hip-hop and new jack swing are employed. But there's no mistaking the fact that the gritty, full-bodied vocals are by the O'Jays. Although not an outstanding album like *Message in Our Music* or *Ship Ahoy*, *Emotionally Yours* definitely has many strong points ranging from the socially aware funk smokers "Respect" and "Something for Nothing" (both of which employ rappers and come across as "Back Stabbers" or "Give the People What They Want" with a touch of Guy!) to the heartfelt balladry and crooning of "If I Find Love Again" "Closer to You" and "Keep on Pleasin' Me." *Emotionally Yours* proves that even at their second best, the O'Jays are far superior to most '90s R&B artists. *—Alex Henderson*

Heartbreaker / 1993 / EMI America ♦♦♦
For *Heartbreaker*, The O'Jays made concessions to changing tastes, adopting drum samples and synthesized backing, and including some new jack swing material. But they wisely didn't tampered with their strength, lush three-part harmonies anchored by the earnest lead vocals of Eddie LeVert. This release contains several intense, urgent ballads, many of them written by group members. Outside of Carlton Hunt's raps on "Trouble"

and "Can't Let You Go," many numbers aren't much different from the classic material that made them superstars in the '70s; that's both part of the music's charm and something that might trouble fans hoping the group would experiment with the vocal arrangements as well as the production. *—Ron Wynn*

Love Train: The Best of the O'Jays / Aug. 9, 1994 / Epic/Legacy ♦♦♦♦♦

All of the band's monster 1972-1976 Philadelphia International hits are here, as well as a couple of small ones. The essay by Robert Palmer is good, but at a mere ten tracks, the selection is unaccountably skimpy. *—Richie Unterberger*

Let Me Make Love to You / Jan. 31, 1995 / Epic/Legacy ♦♦♦

Like *Give the People What They Want, Let Me Make Love to You* is a concept compilation, collecting ten of the O'Jays' most under-appreciated love ballads, including the title track, which was a minor hit, "Stairway to Heaven," and "Listen to the Clock on the Wall." Again, the disc is not a hits collection, but a sampling of some of the group's finest album tracks and forgotten singles, and in that context, it's very enjoyable. *—Stephen Thomas Erlewine*

Give the People What They Want / Feb. 28, 1995 / Epic/Legacy ♦♦♦

In addition to liner notes, a major problem with the first CD configurations of the classic O'Jays albums like *Ship Ahoy* and *Family Reunion* was their brevity. By LP standards, roughly 35-40 minutes was generous; but for CDs, it's undeniably skimpy. In 1995, Sony's reissue-oriented Legacy label was fairly generous when assembling *Give the People What They Want*, a CD containing material from those gems as well as *Back Stabbers* and *Survival*. Everything here is first rate—from the angry socio-political commentary of "Give the People What They Want" and "Rich Get Richer" to the romantic optimism of "(They Call Me) Mr. Lucky," the CD reminds us how consistently superb the O'Jays were during the '70s. It also reminds us of another important fact: under Gamble & Huff, the group's albums tended to contain very little, if any, filler. Most of these pearls—including the moving "How Time Flies" and the biting "Shiftless, Shady, Jealous Kind of People"—weren't even released as singles. *—Alex Henderson*

In Bed With the O'Jays: Greatest Love Songs / Aug. 20, 1996 / EMI ♦♦♦

As if you couldn't guess, this compilation targets the group's most romantic, urban contemporary-oriented efforts, spanning 1976 to 1991. It's not the group at its peak, nor is it an accurate reflection of their diverse output. But it does have a few massive R&B hits, including "Lovin' You," "Darlin' Darlin' Baby (Sweet, Tender, Love)," and "Use to Be My Girl." Most unusual item: their cover of Bob Dylan's "Emotional Yours," from the 1991 album of the same name. *—Richie Unterberger*

Love You to Tears / Jul. 15, 1997 / Volcano ♦♦♦

Live in London / Jun. 30, 1998 / Epic/Legacy ♦♦♦

Recorded in December 1973 at the O'Jays' commercial peak, the live format gave the group chance to stretch, length-wise, beyond the time allotted to them in the studio. Although the disc is 47 minutes, there are only seven songs (six, if you don't count "Introducing the O'Jays"). So you get an eight-minute "Back Stabbers," a six-minute "Love Train," a ten-minute "Sunshine" and a long cruise through "When the World's at Peace," though "Put Your Hands Together" (then a month away from entering the American Top 40) is pretty concise. On the one hand, these live versions don't match the snazzier arrangements, and greater economy, of the studio ones. On the other, you want something a little different from a live album, and this does give you the chance to hear the group elasticize their material, with a live band and, of course, some in-song raps. Whoever thought it was a good idea to do a ten-minute cover of Skylark's "Wildflower," however, was wrong. *—Richie Unterberger*

The Ultimate Collection / 1999 / Marginal ♦♦♦♦♦

This collection contains most of the O'Jays' Imperial/Minit Records sides, one ("I'll Be Sweeter Tomorrow") from their Bell Records stint, and "Miracles," an early recording on Dayco Records. Collectors go crazy over these highly sought after pre-Philadelphia International tracks. The biggest pop record was "Lipstick Traces" led by Walter Williams. The others were awesome in northeast Ohio, including "How Does It Feel," "Lonely Drifter," "Crack Up Laughing," and "Stand in for Love." Two falsetto-led chillers by William Powell ("Oh How You Hurt Me," and "Working on Your Case,") along with the occasional lead from Williams add diversity to Eddie LeVert's frequent leads. While this is not definitive—that would take another CD—it is essential. *—Andrew Hamilton*

The Year 2000/My Favorite Person / 1999 / Capitol ♦♦♦

Classic Philadelphia Years / Jan. 18, 1999 / Music Club ♦♦♦

The rights to Philadelphia International Records (PIR) Masters are obviously available to anyone with money and the wherewithal to master, manufacture, and promote a CD. Get ready for PIR overkill. This 16-song compilation is strange. Only six of the 16 tracks were bona fide hits, but that's not the problem, it's the lesser hits and album tracks that keep this from rising above C level. The jubilant doo woping "Use To Be My Girl," and is the only big crossover hit; the other five did score heavily on the R&B chart. Of those, the dramatic "Lovin' You," and romping "Darlin', Darlin' Baby," are two excellent examples of Philly soul. Many cuts will be unfamiliar to casual fans, and will keep them from spending their benjamins. Particularly when they scan the song titles and find "Back Stabbers," "992 Arguments," "For the Love of Money," "You Got Your Hooks in Me," "Love Train," "Let Me Make Love to You," "Family Reunion," "Sunshine," and other goodies missing. Still, any O'Jay release that includes the smoldering "Your Body's Here With Me (But Your Mind Is on the Other Side Of Town)" can't be all bad. *—Andrew Hamilton*

The Best of the O'Jays: 1976–1991 / Feb. 9, 1999 / The Right Stuff ♦♦♦♦♦

O'Jays fans may find the time period contained in this compilation odd. In 1976, the O'Jays were in the middle of their hitmaking period with CBS-distributed Philadelphia International Records (PIR). In 1985, PIR switched distribution to EMI, the catalog for which is owned by Capitol Records, for which The Right Stuff serves as the reissue arm. The group signed directly to EMI in 1985, remaining until 1993. Though they scored 14 R&B chart hits between 1985 and 1993, The Right Stuff must have felt that there were not enough big hits to justify a compilation of that period. So, the label has licensed ten of the 17 tracks here from PIR, dating back to the 1976 number-one R&B hit "Message in Our Music." From there on, most of the group's R&B Top 40 hits over the next 15 years are included, among them chart-toppers "Darlin' Darlin' Baby (Sweet, Tender, Love)," "Use ta Be My Girl," "Lovin' You," and "Have You Had Your Love Today," though three of their Top 20 hits are missing. With their gruff vocals contrasted by the creamy production style of Kenny Gamble & Leon Huff, the O'Jays on these (and their earlier '70s recordings) proved a valid successor to the pop-soul style pioneered by Motown in the '60s. Their pop crossover appeal was always fitful, and, in fact, only one song here, the gold-selling "Use ta Be My Girl," made the pop Top Ten. But their work was remarkably consistent and, toward the end of this period, even surprisingly diverse, as when they recorded Bob Dylan's "Emotionally Yours" in a gospel style and took it into the R&B Top Ten in 1991. *—William Ruhlmann*

Message in Our Music/Travelin' at the Speed of Thought/ Identify Yourself / Mar. 2, 1999 / WestSide ♦♦♦

★ **The Ultimate O'Jays** / Apr. 10, 2001 / Legacy ♦♦♦♦♦

With few viable alternatives, this can be considered the ultimate O'Jays collection only by default, as it focuses exclusively on recordings from the years 1972-1975, cutting off some reasonable and sometimes very well-known singles from before and after that time frame. Still, this was the period that saw the O'Jays at their commercial and artistic zenith, and these are the songs that most of the public thinks of when the O'Jays' name is mentioned. "Back Stabbers," "Love Train," "I Love Music," "Put Your Hands Together," "For the Love of Money," "Give the People What They Want," and "Livin' for the Weekend" are all on this 16-track compilation, as well as a number of smaller hits and LP-only cuts. It's a solid (and, with 75 minutes of music, good-value) collection documenting both the peak of the O'Jays and the peak of the Philly soul sound in general. *—Richie Unterberger*

For the Love . . . / Sep. 25, 2001 / MCA ♦♦♦

I'll Be Sweeter Tomorrow: The Bell Sessions, 1967–1969 / Apr. 23, 2002 / Sundazed ♦♦♦

The O'Jays' stay at Bell Records, immediately preceding their hookup with the Gamble & Huff production team, saw them land three strong- to mild-charting soul singles. But even though they had nearly a decade of recording under the belt, they really didn't hit their stride until becoming a big part of the Philly sound. With Bell, as documented by this compilation, they were a good sweet soul harmony group, though not one with the kind of ace material and production needed to make them big stars. So this 20-song CD, including all of their Bell 45s and LP tracks (along with five previously unreleased cuts), is something for the serious O'Jays fan or serious '60s soul buff, rather than something on par with their famous '70s work. These are still respectable late-'60s uptown soul productions, sometimes strongly echoing Motown or the emerging Philly soul genre, and featuring strong counterpoint/trade-off harmonies. "I'll Be Sweeter Tomorrow (Than I Was Today)," a Top Ten R&B hit and their biggest Bell single, is the most memorable performance; two lower-charting R&B 45s, "Look Over Your Shoulder" and "The Choice," are also here. Yet it's interesting to hear them venture, if tentatively, into more sinister early sweet soul funk on "That's Alright," and mimic the harder-rocking Temptations sides on "Four for the Price of One" and "Don't You Know a True Love." If you want ultra-sweet soul that's almost sickly sweet, though, you can turn to "Going Going Gone," where they moan in ecstasy about strawberry ice cream chills—quite literally—up and down their backs. *—Richie Unterberger*

The O'Kaysions

f. Wilson, NC

Group / Pop-Soul, Beach, Soul

The O'Kaysions didn't have many hits, but the North Carolina sextet's energetic "Girl Watcher" remains a staple on the Carolina/Georgia/Florida beach circuit. The song actually did a bit better on the pop side, reaching number five there, as opposed to number-six R&B. It was their only chart tune for ABC in 1968. Lead singer Donny Weaver, Ron Turner, Jim Spidel, Wayne Pittman, Jimmy Hennant, and Bruce Joyner began as the Kays. *—Ron Wynn*

● **Girl Watcher** / 1968 / ABC ♦♦♦

David Oliver

d. 1981

Vocals / Urban, Soul

Sweet-singing David Oliver, the son of Jamaican parents, grew up in Florida. He scored on Mercury Records with "MS," which became a staple on quiet storm radio stations, but never scored another significant hit. Oliver started taking singing seriously when he was a high school student of 15; he sung in the school choir with the sopranos because of his naturally high register. Though born and raised in Florida, Oliver made regular trips to Jamaica to keep in touch with his heritage. He sung with vocal groups throughout high school and college and was inspired by major artists like the Temptations and Smokey Robinson.

After college, he joined the Air Force to keep from being drafted by the Army. He stayed five years and was a regular at the service's talent shows. After his tour of duty he moved to Los Angeles in 1967 and joined a racially mixed group called Five Days & Three Nights whose members consisted of other migrants to California; they had a big brassy sound like Chicago, Tower of Power, and Blood, Sweat & Tears; however, contract negotiations with Motown fell through and they disbanded.

After an eight-month association with Redbone ended in 1972 (he recorded *Already Here* with the band), Oliver went solo and worked clubs from L.A. to San Francisco.

Five years later, he got discouraged and took a regular office gig in San Francisco. The office venture didn't last long, and he hooked with another big-band-type group, then joined the Mighty Joe Hicks Band as a singer and stayed until 1975. Mighty Joe recorded the self-titled *Mighty Joe Hicks* on Stax's Enterprise label in 1973. Oliver moved to Jamaica for a year, then renewed an association with Forest Hamilton, who got him the Mighty Joe Hicks gig and recorded *David Oliver* in 1978 with Wayne Henderson at the helm. (Oliver wanted to call the LP "Jamaican Man," but Mercury Records preferred the simpler *David Oliver.*) The single "MS" became a large urban soul hit, and Oliver toured with the R&B major stars. Everything was going well until Oliver unceremoniously died in 1981, a mere three years from the date of his first solo release, silencing a vastly underrated voice. *—Andrew Hamilton*

● **David Oliver** / 1978 / Mercury ♦♦♦

Mind Magic / 1979 / Mercury ♦♦♦

Ollie & the Nightingales

f. 1967, **db.** 1972

Group / Memphis Soul, Soul

This Memphis group included some excellent vocalists, although they didn't enjoy as much success as some other Stax artists. Ollie Nightingale (born Ollie Hoskins), Quincy Clifton Billops Jr., Nelson Lesure, Bill Davis, and Rochester Neal were the original members. Billops had been in the Mad Lads. Their biggest single was "I Got a Sure Thing" in 1968, which made the R&B Top 20. It was also their lone hit. Nightingale left in 1970 and was replaced by Sir Mack Rice. Neal, Billops, and Davis became the Ovations in 1972. *—Ron Wynn*

● **Ollie & the Nightingales** / Aug. 20, 1993 / Stax ♦♦♦♦

Appetizing Southern soul by Ollie & the Nightingales, one of Stax Records' many poorly promoted vocal groups. These 19 tracks (from 1968-1971) come from the pens of some of Stax's most renowned songwriters, including Eddie Floyd, Isaac Hayes, David Porter, Booker T. Jones, Al Bell, Homer Banks, and Mack Rice. Every singer that came through Memphis, TN, chomped a bit from Ollie Haskins' expressive style. A lilting rendition of "I've Never Found a Girl (To Love Me Like You Do)" pricks nerves that are normally dormant; "I'll Be Your Everything" is quintessential Southern soul; they share a Mike with Mack Rice on "Don't Let a Good Thing Go"; and "I Don't Want to Be Like My Daddy" (written by Haskins) puts some family business in the streets. While not a complete overview of Ollie & the Nightingales' career ("I Got a Sure Thing," their first and most popular Stax recording, isn't among the 19 tracks), it's a helluva start. *—Andrew Hamilton*

The Olympics

f. 1958, Los Angeles, CA, **db.** 1966

Group / R&B, Doo Wop, Rock & Roll, Novelty

The Olympics were one of the great L.A.-based acts who managed to score regional hits on the West Coast by balancing upbeat and often humorous novelty R&B tunes with those about popular dances of the day (some of the other West Coast groups who fit this description were the Jay Hawks, the Cadets/Jacks, the Marathons, and the Du-Tones). They are perhaps best remembered for their Coasters-derived "Western Movies," but their other L.A.-area hits include the popular dance number "Baby Hully Gully," "Big Boy Pete" (which stalled out at number-50 pop, but went to number-ten R&B), and "Mine Exclusively."

The Olympics' original lineup—raspy baritone Walter Ward (who sang lead), Eddie Lewis (tenor), Charles Fizer (baritone), and Walter Hammond (baritone)—started out as Walter Ward & the Challengers, waxing "I Can Tell" in 1958. All three baritone leads rarely exploited their low range, preferring to sing in shrill high tones. They changed their name to the Olympics shortly thereafter, hooking up with the songwriting team of Fred Smith & Cliff Goldsmith, who wrote and produced the act's first hit in 1958 for Si Aronson's Hollywood-based Demon Records. "Western Movies," a Coasters-type novelty number, caught on quickly, right around the same time that all of America was preoccupied with Western-Themed movies and TV shows. The single climbed to number-eight pop and number-seven R&B in 1958.

The Olympics then moved—along with Smith and Goldsmith—over to the Arvee label in 1959. For their numerous A-sides (for several labels), the Olympics preferred to issue inner-city generated dance ditties, including the Smith/Goldsmith-penned "(Baby) Hully Gully," "The Philly Dog," "The Slop," and "The Duck" (a local hit for Jackie Lee [aka Earl "Chip" Nelson]). The group only occasionally performed ballads, like the doo wop inspired "Stay Where You Are," and a few rockers like "Shimmy Like Kate" and "Dance By the Light of the Moon." Mostly, the Olympics attempted to duplicate their hit status with novelty songs along the lines of "Western Movies."

Their biggest success in the novelty realm was their remake of "Big Boy Pete," written and first recorded by Don & Dewey for Specialty. Other regional hits included "Little Pedro," "Little Dooley," and "Big Chief Little Foot" (which featured "war whoops"). Others, like the humorous "Dodge City" and "(I Wanna) Dance With the Teacher" sound like teenage West Coast Americana at its most innocent (though at the time, extremist church groups saw nothing innocent about this type of material and often complained that their lyrics were the work of the devil).

Several members of the Olympics also recorded a cover of the Marathons' hit "Peanut Butter," which had been a hit for their producer H.B. Barnum in 1961, waxed for the Checker label. The song was essentially a rewrite of the Olympics' "(Baby) Hully Gully." Arvee sued and acquired the "Peanut Butter" master through contract-infringement litigation. They then rounded up some more singers (including a few Olympics) to record "Peanut"'s successor and album tracks. What makes this more confusing was the fact that the Marathons had some, if not total, personnel overlap with the Vibrations on Checker (who had in 1956 been known as the Jayhawks, who recorded "Stranded in the Jungle" for Flash Records). The same group also performed on-stage as the Marathons. This initially has caused confusion as to whether the two group's shared the same lineup and who did which song and who was in which group at what time.

In total, Arvee released three albums by the Olympics—*Doin' the Hully Gully* (1960), *Dance by the Light of the Moon* (1961), and *Party Time* (also 1961). After the Olympics left Arvee, they scored a couple of hits in 1963 on the L.A.-based Tri-Disc label: the rollicking dance ditty "The Bounce" and "Dancin' Holiday," both produced by Fred Smith. In 1965, they moved over to the Loma label and recorded "Good Lovin'," which failed to connect, but a year later it was remade into a giant hit by the Young Rascals for Atlantic.

In 1966, the Olympics signed with Mirwood, the label run by ex-Vee-Jay executive Randy Wood (and not the Randy Wood from Dot Records). They recorded two hits: "(Baby) Do the Philly Dog" and the gospel-drenched East-side soul single "Mine Exclusively," which inched into *Billboard*'s Hot 100 chart, reaching number 99 in May 1966. Sensing a resurgence of interest in the group, Wood decided to put out an album by the Olympics, but since he had only two minor hits, he opted to have them re-record their old hits from Demon, Arvee, and Tri-Disc for an album called *Something Old, Something New.* (These re-recorded versions have often been included in a vast majority of the reissues and various artist albums where the Olympics appear, much to the annoyance of collectors.) Over the remaining years, the Olympics spawned a host of similar groups (the Contours, the Five Du-Tones, Bull & the Matadors), though they continue to perform at oldies revival shows and around the country. The quartet consists of two original members, Walter Ward and Eddie Lewis. Charles Fizer passed away in 1963 and Walter Hammond retired. Their replacements William DeVase and Kenneth Sinclair have been with them for over 20 years.

After working with the Olympics, Fred Smith worked with Little Caesar & the Romans, and he and Goldsmith later formed Keyman Records. Goldsmith died June 14, 1991, in Burbank, CA. *—Bryan Thomas*

Doin' the Hully Gully / 1961 / Arvee ♦♦♦♦

This album's eight tracks revolve around popular dances or nefarious characters. "(Baby) Hully Gully," a frantic dancer about a popular dance among blacks, got some airplay for the California natives. "The Slop" was one of their typically high-powered zany jams, and was also based on an inner-city dance. "Big Boy Pete" had people singing the street-tough lyrics all across America, and "Boo-Dee-Green" was the 1960s' fascination with a woman's posterior. An entity since the '50s, and still performing in the '90s, the Olympics never had much pop success. *—Andrew Hamilton*

Dance by the Light of the Moon / 1961 / Arvee ♦♦♦

More zany tunes guaranteed to create mayhem from the rambunctious Olympics. The doo wopish "Stay Where You Are," stands out as the rare Olympics' ballad, everything else is upbeat and frantic. "Dance By the Light of the Moon," and "Peanut Butter" (recorded as by the Marathons) have the most commercial appeal. While "Little Pedro," "Little Dooley," and "Big Chief Little Puss"—war-whoops and all—try to duplicate "Big Boy Pete." Oddly includes "Just Like That," by the Robins. Were the Olympics masquerading again? A hokey bass singer makes his presence felt throuhout. *—Andrew Hamilton*

The Olympics Meet the Marathons / 196 / Collectables ♦♦♦♦

With their humorous lyrics, funny voices, and uptempo beats, both the Olympics and the Marathons were in the same vein as the Coasters. They are nowhere near as good however. Apart from their big hits "(Baby) Hully Gully" and "Big Boy Pete" for the Olympics and "Peanut Butter" for the Marathons, the material here is second-rate, mostly vain attempts to recapture the formula that got them their hits or copies of other, better groups like the Coasters or the Drifters. The jokes aren't as good as the Coasters, nor are the singing or the music. Of the two groups, the Marathons get the nod. Their "Talkin' Trash" is very weird; the cackling female vocal will either make you laugh too or reach for the skip button. They are less of a blatant rip-off of the Coasters and might be worth checking out when you have worn out your Coasters records. Until then, look for "(Baby) Hully Gully" and "Peanut Butter" on a doo wop compilation and steer clear of this disc. *—Tim Sendra*

The Olympics Sing / 1976 / Post ♦♦♦♦

A greatest hits compilation by the dancing, clowning Los Angeles natives. It contains their debut (as the Olympics) and biggest hit, "Western Movies"; the novelty went to number-eight pop and number-seven R&B. Raspy baritone Walter Ward sang lead, and the other members included Eddie Lewis (tenor), Charles Fizer (baritone), and Walter Hammond (baritone). Oddly, with three baritones, they rarely exploited their low range, preferring to sing in shrill high tones. Before "Movies," they cut "I Can Tell/The Mambo Beat" as Walter Ward & the Challengers. They never recorded a ballad as an A-side, preferring bouncy, humorous tunes about popular African-American dances: "Hully Gully," "The Philly Dog," "The Duck," and the rollicking "The Bounce." Other tunes include "Big Boy Pete," a popular depiction of a street dude which just missed the pop Top 40, stalling at number 50, but went to number-ten R&B. The high-octane "Mine Exclusively" had a jumpy, dynamic beat like the steppers, but spoke of love; their rare low harmony makes this one a must. Rockers "Shimmy Like Kate" and "Dance By the Light of the Moon" did well for the L.A. natives, who spawned a host of similar groups: the Contours, the Vibrations, the Five Du-Tones, and Bull & the Matadors, to name a few. Many label the Olympics Coasters clones, but the Coasters cut novelty tunes exclusively; the Olympics were exciting, electric dancing daddies. *—Andrew Hamilton*

● **All-Time Greatest Hits!** / 1991 / DCC ♦♦♦♦♦

During their heyday and long after their breakup, the Olympics found themselves being compared to the Coasters more than anyone. While they had their own sound and were far from clones, the Olympics had a lighthearted, fun approach that made comparisons to the Coasters inevitable. Those adjectives certainly describe most of the 26 songs included on *All Time Greatest Hits!*, one of the more comprehensive and thoughtfully assembled Olympics collections available. In retrospect, humorous songs like "Dodge City," "(I Wanna) Dance With the Teacher," "Big Chief, Little Foot" and the 1958 hit "Western Movies" sound like teenage Americana at its most innocent (though at the time, extremist church groups saw nothing innocent in this material). Another high point of this CD (released by DCC Compact Classics in 1991) is the original version of "Good Lovin'," which would become a major hit for the Rascals. Thoroughly entertaining, *All Time Greatest Hits!* is definitely worth acquiring. *—Alex Henderson*

Doin' the Hully Gully/Dance by the Light of the Moon/Party Time / Mar. 1, 1994 / Ace ✦✦✦✦✦

Very Best of the Olympics / Jun. 25, 2002 / Varese ✦✦✦✦
As a group that recorded for about half-dozen labels in its prime, the Olympics' catalog hasn't lent itself well to a comprehensive cross-licensed compilation. Though *The Very Best of the Olympics* has most of the hits that listeners seeking a best-of would want, the absence of the original version of "Good Lovin'" guarantees that this isn't completely satisfactory. There's nothing else they recorded for the Loma label in the mid-'60s either. Other than that, this 17-song compilation does a good job, with all the familiar early Coasters-styled hits: "Western Movies," "(Baby) Hully Gully," "Big Boy Pete," "Shimmy Like Kate," and "Dance By the Light of the Moon." This has an advantage over DCC's *All-Time Greatest Hits!* compilation in that it has a couple small hits they did for the Tri Disc label ("The Bounce" and "Dancin' Holiday") in 1963, and three much more modern uptempo mid-'60s soul sides they did for Mirwood in 1966, including the small hits "Mine Exclusively" and "Baby, Do the Philly Dog." *All-Time Greatest Hits!* doesn't have any of those, but on the other hand it has "Good Lovin'" and considerably more tracks (26) in total. So it's back to the old A-B comparison game if you just want one Olympics CD, ensuring that you're either a little dissatisfied no matter which one you choose or have to spend twice as much money as you'd like to if you break down and get both. Also on this compilation is the Marathons' "Peanut Butter," which used the same backing track as "(Baby) Hully Gully" (and was actually sung by the Vibrations), and a dispensable 1974 soft soul cut, "I'm a Dead Man (Still Walking Around)." *—Richie Unterberger*

Omar

Vocals, Guitar / Club/Dance, Urban, Dance-Pop
Omar's independently released British single, 1990's *There's Nothing Like This*, seemed to guarantee him success in his adopted homeland. The classically trained Omar, descended from Jamaican, Chinese, and Indian stock, had spent most of his life studying in the city of Canterbury and released the laid-back "There's Nothing Like This" on his father's Kongo Dance label. The song's success sparked an intense interest in homegrown British street soul, with record companies gobbling up similar acts. However, when Omar released a critically acclaimed follow-up album, *Music*, it flopped. Omar's new label, Talkin' Loud, blamed the failure on his sophisticated, complex arrangements, so Omar left for RCA. On *For Pleasure*, Omar brought in talents like Stevie Wonder, Lamont Dozier, and Marvin Gaye arranger Leon Ware, resulting in a fusion of British and American soul sensibilities and greater success. The album also contained Omar's first U.S. single, "Saturday." *This Is Not a Love Song* followed in 1997. *—Steve Huey*

There's Nothing Like This / 1990 / RCA ✦✦✦

Music / 1992 / Talkin' Loud ✦✦✦

● **For Pleasure** / 1995 / RCA ✦✦✦✦✦
British soulster Omar's third album is a distinctive delight and a rare element. He collaborates on several tracks, with David Frank, the System (*ESP*), Christina Aguilera, and 98°. Beginning with the oh-too-short "My Baby Says," the album flows into the samba-flavored "I'm Still Standing." "Saturday" has sinewy synth riffs that recall Parliament-Funkadelic's Bernie Worrell. "Keep Steppin'" was inspired by Chicago's step dance movement, and with a remix it could be huge. Underscoring the British respect and appreciation of American R&B and soul music, Omar works with two legends from this genre. "Outside" is culled from an unfinished multi-track tape made in the '70s found in Lamont Dozier's basement. It's smooth soul featuring vintage performances by Ray Parker Jr., Sonny Burke, Jay Graydon, and Sonny Burke. Another Motown alumni, Leon Ware co-writes, contributes backing vocals, and keyboards on the soft pumping "Can't Get Nowhere." The dusky, jazzy "Little Boy" has soft brushes and double bass. Omar's eclectic leanings reminds how much range, personality, and distinctiveness you'll find on pop albums of the past. *—Ed Hogan*

This Is Not a Love Song / Jul. 1997 / RCA ✦✦✦✦
Though he'd been recording for almost ten years, Omar's 1997 album *This Is Not a Love Song* was released into a music world very receptive to new soul music, thanks to the success of artistic vocalists like Maxwell and Erykah Badu. Like albums by those artists, Omar's fourth overall walks the increasingly fine line between spontaneous live instrumentation and pre-programmed electronic productions. *—John Bush*

100 Proof (Aged in Soul)

f. 1969, Detroit, MI
Group / Funk, Soul
100 Proof (Aged in Soul) teamed Detroit area vocalists Steve Mancha (born Clyde Wilson), Eddie Holiday (Eddie Anderson), and Joe Stubbs (the brother of the Four Tops' Levi Stubbs and an alumnus of the Contours and the Falcons). The trio was assembled by the famed writing and producing team of Brian Holland, Lamont Dozier, & Eddie Holland, who in 1967 left the Motown label to set up their own record companies, Invictus and Hot Wax; they signed 100 Proof to the latter, and in 1969 issued the group's debut single, "Too Many Cooks (Spoil the Soup)." The follow-up, "Somebody's Been Sleeping," cracked the pop Top Ten in the fall of 1970; boasting a gritty, earthy approach closer in spirit to Southern soul than the Motor City's trademark sound, the group issued a pair of LPs—*Somebody's Been Sleeping in My Bed* and the 1972 effort *Deliciously Yours*—but never again recaptured the commercial momentum of their first hit, finally dissolving in 1973. The 100 Proof (Aged in Soul) name was briefly resurrected, albeit with an all-new lineup, in 1977. *—Jason Ankeny*

Somebody's Been Sleeping in My Bed / 1971 / Hot Wax ✦✦✦✦
100 Proof (Aged in Soul)—what a name! This Detroit group is classified as one-hit wonders since they only cracked the pop Top 40 once with the alarming "Somebody's Been Sleeping in My Bed." They did, however, have some R&B hits that didn't cross over. The original lineup included Steve Mancha (born Clyde Wilson), Joe Stubbs (Levi Stubbs' brother), and Eddie Holiday. Joe and Steve handle the leads; their voices are so similar that it takes a good ear and lots of listening to discern who's who. This LP is a cornucopia of soul. The title song finds a cheated lover discovering evidence of his woman's infidelity; written by General Johnson (Chairmen of the Board), Greg Perry and Angelo Bond, the song was their second release on the Hot Wax label. Joe Stubbs does a scintillating version of Luther Ingram's "Ain't That Lovin' You (For More Reason Than One)" that's better than the original; Stubbs can be heard persuading his date to stop by his place for some fun, and she does. Steve gets to lead "She's Not Just Another Woman," a lively tune with an odd jumping beat sung in testifying fashion. Ironically, this same recording hit by another Invictus/Hot Wax group called the 8th Day—the same song, track and vocal; it was never released under the name 100 Proof (Aged in Soul). "Too Many Cooks (Spoil the Soup)," their debut single, has a nice horn section that's complemented by a stinging rhythm section. None of the songs are fillers or stiffs; the titles are creative and the lyrics will make you chuckle. The album cover is strange: the front depicts a bird's nest holding one egg with a question mark stamped on it; the back cover depicts an empty nest with a bird lying outside flat on its back, dead. A picture of the group would have been appreciated more. *—Andrew Hamilton*

100 Proof / 1972 / Hot Wax ✦✦✦✦
This is a cleverly done album by the creative hacks at Hot Wax/Invictus Records. Writers/producers Angelo Bond, General Johnson (Chairmen of the Board), Greg Perry, and Ronnie Dunbar share credits in various combinations on six of the LP's eight songs. The other two are "Words" by the Bee Gees and the Association's "Never My Love." Joe Stubbs had left the group by this album, so Steve Mancha (born Clyde Wilson) handles all the leads in his expressive, soul-soaked voice. You don't get much funkier than "Don't Scratch Where It Don't Itch," with its rhyming lyric based around an old saying that means "don't start nothing, and it won't be nothing." The mellow side of 100 Proof comes to fore on "Everything Good Is Bad"; a sweet flute adds some jazzy flavoring to this compelling number that builds in momentum. This is another steaming platter from an underrated act that sold records but never clicked enough with record buyers to gain much of a fan base, probably because Hot Wax never put a picture of the group anywhere on its LPs. (Did the members change that rapidly?) *—Andrew Hamilton*

● **Greatest Hits** / 1990 / Fantasy ✦✦✦✦✦
If one of Stax's artists had gone to Motown and received Eddie Holland's input, it might have sounded something like 100 Proof (Aged in Soul)—a jewel of a group that wasn't nearly as well known as it should have been. For Hot Wax/Invictus, 100 Proof wasn't as commercially successful as Honey Cone, the Chairmen of the Board or Freda Payne. But it certainly wasn't due to a lack of strong material. Full of gems, this collection shows how rewarding things could be when a group with an obvious love of Stax and Memphis soul embraced Holland's sleeker, more elaborate production style. The gritty "Somebody's Been Sleeping in My Bed" was a major hit, but surprisingly, jewels like "Driveway," "90 Day Freeze" and "Too Many Cooks (Spoil the Soup)" were only medium-size hits. "One Man's Leftovers (Is Another Man's Feast)" sounds like a poor person's "Somebody's Been Sleeping in My Bed," but on the whole, this CD shows how exciting things could be when Southern and Northern soul elements were combined. *—Alex Henderson*

Somebody's Been Sleeping in My Bed: The Hot Wax Sessions / 1999 / Sequel ✦✦✦✦✦
Like the 8th Day, 100 Proof (Aged in Soul) were a creation of the Invictus/Hot Wax label—a studio group assembled by Holland-Dozier-Holland to sing the creations of their stable of writers and producers. 100 Proof was more stable than the 8th Day, though they shared Steve Mancha as their lead singer, as well as the single "Too Many Cooks (Spoil the Soup)." They also stuck closer to the big, splashy, early Invictus/Hot Wax sound, never detouring into the funk-rock jams that hampered the second 8th Day record. And, apart from the tremendous "Somebody's Been Sleeping in My Bed," they didn't have singles as brilliant as "She's Not Just Another Woman" or "You've Got to Crawl (Before You Walk)," which the 8th Day had to their credit. What 100 Proof did have was consistency, as Castle's complete collection *Somebody's Been Sleeping in My Bed: The Hot Wax Sessions* proves. Containing their two albums—1971's *Somebody's Been Sleeping in My Bed* and the following year's *100 Proof*—this 22-track collection provides song after song of thrills similar to the hits: songs with big, colorful productions; lots of hooks; and lots of sweet vocals. This is assembly-line soul at its best, a celebration of craft—craft of song and craft of sound. Yes, these records don't define an era the way Motown did, and the songs are often silly, but as a pure rush of sound, these are irresistible. *—Stephen Thomas Erlewine*

112

Group / Urban, Hip-Hop
Equally rooted in gospel, soul and hip-hop, 112 was the first and most successful urban vocal group to emerge from Sean "Puffy" Combs' Bad Boy Records roster. Not only was the group's eponymous 1996 debut popular, but the group could be heard on records by such Bad Boy artists as Puff Daddy. Unlike most artists on Bad Boy, 112's image was clean, pure and wholesome, which helped the group cross over to a more mainstream audience.

The four members of 112—Marvin, Daron, Q and Mike—met each other while attending high school in Atlanta, Georgia. The quartet began to play talent shows at school and local churches, eventually gaining the attention of Courtney Sills and Kevin Wales, who soon became the group's managers. Sills and Wales brought 112 to the attention of

Sean "Puffy" Combs at Bad Boy Records. Combs signed on as the executive producer of 112's eponymous debut album, which featured songs the group co-wrote with such professional songwriters as Stevie J., Wayna Morris of Boyz II Men, and Combs himself. "Only You," the group's debut single, was released in the summer of 1996 and climbed to number three on the R&B charts, peaking at number 13 on the pop charts. *112* was released in late 1996, and it steadily worked its way to gold status as the group's second single, "Come Seem Me," reached number 15 on the R&B charts. *Room 112* followed in 1998 and *Part III* was issued three years later. *—Stephen Thomas Erlewine*

• **112** / 1996 / Bad Boy/Arista ✦✦✦✦
As the first romantic soul group on Puff Daddy's Bad Boy label, 112 at least has the appearance of originality. However, their eponymous debut demonstrates that this is only an appearance—in reality, they are much like a Boyz II Men clone. That's not necessarily bad, actually. 112 have strong voices, and their smooth harmonies are quite seductive, making the lack of originality in their music easy to overlook. A little more variety on *112* would have been nice—the album consists almost entirely of ballads—but the group's sound and Puffy's professional production make it a pleasurable record nevertheless. *—Leo Stanley*

Room 112 / Oct. 20, 1998 / Bad Boy ✦✦
112, Puff Daddy's four-man crew of smooth-crooning R&B loverboys, come on so aggressively sticky and heart-on-sleeve earnest throughout their second album, *Room 112*, that it's often difficult to wade through the torrent of molasses pouring down and through each of the songs. Combining old-school doo wop harmonies with '90s hip-hop trappings—robotic beats, mechanic vocals, half-baked ideas—112 do very little to distinguish themselves from the pack. And because this is a Puffy project, the occasional heavy-handed sample creeps in for an unwelcome visit (the biggest offender here is the use of Shawn Colvin's "Sunny Came Home" during one particularly uninspired tune). The best cut here is "Love Me (Feat. Mase)," a bit of new jack breakdown that swings and hammers with convincing verve and groove, something prominently absent from the rest of the dreary *Room 112*. *—Michael Gallucci*

Part III / Mar. 20, 2001 / Bad Boy ✦✦✦
112 have proven themselves as one of the most successful and enduring acts to emerge from the 1990s urban music explosion, and continue to prove their longevity on their third set, *Part III*. Their second album, *Room 112*, despite the hits "Love Me" and "Anywhere," failed to hint at any artistic progress for the group, but the third effort is a different story. A lot of the sappy ballads that impaired their previous outings are abandoned in favor of edgier, techno-flavored jams, resulting in a more modern and forward-sounding effort. The album's first single, "It's Over Now," is an aching slice of melodrama that proved to be the group's biggest hit to date, and one of the best singles of the year. Other cuts on the album pick up where that one left off, utilizing cutting beats and electronic sounds, such as the album's dance-flavored opener "Dance With Me," the second single "Peaches & Cream," and "All I Want Is You," which is augmented with rock guitars to fine effect. And as always, the group's vocals are nothing short of stellar. Despite some clichéd lyrics (case in point—"Don't Hate Me") and sagging ballads toward the middle of the album (although the ballad "Missing You" is a well-crafted slice of true soul), this set is definitely a step in the right direction for a hard-working group one can happily classify as having evolved. *—Jose Promis*

One Way

f. 1979, Detroit, MI
Group / Quiet Storm, Urban, Adult Contemporary
This was the later identity of the group originally called the Soul Partners. Al Hudson, Alicia Myers, guitarists Dave Robertson and Cortez Harris, bassist Kevin McCord, and drummers Gregory Green and Jonathan Meadows were the original One Way. They first recorded as One Way Featuring Al Hudson before becoming One Way. They were on MCA from 1980 to 1988 and were consistent performers, if not major stars. They were equally skilled at uptempo, danceable numbers and creditable ballads and love songs, even though they never had a great lead singer after Myers departed. They scored five Top Ten R&B hits, with the biggest being "Cutie Pie," which reached number four in 1982. They moved to Capitol in 1988, where they released *A New Beginning* in 1989. *—Ron Wynn*

Love Is . . . One Way / 1981 / MCA ✦✦✦
Abbreviating their name from the earlier One Way Featuring Al Hudson just in time for the 1980s, One Way emerged in 1981 with the grossly overlooked and underrated *Love Is... One Way* LP. Continuing to focus on the smooth vocal harmonies and sweet soul rhythms that had long been their forte, the Detroit group brought the album into the Top 20 in March, their highest spot. With most of the set laying in a cocoon of mid- and slow-tempo urban soul, *Love Is... One Way* meanders from the sleepy and sweet title track to the more emotive "My Lady," which captures an easy, breezy style reminiscent of the Chi-Lites. The latter was rewarded with moderate chart success, while the light-hearted dance groove "Push" shot to number-12 R&B. Elsewhere, "I Didn't Mean to Break Your Heart" finds the band sampling some funk ethics, only to swing 'round a little later on with some classic blues guitar picking and bass thumping on "Wait Until Tomorrow." It's an eclectic, if at times somewhat too smooth, brew, but One Way is so obviously enthralled with their sonic journey that it's hard to criticize. Oddly, despite such cool grooves and their consistent presence in the R&B chart for over a decade, One Way remained inexplicably on the fringes, a fate that is ultimately to the benefit of the soul aficionado, as the band is transformed into a precious, secret jewel, a nifty little nugget for those in the know. *—Amy Hanson*

Shine on Me / 1983 / MCA ✦✦

Lady / 1984 / MCA ✦✦

• **The Best of One Way: Featuring Al Hudson & Alicia Myers** / Apr. 1996 / MCA ✦✦✦✦
Originally, One Way came out as Al Hudson & the Soul Partners and recorded a few interesting, but unsuccessful albums for ABC Records. They were then, and are now, a self-contained act, though the original name suggests a standup vocal group. Essentially, Midwest wonders, they never crossed over, and never got as big as predicted on the R&B circuit, despite having a devastating live act. They should have added their bassist/falsetto tenor, Kevin McCord to the title; he contributes as much as Hudson & Meyers, if not more. This best-of compilation ignores their Al Hudson & the Soul Partner days, and is top heavy with upbeat jams. Like an even handed boxer, One Way could deliver a lethal blow with either hand, being equally as proficient on fast tunes or ballads. The slow jams take a back seat to upbeat cookers, but MCA did include "Something in the Past," and the love happy "Lady You Are" One Way's jams had the juice of a live electrical wire: "Mr. Groove," "You Can Do It," "Pop It," and "Pull Fancy Dancer Pull" represents disco at its best. *—Andrew Hamilton*

Alexander O'Neal

b. Nov. 14, 1953, Minneapolis, MN
Vocals / Urban, Dance-Pop, Retro-Soul
This Minneapolis soul man cut his teeth in the Time but was bounced (for looking "too black") before they signed with Warner Brothers. His tough, ballsy voice has the same grain and range as Otis Redding's. Like that master, Alexander O'Neal is comfortable with pumping dancefloor burners and slinky couch-cuddlers. He's certainly the best singer Jimmy Jam & Terry Lewis have ever produced, and the strength of his material and his robust voice can be heard on releases including 1986's *Hearsay*, 1991's *All True Man*, and 1997's *Lovers Again*. He relocated to Britain, where his efforts had always been better received, and began to set up permanent shop there. His first British-only release, 2002's *Saga of a Married Man*, showed him developing into a smoother and more mature singer compared to his previous output. *—John Floyd*

Alexander O'Neal / 1985 / Tabu ✦✦✦✦✦
Alexander O'Neal wasn't as huge as Luther Vandross or Freddie Jackson; nonetheless, he was among the most exciting male R&B vocalists of the mid- to late '80s. Creatively and commercially, the soul man hit the ground running with this impressive debut album. It's impossible to discuss *Alexander O'Neal* without mentioning the Time—O'Neal is an ex-member of that Minneapolis funk-rock combo, and so are the album's producers (Monte Moir on three tracks, the Jimmy Jam & Terry Lewis team on the others). Also, former Time member Jellybean Johnson is heard on drums, percussion, and guitar. But despite the participation of so many Time graduates, this release isn't nearly as Minneapolis-sounding as it could have been. The intoxicating funk hit "Innocent" is very Time influenced, but for the most part, O'Neal comes across as the epitome of a smooth, romantic soul man—sleek gems like "If You Were Here Tonight," "A Broken Heart Can Mend," and "What's Missing" have more in common with Luther Vandross, Freddie Jackson, and Kashif than with Prince or the Time. While the solo albums that Morris Day and Jesse Johnson provided in the 1980s were consistently Time-minded, that isn't the case with O'Neal's 1985 debut. Some people found that surprising, but then, O'Neal never actually recorded with the Time—when the Time recorded its first LP for Warner Bros. in 1981, O'Neal was long gone. Excellent from start to finish, *Alexander O'Neal* is the singer's most essential album. *—Alex Henderson*

Hearsay / 1986 / Tabu ✦✦✦✦✦
Alexander O'Neal almost achieved the breakout he needed for crossover success with his second album. It cracked the Top 30 on the pop album chart, earned a gold record, and included O'Neal's two strongest uptempo tunes, "Fake" and "Criticize." Jam & Lewis linked the material with "party" dialogue and patter, providing their finest and tightest production for any O'Neal record. The beats were catchy, the songs hook-laden, and O'Neal's voice alternately explosive, sensitive and bemused. *—Ron Wynn*

All Mixed Up / 1988 / Tabu ✦✦

All True Man / Jan. 24, 1991 / Tabu ✦✦✦
Most soul and R&B male vocalists excel at slow, simmering love tunes and merely execute uptempo ones; Alexander O'Neal reverses the process. So it was no surprise that *All True Love* contained several excellent dance-based tunes and no memorable love ballads. Despite some production clutter with multi-tracked female vocalists and overblown strings, O'Neal scored on such numbers as "What Is This Thing Called Love" and "All True Man," prime Jimmy Jam & Terry Lewis numbers. For some reason, Jam & Lewis sought to thematically link several songs on the CD into a portrait of '90s urban angst, without success. *—Ron Wynn*

• **This Thing Called Love: The Greatest Hits of Alexander O'Neal** / Apr. 6, 1993 / CBS ✦✦✦✦✦
While it can be argued that Alexander O'Neal's track record doesn't merit any greatest hits or best-of compilations, that didn't deter Tabu from issuing this compilation. It presented O'Neal's finest uptempo and ballad singles, displaying his ferocity on such cuts as "Fake" and "Criticize," plus his range and passion on "Never Knew Love Like This." *—Ron Wynn*

The Best of Alexander O'Neal / Oct. 1995 / Tabu ✦✦✦✦
Although he has stated his love of Otis Redding, Alexander O'Neal is one of the few R&B singers without an antecedent. *The Best of Alexander O'Neal* covers his work from three regular release albums from 1984 to 1991. The early tracks from the best-of not only trace O'Neal's vocal and stylistic evolution, but also the sound of his chief producers and former Time bandmates Jimmy Jam & Terry Lewis. The bittersweet and melodic "A Broken Heart Can Mend" and "If You Were Here Tonight" still remain as fresh and singular as they were when they hit the radio in the mid-'80s. The songs from O'Neal's sophomore album, 1987's *Hearsay*, are only a cut below. This set includes the killer Time-like romp

"Fake" and the trademark meditative ballads "Sunshine" and "Crying Overtime." For most Alexander O'Neal fans, his name can't be spoken without thinking of his frequent song partner Cherelle. This set also includes their duet "Never Knew Love Like This" that displays their always sexy and wholly believable chemistry. The boast fest "All True Man" (1991) is also here. On the surface, this seems to be the best, but this overview leaves off the beautiful O'Neal/Cherelle classic "Saturday Love." Sure, it never appeared on an O'Neal title, but it sums him up better than the lengthy "Innocent/Alex 9000/Innocent II" does. Although this does have material from only three albums, some fans just may think that this is the best O'Neal album covering the '80s and early '90s. *—Jason Elias*

The Opals

Group / Chicago Soul, Northern Soul

The Opals recorded for four singles for Okeh Records from 1963 to 1965 and also backed Otis Leavill and Major Lance on recordings. Their fame never extended outside the Windy City boundaries despite recording material by Curtis Mayfield, Billy Butler, and sax player Clifford Davis, the brother of producer Carl Davis. Rose Addison (lead singer), Myra Tillison, and a member only remembered as Tootsie were the Opals; the trio made their recording debut in 1963 accompanying Leavill (uncredited) on both sides of his Lucky Records' single: "I Got a Right to Cry" b/w "Rise Sally Rise."

When Carl Davis assumed the A&R duties at OKeh Records the Opals were brought along, along with Davis' assistant Leavill; a young Curtis Mayfield, making a name for himself with the Impressions, contributed independent productions. They backed Major Lance (uncredited) on the B-side "Crying in the Rain" of his number-13 pop and number-12 R&B smash "Hey Little Girl." The spectacular job they did on "Crying" earned them a contract. OKeh issued their debut single late in 1963, two Clifford Davis songs "Losers Weepers" b/w "Take It Right," the latter co-written with Phil Upchurch, and they were off and running. It was followed by Billy Butler's "Does It Matter" in 1964 and Curtis Mayfield's "You Can't Hurt Me No More," later that year.

The Opals backed Major Lance (again uncredited) on Van McCoy's "Everybody Loves a Good Time," released May 1965, but Lance had peaked and the song bubbled under *Billboard*'s Pop 100 at number 109. A final single "I'm Afraid" b/w "Restless Days" dropped in July 1965, Verne Allison and Mickey McGill (the Dells) wrote the latter, but the results were the same; nothing the Opals recorded took off nationally or even regionally and the trio vanished from the music scene. Their sides are available on many compilation albums and are getting more acclaimed and play these days then when first released in the mid-'60s. *—Andrew Hamilton*

The Originals

f. 1966, Detroit, MI

Group / Motown, Urban, Disco, Soul

A Detroit soul vocal group led by Freddie Gorman, the Originals took the R&B world by storm in 1969, although they had worked at Motown for years as invaluable background vocalists. Gorman recorded as a solo for Berry Gordy in 1961 and co-wrote "Please Mr. Postman" for the Marvelettes, and the Originals cut a version of Leadbelly's "Goodnight Irene" for Gordy's Soul subsidiary in 1966 with ex-Falcon Joe Stubbs as lead. But Stubbs had split to form 100 Proof (Aged in Soul) by the time the quartet waxed the beautiful doo wop throwback "Baby I'm for Real," an R&B chart-topper in 1969 that was co-written and lushly produced by Marvin Gaye. The same combination also produced "The Bells," another major hit in 1970. Former solo act Ty Hunter joined the group in 1971, and the Originals continued to chart into the next decade. *—Bill Dahl*

Baby, I'm for Real / 1969 / Motown ✦✦✦✦✦

One classic single—the title track—and lots of filler, performed competently but without distinction. By astutely casting the group in a updated doo wop style that emphasized their complex close harmonies, Marvin Gaye's guidance gave the group the distinctive personality that it previously lacked as well as the commercial success that they so richly deserved. After years of singing in the background, they stepped into the spotlight, and it was worth it the effort. *—John Lowe*

Green Grow the Lilacs / 1969 / Soul ✦✦✦

Naturally Together / 1970 / Soul ✦✦✦

The group's third Motown album didn't fare nearly as well as the previous two, which both made the lower regions of the pop charts. Despite some wonderful production by Clay Murray and fine ballad and uptempo leads from Crathman Spencer and Henry Dixon, they couldn't generate much national action, even though it had one wonderful song in "God Bless Whoever Sent You," which peaked at number-14 R&B. *—Ron Wynn*

Portrait of the Originals / 1970 / Soul ✦✦✦

A fine collection that would have been better without the remakes. Marvin Gaye produced "The Bells," a gorgeous doo wop-influenced ballad with a riveting, spoken bass monologue; it has all the charm of "Baby I'm For Real," another Gaye production, and then some. Members Freddie Gorman, C.P. Spencer, Hank Dixon, and Walter Gaines, with the help of Pam Sawyer wrote "I Like Your Style," a delightful romp that Motown banished to the B-side of "We Can Make It Baby," athough it had the legs to stand on its own. Ironically, Motown released only "The Bells" as a single from this LP, despite other viable candidates like the infectious "Don't Stop Now" and the harmonic heart-tugger "You Want Hearts and Flowers." *—Andrew Hamilton*

Definitions / 1972 / Soul ✦✦✦

This would have been a better LP if the productions weren't so lavish. A prime example is "I'm Someone Who Cares," a good ballad that is overpowered by strings and studio techniques; "Lie No. 2" suffers from the same disorder, and these are the two strongest cuts. A remake of Liz Lands' "Keep Me" is not as good as the original, both were released as singles and both stiffed; Lands' version, however, deserved a better fate. The bouncy "Come Rain or Shine" is cute, but too trite to be taken seriously. Freddie Gorman does a fine lead on "Bridge Over Troubled Water," but the arrangement is too staid to be competitive. The Originals sound better with fewer frills and a sparser setting; their harmonies are warm enough to stand alone without added embellishments. *—Andrew Hamilton*

Game Called Love / 1974 / Soul ✦✦

As far as male R&B vocal groups from Detroit go, the Originals were never considered heavyweights. They weren't in a class with the Temptations, the Dramatics or the Four Tops, but they were a decent group and had their moments. Released in 1974, *Game Called Love* is a competent, if unremarkable, effort that falls into two categories: the funky "Supernatural Voodoo Woman" and the romantic ballads and slow jams that comprise the rest of the LP. Fans of 1970s blaxploitation flicks will know "Supernatural Voodoo Woman" as the theme from *Sugar Hill*, a bloodfest that starred Marki Bey as a woman who hires zombies to avenge the death of her murdered lover. Like 1972's *Blacula*, *Sugar Hill* is a cult classic that merged the horror and blaxploitation genres with campy but highly entertaining results. The infectious "Supernatural Voodoo Woman" should have been a hit single, but it wasn't—and none of the romantic items became hits either. Motown, it seemed, didn't really get behind this album—it didn't make "Supernatural Voodoo Woman" the hit it deserved to be, and it didn't get behind romantic cuts like "Be My Love," "Ooh You (Put a Crush on Me)" and the Originals' cover of Charlie Rich's pop-country smash "Behind Closed Doors." So commercially, *Game Called Love* was a disappointment—and by the late 1970s, it was out of print. *—Alex Henderson*

California Sunset / 1975 / Motown ✦✦

Lamont Dozier wrote and produced every song on this LP for longtime friends the Originals; still, *California Sunset* is a major disappointment. Ty Hunter had replaced C.P. Spencer as the Originals' tenor/falsetto and leads the only memorable song, "Financial Affair." "Fifty Years" is about a couple's hopes that their marriage will last that long—hardly a contemporary item. A couple of songs have intriguing titles but no substance; "Good Lovin' Is Just a Dime Away" and "California Sunset" are quite ordinary. They should have marketed this as a sleeping aid. *—Andrew Hamilton*

Motown Superstar Series, Vol. 10 / 1976 / Motown ✦✦✦✦✦

The Detroit-based Originals began singing in 1966, with tenor vocalists Crathman Spencer and Henry Dixon, bassist Freddie Gorman and baritone Walter Gaines. Marvin Gaye helped bring them to Motown and later wrote or co-wrote three of their singles, including the anthemic "Baby, I'm For Real." That single, their other major hit, "The Bells," and the third Gaye single, "We Can Make It Baby," are among the tunes on this anthology. They weren't a great group, but their two hits are as gripping and wonderfully produced and arranged as any Motown material. *—Ron Wynn*

Down to Love Town / 1977 / Soul ✦✦✦✦✦

Keeping up with the times, the songs on *Down to Love Town* are disco length for those who enjoy dancing uninterrupted for more than three minutes. The most successful single was "Down to Love Town," their biggest record since Marvin Gaye crafted songs for them. The dancer has lead Freddie Gorman's tenor/baritone exhorting everybody to take their bodies down to love town for some good times. Freddie Gorman, Walter Gaines, Henry Dixon, and Ty Hunter's forte were ballads, not tambourine banging, hand clapping, and booty-shaking. Even so, "You Are a Blessing to Me" is a charming, lilting, midtempo beauty. Still, "Call Me Your six Million Dollar Man" is too pretentious to be taking seriously. The guys don't switch leads around as much on this one, with Gorman out front most of the time. *—Andrew Hamilton*

● **The Very Best of the Originals** / Mar. 23, 1999 / Motown ✦✦✦✦✦

Their hits from the late '60s through the mid-'70s, along with some LP cuts, B-sides, and unreleased tracks. The first six songs were produced or co-produced by Marvin Gaye in 1969-1970 (including the hits "Baby I'm for Real" and "The Bells"). These have been sometimes cited as forerunners to his *What's Going On* album, but it would be wrong to view them as a *What's Going On* supplement. They're in much more of a lush, group vocal, sweet soul style, although some traces of ideas Gaye would play with in the early '70s are present, particularly in the way the background voices weave around each other. The one previously unreleased Gaye production, "Just to Keep You Satisfied," would be reworked, with the same backing track and backing vocals but a different lead vocal and lyrics, on Gaye's *Let's Get It On* album. The rest of the tracks are largely in a competent sweet soul mold, also including "Suspicion," a previously unreleased Holland-Dozier-Holland number from 1966 with a more uptempo sound; "Game Called Love," a 1974 cut composed and produced by Stevie Wonder; and "Down to Love Town," a 1976 disco smash. *—Richie Unterberger*

The Essential Collection / 2002 / Motown ✦✦✦

The Orioles

f. 1948, Baltimore, MD, **db.** 1954

Group / R&B, Doo Wop

Led by Sonny Til, the Orioles were the first black vocal group to sing music directly for a black audience. Through their early recordings—which were made in the late '40s and early '50s—the band laid the groundwork for R&B vocal groups and doo wop. The Orioles fused traditional pop songs with gospel sensibilities and arranged blues and gospel material with smooth harmonies, designed to appeal to the broadest audience possible. Based in Baltimore, MD, the Orioles consisted of lead vocalist Sonny Til (born Earlington Carl Tilghman, August 18, 1928; d. December 9, 1981), Alexander Sharp (tenor vocals), George Nelson (baritone vocals), Johnny Reed (bass vocals), and guitarist Tommy Gaither. Originally called the Vibranaires, the group formed when its members were teenagers. They came to the attention of Deborah Chessler, a local merchant who also wrote songs; she would write many of the group's subsequent hits. Chessler became the band's manager and she was able to get the Vibranaires a spot on Arthur Godfrey's *Talent Scouts* television show. Although the group lost to pianist George Shearing, they caught the eye of Jerry Blaine, a New York record company executive, while they were in town for the program.

Jerry Blaine signed the group to his newly created It's a Natural record label and had the band cut "It's Too Soon to Know," a ballad written by Chessler. After they signed their deal with It's a Natural, the band changed its name to the Orioles. In the late summer of 1948, "It's Too Soon to Know" was released on It's a Natural but shortly after the single's release, National Records' Blaine complained about the name of his new label, so he re-released the song on Jubilee Records, a record label he had previously used to release Yiddish comedy records. "It's Too Soon to Know" became a number-one R&B hit and crossed over to number 13 on the pop charts. At the time of its release, no black group had managed to cross over to the pop charts with what was then known as a "race" record. The Orioles immediately followed the success of their debut single with the seasonal "(It's Gonna Be A) Lonely Christmas," which reached the R&B Top Ten at the end of 1948.

"Tell Me So" became the Orioles' second number-one R&B hit in the spring of 1949, beginning a streak of six R&B hit singles that year. In addition to "Tell Me So," the group charted with "A Kiss and a Rose" (number 12, late summer), "I Challenge Your Kiss" (number 11, fall), "Forgive and Forget" (number five, fall), a re-released "(It's Gonna Be A) Lonely Christmas" (number five, winter), and the B-side of "Lonely Christmas," "What Are You Doing New Year's Eve" (number nine, winter).

Following their peak year of 1949, the group ran into tragedy. In 1950, Gaither, Nelson, and Reed suffered an automobile accident that killed Gaither and severely injured the other two members; Nelson quit the group later in the year. As Reed recovered from the accident, the group found replacements for Gaither and Nelson, finally settling on guitarist Ralph Williams and vocalist Gregory Carroll. The new lineup of the band had its first hit in 1952, when "Baby Please Don't Go" reached number eight on the R&B charts. The following year, the group had their biggest hit with "Crying in the Chapel." Released in the summer of 1963, "Crying in the Chapel" spent five weeks on the R&B charts and reached number 11 on the pop charts, eventually going gold; Elvis Presley had a hit with the song 12 years later. Toward the end of the year, the group had another Top Ten R&B hit with "In the Mission of St. Augustine." The single would turn out to be their last hit.

In 1954, the Orioles began to splinter, as Sharp and Reed left to join the Ink Spots. Sonny Til assembled a new lineup, but the group didn't gain much attention. Til continued to lead various incarnations of the Orioles, performing concerts and re-recording the group's old hits, until his death in 1981. George Nelson died some time in 1959 and Alexander Sharp died in the early '70s. In 1995, 40 years after the original lineup of the group disbanded, the Orioles were inducted into the Rock and Roll Hall of Fame. *—Stephen Thomas Erlewine*

Greatest Hits / 1991 / Collectables ♦♦♦

A bit of a ringer, as these aren't the original recordings, but recuts for C.P. Parker's label from 1962. This group of Orioles is an all-star one, however, with members of the Spaniels, the Castelles and the Dreams counted in the lineup. As for the star of the show, Sonny Til sounds very much the way he did some ten years earlier, and the strong backing makes these new versions stand well on their own. Holiday favorites like "What Are You Doing New Year's Eve" and "Lonely Christmas" make this a marvelous addition to the group's scant discography. *—Cub Koda*

★ **Sing Their Greatest Hits** / Nov. 25, 1991 / Collectables ♦♦♦♦♦

This Orioles hit package is about equal to any other that's available, but pales next to the Bear Family boxed set. The now defunct Murray Hill also had a great Orioles box several years ago. Save your money and grab the Bear Family if you really want the real story on the Orioles. *—Ron Wynn*

The Jubilee Recordings / 1993 / Bear Family ♦♦♦♦♦

Six CDs, covering 1948 through 1960, and in that 400-plus minutes you get an overview of the transition of postwar R&B from the black community to the heart of mainstream popular music. Disc one opens with their earliest sides from July 1948, when the quintet was still very heavily influenced by the Ink Spots. The group's music during this period grew rapidly in sophistication; their second session shows a startling level of confidence, the group embellishing the melody and harmony of their songs and transforming them into something new. The sound quality of some of the material on this disc is less than perfect, due to the state of the best available masters. Things get very interesting on disc two, with the first recordings to feature a string section (their first conscious effort at crossing over into the pop market. On disc three, they continued to record in their trademark sophisticated sound, although some songs also capture them at their bluesiest. Disc four catches the group moving into a fully mainstream R&B vogue, as well as Sonny Til's superb duets with Edna McGriff. Disc five covers the period of their biggest hit, "Crying in the Chapel"—by 1953-1954, the Orioles were generally working in a kind of big-band R&B mode, and most of this material, in keeping with their success of the era, did get out. Disc six covers the tail end of the group's original period with Jubilee and then picks up for a coda in the 1960s. This material is a little less focused than much of what has come before, for the Orioles were competing in a crowded new arena of R&B-turned-rock & roll. The notes are fascinating, and the sound, apart from the bulk of disc one, is excellent, improving as the recording dates advance. *—Bruce Eder*

The Orlons

f. 1960, Philadelphia, PA, **db.** 1968

Group / Girl Group, R&B, Pop-Soul, Soul, Novelty

A predominantly female group from Philadelphia, the Orlons had some dance and novelty gems in the early '60s for Cameo-Parkway. Lead vocalist Rosetta Hightower, Marlena Davis, Steve Caldwell, and Shirley Brickley scored with "The Wah Watusi" in 1962; it was a number-five R&B and number-two pop hit, while the follow-ups, "Don't Hang Up" and "South Street," were also Top Ten R&B and pop successes. "Not Me" was their fourth consecutive R&B Top Ten winner in 1963, and it peaked at number-12 pop. It was also their last, although "Cross Fire!" reached number 19 on the pop charts. But their other singles fizzled, and Davis and Caldwell left in 1964, replaced by Audrey Brickley. When Hightower moved to England in 1968, the Orlons disbanded. *—Ron Wynn*

The Wah-Watusi / 1962 / Cameo ♦♦♦♦

• **Biggest Hits** / 1963 / Cameo ♦♦♦♦♦

The Orlons hit with noisy, fun sounding, dance songs. Shirley Brickley, Rosetta Hightower, Marlena Davis and Stephen Caldwell (the lone male), formed the Orlons in their hometown of Philadelphia, at Overbrook High School. Like most Cameo parkway artists, the Orlons became typecast to a particular sound. "I'll Be True," their first recording, flopped although it was a message from a girl to her G.I. boyfriend. So did a follow-up ballad which didn't make this compilation. Cameo Records rethought the marketing of the Orlons and shelved the ballads as A-sides. Their third release, "The Wah Watusi," a rockish, dance ditty soared to number-two Pop; prior to the success of "Watusi," they scored with Dee Dee Sharp by providing the backing on her number-two Pop, and number-one R&B hit, "Mashed Potato Time." The Orlons were blazing, so Cameo released *Biggest Hits* after their three bigger than life recordings. "Don't Hang Up" features Caldwell's growling bass on some humorous fills on an uptempo rocker that did surprisingly well on the R&B chart, settling at number-three, while nesting at number-four Pop. The formula continues with "South Street," another monster that went to number-three Pop and number-four R&B, and contained the same runaway rhythms and vocals on their previous smashes. While the Orlons scored with fast numbers, they excelled on ballads and midtempo R&B numbers. Two good examples are "Dedicated to the One I Love" and "Something's Got a Hold on Me." *—Andrew Hamilton*

Jeffrey Osborne

b. Mar. 9, 1948, Providence, RI

Vocals / Urban, Adult Contemporary, Funk, Quiet Storm, Soul

Jeffrey Osborne began his professional singing career in 1969 with a popular funk and soul group called Love Men Ltd. The band moved to Los Angeles in 1970 and changed its name to L.T.D. Osborne was originally brought on as the drummer and eventually became the lead vocalist. After more than ten years with the band, he decided to pursue a solo career, which produced such Top 40 hits as "Don't You Get So Mad," "Stay With Me Tonight," and "Love Power," which he performed with Dionne Warwick.

Born in Providence, RI, Jeffrey Osborne was the youngest of 12 children and was constantly bombarded with music as he was growing up. He had five brothers and six sisters, some of whom went on to have music careers. His father, Clarence "Legs" Osborne, was a popular trumpeter who played with Lionel Hampton, Count Basie, and Duke Ellington, and died when Jeffrey was only 13. His mother, Wanita, is ancestored by a Pequot Indian sachem. His oldest brother, Clay Osborne, is a singer and pianist, and Billy, another brother, is a songwriter and producer in Los Angeles. But Osborne's father had the greatest influence on his musical career; Clarence "Legs" Osborne turned down many top band offers during his career to be with his family. It was only after receiving his mother's encouragement that Jeffrey left for Los Angeles to play with L.T.D. At the age of 15, he sat in with the O'Jays when the drummer was too tired to play, and went on to play with them for two weeks. It was at a Providence nightclub that fate brought him together with the band Love Men Ltd. in 1969.

Osborne's solo career has brought him five gold and platinum albums, including *Stay With Me Tonight*, *Aymuk*, and *Only Human*. He also recorded an album of duets with popular singer James Ingram, and scored an international hit with "On the Wings of Love" in 1982. Osborne's touring and recording continue to keep him busy much of the time, but he also devotes some of his time to charity work. *—Kim Summers*

• **Jeffrey Osborne** / 1982 / A&M ♦♦♦♦

As vocalist for the group L.T.D., Osborne's booming voice led hits like "Love Ballad," "Where Did We Go Wrong," and "Shine On." The group enjoyed constant success and offered a catalog of well-executed and classic albums including 1977's *Something to Love* and *Togetherness* from 1978. In 1982 it came as a complete shock when Osborne made his solo bid. Unlike countless other acts who did the same thing, his self-titled release proves that it was a great decision. Producer George Duke offered Osborne an up-to-the-minute sound with a collection of great studio players ranging from drummer Steve Ferrone to bassist Louis Johnson. That being said, a few of the tracks here don't play to Osborne's strengths as a committed and slightly quirky vocalist. "New Love" and "Eeenie Meenie" are so proficient yet by the numbers anyone could have sung them. The best tracks on this album give him the needed challenges that make him soar. The first single, the moody and rhythmic "Really Don't Need No Light," co-written by Osborne and David "Hawk" Wolinski, benefits from a string arrangement from George Del Barrio. The ballad "You Were Made to Love" not only perfectly captures Duke's uncluttered and precise production style, it also plays to Osborne's emotionality. The last track, "Congratulations," is a great tearjerker that has Osborne's reserve and intellect making it that much better. This is an impressive solo debut from one of R&B and pop's best vocalists. *—Jason Elias*

Stay With Me Tonight / 1983 / A&M ♦♦♦♦

At this point, some fans might have been hoping that Jeffrey Osborne would return to his former group, L.T.D. If *Jeffrey Osborne* cast doubt on that proposition, *Stay With Me Tonight* made it so that even L.T.D. fanatics didn't want to see it happen. Unlike many R&B acts who either went solo and/or did pop-ish work, Osborne earned raves for retaining his quirky nature with his vocal inflections and ticks intact. The smooth, first single, "Don't You Get So Mad," picks up where *Jeffrey Osborne* and "I Really Don't Need No Light" left off. Osborne's best-sung uptempo George Duke production, "Stay With Me Tonight," clicks from the synths and the Simmons drums to the off-center backing vocals. The best ballad from the album is also one of Osborne's strongest songs. With a strong string arrangement from George Del Barrio, "I'll Make Believe" has Osborne all but living the poignant lyrics and giving them more meaning by accenting the right words and phrases. "We're Going All the Way" is nearly as good. Tracks like "Other Side of the Coin,"

"When Are You Comin' Back," and "Two Wrongs Don't Make a Right" can't help but come off as filler given the excellent songs surrounding them. The best songs here more than make up for any so-so tracks and this is more than recommended. *—Jason Elias*

Don't Stop / 1984 / A&M ♦♦♦

Produced by George Duke, *Don't Stop* was the second in a trio of mid-'80s gold albums from Jeffrey Osborne that included *Stay With Me Tonight* and *Emotional*. The title track was a slab of upbeat '80s rock/pop that successfully broke Osborne out of the ballad mold going. Its follow-up, "The Borderlines," written by keyboardist Raymond Jones (Chic, Whitney Houston, State of Art), made it to number-seven R&B, number-38 pop in late 1984. The tender ballad "Crazy 'Bout Cha" received massive radio play as an album track and remains the singer's most underrated recording. *The X-Files'* Mulder and Scully might play the upbeat UFO-themed "You Can't Be Serious" on their car stereo. The charting single "Let Me Know" is in the mode of Osborne's previous smooth hits. "Don't Stop" and "Borderlines" are on his *Ultimate Collection*. *—Ed Hogan*

Emotional / 1986 / A&M ♦♦

Only Human / 1991 / Arista ♦♦♦

After such George Duke-produced R&B/pop hits on A&M as "On the Wings of Love" and "The Borderlines," Jeffrey Osborne's Arista debut, *Only Human*, was a return to more R&B-oriented material. Wisely, the LP's first single showcased Osborne's special way with a ballad. Produced by Barry J. Eastmond (Freddie Jackson), the halting, dusky "Only Human" was a Top Three R&B smash in late 1990. The singer shows his social consciousness side on the chugging "If My Brother's in Trouble," which was produced by Shep Pettibone and made it to number-11 R&B in the spring of 1991. The Osborne co-written ballad "The Morning After I Made Love to You" (also produced by Eastmond) at times generates the kind of shivers generated by some of his classics with L.T.D. It was the album's third hit single, going to number 24 in the summer of 1991. There are successful flirtations with hip-hop on "Baby Wait a Minute" and a cover of the Roberta Flack hit "Feel Like Making Love" co-produced by Robert Brookins. While it could be argued that Osborne's A&M albums were generally "too pop," he seems absolutely regenerated on *Only Human*, digging his vocal chops into material that accommodates his extensive range. It's a head-scratcher as to why this is his only Arista release (one of his other sides for the label was the tasty Dionne Warwick duet "Love Power"); it would have been very interesting to hear Osborne continue in this mode. Some of the album's tracks are on the Hip-O CDs *Love Songs*, *Ultimate Collection*, and *More of My Best*. *—Ed Hogan*

● **Ultimate Collection** / Sep. 7, 1999 / Hip-O ♦♦♦♦♦

At 17 tracks, containing all of his solo smashes plus selections from L.T.D. where he sang lead, Hip-O's *Ultimate Collection* fulfills the promise of its title, since it does feature all the best-known songs associated with Osborne. *—Stephen Thomas Erlewine*

That's for Sure / Feb. 8, 2000 / Private Music ♦♦♦

The great thing about adult contemporary music is that it provides a format for artists whose place on the pop charts in the '50s, '60s, '70s, and '80s was supplanted by the hip-hop and teenyboppers of the '90s and early '00s. Jeffrey Osborne is one such classic soul voice way past his prime but still cranking out appealing music that can't help but reach emotional depths because his voice is so rich, deep, and powerful. The tunes here are all slickly produced, from the cool and funky ode to love's second chance "2nd Time Around" to the dreamy ballad "That's for Sure." He's never been Barry White, but sexy funk ballads like "Come With Me" make perfect soundtracks to bedroom activities. Yet you can't get around the fact that, as strong as some of these tunes are, they pale next to the closing number, a live rendition of Osborne's first LTD hit "Love Ballad"—which was also made famous by George Benson. The inclusion of this classic serves to remind new listeners that Osborne had a past; but longtime fans may feel a bit sad that none of his work on *That's for Sure* can approach his glories of the past. *—Jonathan Widran*

More of My Best / Jul. 18, 2000 / Hip-O ♦♦♦♦

More of My Best gathers the highlights from Jeffrey Osborne's A&M, Arista, and Capitol releases, including L.T.D. hits like "Never Get Enough of Your Love," "Where Did We Go Wrong," and "Stranger." Top 40 solo hits such as "Soweto," "Room With a View," "In Your Eyes," and his collaborations with Dionne Warwick ("Take Good Care of You & Me") and Najee ("Loving Every Moment") make this collection worthwhile for fans looking to dig deeper into Osborne's work. *—Heather Phares*

Love Songs / Feb. 6, 2001 / Hip-O ♦♦♦♦

Osiris

Group / Funk, Soul

Led by singer Osiris Marsh, Osiris was a fine but obscure soul/funk outfit that was active in Washington, D.C., in the late '70s. The band's influences included Sly & the Family Stone and Funkadelic, and like Earth, Wind & Fire, Osiris was interested in the culture of ancient Egypt. Osiris' debut album, *Since Before Our Time*, came out on Warner Bros. in 1979; unfortunately, the LP received very little attention, and Osiris (which Warner dropped), broke up without ever recording a second album. In addition to lead singer Marsh, Osiris' members included bassist Tony Jones, keyboardist Maceo Bond, saxman Ron Holloway, bassist Tyrone Brunson, guitarist Brent Mingle, drummer Kenny Jones, and percussionist Jimmy "Sha Sha" Stapleton. After Osiris' breakup, Holloway kept busy as a jazz musician and went on to record several hard bop albums for Milestone/Fantasy in the 1990s. *—Alex Henderson*

● **Since Before Our Time** / 1979 / Warner Bros. ♦♦♦♦

Recorded in 1977 and 1978 and released in 1979, Osiris' debut album, *Since Before Our Time*, is a perfect example of a solid soul/funk release that fell through the cracks and did very little commercially. One can speculate on the reasons why this little known LP was ignored. Some might argue that Osiris' Sly Stone-influenced material wasn't disco enough for 1979, but then, Maze and Frankie Beverly had no problem going gold in the late 1970s without jumping on the disco bandwagon. From a commercial standpoint, the problem with *Since Before Our Time* isn't a lack of disco—it's the lack of a really strong single. Tunes like "Damn," "Almost (Never Gets There)" and "Consistency" work well on an album, but they're missing the sort of immediacy that a single would have needed to grab a program director's attention. It's quite possible that some programmers at R&B radio heard *Since Before Our Time* and said, "Interesting album, but where's the single?" Not surprisingly, Warner Bros. dropped Osiris—and it didn't take long for this LP to go out of print and end up in the cutout bins. *—Alex Henderson*

Lee Oskar

b. Mar. 24, 1948, Copenhagen, Denmark

Vocals, Percussion, Harmonica / Fusion, Funk, Jazz-Pop, Album Rock, Soul, R&B

Harmonica player and vocalist Lee Oskar was a charter member of War in the late '60s, when the West Coast group first backed Eric Burdon and later went out on their own. His extended wailing solos became a vital part of War's funk/rock/Latin sound in the '70s and '80s. He made two undistinguished fusion albums as a leader in the '80s and though he remained a part of War, Oskar made his solo debut in 1976 and recorded several albums of solid pop-jazz, R&B, and fusion, among them 1978's fine *Before the Rain* and 1980's *My Road, Our Road*. *—Ron Wynn*

Lee Oskar / 1976 / United Artists ♦♦♦

Lee Oskar's solo career got off to an enjoyable start with this self-titled collection of pop-jazz and instrumental pop/R&B. From this point on, the Danish-born harmonica player had two careers: member of War and solo artist. It's a good thing that Oskar chose to remain in the highly successful War, for his instrumental solo albums were on the esoteric side and lacked War's commercial appeal. Not a huge seller, this album was a creative success more than a commercial one. The album gets off to an impressive start with the haunting "I Remember Home (A Peasant's Symphony)," and Oskar keeps the artistic momentum going with instrumentals that range from the congenial "Sunshine Keri" and the laid-back "BLT" to the funky "Down the Nile." Originally a vinyl LP, *Lee Oskar* was reissued on CD in 1995. *—Alex Henderson*

● **Before the Rain** / 1978 / Elektra ♦♦♦

Here's why all serious music lovers still need a turntable: there are so many worthwhile LPs from the '60s and '70s that will probably never be reissued on CD. Before Avenue Records came into the picture, it seemed unlikely that Lee Oskar's solo albums of 1976-1980 would ever be reissued on CD—labels usually reissue titles they think there is a heavy demand for, and Oskar's solo efforts weren't the mega-blockbusters that War's albums were. But Avenue pleasantly surprised listeners in the '90s by making Oskar's solo output available on CD, including 1978's *Before the Rain*. Did this album outsell War classics like *Why Can't We Be Friends?* and *All Day Music*? Hardly. Reissued in 1995, this mostly instrumental album deserved to come back into print simply because it is good. From a commercial standpoint, the problem with *Before the Rain* is that it's difficult to categorize—is it funk, pop-jazz, quiet storm, or fusion? Arguably, *Before the Rain* is all of those things, and Oskar's harmonica playing is expressive whether he is getting mildly funky on "Steppin'" or being mellow and laid-back on "More Than Words Can Say" and the title track. "Steppin'" certainly isn't typical of funk instrumentals; the tune opens with bagpipes—not exactly an instrument that one ordinarily associates with funk. But then, Oskar is no stranger to multiculturalism; how many harmonica players who were born in Copenhagen, Denmark, went on to play with one of the top soul/funk bands of the '70s? *Before the Rain* may not have set the world on fire when it was first released in 1978, but it was certainly nice too see the album making its CD debut in 1995. *—Alex Henderson*

My Road, Our Road / 1980 / Avenue ♦♦♦

It came as no surprise when Avenue reissued most of War's 1970s albums on CD in the 1990s—many of those albums had been gold and platinum sellers as LPs, and the market for reissues of classic soul and funk was a healthy one. But because Lee Oskar's solo albums of 1976-1980 were far from the huge sellers that War's albums were, it came as a pleasant surprise when Avenue started reissuing them on CD in the 1990s. First released on vinyl in 1980 and reissued on CD in 1995, *My Road, Our Road* was Oskar's third solo album. The highlights of this mostly instrumental pop-jazz/R&B date include the mellow "Up All Night" and the good-natured "Song for My Son" as well as the evocative "My Road" and the moody "Our Road," which features jazz saxophonist Pat Rizzo as well as Brazilian jazz singer Flora Purim. It's safe to say that the vast majority of War fans didn't buy this album; however, it's an enjoyable outing that did receive some attention in the quiet storm market. *—Alex Henderson*

Free / 1981 / Avenue ♦♦♦

● **The Best of Lee Oskar** / Jan. 19, 1999 / Rhino ♦♦♦♦

In the late '70s and early '80s, Lee Oskar recorded several decent solo albums while continuing to be a member of War. The harmonica player/composer was an integral part of War's sound, and his solo albums weren't a major departure from War's more relaxed output. The thing Oskar lacked as a solo artist was major hit singles—his albums tended to sound a lot like War's album tracks, and he never delivered a solo single that had the radio-friendly immediacy of "Why Can't We Be Friends," "All Day Music" or "Slipping into Darkness." Spanning 1976-1983, *The Best of Lee Oskar* isn't a collection of hit singles but paints a likable picture of Oskar as an album-oriented artist. You won't find a lot of hard-driving funk à la "Galaxy" on this 1999 CD—from vocal numbers like "San Francisco Bay" to instrumentals such as "More Than Words Can Say," "Before the Rain" and "Sunshine Keri," this collection emphasizes the laid-back and congenial. None of this material is well known, although Oskar's mellow inclinations earned him some attention in quiet storm circles. For War fans who overlooked Oskar's own albums, *The Best of Lee Oskar* wouldn't be a bad introduction to his solo output. *—Alex Henderson*

Johnny Otis (John Veliotes)

b. Dec. 28, 1921, Vallejo, CA

Leader, Vibraphone, Drums, Vocals, Piano / R&B, Rock & Roll, Jump Blues, West Coast Blues

Johnny Otis has modeled an amazing number of contrasting musical hats over a career spanning more than half a century. Bandleader, record producer, talent scout, label owner, nightclub impresario, disc jockey, TV variety show host, author, R&B pioneer, rock & roll star—Otis has answered to all those descriptions and quite a few more. Not bad for a Greek-American who loved jazz and R&B so fervently that he adopted the African-American culture as his own.

California-born John Veliotes changed his name to the blacker-sounding Otis when he was in his teens. Drums were his first passion—he spent time behind the traps with the Oakland-based orchestra of Count Otis Matthews and kept time for various Midwestern swing outfits before settling in Los Angeles during the mid-'40s and joining Harlan Leonard's Rockets, then resident at the Club Alabam. It wasn't long before the Alabam's owner entreated Otis to assemble his own orchestra for house-band duties. The group's 1945 debut sides for Excelsior were solidly in the big-band jazz vein and included an arrangement of the moody "Harlem Nocturne" that sold well. Shouter Jimmy Rushing fronted the band for two tracks at the same date. Otis' rep as a drummer was growing; he backed both Wynonie Harris and Charles Brown (with Johnny Moore's Three Blazers) that same year.

The Otis outfit continued to record for Excelsior through 1947 (one date featured Big Jay McNeely on sax), but his influence on L.A.'s R&B scene soared exponentially when he and partner Bardu Ali opened the Barrelhouse Club in Watts. R&B replaced jazz in Otis' heart; he pared the big band down and discovered young talent such as the Robins, vocalists Mel Walker and Little Esther Phillips, and guitarist Pete Lewis that would serve him well in years to come. Otis signed with Newark, NJ-based Savoy Records in 1949, and the R&B hits came in droves: "Double Crossing Blues," "Mistrustin' Blues," and "Cupid's Boogie" all hit number one that year (in all, Otis scored ten Top Ten smashes that year alone!); "Gee Baby," "Mambo Boogie," and "All Nite Long" lit the lamp in 1951, and "Sunset to Dawn" capped his amazing run in 1952 (vocals were shared by Esther, Walker, and other members of the group). By then, Otis had branched out to play vibes on many waxings.

In late 1951, Otis moved to Mercury, but apart from a Walker-led version of Floyd Dixon's "Call Operator 210," nothing found pronounced success with the public. A 1953-1955 contract with Don Robey's Peacock logo produced some nice jump blues sides but no hits (though the Otis orchestra backed one of his many discoveries, Big Mama Thornton, on her chart-topping "Hound Dog," as well as a young Little Richard while at Peacock). Otis was a masterful talent scout; among his platinum-edged discoveries were Jackie Wilson, Little Willie John, Hank Ballard, and Etta James (he produced her debut smash "Roll With Me Henry").

In 1955, Otis took studio matters into his own hands, starting up his own label, Dig Records, to showcase his own work as well as his latest discoveries (including Arthur Lee Maye & the Crowns, Tony Allen, and Mel Williams). Rock & roll was at its zenith in 1957, when the multi-instrumentalist signed on with Capitol Records; billed as the Johnny Otis Show, he set the R&B and pop charts ablaze in 1958 with his shave-and-a-haircut beat, "Willie and the Hand Jive," taking the vocal himself (other singers then with the Otis Show included Mel Williams and the gargantuan Marie Adams & the Three Tons of Joy). During the late '50s, Otis hosted his own variety program on L.A. television, starring his entire troupe (and on one episode, Lionel Hampton), and did a guest shot in a 1958 movie, *Juke Box Rhythm.*

After cutting some great rock & roll for Capitol from 1957 to 1959 with only one hit to show for it, Otis dropped anchor at King Records in 1961-1962 (in addition to his own output, Otis' band also backed Johnny "Guitar" Watson on several sides). Later in the decade, Otis recorded some ribald material for Kent and watched as his young son Shuggie built an enviable reputation as a blues guitarist while recording for Columbia. Father and son cut an album together for Alligator in 1982, accurately entitled *The New Johnny Otis Show.* In recent years, the multi-talented Otis added operating a California health-food emporium to his endless list of wide-ranging accomplishments. If blues boasts a renaissance man among its ranks, Otis surely fills that bill. *—Bill Dahl*

Rock and Roll Hit Parade, Vol. 1 / 1957 / Dig ✦✦✦

Here are enjoyable sound-alike covers of popular mid-'50s R&B hits by Otis, singers Mel Williams and Arthur Lee Maye, and the Jayos. *—Bill Dahl*

The Johnny Otis Show / 1958 / Savoy ✦✦✦✦✦

This includes some of the R&B bandleader's earliest and best work (1945-51) for Savoy. The cast includes singers Little Esther and Mel Walker, the Robins, and guitarist Pete Lewis. *—Bill Dahl*

Cold Shot! / 1969 / J&T ✦✦✦

Though Otis' 1969 album wasn't much different from the straightforward R&B he'd been doing for years, it did have some updated rock, soul, and funk influences, due in large part to the presence of his teenage guitarist son, Shuggie Otis. The band is tight and the vocals OK, but it's on the ordinary side as far as such music goes, even if the stew of blues, soul, and funk is reasonably solid. Well, it's not wholly ordinary: "The Signifyin' Monkey Pt. 1" has some daringly profane language for 1969, with the word "motherfucker" cropping up in the very first line and a drawling spoken delivery that anticipated rap. This track's approach, particularly in its lewd language, would be amplified on the Otis album credited to Snatch and the Poontangs the same year, *Snatch and the Poontangs.* [*Cold Shot* and *Snatch and the Poontangs* were combined onto one CD on an Ace reissue in 2002, with the addition of two previously unreleased Snatch and the Poontangs tracks.] *—Richie Unterberger*

Live at Monterey / 1971 / Epic ✦✦✦✦✦

An R&B oldies show with a difference, the artists represented the cream of the crop of jump blues, and in 1970, they were still in fine form. The disc stars Otis, Esther Phillips, Eddie Vinson, Joe Turner, Ivory Joe Hunter, Roy Milton, Roy Brown, Pee Wee Crayton, and Johnny's guitar wielding son, Shuggie. *—Bill Dahl*

New Johnny Otis Show / 1982 / Alligator ✦✦✦

The Capitol Years / 1989 / Collectables ✦✦✦✦✦

Unfortunately now out-of-print, this set anthologizes Otis's late-'50s rise to rock & roll fame, thanks to his shave-and-a-haircut special "Willie and the Hand Jive." Like every other style of R&B Otis drifted into, he excelled at it—"Castin' My Spell," "Crazy Country Hop," "Willie Did the Cha Cha," and "Three Girls Named Molly" are catchy rockers. Otis had a terrific band—guitarist Jimmy Nolen (later James Brown's main axeman), pianist Ernie Freeman, drummer Earl Palmer, and a tight horn section (along with singers Marie Adams and Mel Williams) gave him all the help he could possibly need. *—Bill Dahl*

Creepin' With the Cats: The Legendary Dig Masters, Vol. 1 / 1991 / Ace ✦✦✦

Here are 22 tracks, almost half previously unreleased, from circa 1956-1957 that Otis recorded for his own short-lived Dig label. Not as vivacious as the sides he recorded for Capitol in the late '50s, this is spirited but generic jump blues/R&B, divided evenly between vocals and instrumentals. Occasional cuts like the silly novelty instrumental "Ali Baba's Boogie" stand out from the pack. The one commanding greatest interest is "Hey! Hey! Hey!," which served as the model for Little Richard's version, which in turned was covered by the Beatles in the mid-'60s (as "Kansas City"). *—Richie Unterberger*

★ **The Original Johnny Otis Show** / 1994 / Savoy ✦✦✦✦✦

Here are 27 of the Otis aggregation's best early sides for Savoy and Excelsior, including a slew of the group's early-'50s Little Esther and/or Mel Walker-fronted R&B smashes ("Mistrustin' Blues," "Cry Baby," "Sunset to Dawn"). Jimmy Rushing and the Robins also share vocal duties, as does Otis himself on a jumping "All Nite Long." This is one time when the bonus cuts are on the vinyl version—it contained 32 cuts appearing on a *Completer Disc* that Savoy Jazz reissued at the same time as this CD. The original artwork and liner notes have been reduced so much for the CD that they're unreadable (Pete Welding's essay deserves more respect). *—Bill Dahl*

Too Late to Holler / 1994 / Night Train ✦✦✦✦

This is a more generous selection of late-'40s Swing Time and Excelsior sides, again featuring Swift (who dominates the compilation), Jackson, and Jesse Blivens in front of the powerful Otis orchestra. Very little duplication exists between the two discs. *—Bill Dahl*

Johnny Otis Rock 'N Roll Hit Parade / Oct. 17, 2000 / Ace ✦✦✦

Johnny Otis originally released a 12-song version of this CD in 1957 on his Dig label. That LP centered around the Jayos, a group assembled by Otis that at times included Richard Berry, Jesse Belvin, Mel Williams, Arthur "Lee" Mayes (a future Major Leaguer), Harold Lewis, Sonny Moore, Tony Allen, and others. Nobody brought anything resembling an original song to these sessions; practically all the tunes are remakes or, in some instances, covers, and even the few that aren't sound like something you heard before by someone else. Ace tacked on 12 more tracks (most previously unreleased) for a more thorough perspective of Otis' late-'50s empire. The Jayos did hits by the El Dorados, the Platters, the Drifters, the Penquins, Hank Ballard & the Midnighters, and others, and did them well, but what else would you expect from a lineup of vocal harmony superstars? The Johnny Otis Orchestra pumps out three tracks, and there are tunes by some So Cal singers that are unknown to those outside the region. Jeannie Barnes does tunes made famous by Faye Adams and Ruth Brown; Mel Williams duets with Arthur Lee Mayes on Gene & Eunice's "Ko Ko Mo, I Love You So"; Mayes solos on Little Willie John's "Fever. Tracks by Prince Moreland, Harold Lewis and Mel Williams fill out the interesting compilation. If you just like the original versions of songs this CD won't interest you. But if enjoy good music, regardless of who came first, you'll find this to be a fine collection of '50s R&B/doo wop. The original vinyl LP sells for around $500. *—Andrew Hamilton*

Watts Funky / 2001 / BGP ✦✦✦✦

Whether as an artist, mentor, and/or small-time record label entrepreneur, Johnny Otis was continuing to make some interesting R&B-based music in the late '60s and 1970s, though little of it is familiar to anyone but devoted collectors. *Watts Funky* collects 20 tracks from the late '60s through the mid-'70s that he was involved with, though only about half are billed to either Johnny Otis or the Johnny Otis Show. It's erratic, eccentric, but generally refreshing soul-funk, reflecting the trends of the era, but more idiosyncratic than much of the stuff being put out via more high-profile outlets. Certainly the best track by a country mile is Shuggie Otis' "Strawberry Letter 23," a spaced-out soul ballad that owes a lot to contemporary hippie singer/songwriters as well, and was covered by the Brothers Johnson for a hit in 1977. Shuggie Otis fans will be excited by the inclusion of a couple of previously unreleased cuts from the same era, but actually those are much more ordinary, with "Miss Pretty" sounding a little like Sly Stone as sung by Van Morrison. It's very unlikely you'll have heard of anyone else but the Otises on the disc's artist list, except maybe Preston Love. But there's credible funk by Vera Hamilton on "But I Ain't No More (G.S.T.S.K.D.T.S)," and the Vibrettes sound like they should be singing backup for James Brown funk sides on "The Humpty Dump." There's some pretty humorous, sly late-'60s soul by the Johnny Otis Show on "Country Girl," and Otis himself comes through with some top-drawer jazzy James Brown-ish instrumental funk on "Jaws." *—Richie Unterberger*

Essential Recordings / Jan. 9, 2001 / Cleopatra ✦✦

Alternately a songwriter, performer, bandleader and talent scout, Johnny Otis was a pioneering figure in American R&B. As the 21st century dawned, however, his impressive catalog was largely in disarray. Too few titles were in print, and there seemed to be no single-disc compilation providing an accurate overview of his work. Though, by the title of this 2001 release from Cleopatra Records, it may have seemed like a remedy had arrived, but *Essential Recordings* did little to change the situation. This set misses far too many Otis classics and includes far too many lesser sides to warrant its title. The fact is that the task had been difficult from the outset: Otis recorded for a total of six labels, including his own Dig Records, during his first 14 years alone. The set does get off on the right foot, beginning with the most logical of introductory cuts, "Harlem Nocturne," Otis' big band masterpiece (and a sizable hit) recorded in 1945. Otis had clearly learned a great deal during his tenure with the Count Basie Orchestra, though he quickly struck out on his own, performing jump blues and R&B material. Fans of these styles may enjoy songs like "Low Down Dirty Dog Blues" and slow blues like "Bad Luck Shadow," though they will probably have little patience for crude numbers like "Country Girl" and "The Signifyin' Monkey." Culled from the 1969 *Cold Shot!* set, the songs are notable only for the guitar playing of a young Shuggie Otis, Johnny's gifted son. Add to its many shortcomings an insufficient 33-minute playing time and you end up with a rather unessential offering. *—Nathan Bush*

Cold Shot!/Snatch and the Poontangs / 2002 / Ace ♦♦♦
Two 1969 albums by Otis and his band are combined onto one CD here, though the second of the pair was credited to Snatch and the Poontangs. Though *Cold Shot*, credited to the Johnny Otis Show, wasn't much different from the straightforward R&B he'd been doing for years, it did have some updated rock, soul, and funk influences, due in large part to the presence of his teenage guitarist son, Shuggie Otis. The band is tight and the vocals OK, but it's on the ordinary side as far as such music goes, even if the stew of blues, soul, and funk is reasonably solid. Well, it's not wholly ordinary: "The Signifyin' Monkey Part 1" has some daringly profane language for 1969, with the word "motherfucker" cropping up in the very first line and a drawling spoken delivery that anticipated rap. This track's approach, particularly in its lewd language, would be amplified on the Otis album credited to Snatch and the Poontangs the same year, *Snatch and the Poontangs*. You didn't think that a band with a name like Snatch and the Poontangs was likely to do much touring and get much airplay, did you? The record couldn't have gotten much airplay either, filled to the gills as it was with profane and sexually explicit language. In that sense, it was something of a groundbreaker, with extemporizing as blunt and filthy as almost any to be heard on rap records several decades later. The language was barrier-busting (or should we say ball-busting), much more so than the somewhat faceless blues-soul backup music. Otis did have the wit to rework his "Willie and the Hand Jive" hit as "Hey Shine" (with suitably no-holds-barred lyrics), and the spoken narrative "Two Time Slim," set against lonesome blues guitar, is a little more inventive in its delivery and musical track than much of its surroundings. The wordless "Two Girls in Love (With Each Other)," with its orgiastic female moans and improvised jazz-blues licks faintly in the background, also sticks out for the relative difference in its construction. The CD adds two previously unreleased Snatch and the Poontangs tracks, both of them consistent with the approach purveyed on most of the Snatch and the Poontangs album, though neither are special. *—Richie Unterberger*

Shuggie Otis (Johnny Otis Jr.)

b. Nov. 30, 1953, Los Angeles, CA

Guitar, Producer, Songwriter, Harmonica, Bass, Vocals, Arranger / Funk, Soul, Blues-Rock, Album Rock, Neo-Psychedelia, Psychedelic Soul

Guitarist/singer/songwriter/producer/multi-instrumentalist Shuggie Otis may not be a household name, but his "Strawberry Letter 23" is in the record collections of millions of households. The Brothers Johnson's cover of "Strawberry Letter 23" has sold over a million copies, peaking at number-one R&B and number-five pop on *Billboard*'s charts in summer 1977. It was on their LP *Right on Time*, which went platinum, selling over a million copies, holding the number-one R&B spot for three weeks and making it to number-13 pop in spring 1977. Otis wrote "Strawberry Letter 23" for his girlfriend, who used strawberry scented paper for her letters to him. Another Otis favorite, "Inspiration Information," received substantial airplay in Chicago and other markets, charting number 56 R&B in early 1975.

Born Johnny Otis Jr. on November 30, 1953, in Los Angeles, CA, Otis' formidable musical talents appeared at an early age. He began his professional career around 1965. He played a guitar solo on his bandleader, father Johnny Otis' 1969 number-29 R&B hit, "Country Girl," issued by Kent Records. His guitar skills were so adept that during his teen years, he would have to wear dark glasses and strategically apply black ink between his nose and mouth to appear old enough to perform in clubs with his father.

Signing with CBS Records, Otis began recording virtuoso guitar-laced R&B/West Coast blues sides. His first LP was *Al Kooper Introduces Shuggie Otis* on CBS. Johnny Otis produced 1970's *Here Comes Shuggie Otis*, which was issued on the CBS imprint, Epic Records. Otis' *Freedom Flight* was issued September 1971 and included the original version of "Strawberry Letter 23," the heart-tugging "Someone's Always Singing," "Ice Cold Daydream," and the bluesy "Me and My Woman," co-written by Otis and Gene Barge (known best for his association with Chess Records, Chuck Willis, and Natalie Cole). His LP *Inspiration Information* was issued in October 1974, with Otis playing all of the instruments on jazzy and Latin-tinged R&B numbers. The LP was one of the first releases to showcase the electronic rhythm box then found usually on organs. Besides "Inspiration Information," the LP included the sly "Sparkle City," the sweet ballad "Outtamihead," and the lush, strings-laden "Island Letter," which was the B-side of "Inspiration Information."

George Johnson of the Brothers Johnson was dating one of Otis' cousins and gave Johnson a copy of *Freedom Flight*. Immediately, he liked "Ice Cold Daydream" and "Strawberry Letter 23." The latter song was played at his brother Louis Johnson's wedding during the wedding march. Louis suggested the song to their producer Quincy Jones for an album track. The track's complex guitar solo was played by Lee Ritenour. The Brothers Johnson version is quite close to Otis' original version. Later on in the '90s, Otis played with his own band around northern California and toured extensively. His son, Lucky Otis, played bass with Johnny Otis' band. Shuggie Otis is featured in the book *Alligator Records Presents West Coast Blues*, issued in August 1998 by Milwaukee, WI, publisher Hal Leonard. *—Ed Hogan*

Al Kooper Introduces Shuggie Otis / 1969 / CBS ♦♦♦♦
In 1969, producer/multi-instrumentalist and vocalist Al Kooper added "talent scout" to his already lengthy resumé on the follow-up to the highly successful *Super Session* disc, which had been issued the previous year. One major difference between the two, however, is the relatively unknown cast featured on *Al Kooper Introduces Shuggie Otis*. Both albums again converge with the presentation of top-shelf musicianship and inspired performances. At only 15 years of age, Otis (guitar) is equally potent a performer as the seasoned Kooper (keyboards/guitars). The duo is able to manifest an aggregate of material whose success leans as much on Kooper's experience as it does on Otis' sheer inspired youthful energy. The LP is divided between a side of shorter works (aka "songs") and a few extended instrumentals (aka "blues"). Kooper and Otis steer their house band which includes Stu Woods (bass), Wells Kelly (drums), and Mark Klingman (piano). The tight arrangements aptly reveal Kooper's uncanny ability as a musical conduit. "Bury My Body"—a variation on "In My Time of Dyin'"—has been reworked into a gospel rave-up and features Kooper on one of the album's only vocals. Conversely, "Double or Nothing" is a spot-on re-creation of a Booker T. & the MG's track, which not only retains every Memphis-inspired intonation, but also shows off Otis' ability to cop Steve Cropper's guitar solo note for note. The blues instrumental jams are documented live and presented on this album the way that they originally went down at the recording sessions. The descriptively titled "Shuggie's Old Time Slide Boogie" is endowed with a nostalgic piano/bottleneck slide duet and even features the added production value of manufactured surface noise. Both "12:15 Slow Goonbash Blues" and "Shuggie's Shuffle" are certainly no less traditional, allowing both Otis and Kooper the chance to stretch out and interact in real time. *—Lindsay Planer*

Here Comes Shuggie Otis / 1970 / Epic ♦♦♦♦
Cut when Otis was just 15, 1970's *Here Comes Shuggie Otis* was the second album of blues-based material from the guitar prodigy and Johnny Otis scion. Still a few years shy of his Sly Stone jazz-pop masterpiece, *Inspiration Information*, Otis lets loose on a mix of Hendrix-style instrumentals ("Oxford Gray") and strings- and brass-spiced vocals ("Jennie Lee," a harbinger of things to come). Otis Sr. produced and helped arrange and write (along with Shuggie) the album; and even with some harpsichords and electric pianos in the mix, his and Shuggie's abiding love for R&B is made clear throughout. The variety they show within the form is certainly impressive, as Shuggie expertly navigates through a bit of swamp boogie ("Bootie Cooler"), a psych-tinged groove ("Baby I Needed You"), and some hard-rolling Texas blues shuffle ("The Hawk"). Possibly a shock to listeners only familiar with Otis' sunshine soul-pop hit "Strawberry Letter 23," this album will certainly please fans hip to some expansive blues jamming. *—Stephen Cook*

Freedom Flight / Sep. 1971 / Epic ♦♦♦
Issued in September 1971, *Freedom Flight* teamed Shuggie Otis with a group of ably skilled musicians (including George Duke and the Crusaders' Wilton Felder), giving the virtuoso guitarist a solid foundation to work with. Produced by his father, Johnny Otis, the album is also notable for including the original version of "Strawberry Letter 23." The Brothers Johnson's 1977 million-selling cover adheres pretty close to it. Other highlights are the gentle, musing ballad "Someone's Always Singing," co-written by Otis and Kenny Kahn, and the jukebox-bluesy "Me and My Woman," penned by Otis and Gene Barge.The 2001 CD reissue of Otis' 1974 *Inspiration Information* LP through David Byrne's Luaka Bop label, included two tracks from *Freedom Flight*, the smoking "Ice Cold Daydream" and "Strawberry Letter 23." *—Ed Hogan*

● **Inspiration Information** / Oct. 1974 / Luaka Bop ♦♦♦♦♦
Ignored upon its release in 1974 and celebrated upon its reissue in 2001, Shuggie Otis' fourth and last album *Inspiration Information* exists out of time—a record that was of its time, but didn't belong of it; a record that was idiosyncratic but not necessarily visionary. It was psychedelic soul that was released far too late to be part of any zeitgeist and it was buried at the time. Yet no matter what Luaka Bop's grand poobah David Byrne claims on the sticker—he says Shuggie's "trippy R&B jams are equal to Marvin's and Curtis', but somehow more contemporary sounding... closer to D'Angelo meets DJ Shadow"—this isn't revolutionary. It can occasionally sound modern, such as on the rolling head trip "XL-30," but only because it's the kind of groove Shadow would sample and build on; the slow, liquid instrumental head trips sound the same way. Perhaps that's why it can seem more contemporary—contemporary ears are more attuned to these relaxed, warmly trippy soundscapes. Otis crafted all of this essentially alone, playing each instrument himself, and it's quite clearly a reflection of his inner psyche, and no matter how much it floats and skates upon its own sound, it's a welcoming, inviting sound. But, no matter how much the partisans claim—and their effusive praise is plastered all over the liner notes, with Sean O'Hagan claiming that it shocks you out of a rut, Stereolab's Tim Gane says it is "almost like a new style of music that could've developed but never did"—this isn't revolutionary, even if it's delightfully idiosyncratic. So, don't fall for the hyperbole. This isn't an album that knocks your head off—it's subtle, intricate music that's equal parts head music and elegant funk, a record that slowly works its way under your skin. Part of the reason it sounds so intriguing in 2001 is that there just aren't that many musicians that doggedly pursue their individual vision while retaining a sense of focus. But it isn't a record without precedent, nor is it startling. It's a record for people that have heard a lot of music, maybe too much, and are looking for a new musical romance. [Luaka Bop's reissue contains four fine bonus tracks, including the original version of "Strawberry Letter 23," which the Brothers Johnson later had a hit with. The reissue also replaces the original cover—which is nowhere to be seen in the liner notes—with a "hip," self-consciously retro cover. Also, it has put in the "World Psychedelic Classics" with Os Mutantes, which is slightly misleading and a little unsettling—with that subheading, there's just a little too much self-conscious, scholarly distance at play.] *—Stephen Thomas Erlewine*

Shuggie's Boogie: Shuggie Otis Plays the Blues / 1994 / Epic/Legacy ♦♦♦♦♦

Culled from four albums, except for one previously unreleased track, this *tour de force* is all the more remarkable because the prodigy who produced it was so young. In fact, he recalls during a boyish spoken intro in "Shuggie's Boogie" how he used to wear dark glasses and paint a mustache to look older than his 14 or 15 years when he played in bars in the band of his legendary father Johnny Otis. During the same intro he effortlessly throws off guitar impersonations of T-Bone Walker, B.B. King and Elmore James. This compilation has a few rousing, uptempo numbers, but the highlights are the slow, soulful tunes. One unfortunate omission is the seven-minute "Oxford Gray" from his 1970 album *Here Comes Shuggie Otis*. *—Mark Allan*

In Session: Great Rhythm & Blues / Jul. 23, 2002 / Cleopatra ♦♦

Capitalizing on the unexpected resurgence of acclaim for Shuggie Otis in 2001 due to Luaka Bop's reissue of 1974's *Inspiration Information*, Blues Spectrum/GoldenLane turned out the compilation *In Session: Great Rhythm & Blues* the following year. Despite the appearances—the same photographs from the Luaka Bop edition of *Inspiration* are all over this disc, including the same picture used for both front covers—this is hardly a disc for those newly converted fans, since there is none of the trippy, one-man psychedelic soul that distinguished that record. This is Shuggie, the session-man, from the mid-'70s, when he was playing guitar and co-engineering the *Great Rhythm & Blues Oldies* series for his father, Johnny, who produced this series for Blues Spectrum records. The idea behind the series was simple: Bring a bunch of R&B and blues legends into the studio to record new versions of their classic songs, backed by Johnny Otis' house band, featuring Shuggie on guitar. Not a bad idea on the surface, and it was not unpleasant in practice, but it's also hardly noteworthy, either, since these were pretty much guys doing their hits with a pickup band, captured with indifferent '70s sound. Some of these guys rise above the occasion—Louis Jordan sounds lively, for instance, on both of his cuts—but this is all latter-day recordings by artists past the peak of their game. Sometimes, they update their sound a bit (Richard Berry takes a stab at funk), but most everybody simply brings their trademark sound into the '70s, with a band that's competent but lacking character—and that includes Shuggie, whose playing here is standard blues/R&B licks that are perfectly fine, but never distinctive. It's a very nicely produced package, particularly in how it reproduces the artwork for all of the albums in the series, but the music is what matters and anybody that hears this, either as a fan of the featured artists or Shuggie, will be disappointed by these passable but undistinguished latter-day re-recordings. *—Stephen Thomas Erlewine*

The Ovations

db. 1971

Group / Soul

Despite having only one Top Ten R&B hit, the Ovations were a superb Southern soul trio. The original group featured Louis Williams and made some great ballads that were sung so vividly and produced in such raw fashion that they never reached the wider soul market. Though they reached the R&B charts twice during the late '60s (with "It's Wonderful to Be in Love" and "Me and My Imagination"), the group eventually disbanded. By 1971, a new trio had resurfaced, with former Nightingales Rochester Neal, Bill Davis, and Quincy Clifton Billops Jr. A remake of Sam Cooke's "Having a Party" in 1973 gave them their lone Top Ten R&B hit. *—Ron Wynn*

- **Hooked on a Feeling** / 1972 / P-Vine ♦♦♦♦♦

Sweet Thing / 197 / Vivid ♦♦♦

P

P-Funk All Stars

f. 1981

Group / Funk

After George Clinton disbanded Parliament and Funkadelic at the dawn of the '80s, he embarked on a solo career, but also maintained contact with many of his band alumni in a short-term (at least initially) project dubbed the P-Funk All Stars. Having sorted out various legal and financial difficulties from the initial breakup, Clinton reconvened many of the best musicians from throughout Parliament/Funkadelic history in 1982, including Bootsy Collins, Bernie Worrell, Eddie Hazel, Gary Shider, Dewayne Blackbird McKnight, Walter "Junie" Morrison, David Spradley, and many others—not to mention a guest appearance by Sly Stone. They recorded a fine album, 1983's *Urban Dancefloor Guerillas*, that featured a different lineup on every track; it reached the R&B Top 50 and spawned a chart single in "Generator Pop." The accompanying tour featured many of the same musicians in what was one of the last P-Funk spectacles for quite some time. One of the shows from the tour was released on CD in 1990 by Westbound as *Live at the Beverly Theatre in Hollywood*; Westbound also issued an alternate version of *Urban Dancefloor Guerillas* under the title *Hydraulic Funk*, which restored several tracks to their full, unedited length.

Circa 1989, Clinton revived the P-Funk All Stars name for the group with which he would spend much of the '90s touring. Among these musicians were guitarist/bandleader Dewayne Blackbird McKnight, guitarists Gary Shider and Michael Hampton, bassists Lige Curry and Billy "Bass" Nelson, multi-instrumentalist Rodney "Skeet" Curtis, drummer Frankie "Kash" Waddy, and many others in what became a loose, revolving-door arrangement. With Clinton's musical legacy dominating the hip-hop scene, the group was much in demand during the early '90s, and even played the main stage of the 1994 Lollapalooza tour. Clinton used the All Stars as the backing band on his 1996 album *T.A.P.O.A.F.O.M.*, and subsequently continued to tour with them, putting on marathon shows for a new generation of fans. *—Steve Huey*

● **Urban Dancefloor Guerillas** / 1983 / Uncle Jam ✦✦✦✦

This truly is an all-star affair. Parliament and Funkadelic alumni like Bootsy Collins, Eddie Hazel, Walter "Junie" Morrison, and David Shider, among others, resurface from various stages in the Mothership's time upon earth to contribute to this stylistically sprawling and urbanely funky session; adding to the impressive roll call are high-profile soul and funk guest stars such as Sly "Sylvester Stewart" Stone, Bobby Womack, Fred Wesley, and Maceo Parker. And leading the charge is the master himself, George Clinton. Amazingly, considering all the egos involved, *Urban Dancefloor Guerillas* comes off sounding of a piece. And while the expansive funk found on *Uncle Jams Wants You* and *One Nation Under a Groove* is, for the most part, bypassed here—this album adheres more to the compact and streamlined sound heard on *The Mothership Connection*—*Urban Dancefloor Guerillas* still impresses with sophisticated charts, top playing, and a wealth of rich harmonies. The funk gets nicely mixed up with relatively straightforward cuts like "Pumpin' It Up" and the prescient "Copy Cat" (P-Funk's output, of course, would become a veritable sampling library for the hip-hop community), as well as more experimental numbers like "Catch a Keeper" (co-produced and arranged by Stone) and the Dada-ist funk jam "Hydraulic Pump." And expanding the repertoire nicely, Clinton indulges in the updated doo wop of "One of Those Summers" and some breezy jazz and funk on "Acupuncture." The newer touches may not suit fans loyal to the group's groundbreaking '70s albums, but *Urban Dancefloor Guerillas* is certainly worth checking out for its own brand of inspired funk. *—Stephen Cook*

Live at the Beverly Theatre in Hollywood / 1990 / Westbound ✦✦✦

Originally recorded in 1983, *Live at the Beverly Theatre* was not released until 1990, and, for a long time, remained the most extensive live release from the P-Funk crew. The lineup is impressive, bringing together such P-Funk legends as guitarist Eddie Hazel, bassist Bootsy Collins, and keyboardist Bernie Worrell. The sound quality is crisp and clean, and the songs, which represent virtually all of the classics, are preserved in extended versions. Unfortunately, even with such positives to recommend it, the record isn't an unqualified success. During the first three songs, Maceo Parker, acting as MC, talks over the grooves, introducing the band and pumping up the audience. This may have worked during the show, but on record it quickly becomes grating. And, for a two-CD set, the record is rather short, lasting barely 97 minutes. It would have been nice if the CD version had been filled out with more tracks from the show, especially since P-Funk shows are legendary for lasting upwards of three hours. This set is still worth getting, but, since the release of the multiple P-Funk box sets of live music, it is not nearly as essential as it used to be. *—Victor W. Valdivia*

Ralfi Pagan

Vocals / Latin Soul, Salsa, Boogaloo

Ralfi Pagan passed without making a significant mark in the music industry, but not because he didn't try. Raised on the Lower East Side of New York City, he was part of the city's bubbling salsa scene in the '60s and late '70s. His main body of work—four albums—was waxed for Johnny Pacheco and Gerald Masucci's Fania Records. Though a major player in the studio, he didn't achieve the notoriety of some other Fania artists, known as the Fania All Stars and which included Mongo Santamaria, Johnny Colon, Willie Bobo, Joe Bataan, Ralph Robles, and Bobby Valentine. The label started on a shoestring and couldn't afford to promote its early product across-the-board, but Fania records were hot platters on Latin radio stations.

Pagan was a gifted vocalist. His light, floating tenor was as serenading as Smokey Robinson's, but more ardent when he came down from the clouds. His melodious crooning got some chart action on a remake of Bread's "Make It With You" (1971) for Wand Records (Fania contracted with Wand during this period). Two years later, he scored a minor charter with "Soul Je T'aime" with Sylvia Robinson (now there's a duet made in heaven) on Robinson's Vibration label; but its success was modest at number-39 R&B and 99 pop on *Billboard*. Other singles include "Didn't Want to Have to Do It," "Just for a Little While," and "Come Back Baby." In addition to the four Fania albums, he had an obvious hand in *Ralfi Pagan Presents Johnny Nelson*, which is quite an item among collectors; Low Profile Records also reissued his second Fania album, *Ralfi Pagan With Love*. Examples of Pagan's haunting vocals can be found on ITP Records' *East Side Classics* series. *—Andrew Hamilton*

Ralfi Pagan / 1970 / Fania ✦✦

Owning a falsetto far sweeter than Smokey Robinson or Eugene Record, but with far less strength, Ralfi Pagan was a Latin lover for the salsa set of the '70s. This self-titled record opens with two of the most unrepentant crossover ballads of the era ("Don't Stop Now" and "Who Is the Girl for Me"). Their quaint period charm can't save them from Pagan's odd diction and delivery—though strangely, he does a better job pronouncing his English than most of the other Fania/Tico/Cotique acts then attempting Latin pop like this. Like Michael Jackson later in the '70s, though, he does much better with party songs like the groovy "Latin Soul" and "Ain't No Big Thing," though his frequent attempts to let out a soul shout are misguided at best. *—John Bush*

● **With Love** / 1972 / Fania ✦✦✦

A much better effort than his self-titled debut, *With Love* shows Ralfi Pagan with more command over his voice and with much better arrangements to back him up—by Louie Ramirez on side one and Marty Sheller on the flip. Pagan handles a difficult song like the opener, "Make It With You," with more confidence than he would have earlier, and the strung-out blues guitar during the intro doesn't hurt either. There's hardly any Latin left to this crossover album; it turns out that concentrating purely on pop makes for a much more consistent LP. Surprisingly, only "Make It With You" is a cover, though the others (with songwriting credits to Pagan, Ramirez, Joe Bataan, and Harvey Averne) display a lot of influence from early-'70s soul, pop, and even cocktail jazz. "Latin Soul" is a nice boogaloo change of pace (a bit of a repeat from his earlier LP), and while "Ain't No Big Thing" isn't going to compete with James Brown, it's pleasant enough for a side-two song. No one was confusing him with Smokey Robinson or Curtis Mayfield either, but *With Love* is a notable success from one of Fania's sideline artists. *—John Bush*

I Can See / 1976 / Fania ✦✦

One of Latin music's favorite falsetto balladeers, Ralfi Pagan croons a few mid-'70s favorites on this brief collection of smooth Latin pop. Though Pagan is quite bewitching on covers like "Ooo Baby Baby," "I Could Never Hurt You Girl," and "Just for a Little While," the arrangements (by Louie Ramirez and Marty Sheller) are very tepid. In fact, the music barely deserves the Fania name considering there's practically no hint of Latin percussion other than Bernard Purdie's standard drum kit. Pagan sounds about as emasculated as Michael Jackson on the harder funk of "La Vida," and the CD reissue has a muddy sound and undisguised vinyl transfers. *—John Bush*

Bobby Page & the Riff Raffs

Group / New Orleans R&B, Rock & Roll

The Riff Raffs were a group from Lafayette, LA, that played New Orleans-styled rock and R&B in the late '50s and early '60s. Several of the musicians in the group recorded as solo artists for the Ram label, including singer Bobby Page, singer/pianist Roy Perkins, tenor saxophonist Jimmy "Scatman" Patin, and saxophonist Harry Simoneaux. As singer in Bobby Page & the Riff Raffs, Page did a single in 1958, "Hippy Ti Yo"/"Loneliness," and another in 1962, "Like Twist"/"Tired of Hanging Around." Like the records of everyone in the Riff Raffs, these were typical and rather generic New Orleans-styled rock, with the raucous adaptation of the Cajun song "Hippy Ti Yo" being the highlight. Both sides of the two singles, plus three previously unreleased tracks, appear on the Ace compilation *Roy Perkins*, which has material by Perkins, Page, Patin, and Simoneaux. *—Richie Unterberger*

Earl Palmer

b. Oct. 25, 1924, New Orleans, LA

Drums / New Orleans R&B, R&B, Rock & Roll

Earl Palmer was a first-call drummer on the New Orleans R&B recording scene from 1950 to 1957. Talk about a supreme recommendation—in a city renowned for its second-line rhythms and syncopated grooves, Palmer was the man, playing on countless sessions by all the immortals: Little Richard, Fats Domino, Smiley Lewis, Dave Bartholomew, and too many more to list here.

Born to a mother who was a vaudevillian, little Earl was learning rhythmic patterns as a tap dancer at age four. Such contacts led him to be around drum kits on a regular basis, and it didn't take him long to master them. Bebop jazz was his first love, but R&B and blues paid the bills starting in 1947, when Palmer joined Bartholomew's band. Palmer remained the king of the traps at Cosimo Matassa's fabled recording studio until 1957, when a Shirley & Lee session led to an A&R offer from Aladdin Records boss Eddie Mesner. Palmer found studio work just as plentiful in Los Angeles, making major inroads into the rock, jazz, and soundtrack fields as well as playing on countless R&B dates with his frequent compadres Rene Hall on guitar and saxist Plas Johnson. Occasionally, Palmer would record as a leader—the instrumental "Johnny's House Party" for Aladdin, a couple of early-'60s albums for Liberty.

But even the best session men grapple with a certain sense of anonymity. So the next time you pull out Little Richard's "Tutti Frutti," Smiley Lewis' "I Hear You Knockin'," Lloyd Price's "Lawdy Miss Clawdy," or Fats Domino's "The Fat Man," please keep in mind that it's Palmer feverishly stoking that beat—with a saucy second-line sensibility that drove those songs in fresh, utterly innovative directions. *—Bill Dahl*

Drumsville / 1961 / Liberty ✦✦✦

Percolator Twist / 1962 / Liberty ✦✦✦

This is a strictly-by-the-book album of formulaic twist instrumentals that exhibits precious little of the imaginative rhythmic flair that had previously made Palmer such an in-demand New Orleans session drummer. *—Bill Dahl*

● **The World's Greatest Drummer, Ever!** / May 11, 1999 / Ace ✦✦✦✦✦

This 30-song selection of tracks on which Palmer played in the late 1950s cannot, and does not purport to, tell the whole story of his career. After all, there's only one track apiece from his work with Little Richard and Fats Domino. What this various-artists compilation (only four tracks were actually released under Earl Palmer's name) does, however, is give a pretty good idea of Palmer's early rock & roll contributions via a few well-known hits, a lot of rarities, and a bunch of styles. While Fats Domino's "I'm Walkin'," Bobby Day's "Rockin' Robin," Ritchie Valens' "La Bamba," Thurston Harris' "Little Bitty Pretty One," and Eddie Cochran's "Somethin' Else" are here, most of this is pretty obscure R&B, catching that music's transition to rock. In addition to fairly little-heard sides by Lloyd Price, Richard Berry, and Shirley & Lee, there's hard R&B from Smiley Lewis ("Shame, Shame, Shame"), Amos Milburn, and Charles Brown; gravelly jump & jive from Roy Montrell; Etta James' rock & roll remake of "Dance with Me Henry" (*not* the same as her first and more famous version, "The Wallflower"); instrumental sax rock by Lee Allen; Big T Tyler's insane "King Kong"; Don & Dewey's great harmony romp "Koko"; the rockin' Top Five hit version of "In the Mood" by Ernie Fields; and minor-league rockabilly by Jesse James. The instrumentals cut under his own name are pretty generic stuff ("Johnny's House Party" is a "Honky Tonk" rip), but you'd be checking this out for the cuts graced by Palmer's session drums rather than his own sides anyway. *—Richie Unterberger*

Robert Palmer

b. Jan. 19, 1949, Batley, England

Vocals, Guitar / Blue-Eyed Soul, Pop/Rock, Album Rock, Adult Contemporary

The career of blue-eyed soul singer Robert Palmer was a study in style versus substance. While the performer's earliest work won praise for its skillful assimilation of rock, R&B and reggae sounds, his records typically sold poorly, and he achieved his greatest notoriety as an impeccably-dressed lounge lizard. By the mid-'80s, however, Palmer became a star, although his popularity owed less to the strength of his material than to his infamous music videos: taking their cue from the singer's suave presence, Palmer's clips established him as a dapper, suit-and-tied ladies' man who performed his songs backed by a band comprised of leggy models, much to the delight of viewers who made him one of MTV's biggest success stories.

He first mounted a solo career in 1974, after several years with the Stax-influenced soul group Vinegar Joe. An avowed stylistic experimenter, Palmer recorded albums indebted to reggae and synth-pop as well as more rock-oriented material during the late '70s and early '80s. After teaming with the Duran Duran side project Power Station for the hit singles "Some Like It Hot" and "Get It On," his next solo album (1985's *Riptide*) included the number-one hit "Addicted to Love," the first in a string of videos which offered him in front of a bevy of beautiful women. Two follow-ups, "I Didn't Mean to Turn You On" and "Simply Irresistible," both hit number two. By 1990's *Don't Explain* though, Palmer had returned to the eclecticism of his earliest material and his sales plummeted. *—Jason Ankeny*

Sneakin' Sally Through the Alley / 1974 / Island ✦✦✦✦

Before becoming a slick, sharp-dressed pop star in the 1980s, Robert Palmer was a soul singer deeply rooted in R&B and funk. Those influences are on full display on his debut album *Sneakin' Sally Through the Alley*. With a backing band including members of Little Feat and the Meters, the music has a laid-back groove whether Palmer's covering New Orleans legend Allen Toussaint (the title track) or singing originals ("Hey Julia," "Get Outside"). While the music is tight and solid, it is Robert Palmer's voice that is revelatory—he sounds supremely confident among these talented musicians, and they seem to feed off his vocal intensity. Fans of the Meters or people who want to discover the funky side of Robert Palmer should check this one out. *—Vik Iyengar*

Pressure Drop / 1976 / Island ✦✦✦✦✦

Palmer's own songs (especially the silky "Give Me an Inch" and "Work to Make It Work") and the backing of Little Feat help make this a worthy follow-up to *Sneakin' Sally Through the Alley*. *—William Ruhlmann*

Some People Can Do What They Like / 1976 / Island ✦✦✦

Robert Palmer's third album is a blue-eyed soul disc that sits comfortably alongside *Sneakin' Sally Through the Alley* and *Pressure Drop*. This time, Palmer drops the orchestrations that tarted up portions of *Pressure Drop* in favor of a stripped-down yet stylish sound that shows off his ability to create a romantic, soulful mood. Highlights include "One Last Look," a lush breakup ballad that features a catchy, harmony-drenched chorus, and "Keep in Touch," a romantic tune that highlights Palmer's vocal style at its seductive height over a jazzy yet mellow melody built on a complex background vocal arrangement. Another standout track is "Man Smart, Woman Smarter," a tongue-in-cheek look at the battle between the sexes that deftly blends pop melodicism with reggae rhythms. The downside of *Some People Can Do What They Like* is that it often favors mood over hooks and this leads to music that is listenable yet falls short of being truly compelling: funky mood pieces like "What Can You Bring Me" and "Hard Head" successfully evoke a sultry mood but never take that mood in an interesting melodic direction. Another problem track is "Off the Bone," an effects-drenched instrumental snippet that serves no purpose other than to fill up two minutes of the album's running time. Despite these occasional lapses, *Some People Can Do What They Like* remains a solid and likable outing with enough memorable moments to please anyone who enjoys blue-eyed soul at its most silky and elegant. *—Donald A. Guarisco*

Double Fun / 1978 / Island ✦✦✦

After exploring a sound that filtered blue-eyed soul through excursions into worldbeat, Robert Palmer began to move in a more commercial direction on 1978's self-produced *Double Fun*. The overall sound of the album pushes towards disco (Tom Moulton, a remixer/producer and star of the American disco scene, assisted on a handful of tracks) and a lot of the tracks play up Palmer's love of reggae-styled grooves. The result was a commercial success and produced a Top 20 hit with "Every Kinda People," a catchy call for brotherhood that fleshed out its gentle pop reggae groove with tasteful orchestrations. Elsewhere, Palmer turns up the energy with "Best of Both Worlds," a bass-driven dance tune that shows off his vocal prowess with its cleverly arranged and complex vocal arrangement, and "Night People," an evocative tale of nightlife built on a percolating groove that borders on jazz-funk. The only real problem with *Double Fun* is that it occasionally allows style to overwhelm substance: "Where Can It Go?" has a dreamy ballad sound and "Love Can Run Faster" sports a solid reggae feel, but neither tune has a melody strong enough to keep them from drifting off into the ether. Despite this flaw, *Double Fun* stays afloat thanks to its ability to deftly juggle genres while maintaining an overall consistency to its production style (example: the hard rock guitar riffs that spice up the otherwise dance-oriented "You're Gonna Get What's Coming"). Casual listeners may want to pick up this album's hits on a compilation, but Robert Palmer fans will definitely want to give this album a spin. *—Donald A. Guarisco*

Secrets / 1979 / Island ✦✦✦✦✦

Palmer scored his biggest hit single of the '70s with the uptempo rocker "Bad Case of Loving You (Doctor, Doctor)" on an album that also included a wonderful version of Todd Rundgren's ballad "Can We Still Be Friends." *—William Ruhlmann*

Clues / 1980 / Island ✦✦✦✦

After recording a series of albums that established him as a pop-minded interpreter of soul styles, Robert Palmer surprised fans in 1980 with the stylistic about-face of *Clues*. On this album, he brought his sound into the new wave era by playing up the rock edge to his music, stripping the high-production gloss from his sound, and incorporating synthesizers into the arrangements. The end result became a big hit in the U.K. and paved the way for later international successes like *Riptide* and *Heavy Nova*. *Clues* also produced two notable singles in "Looking for Clues," a clever slice of new wave pop that surprises the listener with an unexpected xylophone solo, and "Johnny and Mary," a moody synth-driven ballad with perceptive lyrics about a doomed romantic relationship. There is also an impressive cover of Gary Numan's "I Dream of Wires" that retains the chilly electronic grandeur of the original while successfully working in an earthier rhythm arrangement that makes the song dance-friendly. Elsewhere, Palmer shows he hasn't abandoned his penchant for soul and ethnic music: "Woke Up Laughing" filters an African-style, chant-like vocal melody through a minimalist electronic production style, and "Found You Now" effectively combines a reggae groove with a deadpan sense of cool that is very "new wave." The end result is a bit short (it clocks in at barely over a half hour), but it remains one of Robert Palmer's strongest and most consistent albums. In short, *Clues* is a must for Robert Palmer fans and worth a spin for anyone into new wave. *—Donald A. Guarisco*

Maybe It's Live / 1982 / Island ✦✦

Pride / 1983 / Island ✦✦

Riptide / Nov. 1985 / Island ✦✦✦✦✦

Here is Palmer's commercial breakthrough, much of it in the hard rock style of his one-shot band Power Station, and featuring the hits "Discipline of Love," "Addicted to Love" (a number-one hit), "Hyperactive," and "I Didn't Mean to Turn You On." *—William Ruhlmann*

Heavy Nova / Jun. 1988 / EMI-Manhattan ✦✦

Robert Palmer cloned his hard rock *Riptide* style for its follow-up, his debut album on EMI, and was rewarded with the number-two hit "Simply Irresistible," even if the formula was beginning to sound thin. *—William Ruhlmann*

● **Addictions, Vol. 1** / Oct. 1989 / Island ♦♦♦♦♦
Thirteen-track compilation containing Palmer's biggest hits, not only the ones on Island but also the Power Station singles and "Simply Irresistible," from Palmer's first EMI album. *—William Ruhlmann*

Don't Explain / Oct. 1990 / EMI America ♦♦

Addictions, Vol. 2 / May 5, 1992 / Island ♦♦♦
Apart from "I Didn't Mean to Turn You On," there are no big hits, only album tracks and failed singles, all of which are quite good. Unfortunately, the majority of the material has been remixed, remade, or has new vocal tracks; the album may sound great, but it isn't an accurate retrospective. *—Stephen Thomas Erlewine*

The Very Best of Robert Palmer / Jan. 28, 1997 / Capitol ♦♦♦
Despite my (yet rationalized) fondness for his 1980 electro-pop hit "Johnny and Mary" (included here), the 16-track collection *The Very Best of Robert Palmer* mostly leaves me cold. Palmer has the tools, but the mechanicals lack potency and soul. Still, if combining mid-'80s hits like "Addicted to Love" and "Simply Irresistible" with a whiff of earlier material, several more recent constructions, and a pair from side project the Power Station sounds like your kind of fun, this disc does the job . . . efficiently. Includes a new cover of the Staple Singers' "Respect Yourself." *—Roch Parisien*

Rhythm & Blues / Jul. 20, 1999 / Pyramid ♦♦

Best of Both Worlds: The Robert Palmer Anthology (1974–2001) / Apr. 30, 2002 / Hip-O ♦♦♦♦♦
There are usually thought to be two phases to Robert Palmer's career: an earlier one running from 1974 to 1983, when he explored New Orleans second-line funk and reggae, backed by members of Little Feat and the Meters and turned out a series of critically acclaimed, modestly successful recordings, and a later one, from 1985 on, when he rode his good looks, some high-fashion videos, and some simplistic hard rock/pop to a series of big hits on his own and with the Power Station. This two-CD set responds to that view by devoting its first disc to the earlier phase and its second disc to the later one. Palmer switched record companies along the way, too, but Hip-O is known for its willingness to license material from other labels, and 15 of the 20 tracks on the second disc come from outside the Universal archives. Along the way, all of the singer's U.S. Top 40 hits are included, though the collection was assembled with Palmer's input, which leads to alterations from the original recordings that fans might not be entirely pleased with. For a couple of earlier compilations, *Addictions, Vols. 1* and *2*, he used remixes of many of his well-known recordings, and those remixes have been retained here. He has also chosen to present three favorites—"Johnny and Mary," "Riptide," and "Looking for Clues"—as 2001 live performances rather than in their original studio recordings. Still, the selection is well-considered. The first disc is a good summation of Palmer's first eight Island albums, and the second disc demonstrates that not all of the second half of his career sounded like "Addicted to Love," that, actually, it was far more varied than the first half. There have been several Palmer compilations, but this one is the most comprehensive yet assembled. *—William Ruhlmann*

Pam & Dodi

f. Detroit, MI
Group / Urban, Contemporary Gospel, Neo-Soul
Pamela Taylor and Audra "Dodi" Alexander comprise Pam & Dodi, a Detroit-based female vocal duo that brings a healthy appreciation of gospel and classic soul to their urban contemporary output. The big-voiced singers, both of whom have impressive ranges, first met in the Motor City in 1996. Taylor and Alexander quickly became close friends and learned that they had a mutual appreciation of gospel and secular R&B; both of them had sung in church extensively. While their self-titled debut album of 2002 isn't a gospel release, per se, some of Pam & Dodi's songs have a spiritual outlook, and the duo has toured with the Clark Sisters (a major gospel/Christian R&B group) as background vocalists.

Taylor and Alexander had been performing together as a duo for a few years when, in 1999, an appearance at a talent showcase led to a deal with Diversified Entertainment Group (a management/production company that has also represented former Brownstone singer turned solo artist Nicci Gilbert). Armed with a demo, Diversified went about trying to get a record deal for Pam & Dodi, and in 2001, the Midwestern duo signed with MCA. That year, Pam & Dodi started recording their self-titled debut album, whose producers range from Randy Jackson (of Jackson 5 fame) to Troy Oliver to Steve "Stone" Huff (known for his work with Avant and KeKe Wyatt). MCA released the album in January 2002. *—Alex Henderson*

● **Pam & Dodi** / Jan. 8, 2002 / MCA ♦♦♦
Back in R&B's golden era—the '50s, '60s, and '70s—gospel was arguably the R in R&B. R&B, like jazz and rock, thrived on blues feeling, but it also owed a lot to the music of the African-American church. The great soulsters of those decades often started out in church choirs, and they maintained their gospel influence when they went secular. In the 21st century, African-American gospel continues to heavily influence R&B. Take Pam & Dodi, for example. A sleek urban contemporary effort with major soul leanings, this self-titled debut album underscores the female duo's gospel roots. The lyrics, for the most part, are secular, although Pam & Dodi do address spiritual concerns on some of the material. They sing about romantic love ("It's Over Now") as well as spirituality ("Forgive Me," "There All the Time"), but while Christianity is an influence, they don't beat listeners over the head with Christian doctrine—therefore, those who are happily committed to Judaism, Islam, Hinduism, or Buddhism won't feel like Pam & Dodi are trying to coerce them into converting to Christianity. Although the production is high-tech and hip-hop-influenced, Pam & Dodi don't do any rapping on this 2002 release—and lovers of classic soul will have no problem pinpointing their baby boomer influences. The Detroit women acknowledge '90s favorites like Mary J. Blige and they also show a strong awareness of Patti LaBelle, Aretha Franklin, and Chaka Khan. Much of the time, Pam & Dodi favor a healthy blend of sweetness and grit—and in that sense they recall the Emotions and Deniece Williams. Some of the songs on this CD are excellent and some are merely decent. But all things considered, *Pam & Dodi* is a promising debut that paints an attractive picture of the Motor City duo. *—Alex Henderson*

The Paradons

f. Bakersfield, CA
Group / Pop, Doo Wop, R&B
The Paradons are know best for the beautiful "Diamonds and Pearls," which reached number 18 on the pop chart in 1960, nine rungs higher than it registered on the R&B chart. The quartet, comprised of friends William Powers and Bill Meyers plus Chuck Weldon and West Tyler, gigged at school dances and local clubs around Bakersfield, CA, singing what the audience requested until a chance to record came about with Milestone Records. Their first session, one night of work, yielded eight sides, including the hit "Diamonds and Pearls" and the B-side "I Want Love." "Diamonds and Pearls" became a favorite on radio stations and generated appearances on *American Bandstand*, the Apollo, the Howard, and other top venues for R&B artists.

Money problems put a monkey wrench in the mix, however, and the group disbanded after disenchantment set in. The follow-up "Bells Ring" failed to do anything, and neither did "Take All of Me" nor "I Had a Dream." The group stayed together less than a year, but Milestone kept issuing Paradons sides until they exhausted the supply. Making rock & roll records, even good ones, didn't prove fruitful for the Bakersfield lads. *—Andrew Hamilton*

The Paragons

f. 1956, Brooklyn, NY
Group / Doo Wop, R&B
Founded in Brooklyn, NY, the Paragons were a black vocal harmony quintet signed to the New York-based Winley label, which was also home to the Jesters ("The Wind"). Julius McMichael (lead), Ben Frazier (first tenor), Donald Travis (second tenor), Ricky Jackson (baritone), and Al Brown (bass) had a distinctive sound with McMichael's high tenor voice as the lead, very much defining this distinctly New York-centered doo wop sound. They began their recording career for Winley with the single "Florence" b/w "Hey Little School Girl," which was released in early 1957 and was a regional hit.

Julius McMichael lasted through three more notable singles, "Let's Start," "Twilight," and "So You Will Know," all of which did well without ever charting nationally, before he exited the lineup to become a member of the Olympics. His replacement in the Paragons' lineup was Bill Witt. The Paragons endured into the early '60s with more lineup changes and label changes as well, to Musicraft and then to Tap. They lucked out with Tap right out of the starting gate when their first single for the new label, "If," charted, which prompted Winley, their original label, to release more material that it was holding on the quintet. The group's success on the charts in the early '60s seemed to presage their subsequent history—the Paragons remained active throughout the 1960s, right into the rock & roll revival, where new audiences, consisting both of old fans of '50s music and new appreciators of harmony vocal groups, discovered the work of this fine, enduring group and boosted their listenership. In more recent years, the group has recorded new versions of their classic material, and continue to play to audiences at rock & roll revival shows. *—Bruce Eder*

The Paragons Meet the Jesters / 1959 / Jubilee ♦♦♦

● **The Best of the Paragons** / Aug. 5, 1993 / Collectables ♦♦♦♦
Here are 14 songs covering most of the high points of the group's history from 1957 into 1962, and all of their hits from this period. The only complaint one can have is that there's no sense to the order of what's here—it certainly isn't chronological, nor is it even programmed to divide the McMichael from the Witt sides. Saving the signature tune "If" for last was probably not wise, either. The desperate, yearning-filled ballad is so far superior, as a performance and a record, to everything else here (fine as all of it is), that it sweeps aside one's favorable impression of everything else here. The group was at its best behind McMichael and Witt doing soaring, ethereal ballads such as "If" and "Twilight," but they weren't any slouches when it came to hot dance numbers—"Doll Baby" and "Hey Little School Girl" are both fast-paced showcases for good humor and healthy, honest lust. The sound is passable, though one can make out some signs of noise and fuzziness (especially on the highs on "Give Me Love"), and it's likely that a new, modern transfer would eliminate many of these problems. A truly comprehensive collection might also have gone to 16 songs and included numbers like their rendition of "Begin the Beguine," not a hit but still a great performance, and "In The Midst of the Night," but this CD will do for all but the most serious fans. *—Bruce Eder*

Mica Paris

b. Apr. 27, 1969, London, England
Vocals / Urban
Though stardom has evaded her, English vocalist Mica Paris has a wonderful voice and individualistic delivery and approach. She sang in the Spirit of Watts gospel group before touring and recording in the late '80s with Hollywood Beyond. She signed with 4th and Broadway/Island in the '80s and then issued her debut *So Good*. Her second LP, *Contribution*, was released in 1990. Paris moved to Polydor for her third LP, *Whisper a Prayer*, in 1993. She also recorded with Will Downing in 1989, doing an updated version of "Where Is the Love." *—Ron Wynn*

So Good / 1989 / Island ♦♦♦
A gospel-influenced soul/pop singer with a fine range and a quality not unlike Natalie Cole, Mica Paris is among the many noteworthy talents to come out of Britain's healthy R&B scene of the 1980s and '90s. Though not a remarkable effort, her debut album,

So Good, was a respectable and decent one indicating that she had much potential. Among the CD's more noteworthy cuts are the haunting "My One Temptation," the jazz-influenced "Sway (Dance the Blues Away)" and the sizzling "Nothing Hits Your Heart like Soul Music" (which also seems like a statement of purpose, and points to Paris' devotion to more traditional R&B elements). Perhaps the song that does the most to test what Paris is truly made of is "Where Is the Love"—forming a duet with Will Downing for this remake of the Roberta Flack/Donny Hathaway classic, the earthy singer makes it crystal clear that she's quite capable of depth. For Paris, the best was yet to come. *—Alex Henderson*

● **Contribution** / 1990 / 4th & Broadway ♦♦♦♦
Mica Paris progressed considerably with her second album, *Contribution*, obviously benefitting from stronger production and better material overall. While hip-hop and house elements assert themselves more, Paris' vocals were still in a traditional R&B vein. This neo-soul approach—hip, up-to-date production combined with down-home, earthy soul singing—almost put Paris on an artistic level with fellow British neo-soul divas Lisa Stansfield and Caron Wheeler. Paris' singing is generally more confident and assured than before, and she soars on everything from the imaginative "South of the River" to a haunting Prince song ("If I Love U 2 Nite") to an unapologetically sentimental remake of Smokey Robinson & the Miracles' "More Love." Like "Where Is the Love" from *So Good*, this '60s Motown classic tests what Paris is truly made of—and makes it clear that she's striving for depth and substance, not superficiality. Rapper Rakim of Erik B. & Rakim is featured on the title song, and the driving "Just to Be With You" was produced by Mantronik (one of rap's unsung heroes). Ironically, higher quality didn't mean higher sales for Paris—*Contribution* didn't do as well as *So Good*. *—Alex Henderson*

Whisper a Prayer / Jun. 8, 1993 / Island ♦♦♦♦
Britisher Mica Paris is the most exciting female vocalist to come along in some time. She hasn't exploded due to the uncertainty and unpredictable nature of the music business. This CD is arguably more satisfying than her stunning debut, *So Good*. My two favorites were co-written by Paris, "Positivity" and "Can't Seem to Make Up My Mind." The productions are divided between Narada Michael Walden and Rod Temperton; Jon Lind produced "Whisper a Prayer," and Paris herself produced "I Bless the Day." Her original version of "You Put a Move on My Heart" sounds better than Tamia's version off Quincy Jones' *Jook Joint* CD. She delivers these songs in her smooth, jazz- and blues-influenced, intense but relaxed style. She has a voice the ears never tired of, and her signature moans will have you writhing in your seat. Unlike her first LP, which scored a minor R&B hit with "My Temptation," none of these excellent songs made much of an impact. *—Andrew Hamilton*

Junior Parker (Herman Parker Jr.)

b. May 27, 1932, Clarksdale, MS, **d.** Nov. 18, 1971, Chicago, IL
Vocals, Harmonica, Leader / Electric Memphis Blues, R&B, Soul-Blues
His velvet-smooth vocal delivery to the contrary, Junior Parker was a product of the fertile postwar Memphis blues circuit whose wonderfully understated harp style was personally mentored by none other than regional icon Sonny Boy Williamson. Little Junior (as he was known then) got his first recording opportunity in 1952 for the Modern label. Parker landed at Sun Records in 1953 and promptly scored a hit with his rollicking "Feelin' Good." Later that year, Little Junior cut a fiery "Love My Baby" and a laid-back "Mystery Train" for Sun, though he moved on to the Duke label before the end of the year. He scored big in 1957 with the smooth "Next Time You See Me," an accessible enough number to even garner some pop spins. Parker developed a breathtaking brass-powered sound that pushed his honeyed vocals and intermittent harp solos with exceptional power. Parker's updated remake of Roosevelt Sykes' "Driving Wheel" was a huge R&B hit in 1961, as was the surging "In the Dark."

Once Parker split from Robey's employ in 1966, though, his hitmaking fortunes declined. His 1966-1968 output for Mercury and its Blue Rock subsidiary deserved a better reception than it got, but toward the end, he was covering the Beatles for Capitol. A brain tumor silenced Junior Parker's magic-carpet voice in late 1971, but his contributions were not forgotten, and he was inducted into the Blues Hall of Fame in 2001. *—Bill Dahl*

Blues Consolidated (Barefoot Rock & You Got Me) / May 1958 / Duke ♦♦♦♦♦
Half Parker, half Bland, all great '50s Texas blues and R&B. *—Bill Dahl*

Driving Wheel / 1962 / Duke ♦♦♦♦
Junior's emerging from his fin-tailed Cadillac on the front of this vintage LP, which contains all kinds of gems not on MCA's CD. For example: an irresistibly upbeat "How Long Can This Go On," the richly arranged blues ballads "I Need Love So Bad" and "Someone Somewhere," Junior's dance hit "Annie Get Your Yo Yo" (all done with Duke's brassy house band), and the New Orleans-cut "The Tables Have Turned" and "Foxy Devil." *—Bill Dahl*

Baby Please / 1967 / Mercury ♦♦♦
Parker traveled back to his old Memphis stomping grounds to cut this quality set for Mercury under Bobby Robinson's supervision with a coterie of the city's hotter young R&B-oriented studio hands: guitarists Reggie Young and Tommy Cogbill, organist Bobby Emmons, and Willie Mitchell's horn section. "Just like a Fish," "Cracked Up over You," and "Sometimes I Wonder" are among its smooth highlights. *—Bill Dahl*

Like It Is / 1967 / Mercury ♦♦♦

Blues Man / 1969 / Minit ♦♦♦

Honey-Drippin' Blues / 1969 / Blue Rock ♦♦♦♦
Junior Parker a Chicago soul singer? Yeah, on at least four cuts of this fine LP for Mercury's Blue Rock R&B subsidiary. "I'm So Satisfied" (penned by Cash McCall), "Ain't Gon' Be No Cutting Aloose" (later covered by James Cotton for Alligator), "You Can't Keep a Good Woman Down," and "Easy Lovin'" stem from a soulful 1969 date in the Windy City. Also aboard: considerably bluesier remakes of Lowell Fulson's "Reconsider Baby" and Percy Mayfield's "What a Fool I Was." *—Bill Dahl*

★ **Junior's Blues: The Duke Recordings, Vol. 1** / 1992 / MCA ♦♦♦♦♦
After the non-success of "Mystery Train" on the R&B charts, Parker jumped contract and signed with Don Robey's Houston-based Duke Records. With his smooth vocal approach, Parker clearly envisioned himself as the next Roy or Charles Brown. But from the evidence of these early sides, it's clear that Robey wanted to piggyback off the success of the Sun sound. Tracks like "I Wanna Ramble" were virtual carbon copies of the "Feelin' Good" riff and Parker's recasting of old favorites like Robert Johnson's "Sweet Home Chicago," Roosevelt Sykes' "Driving Wheel," "Yonder's Wall" and "Mother-In-Law Blues," were all clearly in the down-home vein that Parker felt was too "old timey" for an up-to-date musician/vocalist of his caliber. His first big hit for the label, the horn-driven "Next Time You See Me" is here with others in the same vein, but this otherwise excellent collection is curiously missing "Pretty Baby," Parker's version of Howlin' Wolf's "Riding in the Moonlight," certainly one of his best. *—Cub Koda*

The Mercury Recordings / Nov. 5, 1996 / Collectables ♦♦♦

Backtracking: The Duke Recordings, Vol. 2 / Jun. 16, 1998 / MCA ♦♦♦
This second volume of Parker's best for the Duke label, while leaving off early classics like "I Wanna Ramble," and still delivers on a pile of great early and late tunes for the Houston-based label. Kicking off with the jump blues "Please Baby Blues" and the Howlin' Wolf-like "Can't Understand" from a 1953 session, the early sides vacillate between small rhythm sections with Pat Hare on guitar, to larger ensembles pointing toward Parker's musical future. The early sides reach their peak with the inclusion of "Pretty Baby," recorded in 1956, and Parker's version of Wolf's first single "Riding in the Moonlight." But in two years' time, Junior is recording more R&B-style material like "Barefoot Rock," "You're on My Mind," and culminating in "Annie Get Your Yo Yo" in 1961. "Get Away Blues" from 1965 and "Man or Mouse" from the following year complete the package. As always, Parker's smooth-as-silk voice and Sonny Boy-derived harp playing carry the day, making a strong case for him as a major mover and shaker on the blues scene during this period. *—Cub Koda*

I'm So Satisfied: The Complete Mercury & Blue Rock Recordings / Jul. 21, 1998 / Polygram ♦♦♦

Maceo Parker

b. Feb. 14, 1943, Kinston, NC
Sax (Alto), Leader / Funk, Soul, Soul-Jazz
"Maceo! Blow your horn!" That's how James Brown would dynamically signal his favorite horn player to take another stinging sax solo—and Maceo Parker never once let his boss down. Parker's jabbing workouts in the midst of "Papa's Got a Brand New Bag" and "Cold Sweat" made him a household name among '60s funk fans—not bad for a kid fresh out of college who got the gig primarily because Brown coveted his brother Melvin's drumming chops.

Now Parker is a star in his own right. His Verve albums *Roots Revisited* and *Mo' Roots* impeccably spotlight his soul-drenched alto sax on a sizzling hybrid of funk, R&B, and jazz. And he's brought along his ex-section mates from Brown's band—trombonist Fred Wesley and saxist Pee Wee Ellis—to stoke the almighty groove. The North Carolina product quit Brown several times. Along with his bandmates, Parker mutinied in 1970 to form Maceo & All the King's Men, only to return to the fold three years later; later in the decade, he worked with Parliament/Funkadelic and Bootsy's Rubber Band. But when Brown was incarcerated, Parker was there for him, releasing a rap song that urged the Godfather of Soul's immediate freedom. *—Bill Dahl*

Doin' Their Own Thing / 1970 / Fuel 2000 ♦♦♦
Recorded and released after a mutiny by most of James Brown's late-'60s band, *Doing Their Own Thing* contains 12 slabs of superb early-'70s style funk. Mostly instrumental, radio play for the album and subsequent singles appears to have been blocked by Brown himself. (Credited to Maceo Parker.) *—Rob Bowman*

Us / 1974 / People ♦♦♦

Funky Music Machine / 1975 / El Cello ♦♦

Roots Revisited / 1990 / Verve ♦♦♦♦
Altoist Maceo Parker has spent most of his career in R&B/funk bands, most notably those led by James Brown, George Clinton and Bootsy Collins. This CD gave him a chance to stretch out as a leader and his soulful horn immediately brings to mind Hank Crawford and (to a lesser extent) Lou Donaldson. With a strong backup group that includes Pee Wee Ellis on tenor, trombonist Fred Wesley and Don Pullen on organ, Parker enthusiastically plays over infectious grooves with just one funky departure ("In Time"). *Roots Revisited* is a throwback to the 1960s soul jazz style and Maceo Parker gives one the impression that, if called upon, he could hold his own on a bebop date. *—Scott Yanow*

Mo' Roots / 1991 / Verve ♦♦♦♦♦
The second *Roots* installment, *Mo' Roots* was cut minus Pullen and Collins, leaning a little more toward the instrumental soul side. Three fine originals in conjunction with covers of Ray Charles, Marvin Gaye, Otis Redding, Horace Silver, and Lionel Hampton. *—Rob Bowman*

● **Life on Planet Groove** / Mar. 5, 1992-Mar. 7, 1992 / Verve ♦♦♦♦♦
A scorching album of funky grooves from Maceo Parker, assisted by the rest of the J.B.'s on backing horns. The album was recorded in concert at a restaurant in France, and the crowd seems just as responsive in most ways as any Atlanta mob. Along with the J.B. horns, Vincent Henry accompanies on bass throughout the album/concert. The album starts out with an original Maceo composition, then moves into a pair from his old boss James Brown. After that, there's another Maceo number, a cover of "Addictive Love," a rendition of "Georgia on My Mind," and a composition undertaken by a veritable army of funk veterans. This is probably just about the best solo Maceo Parker album there is, at least until the release of *Funkoverload*. If you're a funk fan, or a soul-jazz fan, this

album might just provide what you need. Maceo on his own always provides a nice collection of soul and funk, and this one is no exception. *—Adam Greenberg*

Funk Overload / Aug. 25, 1998 / What Are Records? ♦♦♦♦

Having steered the mothership and worked as a triggerman for the Godfather of Soul, storied sax man Maceo Parker now brings his own tight rhythm and soul sound to vinyl (er, plastic) in undeniable proof that he's still "got it." Combining his smoking horn with the backing of fellow legends such as trombonist Fred Wesley and new bloods such as son Corey (whose intermittent raps colorfully enhance the album's youthful vibrance), Maceo works through the familiar funk and soul lines of his Parliament and J.B. days and adds new twists to such classics as Marvin Gaye's "Let's Get It On" and "Inner City Blues," Stevie Wonder's "Tell Me Something Good," and Sly Stone's "Sing a Simple Song," while offering a number of his own well-orchestrated and well-seasoned compositions. "Youth of the World" features Maceo on a lead vocal reminiscent of Kool Moe Dee or Kurtis Blow, while "Do You Love Me" rises like Tower of Power before the sultry Chicago lines of closer "Going in Circles." Though Maceo's original lyrical attempts may be a bit immature, his years of experience and hard work shine through with every brassy attack and smooth soul note. *—Matthew Robinson*

Dial M-A-C-E-O / Apr. 18, 2000 / What Are Records? ♦♦♦♦

Ray Parker Jr.

b. May 1, 1954, Detroit, MI

Vocals, Guitar / Urban, Dance-Pop

Guitarist/songwriter/producer Ray Parker Jr. was born in Detroit, MI, and started out as a teenaged session guitarist playing on sessions recorded for Holland-Dozier-Holland's Hot Wax and Invictus Records. He'd also play behind the Temptations, Stevie Wonder, the Spinners, Gladys Knight & the Pips, and other Motown acts when they appeared at the Twenty Grand Club. Later, Parker played on Wonder's albums *Talking Book* (1972) and *Innervisions* (1973). Deciding to become a recording artist, Parker got a deal with Arista Records in 1977. Not confident about his singing ability, he put together a band that included vocalist Arnell Carmichael, bassist/singer Jerry Knight, guitarist Charles Fearing, Larry Tolbert, and Darren Carmichael. However, on record, Parker played most, if not all, of the instruments.

His first LP, *Raydio*, went gold, peaking at number-eight R&B in spring 1978. The LP included the gold, number-five R&B hit single "Jack and Jill" (lead vocal by Jerry Knight), "Is This a Love Thing," and the charting single "Honey I'm Rich." The hits continued with Ray Parker Jr. & Raydio's gold, number-four *Rock On*; the gold, number-six R&B *Two Places at the Same Time* from spring 1980; and the number-one gold record *A Woman Needs Love* from 1981. Then, as Ray Parker Jr., *The Other Woman* held the number-one R&B, number-11 pop spot in spring 1982. One of Parker's biggest hits and best loved songs, "Ghostbusters" parked at the number-one R&B spot for two weeks and the number-one pop for three weeks on *Billboard*'s charts in summer 1984. *—Ed Hogan*

A Woman Needs Love / 1981 / Arista ♦♦♦

This was the last album Parker did with Raydio, and it was a successful outing. It yielded the number-one *Billboard* R&B smash hit "A Woman Needs Love," and an easy-flowing track with lyrics supporting women in relationships that retained its number-one position for two weeks. That single was followed up with "That Old Song," reflecting on the yester-love a girl and boy shared; it peaked at number 26 after 11 weeks. Parker slows down the pace with "Old Pro" and "So Into You." With the latter's title being self explanatory, the former is the tale of a reformed player wanting to settle down. As for dance grooves, Parker exhibits his musicianship on the remainder of the album on tracks like "It's Your Night," (number 73, five weeks), "Still in the Groove," and "All in the Way You Get Down," all creditable compositions. *—Craig Lytle*

The Other Woman / 1982 / Arista ♦♦♦

After three prosperous albums with Raydio, Parker branches out on his own with a successful debut solo release. Not forsaking the sound that spawned a string of hits with Raydio, Parker chalks up two *Billboard* R&B Top Ten singles, the first being "The Other Woman." With its midtempo rhythm and striking electric guitar, it crested at the number-two position for four consecutive weeks, fizzling out after week 19; it also reached the number-four spot on the *Billboard* pop charts. While "Let Me Go," the second release, was a ballad of sorts, it also held a spot on the charts for 19 weeks, peaking at number three. As usual, Parker interjects his vocal sighs on nearly every song, and the third single release, "It's Our Own Affair," is no exception—a midtempo track with an easy-flowing rhythm that reached the 44th position on the charts. The remainder of the album is consistent with the aforementioned releases. The veteran session guitarist does not stray from his musical base; he keeps his compositions simple and production efficient. *—Craig Lytle*

Woman Out of Contol / 1983 / Arista ♦♦

With the proliferation of new music technology, Parker seizes the moment to incorporate some of it on selections like "Electronic Lover," "Invasion" and "N2U2." These are merely experimental endeavors. The highest-charted single on this album was the midtempo "I Still Can't Get Over Loving You," which peaked at number 12 on the *Billboard* R&B charts following an 18-week run. It was succeeded by two lesser-achieving singles: "In the Heat of the Night," (number 64, five weeks) and "Woman Out of Control." The latter is a frail, yet danceable effort; it still maneuvered its way onto the *Billboard* R&B charts for a brief visit at number 71 for four weeks. The former allows Parker to artistically express his trademark moan-and-groan appeal. Selections like "I Don't Wanna Know" and "She Still Feels the Need" never made the charts, but are a good listen. *—Craig Lytle*

After Dark / 1987 / Geffen ♦♦♦

This was the closest Ray Parker Jr. ever came to doing adult soul. His debut for Geffen included the song "I Don't Think That Man Should Sleep Alone." This was his last big hit, and despite the title, said some serious things about male/female intimacy and relationships. Parker's voice sounded more somber, introspective, and varied than on anything before or since. *—Ron Wynn*

I Love You Like You Are / 1991 / MCA ♦♦

Ray Parker Jr.'s big hit days had faded by the time he switched labels to MCA in the early '90s. He made a comeback bid with this album, which had a heavy pop flavor. It did yield him a mild hit with "She Needs to Get Some," although it also generated a little controversy regarding the song's sexual/sexist direction. Parker's vocals were never great, but they seemed more weary than anything else. His past hits had succeeded with him striking either a bemused or a comical/teasing stance; now he sounded tired, detached, and even a little angry. *—Ron Wynn*

● **Greatest Hits** / Oct. 12, 1993 / Arista ♦♦♦♦♦

Though it isn't sequenced in chronological order—in fact, it's sequenced a little bewilderingly—*Greatest Hits* nevertheless is an excellent summation of Ray Parker Jr.'s biggest hits, containing not just solo smashes like "Ghostbusters" and "The Other Woman," but also songs he sang during his time with Raydio. So, even if it could be presented better, it nevertheless gives fans exactly what they need. *—Stephen Thomas Erlewine*

The Heritage Collection / Feb. 8, 2000 / Arista ♦♦♦♦♦

A brief collection of Ray Parker's bubblegum soul hits including the "Ghostbusters" monster from the movie of the same name. Every selection sounds as if it was tailored for 12-year-olds. His only attempts at being hard—"Jamie," "For Those Who Like to Groove," and "Bad Boy"—never quite get there. Still, the charm in lightweights like "You Can't Change That," "Jack and Jill," and "A Woman Needs Love (Just Like You Do)" is contagious. Someone should compile a CD of Ray's pre-Ray Parker Jr. & Raydio recordings; he expressed himself more soulfully as a teenager fronting local Detroit groups like the Vows who waxed "When a Boy Loves a Girl." *—Andrew Hamilton*

Robert Parker

b. Oct. 14, 1930, Crescent City, LA

Vocals, Saxophone / Pop-Soul, New Orleans R&B, R&B, Soul

Robert Parker's dance raver "Barefootin'" was one of the biggest hits to come out of New Orleans during the mid-'60s. Parker played sessions as a saxophonist back in 1949 with the legendary pianist Professor Longhair, and his 1959 solo debut for Ron, "All Night Long," was a scorching two-part instrumental. But Parker's underutilized vocal talents suddenly emerged in 1966, when his highly infectious "Barefootin'" became a giant hit on tiny Nola. Only one other Parker single, "Tip Toe," charted the next year, but Parker remained a popular attraction in his hometown. *—Bill Dahl*

● **Barefootin'** / Nov. 2, 1995 / Collectables ♦♦♦♦♦

Originally issued in 1987 on vinyl by England's Charly, this collection includes Parker's main claim to fame, the 1966 R&B and pop dance smash "Barefootin'"; its flip side, "Let's Go Baby (Where the Action Is)"; both sides of a 1969 single Parker cut for Silver Fox; and a number of '70s recordings the erstwhile sax player waxed for Sansu Enterprises. Much of the CD, including the title cut, is infectious New Orleans R&B of a high caliber, but other tracks find Parker attempting to cut mainstream funk and disco, usually with less-than-inspiring results. If possible, find the Charly release, because Collectables, in their typically shoddy manner, do not bother to provide songwriting credits, let alone track credits or liner notes. A good policy is to buy Collectables only if there is no other anthology of the same material issued anywhere else in the world, no matter what the price difference. *—Rob Bowman*

● **The Wardell Quezergue Sessions** / 2002 / Night Train ♦♦♦♦♦

Let's face it: the name Wardell Quezergue is known only to *hardcore* R&B fans, those that not only seriously study liner notes, but retain information (a common problem for record geeks with too many names and labels floating around in their heads). To translate the title for those that don't already know, Wardell Quezergue was a producer and co-owner of Nola Records, the label that released all 24 of the tracks on Night Train's 2002 Robert Parker reissue, *The Wardell Quezergue Sessions*. Foremost among these, of course, is "Barefootin'," the ebullient dance single that was Parker's one big hit. Along with its flip side, the equally infectious "Let's Go Baby (Where the Action Is)," it's the only number here to have previously been reissued. Previous CD compilations, such as Collectables' *Barefootin': Golden Classics*, sample from several different labels and phases of his career. Although they cover more ground, they don't necessarily provide a better introduction, since most fans of "Barefootin'" are looking for more tunes in that vein, and this collection provides it in spades with 24 tracks of nimble, melodic New Orleans R&B. This is certainly on the lighter side of New Orleans R&B, opting for rolling beats and happy vocals (best illustrated on his covers of "Mr. Pitiful" and "In the Midnight Hour," which are fun, but not nearly as impassioned as those by Otis Redding and Wilson Pickett), and overall effervescent touch, reminiscent of a poppier Lee Dorsey, which can be quite charming. This holds true throughout the collection, even when the quality of the material dips, which it admittedly does: the covers are often misguided, and while the many attempts to recapture the magic of "Barefootin'" are amusing ("The Scratch," "Everybody's Hip Huggin'," "Happy Feet," "Barefootin' Boogaloo," etc.), they wear thin after a while. These do take up a bit more of the track listing than they should, but there are little gems scattered throughout here, such as the wonderful "Heading for a Fall," which makes this not just of interest to serious New Orleans R&B collectors (after all, *all* of this material was impossible to find on CD prior to this), but this is the place to go for those that want more Robert Parker, because it sure is true this all delivers on the sound of "Barefootin'." *—Stephen Thomas Erlewine*

Parlet

Group / Funk

Parlet is essentially a trio (two trios, actually—one with Washington, Wright, and Franklin, the other with Washington, Hayden, and Evans) of backup singers from the

P-Funk mob. The group is similar to the Brides of Funkenstein in that respect, but perhaps a bit less conservative. The group was originally designed as a concept by George Clinton, as a counterpart to his original doo wop group the Parliaments. The original name for the girls group was actually the Parlettes, but it was shortened to try and escape from the Motown sound genre, again by Clinton. By their first release in the spotlight in 1978, *Pleasure Principle*, Parlet was "sexual satisfaction guaranteed, that's what this group is all about" according to Clinton. Under a pile of more energetic funk from the other various components of Uncle Jam's Army, Parlet was hardly able to stand out too readily, peaking on *Billboard*'s R&B chart at number 49, with "Ridin' High," off of *Invasion of the Booty Snatchers*.

Parlet had only two opportunities to show a stage presence, once on a 1978 European tour and again at the L.A. Funk Festivals in 1979. Other than that, they were only holding their positions in front of the backup mikes as the mothership landed. After three albums, the group returned to Clinton's collective fold as backup signers once again, though they may still break loose from time to time for an unrecorded jam of their own. *—Adam Greenberg*

Pleasure Principle / 1978 / Casablanca ♦♦♦

Never let it be said that George Clinton wasn't a busy man in the late '70s. In addition to leading Parliament and Funkadelic (which were essentially the same band with two different names), Clinton produced or co-produced Bootsy's Rubber Band, the Brides of Funkenstein, the Horny Horns, and Parlet. In 1978, he produced Parlet's debut album, *Pleasure Principle*, which is a solid P-Funk-oriented outing, even though it isn't the female trio's best album. This LP finds the Jeanette Washington/Debbie Wright/Mallia Franklin edition of Parlet joined by a lot of familiar P-Funk faces, including Bootsy Collins on drums, Bernie Worrell on keyboards and Fred Wesley on trombone. Not surprisingly, infectious tracks like "Cookie Jar" and "Love Amnesia" are very Clinton-sounding. But *Pleasure Principle* is far from predictable. Clinton opts for variety, producing everything from the moody "Misunderstanding" and the sentimental Northern soul ballad "Mr. Melody Man" (which would not have been out of place on a Love Unlimited or Three Degrees album) to more disco-minded offerings such as "Are You Dreaming?" and the title song. For the most part, Clinton wasn't a disco artist—hardcore funk was his primary focus in the 1970s—but these club-friendly tunes successfully combine P-Funk with disco gloss. "Are You Dreaming?" even has a bit of a Euro-disco outlook, which wasn't the sort of thing that one expected from Clinton in the late '70s. But then, the leader of Parliament/Funkadelic wanted to stretch himself on this LP—and he did. *—Alex Henderson*

• **Invasion of the Booty Snatchers** / 1979 / Casablanca ♦♦♦♦

Parlet's second album, *Invasion of the Booty Snatchers*, found Parliament/Funkadelic leader George Clinton supervising a new edition of the female trio. Jeanette Washington was still on board, but this time, she joined forces with Shirley Hayden and Janice Evans instead of Debbie Wright and Mallia Franklin. However, *Invasion of the Booty Snatchers* (whose title is based on the 1950s sci-fi/horror movie *Invasion of the Body Snatchers*) isn't a radical departure from Parlet's first album, *Pleasure Principle*. Clinton (who produced this 1979 LP with Ron Dunbar) still goes for variety, and Parlet's sophomore album is as unpredictable as their first. While goofy numbers like "No Rump to Bump" and "Huff-N-Puff" are very Parliament-sounding, "Ridin' High" (a minor hit) and the glossy "Booty Snatchers" have more of a disco influence—"Ridin' High," in fact, almost sounds like a marriage of P-Funk and Chic. Meanwhile, the pleasing "Don't Ever Stop (Lovin' Me, Needin' Me)" is a conventional Northern soul ballad—conventional by Clinton's standards, that is. As strong as *Invasion of the Booty Snatchers* is, the LP wasn't a huge multi-platinum seller; many of the P-Funk addicts who bought Parliament and Funkadelic's albums religiously didn't spend a lot of dollars on Parlet. Nonetheless, *Invasion of the Booty Snatchers* is arguably the group's finest and most impressive release. *—Alex Henderson*

Play Me or Trade Me / 1980 / Casablanca ♦♦♦

If 1979's *Invasion of the Booty Snatchers* is Parlet's best and most essential album, *Play Me or Trade Me* runs a close second. This 1980 LP, which George Clinton produced with Ron Dunbar, offers the same Parlet lineup heard on *Invasion of the Booty Snatchers*—Jeanette Washington is joined by Shirley Hayden and Janice Evans. And many of the familiar P-Funk faces are on board, including Bootsy Collins (who plays guitar but doesn't sing), saxman Maceo Parker, and trombonist Fred Wesley. *Play Me or Trade Me*, which was Parlet's third album, isn't quite as diverse as its two predecessors. But if the trio sacrifices some diversity on this record, they don't sacrifice quality—*Play Me or Trade Me* is impressively consistent, and Parlet sounds inspired and focused throughout the LP. Side one is a nonstop P-Funk party; it kicks into high gear with "Help From My Friends" and Parlet keeps the momentum going with "Watch Me Do My Thang" and "Wolf Tickets." Side two, meanwhile, also has a strong P-Funk orientation, although there are hints of Chic on the title track and "I'm Mo Be Hittin' It." And the fact that Chic managed to have some type of influence on one of George Clinton's acts speaks well of the Nile Rodgers/Bernard Edwards team. Back in 1980, Rodgers & Edwards were not music industry veterans; Chic's first album came out in 1977. But they had become extremely influential, and even the mighty Clinton—someone who was incredibly influential himself—is affected by the distinctive Rodgers/Edwards sound on parts of this album. Unfortunately, *Play Me or Trade Me* was the end of the line for Parlet, but at least the group ended their brief recording career on a high note. *—Alex Henderson*

The Best of Parlet / Jun. 7, 1994 / Casablanca ♦♦♦

A collection spanning the short recording lifespan (three albums) of Parlet, one of the offshoot groups from George Clinton's P-Funk mob. Both major lineups of singers in the group are present on this album (the group used one lineup for the first album, then an altered one for the next two), with the earlier group handling four songs, and the later form handling the rest. Really, the group is more notable as background vocalists for the Parliament/Funkadelic endeavors. These tunes, penned mainly by Clinton, work well on the strengths of the vocalists, despite being largely forgettable. For anyone curious about the funk, there are countless other albums available that would be better introductions (notably the *Give up the Funk* compilation of Parliament). This album serves its purpose well, but that purpose is really just the enjoyment of hardcore fans and collectors. *—Adam Greenberg*

Parliament

f. 1970, Detroit, MI, **db.** 1980

Group / Funk, Soul, Psychedelic Soul

Inspired by Motown's assembly line of sound, George Clinton gradually put together a collective of over 50 musicians and recorded the ensemble during the '70s both as Parliament and Funkadelic. While Funkadelic pursued band-format psychedelic rock, Parliament engaged in a funk free-for-all, blending influences from the godfathers (James Brown and Sly Stone) with freaky costumes and themes inspired by '60s acid culture and science fiction. From its 1970 inception until Clinton's dissolving of Parliament in 1980, the band hit the R&B Top Ten several times but truly excelled in two other areas: large-selling, effective album statements and the most dazzling, extravagant live show in the business. In an era when Philly soul continued the slick sounds of establishment-approved R&B, Parliament scared off more white listeners than it courted.

By the time his on-the-move family settled in New Jersey during the early '50s, George Clinton (b. July 22, 1941, Kannapolis, NC) became interested in doo wop, which was just beginning to explode in the New York-metro area. Basing his group on Frankie Lymon & the Teenagers, Clinton formed the Parliaments in 1955 with a lineup that gradually shifted to include Clarence "Fuzzy" Haskins, Grady Thomas, Raymond Davis, and Calvin Simon. Based out of a barbershop backroom where Clinton straightened hair, the Parliaments released only two singles during the next ten years, but frequent trips to Detroit during the mid-'60s—where Clinton began working as a songwriter and producer—eventually paid off their investment.

After finding a hit with the 1967 single "(I Wanna) Testify," the Parliaments ran into trouble with Revilot Records and refused to record any new material. Instead of waiting for a settlement, Clinton decided to record the same band under a new name: Funkadelic. Founded in 1968, the group began life as a smoke screen, claiming as its only members the Parliaments' backing band—guitarist Eddie Hazel, bassist Billy Nelson, rhythm guitarist Lucius "Tawl" Ross, drummer Ramon "Tiki" Fulwood, and organist Mickey Atkins—but in truth including Clinton and the rest of the former Parliaments lineup. Revilot folded not long after, with the label's existing contracts sold to Atlantic; Clinton, however, decided to abandon the Parliaments name rather than record for the major label. One previously recorded Parliaments single, "A New Day Begins," was licensed to Atco in 1969 and became a number-44 hit that May. By 1970, George Clinton had regained the rights to the Parliaments name: he then signed the entire Funkadelic lineup to Invictus Records as Parliament. The group released one album—1970's *Osmium*—and scored a number 30 hit, "The Breakdown," on the R&B charts in 1971. With Funkadelic firing on all cylinders, however, Clinton decided to discontinue Parliament (the name, not the band) for the time being.

Though keyboard player Bernie Worrell (b. April 19, 1944, Long Beach, NJ) had played on the original Funkadelic album, his first credit with the conglomeration appeared on Funkadelic's second album, 1970's *Free Your Mind... And Your Ass Will Follow*. Clinton and Worrell had known each other since the New Jersey barbershop days, and Worrell soon became the most crucial cog in the P-Funk machine, working on arrangements and production for virtually all later Parliament/Funkadelic releases. His strict upbringing and classical training (at the New England Conservatory and Juilliard), as well as the boom in synthesizer technology during the early '70s, gave him the tools to create the synth runs and horn arrangements that later trademarked the P-Funk sound. Two years after the addition of Worrell, P-Funk added its second most famed contributor, Bootsy Collins. The muscular, throbbing bassline of Collins (b. October 26, 1951, Cincinnati, OH) had already been featured in James Brown's backing band (the J.B.'s) along with his brother, guitarist Phelps "Catfish" Collins. Bootsy and Catfish were playing in a Detroit band when George Clinton saw and hired them.

Funkadelic released five albums from 1970 through early 1974, and consistently hit the lower reaches of the R&B charts, but the collective pulled up stakes later in 1974 and began recording as Parliament. Signing with the Casablanca label, Parliament's "Up for the Down Stroke" (number-ten R&B, number-63 pop) appeared in mid-1974 and reflected a more mainstream approach than Funkadelic, with funky horn arrangements reminiscent of James Brown and a live feel that recalls contemporary work by Kool & the Gang. It became the biggest hit yet for the Parliament/Funkadelic congregation. "Testify," a revamped version of the Parliaments' 1967 hit, also charted in 1974. One year later, *Chocolate City* continued Parliament's success: the title track reached number-24 R&B, and "Ride On" also charted.

Clinton & co. ushered in 1976 with the April release of the third Parliament LP in as many years: *Mothership Connection*. Arguably the peak of Parliament's power, the album made number 13 on the pop charts and went platinum, sparked by three hit singles: "P-Funk (Wants to Get Funked Up)" (number-33 R&B), "Tear the Roof Off the Sucker (Give Up the Funk)" (number-five R&B, number-15 pop), and "Star Child" (number-26 R&B). In addition to Bootsy Collins, the album featured two other James Brown refugees: horn legends Maceo Parker and Fred Wesley. Just six months after the release of *Mothership Connection*, Clinton had another Parliament album in the can, *The Clones of Doctor Funkenstein*. Though it only reached gold status, the LP spawned the number-22 R&B hit "Do That Stuff" and the number 43 "Dr. Funkenstein."

Several internal squabbles during 1977 apparently didn't phase Clinton at all; the following year proved to be the most successful in Parliament's history. In January, "Flash Light"—from the Parliament album *Funkentelechy Vs. the Placebo Syndrome*—became the collective's first number-one hit. It topped the R&B charts for three weeks, and was followed by the number 27 single, "Funkentelechy." The LP reached number 13 on the pop charts and became Parliament's second platinum album. Early in 1979, Parliament hit number one yet again with "Aqua Boogie," from its eighth album, *Motor-Booty Affair.* The LP, which stalled at number 23, nevertheless became the group's fifth consecutive album to go gold or better. Parliament's ninth album, *Gloryhallastoopid (Or Pin the Tale on the Funky),* was released later in 1979 and showed a bit of a slip in the previously unstoppable Clinton machine. The group charted in the R&B Top Ten twice during 1980 ("Theme From 'The Black Hole'" and "Agony of Defeet"), but Clinton began to be weighed down that year by legal difficulties arising from Polygram's acquisition of Casablanca. Jettisoning both the Parliament and Funkadelic names (but not the musicians), Clinton began his solo career with 1982's *Computer Games.* He and many former Parliament/Funkadelic members continued to tour and record during the '80s as the P-Funk All Stars, but the decade's disdain of everything to do with the '70s resulted in the neglect of critical and commercial opinion for the world's biggest funk band, especially one which in part had spawned the sound of disco. During the early '90s, the rise of funk-inspired rap (courtesy of Digital Underground, Dr. Dre, and Warren G.) and funk rock (Primus and Red Hot Chili Peppers) re-established the status of Clinton & co., one of the most important forces in the recent history of black music. *—John Bush*

Osmium / 1970 / Invictus ✦✦✦

The first Parliament album as such was a mixed-up mess of an affair—but would anyone expect anything less? The overall sound is much more Funkadelic than later Parliament, if with a somewhat more accessible feel. Things get going with an appropriately leering start, thanks to "I Call My Baby Pussycat," which makes something like "What's New, Pussycat?" seem like innocent, chaste conversation. After a stripped-down start, things explode into a full-on funk strut with heavy-duty guitar and slamming drums setting the way, while the singers sound like they're tripping without losing the soul—sudden music dropouts, vocal cut-ins, volume level tweaks, and more add to the off-kilter feeling. *Osmium*'s sound progresses from there—it's funk's fire combined with a studio freedom that feels like a blueprint for the future. Bernie Worrell's keyboard abilities are already clear, whether he's trying for hotel lounge jams or full freakiness; similarly, Eddie Hazel is clearly finding his own epic stoned zone to peel out some amazing solos at the drop of a hat. As for the subject matter and end results—who else but this crew could have come up with the trash-talking, yodeling twang of "Little Ol' Country Boy" in 1970 and still made it funky with all the steel guitar? Other fun times include the piano and vocal-into-full-band goofy romantic romp of "My Automobile" and "Funky Woman," where over a heavy groove (and goofy Worrell break) the titular character lives with the consequence of her stank: "She hung them in the air/The air said this ain't fair!" Amidst all the nuttiness, there are some perhaps surprising depths—consider "Oh Lord, Why Lord/Prayer," which might almost be too pretty for its own good (Worrell's harpsichord almost verges on the sickly sweet) but still has some lovely gospel choir singing and heartfelt lyrics. *—Ned Raggett*

Up for the Down Stroke / 1974 / Casablanca ✦✦✦✦

Kicking off with one of prime funk's purest distillations—the outrageously great title track, with a perfect party chorus line and uncredited horns (presumably the Horny Horns were involved somehow) adding to the monster beat and bass—*Up for the Down Stroke* finds Parliament in rude good health. As was more or less the case through the '70s, Parliament took a slightly more listener-friendly turn here than they did as Funkadelic, but often it's a difference by degrees. Just listening to some of Bernie Worrell's insane keyboard parts or Bootsy Collins' bass work here is enough to wake the dead. As always, Worrell in particular can suddenly surprise with his delicacy—the soft, understated flow of "I Just Got Back" may have lyrics that could be sung by Jon Anderson, at least at points, but the piano lines have subtle, dreamy grace, the antithesis of Rick Wakeman's masturbations. For that matter, Peter Chase's whistles are downright delightful, goofy, and sweet all at once. Slightly more oddball is "All Your Goodies Are Gone," which has a bit more upfront bite and some downright strange lyrics, delivered with a stoned, breathless tone and backed by unearthly choir arrangements. Eddie Hazel is still listed as present and contributing, though unfortunately not for long after, with Ron Bykowski, Gary Shider, and William Nelson also chipping in as needed. Hazel co-writes two of the songs; it's a pity "The Goose" runs out of steam toward the midpoint of its nine minutes, but it makes for pleasant background music if not Parliament at its unfettered best. In the meantime, Clinton and various familiar voices like Fuzzy Haskins and Grady Thomas keep the weird wigginess of the lyrics flowing. In a nod to the group's past, "(I Wanna) Testify," here simply called "Testify," gets a 1974-era work over. *—Ned Raggett*

Chocolate City / 1975 / Casablanca ✦✦✦✦

"Chocolate City" stands out as a trademark P-Funk moment, with it's languid meandering, rich synth washes, and spoken-word vocals—a perfect way to jump start the album. From there, the album kicks into high gear, moving from one uptempo R&B song to the next, every song driven by Bootsy's slippery bass riffs and most showered with harmonious vocal choruses. Every song has its quirks, with "Let Me Be" being the only song that gets too unconventional for its own good, featuring only synth, piano, and vocals. Most of the other songs are fairly equal, none being lackluster and none being too noteworthy, with the exception of "Together"; this song's soulful chorus drifts momentarily away from the funk for a moment, offering one of the album's most beautiful moments. For the most part, though, this isn't a beautiful album—it's fairly grimy with its funk-infused R&B thumping and worming relentlessly, never taking too much time to worry about catchy hooks. Yet for as understated as this stubborn focus is, never venturing too far into rock, disco, or jamming territory, it's an effective focus, making *Chocolate City* a slight improvement from *Up for the Down Stroke.* There's something rewarding about how consistent and focused this album is, probably because of its amazing lineup featuring Bootsy Collins, Bernie Worrell, and Eddie Hazel. As such, *Chocolate City* won't disappoint those looking for the R&B side of the P-Funk library. *—Jason Birchmeier*

★ **Mothership Connection** / Feb. 1976 / Casablanca ✦✦✦✦✦

The addition of ex-J.B.'s Fred Wesley and Maceo Parker to the Parliament roster on *Mothership Connection* elevated an already mind-blowing band into the best funk band of the '70s, arguably the best funk band ever. With these two funk veterans supplying the horns, Clinton had everything he could ask for in his already stellar group. The opening song, "P-Funk (Wants to Get Funked Up)," harkened back to the opening title track from Parliament's previous album, *Chocolate City,* laying down a languid synth aura for a spoken-word intro. When "P-Funk (Wants to Get Funked Up)" steps into second gear though, bringing in Bootsy's bass, Wesley's horn, Worrell's piano, and a chorus of vocalists, it's fairly evident just how large a step forward *Mothership Connection* is from the conventional R&B roots of *Chocolate City* and *Up for the Down Stroke.* The second song, "Mothership Connection (Star Child)," makes the differentiation glaringly evident, most noticeably when the song enters the cosmic, proto-hip-hop "swing down sweet chariot" bridge with its accompanying melody from beyond. The funk doesn't stop there though, with the remaining five songs keeping the tempo laden with dense interweaving rhythms, peaking on "Give Up the Funk (Tear the Roof Off the Sucker)." In the end, there's no questioning this album's impact, one that is still being felt via rap-induced aftershocks. In addition to its contemporary impact and continued longevity, the album was a massive success for Clinton and company upon its release in 1975, elevating the P-Funk collective to unparalleled heights in terms of audience. Some Parliament albums may be flawless, and others may be innovative, but this is the P-Funk zenith in more ways than one, perfect as well as perennial. *—Jason Birchmeier*

Clones of Dr. Funkenstein / Sep. 1976 / Casablanca ✦✦✦✦✦

Come 1976, and Parliament got up to its usual tricks in that particular incarnation—right down to opening backwards-masked vocal weirdness plus sci-fi scenarios in the "Prelude," where "funk is its own reward." With Bernie Worrell and Fred Wesley splitting the horn arrangements and Clinton and Bootsy Collins taking care of the rest, the result is a concept album of sorts you can dance to. The clones get up and do their thing throughout, and if it's not *The Wall,* then that's all to its benefit. The immediate downside of *Clones* is that it's a fairly one-note record—every groove can just about be exchanged for any other one, unlike the wider variety apparent on other releases. Given Clinton and company's sheer work rate, something likely had to give and this is one of the stress points. There are a couple of stronger songs—"I've Been Watching You (Move Your Sexy Body)" is classic slow jam territory. Not exactly Barry White, but hearing Parliament tone it down just enough pays off, especially with Worrell's drowsy, sensuous horn charts. "Funkin' for Fun," meanwhile, brings the album to a strong, lively end, with just enough in the call-and-response vocals and horns to spark some extra energy into the proceedings. As is the case with most mid- to late-'70s Parliament, things may not be as deep as what was done as Funkadelic, but only those who always explicitly value lyrical worth have any cause to complain. Listening to the silly squeals and burbles on "Dr. Funkenstein" itself is pure fun with sound, while the good doctor's speech is scientific craziness. As one voice says out of nowhere, "Kiss me on my ego!" Special bonus—the utterly goofball cover photo, one of P-Funk's best. *—Ned Raggett*

☆ **Funkentelechy Vs. the Placebo Syndrome** / 1977 / Casablanca ✦✦✦✦✦

Parliament simply poured it on for this amazing album, clearly one of its all-time best. At least one band named itself after a lyric—Urge Overkill, taken from the song "Funkentelechy" itself—while the amount of times this album has been sampled for the music is uncountable. Besides having an absolutely wonderful name, it contained at least three of the finest Parliament tunes ever, including arguably its signature song. "Flash Light," which closes *Funkentelechy* on a riotous high, has it all—a brilliant fake ending, instant singalong value, a synth bassline to kill for from Bernie Worrell, and so much more. As the album ends, so too does it begin, with a stone-cold classic—"Bop Gun (Endangered Species)." Starting with a brisk little guitar figure and beat, it turns into an instant party on all fronts, with great lead vocals and an addictive chorus, the Horny Horns and company hitting the grooves and blasting hard. Worrell's laser noises and shimmering keyboard leads and Cordell Mosson's monster bass squelches send everything all that much more over the top. Another song title says it all—"Sir Nose D'Voidoffunk (Pay Attention—B3M)." Treated with vocoders to an absurd degree, Sir Nose became the legendary enemy of funk, specifically the Starchild, on many a P-Funk recording (that's the two of them on the hilarious cover, the Starchild himself operating the Bop Gun). The throwaway lines in this song are almost legendary in and of themselves, while the music itself is a great slow build and burn rhythm that piles more on as it goes, with singers, horns, and more taking it to a climax. "Funkentelechy" and "The Placebo Syndrome" both have plenty of goodness as well, while "Wizards of Finance" is an amusing retro diversion, helping make *Funkentelechy* the highlight it is. *—Ned Raggett*

Live: P-Funk Earth Tour / 1977 / Casablanca ✦✦✦✦

As amazing as most of the '70s P-Funk albums are, the group was arguably a better live act than a studio act. Once the aggregation's patience and ambition wore thin with studio albums in the late '70s, Clinton was able to sustain his career merely on the merits of live performances, cult-like experiences that were rivaled only by the Grateful Dead's in terms of legacy. Unfortunately, unlike the Dead, Clinton's ensemble never went to excessive lengths to preserve its shows. *Live: P-Funk Earth Tour* stands as the band's only live album from the '70s, when it was at its peak (not counting bootlegs or posthumous imports). To be quite honest, there couldn't have been a better performance chosen for release; this is Parliament at its prime. Recorded in 1977 (the band's zenith) during the infamous "landing of the mothership" tour (its most extravagant), with the Bootsy-Worrell-Wesley-Parker-Hazel-Shider-Hampton lineup (its most talented), and a California audience (its most exuberant), this is almost a perfect document. Unfortunately, for the most part the album doesn't include any Funkadelic material, and at 70 minutes it's a bit brief relative to the band's shows, not leaving much room for extended jams. However, the album compensates by including a 15-minute version of "Dr. Funkenstein" that alludes to the group's potential to turn any song into an epic jam session, and also by including "Landing (Of the Holy Mothership)," a studio-produced three-minute interlude included for conceptual reasons but ultimately functioning better as a P-Funk montage (foreshadowing rap's excessive sampling). Over the years, other live P-Funk recordings have surfaced, but none are as widely available as this one, and none are as succinct. It's all the live P-Funk most fans will need. *—Jason Birchmeier*

Motor Booty Affair / 1978 / Casablanca ♦♦♦♦♦
By this point Parliament was one of the most accomplished and intelligent bands in music. With albums like *Mothership Connection* and *The Clones of Dr. Funkenstein*, George Clinton's druggy and patently eccentric humor often obscured the enviable musicianship throughout. *Motor Booty Affair* is no doubt another classic album and the perfect follow-up to 1977's *Funkentelechy Vs. the Placebo Syndrome*. On *Motor Booty Affair*, Clinton decides to yuck it up more with a great underwater concept and a few of his stronger alter egos, including the rhythmically challenged Sir Nose D' Void of Funk and his friend Rumpofsteelskin. The deft and airy "Mr. Wiggles" has Clinton taking on the persona of Wiggles, the "DJ of the affair" as he says: "Mr. Wiggles here on roller skates and a yo-yo/Acting a fool." The hypnotic "Rumpofsteelskin" has a great bassline and inventive and infectious background vocals. The closest thing to a ballad here is the astrologically savvy "(You're a Fish and I'm A) Water Sign." The well-produced "Aqua Boogie (A Psychoalphadiscobetabioaquadoloop)" with its handclaps and high-pitched basslines basically set the standards for the sound of R&B in the coming decade. The sleeper of the album, "One of Those Funky Things," is filled with timbales, congas, and Bernie Worrell's great synth signatures. The last track, "Deep," has great, understated riffs from the Horny Horns. Although many Parliament efforts can't be fully appreciated unless the whole catalog is nearby, *Motor Booty Affair* stands on its own merits and sustains the laugh throughout. *—Jason Elias*

Gloryhallastoopid / 1979 / Casablanca ♦♦♦
The flaws that kept *Motor Booty Affair* from being in the same league as *Mothership Connection*—that league being near perfection, from beginning to end—became alarmingly more prevalent on *Gloryhallastoopid*. By the time this album was put together in 1979, the classic P-Funk lineup of Bernie Worrell, Bootsy Collins, Fred Wesley, and Maceo Parker had splintered, and when Clinton did manage to get them into the studio, it was never as a unit. This suddenly revolving lineup of second-rate studio musicians in place of a cohesive band plagues this album more than a lack of enthusiasm on Clinton's part or half-hearted songwriting, though those two problems do play a role in this album's failure. Besides "Big Bang Theory" and "Theme From the Black Hole," nothing here is even remotely labored. Simple songs such as "The Freeze" and "Party People" sound as if they were written and recorded in a single session—they're *that* linear and shallow. Furthermore, Clinton insists on dragging these two songs, in particular, out to epic lengths, which is alarmingly futile since the songs never develop or even meander. If you are willing to wade through all the filler on this album, there are two splendid songs here, the aforementioned "Big Bang Theory" and "Theme From the Black Hole" (though "May We Bang You?" has some worthwhile melodies, as well). These two songs follow-up "Aqua Boogie" as obvious moments of funk genius among lackluster filler. But it might be a good idea to seek these songs out on a best-of compilation—nothing else here is worth bothering with. Nowhere else will you find the collective's decline more evident, and it slithers awfully close to brainless disco at times, further affirming its status as a failure. *—Jason Birchmeier*

Trombipulation / 1980 / Casablanca ♦♦
After *Gloryhallastoopid*, most had concluded that George Clinton's P-Funk empire had come to a close. For the most part, they were correct. Clinton's tightly knit unit featuring Bernie Worrell, Bootsy Collins, Fred Wesley, and Maceo Parker as arrangers as well as musicians had splintered. And not coincidentally, Clinton seemed less and less enthused about music, struggling instead with personal issues. Not surprisingly then, *Trombipulation* sounds like a scattered collection of songs composed by an ensemble cast of session musicians—the credits seemingly extend to infinity, as if a new band played every song. Furthermore, Worrell stepped forward to take the helm of Parliament, which explains this album's emphasis on keyboard-driven songs. Bootsy played a minor role as well, but his contributions seem overly self-interested, as if he's writing solo material. In sum, the musicians lack cohesion, and piecing together a rousing funk rhythm demands a tight band, something that just wasn't an option here. "Agony of Defeet" was supposed to be the album's big single, another "Flashlight" or "Aqua Boogie"—but it wasn't even close. In fact, this particular song parodied past Parliament anthems, its funk ineffective, its vocals far from catchy, and its humor undeniably distasteful. If there is one song here worth laboring over, it's "Let's Play House," an obvious Bootsy song. The other songs are all keyboard-driven funk substituting glossy studio polish for the gritty thump of early P-Funk. Arguably a bit more inspired than *Gloryhallastoopid*, though thanks more to Worrell than Clinton, *Trombipulation* concludes the Parliament cycle of albums in a disappointing manner. If you're really curious about latter-day P-Funk, look instead to Funkadelic's *Electric Spanking of War Babies*, a 1981 album that Clinton actually put some heart into. *—Jason Birchmeier*

Greatest Hits (The Bomb) / 1984 / Casablanca ♦♦♦♦♦
Treating Parliament as a singles band isn't entirely fair, since many of their greatest moments came when they pushed the boundaries of funk and soul to their limits. However, George Clinton's vision was often so sprawling that it was often best articulated as individual tracks within the studio, which is what makes *Greatest Hits (The Bomb)* such an effective record. Concentrating solely on Parliament's singles actually illustrates the depth of their vision and influence, since there are no half-baked ideas surrounding these ten stunning songs ("Up for the Down Stroke," "Chocolate City," "Give Up the Funk," "Bop Gun," "Flash Light," "Aqua Boogie"). Of course, their individual albums remain worthy, occasionally essential listening, but as an introduction, *Greatest Hits* does its job effectively, and for some casual fans, it may be all the Parliament they'll ever need. *—Stephen Thomas Erlewine*

☆ **Tear the Roof Off 1974–1980** / May 18, 1993 / Casablanca ♦♦♦♦♦
The Best of Parliament: Give Up the Funk may capture the band's bare essentials, but given the band's penchant for stretching out on extended jams (which included some of their best songs), it's hard to get anything beyond the most basic overview of their work on just one disc. Unless you're a very casual fan, a much better bet is the double-disc *Tear the Roof Off 1974-1980*, whose 25 tracks add plenty of much-needed detail behind the best-known and most-sampled hits. Slightly more party-oriented than Funkadelic, Parliament created the wildest atmosphere of all the projects in the George Clinton oeuvre, full of loopy humor and way-out sci-fi concepts. Parliament was also more of a singles act than the frequently album-oriented Funkadelic, and while Parliament produced its share of classic albums, their material doesn't lose any of its potency when boiled down into compilation form. What's more, *Tear the Roof Off* contains several full-length 12-inch mixes that were never previously available on CD. These are some of the most unstoppable, widely imitated grooves of all time, and they still carry the same impact today, making *Tear the Roof Off* an obvious necessity. *—Steve Huey*

Dope Dogs / 1995 / Hot Hands ♦♦♦
George Clinton's most focused album of the '90s slams a barrel of P-Funk down your throat without even giving you the opportunity to swallow. The P-Funk All Stars get a co-credit on this one, bouncing and funking alongside their leader nearly every step of the way. In typical Clinton fashion, *Dope Dogs* is all over the place: funk, R&B, hip-hop and ass-busting beats cover most of the ground. It all sticks together, however, on a loose-grooved concept about dogs (hasn't most of Clinton's post-"Atomic Dog" stuff been leading to this anyway?), the government and drugs, and how they're tied together in one huge nationwide conspiracy (it makes even less sense on record than it does here). But Clinton always has been about the funk of the matter, and *Dope Dogs* clearly has that, and its tight astro-rhythms, in the right place. *—Michael Gallucci*

★ **The Best of Parliament: Give Up the Funk** / Jun. 6, 1995 / Casablanca ♦♦♦♦♦
To some, boiling Parliament's legacy down to a single-disc collection is the equivalent of heresy, since most fans treat each album as an individual work of art. Still, there is no denying that Parliament was an untouchable singles act, recording some of the greatest soul/funk singles of the '70s. For those listeners that just want an introduction, or only need the hits, *The Best of Parliament: Give Up the Funk* is the ideal choice. A more complete and logical collection than the previous *Greatest Hits (The Bomb)*, *The Best of Parliament* supplies all of the great group's greatest hits, from "Up for the Down Stroke" and "Tear the Roof off the Sucker" to "Flash Light" and "Aqua Boogie." For those that can only handle the funk in moderation, there is no better collection. *—Leo Stanley*

Rhenium / Apr. 16, 1996 / HDH ♦♦
These Parliament Invictus tracks are no newcomers to the reissue market; they've been licensed and packaged for years. And *Rhenium* is yet another coupling. This marked the group's time at Holland-Dozier-Holland's label cutting hybrid soul/funk/acid that was looser than the straight vocal group Parliament on Revilot, less enthralling than Funkadelic on Westbound Records, and nowhere near as funky or compelling as their Casablanca smashes. Some of these first appeared on badly mastered 45s that obliterated much of what took place in the studio. The CD format let you hear the grooves and all the special nuances. Spacy riffs cook on "Breakdown," the torrid "Red Hot Mama," and the scandalous "I Call My Baby Pussycat," which they originally unleashed as Funkadelic as "I Call My Baby Pussycat (I Spell it P-U-S-S-Y)." Odd selections like "Little Ole Country Boy" and "The Silent Boatman" will unnerve all but staunch Parliament/Funkadelic devotees, whose rose-colored glasses will find profoundness and cryptic messages lurking in the lyrics. *—Andrew Hamilton*

The Early Years / Jul. 8, 1997 / Deep Beats ♦♦♦
The Early Years is a repackaging of all of Parliament's recordings for Invictus Records, including their 1970 album *Osmium* and three bonus tracks—"Fantasy is Reality," "Loose Booty" and "Unfinished Instrumental." Parliament hadn't quite refined their sound on *Osmium*, but the record showed promise, and it's interesting for hardcore fans. For any fan who hasn't picked the album up, this is a good way to add it, as well as the rarities, to your collection. *—Stephen Thomas Erlewine*

Funked Up: The Very Best of Parliament / Nov. 5, 2002 / Mercury ♦♦♦♦♦
Funked Up: The Very Best of Parliament is a full-priced, one-disc summation of Parliament's recordings for Casablanca Records (since absorbed into what is now Universal and discontinued, hence the issuance on Universal's Mercury imprint), meant to supplant the 1984 LP compilation *Greatest Hits (The Bomb)* and provide consumers with something in between the more expensive two-CD set *Tear the Roof Off 1974-1980* and the discount-priced *20th Century Masters—The Millennium Collection: The Best of Parliament*. The album's focus, writes annotator Tom Vickers, is "chart success," and it includes among its 16 tracks 14 of Parliament's 19 R&B singles chart entries on Casablanca, including all of their R&B Top 40 hits except "Party People" (which crested at number-39 in *Billboard*). Also included are two album tracks, "All Your Goodies Are Gone" from *Up for the Down Stroke* and "Let's Take It to the Stage" from *Live: P-Funk Earth Tour*. Parliament was more of an albums act than a singles act (and more of a live act than a recording act), and only six of these tracks reached the R&B Top Ten, with two, "Flash Light" and "Aqua Boogie (A Psychoalphadiscobetabioaquadoloop)," hitting number one, while just two, "Tear the Roof Off the Sucker (Give Up the Funk)" and "Flash Light," made the pop Top 20. So, a singles collection makes for a less definitive overview of the group's

career than might be true for others. Hence, if the consumer has a few more bucks to spend, *Tear the Roof Off 1974-1980* is much the preferred compilation. But all of Parliament's big hits and most of its lesser ones are here. *—William Ruhlmann*

The Parliaments

f. 1955, Detroit, MI

Group / Doo Wop, R&B, Soul

The Parliaments were a doo wop group formed by George Clinton in 1955, put together in the back room of a barbershop Clinton was working at with friends Raymond Davis, Clarence "Fuzzy" Haskins, Calvin Simon, and Grady Thomas. Clinton began by modeling the group after Frankie Lymon's group, the Teenagers, but soon moved on to his own sound, which was to evolve heavily in the years to come. The group moved from label to label, releasing 45 after 45 for a time, making *Poor Willie/Party Boys* for APT, *Lonely Island/Cry* for Flip, and *Heart Trouble/That Was My Girl* for Golden World, all the while Clinton was making weekly trips to Detroit to produce for the likes of Roy Handy and the Pets.

In 1967, the Parliaments scored a number-three R&B/number 20 pop ranking on the *Billboard* charts with "I Wanna Testify" for Revilot, and signaled the coming changes in R&B. In 1968, the Parliaments had a dispute with Revilot and refused to continue working for the label. To avoid waiting for some kind of settlement, Clinton hastily renamed the group Funkadelic, with the only musicians listed being the original backing band for the Parliaments. Revilot soon folded and the Parliaments' contract was sold to Atlantic. At this point, Clinton permanently abandoned the doo wop style (to avoid working for Atlantic), though one Revilot recording, "A New Day Begins," was released by Atco in 1969. The group went on to form the basis for Funkadelic, later Parliament, and all things funky that were to follow. *—Adam Greenberg*

● **Testifyin'** / 1995 / Goldmine/Soul Supply ♦♦♦♦

Early Golden World and Revilot Records' tracks when George Clinton, Fuzzy Haskins, Grady Thomas, Calvin Simon, and Ray Davis tried the conventional route. Clinton's bizarre lyrics grab you on "Heart Trouble" "worryation's got a hold on me, I can't think for myself." Only George appears on "I Wanna Testify" backed by the Holidays. The others couldn't afford the trek to Detroit from Plainfield, NJ, that week. Clinton went every Friday to produce other acts and work on Parliament stuff. "All Your Goodies are Gone" clever lyrics' hooks you as much as the slinky vocals, and "The Goose That Layed the Golden Egg" charm lies in its sloop beat and acid-inspired lyrics. They redid both numbers, strobe-light style, on *Up for the Down Stroke.* "Look at What I Almost Missed" sounds unfinished but it still charted on the lower rungs of the R&B chart. A rare falsetto lead carries "I Can Feel the Ice Melting," a big favorite with some. Three of the 18 tracks repeat as instrumentals. The Fellows (a pseudonym) get the credit for "Let's Make It Last." An import, so it takes some effort to find this compilation. *—Andrew Hamilton*

The Pasadenas

Group / Club/Dance, Urban, House, Contemporary R&B, Neo-Soul

The Pasadenas didn't belong in the '80s. The band was caught in a time warp; they bounced between '50s doo wop, '60s Motown, and early-'70s funk and R&B. However, they presented these influences when mainstream pop music had become too shallow and over-produced; instead of sounding dated, the group was actually a refreshing change of pace. The band wasn't given much attention in America, but they were superstars in their native England. Formed by twins David Milliner and Michael Milliner along with Andrew Banfield, Hammish Seelochan, and Aaron Brown, the Pasadenas used to be a dance group called Finesse. In the late '80s they signed with Columbia Records and became the Pasadenas. Not one member overshadowed the other; each of them wrote lyrics and helped with production and arrangements. While their peers, such as Breathe, Johnny Hates Jazz, and Terence Trent D'Arby, also mined soul records from the past, many of the Pasadenas' songs, such as the Smokey Robinson homage "Enchanted Lady," could've been mistaken for the real thing.

The band didn't try to modernize the urban grooves of the '60s and '70s; they simply resurrected the excitement soul music used to bring. In May 1988, the group released their debut single, "Tribute (Right On)." It peaked in the Top Five of the U.K. charts, one of many hits for the Pasadenas. The band's concerts received rave reviews for their tight musicianship and choreographed dance moves. Their first LP, *To Whom It May Concern*, appeared in October 1988, selling in excess of one-million copies. The group's final album, *Yours Sincerely*, was released in 1992. The band landed on the U.K. Top 40 charts five times that year, with the single "I'm Doing Fine" selling more than 200,000 copies. In 2002 Cherry Red Records reissued *To Whom It May Concern* on CD. *—Michael Sutton*

● **To Whom It May Concern** / 1988 / Columbia ♦♦♦

Passion

Group / Club/Dance

Passion was a New York-based disco outfit with a penchant for sensual, extended tracks flavored with funk and Latin rhythms. A brief and unsuccessful stint on AVI—which produced the single "Are You Free Tonight"—was followed by a more fruitful relationship with disco movers-and-shakers Prelude. Their first 12-inch single on the label was 1980's "Don't Bring Back Memories," which gained substantial club play along with its B-side, "In New York"; it was produced by multi-instrumentalist Ray Martinez. In 1982, their biggest club hit, the Kashif-penned "Don't Stop My Love" was released; their final single, the Eric Matthew-produced "You Can't Hide It," was released in 1984. Their only album, *Don't Stop My Love* (initially released under the title *Passion*), later became a popular item among disco collectors, no doubt thanks in part to its notoriously racy cover photo. *—Steve Huey*

● **Don't Stop My Love** / 1984 / Unidisc ♦♦♦

The Passions

f. 1959, Brooklyn, NY

Group / Doo Wop, R&B

An above-average white doo wop ensemble from Brooklyn, the Passions' abilities often exceeded the quality of their material. They began as the Sinceres, then changed their name to the Passions when they began recording in the late '50s. Lead vocalist Jimmy Gallagher, Tony Armato, Albie Gallone, and Vinnie Acierno comprised the group. They never managed either an R&B or pop hit, despite doing sessions for Audicon, Diamond, Jubilee, and Octavia. Their debut for Audicon, "Just to Be With You," made significant impact, but they couldn't sustain the momentum. Another beloved Passions number is "Gloria." *—Ron Wynn*

● **Just to Be With You** / 1992 / Relic ♦♦♦♦♦

Bobby Patterson

b. Mar. 13, 1944, Dallas, TX

Vocals, Bass / Northern Soul, Contemporary Blues, Soul

Like many other Dallas-based blues musicians, Bobby Patterson is a vocalist and multi-instrumentalist who continued the soul-blues tradition of people like Bobby "Blue" Bland, Otis Redding, and Wilson Pickett. But unlike some of these other singers, Patterson has worked in all aspects of the blues record business: as a songwriter, producer, promotion man, and label owner. Patterson began performing when he was ten, playing guitar and drums. While still in his early teens, he formed a band called the Royal Rockers, who won talent contests in and around Dallas. In 1957, one of the talent contests led to a trip to California to track a single for Liberty Records, which was never released. Patterson then went on to nearby Arlington College, where one of his classmates was the son of a local record company owner. In 1962, Patterson recorded "You Just Got to Understand" for Abnak Records. The single wasn't terribly successful, but it convinced the label's owner, John Abnak, to start a soul division, called Jetstar Records. Patterson recorded for Jetstar for the next six years, becoming a talented songwriter, producer, and promotion man in the process. Patterson's regional hits, all self-penned, on the Jetstar label included "Let Them Talk" (also popularized by Little Willie John), "I'm Leroy, I'll Take Her" (with his Mustangs), "Broadway Ain't Funky No More," "T.C.B. or T.Y.A.," "My Thing Is Your Thing," "The Good Old Days," and "I'm in Love With You."

In 1969, after a string of regional hits, Abnak Records folded and Patterson recorded his own self-produced album. Shortly after that, he quit recording under his own name to produce and promote records made by other artists. As a producer, Patterson has worked with Fontella Bass, Chuck Jackson, Ted Taylor, Shay Holiday, Roscoe Robinson, the Montclairs, Tommie Young, and Little Johnny Taylor. Patterson's songs have been recorded by Albert King ("That's What the Blues Is All About") and the Fabulous Thunderbirds, who recorded and had success with his "How Do You Spell Love?" More recently, Patterson has been back on the comeback trail, recording and releasing an album, *Second Coming*, in 1996 on his own Dallas-based Proud Records. *Second Coming* is a good introduction to Patterson's music and still crystal-clear voice, but it's by no means the full story; for that, you'll have to search out his 45 rpm singles. More recently, Wilco's Jeff Tweedy sang Patterson's song "She Don't Have to See You (To See Through You)" on Golden Smog's *Down by the Old Mainstream* album. *—Richard Skelly*

It's Just a Matter of Time / 1972 / Paula ♦♦♦

● **Taking Care of Business** / Nov. 20, 1995 / Kent ♦♦♦♦♦

If there is such a thing as an average 1960s soul singer, Bobby Patterson is it. That's not meant as a putdown, necessarily; it's just the way it is. He drew from both Northern and Southern soul styles, from Motown and Stax, and from other trends. He also wrote and sang competent tunes that sounded like filler in the work of greater artists. Perhaps the difference between Patterson and the hundreds of other similar performers that did one or three singles, is that Patterson had a much lengthier career, putting out singles constantly. This album presents 29 tracks that he did in the mid- and late 1960s, most of which came out as singles on the Jetstar label, although there are a couple of previously unreleased cuts. The material is agreeable but unmemorable, with the occasional number that sticks deeper in the craw, like "If I Didn't Have You," a good pop-friendly Southern soul tune with minor key changes and organ. In a similar vein is "Long Ago," a relatively unknown song with a co-writing credit for Dan Penn. Sometimes it's easy to determine where the inspiration comes from: "You Just Got to Understand" has a sound very much like the Marvin Gaye single "Ain't That Peculiar"; "Soul Is Our Music" is an upbeat brassy number in the Otis Redding-Arthur Conley mold; "I'm Leroy, I'll Take Her" has a boogaloo Joe Tex flavor; "Broadway Ain't Funky No More" rides the James Brown/Dyke & the Blazers train; and "My Baby's Coming Back to Me" has a riff similar to that of the Temptations' "Get Ready." As a warm-up act he wouldn't have been bad, but once the headliners take over, he's definitely just one of the crowd. *—Richie Unterberger*

Soul Is My Music: The Best of Bobby Patterson / Feb. 25, 2003 / Sundazed ♦♦♦♦♦

Rahsaan Patterson

b. 1973, New York, NY

Vocals / Neo-Soul, Urban, Contemporary R&B

Soul vocalist and songwriter Rahsaan Patterson is another in the line of new-school R&B singers (Maxwell, Erykah Badu) with a bit more integrity than most of the chart-toppers during the 1990s. After singing in church from the age of six, Patterson moved with his family from New York to California to star in the children's show *KIDS Incorporated.* He later moved back to the East Coast, resuming his career with small TV roles and assorted commercials, but returned to Los Angeles in the early '90s to record demos and contribute backing vocals to albums by Martika and Brandy, among others. Patterson proved himself a more than competent songwriter as well, penning hits like Tevin Campbell's "Back to the World" and Brandy's "Baby." Those successes finally earned him a recording contract with MCA, which issued his self-titled debut album in early 1997. *Love in Stereo* followed two years later. *—John Bush*

Rahsaan Patterson / Jan. 28, 1997 / MCA ♦♦♦♦
Greatly influenced by Stevie Wonder's recordings of the 1970s, young Rahsaan Patterson showed much promise on his self-titled debut album of 1997. While it's impossible to miss Wonder's considerable influence on slow- and medium-tempo offerings like "Tears Ago," "My Sweetheart" and "Spend the Night," the R&B singer/composer never comes across as a clone and sounds like he's intent on being his own man. One thing Patterson (who was named after jazz innovator Rahsaan Roland Kirk) won't be accused of is favoring style over substance—when many of his contemporaries in the urban contemporary market were heavily into gimmickry, Patterson kept things honest and straightforward on a disc that isn't breathtaking, but is heartfelt and satisfying. *—Alex Henderson*

● **Love in Stereo** / Oct. 19, 1999 / MCA ♦♦♦♦♦
The follow-up to his self-titled debut album, *Love in Stereo* shows that Rahsaan Peterson not only overcame the sophomore slump but triumphed with a very well-crafted album that far surpasses his completely adequate first release. Slick production and strong songwriting help support Peterson's smooth, laid-back style and Stevie Wonder-like vocals. Peterson actually resembles Wonder in more ways than one—"Friend of Mine," for instance, possesses so much early-'70s instrumentation and tone and phrasing reminiscent of his style that it sounds like a lost track from an early Stevie Wonder album. The record as a whole offers the kind of songs concerning love and faith that seem to have been lost since the Wonder era. Peterson is not only paying homage to Wonder in approach, but also in spirit. "Sure Boy" and "The Day" are only two of several other songs on the collection that are extremely well-written with an inspirational edge. Never preachy and always stylish, on *Love in Stereo* Peterson has managed to make an album that should appeal to a broad range of R&B fans. *—Stacia Proefrock*

Patty & the Emblems

f. Camden, NJ
Group / R&B, Soul
Soul group Patty & the Emblems formed in Camden, NJ, around lead singer Patty Russell; they scored their lone Top 40 hit in 1964 with "Mixed-Up, Shook-Up Girl." *—Jason Ankeny*

● **Golden Classics** / Mar. 25, 1997 / Collectables ♦♦♦♦
Patty & the Emblems were the contemporaries of acts like the Sapphires, and just as distinctive. Pat Russell was a soul belter on a par with any woman who ever stepped up to a microphone for Motown (check out her performance on "What's the Use"), and the Emblems could harmonize as sweetly as the Miracles. What's more, they had access to the songwriting talents of Leon Huff, who got them their one big hit ("Mixed Up, Shook Up Girl") and brought them a lot of other worthy material ("Showdown," which sounds a bit like "Heat Wave"; "You Can't Get Away," "The Sound of Music Makes Me Want to Dance," which sounds a bit like "Dancing in the Streets"), usually with clever hooks. Listening to the 20 sides here, it's impossible to fathom why they didn't last. Even where the songs weren't exactly first-rate, the group's style and Russell's voice were capable of carrying the material and making something special out of it. Their sound was not only sweet but bold; Russell projected angst in portions ranging from a trickle to a torrent of emotion, as well as a sultriness that would manifest itself at the strangest, most striking times. The rest of the group were impeccable in their singing, and the backing band always has a great beat and a good, heavy sound—even augmented with strings—that should have made the group a natural for radio play and discotheques. The collection is awesome throughout, and there isn't a bad song here, with the very best, the soaring "I'm So Confused," saved for last. And the sound is superb, one of the best CDs that Collectables has ever issued. *—Bruce Eder*

A Tribute to Patty & the Emblems / 2001 / Philly Archives ♦♦♦♦
The awkward title of this CD is somewhat misleading, implying perhaps that this is a tribute record to the lead singer of Patty & the Emblems, rather than actual Patty & the Emblems recordings. Not to worry, this *is* a compilation of Patty & the Emblems records, most of them from 1964-1968. Their sole song to make any notable commercial impact, "Mixed Up Shook Up Girl," is here, along with 18 other tracks from the mid- to late 1960s that reflect the development of the early Philly soul sound. It's a mix of late doo wop, prime girl group, and '60s pop-soul, pretty attractive for what it is, though the material's only average. "Mixed Up Shook Up Girl," a fine slice of brassy and sassy uptown soul, is the best cut by a fair distance, with some of the others taking some obvious cues from Motown and other soul trends of the day. It's a good listen, nonetheless, for most soul collectors; songs like the ballad "I've Got Nothing to Lose" and the bittersweet "Give Me Time" enduring as examples of the nascent Philly sweet soul sound, with luscious backup harmonies and a careful mix of rock and more orchestral instruments. It would have been nice to have more liner notes (the ones on the sleeve are extremely perfunctory), though dates and songwriting credits are given. There are also five songs recorded by Patty Russell in 1999, shortly before her death, that are slick and unmemorable updates of the vintage soul sound, including a remake of "Mixed Up Shook Up Girl." *—Richie Unterberger*

Billy Paul

b. Dec. 1, 1935, Philadelphia, PA
Vocals / Philly Soul, Soul, Smooth Soul, Quiet Storm, Urban
Billy Paul had a good run in the '70s as an R&B vocalist, though he'd been recording since the '50s, when he debuted on Jubilee. Paul was featured on radio broadcasts in Philadelphia at age 11 and had an extensive jazz background. He worked with Dinah Washington, Miles Davis, and Roberta Flack, as well as Charlie Parker, before forming a trio and recording for Jubilee. His original 1959 recording of "Ebony Woman" for New Dawn was later re-recorded for Neptune as the title of his 1970 LP. He signed the next year with Philadelphia International and scored his biggest hit with "Me & Mrs. Jones" in 1972, topping both the R&B and pop charts. Paul had one other Top Ten R&B single, "Thanks for Saving My Life," in 1974. He remained on Philadelphia International until the mid-'80s. Paul recorded one LP for Total Experience in 1985, *Lately*, and another for Ichiban before announcing his retirement in 1989 in London. *—Ron Wynn*

Ebony Woman / 1970 / Epic ♦♦♦
Billy Paul originally recorded "Ebony Woman" in 1959, but it didn't make much noise. It served as the title track for a good, though uneven, mid-'70s release. Paul never equaled the success of "Me & Mrs. Jones," but was a consistent attraction for Philadelphia International in the early '70s. His albums used the same formula as this one—some adult ballads, one or two dance-oriented tunes, and some in-between numbers that tapped his background as a jazz singer but weren't done in such a sophisticated manner that they angered the R&B faithful. *—Ron Wynn*

Going East / 1971 / Philadelphia International ♦♦♦♦

360 Degrees of Billy Paul / 1972 / Philadelphia International ♦♦♦
Paul's first album for Philadelphia International was straight, club jazz. Sales never got off the ground. This time, Gamble & Huff gave Paul material strong enough to make his sophomore release a viable commercial entity. "Brown Baby's" speaks of people of color making their parents and others proud, the message is positive and correct. "I'm Just a Prisoner," is real, but would have been better served without the string section. It's a stark depiction about a man who has served five years and is contemplating his future. It is about the unsettling fact that he's just a prisoner. Its chilling chorus tells it all—"The cell is cold as hell, you'll never get use to the smell, my bed is hard as wood, I got to fight to keep my manhood," the riveting saga doesn't just end, the fade is lengthy, and features a dejected Paul woefully mourning about the conditions, the situation and the turmoil of prison life. He sounds believable and frustrated belting "Me & Mrs. Jones," a classic that many relate to, and those who don't have no problem being down with the passionate singing and clawing lyrics describing the unapologetic infidelity. His "It's Too Late" is a fine rendition of Carole King's classic. You might not recognize "Let's Stay Together," popularized by Al Green. Paul does it MOR/Jazz style, with a lot of improvising before crooning the original lyrics. It shows versatility, but it's doubtful if people who bought "Jones" appreciated it. A version of Elton John's "Your Song" introduced the Britisher to fans of soul music. Vince Montana's magical vibes punctuate the rhythm, which turns into a lightweight gospel revival. "Am I Back Enough for You" fit in with the times of overt black consciousness, a social message moved along by a perky bongo and clavinet dominated beat, and well-spaced, brassy horn hits. A too staid "I'm Gonna Make It This Time," co-written by Bunny Sigler, marked Paul's second adventure in urban, club jazz on 360 Degrees; this one has bite, and Billy sings it with fire. *—Andrew Hamilton*

Feelin' Good at the Cadillac Club / 1973 / Gamble ♦♦

War of the Gods / 1973 / Philadelphia International ♦♦♦
Billy Paul got reasonably good mileage out of this album, which never had any huge hits but remained on both the pop and R&B charts for several weeks and got good album cut radio airplay. It was well sung, done in stylish and soulful fashion, and had one good message song in "Am I Black Enough For You." It was Paul's second R&B hit and a good follow-up to "Me & Mrs. Jones." *—Ron Wynn*

Billy Paul Live in Europe / 1974 / Philadelphia International ♦♦
Former jazz vocalist Billy Paul found R&B success in the '70s on Philadelphia International doing a mix of anguished ballads, sophisticated originals, and reworked standards. But Paul was not a great live vocalist either as a jazz or soul singer, something that was evident on this mid-'70s set. No matter how polished or well-rehearsed the backing band, Paul's flaws couldn't be covered as smoothly in a concert setting, and they're revealed along with his strengths—timing, a good delivery, and decent range and interpretative skills. *—Ron Wynn*

Got My Head on Straight / 1975 / Philadelphia International ♦♦♦

Let 'Em In / 1976 / Philadelphia International ♦♦
This is a very antiseptic release. Yet, these eight songs keep getting reissued by various companies on two-fer-one compilations, and many always seem to find spots on his greatest-hits collections. Originally released in 1976 on Philadelphia International Records (PIR), there's not much to crow about; "How Good Is Your Game" stiffed as a single, and it's one of the strongest cuts. Still, Paul's vocalizing is so unique that you can't go wrong purchasing anything by him on PIR. Avoid his post-Philly endeavors, they're for fanatics only. *—Andrew Hamilton*

First Class / 1979 / Philadelphia International ♦♦♦♦
A classy parting shot for the "Me & Mrs. Jones" man, but then, all of Billy Paul's recordings on Philadelphia International reeked of class. Knowing that Billy is happiest singing in intimate, smoky night clubs, the producers create a similar atmosphere in the studio. Phil Terry & Phil Pugh's "What a Way to Love" finds Billy crooning in a higher range then normal, and he really works that upper register. Gamble & Huff's "So Good to See You Again" is a finger-snapper complete with some powerful vocals from Paul. Street lyricist extraordinaire Cary Gilbert co-wrote "False Faces" and the confessing "I Got to Put This Life Down." Billy's in great voice on this, his last Philadelphia International LP; he usually sounds kinda muddled, like he's got a mouth full of something.... Isn't it time for a double CD of Billy Paul's best? *—Andrew Hamilton*

Greatest Hits / 1983 / Philadelphia International ♦♦♦♦
Smoky voiced Billy Paul greatest hits compilations' suffer because many of his best efforts were album tracks. Gamble & Huff did a horrible job picking Paul's singles. Some better choices, and his career might have been Hall-of-Famish. "Me & Mrs. Jones" is hands down the brightest of this cuts; Billy sings it as if he has lived it. Updated often, but none compare to Paul's awesome take. I never cared his rendition of "Only the Strong Survive"

originally by Jerry Butler. Besides, it's the Ice Man's song. It would be like Jerry doing "Mrs. Jones," it wouldn't work. "Bring the Family Back," "You're My Sweetness," "Let 'Em In," and "Let's Make a Baby," are OK, but the rest fail to measure up to stronger cuts on his *War of the Gods* LP, or songs cold as "I'm Just a Prisoner," "So Good to See You," "I Was Married," "What a Way to Love," etc. *—Andrew Hamilton*

Lately / Aug. 1985 / Total Experience ✦✦✦

Let 'Em In/Only the Strong Survive / 1999 / The Right Stuff ✦✦

● **Me and Mrs. Jones: The Best of Billy Paul** / Apr. 6, 1999 / Epic/Legacy ✦✦✦✦✦
Too easily dismissed as little more than a one-hit wonder, Billy Paul was in fact one of the most gifted and affecting talents to grace the Philadelphia International stable—the recipient of some of the Gamble & Huff team's most lush and sophisticated productions, his deeply soulful voice bridged the gap between jazz and soul, textured in equal measure by street-smart swagger and touching vulnerability. *Me and Mrs. Jones: The Best of Billy Paul* goes far beyond the classic title track in restoring the singer to prominence, showcasing his versatility via superb covers of pop favorites, including Bob Dylan's "Don't Think Twice, It's All Right"; Elton John's "Your Song"; and Paul McCartney's "Let 'Em In." With the inclusion of R&B chart hits like "Thanks for Saving My Life" and "Billy's Back Home," it all adds up to a definitive portrait of Paul in his prime. *—Jason Ankeny*

Freda Payne

b. Sep. 19, 1945, Detroit, MI
Vocals / Soul, Pop-Soul, Smooth Soul, Vocal Jazz
The multi-talented Freda Payne is best known for her singing career, yet she has also performed in musicals and acted in movies over the years, and briefly was the host of her own TV talk show. Born Freda Charcilia Payne on September 19, 1945, in Detroit, MI, Payne developed an appreciation of music at an early age (due to such sultry jazz singers as Ella Fitzgerald, Sarah Vaughan, and Billie Holiday). Payne's own musical career blossomed soon after, as she began early singing radio commercial jingles, which brought the young vocalist to the attention of several music-biz heavyweights. Berry Gordy Jr. attempted to sign Payne to his then-burgeoning record company, Motown, while Duke Ellington employed Payne as the featured singer with his renowned orchestra for two nights in Pittsburgh, resulting in Ellington offering the teenager a ten-year contract. But in both cases, Payne's mother turned them down.

During the early to mid-'60s, Payne established herself as a fine jazz vocalist, touring the country with both Quincy Jones and Bill Cosby, and issuing a jazz/big band-based album in 1963, *After the Lights Go Down Low and Much More!* In addition to a sophomore effort surfacing three years later, *How Do You Say I Don't Love You Anymore*, Payne enjoyed further exposure via appearances on such TV shows as *Johnny Carson*, *David Frost*, and *Merv Griffin*. But it wasn't until Payne signed on to the Invictus label in 1969 (headed by longtime friends/former Motown songwriters/producers Eddie Holland, Lamont Dozier, & Brian Holland) and issued the fine album *Band of Gold* that she scored her breakthrough hit single, the album's title track, which peaked at number three in the U.S. and topped the chart in the U.K. in 1970.

Although Payne never enjoyed another hit as substantial as "Band of Gold," several other successful singles followed in the early '70s: "Deeper and Deeper," "Cherish What's Dear to You," "You Brought the Joy," and the Vietnam protest song "Bring the Boys Home." Further albums followed throughout the '70s, including such titles as *Contact*, *Reaching Out*, *Payne & Pleasure*, *Out of Payne Comes Love*, *Stares & Whispers*, *Supernatural High*, and *Hot*, which all failed to make an impression on the charts. Payne then switched her attention from music to TV, as she hosted her very own (yet short-lived) talk show in 1981, *Today's Black Woman*. The '90s saw Payne return back to music, as such albums as *An Evening With Freda Payne* and *Christmas With Freda and Friends* were issued, while Payne also landed roles in such movies as *Private Obsession*, *Sprung*, and *Ragdoll*. Payne continued to balance an acting and music career during the early 21st century, as she appeared in the 2000 Eddie Murphy comedy *Nutty Professor II: The Klumps* and the made-for-TV movie *Fire & Ice*, plus issuing an all-new album in 2001, *Come See About Me*. Around the same time, several hits compilations were issued, including such titles as *Band of Gold: The Best of Freda Payne*, *Unhooked Generation: The Complete Invictus Recordings*, and *The Best of Freda Payne: Ten Best Series*. *—Greg Prato*

After the Lights Go Down Low and Much More! / 1963 / Impulse! ✦✦✦✦
By the year 2000, the golden oldie rotation of "Band of Gold" was the main thing keeping the memory of this singer alive. Yet, deep in the catalog of this classic jazz label lies this ambitious, largely successful recording which shows just how diverse and indeed brilliant Freda Payne can be. The album is divided half into big-band tracks, half into small combo. The main presence in both cases is alto saxophonist Phil Woods, and this is one of the few recordings he doesn't turn into a football scrimmage for bebop yardage. There is an incredible wealth of material here, and it is definitely impressive to consider that Duke Ellington wrote a song specifically for the session. It is the singer's confidence and marvelous vocal abilities that steal the show at every turn, but that is not to demean the contributions of top-drawer jazz musicians such as pianist Walter Perkins and guitarist Jim Hall. The record is dominated by Tin Pan Alley material, to be sure, but on the second side some serious jazz is attempted, including a beautiful "Round Midnight" and a version of "Lonely Woman" by Ornette Coleman. When it comes to the latter tune, the author of the liner note seems to be straining to hide his contempt, referring to the song as a "composition" in italics, as if it was too touchy to print such a thing in a regular font. *—Eugene Chadbourne*

How Do You Say I Don't Love You Anymore / 1966 / MGM ✦✦✦

Band of Gold / 1970 / HDH ✦✦✦✦✦
Although much of soul vocalist Freda Payne's early '70s association with the mighty Invictus label would be fraught with stress, her 1970 debut album, *Band of Gold*, was nevertheless a masterpiece of epic proportions. Touted on the sleeve as "people music, for people who like pop, rhythm and blues, ballad, hymns—just about anything," Payne's set certainly reflects that wide range and, while the overall sonic tone of *Band of Gold* reflects her producers' Motown history, especially across songs like "Unhooked Generation" and the Holland-Dozier penned "The World Don't Owe You a Thing," there are other more spontaneous moments here as well. With a majority of the songs co-written by Ron Dunbar, who would go on to become part of the P-Funk empire, "Payne" wowed her audience first with the top hit "Band of Gold" before diving into "Deeper and Deeper." Both are down-tempo love ballads, delivered with a maturity and richness that belies much of the balladeering of the era. Other standouts include the young love remembrances of "Through the Memory of My Mind," which allows Payne's vocals to stay fully in front and even includes a subtle Shangri-Las-y spoken work bridge and the smoky intro'd "This Girl Is a Woman Now." It must be said, however, that the title song—truly one of the greatest soul ballads of all time—so dominates proceedings that it is very easy to overlook these other gems, one reason why *Band of Gold* rarely attracts much attention today. *—Amy Hanson*

Contact / 1971 / Invictus ✦✦✦
Freda Payne's second Invictus album was a significant success, making it onto the pop charts. She found her niche in the early '70s, doing silky, sophisticated pop-soul with excellent production, arrangements, and material supplied by the Holland-Dozier-Holland team. They wisely didn't try to make her a sassy or hard-edged vocalist, putting her voice in string and horn-dominated charts and emphasizing her soothing, lightly sensual side. *—Ron Wynn*

The Best of Freda Payne / 1972 / Invictus ✦✦✦✦✦
Freda Payne had a string of classy, jazz-tinged soul hits for Invictus and HDH in the early '70s. Although she wasn't an earthy or gospel/blues-influenced vocalist, she could be convincing on such cuts as "Band of Gold" and "Bring the Boys Home," one of the more underrated antiwar cuts. This was nice, occasionally memorable pop-soul, and Payne never made better records with any other label. *—Ron Wynn*

Freda Payne / 1974 / MGM ✦✦✦
Payne's brand of glossy pop-soul clicked when she got the right material; even when she didn't, Payne's experience and training as a jazz vocalist made her performances interesting, and that was the case on this collection. The songs are even smoother and more cabaret- and supper-club-oriented than her hits, and show Payne carefully pacing songs, interpreting lyrics, and displaying a soft, yet emphatic vocal style. *—Ron Wynn*

Stares & Whispers / 1978 / Capitol ✦✦

Supernatural High / 1978 / Capitol ✦✦
Skip Scarborough (Earth, Wind & Fire, Con Funk Shun, Patti LaBelle) produced this pleasant collection of disco songs (many of which were club hits), ballads, and midtempo tracks from singer Freda Payne. There's a rousing melody that makes good use of the standard "Happy Days Are Here Again." Other highlights are the stimulating "Pullin' Back," the playful "Tell Me Please," a chugging clavinet-filled "Livin' for the Beat" (co-written by her then-husband Gregory Abbott), the soft "Just the Thought of You" (co-written by Thom Bell), and the jazzy string/sax-woven slow jam "Falling in Love," co-written by Deniece Williams. Payne's sister Scherrie Payne wrote the dynamic "Storybook Romance" and later redid it as half of Scherrie & Susaye on the 1979 Motown LP *Partners*. *—Ed Hogan*

Greatest Hits / Jul. 1, 1991 / Fantasy ✦✦✦✦✦
Fantasy's 11-track *Greatest Hits* doesn't dig much deeper than the hits, but it does contain all six of her charting singles, notably "Band of Gold," "Deeper and Deeper," and "Bring the Boys Home," plus five other fine singles and album tracks from her Invictus recordings. Yes, the aforementioned blockbusters shine the brightest here, but the rest of this is, at its worst, simply pleasant '70s soul, which means there are a few minor gems to be discovered here. *—Stephen Thomas Erlewine*

Live in Concert / Sep. 7, 1999 / Varese ✦✦✦

● **Band of Gold: The Best of Freda Payne** / Nov. 7, 2000 / Music Club ✦✦✦✦✦
Band of Gold: The Best of Freda Payne is a lengthy, comprehensive overview of Freda Payne's peak recordings from the early '70s, including not just hits like "Band of Gold," "Deeper and Deeper," and "Bring the Boys Home." This may seem like a lotta Freda, but her recordings are surprisingly consistent—even when the songs are subpar, the recordings are appealing, as are her performances. There may be more concise collections to appeal to the less-dedicated listener, but for a true appreciation of Payne, this is the disc to get. (Besides, it has an absolutely terrific cover.) *—Stephen Thomas Erlewine*

Come See About Me / Feb. 27, 2001 / Volt ✦✦✦
When Freda Payne signed with the reactivated Volt label in 2000, many of the die-hard soul lovers who knew her for "Band of Gold" and "Bring the Boys Home" were no doubt hoping for an album of Detroit soul and Holland-Dozier-Holland classics. But the veteran singer is more versatile than that. Before she became known for Motor City soul, Payne recorded jazz for ABC/Paramount, MGM, and Bob Thiele's Impulse! label (home of heavyweights like John Coltrane and Pharoah Sanders). Payne is no more an R&B purist than Nancy Wilson (one of her influences) is a jazz purist. Recorded in 2000 and released in 2001, *Come See About Me* contains only a few examples of retro soul. "First Impression" and the title track (a cover of Diana Ross & the Supremes' 1964 smash) recall her soul output of the late '60s and early '70s, but the CD also offers everything from urban and quiet storm to adult contemporary. Payne (who was 55 when this album was recorded) even gets into dance-pop on the anthemic "I Live for New York City." None of the material is straight-ahead jazz, although "Let's Make Beautiful Music," "You Complete Me," and an arrangement of the standard "You Turned the Tables on Me" are the sort of mellow quiet storm offerings that one would expect from Anita Baker. *Come See About*

Me isn't a masterpiece and isn't among Payne's essential albums, but it's a pleasant, enjoyable effort that should please her die-hard fans. *—Alex Henderson*

Unhooked Generation: The Complete Invictus Recordings / Dec. 18, 2001 / Castle ✦✦✦✦✦

Freda Payne was one of the great female soul singers of the early '70s—her voice was powerful enough to rank highly among her contemporaries, but what set her apart was her daring material, its consistency, and the wonderful, ambitious production given her by the Invictus label. All of this is apparent on a mere single-disc collection, but for the best appreciation of the full scope of her achievements, the 41-track collection *Unhooked Generation: The Complete Invictus Recordings* is necessary for any serious soul collection. Though this is a lot to ingest at once, part of the reason for that is that it's dense, layered music; there's a lot going on in the lyrics and music is busy, filled with glorious details that help elevate this music ahead of much of the soul music of the time. As her biggest hits suggest, Payne pushed the subject material of soul further: "Band of Gold" dealt with a marriage falling apart because of male impotence; "Bring the Boys Home" was an anti-Vietnam protest song. This hints at what's covered on the rest of her albums for Invictus, all available here. What's remarkable is how Payne and her team of writers sound fearless throughout these recordings, pushing the boundaries of contemporary soul forward—even if the songs don't cover new thematic ground, or are merely good generic pieces, there's something in the arrangement, production, or performance that elevates it above its peers. So, while this is a lot of music, it's worth exploring—music this rich deserves such an exhaustive, loving presentation and any serious soul fan will be well-served by acquiring this. *—Stephen Thomas Erlewine*

Peaches & Herb

f. 1965, Washington, D.C.

Group / Pop-Soul, Adult Contemporary, Soul, Quiet Storm

Though soul/pop Peaches & Herb was billed as a duo, their group member rotation is more similar to a group's. The original Peaches, Francine Hurd Barker, a Washington, D.C., native, earned the childhood nickname "Peaches" because of her genteel manner. She sang in neighborhood groups and in her teens she became the lead singer for a group named the Keynotes. Starting her own group, the Darlettes, they auditioned for and were signed to D.C.-area label Date Records, where their name was changed to the Sweet Things. Herb Fame, born Herbert Feemster on October 1, 1942, in Washington, D.C., began singing in church at seven and continued singing through the years in neighborhood groups.

After high school graduation, Herb began working at a record store. His friend, Howard University student Freddie Perren, worked at another record store, Sabin's right around the corner. One day in January 1965, producer Van McCoy came into the store Herb worked in to ask about doing in-store promotion for a group he was working with called the Sweet Things. He and Herb began having conversations that lead to Herb auditioning for and signing with Date Records as a solo artist. While in New York recording the two acts, the Sweet Things and Herb Fame, separately, McCoy decided to use some leftover recording time to record Herb & Francine as a duo. The original A-side, "We're in This Thing Together," failed to generate much interest. Then a disc jockey at St. Louis, MO, radio station KATZ flipped the single over and began playing the B-side, "Let's Fall in Love." It became Peaches & Herb's first hit single; it was a remake of a number-one pop hit for Eddy Duchin from 1934 that went to number-11 R&B in December 1966. The follow-up, "Close Your Eyes" written by Chuck Willis, hit number-four R&B, number-eight pop in April 1967.

As the hits continued, the duo earned the nickname the Sweethearts of Soul. Next came "For Your Love" (number-ten R&B, July 1967), "Love Is Strange" (a remake of Mickey & Sylvia's 1956 hit), and "Two Little Kids," written by Chicago soul stalwarts Barbara Acklin, Eugene Record, and Carl Davis. The duo released two hit albums in 1967 *Let's Fall in Love* and *For Your Love*. This same year, Francine "Peaches" Barker tired of the rigors of touring and she was replaced with a succession of "Peacheses" including Marlene Mack, thus initiating a practice that goes on to this day. Voted one of the top soul duos of the day by *Cashbox* magazine, Peaches and Herb continued to have hits: "The Ten Commandments of Love"; Gamble & Huff wrote and produced "United," a 1966 R&B hit for the Intruders; and "When He Touches Me (Nothing Else Matters)," a number-ten R&B hit from spring 1969. The single "It's Just a Game, Love" (from the Jim Brown movie *The Split*), which stalled at number-50 R&B and number pop in summer 1970, was Peaches & Herb's last charting single on Date. Despondent over the act's failing chart success, Herb abruptly quit Peaches & Herb and got a job with the Washington, D.C., Police Department in July 1970.

Then in 1976, Herb decided to re-enter the music business. He found his "new" Peaches in fellow D.C. resident and former model Linda "Peaches" Green through a mutual introduction by Van McCoy. The duo charted again in June 1977 with "We're Still Together" on MCA Records from a self-titled album produced by Van McCoy. The following year, they signed with Herb's old friend, songwriter/producer Freddie Perren's production company MVP Productions. Perren had produced and co-written million-selling hits by the Jackson 5, the Miracles, and the Sylvers, among others. Through him, the duo inked a deal with Polydor Records. Their first Polydor single, "Shake Your Groove Thing," went gold peaking at number-four R&B and number-five pop in late 1978. The creamy ballad "Reunited" seemed an unlikely follow-up to the disco-oriented "Shake." The naysayers watched in shock as "Reunited" earned platinum status, holding on to the number-one spot for four weeks on both the R&B and pop charts during spring 1979. Both are on the platinum album *2 Hot* (released October 1978). The majority of their Polydor hits were written by Perren, Dino Fekaris, Kenny St. Lewis, and Melvin Ragin. Though there were other hits on Polydor, none came close to the success of their early-to mid-'60s Date singles. *—Ed Hogan*

Let's Fall in Love / 1967 / Date ✦✦✦

The first of two albums by the duo Peaches & Herb issued in 1967. This debut LP started slowly as the title track got good response, then exploded when the songs "For Your Love" and "Close Your Eyes" became huge soul hits and even attracted some pop attention. They continued rolling along until 1970, when Barker left to get married. Fame was left without a partner until 1975, when McCoy arranged for Fame to meet and work with Linda "Peaches" Green, reviving Peaches & Herb. *—Ron Wynn*

For Your Love / 1967 / Date ✦✦✦✦✦

The original Peaches & Herb, former sales assistant Herb Fame and vocalist Francine Barker, were teamed by Van McCoy. Their debut album sounded a bit trite at times, but was redeemed by a couple of wonderful duets. This was their second album of 1967, rushed out to keep the momentum going from the response to the two chart hits from their debut. They remained hot with an entertaining version of "Love Is Strange," which had sparkling production and nice harmonies. *—Ron Wynn*

Greatest Hits / 1968 / Date ✦✦✦✦✦

Despite having only been together a little over year and cutting only two albums for Epic, the label rushed out a greatest hits album in 1968. It essentially collected the hits and best tracks from both albums and repackaged them. Peaches & Herb were the ultimate singles act; they weren't versatile enough to do the kind of wide-ranging material necessary to fill an album. *—Ron Wynn*

Peaches & Herb / 1977 / MCA ✦✦

2 Hot! / 1978 / Polydor ✦✦✦

Disco jams and sweet ballads are featured on Peaches & Herb's return to the charts after a long absence. "Reunited," a majestic ballad about lovers getting back together, pulverized the charts, it topped the pop and the R&B Charts, it stayed number one for four weeks running on *Billboard*'s pop 100 Chart. A new Peaches, Linda Green, is featured. Francine Barker was the original Peaches who scored with Herb Fame (Feemster) in the '60s with "Close Your Eyes" and "Lets Fall in Love." This new Peaches oozed sexuality; her voice could raise the dead. Producer Freddie Perren, well aware of the disco rage, balanced their slowies with rump shakers like "Shake Your Groove Thing," and "We've Got Love," two of their better uptempo numbers. "Groove Thing" went to number five in the country and was their biggest record ever until "Reunited." The duo's specialty were ballads, and "Fours a Traffic Jam" is a beauty, Fame's sweet falsetto and Green's sexy phrasings are intoxicating. *—Andrew Hamilton*

Twice the Fire / 1979 / Polydor ✦✦

Peaches & Herb's second album with Freddie Perren at the helm doesn't rate with the spotty *2 Hot!* There's nothing close to "Reunited" to tantalize you, though they try with a remake of Johnny Ace's "I Pledge My Love," the only song here that warrants repeated listens. "Roller Skatin' Mate," which can only be described as bubblegum disco sucks! Others, like "Howzabout Some Love," and "Getting Down, Gettin' Down" aren't much better. After such a good beginning with Perren, the decline came even faster. This one didn't win them many new fans. *—Andrew Hamilton*

The Best of Peaches & Herb / Feb. 6, 1996 / Polygram ✦✦✦✦

This long overdue set coincided with Polygram's mid-'90s reissues of R&B that fell under the corporate umbrella. This 1996 set covers the duo's 1978-1981 work with Polydor. In the late '70s, Herb Fame met up with a new Peaches, Linda Green, and they began a four-year string of hits. The disco classic "Shake Your Groove Thing" perfectly captured the disco's near frantic party vibe. The anachronistic and charming ballad "Reunited" was the duo's biggest hit. What bogs *The Best of Peaches & Herb* down is the remarkable falling off of the quality. The later songs that capitalized on the formula, "Roller Skatin' Mate" and the sweet to the point of nausea "Pledge My Love," are almost as good as the better known songs. But by the time the bland and derivative "Lovey Dovey (Girl & Guy)," "Freeway," and "Surrender" rolled around it is clear producer Freddie Perren was shooting blanks. *The Best of Peaches & Herb* also includes the disco version of "Shake Your Groove Thing." This doesn't offer any tracks from their long gone 1977 MCA album or the instant cutout they did for Columbia in 1983. But for a solid compilation, this is pretty good. *—Jason Elias*

● **The Best of Peaches & Herb: Love Is Strange** / Mar. 12, 1996 / Epic/Legacy ✦✦✦✦✦

The brief, but successful tenure of the original Peaches (Francine Barker) & Herb are recalled in the 16 tracks culled from the duo's 1966-1968 Date Records recordings, including their Top Ten pop hit "Close Your Eyes" and their Top Ten R&B hits "For Your Love" and "When He Touches Me (Nothing Else Matters)." Given the group's love ballad reputation, there are some surprisingly uptempo numbers here, but the focus is always on the vocal interaction between the two singers and their proclamations of romantic commitment, sometimes in the words of such Tin Pan Alley prototypes as Ted Koehler, Cole Porter, and Sammy Cahn. Record-company restrictions mean this set covers only the early hits, and business considerations keep it under 45 minutes (all the releases in Legacy's *Rhythm & Soul* Series contain 16 tracks, which must indicate a ceiling on song publishing expenses), but within those parameters, this is a well-chosen collection. *—William Ruhlmann*

Danny Pearson

b. Racine, WI

Vocals, Bass / Urban, Disco, Soul

Barry White produced teenager Danny Pearson's Top 20 R&B midtempo ballad single "What's Your Sign Girl." The Racine, WI, native was signed to White's Unlimited Gold label distributed through CBS Records. He moved to California in 1974 and was picked by White to be one of the artists to be released on his imprint. An album, *Barry White Presents Mr. Danny Pearson*, was issued. The first single, "What's Your Sign Girl" b/w "Is It Really True Girl" hit number-16 R&B, number-106 pop on *Billboard*'s charts in late 1978. Though none of Pearson's other singles charted, his album was a good debut and is a favorite of soft soul fans. White utilized the same studio band he used on his own million-selling hits as well as the talents of his friend, arranger Gene Page. Page whose credits list Love Unlimited, Johnny Mathis, the Righteous Brothers' "You've Lost That Lovin' Feelin'," various Motown hits, and Jeffree Perry's *Jeffree* album, among others, imbued Pearson's LP with the same kind of shimmering arrangements he'd used on other artists' releases. Besides the aforementioned tracks, other standouts were a cover of White's previous hit "Honey Please, Can't You See," "Say It Again," and Delfonics/Philly soul-tinged "There's No One for Me, but You." Alex Chilton covered "What's Your Sign Girl" on his 1995 Ardent album, *A Man Called Destruction.* *—Ed Hogan*

● **Barry White Presents Danny Pearson** / 1978 / Unlimited Gold ♦♦♦
It was his lucky day when Tony Sepe, Barry White's manager, discovered Danny Pearson camped outside of White's productions offices on Sunset Blvd. Pearson's innocent, teenage soprano flavors eight romantic tracks produced by the maestro of love himself. Pearsons' voice, the complete opposite of Whites' low registers, hit with the astrological question "What's Your Sign Girl"; the *Soul Train* crowd loved the silky ballad with the tired pickup line. Pearson's youthful enthusiasm adds life to the rest of the lush, mushy tracks. The uptempo "Let's Go Dancin' (Let's Go Disco)" a Pearson/White collaboration, is the odd White composition with the word "disco" in its title. Pearson's remake of Loves Unlimited's "Walking in The Rain With the One I Love" deserved to score, White revamped the classic with new lyrics, a wicked bassline, and a long eerie intro. *—Andrew Hamilton*.

David Peaston

b. St. Louis, MO
Vocals, Organ / Adult Contemporary, Urban
David Peaston's inability to gain a foothold on the urban contemporary scene is one of the mysteries of the late '80s and early '90s. His huge, bombastic voice reflects great family roots; his mother Martha Bass was one of the Clara Ward Singers and a great gospel performer, while his sister Fontella Bass has equally distinguished gospel and soul credentials. He started out as a teacher and after being laid off in 1981, Peaston moved from St. Louis to New York. He began doing session work and auditioned for a role in the gospel musical *Don't Get God Started.* He also auditioned for a spot in the Apollo's famous Amateur Night competition. He became a featured attraction on the syndicated *Showtime at the Apollo* in 1988 and eventually landed a deal with Geffen. His 1989 LP *Introducing... David Peaston* was among that year's hottest and most soulful releases, and he also toured with Gladys Knight in America and Gerald Alston in England. Peaston moved to MCA for the 1991 release *Mixed Emotions*, but failed to get the vital crossover exposure or breakout urban hit he needed to get the recognition he deserved. *—Ron Wynn*

● **Introducing... David Peaston** / 1988 / Geffen ♦♦♦♦♦
David Peaston was one of gospel's most demonstrative, majestic talents while working with his family, which included his mother, Martha Bass, and sister, Fontella Bass. He acquired a national television following by dominating the weekly contests on the syndicated *Showtime at the Apollo* and then in 1989 made a huge impression with his debut album on Geffen. While it wasn't an enormous hit, it generated enough publicity and favorable response to get Peaston a spot as the opening act for Gladys Knight. *—Ron Wynn*

Mixed Emotions / 1991 / MCA ♦♦♦
The second album for David Peaston was frustrating and put his career into a spin from which it hasn't recovered. Although he possessed a magnetic, glorious voice with a deep, rich sound ideal for heartache ballads, he also needed quality material with strong lyrics, since he wasn't a songwriter. He didn't get it on this record, and the results were a disappointing collection of throwaway urban contemporary tracks ill-suited to his delivery and approach. *—Ron Wynn*

Pebbles (Perri McKissack)

b. Nov. 6, 1966, Oakland, CA
Vocals / Urban, Dance-Pop
Although dance-pop singer Pebbles scored several hit singles on her own during the '80s, she has become best-known as the manager (and creator) of one of the genre's biggest hit machines the following decade. Born Perri McKissack in Oakland, CA, on November 6, 1966, the singer (who is the cousin of R&B singer Cherelle) got her start in the early '80s as a backup singer for percussionist/band leader Bill Summers and the funk outfit Con Funk Shun, helping co-pen one of the latter band's hits, "Body Lovers." By the end of the decade, however, McKissack was ready to strike out on her own, going by the name Pebbles and signing a recording contract with MCA. The singer's self-titled 1988 debut featured contributions from both Babyface and Michael Sembello (as well as renowned producer L.A. Reid, who Pebbles would eventually marry), and spawned a pair of Top Five hits, "Girlfriend" and "Mercedes Boy," pushing the album to platinum status stateside.

Pebbles' follow-up recording, 1990's *Always*, fared nearly as well, going gold and spawning another Top Five hit with "Giving You the Benefit," while both Salt-N-Pepa and Cherelle made guest appearances on the record. Instead of pursuing her solo career, Pebbles then founded her own record label, Savvy Records, and created the Atlanta, GA-based hip-hop/dance trio TLC (comprised of members Tionne "T-Boz" Watkins, Rozonda "Chilli" Thomas, and Lisa "Left Eye" Lopes). Guiding TLC's career and serving as their manager, the trio became one of pop's biggest hit-making groups by 1994, thanks to their 11-times platinum smash *Crazysexycool.* Pebbles returned back to her solo career in 1995 with her third release overall, *Straight from My Heart.* Although it was a much more mature work (and featured contributions from such producers/songwriters as Sean "Puffy" Combs, Kyle West, and Organized Noize), it failed to match the commercial success of its predecessors. In 2002, a 14-track career overview was released on the Hip-O label with *Greatest Hits.* *—Greg Prato*

Pebbles / 1988 / MCA ♦♦♦
Pebbles surfaced on the scene in 1988 with her self-titled debut album and the two major hits it yielded: "Girlfriend" and "Mercedes Boy." "Girlfriend" continued in the Jody Watley tradition, with hard, urban dance beats and a dramatic story line. "Girlfriend" was also an early hit for Babyface as a songwriter, and, like Karyn White's Babyface-penned hits of the time, possessed an earthy grit which became lost under the adult contemporary gloss found in latter-day Babyface compositions. "Mercedes Boy," a sleek, sophisticated slice of urban dance-pop, proved an even bigger hit than its predecessor, although the version here is somewhat tepid compared to the superior single remix, which can be found on Pebbles' 2000 *Greatest Hits* collection. Pebbles, like her contemporaries Karyn White, Jody Watley, and Paula Abdul, became a big star in the late '80s, but that success could no longer translate to the early '90s, when R&B took a much more aggressive and hard-edged direction. The rest of Pebbles' debut was somewhat pleasurable, but lightweight and rather unmemorable, and a third single, "Take Your Time," failed to ignite the charts, although her two later albums showed a considerable growth in artistry. Regardless, no collection of 1980s dance/pop/R&B would be complete without these two major hits, but the casual fan would be better off with *Greatest Hits.* *—Jose F. Promis*

Always / 1990 / MCA ♦♦♦
Pebbles followed her self-titled LP with *Always*, which went gold and spawned two number-one R&B hits, the gritty "Giving You the Benefit" and the fluttering Pebbles/Babyface duet ballad "Love Makes Things Happen." Salt-N-Pepa appear on the pumping smash "Backyard." The lovely ballad "Always" features her cousin Cherelle and broke the R&B Top 20. The urgent "Say a Prayer for Me" is a lyrical snapshot of '80s-era ills. Other standouts are "Give It to Me," the ethereal ballad "Why Would I Believe," and the sweet, bouncy "Stay With Me." [Some tracks from *Always* are on Pebbles' *Greatest Hits* released by Hip-O/Universal on April 25, 2000, and *Heart of Soul [Polygram]* issued in January 2000.] *—Ed Hogan*

Straight from My Heart / Sep. 12, 1995 / MCA ♦♦♦♦♦
Pebbles was at the height of her career in the late '80s, when she was following the footsteps of Paula Abdul as a lightweight dance-pop diva. For most of the early '90s, her career had suffered as R&B fashions changed, embracing a harder, hip-hop influenced sound. With *Straight from My Heart*, Pebbles attempts to fit into the sound of the mid-'90s and the results are surprisingly successful. Although Pebbles' voice has improved over the years, developing into a seductive, silky instrument, *Straight from My Heart* is more of a showcase for her producers (including Puffy Combs and Organized Noize) than the singer herself. Featuring elements of jazz, funk, and hip-hop, the record is a diverse and soulful catalog of contemporary R&B; even when the songwriting is weak, the record sounds first-rate. *Straight from My Heart* may not have any single as strong as "Mercedes Boy," but it ranks among Pebbles' most consistent efforts. *—Stephen Thomas Erlewine*

● **Greatest Hits** / Apr. 25, 2000 / Hip-O ♦♦♦♦
Pebbles' *Greatest Hits* gathers her most popular singles as well as some of her definitive album tracks. Her four number-one R&B hits—"Girlfriend," "Love Makes Things Happen," "Giving You the Benefit," and "Mercedes Boy"—anchor the album, which also includes "Backyard," her duet with Salt-N-Pepa, "Take Your Time," "Angel," and "Always." Productions by Babyface and L.A. Reid and collaborations with Mario Winans and other singers reaffirm Pebbles' fresh, progressive R&B style. *—Heather Phares*

Ann Peebles

b. Apr. 27, 1947, St. Louis, MO
Vocals / Memphis Soul, Soul, Urban, Contemporary Blues
A diminutive singer with a powerful voice and an even stronger attitude, Ann Peebles was one of the artists who defined Willie Mitchell's legendary Memphis soul label Hi Records, along with Al Green and, later, O.V. Wright. Easily the best female singer in the Hi stable, Peebles ranked among the finest deep Southern soul singers of the decade, notching an instant classic with her 1973 hit "I Can't Stand the Rain." She co-wrote a generous share of her own material with husband Don Bryant, and while she cut plenty of love and heartbreak tunes, her persona was built on the grit and resilient strength she displayed on songs like "I'm Gonna Tear Your Playhouse Down." Peebles wasn't always as appreciated on the charts as her work often merited, especially among pop listeners, but her best recordings hold up among the best of their era.

Peebles was born April 27, 1947, in East St. Louis, MO. Her father was a minister and her mother a singer, and naturally Peebles began singing at a young age in her father's church choir. She also sang with the family group, the Peebles Choir, which had been touring the gospel circuit since Peebles' grandfather founded it a generation earlier. As a teenager, she sang secular music on the St. Louis club circuit, supported and accompanied by her father. There she met blues bandleader Oliver Sain, a local legend, and eventually joined his revue. Peebles caught her big break in 1968 on a trip to Memphis, where she asked to sit in on a club set by trumpeter Gene "Bowlegs" Miller. Miller was already signed to Hi Records at the time, and duly impressed with Peebles' voice, he brought her to Hi house producer Willie Mitchell for a tryout. Mitchell, who was still in the process of shifting the label from country to R&B (and had not yet discovered Al Green), immediately offered Peebles a contract; she was still shy of her 21st birthday.

Mitchell teamed Peebles with singer and house songwriter Don Bryant, seeking a bit more seasoning in her R&B phrasing. Peebles and Bryant soon began writing together, and would also end up dating in 1972. In the meantime, Peebles recorded her debut single, "Walk Away," a song written by Sain that just missed the Top 20 on the R&B chart; the follow-up, "Give Me Some Credit," was also a minor hit. Her fourth single, 1970's "Part Time Love," was her first R&B Top Ten, prompting a reissue of her debut album, *This Is Ann Peebles*, under that title. *Straight From the Heart* (1972) was her first artistically realized LP, however; it featured several minor R&B hits in "I Pity the Fool," "Slipped, Tripped and Fell in Love," "I Feel Like Breaking Up Somebody's Home" (later covered by Bette Midler), and "Somebody's on Your Case," plus the signature album track "99 Lbs." Her hot streak continued with 1973's *I Can't Stand the Rain*, which many critics still regard as her finest work. "I'm Gonna Tear Your Playhouse Down" was a decent-sized hit, and the brilliant title cut—written by Peebles, Bryant, and disc jockey Bernard Miller—became her biggest hit, peaking at number-six R&B and famously becoming a favorite of John Lennon. She also charted with "(You Keep Me) Hangin' On" and "Do I Need You," but more importantly married Bryant in 1974.

In the wake of "I Can't Stand the Rain," Peebles was a star on the soul circuit, even if she never duplicated its commercial success. "Beware," "Come to Mama," and "Dr. Love Power" were all charting singles from 1975's *Tellin' It*, but the rise of disco and the sale of Hi Records in 1977 would conspire against Peebles' career momentum. 1977's *If This Is Heaven* produced only one single in the title cut, which was more polished than Peebles' usual fare; none of the singles from 1979's *The Handwriting Is on the Wall* cracked the R&B Top 50. With Mitchell and most of the Hi house band gone, Peebles took a hiatus from the music business to concentrate on her family.

Peebles reunited with Mitchell in 1989 for *Call Me*, an album released on Mitchell's short-lived new label, Waylo; however, longtime fans generally found it a disappointing comeback overpowered by sterile electronic instrumentation. Peebles returned to a more organic approach by signing with roots label Rounder's Bullseye Blues subsidiary for 1992's *Full Time Love*. Another effort, *Fill This World With Love*, followed in 1996, which featured guest spots from Mavis Staples and Shirley Brown. During the '90s, Peebles guested on several albums by Maria Muldaur. Meanwhile, "I Can't Stand the Rain" was covered by numerous artists, including Tina Turner, and revived by Missy Elliott via sampling on her 1997 smash "The Rain (Supa Dupa Fly)." *—Steve Huey*

This Is Ann Peebles / 1969 / Hi ✦✦

Straight / 1970 / Hi ✦✦✦

Part Time Love / 1971 / The Right Stuff ✦✦✦✦✦
The title track was a masterpiece, and everything else on this dynamic early '70s soul session is a jewel. Ann Peebles may have been the most overlooked great soul singer, male or female, who emerged in the '70s. Hi couldn't strike crossover gold twice, and Al Green was becoming a superstar. But Peebles deserved a better fate than obscurity, as this collection of soul wailers and weepers proves. *—Ron Wynn*

Straight From the Heart / 1972 / Hi ✦✦✦✦✦
A lean, tough set that was not only a triumph for Peebles, but illustrated how the Hi label had surpassed its crosstown Stax rival for quality Memphis soul in the early '70s. The guitars are spare, funky, and bluesy, the horn section punchy, and the material far earthier and down-home than the increasingly formulaic grooves at Stax. There were three modest R&B hits on the album ("Slipped, Tripped and Fell in Love," "I Feel Like Breaking Up Somebody's Home," "Somebody's on Your Case"), much of which was penned by Peebles or her husband Don Bryant. Peebles' vocals were convincingly biting, and she never, unlike many other singers of the era, tried too hard for her own good. The main flaw of the record is its length (26 minutes), which was short even by early-'70s standards. *—Richie Unterberger*

I Can't Stand the Rain / 1973 / Hi ✦✦✦
The title song was an instant classic, and its lyrics are among the most moving and gripping in soul annals. This was Ann Peebles' finest album for Hi Records, and it should have been a massive success. Instead, while it's celebrated in Europe and now considered an anthem, it floundered and barely scraped the pop charts, although the single was her biggest R&B hit. It's sad and ridiculous that the only Ann Peebles session presently available on CD is the one she did for Bullseye Blues in 1992. *—Ron Wynn*

If This Is Heaven / 1977 / Hi ✦✦✦✦✦
Another exceptional album by Ann Peebles, who was cutting remarkable records for Hi in Memphis that no one noticed except for deep soul junkies. Her voice was alternately anguished, angry, defiant, and resigned, while Willie Mitchell and the Hi rhythm section provided minimal, yet spectacular backing. Peebles seldom toured, preferring to stay in Memphis around her family. But she had a voice only surpassed among female soul vocalists by Aretha Franklin and equalled by Carla Thomas. *—Ron Wynn*

The Handwriting Is on the Wall / 1979 / Hi ✦✦✦
Here is some fabulous down-home, earthy soul from Ann Peebles, a Southern treasure. Peebles was the finest female singer to pass through the Hi Records operation, and Willie Mitchell achieved with her the same kind of wonderful records he made with Al Green, although they didn't get identical commercial success. Any and all of the albums Ann Peebles did with Hi are classics; sadly, most of them haven't been reissued. *—Ron Wynn*

Full Time Love / 1992 / Bullseye Blues ✦✦✦
When Ann Peebles returned to the studio after a long absence, little had changed. True, this enriching CD was produced by Ron Levy instead of Willie Mitchell, who had handled all of her classic Hi dates of the 1970s. But for all intents and purposes, *Full Time Love* is state-of-the-art Peebles. Gritty, unpretentious and hard-hitting, this magnificent date throws pop and urban contemporary considerations to the wind and screams "Memphis soul" in no uncertain terms. Peebles still had a monster of a voice, and her singing is as confident as ever on such raw and earthy material as "St. Louis Woman (With a Memphis Melody)," "Read Me My Rights" and "Ain't No Business Like Your Business." But perhaps the most revealing cut is a remix of her biggest hit "I Can't Stand the Rain," which will inevitably be compared to the high standards of the original 1974 version. Played next to the original, this remake sends out a strong message that a first-class soul goddess was still very much in her prime. *—Alex Henderson*

Sings Soul Classics / 1992 / Hi ✦✦✦✦
A compilation of album tracks, B-sides, and unreleased takes recorded during Ann Peebles' 1972-1977 tenure at Memphis soul mainstay Hi Records, *Ann Peebles Sings Soul Classics* consists entirely of covers of soul and R&B classics closely associated with other singers. Normally, this would be a recipe for disaster, but although the underrated Peebles only had a small handful of hits, she's easily among the finest soul singers of her generation. Add in the crack Hi Records session men (making classics for Al Green and O.V. Wright, among others, at the same time), and *Ann Peebles Sings Soul Classics* becomes a fascinating listen. Not all of the songs are the definitive versions, but Peebles has the self-confidence to cop from Aretha Franklin's rearrangement of Otis Redding's "Respect" and the talent to pull it off. The one misstep is the Peter Frampton-style guitar/vocal interlude that mars Peebles' otherwise masterful take on Wright's "You're Gonna Make Me Cry." The gorgeous "(Keep Me) Hangin' On" (not the Supremes tune) more than makes up for that. *—Stewart Mason*

Straight From the Heart/I Can't Stand the Rain / 1992 / Hi ✦✦✦✦✦

Tellin' It/If This Is Heaven / 1992 / Hi ✦✦✦✦✦

Ann Peebles' Greatest Hits / 1995 / MCA ✦✦✦✦✦
Backed by the vaunted Hi rhythm section and produced by Willie Mitchell, this includes her original "Come to Mama" and "I Can't Stand the Rain." These are classics of the '70s Memphis soul idiom. *—Bill Dahl*

Fill This World With Love / 1996 / Bullseye Blues ✦✦✦

St. Louis Woman / 1996 / Hi ✦✦✦✦
St. Louis Woman is a terrific four-disc, 63-track box set covering Ann Peebles' entire career, concentrating (rightly so) on her seminal early-'70s recordings for Hi Records. All of her hits are here, of course, along with underappreciated album tracks, lost singles, B-sides, rarities and a handful of unreleased cuts. Certainly, this isn't the choice for the casual fan—there's simply too much music here—but for the dedicated fan and collector, this is a treasure. *—Stephen Thomas Erlewine*

U.S. R&B Hits '69-'79 / Jun. 25, 1996 / Hi ✦✦✦
U.S. R&B Chart Hits is exactly what it says it is—an excellent collection featuring Ann Peebles' 18 biggest R&B hits, including such classics as "Part Time Love," "I'm Gonna Tear Your Playhouse Down" and "I Can't Stand the Rain." It's arguably the definitive Peebles collection, since it sports a leaner and better track selection than the Right Stuff's 21-track *Best of the Hi Records Years*, which nevertheless is a fine collection in its own right. *—Stephen Thomas Erlewine*

● **The Best of Ann Peebles: The Hi Records Years** / Jul. 23, 1996 / The Right Stuff ✦✦✦✦✦
The Best of the Hi Records Years collects all the highlights from Ann Peebles' creative and commercial heyday, featuring the majority of her hits for the label, including "I Can't Stand the Rain" and "Part Time Love," as well as several terrific lesser-known singles and album tracks. *—Stephen Thomas Erlewine*

This Is Ann Peebles/The Handwriting Is on the Wall / Mar. 4, 1997 / Hi ✦✦✦✦

Teddy Pendergrass

b. Mar. 26, 1950, Philadelphia, PA
Vocals, Drums / Quiet Storm, Urban, Soul, Club/Dance
Teddy Pendergrass started singing gospel music in Philadelphia churches, becoming an ordained minister at ten years old. While attending public school, he sang in the citywide McIntyre Elementary School Choir and in the All-City Stetson Junior High School Choir. A self-taught drummer, Pendergrass had a teen pop vocal group when he was 15. By his late teens, Pendergrass was a drummer for local vocal group the Cadillacs. In the late '60s, the Cadillacs merged with another more-established group, Harold Melvin & the Blue Notes. In 1970, when the Blue Notes broke up, Melvin, now aware of Pendergrass' vocal prowess, asked him to take the lead singer spot. It's no secret that Kenneth Gamble & Leon Huff wanted Marvin Junior of the Dells for their Philadelphia International Records roster. Since the Dells were signed to Chess, they were unavailable. When the gruff 'n' ready vocals of Pendergrass came their way, they eagerly signed the group.

Beginning with "I Miss You," a steady stream of hit singles flowed from the collaboration of Pendergrass and Gamble & Huff: "If You Don't Know Me By Now," "The Love I Lost," "Bad Luck," "Wake Up Everybody" (number-one R&B for two weeks in 1976), and two gold albums, *To Be True* and *Wake Up Everybody*. Unfortunately, the more success the group had, the more friction developed between Melvin and Pendergrass. Despite the revised billing of the group, Harold Melvin & the Blue Notes Featuring Theodore Pendergrass, Pendergrass felt that he wasn't getting enough recognition. Around 1976, Pendergrass left Melvin's Blue Notes and formed his own Blue Notes, featuring Teddy Pendergrass. Briefly, there was some confusion as to which Blue Notes were which. The resolution came when Pendergrass disbanded his Blue Notes in favor of a solo career and Melvin's group signed a recording contract with Source Records, distributed through ABC Records, scoring a hit with "I Want to Be Your Lover."

Pendergrass signed a new contract with Philadelphia International Records in late 1976/early 1977. He burst back on the scene with *Teddy Pendergrass*, a platinum solo debut that included the top-notch singles "I Don't Love You Anymore," "You Can't Hide From Yourself," and "The More I Get the More I Want." Around this time, Pendergrass began to institute his infamous "Ladies Only" concerts. His next three albums went gold or platinum: *Life Is a Song Worth Singing* (1978), *Teddy* (1979), and *Live! Coast to Coast*. The hit single "Close the Door" was used in the film *Soup for One*, where Pendergrass had a small role.

The singer received several Grammy nominations during 1977 and 1978, *Billboard*'s 1977 Pop Album New Artist Award, an American Music Award for best R&B performer of 1978, and awards from *Ebony* magazine and the NAACP. He was also in consideration for the lead in the movie biopic *The Otis Redding Story*. The '70s ended, but Pendergrass kept racking up the hits. *Teddy*, his fifth solo album, went platinum in the summer of 1980 off the singles "Turn Off the Lights," "Come Go With Me," "Shout and Scream," "It's You I Love," and "Can't We Try." *It's Time for Love* gave Pendergrass another gold album in summer 1981, which included the hit singles "Love TKO" and "I Can't Live Without Your Love."

A 1982 car accident left Pendergrass paralyzed from the waist down and wheelchair bound. After almost a year of physical therapy and counseling, Pendergrass returned to the recording scene, signing a contract with Elektra/Asylum in 1983. His ninth solo album, his Elektra/Asylum debut, *Love Language* went gold the spring of 1984. Philadelphia International issued two albums of unreleased tracks, *This One's for You* (1982) and *Heaven Only Knows* (1983). Other albums included *Workin' It Back* (1985), *Joy* (1988, whose title track went to number-one R&B for two weeks), and *Little More Magic* (1993). The latter half of '90s found Pendergrass recording for the Surefire/Wind Up label. *Truly Blessed* (the name of an 1991 Elektra album) is the title of the autobiography Pendergrass co-authored with Patricia Romanowski. *—Ed Hogan*

Life Is a Song Worth Singing / 1978 / The Right Stuff ♦♦♦♦♦
This was the album that convinced anyone who had doubts about the wisdom of Pendergrass leaving Harold Melvin & the Blue Notes that he had made a good decision. Although he only got one R&B hit from the album, there were enough strong ballads and uptempo cuts to show that Pendergrass had the sound, personality, and style to cut it on his own. He would shortly become R&B's greatest male attraction, but in the interim, Philadelphia International was laying the ground work. *—Ron Wynn*

Teddy Pendergrass / 1978 / The Right Stuff ♦♦♦♦♦
The skeptics had their suspicions allayed quickly when Teddy Pendergrass' debut album as a solo singer cracked the Top 40. Its lead single, "I Don't Love You Anymore," was among his best uptempo tunes, and the follow-up ballad "The Whole Town's Laughing at Me" ended any speculation that he was returning to Harold Melvin & the Blue Notes. While many thought the album would launch him to consistent R&B success, almost no one thought he would be R&B's biggest male star in a couple of years. *—Ron Wynn*

Teddy / Jun. 23, 1979 / The Right Stuff ♦♦♦
Teddy Pendergrass scored his greatest hit album with his third solo release, cementing his position at the end of the '70s as the reigning matinee idol and romantic balladeer among male R&B vocalists. This album cracked the pop Top Ten, dominated the R&B charts, and ruled the airwaves through much of 1979. While the overt sexual orientation of a song like "Turn Off the Lights" blinded some to the fact that Pendergrass' animated vocal was as soulful as you'd ever hear outside the gospel/blues/country axis of the South, this album confirmed that Pendergrass had found his niche and would be a dominant singer into the '80s. *—Ron Wynn*

Live! Coast to Coast / Dec. 22, 1979 / Philadelphia International ♦♦
Some artists come across well on live LPs and some average. Pendergrass' fits the latter description. You had to have been there to feel and experience the energy and visual of Teddy live. The audience definitely enjoyed the show, the screaming starts from the moment he's introduced to the finale. "When Somebody Loves You Back" has a cute hook, but goes on too long (more than 12 minutes); the sensuous "Come Go With Me" is bum rushed after a little more than two minutes. Pendergrass' two make-out ballads: "Close the Door," and "Turn Off the Lights" are creamy concoctions. Raps and interviews interspersed throughout the album are distracting. The song selection could have been better—"The Whole Town's Laughing At Me," and "You Can't Hide From Yourself" were omitted. A short Harold Melvin & the Blue Notes' medley is satisfying. Fast tunes balance the slow stuff, but the fast numbers, except for "Do Me," are weak. "Life Is a Song Worth Singing" bores, and "Get Up, Get Down, Get-Funky, Get Loose" annoys. Essential for die-hard Teddy Pendergrass fans and live album freaks only. *—Andrew Hamilton*

TP / 1980 / The Right Stuff ♦♦♦♦♦
Teddy Pendergrass was near, if not at, the pinnacle of a prosperous music career upon this album's release, which spawned two Top Ten singles. "Can't We Try," with its tender introduction, slowly builds into a dramatic vamp in which Pendergrass' domineering baritone clinches each lyric with absolute conviction—an awesome display of vocal power and control. The compassionate number peaked at number three on the *Billboard* R&B charts after 16 weeks. Pendergrass did not lose any steam on the charts. The follow-up single, "Love T.K.O.," came strong. His testimonial lead carried this crafty number to the second position on the charts, holding down that slot for five consecutive weeks before bowing after 18 weeks. However, the best track on this album is the duet with Stephanie Mills; "Feel the Fire," penned by Peabo Bryson, rings with passion and sensuality. Pendergrass and Mills' vocals strikingly contrast each other in an admirable way. The song was never a release, but remains a constant on quiet storm formats. On a few numbers, such as the Ashford & Simpson remake "Is It Still Good to Ya," Pendergrass labors through the verses, struggling to find his form. Though a great song, it does very little for the former Blue Note. Notwithstanding, there are quite a few gems here. *—Craig Lytle*

It's Time for Love / 1981 / Philadelphia International ♦♦♦
Teddy Pendergrass showed no signs of slowing down in the early '80s. This was another R&B smash and crossover hit, again putting him the Top 20. He got two good R&B singles, remained a popular concert attraction, and demonstrated good rapport with Stephanie Mills on several duets. They teamed so well together that Pendergrass eventually appeared on-stage with her during a tour of England. *—Ron Wynn*

This One's for You / 1982 / Philadelphia International ♦♦
In the immediate period after Teddy Pendergrass' tragic, near-fatal car accident, many wondered what would happen to his career. Philadelphia International rushed out a pair of albums containing unissued tracks that hadn't made the cut from past albums. This was the first one, released in the summer of 1982. It actually managed to have two singles crack the R&B Top 40, although neither moved very far beyond that. It was evident on several tracks why they hadn't been issued; the ballads weren't as powerful or sensual, and the uptempo numbers lacked style and hooks. *—Ron Wynn*

Heaven Only Knows / 1983 / Philadelphia International ♦♦
With Teddy Pendergrass undergoing tortuous rehabilitation from his near-fatal car crash, Philadelphia International was faced with the loss of its single greatest star. The company didn't sit back and mourn; they rushed out a pair of albums containing unissued tracks in both 1982 and 1983. This was the second release, and it had a few nice cuts, although it was evident why much of it hadn't been released in the first place. *—Ron Wynn*

Love Language / 1984 / Asylum ♦♦♦
Teddy Pendergrass delighted both R&B and music fans in general when he debuted on a new label with this album in 1984. It was his first album of fresh songs in two years, and Elektra put some muscle behind it. It also helped that he had a good duet with Whitney Houston, a song included in the film *D.A.R.Y.L.*, and generally better material than Philadelphia International had trotted out on the two albums of unissued vault tracks released in the interim. The album made it into the pop Top 40 and was a triumph of the spirit. *—Ron Wynn*

Workin' It Back / 1985 / Asylum ♦♦♦
A most appropriate title, as Pendergrass was making his comeback following the tragic car accident. The album took a long time to make an impact, but finally wound up a modest success. He wasn't able to generate much response to any single, but the fact that he continued his comeback was welcome news, owing to speculation that he was going to retire due to mixed response to his earlier release. *—Ron Wynn*

Greatest Hits / 1987 / Philadelphia International ♦♦♦♦♦
This collection covers Pendergrass' run of big hits from the Philadelphia International era, including "I Don't Love You Anymore," "Close The Door" and "Turn Off the Lights." *—Ron Wynn*

Joy / 1988 / Elektra ♦♦♦
Teddy Pendergrass finally made it back to the top in 1988, when the title track from this album spent two weeks at the head of the R&B list. The song even got mild pop attention, and the album was the first since his accident to really reflect the new Pendergrass sound. He sang in a slower, somber, yet appealing way quite different from the swaggering, openly sexual/macho posturing of the late '70s and early '80s. This was a weary but not beaten Pendergrass, whose manner and delivery underscored the resilient theme in *Joy*'s lyrics. *—Ron Wynn*

Truly Blessed / Mar. 5, 1991 / Elektra ♦♦♦
Teddy Pendergrass' return to recording and performing after the tragic accident that resulted in permanent paralysis was among the greatest stories of the 1980s. Pendergrass had to learn to sing all over again, with restraint, sensitivity and control now his keys rather than volume and presence. This 1991 album wasn't quite as moving as 1988's *Joy*, but it still included several poignant numbers, especially the title track, which addressed his survival, neither downplaying the problems nor overstating his genuine happiness about still being alive. *—Ron Wynn*

The Philly Years / 1994 / Philadelphia International ♦♦♦♦♦
Loaded with every significant track Teddy Pendergrass recorded at Philadelphia International Records, 32 unedited killers. Everything from "I Don't Love You Anymore" to "Crazy About Your Love." Includes the crawlers "Somebody Told Me," "The Whole Town's Laughing at Me," "Close the Door," "Come Go With Me," and "Turn Off the Lights"; the steppers "Do Me," "Get Up, Get Down, Get Funky, Get Loose," "Shout and Scream," and "The More I Get the More I Want"; and pure classics "Is It Still Good to Ya" (a spine tingling duet with Stephanie Mills), "Love TKO," and "You're My Latest, My Greatest Inspiration." All digitally remastered, what else could you possibly want? *—Andrew Hamilton*

You and I / Apr. 15, 1997 / Surefire ♦♦♦
By the late '90s, Teddy Pendergrass was no longer the superstar he once was, due not only to changing fashions but also to the lackluster quality of his music. With 1997's *You and I*, he made an attempt to revive his career, and even though the album is not perfect, he largely succeeds. The material on *You and I* is fairly uneven, but the best moments on the album, including "Let's Talk About It" and the title track, demonstrate that Pendergrass still has the ability to create richly seductive urban soul. It's his best album in years. *—Stephen Thomas Erlewine*

● **The Best of Teddy Pendergrass** / Mar. 31, 1998 / The Right Stuff ♦♦♦♦♦
The Right Stuff's *The Best of Teddy Pendergrass* is a definitive 18-track collection, containing all of his big hits from 1977's "I Don't Love You Anymore" to 1991's "It Should've Been You." In between those two songs, such romantic smooth soul classics as "Can't We Try," "You're My Latest, My Greatest Inspiration," "Close the Door," "Turn Off the Lights," "Love TKO" and "Joy" are heard. Some Top Ten R&B hits, like "Love 4/2" and "I Can't Live Without Your Love," are missing, but the disc remains a near-perfect summary of Pendergrass at the peak of his powers. *—Stephen Thomas Erlewine*

Turn Off the Lights: The Best of Teddy Pendergrass / Jan. 18, 1999 / Music Club ♦♦♦♦♦
Contains all the sensuous, red-light specials that established Teddy Pendergrass as an R&B sex symbol. Delivered in his rough baritone, throbbers "Come Go With Me," "Close the Door," "Turn Off the Lights," "Is It Still Good To Ya," and his theatrical duet with Stephanie Mills' "Feel the Fire," work like aphrodisiacs. Who can't identify with the aching "The Whole Town's Laughing At Me," or the questioning "Be Sure?" The exciting "You Can't Hide From Yourself" has a gospel beat, and is pushed by Pendergrass' fire & brimstone vocal. A good happy feel is evident on "When Somebody Loves You Back," but "Love TKO" is hardly joyous, the beat is hypnotizing, the lyrics agonizing, and Teddy's vocal is full of pain. *—Andrew Hamilton*

Teddy Pendergrass/Life Is a Song Worth Singing / Mar. 2, 1999 / WestSide ♦♦♦

Teddy/This One's for You / Mar. 2, 1999 / WestSide ♦♦♦

It's Time for Love/This One's for You / Aug. 24, 1999 / Right Stuff ♦♦♦

Significant Singles / Nov. 14, 2000 / WestSide ♦♦♦♦♦
Leave it to a United Kingdom record company (WestSide) to release a Teddy Pendergrass compilation that blows its competitors away. This is an as-down-as-it-gets collection of the Harold Melvin & the Blue Notes ex-lead singer's Philadelphia International recordings.

The title's a little misleading—all of these weren't singles, and they missed a few goodies, e.g., "Be Sure"—but, overall, it doesn't get much better than these 28 fuse blowers from Pendergrass in his prime. Losers like "Life Is a Song Worth Singing" were mercifully left off, but it does contains late-night, red-light specials, Holy Ghost-ish wailers, and enough weeping willies to keep you on a binge for days. *—Andrew Hamilton*

The Penguins

f. 1954, Los Angeles, CA, **db.** 1959

Group / Doo Wop, R&B

Best known for their hit single "Earth Angel," the doo wop quartet the Penguins were never able to replicate the success of their only Top 40 hit, but the song became a rock & roll classic. The Penguins formed in 1954, when the members—Cleveland Duncan (lead vocal), Curtis Williams (tenor vocal), Dexter Tisby (baritone vocal), and Bruce Tate (tenor vocal)—were all attending Fremont High School in Los Angeles, CA.

Although he wasn't the lead singer, Williams was the leader of the group. He learned "Earth Angel" from vocalist Jesse Belvin—some sources claim that Williams wrote the song alone, others say he co-wrote the song with Belvin, while others claim Gaynell Hodge, a member of the doo wop group the Turks, wrote the song with the duo (in fact, Hodge won a lawsuit filed in 1956 that gave him a co-writing credit)—and had the Penguins sing the song. Around 1954, the Penguins signed with the local Los Angeles independent label Dootone Records. The group's first single was going to be the uptempo "Hey Señorita," and the ballad "Earth Angel" was going to be the B-side.

Upon the release of the single in the latter half of 1954, Los Angeles radio stations were receiving more requests for "Earth Angel" than "Hey Señorita," and the song soon became the record's A-side. By the beginning of 1955, the single had scaled the national charts, spending three weeks at the top of the R&B charts and peaking at number eight on the pop charts. For the next few years, the Penguins continued to record singles for Dootone Records. Shortly after the success of "Earth Angel," Tate left the group and Randolph Jones became their baritone vocalist. Around 1956, the Penguins left Dootone Records and signed with Mercury Records. After cutting some sides for Mercury, the group moved to Atlantic Records, where they had their second and final hit, "Pledge of Love," which climbed to number 15 on the R&B charts in the summer of 1959. That same year, the group released their only album, *The Cool, Cool Penguins.*

By 1959, the group had returned to their hometown of Los Angeles; shortly after their relocation, they broke up. Over the next four decades, Cleveland Duncan led various incarnations of the Penguins through reunion tours and re-recordings of their hits. In 1963, Duncan, Tisby, and two new members recorded "Memories of El Monte," a song future Mothers of Invention members Frank Zappa and Ray Collins wrote specifically for the group; the single failed to make any impact. Duncan went back to leading new incarnations of the Penguins, while Tisby briefly joined the Coasters. *—Stephen Thomas Erlewine*

The Cool, Cool Penguins / 1959 / Dootone ✦✦✦

Earth Angel / 1990 / Ace ✦✦✦

This is a 21-track anthology from the Dootone label, it's a deeper look at the group's '50s sides and style, built around the title track that sold five-million copies worldwide. *—Hank Davis*

● **Authentic Golden Hits** / 1993 / Juke Box Treasures ✦✦✦✦✦

At long last, a well-thought-out compilation that gathers up all of the group's best sides for Dootone Records, including the original versions of the classics "Earth Angel" and "Hey Señorita" in their original, unedited form. *—Cub Koda*

The Best of the Penguins: The Mercury Years / Jul. 1996 / Mercury ✦✦✦

The Best of the Penguins: The Mercury Years isn't all that it appears to be. Instead of presenting all of the Penguins' hit singles, it only presents the group's Mercury recordings, which means that neither of the two versions of "Earth Angel" on the disc are the original hit single versions, and that the remainder of their classic Dootone sides are missing. What is here is good, but not essential for anyone but hardcore doo wop collectors. *—Stephen Thomas Erlewine*

Ce Ce Peniston

b. Sep. 6, 1969, Dayton, OH

Vocals / Club/Dance, Urban, Dance-Pop

Disco diva Ce Ce Peniston seemed poised to become that genre's reigning crossover attraction. She was born in Dayton, OH, but her family moved to Phoenix when she was nine. Peniston was crowned Miss Black Arizona in 1989 and signed with A&M in the early '90s. Her debut, *Finally*, was a gold album; it peaked at number 36 on the pop charts and even landed a Top Ten pop hit with "Finally" and Top 20 pop single "We Got a Love Thang." After *Thought 'Ya Knew* in 1994, Peniston issued 1996's *I'm Movin' On.* Peniston continued to sing into the new millennium and regularly plays shows in Las Vegas, Atlantic City, and San Francisco. Not entirely part of the mainstream that brought her success in the early '90s, Peniston's work is remixed and remains a favorite in dance clubs around the world. *—Ron Wynn*

● **Finally** / 1993 / A&M ✦✦✦✦

This was the debut album from the former Miss Black Arizona. There is much invigoration within this album. Ce Ce Peniston's vocal versatility from rich, full deliveries on "We Got a Love Thang" to her compassionate intonation on the ballad "Inside That I Cried." This outstanding album spawned five superb singles. The title track "Finally" and "We Got a Love Thang" employ that rapid dancehall groove better known as house music. They respectively claimed number 26 and number 38 on the *Billboard* R&B charts. The gold-selling "Finally" reached number five on the *Billboard* pop charts. "Keep on Walkin'" has a swingin' hip-hop edge with a house music flair. It had the highest outing on the R&B charts at number three. Peniston tenderly caresses the grieving lyric of the percolating ballad "Inside That I Cried." This single sealed the top ten. "Crazy Love" is a midtempo number with an alluring chorus melody enhanced by a brisk string arrangement. It peaked at 31. The label stopped at five, but this album warranted additional releases. Ce Ce Peniston demonstrates her unyielding talent on this entire, solidly produced collection. *—Craig Lytle*

Thought 'Ya Knew / Jan. 25, 1994 / A&M ✦✦✦

Ce Ce Peniston's second album, *Thought 'Ya Knew*, did not deserve the fate it received—that of the dreaded sophomore slump. Her debut album, *Finally*, yielded one of the 1990s' biggest and most unforgettable dance songs, "Finally," making her a huge star among the dance community. The big mistake was trying to market her to an R&B audience, which is what her label did with her sophomore album. The first two singles, "I'm Not Over You" and "I'm In the Mood," were fun, jazzy, finger-snapping R&B cuts, but came nowhere near "Finally" in terms of artistic achievement, dancefloor potential, or chart performance. The third single, "Hit By Love," was closer in spirit to her early dance hits, but by that time the steam had worn off and the song didn't become a hit. This album, however, is definitely not a bad album. It contains several agreeable cuts, including "Searchin'," the clubby "Give What I'm Givin'," the funky, reggae-tinged "Through These Doors," "If You Love Me, I Will Love You," the gospel-infused "I Will Be Received," and the house track "Keep Givin' Me Your Love," which later garnered some attention due to its inclusion in the *Pret-a-Porter* soundtrack. However, this album is not free of filler, most evident on boring, assembly-line ballads like "Forever in My Heart" and "Whatever It Is." Nonetheless, it didn't deserve its lousy fate—Peniston fell victim to misguided marketing on her record label's part. *—Jose F. Promis*

I'm Movin' On / Sep. 9, 1996 / A&M ✦✦✦

20th Century Masters—The Millennium Collection: The Best of Ce Ce Peniston / Apr. 10, 2001 / Interscope ✦✦✦

Many artists in the mid-priced *20th Century Masters: The Millennium Collection* series had already been the subjects of more extensive greatest-hits compilations, but when Ce Ce Peniston's volume was released, it was the only collection of her singles on the market. And, at 12 tracks, it's not a bad overview of the dance club diva's career, either. All of Peniston's major club and urban radio hits are present, including two mixes of her breakthrough smash "Finally," and have been digitally remastered. For those who don't want to purchase Peniston's three albums (to date), this makes a perfect introduction. *—Steve Huey*

The Pentagons

f. 1958, San Bernadino, CA, **db.** 1961

Group / Doo Wop, R&B

The Pentagons are remembered for two 1961 hits, "To Be Loved (Forever)"—which peaked at number 48 nationally—and "I Wonder." The original lineup featured Joe Jones, Carl McGinnis, Bill James, Otis Munson, and brothers Kenneth Goodloe (lead) and Ted Goodloe and formed in 1958 in San Bernardino, CA, northeast of Los Angeles. Some time during this early period, Munson left and James was later replaced by Odie Jones, Joe's brother, making for two sets of brothers in the Pentagons' lineup. A trip to Los Angeles that same year attracted the attention of George Motola's Fleet International, a label Motola owned with Lee Silver. The group recorded their first single, "You'll Be Coming Home Soon," which Motola released under the name the Shields. They were forced to change their name to the Pentagons after discovering a local act from Los Angeles had a hit that year under the same name ("You Cheated").

The group's next single would be the 45 that most doo wop fans and collectors remember them fondly for, the graceful and understated ballad "To Be Loved (Forever)," written by Ken Goodloe. The single was a regional hit in late 1960 and was immediately picked up for national distribution and reissue on Donna Records, a division of Bob Keene's Del-Fi Records. It later broke wide open after it was played on Dick Clark's TV show and in February of 1961, it peaked nationally at number 48 pop.

After this initial glimmer of success, Lester Sill joined Silver and Motola as the Pentagons' managers. The group's next single was another Motola production, "I Like the Way You Look at Me," which was once again licensed to Donna Records. Though not a major hit, it still carried over that string-laden sound the Pentagons were becoming known for. The B-side, "Down at the Beach," written by Joe and Odie Jones, was a minor hit as well (although this happened two years after it was recorded). Beginning with the very distinctive "Billboard March"—a calliope-like flourish heard at the start of a circus and also used in James Darren's number-two 1961 hit "Goodbye Cruel World"—the lyrics of "Down at the Beach" really captured the whole sunny SoCal surf and sand scene—"you look good in your short shorts... I really go for your ta-yan."

After this release, the Pentagons signed to Jamie Records, with whom Sill had connections, causing Keene to lose interest in promoting the Donna-released second single. Their final hit was the Jamie-released "I Wonder (If Your Love Will Ever Belong to Me)" which peaked at number-84 pop in October of 1961, but with no additional hits forthcoming, the group disbanded and faded into obscurity. Lester Sill, incidentally, also produced Duane Eddy's early recordings for Jamie. He passed away on October 31, 1994, in Los Angeles. *—Bryan Thomas*

● **Golden Classics** / Aug. 30, 1994 / Collectables ✦✦✦✦✦

People's Choice

f. 1971, Philadelphia, PA

Group / Philly Soul, Funk, Urban

Vocalist/keyboardist Frank Brunson formed People's Choice in Philadelphia in the early '70s. Drummer/percussionist David Thompson, vocalists Valerie Brown and Marc Reed, guitarists Darnell Jordan and Johnnie Hightower, keyboardists Clifton Gamble and Bill Rodgers, and bassist/vocalist Stanley Thomas were in the original lineup. Despite the vocalists, the group's biggest hits were instrumentals. They were signed to Philadelphia International and worked with Leon Huff on the funk and disco gem "Do It Any Way You

Wanna," among the great pieces of '70s Philly dance music. It was their lone R&B chart-topper, and it peaked at number 11 on the pop charts in 1975. They previously recorded for Phil-L.A. of Soul, and "I Likes to Do It" had reached number nine in 1971. They remained on Philadelphia International until 1982, when they recorded for TPC. They also issued one LP on Mercury, *Strikin'*, in 1984. *—Ron Wynn*

Boogie Down U.S.A. / 1975 / Philadelphia International ♦♦♦♦

If you asked five different R&B experts what the first disco songs were, you might get five different answers. It has been argued that the disco beat was born in Philadelphia in 1972, when Jerry Butler recorded his fast, ultra-danceable version of the Kenny Gamble & Leon Huff classic "One Night Affair" (which had been previously recorded by the O'Jays in 1969). Even if Butler's hit wasn't the very first disco single, it was definitely among the first. It's inaccurate to give Philly all the credit for disco's birth—Isaac Hayes and Barry White, neither of whom are Philadelphians, have been exalted as two of disco's early architects—but the city deserves some of the credit. When Philly soul gave way to Philly disco-soul, one of the groups that got in on the action was the People's Choice. The group's 1975 smash "Do It Any Way You Wanna" is a definitive example of Philly dance music, as are several other disco-funk gems on *Boogie Down U.S.A.*, including "Party Is a Groovy Thing" and the clever "Nursery Rhymes." However, not everything on this 1975 LP (which was produced by Gamble & Huff at Philly's legendary Sigma Sound Studios) is dance-oriented. The playful "Are You Sure" and the ballad "Don't Send Me Away" are pure Philly soul, and the instrumental "Mickey D's" contains jazz overtones. Without question, *Boogie Down U.S.A.* is the most essential LP that the People's Choice recorded in the '70s. *—Alex Henderson*

We Got the Rhythm / 1976 / Philadelphia International ♦♦♦

The People's Choice went through its share of personnel changes in the '70s and '80s. When the Philadelphia outfit recorded *We Got the Rhythm* for TSOP/Philadelphia International in 1976, its lineup included original members Frankie Brunson (lead vocals/keyboards), David Thompson (drums, percussion), and Darnell Jordan (rhythm guitar) as well as more recent additions like Guy Fiske (lead guitar), Roger Andrews (bass), and Donald Ford (keyboards). Despite changes in membership, the People's Choice never had a problem being recognizable; the band was as distinctive on uptempo disco-funk numbers as it was on romantic soul ballads. But there are no ballads on *We Got the Rhythm*, which usually takes dead aim at the dance floor. This vinyl LP (which Kenny Gamble & Leon Huff produced at Philly's famous Sigma Sound Studios) wasn't a huge radio hit, although club DJs found infectious tracks like "Jam, Jam, Jam (All Night Long)," "Cold Blooded and Down-Right Funky," and the instrumental "Movin' in All Directions" to be quite useful. The People's Choice detours into jazz-influenced territory on two sleek Leon Huff instrumentals, "Opus-De Funk" and "A Mellow Mood." Neither are straight-ahead jazz, but they do bring jazz overtones to an R&B foundation. *We Got the Rhythm* isn't as essential as the People's Choice's previous album, *Boogie Down U.S.A.*, but it's a generally pleasing effort that confirmed fans will enjoy. *—Alex Henderson*

● **Golden Classics** / Nov. 5, 1996 / Collectables ♦♦♦♦

Golden Classics isn't so much a greatest-hits collection as it is a repackaging of People's Choice's first album for Philadelphia International, with a few B-sides thrown in for good measure. That album, 1975's *Boogie Down U.S.A.*, recast the sometimes-gritty funk group in the Gamble & Huff mold, featuring a four-on-the-floor pulse and an overall smoother production. Joined here by members of MFSB, it's not surprising that they sound like a tougher version of that group on their crossover pop and R&B hit "Do It Any Way You Wanna." The studio gloss sometimes works against the gruff voice of Frankie Brunson, but ultimately prevails on instrumentals like "Boogie Down USA" and minimal vocal tracks with the lyric reduced to a basic chant, like "Party Is a Groovy Thing." Certainly the strongest album of People's Choice, and as such, the best place to start listening. *—Wade Kergan*

I Likes to Do It / Jun. 27, 2000 / Jamie/Guyden ♦♦♦

Collecting both sides from all four of their 1971-1972 Phil-L.A. of Soul singles, and adding seven previously unreleased songs from the same era, this is notably rawer than their more famous material for TSOP later in the decade. Indeed, it's rawer than almost any soul-funk from the period that had a commercial impact, as three of these cuts did: "I Likes to Do It" made number-nine R&B (and the pop Top 40) in 1971, and "The Wootie-T-Woo" and "Let Me Do My Thing" were low-charting R&B singles. The People's Choice's stock-in-trade at this stage was loose, almost improvised-sounding funky workouts with basic but catchy riffing, semi-scatted vocals, and cool electric-keyboard vamping, often devised by connecting a guitar wah-wah pedal to an organ. The what-ya-play-is-what-ya-hear production is a refreshing contrast to the slicker sounds that were so much more prevalent in early-'70s Philly soul. And that's the way it should have been: when they tried to play conventional vocal sweet soul with strings on "Magic," they sounded far more ordinary. The seven previously unissued tracks (including a much different version of "Magic") are nearly on par with the singles, though perhaps these lean toward more basic riffs and words (this is in a group that favored minimal song construction to begin with). Simplicity can be a virtue, though, and this is damned infectious stuff, really. It's quite a find for early funk fans, to whom this compilation is highly recommended. *—Richie Unterberger*

Perfect Gentlemen

f. 1988, Boston, MA

Group / Contemporary R&B, Urban, Teen Pop

Since he'd already struck gold twice in unearthing and/or producing teen groups, Maurice Starr tried once more in 1990 with Perfect Gentlemen, a trio of Boston youths all between 11 and 13. Corey Blakey, Tyrone Sutton, and Starr's son, Maurice Jr., went out on tour with New Kids on the Block in 1990 and also released *Rated PG* on Columbia. When they landed a Top Ten pop hit with "Ooh La La (I Can't Get Over You)," it seemed Starr had done it again. But they haven't been heard from since. *—Ron Wynn*

● **The Perfect Gentlemen** / 1989 / CBS ♦♦♦♦

Former New Edition and New Kids on the Block producer Maurice Starr found a fresh kiddie group to push into the urban contemporary wars in the early '90s with Perfect Gentlemen. They had the cheekiness and fresh-scrubbed qualities; they just didn't get the songs. Not even Starr could make them into commercial giants. The album did make it into the lower pop rungs, but then stalled. *—Ron Wynn*

Rated PG / 1990 / Columbia ♦♦♦

Freddie Perren

Producer, Arranger / Urban, Disco, Soul, Motown, Funk

Songwriter/producer/keyboardist Freddie Perren's first big break came as a member of the Corporation, the songwriter/producer/arranger collective behind the early Motown hits of the Jackson 5 including their three consecutive number-one pop hits, "I Want You Back," "ABC," and "The Love You Save." The other members were Motown founder Berry Gordy, Fonce Mizell, and Deke Richards. The creative quartet's work appears on many of the Jackson 5's albums. Perren's post-Motown hits include the following number-one pop hits: Yvonne Elliman's "If I Can't Have You," Gloria Gaynor's "I Will Survive," the Miracles' "Love Machine," Peaches & Herb's "Reunited," and the Sylvers' "Boogie Fever."

Shortly after moving to California from Washington, D.C., Perren and bassist Fonce Mizell met guitarist Deke Richards. They wrote a song called "I Wanna Be Free." They thought about shopping the song to Motown acts Gladys Knight & the Pips or Diana Ross. Motown president Berry Gordy suggested some revisions and instead recorded the song on a newly signed teenage five-member brothers singing group from Gary, IN, that he was grooming. "I Want You Back" parked at number-one R&B for four weeks and number-one pop in late 1969. Following was "ABC," the Jackson 5's second consecutive number-one single, topping *Billboard*'s R&B chart and holding down the top spot of its pop chart for two weeks in the spring of 1970. "The Love You Save" (number-one R&B in the summer of 1970) also held down the top spot on the pop charts for two weeks.

From the group's *Third Album* came "Mama's Pearl," which held the number-two R&B/pop spots for two weeks in early 1971. "Goin' Back to Indiana" was never released as a single, but it received an amazing amount of radio play (very unusual in those days) and was the title of the Jackson 5's 1971 ABC-TV special that guest starred Bill Cosby and Tom Smothers. Their 1971 Corporation-produced album *Maybe Tomorrow* boasted the original version of "Never Can Say Goodbye" (number-one R&B/number-two pop for three weeks) and its flip side, the lilting "She's So Good." The Corporation also produced a hit for Martha & the Vandellas, "Bless You." For Michael Jackson, they produced "Ben."

Perren, Mizell, and Richards planned to release albums as the Corporation, but that never happened. Mizell and Perren worked on tracks by Edwin Starr and scored the soundtrack of the 1973 Fred Williamson/American International movie *Hell Up in Harlem*. All three went on to have impressive careers. Freddie Perren produced post-Smokey hits on the Miracles and also produced former Spinners lead singer G.C. Cameron's classic heart-tugging ballad "It's So Hard to Say Goodbye to Yesterday" from the classic 1975 American International movie *Cooley High*. In 1978, Perren signed an old friend from D.C., Herb Fame, and his co-singer, Linda "Peaches" Green, to his production company, MVP Productions. Through him, the duo inked a deal with Polydor Records. Their first Polydor single, "Shake Your Groove Thing," went gold and peaked at number-four R&B and number-five pop in late 1978. While the creamy ballad "Reunited" seemed an unlikely follow-up to the disco-oriented "Shake . . . ," the naysayers were shocked when it earned platinum status, holding on to the number-one spot for four weeks on both the R&B and pop charts during spring 1979. *—Ed Hogan*

The Persuaders

f. 1969, New York, NY

Group / Smooth Soul, Soul, Pop-Soul, Urban

This group made a pair of marvelous heartache ballads in 1971, but have the unfortunate legacy of having their finest cuts turned into pop hits via covers. Lead singer Douglas Scott, whose nickname appropriately was "Smokey," Willie Holland, James Barnes, and Charles Stodghill formed in New York in 1969. They signed with Atlantic in the early '70s and had their lone R&B chart-topper in 1971, the shattering classic "Thin Line Between Love & Hate." It was also their only gold single. The follow-up was nearly as strong; "Love's Gonna Pack Up (And Walk Out)" reached number eight on the R&B charts, but had no crossover appeal. They continued on Win & Lose until 1973, then moved to Atco, where "Some Guys Have All the Luck" was a number-seven R&B single in 1973. It was their final hit, though they kept recording until the late '70s, doing their last session for Calla. Besides the Pretenders re-doing "Thin Line Between Love & Hate," Rod Stewart had a Top Ten pop hit with his version of "Some Guys Have All the Luck" in 1984. *—Ron Wynn*

The Persuaders / 1973 / Atco ♦♦♦♦

While the Persuaders second LP doesn't contain any thing as cold-blooded as "Thin Line Between Love & Hate," or the magnitude of the syncopated "Love's Gonna Pack Up (And Walk Out)," it's a more even affair than their debut. "Peace in the Valley of Love" gets under your skin, you appreciate it, the more you hear the soothing, floater. "Bad, Bold & Beautiful Girl," is the complete opposite, it's boisterous, with a noisy sounding track, and some of the hokiest bass singing since the '50s. The dreamy "What Is the Definition of Love," understated beauty is a quiet storm, Smokey Douglas, shows he can handle the subtle leads, as well as the in your face sagas. "You Still Love Me (After All You've Been Through)" packs a New York wallop, the theatrical drama comes complete with a man to woman rap, and as-if-somebody-died backing vocals by the Persuaders. Smokey recites a laundry list of ordeals that he's put his woman through and sounds surprise when he sings You Still Love Me, You Still Love Me, After All, You've Been Through. *—Andrew Hamilton*

The Best Thing That Ever Happened to Me / 1974 / Atco ♦♦♦
A worthy album by one of New York's most soulful groups. Lead singer Douglas "Smokey" Scott could belt a lyric as convincingly as anyone. Their soulful rendition of "Best Thing Ever Happened to Me" probably surprised Jim Weatherly (the composer) with its earthiness. "Some Guys Have All the Luck," which did well on the charts, sounds better than Rod Stewart's Top Ten remake. They get real on "We're Just Trying to Make It," an epic song about a man, his woman, and their issues. "Stay With Me" is irresistible with its sweet unison backing vocals and building lead. *—Andrew Hamilton*

● **Thin Line Between Love & Hate** / 1974 / Collectables ♦♦♦♦♦
The Persuaders are best-known for their biggest hit song "Thin Line Between Love & Hate," and rightly so. Detailing the moment when relationships breakdown in a storm of suspicion, jealousy and, ultimately, violence, it's a melodramatic masterpiece, one of the greatest soul singles of the '70s, arguably one of the greatest ever. That the rest of their debut album of the same name doesn't live up to such high expectations shouldn't be a surprise, given how good that song is. Still, it's hard to listen to the record and wish there wasn't at least one other song close to its brilliance. That's not to say that there aren't good songs here, or that the group is without talent, because neither statement is true. They have a fairly sold set of material here, and the group is blessed with deep vocal talent, not just in their lead Douglas Scott. What prevents the album from being as transcendent as that record are the twin problems of genericness and inconsistency. Generic shouldn't be read harshly, however—this is "generic" meaning that it's a genre album of its time, trying a little bit of everything from heartbreak ballads, uptempo tunes, lush romance to silly pop-soul and gritty mournful regret. This sampler nature makes it inconsistent, although there are several highlights along the way, notably the second single "Love's Gonna Pack Up (And Walk Out)." As a period piece, it's fine, particularly for those looking to delve deeper into the sound of '70s soul. Those that do pick it up shouldn't expect anything as good as "Thin Line Between Love and Hate," though that itself is worth the price of admission. *—Stephen Thomas Erlewine*

It's All About Love / 1976 / Calla ♦♦♦
The Persuaders tried their luck with Norman Harris, the producer of a host of Philly artists and a carpetbagging Eddie Kendricks; however, little magic resulted from this association. "It's Love" has a lilting charm but no substance—the swirling strings make the song unbearable. Smokey Douglas ad libs to the rhythm on "Count the Ways," but the chorus needs a soul injection. "I Need Love" is a heartfelt, enthusiastic ballad, while "Quickest Way Out" includes a vocal and instrumental version. The Poindexter Brothers offer the klutzy, overarranged "Sure Shot," and "Two Women" suffers from overproduction and only gets interesting when Douglas ad libs à la Teddy Pendergrass. "Hey Sister," written by Rudy Love, stands out as the premier track: Douglas' lead reeks with passion, while the Persuaders chant and chime soulfully in the background. *—Andrew Hamilton*

The Persuasions

f. 1966, Bedford-Stuyvesant, NY
Group / Acappella, Soul
A cappella singing has been part of the African-American musical tradition since the days of slavery. Despite the recent success of the hi-tech a cappella group Take 6, the tradition has suffered a steady decline to the point where it is rare even in gospel circles. The Persuasions, though, are resolutely a cappella. Their chart successes have been minimal (two fleeting R&B entries in 1974-1975), but they carry forward the tradition without appearing ossified. Airplay will probably always elude them—and with it the really big breakthrough—but their music has been a consistently enjoyable sidebar, and never one that has simply reeked of revivalism, remaining fresh through releases like 1993's *Toubo's Song*, 1994's *Right Around the Corner*, and 1996's *Sincerely*. 1999's *On the Good Ship Lollipop* was a foray into children's music, while a year later the group issued *Frankly A Cappella: The Persuasions Sing Zappa* and *Might as Well . . . The Persuasions Sing Grateful Dead*. *—Colin Escott*

Acappella / 1970 / Bizarre ♦♦♦♦♦
This is the first Persuasions release, recorded live in Los Angeles. The sound is a little two-dimensional, but this recording captures the spirit of joy in live harmonizing, which is the very essence of the Persuasions. Includes great takes on the Temptations's "Don't Look Back" and the Drifters's "Up on the Roof," making manifest the intrinsic connection between '50s doo wop and '60s group singing. *—Rob Bowman*

We Came to Play / 1971 / Collectables ♦♦♦♦♦
Better produced than their debut, *We Came to Play* continues what became a formula for the Persuasions—covering '50s and '60s classics (the latter most usually taken from the Motown and Curtis Mayfield portfolios), the occasional Tin Pan Alley standard, and judiciously chosen pop/rock covers. In the '70s, a cappella singing was a lost art the Persuasions were determined to keep alive. *—Rob Bowman*

Spread the Word / 1972 / Capitol ♦♦♦♦♦
Why the Persuasions were never able to generate much action while on commercial labels is a mystery. They made fine albums for A&M and Capitol, but just couldn't get any hits. While it was true that '70s tastes were geared more toward funk, "sweet" soul, and vocal groups with elaborate arrangements and production, there still should have been room for the Persuasions' classic harmonizing. At any rate, this was one of a couple of fine albums they made in the early '70s for Capitol. *—Ron Wynn*

Street Corner Symphony / 1972 / Capitol ♦♦♦♦♦
On this, their highest-charting recording, the Persuasions give more of the same, including gorgeous reworkings of Bob Dylan's "The Man in Me" and The Impressions' "People Get Ready." *—Rob Bowman*

We Still Ain't Got No Band / 1973 / MCA ♦♦♦
Maintaining their high level of consistency, the Persuasions shy away from Motown here and delve into the blues, tackling Jimmy Hughes' "Steal Away" and a medley of Jimmy Reed's "Baby What You Want Me to Do?" and "Bright Lights, Big City." Superb. *—Rob Bowman*

I Just Want to Sing With My Friends / 1974 / A&M ♦♦♦

More than Before / 1974 / A&M ♦♦♦
An often spectacular mid-'70s date by the Persuasions, singing at the peak of their harmonizing powers and on a major label that gave them great production and engineering. Even on songs that weren't first-rate, their interaction, Jerry Lawson's soaring leads, and the bass/baritone support of Jimmy Hayes and Herbert Rhoad were magnificent. *—Ron Wynn*

Live in the Whispering Gallery / 1976 / Hammer N Nails ♦♦

● **Chirpin'** / 1977 / Elektra ♦♦♦♦♦
After two ill-advised albums for A&M with instruments, the Persuasions returned to their a cappella roots. No longer popular enough to chart, the music was in no way diminished. Highlights include a swinging version of the gospel standard "It's Gonna Rain" and a dramatic reading of Tony Joe White's "Willie and Laura Mae Jones." *—Rob Bowman*

Comin' at Ya / 1979 / Flying Fish ♦♦♦

No Frills / 1984 / Rounder ♦♦♦
The Persuasions celebrated their 20th anniversary with this 1986 set blending classics and more contemporary material. They covered vintage songs from the Drifters and Clyde McPhatter, included a lengthy, more modern/dance tune in Candi Staton's "Victim" and added a holiday number with "What Are You Doing New Year's Eve." They brought back former second tenor Joe Russell for four tracks, among them the concluding "Slip Sliding Away." There was also a creditable gospel selection "I Wonder Do You Love the Lord Like I Do." Bev Rohlehr provided an interesting additional element with a woman's voice in the harmonies on six cuts. *—Ron Wynn*

Good News / 1988 / Rounder ♦♦♦

Right Around the Corner / 1994 / Bullseye Blues ♦♦♦♦♦
With *Right Around the Corner*, the Persuasions continue their trademark a cappella vocal stylings reminiscent of a 1950s New York street corner. Yet, through their choice of material and interpretation, the group retains a sense of freshness and vitality absent in many other revivalist groups. Though a song such as "Oh, Heavenly Salvation" is an enjoyable, yet standard, choice, covering Frank Zappa's "Lucille Has Messed My Mind Up" or reworking the overt sexuality of "Little Red Rooster" until it is almost a spiritual, shows just how modern and irreverent the Persuasions can be. *—Steve Kurutz*

Sincerely / 1996 / Bullseye Blues ♦♦♦
Listening to the Persuasions sing can be an enlightening experience. A true a cappella group in the sense that they use no instrumentation other than the human voice, their songs are as rich in tone and texture as any full-scale band. On *Sincerely*, the group pays debt to their street-corner singing roots of the past, while doing much to update an old sound and old material. Jerry Lawson's powerful lead singing dominates the album and its standout tracks such as "Building a Home" and "Five Hundred Miles," while Jimmy Hayes fills out the bottom, adding depth to the sound and taking lead on "Can't Do Sixty No More." *—Steve Kurutz*

Man, Oh Man: The Power of the Persuasions / Jun. 3, 1997 / Capitol ♦♦♦♦♦
Man, Oh Man: The Power of the Persuasions is a terrifc overview of the a cappella group's early-'70s recordings for Capitol. The band was at the peak of their powers during this era, as this stellar retrospective proves. Although *Man Oh Man* doesn't contain their biggest hits, it does contain some of their best work, including covers of "Buffalo Soldier" and "People Get Ready," making it a first-rate retrospective and introduction. *—Stephen Thomas Erlewine*

On the Good Ship Lollipop / May 18, 1999 / Rhino ♦♦♦♦
After more than three decades of spreading the gospel of a cappella, the Persuasions recorded their first album for children. Though it's aimed primarily at the little ones, say one- to five-year-olds, it's hard not to enjoy it no matter your age. There are a host of treats, including "Teddy Bears' Picnic," "A Cappella Fellas" (written for the group by label head and producer Leib Ostrow), and the title track. The story that Jerry Lawson spins to frame "On Top of Spaghetti" is not to be missed. *—Ross Boissoneau*

Frankly A Cappella: The Persuasions Sing Zappa / Apr. 4, 2000 / Rhino ♦♦♦
Frank Zappa gave the vocal group the Persuasions their first chance by signing them to his record label, Straight, in 1969. In 2000, the six-piece a cappella formation recorded a heartfelt tribute to the composer by recording doo wop renditions of a cross section of his songs. Some choices were inevitable, like "The Meek Shall Inherit Nothing," which the group had already performed on the project *Zappa's Universe*, and the already doo woppy "Any Way the Wind Blows" and "Love of My Life." But by adding obscure numbers like "Electric Aunt Jemima" and "Harder Than Your Husband," the Persuasions clearly intended to surprise the fans—and it works. Their inventive arrangements hide many gems, such as the word "duodenum" embedded in the theme from *Lumpy Gravy*. At the end of "Harder Than Your Husband," a man and a woman act out a fight, slipping in the discussion such Zappa conceptual-continuity icons as a sofa, a pair of zirconia-encrusted tweezers, and Frenchie the poodle. The three "Interlude" tracks attempt at experimental dialogues à la *Lumpy Gravy* and are less satisfying, but don't even total a minute. A tribute album would not be complete without special guests: Zappa alumni Bruce Fowler, Bobby Martin, and Mike Keneally contribute to one track each and reappear for "Tears Begin to Fall." Vocal group fans may feel a bit disoriented by this unlikely repertoire and the hermetic references, but Zappa aficionados, especially those who dig the man's doo wop songs, will find *Frankly A Cappella* to be an entertaining work of love. *—François Couture*

Might as Well . . . The Persuasions Sing Grateful Dead / Oct. 10, 2000 / Arista ♦♦♦♦♦
The year 2000 has been a busy year for these veteran, a cappella stalwarts. April saw the release of their highly acclaimed *Frankly A Cappella*, which is the Persuasions' tribute album to the man who gave them their first major-label break, Frank Zappa. The complex vocal arrangements are nothing short of transcendent, fully expressing Zappa's R&B roots with a surplus of soul and creativity. It is a shot from left field that ranks with the Persuasions' very best album, *Chirpin'*. Therefore, one could be forgiven for supposing that *Might as Well: The Persuasions Sing Grateful Dead*, released a scant six months after the Zappa affair, would be an inferior rush job seeking to cash in on the success of its predecessor. One would, thankfully, be quite wrong. The same love, care, and creativity is put into the Grateful Dead tribute as was placed in the Zappa homage. In other words, this release is somewhat expected, and it still delivers. The song choices are more eclectic than might be expected, leaning heavily on the Garcia/Hunter songbook. A special surprise is a little-performed, later-period Garcia/Hunter composition "Lazy River Road." The Persuasions take Hunter's dewy metaphors to church when they harmonize the lyric "All night long I sang love's sweet song/Down where the water flowed/Down along Lazy River Road." Even the obvious covers shine with originality. Lead singer Jerry Lawson delivers "Bertha" as a knock-down soul shout. Bass singer Jimmy Hayes takes the lead on "Ship of Fools," slowing it down to a tantalizing, extended lope. Bob Weir's "One More Saturday Night," on the other hand, is sped up a notch or three and rocked to the rafters. A wise touch is the inclusion of very occasional instrumentation from former Dead keyboardist Vince Welnick on "Ship of Fools" and "One More Saturday Night," and *Aoxomoxoa* sideman Pete Grant on pedal steel for "It Must Have Been the Roses." Former Garcia Old and in the Way bandmate Peter Rowan soulfully trades lead vocal chores with Jerry Lawson on "Sugaree." These guest touches help cement a Dead ambience, even among these mostly R&B arrangements. Thirty-five years into their career and the Persuasions are on a major roll. *—Steve Cooper*

The Persuasions Sing the Beatles / Feb. 26, 2002 / Chesky ♦♦♦♦

Phajja

Group / Urban, Contemporary R&B
A trio made up of two sisters transplanted from Chicago to Boston (Kena and Nakia Epps) and a Boston native, Karen Johnson, Phajja presents a light, classic R&B sound. As teenagers, the Epps sisters focused on studying dance and hoped for theatrical careers—Johnson always had dreams of being a singer. When the sisters moved to Boston, however, their focus changed and they began to pursue singing. They hooked up with Johnson and quickly won a recording contract—their debut album, *Seize the Moment*, was released by Warner Brothers Records in 1997. In 2000 they followed it up with a slickly produced sequel, *Meeting in the Ladies Room*, also issued by Warner Brothers. *—Stacia Proefrock*

Seize the Moment / Jun. 24, 1997 / Warner Bros. ♦♦♦♦

● **Meeting in the Ladies Room** / Oct. 26, 1999 / Warner Bros. ♦♦♦♦
Phajja has made good on all the sizzling promise of their 1997 debut *Seize the Moment*, only this time the talented trio turns up the thermostat by several degrees. This album is about their vision; their take on relationships today. It has a definite feeling and point of view. For *Meeting in the Ladies Room*, Phajja enlisted the expertise of Mario Winans (a member of Sean "Puffy" Combs' hitmen); Rick "Dutch" Cousin, who has worked on projects with Will Smith; production teammates Eric Benet and Demonté Posey; Somethin' for the People; Rappers Lil' Cease and Mr. Bristal, part of the famed Junior M.A.F.I.A. crew, lent their rhyming skills as well. The album's debut single, "Checkin' for Me," is a dramatic telling of a woman's expectations for a little TLC, with all three members trading off on lead vocals. "Slept" is Phajja's first foray into 100-proof hip-hop, with Lil' Cease rockin' the mic. The cleverly written "Hater" features ultra-tight harmonies and jazz overtones, while the dazzling "What's Going On" resembles an R&B opera. Nokio of Dru Hill wrote the verses, and they wrote the bridge. Much edgier than their debut, *Meeting in the Ladies Room* gives both clarity and vision to the trio's message. *—Paul Clifford*

The Pharaohs

f. 1969, Chicago, IL
Group / Jazz-Funk, Funk, Avant-Garde Jazz
The Pharaohs were one of the forgotten treasures of '70s R&B, a freewheeling jazz-funk congregation heavily influenced by Chicago's jazz avant-garde as well as on-the-one funk and African motifs. Unfortunately, they recorded only one album before Earth, Wind & Fire frontman Maurice White (who played in an early version of the Pharaohs) hired several of its members to form the Phoenix Horns, the justly celebrated horn section for Earth, Wind & Fire during the '70s.

The group was formed from several jazz bands active around Chicago's Affro Arts Theater, a community educational collective. One of the bands, the Jazzmen, was formed in the early '60s around trumpeter Charles Handy, trombone player Louis Satterfield, and alto Don Myrick (along with three who didn't survive later conglomerations: pianist Fred Humphrey, bassist Ernest McCarthy, and drummer Maurice White). The other main component of the Pharaohs was the Artistic Heritage Ensemble, who had already recorded one late-'60s LP with cornetist Philip Cohran, a veteran of Sun Ra's Arkestra and AACM. By the time of the Pharaohs' 1971 recording debut *Awakening*, the group included Handy, Myrick, and Satterfield plus Big Willie Woods on trombone, Oye Bisi and Shango Njoko Adefumi on African drums, Yehudah Ben Israel on guitar and vocals, Alious Watkins on trap drums, Derf Reklaw-Raheem on percussion and flute, and Aaron Dodd on tuba. Though the album's astonishing fusion of funk, jazz and Afro-beat earned them an assortment of die-hard fans and critics, the group's abstract inclinations hardly geared them for commercial success.

Back in the '60s, before the Pharaohs were formed, Handy, Satterfield, and Maurice White had often contributed to sessions at Chicago's Chess studios, so when White recorded a demo for a new band he wanted to form, both Handy and Satterfield appeared on it. After he signed to Warner Bros., they also began recording Earth, Wind & Fire material and eventually, were officially hired by White as the Phoenix Horns, with the addition of Pharaohs Yehudah Ben Israel and Rahm Lee, plus Michael Harris. The Pharaohs soldiered on until 1973, but called it quits without recording another studio album. Derf Reklaw became a respected world-jazz leader, while Woods and Dodd both appeared on many soul sessions around Chicago during the '70s. In 1996, the acid jazz label Luv 'N' Haight reissued *Awakening* and also released the 1972 live outing *In the Basement*. *—John Bush*

● **Awakening** / 1972 / Scarab ♦♦♦♦♦
Absolutely one of the finest funk albums of the early '70s, and one of the most unfairly neglected, 1971's *Awakening* is as important and exciting as any of Funkadelic's early albums from the same period. It doesn't have the mordant humor of George Clinton's best work, but these seven lengthy tracks are as powerful as early funk gets. A Chicago-based 11-piece ensemble (many members of which would go on to found Earth, Wind & Fire with Maurice White), the Pharaohs were led by their five-man-strong drum section, which included future world jazz pioneer Derf Reklaw and two percussionists specializing in African drumming. This polyrhythmic powerhouse takes center stage on all of the tracks, even the jazzy, ballad-tempo version of Smokey Robinson & the Miracles' "Tracks of My Tears." Every track is a winner, from the purely Afrocentric "Ibo" to the soulful groove of "Freedom Road," but the winner is the 13-and-a-half-minute closer, "Great House," on which the drums and horn section hurry each other along an expansive, loose-limbed groove while guitarist Yehudah Ben Israel unleashes some acid-style guitar solos similar to what Eddie Hazel was doing on tracks like Funkadelic's "Wars of Armageddon." This is as good as Afro-funk gets. *—Stewart Mason*

In the Basement / Nov. 26, 1996 / Luv N' Haight ♦♦♦♦
The Pharaohs only managed one release during their short lifetime, 1971's masterful *Awakening*. But when the San Francisco-based jazz-funk reissue label Luv 'N' Haight reissued *Awakening* in 1996, they also came out with a brand-new CD of mostly previously unreleased material called *In the Basement*. Most of this album was recorded live in 1972, after the already enormous 11-piece band had grown to include four more players, including a sixth drummer. The live tracks are fascinating, because where *Awakening* sounds like an earthier and more Afrocentric version of Earth, Wind & Fire (which several members of the Pharaohs would go on to found in 1973), the much loopier and more jazz-oriented tracks here sound more like Sun Ra jamming with the P-Funk All Stars. The 11-minute take on the Stylistics' "People Make the World Go Round" is absolutely indescribable, a mix of otherworldly horns and psychedelic guitars over a non-stop African-style groove. Other highlights include the all-rhythm "Drum Suite," a hypnotic blend of organic polyrhythms and chanting, and a stunning cover of Al Green's "Love and Happiness" that's the only studio track here. Not quite as wonderful as *Awakening*, *In the Basement* nonetheless makes one wish that the Pharaohs had lasted longer, just to see what would have happened next. *—Stewart Mason*

Esther Phillips (Esther Mae Jones)

b. Dec. 23, 1935, Galveston, TX, **d.** Aug. 7, 1984, Carson, CA
Vocals / Soul, Pop-Soul, R&B, Ballads, Jazz Blues
Esther Phillips was perhaps too versatile for her own good, at least commercially speaking; while she was adept at singing blues, early R&B, gritty soul, jazz, straight-up pop, disco, and even country, her record companies often lacked a clear idea of how to market her, which prevented her from reaching as wide an audience as she otherwise might have. An acquired taste for some, Phillips' voice had an idiosyncratic, nasal quality that often earned comparisons to Nina Simone, although she herself counted Dinah Washington as a chief inspiration. Phillips' career began when she was very young and by some accounts, she was already battling drug addiction during her teenage years; whenever her problems took root, the lasting impact on her health claimed her life before the age of 50.

Esther Phillips was born Esther Mae Jones in Galveston, TX, on December 23, 1935, and began singing in church as a young child. When her parents divorced, she split time between her father in Houston and her mother in the Watts area of Los Angeles. It was while she was living in Los Angeles in 1949 that her sister entered her in a talent show at a nightclub belonging to bluesman Johnny Otis. So impressed was Otis with the 13-year-old that he brought her into the studio for a recording session with Modern Records and added her to his live revue. Billed as Little Esther, she scored her first success when she was teamed with the vocal quartet the Robins (who later evolved into the Coasters) on the Savoy single "Double Crossin' Blues." It was a massive hit, topping the R&B charts in early 1950 and paving the way for a series of successful singles bearing Little Esther's name: "Mistrustin' Blues," "Misery," "Cupid Boogie," and "Deceivin' Blues." In 1951, Little Esther moved from Savoy to Federal after a dispute over royalties, but despite being the brightest female star in Otis' revue, she was unable to duplicate her impressive string of hits. Furthermore, she and Otis had a falling out, reportedly over money, which led to her departure from his show; she remained with Federal for a time, then moved to Decca in 1953, again with little success.

In 1954, she returned to Houston to live with her father, having already developed a fondness for the temptations of life on the road; by the late '50s, her experiments with hard drugs had developed into a definite addiction to heroin. She re-signed with Savoy in 1956, to little avail, and went on to cut sides for Federal and (in 1960) Warwick, which went largely ignored. Short on money, Little Esther worked in small nightclubs around the South, punctuated by periodic hospital stays in Lexington, KY, stemming from her addiction. In 1962, she was rediscovered while singing at a Houston club by future country star Kenny Rogers, who got her signed to his brother's Lenox label. Too old to be called Little Esther, she re-christened herself Esther Phillips, choosing her last name from a nearby Phillips gas station. Phillips recorded a country-soul reading of the soon-to-be standard "Release Me," which was released as a single late in the year. In the wake of Ray Charles' groundbreaking country-soul hit "I Can't Stop Loving You," "Release Me" was a smash, topping the R&B charts and hitting the Top Ten on both the pop and country charts. Back in the public eye, Phillips recorded a country-soul album of the same name, but Lenox went bankrupt in 1963.

Thanks to her recent success, Phillips was able to catch on with R&B giant Atlantic, which initially recorded her in a variety of musical settings to see what niche she might fill best. It was eventually decided to play up her more sophisticated side and accordingly, Phillips cut a blues-tinged album of jazz and pop standards; her string-laden remake of the Beatles song "And I Love Him" (naturally, with the gender changed) nearly made the R&B Top Ten in 1965 and the Beatles flew her to the U.K. for her first overseas performances. Encouraged, Atlantic pushed her into even jazzier territory for her next album, *Esther Phillips Sings*; however, it didn't generate much response and was somewhat eclipsed by her soul reading of Percy Sledge's "When a Woman Loves a Man" (again, with the gender changed), which made the R&B charts. Nonplussed, Atlantic returned to their former tactic of recording Phillips in as many different styles as possible, but none of the resulting singles really caught on and the label dropped her in late 1967.

With her addiction worsening, Phillips checked into a rehab facility; while undergoing treatment, she cut some sides for Roulette in 1969 and upon her release, she moved to Los Angeles and re-signed with Atlantic. A late-1969 live gig at Freddie Jett's Pied Piper club produced the album *Burnin'*, which was acclaimed as one of the best, most cohesive works of Phillips' career. Despite that success, Atlantic still wanted her to record pop tunes with less grit and when their next attempts failed to catch on, Phillips was let go a second time. In 1971, she signed with producer Creed Taylor's Kudu label, a subsidiary of his hugely successful jazz fusion imprint CTI. Her label debut, *From a Whisper to a Scream*, was released in 1972 to strong sales and highly positive reviews, particularly for her performance of Gil Scott-Heron's wrenching heroin-addiction tale "Home Is Where the Hatred Is." Phillips recorded several more albums for Kudu over the next few years and enjoyed some of the most prolonged popularity of her career, performing in high-profile venues and numerous international jazz festivals. In 1975, she scored her biggest hit single since "Release Me" with a disco-fied update of Dinah Washington's "What a Diff'rence a Day Makes" (Top Ten R&B, Top 20 pop), and the accompanying album of the same name became her biggest seller yet.

In 1977, Phillips left Kudu for Mercury, landing a deal that promised her the greatest creative control of her career. She recorded four albums for the label, but none matched the commercial success of her Kudu output and after 1981's *A Good Black Is Hard to Crack*, she found herself without a record deal. Her last R&B chart single was 1983's "Turn Me Out," a one-off for the small Winning label; unfortunately, her health soon began to fail, the culmination of her previous years of addiction combined with a more recent flirtation with the bottle. Phillips died in Los Angeles on August 7, 1984, of liver and kidney failure. *—Steve Huey*

Memory Lane: The Best Songs Little Esther Ever Recorded / 1959 / King ✦✦✦

And I Love Him! / 1965 / Atlantic ✦✦✦

A collection of "great love songs," *And I Love Him!* leads with the title track, a Beatles cover and an R&B hit, featuring a soft yet tremendously effective performance from the great Esther Phillips. Elsewhere Phillips wears her Dinah Washington influences well, stretching out her voice and exercising it with a sly, nuanced delivery while tackling a few excellent choices for material: "Shangri-La," "Out of the Blue," and "I Wish You Love." Surprisingly, she also exhibits a sure hand with some odd crossovers like "Moonglow & Theme From Picnic," "People," and "Girl From Ipanema." The arrangements, by Ralph Ellis, are definitely geared toward adult pop, but fortunately they're never so ostentatious that they get in the way of Phillips' idiosyncratic voice and gorgeous performances. *—John Bush*

Esther Phillips Sings / 1966 / Atlantic ✦✦✦

Though it lacked a big hit (like 1965's *And I Love Him!*), *Esther Phillips Sings* featured a better set of songs and better charts for her to sing in front of. With the opener "It's All Right With Me" leading the way, Oliver Nelson's seven arrangements bring out the best in Phillips, giving her plenty of space with light instrumentation but filling any available gaps with his strong, brassy orchestra. "A Taste of Honey" and "Just Say Goodbye" are also very successful, leaving the big-band era for a groovier period of swinging traditional pop. There are a few clunkers, mostly the fault of Ray Ellis' overly commercial arrangements on "The Shadow of Your Smile" and "You Can't Go Home Again," but everywhere else Esther Phillips bridges the world of R&B and jazzy pop with finesse and an easy charm. *—John Bush*

Burnin' / 1970 / Atlantic ✦✦✦✦✦

Live at Freddie Jett's Pied Piper / Jan. 31, 1970 / Atlantic ✦✦✦

From a Whisper to a Scream / 1972 / Columbia ✦✦✦✦✦

Her version of "Home Is Where the Hatred Is" became an anthem, plus proved tragically prophetic. *—Ron Wynn*

What a Diff'rence a Day Makes / Jul. 11, 1975 / Columbia ✦✦✦✦

Reading the credits of *What a Diff'rence a Day Makes*, one could easily assume that it is a jazz album. This 1975 LP was produced by Creed Taylor and arranged by guitarist Joe Beck; the other participants range from Michael Brecker on tenor sax, David Sanborn on alto sax, and Randy Brecker on trumpet to Steve Khan on guitar and Don Grolnick on keyboards. With that lineup, Esther Phillips could have easily delivered a first-class jazz album. But *What a Diff'rence a Day Makes* doesn't contain any jazz—not even jazz-funk or soul-jazz. It is, however, an excellent soul/disco outing. This LP is best known for its hit title song, an inspired disco version of a standard that has usually been heard in jazz and pre-rock pop settings. But the song works surprisingly well as disco, and the other tracks are equally impressive. Phillips is as soulful and convincing on the bluesy "I Can Stand a Little Rain" as she is on Gamble & Huff's "One Night Affair" (a Philadelphia soul classic that was recorded by Jerry Butler in 1972 and the O'Jays in 1969) and Ralph MacDonald's "Mister Magic." The latter is the gem that Grover Washington Jr. is best remembered for; while his famous version was instrumental jazz-funk, Phillips' is vocal-oriented soul. It should be noted that most of the jazz musicians who back Phillips on *What a Diff'rence a Day Makes* are not jazz snobs. The Brecker Brothers and Sanborn, for example, have done their share of R&B sessions, and they would probably be the first to tell you that this LP needs to be judged by R&B standards instead of jazz standards. And when R&B standards are applied, it is easy to conclude that *What a Diff'rence a Day Makes* is among Phillips' finest releases. *—Alex Henderson*

Confessin' the Blues / 1976 / Atlantic ✦✦✦✦✦

Here's Esther Are You Ready / 1979 / Mercury ✦✦✦

● **The Best of Esther Phillips (1962–1970)** / Mar. 4, 1997 / Rhino ✦✦✦✦✦

Although former child R&B star Esther Phillips really hit her mature peak in the '60s, commercially she had a hard time finding a niche. "Release Me," her uptown R&B version of a country song, made the pop Top Ten in 1962. But she only dented the charts occasionally over the course of the next decade, despite recording frequently in a number of styles, usually (but not always) for Atlantic. This two-CD, 40-song set is an excellent distillation of work that isn't well known even by R&B devotees, drawing from about half-dozen albums and numerous singles, mostly from Atlantic, but also including 45s she made for Roulette in 1969; about half of the songs on this two-fer, in fact, were never issued on an album. Phillips was to a degree damned by her versatility: too suave and refined to be classified as a straight soul singer, she takes on jazz, pop, show tunes, blues, the Beatles (her gender-morphed "And I Love Him" was a substantial hit), the Rolling Stones, Van Morrison, Bob Dylan, and more. Like Etta James, the Columbia-era Aretha Franklin, and Nina Simone, she was one of those singers that fell between genre cracks: not quite soul, rock, R&B, jazz, pop, or blues, though elements of all those styles were present in her work. Actually, she wasn't quite as good as any of those above-mentioned legends, with a nasal, edgy style that won't be to everyone's taste, somewhat reminiscent (though not as impressive as) Nina Simone's. The smooth arrangements mine the wide territory between Dinah Washington and Dionne Warwick, though again, she wasn't as well-equipped for success with such an approach as those two were. All these caveats aside, if you enjoy the work of any of the reference points listed above, you'll most likely like Esther's work on these recordings as well; she's just not quite in the same Hall of Fame class. *—Richie Unterberger*

Phyrework

Group / Quiet Storm, Funk, Soul

Phyrework was an obscure, little-known soul/funk outfit that recorded for Mercury in 1978. That year, Mercury released the band's self-titled debut album, which was produced by Con Funk Shun guitarist Michael Cooper. Although Con Funk Shun was big at the time, *Phyrework* fell between the cracks and received hardly any attention. The LP included a few examples of tough, hard-driving funk along the lines of the Bar-Kays, although its main emphasis was smooth, sophisticated pop-soul and quiet storm music. When *Phyrework* didn't sell, Mercury dropped the seven-member band, which never recorded a second album. The members of Phyrework included lead singer Clarence Pitts, guitarist Willie Smith, bassist Gerald Calhoun, keyboardist Frank Hames, trumpeter Jim Foster, saxophonist Bill Eden, and drummer John Bryant. *—Alex Henderson*

● **Phyrework** / 1978 / Mercury ✦✦✦

It's safe to say that 99 percent of the world's R&B fans have never heard of Phyrework, an obscure soul-funk band whose 1978 self-titled debut album received very little attention. Mercury/PolyGram didn't give this LP a very aggressive promotional push, and as a result, most R&B fans at the time didn't even know that it existed. Produced by Con Funk Shun guitarist Michael Cooper, *Phyrework* isn't earth shattering but it is generally competent and didn't deserve to be ignored. The record contains a few examples of tough, hard, Bar-Kays-like funk, including "Put Your Hands Up" and "My Funk." But most of the material favors a much smoother, lighter style of pop-soul. Think of the Average White Band performing "Soul Searching" or George Benson singing "Give Me the Night," and you will have an idea what type of sound Phyrework is going for on tunes like "Fly Away," "Make It Last," and "Dance With Me." *Phyrework* takes a sharp left turn on the totally unexpected "Mystic Mariner," a jazz-fusion instrumental that wouldn't have been out of place at a Return to Forever or Larry Coryell session. But make no mistake: this is an R&B release first and foremost. It's too bad the album fell between the cracks. *—Alex Henderson*

Wilson Pickett

b. Mar. 18, 1941, Prattville, AL

Vocals / Soul, Deep Soul, Southern Soul

Of the major '60s soul stars, Wilson Pickett was one of the roughest and sweatiest, working up some of the decade's hottest dancefloor grooves on hits like "In the Midnight Hour," "Land of 1000 Dances," "Mustang Sally," and "Funky Broadway." Although he tends to be held in somewhat lower esteem than more versatile talents like Otis Redding and Aretha Franklin, he is often a preferred alternative of fans who like their soul on the rawer side. He also did a good deal to establish the sound of Southern soul with his early hits, which were often written and recorded with the cream of the session musicians in Memphis and Muscle Shoals.

Before establishing himself as a solo artist, Pickett sang with the Falcons, who had a Top Ten R&B hit in 1962 with "I Found a Love." "If You Need Me" (covered by the Rolling Stones) and "It's Too Late" were R&B hits for the singer before he hooked up with Atlantic Records, who sent him to record at Stax in Memphis in 1965. One early result was "In the Midnight Hour," whose chugging horn line, loping funky beats, and impassioned vocals combined into a key transitional performance that brought R&B into the soul age. It was an R&B chart-topper and a substantial pop hit (number 21), though its influence was stronger than that respectable position might indicate: thousands of bands, black and white, covered "In the Midnight Hour" on-stage and record in the 1960s.

Pickett had a flurry of other galvanizing soul hits over the next few years, including "634-5789," "Mustang Sally," and "Funky Broadway," all of which, like "In the Midnight Hour," were frequently adapted by other bands as dance-ready numbers. The king of that hill, though, had to be "Land of 1000 Dances," Pickett's biggest pop hit (number six), a soul anthem of sorts with its roll call of popular dances, and covered by almost as many acts as "Midnight Hour" was.

Pickett didn't confine himself to the environs of Stax for long; soon he was also cutting tracks at Muscle Shoals. He recorded several early songs by Bobby Womack. He used Duane Allman as a session guitarist on a hit cover of the Beatles' "Hey Jude." He cut some hits in Philadelphia with Gamble & Huff productions in the early '70s. He even did a hit version of the Archies' "Sugar, Sugar." The hits kept rolling through the early '70s, including "Don't Knock My Love" and "Get Me Back on Time, Engine No. 9."

One of the corollaries of '60s soul is that if a performer rose to fame with Motown or Atlantic, he or she would produce little of note after leaving the label. Pickett, unfortunately, did not prove an exception to the rule. His last big hit was "Fire and Water," in 1972. He continued to be active on the tour circuit; his most essential music, all from the 1960s and early '70s, was assembled for the superb Rhino double-CD anthology *A Man and a Half*. *It's Harder Now*, his first new material in over a decade, followed in 1999. *—Richie Unterberger*

It's Too Late / 1963 / Double L ♦♦♦♦
Wilson Pickett like Aretha Franklin, is a Hall-of-Fame member from Detroit who Berry Gordy had the opportunity to record in the early '60s before they achieved fame with other companies but didn't. Gordy's refusal to record Franklin may be confusing, but it's no mystery why he didn't want to deal with the explosive, quick-tempered, sucker-punching Pickett. "If You Need Me," written by Pickett and Robert Bateman & Sonny Sanders (Satintones), is not quite as dynamic as "I Found a Love" recorded as a member of the Falcons, but it's close. It entered the Pop 100 at number-64 Pop, and would have done better if Atlantic hadn't released a cover by Solomon Burke. Burke's rendition made the pop Top 40, and went to number-two R&B in 1962, despite its inferiority to Pickett's electric performance. His blood curdling on-key scream is alive and well on "It's Too Late" the second reason either to seek this out-of-print album, or to locate these songs on CD. Pickett's tent revival delivery touches every nerve on the histrionic ballad. The upbeat "I Can't Stop" sounds Motown-ish, the backing vocals remind you of the Vandellas, former Falcon buddy Willie Schoefield wrote the number. The third single release from this LP "I'm Down to My Last Heartbreak" died a swift certain death toward the end of 1963. "R. B. Special," aka "Robert's Monkey" is an instrumental inspired by Robert Bateman who produced the bulk of this LP. Three labels released this album: Double L, Trip, and Wand as *Great Wilson Pickett Hits*. *—Andrew Hamilton*

In the Midnight Hour / 1965 / Rhino ♦♦♦
Wilson Pickett's first album, from 1965, was a bit of a hodgepodge, including singles from as far back as 1962. Three of these tracks were actually issued as singles by the Falcons (for whom Pickett sang lead) before he started his solo career; others were issued as singles before Pickett broke through as a national star with the title track. This 12-track album doesn't really suffer as a result, however. Besides the all-time classic "In the Midnight Hour," it includes the Mann/Weil-penned single "Come Home Baby," covered by several rock and soul artists; "Don't Fight It," which reached the R&B Top Ten in late 1965; "I'm Gonna Cry," a 1964 single Pickett wrote with fellow soul legend Don Covay; and "I Found a Love," the Falcons single that made the R&B Top Ten in 1962. Working with several collaborators (including Steve Cropper), Pickett himself wrote most of the tunes on this album. The record also featured the first recordings he made with the Stax rhythm section in Memphis—a combination that would yield much fine soul music throughout the rest of the '60s. The 1993 CD reissue of this album features extensive liner notes and session details. *—Richie Unterberger*

The Exciting Wilson Pickett / 1966 / Collectables ♦♦♦♦♦
Less of a hodgepodge than his debut *In the Midnight Hour* album, Pickett's second album established—if there had been any doubt—his stature as a major '60s soul man. The 12 tracks include his monster hits "634-5789," "Ninety-Nine and a Half (Won't Do)," "In the Midnight Hour," and "Land of 1000 Dances" (the last of which was his first Top Ten pop hit). Collectors will be more interested in the non-hit cuts, which are of nearly an equal level. These include covers of the R&B standards "Something You Got," "Mercy Mercy," and "Barefootin'"; several original tunes written in collaboration with Memphis soul greats Steve Cropper, Eddie Floyd, and David Porter; and Bobby Womack's "She's So Good To Me." It all adds up to one of the most consistent 1960s soul albums. The CD reissue of this 1966 record features detailed liner notes and session documentation. *—Richie Unterberger*

The Wicked Pickett / 1966 / Atlantic ♦♦♦♦♦
This is a fabulous album, done when Pickett was in the midst of his best period at Atlantic. It had everything—great songs, wonderful production and arrangements, and a hungry, galvanizing Wilson Pickett hollering, screaming, shouting, and soaring on anything he covered, from ballads to uptempo dance and midtempo wailers. It also has been deleted at present. *—Ron Wynn*

The Sound of Wilson Pickett / 1967 / Atlantic ♦♦♦♦♦
Here is a masterpiece, perhaps his finest '60s album. This wasn't a hits collection, but a batch of great singles. His version of "Funky Broadway" may still be the best; it was certainly the most swaggering and posturing, punctuated by his screams and jubilant cries. Pickett was all over the R&B charts in 1967, and this was one of three albums Atlantic issued on him that year. Each one was a classic. *—Ron Wynn*

I'm in Love / 1968 / Rhino ♦♦♦
No one was expecting a quiet storm album from Wilson Pickett in 1968, and that sure isn't what they got with *I'm In Love*, but the Wicked Pickett sounds a lot more convincing on this album's romantic numbers than anyone would have had a right to expect from one of the baddest cats of Southern soul. Of course, there aren't all that many romantic ballads here, but Pickett's rough-and-ready soul shouting manages to sound just as convincing on "Bring It on Home to Me" and "That Kind of Love" as he does on the pained "Jealous Love" and a properly intense rip through "Stagger Lee." Pickett makes the most of the songwriting contributions from frequent collaborators Bobby Womack and Don Covay, while Tommy Cogbill and his crew of Muscle Shoals session heavyweights offer music which keeps up with Pickett for guts, soul, and drive—no small statement, considering Pickett's richly deserved reputation as one of the strongest and most consistent artists of the period. Like most R&B albums of the period, *I'm In Love* sounds more like a set of tunes than a unified album, but it's a good set of tunes, performed with Pickett's usual high level of passion and skill, and if you're any kind of fan you'll revel in it. Rhino's CD reissue features four bonus cuts, including single mixes for "Jealous Love" and "I've Come a Long Way" and "Believe I'll Run On," which finds Pickett digging into his gospel roots. *—Mark Deming*

Midnight Mover / 1968 / Atlantic ♦♦♦
The title track was another of Pickett's smoking '60s soul singles; he rode the beat perfectly, and then concluded the song with a series of bloodcurdling screams and triumphant exhortations. He turned in several other equally assertive, defiant, and excellent uptempo and ballad performances, continuing a run of great Atlantic albums. *—Ron Wynn*

Hey Jude / 1969 / Atlantic ♦♦♦
Wilson Pickett and the Muscle Shoals session crew with whom he cut most of his best work thankfully had the good sense to not try to go psychedelic when the pop charts went all day-glo in the late 1960s, but that's not to say they didn't make an effort to change with the times. On *Hey Jude*, Pickett and producer Rick Hall decided to throw a couple of recent rock covers into the mix, and while Pickett's version of "Hey Jude" suggests that he isn't entirely sure what it is he's singing about, he still belts it out with his typical level of commitment and builds up to a proper fury at the end; he sounds more comfortable with the neo-biker bombast of "Born to Be Wild", a combination of artist and material that works far better than anyone would have a right to expect. But the most notable change in Pickett's approach for this album was the addition of Duane Allman on guitar; his wirey, blues-accented leads don't overpower the album, but they add a noticeably harder texture to the sound, and that seems to suit Pickett, one of the toughest soul shouters of his time, just fine. Most of the *Hey Jude* is dominated by hard Southern soul numbers like "A Man and a Half" and "Toe Hold," and Pickett, one of the most dependable performers on the 1960s soul scene, gives a typically *con brio* performance on all ten tracks, and the sharp report of the horn section and Allman's blistering guitar makes for music just as potent as the wail of the lead singer, which is not an accomplishment to be sneered at. *—Mark Deming*

Right On / 1970 / Atlantic ♦♦♦
Wilson Pickett encountered a momentary slump in 1970, as this album was his first for Atlantic in many years that stayed locked in the bottom rungs of the pop Top 200 albums. Pickett did get a fluke novelty hit with "Sugar, Sugar," maybe his worst soul smash ever. The album wasn't a total disaster, but everyone forgot about it quickly when Atlantic rushed out *Wilson Pickett in Philadelphia* later that year. *—Ron Wynn*

Wilson Pickett in Philadelphia / 1970 / Atlantic ♦♦♦♦♦
After cutting most of his hits in the laid-back but gritty environs of the Deep South (most notably Memphis and Muscle Shoals), in 1970 Wilson Pickett decided to move with the times and headed to Philadelphia, where his raw, bigger-than-life vocals were paired with the higher-gloss funk of songwriters and producers Kenny Gamble & Leon Huff. It may not have seemed like an ideal match on paper, but in the studio the results were inspired; on *Wilson Pickett in Philadelphia*, Gamble & Huff kept the studio band on the good foot at all times, and Pickett's always passionate and forceful performance added whatever grease that might have been missing from the Philly session cats. (Not that they sound lacking in spirit, as Pickett inspires fiery performances from the band on cuts like "Engine, Engine No. 9" and "Run, Joey, Run".) While a few of the songs aren't quite up to snuff (especially the just-plain-silly "International Playboy"), and Pickett sound a lot better when he's tom-catting than when he's lovelorn (as on "Help the Needy"), the star still fires on all cylinders regardless of the material, and Gamble & Huff create first-class accommodations for his performances without losing touch with Pickett's gritty soul in the process. *Wilson Pickett in Philadelphia* was one of his last truly memorable sets for Atlantic Records; in 1973, he'd leave the label for RCA Victor, and his career as an R&B hit-maker would never truly recover. *—Mark Deming*

Don't Knock My Love / 1971 / Atlantic ♦♦♦
This is his final definitive Atlantic session. The title track was vintage Pickett—a driving, syncopated bass and surging horn arrangement punctuated by his aggressive, spiraling lead and concluding with a robust shout and defiant exhortation. That set the stage for some sharp ballads and a couple of other nice uptempo cuts. "Don't Knock My Love, Pt. 1" was Pickett's last number-one R&B hit and a Top 20 pop smash. He left Atlantic shortly after the album peaked on the charts, returning to RCA and never enjoying similar success again. *—Ron Wynn*

Miz Lena's Boy / 1973 / RCA Victor ♦♦
This has a funny title, and a little bit better material and production for yet another Pickett attempt on RCA. He got a couple of chart hits, although the album itself didn't fare well. But it just wasn't the same; no longer was he roaring and belting out lyrics over a driving beat. Instead, he seemed like a mellow, almost restrained pop/soul type. *—Ron Wynn*

Wilson Pickett's Greatest Hits / 1973 / Atlantic ♦♦♦♦♦
Atlantic issued this Pickett greatest hits anthology to go along with two previous best-of packages that had been released in the late '60s and early '70s. Pickett's personal

problems and feuds with Atlantic studio heads led him to jump ship and head to RCA in 1973. The company rushed this out and kept them scrambling to fill the void because he was back on top and coming off a string of R&B hits and a successful album. As with the other packages, the Rhino set is now the one to grab. *—Ron Wynn*

Live in Japan / 1974 / RCA ✦✦

Tonight I'm My Biggest Audience / 1974 / RCA Victor ✦✦
This is a curious mid-'70s session for Pickett, one that left many people wondering if either he or RCA knew what was happening. The songs were mostly weak ballads or overproduced uptempo pop; Pickett's voice sounded disjointed, and his screams and cries woeful. This was his second RCA album, and it was no surprise when he left the label. *—Ron Wynn*

Join Me and Let's Be Free / 1975 / RCA Victor ✦✦
Wilson Pickett kept trying with RCA, going back to them in the mid-'70s after scoring one more hit album with Atlantic. He tried doing material with less soul and more pop production touches, toned down the familiar screams and cries, and stuck more to the melody. The results were unsatisfying all around. *—Ron Wynn*

Greatest Hits / 1976 / Atlantic ✦✦✦✦✦
Wilson Pickett was one of the most consistently strong performers of the great soul era of the 1960s, but like most R&B artists of the period he was strongest in his singles, not his albums, and while he cut some fine long-players in his day, a quality compilation is still the best place to get started with the Wicked Pickett's raw but passionate music. Originally released in 1973 as a two-LP set, *Wilson Pickett's Greatest Hits* got an upgrade to CD in the mid-'80s, and while it's value has since been supplanted by the more efficient *The Very Best of Wilson Pickett* and the more thorough *A Man and a Half: The Best of Wilson Pickett*, this still pulls together 24 stellar performances from Pickett's glory days (including three recordings from his early group the Falcons). A few of the choices are not especially well advised—while not exactly awful, Pickett's versions of "Sugar, Sugar" and "You Keep Me Hanging On" may be best left to history—but can you really argue with an album that includes "Mustang Sally," "Land Of 1,000 Dances," "In The Midnight Hour," "Funky Broadway," and "634-5789 (Soulsville U.S.A.)"? Not the very best Pickett collection, but still a good one, and fine value for money if you should find it in a bargain bin. *—Mark Deming*

American Soul Man / 1987 / Motown ✦✦
If Wilson Pickett had arrived at Motown 20 years earlier, the reaction would have been frenzied. But by the time he joined them in 1987, the once-great company was in the throes of a horrible slump. Pickett's late-'80s album for them was painful. It wasn't half bad as far as production and arrangements, and Pickett's vocals were better than anticipated. But the songs sounded third-rate, and while he did get one single onto the lower rungs of the charts, "Don't Turn Away," this wasn't the Pickett everyone loved or wanted to hear. *—Ron Wynn*

A Man and a Half: The Best of Wilson Pickett / Apr. 21, 1992 / Rhino ✦✦✦✦✦
A Man and a Half: The Best of Wilson Pickett is a double-disc set that collects the absolute cream of Pickett's early sides with the Falcons and all the highlights of his successful alliance with the Atlantic label. With "Mustang Sally," "In the Midnight Hour," "Ninety Nine & a Half," "Hey Jude," "Land of 1000 Dances," "You're So Fine," and "634-5789" all included, this excellent compilation should be one of the cornerstones of anybody's soul collection. *—Cub Koda*

★ **The Very Best of Wilson Pickett** / Apr. 20, 1993 / Rhino ✦✦✦✦✦
Rhino's 1993 collection *The Very Best of Wilson Pickett* remains the best single-disc anthology of the fiery soul singer's work, choosing 16 of his best tracks for Atlantic and presenting them in excellent remastered sound quality. Pickett never departed all that much from the rough, swaggering vocals that first made his name, but he was utterly electrifying within that style, setting the standard for Southern soul singers behind Otis Redding. All of Pickett's early signature hits—"In the Midnight Hour," "634-5789 (Soulsville, U.S.A.)," "Land of 1,000 Dances," "Mustang Sally," and "Funky Broadway"—lead off the disc in quick succession, capturing the emergence of Southern soul as a viable commercial style. But Pickett is just as charismatic on the rest of the material, nearly all of which made the R&B Top Ten and went underappreciated on the pop charts—he was just too much for white audiences to handle. Pickett did his best to shake up his formula—he cut a near-psychedelic soul tune, "Engine No. 9," with future Philly soul architects Kenny Gamble & Leon Huff; he helped bring Bobby Womack back into the music business by covering his "I'm in Love" and "I'm a Midnight Mover"; and he made some unpredictable cover choices in the Beatles' "Hey Jude," the Archies' bubblegum tune "Sugar Sugar," and Free's "Fire and Water." Fans who want to dig deeper can go for the double-disc *A Man and a Half*, but *The Very Best of Wilson Pickett* is such a concentrated dose of everything that made him great that it should be considered a necessary purchase for anyone who claims to be a fan of real soul music. *—Steve Huey*

It's Harder Now / Sep. 14, 1999 / Bullseye Blues ✦✦✦
"100% Certified Organic" claims the inside cover, and it sure sounds like it. What's more of an issue here, though, than whether or not somebody fired up a sampler during the sessions, is how *good* Wilson Pickett sounds after a dozen years away from the recording studio and more or less out of the spotlight. He's still rough around the edges, still able to belt and wail, and it's almost a revelation—after all, we know James Brown got away with it by keeping going full tilt, which doesn't appear to have been the case with Pickett. Well, never mind, because what we have here is a pretty damn good comeback record. The band, led by Jon Tiven, could perhaps punch it up a bit more on some of the tracks, but when they do hit the mark, they're great, as they are on "Stomp." Looks like we have a bunch of folks here determined to put the "fun" back in funk. *—Steven McDonald*

Pink (Alecia Moore)

b. Sep. 8, 1979, Doylestown, PA
Vocals / Teen Pop, Dance-Pop, Hip-Hop, Club/Dance, Urban
Although she was initially viewed as yet another face in the late-'90s crowd of teen pop acts, Pink quickly showed signs of becoming one of the rare artists to transcend and outgrow the label. Born Alecia Moore on September 8, 1979, in Doylestown, PA (near Philadelphia), Pink received her nickname as a child (it had nothing to do with her later shade of hair dye). She grew up in a musical family and by age 13 was a regular on the Philadelphia club scene, first as a dancer, then as a backing vocalist for the local hip-hop group Schools of Thought. At 14, she began writing her own songs; the same year, a local DJ at Club Fever began allowing her on-stage to sing a song every Friday. Pink was spotted one night by an executive for MCA, who asked her to audition for an R&B group called Basic Instinct; although she got the gig, the group imploded not long after. She was quickly recruited for a female R&B trio called Choice, which signed to L.A. Reid and Babyface's LaFace label on the strength of their demo; however, they too disbanded due to differences over musical direction. During Choice's brief studio time, producer Daryl Simmons asked Pink to write a bridge section for the song "Just to Be Loving You"; impressed with the results, Pink rediscovered her songwriting muse and an equally impressed L.A. Reid soon gave her a solo deal with LaFace.

Pink recorded her solo debut, *Can't Take Me Home*, with a variety of songwriting partners and dance-pop and R&B producers. Released in 2000, the album was a double-platinum hit; it spun off three Top Ten singles in "There U Go," "Most Girls," and "You Make Me Sick." She toured that summer as the opening act for *N Sync, but soon found herself tired of being pigeonholed as strictly a teen act, despite her sassy, forthright persona. As she set about working on her follow-up album, Pink took part in the remake of Patti LaBelle's "Lady Marmalade" featured on the *Moulin Rouge* soundtrack, which also featured powerhouse divas Christina Aguilera, Mya, and Lil' Kim. The song was a massive hit, topping the charts in both the U.S. and U.K. Toward the end of the year, Pink released her next single, "Get the Party Started"; it became her biggest, most inescapable hit to date, climbing into the Top Five. Her accompanying sophomore album, *M!ssundaztood*, quickly went double platinum; it boasted a more personal voice and a more eclectic sound, plus heavy contributions from ex-4 Non Blondes singer Linda Perry, who helped bring some more rock muscle to Pink's sound (as did guest appearances by Steven Tyler and Richie Sambora). *M!ssundaztood* attracted positive critical notices as well, and its second single, "Don't Let Me Get Me," became another fast-rising Top Ten hit. *—Steve Huey*

Can't Take Me Home / Apr. 4, 2000 / La Face ✦✦✦✦
It may be hard to listen to Pink's debut album *Can't Take Me Home* without hearing TLC, specifically their 1999 album *Fanmail*. After all, L.A. Reid and Babyface were the executive producers for both albums, and they decided to use a skittering, post-jungle rhythm for the bedrock of these savvy, club-ready dance-pop productions—a sound exploited expertly on TLC's record. If *Can't Take Me Home* pales next to *Fanmail*, it's not Pink's fault, nor is it because the album is sub-par; it's simply because it follows in the footsteps of a record that's as close to a modern classic as contemporary soul gets. Judged as its own entity, Pink's debut is quite strong, even if it isn't perfect. The production is masterminded by Babyface and L.A. Reid, who oversee such producers as Kevin "She'kspere" Briggs, Terence "Tramp-Baby" Abney, Daryl Simmons, and Tricky (not to be confused with the dark trip-hop genius, of course), and throughout this album, their work sparkles, from the deft layers of drum machines to the sultriness of the slow grooves. For the most part, Pink's performances match that production—she may not be able to deliver ballads with assurance and soul just yet, but she never over-sings. She also not only has an appealing voice, but displays a fair amount of chops. So, with the production and performances in place, that leaves just the songs. While there are no bad cuts on *Can't Take Me Home*, there aren't any knock-out punches, either. They're all fairly well-crafted, but they're more ingratiating than immediate, and if dance-pop should be anything, it should be indelible upon at least the second listen, if not the first. Many of the songs on *Can't Take Me Home* need a few spins before they truly sink in, which is a bit unfortunate. Still, it's not the worst situation in the world, either, especially since a lot of the tunes actually do make an impression with repeated plays. So, *Can't Take Me Home* doesn't really escape many of the pitfalls of a debut, but thanks to LA Reid and Babyface's production and Pink's engaging talents, it's a promising first effort all the same. *—Stephen Thomas Erlewine*

● **M!ssundaztood** / Nov. 20, 2001 / Arista ✦✦✦✦✦
Pink's debut album was a promising collection of dance-pop, easily lumped into the teen pop boon of 2000 since she was young and sang over savvy, skittering club beats. Those comparisons irked—hell, angered—Pink, and she was determined to prove she was real with her second album. So she called up her idol, Linda Perry of 4 Non Blondes fame, to help her rock and write; bared her soul; fought for some artistic control; brought in Steven Tyler; and wound up with *M!ssundaztood*, a title bound to never show up on Internet search engines. This all sounds like the script for a VH1 movie, but the wild thing is that *M!ssundaztood* not only works, it works smashingly—a bewildering amalgam of sounds and attitudes that shouldn't fit together, but defy all odds and do. This record bubbles over with imagination, as hooky pop songs like the title track rub shoulders with glitzy dance-floor anthems like "Get the Party Started" and sexy, swaggering arena rock redux like "18 Wheeler" before delving into weird confessionals like "Family Portrait," "Dear Diary," and "My Vietnam." Forget that this isn't what anybody would have expected Pink to do; it's hard to imagine anybody else that would have the idea and the inclination to blend late-'80s, metal-spiked album rock with modern hip-hop and dance, then dress it up with dazzling modern pop production, all the while not avoiding painful subjects (particularly her dysfunctional family) or melody. If that's not an artistic statement, I don't know what is, and the damn thing is there hasn't been a record in the mainstream this vibrant or this alive in a long, long time. *—Stephen Thomas Erlewine*

The Pips

f. Atlanta, GA

Group / Pop-Soul, Urban, Soul

Although the Pips never had any commercial success on their own, they were famous for the distinctive background harmonies that they provided for Gladys Knight for many years. From 1961's "Every Beat of My Heart" to 1973's "Midnight Train to Georgia" to 1988's "Love Overboard," the Pips backed Knight on one major hit after another. Knight first started working with the Pips in 1952, when she was only eight and formed a quintet with her brother Merald "Bubba" Knight, her sister Brenda Knight, and their cousins William and Elenor Guest. At first, the group's main purpose was entertaining family and friends, but another cousin, James "Pip" Woods, encouraged the quintet to sing professionally and became its booking agent—and by the late '50s, Knight and her relatives were touring with Jackie Wilson and Sam Cooke as an opening act.

Brenda Knight and Elenor Guest left the Pips (whose name was inspired by Woods' nickname of Pip) in 1959, when they were replaced by cousins Langston George and Edward Patten. When George left in 1962, the Pips' most famous lineup—Merald "Bubba" Knight, William Guest, and Edward Patten—was in place. By 1962, Gladys Knight & the Pips had become famous thanks to the 1961 hit "Every Beat of My Heart." Knight temporarily left the group in 1964 when she became pregnant, and the Pips survived by doing background vocals for various artists. Around that time, the Pips recorded some little-known songs on their own, including "Linda," "Bless the One," "To Whom It May Concern," "Walking Around in Circles," and "Darling."

Knight returned in 1965, and the Pips didn't do any more recording on their own until the late '70s. Minus Knight, the Pips recorded two albums for Casablanca: 1977's *At Last... the Pips* and 1978's Bunny Sigler-produced *Callin'*—both of which suffered from inadequate promotion and did very little commercially. After that, the Pips did no more recording on their own. They remained with Knight until 1990—when Knight and the Pips parted company for good that year, she became a full-time solo artist and the Pips retired from music. *—Alex Henderson*

At Last . . . the Pips / 1978 / Casablanca ✦✦

For a time in the late '70s, the Pips—William Guest, Bubba Knight, and Edward Patten—cut their apron strings to Gladys Knight and did this solo release. It wasn't the first time they recorded sans Gladys—they did so in the '60s, prior to Motown when Gladys married and had her first child. Casablanca didn't do its usual powerhouse promotion job on this release. In fact, many are unaware of its existence. Produced by Arthur Wright, the album has a soft, mushy feel with over-dubbed backing harmonies by the Pips. The leads aren't riveting, and coupled with bland songs and arrangements, the results are a grade less than C-level. Three of the seven songs, "At Last My Search Is Over," "Happiness," and "Uncle James" aren't half bad. *—Andrew Hamilton*

● **Callin'** / 1978 / Casablanca ✦✦✦

Callin', the second of two albums that the Pips recorded without Gladys Knight in the late '70s, didn't come out on Philadelphia International but might as well have. This LP was produced by Bunny Sigler, who does most of the writing, and the Pips are backed by the Philly soul-funk band Instant Funk (best known for its major hit "I Got My Mind Made Up"). So not surprisingly, *Callin'* (which was recorded in the Los Angeles suburb of Burbank but mixed at Philly's legendary Sigma Sound Studios) is about as Philly-sounding as it gets. Thanks to Sigler and Instant Funk, the Pips end up having a lot of O'Jays/Harold Melvin & the Blue Notes/Intruders-type appeal; and Sigler can also take credit for the fact that 1978's *Callin'* is a stronger, more satisfying release than 1977's uneven *At Last... the Pips*. As far as Philly soul goes, *Callin'* isn't in a class with the O'Jays' *Survival* or Harold Melvin & the Blue Notes' *To Be True*. But it's definitely respectable, and the Pips are as pleasing on the uptempo selections as they are on the ballad "Anything" (which is easily recommended to anyone who savored the unapologetic crooning of the O'Jays' "Forever Mine"). Now for the bad news: Casablanca gave *Callin'* very little promotion, and the LP died as quick a death as *At Last... the Pips*. *—Alex Henderson*

The Platters

f. 1953, Los Angeles, CA

Group / Doo Wop, R&B, Vocal Pop

The Platters started out as a Los Angeles-based doo wop group with little identity of their own to make them stand out from the pack. They started out making their first records for Federal, a subsidiary of Cincinnati's King Records. These early sides don't sound *anything* like the better-known sides that would eventually emerge from this group, instead merely aping the current R&B trends and styles of the day. What changed their fortunes can be reduced down to one very important name: their mentor, manager, producer, songwriter, and vocal coach, Buck Ram. Ram took what many would say were a run-of-the-mill R&B doo wop vocal group and turned them into stars and one of the most enduring and lucrative groups of all time. By 1954, Ram was already running a talent agency in Los Angeles, writing and arranging for publisher Mills Music, managing the Three Suns—a pop group with some success—and working with his protégés, the Penguins. The Platters seemed like a good addition to his stable.

After getting them out of their Federal contract, Ram placed them with the burgeoning national independent label Mercury Records (at the same time he brought over the Penguins following their success with "Earth Angel"), automatically getting them into pop markets through the label's distribution contacts alone. Then Ram started honing in on the group's strengths and weaknesses. The first thing he did was put the lead vocal status squarely on the shoulders of lead tenor Tony Williams. Williams' emoting power was turned up full blast with the group (now augmented with Zola Taylor from Shirley Gunter & the Queens) working as very well-structured vocal support framing his every note.

With Ram's pop songwriting classics as their musical palette, the group quickly became a pop and R&B success, eventually earning the distinction of being the first black act of the era to top the pop charts. Considered the most romantic of all the doo wop groups (that is, the ultimate in "make out music"), hit after hit came tumbling forth in a seemingly effortless manner: "Only You," "The Great Pretender," "My Prayer," "Twilight Time," "Smoke Gets in Your Eyes," "Harbor Lights," all of them establishing the Platters as the classiest of all. Williams struck out on his own in 1961 and, by the decade's end, the group had disbanded with various members starting up their own version of the Platters. This bit of franchising now extends into the present day, with an estimated 125 sanctioned versions of "the original Platters" out on the oldies show circuit. *—Cub Koda*

Flying Platters / 1958 / Mercury ✦✦✦

Off and running, *Flying Platters* was the Los Angeles warblers' second album for Mercury Records. It features the elegant ones doing what they do best: Platterizing standards. Lead singer Tony Williams' crystal tenor is positively beguiling on "Mean to Me," "Darktown Strutters Ball," "In the Middle of Nowhere," and the LP's only single release—"Only Because." *—Andrew Hamilton*

Flying Platters Around the World / 1959 / Mercury ✦✦✦✦

The Platters are so smooth you don't realized you're being doo-wopped. Along with the Moonglows and the Orioles and others, they were amongst the smoothest purveyors of the beloved vocalizing style. They eloquently employed the technique on the unforgettable "Twilight Time," "It's Raining Outside," "Try a Little Tenderness," and "My Old Flame." Another song, "I'll Take You Home Again Kathleen," is a story in itself. The title is surprisingly popular with songwriters: At least 30 totally different songs have the exact same title. *—Andrew Hamilton*

Encore of Golden Hits / 1960 / Polygram ✦✦✦✦✦

Both the favored group of inspiration point denizens and one of the classiest of doo wop outfits, the Platters transcended their early R&B beginnings in L.A. to become one of the most popular acts of the early rock & roll era. Avoiding the plight of many one-hit doo wop hopefuls, the Platters scored several hits on both the R&B and pop charts. Classics like "The Great Pretender," "Smoke Gets in Your Eyes," "Only You," and "My Prayer" were all long-running hits and, along with nuggets by Elvis, the Drifters, and the Coasters, helped define the burgeoning, postwar youth culture of America. Part of what kept the group at the top from 1955-1960 was the winning combination of Tony Williams' soaring and svelte lead vocals and producer/A&R man Buck Ram's beautiful, crossover-friendly material. This early hits collection on Mercury rounds up the group's best work with Ram, including not only the sides mentioned above, but other gems like "Remember When," "Twilight Time," and "I'm Sorry." Although now eclipsed by recent CDs on Rhino and Mercury, *Encore of Golden Hits* is still a worthwhile title to seek out, especially by those looking for only a brief introduction to the group's prime period. *—Stephen Cook*

Christmas With the Platters / 1963 / Polygram ✦✦✦✦✦

The New Soul of the Platters / 1965 / Mercury ✦✦

Betty Jackson replaced Barbara Randolph in the Platters in 1965, but it's unclear whether it's her or Sandra Dawn (who replaced Jackson) who is singing on this album of preppy tunes that can be purchased from most collectors for less than a five spot in very good condition. No hits emerged and the LP whimpered away quietly before many ardent Platters fans were even aware of its existence. The other members on this recording were Sonny Turner, David Lynch, Nate Nelson, and Herb Reed. *—Andrew Hamilton*

I Love You 1,000 Times / 1966 / Musicor ✦✦

Going Back to Detroit / 1967 / Musicor ✦✦✦

Going Back to Detroit was a complete turnaround from the previous year's *I Love You 1,000 Times*. New lead, Sonny Turner's exciting tenor is the prominent voice, and the material reflects the contemporary mid-'60s Platters, not the originals. "With This Ring" led by Turner, became their most successful Musicor single, soaring to number-14 Pop and number-12 R&B; the song is lively and a complete change, materially, for the Platters, deviating even farther from their patented sound than "I Love You a Thousand Times." Strangely, no other tracks from this album were released as singles—despite the obvious potential of "Get a Hold of Yourself," written by Rodger Hatcher and Johnnie Mae Matthews, and originally recorded by Hatcher on Dotty Records. The same can be said for "Going Back to Detroit," the title track, "Shing-a-Ling-a-Loo" and "I Can't Get Used to Sharing You." This LP is pretty hard to find. Thankfully Musicor has released a best-of CD, but it's not complete, and many of these songs were omitted. *—Andrew Hamilton*

Have the Magic Touch / 1967 / Musicor ✦✦✦

Have the Magic Touch revisits the Platters' '50s roots when, with Tony Williams' classy tenor as the vehicle, they were chart regulars. Old tracks such as "My Prayer," "Alone in the Night," and "Wish It Was Me" dominate, though Williams was long gone when this album came out. His replacement, Sonny Turner, appears once on Luther Dixon and Inez Foxx's "Devri," the last song on the album and, at just under two minutes, the shortest as well. If you're looking for the old Platters, they're here; if you prefer the '60s Platters with Sonny Turner, look elsewhere. The album was originally issued in 1967 on Musicor Records. *—Andrew Hamilton*

The New Golden Hits of the Platters / 1967 / Musicor ✦✦✦

☆ **The Magic Touch: An Anthology** / Oct. 22, 1991 / Mercury ✦✦✦✦✦

A double-disc, 50-track extravaganza from one of the paragons of smooth soul, *The Magic Touch: An Anthology* is the most complete look at the Platters, barring only Bear Family's 1994 box set *Four Platters and One Lovely Dish*. Between 1955 and 1962, the quintet recorded 36 entries that reached the pop charts and they're all here, led by the ones that absolutely *must* be on any effective Platters compilation: "Only You (And You Alone)," "The Great Pretender," "(You've Got) The Magic Touch," "My Prayer," "Twilight Time," "Smoke Gets in Your Eyes," "Harbor Lights," and "Red Sails in the Sunset." That leaves plenty of room for the type of material collectors drool over, like the previously unreleased "Hula Hop" and a rare Tony Williams solo record ("When You Return"), plus obscure Platters versions of songs made famous by others ("The Glory of Love," "Goodnight

Sweetheart, It's Time to Go," "My Old Flame," even an enjoyable stab at "Sixteen Tons"). It's all delivered in the sweetest sound heard yet, with a lengthy booklet and many superb photos. It's the ultimate Platters anthology, and it's everything this important group deserves. *—John Bush*

The Musicor Years / 1995 / Collectables ♦♦♦

The '60s Musicor Platters' featured the magnetic, powerful leads of Sonny Turner a product of Cleveland, OH, and East Technical High School. Turner first recorded with a local group called the Metrotones for Reserve Records. The only resemblance between them and the '50s Platters was their copy cat lineup featuring a female and four guys, and the name. They recorded songs written by Tony Hester, Richard Wylie and Luther Dixon, to name a few. They charted with "I Love You a Thousand Times," "With This Ring" and, to a lesser degree, "Washed Ashore (On a Lonely Island in the Sea)" and "Sweet Sweet Lovin'," while other releases, "I'll Be Home," "Love Must Go On" and "So Many Tears," failed to make an impact. Ironically, the name Platters probably hurt more than it helped. A different name may have made them more viable. Splinter Platters groups were plentiful. Nobody really knew who the official group was. Only die-hards could discern the original group members, surely their new '60s fans couldn't. The Musicor Platters are easily one of the most underrated R&B groups of the '60s, and this compilation CD is a ringing testimonial, with the only odd tracks being the occasional attempt to recapture their patented sound of the '50s. *—Andrew Hamilton*

The Very Best of the Platters 1966–1969 / Jun. 17, 1997 / Varese ♦♦♦

After Tony Williams left the Platters in 1959, a new replacement was found in Charles "Sonny" Turner. But the group's label (Mercury) brought Turner in for album sessions only and kept releasing old tracks with Williams' voice on them as singles, even keeping his name off the liner notes to their new album. It wasn't until their contract was up with Mercury and the group moved on to Musicor Records in 1966 that Turner was allowed to sing on a record by the Platters in his true voice, five to six years after he came on board. This 14-track compilation covers the group's stay at the label between 1966 and 1969, a period of time that saw the Platters recast themselves as a beach-music group ("Washed Ashore [On a Lonely Island in the Sea]") while swimming against the tide of the burgeoning soul music movement. The hits didn't dry up, and "I Love You 1,000 Times," "Devri," "With This Ring," "Sweet Sweet Lovin'" and "I'll Be Home" showed that the group was breaking new ground while still making the charts. This collection chronicles the last stage of the Platters as a recording group of any significance and also features two previously unissued tracks, "Keep on Loving Me" and "Atlanta." Nothing here will ever take the place of the original hits on Mercury (which didn't sound anything like their early recordings for King), but those who want to get the big picture will do well to add this one to the collection. *—Cub Koda*

★ **Enchanted: The Best of the Platters** / Jun. 16, 1998 / Rhino ♦♦♦♦♦

For too many years, there was no single-disc collection of the Platters' greatest hits. Mercury's *Magic Touch* offered two discs' worth of prime material, but it was really too much for anyone outside of serious listeners; it also stopped short of their uneven but occasionally worthwhile Musicor recordings. Rhino's *Enchanted: The Best of the Platters* is the first compilation of the CD era to feature all of their biggest Mercury and Musicor hits on one disc, and it's a stunner. All of their Top Ten pop hits, from "Only You" to "Harbor Lights," are here, along with 18 other charting hits, all in their original hit versions. For any fan, both casual and dedicated, it's essential, since no other compilation features as many hits on one disc and no other compilation is quite so consistently entertaining. *—Stephen Thomas Erlewine*

Platypus

f. 1978, Cincinnati, OH

Group / Disco, Funk

Not to be confused with the late-'90s rock outfit Platypus—which was a side project for Kings X guitarist Ty Tabor—the Platypus examined here was a little known, short-lived funk-disco band that was active in the late '70s. Formed in Cincinnati, OH, in 1978, this Platypus combined its appreciation of the Ohio Players and Parliament/Funkadelic with a lot of disco gloss and sometimes added rock elements. But unlike the Players or Parliament/Funkadelic, Platypus didn't use any horns. In 1978, the five member band signed with Casablanca, which released its self-titled debut LP the following year. But *Platypus* didn't sell, and the outfit broke up without ever recording a second album. Playtpus consisted of Arthur Stokes (lead vocals, percussion), Kerry Rutledge (lead vocals, rhythm guitar), Lloyd Jones (bass), Curtis Sanford (drums, keyboards), and the late Larry "Irfaan" Hines (lead guitar). *—Alex Henderson*

● **Platypus** / 1979 / Casablanca ♦♦♦

In an ideal world, any musician or singer who has talent would be able to make a good living at it. But we don't live in an ideal world and, every year, worthwhile bands fall through the cracks. In the late 1970s one such band was Platypus, a funk-disco unit that couldn't get arrested, and its lack of commercial success is regrettable because this is a decent debut. Released in 1979, *Platypus* has one foot in funk (in some cases, funk-rock) and the other in disco. The Ohio Players and Parliament/Funkadelic are prominent influences, but tracks like "Body and Soul," "Love the Way You Funk," and the opener "Dancing in the Moonlight" have a lot more disco gloss than one expected from either of those bands. At times, Platypus incorporates rock elements, especially on "Street Babies." One thing that separates this LP from a lot of 1970s funk efforts is its complete absence of horns—many of that decade's funk bands were famous for their killer horn sections. But the Isley Brothers were a major exception, and the same goes for Platypus. This enjoyable, if imperfect, LP (which was the band's only album) didn't stay in print for very long. But it's worth hearing if, by some chance, a hard-to-find copy can be tracked down. *—Alex Henderson*

The Players Association

f. 1977, **db.** 1981

Group / Quiet Storm, Urban, Funk, Jazz-Funk, Disco

Led by drummer/arranger Chris Hills, the Players Association was an obscure late-'70s, early-'80s outfit that specialized in a jazz-influenced style of disco-funk. Major jazz musicians like Michael Brecker, David Sanborn, Joe Farrell, and Tom Harrell appeared on its albums, but the New York band never catered to jazz's hardcore; its main focus was disco-funk with jazz overtones, although the Association occasionally detoured into instrumental jazz-pop and quiet storm/NAC music. The Association never became well known, and its recordings received very little radio airplay; however, it did enjoy a small underground following among danceclub DJs. The Players Association signed with Vanguard in 1977, and the band recorded five albums before calling it quits in 1981: 1977's *The Players Association*, 1978's *Born to Dance*, 1979's *Turn the Music Up!*, 1980's *We Got the Groove*, and 1981's *Let Your Body Go*. *—Alex Henderson*

Players Association / 1977 / Vanguard ♦♦

Best known for folk, blues, and jazz, Vanguard tried to cash in on disco's popularity when it signed the Players Association in 1977. The band's jazz-influenced brand of disco-funk didn't make Vanguard huge in the disco field; it's safe to say that the vast majority of Donna Summer, Chic, and Village People fans have never even heard of the Players Association. But this self-titled debut LP did help the band acquire a small following among club DJs. Although not as strong as the Association's subsequent albums, this competent but uneven debut indicated that the band had potential. The club jocks who gave this record some exposure may not have found the Association's covers of Diana Ross' "Love Hangover" or Archie Bell & the Drells' "Let's Groove" mind-blowing, but they admired the band for having an unconventional, recognizable sound and realized that it had potential. Some well-known jazz musicians appear on this largely instrumental CD, including trumpeter Jon Faddis and the late tenor saxman/flutist Joe Farrell; and the band's pleasant version of the Isley Brothers' "For the Love of You" was obviously aimed at the emerging quiet storm and NAC markets. But disco-funk, not smooth jazz, was the forte of the Players Association, whose first album is its least essential. In 1977, the best was yet to come for the Players Association. *—Alex Henderson*

Born to Dance / 1978 / Vanguard ♦♦♦

The list of jazz improvisers who appear on the Players Association's second album, *Born to Dance*, is impressive; tenor saxman Michael Brecker, alto saxman David Sanborn, trumpeter Jon Faddis, and guitarist Steve Khan are among the participants. And percussionist James Mtume, who has jazz credentials but is best known for producing, writing, and performing R&B, is also on board. But despite boasting an impressive lineup, *Born to Dance* is only a slight improvement over the Players Association's self-titled debut album. This isn't a bad album; "How Do You Like It," "Everything's Gonna Be O.K.," "Make It Last All Night," and other tunes that were written or co-written by leader/drummer/ arranger Chris Hills are catchy but unremarkable. The band was capable of a lot more, and it wouldn't live up to its potential until its third album, *Turn the Music Up!* *—Alex Henderson*

Turn the Music Up! / 1978 / Vanguard ♦♦♦

After providing two competent but unremarkable albums—the first in 1977, the second in 1978—the Players Association lived up to its potential on its third album, *Turn the Music Up!* The band's smooth jazz version of Roberta Flack and Donny Hathaway's "The Closer I Get to You" isn't earth-shattering, but the Association really soars on an instrumental interpretation of Chic's "Everybody Dance" and infectious originals like "Ride the Groove" and the title song. Many of the artists who are employed on this 1979 LP are accomplished jazz improvisers, including trumpeter Tom Harrell (who takes his share of solos), tenor saxman Bob Berg, keyboardist Pat Rebillot, and trumpeter Marvin Stamm. But *Turn the Music Up!* shouldn't be judged by jazz standards because it isn't a jazz record per se; most of the material is simply disco-funk with jazz overtones. And from a disco-funk standpoint, *Turn the Music Up!* is exciting more often than not. *—Alex Henderson*

Let Your Body Go / 1980 / Vanguard ♦♦

● **We Got the Groove** / 1980 / Vanguard ♦♦♦♦

The Players Association is a perfect example of a band that improved as it went along. Their self-titled debut album of 1977 is their least essential, but when *We Got the Groove* came out in 1980, it was clear that the Association had gone from competent to excellent. This vinyl LP marked the first time that a Players Association album didn't contain any covers of major R&B and disco hits of the late '70s; all of the material was written by leader/drummer/arranger Chris Hills. The key to excellence in the disco-funk field is finding the perfect groove and working it to death, and Hill's outfit does exactly that on "The Get-Down Mellow Sound," "Dance," "We're Almost There," and the title track. Although the tunes received very little radio airplay, they enjoyed their share of dance club exposure and could easily bring a dancefloor to life. Without question, *We Got the Groove* is the Players Association's most essential album. *—Alex Henderson*

Players Association/Turn the Music Up! / 1998 / Ace ♦♦♦

The Players

Group / Soul

The Players recorded two beautiful ballads that stay in your heart, but the singers on their two soul hits made live duplication of the sound impossible. They were a studio creation that scored in 1966 with the heartfelt "He'll Be Back," a floating ballad about a guy comforting a girl whose man is in Vietnam. It hit instantly on soul stations, but didn't enjoy the same success on pop radio; still, it did make them known far outside of Cook County's limits. Singers on the smoothie were Herbert Butler (lead) and four members of the Dells: Chuck Barksdale, Johnny Carter, Vern Allison, and Mickey McGill. Otha Lee Givens and Tony Lee Johnson were recruited to become actual Players and travel with Butler to promote the record and perform gigs. Minit rushed an album, with the new recruits singing most of the tracks.

A second single, "Glad You Waited" (1966), equaled the beauty of "He'll Be Back," and told of the returning soldier telling his girlfriend how glad he was that she waited faithfully for his return. Allison, Carter, and McGill didn't appear anymore, but the producer still found a need for Barksdale's bass. The Players now consisted of Butler, Johnson, Givins, and Joe Brackenridge. Minit cranked out two more Players singles in 1967, but "That's the Way" and "Get Right" never got off square one. Nothing else ever surfaced from the group built around Herbert Butler's passionate, sweet first tenor. Joe Breckenridge was with the Von Gayels prior to the Players. *—Andrew Hamilton*

● **He'll Be Back** / 1966 / Minit ✦✦✦

The Players—Tony Lee Johnson, Herbert Butler, and Otha Lee Givens—were a sweet singing trio that sounded similar to the pre-Cuba Gooding Main Ingredient, when the late Don McPherson sang lead. Minit rushed this album onto the streets to capitalize on their R&B hit "He'll Be Back," a tearjerker about a girl lamenting because her fellow is serving in Vietnam. The follow-up, "I'm Glad You Waited," was better but slightly less popular; it was an answer to "He'll Be Back," in which the soldier returns home and thanks his lady for waiting patiently. A remake of the Platters' "I Love You a Thousand Times" doesn't compare to the original. Percy Sledge's "When a Man Loves a Woman" gets a strip-down also, as none of the grit and guts displayed by Sledge is evident on the Players' rendition. The rest of the songs are classic filler; they're all right, but lack fire. *—Andrew Hamilton*

Pleasure

f. 1972, Portland, OR, **db.** 1981

Group / Quiet Storm, Disco, Funk, Soul

Best known for its 1979 hit "Glide," Pleasure was a risk-taking, horn driven band that often brought jazz overtones to its funk/soul foundation. Pleasure, which shouldn't be confused with the '90s rock band Pleasure, wasn't huge but enjoyed a small cult following. The band was formed in Portland, OR, in 1972, when guitarist Marlon "The Magician" McClain (born August 8, 1955), lead singer Sherman Davis (born March 15, 1952), and keyboardist Donald Hepburn (born June 30, 1950) joined forces with saxophonist Dennis Springer (born July 21, 1949), bassist Nathaniel Phillips (born December 30, 1955), trombonist Dan Brewster and drummer Bruce Carter (born December 28, 1956). Pleasure was a merger of two Portland outfits: Franchise (which included McClain, Phillips, and Carter) and the Soul Masters (which was Hepburn's band and also included Springer, Smith, and Davis).

The Oregon residents got a lucky break when trombonist Wayne Henderson, a founding member of the Jazz Crusaders, saw them performing in a Portland club—Henderson was impressed with what he heard, and his enthusiasm led to a deal with Fantasy (where he produced four of its six albums) in 1974. Pleasure's debut album, *Dust Yourself Off*, came out on Fantasy in 1975 and was followed by *Accept No Substitutes* in 1976 and *Joyous* in 1977. After *Joyous*, there were a few personnel changes: Brewster left the band, and Donald Hepburn's younger brother Michael (born May 21, 1953) came on board as a keyboardist/lead singer. *Get to the Feeling*, Pleasure's fourth album, came out in 1978 and was followed by 1979's *Future Now*, which contained the hit "Glide." Pleasure's cult following really swore by the band, but it wasn't until "Glide" (which reached number ten on *Billboard*'s R&B singles chart) that the funksters finally scored a Top Ten hit. Trumpeter/flugelhornist Tony Collins (born May 16, 1957) was added to the lineup for *Future Now*, and Doug Lewis came on board as a lead guitarist for 1980's *Special Things*, which was Pleasure's sixth and final album. Unfortunately, Pleasure didn't have any more major hits after "Glide," and in 1981, the band broke up. *—Alex Henderson*

Dust Yourself Off / Jul. 1975 / Fantasy ✦✦✦

When Pleasure's debut album, *Dust Yourself Off*, came out in 1975, the Portland, OR, combo often found itself being compared to the Blackbyrds. It was a valid comparison, to be sure—like the Blackbyrds, Pleasure offered funk and soul with jazz overtones. Both bands recorded for Fantasy, and just as the Blackbyrds' mentor/producer was trumpeter Donald Byrd, Pleasure's was Crusaders trombonist Wayne Henderson (who, like Byrd, started out in hard bop but became very funk-minded in the '70s). But despite all those parallels, Pleasure had a distinctive energy of its own. And while the Blackbyrds had their share of major radio smashes, Pleasure's only major radio hit was 1979's "Glide." Produced by Henderson, *Dust Yourself Off* wasn't a favorite at soul radio but did earn Pleasure a small (and enthusiastic) cult following. Those who, back in 1975, were hip to this LP heard a lot of jazz-tinged potential on invigorating funk items like "Reality," "Music Is My Life," and "Bouncy Lady," as well as the quiet storm ballad "My Love" (which hints at War without being derivative). They also heard it on an unlikely cover of Maria Muldaur's "Midnight at the Oasis," which the band manages to transform into hard funk. Pleasure's funk was tough and gritty—the Oregon residents were as gutsy as Tower of Power and the pre-J.T. Taylor Kool & the Gang, both of which are influences on this LP. In fact, "What Is Slick" is Pleasure's clever response to Tower of Power's "What Is Hip." But as gutsy as Pleasure could be, the band's willingness to incorporate jazz elements gave its funk a certain sophistication. *Dust Yourself Off* didn't go down in history as a multi-platinum blockbuster, but among Pleasure fans, it did go down in history as a promising debut. *—Alex Henderson*

Accept No Substitutes / 1976 / Fantasy ✦✦✦✦

Back in the '70s, AOR radio and soul radio were two very different formats—and not just because one played rock and the other played R&B. "AOR" stood for album-oriented rock, which was an accurate name because that format was, in fact, album-oriented; at AOR, album tracks that were never released as singles could be candidates for heavy rotation. Soul radio, however, was much more singles-oriented—an established soul radio DJ could play some album tracks here and there, but singles were the primary focus. And that wasn't good news for Pleasure, who were more of an album act than a singles act. Pleasure recorded great albums, but for the most part, they didn't have the type of singles that drove program directors wild. *Accept No Substitutes*, Pleasure's second album, is a perfect example of a record that is excellent but, as a rule, didn't blow program directors away. The funk gem "Let's Dance" had the makings of a radio hit, although radio didn't really take notice until the West Street Mob covered it in 1981. At any rate, Pleasure's relatively small group of hardcore fans loved this record. They loved the jazz-tinged funk of "Pleasure for Your Pleasure" and "I'm Mad"; they loved the mellow, laid-back quiet storm outlook of "The Love of My Life." *Accept No Substitutes* did contain one charting single: the hypnotic "Ghettoes of the Mind," which wasn't a huge smash but did become a minor hit and was a favorite at Pleasure's live gigs. Had '70s soul radio been as album-minded a medium as AOR radio, this Wayne Henderson-produced LP might have enjoyed heavy rotation. But in a medium that worshipped singles, *Accept No Substitutes* was fighting an uphill battle. Regardless, most Pleasure fans think of this LP as a highly respectable sophomore outing. *—Alex Henderson*

● **Joyous** / 1977 / Fantasy ✦✦✦✦✦

Pleasure couldn't have asked for a more appropriate producer when, in late 1976, it employed Wayne Henderson on *Joyous*. A band that frequently brought jazz overtones to its funk-soul foundation, Pleasure needed someone who held jazz and R&B in equally high regard—and Henderson easily fit that description. The Texas trombonist first made a name for himself playing hard bop with the Jazz Crusaders, but as the 1970s progressed, he became increasingly R&B-friendly. Henderson was exactly the sort of producer that Pleasure needed, and the band's appreciation of jazz comes through on the uptempo funk numbers (which include "Dance to the Music," "Let Me Be the One," and the title song) as well as the dreamy quiet storm gem "Sassafras Girl." Pleasure brings this vinyl LP to an appealing close with a jazz-funk instrumental titled "Selim," which isn't typical of *Joyous* on the whole—most of the tunes are vocal-oriented. This is a funk-soul record first and foremost, and it is also a classic that underscores Pleasure's risk-taking nature. *—Alex Henderson*

Get to the Feeling / 1978 / Fantasy ✦✦

Future Now / 1979 / Fantasy ✦✦✦✦

Arguably, the members of Pleasure were among the unsung heroes of 1970s funk and soul. The band enjoyed a small but enthusiastic cult following, but one thing that it didn't have was a lot of major hits on R&B radio. For the most part, R&B radio ignored Pleasure, although quiet storm formats did play some of its more mellow album tracks. The exception to that rule came in 1979, when black radio proved to be quite receptive to "Glide." A pearl of a funk single, "Glide" is an infectious party jam that the African-American working class easily related to. The tune isn't really sociopolitical, although it isn't mindlessly fun either—essentially, "Glide" is telling listeners to hang in there and be positive despite the challenges that life presents. And you don't have to be African-American to relate to the song's message. "Glide" was the only song on *Future Now* that could be called a major hit, although it isn't the album's only gem. Those who acquired this 1979 LP also found a lot to admire about jazz-influenced material that ranges from funk smokers like "Nothin' to It" and "Space Is the Place" to the smooth quiet storm offerings "Strong Love" and "Thoughts of Old Flames." Without question, *Future Now* is among Pleasure's most essential albums. *—Alex Henderson*

● **The Greatest of Pleasure** / Jan. 25, 1993 / Fantasy ✦✦✦✦✦

In the 1980s and 1990s, Pleasure's die-hard fans were hoping that Fantasy would reissue its entire catalog on CD. Regrettably, that didn't happen, although Fantasy did assemble this generally excellent collection in 1993. *The Greatest of Pleasure*, as the title indicates, boasts some of the Oregon funksters' most essential work. Naturally, this CD contains "Glide," which was Pleasure's biggest hit—not only is the original hit version from 1979 included, but Fantasy also provides a remix and an interesting, if less than essential, hip-hop remake featuring rapper Psycho (who was a member of the shocking, over-the-top gangsta rap group Insane Poetry). The tracks that *are* essential range from the hit single version of "Glide" to other jazz-influenced 1970s funk smokers such as "Dance to the Music," "The Real Thing," "Joyous," and "Let's Dance" (which wasn't a major hit for Pleasure but became better known when the West Street Mob recorded a cover version for Sugar Hill in 1981). Not that everything on this collection is uptempo; the dreamy "Sassafras Girl" is a fine example of Pleasure's mellow quiet storm side. For those who are seeking an introductory overview of Pleasure's exciting but underexposed Fantasy output, *The Greatest of Pleasure* would be the logical starting point. *—Alex Henderson*

Dust Yourself Off/Accept No Substitutes / Jul. 9, 2002 / Fantasy ✦✦✦✦

P.M. Dawn

f. 1988

Group / Pop-Rap, Alternative Rap, Urban

Comprised of brothers Prince Be (Attrell Cordes) and DJ Minute Mix (Jarrett Cordes), the early-'90s group P.M. Dawn straddled the gap between hip-hop and smooth '70s-style soul, creating an innovative urban R&B that owed as much to pop as it did to rhythm and blues. The brothers recorded their debut single, "Ode to a Forgetful Mind," in 1988, but P.M. Dawn didn't release a full-length album until 1991. The record, *Of the Heart, of the Soul, of the Cross: The Utopian Experience*, was an immediate hit, thanks to the single "Set Adrift on Memory Bliss," which sampled Spandau Ballet's new wave hit "True." Both the album and the single received glowing reviews, as did the 1993 follow-up, *The Bliss Album . . . ?*, which featured the hit singles "I'd Die Without You" and "Looking Through Patient Eyes." In 1995, P.M. Dawn returned with *Jesus Wept*, which received strong reviews but weak sales. *Dearest Christian, I'm So Very Sorry for Bringing You Here. Love, Dad* followed in 1998; by this time, the group had virtually dropped out of sight as a commercial force, even though most corners continued to praise the artistic quality of their work. A greatest-hits compilation, *The Best of P.M. Dawn*, appeared in the summer of 2000. *—Stephen Thomas Erlewine*

★ **Of the Heart, of the Soul and of the Cross: The Utopian Experience** / Aug. 6, 1991 / V2 ✦✦✦✦✦
In the wake of De La Soul, rap group P.M. Dawn's first album samples jazz, whitebread pop soul, adds a dash of Prince's mysticism, embraces melody, and turns inward for surreal (and admittedly often sophomoric) psychedelic lyrics. P.M. Dawn may care about matters of the soul, but on their first album they don't ignore the booty: these are carefully assembled songs, layered with many a chorused vocal or a harpsichord, but all backed up with a solid beat. "A Watcher's Point of View (Dont'cha Think)" stands out here: a bumping sample with scratchy guitars, shimmering acoustic strings, and interweaving lyrics and a chorus. But it was "Set Adrift on Memory Bliss," with its sample from Spandau Ballet's "True," that made it into the charts (it then became the blueprint for following singles, for better or worse). Other successful tracks: "Reality Used to Be a Friend of Mine," "In the Presence of Mirrors," and "On a Clear Day." There's a few missteps, especially on "Shake," a pointless house-like workout. But it's a delicate balance between doe-eyed metaphysics and the dancefloor that the album treads, and it's all the better for it. *—Ted Mills*

The Bliss Album . . . ? / Mar. 23, 1993 / V2 ✦✦✦✦✦
After the breakout pop success of their debut album, P.M. Dawn played up the lush, soothing urban-soul qualities of their sound on the follow-up, *The Bliss Album . . . ?* For all of hardcore rap's hysteria over the duo's gentle demeanor and pop influences, *Of the Heart, of the Soul, and of the Cross* had been a predominantly rap-oriented album. That changes on *The Bliss Album . . . ?*, which downplays Prince Be's rapping (only on about a third of the tracks) in favor of dreamy melodies throughout the songs, not just on the choruses. It's a logical move, since P.M. Dawn's most unique moments were often also their most reflective, and they had an obvious knack for crafting original hooks. *The Bliss Album . . . ?*'s approach also provides more opportunities for the ethereal, layered vocal overdubs that had become one of the duo's signatures. While the results don't quite re-envision hip-hop the way the debut did, they're still tremendously inventive, playing to P.M. Dawn's strengths. The musical landscapes are even more lushly arranged, and the pop numbers positively shimmer thanks to the duo's increasing sense of craft. A couple of the more aggressive rap tracks break up the mood a little, as with "Plastic," a sly rebuttal of the charges leveled by the group's macho detractors. It seems unnecessary, though, since P.M. Dawn's cosmic mysticism and vastly different influences clearly aren't competing on the same turf. Luckily, *The Bliss Album . . . ?* refuses to acknowledge any artificially imposed purist boundaries, continuing to chart new sonic territory and expanding the possibilities in P.M. Dawn's music. *—Steve Huey*

Jesus Wept / Oct. 3, 1995 / V2 ✦✦✦✦
With their third album, *Jesus Wept*, P.M. Dawn doesn't necessarily make a great leap forward. Instead, they make some great refinements. Prince Be's lyrics are just as trippy and cryptic as ever, but they appear more focused, offering a poetic, spiritual worldview that is supported by the lovely, layered music. Using artists like Prince, Stevie Wonder, Marvin Gaye, and the Beatles as starting points, Prince Be creates a unique world assembled equally from soul, pop, hip-hop, and psychedelia. As individual pieces, the songs might not always make much sense, but taken as a whole, they create a singular world that is rich in lush melodies and sumptuous arrangements. Occasionally, P.M. Dawn's ambition gets the best of them and the results sound self-indulgent, not transcendent. However, those moments are few and far between on *Jesus Wept*, the group's best album. *—Stephen Thomas Erlewine*

Dearest Christian, I'm So Very Sorry for Bringing You Here. Love, Dad / Sep. 29, 1998 / V2 ✦✦✦

The Best of P.M. Dawn / Jun. 20, 2000 / V2 ✦✦✦✦✦
Compiled from P.M. Dawn's four albums and the *Senseless* soundtrack *The Best of P.M. Dawn* not only plays like an audio time capsule of slick, tuneful, '90s urban pop, it's a remarkably coherent listening experience. The New Jersey duo's sweet combination of classic silky soul, trip-hop, psychedelia, and pop was one of the most groundbreaking sounds of the decade and influenced countless bands tremendously. All the usual suspects are present and accounted for, beginning with the band's first number one single "Set Adrift on Memory Bliss," an amazingly mature debut tune, and moves forward with two tracks from 1998's relatively obscure *I'm So Very Sorry for Bringing You Here, Love Dad*. A remix of "A Watcher's Point of View" and the rare 7-inch versions of "Reality Used to Be a Friend of Mine" as well as "The Ways of the Wind" are also here. The latter track's single and album versions are included; though they're significantly different, it's a bit redundant. The edgy hip-hop of "A Watcher's . . . ," "Reality . . . ," and "Gotta' Be . . . Movin' on Up," a track from the *Senseless* soundtrack, break up P.M. Dawn's otherwise lush, glossy sound on this hourlong, 14-track disc. Any band that samples Deep Purple, George Michael, and Joni Mitchell has an astonishingly diverse set of influences, but what made P.M. Dawn special is how they incorporated them into music that was uniquely their own. Despite non-existent liner notes and a few omissions, what is here flows smoothly, especially considering the songs were recorded from 1991 to 1999. Like most timeless music, *The Best of P.M. Dawn*'s songs remain fresh, innovative, and enduring. *—Hal Horowitz*

The Pockets

f. 1975, Baltimore, MD
Group / Quiet Storm, Urban
This was a Baltimore group that scored a Top 20 R&B single in 1977, then never repeated the feat while recording for Columbia and ARC until 1979. Lead vocalist Al McKinney, Larry Jacobs, Gary Grainer, Charles C. Williams, Kevin Barnes, George Gray, Irving Madison, and Jacob R. Sheffer comprised the lineup. *—Ron Wynn*

Come Go With Us / 1977 / Columbia ✦✦✦✦
Fueled by the creative production savvy of Verdine White of Earth, Wind & Fire, this album had some impressive selections. The first release from this effort was the aggressively paced single "Come Go With Me." With a progressive rhythm track, energized vocals and a utopian lyric, the number was filled with zest. In spite of its 18-week run on the R&B charts, it only managed to peak at number 17. The second single was the Latin-flavored "Pasado." Likened to the Brothers Johnson, this midtempo number peaked at 65 after only a seven-week run on the charts. On some tracks there is a close resemblance to Earth, Wind & Fire—"One Day at a Time" and "Doin' the Do" fit that bill. The former, penned by White, has that classic "Reasons" rhythm and melody, while the latter has an aggressive rhythm track in the flow of "Getaway." The resemblance to Earth, Wind & Fire certainly doesn't negate the group's excellent performance. Overall, these Baltimore natives come with a nice blend of selections complemeted by the good production work of White. *—Craig Lytle*

Take It on Up / 1978 / Columbia ✦✦✦
Pockets was one of those bands that was supposed to become huge but never did. When Pockets signed with Columbia in 1977, the Baltimore band's supporters insisted that it was destined to become "the next Earth, Wind & Fire." But commercially, Pockets didn't live up to the hype; its biggest hit was the number-17 R&B single "Come Go With Me." Nonetheless, Pockets' material was generally decent and occasionally excellent. Pockets' second album *Take It on Up* isn't as strong as its predecessor *Come Go With Me*, but it's still enjoyable. Earth, Wind & Fire's Verdine White produced the LP with Robert Wright and, not surprisingly, there's a definite EWF influence on "Happy for Love," "Tell Me Why," and other tracks. But that isn't to say that Pockets was an outright clone of EWF—as much as its members admired EWF, Pockets had a recognizable sound of its own. Anyone playing *Take It on Up* next to an EWF album would have no problem telling the bands apart. Unfortunately for Pockets, this LP didn't contain any major singles and was only a modest seller. *—Alex Henderson*

So Delicious / 1979 / CBS ✦✦✦
By the time Pockets recorded its third and final album *So Delicious*, Columbia was feeling frustrated—a band that was supposed to be "the next Earth, Wind & Fire" had never made it any higher than number 17 on *Billboard*'s R&B singles chart and had yet to enjoy a real blockbuster smash. Although Pockets had a small following, supergroup status eluded the Baltimore residents. Pockets' admirers hoped that *So Delicious* would be the group's big commercial breakthrough, but the LP was only a modest seller. While *Come Go With Me* remains Pockets' best and most essential release, *So Delicious* is generally decent—not mind-blowing, but decent. EWF's Verdine White (a brother of Maurice White) produced *So Delicious* with Robert Wright, which is why the strong EWF influence on "How Do You Think It Feels," "Your Heart's in Trouble," and the single "Catch Me" (which hints at "Boogie Wonderland") should come as no surprise. Even on a cover of the Delfonics' "La La (Means I Love You)," EWF's influence asserts itself. But it isn't like Pockets is going out of its way to emulate EWF; rather, the EWF influence is only one element of the band's overall sound. So Pockets didn't suffer from a lack of originality—that wasn't the problem. Pockets' problem was the lack of a major hit, and when this LP didn't sell, the band ended up calling it quits. *—Alex Henderson*

● **Golden Classics** / Nov. 5, 1996 / Collectables ✦✦✦✦
A misleading title, while not "golden classics" these are the best of the Pockets'—a self-contained band from Baltimore—brief run. A career harpooned by misfortune and the complicated dynamics of keeping an eight-piece band intact. Pockets' sound was uplifting, lively, and vibrant; they were equally as adept on ballads, ups, mids, and straight jams. Their lead singer sounded like Lenny Williams, and pulsating rhythms, pumping horns, and honed backing vocals were their identifiers. The 19 songs represent a great overview and include "Come Go With Me," their most successful record, along with picks like "So Delicious," "In the Pocket," "Elusive Lady," and "One Day at a Time." An interesting collection that never bores, no wonder Earth, Wind & Fire took an interest in their career. *—Andrew Hamilton*

The Pointer Sisters

f. 1971, East Oakland, CA
Group / Adult Contemporary, Urban, Dance-Pop, Soul, Pop/Rock, Soft Rock
Versatile Ruth, Anita, June, and Bonnie Pointer regularly scored pop and soul hits throughout the '70s and '80s in a chameleonic variety of styles. Formed in Oakland, with their first successes for Blue Thumb Records blending funky rhythms with a novel nostalgic attitude (beginning with their 1973 revival of Allen Toussaint's "Yes We Can Can"), leading up to their first number-one R&B item in 1975, "How Long (Betcha' Got a Chick on the Side)." Bonnie signed with Motown in 1978 and kicked off her own string of R&B hits with "Free Me From My Freedom/Tie Me to a Tree (Handcuff Me)." (June and Anita also tried the solo route during the '80s, without leaving the fold.)

By 1979, when the remaining trio covered Bruce Springsteen's "Fire," the Pointers were headed in a more contemporary direction on the Planet label, and "He's So Shy" (1980), "Slow Hand" (1981), "Automatic," and the anthemic "Jump (For My Love)" (the last two both 1984) were savvy ditties that blazed trails across the R&B and pop charts. However, the group's success declined during the late '80s, as their records began to sound more formulaic. The Pointer Sisters lost their major-label record contract in the early '90s, and the group began performing on oldies circuits occasionally. In 1995, the trio made a tentative return to the spotlight when they joined a revival performance of the Fats Waller musical *Ain't Misbehavin'*, yet the accompanying soundtrack album failed to gain much attention. *—Bill Dahl*

The Pointer Sisters / 1973 / MCA ✦✦✦
With a big push from their Blue Thumb label, who introduced the band by way of a full-page ad in *Billboard* magazine, the Pointer Sisters took their eponymous debut straight to the top of the R&B charts in summer 1973 on the strengths of their penchant for mixing classic '60s R&B with fresh forward-thinking grooves. Add the sisters' harmonies and complex vocal moves, and there's no doubt the group was destined for a fast rise.

Produced by David Rubinson, *The Pointer Sisters* contained effusive covers that cradled two of the Pointers' own compositions. That remarkable combo, then, allowed the Allen Toussaint classic "Yes We Can Can" to rub shoulders with the original "Jada," a boogie blues-shaded slab of jazz, and a perfect fingerprint of the eclectic style that would define the Pointers' core. That same bent also allowed them to give equal energy to the Willie Dixon gem "Wang Dang Doodle," a song which quickly became a live set favorite, and also to their own "Sugar." Other high points include "River Boulevard," a midtempo vocal that gives way to a light rock riot. It was easy to see exactly where the Pointer Sisters were headed. With talent to spare and an energy that was fresh and unending, this set emerges a cohesive and joyous cabaret, allowing the quartet to do what it does best. Listening to these earliest gems, it's no surprise, then, that the band would spend the better part of the next two decades in the charts. *—Amy Hanson*

That's a Plenty / 1974 / Blue Thumb ✦✦

A strange bird compared to the Pointer Sisters more successful releases on Planet and RCA Records. The Oakland, CA, singers deliver a mixed bag of nostalgia with novelty that defied classification on this early release. The cornucopia of sounds includes the straight country "Fairytale" which was ironically written by two of the Pointer Sisters; the easy listening "Black Coffee" and "Salt Peanuts," a fast jazz scat, a style that saw its best days in the '40s. "Love in Them There Hills," a remake of the tune popularized by the Vibrations provides the only solace for soul aficionados; it rolls for eight and a half pleasurable minutes of sophisticated soul. *—Andrew Hamilton*

Live at the Opera House / 1974 / ABC ✦✦✦✦

Less than six months after delivering their second album, *That's a Plenty*, the Pointer Sisters unleashed an ambitious double, *Live at the Opera House*, recorded at the San Francisco Opera House on April 21, 1974. Backed by a full orchestra as well as their own assortment of rock musicians and produced, in part, by Bill Graham, who they'd left behind to sign to ABC, the set, like their studio material of the time, blisters with standards, clean three-part harmonies, and forgotten-era charm. Dominated by the blues classics "Salt Peanuts," which is interesting if a little shrill at times, and their hit version of the Willie Dixon standard "Wang Dang Doodle" (blended with their own "Hands Up"), as well as the Gamble & Huff classic "Love in Them There Hills," the set moves at quite a clip. And while these covers are bright enough, where the group truly shines is across their own material. "Shaky Flat Blues" is a marvelous down-tempo number imbibed with smoky swing-era sensibilities, a vibe reiterated on the quiet, textured harmonies of "Jada," which dissolves into a raucous spoken-word free-for-all. Also of interest is the unusual, full-on country song "Fairytale," from *That's a Plenty*, which gave the band a number-35 country hit at the end of 1974. Unlike anything else the group would ever record, it's an odd, but understandable inclusion to the set. With a clean live sound, *Live at the Opera House* ebbs and flows across its four packed sides and 15 hefty tracks. It's a delicious moment in time that captures the band at their early best, before they unleashed the pop goddesses within. *—Amy Hanson*

Steppin' / 1975 / Blue Thumb ✦✦✦✦

Keeping their forward momentum at warp speed, the Pointer Sisters brought the effusive *Steppin'* to bear in summer 1975. Having already danced into the spotlight across their first three albums, it was no surprise when the David Rubinson produced LP, which boasted one of the era's best cut-out sleeves (sling back high heeled tap sneakers!), cruised to number-three R&B. Keeping their feet planted firmly in the older soul tradition which had served them so well, the Pointer Sisters continued to look ahead, carving their own niche in a genre soon to be glutted with contenders. This set is a thriller, from the opening funk groove of the number-one hit "How Long (Betcha' Got a Chick on the Side)," which remains a delicious collision of mid period soul, funk and nascent disco, to their energetic cover of Stevie Wonder's "Sleeping Alone" and "Chainey Do," which sports jazz fusionist Herbie Hancock on clavinet. Sparklers like these only serve to whet the Pointer Sisters' own appetite, though, as they work their way through a hefty course of vibes. Their love of early standards blossoms across the smoky sultry six minute "I Ain't Got Nothing but the Blues"—a wonderful tribute to Duke Ellington, sung in medley form and allowing the quartet's vocal harmonies to shine across a big band backdrop. Elsewhere, they take a spin through Allen Toussaint's "Going Down Slowly", which scored them another R&B hit at the end of 1975. And although the Pointer Sisters are now best remembered for the mid-'80s disco soul they plied so well, it's albums like *Steppin'* which best capture the sisters' true spirit. *—Amy Hanson*

The Best of the Pointer Sisters 1978-1981 / 1976 / RCA ✦✦✦✦

Having a Party / 1977 / Blue Thumb ✦✦

This would have to be deemed their first flop album, but there were extenuating circumstances. Bonnie Pointer would soon bolt from the band, and they were also preparing to jump labels. It didn't help that they had a weak crop of songs as well; even Stevie Wonder's writing help couldn't save "Bring Your Sweet Stuff Home To Me." The Sam Cooke cover did make the lower rungs of the R&B charts, but this qualifies as their least memorable album during the 1970s. *—Ron Wynn*

Energy / 1978 / Planet ✦✦✦✦

Now linked with veteran rock producer Richard Perry and signed to his new Planet imprint, the Pointer Sisters rebounded from 1977's mediocre *Having a Party* to blister through *Energy* in late 1978. An absolutely dynamic set of rock standards overflowing with interesting surprises, the LP entered the R&B Top Ten—the first time the group had enjoyed that kind of placement in nearly three years. With a scything guitar intro that charged through the opening "Lay It on the Line," the Pointer Sisters thrust themselves into a remarkable spotlight, proving they wouldn't be slotted as just another R&B vocal act. A take on the mid-period Fleetwood Mac classic "Hypnotized" is a wonderfully slow, bluesy groove—different, but outstanding in its treatment and probably the best song on the album. Elsewhere, "Happiness" is a fine clash of guitar and disco backbeats and "As I Come of Age" (written by Stephen Stills) emerges as one of the album's quieter moments. It was the band's fair, but not great, cover of Bruce Springsteen's "Fire," though, which gave them their biggest hit, reaching number two on the pop charts in early 1979. Although there are some patchy moments to be found, *Energy* was a fresh introduction to a new look for the Pointer Sisters. Confident in themselves and in the process finding their stride, the band crossed over to the mainstream, arriving in style and settling in for another decade. *—Amy Hanson*

Their Greatest Recordings / 1978 / At Ease ✦✦✦

Priority / 1979 / Planet ✦✦✦✦

If the Pointer Sisters caused a puzzled ripple of amazement with the appearance of their rock & roll Planet debut, then they almost certainly broke the dam on 1979's ballsy, bluesed-out *Priority*. Taking rock covers to the next level and operating still under the guidance of producer Richard Perry, the group delivered another sophisticated set, yet this time barely creaked into the Top 50. Hoping to fuel the flames ignited by the success of their earlier Springsteen cover, "Fire," the Pointer Sisters made sure to take the Boss in tow on this new outing with "She's Got the Fever." Slow and smooth with vocals at the front, the song is the epitome of a late-night, low-light classic. But where things become most interesting is across covers of Ian Hunter's "Who Do You Love?," Graham Parker's "Turned up Too Late," and the Rolling Stones' "Happy." Three grimy rock & roll classics by three grungy bands seemed odd fodder for this R&B group, but not only did the Pointer Sisters hold their own on all counts, their own gospel-influenced vocal styles were surprisingly suited to the material. Elsewhere, a cover of British folky Richard Thompson's "Don't Let a Thief Steal Into Your Heart" is magnificent. The band rounds out the mix with a fabulous reevaluation of Bob Seger's "All Your Love." *Priority* is a remarkable, cohesive set. Unfortunately, it left many of the band's old fans a little unsure of where the Pointer Sisters were headed next, and not one song from the LP managed to crack the charts. Nevertheless, it's an interesting and vibrant sidestep in the band's development—before the 1980s took hold and synth-popped them back to the top of the charts. *—Amy Hanson*

Special Things / 1980 / Planet ✦✦✦

Taking everything back a notch from 1979's rock & roll *Priority* LP, the Pointer Sisters slid into mellower waters, pulling from a pool of Burt Bacharach- and Carole Bayer Sager-penned numbers that were well suited to the re-emergence of the group's R&B stylings. And fans obviously liked what they heard, as the album climbed into the Top 20 in the summer of 1980. Hard-rocking riffs have been replaced by elastic basslines and bright brass punches on "Could I Be Dreaming," and it's a perfect cushion for Anita Pointer's rich vocals. A little further on, "Evil" keeps the brass and loops in some wah-wah guitar riffs, while June Pointer's passionate delivery blisters through the melee in this funk-rock hybrid. And, of course, there are several wonderful down-tempo numbers, including the sleepy "This Love Is Too Good to Last" and "Here Is Where Your Love Belongs." But what shoved this LP up the charts was the smash "He's So Shy," which gave the band a number-three hit. Now classic Pointer Sisters, the song edged out of the set and defined the more pop-oriented direction the band would take as the new decade gathered steam. Slow, sensual, and slightly melancholy, it brought synthesizers to the front of the action, putting the band smack in the middle of a musical revolution that itself was on the verge of explosion. Their timing couldn't have been better. *—Amy Hanson*

Black & White / 1981 / Planet ✦✦✦✦

Their fourth album for Planet, 1981's *Black & White*, was also the Pointer Sisters' fourth Top Ten LP. Leaving behind some of the early soul that had taken them through the 1970s, the band now focused on a purer pop. Keeping one foot in the past while gingerly touching the waters of the future, it was a sound that perfectly welded their old intentions to the mainstream diva flag they'd unfurl a little later in the decade. With more than a few major hits already behind them, it was clear that by this time the band was approaching their peak. Across the sweet pop of the opening "Sweet Lover Man," the oddly frenetic harmonies of "We're Gonna Make It," and onto the light rap of "What a Surprise," the sisters were delivering a hammer-punch to the mainstream masses. But the Pointer Sisters were just getting started. The sensuous "Slow Hand," later revamped by country singer Conway Twitty, not only scored the Pointer Sisters a number-two pop hit, but immediately became one of their signature songs. "Fall in Love Again," meanwhile, remained buried deep on side two, but should be considered one of *Black & White*'s highlights. Gritty and funky, this is classic Pointer Sisters, deep and sensuous and shot through with producer Richard Perry's trademark rock & roll spangles. That only left the closing "Should I Do It?," with its old-school doo wop vibe, to close the sonic circle. And while the full impact of *Black & White* was left behind in the wake of what the Pointer Sisters would later be delivering, it remains a classic, as fragile in its breadth and scope as it is dramatic in its vision of the future. *—Amy Hanson*

Greatest Hits / 1982 / RCA ✦✦✦✦

The Pointer Sisters had their run of hit albums on Planet briefly interrupted in the early '80s, when their label rushed out this anthology as their second album of 1982. They were just coming off a huge R&B and pop hit in "Slow Hand," had another song on the R&B charts, and were red hot. This album didn't do much sales-wise, but served to keep their name alive and clear the way for what would prove their biggest album as a group the next year, *Break Out*. *—Ron Wynn*

So Excited / 1982 / Planet ✦✦✦✦

Sandwiched in between the heavy hitting *Black & White* and *Break Out* LPs, the Pointer Sisters's 1982 *So Excited* effort may not have managed the Top Ten, but impacted the scene nevertheless, as the group took three singles into charts that year. The opening, and best remembered track from the set, "I'm So Excited," delivered a punch-drunk, rapid fire snap straight into the dance clubs, following the marvelous, midtempo swing song "American Music" up the charts with a combination of urgent beats and sassy harmony that fall. And, while these songs, along with chart mate "If you Wanna Get Back your Lady" certainly merit their successes, there are several other moments on the album which actually prove more interesting. The Sue Shifrin penned "See How the Love Goes," which is hauntingly reminiscent of Peter Frampton's "Show me the Way," emerged a gorgeously melancholy melody that hovered somewhere between ballad and smooth groover and showcased Anita Pointer's lead vocals perfectly, while the sisters' turned in a surprising cover of Prince's "I Feel for You" two years before Chaka Khan recorded what has become the definitive version. While it's true that the songs on *So Excited* pale markedly in comparison to the best of the Pointer Sisters' remarkable oeuvre, there are still plenty of unexpected guitar solos and heavy harmonies to snap heads to attention. Even in an off year, the group found themselves happily ensconced in the Top 20. That's no small feat. *—Amy Hanson*

Break Out / 1983 / Planet ✦✦✦✦

By the time the Pointer Sisters unleashed their 1983 *Break Out* LP, they had racked up six Top Ten singles spread between the pop and R&B charts. *Break Out* would prove to be their new wave breakthrough, peppering both charts with five further songs—half the album—while the LP itself spent over a year on the charts. Astute performers, the Pointer Sisters had embraced the 1980s' penchant for synthesized sonics wholeheartedly and used them to fine effect across songs that were upbeat and slick, space-age dance grooves that brought a new dimension to the trio's sound. Both "Jump (For My Love)" and "Automatic" were massive hits during early 1984, as both imbibed the sisters' trademark harmonies with fresh grooves that culminated in an appealing blend of old and new. "Neutron Dance," meanwhile, with Ruth Pointer's rich lead vocal laying over an extraordinarily snappy and nearly frenetic melody, did double duty, also featuring in the film *Beverly Hills Cop*. Using those three songs as a springboard, *Break Out* powers on through one groover after another with few surprises, although "Dance Electric" combines a synthesizer straight out Human League territory with a blistering guitar solo and "Easy Persuasion" emerges as a smoky ballad of sorts. Although *Break Out* is a far cry from the Pointer Sisters' earliest intentions, it still charms and pleases. It's a vital part of the early-'80s tapestry, a sonic signpost for the ultimate feel-good generation. *—Amy Hanson*

Contact / 1985 / RCA ✦✦✦

The Pointer Sisters' 13th charting LP, 1985's *Contact*, was an exercise in slick, edgy, synthesized pop with June, Anita, and Ruth Pointer trading vocal duties. Both "Dare Me" and "Freedom," easily the best songs here, peeled off the album and marched straight onto the singles charts. The former was an audacious, rough-and-ready come-on draped in a samba beat, wrapped in period trimmings, and brimming with sharp vocal harmonies. The latter, on the other hand, graced the R&B Top 30 with a quiet, soulful dream, riding a light beat and little instrumentation. Elsewhere, though, the band packs in the punches across a steady flow of uptempo grooves that heavy-handedly overlay synthesizers at almost every turn, most notably on "Twist My Arm," "Back in My Arms," and "Bodies and Souls." Listeners can only take a breather when the Pointer Sisters do, on the more restrained "Hey You" and "Contact." Overall, though, this set is a workout worthy of leg warmers. While it can be said that there is not one thing technically wrong with *Contact*, neither is there anything that stands out as representative of the band at their best. Consummate performers, the trio is in excellent voice, their harmonies as pure as always. But by 1985 they seemed to have hit a plateau, not striving to change, but apparently happy enough to add synth pop R&B to a market already glutted with the stuff. And, ultimately, the set—good as it is—founders in the decade's own miasma. *—Amy Hanson*

Hot Together / 1986 / RCA ✦✦

Jump: The Best of the Pointer Sisters / 1989 / RCA ✦✦✦✦

Jump: The Best of the Pointer Sisters covers their hits for the Planet record label. They had moved beyond their camp/novelty origins and away from their country flirtation, and were comfortable making exuberantly sung, conservatively produced, soul-tinged pop. During this period, they scored a number of crossover smashes, including "Jump," "He's So Shy," "Automatic" and "Slow Hand"; all of their 1980s hits are included on this album. *—Ron Wynn*

Right Rhythm / 1990 / Motown ✦✦

Only Sisters Can Do That / 1993 / SBK ✦✦

Ain't Misbehavin' (The New Cast Recording) / Jan. 16, 1996 / RCA ✦✦✦

The full title of this record is *The Pointer Sisters in Highlights from Ain't Misbehavin'*, and it is billed as "the new cast recording." What all of this explains is that it captures a performance by a newly assembled revival cast of the 1970s musical revue based on 1930s music associated with Fats Waller, a cast consisting of Anita, June, and Ruth Pointer, Eugene Barry-Hill, and Michael-Leon Wooley. Shortly before the album's recording session on October 8, 1995, the show embarked on a national road tour booked to last through most of 1996 and intended to stop on Broadway eventually. In the meantime, the recording finds the always lively Waller material performed with zest. The Pointers started out in the '70s affecting a nostalgic style, and the Waller songs allow them to indulge a talent for theatrical blues and bawdy singing. If they can dance as well as they sing, this edition of *Ain't Misbehavin'* should be a match for earlier ones. *— William Ruhlmann*

The Very Best of the Pointer Sisters: Fire / Jun. 1996 / RCA ✦✦✦✦✦

Over the course of two CDs, *The Very Best of the Pointer Sisters: Fire* runs through every one of the group's biggest hits of the '70s, from their first hit "Yes We Can" through "Fire," and stopping just after their 1983-1984 peak of popularity with "Automatic," "Jump (For My Love)," "I'm So Excited," and "Neutron Dance." Two discs is too much material for anyone but devoted fans, but this is the most complete retrospective available about the Pointer Sisters, and it's hard to imagine that there will ever be another compilation quite so thorough. *—Stephen Thomas Erlewine*

● **Yes We Can: The Best of the Blue Thumb Recordings** / Jul. 15, 1997 / Hip-O ✦✦✦✦✦

Next to LaBelle, the Pointer Sisters were the most unorthodox and adventurous R&B girl group of the mid-1970s R&B scene. (Of course, they'd still be having hits long after LaBelle's 1977 breakup). Beautifully illustrating the siblings' eclectic nature, this CD focuses on their early material for Blue Thumb Records from 1973-1977. Sweaty, passionate hits like "Yes We Can Can," "How Long (Betcha Got a Chick on the Side)," "Going Down Slowly" and "You Gotta Believe" show that they were a first-class soul group, but that's not all they were. The collection also reminds us that they could be equally exciting when it came to blues (Willie Dixon's "Wang Dang Doodle"), jazz ("Cloudburst," "Black Coffee" and Dizzy Gillespie's "Salt Peanuts") and even country ("Fairytale"). One of the most fun tracks is the delightfully silly "Steam Heat," which finds them going on about how rough the winters were in Oakland, CA. One thing the Sisters never lost was their sense of fun, which continued to serve them well on their slicker and much more pop-minded (though equally engaging) hits of the 1980s. But never were they more risk-taking than when they recorded for Blue Thumb. Pop fans who know the Sisters primarily for "Jump" or "Neutron Dance" but might be unaware of their Blue Thumb output owe it to themselves to hear this magnificent collection. *—Alex Henderson*

● **Best of the Pointer Sisters** / Feb. 22, 2000 / RCA ✦✦✦✦✦

RCA's *The Best of the Pointer Sisters* picks up where Hip-O's *Yes We Can: The Best of the Blue Thumb Recordings* leaves off, presenting 18 of the trio's hits for Planet and RCA Records. The collection begins with 1979's "Fire" and ends with "Goldmine," which peaked on the charts in 1987. In between those two songs are such massive hits as "He's So Shy," "Slow Hand," "Automatic," "Jump (For My Love)," "I'm So Excited," and "Neutron Dance." As these hits prove, the Pointer Sisters got a lot smoother once they left Blue Thumb, choosing to record seductive quiet storm ballads and sprightly dance-pop. Fans of the Blue Thumb years may find this a little distasteful, but as this fine collection illustrates, the Pointer Sisters excelled in this area, just as they did with the funkier material for Blue Thumb. Anyone who is a fan of the group's late-'70s and early-'80s hits will not be disappointed by this disc, since it offers a definitive portrait of the Pointer Sisters at Planet and RCA. *—Stephen Thomas Erlewine*

Bonnie Pointer

b. Jul. 11, 1950, East Oakland, CA

Vocals / Quiet Storm, Adult Contemporary, Urban

Bonnie Pointer began her career as one-fourth of the singing Pointer Sisters during the early '70s. She married producer Jeffrey Bowen and started a solo career at Motown in 1978. She released two albums of mostly covers of early Motown hits. Bonnie Pointer left Motown in the '80s, following a dispute over her contract. She moved to Private I Records, where she recorded *If the Price Is Right* in 1984. *—Rick A. Bueche*

● **Bonnie Pointer (Red Album)** / 1978 / Motown ✦✦✦

For Bonnie's first LP on Motown, producer/hubby Jeffrey Bowen brought some new songs to the sessions this time. The most exciting, "Free Me from My Freedom," has a perky rhythm that's accented by a bubbly bass. Zesty backing voices matched Pointer's stinging vocal. However, the anti-women's-lib lyrics didn't go over well in the '70s. She displays softness on "My Everything," a classy ballad that isn't her forte. And she's back in her element on the disco-arranged "Heaven Must Have Sent You," but it doesn't get interesting until she starts growling. Bowen recycles the formula for "I Can't Help Myself" and "Jimmy Mack," but neither compares to the original, though the latter funks hard near the fade. Arresting productions and arrangements set off "I Love to Sing to You" and "More and More"; the midtempo, flamenco-flavored love songs are tastefully done. Smokey Robinson's "When I'm Gone" works better than the other Motown oldies. Bowen's sound worked better on singles and 12-inches; it gets redundant on LPs. *—Andrew Hamilton*

Bonnie Pointer (Purple Album) / 1979 / Motown ✦✦✦

The second solo Motown LP from Bonnie, the cutest Pointer Sister, lacked imagination. Producer Jeffrey Bowen (her husband) only brought one original song "Deep Inside My Soul" to the session, while the rest are remakes of popular Motown recordings. Pointer's version of "I Can't Help Myself" features a clavinet, and a more complex rhythm arrangement than the Four Tops' version. Dressing classics like "Nowhere to Run," "Jimmy Mack," and "Come See About Me" with synthesizers and polyrhythms is okay for a couple of songs, but not an entire album. For a first effort it did well to nest at number 63 on *Billboard*'s Pop Album chart in 1979. *—Andrew Hamilton*

Poonanny

Producer, Vocals / Retro-Soul, Modern Electric Blues

Bawdy blues-singing Joe Poonanny, aka the God Father of the Chitlin' Circuit, came up in Birmingham, AL. His parents' house was across the street from a show bar, and he could look out his window and watch the drummer play, and aspired to do the same, especially after watching *The Gene Krupa Story*. He practiced daily and played his first professional gig at 17. He drummed around for years but wanted something more substantial, so in 1975 he worked behind the scenes operating night clubs and managing bands, but quit in 1981, citing a dislike of the lifestyle. Always the clown, Poonanny built a reputation by singing risqué, double entendre blues tales in clubs and cabarets but didn't record until 1993 when Waldoxy Records released *Poonanny Be Still!* It became a hot item in the South and several more followed, including *The Grindin' Man*, *Ponyrider*, and *That Baby Ain't Black Enough!* *—Andrew Hamilton*

● **Poonanny Be Still!** / 1993 / Waldoxy ✦✦✦✦

Birmingham, AL resident Joe Poonanny had been a fixture on the Southern chitlin' circuit for around 30 years when, in 1993, he finally recorded his debut album, *Poonanny Be Still!* for Malaco's Waldoxy label. Other labels had expressed interest in the blues/soul singer known for his raunchy humor, but allegedly, Poonanny was distrustful of record companies in general and couldn't be persuaded to record an album until Malaco's

Tommy Couch Jr. came along. This fun, highly entertaining CD won't appeal to those who shy away from off-color humor—it isn't as explicit as a 2 Live Crew album, but it isn't exactly gospel either. Clarence Carter's "Strokin'," Latimore's "Let's Straighten It Out" and Denise LaSalle's "Steppin' Out" were perfect choices for Poonanny, whose album has as much to do with Southern R&B as it does with the blues. *Poonanny Be Still!* did especially well in the South—the people who bought this disc were the same people who were into soul-minded bluesmen like Bobby "Blue" Bland, Little Johnny Taylor and the late Z.Z. Hill and blues-friendly souls singers like Carter and LaSalle. With *Poonanny Be Still!* national audiences finally got a chance to hear a talented singer who had gone unrecorded for too long. *—Alex Henderson*

The Grindin' Man / Nov. 22, 1994 / Waldoxy ♦♦♦♦

Joe Poonanny's a throwback, a modern-day purveyor of the raunchy, bawdy recordings of the '40s and '50s that stereotyped R&B for years. "The Devil's music," as some elders called it, changed by the late '50s when R&B cleaned its image and began selling to the masses. "3 People Sleepin' In My Bed" and "Trashy Women" are the tamest selections; others, however, describe love and sex so descriptively they can only be played when kids aren't present. The titles, including "Meatman," "Out Grindin' the Grindin' Man," "Beat Your Meat," "I Ain't Beggin', I'm Buyin'," and "Rump Ringer," say it all. Producer Tommy Couch Jr. gets great performances from all involved. This is first-class party music; an excellent ice breaker for gatherings. *—Andrew Hamilton*

Poonanny / Apr. 1996 / Waldoxy ♦♦

Ponyrider / Aug. 6, 1996 / Waldoxy ♦♦♦

David Porter

b. Nov. 21, 1941, Memphis, TN

Producer, Songwriter / Soul, Memphis Soul, R&B

David Porter is most famous as the songwriting partner of Isaac Hayes during the 1960s. Functioning as house composers for Stax, they penned most of Sam & Dave's hits, including such classics as "Soul Man" and "Hold On! I'm Coming"; they also wrote material for other acts on the roster, such as Carla Thomas, Johnnie Taylor, and the Soul Children. Starting in the late '60s, Hayes became increasingly involved in his own recording career, eventually leading to the end of the partnership. Many soul fans remain unaware that Porter also began to record his own albums for Stax. In fact, in the '60s he had released a few singles for Savoy and Hi under the pseudonyms of Little David and Kenny Cain, and had done a single for Stax itself in 1965, "Can't See You When I Want To." A remake of "Can't See You When I Want To" became a Top 30 R&B hit for Porter, and he cut several albums for Stax in the early '70s, including an ambitious concept LP, *Victim of the Joke?: An Opera* which connected conventional pop/soul tunes with dialogue. By this time he had teamed up with a different songwriting partner, Ronnie Williams, but as a solo artist he ultimately made little impact. *—Richie Unterberger*

● **Gritty, Groovy, & Gettin' It** / 1970 / Enterprise ♦♦♦♦♦

Victim of the Joke?: An Opera / 1971 / Stax ♦♦♦

Victim of the Joke?: An Opera is a concept album of sorts, the songs linked together by dialogue based around a thin romantic plot. The tunes (including both originals and surprising covers of the Beatles' "Help" and the Tin Pan Alley tune "The Masquerade Is Over") are okay, but not special, treading closer to pop-soul than the grittier tone of many of Porter's '60s compositions with Hayes. Porter's voice, again, is okay but unremarkable. While the construction of the LP was a laudably ambitious outing by early '70s soul standards, the results weren't all that interesting; indeed, the thematic "concept" (of a typically rocky love affair) that drives the album is pretty simple and innocuous. *—Richie Unterberger*

Into a Real Thing / Feb. 1971 / Enterprise ♦♦♦

Positive Force

Group / Old School Rap, Electro

An eight-piece funk/soul band consisting of six males and two females (Brenda Reynolds and Vickie Drayton), Positive Force were founded in Pennsylvania through the efforts of Reynolds and Albert Williams. They were discovered by Nate Edmonds, an organist/pianist, writer, arranger, and producer for All Platinum/Stang/Sugar Hill Records, who got them a deal with Sugar Hill. Edmonds, who served as the group's mentor, also played organ with Curtis Knight & the Squires, a band that included Jimi Hendrix, in the mid-'60s. Positive Force's most-successful performance was an uncredited party ambience performance on the Sugar Hill Gang's "Rapper's Delight." However, success under their name eluded them; their debut, "We Got the Funk" (1979), flopped in the States but became a small-ish club hit in the United Kingdom.

Sugar Hill issued an album, *Positive Force*, in 1980 along with a second single, "Especially for You." Again, nothing sales-wise in the States, but they enjoyed a little cult following in the U.K. and appeared on the *Top of the Pops* television show—their first and only taste of stardom. "We Got the Funk" made a second appearance on the U.K. charts as part of a medley from Calibre Cuts; the occasion marked their last chart showing. They reemerged in 1982 as Positive Express for a final album, entitled *Changing Times*, a joint venture by Victory and Sugar Hill Records. After the single "Welcome to the Party" b/w "Not on the Outside" (the Moments' debut hit) stiffed out, they disbanded. Though known for funk, Positive Force/Express had a slow side, which they demonstrated on their albums via tearjerkers like "Today It Snowed." *—Andrew Hamilton*

● **Positive Force** / 1980 / Sugar Hill ♦♦♦

Bobby Powell

Vocals / Soul

Baton Rouge vocalist Bobby Powell recorded a handful of singles for the Whit label in the '60s and '70s. A blind singer, Powell attended Southern University for the Blind before turning professional. His cover of "C.C. Rider" reached number 12 on the R&B charts and was his lone Top 20 hit in 1965. *—Ron Wynn*

Especially for You / 1993 / Ace ♦♦♦

● **Into My Own Thing: The Jewel and Whit Recordings 1966–1971** / Jun. 26, 2002 / WestSide ♦♦♦♦

Into My Own Thing: The Jewel and Whit Recordings 1966-1971 is a 28-track collection containing nearly everything Bobby Powell recorded for Jewel and Whit during the five years indicated in the title. Though this occasionally gets somewhat generic, it's generic in a good way—good, funky Southern soul-blues, with a tight rhythm section and earthy vocals. There's not much variety in material—in Powell's hands, even the Beatles' "A Hard Day's Night" sounds like neo-Stax soul—but it delivers a consistent groove and serious soul-blues fans will find this entertaining. *—Stephen Thomas Erlewine*

Jesse Powell

b. 1971, Gary, IN

Vocals / Urban, Contemporary R&B, Hip-Hop

Jesse Powell grew up singing with his family and in local talent shows. In 1993, Powell met fledgling producer Carl Roland in Kansas City. Upon their arrival in L.A., the two began working together. Powell got his break when Louis Silas Jr. heard him sing at an artist showcase; it was shortly thereafter that Silas signed Powell to a recording contract. The singer's recordings include 1996's *Jesse Powell!*, 1998's *'Bout It*, and 2001's *JP*. *—Craig Lytle*

Jesse Powell / Mar. 12, 1996 / MCA ♦♦♦

Although Jesse Powell's self-titled debut album retained the services of successful writers and producers such as Stokley & Keri Lewis of Mint Condition, Darryl Simmons, Michael Stokes, and Gordon Chambers, it never reached its market's potential. The first single, "All I Need," didn't shake up the charts. With his remake of Enchantment's classic "Gloria," which is unarguably the best track on the CD, Powell is able to demonstrate some of his vocal range. However, he comes up short with style and creativity, lending nothing new to Emanuel "EJ" Johnson's original arrangement and vocal styling. In addition, this track features the original music and background vocals of Enchantment. The remainder of the CD is mixed with midtempo new jack swing rhythms and laid-back ballads that all sound consistent with each other. As Powell's vocals mature, his delivery should become smoother. *—Craig Lytle*

'Bout It / Sep. 8, 1998 / MCA ♦♦♦

While new jack swing was urban contemporary's dominant sound in the late 1980s and early- to mid-'90s, the style that dominated late 1990s R&B was so-called "jeep soul"—slow-grooving, slow-grinding R&B that was appropriate for cruising around in a jeep. Jeep soul didn't return R&B to the type of greatness that characterized it in the 1960s and 1970s, but it had its moments. One release that was appropriate for the late-'90s jeep soul crowd was Jesse Powell's *'Bout It*, which isn't a gem but is generally decent. The singer doesn't incorporate an abundance of rapping (something many jeep soulsters were doing), but his producers do favor a very hip-hop-ish production style on "Up and Down," "I Wasn't With It" and other selections. Powell doesn't provide anything for the dance floor—most of the time, he gets into a comfortable medium-tempo groove, whether he's being romantic or overtly sexual. Not a remarkable CD, but competent and usually likable. *—Alex Henderson*

● **JP** / Mar. 27, 2001 / MCA ♦♦♦

Jesse Powell's third album, *JP*, finds the Gary, IN, native continuing to improve and grow. It isn't that *JP* is a departure from his two previous albums, *Jesse Powell* (1996) and *'Bout It* (1998)—Powell's specialty is still romantic urban contemporary, and even though a few of the tunes are mildly funky, ballads and slow jams are what ultimately define *JP*. The thing that makes *JP* a step forward for the neo-soulster is the quality of the writing; *JP* falls short of remarkable, but romantic items like "Take My Breath Away" (not to be confused with Berlin's 1986 smash), "If I," and the seductive "Go Upstairs" are definitely solid. The album's best track, however, is an inspired remake of the haunting One Way/Al Hudson ballad "Something in the Past." Sadly, urban contemporary is full of singers (both male and female) who get over on attitude or image alone but are sorely lacking when it comes to chops, substance, and vocal range—Powell, however, has genuine talent. The Midwesterner has an impressive range (four octaves, to be exact), and his attractive phrasing sometimes reminds you of former Klique vocalist Howard Huntsberry (who was heavily influenced by Jackie Wilson). Again, *JP* isn't a masterpiece, but it's an enjoyable step forward for Powell. *—Alex Henderson*

The Precisions

Group / Pop-Soul, Soul, R&B

This energetic group from Detroit has a recording career that spreads over at least nine different labels. Beset by personnel changes, the Precisions dropped singles on Strand, Golden Crest, Wild, Highland, and Debra Records from 1960 to 1963. They achieved some regional play by emulating Nolan Strong's falsetto on two D-Town singles: "My Lover Come Back" b/w "I Wanna Tell My Baby" and "You're Sweet" b/w "Mexican Love Song," but enjoyed their best run on Drew Records.

Their lineup consisted of Arthur Ashford, Michael Morgan, William Rodney Prince, Dennis Gilmore, and Robert Lowe; Billy Brooks was also around and may have blended with them on D-Town and Drew at some point. The first Drew single, "A Lovers Plea" b/w "Such Misery," flopped. A second attempt, "Sugar Ain't Sweet," wasn't issued. "Why Girl," the lively lamenter with the gritty tenor lead, got them recognized in the Midwest and the East, expanding their fan base to Cleveland, Detroit, Pittsburgh, and other cities. Martin Coleman, Michael Valvano, and Charles "Cholly" Bassoline wrote "If This Is Love (Than I'd Rather Be Lonely)," a dweller on both the R&B and pop charts, the well-executed song would have passed Motown's quality control with flying colors. It got them television appearances on second-tier dance shows like *Ken Hawkins World of Soul* in Cleveland, *DJ Hops*, and better-paying gigs. The members wrote their fourth Drew single, "Instant Heartbreak (Just Add Tears)," which charted, but not as high as expected. The Drew story ends with "Never Let Her Go," but with no promotion it didn't have a chance and Drew folded.

The same lineup, minus Lowe, switched to Atco Records and hoped to score big. Atco, part of Atlantic, was a giant compared to Drew; plus, they had Coleman, Valvano (ex-Motowners), and Bassoline crafting the material and twisting the control dials. But the change was a disaster. "Into My Life" died upon release; a second, "New York City" b/w "You're the Best," was totally ignored. Their final single is believed to be "Take a Good Look" on Hen Mar. Dennis Gilmore later wrote "Highway to Heaven" with James Dean for the Dramatics. No one has compiled a Precision CD and a good chronicle of their career is overdue. *—Andrew Hamilton*

Pree (Karen Pree)

Vocals / Urban

As Karen Pree, Pree recorded for various labels in the '70s. She had a minor hit "Make Love Last Forever" on Casablanca Records and released the self-titled *Karen Pree* on MCA Records in 1977. The multi-talented singer, songwriter, vocal arranger, and model grew up in Los Angeles, CA. Her Cherokee/Seminole Native American descent is mixed with African-American, German-Jew, and French. Pree's beautiful voice is always in demand as a background vocalist, and she's worked with Quincy Jones, Cornelius Grant, Bobby Taylor, and many others. She toured with Carolyn Crawford, backing Martha Reeves as the Vandellas for a year. She went on to live in Detroit, MI, since 1983, her hubby being producer/songwriter Clay McMurray, a Motown alumni who produced her *A Matter of Fact* album on My Town Records. *—Andrew Hamilton*

• **A Style of My Own** / 1999 / Mytown ✦✦✦✦✦

What a way to bring in the millennium. *A Style of My Own* is a beautiful record—Pree's voice is unique and enchanting, and can warm the coldest heart. She elevates Prince's "I Wanna Be Your Lover" and Maxine Brown's "Oh No Not My Baby," taking both to new plateaus. Captivating romancers like "Lady in Red," "You've Gotten to Me," and "I'm Feeling in Love" are lush and silky, like vintage Smokey Robinson or Ronald Isley. Even the few midtempo and upbeat tracks float like musical bars of Ivory. Pree overdubbed most of the background vocals but gets help on some from Carolyn Crawford, Dee Dee McNeil, and Farrah, Haven, and Blair McMurray. The album also features an ace production job by Clay McMurray and a stunning cover photo by Dan Guttierez. *—Andrew Hamilton*

The Presidents

f. Washington, D.C.

Group / Urban, Pop-Soul, Soul

A sweet soul group from Washington, D.C., the Presidents scored with the infectious "5-10-15-20-25-30 Years of Love." Written by members Tony Boyd and Archie Powell, and produced by Van McCoy, it reached 11 on the pop charts. Billy Shorter completed the trio who called themselves the Presidents because D.C. was home. They sang in three-part harmony, with the lead bursting from the pack to deliver the lyrics, then blending back with the others for a full sound. They had three other releases on Sussex but never cracked the Top 30 again. Two of the Sussex releases, "For You," a beautiful Van McCoy ballad, and "The Sweetest Thing This Side of Heaven," another ballad McCoy had hit with Chris Bartley, were also released by the SpellBinders on Columbia. Before Sussex they recorded for Hollywood and Deluxe records. They later changed their name to Anacostia, after a large low-income development in D.C. As Anacostia, they recorded for Columbia, MCA, Tabu, and Roulette, well into the '80s. *—Andrew Hamilton*

• **5-10-15-20-25-30 Years of Love** / 1971 / Sussex ✦✦✦✦✦

Billy Preston

b. Sep. 9, 1946, Houston, TX

Keyboards, Organ, Vocals, Piano / Soul, Pop-Soul

It's advantageous to get an early start on your chosen career, but Billy Preston took the concept to extremes. By age ten he was playing keyboards with gospel diva Mahalia Jackson, and two years later, in 1958, he was featured in Hollywood's film bio of W. C. Handy, *St. Louis Blues*, as young Handy himself. Preston was a prodigy on organ and piano, recording during the early '60s for Vee-Jay and touring with Little Richard. He was a loose-limbed regular on the mid-'60s ABC TV series *Shindig*, proving his talent as both vocalist and pianist, and he built an enviable reputation as a session musician, even backing the Beatles on their *Let It Be* album. That impressive Beatles connection led to Preston's big break as a solo artist with his own Apple album, but it was his early-'70s soul smashes "Outa-Space" and the high-flying vocal "Will It Go Round in Circles" for A&M that put Preston on the permanent musical map. Sporting a humongous Afro and an omnipresent gap-toothed grin, Preston showed that his enduring gospel roots were never far removed from his joyous approach. *—Bill Dahl*

The Most Exciting Organ Ever / 1965 / Vee-Jay ✦✦✦✦✦

The hyperbole of the title aside, Preston did produce some flamboyant organ solos and keyboard work throughout this album. His use of bass pedals, dazzling intervals, octave jumps, phrases, and chordal maneuvers were impressive. This hasn't been reissued by Vee-Jay, and certainly should be if the label hasn't lost the masters. It's another side of Preston, one that became lost as he gained more and more popularity in the '70s as a singer. *—Ron Wynn*

The Wildest Organ in Town! / 1966 / Capitol ✦✦✦

A late-'60s Capitol set with Preston displaying his jazz/blues side as an organist. Unfortunately, nothing on this album caught fire, even in the R&B community, and Preston would soon go on to work for Ray Charles and the Beatles. His early prowess as a flashy organ equivalent of Jimi Hendrix has been largely forgotten or overlooked, and the fact that this album hasn't been in print for many years hasn't helped. *—Ron Wynn*

Club Meeting / 1967 / Capitol ✦✦✦

Greazee Soul / 1969 / Soul City ✦✦✦

That's the Way God Planned It / 1969 / Apple ✦✦✦✦✦

A great bit of gospel/soul in the title cut, and otherwise a fine record that didn't make Billy Preston a huge star but alerted everyone that he was more than just a talented keyboard player backing the Beatles. This was one of two albums Preston did on the Beatles' Apple label, and while nothing made the charts, it was a good introduction for those unaware of Preston's multiple skills. *—Ron Wynn*

Music Is My Life / 1972 / A&M ✦✦

Everybody Likes Some Kind of Music / 1973 / A&M ✦✦✦

Original Billy Preston: Soul'd Out / 1973 / GNP ✦✦

A moderately interesting set of tracks that GNP issued in the mid-'70s trying to take advantage of the fact that Billy Preston was a huge star at the time. There's nothing here remotely as interesting as any of his hits, but there are bits and pieces that show his skill as a keyboardist and vocalist. It has long since disappeared, and it's no loss to the Preston legacy. *—Ron Wynn*

Live European Tour / 1974 / A&M ✦✦✦✦

In the mid-'70s, A&M Records began releasing live albums by many of its key rock artists (Peter Frampton, Ozark Mountain Daredevils, Flying Burrito Brothers, etc.). Billy Preston's, recorded along his 1973 European tour with a band that included Mick Taylor—moonlighting from the Rolling Stones (from whose lineup he was soon to be liberated)—might be the most impressive of them all, capturing a funky, soulful, soaring, and overall spellbinding performance that embraced just about every side of his work. Preston's rendition of "Let It Be" is the only one that could challenge the original on its own ground, and Preston also turns in killer renditions of his own hits "Will It Go Round in Circles" and "That's the Way God Planned It," a gorgeous organ instrumental version of "Amazing Grace," and a scintillating performance of "Let's Go Get Stoned" (where he gives a loving homage to Ray Charles). The obligatory "Space Race" and "Outa-Space" are also present, the latter expanded into an eight-minute jam that leaves it not too recognizable but still a fair amount of fun as a finale. The sound is excellent and the only flaw might be the fact that there's only 40 minutes of music on this disc, which is an excellent addendum to Hip-O Records' *Ultimate Collection*. As of 2002, *Live European Tour* has been reissued by A&M's Japanese division in killer sound, and is well worth tracking down. *—Bruce Eder*

The Genius of Billy Preston / 1975 / Springboard ✦✦✦

Here is a low-budget anthology that collects some good Preston recordings, but issued them in such a flimsy-sounding package that it diminishes the value. This label may or may not still be in existence, so if they are, perhaps you'll find this around one day. If not, there are better hits and anthologies packages around. *—Ron Wynn*

Whole New Thing / 1977 / A&M ✦✦✦

Well, it really wasn't a whole new thing—just more of the same from the mega-talented singer/songwriter/producer/keyboardist. Except for two tracks produced by Truman Thomas (the thumpin' title track and "Complicated Sayings"), Billy Preston produced the bulk of this satisfying set issued in November 1977. The artist's amazing dexterity is displayed on the honky tonk flavored "Attitudes" and the "Space Race"-ish number-33 R&B hit "Wide Stride." The LP's cornerstone cut is the organ drenched ballad "I'm Really Gonna Miss You." An alternate take was issued as a charting spring 1978 single, which can be found on *The Best of Billy Preston*. Other standouts are "You Got Me Buzzin'," "Touch Me Love," and "You Don't Have to Go." *—Ed Hogan*

Late at Night / 1979 / Motown ✦✦

The Best of Billy Preston / 1988 / A&M ✦✦✦✦

The singer/songwriter/producer/keyboardist extraordinare's greatest-hits set includes the number-one pop singles "Will It Go Round in Circles'" and "Nothing From Nothing," as well as the number-one R&B hits "Outa-Space" and "Space Race"; all were million sellers. The gentle ballad "You Are So Beautiful" was adapted into a gospel song. The included version of the gospel-ish bluesy ballad "I'm Really Gonna Miss You" is the single version and a different take than the one originally issued on *Whole New Thing*. It's a great showcase for Preston's massive talent. *—Ed Hogan*

• **Ultimate Collection** / Mar. 21, 2000 / Hip-O ✦✦✦✦

Hip-O's *Ultimate Collection* may not have the original hit recording of "That's the Way God Planned It," due to licensing restrictions (it was recorded for the Beatles ill-fated label, Apple), but that's about the only thing missing from this near-definitive single-disc set. Over the course of 20 tracks, the collection chronicles every one of Preston's hits, from the funky "Outa-Space," "Slaughter," and "Will It Go Round in Circles" to the smooth, quiet storm soul of his duets with Syreeta ("With You I'm Born Again," "Go for It," "One More Time for Love"). Since it's quite a transition between the two extremes, fans of either side of the spectrum may not enjoy everything here, but it's nevertheless a nearly flawless collection, providing an accurate portrait of Preston's career. It is true that the lesser-known hits aren't as compelling as the smash singles, but this is still an entertaining collection, regardless. *—Stephen Thomas Erlewine*

Billy's Bag / Nov. 6, 2001 / RPM ✦✦✦

It's too bad the otherwise thorough liner notes don't admit to exactly what releases these 13 tracks first appeared upon, or give any songwriting credits. The title is accurate as far as it goes, though, in that these are early Preston sides from the mid-'60s featuring his organ. All of them are instrumental, so they're not too much in line with the vocal soul material he did after reaching fame as a solo artist. If you're looking for instrumental organ '60s soul with dashes of rock, jazz, and gospel, Preston was one of the best at his game, concocting joyful swirls and unpredictable trills that do much to make the basic R&B material swing. What keeps this from being in the same league as, say, Booker T.

& the MG's is the pedestrian nature of that material, which usually sticks to standard R&B progressions, and doesn't do much to redefine the familiar cover tunes, like "Slippin' & Slidin'" and "Shotgun." At its very best, as on "Soul Derby," "The Octopus," and "Let Me Know," he transcends the unmemorable songs by virtue of sheer passionate virtuosity, taking the organ into some pretty adventurous territory with his dense textures and rapid-fire bursts without abandoning a compelling dance groove. *—Richie Unterberger*

The Very Best of the Vee-Jay Recordings / Oct. 22, 2002 / Collectables ♦♦♦

The Pretenders

Group / Northern Soul, Quiet Storm, Soul

The word obscure doesn't aptly describe the Pretenders' brief association with the recording industry. Their recordings were virtually unknown until the reissue of various CDs of Carnival Records recordings. The only Carnival acts to receive any exposure nationally were the Manhattans and Lee Williams & the Cymbals; Carnival's many other releases by a laundry list of artists never saw much action. Carnival was a tiny company that owner Joe Evans ran out of his house; his wife and a part-time employee were his only staff. While running Carnival, Evans also played sax and toured with Motown's road band under the direction of Choker Campbell; ex-Temptation guitarist Cornelius Grant says Evans would promote Carnival recordings while touring and backing the Motown acts.

The Pretenders also suffered because Joe Evans had practically lost interest in the record business. He earned a G.E.D. and started taking college courses at Rutgers University. This action by Evans was directly related to his money makers, the Manhattans, jumping ship; Evans felt betrayed since he had groomed and polished the group from nothing. However, he was persuaded to make another attempt at making records when he heard a tape of the Pretenders that floored him. They had a different name that Evans didn't like so he changed it. The original group was Harry Simpkins, Eugene Cohen, Neil Page, and Valerie Scott. Page and Scott alternated singing lead. Changes came quick. Though Scott appeared on their first recording, a remake of the Manhattans' "I Wanna Be," her husband didn't want her to tour, so she quit. Enter Patricia Tandy who fit right in and had a stronger voice. Their recordings were vocal masterpieces, with exciting harmonies and emotional leads. Three good examples of this are, "For the Rest of My Days," "Hearts Were Made to Love," and an exciting remake of the Manhattans' "I'm the One Love Forgot." They appeared with groups like the Chi-Lites, Kool & the Gang, the Persuaders, the Intruders, Main Ingredient, and the Drifters, mostly in the Washington, D.C., and Philadelphia, PA, areas. Although they never had a record to chart on *Billboard*, the Pretenders were a versatile and talented group. Member Eugene Cohen went on to write and produce, some of his work appears on the Philadelphia International label. *—Andrew Hamilton*

• **Golden Carnival Classics, Vol. 3** / Jun. 25, 1994 / Collectables ♦♦♦

The third in a series of CD releases of Carnival Records recordings by Collectables Records, and this one is the charm. The Pretenders are unknown to many, even the staunchest R&B fans have probably never heard them. They recorded for Carnival, owned by Joe Evans, during the label's waning years when Joe had apparently lost interest. Nine of the 18 cuts are by the Pretenders, whose lineup was comprised of a female and three males. The three Manhattan remakes are better than the originals, particularly "I'm the One Love Forgot"; this slowie overflows with soul. The Manhattans, who later went on to fame with CBS Records, were Carnival's biggest act. Their "For the Rest of My Days" is simply beautiful, the harmonies unbelievably good, ranking with the best. The other cuts on this compilation, save for the Manhattans' rendition of Lee Williams & the Cymbals' "Til You Come Back To Me," are subpar; the Manhattans' version is more laid-back then the Cymbals' emotionally charged original. Oddly, Collectables left the Cymbals version of this beauty off *Golden Carnival Classics: Part 2*, which featured Lee Williams & the Cymbals. Little Royal is represented on two sides and comes off as a bargain-bin James Brown imitator. "I Say Yeah," by the Pets, deserved mentioning because it was one of George Clinton's (of Parliament/Funkakelic fame) first productions; written by George, Joe Evans, Fuzzy Haskins, and Grady Thomas, and produced by Parlar productions in 1965, it's rather dull and shows no indication of the powerful P-Funk vibes to come. Collectables provides no information about the artists or songwriters, which is pretty pathetic. Kent Records out of the United Kingdom has also compiled a series of CDs chronicling Carnival Records and does a much better job. Their CD booklets include information about the artists, Carnival Records, Joe Evans, and songwriting and publishing credits. *—Andrew Hamilton*

Pretty Poison

f. Philadelphia, PA

Group / Urban, Dance-Pop

Vocalist Jade Starling and Whey Cooler co-formed the five-piece Philadelphia dance group Pretty Poison in the early '80s, also featuring guitarist Lou Franco and drummer Bobby Corea (Cooler's younger brother). They recorded for Svengali and Virgin, and their single "Catch Me (I'm Falling)" was a Top Ten pop hit in 1987; it was also featured in the film *Hiding Out*. It peaked on the R&B side at number 13 and was the group's lone hit. *—Ron Wynn*

Catch Me, I'm Falling / 1988 / Virgin ♦♦♦

Major labels in the late '80s and early '90s kept the cutout bins full with this type of release. It had faceless tracks, standard urban contemporary and dance-pop production, forgettable lyrics, and performances that didn't lack earnestness or energy but were expended on flat, lifeless material. The results were predictable. *—Ron Wynn*

• **Greatest Hits, Vol. 1** / Jan. 21, 1997 / Svengali ♦♦♦♦

Kelly Price

Vocals / Urban, Hip-Hop, Contemporary R&B, Dance-Pop

R&B singer Kelly Price spent her early years in the music business behind the scenes, lending backing vocals to records from stars including Mariah Carey, Aretha Franklin, Faith Evans, and Brian McKnight; additionally, she was the featured voice on the Notorious B.I.G.'s "Mo Money, Mo Problems" and Mase's "Feels So Good." In 1997 Price also appeared on Puff Daddy's smash *No Way Out* and was a featured performer on Puffy's subsequent tour. Her solo debut, *Soul of a Woman*, followed in 1998; *Mirror Mirror* appeared two years later. *—Jason Ankeny*

• **Soul of a Woman** / Jun. 23, 1998 / Island ♦♦♦♦

Kelly Price first made her mark as a vocalist on Notorious B.I.G.'s "Mo Money, Mo Problems" and Mase's "Feels So Good," which may give the casual observer the impression that she's a straight-up gangsta. Not so. Price is an urban crooner, much like a streetwise Mariah Carey or a domesticated Mary J. Blige. She has a sweet, smooth voice that's a joy to listen to, but what makes her debut *Soul of Woman* so impressive is that she's not just a singer, she's a talented songwriter as well. *Soul of a Woman* is filled with well-crafted contemporary R&B songs that are melodic, memorable and perfectly delivered. It's an audacious debut from a promising young talent. *—Stephen Thomas Erlewine*

Mirror Mirror / Jun. 27, 2000 / Def Soul ♦♦♦♦

Like Mary J. Blige, Price has a big, bad, beautiful voice. And like Blige, she often chooses smart material to go along with that big, bad, beautiful voice. On her second album, she goes through many R&B motions—over-singing, pallid bedroom songs, tuneless tales—but still manages to sound like a genuinely thrilled diva in the process. Filled with slow jams, slick hip-hop, and gospel, *Mirror Mirror* is a more rounded record than Price's debut. Best is a cover of Shirley Murdock's "As We Lay" played like a Broadway curtain-closer. It reveals Price's penchant for theatricality and demonstrates her warmth as a singer. She puts an individualist's stamp on the album, a looking glass, if you will, into her soul. *—Michael Gallucci*

Lloyd Price

b. Mar. 9, 1933, Kenner, LA

Vocals / New Orleans R&B, R&B, Rock & Roll

Not entirely content with being a 1950s R&B star on the strength of his immortal New Orleans classic "Lawdy Miss Clawdy," singer Lloyd Price yearned for massive pop acceptance. He found it, too, with a storming rock & roll reading of the ancient blues "Stagger Lee" and the unabashedly pop-slanted "Personality" and "I'm Gonna Get Married" (the latter pair sounding far removed indeed from his Crescent City beginnings).

Growing up in Kenner, a suburb of New Orleans, Price was exposed to seminal sides by Louis Jordan, the Liggins brothers, Roy Milton, and Amos Milburn through the jukebox in his mother's little fish-fry joint. Lloyd and his younger brother Leo (who later co-wrote Little Richard's "Send Me Some Lovin'") put together a band for local consumption while in their teens. Bandleader Dave Bartholomew was impressed enough to invite Specialty Records boss Art Rupe to see the young singer (this was apparently when Bartholomew was momentarily at odds with his longtime employers at rival Imperial).

At his very first Specialty date in 1952, Price sang his classic eight-bar blues "Lawdy Miss Clawdy" (its rolling piano intro courtesy of a moonlighting Fats Domino). It topped the R&B charts for an extended period, making Price a legitimate star before he was old enough to vote. Four more Specialty smashes followed—"Oooh, Oooh, Oooh," "Restless Heart," "Tell Me Pretty Baby," "Ain't It a Shame"—before Price was drafted into the Army and deposited unhappily in Korea. When he finally managed to break free of the military, Price formed his own label, KRC Records, with partners Harold Logan and Bill Boskent and got back down to business. "Just Because," a plaintive ballad Price first cut for KRC, held enough promise to merit national release on ABC-Paramount in 1957 (his ex-valet, Larry Williams, covered it on Price's former label, Specialty).

"Stagger Lee," Price's adaptation of the old Crescent City lament "Stack-A-Lee," topped both the R&B and pop lists in 1958. By now, his sound was taking on more of a cosmopolitan bent, with massive horn sections and prominent pop background singers. Dick Clark insisted on toning down the violence inherent to the song's story line for the squeaky-clean *American Bandstand* audience, accounting for the two different versions of the song you're likely to encounter on various reissues. After Price hit with another solid rocker, "Where Were You (On Our Wedding Day)?" in 1959, the heavy brass-and-choir sound became his trademark at ABC-Paramount. "Personality," "I'm Gonna Get Married," and "Come Into My Heart" all shot up the pop and R&B lists in 1959, and "Lady Luck" and "Question" followed suit in 1960.

Always a canny businessman, Price left ABC-Paramount in 1962 to form another firm of his own with Logan. Double L Records debuted Wilson Pickett as a solo artist and broke Price's Vegas lounge-like reading of "Misty" in 1963. Later, he ran yet another label, Turntable Records (its 45s bore his photo, whether on his own sizable 1969 hit "Bad Conditions" or when the single was by Howard Tate!), and operated a glitzy New York nightspot by the same name. But the music business turned sour for Price when his partner, Logan, was murdered in 1969. He got as far away from it all as he possibly could, moving to Africa and investing in nonmusical pursuits. Perfect example: He linked up with electric-haired Don King to promote Muhammad Ali's bouts in Zaire (against George Foreman) and Manila (against Joe Frazier). He indulged in a few select oldies gigs (including an appearance on NBC-TV's *Midnight Special*), but overall, little was seen of Price during the 1970s.

Returning to America in the early '80s, he largely resisted performing until a 1993 European tour with Jerry Lee Lewis, Little Richard, and Gary "U.S." Bonds convinced him there was still a market for his bouncy, upbeat oldies. Price's profile went on the upswing since—he guested on a PBS-TV special with Huey Lewis & the News, and regularly turned up to headline the Jazz & Heritage Festival in his old hometown. *—Bill Dahl*

Lloyd Price: His Originals / 1959 / Specialty ♦♦♦♦♦

Subtitled "My 14 Favorites," this is a nice collection of his very first recordings for Art Rupe's Specialty label in the early '50s. His first hit, "Lawdy Miss Clawdy," is aboard, along with classics like "Mailman Blues," "Oh, Oh, Oh," and "Wish Your Picture Was You." These tracks were cut in New Orleans using the cream of that town's session players, and as such, the music swings with a verve that his later, brassier hits for ABC-Paramount lack, fine as they are. If you want to come in at the start of one of the longer and more varied careers in R&B music, this is the one to pick up. *—Cub Koda*

Mr. Personality / 1959 / ABC ♦♦♦
Recorded in absolutely breathtaking stereo that greatly enhances the brass-heavy arrangements, this LP is worth grabbing any time you run across it. Sure, Lloyd Price sounds off-key on the Tin Pan Alley chestnuts "I Only Have Eyes for You" and "Time After Time," but a forceful "I Want You to Know," the torchy "Dinner for One," and a rocking "Is It Really Love?" make up for the intrusions. *—Bill Dahl*

Mr. Personality Sings the Blues / 1960 / ABC ♦♦♦♦
Blues was no big stretch for the vocalist—his Crescent City output was solidly rooted in the idiom. On this LP, he does a fine job on Eddie Vinson's "Kidney Stew," and Paul Perryman's "Just to Hold My Hand," and his own blasting "I've Got the Blues and the Blues Got Me." *—Bill Dahl*

Sings the Million Sellers / 1961 / ABC ♦♦♦
Lloyd Price sang the hits of the immediate time frame on this long out-of-print album, doing particular justice to "Ain't That Just like a Woman" (then a minor seller for Fats Domino), the Miracles' "Shop Around," the Midnighters' "The Hoochie Coochie Coo," and the Drifters' "I Count the Tears." Uptown soul arrangements by future Motown staffer Gil Askey give Price full-bodied support. *—Bill Dahl*

Greatest Hits / 1982 / MCA ♦♦♦♦♦
Price wasn't content with R&B fame; he yearned for pop acceptance too. He got plenty at ABC-Paramount from 1957 to 1960 (the time frame this 18-song retro addresses). Creating a brassy, accessible sound, Price hit huge with his rock & roll rendition of "Stagger Lee" (here in two versions—original and *American Bandstand*-sanitized) and went all the way pop with the undeniably catchy "Personality." Innovative arrangements and Price's earnest vocals greatly distinguish "Have You Ever Had the Blues?," "Lady Luck," "Three Little Pigs," and "Where Were You (On Our Wedding Day)," and there's a previously unissued "That's Love" to further up the ante. *—Bill Dahl*

★ **Lawdy!** / Aug. 5, 1991 / Specialty ♦♦♦♦♦
Lloyd Price was a teenager when he scored his first hit, "Lawdy Miss Clawdy," for Art Rupe's young Specialty imprint. Backed by trumpeter/arranger Dave Bartholomew's band (featuring special guest Fats Domino on the 88s), Price's song soared to the top of the R&B charts, scoring Rupe his first crossover hit by racking up sales among both white and black audiences. Though Price's time with Specialty was cut short when he was drafted in 1953, he managed nearly 50 storming, pre-rock & roll sides for the label, 25 of which are gathered on *Lawdy.* Though nothing here was as big a hit as his debut, many of these songs easily could have come close were they selected over later Specialty smashes like "Ooh Ooh Ooh" or "Restless Heart." A shout singer with enough edge on his voice to be convincing (even as a teenager), Price's early style was tailor-made for the 45 format. With little thought to pacing himself, the singer seems to approach each number as if it may be his last time at the microphone and, therefore, his last chance at a hit. Though that sense is exactly what makes the music so thrilling, it's also what makes these 25 sides difficult to digest *en masse.* That said, for "Lawdy Miss Clawdy" alone this set is worth it, and the high quality of nearly everything else on hand makes for a desirable package of the singer's early work. *—Nathan Bush*

Lloyd Price, Vol. 2: Heavy Dreams / 1993 / Specialty ♦♦♦♦♦
There is no discernible artistic drop-off on Specialty's encore Price retrospective, distinguished by his classics "Oooh-Oooh-Oooh," "Tell Me Pretty Baby," "Ain't It a Shame?" (not Fats Domino's hit), "Country Boy Rock," and "Why" (he later recut the latter for ABC-Paramount). *—Bill Dahl*

★ **Greatest Hits: The Original ABC-Paramount Recordings** / 1994 / MCA ♦♦♦♦♦
Lloyd Price's recordings of ABC-Paramount were bigger and glossier than his recordings for Specialty, complete with female backing vocals, strings, and pop production. This, of course, means that certain audiences don't consider them as real as his raw, gritty Specialty recordings, and if that's what you're looking for from Price, turn to their excellent compilation, *Lawdy!* But, if you want to hear the second, hitmaking half of Price's career, this is the collection to get, and it provides numerous pleasures. First among those, of course, is the phenomenal "Stagger Lee," a storming version of the classic folk ballad that brought the tale of a murdering outlaw into the pop charts, creating enormous controversy and producing an absurdly sanitized version (known as the Bandstand Version, since it was initially recorded for use on *American Bandstand*). Both versions of the song are here, both terrific (with the original version getting the obvious edge), along with other hits like the yearning "Just Because," the giddy stroll "Personality," the galloping "Where Were You (On Our Wedding Day)?," and a tamer re-recording of "Lawdy Miss Clawdy," along with 12 other sides that might not have been hits, but most are very enjoyable. True, this isn't gutsy R&B like the Specialty sides, but these were meant to be rock & roll hits, and they not only were, they're among the best of their kind from the late '50s. It's Essential music. *—Stephen Thomas Erlewine*

Maxi Priest (Max Elliot)

b. 1962, London, England
Vocals / Smooth Reggae, Contemporary Reggae, Reggae-Pop, Dancehall, Urban, Lovers Rock
Born Max Elliot in Manchester, England, in 1962, Maxi Priest changed his name when he converted to Rastafarianism. He stumbled into a career in reggae when he was discovered while building sound systems. Since then, Maxi Priest became one of the great crossover success stories of the '80s, making chart-toppers on both sides of the Atlantic. A pleasant, easygoing vocal manner coupled with a sexy stage presence have yielded consistent hits—including a cover of "Some Guys Have All the Luck" in 1987 and Cat Stevens' "Wild World" in 1988. Though he initially sang straight, ultra-slick lovers rock, the '90s found him dabbling in dancehall with impressive results. In 1990, he scored a number one pop hit in the U.S. with "I Just Want to Be Close to You" and a Top Ten with "Set the Night to Music," a duet with Roberta Flack. *Man With the Fun*, released in 1996, contained another hit, "That Girl" featuring Shaggy. *—Roger Steffens*

Intentions / 1986 / Charisma ♦♦♦

Maxi Priest / 1988 / Virgin ♦♦♦♦
This bends the reggae-pop equation back toward the crossover side. *—Ron Wynn*

Bonafide / Jun. 1990 / Charisma ♦♦

● **The Best of Me** / 1991 / Charisma ♦♦♦♦♦
The Best of Me collects nearly all of Maxi Priest's pre-1992 U.K. and U.S. singles, and results in a timeless, breezy, and thoroughly engaging album. Maxi Priest doesn't really tackle the heavy social themes that many of his reggae contemporaries do—instead, he sings about love, life, and summertime (what, in other words, is known as "lovers rock"). Included here are nearly all of his U.K. hits, including "Strollin' On," "How Can We Ease the Pain," "Peace Throughout the World," and his cover of "Some Guys Have All the Luck," as well as his near-perfect version of Cat Stevens' "Wild World," which broke him to U.S. audiences, and his funky and immortal 1990 U.S. chart-topper "Close to You." Also included is his hit duet with Shabba Ranks, "Housecall," in which Maxi Priest, with his honey-smooth vocals, completely steals the show, as well as his minor U.S. hit "Just a Little Bit Longer." This CD was released in 1991, after the phenomenal success of "Close to You" and its album *Bonafide*, therefore, later hits such as "Groovin' in the Midnight," "That Girl" (with Shaggy), and his massive duet with Roberta Flack, "Set the Night to Music," don't appear. Until a later and complete hits package is assembled, *The Best of Me*, which also features great pictures, song lyrics, and detailed liner notes, more than fits the bill. *—Jose F. Promis*

Man With the Fun / 1996 / Virgin ♦♦♦
Man With the Fun showcases Maxi Priest's talent for shaping reggae, dancehall and soul into a distinctly pop-oriented and commercial amalgam. *Man with the Fun* happens to be one of Priest's better efforts, simply because the quality of the production and songwriting is uniformly first-rate throughout the record. Of course, there are quite a few mediocre tracks, but the smooth sounds of Priest's voice and the seamless production holds your interest until the album arrives at highpoints like Maxi's duet with Shaggy, "That Girl." *—Leo Stanley*

CombiNation / Jul. 13, 1999 / Virgin ♦♦♦♦
Few artists have explored the possibilities of reggae-pop fusion as successfully as Maxi Priest, who is enormously popular in his native Britain and has achieved a level of stateside success that other reggae artists (with the exception of UB40) can only wish for. His smooth voice and his comfort with soul and hip-hop have only increased his marketability; purists may scoff, but there's no denying his talent. *CombiNation* finds him working in an explicitly soul-influenced style—"What a Woman Needs" and "Wasn't Meant to Be" are seductive smooth groove ballads that have no noticeable connection to any reggae tradition—with frequent detours into muscular hip-hop and dancehall grooves. "Mary's Got a Baby" is a monstrously funky collaboration with Beenie Man (a stripped-down remix ends the album); "Tell Your Man to Take a Walk" takes a similar approach, this time in partnership with the DJ Red Rat. Slow love songs predominate, although they don't provide most of the album's highlights. Recommended. *—Rick Anderson*

The Primes

f. 1955
Group / Doo Wop, R&B
Eddie Kendricks, Paul Williams, Willy Waller, and Kell Osborne, as the Cavaliers, sang in local talent shows with other up-and-coming Birmingham, AL, artists including Frederick Knight, Barbara Lomax (B.T. Express), and Richard Fisher (Jive Five). Kendricks and Williams came to Cleveland, OH, in the late '50s and performed around the area. Williams and Kendricks hooked up with Cleveland natives Paul Hayes and Fred Fluellen but never recorded. With no great haps in Cleveland, manager Milton Jenkins took over the reins and persuaded Williams and Kendricks to move to Detroit. Kell Osborne joined them in Detroit; it's unclear whether Waller trekked from Birmingham too, but Detroiters don't recall him being on the scene. Jenkins christened the trio the Primes, and named a quartet of teenagers—comprising Diana Ross, Mary Wilson, Florence Ballard, and Betty McGlown—the Primettes.

The Primettes struck recording blood first at Lu Pine Records, backing artists like Don Revel and Gene Martin, and even recorded a single, "Pretty Baby." Tiring of gigging in small clubs, Kendricks left for Birmingham but returned shortly afterward; around the same time, Osborne left the Primes to go solo. Two of the Distants—whose downsized lineup consisted of Otis Williams, Melvin Franklin, and Al Bryant—quit, which led to openings for Paul and Eddie, who had befriended the Distants at a house party. The Distants became the Elgins, and secured a deal with Motown, upon which they became the Temptations; already on board was their former sister group, the Primettes, now the Supremes. The Temptations cut their first Motown release on the Miracle label, "Oh Mother of Mine" b/w "Romance Without Finance," and the rest is history. None of the singles Kell Osborne cut on various labels ever charted, though he possessed a marvelous voice that ranged between Eddie's falsetto and Paul's baritone. Some of Osborne's output includes "Little Darling" on Cenco, "The Bells of St. Mary's," and recordings on Brunswick Records. As talented as the Cavaliers/Primes were, no recordings by them are known to exist. *—Andrew Hamilton*

The Primettes

f. 1959, Detroit, MI

Group / Girl Group, Motown, R&B, Soul

The Primettes changed their name to the Supremes, endured a series of flops, and became one of the most successful female vocal groups ever. But before their torrid chart run in the mid-'60s, they were highly sought-after backing vocalists. Their contributions to Bob West's Lu Pine label are documented, but one can also hear them backing obscure artists on a myriad of tiny Detroit-based labels. Diana Ross, Mary Wilson, Florence Ballard, and Betty McGlown were the original Primettes; McGlown married early and became Betty Travis. Ballard formed the group while the members were still in school. Milton Jenkins managed the Primes—Eddie Kendricks, Paul Williams, and Kell Osborne—an exciting trio from Birmingham, AL. Jenkins discovered them in Cleveland and took them to Detroit, where they befriended Ballard, Wilson, Ross, and Travis. Taking them under his wing, Jenkins named them the Primettes, the Primes' sister group.

When she lived in the Belmont area, Ross resided down the street from Smokey Robinson's family and watched the Matadors practice; she was tight with Robinson's sister, Sharon. She begged Robinson, who was making noise with the Miracles, to get them an audition with Berry Gordy. Robinson liked them and promised to tell Gordy. The Motown audition in 1960 was a disappointment; Gordy wasn't exactly wowed with their rendition of the Drifter's "There Goes My Baby," and told them to come back after finishing high school.

Songwriter Richard Morris loved them and introduced them to Bob West, the owner of Lu Pine and its subsidiary labels, who signed the youngsters. Motown was their first love, however, and they hung around 2648 West Grand Boulevard every chance they got, befriending producers, writers, and office staff. They recorded one single on Lu Pine in 1959 that wasn't released until 1964, "Pretty Baby" b/w "Tears of Sorrow." Wilson sings lead on "Pretty Baby" and Ross leads on "Tears of Sorrow." Every member sang lead in the early days, depending on the song. Their talent was obvious—their infectious vocal blend featured Ross' nasal soprano on top and Wilson's alto on the bottom. McGlown left, Barbara Martin replaced her, and Martin stayed until 1963.

The Primettes did so many backing sessions that it's hard to track them all. They accompanied James Dee & a Piece of the Action on "My Pride"; Gene Martin on "Lonely Nights"; Don Revel on "The Return of Stagger Lee"; Wilson Pickett on "Let Me Be Your Boy"; James Velvet on "When I Needed You," "Bouquet of Flowers," "We Belong Together," and "I'm Gonna Try"; Al Garner on "I'll Get Along" and "All I Need Is You"; Walt Jessup on "Roll On"; Eddie Floyd's sessions at Lu Pine; and more, all before Motown. Their labels include Lu Pine, Cub, Correc-Tone, and Pussy Cat.

During all the sessions and little gigs around town, the girls finished school and finally signed with Motown in 1961. Not liking the name the Primettes, Gordy suggested a change, and Ballard came up with the Supremes, which everybody liked. As the Primettes, they recorded some unreleased tracks on Motown, such as "After All" and others, that didn't surface until some 30 years later. They also backed many Motown artists, including Bob Kayli, Mabel John, Pete Hartfield, Stevie Wonder, Don McKenzie, Mary Wells, Marvin Gaye, and Kim Weston. Martin left after the first few non-charting singles to pursue other things, and Ross, Wilson, and Ballard continued as a trio. Soon they began a torrid string of number one hits, commencing with "Where Did Our Love Go." *—Andrew Hamilton*

● **Looking Back** / Apr. 21, 1998 / Ember ♦♦♦

This CD is slightly misleading—it does, indeed, contain seven of eight songs known to have been cut by the Primettes for Lu Pine Records in 1960, although the group is singing backup behind Al Garner on several of these numbers. They're paired here with eight early Eddie Floyd sides, also cut for Lu Pine following the breakup of the Falcons. Primitive as some early Motown recordings seem, these Primettes sides outdo them, essentially doo wop records with an edge, and patterned after the singing of the Chantels. Diana Ross's voice is in evidence, at a very youthful stage, but Florence Ballard (with Mary Wilson and Barbara Martin) is more prominent—"Tear of Sorrow," eerily enough, anticipates the sound and texture of "Please Mr. Postman," even as it borrows some patterns and musical phrases from the Drifters' then-contemporary hit "There Goes My Baby." "Pretty Baby" even seems to appropriate a bit from "Way Over There" by Smokey Robinson & the Miracles. The rest is passionately sung but otherwise undistinguished early '60s girl group style pop—the Primettes had the voices and meshed them well, but needed better songs and a sound of their own, none of which was coming from their manager or Lu Pine Records. Eddie Floyd's sides are more properly representative of his work. The sound quality is fair to good, and somewhat uneven. [British import] *—Bruce Eder*

Prince (Prince Rogers Nelson)

b. Jun. 7, 1958, Minneapolis, MN

Vocals, Keyboards, Drums, Guitar, Bass / Pop/Rock, Club/Dance, Funk, Dance-Pop, Urban, Neo-Psychedelia, Album Rock, Soul, Hard Rock, College Rock

Few artists have created a body of work as rich and varied as Prince. During the '80s, he emerged as one of the most singular talents of the rock & roll era, capable of seamlessly tying together pop, funk, folk, and rock. Not only did he release a series of groundbreaking albums, he toured frequently, produced albums and wrote songs for many other artists, and recorded hundreds of songs that still lie unreleased in his vaults. With each album he has released, Prince has shown remarkable stylistic growth and musical diversity, constantly experimenting with different sounds, textures, and genres. Occasionally, his music can be maddeningly inconsistent because of this eclecticism, but his experiments frequently succeed; no other contemporary artist can blend so many diverse styles into a cohesive whole.

Prince's first two albums were solid, if unremarkable, late-'70s funk-pop. With 1980's *Dirty Mind*, he recorded his first masterpiece, a one-man *tour de force* of sex and music; it was hard funk, catchy Beatlesque melodies, sweet soul ballads, and rocking guitar pop, all at once. The follow-up, *Controversy*, was more of the same, but *1999* was brilliant. The album was a monster hit, selling over three million copies, but it was nothing compared to 1984's *Purple Rain*. *Purple Rain* made Prince a superstar; it eventually sold over ten-million copies in the U.S. and spent 24 weeks at number one. Partially recorded with his touring band the Revolution, the record featured the most pop-oriented music he has ever made. Instead of continuing in this accessible direction, he veered off into the bizarre psycho-psychedelia of *Around the World in a Day* (1985), which nevertheless sold over two-million copies. In 1986, he released the even stranger *Parade*, which was in its own way was as ambitious and intricate as any art rock of the '60s; however, no art rock was ever grounded with a hit as brilliant as the spare funk of "Kiss."

By 1987, Prince's ambitions were growing by leaps and bounds, resulting in the sprawling masterpiece *Sign o' the Times*. Prince was set to release the hard funk of *The Black Album* by the end of the year, yet he withdrew it just before its release, deciding it was too dark and immoral. Instead, he released the confused *Lovesexy* in 1988, which was a commercial disaster. With the soundtrack to 1989's *Batman* he returned to the top of the charts, even if the album was essentially a recap of everything he had done before. The following year he released *Graffiti Bridge*, the sequel to *Purple Rain*, which turned out to be a considerable commercial disappointment.

In 1991, Prince formed the New Power Generation, the best and most versatile and talented band he has ever assembled. With their first album, *Diamonds and Pearls*, Prince reasserted his mastery of contemporary R&B; it was his biggest hit since 1985. The following year, he released his 12th album, which was titled with a cryptic symbol; in 1993, Prince legally changed his name to the symbol. In 1994, after becoming embroiled in contract disagreements with Warner Bros., he independently released the single "The Most Beautiful Girl in the World," likely to illustrate what he would be capable of on his own; the song became his biggest hit in years. Later that summer, Warner released the somewhat halfhearted *Come* under the name of Prince; the record was a moderate success, going gold.

In November 1994, as part of a contractual obligation, Prince agreed to the official release of *The Black Album*. In early 1995, he immersed himself in another legal battle with Warner, proclaiming himself a slave and refusing to deliver his new record, *The Gold Experience*, for release. By the end of the summer, a fed-up Warner had negotiated a compromise which guaranteed the album's release, plus one final record for the label. *The Gold Experience* was issued in the fall; although it received good reviews and was following a smash single, it failed to catch fire commercially. In the summer of 1996, Prince released *Chaos & Disorder*, which freed him to become an independent artist. Setting up his own label, NPG (which was distributed by EMI), he resurfaced later that same year with the three-disc *Emancipation*, which was designed as a magnum opus that would spin off singles for several years and be supported with several tours. However, even his devoted cult following needed considerable time to digest such an enormous compilation of songs. Once it was clear that *Emancipation* wasn't the commercial blockbuster he hoped it would be, Prince assembled a long-awaited collection of outtakes and unreleased material called *Crystal Ball* in 1998. With *Crystal Ball*, Prince discovered that it's much more difficult to get records to an audience than it seems; some fans who pre-ordered their copies through Prince's website (from which a bonus fifth disc was included) didn't receive them until months after the set began appearing in stores. Prince then released a new one-man album, *New Power Soul*, just three months after *Crystal Ball*; even though it was his most straightforward album since *Diamonds and Pearls*, it didn't do well on the charts, partly because many listeners didn't realize it had been released.

A year later, with "1999" predictably an end-of-the-millennium anthem, Prince issued the remix collection *1999 (The New Master)*. A collection of Warner Bros.-era leftovers, *Vault: Old Friends 4 Sale*, followed that summer, and in the fall Prince returned on Arista with the all-star *Rave Un2 the Joy Fantastic*.

Two years later, Prince returned with not only a new album, *Rainbow Children*, but an entirely new outlook on life as a Jehovah's Witness convert. *—Stephen Thomas Erlewine*

For You / Oct. 1978 / Warner Bros. ♦♦

On his debut album *For You*, Prince shows exceptional skill for arranging and performing mainstream urban R&B and funk, but his songwriting remains conventional. Only on the mildly racy "Soft and Wet" does he demonstrate a personal touch, but the song is still more of a promise than a fulfillment. While *For You* isn't a bad record, it is merely a pleasant one, and it offers very little indication of his staggering talents. *—Stephen Thomas Erlewine*

Prince / Oct. 1979 / Warner Bros. ♦♦♦

Expanding the urban R&B and funk approach of his debut, *Prince* is a considerably more accomplished record than his first effort, featuring the first signs of his adventurous, sexy signature sound. Although the album is still rather uneven, a handful of songs rank as classics. "I Wanna Be Your Lover" is excellent lite funk, and "Why You Wanna Treat Me So Bad?" is a wonderful soulful plea, but "I Feel for You," a sexy slice of urban R&B with a strong pop melody, is the true masterpiece of *Prince*, indicating the major breakthroughs of his next album, *Dirty Mind*. *—Stephen Thomas Erlewine*

☆ **Dirty Mind** / Oct. 1980 / Warner Bros. ♦♦♦♦♦

Neither *For You* nor *Prince* was adequate preparation for the full-blown masterpiece of Prince's third album, *Dirty Mind*. Recorded in his home studio, with Prince playing nearly every instrument, *Dirty Mind* is a stunning, audacious amalgam of funk, new wave pop, urban R&B, and pop, fueled by grinningly salacious sex and the desire to shock. Where other pop musicians suggested sex in lewd double entendres, Prince left nothing to hide—before its release, no other rock or funk record was ever quite as explicit as *Dirty Mind*, with its gleeful tales of oral sex, threesomes, and even incest. Certainly, it opened the doors for countless sexually explicit albums, but to reduce its impact to mere profanity is too reductive—the music of *Dirty Mind* is as shocking as its graphic language, bending styles and breaking rules with little regard for fixed genres. Basing the album on a harder, rock-oriented beat than before, Prince tries everything—there's pure new wave pop ("When You Were Mine"), soulful crooning ("Gotta Broken Heart Again"), robotic funk ("Dirty Mind"), rock & roll ("Sister"), sultry funk ("Head," "Do It All Night"), and relentless dance jams ("Uptown," "Partyup"), all in the space of half an hour. It's a breathtaking, visionary album, and its fusion of synthesizers, rock rhythms, and funk set the style for much of the urban soul and funk of the early '80s. *—Stephen Thomas Erlewine*

Controversy / Nov. 1981 / Warner Bros. ♦♦♦
Controversy continues in the same vein of new wave-tinged funk on *Dirty Mind*, emphasizing Prince's fascination with synthesizers and synthesizing disparate pop music genres. It is also more ambitious than its predecessor, attempting to tackle social protest ("Controversy," "Ronnie, Talk to Russia," "Annie Christian") along with sex songs ("Jack U Off," "Sexuality"), and it tries hard to bring funk to a rock audience and vice versa. Even with all of Prince's ambitions, the music on *Controversy* doesn't represent a significant breakthrough from *Dirty Mind*, and it is often considerably less catchy and memorable. Nevertheless, Prince's talents as musician make the record enjoyable, even if it isn't as compelling as most of his catalog. *—Stephen Thomas Erlewine*

☆ **1999** / Feb. 1983 / Warner Bros. ♦♦♦♦♦
With *Dirty Mind*, Prince had established a wild fusion of funk, rock, new wave, and soul that signaled he was an original, maverick talent, but it failed to win him a large audience. After delivering the sound-alike album *Controversy*, Prince revamped his sound and delivered the double-album *1999*. Where his earlier albums had been a fusion of organic and electronic sounds, *1999* was constructed almost entirely on synthesizers by Prince himself. Naturally, the effect was slightly more mechanical and robotic than his previous work and strongly recalled the electro-funk experiments of several underground funk and hip-hop artists at the time. Prince had also constructed an album dominated by computer funk, but he didn't simply rely on the extended instrumental grooves to carry the album—he didn't have to when his songwriting was improving by leaps and bounds. The first side of the record contained all of the hit singles, and, unsurprisingly, they were the ones that contained the least amount of electronics. "1999" parties to the apocalypse with a P-Funk groove much tighter than anything George Clinton ever did, "Little Red Corvette" is pure pop, and "Delirious" takes rockabilly riffs into the computer age. After that opening salvo, all the rules go out the window—"Let's Pretend We're Married" is a salacious extended lust letter, "Free" is an elegiac anthem, "All the Critics Love U in New York" is a vicious attack at hipsters, and "Lady Cab Driver," with its notorious bridge, is the culmination of all of his sexual fantasies. Sure, Prince stretches out a bit too much over the course of *1999*, but the result is a stunning display of raw talent, not wallowing indulgence. *—Stephen Thomas Erlewine*

★ **Purple Rain** / Aug. 6, 1984 / Warner Bros. ♦♦♦♦♦
Prince designed *Purple Rain* as the project that would make him a superstar, and, surprisingly, that is exactly what happened. Simultaneously more focused and ambitious than any of his previous records, *Purple Rain* finds Prince consolidating his funk and R&B roots while moving boldly into pop, rock, and heavy metal with nine superbly crafted songs. Even its best-known songs don't tread conventional territory: the bass-less "When Doves Cry" is an eerie, spare neo-psychedelic masterpiece; "Let's Go Crazy" is a furious blend of metallic guitars, Stonesy riffs, and a hard funk backbeat; the anthemic title track is a majestic ballad filled with brilliant guitar flourishes. Although Prince's songwriting is at a peak, the presence of the Revolution pulls the music into sharper focus, giving it a tougher, more aggressive edge. And, with the guidance of Wendy and Lisa, Prince pushed heavily into psychedelia, adding swirling strings to the dreamy "Take Me With U" and the hard rock of "Baby I'm a Star." Even with all of his new, but uncompromising, forays into pop, Prince hasn't abandoned funk, and the robotic jam of "Computer Blue" and the menacing grind of "Darling Nikki" are among his finest songs. Taken together, all of the stylistic experiments add up to a stunning statement of purpose that remains one of the most exciting rock & roll albums ever recorded. *—Stephen Thomas Erlewine*

Around the World in a Day / 1985 / Paisley Park ♦♦♦
Purple Rain made Prince sound like he could do anything, but it still didn't prepare even his most fervent fans for the insular psychedelia of *Around the World in a Day*. Prince had made his interior world sound fascinating and utopian on *Purple Rain*, but *Around the World in a Day* is filled with cryptic religious imagery, bizarre mysticism, and confounding metaphors, which were drenched in heavily processed guitars, shimmering keyboards, grandiose strings, and layers of vocals. As an album, the record is a bit impenetrable, requiring great demands of the listener, but individual songs do shine through: "Raspberry Beret" is a brilliant piece of neo-psychedelia with an indelible chorus, "Pop Life" is a snide swipe at stardom that emphasizes Prince's outsider status, "Condition of the Heart" is a fine ballad, "America" is a good funk jam, "Paisley Park" is heavy and slightly frightening guitar psychedelia, while the title track is a sunny, kaleidoscopic pastiche of *Magical Mystery Tour*. The problem is, only a handful of the songs have much substance outside of their detailed production and intoxicating performances, and the album has a creepy sense of paranoia that is eventually its undoing. *—Stephen Thomas Erlewine*

Parade (Music from the Motion Picture "Under the Cherry Moon") / May 19, 1986 / Paisley Park ♦♦♦♦♦
Undaunted by the criticism *Around the World in a Day* received, Prince continued to pursue his psychedelic inclinations on *Parade*, which also functioned as the soundtrack to his second film, *Under the Cherry Moon*. Originally conceived as a double album, *Parade* has the sprawling feel of a double record, even if it clocks in around 45 minutes. Prince and the Revolution shift musical moods and textures from song to song—witness how the fluttering psychedelia of "Christopher Tracy's Parade" gives way to the spare, jazzy funk of "New Position," which morphs into the druggy "I Wonder U"—and they're determined not to play it safe, even on the hard funk of "Girls and Boys" and "Mountains," as well as the stunning "Kiss," which hits hard with just a dry guitar, keyboard, drum machine, and layered vocals. All of the group's musical adventures, even the cabaret-pop of "Venus de Milo" and "Do U Lie?," do nothing to undercut the melodicism of the record, and the amount of ground they cover in 12 songs is truly remarkable. Even with all of its attributes, *Parade* is a little off-balance, stopping too quickly to give the haunting closer, "Sometimes It Snows in April," the resonance it needs. For some tastes, it may also be a bit too lyrically cryptic, but Prince's weird religious and sexual metaphors develop into a motif that actually gives the album weight. If it had been expanded to a double album, *Parade* would have equaled the subsequent *Sign o' the Times*, but as it stands, it's an astonishingly rewarding near-miss. *—Stephen Thomas Erlewine*

The Black Album / 1987 / Paisley Park ♦♦♦
Originally scheduled for release in November of 1987—following the double-album *Sign o' the Times* by a matter of months—Prince pulled *The Black Album* weeks before its release, guaranteeing it near-mythic status. Urban legends spread like wildfire: Prince believed it was too bleak to release; Warner Brothers balked at its explicit lyrics; no CDs were ever pressed, and all the LPs were destroyed. That final rumor was certainly untrue, since bootlegs immediately appeared, and when it finally received official release in the fall of 1994, nearly every die-hard fan already had the record. That limited-edition release of *The Black Album* turned out to be a bit anti-climatic, since the album itself isn't a lost masterwork—it's fun, but not much more. If anything, it's a little labored, as Prince works hard to win back the black audience he willfully abandoned after *Purple Rain*. So, he serves up "When 2 R in Love," an urban ballad every bit as nondescript as the genre, and offers "Dead on It," trying to one-up rappers with a mocking attack that winds up as one of the lamest things he ever waxed. The rest of the eight-song album is brilliant pure funk, ranging from the unrelenting "Le Grind," a deliriously lustful plea to supermodel Cindy Crawford, the hyper-tense James Brown workout "2 Nigs United 4 West Compton" to "Bob George," a perverse tale of a macho lunkhead (prince, electronically affecting a deep, idiotic drawl) who discovers his lady just slept with Prince—or "that skinny motherfucker with a high voice," as Bob calls him. All this may not add up to a lost classic, but it is a terrific little record that still delights, even after its mystique has faded. *—Stephen Thomas Erlewine*

☆ **Sign o' the Times** / Mar. 31, 1987 / Paisley Park ♦♦♦♦♦
Fearless, eclectic, and defiantly messy, Prince's *Sign o' the Times* falls into the tradition of tremendous, chaotic double albums like *The Beatles*, *Exile on Main St.*, and *London Calling*—albums that are fantastic because of their overreach, their great sprawl. Prince shows nearly all of his cards here, from bare-bones electro-funk and smooth soul to pseudo-psychedelic pop and crunching hard rock, touching on gospel, blues, and folk along the way. This was the first album Prince recorded without the Revolution since 1982's *1999* (the band does appear on the in-concert rave-up, "It's Gonna Be a Beautiful Night"), and he sounds liberating, diving into territory merely suggested on *Around the World in a Day* and *Parade*. While the music overflows with generous spirit, these are among the most cryptic, insular songs he's ever written. Many songs are left over from the aborted triple album *Crystal Ball* and the abandoned Camille project, a Prince alter-ego personified by scarily sped-up tapes on "If I Was Your Girlfriend," the most disarming and bleak psycho-sexual song Prince ever wrote, as well as the equally chilling "Strange Relationship." These fraying relationships echo in the social chaos Prince writes about throughout the album. Apocalyptic imagery of drugs, bombs, empty sex, abandoned babies and mothers, and AIDS pop up again and again, yet he balances the despair with hope, whether it's God, love, or just having a good time. In its own roundabout way, *Sign o' the Times* is the sound of the late '80s—it's the sound of the good times collapsing and how all that doubt and fear can be ignored if you just dance those problems away. *—Stephen Thomas Erlewine*

Lovesexy / Feb. 1988 / Paisley Park ♦♦♦
It's nearly impossible to judge *Lovesexy* as anything but a hastily assembled substitute for the withdrawn *Black Album*, which does the record a disservice. An exactingly sequenced song cycle—the compact disc didn't have index markings to separate the individual tracks—*Lovesexy* is quite a different record than not only *The Black Album*, but anything else Prince had recorded. Where *Dirty Mind* was single-minded in its lust, *Lovesexy* connects the carnal with spiritual, and the calmness of the music reflects this outlook. Even when the record dips into hard funk, such as on the title track or the single "Alphabet Street," there's a relaxed, casual quality to the music that is shocking after the dense paranoia of *Parade*, *Sign o' the Times*, and *Black Album*. Prince intends to enter a new phase of maturity with such considered music and ambitious lyrical themes, but neither his music nor his lyrics are consistently well-stated over the course of the album. A handful of tracks are worthwhile—the sappy ballad "When 2 R in Love," the moving "I Wish U Heaven," the weird psychedelia of "Anna Stesia" and "Glam Slam," as well as the wonderful "Alphabet Street"—but it is his weakest album since *Controversy*. *—Stephen Thomas Erlewine*

Batman / Jun. 1989 / Paisley Park ♦♦♦
Prince had stumbled commercially with *Lovesexy*, which may be one of the reasons he decided to record the soundtrack for Tim Burton's dark, gothic interpretation of the DC comic *Batman*. Reportedly, the *Batman* album was recorded quickly, and it shows in the loose, offhand nature of the songs, which actually comes as some relief after the big ambitions of all of his records since *1999*. "The Future" and "Electric Chair" are fine, funky one-man efforts, and "Vicki Waiting" is an excellent pure pop song, while "Arms of Orion" is embarrassingly enjoyable sappy mainstream balladry, and "Batdance" is a fun dance-club pastiche of the entire album. Even with these highlights, there are no true classics on the record, and it tends to evaporate in the memory after it's finished—there's no doubt it spent six weeks at the top of the charts because of the blockbuster film. Still, *Batman* sounds fine while it's playing. *—Stephen Thomas Erlewine*

Graffiti Bridge / Aug. 21, 1990 / Paisley Park ♦♦♦
Prince was shooting for the top of the charts with *Graffiti Bridge*, and he missed. The movie was a disaster, causing the soundtrack to sell very poorly. Despite its poor showing,

Graffiti Bridge is not a bad album; in fact, it's often very good. Prince wrote all of the songs, but only performed a little over half the tracks, leaving the rest for the Time, Mavis Staples, and Tevin Campbell. With the exception of the Time's slamming "Release It" and Campbell's "Round and Round," the best songs are the ones Prince performed himself. The George Clinton collaboration "We Can Funk," the psycho-blues of "The Question of U," the sinewy single "Thieves in the Temple," and the pop/rock of "Can't Stop This Feeling I Got," "Tick, Tick, Bang," and "Elephants & Flowers" make *Graffiti Bridge* a thoroughly enjoyable listen. *—Stephen Thomas Erlewine*

Diamonds and Pearls / Oct. 1991 / Paisley Park ♦♦♦
Prince spent the latter half of the '80s courting the pop audience, and by the time of *Graffiti Bridge*, he had lost much of his R&B fan base. As a response, he formed the New Power Generation and recorded *Diamonds and Pearls*, his first record to reconnect with the urban audience since *1999*, as well as his first to acknowledge the hip-hop revolution. Although he still has a problem with rap—"Jughead" is simply embarassing—he manages to skillfully reinvent himself as an urban soulman without sacrificing his musical innovation. The New Power Generation is a more skilled band than the Revolution, and they are able to make Prince's funk jazzier, particluary on "Willing and Able," the breezy "Strollin'" and "Walk Don't Walk." It's clear that these subtly textured songs are where his heart is at, but the songs designed to win back his audience—the slamming dancefloor rallying cry "Gett Off," the sexy T. Rex groove "Cream," the extraordinary Philly soul of the neglected masterpiece "Money Don't Matter 2 Night" and the drippy mainstream ballad "Diamonds and Pearls"—are all terrific pop singles. However, much of the rest of *Diamonds and Pearls* is comprised of middling funk and R&B that sounds less like inspired workouts than stylistic exercises. Even with such weak moments, *Diamonds and Pearls* is a fine record, even though it's only marginally better than *Lovesexy* and *Graffiti Bridge*. *—Stephen Thomas Erlewine*

The Love Symbol Album / Oct. 13, 1992 / Paisley Park ♦♦♦♦♦
The New Power Generation is the most talented and versatile band Prince has ever fronted, and they fulfill their potential on *Symbol*. Although the NPG factored heavily on *Diamonds and Pearls*, it still sounded like a solo Prince album. *Symbol* sounds like a band performing together, working off of each other's strengths and weaknesses. Opening with the dance smash "My Name Is Prince" and the deep funk of "Sexy M.F.," *Symbol* has Prince's best dance tracks since the *Black Album*. But Prince wasn't content; he decided to run the gamut of modern pop/R&B/dance, and the music is uniformly accomplished and excellent. Unfortunately, he also decided to make a "rock soap opera," so the music is saddled with ridiculous lyrics and annoying sound bridges by Kirstie Alley. However, *Symbol* has some of the finest, most inventive music of Prince's career. *—Stephen Thomas Erlewine*

☆ **The Hits 1** / Sep. 14, 1993 / Paisley Park ♦♦♦♦♦
The primary fault with Prince's two-part *Hits* collection is that both volumes are missing some important singles and are sequenced incoherently, thereby failing to give an accurate impression of his astonishing musical growth. However, they do contain enough necessary items to illustrate why he was one of the most influential and gifted musicians of the '80s, as well as providing a reasonable introduction and compilation for casual fans. *Hits 1* contains a good cross-section of his biggest hits—"When Doves Cry" (presented in an edited version), "When You Were Mine," "Let's Go Crazy," "1999," "Sign o' the Times," "Alphabet Street," "Diamonds and Pearls," "7"—plus new items like "Pink Cashmere" and "Nothing Compares 2 U" (a Prince song that Sinead O'Connor took to number one) which are nearly as good as the familiar tracks. However, it provides an incomplete portrait, making *Hits 2* a necessary purchase. *—Stephen Thomas Erlewine*

☆ **The Hits 2** / Sep. 14, 1993 / Paisley Park ♦♦♦♦♦
Like *Hits 1*, *Hits 2* presents an illogically sequenced cross-section of some of Prince's biggest hits and most notorious songs, including "Dirty Mind," "I Wanna Be Your Lover," "Head," "Delirious," "Little Red Corvette," "I Would Die 4 U," "Raspberry Beret," "Kiss," "U Got the Look," "Cream," and "Purple Rain." Two new tracks, "Peach" and "The Pope," are included among the 18 cuts and while they don't match the rest of the songs (or the new cuts on *Hits 1*), they are nevertheless enjoyable. On the whole, *Hits 2* is a slightly stronger collection than its predecessor, but it still gives a rather incomplete portrait—if you buy *Hits 2*, you need to buy *Hits 1*. *—Stephen Thomas Erlewine*

The Hits/The B-Sides / Sep. 14, 1993 / Paisley Park ♦♦♦♦♦
While it isn't a truly comprehensive set, Prince's singles collection does contain most of his biggest hits. The two volumes are available separately or packaged together with a third disc of B-sides; apart from the glorious "Erotic City," the flip sides are only of interest to devoted fans. *—Stephen Thomas Erlewine*

Come / Aug. 16, 1994 / Paisley Park ♦♦
Released after Prince announced his retirement and his intention of never using the name "Prince" again, *Come* is something of a surprise: an album of reportedly all new material, released by "Prince," not "The Artist Formerly Known As Prince." After listening to *Come*, its purpose becomes clear—it's a record fulfilling a contract, nothing more and nothing less. Some of the songs are good, but there's nothing on *Come* that Prince hasn't done before; he even sounds bored on certain tracks. On top of that, the album has no obvious singles, making it a nightmare to sell. Not surprisingly, the album flopped. *—Stephen Thomas Erlewine*

Gold Experience / Oct. 1995 / Warner Bros./NPG ♦♦♦♦
Prince changed his name to an unpronounceable symbol in 1993, but it wasn't until 1995 that he actually released a record credited to that symbol. During those two years, he released a greatest-hits collection, an official version of his much-bootlegged *Black Album*, and a final Prince album, the lackluster *Come*. Throughout 1994, he pressured Warner to release another album, *The Gold Experience*, but the company refused and he staged a public protest in the media, calling himself a slave to the label. By the summer of 1995, the artist and the company had made amends and the record was released in the fall. In a way, *The Gold Experience* lives up to the manufactured hype created while it languished on the shelf. More of a creative rebirth than a change in direction, the record finds Prince and the New Power Generation running through a typically dazzling array of musical styles, subtly twisting new sounds out of familiar forms. Much like *The Love Symbol Album*, it follows a loose concept, interweaving a variety of pop, funk, rock, soul, and jazz styles into a vague story. Song for song, *The Gold Experience* is slightly stronger than its predecessor, as Prince's melodies are more immediate, especially on the Philly soul tribute "The Most Beautiful Girl in the World" and the pure pop of "Dolphin." Also, the band's performance is lively and confident, bringing an effortless virtuosity to funk workouts ("P Control") and fuzzed-out rockers ("Endorphinmachine"), as well as ballads like "Eye Hate U." *The Gold Experience* is somewhat weighed down by interludes that attempt to further the story but wind up interrupting the flow of the music, yet that doesn't stop the album from being Prince's most satisfying effort since *Sign o' the Times*. *—Stephen Thomas Erlewine*

Chaos & Disorder / Jul. 1996 / Warner Bros. ♦♦♦
Like *Come* before it, *Chaos & Disorder* is a contractual obligation album for Prince, a way to get himself out of his contract with Warner Brothers. Unlike *Come*, *Chaos & Disorder* doesn't sound disjointed and pasted together—it's a fun, off-handed throwaway. For the first time since 1987's *Sign o' the Times*, Prince has made a pop/rock album, complete with squealing guitars and sighing melodies. None of the songs qualify as major songs in Prince's canon, but that's part of the record's charm—Prince sounds like he's having a good time, and he could really care less what anyone else has to say. Or, as he puts it in one of the album's best and most careening tracks, "I Rock, Therefore I Am." *Chaos & Disorder* sounds immediate, like the songs were recorded the same day they were written. While that might mean there's a handful of throwaways scattered throughout the album, there are wonderful moments like the stuttering jazz-funk of "Dig U Better Dead," the scathing "Had U," the pscyhedelic clashes of the title track, the heavy rock of "I Like It There" and the beautiful "Dinner With Delores," a rough gem that ranks as one of Prince's simplest and most charming singles of the '90s. So, *Chaos & Disorder* isn't Prince's best or most important work, but it is a really fun listen, especially if you're willing to accept it as what it is—a record that does nothing more than rock. *—Stephen Thomas Erlewine*

Emancipation / Nov. 19, 1996 / NPG/EMI ♦♦♦♦
Emancipation was a critical moment for Prince, one that he designed as an artistic rebirth and, optimistically, as a commercial comeback. In a typically perverse fashion, Prince decided to make the album a triple-disc set running exactly three hours, easily making it the longest album of all-new original material ever released by a popular artist. As the first album he released since leaving Warner Brothers, *Emancipation* was supposed to dazzle, proving that he had not lost any of his creative skills or power. And it does dazzle, but it's hard to digest a full three discs of music, even if it is almost all of high quality. Fortunately, Prince made each disc into a distinct entity in its own right, with the first being the most pop, the second being a song cycle devoted to his new marriage, and the third being a dance/funk extravaganza. Throughout all three discs, Prince tries on a variety of styles, from jazz to R&B, but he doesn't break any new ground; instead, the album is simply reaffirmation of his strengths as a composer and a musician. *Emancipation* doesn't have the bristling, colorful eclecticism of *Sign o' the Times* nor does it have the wildness of early one-man projects like *1999* or *Dirty Mind*, but with its gentle ballads and complex jams, it signals that Prince has evolved into middle-age gracefully. It's a mature effort, to be certain, but in this case that doesn't mean that it's an album bankrupt of ideas—it means that Prince's craft continues to grow. *—Stephen Thomas Erlewine*

Crystal Ball / Mar. 3, 1998 / NPG ♦♦♦
As any die-hard fan knows, *Crystal Ball* was the triple-album set Prince had planned to release in 1987, when Warner forced him to trim it to the double album *Sign o' the Times*. Since then, *Crystal Ball* had become a legendary "lost" album among Prince collectors, and many of its outtakes had circulated on bootlegs for years. So, it didn't come as a complete surprise that Prince revived the title for his own collection of outtakes, which turned out to be the first release on his independent NPG label. Any collector will quibble with the track selection, since there are literally hundreds of known Prince outtakes, and there's no way that a three-disc set could include all the best cuts. Still, this is an impressive sampler that illustrates the true depth of Prince's talents. There may be no hidden masterworks on the level of "When Doves Cry," but the music here is consistently strong and compelling. As a compiler, Prince errs by favoring latter-day recordings over his '80s studio creations, but this is a minor complaint, since he has included such legendary (at least among collectors) songs as "Dream Factory," "Movie Star," "Crucial," "Sexual Suicide," "Days of Wild," and "The Ride." Prince added a full-length album, *The Truth*, as the fourth disc to *Crystal Ball*. Taken on its own terms, *The Truth* is a terrific little record with a similar feel to *Chaos & Disorder*, but with stronger material. Purportedly, it's Prince's acoustic album, but he uses that concept to spring into the blues, tape effects, straight-ahead pop, and soul. It's a joy to hear him work in such a structured form, since it helps him focus his ideas and deliver a tight, enjoyable pop record that offers proof he hasn't lost his gifts. *—Stephen Thomas Erlewine*

New Power Soul / Jun. 30, 1998 / NPG ♦♦
Releasing two multi-disc sets may have been an audacious way to begin his career as an independent artist, but it did nothing to re-establish Prince as a commercial powerhouse. Perhaps that's the reason he released *New Power Soul* (credited to his backing band, New Power Generation, but it's a Prince album in all but name) a mere four months after his mammoth quadruple-disc *Crystal Ball* hit the stores—it was time to release a concise,

focused pop-funk record that proved he could still deliver. And it does, to a certain extent. *New Power Soul* is a tight, focused record, filled with energetic funk workouts and classy, seductive ballads. It's paced to entertain, just like one of his legendary concerts, and there's no shortage of well-crafted songs. The problem is, nothing stands out and makes itself known. Certainly, the album sounds great as it's playing, but it cements Prince's evolution from groundbreaker to craftsman. There are pleasures in his craft, to be sure, but in order to hear them, you have to be a committed fan. *—Stephen Thomas Erlewine*

The Vault: Old Friends 4 Sale / Aug. 24, 1999 / Warner Bros. ✦✦✦
Upon leaving Warner Brothers in 1996, Prince agreed to let the label release a collection of unreleased recordings from his legendary prodigious vaults at some point in the future. Warner unveiled that collection, unimaginatively titled *The Vault: Old Friends 4 Sale*, in the summer of 1999. Instead of an official release for several of Prince's legendary songs though, *The Vault* is a brief collection (under 40 minutes) of ten songs, recorded between 1985 and 1994 according to the liner notes—though they all feel like *Graffiti Bridge* (or maybe *Symbol*) outtakes. That's not a complaint, actually. There's a wonderful carefree feeling to the record, heavy on jazz and light funk, constantly swinging, and nearly always engaging. Only the title track has the necessary weight to announce itself as a major addition to his official catalog, but that doesn't matter since the songs are all enjoyable. After all, it's hard not to be impressed with Prince's songcraft or the casually sophisticated flair to the musicianship throughout the album. That might not be what most observers expected from *The Vault*, but consider this—of these ten songs, eight tracks have never been heavily bootlegged before. That means that even some hardcore followers may not have heard all of this material, which is noteworthy in itself. But the nicest thing about the compilation is that even though it's a minor addition to his catalog, it holds together as an album better than *Come* or *Chaos & Disorder*, the two other Warner-era odds-and-ends collections, or even the tossed-off *New Power Soul*. It's an unassuming, jazzy little record that's damn near irresistible. *—Stephen Thomas Erlewine*

Rave Un2 the Joy Fantastic / Nov. 2, 1999 / NPG/Arista ✦✦✦
Clive Davis convinced Prince to record a star-studded comeback album for Arista in 1999—much like how he coaxed Prince's idol Carlos Santana to revive his career with *Supernatural*. Problem is, Prince isn't willing to fully throw himself into the contemporary mainstream, as Santana did. Instead, he sticks to his guns with *Rave Un2 the Joy Fantastic*, delivering an album that's frighteningly similar to the lackluster *New Power Soul*, only a little slicker and better, and with cameos. *Rave*, like its predecessor, is stilted and canned, clearly the work of one man with guitars, synths, and a drum machine. It's shocking to hear how perfunctory most of the performances are on *Rave*, yet it's stranger to hear Prince gunning for the pop charts. He has funk, a dash of pop, a little bit of rap, and a whole lotta ballads—anything that could result in a crossover hit. There are a couple of cool moments on this overlong, 70-minute album and, curiously, most of those are tracks with superstar collaborators. Prince sounds committed and adventurous on these songs, whether it's the electro-funk "Undisputed," which features a Chuck D rap, the harmonica-laden bluesy pop of "Baby Knows" (harmonica and harmonies by Sheryl Crow), or the utterly delightful, effervescent duet with Gwen Stefani ("So Far, So Pleased"). These songs, along with the passable funk-pop title cut and the ballads "The Sun, the Moon and Stars" and "Wherever U Go, Whatever U Do" are pretty enjoyable, yet their presence highlights how pedestrian the remainder of *Rave* is. Also, these are the kind of songs fanatics appreciate because of their subtleties. So, this is one for the dedicated, like every album he's made since he changed his name to a symbol. *—Stephen Thomas Erlewine*

★ **The Very Best of Prince** / Jul. 31, 2001 / Rhino ✦✦✦✦✦
Even geniuses (maybe especially geniuses) are taken for granted, not seen as geniuses, or only appreciated in small doses. Which is a grandiose way of saying that, no matter how partisans may complain, there are many listeners out there that don't want to delve into the deliriously rich catalog of Prince and would rather spend time with a single disc of all the hits—especially since the first singles compilation was botched, spread too thin over two discs and sequenced as if it were on shuffle play. That doesn't mean that 2001's *The Very Best of Prince* is perfect, even if it is a better hits overview than its predecessor. First of all, Prince had so many hits, and so many of them were so good, that 17 tracks couldn't possibly summarize everything great. After all, this doesn't have Top Ten hits like "Delirious," "Pop Life," "I Could Never Take the Place of Your Man," or "The Most Beautiful Girl in the World" (or the number one "Batdance," for that matter, continuing *Batman* being unofficially written out of his discography), nor does it have such great second-tier hits as "Take Me With U" and "Mountains," or B-sides like "Irresistible Bitch" and "Erotic City," let alone album tracks. What is here are the big songs—"1999," "Little Red Corvette," "When Doves Cry," "Kiss," and so on—all presented in their single edits. And, frankly, that's enough to make this a dynamite collection, perfect for those that just want one Prince disc, and a good, solid listen of some of his best. Besides, this trumps both *Hits* discs by including "Money Don't Matter 2 Night," his best single never to reach the Top 10. *—Stephen Thomas Erlewine*

The Rainbow Children / Nov. 20, 2001 / Redline ✦✦✦
Billed as Prince's most controversial album—at least by his press agency and label—upon its release in the fall of 2001, *The Rainbow Children* was arguably his most curious album to date, which isn't necessarily the same thing as controversial. It could have been controversial, that's for sure, given that it follows his conversion to the Jehovah's Witnesses and that it trumpets his faith, over the most elastic, jazziest backing music he's made. If Prince hadn't marginalized himself through his record company battles, multi-disc sets, and botched superstar comebacks, this could have been genuinely controversial, since people would be paying attention to what he's doing. As of 2001, nobody outside of the die-hards—those who sign up for the Paisley Park subscription service and those that will seek out an album like *The Rainbow Children*, which was initially only available through the Internet—was really paying enough attention to listen to this record, since they were the only ones to sit through the cascade of arcania he turned out after his liberation from Warner. Since they're so deeply immersed in this work, they would realize that musically *The Rainbow Children* is his most cohesive set since *The Gold Experience*, and the only one to really push past his traditional limits since then (which, admittedly, is still much more imaginative). And, you know, that's really too bad, because as a musical experience, this is pretty rich, demonstrating not just that Prince knows no borders, but that his music effortlessly mutates within the course of one song, perhaps drawing from his standard book of tricks—jazz fusion, smooth soul, lite psychedelia, hard rock, and funk general weirdness—but always sounding unpredictable and rewarding. It's too bad, then, that the very thing that inspired the album for its creator is what will turn off even those die-hards that stuck with him this long, seeking out this album—namely, its religious views. It's not that Prince has become a Jehovah's Witness—any objective listener really wouldn't care—but it's that his message doesn't support the music and doesn't fit with the sounds or the approach; it's hard to shut it out, not just because the words are so prominent, but because they're delivered in so many different voices (most distracting of all, the electronically altered basso profundo voice last heard on the decidedly secular "Bob George"), often in short, two-minute songs. This becomes a little overwhelming about halfway through, when the opera comes in on "Wedding Feast," reminding us that this is indeed a concept album, then delving into three eight-minute jams to conclude the record. It all winds up as a bit much, but it doesn't erase the musical facts: this is Prince at his most focused and rewarding in a long time, since *Emancipation* really. Too bad nobody outside of the die-hards cares at this point. *—Stephen Thomas Erlewine*

Princess

Vocals / Urban, Disco
Vocalist Princess sang with Osibisa in the '70s before touring as a background vocalist with several artists, among them Evelyn Thomas and Precious Wilson. She was signed as a solo act to Supreme Records, where the production team of Stock, Aitken & Waterman got her a series of British hits. She didn't fare as well on the American charts, recording for Next Plateau in 1985 and 1986 or 1987 on Polydor. Her best single was "Say I'm Your Number One," which was also her lone Top 20 R&B hit. *—Ron Wynn*

● **Princess** / 1986 / Next Plateau ✦✦✦
Next to the United States, England is the world's largest market for R&B. From Motown in the 1960s to urban contemporary in the 1980s and 1990s, plenty of R&B has been sold in cities like London, Manchester, and Birmingham. A lot of well-known urban artists came out of England in the 1980s, including Soul II Soul, Sade, Junior, Billy Ocean, Five Star, and Loose Ends. Another British R&B artist who was active during that decade was former Osibisa singer Princess, who had a hit in 1986 with the sleek "Say I'm Your Number One." Produced by the prolific Mike Stock/Matt Aitken/Pete Waterman team—which is known for its work with Dead or Alive, Rick Astley, Samantha Fox, Bananarama, and others—Princess' first solo album is generally enjoyable even though it isn't as consistent as it could have been. Princess, an expressive singer along the lines of Evelyn "Champagne" King, Sharon Bryant, and Stephanie Mills, shows a lot of promise on the LP's best tracks, which range from "Say I'm Your Number One" (a Top 20 R&B hit in the U.S.) to the melancholy "After the Love Has Gone" and the funky "Just a Teaze." While some parts of the album are excellent, others are merely decent—at times, Princess coasts on her obvious talents instead of going that extra mile. But, overall, this release leaves listeners with a favorable impression of the singer, who, unfortunately, wasn't as successful in the U.S. as she was in England. *—Alex Henderson*

All for Love / 1987 / Polydor ✦✦✦

The Prisonaires

f. 1953, **db.** 1955
Group / R&B, Doo Wop, Pop
The Prisonaires were just that, five African-American male singers who also happened to be inmates of the Tennessee State Penitentiary in Nashville. Despite what normally would be considered circumstances too onerous to start a pop music career, the Prisonaires were celebrities, albeit briefly, after the recording of the one and only hit record, "Just Walkin' in the Rain," which Sam Phillips released on Sun in 1953—a song that three years later became a million seller for Johnnie Ray. The band was formed by lead singer Johnny Bragg, who had been a penitentiary inmate since the age of 17 after being convicted of six charges of rape. A singer since childhood, Bragg had joined a prison gospel quintet soon after his incarceration, but after a falling out, Bragg took two of its singers, Ed Thurman and William Stewart, each of whom were doing 99 years for murder, and hooked up with recent penitentiary arrivals John Drue (three years for larceny) and Marcell Sanders (one-to-five for involuntary manslaughter), and the Prisonaires were born.

They were discovered by radio producer Joe Calloway, who heard them singing while preparing a news broadcast from the prison. Calloway suggested to warden James Edwards that the group be allowed out to perform on the radio. Edwards, a liberal reform-minded warden who saw this as part of his strategy of rehabilitation, agreed. In the meantime, Bragg was busy selling songs to music publisher Red Wortham, who sent a tape of the Prisonaires' radio performance to Jim Bulliet, a minority shareholder in Sun Records. Bulliet sent the tape to Phillips, and despite his initial reservations (Phillips was not a huge fan of the group's Ink Spots-style close harmony crooning), arranged to have the groups transported under armed guard to Memphis to record. A few weeks later, "Just Walkin' in the Rain" was released and quickly sold 50,000 copies, a small success that was not without long-term ramifications. Peter Guralnick notes that "Just Walkin' in the Rain" was likely the record that captured the attention of a young Elvis Presley as he read about the studio, the label, and more importantly, Phillips. The attendant publicity was more than had been predicted, and soon warden Edwards was allowing the group out on day passes to tour throughout the state of Tennessee. The band became favorites of the state's governor, Frank Clement, and frequently performed for assembled guests at the governor's mansion.

The group never had another hit, and within a year they were finished, the result of the rise of rock & roll and Phillips' preoccupation with a young singer from Tupelo, MS, named Presley. Most of the Prisonaires had no careers outside of the prison with the notable exception of Bragg, who, despite remaining in jail off and on until 1969, recorded some marginal R&B and country for small labels in Nashville. *—John Dougan*

Five Beats Behind Bars / 1979 / Charly ♦♦♦♦

• **Just Walkin' in the Rain** / 1990 / Bear Family ♦♦♦♦♦

Although the Prisonaires are remembered for the song "Just Walkin in the Rain," this collection proves that they were a fine pop/gospel group. Johnny Bragg was a huge fan of the Ink Spots and their lead singer, Bill Kenny, and it's no wonder that much of the material on this disc has that smooth crooning style favored by pre-rock & roll vocal groups. This typically well-researched and documented Bear Family disc includes all of the Sun recordings and unreleased material, which shows the group attempting some hard-ass R&B (e.g., "Surleen" and "Rocking Horse") with mixed results. In terms of their overall output, it's the early stuff that's really compelling, as the Prisonaires proved that they could sing with the best of the vocal groups of the era. Nothing is as good as the title track, but that's a song for the ages, a beautiful piece of pop loneliness infused with near palpable heartbreak. Fans of this type of old-style harmony singing shouldn't pass this up. *—John Dougan*

Process & the Doo Rags

f. Buffalo, NY

Group / Close Harmony, Urban

Produced by Rick James, Process & the Doo Rags looked like a '50s doo-wop group with their "processed" hairdos. Actually, the Buffalo, NY group was in vogue, a part of a brief mid-'80s run of harmonizing vocal groups that also included the Force MDs. The group's lineup was former Rick James backup singer James Hawkins, Stacey Lattimore, Henry Graham, Dennis Andrews, and Michael Gibson. Their charting single, "Stomp and Shout," from their 1985 Columbia LP, *Too Sharp*, became a post-release collectible. The group's hard-to-find 1987 Columbia album was titled *Process and the Doo Rags* with the standout track the optimistic dance track "Stagelights," written by Leroy Burgess and Sonny Davenport and produced by Aleem. Process & the Doo Rags' other charting singles were "I Promise to Remember" and "Call Me Up." *—Ed Hogan*

• **Too Sharp** / 1985 / Columbia ♦♦♦

Rick James protégés Process & the Doo Rags only hung around the music scene long enough to cut *Too Sharp*, an album filled equally with dancers and slow jams. The uptempo numbers are all right, but Process (this refers to a once popular hairstyle worn by black males that used lye concoctions to straighten the hair) & the Doo Rags (scarves used to protect the processed hair from dust, or to hide it when the process began kinking and discoloring) had more of a feel for ballads. Toward that end, "Daddy's Home" and "Thin Line Between Love & Hate" are two songs that can never be redone enough. Their rendition of "The Bells" has all the magic of Marvin Gaye's original production for Freddy Gorman & the Originals. *—Andrew Hamilton*

Professor Longhair (Henry Roeland Byrd)

b. Dec. 19, 1918, Bogalusa, LA, **d.** Jan. 30, 1980, New Orleans, LA

Piano, Vocals, Leader, Arranger / New Orleans R&B, New Orleans Blues, Piano Blues

Justly worshipped a decade and a half after his death as a founding father of New Orleans R&B, Roy "Professor Longhair" Byrd was nevertheless so down-and-out at one point in his long career that he was reduced to sweeping the floors in a record shop that once could have moved his platters by the boxful. That Longhair made such a marvelous comeback testifies to the resiliency of this late legend, whose Latin-tinged rhumba-rocking piano style and croaking, yodeling vocals were as singular and spicy as the second-line beats that power his hometown's musical heartbeat. Longhair brought an irresistible Caribbean feel to his playing, full of rolling flourishes that every Crescent City ivories man had to learn inside out (Fats Domino, Huey Smith, and Allen Toussaint all paid homage early and often).

Longhair grew up on the streets of the Big Easy, tap dancing for tips on Bourbon Street with his running partners. Local 88s aces Sullivan Rock, Kid Stormy Weather, and Tuts Washington all left their marks on the youngster, but he brought his own conception to the stool. A natural-born card shark and gambler, Longhair began to take his playing seriously in 1948, earning a gig at the Caldonia Club. Owner Mike Tessitore bestowed Longhair with his professorial nickname (due to Byrd's shaggy coiffure).

Longhair debuted on wax in 1949, laying down four tracks (including the first version of his signature "Mardi Gras in New Orleans," complete with whistled intro) for the Dallas-based Star Talent label. His band was called the Shuffling Hungarians, for reasons lost to time! Union problems forced those sides off the market, but Longhair's next date for Mercury the same year was strictly on the up-and-up. It produced his first and only national R&B hit in 1950, the hilarious "Bald Head" (credited to Roy Byrd & His Blues Jumpers). The pianist made great records for Atlantic in 1949, Federal in 1951, Wasco in 1952, and Atlantic again in 1953 (producing the immortal "Tipitina," a romping "In the Night," and the lyrically impenetrable boogie "Ball the Wall"). After recuperating from a minor stroke, Longhair came back on Lee Rupe's Ebb logo in 1957 with a storming "No Buts—No Maybes." He revived his "Go to the Mardi Gras" for Joe Ruffino's Ron imprint in 1959; this is the version that surfaces every year at Mardi Gras in New Orleans.

Other than the ambitiously arranged "Big Chief" in 1964 for Watch Records, the '60s held little charm for Longhair. He hit the skids, abandoning his piano playing until a booking at the fledgling 1971 Jazz & Heritage Festival put him on the comeback trail. He made a slew of albums in the last decade of his life, topped off by a terrific set for Alligator, *Crawfish Fiesta*. Longhair triumphantly appeared on the PBS-TV concert series *Soundstage* (with Dr. John, Earl King, and the Meters), co-starred in the documentary *Piano Players Rarely Ever Play Together* (which became a memorial tribute when Longhair died in the middle of its filming; funeral footage was included), and saw a group of his admirers buy a local watering hole in 1977 and rechristen it Tipitina's after his famous song. He played there regularly when he wasn't on the road; it remains a thriving operation.

Longhair went to bed on January 30, 1980, and never woke up. A heart attack in the night stilled one of New Orleans' seminal R&B stars, but his music is played in his hometown so often and so reverently you'd swear he was still around. *—Bill Dahl*

New Orleans Piano / 1972 / Atlantic ♦♦♦♦♦

Here are all 16 of the Atlantic sides from 1949 and 1953 (including a handful of alternate takes) on one glorious disc. Longhair's work for the label was notoriously marvelous—this version of "Mardi Gras in New Orleans" reeks of revelry in the streets of the French Quarter; "She Walks Right In" and "Walk Your Blues Away" ride a bedrock boogie, and "In the Night" bounces atop a parade-beat shuffle groove and hard-charging saxes. *—Bill Dahl*

Rock 'n Roll Gumbo / 1977 / Dancing Cat ♦♦♦♦♦

Recorded in 1974, this album almost never saw the light of day. Fortunately, the master tapes were found and the album was finally issued in 1977. Professor Longhair was a giant in the New Orleans music community, but had not recorded in over ten years when he was convinced to start playing again. From the opening riffs, one can understand the stature of Professor Longhair as a great pianist—he demonstrates that he is equally at home playing rhumba boogie, blues songs, and calypso. He plays New Orleans standards (many penned by himself), but what makes this recording a classic is the chance to hear him play with guitarist Clarence "Gatemouth" Brown. The interplay of these music veterans is mesmerizing. The piano playing is breathtaking, and has a percussive quality unlike any other player before or since. It is hard to believe that Professor Longhair languished in obscurity for so many years after hearing the jubilance of "Mardi Gras in New Orleans," a song that will have you tapping your feet and hands as if you were in the parade. This album is essential for fans of New Orleans music and those aspiring to be rock & roll pianists. *— Vik Iyengar*

Live on the Queen Mary / 1978 / One Way ♦♦♦♦♦

Ask what was Paul and Linda McCartney's *most* important contribution to music, and you just might get the answer—this album, which is also more exciting than anything Wings ever did. Professor Longhair's first live recording came about at a March 24, 1975 party hosted by the McCartneys aboard the Queen Mary in Long Beach, CA. It captures some of the excitement that Ahmet Ertegun and several lesser-known talent scouts found when they came upon Henry Roeland Byrd playing road houses around New Orleans in the late 1940s. Highlights include the rollicking "Mess Around," and the standards "Stagger Lee," "Everyday I Have the Blues," "I'm Movin' On," and his hits "Mardi Gras in New Orleans" and "Tipitina." The lack of instrumental credits prevents one from praising the lead guitarist by name for his playing on "Everyday I Have the Blues" and "I'm Movin' On," but he and the rest of the band still do well backing this legend. *—Bruce Eder*

Crawfish Fiesta / 1980 / Alligator ♦♦♦♦♦

This is probably the best of all the many albums Longhair waxed during his comeback (and likely the last). A tremendously tight combo featuring three horns and Dr. John on guitar delightfully back the Professor every step of the way as he recasts Solomon Burke's "Cry to Me" and Fats Domino's "Whole Lotta Loving" in his own indelible image and roars, yodels, and whistles out wonderful remakes of his own oldies "Big Chief" and "Bald Head." *—Bill Dahl*

Mardi Gras in New Orleans / 1981 / Nighthawk ♦♦♦♦♦

Plenty of rarities are featured on this valuable cross-section of the Professor's early releases. Both sides of the pianist's first two 78s for Star Talent Records are aboard, as well as sides he cut for Mercury, Federal ("Curly Haired Baby," "Gone So Long"), Wasco ("East St. Louis Baby"), Atlantic, and Ebb. *—Bill Dahl*

House Party New Orleans Style / 1987 / Rounder ♦♦♦

Mardi Gras in Baton / 1991 / Rhino ♦♦♦♦

Here are some of the earliest sides from Longhair's rediscovery period (1971-1972), featuring a lot of tunes inexorably associated with him through previous versions and a few ("Jambalaya," "Sick and Tired") that weren't. An added bonus is the magical presence of guitarist Snooks Eaglin, whose approach is every bit as singular as the Professor's was. *—Bill Dahl*

★ **Fess: The Professor Longhair Anthology** / Nov. 16, 1993 / Rhino ♦♦♦♦♦

The rhumba-rocking rhythms of Roy "Professor Longhair" Byrd live on throughout Rhino's 40-track retrospective of the New Orleans icon's amazing legacy. Most of the seminal stuff arrives early on: "Bald Head," the rollicking ode Byrd cut for Mercury in 1950, is followed by a raft of classics from his 1949 and 1953 Atlantic dates ("Tipitina," "Ball the Wall," "Who's Been Fooling You"), the storming 1957 "No Buts—No Maybes" and "Baby Let Me Hold Your Hand" for Ebb, and his beloved "Go to the Mardi Gras" as waxed for Ron in 1959. The second disc is a hodge-podge of material from his 1970s comeback, all of it wonderful in its own way but not as essential as the early work. *—Bill Dahl*

Profyle

f. Shreveport, LA

Group / Contemporary R&B, New Jack Swing, Urban, Hip-Hop

The Shreveport, LA, vocal quartet Profyle consists of a pair of brothers and cousins who grew up together, inspired by the success and positive message of groups like Boyz II Men. They began performing at local talent shows and caught the attention of a promoter during one performance, who introduced them to their future manager, Musa Moore. Moore had the group record their demo tape with producer V. Jeffrey Smith; this tape made its way to Kedar Massenburg, president of Motown Records, who offered Profyle a record contract. The group's debut album, *Whispers in the Dark*, followed in 1999. *—Heather Phares*

- **Nothin' but Drama** / Oct. 17, 2000 / Motown ♦♦♦

Harking back to the late-'80s new jack swing explosion, Profyle's excellent *Nothin' but Drama* album brings together sensual soul strings and light funky hip-hop beats in a classic Teddy Riley sense while also featuring the female-wooing, silky smooth vocals of the group's four crooners. In fact, with Riley actually producing two of the album's tracks (including the smash hit "Liar"), this album sounds almost *too* much like classic Guy or Keith Sweat; it's quite uncanny, as if *Nothin' but Drama* is, in fact, a remnant from the late-'80s new jack heyday. Most will notice this immediately. But to write this album off as merely derivative is to miss the fact that Profyle is making some heartfelt music, even if it retreads familiar ground. The foursome will probably appeal primarily to young women—a fan base that most likely will be too young to even know what new jack swing is—particularly with their sexy looks and posing. So in that sense, Motown Records has put together a wonderful album, pairing Profyle with producers such as Riley and Joe. Similar to how the Backstreet Boys are an uncanny hark back to the New Kids on the Block, it seems that a decade is enough time for a new generation of wistful youths to again soak up such bittersweet music. Still, it's hard to deny the infectious strings of Riley's "Liar," which may be one of his best productions ever. The rest of the album doesn't quite compare to this song, but it comes close at times. If anything though, 14 tracks of sappy romantic purring over candy-coated aural melancholia is a bit too much, without any uptempo Bobby Brown-style numbers to break things up. *—Jason Birchmeier*

Pru (Pru Renfro)

b. Houston, TX

Vocals / Contemporary R&B, Trip-Hop, Urban

The innovative, jazzy singer known as Pru (born Pru Renfro) was raised as the youngest of four children by her mother, Patsy, in Houston's South Park section. Her mother was a free spirit who encouraged Pru's creativity and occasionally brought her to work with her at the nightclub where she tended bar, allowing Pru to perform in between acts. Attending a performing arts high school helped nurture her creative talents and by the time she headed off to college at Texas Southern University, she was well on her way to developing her singing style. She traveled to L.A. hoping to emulate some of the great singers whom she had been recently exposed to, like Cassandra Wilson and Dianne Reeves. She worked in bars and nightclubs frequented by industry mavens in the hope of networking with the powers that be in the music industry.

Her songwriting earned her the first bits of attention and provided a crucial break for her when she was signed by Warner/Chappell Music Publishing and was brought to the attention of Roy Lott at Capitol Records. He was impressed not only with her songwriting skills, but also with her versatile voice, which had developed a unique style that traveled in some of the same directions as the more creative interpreters of R&B, like Lauryn Hill, Macy Gray, and Erykah Badu. Pru polished her singing style while working on tour with the Family Stand and members of Sade's band, and Capitol released her self-titled solo debut in November, 2000. Pru showed off her songwriting skills by penning 12 of the 13 tracks on the album, including the debut single, "Candle," which borrowed lyrical and musical inspiration from Smokey Robinson's "Tracks of My Tears." *—Stacia Proefrock*

- **Pru** / Nov. 7, 2000 / Capitol ♦♦♦♦

As a child growing up in Houston, TX, Pru Renfro could memorize and recite the text of an entire Dr. Suess book. The open-minded, whimsical influence certainly shows on the singer/songwriter's self-titled album *Pru*. She freely mixes hip-hop, Latin, R&B, rock, and trip-hop into a uniquely enticing mix that quickly identifies her as an adventurous artist along the line of Angie Stone, Jill Scott and Lauryn Hill. The ballad "Candles" is a juxtaposition of Smokey Robinson & The Miracles' "Tracks of My Tears." Pru wisely gives Sade's "Smooth Operator a different flavor than the original; bring to the fore the original version's Latin influences more forcefully but still keep it smooth amid popping percussion and fluttery flute runs. The halting ballad "Hazy Shades" recalls "blue light in the basement" old skool slow jams. Other highlights include "Aroma," "183 Miles," "Sketches of Pain," and the movie portion of this enhanced CD. *—Ed Hogan*

Public Announcement

Chicago, IL

Group / Urban, Club/Dance

The onetime backing group for R. Kelly, Chicago's Public Announcement made their solo debut in 1998 with *All Work, No Play*, scoring a Top Ten hit with the single "Body Bumpin' (Yippie-Yi-Yo)." Kelly moved on to contemporary R&B stardom while the group remained in semi-retirement until early 2001 when they released their sophomore album, *Don't Hold Back*. *—Jason Ankeny*

- **All Work, No Play** / Mar. 24, 1998 / A&M ♦♦♦

Public Announcement had been around for years in various incarnations, including one that featured R. Kelly, before they had the opportunity to record their debut album, *All Work, No Play*. Fueled by the infectious single "Body Bumpin' (Yippie-Yi-Yo)," the album is an infectious set of uptempo urban R&B with a distinct hip-hop influence. The group has enough energy to keep the record moving over the dull moments, but their songwriting rarely yields anything as memorable as "Body Bumpin'." Nevertheless, that single is so strong, it indicates that the group could have a bright future, if they had just a few more hooks and a little more discipline. *—Leo Stanley*

Don't Hold Back / Feb. 6, 2001 / RCA ♦♦

Pucho & His Latin Soul Brothers

f. 1959, **db.** 1973

Group / Soul-Jazz, Boogaloo, Latin Jazz, Latin Soul, Hard Bop, Salsa

In the 1960s, no one combined more or less equal elements of jazz, Latin music, soul, and funk as well as Henry "Pucho" Brown. A somewhat forgotten figure until recently, Pucho never achieved the wide recognition of some other Latin jazz performers exploring similar territory, such as Mongo Santamaria, Willie Bobo, and Cal Tjader. Contrary to the assumptions of many listeners, Pucho himself is not Latino, but African-American. As a Harlem teenager, he cultivated loves for jazz, rhythm & blues, and mambo. In the late '50s, he served for several years in the band of pianist Joe Panama. When the band broke up in 1959, Pucho formed a band of his own. Even before he'd cemented his reputation on record, Pucho's band attracted notice from top Latin jazzmen.

Pucho began recording in 1963 and really hit his stride between 1966 and 1970, when he cut over half a dozen albums for Prestige. On these, he helped pioneer a style termed Latin boogaloo, which mixed jazz, New York-style Latin music, R&B/soul, and the sort of funk that was just emerging from James Brown and other performers. Pucho wasn't afraid to mix up his material on his LPs, which placed originals by Pucho & His Latin Soul Brothers next to covers of tunes by Herbie Hancock, the Temptations, the Beatles, Duke Ellington, and John Barry. When his brand of Latin-soul-jazz fusion started to fall from commercial grace in the early '70s, Pucho disbanded the Latin Soul Brothers. In the early '90s, however, Pucho's back catalog began to generate interest in Britain, where he was a hit with the acid jazz crowd, and where several albums were reissued by the Ace label. Happily, he made a return to Latin-soul-jazz-funk with his 1995 comeback effort, *Rip a Dip*. *—Richie Unterberger*

Tough! / Feb. 15, 1966-Nov. 10, 1966 / Prestige ♦♦

A bit more jazz- and pop-oriented than some of his later sessions, with covers of "Yesterday," "The Shadow of Your Smile," "And I Love Her," "Walk On By," and "Goldfinger." However, when Pucho decides to pull out the funky grooves—as he does on "Cantaloupe Island," "Vietnam Mambo," and "Strange Thing Mambo"—he & His Latin Soul Brothers can smoke. Even at its slightest, this is decent mood music. At its best, it's significantly more than that. The CD reissue is a good deal, adding the entirety of the 1966 LP *Saffron Soul*. *—Richie Unterberger*

Saffron Soul / Nov. 8, 1966+Nov. 10, 1966 / Prestige ♦♦♦

As he did on his other 1966 session (*Tough!*), Pucho mixed pop and soul hits with the stronger stuff. That means the best and funkiest pieces—"Aye Ma Ma," "Soul Yamie," and a typically irreverent cover of "Caravan"—are mixed with the likes of "Reach Out I'll Be There" and "Alfie." The entire album has been added to the CD reissue of *Tough!*, so you should look for that disc instead of an original copy of the LP. *—Richie Unterberger*

Shuckin' and Jivin' / 1967 / Prestige ♦♦♦

Heat! / 1968 / Prestige ♦♦♦♦

Super Freak / 1972 / Cubop ♦♦♦♦

The opening track on 1972's *Super Freak* is a brilliant, nearly side-long medley of three tracks from Curtis Mayfield's *Superfly*: the title track, "Pusherman," and, of course, "Freddie's Dead." Heavy, druggy, and psychedelic, with thick organ and wah-wah guitars, the medley sounds more like the psychedelic soul of War or even Funkadelic than the sparkling Latin jazz of Pucho's earlier albums. The rest of *Super Freak* is a little lighter in tone, but this is still the most groove-oriented and least overtly Latin jazz-oriented of this group's albums, trafficking instead in shuffling grooves like "Oak Hurst's Art" and vibes-led ballads like "Judy's Moods" and "One More Day." Latin jazz purists may balk, but this later became a classic of the '90s acid jazz movement, which some sources date to the U.K. hip-hop group Galliano pinching a sample from this album's version of "Freddie's Dead" for the 1989 single "Frederick Lies Still." *—Stewart Mason*

★ **The Best of Pucho & His Latin Soul Brothers** / 1993 / Ace ♦♦♦♦♦

Not only the best overview of Pucho's work, but one of the best Latin jazz recordings available, and certainly one of the best in the nowadays-obscure subgenre of Latin-jazz-soul. It contains 17 tracks from his 1966-1970 heyday, intelligently weighted toward his most dance groove-oriented original material and covers, and eliminating the routine pop covers that filled out some of his LPs. "Canteloupe Island," "Soul Yamie," "Shuckin' and Jivin'," "Maiden Voyage," and "Strange Thing Mambo" are all among his very best cuts. With a running time of 76 minutes, it's a good deal even at import prices. *—Richie Unterberger*

Heat!/Jungle Fire! / Mar. 3, 1995 / BGP ♦♦♦♦

Legends of Acid Jazz: The Best of Pucho & His Latin Soul Brothers / Dec. 3, 1996 / Prestige ♦♦♦♦♦

This is an entirely different set than the British import compilation on Ace called *The Best of Pucho & the Latin Soul Brothers*; only six tracks are found on both CDs. Which one you prefer totally depends upon your individual taste. Soul and rock fans will be far better off with the Ace collection, which concentrates far more heavily on his soul-jazz, R&B, and psychedelic-influenced numbers. The Prestige set focuses on his more sedate, straight jazz side, with tracks taken from his 1967-1970 albums (there's nothing from his first two Prestige records, which have been combined onto one CD on the *Tough!* reissue). This is nicely atmospheric stuff with a Latin lilt, but not Pucho at his funkiest and most adventurous. It's also wholly instrumental, with none of the un-honed but energetic vocals that occasionally adorned his material on cuts like "Shuckin' and Jivin'." *—Richie Unterberger*

Bernard "Pretty" Purdie

b. Jun. 11, 1939, Elkton, MD

Drums / Soul-Jazz, Jazz-Funk, Jazz Blues, Jazz-Pop

An all-time great soul, R&B, funk, and pop drummer, Bernard Purdie's impeccable time and mastery of backbeats and grooves are celebrated. He moved to New York from Maryland in 1960, and recorded with James Brown, King Curtis, and many others.

He was CTI's house drummer in the late '60s and early '70s, and worked with Grover Washington Jr. and George Benson among several others. Purdie toured with Curtis and Aretha Franklin in 1970, and was Franklin's music director until 1975. During his studio days in the early '70s, Purdie recorded with Louis Armstrong and Gato Barbieri along with numerous rock, pop, and soul sessions. He recorded with Dizzy Gillespie in 1980 at the Montreux Jazz Festival and toured with him in 1983. Purdie recorded with Hank Crawford during the early '80s, and continued working steadily into the '90s. He generated a firestorm of reaction in 1993 when he charged it was his uncredited drumming rather than Ringo Starr's on some Beatles tracks. Purdie claimed proof was forthcoming, but none was presented. He made a rare date as a leader for Flying Dutchman in 1972, *Pretty Purdie*, that has long since disappeared. But Purdie can be heard on countless discs by Brown, Franklin, Curtis, Gillespie, and Crawford among many others. *—Ron Wynn*

Soul Finders / 1968 / Camden ✦✦

Purdie Good / 1971 / Prestige ✦✦✦

Even the best session players—and Bernard "Pretty" Purdie is certainly one of those—are not necessarily cut out to lead their own sessions. Indeed, it seems like Purdie's much-vaunted ability to play well in just about any style thrown at him is almost a liability on 1971's *Purdie Good*. Fred Neil's "Everybody's Talkin'" is done in a calypso fashion that does little for the song (although Warren Daniels and Charlie Brown do manage a passable tenor sax duel), and this version of Bobby Bloom's pop hit "Montego Bay" is even more lightweight and middle of the road than the original. Not all of the album is so disposable; the originals "Purdie Good" and "Wasteland" work up some hot jazz-funk grooves, and the ballad "You Turn Me On" has a slinky charm. But the cover of James Brown's "Cold Sweat" sums up the album's problems: the covers are competent enough, but why listen to them when the originals are far superior? At best, the album only barely lives up to its title. *—Stewart Mason*

● **Soul Is . . . Pretty Purdie** / 1972 / Flying Dutchman ✦✦✦✦✦

Shaft / 1973 / Prestige ✦✦✦

Bernard "Pretty" Purdie thinks a lot of himself, as his nickname indicates. And he's not entirely wrong, as his enormous list of stellar studio credits indicates. He deserves to be up there with Hal Blaine, Jim Gordon, and Earl Palmer as one of the great session drummers of all time. But his occasional bouts of musical arrogance—most notoriously his unsubstantiated and frankly rather wacky claim that he, not Ringo Starr, played drums on most of the Beatles' early records—also occasionally get him into trouble. Two of those blunders are on this album. Isaac Hayes' "Theme From Shaft" and Buddy Miles' "Changes" don't need to be covered, period, and if one must make the attempt, only a train wreck like the Ray Conniff Singers' version of "Theme From Shaft" (yes, really) could stand a chance against the majesty of the original. Certainly these limp retreads, apparently aimed at a middle-of-the-road audience that was reaching for hipness but didn't want to be confronted with anything too out there, are utterly unnecessary. There are a handful of good tunes here; although it's unclear what the genial funk groove "Attica" has to do with the 1971 prison riot of the same name, it's got some hot tenor sax solos and a rollicking electric piano solo by composer Neal Creque. Similarly, the mellow and soulful "Summer Melody" has some exquisite electric piano and trumpet over its gentle conga-led groove. An album' s worth of variations on these two themes would have been a minor soul-jazz classic, but unfortunately, Bernard Purdie's overreaching ends up giving him the, um, Shaft. *—Stewart Mason*

Purdie Good/Shaft / 1993 / BGP ✦✦✦✦

James & Bobby Purify

f. 1966, Pensacola, FL

Group / Pop-Soul, Soul

James (born May 12, 1944) and Bobby (born September 2, 1939) of this Southern soul duo were not actually brothers but cousins. James Purify and Robert Lee Dickey joined forces for some classic Southern soul duets during the mid-'60s. Producer Papa Don Schroeder brought the soulful Floridians to Muscle Shoals in 1966 to record at Rick Hall's Fame studios, and the result was the gorgeous midtempo "I'm Your Puppet." The Dan Penn & Spooner Oldham ballad proved their biggest hit for the Bell label, although "Let Love Come Between Us" and their revival of the Five Du-Tones' "Shake a Tail Feather" also made some major noise in 1967. When Bobby mutinied, James went it alone for a while before recruiting a new Bobby (Ben Moore), and they picked up right where the old duo left off. *—Bill Dahl*

James & Bobby Purify / 1967 / Mercury ✦✦✦✦

Like penny candy, the male-recording duo is virtually extinct. Once popular, not many are around these days, only Men at Large comes to mind. You once had: Marvin & Johnny, Don & Juan, Sam & Dave, Santos & Johnny, Sam & Bill, Johnny & Jackie, Two Friends, etc. A James & Bobby Purify act still performs due to the popularity of "I'm Your Puppet" an infectious, loping ballad. This sparkling debut, recorded at the Fame Recording Studios in Muscle Shoals, AL, overflows with blue-plate specials. Relish purifying renditions of the Nightingales' sermonizing "I Got Everything I Need," Otis Redding's "I've Been Loving You Too Long," and Maurice & Mac's "You Left the Water Running." Gritty originals "Wish You Didn't Have to Go," "So Many Reasons," and "Blame Me (Don't Blame My Heart)," hold their own too. *—Andrew Hamilton*

The Pure Sound of the Purifys / 1968 / Bell ✦✦✦

You & Me Together Forever / 1978 / Casablanca ✦✦✦

Do It Right: The Best of James & Bobby Purify / 1985 / Arista ✦✦✦

This collection covers the few hits James and Bobby Purify enjoyed, including "I'm Your Puppet" and "Shake a Tail Feather." They were a good straight soul duo, and were not brothers but cousins. *—Ron Wynn*

● **Shake a Tail Feather: The Best of James & Bobby Purify** / Apr. 23, 2002 / Sundazed ✦✦✦✦✦

You couldn't ask for a better compilation of James & Bobby Purify than this one, which fits no less than 28 songs onto a single disc, all from their prime 1966-1969 Bell era. In addition to a wealth of singles, B-sides, and LP tracks, there are five previously unissued cuts, the whole deal expertly annotated. The duo was harder to fit into a niche than many soul acts of the era; although there have been some comparisons to Sam & Dave, at times their sides were more pop-oriented than what Sam & Dave cut at Memphis, particularly on songs with sophisticated production touches like vibes. At other times, though, they were indeed in the late-'60s Southern deep soul bag; sometimes some doo wop and older R&B influences surfaced; and there's even a reading of the blues classic "You Don't Love Me." It makes for a varied and nice set, though there really isn't anything as instantly memorable as the song that will be always be their calling card, "I'm Your Puppet." If you do like "I'm Your Puppet" in particular, you'll probably go for the half-dozen or so other tracks in which Dan Penn & Spooner Oldham were also involved in the songwriting, like "So Many Reasons" and a version of "You Left the Water Running" that stands up to the better-known one by Otis Redding. For more uptempo numbers, their interpretation of "I Take What I Want," with fuzzy guitar to the forefront, is at least as good as the more famed version by Sam & Dave. *—Richie Unterberger*

Q

Sydney Joe Qualls

b. Jacknash, AR

Vocals / Soul, Disco, Smooth Soul

Sydney Joe Qualls (who is listed as Sidney Joe Qualis on some releases) was a southern-born soul singer who was heavily influenced by Al Green. Signed to Dakar Records in the early '70s after meeting Otis Leavill, he made an impressive showing with singles such as "Run to Me," though by the end of the 1970s, on the Chi-Sound label, he'd begun moving toward a disco sound, which he sustained across several singles and an LP. *I Don't Do This*, a 2002 compilation on the Expansion label, reissued his 1974 Dakar LP *I Enjoy Loving You* and added bonus tracks. *—Bruce Eder*

- **I Don't Do This** / 2002 / Expansion ✦✦✦✦

Sir Joe Quarterman & Free Soul

Group / Funk, Deep Funk, Philly Soul

Joe Quarterman was an unfairly overlooked James Brown-style funk and soul singer. Honing his chops in church choirs and various vocal groups, Quarterman was given the nickname "Sir" in high school, and formed a backing group called Free Soul in 1970. Their first single, "(I Got) So Much Trouble in My Mind," was also their biggest, reaching the R&B Top 30 in early 1973. Quarterman's only LP, *Sir Joe Quarterman & Free Soul*, was released later that year on the small GSF label, and showed Quarterman to be an avatar of the kind of hard, socially conscious funk James Brown often recorded during the early '70s.

Further singles, including "This Girl of Mine (She's Good to Me)" and "Thanks Dad," followed, before Quarterman moved to Mercury in 1974. Unfortunately, the label issued only one single, the fine "Get Down Baby," before letting Quarterman go. Collectables reissued Quarterman's lone album on CD during the '90s, adding several non-LP singles as bonus tracks. *—Steve Huey*

Sir Joe Quarterman & Free Soul / 1973 / GSF ✦✦✦

- **Golden Classics** / Feb. 28, 1995 / Collectables ✦✦✦✦✦

Golden Classics compiles the entirety of Sir Joe Quarterman & Free Soul's only album, along with several non-LP singles recorded for both GSF and Mercury. It's a definitive package—but who's keeping track? The answer is, a cult of fanatical funk collectors who rediscovered Quarterman's extremely hard-to-find, small-label LP, and hailed it as a lost classic. Is it? Well, classic might be stretching it, but it's pretty damn good. There's some excellent straight-ahead dance music, but Quarterman's real specialty is urgent message tracks; he takes on a host of social ills, burning with righteous indignation all the while. There's some uplifting positivity, too, as on the heartfelt tribute "Thanks Dad," but for the most part Quarterman simply sounds as though his frustration is about to boil over. He's a master of the impassioned, roaring vocal style of James Brown, but his range is a bit higher and his timbre smoother. Meanwhile, the razor-sharp backing by Free Soul is somewhere between the J.B.'s and a lower-budget version of Gamble & Huff's plush Philly soul creations. It's deeply and aggressively funky, but layers of keyboards, horns, and wah-wah guitars adorn even the hardest tracks. Quarterman and some of his band-members were jazz-trained musicians, so there's more sophistication and know-how here than you might expect from such a small-scale project. Perhaps that's why the longer tracks tend to be the most exciting ones here: the minor hit single "(I Got) So Much Trouble in My Mind"; the stunningly constructed, eight-minute opus "Thanks Dad"; and the expertly paced buildups of "You Know It's True" and "You're Driving Me." In the end, this material doesn't redefine funk or soul, but it's superbly executed, and not as easy to pigeonhole as it first may seem. The best funk album ever by a guy you've never heard of. *—Steve Huey*

Quazar

f. New Jersey

Group / Jazz-Funk, Funk

Quazar was a ten-piece funk band from the Plainsfield, NJ, area created by Kevin Goins, the brother of Parliament/Funkadelic lead singer and guitarist Glen Goins. Originally known as Eclipse, the band woodshedded for six years before cutting their first and only album, *Quazar*, released September 1978 on Arista Records. The delay was caused by Glen's involvement and commitment with the P-Funk organization. The ball didn't get rolling until Glen quit over money (what else) and had the time to shape the band into an exciting and marketable commodity. The complete lineup consisted of Kevin (guitar, vocals), Richard Banks (keyboards, vocals), Eugene Jackson (bass, vocals), Jefferey Adams (drums), Gregory Fitz (keyboards), Peachena (vocals), Darryl Dixon (saxophone), Monica Peters (trumpet), Daryl De Lomberto (percussion), and Harvey Banks (guitar). Everything went on schedule until Glen's untimely death in 1978 halfway through the recording of their album. Another ex-Parliament/Funkadelic alumni, Jerome Brailey, helped them complete the album for Arista. They opened concerts for Roy Ayers, Cameo, and others but never overcame Glen's death and, without their mentor, faded from the scene. *—Andrew Hamilton*

- **Quazar** / 1978 / Arista ✦✦✦

Quiet Elegance

f. Detroit, MI

Group / Southern Soul, Soul

Quiet Elegance formed in Detroit, MI, with seasoned soul singers Yvonne "Frankie" Gearing, Mildred Vaney, and Lois Reeves. Vaney (aka Mildred Scott) sang with the Glories and Cut Glass with Orthea Barnes (J.J. Barnes' sister) after Quiet Elegance. Reeves replaced Betty Kelly in her sister's group, Martha & the Vandellas, in 1968 and remained until Martha disbanded the group to seek a solo career in 1972. Gearing (the lead singer and catalyst) had sung with the Glories, the Laddins, and the Steinway's; born in Daytona Beach, FL, she grew up in St. Petersburg, FL. Her brother is the late guitarist Johnny Starr, who went on the road with Jackie Wilson's band when he was 13 and later played in Little Richard's band alongside Jimi Hendrix.

They were managed by the Temptations; (Gearing was engaged to Dennis Edwards). Signed to Hi Records, they were produced by Willie Mitchell and Dan Greer and recorded for Mitchell's Hi Records in Memphis, TN. Mitchell recorded them singing mostly Al Green songs; the results were ultra soulful—no girl group cloying—especially "Have You Been Making Out O.K.," but the Temptations didn't want them sounding like female Al Greens, so Greer was brought in to give them a different sound. None of Quiet Elegance's seven Hi singles did much except anchor on the lower rungs of *Billboard*'s R&B chart. Hi strung the 45s out over a five-year period—from 1972 to 1977—and dropped an LP, but they never really surfaced as recording artists. The performing side, however, was roses. Quiet Elegance toured the world many times with Al Green, the Temptations, Engelbert Humperdinck, and Tom Jones.

They disbanded after the Hi contract ran its course. Vaney-Scott and Reeves returned to Detroit. Reeves still gigs occasionally as a Vandella, but mostly works at her full-time day job. After a couple releases with Cut Glass in 1980 for 20th Century Fox Records, Vaney has been quiet. Gearing, however, has stayed active; she cut solo recordings on Beale Street Records before returning to St. Petersburg in 1978 to care for her ailing grandmother and mom and has been an entertaining staple there every since, appearing in nightclubs, concerts, and plays (e.g., *The Best Little Whorehouse in Texas*, where she played Miss Mona's maid and delivered a sassy rendition of "24 Hours of Lovin'").

Like spring flowers, Quiet Elegance's recordings are popping up all over the place, including on CDs: *Complete Quiet Elegance* on Hi/Demon Records and *You've Got My Mind Messed Up* (Hi Records); as well as tracks on the *What's the Question* compilations. *—Andrew Hamilton*

- **You've Got My Mind Messed Up** / 1990 / Hi ✦✦✦✦

These 16 selections include 13 tracks from Quiet Elegance's seven Hi Records singles (one track, "I Need Love," was a B-side twice), with three extra tracks thrown in for your good pleasure. Acting independently, producers Dan Greer and Willie Mitchell whip up a batch of hot, tough Southern sounds that were under-performed when released but are getting recognized decades later. Their interpretations of Al Green's "Tired of Being Alone" and "Have You Been Making Out O.K." (a piece of slow Southern brilliance) are worth the price alone, as are the title track, Betty Crutcher and Bobby Manuel's "Mama Said," "I'm Afraid of Losing You" (their first single), and "How's Your Love Life Baby?" (their final single). Greer is the songwriter, producer, and male lead on "You Brought the Sun Back Into My Life"; he also wrote three other winners. Lead singer Yvonne "Frankie" Gearing's expressive soprano shamelessly exploits the heartfelt lyrics; she's ably accompanied by Mildred Vaney and Lois Reeves' (Martha's sister) strong harmonies. A few tracks ape what the Emotions were doing at the time for CBS Records. *—Andrew Hamilton*

R

The Radiants

Group / Chicago Soul, Pop-Soul, R&B, Soul

The Radiants originated in Chicago in 1960 at the Greater Harvest Baptist Church, where the future Radiants sang in the youth choir. Maurice McAlister assembled the group and sang lead; the other members were Wallace Sampson (baritone), Jerome Brooks (second tenor), Elzie Butler (Bass), and Charles Washington (first tenor). Similar to the Womack Brothers, the guys sang gospel at local churches but also worked on the R&B songs written by McAlister on the side. Green "Mac" McLauren replaced Washington shortly before their first recording session. By 1961, gospel music was a memory, and they started shopping demos to record labels and received nothing but rejections. Motown, among others, turned them down, and so did Chess Records—initially. They eventually signed with Chess and recorded under the tutelage of Billy Davis, aka Tyran Carlo, Berry Gordy's ex-songwriting partner, and former owner of Checkmate Records. Their first release, "Father Knows Best" backed by "One Day I'll Show You," in 1962, stiffed in some cities but was a hit in Cleveland.

Chess followed with "Heartbreak Society"; then in 1963, Chess released "Shy Guy" and "I Gotta Dance to Keep My Baby." All were hit-sounding pieces of wax that failed to sell, probably because of poor promotion. On "Shy Guy," Frank McCollum replaced McLauren Green, who got drafted. By 1964, the Radiants were tripping all over themselves. They had problems galore—so much so that they broke up. Maurice McAlister and Wallace Sampson were the only survivors. In came Leonard Caston Jr., the organist at Greater Harvest Church, who had just gotten out of the Army. A new Radiants group was formed, this time as a trio: McAlister, Sampson, and Caston. McAlister also wrote for other Chess/Checker artists, penning "Soulful Dress" for Sugar Pie DeSanto.

"Voice Your Choice," released late in 1964, is their most popular recording. They duplicated the Impressions' three-part harmony and lead-switching style to perfection. It reached number-51 pop and number-16 R&B on *Billboard*. Chess followed with "Ain't No Big Thing," which slipped the pop charts, only reaching number 91, but did better on the R&B charts, reaching number 14. Again, they displayed some beautiful three-part harmonies, with McAlister and Caston switching off leads. In 1965, Caston left the group to concentrate on songwriting and producing. James Jameson replaced him and appeared on "Baby You Got It"—but the plot thickens: McAlister left shortly after its release. This should have ended the Radiants, but it didn't. Another group, the Confessions, led by Mitchell Bullock, had already recorded "Don't It Make You Feel Kinda Bad," but disbanded before Chess could release it. Billy Davis put Bullock with Sampson and Jameson, and added Victor Caston, Leonard's younger brother, and the Radiants were a quartet again. Chess put out the same record the Confessions had previously recorded, and stamped the Radiants on the label.

Who would know the difference? The record was an emotionally sung wailer but failed to dent the pop chart and only achieved number 47 on the national R&B chart, though it did well where played. "Hold On" did better, climbing to number-68 pop and number-35 R&B in 1968. By this time, their productions were handled by Leonard Caston and later Bobby Miller. Unfortunately, they didn't have any more chart entries and left Chess in 1969, breaking up in 1972.

McAlister went on to record duets with former Radiant Green "Mac" McLauren as Maurice & Mac. "You Left the Water Running" by the two is considered a deep soul classic. Though the Radiants were popular in the Midwest and other areas, Chess never released an album by the group. A few of their cuts can be found on compilation CDs. Chess released ten or 15 singles of the group. Many of their early singles were two-sided hits. "I'm in Love," the flip of "Shy Guy," received quite a bit of airplay, as did "Noble the Bargain Man," the B-side of "I Gotta Dance to Keep My Baby." The latter was written by McAlister and David Clowney aka Dave "Baby" Cortez; you can hear his trademark organ on the recording, driving the rhythm section. Some of the disc jockeys in Cleveland referred to McAlister as Jimmy Durante, because he resembled the inka dinka doo man, a little guy with a big nose, but he could sing and write with the best of them and deserved more. *—Andrew Hamilton*

• **The Regal Theater Presents the Radiants: The Singles Collection 1962–1970** / 2000 / Rack O' Ribs ✦✦✦✦✦

Only the omission of any post-Maurice McAlister Radiants tracks keeps this excellent collection from being Bo Derek's number. It was the labels' choice, and not a bad one really. The post-McAlister Radiants were bogus, and their best release, "Don't It Make You Feel Kinda Bad," a soulful self-pitying tune with stinging lyrics and great harmony, was really done by the Confessions. Chess renamed it and found new guys to masquerade as the Radiants; this was long before the Milli Vanilli fiasco. These tracks feature the original group and their original lead Maurice McAlister, who if nurtured like the Motown artists would have made bold marks in the music industry. Unfortunately, he did his best work for Chess Records who didn't exactly groom their artists. Everything the Radiants recorded with the possible exception of some unknown vault cuts is on this CD. The title is misleading, as not all of the tracks are by the Radiants. Two cuts ("I'd Rather Do It Myself" and "Baby Hang On") are both sides of a solo by McAlister, and nine are deep soul slayers recorded with ex-Radiants original Green "Mac" McLauren as Maurice & Mac. According to McAlister, he made more money touring the South as Maurice & Mac then he ever did with the Radiants. The duo's stark, gutbucket sides are all here including "You Left the Water Running," "Lean on Me," "Lay It on Me," and others. McAlister is heard on many cuts exhorting Green to "Sing it Mac." Their inclusion gives the compilation a Dr. Jekyll/Mr. Hyde feel as the duo's tracks are a complete departure from what the Radiants were about. The Radiants thrilled Midwesterners with catchy creations from McAlister's pen such as "Father Knows Best," "Heartbreak Society," "Shy Guy," and "I Gotta Dance to Keep My Baby"—all on this collection—long before they went national with "Voice Your Choice" and "It Ain't No Big Thing." Rack O' Ribs Records tacked on every B-side including "I'm in Love," "Noble the Bargain Man," and "One Day I'll Show You." They mimic the Impressions on "Whole Lotta Woman" and you won't be able to resist the plugging "Baby You've Got It." What more could you ask for? Chess never released an album by the Radiants so this thorough collection is long overdue. *—Andrew Hamilton*

Baby You Got It: Ultimate Collection / 2002 / Titanic ✦✦✦✦

When Rack O' Ribs Records released *The Regal Theater Presents the Radiants: The Singles Collection 1962-1970*, fans of this underrated and neglected Chicago group literally jumped through hoops. For years, you couldn't find an album or single by them. The Rack O' Ribs CD is a complete account of the Radiants when Maurice McAlister sang lead and wrote most of their material. It's also the only CD that covers McAlister and Green "Mac" McLauren's career as Maurice & Mac. It didn't cover the Radiants after McAlister, the period commencing with "Don't It Make You Feel Kinda Bad," a record credited to them that they didn't record (it was actually done by the Confessions). This collection features some choice cuts by the Radiants when McAlister led them, along with tracks from 1967 to 1971 with the new Radiants, who had a totally different sound. The high points are "Hold On," "Tears of a Clown" (not the Miracles song), "The Clown Is Clever," "Anything You Do Is Alright" (written by Maxine Brown), and some others. Low points are grittier offerings like "Another Mule Is Kicking in Your Stall" and "Ida Mae Foster," which stray too far from their original personae. McAlister rejoined them for a short stint at Twinight Records, who issued "My Sunshine Girl" and "Don't Wanna Face the Truth" in 1971 (included here). The Twinight sides are the only tracks that Chess Records didn't originally issue. Obviously, you need to get this and the Rack O' Ribs disc to complete your Radiants library. The title is misleading; a real ultimate Radiants CD would slap all the old and the new Radiants tracks, sans the Maurice & Mac stuff, on one disk. *—Andrew Hamilton*

Jerry Ragovoy

b. 1935, Philadelphia, PA

Producer, Songwriter, Arranger / Soul, Pop-Soul, Philly Soul

An important behind-the-scenes force behind East Coast soul music, Jerry Ragovoy wrote or co-wrote several classic New York and Philadelphia soul records in the 1960s, often distinguished by a conspicuous gospel feel. The best of these included Garnet Mimms' "Cry Baby," Erma Franklin's "Piece of My Heart," Howard Tate's "Get It While You Can," "Time Is on My Side" (done by Irma Thomas and the Rolling Stones), and Lorraine Ellison's "Stay With Me." Ragovoy also contributed to first-class soul records as a producer and arranger.

A white Jew from Philadelphia, Ragovoy entered record production in 1953 with "My Girl Awaits Me" by the Castelles. He worked at Philly's Chancellor Records (where Fabian and Frankie Avalon had hits) and wrote the Majors' vocal group single "A Wonderful Dream," which made number 22 in 1962. Around this time he began writing some songs with another excellent white soul songwriter-producer type, Bert Berns, including "Cry Baby" by Garnet Mimms, which made number four in 1963. Ragovoy produced Mimms throughout the 1960s, creating a distinctive soul sound that blended churchy vocals and gospel-ish tunes with professional, classy New York studio arrangements. In the mid-'60s he also wrote a song for jazz trombonist Kai Winding, "Time Is on My Side," that was covered by Irma Thomas, and then by the Rolling Stones in a more rock-oriented version that gave them their first U.S. Top Ten hit. "Time Is on My Side," and some other of his best songs, were written under the pseudonym of Norman Meade.

Ragovoy also took a production/songwriting role in the careers of two of the most esteemed cult East Coast soul performers of the late '60s, Lorraine Ellison and Howard Tate. Ellison's "Stay With Me" is a classic example of the Ragovoy style: a slow, emotionally wrenching number which could almost be a gospel song but for the symphonic orchestral production, vocalized passionately and played with a drama with faint echoes of Broadway and opera. Janis Joplin in particular seemed to have a yen for Ragovoy-penned material, covering (with Big Brother & the Holding Company, or as a solo singer) "Piece of My Heart," "My Baby," "Get It While You Can," "Cry Baby," and "Try (Just a Little Bit

Harder)." Ragovoy was not too active after the 1960s, although he did some production for Bonnie Raitt in the 1970s and Francine Reed in the 1990s. *—Richie Unterberger*

The Rainbows

f. 1955, Washington, D.C.

Group / Doo Wop, R&B

One of Washington, D.C.'s pioneering vocal groups, the Rainbows recorded three singles titled after women's names: "Mary Lee," "Shirley," and "Minnie." "Mary Lee" was released on Morgan "Bobby" Robinson's Red Robin label in 1955; the Rainbows on that record consisted of lead singer John Miles, John Berry, and other unknown members who left after the release ran its course. Red Robin leased "Mary Lee" to Pilgrim Records, who promoted it into a small regional hit. For its follow-up, "Shirley" (1956), Berry recruited Chester Simmons and Don Covay to form the lineup most associated with the group. Early articles on Marvin Gaye mentioned him as a member—this was partially true as he, Billy Stewart, James Nolan, Reese Palmer, and others would fill in for ailing, missing, or late members on gigs, but never recorded with the Rainbows. Copies of "Shirley" can be found on three different labels—Pilgrim, Argyle, and Red Robin—but none did it any justice.

D.C. disc jockey Jay Ferry played the Rainbows locally, but DJs in other cities weren't as loving. "Minnie" on Rama Records in 1957 became their swan song, and despite popularity in Washington, the sales were disappointing and the group disbanded. At least four tracks—"Baraboo," "Honey Hush," "Jelly Bean," and "The Bug"—are still rotting in Red Robin's vaults. Covay became a solo act and scored with "Have Mercy" and "See Saw"; he was more successful as a writer and supplied material to many artists. John Berry also took to songwriting, cranking out more than 125 titles registered with BMI; his most successful, "Pony Time," became a hit for Chubby Checker. Simmons and fill-ins Marvin Gaye, James Nolan, and Reese Palmer formed the Marquees. *—Andrew Hamilton*

• **Mary Lee** / Pilgrim ✦✦✦✦

The Raindrops

f. New York, NY

Group / Brill Building Pop, Girl Group, Doo Wop, Rock & Roll

The Raindrops are, on one level, little more than a footnote in the much broader musical careers of Ellie Greenwich and Jeff Barry. On the other hand, as a studio singing group, they assembled one of the more impressive bodies of popular vocal music of the early '60s to come out of that edifice known as the Brill Building, the early-'60s successor to the Tin Pan Alley of the 1920s, which also served as proving grounds for the likes of Phil Spector, Don Kirshner, and numerous other luminaries of American pop/rock.

Jeff Barry (born Jeffrey Adelberg, April 3, 1939, Brooklyn, New York) and Ellie Greenwich (born October 23, 1940, Brooklyn) were from two families related by marriage, and first met when they were age five and four, respectively. Both showed a precocious interest in the creative side of music, and before he was eight years old, Barry (who was influenced heavily by country & western music) had written his first song. Greenwich, who grew up in Levittown, Long Island, began writing songs in junior high school even as she studied music, and led a girl trio called the Jivettes while still in high school—Greenwich's instrument at the time was the accordion. Barry graduated from high school in 1955, put in some army service, and afterward attended City College in Manhattan. Meanwhile, Greenwich released her very first commercial recording in 1958 (under the name Ellie Gaye), entitled "Cha-Cha-Charming," on RCA. Greenwich was studying at Queens College at the time, and one of her professors so disliked the song that he humiliated her in front of a class over it, and she subsequently changed colleges. Barry entered the music business in a more successful manner in 1959 as a songwriter working for E.B. Marks Publishers.

Barry & Greenwich later met once again at a Thanksgiving dinner in 1959—Barry was married at the time, but he introduced Greenwich to a friend, and they started dating. Barry's first big success came along the next year with the song "Tell Laura I Love Her," one of the most haunting and notorious of the teenage "death songs" that became popular in the early '60s—Ray Peterson scored a huge hit with it that year, and soon afterward British pop singer Ricky Valance also recorded it for the English market. By the end of the 1960s, Barry was divorced, and he and Greenwich began dating, writing, and recording demos together at the Brill Building, where Barry's publisher employer was based. Greenwich graduated Hofstra into a publishing career, and, in collaboration with writers like Ben Raleigh (who also worked with Barry) and Tony Powers, got a half-dozen of her songs recorded. Meanwhile, Barry recorded as a singer with several groups, including the Redwoods and the Spartans. Their marital partnership began on October 28, 1963, but their songwriting partnership had to wait, as each was signed to a different publishing company.

Greenwich & Barry finally linked up in business a year later, and spent much of that time collaborating with Phil Spector on such songs as "Da Doo Ron Ron," "Then He Kissed Me," "Be My Baby," and "Baby I Love You." They began recording together commercially with "What a Guy," a song originally intended for a vocal group called the Sensations. Their demo was considered so good that the record company, Jubilee, decided to release it and credit it to "the Raindrops." The demo got to number 41 on the charts, considered a respectable beginning in those days, especially for a nonexistent group. The next Raindrops single, "The Kind of Boy You Can't Forget," got to number 17, an unabashed hit. Now there was demand for the Raindrops. Their self-titled LP was issued by Jubilee in late 1963, which mostly consisted of the best Barry-Greenwich demos punched up with extra overdubbed vocals.

None of the Raindrops' remaining recordings fared any better, partly owing to the fact that they were inevitably competing with other groups on their best material. The arrival of the Beatles in 1964 heralded a wave of British acts that not only had a more powerful sound that teenagers wanted, but could do great covers of Barry-Greenwich songs themselves. The Raindrops' sound turned out to be a little too rooted in the pre-Beatles past, a kiss of death in those days. The Raindrops simply ceased activity, although Barry & Greenwich continued to enjoy hits as songwriters, their real professions in any case. Their most visible work was in association with producer George "Shadow" Morton and the girl group the Shangri-Las ("Remember," "Leader of the Pack," "Out in the Streets"), especially, and Spector ("River Deep, Mountain High"), who was the only American producer who seemingly managed to bridge the gap between the two eras of pop music. *—Bruce Eder*

The Raindrops / 1963 / Jubilee ✦✦✦✦

Album covers and promo pics depict them as a trio, but the Raindrops were contractually a duo comprised of the songwriting couple Ellie Greenwich & Jeff Barry. A crew of session singers accompanied the pair in the studio. This early best-of album features 20 songs mostly written by the pair, including their hits and songs they wrote that hit for others, like "Da Doo Ron Ron," on which they jam better than the Crystals. They even knock off Jesse Stone's "Don't Let Go." The Raindrops are easy to listen to and are prime examples of the simplistic brilliance of early-'60s Brill Building material and teen pop. If not for their songwriting successes and preference to stay behind the scenes, they would have had a string of hits. The camera-shy duo seldom made personal appearances or had write-ups in teen magazines. A later CD with 23 tracks competes with this collection, which is now available on CD as well. *—Andrew Hamilton*

• **The Complete Raindrops** / 1995 / Sequel ✦✦✦✦✦

This is one of the finest compilations of early-'60s girl group-style rock & roll you will ever find, and one of the most instructive, too, in terms of Barry & Greenwich's songwriting. But forget that—it's also about as much fun as any one record could possibly be, its 23 songs all among the most delightful pop/rock ever written. "What a Guy" kicks it off, and it hooks most people who hear it, but there's lots of better stuff here, including "One More Tear" and "You Got What I Like," and the Raindrops' version of "Do Wah Diddy Diddy." The sound is excellent, and the notes, while a little digressive, are as detailed as they get. *—Bruce Eder*

Chuck Rainey

b. Jun. 17, 1940, Youngstown, OH

Guitar, Bass / Jazz Blues, Jazz-Funk, Soul-Jazz

Another instrumentalist more widely associated with soul, pop, funk, and R&B, yet highly respected by jazz musicians, Chuck Rainey's been a star electric bassist since the '60s. While Jaco Pastorius and Stanley Clarke featured flashy, blistering playing and approached electric bass as if they were improvising on a guitar, Rainey's forte has been a heavy, steady pulse and vigorous support, fitting into a rhythm section and locking onto a groove with a vengeance. Rainey studied violin, piano, and trumpet in his youth, then moved from Youngstown to Cleveland at 21. He played electric guitar and bass in various R&B bands, then joined King Curtis' group in New York during 1964.

Rainey's done hundreds of recording sessions since then, but has also done a fair number of jazz dates. He played with Jerome Richardson, Grady Tate, Mose Allison, Gato Barbieri, and Gene Ammons in the late '60s and early '70s, as well as with Eddie "Cleanhead" Vinson at the 1971 Montreux Festival. Rainey toured and played that same year with Aretha Franklin. He moved to Los Angeles in 1972, and worked there with the Crusaders and Hampton Hawes, and recorded with Donald Byrd, Sonny Rollins, and John Handy in the mid-'70s. Rainey recorded in Japan with Hiroshi Fukumura in 1978. He's made two rare dates as a leader for Cobblestone in 1971 and for Hammer n' Nails in 1981. Neither is around today, but Rainey can be heard on many discs by Franklin, Curtis, Rollins, and others. *—Ron Wynn*

• **The Chuck Rainey Coalition** / Sep. 1972 / Cobblestone ✦✦✦

Although Chuck Rainey was among New York's most ubiquitous and in-demand R&B and pop session players of the 1960s and '70s, he didn't record very many albums on his own. *The Chuck Rainey Coalition* gives us a glimpse of the electric bassist in the driver's seat. Rainey doesn't do that much stretching, and most of the time, this collection of instrumental jazz/R&B simmers without really igniting. Nonetheless, there are a few cuts that stand out. Rainey really digs into a funky interpretation of the "Theme from Peter Gunn," and his soul-minded arrangement of "Harlem Nocturne" is fairly imaginative. Meanwhile, uptempo tunes like "Get It Together," "It's Gonna Rain" and "The Lone Stranger" are kind of catchy, though hardly mind-blowing. Overall, this isn't a bad album, but it could have been much better. *—Alex Henderson*

Ram-Z

f. Cincinnati, OH

Group / Contemporary R&B, Hip-Hop

After performing with the likes of Dru Hill, Faith Evans, and 112, this Cincinnati, OH, contemporary R&B trio nailed down Dru Hill's Nokio to produce their debut single, "Let Me Be the One," which featured an appearance by Drag-On and remixes by Kelly G and Bad Boy's Prestige. The single attracted some attention, released on TVT in late 2000, and Ram-Z aimed for commercial success despite the lack of a full-length album. The next year however, saw the release of *Let Me Be the One* in January 2001. *—Jason Birchmeier*

• **Let Me Be the One** / Oct. 24, 2000 / TVT ✦✦✦

Much in the spirit of Sisqó's "Thong Song," Ram-Z's debut single "Let Me Be the One" found its release on this EP, which also features a number of alternate versions, including the radio edit, the instrumental version, and remixes by Kelly G and Prestige. The Cincinnati trio sing with plenty of soul and benefit from some slick production. *—Jason Birchmeier*

Buck Ram (Samuel Ram)

b. Nov. 21, 1907, Chicago, IL, **d.** Jan. 1, 1991, Las Vegas, NV

Songwriter, Producer / Vocal Pop, R&B

Had it not been for an accident at age 15, it's possible that Samuel Ram might have been a concert violinist, or a first-chair player with a symphony orchestra. As it was, thanks to that accident, Buck Ram, as he became known from childhood on, ended up one of the most successful producers, arrangers, managers, and songwriters in R&B, and amassed four decades of enviable achievements in all of those fields.

Born in Chicago in 1907, Buck Ram had a deep and abiding interest in music, especially classical music, from an early age. He taught himself the violin as a boy and was good enough to play in an orchestra in his early teens, until an accident while playing football at age 15 fractured his hand. Still, Ram continued to study classical music, even as he attended the University of Illinois as a pre-law major. Ram's parents were upwardly mobile and had high aspirations for their son. They wanted not only a college graduate but a lawyer in his generation of the family, and he did earn a law degree, and passed the California bar examination in 1933, but he never practiced in the profession. Instead, Ram headed for New York and got a job with Mills Music, a major publishing house.

He became an arranger for an array of big-band performers, and also began writing songs with "Afterglow," for which he provided lyrics in collaboration with Al Stillman to music by Oscar Levant. Ram was primarily active at that time as an arranger, moving up the ladder to the biggest of the bands of this era, including Duke Ellington, Count Basie, and the Dorseys. He also wrote special material for the Cotton Club and other top night spots in New York while writing songs in his spare time—one of them, "At Your Beck and Call," was recorded by Ellington. In 1943, Ram co-wrote "I'll Be Home for Christmas," which became a huge hit for Bing Crosby during Christmas of 1943, repeated that chart success a year later, and established itself as a perennial holiday standard surpassed in popularity only by "White Christmas" and "The Christmas Song." Following the lead of his two collaborators, who were employed by the movie studios, he moved to Los Angeles, where he hooked up with the city's burgeoning music scene.

In 1945, he co-wrote a huge hit, "Twilight Time," for the Three Suns, who were one of the more successful groups based in Los Angeles. He might have been able to capitalize on that hit but for a downturn in his fortunes, owing to ill health that overtook him late in the 1940s. When he returned to the music business in 1952, Ram found that it had changed radically during his absence—the times were hard for jazz performers, while the soft pop business was booming and there was a serious undercurrent of activity in country and R&B, but not the '40s-style R&B with which he'd been familiar. This material was starting to sell to younger audiences and had more of an edge. Ram regrouped by starting a management company, hoping to put his 20 years of experience in the music business to use guiding the careers of some of the new acts that were coming along.

It was during this period that Ram came to discover—though accounts vary as to who actually "discovered" them—the Platters, and subsequently became their manager. The Platters scored a huge hit for Mercury Records in the middle and later part of 1955 with "Only You," one of Ram's own compositions. They followed this up with "The Great Pretender," "My Prayer," "(You've Got) The Magic Touch," "Twilight Time," and a brace of other hits, many of them million sellers and all either written by or arranged and proposed by Ram, who became known at Mercury and around the record industry as the man with the "magic touch." Ram was responsible for polishing the Platters' sound and image and consciously trying to reach a mainstream (that is, adult white) audience with their music. Years earlier than Berry Gordy with the Supremes, Ram was seeing to it that the Platters played the best clubs and the most celebrated venues possible.

The Platters provided Ram with a platform upon which to build his business. Their success lasted into the early-'60s, long past the point where the hits stopped coming, because the Platters under Ram had always cultivated the best venues, where one needed recognition rather than a recent hit to get booked to perform. Over time, as the original members exited, Ram discovered that he still owned a valuable property in the name "the Platters." The group never entirely went out of style, and when the oldies boom hit in the late '60s, Ram was ready and reaped huge amounts of money. *—Bruce Eder*

- **The Magic Touch** / 1960 / Mercury ✦✦

RAMP

f. Cincinnati, OH

Group / Jazz-Funk

A group that was based in Cincinnati and also an acronym for "Roy Ayers Music Productions," RAMP released one album in 1977 that didn't do all that much upon its release. However, decades later, as appreciation for anything bearing the mark of jazz-funk legend Roy Ayers has increased, the album has become a revered rare-groove classic. Supported by the excellent "Daylight" and a version of Ayers' "Everybody Loves the Sunshine," two anti-gravity soul/jazz-funk pearls, the rare album has been known to fetch extremely high prices among collectors. The group—bassist Nate White, drummer John Manuel, guitarist Landy Shores, and vocalists Sibel Thrasher and Sharon Matthews—folded after that album's release. *—Andy Kellman*

- **Come into Knowledge** / 1977 / Blue Thumb ✦✦✦

Randy & the Rainbows

f. 1961, Maspeth, NY

Group / Doo Wop, R&B

Even if you don't know the group by name, if you're the tiniest bit familiar with doo wop you'll still probably recognize Randy & the Rainbows' hit single "Denise." A Top Ten hit, it's one of those feel-good songs that continue to turn up on compilations of the best music from the 1960s. Randy & the Rainbows formed in the Queens section of New York City in 1962. The group included two pairs of siblings, brothers Sal Zero and Mike Zero and brothers Frank Safuto and Dominick "Randy" Safuto. Ken Arcipowski rounded out the quintet. The group evolved from the Dialtones, which in 1959 included the Safutos, Rosalie Calindo, and Eddie Scalla, the Safutos' cousin. After recording during the early '60s for Goldisc, the Safutos hooked up with Arcipowski and the Zeros in 1962 to become Randy & the Rainbows. Backed by the production team that also handled the Tokens, the group put out "Denise" in 1963.

As Randy & the Rainbows, the group never again repeated the success they found with "Denise." They changed names several times and continued to perform at different times as Madison Street, Triangle, and Them and Us. Over the years, the group has shared the stage with such artists as the Spinners, Little Anthony & the Imperials, Tony Orlando, Blood, Sweat & Tears, Freddie Roman, Jay Black, and Pat Cooper. They have also toured with the Beach Boys, Dionne Warwick, and the Four Seasons. The group put out a new album in 2001. As of that year, the Randy & the Rainbows' lineup included original member Mike Zero, Vinny Carella, and Jimmy Bense. *—Linda Seida*

C'mon Let's Go / 1982 / Ambient Sound ✦✦

Remember / 1984 / Ambient Sound ✦✦

- **Play Ball** / May 10, 2002 / WizWorks ✦✦✦

Two performers who were prominent in the 1960s have joined together to bring back a style of popular music that got its start with young singers on the street corners of Philadelphia and Queens: doo wop. Randy & the Rainbows were formed in 1962 and had a big hit with "Denise," which is reprised on this album, connected with Jimmy Wisner, aka "Jimmy the Wiz," for a new release. Wisner was a highly sought after session musician having worked with Judy Collins, Tony Bennett, and other pop luminaries of the time. On this album, Randy & the Rainbows supply the singing, helped exceedingly by top-flight musicians. Wisner supplies the label WizWorks, some of the arrangements, produces, and takes a turn on the Hammond B-3 organ on "Deep Down" and "Joseph." The outcome is a Randy & the Rainbows updated to the 21st century, but still retaining more than a vestige of that wonderful pre-rock harmonic style from the 1950s and 1960s. Although never enjoying the success of their Top Ten hit "Denise," the group has not been hiding out. It has shared the stage with top groups the Four Seasons, Dionne Warwick, Pat Cooper, and others. Good talent rarely ever disappears. Mike Zero, an original member of the group, Vinny Carella, and Jimmy Bense deliver nicely on a play list of 12 tunes, some love songs, others upbeat toe tappers, especially the swinging renditions of "Ain't She Pretty" and "Joseph." The happy music on this CD creates an urge to roll up the rug and do some meaningful dancing, not the senseless, non-directional, self-indulgent gyrations that pass for that lost art these days. Recommended. *—Dave Nathan*

Rare Earth

f. 1967, Detroit, MI, **db.** 1978

Group / Album Rock, Motown, Blue-Eyed Soul, Soul, Psychedelic

Rare Earth began as an R&B band called the Sunliners in Detroit in 1961. Of the musicians who would be part of the band dubbed Rare Earth, only sax player Gil Bridges and drummer/singer Pete Rivera were present. John Persh joined on bass in 1962. Rod Richards became a guitarist with the group in 1966. Keyboardist Kenny James came into the fold the same year. After years of doing the club circuit, the group was picked up by Motown Records as the first act on their new label Rare Earth Records. The company suggested that the band change their name to match the label and the band Rare Earth was born.

When they set out to record their first album, they essentially ran out of material and did a 21-minute rendition of the Temptation's "Get Ready" to fill out the space. The album was making no headway on the charts for a long period of time. So they took the first three minutes of "Get Ready," released it as a single and it made its way into the U.S. Top Ten list, peaking at number four. Pulled along by the success of the single, the album also began to sell, breaking the Top 20, and Rare Earth's career was officially on its way. The second album, *Ecology*, was released in June of 1970, a couple months short of a year after "Get Ready" had been put out. Interestingly enough, *Ecology* was not really the group's second album, but their third. An album entitled *Generation* was recorded as the soundtrack to the film of the same name. When the film stalled at the box office, the album was shelved. Still, *Ecology* would yield not one, but two hit singles. The first was "(I Know) I'm Losing You" (another Temptations cover), which also broke the Top Ten. The second single, "Born to Wander," did not fare quite so well, but did make the Top 20. The album was catapulted to number 15.

Not wanting to lose momentum, *One World* followed almost exactly a year after *Ecology*, and yielded another hit single in a longtime classic, "I Just Want to Celebrate." The song peaked on the pop charts at number seven and the album broke the Top 50. They released a live album in December of the same year. For the next album, *Willie Remembers*, the group insisted on doing all originals, a move that was not common around the Motown camp. Unfortunately, for a band trying to prove a point, the album never reached the type of sales of previous records. Indeed, it stalled out at number 90, and the single "Good Time Sally" didn't even break the Top 50.

Motown tightened the creative grip on the group and original producer Norman Whitfield, who had worked with the group on earlier albums, was brought in to save the day. The resulting album, *Ma*, was released in May of 1973 and fared just a little better than *Willie Remembers*, peaking at number 65. The label was not pleased and sent the group into the studio to record with Stevie Wonder. That pairing did not really gel, though, and only two tracks were recorded, neither of which were released. Instead, the label sought to release another live album, trying to regain the spark that Rare Earth had had. That project also fell by the wayside, though.

What followed was a serious of lineup changes and legal battles, and the group stopped touring altogether in 1974. The following year Rare Earth, in a new lineup, released *Back to Earth*. The album did a bit better than the previous one, reaching number 59 on the charts. The single, appropriately entitled "It Makes You Happy (But It Ain't Gonna Last Too Long)" stalled just outside the Top 100. A disco-oriented excursion entitled *Midnight Lady* was released in 1976, but failed to really go anywhere. To make matters worse, Rare Earth Records was discontinued altogether. The band had broken up by this time. As fate would have it, though, this was not the end of Rare Earth. Instead, Barney Ales, who had presided over Rare Earth Records, started his own label Prodigal Records. He talked the group into reuniting to record the label debut. The resulting album, *Rare Earth*, was released in 1977 and made no real waves in the music business. Rare Earth got things together again for a marathon recording session the following year. That session yielded not one, but two albums. The first was *Band Together*, released in

April of 1978, with *Grand Slam* following in September. Neither of those albums every really took off, either. The group essentially broke up in 1978, although a version of the original lineup was touring all the way into 1983. A different incarnation of the group, with just two original members, still makes the circuits. *—Gary Hill*

Dream Answers / 1968 / Verve ✦✦

Get Ready / 1969 / Motown ✦✦✦
Rare Earth's Motown debut is as well-oiled as a new V-8, and so are its liner notes: "In this age of ego-tripping freak bands, Rare Earth has stood pretty much alone. Each cat stands handsomely tall as if from a fashion rack at Carnaby. They do their gig; do it well—and split." Smirking aside, the band turns in a smoothly harmonized "In Bed" and a chugging rhythm section for "Train to Nowhere." But the core of this release is a live side-long monster version of "Get Ready." It's as driven by the crowd's rapturous response as by the various solos, and the snake-charmer sax improv by Gil Bridges is easily the highlight of the album. *—Paul Collins*

Ecology / 1970 / Motown ✦✦✦
Two strong tracks propelled *Ecology* up the pop charts: the swaggering, bravado-laden "Born to Wander," written by Tom Baird, and a hard-hitting, rocking rendition of the Temptations' "I Know I'm Losing You," written by Cornelius Grant, Eddie Holland, & Norman Whitfield; the epic remake of the latter is almost eleven minutes of pure funk-rock. Lead singer Pete Rivera had a powerful voice, similar to Dennis Edwards, that could sell a song; the percussion and echo vocals accentuate the classic. The guys do a nice job on John Lennon & Paul McCartney's "Eleanor Rigby," and bass player John Persh's "Nice Place to Visit" adds a different twist to Rare Earth's legacy. *—Andrew Hamilton*

One World / 1971 / Rare Earth ✦✦✦
What was necessary for this Motown act was a bit of an identity come the third album, and *One World* did nothing to define the individuals of this sextet. Also, Norman Whitfield's machine shop production on the remake of "(I Know) I'm Losing You" from the previous *Ecology* album was pure genius. They emulate it on "I Just Want to Celebrate," and by doing so they create a diamond in the rough. Woodwind player Gil Bridge's "Someone to Love" shows Brit rock leanings, as does bassist John Persh's "Any Man Can Be a Fool," but it is second-generation watered-down Brit rock, and without the inclusion of their last Top Ten hit, the summer of 1971's "I Just Want to Celebrate" written by non-members N. Zesses and D. Fekaris, the album would've been an instant bargain-bin candidate. The beautiful gatefold painting by England's Roger Dean looks like it inspired 1972's *Bloodrock Passage* album cover, and it probably did. Producer Tom Baird's "The Road" is just dreadful, the production lackluster on a song that was definitely born to wander aimlessly. Guitarist Ray Monette, keyboard player Mark Olson, and conga/ percussionist Ed Guzman actually outdo Baird in a bad way with "Under God's Light," which is even worse than the song that came before it. God may not have been pleased. Pete Rivera's "If I Die" and "The Seed" are filler, while the cover of Ray Charles' "What I'd Say" sounds little like that icon's work, and is one of their weaker arrangements. They should've stretched "I Just Want to Celebrate" across the side of an album à la "Get Ready," but didn't. At least 15 other acts would name their albums *One World* after this album's release, artists from John Denver to Phil Manzanera, so couple that innovation with the beautiful Roger Dean artwork and the superb hit, and you can forgive the other seven tracks. Buy the 45 rpm and stick it inside the album jacket. *—Joe Viglione*

Rare Earth in Concert / 1971 / Motown ✦✦

Willie Remembers / 1972 / Rare Earth ✦✦

Ma / 1973 / Motown ✦✦✦✦
Rare Earth's most satisfying LP, Norman Whitfield wrote and produced all five songs. "Ma," the title track, had been done by Temptations and Undisputed Truth but nobody rocked the sucker like Rare Earth; they jam for 17:17 on the funkiest mama song ever. "Hum Along and Dance," first appeared on the Temptations' *Psychedelic Shack*; Rare Earth gives the groover and update, a rolling organ sets it off. Lead, Gil Bridges brags about his musical ability on the loud, horn dominated stomper "Big John in My Name." A haunting arrangement of "Smiling Faces Sometimes" will make you shiver. And you don't get much more sensual than the soft and lush "Come With Me," where a female simulates an orgasm that puts Donna Summers' exhibition on "Love to Love You Baby" to shame; it's the only new song on the LP, but who's quibbling, Ma is da bomb! *—Andrew Hamilton*

Rare Earth / 1977 / Prodigal ✦✦

Grand Slam / 1978 / Prodigal ✦

Band Together / 1978 / Prodigal ✦✦

Earth Tones: Essential / Aug. 23, 1994 / Motown ✦✦✦✦

Anthology: The Best of Rare Earth / May 23, 1995 / Motown ✦✦✦✦
This compilation is a 36-track, two-CD set chronicling the career of this interesting and too often overlooked group. It covers their entire career, and the extensive booklet included really ties up the loose ends well to provide a vivid picture of the band's career. The lead off track is one recorded by the Sunliners, the original name of Rare Earth. That track is the most different piece on the collection, coming across a very basic and straightforward rock & roll number. The remainder of the album is a bit mixed, but leans more towards the more potent end of the group's recordings. The sound of the material varies from time to time. At best, the band could be seen as a soulful and hard-rocking outfit that really knew how to merge sounds of soul music with hard rock and jazz. At worst they come across as bubble gummy '60s pop. The album includes several previously unreleased tracks. Of course their biggest hit, "I Just Want to Celebrate" is present, as are many other originals and covers by artists such as Smokey Robinson and Ray Charles. For die-hard fans of the band, this is a must have, and it would make a great single buy for the casual Rare Earth listener. *—Gary Hill*

● **The Very Best of Rare Earth** / Aug. 25, 1998 / Motown ✦✦✦✦
Before the rise of the Average White Band in the mid-'70s, the most successful blue-eyed soul unit was Rare Earth (although the Spencer Davis Group was also quite popular). Influenced by Sly & the Family Stone and the artists of Motown as well as 1960s rockers like the Kinks, Rare Earth had a distinctive sound and offered some of the most exciting music of 1969-1973. The Detroit outfit didn't fare as well among black audiences as AWB; Earth recordings that soared to the top of the pop charts only went to number 20 or number 30 on the R&B charts (probably because Earth was much more rock-influenced than AWB). At any rate, this gem-filled CD illustrates just how Earth could be. Spanning 1969-1978, *The Very Best of Rare Earth* boasts such essential hits as "I Just Want to Celebrate," "Get Ready" and "I Know (I'm Losing You)." If much of the material reminds you of Norman Whitfield's work with the Temptations and Edwin Starr, it's no coincidence; Earth often worked with the great Motown producer/songwriter. In fact, "Hum Along and Dance," "Big John" and "Ma" are among the most rock-influenced recordings that Whitfield ever produced. But at the same time, Earth was much too funky for some rock programmers. "Warm Ride" (1978) finds the band being produced by the Bee Gees and taking a stab at disco; the results are decent, though not nearly as strong as its earlier work. Most of the material, however, isn't simply decent—it's excellent. *—Alex Henderson*

Rare Essence

f. Washington
Group / Go-Go, Funk
One of the classic Washington, D.C., go-go bands, Rare Essence carried the torch from the music's early-'80s heyday well into the 1990s. Founded by drummer Quentin "Footz" Davidson, the group debuted in 1981 with "Body Moves," quickly emerging alongside Trouble Funk, E.U., and others among the top go-go bands in the D.C. area; despite countless lineup changes, Rare Essence continued recording and touring regularly throughout the years which followed, seeing many of their albums reissued during the mid-'90s. *—Jason Ankeny*

Get Your Freak On / 1995 / Sounds of the Capitol ✦✦✦

● **Greatest Hits, Vol. 1** / Dec. 12, 1995 / Liaison ✦✦✦✦
Liaison's 1995 greatest-hits release for Rare Essence compiles many of the 12-inch and album mixes that were anthems on the Washington, D.C., go-go circuit throughout the '80s. Their over-the-top, high-intensity live shows had the reputation of being some of the most energetic performances on the circuit—featuring extended workouts, audience call and response, and variations on signature tunes. Opening with their most well-known release, "Body Moves," and working through many a crowd favorite, this compilation serves as a wonderful introduction to those not only unfamiliar with Rare Essence, but those wholly uninitiated to the go-go sound. *—Rob Theakston*

Rare Gems Odyssey

db. 1980
Group / Disco, Funk
Based in Los Angeles, Rare Gems Odyssey was an obscure disco/funk/soul combo that recorded two little-known LPs in the late '70s. The band was formed in 1976, when its six-person lineup consisted of singer Debra Givings, drummer/singer Charles Givings, keyboardist/singer Johnny Ross, guitarist/singer Jimmy Gough, bassist/singer Darryl Coleman, and percussionist/singer Tony Coleman. Produced by Arthur G. Wright, its self-titled debut album came out on Casablanca in 1977; when the LP failed to sell, Casablanca dropped Rare Gems Odyssey. In 1978, the band omitted Odyssey from its name—possibly because it didn't want to be confused with the group Odyssey, which had a major hit with "Native New Yorker" in 1977—and started going by simply Rare Gems. Using that name, it recorded its second album, *Million Dollar Disco*, for the small, L.A.-based California Gold label in 1979. That LP was also plagued by a lack of attention, and in 1980, Rare Gems broke up. *—Alex Henderson*

Rare Gems Odyssey / 1977 / Casablanca ✦✦✦
It's quite possible that 99 percent of the world's R&B lovers have never heard of Rare Gems Odyssey, a little-known disco/funk/soul combo from Los Angeles. Released in 1977, the band's self-titled debut album received very little attention. Only one song on this record (which was produced by Arthur G. Wright) deserves to be called a gem: the hilarious, relentlessly funky "What Is Funk." Grooving to a James Brown-like riff, the members of Rare Gems Odyssey provide six minutes of goofy, wacky jive talk and make "What Is Funk" a classic that would have been worthy of Parliament/Funkadelic. But that's the only great tune on the LP. From disco-funk items like "Psychic Lady" and "Restricted Area" to the soul ballad "Rocky Mountain," the rest of *Rare Gems Odyssey* is mediocre—not terrible, but definitely mediocre. Commercially, the album bombed, and Casablanca gave Rare Gems Odyssey the boot. This LP went out of print in 1978 and is unlikely to ever be reissued on CD. *—Alex Henderson*

● **Million Dollar Disco** / 1979 / California Gold ✦✦✦
After being dropped by Casablanca in 1977, Rare Gems Odyssey changed its name to Rare Gems and resurfaced on the small California Gold label with its second album, *Million Dollar Disco*. This 1979 LP didn't do any better than the band's first album, but it's a competent disco-funk effort. Rare Gems steers clear of ballads and slow jams this time—the disco era was in full swing in 1979, and the Los Angeles residents take dead aim at the dancefloor on pleasant, if unremarkable, tracks like "Love's Hall of Fame," "I Like Disco Music," "Disco Jam," and "Make Your Life So Easy." None of the material is mind-blowing, but none of it is terrible either. Rare Gems' second album (which was produced and arranged by Arthur G. Wright) turned out to be its last; in 1980, the band called it quits. *—Alex Henderson*

The Rascals

f. 1964, New York, NY, **db.** 1972

Group / Blue-Eyed Soul, Pop, AM Pop

The Rascals, along with the Righteous Brothers, Mitch Ryder, and precious few others, were the pinnacle of '60s blue-eyed soul. The Rascals' talents, however, would have to rate above their rivals, if for nothing else than the simple fact that they, unlike many other blue-eyed soulsters, penned much of their own material. They also proved more adept at changing with the fast-moving times, drawing much of their inspiration from British Invasion bands, psychedelic rock, gospel, and even a bit of jazz and Latin music. They were at their best on classic singles like "Good Lovin'," "How Can I Be Sure," "Groovin'," and "People Got to Be Free." When they tried to stretch their talents beyond the impositions of the three-minute 45, they couldn't pull it off, a failure which—along with crucial personnel losses—effectively finished the band as a major force by the 1970s.

The roots of the Rascals were in New York-area twist and bar bands. Keyboardist/singer Felix Cavaliere, the guiding force of the group, had played with Joey Dee & the Starliters, where he met Canadian guitarist Gene Cornish and singer Eddie Brigati. Brigati would split the lead vocals with Cavaliere and also write much of the band's material with him. With the addition of drummer Dino Danelli, they became the Rascals. Over their objections, manager Sid Bernstein (who had promoted the famous Beatles concerts at Carnegie Hall and Shea Stadium) dubbed them the Young Rascals, although the "Young" was permanently dropped from the billing in a couple of years.

After a small hit with "I Ain't Gonna Eat Out My Heart Anymore" in 1965, the group hit number one with "Good Lovin'," a cover of an R&B tune by the Olympics, in 1966. This was the model for the Rascals' early sound: a mixture of hard R&B and British Invasion energy, with tight harmony vocals and arrangements highlighting Cavaliere's Hammond organ. After several smaller hits in the same vein, the group began to mature at a rapid rate in 1967, particularly as songwriters. "Groovin'," "Beautiful Morning," "It's Wonderful," and "How Can I Be Sure?" married increasingly introspective and philosophical lyrics to increasingly sophisticated arrangements and production, without watering down the band's most soulful qualities. They were also big hits, providing some of the era's most satisfying blends of commercial and artistic appeal.

In 1968, almost as if to prove they could shake 'em down as hard as any soul revue, the Rascals made number one with one of their best songs, "People Got to Be Free." An infectious summons to unity and tolerance in the midst of a very turbulent year for American society, it also reflected the Rascals' own integrationist goals. Not only did they blend white and black in their music; they also, unlike many acts of the time, refused to tour on bills that weren't integrated as well. "People Got to Be Free," surprisingly, was the group's last Top 20 hit, although they would have several other small chart entries over the next few years, often in a more explicitly gospel-influenced style. The problem wasn't bad timing or shifting commercial taste; the problem was the material itself, which wasn't up to the level of their best smashes. More worrisome were their increasingly ambitious albums, which found Cavaliere in particular trying to expand into jazz, instrumentals, and Eastern philosophy. Not that this *couldn't* have worked well, but it *didn't*. They had never been an album-oriented group, but unlike other some other great mid-'60s bands, they were unable to satisfactorily expand their talents into full-length formats.

A more serious problem was the departure of Brigati, the band's primary lyricist, in 1970. Cornish was also gone a year later, although Cavaliere and Danelli kept the Rascals going a little longer with other musicians. The band broke up in 1972, with none of the members going on to notable commercial or artistic success on their own, though Cavaliere remained the most active. *—Richie Unterberger*

The Young Rascals / Mar. 28, 1966 / Atlantic ✦✦✦✦✦

The history of '60s rock is littered with stories of great rock classics—the Savages' album, the Thirteenth Floor Elevators' first two albums, the first two Chocolate Watch Band albums—that should have been better known than they were. *The Young Rascals* is that rare example of a genuinely great album that got heard and played, and sold and sold. Apart from the presence of a hit ("Good Lovin'") to drive sales, every kid (and his girlfriend) in any aspiring white rock band on the East Coast in 1966 seemingly owned a copy. And it's easy to see why—the Rascals' debut couples a raw garage band sound with compelling white soul more successfully than just about any record since the Beatles' *Please Please Me*. The band had three powerful singers in Felix Cavaliere, Eddie Brigati, and Gene Cornish, and an attack honed in hundreds of hours of playing dance clubs on Long Island and New York City. The result is a record without a weak moment or a false note anywhere in its 35 minutes: "Do You Feel It" shows them crossing swords stylistically with Smokey Robinson & the Miracles; "Just a Little" and "Like a Rolling Stone" show off their folk-rock chops; and "Slow Down," "Good Lovin'," "Mustang Sally," and "In the Midnight Hour" are all '60s rock & roll classics in these versions. "Like a Rolling Stone," in particular, now seems all the more compelling, pointing the way toward a future that included Hendrix's version of "All Along the Watchtower." The CD is one of Warner Special Products' better sounding reissues, having been remastered by Rhino's Bill Inglot. The original album was on Atlantic, and was one of the label's best-sellers of the mid-'60s. *—Bruce Eder*

Collections / Jan. 9, 1967 / Atlantic ✦✦✦✦✦

The garage-band feel has been banished almost entirely from the group's second album, whose release followed a pair of disappointing singles ("What Is the Reason," "Come on Up"). It also includes their first misjudgment on an album, Gene Cornish's too-quiet, too-introspective, and way-too-languid "No Love to Give," amid an otherwise wonderfully soulful body of music that picks up right where "In the Midnight Hour" from the prior album left off. Most of this record is among the most danceable white rock music of its period—even the Eddie Brigati-sung cover of the then-current pop standard "More" has a certain rocking credibility. Their attempt at bluesy rock & roll, Cornish's "Nineteen Fifty-Six," a bit of a "Kansas City" ripoff, with a pair of crunchy guitar parts and Cornish singing lead, also comes off extremely well. They're even better with the more soulful tracks, however. "Land of 1000 Dances" was the best track on which to end this album, but it was Cavaliere and Brigati's "Love Is a Beautiful Thing" that pointed to the future, showing the group moving toward the mix of sounds and sentiments behind "People Got to Be Free." The CD reissue of this album (originally on Atlantic) has no notes but very good sound. *—Bruce Eder*

Groovin' / Jul. 31, 1967 / Rhino ✦✦✦✦✦

The Rascals move into the era of psychedelia with a vengeance on this album—their best of their entire history—which also retains a soulful core and adds a bit of a Latin beat. The original album on Atlantic was a monster seller thanks to the title track, practically the group's signature tune (number one on the pop charts, number three on R&B), but "Groovin'" was only one small strong point on the album of the same name. "Find Somebody" marked a return to the group's garage band sound with a psychedelic twist, including phased fuzztone guitars and some catchy lyrics and choruses. "How Can I Be Sure" is the second-best-known song off of this album, but it has a fully successful companion piece, "I'm So Happy Now," which applies similar instrumentation to very different (but pleasing) effect. Gene Cornish's "I Don't Love You Anymore" could be the finest pop song in the band's repertory apart from "How Can I Be Sure," with a delectable guitar part, scrumptious melody, and delicious chorus. "You Better Run" was more than a year old when it turned up on this album, and its garage band sensibilities are a bit more primitive than those of "Find Somebody," but it's a great piece of rock & roll. The band turns in one superb Motown cover, "A Place in the Sun," done in a surprisingly subdued fashion. And for a finale, Cavaliere and Brigati turn in an exultant period piece, "It's Love," whose soaring lyrics are matched by guest artist Hubert Laws' flute—alas, his presence would point the way toward less effective, more disjointed work in the group's future, as they moved more deeply into psychedelia. *—Bruce Eder*

Once Upon a Dream / Feb. 19, 1968 / Rhino ✦✦✦

This is a welcomed reissue in Atlantic's Original Sound series, with souped-up audio and a neat reproduction of the original gatefold jacket. It's also a little flawed—only 11 tracks indexed while the jacket says 14. *Once Upon a Dream* is a fascinating record, capturing the Rascals in transition from white soul band to progressive jazz-blues-rock fusion outfit. Working amid the psychedelia flourishes of the post-*Sgt. Pepper* era, this is the Rascals at their most ornate, backed by flutist Hubert Laws, saxman legend King Curtis, and trumpet player Mel Lastie and a string orchestra. "Rainy Day"'s outro, with its mention of peace and love, is the dead giveaway about where the band was heading—luckily, the soulful "Please Love Me" and "It's Wonderful" follow immediately, retaining the toughness and drive of their earlier work; and Felix Cavaliere's "Singin' the Blues Too Long" marks the peak of the band's blues experiments, as well as a compelling foray into jazz, five minutes of surging trumpet and sax, soulful choruses, and searing guitar from the composer/singer. Gene Cornish's "I'm Gonna Love You" is one of the group's strangest tracks up to that time, a mixture of soul and marching band, no less. Not everything here works, by a longshot—the gentle, trippy, sitar-laden "Sattva" is one of the silliest things the band had recorded up to that time; "My Hawaii" is a boring interlude, and the title song is too self-consciously pretty and profound. Those flaws aside, however, *Once Upon a Dream* marked the end of an era, the last Rascals album that could be absorbed casually, without any demanding pretensions or larger messages. *—Bruce Eder*

Freedom Suite / Mar. 17, 1969 / Rhino ✦✦✦

Released in 1969 as a two-record set, *Freedom Suite* showcases the Rascals' hitmaking strengths, but also reveals the weaknesses which prevented the group from becoming more than a singles-oriented band. There are three soulful hit singles included here: the megahit, "People Got to Be Free," which had gone to number one the previous year; its follow-up, "A Ray of Hope," a powerful tribute to Dr. Martin Luther King Jr.; and Felix Cavaliere's statement of faith and hopefulness, "Heaven," a minor hit. However, most of the other songs were considerably more lightweight than that triumvirate, and the entire second record consisted of three meandering instrumental jams. Nonetheless, the lyrics on this album provide an interesting historical documentation of the optimistic "we can change the world" feel of the era in which it was made. *—Jim Newsom*

See / Dec. 15, 1969 / Atlantic ✦✦✦

Felix Cavaliere continued his search for meaning and relevance with this release. The title cut, a track that rocked harder than anything the band had done since its early days, featured distorted electric piano pounding under Cavaliere's optimistic "love's the only thing I see" lyrics. That track and the gospel rave-up "Carry Me Back" were the band's last Top 30 single releases. Although the album didn't do much on the charts, *See* contains some interesting music. "Nubia" has a nice jazz feel and an airy Hubert Laws flute solo; several songs mine the gospel vein; and the band's cover of "Temptation's 'Bout to Get Me" will take any jaded baby boomer back to a slow dance on a sawdust-covered high school gym floor. *—Jim Newsom*

Peaceful World / 1971 / Sundazed ✦✦✦✦

Peaceful World is a wonderful blend of soul, jazz, and funk that never found an audience. Perhaps it was because the positive sentiments expressed in the lyrics were unfortunately becoming passé; perhaps it was the diversity of the two-record set itself. Despite its lack of commercial success, this was an artistic triumph for Felix Cavaliere. With a supporting cast including jazz luminaries Joe Farrell, Hubert Laws, Alice Coltrane, and Ron Carter, Cavaliere creates a musical vision of the *Peaceful World* conjured up by the album's title. The single, "Love Me," which barely cracked the Hot 100, is a piece of funk in a Sly Stone vein. Guitarist Buzz Feiten's "In and Out of Love" is one of those shoulda-been-a-hit-single songs. Many of the tracks, including the side-long (21:25) title track, are mellow jazz excursions. This ambitious album took the Rascals to the place Cavaliere had been headed over the course of the last couple of albums—but, sadly, the fans didn't follow. *—Jim Newsom*

Search and Nearness / Mar. 1, 1971 / Atlantic ✦✦✦

The Island of Real / 1972 / Columbia ✦✦✦
Some of Felix Cavaliere's funkiest songs, Crusaders bassist Robert "Pops" Popwell, the Butterfield Blues Band horn section (with David Sanborn), soulful vocals and jazz solos combine to create another great but overlooked album by the Rascals. With a groove at times like Tower of Power, at others like latter-day Sly & the Family Stone, this, the band's final recording, is worth seeking out. [The CD reissue on Sundazed adds two previously unreleased bonus tracks, the Cavaliere originals "Prove It" and "Love Is a Woman."] *—Jim Newsom*

In Retrospect / 1986 / Raven ✦✦✦✦

The Ultimate Rascals / 1986 / Warner Bros. ✦✦✦✦
A wonderful collection of songs, most of which were major hits for this quartet, *The Ultimate Rascals* was one of the early compilations released when compact discs were still fairly young. As such, the tapes from which this recording was mastered were obviously not first generation, with the resulting subpar sound the disc's only weakness. But, oh, the music: a cornucopia for any baby boomer weaned on AM radio in the mid- to late '60s. The band's development is traced here from the early rock & roll sides, like "Good Lovin'" and "You Better Run," through the blue-eyed soul era of "Groovin'" and "A Girl Like You," to the band's social relevance period, exemplified by "People Got to Be Free" and "A Ray of Hope." During their peak period from 1966-1969, the Rascals cranked out a batch of popular hit singles, and all are here, along with some of their better album cuts. This is the disc that many fans rushed to buy when they first acquired CD players, and it's still a good place to start for the uninitiated. For the true fan, however, the two-disc anthology released in the early '90s is much better. *—Jim Newsom*

Searching for Ecstasy: The Rest of the Rascals, 1969–1972 / 1988 / Rhino ✦✦✦✦

Anthology (1965–1972) / Jul. 14, 1992 / Rhino ✦✦✦✦✦
Boasting all of the Rascals' essential hits as well as many enjoyable album tracks, this two-CD set does a fine job of summarizing the New Yorkers' accomplishments. Whether the Rascals are tearing into rockers like "You Better Run" (covered by Pat Benatar in 1980) and the Olympics' "Good Lovin'" (a frat-rock staple) or expressing their love of soul music (both Northern and Southern) on "Groovin'," "A Beautiful Morning" and "I've Been Lonely Too Long," the package shows us just how dynamic they could be. The Rascals' cover of Wilson Pickett's "In the Midnight Hour" is hard to resist, and it should be noted that their version of Sir Mac Rice's "Mustang Silly" was recorded before the song became a major hit for Pickett. Sadly, things broke down for the Rascals commercially in the early 1970s, but the socially aware soul-pop songs "Love Me," "Saga of New York" and "Brother Tree" show that they still had some creative life left in them. And they indicate that with the right guidance and input (working with someone like Curtis Mayfield, maybe?), the band could have made a comeback and become an important part of the '70s soul-pop scene. From obvious choices to surprises, *Anthology: 1965-1972* is a package that both rock and soul aficionados should savor. *—Alex Henderson*

● **The Very Best of the Rascals** / 1994 / Rhino ✦✦✦✦✦
Although Rhino issued a deluxe two-CD set covering the Rascals a few years ago, this single disc set contains enough essential songs for you to get the point. The Rascals, along with the Righteous Brothers, defined blue-eyed soul singing, making records that were as churchy, earthy, and convincing as anything that came out of the South or Motown in the '60s, backed by tight, anthemic arrangements and excellent combo playing. The 16 cuts include their first hit, "I Ain't Gonna Eat Out My Heart Anymore," and continue on into their flirtation with psychedelia in 1970. The only quibble is their failure to include "Look Around," a socio-political cut from the *Freedom Suite* album that's just a cut below "People Got to Be Free" or "A Ray of Hope." *—Ron Wynn*

All I Really Need: The Complete Atlantic Recordings, 1965–1971 / Oct. 17, 2001 / Rhino Handmade ✦✦✦✦✦

Rasputin's Stash

f. Chicago, IL
Group / Funk
The brainchild of session musician Martin Dumas Jr., Rasputin's Stash was a '70s soul/funk ensemble from the Windy City of Chicago, IL. In the early '70s, Dumas assembled an eight-piece group out of fellow session regulars from the city. Signed early on to the Cotillion label, the group released a self-titled album in 1971 and gradually lost half of their members by the time they recorded their second album for Gemigo, a subsidiary of Curtis Mayfield's Curtom imprint. The quartet—Dumas, Ernest Frank Donaldson, Bruce Butler, and Paul Coleman—shed the possessive of their band name for another self-titled album, released in 1974. Gemigo eventually went under, and the group was shifted over to Curtom proper for a pair of singles released in the latter part of the decade: "Dance With Me" was released as r-Stash in 1977, and "Booty March" was released as Stash the year following. In a distribution switch that saw Curtom move from Warner Bros. to RSO, the label's roster was gutted and Stash was one of the victims. After that, the group opted to quit, but not before they did plenty of shows in New York and their hometown, where they were most appreciated. Throughout the years, Rasputin's Stash and all its following incarnations endured as rare groove favorites. In 2000, the U.K.-based Sequel label issued *The Devil Made Me Do It*, a CD compilation of the group's Gemigo material, including several unreleased cuts that were intended for their third album. *—Andy Kellman*

Rasputin's Stash / 1971 / Cotillion ✦✦✦

Rasputin Stash / 1974 / Gemigo ✦✦✦

● **The Devil Made Me Do It** / 2000 / Sequel ✦✦✦
This disc, released with the help of Castle Music U.K. in 2000, compiles all of Rasputin Stash's Gemigo-era material and adds some previously unreleased material to sweeten the deal. The group featured experienced session musicians who knew how to lay down some loose soul/funk in the vein of early Kool & the Gang, the Meters, and the J.B.'s, while remaining true to their Chicago roots. The lyrical content is limited to getting high and making love, but there's plenty within the grooves—full of slick keyboard work, down-and-dirty basslines, nimble percussion, and the occasional accent of strings—to keep the mind from wandering. Devout fans of all things '70s Chicago would no doubt enjoy this. *—Andy Kellman*

The Ravens

f. 1946, **db.** 1956
Group / R&B, Doo Wop, Vocal Pop
The Ravens were among the pioneering post-World War II R&B groups, and also among the earliest R&B groups named for birds. In both their musicality and their nomenclature, they influenced two generations of performers that followed, as well as sold lots of records in the process. The Ravens originated with Jimmy Ricks (born 1924, Jackson, FL; died 1974, New York, NY), who started singing at an early age. In 1945, he was employed as a waiter at the Four Hundred Tavern and later at an establishment known as the L. Bar, both in New York's Harlem. One of his co-workers was a friend, Warren "Birdland" Suttles, and during moments when the work wasn't too frantic, the two began singing together, to tunes by the Ink Spots, the Mills Brothers, the Delta Rhythm Boys, and other harmony groups whose music appeared on the club's jukebox. They decided to try and form an actual group, searching for two more members that would make up the requisite harmony quartet. The two hooked up with Leonard "Zeke" Puzey and Ollie Jones, and worked up their sound around songs such as "Darktown Strutters' Ball." Choosing the name the Ravens, and thus inaugurating the "bird" group trend in black vocal groups, they were booked into the Club Baton in Harlem, and proved themselves sufficiently talented to rate a national tour, also picking up Howard Biggs, who became their arranger and the composer of much of their original repertory. The Ravens' sound was unusual for its time, featuring bass singer Ricks as the lead voice—this would become their trademark and one of their most often emulated attributes over the next decade.

The group was signed to Hub Records in early 1946, and released their debut single, "Honey" b/w "Lullaby," the latter a Jones original that they'd been performing since putting together their four-man lineup. Jones left the group late in 1946 to join the Cues and was replaced by Maithe Marshall. The Ravens' contract with Hub ended after one year and they jumped to the National label, where they enjoyed an immediate hit with their version of "Ol' Man River," which was perhaps the best of a succession of eight Top Ten R&B hits over the next decade, including "Write Me a Letter" and "Send for Me If You Need Me." By 1948, the Ravens were already an influence on dozens, perhaps hundreds of R&B vocal groups that were coalescing around the variety of sounds that they were bringing to the charts. The Orioles, the Crows, the Swallows, the Swans, and the Wrens followed immediately in their wake, and the trend didn't slacken in the 1950s, as outfits with names like the Penguins continued charting, but the Ravens was where it started. The group continued performing and recording for another seven years, with Marshall and Suttles periodically exiting the lineup at different times, the latter replaced by Joe Medlin and Louis Heyward, and Bubba Ritchie. Their label relationships were nearly as busy as these lineup shifts, from National to Columbia (and OKeh) in 1950, and then to Mercury in 1951. Their move to the latter label resulted in a major lineup change as Jimmy Stewart succeeded as the lead tenor from Puzey, who jumped to the Hi-Hatters—Marshall later followed him into that lineup, as did Heyward for a short period.

Whatever their lineup, the Ravens ascended to the top of their field while at Mercury, although their chart placements didn't always reflect their status as a performing group. They only enjoyed one major chart hit, "Rock Me All Night Long," which got to number eight on the national R&B listings, but the group was commanding a fee of 2,000 dollars a night for their performances during this period. The group, consisting of Ricks, Joe Van Loan, Louis Frazier, and Stewart, moved to Jubilee Records once their Mercury contract ended in 1953. Their four Jubilee singles were released during the period when rock & roll was on the rise and many R&B acts were put in the position of trying to appeal to a wider, whiter youth audience than they'd previously thought of reaching. "Green Eyes" was their biggest hit on Jubilee, in mid-1955—several of their songs from this period show the growing influence of rock & roll, complete with loud sax arrangements and titles such as "Rockin' at the Record Hop."

The beginning of the end for the group came when Ricks began pursuing his goal of a solo career. Their final singles were issued credited to "Jimmy Ricks & the Ravens" or "Jimmy Ricks & the Rickateers." Ricks exited the group in 1956, and the group name was taken over by Van Loan, who purchased the Ravens' name in partnership with their road manager, Nat Margo. Under Van Loan's leadership, the Ravens jumped to Chess Records' Argo imprint that same year. Ricks' influence remained profound into the late '50s, long after the Ravens ceased charting records—the Temptations' Melvin Franklin, in particular, was heavily influenced by Ricks' singing. Ricks remained an active solo performer, moving between the Paris, Decca, and Signature labels before signing with Atlantic Records in 1961, where he recorded with LaVern Baker and Little Esther. By the 1967, when he rejoined Jubilee Records, he'd passed through the Mainstream and Festival Records rosters. Ricks reunited with Warren Suttles in 1971 and re-formed the Ravens, with Gregory Carroll and Jimmy Breedlove filling out the lineup. As an indication of the flexibility of Ricks' singing voice and the respect he commanded even after more than 25 years as an R&B vocalist, he joined the Count Basie band as its vocalist in the early '70s, a capacity in which he was serving at the time of his death on July 2, 1974, at the age of 50. The Ravens never recorded as much as their main rival group, the Orioles, and have never received the kind of comprehensive retrospective accorded the latter group. Their recorded legacies for National, Columbia and OKeh, Mercury, and Jubilee are available but scattered among several releases on various labels. *—Bruce Eder*

The Greatest Group of Them All / 1978 / Savoy ✦✦✦
The Greatest Group of Them All isn't the best title for the Ravens' entry in Savoy's *Roots of Rock and Roll* series. The group was certainly worthy of the claim, but this ballads-heavy collection isn't the best to prove it, and most of the songs aren't even the best of their down-tempo material. Basically for Ravens fans only, this works more as a compilation of the group's later National sides (roughly 1950-1951) plus a few unattributed

odds-and-ends, focused on songs rarely compiled elsewhere. As a result, "Ol' Man River" and "Be I Bumble Bee or Not" are missing, but there are solid runthroughs of the standards "Until the Real Thing Comes Along," "September Song," "Deep Purple," "Lilacs in the Rain," "It's the Talk of the Town," "Who's Sorry Now," and "I've Got the World on a String." It's an interesting collection, but one that has a little trouble coming through on the title's high promises. *—John Bush*

Dreams, Pleas & Blues / Oct. 27, 1998 / Columbia/Legacy ♦♦♦♦
The Ravens were one of the first, if not *the* first, of all of the doo wop groups; numerous groups followed in their wake in the '50s, groups that utilized the basic ground rules the Ravens set into place on their late-'40s recordings for Herb Abramson's National label. Upon leaving National for the greener pastures of major label Columbia in 1950, they made dynamite recordings that unexplainably emerged stillborn in the marketplace, yielding no hits of any kind during their two-year tenure with the label. *Dreams, Pleas & Blues* collects up all the Ravens material—issued, unissued and even one alternate take—and clearly shows that the group was still cutting some mighty fine records, even if their place on the charts was denied largely due to quickly changing trends. Their first session with the Benny Goodman Sextet backing them yielded a cover of Louis Prima's hit "Oh Babe," and already showing the group to be chasing trends rather than creating them, as they had only a couple of years before. The small-jazz-combo backing idea stays with them through "Time Takes Care of Everything" and "Don"t Look Now," while "I"m So Crazy for Love," "Midnight Blues," "Honey I Don't Want You" and "My Baby's Gone" hark back to their earlier National jump blues with a simple, small rhythm section backing. The Ravens tried a little bit of everything to score a hit at Columbia, including hopped-up novelty material like "The Whiffenpoof Song," "That Old Gang of Mine" and "The Calypso Song," and even a precursor to R&B with "I Get All My Lovin' on a Saturday Night," but none of it proved hit-worthy. These aren't the recordings to start your Ravens collection with, but it might not be a bad place to end up. *—Cub Koda*

● **Be I Bumble Bee or Not** / Nov. 28, 2000 / Indigo ♦♦♦♦♦
Excepting only a trio of singles for Hub from 1946, *Be I Bumble Bee or Not* reissues the earliest material recorded by the Ravens, the best of their 1947-1949 hitch with National. That period saw the most chart activity for the quartet as well as the recording of their greatest material, close-harmony gems like the effervescent "Be I Bumble Bee or Not," an understated yet swinging "Ol' Man River," bouncy lovers' requests like "Write Me a Letter" and "Send for Me If You Need Me." Like fellow harmonists the Ink Spots, the Ravens often indulged in standards, and turned in interesting diversions on their versions of "Summertime," "I Don't Know Why I Love You Like I Do," and "Always," plus a pair of holiday favorites: "Silent Night" and "White Christmas." Jimmy Ricks' deep bass is reason enough to hear these songs, and the smooth harmonizing of the rest of the group is the icing on the cake. *—John Bush*

Lou Rawls

b. Dec. 1, 1935, Chicago, IL
Vocals / Soul, Philly Soul, R&B, Vocal Jazz
From gospel and early R&B to soul and jazz to blues and straight-up pop, Lou Rawls was a consummate master of African-American vocal music whose versatility helped him adapt to the changing musical times over and over again, while always remaining unmistakably himself. Blessed with a four-octave vocal range, Rawls' smooth, classy elegance—sort of a cross between Sam Cooke and Nat King Cole—permeated nearly everything he sang, yet the fire of his early gospel days was never too far from the surface. He made his name as a crooner, first by singing jazz standards, then moving on to soul in the mid-'60s, and capped the most commercial phase of his career with a productive stint at Philadelphia International during the latter half of the '70s. Even after his days as a chart presence were over, Rawls remained a highly visible figure on the American cultural landscape, pursuing an acting and voice-over career in addition to his continued concert appearances, and doing extensive charity work on behalf of the United Negro College Fund.

Louis Allen Rawls was born in Chicago on December 1, 1935, and was raised on the city's south side by his grandmother. He sang in the choir at his Baptist church starting at age seven, and became interested in popular music as a teenager by attending shows at the Regal Theatre, with genre-crossing singers like Joe Williams, Arthur Prysock, and Billy Eckstine ranking as his particular favorites. Rawls also tried his hand at harmony-group singing with schoolmate Sam Cooke, together in a gospel outfit called the Teenage Kings of Harmony. Rawls moved on to sing with the Holy Wonders, and in 1951 replaced Cooke in the Highway Q.C.s. In 1953, when Specialty recording artists the Chosen Gospel Singers swung through Chicago on tour, they recruited Rawls as a new member; he made his recording debut on a pair of sessions in early 1954. He later joined the Pilgrim Travelers, but quit in 1956 to enlist in the Army as a paratrooper; upon his discharge in 1958, he returned to the Travelers and embarked on a tour with Cooke. It nearly cost Rawls his life—during the Southern leg of their tour, the car Rawls and Cooke were riding in crashed into a truck. Cooke escaped with minor injuries, but another passenger was killed, and Rawls was actually pronounced dead on the way to the hospital; as it turned out, he spent five and a half days in a coma, did not regain his full memory for another three months, and took an entire year to recuperate.

When Rawls had recovered sufficiently, he switched to secular music and hit the L.A. circuit with a vengeance, performing in clubs, coffeehouses, and any other small venues that would allow him on-stage. During this period, he also landed his first acting role, a small part on the hit detective series *77 Sunset Strip*. In 1962, he was discovered at a coffeeshop near Capitol Records headquarters by producer Nick Venet; at Venet's request, Rawls hastily recorded an audition tape, and wound up with a recording contract. Later that year, Capitol issued Rawls' debut album, *Stormy Monday* (alternately known as *I'd Rather Drink Muddy Water*), a collection of jazz tunes with backing from the Les McCann Trio. The same year, he supplied the impassioned background vocals on Sam Cooke's hit "Bring It On Home to Me." Rawls' next few recordings for Capitol combined jazz, blues, R&B, and pop in varying combinations, sometimes casting him in big-band settings akin to those of his hero Joe Williams. While the results were often rewarding, it was plain that Rawls and Capitol were still searching for a definite direction.

In the meantime, Rawls was revamping his live act by adding lengthy spoken monologues to his songs; these "raps" served as a platform for the singer to discuss social issues and personal experience, not to mention as an attention-getting gimmick that overrode the noise and bustle of the clubs where he performed. 1966's *Live!* captured that distinctive concert presence with a repertoire of mostly jazz and blues (plus a celebrated version of "Tobacco Road"), and proved to be a gold-selling breakthrough hit. However, Rawls found an even more lucrative direction when he made the switch to soul music later that year; his first full-fledged R&B album, *Soulin'*, spawned his first major hit single in "Love Is a Hurtin' Thing," which nearly reached the pop Top Ten and went all the way to number one on the R&B charts before year's end. 1967's "Dead End Street" hit number-three R&B and won Rawls his first Grammy, for Best R&B Vocal Performance; it also teamed Rawls with composer/producer/arranger David Axelrod, who would go on to a legendary career of his own. A 1969 cover of Mable John's "Your Good Thing (Is About to End)" was Rawls' next big hit, although by that time his LP sales had begun to slip a bit; nonetheless, he was still a regular presence on variety shows and on the Las Vegas circuit.

In 1971, Rawls parted ways with Capitol and signed with MGM, where he promptly delivered another one of his greatest successes with "Natural Man." With its subtle message of black pride, "Natural Man" reached the Top 20 on both the pop and R&B charts, and won Rawls his second Grammy. However, much of the material MGM pushed Rawls to record was too lightweight for the singer's standards; disenchanted, he left the label in 1972. It wasn't until 1975 that he caught on with another label, the independent Bell Records, where he recorded an early Daryl Hall/John Oates composition, "She's Gone." Unfortunately, Rawls' version was eclipsed by Tavares' far bigger hit recording of the song, and he soon left Bell to sign with Kenny Gamble & Leon Huff's legendary soul imprint Philadelphia International. With Gamble & Huff's help, Rawls managed to successfully reinvent himself in the lush, orchestrated Philly soul idiom. His label debut, 1976's *All Things in Time*, proved to be the biggest album of his career, reaching the Top Ten and going platinum; likewise, "You'll Never Find Another Love Like Mine" became his biggest hit single ever, topping the R&B charts and zooming to number two on the pop side. Despite Rawls' general taste for mature, adult music, "You'll Never Find Another Love Like Mine" was compatible enough with the emerging disco sound to garner substantial dance-club play as well. The follow-up single, "Groovy People," made the R&B Top 20.

Rawls was a hot commodity once again, and he remained one of Philadelphia International's most successful artists through the rest of the '70s. His 1977 LP *Unmistakably Lou* won him a third Grammy for Best Male R&B Vocal Performance and contained the R&B Top Ten hit "See You When I Git There"; later that year, he continued his artistic and commercial hot streak with *When You Hear Lou, You've Heard It All* and "Lady Love." The title track of 1979's *Let Me Be Good to You* was his last big hit with Philly International, reaching number-11 R&B. The following year, Rawls kicked off what would become a consuming passion for years to come: the Lou Rawls Parade of Stars Telethon, an annual event which eventually raised millions of dollars for the United Negro College Fund.

From the '80s on, Rawls played the part of a well-established entertainer, rather than focusing his energies on maintaining a chart presence. He served a stint on Epic Records from 1982-1986 that proved a commercial disappointment; by then, he was more interested in running the telethon and conducting extensive tours of American military bases around the world. A 1987 reunion with Gamble & Huff produced his final charting single on the R&B side, "I Wish You Belonged to Me." Toward the end of the '80s, Rawls made some recordings for Blue Note, including the Grammy-nominated *At Last* in 1989. During the latter half of the '90s, Rawls returned to his acting career with greater frequency, appearing in the acclaimed *Leaving Las Vegas* (among many other films and TV shows) and also pursuing voice-over work in cartoons like *Hey Arnold* and *Rugrats* (he'd begun this side of his career singing on several *Garfield* specials). Most of his '90s recordings were holiday collections, but 1998's *Seasons 4 U* was a jazzy outing released on his own label. Rawls entered the new millennium by returning to his gospel roots on 2001's *I'm Blessed* (astonishingly, his first solo gospel album) and 2002's *Oh Happy Day*. *—Steve Huey*

Stormy Monday / Feb. 5, 1962+Feb. 12, 1962 / Blue Note ♦♦♦♦♦
Lou Rawls has had a long and commercially sucessful career mostly singing soul, R&B and pop music. Originally a gospel singer, Rawls' first album as a leader (reissued on CD) features him performing soulful standards backed by the Les McCann Trio. Few of the songs have exactly been under-recorded through the years but they sound fresh and lively when sung by Rawls; highlights include "Stormy Monday," "In the Evening" and "I'd Rather Drink Muddy Water." Pianist McCann gets a generous amount of solo space and the reissue has three "bonus cuts" that were being released for the first time. This is still Lou Rawls' definitive recording in the jazz idiom, cut before he went on to more lucrative areas. *—Scott Yanow*

Black and Blue / Oct. 1, 1962-Nov. 1, 1962 / Capitol ♦♦♦
Super blues and jazzy soul by Lou Rawls from an early period on Capitol. He hadn't yet found the hit formula, but was cutting some superb singles. His voice had a resonance and strength developed for years on the gospel trail, and also during his work backing Sam Cooke. Even though he didn't get any hits, it's well worth the cost if you can find this album. *—Ron Wynn*

Tobacco Road / Jul. 29, 1963-Aug. 20, 1963 / Capitol ♦♦♦
His third album for Capitol had a good version of the title track, and tried to mix blues, soul, and R&B. Rawls sang in a strong, rousing manner, turning in both outstanding ballads and good uptempo tunes, but the company wasn't able to promote any song enough for the album to even get on the charts. *—Ron Wynn*

Soulin' / Aug. 1966 / Capitol ♦♦♦♦♦
Lou Rawls began his roll onto the R&B and pop charts with this 1966 work. He was now doing soul material, songs where his gospel background and instincts took over, and he

simply wailed, soared, and shouted, rather than interpreting or working with blues progressions. He scored a huge hit with "Love Is a Hurtin' Thing" and had finally found a successful formula. *—Ron Wynn*

Carryin' On / Dec. 1966 / Capitol ♦♦♦
Rawls got a mild hit from this album with a fine rendition of "On Broadway," but otherwise, it was another example of everything clicking except nothing sold. The production and arrangements were perfectly tailored to his voice, the songs were good, and Rawls sounded confident, assertive, and soulful. Hopefully, Capitol will one day get around to reissuing the entire Rawls catalog. *—Ron Wynn*

Too Much! / May 1967 / Capitol ♦♦♦
Lou Rawls was in the midst of a hot streak at Capitol, scoring smash singles and winning Grammy awards. This was one of three albums he released in 1967, all of which made the pop Top 40 albums chart. It was superbly produced and arranged by David Axelrod, with Rawls being bluesy, soulful, anguished, triumphant, and resigned. He displayed both a variety of moods and a vocal mastery at its peak. *—Ron Wynn*

That's Lou / Aug. 1967 / Capitol ♦♦♦
Rawls topped his success of the previous year with an even bigger hit album. He won a Grammy for "Dead End Street" and got good notices for a follow-up cut about the joys and pains of being a celebrity. David Axelrod gave Rawls the production and arranging support he needed, keeping everything squarely in the background and letting Rawls' voice stay at the center and be the focus of the song. *—Ron Wynn*

Merry Christmas Ho! Ho! Ho! / Sep. 10, 1967 / Capitol ♦♦♦

Feelin' Good / Feb. 1968 / Capitol ♦♦♦
Lou Rawls had enjoyed three smash albums in a row, so it wasn't too surprising when this release failed to equal their success. David Axelrod couldn't work his production magic this time, and there weren't any big hits or tracks Rawls could turn into successes, even though he sang with his normal drive and style. It was inevitable for an artist who was never a trendy vocalist and always depended on first-rate songs. *—Ron Wynn*

You're Good for Me / Jun. 1968 / Capitol ♦♦♦
Produced by David Axelrod with excellent arrangements by H.B. Barnum, *You're Good for Me* is one of Lou Rawls' best Capitol LPs and a good showcase for his earthy vocals. "Down Here on the Ground" was used in the Paul Newman/Strother Martin jail flick *Cool Hand Luke*. "Soul Serenade" and "You're Good for Me" are some tracks that can be found on *Anthology* issued June 6, 2000. *—Ed Hogan*

The Way It Was: The Way It Is / 1969 / Capitol ♦♦♦♦
Unlike collectors of breaks and beats, soul searchers ought to take more than a general interest in Lou Rawls' output from the second half of the '60s. This period proved an immensely productive one, as the artist managed to produce over a dozen records between 1965 and 1970. From a creative point of view, they also tended to get the better out of both Rawls and composer/producer David Axelrod. The latter teamed up with Rawls and was given enough space to develop his own unique ideas, complete with session musicians of his choice and arranger H.B. Barnum. Apart from the singer's smooth but convincing delivery, Axelrod's original approach deserves some credit. The very recognizable guitar and organ parts remain subtle most of the time, careful not to interfere too much with Rawls' delivery. Every now and then though, an element of surprise turns up, whether it's an orchestral outburst, a funky intermezzo, or even a hint of psychedelia. It may leave the listener in bewilderment, after the song continues in its original way. These unexpected twists make most of the Rawls/Axelrod collaborations an exciting listening experience, for you're never quite sure whether a moment like this will turn up. By the time *The Way It Was: The Way It Is* was issued, Axelrod and Rawls had already done a considerable number of albums together. Nevertheless, it's a surprisingly strong set. Interpretations of well-known soul classics like "Fa Fa Fa Fa Fa (Sad Song)" and "When a Man Loves a Woman" get the full Rawls/Axelrod makeover here. The album further contains Axelrod at his peak in the seemingly awkward but brilliantly chosen "Season of the Witch," of Donovan fame. Also included is the sublime "Your Good Thing (Is About to End)," which earned Rawls his third consecutive chart success and would also appear on his next album of the same name. To this day, both albums did not receive a proper release on CD. Too bad, for the album cover is definitely worth a closer inspection: *The Way It Was: The Way It Is* finds the artist appearing from a dark background, tightly dressed in black leather and a stick to match. *—Quint Kik*

You've Made Me So Very Happy / Mar. 1970 / Capitol ♦♦♦♦
Lou Rawls could possibly be mistaken for Mr. Lady Love himself, the guy who hopes to see you when he gets there and wants you to sit down and have a talk with him. Although his contribution to the late-'70s disco era might prove him a companion to the Barry Whites and Manilows of this world, Rawls originally started his career as a gospel-based R&B singer. In terms of chart success, he definitely was an important force behind Philly soul. But initiators Gamble & Huff were nowhere near when he made his first blues and jazz-oriented records. By the middle of the '60s, Rawls joined hands with a young genius named David Axelrod. "Mr. Most Wanted Breaks" produced and composed some of the highest sought after vinyl by crate-digging hip-hop fans. Among these records were a couple of collaborations with Rawls, with whom Axelrod made over a dozen albums between 1965 and 1970. Like most of these, the choice of repertoire for *You've Made Me So Very Happy* consisted almost entirely of songs by different writers, as Rawls was largely known as a performer. The records gradually evolved from jazz to soul and, with this one, they moved into a more rock-oriented territory. Cuts like "Mama Told Me (Not to Come)" and "You've Made Me So Very Happy" are well done, but were already made famous by Three Dog Night and Blood, Sweat & Tears. The latter's rolling piano intro was sampled by De La Soul (for "I Am I Be") and the song undeniably inherits Axelrod's magic touch. Rawls/Axelrod are invincible in reworking Traffic's "Feelin' Alright," a standout track, together with the subtle delivery of "Let's Burn Down the Cornfield." Finally, there's the beautiful "How Can That Be," which Axelrod and Rawls wrote together; though not as memorable as 1967's "Dead End Street," it's still exemplary of what they were capable of. After this album, their fruitful collaboration would be put on hold for more than 30 years. On account of "Loved Boy," the closing piece Rawls did for Axelrod's 2001 comeback album, you wouldn't say their minds ever parted at all. *—Quint Kik*

Silk & Soul / Feb. 1972 / MGM ♦♦♦

A Man of Value / Oct. 1972 / MGM ♦♦♦
Following a string of hits at Capitol Records and the tutelage of producer David Axelrod, Lou Rawls jumped ship to MGM Records. While Rawls was never known for making solid album statements, *A Man of Value* is another record of strong efforts and filler fluff. Rawls charted with the title track in 1972, a song that boasted of his strengths in life and love. Most of the lyrical content on *A Man of Value* is brimming with self-empowerment and a social consciousness Rawls embodied throughout his career, whether covering an American standard or a chart-topper. Songs like "The Politician" and "Walk on In" contain strident soul production that provides the perfect backdrop for Rawls' molasses-thick vocal approach. Rawls adds a soft touch to James Taylor's "Fire and Rain" and reinterprets Stevie Wonder's "Evil" beautifully. Unfortunately, a handful of gems cannot save this album from being just another snoozer in Rawls' catalog. *—Douglas Siwek*

Live at the Century Plaza / 1973 / Rebound ♦♦♦
Rawls covers two songs by the Beatles ("Something," "Golden Slumbers"), swings his way through a four-part blues medley, and finds time to do show-stopping versions of hits like "Love Is a Hurtin' Thing," "A Natural Man" and "Tobacco Road." *—Keith Farley*

All Things in Time / Oct. 1976 / Philadelphia International ♦♦♦♦♦
Shortly before Rawls signed with Philadelphia International, his career had stalled. After a mostly successful stint with Capitol Records, he later signed with MGM and had a big hit with "Natural Man" in 1971. But the hits didn't keep coming and his 1975 Bell album, *She's Gone*, barely made a dent. His 1976 signing with Philadelphia International recharged his career and he immediately became one of the label's most successful acts. *All Things in Time* is his label debut. Rawls was one of the few acts on the label who could do great work with a variety of the producers and arrangers. The biggest track here was the bravado-filled "You'll Never Find Another Love Like Mine." With its subtle Latin rhythms and Rawls' tongue-in-cheek intonations, the songs' inherent nastiness was missed by legions of dancers. "Time" written by Jack Faith and Allan Felder has Rawls doing a pitch-perfect vocal that makes the song sound like a standard. On this album, Rawls also got a chance to do work with the quixotic Bunny Sigler. Both "Need You Forever" and "Frow Now On" have Sigler accentuating Rawls' rougher edges. Unfortunately, all of the tracks aren't great here. Despite Dexter Wensel's imaginative arrangement, "Pure Imagination" could not be saved. *All Things in Time* does end on a great note. On "Let's Fall in Love All Over Again," a song previously done by Billy Paul and Nancy Wilson, Rawls' take is arguably the best version. *All Things in Time* is not only one of Rawls' best albums, it's also one of the finest from Philadelphia International. *—Jason Elias*

Unmistakably Lou / 1977 / Philadelphia International ♦♦♦♦♦
Lou Rawls was riding another hot streak in the late '70s, his career rejuvenated by a string of fine albums and singles on the Philly International label. This was the follow-up to his huge hit LP *All Things in Time*. He only had one R&B chart song from the album, but in ways, his vocals are superior to those on the prior album. Where the Gamble & Huff production team's efforts on the preceding project rivaled Rawls' vocals, he took the spotlight this time, while their arrangements and productions were more on the subdued side. *—Ron Wynn*

When You Hear Lou, You've Heard It All / 1977 / Philadelphia International ♦♦♦♦♦
This is a smooth, often delightful album that kept Lou Rawls squarely in the love/romantic/mellow circle that he'd been scoring in throughout the late '70s. Gamble & Huff were really trimming the productions and keeping things laid-back and casual, while Rawls' emphatic, smoky vocals carried the day. They weren't getting huge pop hits, but were on the R&B charts steadily, and the album just missed the pop Top 40. *—Ron Wynn*

Lou Live / 1978 / Philadelphia International ♦♦♦
Riding high on the success of his mid-'70s soul and R&B dates, Philadelphia International issued this live recording featuring Rawls doing the straight blues, jazzy ballads, and pre-rock standards he normally reserved for clubs and concerts. There were none of the big radio hits here; instead, Rawls covered such songs as "Six Cold Feet of Ground," "Blues for a Four String Guitar," and "Everyday I Have the Blues." It also didn't stay on the charts very long, and Gamble & Huff got back to commercial basics the next time out. Still, it's one of his finest and most representative albums. *—Ron Wynn*

Let Me Be Good to You / May 1979 / Philadelphia International ♦♦♦
Here is an above-average album that did much better than anyone thought it would at the time. The title track just missed the R&B Top Ten, and the album almost made the pop Top 40, although it wasn't on the charts for a long time. Rawls was still singing in a confident, relaxed, earnest, convincing fashion, and the Gamble & Huff production team continued to keep his voice at the forefront and give him miminal arranging support. *—Ron Wynn*

Sit Down and Talk to Me / 1980 / Philadelphia International ♦♦♦
This is a fine late-'70s Rawls album on Philadelphia International. He had temporarily enjoyed some disco success, but had returned to the blend of jazzy pop, soul, and blues that best showcased his skills. While his voice was now deeper and rougher, his timing, delivery, and overall technique had matured to the point where anything he sang was

impressive. Rawls enjoyed a pair of moderate hits from the album and showed that he was still able to turn out quality sessions. *—Ron Wynn*

When the Night Comes / 1983 / Epic ✦✦

This is Lou Rawls' first LP after a lengthy, productive run on Philadelphia International Records. Epic Records tries to keep Rawls commercially viable, but fans of his Kenny Gamble & Leon Huff productions may not appreciate these pop- and country-oriented Ron Haffkine productions. "Upside Down" is so happy-go-lucky that it's reminiscent of "The Candy Man." "Wind Beneath My Wings" is uptempo with a sermonizing rock guitar, but the song works better as a ballad. Producer Ron Haffkine sometimes has Rawls sounding tenor-ish, but the vocalist is more effective singing in the lazy baritone/bass that graced "You'll Never Find Another Love Like Mine" and "Lady Love." "A Couple More Years," "When the Night Comes," "I've Been Him," and "Midnight Sunshine" are failed attempts to corner a piece of the country market. The whole affair reeks of just another session to Rawls, and it doesn't hold a candle to the Philly stuff. *—Andrew Hamilton*

Family Reunion / 1988 / Gamble-Huff ✦✦✦

After wowing listeners with Philadelphia International Records, Kenny Gamble & Leon Huff regrouped with the Gamble & Huff label. It didn't meet with much success, and if this album is any indicator, it's obvious why—they're missing many of the key components that help to create the patented '70s Philly sound. Rawls' rendition of "Family Reunion" doesn't belong in the same room as the O'Jays' marvelous original. The best song, "I Wish You Belong to Me," is vintage Gamble & Huff, a simmering ballad filled with heartfelt lyrics, cooing backing vocals, and a tender vocal from Rawls complete with rap. Three other Gamble & Huff songs—"Two Happy Hearts," "Jealous Lover," and "Today's the Day"—lack punch and substance. They sorely miss Ron Baker (bass) and Norman Harris (guitar); the deceased axe players added so much to the sound of Philly. Also, Kenny Gamble and Thom Bell aren't singing backing vocals like they did, uncredited, on the majority of Philadelphia International's recordings. Sources say they supplemented nearly everybody they produced, including the Stylistics, the O'Jays, Harold Melvin & the Bluenotes, Billy Paul, and the Intruders. Walter "Bunny" Sigler contributed three productions. "It's a Tough Job (Somebody's Got to Do It)" tries to make a statement, but the flaccid production doesn't help. The melodic "When Love Walked in the Door (Hurt Walked out the Other)" attempts to recapture that old magic. However, Sigler's "Who Loves You Baby" suffers from Steve Green's lackluster bass playing; he adds nothing to the flow, but neither does James "D Train" Williams, who plays on some of the other tracks. Where have all the good session bass players gone? Producer Dexter Wansel got an aggressive vocal from Rawls on "Fine With Me," a pleasant midtempo floater that Rawls sings with fire. Jack Faith and Rawls produced "Unchained Melody," a disaster that doesn't become ear-friendly until it's almost over. *—Andew Hamilton*

At Last / Jun. 1989 / Blue Note ✦✦

He's never deserted either blues or jazz, but Lou Rawls hasn't always found a receptive audience for these styles at notoriously conservative major labels. That wasn't the case on this 1989 album, on which Rawls performed straight-ahead jazz and pre-rock pop or blues, and was backed by an all-star lineup including Ray Charles, Cornell Dupree, Steve Khan, Richard Tee and Dianne Reeves. His voice had an exuberance and fervor that spoke volumes about how happy he was in the setting. *—Ron Wynn*

It's Supposed to Be Fun / 1990 / Blue Note ✦✦

The Best of Lou Rawls / Oct. 17, 1990 / Capitol ✦✦✦✦✦

This is a nice collection of Rawls' Capitol singles, which include his number-one hit "Love Is a Hurtin' Thing" and many other fine chart singles, all produced by David Axelrod. Rawls got in a groove during his Capitol years, singing songs that had a soul feel but a jazz and blues base. In some ways, he's never made better songs than his late-'60s and early-'70s stint at Capitol. *—Ron Wynn*

The Legendary Lou Rawls / Feb. 17, 1992 / Blue Note ✦✦✦✦

Portrait of the Blues / Apr. 13, 1992-Oct. 3, 1992 / Capitol ✦✦✦

Love Is a Hurtin' Thing: The Silk & Soul of Lou Rawls / Jun. 3, 1997 / Capitol ✦✦✦✦✦

Here is a strong collection of Lou Rawls' biggest and most soulful singles from his late-'60s Capitol material, *Love Is a Hurtin' Thing* includes classics like "Dead End Street," "Bring It on Home," "Another Saturday Night" and, of course, the title track. Although the set is rather short, every track is a killer. *—John Bush*

The Best of Lou Rawls: Classic Philadelphia Recordings / Nov. 24, 1998 / Music Club ✦✦✦✦✦

The Best of Lou Rawls: The Classic Philadelphia Recordings is an excellent single-disc overview of Rawls' commercial revitalization at the hands of legendary Philly soul producers Kenneth Gamble & Leon Huff, spanning the years 1976-1981. The only problem is that it's now out of print, even in England, the country of its original issue (on the Music Club International label). For some reason, no similar compilation has arrived to take its place; not only that, but more general Rawls anthologies don't license material from this period. So if you can find this, by all means pick it up. Even if the occasional disco inflections sometimes seem at odds with Rawls' smooth, buttery croon, there was arguably never a contemporary trend that fit his sensibility better than Philadelphia soul did. All of Rawls' biggest successes from the period are here: the R&B chart-topper "You'll Never Find Another Love Like Mine," "Groovy People," "See You When I Git There," "Lady Love," "One Life to Live," and "Sit Down and Talk to Me." There are also live renditions of three of Rawls' '60s hits, and more Philadelphia International recordings that flesh out the picture of Rawls' greatest period of commercial popularity. Until another collection is released, keep an eye out for this one. *—Steve Huey*

Unmistakably You/When You Hear Lou, You've Heard It All / 1999 / WestSide ✦✦✦✦✦

All Things in Time/Sit Down & Talk to Me / Mar. 3, 1999 / WestSide ✦✦✦

Let Me Be Good to You/Sit Down and Talk to Me / Aug. 24, 1999 / Right Stuff ✦✦✦

● **Anthology** / Jun. 6, 2000 / Capitol ✦✦✦✦✦

True, this two-CD compilation of 1962-1970 tracks isn't the most balanced Lou Rawls retrospective, as it favors his early soul output and has nothing from his commercial peak in the late '70s with Philadelphia International. It's also true that if you favor Rawls at his earthiest, you'll likely find this the best Rawls compilation available. Not that Rawls ever got too down 'n' dirty, but these are the songs on which his bluesiest leanings came most to the fore, leavened by various degrees of jazz and pop. His three big Capitol hits ("Love Is a Hurtin' Thing," "Dead End Street," and "Your Good Thing (Is About to End)") are all here, but the 33-song program includes a good many other satisfying outings that most listeners will have never heard. There's the previously unreleased 1962 cover of Sam Cooke's "What Makes the Ending"; the odd soul-jazz reading of "It Was a Very Good Year"; and the first-rate soul of 1967's "You Can Bring Me All Your Heartaches." The somewhat weird "Down Here on the Ground" is soul-pop tinged by disoriented psychedelic allusions in the lyrics about wanting to fly, and a bad-trip swirl of strings; co-written by Lalo Schifrin and folk-pop one-hit wonder Gale Garnett, it was used in the *Cool Hand Luke* movie. It's not all soul; indeed, there are a few smoothies like "Willow Weep for Me" and straight jazz interpretations that are among the less interesting selections. On the other hand, cuts like "Dead End Street" and "Blues Is a Woman" show Rawls to be one of the more talented songwriters of hard-luck blues-soul-jazz tunes, though he penned just a handful of the cuts on this anthology. *—Richie Unterberger*

Natural Man/Classic Lou / Oct. 23, 2001 / Polydor ✦✦✦✦

Nobody but Lou/Lou Rawls and Strings / May 7, 2002 / Collectables ✦✦✦✦

Ray, Goodman & Brown

f. 1978

Group / Quiet Storm, Urban

The "sweet" soul trio of Harry Ray, Al Goodman, and Billy Brown scored several hits for All Platinum/Stang Records in the early '70s as the Moments before they became Ray, Goodman & Brown in 1978. They moved to Polygram, where their poignant ballad "Special Lady" topped the R&B charts in 1979 and reached number-five pop. They remained on Polydor until 1981, getting one more Top 20 hit with "Inside of You" in 1980. They moved to Panoramic, then on to EMI, where they got their last Top Ten single in 1986, "Take It to the Limit." They also did background vocals for Sarah Dash on her 1988 LP *You're All I Need*. *—Ron Wynn*

Take It to the Limit / 1978 / EMI America ✦✦✦

Arguably, the sweet singing trio best LP, other than their best of compilations, buttery smooth from beginning to end, with no embarrassing tracks interrupting the flow of non-stop love songs emanating from Harry Ray, Al Goodman, and Billy Brown. The exquisite title cut "Take It to the Limit," is a quiet storm favorite that features all three voices; the contrast, lyrics, and smooth session musicians including Najee combined for an outstanding performance. They croon about love from all angles "Celebrate Our Love," is positive and happy, while "Someone's Missing Your Love," will have you weeping. Harry Ray's lead gets the most play and he doesn't get any better than on "Waiting For Dawn"; his light falsetto delivers the sensitive lyrics of loneliness so tenderly you'd think he was trying to lullaby a baby to sleep. Billy Brown's churchy tenor is outstanding on "We've Got Tonight," my ears are still ringing from some of the high notes. *—Andrew Hamilton*

Ray, Goodman & Brown / 1979 / Polydor ✦✦✦✦

Ray, Goodman & Brown's second Polydor LP is as refreshing as the first. The rapping among the group in order to introduce and end songs harkens back to '50s doo wop; groups singing under street lamps and in hallways would employ the technique to get everybody on the same page. On "Happy Anniversary," a romantic, sentimental ballad, the technique enhances the song. Likewise on the underrated "Shoe Strings," a regretful love refrain with a sweet chorus. The late Harry Ray shines on both with his mesmerizing, buttery falsetto. Billy Brown does "My Prayer," the old Platters tune in straight '50s style. RG&B do more with three voices than most can accomplish with four or five, but they do utilize a fourth voice; Walter Morris rounds out the harmonies on most of their recordings. A different technique is employed on "You," where each member spits out lines on the chorus. The shuffling, reggae beat of "Each Time Is Like the First Time" is irresistible, and shows their versatility. Harry lays his sweet tenor on the romantic "A Part of You," a ballad made for quiet storm formats. An excellent piece of work produced by Vincent Castellano. *—Andrew Hamilton*

Stay / 1981 / Polydor ✦✦

Mood for Lovin' / 1988 / EMI America ✦✦✦

Mood For Lovin' is an unusual Ray, Goodman & Brown LP. An unknown singer, Greg Willis, is credited on the cover—specifically "Ray, Goodman & Brown introducing Greg Willis." This appears to be a Greg Willis solo effort that went bad; some RG&B tracks were added and a little creative packaging took place. Willis sings three tracks, and Harry, Al, or Billy can't be heard of any of them. "Where Did You Get That Body" is Willis' best effort, a girl-watching song that charted R&B. Willis sang in a rough tenor that needed seasoning. "Next Time I'll Now," led by Harry Ray, is a tear-jerker; listen to this after losing someone and you'll bawl like a baby. Jazzman Najee plays a tight, crying sax. Harry forsakes his falsetto and sings natural on "Never Stop Lovin' You," only resorting to his upper register at the end/fadeout. Brown closes the song like Phillipe Wynne did with the Spinners, testifying like a Baptist preacher. Billy Brown leads "Electrified," an uptempo harmonizer that works his versatile tenor. Ex-LaBelle Sarah Dash and Harry Ray duet on

"Don't Make Me Wait"; their voices are similar, and Harry's falsetto is actually higher than Dash's throaty vocals. *—Andrew Hamilton*

• **The Best of Ray, Goodman & Brown** / Feb. 6, 1996 / Polygram ♦♦♦♦
An enjoyable helping of Ray, Goodman & Brown's satiny Polydor sides. Formerly the Moments, their unique style of both singing and rapping made RG&B different from other R&B groups vying for chart space. Having two dynamic leads like Harry Ray and Billy Brown didn't hurt their chances. When you tired of Ray's feather-light tenor, Brown would change the pace with his energetic, gospel-laden leads. Bass/baritone Al Goodman's lower register blends brilliantly with the two tenors. Essential for R&B and doo wop fanatics. This best-of is the ultimate make-out album—play it for that special lady. *—Andrew Hamilton*

James Ray

b. 1941, Washington, D.C.
Vocals / Soul, R&B
The Washington, D.C., native's 1962 hit, "If You Gotta Make a Fool of Somebody," inspired a raft of covers, while one of his lesser-known efforts, "I've Got My Mind Set on You," provided George Harrison with a latter-day big-seller. James Ray's pop-slanted R&B output for Caprice Records, including his less successful follow-up, "Itty Bitty Pieces," was arranged by pianist Hutch Davie. All three of the songs cited above were written by prolific New York tunesmith Rudy Clark. *—Bill Dahl*

James Ray / 1961 / Caprice ♦♦♦

• **If You Gotta Make a Fool of Somebody: Golden Classics** / 1976 / Collectables ♦♦♦♦♦
Collectables' *Golden Classics: If You Gotta Make a Fool of Somebody* may not be as extensive or as well-annotated a collection as one could hope for, it nevertheless is the only collection of James Ray material on CD, and it's quite worthwhile for that. During the early '60s, Ray straddled the line between R&B and pop. His productions and choice of material often favored supperclub crossovers—as the inclusion of "Lazybones," "St. James Infirmary" and "Come Rain or Come Shine" here prove—and even his R&B-oriented material were given elaborate productions similar to Sam Cooke's pop productions. This collection might be tilted toward the supper club, but his sweet voice stands tall throughout this, and his best material—"If You Gotta Make a Fool of Somebody" and "I've Got My Mind Set on You, Pt. 1" (later covered by George Harrison)—prove that Ray was a very good pop-soul singer, and they make this worth hearing. *—Stephen Thomas Erlewine*

Raydio

f. 1977, Detroit, MI, **db.** 1981
Group / Urban
Ray Parker Jr. created Raydio in 1977, with vocalists Arnell Carmichael and Jerry Knight. Knight was the lead singer on the group's first big hit, "Jack and Jill," in 1978. Other group members were Larry Tolbert, Darren Carmichael, and Charles Fearing. He maintained the band until 1981, although they became Ray Parker Jr. & Raydio in 1980. The group had another Top Ten R&B and pop hit with "You Can't Change That" in 1979, and then "Two Places at the Same Time" reached number-six R&B in 1980. They topped the R&B charts in 1981 with "A Woman Needs Love (Just Like You Do)," which also peaked at number-four pop. All their songs and LPs were recorded for Arista. *—Ron Wynn*

• **Raydio** / 1977 / Arista ♦♦♦♦♦
This was the first of three albums from Raydio. On this album, the group consisted of Vincent Bonham, Jerry Knight, Ray Parker Jr. and Arnell Carmichael. Formed and fronted by veteran session guitarist Parker, this album produced three *Billboard* R&B chart singles. Beginning with the Top Ten single "Jack and Jill," Raydio enjoyed national exposure with this single that peaked at number five after 25 weeks on the charts, and it reached the number-eight spot on the pop charts, exceeding sales of 500,000. The less popular releases "Is This a Love Thing" and "Honey I'm Rich" respectively reached the 20th and 43rd positions on the *Billboard* R&B charts. *—Craig Lytle*

Rock On / 1979 / Arista ♦♦♦
To be taken seriously as a R&B group and to shake the stigma of their nursery rhyme hit "Jack and Jill," atheir debut single, Raydio answers the call on this album with two *Billboard* R&B singles. The first of the two is "You Can't Change That," a laid-back yet very danceable track; it features the vocals of the mild-tempered Ray Parker Jr. and the distinctive tenor of Arnell Carmichael. The two alternate throughout the verses, and Carmichael ad libs in the vamp. "You Can't Change That" resided on the R&B charts for 19 weeks, peaking at number three; it also reached the number-nine position on the pop charts. The follow-up single was "More Than One Way to Love a Woman," a midtempo track that made it to the 25th position on the R&B charts after a 13-week run. *—Craig Lytle*

Two Places at the Same Time / 1980 / Arista ♦♦
In addition to Parker's name becoming a headliner alongside Raydio's, this was also his third and final album with the group, spawning three chart singles. The title track, "Two Places at the Same Time," reached its apex at the number-six position on the *Billboard* R&B charts. It was followed by the instrumental dance track "For Those Who Like to Groove," which peaked at number 14 after a 12-week run. "Can't Keep From Cryin'" did not have as much success; after only six weeks of life, it made it to the 57th position on the charts. Other noteworthy dance selections that did not chart are "Until the Morning Comes" and "It's Time to Party Now." Parker also teamed up with the multi-talented Herbie Hancock to pen the unreleased, slow-groovin' "Tonight's the Night." *—Craig Lytle*

Ready for the World

f. 1982, Flint, MI
Group / Quiet Storm, Urban, Funk, Dance-Pop
A Michigan funk band with slight rock leanings, Ready for the World parlayed Melvin Riley's whining vocals and some trendy production into a pair of number-one R&B hits in the mid-'80s for MCA. Riley, Gordon Strozier, Gregory Potts, Willie Triplett, John Eaton, and Gerald Valentine began on their own Blue Lake label before signing with MCA. The label reissued the song "Tonight," and it reached number six on the R&B charts in 1984. They followed it with "Deep Inside Your Love," another Top Ten R&B single, then had their first of two chart-toppers in "Oh Sheila." It got them a huge crossover smash, ultimately topping the pop lists as well. They scored their fourth consecutive Top Ten R&B record with "Digital Display," then had two flop singles before "Love You Down" put them back on top of the R&B world in 1986. It was their last hit and peaked at number-nine pop. *—Ron Wynn*

Ready for the World / 1985 / MCA ♦♦♦♦♦
This troupe from Flint, MI, had a little funk, some rock, and some Prince influence, and enjoyed their best album performance with their mid-'80s debut. They scored four chart hits, including the number-one pop and R&B smash "Oh Sheila." While the whining, nasal vocals of Melvin Riley Jr. could sometimes be irritating, the group didn't do much wrong the first time out. *—Ron Wynn*

Long Time Coming / 1986 / MCA ♦♦♦
Ready for the World scored three more chart hits with their second album, including another number-one R&B hit and Top Ten pop song in "Love Me Down." They continued to milk the funk/pop/Prince connection, and Melvin Riley's vocals hadn't grated on enough people's nerves to derail their success yet. *—Ron Wynn*

Ruff 'N Ready / Sep. 19, 1988 / MCA ♦♦

Straight Down to Business / 1991 / MCA ♦♦♦

• **Oh Sheila! Ready for the World's Greatest Hits** / Sep. 28, 1993 / MCA ♦♦♦♦♦

20th Century Masters—The Millennium Collection: The Best of Ready for the World / Jan. 15, 2002 / MCA ♦♦♦♦
For a midline-priced compilation, this survey of the work of '80s funk band Ready for the World has a lot going for it. At a running time of 73 and a half minutes, much longer than you expect for a disc with such a modest price, it contains all of the group's chart hits as well as "Whose Is It?," the first chart entry by former bandleader Melvin Riley in 1994. To provide variety from the group's regular hits collection, several of the tracks are presented in unusual mixes or edits. The version of "Ceramic Girl" is taken from a 12-inch single and runs nearly nine minutes; "Mary Goes 'Round," "Long Time Coming," and "My Girly" are the single versions; "Straight Down to Business" is a single remix version; "Digital Display" is a radio edit; and "Can He Do It (Like This, Can He Do It Like That)" is taken from a promotional 12-inch single, and is thus making its debut on a commercial release. At the time of their commercial peak, 1985-1986, Ready for the World basically sounded like a Prince clone, aping their Upper Midwest neighbor's funky, synthesized, dance-pop style and his salacious lyrics. Even much later they still sounded like Prince, but they also sounded very dated after trends in R&B music had moved on. But for those who enjoyed them then, this album is a good way to relive their heyday. *—William Ruhlmann*

The Real Thing

f. Liverpool, England
Group / Disco, Funk, Northern Soul
Northern soul had emerged in the north of England when the Real Thing formed in 1970, but the disco/funk/soul quartet couldn't get into the obscure R&B sounds, preferring instead the more progressive soul of the Temptations, Barry White, and funk jams. The Liverpool natives aspired for international success, a dream that went unfulfilled. Original members Chris Amoo, Dave Smith, Kenny Davis, and Ray Lake began by covering and remaking popular American recordings, and experienced payback when Frankie Valli and others covered their number-one British hit "You to Me Are Everything." They cracked Britain's Top Ten for the second consecutive time with "Can't Get By Without You." Their first recording opportunity arose with EMI Records, where they cut their first single, "Plastic Man," the old Temptations song off their *Masterpiece* album; a remake of Tavares' "Check It Out" was the flip. The record didn't open many doors, but they continued thriving on the club circuit. Other EMI singles, including "Listen Joe McGintoo" and "Vicious Circles," were largely ignored.

For unknown reasons, Davis left, and the Real Thing continued as a trio, doing some commercials, as well as live gigs. Their career began to sprout wings when David Essex started producing their initial Pye Recordings. Opening for Essex, they toured all over, even the States, the home of the music they loved. Initial collaborations with Essex, like previous recordings, were turntable hits, but sold few copies. By this time, Amoo's brother Eddie, who had sung with the Chants on Pye, joined the Real Thing. The Liverpool-bred but Ghanaian parentage brothers started writing songs that fleshed out their albums. Later, Loose Ends recorded an Amoo composition, "In the Sky," for their Virgin Records debut in 1980.

The Real Thing hooked up with Ken Gold, and boom, "You to Me Are Everything" aced the British pop chart and placed number-66 pop and number-29 soul in the States. Their first album, titled *The Real Thing*, contained their chart busters and previous singles. The group wanted to call their second LP Liverpool 8, the name of the racially mixed section of Liverpool where they grew up with Asians, Africans, Chinese, Irish, and anyone else who couldn't afford more opulent surroundings. Pye Records didn't like the name, so they compromised with *Four From Eight*, which meant nothing to anyone outside of Britain. The Real Thing continued releasing albums, waxing four for Pye: *Step Into Our World* and *Can You Feel the Force*. PRT Records released *100 Minutes* in 1982, their last regularly scheduled LP. Waxworks Records dropped a live LP in 1998, *The Real Thing Live*; many compilations and best-of albums documenting their career are on the market. *—Andrew Hamilton*

The Real Thing / 1976 / Pye ♦♦♦
Dominated by the monster hit and U.K. chart-topper "You to Me Are Everything," truly one of the benchmark moments in the development of mid-'70s U.K. soul, the Real Thing's fall 1976 debut arrived hot on the heels of their second major smash, "Can't Get by Without You," and between those two songs, everything you need to know about the Real

Thing is on display. Blindingly romantic, gently persuasive, and smooth as a summer sea, *The Real Thing* is as much a showcase for the quartet's Philly-felt vocals as for the material; the moments when they do toughen up, such as the gently cynical "(He's Just A) Moneymaker," are contrarily the weakest tracks, whereas the softer ballads send the romantic's pulse racing. The third of the album's three hit singles, the closing "You'll Never Know What You're Missing," is as fine a promise as anything Gamble & Huff were delivering at this time. But it is "You to Me Are Everything" that remains the album's high point, its unabashed sentiment racing into a soaring chorus that is impossible to shake away. The Real Thing would end the decade as Britain's highest-selling black act of the late '70s. As the best (and best-selling) of their albums, *The Real Thing* accounts for much of their pre-eminence. *—Amy Hanson*

● **The Very Best of the Real Thing** / Sep. 24, 2002 / Castle ♦♦♦♦
The Very Best of the Real Thing collects over a dozen prime moments and chart hits from the Real Thing and adds some pointless remixes at the end for filler's sake. The Liverpool soul band recorded a handful of albums for Pye in the '70s and early '80s and hit the charts in its home country several times with a smooth blend of funk and disco. Unfortunately, the Real Thing only cracked the Top 40 of the American soul chart once with "You to Me Are Everything," which hit the absolute top of the U.K. chart. This compilation covers a lot of ground and includes their most significant material. Apart from their biggest smash, "Let's Go Disco," "Can't Get By Without You," "Whenever You Want My Love," "Can You Feel the Force," and "Boogie Down (Get Funky Now)" are included. This is a fine remastered compilation from a band that developed a strong following in the U.K. and deserved much better in the States. *—Andy Kellman*

Eugene Record

b. Dec. 23, 1940, Chicago, IL
Vocals / Urban, Smooth Soul, Quiet Storm, Soul
Chicagoan Eugene Record became interested in music at an early age, first picking up the guitar. A big influence was his older sister, an accomplished pianist who practiced classical music every day in the living room of his family home. While attending Englewood High School, he formed the Chanteurs and recorded a couple of singles ("You Did That to Me") for Leo Ostell's Renee Records in 1959.

The group's first big break came when member Marshall Thompson ran into Otis Leavill while riding on a city bus. Leavill suggested that the group, now called the Chi-Lites, audition for producer Carl Davis, who signed the Chi-Lites to Brunswick in late 1968, releasing their first national chart hit, "Give It Away," which went to number-ten R&B in early 1969. The double-sided follow-up was "Let Me Be the Man My Daddy Was" backed with "The Twelfth of Never." Davis hired Record to write songs for his Jalynne publishing firm in the late '60s. Record wrote and produced hits for Jackie Wilson ("You Got Me Walking," "Don't Burn No Bridges") and other Brunswick signees.

Collaborating with fellow Brunswick signee Barbara Acklin, Record had a hit with Peaches & Herb's "Two Little Kids." Around this time, he and Acklin wrote the classic melancholy ballad "Have You Seen Her." While going through his catalog of songs for a new album, "Have You Seen Her" got his attention, but he deep-sixed the idea of recording it because it was about five minutes long, which was well over the standard length of a three-minute single. With the success of Stax artist Isaac Hayes' *Hot Buttered Soul* album (with its ten-minute songs), Davis decided to include it on the group's *(For God's Sake) Give More Power to the People* LP. Soul music radio stations and other stations broke the three-minute barrier and played the long album version of the tune. Brunswick released a single version that first went gold, holding the number-one R&B spot for two weeks and hitting number-three pop in 1971, giving the Chi-Lites their first pop hit. In 1976, Record left the Chi-Lites and signed a solo deal with Warner Bros. The first of two Warner Bros. albums, *The Eugene Record* (February 1977) spawned the number-24 R&B hit "Laying Beside You"; the next LP, *Trying to Get to You*, was released a year later. Record kept busy producing former Lost Generation member Lowrell Simon, among many others, and occasionally joining the Chi-Lites on-stage and on record. *—Ed Hogan*

● **The Eugene Record** / 1977 / Warner Bros. ♦♦♦
Eugene Record's debut solo album. The ex-Chi-Lites' lead singer and songwriter/producer, finally freed from an engulfing Brunswick Records contract, takes it easy on the best of his three solo platters for Warner Bros. Records. Record sings in a relaxed, loving mode on some lovely tracks that didn't quite make it. Of the even set, "Laying Beside You," "Overdose of Love," and "Putting It Down," with Barbara Acklin on backing vocals, are the most memorable. *—Andrew Hamilton*

Trying to Get You / 1978 / Warner Bros. ♦♦

Welcome to My Fantasy / 1979 / Warner Bros. ♦♦
Listening to Eugene Record's solo albums takes on a different flavor if you're familiar with his earlier work with the Chi-Lites and his productions for artists like the Artistics, Barbara Acklin, Otis Leavill, and others. To say expectations were high is an understatement. People were expecting Record, the prolific songwriter/producer/singer, to blow up big time. Instead, his solo work has virtually no edge. He's content. Warner Bros. must have fattened his bank account with a big advance because he doesn't sound hungry or hell-bent to come out of the studio with a smash. This is a pleasant album but hardly riveting or essential. One of the best cuts, "Fan the Fire," sounds better by the Impressions, whose version came out around this same period and was produced by Record. *—Andrew Hamilton*

Sharon Redd

b. Oct. 19, 1945, Norfolk, VA, **d.** Jan. 5, 1992
Vocals / Club/Dance, Urban, Disco
Sharon Redd is practically synonymous with Prelude Records, the New York label that released some of the most thrilling dance music of the late '70s and early '80s. Redd released three albums on the label and racked up a number of club hits that have long since become classics with disco and house DJs who continue to rightly view the era with great reverence. While disco was dying during the early '80s, artists like Redd kept the flame alive and also took the form one step further by incorporating more song-based R&B elements.

Prior to becoming a solo artist, Redd—the daughter of a King Records employee, the stepdaughter of a Benny Goodman side musician, and the sister of a songwriter for Kool & the Gang—was involved with theater. During the '70s, both an Australian production of *Hair* and an American production of *The Wedding of Iphigenia* featured Redd in lead roles. After this, she gained more exposure through a popular advertising campaign for Shaffer Beer; this helped her land a background vocalist gig for Bette Midler. Other work followed for Carol Douglas, Bonnie Raitt, Gwen McCrae ("Love Insurance"), and Norman Connors ("You Are My Starship"), and by the end of the decade, she had a solo deal with Prelude. *Sharon Redd* (1980), *Redd Hot* (1982), and *Love How You Feel* (1983) were issued in quick session on the label. Though none of her singles had a huge impact on the R&B charts, the story was much different in clubs, where "Can You Handle It," "Never Give You Up," "Beat the Street," and "Love How You Feel"—just to name a few—were spun with great frequency.

After her third and final Prelude album, Redd slowed down and occasionally did more session work. She re-appeared briefly in 1991 for another solo single, but that would prove to be her final output of note. She succumbed to pneumonia complications on January 5, 1992. Unidisc kept her albums in print in CD format, and a couple anthologies have also kept her material in circulation. *—Andy Kellman*

Sharon Redd / 1980 / Prelude ♦♦♦♦
Sharon Redd was one of the more visible members of the Prelude family during the early '80s, releasing singles and albums with regularity through 1983. Her self-titled debut balances post-disco club music with the extension of '70s soul that many referred to as urban during the '80s. The two lead cuts on the album, "You Got My Love" and "Can You Handle It," are easily the highlights—a 12-inch featuring both songs hit number five on *Billboard*'s club play chart. A young DJ and Prelude employee by the name of François Kevorkian leant his editing and mixing talents to those two songs (arguably the two greatest moments of Redd's career) and helped propel them to their high-chart placement. Redd proves that she's more than competent with ballads on "Leaving You Is Easier Said Than Done" and "You Stayed on My Mind," but it's on the two key tracks and the equally upbeat "Try My Love on for Size" (a surprising non-hit) where she truly shines. The consistency of this album is one major reason why her *Greatest Hits* fails to do her justice. [Unidisc's CD issue adds five alternate mixes and radio edits of "Can You Handle It" and "You Got My Love."] *—Andy Kellman*

Redd Hot / 1982 / Prelude ♦♦♦
Sharon Redd's second album also did some major damage to the club play chart. Working with a new songwriting and production duo—this time it's Eric Matthew and Willie Payne instead of Rodney Brown and Willie Lester—but retaining François Kevorkian's invaluable mixing work, Redd comes out with an album that relies on a fair amount of electronics but loses little of the warmth heard on the less-machine-driven self-titled album. Some people argue that all warmth is lost when a drum kit is replaced by a drum machine, but labels like Prelude were releasing plenty of involving material during the early '80s that incorporated drum programming and synthesizers. The increasing reliance on synthetic instrumentation eventually spawned house music, and this record was part of that evolution. "Never Give You Up" and "Beat the Street" carry on in fine succession from the likes of "Can You Handle It," steeped in disco but never losing touch with song-based R&B roots. The non-singles help make the album add up to one that isn't as well-rounded as its predecessor. However, it's too good to qualify as a full-blown sophomore slump. [Unidisc's CD issue adds a pair of radio edits, as well as an instrumental of "Beat the Street."] *—Andy Kellman*

Beat the Street: The Very Best of Sharon Redd / Aug. 1, 1989 / Unidisc ♦♦♦♦
Unidisc's *Beat the Street: The Very Best of Sharon Redd* includes all the key high points of Sharon Redd's three-album career for the Prelude label. There's "Can You Handle It," "Never Give You Up," "Beat the Street," "Love How You Feel," "You Got My Love," three others, and a lengthy Megamix. Despite the fact that the quantity of tracks makes the disc seem a bit lean, Unidisc made a smart move in avoiding radio edits and instead favoring full-length and extended versions; it's far more preferable to have these songs in their full glory (often mixed to great effect by the great François Kevorkian) than to have them stripped down in order to save space for mediocre album cuts. The only regrettable omission is "Try My Love on for Size," an overlooked track from Redd's excellent debut. Maybe there would've been room for it if the Megamix wasn't so lengthy (16 minutes), not to mention redundant. Seek out Redd's contribution to the Deep Beats series instead. Not only does it include "Try My Love on for Size," but it is also Megamix-free. *—Andy Kellman*

● **Essential Dancefloor Artists, Vol. 3** / Oct. 25, 1994 / Deep Beats ♦♦♦♦
Along with Musique, Inner Life, and D Train, the late Sharon Redd was a valuable part of the Prelude roster, one of the label's most prolific and successful. Her voice couldn't quite be called husky, and it remained powerful without resorting to full-blown wailing or any other form of, "Hey, check my vocal skills" showmanship. She always put the song first, and for that, there are several singles she released during the early '80s that helped define the crack of time that can be referred to as both post-disco and pre-house. This installment of Castle offshoot Deep Beats' *Essential Dancefloor Artists* series collects all the significant slices from Redd's discography and thankfully avoids radio edits. All the club favorites—"Can You Handle It," "Never Give You Up," "Love How You Feel," "Beat the Street," "Liar on the Wire"—are here, as are choice album tracks like "Try My Love on for Size" and her best ballad, "Leaving You Is Easier Said Than Done." This set also doubles as a key compilation for those who are attempting to acquire François Kevorkian's finest mixing jobs without buying all of the original vinyl. *—Andy Kellman*

Love How You Feel / Apr. 22, 1997 / Prelude ♦♦♦
Songwriters/producers Eric Matthew and Willie Payne continued to work with Sharon Redd for her third and final album, *Love How You Feel*. Much of the preceding *Redd Hot* featured a potent balance between synthetic and organic elements, but this third album further abandons live instrumentation. Redd's voice, almost always a dominant force with a near-huskiness, is diminished on most tracks with a liberal amount of echo and a mixing job that makes her sound distant. Combine this with rhythm programming that often sounds stiff and brittle, and you have an album that seems cold and impersonal in relation to Redd's prior releases. "Love How You Feel" performed well on the club charts, but nothing else resonated with club-goers like any of her previous platters. Even a cover of labelmates D Train's "Something's on Your Mind" narrowly misses the mark. Aside from the title track, there are a couple of good moments, like the slithery, aptly titled "Sweet Sensation." Neither a bad nor a particularly good record by any stroke. [Unidisc's CD issue adds a couple alternate mixes to the original running order.] *—Andy Kellman*

Otis Redding

b. Sep. 9, 1941, Dawson, GA, **d.** Dec. 10, 1967, Madison, WI
Vocals / Soul, Deep Soul, Memphis Soul, Southern Soul
One of the most influential soul singers of the 1960s, Otis Redding exemplified to many listeners the power of Southern "deep soul"—hoarse, gritty vocals, brassy arrangements, and an emotional way with both party tunes and aching ballads. He was also the most consistent exponent of the Stax sound, cutting his records at the Memphis label/studios that did much to update R&B into modern soul. His death at the age of 26 was tragic not just because he seemed on the verge of breaking through to a wide pop audience (which he would indeed do with his posthumous number-one single, "[Sittin' On] The Dock of the Bay"). It was also unfortunate because, as "Dock of the Bay" demonstrated, he was also at a point of artistic breakthrough in terms of the expression and sophistication of his songwriting and singing.

Although Redding at his peak was viewed as a consummate, versatile showman, he began his recording career in the early '60s as a Little Richard-styled shouter. The Georgian was working in the band of guitarist Johnny Jenkins at the time, and in 1962 he took advantage of an opportunity to record the ballad "These Arms of Mine" at a Jenkins session. When it became an R&B hit, Redding's solo career was truly on its way, though the hits didn't really start to fly until 1965 and 1966, when "Mr. Pitiful," "I've Been Loving You Too Long," "I Can't Turn You Loose," a cover of the Rolling Stones' "Satisfaction," and "Respect" (later turned into a huge pop smash by Aretha Franklin) were all big sellers. Redding wrote much of his own material, sometimes with the assistance of Booker T. & the MG's guitarist Steve Cropper. Yet at the time, Redding's success was primarily confined to the soul market; his singles charted only mildly on the pop listings. He was nonetheless tremendously respected by many white groups, particularly the Rolling Stones, who covered Redding's "That's How Strong My Love Is" and "Pain in My Heart." (Redding also returned the favor with "Satisfaction.")

One of Redding's biggest hits was a duet with fellow Stax star Carla Thomas, "Tramp," in 1967. That was the same year he began to show signs of making major inroads into the white audience, particularly with a well-received performance at the Monterey Pop Festival (also issued on record). Redding's biggest triumph, however, came just days before his death, when he recorded the wistful "(Sittin' On) The Dock of the Bay," which represented a significant leap as far as examination of more intensely personal emotions. Also highlighted by crisp Cropper guitar leads and dignified horns, it rose to the top of the pop charts in early 1968.

Redding, however, had perished in a plane crash in Wisconsin on December 10, 1967, in an accident that also took the lives of four members from his backup band, the Bar-Kays. A few other singles became posthumous hits, and a good amount of other unreleased material was issued in the wake of his death. These releases weren't purely exploitative in nature, in fact containing some pretty interesting music, and little that could be considered embarrassing. What Redding might have achieved, or what directions he might have explored, are among the countless tantalizing "what if" questions in rock & roll history. As it is, he did record a considerable wealth of music at Stax, which is now available on thoughtfully archived reissues. *—Richie Unterberger*

Pain in My Heart / Jan. 1964 / Rhino ♦♦♦♦♦
This album works on so many different levels, that it's essential listening for at least three categories of buyer—fans of Otis Redding and Stax Records (natch), and more general soul listeners, and also anyone serious about their devotion to the work of the Rolling Stones and any other British invasion bands that covered American soul. *Pain in My Heart* was practically a road map to Mick Jagger and any number of other would-be white soul shouters in the U.K., not just on the title track but also numbers like the hard rocking "Hey Hey Baby." For someone only 22 years old at the time of these sessions, and just two years past his first 45 rpm record, Redding exudes astonishing power, energy and boldness, though it's all packaged with greater restraint than his subsequent records did. This was the only LP that Redding recorded during the lifetime of his idol, Sam Cooke, and his version of "You Send Me" is the least stylized of any of his renditions of Cooke's songs—later on, after Cooke's death, he would throw more of himself into it. The very fact that he was covering Cooke's soul classic shows an essential difference between Redding's and Cooke's early LPs; as Redding was on a soul label, no one tried to make him into a pop singer as that'd done at RCA with Cooke—thus, he was running on all cylinders right out of the starting gate, though he wouldn't get really interesting or show his full depth until two albums later. But even covering Rufus Thomas' "The Dog," Richard Berry's "Louie Louie," Little Richard's "Lucille," or Ben E. King's "Stand By Me," he's already doing 70 percent of what we came to expect from Otis Redding in the years ahead—his writing, apart from "Security," "These Arms of Mine" and "That's What My Heart Needs," was still somewhat less than memorable, but this is still a first-rate debut and a must-own CD. *—Bruce Eder*

The Great Otis Redding Sings Soul Ballads / Mar. 1965 / Rhino ♦♦♦
Otis Redding's second LP only has one major hit on it—his signature tune, "Mr. Pitiful"—but it is a bolder effort than its predecessor, and it also has Redding's original of "That's How Strong My Love Is," which became well known (to the tune of millions of sales) in the hands of the Rolling Stones. Among the less familiar fare, "A Woman, A Lover, A Friend" is a very sweet and compelling blues-based number, while "Your One And Only Man" catches Redding in a jaunty, strutting mode, supported by Steve Cropper's crunchy, slashing guitar and the Mar-Keys' horns; "For Your Precious Love" is a slow, mournful ballad lament that builds in intensity, Bolero-like. And "Chained And Bound" is a compelling mix of blues and gospel-style singing that holds its own in those surroundings. *—Bruce Eder*

☆ **Otis Blue: Otis Redding Sings Soul** / 1966 / Atco ♦♦♦♦♦
Otis Redding's third album, and his first fully realized album, presents his talent unfettered, his direction clear, and his confidence emboldened, with fully half the songs representing a reach that extended his musical grasp. More than a quarter of this album is given over to Redding's versions of songs by Sam Cooke, his idol, who had died the previous December, and all three are worth owning and hearing. Two of them, "A Change Is Gonna Come" and "Shake," are every bit as essential as any soul recordings ever made, and while they (and much of this album) have reappeared on several anthologies, it's useful to hear the songs from those sessions juxtaposed with each other, and with "Wonderful World," which is seldom compiled elsewhere. Also featured are Redding's spellbinding renditions of "Satisfaction" (a song epitomizing the fully formed Stax/Volt sound and which Mick Jagger & Keith Richards originally wrote in tribute to and imitation of Redding's style), "My Girl," and "You Don't Miss Your Water." "Respect" and "I've Been Loving You Too Long," two originals that were to loom large in his career, are here as well; the former became vastly popular in the hands of Aretha Franklin and the latter was an instant soul classic. Among the seldom-cited jewels here is a rendition of B.B. King's "Rock Me Baby" that has the singer sharing the spotlight with Steve Cropper, his playing alternately elegant and fiery, with Wayne Jackson and Gene "Bowlegs" Miller's trumpets and Andrew Love's and Floyd Newman's saxes providing the backing. Redding's powerful, remarkable singing throughout makes *Otis Blue* gritty, rich, and achingly alive, and an essential listening experience. *—Bruce Eder*

The Soul Album / Apr. 1966 / Rhino ♦♦♦♦
Otis Redding's talent began to surge, across songs and their styles and absorbing them, with the recording of *The Soul Album*. In contrast to *The Great Otis Redding Sings Soul Ballads*, which was an advance over its predecessor but still a body of 12 songs of varying styles and textures, rising to peaks and never falling before an intense, soulful mid-range, *The Soul Album* shows him moving from strength to strength in a string of high-energy, sweaty soul performances, interspersing his own songs with work by Sam Cooke ("Chain Gang"), Roy Head ("Treat Her Right"), Eddie Floyd ("Everybody Makes a Mistake"), and Smokey Robinson ("It's Growing") and recasting them in his own style, so that they're not "covers" so much as reinterpretations; indeed, "Chain Gang" is almost a rewrite of the original, though one suspects not one that Cooke would have disapproved of. He still had a little way to go as a songwriter—the jewel of this undervalued collection is "Cigarettes and Coffee," co-authored by Eddie Thomas & Jerry Butler—but as an interpreter he was now without peer, and his albums were now showing this remarkable, stunningly high level of consistency. Also significant on this album was the contribution of Steve Cropper, not only on guitar but as co-author of three songs. Further, as revealed in the remastered Rhino CD, Stax Records was starting to put more into his LPs in thew recording, taking more time and delivering a better, fuller sound than on the two preceding albums, especially where Al Jackson's drums and the Mar-Keys' horns are concerned. *—Bruce Eder*

☆ **Complete & Unbelievable: The Otis Redding Dictionary of Soul** / Oct. 1966 / Rhino ♦♦♦♦♦
Recorded and released in 1966, Otis Redding's fifth album, *Complete & Unbelievable: The Otis Redding Dictionary of Soul* found the rugged-voiced deep soul singer continuing to expand the boundaries of his style while staying true to his rough and passionate signature sound. Redding's ambitious interpretations of "Tennessee Waltz" and especially "Try a Little Tenderness" found him approaching material well outside the traditional boundaries of R&B and allowing his emotionally charged musical personality to take them to new and unexpected places, and while his cover of "Day Tripper" wasn't his first attempt to confront the British Invasion, his invigorating and idiosyncratic take on the Beatles' cynical pop tune proved Redding's view of the pop music universe was broader than anyone might have expected at the time. While Redding's experiments with covers on this set were successful and satisfying, it was on his own material that he sounded most at home, and "My Lover's Prayer" and "Fa-Fa-Fa-Fa-Fa (Sad Song)" are deep Southern soul at its finest, with Redding's forceful but lovelorn voice delivering an Academy Award-worthy performance. And once again, the Stax house band (centered around Booker T. and the MG's and the Memphis Horns) prove themselves both thoroughly distinctive and remarkably adaptable, fitting to the nooks and crannies of Redding's voice with their supple but muscular performances. With the exception of his duet album with Carla Thomas, *Complete & Unbelievable: The Otis Redding Dictionary of Soul* was the last studio album Otis Redding would fully complete before his death, and it proves his desire for a broader musical statement didn't begin when he encountered "the love crowd" at the Monterey Pop Festival in 1967. *—Mark Deming*

King & Queen / Mar. 1967 / Stax ♦♦♦♦♦
Otis Redding never recorded a lighter, more purely entertaining record than *King & Queen*, a collection of duets with Stax labelmate Carla Thomas. In all likelihood inspired by a series of popular duets recorded by Marvin Gaye—indeed, "It Takes Two," Gaye's sublime collaboration with Kim Weston, is covered here—the record serves no greater

purpose than to allow Redding the chance to run through some of the era's biggest soul hits, including "Knock on Wood," "Tell It Like It Is" and "When Something Is Wrong with My Baby,"and while clearly not a personal triumph on a par with either *Otis Blue* or *The Dictionary of Soul*, the set is still hugely succcessful on its own terms. Redding & Thomas enjoy an undeniable chemistry, and they play off each other wonderfully; while sparks fly furiously throughout *King & Queen*, the album's highlight is the classic "Tramp,"where their battle of the sexes reaches its fever pitch in supremely witty fashion. *—Jason Ankeny*

Live in Europe / Jul. 1967 / Rhino ♦♦♦

Live in Europe was the first full-length concert album released on Otis Redding, and the last LP of his work that he lived to see issued. Recorded along the Stax/Volt tour of Europe in March of 1967, it featured Redding backed by Booker T. & the MG's. Their playing, along with that of Wayne Jackson (trumpet) and Andrew Love and Joe Arnold (tenor saxes), is more elegant and elegantly articulated than the work of his usual touring band, and this album is a sort of idealized Otis Redding concert. Some of it lacks the raw excitement of *Live at the Whisky A Go Go* (which was recorded a year earlier than the shows where this album was cut, but not issued until a year later), but in compensation one gets all of the virtuoso flourishes and details that one would expect from this ensemble. The audience, ecstatic at the rare chance to see the soul idol in concert, is very vocal in their enthusiasm for the singer and his songs, and "Fa-Fa-Fa-Fa-Fa (Sad Song)" is practically a singalong number with some finely detailed playing from Booker T. Jones, Steve Cropper, and Al Jackson Jr., who, with Wayne Jackson and company, also add some exquisite grace notes to the finale, "Try a Little Tenderness." Beyond the musical power of his performance, Redding's emotions are practically overflowing as he addresses the crowd in a very personal manner as he introduces "These Arms of Mine." The only flaw in this recording, if there is one, is that it does have only ten songs, but that was the nature of the shows on this tour. *—Bruce Eder*

☆ **The Dock of the Bay** / Feb. 1968 / Atco ♦♦♦♦♦

It was never supposed to be like this: "(Sittin' On) The Dock of the Bay" was supposed to mark a beginning of a new phase in Otis Redding's career, not an ending. Producer/guitarist Steve Cropper had a difficult task to perform in pulling together this album, the first of several posthumous releases issued by Stax/Volt in the wake of Otis Redding's death. What could have been a cash-in effort or a grim memorial album instead became a vivid, exciting presentation of some key aspects of the talent that was lost when Redding died. *Dock of the Bay* is, indeed, a mixed bag of singles and B-sides going back to July of 1965, one hit duet with Carla Thomas, and a pair of previously unissued tracks from 1966 and 1967, respectively. There's little cohesion, stylistic or otherwise, in the songs, especially when the title track is taken into consideration—nothing else here resembles it, for the obvious reason that Redding never had a chance to follow it up. Despite the mix-and-match nature of the album, however, this is an impossible record not to love. Cropper chose his tracks well, selecting some of the strongest and most unusual among the late singer's orphaned songs: "I Love You More Than Words Can Say" is one of Redding's most passionate performances; "Let Me Come on Home" presents an ebullient Otis Redding accompanied by some sharp playing; and "Don't Mess With Cupid" begins with a gorgeous guitar flourish and blooms into an intense, pounding, soaring showcase for singer and band alike. No one could complain about the album then, and it still holds more than three decades later. Reissued on CD by the Atco label through Rhino Records in excellent sound. *—Bruce Eder*

The Immortal Otis Redding / Jun. 1968 / Rhino ♦♦♦

A posthumous release of 11 sides recorded in 1967, showing Otis Redding turning his ability toward the most sophisticated soul music of his career—even the songs with models in earlier works, such as "The Happy Song (Dum-Dum-De-De-De-Dum-Dum)," show a level of articulation and care in the playing that runs circles around Redding's earlier recordings. "Think About It" could pass for the work of an earlier phase in the singer's career, but for the surprisingly elegant piano accompaniment and Redding's more softly nuanced singing. It's a testament to Redding's talent that he left behind enough unanthologized and unreleased tracks to generate four fine posthumous studio albums, including this one. The good tracks are bookended by a pair of masterpieces, "I've Got Dreams to Remember" and the soaring "Amen," of which the latter has been heavily anthologized and the former not heard often enough. *—Bruce Eder*

☆ **In Person at the Whisky A Go Go** / Oct. 1968 / Rhino ♦♦♦♦♦

This album, released posthumously, captured Otis Redding's show at the Whisky A Go Go from April of 1966 in Los Angeles. What is essential here was that it captured Otis Redding's sound in a small club with his own touring band, as opposed to his work on-stage with Booker T. & the MG's—an ideal band, to be sure, which is why they were sent over to Europe with him and why they were at Monterey with him a year later, but not the group that Redding normally worked on-stage with. This album is closer to how Otis Redding sounded in the years coming up and working his way to the top, and the way that his original audience on the chitlin' circuit heard him. The singer and his band (including a pair of tenor saxes, a trombone, and four trumpets, with James Young, Ralph Stewart, and Elbert Woodson pounding out the rhythm on guitar, bass, and drums, respectively, go through roaring versions of "Respect," "I Can't Turn You Loose," "These Arms of Mine," "Pain in My Heart," "Satisfaction" and "Papa's Got a Brand New Bag" and four more, in Redding's only full-length recording in a small-scale setting. They may not have the musical elegance of Booker T. and company, but they create this intense, hypnotic sound that is spellbinding. The set itself lasts less than 40 minutes but the singer and his band are so energetic, that it doesn't feel short or lacking. This album was, in more ways than one, Redding's equivalent to Sam Cooke's *Live at the Harlem Square Club*, and just as essential. Reissued in 1992 on the Atco label through Rhino Records. *—Bruce Eder*

Love Man / Jun. 1969 / Rhino ♦♦♦

While Otis Redding was already one of the biggest stars in soul music when he died in a tragic plane crash in 1967, as is some times the case his star rose considerably after his passing, and this 1969 release dusted off a set of unreleased tracks Redding had cut in 1967, one of which (the title cut) went on to become a sizable chart hit. *Love Man* doesn't hold together quite as well as Redding's best proper albums, such as *Otis Blue* and *Complete & Unbelievable: The Otis Redding Dictionary of Soul*, but it also manages to avoid sounding like a collection of outtakes and leftovers; as an album it's significantly stronger than the average R&B release of similar vintage, due to Redding's indefatigable energy and conviction as a vocalist and the ever-indomitable groove of Steve Cropper, Al Jackson Jr., and the other members of the Stax Records studio crew. If *Love Man* is flawed, it's not a matter of execution so much as material; while Redding's originals are good, none are quite up to the standards of "Cigarettes and Coffee" or "My Lover's Prayer," and covers like "A Lover's Question" and "(Your Love Keeps Lifting Me) Higher and Higher" are not ideally suited to Redding's style. But even the flawed material helps prove just how strong Redding's work was, even under less than ideal circumstances, and *Love Man* makes it clear he never gave less than 110 percent in the studio. *—Mark Deming*

Tell the Truth / Jul. 1970 / Rhino ♦♦♦

When a major artist dies, labels can usually be counted on to release anything and everything the artist had in the can, regardless of quality. In the case of Otis Redding, most of the posthumous releases were of a very high quality. One example is *Tell the Truth*, which was recorded the year he died, 1967, and remained unreleased until 1970. Though it falls short of essential, *Truth* has a lot to excite the soul icon's more devoted followers. Tracks like "I Got the Will," "Snatch a Little Piece," and "Demonstration" are pure Redding—frenzied, passionate, relentlessly gritty Memphis soul that makes no concessions to pop tastes or Northern soul. "Out of Sight" speaks volumes about him—while others would have been afraid to cover a song written and defined by James Brown, Redding confidently tackles the song with splendid results. Redding's last major hit, "Dock of the Bay," indicated that had he lived, he would have explored softer, Northern R&B sounds. But on this album (reissued on CD in the early '90s), it was Memphis all the way. *—Alex Henderson*

Recorded Live / 1982 / Atlantic ♦♦

The first of several attempts to expand the Otis Redding catalog by way of his unissued live recordings, *Recorded Live* was largely ignored when it came out in 1982. Based on tapes from the same shows that yielded *Live at the Whisky A Go Go*, it has since passed into the hands of Fantasy Records' Stax Records imprint, where it was remastered, reconfigured, recompiled, expanded, and generally improved beyond all recognition 11 years later for CD issue as *Good To Me: Live at the Whisky A Go Go, Vol. 2*. *—Bruce Eder*

Remember Me / 1992 / Stax ♦♦♦

One of the better posthumous Otis packages, this brings together tracks recorded between 1963 and 1967, including two alternate takes of the smash "Sittin' on the Dock of the Bay." Far from a batch of leftovers, this features strong material like "I've Got Dreams to Remember," and interesting alternate takes of "Respect," "Come to Me," and "Try a Little Tenderness." After you've absorbed the hits and some of the best of the live material, here's your next stop. *—Cub Koda*

★ **The Very Best of Otis Redding, Vol. 1** / 1993 / Rhino ♦♦♦♦♦

The Very Best of Otis Redding wasn't the first Otis Redding compilation but it is the best of the single-disc collections, distilling the high points across his career (up thru the posthumous hits "(Sitting' On) The Dock of the Bay" and the heartbreaking "I've Got Dreams to Remember") in 16 tracks, every one a musical milestone and a soul music high point of one kind or another. Although aimed at the casual listener and the neophyte fan, there are some astonishing realizations to be had in listening to this disc and looking at the chart placements of the early sides, and realizing just how uniform his musical influence is—"These Arms of Mine" and, especially, "Pain in My Heart," from 1962 and 1963, respectively, sold only a fraction of what his later singles did, yet they've been covered by so many artists since, that they're as familiar as any of the other, bigger hits on this disc. The collection is hardly comprehensive, but all of the major bases are touched, right down to his 1967 hit duet "Tramp" with Carla Thomas. The other advantage, especially for those on a budget, is that this was the first Otis Redding compilation to avail itself of the improved master tape research and analog-to-digital technology of the early '90s. *—Bruce Eder*

Good to Me: Live at the Whisky A Go Go, Vol. 2 / Jan. 25, 1993 / Stax ♦♦♦♦

No Otis Redding fan—not even a casual admirer—could possibly go wrong owning this disc. It needn't be said that there can never be too many Otis Redding live albums, but even allowing for that as a given, this CD—an expanded, somewhat reshuffled version of the LP *Recorded Live*, which appeared to little fanfare in 1982—is worth special attention. Recorded at the same April 1966 dates whence came *In Person at the Whisky A Go Go*, it is a little on the rough side, as singer and band struggle to get completely in sync, but once they do—the version of "I've Been Loving You Too Long" presented here could be the best on record, an extended soul workout that just seems to ratchet up the fever and the tension past the point of no return, so it just seems like Redding is going to float away into the sky because there's no place left for him to go with the song—this reviewer works up a sweat just listening to it. The rendition of "Security" here isn't far behind it, and as neither of those numbers was on the earlier *In Person at the Whisky A Go Go* release, their presence here makes this disc a mandatory purchase. Not everything here comes up to that standard, but even Redding's version of "A Hard Day's Night" is worth hearing. The CD edition has been expanded with the inclusion of an introduction plus versions of three numbers—"I'm Depending on You," "Pain in My Heart," and "These Arms of Mine"—that are already represented on the first album. The sound is excellent and the annotation is thoughtful and informative, all making this disc essential listening for any fan. *—Bruce Eder*

☆ **Otis! The Definitive Otis Redding** / Nov. 9, 1993 / Rhino ✦✦✦✦✦
Anyone who wants to understand the different phases of Otis Redding's career, and the reason for his having made a major impact across the 1960s and beyond, can have no better place to start than *Otis! The Definitive Otis Redding.* There are 73 studio cuts here and the producers have reached back beyond the Atlantic and Stax vaults: They've included numbers like "She's All Right," cut by the Shooters featuring Otis Redding in the summer of 1960 for the Transworld label; "Gettin' Hip," which was done for the Alshire label in 1960; and "Shout Bamalama" by Otis Redding & the Pinetoppers, recorded for Confederate, all prior to Redding's signing with Stax. The selection of studio cuts suggests that the makers thought long and hard about each and every track on this disc—the first three CDs are a mix of single A- and B-sides, coupled with important album tracks, all culminating with "(Sittin' On) The Dock of the Bay." Little or nothing that's essential is missing along the way (though one could argue very persuasively that anything on the albums that Redding released in his lifetime was essential in some respect). The fourth disc is the real killer, however; 23 live songs drawn from the complete range of his concert tapes in the Atlantic (and Stax) vaults, from the Apollo Theater in New York in November of 1963 to his final tour of Europe and the Monterey International Pop Festival in the spring of 1967, including individual tracks that were unheard until the 1980s. An extensive booklet is also included. *—Bruce Eder*

☆ **The Very Best of Otis Redding, Vol. 2** / Apr. 25, 1995 / Rhino ✦✦✦✦✦
Rhino's first Otis Redding volume was perfect within the confines of a 16-song single disc, and a difficult act to follow. *The Very Best of Otis Redding, Vol. 2* is a fine companion volume and fills in some different kinds of gaps. The lion's share of the disc is devoted to 13 more singles, several of which ("I Love You More Than Words Can Say," "Security," "That's What My Heart Needs," "Chained and Bound," "Glory of Love") are, if not definitive, then still all-but-essential. Several posthumous singles are also here, along with two more duets with Carla Thomas. More revealing and representative of the range of Redding's talent, however, are three album tracks that show off Redding applying his talents to the songs of Smokey Robinson, with a rapturous account of "My Girl"; the Beatles, in a ferociously freewheeling, elongated, and essentially re-composed version of "Day Tripper"; and, most notably, Sam Cooke with "A Change Is Gonna Come." The latter, arguably the best recording ever given a Sam Cooke song by anyone other than Cooke himself, might just be the best Otis Redding song never released as a single. The neophyte and the casual listener will love the contents of this disc, and even longtime fans may be impressed with some of the choices. *—Bruce Eder*

Dreams to Remember: The Otis Redding Anthology / Aug. 18, 1998 / Rhino ✦✦✦✦✦
Dreams to Remember: The Otis Redding Anthology presents an interesting dilemma. Certainly, the music on the double-disc set is superb—all of his hits are here, along with a wealth of great album tracks and five live cuts from the Monterey International Pop Festival. The question is, was the collection *necessary*? Casual listeners who just want the hits will be satisfied with the excellent *Very Best of Otis Redding*, while those who want to dig deeper will find the four-disc box *Otis! The Definitive Otis Redding* essential, or will opt for the actual albums. *Dreams to Remember* falls somewhere between the two extremes, containing too much music for the casual listener and not being extensive enough for serious listeners. Perhaps realizing this, Rhino added several tracks here that weren't featured on the box set, but any true collector will have these songs on the original albums. So, *Dreams to Remember* is in limbo—a fine collection that isn't really necessary. It's not a bad choice, to be sure, but *The Very Best of Otis Redding* and *Otis!* are better choices, depending on your tastes. *—Stephen Thomas Erlewine*

Dalton Reed

b. Aug. 23, 1952, Cade, LA, **d.** Sep. 24, 1994, Minneapolis, MN
Vocals / Soul-Blues
Dalton Reed attempted to keep the sweet sound of deep soul alive in the '90s. The Lafayette, LA, singer comes from a gospel background—a prerequisite for success in the genre—and cut his first single for his own little label in 1986. When he was child, Reed sang gospel in church and played trumpet in his high school marching band. Reed fell in love with R&B and soul as a teenager, prompting him to join a few local bands. Soon, he formed his own group, Dalton Reed & the Musical Journey Band. In a short while, the band was playing bars and clubs throughout Louisiana, Alabama, and Texas.

Reed founded his own record label, Sweet Daddy Records, in 1986, releasing his debut single, "Givin' on in to Love," that same year. Within a few years after the formation of Sweet Daddy, Reed and his brother Johnny formed another independent label, Reed Brothers Records. In 1990, Bullseye Blues signed Reed and the label released his debut album, *Louisiana Soul Man*, the following year. Three years later, his second album, *Willing & Able*, appeared. When he wasn't recording, Reed toured, playing concerts throughout America. *—Bill Dahl*

Louisiana Soul Man / Dec. 1991 / Bullseye Blues ✦✦✦
Dalton Reed's *Louisiana Soul Man* establishes the singer as an heir to the deep Southern soul of such artists as Otis Redding, Arthur Conley, and Percy Sledge. Despite the title, there's no hint of cajun music or zydeco on the record—it's pure testifiying from start to finish. The new material is usually quite good, and it should be with songwriters like Doc Pomus, Dr. John, Dan Penn, and Delbert McClinton involved. *Louisiana Soul Man* is for anyone who believed that pure Southern soul died with Otis Redding. *—Thom Owens*

● **Willing & Able** / Mar. 30, 1994 / Bullseye Blues ✦✦✦✦✦
Dalton Reed is a classic gospel-based soul vocalist. There's nothing sophisticated in his approach, staid in his delivery, or polite and detached in his sound. He explodes, attacks, and rips through the 10 tracks on his second Bullseye blues LP, his voice full of animation and expressiveness. These songs are done in the vivid, overwrought manner considered too intense by the urban contemporary tastemakers; you won't hear trendy backgrounds or drum machines on these numbers. This is unapologetic soul from a vocalist who will never appeal to the crossover audience, but is making some of the better R&B in today's market. *—Ron Wynn*

Francine Reed

b. Jul. 11, 1947, Chicago, IL
Vocals / Contemporary Blues, Soul-Blues
Vocalist Francine Reed can't remember a time when she didn't sing. In her youth, the Chicago-born, Phoenix-raised song stylist sang in church and in grammar school. She began singing professionally with her family when she was five and continued into her teens. She got married young and had four children, whom she ended up raising alone. She worked a variety of day jobs and kept her singing career an avocation until 1985, when some friends introduced her to Lyle Lovett. Lovett was interested in finding a female vocalist for his new band and found his singer in Reed. She toured with Lovett for ten years as a member of Lovett's Large Band, and did several TV performances with the Texas singer/songwriter. While her association with Lovett continues, she has embarked on the kind of solo career she always wanted when working the day jobs to support her family. To date, Reed has recorded two albums for the Atlanta-based Ichiban label in 1995 and 1996. Her amphitheater performances with Lovett must have surely had an effect on sales of both of her records. Reed also got a few other nice breaks, including the chance to do some singing for TV commercials. Tom Cruise cranks her album up in a scene from the 1993 movie *The Firm.*

Reed's two albums for Ichiban include *I Want You to Love Me* (1995) and *Can't Make It on My Own* (1996). The former features a duet with bandleader Lovett, while the latter includes a duet with Delbert McClinton. On both albums, Reed continues the tradition already set down by great women soul-blues vocalists like Carla Thomas, Irma Thomas, and Etta James; she returned in 1999 with *Shades of Blue* on the Intersound label. In 2001 following the demise of Ichiban Records, which left her first two records out of print and unavailable, Reed and longtime collaborator Marvin Taylor re-recorded some of her best material live in the studio and released the results as *I Got a Right!... To Some of My Best.* The record business being as unpredictable as it is, Ichiban was resurrected in 2002 and released *American Roots: Blues*, a compilation of her first two records. *—Richard Skelly*

I Want You to Love Me / Apr. 25, 1995 / Ichiban ✦✦✦✦
By the time she released her debut album, Francine Reed had established herself as a fine blues singer through her work with Lyle Lovett. *I Want You to Love Me* proves that she can do it on her own. Lovett drops in for the opening cut, "Why I Don't Know," but this remains Reed's show, and she shows she knows what she's doing. She can sing sultry slow blues, belt out soul, and get down and dirty—in short, she can do it all. Furthermore, she has the songs to prove her talents, relying on classics from Jerry Butler and Muddy Waters, among others. The result is a thoroughly entertaining record from an accomplished artist. *—Thom Owens*

Can't Make It on My Own / 1996 / Ichiban International ✦✦✦

I Got a Right! . . . To Some of My Best / Jul. 31, 2001 / CMO Productions ✦✦✦✦
There aren't many women who can sing the blues like this semi-legendary Atlanta-based belter, and as the title indicates, *I Got a Right!* compiles 13 audience favorites onto one CD. Since the out-of-print original recordings of most of these tunes were tied up in legal wrangling when Ichiban records went under, Reed and longtime collaborator Marvin Taylor simply took the band back into the studio and re-recorded the suckers, boasting proudly in the liner notes that most of these versions came on the first or second take. It's a smart approach that captures the fresh feel of Reed's raucous live shows, where songs like "Been There, Done That" and "One Monkey (Don't Stop No Show)" have earned her a Mae West-like reputation. Fan and friend Willie Nelson stops by for a duet on the lilting, New Orleans-style jazz of "The Night Life," and Reed finds a personal anthem of sorts in the brassy "Wild Women Don't Get the Blues." Her band is in top form here, with a sizzling horn section and smoking guitar solos from Taylor, but Reed is undoubtedly the star of this show, howling, wailing, and growling with every ounce of passion in her soul. If you're a blues fan and don't know Francine Reed, here's a wonderful chance to find out what you've been missing. *—Bret Love*

● **American Roots: Blues** / Apr. 23, 2002 / Ichiban ✦✦✦✦✦

Lula Reed

Vocals / R&B, Soul
A longtime cohort of pianist/producer Sonny Thompson, singer Lula Reed recorded steadily for Cincinnati-based King Records during the mid-'50s after debuting on wax in 1951 to sing Thompson's original version of the moving ballad "I'll Drown in My Tears" (a 1956 smash for Ray Charles as "Drown in My Own Tears").

After serving as Thompson's vocalist at first, the attractive chanteuse was sufficiently established by 1952 to rate her own King releases. She was versatile, singing urban blues most of the time but switching to gospel for a 1954 session. Reed's strident 1954 waxing "Rock Love" was later revived by labelmate Little Willie John. She briefly moved to the Chess subsidiary Argo in 1958-1959 but returned to the fold in 1961 (as always, under Thompson's direction) on King's Federal imprint. While at Federal, she waxed a series of sassy duets with guitarist Freddie King in March of 1962. Another move—to Ray Charles' Tangerine logo in 1962-1963—soon followed. *—Bill Dahl*

● **Blue and Moody** / 1959 / King ✦✦✦✦✦
The longtime protégée of King Records house pianist/arranger/ producer Sonny Thompson possessed a sultry style well-suited to blues ballads in the urban vein and lighthearted upbeat fare—both of which reside on this reissue of her vintage King album. *—Bill Dahl*

Martha Reeves

b. Jul. 18, 1941, Detroit, MI

Vocals / Motown, Soul

Motown's brightest female star after Diana Ross, Martha Reeves was the earthy, gospel-infused counterpart to her rival Ross' uptown sophistication. With her backing group, the Vandellas, Reeves cut some of the brightest, most infectiously danceable R&B of her time. Unfortunately, she didn't fare as well after leaving Motown for a solo career in the '70s, and although she continued to perform for quite sometime, it was mostly on the oldies circuit, looking back over her past glories.

Reeves was born in Eufaula, AL, on July 18, 1941, and before she was even a year old, her family moved to Detroit. As a child, she sang in her grandfather's church and in school, and continued her vocal training through high school. After graduating in 1959, she joined a girl group called the Fascinations, and the following year co-founded the Del-Phis, whose membership included the future Vandellas. They cut a flop single for a Chess subsidiary in 1961; the same year, Reeves won a talent contest as a solo act and got a nightclub engagement performing as Martha LaVaille. There she was noticed by Motown exec William "Mickey" Stevenson, who invited her to stop by the label's offices. Reeves wasn't able to land an audition right away, but did parlay her visit into a secretarial job in the A&R department. She caught a lucky break when backup singers were needed for a recording session as quickly as possible, and so the Del-Phis wound up supporting Marvin Gaye on his first hit, 1962's "Stubborn Kind of Fellow." Stevenson was impressed enough to record a Del-Phis (renamed the Vels) single, "You'll Never Cherish a Love So True ('Til You Lose It)," and released it on Motown's Mel-O-Dy subsidiary. One day, Mary Wells failed to show up for a recording session, and musicians' union rules demanded that a lead vocalist be present on the mike—so secretary Reeves was hastily tapped to sing "I'll Have to Let Him Go." That song went on to become the first single credited to the newly renamed Martha & the Vandellas in 1963; their second single, the ballad "Come and Get These Memories," reached the R&B Top Five.

The rest, of course, was history. Martha & the Vandellas racked up an impressive slate of Motown classics that included the Top Five smashes "(Love Is Like A) Heat Wave" and "Dancing in the Street," plus "Nowhere to Run," "I'm Ready for Love," "Jimmy Mack," and "Honey Chile," all of which made the R&B Top Five. Despite the occasional personnel turnover, and the fact that rivals the Supremes had become Motown's female group of choice, Martha & the Vandellas' run of success continued through 1967. Unfortunately, feeling the pressure to keep up, Reeves developed an addiction to prescription drugs, and in 1968 a bad acid trip prefigured a nervous breakdown that slowed the Vandellas' momentum even further. Although they continued to perform and record for several more years, they never matched the success of old and disbanded in December 1972 after a farewell concert in Detroit.

Meanwhile, Motown decided to transfer its offices from Detroit to Los Angeles. Reeves adamantly refused to move along with them and sued for release from her contract; she eventually won her independence and signed with MCA as a solo artist. She entered the studio with producer Richard Perry and a top session cast, and cut a monstrously expensive album that mixed rock, pop, and R&B covers, both vintage and contemporary. *Martha Reeves* was released in 1974 and sold very disappointingly, especially given its cost. Reeves sank deeper into a host of personal problems until she finally cleaned up and became a born-again Baptist in 1977. That year, she signed with Arista for *The Rest of My Life*, which blended '60s soul with disco-era production; once again, it sold poorly, and Reeves moved to Fantasy for 1978's even more disco-oriented *We Meet Again*, which featured four of her own compositions. After 1980's *Gotta Keep Moving*, Reeves gave up the ghost on her solo career. She spent the early '80s working on various Motown package tours, and eventually put together a new version of the Vandellas. In 1989, she reunited with original Vandellas Annette Sterling and Rosalind Holmes and cut the single "Step Into My Shoes" for British producer Ian Levine's Motor City label. However, she mostly continued make her living on the nostalgia circuit. Reeves was inducted into the Rock and Roll Hall of Fame in 1995. *—Steve Huey*

Martha Reeves / 1974 / MCA ✦✦✦

● **The Rest of My Life** / 1977 / Arista ✦✦✦

Four producers—Tony Silvester, General Johnson, Tony Camillo, and Bert DeCoteaux—working independently resulted in the best post-Motown LP for Martha Reeves to date. The material and arrangements suit her voice and style more than Richard Perry's earlier extravaganza that flopped. While this didn't fare much better commercially, it's more of what we expect from the Detroit diva, and it cost less to produce. Included is Martha's original version of Gwen Guthrie & Pat Grant's "This Time I'll Be Sweeter," a song later popularized by Angela Bofil. Reeves' version of Gamble & Huff's "Now That We Found Love" is one of the better cuts; Martha sings it with as much conviction as the O'Jays, who first waxed it. "Thank You" is an uptempo romp produced by General Johnson, who has Reeves reaching for notes like her former producers at Motown did. Disappointing sales caused Reeves to leave Arista Records after this sole release to take a shot with Fantasy Records and the opportunity to work with ex-Motown producer Henry Cosby. *—Andrew Hamilton*

We Meet Again / 1978 / Milestone ✦✦

As post-Motown Martha Reeves albums go, this one's OK. The title signifies Martha's reunion with former Motown producer Henry Cosby (who, in reality, played an insignificant role in her Motown success). Fantasy gave Martha more creative control than she had enjoyed at Motown, allowing her to pen four of the eight songs here. But for some reason, ex-Motown producers, with few exceptions, lose their magic after leaving Berryland. "Free Again" and "Love Don't Come No Stronger" are adequate dance numbers, but poor sisters to Martha's Motown stuff, and the three ballads are merely decent. Cosby failed to properly capture Martha's reedy soprano; at Motown it was full and vibrant, while at other companies it's thin and shrill. Maybe it's the studio, the musicians, the mastering, who knows? Whatever the reason, Martha Reeves' post-Motown recordings have been less than scintillating. *—Andrew Hamilton*

The Reflections

f. 1962, Detroit, MI

Group / Blue-Eyed Soul, Pop-Soul, R&B

Detroit-based the Reflections were a five-man group schooled in doo wop who scored in 1964 on Ed Wingate's Golden World label with "(Just Like) Romeo and Juliet," written by Bob Hamilton and Freddie Gorman. (Gorman later wrote songs for Motown ("Please Mr. Postman" and "Forever") and formed the Originals, who hit with "Baby I'm for Real.") The Reflections were Phil Castrodale, Ray Steinberg, Tony Micale, Danny Bennie, and Johnny Dean. The group's first recording was a remake of the Five Satins' "In the Still of the Night" on Tigre, which did well in some Midwestern markets. Their Golden World debut, "(Just Like) Romeo and Juliet," cracked the Top Ten before settling at the number-six position.

They recorded seven more 45s for Golden World, but none were as successful as "(Just Like) Romeo and Juliet." "Like Columbus Did" cracked the pop 100, but only by four slots, hanging at number 96. "Poor Man's Son," the Reflections' sixth Golden World single, almost cracked the Top 40 but stopped climbing at number 55. Other singles—"Talking About My Girl," "(I'm Just) A Henpecked Guy," "Shabby Little Hut," "Wheelin' and Dealin'," "Out of the Picture," and their final single, "Girl in the Candy Store"—did nothing. Their producers insisted they use a hokey falsetto sound on their recordings that didn't bode well with the group members.

Problems with Golden World resulted over both creative differences and royalties, so they opted to go with ABC Paramount when their contract time was up. Neither "Adam and Eve" or "Long Cigarette" did well though, so believing the name the Reflections hindered them, the group became High and the Mighty. They released "Escape From Cuba," written by Ritchie Adams and Larry Kusik, but it failed too. Despite a lack of success, they continued singing for years; members Micale and Dean still gigged around the Detroit area in a band called Larados. *—Andrew Hamilton*

● **(Just Like) Romeo and Juliet** / 1964 / Golden World ✦✦✦✦✦

The Regents

f. 1959, New York, NY [The Bronx]

Group / Doo Wop, R&B, Pop

Guy Villari (lead), Sal Cuomo (first tenor), Ernie Maresca (baritone), and Chuck Fassert (second tenor) formed in the Bronx, NY, in 1958 as the Montereys. Signing with Seville Records, they cut two Maresca songs that went unreleased, and soon Donnie Jacobucci replaced a disappointed Maresca. They recorded their demonstration records at the Regents Sound Studios, prompting a name change to the Regents, but their first release didn't happen until 1961, three years after they started.

"Barbara Ann" was recorded in 1958, but more than 50 recording companies said "no," causing them to disband before 1959 rolled around. Jacobucci's younger brother Eddie revived the Regents by accident. His group, the Consorts, lacked original songs for an audition so they cut a version of "Barbara Ann" from an old demo Eddie found around the house. When the owner of Cousins Records heard the song, he decided to put it out, not by the Consorts, but by the Regents. With Eddie replacing Guy, the original group reunited, and Cousins released "Barbara Ann" in March of 1961. The stuttering doo wop became a number-one record in New York; the demand was overwhelming and Cousins leased it to Roulette/Gee for worldwide distribution and saw it soared to number-13 pop and number-seven R&B.

A second single, "Runaround," charted at number-28 pop and number-30 R&B; a third single, "Liar," didn't chart, and neither did a fourth, "Oh Baby." They disbanded but emerged in 1964 as the Runarounds, waxing and releasing five singles on as many labels. The Runarounds were Villari, Fassert, Ronnie Lapinsky, and Sal Corrente; their first single, "Unbelievable," on Nat King Cole's short-lived KC label in 1963 didn't sell nor did their last, "You Lied," on MGM in 1967. Again they separated but reunited as the Regents in 1973 to play the oldie circuit. A copy of "Barbara Ann" on the Cousin label fetches around 1,200 dollars; the same recording on Gee sells for 25 dollars or less. *—Andrew Hamilton*

● **Barbara-Ann** / 1961 / Collectables ✦✦✦✦✦

Barbara-Ann is a straight reissue of the Regents' 1961 album and contains the group's only two hits. "Barbara-Ann" was a Top 15 hit for the group in 1961, but the Beach Boys had even greater success with the song five years later. The Regents' minor follow-up hit, "Runaround," is not the same song with which the Three Chuckles and the Fleetwoods had hits. The album tracks are a mixture of ballads ("Sunday Kind of Love" is covered) and uptempo songs, some of which are original. The Regents were a competent white doo wop group who mostly sang in tune (which is more than you can expect from many of the marginal vocal groups), with five-piece vocal arrangements that made their rockers dense and powerful. Collectables could have added a few bonus tracks to make this a complete anthology of the Regents' Gee recordings, but as it is, *Barbara-Ann* is a good summation of the group's brief career for Beach Boys fanatics and collectors of white doo wop records. *—Greg Adams*

Live at the AM/PM Discotheque / 1964 / Capitol ✦✦

Clarence Reid

b. Feb. 14, 1945, Cochran, GA

Producer / Funk, Soul, Blaxploitation

Singer/songwriter/producer Clarence Reid, like David Bowie and P-Funk's George Clinton, had multiple musical personalities. One was of an earnest Southern soul singer, born February 14, 1945, in Cochran, GA, and recorded for TK Records president Henry Stone's Alston imprint. His *Billboard*-charting singles were "Nobody but You Babe" (number-seven R&B summer 1969, on the Atlantic LP), "Good Old Days" (early 1972), and "Funky Party" (summer 1974). He co-wrote hits for Betty Wright ("Girls Can't Do What the Guys Do"), the million-selling "Clean Up Woman," "Baby Sitter," and "Let Me Be Your

Lovemaker." For Gwen McCrae, Reid co-wrote and co-produced "Rockin' Chair," which reached the pop Top Ten in 1975,

In his other persona, he performed X-rated material under the pseudonym Blowfly. Reid also helped Richard Finch get a job with TK Records and introduced Harry Wayne "K.C." Casey to junkanoo, the festive party music that would be the core sound of Casey and Finch's '70s supergroup KC & the Sunshine Band. Clarence Reid-related releases are *When a Man Cries: The Deep Soul of Scepter/Wand*, in addition to many Blowfly releases. *—Ed Hogan*

● **Dancin' With Nobody But You Baby** / 1969 / Atlantic ♦♦♦

This Henry Stone master (Alston Records) was handled by Atco Records for mass distribution and promotion, which didn't happen to any great extent. If you found this album in a record store north of the Mason-Dixon Line it was because of a shipping foul-up—unfortunate, because it's one of Reid's better endeavors. Recorded at the Zoo Recording Studio in Miami, FL, like most records under Stone's family of labels, the recording was primitive, but in this case appealing. Reid updates "25 Miles," "Shop Around," and "I've Been Trying," and adds some gritty Southern soul via "Nobody but You Baby," "Send Me Back My Money," and "Polk Salad Annie." A prolific writer, Reid never really found his niche as a singer until he ventured into the novelty/party record scene as the outrageous Blowfly. *—Andrew Hamilton*

René & Angela

f. 1977, Los Angeles, CA

Group / Quiet Storm, Urban, Dance-Pop

René & Angela are an early-'80s soul duo from Los Angeles. Before forming in 1977, René Moore—the brother of Rufus' Bobby Watson—played with the Brothers Johnson; Angela Winbush had sung backup vocals for Dolly Parton, Lenny Williams, and Jean Carn. René & Angela had their first R&B hit for Capitol Records in 1980 and proceeded to have seven other hits over the next three years. In 1985, the duo switched to Mercury, where they had the number-one R&B hit "Save Your Love (For #1)" with their first single from the album *Street Called Desire*. Over the next year, the group had three other Top Ten hits—including the number-one R&B single "Your Smile" and the number-two "You Don't Have to Cry"—before pursuing solo careers in the mid-'80s. *—Stephen Thomas Erlewine*

Wall to Wall / Jul. 1981 / Capitol ♦♦♦♦

René & Angela's second Capitol album began to lay the groundwork for their smash fourth release, although it came on another label. *Wall to Wall* had several chart hits including "I Love You More," "Wall to Wall," and "Imaginary Playmates." René and Angela were the ideal singing duo, remaining prominent on the R&B scene throughout 1981 and 1982. Moore was wise enough to content himself with mostly harmonizing while Winbush's soaring, strong voice took the spotlight during the choruses and on the leads. *—Ron Wynn*

Rise / 1983 / Capitol ♦♦♦

With this being the last album the duo would record for Capitol, they still couldn't manage to crack the *Billboard* R&B Top Ten. However, they did come close. Their first release was the dance single "Bangin' the Boogie." With its rapid rhythm and blaring horns, the twosome managed to carry the song to number 33 on the *Billboard* R&B charts. Their follow-up single, "My First Love," had an impressive outing. With its lush string arrangement, the pair deliver a passionate take on a serenely written number, which peaked at number 12 after 18 weeks on the charts. While most of the album features uptempo songs, "Can't Give You Up" is the only midtempo number, and it, like most of the album, suffers from production overkill. *—Craig Lytle*

Street Called Desire / Jun. 1985 / Mercury ♦♦♦♦

The duo of René & Angela were at their peak as hit composers and performers on this album, their debut for Mercury. It included the huge hits "Your Smile" and "Save Your Love (For #1)," both R&B chart-toppers, plus another Top Ten hit in "I'll Be Good." Although they've never been credited with the achievement, long before the new jack swing formula of pairing a rapper with a vocalist or vocal group became fashionable, "Save Your Love (For #1)" featured a guest rap from Kurtis Blow. *—Ron Wynn*

● **The Best of René & Angela: Come My Way** / Oct. 29, 1996 / EMI ♦♦♦♦♦

The Best of René & Angela: Come My Way contains all of the soul duo's hits for Capitol Records, including "I Love You More," "Wall to Wall," "Imaginary Playmates," "My First Love" and "Banging the Boogie." Though the duo's later work for Mercury was more successful, both commercially and artistically, these recordings are entertaining early-'80s soul and contain a couple of fine singles. *—Leo Stanley*

A Street Called Desire and More / May 20, 1997 / Polygram ♦♦♦

René & Angela were Marvin & Tammi with extra soul sauce. The picturesque twosome held nothing back in the studio. Their obvious enthusiasm and for-real emotions makes listening to them a pleasure. This CD doesn't chronicle R&A's entire career; none of the songs from their three Capitol Records LPs are featured. Eight tracks are from the original *Street Called Desire* LP; "Set Me Free" was lifted from the *Jumpin' Jack Flash* soundtrack, and the other five selections are 12-inch versions of five of the original album sides. Essential for any soul music aficionado. The throbbing beat on "I'll Be Good" is mind locking, especially the 12-inch version. Foxy Brown hit 12 years later with "I'll Be" featuring Jay-Z, and that same insatiable beat mesmerized a new generation of fans. The uptempo numbers aren't jokes, but the two ballads, "You Don't Have to Cry" and "Your Smile" (two versions of "Smile"), are outstanding. What makes them work is their unpredictability. No particular, or already determined pattern is set. No attempt is made to divide the lines and choruses equally; each singer unselfishly contributes what's necessary. "Smile" is mostly Angela until Rene repeatedly chants "No other love can light my life, no one can make things right, til my baby smiles." René has more juice on "You Don't Have to Cry," matching alternating verses with Angela—who gives an incredible performance on the heart-stopping ballad. René's brother Bobby Watson (formerly of Rufus) co-produced the sides with Bruce Swedien. "Save Your Love for Number #1" and "Your Smile" both reached number-one R&B; "You Don't Have to Cry" went to number-two R&B, and "I'll Be Good" climbed to number four. *Billboard*'s pop chart proved a tougher nut for R&A to scale, as a number 47 ranking for "I'll Be Good" was their highest number. Due to personal problems and conflicts, René & Angela called it quits and released no more LPs. *—Andrew Hamilton*

Nicole Renee

Vocals / Contemporary R&B, Urban

One of the more promising R&B artists to emerge in the 1990s, Nicole Renee first came to the attention of the urban contemporary world when she was one of the hosts on BET's *Teen Summit*. During her four years with that show, an adolescent Renee did on-camera interviews with quite a few big names in R&B and rap. However, she wasn't planning to pursue a career as an R&B singer when she first joined *Teen Summit*—at the time, Renee was hoping for a career in classical music. But R&B soon became her primary focus, and by 1998 she was signed to Atlantic as an urban contemporary act. That year, Atlantic released Renee's self-titled debut album, in which she did most of the writing, producing, and arranging. *—Alex Henderson*

● **Nicole Renee** / Sep. 15, 1998 / Atlantic ♦♦♦♦

Comparing the soul music of the 1960s and 1970s to the urban contemporary of the 1990s, many Baby Boomers would tell you that R&B isn't what it used to be—and, to be sure, 1990s R&B was full of faceless automatons who went for a cookie-cutter, assembly-line approach. But 1990s R&B wasn't a total waste, and sizable talents like Mary J. Blige, Lisa Stansfield, En Vogue and Lauryn Hill indicated that R&B wasn't something you could close the book on. One of the more promising R&B debuts of 1998 was this self-titled release by Nicole Renee, an interesting singer who often favors a nasal style of singing but can bring to mind Deniece Williams and Ron Isley when she hits the high notes. Renee did most of the producing, arranging and writing herself, although she had some help from Lamont Dozier and Arif Mardin here and there, and even though she uses some samples and drum machines, real instruments are prominent on impressive originals like the alluring "Strawberry," the sentimental "Seems Like Yesterday" and the Isley Brothers-influenced "Let Me Down." Most of Renee's songs are about romantic relationships, but addresses social issues on "Cocaine Lane" and "Ain't Nothin' Changed" (which reflects on the hopelessness and despair of a poor neighborhood). Striving for the organic instead of the mechanical, this album made it clear that Renee had a lot of potential. *—Alex Henderson*

Jeannie Reynolds

d. 1980

Vocals / Disco

Singer Jeannie Reynolds, best known for "The Fruit Song," was the sister of L.J. Reynolds of the Dramatics. Though "The Fruit Song" is her signature song, her highest-charting single was the snappy "The Phone's Been Jumping All Day" on Casablanca Records, which went to number-ten R&B on *Billboard* in summer 1975. Her only other R&B charting single was its follow-up, "Lay Some Lovin' on Me." With its "fruitful" cover, the singer's LP *Cherries, Bananas & Other Fine Things* on Casablanca was issued in June 1976. One single from the LP, "The Fruit Song," written by Lawrence Payton of the Four Tops and Fred Bridges, became a huge disco hit, a post-release collectible, and a steppers standard. Another Casablanca LP, *One Wish*, was produced by Don Davis (Johnnie Taylor, the Dramatics, Marilyn McCoo, and Billy Davis Jr.). Tragically, Jeannie Reynolds took her two children's lives before committing suicide in 1980. *—Ed Hogan*

● **Cherries, Bananas & Other Fine Things** / 1976 / Casablanca ♦♦♦

Rhythm Heritage

f. 1975, Los Angeles, CA

Group / Blaxploitation, Disco, Funk

A Los Angeles studio group that keyboardist Michael Omartian and producer Steve Barri assembled in the mid-'70s, Rhythm Heritage had a pair of television theme hits before fading into obscurity. "Theme From S.W.A.T." topped the pop charts in 1975 and peaked at number-11 R&B, while "Baretta's Theme (Keep Your Eye on the Sparrow)" was a Top 20 R&B and pop single in 1976. Oren and Luther Waters served as group vocalists, but they couldn't keep things going with subsequent follow-ups. *—Ron Wynn*

● **Disco-Fied** / 1976 / ABC ♦♦♦

Rhythm Heritage was never a band in the true sense of the word. Best known for its disco-funk versions of themes from movies and television cop shows, Rhythm Heritage was a group of Los Angeles studio musicians that producers Michael Omartian and Steve Barri threw together. None of its three albums were distinctive—they weren't meant to be. But if you take them for what they are, those albums aren't without their pleasures. Although uneven, Rhythm Heritage's first album, *Disco-Fied*, is arguably its best. This 1976 LP contains its biggest hit, the infectious "Theme From S.W.A.T.," as well as its slick remake of "Baretta's Theme (Keep Your Eye on the Sparrow)," which became the album's second single. Rhythm Heritage's version of the *Baretta* theme isn't the best one—Sammy Davis Jr. and Merry Clayton provided superior versions—but it's still enjoyable. Also noteworthy are Rhythm Heritage's arrangements of Dave Grusin's "Three Days of the Condor" and Duke Ellington's "Caravan," which is devoid of jazz elements in Omartian and Barri's hands. To jazz snobs, recording a glossy disco version of an Ellington standard was musical heresy. But then, Omartian and Barri never claimed that their arrangement of "Caravan" was authentic jazz. Meanwhile, the LP's weaker tracks include "(It's Time To) Boogie Down" and the robotic title song, both of which find Rhythm Heritage sounding like a poor man's Kool & the Gang. But despite its flaws and limitations, *Disco-Fied* is Rhythm Heritage's most fun and memorable album. *—Alex Henderson*

Last Night on Earth / 1977 / ABC ♦♦♦
Rhythm Heritage's second album, *Last Night on Earth*, is best remembered for Michael Omartian and Steve Barri's memorable disco arrangement of the instrumental "Theme From Rocky (Gonna Fly Now)," and the producers are equally enjoyable when they give "Theme From Lipstick" the disco treatment. But this very uneven 1977 LP certainly isn't without its flaws. "Disco Queen" (not to be confused with the Hot Chocolate song) and "Dance the Night Away" (which was written by jazzman Victor Feldman but isn't jazz) are mechanical disco numbers that offer little in the way of feeling or imagination, and a medley of Steely Dan's "Do It Again" and War's "The Cisco Kid" is equally disposable. While side one offers the very things one expected from Rhythm Heritage—disco originals and disco versions of movie themes—side two is a pleasant, if imperfect, surprise. Perhaps Omartian and Barri grew tired of hearing Rhythm Heritage described as mindless; if so, that explains why they tackle social and political issues on side two, which is devoted to a three-song, 17-minute medley called "Last Night on Earth." Reflecting on the world's troubled state, the medley gets off to an impressive start on the assertive "Angry World" but loses some steam on its second and third songs. Nonetheless, Omartian and Barri deserve credit for trying something different—they could have easily made side two a replica of side one. *Disco-Fied* remains Rhythm Heritage's best album (flaws and all), but this sophomore effort does have its moments. *—Alex Henderson*

Sky's the Limit / 1978 / ABC ♦♦♦

Gene Rice

b. Jul. 1950, Baltimore, MD
Vocals / Urban, Contemporary R&B
Contemporary soul singer Gene Rice was born in Baltimore in 1950. Driven by the R&B hit "You're Gonna Get Served," his 1991 debut album *Just for You* earned solid reviews and placed on the R&B charts as well. A self-titled album followed in 1993, but it was his last release for RCA. *—Bil Carpenter*

● **Just for You** / 1991 / RCA ♦♦♦♦♦
Without question, one of the most wrongly neglected R&B releases of 1991 was Gene Rice's *Just for You*—an engaging collection of mostly ballads and slow jams that, for all its high-tech production gloss, is very much a throwback to Teddy Pendergrass' late-'70s, post-Harold Melvin & the Bluenotes solo recordings for Philadelphia International. When the robust, no-nonsense belter digs into such unapologetically romantic slow-burners as "Like I Love You," "You're Gonna Get Served" and "Love Is Calling You"—and provides an inspired interpretation of Carole King's "It's Too Late"—Rice leaves no doubt that he's indeed a Pendergrass disciple, yet projects an appealing personality of his own. Rice makes it abundantly clear that he's a soul singer first and foremost, and refuses to tone down the gospel-ish qualities that many urban-contemporary singers of the '80s and '90s shied away from in the hope of "crossing over" to the pop charts. Rice picks up the tempo for the convincing "I Believe," indicating that as superb a balladeer as he is, he'd do well to change tempos more often. *—Alex Henderson*

Gene Rice / Feb. 1993 / RCA ♦♦
The third of five albums that RCA Records released by multi-talented Gene Rice. This time, Gerald LeVert, Marc Gordon, Chuckii Booker, the Rude Boys, and others help produce and write the nine songs on the set. The consortium didn't help Rice's luck, as none of the songs—save for a remake of Barry White's "I'm Gonna Love You a Little More"—really captivates. Rice's voice, a rich tenor-baritone, overpowers some of the tracks and seems out of place on the hip-hop selections. The grandiose ballad "Come a Little Closer" and the uptempo "Who's Pleasin' You" are not time capsule material but are less mundane than the others. Rice also contributes some keyboards, and Mark Anthony (the Elements) adds some backing vocals. *—Andrew Hamilton*

The Tony Rich Project

Vocals / Contemporary R&B, Urban
Contemporary R&B singer/songwriter Tony Rich first attracted attention as a staff writer at LaFace Records, where he authored hits for acts including Boyz II Men, Johnny Gill, TLC, and Toni Braxton. As the Tony Rich Project, he debuted in 1995 with *Words*, writing, performing, and producing every note of the LP himself; after scoring the Grammy-nominated hits "Like a Woman" and "Nobody Knows," he began work on his sophomore LP, 1998's *Birdseye*. *—Jason Ankeny*

● **Words** / Sep. 26, 1995 / LaFace ♦♦♦♦
Tony Rich's debut album didn't quite fit in with the rigid format of '90s urban R&B. Instead of relying on hip-hop as his foundation, Rich takes elements from soul, blues, pop, and rock, creating a personal brand of new jack R&B. Like Prince, he synthesizes these elements into a distinctive whole. Unlike Prince, his influences are more apparent on the surface, but perhaps that should be expected from a debut. Like many first records, the songs aren't always first-rate, but the best tracks on *Words* stand head and shoulders above much of Rich's competition. What makes *Words* work is Tony Rich's audacity and his talent—he ties together disparate influences with his melodic, soulful songwriting, forming a fresh sound that breathes new life into '90s urban R&B. *—Stephen Thomas Erlewine*

Birdseye / Aug. 11, 1998 / LaFace ♦♦♦♦
Tony Rich made quite a splash with his debut album, *Words*. Like his peers D'Angelo and Maxwell, Rich decided to buck slick contemporary conventions in urban R&B, adhering to the sophisticated styles pioneered by Stevie Wonder, Smokey Robinson and Marvin Gaye. Not only was *Words* a welcome change of pace in a genre that had become too predictable, but it revealed a truly gifted singer-songwriter. Rich's second album, *Birdseye*, proves that the first was no fluke. Branching out from his stylish acoustic love ballads, Rich expands his musical vocabulary by touching on lite-funk, reggae flourishes, pop and soul. Nevertheless, *Birdseye* remains a remarkably romantic record, one of the rare albums whose seduction feels genuine, not prepackaged. It's not only Rich's smooth, soulful voice—it's a combination of his singing, his clean, inviting arrangements, skilled musicianship (he plays every instrument, apart from some guest guitar solos from Eric Clapton) and sturdy, memorable songwriting that makes *Birdseye* such a delight. *—Leo Stanley*

Lionel Richie

b. Jun. 20, 1949, Tuskegee, AL
Vocals, Keyboards / Soft Rock, Adult Contemporary, Urban, Quiet Storm
After leaving the Commodores, Lionel Richie became one of the most successful male solo artists of the '80s, arguably eclipsed during his 1981-1987 heyday only by Michael Jackson and Prince. Richie dominated the pop charts during that period with an incredible run of 13 consecutive Top Ten hits, five of them number ones. As his popularity skyrocketed, Richie moved farther away from his R&B origins and concentrated more on adult contemporary balladry, which had been one of his strengths even as part of the Commodores. After 1987, Richie fell silent, taking an extended break from recording and touring before beginning a comeback toward the tail end of the '90s.

Lionel Brockman Richie Jr. was born on June 20, 1949 in Tuskegee, AL, and grew up on the campus of the Tuskegee Institute, where most of his family had worked for two generations prior. While attending college there, Richie joined the Commodores, who went on to become the most successful act on the Motown label during the latter half of the '70s. Richie served as a saxophonist, sometime vocalist, and songwriter, penning ballads like "Easy," "Three Times a Lady," and "Still" (the latter two became the group's only number-one pop hits). Although the Commodores maintained a democratic band structure through most of their chart run, things began to change when the '70s became the '80s. In 1980, Richie wrote and produced country-pop singer Kenny Rogers' across-the-board number-one smash "Lady," and the following year, Richie's duet with Diana Ross, "Endless Love" (recorded for the Brooke Shields film of the same title), became the most successful single in Motown history, topping the charts for a stunning nine weeks. With the media's attention now focused exclusively on Richie, tensions within the Commodores began to mount, and before the end of 1981, Richie decided to embark on a solo career. Richie immediately set about recording his solo debut for Motown. Titled simply *Lionel Richie*, the album was released in late 1982 and was an immediate smash, reaching number-three on the pop charts on its way to sales of over four-million copies. It spun off three Top Five pop hits, including the first single "Truly," which became Richie's first solo number one. If *Lionel Richie* made its creator a star, the follow-up *Can't Slow Down* made him a superstar. Boasting five Top Ten singles, including the number ones "All Night Long (All Night)" and "Hello," *Can't Slow Down* hit number one, eventually sold over ten-million copies, and won the 1984 Grammy for Album of the Year. Such was Richie's stature that he was invited to perform at the closing ceremonies of the 1984 Olympics in Los Angeles, a spectacular stage event that was broadcast worldwide.

In 1985, Richie put his superstar status to work for a greater good, joining Michael Jackson in co-writing the USA for Africa charity single "We Are the World"; the all-star recording helped raise millions of dollars for famine relief. By the end of the year, he was on top of the charts again with "Say You, Say Me," a ballad recorded for the film *White Nights* but not included on the soundtrack album. The song was slated to be the title track on Richie's upcoming album, but delays in the recording process prevented the record from being released until August 1986, by which time the title was changed to *Dancing on the Ceiling* (in order to promote Richie's next single release). Three more Top Tens followed "Say You, Say Me," as did "Se La," which became the first of Richie's solo singles not to reach the pop Top Ten. Overall, *Dancing on the Ceiling* didn't match the success of *Can't Slow Down*, but it still sold an impressive four-million copies, although Richie's reputation for sentimental ballads was beginning to incur a backlash in some quarters.

Richie's nine-year streak of writing at least one number one single (a feat matched only by Irving Berlin) came to an end in 1987. As a matter of fact, Richie all but disappeared from the music business, simply choosing to take some time off after nearly two decades of recording and performing (or, perhaps, quitting while he was ahead). His silence was broken only in 1992, when Motown released a compilation titled *Back to Front*; in addition to some of his solo hits and a few Commodores tracks, *Back to Front* also featured three new songs, including the number-one R&B hit "Do It to Me" (which wasn't as successful on the pop charts).

Richie wasn't bitten by the recording bug again until 1996, by which time he'd endured his share of personal loss: his father had passed away, and his marriage to wife Brenda—the muse behind some of his most successful ballads—had fallen apart. In approaching his comeback, Richie attempted to update his sound to reflect a decade's worth of developments in urban R&B. The result, *Louder Than Words*, was a moderate success, reaching the Top 30 and going gold. However, it didn't produce any major hit singles, and Richie's nods to new jack swing and hip-hop were criticized as awkward. 1998's *Time* found Richie in a more familiar element, relying on his signature sound with only slight musical updates. However, the album flopped, spending only a few weeks in the lower reaches of the charts. Richie's next album, *Renaissance*, was released to a favorable reception in Europe in late 2000; it was issued in the U.S. in early 2001. *—Steve Huey*

Lionel Richie / 1982 / Motown ♦♦♦♦♦
Lionel Richie was perhaps the dominant songwriter and performer of the early '80s. His overwhelmingly sentimental love tunes were massive crossover hits, and he turned awkwardness into an art form. This was his first big album, and it peaked at number three on the pop album chart, eventually selling over four-million copies and staying on the charts for 140 weeks. *—Ron Wynn*

● **Can't Slow Down** / 1983 / Motown ♦♦♦♦♦
The Lionel Richie gravy train was in full throttle on this second big hit album, which eventually sold over eight-million copies. Richie earned the 1984 Grammy for Album of the Year, and such tunes as "Hello," "Running With the Night," "Stuck on You" and "Love Will Find a Way" were all over the R&B, pop, and even country airwaves. *—Ron Wynn*

Dancing on the Ceiling / 1986 / Motown ♦♦♦♦♦

Lionel Richie had a slump of sorts after the incredible success of *Can't Slow Down.* This record, which came some three years later, only sold four million instead of eight-million copies, stayed atop the pop album charts for only one month instead of two, and only had a few pop hits in "Love Will Conquer All," "Say You, Say Me," "Se La" and "Deep River Woman." *—Ron Wynn*

Back to Front / May 5, 1992 / Motown ♦♦♦♦

On his own and as part of the Commodores, by 1992 Lionel Richie amassed more than enough singles for a greatest-hits collection. Unfortunately, this is one of those compilations that, good intentions aside, falls so flat there's not much point in buying it. By trying to cover his solo material, while touching base with his Commodores fans, and adding some new cuts, no part of his career is well represented. For the record, *Back to Front* lacks "Oh No," "Lady You Bring Me Up," "Ballerina Girl," "You Are," "My Love," "Stuck on You," "Love Will Conquer All," "Se La," and "Dancing on the Ceiling," all Top 40 hits. If Motown had concentrated solely on solo Richie, with another collection of Commodores hits, this could have been a solid, career-topping CD. As it is, it's strong, but hearing such gems as "Still," "Truly," "Say You, Say Me," and "Running With the Night" makes you long to hear the cuts that aren't here. Of the three new songs, "Do It to Me" and "My Destiny" are classic, smooth Richie, but "Love, Oh Love" is very schmaltzy. If you're a casual Lionel Richie fan, this might suffice, but for anyone who truly enjoys pop music, this collection is not worth your money. *—Bryan Buss*

Louder Than Words / Apr. 1996 / Mercury ♦♦♦

After the greatest hits collection *Back to Front* disappeared without a trace in 1992, Lionel Richie spent four years making *Louder Than Words,* his first album for Mercury Records. Although there are some slight attempts to incorporate new jack and hip-hop influences into Richie's sound, *Louder Than Words* relies on his trademark balladeering, which remains his forte. All of the weak moments on *Louder than Words* are ill-advised forays into rap—to put it bluntly, he can rap about as well as Snoop Doggy Dogg can sing. Although the ballads aren't as strong as his late-'70s and early-'80s standards, they are nevertheless pleasant, which makes the record a worthwhile purchase for fans. *—Stephen Thomas Erlewine*

Time / Jun. 23, 1998 / Mercury ♦♦♦

Louder Than Words was the official comeback, the long-awaited return to recording from Lionel Richie, one of the most successful pop stars of the '80s. Perhaps it was inevitable that returning to recording would be difficult—after all, it had been ten years since he had released an album of original material—but *Louder Than Words* turned out to be a bigger disappointment than anyone expected, failing to deliver either musically or commercially. Its failure helped clear the decks for *Time,* Richie's true musical comeback. *Time* doesn't quite match the heights of *Lionel Richie* or *Can't Slow Down,* but it successfully updates his familiar concoction of sweet, seductive ballads and light funk for the late '90s. Whenever he incorporates light hip-hop rhythms here, it sounds less forced, and the dance numbers are often infectious. Similarly, the ballads have strong (albeit sappy) hooks that make them memorable. Don't take Richie's belated version of "Lady," the hit he gave Kenny Rogers, as a bad sign—*Time* is the most satisfying effort he has released in quite some time. *—Stephen Thomas Erlewine*

Renaissance / Mar. 20, 2001 / Island ♦♦

Tommy Ridgley

b. Oct. 30, 1925, New Orleans, LA, **d.** Aug. 11, 1999

Vocals, Piano / New Orleans R&B, Modern Electric Blues, R&B

Tommy Ridgley was on the Crescent City R&B scene when it first caught fire, and he remained a proud part of that same scene until his death in 1999. That was a lot of years behind a microphone, but Ridgley never sounded the slightest bit tired; his 1995 Black Top album *Since the Blues Began* rated as one of his liveliest outings. Ridgley cut his debut sides back in 1949 for Imperial under Dave Bartholomew's direction. His "Shrewsbury Blues" and "Boogie Woogie Mama" failed to break outside of his hometown, though. Sessions for Decca in 1950 and Imperial in 1952 (where he waxed the wild "Looped") preceded four 1953-1955 sessions for Atlantic that included a blistering instrumental, "Jam Up," that sported no actual Ridgley involvement but sold relatively well under his name (incomparable tenor saxist Lee Allen was prominent).

New York's Herald Records was Ridgley's home during the late '50s. The consistently solid singer waxed "When I Meet My Girl" for the firm in 1957, encoring with a catchy "Baby Do Little." From there, it was on to his hometown-based Ric logo, where he laid down the stunning stroll-tempoed "Let's Try and Talk It Over" and a bluesy "Should I Ever Love Again" in 1960. He recorded intermittently after leaving Ric in 1963, waxing a soulful "I'm Not the Same Person" in 1969 for Ronn. Ridgley always remained a hometown favorite even when recording opportunities proved scarce. Happily, *Since the Blues Began* ranked with 1995's best albums, Ridgley sounding entirely contemporary but retaining his defining Crescent City R&B edge. Not long after the appearance of 1999's *How Long,* Ridgley passed away, on August 11th of that year. *—Bill Dahl*

● **The New Orleans King of the Stroll** / 1988 / Rounder ♦♦♦♦♦

Tommy Ridgley was a solid R&B vocalist who was quite successful with novelty tunes and silly songs, but was also a good romantic balladeer. This 15-track collection mostly covers Ridgley material from 1960 to 1964 for the Ric label, and ranges from laments like "Please Hurry Home" and "I Love You Yes I Do" to such comic material and dance-based numbers as "Double Eyed Whammy" and "The Girl From Kooka Monga." Ridgley wasn't as booming or dynamic as some other Crescent City vocalists, but made several nice period pieces and soul tunes, several of which are included on this set. *—Ron Wynn*

She Turns Me On / 1992 / Modern Blues ♦♦♦

Competent contemporary effort that proved Ridgley's voice was still in excellent shape, albeit a less engaging outing overall than his subsequent Black Top release. *—Bill Dahl*

The Herald Recordings / Nov. 30, 1992 / Collectables ♦♦♦♦

There's some very nice late-'50s New Orleans R&B recommending this 17-track collection, along with a few superfluous instrumental backing tracks that could have safely been jettisoned altogether. Ridgley's stint at Herald included the sizzling "When I Meet My Girl," "Baby Do Little," and several more impressive rocking efforts, backed by the esteemed crew at Cosimo's Crescent City studio—saxist Lee Allen, etc. *—Bill Dahl*

Since the Blues Began / 1995 / Black Top ♦♦♦♦

The veteran New Orleans singer remains a contemporary force to be reckoned with. Guitarist Snooks Eaglin, bassist George Porter Jr., and saxist Kaz Kazanoff help Ridgley out on what's easily his finest contemporary release. There are a handful of remakes of his earlier triumphs, but for the most part, he is commendably living in the present, incorporating funk-tinged rhythms into his delectable musical gumbo. *—Bill Dahl*

Riff

f. Paterson, NJ

Group / New Jack Swing, Urban, Dance-Pop

Riff is among several '90s vocal ensembles greatly influenced by classic doo wop and R&B. This New Jersey pop/R&B quintet formed as the Playboys while still in high school, gaining prominence when they sung in *Lean on Me.* Changing their name to Riff, Kenny Kelly, Anthony Fuller, Dwayne Jones, Steven Capers, and Michael Best signed with SBK and released a self-titled debut. After appearances on *The Arsenio Hall Show, The Tonight Show,* and *Soul Train,* the band toured with LL Cool J and Vanilla Ice and then released *To Whom It May Concern.* *—John Bush*

● **Riff** / 1991 / SBK ♦♦♦

Riff came along just before vocal groups began to explode again. They were hurt by erratic material and the fact that they were on a label which had little experience promoting urban contemporary and R&B groups (SBK). This wasn't a bad album, and their vocals and harmonies were often superb, but it died on the vine. Now, this kind of thing dominates the R&B charts, and Riff displayed as much ability on this release as Shai, Boyz II Men, H-Town, Intro, or any number of other hot vocal ensembles. *—Ron Wynn*

To Whom It May Concern / 1993 / ERG ♦♦

Riff isn't quite sure of its direction; some tracks are done in the outdated new jack swing style, complete with tired raps. Others include a barrage of drum tracks and synthesized backbeats in which their vocals must compete for attention with the busy production underneath. Their best tunes are those where their often-impressive harmonies and vocals are allowed to carry the day unencumbered by studio antics. Riff can sing with any vocal ensemble; hopefully, a future album will be fully devoted to that element. *—Ron Wynn*

The Righteous Brothers

f. 1962, California

Group / Blue-Eyed Soul, Brill Building Pop, Pop

They weren't brothers, but Bill Medley and Bobby Hatfield (both born in 1941) were most definitely righteous, defining (and perhaps even inspiring) the term "blue-eyed soul" in the mid-'60s. The white Southern California duo were an established journeyman doo wop/R&B act before an association with Phil Spector produced one of the most memorable hits of the 1960s, "You've Lost That Lovin' Feelin'." The collaboration soon fell apart, though, and while the singers had some other excellent hit singles in a similar style, they proved unable to sustain their momentum after just a year or two at the top.

When Medley and Hatfield combined forces in 1962, they emerged from regional groups the Paramours and the Variations; in fact, they kept the Paramours billing for their first single. By 1963, they were calling themselves the Righteous Brothers, Medley taking the low parts with his smoky baritone, Hatfield taking the higher tenor and falsetto lines. For the next couple of years they did quite a few energetic R&B tunes on the Moonglow label that bore similarity to the gospel/soul/rock style of Ray Charles, copping their greatest success with "Little Latin Lupe Lu," which became a garage-band favorite covered by Mitch Ryder, the Kingsmen, and others.

Even on the Moonglow recordings, Bill Medley acted as producer and principal songwriter, but the duo wouldn't break out nationally until they put themselves at the services of Phil Spector. Spector gave the Wall of Sound treatment to "You've Lost That Lovin' Feelin'," a grandiose ballad penned by himself, Barry Mann, and Cynthia Weil. At nearly four minutes, the song was pushing the limits of what could be played on radio in the mid-'60s, and some listeners thought they were hearing a 45 single played at 33 rpm due to Medley's low, blurry lead vocal. No matter; the song had a power that couldn't be denied, and went all the way to number one.

The Righteous Brothers had three more big hits in 1965 on Spector's Philles label ("Just Once in My Life," "Unchained Melody," and "Ebb Tide"), all employing similar dense orchestral arrangements and swelling vocal crescendos. Yet the Righteous Brothers-Spector partnership wasn't a smooth one, and by 1966 the duo had left Philles for a lucrative deal with Verve. Medley, already an experienced hand in the producer's booth, reclaimed the producer's chair, and the Righteous Brothers had another number-one hit with their first Verve outing, "(You're My) Soul and Inspiration." Its success must have been a particularly bitter blow for Spector, given that Medley successfully emulated the Wall of Sound orchestral ambience of the Righteous Brothers' Philles singles down to the smallest detail, even employing the same Mann-Weil writing team that had contributed to "You've Lost That Lovin' Feelin'." It's a bit of a mystery as to why the Righteous Brothers never came close to duplicating that success during the rest of their tenure at Verve. But they would only have a couple of other Top 40 hits in the 1960s ("He" and "Go Ahead and Cry," both in 1966), even with the aid of occasional compositions by the formidable Goffin-King team. In 1968 Medley left for a solo career; Hatfield, the less talented of the pair (at least from a songwriting and production standpoint), kept the Righteous Brothers going with Jimmy Walker (who had been in the Knickerbockers).

Medley had a couple of small hits in the late '60s as a solo act, but unsurprisingly neither "brother" was worth half as much on their own as they were together. In 1974 they reunited and had a number three hit with "Rock and Roll Heaven," a tribute to dead rock stars that some found tacky. A couple of smaller hits followed before Medley retired from performing for five years in 1976; they've toured the oldies circuit off and on in the 1980s and 1990s. *—Richie Unterberger*

★ **Anthology 1962–1974** / Jul. 1989 / Rhino ♦♦♦♦♦
For some listeners, a double-disc of the Righteous Brothers might seem like overkill, but *Anthology 1962-1974* should silence most skeptics. Over the course of the two discs, it becomes clear that the duo were the finest blue-eyed soul singers of their era. Not only do the hits ("Little Latin Lupe Lu," "You've Lost That Lovin' Feelin'," "Unchained Melody," "Ebb Tide," "(You're My) Soul and Inspiration," "Rock and Roll Heaven") retain their power, there are numerous forgotten gems, like the harder-rocking "Justine" and an excellent version of "This Little Girl of Mine." For listeners who want to dig a little deeper into the Righteous Brothers' music than the hits, they'll be generously rewarded by *Anthology*. *—Stephen Thomas Erlewine*

● **The Very Best of the Righteous Brothers: Unchained Melody** / 1990 / Polydor ♦♦♦♦♦
At 12 tracks, this is considerably lighter than the ambitious double-disc Rhino *Anthology*, and it doesn't cover nearly as much ground (in other words, no "Rock & Roll Heaven" or any other '70s material is here). However, for those listeners that want a straight-up dose of the biggest Righteous Brothers hits, this offers the peaks of their peak, highlighted, naturally, by "You've Lost That Lovin' Feelin'," "Unchained Melody," "(You're My) Soul and Inspiration" and "Little Latin Lupe Lu." *—Stephen Thomas Erlewine*

The Best of the Righteous Brothers, Vol. 2 / 1991 / Curb ♦♦♦
Since *Vol. 1* contained most the duo's biggest hits, the ten-track, budget-priced *Best of Righteous Brothers, Vol. 2* contains leftovers. Only "Rock and Roll Heaven"—which is included in its original version, as well as a 1992 remake—is an oldies staple, while "Give It to the People" and "Dream On" were minor hits. The remainder of the collection is devoted either to forgotten songs or newly recorded covers. Although this isn't bad for a budget-priced disc, there are better collections available, offering more songs and better sound for not much more money. *—Stephen Thomas Erlewine*

The Moonglow Years / 1991 / Polydor ♦♦♦♦
For most listeners, the history of the Righteous Brothers begins in 1964 with the release of "You've Lost That Lovin' Feelin'" and their accompanying move into the more elaborate arrangements favored by Phil Spector (which they later adapted). In point of fact, Bill Medley & Bobby Hatfield had been performing since the start of the 1960s in a variety of group settings, and had been cutting (and charting) singles for two years as the Righteous Brothers before their link with Spector. This CD assembles 28 sides that they recorded for the Moonglow label between late 1962 and mid-1964, and there's not a bad track in the bunch. It also doesn't sound a lot like their subsequent records for Spector's Philles label or the work that followed their split with the producer; there's a lot less polish to the musicianship and the arrangements and it's all played lean and fast, with guitar, bass, and drum accompaniment, and ranges freely between blues, gospel, rock & roll, and R&B, the two singers pulling out all of the stops in terms of putting over the songs. Amid the excellent covers of standards such as "My Prayer," "Let the Good Times Roll," "Georgia on My Mind" (naturally), and a handful of Willie Dixon- & Jimmy Reed-authored classics are a surprisingly large number of originals which hold up well. The producers utilized excellent sources, including undubbed studio masters and original session tapes, and the resulting sound was state of the art at the time and remains impressive even a decade after the release of this CD. *—Bruce Eder*

Cheryl Pepsii Riley

b. Brooklyn, NY
Vocals / Quiet Storm, Urban, Dance-Pop
Cheryl Pepsii Riley topped the R&B charts with the heart-stirring ballad "Thanks for My Child," a tune that connected with and seemed to speak for single mothers the world over. Because of the poignant lyrics, some believed that Riley wrote the song. Actually, "Thanks for My Child" was written by Full Force, the six-man performing/songwriting/production team from East Flatbush/Brooklyn, NY, who had a long run of hits for themselves, Lisa Lisa & Cult Jam, UTFO, Jasmine Guy, Lala, Samantha Fox, and the Weather Girls. Though Riley's interpretation was no doubt enhanced by her ten years as a nurse who worked with handicapped children. The genesis of "Thanks for My Child" began with Full Force member Bowlegged Lou's experience with the complications of his wife's first pregnancy.

As pivotal as "Thanks for My Child" was for the singer's career, it wasn't the first song Lou offered to her. She refused his offer to record "I Wonder If I Take You Home" because she didn't want to spread herself too thin, but after it became a million-selling hit for Lisa Lisa & Cult Jam in 1985, she thought she'd missed her big break. Then Lou offered her "Thanks for My Child." Riley still had her nurse's job when it single went to number one during fall 1988.

The title track single to her debut LP *Me, Myself & I* made it to number-18 R&B in early 1989. Another single, "Every Little Thing About You," peaked at number-55 R&B in later that year. Her second LP *Chapters* was issued and yielded the singles "How Can You Hurt the One You Love" and a cover of Aretha Franklin's 1968 hit "Ain't No Way" (with backing vocals by another FF-produced act, Ex-Girlfriend). Her third album *All That!* was released by Reprise, and featured the singles "Gimme" and "Guess I'm in Love." During the '90s, Riley appeared in nationally touring gospel plays. *—Ed Hogan*

Me, Myself & I / 1988 / Columbia ♦♦♦
Onetime session vocalist Cheryl Pepsii Riley generated lots of discussion with the electrifying single "Thanks for My Child." It singlehandedly elevated her debut album, which was a decent Full Force production adequately showcasing her sizzling voice, even if it didn't always feature standout material. But the single, which some interpreted as an endorsement of unwed mothers, was so declarative in its vocal and compelling in its theme that many overlooked the other flaws on the album. *—Ron Wynn*

Chapters / 1991 / Columbia ♦♦♦♦
Riley's second album was largely a disappointment. She actually sang in even more emphatic fashion than on her debut, but was handicapped by some woeful compositions. The production and arrangements were better than average, and Riley often sounded great, but couldn't turn any of the mediocre material into hits. *—Ron Wynn*

All That! / 1993 / Reprise ♦♦♦

● **Thanks for My Child** / Mar. 23, 1999 / Collectables ♦♦♦♦
A best-of compilation that contains Cheryl Pepsii Riley's defining "Thanks for My Child," which aced the R&B chart in 1988. An '80s theme song if there ever was one, it's hard imagining a '60s or '70s artist hitting with a song about single parenting. Full Force wrote and produced Cheryl's material and at times concocted some good hip-hop with compelling hooks and rhythms to contrast the drama—ballads that were her forte. While not as dynamic or cagey as some female vocalists, she works certain songs right into your inners and imprints them into your memory bank forever. Picks include the title track, "Every Little Thing About You," "Sisters" (a duet with Lisa, Lisa), "Me, Myself and I," "How Can You Hurt the One You Love," and one she co-wrote with Full Force, "(So Glad) This Love Affair Is Over." The tight but sparse productions makes you wonder how Pepsi would fare with stellar session musicians in a studio loaded with the works, and Quincy Jones or Babyface in the production booth. *—Andrew Hamilton*

Teddy Riley

b. Oct. 8, 1967, Harlem, New York City, NY
Producer, Vocals / New Jack Swing, Hip-Hop, Club/Dance, Urban, Dance-Pop
The acknowledged "King of New Jack Swing," producer/songwriter Teddy Riley's enviable list of platinum-laced credits include Guy, the Winans, Joe (the Riley-produced "Stutter" topped both the R&B/pop charts in early 2001), Johnny Kemp, Blackstreet, Keith Sweat, Michael Jackson, Mary J. Blige, Hi-Five, and Al B. Sure among many others.

Born in Harlem, Riley grew up in the St. Nicholas projects. He began playing drums at three years old. At five, Riley picked up the guitar and the trumpet. When he turned eight, he began playing piano for the Little Flower Baptist Church. Later, he began playing in bands around New York. After meeting Kool & the Gang member Royal Bayyan, Riley was introduced to the arts of record production and songwriting. Hooking up with Gene Griffin in the mid '80s, Riley's many talents resulted in platinum hits for Guy—the singing trio that included Riley and brothers Aaron Hall and Damion Hall. One of Riley's early production was Deja's 1988 Virgin LP, *We Belong Together*. In the early '90s, Guy disbanded and Riley formed Blackstreet with Chauncey Hannibal, Dave Hollister, and Levi Little. The self-titled debut album went platinum. Their second album, *Another Level*, followed suite and spawned the million-seller "No Diggity." Tiring of the rigors of big city life, Riley moved to Virginia, opening his state-of-the art Future Recording Studios in the mid-'90s. *—Ed Hogan*

The Rimshots

Group / Disco, Deep Funk, Funk
The Rimshots were the house band at Joe & Sylvia Robinson's All Platinum/Stang label family during the '70s, and also released their own records, mostly on the latter imprint. Led by guitarists and sometime composers and producers Walter Morris and Tommy Keith, their ranks also included drummer Clarence Oliver, bassist Jonathan Williams, and keyboardist Bernadette Randle. Their highest-profile backup appearances were with label flagship artists the Moments, whose Harry Ray & Al Goodman sometimes penned material for them. The Rimshots began releasing their own singles in 1972, when their brand of funk was harder than the disco-flavored sound they would later adopt. Early songs like "Soul Train, Pts. 1 & 2" and "Save That Thing" would go on to become rare collector's items, as would their 1972 debut LP *Soul Train*.

Over the next couple of years, the Rimshots continued to release high-quality, non-LP singles—"Dance Girl," "Harvey Wallbanger," "Who's Got the Monster"—that cemented their future standing as a reliable source for hip-hop samples. By 1975, singles like "Do What You Feel, Pt. 1" and "(7-6-5-4-3-2-1) Blow Your Whistle" were beginning to move the Rimshots into smoother disco territory, and 1976's "Super Disco" and "We've Got You Singing" solidified the transition. 1976 also saw the release of the Rimshots' second album, *Down to Earth*, and the group contributed two tracks to the lesser-known blaxploitation soundtrack *Patty*. In addition to their work as the Stang house band, the Rimshots backed Etta James on her funky blues outing *Etta Is Betta Than Evah*. The 2000 Sequel compilation *7-6-5-4-3-2-1 (Blow Your Whistle)* reissued both *Soul Train* and *Down to Earth*, plus additional non-album material. *—Steve Huey*

Soul Train / 1972 / Sequel ♦♦♦♦

Down to Earth / 1976 / Stang ♦♦♦

● **7-6-5-4-3-2-1 (Blow Your Whistle)** / 2000 / Sequel ♦♦♦♦

Minnie Riperton

b. Nov. 8, 1947, Chicago, IL, **d.** Jul. 12, 1979, Los Angeles, CA
Vocals / Smooth Soul, Chicago Soul, Pop-Soul, Soul, Uptown Soul
The tragic 1979 death of 31-year-old Minnie Riperton silenced one of soul music's most unique and unforgettable voices—blessed with an angelic five-octave vocal range, she scored her greatest commercial success with the chart-topping pop ballad "Lovin' You." Riperton was born in Chicago on November 8, 1947; as a youth she studied music, drama, and dance at the city's Lincoln Center and later contemplated a career in opera. Her pop career began in 1961 when she joined the local girl group called the Gems, signing to the famed Chess label to release a handful of singles as well as lend backing vocals to acts

including Fontella Bass, the Dells, and Etta James. After graduating high school, Riperton went to work at Chess as a receptionist; following the Gems' dissolution, she also signed with the label as a solo act, releasing a single, "Lonely Girl," under the alias Andrea Davis. In 1968, Riperton was installed as the lead vocalist of the psychedelic soul band the Rotary Connection, which debuted that year with a self-titled LP on Cadet Concepts; the singles "Amen" and "Lady Jane" found a home on underground FM radio, but the group failed to make much of an impression on mainstream outlets. While still a member of the Connection, Riperton mounted a solo career; teaming with producer/arranger Charles Stepney and her husband/composer Richard Rudolph, she issued her brilliant debut, *Come to My Garden*, in 1970, but again commercial success eluded her grasp. After the Rotary Connection dissolved in the wake of 1971's *Hey Love*, she and Rudolph took a two-year sabbatical in Florida before relocating to Los Angeles, where she sang on Stevie Wonder's *Fulfillingness' First Finale* and toured as a member of his backing unit Wonderlove.

Wonder agreed to co-produce Riperton's 1974 album *Perfect Angel*, which contained the international blockbuster "Lovin' You"; the record made her a household name, although subsequent LPs like 1975's *Adventures in Paradise* and 1977's *Stay in Love* failed to repeat its success. By this time, however, commercial woes were the least of Riperton's concerns—diagnosed with breast cancer, she underwent a mastectomy in 1976, later becoming a spokesperson for the American Cancer Society and earning a Society Courage Award from then-President Jimmy Carter. Riperton continued performing despite her declining condition, with 1979's *Minnie* the final record completed during her lifetime—she died in L.A. on July 12 of that year. Unreleased vocal tracks with new instrumental backing comprised 1980's posthumous collection *Love Lives Forever*. *—Jason Ankeny*

Come to My Garden / 1969 / GRT ✦✦✦✦✦

Minnie Riperton's solo debut is in many respects her finest hour—devoid of the overly syrupy production that hampers her later work, *Come to My Garden* instead couches her miraculous voice in the elegant arrangements of the great Charles Stepney, striking a perfect balance between romantic melodrama and sensual nuance. Call Stepney's singular approach "chamber soul"—the nimble melodies and insistent grooves swell with orchestral flourishes, while the jazz-inspired rhythms (courtesy of Ramsey Lewis' group) at times evoke Van Morrison's masterpiece *Astral Weeks*. Stepney creates the ideal backdrop for Riperton's soaring vocals, which reveal a subtlety and restraint absent from the glass-shattering bombast of her subsequent performances—the opening "Les Fleurs" (covered decades later by 4Hero) crystallizes the entire record, embracing both intimacy and majesty to haunting effect. *—Jason Ankeny*

Perfect Angel / 1974 / Capitol ✦✦✦✦✦

This is the best Minnie Riperton album, and still the closest she came to stardom. Stevie Wonder chipped in on drums, keyboards, and other instruments, and also wrote several tracks. "Reasons" was her finest uptempo tune, while the title track was a wonderful change-of-pace number. She also got her biggest hit, "Lovin' You," which became a signature tune. *—Ron Wynn*

Adventures in Paradise / 1975 / Epic ✦✦✦

While the follow-up album to *Perfect Angel* didn't prove as successful, it was a good effort. She tried a more mixed crop of songs, doing love ballads, uptempo funk and dance, and even some light pop. Nothing got her back on the charts, but it was still an effective release. Riperton was nearly injured during the photo shoot for the cover when the lion pictured on the album attacked her. Fortunately, she escaped serious injury. *—Ron Wynn*

Stay in Love / 1977 / Epic ✦✦✦

Riperton's final release for Epic had its problems, but still included some solid singles, even though only one charted and it didn't go very far. Riperton had begun to channel her powerful voice and didn't rely so much on the octave-leaping screams and effects. Sadly, she now knew she was suffering from cancer and was working diligently for the American Cancer Society, as well as promoting the album and working on her career. *—Ron Wynn*

Minnie / 1979 / Capitol ✦✦✦

This album was released in the year in which the supreme songstress passed (1979). However, she bestowed upon the listener her gift of voice with a collection of fine songs. The first release was the nostalgic number "Memory Lane." With its sensuous-flowing rhythm, melodious string and horn arrangement, Minnie Riperton strides into the lyric with her silky delivery. The single peaked at number 16 on the *Billboard* R&B charts after a 22 week run. The follow-up single was the vivacious "Lover and Friend." Stevie Wonder's verbal intro bow to a spirited horn introduction. Seasoned with a muted rumbling bassline, a soft texture and supported by a majestic horn arrangement, Minnie Riperton's velvety tone takes charge. She graciously embraces the lyric with style. The single peaked at number 20 after 13 weeks. These were the only two songs to chart from this album, and unfortunately they were more worthy of a better ranking. Nonetheless, they remain staples of R&B radio. It must also be noted that while Minnie Riperton's voice was as silky as the incomparable Billie Holliday's, she had the innate ability to controllably explode into higher octaves without forsaking the beauty of her voice. This admirable quality elevates her to a class of her own. *—Craig Lytle*

Capitol Gold: The Best of Minnie Riperton / Jun. 21, 1993 / Capitol ✦✦✦✦✦

Until 1999's *Free Soul* (Capitol) and 2001's exhaustive but more excellent overall *Petals* (The Right Stuff) came along, *Capitol Gold* offered the best summation of this true original's horribly undervalued solo career. As with *Free Soul, Capitol Gold* leaves a significant gap by excluding the best moments from Minnie Riperton's debut (*Come to My Garden*), an album that was released on GTR. This issue would be rectified by The Right Stuff, a subsidiary of Capitol, for *Petals*. Still, *Capitol Gold* makes for a fine substitute introduction to Riperton; it includes all of her significant singles and a good survey of album tracks that didn't receive the notice they deserved when they were originally released. *—Andy Kellman*

Her Chess Years (50th Anniversary Collection) / Nov. 4, 1997 / Chess ✦✦✦✦

While this compilation is credited to Minnie Riperton, none of the 16 tracks was actually released under her name. Indeed, a more apt title might have been *Best of Minnie Riperton and the Rotary Connection*, as 13 of the songs are Rotary Connection cuts on which she sang lead. The other three date from before the Rotary Connection days, with a couple of tracks by the Gems (a mid-'60s girl group) that bear Riperton's lead vocals, as well as the 1966 single "Lonely Girl," which is actually Riperton solo, but was released under the pseudonym Andrea Davis. The pre-Rotary Connection numbers are fair but unremarkable pop-soul, with Minnie unveiling her stratospheric operatic vocals on "Lonely Girl." The Rotary Connection material is taken from five albums recorded by the group in the late '60s and early '70s; there's nothing from their most famous LP, the self-titled 1967 debut, as Riperton sang no leads on that record (it's been reissued on its own by Chess anyway). This stuff is a very mixed bag, including dubious Cream and Hendrix covers, as well as a ghoulish mauling of "Respect." On the other hand, "Magical World" shows their odd psychedelic-soul-as-MGM-musical production style at its best, and "A-Muse" is a surprisingly pretty, acoustic singer-songwriter type ballad, delivered with sensitivity by Riperton. As a whole, this music isn't so much notable for Riperton's vocals (as wide-ranging as they are) as its eccentric genre-mashing, from a rare period in which mainstream pop and soul tried to be self-consciously avant-garde and eclectic without getting too far out. *—Richie Unterberger*

Free Soul: The Classics of Minnie Riperton / Oct. 27, 1999 / Capitol ✦✦✦✦✦

While there is a domestic two-CD package available of the best of the late Minnie Riperton's work that pretty much captures every single and hit, this entry in Capitol Nippon's *Free Soul* series does a better job in some ways on a single disc. While it is unusual for the *Free Soul* series to focus on a single artist, Riperton is rightfully an exception to that rule as she stood—no, towered—over virtually every other artist in her class with the possible exception of Dusty Springfield, who is now, sadly, also gone. The track list here, 19 in all, features more than a fair share of hits such as "Simple Things," "Lovin' You," "The Edge of a Dream," "Could It Be I'm in Love," "Don't Let Anyone Bring You Down," etc. But in addition to these more well-known cuts, this set goes to the albums themselves for tracks that had been overlooked because they either weren't released as singles or ended up as B-sides, such as "Inside My Love," "Take a Trip," "Perfect Angel," "Feelin' That Your Feelin's Right," and many others. What emerges is a well-rounded portrait of Riperton's considerable gifts, not only as a vocalist but as an interpreter and as an artist who controlled her environment in the recording studio. There isn't a thing here that doesn't ring true as hers. There are a good many Riperton collections out there, but this is the first one to adequately gauge the depth and breadth of the artist. *—Thom Jurek*

● **Petals: The Minnie Riperton Collection** / Feb. 13, 2001 / The Right Stuff ✦✦✦✦✦

Although her 1979 death at 31 still reverberates through pop and R&B, *Petals: The Minnie Riperton Collection* is one of the first sets to successfully celebrate the joy, sensuality and wonder inherent in Minnie Riperton's music. This two-CD set has 34 tracks spanning the years 1966-1979. Unlike other compilations this culls work from all of her styles, including the cutesy but derivative R&B/pop she recorded under the name Andrea Davis. The collection also includes tracks from her stint with the often ho-hum, rock/R&B group Rotary Connection. The challenging and baroque songs from Riperton's first album, *Come to My Garden*, are much better. The tracks including the title, "Les Fleur," "Completeness," and "Expecting" are a collaborative effort between Riperton's husband Richard Rudolph and the brilliant Chicago writer/producer Charles Stepney. A few years down the line, she appeared to be an even more confident singer. Tracks like "Take a Little Trip," "Perfect Angel," and "Lovin' You," all from 1974, were all produced by Stevie Wonder in a relaxed and spare style. This set demonstrates other producers like Stewart Levine, Freddie Perren, and Jeremy Lubbock were also inspired to excellence by the style defined by Riperton and Rudolph. The evocative and powerful "Adventures in Paradise," "Inside My Love," and disco-ish "Young, Willing and Able" all have Riperton's sweetness and intelligence prominent in the mix. The later tracks, including the gorgeous "Memory Lane," finds the formula reaching perfection. Her five-and-a-half octave range is on full display here, and *Petals: The Minnie Riperton Collection* assembles a plethora of definitive songs. *—Jason Elias*

Ripple

Group / Disco, Funk

An interracial Michigan soul-funk band, Ripple had an R&B hit in 1973 with "I Don't Know What It Is but It Sure Is Funky," and made several other recordings for the GRC label in the mid-'70s. They were an eclectic hodgepodge of influences circulating in soul music at the time—sometimes they can sound like a more pop-inclined version of Kool & the Gang, other times they sound like a less distinctive variant of Stevie Wonder. Their brand of funk was neither too raw nor too slick, with liberal pop and jazz influences. Those who like just-pre-disco funk will probably enjoy the group, though their talents were not truly impressive. *—Richie Unterberger*

Ripple / 1973 / GRC ✦✦✦

Sons of the Gods / 1977 / Salsoul ✦✦✦

I Don't Know What It Is But It Sure Is Funky / Nov. 30, 1992 / Collectables ✦✦✦✦

● **But It Sure is Funky!** / 1997 / Southbound ✦✦✦✦

This 21-track compilation includes "I Don't Know What It Is But It Sure Is Funky," as well as other 1973-1974 recordings. There are also eleven previously unreleased tracks, some instrumental (the liner notes do not give exact dates for those, although they sound like they originate from the same era). It's nothing special, but it's good, atmospheric mid-level funk/soul that has some pop appeal without sounding too polished. *—Richie Unterberger*

Hector Rivera

b. Jan. 6, 1933, New York, NY

Keyboards, Arranger / Latin Jazz, Soul

Keyboardist, arranger, and composer Rivera was one of the more renowned performers of the long-neglected '60s sub-genre of Latin soul. Like the more famed Pucho & the Latin Soul Brothers, Rivera blended Latin dance-pop with contemporary soul-funk and jazz, although the jazzy elements were more muted in Rivera's mix than they were in Pucho's. Rivera's fame was not strictly limited to New York Latin dance audiences; in 1967, his single "At the Party" actually made the Top 40 of the national R&B charts.

By that time, Rivera had already been playing for over a decade, beginning in the early '50s, when he joined the band of Elmo Garcia as a teenager. Hector Rivera made his recorded debut as a bandleader in 1957 under odd circumstances—when Garcia didn't have enough material prepared for a planned album, Mercury Records asked if Rivera had anything up his sleeve. The keyboardist did, although he intended on saving it for a solo album; Mercury offered to record him as a solo artist, issuing his debut, *Let's Cha Cha Cha*. Still, over the next few years, Rivera would be known mostly as a sideman to bandleaders Joe Cuba and Pacheco, and vocalist Vincento Valdez.

Rivera made his biggest splash as a bandleader with the 1966 album *At the Party*, with a large band featuring several trumpet players and percussionists (as well as Cachao on bass). If this was not as deep as Machito or as accomplished as Pucho & the Latin Soul Brothers, it was still damn spirited party music, with equal foots in cha-cha and soul. Rivera divided his approach between instrumentals and vocals (he employed several singers, but David Coleman is the one heard most often on the *At the Party* album). The success of the title cut of *At the Party* enabled Rivera to cut several more albums; he also continued to write and arrange, and participated in projects for such top Latin performers as Ray Barretto, Machito, and Tito Puente. *—Richie Unterberger*

● **At the Party . . . Plus** / 1966 / Ace ✦✦✦✦✦

The 1966 *At the Party* album is full of good-natured cha-cha/funk grooves, most of them original compositions, including the good-time hit title track and edgier numbers like "I Got My Eye on You" and "Do It to Me." The British CD reissue (retitled *At the Party... Plus*) adds five worthy bonus tracks from the same era. *—Richie Unterberger*

The Rivieras

Group / Doo Wop, Vocal Pop, Pop, R&B

The careers of Englewood, NJ, natives Homer Dunn, Andy Jones, Ronald Allen, and Charles Cook hadn't reached first base when they met manager of a group named the Avons, who christened them the Four Arts because they favored pop songs. After Warren Lanier rediscovered the quartet, he renamed them the El Rivieras, though they remained unrecorded until Jones met William Fix, the manager of the Ames Brothers. Fix arranged an audition with Marvin Cane and George Paxton, the owners of Coed Records, and the El Rivieras were off and running. They dropped the "El," and debuted as the Rivieras with "I Count Every Star," which entered the pop charts at number 73 in 1958.

Good management kept them working, taking them as far west as Chicago. Their biggest hit, "Moonlight Serenade," reached number 47 in 1959. "Our Love" generated no action, but their fourth release, "Since I Made You Cry," dented the pop charts at number 93 in 1960. Four subsequent releases—"Moonlight Cocktails," "My Friend," "Stay in My Heart," and "El Dorado"—went unnoticed. However, "Moonlight Cocktails" along with "Moonlight Serenade" became popular selections on beach-music compilation albums. Coed released two LPs by the group, *My Silent Love* and *Scarlet Hour*, but after the label folded in 1961, the Rivieras soon faded into the moonlight. In 1992, Relic released the compilation *Moonlight Cocktails* on CD. *—Andrew Hamilton*

● **Moonlight Cocktails** / Jul. 20, 1992 / Collectables ✦✦✦

This is a nice anthology covering the Rivieras' singles on Coed, including the title track and "Count Every Star." Never a huge hit group, they were among the many journeyman doo wop ensembles that plugged away in the 1950s, always one step away from scoring a hit but never quite able to move to the next level. *—Ron Wynn*

The Rivileers

f. Queens, NY

Group / Doo Wop

The Rivileers enjoyed a short (less than two years) recording career from 1954 to 1955. They formed in Jamaica Queens, NY, and at one time included actor Lou Gossett who claims he sung with them on "A Thousand Eyes." Led by Eugene Pearson, the Rivileers most stable lineup consisted of neighborhood and high school buds: Pearson, Milton Edwards, Earl Lennard, Herb Crosby, and Alphonso Delaney. They cut a demo and left it as a resume in a record shop. Sol Rabinowitz (a salesman for a record distributor) heard the multi-song demo and decided to venture into the recording business. Pearson had previously sung with the Embers and co-wrote "Paradise Hill" for them in 1953, a year before the Rivileers first single hit the streets.

Rabinowitz redid the songs with jazz musicians giving the tracks an upscale sound, but after futile attempts at leasing the masters (he cut four), Rabinowitz decided to go it on his own and formed Baton Records. The label's first single (1954) "A Thousand Stars" (written by Pearson) backed by "Hey Chiquita" was credited as Gene Pearson & the Rivileers. Despite limited distribution the record was Top Ten in many cities. Baton followed it up with "Forever" b/w "Darling, Farewell," a hit as well, but not as big. The first two singles bore the catalog numbers Baton 200 and 201, the Rivileers third single "Eternal Love" b/w "Carolyn" catalog number was 205, indicating Rabinowitz had issued three non-Rivileers recordings in the interim. (Buddy Tate and his Band cut Baton single number 202.) Unlike their first two singles the Rivileers' third effort flopped, but Baton scored with the Buddy Tate record.

The following year (1955) saw the release of "For Sentimental Reasons" b/w "I Want to See My Baby," which chocked up some sales, trailed by "Don't Ever Leave Me" b/w "Little Girl" the same year but no more records followed and the group disbanded. Baton reissued "A Thousand Stars" in 1957 with a new flip, "Who Is That Girl," but that was the final shot for the Jamaica Queens hopefuls. Every single after the first was credited as simply the Rivileers. Some unreleased Rivileers' recordings have surfaced, including "Deep Down Inside," a yearning ballad.

Kathy Young & the Innocents had an even bigger hit with "A Thousand Stars" in 1960; Young was only 15 when she redid it, the Los Angeles native was quite familiar with the song cause the Rivileers' original was number one in L.A. in 1954. The song, which also was redone by Britain's Billy Fury (1961), has amassed more than a million performances with B.M.I. Pearson also wrote "Eternal Love" and "Don't Ever Leave Me" for the Rivileers and later sang with the Cleftones (co-writing a few of their songs including "Time Is Running out on Love"); he then replaced Dock Green in the Drifters and sang second tenor on many of their hits from 1962 to 1966. He sandwiched a two-year stint with the military between the Cleftones and Drifters stints and retired as a New York Transit Police Officer in 1987. Delaney is a Reverend but the career paths of the others are unknown. Baton had a couple more hits with the Hearts before Zell Sanders got them, but faded from the scene before the '60s rolled in. The Rivileers regrouped June 6, 1999, for the A Great Day In Harlem event and talked about old times. Eugene Pearson passed April 6, 2000 in Silver Springs, MD, where he relocated after retiring from the New York Transit Authority. *—Andrew Hamilton*

The Rivingtons

f. 1962, Los Angeles, CA

Group / R&B, Novelty

The Rivingtons were a West Coast vocal group featuring Al Frazier, Carl White, John "Sonny" Harris, and Turner "Rocky" Wilson Jr. Though they are best known for their string of early-'60s novelties, the Rivingtons in reality had a rich tradition of doo wop in their background, going back to their original recordings for Federal as the Lamplighters in 1953. They did extensive backup group work throughout the '50s between their own stray releases under a number of different names: the Sharps (singing on the original "Little Bitty Pretty One" and "Over and Over" by Thurston Harris), the Tenderfoots, the Rebels (they do all the backups on the Duane Eddy hits), the Four After Fives, and the Crenshaws. They even sang backup on Paul Anka's first record, credited as the Jacks!

In 1962 they became the Rivingtons and hit pay dirt with their first record, the self-penned "Papa Oom Mow Mow," one of the truly great rock & roll songs to make a virtue of sheer gibberish. They hit the charts again a year later with "The Bird's the Word," capitalizing on a current West Coast dance fad that teenagers were doing to "Papa Oom Mow Mow." A landlocked surf-teen combo from Minnesota called the Trashmen combined the two songs, revved up the beat to warp factor nine, and scored a massive hit with "Surfin' Bird." Despite no further chart success, the Rivingtons' place in rock & roll history (both for the classic performances they recorded and for being the inspiration behind one of the great noise-rock anthems of all time) is assured. *—Cub Koda*

Doin' the Bird / 1963 / Liberty ✦✦✦

Prolific songwriters the Rivingtons—Al Frazier, John Harris, Turner Wilson, and Carl White—penned the bulk of their material, including "Papa Oom Mow Mow," which reached number-42 pop. Its successors ("Mama Oom Mow Mow" and "Kickapoo Joy Juice") failed to improve on the success of "Papa Oom Mow Mow." Singles like "The Bird Is the Word," "Little Sally Walker," and "Surfin' Bird," followed. "Love Pill" and "Long Tall Sally" never hit the charts, and other cuts like "Old Time Love," "Standing in Love Line," and "Have Mercy, Mercy Baby" harkened back to their doo wop days as the Lamplighters and the Sharps. The Rivingtons revised "Papa Oom Mow Mow" on Wand Records in 1973. *—Andrew Hamilton*

● **The Liberty Years** / Jun. 1991 / EMI America ✦✦✦✦✦

If the Rivingtons had done nothing else but record "Papa Oom Mow Mow" and "The Bird's the Word" (the two songs the Trashmen ripped off wholesale for "Surfin' Bird," possibly the most delirious, manic rock & roll song ever created), their place in history would be secured. Amazingly, however, those may not even be the best songs on *The Liberty Years*, a 23-track compilation of just about everything the group recorded for Liberty Records in the early '60s. (The honor may go to the follow-up single, "Mama-Oom-Mow Mow," which is twice as unhinged as the original; "Kickapoo Joy Juice" is a stone classic as well.) Probably the wiggiest of all the vocal harmony groups of the era—only the Cellos, with their immortal "I Am the Japanese Sandman (Rang Tang Ding Dong)," come close—the Rivingtons' best material is performed with a helter-skelter looseness that belies the obvious skill and talent behind the deceptively complex harmonies and rhymes. Even familiar tunes like "Slippin' and Slidin'" and "Long Tall Sally" are transformed. Essential for all fans of late-era doo wop. *—Stewart Mason*

RL

Vocals / Contemporary R&B, Urban, R&B

After two albums with the trio Next, RL launched a solo career with the aid of record industry bigwig Clive Davis. The legendary record exec signed RL to his newly formed J Records label and released a debut album, *RL: Ements*. The album featured one or two sure-shot singles—the Snoop Dogg-Lil' Kim-Battlecat collaboration "Do You Wanna Roll" and the Jermaine Dupri-Erick Sermon collaboration "Got Me a Model"—and other tracks without big-name collaborators. *—Jason Birchmeier*

● **RL: Ements** / Apr. 23, 2002 / J ✦✦✦

Clive Davis took a bit of a gamble when he signed urban vocalist RL to his newly launched J Records label. RL had a good track record, most notably recording two albums with the trio Next in the late '90s. However, few listeners knew RL as a solo artist, probably not even many Next fans, and besides, the group hadn't charted in years. Thus, RL had much to prove, particularly because the market for solo male vocalists was so thin. You get the sense that Davis wanted to make RL another Usher (supported by his decision to hire Jermaine Dupri to produce one of the album's singles), but the result doesn't quite reach that measure. RL is no Usher. But that isn't to say his debut album, *RL: Ements*, proves disappointing. In fact, it's a respectable debut that's unfortunately hurt by a lack of known collaborators. The album's two standout songs, "Got Me a Model" and "Do U Wanna Roll," stand out because of the contributions that Erick Sermon and Jermaine Dupri make on the former and Snoop Dogg, Lil' Kim, and Battlecat make on the latter. Like similar male vocalists such as Nate Dogg and Carl Thomas, RL struggles on his own. He's certainly no singer/songwriter, and his charisma unfortunately isn't as abundant as his poster-boy looks and sultry musings. And unless those looks and musings cause you to swoon, you're left feeling a little bored during the album's long middle stretch, which is devoid of guests. You really want to trust a guy like Davis, but RL doesn't really have anything extraordinary to offer. You're better off sticking to male vocalists like Usher and R. Kelly, who offer a bit more charisma. Singing ability and good looks only go so far, after all—even when Clive Davis is helming your solo debut. *—Jason Birchmeier*

Robert & Johnny

f. New York, NY [The Bronx]

Group / Doo Wop, R&B

A Bronx duo remembered for "We Belong Together," a beautiful harmony ballad that made the Top 40 in 1958, Robert Carr and Johnny Mitchell made about a dozen singles for the Old Town label in the late '50s and early '60s, none of which made remotely as much impact. As one-hit doo wop wonders go, though, they were more interesting than most. They wrote almost all of their material and had a pleasingly distinctive contrast between their closely harmonized voices (one smoky, one nasal). They also covered a more versatile ground than most acts of the genre, proving capable at uptempo bluesy numbers as well as ballads. *—Richie Unterberger*

● **We Belong Together** / 1993 / Ace ✦✦✦✦✦

True, the market for this reissue is mostly limited to doo wop fans, the 27 tracks covering most of the duo's singles and a few unreleased cuts. Despite some occasionally repetitious material (particularly in the ballads), though, it's certainly one of the better single-artist doo wop compilations you're going to come across. "We Belong Together" is here, of course, as well as some surprisingly tough uptempo R&B cuts; the vocals and production are usually first-rate. *—Richie Unterberger*

The Very Best of Robert & Johnny: We Belong Together / May 2, 2000 / Collectables ✦✦✦

Robert Carr and Johnny Mitchell were the doo wop duo Robert & Johnny, releasing several hits in New York for the Old Town label, their biggest being "We Belong Together." Like other doo wop acts whose success arced in the mid- to late '50s, Robert & Johnny sputtered along into the early '60s switching to the Sue label where the door slammed shut on their recording career. This Collectables disc is a fantastic representation of 25 Old Town tracks, the majority written by Carr and Mitchell. *—Al Campbell*

The Robins

f. 1949, Los Angeles, CA, **db.** 1955

Group / Doo Wop, R&B

This Los Angeles vocal group were the forerunners of the Coasters. They began as the Four Bluebirds in 1947, then became the Robins. Ty Terrell, Billy Richards, Roy Richards, and Bobby Nunn were the original members, with Carl Gardner and Grady Chapman adding in 1954. A year later Gardner and Nunn departed to form the Coasters. The Robins had two R&B Top Ten hits. "If It's So Baby" was done with the Johnny Otis Band in 1950 for Savoy, while their best-known number, "Smokey Joe's Cafe," was recorded for Atco in 1955. This was a prototype of the songs that became the Coasters' forte: humorous vehicles with just a dash of cultural insight. *—Ron Wynn*

● **The Best of the Robins** / 1976 / GNP ✦✦✦✦✦

Bert Robinson

Vocals / Quiet Storm, Urban

With a terse, powerful sound and soulful manner, it seemed that Bert Robinson was going to become a force to be reckoned with in urban contemporary circles. His debut LP, *No More Cold Nights*, included the stunning single "Heart of Gold," which reached number five on the R&B chart. Robinson had previously done a duet with Peggie Blu, "All the Way With You." But after a 1989 follow-up, he dropped off the scene. *—Ron Wynn*

● **No More Cold Nights** / 1987 / Capitol ✦✦✦✦✦

I Promise You Love / 1989 / Capitol ✦✦✦

The production chores on singer Bert Robinson's 1989 *I Promise You Love* LP were split between the effort of Attala Zane Giles (who produced his Top Five R&B ballad "Heart of Gold") and his fellow Detroiters One Way. Robinson's vocal sound was in the style practiced by such other singers as Teddy Pendergrass and The Dells' Marvin Junior. He proves adept at handling the LP's slamming tracks—the title track and "Real Thing"—as well as the slow jam "I'll Be So Good to You" (which recalls Pendergrass' "Close the Door") and the edgy "Whip Appeal"-like groover "Sleepin' Alone." *—Ed Hogan*

Janice Robinson

b. Garfield, NJ

Vocals / Contemporary R&B, Singer/Songwriter, Urban

Born and raised in Garfield, NJ, Janice Robinson took to music at an early age. Shyness and loneliness caused by being one of the only African-American kids in a neighborhood of Polish and Italian families, coupled with the rebellion that almost naturally comes to daughters of Baptist preachers, kept her from seriously pursuing her talent until high school. She poured more energy into her craft at Adelphi University where she majored in theater but spent hours secretly composing songs in the music room. After leaving Adelphi, she continued to perform music, playing with a variety of bands from 1989 to 1995. For one year during that time she was on tour with a European dance music band, which taught her a lot about the strain of constant touring but also set her up with a host of international contacts. During one extended stay in Italy, she met Joe Vannelli, who would collaborate with her on some of her first songs, "Children" and "Sweetest Day of May."

In 1994, Robinson had her breakthrough hit, "Dreamer," which she performed with the Italian-based club group Livin' Joy. After that success, she returned to the U.S. and retreated to songwriting, penning songs for Wyclef Jean, Taylor Dayne, Soul Solution, Junior Vasquez, and David Morales-Robinson. A desire to receive more recognition for the hits that she was writing led her to resume her performance career. She was soon signed to Warner Brothers Records, and her first album with them was released in 1999, entitled *The Color Within Me*. The album showcased Robinson's unique vocal style, which crossed rock influences with R&B and also featured an impressive list of supporting musicians, including Jim Keltner, Waddy Wachtel, Ry Cooder, Steve Ferrone, Jimmy Johnson, Michael Landau, and Richard Page. *—Stacia Proefrock*

● **The Color Within Me** / Sep. 7, 1999 / Warner Bros. ✦✦✦✦

Perhaps because she played with various groups for years before making her mark in Europe with Livin' Joy's "Dreamer" in 1994-95, Janice Robinson is not your standard R&B singer. In fact, it would be more accurate to think of her as a rock singer-songwriter. She has assembled a backup band that includes rock veterans like Jim Keltner and Waddy Wachtel and even gotten a wonderful slide guitar performance from Ry Cooder on "Sleeping in the Playground." "Nothing I Would Change" is the autobiographical statement that leads things off, and Robinson remains self-referential in her lyrics. She doesn't really have much to say beyond telling her own, brief story, but she is passionate about that, from the bittersweet hometown reunion of "Dead End Girl" to the memory of racial slurs in "Gracefully Gliding." "Who cares if I'm black or white," she asks on the title track, and she explores miscegenation with an integrationist's fervor in the album closer, "It Really Don't Matter." Those are nervy sentiments at a time when popular music remains as polarized as society at large, and they may make her album difficult to market. But this is an auspicious debut by a talented singer who is also a promising writer. *—William Ruhlmann*

Smokey Robinson (William Robinson)

b. Feb. 19, 1940, Detroit, MI

Producer, Vocals / Motown, R&B, Soul, Smooth Soul, Urban, Quiet Storm

If you're looking for the all-time number-one purveyor of mainstream romantic soul, Smokey Robinson may well be the man, in the face of some towering competition. With the Miracles in the 1960s, he paced dozens of tuneful Motown hits with his beautiful high tenor. As a solo performer from the 1970s onward, he was one of the staples of urban contemporary music. But his singing gifts, as notable as they are, comprise only one of his hats: He's also one of pop's best and most prolific songwriters. As a songwriter and producer, he was the most important musical component to Motown's early success, not only on the hits by the Miracles, but for numerous other acts as well (especially Mary Wells and the Temptations).

Robinson first crossed paths with Motown founder Berry Gordy Jr. in the late '50s in Detroit. In retrospect, this may have been the most important meeting in both men's lives. Robinson needed a mentor and an outlet for his budding talents as a singer and songwriter; the ambitious Gordy needed someone with multi-faceted musical vision. Gordy encouraged and polished Robinson's songwriting in particular in the early days, in which the Miracles were one of many acts bridging the doo wop and early soul eras.

Before solidifying their relationship with the embryonic Motown operation, the Miracles issued a few singles on the End and Chess labels, the most successful of which was "Got a Job." There was no national action for the Miracles until "Shop Around" in late 1960. Gordy withdrew the original single in favor of a faster, more fully produced version of the song; it made number two, doing much not only to establish the Miracles, but to establish the Motown label itself. The song also heralded many of the important elements of the Motown sound, with its gospel-ish interplay between lead and backup vocals, its rhythmic groove, and its blend of R&B and pop.

While Robinson is most often thought of as a romantic balladeer, the Miracles were also capable of grinding out some excellent uptempo party tunes, particularly in their early days. "Mickey's Monkey" (which the group gave an athletically electrifying performance of in the 1964 *T.A.M.I. Show* movie), a 1963 Top Ten hit, is the most famous of these; there was also "Going to a Go-Go" and smaller hits like "I Gotta Dance to Keep From Crying." The 1962 Top Ten hit "You've Really Got a Hold on Me," however, was the key cut in forming Robinson's romantic persona, with its pleading, soaring vocals, exquisite melody, and carefully crafted lyrics. Bob Dylan was impressed enough by Robinson's facility for imaginative wordplay to dub him "America's greatest living poet" (a phrase which has possibly become the most quoted example of one rock giant praising another).

Surveying Robinson's achievements during the 1960s, one wonders if the man ever slept. While the Miracles were never Motown's biggest act at any given time, they were one of its very most consistent, entering the Top 40 25 times over the course of the decade. "I Second That Emotion," "The Love I Saw in You Was Just a Mirage," "The Tracks of My Tears," "Ooo Baby Baby," and "Baby, Baby Don't Cry" were some of their biggest singles, and usually represented Motown at its most sophisticated and urbane. Robinson also was extremely active at Motown as a songwriter and producer for other acts. The number-one singles "My Guy" (Mary Wells) and "My Girl" (Temptations) were each Robinson songs and productions (the latter with fellow Miracle Ronnie White), and Robinson also did some excellent work with the Marvelettes and Marvin Gaye. He also toured with the Miracles, and started a family with the Miracles' female singer, Claudette Rogers, whom he married in 1964. Rogers stopped touring with the group in the mid-'60s, although she continued to sing on their records.

Starting in 1967, the billing on Miracles releases was changed to Smokey Robinson & the Miracles, presaging Robinson's solo career. The group continued to spin out hits until the early '70s, however, getting their only number one in 1970 with the upbeat "The Tears of a Clown" (which had actually been recorded back in 1966). Robinson left the group to go on his own in 1972; the Miracles continued without him with limited success, although they had a number one hit in 1976 with "Love Machine, Pt. 1." Robinson had been made a vice president at Motown near the beginning of his career in 1961. He recorded frequently as a solo artist for Motown in the '70s and '80s, in a considerably mellower vein than his Miracles work, in keeping with the general shift of Motown and soul toward urban contemporary. Robinson, in fact, provided that genre with one of its catch phrases with the title of his 1975 album, *A Quiet Storm*. "Cruisin'" (1979) and "Being With You" (1981) were his biggest solo hits, although artistically and commercially his solo era wasn't nearly as successful as his music with the Miracles. *—Richie Unterberger*

Hi, We're the Miracles / Jun. 1961 / Motown ✦✦✦✦✦

The Miracles' first album is a magnificent debut, filled with impeccable vocal performances, inventive and occasionally brilliant songwriting, and an aching romantic aura. "Shop Around" was the big hit on the record, but another highlight is the group's recut version (also available on the old Miracles' *Anthology* double-disc set) of their single "Way Over There" in a lusher, more beguiling arrangement, which anticipated Phil Spector's "pop symphony" productions with the Crystals, Darlene Love, the Ronettes, and Tina Turner. Smokey Robinson authored or co-authored (with Berry Gordy or fellow Miracle Ronnie White) all but one track here—all are winners, and songs like the ethereal Robinson-White "Heart Like Mine" are worth the price of the disc. They'd do classier, more elaborate work later on, but the youthful verve of Robinson, Claudette Rogers Robinson, Ronnie White, Bobby Rogers, Pete Moore, and Marv Tarplin on these tracks makes this an indispensable record, even for casual fans. *—Bruce Eder*

I'll Try Something New / Jul. 1962 / Motown ✦✦✦✦

The Miracles' second album embraced several different pop and soul idioms in the course of its ten songs with extraordinary aplomb, the group moving from strength to strength while also showing off Gordy's growing musical vocabulary. For the title track, Smokey Robinson's ethereal lead vocal is surrounded by an exquisite chorus (with Claudette, in particular, providing some beautiful effects and a gently comical allusion to the Frankie Avalon song "Venus") and strings that Berry Gordy knew just when to thicken, for an emotional spike in the lyric. "What's So Good About Goodbye" mixed some ravishingly mournful lyrics and deeply emotive performances with a sound that gave equal play to hard electric guitars and a closely recorded violin section. "He Don't Care About Me" is a delightful showcase for Claudette Rogers Robinson in a girl group mode. Those songs and the rest of side one are included on the *35th Anniversary* box, but side two—apart from "If Your Mother Only Knew" (the original B-side of "Way Over There")—has been neglected, which is a shame, because that was the experimental side (truly the "something new" musically to which the LP title could have referred). The quintet's harmonizing soars into what would later become Manhattan Transfer territory in their version of Lerner & Loewe's "On the Street Where You Live," and they bring out equally dexterous and warmer sides of their singing on Cole Porter's "I've Got You Under My Skin"; they also engage in some delightful vocal acrobatics on the Ogden Nash-Kurt Weill "Speak Low." *—Bruce Eder*

Cookin' With the Miracles / Nov. 1962 / Motown ✦✦✦

Their second album shows Smokey and Motown starting to "uptownize" with energetic strings, although it's still one of the Miracles' most uptempo and R&B-oriented efforts. A solid set, with virtually all the material coming from the pens of Robinson and Berry Gordy, although half of the tracks—comprising the best tunes, such as "That's the Way I Feel," "Ain't It Baby," and "Determination"—are available on the Smokey/Miracles box set. [The CD reissue adds "Mighty Good Lovin'" as a bonus track.] *—Richie Unterberger*

The Fabulous Miracles / Feb. 1963 / Motown ✦✦✦

"You Really Got a Hold on Me," one of the Miracles' most popular songs, is the cornerstone of this popular set. Smokey brings his feather-light tenor down a couple of octaves on these sessions, ending his Nolan Strong imitation. Strong, of the Diablos, influenced the young William Robinson; Smokey's first recording was a Nolan Strong remake, "Adios Senorita." Some of Robinson's most brilliant songs—"Such Is Love, Such Is Like," "Happy Landing," "A Love That She Can Count On," and the bouncy "I Can Take A Hint"—provide some serious grooves. Original member Warren Moore is not pictured or featured because of a prior commitment with Uncle Sam. *—Andrew Hamilton*

The Miracles Recorded Live On Stage / Jun. 1963 / Motown ✦✦✦

Short (only seven songs) and amateurish, the recording quality (good for 1963) of *The Miracles Recorded Live On Stage* is very effective. Rock & rollin' "Mighty Good Lovin'" starts the concert on a high note, with Smokey & the Miracles minus Pete Moore—who was in the Service—wailing their hearts out. "A Love She Can Count On," a minor hit, has a blues beat and heart winning lyrics; Smokey emotes near the fade with a rare falsetto wail for emphasis. One of the best tracks here, "Happy Landing," is done at a faster tempo than the studio recording and once again, the sensible words are like pearls of wisdom to young America. One of his most poignant, but overlooked ballads, "I've Been Good to You," is a highlight; he samples a bit of Barbara George's "You'll Lose a Good Thing" on the vamp and heats up the crowd. They sizzle on "What's So Good About Goodbye," an early hit with a hesitating beat and ironic storyline, along with Smokey's passionate lead, and Bobby Rodgers, Ron White and Claudette Robinson's close harmonies make for a heavenly combination. The show-stopping "You Really Got a Hold on Me" sounds better than the studio recording. The underrated "Way Over There" is the finale—it's the ultimate call-and-response song, and the crowd goes wild as the Miracles' work their vocals and visual gyrations. *—Andrew Hamilton*

Christmas With the Miracles / Oct. 1963 / Motown ✦✦✦

Doin' Mickey's Monkey / Nov. 1963 / Motown ✦✦✦

Motown attempts to cash in on the Miracles hit "Mickey's Monkey" by releasing an album of dance tunes, resulting in a fair to middling collection. "I Gotta Dance to Keep From Crying," with its call-and-response opening, shuffling beat, and hot sax break by Thomas "Beans" Bowles, is a gem, as is the Bo Diddley-inspired title cut about a cat named Mickey from out of town. Smokey's self-written "Groovy Thing" is nice filler, but nothing spectacular. Their renditions of dance classics made popular by others—Major Lance, the Orlons Chris Kenner, the Isley Brothers, the Contours and others—are not as compelling as the originals. The huge cartoon character portraying a goofy-looking monkey named Mickey on the cover made this LP a favorite with kids. *—Andrew Hamilton*

Going to a Go-Go / Nov. 1965 / Motown ✦✦✦✦✦

Though its title track ignited a nationwide fad for go-go music, Smokey Robinson & the Miracles' *Going to a Go-Go* LP certainly wasn't just a cash-in effort. It's one of the best records the group put out, and the first six songs make for the best side of any original Motown LP of the '60s (granted, all but one are also available on dozens of Miracles compilations). The four biggest hits were among the best in a set of Miracles archetypes: the throwback to the aching '50s doo wop ballad ("Ooo Baby, Baby"), the flashy uptempo dance song ("Going to a Go-Go"), the dancing-with-tears-in-my-eyes jerker ("The Tracks of My Tears"), and the midtempo orchestral epic ("My Girl Has Gone"). "Choosey Beggar" is one of the sweetest of all Robinson's lead vocals, with stunning background work by the rest of the Miracles. Even the album tracks shine, with "All That's Good" and "Let Me Have Some" working as excellent additions to the program. *—John Bush*

Away We a Go-Go / Nov. 1966 / Motown ✦✦✦

The follow-up to *Going to a Go-Go* probably disappointed the teenagers, offering only a few uptempo dance songs and mostly consisting of odds and ends. It boasted only one pop Top 40 hit, Holland-Dozier-Holland's "(Come Round Here) I'm the One You Need," and never came together the way their classic LPs had. In fact, only four of the songs were Smokey Robinson originals, in part because the Miracles had been so busy on the road. Ivy Jo Hunter, Frank Wilson, and Norman Whitfield took up the slack and contributed material up to par, like the album's other chart entry, Wilson's "Whole Lot of Shaking in My Heart (Since I Met You)." The Miracles also did better than other Motown acts with crossover material; their two Burt Bacharach covers, "Walk on By" and "I Just Don't Know What to Do With Myself," are convincing performances, thanks to Robinson's familiarity with the range required by pop songs. Besides the singles, the other two interesting songs here are their B-sides, both written and produced by the group. Both "Save Me" and "Oh Be My Love" are simply average compositions, but the Miracles make them both winners with thoughtful, caressing performances. *—John Bush*

Make It Happen / Aug. 1967 / Motown ✦✦✦✦✦

The most underrated Miracles LP of the '60s, *Make It Happen* featured a spate of great songs, including three or four that really should've been hits (plus one that only became the group's biggest hit three years after release). Opening with "The Soulful Shack," a grooving dance number that would've fit perfectly on the previous year's *Away We a Go-Go*, the album featured plenty of near-misses, including a pair of delightful good-times dance songs, "My Love Is Your Love (Forever)" and "It's a Good Feeling," plus a great choice for a cover, a tender version of Little Anthony & the Imperials' "I'm on the Outside (Looking In)." The hits really did shine more than any of the other songs, though, marking yet another leap in the level of Smokey Robinson's compositional sophistication. "The Love I Saw in You Was Just a Mirage" is a brilliant twist on a romantic novelty in the Motown mold (with a production that deftly references the British Invasion), while "More Love" is the most sincere lyric and most emotive performance in the group's catalog, a song of reassurance occasioned by several miscarriages suffered by Robinson's wife (and fellow Miracle), Claudette. The capstone, however, was the last song, "The Tears of a Clown," originally written as an uptempo instrumental groover by Stevie Wonder and his producer, Hank Cosby. Robinson's lyric is witty yet sublime, and his lead vocal is one of the best performances of his recording career. One of the biggest misses by the notoriously hit-conscious Motown organization was failing to release this as a single before it became an album hit on British radio in 1970, three years after it first appeared. It shot to the top of the charts on both sides of the Atlantic, and prompted Motown to re-release *Make It Happen* under a new title, *The Tears of a Clown*. *—John Bush*

Special Occasion / Aug. 1968 / Motown ✦✦✦

Another strong LP from Smokey Robinson & the Miracles' late-'60s renaissance, *Special Occasion* was driven by an opening trio of Top 40 hits ("If You Can Want," "Yester Love," the title song), the first of which was not only the biggest hit from the album, but one that illustrated the Miracles could do funky material as well as they did pop. Another gritty composition, "I Heard It Through the Grapevine," was released between the hit versions by Gladys Knight & the Pips and Marvin Gaye and has the quick tempo of Knight's original but more of an uptown feel—a perfect fit for Robinson's falsetto and the group's backing vocals. Robinson's production of the Beatles' "Yesterday" is a stirring cover, stretching out the song to allow for a set of unusually dark harmonies from the Miracles. A few of the album additions are below the quality of most Miracles' songs (Norman Whitfield's throwaway love lyric on "Everybody Needs Love" is particularly embarrassing), but the group made the most of even mediocre songs like Robinson's "Your Mother's Only Daughter" and "You Only Build Me up to Tear Me Down." *—John Bush*

Time Out for Smokey Robinson & the Miracles / Jul. 1969 / Motown ✦✦

Largely produced by Smokey Robinson, *Time Out for Smokey Robinson & the Miracles* pushed four songs into the pop Top 40, but its wide variety of styles made for an album that never came together like a few of the Miracles' classics. The high points were brilliant as usual; "Baby, Baby Don't Cry" is one of the Miracles' best throwback ballads, but with a radical production that makes it a late-'60s classic. Also, Robinson finally got around to recording his landmark composition "My Girl," and "Doggone Right" is a solid performance with an intriguing progression. Still, there's a lot of filler, both of the Motown variety (bland copies of Stevie Wonder's "For Once in My Life" and the Supremes' "The Composer") and of the larger pop world ("Abraham, Martin and John," sung sweetly but sounding inane, and the completely unnecessary "Wichita Lineman"). The only non-hit that's a true success is "Once I Got to Know You (Couldn't Help but Love You)," one of only two songs on the LP where Robinson gave up the production reins. *—John Bush*

Four in Blue / Nov. 1969 / Motown ✦✦✦
Four in Blue, the final Miracles LP of the '60s, was a mixed bag of songwriters and productions encompassing Ashford & Simpson, Mickey Gentile, Deke Richards, and Richard Morris. It followed just four months on from the forgettable *Time Out*, and though it featured no hits of any sort (compared to four for *Time Out*), it did trump its predecessor slightly. Of the four Smokey Robinson originals, "You Send Me (With Your Good Lovin')" and the ballad "A Legend in Its Own Time" are OK, but "Dreams, Dreams" is derivative of past glories and the down-hearted "When Nobody Cares" is only average. Surprisingly, the covers are more intriguing than anything else here; though the production on the group's cover of "Hey Jude" is unobtrusive (at best), Robinson's lead vocal adds a bit to an original that's hard to top, and "You've Lost That Lovin' Feelin'" summons the transcendence of the Righteous Brothers' hit. The closer, a woodwind-led run-through of the Supremes' "My World Is Empty Without You," is interesting but strangely passionless. *—John Bush*

A Pocket Full of Miracles / 1970 / Tamla ✦✦✦
A few good sides make this a fair to middling LP and not one of their best overall. Two single releases, "Point It Out" and "Who's Gonna Take the Blame," did all right but didn't blow up the charts; the latter, a Valerie Simpson & Nickolas Ashford composition, is a teary tale of a girl who turned into a prostitute—heavy stuff for the Miracles. The original version of "Darling Dear" is one of the better tunes here, though a later recording by the Jackson Five is the more popular rendition. Other tunes are competent but fall short of being winners or A-sides. *—Andrew Hamilton*

What Love Has . . . Joined Together / Apr. 1970 / Motown ✦✦✦
A stunning concept album by Smokey Robinson & the Miracles that should have fared better. Notables wrote the six songs, all love ballads: Stevie Wonder, Marvin Gaye, Berry Gordy, Frank Wilson, Bacharach & David, Lennon & McCartney, and Smokey himself. Every selection is a wedding song, and Smokey caresses the lyrics like they were newborns. The heavenly harmonies of the Miracles—Ronald White, Bobby Rogers, Pete Moore, and Claudette Robinson—touch the soul. When they sing Brenda Holloway's "You Made Me So Very Happy," you don't just hear the words; for five minutes and four seconds you experience what lovers feel. The harmonies on "What Love Has . . ." are overwhelming, almost overkill. Smokey drenches more soul onto Marvin Gaye's "If This World Was Mine" then the master himself. The lush arrangements by Smokey and Jerry Long will make you dizzy. Motown didn't release any singles from *What Love Has. . . .* A good photo of Claudette Robinson in a pensive pose graces the back cover. *—Andrew Hamilton*

The Tears of a Clown / Dec. 1970 / Motown ✦✦✦✦

One Dozen Roses / 1971 / Tamla ✦✦✦✦✦
One of their better latter-period albums. Though the singles ("The Tears of a Clown," "I Don't Blame You at All," the lovely "Satisfaction") were the focal points of the set, the real gem is "No Wonder Love's a Wonder," a haunting, socially conscious ballad where Smokey Robinson speaks the lyrics as the Miracles harmonize in the background. It marked one of the few times Robinson ever engaged in social commentary. *—John Lowe*

Flying High Together / 1972 / Tamla ✦✦✦
The last studio album they recorded together as a group, it was produced by Johnny Bristol, who was by then experiencing career problems of his own. Although it was a cohesive, servicable disc, it lacked the clarity that made their earlier records (with Smokey at the helm) so special. Still, it gave the group their last Top 40 hit with "We've Gone Too Far to End It Now," which also cracked the R&B Top Ten. *—John Lowe*

1957-1972 / Dec. 1972 / Motown ✦✦✦✦
A live recording taped over three days at the Carter-Barron Theater in Washington, D.C., of Smokey's farewell tour with the Miracles. The guys were in fine form on this two-record LP that would fit nicely on a CD if Motown ever reissued it. You won't find a smoother ride down memory lane than you'll take on this romantic journey. Smokey & the Miracles' voices waft through the air like jasmine on "Satisfaction." You feel every drop of pain in Smokey's voice as he pleads to his lover on "We've Come Too Far to End It Now." The Miracles' (Warren Moore, Bobby Rogers, Ron White, and Claudette Robinson) harmonies sparkle and glisten like cut diamonds throughout the live performance. From the doo wop-flavored "Bad Girl" to the finger-poppin' "Going to a Go-Go," the stylish group delights the many fans who have loved and supported them over the years. During the introduction, Smokey introduces his replacement Billy Griffin to polite applause; the claps were tentative because nobody wanted Smokey to really leave, hoping they would reconcile and get on with the business of recording and touring—together. *—Andrew Hamilton*

Smokey / Jun. 19, 1973 / Motown ✦✦✦✦✦
Smokey Robinson's first album after splitting with the Miracles remains one of his best, yet it has never received the acclaim it deserves. "Holly" shows the genius of the man; the heart-rending ballad is about a teenage girl who gets strung out on drugs and fast living. Smokey's thoughts are with the Miracles on "Sweet Harmony," a sweet remembrance dedicated to his former bandmates; Robinson salutes his immediate family on the toe-tapping "The Family Song." He sets the bar for lushness with a velvety rendition of Gerry Goffin & Carole King's questioning "Will You Still Love Me Tomorrow," popularized by the Shirelles. And it doesn't get much better than "Baby Come Close," co-written with longtime guitarist Marv Tarplin, who strums some seductive chords to complement Smokey's sweet tenor. *—Andrew Hamilton*

Pure Smokey / Mar. 15, 1974 / Motown ✦✦✦✦
During his solo career, many of Smokey Robinson's best solo efforts are when he writes his own material, which is more personally involved and reflective than his earlier work with the Miracles and others. An exceptionally good, ballad-driven album, its highlight is the modest pop hit "Virgin Man," one of pop and soul music's first attempts to explore male sexual inexperience and insecurity. *—John Lowe*

A Quiet Storm / Mar. 26, 1975 / Motown ✦✦✦✦✦
The genius of William "Smokey" Robinson is immeasurable. As many of his prior songs had shaped R&B and pop music, this album would have a similar effect. The title track became the namesake for a music format. The album itself had three singles hit the charts. Arranged in an intermittent rhythm, "Baby That's Backatcha" ran up the *Billboard* R&B charts to number one inside 16 weeks. It was Robinson's first number-one single since leaving the Miracles. The lyric of the ballad "The Agony and the Ecstasy" hit the Top Ten at number seven, and it was followed by the masterpiece "A Quiet Storm." Although it only managed to seal the Top 25, it has since made a greater impact on the music charts and music industry. Briefly, radio mogul Cathy Hughes, owner of Radio One, was the general manager at Howard University radio WHUR during the early '70s when she created the format "the quiet storm." She used Smokey Robinson's composition as the theme song. Before long, it caught on around the country and evolved into a new market. This album also features the "Wedding Song" which was written for Hazel and Jermaine Jackson's wedding and the "Happy" theme from the movie *Lady Sings the Blues*. *—Craig Lytle*

Smokey's Family Robinson / Feb. 10, 1976 / Motown ✦✦
Smokey Robinson sets up groove-based arrangements that take their tone from Sonny Burke's electric piano rhythms, but his own personal songwriting stamp often gives way to the percolating funk, notably on the single "Open" (number-ten R&B, number-81 pop), which attempts to do what Marvin Gaye did the following year with "Got to Give It Up," but, with its prominent "backup" vocals, only succeeds in confusing the listener. The second side is more ballad-oriented, but there are no great songs even when the focus is on the singer. *—William Ruhlmann*

Deep in My Soul / Jan. 18, 1977 / Motown ✦✦✦
Deep in My Soul is an unusual Smokey Robinson LP in that he only contributed one song, "Vitamin U," a forgettable attempt at disco, though an amusing play on words. Kathy Wakefield and Mike & Brenda Sutton's "There Will Come a Day" uses a similar piano opening to "You Really Got a Hold on Me"; while pleasant, it is far less riveting than the Miracles' classic. The standouts are the tingling "In My Corner" and two Donald Baldwin/Jeffrey Bowen tunes, "If You Want My Love" and "You Cannot Laugh Alone." For years, the latter cut alone made this an essential Smokey Robinson LP. You couldn't find it anywhere else, not even on a 45; Motown has since released it on Smokey's *Motown Legends* collection. The lyrically clever song has a great chorus with Smokey crooning "Your love was crackerjack/A surprise in every pack/A myth a fantasy/A package C.O.D." *Deep in My Soul* only had seven songs, and surprisingly climbed to number 47 on the pop charts, a far better showing than his debut, which peaked at number 70. *—Andrew Hamilton*

Love Breeze / Feb. 21, 1978 / Motown ✦✦✦✦
Take away a bad attempt at trendiness "Why You Wanna See My Bad Side," a dullard "Feeling You, Feeling Me," a metaphoric disaster "Shoe Soul," and *Love Breeze* isn't half bad. The shimmering, floating "Daylight And Darkness" is a mesmerizer depicting his wife's dual personality. Claudette, an ex-wife now, is a Gemini, an astrological sign known for split personalities. Smokey sings the stinging lyrics as if he's trying to penetrate Claudette's soul. The upbeat, romping "Love's So Fine," is a finger snapper that grabs you immediately. A soft, slow "I'm Loving You Softly" reeks of romanticism, while "Trying It Again," an uptempo romper, featuring a looping bassline, has a long, spirited fade with Smokey competing with the bass player for bragging rights. *—Andrew Hamilton*

Where There's Smoke . . . / May 22, 1979 / Motown ✦✦✦
This album was a considerable return to form, Smokey Robinson's most commercially successful solo LP up to this point (and highest-charting record in 11 years), entirely due to the single "Cruisin'" (number-four pop and R&B), his biggest pop hit since "The Tears of a Clown." Motown doesn't seem to have recognized that track's potency, leading off with the flop "Get Ready" (a disco treatment of the old Temptations hit) before turning to "Cruisin'" as a second single several months after the LP's release. *Where There's Smoke . . .* then took off and peaked at number 17, more than six months after first appearing. Although the LP is divided into "Smoke" and "Fire" sides, both sides start out with rhythmic songs and gradually slow down to near-ballad speed, with the sensuous "Cruisin'" the final "Fire" track. In retrospect, the album may be uneven and a touch too disco-ish in places, but in 1979-1980, *Where's There's Smoke . . .* brought Smokey Robinson back into the limelight. *—William Ruhlmann*

Warm Thoughts / Feb. 25, 1980 / Motown ✦✦✦
On his follow-up to "Cruisin'," Smokey Robinson goes right back to that lazy, romantic style with "Let Me Be the Clock" (number-four R&B, number-31 pop), which leads off the aptly named *Warm Thoughts*. Robinson seems to have taken the success of "Cruisin'" as his opportunity to distance himself from disco and return to his more familiar ballad style, even injecting a touch of his old wordplay in "Into Each Rain Some Life Must Fall." Side two begins with the more uptempo "Melody Man," which was arranged, co-written, and co-produced by Stevie Wonder, but for the most part this is the bedroom Smokey Robinson, and that got him to number 14 on the LP chart, his highest solo peak yet. *—William Ruhlmann*

Being With You / Feb. 17, 1981 / Motown ✦✦✦
Smokey Robinson landed his first big album of the 1980s with this release. The title track soared to the top of the R&B charts and stayed there, while it just missed topping the pop

charts. Robinson's wonderful lead vocals, timing, dramatic delivery, and overall technique were as impressive as ever, and he got two more chart hits from the album. It eventually became his most successful LP ever from a commercial standpoint, although his artistic landmark as a solo artist remains *A Quiet Storm.* —*Ron Wynn*

Yes It's You Lady / Jan. 17, 1982 / Motown ✦✦
Surprisingly, having scored his biggest solo success with the self-penned, self-produced *Being with You*, Smokey Robinson turned to an outside producer and outside writers for the follow-up. Both of the singles from *Yes It's You Lady*, which was produced by George Tobin, "Tell Me Tomorrow" (number-three R&B, number-33 pop) and "Old Fashioned Love" (number-17 R&B, number-60 pop) were midtempo rhythm numbers written by Gary Goetzman & Mike Piccirillo. Robinson's own compositions, notably the title track, which would have made a perfect follow-up to "Being with You," were de-emphasized. The result was a retreat from the careful career-building Robinson had been engaged in since 1979; the album peaked at only number 33 after three straight Top 20 LPs. It was as though, having established himself as a solo voice, Robinson was now content to be "Cruisin'." —*William Ruhlmann*

Touch the Sky / Jan. 7, 1983 / Motown ✦✦
Smokey Robinson took back the production reins from George Tobin and reinstated his producing/arranging partnership with Sonny Burke for *Touch The Sky*. The two took a more rhythmic approach, with Burke contributing drums and synthesizers. R&B listeners responded, notably on the title track (number-68 R&B) and "I've Made Love to You a Thousand Times" (number-eight R&B), but Robinson was shut out of the Hot 100, and as a result *Touch The Sky* continued his slide in LP sales, peaking at only number-50 on the pop chart, although it hit number-eight R&B. —*William Ruhlmann*

Essar / May 21, 1984 / Motown ✦✦
Essar marks the low point of Smokey Robinson's solo career. Co-producer and arranger Sonny Burke, a long-time Robinson recording partner, provides nearly all the tracks, dominating the sound with his synthesized keyboards. On songs like "And I Don't Love You" (number-33 R&B), it's hard to identify the result as a Smokey Robinson record. This may help explain why *Essar*, Robinson's second straight album not to generate a Hot 100 pop chart entry, was his lowest charting studio album on the pop LPs list (number 141). But it also flopped with R&B fans, peaking at number 35 and becoming his first album not to generate at least one Top Ten R&B hit. —*William Ruhlmann*

Smoke Signals / Jan. 14, 1986 / Motown ✦✦✦

One Heartbeat / Feb. 24, 1987 / Motown ✦✦✦
Another superb Robinson album. He continued scoring hit singles throughout the 1980s, and this time out, the song "Just To See Her" was another huge pop and R&B smash, and the title track did almost as well. Robinson was thriving, despite the fact that hip-hop was steadily gaining strength, and new jack swing would soon force its way into the urban contemporary spotlight. —*Ron Wynn*

Love, Smokey / Feb. 14, 1990 / Motown ✦✦✦
This is another Smokey Robinson album (executive produced by Iris Gordy, Berry's daughter) and, well, it's definitely one of those discs you can put on for background, or while making out. Lord knows, the man is in fine, fine voice, indeed. However, for all the participation by people of the caliber of George Duke (who produced and appears on several tracks), the album mostly doesn't rise above sweet soul. Only four of the tracks break the groove and become anything else, and those are mostly straight dance grooves. The sound, arrangements, and performances are flawless. The disc has a clean, transparent, and airy sound that's rarely encountered this side of frothy new age discs, while the synthesizer and sampler work is terrific (the non-keyboard instruments, when they appear, are excellent, too). Unfortunately, very few of the songs have any particular immediacy, and none of them stick in the mind the way Smokey Robinson's songs used to—the closest any of these come is "Easy," which has all the classic Motown elements wrapped up together, right down to the Stevie Wonder-style harmonica. More typical is "Unless You Do It Again" (one of two CD-only tracks; the other is "Just Another Kiss"), which sounds for all the world just about how one would imagine Philly soul nowadays—MFSB with the technological edge. The album is basically very smooth, beautifully executed, and sounds good. The question: Is there really a market out there for yuppie soul? The phrase itself seems surely an oxymoron. But, oh, that voice. —*Steven McDonald*

Double Good Everything / 1991 / SBK ✦✦
Smokey's first recording outside of Motown's auspices didn't have fans rushing to record shops. The intro to the rollicking "I Can't Get Enough" reminds you of the Four Tops' "I Can't Help Myself." "Rack Me Back" is a blues song, complete with a guitar solo on the break and sassy lyrics. He tries to get a piece of Lionel Richie's audience with "When a Woman's Cries" which features his light tenor crooning to a piano. He gets back to being Smokey on "You Take Me Away," a pretty love song and the only compelling number here. "Double Good Everything" is a bar rocker that Smokey fans aren't accustomed to; the exotic-sounding "Rewind" is more his style and comes off better. The producer had Smokey singing in too many genres—you got blues, soul, pop, and slivers of country and reggae all in one package. Though pleasant and inoffensive, this will disappoint even die-hard Smokey Robinson fans and won't win him many new ones. —*Andrew Hamilton*

Whatever Makes You Happy: More of the Best . . . / Feb. 16, 1993 / Rhino ✦✦✦✦✦
This is a solid compilation of 18 of the most interesting non-hits from Smokey's (and Motown's) golden era. Culled from 11 albums, this is an intelligent and consistent overview of Robinson's relatively unknown tunes. These cuts show the stylistic evolution of Motown as surely as any greatest hits collection, moving from bluesy, raucous R&B to assembly-line soul to songs reflecting the lyrical and instrumental innovations of the psychedelic era. Robinson's peerless soul songwriting and the Miracles' smooth harmonies remained constant no matter what the era, making this a much more fluid set than you might expect. Ultimately, the songs don't boast hooks quite as memorable as their classic hit singles, despite their similarities in structure and production. The early-'60s tracks are perhaps the record's most interesting, displaying a gritty, almost salacious approach that had yet to be toned down by slicker production values. Dominated by Robinson originals, this collection also includes scattered covers of "Money" and hits by the Temptations and Supremes, as well as the original version of "From Head to Toe," later covered by Elvis Costello. —*Richie Unterberger*

☆ **The 35th Anniversary Collection** / Feb. 22, 1994 / Motown ✦✦✦✦✦
This four-CD boxed set covers every essential track that Smokey Robinson & the Miracles ever recorded, and then some—at least a dozen never previously anthologized tracks are included here, among them the original single versions of "Way Over There" (unavailable elsewhere) and "Shop Around" (which had already been released locally in Detroit when Berry Gordy decided one night to get a session together, punch up the rhythm, and lay down a new version, which became the hit). Even better is the remastering, which runs circles around any previous edition of the Miracles' work, and the annotation—including an essay by Claudette Robinson—that gives credit to all of the participants, including the backup musicians who were seldom if ever mentioned during Motown's heyday. The Smokey Robinson & the Miracles *Anthology* is a fine collection, but this set is the definitive history, and irreplaceable for anyone who genuinely loves the group. —*Bruce Eder*

★ **Anthology** / 1995 / Motown ✦✦✦✦✦
Detroit vocal group the Miracles were a fixture at Motown from day one. Driven by Robinson's superior writing and smooth, silky falsetto, the Miracles placed a stunning 48 singles on the *Billboard* charts, 39 of those with Smokey in tow. Virtually all of them are included on this collection. Songs such as "Ooh Baby Baby," "The Tracks of My Tears," and "The Tears of a Clown" define much that was good about the '60s. The 1995 double-CD reissue is digitally remastered and includes virtually the same tracks, adding a couple previously unreleased songs and extensive liner notes. —*Rob Bowman*

The Ultimate Collection [Smokey Robinson Solo] / Mar. 25, 1997 / Motown ✦✦✦✦✦
While Robinson's solo work pales in comparison to his hits with the Miracles, this 17-track collection of Motown singles uncovers such gems as "Baby Come Close," "I Am I Am," "Cruisin'," "Let Me Be," "The Clock," "Tell Me Tomorrow," "I've Made Love to You a Thousand Times," "One Heartbeat," "Just to See Her," "Everything You Touch," "Baby That's Backatcha," "The Agony and the Ecstacy" and "Open." —*Jason Ankeny*

★ **The Ultimate Collection [Smokey Robinson & the Miracles]** / Feb. 10, 1998 / Motown ✦✦✦✦✦
Motown Records is a bit like the Walt Disney Studios, in the sense that both organizations made a good deal more money in recent decades marketing their histories and reputations than they have in creating very much that's new—indeed, Motown hasn't been an active label, in the sense of recording any new artists, in more than a decade. Apart from its *Anthology* series in the mid-'70s, however, the label seldom came up with anything that could hold a permanent place in a collection, or was reasonably comprehensive. Then came the *Ultimate Collection* series, which was timed to coincide with the first technological upgrade in CD mastering to 20-bit digital audio. This disc has 25 songs that encompass all of the Top Ten hits by Smokey Robinson & the Miracles released between 1960 and 1969 (as well as their 1970 number-one hit, "Tears of a Clown"), but also some of their finest B-sides ("Choosey Beggar," "Who's Lovin' You") and an album track or two of significance, and it also sounded significantly better than any prior hits collection on the group, including the upgraded *Anthology* two-CD set issued just three years earlier. What's more, while it in no way supplants the four-CD *35th Anniversary Collection*, it offers one track that didn't make it onto that set, the second version of "Way Over There," which—though it never charted—is a brilliant piece of writing, singing, and production. After all, "Way Over There" was the very first actual "Motown" single; in fact, it was one of the most ambitious and beautiful records that Berry Gordy ever produced personally—and it did sell a reported 50,000 copies, which was significant enough in helping to keep the fledgling company afloat. That's as much of a "history lesson" as this CD provides, though people will always happily hear history lessons like that. Mostly, it's a gorgeous flood of sound washing over you for 70 minutes, though not quite like you've ever heard these songs—including the gently ringing rhythm guitar on "Tracks of My Tears," the in-your-face drums that open "My Girl Has Gone," and the strings of the Detroit Symphony on "Way Over There," but most of all the silky lead and backing vocals, which have never sounded closer or smoother. The standard is now 24-bit, and someday there may even be a DVD audio or SACD of hits by the Miracles, but for a collection featuring some of their most enjoyable and best-sounding music, no one is going to be cheated by buying this disc. —*Bruce Eder*

Lost and Found: Along Came Love (1958–1964) / Sep. 28, 1999 / Motown ✦✦✦✦
As part of Motown's *Lost and Found* series, this brings together 20 previously unreleased tracks and rarities of prime Smokey & the Miracles from various early time frames in the Motown catalog. Some of the earliest, like "My Mama Told Me," echo Motor City role models Nolan Strong & the Diablos right down to the guitar riffs behind Smokey's uncharacteristically bluesy vocals, while others, like "Please Say You Love Me," splendidly wear their doo wop roots on their sleeves. Here we find the group taking on Broadway show tunes in modern jazz harmonies and *nailing* it on "If I Were a Bell" and "Easy Street." The title track is one of Smokey's patented slow burners. In the rarities department, there's the lost Ron and Bill B-side, "Don't Say Bye Bye," only outdone by "Mr. Misery," a rare lead vocal by Claudette Robinson in the grand girl group style, and a live version of "Shop Around" that's as raw as anything Smokey ever committed to wax. In the final analysis, however, most of the tracks here just make you wonder how material this great could have

languished in unreleased forms for so long. Smokey's worst session is still better than most superstars' best work; here's a whole CD that makes even his leftovers a tantalizing prospect. *—Cub Koda*

Going to a Go-Go/Away We A-Go-Go / Jun. 26, 2001 / Motown ♦♦♦♦♦

Make It Happen/Special Occasion / Jun. 26, 2001 / Motown ♦♦♦♦

Time Out/Four in Blue / Jun. 26, 2001 / Motown ♦♦♦

☆ **Ooo Baby Baby: The Anthology** / Sep. 24, 2002 / Motown ♦♦♦♦♦

There isn't much of a crucial difference between this and the previous Smokey Robinson & the Miracles collection entitled *Anthology*, originally issued in 1973 and then on CD with minor variations in 1995. More to the point, perhaps, about 85 percent of the songs on the two-CD set *Ooo Baby Baby: The Anthology* were also on the more plainly titled *Anthology*, so the differences are kind of cosmetic. *Ooo Baby Baby: The Anthology* has all 28 of their Top 40 hits, so someone looking for the essentials, garnished by a good amount of other material that isn't as familiar, will undoubtedly be satisfied. *Ooo Baby Baby: The Anthology* does have a small but significant edge in the inclusion of the exquisite mid-'60s midtempo ballad "Would I Love You," a great 1964 B-side that somehow escaped inclusion on the CD iteration of *Anthology*. As far as other minor differences that will probably escape detection by the great majority of listeners, there are first-ever stereo mixes of "Whatever Makes You Happy," "I Can Take a Hint," and "Baby Don't You Go"; the first CD appearance of both "I Can Take a Hint" (from the 1963 LP *The Fabulous Miracles*) and a live "I've Been Good to You" (also from a 1963 LP); and new, extended stereo mixes of "You've Really Got a Hold on Me," "Would I Love You," and "I'll Try Something New." However you slice it, it's great soul music, not much less solid than single-disc Miracles collections, though owners of the previous releases titled *Anthology* will not find enough extras here to merit investment. *—Richie Unterberger*

Tad Robinson

b. Jun. 24, 1956, New York, NY

Vocals, Harmonica / Electric Blues, Soul-Blues

Tad Robinson would have fit in snugly with the blue-eyed soul singers of the 1960s. His vocals virtually reeking of soul, he's capable of delving into a straight-ahead Little Walter shuffle or delivering a vintage O.V. Wright R&B ballad. Add his songwriting skills and exceptional harp technique and you have quite the total package. Robinson grew up in New York City on a nutritious diet of Stax, Motown, and Top 40, digging everyone from Otis Redding and Arthur Alexander to Eric Burdon and Joe Cocker. He matriculated at Indiana University's school of music in 1980, fronting a solid little combo on the side called the Hesitation Blues Band that made it up to Chicago now and then (where he soon relocated).

Long respected locally, his reputation outside the city limits soared when he took over as vocalist with Dave Specter & the Bluebirds. Their 1994 Delmark disc, *Blueplicity*, was an inspiring marriage of Robinson's soaring vocals and Specter's tasty, jazz-laced guitar and featured the striking Robinson-penned originals "What's Your Angle," "Dose of Reality," and "On the Outside Looking In." Delmark granted Tad Robinson his own album later that year. *One to Infinity* escorted him even further into soul territory (guests on the set included Mighty Flyers guitarist Alex Schultz, the mystical Robert Ward, and Specter). *—Bill Dahl*

● **One to Infinity** / 1994 / Delmark ♦♦♦♦

Harpist Robinson displays his multi-faceted talents, exploring a multitude of shades of blues and soul. The backing on each song neatly fits the piece—guitarist Robert Ward briefly turns up as a sideman as Robinson proves he's one of the top young vocalists on the contemporary circuit. *—Bill Dahl*

Last Go Round / Sep. 22, 1998 / Delmark ♦♦♦

Vicki Sue Robinson

b. 1955, Philadelphia, PA, **d.** Apr. 27, 2000, Wilton, Connecticut

Vocals / Disco, Hi-NRG

Vicki Sue Robinson turned the disco and pop music world upside down with her rousing 1976 Top Ten pop smash, "Turn The Beat Around." A strong, vibrant vocalist, Robinson's records were among some of the best produced and arranged '70s disco releases with solid beats built on solid songs. Born in Harlem (or Philadelphia) in 1955, Robinson's birth was the result of a union between a black actor and white folk singer. Her professional debut was at the Philadelphia Folk Festival when she was 6. Her eclectic heritage was also reflected in her wide ranging love of different types of music performers. Her favorites included Dinah Washington, Pete Seeger, Woody Guthrie, Laura Nyro, Sonny Terry & Brownie McGhee and Sarah Vaughan.

As a teenager, Robinson appeared in the Broadway hit, *Hair*, and having been discovered by Robert Stigwood (RSO Records, the Bee Gees) she joined the cast of *Jesus Christ Superstar*. Her varied career include stints as a model, waitress and recording with Japanese artists Sadistic Mica Band and Itsuru Shimoda and working at *Ms.* magazine. Signed to RCA Records in the mid '70s by producer Warren Schatz, she had four albums on the imprint, *Never Gonna Let You* (spring 1976), *Vicki Sue Robinson* (fall 1976), *Half and Half* (1978) and *Movin' On* (1979). "Turn the Beat Around," written by Pete and Gerald Jackson reached number-ten pop on *Billboard*'s pop chart in summer 1976, earning Robinson a Grammy nomination for Best Pop Female. Her other favorites include her cover of Bobby Womack's "Daylight" and "Hold Tight." Her movie roles include *Going Home* with Robert Mitchum in 1971 and 1972's *To Find a Man* with Lloyd Bridges.

In between being an in-demand jingles singer, Robinson starred in her own 1999 off-Broadway play, *Vicki Sue Robinson: Behind the Beat*. The play was a continuation of her popular, enticing cabaret show. She happily made the TV talk show circuit, inviting everyone to the show and joyously performed her signature song, "Turn the Beat Around." It's appeared on numerous various artists sets (*Disco Divas: Salute to the Ladies, Turn the Beat Around: Great Disco Hits, 70's Disco Ball Party Pack, Disco Box Sampler, Decades of Dance 60's 70's & 80's, Super Party, Vol.1* and *Millennium Disco Party*) with the 12-inch mix being a part of *Groovin' You: Big 12 Inches* issued May 1999 by BMG/Buddha. In the '90s, her "House of Joy" single was a U.K. dance smash.

At the age of 46, Vicki Sue Robinson died of cancer at her Wilton, CT, home on April 27, 2000. *—Ed Hogan*

● **Never Gonna Let You Go** / 1976 / RCA ♦♦♦♦♦

When "Turn the Beat Around" became a major hit in 1976, many of the people who heard that disco-soul classic on the radio bought the single and skipped Vicki Sue Robinson's debut album, *Never Gonna Let You Go*. But those who did hear the rest of the LP found that most of the other tracks were decent, if unremarkable. Club DJs, unlike radio DJs, didn't play "Turn the Beat Around" exclusively—some of them found "We Can Do Almost Anything" useful and the exuberant, sunny title track (which is arguably the second best song on the album) enjoyed a lot of club exposure. But much of the LP isn't aimed at the dancefloor; "When You're Lovin' Me," "Lack of Respect," and "Wonderland of Love" are competent Northern soul items with a strong Philadelphia influence. At times *Never Gonna Let You Go* sounds like it might have been recorded at Philly's Sigma Sound Studios, but in fact, the album was recorded entirely in New York. *Never Gonna Let You Go* is uneven, but its plusses exceed its minuses—and despite its flaws, it indicated that Robinson had a great deal of potential. *—Alex Henderson*

Vicki Sue Robinson / 1976 / RCA ♦♦♦

Like *Never Gonna Let You Go*, Vicki Sue Robinson's self-titled second album is uneven. Most of the material is decent without being great, but occasionally Robinson soars—and when she soars, she *really* soars. The LP gets off to an impressive start with her classic remake of Bobby Womack's "Daylight," which becomes exuberant instead of moody in her hands. While Womack wanted you to sit down and listen to his version, Robinson's remake is clearly aimed at the dancefloor. Equally impressive are the melancholy "How About Me" and the dramatic disco-soul gem "After All This Time," but for the most part, *Vicki Sue Robinson* isn't mind-blowing. The album's least respectable offering is "Should I Stay," which is nothing more than a poor man's "Turn the Beat Around." Not surprisingly, the guys who wrote "Turn the Beat Around," Pete and Gerald Jackson, also wrote the very similar "Should I Stay." How similar? So similar that if someone else had written "Should I Stay," Pete and Gerald Jackson probably would have filed a lawsuit for copyright infringement. But when you rip yourself off you don't have to worry about feeling the wrath of an intellectual property lawyer. Of course, "Should I Stay"'s lack of creativity doesn't make "Daylight" or "After All This Time" any less appealing. *—Alex Henderson*

Movin' On / 1979 / RCA ♦♦

On her fourth and final album for RCA, Robinson switched from the production of Warren Schatz to T. Life, who also served as co-writer on most tracks. Best-known for his 1970's work with Evelyn "Champagne" King, Life gave Robinson a funkier soul edge on this outing, in the form of grooves like the titletrack, a down-tempo jam with a gospel-esque background arrangement; and the breezy "High on Your Love." Robinson ad-libs more comfortably than on previous efforts, and gives a particularly notable performance on "Can't Accept the Fact." Though not as diverse as its predecessor, *Half and Half*, this set is an impressive effort. *—Justin M. Kantor*

Rockwell (Kenneth Gordy)

b. Mar. 15, 1964, Detroit, MI

Vocals / Urban

Born Kenneth Gordy, Rockwell is the son of Motown Records founder Berry Gordy. He changed his name so as to avoid charges of nepotism, wanting to make it in the music business on his talent alone. He signed to Motown as a solo artist without his father's knowledge, taking his name from his high school band. His first single, the Michael Jackson-esque "Somebody's Watching Me," which featured backing vocals from both Michael and Jermaine Jackson, shot into the Top Ten, hit number one on the R&B charts, and went gold; only then did he reveal his true identity. This, however, was his peak of success; the follow-up single fizzled, as did his next album. *—Steve Huey*

● **Somebody's Watching Me** / 1984 / Motown ♦♦♦♦♦

An impressive debut set with an emphasis on rock instrumentals, Michael Jackson contributes backup vocals. *—Rick A. Bueche*

Captured / 1985 / Motown ♦♦

Nile Rodgers

b. Sep. 19, 1952, New York, NY

Producer, Songwriter, Guitar / Urban, Disco, Soul

A first-rate guitarist, Nile Rodgers was half of the premier '70s production/performance team that was the heart and soul of Chic. New Yorker Rodgers studied classical music and jazz before joining the house band at the Apollo Theater in Harlem. He met bassist Bernard Edwards in 1972 when both were in the Big Apple Band. This group recorded with the vocal group New York City on their single "I'm Doin' Fine Now." The two later wrote and produced major hits for Chic, Sister Sledge ("We Are Family"), Diana Ross ("Upside Down"), and many other groups. Rodgers later gained fame on his own as a producer. He worked with David Bowie, Madonna, Peter Gabriel, Bryan Ferry, Mick Jagger, Al Jarreau, Philip Bailey, Sister Sledge, and Diana Ross. Indeed, the only area Rodgers hasn't been successful in is as a performer; his 1985 LP, *B-Movie Matinee*, fizzled, with the single "Let's Go out Tonight" reaching only number 35 on the R&B charts and completely flopping otherwise. *—Ron Wynn*

Adventures in the Land of the Good Groove / 1983 / Mirage ♦♦♦

Famed producer, writer, and infamous co-conspirator in the disco band Chic, guitarist Nile Rodgers used his solo outings not only to stretch his own wings, but as an extra outlet for the overflow of his talents. Despite the presence of Chic alumni Bernard Edwards and Tony Thompson, a coterie of musicians that included vocalists Rachel Sweet and

Fonzi Thornton (then enjoying his own chart success with "Beverly") ensured that this debut wasn't just a Chic effort in disguise. Sandwiched as it was between that band's own *Tongue in Chic* and *Believer* LPs, *In the Land of the Good Groove* was sure to draw comparisons. Rodgers, though, sidestepped that trap completely, creating a set that was uniquely his own, across a barrage of pop-inflected urban groovers. Although Edwards' elastic basslines are unmistakable, the mood remains squarely uptempo, feel-good without entering the realms of fierce disco. Both the title track and "Rock Bottom" are perfect examples of this catchy energy, while "Yum-Yum" emerges as a spunky contemporary funk song, and Rodgers handles his outstanding R&B ballad, the tender "My Love Song for You," with utmost finesse. *In the Land of the Good Groove* stumbles at times, to be sure, but still emerges a sweet peek at Rodgers' alter-alter-ego. *—Amy Hanson*

● **B-Movie Matinee** / 1985 / Warner Bros. ♦♦♦♦
Released in 1985, *B-Movie Matinee* proved a stellar departure from Nile Rodgers' initial solo outing. Leaving behind the more traditional trappings of his R&B-inflected debut, he instead looked to the synthesized future, driving his organic bass and guitars into what amounted to a concept album of sorts, fueled by memories of lazy Saturday B-movie afternoons. Bright, punchy pop punctuates this set. From the quirky sci-fi of "Plan-9" and the contemporary urban groove on "State Your Mind," which is one of the album's better tracks, Rodgers fills the space with eminently danceable, if somewhat same-y, songs using synthesizer tricks to thrill. "Let's Go out Tonight," meanwhile, proved the album's hot prospect, dipping into the Top 100, giving Rodgers his only solo chart hit. Rounding things out are the ballad "Wavelength" and Rodgers' immaculate instrumentation—most notably the guitar and bass, which bound through the funky "Groove Master" with glee. Perhaps a little too light on substance, *B-Movie Matinee* still manages to please. Being Nile Rodgers can't be easy, as the mere mention of his name conjures such strong sonic images from his Chic canon, and it's hard to ignore those predispositions when listening to his solo material. But that's no detriment to the fine set he's unleashed here. *—Amy Hanson*

Roger (Roger Troutman)

b. Nov. 29, 1951, Hamilton, OH, **d.** Apr. 25, 1999
Keyboards, Vocals / Urban, Funk

Best known as the leader, founder, songwriter, singer, and guitarist of early-'80s funk masters Zapp, Roger Troutman (better known simply as "Roger") also forged a successful solo career. Born November 29, 1951, in Hamilton, OH, Troutman was the fourth child in a family of nine kids, and gravitated toward music at an extremely early age; he was only five years old when he received his first guitar. It wasn't long before the young musician was playing in local bands, including one outfit called the Crusaders at the age of 11, a band that also later included Roger's brother, Lester, on drums. The group broke up in the early '60s, but Roger and Lester stuck together, as Roger became influenced by such R&B legends as B.B. King, Jimmy Reed, Chuck Jackson, and Junior Walker, in addition to such then-current chart-toppers as the Temptations, Wilson Pickett, and the Beatles. By the late '60s, Roger had added Hammond organ to his resumé of instruments, while two other Troutman brothers joined up with Roger and Lester—Tony (bass) and Larry (percussion)—forming Roger & the Human Body.

It wasn't long before Roger and his brothers became enraptured by such funk/rock artists as Jimi Hendrix, the Isley Brothers, Stevie Wonder, and Funkadelic, whose earthy sounds began to reflect in the brothers' own music. Playing shows all over the U.S. and Canada, the group added another Troutman brother to their ranks by 1977, Terry, who went by the nickname of "Zapp," which soon became the group's new name. Shortly thereafter, Bootsy Collins' brother, Phelps "Catfish" Collins, happened to catch a gig by Zapp, who put them in touch with Bootsy, who then brought them to the attention of George Clinton. Clinton promptly signing the group to his own custom label, Uncle Jam (a subsidiary of Columbia Records). Taking Roger and company under his wing, Clinton got the group's leader a performance spot at the first (and only) Funk Awards in December 1979, introducing Roger Troutman as the most talented musician he'd ever seen in his life. His show-stopping performance created a buzz for Zapp's self-titled debut release, issued in 1980 (due to contractual red tape, the album ultimately was not issued via Clinton's label, but through Warner Bros.).

Zapp (who also went by the name of "Zapp & Roger") quickly established themselves as one of funk's finest, issuing such further albums as 1982's *Zapp II*, 1983's *Zapp III*, 1984's *The New Zapp IV U*, and 1989's *Zapp V*; in addition to spawning such hit singles as "More Bounce to the Ounce," "Be Alright," "Dance Floor (Pt. 1)," "Doo Wa Ditty (Blow That Thing)," "I Can Make You Dance (Pt. 1)," and "Computer Love." Along with his Zapp duties, Roger also made time to issue solo albums (mixing R&B standards with originals), including such titles as 1981's *The Many Facets of Roger*, 1984's *The Saga Continues*, 1987's *Unlimited!*, and 1991's *Bridging the Gap*; while scoring such hit singles as a cover of "I Heard It Through the Grapevine (Pt. 1)" and "I Want to Be Your Man."

But by the end of the '80s, the hits and the public's interest in the group began to dwindle. Just as it appeared that Zapp & Roger had fallen off the radar screen by the early '90s, a whole new generation of rap and R&B artists began sampling bits from the group's catalog; including such renowned artists as MC Hammer, Kris Kross, Blackstreet, Michael and Janet Jackson, Ice Cube, Dr. Dre, Tupac Shakur, and Snoop Dogg. As a result, there was a new heightened interest in the Zapp & Roger, as evidenced by the brisk sales of the 1993 17-track collection *All the Greatest Hits*, which obtained platinum certification by 1996. However, tragedy was lurking right around the corner, as Roger was shot to death on April 25, 1999, by his brother Larry (who then turned the gun on himself). In 2002, a reissue of *The Many Facets of Roger* was released via Rhino Records, which included several previously unreleased bonus tracks. *—Greg Prato*

The Many Facets of Roger / Oct. 1981 / Warner Bros. ♦♦♦♦
This is Roger Troutman's first solo release, and it blazes the same trail as the Zapp LPs. Singing through a synthesized vocal box, there's no mistaking Roger's sound. His version of Norman Whitfield and Barrett Strong's "I Heard It Through the Grapevine" is classic, and was a monster on the R&B charts. "So Ruff, So Tuff" continued the maddening dance grooves. But Roger does it all—hence the title of the album; his blues and jazz explorations are top-shelf. A very well-rounded set from a versatile, underappreciated artist. *—Andrew Hamilton*

The Saga Continues / Jun. 1984 / Warner Bros. ♦♦♦
Unique, creative, and the consummate showman, are only a few of the adjectives you could use to describe *The Saga Continues*. Roger uses his vocoder or talk box to great effects on a sizzling, squealing version of Wilson Pickett's "In the Midnight Hour," accompanied by the Mighty Clouds of Joy. A bouncy "In the Mix" soared to number-ten R&B in 1984. Ex-Ohio Players' keyboardist, Billy Beck helps on keyboards, and Maceo Parker adds his usual awesome sax outbursts. Most of the songs were written by Roger and his brother Larry, including "Play Your Guitar Brother Roger," where his playing skills are highlighted. While a solo album, the lineup remains the same as on the Zapp releases, the musical approach remains the same. *—Andrew Hamilton*

Unlimited! / Nov. 1987 / Reprise ♦♦♦
The vocoder-crazed leader of Zapp has made numerous solo albums, but this is the best, powered by enormous synth riffs and the charming "Private Lover." *—John Floyd*

Bridging the Gap / 1991 / Reprise ♦♦

● **All the Greatest Hits** / Oct. 26, 1993 / Warner Bros. ♦♦♦♦♦
As the title suggests, all of the greatest hits and best tracks from the funk outfit Zapp and their lead singer Roger are collected on this single disc, making it the definitive retrospective. *—Stephen Thomas Erlewine*

D.J. Rogers (DeWayne Julius Rogers)

b. Los Angeles, CA
Vocals / Soul, Urban, Contemporary Gospel, Quiet Storm

D.J. Rogers is best known for the tender acoustic piano-based ballad "Say You Love Me," a charting single from his 1976 debut RCA album *It's Good to Be Alive*. Natalie Cole's cover of the song was the first single from her album *Snowfall in the Sahara*, released by WEA/Elektra Entertainment in June 1999. Like most soul singers, DeWayne Julius Rogers began singing and playing piano in church in his native Los Angeles. He later worked with Rev. James Cleveland when he was the director of the Watts Community Choir and a member of the Los Angeles Community Choir. The gospel influence was very evident in Rogers' later secular releases, with many of his songs filled with inspirational messages. After signing with RCA Records, Rogers' debut album *It's Good to Be Alive* was released. Initially gaining radio airplay as an album track, the single "Say You Love Me" peaked at number-51 R&B on *Billboard*'s charts in spring 1976. The 45 was a "turntable hit," meaning that it received a substantial amount of radio play, but for whatever reasons the exposure didn't translate into the single being a big seller.

The lackluster chart success of "Say You Love Me" (and his other RCA releases) lead to Rogers' angry tirades in an article in the premier *Soul* magazine, as he attributed the label's seemingly slothful attitude towards his music as a result of the record division's main purpose as being that of a "tax write-off." After listening to "Say You Love Me," one would have to wonder why the record wasn't a bigger hit. Besides the aforementioned Cole and others, Jennifer Holliday covered the song; her version can be found on *Best of Jennifer Holliday*, UNI/Geffen. Another track from *It's Good to Be Alive* that received radio play was the poignant tale of "Bula Jean," a girl that had beauty that "the world" couldn't see. On "Bula Jean," Rogers' gospel-born fervor was at its peak. On his next album, Rogers began his collaboration with composer/keyboardist/arranger/producer Jerry Peters (co-wrote "Going in Circles" with Anita Poree, a 1969 gold single for the Friends of Distinction and a number-two R&B hit for the Gap Band in 1986). Beginning with a swirling strings intro, "Let Your Life Shine" was Rogers' jubilant single that charted at number-78 R&B, fall 1976. It was included on the 1976 *On the Road Again* LP.

Rogers signed with Lonnie Simmons' Total Experience Records (the Gap Band, Yarbrough and Peoples) and the LP *Love, Music & Life* was issued in 1977. Rogers' first single for the RCA-distributed label, "Love Is All I Need," featured multi-tracked vocals by Deniece Williams ("Free," "Let's Hear It for the Boy," "Too Little Too Late" with Johnny Mathis). The second single was the passionate "Saved By Love." Other highlights were "She Has Eyes for Me," "You Against You," and the pumping "Love Will Make It Better." Signing with Columbia Records, the singer/songwriter finally enjoyed some upper chart success. His highest charting single was "Love Brought Me Back," maybe Rogers' most biographical song. In it, the singer seems to "testify" to his music industry travails. Record buyers heard him, taking the track to number-20 R&B during summer 1978. The follow-up, the playful "All My Love (Pt. 1)" made it to number-87 R&B, late 1978.

Rogers was on Earth, Wind & Fire leader Maurice White's Columbia-distributed label ARC when one of his most enduring tracks, the percolating steppers' favorite "Trust in Me (Pt. 1)" mid-charted at number-68 R&B, spring 1979. The track has a "shucking" string arrangement by Coleridge Taylor Perkinson. The follow-up, "Love Cycles," went to number-44 R&B, spring 1980. Rogers dueted with singer/keyboardist Patrice Rushen on "Givin' It Up Is Givin' Up" from her 1980 Elektra LP *Pizzaazz*. Released as a single, it peaked at number-47 R&B, summer 1980. The album also yielded her number-seven R&B hit "Haven't You Heard." Both tracks are on the 1996 Rhino greatest-hits set *Haven't You Heard—The Best of Patrice Rushen*. Rogers' last charting single was a cover of Kenny Rogers number-five pop hit "She Believes in Me" which charted number-66 R&B.

During the mid- and late '80s, he recorded gospel albums. He co-wrote "My Faith in Jesus" with John Black for gospel artist Keith Pringle ("Call Him Up") and wrote and performed a duet with Pringle on "One More Day." Rogers appeared as a choir member on the 1997 UPN-TV sitcom *Good News*. Another gospel-influenced singer/keyboardist, Billy Preston, was in the cast too. Some of Rogers' RCA/Columbia sides can be found on Collectables Records' 1996 set *D.J. Rogers: Golden Classics*. *—Ed Hogan*

D.J. Rogers / 1973 / Shelter ♦♦♦♦
This early release from D.J. Rogers is one of his best. Cut for the Shelter label in 1973, before Rogers gained some exposure on RCA and Columbia, the eponymous album features plenty of the gospel-inflected soul the singer/producer/arranger would become known

for. In fact, the bulk here is squarely bent on the kind of community-driven positivism found in the black church ("March On," "Where There's a Will"). And the music certainly reflects the lofty sentiments, as strings, choral singing, and urbane soul grooves ensure a truly inspired mix; this blend is especially well essayed on the extended, heaven-bound travelogue "Don't You Want to Ride." A soul classic that's unfortunately still buried in album-bin oblivion. *—Stephen Cook*

It's Good to Be Alive / 1976 / RCA ✦✦✦
Issued in the spring of 1976, *It's Good to Be Alive* was D.J. Rogers' RCA debut after having recorded for Leon Russell's Shelter label. It was a unique mix of soul and gospel that featured the original version of his classic ballad single, "Say You Love Me." Another standout track is the poignant "Bula Jean." Those two, along with the upbeat "Hold on, Be Strong," received radio play. The sparse framework, a rhythm section with a smattering of horns, probably gives Rogers the best showcase for his songs. Some of the album's track can be found on *Golden Classics*. *—Ed Hogan*

On the Road Again / 1976 / RCA ✦✦

Love, Music & Life / 1977 / RCA ✦✦

Love Brought Me Back / 1978 / Columbia ✦✦✦

● **Say You Love Me** / Apr. 1996 / Ichiban/Soul Classics ✦✦✦✦✦
Rogers' brand of gospel-flavored soul was a bit "old school" by the mid- to late '70s, although his work kept pace with mainstream R&B rhythms and production values without making the effort to cross into disco. This is an 18-track compilation of material from the six albums that he cut for RCA and Columbia between 1975 and 1980, including the modest R&B hits "Say You Love Me," "Trust Me, Pt. 1," "She Believes in Me," and "All My Love, Pt. 1"; it's generally best when it cuts closest to his gospel roots. *—Richie Unterberger*

Golden Classics / Nov. 5, 1996 / Collectables ✦✦✦
DJ Rogers' *Golden Classics* is truly a best-of set as it culls tracks from the singer/songwriter/keyboardist's releases on RCA and Earth Wind & Fire founder Maurice White's Columbia-distributed label ARC. The CD not only includes his classic acoustic piano-laced ballad "Say You Love Me" and hit "Love Brought Me Back," but its charming groover follow-up "All My Love," the chugging steppers favorite "Trust Me," the swirling, dynamic "Love Cycles," and the brisk gospel-ish "Let My Life Shine." Besides these singles, there are little-known album gems like the sweet thumper "Sold on You" from the *Love Brought Me Back* LP. Many tracks feature the top-notch skills of bassist Keni Burke. Rogers' other greatest-hits CD is *The Message Man: The Best of DJ Rogers*. *—Ed Hogan*

The Message Man: The Best of DJ Rogers / Feb. 17, 1998 / Columbia/Legacy ✦✦✦
From one of the original pioneers of gospel groove, *The Message Man* includes 13 of D.J. Rogers' greatest hits, including "You Take Me Higher (Brazilian Lover," "Trust Me," "All My Love" and "Love Brought Me Back." *—John Bush*

D.J. Rogers Jr.

Vocals / Neo-Soul
With a career that started with the graphic bump and grind of "Doggy Style," it would be easy to picture D.J. Rogers Jr. as a sultry R&B singer similar to R. Kelly, especially considering the earthy nature of his first hit. However, after contemplating his future in the wake of that song's appearance on the successful soundtrack for *Above the Rim* in 1993, Rogers chose to let his first brush with fame's spotlight wane. Choosing instead to concentrate on his considerable writing skills, the rest of the '90s saw Rogers build a career he was more comfortable with, penning songs for a number of artists including Faith Evans and Carl Thomas. Having inherited the same rich expressive voice that catapulted his father, the senior D.J. Rogers, to fame in the '70s, it seemed inevitable that D.J. Rogers Jr. would return to recording. His return saw him performing with a more organic bent that fit him comfortably in the nascent neo-soul tradition. His debut album, *Emosoul* was released in late 2002. *— Wade Kergan*

● **Emosoul** / Sep. 2002 / Motown ✦✦✦✦
Like Gerald LeVert, D.J. Rogers Jr. is a second-generation soul man with gospel power in his pipes (his father, D.J. Rogers, was a former associate of Rev. James Cleveland and achieved some chart success in the '70s and early '80s). And like LeVert, the younger Rogers concentrates more on his tunes than their settings, eschewing futuristic funk and retro hipness in favor of meat-and-potatoes modern R&B that just sounds good. As a result, Rogers' debut is more than just an ornate jewelry box, containing several gems worthy of the Motown name, including "Wonderful, Beautiful, Amazing," a lovely duet with labelmate India.Arie, and "Don't Miss the Good Stuff," where he testifies in a manner that would do his dad proud. But those tunes, and the several other standouts on *Emosoul*, don't stake their claim to Motown's legacy by self-consciously referencing Berry Gordy's heyday, as is so often the case. Wisely, these songs recall the past in the old-fashioned way: with melodies and grooves solid enough to build a house on, and located firmly in the here and now. *—Dan LeRoy*

The Romancers

Group / Brown-Eyed Soul, Latin Rock, Rock & Roll
In the early and mid-'60s, this group was among the originators of the East Los Angeles Sound, a gritty sort of blue-eyed soul that took root in the Latin-American community in particular. The Romancers' instrumental albums for the Del-Fi label were generic, if solid, sax-driven R&B/rock hybrids, probably good for a high old time at dancehalls, but not that interesting on record. (They did make some vocal recordings for other labels.) Their significance is more historical than musical, as other bands from their neighborhood would take Latino rock to more accomplished heights, particularly Thee Midniters. The Romancers did make their mark known in other ways: they played on the Premiers' hit "Farmer John" and backed the Heartbreakers on an obscure pre-Mothers of Invention single written by Frank Zappa ("Everytime I See You"). Rhythm guitarist Max Uballez also co-produced and arranged Cannibal & the Headhunters' hit "Land of a Thousand Dances." *—Richie Unterberger*

● **The Slauson Shuffle** / 1995 / Del-Fi ✦✦✦
This features instrumental R&B/rock/soul dance tunes, prominently featuring honking sax and chunky guitar rhythms. They were a solid unit, but the material isn't anything special, being far more suitable for live dances or pre-star warmup spots than foreground listening. *—Richie Unterberger*

Rome (Jerome Woods)

b. Benton Harbor, MI
Vocals / Urban, Contemporary R&B
Smooth R&B singer Rome was born Jerome Woods in Benton Harbor, MI. Early on, he sang along with his mother's soul records (Marvin Gaye, Sam Cooke) as well as in the local church choir. He joined an R&B cover band named Fire & Ice while in high school, and traveled around the region performing in local clubs and talent contests as a solo act and with the band. Woods dropped out of Alabama's Oakwood University in 1989 to pursue his dream on the West Coast, and toured with Vesta as a backing vocalist as well as appearing in industry showcases and cable-access programs. Finally, he connected with producers Gerald Baillergeau and Victor Merrit, who sent his demo to RCA Records. The label signed him immediately, and he began working on his debut album in mid-1996. The self-titled LP appeared in April 1997 and soon ascended to number 30 on the album charts, earning gold certification. *Thank You* followed two years later. *—John Bush*

● **Rome** / Apr. 15, 1997 / RCA ✦✦✦✦

Rome 2000: Thank You / Nov. 2, 1999 / JTJ ✦✦✦✦
Rome's second album *Rome 2000: Thank You* features more smooth, romantic ballads from the R&B vocalist, including "Say Yes," "Ain't Nothing Like," and "The Best of Me," while skits and songs like "Throw Your Hands Up in the Air" and "Makin' That Money" add humor and danceability. Overall, it's a well-crafted album of smooth R&B. *—Heather Phares*

The Ronettes

f. 1959, New York, NY, **db.** 1966
Group / Girl Group, Brill Building Pop
Before Phil Spector took them under his wing in the early '60s, the Ronettes had already recorded several singles and were regionally successful. But the Spector-produced records are what everyone remembers, and for good reason—they featured some of his biggest, best productions along with equally impressive songs. Beneath his monumental Wall of Sound, lead vocalist Ronnie Bennett, who would later marry Spector, sang songs of teenage love in a plain, girlish voice; "Be My Baby," the group's first and biggest hit, was the pinnacle of the group's talent, as well as being one of the producer's finest moments. None of their following singles (including "Baby, I Love You," "(The Best Part Of) Breaking Up," and "Walking in the Rain") were quite as successful commercially, although they were nearly as strong artistically.

While Spector was inactive in the mid-'60s, the Ronettes were also inactive; together they re-emerged in 1969 to a small commercial reception. After Ronnie divorced Spector in 1973, she formed a new version of the Ronettes that lasted for three years; after the group disbanded, she launched a solo career. *—Stephen Thomas Erlewine*

Presenting the Fabulous Ronettes Featuring Veronica / 1964 / Phillies ✦✦✦

The Ronettes: The Early Years / 1965 / Rhino ✦✦✦✦✦
The early Ronettes songs weren't as immaculately produced or as evocative as Phil Spector's productions. Their sound was more generic and resembled other girl groups like the Shirelles or Chiffons. They recorded for Colpix and Dimension during 1961 and 1962, with Ronnie Bennett doing most of the leads, while her sister Estelle and cousin Nedra added soothing harmonies and backgrounds. At times, as on "My Guiding Angel" or "You Bet I Would," they came close to the appealing mix of innocence and earnestness that characterized their later (and greatest) tracks. But despite getting material from such songwriters as Jackie DeShannon and Carole King, many of these cuts were more serviceable than classic. Still, this is the foundation for the sound that exploded in the mid-'60s. *—Ron Wynn*

The Greatest Hits, Vol. 2 / 1981 / Masters ✦✦✦
A good 16-track compilation of rare tracks and non-hit singles, highlighted by "I Can Hear Music," "Paradise," and "Is This What I Get for Loving You"; it also has three tracks that Ronnie Spector sang on, but which were credited to the Crystals. The most interesting material, however, is now available on the ABKCO CD. *—Richie Unterberger*

Greatest Hits / 1990 / Spectacular Sound ✦✦✦✦✦
This collection, a pirate from Italy that seems to be legal under the copyright laws there, only contains 15 songs, putting it at a seeming disadvantage next to the authorized *Best of the Ronettes*. That is, until you hear it—for starters, it's in *stereo*! Now, that's not supposed to be the way that Spector intended these to be heard, but the 15 tracks here sound more like the original records than the equivalent songs on the authorized release, with the authentic Phil Spector "Wall of Sound" compression on the bass and the mid-range, the same marvelous sound that used to flow out of a 50-cent transistor radio speaker like something beyond music, like it was hooked directly into a passionate and angst-filled female soul (which it was, in this case Ronnie Spector's), all intact. It hits you here the way fans always wanted this stuff to—check out the drums and the richness of the vocal textures on "I Wonder," and the thick tone of the strings when they come in at the end; Ronnie Spector's up-close-and-personal singing on "Do I Love You," and the bells chiming under the Spector-ized backing; and the horns, bells, chorus with reverb, and Spector's voice all in perfect balance on "Walking in the Rain." What the sources were is anyone's guess, but the "Baby I Love You" mastering here is of demonstration quality, the strumming of the acoustic guitar on an equal footing with the vocal and instrumental overdubs

going on all around it. And "Is This What I Get for Loving You," which has always been an obvious direct model for large sections of Brian Wilson's production on *Pet Sounds*, comes off as clean and sharp here as the remastered *Pet Sounds*. The whole CD is a gem, and an essential addition to any serious Phil Spector collection. *—Bruce Eder*

★ **The Best of the Ronettes** / Sep. 22, 1992 / ABKCO ♦♦♦♦♦

For a couple of years, the Ronettes made music that was as moving and unforgettable as any made during the rock era. Their voices merged sensuality, longing, anguish, and sentimentality, with Ronnie Spector's angelic leads framed by Phil Spector's sweeping production, and the lyrics of Ellie Greenwich, Jeff Barry, Barry Mann, Cynthia Weil, Spector, and others. While such songs as "Walking in the Rain," "Be My Baby," "Baby, I Love You," and "(The Best Part Of) Breaking Up" may seem hopelessly naive and possibly sexist in today's cynical world, they're still classic love poems. Ronnie Spector's voice retains its allure and appeal, and the 18 tracks on this CD will never become dated. *—Ron Wynn*

Rose Royce

f. 1973, Los Angeles, CA

Group / Disco, Funk, Quiet Storm, Urban

Rose Royce—the Los Angeles-based group comprised of Henry Garner (drums), Terral "Terry" Santiel (congas), Lequeint "Duke" Jobe (bass), Michael Moore (saxophone), Rose Norwalt (lead vocals), Kenny Copeland (trumpet, lead vocals), Kenji Brown (guitar, lead vocals), Freddie Dunn (trumpet), and Michael Nash (keyboards)—was actually formed by Copeland and Garner. Both were preparing for graduation from high school, and contemplating their careers. Joined by Dunn and Moore, the two decided to go the route of the music business under the name Total Concept Unlimited (and later as Magic Wand). They auditioned for Edwin Starr, and he hired them as his backup band.

The group's association with Starr enabled them to interact with numerous music industry personalities. One in particular was Motown producer Norman Whitfield. Whitfield gradually became associated with the group by hiring them for recording sessions; the group also worked with Yvonne Fair, the Undisputed Truth, and the Temptations through Whitfield's influence. After a couple of years of seasoning, the group began production on their debut album under Whitfield's supervision. Also during this time, MCA Records was seeking an artist for the soundtrack to the movie *Car Wash*. Whitfield convinced executives that the band was more than competent for the job. So the material that Whitfield had assembled for the group's debut album became the soundtrack's material.

The movie *Car Wash* and the soundtrack were big hits, and they also propelled the group, now known as Rose Royce, into national notoriety. Released in late 1976, the soundtrack featured three *Billboard* R&B Top Ten singles: "Car Wash," "I Wanna Get Next to You," and "I'm Going Down." The former was also a number-one single on the *Billboard* pop charts. To offset any negative rhetoric regarding their legitimacy, the group released its follow-up album, *Rose Royce II: In Full Bloom*, and bloom it did. The group returned to the Top Ten with "Do Your Dance" and "Ooh Boy," silencing all critics. In 1978, they released their third album, entitled *Rose Royce III: Strikes Again!*, and it featued "I'm in Love (And I Love the Feeling)" and "Love Don't Live Here Anymore." Both singles cracked the *Billboard* R&B Top Five.

The group followed with a string of hits that roamed the charts, but never gained the chart status that their previous songs did. They became very popular in England and remained a marquee attraction there through the 90s. *—Craig Lytle*

Car Wash / 1976 / MCA ♦♦♦♦

This double album, the soundtrack to a hit 1976 urban-themed comedy starring Richard Pryor and George Carlin, was also the debut album for funk hitmakers Rose Royce. Although they had already recorded most of a non-soundtrack album prior to *Car Wash*, their producer and Svengali Norman Whitfield insisted that they put that aside when he got the opportunity to write the score for this film. The result was a killer crossover success that made the group's name and proved there was life after Motown for Whitfield. It also produced some serious hit singles: the title track was a clever tune that blended a throbbing disco beat, hypnotic funk riffs from the rhythm section, and an ornate string arrangement to become number-one hit, and "I Wanna Get Next to You" married ethereal strings to a midtempo soul beat to create a classic ballad in the mold of Whitfield's work with the Temptations. The remainder of the album divides its time between funky songs and orchestral-tinged instrumental workouts. In the song arena, standouts include "I'm Going Down," a torchy, dramatically-arranged ballad that features an all-stops-out vocal performance from Gwen Dickey, and "Daddy Rich," a witty portrait of a religious con man that is built on an infectious combination of staccato horns and a relentlessly churning rhythm guitar hook. The masterpiece in the instrumental arena is "Sunrise," a hypnotic ten-minute epic whose effective tension-and-release arrangement that adds and subtracts layers of instrumentation over a pulsating beat to create a thoroughly hypnotic effect. Two album's worth of Rose Royce may be a little too much for the casual listener, but there is no denying that *Car Wash* is both stylishly crafted and intensely funky. It is a required listen for anyone interested in Rose Royce and a solid choice for funk and disco fans alike. *—Donald A. Guarisco*

Rose Royce II: In Full Bloom / 1977 / Whitfield ♦♦♦♦♦

As strong as any of the songs featured on 1976's *Car Wash* soundtrack, Rose Royce's 1977 outing, *II: In Full Bloom*, allowed them to fully shine in their own right and on their own terms. Although their early incarnation as Total Concept Unlimited had paired them with Motown labelmates the Temptations and given them clout in the label stable, it was the addition of powerhouse vocalist Gwen Dickey and continued pairing with über-producer Norman Whitfield that brought the band into their own. Packed with tight funk jams and horn-heavy construction, tempered only occasionally by Dickey's sweet ballads, *II: In Full Bloom* is a disco-funk masterpiece—a pure fusion of both genres that works better than it has a right to, courtesy of both the band's own confidence and Whitfield's artful magic. The wistful and absolutely sublime ballad "Wishing on a Star" opens the set and should have been a chart-heavy hitter. In fact, it reached only number 52 on the R&B charts, proving that the band's fans were truly in the mood to dance. Rose Royce wouldn't disappoint, as the nine-minute funk monster "Do Your Dance" was uncaged. Shaved to a four-minute highlights version, the song gave the band a Top Five R&B hit. The full album version, however, is a far superior workout, while the equally funky "You Can't Please Everybody" and eight-minute epic "It Makes You Feel Like Dancin'" keep the groove moving smoothly. Rose Royce may have shot to stardom with the *Car Wash* craze, but they are far better without the celluloid glitter covering up their own pure gold. *—Amy Hanson*

Rose Royce III: Strikes Again / 1978 / Whitfield ♦♦♦♦

Rose Royce's third album contains two killer ballads: "I'm In Love (And I Love the Feeling)," and the much recorded "Love Don't Live Here Anymore" which Gwen Dickey works like Mary J. Blige wish she could. Norman Whitfield's productions often included doses of classical elements and this album is no exception, the sampling and borrowing occur frequently. "Angel in Disguise" another sweet ballad sounds a bit contrived. As effective on upbeat tunes "That's What's Wrong With Me," "Do It, Do It" and "First Come First Serve," are first-class movers and shakers. A carnival barker on the intro mars the opening cut "Get Up Off Your Fat." *—Andrew Hamilton*

Rose Royce IV: The Rainbow Connection / 1979 / Whitfield ♦♦♦♦

Rose Royce's fourth album, *Rose Royce IV: The Rainbow Connection* marked the end of an era for the Los Angeles-based soul/funk band. Produced by Norman Whitfield, this 1979 effort was the last Rose Royce album to feature Gwen "Rose" Dickey, whose lead vocals had graced such hits as "Carwash," "Love Don't Live Here Anymore," "Ooh Boy," and "Wishing on a Star." The charming singer was among Rose Royce's major assets and fans were sorry to see her go. Rose Royce's Gwen Dickey era ended on a high note with this LP, which finds her excelling on the lush disco hit "Is It Love You're After," as well as the ballad "I Wonder Where You Are Tonight" and sweaty funk jams like "What You Waitin' for" (a Whitfield composition that had been previously recorded by Stargard) and the humorous "Bad Mother Funker." Arguably, "Is It Love You're After" is the most disco-minded tune that the Angelinos ever recorded—while Rose Royce had a lot of grit and was a soul/funk outfit first and foremost, the lush and glossy "Is It Love You're After" is about as disco as it gets. As impressive as Dickey's contributions to *The Rainbow Connection* are, she doesn't sing lead on all of the songs—Kenny Copeland also deserves applause for the lead vocals that he provides on this generally excellent album. *—Alex Henderson*

Golden Touch / 1981 / Whitfield ♦♦♦

Without question, Rose Royce suffered a major loss when lead vocalist Gwen "Rose" Dickey left the band in 1979. But as memorable as her contributions were—as much as fans adored her—1980's *Golden Touch* proved that she wasn't indispensable. Rose Royce still had a gem of a lead singer in falsetto Kenny Copeland and Dickey's female replacement Ricci Benson proved that she was no slouch either. Benson doesn't sound anything like her predecessor, as Dickey's vocals had a girlish sweetness and that isn't the case with the husky-voiced Benson. But the new replacement is charismatic in her own way, and she proves herself to be a deserving addition to the band on the dreamy title song as well as the lovely ballad "And You Wish For Yesterday." Copeland, meanwhile, has some memorable spots on the medium-tempo "Love Is in the Air," the Stylistics-like "Would You Please Be Mine," and the funky "I Wanna Make It With You" (not to be confused with the Bread hit). And all of the singers contribute to "Funkin' Around," a very fun slice of Parliament-influenced P-Funk. *Golden Touch* isn't among Rose Royce's essential albums, but it's a solid, respectable effort that illustrates the band's ability to carry on without Dickey. *—Alex Henderson*

Jump Street / 1981 / Whitfield ♦♦

Stronger Than Ever / 1982 / Epic ♦♦

Music Magic / 1984 / Montage ♦♦♦♦

Streetwave Records originally released this set in 1984. It represents one of the final chapters of Rose Royce's interesting recording career. The tunes are as arresting as any they ever did; but with little promotion, these charming caressers and robotic grooves escaped all but Rose Royce's most fanatical fans' attention. Kenny Copeland's sugary falsetto (he doubles on trumpet) and Ricci Benson's—who replaced Gwen Dickey—striking soprano sparkle throughout. Like good brewed coffee, *Music Magic* is good from the first to the last drop. *—Andrew Hamilton*

Fresh Cut / 1987 / Omni ♦♦♦

When Rose Royce recorded *Fresh Cut* in 1986 the band wasn't nearly as popular as it had been in the late 1970s. They hoped to make a comeback and the Los Angeles residents decided that the way to accomplish that was by being relevant to the urban contemporary scene of 1986. So on *Fresh Cut* Rose Royce works with some of the hot producers of that era (including Nick Martinelli and Arthur Baker) and tries to be more urban contemporary-sounding without being completely unfaithful to its history. Synthesizers and drum machines are more prominent and the horns are decreased without eliminating them. The ballads (which include the emotional "You're My Peace of Mind" and an inspired remake of the Temptations' "Just My Imagination") are excellent, and more uptempo items like "If Walls Could Talk" and "Magic Doll" are enjoyable even though they aren't in a class with Rose Royce's late 1970s funk. One can understand why they changed their sound—it made sense to change with the times. Nonetheless, anyone who savored Rose Royce's classic 1970s output can't help but miss hearing all those horns. But *Fresh Cut* has many more ups than downs, and it's a generally pleasing addition to the band's catalog even though it falls short of essential. *—Alex Henderson*

● **The Very Best of Rose Royce** / Jun. 5, 2001 / Rhino ♦♦♦♦

There has never been a compilation as comprehensive as Rhino's *The Very Best of Rose Royce*, a 16-track trawl through their past that hits from their recordings for MCA and Whitfield, which means it has just about every hit that most fans could want from a collection. In fact, it may be a little long for some listeners, since 16 tracks is a lot of

Rose Royce, but it certainly doesn't leave you wanting more, and it has fine sound and fine notes from A. Scott Galloway, which all adds up to the best collection yet assembled on the disco outfit (and likely one of the best that will ever be assembled). *—Stephen Thomas Erlewine*

Rosie & the Originals

f. 1960, San Diego, CA

Group / Girl Group, Doo Wop, Rock & Roll, R&B

Rosie & the Originals are one of the best-remembered one-shot artists of the early rock era, getting to number five with their 1960 single "Angel Baby." A slow, simple, and primitively recorded and executed doo wop-shaded ballad, it was distinguished from countless other records of the sort by 15-year-old Rosie Hamlin's unnaturally high, thin voice, which got higher-than-high on the periodic wordless "ooh, ooh-oohs" that served as the record's primary hooks.

The single's gotten more notoriety than might be expected considering that the group never had another Top 40 hit. John Lennon cited Rosie as one of his favorite singers in a 1969 interview in *Life* magazine, and recorded the song in the mid-'70s for his *Rock 'n' Roll* oldies collection, although that track wasn't issued until the mid-'80s. In an essay in *Rock Almanac*, Mark Sten even described the song as "generating a robot mantra devoid of embellishment or variation, the perfect underpinning for Rosie's piercing, disembodied-siren vocal. With 'Angel Baby,' rock had regressed as far as it could, some nameless dread loosed within the collective Top 40 mind had run its course and spent itself in a lost mournful wail. 'Angel Baby' was the final moonlit flowering of rock's medieval phase, paean to a purity and innocence on longer possible in the real world."

The band certainly had no thoughts of inviting such intellectual commentary when they formed in San Diego in 1960. Unable to find a recording studio in San Diego, they cut "Angel Baby" in a barn-like building in the farming town of San Marcos, with a radically different B-side, "Give Me Love," with a vocal by Bluford D. Wade. The group had trouble interesting Los Angeles labels in the song (a Hamlin original) until they convinced a department store manager in San Diego to play it. This attracted attention from kids in the store and a record distributor that happened to be there at the time. Through him they got the single "Angel Baby" released on Highland, and at the end of 1960 it shot up the national charts.

Although Rosie & the Originals recorded a few more tracks, they broke up almost immediately after "Angel Baby" made the charts, in a dispute over the terms of a recording contract they were considering signing. In 1961, Jackie Wilson's manager, Nat Tarnopol, got Rosie a contract with Wilson's label, Brunswick. Brunswick did put out a follow-up single, "Lonely Blue Nights," which made number 66, as well as an album and another single, billing the artist solely as Rosie for all the releases. In the meantime Highland put out a couple of Rosie & the Originals 45s with tracks to which they had the rights.

"Angel Baby," however, was one of those accidents of timing and unique material that couldn't be repeated, and none of Rosie's subsequent recordings—which, like "Angel Baby," were usually simple pop/rock ballads with a doo wop feel—could recapture the magic. Hamlin did make another single for the Globe label before leaving the music business to raise a family with her husband, Noah Tafolla, who had been leader and lead guitarist of the Originals. She did some tracks with producer Doug Salma in 1969 in a more updated doo wop/girl group style that remained unreleased until 2000, when the Ace compilation *The Best of Rosie & the Originals* was issued. *—Richie Unterberger*

● **The Best of Rosie & the Originals** / Jan. 25, 2000 / Ace ✦✦✦✦

Rosie & the Originals are among the first early rock acts to come to mind when people think of one-shot artists, so you might think it a bit of a stretch to come up with a 21-song compilation. That it is, combining about a dozen of her early-'60s tracks for Highland and Brunswick—the first of which were done with the Originals, the later of which were done simply as Rosie—with ten previously unissued tracks from a 1969 session. "Angel Baby" was a memorable, unique single, but Rosie Hamlin, who wrote most of the material she recorded, didn't have much else to offer as either a singer or songwriter. Most of her post-"Angel Baby" output was similar and inferior to that hit, often so elementary in content as to be banal. These tracks laid out the same sort of doo wop/pop-rock ballads, exploiting her propensity to hit high, wordless notes that sounded a little like a record rotating at a slightly higher-than-normal speed. "Lonely Blue Nights," her only record to chart (which it did, lowly) besides "Angel Baby," is here, and is so close to "Angel Baby" in structure that one wonders why anyone would be surprised that it didn't rise any higher than number 66. The 1969 sessions are mediocre updates of her transitional doo wop-to-girl group sound, with more modern arrangements (noted session player Jerry Scheff is on bass) that mute whatever charm was heard on the early-'60s sides. As marginal enticements for serious collectors, this includes the wholly uncharacteristic B-side of "Angel Baby," a disorganized, improvised R&B tune on which male R&B singer Bluford D. Wade (who wasn't in the Originals) takes lead vocals. There's also a different, and worse, alternate take of "Angel Baby" that was only issued in the U.K. *—Richie Unterberger*

Angel Baby Revisited / Aug. 28, 2001 / Ace ✦✦

The prior *The Best of Rosie & the Originals* compilation on Ace had already found it a stretch to gather enough material to pad out a full-length retrospective, relying on numerous previously unissued tracks and flop singles to make up the quota. *Angel Baby Revisited*, a collection of odds and ends that didn't make it onto the best-of, really scours too deep and wide to come up with yet another disc's worth of material, much of which really doesn't deserve a hearing. This kind of release is for collectors who want everything, though, not more discriminating listeners. Still, even such collectors may be disappointed to find that only eight of these 23 tracks are from Rosie's early-'60s heyday. Six of those vintage numbers are taken from her 1961 *Lonely Blue Nights* album, and are mediocre light early-'60s pop-R&B, though she sings pretty well on these. The other two are from her rare, and similarly unremarkable, 1962 single on Globe. Few details are given about the origins of the remaining selections, all but one of which date from 2000-2001. Rosie sings alright on these modern recordings, but the material is uninspired (whether remakes of oldies or otherwise), and the production is perfunctory and sometimes ill-suited in its modern instrumentation. When it gets to a cappella versions of "Dedicated to the One I Love" and "Angel Baby" and spoken radio IDs for oldies stations, there seems to be some hidden desperation on the part of the compilers to come up with full-length, if not high-value, product. The one remaining selection is the oddest one: "I Don't Understand," dated as a 1973 Wax World release on the track listing, sounds like it might have been recorded a few years later, with its fairly fetching retro lo-fi production and cross of light soul and adult pop vocal styles. *—Richie Unterberger*

Diana Ross (Diane Earle)

b. Mar. 26, 1944, Detroit, MI

Vocals / Pop-Soul, Soul, Motown, Disco, Urban

As a solo artist, Diana Ross is one of the most successful female singers of the rock era. If you factor in her work as the lead singer of the Supremes in the 1960s, she may be *the* most successful. With her friends Mary Wilson, Florence Ballard, and Barbara Martin, Ross formed the Primettes vocal quartet in 1959. In 1960, they were signed to local Motown Records, changing their name to the Supremes in 1961. Martin then left, and the group continued as a trio. Over the next eight years, the Supremes (renamed "Diana Ross & the Supremes" in 1967, when Cindy Birdsong replaced Ballard) scored 12 number-one pop hits. After the last one, "Someday We'll Be Together" (October 1969), Ross launched a solo career.

Motown initially paired her with writer/producers Nickolas Ashford & Valerie Simpson, who gave her four Top 40 pop hits, including the number one "Ain't No Mountain High Enough" (July 1970). Ross branched out into acting, starring in a film biography of Billie Holiday, *Lady Sings the Blues* (November 1972). The soundtrack went to number one, and Ross was nominated for an Academy Award. She returned to record-making with the Top Ten album *Touch Me in the Morning* (June 1973) and its chart-topping title song. This was followed by a duet album with Marvin Gaye, *Diana & Marvin* (October 1973), that produced three chart hits. Ross acted in her second movie, *Mahogany* (October 1975), and it brought her another chart-topping single in the theme song, "Do You Know Where You're Going To." That and her next number one, the disco-oriented "Love Hangover" (March 1976), were featured on her second album to be titled simply *Diana Ross* (February 1976), which rose into the Top Ten.

Ross' third film role came in *The Wiz* (October 1978). *The Boss* (May 1979) was a gold-selling album, followed by the platinum-selling *Diana* (May 1980) (the second of her solo albums with that name, though the other, a 1971 TV soundtrack, had an exclamation mark). It featured the number one single "Upside Down" and the Top Ten hit "I'm Coming Out."

Ross scored a third Top Ten hit in 1980 singing the title theme from the movie *It's My Turn*. She then scored the biggest hit of her career with another movie theme, duetting with Lionel Richie on "Endless Love" (June 1981). It was her last big hit on Motown; after more than 20 years, she decamped for RCA. She was rewarded immediately with a million-selling album, titled after her remake of the old Frankie Lymon & the Teenagers hit, "Why Do Fools Fall in Love," which became her next Top Ten hit. The album also included the Top Ten hit "Mirror, Mirror." *Silk Electric* (October 1982) was a gold-seller, featuring the Top Ten hit "Muscles," written and produced by Michael Jackson, and *Swept Away* (September 1984) was another successful album, containing the hit "Missing You," but Ross had trouble selling records in the second half of the 1980s. By 1989, she had returned to Motown, and by 1993 was turning more to pop standards, notably on the concert album *Diana Ross Live: The Lady Sings... Jazz & Blues, Stolen Moments* (April 1993).

Motown released a four-CD/cassette box set retrospective, *Forever Diana*, in October 1993, and the singer published her autobiography in 1994. *Take Me Higher* followed a year later, and in 1999 she returned with *Every Day Is a New Day*. *Gift of Love* (2000) was promoted by a concert tour featuring the Supremes, although neither Mary Wilson nor Cindy Birdsong appeared—their roles were instead assumed by singers Lynda Laurence and Scherrie Payne, neither of whom ever performed with Ross during the group's glory days. *—William Ruhlmann*

Diana Ross / Jun. 19, 1970 / Motown ✦✦✦✦✦

Her self-titled debut LP (later retitled *Ain't No Mountain High Enough* after the single became a hit) was arguably her finest solo work at Motown and perhaps her best ever; it was certainly among her most stunning. Everyone who doubted whether Diana Ross could sustain a career outside the Supremes found out immediately that she would be a star. The single "Reach Out and Touch (Somebody's Hand)" remains a staple in her shows, and is still her finest message track. *—Ron Wynn*

Everything Is Everything / Oct. 1970 / Motown ✦✦✦

With her first solo album, Diana Ross proved that she could thrive without the Supremes. Once that matter was decided, she settled into a comfortable pattern of releasing uneven but enjoyable records that didn't stretch her talent too far. There were exceptions, such as the sublime *Lady Sings the Blues*, but her second album *Everything is Everything* pretty much set the pace for the remainder of her solo career. It had a handful of good songs, several covers, and many average tunes from professional songsmiths, all given a contemporary production that inevitably sounds dated several years after the initial release. Since Ross has a great voice and undeniable charisma, the album is entertaining, but very few songs are memorable once the record is completed. Still, the moments where it does work are enjoyable and may be enough to make the album worthwhile, depending on whether you view the glass as half empty or half filled. *—Stephen Thomas Erlewine*

Diana! [Original TV Soundtrack] / Mar. 1971 / Motown ✦✦✦

The very fact that Diana Ross' third album was *Diana! The Original TV Soundtrack* and not a full-fledged studio record was ample proof that she was more concerned with being an all-around entertainer than simply a singer. Fortunately, she was very good as an entertainer, as *Diana!* illustrates. True, a few moments—namely the Bill Cosby and

Danny Thomas sequences and her duets with the comedians—fall flat without visuals, but her showtunes and covers are all quite enjoyable. Nevertheless, they can't help but be overshadowed by the Jackson 5's medley, which captures the group at their dynamic prime. Even if Diana is eclipsed on *Diana!*, the best moments on the record prove that she is a fine showwoman in her own right. *—Stephen Thomas Erlewine*

Surrender / Jul. 1971 / Motown ♦♦♦
A nice early-'70s date from Diana Ross, who at that time was unaffected by her diva/show-business persona and was sticking to singing. She turned in effective, unadorned, soulful leads on several songs, with the title tune cracking the R&B Top 20 and pop Top 40. Ross would later turn to a more exaggerated, self-conscious, mock-sophisticate style, but on her early Motown albums, she retained the mix of innocence, anguish, and sexiness that made her a legendary vocalist. *—Ron Wynn*

Lady Sings the Blues [Original Soundtrack] / Dec. 1972 / Motown ♦♦♦
Her biggest album as a solo act, Diana Ross forever ended any association with the Supremes after this film. She not only got an Oscar nomination and more roles, she really did capture the spirit and flavor, if not the sound and timbre, of Billie Holiday's music; her performance was the film's only saving grace. *—Ron Wynn*

Touch Me in the Morning / Jun. 1973 / Motown ♦♦♦

Diana & Marvin / Oct. 1973 / Motown ♦♦♦♦
By the early '70s, Diana Ross and Marvin Gaye were in completely different creative territories. Ross was settling down as a professional diva, while Gaye was pushing his art forward with *What's Going On*, *Trouble Man* and *Let's Get It On*. What they shared, apart from a mutual admiration, was that they were two of the biggest artists on Motown and that their voices sounded terrific together. So it wasn't entirely surprising that the duo teamed up in 1973 for the *Diana & Marvin* album. Although the album didn't produce any timeless classics, the results were still very good—good enough for the record to be one of Ross' best efforts of the era. The highlights are the three singles ("You're a Special Part of Me," "My Mistake (Was to Love You)," "Don't Knock My Love"), but even the weaker tunes are redeemed by the duo's indelible chemistry, and that's the reason why it's worth a listen. *—Stephen Thomas Erlewine*

Last Time I Saw Him / Dec. 1973 / Motown ♦♦♦
An odd entry into the early-'70s Diana Ross sweepstakes, this album became a hit many months after it was initially issued. It was one of three Ross LPs Motown released in 1973, and it succeeded only after an album of duets between Ross and Marvin Gaye had peaked. The single eventually cracked both the R&B and pop Top 20, and the album became moderately successful nearly a year after its initial debut date. *—Ron Wynn*

Live at Caesar's Palace / May 1974 / Motown ♦♦♦
An entertaining, lavish, and sometimes a bit pretentious concert album from Diana Ross. It was the first album that really presented how a typical Ross live performance sounded, and that proved both complimentary and negative. The staged conversations, often awkward monologues, and rough pacing were balanced by some excellent performances, and the album was produced well enough to keep her voice at the core of the sound. It's not an essential purchase, but it's worth getting if it turns up in an oldies collection. *—Ron Wynn*

Mahogany / Oct. 1975 / Motown ♦♦
As a vehicle for Diana Ross' film career, *Mahogany* wasn't nearly as successful as *Lady Sings the Blues*, not only because it didn't focus on her musical gifts, but because the script was weak. Still, the movie produced one of her biggest and best hits with "Theme from Mahogany (Do You Know Where You're Going To)," a Goffin-Masser tune that was nominated for an Oscar. It's a great song, but most Ross fans will rather pick it up on a collection instead of *Mahogany* since it is the only vocal track on an otherwise monotonous album of instrumental incidental music. *—Stephen Thomas Erlewine*

Diana Ross / 1976 / Motown ♦♦♦♦
Diana Ross landed one of the decade's definitive singles with "Love Hangover," instantly making this a major hit album. While it surprisingly didn't sell as well as some 1980s LPs, the single was a double chart-topper and a huge club hit for much of the next two years. It vaulted the album into the pop Top Ten and even managed to break the follow-up single onto the charts. *—Ron Wynn*

Diana Ross' Greatest Hits / 1976 / Motown ♦♦♦
Not to be confused with *Greatest Hits*, which chronicled her post-Supremes solo hits, *Diana Ross' Greatest Hits* contains the cream of her mid-'70s hits, including "Touch Me in the Morning," "Love Hangover," "Last Time I Saw Him," "Theme from Mahogany (Do You Know Where You're Going To)," "Ain't No Mountain High Enough," "Reach Out and Touch" and "Good Morning Heartache." Although more comprehensive collections, such as *Anthology*, have been released, this remains a good sampler, especially for casual fans who only want hits from this era. *—Stephen Thomas Erlewine*

An Evening With Diana Ross / Jan. 1977 / Motown ♦♦♦♦♦
Recorded live at the Ahmanson Theatre in Los Angeles, *An Evening With Diana Ross* is, in some ways, a definitive Diana Ross album. It may have been recorded in California, but it feels like a Vegas revue, as Diana sings standards, showtunes, forgotten favorites and hits, even telling the Story of Motown and the Supremes in song. It's not necessarily a subtle show, but it is terrifically entertaining, especially if it is viewed as spectacle. More than any other record, this showcases Diana the Diva, and for that alone, it's essential listening. *—Stephen Thomas Erlewine*

Baby, It's Me / Sep. 1977 / Motown ♦♦♦
A moderately successful late-'70s album for Diana Ross. She was evolving into celebrity/stardom status, and her albums were increasingly filled with less soulful, more sophisticated, heavily produced and arranged ballads and light pop. She still sounded glorious on most of them, but now the edge, sensuality, and energy that had made her Motown songs classics was steadily eroding in favor of a more stylized, almost show-business kind of singing. *—Ron Wynn*

The Boss / May 1979 / Motown ♦♦♦
Great dance material is featured, again by Ashford & Simpson. *—Rick A. Bueche*

Diana / May 1980 / Motown ♦♦♦
Coming off four Top Ten hits in three years for their group Chic, producers Bernard Edwards & Nile Rodgers were *the* hot R&B/disco team of the day when they wrote and produced Diana Ross' second album named simply *Diana*. (The first was her 1971 TV soundtrack, *Diana!*) The result was Ross' best-selling album ever, paced by her biggest singles hit yet, "Upside Down," and its Top Ten follow-up, "I'm Coming Out." For the most part, disco productions tended to emphasize the beat over the voice, and it might be argued, but for the billing, Ross had been reduced to guest vocalist on her own album. But it was exactly her struggle to retain an identity beyond the groove that made this music more compelling than Chic's records. *Diana* marked an important comeback for Ross, who had struggled in the late '70s after the early successes of her solo career. She celebrated by leaving Motown for a six-year, five-album sojourn at RCA. *—William Ruhlmann*

All the Great Hits / Oct. 1981 / Motown ♦♦♦♦
Diana Ross is certainly a diva of goddess-like proportions. Whether joined by the Supremes, or out on her own, her voice is unmistakable and powerful, plus she possesses the uncanny ability to take songs penned by others and make them very much her own—to imbibe them with her very soul. This collection of Ross' best-known and loved hits is perfect testament to her massive gift. Working closely with both singer/songwriting duo Ashford & Simpson, as well as producers Nile Rodgers & Bernard Edwards (both of Chic), Ross brought six songs to the top of the pop charts over a decade—all included here. From the early classic gospel-inflected "Reach Out and Touch (Somebody's Hand)" and the empowering chest beater "Ain't No Mountain High Enough," to the lite soul of "It's My House," Ross demonstrates full range. Also featured are the massive club hits "Upside Down" and "I'm Coming Out," cut with Rodgers & Edwards. Strong and uptempo, both songs became disco manifestos across the country in the early '80s and helped to keep the genre alive just a little bit longer. And, of course, this compilation is completed, naturally, with both the sultry throb of "Love Hangover" and the Lionel Ritchie duet "Endless Love." If there is a failing at all, it is within the "Medley (With the Supremes)." This glossy track hits the highlights, but really, why butcher such amazing songs? Any one would be better off slipping a Supremes greatest into the old CD player. But, for the casual listener, this probably hits the spot. It's heavy on the chart-toppers, and a sweet sonic masterpiece by anyone's standards. *—Amy Hanson*

Why Do Fools Fall in Love? / Oct. 1981 / Capitol ♦♦♦
The irony of a 37-year-old woman having a huge hit covering an anthem for a bunch of teenagers aside, Diana Ross enjoyed tremendous success with this early '80s album. It was her second platinum album of the 1980s and eventually did better than any other full album she issued in the decade, except for *Diana*. It also started Ross on a run of youthful hits that would include "Work That Body," "Mirror, Mirror," and the ultimate vanity song, "Muscles." *—Ron Wynn*

Diana's Duets / 1982 / Motown ♦♦♦♦♦
An excellent collection featuring Diana Ross singing with the Temptations, Stevie Wonder, Smokey Robinson, the Supremes, and Marvin Gaye. These songs, all brilliantly produced and arranged, with wonderful lyrics, show how great a vocalist Ross was before she became weighted down with being a star and celebrity. Her delivery, vocal range, lyric interpretations, and performances are amazingly better than what she turned in during the late '70s and '80s. While her album with Marvin Gaye might be her best single duet work, this anthology will more than fill the bill. *—Ron Wynn*

Silk Electric / Oct. 1982 / RCA ♦♦♦
Diana Ross continued her steady pace in the early '80s, scoring a hit single with the curious song "Muscles." She was now established as a stylist and show-business celebrity, and seldom evoked the soulful or sensual air that characterized her past material. The songs were also more elaborately produced, the arrangements designed to accent the carefully calculated pauses, sighs, and coos, and the compositions more suggestive in their lyrics than convincing or compelling. *—Ron Wynn*

Ross / Jun. 1983 / RCA ♦♦
This was a noble, if failed, experiment. Diana Ross teamed up with Steely Dan producer Gary Katz for this, her third outing on RCA. Katz brought in the usual suspects, not only buddies like Michael McDonald and Donald Fagen (each of whom contributed a song and keyboards), but also session aces like Jeff Porcaro and Greg Phillinganes. The result, on the five tracks Katz handled, has that precise, icy sound those guys always get, not a sound that meshes well with Ross. No better are the two tracks contributed by Ray Parker Jr., or Ross's own effort, "Girls," which closes things out. As a result, *Ross* was Diana Ross' first album since 1978 not to even go gold. (Not to be confused with Diana Ross's 1978 album [Motown 907] of the same name.) *—William Ruhlmann*

Swept Away / Sep. 1984 / RCA ♦♦♦
Swept Away went gold on the strength of "Missing You" and the Julio Iglesias duet "All of You," but it nevertheless was one of her best efforts, thanks to restrained production and a solid set of songs highlighted by "Touch By Touch," "Rescue Me," "Swept Away" and "Forever Young." *—Stephen Thomas Erlewine*

Eaten Alive / Aug. 1985 / RCA ♦♦♦
Diana Ross got a lot of mileage from this album, although it didn't duplicate the success she'd enjoyed with *Swept Away*. The title track was a Top Ten R&B hit, thanks in part to

Michael Jackson's presence on background vocals, and another single also made the charts. Ross wasn't the powerhouse she was in the 1970s, but she was still doing well enough to keep making records. *—Ron Wynn*

Portrait, Vols. 1 & 2 / Apr. 1986 / Telstar ✦✦✦✦
The two volumes of *Portrait: Her Greatest Hits* were released as a single package in 1986. When taken together, the two discs result in a good overview of her career from the Supremes to the end of the '70s. Most of *Vol. 1* is devoted to the Supremes, with many of the group's biggest hits ("Where Did Our Love Go," "Baby Love," "Stop! In the Name of Love," "You Can't Hurry Love") featured alongside "Ain't No Mountain High Enough," "Remember Me," "Surrender" and "Love Hangover." The second volume is devoted to such singles as "I'm Still Waiting," "Reach Out and Touch (Somebody's Hand)," "All of My Life," "Theme from Mahogany," "The Boss," "Upside Down," "I'm Coming Out," "It's My Turn" and "Endless Love." It's an entertaining collection, and one of the most comprehensive overviews of her career yet assembled. *—Stephen Thomas Erlewine*

Red Hot Rhythm & Blues / May 1987 / RCA ✦✦✦
Diana Ross made one of her better albums in quite a while, although this late-'80s number didn't fare as well as anticipated. But "It's Hard For Me to Say," co-produced and co-written with Luther Vandross, was the first heartache tune Ross had done in many years with a real, poignant edge to it, while "Cross My Heart" was a decent commercial number. Of course, the tune that ended up making the most noise was "Dirty Looks," another of Ross' patented cute, quasi-sophisticated numbers. *—Ron Wynn*

Workin' Overtime / Jun. 1989 / Motown ✦✦
Diana Ross made a bid for new stardom by returning to Motown with a deal giving her profit participation in the company and creative control in 1989. This album was the first product of that new contract, and the results weren't very encouraging. There were no moderate or even small hits, and the album quickly dropped off both the R&B and pop charts within a couple of weeks of its release. Ross sounded completely lost, and the production, arrangements, and compositions sounded weak and thin next to the dominant new jack and hip-hop works. *—Ron Wynn*

The Force Behind the Power / 1991 / Motown ✦✦
On her first album of the '90s, Diana Ross attempted to keep up with the times, adding light new jack beats and synthesized urban contemporary arrangements. It may have been a good idea in theory, but *The Force Behind the Power* fails in practice. Most of the music sounds too carefully considered, and Ross never quite sounds comfortable with the new sonic surface. Another problem is the material—most of it is simply not memorable. And when there is a good song, like Nick Lowe's "Battlefield," it's destroyed in the arrangements. There are a couple of moments where it seems like it's going to all come together, but for the most part, *The Force Behind the Power* is a bungled attempt at contemporizing Miss Ross. And it's questionable whether such an effort was necessary in the first place. [The U.K. edition of *The Force Behind the Power* has an additional song, "No Matter What You Do," which is a duet with Al B. Sure!.] *—Stephen Thomas Erlewine*

Christmas in Vienna / 1993 / Sony Classical ✦✦

Forever Diana: Musical Memoirs / Oct. 5, 1993 / Motown ✦✦✦
Plagued by inferior sound and a weak track selection, *Forever Diana* is a major disappointment for fans. Only one disc is devoted to the Supremes, with Ross' spotty solo career occupying the other three discs, featuring decidedly poorer sound than previous Motown releases. Besides poor audio, the liner notes are skimpy and incomplete. Ultimately, *Forever Diana* is a wasted opportunity. *—Stephen Thomas Erlewine*

One Woman: The Ultimate Collection / Oct. 1993 / Motown ✦✦✦✦
This compilation attempts to condense Diana Ross's most successful recordings into one 20-song, 71 minute disc. Well, there's good news and bad news. The good news is that Ross (who produced the album, which is to say picked the tracks) has included six of her Supremes recordings from the 1960s (one of them, "Someday We'll Be Together," in a new disco mix) and licensed a few songs from her stay at RCA in the 1980s, making this the most wide ranging of her compilations. The bad news is that she has jettisoned many possible hits (only ten of her 18 chart-toppers are included) in the name of featuring four tracks from the 1990s that do not rank with her best, either aesthetically or in terms of popularity. In other words, Ross has constructed the album as she might a concert—a sprinkling of early Supremes hits, all her biggest solo hits, and what she considers the highlights of her current work. The result is a less than perfect, or "ultimate" portrait, since the selection implies erroneously that a forgettable piece of tripe like the 1991 Top 40 hit "When You Tell Me That You Love Me" is as much a milestone in the Ross catalog as "You Can't Hurry Love" or "Upside Down" (and that Ross remained as significant an artist in 1994 as she was in 1964 and 1974). But the album still makes a good sampler of Ross's entire 30-plus-year career for beginners. *—William Ruhlmann*

50: Diana Extended: The Remixes / 1994 / Motown ✦✦✦
For labels, collections of remixes can be the easy way out—it's easier to remix major hits than to get the artist into the studio to take a chance on some new material. Many have seemed like nothing more than cheap and cynical exploitation. Nonetheless, there's definitely an art to remixing, and with the right DJs, the process can be quite enjoyable. One of the strongest remix albums of the 1990s is *Diana Extended*, which boasts thoughtful and imaginative work by such mixmasters as David Morales, Steve "Silk" Hurley and Frankie Knuckles (rightly exalted as the Godfather of House). "Love Hangover" and "Upsidedown" work impressively well in a house setting, but the biggest surprise of all is hearing Knuckles successfully bring a '90s club sound to "Someday We'll Be Together" (the CD's only Supremes song). For both Ross devotees and dance music enthusiasts, *Diana Extended* is highly recommended. *—Alex Henderson*

Anthology / Sep. 28, 1995 / Motown ✦✦✦✦✦
The double-disc set *Anthology* contains all of Diana Ross' solo hits for Motown Records, from "Ain't No Mountain High Enough" to "Endless Love." It's a comprehensive collection, featuring all of her biggest hits plus many important album tracks and smaller hit singles. Since it doesn't delve too deeply into obscurities and contains all of Ross' most popular songs, *Anthology* is the definitive career compilation for fans who want more than just the standard cuts but are unwilling to explore the original albums or invest in the box set. *—Stephen Thomas Erlewine*

Greatest Hits: The RCA Years / Mar. 25, 1997 / RCA ✦✦✦✦
Diana Ross' glossy 1981-1987 tenure on RCA is the subject of this 18-track collection, which includes her hit tribute to the late Marvin Gaye, "Missing You." Other highlights include her cover of Frankie Lymon & the Teenagers' "Why Do Fools Fall in Love," "Mirror, Mirror," "Swept Away" and a solo version of the chart-topping "Endless Love." *—Jason Ankeny*

Every Day Is a New Day / May 4, 1999 / Motown ✦✦✦
Diana Ross remained a larger-than-life figure throughout the '90s, but she hadn't had a major hit since 1986. *Every Day Is a New Day* was designed to change that. Released in 1999, the record was her most carefully conceived album in years, filled with immaculate productions that appealed either to the dancefloor or adult contemporary radio. The problem is, there wasn't much to recommend in the way of songs. Although the album sounds good, nothing on the album truly catches hold the way even such latter-day hits as "Missing You," "Swept Away" and "Muscles" did. As a result, *Every Day Is a New Day* stands as nothing more than a stylish but failed comeback. *—Stephen Thomas Erlewine*

• **The Motown Anthology** / Mar. 27, 2001 / Motown ✦✦✦✦✦
Up until this release, consumers had a difficult task of finding a definitive compilation highlighting the post-Supremes career of Diana Ross—mainly because there wasn't one. This double-disc set gathers 27 of the diva's finest solo sides, plus an additional 11 tracks that are making their domestic debut. As a retrospective, *The Motown Anthology* succeeds in gathering all of Ross' major singles. Some are available here in a previously unissued form. Such is the case for "Remember Me," "My Mistake (Was to Love You)," and "Lovin' Livin' & Givin'"—from the *Thank God It's Friday* soundtrack. Those looking for chart-toppers should note that *The Motown Anthology* not only delivers rare material, but also all the hits that would render most other collections superfluous. The producers have also hit upon a favorable ratio of hits to rarities. After covering all the bases on the popular and familiar material, the previously unearthed nuggets—which are spread throughout the chronologically organized set—are a treat for both the intense as well as the casual fan. Of particular note is the leadoff track "Time and Love"—a Laura Nyro composition which had been scheduled, and then withdrawn, as Ross' first solo single. The sound is uniformly excellent with the caveat that some of the early recordings on disc one—"Reach Out and Touch (Somebody's Hand)" for example—never were known for their fidelity. Likewise, the sound of mid- to late-'70s tracks such as "Love Hangover" and "The Boss" are marked improvements. Clocking in at over two and a half hours, *The Motown Anthology* is a tremendous value. *—Lindsay Planer*

Stolen Moments: The Lady Sings Jazz & Blues / Mar. 19, 2002 / Motown ✦✦✦✦
Released simultaneously on CD and DVD in 2002 but recorded on December 4, 1992, at New York's Ritz Theatre, *Stolen Moments: The Lady Sings Jazz & Blues* ranks among Diana Ross' finest latter-day performances. This concert, weighing in at a healthy 19 tracks, is a delightful blend of both jazz and blues standards that allows Ross to exercise her remarkable vocal prowess away from the themes for which she is best known. Backed by both a big band and a jazz sextet, Ross absolutely shines across a varied and well-paced set that finds her as at ease with the Gershwins' "Love Is Here to Stay" and "The Man I Love" as on a marvelous rendition of the Billie Holiday classic "Fine and Mellow." It's just a short leap back to Cole Porter's fine "It's Alright With Me." Rounding out the mood are equally nifty versions of "Ain't Nobody's Bizness if I Do," "Don't Explain," and "Them There Eyes." With Ross in her element, obviously enjoying the moment, and with this elegant venue imbued with the smoke and mirrors of yesteryear, her performance utterly transcends a mere concert setting and becomes, truly, the performance of a lifetime. Better perhaps on DVD, where the visual images beautifully enhance the music, *Stolen Moments* on CD is still quite wonderful. What's better than one of R&B's divas diving into those old, gold classics? *—Amy Hanson*

Jackie Ross

b. Jan. 30, 1946, St. Louis, MO
Vocals / Chicago Soul, Pop-Soul, Northern Soul, Soul
Chicago soul diva Jackie Ross was born in St. Louis on January 30, 1946; the daughter of husband-and-wife preachers, she made her performing debut on her parents' radio gospel show at the age of three. Following her father's 1954 death, the family relocated to the Windy City; there the legendary Sam Cooke, a friend of her mother, recruited Ross for his SAR label, where she issued her debut single, "Hard Times," in 1962. Following a stint singing with Syl Johnson's band, she signed to Chess Records, making her label bow with 1964's "Selfish One"; the single fell just shy of the *Billboard* pop Top Ten, and Ross soon issued a follow-up, "I've Got the Skill," as well as an album, *Full Bloom*.

The superb "Take Me for a Little While" followed in 1965; unbeknownst to Ross, however, the same song had been recently recorded by New York singer Evie Sands as well, and although Sands' version for Blue Cat actually came first, Chess' marketing muscle nevertheless ensured that their label's rendition proved more successful. Ross' disgust with the situation, combined with the negligible royalties she received from "Selfish One," soon prompted her to exit Chess, and in 1967 she landed at Brunswick; two years later, she moved to Jerry Butler's Fountain Productions, but failed to recapture her earlier commercial success. *—Jason Ankeny*

● **Full Bloom** / 1964 / Chess ♦♦♦♦
Early diva Jackie Ross had looks, sass, and sex appeal. The poignant "Selfish One," with its creative understated arrangement and sincere vocals, didn't stop climbing the pop chart until it reached the number-11 spot. The follow-up, "I Got the Skill," was just as compelling but failed to chart with the authority of its predecessor. "Skill" had a brassy sound, and the horns exploded on the break. Jackie's rendition of "I Had a Talk With My Man" rivals labelmate Mitty Collier's renowned version. She does two standards, "Misty" and "Summertime," in the gospel-tinged voice that first delighted members of her parents' church (both were preachers). If more consideration had been given to the filler, this debut by Ms. Ross would have been rated higher. Ross' career with Chess lasted only two years; she left in 1966 over an insultingly low royalty check paid to her for "Selfish One." The British CD reissue in 1998 added several bonus cuts to up the track length to seventeen, although unfortunately the liner notes do not make it clear as to when this additional material was recorded and released. —*Andrew Hamilton*

Rotary Connection

f. 1966, Chicago, IL, **db.** 1974
Group / Psychedelic Soul, Psychedelic Pop, Soul, Pop-Soul
Rotary Connection's psychedelic chamber soul continues to sound ambitious and progressive decades after the group's departure. Instantly recognizable from the dramatic string arrangements of Charles Stepney and the five-octave voice of Minnie Riperton, the group released six albums between 1967 and 1971 that combined rock, soul, and psychedelia to theatrical and occasionally transcendental heights. The racially mixed group never really broke out of the Midwest, a region in which they frequently played. Their failure to become more than a regional cult act can be partly attributed to their management's decision to spurn a slot at Woodstock in order to play a more lucrative festival in Toronto. Despite some patchy albums and poor management decisions, Rotary Connection's status as an influential cult group has steadily risen since the '70s.

Marshall Chess, son of Leonard Chess, conceived Rotary Connection in 1967 for Cadet Concept—an upstart subsidiary of his father's Chess label. Chess initially centered the instrumentalists around a trio of musicians from a rock group called the Proper Strangers: drummer Kenny Venegas, bassist Mitch Aliotta and guitarist Bobby Simms. Sidney Barnes, Minnie Riperton and Judy Hauff were added as the vocalists. Upon the group's formation, Barnes was already something of a vagabond; his resumé as a songwriter, background vocalist and solo artist was extensive. Riperton was a veteran of the Chess ranks; she worked as a receptionist in the label's Chicago office, had been a member of the Gems, and released material under the name Angela Davis. Chess musical supervisor Charles Stepney—a legendary composer, arranger, and producer—was brought in to direct the group. He would also implement the skills of studio musicians from the extended Chess family throughout the group's existence, such as drummer Morris Jennings and guitarists Phil Upchurch, Bobby Christian, and Pete Cosey.

Under Stepney's guidance, Rotary Connection recorded and released their self-titled debut album in late 1967. The group's spacious sound was leavened by Stepney's often gorgeous and lilting string arrangements. The album featured both originals (co-written by Stepney and a number of other songwriters, including Barnes and future Riperton spouse Richard Rudolph) and radical covers of the Rolling Stones' "Ruby Tuesday" and Bob Dylan's "Like a Rolling Stone." This became the blueprint for what would follow from the group and, as a stunning (if flawed) debut, the album falls into that old rockist trap of being viewed as the only essential one the group made. That's an unfortunate fact, because the group's key factor—the voice of Minnie Riperton—wasn't truly given a chance to shine until the second album.

The albums *Aladdin*, *Peace* (a Christmas-themed LP), *Songs*, *Dinner Music*, and *Hey Love* were issued between 1968 and 1971. Though the albums include a fair amount of filler, each has some amazingly inspired moments. "Respect," for instance, was a radical re-working of Otis Redding's original; transformed into a duet between Riperton and Barnes, the song's infamous "r-e-s-p-e-c-t" call-out was left out, and the tempo was slowed down to a sultry crawl. *Hey Love*, bizarrely credited to the New Rotary Connection, would become the group's last record. By that time, Riperton already had a solo masterpiece under her belt—1969's *Come to My Garden*. After the group split, Riperton continued her solo career and became one of the most beloved soul vocalists of the '70s. Breast cancer took her life in 1979, when she was just 31 years old. Stepney passed away three years prior, at the age of 43. —*Andy Kellman*

● **Rotary Connection** / 1967 / Chess ♦♦♦♦
The most inexplicable aspect of Rotary Connection's debut is that its strange and experimental qualities are often referred to as charming but dated, while Love's *Forever Changes* (released the same year), a record that is just a shade less bizarre and no more psychedelic, is universally viewed as timeless. There's no mistaking that this is hardly a flawless record—this band, more an experiment than anything else, was only beginning to find its feet. For every cover that radically reshapes the original and either stuns ears or elicits screams of blasphemy ("Like a Rolling Stone"), there's one that falls completely flat in its blandness ("Soul Man"). And for every original that is rife with otherworldly melodies and luscious combinations of countless musical styles ("Memory Band"), there's something like the ghostly "what you've just heard" audio collage/megamix that closes out the album ("Rotary Connection"). The consensus seems to be that this is the only essential record this group released, and that they were such an oddball entity that this is all one can take of them. That's just plain silly, evident from any number of the sparkling moments found on the LPs that followed. Minnie Riperton had yet to take the spotlight she deserved in this group—so in a sense, this could be seen as the *least*-representative Rotary Connection record, as fascinating as it is. Some strange force carried it to the Top 40 of the album chart, not that it was undeserving. —*Andy Kellman*

Peace / 1968 / One Way ♦♦♦♦

Aladdin / 1968 / Cadet ♦♦♦
Aladdin ushered in a bigger and bolder Rotary Connection. The proper follow-up to their debut is also more streamlined and less scatterbrained without shedding the limitless approach that made its predecessor such an intrepid undertaking. Crisp drum breaks, punching horns, and soaring strings are all a part of Rotary Connection's fusion of rock and soul, which shows a greater degree of focus and a decreased reliance on psychedelic flourishes here. This is all for the better and the worse. With less studio indulgences, some of the songs are lacking in character; however, the developments often make for a more confident and powerful sound, and Charles Stepney's string arrangements—the group's most valuable asset after the voice of Minnie Riperton—cut clear through these songs, alternately supporting with luster and leading with dramatic force. The most pleasing development is the more frequent presence of Riperton, whose lead turn during the verses on "I Took a Ride" is so endearingly soft, bewitching, and elegant that the slightly tacky chorus (during which several other voices kick in) does little to diminish her performance. The opening "Life Could" is one of the group's best quasi-Broadway numbers, full of seismic shifts of sound that include everything from squealing guitars to massive drum/horn combinations to trilling flutes to dynamic string tugs. *Aladdin* might not be as solid as its predecessor, but it's a step forward. —*Andy Kellman*

Peace at Last / 1969 / Cadet ♦♦♦

Songs / 1969 / Cadet ♦♦♦♦
The daring covers returned for *Songs*. In fact, the record is nothing *but* covers, including drastic re-castings of three songs from Cream's *Disraeli Gears*. So the creative well was surely drying up for Rotary Connection, right? Wrong. Despite the complete absence of original material, this is a proper Rotary Connection album as much as any other. Their version of Otis Redding's "Respect," like many of their covers, is rendered nearly unrecognizable; slowed to a crawl and stripped of its punctuative chorus of "R-E-S-P-E-C-T/I know what it means to me," Charles Stepney's string arrangement is a subdued but effective smear and Minnie Riperton and Sidney Barnes trade lines, emote in tandem, and twist around each other like they've never done before or since. The song has never sounded more steamy. The slightly eerie tone of the strings that encased "Respect" pop up again for "We're Going Wrong," one of the three Cream covers. The foreboding feel is carried forth with wordless co-ed background vocals that combine with escalating strings. But what really puts a cap on it is the moment when Riperton's voice shoots into a pitch that no theremin can approximate. It's moments like this one that make wading through the group's lapses (a dull, bungled look at "I've Got My Mojo Working," for instance) so worth it. As for those who view the group as blasphemers? Let them cringe. —*Andy Kellman*

Dinner Music / 1970 / Cadet ♦♦♦
The only accurate prediction one could have made before going into a Rotary Connection record was that it would be unpredictable, and attempting to list who the group's peers were to the uninitiated only worked on a song-by-song basis. No other record quite fits this bill like *Dinner Music*. The least-uniform Rotary Connection record—and that's saying a lot—it comes off like a series of tangents with little in the way of cohesion. One moment, they could be jumping in piles of hay on the set of *Hee Haw* ("Country Things"), later on they could be at a packed juke joint ("Stormy Monday Blues"), and then they could be lulling a crowd at the Newport Folk Festival ("Amuse"), or even taking over the BBC Radiophonic Workshop to twiddle with electronics ("Lektricks #2"). The most bizarre song of all is "Merry Prankster," which has all the cracked acoustic pop of late-'60s Arthur Lee until it shifts into an odd tempo and a chorus made from an even odder melody of grunts. The record's best moment is buried in the latter half. "Amuse" is a beautifully folky song sung by Minnie Riperton at her most gentle and arresting. It's nothing but an acoustic guitar and her voice, which effortlessly wraps around your ears despite not taking full advantage of her five-octave range. Altogether, *Dinner Music* is the only record where Rotary Connection's eclecticism worked to their disadvantage. —*Andy Kellman*

Hey Love / 1971 / Cadet ♦♦♦♦
As strong as *Hey Love* is—it's one of Rotary Connection's best records—three of its songs are so rich with full-bloom beauty that you can't help but refer to the group's lack of an adequate single-disc best-of as an extremely unfortunate thing. (Minnie Riperton's *Her Chess Years*, which is dominated by Rotary Connection material, doesn't qualify for its bonkers lack of a couple key songs.) Too many people point to the group's self-titled debut as its only essential release, which means that albums like this remain overlooked. And that means that too many people go on without hearing "If I Sing My Song," "I Am the Black Gold of the Sun," and "Hey Love." On "If I Sing My Song," Richard Rudolph & Charles Stepney play Burt Bacharach & Hal David, and the result belongs in the ranks of that songwriting team for its degree of hummability and the impeccably designed arrangements. "I Am the Black Gold of the Sun" is the apex, the brightest moment in the group's discography; it's an ineffable package of grace, grit, and life-affirming spirit (if your knees don't quake). Virtually anything would seem like a comedown after it, but the title track of the album sounds at points like a precursor to fellow Chicagoan Terry Callier's "Gotta Get Closer to You" and keeps the quality of the orchestra-spiked soul flowing. The rest of the album ranges from fair to good, with a slight edge to the good. That's almost irrelevant, however, given the essential nature of the three aforementioned diamonds. —*Andy Kellman*

Trip One / 1973 / Checker ♦♦

Songs/Hey Love / Oct. 27, 1998 / BGP ♦♦♦♦

Aladdin/Dinner Music / Mar. 9, 1999 / Raven ♦♦♦

Roy-C (Roy Hammond)

Vocals / Soul, Retro-Soul, Urban, R&B
Roy Hammond, from Long Beach, Long Island, sang lead for the Genies, who hit lightly with "Who's That Knocking" in 1958 (number-72 pop); three more Genies singles and the

group disbanded, but Roy was just getting started. He went on to cut an additional single as Roy Hammond & the Genies ("Mama Blow Your Top" on Forum Records), then 32 solo shots as Roy-C and one as Little Frankie on labels including Smash, Black Hawk, Shout, Alaga, Mercury, and Three Gems. He also has accumulated a legacy of 13 albums, plus a compilation on Sequel. What's so amazing about his output is that from 1958 to 1998, the year of his last-known album, he's only hit the chart twice: the lowly Genies hit and "Shotgun Wedding" in 1965 on Black Hawk (the latter nested at number-14 R&B). No other Roy-C recording ever made a national chart.

His first album was *That Shotgun Wedding Man* (1966) on Ember Records. The Mercury albums are *Sex & Soul* (1973), *Something Nice* (1975), and *More Sex & More Soul* (1977). The first Three Gems LP, *I Want to Be Where You Are (All Night Long)*, surfaced in 1984 and the last, *Stella Lost Her Groove Again*, in 1998. Roy composed most of his recordings and has more than 125 titles to his credit. He recorded an album by ex-Temptation Dennis Edwards entitled *Talk to Me*, and also worked on a CD on Bobby Stringer. Shaggy sampled his "Love Me, Love Me" on the soundtrack of *Stella Got Her Groove Back*. *—Andrew Hamilton*

● **Sex & Soul** / 1973 / Collectables ✦✦✦✦✦
Sex & Soul was the first album of pure funky soul that Roy-C recorded in the early '70s. Sounding like a cross between the deep soul of Otis Redding and the smooth production of early-'70s soul, Roy-C sings with grit and passion, investing these songs with true soul. None of the songs are below par, and some are forgotten gems, such as the singles "Got to Get Enough (Of Your Sweet Love Stuff)" and "Don't Blame the Man." All of the songs are delivered with fiery conviction from Mr. C, making it one of the most underrated soul albums of the early '70s. Collectables' reissue makes it even better by adding the singles "If I Could Love You Forever" and "Loneliness Has Got a Hold On Me." *—Stephen Thomas Erlewine*

More Sex & More Soul / 1977 / Ripete ✦✦✦✦✦
As the title suggests, *More Sex & Soul* offers more of what made Roy-C's first album so good—deep soul performed with a modern, early-'70s sensibility. The songs on *More Sex & More Soul* aren't quite as consistent as those on the debut, but there are still a number of terrific moments—"From the Outside Looking In (He Used to Be My Friend)," "You Got Everything I Need," "Show Me Love, I'll Show You Pain," "Don't Let My Love Get Away," "I Want to Love You, Kiss and Hug You" and "Great, Great Grandson of a Slave"—that make this necessary for fans of the first volume. Collectables' reissue includes the bonus tracks "Love Me Till Tomorrow Comes," "Virgin Girl," "Don't Stop Short of Satisfaction" and "Every Woman Has a Right." *—Stephen Thomas Erlewine*

I'm Working Hard for You Baby / Aug. 25, 1998 / Three Gems ✦✦✦✦
The horns and the way Roy-C arrange and mix them grab you immediately. Every cut features die-hard, Southern horns that Roy subs for backing singers, and they're warm, vibrant, and enhance the songs like a fresh coat of paint brightens a room. Roy wrote every song and the titles suggests he wasn't in the best of spirits. The title track, "I'm Working Hard for You Baby," doesn't ring of endearment but of Roy working like a mule to please an expensive, demanding woman. "Everybody's Down on Me," "Somebody Has Taken My Love From Me," and "I'm Hurting" are three heartache specials. A pleasing collection of Southern and deep soul tracks where Roy reminds you of Clarence Carter minus the chuckling and bawdy lyrics. *—Andrew Hamilton*

The Royalettes

f. 1961, Baltimore, MD, **db.** 1969
Group / Soul, Girl Group
This Baltimore quartet was something of a link between the girl group and "sweet soul" styles. Their harmonies were clearly grounded in the early-'60s girl group approach. But they also benefited from pop-oriented, occasionally grandiose production at the MGM label, where they recorded their most successful work. If they sometimes sounded like a female version of Little Anthony & the Imperials' later recordings, it's no coincidence. Little Anthony's producer, Teddy Randazzo, also handled the Royalettes, and wrote much of their MGM material. The Royalettes made some obscure singles for Chancellor and Warner Bros. before being signed to MGM in 1964. Their third single, the lush "It's Gonna Take a Miracle," was by far their most successful outing, stopping just shy of the Top 40. It was destined to be more identified, however, with singer/songwriter Laura Nyro, who made it the title track of her 1971 album of soul covers. In 1982, Deniece Williams took the song into the Top Ten with her own rendition.

The Royalettes did have another small hit in 1965 with "I Want to Meet Him," but never dented the charts again, although MGM spared no expense on their elaborate productions for the group's singles. A final MGM single, produced by Bill Medley of the Righteous Brothers, also failed to get anywhere, and the group broke up by the end of the 1960s, after a final 45 for Roulette. *—Richie Unterberger*

It's Gonna Take a Miracle / 1965 / Celeste ✦✦✦✦✦
In 1966, four completely unknown women from Baltimore, MD, called the Royalettes took the country by storm with their smash "It's Gonna Take a Miracle," a Teddy Randazzo-penned soul/doo wop number that Laura Nyro would cover a few years later. In those days, the single was everything; albums were created around one or two singles to resell the same material and to develop the artists. But there were exceptions. This debut album by the Royalettes is the exception to that rule. Conceived, produced, and arranged by Randazzo, *It's Gonna Take a Miracle* is a masterpiece of the Wall of Sound school of production, with deep nods to the Bacharach-David school of arrangement and songwriting. Randazzo could write with the best of them; no less than eight of the tracks here bear at least his partial signature. The other four, such wonders as Michel Legrand's "Watch What Happens" and Barbara Mason's "When I'm Ready" among them, are all stellar pieces of the puzzle Randazzo and the Royalettes put together. With their silky smooth sound and raw emotional delivery featured atop swirling strings, muted brass and reeds, and shimmering percussions—dig the tubas and glockenspiel on "Watch What Happens," with the swooping chorus and dynamically restrained lead vocal—they were truly was literally lifted by Bacharach for "Goin' Out of My Head." Along with that wondrous title track we get another minor hit with "Out of Sight, Out of Mind" and ten others from that original album. The Japanese have seen fit to issue another single as bonus material with two tracks that Righteous Brother Bill Medley penned for the group called "He Is My Man" and "Take My Love and Hide It From My Heart." This is a classic album of smooth and sweet East Coast soul that sounds like a collision of the Dionne Warwick-styled West Coast silk and New York raw, wall of sound instrumentation. A enduring if little-known classic. *—Thom Jurek*

The Elegant Sounds of the Royalettes / 1966 / Celeste ✦✦✦

● **It's Gonna Take a Miracle: The MGM Sides** / Feb. 1996 / Ichiban/Soul Classics ✦✦✦✦✦
Here are 18 songs from their MGM stint between 1964 and 1966, comprising both sides of their nine singles for the label (some of which were previously unavailable on LP). Though the Royalettes couldn't be considered a major group, their brand of pop-soul was certainly well-produced and competently performed, making this a pleasant listen for '60s soul fans. *—Richie Unterberger*

Ruby & the Romantics

f. 1961, Akron, OH, **db.** 1971
Group / Soul, Smooth Soul, Pop-Soul
One of the great male/female soul vocal groups, Ruby & the Romantics had an epic single in 1963 with "Our Day Will Come." It topped both the pop and R&B charts and for many is the definitive love/angst track. Lead vocalist Ruby Nash Curtis, Ed Roberts, George Lee, and Leroy Fann were the original members when they began in Akron in 1961. The male members had previously been working in a group known as the Supremes. Unfortunately, they never again repeated their chart success, even though they made some other excellent songs, such as 1964's "When You're Young and in Love," as well as "Our Everlasting Love" and "Baby Come Home." By 1966, they completely changed their personnel, with Curtis the only holdover. She then joined Richard Pryor, Vincent McLeod, Robert Lewis, Ronald Jackson, and Bill Evans. Ruby & the Romantics became an all-female group in 1968, as Denise Lewis and Cheryl Thomas now backed Curtis. But it didn't matter, as they never recaptured the magic of "Our Day Will Come." *—Ron Wynn*

● **The Very Best of Ruby & the Romantics** / 1993 / MCA ✦✦✦✦
Smooth pop and MOR offerings by Ruby & the Romantics including original versions of "When You're Young and in Love" and "Hey There Lonely Boy" (redone by Eddie Holman as "Hey There Lonely Girl"). The lovely, lilting "Our Day Will Come" struck gold and hit the number-one spots on the R&B and pop charts. "My Summer Love" features Ruby Nash singing to a sparse musical accompaniment and above the soft harmonies of Ed Roberts, Leroy Fann, George Lee and Ronald Mosley; it cracked the Top 20 (nesting at number 16)—a good showing for a second release. "Hey There Lonely Boy" lacks the fire of Holman's, but the Romantics' original did make the Top 40, stalling at number 27. Despite its stark beauty and melodious hook, "Young Wings Can Fly," their fourth single, failed to enter the Top 40 (braking at number 47). The Akron, OH, natives' fifth single, "Our Everlasting Love," should have done better but stopped at number 64, their worst showing to date. A disturbing trend had developed: each single had done worse than the previous. "Does He Really Care for Me" had a tougher sound than earlier releases but only reached number 87. There are only ten tracks, so some excellent cuts were omitted, particularly "Moonlight and Music." *—Andrew Hamilton*

The Ultimate Collection of Ruby and the Romantics / 2002 / Marginal ✦✦✦✦
At 30 tracks, Marginal's *The Ultimate Collection of Ruby and the Romantics* offers more of the group's output than any other collection available, including their hits "Our Day Will Come," "Hey There Lonely Boy," and "Baby Come Home." Despite the substantial track listing, the album concentrates on the work of the original Ruby & the Romantics lineup, omitting any material by the later incarnations of the group, which included a 1966 version with Ruby Nash Curtis fronting a different group of male vocalists, and a 1968 version that featured two female singers. While this somewhat narrow focus might disappoint completists, fortunately the original lineup did enough worthwhile material to make such an extensive collection enjoyable. On "Daydreaming," "What a Difference a Day Makes," "Heartaches," and several other tracks the group employs the Latin-inspired percussion, shimmering organ, and smooth harmonies that earned them a hit with "Our Day Will Come," but it sounds charming instead of merely repetitive. The group sounds surprisingly earthy on "How Deep Is the Ocean?" especially compared to airy confections like "Two Different Worlds," "Our Everlasting Love," and "When You're Young and in Love." While their version of "I'm Sorry" ends up sounding even squarer than Brenda Lee's original, the dreamy quality the group brings to "Stranger on the Shore" and "Not a Moment Too Soon" recalls their best work. The close harmonies, Spanish guitar, and expressive strings on the lovely, gypsy-tinged "Young Wings Can Fly" and the big, brassy production on "Does He Really Care for Me" make those songs standouts, within the group's overall career as well as this compilation. As lengthy as the album is, *The Ultimate Collection of Ruby and the Romantics* still manages to miss a few of the group's best tracks for their original label, Kapp—which, arguably, calls the title "*Ultimate Collection*" into question even more than the lack of material from their later years. Despite these omissions, this Belgian collection still manages to gather more of Ruby & the Romantics' prime material than the group's other retrospectives, which makes it worth seeking out for anyone looking for a more in-depth retrospective than either *The Very Best of Ruby & the Romantics* or *Greatest Hits* can provide. *—Heather Phares*

The Ruffin Brothers

Group / Motown, R&B
The vocal duo of brothers David and Jimmy Ruffin recorded one LP together for the Soul label in 1970, but were unable to generate much response, even on the R&B circuit. *—Ron Wynn*

• **I Am My Brother's Keeper** / 1970 / Soul ♦♦♦
Motown had a history of recording different artists together, so why not the Ruffin Brothers? Jimmy and David had both enjoyed success; Jimmy charted with "What Becomes of the Brokenhearted," and David had sung with the Temptations and enjoyed a solo hit with "My Whole World Ended." These songs have a harder sound then the brothers usually exhibit as solo artists. Four remakes nest with eight originals. While the former are done well, they won't make you forget the originals. "Didn't I (Blow Your Mind This Time)," the Delfonics hit, is the most interesting of the re-recordings; the Ruffins give the sweet Philly song a rougher edge. Motown released the exciting, uptempo "When My Love Hand Comes Down" as a single, but it failed to establish the brothers as hitmakers. The confessional "Your Love Was Worth Waiting For" and "Got to See If I Can't Get Mommy (To Come Back Home)" are two sweeties; the latter begins with an endearing father to son monologue, and "He Ain't Heavy He's My Brother" is given an epic treatment. David's rough tenor and Jimmy's sweet tenor/baritone mesh well throughout an LP that should have been more successful. *—Andrew Hamilton*

David Ruffin

b. Jan. 18, 1941, Whynot, MS, **d.** Jun. 1, 1991, Philadelphia, PA
Vocals / Motown, Soul, Urban
One of the greatest lead singers the Motown stable ever had, David Ruffin became one of the artistic cornerstones of the Temptations after his lead vocal on "My Girl" (1965) paved the way for such majestic follow-ups as "Since I Lost My Baby" (1965), "Beauty Is Only Skin Deep" (1966), "All I Need" (1967), and "I Wish It Would Rain" (1968). Unfortunately, ever-mounting internal pressures within the group, coupled with Ruffin's swelling ego, led to his dismissal from the group in late 1968. His solo career got off to a promising start with the powerful ballad "My Whole World Ended (The Moment You Left Me)," which cracked the pop and soul Top Ten in early 1969. His last hit to reach the Top Ten was the Van McCoy-produced dance ballad "Walk Away From Love," from 1976. After leaving Motown in 1977, Ruffin recorded for Warner Brothers and later for RCA accompanied by Eddie Kendricks. Unfortunately, Ruffin's career, marred by years of substance abuse and artistic indifference, culminated in his death from a drug overdose in 1991. *—John Lowe*

My Whole World Ended / May 1969 / Motown ♦♦♦♦
A sparkling debut by David Ruffin produced by Johnny Bristol. The title track, "My Whole World Ended (The Moment You Left Me)," had a throbbing midtempo beat and was aided by the Originals' polished backing vocals. The follow-up could have been better chosen; the excellent "I Got to Find Myself a Brand New Baby" should have received more exposure, as well as "World of Darkness" a whoop-'em-up, emotional powerhouse that Motown thankfully included on Ruffin's *Ultimate* CD. Either might have fared better than the overblown "I Lost Everything I Ever Loved," which charted but was saddled by unbelievable lyrics. The loping, melodic "My Love is Growing Stronger" has David screaming à la Wilson Pickett. Only two singles were released from this collection; Motown even chose to neglect the timely, driving, significant "Flower Child," which may have garnered some new fans for David's solo efforts. *—Andrew Hamilton*

Feelin' Good / Nov. 1969 / Motown ♦♦♦
This David Ruffin album was actually issued prior to "My Whole World Ended," but was soon overwhelmed by the success of that single. It hit the pop charts at the end of 1969, but didn't stay there very long. Ruffin was singing with the kind of fierceness, fire, and edge that had been the hallmark of his Temptations hits. He did get one chart single, but the album had been around so long that it couldn't get restarted and soon disappeared. *—Ron Wynn*

Doin' His Thing / 1969 / Motown ♦♦♦

David Ruffin / Feb. 1973 / Motown ♦♦♦
David's self-titled LP is his most unimpressive Motown release. With the exception of Bobby Miller's rip-snorting composition "Blood Donors Needed (Give All You Can)" the material is more Southern soul than traditional Motown. A remake of Harold Melvin & the Blue Notes' "I Miss You" works well, but would have been better if they had included the whole song, Eddie Kendricks joins David at the fade; his contributions are more on Part two, which Motown omitted. While "The Rovin' Kind" is all right, "Common Man" is downright boring regardless of the message; likewise for "A Day in the Life of a Working Man." A remake of Luther Ingram's deep soul classic "(If Loving You is Wrong) I Don't Want to Be Right" captures the pain of the original, but the track is rather bland. For serious David Ruffin fans only; the best tunes here can be found on his *Ultimate Collection. —Andrew Hamilton*

Me 'N Rock 'N Roll Are Here to Stay / Dec. 1974 / Motown ♦♦♦♦
What should have been a breakout, star-establishing album for David Ruffin went virtually unnoticed because it lacked that elusive hit. The title track failed to live up to marketing projections; the rocking tribute to rock & roll's longevity was solid listening, but its blazing fast tempo made it impractical for most dances. His remarkable rendition of "Smiling Faces Sometimes" got relegated to the flip side of "Rock n' Roll." Ruffin sings the Undisputed Truth hit slow and lazy; beginning with a spoken intro, the track has some marvelous instrumental fills and a passionate, pleading vocal from David. The follow-up, "Take Me Clear From Here," was originally a single release by Edwin Starr with a totally different arrangement; Ruffin's version has a strutting, pimpish beat, but it too underachieved. A better choice would have been the explosive "No Matter Where," with its ringing guitar and gospel-inspired vocals. "I Just Want to Celebrate" and "Superstar" are adequate remakes. However, the mysterious, dark, moody "I Saw Her When I Met Her" has to be one of Ruffin's top five tracks, despite the fact that it was never released and was left to languish on the album; Ruffin's pain is real as he sings the note left by his lady saying "I saw you when he met her, I won't ask you to forget her, I saw you when you met her... P.S., pardon my tear stained letter." An excellent Norman Whitfield production that got lost in the shuffle. *—Andrew Hamilton*

Who I Am / Oct. 1975 / Motown ♦♦♦♦
This 1975 release turned into an artistic renewal for the talented, raspy-voiced singer. It couldn't have come at a better time. Throughout the early '70 Ruffin seemed to be missing in action from the charts and was well on the way of being a has-been. *Who I Am* produced, arranged, and conducted by famed New York producer Van McCoy brought Ruffin in the thick of the burgeoning disco sound of the era. The confident title track has Ruffin turning in one of his most flawless performances. The effort's biggest hit, the classic "Walk Away From a Love," found the bass and drums heavy; this Latin-styled track a perfect match for the effortlessly executed vocals. Make no mistake, to his credit McCoy doesn't let up with his early disco production. To that end, great players like Gordon Edwards, Steve Gadd, Eric Gale, and Richard Tee are among the many heavyweight studio players here. Although the mix of didactic lyrics and pure disco arrangements of "It Takes All Kinds of People to Make a World" and "The Finger Pointers" would seem to be lethal, Ruffin's intelligence makes each lyric sing. The album's lone ballad, the gentle and painful "A Statue of a Fool," boasts a first time writing credit for Ruffin and the imagery is poignant and effective. At this time, the single "Walk Away From a Love" earned all of the raves, but to many the total work of *Who I Am* is just as impressive. *—Jason Elias*

Everything's Coming Up Love / May 1976 / Motown ♦♦♦
Another strong David Ruffin/Van McCoy collaboration. The disco-length "Everything's Coming Up Love" has charm despite its bubblegum lyrics; David seems to have enjoyed singing to the bouncy, jubilant track that McCoy extended a tad too much. Second best here is the sentimental "Good Good Times," which Ruffin sings with true emotion; likewise for the churning, tempo-changing "On and Off," a song typical of McCoy's productions on Faith, Hope & Charity. The innocence of "Discover Me" will touch your heart, the pain and passion in Ruffin's voice will have you repeating this one. A blatant attempt at disco, "First Round Knock Out," is the only miscue on an album that made it to number 51 on the pop chart. *—Andrew Hamilton*

In My Stride / Jun. 1977 / Motown ♦♦♦♦
In My Stride is the final Van McCoy/David Ruffin collaboration. McCoy surrounded Ruffin's harsh, expressive tenor with strings, horns, New York studio musicians, and Faith, Hope & Charity's slick backing vocals. So much to choose from... "You're My Peace of Mind" is a deceptive groover, accented by an electric harmonica; "Questions" is an unsung gem, Ruffin at his pleading, inquisitive best. On the ballad side, "Just Let Me Hold You For a Night" is a majestic production and one of David's best leads, a gripper from the first note. But there's more: "Hey Woman" and "Rode By the Place (Where We Used to Stay)" are mature, introspective heartache sagas. It's about time Motown did us a favor and compiled all the Ruffin/McCoy sides on one CD package. *—Andrew Hamilton*

So Soon We Change / 1979 / Warner Bros. ♦♦

Gentleman Ruffin / 1980 / Warner Bros. ♦♦♦♦
As the lead singer of the Temptations, Ruffin was one of the most urbane and charismatic singers around. His work as a solo act was spotty at best. Writers and producers at Motown had Ruffin screaming at the top of his lungs over everything from run over dogs to Dear John letters. A 1970 set with his brother Jimmy Ruffin and a trio of albums with producer Van McCoy in the late '70s were the only respite from a steep artistic decline. Ruffin left Motown in 1977. This 1980 album presents him as more of a lover man and is the follow-up to 1979's *Soon We Change,* also produced by Don Davis. The most striking thing about this effort is Ruffin's voice. Unlike other singers of the raspy/loud type, his voice actually improved and he didn't have to resort to howls to make up for a lost midrange. Producer Don Davis plugged Ruffin into a polished, contemporary R&B setting that featured, among others, Leon Ware and Ronnie McNeir on backing vocals. "I Got a Thing for You has Ruffin coming on smooth and confident as he sings, "Felt the feeling, without a touch." He even has to laugh. The dramatic "Can We Make Love One More Time" shows Ruffin didn't lose his cool while begging. Even the borderline unctuous "Don't You Go Home works even though his "love call" should have made his object of desire head for the exits. *Gentleman Ruffin* is Ruffin's last album as a solo act. Although there are a few weak spots, no comprehensive Rufiin collection should be without it. *—Jason Elias*

David Ruffin & Eddie Kendricks / 1988 / RCA ♦♦♦
This is a gem that slipped through the cracks. Hall & Oates were responsible for securing this deal for the former lead singers of the Temptations and helping to resurrect their stagnant careers by using them to open their shows. I don't understand why "I Couldn't Believe It" didn't do better on the charts, Ruffin leads the explosive, high octane strutter about being dumped, sounding more surprise than hurt; Kendricks contributes occasional lines and soulful backing fills, and a bitchin' sax provides some torchy runs. The beautiful, but agonizing, "One for the Lonely Hearts Club," features Kendricks' weakened, but effective, falsetto. "Goodnight Pillow," led by Eddie, is a bona fide tear jerker, a crying, remorseful sax accents the ache in Kendricks' voice. David shines on "One Last Kiss," one of his most sensitive readings; it deserved a far better fate. RCA didn't even drop it as a single. A remake of Sly & the Family Stone's "Family Affair" is all that; the former Tempts gives Sly's rambling commentary on family business depth and meaning, the rhythms dominated by a resounding bass will have you bouncing. "You Only Get What You Put Out's" positive message needs to be pounded into the heads of everyone by the time they reach eight years of age; a relentless beat and nifty female backing voices complement Ruffin's and Kendricks' soulful vocals. The intense, infectious reggae beat on "Don't Know Why You're Dreaming" will have you longing for Jamaica to experience more of the flavor. RCA dropped the old promotional ball big time on this one. *—Andrew Hamilton*

- **The Ultimate Collection** / Sep. 22, 1998 / Motown ✦✦✦✦✦

For David Ruffin, leaving the Temptations in the early 1970s to pursue a solo career was taking a gamble. Like Eddie Kendricks (who did the same thing), Ruffin was asked whether or not he was sure he wanted to leave such a successful group. But the soul singer had some fine moments as a solo artist, a fact that is illustrated by this CD. Released in 1998, *The Ultimate Collection* focuses on Ruffin's post-Temptations work of the 1970s. There's a lot to admire in this good to excellent anthology, which ranges from his hits "Walk Away From Love" and "My Whole World Ended (The Moment You Left Me)" to a pleasing cover of Harold Melvin & the Blue Notes' "I Miss You." The late soul man was a master of dramatic tearjerkers, and the emotional, heart-on-his-sleeve approach serves him quite well on "Pieces of a Man" (not to be confused with the Gil Scott-Heron song), "World of Darkness" and "No Matter Where." If you've never experienced the pleasures of Ruffin's solo years, *The Ultimate Collection* would be the most appropriate starting point. *—Alex Henderson*

Jimmy Ruffin

b. May 7, 1939, Colinsville, MS

Vocals / Motown, Soul, Urban

The older brother of the Temptations' lead singer David Ruffin, Jimmy enjoyed several huge hits himself in the mid-'60s for Berry Gordy's Soul label. Ruffin first signed with another Motown subsidiary, the short-lived Miracle, in 1961, but it was his convincing vocal on "What Becomes of the Brokenhearted" that made him a star in 1966. He encored with "I've Passed This Way Before" and "Gonna Give Her All the Love I've Got." In 1970 he briefly teamed with David (by then a solo artist) as the Ruffin Brothers and cut a duet remake of Ben E. King's "Stand By Me." He staged an impressive comeback in 1980 on RSO Records with a major pop hit, "Hold On to My Love," that was produced by Robin Gibb of the Bee Gees. *—Bill Dahl*

Jimmy Ruffin Sings Top Ten / Jan. 1967 / Motown ✦✦✦✦✦

Much of Ruffin's best work can be found in this set. In addition to the hits, there is a near-miss in the Smokey Robinson-produced "As Long as There Is L-O-V-E Love" that deserved to be a hit. A proper anthology of his best work is long overdue. *—John Lowe*

The Jimmy Ruffin Way / 1967 / Motown ✦✦✦

Ruff 'n Ready / Mar. 1969 / Motown ✦✦✦

Much weaker than the debut album, primarily because much of the material wasn't up to the debut's standard. The best track here is Norman Whitfield's "Don't You Miss Me a Little Bit Baby," which climbed the lower echelons of the pop charts. *—John Lowe*

The Groove Governor / Sep. 1970 / Soul ✦✦✦

The lesser of his two previous Soul/Motown releases, but still a good effort. "Let's Say Goodbye Tomorrow" has a good chorus and should have done better. The producer employs a spoken intro on Burt Bacharachs' "This Guy's in Love With You," to good effect. "Living in a World I Created for Myself" has hit qualities but failed to make the grade. The backing vocals, aptly done by the Originals, are magnificent throughout. *—Andrew Hamilton*

- **Motown Superstars Series, Vol. 8** / 1973 / Motown ✦✦✦✦

An excellent coupling of David and Jimmy Ruffin's individual solo highlights. A couple of cuts from their unheralded LP together are also included, making this a well-rounded package. Two obscurities from each spice this skimpy but tight compilation: David Ruffin's dramatic, aching "Just Let Me Hold You For a Night," and Jimmy Ruffin's infectious "As Long As There Is L-O-V-E Love." The brothers jell on Ben E. King's "Stand By Me" and the exuberant "When My Love Hand Comes Tumbling Down." *—Andrew Hamilton*

Love Is All We Need / 1975 / Polydor ✦✦✦

20 Golden Classics / 1980 / Motown ✦✦✦✦

Sunrise / 1980 / RSO ✦✦✦

Surprisingly, this Jimmy Ruffin album, produced by Robin Gibb and Blue Weaver, works quite well and is comparable to his Motown releases. The Bee Gees contributed three songs, including "Where Do I Go," written with brother Andy Gibb, on which Jimmy duets with Marcy Levy; the rest are Robin Gibb and keyboardist Blue Weaver's compositions. "Hold On (To My Love)" put Jimmy back on the charts after a long absence. "Changin' Me" has all the ingredients of a hit. The energetic "Jealousy" should have cracked the pop Top 40. *—Andrew Hamilton*

Early Classics / 1996 / Spectrum ✦✦✦✦

While not as thorough a compilation as *20th Century Masters—The Millennium Collection*, this release compiles many of Jimmy Ruffin's well-known early releases, with a few B-sides and unreleased cuts thrown in for good measure. While some of the song selections are questionable (would songs from 1974 truly qualify as early classics for a career that started almost 15 years previous?), musically the results are no less than stellar, as Ruffin's immediately recognizable voice delivers a potent punch with each delivery. *—Rob Theakston*

- **20th Century Masters—The Millennium Collection: The Best of Jimmy Ruffin** / Nov. 6, 2001 / Universal ✦✦✦✦✦

Most of the entries in Universal's *20th Century Masters—The Millennium Collection* series function best as budget collections, perfect for listeners who'd rather not bother paying a few extra dollars for a longer collection. Things are far different for this volume, spotlighting Motown second-line act Jimmy Ruffin, who reached the pop charts several times during the late '60s but never had a solid CD compilation before this one. It certainly leads with the right track, his sole Top Ten entry, the beautiful Motown nugget "What Becomes of the Brokenhearted." And since Ruffin only recorded a few LPs for the label, there's nothing major missing from this set and much that's good: the R&B hits "Don't You Miss Me a Little Bit Baby" and "I've Passed This Way Before," his 1970 cover of "Stand By Me" with brother David as a duet, and one of the best non-hits in Motown history, "As Long as There Is L-O-V-E Love." It's only 11 tracks, but with few other Jimmy Ruffin collections even in print, this is the one to get. *—John Bush*

Rufus

f. 1970, Chicago, IL, **db.** 1983

Group / Funk, Quiet Storm, Soul

One of the most commercially successful funk groups of the '70s, the multi-racial Rufus are today best remembered for launching the career of soul diva Chaka Khan, whose fiery lead vocals were easily the band's focal point. Powered by Khan—who was eventually billed in addition to the group—and an unerring sense of groove, Rufus scored an impressive string of hit singles on both the pop and R&B charts, which lasted through the '70s and up to Khan's official departure in 1983.

Rufus grew out of the Chicago band the American Breed, which had a hit in 1968 with the oldies-radio staple "Bend Me, Shape Me." Guitarist Al Ciner, bassist Chuck Colbert, drummer Lee Graziano, and keyboardist Kevin Murphy had all played in the band at one time or another before forming a new group, originally called Smoke, with vocalists Paulette McWilliams and James Stella. Stella was quickly replaced by lead vocalist/songwriter/keyboardist Ron Stockert, and Colbert by bassist Dennis Belfield; the group changed its name to Ask Rufus, which was later shortened to Rufus. In 1972, drummer Andre Fischer—another former American Breed member—replaced Graziano, and a young female vocalist named Chaka Khan (born Yvette Marie Stevens) replaced McWilliams. Although Khan's dynamic stage presence helped this version of the band take off, Stockert was still the guiding force when they signed with ABC in 1973, and he lent a more pop/rock flavor to the group's self-titled debut, released later that year.

Although the album sold poorly, Rufus gained a fan in Stevie Wonder thanks to their cover of his "Maybe Your Baby." Wonder gave them a new composition, the slowly grinding "Tell Me Something Good," that he'd written specifically with Khan's vocal style in mind. Pulled as a single from their second album, 1974's *Rags to Rufus*, "Tell Me Something Good" was a Top Five smash that turned Khan into a star; she also co-wrote the R&B chart-topping follow-up, "You Got the Love." Clearly, the band had found its niche, and a number of personnel shifts ensued: Stockert left, Belfield was replaced by Bobby Watson, and Ciner was replaced by Tony Maiden. Their funk sensibility thus bolstered, Rufus returned with a strong new album before year's end, *Rufusized*, which spawned two more hits in "Once You Get Started" and "Please Pardon Me (You Remind Me of a Friend)." The billing on 1975's *Rufus Featuring Chaka Khan* made the singer's star power official, and produced one of the group's biggest hits in the R&B number-one "Sweet Thing." Dave "Hawk" Wolinski joined as a second keyboardist for 1977's mellower *Ask Rufus* (the hit was "At Midnight (My Love Will Lift You Up)"), and William "Moon" Calhoun replaced drummer Fischer on 1978's *Street Player*.

Following the release of *Street Player*, Khan made what was perhaps an inevitable move into solo recording with the release of her debut, *Chaka*; despite scoring a significant hit with "I'm Every Woman," she remained an official member of Rufus. Still, the band's next album, *Numbers*, was recorded without her, and upon its release in 1979, it stiffed. Khan was back on board later that year for *Masterjam*, produced by Quincy Jones, and the band (featuring new drummer John "J.R." Robinson) was back on top of the R&B charts with "Do You Love What You Feel." However, Khan split again for 1980's *Party 'Til You're Broke*, and although she returned for 1981's *Camouflage*, Rufus' chart fortunes were slipping away. The George Duke-produced, Khan-less *Seal in Red* bombed, but Khan returned for one last go-round on 1983's *Stompin' at the Savoy*, a double-record set featuring three sides of live material and one side of new studio recordings. One of those new songs, "Ain't Nobody," became Rufus' final number-one R&B hit, and also won a Grammy, allowing the group to end its career on a high note. Her contract up, Khan finally left for good afterwards and became a superstar thanks to a cover of Prince's "I Feel for You." *—Steve Huey*

Rufus / 1973 / MCA ✦✦✦

In 1973, Rufus had yet to start going by the name Rufus & Chaka Khan. The band was still obscure, and the single that made Khan a superstar (1974's "Tell Me Something Good") was still a year away. Khan was handling most of the lead vocals, although keyboardist Ron Stockert was still doing a fair amount of lead singing. It was in 1973 that ABC released Rufus' self-titled debut album, which wasn't the big seller that 1974's *Rags to Rufus*, 1975's *Rufus Featuring Chaka Khan*, and 1977's *Ask Rufus* would be. From a commercial standpoint, the problem with this LP was its lack of a really strong single—there wasn't a "Once You Get Started," a "Sweet Thing," or a "Tell Me Something Good" to drive radio programmers wild. But from a creative standpoint, this is a decent and promising, if imperfect, debut. In 1973, Rufus' original pre-Tony Maiden, pre-Bobby Watson lineup favored an earthy soul/rock blend along the lines of Ike & Tina Turner; in fact, Khan's passionate vocals on "Feel Good," Stevie Wonder's "Maybe Your Baby," and Stephen Stills' "Love the One You're With" point to the fact that Tina Turner was among her early influences. Not that Khan is actually emulating Turner, Aretha Franklin, or anyone else; in 1973, Khan was quite distinctive herself. As time passed, Rufus & Chaka Khan became sleeker and less rock-minded—if your introduction to them was "Once You Get Started" or "Sweet Thing," you might be surprised to hear how rock-minded this LP is. *Rufus* falls short of essential and isn't recommended to those with only a casual interest in Khan's years with the band, but it's an enjoyable debut that certainly isn't without historic value. *—Alex Henderson*

Rags to Rufus / 1974 / MCA ✦✦✦

In many respects the group seems to be feeling their way through this. Luckily, *Rags to Rufus* does feature some can't-miss propositions. The great rock and funk mix of "You've Got the Love" all but sums up what Chaka Khan was going to be doing for the long haul. The biggest hit here, "Tell Me Something Good," is a rare instance of an artist like Stevie Wonder giving away a tune that he could have had a big hit with himself. That being said, it was Khan's playful and sensual vocal that put it over the top. The songs that veer from the formula suffer the most on *Rags to Rufus*. The cutesy "I Got the Wrong Street" and the saccharine "Walkin' the Sun" are duds. Even early on, Khan needed songs that were complicated either lyrically or musically. On Ashford & Simpson's "Ain't Nothin' but a Maybe," Khan displays the maturity and knowing that it took to make the song have that much more emotional weight. *Rags to Rufus* ends on a relaxing note with the tracks, "Look Through My Eyes," "In Love We Grow," and the sultry "Smoking Room." This album is far from perfect, but it's certainly representative of the band's gifts and Khan's vocal power. —*Jason Elias*

Rufusized / 1974 / MCA ✦✦✦✦

In the early '70s, Rufus was one of the most popular and interesting bands in R&B and rock. Of course, the reason was Chaka Khan, who possessed an amazing voice that was well versed in rock and jazz every bit as much as R&B. Their debut went nowhere, *Rags to Rufus* offered two instant classics, and *Rufusized* displayed their skill as album artists. Truth be told, this version of Rufus was nearly a brand-new band, as three members exited and guitarist Tony Maiden and bassist Bobby Watson joined up. The result was a funkier and more talented band who would give Khan the needed earthy and ethereal mix that would make her soar. The sexy and danceable "Once You Started" proves that this version of the band gave off immediate sparks and results. The sneaky and funky "Somebody's Watching You" has Khan displaying even more confidence. After great album cuts like the soothing "Your Smile" and "Pack'd My Bags," *Rufusized* ends on a strong note. The poignant and sophisticated "Please Pardon Me (You Remind Me)" leads into the Maiden and Khan duet cover of Bobby Womack's "Stop on By," which nearly matches the steaminess and wry nature of the original. Often forgotten due to the bigger hits on *Rags to Rufus*, this easily outstrips that album and became of one the band's most-loved efforts. —*Jason Elias*

Rufus Featuring Chaka Khan / 1975 / MCA ✦✦✦✦

One of the most talented bands of the '70s, *Rufus Featuring Chaka Khan* is the groups' fourth release in close to three years. Although this effort doesn't have the epiphanies of 1974's *Rufusized*, *Rufus Featuring Chaka Khan* has them becoming more established as one of the best bands in R&B and pop. The first track, Gavin Christopher's "Fool's Paradise" displays Khan's skill at screaming notes and making complex ideas sound simple, and vice versa. That art is put to work throughout *Rufus Featuring Chaka Khan*. "Everybody's Got an Aura" surely could be dismissed as babble but Khan gives the sentiments a ring of truth even as she shouts, "Everybody's got karma!" The lilting yet propulsive "Circle" has great bass work from Bobby Watson as Khan sings likable and spacy lines, the best being, "My love is like a zero/It is nothing and everything." The albums biggest track, the smoldering "Sweet Thing," has Tony Maiden's gentle guitar and Kevin Murphy's economical electric piano chords. The song is arguably the group's best as Khan's bittersweet vocal provided a standard many singers have attempted to approximate to no avail. The party starters "Have a Good Time" and "Dance Wit Me" both tread familiar ground and pale in comparison to the classic "Once You Get Started." The group even throws in a rare cover for this album. The last track "Jive Talking," is inexplicably slowed to a crawl, therefore, diminishing its appeal. *Rufus Featuring Chaka Khan* perfectly captures their unconventional sound and features Tower of Power on horns and Clare Fischer's string arrangements. This album is one of their best and is recommended. —*Jason Elias*

Ask Rufus / 1977 / MCA ✦✦✦✦

Rufus was one of the most respected groups in the '70s and '80s. Although lead singer Chaka Khan's charismatic vocals were their drawing card, few outfits boasted the skill as Rufus as a band. Songs like "Please Pardon Me," "Sweet Thing," and "Fool's Paradise" are a few of the tracks that displayed the perfect marriage. This 1977 effort is the follow-up to 1975's *Rufus Featuring Chaka Khan*. *Ask Rufus* has the group doing more sophisticated and constantly challenging work with an accent on evocative ballads. The effort's lone dance track "At Midnight (My Love Will Lift You Up)" has the band going for more subtlety. The jazzy "Close the Door" has a confident and gentle vocal from Khan and a beautiful string arrangement from Clare Fischer who offered them throughout this effort. The well-arranged "Earth Song" could be called botched poesy with lyrics like, "Stars what a mystical woman that you've made me," but Khan's charm keeps it from being an overstatement. The best track, the evocative and sensual "Everlasting Love" has great bass and guitar interplay from Bobby Watson and Tony Maiden, respectively, and an appealing earthy and ethereal vocal from Khan. The much loved "Hollywood" has just gotten stronger, with lines like, "Fixed expressions/Smiles worn thin" exhibiting a surprising and apropos world-weary view. The most ambitious song, the evocative "Egyptian Song," has Middle Eastern motifs and a compelling vocal from Khan that pulls it all together. With great keyboard signatures from Kevin Murphy and David "Hawk" Wolinski and Andre Fischer's steady and judicious drumming, *Ask Rufus* is one of their best albums. —*Jason Elias*

Street Player / 1978 / ABC ✦✦✦

Masterjam / 1979 / MCA ✦✦✦✦

As Khan released her first solo album, *I'm Every Woman*, the band released 1978's *Numbers*, sans Khan, and it went absolutely nowhere. *Masterjam* finds them back together, renamed Rufus and Chaka, with Quincy Jones producing the effort. Khan had worked with Jones on his 1978 album, *Sounds... And Stuff Like That*. The most striking thing about *Masterjam* is that is doesn't sound like a trademark *Rufus* effort. Jones' production style is so strong that the band's individual sound is all but lost. It's nothing to cry about, since Jones was at his R&B/pop peak and Rufus couldn't do it any better on their own. The album's first track is "Do What You Love What You Feel," with its subtle horn riffs arranged by Jerry Hey and vocals from guitarist Tony Maiden and Khan. On a track somewhat close to a ballad, the brilliantly arranged "Heaven Bound," Jones gets a good raw vocal from Khan. A frequent Jones collaborator, Rod Temperton, offers the title track and the even better "Live in Me." The album's only low point was a cover of Jones' own "Body Heat." On this version the pace is quickened, inexplicably turned into disco which revealed the lyrics to be paper-thin. Although *Masterjam* was just more of a Quincy Jones album than a Rufus effort, this ended up being one of the groups' last successful full-studio endeavors. —*Jason Elias*

Numbers / 1979 / ABC ✦✦

Party 'Til You're Broke / 1981 / MCA ✦✦

Camouflage / 1981 / MCA ✦✦✦

● **The Very Best of Rufus Featuring Chaka Khan** / Nov. 19, 1996 / MCA ✦✦✦✦✦

The Very Best of Rufus & Chaka Khan contains all of the group's biggest hits, including the number-one R&B hits "You Got the Love," "Sweet Thing," "At Midnight (My Love Will Lift You Up)," "Do You Love What You Feel" and "Ain't Nobody," plus the Top Ten hits "Tell Me Something Good," "Stay," "Hollywood," "Sharing the Love" and "Dance With Me." —*Stephen Thomas Erlewine*

Bobby Rush (Emmit Ellis Jr.)

b. Nov. 10, 1940, Homer, LA

Vocals / Retro-Soul, Modern Electric Blues

The creator of a singular sound which he dubbed "folk-funk," multi-instrumentalist Bobby Rush was among the most colorful characters on the contemporary chitlin' circuit, honing a unique style which brought together a cracked lyrical bent with elements of blues, soul, and funk. Born Emmit Ellis Jr. in Homer, LA, on November 10, 1940, he and his family relocated to Chicago in 1953, where he emerged on the West Side blues circuit of the 1960s, fronting bands which included such notable alumni as Luther Allison and Freddie King. However, as Rush began to develop his own individual sound, he opted to forgo the blues market in favor of targeting the chitlin' circuit, which offered a more receptive audience for his increasingly bawdy material; he notched his first hit in 1971 with his Galaxy label single "Chicken Heads," and later scored with "Bow-Legged Woman" for Jewel.

He appeared on a wide variety of labels as the decade progressed, culminating in the 1979 LP *Rush Hour*, produced by Kenny Gamble & Leon Huff for their Philadelphia International imprint. During the early '80s, Rush signed with the LaJam label, where he remained for a number of years; there his work became increasingly funky and deranged, with records like 1984's *Gotta Have Money* and 1985's *What's Good for the Goose Is Good for the Gander* often featuring material so suggestive he refused to re-create it live. During the mid-'90s, Rush moved to Waldoxy, heralding a return to a soul-blues sound on LPs including 1995's *One Monkey Don't Stop No Show*, 1997's *Lovin' a Big Fat Woman*, and 2000's *Hoochie Man*. In April 2001, his tour bus crashed, injuring several bandmembers and killing one, Latisha Brown. Rush was hospitalized for a short time, then returned home to recuperate. —*Jason Ankeny*

Rush Hour / 1979 / Philadelphia International ✦✦✦✦

Kenny Gamble & Leon Huff produced *Rush Hour*, Bobby Rush's belated full-length debut album, for the Philadelphia International label. By that time, their patented Philly soul sound was out of favor, and they wisely chose not to impose it on Rush. Nevertheless, the album is considerably slicker than any of his Ichiban albums. Oddly, this is hardly a problem, since Rush always favored soul more than blues and had a fondness for funk. The only real flaw with the record is that the material is a bit uneven, but the quality of the performances carries it over rough spots and helps make the record one of the best in his catalog. —*Thom Owens*

Sue / 1982 / LaJam ✦✦✦

What's Good for the Goose Is Good for the Gander / 1985 / LaJam ✦✦✦

Handy Man / 1992 / Urgent! ✦✦✦

Like any of Bobby Rush's '90s recordings for Urgent! and Ichiban, *Handy Man* is a pretty good album that draws from Chicago blues and Southern soul equally. Rush gives some good performances that carry the album through some lame original songs and flat, synth-laden production, complete with robotic drum machines. Of course, this holds true for almost any of Rush's albums, which means you've got to take what you can get, and here you get a couple of good songs balanced by a lot of filler. And Rush fans should be used to that by now. —*Thom Owens*

● **Instant Replays: The Hits** / 1992 / Urgent! ✦✦✦✦✦

Instant Replays: The Hits is a good overview of Bobby Rush's '80s recordings for Urgent! and Ichiban, capturing all of the highlights from such funky, greasy blues albums as *Gotta Have Money* and *What's Good for the Goose is Good for the Gander*. —*Thom Owens*

One Monkey Don't Stop No Show / 1995 / Waldoxy ✦✦

Patrice Rushen

b. Sep. 30, 1954, Los Angeles, CA

Vocals, Keyboards, Piano, Synthesizer / Quiet Storm, Crossover Jazz, Urban

Keyboardist/singer/songwriter/arranger/musical director Patrice Rushen has had an outstanding career with several Top Ten R&B hits, including "Haven't You Heard," "Forget Me Nots," "Feels So Real," and "Watch Out." "Forget Me Nots" was the basis of Will Smith's "Men in Black" from the blockbuster movie of the same name on *Big Willie Style*. R. Kelly's "Remind Me" was sampled from her "You Remind Me," a popular radio-aired LP track from *Straight From the Heart*. Others who have sampled Rushen's music are Def Jeff (Rushen's "Hang It Up") and Zhane ("Groove Thang").

Born September 30, 1954, in Los Angeles, CA, Rushen's parents enrolled her in music classes at U.S.C. when she was three. In her teens, she won a solo competition at the 1972 Monterey Jazz Festival. The attention garnered from this earned her a contract with Prestige Records. After recording three albums and becoming an in-demand session player, Rushen signed with Elektra Records in 1978. Forging an engaging jazz/R&B/funk fusion, she regularly hit the R&B charts. Her five albums for the label were *Patrice*, *Pizzazz*, *Posh*, *Straight from the Heart*, and *Now*. Some of these sides can be found on *Haven't You Heard: The Best of Patrice Rushen*.

In 1993, Rushen signed with Disney's Hollywood Records. Her first and only release was the excellent *Anything but Ordinary*, which yielded the inspiring single "My Heart, Your Heart." Hollywood wasn't satisfied with the album and shelved it. Sin-Drome Records bought the rights to the album and reissued it with the single, and some LP tracks received airplay on R&B and smooth jazz radio stations. Rushen became a member of the jazz collective the Meeting, appearing on several releases. Her busy schedule includes session dates and being the musical director for several different tours and TV specials. 1997's *Signature* found Rushen returning to her jazz roots for this solid album of instrumentals. In fall 2000, Patrice Rushen appeared as a part of Sisters Being Positively Real, an act on Brown Baby Entertainment Group. *—Ed Hogan*

Prelusion / 1974 / Prestige ✦✦✦✦
When a 20-year-old Patrice Rushen recorded her debut album, *Prelusion*, in 1974, she was still four years away from becoming a full-time R&B singer. Instrumental jazz was her main focus, and there was every reason to believe that she would become a major figure in the jazz world. The L.A. native showed considerable promise on this entirely instrumental LP, which is best described as straight-ahead post-bop with fusion references and features such impressive soloists as tenor saxophonist Joe Henderson, trombonist George Bohanon, and trumpeter Oscar Brashear. Playing both acoustic piano and electric keyboards, Rushen brings a strong Herbie Hancock influence to promising originals like "Haw-Right Now," "Shortie's Portion," and "Puttered Bopcorn." Nonetheless, Rushen was an appealing improviser in her own right, and one can only speculate on where her career in jazz might have gone had she not switched to R&B singing in 1978. In 1998, Fantasy reissued *Prelusion* and Rushen's second album, *Before the Dawn*, on a single 77-minute CD; unfortunately, "Puttered Bopcorn" was deleted due to space limitations. *—Alex Henderson*

Before the Dawn / 1975 / Prestige ✦✦✦✦
Patrice Rushen was never a jazz snob or a jazz purist. The pianist/keyboardist grew up listening to R&B and rock, and even her debut album, *Prelusion*—which was the most straight-ahead thing she ever recorded—used electric instruments. So for Rushen, the fusion orientation of her second album, *Before the Dawn*, was a logical progression. While 1974's *Prelusion* was essentially a straight-ahead record with fusion references, 1975's *Before the Dawn* is essentially a fusion album. This generally excellent LP is more commercial than its predecessor, and Rushen doesn't hesitate to bring R&B, pop, and rock elements to her jazz foundation. Purists weren't crazy about *Before the Dawn*, but the fact is that most of the material gives Rushen and her sidemen (who include flutist Hubert Laws and guitarist Lee Ritenour) enough room to stretch out and improvise. The only track that doesn't have a jazz artist's sense of spontaneity is the funk tune "What's the Story," which features singer Josie James and is exactly the sort of thing that Rushen herself would be singing when she signed with Elektra in 1978. Everything else on *Before the Dawn*, however, is instrumental jazz—although instrumental jazz that's mindful of R&B, pop, and rock. *—Alex Henderson*

Shout It Out / 1976 / Prestige ✦✦✦
Barely into her twenties and, on this, her third album, Patrice Rushen's music spoke volumes for her talent and the growth she would endure as a music virtuoso. This album is not smeared with that dated sound of the '70s so many instrumental projects were contaminated with. Instead, Rushen gives her audience a pleasurable collection of songs ranging from jazz, funk and fusion to R&B. While "Let There Be Funk" serves up a modest feel for the groove, "Roll With the Punches" has a rapid rhythm that cooks with precision. As jazzy as they may be, she has moderately paced tracks like "The Hump" and "Stepping Stones"—the former is soul-stirring, and the latter is an easy-listening, melodious number. "Shout It Out," the title track, releases more funk with its delayed cadence. The Los Angeles native gives her testimonial plea on "Sojourn" and has a calming effect on "Yolon." Most of the selections feature vocals. *—Craig Lytle*

Patrice / 1977 / Elektra ✦✦✦
After recording three jazz-oriented albums for Prestige, Patrice Rushen switched to Elektra and gave herself a major R&B/pop makeover with *Patrice*. Even the funkiest parts of *Shout It Out*, the last of Rushen's three Prestige/Fantasy albums, couldn't have prepared listeners for this LP, which finds her taking the commercial plunge and successfully making the transition from jazz instrumentalist to R&B/pop vocalist. As expected, jazz's hardcore audience cried foul: Like Roy Ayers, George Duke, George Benson, and other jazz instrumentalists who took up R&B singing, Rushen was called a sellout and vilified in the jazz media. *Patrice* was trashed by jazz critics. Instead of hating this album because it isn't jazz, however, they should have judged it by R&B/pop standards. When those standards are applied, it becomes obvious that *Patrice* is, in fact, a rewarding R&B/pop effort. *Patrice* demonstrated that she could be an expressive, charming singer, and her writing or co-writing is solid on cuts that range from the funky "Hang It Up" and the lovely ballad "Didn't You Know?" to the socio-political "Changes (In Your Life)." With *Patrice*, the Los Angeles native made it clear that she was as appealing as an R&B/pop singer as she had been as a jazz pianist/keyboardist. *—Alex Henderson*

Posh / 1979 / Elektra ✦✦✦✦
Patrice Rushen entered the 1980s on a high note with *Posh*, her third album for Elektra and sixth album overall. By that time, it seemed unlikely that Rushen would become a full-time jazz instrumentalist again—she was enjoying too much success as an R&B/pop singer. And sure enough, it wasn't until 1997's *Signature* on Discovery that she recorded another instrumental album under her own name. When *Posh* came out in 1980, jazz's loss appeared to be R&B's gain. If you were a jazz lover, it was frustrating to see Rushen—a talented improviser with a healthy appreciation of Herbie Hancock—neglecting jazz. But if you loved sleek, sophisticated R&B/pop, you couldn't help but savor *Posh* and get into such offerings as the exuberant, Emotions-influenced "Look Up!," the vulnerable, slightly Stevie Wonder-ish "I Need Your Love," and the infectious "The Funk Won't Let You Down." Meanwhile, "Time Will Tell" has a bit of a rock edge and may very well be the most rock-influenced tune Rushen has ever recorded. *Posh* is enthusiastically recommended to anyone with a taste for late 1970s and early 1980s R&B. *—Alex Henderson*

Pizzazz / 1980 / Elektra ✦✦✦
When Patrice Rushen was being lambasted by jazz snobs for making the switch from jazz instrumentalist to R&B/pop singer, she was also winning over quite a few people. R&B fans didn't care if she was no longer playing long, improvised piano solos with Joe Henderson or Hubert Laws; they loved her singing, and couldn't have cared less what jazz snobs thought of her new direction. Rushen's profile in the R&B world continued to increase with *Pizzazz*, her second album for Elektra and fifth overall. The song that did the most to make this LP a success was "Haven't You Heard?," a gem of a single that soared to the top of R&B radio play lists and was among Rushen's biggest hits. Many listeners bought *Pizzazz* because of "Haven't You Heard?," and they quickly discovered that the rest of the album was also excellent. Drawing on such influences as Earth, Wind & Fire, Minnie Riperton, Stevie Wonder, and the Emotions, Rushen has no problem holding an R&B lover's attention with treasures that include the funky opener "Let the Music Take Me," the soulful ballad "Settle for My Love," and the perky "Keepin' Faith in Love." *Pizzazz* might have received tongue-lashings from jazz critics, but from an R&B/pop perspective, it's among Rushen's most rewarding and essential albums. *—Alex Henderson*

Straight from the Heart / 1982 / Rhino ✦✦✦
Straight from the Heart is Patrice Rushen's most successful fusion of R&B and jazz. The album doesn't delve too deeply into either R&B and fusion; instead, it charts a light, mellow and soulful middle ground. And the approach was successful: Three of the songs—"Forget Me Nots," "Breakout!," "I Was Tired of Being Alone (Glad I Got Cha)"—were R&B hits, while "Number One" was nominated for a Grammy. Rhino's 1996 reissue of *Straight from the Heart* includes single edits and 12-inch remixes of the album's singles. *—Stephen Thomas Erlewine*

Now / 1984 / Elektra ✦✦✦✦
Listeners expecting a sequel to to her best-selling 1982 album *Straight From the Heart* were in for quite a shock. In the two years between the efforts, Rushen became a proponent of the technology-or-bust ethos of many jazz artists in the early to mid-'80s. Given that thinking, *Now* is both minimal and innovative—with all of its sonic virtues probably not fully appreciated at the time of its release. The album's biggest dance tracks, "Feels So Real (Won't Let Go)" and "Get Off (You Fascinate Me)," are relentlessly polyrhythmic and fulfilling. Rushen, unlike countless other acts, knew how to give synthesizers a sense of panache without the sound seeming artificial. Despite its dancefloor skills, *Now* also takes time out for affairs of the heart. On "Gotta Find It," the buoyant rhythms belie the desperate lyrics and Rushen's meditative vocals. The astute "Heartache Heartbreak" will put a damper on any party as she sings, "Does love mean that I will not be lonely" (a chilling sentiment that's probably too prickly for even Bobby Womack). The infectious "Perfect Love" features both an effortless vocal from Rushen as well as an understated Fender Rhodes solo. During her stint at Elektra, Rushen never made bad albums, but they often had their fair amount of filler. On this effort there isn't any, and the closer you listen the tracks, the more likeable they become. Produced by Charles Mims Jr. and Rushen, *Now* is filled with assiduous grooves and—despite its "trendy" sounds—it has more than stood the test of time. *—Jason Elias*

Watch Out! / 1986 / Arista ✦✦

The Meeting / 1990 / GRP ✦✦✦✦
The selections on this diverse CD (a collaboration featuring keyboardist Patrice Rushen, saxophonist Ernie Watts, bassist Alphonso Johnson and drummer Ndugu Chancler) alternate between soulful jazz, inventive R&B, a bit of funk and ballads. Watts is in top form, and Rushen (who recalls Chick Corea on "Tango" and Herbie Hancock in other spots) shows that she can still play with creativity. A few of the tracks are throwaways, especially "Elements of Mystery" and "Virgin," but overall, the set is a pleasant surprise and is recommended to listeners who enjoy R&B-oriented jazz. *—Scott Yanow*

Anything But Ordinary / Nov. 1, 1994 / Sin-Drome ✦✦✦
In the late 1970s and early to mid-'80s, Patrice Rushen was red hot. Anyone who was seriously into R&B at the time remembers hits like "Haven't You Heard," "Forget-Me-Nots" and "Never Gonna Give You Up." But by the end of the 1980s, the jazz pianist turned R&B singer was in trouble commercially. Switching from Elektra to Arista with 1987's *Watch Out!* proved to be a mistake, and it wasn't until 1994's *Anything But Ordinary* on the small Sin-Drome label that Rushen recorded again under her own name. Though this CD isn't in a class with *Pizzazz* or *Posh*, sleek R&B/pop tunes like "I Do," "My Heart, Your Heart" and "Tell Me" showed that the L.A. native could still hold her own as a singer, composer and producer. Rushen experiments with hip-hop influences on a few selections, but on the whole, the disc is quite similar to her Elektra output. While *Anything* didn't return Rushen to the top of the R&B charts, her more devoted fans were glad to see her back in the studio. *—Alex Henderson*

● **Haven't You Heard: The Best of Patrice Rushen** / 1996 / Elektra/Rhino ✦✦✦✦✦
Nearly every one of Patrice Rushen's R&B hits—including the Top Ten singles "Haven't You Heard," "Forget Me Nots," "Feels So Real (Won't Let Go)," and "Watch Out"—are featured on the single-disc anthology *Haven't You Heard: The Best of Patrice Rushen*. With the exception of "Watch Out," her only Top 40 hit for Arista, the material is entirely drawn from Rushen's heyday at Elektra, when she was fusing jazz with R&B and pop. The songs on *Haven't You Heard* represent the high watermark of her fusions, which makes the compilation both an excellent introduction and a comprehensive career retrospective. *—Stephen Thomas Erlewine*

Signature / Jul. 15, 1997 / Discovery ✦✦

Prelusion/Before the Dawn / Nov. 10, 1998 / Prestige ✦✦✦✦

Brenda Russell

b. Brooklyn, NY

Vocals / Adult Contemporary, Smooth Jazz, Urban, Disco

Born Brenda Gordon, Russell is a soul singer, composer, and keyboardist. Her family moved to Toronto when she was 12. Eventually, she and her husband, Brian Russell, hosted the Canadian TV series *Music Machine*. They moved to Los Angeles in 1973, where they both worked as session musicians. They recorded together under the name Brian & Brenda in 1978, but their music was not received well. After the couple's divorce, Brenda embarked on a solo career. After signing with A&M and releasing two albums, she signed with Warner Bros. and put out *Two Eyes*. Russell then re-signed with A&M and released her most popular album, *Get Here* (1988). "Piano in the Dark" was a Top Five pop and R&B single; she received Grammy nominations for Song of the Year, Best Duo and Best Pop Female Vocalist. EMI signed Russell in 1991 and released *Soul Talkin'*. She has done session work for Barbra Streisand, Elton John, and Bette Midler, and her songs have been recorded by Streisand, Luther Vandross, and Donna Summer, among others. She released *Paris Rain* in mid-2000. *—Steve Huey*

Brenda Russell / 1978 / A&M ✦✦✦✦✦

Upon the release of this album, Russell was not given the praise she was due. However, as the years have passed, her music has become priceless. This album only featured two releases: "So Good, So Right" and "Way Back When." The former is a mellow, jubilant number paced by an acoustic piano and an appeasing arrangement. It landed at number 15 on the *Billboard* R&B charts. The latter is a bouncy midtempo number fueled by a stringent string arrangement, peaking at 42. Fortunately, radio and the public picked up on this indelible album. Of the eight selections, none fall short of being exemplary. The most notable unreleased songs are the progressively jazzy number "In the Thick of It" and the sentimental ballad "If Only for One Night." (Luther Vandross did an outstanding re-make of the latter.) All the selections are arranged and produced with a universal appeal. The album was later re-released with the hit single "Piano in the Dark as a bonus track. Brenda Russell's talent as a musician, writer, arranger and singer is commendable as are the efforts of producer André Fischer. *—Craig Lytle*

Love Life / 1981 / A&M ✦✦✦

Get Here / 1988 / A&M ✦✦✦

Kiss Me With the Wind / 1991 / A&M ✦✦✦

Singer/songwriter Brenda Russell was teamed with mega-producer Narada Michael Walden (Whitney Houston, Mariah Carey, Aretha Franklin) on *Kiss Me With Wind*, a nice fusion of the two talented artists' skills. The propulsive title track combines elements of dance-pop and house music. The whimsical, pulsating "Dinner With Gershwin" is one of the singer's best tracks, and Russell gives one of her most fluid performances; Donna Summer's cover of the song was a Top Ten R&B hit. Furthermore, "Stop Running Away" broke into the R&B Top 40. Russell co-produces a few tracks with André Fischer: "Stupid Love," "Night Train to Leningrad," with its great image-filled lyrics, and the dreamy "Waiting for You," with its lightly sprinkled acoustic guitar by Earl Klugh. Co-written by Matthew Wilder, "Justice in Truth" asks a gentle plea for equality as it ebbs and flows along atop swelling synth string pads. The inspiring, gospel-like "On Your Side" features Toto drummer Jeff Porcano and Yellowjackets members Russell Ferrante and Jimmy Haslip. *—Ed Hogan*

Greatest Hits / Aug. 4, 1992 / A&M ✦✦✦✦

Soul Talkin' / Jun. 1, 1993 / EMI America ✦✦

Paris Rain / Jul. 18, 2000 / Hidden Beach ✦✦✦

● **Ultimate Collection** / Jul. 24, 2001 / Hip-O ✦✦✦✦✦

Hip-O's *Ultimate Collection* essentially lives up to its name, providing 18 hits from her recordings for Horizon and A&M. This, of course, includes her one Top Ten hit "Piano in the Dark," but it also contains a number of songs that made the R&B charts or radio, providing an excellent summary of her career. *—Stephen Thomas Erlewine*

Sade (Helen Folsade Adu)

b. Jan. 16, 1959, Ibadan, Nigeria

Vocals / Sophisti-Pop, Adult Contemporary, Urban, Quiet Storm

When Sade first came on the recording scene in the '80s, her record company, Epic, made a point of printing "pronounced shar-day" after her name on the record labels of her releases. Soon enough the world would have no problem in correctly pronouncing her name. Born Helen Folasade Adu in a village 50 miles from Lagos, the capitol of Nigeria, she was the daughter of an African father and an English mother. After her mother returned to England, Sade grew up on the North End of London. Developing a good singing voice in her teens, Sade worked part-time jobs in and outside of the music business. She listened to Ray Charles, Nina Simone, Al Green, Aretha Franklin, and Billie Holliday. Sade studied fashion design at St. Martin's School of Art in London while also doing some modeling on the side.

Around 1980, she started singing harmony with a Latin funk group called Arriva. One of the more popular numbers that the group would perform was a Sade original co-written with bandmember Ray St. John, "Smooth Operator," that would later become Sade's first stateside hit. The following year she joined the eight-piece funk band Pride as a background singer. The band included future Sade band members guitarist/saxophonist Stuart Matthewman (a key player in '90s urban soul singer Maxwell's success) and bassist Paul Denman. The concept of the group was that there could shoot-offs. In essence, a few members within the main group Pride formed mini-groups that would be the opening act. Pride did a lot of shows around London, stirring up record company interest. Initially, the labels wanted to only sign Sade, while the group members wanted a deal for the whole band. After a year, the other band members told Sade, Matthewman, and Denman to go ahead and sign a deal. Adding keyboardist Andrew Hale, the group signed to the U.K. division of Epic Records.

Her debut album, *Diamond Life* (with overall production by Robin Millar), went Top Ten in the U.K. in late 1984. January 1985 saw the album released on CBS' Portrait label and by spring it went platinum off the strength of the Top Ten singles "Smooth Operator" and "Hang on to Your Love." Her third album, *Promise* (November 1985), featured "Never As Good As the First Time" and arguably her signature song, "The Sweetest Taboo," which stayed on the U.S. pop charts for six months. Sade was so popular that some radio stations reinstated the '70s practice of playing album tracks, adding "Is It a Crime" and "Tar Baby" to their play lists. In 1986, Sade won a Grammy for Best New Artist.

Sade's third album was 1988's *Stronger Than Pride* and featured her first number-one soul single "Paradise," "Nothing Can Come Between Us," and "Keep Looking." A new Sade album didn't appear for four years. 1992's *Love Deluxe* continued the unbroken streak of multiplatinum Sade albums, spinning off the hits "No Ordinary Love," "Feel No Pain," and "Pearls." The new millennium spark a new scene for Sade. She issued *Lovers Rock* in fall 2000 and incoporated more mainstream elements than ever before. Debut single "By Your Side" was also a hit among radio and adult-contemporary listeners. The following summer, Sade embarked on her first tour in more than a decade, selling out countless dates across America. In early 2002, she celebrated the success of the tour by releasing her first ever live album and DVD, *Lovers Live*. *—Ed Hogan*

Diamond Life / 1984 / Epic ♦♦♦♦

Former model Sade made an immediate and huge impact with her 1984 debut album. Her sound and approach were deliberately icy, her delivery and voice aloof, deadpan and cold, and yet she became an instant sensation through such songs as "Smooth Operator" and "Your Love Is King," where the slick production and quasi-jazz backing seemed to register with audiences thinking they were hearing a jazz vocalist. Sade won the Best New Grammy Award for 1984, and *Diamond Life* sold more than two million copies. *—Ron Wynn*

Promise / 1985 / Epic ♦♦♦

Sade's second album improved on the performance of her debut, as "Sweetest Taboo" was a huge hit and "Never As Good As the First Time" landed in both the R&B and pop Top 20. She was once again the personification of cool, laid-back singing, seldom extending or embellishing lyrics, registering emotion, or projecting her voice. This demeanor made her more desirable in the minds of many fans and was perhaps the ultimate misapplication of the notion of sophistication. But this album topped the pop charts and eventually went triple platinum. *—Ron Wynn*

Stronger Than Pride / 1988 / Epic ♦♦♦

After two LPs with little or no energy, Sade demonstrated some intensity and fire on her third release. Whether that was just an attempt to change the pace a bit or a genuine new direction, she had more animation in her delivery on such songs as "Haunt Me," "Give It Up," and the hit "Paradise." Not that she was suddenly singing in a soulful or bluesy manner; rather, Sade's dry and introspective tone now had a little more edge, and the lyrics were ironic as well as reflective. This was her third consecutive multiplatinum album, and it matched the two-million-plus sales level of her debut. *—Ron Wynn*

Love Deluxe / Oct. 20, 1992 / Epic ♦♦♦♦♦

Sade's fourth album included the hit "No Ordinary Love" and marked a return to the detached, cool jazz backing and even icier vocals that made her debut album a sensation. Although Sade's style is more suggestive than hypnotic, and her production and arrangements are in an urbane mode rather than a jazz one, she's maintained her popularity among the fusion and urban-contemporary audiences. This release also included "Mermaid," "Pearls," and "Feel No Pain." *—Ron Wynn*

● **The Best of Sade** / 1994 / Epic ♦♦♦♦♦

By the time this was released in 1994, something unexpected happened. Sade's early work became classic and the later additions boasted even better vocals and songs that nicely improved on the theme. The timeless sound and class always exhibited makes Sade Adu and her band a no-brainer for an appealing compilation. Like Al Green's *Greatest Hits*, *The Best of Sade* doesn't detract from the original albums and is a marker of time, not the end of the act. The ice-princess demeanor and detached vocals worked perfectly for the mid-'80s singles and radio samples "Smooth Operator" and "Your Love Is King." The tracks from the make-or-break second album, *Promise*, seem less dolorous propped up and sequenced for a compilation. The sensual-to-a-fault "The Sweetest Taboo" and "Never As Good As the First Time" both retain their strength here. The songs from *Stronger Than Pride*—"Love Is Stronger Than Pride," "Nothing Can Come Between Us," and the great "Paradise"—all benefit from Ian Cooper's mastering job. This set also includes tracks from Sade's "comeback" CD, *Love Deluxe*, including "Kiss of Life" and "No Ordinary Love." As a bonus, *The Best of Sade* also includes a rare cover of "Please Send Me Someone to Love" from the *Philadelphia* soundtrack. Despite its riches, *The Best of Sade* doesn't include all of the best, since "Maureen" and or "Keep Looking" aren't here. It's a small complaint and *The Best of Sade* is a great overview. *—Jason Elias*

Lovers Rock / Nov. 14, 2000 / Epic ♦♦♦♦♦

Lovers Rock, the title of Sade's first album of the 21st century, could be taken on many levels. Never before has the singer infused more mainstream rock elements (prominent strummed guitars) into her music as evidenced by the first single, "By Your Side." That's not to say that she has eschewed her own tried-and-true brand of smoky, dusky ballads. The singer/songwriter is reunited with co-producer Mike Pela and musician/songwriters Andrew Hale, Stuart Matthewman, and Paul S. Denman; and *Lovers Rock* finds them all in fine form. "Somebody Already Broke My Heart," "Every Word," and "Lovers Rock" are vintage Sade. *—Ed Hogan*

Safire (Wilma Cosme)

b. San Juan, Puerto Rico

Vocals / Sophisti-Pop, Club/Dance, Adult Contemporary, Urban

Although she didn't score as many pop crossovers as groups like Exposé or the Cover Girls, Safire's string of late-'80s club hits helped make her one of Latin freestyle's most popular female performers. Born Wilma Cosme in San Juan, Puerto Rico, she grew up mostly in East Harlem and began her singing career as a session vocalist. She was discovered at an audition for the Cutting Records label, which won her the chance to record the already-waiting single "Don't Break My Heart." Released in 1986, it became an instant freestyle classic, as did the early-1987 follow-up "Let Me Be the One" (which she co-wrote). The success of both singles helped Safire land a deal with Mercury, where she recorded her self-titled debut album. Released in 1988, *Sa-Fire* featured her two previous hits, plus the even more successful "Boy I've Been Told," which was penned by Latin star Marc Anthony, and became a significant success on urban radio and in clubs across the U.S. and Europe. The ballad "Thinking of You," which she also co-wrote, became her biggest pop crossover in early 1989, peaking at number 12 and enjoying substantial radio airplay. Mercury didn't push the dance-oriented follow-up "Love Is on Her Mind" quite as hard, and it stalled her mainstream momentum, though she remained extremely popular in the freestyle community.

Safire's second album, *I Wasn't Born Yesterday*, was released in 1990, around the time that freestyle's presence on the pop charts had begun to diminish. Mainstream dance-pop and house music were taking over its previous audiences, and *I Wasn't Born Yesterday* couldn't perform up to the level of commercial success its predecessor had enjoyed, even despite the house-influenced single "Taste the Bass." With the freestyle scene no longer thriving, Safire remained quiet for a few years. She returned in 1996—signed to Sony and no longer sporting a hyphen—with a more straightforward Latin dance album; *Atrevida* blended salsa with hip-hop rhythms. In 2001, Safire released *Bringing Back the Groove*, a combination of new material and remixes of her past hits. Both "Don't Break My Heart 2002" and the new ballad duet "Can You Stand the Rain" (originally by New Edition, featuring longtime friend Cynthia) landed some airplay among urban and Latin stations. *—Steve Huey*

- **Sa-Fire** / 1988 / Mercury ♦♦♦♦♦

The debut album by the hyphenated vocalist who was physically short (assuming the photo on her album wasn't deceptive) but vocally imposing. She had range, power, and soul, and wasn't afraid to belt out a song or stretch out a lyric. Unfortunately, she didn't really have great (or even good, for the most part) material to embellish. The results didn't get her solo career off to a good start. *—Ron Wynn*

I Wasn't Born Yesterday / 1990 / Mercury ♦♦♦

An erratic, but sometimes arresting second album by a vocalist with little name recognition but above-average talents. Sa-Fire had done some session work in the mid-'80s before getting a shot at being a lead artist. She sang without pretension, put soul and energy into her delivery, and made mundane tracks interesting, but she couldn't salvage another faceless major label release. *—Ron Wynn*

Bringing Back the Groove / Aug. 7, 2001 / Globestar ♦♦♦

Puerto Rican-born Wilma Cosme, known as Safire, brings a collection of her hits, new songs, and remixes to get into the contemporary club scene, starting with a new version of her first smash "Don't Break My Heart," produced by Grammy nominated Tony Moran, getting along with dance/pop singer Cynthia on "Can You Stand the Rain," showing a different side of herself while performing the freestyle ballad "I'm Feeling It Too," without forgetting her 1988 hit single "Boy I've Been Told," composed by Latin star Marc Anthony. Safire's *Bringing Back the Groove* goes through her career, bringing back her best. *—Drago Bonacich*

The Salsoul Orchestra

f. 1974, New York, NY, **db.** 1982

Group / Disco, Philly Soul, Club/Dance

The music world's prime disco big band during the late '70s, the Salsoul Orchestra recorded several of the tightest, chunkiest disco themes of the 1970s, both on its own productions and as the backing group for several prime vocalists. Organized by Vincent Montana Jr. in 1974, the band was an experiment in fusing funk, Philly soul, and Latin music together in a highly danceable discofied style with plenty of room for solos by individual members. With arrangers, conductors, and whole sections of instruments (including up to 18 violinists) contributing to the sound, the Salsoul Orchestra routinely included up to 50 members. Though the Salsoul sound became passé in the wake of disco music's explosion and rapid commercialization during the late '70s, Salsoul was a heavy influence on house music in the 1980s and even the return of disco-inspired electronica during the following decade.

The beginnings of the Salsoul Orchestra (and Salsoul Records) lie with nominal head Vincent Montana Jr. A longtime jazz vibraphonist, bandleader, and session man with Philly soul groups like Harold Melvin & the Blue Notes, the O'Jays, and the Spinners, Montana dreamed of constructing a large studio orchestra which could fuse polished soul and brassy funk with Latin percussion and live strings. In 1974, he was introduced to local entrepreneurs Joe, Ken, and Stan Cayre (who ran a local Latin music label) by Afro-Cuban pianist Joe Bataan. With their blessing (and financing), Montana spent months recruiting dozens of musicians from the streets and studios of New York—including more than a half-dozen percussionists alone. The collective recorded three tracks, which impressed Bataan and the Cayres so much that they decided to form a new label—named Salsoul for its connotations of salsa and soul—to release a full-length LP.

One of the original Salsoul Orchestra recordings, "The Salsoul Hustle," was released in mid-1975 and it placed well on the charts. Salsoul's second single, "Tangerine" (an unlikely cover of a Jimmy Dorsey tune), hit the Top 20 in early 1976 and pushed the eponymous *Salsoul Orchestra* LP to number 14 on the album charts. Follow-up singles like "You're Just the Right Size" and "Nice & Naasty" did moderately well on the charts but soon a glut of similar-sounding material began to flood the market, cheap imitations of the amazing instrumentation of Salsoul Orchestra members—guitarist and producer Norman Harris, bassist Ron Baker, drummer Earl Young, arranger Don Renaldo, percussionist Larry Washington, and vocalists Jocelyn Brown, Phyllis Rhodes, Ron Tyson, Philip Hurt, and Carl Helm. Many Salsoul contributors played on the biggest and best disco tracks of the era, including Trammps, Grace Jones, the Whispers, Loleatta Holloway, and First Choice.

Salsoul's third LP, the slightly amusing *Christmas Jollies*, displayed a predilection towards the growing disco novelty trend. The slip was hardly improved upon with 1977's *Cuchi-Cuchi* (which teamed the Orchestra with Charo) or 1978's *Up the Yellow Brick Road* (a takeoff on *The Wiz*). After disintegrating the Salsoul Orchestra in the early '80s, Vince Montana led the studio group Montana and recorded with several pop stars of the '80s as well as dance inheritors of the '90s like Mondo Grosso and Nuyorican Soul. Though Salsoul records had long been out of print, several were brought back in the mid-'90s, as well as a prescient two-disc retrospective titled *Anthology*. *—John Bush*

The Salsoul Orchestra / Nov. 1975 / Salsoul ♦♦♦

This 1975 album introduced to the world to the slick yet groovy instrumental stylings of the Salsoul Orchestra, a group of Philadelphia session musicians spearheaded by vibes player Vincent Montana. Since many of the musicians (including Montana) also participated in the recordings of MFSB, it's not a big surprise that *The Salsoul Orchestra* explores a similar vein of orchestral soul. The difference between the two is that the Salsoul Orchestra explores a more Latin-oriented style with a heavy emphasis on congas and other forms of exotic percussion. This style is neatly encapsulated in the lead-off track "Salsoul Hustle," which is built on a contrast between a dreamy, string-led melody and a series of funky instrumental breakdowns spiced with conga tattoos. Other highlights in this style include "You're Just the Right Size," which layers sweet orchestrations and a female chorus cooing the title chant over a synthesizer-layered groove while "Salsoul Rainbow" glides forth on a fusillade of congas and wah-wah guitar riffs. On the downside, *The Salsoul Orchestra* occasionally allows their slickness to overpower their R&B backbone and the result is disco-flavored easy listening like "Tangerine" and "Love Letters." Another problem is the album's highlights, as funky as they are, often have a cookie-cutter feel to them: for instance, "Salsoul Hustle" and "Tale of Three Cities" are built on strikingly similar arrangements that hinge on the contrast between string-led flights on fancy and funky grooves from the rhythm section. Despite these shortcomings, *The Salsoul Orchestra* shapes up as a solid disco album that will entertain anyone who enjoys orchestral soul. *—Donald A. Guarisco*

Nice & Naasty / Oct. 1976 / Salsoul ♦♦♦

On their second album, the Salsoul Orchestra enhance the appeal of their string-heavy soul sound by marrying it to a series of tight, hook-laden tunes. The overall feeling of *Nice & Naasty* is very "up" and the album prominently features a number of high-energy tracks tailored for the dancefloor. In fact, the album contains of two of the Salsoul Orchestra's best-ever uptempo tracks: "It Don't Have to Be Funky" moves forward at a double-time speed thanks to a combination of frenetic drumming and an infectious rhythm guitar riff while "Don't Beat Around the Bush" layers the rhythmic, sexy chant of the title over a huge-sounding, thickly-layered drum beat that sounds like it was lifted from a glam rock record. Another uptempo highlight is "Salsoul 3001," a dancefloor stormer that brings "Thus Sprach Zarathustra" into the disco age by marrying its dramatic melody to a frenetic groove anchored by some furious conga drumming. *Nice & Naasty* also improves on the group's debut album by downplaying the easy listening excesses that marred that album: even on soft tracks like "Nightcrawler," the musicians add a rhythmic touch that keeps the album's overall groove moving forward. In fact, the only time *Nice & Naasty* slides toward easy listening is during the "We've Only Just Begun/Feelings" medley, but even that is saved by a clever arrangement that highlights some some lovely vibes work by Vincent Montana. Overall, *Nice & Naasty*'s combination of solid tunes and tight performance make it the Salsoul Orchestra's most consistently entertaining album and a good choice for disco fanatics. *—Donald A. Guarisco*

Christmas Jollies / Nov. 1976 / Salsoul ♦♦

Magic Journey / Jun. 1977 / Salsoul ♦♦

Sadly, the Salsoul Orchestra's third album does not live up to its fanciful title. *Magic Journey* forsakes the consistent feel of the group's past albums in favor of an odd assemblage of material that never comfortably coheres. In fact, it goes all over the map—from soul ("Runaway") to traditional tunes ("Guantanamera") to pure orchestral instrumentals ("Theme From Montreal Olympics, 1976"). The strangest inclusion is a cover of "Short Shorts" that forsakes disco entirely for a '50s nostalgia feel and goofily rewrites the lyrics to mention the members of the band. Another problem with *Magic Journey* is that it allows the "orchestral" to overpower the "soul" in their orchestral soul sound: "Theme From Montreal Olympics, 1976" is a straight orchestral instrumental that is lacking in any kind of R&B content while "Journey to Phoebus" and "Alpha Centuri" feel like outtakes from a science fiction film score instead of the dancefloor material the Salsoul Orchestra is known for. Despite these problems, *Magic Journey* does have its moments: "Getaway" is a high-octane instrumental retooling of the Earth, Wind & Fire classic and "Magic Bird of Fire" transforms musical themes from Stravinsky's "Firebird Suite" into a thrilling and hard-grooving slice of orchestral soul that pulsates with frantic percussion and swirling strings. *The Salsoul Orchestra* also manages to transform the Latin standard "Guantanamera" into a credible midtempo dance track layered with a classy string arrangement. Despite these occasional bright spots, *Magic Journey* is too inconsistent in both the quality of its material and its danceable content to qualify as a solid disco outing. Completists may want to add it to their collection but the casual listener would be better off sampling *Magic Journey*'s highlights on the group's *Anthology* retrospective. *—Donald A. Guarisco*

Cuchi-Cuchi / Nov. 1977 / Salsoul ♦♦

Up the Yellow Brick Road / Mar. 1978 / Salsoul ♦♦

Street Sense / 1979 / Salsoul ♦♦

- **Anthology** / 1994 / Salsoul ♦♦♦♦♦

From the '70s disco big-band comes a double-disc retrospective of their greatest hits and best-known material from "Nice & Naasty," "Don't Beat Around the Bush," "Salsoul Hustle," "Get Happy" and "Tangerine" to "Ooh I Love It (Love Break)." *—John Bush*

Salt-N-Pepa

f. 1985

Group / Hip-Hop, Pop-Rap, Urban

By the late '80s, hip-hop was on its way to becoming a male-dominated art form, which is what made the emergence of Salt-N-Pepa so significant. As the first all-female rap crew (even their DJs were women) of importance, the group broke down a number of doors for women in hip-hop. They were also one of the first rap artists to crossover into the pop mainstream, laying the groundwork for the music's widespread acceptance in the early '90s. Salt-N-Pepa were more pop-oriented than many of their contemporaries, since their songs were primarily party and love anthems, driven by big beats and interlaced with vaugely pro-feminist lyrics that seemed more powerful when delivered by the charismatic and sexy trio. While songs like "Push It" and "Shake Your Thang" made the group appear to be a one-hit pop group during the late '80s, Salt-N-Pepa defied expectations and became one of the few hip-hop artists to develop a long-term career. Along with LL Cool J, the trio had major hits in both the '80s and '90s, and, if anything, they hit the height of their popularity in 1994, when "Shoop" and "Whatta Man" drove their third album, *Very Necessary*, into the Top Ten. *—Stephen Thomas Erlewine*

Hot, Cool & Vicious / 1986 / Next Plateau ♦♦♦

These Queens, NY, natives came on strong when rap was still in its infancy in the mid-'80s. Salt-N-Pepa not only eventually scored massive hits with "Shoop" and "Whatta Man" in the early '90s, but they also paved the way for the countless female rap and soul groups to flood the market. This was their debut, cut for indie Next Plateau label. Produced by

Hurby Luv Bug (aka Hurby Azor, who would be let go after the group's third outing), *Hot, Cool & Vicious* features the trio dressed up in vintage and whimsical old school hip-hop dress. Besides the hit "Tramp" (its B-side, "Push It," would later be remixed and become a huge smash), highlights include "The Showstopper," "I'll Take Your Man," and "My Mic Sounds Nice." *—Stephen Cook*

A Salt With a Deadly Pepa / 1988 / London ✦✦✦
A concept album musically, if not lyrically, this one fleshes out one terrific single, "Shake Your Thang," with a sharpening of the trio's sensibilities and talents. *—John Floyd*

A Blitz of Hits: The Hits Remixed / 1989 / London ✦✦
As remix albums go, Salt-N-Pepa's is fine, but their hit singles lose a bit of their magic in these extended forms. *—Stephen Thomas Erlewine*

● **Blacks' Magic** / Mar. 1990 / London ✦✦✦✦✦
Prior to the release of their third album, *Blacks' Magic,* Salt-N-Pepa were viewed as little more than pop crossover artists. Most of their singles had been rap remakes of old R&B songs, and they hadn't even rapped all that much on their biggest hit, "Push It," which got by on its catchy synth hook. But *Blacks' Magic* was where Salt-N-Pepa came into their own. It wasn't that their crossover appeal diminished, but this time they worked from a funkier R&B base that brought them more credibility among hip-hop and urban audiences. More importantly, they displayed a stronger group identity than ever before, projecting a mix of sassy, self-confident feminism and aggressive—but responsible—sexuality. The album's trio of hit singles—"Expression," "Do You Want Me," and the playful safe-sex anthem "Let's Talk About Sex"—summed up this new attitude and got the group plastered all over MTV. But there was more to the album than just the singles—track for track, *Blacks' Magic* was the strongest record Salt-N-Pepa ever released. Even if there's still a bit of filler here and there, *Blacks' Magic* successfully remade Salt-N-Pepa as their own women, and pointed the way to the even more commercially successful R&B/pop/hip-hop fusions of *Very Necessary.* *—Steve Huey*

Very Necessary / Oct. 12, 1993 / London ✦✦✦✦
While Salt-N-Pepa definitely took their time releasing albums during their career, they returned from a three-year sabbatical in 1993 with *Very Necessary,* a smart album that furthered the progressive femininity that had worked so well for them on *Blacks' Magic.* Unfortunately, *Very Necessary* wasn't as strong of an album as *Black's Magic,* but the female rappers did come prepared with a pair of potent singles capable of carrying the album commercially, "Shoop" and "Whatta Man." Given the success of "Let's Talk About Sex" three years earlier, it's little surprise that Salt-N-Pepa instilled that song's progressive feminine ideology into both "Shoop" and "Whatta Man." Like "Let's Talk About Sex," these two songs aren't overly serious—employing a safe, club-friendly hip-hop rhythm and catchy, radio-friendly vocal hooks—but they do manage to communicate their message of feminine pride and a social norm-challenging view of female sexuality quite effectively without sacrificing any sense of fun. Besides these two obviously contrived singles, there aren't too many other major highlights here, with the exception of "None of Your Business," another song laden with subtle social commentary regarding femininity. Elsewhere, a few songs such as "I've Got AIDS" and "Sexy Noises Turn Me On" are similarly interesting from an ideological standpoint but just aren't that impressive in terms of rapping or production—this can be said for the remainder of the album as well. When you benchmark the best moments on *Very Necessary* against the lesser moments, you get the sense that the group was far more interested in crafting the obligatory crossover singles rather than a solid album from beginning to end. Nonetheless, the album stands only second to *Black's Magic* as the strongest of Salt-N-Pepa's 15-year career. *—Jason Birchmeier*

Brand New / Oct. 21, 1997 / London/Red Ant ✦✦✦
The four years separating Salt-N-Pepa's latter-day blockbuster *Very Necessary* and its successor, *Brand New,* is an eternity in hip-hop. During that time, styles and fashions change rapidly, leaving many artists behind. Salt-N-Pepa suffer from being out of the spotlight for so long—they don't sound in tune with the times, they sound like they're stuck in 1993. However, that isn't necessarily a bad thing, since the group does this kind of thing very well. There isn't anything that stands out like "Whatta Man" or "Shoop," but there's enough strong moments to make it worthwhile for longtime fans. *—Stephen Thomas Erlewine*

The Salty Peppers

Group / Funk, Soul
Earth, Wind & Fire leader Maurice White was a founding member of the Salty Peppers. While a session drummer for Chess Records and a member of the Ramsey Lewis Trio, White started a group with bassist/keyboardist Don Whitehead and vocalist Wade Flemons. The Salty Peppers had a Midwest hit with "La La La"—issued on White's own Hummit Records—and the track was leased to Capitol, which led to a record contract for the group. (The single was "Un Huh Yeah" b/w "Your Love Is Life.") After visiting California several times, White decided to make the move west and quit Lewis' trio. With demo tapes that featured the skills of Chicago multi-talent Donny Hathaway, White began shopping demo tapes (some featuring the skills of Donny Hathaway) around, then signed to Warner Bros., while the Salty Peppers eventually evolved into Earth, Wind & Fire. *—Ed Hogan*

The Salutations

Group / Pop, R&B, Novelty
The Salutations recorded several singles, both novelty cuts and love ballads, for various labels in the early and mid-'60s, but were unable to crack either the pop or R&B charts. The group, which was also known as Vito and the Salutations, recorded for Apartment, Kram, Rayna, Herald, Regina, Rust, Wells, Boom, and Red Boy, with another single coming out on Crystal in 1978. *—Ron Wynn*

Sam & Dave

f. 1961, Miami, FL, **db.** 1971
Group / Soul, Deep Soul, Southern Soul, Memphis Soul
Perhaps no act epitomized soul music as the secularization of gospel more than Sam & Dave. The original pairing of Sam Moore & Dave Prater met in Florida in 1961, and they recorded unsuccessfully for several years before being signed to Atlantic Records in 1965. Atlantic persuaded their Memphis affiliate Stax Records to produce them, and in December that year the writing and production team of Isaac Hayes & David Porter delivered the crisply soulful "You Don't Know Like I Know." Hayes & Porter became the *éminence grises* behind Sam & Dave, much as Holland-Dozier-Holland pulled the strings behind the Supremes. They wrote, they produced—and the result was a string of hits, including "Soul Man," "Hold On! I'm Comin'," and "I Thank You," songs that survive as the very epitome of Southern soul. Certainly, Sam & Dave's hits are among the most soulful ever to crack the Hot 100. Their albums often bore the hallmarks of hasty execution, though. The dissolution of the partnership between Stax and Atlantic virtually sealed the fate of Sam & Dave; there were a few more hits (and, later, a revival of interest thanks to the Blues Brothers), but the glory days were over.

Samuel Moore and David Prater were both raised in the South, where they sang in church as children. During the '50s, they performed in soul and R&B clubs before meeting each other in at the King of Hearts club in Miami in 1961. Moore was hosting an amateur-night contest where Prater was singing. Once Dave forgot the lyrics to Jackie Wilson's "Doggin' Around," Sam coached him through the song. Following that night, the singers became a duo and soon became a popular local Miami act and signed with Roulette Records, releasing a handful of singles. In 1965, they signed with Atlantic Records, but producer Jerry Wexler moved the band to the label's Stax subsidiary.

Working with Stax's house band and songwriters/producers Isaac Hayes & David Porter, Sam & Dave created a body of sweaty, gritty soul that ranks among the finest and most popular produced in the late '60s. The duo's 1966 debut, "You Don't Know Like I Know," kicked off a series of Top Ten R&B hits that included "Hold On! I'm Comin'" (1966), "You Got Me Hummin'" (1966), "When Something Is Wrong With My Baby" (1967), "Soul Man" (1967), and "I Thank You" (1968). However, the duo's career began to unravel in 1968, when Stax's distribution deal with Atlantic ended. Since Sam & Dave were signed with Atlantic, not Stax, they no longer had access to the production team of Hayes & Porter or the house band of Booker T. & the MG's, and their recorded work took a slight dip in quality. Though the switch of labels was unfortunate, what really caused the duo's demise was their volatile relationship. While the duo had enormous creative energy, they frequently fought off-stage. Nicknamed "Double Dynamite," Sam & Dave became famous for their energetic, infectious live performances during the late '60s, which complemented the overall high quality of their studio work. They may have communicated on-stage, but behind the scenes, it was reported that the duo could hardly stand each other's presence. The tension caused Sam & Dave to part ways in 1970, just a few years after their heyday.

During the '70s, Sam & Dave reunited several times to little attention. At the end of the decade, John Belushi and Dan Aykroyd's Blues Brothers routine—which borrowed heavily from Sam & Dave—sparked a resurgence of interest in the duo, and the pair performed a number of concerts during 1980. However, their personal animosity had not faded, and they separated after a performance on New Year's Eve 1981. For the next few years, Prater toured as Sam & Dave with vocalist Sam Daniels. During the mid-'80s, Moore revealed the sources of the duo's tensions in a series of interviews. He disclosed that he had been addicted to drugs during the '70s. Prater was arrested in 1987 for selling crack to an undercover policeman. A year later, he died in a car accident. Moore continued to perform sporadically, most notably on Bruce Springsteen's 1992 album *Human Touch* album. Sam & Dave were inducted into the Rock and Roll Hall of Fame that same year. *—Colin Escott & Stephen Thomas Erlewine*

Hold On, I'm Comin' / 1966 / Atlantic ✦✦✦✦
When the Northern soulsters of Motown were employing strings and pop elements, Sam & Dave rejected pop wholesale and made sure they kept their Memphis soul simple and raw. Their albums never sounded heavily produced, and therein lies much of the appeal of *Hold On, I'm Comin'* (their first album for Atlantic). This wasn't a duo that believed in hiding behind lavish productions. Like the blues and gospel artists who paved the way for soul music, Sam & Dave knew how to seize the moment. From such major hits as "You Don't Know Like I Know" and the title song to solid album tracks like the riveting "It's a Wonder" and the tough yet vulnerable ballad "Just Me," this album epitomizes Memphis soul in all its unpretentious, down-home glory. [A song-for-song reissue of the original LP, the CD version of *Hold On, I'm Comin'* that Atlantic put out in 1991 is rather skimpy by CD standards (as are the CD versions of *Soul Men* and *I Thank You*). Certainly Atlantic could have provided some bonus tracks. Nonetheless, this CD is well worth hearing.] *—Alex Henderson*

Sam & Dave / 1966 / Roulette ✦✦✦
Roulette didn't release this album until 1966—two years after Sam & Dave's last Roulette single. They had become a household name via Stax Records when this hit the market. It is definitive Roulette, containing both sides of their six singles for the label. Roulette featured Dave Prater's baritone/tenor more prominently than Sam Moore's vibrant gospel tenor—Stax featured Moore. They recorded "I Got a Thing Going On," "I Need Love," "No Pain," and "Keep Walkin'" at Criterion Studios in Miami for Henry Stone. And according to Moore they first dropped on either Marlin or TK Records (the Rolling Stones' labels). Their first Roulette release, "I Need Love," written by Moore and Sam Early (not Prater as credited) went unnoticed. A nondescript "No More Pain" did no better. Through Morris Levy (the nefarious owner of Roulette) they kept busy gigging with no hits. According to Moore, "Jackie Wilson hung around the studio and sings background (uncredited) on many of these tracks." A third release, "She's Alright," failed miserably. Only the flowing "It's So Nice While It Lasted" where Prater and Moore's voices blend soulfully

had any juice; it almost broke in 1963. Roulette released the charmer again in 1966 to ride the wave of their Stax hits. *—Andrew Hamilton*

Double Dynamite / 1967 / Atlantic ✦✦✦✦
This was the second Sam & Dave album to enjoy significant crossover appeal. The 1967 record included such hits as "Said I Wasn't Gonna Tell Nobody," "Soothe Me," and "When Something Is Wrong With My Baby." Isaac Hayes & David Porter were now rolling as songwriters, and even though the record didn't attain big pop numbers, the singles clicked with both soul and pop audiences. More importantly, Sam & Dave's teamwork and vocal interaction were establishing them as major stars. *—Ron Wynn*

Soul Men / 1967 / Rhino ✦✦✦✦
Because R&B was such a singles-driven market in the 1960s, many albums released by Stax and Motown were big on filler. But that generally wasn't the case with Sam & Dave's albums, which boasted many gems that weren't released as singles and enjoyed little, if any, radio airplay. Listeners may be surprised to learn that as popular as this twosome was in 1967, *Soul Men* contains only one major single: the anthemic title song and its B-side, the charming "May I Baby." Among the first-class album tracks never released as singles were "Rich Kind of Poverty," the punchy "Hold It Baby," and the gospel-drenched ballads "Just Keep Holding On" and "I've Seen What Loneliness Can Do." For those with more than a casual interest in Memphis soul, *Soul Men* (reissued on CD in 1991) is highly recommended. *—Alex Henderson*

I Thank You / 1968 / Rhino ✦✦✦
Although not quite as strong as *Hold On, I'm Comin'* or *Soul Men*, *I Thank You* serves as a fine illustration of the splendor of Memphis soul. The best known songs on this album (reissued on CD in 1992) are the title song and its infectious B-side, "Wrap It Up." Interestingly, this wasn't an album that contained a lot of major hits, but it does have a lot to admire, including "If I Didn't Have a Girl Like You" (a gem of a ballad), the driving "Ain't That a Lot of Love," and an inspired version of Otis Redding's "These Arms of Mine." As usual, Isaac Hayes' arranging and songwriting is a definite asset for the energetic duo, which really digs right into the material and spares no passion. *—Alex Henderson*

The Best of Sam & Dave / 1969 / Atlantic ✦✦✦✦
During the early '80s, Atlantic released newer compilations from some of the most popular R&B artists from the '60s, including Aretha Franklin and Wilson Pickett. *The Best of Sam & Dave* perhaps works even better. Although the duo's 1969 greatest hits remains definitive from a pop culture and song choice perspective, this boasts superior sound and zero filler. Like all of their compilations of merit, *The Best of Sam & Dave* proves the precision of the backing from Booker T. and the MG's and the duo's most illustrious songwriting team, Isaac Hayes & David Porter. The writing team's masterwork, the amazing and kinetic "Soul Man" was in line with the burgeoning black pride of the time. While other well-known tracks like "When Something Is Wrong With My Baby" and "Hold on, I'm Comin'" are here, *The Best of Sam & Dave* also culls other songs that are just as potent. The humorous "Said I Wasn't Gonna Tell Nobody" and the hard-driving yet quirky "Wrap It Up" all display the singular one-two punch of Moore's narrow and irascible tone pitted against Prater's woebegone baritone. Arguably the best track, the phenomenal "I Thank You" closes the compilation on a high note. Although the duo did switch officially to Atlantic by the early '70s, this compilation stops at the prime Stax material. *The Best of Sam & Dave* had a brief shelf life and was supplanted by more extensive overviews. As a compilation spotlighting the hits, this does the job. *—Jason Elias*

Back at 'Cha! / 1976 / United Artists ✦✦✦
The great soul duo of Sam Moore & Dave Prater made a gallant attempt at a comeback with this mid-'70s release, but the times had changed dramatically, and there wasn't much demand on the urban contemporary horizon for an aging Southern soul duo. Their harmonies were still solid, although the leads and shared vocals were a little on the faded side. It was great to hear the two singing together again, but the combination of changed audience tastes and uneven material proved too much of an obstacle for Sam & Dave to get back in the spotlight. *—Ron Wynn*

☆ **Sweat 'n' Soul: Anthology (1965-1971)** / Jul. 20, 1993 / Rhino/Atlantic ✦✦✦✦✦
Sam Moore and Dave Prather were the ultimate soul duo; one a high-voiced wailer, the other a low-toned blaster. They came together in the mid-'60s to form a superb duo, singing tunes penned by soul's finest writing tandem, Isaac Hayes & David Porter. They made a host of great singles before ego battles broke them apart. This 50-cut, two-disc anthology not only has every song of significance, but plenty of obscure worthwhile items, like a "Stay in School" promo, some overlooked material done with the Dixie Flyers, and a couple of numbers cut by Moore as a solo act in the early '70s. The sound quality, annotation, and song sequencing are as outstanding as the songs themselves. *—Ron Wynn*

★ **The Very Best of Sam & Dave** / Feb. 28, 1995 / Rhino ✦✦✦✦✦
The Very Best of Sam & Dave contains all of Sam & Dave's Top 40 hits, including "You Don't Know Like I Know," "Hold on, I'm Comin'," "Said I Wasn't Gonna Tell Nobody," "You Got Me Hummin'," "When Something Is Wrong With My Baby," "Soothe Me," "Soul Man," and "I Thank You," plus a handful of essential album tracks and B-sides like "I Can't Stand Up for Falling Down." It's an expertly compiled, concise collection that contains everything you need to know. If you need to dig deeper, the double-disc *Sweat 'n' Soul* is essential, but most casual fans will be completely satisfied by *The Very Best of Sam & Dave*. *—Stephen Thomas Erlewine*

Sammie

Vocals / Contemporary R&B, Neo-Soul
Miami's preteen R&B singer Sammie was exposed to music even before he was born. His mother, a former professional singer, sang in the church choir while she was carrying him. Fittingly, Sammie's first singing triumph also occurred at church; at age four, he received a standing ovation for his performance of "Troubles Don't Last Always." Music was never far from Sammie's mind, even at school; teachers would catch him singing under his breath during classes, but encouraged his talent. Eventually, a music teacher from Charles Drew Elementary, a nearby magnet school with a special performing arts program, heard of Sammie's vocal gifts and he transferred there at the start of third grade. Soon after, he formed a vocal group, the Wonder 3, with two junior high boys.

Sammie's music teacher was so impressed with their performances that she sent a videotape of them to the television program *Showtime at the Apollo*, which led to an audition for the group and a 1998 solo performance for Sammie. Ultimately winning the show's finals, Sammie and his mother were contacted by Joyce Irby, an agent connected to Atlanta-based producer/songwriter Dallas Austin, who has worked with Monica and Another Bad Creation. Austin brought Sammie to his studios for some demos and almost a year later, had him return to record his debut album, *From the Bottom to the Top*, which was released in early 2000 by Capitol Records. *—Heather Phares*

● **From the Bottom to the Top** / Mar. 14, 2000 / Capitol ✦✦✦
There's no mistaking little Sammie for Sammy, the post-Pavement indie-rock combo of the mid-'90s. No, Sammie is an urban R&B singer. He's also a kid, not that you'd really be able to tell that from a cursory listen of his debut album, *From the Bottom to the Top*. At times, his voice does sound a little thin, but for the most part, it's surprisingly soulful and convincing—not as stunning and assured as the young Michael Jackson, but certainly a lot better than most child singers. If he's not yet skillful enough to disguise the sometimes uneven material, that's still forgivable, because the tracks that do work, work really well. By and large, those are the songs written and produced by executive producer Dallas Austin, who keeps the beats fresh and light and the hooks strong and catchy—particularly on uptempo numbers like the opener "The Bottom" and "Can't Let Go," featuring Lloyd of N'Toon. That's not to say that other producers and writers come up empty or that Sammie can't handle slower songs—the midtempo soul of "Crazy Things I Do," produced and written by C. "Tricky" Stewart, is proof that he can—but he sounds his most infectious when the beat is a little faster and the hooks are a little sharper. Perhaps that's due to the songwriting, which gets a little undistinguished as the tempo slows, or perhaps it's due to the fact that while Sammie is an impressive talent, he has yet to mature. Either way, the end result is the same: *From the Bottom to the Top* is entertaining, but not always engaging. Still, we have to remember that this is a debut album from a child singer. Judged on that basis, it's charming and, at times, impressive. Sammie does well this time out, and he'll probably do better next time around. *—Stephen Thomas Erlewine*

Santa Esmeralda

Group / Disco, Euro-Dance, Pop
As disco became an important part of the international music business, European producers began working in exotic flavors into the disco beat to create unique and competitive recordings. A good example of this trend is Santa Esmeralda, a Spanish-themed studio group that wove elements of flamenco, salsa, and other Latin musical styles into its Euro-disco sound. Although the group's sound was about as genuinely Spanish as Herb Alpert & the Tijuana Brass (Santa Esmeralda was the brainchild of French record producers), the result was a crossover success that spawned several club-favorite albums and a notable pop hit in the band's Latinized cover of "Don't Let Me Be Misunderstood." *—Donald A. Guarisco*

● **Don't Let Me Be Misunderstood** / 1977 / Casablanca ✦✦✦✦
Santa Esmeralda's debut dropped on Phillips Records in 1977, then Casablanca Records for worldwide distribution; Hot Records reissued it on CD in 1994. Originally titled *Santa Esmeralda Featuring Leroy Gomez*, Casablanca changed the title to capitalize on the hit single "Don't Let Me Be Misunderstood." The old Animals' classic covered an entire side of the original vinyl album, "Esmeralda Suite," was simply a reworking of the hit. Contains three others: a dull ballad "You're My Everything," an elongated remake of "Gloria," that's borderline disco, and the refreshing "Black Pot," a soulful number that uses Spanish guitars, flamenco percussion, and lead guitars to good effect. There's no bonus tracks, so you're getting the original album intact. *—Andrew Hamilton*

Beauty / 1978 / Casablanca ✦✦✦

The House of the Rising Sun / 1978 / Casablanca ✦✦

● **You're My Everything: The Best of Santa Esmeralda** / Dec. 15, 1994 / Hot Productions ✦✦✦✦
The Best of Santa Esmeralda: You're My Everything reveals that the group's recordings have held up quite well. The disc wisely chooses the full-length album versions of the group's tracks, thus allowing the listener to get the full effect of the lush, epic arrangements that characterized the recordings. The uptempo cuts effectively pit pop hooks and melodies against insistently danceable rhythms and are delivered with brio by the studio musicians: "Don't Let Me Be Misunderstood" effectively layers staccato handclaps and horn arrangements out of an Ennio Morricone soundtrack over its stomping dance beat, and "Another Cha Cha" is a bravura disco epic where serpentine horn arrangements duel with percolating salsa rhythms to create dance track that is as suspenseful as it is thrilling. Elsewhere, Santa Esmeralda takes the intensity down a few notches to create some lovely ballads: "Sevilla Nights" is a lush instrumental that creates a mellow, tangibly nocturnal mood, and "You're My Everything" is a heart-tugging ballad highlighted by a gorgeous, lilting flamenco guitar solo. Special note should also be made of the group's vocalists, Leroy Gomez and Jimmy Goings, who keep the music's slick sound from becoming impersonal with their impassioned, rich vocal stylings. In the end, the listener's tolerance for disco will determine how much they get out of *The Best of Santa Esmeralda: You're My Everything*, but anyone who appreciates Euro-disco at its most lush and romantic will enjoy this disc. *—Donald A. Guarisco*

The Sapphires

f. Philadelphia, PA

Group / R&B, Soul

The Sapphires were a trio consisting of Carol Jackson, George Gainer, and Joe Livingston, although Kenny Gamble was also closely associated with the group very early in its history, arranging the vocals on their first album. The trio came out of Philadelphia in the early '60s, where they were signed by producer Jerry Ross and initially released their songs on the Swan label.

The group's first record was the romantic ballad "Where Is Johnny Now," backed with "Your True Love." The backing group for these and other early Philadelphia recordings by the Sapphires included Leon Huff and Thom Bell on keyboards, Bobby Eli on guitar, Joe Macho on bass, and Bobby Martin playing vibes. When this record failed to chart, Ross turned to Gamble for their next single, "Who Do You Love," which reached number 25 on the pop charts. Their next single, "I Found Out Too Late," failed to repeat that success, but its release was accompanied by the issue of the group's first LP. The Sapphires left Swan shortly after the release of a third single, "Gotta Be More Than Friends," moving to ABC-Paramount in 1964, which also led to their recording in New York City. Perhaps not coincidentally, their first ABC single, "Let's Break Up for a While," had a sound reminiscent of the Drifters from this same era.

The group entered its most productive and musically ambitious period during late 1964. The Sapphires' next single, "Thank You for Loving Me," was written by the Brill Building talents of Tommy Boyce, Bobby Hart, and Wes Farrell, and arranged by Jimmy Wisner. Their next single, "Gotta Have Your Love," finally gave the group the second hit they'd been waiting for, with a smooth Motown-type sound and an infectious beat that helped carry it to number 33 on the R&B charts, with an appearance on the pop charts at number 77 in the spring of 1965. The song also featured a trio of background vocalists who would go on to bigger things in the years to come: Valerie Simpson, Nick Ashford, and Melba Moore.

The group was never able to build on this record's success, though not for lack of trying. Their next three singles, "Evil One," "Gonna Be a Big Thing," and "Slow Fizz," all had pleasing hooks and, in the latter case, a wonderfully danceable beat, but failed to sell. "Slow Fizz," released in 1966, marked the end of their contract with ABC-Paramount, and the trio broke up soon after. The Sapphires left behind an extraordinarily high-quality body of work, a match for anything Motown was releasing at the same time. Their lack of staying power on the charts can be attributed largely to many factors, including the vast array of competition from various soul acts at the time—had they maintained a somewhat more consistent sound, or broken nationally a little earlier with a slightly higher profile, they might have achieved the success they deserved. As it was, they left behind a very fine, occasionally stunning body of songs, and provided some valuable early experience for Gamble, Bell, and Huff. *—Bruce Eder*

● **Who Do You Love** / 1964 / Collectables ♦♦♦♦♦

This is from the mid-'60s Philly-group R&B; the album includes the hit title track from 1964. *—Bill Dahl*

The Best of the Sapphires / 1995 / Sequel ♦♦♦♦

Exactly what the title says it is, containing all of the singles and B-sides of consequence, as well as key tracks off of the group's one album for Swan. The sound is excellent throughout, and the track selection is extraordinary—the Sapphires, who were two guys and a girl with sometime backup singers, sang about as sweetly as any Motown group of the era, and had a sound that, if a little stripped-down, was just as sophisticated. Their early records, up through "I Found Out Too Late," have an early-'60s girl group sound, while their records beginning with "I've Got Mine, You Better Get Yours" suddenly start sounding like Motown productions, except that this group was more soulful than the Supremes and fully capable of crossing swords with Martha & the Vandellas. They could also sound like a really soulful version of the Ronettes, but Motown was the most clear and consistent influence by 1964—"Baby You've Got Me" is practically their answer to the Temptations' "Get Ready," while "Hearts Are Made to Be Broken" is more sweetly romantic, showing off the more familiar side of the group's sound. And "Slow Fizz" is one of the greatest dance numbers never to find a national audience. Wherever Carol Jackson is, one hopes she has a copy of this CD. (British import) *—Bruce Eder*

The Satintones

Group / Motown, R&B, Doo Wop

The Satintones were Motown's first group, recording for the company from 1960 through 1961 and releasing six singles. This was during Motown's blues and mundane R&B era, and before the arrival of the jazz-based rhythmic backing of the Funk Brothers; a time when Ivy Joe Hunter led the session musicians, not Earl Van Dyke; a period when Motown released nine bad records for every good one; and a time when disc jockeys cringed at 45s sporting the Tamla or Motown logo. The original group was a quartet consisting of Charles "Chico" Leverett, Sonny Sanders, James Ellis, and Robert Bateman. Chico sang with the Spinners for a minute, and recorded "Solid Sender" on Tamla Records. They became a quintet in 1961, the new lineup consisting of James Ellis, Sonny Sanders, Vernon Williams, Sammy Mack, and Robert Bateman. Depending on who you talk to, Freddie Gorman (Originals) and Brian Holland (hall-of-fame songwriter) sang and recorded with them, but it's unclear if any sides they appeared on were released.

You won't find any of their single releases—"My Beloved," "Motor City," "Tomorrow and Always," "Angel," "I Know How It Feels," and "Zing Went the Strings of My Heart"—on any Motown compilation album. "Tomorrow and Always" created some controversy, and a lawsuit (which Motown lost); the answer song not only answered the Shirelles' hit, it ripped "Will You Still Love Me Tomorrow" off note for note.

All the members enjoyed musical careers before and after the Satintones with the most distinguishing belonging to Sonny Sanders, who went on to become an arranger and songwriter at Ric-Tic/Golden World Records then moved to Chicago, becoming a top arranger and co-writing "Love Makes a Woman" for Barbara Acklin. Bateman produced and wrote Wilson Pickett's early solo sides "It's Too Late" and "If You Need Me," jump-started the Marvelettes' career with "Please Mr. Postman" and "Playboy," and co-wrote Eddie Holland's "Jamie." (The Marvelettes' first album, *Please Mr. Postman*, featured two Satintones remakes, "Angel" and "I Know How It Feels," and one track, "The Feeling Is So Fine," became an obscure single for the Miracles.)

Motown did schedule an album release (The Satintones Sing) in 1961, but it remains unissued; the label does have more than 20 unreleased Satintones tracks in the can, not counting the 12 issued on 45s. Around 1990, the Satintones recorded tracks produced by Ian Levine; surprisingly, Levine's productions of the Satintones are more pleasing than the originals. *—Andrew Hamilton*

Chantay Savage

Vocals / Urban, Club/Dance, Dance-Pop, House

The daughter of a jazz musician, R&B vocalist Chantay Savage grew up in Chicago raised on the sounds of jazz and soul legends like Sarah Vaughan, Chaka Khan, and Marvin Gaye. Inspired by the music around her, Savage began her performing career in earnest when she entered an open mike contest at a local club. Not only did she win the contest eight times, she parlayed this success into gigs as a session musician, singer, and songwriter with artists like Ce Ce Peniston.

Savage's contributions to Peniston's single "We Got a Love Thang" earned her a deal with RCA Records; her 1993 self-titled debut contained more hit singles like "Give It to Ya" and "Don't Let It Go to Your Head." Savage also arranged vocals and sang for artists like Brazen, Associate, and Vertical Hold, along with releasing her second album, 1995's *I Will Survive*, in which she reworked the Gloria Gaynor disco anthem. The album also reflected a more personal, individual side of her talent, which she explored further on 1999's *This Time Around*, on which she wrote all the lyrics and played piano and drums. *—Heather Phares*

Here We Go . . . / May 1993 / RCA ♦♦♦

I Will Survive (Doin' It My Way) / 1995 / RCA ♦♦♦

Savage updates the Gloria Gaynor classic with a funky production job by Steve "Silk" Hurley. *—John Bush*

● **This Time** / Jul. 13, 1999 / RCA ♦♦♦♦

Chantay Savage has demonstrated a continuing development of her craft with each successive release since her debut offering, but this, her third album, far outdistances the other two. Savage is presented here with excellent material on which she uses her impressive "skills" to their best use paying homage to the likes Angela Bofill, Anita Baker, and Chaka Khan along the way by way of her approach and interpretation. This is one of those rare assemblage of songs that is so well sequenced and sung that it is a difficult task to single out outstanding tracks. The production harks back to the day when emotional delivery was placed ahead of perfect phrasing and pitch. Chantay brings you in with each track and makes you feel an integral part of her storytelling. Notable tracks include "My Oh My," "Come Around," and "Just Can't Take This." *—Jaime Ikeda*

Boz Scaggs (William Royce Scaggs)

b. Jun. 8, 1944, Canton, OH

Slide Guitar, Vocals, Guitar / Pop/Rock, Soft Rock, Album Rock, Blues-Rock

After first finding acclaim as a member of the Steve Miller Band, singer/songwriter Boz Scaggs went on to enjoy considerable solo success in the 1970s. Joining former schoolmate Miller in his fledgling group in 1967, Scaggs exited after recording two acclaimed albums with the unit, *Children of the Future* and *Sailor*. With the aid of *Rolling Stone* magazine publisher Jann Wenner, Scaggs secured a solo contract with Atlantic; his soulful self-titled debut failed to find an audience despite winning critical favor, and the track "Loan Me a Dime" later became the subject of a court battle when bluesman Fenton Robinson successfully sued for composer credit.

After signing to Columbia, Scaggs teamed with producer Glyn Johns to record 1971's *Moments*, a skillful blend of rock and R&B which, like its predecessor, failed to make much of an impression on the charts. Scaggs remained a critics' darling over the course of LPs like 1972's *My Time* and 1974's *Slow Dancer*, but he did not achieve a commercial breakthrough until 1976's *Silk Degrees*, which reached number two on the album charts while spawning the Top Three single "Lowdown," as well as the smash "Lido Shuffle." 1977's *Down Two Then Left* was also a success, and 1980's *Middle Man* reached the Top Ten on the strength of the singles "Breakdown Dead Ahead" and "Jo Jo." *—Jason Ankeny*

Boz Scaggs / 1969 / Atlantic ♦♦♦♦♦

Produced by Jann Wenner and featuring crack accompaniment by the Muscle Shoals house band, Scaggs's solo debut is a near-masterwork, mingling the pathos and heartbreak of vintage honky tonk with the celebration and release of Southern soul. The highlights of the album also flaunt its diversity: "Loan Me a Dime," an extended blues dirge, which features some of Duane Allman's finest work, and "Waiting on a Train," Scaggs' marvelous revamping of Jimmie Rodgers' classic hobo song. *—John Floyd*

Moments / 1971 / Columbia ♦♦♦♦

"We Were Always Sweethearts" wasn't a huge hit single, but it was a good one, signaling that Boz Scaggs was a soul man of the first degree. *Moments* places him into a variety of settings, including soul, R&B, blues, country, and beautiful, string-drenched balladry. Side one of the LP is especially strong, the kind whose grooves were worn out by its listeners in the early '70s. The second half of the recording doesn't hold up as well, but the closer, "Can I Make It Last (Or Will It Just Be Over)," is a gorgeous, atmospheric instrumental that pulls at the heartstrings. Although Scaggs' big moment in the commercial spotlight was still a few years away, this recording provides many satisfying musical *Moments*. *—Jim Newsom*

Boz Scaggs & His Band / Dec. 1971 / Columbia ♦♦♦

My Time / 1972 / Columbia ♦♦♦♦

Music critics of the early '70s kept predicting big things for Boz Scaggs, but his records of that period had trouble finding more than a cult audience. *My Time* continued with a mix similar to *Moments* from the previous year, with the opening "Dinah Flo," a great soul-drenched rocker that should have been a hit. In fact, the first three tracks present a powerful opening triumvirate which begs to be heard, with "Full-Lock Power Slide," an air guitarist's dream-come-true. Other high points are Scaggs' definitive cover of Allen Toussaint's "Freedom for the Stallion" and a take on Al Green's "Old Time Lovin'" that gives the original author a run for his money. Considering the success Van Morrison was having working the same territory, it's surprising that this album didn't achieve more in the commercial arena. Its blend of solid '60s soul and bluesy rock is very appealing. However, Boz Scaggs' time was still four years away. *My Time* is a rewarding listen nonetheless. *—Jim Newsom*

Slow Dancer / 1974 / Columbia ♦♦♦♦♦

• **Silk Degrees** / Feb. 1976 / Columbia ♦♦♦♦♦

Both artistically and commercially, Boz Scaggs had his greatest success with *Silk Degrees*. The laid-back singer hit the R&B charts in a big way with the addictive, sly "Lowdown" (which has been sampled by more than a few rappers and remains a favorite among baby-boomer soul fans) and expressed his love of smooth soul music almost as well on the appealing "What Can I Say." But Scaggs was essentially a pop/rocker, and in that area he has a considerable amount of fun on "Lido Shuffle" (another major hit single), "What Do You Want the Girl to Do," and "Jump Street." Meanwhile, "We're All Alone" and "Harbor Lights" became staples on adult contemporary radio. Though not remarkable, the ballads have more heart than most of the bland material dominating that format. *—Alex Henderson*

Down Two Then Left / Nov. 1977 / Columbia ♦♦♦

With 1974's *Slow Dancer*, produced by Johnny Bristol, Scaggs recast himself as a more R&B-infused singer. The 1976 multimillion-selling *Silk Degrees* found Scaggs' switch paying off commercially, displaying enough skills and chops that the odious "blue-eyed soul" tag was deemed passé. This is noticeably more detached than *Silk Degrees*. And although this set is indeed quirky, the often unsurprising production featuring almost-on-cue guitar solos makes this album more "mainstream" than it had to be. "Still Falling for You" kicks the album off and sets the standard for the skilled, seamless production juxtaposed to meandering, almost incoherent lyrics. The melodic "A Clue," the best of the released singles, attains the offhanded cool and tunefulness that most of this set is striving for. Although this set is more soulful throughout than *Silk Degrees*, nothing sticks out like "What Can I Say." More than anything, this album puts the spotlight on Scaggs' romantic views, but they are so all over the road it's hard to tell what he really thinks. On the lush "We're Waiting," a listener may not have an idea of what he's talking about, but his vocal inflections say what the lyrics fail to. After a while, Scaggs seems to give up on making this a statement about love and offers some so-so rockers. In particular, the strongly produced "1993" has Scaggs imagining a drastically changed world as he sings, "Before they take me up/They'll have to alter, alter me." *Down Two Then Left* has a melancholy appeal much like *Al Green Is Love* and Joni Mitchell's *Hissing of Summer Lawns*, but a few concessions prevent this from being in their elite class. *—Jason Elias*

Middle Man / Apr. 1980 / Columbia/Legacy ♦♦♦

Middle Man (1980) was Boz Scaggs' last album for Columbia before an eight-year self-imposed sabbatical. Scaggs nonetheless caps off the decade with equal nods to his '70s hitmaking formulas and the newer, shinier production techniques of the coming decade. The synthesizer rocker "Angel You" and the title track are given the full in-vogue androgynous (i.e., Hall and Oates) treatment, while the opener "Jo Jo" and "Simeone" are pages taken from his *Lowdown*-era grooves that wedded soulful vocals against a flurry of jazz changes. His penchant for the ballad is explored on "You Can Have Me Any Time" and "Isn't It Time," while his seldom-seen rockier side comes up for air on the bluesy "Breakdown Dead Ahead" and "You Got Some Imagination," both featuring stinging guitar from Steve Lukather. Not his best album, but a very timely one. *—Cub Koda*

• **Hits!** / Nov. 1980 / Columbia ♦♦♦♦

Released in 1980, Hits! capitalized on the end of the decade as well as the Scaggs' commercial success from 1976-1980. That's not to say everything is here. The 1972 classic "Loan Me a Dime" is missing, as this concentrates on Scaggs' more radio friendly efforts. From the pre-*Silk Degrees* era, "Dinah Flo" and "You Make It So Hard to Say No" are here. Not surprisingly, this set takes a few tracks from Scaggs' best-selling album *Silk Degrees*. While the sleek and funky "Lowdown" is no doubt here, the underrated "What I Can I Say" strangely didn't make this overview. *Hits!* seemed to stray far from the commercial disappointment of 1978's *Down Two, Then Left* by not including one track. Having "A Clue" on this would have helped in the areas of continuity. *Middle Man*'s biggest hits, "Breakdown Dead Ahead" and "Jo Jo," are included. The best track from *Middle Man*, "You Can Have Me Anytime," is one of Scaggs' strongest ballads. The album also managed to slip in never-a-hit "Miss Sun" that attempted to approximate the sound of a Boz Scaggs hit circa 1980. *Hits!* seems to betray Scaggs' range, and after 1997's *My Time: The Anthology (1969-1997)* gave a more substantive look, this was deemed superfluous. *—Jason Elias*

Come on Home / Apr. 8, 1997 / Virgin ♦♦♦♦

On this prime collection of R&B and blues songs and influences from Scaggs' youth—and four new yet classic-sounding self-penned originals—the blue-eyed soulman eschews the slick production values of his pop chart-toppers such as "Lido" and "Lowdown," instead getting way down and his hands dirty with the honest blood, sweat, and tears of the real down-home blues. Packing in tow drummer Jim Keltner, guitarist Fred Tackett (from Little Feat), and slow-burning, soulful horn arrangements by Willie Mitchell, one of the founding fathers of Memphis soul (and composer of *Come On Home*'s title track), Scaggs' covers of songs originally composed and performed by such legends as Jimmy Reed ("Found Love"), T-Bone Walker (the legendary "T-Bone Shuffle"), Sonny Boy Williamson ("Early in the Morning") and Bobby "Blue" Bland (the thunderous "Ask Me 'Bout Nothing (But the Blues)"), along with "It All Went Down the Drain" (Earl King Johnson), and the smoldering "Your Good Thing (Is About to End)" (David Porter with Isaac Hayes), are absolutely impossible to resist. *Come On Home* is a genuine musical treasure. *—Chris Slawecki*

My Time: The Anthology (1969–1997) / Oct. 7, 1997 / Columbia/Legacy ♦♦♦♦

My Time: Anthology (1969-1997) is an excellent double-disc retrospective of Boz Scaggs' entire career, containing all of his hits, several key album tracks, and a handful of rarities designed to entice the hardcore collector. For any serious fan who wants a comprehensive overview of Scaggs' career, *My Time* is an ideal purchase. *—Thom Owens*

Harvey Scales

Songwriter, Producer, Vocalist / Urban

Songwriter/singer/producer Harvey Scales is best known as the co-writer of Johnnie Taylor's mega-hit "Disco Lady," and he also co-wrote the R&B hit "Love Is Better in the A.M., Pt. 1." In 1961, the Arkansas native formed the Milwaukee-based R&B band Harvey Scales and the Seven Sounds. Influenced by James Brown, the group concentrated on funk. Recording for Lenny LeCour's Magic Touch Records, the band had a hit with "Get Down" b/w "Love-Itis." (The latter track was later covered by rockers the J. Geils Band.) In 1969, the group signed with Chicago-based Chess Records and released the LeCour-produced "The Yolk," "I'll Run to Your Side," and "Leave It for the Trashman" on the label's Cadet imprint. Working with Davis, who was having hits with then-Stax artist Johnnie Taylor, Scales cut sides for the Memphis-based label including "What's Good for You (Don't Have to Be Good to You)" b/w "I Wanna Do It." When Stax became inactive, Taylor signed with Columbia, retaining Davis' services. Recording at Davis' favorite studio (United Sound Studios in Detroit), the producer used the Impressions' "Gypsy Woman" and an African dancer he had seen on a vacation to Spain as a template for a partially finished song ("Disco Baby") that Scales had brought to him. Davis took it to Collins and Worrell, who honed and tightened up the groove, while veteran arranger David VanDePitt did the horn arrangements.

Based on the success of "Disco Lady," Scales was able to secure a recording deal with Casablanca. His 1978 label debut *Confidential Affair* was a collection of disco-laced soul, later a favorite years among dance music and Northern soul devotees. His next Casablanca album was 1979's *Hot Foot: A Funque Dizco Opera*, which included the singles "I Get Off on You" and the 12-inch single "Baby Let's Rock." Scales also co-wrote (with Bunny Sigler) "You're Gonna Get Yours" on Instant Funk's *V* LP and the pro-basketball tribute "Slam Dunk the Funk" on the band's *Looks So Fine* album. *Somebody Else's Somebody* is the title of Scales' 1997 album on Four Sight. *—Ed Hogan*

• **Confidential Affair** / May 1978 / Casablanca ♦♦♦

Harvey Scales co-wrote the first certified platinum single, "Disco Lady" by Johnnie Taylor. The singer/songwriter's 1978 Casablanca Records debut, *Confidential Affair* was a collection of disco-laced soul/R&B music produced by Melvin Griffin. Co-produced by Scales and keyboardist William Scott Harralson, the album has a strong Southern soul vibe running through it. Because of its inventive production, captivating arrangements, and top-notch songs the LP has become a post-release favorite of bluesy, dance/R&B music fans and U.K. Northern soul devotees. The fat, funky single "Shake-A-Matic," is particularly sought after for its chugging beat and flexing Stax-like horn section. Almost eight minutes long, it's similar to Tyrone Davis' lengthy "Get on Up (Disco)," (its shorter single version is on *Best of Tyrone Davis: In the Mood*). Other standout tracks are the child custody ode "Visiting Rights," with such heart-tugging lyrics as "I know life is so much harder without a mother and a father/ if we could just start all over/ but what can I do when another man is visiting you/ visiting rights lonely nights." The sweet, ethereal ballad "Look No Further Than Me," will make you feel all warm inside ("I'll be your leaning post when you're falling down"). *Confidential Affair* closes out with the optimistic "Universal Love," ("the spirit of love never ending/ get aboard this train called freedom") *—Ed Hogan*

Hot Foot: A Funque Dizco Opera / 1979 / Casablanca ♦♦♦

Somebody Else's Somebody / Sep. 23, 1997 / Four Sight ♦♦

The Scarlets

Group / Doo Wop

A '50s R&B vocal group, the Scarlets were the group led by vocalist Fred Parris, before he formed the Five Satins. Based in New Haven, CT, the group cut four highly prized singles for Bobby Robinson's Red Robin label in 1954-1955, notably "Dear One." *—Bill Dahl*

• **Golden Classics** / 1993 / Collectables ♦♦♦♦

The Schoolboys

f. 1955, New York, NY, **db.** 1957

Group / Doo Wop

The Schoolboys sound almost uncannily similar to Frankie Lymon & the Teenagers, but they predate them by close to a year in terms of recording and success. Formed in Harlem's Cooper Junior High School in 1954 or early 1955, with Harold Atley as leader, James Edwards (first tenor), Roger Hayes (second tenor), James "Charlie" McKay (baritone), and Renaldo Gamble (bass), they performed in school talent shows and became popular locally, only to see Atley exit after a few months. He was replaced by Leslie Martin, a boy soprano who had an almost operatic intensity to his singing and intonation. They appeared on *Ted Mack's Original Amateur Hour* and won first prize, which brought them the chance to record soon after, under the aegis of disc jockey Tommy Smalls, who had the popular *Dr. Jive Show* on WWRL in New York—he gave them the name the Schoolboys and got them their recording. Their debut single, "Please Say You Want Me," a slow, moon/June-rhymed ballad featuring Martin's astonishingly powerful boy soprano voice, became a hit in the fall of 1955 and led to a series of releases, notable for the pleading nature of their lyrics, especially the ballads, which were usually backed by songs titled with girls' names. The group was never able to match the success of its debut release, however, and by 1956, the Teenagers Featuring Frankie Lymon, also organized in upper Manhattan, had supplanted them in the minds of the listening public.

The Schoolboys' original lineup disintegrated not too long after their one hit—Renaldo Gamble joined Pearl McKinnon (herself a Frankie Lymon sound-alike) & the Kodaks. By 1957, the Schoolboys were history, their moment having passed to Lymon and company. It is alleged that some of the work credited to the group was really Martin and members of the Cadillacs, rather than his own group. —*Bruce Eder*

Cindy Scott (Sundray Tucker)

Vocals / Motown, Soul, Urban

Cindy Scott is really Sundray Tucker, the vocalist cookin' with Stevie Wonder on "Ordinary Pain" from the *Songs in the Key of Life* album. Raised in north Philadelphia, music runs in Cindy's genes. Lynda Laurence (of the Supremes) is her sister, and her cousins include Thomasina Montgomery (Tammi Terrell) and Bunny Sigler. At 14 she sung in the Pendelles with sister Lynda and later spent two years with the Ordettes (Cindy Birdsong replaced her, and Patricia Holt aka Patti LaBelle was also a member). The name change was to thwart Don Robey, the late, nefarious owner of Duke/Peacock Records.

At 16, as Sandra Kay Tucker, she recorded "Have It Your Way" on Peacock. Her father, Ira Tucker, a member of the Dixie Hummingbirds, showed Sundray's songs to Robey, who signed her to five-year singing and songwriting contracts. The deal soured when Robey refused to record her again, or free her from the stifling contract, so she adopted the alias and recorded incognito. She started collaborating with Leon Huff and others for the City of Brotherly Love Productions and Ben-Lee Records. She even recorded, releasing "What Are You Doin' to Me" as Cindy Scott & the Cousins. She chose the name because she resembled Cindy Birdsong, and Scott was her best friend's surname. In 1967 she worked with Len Barry's old producers, Johnny Madara and Dave White, and had two releases on Veep Records: "I Love You Baby" and Otis Redding's "I've Been Loving You Too Long." When Veep sank, she signed with Neptune Records for two duets with cousin Bunny Sigler.

When the five-year fiasco with Robey ended, she discontinued using Cindy Scott for her real name and joined sister Lynda in Wonderlove. She left Wonderlove to join Ernie Terrell & the Heavyweights, then moved to Miami in 1984 to record for TK and Grace Note Records. She returned to Philadelphia in 1999 and recorded an album for Driving Wheel Records, a small record company in central England, entitled *The Loving Country*, a showcase for her amazing voice. —*Andrew Hamilton*

• **The Loving Country** / Feb. 2000 / Driving Wheel ✦✦✦✦✦

This is David Powner's first production ever, but it sounds like the work of an old pro. Cindy Scott's voice has elements of surprise and excitement similar to those of Chaka Khan. This jamming CD contains uplifting soul and Motown remakes accented by phat bass beats, spirited lead singing, and strong backing vocals featuring Scott and Vera Carey chirping like love birds. On "Remember Me," an awesome bass and high-hat cymbal smashes provide an unforgettable back beat. Her infectious vocals take Linda Clifford's "Runaway Love" to new heights, while well-executed horn hits and synthesizer runs cloud above a mean, intimidating beat. Otis Redding's "I've Been Loving You Too Long," gets a 360-degree rearrangement that has to be heard to be believed. My personal favorite is the sweet, coy "If It Was Me,"—a convincing, heartfelt beat-ballad that tugs at your heart. You will mothball Jackie Moore's "Precious, Precious" after hearing Scott's version, and she does an incredible job on Stevie Wonder's "Signed, Sealed, Delivered (I'm Yours)" as well. Don't get turned off by the remakes; they're often better than the originals. Ian Levine could have used Powner's expertise on his Motorcity project. These 13 delightful tracks include an extended remix of "Remember Me," a sweet reprise of "Runaway Love," a scrump country/soul ballad "Don't Let My Teardrops Bother You," and a better-than-ever version of Smokey Robinson and Ivy Hunter's "Loving Country." —*Andrew Hamilton*

Freddie Scott

b. Apr. 24, 1933, Providence, RI

Vocals, Drums / Pop-Soul, Northern Soul, Soul, Brill Building Pop, R&B

Though he was born in Providence, RI, Freddie Scott had the inflections, delivery, and sound of a classic Southern soul vocalist. Scott attended high school in New York City and later became a songwriter for Columbia Music. He was working there in 1963 when he recorded "Hey, Girl" for Colpix, which became a Top Ten pop and R&B hit. Scott continued on Colpix until the mid-'60s, when he joined Shout. He had his greatest hit there in 1966, the chart-topping R&B wailer "Are You Lonely for Me." Scott continued on Shout until 1970, then recorded for Probe. —*Ron Wynn*

Everything I Have Is Yours / 1964 / CBS ✦✦✦✦✦

Freddie Scott Sings and Sings and Sings / 1964 / Collectables ✦✦

Are You Lonely for Me / 1967 / Shout ✦✦✦

Lonely Man / 1967 / CBS ✦✦✦

I Shall Be Released / 1970 / Probe ✦✦

• **Cry to Me: The Best of Freddie Scott** / Feb. 17, 1998 / Columbia/Legacy ✦✦✦✦✦

One of the sleekest soul senders of the 1960s, Freddie Scott grew a bit rougher as the decade progressed, though his 1966-1968 period with New York's Shout Records still find him in fine form. *Cry to Me* includes 20 tracks, featuring hits like "Are You Lonely for Me Baby" and the title track as well as two previously unreleased tracks. —*John Bush*

Jill Scott

Vocals / Hip-Hop, Neo-Soul, Contemporary R&B

Jill Scott grew up in north Philadelphia and began her performing career reading her own poetry. She was heard by Amir, drummer in the Roots, who invited her to join the band in the studio, resulting in the co-composition "You Got Me," a Top 40 pop hit in 1999. Subsequently, she collaborated with Eric Benet, Will Smith, and Common and broadened her performing experience by touring Canada in a production of the Broadway musical *Rent*. Signed to Steve McKeever's newly formed Hidden Beach Recordings label, she released her debut album, *Who Is Jill Scott? Words and Sounds Vol. 1*, in July 2000. —*William Ruhlmann*

• **Who Is Jill Scott?: Words and Sounds, Vol. 1** / Jul. 18, 2000 / Hidden Beach ✦✦✦✦✦

Though start-up label Hidden Beach and its manufacturer/distributor Sony may have been hoping for another Lauryn Hill in this eloquent young African-American from a Middle Atlantic state, Jill Scott turns out to be something of a hip-hop Patti Smith, a street poet who, on her first album, hasn't quite made the transition from spoken word performances to music, despite an excellent singing voice. With any luck, she will retain her sense of the power of words, since the best parts of this album are the ones when she lets fly, drunk on her verbal virtuosity. Producer Jeff Townes (of DJ Jazzy Jeff and the Fresh Prince fame) and his team of associates from the A Touch of Jazz production company set up sympathetic musical backgrounds for Scott that support her without requiring her to fit her spoken and sung excursions into strict meter. That gives her range to pursue her interests, which include a strong sense of her north Philadelphia neighborhood and such idiosyncratic concerns as food, with many meals listed in detail. But the album has a story to tell, and for the most part it is a love story. Scott describes a relationship from many different angles, including an encounter with her boyfriend's ex in a supermarket ("Exclusively") and her warnings to that girl (or some other) to stay away ("Gettin' in the Way"). She also breaks painfully from an old boyfriend in favor of the new one ("I Think It's Better"), but mostly she celebrates the relationship ("A Long Walk," "He Loves Me (Lyzel in E Flat)," "It's Love," "The Way"). But with "Honey Molasses," things turn sour, and on "Love Rain" and "Slowly Surely," she frees herself, concluding that "One Is the Magic #" and toward the end of the album moving on to social concerns with "Watching Me" and "Brotha." This narrative structure gives Scott ample room to express a variety of emotions and to display her "verbal elation." Like many poets, she sometimes delights in a torrent of words for their own sake, but it's hard to fault her when the result is such a fully articulated world view. There is no existing slot in R&B/hip-hop into which this album fits, which only means a new one will have to be created. [The CD marks a new complexity in the use of bonus and hidden tracks. After the 17th track, "Show Me," there are 26 four-second blank tracks, followed by a 44th track, the bonus song, "Try." One minute after this song ends, there is a hidden selection, an alternate version of "Love Rain" that features Mos Def.] —*William Ruhlmann*

Experience: Jill Scott 826+ / Nov. 20, 2001 / Hidden Beach ✦✦✦✦

What you think of Jill Scott's second album, *Experience: Jill Scott 826+*, is going to depend on how you define the two-hour, double-disc set. Is it, as its title suggests, a live album (recorded mostly on August 26, 2001, in Washington, D.C., hence the "826") plus a bonus disc containing some new studio tracks? Or is it a new studio album with a live disc tacked on? There aren't many artists who can justify the release of a live album after releasing only one studio album, especially when the live album consists almost entirely of material from that one album. The draw here, however, is Scott herself. A performing poet-turned-singer, she clearly knows how to please an audience, and the Washingtonians seem primed, frequently singing along to her songs without prompting and cheering many aspects of the show that can't be appreciated on a mere audio recording of it. If Scott's debut disc found her still in transition from the spoken word to the sung song, she has long since made that shift, and the album is full of vocal pyrotechnics, though, as she herself acknowledges, she talks a lot, even coming off like a standup comic in her defense of her song "Gettin' in the Way." The conceptual unity that tied these songs together on *Who Is Jill Scott? Words and Sounds, Vol. 1* is missing here, but there's no denying Scott's effectiveness as a performer. The "+" disc, however, sounds like a collection of demos for her next album rather than a stand-alone document, even before the extended hidden tracks at the end present alternate versions. (Don't believe the one-minute-and-48-second time listed for the last track; it really runs over 16 minutes.) So, let's call this a satisfying live album with some bonus tracks, a good seasonal stocking-stuffer. —*William Ruhlmann*

Peggy Scott & Jo Jo Benson

f. 1968, **db.** 1973

Group / Soul, Pop-Soul, Southern Soul, Country-Soul

In the late '60s, the female-male duo of Peggy Scott and Jo Jo Benson made the pop Top 40 three times (charting much higher in the R&B section) with a clutch of good-natured Southern pop-soul tunes. Semi-legendary producer Huey Meaux, who had worked extensively with such soul and rock legends as Barbara Lynn and Doug Sahm, was responsible for putting the team together, and produced their first sessions in 1968 in Jackson, MS. After "Lover's Holiday" and "Pickin' Wild Mountain Berries" yielded a couple quick hits, the producer's chair was turned over to Shelby Singleton, who cut a few sessions with the pair in Nashville. Some of these tracks were notable for their fusion of soul and country influences; a few featured top Nashville session men Jerry Kennedy (on guitar) and, more unusually, Pete Drake, perhaps the first white country musician (and certainly one of the few) to play steel guitar on a soul record. Scott and Benson were competent talents, but ultimately would have to be classified as rather-average performers who didn't establish a particularly distinguished or exciting style.

The country influence and the odd sitar-ish guitar tone on several of their records were the most novel things they had going. Under Singleton's guidance, they landed their third hit within a year with perhaps their best track, "Soul Shake," but only managed one more minor hit, "I Want to Love You Baby," before leaving Singleton's SSS International label for Atco. Their relationship already strained, the duo's career petered out after a few obscure singles in the early '70s. Nearly 25 years later, Scott—now known as Peggy Scott-Adams—returned to a recording career with several albums on Miss Butch. —*Richie Unterberger*

Soulshake / Feb. 1969 / Get Back ♦♦♦

Lover's Heaven / Apr. 1969 / SSS ♦♦♦

The Best of Peggy Scott & Jo Jo Benson / Jun. 27, 1995 / Ichiban/Soul Classics ♦♦♦♦
This 20-track comp has all their hit singles, a bunch of flops and B-sides, cuts from their two late-'60s LPs, and four songs from non-album 45s. *—Richie Unterberger*

Lover's Holiday: The Very Best of Peggy Scott & Jo Jo Benson / Feb. 2, 1999 / Collectables ♦♦♦♦♦
A large helping of Peggy Scott and Jo Jo Benson's recordings, a raucous duet who didn't exactly sing into each other eyes like Marvin & Tammi. They're more like the Soul Children; on some cuts Benson sounds like J. Blackfoot. The energetic duo bum rushes every song like ferocious, feeding lions. If a song didn't succeed, it wasn't because of lack of effort on their part. "Lover's Holiday" and "Soul Shake," two chart hits, are interspersed among 22 other grooves that received limited local or regional plays, and in some cases only backyard barbecue and cheat spot spins. *—Andrew Hamilton*

● **The Complete SSS International Recordings** / May 24, 2000 / R.P.M. ♦♦♦♦♦
This purports to contain "the complete 1960s recordings" by the duo, taken from their two albums and the singles, all on the SSS International label. Yet it's missing two songs—the 1969 non-LP singles "Every Little Bit Hurts" and "When the Blind Leads the Blind"—that show up on another compilation, *The Best of Peggy Scott & Jo Jo Benson* (on Soul Classics). That's a minor point, but a significant one for collectors evaluating which of the two they want to buy, or whether they want to buy both. Aside from that quibble, though, this R.P.M. release might be superior, as it contains 26 tracks, while the Soul Classics one only has 19 (although the track annotation on the shorter collection is far superior). That means that *The Complete SSS International Recordings* has nine songs not on the previous compilation, and these are generally up to the standard of everything heard on *The Best of Peggy Scott & Jo Jo Benson.* Those nine cuts include the 1968 B-side "Here with Me," some cuts from their two albums, and one item, "It's the Little Things That Count," that... well, it's not sure where that one comes from, since it's not listed anywhere in the accompanying (and incomplete) discography. The best of the supplementary material might be the gutsy, straight-ahead "Money Don't Satisfy" (though of course there's room for that electric sitar). Imperfections noted, *The Complete SSS International Recordings* does have intriguingly arranged late-'60s soul with touches of country and plenty of electric sitar, and undoubtedly contains more music by the duo than any other release does. *—Richie Unterberger*

Peggy Scott-Adams

Vocals / Retro-Soul, Contemporary Blues
The former Peggy Scott, who toured with Ben E. King as a teenager and hit the Top 40 three times as a duet act with Jo Jo Benson in the 1960s, came back strong in the late '90s after decades of inactivity with "Bill," a wildly popular contemporary blues song about a woman whose man has been fooling around—with another man. Scott had been out of the music business since the late '60s, working as a lounge singer in Pensacola, FL, until she moved to California and married a Compton city commissioner in 1988. Persuaded to return to the studio by songwriter/producer Jimmy Lewis, Scott-Adams recorded *Help Yourself* in mid-1996. One of Lewis' songs was a novelty track which twisted the common complaint of a wife keeping her man faithful. Released as a single initially just to blues radio stations, it also began getting airplay at urban radio and soon gained most-requested status at several larger stations. *Help Yourself* began selling well, prompting the release of *Contagious* later in 1997, and *Undisputed Queen* in 1999. *—John Bush*

● **Help Yourself** / Feb. 1997 / Miss Butch ♦♦♦♦
Help Yourself is a dynamic, exciting comeback album from Peggy Scott-Adams. She is able to breathe new life into blues and soul standards, as well as find new material, like the single "Bill," that fits the bill. The result is a terrific Southern soul album proving that deep soul is far from being dead in the '90s. *—Thom Owens*

Contagious / Nov. 11, 1997 / Miss Butch ♦♦♦

The Undisputed Queen / Jun. 15, 1999 / Miss Butch ♦♦

Live in Alabama & More / May 2, 2000 / Miss Butch ♦♦♦
While only three of the ten tracks are live, this is still a much more satisfying album than Peggy Scott-Adams previous efforts. Of the three live tracks (performed in Montgomery, AL), two suspiciously don't sound all-the-way-live, but they're still enjoyable slices of Southern soul seductively executed in Scott-Adams husky, deep-throated delivery. The seven studio cuts are all worthy, but lack the sweetening horns that define the type of music she's portraying. Peggy emulates Betty Wright on "I'm Getting What I Want," but displays her own unique persona on the rest. The best of the studio jams: "Sweaty Men" (all three mixes) especially, the dark, funky "doggie style mix" and "When I'm With You." *—Andrew Hamilton*

Gil Scott-Heron

b. Apr. 1, 1949, Chicago, IL
Vocals, Piano, Guitar / Poetry, Fusion, Social Commentary, Political Rap
One of the most important progenitors of rap music, Gil Scott-Heron's aggressive, no-nonsense street poetry inspired a legion of intelligent rappers while his engaging songwriting skills placed him square in the R&B charts later in his career, backed by increasingly contemporary production courtesy of Malcolm Cecil and Nile Rodgers (of Chic). Born in Chicago but transplanted to Tennessee for his early years, Scott-Heron spent most of his high school years in the Bronx, where he learned firsthand many of the experiences which later made up his songwriting material. He had begun writing before reaching his teenage years, however, and completed his first volume of poetry at the age of 13. Though he attended college in Pennsylvania, he dropped out after one year to concentrate on his writing career and earned plaudits for his novel, *The Vulture*. Encouraged at the end of the '60s to begin recording by legendary jazz producer Bob Thiele—who had worked with every major jazz great, from Louis Armstrong to John Coltrane—Scott-Heron released his 1970 debut, *Small Talk at 125th & Lennox*, inspired by a volume of poetry of the same name.

With Thiele's Flying Dutchman Records until the mid-'70s, he signed to Arista soon after and found success on the R&B charts. Though his jazz-based work of the early '70s was tempered by a slicker disco-inspired production, Scott-Heron's message was as clear as ever on the Top 30 single "Johannesburg" and the number-15 hit "Angel Dust." Silent for almost a decade, after the release of his 1984 single "Re-Ron," the proto-rapper returned to recording in the mid-'90s with a message for the gangsta rappers who had come in his wake; Scott-Heron's 1994 album *Spirits* began with "Message to the Messengers," pointed squarely at the rappers whose influence—positive or negative—meant much to the children of the 1990s. *—John Bush*

Small Talk at 125th & Lenox / 1970 / Flying Dutchman ♦♦♦♦♦

Pieces of a Man / 1971 / Flying Dutchman ♦♦♦♦♦
After decades of influencing everyone from jazz musicians to hip-hop stars, *Pieces of a Man* set a standard for vocal artistry and political awareness that few musicians will ever match. Scott-Heron's unique proto-rap style influenced a generation of hip-hop artists, and nowhere is his style more powerful than on the classic "The Revolution Will Not Be Televised." Even though the media—the very entity attacked in this song—has used, reused, and recontextualized the song and its title so many times, its message is so strong that it has become almost impossible to co-opt. Musically, the track created a formula that modern hip-hop would follow for years to come: bare-bones arrangements featuring pounding basslines and stripped-down drumbeats. Although the song features plenty of outdated references to everything from Spiro Agnew and Jim Webb to *The Beverly Hillbillies*, the force of Scott-Heron's well-directed anger makes the song timeless. More than just a spoken word poet, Scott-Heron was also a uniquely gifted vocalist. On tracks like the reflective "I Think I'll Call It Morning" and the title track, Scott-Heron's voice is complemented perfectly by the soulful keyboards of Brian Jackson. On "Lady Day and John Coltrane," he not only celebrates jazz legends of the past in his words but in his vocal performance, one that is filled with enough soul and innovation to make Coltrane and Billie Holiday nod their heads in approval. More than three decades after its release, *Pieces of a Man* is just as—if not more—powerful and influential today as it was the day it was released. *—Jon Azpiri*

Free Will / Aug. 1972 / Flying Dutchman ♦♦♦
Gil Scott-Heron's third album is split down the middle, the first side being a purely musical experience with a full band (including flutist Hubert Laws and drummer Pretty Purdie), the second functioning more as a live rap session with collaborator Brian Jackson on flute and a few friends on percussion. For side one, although he's overly tentative on the ballad "The Middle of Your Day," Scott-Heron excels on the title track and the third song, "The Get Out of the Ghetto Blues," one of his best, best-known performances. The second side is more of an impromptu performance, with Scott-Heron often explaining his tracks by way of introduction ("No Knock" referred to a new police policy whereby knocking was no longer required before entering a house, "And Then He Wrote Meditations" being Scott-Heron's tribute to John Coltrane). His first exploration of pure music-making, *Free Will* functions as one of Scott-Heron's most visceral performance, displaying a maturing artist who still draws on the raw feeling of his youth. [The Bluebird reissue from 2001 includes eight alternate takes, best being an alternate of the title track.] *—John Bush*

Winter in America / Sep. 4, 1973+Oct. 11, 1973 / Strata East ♦♦♦
Gil Scott-Heron was at his most righteous and provocative on this album. The title cut was a moving, angry summation of the social injustices Scott-Heron felt had led the nation to a particularly dangerous period, while "The Bottle" was a great treatise on the dangers of alcohol abuse. He also offered his thoughts on Nixon's legacy with "The H2O Gate Blues," a classic oral narrative. Brian Jackson's capable keyboard, acoustic piano and arranging talents helped make this a first-rate release, one of several the duo issued during the 1970s. *—Ron Wynn*

● **The Revolution Will Not Be Televised** / 1974 / Bluebird/RCA ♦♦♦♦♦
Spanning 1970-1972, this superb collection takes us back to Gil Scott-Heron's early years, when he was working with jazz producer Bob Thiele—a man who had been in the studio with everyone from John Coltrane and Pharoah Sanders to Coleman Hawkins. But *The Revolution Will Not Be Televised* isn't a jazz collection per se; it's a collection of innovative R&B and spoken poetry that contains jazz influences and finds Scott-Heron employing such jazz musicians as flutist Hubert Laws and bassist Ron Carter. Like the Last Poets, Scott-Heron has been described as "one of the first rappers"—and while he was hardly the first person to speak in rhyme to music, there are definitely parallels between angry sociopolitical poems like "Whitey on the Moon," "No Knock," and "Brother" and hip-hop commentary from the 1980s. Poetry, however, doesn't dominate this album—most of the selections illustrate Scott-Heron's excellence as a singer, including "Home Is Where the Hatred Is," "Did You Hear What They Said?," and the poignant "Save the Children." One of the collection's less political tracks is "Lady Day and John Coltrane," an R&B classic that articulates how easily jazz can lift a person's spirits. *The Revolution Will Not Be Televised* isn't the last word on Scott-Heron's artistry—he recorded many more treasures after leaving Flying Dutchman for Arista in 1975. But it's one of the collections to acquire if you're exploring his artistry for the first time. *—Alex Henderson*

The First Minute of a New Day / Jun. 1975 / Arista ♦♦♦♦
This follow-up to the righteous and soulful *Winter In America* LP continues with the solid, decidedly left-of-center jazz-R&B that made him a cult figure throughout the '70s. This output, with the opening meditation of "Offering" and the right-on "Ain't No Such Thing as Superman," solidifies Heron's place in the pantheon of jazz poets. Dig the recited (possibly improvised) live take of "Pardon Our Analysis," a follow-up to his seminal

"H2O Blues." And this reissue features four unreleased tracks, including a live medley of "The Bottle/Guan Guanco." *—Tim Sheridan*

From South Africa to South Carolina / Jan. 1976 / TVT ♦♦♦♦
The Gil Scott-Heron/Brian Jackson collaboration was now a formal one, as they were issuing albums as a team. This was their second duo project to make the pop charts, and it included anti-nuclear and anti-apartheid themes, plus less political, more autobiographical/reflective material like "Summer of '42," "Beginnings (The First Minute of a New Day)" and "Fell Together." Scott-Heron was now a campus and movement hero, and Brian Jackson's production and arranging savvy helped make his albums as arresting musically as they were lyrically. *—Ron Wynn*

It's Your World / Nov. 1976 / Arista ♦♦♦♦♦
This Gil Scott-Heron double album, roughly two thirds of which was recorded live in Boston on July 2-4, 1976, makes the most of its Centennial-centric time frame. Between the American flag striped cover art and Heron's spoken word spiel on an eight-and-a-half minute poem/rant "Bicentennial Blues," the album loses little of its impact, regardless of how the years have mildewed once fresh political topics like Nixon, Agnew, and Watergate. Four of its songs are studio recordings ("It's Your World," "Possum Slim," "New York City," and "Sharing"), and even though they're up to Heron's usual jazz/blues/pop standards, the disc is most effective on the concert tracks. As he explains in the 2000 penned liner notes, "The Midnight Band was a compelling live unit" and one listen to the brisk, electrifying, 13-minute rendition of "The Bottle," one of Heron's most penetrating tracks, is all you'll need to understand why. More importantly, like the best protest music, these tunes have lost none of their lyrical edge or incisiveness throughout the years. Musically the band is taut and rehearsed down to the finest time change, yet loose enough to open up on the jams. The heavy Latin percussion/flute/piano—but remarkably guitar-less—sound is equal parts Santana and Mongo Santamaria with a strong jazz current throughout, especially on the John Coltrane tribute "Trane," featuring tenor hornman Bilal Sunni-Ali's fiery lead. Scott-Heron's deep, mellifluous voice is alternately soothing and cutting, infusing the music with heart and soul, while keeping the sound focused even during the longer improvisations. Only a dated '70s drum solo belies the year this was recorded. Chestnuts like "Home Is Where the Hatred Is" explode in extended live versions that become definitive readings of the tunes. Remastered for its reissue, *It's Your World* crackles with energy, presenting an accomplished band at their peak and placing the listener practically on-stage for the live tracks with acoustics that are full, yet airy and spacious. One of Gil Scott-Heron's best albums as well as a compelling musical time capsule, the disc is proof of the artist's musical and lyrical acuity and is a moving listening experience. *—Hal Horowitz*

Bridges / Dec. 1977 / Arista ♦♦♦♦
Gil Scott-Heron, Brian Jackson, and the Midnight Band take a slightly different approach with their 1977 effort, *Bridges.* With less of the gaping and world-infused sound prevalent on previous albums, the songs are more concise and Scott-Heron comes into his own as a singer depending less on his spoken word vocal style. This album may not be one of his better-known releases but the excellent songwriting exposes Scott-Heron at the height of his powers as a literary artist. The social, political, cultural, and historical themes are presented in a tight funk meets jazz meets blues meets rock sound that is buoyed by Jackson's characteristic keyboard playing and the Midnight Band's colorful arrangements. Scott-Heron's ability to make the personal universal is evident from the opening track, "Hello Sunday! Hello Road!," all the way through to the gorgeous "95 South (All of the Places We've Been)." The most popular cut on the album, "We Almost Lost Detroit," which shares its title with the John G. Fuller book published in 1975, recounts the story of the nuclear meltdown at the Fermi Atomic Power Plant near Monroe, MI, in 1966. This song was also contributed to the *No Nukes* concert and album in 1980. Along with the two records that would follow in the late '70s, *Bridges* stands as one of Scott-Heron's most enjoyable and durable albums. *—Jeff Schwachter*

Secrets / Sep. 1978 / Arista ♦♦♦

1980 / Aug. 1979+Oct. 1979 / Arista ♦♦♦♦
1980 can be viewed as a precursor for the venomous rants Gil Scott-Heron would unleash on the eventual Reagan-led White House. Loaded with perceptive and poignant observations on the state of America as it advanced into a new and uncertain decade, *1980* is a powerful final album of the 1970s for Scott-Heron and his partner Brian Jackson. Amazingly, Scott-Heron's focus at the close of the decade is strikingly similar to his focus on his 1970 debut, *Small Talk at 125th & Lennox*; namely that social and political change has yet to come to many Americans, despite the advancements in technology and other seemingly less significant realms. The enemies are the same: nuclear power and big business ("Shut Um Down"), oppressive governments ("Shah Mot"), and racism ("Willing"). On the title track, Scott-Heron's gaze is set on the future with an eye on the past as well. When he sings, "Boogie-Woogie's somewhere in the lost and found," he's not only speaking of the changes in music, but also in popular culture. There is a hint of resentment on his part that this musical style, like other revolutionary African-American innovations, has been progressively stolen, mined, sterilized, and eventually discarded. This is not to say that the music throughout the album is marked by regret or sorrow. The spacey synthesizers, background vocals, and use of horns, along with Jackson's always-extraordinary arrangements, give the album a quality that matches the aura of the period without forgetting past musical styles. The descriptive "Alien (Hold on to Your Dreams)" is the album's most enduring song, vividly portraying the plight of Mexican illegal aliens living in Los Angeles and offering an uplifting refrain. *—Jeff Schwachter*

Real Eyes / Dec. 1980 / Arista ♦♦♦
In 1980, Gil Scott-Heron had a nice opportunity to promote his *Real Eyes* album when he became the opening act on Stevie Wonder's *Hotter Than July* tour. On his own, Scott-Heron usually played small clubs, but opening for Wonder gave him the chance to perform in front of thousands of Wonder fans in major stadiums and sports arenas. Many of Wonder's white fans seemed to be unfamiliar with Scott-Heron (who had never had a major pop hit), while a lot of Wonder's black fans at least knew him for "The Bottle" and "Angel Dust" even if they hadn't bought a lot of his albums. Opening for all those Wonder fans certainly didn't hurt Scott-Heron's career, but it didn't make him a superstar either. While it's possible that some Wonder fans enjoyed Scott-Heron's opening sets enough to go out and purchase *Real Eyes*, most of the people who acquired this LP were already confirmed Scott-Heron fans. Unfortunately, *Real Eyes* lacked a hit single, although the material is excellent nonetheless. As usual, Scott-Heron has a lot of sociopolitical things on his mind—"The Train From Washington" concludes that the working class can't depend on the U.S. government for anything, while "Not Needed" angrily points the finger at companies who consider longtime employees expendable. And the album's less sociopolitical songs are equally memorable. "Your Daddy Loves You" is a touching ode to Scott-Heron's daughter Gia Louise (who was only a child in 1980), and the jazz-oriented "A Legend in His Own Mind" is a humorous, clever put-down of a wannabe "Casanova" who isn't nearly the ladies' man he brags about being. Scott-Heron's love of jazz serves him well on "A Legend in His Own Mind" and the smoky "Combinations," but make no mistake: *Real Eyes* is an R&B album more than anything. *—Alex Henderson*

Reflections / 1981 / Arista ♦♦♦
Although a major across-the-board hit always eluded the poet, singer, and activist Gil Scott-Heron, this album does contains one of his best-known songs. "B-Movie," an extended attack on Ronald "Ray-gun," unleashes 12 minutes of vitriol about the then recently elected president. Beginning with the declaration "Mandate, my ass," it's a laundry list of fears about Reagan, fantasizing that his election meant "we're all actors" in some surreal film. Delivered over a taut funk groove, parts of it are still funny. Elsewhere, Scott-Heron takes an early stab at endorsing firearm control on "Gun"; slows things down for "Morning Thoughts"; and explores reggae's rhythms and revolutionary power on "Storm Music," a direction he'd pursue more fully on his next album, *Moving Target.* The disc also includes a pair of covers that offer varying degrees of success: Bill Withers' "Grandma's Hands" is a natural for Scott-Heron's warm baritone and a bright soul-jazz arrangement from the Midnight Band, but the version of Marvin Gaye's "Inner City Blues," while it swings convincingly, has a lengthy spoken-word riff that fails to embellish on the pain implicit in the original. Overall, *Reflections* doesn't capture Scott-Heron at the peak of his game, though anyone who enjoyed the other works from his Arista period certainly won't be disappointed. *—Dan LeRoy*

Moving Target / Sep. 1982 / Arista ♦♦♦
Gil Scott-Heron's last proper album for more than a decade, *Moving Target* was recorded after a period of intense touring (hence the title) and, perhaps understandably, finds the Midnight Band playing a larger role than usual. It also may reflect the group's travels, as the typical, tastefully jazzy R&B and funk grooves—like set-opener "Fast Lane" and "Explanations"—are supplemented with more exotic sounds. Like Stevie Wonder, for whom he and the Midnight Band opened a tour in 1980, Scott-Heron and his bandmates were experimenting with reggae. "No Exit" has clear echoes of Bob Marley, while "Ready or Not" is a sultry island jam. Both tunes also had themes more personal than political, a shift noticeable elsewhere on the album (even "Washington D.C.," with its seemingly obvious subject, is as much about the resilient spirit of D.C.'s citizens as it's about the city's politicians). That's somewhat surprising, given that Scott-Heron had recently enjoyed success with "B-Movie," a pointed attack on then-president Ronald Reagan. But "Blue Collar" is a populist manifesto that gives shout-outs to working folks in a variety of professions across the fruited plain before concluding with the dispirited chorus, "There ain't no place we ain't been down," and "Black History/The World" offers nearly ten minutes of Afrocentric theorizing, beginning with a spoken introduction that hearkens back to Scott-Heron's sarcastic, poetic beginnings and ends with a simple—some would say simplistic—plea for peace and world change. *—Dan LeRoy*

The Best of Gil Scott-Heron / 1984 / Arista ♦♦♦♦
In 1975, Gil Scott-Heron became the first artist ever signed to Arista Records, but ten years later, he proved expendable when Clive Davis' company dropped him. It was sad to see Arista give Scott-Heron the boot in 1985, although it wasn't surprising—by the mid-'80s, Arista was only interested in superstars, and Scott-Heron was never a superstar. Though the singer commanded a loyal following, it was a small following. Scott-Heron was little-known among pop fans, and although R&B fans knew him for "The Bottle," "Angel Dust," and "Johannesburg," he was never a huge name in the R&B world. Not long before Arista dropped Scott-Heron, it released this LP, which offered one new song ("Re-Ron") but contains mostly previously released material. The only gem from Scott-Heron's pre-Arista years on Flying Dutchman is the 1970s incendiary "The Revolution Will Not Be Televised." Otherwise, *The Best of Gil Scott-Heron* (which spans 1970-1984) spotlights his Arista years and offers some of his most essential recordings for that label, which range from the singles "The Bottle" (a number-15 R&B hit), "Johannesburg" (which went to number 29 on the R&B singles charts), and "Angel Dust" to "Winter in America," "Shut Um Down," and "B Movie" (one of Scott-Heron's angry attacks on President Ronald Reagan). Even if you don't agree with all of Scott-Heron's politics, he was always thought-provoking and was certainly an expressive, captivating R&B singer—it's too bad he ended up spending the second half of the 1980s without any type of label deal. For those who wanted an introductory overview of Scott-Heron's Arista output, this LP was, in the mid-'80s, a logical choice. *—Alex Henderson*

Spirits / Jul. 1994 / TVT ♦♦♦♦♦
With *Spirits,* Gil Scott-Heron made a triumphant return to the studio after a 12-year absence. Though the politically charged R&B singer's voice had deteriorated, much of his

soulfulness comes through. His songwriting is consistently excellent, and songs ranging from "Message to the Messengers" (which advises young rap artists to use their power wisely) to "Work for Peace" leave no doubt that his sociopolitical observations are as sharp as ever. One of the most riveting cuts is "The Other Side," an extended remake of his early-'70s classic "Home Is Where the Hatred Is" (which describes a drug addict's struggle). The East Coaster had been battling addiction himself during his absence from recording, and this heartfelt song isn't for the squeamish. Scott-Heron had successfully dabbled in jazz over the years, and in fact, one of the CD's many strong points are the lyrics he adds to John Coltrane's "Spirits." One cannot help but wish Scott-Heron still had a great voice to go with this material, but even so, *Spirits* is powerful listening. *—Alex Henderson*

Evolution & Flashback: The Very Best of Gil Scott-Heron / Feb. 9, 1999 / RCA ✦✦✦✦
This compilation of work from 1970-1972 finds the master of jazz poetry at his most militant. While the vitality of his approach on "Whitey on the Moon," "Get Out of the Ghetto Blues" and the title track are undeniable, the disc is really notable because it clearly displays the role Gil Scott-Heron played in developing the rap aesthetic. His later, funkier work on such fine albums as "From South Africa to South Carolina" found a better balance between his ideology and a sound groove. *—Tim Sheridan*

Seal (Sealhenry Samuel)

b. Feb. 19, 1963, Paddington, London, England
Vocals / Pop/Rock, Adult Contemporary, Urban, House, Dance-Pop, Club/Dance
Seal emerged from England's house music scene in the early '90s to become the most popular British soul vocalist of the decade. Although his earliest material still showed signs of acid house, by the mid-'90s he had created a distinctive fusion of soul, folk, pop, dance, and rock that brought him success on both sides of the Atlantic.

The son of Nigerian and Brazilian parents, Seal was raised in England. After graduating with an architectural degree, he took various jobs around London, including electrical engineering and designing leather clothing. After a while, he began singing in local clubs and bars. He joined an English funk band called Push, touring Japan with the band in the mid-'80s. When he was in Asia, he joined a Thailand-based blues band. After a short time with that group, he traveled throughout India on his own.

Upon returning to England, Seal met Adamski, a house and techno producer who had yet to make much of an impression within the U.K. Seal provided the lyrics and vocals for Adamski's "Killer," which became a number-one hit in 1990. After "Killer" became a hit, Seal signed a solo record contract. He recorded his eponymous debut album with Trevor Horn, who had previously worked with ABC, Frankie Goes to Hollywood, and the Buggles. The first single pulled from the album, "Crazy," became a number-15 hit in the U.K. and reached number seven in America upon its release in 1991. *Seal* was also a success, reaching number 24 in America and selling over three-million copies around the world. After the success of his debut, Seal took three years to complete his second album. In between the two records, he appeared on the Jimi Hendrix tribute album *Stone Free*, singing on Jeff Beck's version of "Manic Depression."

In the summer of 1994, he released his second album, which was also titled *Seal*. Preceded by the American Top 40 hit "Prayer for the Dying," the album did well upon its release, peaking at number 20 and selling a million copies by the spring of 1995, but it didn't really take off until a year after its release, when "Kiss From a Rose" was featured on the soundtrack to *Batman Forever*. "Kiss From a Rose" became a number-one pop single in America and spent a total of 12 weeks at the top of the adult contemporary charts; the single spent a total of 45 weeks on the adult contemporary charts. Its success sent its parent album, *Seal*, into multiplatinum status; two years after its original release, the album had sold over four-million copies in the U.S. alone. *Human Being* followed in 1998. *—Stephen Thomas Erlewine*

Seal / Jun. 11, 1991 / Sire ✦✦✦✦✦
London singer/songwriter Seal certainly made a name for himself with his eponymous debut despite the comparison to fellow London mate, the raspy-soul Terence Trent D'Arby. But Seal is more relaxed, and his craftsmanship is delicate and well-defined. Lyrical depictions are light, songwriting is personal, and production credits are most impressive. With star-studded work from both Trevor Horn (Tina Turner, Art of Noise, Rod Stewart) and Trevor Rabin (Yes, John Miles), *Seal* is surely a critical hit. Becoming a mainstream radio mainstay for the summer of 1991, the single "Crazy" carried heavy notoriety for Seal and instantly made him a household name. His collaborative effort with Adamski for "Killer" was a massive club hit thanks to it's Hi-NRG strength, but house elements showcased other album tracks such as "The Beginning." Seal is not necessarily a dance innovator so to speak, but he makes for a select crossover artist with impeccable talent worthy of heavy acclamation and critical recognition. The general mood captured on his debut album is refreshing for the early-'90s mediocrity of post-hair metal and manufactured synth bands. His music was a major force throughout the decade and well into the new millennium. With Trevor Horn at his side, it's undeniable. Together they go for exactly what Seal is looking for: the beauty, desire, and simplicity in creating a new sound. Seal is the face and Horn is the face behind it all. *—MacKenzie Wilson*

● **Seal** / 1994 / Sire ✦✦✦✦✦
Fresh from his 1991 self-titled debut, Seal follows up with his again self-titled second release. It's another stunning and moving piece of work, and a musical maturation has obviously taken place. Produced by ex-Buggles frontman Trevor Horn (Pet Shop Boys, ABC, Yes, Tina Turner, Rod Stewart, Frankie Goes to Hollywood), *Seal* is far more enchanting than on his preceding debut with his more than minimal emotion and heartfelt depictions. The warmth is there, sultry and attractive. But Seal is a bit too relaxed at times, making for stripped lyrical stories. Aside from that brief cut, Seal is lush in harmonies and over-the-top melodies. "Don't Cry" flows with luxuriant vibes of hushing vocals and bellowing string arrangements. Showcasing more talent comes "If I Could," the duet between Seal and Canadian folky Joni Mitchell. The elegance of the contemporary "Prayer for the Dying" finally established Seal as a household name after the song became a mainstream radio and television mainstay. The soul is there, hauntingly similar to singer Terence Trent D'Arby. But what's so unique about Seal is his gift of transforming free-flowing songs into quick dancefloor tracks into a transcending step into musical magic. His voice has spell a like that. His second album picks up on such skills. *—MacKenzie Wilson*

Human Being / Nov. 17, 1998 / Warner Bros. ✦✦✦
U.K. pop sensation Seal has become notorious for taking extended breaks between albums (usually up to four years). On his third album, *Human Being*, producer Trevor Horn again joins Seal, and as on his past releases, life's trials and tribulations are used as the basis for the song's subject matter and lyrics (broken relationships, death, etc.). Horn again helps Seal achieve an unbelievably sonically rich album—with each listen, you hear something you didn't before. The moderately paced, grooving opening track, "Human Beings," merges Seal's trademark soothing and crooned vocals with lyrics that deal with the highly publicized deaths of gangsta rappers Tupac Shakur and Notorious B.I.G. Directly after, three instant Seal classics follow—the gentle "State of Grace" and "Just Like You," plus the dance rocker "Latest Craze." Other highlights include the ethereal beauty of "Still Love Remains," the gradually building "Excerpt From," and the moving "Colour." Although Seal fans might grow impatient with such long breaks between albums, the pop perfection of *Human Being* turns out to be well worth the wait. *—Greg Prato*

Marvin Sease

b. Feb. 16, 1946, South Carolina
Vocals / Retro-Soul, Modern Electric Blues, Soul-Blues
Despite a lack of attention from most print sources and other common avenues of publicity in the blues world, Marvin Sease has turned his smooth, X-rated ladies' man persona into a cottage industry complete with merchandising in the Deep South. Sease straddles the line between blues and gospel-drenched soul, much like fellow Southern singers Johnnie Taylor and Tyrone Davis, but his often racy lyrics and concert performances, coupled with the advantages of major-label distribution, have ensured Sease a strong following, particularly among female fans enamored of his signature song and breakthrough jukebox hit, the provocative, innuendo-laced "Candy Licker."

Sease recorded a self-titled LP in 1986 featuring one of his most popular songs, "Ghetto Man," and began working the South's so-called chitlin' circuit of ghetto bars, rural juke joints, and blues festivals. While shopping the LP, released on his own Early label, to record stores, Sease stumbled upon a contact who eventually got him a deal with Polygram, which re-released the LP on London/Mercury in 1987 with the addition of the newly recorded, ten-minute track "Candy Licker." The song became an underground success on jukeboxes across the South; it was too explicit for radio airplay, but audiences—especially female ones—flocked to see Sease in concert. *—Steve Huey*

Marvin Sease / 1986 / London ✦✦✦✦
Marvin Sease hadn't quite perfected his vulgar soul on his eponymous debut album, but he certainly hinted at his new direction with the epic "Candy Licker." That final number pointed the way to the sex-drenched future, but the remainder of the album was relatively tame, as Sease just concentrated on sweaty Southern soul. He may not have found his gimmick, but he was nevertheless a good singer, and since it shies away from carnality, the album may actually be preferable to his later work for more conservative soul fans. *—Thom Owens*

Breakfast / Dec. 1987 / London ✦✦✦
For anyone who loves soul, listening to a Marvin Sease record is likely to be a frustrating experience. There's little questioning that he has a rich, soulful voice and can replicate the sweat-soaked, gritty sound of Stax soul or the bedroom crooning of Al Green at the drop of a hat. It's his subject matter, however, that may make blues and soul fans balk: Sease likes it dirty. Scratch that—he likes it *vulgar*, if "Condom on Your Tongue" and "I Ate You for My Breakfast" are any indication. That can be a problem for anyone with queasy stomachs, since Sease likes to belt out his dirty words, unless it's on the slow songs, where he murmurs his sweet, filthy nothings, presumably to get you in the mood. Musically, there's no way to fault *Breakfast*—it's first-rate retro-soul—but if you don't like nasty pillow talk, chances are the music isn't going to make this *Breakfast* digestible. *—Stephen Thomas Erlewine*

Show Me What You Got / Oct. 8, 1991 / Mercury ✦✦

● **The Best of Marvin Sease** / May 20, 1997 / Polygram ✦✦✦✦
The Best of Marvin Sease is the first comprehensive collection of Sease's best bawdy, funky '70s soul, culled from his four albums for Polygram. Among the 15 tracks are the notorious "Candy Licker" and a single that had never been available on an album prior to this collection. *—Stephen Thomas Erlewine*

Modern Soulman: The Collection / 2001 / Connoisseur Collection ✦✦✦
While he's usually tagged as a blues singer, Marvin Sease's music is more closely rooted in the tradition of Southern soul, with Sease's tales of cheating husbands, housewrecking women, and footloose lover-men cut from the same cloth as the classic sides of Johnny Taylor, Joe Tex, and Otis Redding, even though they're not woven with the same degree of care. *Modern Soulman: The Collection* is a 16-song compilation assembled from material Sease recorded for Jive Records, focusing on his straight-ahead R&B sides rather than the raunchy celebrations of oral sex which brought him much of his American following. As a singer Sease isn't quite in the same league as the artists who most obviously influenced him, but at a time when soul singers in the classic style are becoming a rare commodity, he's not only keeping the tradition alive, he's doing it with no small degree of style and flair, and on his best cuts here Sease sounds impassioned, forceful, and

compellingly gritty, which is to say this collection plays to his strengths. And if Marvin Sease the singer is a few notches stronger than Marvin Sease the songwriter (his songs tend to cover the same ground over and over) or Marvin Sease the producer (his budget-minded reliance on synthesizers and drum machines robs these performances of the weight and feel of classic '60s soul), he's still more than a few paces ahead of the sort of old-school soul artists recording for Malaco or Ichiban these days. If you're looking for Sease in typically lascivious form, *Modern Soulman: The Collection* won't be of much use to you, but if you've wanted to hear him singing at a PG rating for a change, then this disc is the place to go. *—Mark Deming*

Women Would Rather Be Licked / Feb. 6, 2001 / Jive ♦♦♦♦
If you've heard one of his albums, you know Marvin Sease's schtick. He's not just a ribald lover-man, he's really raunchy, delving into double and single entendres for his slow Southern soul grinds. You either dig it or you don't, but if you don't dig it, his 2001 album, *A Woman Would Rather Be Licked*, could change your mind. Yes, all the typical Sease schtick is in place, but his material and performances are more convincing than usual, and the vulgarity level is toned down slightly (however, the Parental Advisory sticker on the cover is still earned—although it's hard to imagine what kid would pick up this album). So, even this doesn't deliver full-on, hardcore Sease, this is one of his most satisfying records, at least on a musical level. *—Stephen Thomas Erlewine*

Jon Secada

b. 1962, Havana, Cuba
Vocals / Adult Contemporary, Latin Pop, Urban, Dance-Pop
Jon Secada (he legally changed his first name from Juan in 1990) immigrated to the U.S. at the age of nine in 1971, settling in Miami where his parents opened a coffee shop. He earned both a B.A. and a M.A. in jazz vocal performance at the University of Miami. Becoming involved with Gloria Estefan's career, he co-wrote six songs on her multi-platinum 1991 album *Into the Light*, among them the number one hit "Coming out of the Dark," and sang backup vocals on her subsequent tour. Then he signed to SBK Records and launched his own career with a self-titled debut record in 1992. With only one album, he became one of the biggest adult contemporary artist of the '90s, selling over six-million albums worldwide. His smooth mix of R&B, pop, and Latin music appealed to a number of different audiences. As well as becoming a huge English-language pop star, he became one of the hottest Latin artists recording in the '90s; *Otro Día Más Sin Verte* (a Spanish-language version of *Jon Secada*) was *Billboard*'s number-one Latin album in 1992 and won a Grammy for Best Latin Pop Album. His second English-language album, *Heart, Soul & a Voice* (1994), sold over a million copies. *Amor* (1995), his second Spanish-language album, won him another Grammy. *Secada* (1997) was a commercial disappointment, and the singer moved to Sony Music's Epic Records where his first duties including writing songs for labelmates Ricky Martin and Jennifer Lopez. In July of 2000, Epic released his label debut, *Better Part of Me*. *—Stephen Thomas Erlewine*

Jon Secada / May 5, 1992 / SBK ♦♦♦♦

Heart, Soul & A Voice / May 24, 1994 / SBK ♦♦♦
While there aren't as many obvious singles on Jon Secada's second album, his voice sounds better than ever, making it a worthwhile sophomore effort. *—Stephen Thomas Erlewine*

Amor / Oct. 10, 1995 / EMI Latin/SBK ♦♦♦
Amor is a collection of Spanish love ballads, sung with grace by Jon Secada. The album is a more subdued and jazzy affair than Secada's previous efforts, proving that he is capable of many different styles as a vocalist. *—Stephen Thomas Erlewine*

Secada / Mar. 25, 1997 / Capitol ♦♦♦
Despite a couple of bland tracks and an overlong running time, *Secada* is a fine return to English-language adult-contemporary pop by Jon Secada. While the songs aren't always distinctive, Secada's voice is clear, pure and lovely, making even the weakest songs tolerable. Only a handful of songs are first-rate—including the single "Too Late, Too Soon"—but the record is pleasant and makes for fine background music. *—Rodney Batdorf*

◐ **The Greatest Hits** / Jul. 27, 1999 / Virgin ♦♦♦♦
Jon Secada really had only one blockbuster album, but he nevertheless was one of the finest adult contemporary singers of the '90s, as *Greatest Hits* proves. Released at the tail-end of his Virgin contract, just before he began recording for Sony Music, *Greatest Hits* covers his first four albums, including not only all of his hits—"Just Another Day," "Do You Believe in Us," "Angel," "I'm Free," "If You Go," "Whipped," "Mental Picture"—but selected highlights from the records themselves. As such, it's a definitive portrait. Secada always sounded good on record, but his material was occasionally uneven. Here, every song connects, making it not only a fine greatest-hits collection, but arguably his best record to date. *—Stephen Thomas Erlewine*

The Seminoles

Group / Blue-Eyed Soul, Doo Wop, R&B, Soul
Early-'50s and -'60s Detroit blue-eyed soul vocal groups usually had great first tenor leads, and the Seminoles were no exception. These smooth harmonizers, led by Joey Finazzo and consisting of members Andy, Al, and Paul (last names unknown), debuted with "Open Your Eyes" b/w "True Love" in 1961 on local hopeful Go Gee Records. The record got their name known around town, and local disc jockeys gave it a few spins, but it was nothing special.

When Roquel "Billy" Davis left Anna Records to form Checkmate Records, he gave the Seminoles a shot. "It Takes a Lot," released May 1962, was starting to do something when Roquel closed Checkmate to take an A&R position with Chess Records (who distributed Anna and Checkmate), leaving the Seminoles in a lurch. Not for long, though—Hi-Lite Records picked up the song and managed to get an area hit for their troubles. A second Hi-Lite release, "Trouble in Mind" b/w "Have You Got Love," bombed. They were the Embers for one release on Act IV Records, "Forever" b/w "You Can Lump It"; when Act IV failed to do anything, the Seminoles took the master to Midtown Records who re-released the sides as the Seminoles. It didn't matter, the single still failed to ignite and the Seminoles disbanded. Finazzo later toured with the New World Symphony and sang with the Larados, whose members also include the Reflections' lead singer Tony Micale, John Dean, and two original Larados members. *—Andrew Hamilton*

The Sensations

f. 1954, Philadelphia, PA
Group / Doo Wop, R&B, Soul
A Philly vocal group who were originally known as the Cavaliers in 1954, the Sensations initially featured dual lead vocalists Yvonne Mills Baker and Tommy Wicks. They enjoyed two Top 40 R&B hits in that vein, the biggest being "Please Mr. Disc Jockey" for Atco in 1956. They changed their style and lineup in 1961, with Baker and bass vocalist Alphonso Howell from the original band being joined by Richard Curtain and Sam Armstrong. They scored their biggest hit with "Let Me In," which reached number two on the R&B charts (number-four pop) for Argo in 1962. *—Ron Wynn*

The Sequence

f. Columbia, SC
Group / Old School Rap, Urban, Electro
The Sequence hailed from Columbia, SC, and consisted of Angie Brown Stone, Cheryl Cook, and Gwendolyn Chisolm. Recording for Joe & Sylvia Robinson's Sugarhill Records label, they hit with "Funk You Up" in early 1980; "Funky Sound (Tear the Roof Off)," a remake of Parliament's 1976 gold single "Tear the Roof Off the Sucker" in summer 1981; and "I Don't Need Your Love (Pt. 1)" from spring 1982. Their two charting LPs were both titled *The Sequence*. Angie Stone sang lead on Vertical Hold's 1993 Top 20 R&B hit "Seems You're Much Too Busy" and had a gold single with "There's No More Rain in This Cloud" from her 1999 gold album *Black Diamond*. *—Ed Hogan*

Sugar Hill Presents the Sequence / 1980 / Sugarhill ♦♦♦
No doubt, Salt-N-Pepa emulated the Sequence, who preceded them as tough rap divas. The lineups and attitudes are similar, and none of the curvy rappers comes off as passive, unliberated women. Gwendolyn (Blondie) Chisolm, Cheryl (Cheryl the Pearl) Cook, and Angela (Angie B) Brown, b.k.a. Sequence were street-wise, gritty and butter-bred. "Simon Says" has a contagious, comical beat that's made for disco. Showing they do more than rap, they break off in "The Times When We're Alone," a slow and sensual winner. The nursery rhyme raps on "We Don't Rap the Rap," with its energetic beats, are like dancing pills. *Sesame Street*-like sounds continue, lyrically anyway, on "Funk a Doodle Rock Jam," infants must have loved this one, they could pronounce some lyrics, particularly "doodle." Heavy beats and well-spaced horns, married with Sequence's three part harmonies and leads, keeps you rocking until the end. The group borrowed from Parliament's "Give Up the Funk" and came up with "Funky Sound" where Blondie, Angie B and Cheryl the Pearl take turns busting bodacious raps. *—Andrew Hamilton*

The Sequence / 1982 / Sugarhill ♦♦♦♦
The Sequence's second album contains all of the same funky, soulful grooves they busted on *Sugar Hill Presents the Sequence*. It's almost an even split between the ballads and hip-hop numbers: "I Don't Need Your Love," a wailing beauty, pulled up lame at number 40 on *Billboards'* R&B chart in May of 1982, a poor showing for one of their best performances; "Love Changes," led by Angie B, is seven plus minutes of gut-wrenching soul searching; "Unaddressed Letter" is an unexpected piece of traditional soul that works like a charm; James Brown's "Cold Sweat" gets a makeover and a new feel; and finally, "Funk That (You Mothers)" and "Get It Together" are hip-hoppers accented with hot raps. *—Andrew Hamilton*

● **The Best of the Sequence** / Dec. 17, 1996 / Deep Beats ♦♦♦♦
Many aren't aware of neo-soul singer Angie Stone's roots in the Sequence, a versatile female trio that recorded for Sugarhill during the early '80s. The Sequence only cut two albums, but they made enough impact to inspire the likes of Salt-N-Pepa, who obviously took a thing or two from this group and became much more popular in the process. Put together by Sequel's Deep Beats offshoot, *The Best of the Sequence* culls a dozen tracks from 1980's *Sugar Hill Presents the Sequence* and 1982's *The Sequence*, and includes their three Top 40 black singles: "Funky Sound (Tear the Roof Off)," "I Don't Need Your Love," and "Funk You Up." Though it seems like it might've been preferable to simply combine the group's two albums on one disc, this anthology does an admirable job of leaving off the filler from those albums and concentrating on highlights. This lean disc also demonstrates the group's ability to gracefully switch gears from funk to soul to rap. *—Andy Kellman*

The Sequins

Group / Girl Group, Pop, R&B, Soul
The Sequins said "Hey Romeo" and record buyers responded, giving the teenaged singing trio a Top 40 R&B hit. Consisting of Veronica "Ronnie" Gonzalez, Linda Jackson, and Dottie Hayes, the Sequins were all students at Chicago's Harlan High School. After winning first prize at a talent contest at the legendary Regal Theater, the group began performing in area clubs. During one club appearance, they were spotted by the husband and wife team of Bill & Denise Jones, owners of Crajon Productions. Crajon was a contradiction of the first three letters of Denise's maiden name Craig and her husband's last name, and the independently distributed label was started from the couple's home around 48th and Langley Avenue on the city's South Side. Denise Jones recorded herself under the name Denise LaSalle (the 1971 gold number-one single "Trapped By a Thing Called Love"). For the bulk of her releases and the ones on Crajon, LaSalle utilized the

services of Memphis, TN, producer Willie Mitchell, who would go on to have gold- and platinum-laced success with Al Green.

The Sequins' first release on Crajon's label was "Hey Romeo" b/w "I've Got to Overcome" and it went to number 32 on *Billboard*'s R&B charts in late summer 1970. The singers went on a national tour, performing at New York's Apollo Theater and other major venues. The follow-up on the medium sky-blue colored Crajon imprint was "The Third Degree" b/w "Someday You'll Be Mine," released in spring 1971. The silky ballad was recorded in Memphis with Mitchell utilizing the same subdued style and instrumentation (the Memphis Horns and the Hi Records Rhythm Section in a low-key mode and crying strings) he would use on Al Green in the next year or so. "The Third Degree" received radio airplay in Chicago and other markets. This led to the trio's appearance on a pre-nationally syndicated *Soul Train* with Don Cornelius on WCIU-TV channel 26 (sponsored by Joe Louis Milk). Another Crajon release, "It Must Be Love," was a regional hit in the summer of 1973, the year LaSalle relocated to Memphis, later marrying James Wolf and moving to Jackson, TN, where she began recording for the city's Malaco label in 1983.

With Crajon defunct, the Sequins drifted into private life. Other Sequins singles were "It Must Be Love," written by Philip Mitchell (Ben E. King and the Average White Band's "Star in the Ghetto"), b/w "You Flunked Out" on Crajon; "Hideaway" b/w "I Ain't Gonna Cry No More" on the Terrace label; and "Who Says You Can't Jerk" b/w "I'll Be Satisfied" and "Don't Fall in Love." *—Ed Hogan, AMG*

The Serenaders

f. 1956

Group / Motown, Soul, R&B

Even the most avid Motown fanatics are unaware of the Serenaders, yet the New York-based group cut their final single on Motown's VIP label. Forming in 1956, the central figures were George Kerr, Sidney Barnes, and Timothy "Andre" Wilson, and various other members serenaded in out and out over the years. They debuted on Chock Full of Hits records with "Never Let Me Go" b/w "I Wrote a Letter" in 1957. When it started to move, MGM records acquired it for mass distribution in 1958. It sold enough locally to get the guys another shot at MGM, but "Dance, Darling Dance" b/w "Give Me a Girl" (1958) never got to first base and the associated ended. In 1959, they dropped "How Do You Mend a Broken Heart" on the Cross Country label, but sales were disappointing.

The lion's share of the Serenaders' material was written by George Kerr with some collaborations with Sidney Barnes and others. Later in 1959, they moseyed over to Rae-Cox records for one release, "My Girl Flip Flop" b/w "Gotta Go to School," two good well-sung novelty types that failed to register. The members splintered, but the core members stayed in touch, and after many false starts and unfulfilled promises got another chance in 1963 on Riverside records with "Adios My Love" b/w "Two Lovers Make One Fool." They never sold well outside the New York/Jersey/Philly area. What should have been a big break with Motown became a major letdown. Signed by Raynoma Gordy out of Motown's New York office, the Serenaders never got a real shot. Even though they were blessed with George Kerr, a songwriting fool, and the major reason Raynoma signed them in the first place; Sidney Barnes, also a constant writer, with a vocal range from first tenor to bass, and Timothy Wilson, who sounded like Little Anthony.

Motown finally released the Serenaders' "If Your Heart Says Yes," a Kerr/Barnes composition, on its VIP label in 1964; it possessed loads of charm, and with promotion could have went places, but neglect caused it to flop miserably. You won't find it on any of the many Motown compilations albums, cassettes, or compact disks. Temptations Eddie Kendricks and Elbridge Bryant sang with the Serenaders on the A-side and its flip "I'll Cry Tomorrow." Shortly after that, they broke up. Timothy Wilson married Raynoma's sister Alice; Wilson previously sung with Tiny Tim & the Hits on Roulette records. Sidney Barnes did some solos and got into producing, as did George Kerr who was more successful. Kerr produced Linda Jones' "Hypnotized," and stellar sides for the Whatnauts, the O'Jays, the Moments, Lonnie Youngblood, and others, in addition to singing with Little Anthony & the Imperials on their New Time recordings. *—Andrew Hamilton*

The Servicemen

Group / Soul, Northern Soul

The mysterious Servicemen released three records on as many labels between 1966-1967 on Wind Hit, Chartmaker, and Patheway Records respectively. Probable members were James Mitchell and Hadley D. Murrell, who wrote the groups' recordings. They debuted with "I Need a Helping Hand" b/w "Are You Angry" in 1966 and followed it with "Sweet Magic" b/w "Connie" the same year; it all ended with "My Turn" b/w "I Need a Helping Hand" in 1967. The Servicemen—who probably were in the military, therefore the name—fell off the face of the earth musically. Little did they know that "I Need a Helping Hand" and "Sweet Magic" would become top Northern soul plays and still sought by collectors more than 30 years after appearing. *—Andrew Hamilton*

Shai

Group / Urban, Club/Dance, House

At the end of 1992, the four-man urban contemporary vocal group Shai shot to the top of the R&B and pop charts with their debut album, *If I Ever Fall in Love*, and its number one title track. Although they sometimes lack quality material, the smooth silkiness of their voices usually makes such weaknesses easy to ignore; the group has remained hot on the R&B charts, even if they haven't duplicated the pop success of their first single. *—Stephen Thomas Erlewine*

• **If I Ever Fall in Love** / 1992 / Gasoline Alley ♦♦♦♦♦

Apart from the gorgeous title track, most of the material on *If I Ever Fall in Love* is underdeveloped; although Shai sounds terrific, their material doesn't match their vocal talents. There are occasional signs of promise, but the single is the only flat-out impressive track here. *—Stephen Thomas Erlewine*

The Place Where You Belong / 1994 / MCA ♦♦

Blackface / Sep. 26, 1995 / Gasoline Alley ♦♦♦

Overall, Shai's follow-up to their breakthrough album *If I Ever Fall in Love* is a stronger record than their debut, featuring more complete songs and smoother harmonies. The first half of the disc is devoted to seductive slow numbers, while the second part is dominated by deep bass grooves. While there's nothing as strong as "If I Ever Fall in Love" on *Blackface*, it is a better album, demonstrating that the band is continuing to grow. *—Stephen Thomas Erlewine*

20th Century Masters—The Millennium Collection: The Best of Shai / Aug. 14, 2001 / MCA ♦♦♦♦

Shai's *20th Century Masters* may not contain every hit the group ever had, but it has all of the big ones, making this an excellent choice for listeners who want simply the basics. *—Stephen Thomas Erlewine*

Shalamar

f. 1976, New York, NY, **db.** 1991

Group / Urban, Disco, Soul

Shalamar was the creation of Dick Griffey, the booking agent for the television R&B program *Soul Train*, and British R&B producer Simon Soussan. The group's first single, the 1977 Motown medley "Uptown Festival," featured a bevy of faceless studio musicians; once it became a hit, Griffey decided to form a performing group under the name Shalamar. Through *Soul Train*, Griffey found Jody Watley, Jeffrey Daniels, and Gerald Brown, the three vocalists that became Shalamar; Brown was quickly replaced by Howard Hewett in 1978.

Shalamar's string of poppy dance-soul hits began in 1979 with "Take That to the Bank"; later that year, "The Second Time Around" hit the Top Ten. Throughout the early '80s the group were favorites on the U.S. R&B scene, as well as scoring a number of British hit singles. Watley and Daniels left the group in 1982 and were replaced by Delisa Davis and Micki Free in 1984; Watley went on to stardom as a solo act. The following year Shalamar won a Grammy award for "Don't Get Stopped in Beverly Hills," which was featured in *Beverly Hills Cop*. Hewitt left for a solo career in 1986, signaling the end of the band's career as hit-makers. Sidney Justin replaced Hewitt and the group recorded 1987's *Circumstantial Evidence*, which was a commercial disappointment. The group faded away soon after the release of 1990's *Wake Up*. *—Stephen Thomas Erlewine*

Uptown Festival / 1977 / Soul Train ♦♦

Shalamar's debut album *Uptown Festival* is a dated set of shamelessly pandering disco that became a hit on the basis of the title track, a clever medley of old Motown hits. "Uptown Festival"—and its less-successful follow-up, a cover of Smokey Robinson's "Ooh Baby Baby"—were hits simply because they grafted a familiar melody to a disco beat, not because they represented any innovation. The remainder of *Uptown Festival* suffers from a similar fate. Shalamar sing as if the lyrics meant something, but the music on the record is so stilted, the album sounds lifeless. Occasionally, such as the opening cut "Inky Dinky Wang Dang Doo," the music is kitschy fun, but more often than not, it is simply an artifact of its times. *—Stephen Thomas Erlewine*

Disco Gardens / 1978 / RCA ♦♦♦

Uptown Festival was Shalamar's first album, but *Disco Gardens* was Shalamar's first worthwhile album. To say that there was a world of difference between the two might be an understatement. Much of *Uptown Festival* had a robotic, impersonal quality, and it was obviously the work of a manufactured studio act. But when Shalamar introduced its Jody Watley/Jeffrey Daniels/Gerald Brown lineup on its second album, *Disco Gardens*, it started feeling like an honest-to-God group with a real identity. This decent-to-excellent album had a pearl of a hit single in "Take That to the Bank," and almost as appealing are the irresistibly funky "Tossin', Turnin', Swingin'" (which should have been a hit single as well) and the catchy "Shalamar Disco Gardens." Although Howard Hewett had yet to join the group, Shalamar had developed a recognizable soul-pop sound. *Disco Gardens* turned out to be Brown's only album with Shalamar, and in 1978, the arrival of his replacement, Mr. Hewett, would be the icing on Shalamar's cake. *—Alex Henderson*

Big Fun / 1979 / Solar ♦♦♦♦

With its third album, *Big Fun*, Shalamar unveiled its best-known and most successful lineup. Jody Watley and Jeffrey Daniels were still on board, but Gerald Brown had been replaced by the charismatic Howard Hewett. Both creatively and commercially, this album would take Shalamar to new heights and establish the trio as one of the best soul-pop units of 1979-1983. The single that made Hewett famous and really sent Shalamar into orbit was "Second Time Around," but the classic Hewett/Watley/Daniels lineup also excels on everything from the insistent "Right in the Socket" to the playfully funky "Take Me to the River" (not the 1974 Al Green classic) and the smooth, Philadelphia soul-type ballad "Let's Find the Time for Love." [Definitely one of Shalamar's essential releases, *Big Fun* was reissued on CD by The Right Stuff in 1996.] *—Alex Henderson*

Three for Love / 1981 / Capitol ♦♦♦♦♦

The Howard Hewett/Jody Daniels/Jeffrey Daniels edition of Shalamar was in excellent form on *Big Fun*, *Friends* and *The Look*, but if one had to pinpoint the group's best release ever, the hands-down winner would have to be its fourth album, *Three for Love*. With Leon Sylvers III producing and members of Shalamar and Lakeside contributing to the writing, all of the pieces fell into place quite nicely. Shalamar enjoyed major hits with the irresistible "Make That Move" and the sentimental ballad "This Is for the Lover in You," and every bit as strong are the funky "Pop Along Kid" and the dreamy "Somewhere There's a Love." [A non-musical point: when The Right Stuff reissued *Three For Love* on CD in 1997, the liner notes stated "copyright 1978," but in fact, the album wasn't released until late 1980; there's no way *Three for Love* could have even been recorded in 1978 because Hewett had yet to join Shalamar. But the main thing is the music, and the CD reissue certainly sounds great.] *Three for Love* is soul-pop heaven. *—Alex Henderson*

Go for It / 1981 / Solar ✦✦✦
Coming on the heels of two Top Ten LPs, Shalamar's 1981 *Go for It*, their second album of the year, barely stumbled into the Top 20, reflecting the band's own brief mid-career slump. Still intent on delivering uptempo R&B hinging on urban beats, disco strings, and funky interludes, Shalamar was suffering from the beginning of inter-band strife that would eventually find both founder members, Jody Watley and Jeffrey Daniels, leaving the group for the less-stressful pastures of solo work. And although only one song, the bright-popped but bland "Sweeter As the Days Go By," broke away to enter the charts, there are still some fine moments across the LP. "Go for It," which uses strings and a remarkably fluid bass to marvelous effect, is particularly strong and it's surprising that it wasn't tagged for a single. This, in turn, is well complemented by the edgy James Ingram-penned "You've Got Me Running," while "Talk to Me," co-written by Watley, is a smooth piece of funk-inflected R&B. Elsewhere, though, the band degenerates into the fairly generic slow-movers "Good Feelings" and "The Final Analysis," which features singer Stephanie Mills, both causing *Go for It* to fumble as often as it flies. *—Amy Hanson*

Friends / 1982 / Solar ✦✦✦
Although the group had been around since the late '70s, Shalamar didn't really gel until vocalist Howard Hewett joined original members Jeffrey Daniel and Jody Watley. While *Friends'* predecessor, *Three for Love*, offered more hits, *Friends* is a sometimes-cautious though fulfilling continuation of the style. The biggest hit and leadoff track, "A Night to Remember," successfully mixes a subtle flash and a bittersweet melody that made the track an instant classic. As disco was long gone at this point, *Friends* represents the production style inherent in Solar and a fair amount of R&B of the time. "I Don't Wanna Be the Last to Know" coasts on the same smooth sound of their 1981 hit, "The Lover in You." At this point, the separate skills of the trio were beginning to supersede the act. Hewett ably handles the hooky and insinuating ballad "I Just Stopped By Because I Had To." The textbook Solar style and Leon F. Sylvers III's production on "There It Is" get back to the trio harmonies and aesthetic. *Friends* is not only an assured Shalamar, a fact that was a given with this version of the group, it's also a great representation of the Solar sound and early-'80s R&B. *—Jason Elias*

The Look / 1983 / Solar ✦✦✦
The Look found Shalamar incorporating elements of new wave pop into their stylized dance funk, as demonstrated by such glossy pop-funk as "Dead Giveaway" and "No Limits (The Now Club)." The sound is appealing on such uptempo numbers, but the ballads are slightly weaker, lacking strong, memorable hooks. Similarly, the funk numbers tend to blend together after certain point, but *The Look* remains an entertaining artifact of its era. *—Leo Stanley*

Love for Love / 1983 / Solar ✦✦✦

Heartbreak / 1984 / Solar ✦✦✦
With Jody Watley and Jeffrey Daniels having left Shalamar and been replaced by singer Delisa Davis and guitarist/Prince admirer Micki Free, Howard Hewett unveiled a new Shalamar lineup on *Heart Break*. Although the loss of Watley and Daniels was quite a loss for the group, it wasn't a fatal blow. In fact, *Heart Break* was good enough to indicate that there might be life after Watley and Daniels for Shalamar, mainly because the trio still had Hewett's talent and charisma to rely on. Hewett is clearly the one holding down the fort on *Heart Break*, which finds Shalamar continuing to incorporate new wave elements. *Heart Break* (which The Right Stuff reissued on CD in 1998) boasted the wildly infectious, rock-influenced hit from *Footloose* "Dancing in the Sheets," and the combination of soul-pop and new wave also proved quite appealing on "My Girl Loves Me," "Don't Get Stopped in Beverly Hills" and the George Duke-produced "Amnesia." Also impressive is Howard and Davis' charming duet on the ballad "Whenever You Need Me." As it turned out, *Heart Break* would be Hewett's last album with Shalamar, as well as the last decent Shalamar album. *—Alex Henderson*

Circumstantial Evidence / 1987 / Solar ✦✦✦

Wake Up / 1990 / Solar ✦✦

The Greatest Hits Collection: A Night to Remember / May 1998 / Spectrum ✦✦✦✦

• **The Greatest Hits** / Jul. 27, 1999 / Capitol ✦✦✦✦✦
The Right Stuff's *Greatest Hits* comes close to being the definitive Shalamar hits collection. Every one of their biggest hits—"Uptown Festival (Pt. 1)," "The Second Time Around," "Make That Move," "A Night to Remember," "Dead Giveaway," "Dancing in the Sheets," "Games"—are present, in their best-known mixes. Some dedicated fans might notice that a song or two is missing, but all the biggest best singles are here, making it a very entertaining compilation ideal for casual and dedicated fans alike. *—Stephen Thomas Erlewine*

The Shangri-Las

f. 1963, Queens, NY, **db.** 1969
Group / Brill Building Pop, Girl Group, Rock & Roll
Along with the Shirelles and the Ronettes, the Shangri-Las were the greatest girl group; if judged solely on the basis of attitude, they were the greatest of them all. They combined an innocent adolescent charm with more than a hint of darkness, singing about dead bikers, teenage runaways, and doomed love affairs as well as ebullient high school crushes. These could be delivered with either infectious, handclapping harmonies or melodramatic, almost operatic recitatives that were contrived but utterly effective. Tying it all together in the studio was Shadow Morton, a mad genius of a producer who may have been second in eccentric imagination only to Phil Spector in the mid-'60s.

Originally the Shangri-Las were comprised of two pairs of sisters from Queens, NY (identical twins Marge and Mary Anne Ganser and siblings Mary and Betty Weiss). They had already recorded a couple of obscure singles when they were hired by George "Shadow" Morton to demo a song he had recently written, "Remember (Walkin' in the Sand)." The haunting ballad, with its doomy "Moonlight Sonata"-like piano riffs, wailing lead vocal, and thunderous background harmonies, seguing into an a cappella chorus backed by nothing except handclaps and seagull cries, made the Top Five in late 1964. It also began their association with Jerry Leiber & Mike Stoller's Red Bird label, which would handle the group for the bulk of their career. The quality of Morton's work with the Shangri-Las on Red Bird (with assistance from Jeff Barry and Artie Butler) was remarkable considering that he had virtually no prior experience in the music business. The group's material, so over-the-top emotionally that it sometimes bordered on camp, was lightened by the first-class production, which embroidered the tracks with punchy brass, weeping strings, and plenty of imaginative sound effects. Nowhere was this more apparent than on "Leader of the Pack," with its periodic motorcycle roars and crescendo of crashing glass. The death-rock classic became the Shangri-Las' signature tune, reaching number one.

Several smaller hits followed in 1965 and 1966, many of them excellent. "Give Him a Great Big Kiss" proved they could handle more conventionally, bubbly girl-group fare well; "I Can Never Go Home Anymore," a runaway tale that took their patented pathos to the extreme, would be their third and final Top Ten hit. These all show up on oldies collections, but lots of listeners remain unaware of the other fine singles in their catalog, like the moody "Out in the Streets," the dense orchestral swamp of "He Cried" (which cuts Jay & the Americans' original, "She Cried," to pieces), and another teen death tale, "Give Us Your Blessings." Some of their best songs, in fact, were B-sides; "Dressed in Black," yet another teen death drama, had a marvelously hushed and damned atmosphere, and "Paradise" was co-written by a young Harry Nilsson. Their most unusual single of all was "Past, Present and Future," which didn't feature a single sung note, presenting a somber spoken monologue and occasional spoken background chants over a classical piano track reminiscent of "Remember (Walking in the Sand)." It was too unconventional to rise above the middle of the charts, especially given that the narrative could quite possibly be construed as the recollections of an assault/rape victim.

Unlike some girl groups, the Shangri-Las were dynamic on-stage performers, choreographing their dance steps to their lyrics and wearing skin-tight leather pants and boots that were quite daring for the time. Their real lives, however, were not without elements of drama themselves. Their constant personnel changes baffle historians; sometimes they are pictured as a trio, and sometimes one of the members in the photos is clearly not one of the Weiss *or* Ganser sisters. Worse, the Red Bird label ran into serious organizational difficulties in the mid-'60s, and wound down its operations in 1966. The group moved to Mercury for a couple of dispirited singles, but had split by the end of the 1960s. Shadow Morton went on to an interesting, erratic career that included involvement with Janis Ian, the New York Dolls, and Mott the Hoople. Mary Anne Ganser died of encephalitis in 1971.

Even today, the Shangri-Las' history remains somewhat murky and mysterious; the original members have rarely reunited for oldies shows or talked to the press. The situation was exacerbated by frustratingly substandard reissues of their Red Bird work, which made it impossible to collect all of their fine sides without buying numerous packages, many of which boasted shockingly shoddy sound quality. Happily, the situation was rectified in the mid-'90s with excellent, comprehensive compilations of the Red Bird material in both the U.K. and U.S. *—Richie Unterberger*

Shangrilas '65 / 1965 / Charly ✦✦✦✦

Leader of the Pack / 1983 / Charly ✦✦✦
Not a bad collection of this edgy girl group's best sides, particularly "Remember (Walking in the Sand)" (which got a new lease on life when it appeared in the movie *Goodfellas*) and, of course, the classic title track. This is hardly a definitive career retrospective, however, as it's missing "Give Him a Great Big Kiss," "Sophisticated Boom Boom," and "Past, Present, and Future" (among others). On the other hand, many of the more extensive collections—this one has only ten tracks—lack "So Much Love," "Shout," and "Goodnight My Love." Although Polygram's *Leader of the Pack* does include "Give Him a Great Big Kiss," it's missing "Remember," so this one is probably the better bet. At the very least, there's no filler here. *—Kathleen C. Fennessy*

Golden Hits of the Shangri-Las / 1984 / Mercury ✦✦✦✦✦
It includes all the eerie three-minute melodramas from one of the all-time great girl groups: "Leader of the Pack," "Remember," "I Can Never Go Home Anymore," and "Past, Present, and Future." *—George Bedard*

Collection: 20 Greatest Hits / 1993 / Masters ✦✦

• **Myrmidons of Melodrama** / 1994 / RPM ✦✦✦✦✦
Until the release of this import, there had never been a truly satisfactory Shangri-Las anthology; in fact, the group had been subject to worse piecemeal mangling than almost any other significant act of the 1960s. This 33-track production finally sets the record straight, including all of the significant A-sides, B-sides, and album tracks they recorded for Red Bird between 1964 and 1966, as well as an earlier single for a different label, and four radio commercials. Includes every one of their hits, but anyone who likes those will be enchanted by quite a few of their more obscure numbers here: "Dressed in Black," "Paradise," "It's Easier to Cry," "Never Again," and "Heaven Knows" are all first-class (if sometimes mordant). Not everything is up to that level, but enough is to make a case for them as one of the very best girl groups, and the good sound and thorough liner notes are significant bonuses. It may be more extensive and expensive than some fans wish, but don't settle for the numerous skimpy/rip-off domestic compilations, all of which manage to leave off some key tunes; this is the definitive document. *—Richie Unterberger*

• **The Best of the Shangri-Las** / Jun. 18, 1996 / Mercury ✦✦✦✦✦
This 25-song best-of actually covers most of their discography, containing all of the chart singles, and notable misses and B-sides like "Paradise" and "Dressed in Black." An excellent package, but the British *Myrmidons of Melodrama* is just a bit better, assembling a few more of their Red Bird tracks, including a couple of pretty notable ones ("It's Easier

to Cry" and "The Boy") that this domestic anthology omits. The Mercury CD does have their rare (but unexceptional) final two singles, which don't appear on *Myrmidons of Melodrama*. *—Richie Unterberger*

Myrmidons of Melodrama / Apr. 2, 2002 / RPM ♦♦♦♦♦
Although this is extremely similar to the 1994 CD Shangri-Las compilation on RPM bearing the same title, there are some small differences that might give you pause for consideration if you're either choosing between the two of them or considering "upgrading" with the new version. One of their two rare pre-Red Bird singles, "Wishing Well"/"Hate to Say I Told You So," has been dropped from the track lineup, as has their cover of the Chantels' "Maybe." In their place is the less impressive of the other pre-Red Bird 45s, "Simon Says"/"Simon Speaks," a live (or perhaps pseudo-live) early soul-pop novelty effort. In addition, seven songs, including several of their biggest hits, are heard in stereo. Close listening reveals some difference between those and the more commonly heard versions, like a longer fade on "Remember (Walkin' in the Sand)" and an extra instrumental bar after the crash on "Leader of the Pack" (which actually diminishes that classic's impact slightly). There's a new cover and longer, updated liner notes. All this doesn't necessarily add up to an improvement. It's good to have the rare "Simon Says"/"Simon Speaks" single available at last, but you still need "Wishing Well"/"Hate to Say I Told You So" and the two post-Red Bird 1966-1967 Mercury singles (available on Mercury's *The Best of the Shangri-Las* CD) to assemble all of the group's important rarities. More embarrassingly, the running order of tracks 24 through 28 play in a different sequence than that listed on the cover. And most importantly, you still need to buy no less than three CDs—Mercury's *The Best of the Shangri-Las* and both RPM configurations of *Myrmidons of Melodrama*—to get everything of interest by the group. That's a luxury that most fans would agree should somehow have been covered by a more affordable, convenient two-CD set if possible. If for some reason this is the only Shangri-Las comp you can lay your hands on, though, it's a very good one, including all of their big hits, several fine semi-forgotten low-charting singles, several other worthy obscure cuts, and additional assorted rarities. *—Richie Unterberger*

Shanice (Shanice Wilson)

b. May 14, 1973, Pittsburgh, PA
Vocals / Teen Pop, Urban, Dance-Pop
A member of the Motown label roster during the 1990s, R&B singer Shanice was best known for her infectious smash "I Love Your Smile." Born May 14, 1973, Shanice Wilson entered show business virtually as a toddler, appearing in a number of musicals and television commercials; by 1984 she was a regular on the series *Kids Incorporated*, and soon after performed on the program *Star Search*. Her appearance there caught the eye of A&M Records, and at the age of 11 Shanice was under contract to the label. She issued her debut *Discovery* in 1987, scoring a pair of minor hits with the singles "(Baby Tell Me) Can You Dance" and "No 1/2 Steppin'." Signing to Motown in 1990, she teamed with producer Narada Michael Walden and recorded *Inner Child*, scoring with the hit "I Love Your Smile" as well as "I'm Cryin'" and "Lovin' You." Shanice subsequently appeared on a number of movie soundtracks, including *Boomerang* and Disney's *Pocahontas*, dueting with Jon Secada on "If I Never Knew You." Her third solo LP, *21 . . . Ways to Grow*, appeared in 1994, followed five years later by her self-titled La Face label debut. *—Jason Ankeny*

Discovery / 1987 / A&M ♦♦♦

Inner Child / 1991 / Motown ♦♦♦
Shanice sure has an impressive voice, including the ability to sing falsetto à la Mariah Carey and Minnie Riperton. In fact, Shanice performs a version of Riperton's "Lovin' You," which is somewhat faithful to the original. Fortunately, even though Shanice was just a teenager when she recorded this album, she doesn't overindulge in the falsetto like Carey did on her early releases. Unfortunately, she does overindulge in rapping, which is not her particular strength. Standout tracks include the hit "I Love Your Smile" and "Silent Prayer," featuring the great voice of Johnny Gill. It's a nice set produced by Narada Michael Walden. *—Tim Griggs*

21 . . . Ways to Grow / Jun. 21, 1994 / Motown ♦♦

Shanice / Mar. 9, 1999 / La Face ♦♦♦

● **Ultimate Collection** / Nov. 16, 1999 / Polygram ♦♦♦♦
Ultimate Collection collects the R&B singer's best singles and album tracks from the late '80s to the mid-'90s, including her early hits "(Baby Tell Me) Can You Dance" and "No 1/2 Steppin'" and the 1991 chart-topper "I Love Your Smile." "I'm Cryin'," "I Wish" and "Turn Down The Lights" are among the other singles gathered in this retrospective. *—Heather Phares*

Shannon (Brenda Shannon Greene)

b. 1958, Washington, D.C.
Vocals / Hi-NRG, Electro, Urban, House, Dance-Pop
Singer Shannon hit gold with the trendsetting, pulsating dance classic "Let the Music Play" and other similar-sounding hits in the mid-'80s. Born Brenda Shannon Greene in Washington, D.C., in 1958, she grew up in Brooklyn and while at college, joined the New York Jazz Ensemble as a singer. While a member, she met drummer Lenny White and sang with Brownstone, which led to some recording. One single, 1983's "Let the Music Play," was issued on the New York-based dance label Emergency Records as a 12-inch single with Shannon listed as the artist. Produced by Mark Liggett and Chris Barbosa, the track's upfront heavy, staccato beats and synth bass marked it as an electro single. The record became a monster club hit, pumped its way up to the pop Top Ten, and sold a million copies. Her debut album titled *Let the Music Play* was issued in February 1984 and went gold, peaking at number-32 pop in March 1984. Shannon followed that up with the Top Ten R&B hit "Give Me Tonight" and "My Heart's Divided."

Do You Wanna Get Away was the title of her second Mirage album, issued in May 1985. The title track single hit number-13 R&B in spring 1985. Her third album *Love Goes All the Way* was released on Atlantic in 1986, with the singles "Dancin'," "Criminal," and "Prove Me Right." Shannon's career was remarkably short-lived, however, due in part to the closing of Emergency Records, some litigation surrounding "Let the Music Play," the decline of dance-oriented radio stations, the loss of club airtime on mainstream radio stations, and the inevitable "Let the Music Play" sound-alike clones that surfaced. Nevertheless, Shannon appeared on a 1999 segment of VH1's *Where Are They Now*, vowing to return to the top of the charts; the following spring she released the album *The Best Is Yet to Come*. *—Ed Hogan*

● **Let the Music Play** / Feb. 1984 / Mirage ♦♦♦♦♦
Shannon wasn't a great singer-as far as dance divas go, she didn't have the chops of Gloria Gaynor, Thelma Houston, Claudja Barry, Donna Summer or Loleatta Holloway. Shannon was merely a competent singer, but a competent singer who sometimes had great material and great producers to work with. And thanks to the production team of Mark Liggett & Chris Barbosa, Shannon's debut album, *Let the Music Play*, has a lot going for it. Liggett & Barbosa give the album an attractive, high-tech sound, and some of the songs that Shannon embraces are excellent. Released in late 1983, the haunting title song went down in history as a dancefloor classic—and club gems like "Give Me Tonight" and "My Heart's Divided" (both of which Barbosa co-wrote) are almost as strong. Shannon successfully ventures into pop-rock territory on "One Man," although she isn't very convincing on the ballads "It's You" and "Someone Waiting Home"—ballads and slow jams were never her strong point. But for the most part, *Let the Music Play* underscores Liggett & Barbosa's ability to make Shannon sound good. *—Alex Henderson*

Do You Wanna Get Away / May 1985 / Mirage ♦♦♦
The dance-pop and urban contemporary markets can be incredibly fickle, and no one knows that better than Shannon. The singer was quite popular from 1983-1985, but by the end of the 1980s, she was considered a has-been. And that's regrettable because even though Shannon wasn't in a class with big-voiced dance divas like Loleatta Holloway and Gloria Gaynor, she was a likable singer who provided her share of infectious dance grooves. Produced by the Mark Liggett & Chris Barbosa team, Shannon's second album, *Do You Wanna Get Away*, was among the most memorable dance-pop/urban releases of 1985. Liggett & Barbosa generally served Shannon well on her first album, *Let the Music Play*, and they also do right by her on this generally pleasing sophomore effort. Anyone who seriously craves dance music would have a hard time not moving to the hit title song, the haunting "Stop the Noise" or Shannon's remake of Foreigner's "Urgent." Shannon doesn't fare as well on the slow jam "Bedroom Eyes"—ballads and slow jams had a way of illustrating her limitations as a vocalist—but most of the time, Shannon, Liggett & Barbosa are a strong combination on the singer's second album. *—Alex Henderson*

Love Goes All the Way / Oct. 1986 / Atlantic ♦♦♦
Going for a decidedly more pop direction on her junior album, Shannon and producers Robbie Buchanan, Patrick Adams and Russell Taylor enhanced her club-friendly style with edgier, more universal strokes. Artistically, the concept worked reasonably, but commercially, it was ill-fated—perhaps this merging of club and pop was ahead of its time. The single "Prove Me Right" made a tiny dent on the R&B charts, but its clever synchronizing of rock guitars and synthesizers with a dancefloor-ready bottom deserved much more exposure. Equally overlooked, the emotive (if slightly glossy) title track brings to mind a merging of a Chaka Khan melody and a Whitney Houston arrangement. True, Shannon doesn't have nearly as much vocal power as either diva, but her restrained, sensitive treatment of the lyric is ultimately just as real. Ironically, the two pure dance numbers that are contained, "Dancin'" and "Sabotage My Heart," don't live up to the caliber of earlier hits like the perennial favorite "Let the Music Play" and "Do You Wanna Get Away." They're produced only somewhat satisfactorily, and the melodies don't pack much punch. Otherwise, the mixture of pop, R&B and dance is a success. *—Justin Kantor*

Dee Dee Sharp (Dione LaRue)

b. Sep. 9, 1945, Philadelphia, PA
Vocals / Philly Soul, Soul
Dee Dee Sharp hit the biggest with her first record for the Cameo/Parkway label, a blessing that pigeonholed the Philly songstress as a teenybopper forever to be identified with her number-one smash from 1962, "Mashed Potatoes Time." Living in Philadelphia, the home of Dick Clark's *American Bandstand* helped her career; she appeared on the syndicated teen dance show many times from 1962 to 1981. The first black female teen idol, Sharp also became a fixture on Clark's Caravan of Stars tours, and a familiar face in the popular *16* magazine. Born Dione LaRue on September 9, 1945, she played piano from an early age, and directed choirs at her grandfather's and other churches in Philadelphia. After her mother suffered debilitating injuries from a car accident when LaRue was only 13, she gained a job as a background singer and developed the skills to work on sessions by Lloyd Price, Frankie Avalon, Fabian, Bobby Rydell, Jackie Wilson, and Chubby Checker.

Lady luck helped when her vocals were added to Chubby Checker's "Slow Twistin'" (1962) making it a duet. Her first solo session was scheduled the next day—the "Mashed Potatoes Time" session—and at 17, Dione LaRue was became an overnight sensation. Producers Kal Mann & Bernie Lowe didn't like LaRue's name so they created Dee Dee Sharp, since everyone called her D and she sang in D sharp. Smaller hits followed: "Gravy (For My Mashed Potatoes)," "Ride," "Do the Bird," "Wild," "Willyam, Willyam," "Never Pick a Pretty Boy," and "I Really Love You" in 1965—Sharp's first R&B record. None sold like her first, but the young singer did all right. She appeared on *American Bandstand* to promote every release; Cameo promoted her as pop so she didn't see much of the chitlin' circuit; the label also sent her to modeling and charm school.

Sharp and Checker hooked up and recorded an album together entitled *Down to Earth*, one of nine LPs that Cameo issued on Sharp (all with blinding colorful colors).

Languishing record sales prompted her exit from Cameo to Atco/Atlantic Records. The Atco deal materialized partly because the label was trying to snag her soon-to-be husband Kenny Gamble to produce records, and used Sharp as bait. Three singles appeared (from 1966-1968) including a duet with Ben E. King ("Whatcha Gonna Do About It"). The tracks, done mostly in Memphis, were harder than the Cameo sides, but the promotion wasn't there. Displeased at Atco's efforts, Sharp, Gamble, and Leon Huff started Gamble Records in 1967, which issued three Dee Dee Sharp singles. Two more appeared on Gamble & Huff's TSOP label, including the LP *Happy 'Bout the Whole Thing.* She then signed with Philadelphia International (PIR)—as Dee Dee Sharp-Gamble—for five singles and "Conquer the World Together," a duet with Bunny Sigler (as David Siqler).

Sharp also collaborated (uncredited) on many of the songs on Gamble Records, but by the time her second PIR album came out, she had begun divorce proceedings, finalized by 1980. A new earthier, sophisticated, foxy Sharp emerged after the Cameo recordings, but nothing happened. While Checker made a career cutting dance hits and became an international superstar, Sharp's career lacked the horsepower, though she maintained good visibility via television, tours, concerts, and club dates that took her around the world. Besides her many television spots, she appeared in films including *Desperately Seeking Susan, Don't Knock the Twist, Hairspray, Sister Act,* and *Troop Beverly Hills.* A beauty, Sharp remarried (to Bill Witherspoon) and has been linked romantically with Gene Chandler, Muhammad Ali, and David Ruffin. Sharp enjoyed a fruitful career, despite minimal chart action after 1966. And except for some racial incidents in the South experienced by many African-American performers in the era, she emerged unscathed, un-addicted, and unscarred. *—Andrew Hamilton*

Down to Earth / 1962 / Cameo ✦✦✦

It's Mashed Potato Time / 1962 / Cameo ✦✦✦✦

Happy 'Bout the Whole Thing / 1976 / Philadelphia International ✦✦

Dee Dee Sharp is best known for "Mashed Potato Time" and "Do the Bird," Top Ten hits in the early '60s. This mid-'70s Philly sound outing has pop leanings that infiltrate the disco so important to the dance music empire of Sharp's husband, Kenneth Gamble. "Love Buddies" is an interesting concept seeing that much of the Philly sound was club oriented, and this first song is the only one penned by Kenneth Gamble & Leon Huff. "Touch My Life" is an adequate tune by James Mendell, but it's Sharp's exquisite voice that really shines, taking over the material and making the entire album listenable. The familiar sounds Sharp creates are a perfect marriage with the Philadelphia sound. Thankfully, she gets the chance to break out of the TSOP formula. The cover of Stan Vincent's "Ooh Child" is sublime, and her cabaret co-write with Mendell on "Real Hard Day" is strong, music that Whitney Houston could send up the charts. "Make It Till Tomorrow," the second of three songs co-written by Dee Dee Sharp, shows a maturity and style, a voice that is always welcome on the radio. Hearing her distinctive and happy cover of the 10CC hit stretch over five minutes and 17 seconds—the longest track on the record—is a delight. Sharp looks stunningly beautiful on the cover and inside photos, and the sounds she emits are superb. She takes the less than perfect "Share My Love" and gives it her best, bringing it to a plateau it simply couldn't reach in lesser hands. Six of the nine titles are written or co-written by associate producer James Mendell, his "Best Thing You Did for Me" a beautiful pop conclusion to this elegant collection. *—Joe Viglione*

● **The Cameo Parkway Sessions** / 1979 / London ✦✦✦✦✦

The Sharpees

Group / R&B, Soul

Recording on George Leaner's One-derful records in Chicago, IL, the Sharpees, like everyone on the label, recorded in a fashion not normally associated with the Chi-town sound, delivering a harder brand of soul that married a myriad of styles. The members were Vernon Guy, Horse O'Toole, Herbert Reeves, and Benny Sharp (guitarist). Stacey Johnson, who also recorded solo for Leaner, joined the Sharpees after their debut "Do the 45" b/w "Make up Your Mind," replacing O'Toole. A second single released in November of 1965, "Tired of Being Lonely," defined their sound of windy male backing harmonies accompanied by females with an unspectacular but competent second tenor lead. A third single from April of 1966, "I've Got a Secret," failed to shake up the charts, and neither did a final One-derful release "My Girl Jean" b/w "The Sock" three months later.

Dormant for three years, they resurfaced on record in 1969 with "Music (I Like It)" on Midas Records as Benny Sharp & the Sharpees. Collectors find anything done on One-derful fantastic, and the Sharpees' recordings can be found on various vinyl and CD compilations that trumpet the One-derful family of labels. O'Toole and Reeves previously sang with the Arabians. Reeves died in January of 1972. *—Andrew Hamilton*

Marlena Shaw

b. Sep. 22, 1942, New Rochelle, NY

Vocals / Mainstream Jazz, Jazz Blues, Jazz-Pop, Ballads, Vocal Pop, Soul

Marlena Shaw is among the most versatile and charismatic jazz vocalists on the scene today. Her performances are marked by an artful blend of pop standards and straight-ahead jazz tunes. Her extroverted stage presence gives her an edge over other vocalists, and clearly, singing live before an audience is where she feels most comfortable.

After her uncle Jimmy Burgess introduced her to the recordings of Dizzy Gillespie and Miles Davis, she caught the jazz bug and purchased records by Al Hibbler, a vocalist who had a big influence on her singing style. When she was ten she performed at Harlem's Apollo Theater, and despite the enthusiastic reception she received in front of one of the world's toughest audiences, her mother refused to let her go on the road with her uncle, a trumpet player. Shaw attended the State Teachers' College in Potsdam, NY, but later dropped out. For some time in 1963 she worked around New England with a trio led by Howard McGhee. By the mid-'60s she was performing regularly for audiences in the Catskills, Playboy clubs, and other New York area clubs. In 1966, she recorded "Mercy, Mercy, Mercy" for Cadet Records, and the single sold very well for an unknown singer. The single's success, a rare vocal version of the tune, prompted executives at Cadet to encourage her to record a whole album for the label in 1967. The diversity of styles, including blues, jazz, and pop standards, is reflected in the album's title, *Out of Different Bags.* Through her accountant, she was brought to the attention of bandleader Count Basie, and she ended up singing with the Basie band for four years.

In 1972, after leaving the Basie Orchestra, Shaw was the first female vocalist signed to Blue Note Records, and she toured for a while with the late Sammy Davis Jr. Shaw recorded five albums and several singles for Blue Note, and critics likened her singing style to Dinah Washington and Sarah Vaughan. At her club shows, Shaw dazzled audiences with her intoxicating blend of straight-ahead jazz, soul, pop, and classic R&B, but her recordings will also satisfy fans of traditional jazz who have no prejudices about blues and R&B. *—Richard Skelly*

Spice of Life / 1969 / Cadet ✦✦✦✦

Marlena Shaw's penchant for stylistic variety is certainly evident on this, her sophomore release. Cut for the Cadet label in 1969, *Spice of Life* ranges from soul and proto-funk to jazz and MOR-hued material. Shaw shines throughout, showing her power on politically charged, Aretha-styled cuts like "Woman of the Ghetto" and "Liberation Conversation," while also delivering supple interpretations of such traditional jazz fare as "Go Away Little Boy" (shades of Nancy Wilson). And with a gutsy take on "Stormy Monday," it's clear Shaw doesn't shrink from the blues either. Across this sound spectrum, arrangers Richard Evans and Charles Stepney envelope Shaw in unobtrusive yet exciting pop-soul environs, throwing kalimba runs (a few years before Earth, Wind & Fire picked up on the instrument), psych guitar accents, and bongo-fueled organ riffs into the mix. Their widescreen touch is particularly well essayed on strings-and-brass standouts like the Bacharach-inspired Barry Mann & Cynthia Weil composition "Looking Through the Eyes of Love" and Ashford & Simpson's "California Soul" (a classic reading heavily favored by the crate-digging set). A perfect way to get familiar with Shaw's impressive early work. *—Stephen Cook*

Who Is This Bitch, Anyway? / 1974 / Blue Note ✦✦✦✦

Just a Matter of Time / 1976 / Blue Note ✦✦✦

Sweet Beginnings / Sep. 1977 / Columbia ✦✦✦✦

After being the most popular female vocalist at Blue Note, with 1974's *Who Is This Bitch, Anyway?,* Shaw often did material that didn't suit her well. Her take on Roberta Flack's "Feel Like Making Love" springs to mind as an instance of Shaw's apparent boredom. Shaw was always an artist who needed to be mentally engaged or the proceedings would be like pulling teeth. This effort finds her challenged, taking on many styles and in amazing voice. *Sweet Beginnings,* her first effort for Columbia, finds her again teamed with producer Bert DeCoteaux. The album's biggest hit was Shaw's tasteful jazz take on Gerry Goffin & Carole King's "Go Away Little Boy. Although her strength is well known, on that track, Shaw's sweetness keeps the assertiveness from being tedious. On the song after giving ultimatums, she finally says, "Do you think you can get a job by Thursday?" *Sweet Beginnings* is one of those efforts that picked up momentum as it went along. The title track is effortless. In the middle of R&B and disco, it more than shows off her assured and sensual vocals. Perhaps the best part of *Sweet Beginnings* is how Shaw's charisma takes over and the lyrics were almost secondary. Both "Look at Me, Look at You" and "Johnny" have Shaw taking on a lighter touch, as each line she sings is emotive and affecting. The album's last track, the brassy, big-band styled "I Think I'll Tell Him" written by Thom Bell & Linda Creed has Shaw almost thrilled to tell her husband that she had been cheating as she sings, "I couldn't help myself sweet baby." *Sweet Beginnings* benefits from a sympathetic production job from Bert DeCoteaux and is one of Shaw's most enduring efforts. *—Jason Elias*

Take a Bite / 1980 / Columbia ✦✦

Like Dee Dee Bridgewater, Marlena Shaw started out as a jazz singer but made a long detour into R&B before returning to her straight-ahead jazz roots. *Take a Bite* was among the albums that Shaw recorded during her R&B period, and this 1979 LP is her most disco-friendly release. Of course, 1979 was the perfect time for her to be disco-friendly—that was the year that gave us classics like Gloria Gaynor's "I Will Survive," Donna Summer's "Bad Girls" and Chic's "Good Times." Many of the soul and disco enthusiasts who bought this record didn't associate Shaw with Count Basie, but the jazz world did—and not surprisingly, myopic jazz snobs believed that Shaw had committed heresy, treason and blasphemy by embracing disco. Some of them probably thought that an exorcism was in order. But truth be told, *Take a Bite* is nothing for the former Basie vocalist to be ashamed of. This LP shouldn't be judged by jazz standards because it doesn't pretend to be jazz; it is, however, an enjoyable disco/soul outing. Shaw takes dead aim at the dance floor with "Suite Seventeen," an extended disco medley that takes up all of side one. "It Was a Very Good Year" is the medley's main song, although "Suite Seventeen" also includes everything from Diana Ross' "Touch Me in the Morning" to Sam & Dave's "I Thank You." A gem that was defined by Frank Sinatra, "It Was a Very Good Year" started out as a traditional pop ballad but works surprisingly well as uptempo disco. Side two, meanwhile, makes some dancefloor moves but also contains a gospel-drenched soul ballad titled "I'll Be Your Friend." *Take a Bite* isn't among Shaw's essential albums, but it's a decent record that fans of late-'70s disco will appreciate. *—Alex Henderson*

Let Me in Your Life / 1982 / South Bay ✦✦✦

In 1982, Marlena Shaw had yet to make her return to straight-ahead jazz singing. R&B was her main focus, but she had gotten away from the sort of outright disco she had embraced in the late '70s. It was that year that the singer recorded *Let Me in Your Life,* an enjoyable urban-contemporary effort that came out on the short-lived South Bay label. Although this rare LP was ignored by radio and didn't do much commercially, it boasts some noteworthy participants: Johnny Bristol and Webster Lewis are the producers, and the musicians include percussionist Paulinho Da Costa and the late alto saxophonist Don

Myrick (best known for his years with Earth, Wind & Fire's Phoenix Horns). The material isn't outstanding, but it's decent; in fact, the ballad "Next Time I Fall in Love," the sleek "Never Give Up on You," and the funky single "More Room at the Top" might have become hits if they had enjoyed the promotional push of a larger label. But unfortunately, the L.A.-based South Bay Records was unable to do as much for Shaw as it would have liked to. *—Alex Henderson*

The Best of Marlena Shaw / Mar. 25, 1997 / Blue Note ♦♦♦♦
Fueled by highly sought fusion musicians of the era (Harvey Mason and Ron Carter are among the many who make appearances) and brilliant production, Marlena Shaw gracefully fuses modern-day funk and soul with her jazz background. Shaw's unique vocal delivery and ability to glue all of these elements together helped to further Blue Note's status into mainstream R&B territory. Nowhere is this more prevalent than her rendition of Marvin Gaye's classic "Save the Children." Calling this compilation *The Best of Marlena Shaw* is somewhat inaccurate, as it's culled from her tenure at Blue Note records from the early '70s and has many of her early Cadet recordings notably absent. However, this should not deter new listeners from giving this a spin, as the performances are predominately top-notch. *—Rob Theakston*

● **Go Away Little Boy: The Sass and Soul of Marlena Shaw** / Apr. 6, 1999 / Columbia/Legacy ♦♦♦♦
Marlena Shaw is one of Columbia's best signings, as she came to the label after the classic 1975 LP *Who Is This Bitch, Anyway?* In short order, Shaw continued to do great work, with a new accent on disco and less jazz-accented R&B. While quite a few compilations get tracks from before or after the artist's tenure there, this concentrates on three late-'70s titles, *Sweet Beginnings, Acting Up,* and *Take a Bite.* The tracks from *Sweet Beginnings* remain the best. Urbane, perfectly sung tracks like "Sweet Beginnings," "Yu-Ma/Go Away Little Boy," and the brassy "I Think I'll Tell Him" provide high points few singers are ever able to accomplish. Later songs "I'm Back for More," "Moonrise," and "The Rhythm of Love" pale in comparison to the work from *Sweet Beginnings.* If anything, *Go Away Little Boy: The Sass and Soul of Marlena Shaw* shows how daring Shaw is. Shaw paired herself with producers and arrangers including Bobby Bryant, Meco Monardo, and Harold Wheeler. While the results could have been disastrous, Shaw came out unscathed. The uncut and sensual disco of "Love Dancin'" to the playful "No One Yet" prove that it was a great move, as Shaw's voice again is vibrant and sensual. This 1999 set was the first time that Shaw's knowing, great, and dancy disco cover of "Touch Me in the Morning" made it to CD. Despite the great artist it spotlights, this set does miss Shaw essentials like "Don't Ask Me to Stay Until Tomorrow," "Johnny," and "Look at Me, Look at You." Even without some songs, this does capture Marlena Shaw's edge. *—Jason Elias*

The Shells

f. 1956, Brooklyn, NY
Group / Doo Wop, R&B
The Shells—led by Nate Bouknight (aka "Little Nat")—scored with a Top 30 hit with "Baby Oh Baby," charting for the tiny Johnson label in 1957. The group—Bouknight, Randy "Shade Alston (tenor), Bobby Nurse (tenor), Danny Small (bass), and Gus Geter (baritone)—continued to wax impressive 45s into the early '60s without much commercial interest, including 1958's "Sippin' Soda" and 1959's "She Wasn't Meant for Me."

In 1960, "Baby Oh Baby" was given a rare second chance when record collectors/archivists/reissue producers Donn Fileti and Wayne Stierle reissued the track to give it a second chance, hitting the pop charts on its second time around, charting at number 21. The Shells then made a hasty comeback, recording a mix of soul and pop standards as well as straight-ahead doo wop, such as "Be Sure My Love" and "So Fine." In 1961, another fine effort, "Explain It to Me" was released, and in 1962, the quintet cut the popular "Happy Holiday" with Ray Jones (aka Ray Lamont Jones) taking over lead vocals. In 1963, the Josie label paired the group together with the Dubs for half an LP, *The Dubs Meet the Shells*, a battle of the bands album in the tradition of *The Paragons Meet the Jesters*). *—Bryan Thomas*

● **Golden Classics** / 1989 / Collectables ♦♦♦♦♦

Badder Than Badd / 1993 / Juke Box Treasures ♦♦♦♦♦
Another entry in JBT's a cappella series, this collects 20 studio tracks of the group doing a mixture of original material penned by producer Wayne Stierle as well as several genre classics. *—Cub Koda*

Shep & the Limelites

f. 1961, Jamaica, NY, **db.** 1966
Group / Doo Wop
Shep & the Limelites' name will forever be etched in rock & roll history for recording the endearing "Daddy's Home," a tender ballad about returning from war that soared to number two on the pop charts in May 1961. James Sheppard's career began with the Heartbeats, a band from Jamaica, Queens, NY. (They were the Hearts until a female group from Harlem with the same name scored a minor hit called "Lonely Nights" in early 1955.) The Hearts would mimic songs by the Orioles, the Ravens, Five Keys, the Moonglows, the Larks, the Flamingos, and others. When not rehearsing, they competed with wannabes in parks and under street corner lamps. During one encounter they battled a group led by James Sheppard; impressed, the Hearts asked Sheppard to be their new lead.

The acquisition of Sheppard helped the Hearts twofold: not only could he blow, he also wrote gorgeous ballads. Shortly after he joined the Hearts, they became the Heartbeat Quintet and started playing clubs, weddings, graduations, ceremonies, and basement parties. Jazz saxophonist Illinois Jacquet befriended them and let them rehearse in his basement. Jacquet's brother arranged their first recording opportunity. "Tormented," a ballad written by Sheppard, was released on Network Records in Philadelphia, but lack of promotion killed any chance of success. After shortening their name to the Heartbeats, they came to the attention of William Miller, who worked for Hull Records. He introduced the quintet to owner Bea Caslin, who was impressed by their tight harmonies and Sheppard's songwriting skills; the group was soon signed to the label. Three initial releases sold well, particularly the magnificent "Your Way"; all were ballads written by Sheppard.

The minor successes of the recordings encouraged Hull Records to invest in professional choreography to tighten the band's stage presentation. Appearances at premier New York venues like the Brooklyn Fox and the Apollo had become common. To the surprise of Hull Records, fans called radio stations in record numbers demanding to hear the flip of "Baby Don't Go," the exquisite "A Thousand Miles Away." Sheppard's craving for an ex-girlfriend who moved to Texas had inspired "A Thousand." Not only did the song do well locally and regionally, it started selling nationwide. Bookings poured in, providing appearances with luminaries like Ray Charles, B.B. King, and the Flamingos. Touring, however, didn't prove lucrative, as they experienced an inordinate share of misfortunes including vehicle breakdowns and promoters leaving with the proceeds. "Daddy's Home" would be the Heartbeats' final Hull Record release.

Bea Caslin then sold the Heartbeats' contract and the publishing rights to the Roulette Record conglomerate. "I Won't Be the Fool Anymore" came out on Rama Records in 1957; after another Rama release, Roulette switched them to Gee Records, and eventually to Roulette itself. "500 Miles to Go" and "After New Year's Eve" were the most successful commercially, while "Down on My Knees" was the most notable artistically. Problems within the group began to show: the last straw came when Sheppard passed out at the microphone in Philadelphia, and bandmate Al Crump sang the lyrics until Sheppard was able to continue. The group wanted to break up after this embarrassment but had commitments, so the group sang on gigs as a quartet doing standards, and Sheppard appeared afterward to sing the Heartbeat hits. They did their last gig in 1959 at the Howard Theater in Washington, D.C., and Sheppard opened a restaurant in Jamaica, Queens, singing solo on the side.

Two years after the the Heartbeats' demise, Sheppard met some old friends—Clarence Bassett and Charles Baskerville of the Videos—and formed Shep & the Limelites. Bassett had also warbled with the Five Sharps. After two flops on Apt. Records, Shep returned to Hull Records and Caslin signed them on the spot. "Daddy's Home" was Shep & the Limelites' first Hull release and it nearly aced the pop chart, stopping at number two. (Ricky Nelson's "Travelin' Man" kept it from the top spot.) Hull released 12 Shep & the Limelites singles between 1961 and 1965. "Our Anniversary" went to number-seven R&B in 1962 and was their only other chart success. Personal differences caused the Limelites to disband by 1966. Baskerville joined the Players, and Bassett sang with the Flamingos and later Creative Funk. Sheppard reunited with the Limelites in 1970 to perform on the oldie revival circuit, but this quickly ended when Sheppard was found on January 24, 1970, shot to death in his car on the Long Island expressway. *—Andrew Hamilton*

● **Daddy's Home to Stay** / Nov. 24, 1998 / WestSide ♦♦♦♦
Shep & the Limelites would have been your average garden-variety late-'50s/early-'60s doo wop group had it not been for the massive talents of their visionary lead singer James Sheppard. Sheppard was the group's songwriter, but more of a storyteller, using connecting themes between songs to create an overall bigger thing, an R&B song cycle, if you will. As the leader of the Heartbeats, he wrote and had hits with "A Thousand Miles Away" and "500 Miles to Go," sentiments that gave his new group a massive "follow-up" hit in "Daddy's Home" and others extending the theme. This two-disc, 44-track set brings together the A- and B-sides of every single, many alternate takes and previously unissued demos to give the most complete overview of this amazingly underrated trio. Many of the master tapes have been remixed to stereo for the very first time and sound wonderful, and there's studio chatter galore on the unissued material. If you only think of Shep & the Limelites as a one-hit wonder, here's exactly where you should go to reassess your thinking. One of doo wop's best-kept secrets. *—Cub Koda*

Daddy's Home: The Very Best of Shep & the Limelites / Jan. 16, 2001 / Collectables ♦♦♦
At 39 tracks long and two discs strong, *Daddy's Home* is only slightly less thorough than the previous anthology *Daddy's Home to Stay.* Still, this collection provides all of the hits as well as demos, outtakes, and alternate versions of songs such as "Why, Why Won't You Believe Me," "This I Know," and "Don't Let Our Love Slip By." "What Did Daddy Do," "Two Loving Hearts," and, of course, "Daddy's Home" are some of this extensive collection's highlights. *—Heather Phares*

The Sheppards

f. 1959, **db.** 1969
Group / Doo Wop, R&B, Soul
An unjustly neglected Chicago sextet boasting twin lead vocalists, the Sheppards bridged the era of doo wop and soul, like the Impressions and the Dells, but never gained the hits to match their excellent recordings. Unlike their more successful contemporaries, they never spent much time at any one label, despite the management and patronage of their namesake: producer and Chicago-area entrepreneur Bill "Bunky" Sheppard. They never entirely let go of the '50s doo wop sound then going out of fashion during the '60s, and though it cost them at the time with record-buyers, the Sheppards recorded dozens of memorable sides.

The origins of the group, as with many of the doo wop era, lie with an assortment of different bands, only some of whom ever recorded. The first group to appear under the Sheppards' name was a South Side unit previously known as the Cavaliers, managed, obviously, by Sheppard and headed by Andre Williams (the legendary soul eccentric later to record for Fortune and produce for Motown). After a pair of singles during 1955-1956 (for Theron and United), this group dissolved, and only one of the members, James Dennis "Brother" Isaac, ever recorded for the Sheppards again. By 1959, a new version of the Sheppards formed from the members of two groups: the Bel-Aires (including Isaac, Millard Edwards and Jimmy Allen) and the Ballads (Murrie Eskridge, O.C. Perkins, and a barely teenaged guitarist named Kermit Chandler).

The Sheppards were among the first signed to Apex, a new label of Sheppard's, and the group's first session in January 1959 yielded one of their highest peaks, the doo wop classic "Island of Love." Propelled by the smoky lead of Millard Edwards, the song became a regional hit—though it never reached the national charts—and earned the Sheppards entry into the local touring circuit. The group recorded six more singles for Apex, with Edwards trading leads with the sweet gospel tenor of Murrie Eskridge, but still failed to reach the charts. The closest, an excellent time-stopping ballad called "Tragic," did earn them a spot on *American Bandstand* though.

After their stint on Apex, the group moved to another Sheppard-affiliated concern, Pam and Wes (both co-owned with Carl Davis), for a pair of singles. Their two best chances for chart action came in 1961 when Vee-Jay picked up "Glitter in Your Eyes," and in 1963 when OKeh issued "Walkin'," but neither influenced record-buyers. Edwards subsequently dropped out and the Sheppards recorded only a few more sessions, including a 1966 date for ABC-Paramount and a 1969 date for Sharp. A few ex-Sheppards recorded solo material, including Edwards (a 1966 single for Constellation under the name Mill Evans) and Isaac (a 1969 single for Sheppard's Bunky label). In 1980, more than ten years after their last recording session, they earned a bit of attention when critic Jay Cocks included a Sheppards reissue on his Top Ten list published in *Time* magazine. *—John Bush*

The Sheppards / 1964 / Solid Smoke ♦♦♦♦♦

Golden Classics / 1989 / Collectables ♦♦♦♦♦

Until WestSide's *Bunky's Picks* was released, Collectables' *Golden Classics* was the best CD collection of the trailblazing recordings of the Sheppards. Even with that 25-track collection on the market, this is still a very good set, containing 18 of the group's best—all of their essentials, really—in a domestically available set. The packaging and sound isn't quite as good as those on the WestSide release, but the music remains tremendous and exciting, finding the Sheppards pushing past doo wop and into soul with their passionate, beautiful R&B. *—Stephen Thomas Erlewine*

★ **Bunky's Picks** / Oct. 13, 1998 / WestSide ♦♦♦♦♦

WestSide's *Bunky's Picks* is the best collection ever assembled on the Sheppards, an under-appreciated and pioneering sextet from Chicago. As Bill Dahl points out in his excellent liner notes, the Sheppards legacy was largely ignored until Solid Smoke reissued their music on a vinyl collection in 1980, named by *Time* critic Jay Cocks as one of the Top Ten albums of that year. This fact illustrates not just that this music lasts, but that it's perhaps even easier to respect its achievement and power years later, when it's possible to put it into perspective with what came before and since. With that hindsight, it's not hard to hear this group as a pivot point for the music—a harmony group with its roots in doo wop, but tackled a number of different sounds, including rock, pop and blues, and helped point the direction toward soul. This doesn't necessarily mean they were influential. They were based in Chicago and were rarely heard outside of that area, and while their manager and namesake Bunky Sheppard was a major figure on the scene, managing numerous other groups (most notably the Esquires), it's hard to tell if this group in particular was influential on the musicians of the '60s. That said, the music stands as prescient, tremendous music; perhaps the very fact that it was created and exists in a vacuum makes it all the more remarkable. Throughout these 25 songs, many doo wop traits surface, but it's hardly street-corner harmony, due to the instrumentation, vocal arrangements and how pop hooks, humor, flashes of blues guitar, sweet melodies and strings all combine in different ways to suggest the Chicago soul of the '60s. Based on these songs, it sounded as if they could have done anything, but they also managed to seem slightly behind and ahead of their time, so they never made waves at the time. Looking back, this is absolutely stellar music. Cocks wasn't kidding when he named this among the best 1980 had to offer. *Bunky's Picks* ranks among the best 1998 had to offer, too, and whenever you hear this for the first time, this will be among the best music you'll hear all year, too. *—Stephen Thomas Erlewine*

The Sherrys

Group / Rock & Roll, R&B

The Sherrys were a short-lived girl group with a rich, soulful sound, built around dance numbers that they performed with extraordinary exuberance, organized by Philadelphia singing star Little Joe Cook. A veteran of gospel and R&B, Cook had led a group called the Thrillers from the mid-'50s until 1961, when he began putting a group together around his two daughters, Delphine and Dinell Cook, their cousin Charlotte Butler, and Delores "Honey" Wiley. At one point early in the days of the group's formation, future Motown star Tammi Montgomery (later Terrell) was a member. The group spent a lot of its early days backing other Philadelphia-based acts, including Bobby Rydell, on their recordings. Their big moment as a recording act in their own right came when a dance craze arose in New Orleans called the Popeye—initially, the dance was done to Chris Kenner's "Something You Got," but Eddie Bo soon came along with "Check Mr. Popeye," which became a major seller in New Orleans. By early 1962, the dance was being touted as a rival to the Twist, with acts as different as Huey "Piano" Smith & the Clowns and Chubby Checker starting to push it.

Cook, who'd seen his own recording of "Let's Do the Slop" become a serious regional hit in 1956, knew a good prospect when he saw it and had the Sherrys record "Pop Pop Pop-Pie," written by producers Johnny Madera and Dave White and aimed at the dance crowd. *American Bandstand* then featured the group and the record heavily, and the single (issued on Guyden) charted in October of 1962, for an eight week run that carried it up to number 35 nationally on the pop charts and to number 25 on the R&B lists. The group's success was short-lived, however, as they never came up with a suitable follow-up—their "Slop Time" didn't chart nearly as well.

A superb album, *At the Hop With the Sherrys*, made up almost entirely of Madera-White songs, appeared on Guyden in early 1963, but it undeservedly disappeared without leaving much of a trace. Ironically, while the Sherrys' moment in the sun in the U.S. proved to be both brief and over, their records were extremely popular and enduring in Europe, where audiences devoured their authentic soul-dance sound. The quartet ended up touring overseas twice, with great success. They might've regained their career momentum in America, but for a series of personnel and business difficulties that ensued over the next several months. Delphine, the younger Cook daughter, married, and then Butler left the act soon after. Cook held a version of the Sherrys together to fulfill bookings, but during a successful engagement in Boston, the group—now a trio—decided to get a new manager. Their history came to an end with this decision, because Cook owned the name the Sherrys. The trio, deprived of the name under which they were known, was never heard from again, and the Sherrys became part of pop music and dance history. *—Bruce Eder*

● **Pop Pop Pop-Pie** / 1996 / Bear Family ♦♦♦

The Shirelles

f. 1958, Passaic, NJ, **db.** 1982

Group / Brill Building Pop, Girl Group, Pop

The Shirelles were instrumental in defining the girl group sound, and were one of the style's most successful acts between 1960 and 1963, when they placed six singles in the Top Ten. Bridging doo wop and uptown New York pop-soul, the group projected a beguiling mixture of tenderness and innocence that was grounded in R&B as much as pop/rock. Forming as high school classmates in New Jersey, the Shirelles came under the wing of manager Florence Greenberg, who also ran the Scepter label. Many of their classic early sides featured innovative, occasionally string-laden production by Luther Dixon, who also penned several of their greatest songs. Top Brill Building pop songwriters like Goffin-King, Bacharach-David, and Van McCoy also supplied the group with material. "Will You Love Me Tomorrow," "Baby It's You," "Foolish Little Girl," "Soldier Boy," "Dedicated to the One I Love," and "Mama Said" were their biggest hits, but they also cut a number of less-famous sides, including "Boys," which (like "Baby It's You") was covered by the Beatles on their first LP. After mid-1963, the Shirelles were unable to dent the Top 40, although they recorded several songs, including the original version of "Sha La La" (covered for a hit by Manfred Mann). The group recorded well into the '70s, updating their sound into a more soul-oriented mode. *—Richie Unterberger*

Baby It's You / 1962 / Sundazed ♦♦♦

The best songs on here—the title track, "Big John," "A Thing of the Past," "Make the Night a Little Longer," "Soldier Boy," and "Putty in Your Hands"—are available on the Rhino best-of double album. Still, it's a pretty solid effort for its day, featuring state-of-the-art orchestral early-'60s New York girl group production and decent songwriting. *—Richie Unterberger*

A Shirelles & King Curtis Give a Twist Party / 1962 / Sundazed ♦♦

This was a rather strange concept for an early-'60s album, pairing the Shirelles, then at the peak of their success, with R&B/soul sax great King Curtis. It's not so much a collaboration as an alternation; Curtis gets three instrumentals to himself, and sings "I Got a Woman" and another cut. King does duet with the girls on "I Still Want You," and the Shirelles handle the rest of the material, mostly written by their chief producer/songwriter Luther Dixon, in a much more uptempo vein than their famous singles. No hits on this record, which is respectable but not terribly exciting, and a bit schizo in concept. *—Richie Unterberger*

Anthology (1959–1964) / 1986 / Rhino ♦♦♦♦♦

In the course of eight years, Rhino came out with two separate but very similar Shirelles anthologies. The first was 1986's *Anthology: 1959-1964*, followed by *The Very Best of the Shirelles* in 1994. Both are 16-song CDs, and many of the essential hits that were included on *Very Best* were also found on this CD, including "Tonight's the Night," "Dedicated to the One I Love," "Mama Said," and "Will You Love Me Tomorrow" (as well as "Boys," "A Thing of the Past," "Soldier Boy," and "Big John"). The main reason *Very Best Of* has a slight edge over this disc is because of its inclusion of the 1958 doo wop classic "I Met Him on a Sunday (Ronde-Ronde)," which is missing from *Anthology*. Both CDs, however, are full of gems that would greatly influence countless girl groups. These songs were undeniably seminal, and the late-'50s/early-'60s harmonies of the Shirelles would directly or indirectly influence everyone from the Supremes, the Marvelettes, the Shangri-Las, and Martha & the Vandellas in the 1960s to LaBelle, First Choice, the Three Degrees, and the Pointer Sisters in the 1970s. How many groups who influenced the Go-Gos and Blondie also had an impact on En Vogue? The importance of the Shirelles hits found on this CD cannot be overstated. *—Alex Henderson*

The Best of the Shirelles / 1992 / Ace ♦♦♦♦♦

This album consists of 32 Shirelles classics. Before the Supremes, the Shirelles was the definitive female vocal group—everybody's sweethearts—who waxed songs by the best writers the Brill Building had to offer. Their recordings don't sound dated like the vast majority of tunes from that era do today. Still strong are "Dedicated to the One I Love," "Tonight's the Night," "Will You Love Me Tomorrow," "Baby It's You," "Soldier Boy," plus a whole slew of just as good, but not as well known, masterpieces. *—Andrew Hamilton*

For Collectors Only / 1995 / Collectables ♦♦♦♦

Having 68 songs spread among three CDs may seem like a little more of the Shirelles than most listeners want, but the truth is that even the group's non-hit singles were so strong (especially the heartbreaking misses from late 1963 onward) that it's hard to speak of overkill, even in addressing relatively casual fans—they will find plenty to like here, far beyond "Mama Said," "Soldier Boy," and "Will You Love Me Tomorrow." If everything isn't on the level of soaring passions exhibited in "Tonight's the Night," it's still all nicely crafted and beautifully sung early-'60s pop-soul, some of which had a profound influence on white rock & roll when the Beatles took two of the group's songs, "Boys" and "Baby It's You," and added them to their stage repertory and, by extension, to their debut LP. More British Invasion influence can be found on disc two, with "It's Love That Really Counts," which became a key part of the repertory of the Merseybeats. But going into 1964 and songs like "Till My Baby Comes Home," the group was still producing superb music, even if relatively few people were buying the records by then. This set is a reminder of just how far the quality of the Shirelles' work extended beyond those hit singles, even when they started becoming highly derivative (as on "Bright Shiny Colors," which borrows its opening and chorus from "I Count the Tears"), right up through the very Motown-sounding "Last Minute Miracle," their final charting record. One comes away with the realization that, if the Shirelles didn't always make great records, or the most original-sounding music, they almost never issued anything that wasn't a lot of fun to hear, and was often diverting in the bargain. The sound throughout is very good if not exceptional, and most of this set is derived from the stereo versions of the masters, which are good and loud and do reveal a wealth of detail in the playing and singing. There are only a few complaints—the producers either didn't (or couldn't) reach back to the MCA-owned original version of "I Met Him on a Sunday" and the group's two other early, pre-Scepter records releases; there's also no discography, or even a list of release dates; and the notes only address a small portion of the songs included here. But this is still nearly three hours of always enjoyable, sometimes enlightening listening. *—Bruce Eder*

Lost & Found / Dec. 1, 1995 / Ace ♦♦
Here are 29 songs from the Scepter vaults, most not released when the Shirelles were active (a few found their way onto flop singles, as well as the 1965 album *Swing the Most*). Even Shirelles fans might find this album disappointing, though it's a long way from horrible. Much of the material was probably recorded after their 1960-1963 prime (the source dates remain vague). This era often found them trying to emulate commercial pop-soul trends (particularly Motown) without much personality, and without the benefit of distinctive material. Goffin-King, Bacharach-David, David Gates, and Ashford-Simpson gave the group (little-known) compositions during this era. But while the results were competent, they were forgettable, despite the odd better-than-average track like the pleading "Remember Me," or the soulful "I'm Yours." *—Richie Unterberger*

★ **25 All-Time Greatest Hits** / Jul. 27, 1999 / Varese ♦♦♦♦♦
This is an excellent 26-song single-disc collection that has all of the significant hits and several very fine low-charting 45s and B-sides. Some good tracks are missing, however, notably "Putty" (which the Yardbirds covered) and Goffin-King's "Make the Night a Little Longer." Rhino's *Anthology* double LP still has a tiny edge in song selection if you can find it, but if you're not real picky this is certainly a quality summary of their career highlights. There are also a few items that don't show up on all the best-ofs, like the 1961 B-side "The Things I Want to Hear" and the small 1964 hit "Thank You, Baby." *—Richie Unterberger*

Shirley & Lee

f. 1951, New Orleans, LA, **db.** 1963
Group / New Orleans R&B, R&B
Shirley Goodman & Leonard Lee, born just ten days apart in 1936, scored three massive R&B hits before either one of them were both 20 years old: "Feel So Good," "Let the Good Times Roll," and "I Feel Good" were all written by the talented young couple. They had one trait in common among their recordings; this New Orleans-based duo almost never sang in harmony, let alone together at all. Their contrasting male-female duet style was later influential on early ska and reggae productions from Jamaica. Shirley & Lee recorded extensively for Eddie Messner & Leo Messner's L.A.-based Aladdin label. The Messners—along with former NBC radio exec. Lew Chudd's Imperial Records and Art Rupe's Specialty—seemed to have a knack for signing talent straight out of the Crescent City.

Shirley & Lee's debut single, "I'm Gone," was written and produced by Dave Bartholomew, Imperial's writer/arranger/producer/A&R man and a major contributor to New Orleans-style R&B. (It was Bartholomew's production work with Fats Domino which utilized that talents of a great house band—pianist Allen Toussaint, bassist Frank Fields, drummer Earl Palmer, and saxophonists Lee Allen, Alvin "Red" Tyler, and Herb Hardesty—that elevated nearly everything he worked on to "legendary" status.) With their backing "I'm Gone" went on to become a major R&B hit in the fall of 1952.

Early in their careers, Shirley & Lee became known as "the Sweethearts of the Blues," a nickname given not for their personal relationship, but for their romantic sagas of their songs, which often bordered on telling a fictional soap-opera storyline about two lovers. Their fans would buy the singles simply to keep up with the continuing story of the two sweethearts. The story continued with the very next single, "Shirley Come Back to Me," a heartbreaker released in early 1953, followed by "Shirley's Back," later that year. This happy theme continued through the happy ending for the next single, "The Proposal" b/w "Two Happy People." By the end of the year, Aladdin was reveling in success of the story of Shirley & Lee. Of course, the couple in the songs had already been apart and were now back together, so they had to shake things up with the next release, called "Lee Goofed," and followed that with "Confessin'" but by now the audience seemed to be tiring of the soap opera, so Shirley & Lee moved on to new lyrical subject matter.

Messner decided to try something new for the duo in May of 1955, issuing a medium-tempo rocker called "Feel So Good." The song featured full vocal group backup (reportedly by the Spiders) and did well, but it was the bluesy B-side, "You'd Be Thinking of Me," that put the duo back on the R&B hit charts. "Lee's Dream" also charted. In early 1956, Aladdin released the duo's slow blues ballad, "A Little Word," which received good airplay, but sales weren't spectacular. Trying to get back on track, Aladdin finally opted to issue a full-length album, *Let the Good Times Roll*, in December. It was reissued two years later on Score, Aladdin's budget label.

By the middle of 1957, Shirley & Lee were back on top, this time with the biggest hit in their careers. Goodman and Lee borrowed one of New Orleans' most familiar refrains and built a rocking tune around it called "Let the Good Times Roll." The recording was an instant smash and received substantial airplay, climbing up the charts in the process. It sold well-over one million copies and for more than 40 years has been a staple of oldies play lists. To date, there are over a hundred cover versions of the song, but most still prefer the original. The pair stayed on Aladdin into 1959 before moving to Warwick, where they ended up re-recording "Let the Good Times Roll." Other tunes followed—"I Feel Good" and "The Flirt" among them—but like many acts, Shirley & Lee were never able to recapture the nationwide success of their biggest hit. After a few final singles in 1962-1963, this time for Imperial—Aladdin and Imperial continued their rivalry and tried to one-up each other until Aladdin was acquired by Imperial outright—the "Sweethearts of the Blues" decided to call it a day.

In 1974, Shirley Goodman reappeared on the R&B scene, this time paired with studio musicians—they called themselves Shirley & Company—for "Shame, Shame, Shame," released on the Vibration label. (The song also featured Jesus Alvarez supplying lead vocals). The disco-fied hit topped the R&B charts at number one that summer and peaked at number 12 on the pop charts. It was written by producer Sylvia Robinson, who had also been part of a successful '50s duo, Mickey & Sylvia, with Mickey Baker. Robinson also penned Goodman's less successful follow-up "Cry, Cry, Cry." They issued one more single on Vibration, then dropped out of sight. Leonard Lee passed away on October 23, 1976. *—Bryan Thomas*

Let the Good Times Roll / 1956 / EMI America ♦♦♦

The Legendary Masters Series, Vol. 1 / Mar. 16, 1990 / Collectables ♦♦♦♦♦
Shirley & Lee were responsible for a few enduring classics of New Orleans rock & roll, particularly "Let the Good Times Roll," which topped the R&B charts and crossed over to the pop Top 20 in 1956. Shirley Goodman's helium voice is simply unforgettable, and her partner, Leonard Lee, was a talented teenage songwriter. *The Legendary Master Series, Vol. 1* is a reissue of a deleted 1991 anthology, and contains all of the duo's Aladdin hits and more with extensive notes and annotation. Serious collectors may wish to seek out Bear Family's four-disc box set of Shirley & Lee's complete Aladdin recordings, but most buyers will be content with this excellent distillation. *—Greg Adams*

Sweethearts of the Blues / Mar. 18, 1997 / Bear Family ♦♦♦♦♦
Many folks only know New Orleans R&B through the teenage singing and songwriting duo of Shirley Goodman & Leonard Lee, who penned and recorded the definitive version of the most explosive party tune of all time (with the possible exception of "Great Balls of Fire" that came six years later), "Let the Good Times Roll." Given the fact that this box set is four CDs in length, anyone who believes that Shirley & Lee were mainly responsible for that smash hit alone have incomplete knowledge of the duo. Here are 113 performances that include all of their singles, outtakes, albums, and unreleased and rehearsal tracks, which serve not only as a chronology of the pair's contribution to the Crescent City's R&B tradition, but as a portrait of the studio scene and its players who were already changing musical history. This set has all the chapters of their "Sweethearts of the Blues" story on disc one and then gets deep into their scorching, risqué, utterly moving, and joyous R&B tracks. The "Sweethearts of the Blues" moniker was concocted by Aladdin, their label, as a way of getting regional fame based upon the success of their first single, "Sweethearts" and "I'm Gone." When they had the "Sweethearts" angle in place, Shirley & Lee began to write songs to match the chapters in a love affair. With "I'm Gone," the first chapter was written; next came "Shirley, Come Back to Me," which was followed by "Shirley's Back" (the alternate take of which is the better of the two), "So in Love," "The Time Has Come," "I Love You So," "The Proposal," and "Two Happy People," before Lee got sick of it and wrote "Lee Goofed." The folks in New Orleans and throughout the regional South followed the pair's antics on record and Aladdin's scheme worked. Shirley & Lee even had a stage routine to go with the songs! This set documents Shirley & Lee's regional successes and their gradual national buildup, which broke down popular culture's door nationwide with "Let the Good Times Roll." Finally, the appeal of the pair was noticed in terms of the raw excitement they provided. The record broke out of New Orleans like a rocket and didn't stop for years. DJs everywhere were playing the hell out of it until about 1960, four years after it was released! The pair's edgy, sharp voices enunciated perfectly above the crackling din of the Crescent City's finest musicians.

And that's the other part of the story—that many players, such as Dave Bartholomew (who first recorded them commercially), Earl Palmer, Alvin "Red" Tyler, Lee Allen, James Booker, Frank Fields, Herbert Hardesty, Wardell Quezergue, and many others played on dozens of these records. Bartholomew, Palmer, Tyler, and Allen appear on almost everything here! The cream of the crop in New Orleans backed these two singer/songwriters. And as a unit, the combination was unbeatable, as the Aladdin, Warwick, and Imperial sides all attest. Just check the deep horn section swing on "When I Saw You," or hear Allen check out of the stratosphere on "The Reason Why" and "Why Did I," or Booker's flailing arpeggios on "Honey Bee." When listening to this box, a foggy part of American musical history begins to reveal itself, the other side of the rock & roll coin that white Americans were obsessed with in Elvis, Jerry Lee Lewis, and fakes like Pat Boone and Frankie Avalon. This is the other side, a musically diverse and challenging catalog that drove black audiences wild all over America under the noises of white kids who would have flipped if they'd only had the opportunity to hear Shirley & Lee. New Orleans, being what it is, would probably have remained unchanged, but it might have gotten a different kind of attention for its musical wealth in the same way that Memphis did, where its musicians would be regarded as kings throughout the rest of the world—and not just among other musicians. But these are all big "ifs." Shirley & Lee created an atmosphere conducive to asking those kinds of questions while listening, but this collection does plenty more—for starters, it makes you get your damn shoes off, take your loved one in your arms, and begin to slip and shimmy all over the floor until.... There is no higher tribute for great R&B music than to inspire people to dance and to get busy, and this music certainly does that. *—Thom Jurek*

● **Let the Good Times Roll** / May 2, 2000 / Ace ♦♦♦♦♦
The track listing of this 30-song disc is based on the 1973 double-LP Shirley & Lee compilation in United Artists' *Legendary Masters* series, with "I Feel Good" substituted for "Do You Mean to Hurt Me So." Spanning their 1952-1959 work for Aladdin, it's comprehensive enough to serve as a best-of, particularly as it included the four songs that are by far their most famous cuts: "Let the Good Times Roll," "I'm Gone," "I Feel Good," and "Feel So Good." As the American best-of CD compilation *Legendary Masters* (issued first

on EMI America, then on Collectables) has only 20 numbers, one might presume that this 30-track anthology has the edge. It doesn't make the *Legendary Masters* CD redundant, though, as *Legendary Masters* has seven songs that don't appear here. At any rate, *Let the Good Times Roll* will almost certainly be a sufficient overview of the duo's prime output for those who haven't picked up a Shirley & Lee greatest hits anthology yet. Truth to tell, for most listeners 30 Shirley & Lee songs is more than enough, as the accomplished, good-timey New Orleans R&B/rock groove gets pretty similar-sounding over the course of an hour-plus. One thing you could note is how the contrasting male-female duet style of Shirley & Lee was influential on early ska and reggae productions from Jamaica; listen to "Marry Me" for one instance in which Shirley & Lee themselves played calypso/Caribbean rhythms. It's also interesting to note that almost all of the material on this disc was self-penned, an impressive feat for teenage R&B singers of the '50s. *—Richie Unterberger*

Shirley & Company

f. 1974, **db.** 1976

Group / Disco, Funk

Almost 23 years after teaming with Leonard Lee, Shirley Goodman reappeared on the R&B scene. This time she was paired with studio musicians on "Shame, Shame, Shame," with Jesus Alvarez supplying lead vocals. The song topped the R&B charts and peaked at number 12 on the pop side in 1975 for Vibration Records. It was written by Sylvia Robinson, who had also been part of a successful '50s duo with Mickey Baker. Robinson also penned the less successful follow-up "Cry Cry Cry." Shirley & Company issued one more single on Vibration, then dropped out of sight. *—Ron Wynn*

• **Shame Shame Shame** / 1975 / Vibration ✦✦✦

An eclectic mix of funk, disco, Caribbean, moody R&B, and pop influences, this hidden gem of an album followed the surprising comeback success that Shirley Goodman—one-half of legendary 1950s duo Shirley & Lee—enjoyed with the single of the same name. Penned and produced by Vibration founder Sylvia Robinson, "Shame, Shame, Shame" was one of the earliest examples of disco, following in the footsteps of efforts like George McCrae's "Rock Your Baby" and the Hues Corporation's "Rock the Boat," but with a notably soulful grip. The tune's nifty guitar strolls, spirited piano licks, and persistent percussion, combined with the utter enthusiasm of Goodman and male vocalist Jesus Alvarez, make for a hard-to-resist concoction. The album isn't limited to the fiery antics of that song; all of its selections share a common feel-good vibe. Perhaps the most celestial moment is the endearing, easily coaxing "I Gotta Get Next to You"; it's truly rare to find a ballad so simultaneously soulful and relaxed. Additionally, both "Love Is" and "I Guess Things Have to Change" are sprightly, mellow numbers with fluid horn arrangements and vocal lines that showcase Alvarez's impressive writing skills. Goodman co-wrote several tunes as well: the reggae-influenced "Jim Doc Kay" and the sassy "Keep on Rolling On." The two vocalists trade verses on a number of tunes, making for a unique, well-rounded sound. "Cry, Cry, Cry" and "Disco Shirley," two takeoffs on the initial hit, were released as follow-up singles that didn't fare so well. In 1976, Vibration also released a non-album single, "I Like to Dance," featuring Goodman paired with a new male vocalist (surprisingly, Collectables didn't include this on its CD reissue). Perhaps if one of the album's more divergent efforts had been chosen as a single instead, success wouldn't have been as fleeting. *—Justin M. Kantor*

Shotgun

f. Detroit, MI

Group / Funk, Urban, Soul

This was a Detroit funk group whose enthusiasm didn't pay off in hit singles. Trumpeter Richard Sebastian, saxophonist Greg Ingram, keyboardist/lead guitarist Billy Talbert, guitarist Ernest Latimore, bassist Larry Austin, drummer/vocalist Tyrone Steels, and percussionist Leslie Carter made entertaining songs in the best Ohio Players/Slave/Cameo mode but never could land the elusive hit. They also toured with Rick James while recording for ABC, MCA, and Montage in the late '70s and early '80s. *—Ron Wynn*

• **Shotgun** / 1977 / ABC ✦✦✦

This six-man funk outfit's debut album showcased two single releases. "Hotline" is a moderately paced funk cut with lyrics that are somewhat vague with regard to the song's message; the number peaked at number 87 after seven weeks on the *Billboard* R&B charts. "Mutha Funk" is a pumpin' number which lives up to its title; however, the single only managed a number-67 ranking after staying on the charts one week longer than the album's initial release. Most of the vocals are poorly arranged. As funky as this group's music is, many cuts are heavily doused with rock & roll. *—Craig Lytle*

Good, Bad and Funky / Jan. 1978 / ABC ✦✦

Shotgun was a band that never lived up to its potential—not creatively, not commercially. The Detroit outfit never enjoyed a major hit, nor did it provide any albums that were truly mind-blowing. But the potential for greatness was definitely there, and with the right guidance and direction, it might have developed into something special. Unfortunately, ABC's A&R department let them settle for competent instead of pushing it to excel. Although their second album, *Good, Bad and Funky*, isn't bad, it isn't great either. Everything on the 1978 LP is merely decent; this is true of the hard funk offerings (which include "Fire It Up" and the title song) as well as sleeker sophisticated funk ("I'm All Strung Out," "Love Attack," and "Danger of the Stranger"), and the smooth Northern soul ballad "I Wish I Could See You Again." Throughout the record, one finds himself/herself admiring Shotgun's attractive sound—which is best described as a combination of the Ohio Players, the Bar-Kays, and Cameo—while knowing that the writing could be stronger. Again, *Good, Bad and Funky* isn't bad, but Shotgun was capable of a lot more. *—Alex Henderson*

Shotgun III / Feb. 1978 / MCA ✦✦✦

In the 1970s, it wasn't uncommon for a funk band to be totally self-contained—meaning that it did all of its own writing, playing, producing, and arranging. Shotgun wasn't totally self-contained; the Motor City combo worked with outside producers and brought in guest musicians. However, Shotgun did most of its own writing, which was a problem because its members weren't great composers. The band had an attractive sound, but most of its writing was merely competent. Take *Shotgun III*, for example; all of the songs that they wrote for their third album are adequate, but none are remarkable. The hard funk jams (which include "Skate," "Big Legs," and "Midnight Breakdown") are competent, and so is the romantic Northern soul ballad "Special Lady." However, Shotgun never excels and never achieves the greatness it was capable of. Shotgun was hoping that this 1979 LP would contain a major hit, but commercial success continued to elude the Detroit funksters, who settled for beer when they should have been pouring champagne. *—Alex Henderson*

Shotgun IV / 1980 / MCA ✦✦✦

After recording three albums for ABC, Shotgun moved to MCA with its fourth album, *Shotgun IV*. This 1980 LP also marked a few personnel changes; trumpeter William Gentry and drummer Robert Resch were gone, and trumpeter/trombonist Rickey Sebastian (who also contributed some lead and background vocals) came on board. Neither the personnel changes nor the label switch had much of an impact either creatively or commercially—the band still couldn't score a major hit, and it still provided a lot of material that was adequate but not remarkable. Hard funk items like "Come On and Dance," "I Want You," and "Go Head" are catchy enough, but Shotgun still had yet to qualify as funk royalty. However, this album does contain the Detroiters' most memorable ballad: "Standing in Need of Love." Funk, not ballads, was the band's main focus, but "Standing in Need of Love" points to the fact that Shotgun could, on occasion, deliver an enjoyable Northern soul ballad. None of the songs on this LP are bad—Shotgun never recorded a bad album, but unfortunately, it never recorded a great one either. *—Alex Henderson*

Kingdom Come / 1980 / MCA ✦✦

The Show Stoppers

f. Philadelphia, PA

Group / Pop-Soul

The Show Stoppers were Philadelphians, and recorded in the States, but had their only hit courtesy of the United Kingdom. Two sets of siblings made up the quartet: Timmy and Earl Smith, and Alec and Laddie Burke (brothers of popular soul man Solomon Burke). They formed at Germantown High School and rehearsed religiously under the guiding hand of the elder Burke. All were either 18 or 19 years old when "Ain't Nothing but a House Party" broke in England. Written by Joseph Thomas and produced by Del Sharah, that dance song was first released on Showtime Records, a small local company, and sold around 40,000 copies in the Philadelphia area. Showtime didn't have the means or the inclination to release the record nationally. That would have been it, but producer Jerry Ross purchased the master from Showtime and released it on his newly founded Heritage Label, distributed by MGM Records.

Ross even came onboard as the group's co-manager, and produced more sessions for the exciting act, who more than lived up to their name. Bad luck followed, however, and subsequent releases, "Eeny Meeny," "What Can a Man Do," and "How Easy Your Heart Forgets" flopped. DJs in England soon began spinning "Ain't Nothing but a House Party" though, and created demand not only for the record but for live appearances as well. Unfortunately, the real Show Stoppers were beaten to the punch by bogus groups performing in Europe pretending to be the Show Stoppers. (The group later known as the Persuaders, who would later score with "Thin Line Between Love and Hate," did an entire European tour as the Show Stoppers.) The authentic Show Stoppers eventually traveled to Europe and were well-received. Although two of the members were brothers of Solomon Burke, it didn't seem to help the group. They were victims of bad management and probably never saw much money for their efforts. Disappointed, the electrifying act called it quits and never surfaced again. *—Andrew Hamilton*

The Showmen

f. 1960, Norfolk, VA, **db.** 1968

Group / Pop-Soul, New Orleans R&B, Soul, Beach

The Showmen were one of the R&B groups to bridge the gap between doo wop and soul in the early '60s, creating a buoyant, energetic fusion of harmonies and propulsive R&B beats. The group only had one hit, "It Will Stand," which charted both in 1961 and in 1964, but their lead singer, General Johnson, went on to greater success as the leader of the '70s soul group Chairmen of the Board.

Formed in Norfolk, VA, in the early '60s, the Showmen consisted of Johnson (born Norman Johnson, May 23, 1943), Leslie Felton, Gene Wright, Dorsey Wright, and Milton Wells. In 1961, the group signed with Minit Records, which was based in New Orleans. Their first single was a rock & roll anthem, "It Will Stand." Released in the fall of 1961, "It Will Stand" was a hit, particularly on the East Coast and in the New Orleans era, but it only peaked at number 61 on the pop charts. Nevertheless, the song's popularity never decreased and it became a hit three years later, when re-released on the Imperial label. On its second release, the single peaked at number 80 on both the R&B and pop charts. Between the two chart appearances of "It Will Stand," the Showmen kept recording and performing. During this time, they had no national hits, but "39-21-46" became a significant regional hit. In 1965, the group signed with Swan Records, but none of the ensuing singles became hits.

In 1968, Johnson left the band and moved to Detroit, where he formed the Chairmen of the Board, who would later have hits with "Give Me Just a Little More Time," "(You've Got Me) Dangling on a String," and "Everything's Tuesday" in the early '70s. In the three decades after the breakup of the Showmen, "It Will Stand" and "39-21-46" remained popular on the East Coast "beach music" scene and Johnson would later return to this area, carving out a living as a local performer. *—Stephen Thomas Erlewine*

Some Folks Don't Understand It / 1962 / Charly ♦♦♦

● **It Will Stand** / Apr. 24, 1990 / Collectables ♦♦♦♦♦

Collectables' collection *It Will Stand* hardly stands as a complete overview of the fine vocal group's work. Still, at 16 tracks, it stands as the closest available in the CD age, especially since it focuses on their best, most popular work for Minit records. This means it bypasses their handful of sides for labels like Swan and Itzy and several smaller imprints, but it does have three tracks cut for Instant, along with five previously unissued tracks (including alternate takes). Complete, it may not be, but it's satisfying all the same, capturing why the group is beloved by many collectors of vocal harmony and beach music. Foremost among their jewels, of course, is the title track, a swinging testament to rock & roll's lasting impact. It may only have been a small hit upon its initial release in 1961, gaining a few more fans in its 1964 re-release, but it's a cult favorite, thanks to its sweet tribute to rock & roll and to lead singer General Norman Johnson's powerhouse lead vocals. Johnson later came to prominence as the leader of the Chairmen of the Board, where his stuttering exuberant vocals propelled the group to several hits including "Give Me Just a Little More Time," but his vocals are nearly as good here, illustrating how this band were one of the key acts in the transition between doo wop and soul. The harmonies, and several of the songs, are very much in the tradition of late-50s street-corner harmony, but Johnson's forceful vocals and the bouncy uptempo material are much closer to the pop-soul that would later form the core of mid-'60s soul. Yes, a few of the songs are a little generic, but many are either dynamic or romantic, which is why this collection is necessary for serious soul listeners until a better, logical, more comprehensive compilation comes along. *—Stephen Thomas Erlewine*

Side Effect

f. 1972, Los Angeles, CA

Group / Funk, Disco

If the O'Jays, the Dramatics, or Bloodstone had added a female singer and incorporated bebop-influenced harmonies, they might have sounded something like Side Effect—a distinctive soul and funk vocal quartet of the '70s and early '80s. Side Effect was never a big name in R&B—and its material wasn't as consistently strong as that of the O'Jays—but it did have a recognizable and appealing sound. The group was formed in Los Angeles in May 1972, when it started out as an all-male trio and consisted of Louis Patton, Gregory Matta, and leader Augie Johnson. The latter had been singing since childhood—in fact, Johnson was among the kids who sang on Frank Sinatra's 1959 hit "High Hopes." Side Effect became a quartet when, in 1974, Johnson, Patton, and Matta decided to add a female vocalist and hired L.A. native Sylvia Nabors. In 1975, Side Effect signed with Fantasy and recorded its self-titled debut album, which was, like subsequent efforts, produced by Wayne Henderson of Crusaders fame. By the time Side Effect recorded its second album, *What You Need*, in 1976, Nabors had been replaced by Helen Lowe. Then, in 1977, Lowe was replaced by Sylvia St. James, who recorded with the group in 1977 and 1978. St. James' subsequent replacement was Miki Howard, a talented singer who sang with the group for a few years before signing with Atlantic in 1986 and becoming well known as a solo artist. *—Alex Henderson*

Side Effect / 1976 / Fantasy ♦♦♦

With a lineup consisting of Augie Johnson, Louis Patton, Gregory Matta and Sylvia Nabors (the first of its four female vocalists), Side Effect showed some promise on this self-titled debut album. The LP was produced by trombonist Wayne Henderson, who seemed like the ideal producer for the group. Best known for his years with the Crusaders/Jazz Crusaders, Henderson had strong soul and jazz credentials, so he was a very logical choice for a group whose goal was to bring bebop-influenced harmonies to soul and funk. Although not remarkable, this album is decent. When Side Effect dives into the catchy funk of "Baby Love (Love You Baby)" and "What the Heck, Let's Discotheque," plus the silky ballad "Oh, Baby," you can hear how much potential the group had. *—Alex Henderson*

What You Need / 1976 / Fantasy ♦♦♦♦

Side Effect reached its creative peak with the Wayne Henderson-produced *What You Need*, which was the group's second album as well as its best one. This time, the songs weren't simply decent—they were excellent, and Side Effect had a gem of a female vocalist to help bring them to life. The quartet's new female singer was Helen Lowe, who had replaced Sylvia Nabors. While Nabors was competent, the brassy, big-voiced Lowe was a treasure—and she shows herself to be major asset on the hit "S.O.S." and a remake of Ronnie Laws' "Always There," which was originally a soul-jazz instrumental in 1975 but becomes a gutsy vocal tune thanks to added lyrics by Paul Allen. Equally strong are the funky "Honky Tonk Scat," the mournful ballad "Changes," and a cover of the Crusaders' "Keep That Same Old Feeling." Regrettably, *What You Need* was Lowe's only album with Side Effect, and it's equally regrettable that she didn't go on to become huge as a solo artist. *—Alex Henderson*

Goin' Bananas / 1978 / Fantasy ♦♦♦

Helen Lowe's replacement, Sylvia St. James, joined Side Effect with its third album, *Goin' Bananas*, which fell short of the excellence of *What You Need*, but is generally decent. Although Lowe's departure was a major loss for the group, St. James shows herself to be an expressive and capable vocalist on the catchy "Private World," the title tune (a goofy yet infectious funk song), and an interpretation of "Cloudburst" that is probably the group's most jazz-oriented offering ever. Augie Johnson, meanwhile, has a charming lead vocal on "Open Up Your Heart." Though Side Effect didn't have a lot of major hits, the funky single "It's All In Your Mind" made it to number 18 on *Billboard*'s R&B singles chart. For this LP, Side Effect went all out with the bananas gimmick—St. James was depicted in a Carmen Miranda-like getup, and Fantasy pressed the LP on yellow vinyl. *—Alex Henderson*

Rainbow Visions / 1979 / Fantasy ♦♦♦

After the Rain / 1980 / Elektra ♦♦♦

Side Effect entered the '80s with its fifth album, *After the Rain*, which found Miki Howard replacing Sylvia St. James and becoming the group's fourth female singer. It also found Side Effect switching to Elektra after four albums with Fantasy, and it marked the first time a Side Effect album wasn't produced or co-produced by Wayne Henderson (Augie Johnson serves as producer this time). Despite all these changes, *After the Rain* isn't a radical departure from *Rainbow Visions*. Side Effect's distinctive sound was still something to admire, but on the whole, the quartet still didn't have five star material to go with that sound—and it was still unable to hit big commercially. Nonetheless, this isn't a weak album. Material ranging from the exuberant "The Thrill Is Gone" (which has a Philadelphia type soul/disco appeal) and the insistent "Black Beauty," to the silky ballad, "Close to Me," is enjoyable, and "Pretty Baby" is a rare example of Side Effect delivering a 12-bar blues. Also noteworthy is the group's disco take on the Beatles' "Eleanor Rigby." *After the Rain* is a likable LP that has more plusses than minuses, but even so, it's still clear that the group wasn't living up to its enormous potential. *—Alex Henderson*

● **Greatest Hits** / 1981 / Fantasy ♦♦♦♦♦

Side Effect/What You Need / Jul. 9, 2002 / Fantasy ♦♦♦

Bunny Sigler

b. Mar. 27, 1941, Philadelphia, PA

Producer, Keyboards, Guitar / Philly Soul, Disco, Soul

Born in Philadelphia, Bunny Sigler spent his formative years singing at various churches. In his teens, he sang in doo wop groups like, the Opals. Despite all of this involvement, Sigler's real aspiration was to be a professional basketball player. But that ambition was squelched when he injured his leg. Seeing that he he'd have to look at singing in a different light, Sigler threw himself into music with a passion, recording for various local labels and singing and playing guitar and piano in area nightclubs.

Sigler was brought to the attention of independent producers John Medara and Dave White by Leon Huff. Impressed, they signed him to a deal that led to the release of Sigler's first album, *Let the Good Times Roll* on Cameo Parkway. The first single, "Girl Don't Make Me Wait," received both R&B and pop airplay. The title track (originally a hit for Shirley & Lee) was the second single and was making a respectable showing on the R&B/pop charts (number 20 and number 22, respectively) when Cameo Parkway suddenly folded. While waiting for his Cameo Parkway contract to lapse, Sigler began hanging around the hallways of Gamble & Huff Productions, singing and strumming guitar, leading Kenny Gamble to suggest that Sigler try to write some songs with Ugene Dozier. Around 1970, Gamble & Huff Productions became Philadelphia International Records. When Dozier left the label, Sigler inherited his office. Sigler's songwriting break came when a tune he co-wrote with Phil Hurtt, "Sunshine," was released as a follow-up single to the O'Jays' million-selling "Back Stabbers." The O'Jays' follow-up album, *Ship Ahoy*, had Sigler's first solo-written song, "You Got Your Hooks in Me," and the Sigler/Gamble tune "Don't You Call Me Brother." Sigler's songs, productions, piano, and background vocals are sprinkled throughout the Philadelphia International Records catalog.

Sigler began to look for a group to develop and met the TNJs, a vocal group that built up a strong reputation around the Tri-State area. Backing the TNJs was a band called Instant Funk. In 1972, Sigler was given the go-ahead by PIR to start cutting tracks on himself as a singer and brought Instant Funk and the TNJs into the studio. PIR issued two albums by Sigler in 1974, *That's How Long I'll Be Loving You* and *Keep Smilin'*, and *My Music* in 1976. Though most tracks on Sigler's PIR albums have backing tracks by MFSB, a significant number (including the whole *My Music* album) feature the Instant Funk rhythm section. With the Philly soul sound so hot, Sigler got a chance to work with a number of acts as a writer and/or producer, including the Whispers, Ecstasy, Passion & Pain, and Carl Carlton. He cut tracks for artists on Curtis Mayfield's Curtom label, including Mayfield himself ("Trippin' Out"), and made a duet album with Barbara Mason. In 1976, Sigler got Instant Funk an album deal with Gamble & Huff's TSOP label. The album, *Get Down With the Philly Jump*, had two singles that were popular in the disco clubs, the title track and "It Ain't Reggae (But It Sho Is Funky)."

In 1978, Sigler, bringing along Instant Funk, switched to Gold Mind, a label started by MFSB guitarist Norman Harris and distributed by Salsoul Records. Just like at PIR, Sigler and Instant Funk worked with the acts on Salsoul—Loleatta Holloway, Double Exposure, and First Choice—as well as acts on other labels. In the early '80s, Salsoul ceased operations. Sigler continued to write and produce, hitting with "Somebody Loves You Baby" (co-written with Eugene "Lambchops" Curry), a million-seller for Patti LaBelle, and taking Shirley Jones, formerly of PIR sister act the Jones Girls, to number-one R&B with "Do You Get Enough Love" in August of 1986. *—Ed Hogan*

Let the Good Times Roll / 1967 / Parkway ♦♦♦

Philly soul singer Bunny Sigler's first LP carried the name of his summer 1967 hit cover of Shirley & Lee's "Let the Good Times Roll." Issued by Philadelphia, PA-based Cameo Parkway and produced by John Medara and Dave White (Len Barry's "1-2-3"), the cover photo of *Let the Good Times Roll* featured Sigler with a smiling, whimsical expression on his face on a sunny day in the Alice in Wonderland section of New York City's Central Park. The inference was to the hurried white bunny rabbit in the classic Lewis Carroll book. Future Philadelphia International Records co-owner Leon Huff played piano, wrote the beautifully bombastic first single "Girl Don't Make Me Wait," and did some arranging on the LP. Lennon and McCartney's "Yesterday" gets a bluesy, horns-punctuated reworking. Besides the rollicking "Let the Good Times Roll," another single was the Little Richard-ish "Lovey Dovey," the U.K. Northern soul favorite. The bluesy "Sunny Sunday" is enlivened by vibraphonist Vince Montana. Standout tracks are the Stax-flavored ballad "It's Up to the Women and the comin-ta-get-ya Motown flourishes of "Follow Your Heart."

"Always in the Wrong Place (At the Wrong Time)" foreshadows the everyman poignancy of "Somebody Free" found on 1974's *That's How Long I'll Be Loving You.* There are no original songs by Sigler on *Let the Good Times Roll* because he hadn't started writing songs. His introduction to the art of songwriting happened in 1968 while he was hanging around the offices of the just-opened Gamble & Huff Productions. *—Ed Hogan*

That's How Long I'll Be Loving You / 1974 / Philadelphia International ♦♦♦
After co-writing hits for Joe Simon (the 1971 million-seller "Drowning in a Sea of Love") and the O'Jays ("Sunshine," "You Got Your Hooks in Me") among many others, singer/songwriter/producer Bunny Sigler was given the opportunity to record his debut album for Gamble & Huff's Philadelphia International Records. The result, *That's How Long I'll Be Loving You,* is one of the artist's most beloved albums with MFSB and Instant Funk in fine form. Several of the album's tracks can be found on a 1996 Sony Legacy CD *The Best of Bunny Sigler: Sweeter Than the Berry* and the 1998 Sony CD *Bunny Sigler.* "That's How Long I'll Be Loving You," along with Sigler's first single, the soft, sweet "Regina," is on the 1997 Sony CD set *Philly Sound (1966-1976): Kenny Gamble & Leon Huff.* The brassy opener, "Things Are Gonna Get Better," bops along enwrapped by a jovial vocal by Sigler. The doo wop-flavored "Picture Us" has one of Sigler's most emotive vocals and soaring, angelic background vocals. Along the same lines is the richly arranged "That's How Long I'll Be Loving You " that says: "Till the stars fall from the sky/till babies no longer cry/that's how long I'll be loving you." Sigler's churchy ballad cover of the O'Jays' million-selling hit "Love Train" is absolutely beautiful, emphasizing the brotherly/sisterly love ethic of the song bolstered by Instant Funk and crisp harmonies by the TNJs. The steppers track "Your Love Is Good" opens with the popping sound of champagne being uncorked. Domestic disputes are given a rollicking, bluesy, brassy take on "I Lied"; listen for the mid-'70s gas shortage reference as the track fades. The gospel-ish ballad "Somebody Free" has the same heart-tugging appeal that Sigler evoked on "Always in the Wrong Place (At the Wrong Time)" from *Let the Good Times Roll.* *—Ed Hogan*

Keep Smilin' / 1975 / Philadelphia International ♦♦♦♦♦
Bunny Sigler's *Keep Smilin'* LP was rush-released to capitalize on the fast-breaking (fast-selling) title track single. Several tracks on *Keep Smilin'* were first included on *That's How Long I'll Be Loving You* released earlier that year. The Philly soul singer/songwriter/producer was trying to quickly follow up his Top 30 R&B churchy ballad cover version of the O'Jays gold hit, "Love Train." The difference between the two albums is the outstanding two tracks that feature Instant Funk: "Keep Smilin'," "Sweeter Than the Berry." Co-written by Sigler and Allan Felder, the pumpin' "Keep Smilin'," is one of Sigler's best.), Sigler later produced a cover of the tune on guitarist Gzabo Szabo's excellent 1976 Mercury LP, *Nightflight* with that version becoming a steppers classic. The bluesy "Sweeter Than the Berry," has punching horns and a *nassty* break that features Sigler, bassist Raymond Earl and the late-night wailing sax of Sam Peake. Another single, the thumpin', brassy, fun-filled "Shake Your Booty," was starting to gain interest before it was quelled by protest over its title. Oddly, no such protest was waged against the similarly titled "Shake Your Booty." Several of the album's tracks can be found on 1996 Sony Legacy CD *The Best of Bunny Sigler: Sweeter Than the Berry* and on the 1998 Sony CD, *Bunny Sigler* and the 1997 Sony CD set *Philly Sound (1966-1976): Kenny Gamble & Leon Huff.* *—Ed Hogan*

My Music / 1976 / Philadelphia International ♦♦♦
Philly soul artist/producer Bunny Sigler's third album for Gamble & Huff's Philadelphia International Records label, *My Music* marked the first time he used his protégé band Instant Funk on an entire album. Sigler seems better for it since he lets his creativity fill the album with engaging surprises. The opener, "I'm the Bunny From the Other Side of the Ocean," is filled with humor, jokey asides, and a tight horn section. The thumpin' percolating title track, co-written by Sigler, Leon Huff, and McFadden & Whitehead ("Ain't No Stoppin' Us Now"), slowly builds instrument by instrument as Sigler directs each band member to come in, then the whole funk lesson becomes peppered with James Brown-ish horn riffs. The effervescent "Thank You Baby for Last Night" and the laid-back bounce groover "Come on and Dance, Dance, Dance" are nice numbers to kick back with. Sigler eccentricities come to the forefront on the street-slick Sigler/T.Life song "Ladies Man" and the samba-flavored "Calling Me Back," which has sharp lyrics. The lush, sweepingly romantic "Somebody Loves You," co-written with Life and arranger Richard Rome (aka Richie Rome), testifies to the redemptive power of love. Going into the 21st century Sigler's fans would ask him when he was going to re-record the song or when the original version would be available on CD. He co-wrote (with Eugene "Lambchops" Curry) the similarly themed "Somebody Loves You Baby (You Know Who It Is)," a 1991 million selling single for Patti LaBelle from her *Burnin'* album. Sigler's brother, Jimmy Sigler, wrote the joyous "Can't Believe That You Love Me." One track from this album, the introspective slow jam/Opals tribute "Just Let Me Love You Tonight," is on the 1996 Sony Legacy CD, *The Best of Bunny Sigler: Sweeter Than the Berry.* *—Ed Hogan*

Locked in This Position / 1977 / Curtom ♦

Let Me Party With You / 1978 / Gold ♦♦♦
This originally appeared in 1978. Marvin Gaye's "Got to Give It Up" inspired both "Let Me Party With You" and "Don't Even Try (Give It Up)." The soulful "Your Love Is So Good" shakes the imitation, while "I Got What You Need" slows the collection's frantic pace. "I'm a Fool" swirls and whistles like Sigler's work with Instant Funk. Unfortunately, the fillers equal the thrillers. *—Andrew Hamilton*

I've Always Wanted to Sing . . . Not Just Write Songs / 1979 / Gold ♦♦♦

Not Just Write Songs / 1979 / Gold Mind ♦♦♦
For *(I've Always Wanted to Sing) Not Just Write Songs,* his follow-up LP to his hit *Let Me Party With You* album, Bunny Sigler had a bigger production budget to work with. There are strings and (orchestrated) horns laced throughout the release. Yet it was the more sparser tracks that got the most attention. The first single, the funky, disco-ish "By the Way You Dance (I Know It Was You)," cracked the R&B Top 40. The double entendre-filled "I'm Funkin' You Tonight (With My Music)" made the album a favorite among funk fans and club goers. Sigler's late-night supper club leanings come through on the echo-drenched ballads "Cry My Eyes Out" and "Half a Man." Repeating guitar lines are used effectively on the bouncy "Simple Things You Do," and Sigler's late dad can be heard singing on the drivin' "Glad to Be Your Lover," for a funny, touching effect. *—Ed Hogan*

Let It Snow / 1980 / Salsoul ♦♦♦
Bunny Sigler let his fertile, prolific imagination run wild for his final Salsoul album, *Let It Snow,* issued in June 1980 with the end results being fun, funny, and funky. The first single, "Super Duper Super Man," has great cartoonish sound effects and the chant: "I don't like Kryptonite/but I like Lois Lane and some serious tympani rolls." The snap-laced, quiet storm-ish title track—not the holiday standard—seductively swirls around in a frosty mix of echoing "oohs" and lazy don't-give-a-darn guitar lines. The track became a steppers standard, so copies of *Let It Snow* maybe extremely hard to find. "Girl You're Driving Me Crazy" skates along on a hi-hat, a sense of wacky humor, and a great horn and string arrangement by Lenny Pakula. "Dis Away Dat Away" thumps along with a gonging electronic beat, shimmying funky rhythm guitar breaks, and kazoos (yes, kazoos, as on his *Let Me Party With You* LP). Sigler and Instant Funk sounded like they had a lot of fun recording this jam. The snappy, joyous "Since the Day I First Saw You" is one of the most engaging tracks he has ever done. The multi-talented Philly soul veteran's brother, Jimmy Sigler, wrote the sparse, organ-laced, balladic single, "How Can I Tell Her It's Over." The album closer, the explosive, extremely hyper "Slow Down," reflects Sigler's agony while trying to keep up with his wayward woman. On some copies of *Let It Snow* you'll see a song listing for "Rise," but you won't find the track on the actual record. Oddly, his cover of Herb Alpert's 1979 pop hit was never released. Still, *Let It Snow* is one of Sigler's best LPs. *—Ed Hogan*

● **The Best of Bunny Sigler: Sweeter Than the Berry** / Mar. 12, 1996 / Epic/Legacy ♦♦♦♦♦
Sweeter Than the Berry collects the biggest hits from Philly soul singer Bunny Sigler on a single disc. It's a thoroughly entertaining retrospective and the only disc many Sigler fans will ever need to own. *—Stephen Thomas Erlewine*

The Silhouettes

f. 1957, Philadelphia, PA
Group / Doo Wop, R&B
To most listeners, the Silhouettes are another one of rock & roll's one-hit wonders, another of those R&B harmony vocal groups that scored big once (with "Get a Job") and never repeated that trip up the charts. And that is true—they never scored a second nationally charting single. But they did carry on a lot longer than most people think, continuing to perform and even record right to the end of the 1960s. Additionally, the impact of "Get a Job," a song that was written by group member Richard Lewis (and credited to all four Silhouettes), is astonishing to contemplate as a popular culture flash point. It became, for many listeners, the quintessential doo wop song—or, at least, one of a handful of songs thought of automatically when the musical term is mentioned (although some purists also loathed the song for its seeming burlesque of doo wop's attributes). More than that, it inspired good work and imitation in others; the Miracles were one of several groups that delivered "answer songs" to "Get a Job."

The Silhouettes' history went back five years earlier than "Get a Job," to the early '50s, when Earl Beal and Raymond Edwards formed a gospel group called the Balladeers, who performed in the Philadelphia area and recorded a pair of singles in 1954. That same year, Bill Horton joined as lead singer, replacing original Balladeer Clarence Basil, and a little later the group changed their name to the Gospel Tornadoes. More personnel changes followed, and in 1956 Rick Lewis joined. Lewis had not only sung with different gospel outfits since the early '50s, but had started writing songs while he served in the U.S. Army. The group was popular but was barely making any kind of a living at all performing gospel, and it was with those circumstances that Lewis convinced them to give rock & roll a try.

The Gospel Tornadoes became the Thunderbirds. They tried without success to get a record out until they crossed paths with disc jockey Kae Williams, who was trying to start up a label of his own in Philadelphia and liked what he heard one night at a club where they were performing. The group was signed to his Junior Records label and cut its first single in the fall of 1957—the intended A-side was the original ballad "I Am Lonely," backed with an upbeat tune that Lewis had written after getting out of the army entitled "Get a Job." Just as they were preparing to cut the record, they also learned of another outfit called the Thunderbirds that had a prior claim on the name—in response, at the suggestion of Earl Beal, they changed their name once again, borrowing the title of a 1957 hit by the group the Rays called "Silhouettes."

"I Am Lonely" b/w "Get a Job" came out on Junior Records in November of 1957. The song was picked up by Dick Clark for play as an almost certain hit on *American Bandstand* that same month. "Get a Job" was hard to resist, with strong singing, a great beat, and an array of a half-dozen memorable hooks (starting with the "yip-yip-yip" opening), and even a memorable tenor sax break by Ronnie McGill. The record eventually topped both the *Hot 100* and the R&B charts in *Billboard* magazine, only the third doo wop single to reach number one in the pop listings. The Silhouettes' second single, "Headin' for the Poorhouse" b/w "Miss Thing," was far less successful, although it did generate some airplay in early 1958. The next two singles were issued nationally by Ace Records, and both sold respectably without ever charting nationally. By the end of 1958, Bill Horton and Raymond Edwards left the group, while Lewis and Beal soldiered on with two new members, John "Bootsie" Williams on lead vocals and Cornelius "Brother" Brown as bass.

Things began looking up when the reconstituted Silhouettes were signed by producer Jerry Ragavoy, who got three modestly successful records out from them. By 1963, they were back with Kae Williams, who tried to repeat the "Get a Job" formula and sound with "Rent Man." It failed to chart, although it did sell locally when released through Junior Records. By 1966, the group, revamped yet again, was being billed as the New Silhouettes. In 1968, the first album ever issued of Silhouettes material, *The Original and New Silhouettes '58/'68 Get a Job*, showed up on the Goodway label. It was made up of classic Silhouettes material and new songs cut by the current lineup. *—Bruce Eder*

● **Get a Job** / 1996 / Collectables ♦♦♦♦

Here are 13 songs by the original and the earliest change of lineup, in stunning sound. The title tune has such an edge here, in booming sound, that hearing it is a refreshing experience. The thunderous bass and a drum beat, stolen from a roadhouse strip act, comes through loud and clear beneath those larger-than-life vocals—which makes this some of the busiest doo wop singing of its period. There aren't any other hits here, but a good part of the material sold well locally at the time and remains enjoyable, the efforts to emulate "Get a Job" (right up through "Rent Man") are entertaining, and the soaring "I Sold My Heart to the Junkman" is worth the price almost by itself. The notes by Todd R. Baptista are astonishing in their care and detail—anyone buying this because of the one hit is likely to end up loving the Silhouettes. *—Bruce Eder*

Silk

f. Philadelphia, PA

Group / Philly Soul, Funk

The '70s R&B trio Silk was one of the many groups to arrive from that genre in the wake of classic Motown and during the heyday of their native Philadelphia scene. The group was never as famous as most of their contemporaries, but they still managed to release two albums before they disbanded in the late '70s, 1976's *Smooth as Silk* and 1977's *Silk*. *—Bradley Torreano*

Smooth as Silk / 1976 / Prelude ♦♦♦♦

Silk was comprised of ex-Independents ("Leaving Me") Maurice Jackson and Aaron "Eric" Thomas, along with Arthur Reid. If price was the barometer, this should be a great album by a great group—the nine tracks sell for 20 dollars discounted online, with their first single, "Party 1 & 2," at six minutes and 21 seconds, the longest. While not worthy of its inflated price, it's alright. David Porter (Isaac Hayes' old collaborator ("Soul Man")) produced the LP in Jackson, MS, at Tommy Couch's renowned Malaco Studios with mostly Memphis musicians. Except for Porter's Southern jerker "Ain't No Need of Crying," Silk members wrote all the tunes, including jewel-case gems "I Know I Didn't Do You Wrong," which is sweet, gutty, and sincere, and "Let Him Go," which is lilting and passion-filled. And listeners won't skip past the LP's best dancer, "Give Yourself to Me," or the uplifting "Live While You Can." *—Andrew Hamilton*

Silk / 1977 / Prelude ♦♦♦

● **Smooth as Silk/Silk** / Apr. 23, 1996 / Sequel ♦♦♦♦

Silk

f. 1992

Group / Urban, Dance-Pop, Club/Dance

This '90s R&B vocal group should not be confused with the late-'70s Philadelphia band, which was a funk-oriented unit, or the vocal trio Silk from Los Angeles. Timothy Cameron, Jimmy Gates Jr., Jonathen Rasboro, Gary Jenkins, and Gary Glenn issued their debut LP, *Lose Control*, in 1992 and have excited urban contemporary audiences, particularly women, with their engaging harmonies and aggressively suggestive material. Their single "Freak Me" was a huge hit in 1993; two years later, the group issued a self-titled LP for Elektra, followed in 1999 by *Tonight*. *Love Session* appeared in spring 2001. *—Ron Wynn*

● **Lose Control** / 1992 / Elektra ♦♦♦♦

New jack vocalist/producer Keith Sweat helped mold the ensemble Silk in his own image on their debut. He wrote or co-wrote eight of the 10 tracks, produced or co-produced every cut, sang the lead on "Happy Days," and either did background vocals or played on all the numbers (doing both on several). The quintet demonstrated nice harmonizing and competent vocal skills on most songs, although they hadn't yet developed a cohesive identity or first-rate vocalist. Silk scored hits with the smash "Freak Me" and "Happy Days." The best numbers highlighted their roots in '70s soul and '50s doo wop. It wasn't a spectacular debut, but a promising one. *—Ron Wynn*

Silk / Nov. 28, 1995 / Elektra ♦♦♦

Like TLC, Silk balances the line between seductive soul and hip-hop informed funk on their self-titled debut. Vocally, the group is impressive, as is much of the production, which is seamless without being overly slick. The only problem with *Silk*, then, is the wildly uneven material. *—Stephen Thomas Erlewine*

Tonight / Mar. 23, 1999 / Elektra/Asylum ♦♦♦

There's a saying that most pop music is about romance, so it's logical that a good portion is also about sex. If you listen to Silk, however, it would be fair to say that 95-100 percent of their music is about sex. Ever since their debut, *Lose Control*, they have showed little inclination to sing about anything other than sex, coming on like disciples of early R. Kelly, crossed with a bit of Barry White and Boyz II Men. Through three albums, they haven't changed their modus operandi one bit, which makes *Tonight* a little predictable. If you're at all familiar with the previous two records, you know what to expect lyrically and musically from every track on the record and, chances are, you won't be too disappointed by this slightly overproduced, ballad-heavy set. The uninitiated may find the constant sex talk a little ridiculous and monotonous, but they'll likely groove on Darryl "Delite" Allamby's production, which updates classic '70s soul and funk. It can be a little glossy and glib, as well as a little lightweight in the songwriting department, but that Allamby production makes *Tonight* fairly effective romantic mood music—even with Silk's vocal histrionics. *—Stephen Thomas Erlewine*

Love Session / Jun. 12, 2001 / Elektra/Asylum ♦♦

Silver Convention

f. 1974, Munich, Germany

Group / Disco, Soul

Best remembered for their disco smash "Fly Robin Fly," the Munich, Germany-based ensemble Silver Convention was formed by producers Silvester Levay & Michael Kunze, debuting in 1975 with the LP *Save Me* and scoring a U.K. hit with the title track. After topping the American charts with "Fly Robin Fly," Levay and Kunze recruited a trio of vocalists—Linda Thompson (not to be confused with the same-named singer and wife of guitarist Richard Thompson), Ramona Wolf, and Penny McLean—who began appearing publicly under the Silver Convention banner; they were featured on the follow-up, "Get Up and Boogie (That's Right)," which was also a smash in 1976. While another single, "Telegram," proved a success that same year in the annual Eurovision Song Contest, Silver Convention's popularity quickly faded, and by the end of the decade the group was no more. *—Jason Ankeny*

Save Me / 1975 / Midland Int. ♦♦♦♦♦

In 1975, Munich was quickly becoming one of Europe's top cities for disco. That year, the Giorgio Moroder/Pete Bellotte team produced Donna Summer's breakthrough hit "Love to Love You, Baby" in Munich, and it was also in 1975 that the Munich-based Silver Convention hit big with "Fly, Robin, Fly," one of the gems that defined the Euro-disco sound. Some listeners were happy just having the "Fly, Robin, Fly" single, but for serious Euro-disco enthusiasts, the Silver Convention's debut album *Save Me* is essential. While American radio stuck to "Fly, Robin, Fly," dance-club DJs also found a lot to admire about glossy, strings-laden ear candy like "Tiger Baby," "I Like It," and "Another Girl." The lavish production of Michael Kunze & Silvester Levay (who were the brains behind the Silver Convention) is consistently attractive, and Levay's string arrangements give the impression that he was a big admirer of Barry White, Isaac Hayes, and Gamble & Huff. Nonetheless, *Save Me* doesn't sound derivative. In fact, the Silver Convention was quite distinctive itself and had a uniquely European take on American soul-pop and disco. Arguably the group's most essential release, *Save Me* is a dance classic. *—Alex Henderson*

Silver Convention / Jan. 1976 / Midland Int. ♦♦♦

Although not quite as strong as *Save Me*, the Silver Convention's self-titled second album is a respectable, if uneven, Euro-disco effort that boasts the disco smash "Get Up and Boogie." In the U.S., "Get Up and Boogie" was the only tune on the LP that enjoyed a lot of radio airplay. But dance club DJs weren't about to play that single exclusively; they also gave a lot of exposure to high-gloss cuts that range from the lush "San Francisco Hustle" and the mildly funky "No No Joe" to the dreamy "You Got What It Takes (To Please Your Woman)" and the clever "Play Me Like a Yo-Yo." On a few tracks, the Silver Convention tries to demonstrate that it can sing more than Euro-disco. "The Boy With the Ooh La-La" is a playful pop-reggae number, while "Thank You, Mr. D.J." is an unremarkable pop ballad. But Euro-disco is what the Silver Convention did best, and it is the style that dominates this generally decent sophomore effort. *—Alex Henderson*

Madhouse / Feb. 1976 / Midland Int. ♦♦♦♦

If you looked at one of the Silver Convention's publicity shots in 1976, you would have seen a picture of vocalists Penny McLean, Ramona Wolf, and Rhonda Heath. But Michael Kunze & Silvester Levay were running the show. They founded the group and took care of the producing and songwriting—McLean, Wolf, and Heath were essentially there to carry out Kunze and Levay's ideas. And on the Silver Convention's third album, *Madhouse*, Kunze & Levay decided to play up the funkier elements in the group's Euro-disco sound. There are plenty of swirling strings on this 1976 LP, and the production is still ultra-slick. Even so, "The World Is a Madhouse," "Plastic People," and "I'm Not a Slot Machine" are among the Silver Convention's funkier offerings—certainly not funky in a LaBelle or Pointer Sisters type way, but funky by the Silver Convention's Euro-disco standards. And on "Everybody's Talking 'Bout Love" (one of the group's best singles), Kunze & Levay sound like they're really trying to connect with fans of female Northern soul groups like First Choice and the Three Degrees. *Save Me* remains the Silver Convention's most essential album, but *Madhouse* runs a close second. *—Alex Henderson*

Golden Girls / 1977 / Midsong ♦♦♦

● **Get Up and Boogie With Silver Convention: Their Greatest Hits** / 1977 / Music Club ♦♦♦♦♦

In the late '70s, different "best-of" collections by the Silver Convention came out in different countries. One of them was this British LP, which came out in 1977 and offered a concise 15-song overview of the German group's 1975-1977 output. The Silver Convention was quite popular among British disco enthusiasts, so it came as no surprise when Magnet assembled this collection. Most of the Munich residents' essential recordings are provided, including "Fly, Robin, Fly," "Telegram," "Get Up and Boogie," "Always Another Girl," and "I Like It," as well as "Tiger Baby," "Save Me," and "Everybody's Talking 'Bout Love." Only a few of these gems were major radio hits in the U.S., although the Silver Convention enjoyed a lot more radio airplay in Western Europe. And even if a particular song on this album wasn't a radio favorite in Europe, chances are that it received a lot of exposure in dance clubs. Although *Greatest Hits* was primarily for British listeners, copies of the LP made it to the U.S. as an import, and in 1999, Music Club reissued the collection on CD. *—Alex Henderson*

The Best of Silver Covention: Get Up and Boogie / Dec. 15, 1994 / Hot Productions ♦♦♦♦♦

To a large portion of America's 1970s radio listeners, the name Silver Convention is synonymous with "that one-hit-wonder group that sang 'Fly, Robin Fly'." Indeed, the number-one pop- and R&B-charting disco jaunt was to be the group's most successful single, followed closely by the similar-sounding number two hit "Get Up and Boogie." But on the strength of that classic, the German studio conglomerate—spearheaded by producer Michael Kunze and arranger Silvester Levay—released a total of five albums during the latter part of the '70s and came up with a bundle of international dance hits. Not surprisingly, oodles of CDs compiling these ditties started surfacing with the disco nostalgia of the early '90s. Given that much of the group's material relies on formula—steady disco backbeat, dramatic strings, and inviting melodic lines sung in unison—there aren't many differences between most of these collections that will stand out to the average listener. But this collection by Hot Productions is the most hit-laden of the pack and wisely includes the full-length versions of the most important tunes. "Fly, Robin Fly" and "Get Up and Boogie" are each included in nearly eight-minute formations, and ardent disco fans will appreciate the inclusion of staples like "Save Me," "Always Another Girl," "Telegram," and "Spend the Night With Me." An additional smattering of nine internationally charting singles and various album tracks round things out. With 15 tracks total, this collection is a consistent, well-rounded representation of what made Silver Convention more than a one-hit wonder. *—Justin M. Kantor*

Joe Simon

b. Sep. 2, 1943, Simmesport, LA

Vocals / Deep Soul, Southern Soul, Pop-Soul, Soul, Country-Soul

His plaintive baritone equally conversant with R&B and country phrasing, Joe Simon married the two genres with startling success during the late '60s, adapting Nashville material to the soul sound and repeatedly coming up a winner. Simon began recording in the Bay Area, but a switch in recording sites (first to Muscle Shoals for Vee-Jay and then to Nashville, upon signing with disc jockey John Richbourg's Sound Stage 7 label in 1966) heightened his national appeal. With easy access to prime country-oriented material, Simon soon found his true calling, scoring major hits with "Nine Pound Steel," "(You Keep Me) Hangin' On," and the number-one R&B smash "The Chokin' Kind," penned by Music Row tunesmith Harlan Howard.

Still dabbling in country covers after switching to the Spring imprint in 1970, Simon was even more successful when assigned to Philadelphia wizards Kenny Gamble & Leon Huff, who produced the moody "Drowning in the Sea of Love" the next year. Simon tried his hand at disco in 1975 with the sizzling "Get Down, Get Down (Get on the Floor)" and "Music in My Bones," two of the most palatable artifacts of the era. Simon eventually retired from active performing to devote his life to the church. *—Bill Dahl*

Pure Soul / 1967 / Sound Stage 7 ♦♦♦

Joe Simon established himself as a poignant, folksy, yet urgent vocalist with his debut album on the Sound Stage label. He was then working with the great disc jockey John "R" Richbourg, who helped him find the right blend of soulful ardor and countrified narrative. While neither "Teenager's Prayer" nor "Nine Pound Steel" hit the charts, they laid the groundwork for Simon's monster hits that followed two years later. This album has long been deleted; look for it on collector's auction lists or in used record stores. *—Ron Wynn*

No Sad Songs / 1968 / Sound Stage 7 ♦♦♦

Joe Simon's second album predated his big soul hits, but contained superb vocals and some wonderful country-tinged numbers. His voice was as smooth as glass and had the perfect mix of down-home wit and intensity. He glided through his lyrics, never screaming or wailing, yet still turning ballads into expressive triumphs and caressing the groove while punctuating the lyrics on the uptempo numbers. *—Ron Wynn*

The Chokin' Kind / Jun. 21, 1969 / Sound Stage 7 ♦♦♦♦

There's something about Joe Simon's rich, burnished voice that sounds as smooth as a glass of 12-year-old bourbon, and feels just as appropriate on a sad and lonely day. In some respects, Joe Simon could be called Roy Orbison of soul music—there's a naturally sorrowful tone in Simon's voice that shines clearly through even the most upbeat material, and both singers had obviously learned more than a little from the sounds of classic country. *The Chokin' Kind*, the first of three albums Joe Simon would crank out in 1969, features three tunes written by the great C&W tunesmith Harlan Howard, and all three (especially the title cut) serve as superb examples of the clear if little-examined kinship between soul and country, inspiring truly stellar performances from Simon. Much of the rest of the album is padded out with covers, and while one might imagine it would take a brave man to cover Otis Redding, Glen Campbell and the Five Satins on the same LP, Simon brings his own style and personality to each song, no matter how familiar they may be in other contexts. Like many soul long-players of the 1960s, *The Chokin' Kind* is more a collection of songs that a unified work, but the consistent strength of Simon's performances makes it fine listening from start to finish. *—Mark Deming*

Better Than Ever / 1969 / Sound Stage 7 ♦♦♦

The hardworking Joe Simon cut three albums in 1969 (admittedly, this was back in the day when a pop album rarely ran over 35 minutes, but that's still an impressive amount of material in the space of twelve months), and if *Better Than Ever* found Simon running a bit short on top-shelf material, as a vocalist he was still hitting his targets dead center. Unfortunately Simon and his producers weren't able to scare up any Harlan Howard compositions for this set (which always showed off Simon's subtle but deeply affecting vocal style to his best advantage), and the album's take on Mac Davis' "In the Ghetto" never quite gets into gear, but otherwise Simon's performances range from strong to stellar on this set, and the production shows a touch more polish than on Simon's earlier sessions which mirrors the strength of his voice without overpowering it. "Straight Down to Heaven," "Wounded Man," and "Silver Spoons and Coffee Cups" are outstanding examples of Southern soul at it's most beautifully sorrowful, "When" is a topical "peace and brotherhood" number which has worn better than most, and "Rainbow Road" (witten by Dan Penn & Donnie Fritts) is a simply masterful example of Simon making the most of a thick slice of country soul (even if Arthur Alexander's later recording topped it). Not quite top shelf Joe Simon, *Better Than Ever* is still good enough to please anyone who loves Southern soul at its best. *—Mark Deming*

Drowning in the Sea of Love / 1972 / Southbound ♦♦♦♦♦

There's an old saying "You can take a person out of the country, but you can't take the country out of the person." Kenny Gamble & Leon Huff surrounded Joe Simon with MFSB, hot songs, and Bobby Martin's arrangements, & Simon still comes off sounding country, but in a positive vein. "Drowning in the Sea of Love" shot up the charts, settling at number-three R&B and number-11 pop, and was a certified million-seller. This album is the most successful of Simon's career. "Pool of Bad Luck" nearly duplicated the success of "Drowning"; both songs were similar to productions Gamble & Huff were doing with Jerry Butler. Simon's thick Southern drawl didn't discourage record buyers at all; "I Found My Dad" is the most country-based song on the album, with the same flavor as his past R&B number-one hit "The Choking Kind." The ballads are as effective as the uptempo numbers; "If" and a remake of the Stylistics' "You Are Everything" demonstrate Simon's versatility. Though an unusual marriage at first glance (similar to when Holland-Dozier-Holland announced they were going to produce Junior Walker), it worked extremely well, producing some of the best songs of Simon's career. *—Andrew Hamilton*

Mood, Heart and Soul / 1974 / Polydor ♦♦♦

If the marriage of soul and country sends you, then *Mood, Heart and Soul* will take you there in style. Joe Simon's aching rendition of Gladys Knight & the Pips' "Neither One of Us" cuts painfully to the bone. The soul runs deep on "Walking Down Lonely Street" and "I'm in the Mood for You," while "I'm Still There" and others have a strong country flavor. The lilting hooks on "Good Time Charlie's Got the Blues" and "Covering the Same Old Ground" are as infectious as Simon's drawl. *—Andrew Hamilton*

A Bad Case of Love / 1978 / Spring ♦♦♦

Love Vibrations / 1979 / Spring ♦♦♦♦

Released in 1978, *Love Vibrations* is an often-perfect merge between the hard-driving version of the Philly sound and the folksy yet not ingratiating style of Joe Simon. Of course, Simon was no stranger to the production style. In the early '70s he got his biggest singles from the Kenny Gamble & Leon Huff productions of "Drowning in the Sea of Love" and "Power of Love." The songs, while good, did have Simon coming off like a cornpone Jerry Butler. *Love Vibrations*, mostly produced by Norman Harris, does a better job at capturing Simon's quirkiness. Only the title track and "Going Through These Changes" flop outright. The remaining songs more than make good on the synthesis of the participants involved, which also include Ron Tyson, Ron "Have Mercy" Kersey, and Lester Snell. Simon effortlessly nails the album's lone ballad, the hooky gem "Can We Come and Share in Love," a song originally done by the Temptations in 1977. The hilarious "I Can't Stand a Liar" has Simon unabashedly peeved, with a sedulous guitar and sneaky horns driving the point home. The album's best song, "If You Got the Time (I've Got the Place)," like the best tracks here, slides the equation more toward Philly, as the arrangement is a perfect fit for Simon's voice. "It Must Love" possesses a great bridge and is almost as good. While a few tracks do take the wind out of the sails of this effort, *Love Vibrations* is an absolute necessity for fans of the late-'70s Philly sound and Simon. *—Jason Elias*

The Sounds of Simon/Simon Country / 1990 / Southbound ♦♦♦♦

Mood, Heart and Soul/Today / 1991 / Southbound ♦♦♦

Greatest Hits: The Spring Years, 1970–1977 / 1997 / Ace ♦♦♦♦♦

Of all the soul singers who got their first hits during the 1960s, Joe Simon proved to be one of the most adaptable to the sweeter and slicker sounds of the 1970s. This 23-track compilation, covering his output at the Spring label, is not necessarily the best Simon anthology, omitting as it does his less elaborately produced work of the 1960s, which some find preferable to his Philly soul outings. It does, however, feature all his major pop hits of the era—"Drowning in the Sea of Love," "Power of Love," "Your Time to Cry," "Get Down, Get Down," and "Theme From Cleopatra Jones"—as well as a number of singles that only made a strong impression on R&B audiences, like his cover of Kris Kristofferson's "Help Me Make It Through the Night." As usual with this sort of overview, the music gets more tedious the further you get into the disco era, but it's certainly a good pickup for those who like their soul with a bow tie on it. *—Richie Unterberger*

Mr. Shout / 1997 / Ace ♦♦♦

If Simon had for some reason not recorded much after the mid-'60s, this is how he would be remembered: a soul journeyman, one of many good singers in search of a style and excellent material. Of course, he found that in the latter half of the 1960s. But on this 24-track compilation of sides for Hush, Vee-Jay, and other labels in the early and mid-'60s, we hear a good but derivative singer; "The Whoo Pee," for instance, is a clear Junior Walker knockoff. This is more explicitly gospel and roots R&B-influenced than his famous work, and while the tunes are serviceable, there's nothing that stands out as arresting, or even something that especially deserved to be a hit with better luck. It's certainly a useful disc for historians; it even has some previously issued cuts, as well as three songs he recorded with the Goldtones in 1959 and 1960. Interestingly, several of the early-'60s sides benefit from songwriting and musical accompaniment by Johnny Heartsman, who would eventually make a name for himself as a blues artist. *—Richie Unterberger*

● **Music in My Bones: The Best of Joe Simon** / Nov. 11, 1997 / Rhino ♦♦♦♦♦

Music in My Bones: The Best of Joe Simon is a superb 20-track collection that contains the best of the soul singer's recordings between 1966 and 1976. During those ten years, he recorded for Sound Stage 7, Spring and Warner, and had 13 Top-Ten R&B hits, all of which are included on this collection. Simon was one of the best country-soul and smooth soul singers, as evidenced by such hits as "The Chokin' Kind," "Your Time to Cry," "Drowning in the Sea of Love," "Power of Love," "Step By Step," "Theme From Cleopatra

Jones," "Get Down, Get Down (Get on the Floor)," and "Music in My Bones," and there is no better place to listen to his music than on this excellent collection. *—Stephen Thomas Erlewine*

The Chokin' Kind/Better Than Ever / May 11, 1999 / Monument ♦♦♦♦
This two-fer CD (which replicates a double-LP reissue from 1976) pulls together two strong albums Joe Simon recorded in 1969 onto one disc. While *The Chokin' Kind* sounds a bit more spare in terms of its arrangements and production and *Better Than Ever* lacks any songs written by Harlan Howard, for the most part these two albums fit together quite well; both sets are steeped in Southern soul with a pronounced C&W influence, and both make the most of Simon's strong, sad and smoky voice. Both halves of the disc are also seasoned with a healthy selection of covers, and if Simon doesn't exactly cut Otis Redding on "(Sittin' On) The Dock of the Bay" or Glen Campbell on "Wichita Lineman," he brings qualities to both that set them apart from the better known originals. And Joe Simon is at the top of his form on all 22 tracks; impassioned without overplaying his hand and displaying a disarming emotional honesty that brings a touch of sorrow to even his most optimistic moments, this is stuff anyone who loves Southern soul will fall for. Strong material well presented (except for some audio anomalies on "Wounded Man"), this isn't quite as useful for beginners as Rhino's superb *Music In My Bones: The Best of Joe Simon*, but anyone with a taste for Simon's early work will love it. *—Mark Deming*

Monument of Soul / Apr. 3, 2001 / RPM ♦♦♦♦
Monument of Soul is a comprehensive collection of Joe Simon's 1966-1972 releases on the Sound Stage 7 label, including nearly everything that he put out on singles through the company during that period. Among them are all of his R&B and pop chart hits on Sound Stage 7, which in Simon's case were quite numerous—16 in all, even if just a couple of them ("The Chokin' Kind" and "You Keep Me Hanging On") got into the Top 40. Simon's Sound Stage 7 period is underrepresented by the singer's best career retrospective, Rhino's *Music in My Bones: The Best of Joe Simon*, so this is a welcome in-depth view of the earlier era. And, for listeners who prefer his Nashville soul stint to his slicker Philly soul and disco productions of the '70s, this will probably be the Simon CD they'll want most. Simon was not quite on the Hall of Fame level of soul singers, but he was on the next level down, and he pretty consistently delivered the goods, even on B-sides, of which there are quite a few on this disc. He was better on the countrified ballads than he was on the midtempo chuggers, both because these suited his style better, and because such material stood in bolder relief when juxtaposed with much late-'60s soul. "I Worry About You" and "San Francisco Is a Lonely Town" are two of the overlooked slow-burners on this anthology, though some relatively unknown uptempo belters are worthy of attention too, like "Travellin' Man." *—Richie Unterberger*

Valerie Simpson

b. Aug. 26, 1946, New York, NY [The Bronx]
Vocals, Songwriter, Piano / Urban, Smooth Soul, Soul
Teaming with husband Nickolas Ashford, Valerie Simpson co-wrote numerous soul hits before the pair began a fabulously successful performing career of their own in the early '70s. Ashford & Simpson wrote for the likes of Chuck Jackson and Ray Charles before joining the production staff at Motown and creating hits for many of the company's top acts, notably Marvin Gaye and Tammi Terrell. They tallied their own first soul hit in 1973 for Warner, racking up a solid string of smashes that include "Don't Cost You Nothing" (1978), "Found a Cure" (1979), "Street Corner" (1982), and "Solid," the duo's first R&B chart-topper in 1984. *—Bill Dahl*

Valerie Simpson Exposed / 1971 / Motown ♦♦♦

Valerie Simpson / 1972 / Motown ♦♦♦

● **The Best of Valerie Simpson** / 1991 / Motown ♦♦♦

Simtec & Wylie

f. Chicago, IL
Group / Soul
Walter "Simtec" Simmons and Wylie Dixon, an explosive Sam & Dave-ish act, had a few soul hits in the late '60s and early '70s as Simtec & Wylie. Though exciting live, the duo never hit the charts as big as Gene Chandler's other duo discovery, Mel & Tim ("Backfield in Motion"), but it wasn't because of lack of effort. Simtec was born in Chicago (born December 23, 1944) but moved to Orrville, AL, when he was six (he attended Rocky Branch Elementary and Keith High), but returned to the South Side of Chicago at 14 and completed his schooling at Bowen High. He also studied accounting and income tax law at Loop Junior College. A South Side Chicago group, the Vermaharms, was Simtec's springboard into music. Besides him, the members were James Bingham, Mathews Whitfield, and Mel Tucker. After the group disbanded, guitarist Simtec , and his brother, bassist Ronald, who plays bass, caught the ears of Chicago DJ Herb "Kool Gent" Kent, who asked the siblings to put some music to a rhythm emanating from the rhythm machine Kent was playing at a record shop. The result was "T-Box," a local hit that prompted Simtec to whip up a band and name it after the record: Simtec Simmons & the T-Boxes.

The T-Boxes became the backing band for Simtec & Wylie, who cut their first record "Socking Soul Power" (shades of James Brown) under that name in 1969 on Toddlin' Town Records. Two releases for Shama Records in 1970, "Do It Like Mama" and "Gimme Some of What You Got," followed. Wylie Dixon was a gospel-based singer who worked with Sonny Thompson at King Records with the Big Wheels, a secular group consisting of himself, James Carr, Bobby Pointer, and Robert Goley. Dixon has sadly passed and little is known about his upbringing. He often collaborated with the Simmons brothers on songs.

Simtec & Wylie enjoyed their most popular recordings in 1971 on Mr. Chand: "Gotta Get Over the Hump" and "Bootleggin'." Those songs prompted the release of their only album, *Gotta Get Over the Hump*, which saw daylight on Mr. Chand. "Cross That Bridge" b/w "What's Good to You" (1973) doesn't appear on the album, nor do a couple of B-sides. They recut "Gimme Some of What You Got" b/w "Put an Extra Plus in Your Love," and Atlantic Records released it as a 12-inch.

Simtec produced other acts during this period, including the girl group Krystal Generation, who toured with the Simtec & Wylie Revue. He also contributed, along with Dixon and Ronald Simmons, to Gene Chandler and Jerry Butler's *One and One* album. An accomplished songwriter, Simtec has 50 titles cleared with B.M.I.

In 1975, Simtec went solo with "Classified Crazy Man"/"Some Other Time" on Innovation 2. In 1977, he cut a self-titled album on AVI Records that's hard to find. Simtec later became involved in real estate and ran Supreme Realty in Chicago. *—Andrew Hamilton*

● **Gettin' Over the Hump** / 1971 / Mr. Chand ♦♦♦
Chicago's Sam & Dave's first and only album contains some righteous riffs, including their pull-yourself-up-by-your-bootstraps anthem "Gotta Get Over the Hump" and "Bootleggin'." The most interesting cut is the duo's funky remake of Rod Stewart's "Maggie May." Part of their backing band—Ronald Simmons, Bobby Pointer, and Fred White—became a part of Southside Movement, who started a little commotion with "I've Been Watching You" in 1973. This same album was reissued in 1971 on Mercury Records as *Bootleggin'*. *—Andrew Hamilton*

Sisqó (Mark Andrews)

b. Baltimore, MD
Vocals / Urban, Pop-Rap
Even before Sisqó became an overnight superstar in summer 2000 with the infamous "Thong Song," he was no stranger to success. Not many may have recognized his name, but his voice was no doubt familiar, since he was a member of the massively successful '90s R&B group Dru Hill. Long before Sisqó dyed his hair and tattooed his body, he was born Mark Andrews in Baltimore, MD. He co-founded the group Dru Hill in 1995 with high school friends Jazz, Nokio, and Woody and saw their debut album released in 1996, instantly notable for Keith Sweat's production work. But Dru Hill quickly became noteworthy themselves with "Tell Me," a huge R&B hit. Two years later in 1998, Sisqó again graced the airwaves with the second Dru Hill album, *Enter the Dru*. After the success of this album, it didn't take long for the prolific young artist to bounce back the following summer with his solo album, *Unleash the Dragon*. The album's hit singles propelled it to multiplatinum success, setting the stage for Sisqó's forays into acting. He first appeared in the teen comedy *Get Over It* before signing a development deal with NBC television and a five-picture deal with Miramax.

By the end of 2000, Sisqó was not only a music star but also a teen phenomenon because of his youthful looks, toned body, trendy clothing, and stylish hair—and his omnipresence on MTV obviously didn't hurt. Following commercially successful guest appearances on DMX's "What These B*****s Want" and Lil' Kim's "How Many Licks" that kept him in the spotlight while he spent time in the studio, Sisqó re-emerged in the summer of 2001 with *Return of Dragon*, his attempt to prove that "Thong Song" wasn't just a novelty success. *—Jason Birchmeier*

● **Unleash the Dragon** / Nov. 30, 1999 / Def Soul ♦♦♦
By the end of his debut solo album, Dru Hill's finest singer Sisqó has beaten the same rhythmic pattern, which is churned in and out of nearly every song, into the ground. Loaded with whispered bedroom moans, which have become late-'90s R&B clichés, *Unleash the Dragon* is short on any real songs to justify the pointless replay of these familiar grooves. Only when he actually unleashes his inner dragon, like on the club thumper "Thong Song," does Sisqó sound at all like the ferocious soulman he fancies himself to be. There's also little distinction among the guest spots here (though Make It Hot's turn on the jittery "Got to Get It" offers some sparks). And once the beats—which borrow heavily from the contemporary R&B playbook—are programmed, there's little for Sisqó to do but coast along the grooves, with all the conviction and commitment of a soul robot. *—Michael Gallucci*

Return of Dragon / Jun. 19, 2001 / Def Soul ♦♦♦
Sisqó's second solo album, *Return of Dragon*, follows up a debut that unexpectedly shot to the top of the charts a year earlier and remained there, week after week. That debut album, *Unleash the Dragon*, was almost solely powered by an omnipresent summer anthem in "Thong Song"—a difficult feat to duplicate, an even more difficult feat to top. But even if *Return of Dragon* doesn't have a surefire novelty hit like "Thong Song" on it, it still has enough firepower to carry Sisqó back to the top of the charts. It's a safe record, no doubt, offering only ten full-length songs and an ensemble cast of songwriters and producers. But regardless of how few risks Sisqó takes on this album, the result is commendable, an energetic, slick, and stylish album with plenty of subtle sex and overt gloss—everything early-2000s pop listeners demand in their superstars. To be honest, though, pop fans aren't looking for well-crafted albums but rather dynamite singles. And this album has its fair share. In fact, somewhere around half of these ten songs could function as hit singles in 2001, with "Can I Live," "Dance for Me," and "Close Your Eyes" being the most obvious choices. In particular, "Can I Live" stands out on the album mostly because of its over-the-top execution; here, the timeless Teddy Riley takes the reigns with songwriting partner D'Wayne Jones, crafting a jittery Timbaland-style beat and working various members of Sisqó's new affiliates, the Dragon Family, into the song. Yet while "Can I Live" stands out as a step in a new direction for Sisqó, "Dance for Me" takes a look back to "Thong Song," resulting in a similarly sexy dancefloor anthem that is just dying for a sleazy, near-naked-dancers-everywhere MTV treatment. In short, Sisqó gives you exactly what you want—assuming you liked his debut album—offering a can't-miss collection of should-be hits and even more of his ceaseless crooning. *—Jason Birchmeier*

Sister Sledge

f. 1971, North Philadelphia, PA
Group / Urban, Disco, Smooth Soul, Quiet Storm, Soul
Best known for their work with Chic in the late '70s, siblings Debbie, Kim, Joni, and Kathy Sledge—collectively Sister Sledge—reached the height of their popularity during the

disco era but had been recording since the early '70s and were still active several decades later. The group was formed in Philadelphia in 1971, when the sisters' ages ranged from 12 to 16, and they recorded their first single, "Time Will Tell," for the Philly-based Money Back label. (For the first few years, the group called itself Sisters Sledge.) In 1972, Sister Sledge signed with Atco and recorded its second single, "Weatherman," which was followed by the Jackson 5-like "Mama Never Told Me" in 1973.

Sister Sledge's first national hit came in 1974, when "Love, Don't You Go Through No Changes on Me" reached number 31 on the R&B charts and the Philadelphians recorded their debut album, *Circle of Love*. Their second album, *Together*, was released in 1977 and contained the number 61 R&B hit "Blockbuster Boy." It wasn't until 1979, when Chic leaders Nile Rodgers & Bernard Edwards produced *We Are Family*, that Sister Sledge really exploded commercially. "He's the Greatest Dancer" and *We Are Family*'s title song both soared to number one on the R&B charts, and the latter (a number-two pop smash) was adopted as a theme by the World Series-winning Pittsburgh Pirates.

Sister Sledge's next album, *Love Somebody Today* (1980), was also produced by the Rodgers & Edwards team, and the single "Got to Love Somebody" became a number-six R&B hit. In 1981, Sister Sledge switched producers and worked with Narada Michael Walden, who produced 1981's excellent *All American Girls*. The title song was a number-three R&B hit, and in 1982, Sister Sledge had a number-14 R&B hit with a cover of Mary Wells' "My Guy" that appeared on *The Sisters*. But after that, the foursome's popularity faded, and it never had another Top 20 hit in the U.S.—although 1985's "Frankie" (a number-32 R&B hit in the States) became a pop number-one hit in England. Sister Sledge left Atlantic for good in 1985. Epic released Kathy's debut solo album, *Heart*, in 1992, and 1997 found the sisters recording a risk-taking date, *African Eyes*, arguably one of the finest albums they ever recorded. *—Alex Henderson*

Circle of Love / 1975 / Atlantic ♦♦♦
When Sister Sledge recorded their debut album *Circle of Love* in 1974, all four members of the group were still in their teens—Debbie Sledge, the oldest member, was 19, while the youngest, Kathy, was only 15. However, there's nothing bubblegum about *Circle of Love*. If Sister Sledge sounded like a female equivalent of the early Jackson 5 on 1973's "Mama Never Told Me," this vinyl LP found the Philadelphians sounding more like a younger version of the Three Degrees (who were also from Philly). This LP had a gem of a single in the haunting "Love, Don't You Go Through No Changes on Me," which wasn't huge but did reach number 31 on the R&B charts. The rest of the album isn't that strong, nor is it in a class with Sister Sledge's late-'70s/early-'80s work with Chic and Narada Michael Walden. Nonetheless, it's a decent, if uneven, collection of Philly soul, and the siblings handle themselves well on material ranging from the Gamble & Huff-minded "Pain Reliever" and the charming "Cross My Heart" to the Thom Bell & Linda Creed ballad "Give in to Love." Out of print since the 1970s, *Circle of Love* isn't among Sister Sledge's essential albums, but it has historic value. *—Alex Henderson*

Together / 1977 / Cotillion ♦♦♦

We Are Family / 1979 / Cotillion ♦♦♦♦♦
Before 1979's *We Are Family*, Sister Sledge wasn't a huge name in the R&B/disco world. The group had enjoyed a small following and scored a few minor hits, including "Love, Don't You Go Through No Changes on Me" in 1974 and "Blockbuster Boy" in 1977. But it wasn't until *We Are Family* that the Philadelphia siblings finally exploded commercially, and the people they have to thank for their commercial success are Chic leaders Nile Rodgers & Bernard Edwards. The Rodgers & Edwards team handles all of the writing, producing, and arranging on this album; so not surprisingly, almost everything on *We Are Family* is very Chic-sounding. That is true of the sexy "He's the Greatest Dancer" and the anthemic, uplifting title song (both of which soared to number one on the R&B charts), as well as excellent album tracks like the lush "Easier to Love," the perky "One More Time," and the addictive "Thinking of You." The least Chic-sounding tune on the album is the ballad "Somebody Loves Me," which favors a classic sweet soul approach and is the type of song one would have expected from Thom Bell, Gamble & Huff, or Holland-Dozier-Holland rather than Rodgers & Edwards. Meanwhile, the intoxicating "Lost in Music" (a number-35 R&B hit) is about as Chic-sounding as it gets. When Rhino reissued *We Are Family* on CD in 1995, it added four bonus tracks, all of which are remixes of either the title song or "Lost in Music." These remixes are intriguing; it's interesting to hear late '70s classics turned into high-tech 1990s dance-pop. But they are less than essential, and the original versions are by far the best—how can you improve on perfection? Both creatively and commercially, *We Are Family* is Sister Sledge's crowning achievement. *—Alex Henderson*

Got to Love Somebody Today / 1980 / Cotillion ♦♦♦♦♦
A decline was inevitable after the platinum across-the-board success of *We Are Family*, but *Love Somebody Today* wasn't quite the dropoff many claimed at the time. Nile Rodgers & Bernard Edwards again properly kept the emphasis on their harmonies, interaction and vocal flexibility, and provided them with more fine material. But this time around, only "Got to Love Somebody" managed to click. The anti-disco backlash was in full bloom, and fine singles like "Easy Street," "How to Love" and "Reach Your Peak" were completely ignored. R&B stations reacted in a lukewarm fashion as well, even though "Reach Your Peak" did prove a moderate R&B hit. *—Ron Wynn*

Love Somebody Today / 1980 / Cotillion ♦♦♦
Although Sister Sledge had already peaked with their 1979 powerhouse *We Are Family* LP, they returned in the first half of 1980 with *Love Somebody Today*. Not quite as successful as its predecessor, but still showcasing the group's remarkable vocal strength, the album foundered primarily because it hit the brick wall laid down by the burgeoning disco backlash, but still managed to peak at number seven on the R&B charts in March. Partnered for the second go-round with Chic's Bernard Edwards & Nile Rodgers, who wrote and produced all the songs, Sister Sledge spun out a sophisticated, slick set of smooth, midtempo R&B that concentrated on the sisters' vocals, leaving the musical arrangements in the background. Both the title track, which proved the album's only major hit, and the melancholy "You Fooled Around" emerged as the set's high points. Elsewhere, "Reach Your Peak" is a surprising combination of disco and jazz, leaving both "I'm a Good Girl" and "How to Love" to weigh in on the ballad front. It would have been hard for Sister Sledge to surpass the monstrously good one-two punch of "We Are Family" and "He's the Greatest Dancer." And, not surprisingly, much of *Love Somebody Today* sounds flat in comparison. But still, the sounds of Sister Sledge at the peak of their star power are better than much of the pap that passed for pop at the time. *—Amy Hanson*

All American Girls / 1981 / Cotillion ♦♦♦
After recording two albums under the direction of Chic leaders Nile Rodgers & Bernard Edwards, Sister Sledge surprised the R&B world by working with Narada Michael Walden on *All American Girls*. The Philadelphia siblings had become identified with the Chic sound, and were ready for a change. It was a gamble that paid off artistically more than commercially. Far from a bomb but not as successful as it deserved to be, the album boasts its share of gems, including the hit title song (which, ironically, does have a few Chic-ish touches), the rock-influenced "He's Just a Runaway" and the infectiously funky "Make a Move." Interestingly, "Runaway" didn't became a hit until given a reggae remix that isn't nearly as exciting as the version heard on *All American Girls*, clearly one of the group's finest accomplishments [reissued on CD in 1995 with informative liner notes by music journalist Gary Jackson]. *—Alex Henderson*

The Sisters / 1982 / Cotillion ♦♦♦
Keeping to their regular routine of releasing an album a year, Sister Sledge emerged in 1982 with *The Sisters*, their first self-produced effort. Keeping their disco-fied R&B in place, the sisters added a few contemporary kicks to hold their own in a decade fast leaving them behind. The move proved correct, as the group was rewarded with another Top 20 hit. The punchy, horn-heavy, and lightly funky "Super Bad Sisters" not only opens the album in fine style, but also adds a surprising sonic update via a rap from Kenneth and James Williams. Following that feat, though, the rest of the set settles down to soft-edged R&B and mediocre ballads. A less-than-stellar remake of the Mary Wells classic "My Guy" managed to reach number-14 R&B, while a passable duet between Kathy Sledge and David Simmons actually emerges as one of *The Sisters*' best moments. "Jacki's Theme: There's No Stopping Us," meanwhile, brought the set to a close with its quirky, snap-happy disco grooves. At the end of the day, and despite the fact that it's obvious that the band was still full of good ideas, *The Sisters* just doesn't reach its full potential. It could be that the band was too far out of its time and place, or that it just didn't have enough oomph to keep its edge, or perhaps it just suffered from production jitters. But ultimately, there are far finer ways to sample the remarkable talents of this R&B powerhouse. *—Amy Hanson*

Bet Cha Say That to All the Girls / 1983 / WEA ♦♦
With veteran jazzman-turned-funker George Duke at the production helm and a plethora of well-known musicians—including Al Jarreau, Michael Sembello, and Jeffrey Osborne—arrayed behind them, a late-in-the-day Sister Sledge released *Bet Cha Say That to All the Girls* to moderate success in 1983. While the band's blend of light urban dance was certainly urbane, the sisters were well past the days of the powerhouse R&B diva posturing that brought them to the top of the charts in the 1970s. Sister Sledge was instead bent on bright pop. Leading with the strong charting single "B.Y.O.B. (Bring Your Own Baby)," the rest of *Bet Cha Say That to All the Girls* unreeled in much the same manner. The superb harmonies and lush strings and horns swing from smooth R&B to light funk and back to classic mainstream pop with ease, as the beautiful ballad "Once in Your Life" and the funky closer "Thank You for the Party," as well as the title track, emerge as the album's real highlights. With perhaps a little too much emphasis placed on a light, bright sound which ultimately sacrifices substance, it's no surprise that this set foundered. Too much sugar can spoil even the sweetest dessert. *—Amy Hanson*

When the Boys Meet the Girls / 1985 / Atlantic ♦♦♦
Their last album to hit the charts, 1985's *When the Boys Meet the Girls* found Sister Sledge attempting to return to past form as they brought Chic's Nile Rodgers back on-board to produce and perform. And although the move would ultimately prove ineffective, as the album appeared and hovered just out of the Top 50, this easy pairing returned the sisters to an earlier edge. With the title track backed by an eclectic arrangement, those classic punchy Sister Sledge vocals were pushed well into the front of the action. The album birthed two further standouts, as both "Frankie," which is spun to become reggae-lite, and the heavily Rodgers-influenced club hit "Dancing on the Jagged Edge" rippled off the grooves. The latter, just barely limping to a paltry number-73 R&B, would prove the band's last hit until their comeback in the early '90s. Elsewhere, the Kathy Sledge-led ballad "You Need Me" emerges the best of the bunch, while the snappy "Peer Pressure" wades into wave territory, leaving the frenetic and not-quite-pleasing "Hold out Poppy" well out of the loop. *When the Boys Meet the Girls* is a fine effort, but this late in the day it just doesn't pull enough tricks out of the hat to make it worthwhile. And even through it's a major step up from their last effort, Sister Sledge is far better sampled across their earlier R&B heyday. *—Amy Hanson*

● **The Best of Sister Sledge (1973–1985)** / Sep. 1, 1992 / Rhino ♦♦♦♦♦
Sister Sledge evolved quite a bit during the 12 years documented on this 1992 collection, which traces the Philadelphians' evolution from bubblegum soulsters to sexy but wholesome disco-era darlings to struggling urban-contemporary act. After early numbers like "Mama Never Told Me" and "Love Don't You Go Through No Changes on Me" (both recorded at a time when the sisters were still in their teens and came across as sort of a female Jackson 5), they dive headfirst into disco/soul with "Cream of the Crop" (an

underrated, Philly-sounding pearl) and finally hit the big time with the Chic-produced mega-hits "We Are Family" and "He's the Greatest Dancer." One hears Sledge entering the '80s on a high note with "Got to Love Somebody" but by the middle of the decade sounding less inspired on the singles "Frankie" and "Dancing on the Jagged Edge." One of the collection's most disappointing tracks is the reggae remix of "He's Just a Runaway." While it's true that this is the version that became a medium-size hit, the more rock-ish version found on *All American Girls* packs a much greater punch. But despite a few weak spots here and there, this is a gem-laden CD that paints a generally impressive picture of the group. *—Alex Henderson*

African Eyes / 1997 / Fahrenheit ♦♦♦
One of Sister Sledge's finest achievements came in 1997, when the Philadelphia siblings recorded the overlooked *African Eyes.* While Sister Sledge had long since passed its commercial peak, this CD made it clear that the group still had a lot to say musically. Reflective and highly spiritual, *African Eyes* often recalls Earth, Wind & Fire's '70s output and sometimes combines soul and funk with elements of world music. In fact, the uplifting tone of "World Rise & Shine," "The Unraveling" and "Walking in the Light" gives us an idea what Sister Sledge might have sounded like if the sisters had worked with Maurice White in the late '70s instead of various Philadelphia producers and Chic leaders Nile Rodgers & Bernard Edwards. Some of the material, however, isn't EWF-ish, but instead, offers an unlikely blend of R&B and folk. Folk-ish touches find their way to "Love's Abyss" and "Cry for Sowetto," a beautiful reflection on the political evolution of South Africa. But as much as *African Eyes* has going for it, the album was ignored by commercial radio and failed to do very much commercially. In fact, it's safe to say that the vast majority of listeners who bought *We Are Family* and *All American Girls* didn't even hear about the album's release. *—Alex Henderson*

Free Soul: The Classics of Sister Sledge / Aug. 8, 2000 / Atlantic ♦♦♦♦
An ample serving of Sister Sledge, but hardly a hunger buster; 18 tracks doesn't exactly constitute an all you can listen to buffet, and some lesser A-sides, i.e., their update of "My Guy," is outside looking in. This is noted because if you want this baby you're gonna spend around $50—after factoring in shipping and handling—if you cop from an Internet retailer, and probably more if you don't. Where's Napster when you need them? For that piggy bank-busting price you get most that you expect, some you don't, and a few pre- and post-Nile Rodgers & Bernard Edwards tracks. Alright, but you can get the gist of Sister Sledge much cheaper by looking for something that say "greatest hits" or "best-of." This is a Japanese import; those import taxes must be a real mutha. *—Andrew Hamilton*

The Sisters

Group / Girl Group, Latin Soul
Chicano girl group the Sisters teamed East Los Angeles siblings Rosella, Ersi, and Mary Arvizu. Discovered by producer Billy Cardenas, the trio signed to Del-Fi Records; their debut session, recorded at the famed GoldStar studios with future Love members Arthur Lee and John Echols among the session players, generated a fine 1964 rendition of the oft-covered "Gee Baby Gee"; the follow-up, the Sisters' take on the Jessie Hill classic "Ooh Poo Pah Doo," featured Ersi on lead (Rosella typically assumed the helm), but like its predecessor failed to catch on at radio. The group's final single, 1965's Sam Cooke cover "I Love You (For Sentimental Reasons)," was also the last official Del-Fi release; although the Sisters soon disbanded, Ersi eventually scored a belated chart hit as a member of the Latino rock combo El Chicano, whose instrumental "Viva Tirado" cracked the pop Top 30 in the spring of 1970. *—Jason Ankeny*

Six Teens

f. 1956, Los Angeles, CA
Group / Doo Wop, R&B
The Six Teens' name derived from the average age of the six members divided by six; Ed Wells was the oldest at 17, and Trudy Williams the youngest at 12. Like most teenage groups of that era, they were inspired by Frankie Lymon & the Teenagers. Originally the Sweet Teens, they recorded one single under that name ("Don't Worry About a Thing" for Flip Records in 1956), with Wells singing lead on the first recording but Williams taking the helm for subsequent releases. The first Six Teens single, "A Casual Look," became their biggest hit. Flip's owner picked "Teenage Promise" but the disc jockeys flipped it, and it went to number 25 on the pop charts and number-seven R&B.

The group began performing and spent much of the summer of 1957 performing in Hawaii. "Send Me Flowers," their second release, was number one there, but their third record, "Only Jim," did nothing to advance their career. The fourth, "Arrow of Love," showed at number 80, and when Flip began marketing the Six Teens to teenyboppers, their songs and lyrics became unbelievably trite. Tunes like "Stop Playing Ping Pong With My Little Heart" had no chance for success, and a personnel shakeup did nothing to stabilize the group. In 1957, the Six Teens recorded "My Surprise," credited to the Six Teens featuring (14-year-old) Trudy Williams. Three final recordings failed to chart, but they continue performing with different members until the late '60s. They have since regrouped and performed on the doo wop circuit, releasing a CD of new recordings on Lacoriha Records, *The Six Teens Greatest Hits.* *—Andrew Hamilton*

• **A Casual Look: The Flip Recordings** / May 7, 2002 / Ace ♦♦♦
The Six Teens only had one substantial hit, 1956's "A Casual Look," but made, like many such groups of the time, a surprising number of records. Both sides of all dozen of their 1956-1960 singles are on this CD, as well as a fast version of "A Casual Look"'s B-side, "Teenage Promise," that was first issued in 1961 as credited to Trudy and Louise. There's an appealing innocence to the group, particularly Trudy Williams' vocals, and it's impressive that almost all of their songs were written by a member, Ed Wells. This cannot obscure, however, the general formulaic mediocrity of the material, which usually sticks to simple doo wop ballads at their most innocuous. There's an occasional glimpse of something a little more interesting, like a bit more sophisticated melody in the 1956 B-side "My Special Guy," lusher-than-usual harmonies on "Oh It's Crazy," and the addition of strings on their final sides in what sounds like a conscious or unconscious attempt to emulate acts like the Skyliners and (on "So Happy") the duets by Brook Benton and Dinah Washington. For almost everyone, however, the presence of "A Casual Look" on oldies collections (though it's shown up on surprisingly few of those) will be enough. As usual, Ace's liner notes supply more information about the group than you'll find anywhere else, including comments on each track. *—Richie Unterberger*

Skull Snaps

Group / Funk
Skull Snaps were a mysterious funk group that lasted long enough to record and release a self-titled 1973 album before apparently disbanding. Since its small-time release on the GSF label, *Skull Snaps* has become one of the more legendary rare funk records, having been sampled countless times on rap records. Gang Starr's "Take It Personal," Camp Lo's "Cooley High," Ol' Dirty Bastard's "Hippa to da Hoppa," Lords of the Underground's "Funky Child," and Diamond D's "Sally Got a One Track Mind" represent just a handful of the tracks that have put the drums from "It's a New Day" to use. Charly later issued the album on CD in the '90s, to the amazement of those who had paid triple figures for the original LP. *—Andy Kellman*

• **Skull Snaps** / 1973 / Charly ♦♦♦
Original vinyl copies of Skull Snaps' one and only LP continue to exchange hands on the rare groove market for three figures. There are two reasons for this: one, it's rare, and two, the drum breaks from the album have been feasted upon for samples so frequently that samples of the samples have likely been sampled. It's not that the album is spectacular—it's merely a decent early-'70s funk record from some accomplished musicians who don't exactly leave a trademark of their own throughout its nine songs. This soul-drenched funk album is most notable for the drums of "It's a New Day." It's the album's strongest cut, and the opening drum pattern is as ubiquitous they come—you can hear it get put to re-use in well over two dozen popular rap songs. Anyone who likes hard funk will find much to like—the vocals are gruff, the rhythms are tough yet nimble (the drums are crisp and smacking throughout), and the subject matter takes on everything from pimps to romance to everyday relationships. [Charly reissued the album on CD in 1995.] *—Andy Kellman*

The Skyliners

f. 1959, Pittsburgh, PA
Group / Doo Wop, Pop
This Pittsburgh vocal group made a magnificent heartache ballad in 1959, "Since I Don't Have You." It remains among R&B's ultimate agonizing triumphs, and Chuck Jackson later did an equally gripping version. Jimmy Beaumont was the lead vocalist, with Janet Vogel, Wally Lester, Joe VerScharen, and Jackie Taylor. Beaumont, Taylor, and Lester had been in the Crescents, while Vogel and VerScharen were alumni of the El Rios. Their follow-up, "This I Swear," was a creditable effort that peaked at number 20 on the R&B charts, but few remember it. Oddly, "Since I Don't Have You" only reached number three on the R&B side and number 12 on the pop charts. But it's certainly one song for whom the numbers really don't come close to telling the story. The Skyliners had two chart singles on Calico and then had one other song reach the R&B Top 40 in 1965, "The Loser," for Jubilee. *—Ron Wynn*

The Skyliners / 1978 / Tortoise ♦♦♦

• **The Greatest Hits** / 1986 / Original Sound ♦♦♦♦♦

Since I Don't Have You / 1991 / Ace ♦♦♦♦♦
The Skyliners were among the more dramatic, theatrical white doo wop groups. Their hit "Since I Don't Have You" has been covered by numerous performers, and it's among the 21 singles featured on this Ace anthology covering numbers recorded for Calico and Laurie. Jimmy Beaumont's tremendous leads distinguished "I Swear," "It Happened Today," and the title track, among others. It's no surprise that such flamboyant performers as Patti LaBelle and Chuck Jackson are big Skyliners fans. *—Ron Wynn*

40th Anniversary Edition / May 11, 1999 / Collectables ♦♦♦♦♦
More than one person has called the Skyliners the greatest vocal group of all time, and although every act has their fans, that kind of praise is telling. The group's 1959 hit "Since I Don't Have You" is one of the most sublime, mood-setting singles of its era, and it's no wonder it has been so widely used in motion pictures. *40th Anniversary Collection* is a two-disc set filled with 40 cross-licensed tracks that trace the group's history from the '50s through the '70s, including every chart hit along the way. The attention to detail makes this one of the best packages Collectables has assembled. Many buyers will be content with a simple best-of collection, but *40th Anniversary Edition* is an excellent expanded anthology for those who want to take a closer look than a single disc can provide. *—Greg Adams*

Skyy

f. Brooklyn, NY
Group / Quiet Storm, Urban, Disco
A New York City octet, one of three funk and/or disco bands in which producer/keyboardist Randy Muller was involved. The original lineup featured Denise, Delores, and Bonny Dunning as vocalists, with guitarists Solomon Roberts and Anibal Anthony Sierra, keyboardist Larry Greenberg, bassist Gerald Lebon, and drummer Tommy McConnell. Muller organized the group and they recorded for Salsoul from the late '70s until 1984. Their biggest hit was "Call Me" in 1981, an R&B chart-topper. They could do sweeping funk tracks, dance-oriented cuts, or light ballads, although they never enjoyed the crossover success of a group like Atlantic Starr. They moved to Capitol in 1986 and

enjoyed their biggest hit in quite some time with "Givin' It (To You)," a Top Ten R&B single. They recorded *Start of a Romance* for Atlantic in 1989 and landed another hit with "Real Love." Their most recent release was *Nearer to You* in 1992. *—Ron Wynn*

Skyy / 1979 / Salsoul ✦✦✦✦
This was the debut album for this self-contained octet. Their first release was the dance number "First Time Around." It was a mixture of funk and disco. A very lengthy musical track with some vocals added here and there; ideal for a party. It sealed the top 20 inside 14 weeks. It was followed by "Let's Turn It Out." Funk was the focus here for the Brooklyn-based band. Chanting party vocals, improvising solos and Solomon Roberts master of ceremonies wail keep this groove on the move. However, it was only on the charts for nine weeks peaking at number 65. A bona fide party song, as are most of these selections and solid ones they are. "Stand By Me" is the only ballad; it's trimmed in a pop texture. Though disco was on its last leg, its popularity still warranted groups including it in their repertoire and Skyy had its share. *—Craig Lytle*

Skyway / 1980 / Salsoul ✦✦✦
The second album from the Brooklyn-based octet featured two releases: "High" and "Skyyzoo." The former is a moderately-paced groove showcasing the unison vocals of the Dunning sisters. Lightly arranged with an unruffled rhythm track and some guitar licks, the strings and horn complement this laid-back dance number. The single peaked at 13 after 16 weeks on the *Billboard* R&B charts. The follow-up, "Skyyzoo," was more of a antic-driven number. With its hyped vocals and various music gadgets, the song was an invitation to the dancefloor. It peaked at number 32 on the charts after 11 weeks. The remainder of the album falls in line with these two singles save the ballad "Who's Gonna Love Me" and "Music Music," which swings the way of rock with its heavy electric guitar and slashing vocals. *—Craig Lytle*

Skyyport / 1981 / Salsoul ✦✦✦✦
In the late 1970s and early 1980s, producer Randy Muller was best known for two things: being a member of Brass Construction and working with Skyy. Both bands favored a funk/disco approach that brought many dancefloors to life, but there were some major differences between the two East Coast outfits. For one thing, Skyy had three female vocalists. Plus, Skyy was a lot more consistent. While Brass Construction recorded its share of albums that were uneven or disappointing, Skyy was usually reliable—more often than not, one could safely assume that the latter would deliver a first-rate party album. *Skyyport* is no exception. This 1980 release was the band's third album, and the party people who had acquired Skyy's two previous albums were not disappointed. The LP gets off to an impressive start with the hit "Here's to You" (written by Muller), and they keep the creative momentum going with equally infectious funk dance numbers like "Superlove" (another hit single that Muller wrote) and "Take It Easy." So, if Brass Construction and Skyy both had Muller's input, why was the latter so much more consistent? It all came down to chemistry—he had a more consistently productive relationship with Skyy, which is interesting when you consider that Muller was actually a member of Brass Construction. Though he co-produced *Skyyport* and other band releases with Skyy's Soloman Roberts Jr. and did a lot of writing for the band, he was never an actual member. One of the *Skyyport* offerings that he didn't write is the ballad "For the First Time," which Roberts contributed. Although ballads weren't the group's forte, the tune is pleasant enough. However, it is the uptempo funk/dance numbers that ultimately define *Skyyport* and make it one of Skyy's best releases. *—Alex Henderson*

Skyy Line / 1982 / Salsoul ✦✦✦

Skyylight / 1983 / Salsoul ✦✦✦

Start of a Romance / 1989 / Atlantic ✦✦✦
Following in the footsteps of both Brass Construction and B.T. Express, latter-day funk band Skyy spent the better part of the 1980s honing its sound, keeping the funk-fueled ethics and infusing the beat with catchy disco. *Start of a Romance*, released in 1989, found the band now on Atlantic and clawing its way back into America's psyche after a three-year silence, hitting the streets with an album of light funk and dance ballads. The title track abounds with a big beat technique, while the slightly skewed tempo behind the lush vocal harmonies sets the pace for what unfolds as slick and sophisticated dance-pop. It's a technique that the band would employ to its advantage across the entire set—while it can be argued that "Start of a Romance" is just another late-'80s dance song, there's enough push and pull within the bars to create an interesting rhythm. Elsewhere, Skyy brought the marginally soppy "Real Love," with its emphatic spoken word break, into the charts as easily as it employed the mainstream's burgeoning love of scratching within "Sending a Message." Although the album enjoyed more than moderate success, by this time the members of Skyy found themselves supplanted by the similar strains of the likes of both Janet Jackson and Paula Abdul. The band would drop from sight shortly after, not to reappear until 1992. *—Amy Hanson*

Nearer to You / 1992 / Atlantic ✦✦✦✦✦

● **Greatest Hits** / Jul. 23, 1996 / Capitol ✦✦✦✦✦

Slave

f. 1975, Dayton, OH
Group / Disco, Funk
Arguably the hottest of the '70s Ohio funk bands, Slave had a great run in the late '70s and early '80s. Trumpeter Steve Washington formed the group in Dayton in 1975. Vocalist Floyd Miller teamed with Tom Lockett Jr, Carter Bradley, Mark Adams, Mark Hicks, Danny Webster, Orion Wilhoite, and Tim Dozier. Vocalists Steve Arrington and Starleana Young came aboard in 1978, with Arrington ultimately becoming lead vocalist. Their first big hit was the thumping single "Slide" in 1977 for Cotillion, where they remained until 1984. Their best tracks were lyrically simple and at times silly, but the arrangements and rhythms were intense and hypnotic. Other Top Ten R&B hits were "Just a Touch of Love" in 1979, "Watching You" in 1980, and "Snap Shot" in 1981. Young, Washington, and Lockett departed to form Aurra in 1979. Arrington himself left in the early '80s.

They added Charles Carter, Delburt Taylor, Sam Carter, Kevin Johnson, and Roger Parker as replacements and continued on, though much less successfully, into the late '80s. They moved to Atlantic for one LP in 1984, then switched to the Atlanta-based Ichiban in 1986 for singles and LPs that were just a shade of the former vibrant Slave sound. Their most recent release was *The Funk Strikes Back* in 1992. Rhino issued *Stellar Funk: The Best of Slave*, a first-rate anthology of their finest cuts, in 1994. *—Ron Wynn*

Slave / 1977 / Rhino ✦✦✦✦
The debut album from the Ohio-based funk aggregate was a grand success, all of which resulted in the release of one single, "Slide." Being the only single released from the album, "Slide" had no problem gaining airplay with its gothic introduction, animated vocals, and rumbling bassline. The funk anthem claimed the number-one spot on the *Billboard* R&B charts inside of 20 weeks. The other cuts on the album continue the aggressive funk assault, but with subtle passion and their own distinctive arrangements. The exception is "Son of Slide," which is identical to the album's big hit, except that it's an instrumental save a brief chorus chant. The only ballad is "The Happiest Days," a sweet soul song arranged in the vein of the Ohio Players with its horns, lead and backing vocals. *—Craig Lytle*

The Hardness of the World / 1977 / Cotillion ✦✦✦✦
As funky as they were, Slave had a distinctive smoothness to their music. Here on their second album, the self-contained ten-member band assembled an engaging mix of songs. This collection featured two releases. The first was "The Party Song." Arranged around a swinging funk track and chanting vocals in unison, group leader Steve Washington invokes a jazzy trumpet interlude. The single peaked on the *Billboard* R&B charts at number 22 after an unjust ten weeks. The second release was "Baby Sinister," also spiced with that '70s funk sound. While it has a similar arrangement to "The Party Song," it retains more use of the synthesizer. It peaked at number 74 after a mere four weeks. While their vocals are not as sharp on most selections, the group compensates with their musical ability and impressive arrangements. "We Can Make Love" is the only ballad on the album, and an outstanding ballad it is. It would be a great addition to any quiet storm format. *—Craig Lytle*

The Concept / 1978 / Cotillion ✦✦✦✦
The amazing aspect about bands from Dayton is originality, there's no defining thread or sound to speak of, each group is unique. A short list of Dayton bands include the Ohio Players, Zapp, Lakeside, Sun, and Heatwave. Where's the trademark Dayton sound? Slave may be the most underrated of all, their brand of electronic, funk/soul, techno sound made for great albums. "Stellar Fungk" the title track (yes they spelled funk that way) is stimulating head music, enhanced by brain probing lead guitarist Marc "Drac" Hicks, powerful basslines from Mark Adams, and some ear popping synthesizer work by Carter Bradley. The title *The Concept* is misleading, the only concept to this fine collection of grooves and funky sounds is getting your boogie on. *—Andrew Hamilton*

Just a Touch of Love / 1979 / Cotillion ✦✦✦✦✦
In 1977, Slave's self-titled debut album (which boasted the number-one R&B smash "Slide") earned the Dayton outfit a reputation for playing sweaty, aggressive, in-your-face funk. But when Slave provided its fourth album, *Just a Touch of Love*, in 1979, it was clear that the Midwesterners were determined to soften their approach. "Funky Lady (Foxy Lady)," "Roots," and the hit title song (all of which boast Steve Arrington on lead vocals) were definitely the work of a smoother, sleeker Slave—and yet, the band still had plenty of grit. This excellent album left no doubt that Slave was still a funk band, although it wasn't as in-your-face as the Slave that gave listeners "Slide" and "Screw Your Wig on Tite" in 1977. Arrington, who first recorded with Slave on 1978's *The Concept*, played a major role in its evolution—and two other lead vocalists who make important contributions to this LP are Starleana Young and Curt Jones (both of who went on to form Aurra, the group that hit big with "Are You Single" in 1981). Arrington, Young, and Jones weren't original members of Slave, but all of them proved valuable when Slave opted to embrace a smoother style of funk. And all of them do their part to make *Just a Touch of Love* one of Slave's finest albums. *—Alex Henderson*

Stone Jam / 1980 / Rhino ✦✦✦
The funk of the late 1970s and early 1980s can be divided into two main categories: hardcore funk (Parliament/Funkadelic, Cameo, Rick James, the Gap Band, the Ohio Players) and the type of smoother, so-called "sophisticated funk" associated with Rufus & Chaka Khan, Average White Band, Chic and Teena Marie. Slave first made a name for itself nationally playing the sweatiest, hardest funk, but when singer/drummer Steve Arrington's role in the Dayton, OH, outfit increased, Slave shifted to more of a "sophisti-funk" approach. Except for "Sizzlin' Hot" and the title song, there's little on Slave's fifth album, *Stone Jam*, that can be called hardcore funk. From the laid-back hit "Watching You" to addictive jams like "Dreamin'," "Feel My Love" and "Let's Spend Some Time," this sleeker, consistently melodic Slave is every bit as appealing as the Slave that gave us such aggressive gems as "Slide" and "Screw Your Wig on Tite." Arrington's lead vocals played a major role in the success of this gold album (which Rhino reissued on CD in 1997), and the sexy lead singing of Starleana Young (who would soon make Aurra successful) certainly didn't hurt things either. *—Alex Henderson*

Show Time / 1981 / Atlantic ✦✦✦✦✦
Released in 1981, *Show Time* was the last album that Steve Arrington recorded with Slave. The singer/drummer had been a valuable part of the Dayton funk combo, providing lead vocals on such hits as "Watching You" and "Just a Touch of Love." So you can say that *Show Time* (which was produced by Jimmy Douglass) was the end of an era for Slave.

Creatively, the band was on quite a roll during its Arrington era, and those who had savored 1979's *Just a Touch of Love* and 1980's *Stone Jam* found this LP to be equally strong. From "Smokin'" and "Funken Town" to the single "Snap Shot," *Show Time* proved to be a consistently rewarding addition to Slave's catalog. All of the tracks are immediately recognizable as Slave offerings; during its Arrington period, Slave favored a very distinctive style of funk that was sleek and gritty at the same time. And even though Arrington wasn't an original member—he didn't start recording with the band until its third album, *The Concept*—he was a main ingredient of the Slave sound from 1978-1981. *Show Time* is recommended to funk addicts without hesitation. *—Alex Henderson*

Visions of the Lite / 1982 / Cotillion ♦♦

Bad Enuff / 1983 / Cotillion ♦♦♦

After 1982's disappointing *Visions of the Lite*, it was logical to assume that Slave was past its prime. But the Dayton funksters' next album, *Bad Enuff*, turned out to be a pleasant surprise. Although it falls short of remarkable, this solid, pleasing album was a definite improvement over *Visions of the Lite*. *Bad Enuff* isn't in a class with *The Concept*, *Just a Touch of Love*, or *Stone Jam*, but it's an enjoyable, satisfying record—and unlike *Visions of the Light*, it proved that there could be life after Steve Arrington for Slave. This Jimmy Douglass-produced LP found the band unveiling a new lineup; original members Mark Adams (bass), Danny Webster (lead vocals, lead guitar), and Floyd Miller (lead vocals) were joined by several newcomers, including lead singers Eugene Jackson and Wayne Foote, keyboardist Kenny Hairston, saxman Albrey Rivers, and trumpeter Kenny Anderson. Despite all the personnel changes, Slave is instantly recognizable as Slave on lively, infectious offerings like "Bad Girl," "Rendezvous," and the single "Shake It Up." While *Visions of the Light* had listeners lamenting Arrington's departure from Slave, *Bad Enuff* proved that it could get along without him. *Bad Enuff* isn't recommended to casual listeners, who would be better off sticking with the Midwesterners' essential 1977-1981 work. But it isn't a bad album to have in your collection if you're among Slave's die-hard fans. *—Alex Henderson*

New Plateau / 1984 / Cotillion ♦♦

Rebirth / 1991 / Ichiban ♦♦

● **Stellar Funk: The Best of Slave** / Feb. 22, 1994 / Rhino ♦♦♦♦♦

The most remarkable thing about Slave's music through its career was its commitment to simplicity. Sparse, yet dense arrangements in which everything wrapped itself around a potent bass melody and simple songwriting formula. No ostentatious production or over-the-top divas in acrobatic vocal hysterics. These were tight, jam-packed songs designed to make you move. *Stellar Funk* captures the best moments of Slave's career and some of the most hypnotic funk ever to come out of Ohio, or the '70s for that matter. *—Rob Theakston*

Kathy Sledge

b. Jan. 6, 1959, Philadelphia, PA

Vocals / Club/Dance, Urban, Disco, Funk, Soul, House

Kathy Sledge sang lead on Sister Sledge's hits "He's the Greatest Dancer" and "We Are Family." The Sledge sisters—Debbie, Joni, Kim, and Kathy—released their first single in 1971 on the Money Back label. A few years later, Sister Sledge signed with Atlantic Records' Atco subsidiary. The quartet was teamed with the hit production duo of former Main Ingredient Tony "Champagne" Silvester and Bert "Super Charts" DeCoteaux. Their first major label single, the dazzling "Love Don't Go Through No Changes on Me"—written by Patrick Adams and actress Fay Hauser—b/w the tender ballad "Don't You Miss Him" was a hit in late 1974. Both were included on their debut LP *Circle of Love*. In the group's encircled album cover photo, a teenaged, pig-tailed Kathy is all smiles. On *Circle of Love*'s ballads "Cross My Heart," "Don't You Miss Him," and "You're Much Better Off Loving Me," there are traces of the supple earthy, sexiness that Kathy would later exhibit. After being transferred to Atlantic's Cotillion label, Sister Sledge worked with Silver Convention producers Michael Kunze and Silvester Levay, who wrote most of the songs for their 1977 LP, *Together*.

The hit/songwriting/production duo of guitarist Nile Rodgers and bassist Bernard Edwards of Atlantic Records act Chic were told by Atlantic that they could work with anyone on their roster. Rodgers & Edwards chose one of the label's lesser-known acts, Sister Sledge. Their first single with Rodgers & Edwards, issued on Atlantic's Cotillion label, was "He's the Greatest Dancer," which hit number-one R&B and number-two pop on *Billboard*'s charts in spring 1979. "We Are Family," the title track of Sister Sledge's third album, had already received massive dance club and radio play when it was issued as a single, giving the group a number-one R&B and number-two pop hit in summer 1979. The track was adopted by the 1979 World Series-winning Pittsburgh Pirates and numerous other organizations, and it became a standard tune for family reunions. The *We Are Family* LP went platinum, peaking at number-three pop in spring 1979. The Rodgers/Edwards-produced follow-up LP, *Love Somebody Today*, boasted the singles "Got to Love Somebody" b/w "Good Girl Now," the perky "Reach Your Peak," and "Let's Go on Vacation." The title track to their 1981 LP *All American Girls* went to number-three R&B in early 1981.

In 1992, Kathy Sledge signed with Epic Records as a solo artist. For her first LP, Sledge enlisted top-flight producers. The album, *Heart*, featured the singles "Take Me Back to Love Again" and the ballad "All of My Love." The remix of "Take Me Back to Love Again" was a huge dance hit. The album's inspiring title track was released as a single and became a dance hit. After she left Epic, Sledge recorded several dance hits for other labels. *—Ed Hogan*

● **Heart** / 1992 / Epic ♦♦♦

Absent from the national scene since 1985, Kathy Sledge assembles an impressive lineup of producers and session musicians. However, the result is not as fruitful as expected. The album featured the singles "Take Me Back to Love Again" and "All of My Love," respectively peaking at number 24 and number 57 on the *Billboard* R&B charts. The former has a progressive rhythm with flashbacks of disco, and the latter is a comforting ballad. Kathy Sledge's coarse, yet agile vocals remain as inviting as they did when she sang with her sisters. While there is no knockout song, all selections have good production. *—Craig Lytle*

Percy Sledge

b. Nov. 25, 1941, Leighton, AL

Vocals / Soul, Deep Soul, Southern Soul, Country-Soul

Percy Sledge will forever be associated with "When a Man Loves a Woman," a pleading, soulful ballad he sang with wrenching, convincing anguish and passion. Sledge sang all of his songs that way, delivering them in a powerful rush where he quickly changed from soulful belting to quavering, tearful pleas. It was a voice that made him one of the key figures of deep Southern soul during the late '60s. Sledge recorded at Muscle Shoals studios in Alabama, where he frequently sang songs written by Spooner Oldham & Dan Penn. Not only did he sing deep soul, but Sledge was among the pioneers of country-soul, singing songs by Charlie Rich and Kris Kristofferson in a gritty, passionate style. During the '70s, his commercial success quickly faded away, but Sledge continued to tour and record into the 2000's.

While he worked as a hospital nurse in the early '60s, Sledge began his professional music career as a member of the Southern soul vocal group the Esquires Combo. On the advice of local disc jockey Quin Ivy, he went solo in 1966. Ivy fancied himself a record producer and he agreed to help shape Sledge's song "When a Man Loves a Woman" into a full-fledged single, hiring Spooner Oldham to play a distinctive, legato organ phrase. Ivy released the single independently and quickly licensed it to Atlantic Records, who quickly bought out Sledge's contract. "When a Man Loves a Woman" became a huge hit in the summer of 1966, topping both the pop and R&B charts. It was quickly followed that year by two Top Ten R&B hits, "Warm and Tender Love" and "It Tears Me Up," which were both in the vein of his first hit. Although few of his subsequent singles were hits—only "Take Time to Know Her" reached the R&B Top Ten in 1968—many of the songs, which were often written by Dan Penn and/or Oldham, were acknowledged as classics among soul aficionados.

Despite his strong reputation among deep soul fans, Sledge's sales had declined considerably by the early '70s, and he headed out on the club circuit in America and England. In 1974, he left Atlantic for Capricorn Records, where he surprisingly returned to the R&B Top 20 with "I'll Be Your Everything." Instead of re-igniting his career, the single was a last gasp, as far as chart success was concerned. Over the next two decades he continued to tour, and in the late '80s, "When a Man Loves a Woman" experienced a resurgence in popularity, due to its inclusion in movie soundtracks and in television commercials. Following its appearance in a 1987 Levi commercial in the U.K., the single was re-released and climbed to number two. Two years later, he won the Rhythm & Blues Foundation's Career Achievement Award. Sledge was able to turn this revived popularity into a successful career by touring constantly, playing over 100 shows a year into the '90s. In 1994, he released *Blue Night*, his first collection of new material in over a decade, to uniformly positive reviews. *—Stephen Thomas Erlewine*

When a Man Loves a Woman / 1966 / Collectables ♦♦♦♦♦

This is a country-soul masterpiece. The title track remains among the most beloved, anthemic explanations of love's impact and travails ever written or performed. Had Sledge never made another song, he would still deserve kudos just for that one. But he continued to score with more simple, heartfelt, unsophisticated stories about disappointment, pain, rejection, and perseverance. *—Ron Wynn*

The Percy Sledge Way / 1967 / Atlantic ♦♦♦

This late-'60s album contains hard-hitting, memorable country-soul testimonies from Percy Sledge, who had hit his stride at Atlantic. His narratives were perfectly paced, written with irony and insight, and sung with the ideal mixture of crunching soul and country wit and wisdom. *—Ron Wynn*

Take Time to Know Her / 1968 / Collectables ♦♦♦

The title track was another smashing Sledge gem, while the remainder of the album continues his evocative country-soul tales of woe and heartache. Sledge's late-'60s Atlantic singles and albums were landmarks in the genre; they should have been major country events just as Ray Charles' earlier cuts, but were simply too rooted in black nuance to get any shot with the unimaginative types running country radio (although to be fair, there were also some great country songs in the period that should have been aired on soul stations). The songs were produced and arranged with the right amount of care and sensitivity, never intruding or crowding Sledge as his stories unfolded. *—Ron Wynn*

I'll Be Your Everything / 1974 / Capricorn ♦♦♦

Some wonderful country-soul from Percy Sledge, whose throaty, energized, wonderfully Southern delivery hadn't lost either its earthiness or its zeal, but was so regional that it was losing its appeal to the cosmopolitan, urban types gaining hegemony in black music circles. Sledge delivered several grainy, earnest country-soul weepers and wailers when he moved to Capricorn in the mid-'70s, but they didn't generate much attention anywhere beyond the South. *—Ron Wynn*

★ **It Tears Me Up: The Best of Percy Sledge** / Apr. 21, 1992 / Rhino/Atlantic ♦♦♦♦♦

Percy Sledge's first single, "When a Man Loves a Woman," was an instant masterpiece of deep Southern soul, so powerful and so distinctive it made him a star overnight and helped to quickly establish Muscle Shoals, AL, as one of the major recording centers in the Southern music scene. However, "When a Man Loves a Woman" was such a big hit that it tended to overshadow everything else Percy Sledge did from that point onward; while he had a handful of smaller hits and still records and tours, few people outside of soul obsessives are aware of the full scope of his recording career. *It Tears Me Up: The Best of Percy Sledge*, a typically well-assembled compilation album from Rhino Records, features 23 songs Sledge cut for Atlantic during the 1960s and makes an excellent case for the consistent strength of Sledge's Atlantic catalog. While Sledge specialized in sad songs of love gone wrong, he certainly knew how to make the most of such material, and his stellar, heart-tugging performances of "Take Time to Know Her," "Warm and Tender Love," "It's All Wrong but It's Alright," and the title tune prove that Sledge had more than one brilliant performance in his repertoire. Great stuff, and certainly the best Percy Sledge collection available. *—Mark Deming*

Very Best of Percy Sledge / Feb. 3, 1998 / Rhino ✦✦✦✦✦
The Very Best of Percy Sledge is an excellent 16-track collection that features his biggest hits from 1966-1994. The disc concentrates on his classic '60s hits, including "When a Man Loves a Woman," "Warm and Tender Love," "It Tears Me Up," "Baby, Help Me," "Out of Left Field," "Cover Me," "Take Time to Know Her," "Sudden Stop," and "I'll Be Your Everything," as well as the alternate version of "When a Man Loves a Woman" where the horns are in tune. While the latter-day tracks didn't need to be included on the collection, the disc remains a concise, affordable summation of Sledge's peak period and is a fine introduction to the legendary R&B vocalist. *—Stephen Thomas Erlewine*

Sly & the Family Stone

f. 1967, San Francisco, CA, **db.** 1975

Group / Soul, Psychedelic Soul, Pop/Rock, Funk

Sly & the Family Stone harnessed all of the disparate musical and social trends of the late '60s, creating a wild, brilliant fusion of soul, rock, R&B, psychedelia, and funk that broke boundaries down without a second thought. Led by Sly Stone, the Family Stone was comprised of men and women, and blacks and whites, making the band the first fully integrated group in rock's history. That integration shone through the music, as well as the group's message. Before Stone, very few soul and R&B groups delved into political and social commentary; after him, it became a tradition in soul, funk, and hip-hop. And, along with James Brown, Stone brought hard funk into the mainstream. The Family Stone's arrangements were ingenious, filled with unexpected group vocals, syncopated rhythms, punchy horns, and pop melodies. Their music was joyous, but as the '60s ended, so did the good times. Stone became disillusioned with the ideals he had been preaching in his music, becoming addicted to a variety of drugs in the process. His music gradually grew slower and darker, culminating in 1971's *There's a Riot Going On*, which set the pace for '70s funk with its elastic bass, slurred vocals, and militant Black Power stance. Stone was able to turn out one more modern funk classic, 1973's *Fresh*, before slowly succumbing to his addictions, which gradually sapped him of his once prodigious talents. Nevertheless, his music continued to provide the basic template for urban soul, funk, and even hip-hop well into the '90s.

Sly Stone (born Sylvester Stewart, March 15, 1944) and his family moved from his home state of Texas to San Francisco in the '50s. He had already begun to express an interest in music, and when he was 16, he had a regional hit with "Long Time Away." Stone studied music composition, theory, and trumpet at Vallejo Junior College in the early '60s; simultaneously, he began playing in several groups on the Bay Area scene, often with his brother Fred. Soon, he had become a disc jockey at the R&B station KSOL, later switching to KDIA. The radio appearances led to a job producing records for Autumn Records. While at Autumn, he worked with a number of San Franciscan garage and psychedelic bands, including the Beau Brummels, the Great Society, Bobby Freeman, and the Mojo Men.

During 1966, Stone formed the Stoners, which featured trumpeter Cynthia Robinson. Though the Stoners didn't last long, he brought Robinson along as one of the core members of his next group, Sly & the Family Stone. Formed in early 1967, the Family Stone also featured Fred Stewart (guitar, vocals), Larry Graham Jr. (bass, vocals), Greg Errico (drums), Jerry Martini (saxophone), and Rosie Stone (piano), who all were of different racial backgrounds. The group's eclectic music and multiracial composition made them distinctive from the numerous flower-power bands in San Francisco, and their first single, "I Ain't Got Nobody," became a regional hit for the local label Loadstone. The band signed with Epic Records shortly afterward, releasing their debut album, *A Whole New Thing*, by the end of the year. The record stiffed, but the follow-up, *Dance to the Music*, generated a Top Ten pop and R&B hit with its title track early in 1968. *Life* followed later in 1968, but the record failed to capitalize on its predecessor's success. "Everyday People," released late in 1968, turned their fortunes back around, rocketing to the top of the pop and R&B charts and setting the stage for the breakthrough success of 1969's *Stand!*

Featuring "Everyday People," "Sing a Simple Song," "Stand," and "I Want to Take You Higher," *Stand!* became the Family Stone's first genuine hit album, climbing to number 13 and spending over 100 weeks on the charts. *Stand!* also marked the emergence of the political bent in Stone's songwriting ("Don't Call Me Nigger, Whitey"), as well as the development of hard-edged, improvisational funk like "Sex Machine." The Family Stone quickly became known as one of the best live bands of the late '60s, and their performance at Woodstock was widely hailed as one of the festival's best. The non-LP singles "Hot Fun in the Summertime" and "Thank You (Falettinme Be Mice Elf Agin)" b/w "Everybody Is a Star" became hits, reaching number two and number one, respectively, in late 1969/early 1970. Both singles were included on *Greatest Hits*, which became a number-two record upon its fall 1970 release. While the group was at the height of its popularity, Sly was beginning to unravel behind the scenes. Developing a debilitating addiction to narcotics, Stone soon became notorious for arriving late for concerts, frequently missing the shows all together.

Stone's growing personal problems, as well as his dismay with the slow death of the civil rights movement and other political causes, surfaced on *There's a Riot Goin' On*. Though the album shot to number one upon its fall 1971 release, the record—including "Family Affair," Stone's last number-one single—was dark, hazy, and paranoid, and his audience began to shrink slightly. During 1972, several key members of the Family Stone, including Graham and Errico, left the band; they were replaced by Rusty Allen and Andy Newmark, respectively. The relatively lighter *Fresh* appeared in the summer of 1973, and it went into the Top Ten on the strength of the Top Ten R&B hit "If You Want Me to Stay." Released the following year, *Small Talk* was a moderate hit, reaching number 15 on the charts and going gold, but it failed to generate a big hit single. *High on You*, released in late 1975 and credited only to Sly Stone, confirmed that his power and popularity had faded. "I Get High on You" reached the R&B Top Ten, but the album made no lasting impact.

Disco had overtaken funk in terms of popularity, and even if Sly wanted to compete with disco, he wasn't in shape to make music. He had become addicted to cocaine, his health was frequently poor, and he was often in trouble with the law. His recordings had slowed to a trickle, and Epic decided to close out his contract in 1979 with *Ten Years Too Soon*, a compilation of previously released material that had the original funky rhythm tracks replaced with disco beats. Stone signed with Warner Brothers that same year, crafting the comeback effort *Back on the Right Track* with several original members of the Family Stone, but the record was critically panned and a commercial failure. In light of the album's lack of success, Stone retreated even further, eventually joining forces with George Clinton on Funkadelic's 1981 album *The Electric Spanking of War Babies*. Following the album's release, Stone toured with Clinton's P-Funk All-Stars, which led him to embark on his own tour, as well as a stint with Bobby Womack. The culmination of this burst of activity was 1983's *Ain't But the One Way*, an album that was ignored. Later that year, Stone was arrested for cocaine possession; the following year, he entered rehab.

Stone appeared on Jesse Johnson's 1986 R&B hit "Crazay." The following year, he dueted with Martha Davis on "Love & Affection" for the *Soul Man* soundtrack; he also he recorded "Eek-a-Bo-Static," a single that didn't chart. Stone was arrested and imprisoned for cocaine possession by the end of 1987, and he was never able to recover from the final arrest. Stone continued to battle his addiction, with varying degrees of success. By his 1993 induction to the Rock and Roll Hall of Fame, he had disappeared from public view. Following his appearance at the induction ceremony, he was found living in a sheltered-housing complex. Avenue Records gave Stone a recording contract in 1995, but nothing would be recorded. *—Stephen Thomas Erlewine*

Whole New Thing / 1967 / Epic/Legacy ✦✦✦
Their debut album is more restrained and not nearly as funky or psychedelic as their subsequent efforts, owing far more to traditional soul arrangements. These aren't *that* traditional, though; Sly is already using goofier and/or more thoughtful lyrics than the soul norm, and taking some cues from rock in his adventurous and unexpected song construction. The Family Stone, similarly, aren't as innovative as they would shortly become, but are already a tight unit, particularly in the interplay between lead and backup vocals and the sharp horn riffs. The CD reissue adds a previously unissued track, "What Would I Do." *—Richie Unterberger*

Life / 1968 / Epic/Legacy ✦✦✦✦✦
Just a matter of months after *Dance to the Music*, Sly & the Family Stone turned around and delivered *Life*, a record that leapfrogged over its predecessor in terms of accomplishment and achievement. The most noteworthy difference is the heavier reliance on psychedelics and fuzz guitars, plus a sharpening of songcraft that extends to even throwaways like "Chicken." As it turns out, *Life* didn't have any hits—the double A-sided single "Life"/"M'Lady" barely cracked the Top 100—yet this feels considerably more song-oriented than its predecessor, as each track is a concise slice of tightly wound dance-funk. All the more impressive is that the group is able to strut their stuff within this context, trading off vocals and blending into an unstoppable force where it's impossible to separate the instruments, even as they solo. The songwriting might still be perfunctory or derivative in spots—listen to how they appropriate "Eleanor Rigby" on "Plastic Jim"—but what's impressive is how even the borrowed or recycled moments sound fresh in context. And then there's the cuts that work on their own, whether it's the aforementioned double-sided single, "Fun," "Dynamite!," or several other cuts here—these are brilliant, intoxicating slices of funk-pop that get by as much on sound as song, and they're hard to resist. *—Stephen Thomas Erlewine*

Dance to the Music / Apr. 27, 1968 / Epic/Legacy ✦✦✦
Sly & the Family Stone came into their own with their second album, *Dance to the Music*. This is exuberant music, bursting with joy and invention. If there's a surfeit of classic material, with only the title track being a genuine classic, that winds up being nearly incidental, since it's so easy to get sucked into the freewheeling spirit and cavalier virtuosity of the group. Consider this—prior to this record no one, not even the Family Stone, treated soul as a psychedelic sun-splash, filled with bright melodies, kaleidoscopic arrangements, inextricably intertwined interplay, and deft, fast rhythms. Yes, they wound up turning "Higher" into the better "I Want to Take You Higher" and they recycle the title track in the long jam "Dance to the Medley," but there's such imagination to this jam that the similarities fade as they play. And, if these are just vamps, well, so are James Brown's records, and those didn't have the vitality or friendliness of this. Not a perfect record, but a fine one all the same. *—Stephen Thomas Erlewine*

☆ **Stand!** / May 3, 1969 / Epic ✦✦✦✦✦
Stand! is the pinnacle of Sly & the Family Stone's early work, a record that represents a culmination of the group's musical vision and accomplishment. *Life* hinted at this record's boundless enthusiasm and blurred stylistic boundaries, yet everything simply gels here, resulting in no separation between the astounding funk, effervescent irresistible melodies, psychedelicized guitars, and deep rhythms. Add to this a sharpened sense of pop songcraft, elastic band interplay, and a flowering of Sly's social conscious, and the result is utterly stunning. Yes, the jams ("Don't Call Me Nigger, Whitey," "Sex Machine") wind up meandering ever so slightly, but they're surrounded by utter brilliance, from the rousing call to arms of "Stand" to the unification anthem "Everyday People" to the unstoppable "I Want to Take You Higher." All of it sounds like the Family Stone, thanks not just to the communal lead vocals but to the brilliant interplay, but each track is distinct, emphasizing a different side of their musical personality. As a result, *Stand!* winds up infectious and informative, invigorating and thought-provoking—stimulating

in every sense of the word. Few records of its time touched it, and Sly topped it only by offering its opposite the next time out. *—Stephen Thomas Erlewine*

★ **Greatest Hits** / Nov. 21, 1970 / Epic ✦✦✦✦✦

Released in 1970, during the stopgap between *Stand!* and *There's a Riot Goin' On*, *Greatest Hits* inadvertently arrived at precisely the right moment, summarizing Sly & the Family Stone's joyous hit-making run on the pop and R&B charts. Technically, only four songs here reached the Top Ten, with only two others hitting the Top 40, but judging this solely on charts is misleading, since this is simply a peerless singles collection. This summarizes their first four albums perfectly (almost all of *Stand*, outside of the two jams and "Somebody's Watching You," is here), adding the non-LP singles "Hot Fun in the Summertime," "Thank You (Falettinme Be Mice Elf Agin)," and "Everybody Is a Star," possibly the loveliest thing they ever recorded. But, this isn't merely a summary (and, if it was just that, *Anthology*, the early-'80s comp that covers *Riot* and *Fresh* would be stronger than this), it's one of the greatest party records of all time. Music is rarely as vivacious, vigorous, and vibrant as this, and captured on one album, the spirit, sound, and songs of Sly & the Family Stone are all the more stunning. Greatest hits don't come better than this—in fact, music rarely does. *—Stephen Thomas Erlewine*

☆ **There's a Riot Goin' On** / Nov. 20, 1971 / Epic ✦✦✦✦✦

It's easy to write off *There's a Riot Goin' On* as one of two things—Sly Stone's disgusted social commentary or the beginning of his slow descent into addiction. It's both of these things, of course, but pigeonholing it as either winds up dismissing the album as a whole, since it is so bloody hard to categorize. What's certain is that *Riot* is unlike any of Sly & the Family Stone's other albums, stripped of the effervescence that flowed through even such politically aware records as *Stand!* This is idealism soured, as hope is slowly replaced by cynicism, joy by skepticism, enthusiasm by weariness, sex by pornography, thrills by narcotics. Joy isn't entirely gone—it creeps through the cracks every once and awhile and, more disturbing, Sly revels in his stoned decadence. What makes *Riot* so remarkable is that it's hard not to get drawn in with him, as you're seduced by the narcotic grooves, seductive vocals slurs, leering electric pianos, and crawling guitars. As the themes surface, it's hard not to nod in agreement, but it's a junkie nod, induced by the comforting coma of the music. And damn if this music isn't funk at its deepest and most impenetrable—this is dense music, nearly impenetrable, but not from its deep grooves, but its utter weariness. Sly's songwriting remains remarkably sharp, but only when he wants to write—the foreboding opener "Luv N' Haight," the scarily resigned "Family Affair," the cracked cynical blues "Time," and "(You Caught Me) Smilin'." Ultimately, the music is the message and while it's dark music, it's not alienating—it's seductive despair, and that's the scariest thing about it. *—Stephen Thomas Erlewine*

☆ **Fresh** / Jun. 30, 1973 / Epic ✦✦✦✦✦

Fresh expands and brightens the slow grooves of *There's a Riot Goin' On*, turning them, for the most part, into friendly, welcoming rhythms. There are still traces of the narcotic haze of *Riot*, particularly on the brilliant, crawling inversion of "Que Sera Sera," yet this never feels like an invitation into a junkie's lair. Still, this isn't necessarily lighter than *Riot*—in fact, his social commentary is more explicit, and while the music doesn't telegraph his resignation the way *Riot* did, it comes from the same source. So, *Fresh* winds up more varied, musically and lyrically, which may not make it as unified, but it does result in more traditional funk that certainly is appealing in its own right. Besides, this isn't conventional funk—it's eccentric, where even concise catchy tunes like "If You Want Me to Stay" seem as elastic as the opener, "In Time." That's the album's ultimate charm—it finds Sly precisely on the point where he's balancing funk and pop, about to fall into the brink, but creating an utterly individual album that wound up being his last masterwork and one of the great funk albums of its era. *—Stephen Thomas Erlewine*

Small Talk / 1974 / Epic ✦✦✦

A new bass player and drummer signaled a toned-down Family Stone sound. Partially in keeping with changes in much of popular music in the early '70s, and maybe the result of marriage and a child, Sly became more introspective, quieter, and calmer, even employing a string section on various cuts. A less exhilarating album than earlier efforts, there is still much of merit here, including the Top Ten R&B hit "Time for Livin'." *—Rob Bowman*

High on You / Nov. 8, 1975 / Epic ✦✦✦

The first album attributed to Sly Stone rather than Sly & the Family Stone, *High on You* didn't exactly resurrect the troubled artist's sinking career, but it does remain one of the better straight-up funk albums of the '70s. Released during the same mid-'70s era that spawned vibrant funk albums such as the Commodores' *Machine Gun*, Parliament's *Up for the Down Stroke*, and the Ohio Players' *Skin Tight*, along with the first Graham Central Station albums, *High on You* seems somewhat like a genre exercise for Sly—rather than trailblazing new sounds like he did five years earlier, he's now a bit behind the times. Still, even though Sly isn't doing anything incredible here, he performs a highly competent series of succinct, well-crafted funk songs with plenty of pop accessibility and a bit of soul embedded in his vocals. It's worth noting that the album's title track was an impressive single, peaking at number three on the R&B chart and even making an appearance on the pop chart—though rarely mentioned, "High on You," remains one of Sly's career highlights. Elsewhere, "Crossword Puzzle" stands out with its distinct horn hook and numerous background vocals, while the gentle "That's Lovin' You," the album's sole ballad, cools things down a bit. After these first three highlights, the album's quality dips a bit, though the funk level remains high. Undoubtedly Sly's best post-*Fresh* album alongside the better moments on *Small Talk*, *High on You* isn't nearly as accomplished as his great late-'60s/early-'70s run of albums, though it deserves more respect that it has garnered with time. While most have lazily written this album off, lumping it together with Sly's other post-*Fresh* efforts, it's actually a respectable '70s funk album that is also his most underrated. *—Jason Birchmeier*

Heard Ya Missed Me, Well I'm Back / Dec. 18, 1976 / Epic ✦✦

As distasteful as the lighthearted album cover to *Heard Ya Missed Me, Well I'm Back* is, with Sly sporting a clownish smile and an assortment of lame instruments, it's very analogous to the album itself. Like the cover photo, sure to make any fan of his more accomplished work cringe, the music on this album found the struggling artist trying to shroud his underlying problems with a shallow façade characterized by a fun, carefree attitude. Every song on the album is cheery and upbeat, with many professing an untroubled, optimistic demeanor, most obviously apparent on the album's sole single, "Family Again," and its "feels like family again" hook. But no matter how much Sly tried to comfort his fans and critics, exuding an optimistic façade and addressing his audience in the album-opening title track ("If you ever thought I'd leave you/paranoia put it on your mind/here I am in live and livin' colors/one or maybe both of us were blind"), it's fairly obvious to anyone familiar with his body of work that something's wrong. To put it bluntly, Sly had went from being one of the most admired artists in all of music, an artist whose significance spans decades, to being an acknowledged failure—that's a pretty big problem. With the aid of longtime bandmate Cynthia Robinson dominating the music with her trumpet-led arrangements and the official return of the Family Stone, Sly wrote a rather simple album with a pop hook for every song. There's no sense of funk, and the soul aspect is forced and near mechanical. It almost seems as though Sly and Cynthia regressed to the simple sound of their first two albums; unfortunately, while those albums found them inspired, here they're unsure of themselves, arguably scared, and it results in a horribly tentative album. *—Jason Birchmeier*

Back on the Right Track / Nov. 3, 1979 / Warner Bros. ✦✦

By the late '70s, Sly had been so thoroughly written off as a has-been that few listeners checked out this effort. Nor have listeners been inspired to rediscover the album, since his late-'60s/early-'70s classics cast such a huge shadow over his subsequent work. It comes as somewhat of a surprise, then, to find the basic Stone soul/rock/funk foundation still firmly in place here. There were two problems: the foundation didn't make any notable advancements on the territory he'd already mapped out by the early '70s, and the songs themselves weren't that special, sounding more like basic vamps or promising scraps than fully baked ideas. Judged solely on its own terms, it's actually a respectable slice of funk; it's only when stacked against Stone's other works that the disappointment becomes intense. The album has been reissued in Britain (as Charly 8033) with a couple of outtakes added as bonus tracks. *—Richie Unterberger*

★ **Anthology** / 1981 / Epic ✦✦✦✦✦

Anthology essentially replicates the previous collection *Greatest Hits* and adds singles from *There's A Riot Goin' On* and *Fresh* to the end of the album. Where *Greatest Hits* didn't follow chronological order, *Anthology* presents every single in the order they were released—and, with the exception of the latter-day singles and the inclusion of "Don't Call Me Nigger, Whitey," that is the major difference between the two collections. *Anthology* goes for a sweeping, definitive overview, while *Greatest Hits* is a brief blast of 12 of the finest singles of the rock & roll era. Either compilation functions as an excellent introduction, but *Anthology* is more comprehensive, giving it the edge as a first purchase. *—Stephen Thomas Erlewine*

Ain't But the One Way / 1983 / Warner Bros. ✦

After his stint as George Clinton's sidekick, Sly Stone returned for his second Warner album, *Ain't But the One Way*. His poor Warner debut, *Back on the Right Track* (1979), had unanimously proved that Sly's dismal mid- to late-'70s stint with Epic was no fluke, and this 1983 follow-up didn't do anything to change his painful decline into oblivion. Expectations definitely weren't high for this album; in fact, few even noticed its release. But it is worth noting that Sly had been working with Clinton during the early '80s, contributing to the final Funkadelic record, *The Electric Spanking of War Babies* (1981), and also did some touring with the P-Funk ensemble. Unfortunately, Sly failed to bring any P-Funk influence to this album; it's a shallow record of half-hearted songwriting and little musicianship. By this point in his career, he had sunk so low as to emulate contemporary artists that had once looked to him as an influence; his attempt (if you even can call it that) to make a trendy, early-'80s, studio-polished album doesn't work either, though, resulting in an album that is a failure from beginning to end with few moments of hope or inspiration. In fact, it's a downright depressing album to listen to. Sly's timid lack of confidence is glaringly obvious, and his total loss of musicianship is almost embarrassing. The final nail in the coffin, this album is a morbid finale to a once-brilliant career for Sly, like watching a loved one die in pain. Even die-hard fans should avoid this. *—Jason Birchmeier*

Dance to the Music / 1991 / Thunderbolt ✦✦

With the exception of Ace's *In the Studio With Sly Stone*, the import compilations of Sly's pre-1967 work seem determined to keep such trivial information as sources of material and dates secret. So we'll have to guess that most of the ten tracks on *Dance to the Music* come from the early '60s, even before Stone started working at Autumn Records (a couple, "Help Me With My Broken Heart"/"Long Time Alone," were definitely released as a solo single). Most of these have a late-period doo wop feel, and although the songs aren't that noteworthy, Sly sings well, and there's a nice pop/R&B feel to the production. It's a curiosity that fills out the puzzle of Sly's pre-Family history. A couple of tracks obviously date from his later, more sophisticated Autumn productions, like the female-sung "Honest," which has also appeared on other compilations. *—Richie Unterberger*

Family Affair / 1991 / Thunderbolt ✦

Beware of this deceptively titled, quasi-legal import. Sly Stone did indeed work with the Mojo Men, a minor San Francisco band, as a producer in the mid-'60s. No less than 11 of the 15 cuts here are not Sly, but mid-'60s Mojo Men tracks, available in much better fidelity on Sundazed's *Whys Ain't Supposed to Be* reissue (which has more songs to boot). This disc does end with three outtake-sounding Sly Stone tracks of obscure vintage (there are no liner notes). An educated guess would put them circa 1967, but they're not that interesting in any case. *—Richie Unterberger*

In the Still of the Night / 1991 / Thunderbolt ✦✦

The two years or so before Sly Stone signed to Epic saw him lay down a myriad of hazily documented official and unissued recordings. Now available on a variety of labels, *In the Still of the Night* has 17 of them, most seeming to date from his days as a producer at Autumn in the mid-'60s (the liner notes are of little help). These are mostly sketches, really, of primary interest to Sly historians: some soul covers, some instrumental R&B vamps, and tentative originals that show Stone approaching his singular rock/soul fusion. There's a good deal of duplication with other packages of early Sly material, and it's much less thoughtfully assembled than the best of those (Ace's *In the Studio With Sly Stone*). *—Richie Unterberger*

Precious Stone: In the Studio With Sly Stone 1963–1965 / Sep. 13, 1994 / Ace ✦✦✦

Before forming the Family Stone, Sly Stone gained a lot of experience in the studio as the virtual in-house producer for the San Francisco-based Autumn label. The sessions he worked on during this era (performed by both himself and other artists) have appeared on numerous scattershot compilations. This 28-song anthology is the most comprehensive and intelligently assembled of these, including Sly solo performances, Sly collaborations with Billy Preston, and obscure soul-pop sides by Bobby Freeman, Gloria Scott, George & Teddy, and others. Over half of the cuts were previously unissued, and the lengthy liner notes provide an in-depth overview of his early accomplishments. Only serious collectors should seek this out, though. While Autumn afforded Stone the opportunity to experiment in the studio and devise various primitive collisions of soul and pop, his compositional, instrumental, and vocal skills were still in a very formative (if very promising) stage. Much of this is routinely pleasant, if lightly eccentric, period pop-soul, with occasional bursts of inspiration like Sly's wild scat vocals on "Scat Swim," and the folk-rockish "As I Get Older," and a few songs that would be reworked for inclusion on the first couple of Family Stone albums. *—Richie Unterberger*

Slyest Freshest Funkiest Rarest / 1995 / Magicalmystery ✦✦

In 1967, before signing to Epic, Sly cut four tracks at Leo Kulka's Golden State Recorders studio—"Can't Turn You Loose," "I Ain't Got Nobody," "Take My Advice," and "Life of Fortune and Fame." All of those are here, plus 20—yes, 20—outtakes of instrumental backing tracks for those four tunes. So what you have here, basically, is the kind of thing that's better-suited for a small-circulation bootleg for rabid fans than general release. The four primary tracks do have their interest: "Can't Turn You Loose" is direct evidence of Stone's soul roots, "Life of Fortune and Fame" shows his lyrical ambitions starting to flower, and "I Ain't Got Nobody" offers intriguing proof that Santana weren't the only San Francisco rock band around that devised rearrangements of that Latin-soul-jazz tune. The instrumental outtakes, most of which are pretty brief, are more suited for scholarly listening than entertainment, though Sly-heads may find the insight it affords into the young maestro's working methods interesting. If you can do without these outtakes, the four complete tracks are also available on such other shadowy reissues of early Sly material as *In the Still of the Night* and *Spotlight on Sly and the Family Stone*. *—Richie Unterberger*

Who in the Funk Do You Think You Are: The Warner Bros. Recordings / Aug. 16, 2001 / Rhino Handmade ✦✦✦

By the time Sly Stone—with a revamped version of the Family Stone—released his two Warner Bros. albums, *Back on the Right Track* and *Ain't But the One Way*, he had been dismissed as a drugged-out has-been, with his best days past him. The latter part was most certainly true, since he was not only worn out, it would have been hard for most musicians to reach the peaks of *Stand!*, *There's a Riot Goin' On*, and *Fresh*, not to mention his unbelievable singles of the late '60s. But the truth was Sly was running on near-empty, barely able to keep afloat during a series of personal trouble and addictions. In retrospect, that makes these Warner recordings all the more remarkable—not because they're great, but because they're competent, enjoyable, period-piece funk. That's a testament to the sheer size of his genius—even amidst all the trouble he made pretty good music. Not great, to be sure, but neither of these records are disasters, which is more evident now than it was at the time. This still isn't music that packs any revelations, and there's not much depth in the music, apart from "The Same Thing (Makes You Laugh, Makes You Cry)," but it's surprisingly enjoyable, considering its reputation, and the presentation and packaging is first-rate, making this a nice collectors piece. *—Stephen Thomas Erlewine*

Sly, Slick & Wicked

Group / Smooth Soul, Urban, Disco, Soul

Sly, Slick & Wicked's musical journey defies belief; one single in the early '70s, one in 1976 that was re-released in the early '80s, then nothing until 1996 when they dropped *Confessin' a Feeling*, a CD on ITP Records. The Los Angeles-based group has no connections with a group with the same name based out of Cleveland that began recording around the same time.

The original members were Thomas Hawkins (aka Sonny Daye), Larry Lewis, and Donny Everheart. Daye, a native of Texas, founded the group in East Los Angeles in 1969. "Confessin' a Feeling" b/w "Love's Gonna Pack Up" on Bad Boys Records sold well in the southwestern part of the States, but was unknown virtually everywhere else. Their next single, "Tonight's the Nite came out in 1976; the same song came out again by them in 1981. It's possible Bad Boys released a couple more singles that went unnoticed. In 1981, Bad Boys Records re-released "Tonight's the Nite" with the hokey-sounding "We're Sly, Slick, & Wicked... Wicked" on the flip side; the A-side was all right, but side B was an out-of-character joke. Nobody talks about what happened between the long recording intervals, but they regrouped in 1991 to become a hot item on oldies shows in Southern Cali and other locales. From the start they modeled themselves after R&B groups like the Delfonics, Moments, Mighty Marvelows, Intruders, Masqueraders, Blue Magic, and Bloodstone. They broke out in 1996 with the Alan Beck-produced *Confessin' a Feeling*, a marvelous disc loaded with crisply done R&B oldies, featuring a live rendition of "Confessin' a Feeling." It quickly became an underground favorite. Daye sung all the leads, except for "Strange Feelings" (Larry Lewis) and the old Jive Five tune "What Time Is It" (led by Donny "Doc" Everheart). Eddie Stovall and Freddie Holiday supplemented the trio on backing vocals.

In 1999 ITP released a second CD, *Tonight's the Nite*. Titled after their old 45, it featured a second feast of immaculately done oldies including the Incredibles' "I'll Make It Easy," the Notations' "I'm Still Here," the Moments' "Not on the Outside," and Betty Everett's "There Come a Time." The original version of "Tonight's the Nite features Ron Crowder with Daye, and Freddie Lewis sings the falsetto lead on "Not on the Outside" and Eddie Holman's "This Can't Be True" while Larry Lewis does the Younghearts' "(Me and You) You and I" and "I'm Still Here." The group that took its name after Lost Generation's hit "Sly, Slick & Wicked" most certainly deserves the title "The Kings of Underground Oldies." *—Andrew Hamilton*

● **Confessin' a Feeling** / Apr. 6, 1996 / ITP ✦✦✦✦✦

Harmony lovers will love this throwback by Sly, Slick & Wicked (SSW), despite some flaws, it's as refreshing as a cold citrus drink on a hot humid day. This is a different group than the SSW who recorded for Ju-Par & People Records. This SSW formed in Los Angeles, CA, Thomas Hawkins (aka Sonny Daye) handles most of the leads, backed by Larry Lewis, and Donny Everheart. Eddie Stovall & Freddie Holiday supply additional vocals in the studio. They debuted in the '60s and released "Confessin' A Feeling" in 1972, it did well in the Southwest. The updated live version captures them serenading the ladies. Overall, the productions lack the tightness and intensity of the originals, and SSW often flubbed lyrics. But Charles Crews (producer) always manages to captures the essence of these arresting ballads, keeping the orchestration sparse, and never allowing anything to overshadow the vocals. The tempo on "Ain't No Big Thing" is faster than the original, and SSW can't compete with the Radiants' crisp, gospel inspired harmonies, but it will do until someone releases a CD by the Radiants. "That Day When She Needed Me," originally done by the Contours, lacks Motown's touch, but SSW does justice to the slinky, doo wop ballad. Credits list Hunter/Stevenson, but Smokey Robinson actually composed the song. They excel on "Strange Feeling," a minor hit for Billy Stewart, the Persuaders' "Thin Line Between Love and Hate," the Masqueraders' "I Ain't Got To Love Nobody Else," and delivers a silky rendition of Lost Generations' "Sly, Slick & Wicked." The pluses far outweigh the minus, on *Confessing a Feeling*. *—Andrew Hamilton*

Tonight's the Night / Mar. 16, 1999 / ITP ✦✦✦✦

Three years after releasing *Confessing a Feeling*, Sly, Slick & Wicked (SSW) returns with more moldy oldies. The mundane title track "Tonight's the Nite," dropped in 1976, and features Sonny Daye (aka Thomas Hawkins) and Ron Crowder. Freddie Davis' satiny falsetto sounds fresh on "Not on the Outside" (Moments), and "This Can't Be True Girl" (Eddie Holman). Founding member Larry Lewis leads "Me and You (You and I)," an obscure Younghearts recording, and "I'm Still Here." SSW perform two Marvelows' songs: "I'm Without a Girl," and the harmonious "When the Morning Comes" the LP's best track. Smoldering versions of Betty Everett's "There'll Come a Time," Billy Stewart's "Sitting in the Park" and the Incredibles' sobbing "I'll Make It Easy" are first-class pleasers. *—Andrew Hamilton*

Huey "Piano" Smith & the Clowns

b. Jan. 26, 1934, New Orleans, LA

Piano, Songwriter / New Orleans R&B, R&B

Huey "Piano" Smith was an important part of the great New Orleans piano tradition, following in the footsteps of Professor Longhair and Fats Domino to take his place among the Crescent City's R&B elite. He was also one of R&B's great comedians, his best singles matching the Coasters for genial, good-time humor, although his taste often ran more towards nonsense lyrics. Smith's sound was too earthy to match the pop crossover appeal of Domino or the Coasters, which limited his exposure, and he couldn't match the latter's amazing consistency, lacking their reliable supply of material. But at the peak of his game, Smith epitomized New Orleans R&B at its most infectious and rollicking, as showcased on his classic signature tune "Rockin' Pneumonia and the Boogie Woogie Flu."

Huey Smith was born in New Orleans on January 26, 1934, and began playing the piano at age 15. At the dawn of the '50s, Smith backed New Orleans guitar legends Earl King and Guitar Slim, and quickly became a popular session pianist, playing on records by the cream of the New Orleans R&B scene: Smiley Lewis (the classic "I Hear You Knockin'"), Lloyd Price, and Little Richard. During the mid-'50s, Smith began leading his own band, the Clowns, which usually featured popular local blues singer and female impersonator Bobby Marchan on lead vocals. Smith & the Clowns signed with the Ace label and scored a breakout Top Five R&B hit in 1957 with "Rockin' Pneumonia and the Boogie Woogie Flu," which despite becoming a classic rock & roll standard didn't even make the pop Top 40, thanks to reticent white radio programmers. The following year, Smith scored his biggest hit with the double-sided smash "Don't You Just Know It"/"High Blood Pressure," which reached the pop Top Ten and the R&B Top Five. In 1959, Smith cut the original tune "Sea Cruise," and seeking pop radio airplay, Ace had white teenage R&B singer Frankie Ford overdub his own vocal onto Smith's backing track; the result became a nationwide hit.

Smith cut a few novelty numbers in an attempt to duplicate the success of "Rockin' Pneumonia," some even using the same type of illness joke ("Tu-Ber-Cu-Lucas and the Sinus Blues," for example). It didn't work, and Marchan left the Clowns after scoring a solo hit with "There Is Something on Your Mind" in 1960; he was replaced by female singer Gerri Hall and male vocalist Curley Moore. Smith switched briefly to the Imperial label, then returned to Ace for one last chart single in 1962, "Pop Eye." Smith spent part of the '60s recording for Instant and touring not only with the Clowns, but alternate groups the Hueys and the Pitter Pats as well. Unable to return to the charts, he eventually converted to the Jehovah's Witnesses and left the music industry permanently. *—Steve Huey*

Having a Good Time / 1959 / Edsel ✦✦✦✦✦
No collection of leftovers here, Huey "Piano" Smith's album debut featured the hits "Rockin' Pneumonia and the Boogie Woogie Flu," "High Blood Pressure," and "Don't You Just Know It" along with Crescent City favorites like "Little Liza Jane," "Don't You Know Yockomo," "Just A Lonely Clown," and Bobby Marchan's "Little Chickee Wah Wah." As a budget-priced collection, this one's hard to turn down. An essential building block for any New Orleans collection. *—Cub Koda*

'Twas the Night Before Christmas / 1962 / WestSide ✦✦✦✦

Having a Good Time With Huey "Piano" Smith & His Clowns / 1997 / WestSide ✦✦✦✦✦
Next to Professor Longhair and Fats Domino, no one better typified the New Orleans piano style than the work of Huey "Piano" Smith. This 24-track, single-disc compilation is the first proposed installment of Huey and the Clowns' tenure with the Jackson, MS-based Ace label, home to his biggest hits. Kicking off with parts one and two of his first hit, "Rockin' Pneumonia and the Boogie Woogie Flu" (although the second part used here seems one overdub away from the single version issued), more obscure but equally worthwhile items like "Little Liza Jane," "Just a Lonely Clown," "Would You Believe It (I Have a Cold)" and "She Got Low Down" sit comfortably next to the hits ("High Blood Pressure," "Don't You Just Know It," "Tu-Ber-Cu-Lucas and the Sinus Blues," "Don't You Know Yockomo" and "Pop-Eye"), making this volume a perfect introduction to the music of this Crescent City genius. Transfers are as crisp as you could ask for, and the packaging and liner notes are equally fine. *—Cub Koda*

● **This Is Huey Piano Smith** / Apr. 21, 1998 / Music Club ✦✦✦✦✦
For years, Huey "Piano" Smith lacked a comprehensive overview of his recording career, and no compilation ever appeared on CD in the United States. The budget-line label Music Club rectified that situation in 1998 with the release of *This is Huey Piano Smith*, an 18-track collection that features all of his hit singles for Ace plus several failed singles and New Orleans staples. Smith's hits and standards—"Rockin' Pneumonia and the Boogie-Woogie Flu," "Don't You Just Know It," "High Blood Pressure," "Pop-Eye," the original version of "Sea Cruise," with his vocals instead of Frankie Ford's—are so good that it's an inevitable disappointment to find many of the songs here are blatant attempts to get back on the charts ("Tu-Ber-Cu-Lucas and the Sinus Blues," "Would You Believe It (I Have a Cold)"). These fall flat, as do a couple of the other cuts, but unfortunately, that's an accurate portrait of Smith's career—he had a handful of wonderful, essential songs and was a hell of a performer, but he wasn't a consistent hitmaker. Nevertheless, the strong stuff is so good—even essential—that this is still highly recommended for New Orleans R&B fans and R&B fans in general.*—Stephen Thomas Erlewine*

Havin' Fun With Huey "Piano" Smith: More of the Best / Mar. 3, 1999 / WestSide ✦✦✦✦
The second part of Ace Records combing through their Huey "Piano" Smith vault, *More of the Best* includes 24 tracks of new-to-disc songs and unreleased recordings, with vocalists including Bobby Marchan and Curley Moore, as well as Smith himself. *—Keith Farley*

That'll Get It (Even More of the Best) / Aug. 24, 1999 / WestSide ✦✦✦✦
The third volume of WestSide's retrospective into the music of Huey "Piano" Smith yields even more amazing treasures. It seems as if Huey never stopped recording and recording in every conceivable configuration it seems, as sideman, leader, songwriter, backing up young singing hopefuls, and beyond. With the advent of recording band tracks separately from vocals (the beginnings of stereo recording), label owner Johnny Vincent could take Huey's old tracks and try new vocals on them and in many cases that's what we have here. But also along the way are another brace of Ace and related label singles and album tracks that go just that further in making the case for Huey being one of the most influential and prolific of all New Orleans musicians. Not the place to start your Huey "Piano" Smith collection, but definitely not a bad place to end up. *—Cub Koda*

Melvin Smith

b. 1936, Atlanta, GA
Vocals, Guitar / R&B
Anyone reading this can be forgiven for not knowing much about Melvin Smith. Indeed, if more than a few thousand listeners even remember the name of "Looped," his most popular recording of the early '50s, that would be amazing. In a 15-year recording career, Smith never charted a record nationally; he wrote songs, but not one of them was a hit in any form for him or anyone else; he never sang with any bands that became famous; and he wasn't an influence—so far as anyone knows—on any major rock or R&B acts that followed in his wake.

None of that, however, means that his music isn't worth hearing or as enjoyable as any other R&B of the same era. Stylistically, he stood somewhere midway between Roy Brown and Louis Jordan, and aside from Piano Red, he was just about as strong an R&B singer as RCA had on its roster during the early '50s. It wasn't his "fault" that he never had a hit, and it is to RCA's credit that they stood by him through three years and 32 recorded sides. Smith was born in Atlanta in 1936, the son of Samuel and Minnie Smith, fourth in a family of nine children. Samuel Smith, a truck driver, abandoned the family in the mid-'40s, and all nine children were raised by their mother, a hotel chambermaid. Melvin began listening to music at an early age, and among his favorite singers growing up were Roy Brown, Wynonie Harris, and Jimmy Witherspoon. By the time he was in his early teens, Smith was winning talent contests in the Atlanta area and singing regularly with a group called the Arstell Allen Sextet.

In early 1951, a group of RCA-Victor executives came to Atlanta in search of talent to expand their R&B roster. They were referred to Smith, then 15 years old, and were suitably impressed. On January 11, 1951, Smith had his first recording date, fronting saxophonist/bandleader Clyde W. "Blow Top" Lynn & His House Rockers on four songs. Their first single, "Reliefin' Blues" backed with "School Boy Blues," was released to little notice in March of that year. Smith's career was now in high gear, with regular shows outside of Atlanta spaced in between odd jobs and school whenever he could fit it in—he was finally expelled from school sometime in 1951. By the end of that year, he was known as "Little Melvin" and was singing with Tommy Brown's Maroon Notes. In the meantime, he recorded a further four songs with Lynn and his band in the spring of 1951.

The first resulting single, "Rampaging Mama" backed with "Real True Gal" (the latter co-written by Smith), also failed to chart. By January of 1952, Smith was back in the studio with a new band, in a session that generated the critically well-received but poor-selling Smith-authored "California Baby"/"Everybody's Got the Blues." RCA was still convinced that Smith had what it took to succeed, however, and in late March of 1952, they brought him to New York for a recording session with some of the top players of the period, including jazz legend Tyree Glenn on trombone, Taft Jordan on trumpet, Eddie Barefield on sax, and leader Howard Biggs at the piano. The result was Smith's most critically acclaimed single, "Looped," which managed to become a regional hit and elicited a rival cover version.

Somehow, "Looped" never broke out, and Smith and RCA were left to look back on another promising failure. The session did bring Smith to New York, however, and some very enjoyable and lucrative club dates. These were good times for Smith, despite his stagnant recording career, singing before bigger and more appreciative audiences than ever before. Unfortunately, RCA saw the need to make some changes in Smith's sound, and his next sessions featured the presence of a trio of backup pop singers whose voices were too prominent for the song's own good. The single "Sarah Kelly (From Plumnelly)" flopped. Smith's recording career continued with RCA for another two years without any success, and he was finally dropped by the label in early 1954.

Smith was only 18 years old, however, and hardly done singing. He had moved to Philadelphia the previous year, and for the next decade, he fronted a quintet called the Nite Riders, whose membership included pianist/composer Van Walls ("Chains of Love"). He was signed to Apollo Records and later recorded for Sound/Teen, Swan, Cameo, and Sue Records. Smith and the group reached the pinnacle of their success in the late '50s, playing an extended engagement at the Wagon Wheel club in midtown Manhattan, and also enjoyed considerable popularity in Canada and Boston.

Smith continued working into the 1970s and early '80s with a variety of bands. In his late forties, at the beginning of the 1990s he decided to quit in favor of a federal civil service job while he still had his health and some good memories of a few great times and records of which he was proud. *—Bruce Eder*

● **At His Best** / 1994 / Bear Family ✦✦✦✦✦
Only Bear Family Records would think of bringing out a two-CD set of the complete early-'50s sides of an artist who never had a single record on the charts. The 32 RCA-Victor sides here are all good, and a few, like "School Boy Blues," "Reliefin' Blues," "Rampaging Mama," and "Looped" (all from just the first disc) are as fine examples of R&B as you can find during that era. The first eight songs comprise Melvin Smith's recording history fronting Blow Top Lynn & His House Rockers, who play a hard, sax-driven brand of R&B (with some romping piano by Tom Patton and a hot trumpet solo by W.M. Bostic on "Reliefin' Blues"), with at least one song ("They Ain't Gonna Tell It Right") that sounds like a lost Louis Jordan classic—not bad for a 15-year-old vocalist. The second four sides are smoother than the first, and the best of them, "Rampaging Mama," is a masterpiece. He was nearly as strong on slow songs like Lynn's "Homesick Blues" as he was on the jump numbers like "Rampaging Mama," calling up images of Roy Brown at his best. His own "Everybody's Got the Blues" is a pretty impressive piece of songwriting for a 16-year-old, as well as a great number. "Looped" and the other New York-recorded numbers show greater sophistication than the earlier Atlanta songs—they're smooth and their sound is nice and spread out, with lots of room for electric guitar, a solid jazz-type backup on trumpets and trombones, and a really "produced" sound that brings out the most powerful and expressive sides of Smith's singing. He was about the same age as Little Richard—who also recorded for RCA around this time—but a more developed artist. "Baby I'll Be There" is a beautiful R&B ballad, and gives Smith a chance to stretch out vocally, which he exploits to the fullest, while "I'm Out of My Mind" is the kind of jumping, honking blues number that probably brought many a house down at his shows during this era. "Business Man's Blues," which closes disc one, is one of eight 1994 discoveries unearthed here for the first time. Even the weakest track here, "Sarah Kelly," has a great beat and a lusty, raunchy performance by Smith, marred only by the pop singers handling the choruses. "Six Times Six," by contrast, from the very same session, is the kind of lusty number that lots of white kids started tuning in to black radio stations to hear around this time. The later tracks, from 1953-1954, are good as recordings, with Smith's voice finally sounding almost larger-than-life on numbers of "I Don't Have to Hunt No More" and "Every Pound," although the songs themselves lack the quality of the 1951-1952 sessions. *—Bruce Eder*

O.C. Smith (Ocie Lee Smith)

b. Jun. 21, 1932, Mansfield, LA, **d.** Nov. 23, 2001, Los Angeles, CA
Vocals / Country-Soul, Soul, Vocal Jazz, R&B
O.C. Smith began as a jazz vocalist and later moved into country and R&B. The Louisiana vocalist was hired to replace Joe Williams in Count Basie's band in the early '60s after cutting some unsuccessful records for Cadence and others in the '50s. He sang with Basie's band from 1961 to 1963. Following a period where he sang country and even had a hit with "Son of Hickory Holler's Tramp," Smith moved into soul. His biggest hit was "Little

Green Apples," which was number two on both the pop and R&B charts in 1968. His other big R&B single was "Daddy's Little Man," which reached number nine in 1969. Smith stayed on Columbia until 1974, but didn't score any more big records. He moved to Caribou in 1976 and recorded later for Shady Brooks, Family, Motown, and Rendezvous. In 1985 he began to balance his work in the recording studio with his new passion for Christian ministry, but despite the fact that he founded his own church in Los Angeles, The City of Angels Church of Religious Science, he continued to perform and record until the time of his death on November 23, 2001. *—Ron Wynn*

The Dynamic O.C. Smith / Apr. 1966 / Columbia ✦✦✦✦✦

Hickory Holler Revisited / 1968 / Columbia ✦✦✦

O.C. Smith at Home / 1969 / CBS ✦✦✦

O.C. Smith at Home was the finest showcase for the singer's warm, baritone vocals. Produced by Jerry Fuller, the LP's songs revolved around home and heart. The LP cover featured the singer walking with a little boy. The second single, the rousing, dynamic "Daddy's Little Man," hit *Billboard's* charts in fall 1969. Its flip side was the driving, horn-accented soap opera-themed "If I Leave You Now." The lushly orchestrated "The Learning Tree" was the opening title theme of the family drama movie directed by Gordon Parks. "Friend, Lover, Woman, Wife" cracked the R&B Top 25. All of this musical magic was wrapped up in the great arrangements of H.B. Barnum. Some of the LP tracks appeared on his *O.C. Smith's Greatest Hits*. *—Ed Hogan*

Help Me Make It through the Night / 1971 / Columbia ✦✦✦

● **O.C. Smith's Greatest Hits** / 1976 / Embassy ✦✦✦✦

This early O.C. Smith compilation contains the most significant recordings of the country-pop singer's career, including "Son of Hickory Holler's Tramp," a moving song with hurtin' lyrics about growing up in a small township with a loose mother, along with "Little Green Apples," "Daddy's Little Man," and "Honey (I Miss You)"; 11 in all, but later CD compilations make this out-of-print album a dinosaur. *—Andrew Hamilton*

Love Changes / 1982 / Motown ✦✦

Hickory Holler Revisited/For Once in My Life / Jan. 21, 2003 / Collectables ✦✦✦✦

Will Smith

b. Sep. 25, 1968, West Philadelphia, PA

Vocals / Urban, Hip-Hop, Pop-Rap

Beginning his career during the mid-'80s under the name the Fresh Prince, by the following decade rapper Will Smith was one of the biggest superstars of his time—not only a pop music sensation, he also conquered television and eventually feature films, starring in a string of box-office megahits. He was 16 when he met aspiring DJ Jeff Townes; joining forces as DJ Jazzy Jeff & the Fresh Prince, in 1987 the duo issued their debut record *Rock the House*, scoring a hit with the single "Girls Ain't Nothing but Trouble." Propelled by the smash "Parents Just Don't Understand," DJ Jazzy Jeff & the Fresh Prince broke into the mainstream a year later with *He's the DJ, I'm the Rapper*, one of the first hip-hop LPs to achieve double-platinum status. Clean-cut, witty, and easygoing, the duo's bubblegum approach was a stark contrast to the dominant, harder-edged rap sound of the period; viewed as a non-threatening alternative to their peers, they received the parental seal of approval, and their appeal spread across racial lines as well.

Soon Hollywood began taking notice of Smith's success; in 1990, he was tapped to star in *The Fresh Prince of Bel-Air*, a sitcom for NBC. In 1995, Smith co-starred in the action film *Bad Boys*, a major box office hit; it set the stage for his leading role in 1996's *Independence Day*, the summer's biggest smash. A year later, he starred in *Men in Black*, again the box-office champ of the summer season; recording for the first time under his given name, he also scored a smash with the movie's rap theme. Smith's debut solo LP, *Big Willie Style*, also appeared in 1997, notching the hit "Gettin' Jiggy Wit It." *—Jason Ankeny*

Big Willie Style / Nov. 25, 1997 / Columbia ✦✦✦✦

Will Smith wisely decided not to change his style too much on *Big Willie Style*, the first record he released since becoming a major movie star with appearances on *Independence Day* and *Men in Black*. Instead of trying to toughen his image, Smith continued with the friendly, humorous pop-rap that has been his trademark since *He's the DJ, I'm the Rapper*. Of course, he gives the music a glossy modern sheen (ironically based on early-'80s funk) in order to prove that he's still hip—and it works. Sure, there's filler scattered all the way the through the album, but the best moments—the disco-thumping "Gettin' Jiggy Wit It," the Larry Blackmon duet "Candy," the ballad "I Loved You," and the riotous "Men in Black"—rank among his best singles. *—Stephen Thomas Erlewine*

Willennium / Nov. 16, 1999 / Columbia ✦✦✦✦

By the time Will Smith released *Willennium* in November 1999, it was fashionable to put him down, especially since he was recovering from his first major stumble, the overblown *Wild Wild West*. Probably just the fact that he was everywhere made certain spoilsports long to take him down a notch, but *Wild Wild West* wasn't a mess because of him; in fact, he provided the only glimmers of fun in the whole misguided mess, through sheer star power. And that star power drives *Willennium*, turning it into a bold, brassy delight. Smith just doesn't care what anyone thinks; he knows he's a superstar, and he revels in his status. He likes to make fun music, and he likes to make it on a grand scale. Furthermore, he has no shame about entertaining. Consequently, *Willennium* is a gonzo pleasure in the way only a handful of big-budget pop albums can be: gaudy, giddy, infectiously silly, and proudly over-the-top. Case in point, its de facto title track, "Will 2K." Smith and his producers picked the Clash's "Rock the Casbah" as the foundation for an end-of-the-century party jam, a move so mind-bogglingly unpredictable that it's hard not to smile. And that spirit carries throughout the album, as Smith drops lyrical and musical allusions that are at once well-known and totally out of left field. All of this is done to bright, joyful party music that celebrates its big beats and big hooks. Smith isn't quite as convincing when it comes to slow jams, but still his charm shines through. But the heart of the album lies in the uptempo dance numbers, since they're what make *Willennium* irresistible. And this is one of the rare times that an abundance of cameos enhances the spirit of an album, making *Willennium* feel like a Y2K blowout where everyone is invited. *—Stephen Thomas Erlewine*

Born to Reign / Jun. 25, 2002 / Columbia ✦✦✦✦

It'd be inaccurate to call Will Smith's third album the musical equivalent of *Ali*—a bid for artistic credibility from an artist so assured and smooth, it's been easy to pigeonhole him as merely a pop artist—but given the range and harder edge on *Born to Reign*, it's hard not to think of it at first. Make no mistake, this is *not* as serious as *Ali*, nor is it a record whose first intent is to enlighten and educate (this is not a KRS-One or Wyclef Jean project). It's a fun, pop-leaning record, much like his first two records, and never is it afraid to return to the sounds and styles that brought the former Fresh Prince (deserved) big hits, but among comfortably familiar jams, Smith stretches his legs. Some of the hip-hop hits harder; there's a touch of reggae; he even appropriates a bit of a Ricky Martin vibe on "I Can't Stop." It's a small but significant change, and while it doesn't result in a record that flows as effortlessly, or giddily, as *Willennium*, it's easy to appreciate the effort to stretch, because even if all the experiments aren't necessarily successful (sometimes, the idea is better than the execution), it does reinvigorate the Smith signature pop-rap sound (apart, oddly, from the theme for *Men in Black 2*, "Black Suits Comin'," the only cut in this vein to fall flat), and results in another solid record from Smith. Maybe not as consistent as its predecessors, but still enjoyable in its familiar turf, while provoking admiration for its ambition, even when it's not always satisfying. Not a bad way to stretch. *—Stephen Thomas Erlewine*

● **Greatest Hits** / Nov. 26, 2002 / Columbia ✦✦✦✦✦

In retrospect, the point at which Will Smith went too far was with 1999's "Freakin' It," on which, over samples from "Love Hangover" and "Rapper's Delight," he boasted of his movie earnings, defended himself against charges of being a "soft" rapper, and criticized his peers. It was hard to dispute any of his arguments (though the citation of the American Music Awards as an example of his superiority seemed a bit of a stretch), but the song also emphasized—in the wrong way, as far as fans were concerned—how far Smith had come from Philadelphia, and it flopped. After that, his movies and records had to struggle more for attention. All careers go through peaks and troughs, however, and this collection of Smith's musical high points makes the case for his popularity, dating back to the late-'80s days of DJ Jazzy Jeff & the Fresh Prince, whose work is licensed from Jive Records for one-third of the tracks here. Not all of the early duo's hits are included, but the signature ones, particularly the breakout "Parents Just Don't Understand," are. In a sense, this is Smith at his most appealing, using rap to create novelty records that reveal the comic sense that later would light up movie screens. He remains engaging through solo hits like "Men in Black" and "Getting' Jiggy Wit It," even if he already seems to be starting to believe his press clips. By this point, the musical career has become an appendage of the movie career, and movie stardom begins to inform the raps, culminating in the defensiveness of "Freakin' It." Along the way, however, there is some clever writing, always put across by Smith's expansive personality, which enabled him to swim against the current of contemporary rap, at least for a time. *—William Ruhlmann*

Smooth Approach

Group / Quiet Storm, Urban

Based in Cleveland, OH, Smooth Approach packs a duel wallop, incorporating harmony and passionate leads with slick steps and moves reminiscent of the Temptations. Jeffrey "Jeff Tight" Roberson, Kerry Willis, Phlanoid "Jay Dee" Dismuke, and Lawrence "Big L" Harris comprise Smooth Approach. Their first CD, the self-titled *Smooth Approach*, dropped in 1996 on Executive Hits Records. It featured, among its nine selections, the single "Never Enough" and an update of Switch's "I Wanna Be Closer." In 1997 they released a cassette *Push 'Em Up* that featured five versions of the title track and two additional songs: "Never Enough" and "Don't Worry." They've opened for 702, the O'Jays, MC Lyte, K-Ci & JoJo, Zhane, and Ginuwine. Smooth Approach performances include appearances at the Rock and Roll Hall of Fame, the Music Hall with Men at Large, the Rappers Ball in Akron, a concert with the Rude Boys in Dayton, and stints at Club Flava and Cafe Echelon in Atlanta, GA, and many more.

Tight has the most experience. At the age of nine he played drums for his older brothers' group, Cash. His first performed on a show that headlined Al Hudson and One Way. Cash's lineup was Dennis and Danny Roberson (twins), and Jimmy Fleming. Their singles include "I Love You Still," on Greedy Records, and "Hot Thing" and "I Wanna Be Loved By You," both on the Casbar label. Tight graduated from John Adams High School, then Ohio University with a major in sports science and a minor in music & fine arts. He's a member of Phi Beta Sigma. Willis graduated from Warrensville Heights High and then served in the Marines for four years. As a youth he served as a Hula Boy, a troupe that won many dance contests throughout the city. Willis works for Ameritech in communications. Jay Dee comes from Ashtabula, OH, about 60 miles east of Cleveland. He graduated from St. Johns Catholic High School and Kent State University with degrees in chemistry and medical technology. Jay Dee's a member of Kappa Alpha Si and works as a medical technologist for Cleveland Clinic. Big L comes from Jefferson, OH, and graduated from Jefferson High. He attended Heidelberg College in Tiffin, OH, and majored in vocal performance. He toured the U.S. with the Acapella Choir and sings with the All-Country Choir in Ashtabula, OH. He comes from a musical family that includes his sisters, the Harris Sisters, and a brother James. *—Andrew Hamilton*

Smooth Approach / 1996 / Executive Hits ✦✦✦

● **You Got It** / 1999 / Executive Hits ✦✦✦✦

Cleveland-based Smooth Approach lives up to their name on *You Got It*, their sophomore CD for Executive Hits Records. This 18-song collection makes good use of polyrhythms on uptempo tracks, as well as Q-Nice—C-town's hottest rapper. A stalking beat paints the scenario for "Are You Down For Me," which features a cameo from Q-Nice. The first ten cuts consist of upbeat, hip-hop tracks: "Push 'Em Up," "Everybody on the Floor (Keep Dancing)," which samples "Good Times," by Chic, and "Keep It Real," accented by Sky Boy's scathing rock guitar, are rump shaking delights. Smooth Approach's, *For Lovers Only* show, begins with the romantic "Don't Worry." "By The Sea," an eerie, pop ballad featuring airy vocal blends with an a cappella fade. A sensitive "Gentle" exemplifies the urban beat ballad that has worn out its welcome. "Never Enough," a floater driven by sweet harmonies and created by Kevin Flourney, is one of two songs not created by Jeff "Tight" Roberson. Roberson, along with Kerry Willis, Jay Dee Dismuke, and Lawrence "Big L" Harris make up Smooth Approach. A lush remake of Switch's "I Wanna Be Closer," displays the group's smooth, silk, satiny sound. *—Andrew Hamilton*

The Solitaires

Group / Doo Wop, R&B

Best remembered for their hit "Walking Along," Harlem doo wop group the Solitaires was formed in 1953 by ex-Vocaleer Herman Curtis in tandem with tenor Buzzy Willis and bass Pat Gaston, who together previously teamed in the Crows. Three former members of the Mello-Moods—tenor Monte Owens, baritone Bobby Baylor, and pianist Bobby Williams—completed the founding lineup, which soon signed with the Old Town label to issue a series of lushly atmospheric local hits including "Wonder Why," "Blue Valentine," and a cover of Bing Crosby's "I Don't Stand a Ghost of a Chance With You." With Curtis' 1955 exit, new lead Milton Love (formerly of the Concords) steered the Solitaires to greater success with "The Wedding," followed in 1956 by the lovely "The Angels Sang"; a year later "Walking Along" became the group's biggest hit.

Personnel changes consistently plagued the Solitaires in the years to follow, however, and over time the group's uniquely romantic approach was supplanted by a sound clearly influenced by the Coasters; in the wake of their final recordings from 1961, the current roster disbanded, with Willis later working for labels including RCA and MGM. Various Solitaires lineups toured the oldies circuit in the decades to come. *—Jason Ankeny*

- **Very Best of the Solitaires: Walking Along** / Jan. 25, 2000 / Collectables ♦♦♦♦

Somethin' for the People

Group / Club/Dance, Urban, Dance-Pop, Hip-Hop

The R&B production/recording trio Somethin' for the People was formed in Los Angeles in 1990 by Oakland, CA, natives Curtis "Sauce" Wilson and Jeff "Fuzzy" Young, along with L.A.-based Rochad "Cat Daddy" Holiday. After writing songs and recording demos for several years, the three hit pay dirt when they were asked by producers Denzil Foster and Thomas McElroy to write a song for their artist Samuelle. Somethin' for the People signed a contract with Capitol Records in 1993, releasing their self-titled debut album that year. They also wrote songs for Brandy, En Vogue, and UNV.

Somethin' for the People had hopped labels by 1996, and their debut LP was reissued on Warner Bros. The trio's second album, *This Time It's Personal*, was released in September of 1997. It spawned the gold-selling, Top Five pop and R&B hit "My Love Is the Shhh!" While attempting to craft a follow-up, Sauce, Fuzzy, and Cat Daddy were kept busy producing tracks for Will Smith's hit album *Big Willie Style* and Adina Howard's *Welcome to Fantasy Island*. But they finally released another album of their own, *Issues*, in July of 2000. *—John Bush*

- **Somethin' for the People** / Jun. 21, 1993 / Capitol ♦♦♦

This Time It's Personal / Sep. 23, 1997 / Warner Bros. ♦♦♦

Somethin' for the People's second album *This Time It's Personal* finds the West Coast trio expanding their sound, creating a sexy blend of hip-hop and contemporary soul. Despite their attempts to make the music "personal," the album offers more surface pleasures than substance, but their sound is often alluring enough to make such problems minor. *—Leo Stanley*

Issues / May 16, 2000 / Warner Bros. ♦♦♦

Somethin' for the People has functioned most successfully as a writing/production team for other artists, but in 1997 the trio finally scored a major hit of their own with "My Love is the Shhh!" Three years later, they were back with an album that touches most of the bases in contemporary R&B/hip-hop, combining a strong melodic sense with distinctive rhythm tracks and mixing silky vocals, courtesy of band member Jeff "Fuzzy" Young, with raps performed by a series of guest stars. Lyrically, the group also pursues the usual subjects, from bedroom pleas ("Can We Make Love") to that ever-popular rap theme, "you wouldn't look at me when I wasn't rich and famous but now that I am you want me and I'm not having any" ("Now U Wanna"). The chart single "Bitch With No Man" has the same subject as the 1965 Supremes hit "Back in My Arms Again," questioning the romantic advice given to one girl by her girlfriends who are themselves unhappy in love. In this case, it's the boyfriend, not the girl herself who doubts the friendly advice, and with the increase in vulgarity over 35 years, he calls the friend not only a bitch, but also a "psycho 'ho'." It's a term the listener may recall three tracks later when Somethin' for the People turns thoughtful on "Things Must Change," a muddled social commentary that, among other things, deplores the use of the epithet "whore." As such a contradiction suggests, the trio is less than certain about its feelings. They open the song criticizing drug dealers, for example, only to apologize quickly and add, "I got friends that hustle, too." As such, the bland clichés that make up the chorus are not reassuring, though perhaps the songwriters' statement that they are trying to figure these things out should be accepted at face value. Unlike many current hip-hop albums, which change style from track to track depending on what production team is in charge, *Issues* has a consistent sound and approach throughout. It isn't breaking new ground, but it is a state-of-the-art example of the form. *—William Ruhlmann*

S.O.S. Band

f. 1977, Atlanta, GA, **db.** 1989

Group / Urban, Funk, Soul

The S.O.S. Band hit with a two-million selling single, "Take Your Time (Do It Right)," their first time out, before having several hit singles written and produced by Jimmy Jam & Terry Lewis. The Atlanta, GA-borne band was started in 1977, when keyboardist/vocalist Jason Bryant, saxophonists Billy Ellis and Willie Killebrew, guitarist Geno Speight, bassist John Simpson, drummer James Earl Jones III, and lead vocalist Mary Davis formed a group called Santa Monica that played at Atlanta nightclub the Regal Room. Their manager, Bunny Jackson-Ransom (who later managed Cameo) sent a demo to Clarence Avant, head of Tabu Records. After signing the band to Tabu, Avant suggested that the band work with songwriter/producer Sigidi Adullah. Adullah was curious as to why an Atlanta-based band named itself Santa Monica. Keyboardist Jason Bryant replied that the band had an enjoyable concert in Santa Monica, CA. Adullah then came up with a new band name, the S.O.S. Band, with S.O.S. standing for "Sounds of Success."

Adullah produced and co-wrote "Take Your Time (Do It Right)" with Harold Clayton, which went platinum, parking at number-one R&B for five weeks and peaking at number-three pop on *Billboard*'s charts in spring 1980. The debut LP, *S.O.S.*, went gold, selling over 800,000 copies and holding the number-two R&B spot for three weeks. While the band was on its world tour, trumpeter/vocalist/percussionist Abdul Ra'oof joined them. Their second album, *Too*, went to number-30 R&B in summer 1981. On the band's third LP, *S.O.S. III*, they worked with producer Leon Sylvers III and the Time's Jimmy Jam & Terry Lewis. The breaking single, "High Hopes," hit number-25 R&B in the fall of 1982 while the album went to number-27 R&B in late 1982.

On their fourth LP, *On the Rise*, Jam & Lewis took over the production chores. Scoring with the slammin' number-two hit "Just Be Good to Me" and the number-five beatbox ballad "Tell Me If You Still Care," *On the Rise* became their second gold album hitting number-seven R&B in summer 1983. The formula continued working: *Just the Way You Like It* went to number-six R&B in fall 1984 (included the number-six R&B single "Just the Way You Like It") and *Sands of Time* went gold and hit number-four R&B in spring 1986 (included the number-two R&B hit "The Finest"). Many of these releases as well as the sound of early releases of Chicago-born house music helped to popularize the now-classic sound of Roland drum machine, the TR-808. In 1987, vocalist Mary Davis left the S.O.S. Band to pursue a solo career. The band recorded two more albums, *Diamonds in the Raw* (number-43 R&B in fall 1989) produced by Eban Kelly and Jimi Randolph and *One of Many Nights* produced by Curtis Williams.

In August 1994, former lead vocalist Mary Davis reunited with Abdul Ra'oof and Jason Bryant, together they reconstructed a new band with the same funky S.O.S. sound, appearing on comedian Sinbad's HBO concert specials and Rhino's new music various artists set, *United We Funk* issued October 5, 1999. *—Ed Hogan*

- **S.O.S.** / 1980 / Tabu ♦♦♦♦

One of 1980's most promising R&B debuts came from the S.O.S. Band, whose debut album is a classic. This sleek yet gritty album went gold in the U.S. (which isn't counting sales in Europe), and the infectious "Take Your Time (Do It Right)" soared to number one on *Billboard*'s R&B singles chart. It isn't hard to see why the S.O.S. Band's first album was a hit; all of the tracks are excellent. That is true of uptempo funk-dance gems like "Take Your Time (Do It Right)," "S.O.S. (Dit Dit Dit Dat Dat Dat Dit Dit Dit)," "Love Won't Wait for Love," and "Take Love Where You Find It," as well as the melancholy soul ballad "What's Wrong With Our Love Affair?" In 1980, there were plenty of inconsistent albums that failed to live up to the promise of an exciting single, but the S.O.S. Band's debut isn't one of them. Those who bought this LP after hearing "Take Your Time (Do It Right)" on the radio were not disappointed by the other tracks—they were happy to learn that the S.O.S. Band's first album is impressively consistent. And they also discovered that the Atlanta outfit had a major asset in lead singer Mary Davis, an expressive, big-voiced belter who demonstrated that she could handle uptempo material and ballads equally well. Not all of the S.O.S. Band's subsequent albums were consistent, but this release is superb as well as essential. *—Alex Henderson*

Too (S.O.S. 2) / 1981 / Tabu ♦♦♦

When a debut album is as promising as the S.O.S. Band's first album, one fears the possibility of a sophomore slump—meaning that the second album won't live up the promise of the first. *Too*, the S.O.S. Band's second album, does, in fact, find the Atlanta residents experiencing a bit of a sophomore slump. But "bit" is the operative word; *Too* is far from a disaster. While the S.O.S. Band's self-titled debut album of 1980 was superb, this 1981 follow-up is merely decent. And in that sense, the LP is somewhat of a disappointment—but certainly not a major disappointment. "Do It Now," "It's a Long Way to the Top," and other uptempo funk-dance singles are likable and catchy; they just aren't exceptional. If the S.O.S. Band's first album was the funk-dance equivalent of champagne, *Too* is more like a beer. And when you have come to expect champagne, beer is a letdown—even if it is a beer of decent quality. But all was certainly not lost for the S.O.S. Band. A few years after *Too*, the Atlanta residents joined forces with the hit-producing songwriting team of Jimmy Jam & Terry Lewis—and that alliance resulted in a creative and commercial revitalization for the S.O.S. Band. Again, *Too* isn't a bad album, but it isn't among the Atlantans' essential releases and is only recommended to collectors and hardcore fans. *—Alex Henderson*

S.O.S. Band III / 1982 / Tabu ♦♦♦

Following a mediocre second album, 1982's *S.O.S. Band III* is the sound of the S.O.S. Band regaining their equilibrium, a tight set that capitalized on the slick style of newly recruited producers Ricky Sylvers & Gene Dozier, and made the Top 30 in December 1982. It's driven primarily by uptempo, funk-inflected R&B that utilized the early '80s tricks of the trade for pizzazz, with just a few ballads to temper the tide. Naturally, the set shines brightest among the thumpers because, as sweet as the ballads could sound, the group was always fiercest when agitating the dancefloor. (That said, they brought a beautiful ballad, "Have It Your Way," into the charts early in 1983.) The single "High Hopes," written by James (Jimmy Jam) Harris & Terry Lewis (who would, of course, go on to produce the band), pairs a catchy hook with a quirky, synthesized flavor that is completely representative of the sound that band and songwriters alike were honing. The process was repeated to lesser effect across "Can't Get Enough," while "Looking for You" and "Groovin' (That's What We're Doin')" put the boys back in smoother R&B-flavored waters. Although it's patchy in places, *III* can still be counted a success, the smooth ride across a slight stumble that would ultimately heave them to the top of the charts for another three years. *—Amy Hanson*

On the Rise / 1983 / Tabu ✦✦✦✦

After a strong start at the beginning of the 1980s, the S.O.S. Band quickly hit that rut which is so sadly common among young bands needing a second shot of gold and, by 1983, they were teetering on the edge of an oncoming oblivion. It is to their ever-lasting credit that not only were they able to pull out of the nosedive, they did it with such aplomb that *On the Rise* could easily have been retitled *Back on Top*. Teaming with hot writing/ production team of Jimmy Jam & Terry Lewis, a completely revitalized S.O.S. Band found themselves firmly on the top of the charts and in the public eye. Hip, slick, and full of dance tricks, the band infused *On the Rise* with enough '80s synth sounds to break through in the clubs, while keeping their funk roots intact. Energized throughout, the set hardly slows down for a moment. From "For Your Love" and the stellar second side opener, "I'm Not Runnin'," to the Motown soul stylings of "Who's Making Love," the S.O.S. Band proved they still had their moves. The album spun two songs into the top of the R&B charts—"Tell Me If You Still Care" reached number five, while the showstopping "Just Be Good to Me" dropped in at number two, not only becoming one of 1983's defining songs, but also returning the band to the spotlight in 1991, when the English house band Beats International revisited the grooves across their smash "Dub Be Good to Me." *On the Rise* is the sound of a band finding their feet again—and knowing what to do with them once they'd found them. *—Amy Hanson*

Just the Way You Like It / 1984 / Tabu ✦✦✦

The signs of decline were all over this 1984 S.O.S. release. Even though they scored two big hits, with the title track checking in at a lofty number six, the exuberance and energy were fading, and rumors about Mary Davis' departure were denied (she left after the next record). The group funk sound was losing its appeal, and the Jam/Lewis combo was beginning to stretch itself too thin. *—Ron Wynn*

Sands of Time / 1986 / Tabu ✦✦✦

The S.O.S. Band had their last fling with chart success on this 1986 album, which was the swan song for Mary Davis. "The Finest" hearkened back to the glory years, with its jaunty arrangements, collective vocals, and catchy production. Everything else was efficiently sung and assembled, as Jam & Lewis wrung the last commercial drop out of the formula. *—Ron Wynn*

Diamonds in the Raw / 1989 / Tabu ✦✦✦

By the time 1989's *Diamonds in the Raw* hit the racks, the S.O.S. Band had been chart-toppers for the better part of a decade. And though no one really expected much of the S.O.S. Band, they still had something to prove, and pulled off a hat trick of mammoth proportions, delivering a slick, sophisticated set. With vocalist Chandra Currelly stepping behind the mike alongside Fredi Grace and the production helmed by Curtis Williams (ex-Kool & the Gang), the stage was set for success. This stellar moment was tragically marred, however, by the untimely death of saxophonist Billy Ellis shortly before the record's completion. The album, then, was given to the fans in tribute. From the opening "I'm Still Missing Your Love" through the jazzy "Goldmine" and on to the edgy harmonies of "Secret Wish," it just doesn't get much tighter. The honeyed ballad "Hold Out," meanwhile, showcases the S.O.S. Band's quieter side and, as the last recording Ellis made before his death, becomes a fitting and poignant tribute. It's only the lackluster "Crossfire, Pts. 1-2" that lets the set down, but buried as the closer, it's easy to skip. That the band had maintained its style and grace is without question. That it had outstayed the musical tide in the United States is also true. Sales remained fairly sluggish stateside, but the S.O.S. Band took *Diamonds in the Raw* and sparkled across Europe, where the album proved a massive hit, giving way to the live *Escape* LP recorded in Amsterdam. *—Amy Hanson*

One of Many Nights / 1991 / Tabu ✦✦

The Best of S.O.S. Band / Oct. 1995 / Tabu ✦✦✦✦

Like all greatest-hits or best-of compilations, this one is missing some key ingredients, namely "S.O.S. (Dit Dit Dit Dat Dat Dat Dit Dit Dit)" and "Just The Way You Like It." Since the band didn't record tons of material and was only active a short time, the omissions are hard to fathom. It's not like they didn't have room on the CD; only ten songs are compiled here. Jimmy Jam & Terry Lewis are well represented with eight songs. Despite the omissions, this is still good listening. Mary Davis' vocals are irresistible; she can do it all. On "Take Your Time (Do It Right)," she shows her funk side, matching the driving, disco-like beat with some powerful vocals. On "Tell Me If You Still Care," she sings in a softer voice, similar to a Smokey Robinson production for Mary Wells. She sings "Just Be Good to Me" with so much conviction that you believe she wrote it. Members of S.O.S. were Jason "T.C." Bryant (keyboards, vocals), Billy Ellis (saxophone, keyboards, vocals), Mary Davis (vocals, percussion), James Earl Jones III (drums, vocals, 1980-1981), Willie "Sonny" Killebrew (saxophone, flute, vocals), Geno Speight (lead guitar), John A. Simpson (bass guitar, vocals), Abdul Ra'oof (trumpet, flugelhorn, percussion, 1982-1986), and Jerome "JT" Thomas (drums, percussion, 1982-1986). *—Andrew Hamilton*

Soul Brothers Six

f. Rochester, NY

Group / Pop-Soul, Funk, Soul

This hard-hitting soul group formed in Rochester, NY, consisting of the multi-talented Willie John Ellison, along with Lester Freeman, Vonell Benjamin, and Charles, Moses, Sam, and Harry Armstrong. (That's seven, but one of the Armstrong brothers' bounced early.) They debuted with "Stop Hurting Me" on Fine Records (1965) and another on Lyndell Records (1966) typo-credited to the Sold Brothers Six. A Philly DJ introduced them to Jerry Wexler of Atlantic Records, and they had a small hit with "Some Kinda Wonderful" (written by Ellison) in 1967; it was their most successful record, making it into the Top 100 at number 91. The Fantastic Johnny C took it four slots higher the following year; and Grand Funk Railroad outdid 'em all by rocking it to number-three pop in 1974.

John Ellison, a coalminer's son, grew up in West Virginia. He learned to play guitar and wrote his first songs when he was 13, later moving to New York City and then Rochester. Soul Brothers Six cut two records on two tiny labels before inking with Atlantic on the strength of Ellison's "Some Kinda Wonderful." But sales of follow-ups—"You Better Check Yourself," "Your Love Is Such a Wonderful Love," "Thank You Baby for Loving Me," and "Drive"—were embarrassing and Atlantic dropped the group before the end of the decade.

Around this time, Joe Johnson, James Johnson, Charles Pevy, and Eddie Reno replaced the Armstrong Brothers, who left disgusted and soured by the Atlantic ordeal. This new lineup waxed three singles on Phil-L.A. of Soul from 1972 to 1974: "Funky, Funky Way of Making Love," "You're My World," and "Let Me Do What We Ain't Doin'." None hit nationally but they worked steadily throughout the country anyway. A substantial royalty check from Grand Funk Railroad's rendition of "Some Kinda Wonderful" revitalized Ellison's songwriting juices. He secured a deal with a small label in Rochester, and scored a Carolinas beach hit that did some business in Europe as well. Ellison has cut two solo albums to date, appeared in the A&E movie *Rev*, and marketed a Some Kinda Wonderful spice via the Allen Beef Company. *—Andrew Hamilton*

The Soul Children

f. 1968, Memphis, TN

Group / Soul, Memphis Soul

A two-man, two-woman vocal group with a penchant for recording soap-opera ballads dealing with adultery, the Soul Children were signed to Stax Records in the late '60s and first clicked on the soul charts with the multi-part "The Sweeter He Is." Their biggest hit came in late 1974 with "I'll Be the Other Woman," which dented the pop Top 40. After Stax closed its doors in 1975, they recorded for Epic and later some uptempo dance singles for Fantasy's reactivated Stax label. *—John Lowe*

The Soul Children / 1968 / Stax ✦✦✦

Genesis / 1972 / Stax ✦✦✦

A respectable record that, even more than many Stax albums from the late '60s and early '70s, has a substantial gospel influence. Gospel was an influence in just about every soul record, of course, but you really hear it with this quartet, especially in the opening, eight-minute "I Want to Be Loved." The mood is funky but a bit more low-key and subdued than was the case on many such LPs of the time, which is a plus—it makes the record stand out from the crowd a little. The presence of different male and female lead singers, and shared leads within the same song, also gives it some welcome variety, even if the group didn't have what it took to be considered among the top tier of soulsters, either in terms of vocals or material. J. Blackfoot's hoarse, scratchy leads (like a muted mixture of James Brown and Otis Redding) provide the most distinctive voice. And it's his lead that paces "Hearsay," the album's upbeat hit single, which made number five on the R&B charts and the middle of the pop charts. The album was paired with 1974's *Friction* on a single-disc CD reissue. *—Richie Unterberger*

● **Chronicle** / 1979 / Stax ✦✦✦✦✦

This is an especially fine collection of their singles for Stax, from a group who had great records but were not stars in the truest sense. One track worth hearing is their 1973 near-miss "It Ain't Always What You Do (It's Who You Let See You Do It)." *—John Lowe*

The Soul Children/Genesis / 1990 / Stax ✦✦✦

The Soul Children/Best of Two Worlds / Apr. 28, 1995 / Stax ✦✦✦✦

Here are two vintage albums by the Soul Children for the price of one CD. Half the productions are by their mentors Isaac Hayes & David Porter, the other half by Porter and his subsequent partner Ronnie Williams. Deep soul sagas the magnitude of "I'll Understand," "Move Over," and "Tighten Up My Thang" provided the paradigm for future Soul Children producers. The Porter & Williams productions are more consistent, but none are as brilliant as the few gems by Hayes & Porter. But whatever the Soul Children sing, their golden voices make even the most hackneyed cuts interesting. *—Andrew Hamilton*

Genesis/Friction / Jan. 1, 1999 / Stax ✦✦✦

The Soul Clan

f. 1969

Group / Soul, Southern Soul

A short-lived but legendary supergroup comprised of some of the biggest name in '60's soul, the Soul Clan's proper recording career amounted to a mere two songs, but the act's lineup was enough to make any R&B aficionado take notice—Solomon Burke, Arthur Conley, Don Covay, Ben E. King, and Joe Tex. At the height of their fame, Burke, Covay, Tex, Otis Redding and Wilson Pickett (all of whom recorded either for Atlantic Records or its affiliated labels) were good friends, often toured together, and would sometimes pop up at each other's shows. Both Burke and Covay began bandying around the idea of working together as a show of musical solidarity; Burke saw the collaboration as a stepping stone towards building an autonomous African-American business empire, while Covay, more successful as a songwriter than a performer, hoped to promote his own career alongside of his friends. While the idea simmered for some time, it wasn't until 1968 that the project finally took flight; by this time, Redding had died in a tragic airplane crash, and Pickett developed cold feet, supposedly uncomfortable with Burke's grandiose financial plans, so Conley and King stepped in to replace them.

The group recorded a single, "Soul Meeting" b/w "That's How I Feel," which was intended as a trailer for a later album and tour, but the single failed to make a serious impression on the charts, and Atlantic pulled their financing towards further recording (Burke has subsequently said he believes Atlantic purposefully let the record fail to prevent the artists from gaining too much power). A Soul Clan album did emerge, but it simply combined the two sides of the single with solo tracks by the various stars, and ended the group's recording career the same year it began. In 1981, the group reunited for a live concert in New York City (with Pickett stepping in for Arthur Conley, who was in Europe at the time), but it was the last time they would work together; Joe Tex died in 1982. *—Mark Deming*

● **Soul Meeting** / 1969 / Atco ✦✦✦✦✦
Sure, it doesn't live up to the billing; with Solomon Burke, Arthur Conley, Don Covay, Ben E. King, and Joe Tex all together on the same session, any soul fan worth his or her salt is going to expect a masterpiece, and the two-song repertoire of the Soul Clan falls a bit short of that description. But that's not to say they aren't two pretty great songs (with Don Covay and Bobby Womack once again demonstrating their gifts as songwriters), and the assembled talent performs at their agonized, churchy best on "That's How It Feels," while getting down on the rockin' and uptempo "Soul Meeting." To listen to these songs, it sounds as if the Soul Clan was an idea as much as a singing group, but it was such a good idea—and the two songs that resulted were strong enough—that you can't help but wonder what could have been if these guys had a bit more time to work together (and had actually been in the same studio together when they cut these songs; due to schedule commitments, some of the artists cut their vocals in different studios at different times). The Soul Clan's album doesn't do a thing to build on the magic of that 45—the set is simply padded out with solo hits by the five headliners—but anyone with an interest in vintage soul will want to lend an ear to the small but impressive legacy of the Soul Clan. (Incidentally, "That's How It Feels" appears on several compilation albums—most economically on the soundtrack to the film *Another Day in Paradise*—while "Soul Meeting" can be found on *The Very Best of Solomon Burke*.) *—Mark Deming*

Soul for Real

f. 1992

Group / New Jack Swing, Urban, Club/Dance

An R&B quartet comprised of the four Dalyrimple brothers—Brian, Chris, Dre, and Jason—Soul for Real formed in 1992, though the siblings had spent many hours singing in their church choir. Signed to Uptown Records, Soul for Real debuted in early 1995 with *Candy Rain*; by the end of the year, the album had gone platinum and reached number 23 on the album charts. After touring both America and overseas, the group worked with producers Heavy D and Sean "Puffy" Combs to record *For Life*. 1999 saw the release of a third album, *Heat*. *—John Bush*

● **Candy Rain** / Mar. 28, 1995 / Uptown ✦✦✦✦
The title track to Soul for Real's debut album was a monster hit, and it's easy to see why—the vocal group sounds sultry and seductive and the production is smooth. However, it's the only knockout on the album. Although the group are undoubtly fine singers, they don't have the strength to make mediocre material convincing. *—Stephen Thomas Erlewine*

Heat / May 18, 1999 / Warlock ✦✦✦
Soul for Real's third album *Heat* reveals the growth that the band experienced in the three-year interim since *For Life*. A more diverse outing than their previous works, *Heat's* songs reflect the romantic side of the four Dalyrimple brothers with "Into You" and "I Want You," their upbeat side on "Can't Wait" and "Party All Night," as well as their serious side on songs like "Hymn." But as with all their work, Soul for Real's smooth, inspiring harmonies ignite *Heat*'s hottest moments. *—Heather Phares*

Soul Generation

Group / Soul

A long running New Jersey vocal quartet, Soul Generation started in the early '70s with Cliff Perkins, Jeff Burgess, Herman Hammond, Earl Davenport. Later the group was continued by Perkins, this time joined by Ted West and Veda LaRue. They kept busy working with producer Tony Camillo, adding harmony vocals and arranging productions at his studio. The group recorded an album and had one top 40 R&B hit in 1972, "That's the Way It's Got to Be (Body and Soul)" for Ebony Sounds Records before a late-'70s move to Buddah Records. *—Wade Kergan*

The Soul Generation: A Golden Classic Edition / 1993 / Collectables ✦✦✦
Here are 20 tracks, ballads and shufflers, with a feeble attempt at social commentary, "Black Man." A sweet falsetto similar to the Younghearts' Ronnie Preyer leads more than half the songs; a David Ruffin-ish tenor cranks out the rest and serves as a balance to the syrup. Some digression occurs on "What's in It for Me," which is loaded with studio tricks; "Wait So Long" mimics a Thom Bell production; and "I've Got That Lovin' Feelin'" reverses the theme of the Righteous Brothers' "You've Lost That Lovin' Feelin'." "Super Fine," "I Don't Know Why," and "Ray of Hope" are stellar representations. A fine singing group, but nobody, including producer Paul Kyser, had the Midas Touch and the Soul Generation never enjoyed a national R&B hit. *—Andrew Hamilton*

● **Battle of the Bands: Round 3** / Nov. 4, 1997 / Sequel ✦✦✦✦
Sequel Records pits two popular East Coast groups in a mythical musical confrontation. Soul Generation comes out jabbing with their Ebony Sound recordings with two B-sides—"Mandingo Woman" and "Young Bird"—the only omissions. They rely heavily on a candy falsetto and use a more pleasing second tenor sparingly. "Body & Soul" is sugary and over-arranged, but the saccharin works on "Praying for a Miracle," "Million Dollars," "Wait So Long," and the Young Rascals' "Ray of Hope." Answering the bell with more firing power, fueled by member Glenn Dorsey's songs, and a more charismatic falsetto, the Joneses win this match hands down with pleasers like "Baby (There's Nothing You Can Do)," "Pretty, Pretty," "Mary, Mary," and "Pull My String." The Joneses don't subject you to falsetto overkill and feature a second tenor on many songs. *—Andrew Hamilton*

Soul II Soul

f. 1989, London, England

Group / Club/Dance, Urban, House, Dance-Pop, Acid House

Led by producer/vocalist/songwriter DJ Jazzie B., Soul II Soul was one of the most innovative dance/R&B outfits of the late '80s, creating a seductive, deep R&B that borrowed from Philly soul, disco, reggae, and '80s hip-hop. Originally featuring Jazzie B., producer/arranger Nellee Hooper, and instrumentalist Philip "Daddae" Harvey, the musical collective came together in the late '80s. The group had a residency at the Africa Centre in London's Covent Garden, which led to a record contract with 10, a subsidiary of Virgin. Two singles, "Fairplay" and "Feel Free," began to attract attention both in clubs and in the press.

Featuring the vocals of Caron Wheeler, Soul II Soul's third single "Keep on Movin'," reached the U.K. Top Ten in March of 1989. Released in the summer of 1989, "Back to Life" also featured Wheeler and became another Top Ten hit. Soul II Soul released their debut album, *Club Classics, Vol. I*, shortly afterward. The album was released in America under the title *Keep on Movin'*; both "Keep on Movin'" and "Get a Life" became substantial hits, propelling the album to double-platinum status. Wheeler left the group before the recording of the group's second album, *Vol. II: 1990—A New Decade*. The album debuted at number one in the U.K., yet it caught the group in a holding pattern. Hooper soon left the collective, leaving Jazzie B. to soldier on alone. Hooper went on to work with several of the most influential and popular acts of the early '90s, including Massive Attack (*Blue Lines*), Björk (*Debut* and *Post*), Madonna (*Bedtime Stories*), and U2 ("Hold Me, Thrill Me, Kiss Me, Kill Me"). In 1992, Soul II Soul released *Vol. III: Just Right*, to both lukewarm reviews and sales. After the compilation *Vol. IV: The Classic Singles*, the group's next studio album (*Vol. V: Believe*) appeared in 1995. *—Stephen Thomas Erlewine*

● **Keep on Movin'** / Jun. 1989 / Virgin ✦✦✦✦✦
When American urban-contemporary radio was bombarding its listeners with one Guy clone after another in the late '80s and early '90s, British neo-soulsters like Soul II Soul, Lisa Stansfield, and the Chimes offered highly creative and gutsy alternatives. With influences ranging from Chic to hip-hop to African music, Soul II Soul's debut album, *Keep on Movin'* (titled *Club Classics, Vol. I* in its original British incarnation), was among the most rewarding R&B releases of 1989. Soul II Soul leader/producer/composer Jazzie B. takes one risk after another—all of which pay off. The group enjoyed major hits with the Chic-influenced gems "Keep on Movin'" and "Back to Life" (both of which feature the gifted Caron Wheeler), and equally superb are the African-influenced reflections of "Dance" and "Holdin' On," the soulful grit and intensity of "Feel Free," and the hypnotic house music of "Happiness." Though Wheeler was Soul II Soul's best-known singer and went on to enjoy a career as a solo artist, Rose Windross and Do'Reen (both expressive soul divas) also do their part to make *Keep on Movin'* the artistic triumph that it is. *—Alex Henderson*

Vol. II: 1990, A New Decade / May 21, 1990 / Virgin ✦✦✦✦
When a debut album is as promising as Soul II Soul's *Keep on Movin'*, there are always fears of a sophomore slump—meaning that the second album won't live up to the promise of the first. But *Vol. II: 1990, A New Decade*, Soul II Soul's sophomore album, isn't the least bit disappointing. Although *Keep on Movin'* (which was titled *Club Classics, Vol. I* in England) remains the British outfit's most essential release, this is an excellent follow-up. Soul II Soul suffered a major loss when singer Caron Wheeler left to pursue a solo career after *Keep on Movin'*; it was a major blow, but certainly not a fatal one. Jazzie B.'s collective fares well without her on sleek urban/dance/neo-soul grooves like "Missing You" (which boasts a guest appearance by British dance diva Kym Mazelle), "People," and the haunting "A Dream's a Dream." Jazzie realized that Wheeler's departure was a big loss for Soul II Soul, and when the time came to record a second album, he filled the void by featuring talented, expressive female vocalists such as Victoria Wilson-James, Lamya, and Marcia Lewis. However, not every tune on this CD employs a vocalist. "Courtney Blows" (just to give one example) is an acid jazz instrumental that features British jazz saxophonist Courtney Pine; the tune isn't hard bop or straight-ahead jazz, but it's a pleasing example of dance music with jazz overtones. Again, *Keep on Movin'* is Soul II Soul's most essential album, but *Vol. II: 1990, A New Decade* is also well-worth the price of admission. *—Alex Henderson*

Vol. III: Just Right / Apr. 13, 1992 / Virgin ✦✦

Vol. IV: The Classic Singles 1988–1993 / Dec. 6, 1993 / Virgin ✦✦✦✦✦
This compilation captures the essence of ultra-sophisticated R&B and house music at a turning point, before the sample-heavy storm of American R&B took over in the early '90s. Soul II Soul brought an organic feeling to their music, which shines through on this stellar compilation. The music was sleek, the vocals were clear, and the beats were irresistible. This collection assembles the hits and singles from the ever-evolving act's first three albums. "Back to Life," the group's biggest stateside hit, is included in its single form, which was dramatically different from the original album version, which made many purchasers of *Keep on Movin'* very disappointed when they realized the song they heard on the radio was clearly not the one on the album. Other singles, such as "Jazzie's Groove" and "A Dream's a Dream" are also included in their radio/video versions. The album includes their other big hit, "Keep on Movin'" (unfortunately in an edited form—the full-length album version was better), as well as other key singles, such as the rousing "Joy," the gritty club hit "Fairplay," and the ballad "Move Me No Mountain." From slick

R&B ballads to Philly-inspired soul, from hip-hop to house music, Soul II Soul's hit collection offers up a musical smorgasbord that neatly highlights the outfit's greatest successes. *—Jose Promis*

Vol. V: Believe / Aug. 11, 1995 / Virgin ✦✦✦
Six years after they revolutionized R&B and soul with their debut album, *Keep on Movin'*, Soul II Soul returned with *Vol. V: Believe.* Since their debut, the soul collective had been struggling to regain their position as musical innovators; in the process, they turned out two confused albums that had their moments, but nothing quite as stirring as their initial singles, which were collected on the British-only *Volume IV: The Classic Singles. Believe*, their fourth album of original material, doesn't necessarily make a case for Soul II Soul as pioneers in the mid-'90s, but it does represent something of a comeback. Where their two previous albums were muddled affairs, *Believe* is clear and confident, filled with fully formed songs. It helps that Jazzie B., the leader of the group, has persuaded former members Caron Wheeler and Penny Ford to make appearances on the album and has recruited some genuine new talent that helps spark him into recording his best music since the group's debut. Granted, it doesn't push down many boundaries, but *Believe* fits comfortably into the laid-back, jazz-saturated grooves of '90s R&B. *—Stephen Thomas Erlewine*

Time for Change / 1997 / Island ✦✦

Club Classics, Vol. 1: 10th Anniversary Edition / May 18, 1999 / Virgin ✦✦✦✦✦
This tenth anniversary reissue of Soul II Soul's groundbreaking debut album provides a good opportunity to look back and see how influential it really was—these dark, jazz-inflected grooves still resonate in the deep house, acid jazz and illbient music of the late '90s. And even if "Keep on Movin'," the album's lead track and centerpiece, is way overrated as a song, Caron Wheeler's voice still cuts through it shiningly; Rose Windross isn't far behind Wheeler on the more substantial "Fairplay." Bandleader Jazzie B., on the other hand, is a great arranger and a passable rapper (at his best on the very fine "Feelin' Free," which features the future members of Massive Attack on background vocals), but his singing sounds pretty sorry in this company. But the vocals are less important than the grooves, of course, and these are consistently excellent, often spiced up with jazz flute or buoyed by the strings of the Reggae Philharmonic Orchestra. The reissue adds an extra 30 minutes of remixes, including a great drum n' bass treatment of "Keep on Movin'" and an equally compelling remix of the Caron Wheeler showcase "Back to Life (However Do You Want Me)." *—Rick Anderson*

The Soul Stirrers

f. 1927, Trinity, TX
Group / Traditional Gospel, Black Gospel, R&B, Soul
Indisputably among the premier gospel groups of the modern era, the Soul Stirrers pioneered the contemporary quartet sound. Pushing the music away from the traditional repertoire of jubilees and spirituals towards the visceral, deeply emotional hard gospel style so popular among postwar listeners, the group's innovative arrangements—they were the first quartet to add a second lead—and sexually-charged presence irrevocably blurred the lines between religious and secular music while becoming a seminal influence on the development of rock & roll and soul, most notably by virtue of their connection to the legendary Sam Cooke. The Soul Stirrers' classic early lineup included baritone Senior Roy Crain, bass Jesse Farley, baritone T.L. Bruster, second lead James Medlock and, most notably, lead R.H. Harris, whose high, crystalline voice remains the inspiration for virtually all great male quartet leads to follow since.

After moving to Chicago, they began shifting away from the signature tight harmonies and compact songs of traditional gospel towards a harder style distinguished by shifting leads and performances elongated to increase their emotional potency; they also began performing new material from the pens of Thomas A. Dorsey, Kenneth Morris and others. Throughout the 1940s, the Soul Stirrers' reputation grew; not only were they constantly on tour, but they booked most of the major gospel programs in the Chicago area. They recorded over two dozen tracks for Specialty in 1950 before Harris quit the group that same year; many predicted a dire future, especially when it was announced that his replacement was a relatively unknown 20-year-old named Sam Cooke. When Cooke made his recording debut with the Soul Stirrers in 1951, however, any reservations were quickly dispelled—blessed with a gossamer voice even sweeter and more graceful than Harris', he would take the group to even greater heights than before. *—Jason Ankeny*

Jesus Be a Fence Around Me / 1961 / S.A.R. ✦✦✦✦✦

Gospel Pearls / 1962 / S.A.R. ✦✦✦✦✦
Here is strong lead work from Cooke, Outler, Harris and Leroy Crume. Also features the Gospel Paraders. *—Opal Louis Nations*

☆ **The Original Soul Stirrers Featuring Sam Cooke** / 1964 / Specialty ✦✦✦✦✦
The split between the secular and spiritual in black music has not only caused controversy, but has been the springboard for some of the best gospel, R&B, soul, and even hip-hop records to come out in the last 50 years; Ray Charles, Sam Cooke, Little Richard, and Al Green certainly come to mind in relation to seemingly irreconcilable allegiances to God and the commercial spotlight. Cooke's own move into the soul music field (in fact, he practically created the style) certainly caused major problems for fans of his first group and gospel music's own vocal royalty, the Soul Stirrers; it was one thing to sing sexy in church, but to embrace rock & roll with songs like "Having a Party" and "Shake" was tantamount to blasphemy. This fine Soul Stirrers collection reveals what some of the fuss was about, as Cooke is featured on a handful of the group's innovative and highly expressive gospel hits. At times sharing the mike with second lead Paul Foster, Cooke soars with angelic soulfulness on hits like "Wonderful," "Touch the Hem of His Garment," and "I'm So Glad (Trouble Don't Last Always)." Beyond the cuts featuring Cooke, the record also spotlights the talents of Cooke's replacement and future soulster Johnny Taylor as well as veteran group member R.H. Crain. There's also plenty of fine, post-Cooke material like "Feel Like My Time Ain't Long." Check this collection out before picking up Cooke's popular records and see why "soul music" has been a part of the church all along. *—Stephen Cook*

★ **The Soul Stirrers** / 1964 / Specialty ✦✦✦✦✦
Specialty's *Soul Stirrers* is a wonderful, definitive collection that contains the best moments from the seminal gospel group, including material recorded with all four lead vocalists—Sam Cooke, Johnnie Taylor, R.H. Harris and Paul Foster. *—Leo Stanley*

Heaven Is My Home / 1988 / Specialty ✦✦✦

Jesus Gave Me Water / 1992 / Specialty ✦✦✦
Sam Cooke was only a tender 19 years of age when he was tapped to replace R.H. Harris as the lead singer of legendary gospel group the Soul Stirrers. Cooke's break came when Soul Stirrer baritone R.B. Robinson saw him perform with the Highway QCs and decided to take the young singer under his wing. Well, if this recording is any indication, Cooke was already the master and everyone else, students. Cooke gives a command performance running in and out of the Stirrers' characteristically solid backing. Never sounding better, he lends energy and sense of teenage desperation to this set of gospel classics and originals. Especially outstanding are the tracks "I'm on the Firing Line," "Jesus Will Lead Me to That Promised Land," and the brilliantly arranged "Jesus Paid the Debt." It wouldn't be until 1958 that Sam Cooke would break into the pop charts, but this record reveals he was a consummate performer. As a total unknown suddenly thrust into leading the most popular gospel group in America, Cooke breaks not a sweat. An excellent, though largely forgotten, record. *—Brian Whitener*

☆ **Shine on Me** / Jul. 29, 1992 / Specialty ✦✦✦✦✦
Robert Harris was undoubtedly one of the great voices and stylists of the genre, and his performances on this disc go a long way to justifying the claim that he was the greatest of them all. Every track on here is a gem of beauty, tone and commitment. But the kick-off track on this compilation, an alternate take of their two-part single, "By and By," is absolutely devastating in its use of shading, dynamics, and unrelenting fervor in getting its message across. The Soul Stirrers lock the groove down mightily, chiming up on those low seventh chords like twelve feet of concrete. Harris, as the old saying goes, sings his rear end off on this one, and, as transcendent moments go, this one is in a class all by itself. If the issued versions included here are slightly less subdued and don't quite hit as high a quotient on the fervor meter, so what?—we should be grateful enough that this performance has survived. If impassioned gospel is your thing, boy, are you gonna love this. *—Cub Koda*

The Soul Survivors

f. 1967, **db.** 1968
Group / Pop-Soul, Soul
The Soul Survivors' only giant hit, "Expressway to Your Heart," was one of the first notable productions by Philadelphia wizards Kenny Gamble & Leon Huff in 1967. Although they were white, the Soul Survivors adopted a convincing R&B sound for their early singles on Crimson. Gamble & Huff loaded "Expressway to Your Heart" with honking horns and other automotive sound effects, but the record's principal strength lay in its soulful vocals and pounding beat. After a less successful follow-up, "Explosion in Your Soul," the band faded but returned for one more hit in 1974. *—Bill Dahl*

● **When the Whistle Blows Anything Goes** / 1967 / Collectables ✦✦✦✦✦
This features the first band to help establish the Gamble & Huff combine. They were a great white soul ensemble. *—Ron Wynn*

Take Another Look / 1968 / Atco ✦✦✦
The Soul Survivors flamed out quite quickly, but their second album wasn't a bad bit of blue-eyed R&B. They could do effective hard-driving dance tunes or decent ballads, and while Gamble & Huff hadn't yet become legends, they provided workmanlike production and arrangements. What stopped the Soul Survivors was the fact that they were merely a good band, and in an era loaded with great ones, they couldn't generate enough "Expressway to Your Heart" gems to maintain audience interest. *—Ron Wynn*

The Soul Survivors / 1975 / T S O P ✦✦✦
Do not be fooled someday, if this pops up, into thinking that you'll be grabbing a lost treasure. By the mid-'70s, the bloom had long since come off the Soul Survivors' rose. They tried to regroup, signing with one-time mentors and producers Gamble & Huff's label. Only Richard and Charles Ingui from the original troupe were in this edition, and they simply didn't have the old magic. Even if they had, it's highly doubtful that '60s-style blue-eyed soul would have meant much in the mid-'70s. *—Ron Wynn*

Soul Train Gang

Group / Urban, Disco, Soul
In the early '70s, the dancers on Don Cornelius' hit television program *Soul Train* were known as the Soul Train Gang. But they became the Soul Train Dancers in 1975, when Cornelius and Dick Griffey co-founded Soul Train Records—which evolved into Solar Records, home to Lakeside, Shalamar, the Whispers and others—and decided to name an R&B vocal quintet the Soul Train Gang.

Consisting of Gerald Brown, Terry Brown, Judy Jones, Patricia Williamson (replaced by Denise Smith in 1976) and Hollis Pippin, the Soul Train Gang recorded its debut album, *Don Cornelius Presents the Soul Train Gang*, in 1975. Produced by Cornelius and Griffey, the LP included "Soul Train '75," one of the many themes from *Soul Train.* (The previous theme had previously been MFSP's famous "TSOP" on Philadelphia International.) In 1976, the Soul Train Gang recorded its second album, *The Soul Train Gang*, which was produced by Norman Harris and recorded mostly in Philadelphia. Not surprisingly, Cornelius and Griffey hoped they could use *Soul Train*'s popularity to make the Soul Train Gang a hit. But while both albums were decent examples of '70s soul and funk, neither made the Soul Train Gang a big name in the R&B world. After the quintet's breakup in 1977, Brown went on to join Shalamar the following year, replacing original Shalamar member Gary Mumford. Brown appeared on Shalamar's second album, *Shalamar Disco Gardens*, and the hit single "Take That to the Bank" before being replaced by Howard Hewett in 1979. *—Alex Henderson*

● **Don Cornelius Presents the Soul Train Gang** / 1975 / Soul Train ♦♦♦
When Don Cornelius' *Soul Train* caught on in the early '70s, the show was often described as the African-American equivalent of *American Bandstand*, and Cornelius often found himself being exalted as the R&B world's version of Dick Clark. Back then, there was no BET, so a weekly syndicated program focusing primarily on R&B meant a lot to the African-American community. In 1975 Cornelius branched out into recording when he formed Soul Train Records with Dick Griffey, and the two produced this debut album by the Soul Train Gang. The group never became huge, and the record didn't establish Soul Train Records as another Motown or Philadelphia International. However, Griffey *did* become a major-league record mogul after Soul Train Records evolved into Solar Records (minus Cornelius) several years later, putting out smash hits by the Whispers, Lakeside, Shalamar, Dynasty, and others. Although a bit uneven and not exactly earth-shattering, this LP is a likable example of '70s soul that boasts such talented arrangers as Stevie Wonder and Gene Page. Side one focuses on uptempo material, with cuts that include the gritty "Garbage Can," the funky "I Can Do It All Night," and the Philadelphia International-like "Soul Train '75," one of the various themes from *Soul Train*. But ballads are the focus of side two, which ranges from the jazzy, Minnie Riperton-ish "Music on My Mind" to the Stylistics-like "Fairytales." It's true that everyone has to start somewhere—and for Soul Train Records this LP was a decent start, if an imperfect one. *—Alex Henderson*

The Soul Train Gang / 1978 / RCA ♦♦♦
For its second and last LP, the Los Angeles-based Soul Train Gang traveled across the U.S. to Philadelphia's legendary Sigma Sound and enlisted Norman Harris, who had been producing major hits for Blue Magic and the Spinners in that very studio. While parts of the Soul Train Gang's first album were influenced by the Philly sound, *everything* on this album is Philadelphia-sounding. With Harris producing and Bobby Martin helping with the arranging (Don Cornelius and Dick Griffey are listed as executive producers), the Philly influence is impossible to miss on romantic cuts like "All My Life (I Wanna Live With You)" and the Blue Magic-minded "If It Takes All Night," as well as uptempo offerings such as "Country Girl" and the funky "Soul Train Theme," which in 1976, replaced "Soul Train '75" as the program's theme music. ("Soul Train '75" had replaced MFSB's famous "TSOP"). Despite *Soul Train*'s popularity and despite the popularity of the Philly sound, this LP wasn't a huge seller. Nor is it an album that lovers of Philly soul would consider essential. But it's a decent, if less than remarkable, footnote in the history of '70s R&B. *—Alex Henderson*

S.O.U.L.

Group / Funk, Jazz-Funk, Soul
Originating in Cleveland, OH, S.O.U.L. stood for "Sounds of Unity and Love." The members were Lee Lovett (bass), Gus Hawkins (sax/flute), Paul Stubblefield (drums), and Walter Winston (guitar). Larry Hancock (vocals/organ) was added in 1971 and Bernard (Beloyd) Taylor (guitar) replaced Winston in 1972. All had been involved in music before the formation of S.O.U.L. The fellows entered a battle-of-the-bands contest in 1970, sponsored by the May Company department store in Cleveland, WHK radio station, and Musicor Records. The group won the first prize of 1,000 dollars and a recording contract with Musicor. They traveled to New York City in 1971 and recorded a 45 entitled "Down in the Ghetto Parts I & II" which exceeded the expectations of Musicor by doing so well regionally. They cut a second single, then were invited back to New York to record an album. *What It Is* consisted of seven tracks and illuminated the versatility of the band. They did covers of jazz and funk tunes to augment their two singles. It did quite well, cracking the Top 40 album spot on *Billboard*'s soul album chart and nesting there for two months. The album was released in the United Kingdom and other European countries in the early '90s on the BGP label where S.O.U.L. is a cult figure.

Bassist Lee Lovett was born in Detroit but moved to Cleveland in the late '50s. He led a popular band entitled Lee Lovett and the Dynamic Sounds in the '60s who played live gigs and backed some local acts in the studios. Sax/flute player Gus Hawkins was born in Oakwood, where minorities were as scarce in the '50s and '60s as Dixie Peach hair dressing. It was an upper-middle-class village about 13 miles from Cleveland. He learned to play tenor sax in Oakwood's schools as a member of the band. Leaving school in the '60s, he moved to Cleveland and joined the Futuretones.

Around the time S.O.U.L. began work on their third LP, Winston quit the group and was replaced by Bernard "Beloyd" Taylor. Beloyd's birth place is a mystery, but he grew up in Cleveland. With Taylor, they enjoyed their most successful single, "This Time Around," which made the Top 50 R&B. The next release, "The Jones," written by Lee Lovett, entered the Top 100 and hung around for ten weeks. After a few more releases the guys split up, going their separate ways. Gus Hawkins went to school and became a phlebotomist, then worked at the Cleveland Clinic before moving to Atlanta, GA, to work and raise his family. Paul Stubblefield joined a ten-member group called the Rasts, recording and touring before becoming a member of the Murphys (a lounge act). He also toured with various versions of the Ink Spots and the Platters before moving to Phoenix, AZ. Taylor moved to Los Angeles and wrote "Get Away" for Earth, Wind & Fire in 1976. He also recorded solo for 20th Century Records and later toured with Earth, Wind & Fire. Lee Lovett stayed in Cleveland and recorded tracks with other groups.

Hancock has been active since the breakup of S.O.U.L., recording with two versions of Truth. The first group featured Hancock, Al Boyd, Leo Green, and Russell Watts. Al Boyd later co-wrote "Shakey Ground" for the Temptations (it was redone by Phoebe Snow). Truth recordings failed to chart and two members left, leaving Hancock and Green as Truth's only members. The two recorded an album on Devaki Records as Truth, entitled *Coming Home*, that fail to grab the public when released. Interestingly, Dennis Edwards had been kicked out of the Temptations and was hanging around Cleveland and played a big part in the *Coming Home* album. Hancock ventured back out to California and recorded for Decca Records including a duet with Alfie Silas before returning to Cleveland. He also sang with one of the Platters groups. Lead singer Sonny Turner ("With This Ring") is a Clevelander and they knew each other well. *—Andrew Hamilton*

What Is It / 1971 / BGP ♦♦♦

Can You Feel It / 1972 / BGP ♦♦♦

● **What Is It/Can You Feel It** / 1996 / BGP ♦♦♦
Both of S.O.U.L.'s LPs, *What Is It* and *Can You Feel It*, are compiled on this two-fer release from the BGP label. *—Jason Ankeny*

Jimmy Soul

b. Aug. 24, 1942, Weldon, NC, **d.** Jun. 25, 1988, New York, NY
Vocals / R&B, Soul
Born on August 24, 1942, in Weldon, NC, Jimmy Soul became a preacher at the age of seven and performed gospel as a teenager, becoming known locally as "the Wonder Boy." His talent was noticed by Frank Guida, engineer of the legendary Norfolk sound, and was recruited to record some of the calypso-based songs that Guida had hand-picked for one of his other hit artists, Gary "U.S." Bonds. Soul's only two charting hits were both Bonds' cast-offs, 1962's "Twistin' Matilda" and 1963's number one hit "If You Wanna Be Happy." That song, with its upbeat, vibrant Caribbean sound, was a huge success and prompted Soul to try to re-create the success of his hit with some fairly derivative West Indian songs such as "Treat 'Em Tough" and "A Woman Is Smarter in Every Kinda Way," but he failed to chart again and later joined the Army, giving up his career in music. He died of a heart attack on June 25, 1988, at the age of 45. *—Stacia Proefrock*

If You Wanna Be Happy / 1963 / SPQR ♦♦

Jimmy Soul and the Belmonts / 1963 / Spinorama ♦♦

● **The Best of Jimmy Soul** / 1992 / Rhino ♦♦♦♦♦
Jimmy Soul wasn't the most original or varied of soul singers, but he had a light touch and effervescent charm that made his singles perfect for beach parties. Rhino's *The Best of Jimmy Soul* contains his 18 best singles, including not only "If You Wanna Be Happy," but a lot of rewrites of that song, such as "My Baby Loves to Bowl." Nothing is as good as that big hit, and this is awful samey, but it keeps its mood grooving from start to finish, and provides a good time—provided that you're looking for sound, not songs. *—Stephen Thomas Erlewine*

If You Wanna Be Happy: The Very Best of Jimmy Soul / Feb. 20, 1996 / Ace ♦♦♦♦
Even though it contains a bunch of the same material, Ace's *If You Wanna Be Happy: The Very Best of Jimmy Soul* trumps the Rhino collection, since it cuts out novelties and has a sharper track selection. This still is a lot of Jimmy Soul, probably too much for most listeners, but if you're serious about your pop-soul, this is the Jimmy Soul collection to get. *—Stephen Thomas Erlewine*

Sound Experience

Group / Funk, Deep Funk, Soul
Sound Experience was a tight, hard-driving funk ensemble with a flair for uptempo grooves and aggressive, mind-bending guitar work drenched in fuzz and wah-wah effects. Composed of lead vocalist Arthur Grant, Leroy Frailing, Johnny Groman, Gregory Holmes, James Lindsey, Melvin Miles, Anton Scott, and Reginald Wright, the rather large group formed at Baltimore's Morgan State College in 1970 and quickly built a local following. During the early '70s, the group hooked up with producer Stan Watson and his Philly Groove/Soulville labels, and moved to Philadelphia to record with him. Early sides like "40 Acres and a Mule" and "Blow Your Mind" displayed the influence of early Funkadelic, but by the time of their first album, 1974's *Don't Fight the Feeling*, their sound was a bit smoother around the edges. The title cut was a minor hit, and "Devil With the Bust" became an oft-sampled breakbeat classic in the years to come; other singles included "You've Broken My Heart" and 1975's "Boogie Woogie." Although their recorded output was limited, Sound Experience enjoyed an enduring cult following among funk collectors; Collectables issued the career overview *The Soulville Collection* on CD in 1994, and acclaimed director Paul Thomas Anderson used the track "J.P. Walk" in his adult-film saga *Boogie Nights*. *—Steve Huey*

Don't Fight the Feeling / 1974 / P-Vine ♦♦♦

● **The Soulville Collection** / Jun. 25, 1994 / Collectables ♦♦♦♦
This compilation covers the short career of Sound Experience, a large funk ensemble reminiscent of the Ohio Players who knocked out some impressive jams during their brief recording career. The surprising thing about this group's sound is the driving, rock-oriented style utilized on the uptempo tracks: songs like "Don't Fight the Feeling" and "40 Acres and a Mule" prominently feature loud, fierce electric guitar lines among the expected driving basslines and jazzy horn arrangements. Sound Experience have also become something of a cult item thanks to songs like "Devil With the Bus," a clavinet-fueled track that balances a smoothly harmonized chorus with some throbbing, percussive rhythms, and "J.P. Walk," an instrumental epic that builds from some meditative electric piano lines into a horn-laden opus that features some tasty synthesizer solos on its tag (trivia note: this tune gained new notoriety when it was used as soundtrack music for the mock-porn films in *Boogie Nights*). Other tracks show the group had a winning way with ballads: "He Don't Really Love You" is an elegant track that effectively blends a gospel-styled piano melody with lush string orchestrations and "You Don't Know What You're Doing" is an anguished slow groove that highlights the group's

strong grasp of slick, heart-tugging vocal harmonies. Some of the lesser tracks value groove over melody, but the arrangements and musicianship are so tight that funk fans won't care and all of the songs sport plenty of catchy riffs. All in all, *The Soulsville Collection* is an engaging portrait of a lesser-known funk group who are worthy of investigation by fans who have worn out their Ohio Players and J.B.'s albums. *—Donald A. Guarisco*

Sounds of Blackness

f. 1971, St. Paul, MN

Group / Contemporary Gospel, World Fusion, CCM, Urban

Sounds of Blackness, a 40-person choir and ten-piece orchestra led by Gary Hines, combined traditional African music with urban soul to become one of the most distinctive and popular contemporary gospel groups. Russel Knight formed the group that would prove to be the origins of Sounds of Blackness in 1969 at St. Paul, Minnesota's Macalester College in 1971. It wasn't until 1971, when Hines was hired as their musical director, that the group developed its own identity. Hines opened the group up to the entire community, and expanded their musical scope to concentrate on all aspects of black music. He designed the group as a way to embrace all manners of African-American music and create rich, diverse music to celebrate God and the human spirit, as well as make social statements. With their new direction in mind, the group renamed itself Sounds of Blackness.

Partially by choice, Sounds of Blackness remained a regional attraction until 1989, when Jimmy Jam & Terry Lewis, the hot Minneapolis-based production team, brought Janet Jackson to one of their concerts. Jackson's enthusiastic response inspired Jam & Lewis, who were already in negotiations with Sounds of Blackness, to sign the group to Perspective/A&M immediately. The group's national debut album, *The Evolution of Gospel*, was largely produced by Jam & Lewis and received strong reviews. *—Stephen Thomas Erlewine*

● **The Evolution of Gospel** / 1991 / Perspective ♦♦♦♦

Though from beginning to end one of the best gospel albums of its era, *The Evolution of Gospel* became and remains noteworthy because of three songs in particular: "Optimistic," "The Pressure," and "Testify." These three songs rocketed to the upper reaches of the R&B charts in 1992, all three entering the Top 20 and "Optimistic" peaking at number three—remarkable numbers for such unashamed gospel music. And these weren't flukes or novelty hits. No, these were amazing songs that captured the spirit of the time, in particular the new jack swing production sound that was all the rage in the early '90s. Furthermore, it didn't hurt that Sounds of Blackness teamed with the hottest production team of the time for these songs, Jimmy Jam & Terry Lewis, who were in the process of producing Janet Jackson's *Rhythm Nation* at the time. The result was three definitive songs that synthesized Jam & Lewis' incredibly dense rhythms with Sounds of Blackness' uplifting gospel technique. The remainder of the album unfortunately didn't feature Jam & Lewis' production, but group mastermind Gary Hines obviously knew he had a winning formula and stuck with the new jack motifs, even if he's a second-rate Teddy Riley at best. As a further testament to this album's monolithic status, it's important to note that much of this album remains as charged as it did at its prime, while all the other Bobby Browns and Color Me Badds of the time admittedly haven't aged nearly as well. Sounds of Blackness never could duplicate the success of *Evolution of Gospel*, the undisputed zenith of the group's career. *—Jason Birchmeier*

Africa to America: The Journey of the Drum / Apr. 19, 1994 / Perspective ♦♦♦♦

Nothing on *Africa to America* tops the shining moments—"Optimistic" and "Testify"—on Sounds of Blackness' debut, *Evolution of Gospel*. However, all things considered, *Africa to America* is probably the better album. And if it's not the better album, it's surely the more consistent of the two. Where Jimmy Jam's & Terry Lewis' efforts were somewhat limited on *Evolution of Gospel*, with the exception of the album's highlights, the producers devoted themselves to this 1994 follow-up, producing not just a few great songs but rather numerous great songs: "I Believe," "I'm Going All the Way," "Black Butterfly," "Everything Is Going to Be Alright," and "The Harder They Are, the Bigger They Fall," in particular. And while these songs don't depart too far from the potent new jack swing-meets-gospel sound of "Optimistic," that's a *good* thing—Jam & Lewis were on top of their game at the time and brought no shortage of their trademark dense percussive rhythms to *Africa to America*. So, even if the production sounds a little calculated and perhaps even outdated for its time, it made for some amazing songs. It wasn't until subsequent albums that it became evident just how integral Jam & Lewis were to Sounds of Blackness' success. Along with *Evolution of Gospel*, *Africa to America* remains the group's pinnacle. With Jam & Lewis, Sounds of Blackness sounded fresh and relevant; without the duo, they sounded like any other gospel group. *—Jason Birchmeier*

Time for Healing / May 5, 1997 / Perspective ♦♦♦

The Very Best of Sounds of Blackness / Oct. 23, 2001 / A&M ♦♦♦♦

Up until the time of *The Very Best of Sounds of Blackness*' release in late 2001, you headed straight to *Evolution of Gospel* if you wanted to hear Sounds of Blackness. That album had the group's biggest hits—"Optimistic," "Testify," and "The Pressure"—songs that not only scaled the R&B charts but partly defined an era. And, for many listeners, this was all the Sounds of Blackness they needed. Yet to write off the post-*Evolution of Gospel* Sounds of Blackness would be a mistake. Granted, the group never did deliver anything that would measure up to "Optimistic." However, they did come close. The group's 1994 follow-up, *Africa to America*, also featured Jimmy Jam & Terry Lewis as producers as *Evolution of Gospel* did. So, as a result, there's no shortage of great moments on that album, many of which are featured here. In fact, the bulk of this best-of comes from *Africa to America*. And while Sounds of Blackness' other albums for the Perspective label—*The Night Before Christmas* and *Time for Healing*—are ignored for the most part, that's not such a bad thing—they aren't particularly impressive albums and their absence makes more room for selections from *Evolution of Gospel* and *Africa to America*. There's also a soundtrack contribution here from the 1992 *Mo' Money* soundtrack, "Joy," another Jam & Lewis production. It's this emphasis on the group's work with Jam & Lewis that takes center stage on this best-of and rightfully so—Sounds of Blackness never sounded quite as impressive without Janet Jackson's trademark producers behind the boards. So, even if this best-of leans heavily toward the Jam and Lewis productions, you really can't complain. *—Jason Birchmeier*

Southside Movement

Group / Chicago Soul, Funk, Soul, Disco

The Southside Movement was a Chicago-based funk and soul octet which recorded in the early '70s. Made up of vocalist Melvin Moore, guitarist Bobby Pointer, keyboardist Morris Beeks, bassist Ronald Simmons, drummer Willie Hayes, alto saxophonist Milton Johnson, trumpeter Steve Hawkins, and trombonist Bill McFarland, the group got its start as the backing band for the Sam & Dave-styled soul duo Simtec & Wylie. They later signed with the Wand label and issued their self-titled debut album in 1973; it produced a Top 20 R&B hit in the breakbeat classic "I've Been Watching You," which was sampled heavily by a future generation of hip-hoppers (including the Beastie Boys on "So What'cha Want"). The follow-up single "Can You Get to That" also charted, and the band subsequently moved to the 20th Century label. Their sophomore album *Movin'* appeared in 1974, but despite another much-sampled item in "Save the World," it didn't match the group's earlier success. "Bus Stop" (1975) was a minor hit, and the high-quality accompanying album, *Moving South*, spawned a second single in "Do It to Me." However, the Southside Movement broke up later that year. Collectables' CD-era compilation *The Very Best of Southside Movement: I've Been Watching You* concentrates mostly on their first album. *—Steve Huey*

The South Side Movement / 1973 / Wand ♦♦♦

● **The Very Best of Southside Movement: I've Been Watching You** / Jan. 5, 1998 / Collectables ♦♦♦♦♦

The Very Best of Southside Movement: I've Been Watching You is a ten-track overview of the disco band's career, containing the entirety of their original debut album, which featured the hit singles "I've Been Watching You" and "Can You Get to That." The group didn't have much beyond those two singles, and even those will be of interest primarily to disco specialists, but for those who like the hits, there are a couple of enjoyable, similar-sounding songs on the album. *—Stephen Thomas Erlewine*

Bob B. Soxx & the Blue Jeans

f. 1962

Group / Girl Group, Pop, Brill Building Pop, R&B

Bob B. Soxx & the Blue Jeans were an early-'60s studio group assembled by producer Phil Spector that featured singers Bobby Sheen (b. 1943, St. Louis, MO), Darlene Love, and Fanita James (the latter two were former members of the Blossoms). The group had a Top Ten pop and R&B hit with a cover of "Zip-A-Dee-Doo-Dah," the Oscar-winning song from the 1946 Walt Disney film *Song of the South*, in the winter of 1962-1963. Later hits were "Why Do Lovers Break Each Other's Heart?" and "Not Too Young to Get Married." Love and James were replaced by Gloria Jones and Carolyn Willis in 1964. Love has continued as a successful singer and actress. Sheen has toured as a member of the latter day Coasters. *—William Ruhlmann*

● **Zip-A-Dee-Doo-Dah** / 1963 / London ♦♦♦

The Spaniels

f. 1952, Gary, IN, **db.** 1974

Group / Doo Wop, R&B

The Spaniels are best known for their massive 1954 hit, "Goodnight, Sweetheart, Goodnight" (number-five R&B). They were the first successful Midwestern R&B group, coming from Gary, IN, by way of Chicago. Lead vocalist James "Pookie" Hudson was a graceful lead singer who influenced many who came after him, most notably Aaron Neville. They were also one of the first (if not the first) R&B groups to perform with the lead singer on one microphone and the rest of the group sharing another, and initiated a trend toward using tap dance routines in live shows. Their often a cappella recordings showcase the purity of a sound and style uniquely their own. It was also the Spaniels who partially brought about the formation of one of R&B's legendary labels, Vee-Jay, which became one of the most successful black-owned record companies in the country.

The story of how the Spaniels came to prominence begins in late 1952, when lead singer Hudson was convinced by four of his Roosevelt High classmates—Ernest Warren (first tenor), Opal Courtney Jr. (baritone), Willie Jackson (second tenor), and Gerald Gregory (bass) to join them for a school talent show. They had debuted as Pookie Hudson & the Hudsonaires for the Christmas show and fared so well they decided to continue. Not wanting to join the bird group club (Orioles, Ravens, etc.), they decided on the name Spaniels. In the spring, the group visited the local record shop owned by James and Vivian Bracken, who had begun developing a record label called Vee-Jay Records. They soon moved their operation to Chicago, in a garage off 47th Street (later they would relocate to offices at 1449 South Michigan Avenue). The Spaniels were one of the first two artists signed to the label (the other was blues guitarist Jimmy Reed). On May 5, 1953, the Spaniels recorded "Baby It's You," released in July. On September 5, "Baby" hit number ten on the national R&B best-seller charts.

The Spaniels' next session produced additional singles, including "Goodnight, Sweetheart, Goodnight," which took off in March 1954, but it took about six months for the record to break nationally, charting at number five on the R&B charts. Its success prompted the McGuire Sisters to cover it for the "white" market, stealing a lot of the Spaniels' thunder when their version landed in the Top Ten (number seven). The Spaniels' next single, "Let's Make Up," earned more for songwriter Hudson as someone else's B-side when it appeared on the flip of the Top 20 hit "The Ballad of Davy Crockett" (number 14, 1955). On June 11, 1954, the Spaniels made the first of numerous appearances at the

Apollo Theatre and began touring the greater Midwest. Another single, "You Painted Pictures," reached number-13 R&B in October.

After Opal Courtney Jr. was drafted, Vee-Jay A&R man and Spaniels producer Calvin Carter was pressed into service during their road trips for a few months until James "Dimples" Cochran took over permanently. Shortly thereafter, Ernest Warren was drafted and the group continued recording as a quartet. Two subsequent Spaniels singles failed to connect. Disappointed, Pookie Hudson and Willie Jackson both decided to leave the group. The Spaniels bravely continued on, with Carl Rainge (lead), Gerald Gregory (bass), James Cochran (baritone), and Don Porter (second tenor). This contingent lasted for only one single until Pookie rejoined.

In April 1957, Vee-Jay released the first full-length album, *Goodnight, It's Time to Go.* By mid-summer, the group was back to turning out terrific singles. Incidentally, around this same time Hank Ballard (of Hank Ballard & the Midnighters) had just re-written the Drifters' 1955 number-two pop hit "What'cha Gonna Do"—already a revision of an old gospel tune, "What're You Going to Do"—and offered his rewrite, called "The Twist," to the Spaniels, but they passed on it. It later became a number one hit for Ernest Evans, who recorded it under the name Chubby Checker. By 1960, the Spaniels were Hudson, Ernest Warren, Gerald Gregory, Bill Carey, and Andy McGruder (former lead of the Five Blue Notes). They recorded the group's last Vee-Jay single "I Know" in 1960; it reached number-23 R&B that summer. Meanwhile, Vee-Jay Records issued a second full-length album.

A year later, McGruder and Gregory left the group, and the group broke up briefly after trying to sort out what to do. Road manager Ricky Burden took over on bass for the group's recording for Neptune. Hudson did a few solo sides for Jamie and in 1962 recorded with the Imperials (minus Little Anthony) for Lloyd Price's Double-L label. In the late '60s, Hudson formed his own North American Records and issued "Fairytales," which was picked up by Nat McCalla's Calla Records (distributed by Roulette). It became Pookie's last charting single (number-45 R&B) in the fall of 1970.

Two more singles were issued in the early '70s with a new Spaniels lineup: Hudson, Charles Douglas (first tenor), Alvin Wheeler (second tenor), Alvin Lloyd (baritone), and former guitarist for the group Pete Simmons (bass). He was later replaced by Andrew Lawyer (the Truetones) when the group recorded a remake of "Goodnight, Sweetheart, Goodnight" for Buddah. Their last release was for Henry Farag's Canterbury label of Gary, IN, in 1974. Hudson and the Spaniels remained active and were one of the more in-demand acts on the oldies circuit. Pookie Hudson is still performing with a Spaniels group. Courtney and Willie Jackson are also alive. Gregory died in the '90s. *—Bryan Thomas*

The Ultimate Acapella Collection / 1993 / Juke Box Treasures ♦♦♦
Of all the early vocal groups working in the doo wop style, The Spaniels never really changed theirs when rock & roll came into being. These Acapella recordings showcase the purity of their sound and style and makes an excellent companion volume to their more celebrated Vee-Jay recordings. *—Cub Koda*

● **Goodnight, Sweetheart, Goodnight** / 1993 / Vee-Jay ♦♦♦♦♦
This 25-track overview featuring some of the greatest doo wop sides ever recorded from this legendary Chicago group. "Pookie" Hudson's vocals is one of the great treats this genre has to offer. Highlights include then title track, "Baby, It's You," and great versions of the standards "Red Sails in the Sunset' and "Stormy Weather." *—Cub Koda*

40th Anniversary 1953–1993 / 1995 / Collectables ♦♦♦♦
Although the sound quality and presentation could be better on *40th Anniversary 1953-1993*, it's a good single-disc collection, featuring 20 tracks, including all of the group's hits, plus several rarities and remixes. *—Stephen Thomas Erlewine*

Phil Spector (Harvey Phillip Spector)

b. Dec. 26, 1940, New York, NY [The Bronx]
Producer, Songwriter / Brill Building Pop, Girl Group, Pop, Rock & Roll, Baroque Pop
Strictly speaking, Phil Spector wasn't even a performer—he's a musician, but he very rarely released records under his name. However, as a producer—and, to a significant extent, songwriter, label owner, and session player—he has influenced the course of rock & roll for more than all but a handful of performers. The Wall of Sound that he perfected in the early '60s opened unlimited possibilities for arrangements and sound construction in rock and pop, and his brilliant talents imprinted the discs that he produced with an artistic vision that was much more attributable to him than the talented performers with whom he worked.

Spector entered the record business in 1958 as songwriter, guitarist, and backup singer for the L.A. group the Teddy Bears, who landed a left-field number one with their first release, "To Know Him Is to Love Him." The Teddy Bears couldn't follow their hit up and soon disbanded, but Spector almost immediately moved to New York and became a songwriter and producer. After producing a few hits, he founded his own label, Philles, and ran off a series of brilliant smashes, primarily with girl groups the Crystals and the Ronettes.

To an extent that had never been imagined in rock & roll, Spector pumped his records full of orchestration—strings, horns, rattling percussion—that coalesced into teenage symphonies, never overwhelming the material or the passionate vocals. Often called a mad genius because of his eccentric and temperamental behavior, Spector's idiosyncrasies were almost always validated by the artistic and commercial results of his sessions, which combined dozens of instruments and innovative production techniques into end products which only he could combine into works of art. His influence was immense, not only in the dozens of imitation Wall of Sound productions (some very accurate and worthy, it must be added) that flooded the market between 1962 and 1965, but as an inspiration to Brian Wilson of the Beach Boys, Rolling Stones producer Andrew Loog Oldham, and others.

Spector was hip to the British Invasion before it had even reached the U.S., befriending the Beatles and Rolling Stones, but had nearly as much trouble as the rest of the industry in maintaining his success. Self-contained bands were writing more adventurous material and finding more adventurous sounds, and Spector's teen operas were becoming out of fashion, although he enjoyed a lot of success with blue-eyed soul duo the Righteous Brothers in the mid-'60s. After the failure of Ike & Tina Turner's 1966 single "River Deep, Mountain High"—which he always considered among his greatest achievements, blaming a vengeful U.S. music industry for its poor sales (although it was a big hit in Britain)—he retired to his L.A. mansion, marrying Ronnie Bennett, lead singer of the Ronettes.

Spector re-emerged in the late '60s and was hired by the Beatles to do post-production on their controversial *Let It Be* album; critics and Paul McCartney himself found his work faulty, although it must be pointed out that the material he was given to work with didn't rank among the Beatles' best. He then produced George Harrison and John Lennon's first solo albums; though these were artistic triumphs, they were hardly Spector productions in the classic sense, owing much more of their success to the talents of the performers than the producer. After that, he was active only sporadically, producing isolated albums by Dion, Leonard Cohen, and the Ramones. He became one of rock's most legendary recluses, rarely appearing in public, but his accomplishments cast a shadow over all performers and producers who aspire to create works of art in the studio. *—Richie Unterberger*

☆ **A Christmas Gift for You From Phil Spector** / 1963 / ABKCO ♦♦♦♦♦
Featuring Phil Spector's "Wall of Sound" in its prime and his early stable of artists, the Ronettes, Crystals, Darlene Love, and Bob B. Soxx & the Blue Jeans, this stands as inarguably the greatest Christmas record of all time. Spector believed he could produce a record for the holidays that would capture not only the essence of the Christmas spirit, but also be a pop masterpiece that would stand against any work these artists had already done. He succeeded on every level, with all four groups/singers recording some of their most memorable performances. This is the Christmas album by which all later holiday releases had to be judged, and it has inspired a host of imitators. [Note: This CD is available separately and as part of the highly recommended four-CD box set, *Phil Spector: Back to Mono (1958-1969)*.] *—Dennis MacDonald*

Early Productions 1958–1961 / 1983 / Rhino ♦♦♦♦
A sampling of Spector's earliest work, generally more pop-oriented, sappy, and far less distinguished than his early and mid-'60s classics. The Teddy Bears' "To Know Him Is To Love Him," and Gene Pitney's "Every Breath I Take," The Paris Sisters' "I Love How You Love Me," and Curtis Lee's "Pretty Little Angel Eyes" are fine hits that reveal much of the talent that would fully blossom on his Philles singles. The other tracks, including rarities by the Ducanes, Kell Osborne, and Spector's Three, suffer from weak songwriting, and would be downright dispensable if not for their historical significance. *—Richie Unterberger*

★ **Back to Mono (1958–1969)** / Nov. 12, 1991 / ABKCO ♦♦♦♦♦
At the time *Back to Mono* was released in 1991, Phil Spector's reputation as one of pop's great visionaries was intact, but there was no way to hear his genius. It wasn't just that there were no collections spotlighting his productions, there weren't collections of artists he produced. It wasn't until *Back to Mono* that there was a thorough overview of Spector's greatest work, and while it's not without flaws, it still stands as one of the great box sets. Some may complain that there are no selections from his superstar '70s productions for John Lennon, George Harrison, Leonard Cohen, and the Ramones, but that's for the best, since their presence would have been incongruous, taking attention away from the music that forms the heart of Spector's legacy. All of that music is here, not just on the first three discs, all devoted to singles, but also on the fourth disc, his seminal 1963 holiday album, *A Christmas Gift for You*, which isn't just the greatest rock Christmas album, but a crystallization of his skills. It could be argued that the song selection overlooks some obscure fan favorites, such as "Do the Screw," but that's simply nitpicking, because what's here are all the great Spector records, which were hardly just great productions, they were great songs as well. As the set plays, it's hard not to be stunned by the depth of the material and clarity of Spector's vision for his famed Wall of Sound, whether you've heard these songs hundreds of times or not at all—especially because they gain power when grouped together. Many producers have been credited as the true creative force behind many rock records, but usually that's hyperbole. In Spector's case, it wasn't, as this set gloriously proves. *—Stephen Thomas Erlewine*

Ronnie Spector (Veronica Bennett)

b. Aug. 10, 1947, New York, NY
Vocals / Rock & Roll, Girl Group, Pop/Rock
Ronnie Spector, born Veronica Bennett on August 10, 1943 in New York, NY, became famous as a member of the Ronettes, a girl group featuring her sister Estelle Bennett and cousin Nedra Talley. The group made a string of unsuccessful records in the early '60s before hooking up with Phil Spector in 1963 and releasing smash hits like "Be My Baby," "Walking in the Rain," "Do I Love You," and "I Can Hear Music." Ronnie fell in love with Spector and they were married in 1968. The Ronettes' career was stalled at this point and (at Phil's insistence) Ronnie gave up her musical aspirations, releasing only "You Came, You Saw, You Conquered" in 1969 for A&M and "Try Some Buy Some," which was written by George Harrison and featured all four Beatles, for Apple in 1971 After her marraige to Spector broke up in 1974, Ronnie tried to recapture her chart success, forming a new edition of the Ronettes for a couple of flop singles, releasing many solo singles including the great Billy Joel-penned "Say Goodbye to Hollywood" (which has Bruce Springsteen and the E Street Band providing the music), and two poor-selling solo albums (1980's *Siren* and 1987's *Unfinished Business*). She did have a hit with "Take Me Home Tonight," her 1986 duet with Eddie Money.

In 1990 she published her autobiography *Be My Baby: How I Survived Mascara, Miniskirts and Madness*, which sparked new interest in Ronnie. She didn't release any records in the 1990's but did appear on many compilations and soundtracks. In 1999 Ronnie Spector returned to the studio to record new solo material. The Joey Ramone-produced *She Talks to Rainbows EP* was released on Creation in the U.K. and *Kill Rock*

Stars in the U.S. to much critical acclaim. Featured on the disc were a duet with Joey on "Bye Bye Baby" and a version of the Beach Boys' "Don't Worry Baby," which Brian Wilson had originally written for her. Ronnie Spector spends her time occasionally performing and mostly living the quiet life in Connecticut with her husband and two sons. *—Tim Sendra*

Siren / 1980 / Polish ✦✦✦

There are many extraordinary things about Ronnie Spector's *Siren* album. It was conceived and produced by the legendary Genya Ravan (aka Goldie Zelcowicz) of one of the first all-girl bands, Goldie & the Gingerbreads. It has a street feel much like Ronnie Spector's solo concerts over the years. And it has pretty much a cast of thousands. Well, if not thousands, more session people scattered over one album than Phil Spector would put on one song. It is an important piece of Ronnie's musical legacy which bridges the gap between *The Ronettes Sing Their Greatest Hits* to the 1995 collection of her '70s/'80s material on Sony, the *Dangerous* re-release on Australia's Raven Records. One of the Ramones biggest selling albums, if not their biggest, was the one produced by Phil Spector. Genya Ravan's choice of the Ramones song "Here Today, Gone Tomorrow" is brilliant. They may have been headbangers, but they were Ronnie Spector fans. Members of Johnny Thunders' Heartbreakers, the Dead Boys, and Mink DeVille must have been honored to appear on this, and the musical integrity and heart is there, for sure. The problem here was the timing. The new wave was just cresting with Willie Alexander, producer/singer Genya Ravan, Ian Hunter, Mink DeVille, the Shirts, and so many others releasing substantial records that mainstream radio turned its back on. If the Runaways members didn't break through, they were still "underground." When Joan Jett hit, she became the "mainstream." And here's the classic '60s voice which ruled on Top 40 for five hit records in 1963 and 1964 rocking out with the best of them on songs like "Settin' the Woods on Fire" with backing by the Diamond Dupree Band, or singing to the reggae beat of the Bahama Mama Band on Roger Cook's "Let Your Feelings Show." This is a dynamic and diverse album with even Janis Joplin/Merrilee Rush/Troggs songwriter Chip Taylor weighing in on "Any Way That You Want Me." If Phil Spector overproduced to good effect, Genya Ravan purposely underproduced, choosing instead to let flavors of different musicians paint the fabric behind Ronnie Spector. In her book *Be My Baby* on page 248, Ronnie says "Genya was a strong producer who knew what she wanted, just like Phil." High praise indeed. This album came after Ronnie's exquisite "Say Goodbye to Hollywood" and before the Columbia *Unfinished Business* album, both neatly compiled on the aforementioned *Dangerous* disc on Raven. "Happy Birthday Rock & Roll" has the magic, and the other singles released by Ronnie during the '70s would be nice additions to *Siren* on an extended CD package. *—Joe Viglione*

Unfinished Business / 1987 / Columbia ✦✦

Dangerous, 1976–1987 / Feb. 1996 / Raven ✦✦✦

Ronnie Spector's vocal work on the "Miami" Steve Van Zandt tune "Baby Please Don't Go" is amazingly perfect, overshadowed only by the majesty of the opening track, "Say Goodbye to Hollywood." The two songs were on a 1977 Epic single and they are the highlight of this superb collection released by the Raven label out of Australia. *Dangerous* is a compilation that features the various sides Spector cut for Columbia. The Top Five hit "Take Me Home Tonight," released in 1986 as a duet with Eddie Money, was the only one of his ten hits to land that high on the charts. It is also Spector's second biggest career hit under "Be My Baby," which, of course, is what she sings in this tune. Her other track with Eddie Money, "Who Can Sleep," provides more proof that she brought the best out of Money. "Who Can Sleep" works in the same way that "Baby Please Don't Go" grabs you—with slow-moving intensity. Her cameo on a Southside Johnny & the Asbury Jukes album, "You Mean So Much to Me," sounds like the duet that it is in the context of this album. These five performances precede the re-release of her *Unfinished Business* album, and the music flows almost seamlessly. "Love on a Rooftop" is the girl group stuff fans expect, exquisitely produced for Columbia. "Dangerous" is where the Go-Go's should've gone to reinvent themselves, and that Spector tips her hat to the new gals on the block is impressive. Elvis Presley's "Burnin' Love" is put to a dance beat, and it works. What's important about this cover is that it takes Spector away from the elements producers and fans had locked her into. The track "Unfinished Business" is modeled after Hall & Oates' 1984 number one single "Out of Touch." The track, like most of this record, is terrific. The Ronettes' immortal first album and Spector's *Siren* LP, produced by girl group pioneer Genya Ravan, were the only full length albums by this rock legend. *Dangerous* is an important and elegant addition to the small output. Glenn A. Baker co-conceived and compiled this treasure, and his liner notes are meticulous, covering all the 45s, album tracks, and unreleased titles Spector recorded along the way. That material is also top-notch and would have made a nice second CD, but with 77 minutes here, including an 18-minute interview with Spector, it's hard to complain. "True to You," "Heart Song," and the dainty "When We Danced" (which has the charm of a Harriet Schock record) are all serious contributions to the Spector catalog. "Good Love Is Hard to Find" is a modern "Walking in the Rain" meets Bob B. Soxx & the Blue Jeans, a definite and worthwhile tribute to Phil Spector. A live version of "You Mean So Much to Me" concludes the musical portion of the program, providing the listener with more of the star power that drives this set. Without Ronnie Spector's unique voice, the record would misfire. Billy Joel contributes to the superior liner notes, exposing his fanatical appreciation. Some may disagree with the opinion that "Say Goodbye to Hollywood" is Joel's finest achievement, but it explodes off this disc and is the perfect opening track. To have it here, lovingly compiled, is a dream come true. *—Joe Viglione*

She Talks to Rainbows / Feb. 23, 1999 / Import ✦✦✦✦✦

This EP was originally issued by Creation Records in the U.K. With that in mind, though it's a little weird to hear the original teenager singing her songs through a Jesus and Mary Chain-style wall of sound filter, it works like a charm. The Joey Ramone-penned "She Talks to Rainbows" and the "Be My Baby"-ish "Bye-Bye Baby," a duet with Ramone, is perfect for the pair. What a a thrill to hear Spector sing the Brian Wilson song she inspired, "Don't Worry Baby." This one might just be the version of Johnny Thunders' "You Can't Put Your Arm Around a Memory" that his fans have hoped would materialize. Daniel Rey uses the same heavy hand he used on the Ramones and White Zombie but original tough chick Spector can handle it. "I Wish I Never Saw The Sunshine," recorded for English television tops off this extraordinary "comeback." *—Denise Sullivan*

Benny Spellman

b. Dec. 11, 1931, Pensacola, FL

Vocals / New Orleans R&B, R&B

The deep bass voice of New Orleans R&B vocalist Benny Spellman boomed through loud and clear on many early-'60s Allen Toussaint productions, but he enjoyed a major hit of his own in 1962, "Lipstick Traces (On a Cigarette)." Spellman spent some time with Huey "Piano" Smith & the Clowns before signing with Minit, where Toussaint utilized his deep pipes to full advantage as a backing vocalist behind Ernie K-Doe on "Mother-in-Law" and countless others. The Rolling Stones covered "Fortune Teller," the flip side of this hit. Spellman recorded through much of the '60s, his "Word Game" turning up on Atlantic in 1965, before he took a day gig as a beer salesman. *—Bill Dahl*

● **Fortune Teller** / 1988 / Collectables ✦✦✦✦✦

Though Collectables' presentation certainly leaves something to be desired—it's one of their early titles and it lacks extensive packaging—they still should be commended for having the only Benny Spellman collection available on CD. Many of his tracks are available on various artists collections, but this is the only disc available under his own name, and the 16-track collection proves that he was one of the finest New Orleans vocalists of the early '60s. His smooth baritone found a perfect fit with Allen Toussaint' s typical earthily elegant production, and he had a great set of material, too, highlighted by the hits "Fortune Teller" and "Lipstick Traces (On a Cigarette)." The others tunes may not be hits, but they're worthy additions in that tradition, making this a necessary set for New Orleans R&B fans. *—Stephen Thomas Erlewine*

The Spiders

f. 1953, New Orleans, LA, **db.** 1957

Group / New Orleans R&B, R&B

New Orleans R&B was best known for its solo artists, but the Spiders rank among the Crescent City's pre-eminent vocal groups, and were certainly the best the city produced during the '50s. The Spiders actually began life circa 1947 as a gospel group called the Zion City Harmonizers; they later changed their name to the Delta Southernaires, and made a few recordings and radio appearances from 1952-1953. With encouragement from legendary New Orleans studio head Cosimo Matassa, the group switched to secular R&B and signed with Imperial in late 1953. The newly christened Spiders were centered around brothers Hayward "Chuck" Carbo and Leonard "Chick" Carbo, the latter a bass singer who sometimes split lead vocals with his brother; the other members of the quintet were Joe Maxon, Matthew West, and Oliver Howard. Their first single, "I Didn't Want to Do It," went to number three on the R&B charts in early 1954, and other sides like "You're the One," "Tears Begin to Flow," and "I'm Slippin' In" were top sellers as well, making the Spiders a hot concert draw.

Maxon and West both left the group in 1955 and were replaced by Bill Moore and Issacher Gordon. The Spiders' string of R&B Top Tens continued that year with "21" and the Dave Bartholomew-penned "Witchcraft," their second Top Five hit and biggest overall seller (it was later covered by Elvis Presley). Imperial began grooming Chuck Carbo for a solo career in 1956, which caused dissent within the group; by the end of the year, Chick Carbo had signed to Atlantic as a solo artist himself, and the Spiders effectively dissolved. A final single in 1957, "That's My Desire," failed to catch on, as did a posthumous from-the-vaults release in 1960, "Tennessee Slim." Neither of the Carbo brothers scored any significant chart hits, although Chuck did return in the late '80s and early '90s, cutting an album for Rounder in 1993. Chick passed away in 1998. *—Steve Huey*

● **The Imperial Sessions** / 1993 / Bear Family ✦✦✦✦✦

The Spinners

f. 1961, Detroit, MI

Group / Soul, Smooth Soul, Quiet Storm, Philly Soul, Pop-Soul, Disco

The Spinners were the greatest soul group of the early '70s, creating a body of work that defined the lush, seductive sound of Philly soul. Ironically, the band's roots lay in Detroit, where they formed as a doo wop group during the late '50s. Throughout the '60s, the Spinners tried to land a hit by adapting to the shifting fashions of R&B and pop. By the mid-'60s, they had signed with Motown Records, but the label never gave the group much consideration. "It's a Shame" became a hit in 1970, but the label continued to ignore the group, and dropped the band two years later. Unsigned and featuring new lead singer Philippe Wynne, the Spinners seemed destined to never break into the big leagues, but they managed to sign with Atlantic Records, where they began working with producer Thom Bell. With his assistance, the Spinners developed a distinctive sound, one that relied on Wynne's breathtaking falsetto and the group's intricate vocal harmonies. Bell provided the group with an appropriately detailed production, creating a detailed web of horns, strings, backing vocals, and lightly funky rhythms. Between 1972 and 1977, the Spinners and Bell recorded a number of soul classics, including "I'll Be Around," "Could It Be I'm Falling in Love," "Mighty Love," "Ghetto Child," "Then Came You," "Games People Play," and "The Rubberband Man." Wynne left in 1977 and the Spinners had hits for a few years after his departure, but the group will always be remembered for its classic mid-'70s work.

Originally, called the Domingoes, the Spinners formed when the quintet were high school students in the Detroit suburb of Ferndale in 1957. At the time, the group featured Bobbie Smith, Pervis Jackson, George W. Dixon, Billy Henderson, and Henry Fambrough.

Four years later, they came to the attention of producer Harvey Fuqua, who began recording the group—who were now called the Spinners—for his Tri-Phi Records. The band's first single, "That's What Girls Are Made For," became a Top Ten R&B hit upon its 1961 release and featured Smith on vocals. Following its release, Dixon was replaced by Edgar "Chico" Edwards. Over the next few years, the group released a series of failed singles, and when Tri-Phi was bought out by Motown in the mid-'60s, the Spinners became part of the larger company's roster. By that time, Edwards had been replaced by G.C. Cameron. Though the Spinners had some R&B hits at Motown during the late '60s, including "I'll Always Love You" and "Truly Yours," they didn't have a genuine crossover success until 1970, when Stevie Wonder gave the group "It's a Shame." Motown never concentrated on the Spinners, and they let the group go in 1972. Before the band signed with Atlantic Records, Philippe Wynne replaced Cameron as the group's lead vocalist. Wynne had previously sung with Catfish and Bootsy Collins.

At Atlantic Records, the Spinners worked with producer Thom Bell, who gave the group a lush, seductive sound, complete with sighing strings, a tight rhythm section, sultry horns, and a slight funk underpinning. Wynne quickly emerged as a first-rate soul singer, and the combination of the group's harmonies, Wynne's soaring leads, and Bell's meticulous production made the Spinners the most popular soul group of the '70s. Once the group signed with Atlantic, they became a veritable hit machine, topping the R&B and pop charts with songs like "I'll Be Around," "Could It Be I'm Falling in Love," "One of a Kind (Love Affair)," "Ghetto Child," "Rubberband Man," and "You're Throwing a Good Love Away." Not only were their singles hits, but their albums constantly went gold and charted in the Top 20.

Wynne left the band to pursue a solo career in 1977; he was replaced by John Edwards. Though none of Wynne's solo records were big hits, his tours with Parliament-Funkadelic were well-received, as were his solo concerts. In October 1984, he died of a heart attack during a concert in Oakland, CA. The Spinners, meanwhile, had a number of minor hits in the late '70s, highlighted by their disco covers of "Working My Way Back to You" and the medley "Cupid/I've Loved You for a Long Time." During the early '80s, they had several minor hits before fading away from the charts and entering the oldies circuit, reprising their earlier material for 1999's new studio effort *At Their Best*. *—Stephen Thomas Erlewine*

2nd Time Around / 1970 / VIP ♦♦♦

The Spinners began making some soul noise in 1970, when Stevie Wonder produced a pair of hit singles for them. "It's a Shame" was their first Top Ten R&B song since 1965, and was the swan song for G.C. Cameron as lead vocalist. Phillipe Wynne stepped in and shortly after made everyone forget (who remembered) that Cameron was ever in the band. The follow-up tune, "We'll Have It Made," wasn't bad either. *—Ron Wynn*

Spinners / 1972 / Rhino ♦♦♦♦♦

This is a superb album, arguably their finest, though not their biggest, crossover work. The Spinners teamed with Thom Bell and made Motown look stupid with this album of glorious anthems. "I'll Be Around" and "Could It Be I'm Falling in Love" ended any discussions, mentions, or even thoughts of their former lead singer G.C. Cameron, as Philippe Wynne was emerging as the king of immaculate, sophisticated soul. They had three R&B chart toppers from this album and were now dominating the Motown acts they once idolized. *—Ron Wynn*

The Best of the Spinners / 1973 / Motown ♦♦♦♦♦

Yet another Motown collection (that makes at least three for a group that only had four hits from 1965 to 1971) of Spinners singles. It's not as extensive as the anthology, so if you only want hits, they're available. Otherwise, take your pick between it and the others. *—Ron Wynn*

Mighty Love / Jan. 1974 / Rhino ♦♦♦♦♦

Philippe Wynne's twisting, soulful, frequently captivating voice was at its finest on this 1974 album. The title track was a smash in edited single form, and the extended album version contains marvelous Wynne ad-libs and exchanges nicely contrasted by the group's harmonizing. The album contains many other fine songs, like "Ain't No Price on Happiness" and "I'm Coming Home," and was their second Atlantic release. It equaled the gold-selling pace of its predecessor and cemented the Spinners' status as R&B stars. *—Ron Wynn*

New and Improved / Feb. 1974 / Rhino ♦♦♦♦

The Spinners were on a roll; after years of neglect at the hands of Motown, their ship just kept coming in, and in, and in with Atlantic Records. *New and Improved* is an absolute classic, yet it gets less run than some of their other LPs. Everything from the romanticism of "Smile We Have Each Other," a real tearjerker, to the self-assured, driven "I've Got to Make It on My Own" is on board, and it all works. "Sadie," a song about the death of a mother, became a signature song for the Spinners; it was revived in the '90s by R. Kelly, who introduced it to new fans, many of whom thought he created the touching tribute. Dionne Warwick struts her soul on "Then Came You," accompanied by Bobby Smith; it's a mover from the first note. A strong effort from Thom Bell and the Spinners. *—Andrew Hamilton*

Live / 1975 / Atlantic ♦♦

A nice concert album that did much better than anticipated. It featured extended versions, concert ambience, and exuberant harmonies and treatments of familiar numbers. Like most live dates, it had its padding and filler, but as a portrait of an R&B institution doing its thing before the faithful, it was well worth the cost of a double album. *—Ron Wynn*

Pick of the Litter / 1975 / Rhino ♦♦♦♦♦

The Spinners were rolling in the 1970s, and this proved to be their biggest album ever. It peaked in the pop Top Ten at number eight, and they racked up four consecutive R&B Top Ten singles, including the chart-topper "They Just Can't Stop It (The Games People Play)." Philippe Wynne sang with an amazing mix of class and fire, sophistication and earthiness that hadn't been heard in soul circles for years. Of course, this is now out of print. *—Ron Wynn*

Happiness Is Being With the Spinners / 1976 / Atlantic ♦♦♦

As 1975's classic *Pick of the Litter* seemed to garner its strength from melancholy and faultless arrangements, this 1976 studio follow-up often wallows in style over substance and platitudes. The pretty but vacuous "Now That We're Together" is all over the road and has inane lyrics like, "You're such a great crowd/Why don't you sing loud." Other tracks "You're All I Need in Life" and "If You Can't Be in Love" all put into practice arrangements and themes that were better executed on *New and Improved*. Although things get a little mushy here, producer Thom Bell and the Spinners do have their moments here. The highly danceable and infectious "Rubberband Man" breaks out of this effort's stodgy surroundings and gave lead singer Philippe Wynne plenty of room for his skilled scatting and effortless riffing. The best non-hit on this effort is "Toni My Love." The song is jazzy rumination on a mature relationship and it's the only track that's skilled enough to stand tall on *Pick of the Litter*. Despite the few high points, *Happiness Is Being With the Spinners* winds down before any of its predecessors did. The best of the last tracks, "The Clown" is a little overwrought and Philippe Wynne sounds like his hands are tied. *Happiness Is Being With the Spinners* is one of the first Bell efforts to be partially recorded at Kaye Smith Studios in Seattle, WA, and was mastered at A&M Studios rather than Philadelphia's Sigma Sound. That fact arguably changed the winning formula and for the most part this falls short of the work that came before it. *—Jason Elias*

8 / 1977 / Atlantic ♦♦

The switch between lead singers presented its shares of woe. Whereas Philippe Wynne fit neatly in Thom Bell's production style, at this point Bell had no idea what to do with new lead singer John Edwards. Coupling that indisputable fact with the continuing decline of the songwriting, *Spinners/8* isn't the most proficient album to come down the pike. Not everything's bad here, however. Bobbie Smith's playful lead on the well-produced "I'm Gonna Getcha" starts things off on a deceptively blithe note. With lyrics like "Count the days you can still run free" and "There's no escaping me now," stalking never sounded so mellifluous. While "I'm Tired of Giving" and "Painted Magic" are nonsensical retreads, the best parts of *Spinners/8* had Bell tinkering with his style to accommodate Edwards' booming and all-encompassing vocals. Enlivened by Edwards' firepower and command, "You've Got the Love I Need" is on the track as he sings/shouts, "You've got me walking/Talking to myself." The charming and anachronistic "Heaven on Earth (So Fine)" is the only single release from this effort and later showed up on their 1991 anthology *A One of a Kind Affair*. While the Edwards-led "Back in the Arms of Love" and "Easy Come, Easy Go" are locked into the old style, the last track attempts a new sound. The synth-adorned ballad "Baby I Need Your Love (You're the Only One)" has smooth harmony and the minimal backing gives Edwards a great chance to vamp loudly near the end. Unfortunately, the bad outweighs the good here, making *Spinners/8* the most problematic album Bell produced for the group. *—Jason Elias*

Yesterday, Today & Tomorrow / 1977 / Atlantic ♦♦♦

During the '70s, the Spinners' pairing with Philadelphia producer Thom Bell resulted in some of the most fulfilling and immaculately produced albums of the era. The pairing brought the group six gold singles and five gold albums. *Yesterday, Today & Tomorrow* in effect drew the hitmaking ways to a screeching halt. The group had declined shortly after 1975's *Pick of the Litter*. That was perfectly acceptable. Both *Mighty Love* and *Pick of the Litter* were two of the best albums of the '70s so there wasn't anywhere to go but down. The lyrical decline that was evident on this album's predecessor, *Happiness Is Being With the Spinners*, is even clearer here. In fact, most of the sessions on this album were recorded at the same time as *Happiness Is Being With the Spinners*. The problems with this were seen immediately. "Me and My Music" like most songs about the joys of the music are always danger zones and folksy rural asides of lead singer Philippe Wynne made it even more cloying. The elegiac "I'm Riding Your Shadow Down to Love" is so beautifully arranged—from the strings to the near three-dimensional harmony—that it made it easy to overlook the incoherent lyrics. As for hit potential, the likable "You're the Love of My Life" was this album's best shot at a hit single but was left unreleased. Not that it would have made much of a difference at this point. This was Philippe Wynne's swan song and the fact that he was ready to barrel out the door put a damper on the festivities. Both "Just to Be With You" and "Throwing a Good Love Away" recall his past glories without half of the charm. In an odd note, on the track "Honey, I'm in Love With You" produced and arranged by Thom Bell's brother Tony Bell, is a good-natured song that seemed custom made for Philippe Wynne, but he's not even on it. The lead on the track is John Edwards. He attempts Wynne's aphorisms and rhythm style before giving up and unleashing high-pitched wails and his own barrage of ad-libs. Taken on its own, *Yesterday, Today & Tomorrow* is a good effort, but the Spinners' earlier '70s efforts are where the consistently great work is found. *—Jason Elias*

The Best of the Spinners / 1978 / Atlantic ♦♦♦♦♦

The Spinners lost lead singer Philippe Wynne in 1977, as he left to join Parliament/Funkadelic. While they were getting replacement John Edwards acclimated, Atlantic issued this greatest-hits LP containing all the gems with Wynne as their lead singer. Until the Atlantic two-CD set was issued, this was a definitive work, and it's still as complete a single album package as available. It includes "Could It Be I'm Falling in Love," "How Could I Let You Get Away," "Mighty Love," "Rubberband Man," and "One of a Kind (Love Affair)," among others. *—Ron Wynn*

Dancin' and Lovin' / 1979 / Rhino ♦♦♦

While soul purists recoiled in horror, the Spinners climbed off the ropes and soared back into the spotlight by recasting themselves as a modified dance/crossover band with soul/R&B influences. It worked in the short run, as their remake of the Four Seasons'

"Working My Way Back to You," mixed with their own wailer, "Forgive Me Girl," made a nice sandwich at number-two pop and number-six R&B. It took nearly a year, but they were revived. While they wore the formula out with a similar follow-up, it gave them a fresh start and the necessary credibility to eventually return to their customary sophisticated soul. *—Ron Wynn*

From Here to Eternally / 1979 / Atlantic ♦♦♦

Yesterday, Today & Tomorrow all but ended the group's string of classics. And this album's predecessor, *Spinners #8,* rightfully put a big scare into their biggest fans. The good news is that *From Here to Eternally* shows things did get better. A few of the best tracks are easily the best songs Thom Bell and the Spinners had been involved with since *Pick of the Litter.* Admittedly it does a take awhile to get to them. The too smooth and lyrically barren tracks, "It's Natural Affair" and "Don't Let the Man Get You," are so interchangeable they cancel one another out. While those embarrassments don't bear thinking about, the best tracks have lead singer John Edwards working his magic with his excitable persona. He survives the potential treacle of the ballad "A Plain and Simple Song" by giving a flat-out believable and melisma-filled performance. On the melodic and disco-styled "Are You Ready for Love," Edwards' voice finally meshes with Bell's patently effervescent production. The effort's only released single, "If You Wanna Do a Dance (All Night)," comes off like a more languid "Rubberband Man." The track has Edwards doing a commanding lead, and as he calls out "Henry, Billy" on the fade, you know he's the right guy for the gig. The last track, "Once You Fall in Love" has interesting production values and was a great way to close the album. While it is true *From Here to Eternity* didn't help the Spinners that much commercially, it features a few underrated gems and some good to great production by Bell. *—Jason Elias*

Love Trippin' / 1980 / Atlantic ♦♦♦

Labor of Love / 1981 / Atlantic ♦♦♦

The Spinners began to slide again with this release, following two consecutive big albums. The problem was that they had established an identity that had crossover and pop types thinking they were just a cover band. When they returned to the ebullient soul ballads and uptempo tunes that had been their forte since the 1960s, the trendy types moved on to the next fashionable thing. Meanwhile, the R&B landscape was shifting, and they were caught in the move. They also went to the medley well one more time with "Yesterday Once More/Nothing Remains The Same." *—Ron Wynn*

Grand Slam / 1982 / Atlantic ♦♦

Lovin' Feelings / 1985 / Mirage ♦♦

Down to Business / Sep. 1989 / Volt ♦♦♦

The Spinners made a bid for renewed stardom on a soul independent when they signed with the revived Volt in 1989. Unfortunately, they also found out quickly that being on Volt didn't mean in the late '80s what it meant in the '60s and '70s. Despite a representative effort, with some excellent harmonizing and fine, soulful leads from John Edwards, they couldn't even get a nibble from urban contemporary radio. They're still working the nostalgia/oldies circuit, but this one was a shocker all around. *—Ron Wynn*

Can't Shake This Feeling / 1990 / Atlantic ♦♦♦

☆ **One of a Kind Love Affair** / Nov. 5, 1991 / Rhino ♦♦♦♦♦

Spanning from their first single, 1961's "That's What Girls Are Made For," to their last charting single more than 20 years later, *One of a Kind Love Affair—The Anthology* is the definitive Spinners collection. The bulk of the two-CD compilation is the group's work with Thom Bell during the mid-'70s, easily the best work they ever recorded and arguably the finest Philly soul singles. All of the Spinners' major hits are here, as are excellent, informative liner notes (including complete personnel and discography). *—Stephen Thomas Erlewine*

★ **The Very Best of the Spinners** / Apr. 20, 1993 / Rhino ♦♦♦♦♦

The Spinners were rivaled only by the O'Jays as the greatest Philly soul group, and for that matter the greatest vocal group of the '70s. For listeners who don't want to dig as deeply as the excellent double-CD anthology *One of a Kind Love Affair,* Rhino's *The Very Best of the Spinners* is a stellar single-disc career summary that offers a concentrated dose of the group's sweet soul magic. It also serves as a primer on the best work of Thom Bell, Philly soul's "other" great producer besides the legendary Gamble & Huff team. Incredibly, every one of the 16 tracks here—culled from 1970-1980—reached the R&B Top Ten, and half went all the way to number one on either the pop or R&B lists. As this collection demonstrates, the Spinners' massive popularity was well-deserved. Built around the magnetic leads of Philippe Wynne, their records were tastefully, elegantly romantic, full of adult heartache and longings as complex as the group's shifting harmonies. The compilers also license the pre-Wynne Motown hit "It's a Shame," co-written by Stevie Wonder, and include two disco-tinged medleys that returned the Spinners to the Top Ten for the last time at the close of the '70s. But the Wynne material is really the backbone of their output, and Thom Bell's gorgeous production frames his voice with just the right amount of sweetness. There's more to discover on *One of a Kind Love Affair,* but *The Very Best of the Spinners* is so solid from top to bottom that it's hard to argue with; one or the other is a necessary purchase for anyone even remotely interested in '70s soul. *—Steve Huey*

The Very Best of the Spinners, Vol. 2 / May 27, 1997 / Rhino ♦♦♦♦

The Very Best of the Spinners, Vol. 2 rounds up the lesser-known hits that didn't make the first volume, plus selected album tracks, including "Heaven on Earth," "You're Throwing a Good Love Away," "Love or Leave," "Wake Up Susan" and "Easy Come, Easy Go." *—Stephen Thomas Erlewine*

The Springers

Group / Soul, Northern Soul, R&B

The Springers from Cleveland, OH (there was a Philadelphia group with the same name), started recording in the mid-sixties but had a dated sound. Their first (at Way Out Records) single "I Know Why," was a minor R&B hit in 1964; the slow, dripping doo wop was the labels' biggest record and earned the Springers a week long gig at New York's famed Apollo Theater. Lester Johnson and Ike Perry, of Ike Perry & the Lyrics, produced the harmonic ballad written by Johnson, and Tyrone Henry, one of the Springers. The other members were Jeff Crutchfield, who became Jeff Dale with the Springers, James Dodson (Sahibs, Crown Imperials), James McClain, and another member nobody can recall. They resided in Cleveland's Wade Park area; Crutchfield was born in Memphis, TN but moved to Cleveland with family when he was 12.

Way Out issued a second single, similar to the first, "Why," written by Henry & McClain, in 1965; A third and final single appeared later in 1965, but "It's Been A Long Time" b/w "You Can Laugh," didn't generate much action and no more singles were issued. The Springers kept going, gigging at places like the Spaghetti Inn on Wade Park, the Red Carpet, the Circle Ballroom, and occasional treks to a club in Lorain, OH. There are some unreleased tracks laying around somewhere, a female who lived on Ansel Road, wrote songs that the Springers recorded but that remains unreleased.

Where are they now? Jeff Crutchfield was murdered, Dodson worked for Ford; the whereabouts of Henry, McClain and the mystery member is unknown. Crutchfield operated a barbecue joint on the corner of 79th & Holton called Jeff & Al's, in the late '60s for a short time. It's unclear whether Al was the mystery member. Crutchfield's uncle Walter Crutchfield sang with the Futuretones, the group that spawned Charles Hatcher (Edwin Starr), and the late Russell Evans, the O'Jays' guitarist. *—Andrew Hamilton*

● **The Best of the Springers: Nothing's Too Good for My Baby** / Apr. 23, 2002 / Jamie/Guyden ♦♦♦♦

The Springers didn't have as much personality or distinction as many better-known soul groups from Philadelphia or elsewhere, and some of their recorded efforts were ordinary. Still, groups that are unknown, not major innovators, and not stylistically immediately identifiable can still produce some good sounds. *The Best of the Springers: Nothing's Too Good for My Baby* (a deceptive title considering that they put out hardly anything and never had hits) can be confidently recommended to anyone who likes good, well-produced '60s Philly soul or is interested in the roots of the sound in which the likes of Thom Bell (who arranged at least some of these cuts) got their feet wet. Of these 16 sides (all recorded in 1965 and 1966), ten tracks (some alternate versions) were previously unissued and six were released on rare singles, though it's unclear from the notes whether these constituted *all* their official singles. A couple of the catalog numbers in the track listings are attached to just one song, leaving one to wonder whether the B-sides were omitted or these were 45s on which the group was only featured on one side. The rather vague if lengthy interview with producer and label owner Thaddeus Wales that comprises most of the liner notes adds to the confusion when he states that he only put out four songs by the group. Leaving aside such issues for those who lose sleep over such inconsistencies, "Nothing's Too Good for My Baby" is the song that's attracted attention (and astronomical prices) in the soul collecting circuit, with its lightly danceable beat and slightly jazzy harmonies and chord progressions. But the Springers were also very adept at tuneful ballads, some sprinkled with the doo wop-derived harmonies that Philadelphia was known for, others (like "(I Want You) Every Night and Day") in a snazzier, moodier, more sophisticated frame of mind. At other times they get into a slightly harder groove with echoes of bluesy funk; "(You're Drawing Me) Closer and Closer" and "Hold On" drift toward the raucousness of the likes of Bobby "Blue" Bland and the Isley Brothers. *—Richie Unterberger*

Dusty Springfield (Mary Isabel Catherine Bernadette O'Brien)

b. Apr. 16, 1939, Hampstead, London, England, **d.** Mar. 2, 1999

Vocals / Pop-Soul, Blue-Eyed Soul, British Invasion, Smooth Soul, Soul

Britain's greatest pop diva, Dusty Springfield was also the finest white soul singer of her era, embracing everything from lushly-orchestrated pop to gritty R&B to disco with unparalleled sophistication and depth. She was born Mary O'Brien on April 16, 1939; after completing her schooling she joined the Lana Sisters, a pop vocal trio which issued a few singles on Fontana before dissolving. In 1960, upon teaming with her brother Dion and his friend Tim Field in the folk trio the Springfields, O'Brien adopted the stage name Dusty Springfield; thanks to a series of hits the group was soon the U.K.'s best-selling act. In 1963 she left the Springfields at the peak of their fame to pursue a solo career. Her first single, "I Only Want to Be With You," quickly reached the British Top Five. Propelled by hits like "Wishin' & Hopin'" by the end of 1964 Springfield was arguably the biggest solo act in British pop. In1966, she scored her biggest international hit with the devastating ballad "You Don't Have to Say You Love Me." In 1968, she traveled to Memphis to record *Dusty in Memphis,* which remains her masterpiece, a perfect marriage of pop and soul stunning in its emotional complexity and earthy beauty. The album and its fine 1970 follow-up *A Brand New Me* unfortunately were commercial failures, as was another critical success, 1973's *Cameo.*

Springfield spent the mid-'70s mostly outside of music while battling substance abuse problems. A comeback was orchestrated in 1987 when she collaborated with techno-pop innovators the Pet Shop Boys on a duet titled "What Have I Done to Deserve This?" The single was a global blockbuster, peaking at number two in both the U.S. and the U.K. Neil Tennant and Chris Lowe also agreed to produce a handful of tracks for 1990's *Reputation,* which became Springfield's best-selling new album since her '60s-era peak. Breast cancer detected during sessions for 1995's *A Very Fine Love* eventually took her life on March 2, 1999; just ten days later, she was inducted into the Rock and Roll Hall of Fame. *—Jason Ankeny*

Stay Awhile – I Only Want to Be With You / Jun. 1964 / Mercury ♦♦♦♦♦
Her most rock & roll-oriented album, and one of the finest solo rock albums of the mid-'60s. Besides the two hit title tracks, Dusty covers various American soul and pop tunes that usually rank at least equal to the originals, in some cases totally outclassing them. In particular, she improves upon "24 Hours From Tulsa," "Anyone Who Had a Heart," "You Don't Own Me," and "When the Lovelight Starts Shining Through His Eyes." The production is the most credible approximation of the Phil Spector wall of sound ever managed in the U.K., with full brass and strings, soulful female backup choruses, and pounding piano and drums. Also includes a first-rate Springfield original, "Somethin' Special." *—Richie Unterberger*

Dusty / Oct. 1964 / Mercury ♦♦♦
Although not quite as good as her first American LP, *Dusty* is a good mix of soul/R&B covers and orchestrated pop/rock in the manner of early Dionne Warwick. Standouts include the cover of Bacharach-David's "I Just Don't Know What to Do With Myself" (a British hit), "All Cried Out," and the epic ballad "Summer Is Over," which foreshadows the style she'd use on her later hit "You Don't Have to Say You Love Me." [The 1999 Mercury CD reissue adds three rare bonus tracks: the Stax soul tune "Every Ounce of Strength" (a 1966 U.K. B-side), the 1966 B-side "I'm Gonna Leave You," and an unreleased cover of Gloria Jones' soul stormer "Heartbeat."] *—Richie Unterberger*

Ooooooweeee!!! / Mar. 1965 / Mercury ♦♦♦♦
Springfield's second U.S. album is another hybrid work, but for different reasons. The tracks, of which two ("You Don't Own Me," "When the Lovelight Starts Shining Through His Eyes") are repeated from her debut, were cut in London and in Nashville, the latter under the direction of Shelby Singleton Jr. The Singleton-produced numbers, except the girl groupish "Now That You're My Baby," are better R&B, more raw and less dignified in their playing (Springfield in the early days had to fight to get the sound she wanted from her backing musicians), and mix well with the London-based material. In fact, "Lovelight" works better here than it did on the earlier album, for *Ooooooweeee!!!* is overall a more soul-oriented album. The bonus tracks are a significant enhancement—"Go Ahead On," cut by Springfield backed by the Echoes is a fine piece of Brit-beat R&B; her version of Aretha Franklin's "Don't Let Me Lose This Dream" is a harbinger of Springfield's real musical direction, while "I Will Always Want You" is a throwback to the sound of her first album, in a broad, big-voiced, heavily orchestrated style. *—Bruce Eder*

Ev'rything's Coming Up Dusty / Sep. 1965 / BGO ♦♦♦♦♦
Dusty Springfield's second British LP was roughly equivalent to the American *You Don't Have To Say You Love Me* album, which appeared ten months later in the United States and had the title hit and one other song ("Little By Little") added, and three of the U.K. edition's songs stripped off. The British version also appeared as a gatefold, filled with a series of beautiful photographs and extensive notes. More to the point, this second album presented a more mature Dusty Springfield, doing songs by Leslie Bricuse and Anthony Newley, Randy Newman et al., although all of the material here—even "Who Can I Turn To," from the music The Roar of the Greasepaint—still has a soulful edge. Moreover, she scales new heights of passion on Rod Argent's "If It Don't Work Out" and the ethereal "That's How Heartaches Are Made," and seems close to bursting her lungs on Gerry Goffin & Carole King's "I Can't Hear You." Something more than half of this album—mostly the uptempo numbers—was recorded with her on-stage backing group the Echoes, and they have a nice, lean band sound that was also a departure from the lushly orchestrated, outsized production of her early singles sides. The whole record comes off as perhaps the greatest Motown album that was never made by Motown, and has a pleasing unity in its British form that the U.S. version lacks. [This album has been reissued twice on CD, first in 1990 from BGO Records and again, in 1998, from Philips Records in England, augmented with eight bonus tracks, all songs that she recorded in September of 1964 with producer Shelby Singleton and arranger Ray Stevens, most of which turned up in America on the *Ooooooweeee!* album, but three of which were unreleased in England until the issue of the Philips CD.] *—Bruce Eder*

You Don't Have to Say You Love Me / Jul. 1966 / Mercury ♦♦♦♦♦
If you overlook the title track, a pop hit in the manner of "Stay Awhile" et al., this is Springfield's best R&B album of her early career. "Won't Be Long" shows Springfield as a soul-shouter par excellence, now with the backing to match, a reasonable fascimile of an authentic American sound, and she alternates with her softer ballad singing. But whether she's covering songs by Goffin-King ("Oh No! Not My Baby," "I Can't Hear You"), Burt Bacharach ("Long After Tonight Is Over"), Randy Newman ("I've Been Wrong Before"), or Ragavoy & Russell ("It Was Easier to Hurt Him"), she makes it come out in her most alluring R&B style. There are a few breaks in the mood, like a less than compelling "La Bamba" and a rendition of "Who Can I Turn To" that's close in spirit to Dionne Warwick at her poppiest, but generally Springfield is consistently superb here, even elevating Rod Argent's "If It Don't Work Out" in an achingly soulful rendition. The 1999 Mercury reissue contains a trio of tracks never before issued in the U.S. "Doodlin'" and "Packin' Up" are lively enough, and the latter features an uncredited guitar solo, a first on a Springfield record and a fine counterpoint to her lusty, shouted performance, but the real jewel is her poignant, lyrical rendition of "That's How Heartaches Are Made." *—Bruce Eder*

Dusty Springfield's Golden Hits / Oct. 1966 / Mercury ♦♦♦♦

Where Am I Going / Nov. 1967 / Philips ♦♦♦♦

The Look of Love / Dec. 1967 / Mercury ♦♦♦
A true mixed bag, from the sensual title track to the melodramatic "If You Go Away," and some fine soul stylings in between, most notably "Small Town Girl" (check out the choruses) and "I've Got a Good Thing." The latter is one of four choice bonus tracks on this, the last of Springfield's Philips albums to be released in America (she signed with Atlantic in the U.S. soon after, and the label declined to release most of her Philips output here)—"I'll Try Anything" makes its first U.S. appearance in stereo, and the CD ends with the previously unissued, very dramatic "It's Over." *—Bruce Eder*

★ **Dusty in Memphis** / Mar. 1969 / Mercury ♦♦♦♦♦
Sometimes memories distort or inflate the quality of recordings deemed legendary, but in the case of *Dusty in Memphis*, the years have only strengthened its reputation. The idea of taking England's reigning female soul queen to the home of the music she had mastered was an inspired one. The Jerry Wexler/Tom Dowd/Arif Mardin production and engineering team picked mostly perfect songs, and those that weren't so great were salvaged by Springfield's marvelous delivery and technique. This set has definitive numbers in "So Much Love," "Son of a Preacher Man," "Breakfast in Bed," "Just One Smile," "I Don't Want to Hear About It Anymore," and "Just a Little Lovin'" and offers exquisite mastering, informative notes, and an unreleased version of "What Do You Do When Love Dies." It's truly a disc deserving of its classic status. In 1999, Rhino upgraded *Dusty in Memphis* with a deluxe edition that retained the original album, the three bonus tracks from the same era that appeared on its first CD reissue of the record, and 11 further bonus tracks, the new material dating from 1970-1971. It isn't quite accurate to lump those early-'70s cuts into Dusty's "Memphis" era, since they were recorded in New York and Philadelphia and don't have as much of a soul orientation. "Cherished" and "Goodbye" were produced by Gamble & Huff in early 1970 and are good pop-soul numbers. The rest of the sides were produced by Jeff Barry in 1971 and are more pop in flavor, including covers of Bread's "Make It With You" and Carole King's "You've Got a Friend." These Barry-overseen efforts are okay pop-soul, but lacking in truly memorable songs or inspired playing, especially in comparison to the original *Dusty in Memphis* tracks. *—Ron Wynn & Richie Unterberger*

A Brand New Me / Nov. 1970 / Rhino ♦♦♦♦♦
Sticking with the soul stylings of her stellar *Dusty in Memphis* recording, Springfield takes her sensual huskiness north to the City of Brotherly Love for this 1970 slice of Philly soul. Doing incredible justice to a batch of top-quality Gamble & Huff songs, Springfield trades in the Stax-inspired swamp grit of her Memphis album for the urban soul kaleidoscope of *A Brand New Me*. Surrounded by angelically funky string and horn charts from guitarist Roland Chambers and Thom Bell (along with Gamble & Huff, Bell can be counted as an architect of Philly International sound), Springfield sounds positively liberated ranging through the gospel pop closer "Let's Talk It Over," an Aretha-inspired "Silly, Silly Fool," and the Bacharach-styled ballad "Joe." These get topped off by the upbeat Jackson 5 knockoff "Bad Case of the Blues" and covers of two of Jerry Butler's best Mercury hits, "Lost" and "A Brand New Me." Along with *Dusty in Memphis* and her early *You Don't Have to Say You Love Me* record, *Brand New Me* figures into Springfield's handful of really top-notch albums. [Available as an import CD with bonus tracks.] *—Stephen Cook*

From Dusty With Love / Nov. 1970 / Philips ♦♦♦

See All Her Faces / Nov. 1972 / Philips ♦♦♦
Never released in the US, *See All Her Faces* was a hodge-podge of tracks from the late 1960s and early 1970s, some of which had previously appeared on Atlantic singles in the States, although it did have some good moments. One of those was the bossa nova-influenced title track, and she does another bossa nova-flavored number, "Come for a Dream," co-written by Antonio Carlos Jobim. As always there were some really straight orchestrated pop ballads, like "I Start Counting," and something that sounded like an attempt to emulate whatever was happening at Motown at the moment ("Girls It Ain't Easy"). There were also some deep soul-speckled outings (the 1969 single of Tony Joe White's "Willie & Laura Mae Jones," Goffin-King's "That Old Sweet Roll (Hi-De-Ho)"), and some half-decent cuts from early-'70s singles that Ellie Greenwich & Jeff Barry helped write ("What Good Is I Love You," "Nothing Is Forever"). Eight of the tracks are on Rhino's compilation of 1968-1971 British recordings, *Dusty in London*; all but one ("Girls Can't Do What the Guys Do") of the six remaining tracks appears as one of the bonus cuts on Rhino's reissues of *Dusty in Memphis* and *A Brand New Me*. If you live in the U.S., picking up all of these Rhino reissues, rather than hunting for the *See All Her Faces* album, seems like the way to go. *—Richie Unterberger*

Cameo / Apr. 1973 / Dunhill ♦♦♦♦

Reputation / Jul. 1, 1991 / Alex ♦♦♦
In 1990, after almost a decade's absence from the new-release lists and an even longer time away from the charts, Dusty Springfield re-emerged with *Reputation*. A partial collaboration with the Pet Shop Boys, it proved to be her most satisfying record in 15 years and sold better than anything that she'd released since the '60s. The late-'80s synth pop sound melded perfectly with Springfield's still very expressive, powerful, and soulful singing—Dan Hartman handled the producing chores on four of the cuts, Andy Richards on one, and the album has a unified sound, at once airy and dense, soaring and deep. The best cuts, however, are the five produced (and, in all but one case, written) by Neil Tennant and Chris Lowe of the Pet Shop Boys. Much as Robert Fripp may have been put on this earth first and foremost to produce the Roches, Tennant & Lowe's collaborations with Springfield are as satisfying and unified and whole as she ever achieved working with Jerry Wexler, Thom Bell, and Roland Chambers 20 years earlier. She seems to reach that much higher and also that much deeper inside of herself on "In Private" and "Daydreaming" to much subtler effect; those cuts are very much of a piece with her best work on the *Dusty in Memphis*, *A Brand New Me*, and *Cameo* albums, just later links in the same chain, and their effect is to leave the listener breathless and delighted with their sheer beauty as recordings, as well with as her performance. *—Bruce Eder*

Anthology / Sep. 23, 1997 / Mercury ✦✦✦✦✦
Weighing in at three discs, *Anthology* sets out to be the definitive Dusty Springfield compilation and it damn near achieves its goal. While the size of this set makes it a little impractical for fans that just want the hits, anyone that wants to dig deeper into her career will discover that she was one of the most consistent interpretive singers of the '60s, capable of sweet girl group pop, lush orchestral pop, and blue-eyed soul. Bypassing her early records with the Springfields and starting with her solo career in 1963, *Anthology* hits all the high points and features a number of fine forgotten gems as well, making it essential for serious fans of Dusty, '60s pop, and blue-eyed soul. *—Stephen Thomas Erlewine*

★ **The Very Best of Dusty Springfield** / Apr. 21, 1998 / Mercury ✦✦✦✦✦
The Very Best of Dusty Springfield is an ideal compilation, featuring 20 songs from Dusty's prime period of 1963 through 1969. All of the hits—"I Only Want to Be With You," "Wishin' and Hopin'," "Son of a Preacher Man," "I Just Don't Know What to Do With Myself," "A Brand New Me"—are here, along with several lesser-known singles and album tracks that illustrate the full range of her talent. The triple-disc *Anthology* may be more comprehensive and thereby suited for collectors, but this excellent set is the ideal choice for casual fans, since it captures one of the greatest pop singers of the '60s at her very best. *—Stephen Thomas Erlewine*

Dusty in London / Feb. 16, 1999 / Rhino ✦✦✦✦
In the late 1960s and early 1970s, Springfield had an unusual arrangement whereby Philips released her records everywhere in the world except the United States, where they appeared on Atlantic. Atlantic chose to release only 1968-1971 material that was recorded in the U.S., meaning that quite a few tracks she recorded in Britain during this time went unreleased stateside. This collects 24 of those songs Springfield recorded in the U.K. between 1968 and 1971, only a few which had appeared in the U.S. before. Although this is not as soul- and R&B-oriented as the material Atlantic recorded with her in America during this era, in truth it's not always that far removed in sound and spirit from what you'll hear on the Atlantic albums *Dusty in Memphis* (1969) and *A Brand New Me* (1970). You can't get much more soulful than "Piece of My Heart," for instance, a good cover of which leads off the collection. Overall, though, it takes in a broader range of pop styles than Springfield did with her American/Atlantic recordings, from covers of the Rascals ("How Can I Be Sure") and Goffin-King ("Wasn't Born to Follow") to Charles Aznavour, Leon Russell, Jimmy Webb, Bacharach-David, and Antonio Carlos Jobim. Most of it's taken from the British albums *Dusty Definitely* (1968) and *See All Her Faces* (1972), and it's lower on standout performances than the familiar Atlantic albums are. The singing is almost always involved and committed, but sometimes the material is pedestrian. The highlights are very good, however, including Randy Newman's "I Think It's Going to Rain Today," the beautiful string ballad "Morning," and the bossa nova-spiced "See All Her Faces." This is worth hearing if you like Springfield a lot; just don't gear up for an extraordinarily consistent or essential listen. *—Richie Unterberger*

Beautiful Soul: The ABC/Dunhill Collection / Feb. 6, 2001 / Hip-O ✦✦✦
Hip-O's *Beautiful Soul: The ABC/Dunhill Collection* is an exhaustive retrospective of Dusty Springfield's early-'70s stint at Dunhill records, containing the entirety of the 1973 *Cameo* album, plus all the completed material from the unreleased 1974 album, *Longing*. After she signed to Dunhill in 1972, Springfield relocated to California to cut the material, and, appropriately these are Californian productions of their time, filled with studio pros (Larry Carlton, Hal Blaine, Bernard Purdie, Joe Venuto), a warm lush production, and soft rock, written by such songwriters as Alan O'Day, David Gates, Melissa Manchester, and Ashford & Simpson. In other words, this is not the Dusty of *Dusty in Memphis* and *A Brand New Me*, although a cover of Van Morrison's "Tupelo Honey" has an appropriate Southern flair and Ashford & Simpson's "I Just Wanna Be There" is smoothly seductive. All this means that some fans will not warm to this and, admittedly, some of the music is a little slight, but it works on two different levels. First, it's simply a good pop artifact, evoking its era with high-class performances and classy productions, appealing to the kind of listener that finds "Learn to Say Goodbye"'s status as the theme from the ABC Movie of the Week *Say Goodbye, Maggie Cole* to be a virtue. More importantly, this finds Springfield exploring more adventurous material, particularly on *Longing*, where she tackles Janis Ian's "In the Winter" and Margie Adams' lesbian love song, "Beautiful Soul." Therefore, this compilation winds up being as a historical exercise, both for Springfield diehards and early-'70s fanatics, but it'll please both camps equally, since they'll both find its flaws somewhat charming. *—Stephen Thomas Erlewine*

Pamala Stanley

Vocals / Dance-Pop, Club/Dance, Disco, Hi-NRG
Pamala Stanley was never well known in the pop or R&B markets, but in dance music, the singer was held in high regard in the late '70s and early to mid-'80s. A native and resident of Dallas, Stanley first grabbed the attention of dance/club DJs in 1979, when she recorded her debut album, *This Is Hot*, for EMI. The LP fared well in Latin and gay clubs, both of which proved to be equally receptive to three singles she recorded in the '80s: "I Don't Want to Talk About It" in 1983, "Coming Out of Hiding" in 1984, and the rock-influenced "If Looks Could Kill" in 1985. The latter was recorded that same year by Heart, who approached the song as arena rock instead of dance-pop. After that, Stanley retired from music to be a full-time mother, much to the dismay of her fans. In 1990, Beachwood released *Coming Out of Hiding: The Sequel*, a CD containing remixes of Stanley's club hits, and in the mid-'90s, "Coming Out of Hiding" received a folk-rock makeover from the New York-based female group Her Sister. *—Alex Henderson*

● **Coming Out of Hiding . . . The Sequel** / 1990 / Beachwood ✦✦✦✦
Though Pamala Stanley hasn't enjoyed much exposure on commercial radio, she has been a favorite in dance clubs since the disco era. After a string of club hits in the late 1970s and early to mid-'80s, Stanley put her singing career on the back burner to concentrate on motherhood. But even when she wasn't being recorded, the Dallas native's music was kept alive in clubs (especially gay and Latino establishments) thanks to enthusiastic DJs. *Coming Out of Hiding*, a collection of remixes released in 1990, is the closest thing available to a Stanley anthology. From the disco-era hit "This Is Hot" to '80s club smashes like the rock-influenced "If Looks Could Kill" (also recorded by Heart), "Coming Out of Hiding" (embraced in the mid-'90s by New York folk-rockers Her Sister), and "I Don't Want to Talk About It," all of her essential material is here. This is a CD that disco and dance music aficionados shouldn't miss. *—Alex Henderson*

Lisa Stansfield

b. 1965, Rochdale, United Kingdom
Vocals / Club/Dance, Dance-Pop, Urban
English vocalist Lisa Stansfield was the lead singer of the group the Blue Zone and featured on Coldcut's "People Hold On" in 1989. She zoomed into the spotlight with *Affection* in 1990. The album went platinum and earned her a number-three pop and number-one R&B single with "All Around the World." *Affection* and its follow-up, *Real Love*, were deeply influenced by the '70s disco sound of Barry White, from arrangements to mood and even Stansfield's own technique. After a long hiatus, she returned with a self-titled effort in 1997. The *#1 Remixes* EP followed a year later. *—Ron Wynn*

● **Affection** / 1989 / Arista ✦✦✦✦✦
When Lisa Stansfield took the R&B world by storm with her melancholy, Barry White-influenced single "All Around the World," it was obvious that not since Teena Marie had a white female singer performed R&B so convincingly. Though she didn't shy away from hip-hop and house-music elements, *Affection* leaves no doubt where the British singer's heart lies—sleek yet gritty '70s R&B. Though the retro leanings of such updated soul treasures as "You Can't Deny It" and "What Did I Do to You" are obvious, Stansfield's producer keeps things very fresh sounding by embracing a decidedly high-tech and very late-'80s/early-'90s production style. Though essentially a soul diva, Stansfield has a disco masterpiece in the love-and-togetherness anthem "This Is the Right Time." *—Alex Henderson*

Real Love / 1991 / Arista ✦✦✦
Expectations ran incredibly high when the time came for Lisa Stansfield to deliver a second album, but unfortunately, she didn't escape the infamous sophomore slump. *Real Love*, although far from a bad album, clearly falls short of *Affection*'s unmitigated excellence. Nonetheless, there are some definite gems here—including the poigant and heartbreaking ballad "All Woman," the spunky "Soul Deep," and the sleek "Set Your Loving Free." While most of *Real Love* is at least decent and is far superior to most '90s R&B, Stansfield is a major talent who—as the outstanding *Affection* quite clearly demonstrated—can do much better than "merely" good. *—Alex Henderson*

So Natural / 1993 / Arista ✦✦✦

Lisa Stansfield / Apr. 15, 1997 / Arista ✦✦✦✦
Lisa Stansfield's long-awaited eponymous fourth album finds the blue-eyed soul singer at the top of her game, turning in a stylish set of smooth, disco-inflected dance-pop. The songs, from a cover of Barry White's "Never, Never Gonna Give You Up" and "Never Gonna Fall" to the ballad "I Cried My Last Tear," are uniformly strong and Stansfield's voice is seductive and sexy, making the album a small gem in her catalog. *—Stephen Thomas Erlewine*

Swing [Original Soundtrack] / 1999 / RCA Victor ✦✦✦✦
A gem of a soundtrack, sung primarily by this British soul singer. The bright, sassy arrangements are fine showcases for her confident, take-charge vocals. She's also in on the writing of five of the album's 15 songs. Veteran English singer and occasional Van Morrison collaborator Georgie Fame guests on a couple of numbers. The band includes former Bruce Springsteen saxman Clarence Clemons, who appears in the movie with Stansfield. Even if the movie stinks, there's the music to remember. *—Mark Allan*

Face Up / Jul. 3, 2001 / Arista ✦✦✦
Face Up is Lisa Stansfield's first offering for the new millennium, and on this disc she treads similar waters as on previous albums, except for a few more adventurous outings. The album's first single, "Let's Just Call It Love," incorporates the British garage 2step beats introduced to Americans and popularized earlier in 2001 by fellow Brit Craig David, and makes for an unusual but interesting leadoff single. The album's opener, "I've Got Something Better," is classic, funky Lisa Stansfield at her best, and the song gets more and more fun with each repeated listening. Other standouts include the Burt Bacharach-ish showstopping ballad "How Could You?," the pleading "Don't Leave Now I'm in Love," and the set's most obvious hit, the breezy, disco-laced anthem "8-3-1." The title track is the album's requisite Barry White tribute, and the album's irresistibly funky closer, "All Over Me," is this set's answer to her previous album's "The Line." This disc does have its share of filler, including the Destiny's Child-sounding "Boyfriend," which is quite immature for a sophisticated gal like Lisa, and the silly ditty "Candy." Stansfield's pipes get quite gritty on the ballad "Didn't I," and "Wish on Me" is as sensitive and acoustic as the "Rochdale Queen" gets. Once again, this reliable singer, without straying too far from her signature formula, delivers a high-quality set, despite the presence of a few dull moments. *—Jose F. Promis*

The Staple Singers

f. 1951, Chicago, IL
Group / Soul, Traditional Gospel, Southern Gospel, Black Gospel, Country-Soul
The Staples' story goes all the way back to Winona, MS, in 1915. It was then and there that patriarch Roebuck Staples entered the world. A contemporary and familiar of Charley Patton, Roebuck quickly became adept as a solo blues guitarist, entertaining at local dances and picnics. Gradually drawn to the church, by 1937 he was singing and

playing guitar with a spiritual group based out of Drew, MS, the Golden Trumpets. Moving to Chicago four years later, he continued playing gospel music with the Windy City's Trumpet Jubilees. A decade later Pops Staples (as he had become known) presented two of his daughters, Cleotha and Mavis, and his one son, Pervis, in front of a church audience, and the Staple Singers were born.

The Staples recorded in an older, slightly archaic, deeply Southern spiritual style first for United and then for Vee-Jay. Pops and Mavis Staples shared lead vocal chores, with most records underpinned by Pops' heavily reverbed Mississippi cotton-patch guitar. In 1960 the Staples signed with Riverside, a label that specialized in jazz and folk. With Riverside and later Epic, the Staples attempted to move into the then-burgeoning white folk boom. Two Epic releases, "Why (Am I Treated So Bad)" and a cover of Stephen Stills' "For What It's Worth," briefly graced the pop charts in 1967.

In 1968 the Staples signed with Memphis-based Stax. The first two albums, *Soul Folk in Action* and *We'll Get Over*, were produced by Steve Cropper and backed by Booker T. & the MG's. The Staples were now singing entirely contemporary "message" songs such as "Long Walk to D.C." and "When Will We Be Paid." In 1970 Pervis Staples left and was replaced by sister Yvonne Staples. Even more significantly, Al Bell took over production chores. Bell took them down the road to Muscle Shoals, and things got decidedly funky.

Starting with "Heavy Makes You Happy (Sha-Na-Boom Boom)" and "I'll Take You There," the Staples counted 12 chart hits at Stax. When Stax encountered financial problems, Curtis Mayfield signed the Staples to his Curtom label and produced a number-one hit in "Let's Do It Again." The Staples went on to continued chart success, albeit less spectacularly, with Warner, through 1979. One more album followed on 20th Century Fox in 1981. After a three-year hiatus, they signed a two-album deal with Private I and hit the R&B charts five more times, once with an unlikely cover of Talking Heads' "Slippery People." The Staple Singers found a new audience in 1994 when they teamed with Marty Stuart to perform "The Weight" on the *Rhythm, Country and Blues* LP for MCA. Sadly, Pops passed away on December 19, 2000, shortly after suffering a concussion due to a fall in his home. *—Rob Bowman*

Uncloudy Day / 1959 / Vee-Jay ✦✦✦✦✦
This is classic folk-rooted gospel from this mixed group with stinging Delta guitar and Stunning harmonies. *—Opal Louis Nations*

Swing Low Sweet Chariot / 1961 / Vee-Jay ✦✦✦✦✦

Hammer and Nails / Oct. 1962 / Riverside ✦✦✦
This is fine material, beautifully recorded and produced. *—Opal Louis Nations*

Freedom Highway / 1965 / Columbia ✦✦✦
Here is classic live in-church Epic recordings from the height of the civil rights movement of 1965. *—Opal Louis Nations*

Pray On / 1968 / Frank Music ✦✦✦✦✦
The Staple Singers recorded ten 78s over a four-year period for Chicago's Vee-Jay. These have been reissued countless times in various forms. The Charly CD is simply the most recent. For Vee-Jay, the Staples recorded a number of Pops Staples originals as well as radical rearrangements of standards. Pops Staples and Mavis Staples shared the lead singing chores, with Pervis and Cleotha Staples moaning in the background. It's superb gospel shouting. *—Rob Bowman*

Soul Folk in Action / 1968 / Stax ✦✦✦
This is one you are probably going to have to search out, but this gem is worth all the effort. First, take the stunning voices of the Staple Singers, with the closely blending harmonies that can only come from the years of a family singing together. Put in the crack vibrato guitar of Pops (he was a blues player early on), add in a top-notch rhythm section that play as close as it gets, and throw in the Memphis Horns. Then add some material that was just about custom-tailored for them, mixed and mastered by Steve Cropper, and you have the makings of a fantastic disc. Still, how many times have we seen all the right ingredients and been disappointed? Not this time. The only disappointment might come from the brevity of the disc; you just want it to continue. The power and majesty that these voices carry come as close to heaven as can be felt here on earth. They are truly performers who give their all. There are few performers who could rival Otis Redding, and to try and do one of his songs while he was still alive was almost considered sacrilege, yet listen to what they do with "(Sittin' On) The Dock of the Bay." It is a completely different take, yet it loses absolutely nothing and in fact gains a new dimension with their controlled power. True, it probably helps that Steve Cropper, the co-writer of the song, is leading the backing band. Two of the highlights of an incredibly strong disc are "Slow Train," for its slow adept building of potency, and "The Weight." It is a vital testament to belief and love, and you will thank yourself for following a hunch. *—Bob Gottlieb*

We'll Get Over / 1970 / Stax ✦✦✦
Their second Stax release was similar to *Soul Folk in Action*. The album's highlight is Randall Stewart's "When Will We Be Paid?" *—Rob Bowman*

The Staple Swingers / 1971 / Stax ✦✦✦
The Staples' first album produced by Al Bell and recorded in Muscle Shoals hit the winning formula. Other changes saw Pervis Staples departing just before the album was recorded and being replaced by sister Yvonne Staples. Everything was now in place for the Staples' golden years. Three songs, "Heavy Makes You Happy," "Love Is Plentiful," and "You've Got to Earn It," all charted. *—Rob Bowman*

Be Altitude: Respect Yourself / 1972 / Stax ✦✦✦
This is the Staples' finest single album, containing three Top Ten R&B hits, "Respect Yourself," "I'll Take You There," and "This World." The first two also were pop Top 20s, "I'll Take You There" going all the way to number one. *—Rob Bowman*

Be What You Are / 1973 / Stax ✦✦✦
By the early '70s, despite a roster that included the Dramatics and Isaac Hayes, Stax Records was winding down. The Staple Singers, signed to the label in the late '60s, always provided hit singles and respected album efforts. Despite their gospel beginnings, the Staple Singers' biggest draws became Pops Staples' blues-based "devil's music" guitar and Mavis Staples' breathy and sexy vocals. Their 1972 album, *Be Altitude: Respect Yourself*, all but set the template for their subsequent work. *Be What You Are* in some respects is an often overly cautious follow-up. The first single, "If You're Ready (Come Go With Me)," comes off as a softer take on "I'll Take You There." While the implications of having a narrow lyrical scope did impede the group somewhat, *Be What You Are* has the group mining familiar terrain with minimal wear. Tracks like "Love Comes in All Colors," "Tellin' Lies," and the masterful "Touch a Hand, Make a Friend" are all strong and well-produced tracks in the group's rural yet urbane style. The effort's lone cover of Bill Withers' "Grandma's Hands," despite Mavis Staples' lead, comes up short due to the perfection of the Withers original. Mavis Staples also gets two solo efforts here, including Bettye Crutcher's tough "Drown Yourself" and the spare "Heaven." *Be What You Are* isn't as strong or innovative as its predecessor, but it is a cohesive album and a must-have for fans. *—Jason Elias*

City in the Sky / 1974 / Stax ✦✦✦
City in the Sky, the final LP that the Staple Singers made with Stax Records, features the same socially conscious lyrics and powerful singing that had become their trademark before the album's 1974 release. While the original recording didn't have the kind of explosive singles like "Respect Yourself" and "I'll Take You There" that helped them become legends of soul music, this is by no means a weak album. The opener "Back Road Into Town" seethes with energy and anger-tinged pride, while "Washington We're Watching You" combines that same message of anger and pride with organ and horn-driven funk. The Staple Singers return to the gospel style that had begun their musical career nearly 20 years before with "Who Made the Man,"—perhaps the strongest song on the album, alternating between gentle invectives by Pops Staples and powerful harmonic blasts by Mavis, Cleotha, and Yvonne. Overall, the album combines a classic Stax-influenced soul sound with a strong message, making it an essential part of the Staples Singers' catalog. [The 1996 CD reissue of *City in the Sky* features four bonus tracks, including "Oh La De Da" and live versions of "I Like the Things About You," "Respect Yourself," and "I'll Take You There."] *—Stacia Proefrock*

Let's Do It Again / 1975 / Spy ✦✦✦
As Stax neared bankruptcy, the Staples signed with Curtis Mayfield's Curtom label for this soundtrack album. The title track was a number-one hit and "New Orleans" reached number 70, returning the Staples to the upper echelons of the charts for the last time. *—Rob Bowman*

Unlock Your Mind / 1978 / Warner Bros. ✦✦✦

Chronicle / 1979 / Stax ✦✦✦✦✦
Released in 1979, *Chronicle* remains a near-definitive overview of the Staple Singers' time at Stax Records, containing 12 tracks including such classic soul singles as "Heavy Makes You Happy (Sha-Na-Boom-Boom)," "You've Got to Earn It," "Touch a Hand (Make a Friend)," "If You're Ready (Come Go with Me)," "Be What You Are," "Respect Yourself" and "I'll Take You There." *—Stephen Thomas Erlewine*

★ **The Best of the Staple Singers** / Oct. 17, 1990 / Stax ✦✦✦✦✦
The best and most famous cuts from their glory years at Stax. Includes their massive hits "Respect Yourself" and "I'll Take You There"; less famous but similar gospel-funk fusions like "Touch a Hand (Make a Friend)" and "Heavy Makes You Happy (Sha-Na-Boom Boom)"; and less expected items like a cover of "(Sittin' On) The Dock of the Bay." It does not, however, have their 1975 number-one single "Let's Do It Again," which they recorded just after cutting their ties to Stax. *—Richie Unterberger*

Great Day / Oct. 15, 1991 / Milestone ✦✦✦
This two-album Fantasy reissue is an anthology of the material the Staples recorded for Riverside between 1960 and 1963. For Riverside, the Staples recorded mostly gospel but the shouting was toned down a bit. A few modern-day "message" songs make their way into their repertoire as well, including Bob Dylan's "Masters of War." Not quite as cataclysmic as their Vee-Jay material but still essential. *—Rob Bowman*

Uncloudy Day/Will the Circle Be Unbroken / 1992 / Vee-Jay ✦✦✦✦✦
The Staple Singers brilliantly fused gospel, folk, blues, and soul into a cohesive, commercially potent sound in the '50s and '60s. They perfected this approach during their tenure at Vee-Jay, the first label that fully presented their harmonies and allowed the twangy, expert guitar licks of Roebuck "Pops" Staples to be heard in the group's mix. This single disc contains two pivotal Staples albums; *Uncloudy Day* includes such gospel favorites as "I Know I Got Religion" and "Let Me Ride," while *Will the Circle Be Unbroken* offers the splendid title track, plus masterpieces like "Pray On" and "Come Up in Glory." *—Ron Wynn*

The Very Best of the Staple Singers, Vol. 1: Live / Mar. 3, 1998 / Collectables ✦✦✦
Here is 1950s Vee-Jay classics with Pops' Delta guitar and Mavis' deep, compelling vocals. *—Opal Louis Nations*

The Very Best of the Staple Singers, Vol. 2: On My Way to Heaven / Mar. 3, 1998 / Collectables ✦✦✦
This is the cream of the cream. It features their choice Vee-Jay sides. *—Opal Louis Nations*

Mavis Staples

b. 1940, Chicago, IL

Vocals / Contemporary Gospel, Soul, Urban, Country-Soul

Born in 1940 in Chicago, most of Mavis Staples' career has been as lead singer for the Staple Singers. She first recorded solo for Stax subsidiary Volt in 1969. Subsequent efforts included a Curtis Mayfield-produced soundtrack on Curtom, a disappointing nod to disco for Warner in 1979, a misguided stab at electro-pop with Holland-Dozier-Holland in 1984, and an uneven album for Paisley Park. Staples has a rich contralto voice that has neither the range of Aretha Franklin nor the power of Patti LaBelle. Her otherworldly power comes instead from a masterful command of phrasing and a deep-seated sensuality expressed through timbre manipulation. Both the Staple Singers and Mavis found fresh audiences stemming from their participation on the CD *Rhythm, Country and Blues*, and in 1996 she issued *Spirituals & Gospel: Dedicated to Mahalia Jackson*. *—Rob Bowman*

Mavis Staples / 1969 / Volt ♦♦♦
A powerhouse soul belter and wailer, Mavis Staples doesn't have to play second fiddle to anyone, including Aretha Franklin, when it comes to pure, house-rocking, testifying authority. She's seldom gotten a complete album of quality material, but on this 1969 debut, she took half-baked material and made it memorable. "I Have Learned To Do Without You" wasn't a classic, but her vocal made it mighty close. *—Ron Wynn*

Only for the Lonely / 1970 / Stax ♦♦♦

A Piece of the Action / 1977 / Curtom ♦♦♦
Music by Curtis Mayfield is featured on the soundtrack album from the 1977 movie *A Piece of the Action*, which starred Bill Cosby and Sidney Poitier. After composing scores for *Superfly*, *Let's Do It Again*, *Claudine*, and *Short Eyes*, movie scores were old hat to Mayfield, but nothing clicked this time around. Supposedly, this was originally Roberta Flack's project (or this was told to Mavis Staples to motivate her). Staples got a call to add her vocals to tracks Mayfield had finished except for some sweetening. But it's hard—no, impossible—imagining Flack singing these funky songs, so the story about her cancelling out of the project because of personal problems seems far-fetched. In addition, Mayfield's manager, Marv Stuart, told Staples he was paying her half what was promised Flack; this was intended to further ignite Staples, who insisted on and received what was (supposedly) offered Flack. These were mind games to get Staples chomping at the bit. As further motivation, Mayfield insisted that the vocals be completed in only three days. Artistically, the psyche job worked; the album is one of the '70s overlooked gems. Warner Bros. (Curtom's distributor) simply fumbled the ball. They soured on the project when the title track only managed a scrawny showing of 47 on the R&B chart. Though a commercial failure, the album is loaded with funky joints ("Chocolate City," "Orientation") and sexual innuendo pieces ("Getting Deeper," "Koochie, Koochie, Koochie," "Good Lovin' Daddy"). For eye candy, the album features a Vogue quality picture of Staples that's so sweet you'll kiss the cardboard cover. *—Andrew Hamilton*

Mavis Staples / 1984 / HDH ♦♦♦
Like most of their projects after the demise of Invictus and Hot Wax Records, Eddie & Brian Holland miss the mark. Whatever they were trying to accomplish didn't materialize on this unfortunate set of a baker's dozen tunes, which also features productions by Steve Cropper, who produced Mavis Staples and the Staple Singers at Stax Records. Not terrible, but there's nothing that is exciting either. "Love Gone Bad" (number-75 R&B 1984) was the sole single, and it's not the Chris Clark recording written by Holland-Dozier-Holland, but an inferior version written by Brian & Eddie Holland, minus Lamont Dozier. But since Mavis Staples had creative input in this project, which started as a joint venture with Carolyn Franklin, it's one of her favorites. Initially, Franklin and Staples were going to fund the project with a businessman's money and hawk it to a label when the Hollands entered the scenario. The album didn't come out when it was completed, but years later (1984) to a thudding silence; the single surfaced earlier on Phono. Franklin, Aretha Franklin's baby sister, wrote two songs: "It Only Happened" and "Beat Well Done." With the names involved, this should have been so much sweeter; instead it's like a bland bowl of pudding. *—Andrew Hamilton*

Time Waits for No One / 1989 / Paisley Park ♦♦♦
Prince took a great interest in Mavis Staples after she provided him rousing background vocals and appeared in the 1990 film *Graffiti Bridge*. He signed her to his label and wrote and produced some of the tracks on this disc. Unfortunately, it enjoyed little impact saleswise, although Staples soared, shouted and roared with splendor. But her sound and approach were so soulful that it seemed out of place in the detached setting of urban radio. There were both fiery message tracks and blistering love songs, with Staples' assertive, tender and intense vocals. However, not even Prince's name could break the embargo on acts considered too old-school for modern audiences. *—Ron Wynn*

Don't Change Me Now / 1990 / Ace ♦♦♦♦♦
Mavis Staples' solo career has been largely undistinguished. *Don't Change Me Now* pulls together most of her better efforts, being a composite of Staples's two Volt solo albums, *Mavis Staples* and *Only for the Lonely*, recorded for Stax subsidiary Volt in 1969 and 1970, respectively. Ace has added a number of originally unreleased tracks to this collection. The liner notes are well written and the sound is fine. *—Rob Bowman*

• **Only for the Lonely [Compilation]** / Mar. 21, 1993 / Stax ♦♦♦♦♦
This 21-track anthology collects songs recorded in 1969 and issued on three albums. The roster includes a strong duet with Johnnie Taylor called "That's The Way Love Is" and her signature tune, "A House Is Not a Home." Steve Cropper produced and arranged 11 cuts, with Don Davis producing another eight. Staples' energy, delivery, timing and technique were consistently awesome. Unfortunately, only a few of these songs got much attention outside R&B circles, but their quality shows Staples' greatness as a soul vocalist. *—Ron Wynn*

Spirituals & Gospel: Dedicated to Mahalia Jackson / Nov. 5, 1996 / Verve ♦♦♦♦
Recorded in Louisiana, not terribly far from Mahalia Jackson's birthplace, this is a 13-song tribute to the legendary Queen of Gospel. Staples leads all the tracks with Lucky Peterson on the Hammond B-3 organ. This is a very bare-bones set, and after the fourth song, "If I Could Hear My Mother Pray Again," the format becomes boring and the songs begin to sound similar. There's nothing unique about these arrangements: Peterson's riffs are fun the first couple of times but quickly grow repetitive, and the choice of songs is decidedly depressing—"Nobody Knows the Trouble I've Seen," "Swing Low, Sweet Chariot"—and although Staples sings them with zeal, the overall package lacks the flair, creativity and sense of celebration such a project should connote. *—Bill Carpenter*

Roebuck "Pops" Staples

b. Dec. 2, 1915, Winona, MS, **d.** Dec. 19, 2000
Vocals, Guitar / Soul, Black Gospel, Blues Gospel, Funk, Country-Soul
The patriarch of one of music's most successful families, Pops Staples worked with everyone from Robert Johnson to Curtis Mayfield. Roebuck Staples was born December 2, 1915, in Winona, MS; a close friend of Charley Patton, he also played not only with Johnson but also such legends as Son House and Robert Jr. Lockwood, becoming a top-notch blues guitarist in the process. Increasingly drawn to the church, he joined the gospel group the Golden Trumpets in 1937, and upon relocating to Chicago in 1941, he signed on with the Windy City's Trumpet Jubilees; by the following decade, Staples was regularly performing at services in the company of his daughters Mavis and Cleotha and son Pervis, and soon they began appearing professionally as the Staple Singers.

While originally a gospel group, the family achieved their first commercial success with a more contemporary soul sound honed during the late '60s while signed to the Stax label; by the early '70s, the Staples even moved into funk, scoring a major pop hit with "I'll Take You There." After signing with Mayfield's Curtom label, they also found success with "Let's Do It Again." Pops Staples did not pursue a solo career prior to releasing 1992's *Peace to the Neighborhood*, which returned him to his blues and gospel roots. Its follow-up, 1994's *Father Father*, earned a Grammy for Best Contemporary Blues Album. Staples also appeared in several films, including 1998's *Wag the Dog*. Late in 2000, Staples suffered a concussion after a fall in his home; shortly thereafter, on December 19, he passed away at the age of 85. *—Jason Ankeny*

• **Peace to the Neighbourhood** / 1992 / Pointblank ♦♦♦♦
77-year-old Pop Staples puts a lot of younger performers to shame with his integrity-laden solo release *Peace to the Neighbourhood*. The founder of the Staples Singers combines joyous soul and gospel with swampy funk and blues. Of course, it doesn't hurt to have the rest of the Staples, and admirers Bonnie Raitt, Jackson Browne, and Ry Cooder along for the ride. Includes the street-wise, anti-drug-culture "Miss Cocaine." *—Roch Parisien*

Father Father / 1994 / Pointblank ♦♦♦
Pops Staples was 79 when he recorded *Father Father*, which was only his second solo album. The patriarch of the Staples family was always a team player, and providing solo albums was something he didn't do until he was well into his 70s. Although *Father Father* won Staples a Grammy for Best Contemporary Blues Album, this isn't strictly a blues offering—true to form, *Father, Father* is the work of an artist who had long had one foot in secular music and another in gospel. This CD, in fact, has as much to do with gospel and R&B as it does with the blues. Staples' secular side is heard on his cover of Bonny "Mack" Rice's "Getting Too Big for Your Britches," but the singer's spirituality asserts itself on everything from "Glory Glory" and the traditional "Jesus Is Going to Make Up My Dying Bed" to a remake of the Impressions' civil rights anthem "People, Get Ready." To be sure, Staples' voice had declined considerably over the years—comparing his performances on this album to his work with the Staple Singers in the 1960s and 1970s, it becomes obvious just how much his voice had thinned out. Even so, Staples manages to deliver an enjoyable and meaningful album, but one that—despite its assets and Grammy-winning status—is less than essential. Not for the casual listener, *Father, Father* is primarily for completists and die-hard fans. *—Alex Henderson*

Stargard

f. 1976, **db.** 1983
Group / Disco, Funk, Urban, Soul
Heavily influenced by LaBelle and the Pointer Sisters, Stargard was a female R&B vocal group that was best known for providing the theme song from the 1977 film *Which Way Is Up*. Rochelle Runnells, Debra Anderson, and Janice Williams—who comprised Stargard's original three-woman lineup—didn't go for the type of breathy, sweet, girlish vocals that the Supremes and the Three Degrees were known for. Like LaBelle and the Pointer Sisters, Stargard favored robust, aggressive belting and brought a gospel-like passion to its funk, soul, and disco. Stargard signed with MCA in 1977, when its first single, the ultra-funky "Theme From 'Which Way Is Up'" (a Norman Whitfield gem), soared to number one on the R&B singles charts. Stargard's self-titled debut album came out in early 1978, and later that year, MCA released the trio's sophomore effort *What You Waitin' For*. That album's funky title track (also written by Whitfield) became a Top Ten R&B hit, but after that, Stargard lost its commercial momentum. In 1979, Stargard left MCA for Warner Bros. and recorded its third album, *The Changing of the Gard*, which was produced by Robert Wright and Earth, Wind & Fire's Verdine White (Maurice White's brother) and contained the single "Wear It Out." That superb album had the makings of a smash, but regrettably, it didn't do nearly as well as it should have. In 1980, Anderson left the group, and Runnells and Williams decided to carry on as a duo instead of hiring a replacement. As a duo, Runnells and Williams recorded 1981's Norman Whitfield-produced *Back 2 Back* for Warner Bros. and 1982's *Nine Lives* (which Runnells produced) for MCA. Both of those LPs received very little attention, and in 1983, Stargard broke up. *—Alex Henderson*

Stargard / 1978 / MCA ♦♦♦
When Stargard soared to number one on the R&B singles charts with "Theme From 'Which Way Is Up'" in late 1977, the female trio was hyped as "the next LaBelle"—and Rochelle Runnells, Debra Anderson, and Janice Williams also found themselves being compared to the Pointer Sisters. LaBelle and the Pointer Sisters are, in fact, valid comparisons because Stargard was among the grittier female R&B groups to emerge in the late 1970s. If you wanted the sort of breathy sweetness that the Supremes and the Three Degrees were known for, you wouldn't get it from Stargard—like LaBelle and the Pointer Sisters, Stargard favored robust, gospel-minded belting. Regrettably, Stargard only had a

few major hits and wasn't as big as it should have been, although the funk-soul trio's recording career got off to a promising start with this 1978 LP (which was produced by Mark Davis). Those who bought *Stargard* because of "Which Way Is Up" found the rest of the album to be quite solid; the threesome brings as much conviction to exuberant, uptempo numbers like "Smile" and "Disco Rufus" as it does to the ballads "Love Is So Easy" and "Don't Change." Surprisingly, "Which Way Is Up" turned out to be the album's only major hit. But even so, one could hear a tremendous amount of potential on this excellent debut. *—Alex Henderson*

What You Waitin' For / 1978 / MCA ✦✦✦✦✦
It was a very sad day for R&B when, in early 1977, LaBelle broke up. Inevitably, Patti LaBelle wanted a solo career, but even so, LaBelle's breakup was a bitter pill for R&B lovers to swallow. And when Stargard was burning up the R&B charts with "Theme From 'Which Way Is Up'" in late 1977 and early 1978, some people tried to fill the void by hyping Stargard as "the next LaBelle." But while Debra Anderson, Rochelle Runnells, and Janice Williams were heavily influenced by LaBelle and the Pointer Sisters and shared LaBelle's love of wild, outrageous space costumes, Stargard was an appealing group in its own right. The trio showed no signs of a sophomore slump on its second album, *What You Waitin' For*, which was produced by Mark Davis. The title song (a funk gem that was written by Norman Whitfield and was also recorded by Rose Royce) became a Top Ten R&B hit, and Stargard is equally exciting on album tracks that range from the melancholy ballad "Blue Rain" to gutsy funk items like "Never Take You Back," "Sensuous Woman," and the Parliament-influenced "Starbob." This LP ends on a surprising note with the moody "Chameleon Lady," which is the most jazz-minded thing that ever came from Stargard—a group that was best known for funk and soul. It's regrettable that the title song was this LP's only major hit; two or three of the album's other songs should have been big hits as well. But be that as it may, *What You Waitin' For* is excellent from start to finish. *—Alex Henderson*

• **The Changing of the Gard** / 1979 / Warner Bros. ✦✦✦✦✦
The Changing of the Gard was an appropriate title for Stargard's third album because it was, in some respects, a departure from the female trio's two previous albums. With this LP, Stargard switched from MCA to Warner Brothers—and while *Stargard* and *What You Waitin' For* were both produced by Mark Davis, *The Changing of the Gard* found Rochelle Runnells, Debra Anderson, and Janice Williams working with Robert Wright and Earth, Wind & Fire's Verdine White. So, not surprisingly, Stargard becomes a bit more Earth, Wind & Fire-ish at times, and the Wright/White team gives the group a sleeker sound on gems like "Take Me Back," the ballad "(Once in a Lifetime) Dream Come True," and the exuberant single "Wear It Out." But Stargard still has plenty of grit and passion; like EWF's 1970s recordings, *The Changing of the Gard* manages to sound polished and gritty at the same time. Those who expect Stargard to provide uninhibited, extroverted party jams won't be disappointed by "Footstompin' Music," "Put on Your Rollerskates," and other funk smokers. Now for the bad news: this vinyl LP didn't do nearly as well as it should have. While *The Changing of the Gard* is full of pearls that deserved to be major hits, this record didn't receive as much attention as Stargard's two previous albums. It goes without saying that justice doesn't always prevail in the music world, and *The Changing of the Gard* is a perfect example of a fine album being a commercial disappointment. *—Alex Henderson*

Back 2 Back / 1981 / Warner Bros. ✦✦✦
When Debra Anderson left Stargard in 1980, Rochelle Runnells and Janice Williams didn't hire a replacement—instead, they decided to carry on as a duo. Released in 1981, *Back 2 Back* was Stargard's first album as a duo, second album for Warner Brothers, and fourth album overall. Losing Anderson wasn't a fatal blow for Stargard; Runnells and Williams could sing their heads off. Nonetheless, *Back 2 Back* was the first Stargard album that fell short of excellent. Produced by Norman Whitfield, this vinyl LP isn't unlike the records that he produced for Rose Royce in the late 1970s—and it has more in common with *Stargard* and *What You Waitin' For* (the group's first two albums) than 1979's sleeker *The Changing of the Gard*. Runnells and Williams were hardly strangers to Whitfield's work; the legendary producer/songwriter wrote Stargard's two biggest hits, "What You Waitin' For" and "Theme From 'Which Way Is Up'." But Whitfield, for all his credentials, doesn't do all that much for Stargard on *Back 2 Back*. This isn't a terrible album; it's generally competent, but it's uneven and unremarkable. Funk tunes like "High on the Boogie," "It's Your Love That I'm Missin'," and "Back to the Funk," although mildly catchy, are quite formulaic and sound like recycled versions of "What You Waitin' For." The album's most memorable tracks are its ballads, which include Runnells' "Just One Love" and David Gates' "Diary." But even the LP's best offerings don't prevent the listener from feeling disappointed—especially when considering how superb Stargard's previous album, *The Changing of the Gard*, was. *Back 2 Back* is only recommended to completists. *—Alex Henderson*

Nine Lives / 1982 / MCA ✦✦✦

Brenda K. Starr

b. Oct. 15, 1966, New York, NY [Manhattan]
Vocals / Freestyle, Urban, Club/Dance, Salsa, House, Dance-Pop
New York-born singer Brenda K. Starr had the opportunity to make her first demo at the age of 12. Two years later, Starr was signing up for her first record deal and climbing music charts with Grammy-nominated pop ballad "I Still Believe" and a club/dance song called "What You See Is What You Get." Brenda K. Starr decided to turn to tropical music after meeting label executive José Armand Jr. Starr made her Spanish-language debut with the release of *Te Sigo Esperando*, which was produced by Humberto Ramírez and featured the hit single "Herida." Univision's lo Nuestro-nominated *No Lo Voy a Olvidar* followed in 1998. *—Drago Bonacich*

Brenda K. Starr / 1987 / MCA ✦✦✦
A generally consistent effort with a few uninspired moments, Starr's breakthrough album embodies both the good and bad aspects of late-'80s synth-driven dance-pop. At its peak, the set is bright and zesty, with irresistible hooks and danceable rhythms ("What You See Is What You Get") or passionately dramatic and heartfelt ("I Still Believe"). So, it's fitting that both of those numbers became Top 40 pop hits. At its low point, the album suffers from banal arrangements and clichéd melodies ("All Tied Up" and "Drive Another Girl Home," though the latter is commendable for its unique delivery of an anti-drunk-driving message within a pop context). The most consistent factor of *Brenda K. Starr* is, in fact, Starr, who gives honorable energy and vitality to each number—rising above the weaker moments. Musically, the album's stronghold lies in its exploration of several subgenres: freestyle; smooth, midtempo R&B; straightforward club sounds; and radio-friendly pop. That wasn't the case with her 1985 debut album, *I Want Your Love*; but it can also be argued that the latter had a rawer, less polished quality that made it more endearing at times. *—Justin M. Kantor*

• **By Heart** / 1991 / Epic ✦✦✦✦✦
With an abundance of producers and writers, *By Heart* strived to pick up where Starr's breakthrough sophomore set, *Brenda K. Starr*, left off. Deodato and Stephen Broughton Lunt, who had produced her Top 40 hits "I Still Believe" and "What You See Is What You Get" were called upon once more; and the services of Rick Wake, Guy Roche, Michael Jay, and Richard Scher were also enlisted to diversify the palette. Somehow, there is a consistency amongst the various production and songwriting values. Especially notable are the down-to-earth call to unity, "What If," a soulful pop midtempo number; the endearing and poignant ballad "Never Let You Go" (melody and lyrics penned by Starr); and the heartwarming title track. But there isn't necessarily always strength in numbers. Several entries—notably the generic club number "Let's Go Undercover" and the disposable, contrived cheese-pop of "Wake Up the Neighbors"—fall prey to the unimaginative banality that hindered a good portion of Starr's 1987 set. But that problem is considerably brief on *By Heart*, given the impressive mixture of both coveted and newcomer contributors and a good balance of slow and fast tempos. For the first time, here Starr gets to shine over a sizeable production budget and define her ability to adapt to a number of vocal contexts—from freestyle ("What Goes On") to R&B balladry ("You Touch Me in All the Right Places") to pure pop (the only single release, "If You Could Read My Mind"). Unfortunately, the album's repeatedly delayed release and an obvious lack of promotional muscle when it finally did hit shelves prevented it from going anywhere—and Starr was dropped from the label shortly after its release. She has since carved a successful second career for herself as a salsa songstress; and for those fans looking for a nice taste of her earlier English-language material, *By Heart* is the best start. *—Justin M. Kantor*

Edwin Starr (Charles Hatcher)

b. Jan. 21, 1942, Nashville, TN, **d.** Apr. 2, 2003, Nottingham, England
Vocals / Pop-Soul, Motown, Soul, Northern Soul, Psychedelic Soul
Rightly revered for the storming protest classic "War," Edwin Starr didn't really need another hit to achieve legendary status in soul circles, so electrifying was that single performance. Starr first made his name as "Agent Double-O-Soul," and when his contract was transferred to Motown, he instantly became one of the roughest, toughest vocalists on the crossover-friendly label, with his debt to James Brown and the Stax soul shouters. Even if nothing else ever matched the phenomenon of "War," Starr had several Top Ten hits on the R&B charts over the late '60s and early '70s, and also enjoyed a brief renaissance during the disco era.

Starr was born Charles Hatcher in Nashville, TN, on January 21, 1942; his cousin was deep soul singer and songwriter Roger Hatcher. He grew up in Cleveland and formed a doo wop quintet called the FutureTones while still in high school. They won numerous local talent competitions and even recorded a single for a small label, but Starr was drafted into the military in 1960, stalling the group's momentum. When he returned in 1962, he tried to get things going again, but to no avail; instead, he wound up joining Bill Doggett's group as a featured vocalist in 1963. Two years later, Starr wrote what he felt was a surefire hit in the spy-themed "Agent Double-O-Soul," and left Doggett's band to sign with Ric-Tic Records and settle in Detroit. "Agent Double-O-Soul" hit the R&B Top Ten later in 1965, and just missed the pop Top 20. Starr capitalized on the song's novelty appeal by appearing on-stage in a spy costume complete with toy gun, but proved he was no one-trick pony by returning to the Top Ten a year later with "Stop Her on Sight (S.O.S.)."

Motown head Berry Gordy subsequently bought out Ric-Tic and took over its artist roster, with Starr the crown jewel. Contract negotiations took some time, but Starr rebounded with his biggest hit yet in 1969's "25 Miles," which reached the Top Ten on both the pop and R&B charts. The follow-up, "I'm Still a Struggling Man," wasn't as successful, and Starr was something of a forgotten man for several months. When he returned to the studio, it was with producer Norman Whitfield, who'd been reinventing the Temptations as a psychedelic soul act. Whitfield had co-written a strident anti-war protest song, "War," for the Temps' *Psychedelic Shack* LP, and in spite of growing demand for a single release, Motown didn't want the group to take such an aggressive stance. Whitfield recut "War" with Starr, and the resulting version was arguably the most incendiary song Motown ever released. It zoomed to the top of the pop charts in 1970, and its chorus—powered by Starr's guttural delivery—remains a catch phrase even today.

The follow-up single, "Stop the War Now," was blatantly derivative, but made the R&B Top Five anyway, and Starr went on to land another significant hit with "Funky Music Sho' Nuff Turns Me On." In 1974, he handled the soundtrack to the blaxploitation film *Hell Up in Harlem*, a sequel to the James Brown-scored *Black Caesar* (Brown had originally been slated to do the follow-up as well). The lack of promotion signaled that Starr's days with Motown were likely numbered; he charted again in 1975 with "Pain," and bade farewell to the label with "Who's Right or Wrong." He recorded albums for small labels, including 1975's *Free to Be Myself* on Granite and 1977's *Afternoon Sunshine* on GTO, before finding a new home on 20th Century in 1978. Here he briefly reinvented himself as a disco singer, scoring his biggest hits in years with 1979's "Contact" and "H.A.P.P.Y. Radio"; his final release with the label came in 1980.

Starr moved to the U.K. during the '80s, recording a Marvin Gaye tribute album for Streetwave and a handful of singles for Hippodrome over 1985-1986. His participation in the Ferry Aid charity project led to a deal with Virgin and a session with the hot production team of Stock, Aitken & Waterman, but he didn't take to their high-tech dance-pop style and instead moved to Ian Levine's Motown revival label Motorcity from 1989-1991. Since then, he's guested on dance remakes of his past hits by Utah Saints ("Funky Music") and Three Amigos ("25 Miles"). *—Steve Huey*

Soulmaster / 1968 / Motown ✦✦✦✦✦
Edwin Starr was never able to hit a groove while at Motown. He made some good and a few great tracks, but just couldn't get the steady stream of great material and hit records that made many others at Motown household names. This was arguably his best album; it included both Gordy and Ric-Tic singles like "Agent Double-O-Soul." It shows that at times Starr could be as riveting and exciting as any male singer on the soul circuit; he was simply unable to consistently maintain that level. *—Ron Wynn*

Just We Two / 1969 / Motown ✦✦✦
Motown Records was famous for pairing their artists on duets. Usually they placed an established artist with an unknown (Marvin Gaye with Kim Weston and Tammi Terrell, or Billy Preston with Syreeta). At other times, Motown paired two established artists, such as Gaye and Mary Wells, the Temptations and the Supremes, and the Supremes and the Four Tops. Edwin Starr (born Charles Hatcher) was hot at the time, so to maximize profits, Motown teamed the Cleveland soul singer with Blinky Williams, an unknown singer. The results, other than the moving "We'll Find a Way," are disappointing. Edwin sounds uncomfortable and disinterested. Even his brilliant, chirpy "Oh How Happy" comes off limp, and "I'm So Thankful," a little-known Ikettes tune, embarrasses the original. Blinky seems more comfortable with the arrangements than Edwin, but when they blend their voices, you want to cover your ears. The two sound like yodeling cocker spaniels on "Ooh Baby Baby." This was not a match made in heaven. *—Andrew Hamilton*

War & Peace / 1970 / Motown ✦✦✦✦✦
Edwin Starr went from run-of-the-mill second-level act to hitmaker with this 1970 album, without question his finest. Norman Whitfield gave Starr the chance to cut a song that had been intended for the Temptations. They later did a version of "War," but Starr completely vaporized their rendition to the extent that most people today think he wrote it. Starr was now a celebrity and briefly in Motown's top echelon. The fact that everything else on the album is only fair to average didn't even matter in the scope of things. *—Ron Wynn*

Involved / 1971 / Motown/Gordy ✦✦✦
It's amazing that Edwin Starr had any voice at all after recording these songs. Producer Norman Whitfield had the explosive singer hitting incredible notes in the studio. A follow-up to his number-one "War," the jammin' "Stop the War Now," which many fluffed off as a copy cat, is actually its own brand of poison. From Starr's opening line, "Make the Sign of Peace," and "Sing Now!" It's a nonstop rocker that suffered from comparisons to "War." Unbelievable, but "Funky Music Sho Nuff Turns Me On" reaches even higher decibels. Norman had the session musicians playing fast, funky and reckless, as Edwin belted, at the top of his lungs, his love for low-down grooves. Whitfield recorded the same songs by different artists, so it didn't surprise me to hear Edwin doing the Temptations' "Ball of Confusion," which employs a motor-booty beat to drive home its socially significant lyrics. The Miracles' "Way Over There" was first released on Edwin's debut Motown LP; the brain trust at Hitsville U.S.A. decided to include it here also. And it's easy to see why, it has the same driving beat that is prevalent on this LP. The only cooling points are versions of Sly & the Family Stone's "Stand," and a soulful rendition of George Harrison's "My Sweet Lord." *—Andrew Hamilton*

Hell Up in Harlem / 1974 / Motown ✦✦✦✦
With productions and songs from Freddie Perren and Fonce Mizell, *Hell Up in Harlem* is the scathing and soulful soundtrack of the motion picture starring Fred Williamson. This was Edwin Starr's last album for Motown which probably accounts for the woeful lack of promotion. Two singles were released, *Hell Up in Harlem*, the first, should have remained an album cut, as its appeal was limited, despite a dogmatic vocal by Edwin. However, the follow up, "Big Papa," should have been a monster. Written by Freddie Perren, it has the same power, forcefulness and drive of numbers that Norman Whitfield had produced on Rare Earth and the Temptations. The flips of both singles, "Don't It Feel Good to Be Free" and "Like We Used to Do," are mellower than the push sides. The bone picker, however, is "Easin' In," a great midtempo number with cool backing vocals, and a great reading from Starr, it has chart buster written all over it, yet Motown never released it as a single. Mind boggling, since Starr's final single for Berry's empire, "Who's Right or Wrong," backed with "Lonely Rainy Days in San Diego," dropped six months after "Papa," but doesn't rate with "Easin'." Even more puzzling is why Phillips, which owns the Motown masters, hasn't reissued this winner on CD. *—Andrew Hamilton*

Hits of Edwin Starr / 1974 / Motown ✦✦✦✦
This highly explosive Edwin Starr compilation contains nearly every significant track by the soul singer, including his best Ric-Tic recordings': "Stop Her on Sight," "Back Street," "Headline News," and "Agent Double-O-Soul." Features "Soul Master," the super cool title track from his debut Motown LP. Known as a screamer and shouter at Motown, these 18 tracks support that assessment. A monster in the studio under producer Norman Whitfield, Starr's powerful vocals' push unmercifully on "25 Miles," "Cloud Nine," "You've Got My Soul on Fire," "Funky Music Sho Nuff Turns Me On," and "Way Over There." "War" and "Stop the War Now," two anti-war songs, are fused together—it gets so good you'll be making peace signs as they play. "There You Go," a smooth beat ballad, is the mellowest track and seems out of place among these funky tracks. Would have preferred "Big Poppa" to the jaunty "Gonna Keep on Trying Till I Win Your Love," which works better as a ballad. A fine collection of Starr's most prolific years. *—Andrew Hamilton*

Free to Be Myself / 1975 / Granite ✦✦✦

Edwin Starr / 1977 / GTO ✦✦

Clean / 1978 / 20th Century ✦✦✦
In the late '70s, Edwin Starr was adjusting to the disco era, like many other soul and R&B vocalists. He hadn't gotten fully comfortable with bustling dance tracks, but this album helped ease the transition. It laid the groundwork for Starr's next LP, in which he returned to prominence and found a way to accomodate the demands of the dancefloor without sacrificing his own integrity. *—Ron Wynn*

Ear Candy / 1980 / 20th Century ✦✦✦

Stronger Than You Think I Am / 1980 / 20th Century ✦✦✦

The Best of Edwin Starr / 1981 / 20th Century ✦✦✦
Starr's best Motown singles were jubilant, energetic, and emancipating in their power and vocal brilliance. He didn't make enough to justify a greatest hits collection or anthology, but if you don't have the singles and want to get them, as well as some decent follow-up singles and album cuts, this will be worth the purchase. *—Ron Wynn*

Stop Her on Sight / 1997 / Castle ✦✦✦

● **The Very Best of Edwin Starr** / Aug. 25, 1998 / Motown ✦✦✦✦✦
Edwin Starr was at the height of his creative powers in the 1960s and early to mid-'70s, when he did much of his best work for Motown. Released in late 1998, this CD spans 1965-1974 and boasts many of his essential Motown hits. Starr was very much a product of Northern soul, and yet, he sometimes showed an awareness of the sweaty, rough-and-tumble soul that Stax Records was recording down in Memphis. "If My Heart Could Tell the Story," "Stop Her on Sight (S.O.S.)," and "I'm Still a Struggling Man" are pure Detroit; the sweetness and honey-coated harmonies that defined a lot of Motor City and Northern R&B are very much a part of these classics. But Starr's tougher side asserts itself on "25 Miles" and the angry protest song "War," both of which demonstrate that when he wanted, Starr could be every bit as gritty as Memphis shouters like Otis Redding and Sam Moore. If you're seeking an introduction to Starr's talents, this disc would be the best choice by far. *—Alex Henderson*

Agent Double-O-Soul: The Ultimate Live Performance / Mar. 28, 2002 / Cargo ✦✦✦
At no point in the track listing or liner notes is the important information as to what date or dates this live material was recorded divulged. That's not the greatest of signs; if it was a relic from Starr's commercial prime, they'd be sure to plaster that date very prominently in the package. An educated guess would place it as having been recorded shortly before the CD's 2002 release date, and certainly it postdates his 1960s-1970s salad days. But really, who can speculate on an exact date for sure, leaving hapless reviewers no option but to look a bit like buffoons? Anyway, even working on the near-certain assumption that this is from the 1990s or early 2000s, it's better than you might expect, though not a necessary addition to your Starr library. Starr is in good voice and high energy and the band is punchy and competent, though not up to Booker T. & the MG's' level or anything like that. He gets the big hits—"25 Miles," "S.O.S.," and "War"—out of the way right away, throws in covers of "My Girl" and "Let's Stay Together," and makes occasional outings into disco arrangements that the soul fans who comprise the majority of his constituency might not dig. It's respectable, but not something you'll put on nearly as often as his best vintage discs. *—Richie Unterberger*

Candi Staton

b. Mar. 13, 1940, Hanceville, AL
Vocals / Contemporary Gospel, Country-Soul, Urban, Disco, Soul, Quiet Storm
Born March 13, 1940, in Hanceville, AL, Candi Stanton sang with the Jewell Gospel Trio as a teenager. They toured the traditional gospel circuit in the 1950s with the Soul Stirrers, C.L. Franklin, and Mahalia Jackson. They recorded several sides for Nashboro, Apollo, and Savoy Records between 1953 and 1963. In 1968 Staton launched solo career as a Southern soul stylist, garnering 16 R&B hits for Rick Hall's legendary Fame Studios and gaining the title of First Lady of Southern Soul for her Grammy-nominated R&B renditions of country tunes "Stand By Your Man" and "In the Ghetto." In 1975 Staton saw Southern soul falling out of fashion and began collaborating with producer Dave Crawford, who propelled her into a disco diva with dance songs such as "Young Hearts Run Free" and "Victim." In 1982 Staton had been disgruntled with Warner Brothers' passing interest in her career and a career slump, so she returned to the gospel field. She and her husband, John Sussewell (drummer for Ashford & Simpson), founded Beracah Ministries in Atlanta with help from Jim and Tammy Bakker's PTL Ministries. She has since recorded eight popular gospel albums, two of which have won Grammy nominations. In 1992 she was back in the pop mainstream with a Top Ten British hit, "You Got the Love," a club-styled dance hit which sold two-million copies abroad. Since joining Intersound Records in 1995, Staton has begun to sing some of her old R&B hits again and recorded some new message-oriented pop songs while gaining a new title, the Sweetheart of Soul. In 2000, she released her 11th album, *Here's a Blessing*. *—Bil Carpenter*

I'm Just a Prisoner / 1969 / Fame ✦✦✦✦✦
Recorded at Rick Hall's Muscle Shoals studios, this set embodies the essence of Southern soul—a hybrid of country, R&B and the blues. This long-out-of-print set features the novelty tune "I'd Rather Be An Old Man's Sweetheart (Than a Young One's Fool)" and a killer cover of O.V. Wright's "That's How Strong My Love Is." *—Bil Carpenter*

Young Hearts Run Free / 1976 / Warner Bros. ♦♦♦
This is a reissue of Staton's 1976 pop breakthrough which also features her signature song, the title tune. Recorded at Sound Studios in L.A., it was her first album recorded outside of Muscle Shoals. The set was produced by the late Dave Crawford and marked Staton's exodus from the world of gritty Southern soul to the classy world of urban soul and dance music. The album featured fine ballads such as the whispery "Summertime With You," "What a Feeling," a coming of age tale, and Al Green's "Living For You." The dance tracks "Destiny" and "Run to Me" were too formulaic and similar to "Young Hearts" to merit discussion. The set also featured the rocking "I Know," and the laid-back "You Bet Your Sweet, Sweet Love," with background vocals by Deniece Williams, and Ray Parker Jr. on guitar. *—Bil Carpenter*

Love Lifted Me / 1988 / Beracah ♦♦♦♦♦

Stand Up and Be a Witness / 1990 / Beracah ♦♦♦

I Give You Praise / 1993 / Beracah ♦♦♦

It's Time / Oct. 1995 / Intersound ♦♦♦♦
Here are ten songs covering a wide range of musical styles. This set was produced by Staton's son, Marcus Williams, who is a flawless and in-demand session drummer. As a result, the production is very slick and clean. It features Staton's autobiographical number-one gospel hit "Mama," which was actually more of a Southern pop song than gospel. The album was diverse, with "I'm Changed" and "Born Again" sounding as though they were cut from a page in the Ward Singers' 1950s songbook. "The Blood" and "I Want to Grow" express light jazz elements, while "Rapture Me" is pure funk. *—Bil Carpenter*

★ **The Best of Candi Staton** / Nov. 1995 / Warner Archives ♦♦♦♦♦
This is a long-overdue compilation of the soul siren's best-known '70s dance hits, featuring "Victim," "When You Wake Up Tomorrow," "Run to Me," and her signature tune "Young Hearts Run Free." Also included on the 14-song set is a previously unissued Southern soul ballad entitled "He's Making Love to You (But He's Thinking of Me)." The set also features four of Staton's last recordings with renowned soul producer Rick Hall on the erotic "As Long as He Takes Care of Home" and the torchlike "Here I Am Again" ballad. The set is rounded out with lesser-known dance tracks and album tracks from between 1974 and 1980, such as the quiet storm ballads "One More Chance on Love" and "Halfway to Heaven." The album closes with a very traditional, almost a cappella reading of "Precious Lord" with just piano and background singers. *—Bil Carpenter*

Cover Me / 1997 / CGI ♦♦♦♦
This is a traditional-style, 12-song concept album of gospel remakes of pop and gospel songs such as Simon & Garfunkel's "Bridge Over Troubled Water" and Sam & Dave's "Hold on, I'm Comin'." The other remakes include new versions of early gospel favorites such as the Harmonettes' "Old Landmark" and "I Will Trust in the Lord." Staton also remakes her 1987 gospel hit "The First Face I Want to See" with raspy-voiced Joe Ligon of the legendary Mighty Clouds of Joy. The album also includes four bonus original compositions, such as the country-styled "Tears That Mama Cried." A stunning, eclectic mix of gospel, pop and soul. *—Bil Carpenter*

Charles Stepney

d. May 17, 1976, Chicago, IL
Producer, Arranger / Chicago Soul, Uptown Soul, R&B, Soul
The formidable skills of arranger/producer Charles Stepney are heard on gold and platinum hits by the Dells and Earth, Wind & Fire, as well as artistic Chicago soul by acts ranging from Rotary Connection to Terry Callier. While a staff arranger and producer at Chicago-based Chess Records, where he worked with a pre-stardom Minnie Riperton, his biggest successes were the sides he cut with the Dells. Soon after the group hit in 1965 with the classic "Stay in My Corner" on Vee-Jay Records, the label folded. The Dells, who had recorded for Chess before going to Vee-Jay, returned to the label in summer 1966, where they began working with producer Billy Davis and arranger Phil Wright.

In summer 1967, Chess assigned the Dells to their Cadet imprint. Staff producer Bobby Miller and arranger Stepney picked the group to work with after a meeting with Leonard Chess. Their collaboration with Miller and Stepney yielded a hit single, "O-O, I Love You," in late 1967. The next year, their career-making fast-selling album *There Is* was issued. The title track b/w the Motown-ish "Show Me" peaked at number-11 R&B, number-20 pop in early 1968, and "Wear It on Your Face" went to number-27 R&B in spring 1968. The *There Is* LP hit number-29 pop in summer 1968.

The hits continued: a six-minute remake of "Stay in My Corner," "Always Together," "Does Anybody Know I'm Here," the medley "I Can Sing a Rainbow"/"Love Is Blue," a remake of their Vee-Hay hit "Oh What a Night," an uptempo cover of Otis Redding's "Sitting on the Dock of the Bay," and "Open Up Your Heart."

In 1970 Stepney took over the production duties for the Dells. The 1971 album *Freedom Means* spawned the hit single "The Love We Had (Stays on My Mind)" (number-eight R&B, summer 1971). The group recorded two more LPs with Stepney, *The Dells Sing Dionne Warwicke's Greatest Hits* (May 1972) and *Sweet as Funk Can Be*. In the '70s, Stepney was reunited with former Chess session drummer Maurice White, who founded the '70s supergroup Earth, Wind & Fire (EWF). Along with White and Philip Bailey, he co-wrote the classic ballad "Reasons," an extremely popular track from EWF's 1975 double-platinum LP *That's the Way of the World* that was curiously never a single. In addition to the soul-stirring title track, White, Stepney, and Verdine White wrote the track "Yearnin', Learnin'" for *That's the Way of the World*, which held the number-one pop spot for three weeks in spring 1975, was the soundtrack of a Sig Shore-produced movie that featured EWF, and included the gold number one single "Shining Star." The trio also wrote the radio-aired LP track "Imagination" from the double-platinum LP *Spirit*, which also boasted the gold single "Getaway." Stepney then died May 17, 1976, in Chicago, IL, at the age of 43. *—Ed Hogan*

Amii Stewart

b. 1956, Washington, D.C.
Vocals / Disco, Club/Dance
Washington, D.C., vocalist Amii Stewart came whooping and shouting into the spotlight with an amazing though unconventional cover of Eddie Floyd's "Knock on Wood." Her boisterous vocal, coupled with a non-stop arrangement and equally unrestrained backing vocals, topped the pop charts in 1979 and reached number six on the R&B side. Stewart, who was in the Broadway musical *Bubbling Brown Sugar*, did another remake as a follow-up, the Doors' "Light My Fire," backed by "137 Disco Heaven." It dissipated the initial momentum of the lead single, and things went downhill from there. Stewart later moved to Italy and had some singles issued on international labels before trying again in America on RCA in the mid-'80s. Her 1985 single "Friends" for Emergency just missed the R&B Top 40. *—Ron Wynn*

I'm Gonna Get Your Love / 1981 / Handshake ♦♦♦
A slightly altered version of Stewart's European release *Images* (replacing her pop-disco rendition of "Great Balls of Fire" and "Love Is Bad for Your Health" with two funkier, R&B-rooted numbers), *I'm Gonna Get Your Love* largely expands the scope covered on Stewart's first two albums and is a close second to the album that would follow. Particularly engaging are the title track, a bountiful dancefloor number produced by Raymond Reid and William Anderson of Crown Heights Affair; the saucy, spunky "Why'd You Have to Be So Sexy; and the exotic "Premiere." Meanwhile, the remakes of "Where Did Our Love Go" and "My Guy, My Girl"—the latter a duet with Johnny Bristol in which the two singers trade countermelodies from the Mary Wells and Temptations classics—are genuine in intention, but their arrangements aren't very cohesive. Even during these weaker moments, Stewart remains in top vocal form. Her next album, 1983's *Amii Stewart*, would up the ante with more consistent material and production to back up her chops. But with the singer's impressive balance of elegance and intensity and a diverse selection of styles, *I'm Gonna Get Your Love* is certainly worth investigation. *—Justin M. Kantor*

Amii / 1986 / Teldec ♦♦♦♦
While Stewart is primarily recognized in the U.S. for her late-'70s disco remakes of "Knock on Wood" and "Light My Fire," her '80s and '90s output is artistically more viable. This 1986 outing—one-half produced by Giorgio Moroder, the other by the team of Bob Bolland & Ferdi Bolland—is one of the highlights. Stylish tracks such as the funky "Love Ain't No Toy" and the contagious pop number "Lover to Lover" would have fared well within the U.S. market, but the album never made it to these shores. Stewart sounds energetic and fresh throughout, and even if the songs themselves are not always knockouts, they come off stronger than the substandard material which graced some of her earlier efforts, and are better produced. *—Justin M. Kantor*

Magic / 1992 / RTI ♦♦♦

● **The Best of Amii Stewart: Knock on Wood** / Jul. 16, 1996 / Hot Productions ♦♦♦♦
The Best of Amii Stewart: Knock on Wood is a 14-track collection that contains all of the disco singer's hits, as well as several cult favorites, including "Knock on Wood," "You Really Touched My Heart," "Light My Fire/137 Disco Heaven," "Bring It on Back to Me," "Paradise Bird," "Jealousy," "Right Place, Wrong Time" and "Friends." "Knock on Wood" is a strong disco single, but the remainder is hit-and-miss, and is primarily of interest to disco completists. *—Stephen Thomas Erlewine*

Billy Stewart

b. Mar. 24, 1937, Washington, D.C., **d.** Jan. 17, 1970, Neuse River, NC
Vocals, Piano, Drums / Soul, Pop-Soul, R&B, Beach
Pianist and singer Billy Stewart was a distinctive and influential R&B vocalist whose stuttering delivery and word-repetition technique borrowed liberally from the jazz practice of scat singing. Born in Washington, D.C., in 1937, Stewart started singing publicly with his mother's group, the Stewart Gospel Singers, as a teenager. He moved into secular music by filling in occasionally for the Rainbows, a D.C.-area vocal group led by future soul star Don Covay; like fellow Rainbows substitute Marvin Gaye, Stewart never recorded with them. Despite winning a local talent contest with a unique rendition of Gershwin's "Summertime," Stewart was first discovered as a pianist, not a singer—while passing through on a tour, Bo Diddley heard him playing backstage and offered him a job as a backing musician. Thanks to his connection with Diddley, Stewart cut his first solo single, "Billy's Blues," for Chess in 1956. He moved to OKeh in 1957 and recorded "Billy's Heartache" backed by the Marquees, another D.C.-area group featuring Gaye.

Stewart would not return to his solo career until 1962, when he returned to Chess and cut a song called "Fat Boy," a nickname he'd acquired for straightforward reasons. He scored his first charting single on the R&B side with "Reap What You Sow," recorded at the same session, and began to hit his creative stride with the warm "Strange Feeling" in 1963. The following year's "Count Me Out" was only a regional hit, but Stewart broke through in 1965 with two lovely R&B ballad hits, "I Do Love You" (which became the title track of his first album) and "Sitting in the Park." Stewart toured heavily behind those two successes, and also charted the following year with "How Nice It Is" and "Because I Love You." Later in 1966, he returned to the Chess studio to cut an album of jazz and pop standards, *Unbelievable*. Stewart's unique vocal stylings were in full flower, earning him the new nickname "Motormouth," and his revisitation of "Summertime" landed in the Top Ten on both the pop and R&B charts; it still ranks among the more radical reinterpretations of the oft-recorded warhorse. A waxing of Doris Day's "Secret Love" just missed the R&B Top Ten. However, the hits subsequently dried up, and Stewart's weight problem had worsened into diabetes. In 1969, he suffered minor injuries in a motorcycle accident, but the real tragedy struck on January 17, 1970, when the car Stewart was driving went off the road and plunged into the Neuse River in North Carolina, killing Stewart and the three bandmembers riding with him. He was not quite 33. *—Steve Huey*

I Do Love You / 1965 / Chess ♦♦♦♦♦
Billy Stewart's greatest album and song were both contained on this fine recording from the mid-'60s. "I Do Love You" was that rare anguished testimonial that never became vapid, sappy, or overly sentimental, and was compelling and captivating throughout Stewart's marvelous leads and the piercing harmonies. The album also contained other gems like "Fat Boy," "Reap What You Sow," and "Sitting in the Park." Maybe someday this album will be reissued intact, after Stewart's hits have finally been recycled to death. *—Ron Wynn*

Unbelievable / 1966 / Chess ♦♦♦♦♦
The second legitimate Billy Stewart album that wasn't a later rehash or repackaged collection. It was issued in 1966 and contained some magnificent numbers, among them the great "Summertime," "Foggy Day," "Moon River," and "Misty." Chess kept priming the pump after Stewart's tragic death, repeatedly putting these songs onto different anthologies and collections. They were sung with beauty, dignity, and passion, and should be heard in the manner they were released. *—Ron Wynn*

Old Standards, New Tricks / Apr. 1967 / Chess ♦♦♦♦♦
Billy Stewart sang more than pleading, anguished love ballads. He was a good crooner in the classic supper club/cabaret fashion, and that was the focus of this collection of jazz-based pop and pre-rock numbers done by Stewart at various points in the 1960s. The *tour de force* was "Summertime," a stuttering, rumbling improvisation with him stretching out in the middle and concluding with a flourish. This has been out-of-print for quite a while. *—Ron Wynn*

Teaches Old Standards, New Tricks / Aug. 1967 / Chess ♦♦♦
This is merely a rehash of the same material featured on *Old Standards, New Tricks*, but Stewart's singing certainly makes it worthwhile. It's been long gone and probably isn't destined to return. *—Ron Wynn*

Billy Stewart Remembered / 1970 / Chess ♦♦♦♦♦
When Billy Stewart's car plunged into a river in 1970, soul music lost a legendary stylist. He didn't enjoy sustained commercial success, but possessed one of the genre's signature voices. Unfortunately, shortly after his death and ever since, his songs have been repeatedly savaged, recycled, repackaged, and reissued. This was the first of a series of collections, some good, some horrid. This has long since vanished, so it's almost irrelevant, but it was a decent compilation of his material. *—Ron Wynn*

Cross My Heart / 1976 / Chess ♦♦♦
Issued four years after Stewart's fatal automobile accident, this album features the D.C. native's recordings from 1965 to 1970. Highlights are two classics: "Cross My Heart" (1967), and his last great composition, the understated ballad "How Nice It Is" (1965). Nothing else ranks as high, but the lilting "I'm in Love (Oh Yes I Am)," "Why Do I Love You So," "Tell It Like It Is," and "By the Time I Get to Phoenix" are good also-rans. *—Andrew Hamilton*

• **One More Time: The Chess Years** / Oct. 1990 / Chess ♦♦♦♦♦
When you hear Bo Diddley's opening guitar on "Billy Blues," you know you're listening to something special. Billy Stewart ices the cake with a hiccupping, apologetic vocal. That lovely guitar melody was plagiarized and reappeared as "Love Is Strange," a big hit for Mickey & Sylvia. It doesn't get much better than "Strange Feeling," a warm floating song about the joys of new love. "I Do Love You" is a creamily concocted ballad—he sings as if in a trance, playing off excellent backing blends by uncredited male vocalists. Stewart dazzles again on "Sitting in the Park"; the slow ballad speaks of utter rejection, sitting in a park waiting on your chick, and she never shows. The backing is majestic, and pushes Stewart to unthought-of heights, such as "Love Me," where he sounds uncompromisingly happy. If you like cool midtempo ditties then you'll go for "How Nice It Is," an R&B charter. The lovely "I Cross My Heart" is a tearjerker; it sounds like the Dells on backing vocals with Stewart crooning like he was born to hurt, his soulful howl on the fade will make you tingle. Better known to some are his revitalization of pop/MOR standards "Summertime" and "Secret Lover." You get the full unedited dose of the former. He does it his way, performing complete makeovers on both. "Golly Golly Gee" and "I'm in Love (Oh, Yes I Am)" deserve honorable mention for being borderline great. The latter is similar in feel and melody to "I'm Gonna Make You Love Me" by the Supremes & the Temptations. Stewart was one of a kind (Otis Redding's singing style and stage performance was probably influenced by the late, great Billy Stewart). *—Andrew Hamilton*

Hits and Rarities / 1996 / Marginal ♦♦♦♦
Definitely the longest Billy Stewart collection (occasionally) available, *Hits and Rarities* comes from the same Belgian label responsible for nearly a dozen volumes in the solid *Soul Patrol* nuggets series. Even with 26 tracks, though, the set was forced to trade in a few of his more widely known songs ("Strange Feeling," "Reap What You Sow," "Love Me") for some seriously deep-cover obscurities like "Temptation" (the Tin Pan Alley standard), "I'm No Romeo," "A Fat Boy Can Cry," "Fat Boy's Boogaloo," and a groovy popcorn instrumental called "Scramble." Also included are the long version of "Summertime" and a great mono version (with organ) of "Fat Boy." It's very tough to find (as are all the label's quasi-bootleg releases), but well worth picking up by fans who can't get enough from one of the '60s' most distinctive soul singers. *—John Bush*

Jermaine Stewart

b. Chicago, IL, **d.** Mar. 17, 1997
Vocals / Dance-Pop, Club/Dance, Urban, Disco
An Ohio singer/dancer, Jermaine Stewart was on *Soul Train* as a teen during the years it was in Chicago. He later did background vocals for Shalamar, Millie Jackson, Tavares, the Temptations, and Boy George before getting his own deal with Arista in the mid-'80s. He had three Top Ten R&B hits with Arista from 1984-1988, but his biggest hit, "We Don't Have to Take Our Clothes Off," was an R&B dud despite making it to number five on the pop charts. He died in 1997. *—Ron Wynn*

Word Is Out / 1984 / Arista ♦♦♦
Four years before he hit big in America with the chaste smash "We Don't Have to Take Our Clothes Off," ex-Shalamar backing singer Jermaine Stewart debuted with a set of songs that probably should have brought him widespread success sooner. Crisply produced by Peter Collins, and with a bit of songwriting help on "In Love Again" by Culture Club's Mikey Craig (Stewart had added backing vocals to the group's *Colour By Numbers* album the year before), *The Word Is Out* is a winning combination of pop smarts and electro-dance grooves; it was an R&B hit, but also includes several tunes with crossover potential. The title track, with its crunching, big-beat chorus, is one, and the sleek, sexy club cut "I Like It" is another, while the lack of a backbeat is probably all that kept the brilliant piano ballad "Brilliance" from breaking through. Sometimes the nods to the hit parade are a bit too overt: the pumping beat and squealing rock guitar of "Get Over It" crowd Shalamar's "Dancing in the Sheets" a bit, and "Debbie," with its twangy hook, has a definite "Footloose" feel. But Stewart's energy and warmth make it impossible to dislike any of these ten skillful songs, and later fans who missed this early chapter in his development are in for a pleasant surprise on first listening. *—Dan LeRoy*

• **Frantic Romantic** / 1988 / Arista ♦♦♦♦♦

Set Me Free / 1992 / Reprise ♦♦♦

Angie Stone

Vocals, Songwriter, Keyboards / Neo-Soul, Urban, Contemporary R&B
Singer/self-taught keyboardist/prolific songwriter Angie Stone's first claim to fame was being the lead vocalist on Vertical Hold's smooth urban dance track "Seems You're Much Too Busy." The A&M single hit number-17 R&B during summer 1993. Going solo, her debut album *Black Diamond* was issued September 1999 by Arista Records. There's definitely an ol' school and autobiographical vibe throughout the enchanting "keeping it real" release that's exemplified by her hit ballad "No More Rain (In This Cloud)," which has samples from Gladys Knight & the Pips' "Neither One of Us (Wants to Be the First to Say Goodbye)." Stone has collaborated with Mary J. Blige, Jill Jones, D'Angelo, and hit producer Malik Pendleton, among others. Contributing to *Black Diamond* are Lenny Kravitz ("Green Grass Vapors"), former Tribe Called Quest member Ali Shaheed Muhammad ("Bone 2 Pic [Wit U]"), Stone's co-producer Aaron "Freedom" Lyles, Rex Rideout, Phil Temple, Gary Deveaux, DJ U-Neek, and Russell Elevado. The title of the first single, "No More Rain (In This Cloud)," was taken from a rebuffing phrase that her father would use when Stone would sometimes ask him for money: "There's no more rain in this cloud." Stone's ex-boyfriend D'Angelo (who also has a lot of ol' school influences in his hits) guests on "Everyday."

The Columbia, S.C., native began singing gospel music at a young age at First Nazareth Baptist Church. Her father, a member of a local gospel quartet, would take his only child to see performances by gospel artists such as the Singing Angels and the Gospel Keynotes. During her youth, Stone wrote poetry, played sports, and after high school graduation was offered college basketball scholarships. She also performed solitary "mirror concerts" in her bedroom while her recordings of her musical heroes, Aretha Franklin, Donny Hathaway, Smokey Robinson, and Marvin Gaye, played in the background. Later on *Black Diamond*, Stone would do a gender bender cover of Gaye's "Trouble Man," the title track from the soundtrack of the 1972 Robert Hooks/Paul Winfield 20th Century Fox movie—Gaye's sole soundtrack release.

While working dead-end jobs, Stone began saving money to record her own demos at a local studio called PAW. She joined Gwendolyn Chisolm and Cheryl Cook in the rap trio the Sequence who recorded hits for Joe & Sylvia Robinson's (she of "Pillow Talk" fame) Sugarhill Records: "Funk You Up," a remake of Parliament's hit "Tear the Roof Off the Sucker" called "Funky Sound (Tear the Roof Off)," and "I Don't Need Your Love (Part One)." Soon after, Stone was working with futuristic rappers Mantronix and rocker Lenny Kravitz and formed neo-soul trio Vertical Hold, who first charted with the Criminal single "Summertime" (number-82 R&B in summer 1988). Besides "Seems You're Much Too Busy," the group's self-titled A&M album spawned the charting single "ASAP." Standout tracks on *Black Diamond* are "Heaven Help," "Man Loves His Money," "Life Story," and "Visions," which includes a sample from Ramsey Lewis and Earth, Wind & Fire's "Sun Goddess." To the list of super-talented ol' school-flavored female singers with unique feminine perspectives (Erykah Badu, Lauryn Hill), add the name of Angie Stone. *—Ed Hogan*

Black Diamond / Sep. 28, 1999 / Arista ♦♦♦♦
A backup singer, an occasional producer, and once the leader of an all-girl singing group, Angie Stone presents an impressive fusion of classic soul, '80s funk, and '90s hip-hop in her solo debut *Black Diamond*. Purposefully positive, the album chronicles Stone's journeys maintaining personal faith and loving relationships resplendent with new takes on traditional soul sounds. Stone supports her songwriting and vocal talents with help from A-list musicians/writer/producers such as Lenny Kravitz and D'Angelo. The sophisticated mix is elevated by Stone's incredible voice. With a continuous easy groove, she never resorts to cheap vocal acrobatics to showcase her gifts. With nods to Roberta Flack and Chaka Khan and stylistic similarities with Lauryn Hill, Stone sings of the possibilities of love and life's challenges with "Life Story" and the beautiful standout single "No More Rain." When Stone reaches for a funkier, dirtier groove, the result is riveting. "Love Junkie" and "Man Loves His Money" are as sexy as any Prince song with interesting guitar solos and funky basslines. And even when she's calling out dishonest lovers everywhere on "Bone 2 Pic" and "Just a Pimp," she makes it sound like the offenders should be ashamed for dissing such a sexy woman. Stone's sensual soul is a refreshing and much-needed alternative to silicone-coated R&B and cartoonish rap, and should satisfy fans of soul, R&B, rap, rock, and any other genre. *—Theresa E. LaVeck*

• **Mahogany Soul** / Oct. 16, 2001 / J-Records ♦♦♦♦
Accomplished neo-soul queen Angie Stone's second solo outing, *Mahogany Soul*, delivers more of the organic, gritty, rootsy yet sophisticated soul which put her on the map as

a solo artist. The production is great and the songs are funky, mature, and intelligent, but when she truly shines is when she actually spreads her wings and glides away from her neo-soul trappings, which she manages effortlessly. The album's true gem is the smoldering, gorgeous, aching "Wish I Didn't Miss You," which pulls forward with an unstoppable beat and features a stellar, yearning performance from Miss Stone. Other highlights include the mesmerizing first single (produced by Raphael Saadiq), "Brotha," which draws the listener in with its atypical, almost hypnotizing beat. "Snowflakes" is a lighter-than-air, breezy winner, and her duet with Musiq Soulchild, "The Ingredients of Love," is silky, funky, and sweet. The album tends to wane toward the second half, with just a little too much emphasis on the neo-soul recipe, but nonetheless remains engaging with other winners like "20 Dollars," the sweet and easy "Life Goes On," and the organ-enhanced "Time of the Month" popping up to maintain the listener's interest. Despite a few lulls, *Mahogany Soul* stands as one of the best R&B albums of 2001 and keeps the listener anxiously waiting to see what Angie Stone will do next. *—Jose F. Promis*

Jesse Stone (Charles E. Calhoun)

b. Nov. 16, 1901, Atchison, KS, **d.** Apr. 1, 1999, Altamonte Springs, FL
Piano, Songwriter / R&B, Rock & Roll
Songwriter Jesse Stone wrote the classic rock songs "Shake Rattle and Roll," "Don't Let Go," "Flip Flop and Fly"—co-written with Lou Willie Turner—and "Your Cash Ain't Nothing but Trash." Stone, who also wrote songs under the pseudonym Charles E. Calhoun, was a key player in the development of R&B, rock & roll, and such pioneering Atlantic Records artists as Ray Charles, Ruth Brown, Big Joe Turner ("Flip Flop and Fly," number-two R&B), the Drifters, and the Clovers ("Your Cash Ain't Nothing but Trash").

Born in Atchinson, KS, November 16, 1901, Stone was the leader of a jazz band during the 1920s that included saxophonist Coleman Hawkins. Around 1936, jazz legend Duke Ellington assisted Stone in getting a booking at New York City's Cotton Club. Later, Stone became a staff arranger/composer/comedy writer at the city's Apollo Theater. Stone joined Atlantic Records as a staff producer/songwriter/arranger in the late '40s. During that decade, Stone's original song "Idaho" was covered by Guy Lombardo and sold three-million copies. Trailblazing rock & roll band Bill Haley & His Comets recorded Stone's "Shake Rattle and Roll" and the single sold a million copies. Epic Records star Roy Hamilton covered Stone's "Don't Let Go," taking it to number-two R&B in early 1958. "Don't Let Go" was also covered by Isaac Hayes, whose dazzling disco string- and horn-laced version on Polydor Records hit number-11 R&B in fall 1979. *—Ed Hogan*

- **Jesse Stone Alias Charles "Chuck" Calhoun** / 1996 / Bear Family ✦✦✦✦

The Street People

Group / Pop-Soul, Disco, Bubblegum
A New Jersey group produced by Ray Dahrouge; their first single surfaced in 1974 on Spring Records; but "I Wanna Get Over" never ignited and Ray switched them to Vigor Records for five singles and an album issued from 1974 to 1977. The Street People were Roy Daniels, Milton Daniels, Tom Williams, Joe Gardner, and Rick Johnson. The clubs were the aim of their first Vigor single "Never Get Enough of Your Love"; it was followed by "You're My One Weakness Girl" in 1976. A third single "I Wanna Spend My Whole Life With You," flopped. The fourth single proved the charm "I Wanna Slow Dance With You Baby," is Street People's most memorable recording, though its success was only regional. A final single "Liberated Lady" b/w "Rerun From An Old Time Movie," did nothing and they disbanded. Their sole album Street People, contains all the Vigor singles. Joe Gardner sung with the Valtairs prior to Street People with Harry Ray (Moments, Ray, Goodman & Brown). *—Andrew Hamilton*

Street People / 1976 / Vigor ✦✦✦

- **Greatest Hits** / Mar. 3, 1994 / Unidisc ✦✦✦

The title of this CD is misleading—these are the same songs that comprised the Street People's first and only album on Vigor Records, and Unidisc did not uncover any unreleased gems in Vigor's vaults. "Greatest Hits" is a dubious term, since the Street People didn't have any hits, the closest being "I Wanna Slow Dance With You Baby," a regional charter that received some exposure along the East Coast. Casual fans west of Philadelphia have probably never heard of the Street People; Ray Dahrouge's productions are too pop for R&B radio stations, and the uninspired Sesame Street-sounding vocal arrangements will have you craving bubble gum—"Don't Leave Me Hanging (When You Hang Up)" exemplifies this. Yet there's a charming element to these songs that makes them palatable. *—Andrew Hamilton*

Strikers

f. New York, NY
Group / Club/Dance, Disco, Funk
This New York group had some disco/club hits in the early '80s for Prelude. Drummer Milton Brown, bassist Willie Slaughter, keyboardist Howie Young, guitarist Robert Gilliom, saxophonist Darryl Gibbs, and lead vocalist Ruben Faison had their first success with "Body Music" in 1981. It reached the R&B Top 30. The follow-up, "Inch by Inch," flopped, but the Strikers' single "Contagious," in 1982, was another club winner. Brown eventually became Warp 9's lead singer. *—Ron Wynn*

The Strikers / 1978 / Sequel ✦✦✦✦

Body Music / Sep. 1982 / Prelude ✦✦✦

- **Greatest Hits** / Jun. 5, 1992 / Unidisc ✦✦✦✦✦

Sylvia Striplin

Vocals / Urban, Funk
Vocalist Sylvia Striplin joined Aquarian Dream for the jazz-funk/disco group's second album and stayed with them through their early-'80s breakup. Shortly after that, she became associated with Roy Ayers and his Uno Melodic label; not only was she part of the short-lived Eighties Ladies project guided by Ayers (which released a lone album, *Ladies of the '80s*, on Uno Melodic in 1980), but she also released some solo material with significant help from the jazz-funk legend. An excellent single with "Give Me Your Love" as the A-side and "You Can't Turn Me Away" was released by 1980 on Uno Melodic. A follow-up album was released roughly a year after the single. Though Striplin never attained mainstream success, her sweet voice is instantly recognized by devout fans of jazzy R&B and those who made up England's "rare groove" scene of the early '90s. *—Andy Kellman*

- **Give Me Your Love** / 1980 / Charly ✦✦✦✦

Sylvia Striplin's biggest year was 1980. Fresh from her brief but crucial role in Norman Connors' Aquarian Dream, another essential figure in the jazz-funk phenomenon, Roy Ayers, provided multiple outlets for the sweet-voiced singer. In the same year that saw Striplin release an album with Ayers' Eighties Ladies' project, she also broke out with a solo album. Both of these albums were issued on Ayers' Uno Melodic label, and while they didn't reach full-blown crossover status on the R&B charts, they have long since become rare groove favorites. Ayers produced and arranged this affair, but Striplin truly is the star; her voice is neither booming nor wailing, maintaining a youthful but powerful sweetness throughout eight songs that stick to sophisticated R&B constructs. Not a single track is weak, but a few stand out: the slinky, oft-sampled "You Can't Turn Me Away" (thanks in large part to the odd squelching effects) shows Striplin at her most sultry; "Give Me Your Love" is an irresistible uptempo number full of drive and punch; and the low-key and feather-light "All Alone" benefits from subtle string arrangements. Whether you're an Ayers fan or an early-'80s R&B nut, you can't afford to overlook this album. *—Andy Kellman*

Barrett Strong

b. Feb. 5, 1941, Westpoint, MS
Vocals, Songwriter / Motown, R&B, Soul
A pivotal figure in Motown's formative years, singer/composer Barrett Strong was a key associate and friend of Berry Gordy. It was his hit "Money (That's What I Want)" for Anna Records in 1960 that provided vital capital for Gordy to expand his operation. The song gave Strong his only major hit as a vocalist, reaching number two on the R&B charts and barely missing the pop Top 20. During the late '60s and early '70s, Strong collaborated with Norman Whitfield on some historic songs that included Marvin Gaye's "I Heard It Through the Grapevine" and "Too Busy Thinking About My Baby," the Temptations' "Papa Was a Rolling Stone" and "Ball of Confusion," Edwin Starr's "War," and "Take Me in Your Arms and Love Me" for Gladys Knight & the Pips, which he also co-wrote. Strong left Motown when the label moved to Los Angeles in 1972, and he signed with Epic.

After one failed single, Strong moved to Capitol, where he had the LP *Stronghold* released in 1975 and later *Live & Love* in 1976. Though it wasn't a hit, his song "Man Up in the Sky" was a '70s soul gem. Johnny Bristol later re-recorded it. Strong continued into the '80s, recording "Rock It Easy" for an independent label and writing and arranging "You Can Depend on Me," which was included on the Dells' *The Second Time* LP in 1988. *—Ron Wynn*

Stronghold / 1975 / Capitol ✦

- **Live & Love** / 1976 / Capitol ✦✦✦

This is light-years ahead of his Capitol debut, the amateurish, weak *Stronghold*; *Live & Love* has better songs, arrangements, and instrumentation. He adequately revives his only hit "Money (That's What I Want)" and Eddie Floyd's "Knock on Wood." The excellent "Man Up in the Sky" had hit potential, a moving number with a spiritual theme; Johnny Bristol's version of this Barrett Strong/Billy Always composition achieved some popularity in Europe, and most people associate the song with Bristol. A good effort, but people expected more from the co-writer of classics the stature of "Ball of Confusion," "War," "Friendship Train," "Too Busy Thinking About My Baby," and others. *—Andrew Hamilton*

Nolan Strong & the Diablos

b. Jan. 22, 1934, Scottsboro, AL, **d.** Feb. 21, 1977, Detroit, MI
Vocals / R&B, Detroit Blues
The Diablos with their 1954 classic "The Wind" are revered among R&B and doo wop lovers. The group had a unique sound, centered around the high ethereal lead tenor voice of Nolan Strong. Besides "The Wind," the Diablos were known for many songs, such as "Adios My Desert Love," "Can't We Talk This Over," "Mambo of Love," "If I," "Harriet," "I Am With You," "Goodbye Matilda," "I Wanna Know," "Beside You," "Mind Over Matter," and many more.

The group formed in Detroit around 1950 and originally consisted of Strong (lead tenor), Juan Guieterriez (tenor), Willie Hunter (baritone), Quentin Eubanks (bass), and Bob "Chico" Edwards (guitar). The Diablos name is said to have come from a book, *El Nino Diablo* (The Little Devil), that Strong was reading for a high school book report. In 1954, the Diablos went in to Detroit's Fortune Record Studios to cut some demo sides, with the hopes of furthering their career. Their hopes were realized even more quickly than they expected. Those demos obviously impressed Jack and Devora Brown, owners of Fortune, who immediately signed the group to record for their label. Their first recording for Fortune was the Devora Brown-penned "Adios My Desert Love," a cha cha-flavored tune. But it was their second Fortune outing which would establish the group among the R&B legends. Written by the group members, "The Wind" had a haunting sound, with the group chanting "blow wind" in harmony behind Strong's delicate tenor lead, and smooth and sexy talking bridge. Following the release of "The Wind," Guieterriez and Eubanks left the group, to be replaced by Nolan's brother Jimmy on tenor and George Scott on bass. Over the next two years this configuration of Diablos would turn out several records, including "Route 16," "Do You Remember What You Did," "Daddy Rockin' Strong," "The Way You Dog Me Around," "You Are," and "A Teardrop From Heaven."

By late 1956, more changes were in store for the Diablos. Scott decided to leave the group about this time to join Hank Ballard & the Midnighters—and again the Diablos were in need of a bass. Enter Jay Johnson, who was introduced to Strong through fellow Fortune artist Andre Williams. Although not quite 17 at the time, Johnson was already a veteran singer, having sung bass with Williams' "new" group on "Bacon Fat," "Just Because of a Kiss," "Mean Jean," and "Bobby Jean." (Williams' "new" group consisted of Gino Parks, Bobby Calhoun, Steve Gaston, and Johnson.)

Strong was impressed and the Diablos had their new bassman. Johnson's first session with the Diablos was on "Can't We Talk It Over" and "Mambo of Love," recorded in late 1956 and released in 1957. By the time the first *Fortune of Hits* album came out, Johnson had already replaced Scott with the group. Unfortunately, the picture on the album cover didn't reflect this change, and shows the group with Scott instead of Johnson. This oversight may be a factor in many believing that Johnson didn't join the group until several years later. In fact, Johnson is heard on bass on more Diablos recordings than either Eubanks or Scott. Among these are: "Beside You," "Mind Over Matter," "Everything They Said Came True," "Welcome Baby to My Heart," "I Wanna Know," "If I Could Be With You," "Since You're Gone," "Harriet," "Harriette It's You," "I Am With You," "Are You Making a Fool Out of Me," "You're My Happiness," "Village of Love," "For Old Times Sake," "My Heart Will Always Belong to You," and "Come Home Little Girl." On "Village of Love," Johnson also provided the bass on the original Fortune version by Nathaniel Mayer & the Fabulous Twilights.

Also in late 1956, about the time Johnson joined the group, Strong received a call from Uncle Sam and was soon off to the service for a two-year stint. While Nolan was in the service, the Diablos released one single without him, "Harriet," backed with "Come Home Little Girl," featuring Hunter on lead. Without Strong, the Diablos' magic seemed to be missing and the record received little fanfare. After Strong returned from the service, the group recorded "Harriette It's You." But when Nolan came back from the service, things weren't quite the same. Fortune was focusing more of their attention on Strong, and not the Diablos group. In 1954, records showed "The Diablos Featuring Nolan Strong." Then billing changed to "Nolan Strong & the Diablos," and by 1962, when "Mind Over Matter" was climbing the charts, the label just read "Nolan Strong," although the Diablos were on the record, as prominent as ever. This lack of recognition along with financial inequities (lack of royalties and unequal pay to the group members versus Strong), inevitably lead to the group's demise.

Just as Strong had been influenced by Clyde McPhatter, he in turn would be influential to Smokey Robinson. And Robinson was not the only one at Motown to have an appreciation for Nolan Strong & the Diablos. Berry Gordy had wanted to bring the Diablos into his fast-growing Motown complex. Gordy reportedly offered Jack and Devora Brown 5,000 dollars for the Diablos contract, but the Browns countered with 15,000 dollars and the deal never transpired. Later, Gordy would cover the Diablos' "Mind Over Matter" on his Mel-O-Dy label with a group called the Pirates (aka the Temptations).

But where one story ends, another begins. As the Diablos were dissolving, the Velvet Angels were forming. The group would include Diablos alumni Johnson and Hunter along with Calhoun (baritone) and Cy Iverson (tenor). Iverson had gone to high school with Johnson, and Calhoun had recorded with Johnson as part of Williams' "new" group on Fortune. Tired of being devils (diablos is Spanish for devils), they decided angels would be a better name. Velvet was added to describe their smooth and velvety harmonies, calling to mind groups like the Mills Brothers and Ink Spots. The Velvet Angels performed at clubs around Detroit and across the border in Canada, while perfecting their material. They then traveled to New Jersey in search of greater opportunity. Soon after setting up residence in Jersey City, they found an ad for a talent show in the local paper. As luck would have it, they performed at show and won! Frank Sheldon, the show sponsor and owner of the Tender Trap club in Fairview, N.J., was looking for this type of group. The Velvet Angels were talented and versatile doing a mix of R&B, pop, gospel, and soul music, and doing them all a cappella. Things were starting to happen for the Velvet Angels; they were hired to do commercials for Lionel Trains, but unfortunately their manager became ill and that deal fell apart.

And right about here is where the Velvet Angels' story gets very interesting and also somewhat confusing. Nolan had remained on good terms with Hunter and Johnson and had talked about reuniting with them. In 1963, Strong came to New Jersey and spent some time with the group, rehearsing and appearing with them at the Tender Trap. Some of these rehearsal sessions at their hotel (the Madison Hotel in Jersey City, N.J.) were recorded on a basic home tape recorder. A young man named Angelo Pompeo made the acquaintance of some of the group members and eventually purchased some of the rehearsal tapes. Johnson was not there at the time of the "deal," nor aware of it until after the fact. The tapes soon found their way to Eddie Gries, who would issue some of the tunes as singles on his Medieval label.

And so in 1964 "I'm in Love" b/w "Let Me Come Back" was issued as Medieval 201. Both sides highlighted the bass work of Johnson, with a bass lead on "Let Me Come Back," and an incredible driving bass on "I'm in Love" (also released as Co-Op 201). Interestingly, the Medieval record credits "Strong" as the writer while the Co-Op version credits "Calhoun-Hunter-Johnson-Iverson." The singles were well received at the time by a subculture of doo wop collectors that had developed in the metropolitan New York City area, but garnered little notice elsewhere. And yes, Strong is heard on these tapes but mostly as a background singer, although he did lead vocal on "Fools Rush In." More Velvet Angels material was released later through Gries on the Relic *Best of Acapella* series, as well as his *Acappella Showcase Presents the Velvet Angels* LP, also on Relic. The picture of the Velvet Angels that appears on the Relic Velvet Angels album incorrectly identifies Johnson (third from left) as Strong.

In 1964, the group disbanded. Calhoun indicates he went south and did some work with Stax Records. Iverson and Hunter returned to Detroit. Johnson stayed on for a time in New Jersey, continuing to perform solo at the Tender Trap, but also found his way back to Detroit. Upon his return, he joined Detroit's Five Monarchs, but did not record with them. In the late '60s Johnson formed the soul group the Four Sonics, releasing two singles in 1968 on Detroit's Sport label. The group recorded through the mid-'70s. In 2002, Johnson was still an exciting stage performer, and has performed recently with Nathaniel Mayer, reprising his "Village of Love" work. Jimmy Strong passed away January 29, 1970, at age 34. His brother Nolan would join him on February 21, 1977, at age 43. Hunter, Edwards, and Eubanks are also deceased. *—Jim Dunn & Nikki Gustafson*

● **Fortune of Hits, Vol. 1** / 1961 / Fortune ✦✦✦✦✦
Nolan Strong's high-tenor voice was a huge influence on many Detroit singers, most notably Smokey Robinson. *Fortune of Hits, Vol. 1* collects some of the legendary singles Strong recorded with the Diablos during the '50s. A doo wop classic, "The Wind" is probably the best-known of these; with a truly unique and haunted sound, its chief strength lies in the vocal interplay of Strong and the rest of the group, who counter his shimmering lead with a harmony chorus of "blow wind." Other highlights include the blues-based "The Way You Dog Me Around" and another ballad, "A Teardrop From Heaven." All of their songs share a quality of discovery and should be sought out by anyone interested in soul and R&B. *—Wade Kergan*

Fortune of Hits, Vol. 2 / 1962 / Fortune ✦✦✦✦✦
This is the companion piece to *Fortune of Hits—Vol. 1*. *—Cub Koda*

Daddy Rock / 1963 / Fortune ✦✦✦
It's a great batch of rare and unreleased sides. *—Cub Koda*

Mind over Matter / 1963 / Fortune ✦✦✦

Stuff

Group / Urban, Funk
Under the leadership of bassist Gordon Edwards, several of the most prolific studio players around teamed together to form an all-star rhythm section that on a part-time basis operated as an independent group. Back around 1967, Edwards put together the Encyclopedia of Soul and during the next decade, the group (which just played together on an occasional basis) evolved into Stuff. Such musicians as drummer Billy Cobham and Jimmy Johnson and altoist David Sanborn passed through the group. By the time of its initial recording in 1975, the lineup was set: Richard Tee on organ, electric piano, and acoustic pianos, both Eric Gale and Cornell Dupree on guitars, bassist Edwards, and drummer Steve Gadd; Christopher Parker was occasionally with the group on second drums and percussion. Although the band, which consisted of masterful accompanists, often sounded like a "music minus one" ensemble (as if they were waiting for the main soloist to show up), Stuff was quite popular for a few years, recording four albums for Warner Bros. and having occasional reunions in the '80s. *—Scott Yanow*

Stuff / 1976 / Just Sunshine ✦✦✦
Stuff never won the respect of bop snobs, but that isn't what they were going for. The band's specialty was an accessible, groove-oriented blend of jazz, R&B, and pop, and not everyone who bought their records was a jazz expert. Though some of Stuff's fans knew a lot about jazz, others were Average White Band or Chaka Khan fans who bought the occasional Grover Washington Jr. album. Stuff's LPs weren't amazing, but they were generally likable. That is the case with this self-titled debut album, which was produced by Herb Lovelle and Tommy LiPuma and earned the band a loyal following in 1976. While congenial tunes like "Reflections of Divine Love" and "Foots" aren't breathtaking, they're pleasant and easy to like. Guitarist Eric Gale, drummer Steve Gadd, and other Stuff members were capable of a lot more. Nonetheless, the band's recording career was off to a decent, if unremarkable, start with this 1976 LP. *—Alex Henderson*

More Stuff / 1977 / Warner Bros. ✦✦✦
Stuff's sophomore album *More Stuff* was quite similar to its first LP. Once again, the band offered a pleasant and good-natured, if unremarkable, blend of jazz, R&B, and pop. Many jazz critics gave this record negative reviews, attacking it for being commercial and groove-oriented. But Stuff never claimed to be Art Blakey & the Jazz Messengers and tunes like Eric Gale's "Honey Coral Rock" and Cornell Dupree's "Subway" weren't meant to be straight-ahead bop. Stuff wanted to attract R&B and pop fans as well as jazz fans, and its members would have been happy to learn that someone who was into Marvin Gaye and Tyrone Davis also appreciated *More Stuff*. The fact that Stuff produced this LP with Charlie Kipps and the late Van McCoy says a lot; McCoy enjoyed one of disco's definitive smashes with 1975's "The Hustle," and he was also the guy who wrote Gladys Knight & the Pips' 1964 hit "Giving Up." So there was no way that an album McCoy coproduced was going to be a serious bop record. *More Stuff* isn't a masterpiece, although it's a decent LP that fared well in the crossover/NAC market. *—Alex Henderson*

Live Stuff / 1978 / Warner Bros. ✦✦✦

Stuff It / 1978 / Warner Bros. ✦✦✦✦
The fact that there is a dozen people credited for backing vocals on this album, but no one for lead, says a lot. There is actually only one song, "Talkin' About My Love for You," with solo vocals, and the rest are instrumental, sometimes with vocal choruses. This could give a feeling of a karaoke record, but getting used to it one will find the tracks with backing vocals the album's strongest; for example, the introductory "Mighty Love," with the groove slowly building up to an irresistible frenzy. And the extremely skilled ensemble manages to do this trick even when conditions seem really bad, like in "Dance With Me," starting out with lazy synth strings, a bossa rhythm, and quiet backing vocals. When listeners dance to the funky beat at the end of the song, they are likely to have forgotten what it sounded like in the beginning. And Stuff is obviously not about writing durable songs, but doing party music with a highly competent band, and this time including a whole lot of gospel in the jazz-funk. The only time Stuff is disappointing is when they don't raise the tempo. "Rainbows" and "Gordon's Theme" may be important for the balance of the album, but are actually a bit boring, though the latter has some comic ingredients. But that is followed up by the magnificent "Talkin' About My Love for You." And it has been said before, but this *will* make everyone dance. *—Lars Lovén*

Live in Japan / 1979 / Warner Bros. ✦✦

Live from New York / 1980 / Warner Bros. ✦✦✦
After releasing their last studio album in 1978, Stuff released three live albums in only two years. Wisely enough, they concentrated on up- and midtempo songs for this, the last one—wisely, because in their slick instrumental ballads, Stuff was often dangerously close to playing background music (they actually never ran totally clear of that risk). But on the whole, the instrumental funk found on this album has more in common with the first studio album than with later gospel- and soul-influenced releases. There are no horns, for example, which is unlucky because the horns did do a lot to lift the music on *Stuff It*, and the same can be said about the lack of vocals. There is more percussion than before though, as skilfully played as can be expected, and overall the band proves to be just as tight live as in the studio, and even more groovy. This may have been the band's last album ever, but the music is still intensely happy, though in the case of Stuff, that is more of a generic statement than a statement about mode. Happiest is the live version of "The Real McCoy," actually happy enough to position itself on an imaginary Stuff Top Five list, but the energetic medley "Love the Stuff—Ain't No Mountain High Enough" isn't far behind. *—Lars Lovén*

● **The Right Stuff** / Jul. 9, 1996 / Warner Bros. ✦✦✦✦✦
The Right Stuff takes some of the high points of this jazz-funk supergroup's all-too-brief career and compiles them into one tidy little package. Sharp musicianship, crisp production, and creative songwriting make up for some of the off-key moments of vocal delivery, but the band really gets rocking with their 11-minute disco-tinged workout of Stevie Wonder's classic "Signed, Sealed, Delivered (I'm Yours)." Most of their records have been out of print for quite some time, so unless you are a daring collector this compilation is definitely the way to go. *—Rob Theakston*

The Stylistics

f. 1968, Philadelphia, PA, **db.** 1980
Group / Smooth Soul, Quiet Storm, Philly Soul, Soul
After the Spinners and the O'Jays, the Stylistics were the leading Philly soul group produced by Thom Bell. During the early '70s, the band had 12 straight Top Ten hits, including "You Are Everything," "Betcha by Golly, Wow," "I'm Stone in Love With You," "Break Up to Make Up," and "You Make Me Feel Brand New." Of all their peers, the Stylistics were one of the smoothest and sweetest soul groups of their era. All of their hits were ballads, graced by the soaring falsetto of Russell Thompkins Jr. and the lush yet graceful productions of Bell, which helped make the Stylistics one of the most successful soul groups of the first half of the '70s.

The Stylistics formed in 1968, when members of the Philadelphia soul groups the Monarchs and the Percussions joined forces after their respective band dissolved. Thompkins, James Smith, and Airrion Love hailed from the Monarchs; James Dunn and Herbie Murrell were from the Percussions. In 1970, the group recorded "You're a Big Girl Now," a song their road manager Marty Bryant co-wrote with Robert Douglas, a member of their backing band Slim & the Boys, and the single became a regional hit for Sebring Records. The larger Avco Records soon signed the Stylistics, and single eventually climbed to number seven in early 1971. Once they were on Avco, the Stylistics began working with producer/songwriter Thom Bell, who had previously worked with the Delfonics. The Stylistics became Bell's pet project and with lyricist Linda Creed, he crafted a series of hit singles that relied as much on the intricately arranged and lush production as they did on Thompkins' falsetto. Every single that Bell produced for the Stylistics was a Top Ten R&B hit, and several—"You Are Everything," "Betcha By Golly, Wow," "I'm Stone in Love With You," "Break Up to Make Up," and "You Make Me Feel Brand New"—were also Top Ten pop hits.

Following "You Make Me Feel Brand New" in the spring of 1974, the Stylistics broke away from Bell and began working with Van McCoy, who helped move the group towards a softer, easy listening style. In 1976, they left Avco and signed with H&L. The group's American record sales declined, yet they remained popular in Europe, particularly in Great Britain, where "Sing Baby Sing" (1975), "Na Na Is the Saddest Word" (1975), "Can't Give You Anything" (1975), and "Can't Help Falling in Love" (1976) were all Top Five hits. The Stylistics continued to tour and record throughout the latter half of the '70s, as their popularity steadily declined. In 1980, Dunn left the group because of poor health, and he was followed later that year by Smith. The remaining Stylistics continue performing as a trio on oldies shows. *—Stephen Thomas Erlewine*

The Stylistics / 1971 / Amherst ✦✦✦
The brilliant album that got everything started. Heads turned, people snapped to attention (women especially), and the "sweet" soul fraternity was turned on its head when this five-member group featuring the sugary, sweeping falsetto of Russell Thompkins Jr. hit the scene with such singles as "Betcha By Golly Wow," "People Make the World Go Round," and "Stop, Look and Listen to Your Heart." His delivery, shimmering style, and brilliant pacing and control temporarily rendered almost every other "sweet" soul vocalist and group speechless; pretty soon, the Delfonics, Blue Magic, Moments, and others would fight back, but in 1972, everyone was playing catchup to The Stylistics. *—Ron Wynn*

Round 2 / 1972 / Amherst ✦✦✦✦✦
This was the Stylistics' sophomore album and it spawned three *Billboard* R&B Top Ten singles: "I'm Stone in Love With You," "Break Up to Make Up," and "You'll Never Get to Heaven (If You Break My Heart)." The first two even cracked the Top Ten on the pop charts. Furthermore, there is much here to savor. The vocal quintet's version of the Carole King classic "It's Too Late" never soars or dips—it just soothes in spite of the fateful lyric. "Children of the Night" imparts a similar mood but with a different lyrical content. The two selections "Peek-A-Boo" and "You're As Right As Rain" are Stylistics originals. First tenor Russell Thompkins Jr., who leads on all the aforementioned songs, seems to effortlessly reach each note and hold it as long as necessary. Although only the first three hit the charts, all of the songs referenced are radio favorites. As superb as the group was vocally, the production work of Thom Bell is commendable as well. *—Craig Lytle*

Rockin' Roll Baby / 1973 / Amherst ✦✦✦✦
The last of the Stylistics' Thom Bell productions is just as essential as the first two. This one is slightly harder to find as it has not been reissued in the States. It has been reissued by a United Kingdom company however, and can be purchased via online music stores. The title cut is possibly the fastest record the sweet Philly crooners ever recorded. The late Linda Creed's lyrics fit the speedy rhythm track like custom gloves and lead singer Russell Thompkins enunciates every word clearly, making a lyric sheet unnecessary. Kenny Gamble collaborates with Bell on "Payback Is a Dog," a what-goes-around-comes-around song performed in the Stylistics' classic style. Normally writers for the Spinners, Bruce Hawes, Chester Simmons, and Joe Jefferson contributes the questioning "Could This Be the End," a ballad that Thompkins precise falsetto works to perfection. Everybody knows "You Make Feel Brand New," Airrion Love begins the stately love song, and Thompkins takes it home shining brightly, hitting the notes with the precision of a diamond cutter. With Thompkins it's all about technique, on the Bell sides he was always restrained, just once you wanted him to cut loose and let that falsetto go hog wild. Overall, not as compelling as the first two Bell productions, but a far cry better then anything that came after it. *—Andrew Hamilton*

Greatest Love Hits / 1974 / Amherst ✦✦✦✦✦
Another anthology, this one covering the beautiful love songs and romantic ballads that were the Stylistics' specialty. These are all magnificent, some of the finest sentimental soul that's ever been recorded. But it's also been issued before, and Amherst's mastering isn't anything to write home about, especially the way they tend to wash out Russell Thompkins Jr.'s high notes. *—Ron Wynn*

Let's Put It All Together / 1974 / Avco Embassy ✦✦✦
Their finest album, The Stylistics climbed the "sweet" soul mountain in 1974. "You Make Me Feel Brand New" and the title cut were among the year's prime love/romance numbers, and Russell Thompkins Jr. had nudged past Blue Magic's Ted Mills and the Delfonics' Hart brothers as the falsetto voice of choice among female fans. Their run on Avco, with Thom Bell at the production helm, was one of the greatest in modern soul annals. *—Ron Wynn*

Heavy / 1974 / Avco Embassy ✦✦✦
The magical union between the Stylistics and producer/writer Thom Bell ended with this album, but the legacy had included a string of fabulous hit singles and arguably the greatest "sweet" soul productions of all time. Russell Thompkins Jr. was in his prime as a lead vocalist, and while this album didn't have any blockbusters like its predecessors, it still had plenty of exquisitely sung, nicely harmonized ballads and love tunes. *—Ron Wynn*

The Best of the Stylistics / 1975 / Amherst ✦✦✦✦✦
Any of their collections are good, but this one features their biggest and best hits, including "I'm Stone in Love with You," "Rockin' Roll Baby," "Betcha by Golly Wow," and "You Make Me Feel Brand New." *—Cub Koda*

Thank You Baby / 1975 / Avco Embassy ✦✦✦
The group's decline began with this album, their next to last on Avco and their weakest to that point. Thom Bell's departure hastened the slump, for such songs as "Can't Give You Anything (But My Love)" and "Thank You Baby" lacked the lyrical insight, flow, and rhyme scheme that characterized their past triumphs. Russell Thompkins Jr., didn't seem as focused or effective, and the backing was feeble, as were the arrangements. *—Ron Wynn*

You Are Beautiful / 1975 / Avco Embassy ✦✦
The Stylistics' slump continued as they concluded the Avco years with this 1975 album. It was clear from the content of "Day the Clown Came to Town" and "Na-Na Is the Saddest Word" how much they missed Thom Bell. Russell Thompkins Jr., was merely competent, and sometimes sounded dispirited, as did the remaining members behind him. The production, arrangements, and compositions ranged from routine to banal, and the entire affair was a sorry way for a great group to leave a label after several wonderful years. *—Ron Wynn*

In Fashion / 1978 / Mercury ✦✦
The Stylistics' late-'70s slump continued with this album. The uptempo tunes were completely flat, while the ballads often had a good lead vocal from Russell Thompkins Jr., and solid harmonizing behind him, but were sabotaged by third-rate lyrics or even worse production and arrangements. *—Ron Wynn*

Wonder Woman / 1978 / H&L ✦✦
The Stylistics' tenure on Mercury wasn't memorable. They couldn't find the right songs and couldn't get their albums or singles in the right hands, or aired on radio. This album actually had some nice tracks; the title cut was fine, and "First Impressions" made the charts. But the overall product was limp, and the group didn't remain with Mercury very long. *—Ron Wynn*

Love Spell / 1979 / Mercury ✦✦
The Stylistics showed signs of life with this late-'70s effort. Their vocals were once more vigorous and assertive, while Russell Thompkins Jr. reached back and began singing with the soaring force and might that had characterized their best songs. They still didn't have top-flight, or even good material, and the production and arrangements were again dreary. But at least the group didn't sound ready to call it a career. *—Ron Wynn*

Hurry up This Way Again / 1980 / Philadelphia International ✦✦✦
The Stylistics' last album to hit the pop charts, this eased them into the 1980s on somewhat solid ground. While the "sweet" sound was no longer a force in black music, they had regrouped with a deal on TSOP, and the title cut garnered them one final Top 20 R&B hit. It was the end of an era, as delicately sung, innocently written pop and "sweet" soul would soon be relegated to the graveyard of nostalgia. *—Ron Wynn*

Closer Than Close / 1981 / Philadelphia International ♦♦♦
A nice, though slightly disappointing album that saw The Stylistics fail to regain the chart momentum they had enjoyed in the 1970s, despite getting superior production and decent songs from the Gamble & Huff team. "Sweet" soul had pretty much run its course by the early '80s, and urban contemporary radio hadn't yet stratified to the degree where the group could have been marketed to no-rap outlets. But the vocals were above-average, and Russell Thompkins Jr. had emerged from his late-'70s funk and was again singing with flair, expressiveness, and conviction. *—Ron Wynn*

1982 / 1982 / Philadelphia International ♦♦♦
The Stylistics didn't always get hits when they were with Gamble & Huff, but their albums sure sounded great. That was the case with *1982*. But the superb production and mastering aside, this was the least interesting, off-centered album the group did while at TSOP. There wasn't one song that charted, nor were there any that deserved to be hits, which was almost shocking considering the parties involved. *—Ron Wynn*

Some Things Never Change / 1985 / Streetwise ♦♦♦
After a three year hiatus from recording, the Stylistics return with keyboardist/songwriter Raymond Johnson as a new member and a marginal effort as far as the material is concerned. The title track was the first release. While the song is privileged to have Russell Thompkins Jr. and Airrion Love express its lyric, the song offers both very little in return. The same goes for the follow-up single "Give a Little Love." Respectively, both peaked at 47 and 86 on the *Billboard* R&B charts. It appears that the producers, brothers Maurice Starr and Michael Jonzun of New Edition fame, tried to re-kindle the sound that made the Stylistics popular during the early '70s. However, the songs lack the articulate penmanship and buoyant production. *—Craig Lytle*

Love Talk / 1991 / Amherst ♦♦♦
Although they were at least 14 years past their creative and commercial peak when the small, Buffalo-based Amherst label released *Love Talk* in 1990, the Stylistics proved that they could still be enjoyable on this decent release. The CD isn't in a class with their remarkable work with Thom Bell & Linda Creed in the mid-'70s, but it isn't anything to be ashamed of either. "I Don't Need This" finds the group embracing new jack swing (and even doing some rapping!) with surprisingly unpretentious results, but for the most part, the Philadelphians don't go out of their way to appeal to 1990's urban contemporary market. Silky offerings like "I Just Don't Know What to Do," "Me—U equals Blue" and a cover of the Willie Nelson hit "Always on My Mind" aren't all that different from the type of sweet soul they were embracing 17 years earlier. Russell Thompkins' falsetto had held up well over the years, and he could still be quite charismatic. But the little-known CD was pretty much ignored by urban radio, and in fact, many die-hard Stylistics fans didn't even know that it existed. *—Alex Henderson*

Love Is Back in Style / Jul. 29, 1996 / Marathon ♦♦♦
A few tracks into this and you'll think you're listening to a reunion of the Stylistics and Thom Bell. With few exceptions, the interest of some Stylistics fans waned after their trio of Bell-produced albums. This one, however, surrounds the group with elegance and first-class Philly songs and arrangements. Russell Thompkins' effortless falsetto never sounded better, and the same is true for Herb Murrell, and Airrion Love, whose deeper register takes "Love Can Heal a Wounded Heart" to lofty heights. As much as Herb Murrell preaches against rap at live concerts, they include one here by Biggy Smallz on the remix version of "She's All That." There are too many keepers among the 12 tracks to single out favorites, but if you enjoyed the early Stylistics, you'll love this well-crafted and well-executed gem. *—Andrew Hamilton*

● **The Best of the Stylistics** / Dec. 28, 1999 / Spectrum ♦♦♦♦♦
Here are 18 of the Stylistics' creamiest recordings featuring a good helping of Thom Bell productions and ample portions of Hugo & Luigi's efforts. The different styles are quite evident: Bell has Russell Thompkins' soaring falsetto under complete control while Hugo & Luigi allow him to fly off the handle every once in a while. The H & L tunes didn't set the states on fire, but "Star on a TV Show," "Funky Weekend," and "Can't Give You Anything but Love" exploded in Europe. "You're a Big Girl Now," produced by Marty Bryant, shows yet another side of the talented Philly group and contrasts with Bell's stately productions, such as "You Make Me Feel Brand New," "You'll Never Get to Heaven," "You Are Everything," "Betcha By Golly Wow," and "Stone in Love With You." *—Andrew Hamilton*

The Sugarman 3

f. 1997
Group / Deep Funk Revival, Soul-Jazz
New York City retro-funk combo the Sugarman 3 was formed by saxophonist Neal Sugarman in the spring of 1996 following his return from New Orleans, where he backed artists including Eddie Henderson and Mike Longo. Teaming with organist Adam Scone (a onetime protégé of Ben Dixon) and longtime Brother Jack McDuff drummer Rudy Albin, the trio—inspired by the vintage jazz-funk sounds of the 1960s—quickly emerged as a club favorite, and with guitarist Coleman Mellett, the Sugarman 3 recorded their 1998 Desco label debut *Sugar's Boogaloo*. A single, "Cherry Pickin'," preceded the release of the combo's second album, *Soul Donkey*. *Sweet Spot*, a compilation of the previous two albums, appeared in spring 2001. That fall the band met with former Desco Records owner Gabriel Roth and producer Bosco Mann to form Daptone Records, label that would reflect their interests and act as a platform for Sugarman 3 albums. The first of these projects appeared in the summer of 2002, when Sugarman 3's *Pure Cane Sugar* arrived in stores. *—Jason Ankeny*

● **Sugar's Boogaloo** / 1998 / Desco ♦♦♦♦
The Sugarman 3's debut album, *Sugar's Boogaloo*, is a slice of vintage Blue Note-style soul-jazz, with alto saxophonist Lou Donaldson being perhaps the most obvious touchstone. The music is primarily driven by groove and rhythm, with Neal Sugarman's melodic, R&B-based saxophone providing most of the leads. Sugarman's playing stays solidly within the groove, so jazz fans looking for improvisational fireworks will probably not find *Sugar's Boogaloo* as interesting as the artists who influenced it. But fans of earthy, greasy jazz-funk and rare groove will delight in the fact that this music is being revived—and in such danceable, soulful fashion. *—Steve Huey*

Pure Cane Sugar / 2002 / Daptone ♦♦♦♦
Picking up where their 7-inch singles left off, Sugarman 3 provides 11 memorable, booty-shaking moments on this 2002 release. Although Sugarman 3 has received many Jon Spencer comparisons from indie rock circles, *Pure Cane Sugar* is a slick and soulful slab of raw R&B that carries little of the screaming and noise of Spencer's outfit. Instead, they harness the sharp timing of funk and produce intensely groovy instrumentals with the occasional guest vocalist making an appearance. The best use of a singer is "Take It As It Comes," a James Brown-style number that uses a tight horn part to drive the song along while Sugarman 3 jams away in all their funky glory. Other highlights include the midtempo groove of "Pure Cane," the Motown-esque "Modern Jive," and the saxophone extravaganza "Country Girl." The key to Sugarman 3's magic is the tension they manage to pull out of these songs, making each glorious breakdown seem like a genuine release. Soulful, swaggering, and fun, *Pure Cane Sugar* is a fantastic modern funk release that journeys into the complicated rhythms and basslines of the genre's heyday and comes back ready to dance. *—Bradley Torreano*

Donna Summer

b. Dec. 31, 1948, Boston, MA
Vocals / Disco, Club/Dance, Urban
Donna Summer's title as the "Queen of Disco" wasn't mere hype—she was one of the very few disco performers to enjoy a measure of career longevity, and her consistent chart success was rivaled in the disco world only by the Bee Gees. Summer was certainly a talented vocalist, trained as a powerful gospel belter, but then again, so were many of her contemporaries. Of major importance in setting Summer apart were her songwriting abilities and her choice of talented collaborators in producers/songwriters Giorgio Moroder and Pete Bellotte, which resulted in a steady supply of high-quality (and, often, high-concept) material. But what was more, few vocalists could match the sultry, unfettered eroticism Summer brought to many of her best recordings, which seemed to embody the spirit of the disco era perfectly. The total package made Summer the ultimate disco diva, one of the few whose star power was even bigger than the music.

Donna Summer was born LaDonna Andre Gaines on December 31, 1948, and grew up in Boston's Mission Hill section. Part of a religious family, she first sang in her church's gospel choir, and as a teenager performed with a rock group called the Crow. After high school, she moved to New York to sing and act in stage productions, and soon landed a role in a German production of *Hair*. She moved to Europe around 1968-1969, and spent a year in the German cast, after which she became part of the *Hair* company in Vienna. She joined the Viennese Folk Opera, and later returned to Germany, where she settled in Munich and met and married Helmut Sommer, adopting an Anglicized version of his last name. Summer performed in various stage musicals and worked as a studio vocalist in Munich, recording demos and background vocals. Her first solo recording was 1971's "Sally Go 'Round the Roses," but success would not come until 1974, when she met producers/songwriters Giorgio Moroder and Pete Bellotte while working on a Three Dog Night record. The three teamed up for the single "The Hostage," which became a hit around western Europe, and Summer released her first album, *Lady of the Night*, in Europe only. In 1975, the trio recorded "Love to Love You Baby," a discofied re-imagining of Serge Gainsbourg and Jane Birkin's lush, heavy-breathing opus "Je T'aime... Moi Non Plus." Powered by Summer's graphic moans, "Love to Love You Baby" became a massive hit in Europe, and drew the attention of Casablanca Records, which put the track out in America. It climbed to number two on the singles charts, and became a dance-club sensation when Moroder remixed the track into a 17-minute, side-long epic on the LP of the same name.

In the wake of "Love to Love You Baby," albums (as opposed to just singles) became an important forum for Summer and her producers. The 1976 follow-up *Love Trilogy* contained another side-long suite in "Try Me (I Know We Can Make It Work)," and demonstrated Moroder and Bellotte's growing sophistication as arrangers with its lush, sweeping strings. *Four Seasons of Love*, released later in the year, was a concept album with one track dedicated to each season, and 1977's *I Remember Yesterday* featured a variety of genre exercises. Despite the album's title, it produced the most forward-looking single in Summer and Moroder's catalog, the monumental "I Feel Love." Eschewing the strings and typical disco excess, "I Feel Love" was the first major pop hit recorded with an entirely synthesized backing track; its lean, sleek arrangement and driving, hypnotic pulse laid the groundwork not only for countless Euro-dance imitators, but also for the techno revolution of the '80s and '90s. It became Summer's second Top Ten hit in the U.S., and she followed it with *Once Upon a Time*, another concept album retelling the story of Cinderella for the disco era.

Summer's albums were selling well, bolstered by her popularity in the dance clubs, and she was poised to become a major pop hitmaker as well. Her acting turn in the 1978 disco-themed comedy *Thank God It's Friday* produced another hit in "Last Dance," which won her a Grammy for Best Female R&B Vocal (as well as an Oscar for songwriter Paul Jabara). Doubtlessly benefiting from the added exposure, the double-LP set *Live and More* became Summer's first number-one album later that year. It featured one side of new studio material, including a disco cover of the psychedelic pop epic "MacArthur Park" that became her first number-one pop single early the next year. Her 1979 double-LP *Bad Girls* featured more of her songwriting contributions than ever, and went straight to number one, as did the lusty singles "Bad Girls" and the rock-oriented "Hot Stuff," which made Summer the first female artist ever to score three number-one singles in the same calendar year. Her greatest-hits package *On the Radio* also topped the charts, the first time any artist had ever hit number one with three consecutive double-LPs; the newly recorded title track became another hit, and Summer's duet with Barbra Streisand, "No More Tears (Enough Is Enough)," became her fourth number-one single.

At the peak of her success, Summer decided to leave Casablanca, and became the first artist signed to the new Geffen label. Sensing that the disco era was coming to a close, Summer attempted to modify her style to include more R&B and pop/rock on her first Geffen album, 1980's *The Wanderer*, the album and its title track were both hits. Not wanting to alienate her core audience, Summer returned to pure dance music on an attempted follow-up; however, Geffen deemed *I'm a Rainbow* not worthy of release (it was finally issued in 1996). Instead, Summer ended her collaboration with Moroder and Bellotte and teamed up with Quincy Jones for 1982's *Donna Summer*. "Love Is in Control (Finger on the Trigger)" was a significant hit, but none of its follow-ups did very well. With producer Michael Omartian, Summer moved back into post-disco dance music and urban R&B with 1983's *She Works Hard for the Money*; its title track was a smash and became a feminist anthem of sorts. However, with her career momentum slowing, it also marked the end of Summer's prime. Despite winning a gospel Grammy for "Forgive Me," Summer's 1984 follow-up *Cats Without Claws* flopped, as did the 1987 comeback effort *All Systems Go*. Hiring the British production team of Stock, Aitken & Waterman, Summer scored her last major success with the 1989 Top Ten single "This Time I Know It's for Real," from the album *Another Place & Time*; around the same time, she began denouncing her earlier, "sinful" disco material. The lackluster, urban-styled *Mistaken Identity* (1991) effectively killed her career momentum, and none of her new '90s albums produced that elusive hit. However, she did make some noise on the dance charts with "Melody of Love," from the excellent 1994 retrospective *Endless Summer*, and reunited with Moroder for the 1997 non-LP single "Carry On," which won the inaugural Grammy for Best Dance Recording. Summer subsequently signed a deal with Sony, which primed her for re-establishment with the 1999 greatest-hits live album *VH-1 Presents: Live and More Encore!*; it featured the new song "I Will Go With You (Con Te Partiro)," which had some success on the dance charts. *—Steve Huey*

Lady of the Night / 1974 / Basart ✦✦✦

Love to Love You Baby / Sep. 1975 / Casablanca ✦✦✦✦✦
"Love to Love You Baby"'s 16:50 of arousal and refill—ticklishly sensitive rhythm and fusion—threw disco into a tizzy overnight, but the tonally starved blues-of-isolation on the B-side isn't to be missed, either: the broken promises Summer bemoans in "Full of Emptiness"; "Need-A-Man Blues," with its unrequitedly sexy guitar rhythm as out of range of Summer's voice as she of satisfaction; the imaginary seaside hold-me in "Whispering Waves"; and "Pandora's Box," where Summer and guitar scream icily at one another as they turn their backs on each other's body music. Hunger without recourse; essential disco. *—Michael Freedberg*

Love Trilogy / Mar. 1976 / Casablanca ✦✦✦
Summer's quizzical "Try Me," "I Know," and "We Can Make It" wings her nervous little falsetto from risk to dare and from dare to mad hope, and her rhythm section gropes from testy touch beats to tightrope-walkers' guitar figures and safety-net harmonies. The second side substitutes dance with imaginary lovers for the debut album's love starvation blues. Don't dismiss its subtle mood poems the way fans of "Love to Love You" sped right past the B-side of Summer's debut; the flightier Summer plays a rhythm, the dicier her resolution. *—Michael Freedberg*

Four Seasons of Love / Oct. 1976 / Casablanca ✦✦✦
One's inclined to resist this package of self-conscious stardom concepts—the LP sports its own 1977 calendar featuring La Summer dressed up as winter, spring, summer, and Marilyn Monroe vamping on the subway grating (fall, I guess), and the four "seasonal" dancey suites promise more and say less than Summer's intimate touch-me's deliver without any hype. Fortunately the music has a mind of its own. The rhythms push and go poof as delicately as ever, the horn section mutes and jazzes the melody, the beats stop, run, and stop again when ever they damn please, and Summer falsettoes in private rapture as she smooches oohs and ahs onto the mix like lipstick traces. Oh, rapture.*—Michael Freedberg*

I Remember Yesterday / May 1977 / Casablanca ✦✦✦
Donna Summer continued her climb to superstardom with this late-'70s album, her first since the attention-grabbing *Love To Love You Baby* album in 1975 to crack the pop Top 20. The single "I Feel Love" was her second Top Ten R&B and pop hit, and paved the way for Summer to emerge shortly after as disco's reigning queen. *—Ron Wynn*

Once Upon a Time / Nov. 1977 / Casablanca ✦✦✦
Summer and her liberators have created one audience and redefined another, and this record's four sides of dreamworlds without end sometimes manipulate each audience. The candy-girl music of "Fairy Tale High," "Queen for a Day," and "If You Got It, Flaunt It" explicitly recognizes her newly created gay audience, a daring acknowledgement coming from a mainstream pop star. As for her redefined audience of naive young things who live in the suburbs and dream of romance, adventure and sex while they search for identity, Summer works her music into a true-to-life Cinderella story staged as four acts of impatient pulse, delirious space noise, wish-upon-a-star voice monologues, and motion. *—Michael Freedberg*

Live and More / Sep. 1978 / Casablanca ✦✦✦
After becoming the queen of disco thanks to orgasmathon hits like "Love to Love You Baby" and "I Feel Love," Donna Summer topped off her five-year rise to fame with this live set. Certainly not a contender for first-disc choice, *Live and More* still works quite well as a '70s sampler for the converted. And since disco was the party music par excellence, the album's feel is one of a all-nighter in action. Featuring her signature hits and a fat chunk of disco tracks from the *Once Upon a Time* record, sides one and three solidify Summer's reputation as one of the most exciting and slick singers on-stage. Balancing out the requisite dance material, Summer spends side two waxing nostalgic via a pop standards medley ("The Man I Love," "I Got It Bad and That Ain't Good," "Some of These Days") and some nice jazz and blues-imbued fare of her own. And ending the album on a very high note, Summer indulges in "McArthur Park Suite," a classic long-player that bookends two of Summer and producer Giorgio Moroder's pop disco numbers with a dance-friendly take on Jimmy Webb's monumental classic. Along with cloud-walking bouncers like "I Love You" and "Last Dance," this closing piece finds Summer at her sophisticated and tuneful best. There's nothing here to eclipse the original versions of these cuts—save for the Webb cover, which is new—but the Summer faithful will nonetheless want to pick up this very enjoyable concert recording. *—Stephen Cook*

Bad Girls / May 1979 / Casablanca ✦✦✦✦✦
Summer defined "feminine" for an age in love with femininity and made the disco experience an adventure, even for those who had trouble learning how to fantasize. Now, on her third two-record set in two years, she has altered her outlook on femininity and changed her mind about the adventure. The disco queen becomes a streetwalker ready to sell her voice to any guy (read: producer) for a dime ("Bad Girls," "Hot Stuff") or anyone at all blindly searching for a lover they'll never find ("Sunset People"). *—Michael Freedberg*

Walk Away: The Best of Donna Summer (1977–1980) / 1980 / Casablanca ✦✦✦✦✦
A collection of later Donna Summer material, including such song as "Winter Melody," "I Feel Love," and "Bad Girls." Although disco was beginning to peak, Summer was riding high, dominating the R&B and pop charts. In some ways, these songs were more varied than her pre-1977 cuts, because only "Love to Love You Baby," from her Oasis material, was a major hit. *—Ron Wynn*

The Wanderer / Oct. 1980 / Geffen ✦✦✦✦✦
This first post-Casablanca set has a hard-rock edge that shines best on the title cut, "Cold Love," and "Night Life." *—Bil Carpenter*

Donna Summer / Jul. 1982 / Geffen ✦✦✦
The follow-up to Donna Summer's first big Geffen album did reasonably well and proved to be the lull before the storm. "State of Independence" just missed being a hit, and "Woman In Me" cracked the pop and R&B Top 40, although it wasn't a smash. But the album mostly reaffirmed that Summer was back in stride and hadn't merely scored a fluke with her previous release. *—Ron Wynn*

She Works Hard for the Money / Jun. 1983 / Casablanca ✦✦✦✦✦
Summer's brassy, matter-of-fact mezzo does not play the sexy sanctified diva, and her musicians' crisp loud beats don't evoke rapture or delirium. Instead, she and her rhythm men live up to the title of "She Works Hard for the Money." Here's praise for a waitress's 12-hour workday that sums up Summer's own post-dance queen job status as well as disco fans' own spotlighted lives and maintains the pressure from the steel-and-synth riffs of "Stop, Look & Listen" to the impatient tenderness of "People, People." No one writes about love with as mesmeric a sense of wonder as Summer confesses in "Love Has a Mind of Its Own," "Unconditional Love," and "I Do Believe (I Fell in Love)." *—Michael Freedberg*

Cats Without Claws / 1984 / Warner Bros. ✦✦

All Systems Go / 1987 / Geffen ✦✦

Mistaken Identity / 1991 / Atlantic ✦✦✦
Teamed with Keith Diamond, Summer returned in 1991 to aggressive dance music of her late-'70s records on "Work That Magic," "Be My Fred Astaire," and "What Is It You Want?" Also included is the acoustic ballad "Heaven Is Just a Whisper Away" and the pop anthem "Let There Be Peace." *—Bil Carpenter*

The Donna Summer Anthology / Sep. 21, 1993 / Casablanca ✦✦✦✦✦
Donna Summer's two-CD *Anthology* is by far the most exhaustive compilation available on the disco diva. This two-CD set includes most of Summer's hits, from her earliest "Love to Love You Baby" to her '90s dance single "Carry On." The music flows from early to classic disco and '80s pop, rock, R&B, and adult contemporary. Also included are two tracks ("I'm a Rainbow" and "Don't Cry for Me Argentina") from her 1981 album *I'm a Rainbow*, which wasn't released until 1996. However, a couple of sore points keep this collection from having a perfect rating. First, some of the edits are a little awkward. One only wishes that the longer, five-minute edit of "Love to Love You Baby" were included as opposed to the severely truncated version found here. The promo single version of "MacArthur Park" is included, and "Heaven Knows" suffers from an early fade-out. Then there are the omissions—"The Woman in Me," "Walk Away," "Winter Melody," "Who Do You Think You're Foolin'," "Dinner With Gershwin," and "Love's About to Change My Heart" are nowhere to be found. All of this only highlights the fact that an ultra-exhaustive, three-CD box set on this star would be a welcome addition. But, for now, with so many other hit collections on the market, this clearly stands as the best, and also stands as a testament to a time gone by. As an added bonus, the liner notes and photographs are nothing short of excellent. Finally, the versions of "Hot Stuff" and "Bad Girls" included here are the 12-inch mixes. *—Jose F. Promis*

★ **Endless Summer** / 1995 / Casablanca ✦✦✦✦✦
With '70s and disco nostalgia taking the U.S. by storm in the early to mid-'90s, it wasn't surprising that Mercury/PolyGram saw Donna Summer's recordings as a way to make a quick dollar. What is surprising is that the label came out with this single-disc best-of collection only a year after releasing the two-CD set *The Donna Summer Anthology* in 1993. Why was another greatest-hits package needed? Though not definitive, this CD does contain many of Summer's essential material. From the erotic club diva of "Love to Love You Baby," "Could It Be Magic," and "I Feel Love" to the Vegas-like pop star of "On the Radio," "Last Dance," and "Dim All the Lights," the Queen of Disco is as charismatic as she is cutting-edge. And Summer still sounds incredibly fresh on 1989's infectious "This Time I Know It's for Real" and 1994's previously unreleased "Melody of Love." It would have been preferable to hear many of these songs in their

extended versions (as opposed to the shorter ones provided here), but then, a label can only fit so much on a single disc. Although *The Donna Summer Anthology* is more comprehensive, *Endless Summer* can work well as a shorter introduction to her innovations. *—Alex Henderson*

Greatest Hits / Sep. 15, 1998 / Mercury ✦✦✦✦✦
There are Donna Summer collections available for any level of fan. For hardcore fans, there's the double-disc set, *The Donna Summer Anthology.* For casual fans wanting a solid collection that digs a little deeper than a basic hits compilation, there's the very fine *Endless Summer: The Very Best of Donna Summer.* Then there's *Greatest Hits,* a bare-bones collection that contains her 12 biggest hits, from "Love to Love You Baby" to "She Works Hard for the Money," all presented in their single edits. Only listeners who want just the singles will want *Greatest Hits,* since the other compilations provide a better, more thorough overview, but they will be quite pleased with the end result. *—Stephen Thomas Erlewine*

VH-1 Presents: Live & More Encore! / Jun. 22, 1999 / Epic ✦✦✦
Though Donna Summer is one of the most talented vocalists of the past 25 years, this VH-1 concert is not one of her most musically adventurous efforts. Blending past hits ("On the Radio," "She Works Hard for the Money") with standards like "MacArthur Park," the album is meant to provide a graceful re-introduction of Summer who inked a deal with Sony shortly before this album's recording. So much has changed since her late-'70s heyday that on *VH-1 Presents* you can feel Summer gathering up stalwart fans, digging her heels in and getting prepared to fight her way back into the fickle pop consciousness. But if any disco diva has the power to make a comeback, it's Summer and her ballsy voice. *—Steven Kurutz*

Sun

f. Dayton, OH
Group / Funk, Disco
Another of the many Dayton funk bands that emerged in the '70s, Sun didn't enjoy as much success as their counterparts. Vocalist Nikki Buzz, guitarist Randy Fredrix, bassist Clyde Isom, and drummer Timmy Hollans recorded prolifically for Capitol from 1976 to 1984, but just couldn't score a major hit. The closest they came was "Sun Is Here," which made it to number 18 on the R&B charts in 1978. They made one last try with *Air City* in 1984, but it flopped. *—Ron Wynn*

• **Live On, Dream On** / 1976 / Capitol ✦✦✦✦
From Cleveland to Dayton to Cincinnati, Ohio had an abundance of horn powered funk bands in the 1970s. If Philadelphia and Detroit were best known for sophisticated Northern soul, Ohio's major cities were famous for hardcore funksters like the Ohio Players, Bootsy's Rubber Band, the Dazz Band (originally Kinsman Dazz), Slave, and Lakeside. Dayton was the home of Sun, a funk combo that showed a lot of promise in the beginning but didn't get nearly as far as it should have commercially. Sun's output was inconsistent—some of its material was excellent, much of it was merely competent. But the band's recording career got off to a fairly promising start with 1976's *Live On, Dream On,* which boasted the sweaty funk gem "Wanna Make Love." Unfortunately, many of the people who bought the single passed on this good-to-excellent LP, and that was a mistake because a lot of the other material is almost as strong. While "Wanna Make Love" is lusty and carnal, a more spiritual, Earth, Wind & Fire-ish outlook defines funk items like "They're Calling for More," "Tell the People," and the title song. Meanwhile, Sun's romantic side successfully asserts itself on the haunting ballad "My Woman." *Live On, Dream On* (which Capitol re-released as *Wanna Make Love* several months later) falls short of perfect, but for the most part, it is among Sun's stronger, more memorable albums. *—Alex Henderson*

Sun Power / 1977 / Capitol ✦✦✦
In the 1980s, R&B was all about downsizing—instead of hiring a lot of musicians for a session, one producer could do everything himself/herself with synthesizers and drum machines. But when Sun recorded its second album, *Sun Power,* in 1977, "the more, the merrier" was the attitude of many R&B acts. So it wasn't surprising that the Dayton funk band Sun added three new members for this LP: Gary King, Ernie Knisley, and Bruce Hastell. With that new ten-man lineup, Sun got away from the spiritual, Earth, Wind & Fire-ish vibe that characterized much of its first album, *Live on, Dream On,* and emphasized escapist party music. The tune that Sun was best known for, "Wanna Make Love," was carnal in nature, and that fact obviously wasn't lost on the Midwestern funksters when they wrote "Organ Grinder," "Boogie Bopper," and "Light Me Up" (all of which deal with matters of the flesh) for this LP. Sun was hoping for another hit, but unfortunately, *Sun Power* didn't contain any major singles. None of the funk jams were big hits, nor was the jazzy quiet storm ballad "Time Is Passing." *Sun Power* (which Capitol released on yellow vinyl) falls short of remarkable, but it's a solid, enjoyable effort that should have done better. *—Alex Henderson*

Sunburn / 1978 / Capitol ✦✦✦
Sun's third album, *Sunburn,* found the Ohio funk band going through some major personnel changes. Six guys (Bruce Hastell and original members Dean Hummons, Chris Jones, Hollis Melson, Shawn Sandridge, and John Wagner) left after 1977's *Sun Power,* and five new members (Robert Arnold, Nigel Boulton, Sonnie Talbert, Keith Cheatham, and Curtis Hooks) came on board. Gary King and Ernie Knisley (both of whom joined Sun with *Sun Power*) remained, as did original members Byron Byrd and Kym Yancey. So by its third album, the group only had two of its original members. But creatively, that isn't a problem on *Sunburn,* which is one of the band's more consistent and memorable records. Most of the material is rewarding, and that includes gritty funk jams like "You're the One," "Sun of a Gun," and "Sun Is Here" (a number-18 R&B hit) as well as the sentimental, Temptations-like slow jam "When You Put Your Hand in Mine" and the smooth Northern soul ballad "I Had a Choice." When a band loses six of its members in one fell swoop, there is cause for concern—if you had been either Sun's manager or a Capitol A&R person in the late 1970s, imagine how you would felt upon learning that over half of its members were leaving and being replaced. But as it turned out, they weathered that storm nicely on *Sun Power,* one of their best releases. *—Alex Henderson*

Destination: Sun / 1979 / Capitol ✦✦✦
Sun had high hopes for its fourth album, *Destination: Sun,* which came out in 1979. The Dayton funksters had enjoyed two hits—"Wanna Make Love" in 1976 and "Sun Is Here" in 1978—but they had yet to come out with a blockbuster album that would go double or triple platinum and give them supergroup status. Unfortunately for Sun, *Destination: Sun* wasn't that album. The infectious funk single "Radiation Level" wasn't the hit it should have been, and the LP didn't receive very much attention. But while *Destination: Sun* isn't a masterpiece (except for "Radiation Level"), it's a generally enjoyable record. Catchy funk items like "Deep Rooted Feeling (Stand Up)" and "Pure Fire" didn't make Sun as big as the Commodores or the Bar-Kays; nor did the soul ballad "Baby, I Confess" or the perky, Earth, Wind & Fire-ish "Hallelujah Spirit" (which is somewhat similar to EWF's "Sing a Song"). But they're still decent. The weakest tune on the LP is "I Want to Be With You (Forever)," a pop/R&B ballad that tries to emulate the Commodores' "Three Times the Lady" and ends up being much too mushy for its own good. Nonetheless, *Destination: Sun* has more plusses than minuses, and it's a shame that the record didn't enjoy more attention. *—Alex Henderson*

Sun Over the Universe / 1980 / Capitol ✦✦✦

Force of Nature / 1981 / Capitol ✦✦✦
Sun was definitely a revolving door in the late '70s and early '80s. By the time the band provided its third album, *Sunburn,* in 1978, Kym Yancey and head honcho Byron Byrd were the only remaining original members. And when Sun recorded its sixth album, *Force of Nature,* in 1981, only Byrd remained from its original lineup. Yancey left after 1980's *Sun Over the Universe,* and this LP marked the arrival of two newcomers: bassist Don Taylor and rhythm guitarist Anthony Thompson. Despite all those personnel changes, Sun always managed to sound like Sun—something it can thank Byrd and Beau Ray Fleming for. Together, Byrd and Fleming (who wasn't an actual member) produced all of Sun's Capitol LPs, which is why the Sun of 1981 was recognizable as Sun even though it had only one original member left. But *Force of Nature* is a departure from Sun's previous albums in one sense: Byrd handles all of the writing himself this time, and the material he gives his band to work with is competent but not mindblowing. "This Is What You Wanted," "Jamming in Brazil," and "Reaction Satisfaction (Jam Ya'll: Funk It Up)" aren't funk masterpieces—they aren't in a class with early-'80s treasures like Rick James' "Ghetto Life," Cameo's "Shake Your Pants," or the Gap Band's "Burn Rubber on Me," but they're still fairly catchy (if predictable and not terribly imaginative). Similarly, "It Seems So Hard" is a pleasant soul-pop ballad even though no one would mistake it for a Gamble & Huff treasure. *Force of Nature* isn't for casual listeners, but the band's small following found that it had more plusses than minuses. *—Alex Henderson*

Let There Be Sun / 1982 / Capitol ✦✦

• **Greatest Hits** / Jun. 30, 1998 / Capitol ✦✦✦✦
If you're a Sun fan or just a plain old stomp-down '70s funk freak, at under ten dollars via online shops, this 17-track greatest-hits package is a bargain; if you're not, a buck will seem excessive. The Dayton, OH-based, band-patented groove gets a little tired after so many tracks; the occasional ballad breaks the monotony and keeps your interest from dissipating, but this is dancing, not listening, music. *—Andrew Hamilton*

Sunbear

Group / Funk, Soul
Singer/drummer Arnie Oliver, aka Ahaguna G. Sun, and singer/guitarist Werner "Bear" Schuchner comprised Sunbear, a little-known soul/funk vocal duo that recorded in Los Angeles in 1977. Earth, Wind & Fire was a heavy influence on Sunbear, and there were also hints of Tower of Power and El Chicano in their sound. In 1977, Sunbear recorded its self-titled debut album for Don Cornelius and Dick Griffey's Soul Train Records, which evolved into Solar Records after Cornelius' departure in 1978. Sunbear broke up without ever recording a second album, and Oliver and Schuchner both went on to pursue other activities in the R&B world. Oliver became a member of Frankie Beverly's Maze, while Schuchner played guitar on albums by the Whispers, the Soul Train Gang, High Inergy, and others. In 1980, the Whispers recorded Sunbear's ballad "Fantasy" for their hit album *Imagination.* *—Alex Henderson*

• **Sunbear** / 1977 / Soul Train ✦✦✦
From 1975-1978, Dick Griffey and *Soul Train* host Don Cornelius co-led Soul Train Records, which evolved into Griffey's Solar Records after Cornelius' departure in 1978 and proved to be one of the hottest R&B labels of the late '70s and early- to mid-'80s. When Griffey and Cornelius were still working together and Soul Train Records had yet to become Solar Records, the company went through a trial and error process. Soul Train Records had some hits—including Shalamar's "Uptown Festival" in 1977 and the Whispers' "Living Together (In Sin)" in 1976—but it wasn't the Motown-like powerhouse that Solar would be. The company was still finding its way in 1977, when it released Sunbear's self-titled debut album. Commercially, this LP was a major disappointment, and that's regrettable because it's a generally decent, if less than spectacular, soul/funk outing. Sunbear had a likable sound, and the band's appreciation of Earth, Wind & Fire and Tower of Power (among others) comes through on funk items like "Don't Overlook the Feelings" and "I Heard the Voice of Music Say." The best thing on the album, however, isn't a funk smoker—it's the dreamy soul ballad "Fantasy," which shouldn't be confused with the Earth, Wind & Fire favorite. Had Sunbear's "Fantasy" been released as a single, perhaps it would have been a hit. In 1980, the song reached a much larger audience when the

Whispers recorded it on *Imagination*, one of their strongest and most successful albums. And by that time, Sunbear was history. This LP, which Sunbear produced with Griffey and Cornelius, went out of print when Soul Train Records evolved into Solar in 1978. *—Alex Henderson*

Sunday's Child

f. Los Angeles, CA

Group / CCM, Soul

A talented teenage group that formed in Los Angeles, CA, the members were Ilene Anderson, Mary Lou Anderson, and the incredible Renee "Ren" Woods. The sky was the limit for this promising group which began as the Soul Five, inspired by the Jackson 5. Two members dropped and the remaining members switched to Sunday's Child. Sammy Davis Jr. took them under his wing and was partly responsible for securing them a deal with Reprise Records, where they recorded their only album, *Sunday's Child* in 1970. None of the singles from the LP hit, and the album itself, despite being spirited and heartfelt, went virtually unnoticed, and Sunday's Child disbanded without fanfare. Their most memorable gig was an appearance with Sammy Davis Jr. at Carnegie Hall in New York, NY. Woods became a successful and prolific character and sometimes a featured actress in movies and television and also on live stage. *—Andrew Hamilton*

● **Sunday's Child** / 1970 / Reprise ✦✦✦✦

Reprise Records let this fantastic album by three Southern California teenagers—16-year-old Ilene Anderson, 14-year-old Mary Lou Anderson, and 13-year-old Renee "Ren" Woods—gather dust in warehouses. The teens give every selection a rich gospel flavor, excelling on a medley comprised of "I Found a Love," "Yes I'm Ready," "You're Good for Me," and "Wichita Lineman." They show reverence but no fear in tackling "My Song," popularized by Aretha Franklin, the Bee Gees' "To Love Somebody," and Paul McCartney's "Maybe I'm Amazed." This is an item that Reprise should reissue on CD pronto; as it is, if you can't find a copy at a garage sale or resale store, you're out of luck. Dynamo lead singer Ren Woods later recorded solo on many labels including Elektra and CBS/ARC, and she has enjoyed a long acting career in television and movies. *—Andrew Hamilton*

The Sunlovers

Group / Soul

An obscure Los Angeles-based group that recorded five singles on three labels. The members were Huey Bell Jr., Louise Bell, John Gibson, and Lawrence Ivey. They debuted June 1967 with "My Poor Heart" on Mutt & Jeff Records, which started taking off in Southern/Northern California and surrounding States. The label leased it to Breakthrough Records a month later and released another Sunlovers' single with the same catalog number entitled "You'll Never Make the Grade" with the same flip, "This Love of Ours," a sweet ballad. "My Poor Heart" was more mellow than the uptempo "You'll Never Make . . . ," an uptempo dancer. Neither became more than a local/regional success, nor did a third Mutt & Jeff single "I'll Treat You Right." "Main Street" on Revue Records in 1969 appears to be their final release. Foreign and domestic labels are quite aware of the Sunlovers and you'll find their few tracks on many compilation albums via labels like Goldmine/Soul Supply, Presto Bar, Dynamite, etc. *—Andrew Hamilton*

The Supremes

f. 1961, Detroit, MI, **db.** 1977

Group / Motown, Soul, Pop-Soul, Girl Group, Uptown Soul

The most successful black performers of the 1960s, the Supremes for a time rivaled even the Beatles in terms of red-hot commercial appeal, reeling off five number-one singles in a row at one point. Critical revisionism has tended to undervalue the Supremes' accomplishments, categorizing their work as more lightweight than the best soul stars' (or even the best Motown stars'), and viewing them as a tool for Berry Gordy's crossover aspirations. There's no question that there was about as much pop as soul in the Supremes' hits, that even some of their biggest hits could sound formulaic, and that they were probably the black performers who were most successful at infiltrating the tastes and televisions of middle America. This shouldn't diminish either their extraordinary achievements or their fine music, the best of which renders the pop vs. soul question moot with its excellence.

The Supremes were not an overnight success story, although it might have seemed that way when they began topping the charts with sure-fire regularity. The trio that would become famous as the Supremes—Diana Ross, Mary Wilson, and Florence Ballard—met in the late '50s in Detroit's Brewster housing project. Originally known as the Primettes, they were a quartet (Barbara Martin was the fourth member) when they made their first single for the Lupine label in 1960. By the time they debuted for Motown in 1961, they had been renamed the Supremes; Barbara Martin reduced them to a trio when she left after their first single. The Supremes' first Motown recordings were much more girl group-oriented than their later hits. Additionally, not all of them featured Diana Ross on lead vocals; Flo Ballard, considered to have as good or better a voice, also sang lead. Through a lengthy series of flops, Berry Gordy remained confident that the group would eventually prove to be one of Motown's biggest. By the time they finally did get their first Top 40 hit, "When the Lovelight Starts Shining Through His Eyes," in late 1963, Ross had taken over the lead singing for good.

Ross was not the most talented female singer at Motown; Martha Reeves and Gladys Knight in particular had superior talents. What she did have, however, was the most purely pop appeal. Gordy's patience and attention paid off in mid-1964, when "Where Did Our Love Go" went to number one. Written by Holland-Dozier-Holland, it established the prototype for their run of five consecutive number-one hits in 1964-1965 (also including "Baby Love," "Stop! In the Name of Love," "Come See About Me," and "Back in My Arms Again"). Ross' cooing vocals would front the Supremes' decorative backup vocals, put over on television and live performance with highly stylized choreography and visual style. Holland-Dozier-Holland would write and produce all of the Supremes' hits through the end of 1967.

Not all of the Supremes' singles went to number one after 1965, but they usually did awfully well, and were written and produced with enough variety (but enough of a characteric sound) to ensure continual interest. The chart-topping (and uncharacteristically tough) "You Keep Me Hangin' On" was the best of their mid-period hits. Behind the scenes, there were some problems brewing, although these only came to light long after the event. Other Motown stars (most notably Martha Reeves) resented what they perceived as the inordinate attention lavished upon Ross by Gordy, at the expense of other artists on the label. The other Supremes themselves felt increasingly pushed to the background. In mid-1967, as a result of what was deemed increasingly unprofessional behavior, Ballard was replaced by Cindy Birdsong (from Patti LaBelle & the BlueBelles). Ballard became one of rock's greatest tragedies, eventually ending up on welfare, and dying in 1976.

After Ballard's exit, the group would be billed as Diana Ross & the Supremes, fueling speculation that Ross was being groomed for a solo career. The Supremes had a big year in 1967, even incorporating some mild psychedelic influences into "Reflections." Holland-Dozier-Holland, however, left Motown around this time, and the quality of the Supremes' records suffered accordingly (as did the Motown organization as a whole). The Supremes were still superstars, but as a unit, they were disintegrating; it's been reported that Wilson and Birdsong didn't even sing on their final hits, a couple of which ("Love Child" and "Someday We'll Be Together") were among their best.

In November 1969, Ross' imminent departure for a solo career was announced, although she played a few more dates with them, the last in Las Vegas in January 1970. Jean Terrell replaced Ross, and the group continued through 1977, with some more personnel changes (although Mary Wilson was always involved). Some of the early Ross-less singles were fine records, particularly "Stoned Love," "Nathan Jones," and the Supremes-Four Tops duet "River Deep—Mountain High." Few groups have been able to rise to the occasion after the loss of their figurehead, though, and the Supremes proved no exception, rarely making the charts after 1972. It is the Diana Ross-led era of the 1960s for which they'll be remembered. *—Richie Unterberger*

Meet the Supremes / Oct. 1962 / Motown ✦✦✦

The romantic and sentimental "Your Heart Belongs to Me," written by Smokey Robinson, should have been the Supremes' first hit. It's every bit as charming as his chartbusters for Mary Wells. Diana Ross' sweet tender lead, assisted by Mary Wilson and Florence Ballard's warm harmonies, could melt icebergs. Ross vocals on "Who's Lovin' You" are intense and bluesy; Wilson leads the soulful "Baby Don't Go"; and Ballard leads the raucous "Buttered Popcorn," a tune more suited for the Contours. "I Want a Guy," their first recording, had been done by the Marvelettes—the backing voices are buried, and Ross' voice sounds whiny and high-pitched. This song, along with the '50s-sounding "He's Seventeen," are the only bummers. Ballard shines again on "Let Me Go the Right Way," delivering a tough vocal on top of Ross and Wilson's enthusiastic vocals. "Time Changes Things," written by Brian Holland, Lamont Dozier and Janie Bradford, was a forerunner to later efforts by Holland-Dozier-Holland. Blues lovers will relish the torching "Play a Sad Song." "Never Again" is straight '50s doo-wop; if you didn't know, you would think it was the Chantels. *—Andrew Hamilton*

Live at the Apollo / 1964 / Motown ✦✦✦✦✦

Where Did Our Love Go? / Aug. 1964 / Motown ✦✦✦✦✦

Diana Ross' sweet innocent lead, and Mary Wilson and Florence Ballard's cool "ooh"s and "aah"s made "Where Did Our Love Go" a smash. Other goodies like "When the Lovelight Starts Shining Through His Eyes," the metaphor-ridden "A Breathtaking Guy" and "Run, Run, Run" had an undeniable charm, but with "Where Did Our Love Go," Lamont Dozier & Eddie and Brian Holland took control and kept the trio on top for years (much to the disappointment of the Marvelettes, who turned the song down in favor of "Too Many Fish in the Sea"). The tender "Baby Love" zoomed up the charts light a laser shot. And despite covers, most notably by Nella Dodds, "Come See About Me" established the Supremes as household names. *Where Did Our Love Go* is loaded with lovely concoctions: "I'm Giving You Your Freedom," which features a pretty understated guitar; the dramatic "Standing at the Crossroads of Love," like "Freedom" and the rolling "Ask Any Girl," would have been A-sides for most groups but were fillers and B-sides for the Supremes. This LP climbed the charts like their singles, reaching the number-two rung on *Billboard*, and is Motown's most successful LP to date. *—Andrew Hamilton*

A Bit of Liverpool / Oct. 1964 / Motown ✦✦✦

The Supremes Sing Country Western & Pop / Feb. 1965 / Motown ✦✦✦

The Supremes made a series of change-of-pace albums designed to show off their versatility as all-around entertainers in contrast to the pop/R&B style of their hit singles. The concept here seemed to be to reveal the group's affinity for country standards like Willie Nelson's "Funny How Time Slips Away," the leadoff track. But Motown must have decided not to let much of the song publishing out—seven out of 11 songs were written by producer Clarence Paul, either alone or with 14-year-old Stevie Wonder or company president Berry Gordy. As a result, the collection has an ersatz quality—Nashville by way of Detroit. [Originally released on LP as Motown 625 on February 22, 1965, *The Supremes Sing Country Western & Pop* was reissued on CD as Motown 0327 on June 14, 1994.] *—William Ruhlmann*

We Remember Sam Cooke / Apr. 12, 1965 / Motown ✦✦✦

The Supremes were hot in the mid-'60s, and Motown tried to capitalize on the trio's success. And why not? *Where Did Our Love Go?* almost aced the Pop 200 album chart, zooming to number two. Its successor, *More Hits by the Supremes*, did almost as well (it went to number six). An album of British remakes titled *A Bit of Liverpool* surprised everyone by going to number 21—unheard of achievements for an R&B or soul act—so an album with America's darlings singing songs by the late Sam Cooke seemed a good bet. But despite its relevance—Cooke was killed in December 1964—it only went to number 75. The public took this baby for granted and so did Motown, who didn't even release a single from this collection. The Supremes performed a Sam Cooke medley on the successful (number 11) *The Supremes Live at the Copa* to heartfelt applause. Diana Ross, Mary Wilson and Florence Ballard's sweet renditions of "You Send Me," "Cupid" and "Bring It on Home to Me" sound like winners, not to mention the party animals: "Chain Gang," "Shake," "Having a Party" and the delightful "Wonderful World." *—Andrew Hamilton*

The Supremes at the Copa / Nov. 1965 / Motown ♦♦♦

The Supremes at the Copa suffers from its inclusion of numerous standards that pre-date rock & roll, likely in an attempt to appeal to the New York show's conservative audience. Compared to the group's own signature tunes and a medley of Sam Cooke songs, these others seem to fall very flat. Even the audience seems to react more enthusiastically to the opening strains of "Baby Love" and "Come See About Me." After listening to this recording, it becomes clear that they would have been crazy not to—in this live setting the tunes take on an added ferocity and highlight the astounding songwriting and musicianship that was so central to Motown's success. *—Brian Egan*

Merry Christmas / Nov. 1965 / Motown ♦♦♦♦

I Hear a Symphony / Feb. 1966 / Motown ♦♦♦♦♦

I Hear a Symphony has some great soul numbers on it, mostly by the Holland-Dozier-Holland songwriting team, including not only the title track but also "Any Girl in Love (Knows What I'm Going Through)," "My World Is Empty Without You," and "He's All I Got"—the latter is one of the greatest album tracks the group ever recorded, with stunning vocals by Mary Wilson and Florence Ballard behind Diana Ross, showing the trio in just about its peak form. Other parts of *I Hear a Symphony* seem to take its title track almost literally, with the inclusion of the majestic "Unchained Melody" and the Bach-based "A Lover's Concerto"; the latter, in particular, is a Diana Ross *tour de force*, with very sweetly understated accompaniment by Wilson and Ballard. And elsewhere, Berry Gordy was pushing his vision of the Supremes as a mainstream pop trio, covering "A Stranger in Paradise," "With a Song in My Heart," "Without a Song," and "Wonderful, Wonderful." None of these are bad, but neither are they terribly distinguished—the group even adds a certain fresh sparkle to "Wonderful, Wonderful," but realistically, people were paying their money for the Holland-Dozier-Holland and Eddie Holland-authored songs, any of which would have made about as fine singles as anything the trio ever put out, and all of which are still a chunk of the best part of the group's legacy. *—Bruce Eder*

Supremes A' Go-Go / Aug. 1966 / Motown ♦♦♦♦

Supremes A' Go-Go was the group's first number-one pop album, propelled to that place with help from a chart-topping single ("You Can't Hurry Love") and a marketing ploy that generated an irresistible song lineup. And along with *The Supremes Sing Holland-Dozier-Holland*, *Supremes A' Go-Go* has held its value better than almost any of the trio's most successful albums (which excludes *We Remember Sam Cooke*)—in fact, back in the days when vinyl was the only game in town, used copies of this record sold faster and better than any of their other common '60s LPs, and for good reason. Various hits compilations had skimmed the most familiar songs off of *Where Did Our Love Go*, *I Hear a Symphony*, etc., but the very concept behind *Supremes A' Go-Go*—getting the group to cover some of the top hits of other (mostly Motown) acts—dictated that every song on this album was familiar in name, and only "You Can't Hurry Love" was culled for any hits packages. There was a lot to recommend it musically, including the trio soaring rendition of "Shake Me, Wake Me" and a version of "Get Ready," which, even if it was no threat to the Temptations, still could have been a hit. Similarly, "Baby I Need Your Lovin'" and "I Can't Help Myself" will always belong to the Four Tops, but Diana Ross, Mary Wilson, and Florence Ballard throw themselves into both (in a less weighty version of the former) with enough spirit to make them work as album cuts; "Money" is diverting if less successful, and "Come and Get These Memories" is worth checking out just to hear Florence Ballard and Mary Wilson step forward. And even the non-Motown covers, like "These Boot Are Made for Walkin'" and "Hang on Sloopy," make worthwhile listening, with Ross turning in a surprisingly strong, passionate performance on the latter. A number-one album in its time on the pop and R&B charts, *Supremes A' Go-Go* also benefited from the fact that there were no pop standards or slow ballads here, just solid R&B dance numbers. *—Bruce Eder*

The Supremes Sing Holland-Dozier-Holland / Jan. 1967 / Motown ♦♦♦♦

Anchored by two of their most popular recordings, "You Keep Me Hanging On," and "Love Is Here and Now You're Gone," this LP features Holland, Dozier & Holland (HDH) compositions and productions, and it ranks among their best. The Supremes' renditions of songs popularized by label mates illustrate the interchangeability of HDH's songs. Ross' soprano may not have the bite of Ron Isley's tenor, but she still does a better than average job on "I Guess I Always Love." Two Four Tops' remakes, "I'll Turn to Stone," and "The Same Old Song," are just as groovy as the originals. An update of Martha & Vandellas' "Love Is Like a Heat Wave" fails to live up to the dynamics of the original. The Vandellas' version was special, while this one comes off like another song for the session. "Mother You, Smother You" is too formulaic, but the singing and lyrics place it well above what other girl groups were releasing at the time. Ditto for "Going Down for the Third Time." A Supremes' album track would be an A-side for most artists. The prolific writers did an excellent job on their namesake LP, which turned out to be the last of the great Supremes albums. *—Andrew Hamilton*

The Supremes Sing Rodgers & Hart / Jun. 1967 / Motown ♦♦♦♦

☆ **Diana Ross and the Supremes' Greatest Hits** / Sep. 1967 / Motown ♦♦♦♦♦

Although all of these 20 songs were credited to the Supremes when they were released between 1963 and 1967, this album marked the first LP on which the group was billed as "Diana Ross & the Supremes." However you credit it, this out-of-print double-LP contains the bulk of the best of the Supremes, no less than 10 number-one hits from "Where Did Our Love Go" to "The Happening," and thus some of the most popular music of the 1960s. Ross and the Supremes, together and separately, continued to score afterwards, but this was their peak. *—William Ruhlmann*

Reflections / Mar. 1968 / Motown ♦♦♦

Their last album with Holland-Doizer-Holland at the creative helm, it was apparent that both parties were battling creative fatigue and were exhibiting the appropriate scars at the time. But aside from the then-innovative title song and the jazzy "In and Out of Love," there's nothing much to get excited about. [Note: the CD version contains two extra tracks, one being a lackluster rendition of "Stay in My Lonely Arms" that pales next to the Elgins' original]. *—John Lowe*

Funny Girl / Aug. 1968 / Motown ♦♦♦

Live at London's Talk of the Town / Aug. 26, 1968 / Motown ♦♦♦

Even as they released a steady stream of pop/R&B classics in the 1960s, the Supremes tried as a live act to escape the chitlin' circuit and the teen tours and graduate to the sophisticated supper clubs, a goal they achieved when they played the Copacabana. By the time the renamed Diana Ross & the Supremes played the Talk of the Town in London, they were backed by an orchestra and were presenting most of their material in abbreviated medley form. (This album contains no less than *five* medleys.) Ross was attempting jokes in the brief moments between musical sequences, and the song list was weighted as much with MOR standards like "Here" as it was with Supremes hits, an uneasy mixture. The live versions of the hits provided an object lesson in the importance of the Motown house band: Here, the tempos were rushed, the groove was gone, and Ross and Company were frantic to keep up. For all the razzle dazzle, though, the girls did manage to approximate a slick Las Vegas style, which makes the album a harbinger of the future. [Originally released on August 26, 1968, as Motown 676, *Live At London's Talk of the Town* was reissued in 1994 as part of the Motown Master Series as Motown 0328.)] *—William Ruhlmann*

Love Child / Nov. 1968 / Motown ♦♦♦♦

Through 1964 to 1967 the Supremes were Motown's biggest act. Singles like "Where Did Our Love Go," "Back in My Arms Again," and "You Keep Me Hanging On" defined the label's pop prowess and the quirky appeal of talented lead singer Diana Ross. By 1968, the group not only lost member Florence Ballard, but also Holland-Dozier-Holland who had written and produced all of their big singles. Cindy Birdsong joins Mary Wilson and Ross for this 1968 effort and the group name was officially changed. Although it's always fun to hear Ross & the Supremes, the most interesting thing about this effort is its production. With a lack of consistently great songs, *Love Child* had to rely on hooks, choruses, and production values rather than magical songs. The well-produced and controversial title track proved how good Ross is with melodrama. "How Long Has That Evening Train Been Gone" has a great bassline from James Jamerson and Ross oddly having a lot of fun with her supposedly dire romantic prospects. The warm cover of Bobby Taylor & the Vancouvers' classic "Does Your Mamma Know About Me" sticks close to the original with good results. Ashford & Simpson offer two of their early tracks, the album's first single "Some Things You Never Get Used To," and the graceful "You Ain't Livin' Until You're Lovin'." For the most part, *Love Child*'s tracks seem to run together but this offers the late-'60s Motown sound without gimmicks and is more than recommended. *—Jason Elias*

T.C.B. / Dec. 1968 / Motown ♦♦♦

Surprisingly, this television soundtrack featuring the Supremes and the Temptations soared to the pinnacle—number one; a studio album by them released earlier climbed to number two on *Billboard*'s pop Album Chart. More than three decades later, however, *T.C.B.* is unlistenable. Still, it proved a good vehicle for both groups, and accomplished its goal by helping them crossover, along with getting them gigs in Las Vegas Casinos, and prestigious high paying clubs like the Copacabana. Watching the two groups interact and sing these songs on the television special was more enjoyable then listening to the record. *T.C.B.* is watered-down Temptations and Diana Ross & the Supremes. The songs, even the hits, sound campy; the big band didn't help. If a current Urban Contemporary artist released a CD like this today they would be crucified by their fans and magazines like *Vibe*, *Source* and *Rolling Stone*. But it worked, fans bought this album, and a bigger untapped audience discovered the versatility of arguably the best male, and the best female vocal group of all time. *—Andrew Hamilton*

Let the Sunshine In / May 1969 / Motown ♦♦♦

Cream of the Crop / Nov. 1969 / Motown ♦♦♦

The final Diana Ross & the Supremes' album before Ms. Ross' departure, a duet LP with the Temptations (the second for the two groups) came out the same month. This rag tag bunch of vault dwellers and passed over tunes written by the company's third and fourth tier writers and producers has a misleading title: there are few creams and it's a bad crop. The sole star is their scintillating remake of Johnny & Jackey's forgotten "Someday Will Be Together"—their last hurrah, and a few other honorable mentions, namely "The Young Folks" and "You Gave Me Love." Despite the shortcomings, it wrangled it way to number 33 on *Billboard*'s Pop Chart. *—Andrew Hamilton*

Right On / Apr. 1970 / Motown ♦♦♦

"Up the Ladder to the Roof" opens the album with enticing voices and Frank Wilson's underappreciated first-class production. *Right On* is a textbook on how to come back from the brink of disaster. The Supremes achieved something the Doors, Big Brother & the Holding Company, Creedence Clearwater, the Guess Who, and so many others could not, go Top Ten and survive the loss of the star who the world recognized and assumed was the key element of their success. Even more stunning is that they did it two months before Diana Ross would go Top 20 with her first solo hit. Jean Terrell brought a terrific voice and new emotion to a group that would rack up eight Top 40 hits without Diana

Ross. This is not your Holland-Dozier-Holland Supremes; Wilson creates a sublime stereo mix for the debut single, a wonderful-to-this-day headphone mix with sounds swirling left and right. The follow-up single, "Everybody's Got the Right to Love," went Top 25 with its politically correct theme and clever R&B pop flavors. It gives Mary Wilson and Cindy Birdsong a chance to use their voices to interact with Terrell, creating a true group sound. A new team, a united front. Where producer Wilson would give the girls cover tunes to sing on the follow-up—which came eight months after this debut—they experiment with all sorts of styles on *Right On*. Among its generous selection of 12 titles, "I Got Hurt" gives a nod to the Honeycombs, "Baby Baby" seems to be a response to Diana's vocal work on "Where Did Our Love Go," and the Supremes take on the sounds of Dionne Warwick with "Then I Met You" (Warwick later hitting with "Then Came You," but this is more the Warwick of Bacharach/David, not the Philly sound). "Bill, When Are You Coming Back" is the Fifth Dimension meets Martha & the Vandellas by way of Laura Nyro. This is Frank Wilson and the Supremes having fun, and *Right On* holds up today as a solid pop album that is both adult contemporary and girl group pop. "But I Love You More" ends side one, a powerful composition co-written by producer Wilson, performed with enthusiasm by the Supremes. They would rack up four hits in 1970, double the tally by Diana Ross, and between 1971 and 1976 an additional four Top 40 titles. Eight hit singles is a major accomplishment for any recording act, more so for one that endured after the departure of a superstar. *Right On* is thoroughly enjoyable. *—Joe Viglione*

Farewell / May 1970 / Motown ♦♦♦♦
Presented here in all its magic and splendor is the last recorded show of the super singing group, Diana Ross & the Supremes. The Supremes sing their greatest hits and a plethora of classic melodies in front of a live audience in Las Vegas during their *Farewell* tour, January 14, 1970. In their last performance at the Frontier Hotel, the Supremes sang with vibrancy and a unique and unmatched harmony that seemed to uplift and sweep the fans off their feet. Soulful and passionate tunes such as "Stop! In the Name of Love," "Come See About Me," "My World Is Empty Without You," and "Baby Love" are featured on the first side of this double-record collection, marking the pure delight and colorful charisma of the group's early career. Covers such as "Lady Is a Tramp" and "Can't Take My Eyes Off You" reflect the soulful times during the height of Motown's success. "Reflections," Ross' personal favorite, closes out the first set with fervent energy. The Supremes' enthusiasm is very identifiable on "Love Child" and the great hit sung by the 5th Dimension, "Aquarius." Many Rodgers & Hart tunes are featured in this exciting collection, and sung by the Supremes like only they can, spinning the melodies with their unique trademark harmony and youthful vigor. "Falling in Love With Love" and "The Lady Is a Tramp" bring a sophisticated and jazzy '30s flavor to the gig. The group closes out this memorable performance with "Someday We'll Be Together," granting faith and some hope to those who hoped the Supremes would return in the near future. As is turned out, this was the last live performance of the legendary trio. Producer Deke Richards did a good job capturing the essence of the Supremes, their tight harmonies and self esteem, on record. This can be a perfect fit for anyone's record collection, especially fans of '60s Motown. *—Shawn M. Haney*

The Magnificent 7 / Sep. 1970 / Motown ♦♦♦
Neither anticipation nor expectation were as high with this pairing as they were when Motown recorded the Supremes and the Temptations together at the peak of their careers. The Supremes were minus Diana Ross, and like the Four Tops, were no longer automatic Top 40 crashers. Their waning careers made many overlook these recordings featuring Levi Stubbs and Jean Terrell's exhilarating leads. The combo cut three albums and each has it moments. This, the best-selling one, reached number 113 on *Billboard*'s Top 200 album chart and glistened with an update of Ike and Tina Turner's "River Deep, Mountain High." With the exception of "Knock on My Door," the whole LP consists of remakes, including "Stone Soul Picnic" (the 5th Dimension), "For Your Love" (Ed Townsend), "Ain't Nothing Like the Real Thing" (Marvin Gaye & Tammi Terrell), "It's Got to Be a Miracle (This Thing Called Love)" (Marvin Gaye and Kim Weston), and fiery versions of "Together We Can Make Such Sweet Music" (the Spinners) and Sly Stone's "Everyday People." *—Andrew Hamilton*

New Ways But Love Stays / Oct. 1970 / Motown ♦♦♦

The Return of the Magnificent Seven / Jun. 1971 / Motown ♦♦♦
The Supremes and the Four Tops' first album crept to number 113 on *Billboard*'s Top 200 Albums survey and produced a moderate hit, prompting Motown to go to the well again with *The Return of the Magnificent Seven* (three Supremes and [four] Tops). Remakes dominated the first LP, but this time they sing more originals. While "You Gotta Have Love in Your Heart" did a little action, it was a mere blip on a radar screen compared to what was expected. And others like "I'll Try Not to Cry," "I Wonder Where We're Going," and an update of "I Can't Believe You Love Me," originally by Tammi Terrell, went unnoticed. Like their first LP, Motown issued one single and passed on the rest. Sales were disappointing; it stumbled to number 154, 41 slots lower than the original. But like the original, Jean Terrell's and Levi Stubbs' leads are invigorating. Atlantic Records later paired Stubbs (and the Four Tops) with Aretha Franklin for some dizzying dramas, i.e., "Make It With You," that also failed to gain a mass audience. *—Andrew Hamilton*

Touch / Jun. 1971 / Motown ♦♦♦
Perhaps the weakest in the trilogy of the Frank Wilson-produced albums (a fourth, *Promises Kept*, was shelved), the album is redeemed by a few good songs, most notably the Clifton Davis-penned "Here Comes the Sunrise" and "Johnny Raven." The title track, however, marks the first time Mary Wilson shared the lead vocals with Jean Terrell (Wilson's unfamiliarity with the record-buying public may be the reason why the title track flopped when released as a single). *—John Lowe*

Dynamite / Dec. 1971 / Motown ♦♦♦
The last of three albums together finds the Supremes and the Four Tops' producers reverting back to the formula of the first and most successful of the three with this set of remakes. "It's Impossible" builds on New Birth's recording and "Hello Stranger" is a melter; Jean Terrell syncs her soprano to your heart on this soul/pop classic where she swaps lead lines with Levi Stubbs. They get sweaty on Stephen Stills' "Love the One You're With" and gel on Marvin Gaye & Tammi Terrell's "Good Lovin' Ain't Easy to Come By" and "If I Could Build My World Around You." The last track, "Do You Love Me Just a Little Honey," is as creamy as "Hello Stranger" and as aching as the original by Gladys Knight & the Pips. *Dynamite* gassed at number 160 on *Billboard*'s pop 200 chart, six rungs lower than their second together and 47 shy of their debut, *The Magnificent Seven*. *—Andrew Hamilton*

Floy Joy / May 1972 / Motown ♦♦♦
An interesting but erratic set, co-written and produced by the prolific Smokey Robinson, then undergoing a transition phase in his career (he was getting ready to exit the Miracles). As usual, the highlights were the singles, particularly "Automatically Sunshine" and the bouncy title track. Unfortunately, there wasn't enough promotional push to maintain the group's viability, and thus a commercial decline reigned unchecked until the group disbanded in 1977. *—John Lowe*

The Supremes Arranged and Produced by Jimmy Webb / Oct. 1972 / Motown ♦♦♦

☆ **Anthology: The Best of Diana Ross & the Supremes** / May 1974 / Motown ♦♦♦♦♦
When it was released in 1974, Motown's Diana Ross & the Supremes' *Anthology* was the most comprehensive compilation yet issued on one of the 1960s' most popular groups. A 35-track triple LP, it superseded the 1967 double-LP *Greatest Hits*, including 17 of that album's 20 tracks, as well as the 1969 *Greatest Hits, Vol. 3*, all of which was repeated. All 27 of the Supremes' R&B hits between 1962 and 1969 were featured, as well as 28 of their 30 pop chart entries. That represented a formidable chunk of the decade's biggest hits, among them the chart-toppers "Where Did Our Love Go," "Baby Love," "Come See About Me," "Stop! In the Name of Love," "Back in My Arms Again," "I Hear a Symphony," "You Can't Hurry Love," "You Keep Me Hangin' On," "Love Is Here and Now You're Gone," "The Happening," "Love Child," and "Someday We'll Be Together." The lengthy album also found space for some of the group's musical experiments, devoting a five-song side, dubbed "Versatile Stylists," to material culled from the albums *A Bit of Liverpool, The Supremes Sing Country Western & Pop, We Remember Sam Cooke, The Supremes Sing Rodgers & Hart*, and *Diana Ross and the Supremes Sing and Perform "Funny Girl."* They made for an interesting interlude, but the heart of the matter remained the Supremes' brilliant interpretations of the Holland-Dozier-Holland hits of the mid-'60s, which were all here. [Motown continually revised its *Anthology* series over the years, putting out successive Diana Ross and the Supremes editions in 1986, 1995, and 2001 that expanded upon and altered the conception of the original. These albums have their own listings.] *—William Ruhlmann*

The Supremes / May 1975 / Motown ♦♦
Their first studio album in nearly three years was a disappointment. By then Jean Terrell left the group, powerhouse singer Scherrie Payne (a former vocalist with the group the Glass House) replaced her and Mary Wilson took charge of the group, splitting leads with Payne. The result was a collage of production approaches that don't seem to jell as a unified whole. Another problem was that Mary Wilson wasn't (then) a particularly distinctive lead singer. (It wasn't until her 1979 self-titled solo album with Motown that she began to gain a clearer musical idenity.) The album's failure sent them scurrying back to the drawing board, quite appropriately as the album did nothing to establish a distinctive musical idenity for the group. *—John Lowe*

High Energy / Apr. 1976 / Motown ♦♦♦
Perhaps the most vigorous (and best) album of their latter-day career, it helped that Payne was established as the centerpiece of the group. Also, multi-octative-voiced Susaye Greene replaced Cindy Birdsong in the group, though producers used her voice more for coloration than for substance. It also helped that Brian & Eddie Holland returned to the production helm, though they were past their artistic prime. A sturdy dance-oriented album, it is highlighted by the hard-driving dance hit "I'm Gonna Let My Heart Do the Walking," which became their last Top 40 hit in 1976. *—John Lowe*

Mary, Scherrie and Susaye / Oct. 1976 / Motown ♦
Things started to go downhill when they recorded this effort. This time they alternated leads (Payne on the uptempo tunes, Wilson and Greene on the ballads) and the Holland brothers continued on as producers. While Susaye Greene gets a chance to show off her power and range, Mary Wilson comes off as competent yet colorless. Although they had a minor hit with the disco number "You're My Driving Wheel," by then they'd lost their distinction and became an anonomyous echo of their former glory, as interchangable as the next group on the block. Sad. *—John Lowe*

Greatest Hits With Mary Wilson / 1983 / Motown ♦♦♦
A curiously titled album that is essentially a collection of post-Diana Ross & the Supremes recordings that include some Four Tops pairings. You would think all the tracks Mary Wilson led with the Supremes would be included, but they're not. If you're going to include Wilson's name in the title, they should be on here. Most of these cuts are familiar to all but there are some pleasant surprises like "Together We Can Make Such Sweet Music," recorded with the Four Tops, a song originally recorded by Joe Towns on Detroit's microscopic, short-lived Top Dog Records. Wilson sings in a sexy alto that can be heard oozing some enticing lines on the crackling, uptempo "Floy Joy." Though she's credited in the title, Mary takes a back seat to Jean Terrell, who sings most of the leads. *—Andrew Hamilton*

Compact Command Performances: 20 Greatest Hits / Feb. 1984 / Motown ♦♦♦

At the time of its release in 1984, *Compact Command Performances: 20 Greatest Hits*, credited to Diana Ross & the Supremes, was the only single-disc compilation covering the Supremes' entire career as hitmakers, from 1963 to 1971. More than a decade later, it remained the best such collection. The 1967 double-LP *Greatest Hits* (now divided into two volumes) was arguably a stronger set of songs because the quality of the group's music declined in the late '60s and '70s, and the various versions of the *Anthology*, whether triple-LP or double-CD, were more comprehensive. But this album fulfilled the purpose of sampling most of the Supremes' biggest hit singles from all three of their notable lineups: the original trio of Ross, Mary Wilson, and Florence Ballard (1961-1967); the rebilled Diana Ross & the Supremes, with Wilson and Cindy Birdsong (1967-1970); and the post-Ross Supremes, Wilson, Birdsong, and Jean Terrell. It featured 17 of the group's 20 Top Ten pop hits (leaving out "The Happening," "In and Out of Love," and "I'm Livin' in Shame" in favor of "When the Lovelight Starts Shining Through His Eyes," "I'll Try Something New," and "Nathan Jones," all of which made the Top 40). As one of the early CDs, the album, with tracks "transferred directly to digital from the original masters," sounds generally good, but has nothing like the spectacularly improved sound achieved on later compilations of the same material. In fact, "I Hear a Symphony," inexplicably, is in mono, and there is a drop-out in "Love Is Like an Itching in My Heart." —*William Ruhlmann*

25th Anniversary / Mar. 1986 / Motown ♦♦♦

The Supremes were signed to Motown in January 1961, and the 25th anniversary of that event provided the hook for yet another compilation. This one is a triple-LP/ double-CD set, one half of which, or 20 tracks, is given over to the group's biggest hits of the Diana Ross era, from "When the Lovelight Starts Shining Through His Eyes" (1963) to "Someday We'll Be Together" (1969). The other half of the album consists of previously unreleased material from the same period. Motown used to cut tons of songs on its major groups compared to what was released, and here we have outtakes from the *Rodgers & Hart* album (initially planned as a double-LP), from the never-released *Disney Classics* album, and from other sessions (some of the tracks later reworked into released songs), plus movie and promotional appearances, including an interview and commercials. All of that makes this a good album for collectors to seek out, though there's nothing revelatory. [Originally released in March 1986 as a triple-LP by Motown as Motown 5381, *25th Anniversary* was reissued in on October 14, 1986, as a double-CD by Motown as Motown 6193.] —*William Ruhlmann*

70's Greatest Hits & Rare Classics / 1991 / Motown ♦♦♦

A rather ragtag greatest-hits collection. The Supremes' changing lineups didn't help give this collection any continuity—nor did the countless producers. Smokey Robinson and Frank Wilson's productions come off better then the others. Wilson produced "Up the Ladder to the Roof," "Stoned Love," and "Everybody's Got the Right to Love," all led by Jean Terrell's biting soprano. "Floy Joy" and "Automatically Sunshine" are the two Smokey productions. Robinson gave the Supremes a coy, cute sound accented by stamping beats and heavy echo in the backing vocals. The first incarnation of new Supremes were Jean Terrell, Mary Wilson, Cindy Birdsong, and later Lynda Lawrence. Later, on "I'm Gonna Let My Heart Do the Walking," and "You're My Driving Wheel," the members were Mary Wilson, Lynda Lawrence, Scherrie Payne, and Susaye Greene. All could sing lead—a classic example of too many cooks spoiling the soup. —*Andrew Hamilton*

Anthology: The Best of Diana Ross & the Supremes / 1995 / Motown ♦♦♦♦

Motown Records' *Anthology* series, first introduced in the 1970s, presented three-LP sets devoted to the work of its major artists, among them, of course, Diana Ross & the Supremes, who got a 35-track treatment in 1974, chronicling their chart hits and a handful of their more adventurous stylistic forays. About 12 years later, Motown brought out a second *Anthology* of the group for the CD era, expanding to 50 tracks and including recordings by the post-Diana Ross version of the Supremes. Another nine years on, here is yet another variation on the formula. This 52-track Diana Ross & the Supremes *Anthology* adopts the same basic chronological approach as its predecessors, and like the 1986 album includes Supremes songs from the '70s, taking the group from 1961 to 1976. (Ross bid farewell at the start of 1970.) Compiler Bill Inglot is not interested in hearing the Supremes cover Rodgers & Hart; rather, in addition to including all their Top 40 pop hits, he has sought out album tracks in the same style as their successful singles, songs like "Mother Dear" and "He's All I Got," written by Holland-Dozier-Holland, that one can easily imagine having joined their list of hits. (The sole unreleased track is a fascinating public service announcement written and produced by Phil Spector, "Things Are Changing.") This gives the album stylistic consistency, at least through its first disc, though the continuing decision to lump the post-Diana Ross material in at the end remains questionable. But the most bizarre aspect of this *Anthology* is the choice of presenting most of the tracks in monophonic sound. That sound is punchy, reminiscent of 1960s AM radio, but it's not as though there weren't stereo versions of these recordings, and when a few stereo mixes are introduced on the second disc, they stick out. —*William Ruhlmann*

★ **The Ultimate Collection** / Oct. 7, 1997 / Motown ♦♦♦♦♦

For those who believe the Supremes' best work can be found within the bounds of their many hits, this edition of Motown's solid, late-'90s repackaging job will be the collection to get. Covering the seraphic vocal group's prime stretch, the 25-track set (nine short of the previous—and arguably still superior—*Anthology* package) includes all the big hits, plus two fine Temptations collaborations ("I'm Gonna Make You Love Me," "I'll Try Something New") and relative obscurities from the latter days ("The Composer," "No Matter What Sign You Are"). Featuring top-drawer production by Holland-Dozier-Holland, label-chief Barry Gordy, Frank Wilson, and a young Ashford & Simpson, Diana Ross & the Supremes' *Ultimate Collection* makes for a very enjoyable way to get cozy with one of soul music's most regal vocal-harmony groups. —*Stephen Cook*

Supremes / Aug. 29, 2000 / Motown ♦♦♦♦

The Supremes were Motown's most popular act, so there was much anticipation for a comprehensive box set, especially since Motown waited many years to assemble one. So, the question is, was the wait worth it? Almost. It's a lavish set, spanning four discs (five, if you include the limited-edition live bonus disc included with the first 25,000 sets), housed in a red-velvet plated book and boasting a 70-page booklet, plus alternate takes, original 45 mixes, and other rarities. The devil is in the details, though. Rarities are substituted for original hit versions; for instance, the original versions of "Stop! In the Name of Love" and "Love Is Here and Now You're Gone" are not here. Then, there are the little omissions, like noting Elvis Costello's cover of "Remove This Doubt" in a list of great Supremes covers, but not including the original. These curious choices, along with the decision to devote the fourth disc to post-Diana Ross material, makes the set feel a little incomplete even though it covers a tremendous amount of ground. There are some classic cuts missing, and it's not a good thing that some of those missing items are the single versions of the hits. Still, it's hard not to like *The Supremes* as a set for hardcore fans, who will thrill to the different mixes and alternate versions, unreleased photos, Top Ten Lists, and illustrated discographies. But for the listener looking for one exhaustive set containing all the Supremes they'll ever need, this set falls short of the mark. In fact, for that kind of listener, a good double-disc hits compilation remains a preferable choice over this set. —*Stephen Thomas Erlewine*

☆ **Anthology** / Dec. 18, 2001 / Motown ♦♦♦♦♦

This release marks the fourth time a Supremes collection titled *Anthology* has hit the racks. Fans can be forgiven for getting confused, even aggravated, as to which one should be selected above others, as all of them contain the basic big hits for which the group is known. Motown keeps tweaking the precise track lineup with each edition, however, as they have for this two-CD, 50-track set. First off, if you're starting from scratch and just want a good greatest-hits collection, this is very good, and you won't have any regrets after purchase. The key thing to keep in mind is that it covers only the Diana Ross years, and doesn't reach into the 1970s for the clutch of hits the group landed without her. It has all of their 1960s chart singles, though, including duets with the Temptations and some low-charting ones that aren't familiar, from 1962's "Your Heart Belongs to Me" to 1969's "No Matter What Sign You Are." Along the way are some odd B-sides, album tracks, and rarities, like their early-'60s singles "I Want a Guy" and "Buttered Popcorn," and their Phil Spector-produced 1966 public service announcement "Things Are Changing." The ten covers at the end grouped under the heading "Supreme Stylists" are padding, as the group takes a shot at material from the Beatles to Disney and Broadway, but they do reflect an aspect of the Supremes that was represented on their albums and in their live performances. As for the three previously unreleased items here, you've gotta be real hardcore to shell out for the whole set if you already have most of the songs, as they comprise an extended version of "Love Is Like an Itching in My Heart," an alternate mix of "You Keep Me Hanging On," and a stereo mix of "He." Also, the version of "Buttered Popcorn" is the first pressing, and was previously unavailable on album. —*Richie Unterberger*

The Supremes Sing Rodgers and Hart: The Complete Recordings / Mar. 26, 2002 / Motown ♦♦♦♦

This greatly expanded version of *The Supremes Sing Rodgers and Hart* was issued in 2002. The single CD includes all 25 unique recordings that the ladies made during those sessions—including two previously unissued sides: "I Could Write a Book" and a medley of "The Lady Is a Tramp" and "Let's Get Away From It All" from their legendary Copa performances. The somewhat unlikely appearance of an album's worth of show tunes from a group primarily known for R&B and pop music proves once again that Motown was producing artists and concepts that reached far beyond that of other record labels. *The Supremes Sing Rodgers and Hart* began as a multimedia spinoff based on the female vocal trio's appearance on the prime time ABC TV special *Rodgers and Hart Today* during the summer of 1966. Although the original idea that included a double LP was scrapped, the dozen tracks that made the cut are indeed the *crème de la crème* of savory and sophisticated stage and screen showstoppers with '60s soul. The naturally dramatic vocal delivery of the Supremes—Diana Ross, Mary Wilson, and Florence Ballard—was an obvious key to the success of their chart-topping hits "Stop! In the Name of Love," "Where Did Our Love Go," and "You Can't Hurry Love." Additionally, the trio had incorporated show tunes into both its stage performances and recordings. So, the concept was not as foreign as first impressions might infer. The mix of traditional and modern arrangements also lends to the ageless quality of the music. The album is bookended by the lavishly orchestrated "The Lady Is a Tramp" and "Blue Moon"; however, the whole of pop music is explored in between. The intimate jazz leanings of "My Funny Valentine" and "Thou Swell" foreshadow the role Ross would play in *Lady Sings the Blues*. There are also a few instances of the fusion between the hip-shakin' Motor City R&B magic that had become synonymous with Motown and the songwriting craftsmanship of Richard Rodgers and Lorenz Hart. The uptempo "My Heart Stood Still" and "This Can't Be Love" mirror the funky and contemporary rhythms of "You Keep Me Hanging On." The perky "Mountain Greenery" has a bossa nova influence, with the trio's cherubic and spry vocals gently peppering the melody. These recordings also marked a historical milestone for the Supremes. Not only would this project be the last time the trio would receive group credit—as all future releases involving Ross would give her top billing—but sadly, these also turned out to be the final studio recordings made by the original lineup. Shortly after a final run of shows at the Copa in New York, Flo Ballard would be replaced by Cindy Birdsong. —*Lindsay Planer*

The '70s Anthology / Oct. 29, 2002 / Motown ♦♦♦♦♦
This two-disc set, running as long as CDs allow, provides a comprehensive look at the second and final decade of the Supremes, the era after lead singer Diana Ross left, when sole original member Mary Wilson juggled personnel changes and struggled with Motown Records and the changing musical times to try to maintain the group's success. She did that with some degree of effectiveness, especially in the first few years. It's apparent that Motown did make some efforts to support the Supremes, providing Smokey Robinson and Stevie Wonder as at least occasional writer/producers, with their old hitmakers—Brian Holland, Lamont Dozier, and Edward Holland Jr.—even coming back in toward the end. The result was a batch of hits, including the R&B chart-topper "Stoned Love," through mid-1972. It is not clear why the group had no album releases in 1973 or 1974, and Wilson in her liner notes doesn't seem to know, either. But by the time they returned to recording in 1975, despite the efforts of the Holland brothers and a series of disco-styled recordings that scored in the dance clubs, the old momentum was lost, especially as the lineup changed, with lead singer Jean Terrell giving way to Scherrie Payne, and the Supremes disbanded in 1977. On the hits, select album tracks, and some revealing previously unreleased material, one can hear the group's development. Their versions of well-known songs by others—Stephen Stills' "Love the One You're With," Joni Mitchell's "All I Want," Bread's "Make It With You," the Jackson 5's "Never Can Say Goodbye"—are illuminating, and hits like "Up the Ladder to the Roof" and "Floy Joy" hold up well. The later editions of the Supremes may not rank with the Diana Ross-led '60s version, but this collection demonstrates that they had their own appeal. *—William Ruhlmann*

Al B. Sure! (Al Brown)

b. Boston, MA

Vocals / Urban, New Jack Swing

During the late '80s, Al B. Sure! enjoyed a brief run as one of new jack swing's most popular romantic singers. Born Al Brown in Boston, he grew up in Mount Vernon, NY, listening to smooth crooners like Marvin Gaye and Johnny Mathis; he later became interested in rap and added that skill to his vocal repertoire. At age ten, he and a friend performed on a song written by Ellie Greenwich for the soundtrack of *Sesame Street*, and later he began writing songs with his cousin Kyle West. While in high school (where he quarterbacked the football team), he became friends with Edward Ferrell, aka DJ Eddie F, who was working with rapper Heavy D at the time. Eddie F introduced the still-teenaged Al B. Sure! to Heavy D's manager/Uptown labelhead Andre Harrell, who had him sing backing vocals on several Heavy D tracks and helped him get a deal with Warner Brothers.

Featuring production from DJ Eddie F and a number of co-writes with West, Al B. Sure!'s debut album, *In Effect Mode*, was released in 1988 and became a platinum-selling sensation thanks to the single "Nite and Day," which reached the Top Ten on the pop charts and topped the R&B charts for three weeks. The follow-up "Off on Your Own (Girl)" was also a number-one R&B hit, and he became a bona fide star among urban audiences, though he didn't remain a presence on the pop charts. His second album, *Private Times... and the Whole 9*, appeared in 1990 and produced another R&B number one in "Misunderstanding," as well as a duet with Diana Ross called "No Matter What." His third album, 1992's *Sexy Versus*, wasn't as successful, and he took a hiatus from recording, eventually landing a vice president position at Motown. In 1996, he survived a potentially nasty car accident in New York, and in 2002, he began hosting a quiet storm-style radio show in the San Francisco Bay Area, although rumors of a new album remained unsubstantiated. *—Steve Huey*

● **In Effect Mode** / May 3, 1988 / Warner Bros. ♦♦♦♦♦
Here is supple hip-hop soul crooning comes from this teen prodigy. "Nite and Day," a huge hit from the summer of 1988, is a must-own. *—John Floyd*

Private Times & the Whole 9 / Oct. 16, 1990 / Warner Bros. ♦♦♦
Al B. Sure's second album pretty much picks up where the first left off, providing plenty of new jack funk and urban slow cookers. There's not much personality here, however. Al and his crew seem determined to stick to formula, which ultimately fails to generate much heat. That means some decent songs (specifically, "Misunderstanding," "Had Enuff?," and a silky duet with Diana Ross, "No Matter What") get lost in the mix. *—Michael Gallucci*

Sexy Versus / 1992 / Warner Bros. ♦♦♦
The third album from Al B. Sure is more moody than its predecessors, more concerned with stoking the bedroom flames than providing any internal heat. The result is a fine boudoir record but a boring listen otherwise. Songs like "Right Now," "Natalie," and "I Don't Wanna Cry" do their best to keep the fire burning, but its one-note blandness and one-track mind eventually can't overcome the overriding dullness of the grooves. Small surprise that little has been heard of Al since. *—Michael Gallucci*

Surface

f. New Jersey

Group / Urban, Dance-Pop, Disco

When you think of the group Surface, the term disco dancefloor doesn't come to mind. The '80s soft soul vocal trio known for such lush ballads as "Closer Than Friends" and the million-selling singles "Shower Me With Your Love" and the number-one pop hit "The First Time" had one of its first charting records as artists signed to dance music pioneer Salsoul Records. "Falling in Love," co-written by Surface member David Conley, doesn't have much in common with the aforementioned titles other than the group name and a (presumably) Conley flute solo. The single made it to number-84 R&B in summer 1983 and the U.K. pop charts. Singer Bernard Jackson who grew up in Stamford, CT, got into the music business through his cousin who lived in New York. Seizing the opportunity, he relocated to New York and began performing around the city. While doing a show in Stamford, his godfather suggested that he contact his nephew David Townsend who was also in the music business. Townsend, a former touring guitarist for the Isley Brothers, was the son of singer/songwriter/producer Ed Townsend who had a hit with "For Your Love" in summer 1958 and wrote the Impressions' "Finally Got Myself Together (I'm a Changed Man)" and co-wrote Marvin Gaye's "Let's Get It On."

Around 1973, Townsend joined a band called the Port Authority where he met David "Pic" Conley. Townsend, whose father shared hit songwriting tips with him, began writing songs with Conley. After Townsend and Conley met Jackson it was decided that they'd write songs together. The trio became staff writers for EMI Music. Their songs were covered by New Edition ("Let's Be Friends" from their 1985 MCA LP *All for Love*) and Sister Sledge ("You're So Fine"). The trio became performers using the name Surface and moved to Los Angeles. An EMI Music executive brought one of their songs, "Let's Try Again," to the attention of Larkin Arnold of Columbia Records. Arnold's previous successes include Natalie Cole and Peabo Bryson. He signed the group to Columbia and their first single "Let's Try Again" charted number-80 R&B in late 1986.

The debut album *Surface* included the smooth and sweet "Happy," which hit number two R&B for two weeks in early 1987, "Lately" (number eight R&B), and the reissued "Let's Try Again." The next LP, *2nd Wave* yielded "I Missed" (number-three R&B), "Closer Than Friends" (number-one R&B for two weeks in early 1989), the wedding standard "Shower Me With Your Love" (gold, number-one R&B/number-five pop), "You Are My Everything" (number-one R&B for two weeks), and "Can We Spend Some Time" (number-five R&B). Jackson brought the sheet music to a song he had written in 1986 to his friend, songwriter Brian Simpson, who had a recording studio in his garage. After listening to the finished demo tape, Jackson thought that he had a hit. Hiring a mobile 24-track recording studio truck to capture his vocal in the best professional conditions, Jackson sang "The First Time" in Simpson's house. "The First Time" was the first single from Surface's *3 Deep* album and went gold hitting number-one R&B and holding the number-one pop for two weeks in early 1991.

While "The First Time" was topping the charts, Surface was one of the presenters at the American Music Awards and were enthusiastically congratulated. The hits continued with "All I Want Is You" (number-eight R&B, early 1991) and "Never Gonna Let You Down." "You're the One" billed as Surface featuring Bernard Jackson made it to number-24 R&B, summer 1991. The group's last charting single was "A Nice Time for Lovin'" included on their 1991 greatest hits LP *The Best Surface: A Nice Time for Loving*. Conley and Townsend also produced sides on Rebbie Jackson ("Reaction") that are on *The Rebbie Jackson Collection* from U.K. label Expansion distributed by Sony/3MV. *—Ed Hogan*

Surface / 1987 / Columbia ♦♦♦
The trio Surface became a hit act in the late '80s, doing soft, overly sentimental love tunes with a self-effacing, subdued style. David Conley, David Townsend, and Bernard Jackson weren't great vocalists, but did nice harmonies. Their songs wouldn't win any lyric awards, and the production and arrangements were rather predictable, but this album put them in the R&B spotlight. *—Ron Wynn*

2nd Wave / 1989 / Columbia ♦♦♦♦♦
Here is a good follow-up album for the New Jersey trio, who were hot tickets at the end of the 1980s. They were a nice harmonizing three-member unit, but didn't have an Eddie LeVert to punctuate things, and they weren't consistently productive songwriters or performers. Still, "Shower Me With Your Love" and "You Are My Everything" filled the airwaves in 1988 and 1989. *—Ron Wynn*

3 Deep / 1990 / Columbia ♦♦♦

The Best Surface: A Nice Time for Loving / 1991 / Columbia ♦♦♦♦♦
Their reign as R&B love champs didn't last very long. The trio Surface ran out of steam in the early '90s, and Columbia opted to circle the wagons and get what they could from this greatest hits collection. It reveals the New Jersey trio as a competent singing group without a dynamite leader. Their hits were pleasant and certainly conducive to late-night romantic situations, but weren't substantial enough to sustain their careers once they fell off the charts. *—Ron Wynn*

● **The First Time: The Best of Surface** / Aug. 21, 2001 / Sony ♦♦♦♦♦
Although they had a number of R&B hits during the late '80s, Surface didn't cross over into the pop mainstream in any notable way. They scraped the bottom reaches of the charts a few times, but they never had a breakout hit that would establish them as stars. Listening to Columbia/Legacy's definitive retrospective *The First Time: The Best of Surface*, it's possible to hear why they didn't break out—they simply didn't have a song that would break them big. That doesn't mean that they were a bad group, since they were very competent within their genre and several hits here are very pleasant late-'80s urban cuts, either on the ballad or dance side. But there's nothing particularly striking, nothing with a hook that would send the band soaring up the pop charts. Still, if you happen to be a fan, either of the group or of this sound, this is a pleasing listen, and a very representative overview of what Surface achieved. *—Stephen Thomas Erlewine*

The Swallows

f. 1946, **db.** 1958

Group / Doo Wop, R&B

The Swallows are best remembered for "Dearest" (number-nine R&B in August 1951) and a handful of other great doo wop tunes. The group—like their neighborhood influences the Vibranaires—were from Baltimore, MD, and began singing shortly after, forming in 1946. Originally called the Oakateers, by 1949 the group was renaming themselves the Swallows (in deference to Baltimore's hugely successful Orioles). The original lineup featured lead tenor vocalist Lawrence Coxsen and Irving Turner, but by the late '40s, both were gone. Tenor lead Eddie Rich was Coxson's replacement, joining Frederick Johnson, Herman "Junior" Denby (baritone, tenor, and string bass), Norris "Bunky" Mack (bass vocals, guitar, piano, drums), and Earl Hurley. After a number of local gigs in the Baltimore area, they came to the attention of King Records of Cincinnati in 1951. A recording session produced their first single, "Dearest" (King 4458). It climbed to number nine on the R&B charts in August 1951 and was a big seller in the both San Francisco and Oakland, which led to the group's first tour (with the Count Basie Orchestra and vocalist Earl Williams).

Other singles failed to top the success of their initial outing, although "It Ain't the Meat (It's the Motion)," the ribald jump B-side of their third single, was a big seller in the South, especially in Georgia and the Carolinas. Sometimes Junior Denby took over singing lead chorus. They also released a version of the pop standard "I Only Have Eyes for You," predating the Flamingos' version by six years. (Interesting note: as an added bit of circumstance, the Flamingos were originally known as the Swallows until they discovered the King group had first dibs on the name.)

The group continued to tour the U.S. extensively, while King released additional singles. Their last single for King was "I'll Be Waiting" (King 4676). Shortly after leaving the label, the group disbanded, then re-formed again with Earl Hurley (lead), Eddie Rich, original late '40s member Irv Turner, and new Swallows Al France, Ernie "Buddy" Bailey (not the Clovers' Bailey), and "Money" Johnson. By the spring of 1954, the new lineup recorded for Lexy "Flap" Hanford's After Hours label, but the group disbanded shortly afterwards, for a second time. In 1956, France and Turner were replaced by Bobby Hendricks and Buddy Crawford, but no recordings are credited to this contingent. The group went on hiatus afterwards.

In 1958, the Swallows came together with original members Eddie Rich and Earl Hurley, Bailey, Johnson, and new Swallow Calvin Collette. They signed with Syd Nathan's Federal label (based in Cincinnati at the time), who issued four sides, including a cover of Bobby Hendricks' "Itchy Twitchy Feeling" (which just barely touched the national pop charts in late 1958). Soon afterwards, the Swallows called it quits after more than a decade of making music. *—Bryan Thomas*

● **Dearest** / 1991 / Charly ✦✦✦✦✦

Swamp Dogg (Jerry Williams)

b. Jul. 1942, Portsmouth, VA

Vocals, Keyboards, Piano, Producer / Soul, Soul-Blues, Blues-Rock, R&B

One of the great characters in rock and soul music is Jerry Williams, better known as the eccentric, idiosyncratic, and always entertaining Swamp Dogg (no relation to Snoop Doggy Dogg). A Virginia native, Williams invented his own legend by claiming that he had little proper schooling, only to wake up one day and find himself a musical genius (his words). Actually, Williams is very talented, and an early association with Jerry Wexler and Phil Walden led to him working for a number of years as a producer, engineer, and occasional songwriter with Atlantic in the '60s. At decade's end, however, he decided that the time was right to unleash Swamp Dogg's singular view of the world on an unsuspecting public.

The initial result was one of the most gloriously gonzo soul recordings of all time, *Total Destruction to Your Mind.* Along with living up to its title, it was a renegade chunk of not-quite-commercial music, with an unforgettable (though fuzzy) cover shot of the portly Dogg in his underwear. Although undeniably great, *Total Destruction to Your Mind* is one of the most obscure soul records ever made. That, however, has nothing to do with the music, which rocks in a way reminiscent of Solomon Burke or Wilson Pickett. The album's charm may have to do with Dogg's world view: part libertarian politics; part Zappa-style critiques of commerciality and capitalism; and part horny male, the latter defining for better and worse his view of women. Although he spent years working in the industry, Dogg was simply not the standard-issue soul type. And that was good. Dogg continued to make records, albeit infrequently, after 1969, some good, a few great, and most all extremely difficult to find. With contemporary soul sounding increasingly mannered and sterile, Dogg's yelling, screaming, and general craziness is missed. Thankfully, he hasn't disappeared for good, although he only makes records when he feels like it. His release, *Surfin' In Harlem,* came out in 1991. And as is often the case with quirky "legends," what he's up to at any given time is the source of wild speculation. It would be wise to not count him out; just when you think this Dogg is down and out, he sneaks up and bites you. *—John Dougan*

Total Destruction to Your Mind / 1970 / Canyon ✦✦✦✦✦

The title track is a slam-bangin' chunk of rock and funk that's pushed by a great session band including guitarist Jesse Carr and drummer Johnny Sandlin, and is easily Dogg's finest moment on record. But the rest of this is great too, ranging from the consumer nightmare "Synthetic World" to the paternity blues of "Mama's Baby, Daddy's Maybe." Plus, Dogg is a great singer, and his dizzying range gets a workout on these songs. *—John Dougan*

Swamp Dogg (Rat On) / 1971 / Elektra ✦✦✦✦✦

The cover of this LP—Swamp Dogg riding a white rat, hands raised and fists clenched in triumph—lets you know that you're not in for any ol' R&B record, even before the needle hits the grooves. It's a satisfying continuation of the eclectic soul-singer-songwriter mix of his debut. Vocally, Swamp Dogg sounds like a cross between General Johnson (of Chairmen of the Board) and Van Morrison; as a songwriter, he's his own man. With the exception of Sly Stone, no other soul men of the period were investigating controversial topics with such infectious musicality and good humor. He takes on promiscuity with unbridled frankness in cuts like "Predicament #2," and bemoans the eternal delay of American justice for minorities in "Remember I Said Tomorrow," and twists Irving Berlin's "God Bless America" into a protest song (and also, bizarrely, covers the Bee Gees' "Got to Get a Message to You"). None of this endeared him to industry insiders, and Swamp Dogg was dropped by Elektra after the album's release. [It's long been out of print, but in the U.K. Charly has reissued it on CD on a two-fer with *Total Destruction of Your Mind*.] *—Richie Unterberger*

Cuffed, Collared and Tagged / 1972 / Edsel ✦✦✦✦✦

Gag a Maggot / 1973 / Stonedogg ✦✦✦✦✦

Another great album title, another tiny label, another great record long forgotten. Not as consistently manic as *Destruction, Maggot* is as ferocious sounding and does have a good cover of Wilson Pickett's "In the Midnight Hour." Never one to let a love lyric go by without a sarcastic twist, Dogg's love song here is called "I Couldn't Pay For What I Got Last Night." *—John Dougan*

Have You Heard This Story? / 1974 / Island ✦✦✦

I'm Not Selling Out, I'm Buying In / 1981 / Takoma ✦✦✦✦✦

After years of keeping a low profile, Dogg emerged from out of nowhere with this fine record. Instead of streamlined hard soul, this record carries a rock & roll clout that keeps even its most banal moments ("Wine, Women and Rock 'n' Roll") from terminal tedium. Song title highlight: Dogg's duet with Esther Phillips, "The Love We Got Ain't Worth Two Dead Flies." Kind of says it all, doesn't it. *—John Dougan*

Uncut & Classified / 1981 / Charly ✦✦✦

Unmuzzled / 1983 / Charly ✦✦✦

● **Total Destruction to Your Mind/Rat On** / 1991 / Charly ✦✦✦✦✦

These two early Swamp Dogg albums were unheralded landmarks of early '70s soul; Charly has now combined both of them onto a single-disc CD reissue. The liner notes seem to have been written by someone who speaks English as a third language, but that minor gripe aside, this probably contains the singer's most significant work. *—Richie Unterberger*

Surfin' in Harlem / Oct. 31, 1991 / Volt ✦✦

● **The Best of 25 Years of Swamp Dogg** / Mar. 5, 1996 / Pointblank ✦✦✦✦✦

The 18-track retrospective *Best of 25 Years of Swamp Dogg* collects many of the highlights from his scattershot career. Concentrating on his '80s output, the compilation doesn't provide a definitive portrait of the warped blues and soul man, but it does offer enough of his best material to make it an excellent introduction. *—Stephen Thomas Erlewine*

Swamp's Things: The Complete Calla Recordings 1966–1967 / May 2, 2000 / WestSide ✦✦✦✦

A collection of Swamp Dogg's '60s Calico sides, making their first time on CD appearance with the bonus of a whole album's worth of new-to-CD '70s recordings. The first ten tracks were released as Jerry Williams or Little Jerry Williams while the remainder came out under the sobriquet of Swamp Dogg. Highlights include "Eat the Goose (Before the Goose Eats You)," "Call Me Nigger," "Paradoxical (No Bugles)," "Baby, Bunny, Sugar, Honey," "Philly Duck," and "Baby You're My Everything." A stellar collection of '60s and '70s soul-funk. *—Cub Koda*

The Swan Silvertones

f. 1938, Coalwood, West Virginia

Group / Traditional Gospel, Black Gospel, Southern Gospel, R&B

The Swan Silvertones are one of the premier gospel groups of all time. The a cappella quartet Four Harmony Kings was created by tenor Claude Jeter in 1938 in Coalwood, WV, but the name was changed to the Swan Silvertones when they began a 15-minute radio show in Knoxville sponsored by the Swan Bakery Company in 1942. They developed a national reputation during their contract with King Records from 1946 to 1951, recording some 21 songs, mostly in the jubilee gospel style. They joined Specialty Records from 1951 to 1953, but issued only four singles (in a more contemporary, harder style) before they were dropped. The group really came into their own when they signed with Vee-Jay and recorded with that label from 1956 through 1964. During their years at Vee-Jay, the main members of the group were tenor (and falsetto) Jeter, baritone John H. Myles, tenor/arranger Paul Owens and bass William Conner, with a few other singers moving through the group during that time.

The smoother Vee-Jay sound is probably due to arranger Owens, who joined the group in 1952. Influenced by jazz vocal groups like the Four Freshmen and the Hi-Los, Owens smoothed out the sound and made it more contemporary, even progressive. Starting in 1956, the group began adding instruments to what had been a purely a cappella sound, including several jazz sidemen. Perhaps their greatest hit was "Oh Mary Don't You Weep," released in 1959; Claude Jeter intones the phrase "I'll be a bridge over deep water, if you trust in my name" that inspired Paul Simon to compose "Bridge Over Troubled Water" some years later. When Vee-Jay closed in 1965, the group moved to HOB Records, where they did one last album before Claude Jeter left to record on his own and focus on his ministry. *—Michael Erlewine*

The Swan Silvertones / 1959 / Vee-Jay ✦✦✦✦

Singin' in My Soul / 1960 / Vee-Jay ✦✦✦✦✦

The Swan Silvertones' second Vee-Jay LP is an impressive collection of gospel singing dominated by the compositions of Rev. Claude Jeter, particularly "Rock My Soul," which went on to greater renown. The group's reverent fervor is underscored by their sense of dread, notably on the terrifying "Sinking Sand," in which they confess that they fear the instability of the ground beneath their feet. As much as the songs themselves, of course, it is the group's impassioned singing that makes *Singin' in My Soul* another classic gospel album from the Swan Silvertones. *—William Ruhlmann*

☆ **Let's Go to Church Together** / 1964 / Vee-Jay ✦✦✦✦✦

This is quintessential Swan Silvertones at their peak. Songs like "Love Lifted Me," and "I'll Be Satisfied"—12 songs from a single session in 1964 have captured some of the finest work of this legendary group. This makes for deep satisfying listening. *—Michael Erlewine*

Get Right With the Swan Silvertones / 1982 / Rhino ✦✦✦✦

A reissue of various '50s and '60s singles and album sides plus two unissued cuts. Lead vocal dynamics from Rev. Claude Jeter, Paul Owens, and Louis Johnson. This well-rounded and amply annotated cross-section deserves serious consideration. *—Kip Lornell*

☆ **The Best of Swan Silvertones** / Oct. 17, 1990 / Chameleon ✦✦✦✦✦

★ **The Swan Silvertones/Singin' in My Soul** / Oct. 1993 / Vee-Jay ✦✦✦✦✦
Here is one CD with two classic Vee-Jay albums (24 tracks) of vintage Swan Silvertones. The tracks from both albums came from six sessions for Vee-Jay, when the group was at its creative peak. The album *Swan Silvertones* is perhaps the single best album they ever put out, containing 12 tunes including their hit "Oh Mary Don't You Weep," "How I Got Over," "My Rock," "The Lord's Prayer," "When Jesus Comes," and "Great Day in December"—all incredible musical experiences. The music continues from the album *Singin' in My Soul*, featuring 12 more prime Vee-Jay cuts including "End of My Journey," "Jesus is Alright With Me," and their version of "Rock My Soul." *—Michael Erlewine*

Hallelujah: A Collection of Their Finest Recordings / May 18, 1999 / Music Club ✦✦✦✦
This 15-track collection brings together both live and studio recordings made for the HOB label. Both of the famous leads with the group—the Rev. Claude Jeter and Louis Johnson—are featured on tracks like "Only Believe," "I Love the Lord," "Home in that Rock," "Call Him Up," "Jesus, I Love You," their two magnificent voices dueting on "Leaning on Jesus," "In My Heart" and "He's My Friend." The live tracks on here literally sweat with emotion and fervor. It's a nice set. *—Cub Koda*

☆ **Pray for Me/Let's Go to Church Together** / 2000 / Collectables ✦✦✦✦✦
The Swan Silvertones perfected their shimmering, explosive vocals while on Vee-Jay Records from 1956-1964. The elastic, dazzling falsetto of Claude Jeter, which was later adapted and reworked by Al Green, was contrasted by any number of powerful second lead singers within the group: Paul Owens, Louis Johnson, or Azell Monk. The songs on this disc, with one exception, cover the Silvertones' last great period and offer resounding harmonies, soaring leads, and remarkable music. The lead selection, "Sinners Crossroad," is actually the Silver Quintette, an Indiana group probably most famous for having on its roster two future soul stars in Roscoe Robinson and Joe Henderson. *—Ron Wynn*

Bettye Swann

b. Oct. 24, 1944, Shreveport, LA
Vocals / Pop-Soul, Soul
Los Angeles soul vocalist Bettye Swann scored a number-one R&B hit in 1967 with her lilting midtempo "Make Me Yours." Swann began recording for the Money label in 1964 and found herself on the charts the next year with "Don't Wait Too Long." After "Make Me Yours" made her some money on Money, she stopped off at Capitol long enough to enjoy a hit with "Don't Touch Me" in 1969 and then settled in at Atlantic, where she notched several soul hits during the early '70s (including "Victim of a Foolish Heart"). *—Bill Dahl*

Make Me Yours / 1967 / Collectables ✦✦✦

The Soul View Now / 1968 / Capitol ✦✦✦✦

Don't You Ever Get Tired of Hurting Me / 1969 / Capitol ✦✦✦

● **The Money Recordings** / Jul. 31, 2001 / Kent ✦✦✦✦
All of the material known to exist by Bettye Swann in the vaults of the Money label is found on this 24-track compilation. It has all of her 1965-1968 singles for the company, as well as a few songs released on her 1967 *Make Me Yours* LP, and nine previously unreleased tracks (two of which are just remixes, half a dozen of which are alternate versions). It's satisfactory, but not thrilling, mid-level soul, shaded a little toward the mainstream Motowny pop-soul side of things, though not overbearingly so. Swann did write most of her material, yet there wasn't much particularly striking (or inadequate) about her songs and vocals. Even non-intense soul listeners would have little trouble placing the material in the 1966-1967 time frame, so much is it like the standard soul fare of the era. Once in a while, particularly on the slightly earlier-sounding cuts, there are hints of a gutsier and more satisfyingly bluesier bent, as on "The Heartache Is Gone," "What Can It Be," and especially "I Will Not Cry." "Lonely Love," though a 1967 single, has the slight girl group flavor more associated with some soul records from circa 1964, as does the previously unissued "The Dance Is Over." *—Richie Unterberger*

Keith Sweat

b. Jul. 22, 1961, New York, NY
Vocals / Urban, New Jack Swing, Club/Dance
Keith Sweat is a Harlem-born R&B singer/songwriter who released his debut album, *Make It Last Forever*, at the end of 1987. The album sold over three-million copies, spawning the hits "I Want Her" (number-one R&B, number-five pop), "Something Just Ain't Right" (number-three R&B), "Make It Last Forever" (number-two R&B), and "Don't Stop Your Love" (number-nine R&B). It was followed in June 1990 by *I'll Give All My Love to You*, another million-seller, that featured the hits "Make You Sweat" (number-one R&B, number-14 pop), "Merry Go Round" (number-two R&B), "I'll Give All My Love to You" (number-one R&B, number-seven pop), and "Your Love, Pt. 2" (number-four R&B). Sweat's third album was *Keep It Comin'*, an R&B chart-topper at the end of 1991, whose title track was another number-one R&B hit. In 1994 he returned with *Get Up on It*; a self-titled release followed in 1996, and two years later he issued *Still in the Game* and *Didn't See Me Coming* in fall 2000. *—William Ruhlmann*

Make It Last Forever / 1987 / Elektra ✦✦✦✦✦
Produced by Teddy Riley, Keith Sweat's debut *Make It Last Forever* exploded all over urban and pop stations and remains the brightest star in Sweat's galaxy of LPs. Sweat's pleading, whining tenor adroitly draws you into every song, demanding an emotional commitment. Who can't relate to "Something Just Ain't Right" and "Right and a Wrong Way," two tense, stunning realizations. The hip-hop beats and plucky guitar of "I Want Her" put new jack swing on the map; it was Sweat's first single release and topped *Billboard*'s R&B chart the week of January 30, 1988. All eight tracks are impressive, with his rendition of Tony Hester's "In the Rain," popularized by the Dramatics, equaling and possibly surpassing the original. *—Andrew Hamilton*

● **I'll Give All My Love to You** / 1990 / Elektra ✦✦✦✦✦
The glut of faceless, interchangeable new jack swing artists plaguing urban contemporary radio in the early 1990s served one useful purpose: they reminded us how exciting the originators of the style (Guy, Bobby Brown and Keith Sweat, among others) could be. When Sweat's overdue sophomore effort, *I'll Give All My Love to You*, was released in 1990, it exposed countless new jack automatons for the unimaginative frauds they were. Though not quite as strong as 1987's *Make It Last Forever*, this is a respectable disc that sounds consistently heartfelt and sincere. The hard electro-funk groove of "Make You Sweat" is likable enough, but ballads and slow jams like "Just One of Them Things" (a duet with Gerald LeVert), "I Knew That You Were Cheating" and "Merry Go Round" are where the Harlem native really shines. For all its high-tech production gloss and use of hip-hop elements, this self-produced CD reminds us that Sweat is quite aware of the great soul music of the 1970s. *—Alex Henderson*

Keep It Comin' / 1991 / Elektra ✦✦

Get Up on It / 1994 / Elektra ✦✦✦
After scoring massive success with his first two albums, *Make It Last Forever* and *I'll Give All My Love to You*, Keith Sweat's third album, *Keep It Comin'*, signaled something of a creative and commercial slump for the new jack pioneer, which continued through 1994's *Get Up on It*. However, *Get Up on It* is not a bad album by any means. In fact, the set is classic Keith Sweat, filled to the brim with the pleading ballads that made this Harlem crooner so popular. Sweat began to utilize female background vocals, courtesy of Kut Klose, to full effect on this album, especially on the hit title track (one of the album's shining moments), a trend that he perfected on his huge 1996 self-titled comeback album. So *Get Up on It* finds Sweat in a stage of transition, leaving the formula that began to grow stale on *Keep It Comin'* and beginning to feature female backing vocals at center stage, somewhat similar to what Barry White and Luther Vandross had done before him. *Get Up on It* churned out two other singles, the uptempo yet slightly unimaginative "How Do You Like It?" (which, as the set's lead single, didn't really work to catapult the album to massive early sales) and the big ballad "When I Give My Love," which is pure Keith Sweat. Other standouts include "Put Your Loving Through the Test," featuring the late Roger Troutman, and "Telephone Love." For fans of classic Keith Sweat, R&B ballads, and midtempo grooves, this album will do, although it doesn't rank as one of the more essential pieces in this artist's enduring catalog. *—Jose F. Promis*

Keith Sweat / Jun. 25, 1996 / Elektra ✦✦✦
In a way, it's ironic that an album entitled *Keith Sweat* is crammed with guest stars, thereby attracting attention away from the man himself. No matter. Sweat turns in a typically stylish and sophisticated set of urban soul and new jack R&B, all highlighted by his silky singing. Sweat's main talent is for smooth ballads, and *Keith Sweat* is filled with excellent selections, including the seductive "Come With Me," which features guest vocals by Ronald Isley. The album does bog down a bit with uneven material, but its highpoints are as captivating as any of Sweat's previous work. *—Leo Stanley*

Just a Touch / 1997 / Elektra ✦✦✦✦
Keith Sweat keeps coming up with the goods, and *Just a Touch* continues his string of gold LPs—rightly so, as all 12 cuts are carefully crafted. "Twisted" took the charts by storm; backed by protégés Kut Klose, the midtempo number includes a cameo rap by Pretty Russ. Guest appearances by Gerald LeVert, Aaron Hall, and Buddy Banks give the fresh "Funky Dope Lovin'" a 3-D appeal; Sweat can blend with anybody. He updates Slave's "Just a Touch" by adding some slick new beats, as well as Traci Hale on backing vocals. Sweat duets with Althena Cage on "Nobody," a dramatic saga and the most compelling track on the CD. Like many of his contemporaries, Keith plays the Ron Isley card on "Come With Me"—decent, but it fails to live up to Ron Isley collaborations with notables like R. Kelly. Pretty Russ, Tizone, and Lil Bud all break off raps on the sensual, erotic "Freak With Me." There seems to be no bottom in Keith Sweat's well. He was one of the most prolific artists of the '90s and showed no signs of slacking off entering the millennium. *—Andrew Hamilton*

Still in the Game / Sep. 22, 1998 / Elektra ✦✦✦

● **Singles Collection** / Apr. 18, 2000 / WEA International ✦✦✦✦

Didn't See Me Coming / Nov. 14, 2000 / Elektra ✦✦✦✦
When Keith Sweat first appeared, some folks didn't know what to make of him because of his unique style. Like Teddy Riley, Sweat was a pioneer of new jack, the genre that helped lay the foundation for the R&B/hip-hop and street music of the '90s. On his first album of the 21st century, *Didn't See Me Coming*, the singer showcases his versatility and adaptability. The sinewy "Whatcha Like" seductively slinks along. The softly chugging "Real Man" has Sweat singing to a woman who's out to get his ends that "you wouldn't know a real man if he was staring in your face." "Caught Up" is a vintage Keith Sweat slow jam with its "I was played" theme and its on this track the singer's vocal maturity is probably most apparent. Sweat supplies the album with some of his trademark "beggin'" songs in "Only Wanna Please You" and "Why U Treat Me So Cold." Lil Mo shares vocals with the singer on the "lonely superstar" duet ballad, "I'll Trade (A Million Bucks)." Sweat duets with David Hollister on the "money can't buy ya love"-themed "Don't Have Me." After five platinum albums (three of which went multi-platinum), two gold singles (four number-one R&B, two Top Ten pop), and this fine addition, those who didn't see Keith Sweat coming will have "to recognize." *—Ed Hogan*

Rebirth / Aug. 13, 2002 / Elektra ✦✦✦
It's not a comeback because he's been putting out records consistently since the late '80s, and it's not really a creative reawakening since he hasn't changed anything about his game. In the end, *Rebirth* is really just another Keith Sweat album, and it's a tribute to one of the leading soul men of the '80s and '90s that he can continue making records as smooth and as vigorous as this one 15 years down the road. He produces about half

of the songs, while co-producer Roy "Royalty" Hamilton takes most of the first few. Other than a few carefully placed samples, there aren't many nods to contemporary rap, just the same midtempo chug over loving/pleading songs like "I Want You," "Gots to Have It," "Ladies Night," and "One on One." Sweat is still in great voice, and it's his personality that carries *Rebirth*, even when it sounds similar to his work in the past. *—John Bush*

The Sweet Inspirations

f. 1963, **db.** 1979
Group / Pop-Soul, Soul
If one was cutting a soul, R&B, pop, rock, or girl group record in New York in the '60s and needed female backup vocals, chances are they'd try to get the Sweet Inspirations first. The group found their way onto numerous recordings, including hits by the Drifters, Van Morrison, Wilson Pickett, Solomon Burke, Garnett Mimms, and most famously, Aretha Franklin (with whom they sometimes toured).

The group evolved from the '50s gospel group the Drinkard Singers. At various points soul singers Doris Troy, Judy Clay, Dionne Warwick, and sister Dee Dee Warwick were members. By the time they began to record on their own in 1967, their leader was Cissy Houston (mother of Whitney), and the women were renamed the Sweet Inspirations. As an Atlantic recording act, the group cut some fine sides that rank among the clearest illustrations of the close links between soul music and gospel harmony. Usually sticking to material by famed soul and pop songwriters, they had about a half-dozen moderate R&B hits in the late '60s; the biggest, "Sweet Inspiration," was a Top 20 pop single. Houston left the group at the end of the '60s and the Inspirations left Atlantic in the early '70s, sometimes working with Elvis Presley and recording an album for Stax in 1973. *—Richie Unterberger*

Songs of Faith & Inpsiration / 1968 / Atlantic ♦♦♦♦

Sweets for My Sweet / 1969 / Atlantic ♦♦♦
Originally released in 1969 by Atlantic Records, *Sweets for My Sweet*, the Sweet Inspirations' fourth album, burns rubber in CD format. Elvis Presley's favorite female backing vocalists turn "Chained" (made famous by Marvin Gaye) into a fiery testimonial; Gaye was serious, but these ladies sound ready to die for their men. Other selections that make your hair stand up are Joshie Armstead, Nickolas Ashford, and Valerie Simpson's "Don't Go," the title track (an old Drifters hit), Eddie Hinton's "Always David," and William Bell and Booker T. Jones' "Everyday Is Like a Holiday." A gratifying girl group with a full sound that hits the spot every time. *—Andrew Hamilton*

The Estelle, Myrna and Sylvia / 1973 / Stax ♦♦♦♦
Though Cissy Houston was long gone from the group by the time they made this album, it's a fine set of gospel-pop-soul, with arrangements that manage to be sophisticated without getting slick. Co-produced by David Porter and Ronnie Williams, who as a pair also wrote most of the material; the songs are good and varied, the vocals and harmonies emotive and ebullient. [The CD reissue adds two hits that they recorded for Atlantic in 1967 with Houston in the lineup ("Why (Am I Treated So Bad)" and "Sweet Inspiration").] *—Richie Unterberger*

Hot Butterfly / 1979 / RSO ♦♦

● **The Best of the Sweet Inspirations** / Nov. 22, 1994 / Ichiban/Soul Classics ♦♦♦♦♦
Here is a solid retrospective of their Atlantic years (1967-1971), including all the hits and several misses. A lot of the songs were cut at Muscle Shoals, Memphis, or Atlantic Studios, and accordingly the arrangements have a deep soul flavor characteristic of Atlantic's late-'60s releases (although they worked briefly in Philadelphia in 1969 for a Gamble-Huff-flavored sound). Includes covers of songs by Isaac Hayes, Roebuck Staples, Dan Penn, and Gamble & Huff, all of which they make their own with lovely harmonies and imaginative interpretations. *—Richie Unterberger*

Sweet Sensation

f. Manchester, England
Group / Smooth Soul, Urban
Not to be confused with the late '80s American dance act of the same name, Sweet Sensation were an eight-man British soul band from Manchester, England, cast very much in the then-popular mold of the Philly sound, who broke through in 1974 following an appearance on the television talent show *New Faces*. There they were discovered by British pop impresario Tony Hatch, a panelist on the show. It was Hatch who landed the group a deal with Pye Records but, despite his patronage, the group's first single, "Snow Fire," was a total non-starter. In September 1974, however, "Sad Sweet Dreamer"—co-produced by Hatch and songwriter Desmond Parton—rocketed to the top of the U.K. chart and also cracked the U.S. Top 20. A soaring soul ballad heavily influenced by the Stylistics, and led by lead vocalist Marcel King's ethereal falsetto, "Sad Sweet Dreamer" was quickly followed by "Purely by Coincidence," which rose to number 11 in the New Year.

However, an eponymous debut album failed to move in Britain (it made number 163 in America), and the group's next single, "Hide Away From the Sun," certainly lived up to at least half of own title. Undeterred, Sweet Sensation released a string of further singles, including "Mr Cool," "Sweet Regrets," and "Mail Train" during 1975-1976, while 1977 saw the group competing to represent the U.K. in that year's Eurovision Song Contest. Out of a dozen acts, "You're My Sweet Sensation" finished in a lowly eighth place in the British final. That was very much the group's last hurrah, and they were dropped by Pye soon after. *—Amy Hanson*

● **Sad Sweet Dreamer** / 1975 / Pye ♦♦♦
With the 1975 debut of *Sad Sweet Dreamer*, Sweet Sensation became Manchester, England's answer to the Stylistics. And, finding themselves riding high with the trans-Atlantic Top 20 title track, ultimately turned in a neatly stylized collection of smooth pop-soul that suggests transplanting the Sound of Philadelphia to the industrial northwest of England wasn't such an odd thing to do. Certainly Marcel King lacks for nothing in the lead vocal department, his molten falsetto wraps itself seamlessly around ten generally excellent songs, while the harmonic backwash created by the remainder of the group becomes almost orchestral around him. And if the production might not be as perfect as the best of Gamble & Huff, at times, it's certainly as haunting. "Emptiness Filled with Love" and "Sad Sweet Dreamer," which scored the band a U.K. number one, itself are minor masterpieces of aching romanticism, by whichever contemporary standards you care to measure them, while "Snow Fire," too, catches the ear with slick hooks and effervescent harmonies. "Purely by Coincidence," the U.K. hit follow-up to "Sad Sweet Dreamer," is another jewel—the best of the album's more uptempo numbers, it also indicates that, with less slavish guidance and more practiced production, Sweet Sensation could at least have drawn level with the Real Thing in the British public's estimation. (America, on the other hand, simply preferred another real thing altogether.) *—Amy Hanson*

Switch

f. 1975, Mansfield, OH, **db.** 1984
Group / Funk
Another Ohio funk band, they began as First Class in 1975. Jermaine Jackson discovered the group that included lead vocalist Phil Ingram and Bobby DeBarge, Greg Williams, Tommy DeBarge, Eddie Fluellen, and Jody Sims. They had a huge hit in 1978 with "There'll Never Be," a Top Ten R&B single. They also had two others during their tenure on Gordy, "I Call Your Name" in 1979 and "Love Over and Over Again" in 1980. Phillip Ingram went on his own in 1980, and Bobby and Tommy also departed to join the family group DeBarge. Percussionist/vocalist Renard Gallo and Gonzales Ozen and keyboardist Attala Zane Giles were their replacements. They left Gordy for Total Experience in 1984, cutting the LP *Am I Still Your Boyfriend?* *—Ron Wynn*

Switch / 1978 / Gordy ♦♦♦
The successful debut album from the self-contained sextet introduced the R&B community to an exciting, soulful sound. This album consisted of quality uptempo and midtempo tunes. Their first release, "There'll Never Be," graced the *Billboard* R&B charts for 26 weeks, peaking at number six. The moderately paced single features creative background vocals, inviting horn arrangements, and the high-pitched falsetto of Bobby DeBarge, who also co-wrote the track with the Bewley Brothers. As mellow as the aforementioned single is, the follow-up "I Wanna Be Closer" is even more comforting. Written, arranged and produced by Jermaine Jackson, the single peaked at number 22 after 13 weeks. Featuring three-part harmonies and a soulful introduction, it also showcased the articulate lead vocals of Phillip Ingram (baritone) and Bobby DeBarge. This is a good collection. *—Craig Lytle*

Switch II / 1979 / Gordy ♦♦♦♦♦
Switch's sophomore album picks up where the group's debut left off. Scintillating harmonies and torching leads by Phil Ingram and Bobby DeBarge make "Calling on All Girls," written by Jermaine Jackson, a standout. Equally as captivating is the roller coastering "I Call Your Name," written by Bobby Debarge, a song that aptly depicts teenage infatuation. They handle uptempo material with aplomb, too. Check out the groove on "Best Beat in Town, and the urgency and realness of "You're the One for Me." A bright yellow album cover depicts Switch dressed in fly outfits and enjoying the California sun. The guys from Akron, OH and Grand Rapids, MI had it going on, and probably thought the phat grooves and adulation would never stop. *—Andrew Hamilton*

Switch V / 1980 / Gordy ♦♦♦
With two *Billboard* R&B Top Ten singles under their belts, it was thought that Switch was on its way to becoming an urban mainstay. However, a personnel shuffle brought about the exit of Bobby DeBarge and brother Tommy and introduced Terrance Gaines and Attala Zane Giles. Bobby was the group's marquee attraction with his naturally high tenor, in addition to being a superb songwriter and producer. Before his exit, he did sing lead on and produce the track "I Luv It," not his best work. Unlike their previous albums, this one does not revel in those tender, heart-moving melodies. The two featured singles were the uptempo "I Do Love You" and the laid-back "Call on Me." Both are credible tracks, but they don't retain that Switch aura. The singles peaked on the *Billboard* R&B charts at number 73 and number 70, respectively. The group was obviously trying to redefine its sound and image, but it was too little too late, as this would be their last album for the Motown family. *—Craig Lytle*

This Is My Dream / 1980 / Gordy ♦♦♦
This album does not have the same magic that the group's debut release generated; it's lacking those harmonious background vocals, grand arrangements and dynamic lead vocals. Several numbers try to rekindle that aura. "This Is My Dream" has an inviting arrangement, as does "You and I" (*Billboard* R&B number 57), which also touches on the sentimental side. "What a Feeling" is reminiscent of Con Funk Shun's uptempo grooves. Nonetheless, it is a superb party track, and "Love Over and Over Again" comes closest to that Switch sound, compliments of lead singer Bobby DeBarge. With his naturally high tenor, Bobby DeBarge (older brother of El DeBarge) carried the song to number nine on the *Billboard* R&B charts. *—Craig Lytle*

● **The Best of Switch** / 1991 / Motown ♦♦♦♦♦
Big things were expected when Grand Rapids natives Bobby and Tommy DeBarge merged with Akronites Jody Sims, Gregory Williams, Eddie Fluellen and Phil Ingram to form Switch. Switch was Fluellen, Ingram, Williams and Sims' second shot at stardom; they had previously been part of White Heat, which recorded an album for RCA Records that Barry White produced. A beautiful trumpet, soaring three part harmonies, and romantic lyrics tenderly sung by Bobby DeBarge and Phil Ingram help to make "I Wanna Be Closer" irresistible; the dazzling ballad was written and produced by Jermaine Jackson. The bubbling "There Never Be" was the opposite, fast and full of vocal gymnastics; the love vow became the first hit out the box for the young men. A pounding "Best

Beat in Town" fit right in with the times, drummer Jody Sims co-wrote the mover with Bobby and Tommy, and can be heard adding percussions to the pounding beat. "I Call Your Name" commands attention every time it's played on "for lovers only" programs; Bobby DeBarge's unique scat singing is featured along with his mercurial falsetto, on the flowing, airy number. Equally as compelling, is the slower "Love Over and Over," the moving "You And I," a good wedding song, and the thumping, emphatic "I Do Love You." Switch was bad, and that means good. It's about time Motown dropped a good 18-plus-song CD on Switch like they did with DeBarge. *—Andrew Hamilton*

SWV

f. 1990

Group / Urban, New Jack Swing, Dance-Pop, House

With their Teddy Riley-produced 1992 debut, *It's About Time*, the all-female new jack swing trio SWV scored a string of Top Ten R&B hits that established them as one of the most popular urban R&B groups of the '90s. SWV (their name is an acronym for Sisters With Voices) is comprised of three school friends: Coko (born Cheryl Gamble), Taj (born Tamara Johnson), and Lelee (born Leanne Lyons). All three vocalists sang in church as children, which is where they learned how to harmonize. A demo tape the group assembled caught the attention of producer Teddy Riley, a former member of Guy and arguably the father of new jack swing. Prior to SWV, Riley helped establish the careers of Jodeci and Mary J. Blige. Riley's luck didn't wear out with SWV—he helped the group craft their debut, *It's About Time*, which went double platinum within its first year of release.

The release of *It's About Time* was preceded by "Right Here" in the fall of 1992. The single reached number 13 on the R&B charts, but it was the number-two hit, "I'm So Into You," that established the trio as a commercial force early in 1993. It was followed by two number-one R&B singles in a row: "Weak" and "Right Here/Human Nature," a remix of their first single that featured samples of Michael Jackson's hit, "Human Nature." "Weak" also hit number one on the pop charts; "Right Here/Human Nature" reached number two on the pop charts. One other Top Ten R&B hit from *It's About Time*, "Always on My Mind," followed late in 1993. "Anything," SWV's contribution to the soundtrack for *Above the Rim*, became a Top Ten R&B hit in the spring of 1994. Also in the spring of 1994, SWV released *The Remixes*, which went gold by the end of the year. In the summer of 1995, the trio lent vocal harmonies to Blackstreet's Top 40 R&B hit, "Tonight's the Night."

In 1996, SWV returned with *New Beginning*, which was preceded by the number-one R&B hit, "You're the One." *Release Some Tension* followed in 1997, and two years later the group's past successes were recalled on their *Greatest Hits*. *—Stephen Thomas Erlewine*

It's About Time / Oct. 27, 1992 / RCA ♦♦♦♦♦

SWV (Sisters With Voices) electrified the urban contemporary world with *It's About Time*. Their deep, sensual harmonies, sometimes naughty lyrics and aggressive style immediately struck a responsive chord, particularly among male fans. Their CD shows their versatility, as they handled new jack tunes, romantic ballads like "It's About Time," and sassy, innuendo-laden fare such as "Blak Pudd'n" and "That's What I Need." Their hits "Weak" and "Right Here" had the same blend of heat and vulnerability that underscore the best En Vogue material, and even though this CD was padded by remixes and repeats, it was still among the finest debuts issued in 1992. *—Ron Wynn*

New Beginning / Apr. 1996 / RCA ♦♦♦♦

As a title, *New Beginning* may be something of an overstatement—after all, it is only SWV's second album. Nevertheless, the group does take a different approach on *New Beginning*, backing away from the new jack grooves that dominated their debut and exploring a more direct, organic R&B vibe. They haven't left hip-hop behind, but they've added a new array of sonic textures that gives their music added depth. But the true strength of *New Beginning* is the vocal capabilities of SWV—they can handle smooth soul like "Don't Waste Your Time" as easily as the funk of "Whatcha Need." There may be a couple of weak spots on the album, but the trio's considerable talents make those moments easy to forgive. *—Stephen Thomas Erlewine*

Release Some Tension / Jul. 29, 1997 / RCA ♦♦♦

● **The Best of SWV** / Nov. 6, 2001 / RCA ♦♦♦♦♦

By the time *The Best of SWV* surfaced, the urban trio had long disappeared from the top of the charts after having scored tremendous success in the early '90s. This collection gathers up the trio's best hits from that golden era, reminding you just how wonderful SWV was for their time, even if time and changing trends made you forget about them. Rather than skim through the group's spotty albums, it's best to head straight for this best-of. Everything you need is here, succinctly gathering up the songs that made SWV one of the most successful urban acts of the early '90s. *—Jason Birchmeier*

Sybil

b. New Jersey

Vocals / Disco, Club/Dance, House

An excellent vocalist and one of the finest among disco divas, New Jersey singer Sybil has come close to pop stardom but has not yet attained it. She worked with Ce Ce Rogers in Ce Ce & Company before signing with Next Plateau. Though her songs have been well received by club audiences, R&B fans have been slower to warm to her cool but expertly sung numbers. She got the best general response to her remake of "Don't Make Me Over" in 1989. Her other songs didn't reach the R&B Top 40. Sybil signed with the Stock, Aitken & Waterman team in 1990, and the single "Make It Easy on Me" was issued shortly afterward. In 1993, she released *Doin' It Now* for Next Plateau. *—Ron Wynn*

● **Greatest Hits** / Mar. 11, 1997 / Next Plateau ♦♦♦♦

In addition to the hits "Falling in Love," "The Love I Lost," "Crazy 4 U" and "Let It Rain," Sybil's *Greatest Hits* features remixes of "When I'm Good and Ready" and "My Love Is Guaranteed." *—Jason Ankeny*

The Sylvers

f. 1972, Memphis, TN

Group / Disco, Funk

Among the more popular family acts on the '70s R&B circuit, Memphis' Sylvers recorded for Pride, MGM, Capitol, Casablanca, and Geffen during their 13-year chart run. No less than nine of the ten brothers and sisters in the family—Olympia, Leon, Charmaine, James, Edmund, Ricky, Angie, Pat, Foster—performed in the group that was viewed as a Southern version of the Jackson 5. Their 1972 Pride single "Fool's Paradise" got things going in the right direction, reaching number 14 on the R&B charts. They had three other Top Ten R&B hits in the '70s, but their biggest song was "Boogie Fever" in 1975. It perfectly captured the disco spirit and topped both the R&B and pop charts that year. "Hot Line" was another Top Ten on both lists in 1976, and their second biggest single. They scored another Top 20 R&B single on Casablanca in 1978, "Don't Stop, Get Off," but the charming qualities of their earlier material seemed more calculated. They couldn't recapture the spark during their mid-'80s period on Geffen. *—Ron Wynn*

The Sylvers / 1972 / Pride ♦♦♦

The Sylvers II / 1973 / Pride ♦♦♦

The Sylvers III / 1974 / MGM ♦♦♦

Showcase / 1976 / Capitol ♦♦♦♦

If the Jacksons could do it and the Osmonds could do it, then, by gosh, so could the Sylvers. By the mid-'70s, this multi-talented, nine-member family group was recording veterans. And having peppered the R&B charts with singles in the early part of the decade, the Sylvers would take the top spot with the seminal proto-disco "Boogie Fever" in 1975. Produced by Freddie Perren, who had already brought magic to the Jackson 5, "Boogie Fever" had all the right stuff. And while the song draws easy comparisons to Perren's work with the Jacksons, it also stands strong in its own right. It was catchy, hooky, well-harmonized, and would set the primary tone for 1976's *Showcase*. However, although Perren gave the band a bona fide hit, his style also firmly entrenched the band on the bubblegum road—a path they would not truly depart from until later in the decade. That said, while both "The Roulette Wheel of Love" and "Ain't No Good in Goodbye" are firmly stamped with Perren's style, there is much more percolating across the album. Leon Sylvers, who would later find success with the famed Solar label, demonstrated a genuine flair for funk as he wielded his pen for "Clap Your Hands to the Music" and "Freestyle." The latter, which opens side two, is a particularly juicy, enthusiastically sung, and horn-heavy jam that allies itself more to the funk of Kool & the Gang than to Motown soul. *Showcase* mishmashes its sounds, and while the result is good, it really does feel at times like a revue—a little bit funky, a little bit soul. But that's its only real failing. For the most part, the Sylvers have enough kick to keep the groove going all night long. *—Amy Hanson*

Something Special / 1976 / Capitol ♦♦♦

Something Special, released in late 1976 and featuring an interesting fold-over sleeve, proved to be the Sylvers' best-selling album, reaching number-13 R&B and remaining in the charts for nearly half a year, despite the fact that the band had already scored the previous year with their best-known song, "Boogie Fever." Still, this is a strong set, dominated by the smoothly arranged, wholesome R&B songs that this large family band was known for. Two songs peeled off the LP and onto the singles charts: "Hot Line" is an innocent, dirty-sweet crush of a song wrapped in strings with Motown overtones, while "High School Dance" keeps the traditional Sylvers sound but pulls a few funky tricks out of its bag as well, including a full-horn arrangement. But they're not done yet, as they move on to the well-intentioned (but weak) "Disco Showdown." Elsewhere, the storm is tempered by a handful of ballads as the boys take on "That's What Love Is Made Of" and the girls reciprocate with the very fine "Got to Have You (For My Very Own)." At the end of the day, *Something Special* emerges as a fine LP, albeit one with limited staying power. Is the band proficient? Yes, they are. Is the LP well done? Yes, it is. But, like the Jackson 5, the Osmonds, or even the Carpenters to some extent, family appeal is utterly charming in small doses, but wears out its welcome long before both sides play through. *—Amy Hanson*

New Horizons / 1977 / Capitol ♦♦♦

Their last LP for Capitol before jumping to Casablanca and disco guru Giorgio Moroder, *New Horizons* found the Sylvers a silver-suited septet, jetting off into the sunset atop a Meconian spaceship bound for who knows where. Now self-produced, the Sylvers had their sound and style well in hand, able to present a cohesive and slick set of soft R&B with ease. *New Horizons* leapt onto the charts with softer, subtle songs this time around, including both the jazzy title track, which focused on the vocal harmonies, and "Another Day to Love," which used the same format but took the vibe way down with strings that cushioned the harmonies. And, of course, because everyone and their grandmother were enraptured with the disco monster, the band seemed to have more fun breaking a sweat across the light strains of "Star Fire" and the remarkably funky "Charisma," while the horn-laden "Dressed to Kill" emerges as one of the finest songs in sight. Divided between these two distinct styles, the Sylvers once again churned through a competent set that can't be faulted. However, there's nothing here that really stands out, either. It's fine R&B, but it's clear they had nearly overstayed their welcome. *—Amy Hanson*

Forever Yours / 1978 / Casablanca ♦♦♦

Leon F. Sylvers III made his producing debut on the Sylvers' Casablanca Records debut, *Forever Yours*. It was his and the rest of the family's chance to break away from the bubblegum soul sound that was fostered by producer Freddie Perren that had resulted in the gold single "Boogie Fever" and the hits "Cotton Candy," "Hot Line," and "High School Dance"; it also gave them the opportunity to write their own material. The lead single/Top 20 R&B hit "Don't Stop Get Off" was thick funk sprinkled with a JB-like horn section and replete with the then-popular "woop woop" chant. Other highlights are the luscious cover of Smokey Robinson and the Miracles' "Swept for You" and the sweepingly romantic "Forever Yours" with its Smokey-ish lyrics: "Until the mountains turn to sand/you can always take my hand." Both were popular radio-aired LP tracks. Another standout is the Latin-tinged slacker funk of "Play This One Last Record" with its croaky spoken asides. "Don't Stop Get Off" is also on *Boogie Fever: The Best of the Sylvers*. *—Ed Hogan*

Disco Fever / 1979 / Casablanca ♦♦

Concept / 1981 / Solar ♦♦

● **Boogie Fever: The Best of the Sylvers** / 1995 / Razor & Tie ♦♦♦♦
Boogie Fever: The Best of the Sylvers is a definitive 16-track collection that contains all of the group's hits, from "Fool's Paradise" to "Falling for Your Love." In between, the Top Ten R&B hits "Wish That I Could Talk to You," "Boogie Fever," "Hot Line" and "High School Dance" are heard, as are a number of smaller hits. Not all of the songs are as infectious or memorable as the big hits, but they're solid disco and soul cuts. And there's never been a collection of Sylvers material as strong as this excellent disc. *—Stephen Thomas Erlewine*

Classic Masters / Jan. 29, 2002 / Capitol ♦♦♦♦
Next to Razor & Tie's 1995 collection *Boogie Fever* (which went out of print not long after its release), Capitol's 2002 collection *Classic Masters* is the best overview of the nine-piece disco band's career, containing all of their biggest hits on a snappy 12-track collection. Not everything is as good as "Boogie Fever," and some of these tunes now sound a little silly, but it still all sounds pretty fun, particularly for those that like the hits. They might not find hidden gems here, but they'll likely groove along with the record rather enjoyably. *—Stephen Thomas Erlewine*

Sylvester

b. Sep. 1944, Los Angeles, CA, **d.** Dec. 16, 1988, San Francisco, CA
Vocals, Keyboards / Disco, Hi-NRG, Funk
Along with the Village People, '70s disco artist Sylvester was one of the few artists of the era not afraid to openly acknowledge his homosexuality. Born Sylvester James during September 1944 in Los Angeles, CA, Sylvester was introduced to music at an early age by his grandmother, Julia Morgan, who was a jazz singer. While still a youngster, Sylvester began singing in gospel groups, while finding further inspiration from the likes of Bessie Smith and Billie Holiday, among others. After relocating to San Francisco in the late '60s, Sylvester began to perform in a musical production called *Women of the Blues*, before becoming the star attraction of a transvestite vocal group called the Cockettes in the early '70s. After leaving the band in 1973, Sylvester signed on with the Hot Band and issued such releases as *Scratch My Flower* and *Bazaar* the same year. Sylvester's dance-happy funk style eventually transformed into disco, as his flamboyant and over-the-top stage act created quite a following for the singer in the San Francisco area. He also issued some of his best-known recordings around the end of the decade—1977's *Sylvester* and 1979's in-concert *Living Proof*—while racking up such popular disco hits as "You Make Me Feel (Mighty Real)" and "Dance (Disco Heat)."

1979 saw Sylvester receive three *Billboard* awards and another for Best Male Disco Act from Disco International Magazine, as well as landing a bit part in Bette Midler's 1979 movie, *The Rose*. But by the dawn of the '80s, disco was being considered increasingly passé and the singer's career began to slow down (funny enough, Sylvester's backup singers, Martha Wash and Izora Rhodes, would go on to form the Weather Girls, and score one of 1982's big dance hits with "It's Raining Men"). Although he continued to issue albums throughout the '80s, Sylvester's career came to an abrupt and tragic end on December 16, 1988, when he died from AIDS-related complications. Despite his passing, Sylvester's music remains popular on dancefloors worldwide, while "You Make Me Feel (Mighty Real)" has been covered over the years by three separate artists: former lead singer of Bronski Beat and the Communards Jimmy Somerville (on his 1989 solo debut *Read My Lips*), comedian/actor/singer Sandra Bernhard (on her 1994 release *Excuses for Bad Behavior, Pt. 1*), and by former Ten City lead singer Byron Stingily (on his 1998 solo debut, *The Purist*), whose version hit number one on the U.S. dance chart the same year. *—Greg Prato*

Scratch My Flower / 1973 / BTS ♦♦♦

Bazaar / 1973 / BTS ♦♦♦

Sylvester / 1977 / Fantasy ♦♦♦♦
With his more rock-based work with the Hot Band laid to rest (no more Neil Young or Procol Harum covers), Sylvester headed down the soul and disco route with this self-titled album and never looked back. It didn't take long at all for him to hit his stride, evidenced by Ashford & Simpson's dynamic "Over and Over"—a disco single full of memorable blips of horns that went over better in the U.K. than the U.S.—but the album has its growing pains. The remainder moves through smooth and uptempo soul, with resonating moments equaled by those that pass by without much notice. Longtime Sylvester associates Martha Wash and Izora Rhodes are in tow, providing complementary background vocals that would lead to their Two Tons and Weather Girls projects. Regardless of its shortcomings, Sylvester left plenty of evidence with this record that a major talent was about to crack. [Fantasy combined this album with 1981's *Too Hot to Sleep* in 1999; somewhat confusingly, Fantasy simply titled the disc *Too Hot to Sleep*.] *—Andy Kellman*

Living Proof / Feb. 1979 / Fantasy ♦♦♦♦♦
Rockers who dismissed disco in general as cold and mechanical never seriously listened to Sylvester, a passionate, captivating singer who had a magnificent range and was consistently mindful of disco's soul and gospel roots. In the late '70s, disco-oriented artists generally shied away from live albums because of their lack of dance club appeal. But like Donna Summer, the colorful Sylvester was an exception. *Living Proof*, recorded at the San Francisco War Memorial Opera House, documents a varied and unpredictable performance showing that Sylvester was far from one-dimensional. While he probably inspired dancing in the aisles with sweaty versions of such dancefloor favorites as "You Make Me Feel (Mighty Real)," "Dance (Disco Heat)" and "Body Strong," he shows how expressive a balladeer he could be on "Sharing Something Perfect Between Ourselves" and interpretations of Billie Holiday's "Lover Man" and Patti LaBelle's "You Are My Friend." Emotionally, Sylvester wasn't one to hold back, and that honesty serves him impressively well on this excellent CD. *—Alex Henderson*

Sell My Soul / 1980 / Fantasy ♦♦♦♦
Although the singularly named Sylvester reached his apex with 1978's disco anthem "You Make Me Feel (Mighty Real)," *Sell My Soul*, released in 1980, is packed with a wonderful assortment of easy, breezy dance classics which readily tipped the whole package into the pop Top 50 that fall. Driven by strings and pulsing, synth-edged disco beats, the songs on *Sell My Soul* are brought to life thanks to Sylvester's mighty, mighty voice. Sweet and sexy, it rumbles as often as it breaks into his soaring trademark falsetto. Either way, it lends a shine to the set that couldn't be reproduced by anyone else. Both "I Need You" and "I'll Dance to That" are uptempo, feel-good groovers. The title track, meanwhile, is a heavier affair—still upbeat, but more textured, adding a nice looping bass and outstanding backing vocals from Delores and Carl Hall. In fact, that's the formula that winds its way across the set, although an impassioned reiteration of the magnificent "Cry Me a River" is a quick-stepping, gospel-inflected romp that stands outside the pack, thanks in part to the fierce brass which trails the vocals, while "My Life Is Loving You" is a tender, emotive, end-of-the-night ballad. Ultimately, although it runs the risk of becoming just another clutch of lite pop, *Sell My Soul* is another stunner from one of dance music's most underrated artists. Consigned to the one-hit wonder bin by most, Sylvester gave more chops to what became *de rigueur* in the late-'80s/early-'90s acid house dance set than most give him credit for. And this oft-overlooked album is the proof in the pudding. *—Amy Hanson*

Too Hot to Sleep / 1981 / Fantasy ♦♦♦♦
Many overlook the fact that Sylvester was as much of a soul artist as he was a disco artist, what with his gospel roots and his ability to wrap his voice around a slow, deliberate arrangement. That's a shame, since there are soul-loving disco haters who simply avoid Sylvester's records for his disco connections, not to mention his sexual orientation. He was one of the most versatile artists of his time, singing deeply and sensually ("Thinking Right") one moment and then reaching up for a type of falsetto that will either cause your goose pimples to rise or make you run for shelter ("Can't You See"). *Too Hot to Sleep* is one of his most refined and laid-back albums, a consistent but unremarkable one that puts a spotlight on his crooning (best heard on his version of "Ooo Baby Baby"). The problem with this record is that it seems too much like a compromise. It's lacking in personality and hardly captures all of what makes Sylvester Sylvester. [Fantasy reissued this album in 1999 and combined it with 1977's *Sylvester*; *Too Hot to Sleep* was retained as the title.] *—Andy Kellman*

All I Need / 1982 / Megatone ♦♦♦
Sylvester was on the downside of his career in the mid-'80s. He still had the glorious tones and booming voice, but was now floundering, with his high-energy brand of disco out of fashion. Sylvester tried to fashion a comeback by mixing in lightweight pop arrangements and production while singing his old fashion. The results were not encouraging, but that wasn't because the songs lacked style; they were just the wrong things for the time. *—Ron Wynn*

Greatest Hits / 1983 / Fantasy ♦♦♦♦♦
With several outdated Sylvester collections on the market, this hard to find Canadian import is by far head and shoulders above the rest. For example, 1989's *Original Hits* unbelievably left off "Do You Wanna Funk," one of his signature hits, and other collections, such as *12 by 12*, leave off "You Make Me Feel (Mighty Real)." Therefore, this Canadian collection stands as the definitive Sylvester hits package, containing the full-length versions of his dancefloor classics. *Greatest Hits* includes his three American Top 40 hits, including the aforementioned pair and an 11-minute version of "I (Who Have Nothing)," as well as his U.K. hits, which include "Stars" and "Band of Gold." Additionally, the collection boasts excellent audio quality and live tracks such as "You Are My Friend," but unfortunately lacks detailed liner notes and photographs, which would have been interesting, especially considering Sylvester's colorful, inspirational, and ultimately short-lived life. So, for those wanting a comprehensive collection of Sylvester's music and an excellent testament to the bygone era of disco music, this rare double album is the way to go. *—Jose F. Promis*

Call Me / 1984 / Megatone ♦♦

M-1015 / 1984 / Megatone ♦♦

Mutual Attraction / 1987 / Warner Bros. ♦♦
The final album issued before Sylvester's death wasn't a distinguished effort from anyone. He was dispirited and sounded like a shell of himself. The vocals had no power, color, authority, or conviction, while the uptempo cuts were wooden and the ballads deadly. Anyone who remembered the great Sylvester cuts was embarrassed, and his tragic death didn't make things any better. *—Ron Wynn*

● **Original Hits** / 1989 / Fantasy ♦♦♦♦
Original Hits sums up disco sensation Sylvester's years (1977-1981) with the Fantasy label. These years include most of the artist's most important output, particularly dancefloor hits like "You Make Me Feel (Mighty Real)," "Dance (Disco Heat)," and "Body Strong." In addition to these stellar dance tracks, songs like "Cry Me a River" and a live version of "You are My Friend" emphasize Sylvester's warmth and soulfulness. The album is shorter and less comprehensive than Fantasy's earlier *Greatest Hits* compilation, but all the same offers a good and, since it's one CD rather than two, likely more affordable introduction to one of the most exciting and energetic figures of the disco era. *—Ben Tausig*

Too Hot to Sleep / Aug. 17, 1999 / Fantasy ♦♦♦
In 1999, Fantasy reissued Sylvester's first and last albums for the label—*Sylvester* (1977) and *Too Hot To Sleep* (1981)—on this 74-minute CD. Both sessions point to the fact that no artist was no more consistently mindful of disco's Northern soul and gospel roots than Sylvester, who made sure that his albums were as listenable as they were danceable. This CD is full of dancefloor classics—club hounds of the Disco Era were well aware of infectious gems like "Over and Over," "Down Down Down" and "Change" from *Sylvester* and "Give It Up (Don't Make Me Wait)" from *Too Hot to Sleep*. But Sylvester wasn't recording strictly for clubs, and his talents as a soulful, charismatic provider of slow jams and ballads are evident on "Loving Grows Up Slow," "Tipsong" and a superb cover of Smokey Robinson & the Miracles' "Ooh Baby Baby." Of course, Sylvester didn't escape the wrath of the knee-jerk disco bashers of the late 1970s and early 1980s, who saw disco as robotic and mechanical and refused to believe that any disco artist could be warm, personal and expressive—all of the things that Sylvester's albums were. But time would be kind to disco. While many rockers of the late 1970s jumped on the death-to-disco movement, disco spelled "legitimacy" and "hipness" to a lot of Generation X rockers of the 1990s. And if those Gen-Xers are basing their opinions on excellent CDs such as this one, it's easy to understand why they feel the way they do. *—Alex Henderson*

Sylvia

b. May 29, 1936, New York, NY
Vocals, Producer, Songwriter / Disco, Urban, Soul, Quiet Storm, Hip-Hop
Going strictly by the chart book, Sylvia was a one-hit wonder, hitting number-three pop (and number-one R&B) with her 1973 single "Pillow Talk," a slice of proto-disco bedroom funk. Few other one-hit wonders, however, had a career as multi-dimensional as Sylvia Robinson's. For one thing, she was actually no stranger to the hit parade when "Pillow Talk" started to catch on. In the 1950s, she'd been one-half of the rock & roll duo Mickey & Sylvia, remembered for eternity for their classic "Love Is Strange." As a one-named solo artist 15 years later, Sylvia would help lay the ground for disco, urban contemporary, and even rap with her cooing whispers and orgasmic sighs. Murmuring about romantic love with a seductive come-on that was pretty bawdy by early-'70s standards, she was the yin to Barry White's yang, if you will, offering a kinder, gentler brand of between-the-sheets soul from a feminine viewpoint. Unlike many of the singers who would follow a similar path, Sylvia was no producer's tool: she played guitar and co-wrote and co-produced most of her material, which was released on a record company run by her and her husband Joe. In the late '70s and early '80s, she would play a crucial role in the birth of rap as the co-founder of Sugar Hill Records.

"Pillow Talk" began life as a song that Sylvia hoped to pitch to Al Green. After nothing came of that plan, she issued it herself on the Vibration label, an imprint of the All Platinum company that she had founded with her husband in the late '60s in New Jersey. It would be her only major pop crossover hit, but she did have a handful of small R&B hits in the mid-'70s in a similar vein, her hushed sexy whispers backed by laconic funk-cum-disco grooves and occasional strings. Not nearly as risqué as Millie Jackson, this was nonetheless fairly forthright stuff for its era; when she pushed it to the limit, it could have passed for some of the milder routines on phone-sex lines. In this sense, she could be considered as a precursor not only to rap, but to R&B performers like Prince who would make plainly stated lust a centerpiece of their compositions. While her Sugar Hill activities took most of her time by the 1980s, she still found some time for recording, making the middle of the R&B charts again with a rap tune, "It's Good to Be the Queen." *—Richie Unterberger*

• **Pillow Talk: The Sensuous Sounds of Sylvia** / Aug. 20, 1996 / Rhino ♦♦♦♦♦
Here is a 20-track compilation drawn primarily from her mid-'70s albums, adding four songs from non-LP singles of the era, and a couple of cuts from 1982 Sugar Hill singles. It can get a little gooey over the course of its 79 minutes, not to mention a bit comically unsubtle at times. Her cover of Marvin Gaye's "You Sure Love to Ball," to take one example, would be raunchy enough to ruin the day of many a Republican delegate even 20 years later, when such sexual come-ons are far more commonplace on the radio. It's not all candlelight-on-the-way-to-the-bedroom stuff, though. "My Thing" (the flip of "Pillow Talk") proves she could sing fairly straight soul when given the inclination, and "Sunday" and "Not on the Outside" are sparsely produced ballads, sung with great tenderness. They make one wish that Sylvia had pursued a somewhat more versatile direction during the '70s, but there's no question that the "Pillow Talk" was bringing in the bacon, and this compilation supplies it in droves. *—Richie Unterberger*

The Symphonics

f. 1964, Philadelphia, PA
Group / R&B, Soul
A Philadelphia-based group with very solid instrumental support and an infectiously upbeat sound, the Symphonics had the honor of being only the second act signed to Curtom Records in 1968, during the company's formative months—it was also the group's misfortune to join Curtom when the label had no national distribution. Their single "When I Grow Old" b/w "Guilty" was the company's second release, principally in Chicago and other local markets. They were unable to come up with a follow-up for Curtom, although they subsequently cut singles for the Brunswick label. *—Bruce Eder*

Syreeta (Rita Wright)

b. Feb. 28, 1946, Pittsburgh, PA
Vocals, Songwriter / Soul, Motown
Some performers, such as Florence Ballard, were ground up in the Motown hit-making machine—and a few, like Syreeta, found their callings and success in other parts of the music business. Born in Pittsburgh, Rita Wright had her sights set on a performing career, and luckily her family moved to Detroit when she was in her teens and she had the talent to back up the goal. She came to the company as a secretary and was later discovered by Brian Holland, one third of the Holland-Dozier-Holland songwriting team, who began using her as a backup singer on various records and brought her to Berry Gordy's attention. He was so impressed with Wright's voice that he signed her up and later gave her a song, "I Can't Give Back the Love I Feel for You," co-authored by Holland, Ashford, & Simpson, that originally had been intended for Diana Ross. In Wright's hands (credited to Rita Wright), the single did well enough, especially overseas, where she later discovered she had a serious following. Wright later met and fell in love with Stevie Wonder, and the two were married in September of 1970—by that time, she was using the name Syreeta, which is how she became best known to the public.

The personal union lasted only two years, but it led her into a new area of music, as a lyricist. Wonder began setting her poems to music, and she realized that she was able to write songs; their collaboration as composers and artists outlasted the marriage by three years, and led to some superb work in both departments. Their subsequent hits together included "If You Really Love Me," "Signed, Sealed, Delivered," and "It's a Shame"—her biggest hits, "Spinnin' and Spinnin'" and "Your Kiss Is Sweet," were also Wonder/Wright collaborations. Syreeta released her first album under that name in 1972, on the Motown MoWest imprint—*Syreeta*, produced by Stevie Wonder, was one of the more beautifully made records issued by the label in the 1970s and gave her voice the first fully realized showcase it ever had. They issued two more albums together, and she remained with the label for nine more years, as part of the tiny group of "inside" artists (along with her ex) who were more than just business acquaintances. She scored a number-five hit in 1980 with the ballad "With You I'm Born Again," a duet with Billy Preston, and also recorded duets with Jermaine Jackson, among other artists on the label, during the early '80s. Syreeta retired from full-time music work in the mid-'80s in order to devote herself to her personal life and family, but she remains a much-loved artist from Motown's silver age. *—Bruce Eder*

Syreeta / 1972 / MoWest ♦♦♦♦
This album represented the solo debut of Syreeta, a Motown staffer who was one of Stevie Wonder's most important collaborators during his early '70s renaissance. Fittingly, Wonder returned the favor by producing this album and writing or co-writing several of its songs (he is also notably present in the background vocals of several of the tracks). As a result, the album utilizes the same experimental approach to R&B music that defined his early '70s work, blending conventional string-sweetened '70s soul with ventures into synthesizer-inflected funk. Highlights include "Black Maybe," a jazz-inflected ballad with socially conscious lyrics, and "Baby Don't You Let Me Lose This," a gently-percolating midtempo number that benefits from an infectious chorus and some sleek synthesizer textures. There is also a strong cover of the Smokey Robinson classic "What Love Has Joined Together" that provides an excellent showcase for Syreeta's emotionally-rich vocals. Unfortunately, this experimental approach occasionally fails to pan out: the big misstep is a badly-misjudged cover of the Beatles' "She's Leaving Home" that suffers from a gimmicky production featuring annoying voicebox-treated vocals on the chorus. Another problem with the album is that it fails to build a cohesive sense of flow from song to song, resulting in an album that feels more like a loose collection of songs instead of a proper album. Despite these problems, *Syreeta* offers enough likable soul music to make it worth a spin for anyone interested in Syreeta and the rare Stevie Wonder tunes it includes make it a necessity for his hardcore fans. *—Donald A. Guarisco*

• **Stevie Wonder Presents Syreeta** / Dec. 1974 / Motown ♦♦♦♦♦
After a promising but uneven debut, Syreeta summoned her creative strengths and worked in tandem with creative partner Stevie Wonder to produce another album in 1974. The result was *Stevie Wonder Presents Syreeta*, the most delightful and consistent album of her career. As with *Syreeta*, this album pursues a combination of smooth soul tracks ideally suited to Syreeta's silky vocal range and more experimental outings that are creatively in line with Wonder's then-current solo work. However, the eclecticism that weighed down *Syreeta* is transformed into a strength on *Stevie Wonder Presents Syreeta*: The tracks pursue a dazzling array of different pop-soul styles, but everything is kept in check by solid performances from everyone involved and tight arrangements that keep the album's hook-filled songs on track. Highlights on the first side include "Spinnin' and Spinnin'," a clever tune that uses a spiraling, carnival-styled keyboard motif to bring its tale of an unwieldy relationship to life, and "Come and Get This Stuff," a funky pop number built on an infectious sing-along chorus. Another notable track is "Cause We've Ended As Lovers," a delicate breakup ballad with a stunning, ethereal vocal from Syreeta. On the second side, a majority of the running time is devoted to an *Abbey Road*-style medley of short tracks. Everything here is catchy and well-arranged, but the highlight is "I Wanna Be By Your Side," a heart-melting romantic duet between Syreeta and fellow Motown solo artist G.C. Cameron. All in all, *Stevie Wonder Presents Syreeta* is the shining moment of Syreeta's solo career and a lost highlight of 1970s soul in general. Any fans of Stevie Wonder owe it to themselve to track this album down because it makes a worthy companion to albums like *Talking Book* and *Innervisions*. *—Donald A. Guarisco*

One to One / 1977 / Motown ♦♦♦
As Rita Wright she released one of *Motown*'s best underrated singles, Ashford & Simpson's "I Can't Give Back the Love That You Feel for Me." By the early '70s she married Stevie Wonder and wrote the lyrics to such classics as "Blame It on the Sun" and "If You Really Love Me." Her first album release was late 1974's *Stevie Wonder Presents Syreeta*. While that effort featured all of the tracks as collaborations between Wonder and Wright, *One to One* has her co-writing five of the tracks here, and this album is produced by Leon Ware. Wright and Ware's romantic and hooky "I Don't Know" is nearly brilliant, but runs overlong. "Don't Cry" also has time concerns, but it is the perfect pitch for Wright's voice and has a great saxophone solo from Gary Bartz. The emotional "I Too Am Wanting," like all of the Wright and Ware collaborations, suggests that the two had the potential of being a good writing team. Wonder's "Harmour Love" from 1975 shows up here, but it's not one of his strongest songs or productions. While *One to One* does have the requisite, pensive and sensual sound of intelligent late-'70s R&B efforts, it was released a little too late to capitalize on its virtues. *—Jason Elias*

Rich Love Poor Love / 1977 / Motown ✦✦

The Best of Syreeta / 1981 / Motown ✦✦✦
A good collection, but glaring omissions like "Quick Slick," "What Love Has Joined Together," "Tiki, Tiki Donga," "Heavy Day," and "Rich Love Poor Love" keeps it from being essential. Syreeta dueted with Billy Preston and G. C. Cameron but only three made the final 18—"With You I'm Born Again," "Go for It" (Preston), and "Let's Make a Deal" (Cameron). A duet with Smokey Robinson came after this LP was released. Nothing from a second LP with Billy Preston made the grade nor did her two contributions to the *Loving Couples' Soundtrack.* It contains both sides of her Gordy debut as Rita Wright: "I Can't Give Back the Love" and "Something on My Mind," and other delectables, but the omissions leave a bitter taste. *—Andrew Hamilton*

● **The Essential Syreeta** / Apr. 17, 2001 / Spectrum ✦✦✦✦✦
The reissue labels were never very kind to Syreeta, resulting in the sad fact that compilations remain the best (if not the only) way to hear what made her recordings so special. *The Essential Syreeta* is the best of a tiny lot, with a passable selection of material from her '70s and '80s records. For some unknown reason, the compilers virtually ignored her fine 1972 debut; only two songs are included, one of them (fortunately) her sweet, grooving remake of Stevie Wonder's "I Love Every Little Thing About You" (first heard earlier that year on Stevie's *Music of My Mind*). The collection does a much better job with 1974's *Stevie Wonder Presents Syreeta*, presenting her best songs ("Spinnin' and Spinnin'" and "Your Kiss Is Sweet," both written with Wonder) as well as three other solid tracks. Most of the rest comes from the period 1977 to 1981, when she recorded some good work—like the R&B hits "Harmour Love" and "Let's Make a Deal"—but never approached her early-'70s heyday. The final blow is the absence of "With You I'm Born Again," her fine hit duet with Billy Preston from 1981. Yes, it's recommended, but that's only until a real compilation comes along. *—John Bush*

The System

f. 1982, **db.** 1989

Group / Urban, Dance-Pop, Electro

Pioneering synth duo the System rode the '80s wave of emerging synth/MIDI music technology to help lay the foundation for contemporary electronic popular music with their upfront, unapologetic use of synths and intelligent songwriting. In the early '80s, singer Mic Murphy and keyboardist David Frank met in New York. Collecting on studio time that he had bartered for in exchange for playing on sessions, Frank asked Murphy to join him in the studio to work on some ideas. After their overnight session, Murphy took the master tape to an engineer friend that transferred the tape onto a 12-inch lacquer record. The duo took the record to Atlantic's Mirage Records and were signed right away.

Their 1982 single "You Are in My System" quickly became the rage on both the dancefloor and on urban-formatted radio, leading to the release of *Sweat* on Mirage/Atlantic. Other tracks from the album got dancefloor attention, such as "Sweat" and "I Can't Let Go." Their next album, *Experiment*, included the infectious "I Just Want to Make You Feel Good," the sweet ballad "Promises" b/w "X-periment," and the stunningly passionate "I Can't Take Losing You." In 1986, the duo performed the title album track/hit single "The Pleasure Seekers" on *Miami Vice.* The LP contained "Groove" precursor "This Is for You," which was the second single. The System had a great year in 1987, giving them their biggest hit. The title track of their album *Don't Disturb This Groove* went to number-one R&B and number-three pop. The tune was also used as the basis of one of the last tracks released by Tupac Shakur. The next release *Midnight Lover* cracked the pop Top 20. Their fresh approach put the System in high demand as producers, songwriters, and musicians. They can be heard on Chaka Khan's cover of Prince's "I Feel for You" and Mtume's "Juicy Fruit" (both million-sellers). The record was later used by the Notorious B. I. G. for his gold record "Juicy." The list continues with Phil Collins' "Sussudio," Angela Bofill's "Can't Slow Down," Pauli Carmen's "Dial My Number," Ashford & Simpson, and Jeff Lorber's "Step by Step." They contributed to the movie soundtracks for two Eddie Murphy blockbusters, *Beverly Hills Cop* and *Coming to America* (the title track went Top Ten pop). Even though it seemed that everyone wanted to work with the System, the pair decided not to spread themselves too thin and turned down a lot of offers. They opened their own recording studio called Science Lab Music.

1989's *Rhythm and Romance* ("Midnight Special," "Have Mercy," "Soul to Soul") was the duo's last album. During early 1991, Mic Murphy released a solo album on East West called *Touch* ("Fit to Be Tied") which had a lot of System overtones. Frank did concert dates backing Annie Lennox during the recording of her *Live in Central Park* CD and video (Arista) among others. He's also active in production, working with Omar, Dionne Farris, female pop vocal trio Wild Orchid, and Rebbie Jackson. *—Ed Hogan*

Sweat / 1983 / Mirage ✦✦✦
Mic Murphy and David Frank created a new group mixing funk and technology in the early '80s. While the debut wasn't a huge pop hit, it made an immediate impact in the R&B community. The synthesized backbeat of "You Are in My System" rose up the charts and made Murphy and Frank the hot R&B production tandem of the day. The rest of *Sweat* wasn't quite as successful, but it had already launched them into stardom. *—Ron Wynn*

X-Periment / 1984 / Polydor ✦✦✦
The System's sophomore album set the Big Apple duo well apart from the growing pack of electro-dance duos that proliferated in the mid-'80s. While Mic Murphy made a distinctive and soulful frontman, it was keyboardist David Frank's mastery of studio technology that gave the System its edge; *X-Periment* showed that his only rivals in creating the hip-hop-flavored dance music of the day were producers Arthur Baker and John Robie. The supple grooves here wiggle well beyond the disco lockstep of the band's debut, and the incredibly busy mixes make for consistently entertaining listening. If there's a weakness, it's that, as on the first album, the melodies are often sketchy, and songs like "Dangerous" lean too heavily on Frank's studio wizardry. However, *X-Periment* also contains two of the System's best-ever tunes, both written with guest guitarist (and Madonna sideman) Paul Pesco. "Promises Can Break" is a sweet showcase for Murphy, tipping the group's trademark balance between hi-tech and humanity firmly in favor of the latter, and "I Wanna Make You Feel Good" is even better, a far superior rethink of "You Are in My System," the band's big hit from its debut. Beneath the layers of squiggly synths and crackling electronic percussion is a Prince-ly pop song that deserved to be a breakout hit—something that eluded the System until 1987's more restrained "Don't Disturb This Groove." *—Dan LeRoy*

Pleasure Seekers / 1985 / Mirage ✦✦✦
The System's scintillating synth tonal accents seemed to mirror the quicksilver '80s era ascendancy of the microchip in every facet of everyday life. The pioneering synth duo of keyboardist David Frank and singer Mic Murphy first came to fame for their innovative dance single "You Are in My System" and had a 1987 hit with "Don't Disturb This Groove." On their 1985 album *The Pleasure Seekers*, The System continue to shape and influence synth-based R&B/pop music. The duo performed the propulsive title track single on an episode of the hit NBC series *Miami Vice.* The smooth, warm "This For You" could be described as a midtempo forerunner to "Don't Disturb This Groove." Other standouts are "Big City Beat," "It Takes Two," "Love Won't Wait," and "I Don't Run From Danger." [*The Pleasure Seekers* was reissued on CD in 2000 as a Japanese import by WEA International. During the same month, The System's Orpheus Music/Avex USA debut album *ESP* was released.] *—Ed Hogan*

● **Don't Disturb This Groove** / 1987 / Atlantic ✦✦✦✦
The title cut was Mic Murphy and David Frank's greatest record, a catchy title, decent vocals, and outstanding rhythm track, making it both a club and radio staple throughout 1987. It was also a high water mark for their techno-funk; this was their last record to make such an impact. Techno-funk was being supplanted by hip-hop, dancehall, new jack swing, house and hip-house. But while it lasted, Murphy and Frank were on the R&B throne. *—Ron Wynn*

Rhythm & Romance / 1989 / Atlantic ✦✦

ESP / Jun. 20, 2000 / Town Sound ✦✦✦
The System was way ahead of its time with their early embrace of MIDI/synth technology and the otherworldly sounds they could produce. Coupling that with top-notch songwriting skills, the duo scored a number-one R&B/number-three pop hit with "Don't Disturb This Groove" from the album of the same name. At the end of the '80s, singer Mic Murphy and keyboardist David Frank parted ways. Frank went on to co-write and co-produce multi-platinum hits with Steve Kipner: Christina Aguilera's "Genie in a Bottle" and 98 Degrees' "The Hardest Thing." The start of the 21st century finds Frank and Murphy reunited, bringing about new music from one of pop music's most unique combination. On their Orpheus Music/Avex USA debut, *ESP*, the System evolves in order to make music for a new millennium. Gone are the dazzling, hyperactive synth sounds found on past albums such as *The Pleasure Seekers.* Now the System's sound is sparser (more sonically similar to Frank's work on Omar's *For Pleasure* and *This Is Not a Love Song*) but no less engaging. Standouts are the swirling romantic "... Groove"-like "Heaven in Your Eyes," the ode to commitment "As God Is My Witness," the bass-bouncy "Supernatural," the chugging "Midnight Train," and the steppers cuts "Love's Deja Vu," "Good As Gold," and "Soul Food." Their classic "You Are in My System" is revisited as "You Are in My System Version," a tasty slice of trip-hop, just as engaging and pleasingly propulsive as ever with a rap by Prodigy of Mobb Deep. After one listen to *ESP*, you won't need to be a mind reader to know that the System, David Frank, and Mic Murphy are E-lectro S-oul P-ioneers! *—Ed Hogan*

T

T-Connection

f. 1975, Nassau, Bahamas

Group / Disco, Funk

Bahamian vocalist, guitarist, and keyboardist T-Coakley formed T-Connection in the '70s. His brother Kirkwood Coakley joined him on bass and drums, with drummer/percussionist Anthony Flowers and guitarist David Mackey as the other members. They quickly became enormously popular in the Bahamas and Caribbean before moving to Miami and signing with TK. Their single "Do What You Wanna Do" was a disco anthem, and one of the first 12-inch singles issued domestically. They recorded for TK until 1980, then signed with Capitol. They released four more LPs with Capitol from 1980 to 1984, but were unable to regain their earlier momentum, although they remained popular with international dance audiences. *—Ron Wynn*

Magic / Apr. 1977 / RCA ✦✦✦

In the late 1970s, T-Connection was one of those bands that had one foot in funk and the other in disco. The Miami residents weren't nearly as gritty as Parliament/Funkadelic or Cameo, but they had more grit and toughness than glossy Euro-disco acts like Silver Convention, Love & Kisses, and the Munich Machine. T-Connection's albums were uneven, but the band could be exciting when it came up with the right groove. Released in 1977, their first American album, *Magic*, isn't perfect but has more plusses than minuses. The vinyl LP gets off to an impressive start with "Do What Ya Wanna Do," the infectious disco-funk anthem that T-Connection is best remembered for. And the band keeps side one's creative momentum going with the glossy instrumental "Disco Magic" (a favorite in dance clubs) and the exuberant, Caribbean-flavored "Go Back Home" (which reflects leader T. Coakley's Bahamian background). Side two, meanwhile, isn't quite as consistent but has some noteworthy tracks, including "Got to See My Lady" (another club hit) and the sociopolitical "Crazy Mixed Up World," which was a departure from the escapist get-down-and-party vibe that T-Connection was known for. All things considered, *Magic* is among the band's more memorable releases. *—Alex Henderson*

On Fire / Jan. 1978 / TK ✦✦✦

An album featuring disco and light pop tunes. T-Connection, more than anything else, had a knack for disco. The only single to chart from this outing was the title track "On Fire." Flavored with electric guitar solos, percussion solos and hyped vocals, this brisk number cracked the *Billboard* R&B Top 30 at number 27 after 15 weeks. Other disco cuts also include "Let Yourself Go," "Cush" and "Playing Games." With the exception of being tagged a disco unit, their music is more pop-oriented than R&B. *—Craig Lytle*

T-Connection / 1979 / TK ✦✦✦

Totally Connected / Nov. 1979 / TK ✦✦

The Best of T-Connection / 1995 / Hot ✦✦✦✦

This is miles ahead of T-Connection's diluted regular releases which suffered from an overabundance of weak material. These tracks feature the group at their best, especially on "Do What You Wanna Do," "Disco Magic," "Go Back Home," "On Fire (Getting Higher)," and "At Midnight." A good cherry picking of T-Connections' finest. *—Andrew Hamilton*

The Best of T-Connection: Everything's Still Cool / Jan. 28, 1997 / EMI ✦✦✦

The title is misleading: this has none of what they did for TK in the 1970s, and is entirely composed of material from the first half of the 1980s. In fact, all but one of the 14 tracks is taken from two albums (1981's *Everything is Cool*, 1982's *Pure & Natural*). The music is caught somewhere between disco, urban contemporary, and soul—which is another way of saying that it's pretty lacking in personality. *—Richie Unterberger*

● **Classic Masters** / Mar. 26, 2002 / Capitol ✦✦✦✦

The recording career of the '70s/'80s disco/funk band T-Connection was evenly divided between the TK subsidiary Dash Records (its catalog now controlled by Rhino, which is owned by the major label Warner) and Capitol Records (owned by the major label EMI); the group recorded four albums and scored four R&B singles chart entries for each company. *The Best of T-Connection* (1995) compiled the Dash material and 1997's *The Best of T-Connection: Everything's Still Cool* compiled the Capitol material, but until now no compilation has combined the two catalogs. For their midline-priced, digitally remastered *Classic Masters* collection, Capitol has licensed three of the Dash tracks, making this the best best-of yet released on T-Connection. It still isn't perfect, however. The ratio of three Dash recordings to nine Capitol ones is just about the opposite of what you'd want, given that the Dash period was more successful, artistically and commercially, for the group. Two of the Dash R&B chart entries, "At Midnight" and "Saturday Night," are missing. Compiler Cheryl Pawelski, who has handled the entire *Classic Masters* series for Capitol, takes a methodical approach, presenting the material in chronological order and favoring singles. Where a group doesn't have enough chart singles to fill up the requisite 12 tracks, she opts for singles that didn't make the charts. In the case of T-Connection, that means five non-charting Capitol singles, some of them from albums that didn't chart, either. T-Connection evolved from a disco band with an island inflection to an anonymous funk group grinding out forgettable, bass-heavy groove tunes, and there are too many of those here. *—William Ruhlmann*

T. Life (Theodore Life Jr.)

b. Philadelphia, PA

Producer, Songwriter, Vocals, Guitar / Urban, Club/Dance, Quiet Storm, Pop, Soul

Sometimes credited as T. Life or Theodore Life, the producer/songwriter/guitarist/vocalist's songs and guitar licks can be found on various tracks in Gamble & Huff's Philadelphia International Records catalog and numerous sides he tracked with fellow Philly soul singer/songwriter/producer Bunny Sigler and his backup band Instant Funk.

The Jacksonville, FL, native played in a band called Raw Soul that went on to become Maze Featuring Frankie Beverly. Relocating to Philadelphia, Life became part of the thriving Philadelphia music scene of the '70s, performing with the band Spiritual Concept. Signed to Gamble & Huff's music publishing firm Mighty Three Music, Life's songs were covered by PIR artists such as the Intruders ("Memories Are Here to Stay," "Plain Old Fashioned Girl"), several songs on Instant Funk's 1976 debut album *Get Down With the Philly Jump* (the title track, "Give Me Your Love," "So Glad I'm the One"), Bunny Sigler (the sweepingly romantic ballad "Somebody Loves You," "Ladies Man," "Woman, Woman, Woman," the title track of his 1977 Curtom LP *Locked in This Position*), and the Ebonys (the steppers classic "Life in the Country"). They can also be also found on releases by non-PIR artists such as Carl Carlton ("Universal Girl," "Let's Groove," "Spend the Night"), the Spinners (the radio-aired LP track "All That Glitters Ain't Gold"), and Eddie Kendricks (the tropical-flavored "Get It While It's Hot").

In the mid-'70s, Life signed Evelyn "Champagne" King to a production deal and began gathering song material for the teenager with the grown woman's voice, namely a song demo from John Fitch and Reuben Cross called "Shame." Getting a deal with RCA Records, "Shame" began gaining radio airplay in 1977. The follow-up, "I Don't Know If It's Right," went gold, as did "Smooth Talk," which peaked at number-14 pop in summer 1978 and sold almost 900,000 copies. Life also produced LPs on Kalyan, the 14-man soul/calypso band from Trinidad (*All the Way Live*), hard funk/rock band Thomas Bucknasty, Vicki Sue Robinson, and London Records act the Beck Family. Some Life-related singles are Mystique's steppers cut "Is It Really You," Teddy Pendergrass' cousin N'cole's "Gonna Need This Love," and Vicki Sue Robinson's "Can't Accept the Fact."

Life became an RCA recording artist in August 1978 with the release of *That's Life*, produced by Al Garrison. Life's studio bandmates Instant Funk are featured on the sparse, beautiful ballad "I Found My Way," which has background vocals by a pre-stardom Luther Vandross and enchanting acoustic piano; the funk/rock single "Tell Me"; and the catchy "Games." Other standout tracks are the lilting island-ish ballad "Another Story" and funky horn-laden title track. The title track single from his second LP, *Something That You Do to Me (Keeps Turning Me On)*, was released on Arista in the early '80s with it becoming a disco hit and a post-release 12-inch collectible. *—Ed Hogan*

● **That's Life** / Aug. 1978 / RCA ✦✦

T. Life, the producer of Evelyn Champagne King's gold single "Shame," made his solo recording debut with *That's Life* on the same label as his protégé, RCA Records, in summer 1978. The album was produced by Al Garrison, who remixed "Shame," with David Todd. The vocalist/guitarist/songwriter features his studio bandmates Instant Funk on three tracks: the rock/funk-ish first single "Tell Me," the sinewy "Games," and the sparse, gentle ballad "I Found My Way." On the latter, listen for vocals (background) by a pre-stardom Luther Vandross. Other standouts are the slick, punchy horn-laced second single "Short Changed," the tight thumpin' bass-dominated title track, and the lilting, reggae-flavored "Just Another Story." Those expecting Life's LP to be in the mode of tight disco funk of "Shame" will be surprised to hear an adventurous fusion of R&B, funk, rock, island, and acoustic jazz. Life dabbled more with rock funk fusion on the 1979 RCA LP *Blast-O-Funk* by the band Thomas Bucknasty. He also had an '80s Arista LP, *Something That You Do to Me Keeps Turnin' On*, whose title track was a dance favorite. *—Ed Hogan*

Something That You Do to Me Keeps Turnin' On / 1981 / Arista ✦✦

Philly soul singer/songwriter/producer T. Life's (Evelyn Champagne King's gold single "Shame") second album, *Something That You Do to Me Keeps Turnin' On* wasn't as rock-oriented as his first LP, *That's Life*, but it was no less eclectic. Life's frequent collaborator George Andrews is on hand to supply his usual dazzling arrangements. The pumping, punchy horn-laced title track was a dance hit and the extended not-available-to-retail 12-inch version became a post-release collectible. "Shame" saxophonist Sam Peake weaves through the low-toned funky, atmospheric "Smokin'." "Don't Let This Be the Last Time" has player piano, almost show tune-like quality to it. The reggae-ish "Let Him Go" has beautiful, bombastic horns.The lovely, crystalline ballad "Don't Wanna Be Lonely" has an exotic, Oriental flavor. "Wouldn't You Know" is funky while having striking vocal counterpoint. *—Ed Hogan*

Ta Mara & the Seen

db. 1989

Group / Urban

Best known for their 1985 hit "Everybody Dance," Ta Mara & the Seen were among the many acts that came out of Prince's Minneapolis funk/rock scene in the 1980s—a scene that the Time, Morris Day, Sheila E., Jesse Johnson's Revue, Vanity 6, Apollonia 6 and Mazarati and the Family were also associated with. Lead singer Ta Mara was born in Kenitra, Morocco and lived there as a child before moving to Minneapolis with her family at the age of seven. Growing up in Minneapolis, the singer learned to play several instruments, including piano, guitar, and drums. After reaching adulthood, she started working with local acts such as the Doug Maynard Band and the T.C. Jammers. Ta Mara also had her own band, which was eventually named the Seen and included bassist Keith Woodson, guitarist Oliver Leiber, keyboardist Gina Fellicetta, and drummer Jamie Chez.

In the early '80s, Ta Mara caught the attention of Time guitarist Jesse Johnson, who helped Ta Mara & the Seen get a deal with A&M and produced their self-titled debut album in 1985. The funky "Everybody Dance" became a major hit, but unfortunately, Ta Mara & the Seen would go down in history as one-hit wonders. In 1988, Johnson produced their second A&M album, *Blueberry Gossip*, which was a commercial disappointment and received very little attention. Ta Mara & the Seen's second album turned out to be their last; dropped by A&M, the band broke up in 1989 without ever recording a third album. *Ta Mara & the Seen* and *Blueberry Gossip* are both out of print. *—Alex Henderson*

● **Ta Mara & the Seen** / 1985 / A&M ✦✦✦✦

When Ta Mara & the Seen's self-titled debut album came out in 1985, the Minneapolis funk-rock sound was huge. Countless artists who had no connection to Minneapolis were trying to cop that sound and emulate Prince or the Time, but as a rule, the best Minneapolis grooves came from the Minneapolis artists themselves. Produced by Jesse Johnson, this LP is among the stronger Minneapolis-style funk/rock efforts that came out in 1985. Lead vocalist Ta Mara, who isn't black but sounds like she could be, showed a lot of promise on this album. The LP is best known for the infectious funk hit "Everybody Dance," but Ta Mara is also quite appealing on songs that range from the playful "Summertime Love" to the sweaty "Thinking About You" and the melancholy "Long Cold Nights." Because *Ta Mara & the Seen* is out of print, fans of the Minneapolis funk/rock sound are advised to grab it at once if they come across a copy. *—Alex Henderson*

Take 6

f. 1985, Alabama

Group / Acappella, Urban, Contemporary Gospel

With its roots in gospel, doo wop, and the sophisticated jazz-influenced singing groups of mid-century America like the Hi-Los, the a cappella vocal group Take 6 is both a throwback to an earlier, more genteel era of American music and a precursor for a number of black male pop groups of the '90s (most notably Boyz II Men). Its members include David Thomas, Alvin Chea, Cedric Dent, Mark Kibble, Claude V. McKnight III, and Joey Kibble (who replaced Mervyn Warren). McKnight and Mark Kibble caught the a cappella bug at Alabama's Oakwood College in the early '80s, forming a vocal group that solidified into Take 6 when singer/arranger Warren joined up in 1985. They signed a pact with the Reunion label in 1988, recording arrangements of Negro spirituals and newly composed material on their first album, *Doo Be Doo Wop Bop!*

They were quickly picked up by Warner Bros.' Reprise label, for whom they started making smooth yet vocally adventuresome albums that defy pigeonholing other than the all-purpose a cappella label. Take 6 has also recorded Christmas carols, toured with Al Jarreau, appeared on Quincy Jones' all-star *Back on the Block* album, and on *Join the Band* (1994) they used instrumental backing for the first time. However, 1996's *Brothers* album indicated a turn toward commercial, sound-alike soul music that threatened to rob Take 6 of its unique identity. *So Cool* followed in 1998, with *We Wish You a Merry Christmas* appearing a year later. The new millennium was a time of rejuvenation. *Beautiful World*, released in April 2002, showcased an incredible instrumentation and Take 6's new musical approach. *—Richard S. Ginell*

★ **Take 6** / 1988 / Reprise ✦✦✦✦✦

The debut recording by Take 6 is still their finest set. Comprised of six singers performing a cappella, Take 6's message was always strictly gospel, but their advanced harmonies, impressive ranges, and swinging style often crossed over stylistically to jazz. Some of their ensembles are quite remarkable on this CD, and their interpretations of originals and such songs as "Oh Mary, Don't You Weep," "Get Away, Jordan," and "He Never Sleeps" invigorate both gospel music and the legacy of jazz vocal groups. A classic set. *—Scott Yanow*

So Much 2 Say / 1990 / Warner Alliance ✦✦✦✦✦

Take 6's second recording is almost the equal of their first. The six singers (Mark Kibble, Claude V. McKnight III, Cedric Dent, David Thomas, Mervyn E. Warren and Alvin Chea) perform some near-miraculous ensembles on a variety of original material, all of which contains gospel-oriented lyrics. Take 6's first two CDs are their strongest, before the innovative group started to water down both their message and their jazz-influenced harmony sound with the addition of occasional instruments. *—Scott Yanow*

Join the Band / 1994 / Warner Alliance ✦✦✦

This gospel-infused, jazz-inspired sextet shows all the little boy vocal harmony groups how it's done. The lyrics are geared towards God, but the slick, bubbly production is cool and soulful R&B all the way. Their picture-perfect, rhythmically fascinating voice texturing certainly doesn't need any embellishment; however, on hand to lend support are Stevie Wonder, Ray Charles, Kirk Whalum, and Gerald Albright. In light of all the self-contained artistic brilliance, it's sad that they resorted to the commercialism of a bland David Foster ballad and a Queen Latifah rap. Top cuts include "Biggest Part of Me" (remake of the old Ambrosia hit), "It's Gonna Rain," and "I've Got Life." *—Jonathan Widran*

Brothers / 1996 / Warner Alliance ✦✦✦

The Greatest Hits / Jul. 20, 1999 / Reprise ✦✦✦✦

There are numerous musical styles represented on this compilation. Gospel, befitting the group's Seventh Day Adventist background, is the genre most represented. On "Oh Thou That Tellest Good Tidings to Zion," the group is joined by Stevie Wonder. "A Quiet Place," while a hymn, is delivered as if it came from the Top Ten pop song chart. Jazz, albeit smooth, is represented by the Quincy Jones-produced "Setembro," featuring such contemporary jazz luminaries as George Benson, Herbie Hancock, and Gerald Albright. Sarah Vaughan is also listed on the playbill. But if she is in fact there, it is as a background singer; her voice is overwhelmed by the vocal group, synthesizers, keyboards, and the other electronic wizardry dominating this cut. Albright's alto is given a few measures, providing some musical substance to this tune. Smooth jazz has another entry with "U Turn," from the Joe Sample album *Spellbound*. The harmonic gifts of Take 6 are best displayed by those songs having a R&B, gospel flavor. "One and the Same," featuring gospel and R&B diva CeCe Winans, is an album highlight. The 1960s singing style of the Temptations is brought to mind with "The Best Stuff in the World Today Café." On "Spread Love," another gospel influenced R&B number, Take 6 uses the Hal David/Burt Bacharach song "What the World Needs Now" to bridge choruses, with good results. The session ends with the lone tribute to vocalese, "So Much 2 Say." The album is a fine compilation from previous Take 6 recordings, and should appeal to fans of this popular and erstwhile crossover singing group. *—Dave Nathan*

Beautiful World / Apr. 23, 2002 / Warner Bros. ✦✦✦✦

With intelligence, imagination, passion, and skill, Take 6 offers an unprecedented convergence of a cappella vocal artistry with solid instrumental accompaniment on *Beautiful World*. Produced by the highly talented Marcus Miller (of Miles Davis' electric period fame) and fueled by the intriguing messages delivered on 13 great songs from the pop, gospel, and soul styles, *Beautiful World* is overflowing with inventive lyricism and catches the listener up in Take 6's musical stories. The title track is performed with new lyrics to the verses that give it an actual gospel message, a departure from the tongue-in-cheek cynicism of the original song released as "I.G.Y. (What a Beautiful World)" by Steely Dan. David Thomas sings a very beautiful "Fragile"—the pop hit made famous by Sting—with such reverence and feeling that he transcribes the song's impact for a new generation of soul/gospel enthusiasts. On "Takin' It to the Streets," the addition of alto saxophone riffs by David Sanborn alongside the six-man group's vocal harmonizing makes it even more enjoyable. Alvin Chea's vocal bass "walkin'" style of a cappella singing is the perfect alter ego for Marcus Miller's explorative "talkin'" bass guitar lines that have been heard around the world. Joey Kibble's fresh reprise on "Grandma's Hands" is uplifting, containing spiritual encouragement that, along with a ripe saxophone interpretation of the refrain, makes this song a pick. The multiple award-winning group's classic African-American gospel-based interpretations of some of the most enjoyable music of the 20th century—combined with new instrumental dimensions—make *Beautiful World* an excellent addition to your listening pleasures. *—Paula Edelstein*

Tamia (Tamia Washington)

b. May 9, 1976, Windsor, Ontario, Canada

Vocals, Songwriter / Urban, Contemporary R&B

Tamia is an urban R&B singer/songwriter who released her self-titled debut album in the spring of 1998. A native of Canada, Tamia got an early start in the music industry, singing on "You Put a Move on My Heart," the first single from Quincy Jones' 1994 hit album *Q's Jook Joint*, when she was only a teenager. That paved the way for the release of her debut album in 1998.

Tamia was born and raised in Windsor, Ontario. As a child, she took acting and singing lessons, eventually performing in a number of local choirs and theatrical presentations. She soon earned a reputation and several awards, including the YTV Vocal Achievement Award in 1993. The following year, she won the Steve Ross Music Scholarship at the American Academy of Achievement's Annual Salute to Excellence in 1994. That same year, she attended a party her manager Brenda Richie held for Luther Vandross. At that party, she met Quincy Jones, who became taken with Tamia's talent. By the end of the year, she had sung "You Put a Move on My Heart" for Jones' new album, *Q's Jook Joint*. The song became a Top Ten R&B hit and earned her a Grammy nomination for Best Female R&B Vocal Performance; another song on the album, a duet with Babyface entitled "Slow Jams," was nominated for Best R&B Performance by a Duo or Group. She also sang "Missing You" with Brandy, Gladys Knight, and Chaka Khan on the soundtrack for the 1995 film *Set It Off*. "Missing You" was also nominated for a Grammy, making for a total of three nominations for Tamia before she had even released an album.

Such exposure, plus nominations from the NAACP Image Awards and the Soul Train Music Awards, made Tamia a hot commodity in the music industry. She carefully crafted her debut album over the course of 1996 and 1997, taking time out to play a small role in *Speed II: Cruise Control* in 1997; she also sang "Make Tonight Beautiful" for the soundtrack. Tamia finally released her debut album, *Tamia*, in April 1998. The album boasted an impressive list of collaborators and producers, including Jermaine Dupri, Keith Crouch, Tim Kelly & Bob Robinson, Stevie J., Mario Wynans, and Quincy Jones. Two years later and newly signed to Elektra, Tamia released her sophomore effort *A Nu Day*, featuring production collaborations from Missy Elliott, Dallas Austin, and Shep Crawford. *—Stephen Thomas Erlewine*

● **Tamia** / Apr. 14, 1998 / Qwest/Warner Bros. ✦✦✦

Although it suffers from some uneven material, Tamia's eponymous debut album is an appealingly stylish collection of contemporary urban soul. Usually, her seductive voice can make the mediocre songs enticing, but the album truly soars when she has a strong song, like "Imagine." It's moments like these that indicate Tamia has true potential. *—Leo Stanley*

A Nu Day / Oct. 10, 2000 / Elektra/Asylum ✦✦✦

Canadian-born chanteuse Tamia's second album, *A Nu Day*, is a nice pop-R&B record that doesn't set off to break much new ground. She has more of a traditional singer's voice (à la Vanessa Williams) than the guttural growls of many of her day's R&B contemporaries. That said, this album provides for a pleasurable and unchallenging listening experience. As was the norm for that day and age, the album contains its share of mandissing tunes, notably the two openers, "Dear John" and the set's first single, "Can't Go for That," which is also offered as the set's closer, in remix form, sampling the Hall & Oats hit from which it's inspired. There's also an adequate cover of the old DeBarge hit "Love Me in a Special Way." Some of the set's strongest material, however, includes funkier tunes penned by Dallas Austin, "Go," and Missy Elliott ("Wanna Be," arguably the set's biggest highlight). Dubious offerings include "Un'h—to You," which may sound somewhat funky, but the over-sexed lyrics come off sounding more awkward than legitimate (imagine Vanessa Williams singing about "finding her spot"). Another song, "Long Distance Love," tries awkwardly to make poetry out of lyrics that include the words "AT&T," "Bell Atlantic," and "Sprint," with awkward commercial-sounding results that only serve to date and cheapen this otherwise engaging set. Regardless, Tamia's voice is a pleasure to the ear, and the set boasts its share of strong songs. Other notables include "Stranger in My House" (the second single) and "If I Were You." *—Jose Promis*

The Tams

f. 1959, Atlanta, GA, **db.** 1973
Group / Northern Soul, Beach, Soul
A "beach" music favorite, Atlanta's Tams were among the more popular uptempo soul groups of the '60s, although they were never able to break Motown's pop stranglehold. Joseph Pope's gravelly voiced leads were their selling point. He was joined by his brother Charles, Robert Smith, Floyd Ashton, and Horace Key. They began on Swan in 1960, then landed their first hit with "Untie Me" for Arlen in 1962. It peaked at number 12 on the R&B charts (number-11 pop). They moved to ABC-Paramount the next year, where they remained until 1968. They scored their biggest hit in 1963 with "What Kind of Fool (Do You Think I Am)." But many soul fans regard 1968's "Be Young, Be Foolish, Be Happy" as their ultimate hit, although it only reached number 26 on the R&B charts. *—Ron Wynn*

● **The Best of the Tams** / Jan. 23, 1995 / Ripete ✦✦✦✦
Here are 14 songs from singles that they recorded for ABC-Paramount between 1963 and 1969, their most productive era. Includes "What Kind of Fool (Do You Think I Am)," "Be Young, Be Foolish, Be Happy," and a few late-'60s songs by Joe South. Decent, somewhat retro-flavored (even for the time) soul with heavy pop and doo wop influences, sounding at times like a very unschooled variation of the early Impressions. Unfortunately, this doesn't include their early-'60s hit "Untie Me," which was recorded before the group joined ABC-Paramount. *—Richie Unterberger*

Dancing Mood / 1996 / Ring of Stars ✦✦✦✦
Perennial favorites of beach music fans, the Tams were a group who knew how to balance the sweet, smooth sounds of their harmonies and (mostly) upbeat material with the passionate grit of Joseph Pope's vocals, who had a knack for sounding emphatic without overstating the case. Masters of sweet soul with a Southern sense of laid-back enthusiasm, the Tams have been a phenomenon in Georgia and the Carolinas since the early '60s, and *Dancing Mood* pulls together a whopping 30 of their classic tracks, most of them dating from their early days with Arlen Records, but also including some important later material cut for ABC-Paramount and 1-2-3. While this collection suffers from less-than-attractive packaging, inadequate liner notes, and skimpy information on the where-and-when of the individual tracks, as a collection of the Tams at their best, *Dancing Mood* does the job quite well, chronicling both Pope's often lovelorn vocals as well as the sharp songwriting (often from Joe South) and imaginative arrangements that make these sides memorable. Sound quality varies from cut to cut, though most of it's quite good. The packing prevents this from being the definitive Tams disc, but *Dancing Mood* is still a far better-than-average summary of this classic group's big hits and worthy lesser-knowns. *—Mark Deming*

Tashan

b. 1963, New York, NY
Vocals / Urban, Hip-Hop, Club/Dance
A first-rate soul and R&B vocalist, Tashan has had the misfortune of being stylistically in the wrong era. His sound is too earthy and raw for the urban contemporary mainstream, yet not Southern and bluesy enough for the Southern market. While he is also well-versed in hip-hop and rap via his New York upbringing, his Def Jam LPs have included some blistering duets with Alyson Williams. Tashan started off in the mid-'80s by writing and producing "Yours for a Night," which was recorded by rappers Whodini. He was signed to Def Jam/Columbia in 1985 and *Chasin' a Dream* was released in 1986. *On the Horizon* followed in 1989. Neither attracted widespread commercial interest, though he is more popular in England. His third album was released in 1994. *—Ron Wynn*

Chasin' a Dream / 1986 / Def Jam ✦✦✦

● **On the Horizon** / 1989 / Original Black ✦✦✦✦✦
A sleeper from a deep-voiced crooner, he wants to rewrite *What's Going On.* On "Black Man," "Save the Family," " and a few others he actually succeeds. *—John Floyd*

For the Sake of Love / Jun. 1992 / Columbia ✦✦✦

A Taste of Honey

f. 1971, Los Angeles, CA
Group / Disco, Quiet Storm
A Taste of Honey had two huge hits that were very dissimilar from each other—"Boogie Oogie Oogie" and a cover of Kyu Sakamoto's 1963 gold hit "Sukiyaki." The former was foot-stomping disco and the latter was languid and lush. Around 1971, singer/bassist/guitarist Janice Marie Johnson and keyboardist Percy Kibble decided to start a band after meeting at an audition for vacation cruise gigs for Princess Cruises. Taking their group name from one of their favorite songs, the band added several friends to the lineup and began playing Southern California bars and military bases in the U.S. and abroad. Their lead singer Gregory Walker quit to join Santana and guitarist Hazel Payne was added. After meeting with producer Fonce Mizell and his brother Larry, the group was signed to Capitol Records.

The group's first single, "Boogie Oogie Oogie," was inspired by an unresponsive audience during a date at a military base; Johnson believed the crowd was chauvinistic toward the group's two female guitar players. The notorious bass solo intro came about when Johnson was warming up before the recording session, unaware that she was being recorded. The single sold more than two-million copies and topped *Billboard's* charts for three weeks in fall 1978. The follow-up single, the slinky and funky "Do It Good," went to number-13 R&B and number-79 pop, and *A Taste of Honey* went platinum.

After hearing Linda Ronstadt's version of Smokey Robinson's "Ooh Baby Baby," Johnson decided that the group (now Johnson and Payne) should remake a classic song. In their pre-Capitol days, Johnson used to sing the lyrics to Sakamoto's "Sukiyaki" when the group toured Japan and performed at the Yamaha Song Festival). She contacted her Japanese sub-publisher, whom in turn contacted the original writers, Rokusuke EI and Hachidai Nakamura, to get permission to redo the song with English lyrics. Two translators were employed, and one of them came up with lyrics that were close to the maudlin theme of the original song, translated into English as "I Look Up When I Walk." Johnson decided to add her own original lyrics to the song. At first she thought her lyrics were too simple, but producer George Duke encouraged her to write from her heart. A publishing rights dispute almost stopped the song from being released. After it was recorded, Johnson found out that one of the original writers had signed his rights away years before. His publisher had Johnson give up all songwriting and publishing rights to her new version before Capitol was able to release it. The bassist relented, knowing that this song would be the one to take A Taste of Honey out of the disco category. But Capitol wasn't too keen on "Sukiyaki," promising to release it as a single but then releasing "Rescue Me" (number-16 R&B, summer 1980) and "I'm Talkin 'Bout You" (number-64 R&B, late 1980).

Others discouraged Johnson for donning Japanese attire and doing a fan dance while performing the song. Forced by album track radio play, the label finally released "Sukiyaki" as a single, which went to number-one R&B, number three pop in spring 1981. The *Twice as Sweet* LP went to number-36 pop in spring 1981. After "Sukiyaki" was a hit, the duo went to Japan and toured with Kyu Sakamoto. A Taste of Honey also covered Smokey Robinson and the Miracles' "I'll Try Something New." Johnson released a solo Capitol LP, *One Taste of Honey,* which yielded a charting single, the softly "Sukiyaki"-ish "Love Me Tonite," number-67 R&B, summer 1984. The Burger King national fast food chain began using "Boogie Oogie Oogie" in a national TV ad campaign in summer 1999, introducing another generation to the late-'70s smash. The track has also been sampled by hip-hop and rap artists MC Lyte, Mac 10, and others. Around the same time, Johnson announced plans for an EP, *Hiatus of the Heart,* for her own Tastebuds label to be released in 2000. She also said she had projects with Ice Cube and Con Funk Shun founder Felton Pilate. Payne tours Japan with her own Top 40 band. Percy Kibble died in 1999. A Taste of Honey's greatest hits can be found on *Anthology* (One Way, 1995) and "Sukiyaki" is listed on *Smooth Grooves, Vol. 7: A Sensual Collection* (Rhino, 1996). *—Ed Hogan*

A Taste of Honey / 1978 / Capitol ✦✦✦✦
Because A Taste of Honey's first major hit, "Boogie Oogie Oogie," was a lighthearted, escapist piece of ear candy, rock critics of the late '70s didn't take the group seriously and tended to dismiss Janice Marie Johnson and Hazel Payne as producers' puppets. But they were far from that: In addition to being expressive singers, Johnson and Payne were talented, versatile musicians and songwriters. Anyone who gives this self-titled debut album a serious listen will quickly realize you can't lump Honey in with the type of disco acts that were, in fact, invented by producers or A&R teams. To the more knowledgeable listener, it's also apparent that *A Taste of Honey* has as much to do with soul and funk as it does with disco. Although "Boogie Oogie Oogie," which became one of the disco era's major anthems, is the gem that made this album sell over one-million units in the U.S., it isn't the record's only highlight. Equally impressive are tracks that range from the gritty, funky "You" to the dreamy "Sky High" and the haunting "World Spin." Meanwhile, "You're in Good Hands" is a '60s-flavored soul ballad that should have been a hit (Honey didn't have a hit ballad until "Sukiyaki" in 1980). Produced by Fonce and Larry Mizell, *A Taste of Honey* is excellent from start to finish. *—Alex Henderson*

Another Taste / 1979 / Capitol ✦✦✦✦
Inevitably, many groups will suffer from the dreaded sophomore curse—they'll impress you with a promising debut album, only to disappoint you with an inferior second album. But Taste of Honey didn't let its audience down on its generally impressive sophomore effort, *Another Taste.* While this album didn't contain a chart-topper hit like "Boogie Oogie Oogie," the addictive "Do It Good" did reach number 13 on the R&B charts. *Another Taste* is full of irresistible soul-disco grooves, which range from the lush "Dance" and the dreamy "The Rainbow's End" to the exuberant "Take the Boogae or Leave It." Because "Boogie Oogie Oogie" had sold two-million copies, it stands to reason that Capitol would, in 1979, encourage Honey to give this album a lot of dancefloor appeal. But to their credit, Janice Marie Johnson and Hazel Payne don't try to turn any of the dance numbers into a remake of "Boogie Oogie Oogie"; in fact, they deserve high marks for making this album as unpredictable as it is. And while uptempo material dominates *Another Taste,* "Let's Begin" and "Your Love" remind us how appealing the group's slow jams could be. *—Alex Henderson*

Twice as Sweet / 1981 / Capitol ✦✦

Anthology / 1995 / One Way ✦✦✦✦

Beauty & the Boogie / Jun. 3, 1997 / Capitol ✦✦✦

● **Classic Masters** / Jan. 29, 2002 / Capitol ✦✦✦✦
Capitol records recognized that Universal had a good thing going on with their *20th Century Masters* series, realizing that it was a perfect way to offer new greatest-hits collections in a classy, eye-catching fashion. Fortunately, they also learned from the mistakes

of Universal (who took a while to get off the ground with their initial volumes of the series) and began rivaling the overall quality of latter-day volumes of *20th Century Masters* with the initial volumes of their own series, *Classic Masters*. Case in point is Taste of Honey's edition of the series. What's nice about it is that it does its job cleanly and stylishly, offering all of the group's hits, along with selected highlights, in 12 crisply remastered tracks. Yes, some fans could want a more thorough compilation, but they would have to be serious listeners. For the majority of listeners, though, this delivers everything they need in a very good greatest-hits package—and it's quite representative of the rest of this fine line. *—Stephen Thomas Erlewine*

Howard Tate

b. 1938, Macon, GA

Vocals / Soul, Northern Soul, Pop-Soul

Highly regarded by soul music cultists, and virtually unknown by anybody else, Howard Tate had some minor success with the Verve label in the late '60s. The singer brought a lot of blues and gospel to his phrasing, but what made him palatable to the modern R&B (and, to a lesser degree, pop) audience was the Northeast soul production of Jerry Ragovoy, who also wrote much of Tate's material. Howard made the R&B Top 20 three times in the late '60s (with "Ain't Nobody Home," "Stop," and "Look at Granny Run Run"). However, he's most famous to rock audiences as the original performer of "Get It While You Can," which became one of Janis Joplin's signature tunes.

Before establishing himself as a solo performer, Tate sang with the Gainors, a North Philadelphia doo wop group that also included future soul star Garnet Mimms. In the early '60s, he was the vocal frontman for Bill Doggett, the organist famous for the instrumental hit "Honky Tonk." Jerry Ragovoy was urged to check out Tate by a member of the Enchanters, Garnet Mimms' backup singers. He recorded about ten singles with Tate between 1966 and 1969, the first for the small Utopia label, the rest for Verve.

Tate moved on to Lloyd Price's Turntable label, for which he recorded a few singles in the late '60s and early '70s. From there he chalked up a short stint with Atlantic, which saw a few other 45s and a critically well-received album, but again little commercial success. A final 1974 single for Epic was his swan song. Always somewhat of a mysterious figure, he hasn't been seen since the early '80s. His music has received its greatest exposure via cover versions: Jimi Hendrix and Hugh Masekela did "Stop," Ry Cooder covered "Look at Granny Run Run," B.B. King recorded "Ain't Nobody Home," and rappers Brand Nubian sampled "Look at Granny Run Run." And of course Joplin (who also raided the Ragovoy catalog for "Try (Just a Little Bit Harder)," "Cry Baby," and "My Baby") did "Get It While You Can" in a manner closely derived from Tate's interpretation. *—Richie Unterberger*

Get It While You Can / 1966 / Verve ✦✦✦✦✦

This is a fine Jerry Ragovoy production and soulful, wailing vocals from Tate. Includes original versions of "Get It While You Can" and "Look at Granny Run Run." *—Christine Ohlman*

Howard Tate / 1972 / Atlantic ✦✦✦✦

Here is some gritty, no-frills Southern soul from Howard Tate, who never quite achieved the highs on Atlantic he had reached with Verve or Lloyd Price's Turntable label. He put plenty of emotional punch and fire into these numbers, but couldn't elevate them or make them hits. *—Ron Wynn*

Reaction / 1981 / Turntable ✦✦✦

A good album of vintage Southern soul, delivered with conviction and earnestness by Howard Tate. At his best, Tate's blend of gospel-tinged shouting and wailing and countrified inflections and delivery put him close to Percy Sledge. But he just wasn't able to get over the hump, mainly because he never had a full album's worth of consistently solid material, and also seldom recorded for labels with any foothold in the R&B/soul market. *—Ron Wynn*

● **Get It While You Can: The Legendary Sessions** / Jun. 20, 1995 / Mercury ✦✦✦✦✦

Tate's entire Verve output, condensed into a tidy 17-track compilation, including all of his late '60s singles for the label, and one previously unreleased track. It's solid period soul with a slight eclectic bent for the blues, gospel, and some pop influences. *—Richie Unterberger*

Pam Tate

Vocals, Arranger, Producer / Urban, Contemporary Blues

A soul-styled vocalist, Pam Tate released two albums (1991's *Die Happy* and 1994's *Dancing on the Pyramids*) for the Left Field label. *—Ron Wynn*

● **Die Happy** / Aug. 19, 1991 / Left Field ✦✦✦✦

Armed with a big voice and a soulful outlook, Pam Tate successfully tackles R&B, jazz and blues on her debut album, *Die Happy*. It's regrettable that this self-produced outing bombed commercially, for the singer shows a fair amount of promise. Tate is convincing as a sassy, bluesy R&B shouter on "A Woman Scorned," "Counting the Hours" and "Step in the Wrong Direction," and she's equally appealing when she turns around and takes a dusky, nocturnal, jazz-minded approach on the title song, "Shadow of a Doubt" and the lonely torch song "Once in a Blue Moon." Tate proves herself to be the type of singer who would have no problem tackling Bobby "Blue" Bland's songs one minute and paying tribute to Joe Williams or Count Basie the next, but on *Die Happy*, Tate does all of the writing herself—and she isn't half bad as a composer. One hoped that eventually, Tate would become better known, because a singer this good shouldn't be so obscure. *—Alex Henderson*

Tommy Tate

b. Sep. 29, 1944, Homestead, FL

Vocals / Southern Soul, Soul, Urban, R&B

Florida vocalist Tommy Tate is a consistent, if unspectacular, Southern soul wailer. He debuted on Rise in 1964, and continued recording for OKeh, Verve, and Big Ten before joining the Nightingales at Stax in 1970. He returned to the solo scene a couple of years later, recording for Koko. He had a Top 30 R&B single with "School of Love" in 1972, and it has been his only substantial hit. But Tate has kept plugging, working in Mississippi clubs and recording for Juana, Sundance, and other independents. His most recent release was *Love Me Now* for Ichiban's subsidiary label Urgent! in 1992. *—Ron Wynn*

● **Love Me Now** / Sep. 9, 1992 / Urgent! ✦✦✦

Tommy Tate tried his luck with the Urgent! label, an Atlanta-based company distributed by Ichiban. He had some nice, but dated material done in vintage 1960s and '70s soul style. They attempted at times to update the framework with drum machines and other trappings, but wound up with another strictly regional item, although it's not that bad for fans of the genre. *—Ron Wynn*

Tavares

f. 1964, New Bedford, MA

Group / Disco, Pop-Soul, Quiet Storm, Funk, Soul

The five-brother singing group Tavares may be best known for such uptempo hits as the million-selling single "Heaven Must Be Missing an Angel," "More Than a Woman," and "Whodunit," but they first came to national attention with the luscious ballad "Check It Out." Their crisp vocalizing and clean-cut, young-men-next-door image made them favorites on TV shows starring Johnny Carson, Mike Douglas, and Dick Clark's *American Bandstand*. In 1974, Tavares also had the first hit version (number-one R&B) of "She's Gone" written by the then relatively unknown duo of Daryl Hall and John Oates. Hall & Oates scored a number-seven pop hit with the song in 1976.

The Tavares brothers—Arthur Tavares, Ralph Vierra Tavares, Perry Lee Tavares, Antone Tavares, and Feliciano Tavares nicknamed "Pooch," "Tiny," "Chubby," and "Butch"—started the group in 1964 as Chubby & the Turnpikes in New Bedford, MA. Their grandparents taught them traditional Cape Verde folk songs, while their older brother John schooled them on doo wop singing. In 1969, the group became Tavares. They began singing in New England clubs and were signed to Capitol Records in 1973. Their debut album, *Check It Out*, was issued in early 1974. The title track slow jam single went to number-five R&B on *Billboard*'s charts in summer 1973. The next single, the ballad "That's the Sound That Lonely Makes," hit number-ten R&B in early 1974. *Check It Out* was followed by *Hard Core Poetry* in summer 1974, helmed by songwriting/production duo Dennis Lambert & Brian Potter (the Four Tops' "Aint No Woman Like the One I Got").

It listed the soaring number-ten hit "Too Late," the number-one hit "She's Gone," and "Remember What I Told You to Forget," which hit number-four in 1975. Lambert & Potter produced *In the City* (summer 1975), which yielded the driving number-one hit "It Only Takes a Minute," "Free Ride" (a 1973 pop smash for the Edgar Winter Group), and "The Love I Never Had." Take That's 1993 cover of "It Only Takes a Minute" was a U.K. hit. Tavares' album *Sky High!* (spring 1976) was the group's first collaboration with producer Freddie Perren. Perren seemed to have an affinity for family singing groups, having had hits with the Jackson 5 ("I Want You Back," "ABC," "The Love You Save") as a member of the Motown arrangers/songwriters/producers collective The Corporation, and would later go to have hits with the Sylvers ("Boogie Fever"). *Sky High!* boasted the sparkling number-three R&B hit "Heaven Must Be Missing an Angel (Part 1)" from summer 1976. Their fifth LP, *Love Storm* was issued in spring 1977 and included the clever number-one R&B hit "Whodunit" in spring 1977.

"More Than a Woman" was specifically written for Tavares by the Bee Gees and was issued as a single from the 11-million-selling *Saturday Night Fever* soundtrack. "More Than a Woman" was also on their *Future Bound* LP released in spring 1978. A greatest hits set, *The Best of Tavares*, was released in fall 1977. On 1979's *Madame Butterfly* LP, the group worked with Philly soul arranger/producer Bobby Martin (the Manhattans, L.T.D.). The sweet ballad "Never Had a Love Like This Before" went to number-five R&B in early 1979. In 1994, Canadian label Unidisc released *The Best of Tavares Revisited*, which had re-recordings by the group of their past hits. *—Ed Hogan*

Check It Out / Jan. 1974 / Capitol ✦✦✦✦

From Earth, Wind & Fire and L.T.D. to the O'Jays and the Dramatics, many of the great soul outfits of the 1960s and 1970s paid more than their share of dues. None of those groups were overnight sensations, they struggled a long time before becoming huge, and the same can be said about Tavares. The Boston vocal group was formed in 1964, and it wasn't until 1973 that Tavares finally landed a deal with a major label. But there is one important difference between Tavares and those other soulsters; unlike EWF (which didn't really start to achieve supergroup status until its fifth album) or the O'Jays (which recorded its share of commercially unsuccessful records before becoming famous at Philadelphia International), Tavares made it big with its first album. Capitol didn't screw around when it signed the Tavares siblings in 1973; making sure that they hit the ground running, Capitol united them with singer/composer/producer Johnny Bristol on their debut album, *Check It Out*. Known for 1970s hits like "You and I" and "Hang on in There, Baby," Bristol was a master of smooth, sophisticated Northern soul, and he proves to be a major asset to Tavares on gems like "Strangers in Dark Corners," Billy Preston's "Little Girl," "That's the Sound That Lonely Makes" (a number-ten R&B hit), and the romantic title song (which reached number five on the R&B singles charts). Before *Check It Out*, Tavares was considered a noteworthy local attraction in the Boston area. When this excellent album took off, the quintet became famous all over the U.S. *—Alex Henderson*

Hard Core Poetry / Sep. 1974 / Capitol ✦✦✦✦✦

Because Johnny Bristol served Tavares so well on its debut album, *Check It Out*, it was logical to assume that he would be producing the group's next project. Instead, Tavares switched producers on its second album, *Hard Core Poetry*, and joined forces with the Dennis Lambert/Brian Potter team. Having worked with the Four Tops and others, Lambert & Potter had an impressive track record when it came to Northern soul, and they do right by Tavares on this excellent sophomore effort. In addition to producing the LP, Lambert & Potter handle most of the writing. The only track they didn't write is a cover of

Hall & Oates' "She's Gone," which became a number-one R&B hit for Tavares. All of the other tracks are Lambert/Potter compositions, and their writing is excellent on material that ranges from the dramatic "Too Late" and the sentimental "Remember What I Told You to Forget" (a number-four R&B hit) to the inspiring "Someone to Go Home To." Full of gems, *Hard Core Poetry* is among Tavares' most essential albums. *—Alex Henderson*

In the City / 1975 / Capitol ♦♦♦♦♦
The Tavares brothers' creative and commercial winning streak continued with their third album, *In the City*. This excellent 1975 release marked the second time that they worked with the Dennis Lambert/Brian Potter team, which produced the record and wrote half of the songs (including the hit ballad "The Love I Never Had" and the funky number-one smash "It Only Takes a Minute"). Lambert & Potter had done well by Tavares on their second album, *Hard Core Poetry*, and their input proves to be just as valuable this time around. The songs that Lambert & Potter didn't write range from Tavares' gritty title song (a bittersweet ode to urban life) to inspired covers of the Edgar Winter Group's "Free Ride" (which gives us a rare chance to hear Tavares performing rock & roll) and the Average White Band's smooth "Nothing You Can Do." The latter wasn't among AWB's major hits, although it should have been. Like *Check It Out* and *Hard Core Poetry*, *In the City* is undeniably essential. *—Alex Henderson*

Sky High! / 1976 / Capitol ♦♦♦♦
Thanks to producer Freddie Perren, Tavares acquired a lot of disco gloss on their fourth album, *Sky High!* The producers Tavares had worked with on previous efforts—first Johnny Bristol on *Check It Out*, then the Dennis Lambert/Brian Potter team on *Hard Core Poetry* and *In the City*—saw them as primarily a Northern soul vocal quintet. Perren didn't forget about Tavares' Northern soul heritage, but he made sure that the uptempo selections would appeal to disco audiences in a major way. The joyous "Heaven Must Be Missing an Angel" (a number-three R&B hit) and the equally exuberant "Don't Take Away the Music" became dancefloor favorites, and pop fans who knew Tavares for those gems started to think of them as a disco group instead of a soul group. But it would be a mistake to believe that *Sky High!* isn't relevant to soul; in fact, "To the Other Man" and "Guiding Star" are exactly the type of smooth Northern soul ballads that had put Tavares on the map in 1973 and 1974. And "Don't Take Away the Music," like the Trammps' best recordings, is a perfect marriage of Philadelphia soul and Philadelphia disco—it has just the right blend of grit and gloss. *Sky High!* may not be quite as essential as *Hard Core Poetry*, *Check It Out*, or *In the City*, but it was certainly a rewarding and often fun addition to Tavares' catalog. *—Alex Henderson*

The Best of Tavares / 1977 / Capitol ♦♦♦♦
This was the best introduction to Tavares until well over a dozen other anthologies—some better, most not—arrived in a seemingly endless succession throughout the '90s and early 2000s. This vinyl release consisting of nine songs sticks to the basics, including "Heaven Must Be Missing an Angel" (*Billboard* number-one club play), "More Than a Woman" (number-32 pop), "She's Gone" (number-one black singles), "It Only Takes a Minute" (number-one black singles), and "Check It Out" (number-five black singles). This should not be confused with a similarly titled compilation in Capitol's *Capitol Gold* series, released on CD in the mid-'90s. *—Andy Kellman*

Love Storm / 1977 / Capitol ♦♦♦
The Tavares brothers' debut album, *Check It Out*, established them as soul stars, and when they delivered their fourth album, *Sky High!*, in 1976, they became disco stars as well—at least for a few years. The man Tavares has to thank for its popularity in the disco world from 1976-1978 is Freddie Perren, who made sure that *Sky High!* had both soul appeal and disco appeal. And Perren did the same thing when he produced Tavares' fifth album, *Love Storm*. Perren brings a fair amount of disco gloss to the major hit "Whodunit" and the Latin-tinged "Watchin' the Woman's Movement," but the 1977 LP also has plenty of unapologetic soul crooning. Those who were initially sold on Tavares because of their romantic ballads and slow jams won't be disappointed by "Keep in Touch," "Out of the Picture," the Blue Magic-like "Fool of the Year," or a heartfelt cover of Jesse Belvin's 1956 doo wop hit "Goodnight, My Love." Also memorable is Tavares' cover of the Jim Weatherly song "The Going Ups and the Coming Downs," which Gladys Knight & the Pips had recorded in 1974. *Love Storm* isn't among Tavares' essential albums, but it's a decent, satisfying effort that the group's hardcore fans will enjoy. *—Alex Henderson*

Future Bound / 1978 / Capitol ♦♦♦
Released in 1978, *Future Bound* was the third album that Freddie Perren produced for Tavares and was the group's sixth album overall. Once again, Perren sees to it that Tavares provides a healthy blend of uptempo dance numbers and romantic soul ballads. Those who savored "Heaven Must Be Missing an Angel" shouldn't have a problem getting into exuberant disco-soul items like "Slow Train to Paradise," "The Ghost of Love," and Tavares' hit version of the Bee Gees' "More Than a Woman" (which was available on the *Saturday Night Fever* soundtrack several months before *Future Bound* came out). Meanwhile, "Feel So Good" and "All I See Is You" are caressing Northern soul ballads that would have fit right in on a Stylistics, Delfonics, or Moments album. What was true of 1977's *Love Storm* is true of 1978's *Future Bound*: It falls short of essential but is a pleasing, likable LP nonetheless. *—Alex Henderson*

Madame Butterfly / 1979 / Capitol ♦♦♦♦
Pop fans who associate Tavares with "Heaven Must Be Missing an Angel" and the Bee Gees' "More Than a Woman" tend to think of it as a disco group. But Tavares' roots were Northern soul, and it was a classic Northern soul approach that first sent the Bostonians to the top of the R&B charts, not until Tavares' fourth album, *Sky High!*, did the quintet start to acquire a reputation as a disco act. With 1979's *Madame Butterfly*, Tavares seemed to be going out of its way to live down its disco reputation. The material is straight-up Northern soul, and nothing on this hell bent for R&B album is as disco-minded as "Heaven Must Be Missing an Angel" or "More Than a Woman." If you notice that much of *Madame Butterfly* is very Philadelphia-sounding, it's no coincidence, this excellent LP was produced by Bobby Martin, a Philadelphian who was highly regarded in Philly soul circles. Anyone who has spent hours and hours listening to the O'Jays, Harold Melvin & the Blue Notes, and the Intruders should have no problem getting into solid offerings like "My Love Calls," "Straight from the Heart," and the major hit "Never Had a Love Like This Before." If, in 1979, you were hoping to hear Tavares performing a lot of disco, you were bound to find *Madame Butterfly* disappointing. But those who wanted Tavares to stick to pure, unadulterated northern soul agreed that working with Martin was a very wise move. *—Alex Henderson*

Love Uprising / 1980 / Capitol ♦♦♦
It's easy to complain when a major label screws up, one could write a book about all of the talented artists who have been victimized by corporate politics and bad decisions, or all of the A&R people who forced artists to work with the wrong producer and made them record material that was totally wrong for them. But when a major label does right by an artist, it should get credit, and, for the most part, Capitol did right by Tavares. Thanks to Capitol, Tavares hit the ground running (both creatively and commercially) with its debut album of 1973, *Check It Out*. And all of its subsequent Capitol releases were either decent or excellent. Tavares' seven-year stay at Capitol ended with 1980's *Love Uprising*, which was produced by Benjamin Wright. While Wright had produced three songs on Tavares' last album, *Supercharged*, he handles all of the producing on *Love Uprising*. Under Wright's direction, the Tavares siblings deliver a vinyl LP that is enjoyable but not mind-blowing. All of the material is decent—none of it is bad, but none of it is fantastic either. Unlike *Hard Core Poetry*, *Check It Out*, and *In the City*, *Love Uprising* isn't among Tavares' essential albums and isn't recommended to casual listeners. But it's worth searching for if you consider yourself a hardcore fan of the group. *—Alex Henderson*

Supercharged / 1980 / Capitol ♦♦♦

New Directions / 1982 / RCA ♦♦

The Best of Tavares Revisited / 1994 / Unidisc ♦♦♦
Sometimes when artists from a music genre's classic era try to remake their own best-known sides, it's an embarrassing affair. Either the artist's skills and/or backing accompaniment can't match the passion or expertise of the original recordings or the tracks end up being a misguided exercise in being "current" or "hip" in an effort to bring the artist "back to the top of the charts!" Such is not the case with Tavares' *The Best of Tavares Revisited*, a 1994 release from Quebec label Unidisc. The brothers bring vitality and authenticity to their reinterpretation of their biggest '70s-era hits. Though the album uses modern musical technology, the emphasis remains on Tavares' time-honed vocal skills. As produced by the group—Eric Mathew, Daryl Payne, Robert Matichak, Gino Crescenza, Maurizio Nall—the album is an excellent example of how a remake set should done. *The Best of Tavares Revisited* makes one want to see the group live. *—Ed Hogan*

● **Capitol Gold: The Best of Tavares** / Jul. 23, 1996 / Capitol ♦♦♦♦♦
As prolific as Tavares was during the latter half of the '70s and the early half of the '80s, its compilations outnumber its proper studio albums. It's nearly impossible to consider all of the band's compilations without getting cross-eyed and confused, but *Capitol Gold: The Best of Tavares*—released in 1996—remained the best of the crop through 2002. The group had a remarkable run during the late '70s; "Check It Out," "Don't Take Away the Music," "Heaven Must Be Missing an Angel," "It Only Takes a Minute," "Never Had a Love Like This Before," "Remember What I Told You to Forget," "She's Gone," "That's the Sound That Lonely Makes," "Too Late," and "Whodunit" scaled the Top Ten of one *Billboard* chart or another (usually the black singles chart). Every one of those songs can be found here, and so can lower-charting singles and some scattered album tracks. *—Andy Kellman*

Greatest Hits / 2000 / EMI ♦♦♦
As Tavares' greatest-hits CDs go, one might overlook this one or one might not. While all their major hits are here unedited, some choice ones (e.g., "Is It Too Late" and "Remember What I Told You to Forget") are not. Instead, EMI chose some tracks not often available on these sets (e.g., "Slow Train to Paradise" and "The Ghost of Love"). So, depending on your likes and dislikes you may choose this best-of package over some other ones by the New England-bred brothers, especially if you're trying to accumulate all the cuts by the talented siblings who first burst on the recording scene as Chubby & the Turnpikes. *—Andrew Hamilton*

Classic Masters / Mar. 26, 2002 / Capitol ♦♦♦♦
Tavares scored 12 pop single chart entries (not counting the B-side "My Ship") between 1973 and 1980, and all 12 are presented in chronological order on this midline-priced, digitally remastered best-of, from "Check It Out" to "Bad Times," and including the gold-selling "Heaven Must Be Missing an Angel" and the group's contribution to the *Saturday Night Fever* soundtrack, "More Than a Woman." The sequencing allows an appreciation of Tavares' evolution from a vocal group of soul balladeers to disco stars. The selection strictly serves their pop crossover fans; they scored many more hits on the R&B charts, but none of the singles that failed to make the pop charts are included, not even "Never Had a Love Like This Before," which was a Top Five R&B hit. There are more thorough Tavares compilations at full price, but for the money this is an excellent overview of their career. *— William Ruhlmann*

Bobby Taylor & the Vancouvers

f. Feb. 18, 1936, Vancouver, British Columbia, Cana
Group / Soul, Motown, R&B
A San Francisco nightclub launched one of the most exciting bands to come out the Northwest. Tommy Chong and Bobby Taylor formed Four Niggers & A Chink from Little Daddie & the Bachelors, who originated from the Shades, a Calgary/Edmonton based

group. Little Daddie & the Bachelor's recorded a couple singles, including "Too Much Monkey Business" out of Vancouver, British Columbia. The offensive name killed the fan base that Little Daddie & the Bachelors had built. It's unclear whether Bobby Taylor was a member of the Bachelors—Tommy Milton, Donald Mallory, Chong, and Wes Henderson, but he was with the latter group who changed their name weekly around the same theme: Four Colour Fellas and a Chinese Lad ... Four N's and a C, before settling on Bobby Taylor & the Vancouvers. The original Vancouvers, in addition to Chong and Taylor, were Wes Henderson (guitar), Robbie King (keyboards), Ted Lewis (drums), and Eddie Patterson (bass).

They rebuilt their fan base by doing spirited, rock-ish versions of Motown hits. Jimi Hendrix played with them at one point for a year (prior to his stint with the Isley Brothers), mainly at Seattle's Black and Tan Club, but was fired because his solos were too long and loud. Mary Wilson and Florence Ballard heard the band when they played at Chong and Taylor's after-hour joint, the Elegant Parlor in Vancouver; Berry Gordy was contacted and the group signed with the hot recording company. It turned out to be a horrible mistake, but if they hadn't, would they have ever emerged from the Northwest?

Taylor was a veteran when he inked with Motown in 1967, he was born February 18, 1936, making him 31 at the time of the signing. Born in North Carolina, his folks moved to Washington, D.C., where he grew up in a public housing project and sang doo wops with friends on the street corners, sometimes joined by a tall, skinny kid named Marvin Gaye. Taylor's father was a full-blooded Native American and his grandfather, who had a singing group, was Puerto Rican. The Taylors knew all the musicians and their home was used as a resting place and motel for many artists who came through the district. Taylor and friends traveled to Brooklyn, NY—the Fort Green Projects—to doo wop with locals who became Little Anthony & the Imperials and Frankie Lymon & the Teenagers; but nothing happen until he migrated West and connected with Chong.

Motown got Bobby & the Vancouvers' name out there, but things were never right. They suffered the same indignation as the Isley Brothers and were viewed as carpet bagging, newcomers, and were igged, by Taylor's account, by "90 percent of the artists." And to add salt to an open wound: Johnny Bristol didn't like Tommy Chong, who was married with a kid and a die-hard pot smoker. Taylor left the group some time after the first album, which contained their hit "Does Your Mama Know About Me" (number 29, 1968), and two lesser smoothies: "Malinda" and "I Am Your Man." The Vancouvers were reduced to backing blue-eye soul singer Chris Clark on gigs. A Canadian, Chong needed Green Cards for himself and the bass player and was fired by Clark (actually Bristol) when he left in the middle of a gig for a Green Card interview.

Taylor "discovered" the Jackson 5 who were billed with him for a ten-day stint at Chicago's Regal Theater. He took them back to Detroit and put them up in his apartment while he prepped them for an audition with Motown. He was living in a mostly lily white apartment building at the time and when management saw all the little black kids running around, they kicked Taylor and the Jacksons out. Motown released his solo album, *Taylor Made Soul*, on Gordy; a good album that met with disinterest. Some of its titles, however, ("I've Been Blessed," "Don't Be Afraid," "Out in the Country," and "Eleanor Rigby") were bona fide. A second album was reportedly recorded but never issued.

The Jacksons passed their audition with distinction and Taylor was busy flying to Los Angeles to record them. His productions with the Jackson 5, except for some tracks that appeared on their debut album, were shelved for years. Taylor cut mostly old soul tunes with them to demonstrate their singing skills. But Berry Gordy wanted a contemporary sound that would cross over to all segments, so he created the Corporation with Deke Richards, Fonce Mizelle, Freddie Perren, Taylor, and himself. Taylor worked on the first three Jackson 5 hits, but got no credit. He was out by 1970; according to many, Taylor was a bear to get along with. The Jackson 5 situation caused IRS problems for Taylor and he subsequently sued Motown for unpaid royalties, won the suit, but supposedly never got paid. Tommy Chong hooked up with Cheech Marin and became comedians and actors who glorified marijuana use. The rest of the Vancouvers continued in bands and worked day jobs. After Motown, Taylor recorded for Epic, Playboy, and Philadelphia International Records (never issued); none were as successful as his Motown releases.

He developed throat cancer and relocated to Columbus, OH, where he lived with his mother for years before returning West and settling in the San Jose, CA, area. He was part of Ian Levine's near 900-track Motorcity project, cutting one of the Britisher's best songs and tracks—"Cloudy Day," a stupendous ballad. He has formed Bobby Taylor & the New Vancouvers and reportedly performs occasional gigs in the San Jose area. Little Daddie & the Bachelor's tracks—featuring Tommy Chong's rock guitar licks—can be found on *Northwest Killers, Vol. 2* 1964-1965 ("Come on Home"), and *History of Vancouver Rock and Roll, 2*, which features "Junior's Jerk." Another track, "Valley of Tears," is also floating around on a compilation. *—Andrew Hamilton*

• **Bobby Taylor and the Vancouvers** / 1968 / Gordy ✦✦✦✦

A marvelous but underrated collection by Bobby Taylor & the Vancouvers, one of the few mixed groups to record for Motown. Tommy Chong, later of Cheech & Chong fame, was a member and co-wrote their biggest record, "Does Your Mama Know About Me," a song about an interracial relationship. Though their biggest hit was a ballad, they built their reputation by singing spirited live versions of Motown and soul classics. Bobby's tenor dripped with soul, as his crooning on Ashford & Simpson's "I Am Your Man" attests. "Malinda," one of Smokey Robinson's catchiest songs, will have you singing along with the chorus. A good version of the Temptations' "Fading Away" and the Fantastic Four's "You Gave Me Something" will have you finger-snapping and hand-clapping. *—Andrew Hamilton*

Taylor Made Soul / 1969 / Gordy ✦✦✦

Bobby Taylor goes solo with mixed results. Taylor's emotional tenor has a thin, wiry quality that works well when matched up correctly. However, without the Vancouvers' wall-paper harmonies, Bobby strays from the melodies. None of the album six remakes are as good as the originals, and that includes "Eleanor Rigby." At times, he seems to be trying to out-sing the orchestration. Technically, the mixes could have been better. I can't detect Motown's ace session groups, the Andantes and the Originals, and that may be part of the problem. OK, but not on par with the album he waxed with the Vancouvers. *—Andrew Hamilton*

Debbie Taylor

Vocals / Soul

Obscure soul singer Debbie Taylor made her first recordings for Decca in 1968, and moved on to GWP the following year. Her most collectible output came via a 1972 stint on Today, a label run by producer/writer Patrick Adams. Her lone album, *Comin' Down on You*, featured the singles "Too Sad to Tell" and "No Deposit, No Return," neither of which brought her much commercial success despite the generally high quality of her performances. *—Steve Huey*

Gary Taylor

b. Los Angeles, CA

Vocals, Bass, Guitar / Quiet Storm, Adult Contemporary

Known as the "Master of the Quiet Storm," bassist Gary Taylor played sideman on dozens of albums during the 1960s, '70s, and '80s, and became a fixture of his own on adult contemporary radio with his own recordings, beginning with 1991's *Take Control*. Albums followed for Sindrome and Morning Crew during the '90s. *—John Bush*

• **Compassion** / 1981 / Virgin ✦✦

Gary Taylor switched from A&M to Virgin with this late-'80s album. It contained a pair of above-average productions and performances with "Tease Me" and "Love to the Limit." The only thing missing was sustained interest from the audience. The title track cracked the R&B Top 40, but didn't last, and Taylor wasn't able to get the breakout track that might have given him a shot at solo stardom. He continued to crank out singles, with The Manhattans, Mac Band, and Lalah Hathaway all recording his songs after this album. *—Ron Wynn*

Take Control / 1991 / Valley Vue ✦✦

A decent set of urban contemporary tracks by a prolific composer, producer, and performer. Gary Taylor had written material for Marlena Shaw, Michael Wycoff, the Whispers, Vesta Williams, and many others, as well as doing his own A&M and Virgin albums. This release generated more noise in England than in America. He had several moderate English hits, among them "Time After Time" and "I Live 4 U." Like Taylor's other albums, there were too many styles displayed with little regard for pacing, thematic unity, or the audience. He certainly has talent, but has yet to harness it in a manner that both showcases his skills and gets him noticed. *—Ron Wynn*

James Taylor Quartet

b. London, England

Producer, Organ (Hammond) / Acid Jazz, Club/Dance, Soul-Jazz

Reportedly the band whose music coined the term acid jazz (when a British journalist struggled to describe it), the James Taylor Quartet has explored spy-soundtrack soul-jazz and funk since the group's beginnings in the mid-'80s. Originally playing the Hammond B-3 organ in the U.K. mod revival band the Prisoners, James Taylor formed his own jazz quartet in 1985 and began playing music similar to the rare-groove jazz-funk then in vogue around London. By the early '90s, that movement had spawned acid jazz and the James Taylor Quartet found itself at the forefront of a vibrant young club scene, even though Taylor was a decade-long veteran by that time.

The Prisoners had emerged from Kent in 1982, and released two albums, *A Taste of Pink* and *The Wisermiserdemelza*, before Taylor quit in the mid-'80s (the group imploded after just one more studio album). Taylor quickly formed a quartet around ex-Prisoner Allan Crockford on bass, drummer Simon Howard, and James' own brother David on guitar. The James Taylor Quartet recorded for several small labels during 1985, but a 1986 session for Radio 1 DJ John Peel got the group signed to Re-Elect the President Records, which released a 1987 mini-LP of covers, *Mission Impossible*. After *The Money Spyder* appeared that same year, the James Taylor Quartet moved to Urban/Polydor for 1988's *Wait a Minute*. Not long after, however, Howard and Crockford left to play with another ex-Prisoner, Graham Day, in the Prime Movers. Now just a duo, James and David began recruiting studio musicians to fill in the instrumental gaps from album to album, later building the band up to a sextet (though the name stayed the same) with John Willmott on saxophone and flute, bassist Gary Crockett, drummer Neil Robinson, and trumpeter Dominick Glover. A contract with Acid Jazz Records resulted in increased American distribution through Hollywood Records, which reissued *Mission Impossible* and *The Money Spyder* as well as the group's 1995 album *In the Hand of the Inevitable*. *The Penthouse Suite* and *(A Few Useful Tips About) Living Underground* both followed in 2000. *Bigger Picture* was issued earlier the next year. *—John Bush*

• **Mission Impossible** / Apr. 1987 / Hollywood ✦✦✦✦✦

The riotous and distinctly '60s-era sound of *Mission Impossible* breaks through the gates from the first note of the Herbie Hancock classic theme for "Blow Up," and sprints confidently forward from there. Not to be confused with the "You've Got a Friend" folk-rocker, this James Taylor is a virtuoso on the Hammond B-3 organ with a gifted ear for arranging. As a sidenote, this is a great band to see live, with Taylor fiercely soloing with one hand while pouring vodka for the audience with the other. This little gem on Hollywood Records is great party music; for a scant 33 minutes, Taylor and his bandmates crank and twang their way through a checklist of classic film fodder and hipster motifs, like "Alfie," "One Mint Julip," and *The Graduate*'s "Mrs. Robinson," to name a few. The title cut of *Mission Impossible* is simply fantastic—every bit as dangerous and twice as exciting, even on a shoestring budget. Using old mixers and recording equipment, the production value of this disc is a dead ringer for an album 40 years older than it is, adding an extra level of cheeky fun for the listener. John Barry's theme to *Goldfinger* has never sounded more raw—admittedly some of the snarl may be gone, but the quartet's slant on things transforms it into a distracted go-go dance of caution. Also included are three of his own compositions that are every bit as catchy as the giants around him (check out "The Stooge" for proof). The energy is undeniable, with the feel of live recordings in all their unpolished glory. Admittedly there is not a lot of varying instrumentation here—every track is organ, guitar, drums, and bass (though "Alfie" features a jazzy saxophone for the melody). Consequently the palette is a bit narrow, but the niche it finds is a triumph in the rebirth of cool. *—Glenn Swan*

The Money Spyder / Aug. 1987 / Hollywood ♦♦♦♦
Constructed as a mock soundtrack, *The Money Spyder* does a good, convincing job at capturing the flavor of '60s spy flicks with its blend of jazzy rhythms, swelling Hammond organs, and dark, tasty guitar licks. The group gets a Booker T. & the MG's-meets-the Ventures sound on this set of instrumentals, with some Lalo Schifrin and film noir jazz thrown in the blender. Marketed as part of Hollywood Records' *Acid Jazz* line, it could catch the coattails of the lounge/space-age pop revival as well (though the JTQ have been doing this sort of stuff for years). *—Richie Unterberger*

Get Organized / 1989 / Polydor ♦♦♦♦♦
On this, their fourth studio album, you are treated to the unexpected missing link between James Taylor Quartet's early mod-cum-spy theme sound and the later polished acid jazz feel (which carried the band through to be the respected pioneer figures they are today) without sounding exactly like either of them. Having landed themselves with the big-budget U.K. label Polydor, James Taylor found he could indulge himself with the best in big jazz-funk sounds, employing what sounded suspiciously like more than a "quartet" to produce a collection of bold and brassy numbers that escalated the sounds of Johnny Hammond and Booker T. into the late '80s. The album begins as it finishes, with a touching yet relentless jazz-rock instrumental groove combining clever chord structures and strong piano flourishes gliding over, of course, Taylor's trademark whirring Hammond organ. As ever, it's with this tool that Taylor guides the listener's focus (hence the title), on this record especially, as all but two of the songs are instrumental, a fact you would only subliminally realize as the organ and brass lay down strong melodies. In fact, the only real inclusion of vocals comes courtesy of Cleveland Watkiss on "It Doesn't Matter," a feel-good jive-inspired midtempo track, and the anthemic "Breakout," which gives the band a brief chance to exercise their vocal chords. Elsewhere, the listener is treated to cool modern boogaloos and bossa novas as Taylor proves he's more than just adept on the ivories, but a capable arranger as well. *—Owen Guthrie-Jones*

In the Hand of the Inevitable / 1995 / Acid Jazz ♦♦♦

Creation / May 27, 1996 / Acid Jazz ♦♦♦♦
This Britster mixes up intelligent funk and thumpin' jazz for a truly classic album that should be placed in history as a revitalizing step for the jazz idiom. Taylor knocks out notes on a Hammond Organ and more sounds come from drums, bass, trumpet, guitar, sax and flute. While "acid jazz" supposedly was coined to describe James' output, it certainly does not carry the image of the jump-soul/hot jazz stew bubble in this cauldron. Taylor himself spells out the secret recipe: "Rude, hard funk—like all the Blaxploitation movies and cop shows—that's what we're aiming for." *—Thomas Schulte*

(A Few Useful Tips About) Living Underground / Nov. 14, 2000 / Acid Jazz ♦♦♦♦
The mostly instrumental albums of British keyboardist James Taylor are as diverse as they are accomplished, running the spectrum between skinny-necktie '60s (*The Money Spyder*) and contemporary jazz (*In the Hand of the Inevitable*). This time he hits an especially satisfying nostalgic niche: a faithful jazz-rock fusion that hearkens back to the classic '70s TV cop shows and the high standards of the Mahavishnu Orchestra, Weather Report, Herbie Hancock's Headhunters, and various other sorely missed demi-gods of the genre. Taylor lays triple-thick hot fudge on most of the tracks in *(A Few Useful Tips About) Living Underground*—the original (and superior) import version of the album that would later become the U.S. release *Creation*, trading out a few tracks along the way. "Selectivity" crashes through the speakers with polished brass arrangements, congas, and rhythm guitar, and "Creation (Fanfare for a Third Millennium)" belts out fantastic energy, with blistering keyboard solos on the Hammond B-3. "Staying Active" only adds fuel to the fire, an uptempo and relentless show-stopper that makes the ears sweat. "It's Your World" is a groovy, soulful stroll along a Malibu sunset, and "The Theme From Dirty Harry" turns Lalo Schifrin's original score into a relentless chase with burning flute solos and Latin jazz pounding through the veins. "Summer Fantasy" features a synth melody line cruising the streets in the spirit of Chuck Mangione as an undercover vigilante with great sideburns. "Check It Out" is a celebration in clichés—a low-rider Cadillac stuffed with gold chains, fur coats, lovely ladies, turntable scratches, and the spirit of Bootsy Collins at the wheel—even stiff necks will loosen up as the groove chugs along. Here, there, and almost everywhere, Taylor's production values are crisp without being dry, striking the perfect balance between yesterday's live improvisational energy and today's front-row center-stage acoustics. With solid musicianship at every turn and a commitment to excellence, this album is delightfully retro without being a joke. Simply put, it makes you feel good. *—Glenn Swan*

A Bigger Picture / Feb. 13, 2001 / Instinct ♦♦♦
The Bigger Picture is a polished production performed by the legendary James Taylor Quartet. This is the 12th release in the quartet's 15-year career and should embrace both new and old fans because of their savory mix of funk, soul, jazz, and groove that is brought to life by excellent arrangements and a brand new singer, Yvonne Yaney. Along with additional help from a master of the vibes, Roy Ayers, the James Taylor Quartet consistently evokes their modern groove on 13 songs—12 of them either written or co-written by Taylor. Taylor's brand of funk on Bobby Womack's "TKO" is given a fresh treatment with Yaney's smooth vocals. "Chasing Dragons" is a synth smash, with excellent keyboards and organ by Taylor rounded out by excellent solos from John Willmott on flute and Dominick Glover on trumpet. On the final three selections, labeled "The Smaller Picture," Taylor provides a generous anointment of synthesized sounds on "Decoding the Pyramids," "First Time," and "Change Your Mind." *—Paula Edelstein*

James "J.T." Taylor

b. Aug. 16, 1953, Morristown, NJ
Vocals, Engineer / Urban
The lead singer for Kool & the Gang from 1979 to 1988, James "J.T." Taylor presided over the group's commercial—if not artistic—peak of the early to mid-'80s, later moving on to a solo career. Born August 16, 1953, Taylor joined Kool & the Gang at a point when the pioneering funk band was beginning to lose steam amidst the rise of disco. Five years after their last hit, the group enlisted both producer Eumir Deodato and Taylor and re-entered the Top Ten in 1979 with the decidedly disco-slanted "Ladies Night," a track which topped the R&B charts. The following year, Kool & the Gang delivered its first number-one hit on the pop charts, "Celebration." Although Top Ten placements were frequent from 1982 through 1987, Taylor left the band for a solo career in 1988, thanks in large part to the success. (One monument to his impact with Kool & the Gang is that the group recruited three people to replace him—Sennie "Skip" Martin III, Gary Brown, and Odeen Mays.)

After signing to Epic Records in 1988, Taylor found a hit on his first at-bat: a duet with Regina Belle called "All I Want Is Forever." The theme song to the Gregory Hines film *Tap*, it reached number two on the R&B charts, but was unable to cross over to the pop charts. Taylor recorded three albums for MCA during the early '90s, failing to trump the success of "All I Want Is Forever," though "Long Hot Summer Night" made it to the R&B Top 20 in 1991. After a lengthy hiatus, he resurfaced in mid-2000 with *Brand New Me*. *—John Bush*

Master of the Game / 1989 / MCA ♦♦♦
Former Kool & the Gang frontman James "J.T." Taylor's solo debut is a slick, tight set crammed with snappy uptempo R&B grooves. Even out of a funk context, his voice is unmistakable, blending just as well across this new sound as it ever did across the massive grooves of old. Although none of the songs were able to shake their way into the charts, there are still some neat nuggets to be found, most notably on the smooth "Sister Rosa" and the fat-bassed, brass-punched funk of "Kiss My Face." Both the slightly Latin-inflected "Lay Awake at Night" and the closing "The Promised Land" weigh in with equal aplomb. Where Taylor fumbles is on the ballads "Master of the Game" and "Romancia." Both showcase the singer's outstanding voice but are short on overall substance and ultimately fall flatter than they should. An album of absolute technical finesse, *Master of the Game* suffers mostly because it came too late in the day to make any impact at all. The songs are enjoyable, but don't have any of the real fire listeners expect of a vocalist of Taylor's caliber. Perhaps if he'd struck his path earlier in the decade this debut would have been startling rather than standard. *—Amy Hanson*

Feel the Need / 1991 / MCA ♦♦♦♦

● **Greatest Hits** / Apr. 17, 2001 / Hip-O ♦♦♦♦
Hip-O's 2001 *Greatest Hits* collection pulls off a nifty trick by balancing J.T. Taylor's solo hits with duet numbers and sides he fronted with Kool & the Gang. So, while this technically isn't a retrospective of his solo career, this is what people looking for the best of Taylor should turn to, since it has his best performances, whether he's singing "Too Hot" and "Joanna" with Kool & the Gang, "All I Want Is Forever" with Regina Belle, or "Long Hot Summer Night," "Feel the Need," or "Baby I'm Back" by himself. Again, this shouldn't be seen as a retrospective of his solo recordings, but anybody wanting Taylor at his best should probably go here. *—Stephen Thomas Erlewine*

Johnnie Taylor

b. May 5, 1938, Crawfordsville, AR, **d.** May 31, 2000, Dallas, TX
Vocals / Soul-Blues, Soul, Southern Soul, Disco, Deep Soul
Young gospel phenom, gritty Stax/Volt soulster, lady-killing balladeer, chart-topping disco king, Southern soul-blues stalwart—Johnnie Taylor somehow always managed to adapt to the times, and he parlayed that versatility into a recording career that lasted nearly four decades. Nicknamed the "Philosopher of Soul" during his Stax days, that version of Taylor is best remembered for his 1968 R&B chart-topping smash "Who's Making Love," but far and away his biggest success was 1976's across-the-board number one "Disco Lady," the first single ever certified platinum (which at the time meant sales of over two-million copies). When the national hits dried up, Taylor wound up as one of the most prolific artists on the Malaco label, a refuge for many Southern soul and blues veterans whose styles had fallen out of popular favor by the '80s. Taylor called Malaco home for over 15 years, and kept on recording and performing right up to his passing in 2000.

Johnnie Harrison Taylor was born in Crawfordsville, AR, on May 5, 1938; he grew up mostly in nearby West Memphis. He began singing in church as a young child, and later moved to Kansas City, where he performed with a gospel group called the Melody Kings; it was through this outfit that he initially met and befriended Soul Stirrers frontman Sam Cooke. In 1953, Taylor left home and moved to Chicago, where he joined the doo wop group the Five Echoes; shortly thereafter, he began performing concurrently with the gospel group the Highway QCs, which had once been home to Sam Cooke. In 1957, Taylor would replace Cooke in the hugely influential Soul Stirrers, after Cooke departed for a career in secular music.

After four years with the Soul Stirrers, Taylor escaped gospel music's waning popularity and followed Cooke into the world of secular soul, becoming the first artist to sign with Cooke's label, Sar, in 1961. Taylor released a few singles on Sar and another Cooke label, Derby, over the next few years, including the minor R&B hit "Rome (Wasn't Built in a Day)." Unfortunately, Cooke was murdered in late 1964, and his labels folded, leaving Taylor without a record deal. He returned to the Memphis area and signed with the enormously popular Stax label in 1965, debuting early the following year with "I Had a Dream." Taylor scored a few minor R&B hits over the next few years, including "I Got to Love Somebody's Baby," "Somebody's Sleeping in My Bed," and "Next Time." He hit it big in late 1968 with the gritty, funky "Who's Making Love," his first number-one R&B hit, which also made the pop Top Five. Taylor was able to land some decent-sized follow-up hits in the years to come, among them "Take Care of Your Homework," "Jody's Got Your Girl and Gone," "Steal Away," and "I Am Somebody." By the early '70s, Taylor's bread and butter had become smooth, elegant crooning, as typified by his 1973 album *Taylored in Silk* and his two attendant ballad smashes, "I Believe in You (You Believe in Me)" and "Cheaper to Keep Her."

When Stax went bankrupt in 1975, Taylor moved over to CBS/Columbia, debuting in 1976 with the album *Eargasm*. Its first single, "Disco Lady," was an instant smash, capturing the spirit of the era and selling over two-million copies (although some soul fans still debate whether it was a *true* disco song). "Disco Lady" was Taylor's first number-one pop hit, despite losing airplay over its supposedly suggestive lyrics, and it proved such a phenomenon that CBS eagerly pushed him to record more disco-oriented material, something Taylor wasn't extraordinarily comfortable with. He recorded several more albums for the label through 1980, but never came close to duplicating the success of "Disco Lady," and left to sign with the smaller Beverly Glen imprint in 1982.

Taylor recorded one album for Beverly Glen, 1982's *Just Ain't Good Enough*, which produced a minor R&B hit in "What About My Love." Still searching for a home more in line with the environment at Stax, Taylor soon jumped to Malaco Records, a Southern label dedicated to preserving the region's classic soul and blues sounds (albeit sometimes with a bit less grit than in days of old). Debuting with 1984's *This Is Your Night*, Taylor and Malaco clicked right away, and he wound up recording a total of 12 albums for the label over the next 15 years, ranking as one of their best-selling artists. Taylor's style during this era had evolved into a hybrid of soul and blues, with more emphasis on the latter than at any other point in his career; he continued to tour steadily through the '80s and '90s, and landed a few more singles on the lower reaches of the R&B chart up until 1990. In 1996, his album *Good Love!* topped the *Billboard* blues chart. Taylor's final album was 1999's *Gotta Get the Groove Back*; on May 31, 2000, he suffered a heart attack at his home in Duncanville, TX (a suburb of Dallas), and died at the hospital. *—Steve Huey*

Wanted: One Soul Singer / 1967 / Atlantic ✦✦✦✦

Johnnie Taylor set the tone for his recording career at Stax with *Wanted: One Soul Singer*, a consistently gritty collection of blues and raw, hard-hitting Memphis soul. In addition to his appealing medium-sized hits "Just the One I've Been Lookin' For" and "I Had a Dream," *Wanted* (reissued on CD in 1991) boasts pleasant surprises ranging from the addictive "Toe-Hold" to gutsy versions of Merle Travis' "Sixteen Tons" and the standard "Blues in the Night." Adding lyrics to Herbie Hancock's "Watermelon Man," Taylor removes the song's jazz elements and turns it into pure Southern R&B. When *Wanted* was released, Taylor (who has occasionally been confused with bluesman Little Johnny Taylor) had yet to become the soul-radio fixture that "Who's Making Love" would make him, but these solid performances show that he was definitely on the right track. *—Alex Henderson*

Who's Making Love . . . / 1968 / Stax ✦✦✦✦✦

The Johnnie Taylor Philosophy Continues / 1969 / Stax ✦✦✦

Shows the former Soul Stirrer's versatility, but a mediocre effort overall for Johnnie. Producer Don Davis' attempt to widen Taylor's appeal resulted in an album of watered-down Southern soul. Fans didn't expect Taylorized versions of "Love Is a Hurting Thing," "Who Can I Turn To," or "Games People Play," nor were they appreciated. He charted with "I Could Never Be President," but the song's appeal escapes some, even though David Ruffin redid it on his *Doin' His Thing* album. "Love Bones" and "It's Amazing" are the best soul offerings, but "I Had a Fight With Love" and "Separation Line" are mundane and formulaic. Taylor's rendition of Parliament's "I Wanna Testify" made an impact on the charts, and is interesting, but his voice was worthy of better. Everybody and their mama must have recorded "It's Your Thing," but none seem to be able to touch the Isleys' stomping original. *—Andrew Hamilton*

Raw Blues / 1969 / Stax ✦✦✦✦✦

While the "Raw" part of the title may be overstating the case just a bit, "Blues" describes this disc pretty well, thank you—on his fourth album, Johnnie Taylor shifts his focus away from Stax's trademark Southern soul stylings towards leaner and grittier blues-based performances, a style he'd already shown a knack for on his earlier sets. *Raw Blues* still walks a line between soul and blues, with the sweet-and-sour tone of The Memphis Horns sometimes stacking the deck in favor of the former, but "Part Time Love," "Hello Sundown" and "You Can't Keep A Good Man Down" generate a potent late-night mood vibe which match the downcast authority of Taylor's voice. And if the always air-tight performances of the Stax studio crew (including Steve Cropper and Isaac Hayes) pack enough heat to turn "You Can't Win With a Losing Hand" and "That Bone" into potent dancefloor material, Taylor's rough but passionate delivery never lets this get too close to the Land of the Slick. A strong and heartfelt set that serves as an important precursor to Taylor's later blues-oriented sets for Malaco. *—Mark Deming*

Greatest Hits / 1970 / Stax ✦✦✦✦✦

A nice single-album collection of Taylor's best Stax hits to that point. Until the *Chronicle* retrospective, this was the best bet for those who only wanted a reasonable batch of his hits. It's still worth getting, although the *Chronicle* CD has everything and some great liner notes as well. *—Ron Wynn*

Rare Stamps / 1970 / Stax ✦✦✦

An early Taylor album on Stax, this mixes hard-hitting blues with scorching soul ballads and quickly showed that Taylor was capable of being a strong hit artist. While this lacked the staying power or vocal integrity of *Raw Blues*, it was still a marvelous album, one that should be reissued pronto. *—Ron Wynn*

One Step Beyond / 1971 / Stax ✦✦✦✦

Cut in the middle of Taylor's late-'60s and early-'70s stay at Stax, *One Step Beyond* qualifies as one of the singer's best LPs. Captured in his Southern soul prime, Taylor lets loose on fine mix of gospel-inspired ballads ("I Don't Want to Lose You"), countrified midtempo burners ("Party Life"), and breezy stings-and-horns soul ("Will You Love Me Forever"). And, yes, there are such unforgettable hits as "I Am Somebody" and an amazing reading of the jazz standard "Time After Time." A must-have for all Taylor fans. *—Stephen Cook*

Taylored in Silk / 1973 / Stax ✦✦✦✦✦

Perhaps Taylor's best pure soul release, this contains the shattering "We're Getting Careless With Our Love" and the equally bittersweet/humorous "Cheaper to Keep Her." Taylor was in peak form as a vocalist, and was getting superb productions, arrangements, compositions, and musical backing from the Stax braintrust. *—Ron Wynn*

Super Taylor / 1974 / Stax ✦✦✦

Johnnie Taylor continued churning out steamy wailers, creditable weepers and heartache songs, and ripping up the soul circuit in the mid-'70s. His grainy, blues- and gospel-tinged lead vocals were dynamic on uptempo tunes, and alternately poignant, anguished, prophetic, or hurt on ballads. *—Ron Wynn*

Eargasm / 1976 / Columbia ✦✦✦

Johnnie Taylor's biggest hit album also proved his undoing. Stax had collapsed, and he ended up on Columbia's roster. The disco boom was beginning, and Taylor had the perfect single. "Disco Lady" was vocally quite similar to his earlier material, but its lyrics embraced the hedonism and dance-your-troubles-away ethic of the era. It was not only a number-one hit, but *the* song of the year for 1976, and Taylor was shoved into territory he wasn't comfortable in. The rest of the album was standard soul, but this was overlooked in the rush. Taylor eventually left the label after subsequent attempts to pigeonhole him as a dance singer bombed. *—Ron Wynn*

● **Chronicle: The 20 Greatest Hits** / 1977 / Stax ✦✦✦✦✦

Johnnie Taylor's career covered enough ground (and enough different record labels) that trying to sum it up on a single disc would really take some doing, and *Chronicle: The 20 Greatest Hits* is not the CD designed to do that job. Despite the title, *Chronicle* is a collection focusing exclusively on Taylor's work for Stax, meaning his disco-funk material for Columbia (including his biggest chart hit, "Disco Lady") doesn't make the cut; neither do his late-period soul-blues recordings for Malaco, nor his early gospel material with the Highway QCs or the Soul Stirrers. But if you're looking for a single-disc anthology of Taylor's best stuff for Stax, this CD will give you what you need; it includes several late-'60s/early-'70s hits, including "Who's Makin' Love?," "Cheaper to Keep Her," and "Stop Doggin' Me," as well as a number of lesser-known classics that capture the gruff but heartfelt vocal style and "learned-it-the-hard-way" lyrical perspective that were the hallmarks of Taylor's work. Deciding which Johnnie Taylor collection to get is largely a matter of deciding which part of Taylor's career you're most interested in, but if you want a solid dose of his Southern soul sides for Stax, then *Chronicle: The 20 Greatest Hits* is just what you need. *—Mark Deming*

Rated Extraordinaire / 1977 / CBS ✦✦✦

A decent follow-up to his huge hit album *Eargasm*, although the danger signs were already in the air. It did have some fine ballads, such as "I'm Just a Shoulder to Cry On" and "Love Is Better in the A.M. (Pt. 1)," but it became evident that Columbia wanted another "Disco Lady" and not only didn't have one, but didn't even have the singer they thought they had. Disenchantment would quickly take its toll. *—Ron Wynn*

Reflections / 1977 / RCA ✦✦✦

This obscure Johnnie Taylor album fell between two other 1977 releases: *Rated X-Traordinaire* and *Disco 9000*. The latter two came out on CBS, this one RCA. Don Davis handled the productions, and the songs are by some of Detroit's best songsmiths, including Barrett Strong. CBS issued at least three albums by Taylor after this bump-in-the-road effort by RCA. *Reflections* features Taylor's R&B hit "Stop Half Lovin' These Women" and is gutsier and more even than his CBS albums, but not as rootsy as his Sar, Stax, or Malaco recordings. With material like "Wanting What You Can't Have (Having What You Don't Want)," "I Worry About You," and a soul remake of "Never My Love," he becomes the blues wailer again. *—Andrew Hamilton*

Disco 9000 / 1977 / Columbia ✦✦

The soundtrack of the movie *Disco 9000* (later retitled *Fass Black* after the blaxploitation flick's main character). Johnnie Taylor had a small part —performing "Disco Lady"—in the less-than-thrilling box-office flop. Incidentally, "Disco Lady" is not part of the soundtrack. Sony records issued an album with this title in 1998 that is essentially a "best of Johnnie Taylor at CBS" CD and not the original soundtrack. This seven-track album contains two prototype soundtrack instrumentals; the other material, especially the formulaic "Disco 9000," is not Taylor's best. However, "I Love You Woman," "Right Now," and "I Don't Know What I'd Do Without You," are OK bluesers with contemporary productions. *—Andrew Hamilton*

Ever Ready / 1978 / CBS ✦✦✦

Things were beginning to get ugly for Johnnie Taylor at Columbia, following a period when he enjoyed remarkable success. But the success of "Disco Lady" fooled executives into thinking Taylor could repeat that kind of pop performance when his style was straight gospel-tinged soul with a dollop of blues flavor. Taylor was recording songs he didn't believe in, care about, or was suited to sing, and it showed. This was his next to last album with Columbia. *—Ron Wynn*

She's Killing Me / 1979 / CBS ✦✦

New Day / 1980 / CBS ✦✦

Just Ain't Good Enough / 1982 / Beverly Glen ✦✦✦✦✦

Just Ain't Good Enough is an album Taylor released on the short-lived Beverly Glen label in 1982. The record spawned two R&B hits for Taylor—"What About My Love" and "I'm So Proud"—and peaked at number 19 on the R&B charts. It's a solid effort that fits sound- and style-wise alongside his six albums for Columbia. Taylor, dissatisfied with the label's promotion of the record, would soon leave for Malaco, but this is the missing link in the chain, and an album well worth hearing. *—Cub Koda*

This Is Your Night / 1984 / Malaco ♦♦♦
Johnnie Taylor departed Beverly Glen and made an immediate and welcome impact with his debut at Malaco. They continued having him do evocative ballads like the title cut, mixed in a few uptempo wailers, and were close to putting Taylor back in the ball game. They weren't able to duplicate their Z.Z. Hill success, but Taylor was making music and singing tunes that he felt and believed in, and the results were obvious. *—Ron Wynn*

The Best of Johnnie Taylor on Malaco, Vol. 1 / 1984-1992 / Malaco ♦♦♦♦
Given how much of a fixture Johnnie Taylor was on black radio in the 1960s and early to mid-'70s, it's ironic that one of his best-of collections doesn't contain an abundance of hit singles. Rather, the focus of this CD is the veteran soul man's work for Malaco in the 1980s and '90s. Taylor may have been long past his peak commercially when these songs were recorded, but artistically, he still sounds like he's very much in his prime. Malaco's choices are generally excellent. Selections like "Don't Make Me Late," "Still Called the Blues" and "Everything's Out in the Open" show why Taylor has fared so well creatively at the label, which has encouraged him to continue taking a classic soul approach instead of catering to the urban contemporary market (something he has pretty much ignored). For listeners who haven't been exposed to his Malaco output, this collection is the logical starting point. *—Alex Henderson*

Wall to Wall / 1986 / Malaco ♦♦♦
Johnnie Taylor begin to express some frustration with Malaco in the late '80s, most of it due to their inability to get him a major hit. It's doubtful if Stax in its prime could have gotten hard-edged Southern soul aired on urban radio in the late '80s, but they gave it a shot. The title cut was a good uptempo tune, produced in a less Stax/Volt manner than usual, while they added some synthesized and drum machine textures to try to meet radio requirements. It didn't work, but it wasn't a sellout either. *—Ron Wynn*

Lover Boy / 1986 / Malaco ♦♦♦
The title tune was a nice change of pace, part mocking and part confrontational. Otherwise, it was a standard Taylor record on Malaco—lots of fine, earnest gospel/soul singing with blues underpinnings, expert production and arrangements, and one or two songs that might have become staples in the '60s or '70s. But you can't help feeling that time has passed many of the Malaco (and Ichiban) artists by. *—Ron Wynn*

In Control / 1988 / Malaco ♦♦♦

Crazy 'Bout You / 1989 / Malaco ♦♦♦♦
Like most of his Malaco CDs, *Crazy 'Bout You* is an inviting soul date recalling his early to mid-'70s triumphs for Stax. Pouring his heart into everything from the lustful "Dance Floor to the Back Door" to the amusing "She's No Lady" to the sweaty "Money's Running Funny," it's obvious that unlike other R&B veterans, he isn't about to alter his time-tested approach in order to appeal to the whims of trendy urban radio. At 50, Taylor comes across as a seasoned, assured storyteller who knows what his strong points are and is sure to zero in on them. *—Alex Henderson*

Little Bluebird / 1990 / Stax ♦♦♦
The vaults at Stax are wide open these days. While Fantasy is nowhere near as bad about scavenging and issuing half-hearted material, they sometimes release things that have limited value. There are some good songs on this Taylor session, but also some that could have easily remained where they were. The backing, production, and vocals are superior to several of the compositions and arrangements. *—Ron Wynn*

I Know It's Wrong, But I . . . Just Can't Do Right / Sep. 4, 1991 / Malaco ♦♦♦
Even when they aren't outstanding, Johnnie Taylor's '90s albums on Malaco are usually satisfying. None of his Malaco dates of the '80s and early to mid-'90s were weak or disappointing, and are at least worthwhile. *(I Know It's Wrong, But I . . .) Just Can't Do Right* doesn't qualify as one of Taylor's all-time best albums, but it's an above-average effort with many strong points. Whether going for a '60s-like Southern soul approach on "Guilty As Charged" and "Crazy Over You" or a smoother, more Philly-ish '70s-type sound on the moving "Only My Woman Can," Taylor comes across as a seasoned soul man who uses decades of solid experience to his advantage. Though not essential, this is a CD that Taylor's more devoted fans will want. *—Alex Henderson*

Real Love / 1994 / Malaco ♦♦♦

● **Rated X-Traordinaire: The Best of Johnnie Taylor** / Mar. 12, 1996 / Columbia/Legacy ♦♦♦♦♦
The 16-track *Rated X-Traordinaire* sets out to rescue the reputation of the Johnnie Taylor of 1976-1980, the period that began with his biggest smash, "Disco Lady," but that found him, so the conventional wisdom goes, a Southern soul man set adrift on the disco wave. Annotator Kalamu ya Salaam argues that "Disco Lady" is not a disco song, and backs this up by noting that the track actually was played by members of Parliament-Funkadelic. True enough, though that only applies to Taylor's debut Columbia album, *Eargasm*. Elsewhere, Taylor did drift, from Muscle Shoals tracks that updated his Stax Memphis sound to tracks that sounded like Marvin Gaye. The early years, 1976 and 1977, were more accomplished than the later ones, and that's where compilation producer Leo Sacks focuses, with 12 of the 16 tracks coming from then. In so doing, he ignores R&B chart singles like "Keep on Dancing" and "Ever Ready," but he satisfies the "best-of" title. *—William Ruhlmann*

Good Love! / Jul. 1996 / Malaco ♦♦♦♦
Good Love! is an excellent latter-day record from Johnnie Taylor, illustrating that the singer has lost very little of his soulful power. Although the production may be a little to slick for some tastes, Taylor's gutsy singing makes the music sound gritty, and very few modern-day Southern soul albums have a collection of songs this consistently strong. In other words, *Good Love!* is everything any Johnnie Taylor fan could hope for from a modern-day soul record. *—Leo Stanley*

Lifetime / Oct. 24, 2000 / Stax ♦♦♦
Taylor gets honored with a three-CD box set for this career retrospective. And it truly is a career retrospective: it spans 1956-1999 and includes a good deal of material that he did for other labels before and after his lengthy Stax stint. It's true that you have to be a pretty deep Taylor fan to commit to nearly four hours of his music. It's also true that even if you are a big Taylor fan, you're likely to need some patience to last through some of the average cuts, or his stylistic transition from gospel to soul to disco and retro-soul. Overall, however, it's a fine commemoration of an important if not quite great soul star. The most valuable components of the set are found on disc one, which kicks off with a half-dozen gospel tunes from his stints with the Highway QCs and the Soul Stirrers in the late '50s, moving into some of his soul sides for Sam Cooke's SAR label in the early '60s. For the remainder of disc one and some of disc two, there are plenty of fine soul-blues cuts from his early days at Stax in the mid- to late '60s that will be familiar to relatively few listeners, his fine soul-blues-gospel vocal blend resulting in some of his finest work. As time wore on—even starting in the early '70s—Taylor's material got duller and more homogenized, though there were always some highlights to perk up your ears. Unsurprisingly, then, like most box sets, this gets less interesting the closer it draws to the finish line, although wisely his late-'70s Columbia era (yes, "Disco Lady" is here) and post-'70s Malaco output is represented by a mere four cuts each. Ultimately, it's a well-done summation of Taylor's legacy, with an accompanying 50-page booklet including essay, discography, and photos. *—Richie Unterberger*

Little Johnny Taylor (Johnny Lamont Merrett)

b. Feb. 11, 1943, Gregory, AR, **d.** May 17, 2002, Conway, AR
Vocals / R&B, Soul, Soul-Blues

Some folks still get them mixed up, so to get it straight from the outset, Little Johnny Taylor was best known for his scorching slow blues smashes "Part Time Love" (for Bay Area-based Galaxy Records in 1963) and 1971's "Everybody Knows About My Good Thing" for Ronn Records in Shreveport, LA. This Johnny Taylor was definitely not the suave Sam Cooke protégé who blitzed the charts with "Who's Making Love" for Stax in 1968; that's Johnnie Taylor, who added to the confusion by covering "Part Time Love" for Stax. Another similarity between the two Taylors: Both hailed from strong gospel backgrounds. Little Johnny came to Los Angeles in 1950 and did a stint with the Mighty Clouds of Joy before going secular. Influenced by Little Willie John, he debuted as an R&B artist with a pair of 45s for Hunter Hancock's Swingin' logo, but his career didn't soar until he inked a pact with Fantasy's Galaxy subsidiary in 1963 (where he benefited from crisp production by Cliff Goldsmith and Ray Shanklin's arrangements).

The gliding midtempo blues "You'll Need Another Favor," firmly in a Bobby "Blue" Bland mode, was Taylor's first chart item. He followed it up with the tortured R&B chart-topper "Part Time Love," which found him testifying in gospel-fired style over Arthur Wright's biting guitar and a grinding, horn-leavened downbeat groove. The singer also did fairly well with "Since I Found a New Love" in 1964 and "Zig Zag Lightning" in 1966.

Taylor's tenure at Stan Lewis' Ronn imprint elicited the slow blues smash "Everybody Knows About My Good Thing" in 1971 and a similar witty hit follow-up, "Open House at My House," the next year (both were covered later by Z.Z. Hill for Malaco). While at Ronn, Little Johnny cut some duets with yet another Taylor, this one named Ted (no, they weren't related either). Little Johnny Taylor died on May 17, 2002, at Conway Regional Medical Center in Conway, AR. *—Bill Dahl*

Part Time Love / 1962 / Ronn ♦♦♦♦♦
Soulful Little Johnny Taylor's brand of shuffling R&B/Blues is exploited fully on this reissue of his debut album originally released on Galaxy Records in 1962. The grandiose horns are spectacular and impressive, and the lyrics express real-life, down-to-earth love dramas. A signifying blues guitar makes both draggers "Part Time Love" and "Found a New Love" totally mesmerizing. There's not a hint of mere filler among the ten tracks. "Junkie for Your Love," the harmonic "True Lovin'," "You're Gonna Need Another Favor," and "I Don't Want It All," each effectively portray the blues style that Taylor helped establish. *—Andrew Hamilton*

Little Johnny Taylor / 1963 / Galaxy ♦♦♦♦
Terrific brass and heavy charts by Ray Shanklin push Taylor's soulful pipes heavenward on this great LP that includes hit "Part Time Love." *—Bill Dahl*

Everybody Knows About My Good Thing / 1970 / Ronn ♦♦♦♦
A great simmering soul-blues album. Two R&B hits—"It's My Fault Darling" and the ironic two-part title cut, later revived by Z.Z. Hill—share microgroove space with eight more solid efforts, supervised by Miles Grayson (who co-wrote a good deal of the album). *—Bill Dahl*

Open House / 1973 / Ronn ♦♦♦

Super Taylors / 1974 / Ronn ♦♦♦

I Shoulda Been a Preacher / 1981 / Red Lightnin' ♦♦♦♦♦
Only his pastor knows that for sure, but this is one wailing collection. It contains the hottest gospel-tinged singles Little Johnny Taylor cut for Galaxy, and anyone turned off by the tepid material coming out for Ichiban should consult these before hopping off the bandwagon. *—Ron Wynn*

● **Greatest Hits** / 1991 / Fantasy ♦♦♦♦♦
The gospel-tinged and decidedly soul-inflected 1963-1968 blues sides of Little Johnny Taylor on Galaxy Records benefitted from marvelous horn-powered arrangements by Ray Shanklin that brilliantly pushed Taylor's melismatic vocals. Naturally, the impassioned "Part Time Love" is included, along with the Bobby "Blue" Bland-tinged

midtempo groover "You'll Need Another Favor," a delicious "Since I Found a New Love," and the blistering "You Win, I Lose." There are 17 tracks in all, many of them bolstered by Arthur Wright's stinging guitar. *—Bill Dahl*

Ted Taylor

b. Feb. 16, 1934, Okmulgee, OK, **d.** Oct. 2, 1987, Lake Charles, LA

Vocals / Soul-Blues, Soul, Northern Soul

Soul-blues singer Ted Taylor unleashed his stratospheric, falsetto-driven voice on a wide variety of material during the 1950s, '60s, and '70s, his gospel heritage never far from the surface. Taylor first entered the studio as a member of the Cadets and Jacks, a Los Angeles R&B vocal group with two names that recorded for Modern. By the late '50s, Taylor was signed to Ebb, and a myriad of other imprints soon followed (notably Duke, where he waxed his first version of the sugary ballad "Be Ever Wonderful"), OKeh (his sides for the Columbia subsidiary were done in Chicago and Nashville), and Ronn, where he spent nearly a decade. A car wreck claimed his life in 1987. *—Bill Dahl*

Be Ever Wonderful / 1963 / Laurie ✦✦✦

A remake of Ted's classic ballad and several more with a malaco soul/blues feel. *—Bill Dahl*

You Can Dig It / 1970 / Ronn ✦✦✦✦✦

Here is classic Muscle Shoals-cut soul LP that cries out for CD reissue. *—Bill Dahl*

● **Ted Taylor & Little Johnny** / 1974 / Ronn ✦✦✦✦✦

Keeping My Head Above Water / 1978 / MCA ✦✦✦

Soul-singin' Ted Taylor employs his airy falsetto on uptempo and ballad tracks in an obvious attempt to spread his talents to the masses. He updates his signature song "Be Ever Wonderful," losing none of the original's richness. On the upbeat "Double My Money Bags," his stratospheric false voice sounds Bee Gee-ish, and "Keeping My Head Above Water" is a good attempt at emulating the Stylistics' Russell Thompkins. "Born on the Wrong Side of Temptation" has a fast disco beat, similar to what Salsoul Records was doing with Eddie Holman. The other beaters and ballads are equally as pleasing, a good effort that never got recognized. *—Andrew Hamilton*

Willie Tee

b. Feb. 6, 1944, New Orleans, LA

Vocals, Piano / New Orleans R&B, Soul, Beach

New Orleans vocalist Willie Tee hasn't been a consistent hit artist, but ranks among the city's most productive and diversified performers. An excellent pianist and vocalist, Tee formed the Seminoles with his brother Earl and began recording for AFO in 1960. He had a Top 20 R&B hit with "Teasin' You" for Atlantic in 1965 and produced sessions for Margie Joseph and the Wild Magnolias. Tee has backed almost every major New Orleans name over the past three decades, and has been a familiar face at recording sessions and in concerts at Crescent City spots. *—Ron Wynn*

● **Anticipation** / 1976 / United Artists ✦✦✦

Back in Time / 2002 / BK ✦✦✦

The Temprees

f. 1970, Memphis, TN

Group / Memphis Soul, Soul

A Memphis soul vocal trio. This polished group formed in 1970 and recorded for We Produce, a Stax offshoot. Bandmembers Harold "Scotty" Scott, Jasper "Jabbo" Phillips, and William Norvell Johnson rode a sumptuously produced remake of the often-covered 5 Royales/Shirelles standard "Dedicated to the One I Love" onto R&B play lists in 1972. After "Love's Maze" made a little noise as a follow-up, the trio moved to Epic for their final hit in 1976, the entirely self-explanatory "I Found Love on a Disco Floor." *—Bill Dahl*

Lovemen / 1972 / We Produce ✦✦✦✦

The Memphis, TN, balladeers' finest LP. Lead singer Jasper "Jabbo" Phillips, Dale Juan Calvin, and Harold Scott put the "l" in "lush." Only two fast numbers are on *Lovemen.* "Explain It to Her Mama" and "My Baby Love" are both tight, but are not the caliber of the slow jams. Without a lot of fanfare, the Temprees recorded some of the '70s' sweetest soul music. "If I Can Say What's on My Mind" really hits home; men and women can relate to the message which depicts the innocence of attraction and the inability to say what you really mean. "Girl I Love You, You Love Me" is a love vow with an exclamation point; it sounds like a lyric you'd write after a passionate love session. Their version of "Dedicated to the One I Love" is the definitive version; you won't find a better rendition of the super ballad and quiet storm staple. They're too tender to be dudes on "Love ... Can Be So Wonderful," a silky-smooth soul waltz powered by a prominent organ that will rip your heart out. *—Andrew Hamilton*

Love Maze / 1974 / We Produce ✦✦✦

Three / 1975 / Stax ✦✦✦

The Best of the Temprees / 1984 / Stax ✦✦✦✦

The three Memphis, TN natives specialized in tearjerking, sentimental ballads led by the airy falsetto leads of Jasper (Jabo) Phillips and complemented by Harold "Scotty" Scott and Del "Deljuan" Calvin's heavenly harmony blends. "Love ... Can Be So Wonderful" and "I'm For You" are light, sweet romantic excursions. Many believed the Temprees were from Philadelphia, PA, but I never saw the connection. A Temprees recording consisted of vocals and a simplistic rhythm track; horns and strings were used sparingly, unlike Philly sessions, which were elaborate in comparison. On "Love Maze," a three-hearts-in-a-tangle ballad, a gripping falsetto shares the lead with a buttery tenor on the for-lovers-only selection. "A Thousand Miles Away," originally done by the Heartbeats, is competent but doesn't equal or surpass the original—then again, I've never heard a version that did. The uptempo arrangement of the MOR classic "At Last" leaves me cold. They obviously recorded the toe-tappers to break the monotony of the soft stuff. My only beef is that Stax/Fantasy Records left "Love Between a Boy and Girl" off this best-of compilation—and that's an unforgivable, downright shame. *—Andrew Hamilton*

● **Dedicated to the One I Love** / 1994 / Stax ✦✦✦✦

Led by the late Jasper "Jabbo" Philips' sweet falsetto, the Temprees excelled at singing heart touching sweet Southern jerkers. Representative of that infectious sound are "Dedicated to the One I Love," "If I Could Say What's on My Mind," and "I Love You, You Love Me." Jabbo forsakes the falsetto for a natural tenor similar to the Newcomers' Bertram Brown on "Your Love Is All I Need," the midtempo "I Love, I Love," "You Make Me Feel So Good Baby," and James Taylor's "Don't Let Me Be Lonely Tonight/A Love Song." Mid and ups flow with their sugary ballads to provide a more even and enjoyable set than their *The Best of the Temprees'* compilation. *—Andrew Hamilton*

The Temptations

f. 1960, Detroit, MI

Group / Motown, Soul, Pop-Soul, R&B, Smooth Soul, Psychedelic Soul

Thanks to their fine-tuned choreography—and even finer harmonies—the Temptations became the definitive male vocal group of the 1960s; one of Motown's most elastic acts, they tackled both lush pop and politically charged funk with equal flair, and weathered a steady stream of changes in personnel and consumer tastes with rare dignity and grace. The Temptations' initial five-man lineup formed in Detroit in 1961 as a merger of two local vocal groups, the Primes and the Distants. Baritone Otis Williams, Elbridge (aka El, or Al) Bryant, and bass vocalist Melvin Franklin were longtime veterans of the Detroit music scene when they joined together in the Distants, who in 1959 recorded the single "Come On" for the local Northern label. Around the same time, the Primes, a trio comprised of tenor Eddie Kendricks, Paul Williams (no relation to Otis), and Kell Osborne, relocated to the Motor City from their native Alabama; they quickly found success locally, and their manager even put together a girl group counterpart dubbed the Primettes. (Later, three of the Primettes—Diana Ross, Mary Wilson and Florence Ballard—formed the Supremes).

In 1961, the Primes disbanded, but not before Otis Williams saw them perform live, where he was impressed both by Kendricks' vocal prowess and Paul Williams' choreography skills. Soon, Otis Williams, Paul Williams, Bryant, Franklin, and Kendricks joined together as the Elgins; after a name change to the Temptations, they signed to the Motown subsidiary Miracle, where they released a handful of singles over the ensuing months. Only one, the 1962 effort "Dream Come True," achieved any commercial success, however, and in 1963, Bryant either resigned or was fired after physically attacking Paul Williams. The Tempts' fortunes changed dramatically in 1964 when they recruited tenor David Ruffin to replace Bryant; after entering the studio with writer/producer Smokey Robinson, they emerged with the pop smash "The Way You Do the Things You Do," the first in a series of 37 career Top Ten hits. With Robinson again at the helm, they returned in 1965 with their signature song, "My Girl," a number-one pop and R&B hit; other Top 20 hits that year included "It's Growing," "Since I Lost My Baby," "Don't Look Back," and "My Baby."

In 1966, the Tempts recorded another Robinson hit, "Get Ready," before forgoing his smooth popcraft for the harder-edged soul of producers Norman Whitfield and Brian Holland. After spotlighting Kendricks on the smash "Ain't Too Proud to Beg," the group allowed Ruffin to take control over a string of hits including "Beauty's Only Skin Deep" and "(I Know) I'm Losing You." Beginning around 1967, Whitfield assumed full production control, and their records became ever rougher and more muscular, as typified by the 1968 success "I Wish It Would Rain." After Ruffin failed to appear at a 1968 live performance, the other four Tempts fired him; he was replaced by ex-Contour Dennis Edwards, whose less polished voice adapted perfectly to the psychedelic-influenced soul period the group entered following the success of the single "Cloud Nine." As the times changed, so did the group, and as the 1960s drew to a close, the Temptations' music became overtly political; in the wake of "Cloud Nine"—its title a thinly veiled drug allegory—came records like "Run Away Child, Running Wild," "Psychedelic Shack," and "Ball of Confusion (That's What the World Is Today)."

After the chart-topping success of the gossamer ballad "Just My Imagination (Running Away With Me)" in 1971, Kendricks exited for a solo career. Soon, Paul Williams left the group as well; long plagued by alcoholism and other personal demons, he was eventually discovered dead from a self-inflected gunshot on August 17, 1973, at the age of 34. In their stead the remaining trio recruited tenors Damon Harris and Richard Street; after the 1971 hit "Superstar (Remember How You Got Where You Are)," they returned in 1972 with the brilliant number-one single "Papa Was a Rolling Stone." While the Tempts hit the charts regularly throughout 1973 with "Masterpiece," "Let Your Hair Down," and "The Plastic Man," their success as a pop act gradually dwindled as the 1970s wore on. After Harris exited in 1975 (replaced by tenor Glenn Leonard), the group cut 1976's *The Temptations Do the Temptations*, their final album for Motown. With Louis Price taking over for Edwards, they signed to Atlantic, and attempted to reach the disco market with the LPs *Bare Back* and *Hear to Tempt You.*

After Edwards returned to the fold (resulting in Price's hasty exit), the Temptations re- entered the Motown stable, and scored a 1980 hit with "Power." In 1982, Ruffin and Kendricks returned for *Reunion*, which also included all five of the current Tempts; a tour followed, but problems with Motown, as well as personal differences, cut Ruffin's and Kendricks' tenures short. In the years that followed, the Temptations continued touring and recording, although by the 1990s they were essentially an oldies act; only Otis Williams, who published his autobiography in 1988, remained from the original lineup. The intervening years were marked by tragedy: after touring in the late '80s with Kendricks and Edwards as a member of the "Tribute to the Temptations" package tour, Ruffin died on June 1, 1991, after overdosing on cocaine; he was 50 years old. On October 5, 1992, Kendricks died at the age of 52 of lung cancer, and on February 23, 1995, 52-year-old Franklin passed away after suffering a brain seizure. In 1998, the Temptations returned with *Phoenix Rising*; that same year, their story was also the subject of a well-received NBC television miniseries. *Ear-Resistable* followed in the spring of 2000. *—Jason Ankeny*

Meet the Temptations / Mar. 1964 / Motown ♦♦♦♦♦
The Temptations' first LP, released three years into the group's history with Motown, is also a great record, even though it wasn't really an album so much as a collection of their early singles, hooked around their then new hit, "The Way You Do the Things You Do." Those expecting the classic Temptations sound should also be aware that David Ruffin is absent from all of the tracks except "The Way You Do the Things You Do," which was cut just after he joined, replacing Elbridge "Al" Bryant. Thus, the 14 cuts on this CD (12 off the original album plus two bonus tracks) represent the evolution of the act and its sound, as well as a succession of producers—Andre Williams and Mickey Stevenson on "Oh, Mother of Mine" and "Romance Without Finance," the group's earliest 45 pairing, issued on the short-lived Miracle label; Norman Whitfield, for one single; Berry Gordy and Smokey Robinson; and finally Robinson. The differences are fascinating—"Oh, Mother of Mine," sung by Paul Williams and Eddie Kendricks sharing the lead, has an exuberant doo wop-based sound mixed with a serious soulful quality that would eventually define the group; "Romance Without Finance" is a little less derivative, with a heavier, fuller band sound (especially the guitars), but both tracks are rooted in a fast dance beat, in keeping with the tastes of the times (early 1961), and neither had the hooks to make it distinctive unto itself. Several of the Gordy-produced numbers seem highly derivative of other, more familiar songs by other acts—"Paradise" sounds like the Four Seasons covering Maurice Williams' "Stay," and "Isn't She Pretty" comes off like a rewrite (albeit a very pretty one, no joke intended) of the Isley Brothers' "Respectable." These and other Gordy written and produced numbers are attractive enough, but not special as songs or productions, despite some excellent singing. One group composition, "Check Yourself," produced by Gordy, is interesting for its abrupt tempo change, and features a beautifully expressive Paul Williams lead vocal. But the Smokey Robinson cuts are where the group's sound blossoms; their harmonies suddenly soaring elegantly with Williams' voice cutting through the center while an understated but fully integral band sound provides the foundation. Coupled with his songwriting, those numbers and Robinson helped put the Temptations on the charts—and well up on the charts—after three years of failure. [The sound on the 1999 reissue of this album is excellent and then some (the Earl Van Dyke Band never sounded better), and the notes, although minimal, give some frame of reference for the album's release. An excellent mid-priced release that will delight fans and casual listeners.] *—Bruce Eder*

The Temptations Sing Smokey / Feb. 1965 / Motown ♦♦♦♦♦
This was only the group's second LP, and it was an extremely strong one, built around two monster hits ("My Girl" and the previously recorded "The Way You Do the Things You Do") and one close runner-up ("It's Growing"), plus a brace of some of the best songs in the Motown catalog, including renditions of "You Beat Me to the Punch," "What's So Good About Good Bye," "You've Really Got a Hold on Me," and "Way Over There." All are done in a style unique to the Temptations, with arrangements that are distinctly different from the familiar versions by other Motown acts, and all worthwhile. The original CD version, released in the mid-'80s, was a major disappointment; in 1998, it was remastered in 24-bit digital audio, giving it vastly superior sound quality (the 1998 copyright on the back is the giveaway, along with the reference to Polygram as owner of Motown); it was the first of the classic individual Motown albums already out on CD to get this treatment. The stereo separation on the reissue is very sharp, the sound is a lot closer and louder, and the detail is startling, right down to the rhythm section, parts of which, on "Baby, I Need You" and "My Girl," stand out in astonishingly sharp relief. The bass on the latter is so solid it's scary, and the disc is worth owning almost as much for the sound as the music, just to show what we've been missing on those earlier CDs. *—Bruce Eder*

Temptin' Temptations / Nov. 1965 / Motown ♦♦♦♦♦
The Temptations' third album for Motown's Gordy subsidiary in 1965 kept the hit streak alive with the inclusion of "Since I Lost My Baby," "My Baby," "Don't Look Back" and "Girl (Why You Wanna Make Me Blue)." As a matter of fact, this album churned out seven chart hit singles—or rather, they were included on this collection, as singles wagged the album dog back in those days. Either way, Smokey Robinson produces the lion's share of tracks (six) on here, including "You've Got to Earn It," "I'll Be In Trouble" and "You're the One I Need." The album also introduces Ivy Jo Hunter and Mickey Stevenson's production work on "Just Another Lonely Night" and "Born to Love You" and future producer Norman Whitfield on "The Girl's Alright With Me," "I Gotta Know Now" and "Everybody Needs Love." Another classic album by the original group. *—Cub Koda*

Gettin' Ready / Jun. 1966 / Motown ♦♦♦♦
The Tempts' 1966 album sported not only two of their biggest hits (Smokey Robinson's "Get Ready" and Holland & Whitfield's "Ain't Too Proud To Beg"), but also moved the group from Smokey producing the group over to Norman Whitfield. In addition to the original 12-track lineup (all in original stereo except for "Say You," preserved off the original mono master), there's two bonus tracks cut in 1963, featuring a Paul Williams-led group on "Give It Up" and "The Man Who Don't Believe In Love," the latter produced by early pre-Motown alumnus Marv Johnson. *—Cub Koda*

Greatest Hits, Vol. 1 / Nov. 1966 / Motown ♦♦♦
As the first Temptations hits package Motown released, *Greatest Hits, Vol. 1* appeared a little over two years into the group's career, but it remains an excellent hits collection. Not all of the 12 tracks were giant hits—"The Girl's Alright With Me," "Since I Lost My Baby," "It's Growing" and "I'll Be in Trouble" never became as ubiquitous as "The Way You Do the Things You Do," "My Girl," "Ain't Too Proud to Beg" and "Get Ready," all of which are included here—but the lesser-known tracks are terrific in their own right and help make the album a dynamic experience. Nevertheless, those minor hits and album tracks date *Greatest Hits*, illustrating that it was released during the group's extraordinary run. They also mean that anyone looking for a definitive single-disc collection should look to the latter-day collections, which contain all the hits from this album and *Greatest Hits, Vol. 2* and thereby offer a better bargain for the casual fan. *—Stephen Thomas Erlewine*

TV Show / 1967 / Gordy ♦♦

Temptations Live! / Mar. 1967 / Motown ♦♦♦
Capturing live rock or soul performances professionally for commercial release was still more art than science on October 3, 1966, when this album was recorded at the Roostertail's Upper Deck in Detroit. Technically, *Temptations Live!* has its flaws—balance problems and leakages—but the remastering has compensated for these problems extraordinarily well, and the performance always had about as much energy as any other three albums of the same era. And as fine as their studio sound was, that energy was something that could only be captured in concert. In fact, they fare better than almost any other Motown act of the period on this live album. Berry Gordy always encouraged his acts to try to "mainstream" their sound in concert—which meant the Supremes did numbers from contemporary Broadway shows when they cut live albums—but the Temptations were one act that could get away with this repertory and not seem arch or artificial on-stage—Paul McCartney's "Yesterday" (he must've gotten the biggest kick out of the Temptations covering one of his songs) and Jerome Kern and Oscar Hammerstein's "Old Man River" just flow out as part of the show, sandwiched between the Smokey Robinson numbers. The producers compensated for the original album's flaws by going back to the unedited tape, which yielded yet another bonus—in addition to the released album, they found the original finale of "The Way You Do the Things You Do" (which would have made the LP too long) that puts a killer cap on a superb concert recording and fills a gap in their recorded history. The notes are fully detailed as well—always a nice bonus on a mid-priced CD. *—Bruce Eder*

In a Mellow Mood / Jul. 1967 / Motown ♦♦♦
The Temptations moved into world of jazzy pre-rock pop and showed that great singers can handle anything. While many soul fans were surprised that they issued an album with versions of "Ol' Man River," "Somewhere" and "Taste of Honey," they were hooked once they heard it. This recording was another indication of how much Berry Gordy wanted to show mainstream audiences that Motown acts were versatile. *—Ron Wynn*

With a Lot o' Soul / Jul. 1967 / Motown ♦♦♦♦♦
This was the Temptations' seventh hit album in a row, released as Gordy 922 in July of 1967. It shows them—and the Motown Sound—moving in a more modern direction. Sporting the hits "(I Know) I'm Losing You" and "All I Need," it also features some first-rate vocal exchanges between Eddie Kendricks & David Ruffin on "You're My Everything." Other highlights include the Smokey Robinson-written and -produced "Don't Send Me Away," "Now That You've Won Me" and "No More Water in the Well," plus Ivy Jo Hunter's "Sorry Is a Sorry Word," while Norman Whitfield checks in for six of the production credits on here, especially effective on "Loneliness Made Me Realize) It's You That I Need" and "Two Sides to Love." Considered by many to be their best recording of the '60s, this is a very strong addition to anyone's Motown/R&B/soul music collection. *—Cub Koda*

Wish It Would Rain / Apr. 1968 / Motown ♦♦♦♦♦
The Temptations were at the peak of their popularity as Motown's flagship act (well, if it wasn't the Supremes, it was the Tempts) in 1968 when they cut *Wish It Would Rain*, and if the album doesn't hold any great surprises in terms of material, production, or performance, it's also a consistently strong set which demonstrates just what made this group so popular. The Temptations were on the cusp of a number of changes when these sessions were recorded—a year later, David Ruffin would be out of the group, Dennis Edwards would take his place, and Norman Whitfield would nudge the group into the direction of rock-oriented guitars and neo-"protest" lyrics—and so *Wish It Would Rain* unwittingly became one of the group's last proper gestures toward sweet soul. And the Temptations certainly gave it a beautiful send-off; "I Could Never Love Another (After Loving You)", "Please Return Your Love to Me" and the title cut are all musical heartache at its most satisfying, with keening string charts and heart-wrenching harmonies, and "Fan the Flame" and "He Who Picks the Rose" showed the group could put the same emotional power into uptempo dance-friendly material. *Wish It Would Rain* never quite sounds like one of the Temptations' most ambitious albums, but it does capture a group of gifted professionals (both in front of the microphones and behind the scenes) working at the peak of their skills, and the results are impassioned, satisfying, and beautifully crafted; if you like the Temptations at all, this is an album you'll cherish. *—Mark Deming*

The Supremes Join the Temptations / Nov. 1968 / Motown ♦♦♦♦♦
What more could you want, two great groups, 11 great songs, and classic Motown productions. Contains the super groups' big hit "I'm Gonna Make You Love Me" and the equally effervescent "I'll Try Something New." But the goodies don't stop there: Check "Try It Baby," a remake of Marvin Gaye's hit, done this time with bass Melvin Franklin groaning lead lines to Diana Ross' soprano; Diana and Dennis Edwards re-create Marvin & Tammi on a rousing version of "Ain't No Mountain High Enough"; smooth tenor-singing Otis Williams does a silky rendition of "This Guy's in Love With You"; and Paul Williams is forever Paul as the prominent voice on "Then," an old Four Tops album cut. Originally released in 1969, this is a CD every Temptations, Diana Ross & the Supremes, and Motown fan should have. A Holland import combines this and a following album by both groups on one CD—21 tracks of these delicacies. *—Andrew Hamilton*

Live at the Copa / Dec. 1968 / Motown ♦♦♦♦
David Ruffin is history as a Temptation, and his replacement Dennis Edwards shows his stuff on this live recording of a Copacabana performance. This is on a par with their

previous live album, *The Temptations Live*. They successfully combine their hits with songs from the *In a Mellow Mood* LP, making for an entertaining, well-rounded set. Eddie Kendricks was never in finer voice than here, emoting and pleading on "Please Return Your Love to Me," while showing his ability to sing standards on "With These Hands." Paul Williams' rendition of "The Impossible Dream" is appealing to even the most die-hard fans of soul music; you can almost see Williams sweating as he reaches for the notes and belts out the theme from *Man of La Mancha*. He also treats the crowd to his popular version of "For Once in My Life." Bass singer Melvin Franklin gets a rare lead and sings his crowd-pleasing "I Truly Believe," the popular flip side of "I Wish It Would Rain." Otis Williams handles the introductions, but the roar comes when newbie Edwards take the lead with his powerful, churchy voice. He makes "I Could Never Love Another (After Loving You)" his own; you completely forget David Ruffin's original version. A powerful statement from the Temptations. *—Andrew Hamilton*

Cloud Nine / Feb. 1969 / Motown ✦✦✦✦✦
Best known for their silky soul vocals and smooth-stepping routines, the Temptations were firmly entrenched as the undisputed kings of Barry Gordy's Motown stable when cutting-edge producer Norman Whitfield walked into the studio and announced that it was time to shake things up. The resulting freakout became the first half of the stellar *Cloud Nine*, an album that would become one of the defining early funk sets, with songs that not only took Motown in a new direction, but helped to shape a genre as well. On one side and across three jams, Whitfield and the Temptations would give '70s-era funk musicians a broad palette from which to draw inspiration. The title track, with its funky soul bordering on psychedelic frenzy, was an audacious album opener, and surely gave older fans a moment's pause. Only two more songs rounded out side one: an incredibly fresh take on "I Heard It Through the Grapevine," which jazzed up the vocals, brought compelling percussion to the fore, and relegated the piano well into the wings, and "Run Away Child, Running Wild," an extravagant nine-minute groove where the sonics easily surpassed the vocals. After shaking up the record-buying public with these three masterpieces, the Temptations brought things back to form for side two. Here, their gorgeous vocals dominated slick arrangements across seven tracks which included "Hey Girl" and the masterful "I Need Your Lovin'." Funk continued to percolate—albeit subtly—but compared to side one, it was Temptations business as usual. It was this return to the classic sound, however, which ultimately gave *Cloud Nine* its odd dynamic. The dichotomy of form between old and new between sides doesn't allow for a continuous gel. But the brash experimentation away from traditional Motown on the three seminal tracks which open the disc shattered the doorway between past and present as surely as the decade itself imploded and smooth soul gave way to blistering funk. *—Amy Hanson*

The Temptations Show / Jul. 1969 / Motown ✦✦✦
While any album that contains the baggage of guest "celebrities" Kaye Stevens and George Kirby putting in their two cents' worth on "When I Lay My Burden Down," can't be judged a complete success, this still has enough creditable performances to overcome that fiasco. The group was in turmoil behind the scenes, but you wouldn't know it from the organization, class, and charm they display on this television outing. *—Ron Wynn*

Puzzle People / Sep. 1969 / Motown ✦✦✦
Both the Temptations and producer Norman Whitfield were at the top of their form with 1969's *Puzzle People*, which captures the group in the midst of their rock-influenced "socially conscious" period. While the lead-off cut, "I Can't Get Next to You," was a potent R&B dancefloor filler, elsewhere the album was dotted with "relevant" tunes such as "Message From a Black Man" (not nearly as militant as it sounds), "Don't Let the Joneses Get You Down," and the "life-in-prison" epic "Slave," complete with plenty of fuzztone and wah-wah and enough panning to make George Clinton dizzy. But while the material and the production is a bit dated, *Whitfield* and his crew certainly caught the Funk Brothers on a great run when they cut these sessions, with the musicians blending the swagger and confidence of rock with a soundly funky undertow and chops to spare. And as for the Temptations themselves, if new lead vocalist Dennis Edwards lacked the élan of David Ruffin, he had power to spare, and the group's harmonies and shared vocals found room for both smooth precision and streetwise grit. While short on hits past the opening track (and padded with well-executed but hardly essential covers of "Hey Jude" and "Little Green Apples," *Puzzle People* is still the work of a great vocal group firing on all cylinders and getting inspired support in the studio, and it's one of the group's strongest late-'60s efforts. *—Mark Deming*

Psychedelic Shack / Mar. 1970 / Motown ✦✦✦✦
With everything the Temptations released pretty much guaranteed to turn to gold, not to mention platinum for that matter, even their tripped-out forays into sweet '60s psychedelic experimentation were sure to fire a string of hits. Norman Whitfield-produced *Psychedelic Shack* (1970)—while perhaps a system shock to those fans who grooved to the band's lame-suited, Motown dance-routined R&B classics—was a magnificent stretch into an epic and ultimately emerged as another in a long line of enduring sets. Deviating from form across the first songs, it was with the whimsical and willful title track (and a big thanks to the band from Georgia retro-ists the B-52's, who took their own homage, "Love Shack," to the top of the charts in 1989) that the Temptations broke their own mold with the acid-drenched party chant: "Psychedelic shack/That's where it's at." Opening that door and venturing outside the nonstop celebration, the band retains that vibe while returning to a slightly more staid stance on "Hum Along and Dance," leaving both the oddly paced "You Make Your Own Heaven and Hell Right Here on Earth" and the totally tripped-out "Take a Stroll Thru Your Mind" out on their own plane entirely. With such a strong collection of songs, it couldn't get much better than that. But, of course, it does, as the Temptations blister through the groovers "It's Summer" and "Friendship Train." And that, of course, just leaves the Whitfield-penned classic "War" to round out the mix. While fellow Motown-er Edwin Starr has etched what is now considered to be the definitive version of the song into the history tablets, the Temptations certainly took their own inspiration and added a unique spin as well. Not much else can be said, except that this is an absolutely outstanding album—one which has stood the test of time, sounding as fresh as it did upon initial release. And for those who still suffer the scratchy vinyl, a 2002 CD reissue of the album on Dutch Motown finds *Psychedelic Shack* cunningly paired with the similarly superlative *All Directions* in a neat two-disc package. *—Amy Hanson*

Greatest Hits, Vol. 2 / Sep. 1970 / Motown ✦✦✦
Greatest Hits, Vol. 2 is a 12-track overview of the Temptations' late-'60s recordings, containing such hits as "Cloud Rain," "I Wish It Would Rain," "Ball of Confusion," "(I Know) I'm Losing You," "I Can't Get Next to You," "You're My Everything," "Runaway Child, Running Wild" and "Psychedelic Shack." Like its predecessor, *Vol. 2* balances hits with lesser-known tracks ("Don't Let the Joneses Get You Down," "(Loneliness Made Me Realize) It's You That I Need"), and that makes the collection less interesting to casual fans who only want hits. They'll be better served by latter-day collections which feature hits from both *Vol. 1* and *Vol. 2*, but this album remains a solid summation of the Temptations' late-'60s singles. *—Stephen Thomas Erlewine*

The Sky's the Limit / Apr. 1971 / Motown ✦✦✦
Eddie Kendricks said so long to the Temptations on this early-'70s album, with the glorious "Just My Imagination" being his swan song. The song that everyone missed was their lengthy, imaginative version of "Smiling Faces Sometimes," which wasn't a huge hit for them, but became a smash for the Undisputed Truth. Although they were successful with Damon Harris replacing Kendricks, things would never be the same. *—Ron Wynn*

Solid Rock / Jan. 1972 / Motown ✦✦✦
Solid Rock spawned two hits, the rockish "Superstar (Remember How You Got Where You Are)" written by Barrett Strong and Norman Whitfield with David Ruffin foremost on their minds, and "Take a Look Around," a slow lilting social commentary number featuring Richard Street and Damon Harris. Whitfield put a totally new arrangement on "Stop the War Now," popularized Edwin Starr and turned the rocker into a mammoth head song. It begins with bass singer Melvin Franklin reciting the Lord's Prayer on top of a slow syncopated beat before mushrooming for more than 15 minutes into some classic-'70 psychedelic music wherein Whitfield made good use of his bag of studio tricks. Every time you listen you hear something new. It was not for everybody though, as many thought it was a waste of space and weird beyond comprehension. A rendition of Bill Withers' "Ain't No Sunshine" is one of the better cuts, Street and Harris again take turns at lead, while the others perform their background gymnastics. Whitfield was known for recording the same song with different Motown artists, varying the arrangements to keep them from sounding similar, but on "It's Summer" he went one better by recording the same song on the same group twice; this version has Dennis Edwards singing lead, the previous version was led by Melvin Franklin, both versions are equally as effective, on this rendition Franklin's low bass plays a prominent role in the background, and the Temptations' harmonies are heavenly. Two other cuts, "The End of Our Road," and "What It Is," are indistinguishable remakes. "Smooth Sailing" led by Damon Harris, is an upbeat tune about being in love that lacks bite and is saddled with adolescent lyrics. *—Andrew Hamilton*

All Directions / Jul. 1972 / Motown ✦✦✦✦✦
A monster album, the one that put them back in the spotlight and signaled that Norman Whitfield had saved the day. Damon Harris had replaced Eddie Kendricks, and there were many doubters convinced the band was finished. Instead, Whitfield revitalized them via the majestic single, "Papa Was a Rolling Stone." Despite its length, Whitfield's decision to open with an extensive, multi-layered musical suite and tease listeners was a master stroke. By the time Dennis Edwards' voice came rushing in, no one would dare turn it off. The single, as well as "Law of the Land" and others, ended the funeral arrangements that had been prepared for the Temptations. *—Ron Wynn*

Anthology / Feb. 1973 / Motown ✦✦✦✦✦
Since supplanted by a few new anthology releases, this initial Temptations overview will still be an attractive slice of soul history for bargain-bin-minded music-lovers. Spanning close to ten years, the 41 tracks here cover the group's prime, from the early Smokey Robinson hits ("The Way You Do the Things You Do," "My Girl") on through Norman Whitfield's incredible run of smashes circa 1966-1972 ("Ain't Too Proud to Beg," "I Wish It Would Rain"). And that's not to forget such pinnacles of psych-soul as "Ball of Confusion," "Cloud Nine," "Psychedelic Shack," and "Papa Was a Rolling Stone." Essential listening for novice and expert crate-diggers alike. *—Stephen Cook*

Masterpiece / Feb. 1973 / Motown ✦✦✦
Norman Whitfield was always the Motown producer who had the most daring creative vision for the Temptations; he was the man who helped them turn psychedelic (well, sort of) with "Cloud Nine" and "Psychedelic Shack", and when the group's career had hit a slump in the early 1970s, he brought them back to the top of the charts with the brilliantly realized "Papa Was a Rolling Stone". After the latter tune had become a smash, Whitfield and the Temptations set out to make their most ambitious project to date, but in many ways, *Masterpiece* sounded more like a Norman Whitfield solo album with the Tempts adding occasional vocals; the album's long, carefully layered tunes, complete with sweeping string charts and cleanly punctuated horn lines, have the widescreen splendor of a big-budget movie, and while it's inarguably impressive to hear, the featured artists often seem to be lost in the shuffle. It doesn't help that while the album is musically impressive, several of the songs are lyrically cut-rate, especially the cliché-ridden "Ma" and "Plastic Man," a ho-hum critique of hypocrisy, and while the Temptations deliver their material with conviction and typically peerless vocal skill, it's not enough to disguise the fact this album overshoots its target. While still better than the average Motown effort of

the period, *Masterpiece* never quite becomes the triumph it obviously wants to be, proving once again that a "Masterpiece" usually occurs as a matter of serendipity rather than careful design. *—Mark Deming*

Zoom / Dec. 1973 / Motown ♦♦♦♦

Zoom is the final Norman Whitfield/Temptation Motown collaboration. Whitfield composed all seven songs without help from former writing partner Barrett Strong. Why Motown hasn't re-released this compilation on cassette or CD is an unsolved mystery; sure it lacked the big hit, but the LP is a smoker. Dennis never sang harder than he does on "Let Your Hair Down" and "You Got My Soul on Fire"; both songs are lightning fast, and the pulsating rhythms overshadow any melody the songs may have. Damon Harris does his Eddie Kendricks imitation on "I Need You," a pleasant ballad that lacks bite. "Heavenly," led by Richard Street, should have been a significant record, but Motown dropped the ball big time on this one. The *pièces de résistance* here are the title track, a powerful explosion of social commentary about America entitled "1990," and the futuristic masterpiece "Zoom," where the Tempts take the listener with them on an imaginary flight to the moon via Norman Whitfield's bag of tricks. *—Andrew Hamilton*

Song for You / Jan. 1975 / Motown ♦♦♦

By 1975, the Temptations were a much different group with both David Ruffin and Eddie Kendricks out of the lineup. Dennis Edwards was now singing lead, and only Melvin Franklin and Otis Williams existed from the original group. The group was far more of a funk mind, and this set proves it. The big hit on here was "Happy People," with the Tempts backed up by the Commodores, listed as "the Temptations Band" on the second part instrumental version. For ultra-funk, though, it's hard to beat "Glasshouse" and "Shakey Ground," which features guitar and bass work from P-Funk alumni Eddie Hazel and Billy Nelson. But they didn't leave their ballads entirely in the good old days, as the satin-drenched "Firefly," "Memories" and the title track clearly show. Produced by Jeffrey Bowen, this thing has "'70s" stamped all over it. In the case of the Tempts, that's good. *—Cub Koda*

House Party / Nov. 1975 / Gordy ♦♦♦

Longtime producer/writer Norman Whitfield left Motown in 1974 to start his own label at Warner Brothers, while his primary group, the Temptations, stayed behind. In his absence the group was desperately searching for a style and new producers. This 1975 set collects both so-so sessions from 1974 as well as cuts made to bide time between *A Song for You* and 1976's *Wings of Love*. Releasing an album of "leftovers" for a group of the Temptations stature is still a little silly, but Motown thought it was a good idea in case anyone would forget them in the course of a year. The 1974 songs are the lowlights: "It's Just a Matter of Time" and a cover of Bobby Womack's "Can't Stop a Man in Love" were dated by the time tracks were laid. The Steve Cropper produced tracks, "Johnny Porter" and "The Ways of a Grown Up Man" attempts to attain the Whitfield production aesthetic with little success. This album's best tracks were recorded in 1975. The well-produced gaudy funk of Eddie & Brian Holland's "Keep Holding On" gave lead singer Dennis Edwards plenty of room to wail. That track, along with the smooth "Darlin' Stand By Me (Song For My Woman)," landed on the groups 1994 *Emperors of Soul* box set. The album's best track, the ballad "If I Don't Love You This Way," is warm, early '70s Motown benefiting a strong lead from Richard Street. Despite the good tracks *House Party* is not one of the group's essential albums. *—Jason Elias*

Wings of Love / Mar. 1976 / Gordy ♦♦♦

The Temptations Do the Temptations / Aug. 1976 / Gordy ♦♦♦

The Temptations were going through some personnel and transitional changes during this period, and it's reflected in the selections. On this album, the Tempts emerge with a new falsetto lead singer in Glenn Carl Leonard; Dennis Edwards rejoins the group after a brief absence, while Richard Street and mainstays Otis Williams and Melvin Franklin complete the lineup. The title of this album is deceiving; it would have one think that these are songs the group recorded on prior albums. But to the contrary, these are songs assembled specifically for this recording, never before recorded by the Tempts. During a period when they were struggling to remain a quintet, they were also struggling to find material that was appealing to their audience and conducive to their sound. They managed to assemble a series of songs that featured only one single, "Who Are You," to appear on the *Billboard* R&B charts (number 22, 12 weeks). The single is dance-oriented, with Dennis Edwards on lead, but it's not the best single from the album. "Why Can't You and Me Get Together" is a spendidly arranged composition set in an uptempo, finger-snapping groove with a full orchestra introduction and interlude with co-leads by Leonard (falsetto) and Street (baritone). And for a more mellow mood, "I'm on Fire (Body Song)" is a romantic, gentle-flowing ballad that allows Leonard to express urgency and impatience in each lyric. *—Craig Lytle*

Hear to Tempt You / 1978 / Atlantic ♦♦♦

When the Temptations left Motown in 1977 the group weighed offers from Warner Bros. and Philadelphia International before settling for Atlantic. The album seemed doomed from the start. Temptations lead Dennis Edwards had already left the group and was replaced by Louis Price. This album was released in late 1977 and was a fixture of the cutout bins by the early '80s. Ron Baker, Norman Harris, and Trammps member Earl Young, collectively known as Baker-Harris-Young, produced this album. They were known for their grittier variant of Philly soul/disco but often they play it too safe here. The fact that the Temptations did their vocals in New York rather than Philadelphia does diminish the Philly credentials a bit. The two singles from the album, "Think For Yourself" and the bittersweet "In a Lifetime," are the best at mixing the Temptations' with the Baker-Harris-Young production style. The ballads led by the smooth baritone of Louis Price, "Can We Come and Share in Love" and "Let's Live in Peace," also display the rich harmonies in this particular lineup. Unlike other efforts, *Hear to Tempt You* features all of the members getting a lead vocal. "I Can Never Stop Loving You," with bass Melvin Franklin, is a melodic ballad that gives Franklin a rare romantic lyric. *Hear to Tempt You* was released shortly before Baker-Harris-Young began to update their sound. This effort lacks the confidence of late-'70s like-minded albums from the Trammps and Eddie Kendricks. Fans of both the Temptations and the Philly sound may find this an imperfect alliance. *—Jason Elias*

Bare Back / 1978 / Atlantic ♦♦

Other than Richard Streets' energetic lead on the risqué "Bare Back" and Glenn Leonard's glowing falsetto on "Ever Ready Love," there's not much to recommend on the Temptations' second Atlantic record release. Producers Brian & Eddie Holland didn't give Louis Price, who took Dennis Edwards' place, much to show his skills on. Overall, the songs are arguably the weakest ever recorded by the Tempts. After this, the Tempts returned to Motown, their mouths filled with humble pie. *—Andrew Hamilton*

Power / Apr. 1980 / Motown ♦♦♦

Struggling to rekindle the magic that kept them atop the charts, the group was, for the most part, missing in action on this album. Nonetheless, the five vocalists did hit the charts with the title track, "Power." The single is groomed around a poppin' bassline that's blended with Melvin Franklin's natural bass. Glenn Leonard, Dennis Edwards and Richard Street share lead on the single, which peaked at number 11 on the *Billboard* R&B charts after 13 weeks. In spite of its ranking, the single is not as worthy as some of the group's other songs of comparable ranking. An honorable mention is "Isn't the Night Fantastic." With Richard Street out front, the Tempts groove their way through this inviting track. "Shadow of Your Love" has a tendency to deviate from its original feel, as do some of the other selections, but "Go For It," also a ballad, stays its course with Leonard on lead. The group's vocal skills remain keen. *—Craig Lytle*

The Temptations / Aug. 1981 / Motown ♦♦♦

The Temptations waited nearly ten years to work with '70s hit-making producer Thom Bell. While the Temptations sound as impeccable as ever, the compositions lacked the magic for which the quintet was known among their R&B followers. This collection of songs leans more toward the pop format. "Aiming at Your Heart" is an uptempo, home-grown R&B cut featuring Richard Street and Glenn Leonard on lead vocals, and it was the only single to crack the *Billboard* R&B charts (number 36, 13 weeks). While Street gets gritty with his blaring baritone, Leonard's contrasting falsetto blossoms with agility as the two storm their way through the vamp. Melvin Franklin takes center stage on "What Else," a beautifully written number with a bright melody and a Temptations-style arrangement. Franklin's distinguishable bass sails through this mellow tune. While all the songs are worthy, the album should have been marketed to a crossover audience. *—Craig Lytle*

Reunion / 1982 / Gordy ♦♦♦

Reunion is a very good Temptations album that could have been great. Kenny Gamble & Leon Huff were originally rumored to produce this reunion of Eddie Kendricks and David Ruffin with the current crop of Temptations. However, the two sides couldn't get the deal done. So Motown rationed out the production assignments to in-house producers, Rick James, Smokey Robinson, and others. Seven voices sang on these tracks besides Kendricks and Ruffin; they were: Dennis Edwards, Glenn Leonard, Richard Street, Melvin Franklin, and Otis Williams—a mini-choir. Considering the voices on hand, they should have spread the leads around. Of the seven tracks, Dennis Edwards sings six and David Ruffin one, the very ordinary "You Better Beware," written by money man Barrett Strong. Ruffin's vocal sounds rough and appears to strain trying to reach some notes. Punk-funker Rick James' epic "Standing on the Top" production is the most popular track here, with its dead-on beat, blaring horns, and multiple voices; Rick James himself joins the Tempts on this festive song. Kendricks' bluesy falsetto lines on the fade are like cherries topping a sundae. Relishing the opportunity to produce Dennis Edwards, Smokey writes two beauties for the churchy belter: the introspective, engaging "Backstage" and the understated "More on the Inside," the second release from this set. Kerry Gordy, one of Berry Gordy sons, co-wrote two in-your-face cold-blooded stompers, the so-true "Money Hards to Get" and the frantic "Lock It in the Pocket," both excellent and both left for dead on the album. Edwards displays his balladry ability on a stunning rendition of "I've Never Been to Me" originally done by Charlene. Not a bad album, but the product doesn't equal the sum of the voices and producers. Why wasn't Eddie Kendricks given a lead? Or Richard Street and the Kendricks-sounding Glenn Leonard? Fans would have loved to hear the two falsettos featured on a song, or Kendricks and Ruffin co-leading as they did on "You're My Everything" and the lesser-known but just as brilliant "Born to Love," from *Temptin' Temptations*. While we're playin', a gospel jam would have been a rip-snortin' inclusion (or conclusion); with seven voices, the results would have been breathtaking. *—Andrew Hamilton*

Surface Thrills / 1983 / Motown ♦♦

Producer/writer Dennis Lambert had tunnel vision when it came to the Temptations: Dennis Edwards was the only Temptation Lambert could see, and the other members seemed to be in his way. Eight tracks comprise *Surface Thrills*, and Edwards sings them all. This could very well have been a Dennis Edwards solo album; Edwards left the group after this to record solo, with Lambert (who else) producing. *Surface Thrills* is one of the least thrilling LPs of the Temptations' career. Only "Love's on My Mind Tonight" saves it from being a straight turkey. "Surface Thrills" did nothing when released as a single; the other songs are unmemorable, formulaic productions that lack substance and charm. *—Andrew Hamilton*

Back to Basics / Oct. 1983 / Motown ♦♦♦

Truly for You / Oct. 1984 / Motown ♦♦♦

The album that preceded this one (*Back to Basics*) introduced the group's new falsetto lead, Ron Tyson, who is also a remarkable tenor. To fill the departure of Dennis Edwards, this release introduces the electrifying vocals of Ali-Ollie Woodson. As talented, competitive and competent as Edwards is, Woodson's sound is not only refreshing to fans of the Tempts, but to the music industry overall. The smash hit on this release was "Treat Her Like a Lady," a soulful, dance composition that entails some dazzling backgrounds led by Woodson's fiery approach to the melody and the ligthnening squeal of his trademark falsetto. The single was treated very well by the *Billboard* R&B charts, peaking at number two for two consecutive weeks after 21 thriving weeks. The title track, "Truly for You," retains much of that Temptations magic with its affectionate harp-like guitar rhythms, a romantic confession conveyed in a sincere tone and Ron Tyson's agile, flowing vocals that express the lyrics with honesty and grace. The single made its mark at number 14 on the *Billboard* R&B charts inside of 13 weeks. *—Craig Lytle*

Touch Me / 1985 / Gordy ♦♦♦
With Ali-Ollie Woodson's polished vocals, the Temptations scored a *Billboard* R&B Top 20 hit with "Do You Really Love Your Baby." Penned by Luther Vandross and Marcus Miller, the Tempts gratefully reap the rewards of Vandross' crafty style. Woodson and Ron Tyson switch off on lead. With a mixture of urban and pop rhythms, the single peaked at number 14 after 15 weeks. The title track, "Touch Me," is a moderately slow number with a thumping bassline featuring Woodson out front on vocals. "Don't Break Your Promise to Me" has a gospel-seasoned rhythm track with Tyson and Woodson on lead and also featuring female guest vocalist Alfie Silas. Though it was not a release, "Magic" has a certain sophistication about it. Woodson patiently caresses each lyric with his dapper vocals. The overall arrangement allows the Tempts to interject their splendid vocal presence. Not as worthy as its predecessor *Truly for You*, this album still does have its moments. *—Craig Lytle*

25th Anniversary / 1986 / Motown ♦♦♦

To Be Continued . . . / 1986 / Motown ♦♦♦
Although it contained the super "Lady Soul," this was still far from a good Temptations album. It had uneven material, some poorly produced uptempo tunes, and some of the least distinguished harmonies and leads ever heard on a Temptations LP. Fortunately, it also had the title track and "Someone," decent enough songs to keep it from being a complete flop. *—Ron Wynn*

Together Again / 1987 / Motown ♦♦♦
The last Temptations album to make even a little bit of noise on the pop chart, this wasn't quite the bomb it seemed. Both "I Wonder Who She's Seeing Now" and "Look What You Started" are solid R&B tunes, and were greeted with relief by an audience that thought things were almost over after hearing some of the other Temptations singles. They weren't back in peak form, but they were still standing. *—Ron Wynn*

Special / 1989 / Motown ♦♦♦
Things sounded bleak for the Temptations on this 1989 release. Not only didn't it generate any hits, but the rotating personnel, feeble production, weak songs and arrangements, and general malaise certainly didn't justify slapping a title like *Special* on it. Perhaps Dennis Edwards knew what was happening when he left for the third time a year before this was issued. *—Ron Wynn*

Psychedelic Shack/All Directions / 1990 / Motown ♦♦♦

Song for You/Masterpiece / 1990 / Motown ♦♦♦

Milestone / 1991 / Motown ♦♦
One of the most forgettable records in the Temptations' long and illustrious history. The personnel was unsettled, and seldom has the group ever issued an album with absolutely nothing having a remote shot at being a hit. Ali-Ollie Woodson didn't make anyone forget the group's legacy of great lead vocalists. *—Ron Wynn*

Hum Along and Dance: More of the Best (1963–1974) / Feb. 16, 1993 / Rhino ♦♦♦♦
This 18-track compilation contains Temptations B-sides, non-hit cuts and obscure sides recorded from 1963-1974. It includes such sumptuous ballads as "What Love Has Joined Together" and "Gonna Keep on Trying Till I Win Your Love," plus uptempo wailers and an occasional dud ("Stop The War Now"). The early tracks show the group evolving from its doo wop roots into soul's premier group. While the cuts on this disc aren't the ones that made the Temptations popular music institutions, they're still a vital part of their legacy. *—Ron Wynn*

Emperors of Soul / Sep. 20, 1994 / Motown ♦♦♦♦♦
The Temptations were unquestionably one of Motown's greatest groups, recording a large number of classic singles. They were also one of the handful of Motown groups that were able to successfully make the transition from the '60s to the '70s, giving them a sizable amount of quality material from both decades. *Emperors of Soul*, a lavishly produced five-CD box set, draws from the Temptations' entire career, treating all aspects of it with equal respect. For the dedicated fan, the box set is a treasure—the sound is great and there are numerous rarities. However, for most listeners, it is simply too much music, featuring too many unfamiliar songs. *—Stephen Thomas Erlewine*

☆ **Anthology** / May 23, 1995 / Motown ♦♦♦♦♦
A definitive overview of the Temptations' career at Motown, *Anthology* was first released on LP in 1973, revamped in 1986, and updated once again for the CD era in 1995, with modern remastering technology and new packaging. The 1995 version tinkers with the selections a bit, appends a few later singles released after the original issue, and adds a few extra, lesser-known items from their earlier years, including the previously unreleased "Lullaby of Love." Since it's difficult to encapsulate the Temptations' accomplishments on just one disc—they remained consistent and viable hitmakers well into the '70s, totally reinventing their sound in the process—*Anthology* should really be considered the best available summation of their career. The two discs split up the Tempts' two major phases pretty neatly. Kicking off with their breakthough hit "The Way You Do the Things You Do," the first disc covers their years as the epitome of the Motown sound, while the second sums up their transformation into a funky psychedelic soul outfit at the close of the '60s. All the key hits are here, including a few major R&B-chart smashes that were left off *The Ultimate Collection*; plus, the liner notes offer a detailed history of the group, right down to listings of every lead singer on each individual track. It all makes for a tremendous package and an amazing two-and-a-half hours of music. *Anthology* is the ideal choice for any listener who wants to dig deeper than the single-disc *Ultimate Collection*, but doesn't want to spring for the five-disc *Emperors of Soul* box; unfortunately, as of early 2003, it had gone out of print again. *—Steve Huey*

For Lovers Only / Sep. 26, 1995 / Motown ♦♦♦♦
Arguably the Temptations' best album since *Truly For You* dropped in 1984, *For Lovers Only* is not the Temptations' first album of standards. This set of classics is different than *Temptations in a Mellow Mood*, where they acquiesced to the material, giving relatively straight readings, and never deviated far from the songs' popular arrangements. The only things the standards on *For Lovers Only* have in common with the originals are the titles and the lyrics, the arrangements are completely different, and the tempos are changed. The Temptations sing with this much enthusiasm in years. The main shortcoming of this record is that the lead singers for the particular songs aren't listed in the CD Booklet; this is essential information, since the group has gone through so many changes. Richard Perry outdid himself with this production, he expertly captured the essence of the Temptations, regardless of the members, in these songs. Their signature vocal blend is emphasized at every turn, and why not, it's what brought throngs of fans into their fold in the first place. He didn't concentrate on one lead singer, like others have in the past. The Temptations were initially marketed as a group of five capable lead singers and that's what you get with this excellent collection. Credit also goes to Jimmy Varner who assisted in the production, all the vocals and arrangements were done by the Temptations. *—Andrew Hamilton*

One by One: The Best of Their Solo Years / Mar. 19, 1996 / Motown ♦♦♦
An interesting concept for a compilation, devoted to the most significant solo tracks by Temptations vocalists David Ruffin, Eddie Kendricks, Dennis Edwards, and Paul Williams. In other words, this two-CD, 35-track compilation isn't really a Temptations CD at all, although it's more appropriate to list it under their entry than anywhere else. The ex-Tempts' solo outings had their high points, like David Ruffin's Top Ten hit "My Whole World Ended (The Moment You Left Me)," and Eddie Kendricks's "Keep on Truckin'." But overall, this isn't anything special, with a pleasantly generic late-period Motown sound that sometimes begs the inevitable unfavorable comparisons with the Temptations' own work, from the perspectives of both material and execution. Kendricks comes off best here, but Motown fans will be interested in the chance to track down many obscure minor hits and flops by the singers, and even a few unreleased cuts. It's too late to do anything about it, but the best of these solo hits would have been far more appropriate selections for the *Emperors of Soul* box than most of the group-performed post-"Papa Was a Rolling Stone" material that made the cut. *—Richie Unterberger*

★ **The Ultimate Collection** / Mar. 25, 1997 / Motown ♦♦♦♦♦
With the exception of Stevie Wonder and Marvin Gaye, one would be hard pressed to name a Motown act who went through as many creative shifts as the Temptations. While Wonder's and Gaye's changes of direction were a product of their own creative rebellion against Berry Gordy's brilliant but often formulaic vision, the Temptations seemed to be the label's official "keeping up with the times" artists, starting out as interpreters of Smokey Robinson's silky-smooth sweet soul confections and going on to embrace rock guitars, work with members of Funkadelic, and be produced by Rick James, all while holding onto their trademark vocal style. The length and breadth of the Temptations' career would make it practically impossible for a single-disc career retrospective to be truly comprehensive, and *The Ultimate Collection* is missing a few essential tracks (most notably "Psychedelic Shack" and "Runaway Child, Running Wild"), and two latter-day hits, "Treat Her Like a Lady" and "Error of Our Ways," don't exactly bring this set to a triumphant conclusion. But if you're only going to own one Temptations disc, *The Ultimate Collection* is a very good one to get; it includes the majority of the group's biggest hits, the remastering sounds great, and the chronological sequence gives a fine picture of the group's constant musical evolution. *The Ultimate Collection* isn't the last word on the Temptations, but it's a splendid starting point to their music, and will add a satisfying portion of sweet-and-sour soul to your next party. Special added attraction: a rare a cappella take of "My Girl" is included as a bonus. *—Mark Deming*

Phoenix Rising / Aug. 18, 1998 / Motown ♦♦♦
Three years after the brilliant *For Lovers Only* and two personnel changes, the Temptations dished out *Phoenix Rising*. Ali-Ollie Woodson and Theo Peoples were replaced by Harry McGilberry Jr. and Barrington Scott Henderson. The album gets off to an excellent start with "Stay," a lilting, midtempo mood setter that samples the opening riffs of "My Girl"; the red-light special became their highest charting singles in years. "How Could He Hurt You," is one of those good, questioning ballads that always find a way into your heart. These new Temptations are all right, but none are comparable to the squalling Temptation tenors of the past. Voices reaching the magnitude of David Ruffin's, Dennis Edwards', Ali Woodson's and Richard Street's are sorely missed. Otis Williams seems to have found his niche doing interludes between songs, it would be interesting to see if they would incorporate Williams' eloquent love talks into their stage act. Ron Tyson sings effortlessly in a honey-laden falsetto on "Tempt Me," which, other than "Stay," is the most arresting number here. Tyson displays his natural tenor before sliding into a cloud high falsetto, the backing voices are a thing of beauty as they weave in, out and around Ron's deft delivery and the bass dots in and out placing exclamation points everywhere. "If I Give You My Heart" features a Williams rap and has a pop-ish beat; the tenor tries

to cut loose but may have been restrained by producer Narada Michael Walden. When listening to "Take Me in Your Arms" it helps to imagine Ruffin, Edwards or Woodson on lead. The midtempo songs, for the most part, outshine the ballads. "That's What Friends Are For" (not the Dionne Warwick song) has a def, stepping beat but changes tempos on the chorus and becomes annoying until it gets back to that "Da, Da, Da" beat. The baritone voice on an occasional lead is sorely missed, Temptations albums used to feature a baritone voice distinct from the tenor not only in register, but in style and phrasing, now the voices are too similar. Still, not a bad silver platter when you take the personnel changes into consideration. *—Andrew Hamilton*

Lost and Found: You've Got to Earn It (1962–1968) / Sep. 28, 1999 / Motown ♦♦♦♦
As one of the entries in Motown's *Lost and Found* series, this is a 20-track major find of largely unreleased Temptations material. It all originates from the early golden period of the group's history, with Eddie Kendricks and David Ruffin finding their groove with each track, redefining soul history while searching for a hit. Several tunes would go through lyric and arrangement changes in Motown's rigid back-to-the-factory production methods, and some of the tunes aboard ("Last One Out Is Brokenhearted," "Camouflage," "Forever in My Heart," and "We'll Be Satisfied") are in their early incarnations. There are also alternate versions of the title track, "Ain't Too Proud to Beg," and a live performance at the Fox Theater of "My Girl," announced on-stage as their newest single. Here's a treasure trove of rare Temps tracks from the good old days; far from a pack of leftovers, in all honesty it doesn't get much better than this. *—Cub Koda*

Psychedelic Soul / 2000 / Spectrum ♦♦♦♦♦
Once Norman Whitfield caught the reins of Motown's strongest act (and the one closest to Berry Gordy's heart), he recorded hit after hit, stretching from 1968's "Cloud Nine" to 1973's "Masterpiece." But despite some seriously groovy covers, the Temptations' LPs of the era suffered from Motown's unwillingness to ever commit fully to any one direction: 1969's *Puzzle People* included both the defiant anthem "Message From a Black Man" and a cover of Roger Miller's "Little Green Apples." Britain's Spectrum remedied the situation with its 2000 compilation *Psychedelic Soul*, not just a hits collection from the Whitfield years but a nearly definitive look at his best productions for the Temptations. Included are not only all the obvious biggies from the era—"Papa Was a Rollin' Stone," "Psychedelic Shack," "Runaway Child, Running Wild," "Ball of Confusion," "Cloud Nine," and "Masterpiece"—but a host of great middle-level hits ("Don't Let the Joneses Get You Down," "Message From a Black Man," "You Make Your Own Heaven and Hell Right Here on Earth") and intriguing album tracks like "Ungena Za Ulimwengu (Unite the World)" and "Funky Music Sho Nuff Turns Me On." All of them hang together really well (much better than any of the albums, barring 1973's *Masterpiece*), and despite the small caveat of an occasionally baffling running order, *Psychedelic Soul* is the best way to hear some of the grooviest, most ambitious music ever recorded for Motown. *—John Bush*

Ear-Resistable / May 16, 2000 / Interscope ♦♦♦♦

Meet the Temptations/Sing Smokey / Dec. 19, 2000 / Motown ♦♦♦

Wish It Would Rain/In a Mellow Mood / Jan. 16, 2001 / Motown ♦♦♦

Original Lead Singers of the Temptations / Jun. 12, 2001 / Eagle ♦♦
This reunion album of sorts finds the original singers for the Temptations revisiting some of their biggest hits for Motown in the mid- to late '60s. They choose mostly the obvious: "My Girl," "Papa Was a Rolling Stone," "The Way You Do the Things You Do," "Cloud Nine," "Ball of Confusion (That's What the World Is Today)," and so on. Fans of the group's late-'60s/early-'70s material will be happy to see a perhaps surprising number of songs from that era, such as "Masterpiece" and "Psychedelic Shack." But as promising as the track listing makes this album seem, one can't help but feel a little disappointed by the music itself. Yes, the guys still can sing up a storm, but the shoddy backing music really makes listeners realize how integral Motown's in-house musicians were with their patented Motown sound. Listeners who are just plain happy hearing the guys and could care less about how authentic these re-recordings are should by all means check this out. Otherwise, it's probably best to dust off the originals when the craving strikes. *—Jason Birchmeier*

Awesome / Nov. 20, 2001 / Universal ♦♦♦
As the Otis Williams-fronted Temptations learned with *Ear-Resistible*, the group's surprisingly successful album from a year earlier, it's best to play it safe and stay true to the times. And that's precisely what Williams does on *Awesome*, an album that models itself after *Ear-Resistible*. There are mostly ballads here and some innocent concessions to the hip-hop audience. Overall, though, this is the Temptations sounding like the Temptations, albeit a tender yet resilient Temptations. There aren't any "Papa Was a Rolling Stone"s here and there aren't any "Cloud Nine"s, just sappy, utopian love songs and some extra-lite music lingering safely in the background. This is how sequels should sound—modestly like their predecessors. However, the modest sense of submission makes *Awesome* less rewarding than *Ear-Resistible*. There are few surprises, and the few surprises you do encounter are more calculated than inspired—the calling card of a, perhaps unfortunately, content veteran act. *—Jason Birchmeier*

My Girl: The Very Best of the Temptations / Apr. 16, 2002 / Motown ♦♦♦
At the time of the release of this two-disc Temptations compilation, Motown had in print a five-CD box set, *Emperors of Soul*; a one-disc *Ultimate Collection*; and two volumes of the midline-priced *20th Century Masters: The Millennium Collection* on the group (not to mention umpteen older, out-of-print comps). So, this TV-advertised set must have been meant to satisfy the fan for whom *The Ultimate Collection* wasn't enough, but the box set too much. But it was also meant for fans who had taken notice of the vintage group recently, since it emphasized 1990s recordings, particularly in special mixes, and was highly selective about what older songs were included, opting for the better-remembered ones over an actual hits selection based on chart rankings. That could make it a frustrating set for the long-lived Temptations fan, who would notice that only 26 of the group's 43 R&B Top Ten hits were included among the 36 tracks, especially when there was room on the first disc, which ran less than an hour, for several more songs. The collection was an odd combination of rarities, such as previously unreleased stereo mixes of two early singles ("Dream Come True" and "I Want a Love I Can See"), the Temptations' most famous 1960s hits, and some miscellaneous recordings. Particularly short-changed was the mid-'70s, with only three of the nine consecutive Top Ten R&B hits the Temptations scored from mid-1973 to early 1976 included. Since the group's personnel changed in revolving-door fashion after the early '70s, the result was that much of the second disc sounds like it was made by many different male vocal groups instead of one. While you could see what the compilers were going for here, the album was hardly an ideal Temptations compilation. *—William Ruhlmann*

The Temptones

f. Philadelphia, PA

Group / Blue-Eyed Soul, Soul, Rock & Roll

The Temptones were a blue-eyed soul group from Philadelphia, PA. Their recording career began while they attended college and lasted less than two years, from 1966 to 1967. Daryl Hall, who went on to superstardom with John Oates, debuted with the Temptones as their lead singer. The other members were Barry Glazer, Ken Halpern, Brian Utain, and Paul Fogel (considered the fifth Temptone). Oates joined the group toward their end playing rhythm guitar on live gigs; he never recorded with the Temptones. The guys came in second on a James Brown Talent Show in Philadelphia at the Uptown Theater. The Godfather held the contest during his two-week engagement. The prize was a little cash and a recording contract with Arctic Records. Their contracts were signed as individuals and Gamble & Huff and Jimmy Bishop produced the recordings. According to Glazer, they would rehearse the songs then cut them live at Sigma Sound Studios in Philadelphia—no overdubbing. Two recordings were released. Both stiffed and the association with Arctic ended. The group disbanded when one member left and another got drafted.

They were more popular live than their recordings, however. They played many gigs including two Freedom Shows in Philadelphia, the Uptown Theater, and several television shows including *The Jerry Blavatt Show*. Music comrades were the Vibrations, the Delfonics, the Intruders, the Temptations (Glazer called the late Paul Williams their sponsor), and fellow blue-eyed soul men, the Magnificent Men. Group members recall being booed when they first came on-stage but always were applauded after being heard. Happy times included singing "Old Man River" (Temptations-style) in Philly at the Freedom Show for 10,000 people. Glazer went on to own a photo-processing lab, Paul Fogel became a doctor, and Daryl Hall became a star. In 1996, Bear Family Records in Germany released a 21-track CD of Temptone recordings. Some of the tunes are the Radiants' "Voice Your Choice," the Impressions' "I've Been Trying," and many Temptations songs. *—Andrew Hamilton*

• **The Temptones** / Apr. 16, 1996 / Bear Family ♦♦♦♦

Ten City

f. 1987, Chicago, IL

Group / Dance-Pop, Club/Dance, House

The Chicago vocal group Ten City was one of the few house units to enjoy mainstream exposure during the late '80s and early '90s. Originally called Ragtyme, the trio was formed by vocalist Byron Stingily, guitarist Herb Lawson, and keyboard player Byron Burke, all under the aegis of producer extraordinaire Marshall Jefferson. After signing with Atlantic in the late '80s, Ten City's debut LP, *Foundation*, included the singles "Right Back to You" and "That's the Way Love Is," both of which received a good response in R&B and dance circles. *State of Mind* and *No House Big Enough* followed in 1990 and 1992, though Atlantic dropped them soon after. Just after release from their contract, the single "Fantasy" (written with Masters at Work) did well on the club scene, but by the time Ten City released their third album, *That Was Then, This Is Now*, the buzz had disappeared. The group rapidly disintegrated, though Stingily went on to a solo career. *—Ron Wynn*

Foundation / 1989 / Atlantic ♦♦♦♦
Retro and proud of it, Ten City was among the most impressive "deep house" acts to come out of Chicago in the late '80s. Like others playing deep house, these guys enthusiastically recall the great soul/disco of the mid- to late '70s and make no secret of their love of that era. Ten City clearly realizes that the best disco emphasized vocal personality as well as danceability, and like the music of the Trammps, Tavares and Double Exposure before them, *Foundation* is appropriate for listening as well as dancing. "That's That Way Love Is" (City's best known single), "Suspicious," "Devotion" and other songs on this absorbing debut album aren't simply about the beat and the track, but also the rich vocals that would have sounded great even if Ten City had gone a cappella. *Foundation* was a smash in the clubs, but unfortunately didn't do that much in the R&B or pop markets. This is a group that deserves to be much better known. *—Alex Henderson*

State of Mind / 1990 / Atlantic ♦♦♦♦
In the 1980s and 1990s, house music was as diverse as hip-hop. Depending on your preferences, you could find anything from amelodic, rave-friendly acid house (which lacked a song structure and often consisted of nothing more than a track and scattered samples) to ultra-melodic deep house artists like Chanelle, Adeva, and Jeanne Harris. Another act that epitomized deep house was Ten City, whose second album, *State of Mind*, came out in 1990 but owes a major artistic debt to the disco-soul of the mid- to late 1970s. Think of that era's most soul-drenched disco—Loleatta Holloway, Double Exposure, Linda Clifford, etc.—and you will know where Ten City is coming from on this sophomore effort, which isn't as consistently strong as 1989's *Foundation* but still has a lot going for it. The CD's best songs are flat-out excellent, including "Whatever Makes You Happy," "Nothing's Changed," "Destiny," and "It Ain't No Big Deal." But some of the other tunes are merely

decent. Unlike *Foundation*, this release is a bit uneven, although its plusses exceed its minuses by far. *State of Mind* isn't Ten City's best or most essential album, but it's worth acquiring for those who like their house music with a lot of soul. *—Alex Henderson*

- **The Best of Ten City** / Oct. 30, 2001 / Ibadan ✦✦✦✦✦

Despite a raft of club hits, Chicago's Ten City were never the most likely candidates for a greatest-hits compilation. Of course, the concept is no less welcome, though, and Ibadan does it up really well. Leading off with the club mix of "Devotion," *The Best of Ten City* captures the best versions of Ten City's best tracks, like extended mixes of "Right Back to You" and "That's the Way Love Is" or demo mixes of "Only Time Will Tell" and "My Peace of Heaven." With Ten City reissues nowhere to be seen and compilation appearances few and far between, this collection is a good place to round up some of the best Chicago house vocals ever recorded. *—John Bush*

Tammi Terrell (Thomasina Montgomery)

b. Apr. 29, 1945, Philadelphia, PA, **d.** Mar. 16, 1970, Philadelphia, PA

Vocals / Motown, Soul

Singer Tammi Terrell joined forces with the immortal Marvin Gaye to create some of the greatest love songs ever to emerge from the Motown hit factory; sadly, their series of classic duets—"Ain't No Mountain High Enough," "Ain't Nothing Like the Real Thing," and "You're All I Need to Get By" among them—came to an abrupt and tragic halt with her premature death. Terrell was born Thomasina Montgomery in Philadelphia on April 29, 1945; after winning a number of local talent contests, by the age of 13 she was regularly opening club dates for acts including Gary "U.S." Bonds and Patti LaBelle & the BlueBelles. In 1961, she was discovered by producer Luther Dixon and signed to Scepter. Credited as Tammy Montgomery, she made her debut with the single "If You See Bill," followed early the next year by "The Voice of Experience." After James Brown caught Terrell's live act, she was signed to his Try Me label, issuing "I Cried" in 1963 and also touring with his live revue. "If I Would Marry You" appeared on Checker a year later, during which time she also studied pre-med at the University of Pennsylvania.

While performing with Jerry Butler in Detroit in 1965, Terrell was spotted by Motown chief Berry Gordy Jr., making her label debut with "I Can't Believe You Love Me." When subsequent outings "Come on and See Me," "This Old Heart of Mine (Is Weak for You)," and "Hold Me Oh My Darling" earned little notice, she was paired with Gaye, who previously recorded duets with Mary Wells and Kim Weston. His chemistry with Terrell was immediate and in 1967, they entered the pop Top 20 with the magnificent "Ain't No Mountain High Enough," the first in a series of lush, sensual hits authored by the husband-and-wife team of Nickolas Ashford & Valerie Simpson. "Your Precious Love" cracked the Top Five a few months later and in 1968, the twosome topped the R&B charts with both "Ain't Nothing Like the Real Thing" and "You're All I Need to Get By." The success of these later hits was nevertheless tempered by Terrell's off-stage travails—after an extended period of severe migraine headaches, in 1967 she collapsed in Gaye's arms while in concert at Virginia's Hampton-Sydney College, and was diagnosed with a brain tumor.

Although the tumor forced Terrell to retire from performing live, she continued to record with Gaye even as her health deteriorated; however, as time went on, Valerie Simpson herself assumed uncredited vocal duties on a number of hits, including 1969's "Good Lovin' Ain't Easy to Come By" and "What You Gave Me." (For several other tracks, Gaye's vocals were added to pre-existing Terrell solo recordings.) In all, Terrell endured eight operations, ultimately resulting in loss of memory and partial paralysis; she finally died in Philadelphia on March 16, 1970. Gaye was so devastated by her decline and eventual passing that he retired from the road for three years; her loss also contributed greatly to the spiritual turmoil which informed his 1971 masterpiece *What's Going On*. At the time of her death, Tammi Terrell was just 24 years old. *—Jason Ankeny*

Irresistible / 1968 / Motown ✦✦✦✦✦

Tammi Terrell had a sexy, hypnotic voice and alluring sensibility that not only made her an ideal partner for Marvin Gaye, but could have resulted in substantial impact as a solo singer. This album includes her finest solo single, "I Can't Believe You Love Me," and some other interesting numbers, although Terrell never received any songs for herself that matched what she did with Gaye. *—Ron Wynn*

Marvin Gaye & Tammi Terrell: Greatest Hits / 1970 / Motown ✦✦✦✦✦

This is actually a greatest hits LP for Marvin Gaye & Tammi Terrell, and there's little more that needs to be said about these numbers—the writing of Ashford & Simpson and the vocals of Gaye and Terrell were an epic collaboration. "Ain't No Mountain High Enough," "Ain't Nothing Like the Real Thing," "If This World Were Mine," and the list continues, classics each and every one. *—Ron Wynn*

The Story of Tammi Terrell / 1999 / Marginal ✦✦✦✦✦

This is a great import of Thomasina Montgomery (Tammi Terrell) sides. Included here are early recordings such as "Sinners Devotion" with the Shirelles on background vocals, "It's Mine" with a group called the Voice of Experience, and the three recorded on one of James Brown's labels: "Big John," "If You See Bill," and "I Cried." The collection also contains the best of her solo Motown album with "I Can't Believe You Love Me," "Come on and See Me," "Baby Don't You Worry," and "Tears at the End of a Love Affair." Further highlights are the three B-sides and/or album cuts "Two Can Have a Party," "I Can't Help but Love You," and "This Poor Heart of Mine." Seven duets with Marvin Gaye conclude this outstanding compilation. A whopping 28 songs are more than enough to satisfy the most voracious Tammi Terrell appetite, and the only fault is Marginal's below-standard mastering. *—Andrew Hamilton*

- **Essential Collection** / Aug. 14, 2001 / Spectrum ✦✦✦✦✦

Setting aside *Marvin Gaye & Tammi Terrell's Greatest Hits* and *The Complete Duets* (which anthologizes and collects, respectively) her 1967–1969 material with Marvin Gaye, *The Ultimate Collection* is the best Tammi Terrell retrospective available. Thankfully including just one duet with Gaye, this Spectrum compilation features 17 solo tracks—virtually all the material Terrell recorded at Motown on her own (even a solo version of her duet hit "Two Can Have a Party"). Beginning with her Motown debut "I Can't Believe You Love Me" and "Come on and See Me," her twin R&B hits during 1966, *The Ultimate Collection* proves Tammi Terrell recorded a lot of glorious solo material for Motown. She usually worked with Johnny Bristol and Harvey Fuqua, who made her a stunning alternative to Diana Ross or Martha Reeves with standouts like her cover of the Isleys' "This Old Heart of Mine (Is Weak for You)" or "Tears at the End of a Love Affair." The final song, included presumably just for comparison, is one of her finest Marvin Gaye duets: "Ain't No Mountain High Enough." *—John Bush*

Joe Tex (Joe Arrington Jr.)

b. Aug. 8, 1933, Rogers, TX, **d.** Aug. 13, 1982, Navasota, TX

Vocals / Soul, Funk

Joe Tex made the first Southern soul record that also hit on the pop charts ("Hold What You've Got," in 1965, made number five in *Billboard*). His raspy-voiced, jackleg preacher style also laid some of the most important parts of rap's foundation. He is, arguably, the most underrated of all the '60s soul performers associated with Atlantic Records, although his records were more likely than those of most soul stars to become crossover hits.

Tex was born Joseph Arrington Jr., in Rogers, TX, in 1933, and displayed his vocal talent quickly, first in gospel, then in R&B. By 1954, he'd won a local talent contest and come to New York, where he recorded a variety of derivative (and endlessly repackaged) singles for King, some as a ballad singer, some as a Little Richard-style rocker. Tex's career didn't take off until he began his association with Nashville song publisher Buddy Killen, after Tex wrote James Brown's 1961 song "Baby You're Right." In 1965, Killen took him to Muscle Shoals, not yet a fashionable recording center, and they came up with "Hold What You've Got," which is about as close to a straight R&B ballad as Tex ever came. It was followed by a herd more, most of which made the R&B charts, a few cracking the pop Top 40.

Tex made his mark by preaching over tough hard soul tracks, clowning at some points, swooping into a croon at others. He was perhaps the most rustic and back-country of the soul stars, a role he played to the hilt by using turns of phrase that might have been heard on any ghetto street corner, "One Monkey Don't Stop No Show" the prototype. In 1966, his "I Believe I'm Gonna Make It," an imaginary letter home from Vietnam, became the first big hit directly associated with that war. His biggest hit was "Skinny Legs and All," from a 1967 live album, his rapping pure hokum over deeply funky riffs. "Skinny Legs" might have served as a template for all the raucous, ribald hip-hop hits of pop's future. After "Skinny Legs," Tex had nothing but minor hits for five years until "I Gotcha" took off, a grittier twist on the funk that was becoming disco. He was too down-home for the slickness of the disco era, or so it would have seemed, yet in 1977, he adapted a dance craze, the Bump, and came up with the hilarious "Ain't Gonna Bump No More (With No Big Fat Woman)," his last Top Ten R&B hit, which also crossed over to number 12 on the pop chart.

In the early '70s, Tex converted to Islam and in 1972 changed his offstage name to Joseph Hazziez. He spent much of the time after "Ain't Gonna Bump" on his Texas farm, although he did join together with Wilson Pickett, Ben E. King, and Don Covay for a reformed version of the Soul Clan in 1980. He died of a heart attack in 1982, only 49 years old. Killen, King, Covay, Pickett, and the great songwriter Percy Mayfield served as pallbearers. *—Dave Marsh*

Hold on to What You've Got / Jan. 1965 / Atlantic ✦✦✦✦

For the most part, this early long-player from Joe Tex favors the goofier side of his musical personality rather than the home-truth moral lessons which often dominated much of his work. While "One Monkey Don't Stop No Show," "You Better Get It" and the title tune all offer heartfelt advice on love and life, the Caribbean-flavored "I'm Not Going to Work Today" and the Roger Miller-turned-hawk anthem "Are We Ready" both aim squarely for the funny bone, as does the exasperated "You Can Stay," a rant against noisy neighbors, while the slinky "You've Got What It Takes" confronts a seriously sexy woman with an appreciative smile. Of course, being the country boy that he was at heart, Joe Tex's comic numbers are still seasoned with friendly advice on living a better life, but Tex's warm, emphatic delivery and the easy-going but potently soulful accompaniment ensures that Tex doesn't sound preachy so much as he recalls a neighbor down the way ready to offer some helpful words to a friend in need. A consistently enjoyable album from one of the most distinctive artists of Southern soul. *—Mark Deming*

I've Got to Do a Little Better / 1966 / Atlantic ✦✦✦

Another rock-solid album from Joe Tex, *I've Got to Do a Little Better* was his third full-length release of 1966, but Tex showed no signs of slowing down or losing his breath on these twelve songs. *I've Got to Do a Little Bit Better* revisits Tex's traditional themes, namely holding on to your man (or woman) ("A Woman Sees a Hard Time (When Her Man Is Gone)," "S.Y.S.L.J.F.M. (The Letter Song)"), playing fair with others ("Lying's Just a Habit, John" and the title tune), and being true to yourself ("Papa Was, Too," which bears more than a passing resemblance to the Otis Redding/Carla Thomas hit "Tramp"), while "I Believe I'm Gonna Make It" is one of the strangest R&B tunes to surface concerning the war in Vietnam (in which Joe, after getting a letter from his baby, is so filled with love and patriotic fervor that he leaps from his foxhole to gun down several Vietnamese). Buddy Killen's production is admirably malleable, knowing when to go for subtlety and when to rave on, and Tex's rich and passionate tenor rings out clear and true on each and every tune. One of the very best albums of Tex's Southern soul period, *I've Got to Do a Little Bit Better* suggests the kind of care and careful thought that rarely went into LPs of the period, and it's well worth seeking out for fans. *—Mark Deming*

The Love You Save / 1966 / Atlantic ✦✦✦

Joe Tex was at the top of his game as the down-home philosopher of Southern soul when he cut *The Love You Save*, one of three (!) albums Tex would release in 1966. Tex's warm and passionate tenor is in superb form on these tunes, and his songs, which offer plenty of advice on keeping your relationship in good shape ("Build Your Love (On a Solid Foundation)"), keeping up with the Joneses ("Funny Bone"), understanding what you want out of life ("I'm a Man"), and various other topics of importance, are solid, funny, and bear the sing of truth. Buddy Killen's production is the perfect marriage of Deep South vibe and East Coast polish, and all twelve songs hit the bullseye (including an idiosyncratic but beautifully executed cover of "Heartbreak Hotel." Great stuff that any fan of Southern soul should have on their want list. *—Mark Deming*

The New Boss / 1966 / Atlantic ♦♦♦♦♦

While he was one of the leading lights of the Southern soul scene of the 1960s, Joe Tex never made a secret of his fondness for country music, and on his 1966 set *The New Boss,* Tex allowed his C&W influences to shine more brightly than usual, covering Roger Miller's "King of the Road" and Bobby Bare's "Detroit City" in a style that was faithful to the sound and feel of the originals while adding a soulful edge all his own to the tunes. And while that was the end of the C&W covers on *The New Boss,* they also fit right in alongside the very Southern preachments of "A Woman (Can Change a Man)" and "Don't Make Your Children Pay," though "C.C. Rider," "Stop, Look and Listen" and "What in the World" are also on hand for those looking for more dance-friendly fare. As usual, Tex's warm and incisive vocals cut to the emotional core of these songs in a way that's honest, human and thoroughly compelling, and the production, subtle and supportive without being intrusive, is just what the material called for. At eleven tracks, *The New Boss* is a bit light in the value-for-money department, but Joe Tex's performances ensure that what's here is choice. *—Mark Deming*

Greatest Hits / 1967 / Curb ♦♦♦

Here is an early-'90s anthology that contains most of Joe Tex's significant hits. They're remastered in a rather dry fashion, but if you didn't have them already, it's worth getting, since there hasn't yet been a comprehensive Joe Tex box set and probably won't be anytime soon. *—Ron Wynn*

Live and Lively / Feb. 1968 / Atlantic ♦♦♦♦♦

This is a fantastic reproduction of a 1968 show—who knows how much overdubbing was done, and when the feel is this spontaneous and funky, who cares? He tears up stuff like "Get Out of My Life, Woman," "Love is a Hurtin' Thing," and even "That's Life." But the real meat is in his hits: "Skinny Legs and All" is a true climax, but only because part of what it follows is "A Woman's Hands," "Papa Was, Too," and other originals, all of them topping the standards. Arguably the definitive Joe Tex document. (The liner notes, by a St. Louis DJ, are among the worst in even the shabby history of '60s R&B notes, but that just makes them funnier.) *—Dave Marsh*

Soul Country / Jul. 1968 / Atlantic ♦♦♦

Here is a 1968 set recorded in Memphis and Nashville. It features only one Tex original, "I'll Never Do Wrong." The rest are remakes of period hits: "Ode to Billie Joe" and "Skip a Rope" are inspired selections, "Funny How Time Slips Away" one of his greats, "Dark End of the Street" inevitable, Roger Miller's "Engine Engine Number Nine" and the budding standard "Green Green Grass of Home" worth trying. But Joe Tex singing "By the Time I Get to Phoenix" and "Honey"? Dated barely begins to describe it. *—Dave Marsh*

Happy Soul / 1969 / Atlantic ♦♦♦♦

Here is generic Joe Tex in Memphis from 1969. But there's still an awful lot of funky music here, and a storehouse of folksy sagacity ("Go Home and Do It," "Take the Fifth Amendment," "Keep the One You've Got") that deserved preservation. "You Need Me Baby" and "That's Your Baby" are the hits. *—Dave Marsh*

Buying a Book / 1969 / Atlantic ♦♦♦♦♦

This is a 1969 Memphis session that produced a big hit from the title track's folk wisdom, a truly hilarious moment in "It Ain't Sanitary," and vintage Tex in "Grandma Mary," "Get Your Lies Together," and "The Same Things You Did to Get Me." Funny, funky, and as deep as it wants to be. *—Dave Marsh*

Joe Tex With Strings and Things / 1970 / Atlantic ♦♦♦♦

The title has all the earmarks of a disaster but the contents mainly serve to demonstrate how indomitable Tex was. "You're Right, Ray Charles" is classic Tex, and "(When Johnny Comes Marching Home Again) I Can't See You No More" isn't far behind. Maybe it's just that in 1970 no combination of a great singer and the rhythm section assembled at American Studios in Memphis could do wrong. *—Dave Marsh*

From the Roots Came the Rapper / 1972 / Atlantic ♦♦♦♦♦

This has a prescient title, and an accurate one. This is both rootsy and, in its use of rhythmic dialogue (not all that uncommon for Tex, of course), a prophecy of hip-hop to come, especially the Southern blend of the turn of the century. *—Dave Marsh*

I Gotcha / 1972 / Dial ♦♦♦♦

The world was beginning to wake up to funk as a basic musical language, and one result was that the title track and "You Said a Bad Word" from this 1972 album became huge hits in both R&B and pop. What did the pop audience make of album tracks like "Bad Feet," let alone "God of Love"? Probably not as much as it could have, but these days, it sounds like a miraculous synthesis of gospel into the onrushing craziness of music's maddest decade. *—Dave Marsh*

Spill the Beans / 1972 / Dial ♦♦♦

Another Man's Woman / 1977 / Powerpak ♦♦♦

Bumps & Bruises / 1977 / Epic ♦♦♦

For one shining moment, disco and funk came together to produce a last big hit for Joe Tex, who was more than worthy of it. Trivial next to his greatest material, but he loved that big fat woman at least as much as the one with the scrawny legs, and it shows through, which is all fans of the form will ask. *—Dave Marsh*

Rub Down / 1978 / Epic ♦♦♦

This is a desperate attempt to let the rhythm dominate the vocalist. In their desperation to connect with a vastly changed R&B marketplace, these are the only embarrassing lyrics Tex ever sang. *—Dave Marsh*

He Who Is Without Funk Cast the First Stone / 1979 / Dial ♦♦♦

Richard Pryor meets P-Funk, down-home. Tex's still telling the most basic truths: "Finger Popped Myself into the Poor House" and "Who Gave Birth to the Funk" speak for all the soul men virtually wiped out by 1978, when disco seemed to rein over all (so much so that by now Dial was distributed by the Miami dance label TK). The remake of "Hold What You've Got" is horrid, but "Music Ain't Got No Color" *is* the truth. *—Dave Marsh*

London Collector: Super Soul / 1979 / London ♦♦♦

A better anthology than some of the low-budget, slipshod efforts that have been trotted out in his name. This contains both Tex's novelty material and some of his finest country/soul hits. Its only drawback is availability; this will only be in the bigger stores, while the Rhino and an Ichiban package have wider distribution, and the Rhino slightly superior sound. *—Ron Wynn*

Hold On! It's Joe Tex / 1983 / Checker ♦♦♦♦

Early pre-Dial Records sides recorded on Anna and Chess Records that include Tex's two-part rendition of "All I Could Do Was Cry," and his answer to Jerry Butler's "He Will Break Your Heart," "I'll Never Break Your Heart." You also get an earful of Joe's early gems like "Baby You're Right," "You Keep Her," and "Ain't I A Mess." *—Andrew Hamilton*

I Believe I'm Gonna Make It: The Best of Joe Tex / 1988 / Rhino ♦♦♦♦♦

This is first-rate country-soul, sung with the just the right blend of whimsy, worry, and relief. Joe Tex was routinely turning out excellent cuts throughout the mid-'60s, but it wasn't until his novelty/disco tunes of the mid-'70s that he finally attained any widespread recognition. *—Ron Wynn*

Show Me: The Hits . . . & More / Oct. 12, 1992 / Ichiban ♦♦♦♦

While he could spin a mean yarn, Tex was also a mournful, moving vocalist whose convincing delivery on country-soul ballads was sorely underrated. This 18-track collection includes some of Tex's biggest hits, fine covers of "Dark End of the Street" and "You're Right," plus several Tex originals such as "I Want to Do Everything For You," "Same Old Soup," and "King Thaddeus." While there are some notable and surprising exclusions, it's a representative Tex collection, but isn't as complete as Rhino's single-disc anthology from 1988. *—Ron Wynn*

Golden Classics / 1993 / Collectables ♦♦♦♦♦

It's cursorily packaged and randomly organized, but there are two dozen slabs of Tex's soul here, a slightly off-kilter selection that finds room for "Don't Make Your Children Pay," "Grandma Mary," but omits no important hit except "Ain't Gonna Bump No More." The notes are not extensive but they are a good stylistic history of the music. *—Dave Marsh*

Bump to the Funk / Apr. 25, 1995 / Charly ♦♦♦♦

Bump to the Funk is an informative and wide-reaching compilation of one of R&B's most underrated talents. Unlike other compilations, *Bump to the Funk* thankfully shows Tex for the nut he could be. The tracks "Anything You Wanna Know," "You Need Me Baby," and "We Can't Sit Down" display his singular wit juxtaposed to the classic Fame/Muscle Shoals sound. The loose-limbed "You're Right, Ray Charles" has Tex all but detailing his musical shift as he sang "I'm going to Memphis y'all/get me a band/find me a funky bass player/funky drummer and a good guitar player." *Bump to the Funk* subsequently and skillfully compiles some of Tex's most potent dance tracks and a few curious misses. Innovative tracks like "Give the Baby What She Wants," "You Said a Bad Word," and the million-seller "I Gotcha" proves that Tex was only second to James Brown at cutting pure Southern tracks that were challenging, extremely danceable, and, in Tex's case, increasingly eccentric. The single version of "Ain't Gonna Bump No More (With No Big Fat Woman)" is the best joke he never wrote and still retains it's humor and charm. This set also includes the hilarious B-side "I Mess Up Everything I Get Me Hands On," which has Tex calling himself "the world's biggest goof-off" and taking the drastic step of finding a surgeon to cut his hands "off down to the wrist bone." *Bump to the Funk* also includes a few of Tex's later tracks. "Who Gave Birth to the Funk" and "Stick Your Key In (And Start Your Car)" have Tex and producer Buddy Killen fresh out of jokes and convincing dance patterns. Those fans who like to hear a lot of Tex's somewhat odd tracks won't be let down with this compilation. *—Jason Elias*

The Very Best of Joe Tex / Nov. 19, 1996 / Rhino ♦♦♦♦♦

An old friend of mine once said he considered listening to Joe Tex a viable alternative to seeing a marriage counselor; it was his opinion if you sat down with Joe's records and heeded his advice on keeping a happy home, chances were good you'd end up doing the right thing. And while Joe Tex had a great voice (a rich tenor whose openness and warmth tended to belie its strength and agility) and cut some of the most engaging Southern soul sides of the 1960s (as well as some potent '70s funk), what really set him apart were his songs, which with humor, charm and down-home horse sense offered plenty of hard-won advice on dealing with the ups and downs of life and love. While the albums Tex cut for Atlantic in the 1960s are consistently strong and worth hearing, many are not widely available in the U. S.; fortunately, this 16-cut sampler brings together many of biggest and most memorable hits, including "Skinny Legs And All," "You Got What It Takes," "The Love You Save (May Be Your Own)," and "S.Y.S.L.J.F.M. (The Letter Song)," as well as a few of his best latter-day dance tracks, such as "I Gotcha" and the memorably titled "Ain't Gonna Bump No More (With No Big Fat Woman)." *The Very Best of Joe Tex* is a fine introduction to an artist well worth your attention; it's better than watching *Dr. Phil,* and you can dance to it, too! *—Mark Deming*

• **25 All Time Greatest Hits** / Mar. 21, 2000 / Varese ♦♦♦♦♦
If you're set on having the best available Joe Tex CD anthology and you already have the 1996 16-track Rhino comp *The Very Best of Joe Tex*, it might vex you to learn that all 16 of those songs are on this 25-song anthology, making the Rhino disc redundant should you decide to upgrade. If you *don't* have a Joe Tex CD anthology yet, though, you're in luck, as this definitely supersedes others as the greatest-hits collection of choice. All but one of these songs (the 1965 B-side "Don't Let Your Left Hand Know") was a chart single, and aside from the 1977 hit "Ain't Gonna Bump No More (With No Big Fat Woman)," all are from his prime 1965-1972 period. Of the songs not on the Rhino disc, highlights are the 1965 slowies "You Better Get It" and "A Woman Can Change a Man," and the aforementioned "Don't Let Your Left Hand Know," an odd soul-pop tune with folky guitars and harmonies straight off a Rooftop Singers record. Also, "A Woman's Hands" (a small 1967 hit) is a good example of Tex's preaching style. Then there's 1968's "You Need Me Baby," in which Tex disses a stud who was the best athlete in town and left to become a big success, maintaining that he [Tex] is still a better catch for the woman whom the stud left behind, since he'll love her children. Heck, all of the songs not on the Rhino disc are worthwhile additions. There's no telling if this will remain the definitive Tex compilation if his catalog continues to get passed around, but there's a good chance that it won't be surpassed. *—Richie Unterberger*

Greatest Hits / Aug. 22, 2000 / 7-N ♦♦♦

Oh Boy Classics Presents Joe Tex / Jun. 26, 2001 / Oh Boy ♦♦♦♦
Here are 14 fundamental hits, mainly from the Atlantic soul period, starting with "Hold What You've Got" and with a brief diversion to the disco-funk of "I Gotcha." This is Tex as pared down to his essence as you'll find. Notes are by the great Memphis producer/songwriter Chips Moman, but, unfortunately, they're just one paragraph long. *—Dave Marsh*

From the Roots Came the Rapper [Expanded] / 2002 / Kent ♦♦♦
The first ten tracks of this CD comprised the totality of Tex's 1971 Atlantic LP *From the Roots Came the Rapper*. This isn't exactly a straight reissue of that record, though, since it tacks on ten additional tracks recorded in the early '70s. The era this material represents wasn't an artistic or commercial high-water mark in Tex's career, although it's OK. Like his late-'60s sides, it bridges smooth soul with funk and anticipates rap, though it's a little lusher than his slightly earlier stuff. From *From the Roots Came the Rapper* itself, a highlight is the epic eight-minute version of "Oh Me Oh My (I'm a Fool for You Baby)," which naturally includes some extended spoken sections. That and the similarly constructed 11-minute cover of "I'll Never Fall in Love Again" make you wonder whether there was some influence traveling back and forth between Tex and Isaac Hayes. The rest of that LP had fair, and not great, good-natured yet earthy soul with a bit more of a slick Northern production influence than his '60s records. Tex himself, surprisingly, wrote just one of the tunes, though the other writers included stalwarts Jerry Williams Jr. (aka Swamp Dogg) ("The Baby Is Mine") and Don Covay ("I Can Do It Better"). The ten additional bonus tracks appeared on early-'70s Dial singles and the LPs *I Gotcha* and *JT Spills the Beans*, with one of them ("Lesley") previously unreleased; 1975's "Under Your Powerful Love" is the only cut dating from after 1972, and its early disco feel makes it a little out of place. The early-'70s tracks are OK, characteristic soul-gospel-funk Tex. But there's a sense that he's going over ground he tilled several times before, and not with the same sense of excitement as the first or second time around. The funk-rap flavor gets tangiest on the 1972 single "King Thaddeus." *—Richie Unterberger*

The Complete Dial Recordings, Vol. 4: Happy Soul/Buying a Book / May 21, 2002 / RPM ♦♦♦♦

The Complete Dial Recordings, Vol. 3: Live and Lively/Soul Country / May 21, 2002 / RPM ♦♦♦♦

Carla Thomas

b. Dec. 21, 1942, Memphis, TN
Vocals / Memphis Soul, Southern Soul, Soul
In the glorious decade and a half of sound that was Stax in the '60s and early '70s, Carla Thomas was the Queen of Memphis Soul. She was born in Memphis in 1942, and 18 years later she recorded a duet with her father Rufus Thomas, giving the fledgling Satellite label its first taste of success with the regional hit "Cause I Love You." As her 18th birthday drew nigh, she cut her first solo single, the teen ballad "Gee Whiz (Look at His Eyes)." Written a few years earlier and rejected by Vee-Jay in Chicago, it gave Satellite its first national hit, breaking the Top Ten mark on both the R&B and pop charts. Shortly thereafter Satellite became Stax, and Carla proceeded to claw her way onto the national charts another 22 times with such immortal slices of soul as her answer song to Sam Cooke, "I'll Bring It on Home to You," as well as "Let Me Be Good to You," "B-A-B-Y," "Tramp" (with Otis Redding), and "I Like What You're Doing to Me." Carla released six solo albums and, with Redding, one duet album on Stax between 1961 and 1971. *—Rob Bowman*

Gee Whiz / 1961 / Atlantic ♦♦♦
Thomas' first album was built around the huge title hit, and also included her follow-up single, "A Love of My Own," which reached the R&B Top 20, although it wasn't nearly as popular as "Gee Whiz (Look at His Eyes)." The record is far more pop-oriented than the sound for which Stax would become known, with both the material and the arrangements showing substantial influences from pop standards, doo wop, and even (particularly in the songs with backup vocals by the Anita Kerr Singers) Nashville country. That doesn't make it a bad record at all, just not one that listeners familiar with the Stax sound, or even Thomas' later Stax records, might expect. Though Thomas herself wrote some of the songs, about half of the tracks are covers of pop standards ("(I'm Afraid) The Masquerade Is Over") and still-recent rock/R&B hits like the Drifters' "Dance With Me" and "Fools Fall in Love" and the Five Satins' "To the Aisle." Also onboard is a composition by Carla's dad, Rufus Thomas, and a song and a half by famed Memphis producer Chips Moman, who produced five of the tracks. [The 2002 CD reissue adds an alternate version of "Promises."] *—Richie Unterberger*

Carla / 1966 / Rhino ♦♦♦♦♦
Paired with Stax writing whiz-kids Isaac Hayes & David Porter, Thomas had her greatest chart run, beginning with the hit "B-A-B-Y" and continuing with "Let Me Be Good to You." Both of those appear here, alongside evocative slabs of country-soul in covers of Hank Williams' "I'm So Lonesome I Could Cry" and Patsy Cline's "I Fall to Pieces." For good measure, Thomas also tries her hand at the blues with covers of Howlin' Wolf's "Little Red Rooster" and Jimmy Reed's "Baby What You Want Me to Do?" *—Rob Bowman*

Comfort Me / 1966 / Rhino ♦♦♦♦♦
A collection of 12 tracks recorded over a year and a half, *Comfort Me* showcases Thomas in the midst of the developed Stax sound. Backed by Booker T. and the MG's and the Mar-Key horns, Thomas turns in fine covers of Baby Washington's "Move on Drifter," and the Marvelettes' "Forever," the Shirelles' "Will You Love Me Tomorrow?," the Everly Brothers' "Let It Be Me," Jackie DeShannon's "What the World Needs Now," the Toys' "Lover's Concerto," and Barbara Mason's "Yes I'm Ready," coupled with a number of efforts by Thomas herself, Steve Cropper, and Eddie Floyd. The highlight is the Cropper-Floyd title cut, with utterly gorgeous backing by Gladys Knight & the Pips. *—Rob Bowman*

The Best of Carla Thomas / 1969 / Atlantic ♦♦♦♦♦

The Queen Alone / 1969 / Rhino ♦♦♦♦♦
Carla Thomas was more than deserving of her title "The Queen of Memphis Soul," but she was hardly oblivious to the sleeker, more pop-influenced sweet soul and uptown soul coming out of Detroit, Philadelphia and Chicago. One of her strongest albums, *The Queen Alone* isn't the work of someone who took a Memphis-only approach, but of someone who was well aware of what Gladys Knight, Dionne Warwick, Martha Reeves and others were up to. What's surprising is the fact that this album (reissued on CD in 1992) contains only two hits: the playful "Something Good (Is Going to Happen to You)," which made it to number 29 on *Billboard*'s soul singles chart, and the idealistic, gospel-influenced ballad and number-11 R&B single "I'll Always Have Faith in You." Songs ranging from the sweet and vulnerable "I Want to Be Your Baby" to the remorseful "All I See Is You" and the pessimistic "Any Day Now" (a song co-written by Burt Bacharach) weren't singles, but it wasn't for a lack of heartfelt singing. Drawing on both Southern and Northern soul, *Queen* is a pleasant reminder that they were equally attractive options. *—Alex Henderson*

Memphis Queen / May 1969 / Stax ♦♦♦
Half recorded in Memphis with the usual stellar Stax crew and half recorded in New York with local session musicians (all overdubbed in Detroit), *Memphis Queen* finds Thomas and the Stax label in transition. Motown alumnus Don Davis handled production, draping many cuts in large, lush orchestral settings. "I Like What You're Doing (To Me)" was a Top Ten R&B hit, and three other tracks had brief chart runs. [In 1997, this was reissued on a single-disc CD that also included her 1971 album *Love Means*.] *—Rob Bowman*

Love Means Carla Thomas / 1971 / Stax ♦♦♦
Thomas had gone in a Memphis-meets-Motown direction on her previous album (*Memphis Queen*), and *Love Means* continued in that vein, with much more pop-conscious production (mostly courtesy of her keyboardist brother Marvell) and material that sometimes recalled Diana Ross. Thomas herself has noted that "we wanted a good listening album to send to [people like] Johnny Carson." While these sound like bad omens, in the event it's a pretty good pop-soul LP, coming off like Diana Ross with more grit. There weren't any obvious singles, which helped accelerate her commercial downfall at Stax, though one of the worst tracks—"You've Got a Cushion to Fall On," a dated stand-by-your-man piece—was a small hit. [In 1997, this was reissued on a single-disc CD that also included her 1969 album *Memphis Queen*.] *—Richie Unterberger*

Chronicle: Their Greatest Stax Hits / 1979 / Stax ♦♦♦♦
Rufus & Carla Thomas helped launch the Stax era, both individually and as a team. Thomas bought his daughter to Stax in the hopes of finding suitable material, and she soon had "Gee Whiz" soaring to the top. Had Carla chosen to tour extensively, she might have been a great star in Aretha Franklin's class; she sang with equal ferocity and power during this period. Rufus Thomas parlayed his dance/novelty tracks into international superstardom, but he was also a fine straight soul vocalist. This album splits its bill between the two, offering each a side to showcase their hits. *—Ron Wynn*

Hidden Gems / 1992 / Stax ♦♦♦

• **Gee Whiz: The Best of Carla Thomas** / Jul. 19, 1994 / Rhino ♦♦♦♦♦
Gee Whiz: The Best of Carla Thomas is a wonderful 22-track collection of her seminal recordings for Atlantic and Stax, featuring all of her biggest hits—"Gee Whiz," "I'll Bring It Home to You," "B-A-B-Y," "Tramp," "I Like What You're Doing (To Me)"—as well as a terrific selection of lesser-known singles and album tracks. *—Stephen Thomas Erlewine*

Sugar / Sep. 30, 1994 / Stax ♦♦♦
A collection of odds and ends from the late '60s and early '70s, including some obscure Stax singles, duets with Pervis Staples and Johnnie Taylor, and three live numbers from the *Wattstax* soundtrack. It's not the first (or second) Carla Thomas collection you should pick up, but it's solid material. Donny Hathaway and Chips Moman each produced a couple of the singles spotlighted here (A-sides and B-sides are included), adding moderately ambitious variations on the standard Stax sound. *—Richie Unterberger*

You Thrill My Soul / Sep. 5, 1995 / Stax ♦♦♦
Color this: collectors item. *You Thrill My Soul* features early female and girl group recordings originally released on Stax Records. Only Carla Thomas emerged from these artists as a hit maker, but unfortunately–for casual fans–none of them are included. Wendy Rene

(the Drapels) warbles like Frankie Lymon on a few non-sellers. Deanie Parker, who later hit somewhat as a songwriter, not a singer, does a few tracks. Barbara Stephens, a talented singer, never busted a grape and vanished after these early efforts bricked. The Tonettes, comprised of Oscar Toney Jr.'s three sisters, held on a bit longer as the Charmels but with little success. For a costly CD, there's not a hit among its 24 tracks, but there are enough interesting selections to appease the most ardent soul music lover, including some early Chips Moman stuff, who left Stax before the serious cooking began. *—Andrew Hamilton*

Evelyn Thomas

b. 1953, Chicago, IL

Vocals / House, Hi-NRG, Disco, Dance-Pop

Evelyn Thomas was discovered in her hometown of Chicago, IL, by Ian Levine in 1975. Levine had come to America to discover talent for his newly formed Voltafine Production Company. His goal was to record American soul singers and lease the masters to major recording companies. Thomas, an ex-gospel singer, sung in a plain, unemotional voice that masked her ethnicity; Thomas is a black singer who sounds white, by design or by chance. Impressed by her voice and willingness, Levine cut some tracks and secured a deal for her with 20th Century Records. During this period, Levine was a constant victim of rip-offs and threats, but persevered to realize his dream, often having to call up friends and relatives for loans via Western Union for payoffs and to complete sessions. Ian Levine and Danny Leake produced Thomas' first 45 single, "Weak Spot," which was arranged by Paul Wilson and soon entered the U.K.'s Top 50.

The success of Thomas' record and others prompted Voltafine to fly their American artists to England to appear on *Top of the Pops*, in hopes of breaking the recordings on Britain's pop charts. Thomas came over with fellow Chicagoans and Voltafine artists Barbara Pennington and L.J. Johnson. The appearances went well but the records never crossed, nor did they do anything in the States. Still, "Weak Spot" sold 70,000 copies, pretty good for a debut. After returning to Chicago, the threesome was soon flown back to England to tour the Northern soul clubs; this event was promoted by Terry King and was called the Chicago Soul Review. 20th Century welcomed Thomas with open arms and did all they could to help her while she was in England. Thomas went over well at the clubs, being blessed with a perpetual smile and a bluesy voice that Levine and Leake could transform to gutless pop/disco in a New York minute. Financially, the tour was a failure, drawing well in the northern areas but failing miserably in London proper.

"Doomsday," Thomas' follow-up, didn't do as well as her debut, entering the chart and dropping out, only to re-enter again for a pit stop before disappearing completely; it sold less than half of what "Weak Spot" did. Back in the studios, Voltafine cut the Gloria Gaynor-influenced "Love Is Not Just an Illusion" and "My Head's in the Stars" for Thomas. Then came problems with an ex-manager who informed Levine that he was Thomas' manager under contract, and demanded that Thomas' royalties and contracts go through him. Levine insisted he had a valid contract, that is, until he was taken on a scary car ride in a Mercedes with Thomas' ex-manager, who now wanted 2,000 dollars for compensation. After some scurrying around and many phone calls, the ex-manager was satisfied and Thomas was again Levine's artist.

Over the years, Thomas proved to be one of Levine's most prolific artists. To date, five CDs have resulted from the chance union of this Brit and American: *The Best of Evelyn Thomas, Have a Little Faith in Me, High Energy, I Wanna Make It on My Own*, and *Standing at the Crossroads*. Thomas' sweet, innocent voice can also be heard on some Redemption tracks when the group was billed as Redemption Featuring Evelyn Thomas, and her singles are included on many compilation CDs. A pretty good run for an American singer who never had a hit or significant record in her own country. *—Andrew Hamilton*

I Wanna Make It on My Own / 1979 / Casablanca ♦♦♦

Merely five tracks long, Chicago crooner Evelyn Thomas' debut "album" is a thoroughly pleasant if not entirely remarkable effort. By this point, the singer had scored several Top 40 U.K. hits in the Northern soul vein; for *I Wanna Make It on My Own*, that focus was maintained—but disco elements were added for commercial measure. But it's the simultaneously effervescent and mellow horn and string arrangements that set the songs apart from other typical dancefloor fodder. It's easy to relax or groove to "It's the Magic of Your Touch," especially with the distinctive stamp of Thomas' eager, down to earth vocal approach and the background singers' equally spirited musings. Meanwhile, "Back to Reality" is sublimely funky, and the title cut sets themes of freedom and imprisonment in love to a chirpy, pre-Hi-NRG background. Melodically, though, the songs aren't nearly as consistent and engaging as those found on the follow-up set, *Have a Little Faith in Me*. Tracks on the latter, such as "Love's Not Just an Illusion" and "My Head's in the Stars," have an energy that *I Wanna Make It on My Own* lacks. Here, the sound is less discernible from a handful of other projects crafted by producer Ian Levine around the same time—for artists such as Barbara Pennington, L.J. Johnson, and Doris Jones. *—Justin M. Kantor*

Have a Little Faith in Me / 1979 / Hot Productions ♦♦♦♦♦

With a robust set of pipes, dance diva Evelyn Thomas offered a wealth of bona fide disco and Hi-NRG jammers from the mid-'70s through the mid-'90s. On this second full-length effort originally released on Avi in 1979, she is in her prime. The kinetic title cut is an all-out party via its vibrant vocal melodies and arrangements, perky strings, fluid, Latin-tinged percussion, and insinuating chord changes. Thomas' delayed attacks and anticipation are colorful here, too, as they are on the unique and beautiful "Love's Not Just an Illusion" and "My Head's in the Stars." Originally a four-cut album (all of the songs being in the six-and-a-half to eight-and-a-half-minute range), Hot Productions added five non-album tracks to its 1996 CD release of *Have a Little Faith in Me*. The singer's first two singles, "Weak Spot" and "Doomsday" (from 1975 and 1976, respectively), are included, as well as "Summer on the Beach," "Love in the First Degree," and the mostly instrumental "Sleaze." With the exception of the monotonous moaning and percussion of "Sleaze," it's an invigorating listen throughout. *—Justin Kantor*

High Energy / 1984 / Record Shack ♦♦

Standing at the Crossroads / 1987 / Hot Productions ♦♦♦

● **The Best of Evelyn Thomas** / 1991 / Hot Productions ♦♦♦♦♦

The Best of Evelyn Thomas contains 13 songs, including her big hit "High Energy," as well as cult favorites like "How Many Hearts," "Masquerade," "Heartless," "Love in the First Degree," "No Win Situation," "Weak Spot," "Doomsday" and "Have a Little Faith in Me." *—Stephen Thomas Erlewine*

Irma Thomas

b. Feb. 18, 1941, Ponchatoula, LA

Vocals / New Orleans R&B, Soul, Contemporary Gospel

Radiating an outgoing joy that's inevitably at the heart of her infectious vocal delivery, Irma Thomas has no rivals as the Soul Queen of New Orleans. Working at a Crescent City nightery as a waitress in 1959, Thomas sat in one night with Tommy Ridgley's band and made such a favorable impression that the veteran bandleader hustled her into the studio shortly thereafter to wax her first hit for the Ron label, the driving "Don't Mess With My Man." She joined forces with producer Allen Toussaint to make some of her most moving outings for Minit Records during the early '60s, notably "It's Raining," "Ruler of My Heart," and "Cry On," before venturing to the West Coast, where she cut both her biggest seller, the lushly produced "Wish Someone Would Care," and her best-known song, the original "Time Is on My Side"—and she's still bitter enough about the Rolling Stones' cover stealing her thunder to discourage requests for the tune.

The highly adaptable chanteuse also made some sizzling soul at Rich Hall's Muscle Shoals studio for Chess in the summer of 1967 before cooling off for a while during the '70s. But she's back now, as radiant as ever—and for convincing proof, listen to her buoyant 1990 concert performance on Rounder, *Live! Simply the Best*. Now that's truth in packaging! Thomas finally fulfilled a lifelong ambition in 1993 by recording her first gospel release. *Walk Around Heaven* was as magnificently sung and emotionally convincing as any of her classic New Orleans soul cuts. Thomas followed the album in 1997 with *The Story of My Life*, which featured several songs written by Dan Penn. She continued this trend with 2000's *My Heart's in Memphis: The Songs of Dan Penn*. *—Bill Dahl*

Wish Someone Would Care / 1964 / Imperial ♦♦♦♦♦

Irma Thomas has been New Orleans' reigning soul queen since the early '60s, and this landmark album was her most stunning and complete session. It didn't make her a national star, but it showed vulnerability as captivating as lust, anger or pain. Thomas' voice seemed deliberately frail at times, but she made "Time Is on My Side" and "I Wish Someone Would Care" remarkable triumphs. There were many other fine songs, such as "I Need Your Love So Bad," "Please Send Me Someone to Love" and "Break-A-Way." It remains one of the greatest soul albums ever recorded. *—Ron Wynn*

Take a Look / 1968 / Imperial ♦♦♦

The songs from Irma Thomas' Imperial sessions are timeless and magnificent; they've also been constantly reissued and are available all over the place. That reduces the value of this anthology, one of two that were issued featuring her Imperial cuts. Every significant song from both of these releases has subsequently been compiled and issued on the EMI domestic CD package. *—Ron Wynn*

Safe With Me / May 1981 / Paula ♦

Break-A-Way: The Best of Irma Thomas / 1986 / EMI America ♦♦♦♦♦

New Orleans' finest female vocalist has been featured on several anthologies. This was one of the better domestic packages of its era, containing her finest material from the early and mid-'60s, such as the majestic "It's Raining," "Time Is on My Side, " and "I Wish Someone Would Care." If you haven't already gotten these, you're seriously deficient, but at least you can get them at a reasonable price. The mastering is excellent. *—Ron Wynn*

The New Rules / 1986 / Rounder ♦♦♦

The Way I Feel / 1988 / Rounder ♦♦♦♦♦

Irma Thomas deserves hits and wider exposure more than almost any other R&B vocalist you could name. While the material on this album was uneven, she retained her credibility regardless. It took real guts to cover "Dancing in the Street" and "Baby I Love You," and even more talent not to be subsumed by their history. She's vibrant on "Old Records," hard-hitting on "You Don't Know Nothin' About Love" and poignant on "Sorry Wrong Number," "Sit Down and Cry" and "I'll Take Care of You." *—Ron Wynn*

Something Good: Muscle Shoals / 1990 / Chess ♦♦♦♦♦

Thomas' brief liaison with Chess in 1967 saw her, like labelmates Laura Lee and Etta James, record in Muscle Shoals' Fame studios to tap into the Southern/deep soul grooves that were one of the hottest tickets in soul music at the time. Commercially, these sessions (all recorded in June and July of 1967) weren't a success. It's also fair to say that they don't rate as her finest work of the '60s; her early New Orleans sessions, along with her pop/rock sides of the mid-'60s, featured both stronger material and more suitable accompaniment. That's hardly a knock, though; these were solid soul performances paced by Thomas' habitual excellent, committed vocals. But there's a bit of a generic Stax/Volt feel, and not much of the material (which features several compositions by Otis Redding and the Spooner Oldham-Dan Penn team) leaps out and grabs you. It's still worth finding if you're an Irma fan, with 14 tracks that include several Chess singles and nine songs recorded for an unreleased LP that were previously unavailable in the U.S. *—Richie Unterberger*

Live: Simply the Best / 1991 / Rounder ♦♦♦♦♦

Irma Thomas has long been an institution in New Orleans-based R&B. This live CD is both a strong introduction to her powerful voice and a summation of her career up to 1990, mixing together remakes of some of her mid-'60s recordings with more current material. Cheered on by an enthusiastic crowd, Irma Thomas sounds inspired and in her prime for the consistently passionate set. Of the highlights, "Hip Shakin' Mama" is a humorous blues, "I Needed Somebody" is especially soulful (if overly repetitive near its conclusion), "It's Raining" is memorable and the "Second Line Medley" effectively mixes in a touch of Dixieland with R&B. An excellent introduction to the talented Irma Thomas. *—Scott Yanow*

☆ **Time Is on My Side: The Best of Irma Thomas, Vol. 1** / Apr. 21, 1992 / EMI America ✦✦✦✦✦

Here are 23 representing the cream of Irma Thomas' brilliant Minit/Liberty years (1961-1966), when her reputation as "The Soul Queen of New Orleans" was built. Virtually all her best-known tunes are here—"Wish Someone Would Care," "Ruler of My Heart," "It's Raining," and "Time Is on My Side" (covered note-for-note by The Stones). Beautiful singing from one of the first ladies of soul music. Essential. *—Christine Ohlman*

Walk Around Heaven: New Orleans Gospel Soul / Oct. 1993 / Rounder ✦✦✦

During R&B's glory years—the 1950s, '60s and '70s—the African-American church provided one great singer after another. Church choirs served as a magnificent training ground for so many of the great soul shouters, and it clearly had a positive effect on Irma Thomas (arguably the greatest female soul singer to come out of New Orleans). At 52, Thomas celebrated her gospel heritage with this solid, heartfelt CD. Thomas' voice had held up quite well since the 1960s, and she brings an impressive range and a seemingly endless supply of emotion to songs like "Where We'll Never Grow Old," "Ask What You Will" and "Careful Hands." *Walk Around Heaven* reminds us that as impressive as her contributions to secular soul have been, Thomas hasn't forgotten the church. *—Alex Henderson*

★ **Sweet Soul Queen of New Orleans: The Irma Thomas Collection** / Feb. 20, 1996 / Razor & Tie ✦✦✦✦✦

This 23-track collection of early and mid-'60s sides largely duplicates the material on EMI's *Time Is on My Side* collection, with some additions and subtractions. The EMI set has a very slight edge, though for most listeners either compilation will do the job. It's too bad somebody doesn't take the plunge and issue an 80-minute CD documenting this era; as it is, serious Irma fans will need to get each best-of, as each contains tracks not on the other. *—Richie Unterberger*

Time Is on My Side / Nov. 5, 1996 / Kent ✦✦✦✦✦

In its original LP incarnation circa 1983, Kent's *Time Is on My Side* was a solid 16-track compilation of Irma Thomas material from the mid-'60s, most of it duplicated by the more extensive CDs on EMI and Razor & Tie. By the time of its CD release in 1996, however, it boasted more tracks than both of them, with seven songs not appearing on either of the other collections. Those tracks are worth hearing, particularly the gutsy soul-pop concoction "Baby Don't Look Down," one of Randy Newman's earliest compositions. *—Richie Unterberger*

The Story of My Life / Feb. 11, 1997 / Rounder ✦✦✦✦

The Story of My LIfe stands out among latter-day Irma Thomas albums not only because she gives a consistently excellent performance, but because the record boasts three new songs from Dan Penn, who wrote some of the greatest soul songs of the '60s. While his new songs ("Hold Me While I Cry," "I Count the Teardrops," "I Won't Cry for You") aren't quite as strong as his best, they are nevertheless wonderful contemporary soul numbers, and they help make the record, the remainder of which is comprised of covers and slightly weaker new numbers, one of Thomas' best latter-day albums. *—Stephen Thomas Erlewine*

My Heart's in Memphis: The Songs of Dan Penn / Aug. 8, 2000 / Rounder ✦✦✦

Dan Penn is one of the great Southern soul songwriters, and Irma Thomas is one of the great soul singers, so devoting an entire album to Penn songs was a good idea. Actually, Penn didn't so much write the material as co-write it; he composed every track with one or more co-writers, with Thomas herself getting in on the act on a couple. Four of the 13 tunes are actually interpretations of songs that have been around for a long time (such as "I'm Your Puppet" and "Woman Left Lonely"), but otherwise they were done specifically for this album. So is the result godhead? No, though it's okay. Thomas sings very well—it's been pretty rare that she *hasn't* sung well, on anything—and has a good sense of staying within herself where a lot of singers would over-emote, as on "If You Want It, Come and Get It." Recorded in Memphis (noted frequent Penn associate Spooner Oldham plays keyboards on several cuts), there's a laid-back modern soul feel that gets too laid back at times and not fiery on enough occasions. It's respectable modern soul, slicker than purists would like, but not annoyingly so. The newly written songs are alright, but again not amazing. Thomas' vocals are the highlight, as they should be. *—Richie Unterberger*

If You Want It, Come and Get It / Apr. 10, 2001 / Rounder ✦✦✦✦✦

It's a crime that soul singer Irma Thomas isn't a household name. Her recordings for the Minit and Chess labels in the 1960s and 1970s remain classics of the genre, and one of her compositions, the torchy "Time Is on My Side," was a big hit for a young British band called the Rolling Stones. She took some time off to raise a family, but came back on the scene in the late '70s, and in 1984 she teamed up with producer Scott Billington to make a series of albums for the Rounder label. The songs collected here were all recorded between 1985 and 1999, and all but one were previously released on those earlier albums. Thomas' singing style and the playing of her various backing musicians is so consistent, though, that it's almost impossible to tell which tracks were recorded when; every one partakes of that joyful mix of New Orleans steam and chugging Memphis soul that has become her trademark. The songs are all classics—the Dan Penn composition "If You Want It, Come and Get It," Paul Kelly's "The New Rules," Doc Pomus and Dr. John's "I Never Fool Nobody but Me." And there's even a gospel tune, the exuberant "Yield Not to Temptation" (with backing vocals by Marcia Ball and Tracy Nelson). Any fan of soul music ought to own all of the albums from which this collection was taken, but this disc is a good place to start. *—Rick Anderson*

Jamo Thomas

Vocals / Northern Soul, Soul, Funk

Best known for his hit "Bahama Mama," Jamo Thomas was one of the few Bahamian artists to achieve significant—if fleeting—recognition in America during the 1960s. He came to Chicago during the early '60s and cut his first single, "Stop the Baby," for the Conlo label, produced by Jerry Butler. He moved to the Sound Stage 7 label in 1965, which led to the recording of "Bahama Mama" in Memphis, which became a hit. In 1966, he met Eddie Thomas, Butler's former driver and now an executive with ABC-Paramount, who was starting to cut records for his own Thomas label (a de facto companion label to Curtis Mayfield's Windy C and Mayfield imprints), and recorded Thomas doing a version of Luther Ingram's "I Spy (For the FBI)," a smooth and rousing piece of soul music that became an international hit. Thomas later recorded for Chess and Decca before moving to Philadelphia, where he recorded for the Perception label, including "Shake What You Brought With You" and "You Just Ain't Ready."

Thomas later recorded for the MCA and Nassau labels. He stopped recording his own material after 1976, but in 1979, he provided the introduction to "Scream" by Larry Graham and Graham Central Station on the *Star Walk* album (Warner Bros.). Thomas re-emerged in the 1980s as an arranger on a gospel recording by Ella Washington. He also turned up on a Chess/P-Vine LP called *The Real Chicago Blues Today: 60's Style.* A video clip of Thomas performing appears on the third volume of *Northern Soul Videos*, in conjunction with the Poppies, Otis Redding, Willie Mitchell, Esther Phillips, and Cleo Randle. *—Bruce Eder*

Lillo Thomas

b. Brooklyn, NY

Vocals, Songwriter / Urban

Lillo Thomas was a world-class sprinter at 16, setting the world record for the 200 meters at 20.8 seconds. But an automobile accident in Brazil prevented him from appearing in the 1984 Olympics, for which he had qualified. Thomas left athletics behind for music, and toured with comedian Eddie Murphy in 1985. He became a successful session vocalist, doing vocals on releases by Evelyn "Champagne" King, Kashif, James Ingram, George Benson, and Melba Moore, among others, while also writing "Mind Up Tonight" for Moore. He landed his own solo deal with Capitol, and began getting singles on the charts. "Your Love's Got a Hold on Me" was his first Top 20 R&B single in 1984, and Thomas enjoyed his biggest year in 1987 with three Top Ten R&B hits. "I'm in Love" reached number two and remains his most successful single. Thomas collaborated with Paul Laurence on songs recorded by Freddie Jackson and Moore. He has also successfully acted and painted. *—Ron Wynn*

Let Me Be Yours / 1983 / Capitol ✦✦✦✦

The debut album from the former track star generated two *Billboard* R&B singles. "(You're A) Good Girl" is a midtempo number that employs a danceable rhythm and enchanced with icy background vocals and scintillating guitar rhythms. It crested at 22 on the charts. With added studio gimmickry and vocal antics, "Who Do You Think You Are," also a dance cut, peaked at number 68 on the charts. The Brooklyn native lays down his own rendition of the Temptations classic "Just My Imagination." Thomas injects his own lyric throughout several parts of the song without forfeiting the song's natural beauty. While he does not have explosive vocals, Lillo Thomas does possess vocal savvy and an uniqueness to his style to deliver a excellent album. *—Craig Lytle*

All of You / 1984 / Capitol ✦✦✦

● **Lillo** / 1987 / Capitol ✦✦✦✦✦

The Best of Lillo Thomas / 1996 / Brunswick ✦✦✦✦

A suave, smooth best-of compilation from Lillo Thomas, at least they didn't call it a greatest-hits set, since he had few of them. Thomas recorded mostly ballads and midtempo floaters in his light tenor/falsetto. His renditions of "My Girl," and "Just My Imagination" are smooth, fluid and majestically done, many can't distinguish his version of "Imagination" from Eddie Kendricks' original. Sugar plums like "Downtown," "Sexy Girl," and "Sweet Surrender" achieved some recognition for Thomas along the Eastern Seaboard. His rendition of Otis Redding's "I've Been Loving You Too Long (To Stop Now)" is a surprise, but Lillo pulls off the deep soul classic, despite the frailties of his voice. "All of You (Can't Take Half,)" a duet with Melba Moore, is more familiar to many then his solo sides. *—Andrew Hamilton*

Rufus Thomas

b. Mar. 26, 1917, Cayce, MS, **d.** Dec. 15, 2001, Memphis, TN

Vocals / Memphis Soul, Southern Soul, R&B, Soul, Electric Memphis Blues, Modern Electric Blues, Funk

Few of rock & roll's founding figures are as likable as Rufus Thomas. From the 1940s onward, he has personified Memphis music; his small but witty cameo role in Jim Jarmusch's *Mystery Train*, a film that satirizes and enshrines the city's role in popular culture, was entirely appropriate. As a recording artist, he wasn't a major innovator, but he could always be depended upon for some good, silly, and/or outrageous fun with his soul dance tunes. He was one of the few rock or soul stars to reach his commercial and artistic peak in middle age, and was a crucial mentor to many important Memphis blues, rock, and soul musicians.

Thomas was already a professional entertainer in the mid-'30s, when he was a comedian with the Rabbit Foot Minstrels. He recorded music as early as 1941, but really made his mark on the Memphis music scene as a DJ on WDIA, one of the few black-owned stations of the era. He also ran talent shows on Memphis' famous Beale Street that helped showcase the emerging skills of such influential figures as B.B. King, Bobby "Blue" Bland, Junior Parker, Ike Turner, and Roscoe Gordon.

Thomas had his first success as a recording artist in 1953 with "Bear Cat," a funny answer record to Big Mama Thornton's "Hound Dog." It made number three on the R&B charts, giving Sun Records its first national hit, though some of the sweetness went out of the triumph after Sun owner Sam Phillips lost a lawsuit for plagiarizing the original Jerry Leiber & Mike Stoller tune. Thomas, strangely, would make only one other record for Sun, and recorded only sporadically throughout the rest of the 1950s. Thomas and his daughter Carla would become the first stars for the Stax label, for whom they recorded a duet in 1959, "'Cause I Love You" (when the company was still known as Satellite). In the '60s, Carla would become one of Stax's biggest stars. On his own, Rufus wasn't as successful as his daughter, but issued a steady stream of decent dance/novelty singles.

These were not deep or emotional statements, or meant to be. Vaguely prefiguring elements of funk, the accent was on the stripped-down groove and Rufus' good-time vocals, which didn't take himself or anything seriously. The biggest by far was "Walking the Dog," which made the Top Ten in 1963, and was covered by the Rolling Stones on their first album.

Thomas hit his commercial peak in the early '70s, when "Do the Funky Chicken," "(Do The) Push and Pull," and "The Breakdown" all made the R&B Top Five. As the song titles themselves make clear, funk was now driving his sound rather than blues or soul. Thomas drew upon his vaudeville background to put them over on-stage with fancy footwork that displayed remarkable agility for a man well into his 50s. The collapse of the Stax label in the mid-'70s meant the end of his career, basically, as it did for many other artists with the company. In 2001, Rufus Thomas was inducted into the Blues Hall of Fame. Later that year, on December 15, he died at St. Francis hospital in Memphis, TN.—*Richie Unterberger*

Five on Eight / 1963 / Cameo ✦✦✦

Walking the Dog / 1964 / Rhino ✦✦✦✦✦

One of the artists who defined Memphis soul and put Stax Records on the map, Rufus Thomas is known for liking his R&B hard-edged, gritty and earthy. That approach served him impressively well on his debut album *Walking the Dog*. In contrast to the sleeker, more elaborate production style favored by the Northern soulsters of Motown, Thomas rejects pop elements altogether and thrives on rawness on his hits "Walking the Dog" and "The Dog," as well as inspired versions of "Land of 1000 Dances" (which became a major hit for Wilson Pickett), Lee Dorsey's "Ya Ya" and John Lee Hooker's "Boom Boom." Thomas was in his mid-40s when these fun, infectious recordings were made, and he definitely lives up to his title "The World's Oldest Teenager" (a title later given to Dick Clark as well). Reissued on CD in the early 1990s, *Walking the Dog* is an album Memphis soul aficionados shouldn't overlook. —*Alex Henderson*

Do the Funky Chicken / Jun. 1969 / Stax ✦✦✦

Thomas' first album following Stax's break from Atlantic had "Do the Funky Chicken" at its centerpiece, so the emphasis upon good-humored dance tunes was unsurprising. There were some weird moments, particularly the down-and-bestial seven-minute update of "Sixty Minute Man" (on which Rufus sounds like he's singing in tongues), a remake of "Bear Cat," and a two-part version of "Old McDonald Had a Farm." Still, the slightly goofy uptempo arrangements can get a little tiresome, and as his best hits from the period are better than the album-only tracks, almost everyone should just stick with a compilation. The CD adds seven bonus tracks from 1968-1974 singles, which are OK but not essential; Eddie Floyd's "Funky Mississippi" (from 1968) is about the best. —*Richie Unterberger*

Did You Heard Me? / 1971 / Stax ✦✦✦

Signed to Satellite in 1959, before it became Stax, Rufus Thomas could be counted on to provide some of the hardest, unabashedly Southern music in the history of the label. Big hits like 1964's "Walking the Dog" and 1970's classic "Do the Funky Chicken" all but helped typify the quirky and potent Stax sound. As his label was going through many reconfigurations and styles in the early '70s Thomas didn't change too much and continued to do uptempo tracks with a suitably updated production. This 1971 album offers prime Thomas having great chemistry with the members of Isaac Hayes' band of the time. "(Do the) Push and Pull, Pts. 1 and 2" has Michael Toles' lazy, country styled guitar riffs and the steady rhythm section of bassist James Alexander and drummer Willie Hall. The other hit singles, "The Breakdown Pts. 1 & 2" and "Do the Funky Penguin Pts. 1 & 2 have Charles Pitts' humorous guitar effects that helped to make the songs even more kinetic. On the track Thomas manages to pose the album's title question not once but 12 times. The last song recorded from the sessions, Thomas' ode to gambling "6-3-8" has sneaky horn charts and a booming bassline. A warbled cover of the standard "(I Love You) For Sentimental Reasons" is the only dud here. Although a few disposable tracks weighs down the effort, *Did You Heard Me?* more often than not has Thomas on his game. —*Jason Elias*

Doing the Push and Pull Live at P.J.'s / 1971 / Stax ✦✦✦

One of only a couple of Rufus Thomas albums that actually cracked the pop charts, this featured live versions of "Do the Funky Chicken" and "(Do the) Push and Pull," plus warhorses like "The Preacher and the Bear" and "Night Time is the Right Time." The label also stuck the recent number-one hit "Walkin' the Dog" onto the album from its prior release, an unnecessary move and one that couldn't get it any more pop action than it enjoyed. —*Ron Wynn*

The Crown Prince of Dance / 1972 / Stax ✦✦✦✦✦

The "world's oldest teenager" was springy, sassy, and jubilant when he cut this date in the early '70s. Thomas, whose career goes back to the days of the Rabbit Foot Minstrels, made some brilliant novelty cuts for Stax in the 1970s. He simply went into the studio and clowned, backed by the great Stax session pros. The results are comic gems, numbers that are purposefully lightweight and succeed without sounding sappy. —*Ron Wynn*

If There Were No Music / 1977 / Avid ✦✦

I Ain't Gettin' Older, I'm Gettin' Better / 1977 / Avid ✦✦

Jump Back / 1984 / Edsel ✦✦✦✦✦

This is the best compilation of his early Stax sides. The 16 tracks include "Walking the Dog," "The Dog," and some lesser-known songs in the same league, some of which ("Jump Back," "All Night Worker," "Sister's Got a Boyfriend," "Sophisticated Sissy") made the rounds via cover versions by both black and white artists. —*Richie Unterberger*

That Woman Is Poison! / 1988 / Alligator ✦✦✦

Here is a masterful comeback album from a blues and soul veteran who was assumed to be ready for the retirement home. Rufus Thomas went back to the comic blues that had been his forte in the 1950s, and the edge in his voice and defiance in his tone proclaimed that he wasn't finished yet. After years of taking heat from purists for not issuing enough "real" blues albums, Alligator didn't get nearly enough credit for being the only label to give Rufus Thomas a fair shot in the 1980s. —*Ron Wynn*

Can't Get Away from This Dog / 1992 / Stax ✦✦✦

Can't Get Away from This Dog gathers 20 previously unreleased Rufus Thomas recordings from the Stax vaults. Stylistically, fans won't find any surprises—this is still hard-hitting, hard-driving Memphis soul—but they'll find a couple of hidden treasures, such as versions of "Wang Dang Doodle," "Reconsider Baby" and "Barefootin'," as well as alternates of "Walking the Dog," "Jump Back" and "Can Your Monkey Do the Dog?" Some of Thomas' original material is a little thin—there's only so many times you can work the word "dog" into a song title, after all—but this is a surprisingly successful collection of rarities that will not only satiate die-hards, but will entertain casual fans as well. —*Stephen Thomas Erlewine*

Did You Heard Me?/Crown Prince of Dance / 1995 / Stax ✦✦✦

This pairs up two of Thomas' original Stax albums on one compact disc. The first ten tracks emanate from 1970 and 1971 sessions that produced the *Did You Heard Me?* album, featuring the hits "(Do the) Push and Pull, Pts. 1 and 2" and "Do the Funky Penguin." The follow-up, 1972's *The Crown Prince of Dance*, wasn't as successful musically or sales-wise, but features plenty of Thomas' funky dancefloor rave-ups like "Funkiest Man Alive," "The Funky Bird," and a nice duet with daughter Carla Thomas on "Steal a Little." This would end up being Thomas' last album for the label before it went under, and it still holds up well. —*Cub Koda*

Rufus Thomas Live! / Oct. 1995 / Stax ✦✦

● **The Best of Rufus Thomas: Do the Funky Somethin'** / Apr. 1996 / Rhino ✦✦✦✦✦

Overdue career-spanning collection of his best material, centering around his Stax hits from the '60s and early '70s. The whole "dog" series of novelty dance songs from 1963-1964 is here, as well as the hit "Jump Back" and a clutch of Stax singles that weren't hits, but became pretty well-known anyway, like "Sister's Got a Boyfriend" and "Sophisticated Sissy." There are also the early-'70s funk dance hits "Do the Funky Chicken," "(Do the) Push and Pull," "The Breakdown," and "Do the Funky Penguin," a couple of '60s duets with his daughter Carla, and his 1953 blues single "Bear Cat (The Answer to Hound Dog)," the first hit on Sun Records. A few other compilations have gone into specific phases of his career in greater depth, but this is certainly the best overview of a man who offered some of the funkiest and funniest Memphis soul around. —*Richie Unterberger*

Funky Chicken / 1997 / Stax ✦✦✦

Rufus Thomas would storm the soul charts in 1970, scoring three hits, two of them in the Top Ten. The title track and his number one smash "(Do the) Push and Pull" were identical—dance-based novelty tunes featuring Thomas' manic instructions and bluesy shouts backed by surging, horn-based soul and funk from the Stax band. It wasn't earth-shaking, just fun, brilliantly produced and arranged stuff. —*Ron Wynn*

The Funkiest Man / 2002 / Stax/Ace ✦✦✦

This compilation gathers 18 of Thomas' funk-oriented songs from 1967-1975, though only a few '60s sides are here. His biggest funk hit of all, "Do the Funky Chicken," is *not* here, and though the liners point out that the song is available on other Ace compilations, why not put it on here anyway? In its favor, there's little overlap between this anthology and the Stax CD *Funky Chicken*, a reissue of his 1969 LP *Do the Funky Chicken* with seven bonus tracks from his 1968-1974 singles. This also has his three big follow-up hits to "Do the Funky Chicken": "(Do the) Push and Pull (Pt. 1)," "Do the Funky Penguin (Pt. 1)," and "The Breakdown (Pt. 1)." To its detriment, however, the novelty dance funk grooves just get unimaginative, even monotonous, in such a concentrated dose, getting into spin-offs like "Funky Robot (Pt. 1)," "Do the Double Bump," "The Funky Bird," "Funky Mississippi," and so forth. Rufus Thomas is cool, but he's not James Brown (though the scratchy guitar and jerky rhythms of 1972's "Itch and Scratch (Pt. 1)" certainly owe a lot to Brown), nor are the backup musicians. When it stretches back as far as 1967 for "Sophisticated Cissy," there's a refreshing injection of more soul-grounded chops, female backup vocals, and horns. Two of the songs, "I'm Getting Better" and "Memphis Train '75," were previously unreleased. Incidentally, this British release is unavailable for sale in North America. —*Richie Unterberger*

Timmy Thomas

b. Nov. 13, 1944, Evansville, IN

Producer, Keyboards, Vocals, Piano / Funk, Soul, Disco

Timmy Thomas is notable for having been a major one-hit wonder with "Why Can't We Live Together?," a song distinguished by its stripped-down production—soulful organ, played seemingly improvisationally over a rhythm from a primitive drum machine, with Thomas' impassioned vocals layered over both. The result was a 1973 hit for Thomas and for TK Records subsidiary Glades. While Thomas had released records before "Why Can't We Live Together?," and continued to release them afterwards, none of them garnered much in the way of sales. He continued to work on sessions for TK Records artists (including Gwen McCrae and Clarence Reid's alter-ego, Blowfly) and could be spotted in the '90s working as a producer for LaFace Records. —*Steven McDonald*

Why Can't We Live Together / 1974 / Glades ✦✦

This album originally dropped on Glades records following Thomas' million-selling "Why Can't We Live Together," which qualifies as the cheapest Top Ten hit ever made. The session consists of Timmy Thomas singing and accompanying himself on organ. The rest of the album is almost as sparse. If you like a lot of production, you won't find it here. Remakes of "The First Time Ever I Saw Your Face" and the Chi-Lites' "Coldest Days of My Life" won't make you ditch the original versions. And with the exception of the title track, the originals are forgettable. *—Andrew Hamilton*

Magician / 1977 / TK ✦✦

● **Why Can't We Live Together: The Best of the TK Years 1972–1981** / May 19, 1998 / WestSide ✦✦✦

Timmy Thomas was definitely not over produced. Usually his recordings consisted of Thomas playing organ and singing, accompanied by a drum machine. The formula worked on "Why Can't We Live Together," a million-selling message song. Lightning, however, didn't strike twice—he never had another one as successful. Sparseness works sometimes, but after 20 tracks the holes become gaping; Thomas is easier to embrace on a shorter set. "Ebony Affair," a duet with Betty Wright; "People Are Changin'"; "Sweet Brown Sugar"; "Freak In, Freak Out"; "Dizzy, Dizzy World"; and "Fox With the Box" provide some good moments, but nothing earthshaking or essential. *—Andrew Hamilton*

Gina Thompson

b. Vineland, NJ

Vocals / Urban, Hip-Hop, Contemporary R&B

Comparable to Missy Elliott, Faith Evans, and the late Aaliyah, Gina Thompson is among the hip-hop-drenched urban contemporary female vocalists who emerged in the '90s. Thompson grew up in Vineland, NJ, where she began singing as a child. She kept singing as a teenager, and by the time she graduated from high school, Thompson had become the first black homecoming queen in the history of her high school. In 1995, Thompson signed with Mercury/PolyGram, which released her debut album, *Nobody Does It Better*, the following year. The album's producers included Stevie J. (not to be confused with Stevie V or Stevie B) and Bad Boy Entertainment leader Sean Puffy Combs aka Puff Daddy aka P. Diddy, who had become one of the most famous (and controversial) producers in both rap and urban contemporary.

One of the songs that Puff Daddy produced for Thompson's first album was "The Things That You Do," which featured Elliott and gave the Virginia singer/rapper some valuable exposure. In 1996, Elliott had yet to become a superstar vocalist; she was still a behind-the-scenes songwriter/producer and was best known for working with Aaliyah and producer Timbaland. "The Things That You Do" was a major step forward for Elliott the vocalist (as opposed to Elliott the songwriter/producer), and thanks to Thompson's single, more people started to think of Elliott as a vocalist and not just a behind-the-scenes person. "The Things You Do" helped pave the way for the tremendous acceptance of Elliott's debut solo album, *Supa Dupa Fly*, which Elektra released in 1997.

Thompson didn't write "The Things That You Do," although she co-wrote three of the other songs on *Nobody Does It Better*: "Freak On," "Without You," and "Strung Out." *Nobody Does It Better* turned out to be Thompson's only album for Mercury/PolyGram; a few years later, Thompson's association with Elliott led to a deal with Elektra. In 1999, Elektra released Thompson's second album, *If You Only Knew*. The album's guests included Elliott as well as Los Angeles singer Montell Jordan (best known for his 1995 smash "This Is How We Do It"), DJ Jazzy Jeff (as in DJ Jazzy Jeff & the Fresh Prince), and Philadelphia rapper Beanie Sigel. *—Alex Henderson*

Nobody Does It Better / Aug. 13, 1996 / Mercury ✦✦✦

● **If You Only Knew** / Sep. 21, 1999 / Elektra ✦✦✦✦

Gina Thompson's *If You Only Knew* marks her debut for Elektra Records and features more of the attitude she displayed on her first single with Missy Elliott, "The Things That You Do." Elliot reappears on *If You Only Knew*'s "Ya Di Ya," and the album also features guest performances from Beenie Siegel and Jon B. From slinky, seductive songs like "Don't Take Your Love Away" and "Caught Up" to attitude packed tracks like "You Can't Play Me," *If You Only Knew* showcases Thompson's versatility as a singer, songwriter and co-producer. *—Heather Phares*

Tony Thompson

b. Waco, TX

Vocals, Drums / Urban, Dance-Pop

Tony Thompson, the vocalist for R&B act Hi-Five, was born in Waco, TX, and raised in Oklahoma City. He began singing solos in the local church choir at the age of eight. He was noticed by a producer and invited to cut a demo with Roderick Clark, Russell Neal, Marcus Sanders, and Toriano Easley, acquaintances from his days in Waco. The group signed with Jive Records in 1990. The quintet's self-titled debut album went multi-platinum and spawned several hits, including "I Like the Way (The Kissing Game)," "I Can't Wait Another Minute," and "Just Another Girlfriend." *Keep It Goin' On* with "She's Playing Hard to Get" and "Quality Time" came in 1992. *Faithful* appeared the following year. Thompson's solo debut, *Sexsational*, was released on Giant in 1995. *—John Bush*

● **Sexsational** / 1995 / Giant ✦✦✦

Tony Thompson began his career with the teen-R&B sensations Hi-Five, responsible for the hit single "I Like the Way (The Kissing Game)." With his first solo album, *Sexsational*, the 19 year-old Thompson tried to establish himself as a viable solo artist, as well as a sex symbol, as the title of the album implies. In his favor, he knows talent when he hears it. Thompson brought together an impressive list of writers and producers (Babyface, Puffy Combs, DeVante Swing, among others), and left them to create backdrops for his sweet falsetto voice. However, most of the behind-the-scenes musicians fail to come up with distinctive material, which hurts *Sexsational* considerably. When given the right material, Thompson is convincing, but he isn't powerful enough to rescue weak songs. A few songs, like "I Wanna Love Like That" and a cover of Stevie Wonder's "My Cherie Amour," work but *Sexsational* is by and large unfulfilling. *—Stephen Thomas Erlewine*

Fonzi Thornton (Alfonso Thornton)

b. New York, NY

Vocals / Urban, Quiet Storm

Born Alfonso Thornton in New York City, Fonzi Thornton became a background vocalist behind Luther Vandross. He toured the world and can be heard on the singer's gold and platinum albums. He also can be heard doing background vocals on various releases including those by Chic. In 1983, Thornton got a solo deal with RCA Records. Thornton co-wrote and co-produced his debut LP, *The Leader*, with RCA executive Robert Wright. Issued in spring 1983, the urban pop LP yielded the percolating, perennial dance favorite "Beverly," which made it to number-43 R&B on *Billboard*'s charts in spring 1983. Chic's Nile Rodgers & Bernard Edwards appear on the LP. Thornton and Wright also co-wrote and produced his second RCA LP, *Pumpin'*, released in summer 1984, which was more reflective of the dance/rock of the time. *—Ed Hogan*

● **The Leader** / 1983 / BMG ✦✦✦

THP Orchestra

db. 1980

Group / Euro-Dance, Disco

Led by producers Ian Guenther and Willi Morrison, the THP Orchestra was a Euro-disco outfit that recorded in Toronto, Canada in the late '70s. THP wasn't actually based in Europe, although its three albums reflected the Guenther/Morrison team's appreciation of the type of sleek and glossy (but sometimes funky) dance music was coming out of Germany, France, and other European countries at the time. THP made its vinyl debut in 1977, when it recorded *Two Hot for Love!* for Butterfly. The LP was ignored by pop/Top 40 radio in the U.S., but that didn't prevent it from becoming a club hit. THP, whose line-ups varied from one album to the next, provided its second album, *Tender Is the Night*, for Butterfly in 1978 before switching to Atlantic in 1979 and recording its third album, *Good to Me*. By that time, Guenther and Morrison had dropped "Orchestra" from the band's name and were simply going by THP. *Good to Me* turned out to be THP's final album; by 1980, THP had called it quits. *—Alex Henderson*

● **Two Hot for Love!** / 1977 / Butterfly ✦✦✦

Throughout the history of dance-pop, there have been club artists and radio artists. Donna Summer, the Village People, Chic, Gloria Gaynor, and Madonna are perfect examples of radio artists; although they were extremely popular in dance clubs, they enjoyed extensive radio airplay and reached a lot of people who weren't necessarily major club hounds. Those artists became a part of mainstream pop culture, whereas club artists are more underground—they cater to clubs, and if commercial radio ignores them, so be it. In the late '70s, the THP Orchestra was the epitome of a club act. *Two Hot for Love!*, THP's first LP, was generally ignored by radio but gave the Euro-disco outfit a small but enthusiastic club following. DJs were especially fond of the title song, which lasts almost 16 minutes and takes up all of side one. Boasting a sweaty, intoxicating performance by singer Barbara Fry, "Two Hot for Love!" is an orchestral Euro-disco masterpiece. Side two, meanwhile, is devoted to instrumentals, the strongest of which is an arrangement of Luis Bonfa's "Manha de Carnival." The Bonfa standard is generally associated with Brazilian pop-jazz and bossa nova, although it works surprisingly well in a Euro-disco setting. The other instrumentals on side two (including the dramatic "Early Riser" and the playful "Crazy Crazy") are pleasant, if unremarkable. Produced by THP leaders Ian Guenther and Willi Morrison, this decent-to-excellent LP isn't for the casual disco fan but is worth hearing if you're a seasoned disco addict. *—Alex Henderson*

Tender Is the Night / 1978 / Butterfly ✦✦✦

In the 1980s, dance-pop went totally high-tech—rather than hire a lot of musicians, a producer could easily act as a one-man (or one-woman) band and program all of the synthesizers, sequencers, and drum machines himself/herself. That was a major departure from the late '70s, when disco producers typically used a lot of musicians and favored lavish string and horn arrangements. The THP Orchestra was an orchestra in the true sense of the word—at least in the beginning. On THP's second album, *Tender Is the Night*, producers Ian Guenther and Willi Morrison oversee a lineup that includes vocalists Phyllis and Helen Duncan, a rhythm section, five horn players (including Canadian jazz trombonist Ian McDougall), and no less than ten string players. That didn't impress radio DJs, who ignored the LP. But in dance clubs, *Tender Is the Night* was a hit. Club jocks who favored the European disco sound were quick to play exuberant, ultra-danceable numbers that range from the clever "Weekend Two Step" to the lush title song and the funky, if mechanical, "Music Is All You Need." The glossy "Half as Nice" is much too sugary and campy for its own good, although the other songs are decent. Like THP's first record, *Two Hot for Love*, this LP isn't recommended to those who have only a casual interest in late-'70s Euro-disco. But it's worth having in your collection if you're a serious fan of this type of music. *—Alex Henderson*

Good to Me / 1979 / Atlantic ✦✦✦

At the turn of the millennium, THP's Euro-disco recordings of the late 1970s sound incredibly dated. But dated isn't necessarily bad; for those fond of a particular era, it can actually be a good thing. And for anyone fond of the disco era, THP is a name that's worth knowing. Not everything that THP recorded was great, but it did record the occasional gem and was at least decent most of the time. *Good to Me*, THP's third and final album, found the Canadian outfit switching to the Atlantic label and changing its name—what had been the THP Orchestra in 1977 and 1978 became just plain THP in 1979. However, *Good to Me* isn't terribly different from the THP Orchestra's two previous albums; producers Ian Guenther and Willi Morrison ditched the huge string section and hired Joyce Cobb as their new female singer but continued to emphasize state-of-the-art Euro-disco. Cobb, a big-voiced belter, handles herself well on European-flavored tracks like "Dancin' Forever," "Dancin' Is Alright," and the title song. But not everything on this LP has the European sound; on "Two Hearts, One Love" and "Who Do You Love," Cobb detours into more of a disco-soul approach à la Gloria Gaynor, Thelma Houston, or Loleatta Holloway. With the right promotion on Atlantic's part, those two songs could have easily become radio hits. But unfortunately, Atlantic didn't really get behind this LP, which went out of print not long after it was released. Nonetheless, *Good to Me* did enjoy some club exposure, and it isn't a bad record to have in your collection if you're a die-hard disco fanatic. *—Alex Henderson*

The Three Degrees

f. 1963, Philadelphia, PA

Group / Philly Soul, Disco, Smooth Soul, Soul

Philly soul vocal group the Three Degrees started in 1963 in Philadelphia, PA. They were discovered by producer and songwriter Richard Barrett. Barrett was a key force for 1950s groups the Chantels, Little Anthony & the Imperials, Frankie Lymon & the Teenagers, and his own group the Valentines. The original lineup was Fayette Pickney, Shirley Porter, and Linda Turner. Barrett recorded this lineup on their first single, "Gee Baby (I'm Sorry)." In 1963, Linda Turner and Shirley Porter left the group and were replaced by Helen Scott and Janet Jones. Around this time, Barrett began managing and producing Sheila Ferguson who was a high school friend of Scott. Barrett got deals for both the group and Ferguson with Swan Records. By 1966, Helen decided to leave the group and become a housewife. Sheila Ferguson took her place. She sang backup on all the Three Degrees' Swan recordings, as did the Three Degrees for her solo singles. In 1967, Valerie Holiday joined the group, while Janet Jones departed. Over the next four years, both the Three Degrees and Ferguson released many singles.

In 1970, now signed to Roulette Records, the Three Degrees scored their first national chart hit with a remake of the Chantels' "Maybe" with Scott taking the lead vocals. It went to number-four R&B in summer 1970. The follow-up, "I Do Take You," peaked at number-seven R&B. Barrett got the group short-term deals with Warner Bros., Metromedia, and Gamble & Huff's Neptune Label. The group had a cameo in the classic 1971 movie *The French Connection* starring Gene Hackman and toured with Engelbert Humperdink. In 1973, Barrett worked a deal with Gamble & Huff's Philadelphia International Records (PIR). The Three Degrees' first PIR single was "Dirty Ol' Man," a disco hit. A short time later, Don Cornelius, producer and host of TV's *Soul Train*, approached Gamble & Huff about coming up with a new theme song for his hit syndicated show. The Three Degrees were asked to do vocals at the end of the show's new theme track. After some airings, public demand forced the TV show's theme to be released as a single. "TSOP (The Sound of Philadelphia)" by MFSB featuring the Three Degrees went gold hitting number-one R&B and holding the number-one pop for two weeks during spring 1974. Meanwhile, a previously released Three Degrees single, "Year of Decision," stalled at number-74 R&B.

Another MFSB/Three Degrees single, "Love Is the Message," peaked at number-42 R&B in the summer of that year. In the summer of 1974, PIR released another single on the group, "When Will I See You Again." The single went platinum, selling over two-million copies, going to number-four R&B and number-two pop around September 1974. Their PIR debut album, *The Three Degrees*, was released at the end of 1974. The follow-up, "I Didn't Know," written and produced by Bunny Sigler, went to number-18 R&B in early 1975. The group performed the song on a guest appearance on the hit NBC show *Sanford and Son*. Their only other charting PIR single was "Take Good Care of Yourself" (number-64 R&B in summer 1975).

Around 1976, Pickney left the group and was replaced by returning member Helen Scott. CBS released their album *Standing Up for Love* in the U.S. in 1977. In 1978, the Three Degrees were signed to European label Ariola Records. The group recorded three LPs for the label. Longtime favorites in the U.K., the group performed at Buckingham Palace for Prince Charles' 30th birthday party and they were guests at his wedding to Princess Diana. During the first half of the '80s, the Three Degrees released U.K.-issued albums, *Album of Love* and *Live in the UK* and singles, "Liar" and "A Sonnet to Love." Stock/Aitken/Waterman produced a 1985 U.K. chart hit, "The Heaven I Need," on the group for Supreme Records. In 1986, Sheila Ferguson left the group. With Helen Scott, Valerie Holiday, and Victoria Wallace, the group recorded an album for Ichiban Records, *...And Holding*. The act recorded another live CD with Billy Paul and Harold Melvin & the Bluenotes during a TSOP tour in the summer of 1989. Scott, Holiday, and new member Cynthia Garrison recorded three albums in the 1990s. *—Ed Hogan*

Maybe / 1970 / Roulette ♦♦

The Three Degrees / 1974 / Philadelphia International ♦♦♦♦

The divas of Gamble & Huff's Philadelphia International stable, the Three Degrees debuted their self-titled album for the label in 1973 before they hit the mainstream with MFSB and "TSOP" the following year. And, although they are so often piggybacked on that glory, it's important to remember that this remarkable trio was already established as one of the country's premier female vocal groups. With successful sides for Roulette already under their belt, *The Three Degrees* found them combining their already tried and true R&B style with Gamble & Huff's trademark orchestral, instrumental flourish. It was a heavenly marriage that easily, and obviously, brought the band into the Top 40. With the lion's share of "good" material crowded on side one, the set is highlighted by the opening "Dirty Ol' Man," which brought the band's harmonies cascading over the opening strings before they descended into edgier waters. Following apace is a wonderful version of "A Woman Needs a Good Man," before closing with "When Will I See you Again"—the gorgeous, breathless ballad that nearly topped the charts in 1974. Elsewhere, the band tempers the obvious and silly "I Like Being a Woman" with the overlooked gem "If and When." The song, one of several written by Philly International bigwig Bunny Sigler, is a rough-and-tumble ballad that heats up by merging classic '70s rock elements with the Three Degrees' girl group ethics. Although it's ultimately patchy in places, *The Three Degrees* was a fine introduction for the partnership between the band and the label that would put them on the map. A fine bridge between sugary soul and the sexy disco strings lurking in the band's future. *—Amy Hanson*

International / 1975 / Philadelphia International ♦♦♦

Now past their "TSOP" apogee and working well with producers Gamble & Huff, the Three Degrees bounded back into the Top 40 with 1975's *International*. Working across a slick set dominated by Gamble & Huff-penned songs that provided a smooth vehicle for the trio's powerhouse vocals, the Three Degrees took the pleasing "Take Good Care of Yourself" into the charts. But despite the evidence of a fine performance, it never really feels like the band really hit its stride. Both "Long Lost Lover" and the very Motown-ish "Loving Cup" are pleasant efforts but, as the songs unfold, the band seems to stagnate across an apparently endless supply of ballads. Even a reprisal of "TSOP" and a cover of Marvin Gaye's 1973 classic "Distant Lover" don't manage to stir the old heartstrings. Although they'd revamp and revive across later efforts for Ariola, the bandmembers were running out of steam in the confines of the Philadelphia International format. Stripped of their earlier fire and spark, it's obvious the Three Degrees really didn't have anything fresh to offer. However, that's not to say that this album isn't without merit—after all, it did carve a respectful niche for itself. In another time and place, *International* would probably crackle with effervescence but, in retrospect, there are far better ways to sample this wonderful trio. *—Amy Hanson*

Live / 1975 / Philadelphia International ♦♦♦♦

Although they were certainly guilty of some lackluster moments on their studio albums, the Three Degrees were another entity entirely when performing live. On-stage and in front of an audience, they were charged, bounding through snappy sets with phenomenal energy. This 1975 concert, recorded with a full orchestra in Leicester, England, is that pudding's proof. And, being 1975, the band covers all its hits, powering through "TSOP," "When Will I See You Again," and "Dirty Ol' Man" with an easy, breezy style that's a refreshing lift after some more forced moments on the preceding *International*. But things get really interesting on some inspired and often off-kilter choices included in the set, as listeners hear the band break out of its Philadelphia International cocoon. As a treat for their English audience, according to the band's between-song patter, the Three Degrees punch up Elton John's then-current hit, "Don't Let the Sun Go Down on Me," turning it into a quick-stepping R&B-styled groover. Stevie Wonder's "Living for the City," combined with "For the Love of Money," receives similar treatment, while the trio's rendition of the Edgar Winter Group's roots rock classic "Free Ride" takes first place in the oddest cover ever category. It's a wild and well-thought-out set, spotlighting the Three Degrees where they are most comfortable and at their best. The sound is clear and clean, sacrificing some vicarious energy by mixing the obviously enthusiastic audience down but not quite out of the experience. It's a timeless treat. *—Amy Hanson*

Take Good Care of Yourself / 1975 / Philadelphia International ♦♦♦

Standing Up for Love / 1977 / Philadelphia International ♦♦♦

3-D / 1979 / Ariola ♦♦♦

... And Holding / 1989 / Ichiban ♦♦♦

Long after the Three Degrees' popularity had faded in the United States, the Philadelphia natives remained visible in their new home of England. Instead of sticking with the type of Philly soul and disco they embraced during the 1970s under the insightful direction of Kenny Gamble & Leon Huff, they changed with the times and embraced more high-tech urban contemporary sounds. Sounding like it was tailor-made for urban radio, *...And Holding* is hardly their finest hour. Though a remake of Jerry Butler's "Make It Easy on Yourself" is fairly likable, automatic pilot numbers like "Tie U Up," "Are You That Kind of Guy" and "Vital Signs" are as contrived as they are pedestrian. To be sure, a compilation of the trio's Philadelphia International material would be a much wiser investment. *—Alex Henderson*

● **The Best of the Three Degrees: When Will I See You Again** / 1996 / Epic/Legacy ♦♦♦♦♦

In the '70s, the Three Degrees bridged the gap between Philly soul and disco, moving from lush soul to seductive dance music within the course of their career. Although they had a few hits in the mid-'60s as R&B vocal group, their career didn't really take off until the mid '70s, when they signed to Philadelphia International and Gamble & Huff began producing their records. *The Best of the Three Degrees: When Will I See You Again* covers the trio's time at Philadelphia International, when they had a number-one pop hit with "TSOP (The Sound of Philadelphia)" and a number-two pop hit with "When Will I See You Again," in addition to a string of minor R&B hits. Although their sound was always pleasing, the Three Degrees didn't have quite enough depth in material to make this 14-track compilation consistently engaging. There are a couple of forgotten gems—including the minor hit "Love is the Message"—but the collection feels too comprehensive for some listeners. Still, *When Will I See You Again* is the ideal starting point for anyone interested in the Three Degrees—it boils down their best moments, from both singles and album, to one disc. *—Stephen Thomas Erlewine*

The Roulette Years / Jan. 1996 / Sequel ♦♦♦♦

Satiny, ear-pleasing sound checks from Philly's elegant Three Degrees. These '60s tracks preceded a scintillating run on Philadelphia International Records. *The Roulette Years* is loaded with phat remakes like "Maybe," "Who Is He and What Is He to You," "Ebb Tide," and "Trade Winds." The 22-songs encompass the best of their early years, and is essential for fans wanting another side of the "TSOP" and "When Will I See You Again" songbirds. *—Andrew Hamilton*

Gee Baby I'm Sorry: The Best of the Swan Years / Oct. 21, 1997 / Collectables ♦♦♦

Gee Baby, I'm Sorry: The Best of the Swan Years collects 15 highlights from the Three Degrees' early years, before they signed to Philadelphia International and became stars. In fact, this collection doesn't even feature the group's Roulette singles, which did include two Top Ten R&B hits, "Maybe" and "I Do Take You." Instead, *Gee Baby, I'm Sorry* chronicles the group's little-known girl group recordings for Swan in the mid-'60s. Only two singles, "Gee Baby" and "Look in My Eyes," became minor hits, which is one reason why these recordings have been ignored, but another, more prominent reason is that the label went bankrupt and they subsequently disappeared. Even though these aren't perfect, these recordings don't deserve to be ignored, since they capture the Three Degrees as a good girl group. They weren't an exceptional girl group—they certainly flourished under the direction of smooth Philly soul producers Gamble & Huff—but they were good, and this collection will satisfy many hardcore girl group collectors, even if the material is rather uneven. *—Stephen Thomas Erlewine*

Greatest Hits / Jan. 29, 2002 / Goldies ✦✦✦✦✦
A super-sizing of this long-running but under-publicized group's productive years—from 1970 to 1979—on Roulette, Philadelphia International, Epic, and Ariola Records. Only diehards will miss earlier (excluded) sides from 1965 to 1969 on Swan, ABC, Warner Bros., Metromedia, and Neptune. This set beams up their hits: "TSOP," "When Will I See You Again," "Maybe," "Dirty Old' Man," "Long Lost Lover," etc. and spans to include scorching renditions of New York City's "I'm Doing Fine Now," Marvin Gaye's "Let's Get It On," and Aretha Franklin's "Do Right Woman, Do Right Man." Essential for girl group fans, and a good buy for casual fans. *—Andrew Hamilton*

3LW

f. 1999
Group / Teen Pop, Urban
The young women that shape the R&B trio 3LW (Three Little Women) are Naturi Naughton, Kiely Williams, and Adrienne Bailon, and together they compose the healthy pop sound similar to the soulful poise of Destiny's Child, TLC, and Blaque. Each of them, however, hail from different backgrounds and their musical influences span a wide spectrum. The initial formation of the group was pulled together by Michelle Williams, mother of Kiely. She wanted a singing outlet for her daughter, and to make her daughter's wishes a reality, she held auditions and hand-picked each member for 3LW and became the manager of the group. 3LW was official.

New Jersey-native Kiely Williams started embracing the entertainment industry at age five. Her beginning moment in show business was for a TV pilot directed by Robert DeNiro, but the desire to sing came later. Naturi Naughton, also of New Jersey, had been singing in the church choir since the age of five, but Adrienne Bailon's rise to performing took an interesting shape. Bailon, who is of Puerto Rican and Ecuadorian background, grew up listening to her singer/songwriter father who emigrated from Ecuador to the States in hopes of scoring a better career deal in professional singing. Enjoying Latin tinges of salsa and Cumbia, she grew up listening to music and relishes the pioneering careers of Celia Cruz and La Lupe, but also appreciates the Latin newcomers like Marc Anthony and La India. Prior to joining 3LW, Bailon was spotted by Ricky Martin while singing with her church choir at a conference at Madison Square Garden. Hand-picked by the Latin superstar himself, Bailon had the opportunity to sing backup for Martin's performance that same evening.

In fall 2000, the girls also got a chance to act, playing an all-female group called Blue Mascara in an episode of the Nickelodeon series *Taina* and they also contributed their track "Til I Say So" to the 2000 teen flick *Bring It On*, featuring Kirsten Dunst. Signed to Epic, 3LW were becoming *TRL* mainstays at the time of their self-titled debut in fall 2000. Two years later, the ladies of 3LW added vocals to Bone Thugs-N-Harmony's summer smash "Get Up and Get It." They also spent most of summer 2002 recording and tweaking a second album, *A Girl Can Mack*. In August, founding member Naturi Naughton announced that she had been forced out of 3LW just a month shy of *A Girl Can Mack*'s release date and was soon replaced by vocalist Jessica Benson. *—MacKenzie Wilson*

● **3LW** / Nov. 14, 2000 / Epic ✦✦✦✦
On their million-selling debut single "No More (Baby I'm a Do Right)," female trio 3LW ("Three Little Women") leapt to the forefront with a fresh sound that deftly mixes hip-hop/R&B and pop. It's included on their self-titled debut album which has a sweet undercurrent of old-school craftsmanship. That is not to say that 3LW is retro; they're surrounded by melodically inventive uses of MIDI-based music. Standouts are "Is You Feelin' Me," "More Than Friends (That's Right)," "Crush on You," and the tender ballads "Curious," the inspiring "Ocean," and "I'm Gonna Make You Miss Me." The group's strong vocals and an overall adventurous vibe supplied by the album's producers and songwriters makes *3LW* a pleasure. *—Ed Hogan*

Three Million

Group / Disco, Dance-Pop
Three Million were siblings Wanda "Doll" Butler and Larry Butler and acquaintance Mark King, the same trio that recorded as Unity for United Artists Records. Doll and Larry originated Odds & Ends along with their younger brother Jim Grant. According to Larry, the name changes were a result of not owning them legally; with Three Million they corrected the problem and got the legal right to use and maintain the name. Doll came up with the moniker which means they wanted to make three million dollars or to look like three million bucks on-stage. Their manager, Eugene Lawson, worked a deal with Cotillion Records for a couple of 12-inch disco records. The first, "I've Been Robbed" (1983), was huge in New York City and parts of Jersey, but didn't score in Philly or elsewhere because, according to Larry, "Lawson pulled it." And he believes the reasoning was because Lawson wanted to concentrate on a record he was pushing on his Drema label. In 1984, Cotillion released "I've Got the Hots (For You)," a straight disco number that received some club spins, but Cotillion let them languish and didn't release any other recordings by them.

Doll moonlighted and took gigs as they came; she and another female vocalist once backed Major Harris at a local club. The gig nearly fell through when Harris didn't arrive when expected; Doll had to make a hasty mission to get an inebriated "Mr. Love Won't Let Me Wait" out of the arms of his current lady so she could get paid that night. Doll went solo after firing Larry for losing a tape she needed for a session. Reverend Reggie Wilder became her third manager and things were clicking but ended abruptly when Wilder passed in 1994. Some good solo material, especially "If You Believe," remained unreleased. Inactive since the death of Wilder, she still believes her three million dollars are waiting for her to deposit. Her husband was killed in North Philly in 1991, leaving her with two sons: Dale and Keith (now grown); she goes by her marital name, Wanda Maultasby. Larry left the biz in 1991 to support his family, and Mark recovered from two operations and plays piano at his church. *—Andrew Hamilton*

The Three Reasons

Group / Northern Soul, Soul
After two Carnival records singles, the Three Reasons—Kenneth Ruffin, Bruce Carter, and Robert Draden—faded into oblivion. Neither "Go Right On," released in 1971, nor "Take Me Back" in 1972 ignited. A shame because the former was a "you made your bed now lie in it" with a lilting chorus; the latter, an engaging plea with opening doo dah, doo dah, doo dah's, high-end harmony, and a falsetto lead was joined by a rougher tenor mid-song to drive home the point. Kenny Ruffin's wife, Shirley, wrote both of the Delfonics-flavored softies. Ruffin recorded a solo single for Carnival in 1968. "I'll Keep Holding On" b/w "Cry, Cry, Cry" was totally different from the Three Reasons sides. A hard, anguished tenor distinguishes both, and Ruffin, not his wife, wrote both sides. Ruffin penned "I Am the Man for You Baby" for the Turner Brothers, "Can't Lose My Head" for George Blackwell, and "Hang My Head and Cry" on the Big Boys for Warner Bros.

With nearly 30 registered compositions, Ruffin's most successful was the Moment's "I Do" (1969), which featured Billy Brown doing the lead and background parts; Harry Ray and Al Goodman weren't even in the studio. He also wrote "She's Gone to Another," a grieving ballad where the lead bemoans over being dumped, for the Whatnauts. The Three Reasons' singles were promising, but the group was short lived. Even sadder, they only recorded two sides for Carnival; the B-sides were instrumentals. *—Andrew Hamilton*

Johnny Thunder (Gil Hamilton)

b. Aug. 15, 1941, Leesburg, FL
Vocals / Soul, R&B
In 1963, Johnny Thunder, born Gil Hamilton, scored the only hit of his career. "Loop de Loop" was essentially a nursery rhyme set to music. The public loved it, and it assailed to the lofty perch of number four on the pop charts. Only "Hey Paula" at number one, "Walk Right In," and Bobby Vee's "The Night Has a Thousand Eyes" at number three, prevented it from being the top record during the week of February 9, 1963.

Born August 15, 1941, in Leesburg, FL, Johnny Thunder started singing in church, high school, and on street corners. Nothing was happening in Florida in the late '50s, so Thunder moved to New York City under the advice of a friend who worked as the road manager for the Drifters. Thunder even sung with the famous Atlantic Record group for a few months prior to Ben E. King leaving to go solo. After the stint, he started recording under his birth name for Capitol and Fury Records, but had no success. To keep the rent paid and food in his belly, he made himself useful as a studio background vocalist working with then-unknowns Dionne Warwick, Luther Vandross, Cissy Houston, and others. Thunder's high mellow resonant tenor always lifted him above the others. One of his Capitol releases was "Tell Him," the same song which became a hit for the Exciters months after his version had died. (The Exciters' members included the boisterous voice of Brenda Reid, who's the mother of Antonio "L.A." Reid, who became a songwriting and record producing force with Babyface in the '80s, '90s, and 2000s.)

Producer/songwriter Teddy Vann came up with "Loop de Loop," a song that Thunder thought was a joke. Vann even suggested the name change from Gil Hamilton to Johnny Thunder. None of his following releases came close to equaling the success of "Loop": "The Rosey Dance" failed to enter the Top 100, stopping at number 122; Bert Bern's "Everybody Do the Sloopy" did much better, but its showing at number 67 was still unimpressive. Like most singers, Thunder didn't like the stuff he recorded, but did it hoping lightening would strike twice. He continued recording throughout the '60s, waxing sides for Calla, Vee-Jay, and United Artists Records; the Vee-Jay 45 dropped under his birth name. In the '70s, he recorded sides for Arista, but again, no hits. He recorded one album, *Loop de Loop*, on Diamond. *—Andrew Hamilton*

Loop de Loop / 1963 / Diamond ✦✦✦
A quick cash-in effort number-four chart placement of the title track in early 1963, this album suffers from too much sameness, though Johnny Thunder is a good singer. Producer Teddy Vann, who wrote (or, more properly, adapted) "Loop De Loop" as an R&B-type song, wrote all but one other cut on this album, and attempted to give the same kind of treatment to "Al-La-Wetta," "All 'Round in a Circle," etc., without similar commercial results. It is a good midtempo R&B album, however, and marked an early success for the songwriting of Al Kooper, who co-authored the only non-Teddy Van composition here, "The Chain"—according to Kooper, he and his songwriting partners worked in the same building where Thunder did, and the song was written for him because they thought they had a shot at getting covered, which it was. Kooper and his partners Irwin Levine and Bob Brass had far greater success with the song "This Diamond Ring" later in the year (ironically, a song written with the Drifters in mind, and Thunder had briefly sung with the Drifters). *—Bruce Eder*

● **Loop de Loop: The Very Best of Johnny Thunder** / Jul. 28, 1998 / Collectables ✦✦✦
Not to be confused with Johnny Thunders, the legendary junkie guitarist of the New York Dolls and Heartbreakers, Johnny Thunder was a dynamic R&B and rock & roll singer who originally sang as a backing vocalist for the Drifters and the Ink Spots. He had a hit in 1963 with "Loop de Loop," and an infectious dance number reminiscent of Hank Ballard or a more soulful Chubby Checker. Although he had another minor hit a few years later with "Make Love to Me," a duet with Ruby Winters, during the early '60s he wasn't able to successfully follow up "Loop de Loop." Nevertheless, even if they didn't chart, a few of his subsequent singles were pretty good, as evidenced by Collectables' *Loop de Loop: The Very Best of Johnny Thunder*. It's certainly not flawless—a few of the

songs are shameless attempts to replicate "Loop de Loop," and others are simply silly—but for archivists of early-'60s R&B and rock, it's worth a listen. —*Stephen Thomas Erlewine*

Bobby Thurston

b. Washington, D.C.

Vocals / Disco

Soul singer Bobby Thurston was a native of Washington, D.C., and got his start singing and playing congas with a group called Spectrum Ltd. in his high school years. He caught his break when writers/producers Willie Lester and Rodney Brown heard him sing live, and signed him as part of their attempt to forge a stable of artists in the vein of Philadelphia International. Thurston recorded his first album, *Sweetest Piece of the Pie*, in 1978, and it was very much in the smooth, mellow Philly soul vein, with help from keyboardist/arranger Al Johnson. Thurston's subsequent recordings for Prelude were more consistently disco-oriented, starting with 1980's double-sided 12-inch club smash "You Got What It Takes"/"Check Out the Groove." The accompanying LP, *You Got What It Takes*, became his biggest seller, but the 1981 follow-up, *The Main Attraction*, was less successful, and Thurston faded from view as disco died out. —*Steve Huey*

You Got What It Takes / 1980 / Epic ♦♦♦

"You Got What It Takes" is not the old Marv Johnson song, but a new concoction that incorporates Thurston's nondescript tenor over a peppy disco-length track. "I Wanna Do It with You," supposedly about dancing, samples Thurston's lead on a pulsating track with nice changes; the female voices sing with vigor, and Rodney Brown's guitar solo and Al Johnson's maniacal keyboarding will have your ears ringing. Also includes the first-class booty song "I Want Your Body" and a pedestrian remake of Billy Stewart's "Sitting in the Park." —*Andrew Hamilton*

The Main Attraction / 1981 / Epic ♦♦♦

● **You Got What It Takes/The Main Attraction** / Jun. 10, 1997 / Deep Beats ♦♦♦

Thurston's first LP, 1982's *You Got What It Takes*, is also his best collection of lite, white-boy funk; as an added bonus, this reissue also features his follow-up, 1981's *Main Attraction*. —*Jason Ankeny*

Tierra

f. 1972, East Los Angeles, CA

Group / Latin Pop, Brown-Eyed Soul, Latin Rock, Urban

An early-'70s spin-off group from El Chicano, Tierra kept plugging away until 1980, when they scored some brief success on the R&B charts doing Afro-Latin-flavored soul covers. Guitarist Rudy and trombonist/percussionist Steve Salas had both been in El Chicano. They teamed with keyboardist Joey Guerra, bassist Steve Falomir, drummer Philip Madayag, percussionist Andre Baeza, and Bobby Navarrete on reeds. Their cover of the Intruders' "Together" cracked the R&B Top Ten in 1980 and reached number 18 on the pop charts. It was their lone big hit, although their remake of the Delfonics' "La La Means I Love You" did make the R&B Top 40 in 1981. The group returned in the early '90s with *Tonight* in 1993 and *A New Beginning* two years later. —*Ron Wynn*

Tierra / 1973 / 20th Century ♦♦♦♦

Tierra was a spinoff of El Chicano, a risk-taking band that fused soul, jazz, rock, and Latin music and gave us the hits "Viva Tirado" and "Tell Her She's Lovely." So, not surprisingly, Tierra was very El Chicano-influenced in the beginning. By the time it recorded the 1978 single "Gonna Find Her," Tierra had fashioned a very distinctive style of brown-eyed soul. But when it recorded *Tierra* in 1973, the East L.A. band was still searching for an identity. This vinyl LP, which Salsoul reissued in 1981, isn't as focused or inspired as 1980's *City Nights*—it's an uneven record, although a generally competent one. Even though Tierra was still finding its way in 1975, one hears some potential on soul-pop offerings like "Don't Be So Sure" and "Knowing You, Loving You" as well as the salsa tune "Baila Simon" and the jazz fusion instrumental "Sun God." Also noteworthy is the poignant "Land of the Free," which describes the struggle that a poor Mexican immigrant faces after his arrival in the U.S.—the song addresses the sort of conditions that activist Cesar Chavez dedicated his life to improving. Although it has its moments, *Tierra* is the work of a band that, in 1975, still had some developing to do. Nonetheless, collectors will find this LP interesting. —*Alex Henderson*

City Nights / 1980 / Boardwalk ♦♦♦♦♦

Outside of the Mexican-American community, Tierra is considered a one-hit wonder—the band's only major national hit was its 1980 cover of the Intruders' "Together," which reached the Top Ten on the R&B singles charts. But among Mexican-Americans, the East L.A. band enjoyed a devoted cult following. Released in 1980, *City Nights* is a soul-oriented classic that sometimes detours into Latin-flavored grooves. Anyone with a taste for sweet Northern-style soul should make a point of hearing Tierra's version of "Together" as well as the sentimental "Memories" and the romantic ballad "Gonna Find Her" (which had been released as a single in 1978). Tierra successfully mixes funk-soul with salsa on "Latin Disco" and "Time to Dance," and the Chicano band turns to swing with catchy results on "Zoot Suit Boogie"—an instrumental that fondly recalls the days when pachucos were the party animals of East L.A. Without question, *City Nights* is Tierra's most essential album. —*Alex Henderson*

● **Greatest Hits** / Jul. 25, 2000 / Thump ♦♦♦♦♦

Tierra's *Greatest Hits* collects the Latin R&B group's most memorable songs, including the Top 20 hit "Together." "Gonna Find Her," "Barrio Suite," "Margarita," "Sonya," and a live version of "Vamanos Pa Monte" round out this best-of compilation, which is a good introduction to Tierra's unique Latino soul sound. —*Heather Phares*

Justin Timberlake

b. Memphis, TN

Vocals / Teen Pop, Dance-Pop, Adult Contemporary, Urban

As both a member of *NSYNC and a solo artist, Southern superstar Justin Timberlake has played a major role in the teen pop explosion of the '90s and 2000s. Like similar teen pop favorites—who have included the Backstreet Boys, C-Note, Christina Aguilera, Hanson, the Spice Girls, and Britney Spears—Timberlake usually doesn't get much respect from rock critics (who, in many cases, tend to be very alternative-minded and anti-commercialistic). Regardless, he is adored by millions of fans, many of whom have been adolescent girls. Over the years, the teen market has had a lot of different sounds. In the '70s, for example, artists like Donny Osmond, the Partridge Family, David Cassidy, and the DeFranco Family were aimed at teens—those were the bubblegum popsters one typically read about in *Tiger Beat* magazine back then. But Timberlake is part of the more modern school of teen pop, which is mindful of dance-pop, urban contemporary, and hip-hop and got started with the rise of New Kids on the Block, Debbie Gibson, and Tiffany in the late '80s. New Kids, in fact, were the male group that paved the way for *NSYNC as well as the Backstreet Boys and Take That (who were meant to be a British equivalent of New Kids). And just as *Tiger Beat* (the bible of bubblegum) was obsessed with the New Kids in the late '80s, it would become equally obsessed with *NSYNC and the Backstreet Boys in the '90s.

Like Spears (who Timberlake became romantically involved with), Aguilera, and *NSYNC's JC Chasez, Timberlake got his start on the Disney Channel's '90s version of *The Mickey Mouse Club*. Timberlake and Chasez were on *The Mickey Mouse Club* simultaneously in their pre-*NSYNC days, and they kept working together when *NSYNC was formed. *NSYNC got started in Orlando, FL, in 1996, when Timberlake and Chasez teamed up with Lance Bass, Chris Kirkpatrick, and Joey Fatone. Released by RCA/BMG in 1998, the vocal quintet's self-titled debut album sold millions of copies in both the U.S. and Europe and contained the smash hits "I Want You Back" and "Tearing Up My Heart." *NSYNC's second album, *No Strings Attached*, was released on Jive in 2000 and was even more commercially successful; *No Strings Attached* went double platinum in only one week, and the singles "Bye Bye Bye" and "This I Promise You" became major hits.

Jive released *Celebrity*, *NSYNC's third album, in 2001, and after that, Timberlake started recording as a solo artist. The singer had performed live as a solo artist before *NSYNC, but it wasn't until the early 2000s that he actually recorded an album as a solo act. *Justified*, Timberlake's first solo album, was released on Jive in November 2002. "Like I Love You," the album's first single, became a major hit and was followed by a second single, "Cry Me a River" (not to be confused with the melancholy Arthur Hamilton standard that was a hit for the late jazz singer/actress Julie London in 1955). —*Alex Henderson*

● **Justified** / Nov. 5, 2002 / Jive ♦♦♦

Growing up is hard to do, as any teen pop idol will attest. Still, showbiz kids are nothing if not savvy, so they know it's better to make the jump than to idle as an idol, no matter how hard that jump may be—and no matter how hard they try, it's hard to judge the distance, and they may miss their mark. With his debut solo album, *Justified* (face it, that title was a given), Justin Timberlake misses his mark slightly; he hits much closer than fellow *Mickey Mouse Club* alum Christina Aguilera did with her *Stripped*, but he's uneasy as a suave, mature lover-man, particularly because much of his stance is borrowed directly (and rather improbably) from Michael Jackson. JT—a shorthand nickname that's distressingly inevitable—shamelessly borrows from Jacko, from the *Thriller*-era getup and poses, to the sharply modernized spin on the classic *Off the Wall* sound. To be sure, the sound of the Neptunes productions which dominate *Justified* is the best thing about the album; they have a lush, sexy, stylish feel that is better, more romantic than most modern R&B. Too bad they're delivered by such a cipher. Though he's turned into a technically skilled vocalist, he's still too much of a showbiz kid—all technique and surface, not much substance. His falsetto may be smooth, but it's utterly without character, which unfortunately describes the songs too: pretty on the surface, but devoid of memorable hooks. This means that what truly stands out is when he breaks from form and tries to prove how street and hip he is, delivering awful entendres like "I can think of a couple of positions for you" and "get real wet if you know what I mean" and exhorting the fellas and ladies to sing separately in a cringe-worthy affectation on "Senorita." When he sings that he'll "have you nekkid by the end of the song," he doesn't sound like a seductor, he sounds like a kid actor awkwardly assuming a new persona. This isn't without merit—the sound, apart from some flop Timbaland productions (which he redeems with the slinky funk of "Right for Me"), works well, and if these cuts were songs instead of tracks, his bland falsetto would be fine. This sure isn't the musical immolation of Christina's ugly *Stripped*. Unlike that album, this suggests a direction Timberlake could follow in the future, given stronger songwriting collaborators. But *Justified* is just sound and posturing, with no core. [Bad packaging alert: The foldout booklet for *Justified* is merely stuck into the digipak for the album, with no sleeve or slot to house it; it's guaranteed to get beat up or lost.] —*Stephen Thomas Erlewine*

The Time

f. 1981, Minneapolis, MN

Group / Funk, Urban, Dance-Pop

From their origins as Prince's first pet project to their self-produced funk-rock oeuvre, the Time has been a fascinating and outrageous congregation. Vocalist Morris Day infused his cocky, swaggering personality into dance hits that would make Rufus Thomas envious, and, unlike most of the competition, the band managed to do something unique with Prince's genre-busting innovations. The Time broke up in the late '80s, with Day going on to a somewhat disastrous solo career, Jesse Johnson crafting two dazzling solo albums, and Jimmy Jam & Terry Lewis becoming one of the most successful production teams this side of Gamble & Huff, working with everyone from Full Force and Janet Jackson to the S.O.S. Band and Human League. The group re-formed in 1990 and released the excellent *Pandemonium*. *—John Floyd*

The Time / 1981 / Warner Bros. ♦♦♦

The Time's 1981 debut album found the group of Minneapolis-based Prince affiliates in a formative stage, blending synthesizers with guitars, humor with sex, and rock with funk. This amalgam of seemingly juxtaposing elements wasn't anything incredibly innovative, particularly when one looks at '70s groups such as the Ohio Players or Funkadelic. But even if the Time are merely co-opting a '70s funk approach, they're instilling an undeniable '80s aesthetic—more studio polish, more prominent use of synthesizer, an emphasis on vanity, and more overt sexual innuendoes. So even if this self-titled debut isn't entirely realized in terms of musical direction, the Time has no doubt stumbled onto something exciting here, particularly given the album's 1981 release date. Furthermore, with "Give It Up," they offer a fully blossomed moment of brilliance among the other five formative songs; this song in particular sums up everything wonderful and worthy of praise about the Time and why they were so influential if not popular: the group's densely layered funk riffs anchored by Terry Lewis' basslines, the dirty-minded lyrics, the catchy singalong chorus, Morris Day's quirky charisma, Jesse Johnson's manic guitar solos, the dual synthesizers, and the underlying near-mechanical drum sound. Furthermore, the song stretched itself to epic lengths, leaving plenty of time for jamming. Nothing else on this album quite compares, though "Cool" molds itself similarly, stretching itself to epic lengths. The shorter songs here aren't really that effective, particularly the ballads—it's clear even at this point that the group's strengths lie in their instrumentation and not Morris Day's songwriting. Though this isn't a perfect album, none of the Time's small handful of albums were. "Give It Up" by itself makes this self-titled debut worth seeking out; consider the other five songs a bonus. *—Jason Birchmeier*

● **What Time Is It?** / 1982 / Warner Bros. ♦♦♦♦♦

Despite only releasing three albums in the early '80s, the group thought of primarily as Prince's opening act by many at the time proved to be an influential group in retrospect. And if there is one album that illustrates why the Time deserve such praise, it's *What Time Is It?* First of all, the group only released a trilogy of early-'80s albums, with the other two—*The Time* (1981) and *Ice Cream Castle* (1984)—each somewhat flawed. Thankfully, *What Time Is It?* proves itself to be a perfect medium. The group's patented aesthetic that first became clear on "Give It Up" from their formative debut album blossoms here, and the ridge between Morris Day's wannabe-Prince megalomania and the musicians' enormous talents hasn't quite become an issue yet. Secondly, the group doesn't try anything too ambitious here; in fact, they almost seem to rewrite their debut album, fixing its flaws and expanding upon its strengths. Again, they offer six songs, this time going with more epic jam-orientated songs. Furthermore, Morris Day even manages to offer a respectable ballad with "Gigolos Get Lonely Too." But, for the most part, the Time are at their best when they're jamming—which they do plenty of here—and not when Day is singing or indulging in one of his many ideologically questionable skits. But what makes this album the Time's best isn't so much its highlights but rather its lack of poor moments. Both *The Time* and *Ice Cream Castle* have moments of brilliance that rival even this album's best; however, those two albums are burdened by lackluster moments—this album has none. From beginning to end, *What Time Is It?* is nothing but fun music, driven largely by brilliant funk riffing and also by some catchy hooks. *—Jason Birchmeier*

Ice Cream Castle / 1984 / Warner Bros. ♦♦♦

The final album released before the Time splintered into pieces for the remainder of the '80s, *Ice Cream Castle* provides ample evidence in regard to both the group's undeniable talents and also the personal issues that ultimately led to their demise. On the one hand, *Ice Cream Castle* finds the Time perfecting their patented style of synth-heavy funk-rock; while their previous two albums saw their music blossom, here it sounds fully realized. Never once does the band sound tentative, churning out densely layered riffs with near-reckless abandon when given the chance. In particular, Jesse Johnson steals the spotlight at times with his '80s-style guitar solos, complementing the rhythm section's synth funk with his rock aesthetic. Yet on the other hand, as tempting as it is to praise the Time for hitting their stride with *Ice Cream Castle*, Morris Day's egocentric indulgences ruin what very well could be the group's best album; you can feel the ridge dividing his megalomania from the remaining group's rapport. When Day keeps his antics to a minimum and lets the group jam—such as on "Ice Cream Castles," "My Drawers," and "Jungle Love"—it becomes quite clear why this group is so revered: at this point in their short-lived career, they can play circles around any other '80s funk band. But then there are the obvious Day vehicles—"Chili Sauce," "If the Kid Can't Make You Come," and "The Bird"—three songs that find the singer/songwriter's charismatic mania frustratingly eclipsing the band's efforts with his tasteless belligerence. In retrospect, this flawed album does have some brilliant moments worth seeking out; it's just unfortunate that a few self-centered moments on Day's part, and to a lesser degree overproduction, sour what could very well have been the Time's crowing achievement. *—Jason Birchmeier*

Pandemonium / Jun. 1990 / Paisley Park ♦♦♦

How frustrating it is that one of the most vital and dynamic bands of the 1980s, the Time, broke up after only three albums. When the Time reunited in 1990 after a six-year absence from the studio, there was excitement as well as cautious optimism in the R&B world. The big question: Would the chemistry still be there? And the answer turned out to be a definite "yes." Humorous, inventive, and unapologetically funky, *Pandemonium* is an excellent party album that's every bit as strong as its three predecessors. Leader Morris Day is as amusing and confident as ever, and the distinctive unit still used the influence of George Clinton and mentor Prince to great artistic advantage. Those who savored the Time's three previous albums will find that on gems like "Chocolate," "Jerk Out," and the rock-influenced "Blondie" (a fine vehicle for Jesse Johnson's electric guitar), the old magic asserts itself without hesitation. This is a disc that no fan of the Minneapolis sound should be without. *—Alex Henderson*

Timex Social Club

f. 1982, **db.** 1987

Group / Dance-Pop, New Jack Swing, Old School Rap

The forerunner to Club Nouveau, the Timex Social Club had one huge hit in 1986, the R&B chart-topper "Rumors." It peaked at number-eight pop, and featured Michael Marshall's vocals. The two follow-up singles, "Thinkin' About Ya" and "Mixed Up World," both made the R&B Top 20, but producer Jay King shortly afterward formed his own band, Club Nouveau, and the Timex Social Club disbanded. *—Ron Wynn*

● **Vicious Rumors** / 1987 / Danya ♦♦♦♦

Titiyo (Titiyo Jah)

b. 1967, Stockholm, Sweden

Vocals / Swedish Pop/Rock, Club/Dance, Dance-Pop, Hip-Hop

The title of Sweden's Queen of Soul might not seem one of modern music's most coveted crowns but, in Sweden itself, there is little doubt that Titiyo not only merits all the acclaim lavished by her homeland, but that international acclaim has already demolished borders across much of Europe too. Titiyo Jah was born in Stockholm in 1967, the half sister of singer Neneh Cherry—their father is Sierra Leone-born percussionist Ahmadu Jah of the Africa Hi-Life Orchestra. It was Cherry who first pointed Titiyo in the direction of performing, encouraging her to sing and prompting her, too, to seek out musical directions that Swedish pop had rarely visited in the past. By 1987, Titiyo was fronting her own band, performing rare groove covers on the Stockholm circuit before signing to the local Telegram label in 1989.

Titiyo scored her first hit that June, when "Talking to the Man in the Moon" climbed to number six on the Swedish chart. "After the Rain" reached number 13 in November and the following summer brought Titiyo's self-titled debut album. It reached number three and also brought her to the attention of American audiences, via a well-received Arista release. An imminent breakthrough, however, was placed on hold when Titiyo withdrew for two years to raise her newborn first child; it was September 1993 before she resurfaced, with a cover of Aretha Franklin's "Never Let Me Go," a number-25 Swedish hit. *This Is Titiyo*, her second album, followed in 1993. Featuring guest appearances from both of her parents (Titiyo's mother is an accomplished pianist), the album spun off further hits "Back and Forth" and "Tell Me I'm Not Dreaming" and, even before Titiyo made her London debut at the Astoria in February 1994, garage remixes of several tracks were established club favorites.

Over the next two years, Titiyo's activities were largely confined to guest work. She appeared with the Blacknuss All Stars ("It Should Have Been With You") and Stakka Bo & the Flesh Quartet ("We Vie"), and duetted with sibling Eagle-Eye Cherry on a track from the *Best Laid Plans* movie soundtrack, "Worried Eyes." Her own next album, *Extended*, finally arrived in late 1997, a self-produced/composed epic highlighted by the hit single "Josefin Dean." As usual, another lengthy silence followed the album's release, a four-year gap that was finally broken in 2001 by *Come Along*. Recorded with the songwriting team of Peter Svensson (the Cardigans) and Jocke Berg (Kent), and produced by Tore Johansson, *Come Along* received a U.S. release (through Lava) in October 2002. *—Dave Thompson*

Titiyo / 1991 / Arista ♦♦

● **Come Along** / Oct. 15, 2002 / Lava ♦♦♦♦

While Titiyo might never re-create the sheer visceral shock of her debut album, still nobody could ever accuse Sweden's Queen of Soul of standing still. Following up from the self-produced excursion that was her third album, Titiyo now links with Cardigans/Kent supremos Peter Svensson and Joakim Berg for an album that carves her so-remarkable voice into its rockiest surroundings yet. She credits her recent discovery of Radiohead, Jeff Buckley, and even Soundgarden for pushing her in this new direction, and that may be. The influence that hangs most heavily, however, is another Svensson/Berg project, Paus; indeed, *Come Along* started life as nothing more than an English-language revision of that entire album. Instead, the pair presented her with an entire new collection of songs and wound up with a set that leaves Paus itself in the dust. The opening title track sets the scene, a sultry post-blues number infused with just enough of Titiyo's trademark dance sensibility to mask (but never bury) the distinctly PJ Harvey-esque feel of the song itself. Later, "My Heart Won" takes a similar brew, but this time has no compunction whatsoever about pushing Titiyo into some defiantly scratchy territory, even as it continues to acknowledge her urban R&B roots and reputation. A few nods in the general direction of trip-hop also offer respite to fans puzzled by the omnipresent guitars, while "Last Time" is a showstopping ballad that would have sounded great on any of her past albums—a point that is proven by the bonus addition of "Josefin Dean" (from 1997's *Extended*) to U.S. pressings of *Come Along*. A major European hit at the time, it's a swirling blues that, at the time, posited one of several future directions suggested by that album. Its seamless inclusion on *Come Along* suggests Titiyo took the correct one. *—Dave Thompson*

TLC

f. 1991, Atlanta, GA

Group / Hip-Hop, Urban, Club/Dance, Dance-Pop

TLC was one of the biggest-selling female R&B groups of all time, riding a blend of pop, hip-hop, and urban soul to superstardom during the '90s. Tionne "T-Boz" Watkins, rapper Lisa "Left Eye" Lopes, and Rozonda "Chilli" Thomas managed to appeal equally to pop and R&B audiences, blending catchy hooks and bouncy funk with a sassy, sexy attitude. Initially, their image was equal parts style and spirit, bolstered by a flamboyant, outrageous wardrobe. As time passed, they became equally well known for their chaotic personal lives, leaving a trail of headlines that read like a soap-opera plot: arson, rehab, bankruptcy, serious illness, high-profile romances, and countless intra-group squabbles.

After their star-making second album, *CrazySexyCool*, TLC fell into disarray, taking over four years to record the follow-up *Fanmail*; even so, they returned more popular than ever, and the hits kept on coming. Unfortunately, tragedy struck in early 2002, when Lopes was killed in a car accident in Honduras.

TLC was formed in Atlanta, GA, in 1991, when Watkins and Lopes decided to split off from another all-female group. In short order, they met Thomas, locally based producer Dallas Austin, and '80s R&B singer Pebbles, who became their manager. They quickly scored a record deal with L.A. Reid and Babyface's new label, LaFace, and in 1992 issued their new jack-styled debut album *Ooooooohhh... On the TLC Tip*. The video for the sexy, aggressive lead single "Ain't 2 Proud 2 Beg" established their quirky, colorful fashion sense, and true to her nickname, Lopes stirred some attention by wearing a condom over her left eye to promote safe sex. The song became a Top Ten hit, as did its follow-ups, the ballad "Baby-Baby-Baby" (a number-two hit) and "What About Your Friends." TLC was definitely a success, but they weren't quite stars yet, and it remained to be seen whether they could maintain their momentum over the long haul.

Not long before the release of their second album in late 1994, Lisa Lopes was arrested on arson charges. In an alcohol-fueled fit of rage, Lopes vented all the frustrations from her often-stormy relationship with NFL wide receiver Andre Rison, burning his Atlanta mansion to the ground and vandalizing several of his cars. Lopes' lawyers claimed that she had a drinking problem, and while Lopes herself wasn't happy with that defense, she avoided jail time with a sentence of five years' probation; she was also later admitted to an alcohol rehab program. All the publicity certainly didn't hurt *CrazySexyCool*, which became a blockbuster success, albeit for other reasons. Taking a cue from Salt-N-Pepa's makeover on *Very Necessary*, *CrazySexyCool* toned down the boisterousness of their first record in favor of a smoother, more mature presentation; they were still strong and sexual, but now fully adult as well, and were more involved (especially Lopes) in crafting their own material. The slinky lead single "Creep" became TLC's first number-one pop hit, topping the charts for four weeks. It was followed by three more Top Five singles: "Red Light Special," "Waterfalls" (which became their biggest hit ever, spending seven weeks at number one), and "Diggin' on You." TLC was a bona fide phenomenon, and their stylish videos and live performances kept upping the ante for outrageous fashion sense. *CrazySexyCool* eventually sold over 11-million copies in the U.S. alone, and won a Grammy for Best R&B Album.

All was not well, however. In 1995, TLC filed for bankruptcy, claiming debts of over 3.5-million dollars, in part stemming from Lopes' insurance payments over the arson incident. They also claimed they hadn't seen their fair share of royalties from *CrazySexyCool*; LaFace countered that they were simply trying to get a bigger contract. TLC did wind up splitting from Pebbles' management company over the money issues (not helped by the fact that Pebbles' marriage to LaFace head L.A. Reid had gone through a nasty breakup). What was more, it was announced that for some time, Watkins had been battling sickle cell anemia, which sapped her energy and often made performing difficult. TLC spent much of 1996 getting their financial affairs in order, and was set to re-enter the studio in the summer of 1997. The sessions had trouble getting off the ground, though, thanks to the group's public spat with producer Dallas Austin, claiming that his fee was far too high; not only had Austin played a significant role in the creation of their music, but the split was all the more awkward because he and Thomas had just had a son together. It took until early 1998 to finally resolve the producer situation, and Austin wound up handling the vast majority of the record. Still, it took quite some time to put together; Lopes announced in the summer of 1998 that she was working on a solo record, and Watkins tried her hand at acting with an appearance in the Hype Williams-directed *Belly*. All the delays, tension, and side projects fueled rumors of the group's impending breakup.

TLC's third album was finally released at the beginning of 1999. The hotly anticipated *Fanmail* debuted at number one, and its first single "No Scrubs"—a dismissal of men who didn't measure up—topped the charts as well for four weeks. The critically acclaimed follow-up, "Unpretty," tackled unrealistic beauty standards, and spent three weeks at number one. *Fanmail* wound up going six-times platinum, and won another Best R&B Album Grammy. As TLC prepared to tour in late 1999, tensions between the individual members spilled over into a public feud; Watkins and Thomas criticized Lopes for putting herself before the group, and Lopes responded by blasting TLC's recent music and challenging her bandmates to record solo albums, so that fans could see who the real talent lay with. The blowup was only temporary, but rumors about TLC's future continued to swirl. Lopes continued to publicize her upcoming solo project, and Thomas eventually began working on her own album as well. Watkins married rapper Mack 10 in the summer of 2000, and had their first child not long after. Meanwhile, tabloid favorite Lopes continued to make headlines when she disappeared for over a week, missing a family function and a press conference (she turned out to be with a new boyfriend).

In 2001, TLC somehow managed to regroup and enter the studio together to work on material for a new album. That summer, a report surfaced that Lopes had postponed a wedding with, of all people, Andre Rison. Meanwhile, her solo debut, *Supernova*, was scheduled for release and then scrapped on several occasions; it eventually came out overseas, but domestically Arista pulled the plug. Meanwhile, TLC's recording halted while Watkins was hospitalized from complications with her anemia. At the beginning of 2002, Lopes announced that she had signed a solo deal with the infamous Suge Knight's new label Tha Row, for which she would begin recording a follow-up to the unreleased *Supernova* under the name N.I.N.A. (New Identity Non-Applicable). Sadly, she would never get the chance. Vacationing in her favorite getaway spot, Honduras, Lopes was driving a rented SUV with at least seven (possibly eight) passengers. Reportedly speeding, she lost control of the vehicle, which flipped over; she was the only member of the party to be seriously injured, and died from severe head trauma on April 25, 2002. The surviving members of TLC completed the album they'd begun before Lopes' passing, titled *3D*, and released it to positive reviews. *—Steve Huey*

Ooooooohhh . . . On the TLC Tip / Feb. 25, 1992 / LaFace ✦✦✦
TLC's debut album was a well-produced but inconsistent effort, with the three hit singles—"Ain't 2 Proud 2 Beg," "Baby-Baby-Baby," and "What About Your Friends"—being the catchiest and most memorable songs on the album. *—Sara Sytsma*

● **CrazySexyCool** / 1994 / LaFace ✦✦✦✦✦
On their second album, TLC downplays their overt rap connections, recording a smooth, seductive collection of contemporary soul reminiscent of both Philly soul and Prince, powered by new jack and hip-hop beats. Lisa Lopes contributes the occasional rap, but the majority of *CrazySexyCool* belongs to Tionne Watkins and Rozonda Thomas. While they aren't the most accomplished vocalists—they have a tendency to be just slightly off-key—the material they sing is consistently strong. As the cover of Prince's "If I Was Your Girlfriend" indicates, TLC favors erotic, midtempo funk. Yet the group removes any of the psychosexual complexities of Prince's songs, leaving a batch of sexy material that just sounds good, especially the hit singles. Both "Creep" and "Red Light Special" have a deep groove that accentuates the slinky hooks, but it's "Waterfalls," with its gently insistent horns and guitar lines and instantly memorable chorus, that ranks as one of the classic R&B songs of the '90s. *—Stephen Thomas Erlewine*

Fanmail / Feb. 23, 1999 / LaFace ✦✦✦✦
CrazySexyCool was one of those records that defined an era. Few records before it combined hip-hop and classic soul songwriting quite as intoxicatingly or gracefully—the performances and productions were utterly seamless. It would have been difficult to top anyway, but TLC had it doubly bad, since a number of behind-the-scenes problems delayed a sequel for nearly five years. As with any eagerly anticipated record, that follow-up, *Fanmail*, arrived with too many expectations. And initially, it may be disappointing to realize TLC doesn't forge new ground with *Fanmail*, but after a few spins, it settles in that nobody else makes urban soul quite as engaging as this. Not that it was easy to make this record, as the head-spinning list of collaborators indicates. Almost ten producers worked on the record, all trying to replicate the easy, appealing sound of *CrazySexyCool*. And "replicate" is the right word, since there are no new innovations on *Fanmail*, apart from a few lifts from the Timbaland book of tricks. Nevertheless, that may be for the best, since TLC and their army of producers have spent time crafting the songs and productions, turning *Fanmail* into a record that almost reaches the peaks of its predecessor. By the end of the record, it appears that they can do it all—funky, hip-hop-fueled dance-pop, seductive ballads, and midtempo jams—and they can do it all well. Other groups try to reach these heights, but they don't have the skills or the material to pull it off quite so well. True, the five-year wait felt interminable, and they're now standard-bearers instead of pioneers, but if takes TLC as long to make a sequel to *Fanmail*, so be it—they have one of the best track records in '90s urban soul. *—Stephen Thomas Erlewine*

3D / Sep. 17, 2002 / LaFace ✦✦✦✦
How good is TLC? So good that they survive the tragic, early death of a key member—Lisa "Left Eye" Lopes was killed in a car accident during the recording of *3D*—with grace and style, turning out a record that sits comfortably next to their modern classics, *CrazySexyCool* and *Fanmail*. Perhaps surviving members Chilli and T-Boz spend a little too much time in the lyrics paying tribute to their colleague, but it's easy to glide past that and just concentrate on the strong songwriting and stylish production. Like their previous albums, the particulars don't matter as much as the overall impression. No member of TLC has an astounding voice, but their skills are exploited to the hilt, since the material not only suits them, it's melodic, memorable, and grows in stature with each play. Best of all, the production plays to the strength of the song, balancing the group's character and abilities with the hooks and character of the song. Perhaps *3D* doesn't blaze trails like their other albums, but it never plays it safe and it always satisfies, and it's one of the best modern soul albums of 2002. A bittersweet triumph, perhaps, but it's better to go out on a positive note. *—Stephen Thomas Erlewine*

Today

f. 1989, Englewood, NJ, **db.** 1991
Group / Urban
Motown promoted Today as the new Four Tops in the late '80s, though the group had company. The Boys were pushed as the new Jacksons and the Good Girls the new Supremes. Today and the Boys enjoyed number-one R&B hits, while the Good Girls charted with a few singles but never reached the pinnacle. Today—Frederick Lee "Bubba" Drakeford, Larry Singletary, Wesley Adams, and Larry McCain—were childhood friends from Englewood, NJ. They formed as the Gents around 1984 and befriended a record company executive at an anti-drug benefit who arranged a meeting with the then virtually unknown Teddy Riley, who renamed them Today. Reportedly, Today was the first group that Riley produced. Riley was producing for MCA Records and secured a deal for Today. The head of MCA's urban division, Jheryl Busby, was making an upward corporate move to Motown Records to replace the departing Berry Gordy Jr. as the president. (Gordy became chairman of the board.) Busby came loaded for bear. He brought Today, the Boys, the Good Girls, Milira, Rich Nice, MC Trouble, and others with him. They were labeled the New Motown Artists and toured the States with a fantastic live show headlined by the Boys that sequenced from artist to artist with virtually no waiting time between acts.

Things looked rosy. Today's first single, "Him or Me," charted. But their second single, "Girl I Got My Eyes on You," rose to the top of *Billboard*'s R&B survey April 8, 1989; the Boys' second number one, "Lucky Charm," preceded it at the top April 1, 1989 (also for one week). A third single, "Take It Off" (also released as a 12-inch), didn't meet any of its projected sale forecasts, nor did "You Stood Me Up"; all bounced from the group's debut Motown album, *Today*. Things didn't look so rosy anymore. Like the Boys and the Good Girls, Today resented the way they were being produced and promoted. Riley headed their first album but was missing in action on the group's second and final Motown album, *The New Formula*—whose title speaks volumes. The second LP flopped. The only bankable thing from it was the single "Why You Get Funky on Me" (March 1990). Surprisingly, shortly after the New Motown Artists-heralded tour, all the acts involved seemingly dropped off the face of the earth. (MC Trouble suffered a brain tumor.)

Today, who recorded as the Gents on Positive Image Records prior to Motown ("For You and My Baby") (1984), disbanded. The Gents' lineup differed slightly. The members were Drakeford, McCain, William McNeir, Ronald Scruggs, a guy identified only as Harold, and Bernard Bell. Bell sang background vocals on Today's final Motown album. Using his street holler Big Bub, Drakeford started a successful solo career, enjoying hit singles off his first solo album on East West Records, *Comin' at Cha* (1992), which he followed with LPs on Universal and Flavor Unit Records. He went on to produce others and make his ample pipes available for backing sessions. Singletary did vocal arrangements and wrote songs for other acts including F.A.T.E. and Big Bub. And, with Adams and McCain, wrote songs and made demos in an attempt to get a deal as a trio. *—Andrew Hamilton*

Today / 1989 / Motown ✦✦

A relentlessly positive album of assembly-line Christian R&B anchored by synthesizer and rhythm tracks that come too much out of the box. The vocals almost manage to get carried away by joy and passion, but in the end the machinery ties the voices down in the temporal plane, leeching the spiritual enthusiasm. *—Steven McDonald*

● **The New Formula** / 1991 / Motown ✦✦✦

The New Jersey aggregation came close to breaking out of the pack with their second album, but just couldn't get over the hump. Despite good production and a pair of decent singles in "Why You Get Funky on Me" and "Every Little Thing About You, " they failed to click with the urban audience. *—Ron Wynn*

Kim Tolliver

b. Lebanon, TN

Vocals / Deep Soul, Soul

Soul singer Kim Tolliver was born in Lebanon, TN, but her formative years took place in Cleveland, OH's Hough area. She built a reputation wowing local bar patrons with dramatic interpretations of blues and soul songs, and gigged for years before recording her first single. The slow torching "In Return for Your Love" came out on Don Robey's Sureshot label in 1967 and quickly disappeared. Her next four recordings were products of Jack Taylor's Rojac Records, located in New York City. These Southern-fried soul offerings are considered gems, perhaps the best of her career, by those who have heard them. They include the gospel-laden "I'll Try to Do Better"; "Tuesday Child" and its B-side, "Cop My Stuff"; "Let Them Talk"; and "Driving Me Into the Arms of a Stranger." She gigged a lot during this period, as far away as Australia, and once did 102 days in Auckland, New Zealand, with obscure soul singer Lou Ragland.

Her next singles appeared on Gar Records—"I Caught You" is an uptempo, humorous mimic of Joe Tex's style. The second Gar single, "Got Myself Together," has a sweet Southern hook. The Gar and some Rojac singles were written and/or produced by Fred Briggs, who became her third husband. Her first husband, blues singer Rex Robinson, died in an automobile accident while coming home from a gig in Lorain, OH; second hubby Leroy Grafenreed owned and operated a barbershop in Cleveland. Briggs had produced and written for, among others, the Dells, Margie Joseph, the Goodies, and Johnny Taylor, and had recorded himself as Coldwater Stone. Under Briggs' tutelage, Tolliver enjoyed a prolific period. She cut "How Long Can I Keep Holding on, Pts. 1 & 2" on Superheavy Records as Big Ella. She cut her first album, *Passing Clouds*, on Fantasy Records as Kimberly Briggs in 1972, and waxed her second LP, *Come and Get Me*, on Chess Records a year later as Kim Tolliver.

Neither label promoted the pleasing LPs and both were deleted before most knew they existed. In 1975, she cut "I Don't Know What Foot to Dance On" on Castro Records as Kim Tolliver; the disco dancer, written by Briggs and Andrew Hamilton, was popular in England's Northern soul clubs. In 1968, Pathfinder Records released the dramatic "Standing Room Only," which suffered the same dismal fate as previous releases. Though her recordings bombed, she kept active in local clubs like the Chaz Bo, the Spaghetti Inn, the Music Box, and Gleasons. She had a following in Buffalo, where she played the Revilot Club. She reunited with Jack Taylor on his newly formed Tay-Ster Records for her final two 12-inch releases: a reworking of "Let Them Talk" and "Where Were You." Tolliver sang hard like Eddie LeVert and Linda Jones, and could work a crowd into a frenzy. Disgruntled by her lack of success coupled with her separation from Briggs, Tolliver put music down for real estate, and with the help of her companion, and sons, Daryl and Andrew, made a comfortable living. The '90s found the once-vibrant singer suffering from Alzheimer's. Fred Briggs suffered a stroke. Kim's unsuccessful recordings have become sought-after treasures for collectors. A bootleg CD titled *The Torrid Tolliver* contains 18 tracks and includes all her singles, except the Castro release, and the choicest cuts from her two albums. *—Andrew Hamilton*

● **Come and Get Me, I'm Ready** / 1973 / Chess ✦✦✦

Kim Tolliver sings hard, in the mold of Linda Jones. She attacks a song the way Eddie LeVert (O'Jays) does. Tolliver's, best recordings can only be found on 45s issued by rinky dink companies like Rojac, Pathfinder, Sureshot, Gar and Castro Records. None achieved any degree of success, though they made her a cult favorite among die-hard soul collectors, especially in Europe. This is Tolliver's first LP, she recorded a second as Kimberly Briggs on Fantasy Records that is equally as obscure. Rumor says there's a homemade CD of Tolliver's recordings, which includes the Rojac singles, floating around Europe. Tolliver, and husband Fred Briggs, either collaborated or wrote solo, seven of the nine tracks. The two they didn't write, "I'm Losing This Feeling," and "She Don't Know You (Like I Do)," are Willie "Little Beaver" Hale, and Clarence Reid compositions, respectively, and are easily the best songs. Fred Briggs wrote "The Way He Used To," a deep soul classic enhanced by Tolliver's powerful vocal hysterics. (Fred Briggs recorded a few singles himself as Coldwater Stone.) Country music lovers will enjoy "The Other Side of Town" written by Tolliver under her married name, D. K. Briggs. Midtempo tracks and dancers like "Learn to Get Along Without You" dominate the tracks. The negatives: too many strings, and production overkill. Four different locations were used for over-dubs and re-mixings. Mystifying but true, Chess never released a single from this album. *—Andrew Hamilton*

Oscar Toney Jr.

b. May 26, 1939, Selma, AL

Vocals / Southern Soul, R&B, Soul, Deep Soul

Oscar Toney Jr. recorded some soulful sides for Bell Records in the late '60s that will forever etch him into soul music lovers' memories. The emotive singer born May 26, 1939, in Selma, AL, was raised in Columbus, GA. He sung gospel in church and high school with a group he called the Sensational Melodies of Joy. After high school he ventured into secular music with the Searchers waxing "Wow Wow Baby" b/w "Ooo-Wee" on Class Records in 1958. They kept searching doing local and regional gigs and in 1961 cut a final recording, "Yvonne" b/w "Little Wanda," on Max Records. Like the first, the public and radio stations ignored it and the Searchers disbanded. Three years later Toney soloed with "Can It All Be Love," produced by Bobby Smith in Macon, GA, but released on Cincinnati's King Records; it too went unnoticed.

He befriended DJ/Producer Papa Don Schroeder in Pensacola, FL, who produced recordings on Mighty Sam McClain and James & Bobby Purify. He kept Toney around to fill in for either James or Bobby when one couldn't make a gig. Overwhelmed by Toney's vocal ability, Papa Don signed him to a production deal with Bell Records in 1967. Not messing around, Schroeder took Toney to legendary producer Chips Moman in Memphis, TN, and hit the first time out with a moving rendition of Jerry Butler & the Impressions' "For Your Precious Love"; it cracked the R&B Top Ten, settling at number four, and the pop Top 40, nesting at number 23. Its success prompted King Records to release the previously unreleased "I Found True Love." None of his subsequent recordings did as well. A revival of Bobby "Blue" Bland's "Turn on Your Love Light" went to number-37 R&B and number-65 pop late in 1967. Bell released four singles on Toney in 1968; all flopped, except another remake, this time a Clyde McPhatter song, "Without Love (There Is Nothing)," which barely made the charts. Bell dropped one more Toney single in 1969, "Down in Texas" b/w "Ain't That True Love." The association dissolved when Schroeder left the business.

He signed with Phil Walden's Capricorn Records in 1970, which resulted in "Down on My Knees." Capricorn got it played in the South, but couldn't get the sucker aired anywhere else. Three more singles bombed and by 1973 the Capricorn deal was history. Toney rarely worked a full-time job during his quest for musical fame and fortune. He earned his supper gigging; many times he visited England, where Northern soul fans appreciated his deep soul ballads far better than the fickle fans in the States. Contempo Records' boss John Abbey signed Toney to the label. Abbey also attempted to revitalize the careers of J.J. Barnes, and other American soul singers. Six Contempo 45s and one LP resulted in zilch sales. Before the '80s rolled in, Toney left secular music; 23 years of trying only produced one substantial hit, and the wailing soul singer returned to his first love, gospel music. *—Andrew Hamilton*

For Your Precious Love / 1967 / Bell ✦✦✦

● **Oscar's Winner** / Oct. 13, 1998 / WestSide ✦✦✦✦✦

While not definitive—it only includes the songs he cut with Papa Don Schroeder—this is still the best collection of Oscar Toney Jr. available. The 18 tracks feature remakes of the Impressions' "For Your Precious Love," Chuck Jackson's "Any Day Now," Aretha Franklin's "Do Right Woman—Do Right Man," Jerry Butler's "He Will Break Your Heart," and Bobby "Blue" Bland's "Turn on Your Lovelight." Toney's emotive baptismals stamp every cut, including stirring renditions of "The Dark End of the Street," "That's All I Want From You," and "You Can Lead Your Woman to the Altar." *—Andrew Hamilton*

For Your Precious Love / Feb. 2001 / Sundazed ✦✦✦✦

Including the entirety of Toney Jr.'s 1967 LP *For Your Precious Love*, this CD reissue is really a survey of his entire late-'60s Bell output, as it adds nine bonus tracks from 1967-1968. Issued in the wake of Toney Jr.'s hit cover of "For Your Precious Love," this is mostly filled with covers of soul oldies and then current soul songs, including "Dark End of the Street," "Moon River" (again following the Jerry Butler version), "Do Right Woman—Do Right Man," "Turn on Your Love Light," and "Any Day Now." Toney specialized in updated, well-produced (sometimes orchestrated) versions of familiar soul tunes, and while he sang them well, the format was kind of retro and unoriginal, even in 1967. Top Southern soul session guys Tommy Cogbill (bass), Reggie Young (guitar), Bobby Emmons (keyboards), and Chips Moman (engineer) provide accomplished backing for Toney's emotional vocals, which have traits in common with both Jerry Butler and (more strongly) Otis Redding, and favor ballads. Toney did contribute one original to the LP, "Ain't That True Love," and the good-time "No Sad Songs" would be covered a year later by Joe Simon. This CD adds seven songs from 1967-1968 Bell singles, as well as the previously unreleased demo "Gettin' Ready for the Heartbreak" and an alternate take of his 45 "You Can Lead Your Woman to the Altar." The non-LP singles are respectable, yet not outstanding, Southern deep soul efforts, a bit poppier than Stax's product. These are again at their best at their slowest, when they're comparable in some respects to Otis Redding's ballads. *—Richie Unterberger*

Tony! Toni! Toné!

f. 1987, Oakland, CA

Group / Urban, Hip-Hop, Neo-Soul, Contemporary R&B, New Jack Swing

Brothers Dwayne and Raphael Wiggins and cousin Timothy Christian have proven themselves durable guardians of the soul and funk tradition, while also infusing their music with enough contemporary devices to remain popular. This Oakland trio scored a number-one R&B hit right out of the box in 1988 with "Little Walter," a song that generated some criticism from gospel audiences for its use of the melody from "Wade in the Water." But they've since been able to keep things going on their own, as their LPs, *The Revival* in 1990 and *Sons of Soul* in 1993, have also been enormously successful. Tony! Toni! Toné! released their fourth album, *House of Music*, in the fall of 1996. *—Ron Wynn*

Who? / Jan. 1988 / Wing ✦✦✦

Dwayne and Raphael Wiggins, along with cousin Timothy Christian, made a quick and lasting impact with their 1988 debut album. The lead single, "Little Walter," used the melody from "Wade in the Water" and laid out in vivid detail the rise and fall of a comrade who lacked control and direction. It proved a huge R&B hit and got moderate pop attention, but it helped establish the trio and their creative mix of vintage soul and contemporary hip-hop and new jack production. "Baby Doll" and "For the Love of You" also got sizable pop attention, and Tony! Toni! Toné! were on their way. *—Ron Wynn*

The Revival / Apr. 1990 / Wing ♦♦♦♦♦
One of the more distinctive R&B groups of the late 1980s and early 1990s, Tony! Toni! Toné! has managed to appeal to urban contemporary audiences while expressing its love of 1970s soul and funk. As high-tech as things get on its sophomore effort *The Revival*, the Oakland trio never fails to sound organic and soulful. Funk smokers like "The Blues," "Oakland Stroke," "Let's Have a Good Time" and "Feels Good" (a major hit) may use technology extensively, but the soulsters always sound like they're in control of the technology (as opposed to it controlling them). Drawing on influences ranging from Sly & the Family Stone, Parliament/Funkadelic and Prince to Digital Underground, Tony! clearly likes its funk down and dirty. And yet, the group sounds equally inspired on such laid-back, mellow slow jams as "I Care" and the hit "It Never Rains (In Southern California)." Many of the urban contemporary releases of 1990 were gutless and homogenized, but *The Revival* is an album that had commercial appeal, as well as artistic integrity. *—Alex Henderson*

Sons of Soul / Jun. 22, 1993 / Mercury ♦♦♦♦♦
With their third album, Tony! Toni! Toné! received their greatest chart success, without compromising their music; it was still the finely crafted, highly eclectic and funky pop-soul that distinguished their first two albums, while the band's songwriting and playing had improved. The result was the band's most successful album yet, both commercially and successfully. *—Stephen Thomas Erlewine*

House of Music / Nov. 19, 1996 / Mercury ♦♦♦♦
When Tony! Toni! Toné! finally delivered *House of Music*, their follow-up to their 1993 breakthrough *Sons of Soul*, their influence was beginning to be apparent, as younger soul singer/songwriters like Tony Rich and Maxwell began reaching the R&B charts. Like Tony! Toni! Toné!, Rich and Maxwell relied on traditional soul and R&B values of songwriting and live performances, discarding the synth-heavy productions of the late '80s and early '90s. But, as *House of Music* makes clear, the difference between the Tonies and their successors is that they know how to seamlessly incorporate hip-hop and new jack swingbeat into their essentially traditional sound. Embellishing soul and funk with slamming '90s beats, Tony! Toni! Toné! sounds modern, and they can successfully accomplish their fusion of the traditional and contemporary. More importantly, they can do this within the framework of memorable, catchy songs, whether its the party funk of "Let's Get Down" or the balladry of "Let Me Know." *—Leo Stanley*

● **Greatest Hits** / Oct. 28, 1997 / Mercury ♦♦♦♦♦
Although it's a little early for Tony! Toni! Toné! to have a *Greatest Hits*, this single-disc compilation is nevertheless an excellent summary of their four albums, containing all of the trio's big hits ("If I Had No Loot," "Little Walter," "Feels Good," "It Never Rains (In Southern California)," "Anniversary," "Baby Doll," "The Blues," "Whatever You Want"), plus the new single "Boys and Girls." In the process, it makes a convincing argument that they were one of the best contemporary R&B bands of the early '90s. *—Stephen Thomas Erlewine*

The Topics

Group / Northern Soul, Soul
The Topics hung tough from 1966 to 1987, recording mainly for small New York recording companies. Beginning as the Uniteds, they signed with Chess Records in 1965 with a lineup of Ronald McCoy, Vaughn Curtis, Wesley "Bobby" Adams, and Gerald Jones. Richard and Bobby Poindexter cut their first demo on Chess, but "Come Back Baby" and "Baby, Baby Yes I Love You" remain unissued, and they left after four months.

Now a trio comprising McCoy, Curtis, and Adams, they signed with Joe Evans' Carnival/Chadwick labels as the Cymbals. But Evans wanted to use that name on another group, so they became the Topics. Their debut, "I Don't Have to Cry" (1966), didn't chart, nor did a second, "Hey Girl Where Are You Going," in 1967, with a new member, Charles "Charlie" Stodghill. They stayed at Carnival for two years, leaving due to inactivity and because Evans was more interested in McCoy's songwriting skills than the Topics' singing abilities. McCoy wrote labelmates Lee Williams & the Cymbals' two biggest hits, "I Love You More" and "Peepin' Through the Window." Stodghill left to join the Persuaders, and appeared on "It's a Thin Line Between Love and Hate." Robert Lewis replaced Stodghill and the quartet recorded some sides earmarked for either Musicor or Atlantic Records, but the Lou Courtney productions never saw daylight. Danny Evans, who sang with the Larks ("The Jerk"), became their manager. In 1968, an opportunity came to tour England, but once across the pond the promoter demanded they front as the Fabulous Impressions to give the tour name recognition. "We don't have a name act, and we need one to draw people," barked the promoter.

According to McCoy, the promoter issued an ultimatum, and told the group that they must either masquerade as the Impressions or go home unpaid. They toured England later as the Topics, but McCoy didn't make the second trip because of the flu and skepticism—after all, the first tour was a disaster. They severed ties with Danny Evans after he got caught promoting bogus Aretha Franklins and James Browns in Florida and Texas; there was a big article in *Jet* magazine about these incidents. The Topics are remembered by East Coast fans for "All Good Things Must End," a heart-tugging ballad recorded on Heavy Duty Records in 1972 that became huge in the New York/Jersey area, but received practically no exposure anywhere else. The revamped Topics now consisted of McCoy, Curtis, Robert Radcliffe, and Yvonne McCoy (Ronald McCoy's wife). More than 30 people sang with the Topics. McCoy said, "The constant recruiting was essential; you had to be ready for unexpected gigs, members were flighty, and I needed substitutes to fill in."

The Heavy Duty deal proved lightweight, and Brothers III Records issued "Please Take This Heart of Mine" (1972), but it only got a few local spins. Mercury Records released the Topics' "Booking Up Baby" in 1973, but it did nothing; nor did a final single on Noodle Records, entitled "God and You," in 1976 that was also recorded by Loreli. An album worth of material on T.S.G. Records remained unissued. Brothers III Records released an LP entitled *All Good Things* in 1974 by the Topics that was reissued on CD by Japan's P-Vine label in 1999, with additional tracks by other Brothers III artists: the Electras, Marion Butler, Loreli, and Empress Kilpatrick. The reissued album was renamed *The Topics and Friends: All Good Things*. McCoy kept the Topics viable and never stopped trying. At one point, he took ill and was falsely diagnosed with cancer; doctors told him he had six months to live. He made plans to move to Ohio but never did.

Regrouping, McCoy performed and recorded briefly in 1986-1987 with his wife and daughter in a group called Triple Threat. After that, he decided to sing solo. Many of the Topics died: Bobby Adams was fatally shot in a bar defending Charles Stodghill, who got into an argument with someone, and Stodghill later fell ill and died at Jacoby Hospital in the Bronx. Robert Lewis, who joined Ringling Brothers, died also; Vaughn Curtis suffered a stroke in 2000 but remained alive. *—Andrew Hamilton*

All Good Things / 1974 / Brothers III ♦♦♦
The Topics, hot stuff in New York, NY, and parts of New Jersey, rarely got heard anywhere else. They previously recorded for Carnival Records, but these later cuts produced by Bruce Clark are superior. Member and main writer Ronald McCoy handles most of the leads; Vaughn Curtis led most of their Carnival sides. The 11 tracks include "Wichita Lineman" coupled with "Rainy Night in Georgia," a semi-masterpiece arranged by Dennis Williams, and a cold-blooded rendition of "Giving Up," the old Gladys Knight & the Pips hit. "All Good Things Can't Last" had R&B Top Ten magic, but lack of funds killed its chances of becoming a significant record; the lilting mourner reigns as their most popular recording. "You've Got the Power," is uptempo, with multi-vocalists including Robert Radcliffe and Yvonne McCoy contributing lead lines. Slow, midtempo romancers and lamenters like "Gotta Get You Back" and "Your Love Comes Slower Than Never" and harmony checks like "Please Take This Heart of Mine" are preferable. Yvonne leads "God and You," a romantic cruiser that was also recorded by Loreli. *—Andrew Hamilton*

● **The Topics and Friends: All Good Things** / 1999 / P-Vine ♦♦♦♦
Japanese reissue of the Topics' 1974 album, *All Good Things*, fleshed with additional Bruce Clark productions. The Electras will remind you of Southern soul storyteller Ann Sexton on "Another's Man Woman." Easy male vocals accompany Marion Butler soft, subtle lead on "What Is Love"; she shows a different side on J. R. Bailey's uptempo "Am I Ever Gonna See My Babe Again." Loreli, another female group, does "God and You," also done by the Topics; good luck trying to pick a favorite version. "Everybody's Got a Good Thing" by Loreli and Empress Kilpatrick begins dark and somber then modulates into something special spiced by a sinewy, sensuous Sarah Vaughn-ish lead. Harmony lovers will want "All Good Things Can't Last" on that slow jam tape to play in the car. A medley of "Wichita Lineman"/"Rainy Night in Georgia" and their updated "Giving Up" are quiet storm specials. "Please Take This Heart of Mine" has a chorus similar to Mary Wells' "Never, Never Leave Me," but the harmonies are pure Topics. *—Andrew Hamilton*

Total

f. New York, NY
Group / New Jack Swing, Urban, Hip-Hop, Club/Dance
The "New Jill Flava" trio Total comprised singers Kima, Pam, and Keisha; signed to Sean "Puffy" Combs' Bad Boy Entertainment label, they first attracted attention backing the Notorious B.I.G. on his hits "One More Chance" and "Juicy," soon after scoring their own hit with the single "Can't You See" from the soundtrack to the film *New Jersey Drive*. Total's self-titled debut LP followed in 1996, launching the hits "No One Else," "Kissin' You," and "Do You Think About Us?" The single "Trippin'" preceded the release of Total's second LP, 1998's *Kima, Keisha & Pam*. *—Jason Ankeny*

● **Total** / Jan. 30, 1996 / Bad Boy ♦♦♦♦
Total first gained attention as the backup vocalists for the Notorious B.I.G., singing on his hits "One More Chance" and "Juicy." After releasing a hit single, "See," from the *New Jersey Drive* soundtrack, the girl group released their self-titled debut. While the album is simply too long to sustain the quality of "See" and "No One Else," most of the record is filled with deep, seductive funk that follows through on the group's promise. *—Stephen Thomas Erlewine*

Kima, Keisha & Pam / Oct. 27, 1998 / Bad Boy ♦♦♦
On their second album, these '90s soul sistas sex up their lives, and everything around them, quite a bit, turning their fairly standard take on the hip-hop girl group into a late-night bath of delight. But by inviting a who's-who roster into the tub with them (producers here include Missy Elliott, Sean "Puffy" Combs and Heavy D., among others), Total—the Kima, Keisha and Pam of the title—are barely heard. Brimming with the sounds of the world around it, *Kima, Keisha & Pam* is a studio-powered album that loses its individuality while trying desperately to be a part of the streets and scene. The best track, "Trippin'," is an Elliott-produced slice of robotic R&B that combines the gals' sweet harmonies with state-of-the-soul-art studio savvy. But an album's worth of the sexy same unveils Total's ultimate limitations. *—Michael Gallucci*

Allen Toussaint

b. Jan. 14, 1938, New Orleans, LA
Producer, Keyboards, Piano, Vocals / R&B, New Orleans R&B, Soul, Southern Soul
Producer, songwriter, arranger, session pianist, solo artist—Allen Toussaint has worn all these hats over the course of his lengthy and prolific career, and his behind-the-scenes work alone would have been enough to make him a legend of New Orleans R&B. Thanks to his work with numerous other artists, Toussaint bore an enormous amount of responsibility for the sound of R&B in the Crescent City from the '60s on into the '70s. His

productions kept with the times, moving from rollicking, earthy soul in the '60s to gritty, rambunctious funk in the '70s. As a composer, Toussaint proved himself a consistent hit-maker, penning more than a few gems that have since become R&B standards and been covered by countless artists working in many different styles. In keeping with that across-the-board appeal, Toussaint has worked in some supporting capacity for a wide variety of rock and blues legends, particularly from the '70s on. On top of all that, Toussaint waxed his own records from time to time, enjoying a creative peak in the '70s with several albums that highlighted his laid-back vocals and elegantly funky piano work. Even if he wasn't always the most visible figure, Toussaint's contributions to New Orleans music—and to rock & roll in general—were such that he earned induction into the Rock and Roll Hall of Fame in 1998.

Toussaint was born January 14, 1938, in New Orleans, and began learning piano at age seven, inspired by Professor Longhair; his style later grew to include elements of Fats Domino, Huey "Piano" Smith, and Ray Charles. As a teenager, he played in a band called the Flamingos with bluesman Snooks Eaglin. Toussaint caught his first professional break at age 17, when Earl King tapped him to fill in for Smith at a live gig. Not long after, famed producer/songwriter Dave Bartholomew—whose role in New Orleans R&B during the '50s was fairly analogous to Toussaint's later career—hired him to lay down the piano parts at a Fats Domino recording session for which Domino himself was unavailable. Bartholomew made regular use of Toussaint, most notably on further sessions for Domino and Smiley Lewis, and demand for the young pianist's services grew quickly, especially after he first displayed his talent as an arranger on saxman Lee Allen's biggest hit, "Walkin' With Mr. Lee." In 1958, Toussaint recorded an instrumental album for RCA called *The Wild Sound of New Orleans*, under the alias Tousan; one of his original compositions for the record, "Java," went on to become a smash hit for Dixieland jazz trumpeter Al Hirt five years later. Toussaint also began writing under the pseudonym Naomi Neville, after his mother's maiden name.

In 1960, Toussaint was hired by Joe Banashak as an A&R man for the brand-new Minit label; in practice, he wound up masterminding most of the label's recording sessions. It was here that Toussaint truly began to build his legend. His first national success as a producer came with Jessie Hill's R&B Top Five smash "Ooh Poo Pah Doo" in 1960, and the classic hits came fast and furious after that: Ernie K-Doe's pop and R&B number-one "Mother-in-Law" (a Toussaint composition), Benny Spellman's "Fortune Teller," and "Lipstick Traces (On a Cigarette)" (both Toussaint tunes written as Naomi Neville, with the former later covered by the Rolling Stones), Chris Kenner's original version of "Land of 1000 Dances," Lee Dorsey's "Ya Ya," and numerous sides with New Orleans Soul Queen Irma Thomas. Toussaint's singular touch on all these records redefined the sound of New Orleans R&B for a new decade. When Banashak left Minit to found another label, Instant, Toussaint went with him to fulfill much the same duties; he also freelanced elsewhere, most prominently with Dorsey's recordings for the Fury label, and cut a few low-profile singles of his own, mostly for Seville. In 1963, Toussaint was drafted into the military, during which time he recorded with his backing band the Stokes while on leave; one of their tunes, the Naomi Neville credit "Whipped Cream," was covered by Herb Alpert in 1965 for an instrumental hit, which was in turn later adopted as the theme for TV's *The Dating Game*.

Upon his discharge in 1965, Toussaint teamed up with fellow producer Marshall Sehorn to form a production company and record label, Sansu Enterprises. Sansu recorded the likes of Betty Harris, Earl King, Chris Kenner, and Lou Johnson, among others, often leasing their singles to larger labels for official release. Their most profitable association was with Lee Dorsey, who returned to the upper reaches of the R&B charts with Toussaint-penned hits like "Ride Your Pony," the oft-covered "Get Out of My Life Woman," the immortal "Working in a Coalmine," and "Everything I Do Gonh Be Funky (From Now On)" (covered by jazzman Lou Donaldson). In 1966, Sansu also engaged the services of a house band dubbed the Meters, who supplied backing for nearly all of the company's productions; after the Meters started making their own records in 1969 (produced by Toussaint), they developed into arguably the top instrumental funk ensemble of the '70s outside of the J.B.'s.

In 1971, Toussaint recorded his first solo album in over a decade for Scepter, calling it simply *Toussaint* (it was later reissued in the U.K. as *From a Whisper to a Scream*, after its best-known track). The following year, he moved up to Reprise for *Life, Love and Faith*, and he and Sehorn opened a state-of-the-art recording studio in New Orleans called Sea-Saint, which became the site for most of his subsequent projects. In addition to his solo records, Toussaint was getting more high-profile offers for outside work during the first half of the '70s. He did horn arrangements for the Band, Paul Simon, Little Feat, and Sandy Denny, and his continued work with the Meters was moving him into contemporary funk with a harder edge than his own albums. In fact, he wound up producing two of New Orleans' greatest funk records: Dr. John's Top Ten hit "Right Place, Wrong Time" and LaBelle's number one disco-funk smash "Lady Marmalade."

In 1975, Toussaint released what many regarded as his finest solo album, *Southern Nights*; the title track went on to become a huge hit for country-pop superstar Glen Campbell, and "What Do You Want the Girl to Do?" was covered by Boz Scaggs, Lowell George, and Bonnie Raitt. In 1976, Toussaint produced the Meters-related group the Wild Tchoupitoulas, whose self-titled debut was hailed as a classic of New Orleans funk. The record's experimentalism signaled a growing desire to branch out in the Meters camp, though, which would soon cause the band's split with Toussaint and, eventually, each other. The absence of their unerring sense of groove was noticeable on Toussaint's final solo LP for quite some time, 1978's *Motion*. Toussaint's activities tailed off in the years that followed; he still produced, arranged, and played piano on selected projects, which included albums by blues artists Etta James and Albert King, and rockers Elvis Costello and Joe Cocker, among others. In the meantime, his extensive song catalog was still mined regularly for cover material; the Lee Dorsey period was the most fertile, not just for "Working in a Coalmine" (Devo, the Judds), but lesser-known items like "Yes We Can" (the Pointer Sisters), "Sneakin' Sally Through the Alley" (Robert Palmer), and "Freedom for the Stallion" (the Oak Ridge Boys, among others). In addition, "Play Something Sweet (Brickyard Blues)" was a hit for Three Dog Night, and Bonnie Raitt cut a well-received version of "What Is Success."

The release of *The Allen Toussaint Collection* (1991), featured a fine overview of his major-label recordings in the '70s. In 1996, Toussaint formed a new label, NYNO, and recorded a full album of new material at his Sea-Saint studio, titled *Connected*. Toussaint also began recording newer Crescent City artists in hopes of preserving the classic New Orleans sound. He was inducted into the Rock and Roll Hall of Fame in 1998 in the non-performer category. *—Steve Huey*

The Wild Sound of New Orleans / 1958 / Edsel ✦✦✦✦✦

His debut album, featuring a killer band, storming second-line instrumentals, and Toussaint's rolling 88s. *—Bill Dahl*

Toussaint / 1971 / Scepter ✦✦✦

New Orleans production and performing wizard Allen Toussaint launched his solo career with this early-'70s release. But for some strange reason, the same performer who's written and produced marvelous material for Irma Thomas, Lee Dorsey, Chocolate Milk, and General Johnson among others, was never able to score the same success working as a lead act. There was nothing on this album even in the same arena as his classic R&B tunes, and throughout Toussaint's run of solo releases, only the song "Southern Nights," which Glen Campbell made a hit, could be even mentioned in the same sentence with Toussaint classics like "Ride Your Pony" or "It Will Stand." *—Ron Wynn*

Life, Love and Faith / 1972 / Reprise ✦✦✦

Bomp City / 1973 / Reprise ✦✦✦

Southern Nights / 1975 / Reprise ✦✦✦✦✦

Motion / Aug. 1978 / Warner Bros. ✦✦✦

A nicely produced, competently performed, but disappointing album by New Orleans giant Allen Toussaint. He seemed unable to find a groove or a sound, dabbling in pop, light R&B, rock, and mild funk, but never coming close to duplicating prior magical productions or compositions. This was perhaps Toussaint's least impressive material, and was especially surprising in light of the artistic success of his prior Warner Bros. album *Homage*. *—Ron Wynn*

★ **The Allen Toussaint Collection** / Apr. 30, 1991 / Reprise ✦✦✦✦✦

Allen Toussaint's contribution to New Orleans R&B is indelible and his presence can be felt throughout classic recordings from the late '50s, '60s, and beyond. His name, though, is the province of connoisseurs, those who peruse album jackets looking for who wrote that great song or wrote out that phenomenal arrangement. Many who know his name may not even know that he was a solo recording artist, partially because his discography is a little confusing, as he cut for little New Orleans record labels, then signed with Reprise, before returning to sporadic waxings for indies. Of all the albums and compilations that have poured onto the market, the best, by far, is Reprise's *The Allen Toussaint Collection*, even if it spotlights just a small portion of his career—namely, his '70s recordings for Reprise. True, this doesn't have all the great songs he's written, or records he's made, but it does provide an irresistible, comprehensive overview of his best albums. These aren't nearly as gritty as any of his productions of the '60s, lacking the earthiness of, say, Lee Dorsey or the down-and-dirty grind of the Meters. Instead, it's elegant, *sexy* music—witness how "From a Whisper to a Scream" eases its way out of the speakers as the collection begins, seducing the listener, not hitting them in the gut. Even the funkiest moments here have style and are delivered subtly, which only makes them funkier, while putting such stylistic detours as the trippy "Southern Nights" into perspective. The individual albums Toussaint made for Reprise range from very good to excellent, yet this simply named collection eclipses them all, since it has all the best moments, expertly sequenced. It may be softer than his famous productions, but it's every bit as good and essential; in fact, it's one of the greatest greatest-hits albums of '70s soul, funk, and R&B. *—Stephen Thomas Erlewine*

The Complete "Tousan" Sessions / 1992 / Bear Family ✦✦✦✦✦

Bear Family's *The Complete "Tousan" Sessions* compiles material Allen Toussaint recorded between 1958 and 1963—namely, a 1958 instrumental album for RCA called *The Wild Sound of New Orleans*, plus several very rare singles he recorded for the small label Seville. Though they were cut for different labels, the sound is basically the same: lively, jumping instrumentals which effectively showcase Toussaint's remarkable skill at the piano. If you're looking just to hear him play, this is the best bet, since his piano is always at the forefront, whether he's vamping, strutting, or tearing loose with nimble leads. As a listening experience, though, it can get a little samey; it's performed well, but there's not much variety in the style or approach, and only "Java," which Al Hirt later popularized, sticks out as a song. Still, it's an entirely pleasant listen and for serious collectors of New Orleans R&B it's worth seeking out, even if you don't play it that much, since it captures Toussaint in a relatively rare setting, pounding out jukehouse instrumentals. *—Stephen Thomas Erlewine*

Connected / May 7, 1996 / NYNO ✦✦✦✦✦

Allen Toussaint's name became synonymous with New Orleans music, even though he didn't seem to "do" the records his name was on as producer, arranger, or writer on records by artists such as Ernie K-Doe or Irma Thomas. This is his first studio album in at least a decade, and it is a very worthy effort of all self-penned songs that seem to be a mix of old and new (if not in age, at least in feel). He is supported by an extremely worthy cast of the finest New Orleans musicians. Funky material like "Funky Bars," "Ahya," and the rolling gait of "Oh My" stands next to much softer pieces that require a more versatile voice. There are times when his voice doesn't have that reaching pain, for instance, that Aaron Neville gave to "Wrong Number." On most cuts, his easy delivery is just what is called for, and his rollicking piano is always perfectly matched to the song. This is not a disc of memories, though it may bring up a few, it is fresh new funk and roll from the city where American music has always stretched to new levels. *—Bob Gottlieb*

A Taste of New Orleans / Mar. 9, 1999 / NYNO ♦♦♦
A 12-cut sampler of artists on Allen Toussaint's NYNO label, which is devoted to contemporary New Orleans music, and produced by Toussaint himself. All of these tracks are on single-artist NYNO albums, so it's more a promo for the company than a cohesive anthology. There's jazz from Amadee Castenell, gospel from Raymond Myles, reggae from Cool Riddims & Sista Teedy, updated old-time jazz from the New Birth Brass Band and good ol' New Orleans R&B from Toussaint, James Andrews and others. Toussaint is doing a noble service by recording New Orleans musicians, but this is not going to convince anyone that the city is headed for a new golden age. The traditional-style New Orleans cuts are pleasantly familiar and unexceptional, while others seem to be trying too hard to add contemporary pop seasoning to New Orleans music, as if figuring that it might somehow help them get played on the radio. *—Richie Unterberger*

Tower of Power

f. 1967, Oakland, CA
Group / Funk, Quiet Storm
The renowned horn-driven funk outfit Tower of Power has been issuing albums and touring the world steadily since the early '70s, in addition to backing up countless other musicians. The group's leader since the beginning has always been tenor saxophonist Emilio Castillo, who was born in Detroit, but opted to pursue his musical dreams in Oakland, CA. It was in Oakland that Castillo put together a group called the Motowns, which as its name suggested, specialized in '60s-era soul. Castillo teamed up with a baritone sax player (and Motowns fan) Stephen "Doc" Kupka, and soon the Motowns had transformed into Tower of Power (one of the first tunes the duo penned together was "You're Still a Young Man," which would eventually go on to be one of the TOP's signature compositions). Tower of Power played regularly in the Bay Area throughout the late '60s, as its lineup often swelled up to ten members, including such other mainstays as Greg Adams on trumpet and vocals and Rocco Prestia on bass. By 1970, the funk outfit had inked a recording contract with Bill Graham's San Francisco Records, resulting in the group's debut the same year, *East Bay Grease*, which failed to make an impression on the charts as TOP was still trying to find their own sound.

But it all came together quickly for the group, as 1972's *Bump City* would touch off a string of classic hit releases, including 1973's self-titled release (which included another one of the group's most enduring tunes, "What Is Hip?"), 1974's *Back to Oakland*, plus 1975's *Urban Renewal* and *In the Slot*. While Tower of Power remained a must-see live act, the quality of their subsequent records became erratic, resulting in some admirable releases (*Ain't Nothin' Stoppin' Us Now, Live and in Living Color*) and several uninspired albums that are best skipped over (*We Came to Play, Back on the Streets*).

Despite the dip in the quality of their albums, Tower of Power remained a much in-demand backing group for some of pop/rock's biggest names, including Elton John, Santana, Bonnie Raitt, Huey Lewis, Little Feat, David Sanborn, Michelle Shocked, Paula Abdul, Aaron Neville, Aerosmith, Michael Bolton, Billy Preston, PiL, Rod Stewart, Toto, Merl Saunders, and others. Tower of Power remains very active to this day, keeping up a brisk touring schedule and issuing such new albums as 1999's *Soul Vaccination: Live*; while several compilations were issued around the same time: Rhino's double disc *What Is Hip?: The Tower of Power Anthology* (1999) and *Very Best of Tower of Power: The Warner Years* (2001), plus Epic/Legacy's *Soul With a Capital "S": The Best of Tower of Power* (2001). *—Greg Prato*

East Bay Grease / 1970 / Rhino ♦♦♦
The first Tower of Power album, when the band was only honing its concept and seeking a lead singer. On some songs, notably "Sparkling in the Sand," you can hear the group beginning to come together. They already had a fine horn section, and were only some good arrangements away from becoming one of the best pop and soul bands in the nation. The vocals were uneven, although Rick Stevens would later emerge as the prime vocalist. Despite its flaws, it's worth having because the diamond was being cut on these selections. It's recently been reissued on CD. *—Ron Wynn*

Bump City / Nov. 1972 / Warner Bros. ♦♦♦
The second Tower of Power LP, *Bump City* was the first to make any impact. The group went to Memphis, cut their first great single in "You're Still a Young Man," and learned firsthand about funk and soul. The production and arrangements were much improved over the debut album, as was the engineering and overall technical quality. Their lines were crisper, the unison and ensemble passages much sharper, and they were beginning to round into shape. *—Ron Wynn*

Tower of Power / 1973 / Warner Bros. ♦♦♦♦♦
The Tower of Power finally found their ideal lead singer on this album. Lenny Williams came aboard and gave them both the uptempo belter and convincing balladeer they had previously lacked. They landed their biggest single hit, "So Very Hard to Go," and also had two other top tunes in "What Is Hip" and "This Time It's Real." The arrangements and production were also excellent, and the horn section was at its explosive best. *—Ron Wynn*

In the Slot / 1975 / Warner Bros. ♦♦♦
In the Slot came off a four-year string of classic singles and albums. As *Bump City* era lead singer Rick Stevens exited, the phenomenal Lenny Williams replaced him. With Williams, Tower of Power became a hit-making machine as albums like *Back to Oakland* and *Urban Renewal* became R&B standards. *In the Slot* marks the first album of vocalist Hubert Tubbs. he possessed a throaty more muscular voice a few shades lower than his predecessor. While it was serviceable, Tubbs' voice didn't have the same grace and agility as Williams'. On the rollicking "Just Enough and Too Much" the difference is slight and the track is one of the band's most potent tracks. The ballads were where the contrast is most striking. "As Surely As I Stand Here" and the "The Soul of a Child" display not only a drop off in lyrical quality, but also the clearest indication that the band did indeed miss Williams' skill at making even bromides ring. Oddly enough, the great and too brief B-side "Stroke '75" wasn't included here. After many failed attempts, band and singer do end up on the same page. On "Drop It in the Slot" and "On the Serious Side" the groups' trademark rhythm section and the horns come on stronger and match Tubbs' more volatile style. This effort in effect put an end to the string of "classic" albums from the group. *In The Slot*, despite its enviable firepower, finds the band missing Lenny Williams' skill at putting all of the pieces together. *—Jason Elias*

Urban Renewal / 1975 / Warner Bros. ♦♦♦♦♦
Tower of Power was very much in its prime in 1974, when the Bay Area outfit tore up the soul charts with the outstanding *Urban Renewal*. Lenny Williams, a passionate, wailing, gospel-influenced dynamo of a singer, had joined Tower the previous year, and worked out remarkably well—whether digging into tough funk or romantic ballads, Williams is in top form. Funk doesn't get much more invigorating than horn-driven gems like "Maybe It'll Rub Off," "Give Me the Proof" and "Only So Much Oil in the Ground" (a commentary on the mid-'70s energy crisis), and soul ballads don't get much richer than "Willing to Learn" and "I Won't Leave Unless You Want Me To." Tower (an influence on everyone from L.T.D. to the Average White Band) recorded a number of essential albums in the '70s, and *Urban Renewal* is at the top of the list. *—Alex Henderson*

Ain't Nothin' Stoppin' Us Now / 1976 / Columbia ♦♦♦
Edward McGhee turned in mostly above-average performances on their first post-Lenny Williams release, but it was the beginning of the end. With funk losing its foothold among R&B audiences, they couldn't keep it together. McGhee was an energetic, exuberant vocalist who held his own on uptempo tunes like "You Ought to Be Havin' Fun" and the title song, but lacked Williams' range or tonal quality on ballads. The group always had a weakness for ponderous message cuts, and "Can't Stand to See the Slaughter" and "While We Went to the Moon" were well-intentioned but clumsy tracks. This was almost the Tower of Power's swan song. *—Ron Wynn*

Live and in Living Color / 1976 / Warner Bros. ♦♦♦♦
The band's final album for Warner Bros. before it decamped to Columbia, the absolutely stunning 1975 *Live and in Living Color* ensured that Tower of Power left in a blaze of glory. Recorded at Sacramento Memorial Auditorium and Cerritos College, the group brought what remains one of the era's finest live albums to glorious fruition. Leaving behind the dismal soul of its previous *In the Slot*, the band fell back on its two great strengths—classy live performance and unerring funk. With every ounce of the group's full energy packed into the grooves and a little more added for emphasis, *Live* squeezes out five tracks of epic proportions. Reaching back to its debut LP, *East Bay Grease*, Tower of Power jammed on a majestic 23-minute rendition of "Knock Yourself Out" and the sleepy classic "Sparkling in the Sand," before continuing its sonic domination across two songs pulled from *Bump City*. "Down to the Nightclub (Bump City)" is effusive, while "You're Still a Young Man" is an absolutely outstanding performance of one of TOP's finest songs—and judging by the audience enthusiasm, it packed as much power in 1976 as it did in 1972 (and indeed, still does today). Courageously, only one track, "What Is Hip?," emerges from the group's most successful era, but with its rock riffing slices and roiling organ solo, you really don't need anything else—it stands well as a lone representative of what many hail as TOP's finest hour. There's nothing to fault here except, possibly, the decision to release a mere single disc at a time when live double albums were becoming *de rigueur*, a move guaranteed to leave listeners crying for more. But perhaps that was the intent all along—too little is always sweeter than too much. *—Amy Hanson*

We Came to Play / 1978 / Columbia ♦

Back on the Streets / 1979 / Columbia ♦

Direct / 1988 / Sheffield Lab ♦
An album most interesting for being directly recorded to digital by Sheffield Labs. The Tower of Power have seldom sounded more vapid, devoid of rhythmic intensity, or leaden than they did on this set, whose pristine quality only served to illuminate the group's colorless performances. *—Ron Wynn*

Power / Apr. 1988 / Cypress ♦♦

Monster on a Leash / Mar. 1991 / Epic ♦♦♦
In contrast to the many soul veterans who who have turned to urban contemporary sounds in the hope of staying on the staying on the charts, Tower of Power has stuck with the type of horn-driven, live-sounding funk and soul that put the Bay Area band on the map. Tower was long past its prime by the time *Monster on a Leash* was released in 1991, and had experienced its share of personnel changes. Lead singer Tom Bowes, although a passionate and competent belter, is hardly on a par with Lenny Williams. Even so, this is a respectable and decent effort from a band that remained artistically viable by staying true to itself. Unapologetically '70s-sounding, the album falls short of the unmitigated excellence of *Back to Oakland* and *Urban Renewal*, but isn't significantly different in its approach, content or attitude. While novices would do better to start with either those gems, this is an album that die-hard Tower enthusiasts shouldn't pass up. *—Alex Henderson*

TOP / 1993 / Epic ♦♦♦♦
This 1993 effort marked a strong comeback for the group, who started with 1991's *Monster on a Leash*. *TOP* continues the formula with great results. The reason for the revitalization can be directly attributed to the energetic, Stevie Wonder-influenced lead singer, Tom Bowes. The hard-driving, James Brown-derived funk of "Soul With a Capital S" and "I Like Your Style" update the band's classic horn-driven sound and is augmented by not only Bowes but Francis "Rocco" Prestia's amazing and soulful bass work. The ballads—like "Quiet Scream," "Please Come Back to Stay," and arguably the best, "Come to a Decision"—underscore the fact that this version of Tower of Power was the first in years that was equally adept with slower songs and uptempo offerings. *TOP* also has other members doing lead vocal chores. Group co-founder Emilio Castillo leads on the

hammy and fun "Come on With It" and guitarist Carmen Grillo assumes lead on the melodic and smooth "You." Former member, saxophonist Lenny "L.P." Pickett, shows up for five tracks. Produced by Castillo, *TOP* not only made an album to stand with *Monster on a Leash*, but also other classics like *Urban Renewal* and *Ain't Nothing Stopping Us Now*. *—Jason Elias*

What Is Hip?: The Tower of Power Anthology / Aug. 31, 1999 / Rhino ✦✦✦✦✦
Having played on hundreds of hit records, it was only fitting that this Oakland-based group of studio hornmen should strike out on their own and this two-disc anthology from Rhino captures the ups, downs, ins, and outs of TOP's 30-year career. In many ways, the group retrospective is not just a document of the group's evolving sound, but a microcosm of the changing sound of R&B throughout the '70s and '80s. The soul band sound of early tracks like "Knock Yourself Out" sound as if the group is doing a muscular workout at a soul music revue and the oily R&B of "Back on the Streets Again" and "Down to the Nightclub" perfectly reflects the post-Motown pre-disco period of early-'70s rhythm and blues. As the songs progress the band goes on to dabble in funk ("You Got to Funkifize"), jazz soul ("Sparkling in the Sound"), and disco before ultimately (and unfortunately) giving way to the slick, hollow production standards of the '80s. Throughout the 35 tracks, however, singer Lenny Williams' voice sparkles and the group's tight musicianship, being honed through years of session work, is undeniable. At two discs, Rhino has made sure not to stretch the music thin and with a relative cost, the anthology is a good entrance to TOP's long career. *—Steve Kurutz*

Dinosaur Tracks / 2000 / Rhino Handmade ✦✦

● **The Very Best of Tower of Power: The Warner Years** / Jul. 17, 2001 / Rhino ✦✦✦✦✦
Usually, it's not a good sign if a band is generally known for augmenting artists instead of their own records, but Tower of Power was really a very good horn section, and they did make records that held their own. Of course, "What Is Hip?" was the biggest single they ever had, but they also had several other smaller hits that captured their sleek, stylized soul-funk quite well, such as "Soul Vaccination." Pretty much all of those songs are captured on Rhino's 2001 anthology *The Very Best of Tower of Power: The Warner Years*, which spans 16 tracks and contains almost all the highlights of their '70s records. Yes, the 1999 double-disc set *What Is Hip?* is more comprehensive, but that's really for serious listeners. For listeners that want a lean dose of the TOP's prime, this is the best collection on the market. *—Stephen Thomas Erlewine*

Soul With a Capital "S": The Best of Tower of Power / Feb. 26, 2002 / Epic/Legacy ✦✦✦
The crucial subtitle missing is that this is the best of Tower of Power on Columbia, not a career-spanning anthology that takes in their material with other labels. Since their most popular stuff was done for Warner Brothers, that creates quite a problem when you're representing this material in particular as their best. With the understanding that this disc is limited to their Columbia catalog, it's a decent selection, through chronologically haphazard, drawing from the '90s, the late '70s, and nothing else. For the most part it's competent funk, a little too heavy on the feets-don't-fail-me now braggadocio, as on "Attitude Dance." Yes, there are versions of their well-known "So Very Hard to Go" and "What Is Hip?," but take caution: these are 1998 live recordings, not the famous originals. There's a previously unreleased alternate mix of "I Love That Girl So Much" from the sessions for their 1979 album, *Back on the Streets*, and it would be a pretty heavy price to pay for the whole disc just to get that one track, even for insistent completists. *Very Best of the Warner Years* and the more extensive *What Is Hip?* remain far better best-of compilations on this band. *—Richie Unterberger*

Carol Lynn Townes

Vocals / Dance-Pop, Disco
Dance/disco vocalist Carol Lynn Townes had a pair of mild hits in the mid-'80s that were featured in soundtracks. Both "99 1/2" and "Believe in the Beat" were part of the music for *Breakin'* and *Breakin' 2: Electric Boogaloo*, respectively. Neither was a rousing hit, although "99 1/2" made the R&B Top 30. *—Ron Wynn*

● **Satisfaction Guaranteed** / 1985 / Polydor ✦✦✦✦
Light years away from the deep soul style of Townes' 1970s recordings with Fifth Avenue, this sharp solo debut thrives on hook-friendly Hi-NRG dance numbers. Townes delves into the catalogs of dance staples Donna Summer, Sylvester, and Alton McClain & Destiny as well as classic soul group the Stylistics. Her cover of Destiny's "99 1/2" and Sylvester's "Trouble in Paradise" set things off, and are the set's most dynamic entries. The vibe is consistently fun, with passionate electric guitars melding cleverly with the synthesized percussion and keyboards. Not to mention, the singer's wholehearted delivery rests oodles of notches above dance-pop peers Madonna and Lisa Lisa in quality. On a more understated note, there's the moody electro-funk swing of the title track and a take on the Stylistics' "People Make the World Go Round"—the latter not being very convincing. Both "99 1/2" and "Believe in the Beat" were featured on the *Breakin'* soundtracks; and "I Freak for You" was also released as a single. The latter was a predictable, rather dry choice (considering it's patterned after the *Breakin'* sound and doesn't boast a distinctive melody, by comparison) and resulted in no chart success for the album. Perhaps one of the edgier, aforementioned cuts would've set more dancefloors afire. *—Justin M. Kantor*

Try Me Out / Jul. 1987 / Polydor ✦✦✦
Where Carol Lynn Townes' first solo outing delights with fiery dance grooves, her sophomore effort pleases with understated, but sassy, midtempo selections and unconventionally soulful ballads. Her vocals are incendiary on the moody houser "You Keep Runnin' Back"; while consistently jazzy on the heartwarming "We Started Out as Friends" and ultra-sexy "I Don't Know What I'd Do." The singer produced and co-wrote the latter effort, along with the funky, simile-filled "Disposable World." With writing that's simple and gets straight to the point, she utilizes impressive imagery that the album's other writers lack. "Disposable World" opines: "Nobody wants to stay together/They think that permanence is a bore ... Like your cigarette lighter/relationships go out the door ... Not like your Good News razor/Your old blue blazer/I wanna be a permanent girl." And to go with it, it's got a unique synth groove that further proves the point of its lyric. The melodies and arrangements of the tracks here aren't as dynamic as those on *Satisfaction Guaranteed*; rather, it's the fluid grooves and creative vocal nuances throughout that result in a fulfilling listening experience. *—Justin M. Kantor*

Toya (Toya Rodriguez)

b. St. Louis, MO
Vocals / Urban, Contemporary R&B, Hip-Hop
The popularity of Dirty South-style rap artists has helped put St. Louis on the musical map, especially following the huge success of Nelly's *Country Grammar* album. The city's true musical style lies somewhere between the South and the Midwest, though, with a diverse collection of artists who draw as much inspiration from Chicago as Atlanta. Born and raised in St. Louis, Toya (born Toya Rodriguez) was mentored by the same people who helped Nelly achieve fame, but used that help to produce an album in her own unique style. After a childhood spent singing in church and school, Toya was attending St. Louis University on scholarship, working two jobs, and writing songs and recording demos in her spare time when she made arrangements to sing for Nelly's managers, Tony Davis and Courtney Benson. She sang a gospel song, "I Won't Complain," on a Friday, and the pair were so impressed that they asked her to give them two new songs by the end of the weekend. Despite having to work that weekend, Toya put two songs together with the help of her longtime friend and manager, Harold Guy, and a professional songwriter. The songs were played for L.A. Reid of Arista Records and he liked them so much that he flew her to New York to audition.

That audition led to a recording contract and the release of her self-titled debut album in the summer of 2001. With its first single, "I Do," the album made an impressive impact amidst a sea of releases from other baby divas, in part because of the stylistic diversity of its songs that ranged from hip-hop influenced R&B numbers to jazzy ballads and dance tunes. Guest appearances by Murphy Lee of the St. Lunatics and Penelope also helped give the album a unique St. Louis flavor. *—Stacia Proefrock*

● **Toya** / Aug. 7, 2001 / Arista ✦✦✦✦✦
Another excellent female urban soul album from the summer of 2001, Toya's eponymous debut album—like the 2001 albums by Blu Cantrell, Alicia Keys, and the sadly departed Aaliyah—is a savvy combination of classic soul conventions, innovative production, strong songwriting, and fine, understated singing. Of the aforementioned albums, Toya's is the closest to the urban mainstream, but where many of her peers favor songs and performances that are all surface, this record still has style, but it's enhanced by uniformly strong songs, good sequencing, fine singing, and sharp production masterminded by executive producer Antonio "L.A." Reid. Compare this record to Reid's work with Usher on *8701*, and the difference becomes apparent—Usher may show off more, but Toya's more seductive, even on neo-disco songs like "Think." This also sets a mood, but there's a lot of variety within the mood and within the album's songs, resulting in a record that's not just a fine debut, but one of the best urban records of 2001. *—Stephen Thomas Erlewine*

The Toys

f. 1961, Jamaica, NY, **db.** 1968
Group / Brill Building Pop, Soul, Girl Group, R&B
Barbara Harris, Barbara Parritt (both originally from North Carolina), and June Montiero attended Woodrow Wilson High School in Jamaica, NY; they decided to form a group one day at Parritt's sister's house. The trio got together after school, sang on corners, and entered talent shows. After graduation, they were eager for more, and made trips to 1619 Broadway, more commonly known as the Brill Building, seeking work as background vocalists. Vince Marc discovered the warblers at a talent show and introduced them to Sandy Linzer and Denny Randell, who signed them to their Genius Incorporated label and brought them to the attention of record producer Bob Crew. The Toys came on like gangbusters, scoring with an adaptation of Johann Sebastian Bach's Minuet in G, a five-finger piano exercise titled "A Lover's Concerto," written and produced by Linzer and Randell. The song scorched the R&B (number four) and pop (number two) charts, and went to number five in the U.K., selling over a million copies in 1965. Sadly, it was all over by 1968; the girls had differences and went their separate ways.

They initially recorded four songs, with "Concerto" being the last of the four and the only one that was done in one take. The other three were rehearsed by the girls for weeks and labored over in the studio, while their shining star was a throw in. Little did they know the throw in would become the monster hit. The success overwhelmed the girls. Vince Marc whisked them off on a world tour, putting his wife's (Barbara Chandler) career on hold while he and the girls traveled all over Europe and were mobbed by crowds of admirers. Dyno Voice was not pleased with the events; they wanted the Toys back in New York to record more tracks. They eventually returned to the States and recorded the remaining sides for *The Toys Sing a Lover's Concerto and Attack!*, a truly marvelous compilation and one of the best pairings of artist and producer in rock & roll's history. Harris handled most of the leads but Parritt and Montiero were hardly slouches—both excelled when thrust into the spotlight: Montiero on "Yesterday" and Parritt on "Hallelujah." It remains a mystery why this great album only peaked at number 92 pop in 1966.

The Toys appeared on many musical television programs, including *Shindig*, *Hullabaloo*, *American Bandstand*, *Hy Lit*, *Where the Action Is*, *Clay Cole*, and *Upbeat*. Dyno Voice released "Attack" as the follow-up and watched it soar to number-18 pop. They even had a cameo spot in the film *It's a Bikini World*, which also featured the Castaways, the Animals, and the Gentrys. Two more releases charted in 1966, they switched to Philips Records for several singles in 1967, and then moved to Musicor where they had their last chart hit in 1968 ("Sealed With a Kiss," number-112 pop); the group split shortly afterward. Parritt and Montiero joined fake Marvelettes groups (there were about five fake

Marvelette groups doing gigs at the time). Harris married a musician (Kenneth Wiltshire) and sung with bands doing the NY bar scene. Harris reformed the Toys in the '90s for oldies reunion gigs, and with her husband's help, cut a solo CD titled *Barbara Now.* Her two enterprising sons financed her CD from their computer business' profits. Parritt and Montiero live in Queens and both still perform. Sundazed Records compiled an excellent CD of the Toys' recordings that includes the gems from the first LP as well as many of their later singles. *—Andrew Hamilton*

● **Sing "A Lover's Concerto" and "Attack!"** / 1967 / Sundazed ♦♦♦♦
The influence of the Toys is evident when one sees the group listed as the first "tribute" on page 49 of the Supremes four-CD box set on Motown. The Supremes' own "I Hear a Symphony," released October 6, 1965, was a tribute to the tribute, if you will. It says a lot about the competition as the Toys hit number two on the charts that very week, pushing the Supremes, Diana Ross, and the production team of Holland-Dozier-Holland to one of their greatest heights. The re-write of Bach, with its boss production, is a sweeping pop sensation. And the album's 14 tracks play like the Ronettes' first and only official release, a magnificent statement of vocal harmony and pretty melodies. The songwriter/production team of Sandy Linzer and Denny Randell for Bob Crewe Productions adds that remarkable Four Seasons punch to the music. A little of the boy group sound, classical music, and a refreshing collection of melodies that the airwaves were, somehow, denied. "This Night," "Back Street," solid dance hall/radio hits that never got to reign the way "Lover's Concerto" and, to a lesser degree, "Attack" climbed the Top 40. "Attack" is a brilliant song that sounds like a tribute to Frankie Valli. The Dyno Voice album, re-released on Sundazed, is augmented by singles "Baby Toys" and "May My Heart Be Cast Into Stone," songs that lead soprano Barbara Harris said were recorded for the second, unreleased Toys disc slated for Dyno Voice. The musical camaraderie on "Baby Toys" is amazing. These voices carry. Both singles are a welcome addition to this album, and they should've been huge. June Montiero's vocal on The Beatles' "Yesterday" bridges the gap between the Vegas and new wave arrangement. Perhaps that marriage of underground rock with middle of the road pop is what makes the girl group genre so perpetually inviting. The first track on the disc, "Can't Get Enough of You Baby," is reminiscent of the Cake, a band that couldn't crack the *Billboard* Top 40 as the Toys did, but deserved to. "Hallelujah," not the fun Sweathog tune from 1971, but a wonderful song that should've hit, with a delicious lead vocal by Barbara Parritt. The Toys were formidable beyond their two Top 20 hits; "This Night" is a fine example. The girls continue to practice and tour with Richard Nader's rock & roll packages. Harris, with a strong solo record *Barbara Now,* speaks highly of Nader and his events. This CD, with its bonus tracks and replication of the original disc and liner notes, is classic pop. *—Joe Viglione*

The Trammps

f. 1973, Philadelphia, PA, **db.** 1980
Group / Disco, Soul
Disco's most soulful vocal group began in the '60s as the Volcanos, and were also called the Moods. Gene Faith was the original lead vocalist, with Earl Young, Jimmy Ellis, guitarist Dennis Harris, keyboardist Ron Kersey, organist John Hart, bassist Stanley Wade, and drummer Michael Thomas. But by the time they'd gone through various identities and emerged as the Trammps in the mid-'70s, the lineup featured lead vocalist Ellis, Harold and Stanley Wade, Robert Upchurch, and Young. A snappy revival of Judy Garland's '40s tune "Zing Went the Strings of My Heart" was their first chart single, reaching number 17 on the R&B list in 1972. Despite their well-deserved reputation and boisterous, jubilant harmonies and sound, the Trammps were never huge commercial successes even during disco's heyday. Indeed, they had only three R&B Top Ten hits from 1972 through 1978, and such wonderful records as "Soul Bones," "Ninety-Nine and a Half," and "I Feel Like I've Been Livin' (On the Dark Side of the Moon)" stiffed on the charts though they were beloved by club audiences and R&B fans alike.

Their only huge hit was "Disco Inferno" in 1977, which was a number-nine R&B single in 1977 and was also featured in *Saturday Night Fever.* Yet it missed the pop Top Ten, peaking at number 11. But the Trammps' prowess can't be measured by chart popularity; Ellis' booming, joyous vocals brilliantly championed the celebratory fervor and atmosphere that made disco both beloved and hated among music fans. *—Ron Wynn*

Trammps / Jul. 1975 / Philadelphia International ♦♦♦
The Trammps' first album was viewed as an early disco effort, and while there is a good amount of disco here, it's fair to say that it's pretty Philly soul-rooted disco. The group were not an entirely faceless front for dance tracks, but a pretty solid harmonizing soul outfit, even if the mid-'70s Philly soul backing grooves are a little generic (if very accomplished). Three of these cuts had already been small R&B hits—"Love Epidemic" (which seems to take no small inspiration from both the O'Jays' "Love Train" and James Brown's "Night Train"), "Where Do We Go From Here," and "Trusting Heart"—though actually some other songs ("Stop and Think," "Save a Place," the B-side "I Know That Feeling") sound at least as worthy of single release. Away from the soul-funk-disco train, there was silky pillow talk balladry ("Every Dream I Dream Is You," "Down Three Dark Streets") and a lightly discofied cover of the Isley Brothers' "Shout," though it might have been the instrumental "Trammps Disco Theme" that pointed most firmly to their future successes. [The 2002 CD reissue on Epic/Legacy adds three bonus tracks from the 1977 album *Disco Champs* that were actually recorded in 1973 and 1974, one of them an extended version of "Love Epidemic."] *—Richie Unterberger*

Where the Happy People Go / Apr. 15, 1976 / Atlantic ♦♦♦
If the Trammps were assembled to only perform disco songs, this album supports that notion—in a good way. Every selection here rings with disco. Even though there are no ballads or moderate grooves, the Trammps still come across with some smooth vocals and invigorating rhythms. The first release from this dance album was the melodic "That's Where the Happy People Go." It broke into the *Billboard* R&B Top 20 at number 12, staying on the charts for 16 weeks. The second single was the busier "Soul Searchin' Time." A bit more rapid than its predecessor and also more instrumentally involved, it came with a social message. With the exception of one non-vocal track, "Love Is a Funky Thing," everything here is uptempo disco. *—Craig Lytle*

The Trammps III / Nov. 10, 1977 / Atlantic ♦♦♦
Cranking out three albums in the space of two years, *The Trammps III* richly displays more innovation from disco's most popular group. That's the good news. The bad news is that by 1977, a countless number of other acts had also joined the disco bandwagon. To make matters worse, their 1976 classic "Disco Inferno" was beginning to pick up even more steam consequently making their subsequent efforts barely heard. Although the group was often thought of as lesser than the O'Jays and Harold Melvin & the Blue Notes, the majority of their '70s work often holds up better than their contemporaries. *The Trammps III* introduces more creative arrangements as well as a batch of smooth ballads. "The Nights the Lights Went Out" finds the guys taking advantage of New York's 1977 power outage. While the track could have been gimmicky, it's one of Norman Harris' best productions and arrangements. "People on the World, Rise" is an unfocused dancefloor plea. When they sing, "Just let the world be dancefloor people," it's this close to self-parody. While the Trammps aren't on the short list of balladeers, *The Trammps III* has them at least thinking about love. The winning "Living the Life" and "It Don't Take Much" is reminiscent of the group's work on Golden Fleece and Buddah. Both tracks feature the softer-voiced Robert Upchurch assuming lead duties from the irascible Jimmy Ellis. *The Trammps III* is an interesting effort from one of R&B's most overlooked artists. *—Jason Elias*

The Legendary Zing Album / 1978 / Buddah ♦♦♦
The Trammps had a few modest hits on Buddah: "Zing Went the Strings of My Heart," which featured Earl Young's seasoned bass voice on lead; "Penquin at the Big Apple"; and a disco version of the Dominoes' erotic "Sixty Minute Man." When their contract ended, Young, Ron Baker, and Norman Harris left to form Golden Fleece Records, the Trammps' new home. After a few singles on Golden Fleece, which were not as good as the stuff here, Buddah brought in hired gun, disco mix master Tom Moulton to redo the Trammps' singles and unreleased songs that resulted in *The Legendary Zing Album.* The best of the rest include "Hold Back the Night," "Scrub Board" (an instrumental), and "Pray All You Sinners." *—Andrew Hamilton*

The Whole World's Dancing / 1979 / Atlantic ♦♦♦

● **This Is Where the Happy People Go: The Best of the Trammps** / 1994 / Rhino ♦♦♦♦♦
Due to all the great funk, R&B, and soul bands of the '70s, it's easy to overlook many of the lesser-known (but just as great) bands. Such is the case with the Trammps. Best known for their smash hit from the *Saturday Night Fever* Soundtrack, "Disco Inferno" (their only Top 20 appearance on the pop charts), the group had many other hits on the R&B charts, which were just as deserving of crossover success. Just about any track from the excellent *This Is Where All the Happy People Go: The Best of the Trammps* compilation is a solid example of '70s R&B at its finest and most expertly crafted. Many overlooked and forgotten gems reside here, such as "Hold Back the Night," "Trammps Disco Theme," "That's Where the Happy People Go," and "Zing Went the Strings of My Heart." Admittedly, the Trammps did seem to jump on the disco bandwagon, like so many other bands from this era, but the quality of the music never suffered. For a representation of some of the finest music the '70s had to offer, *The Best of the Trammps* simply can't be beat. *—Greg Prato*

The Treniers

f. 1947
Group / Jump Blues, R&B
Featuring twin brothers Cliff and Claude Trenier, the Treniers helped link swing music to rock & roll with their brand of hot jump blues in the late '40s and early '50s. To the latter-day listener, their early-'50s singles sound closer to swing than rock; indeed, Cliff and Claude had once sung with the Jimmie Lunceford Orchestra. The group did anticipate some crucial elements of rock & roll, though, with their solid, thumping beats, their squealing saxophone solos, and their song titles, such as "Rocking on Sunday Night," "Rockin' Is Our Business," and "It Rocks! It Rolls! It Swings!." The Treniers' brand of swing-cum-R&B was undoubtedly an influence on Bill Haley, who saw them when both acts were playing summer shows in Wildwood, NJ. They had work recorded for OKeh in the early '50s; by the middle of the decade, their sound was more R&B-oriented. Like many early R&B pioneers, they were unable to find success in the rock & roll era, though they appeared in a few of the first rock & roll films. *—Richie Unterberger*

The Treniers on TV / 1955 / Epic ♦♦♦

Cool It Baby / 1988 / Bear Family ♦♦♦♦♦

Hey Sister Lucy / 1988 / Bear Family ♦♦♦♦♦

● **They Rock! They Roll! They Swing!: The Best of the Treniers** / Feb. 28, 1995 / Epic/Legacy ♦♦♦♦♦
Led by identical twins Cliff and Claude Trenier, the Treniers were a joyously crazed R&B group whose style suggested a middle ground between Louis Jordan's swingin' boogie and the more stylized approach of Ray Charles' early sides, but with less ballast and more frantic energy than both of those acts put together. While the Treniers released their first records through Mercury, the group's best recordings were cut for the OKeh label between 1951 and 1955, and *They Rock! They Roll! They Swing!: The Best of the Treniers* collects 15 classic sides from the OKeh vaults (among them their duet with baseball star Willie Mays, "Say Hey (The Willie Mays Song)," and the gotta-hear-it-to-believe-it "Poontang") along with five equally potent unreleased cuts. Whether they were chasing women, getting drunk on patent medicine, or simply celebrating their own monumental coolness, the Treniers were one group who knew how to get the party started, and *They Rock! They*

Roll! They Swing! is both a fine introduction to their fine sounds and a fitting soundtrack for your next bash. All 20 tunes have been expertly remastered and sound great, while Nick Toshes (who wrote a superb appreciation of the Treniers in his book *Unsung Heroes of Rock 'n' Roll*) contributes informative and entertaining liner notes. *—Mark Deming*

Ralph Tresvant

b. May 16, 1968, Boston, MA

Vocals / Urban, Contemporary R&B

Ralph Tresvant sang lead on New Edition's hits and had his own gold number one R&B hit with the silky "Sensitivity." He was the last member to release a solo project of his own. All of the group's previous members had number one R&B hits: Bobby Brown with "Girlfriend " and Ricky Bell, Michael Bivins, and Ronald DeVoe as Bell Biv DeVoe (aka BBD) with "Poison." Besides this, Tresvant had New Edition's formidable chart success to contend with: four number-one R&B singles, "Candy Girl" (gold), "Cool It Now," "Mr. Telephone Man," and "Can You Stand the Rain." Could Ralph Tresvant have hits after New Edition as a solo artist? But then again having Tresvant's record come out after his previous bandmates could be an advantage because he could gauge what his music should be like based on the response of the fans.

Born May 15, 1968, to Patricia Ann Tresvant and Ralph Tresvant Sr., Ralph Tresvant grew in the Roxbury section of Boston. He joined Bobby Brown, Ricky Bell, Michael Bivins, and Ronald DeVoe in a group formed by producer/songwriter Maurice Starr. Starr's concept was to form a group that was basically a "new edition" of the Jackson 5. Paradoxically, Motown founder Berry Gordy wanted to mold the Jackson 5 into a "new edition" of Frankie Lymon & the Teenagers. Signed to StreetWise Records, the group scored with "Candy Girl." The hits continued with "Is This the End" (number-eight R&B), "Lost in Love" (number-six R&B), "Count Me Out" (number-two R&B for two weeks), "Earth Angel" from the movie *Karate Kid Part 2* (number-three R&B), "Once in a Lifetime Groove" from the Gregory Hines/Billy Crystal movie *Running Scared* (number-ten R&B), "Tears on My Pillow" with Little Anthony of Little Anthony & the Imperials, "If It Isn't Love" (number-two R&B, number-seven pop), "You're Not My Kind of Girl" (number-three R&B), and "Crucial" (number-four R&B).

Signing to MCA Records as a solo artist, Tresvant expressed his apprehension about becoming a solo artist and trying to match his previous successes in various interviews. Producers/songwriters Jimmy Jam & Terry Lewis felt confident in Tresvant's abilities having work with him on the group's double-platinum LP *Heartbreak*. They had him sing the lead and background vocals on the song they had written for him, "Sensitivity." "Sensitivity" sold over a million copies, going to number-one R&B and number-four pop on *Billboard*'s charts in fall 1990. His solo debut, *Ralph Tresvant*, was released November 27, 1990, and went platinum, parking at number-one R&B for two weeks. The LP also yielded the charting hits "Stone Cold Gentleman," "Do What I Gotta Do," and "Rated X." For Jam & Lewis' Perspective Records, Tresvant sang on the 1992 hit "The Best Things in Life Are Free" issued as "Luther Vandross and Janet Jackson with BBD and Ralph Tresvant." That was followed by his own hit single, "Money Can't Buy You Love," from the Damon and Marlon Wayans movie *Mo' Money*. The singer appeared in the movie *House Party 2*. Tresvant was on the 1996 New Edition reunion album, *Home Again* and there was a 1998 MCA Special Products CD *It's Goin' Down*. *—Ed Hogan*

• **Ralph Tresvant** / 1990 / MCA ✦✦✦✦✦

With Bobby Brown, Bell Biv DeVoe and Johnny Gill all doing quite well outside of New Edition in 1990, it wasn't surprising that colleague Ralph Tresvant pursued a solo career. This self-titled R&B/pop release isn't as distinguished or as confident as the music Brown, BBD and Gill had been doing on their own, but it has its moments, including the smooth ballad "I Love You (Just For You)," the nice-guy manifesto "Stone Cold Gentleman" and the new jack swing tune "Public Figure (Ordinary Guy)." Some of urban contemporary's hottest producers (Jimmy Jam & Terry Lewis and Wolf & Epic, among others) are employed, and yet, the overall results aren't as strong as one might expect. None of the material is really bad; it's just that most of it isn't that far above average. *—Alex Henderson*

It's Goin' Down / 1994 / MCA ✦✦

On this follow-up to his solo debut, Ralph Tresvant attempts to show he is a bad mutha, but fails. Of course, it's difficult to be a badass when you have a voice similar to Michael Jackson (Jacko certainly failed at being bad). Unfortunately, except for three of the tracks produced and written by the great production team of Jimmy Jam & Terry Lewis, Tresvant chose to write and produce the majority of the album himself—bad choice. Much like Janet Jackson's releases, it's amazing the quality difference between the Jam & Lewis tracks compared to the self-produced and written tracks. Tresvant destroyed whatever promise he showed on his self-titled debut release by "It's Going Down." *—Tim Griggs*

Trin-I-Tee 5:7

Group / Contemporary Gospel, Urban

During the late '90s as the urban sounds of TLC and En Vogue stormed up the charts, Trin-I-Tee 5:7 offered a similar style of smooth harmonizing over uptempo beats, except with a strong gospel message. Following a promotional EP release, the trio, originally comprised of Chanelle Hayes, Terry Brown, and Angel Taylor, debuted in summer 1998 with its self-titled album, released by B-Rite. The album notably featured production work by R. Kelly, who was one of urban music's dominant hitmakers at the time. A year later Trin-I-Tee 5:7 returned with its second album, *Spiritual Love*, which again featured production work by Kelly. The trio's makeup artist, Adrian Anderson, had replaced the departed Brown by this point, solidifying the lineup. In 2002 Trin-I-Tee 5:7 delivered *The Kiss*. *—Jason Birchmeier*

Trin-I-Tee 5:7 / Jul. 14, 1998 / Interscope ✦✦✦

While it may not be entirely successful, Trin-I-Tee 5:7's eponymous debut album is an admirable attempt to bring the cool, new jack R&B stylings of TLC to contemporary gospel. Since the sound is so sexy, it's a little strange to hear it in a sacred setting, but the tracks that do work on *Trin-I-Tee 5:7* prove that this was a risk worth taking. *—Stephen Thomas Erlewine*

• **Spiritual Love** / Oct. 19, 1999 / Interscope ✦✦✦

Spiritual Love, the sophomore effort from urban gospel trio Trin-I-Tee 5:7, again features a number of fine moments that equal the best of their debut; the juxtaposition of sexy, slinky, urban R&B grooves with non-secular subject matter still seems a bit odd—form not matching up with content—but Christian music fans will be happy to have a sound they enjoy with the messages they respect. *—Steve Huey*

The Kiss / Jun. 25, 2002 / Gospocentric ✦✦✦

Destiny's Child pays lip service to God on occasional tracks, but Adrian Anderson, Angel Taylor, and Chanelle Hayes are gospel's answer to that group and are more the real deal. They combine the same picture-perfect harmonies, with thumping soul grooves by a sea of top producers, but are focused on the Lord 24/7. Not that they're beyond wanting to be as commercial as possible—the opening track is a remix of the final song, "Holla," featuring a slightly thicker groove and a rap interlude. There is certainly a fair amount of straightforward praise songs, including the seductive and danceworthy old-school soul-vibing "Dance Like Sunday." But what sets Trin-I-Tee 5:7 apart is the interesting lyrical approaches, which tackle themes beyond the usual repetitive worship lines listeners have all heard. The ballad "Lord" tackles the issues of people using God for bad purposes and people with the best intentions going astray. A title like "With a Kiss" would mean late-night seduction for Destiny's Child, but here is an acoustic guitar-driven reading of the relationship between Jesus and Judas, and the Betrayal. The midtempo advice-oriented tune "What He Wants" addresses the difficulties of romantic temptation and urges listeners to follow God rather than worry about pleasing people. There's also a gentle anthemic reading of "People Get Ready," an important song that deserves a new generation of listeners. Often, spoken word interludes seem pretentious, but here they show the happy spirit of the girls making the music. And that's what it's all about, isn't it? *—Jonathan Widran*

Trouble Funk

f. 1978, Washington, D.C., **db.** 1984

Group / Go-Go, Funk, Disco

Miles off the radar of popular music during the early '80s, Trouble Funk energized their D.C. home with the sound of go-go music, an uproarious blend of swinging, uptempo '70s funk and a '60s-style horn section. The band formed in 1978, and the lineup coalesced around drummer Emmett Nixon, percussionists Mack Carey and Timothius Davis, guitarist Chester Davis, bassist Tony Fisher, trombone players Gerald and Robert Reed, trumpeter Taylor Reed, keyboard player James Avery, and saxophonist David Rudd. Trouble Funk earned a loyal fan base for their notoriously can't-miss live act, a raw, party friendly version of dance and funk with few songs but plenty of extensive jams organized around audience-friendly vocal tags and call-out hooks.

The first go-go record released *outside* of D.C., Trouble Funk's 1982 debut *Drop the Bomb* appeared on Sugarhill, the same label then championing early hip-hop. (The two styles had very similar origins, in the breakbeat culture of urban block parties.) Though the band's second album, *In Times of Trouble*, appeared only on the local label D.E.T.T., Trouble Funk earned national distribution with a prescient concert record, 1985's *Saturday Night (Live from Washington, D.C.)*, released through Island. After taking the live act nationwide and even worldwide (they played the 1986 Montreux Jazz Festival), Trouble Funk returned in 1987 with the boundary breaking *Trouble Over Here, Trouble Over There*, featuring sympathetic heads like Bootsy Collins and Kurtis Blow. It was a bit of a stylistic misstep, however, and Island released the group from its contract. Undeterred, Trouble Funk kept on grooving around the city, playing often, even into the '90s, for nostalgic party goers as well as the musically curious. *—John Bush*

Live / 1981 / Infinite Zero ✦✦✦✦✦

There are no actual songs contained on Trouble Funk's *Live*; there are four near-15-minute jams, but they prove to be just as magical and rewarding as their compact songs (for Trouble Funk's more accessible tunes, check out the *Early Singles* compilation on Infinite Zero). Although the band never caught on nationally, for reasons unknown, they were huge in the Washington, D.C. area. And like other funk specialists (Graham Central Station, Funkadelic, etc.), Trouble Funk songs were infectious rave-ups that instantly created a party-like atmosphere. The group could really stretch out in concert, and although it may sound like a cliché, *Live* is the closest you can come to the Trouble Funk concert experience without actually attending one of their shows. Each of the four album sides twist, turn, bounce, groove, and breathe. There's lots of crowd chanting (done amazingly on cue), superb drumming/percussion (courtesy of Timothy Davis, Mack Carey, and Emmett Nixon), and rubbery synthesized sounds. The energy never dips, and the group is constantly inspired and at their peak. Also included are interesting liner notes from an unlikely Trouble Funk fanatic, Henry Rollins. *—Greg Prato*

Drop the Bomb / 1982 / Sequel ✦✦✦✦✦

Masters of Washington, D.C.'s '80s go-go craze, Trouble Funk brought early hip-hop (the group was part of Sugarhill Records) to the dancefloor with deep bass, propulsive rhythms, and party lyrics. Being even more inspired by '70s funk bands like Chic, Cameo, and the Gap Band than either the Sugar Hill Gang or Grandmaster Flash, Trouble Funk and other go-go acts like E.U. and Chuck Brown used the MC to conduct party-time call-and-response sessions and not generally for street poetry raps à la Melle Mel and Kurtis Blow. A celebratory atmosphere certainly prevails on Sequel Records' fine Trouble Funk collection *Drop the Bomb*, with many of the band's prime dance hits like the title track, "Get on Up," and "Let's Get Hot" being featured in their extended versions. The band's nasty synth licks, up-front percussion, and sinewy funk guitar lines keep the music pumping throughout, while both the go-go/rap hybrid "Pump Me Up" and Barry White-inspired soul ballad "Don't Try to Use Me" show off the group's musical flexibility.

The set is rounded out with the ten-minute, bring-the-house-down jam "Supergrit," which nicely incorporates the funk of Kool & the Gang and Earth, Wind & Fire into the go-go mix. This is a great introduction to both Trouble Funk's music and the go-go sound. *—Stephen Cook*

Saturday Night (Live from Washington, D.C.) / 1985 / Island ♦♦♦

The Bomb Has Dropped / 1987 / Castle ♦♦♦

One of the first CD compilations of Trouble Funk's classic sides for Sugarhill, it has now been superseded by much better and more thorough retrospectives. However, there's no denying that all the essential tracks are here, in uncut form. "Pump Me Up," "Hey Fellas," and "Drop the Bomb" are all pure go-go, recognizable now as the source of numerous samples, and as funky as the genre got. On the other hand, the liner notes are scant, the sound tinny with very little bass, and the compilation ends on a ballad, "Don't Try to Use Me." Not terrible, but only serves to point out what they were really good at. *—Ted Mills*

Trouble Over Here, Trouble Over There / 1987 / Island ♦♦♦

● **Early Singles** / Mar. 11, 1997 / Warner Bros. ♦♦♦♦♦

While Chuck Brown & the Soul Searchers were longer lived and E.U. scored the biggest national hit, Trouble Funk was the best and most interesting group to come out of the Washington, D.C., go-go scene, and its relentless pursuit of the good groove, propelled by buoyant horn charts, P-Funk-inspired keyboard lines, and tireless percussion jams, was a potent and satisfying reminder in the dying days of the disco era of just how joyous, muscular, and human good dance music could sound. This compilation (released by former D.C. resident and longtime fan Henry Rollins—yep, *that* Henry Rollins) features eight cuts from the band's early, self-released 12-inch singles, where Trouble Funk could stretch out its tracks to eight to ten minutes without outside influences urging the band to shoot for something more commercial or radio-friendly; this is go-go with enough grease for purists and enough groove to win converts, including the epochal "Supergrit," "So Early in the Morning," and an idiosyncratic reworking of Kraftwerk's "Trans Europe Express." A valuable archival release that will also give you enough fuel to set the dancefloor burning all night long. *—Mark Deming*

● **Droppin' Bombs: The Definitive Trouble Funk** / Aug. 25, 1998 / Harmless ♦♦♦♦♦

Believe the title—this two-CD best-of is the definitive collection by the most creative group to emerge from the Washington, D.C., go-go scene. Selected by the group itself, the songs don't sound like calls to party hearty as much as recorded parties with bassist Tony Fisher as the gruff-voiced but cordial host leading the rapped call-and-response chants over potent funk grooves. But Trouble Funk's real strength lies in its savvy command of dynamics and the creative variety the band melds with the percussive power of the cowbell and conga-laden go-go rhythm. "Drop the Bomb," "Let's Get Small," the convincing go-go adaptation of Kraftwerk's hit "Trans-Europe Express" on "Trouble Funk Express," the explosive opening to "Say What," and the monster horn riff driving "Hey Fellas" are just a few of the many highlights. Even two mediocre ballads can't derail the momentum of *Droppin' Bombs*, which clearly demonstrates how Trouble Funk and go-go were the mid-'80s missing link between George Clinton's Parliament-Funkadelic mob and the rap crews that flourished later in the decade. *—Don Snowden*

All the Way Live / 2000 / Swollen ♦♦♦♦

E Flat Boogie / 2000 / Funky Delicacies ♦♦♦♦♦

Given the volatility of the late '70s in popular music in general and urban music in particular, this first of three volumes documenting the history of the Washington, D.C., area's Trouble Funk is more than welcome. Unlike the Island compilation that focuses only on the band's work either recorded with or licensed by the label, this first Funky Delicacies disc concentrates on the earliest go-go material from the band's own D.E.T.T. label, from the first single, "E Flat Boogie," on to "Pump Me Up," all of which were issued only on 12-inch or, bizarrely enough, on cassette. From the opening bars of "E Flat Boogie," it's easy to see why Trouble Funk is one of the most sampled groups in history. The deep, backbone-slipping basslines illuminate the very idea of the word funk. The multiple drummers—two trap kits and two percussionists who were interchangeable—set Trouble Funk apart, even from the alleged go-go music originators, Chuck Brown & the Soul Searchers. The horn section may have had Tower of Power's tight lines, but it had a raw punch all its own. Tracks like "Let's Get Small," which became an anti-drug anthem with its call-and-response choruses and verse lines, also became a funk anthem. There is no party jam like this one, with harmonicas cascading through a mix that is dominated by a crushing rhythmic attack and down-and-dirty keyboards. "Pump Me Up" is totally worthy of its name, and signifies the rhythm track that was the basis for later classics such as "Paint the White House Black." "Trouble Funk Express" pays a perverse nod to Kraftwerk's "Trans-Europe Express" before tearing down the German group's puny attempts at rhythm consciousness with pure go-go chaos that splinters the synthesizers in the background. Also on board are "So Early in the Morning," "Hey Fellas," and instrumental versions—which are far from add-ons—of the first three tracks, making this an exceptional compilation. It'll be tough to wait for the other two. *—Thom Jurek*

Doris Troy

b. Jan. 6, 1937, New York, NY

Vocals / Pop-Soul, Soul

Surely one of the most talented one-hit wonders of the rock era, Doris Troy hit the Top Ten with "Just One Look" in 1963, but also recorded many other fine pop-soul sides for Atlantic between 1963 and 1965. Unlike many soul performers of the time, Troy wrote most of her own material (under the pseudonym Payne), and had already written for other artists and sung backup with Dionne and Dee Dee Warwick and Cissy Houston on New York soul records before striking out on her own. More melodically ambitious and stylistically eclectic than many of her peers, her Atlantic sides blend elements of gospel, girl group, blues, and pop into a rich New York soul sound. Troy never reached the charts again after "Just One Look," but was more appreciated in England, where she toured occasionally and where the Hollies covered her "What'cha Gonna Do About It" on their first album. Moving to Britain, she recorded an album for Apple in 1970 with assistance from George Harrison and Billy Preston. In the early '70s, she sang backup vocals for British rock groups in addition to recording a couple more albums. In the '80s she starred in *Mama I Want to Sing*, a musical based on her life story. *—Richie Unterberger*

Just One Look / 1963 / Atlantic ♦♦♦

Doris Troy's debut album contains her number-ten pop hit "Just One Look," along with an assortment of other fine tracks; seven of the 12 songs are composed by Troy and Gregory Carroll, with Rex Garvin helping on a couple. And while Troy's rendition of "Stormy Weather" won't overwrite the great torch singers' versions, this is still a fine album. Atlantic gave Doris ample input to display her songwriting and warbling skills, but she never had another hit. Sometimes it's best to go with the hot producers and writers. *—Andrew Hamilton*

Doris Troy / 1970 / Capitol ♦♦♦

An all-star cast supported Troy on her lone Apple effort: George Harrison, Billy Preston, Peter Frampton, Stephen Stills, Klaus Voormann, Jackie Lomax, Eric Clapton, Leon Russell, and Delaney & Bonnie all contributed, and Harrison, Stills, Lomax, Preston, Voormann, and Ringo Starr pitched in on the songwriting, though Troy wrote or co-wrote most of the songs. Well-received by some critics, it really doesn't add up to the sum of its parts. Troy is in great voice, but much of the material is pedestrian, and the heavy rock/soul arrangements often have an over-beefy, early-'70s super-session feel. It works best when Troy puts the brakes on the hard rock to deliver emotional, slower soul tunes. [The CD reissue adds five interesting cuts from non-LP singles and outtakes.] *—Richie Unterberger*

Rainbow Testament / 1972 / Polydor ♦♦♦♦

Two years after Doris Troy's critically acclaimed album on Apple, the voice which made records by the Rolling Stones, Sky, Tom Jones, Humble Pie, Carly Simon, and, especially, Pink Floyd's *Dark Side of the Moon*, among many, many others, so very extra special, is in full command as Doris Troy & the Gospel Truth perform at the Rainbow Theater in London. Gospel originals like Troy's "Morning Train" and "My Father's House" are electrifying, and the singer's friends Claudia Lennear and Rufus Thomas show up, adding to the fun and festive atmosphere. There's an incredible wall of sound with the combination of horn players, percussion, Hammond organ, piano, singers, and master of ceremonies, Doris Troy, inviting notables like the New Seekers up on-stage. The singer told *AMG* "I love that album. It was live. We had a really great time. The audience was fantastic." You can feel the high-energy vibe on Gene MacLellan's "Put Your Hand in the Hand," as well as all over the tremendous rendition of Joe South's 1969 hit "Games People Play." It's slowed down and soulful with the simply amazing vocal prowess of Troy creating a definitive version of the multi-format songwriter's chestnut. South had Deep Purple putting the hard rock stamp on "Hush," Lynn Anderson taking "Rose Garden" country, and produced slick pop for Billy Joe Royal, but this performance must have given the veteran songwriter chills when he first heard it. Released in 1972 on Polydor Records in Germany, the album design is very classy, a photo of "Mama Troy" on the cover, a positive message throughout the music and the uplifting poem on the back cover with thoughts like "We believe the world's a friendly place/We believe in all our many blessings... We believe we're helped by hidden powers" bringing the message home. A driving Taylor/Clinton title, "(I Wanna) Testify" opens the album contrasted with the Doris Troy original "Steal Away," voices swelling and Jimmy Helms taking a vocal lead along with the star. Troy arranged and produced this highly collectible album, her work sought after on eBay and at record shows, and justifiably so. A classic performance by an important and multi-talented artist, *The Rainbow Testament* by Doris Troy & the Gospel Truth deserves to be expanded and re-released. *—Joe Viglione*

● **Just One Look: The Best of Doris Troy** / Aug. 23, 1994 / Ichiban/Soul Classics ♦♦♦♦♦

This 21-track anthology of her 1963-1965 Atlantic sides is as comprehensive as one could ask for. It includes all of her singles, her rare album, three cuts only issued on British singles, and her rare 1965 single for the Calla label, "I'll Do Anything (He Wants Me to Do)." Besides "Just One Look," there are quite a few other downright excellent lost gems here: "What'cha Gonna Do About It," the bluesy "Draw Me Closer," the driving "You'd Better Stop" (with a fierce guitar break that sounds like a young Jimmy Page), and the soulful wall of sound on "I'll Do Anything." "How My Heart Aches" is a special standout that ranks among the very finest wrenching, melancholy soul ever waxed. Much more than a collector's item, this proves Troy to be a genuinely overlooked major talent. *—Richie Unterberger*

The Andrea True Connection

b. Nashville, TN

Vocals / Disco

Singer Andrea True was among the most fascinating characters to emerge from the disco era—a former porn star, she was best known for the smash "More, More, More," one of the truly classic club hits of its time. Born and raised in Nashville, during the late '60s True relocated to New York City to pursue a career in acting. Outside of work as an extra in a handful of mainstream films, she enjoyed little success; eventually, she was forced to turn to X-rated material. While in Jamaica in 1975, she recorded the sensual "More, More, More" with producer Gregg Diamond; the track—credited to the Andrea True Connection—was then licensed to Buddah Records and remixed by Tom Moulton, and upon its release ultimately reached the number-four slot on the U.S. pop charts. An LP, also titled *More, More, More*, soon followed, but after the sophomore effort *White Witch* failed to match True's early success, her recording career was essentially over. *—Jason Ankeny*

More, More, More / 1976 / Buddah ♦♦♦
Resplendent in Gregg Diamond's swirling "Love Boat Theme" mix of disco beats, strings, Latin percussion, and horns, the Andrea True Connection's debut is a classic bit of polished dancefloor kitsch (also deserving credit is Tom Moulton, who remixed the album just prior to release). True's star rose considerably with the chart-topping title track (one of the most impressive of many one-hit disco wonders of the era), but this would prove to be an anomaly in light of the dismal sales of her sophomore album, *White Witch*. Considering True's highly mixed and less-than-amazing vocal talents, though, a single splash is all one could have probably hoped for. And adding to the quality of "More, More, More" (featuring Diamond's lovely trumpet and cow bell instrumental breaks), there is the peppy, pop-disco of "Party Line," the slicked-up boogaloo cut "Keep It Up Longer," and two fine extended tracks: the jazz-inflected, Philly soul-wise "Fill Me Up (Heart to Heart)" and the fleet and airy "Call Me" (probably the most *Love Boat*-esque of the lot). Something of a classic from the disco catalog, *More, More, More* makes good on its one giant hit with a highly enjoyable and urbane array of dance tracks. *—Stephen Cook*

White Witch / 1978 / Arista ♦♦♦
Technically, Andrea True wasn't a one-hit wonder because 1976's "More, More, More" wasn't her only hit—the porn actress turned disco diva also enjoyed a lot of dance club exposure with "N.Y., You Got Me Dancing" and "What's Your Name, What's Your Number" in 1978. But it is safe to say that her career in music was short-lived, and that "More, More, More" was her only major pop/Top 40 hit. Released in 1978, *White Witch* was True's second album as well as her last. This LP finds True experiencing the infamous sophomore slump—while *White Witch* isn't a bad album, it falls short of the excellence her first album, *More, More, More*. There are a few gems, including the Michael Zager-produced "What's Your Name, What's Your Number" and the exuberant, Gregg Diamond-produced "N.Y., You Got Me Dancing"—both of which are exercises in unapologetically campy fun. Also enjoyable is True's trashy cover of Lou Reed's "Sally Can't Dance." But the other material is unremarkable. While Diamond saw to it that *More, More, More* was consistently strong, *White Witch* is wildly uneven—the fact that The Right Stuff's 1997 collection *More, More, More: The Best of the Andrea True Connection* contains five songs from True's first album and only two from her second really lets you know how uneven *White Witch* is. This LP is strictly for die-hard disco collectors. *—Alex Henderson*

• **More, More, More: The Best of the Andrea True Connection** / Aug. 26, 1997 / Capitol ♦♦♦♦
When one thinks of the disco era, Andrea True's 1976 smash "More More More" is one of those songs that immediately comes to mind. The former porno star turned disco diva didn't have nearly as many hits as Donna Summer, the Bee Gees or the Village People—in fact, she only recorded two albums, 1976's *More More More* and 1978's *White Witch*. But even so, no discussion of disco is complete unless True's name is mentioned, and no disco collection is complete without the songs on this 1997 CD. While the sexy title song was True's biggest radio hit, glossy numbers like "N.Y., You Got Me Dancing," "Keep It Up Longer" and "Call Me" brought more than a few dance clubs to life. These very European-sounding classics (most of them produced by Gregg Diamond) weren't about social relevance or intellect; their only goal was escapist, campy fun. And True accomplished her goal without apology. *—Alex Henderson*

Truth Hurts

Vocals / Urban, Contemporary R&B, Hip-Hop
Urban vocalist Truth Hurts began her career in grand fashion with the aid of Dr. Dre. The enormously successful West Coast rap producer signed her to his Aftermath label in the wake of his chart-topping productions for Mary J. Blige ("Family Affair") and Eve ("Let Me Blow Your Mind"), around the same time Dre presented his former songwriting partner Knoc-Turn'al and the return of golden-age legend Rakim. Just as he did for those two, Dre crafted a sure-fire lead single for Truth Hurts, "Addictive." Though Dre doesn't actually produce the song himself—DJ Quik does—he applied his stamp of approval, arranging for Rakim to duet with Truth Hurts and getting the song incredible exposure on both radio and MTV. *—Jason Birchmeier*

• **Truthfully Speaking** / Jun. 25, 2002 / Interscope ♦♦♦
Truth Hurts is not just another contemporary R&B vocalist to compare to Alicia Keys or Ashanti. For one thing, the executive producer on her debut *Truthfully Speaking* is Dr. Dre, and the album was released on his Aftermath sublabel of Interscope. She also benefits from a laundry list of the best commercial hip-hop trackmasters around: Dre, DJ Quik, Timbaland, even R. Kelly. Despite this star-studded credit list, *Truthfully Speaking* is a bland record; Truth Hurts' vocals, while evocative and rangy, aren't incredibly strong (especially when she's stretching a note), and she usually needs a backup chorus to keep the songs sounding good. The single "Addictive" is bizarre, with an Indian filmi vocal sample sounding stronger than Truth Hurts herself, and a brief appearance by Rakim strictly phoning it in. A few of the productions make for good tracks, though most of the time Truth Hurts struggles to keep up with the best in the contemporary R&B field. *—John Bush*

Truth

f. 1976, Cleveland, OH
Group / Urban, Smooth Soul
Truth was a Cleveland group created by ex-O'Jay Bobby Massey that formed around 1976; the original lineup consisted of Larry Hancock, Leo Green, Al Boyd, and Russell Watts. They cut "Excedrin Headache #24" b/w "Come Back Home" on Sound of Cleveland Records, the latter, a ballad written by Massey, Boyd, and Walter Johnson, clones the O'Jays' dramatic ballad sound. Truth's members were musical veterans. Hancock wrote "Working on Your Case," for the O'Jays in-between studies at Thomas Edison High, and later recorded "Gotta Find Myself a Girl" and "Glad I Found You" with the Intertains on Uptown Records (1966-1967); he fronted S.O.U.L. in the early '70s ("This Time Around"). Boyd and Green started with the Imperial Wonders, a flashy group patterned after the Temptations who recorded good but neglected tunes including "Trying to Get to You," "Turned Around Over You," and "Just a Dream"; Boyd also sung with the Rotations, who released a couple of singles.

When Otis Williams booted Dennis Edwards from the Temptations in 1977, Edwards moved to Cleveland and gigged at his late Uncle's construction company. He teamed with Massey and Truth members for one helluva road show that included Margaret Foxworth. They recorded *Coming Home* on Devaki Records; two singles, "Understanding" and "Coming Home," both co-written by Edwards, received some local play.

When it hit the streets, only Hancock and Green were on the cover. The liner notes say that Will Thomas, William Grover, Phil Coghill, Doris Wallace, and Foxworth assisted on vocals. Actually, Wallace only did a talking part on "Coming Home"; she didn't sing. People at the sessions insist that Watts and Boyd also contributed vocals. Coghill had sung with the short-lived True Movement ("Lovely Way to Meet"), who evolved into Avatarr ("I'm So Glad I Found You"). It didn't matter, the singles never clicked nationally and didn't make that big of a splash in Cleveland. When Edwards returned to the Temptations he took "Coming Home," which appeared on their *Power* album as "I'm Coming Home," with the writing credited to the Temptations. Hmmmm?

By 1980, Truth was history. Hancock remained involved in music and has appeared in a Broadway play. Boyd became a staff writer at Motown; his biggest cut was "Shaky Ground" on the Temptations, a song Phoebe Snow took to even greater heights. Foxworth backed Reverend Al Green on occasion, something she did before Truth, and ran a bar in Cleveland. The others became Joe lunch buckets. *—Andrew Hamilton*

• **Coming Home** / 1980 / Devaki ♦♦♦
Larry Hancock and Leo Green represent Truth on the album cover but the Truth on this album also includes Will Thomas, Phil Coghill, William Grover, and Margaret Foxworth. Originally a quintet, they cut "Excedrin Headache #24" b/w "Come Back Home" (not included here) which got played in their hometown of Cleveland and not much anywhere else. Green sings in a husky baritone, and Hancock has a cutting tenor. "Comin' Home," co-written by Dennis Edwards, is the most exciting track. Edwards, on a hiatus from the Tempts, took the song with him when he rejoined the legendary band (who recorded it on their *Power* album, with the Temptations' name credited as the songwriters). The rest of the songs are decent; "It's Gonna Take a Miracle," "International Dancing," and "Understanding" are the most memorable. *—Andrew Hamilton*

Tommy Tucker (Robert Higginbotham)

b. Mar. 5, 1933, Springfield, OH, **d.** Jan. 17, 1982, Newark, NJ
Vocals, Piano / R&B, Soul-Blues
When Tommy Tucker ordered his lady to "put on her hi-heel sneakers" in 1964, the whole world was listening, judging from the myriad of covers and sequels that followed in its wake. Robert Higginbotham (Tucker's legal handle) grew up in Springfield, getting his little fingers accustomed to the ivories by age seven. Tucker joined saxist Bobby Wood's band in the late '40s as its piano player. When vocal groups became the rage, the band switched gears and became the Cavaliers, a doo wop outfit that remained intact into the late '50s. Tucker put together his own combo after that to play bars in Dayton, his personnel including guitarist Weldon Young and bassist Brenda Jones.

The trio eventually relocated to Newark, NJ, setting Tucker up for his debut solo session in 1961 for Atco. "Rock and Roll Machine" was issued as by Tee Tucker and already exhibited the gritty, Ray Charles-inflected vocal delivery that Tucker later used to great advantage. His traveling companions did pretty well for themselves, too: renamed Dean & Jean, they hit big in 1963-1964 with the lighthearted duets "Tra La La Suzy" and "Hey Jean, Hey Dean" for Rust Records.

Tucker fortuitously hooked up with Atlantic Records co-founder Herb Abramson, who was working as an independent R&B producer during the early '60s. Among their early collaborations was the lowdown Jimmy Reed-style shuffle "Hi-Heel Sneakers" (Dean Young was the nasty lead guitarist). Abramson leased it to Checker Records and watched it sail to the upper reaches of the pop charts in early 1964. A terrific Checker LP and a trip to Great Britain were among the immediate upshot for the organist. R&B star Don Covay co-wrote Tucker's follow-up, "Long Tall Shorty," an amusing tune in a similar groove. It barely scraped the lower end of the charts, and Tucker never scored another hit. That didn't stop Abramson from trying, though—he produced Tucker singing a soulful "That's Life" in 1966 for his own Festival label, while "Alimony," another standout Checker 45, certainly deserved a better reception than it got in 1965.

Although the majority of his waxings were under Abramson's supervision, Tucker did travel to Chicago in 1966 to record with producer Willie Dixon in an effort to jump-start his fading career. "I'm Shorty" had Dixon contributing harmony vocals and Big Walter Horton on harp, but it didn't do the trick. Abramson admirably stuck by his protégé, recording him anew for at least another decade, but most of the mixed results just gathered dust in his vaults. Tucker was still musically active when he died, a relatively young man, in 1982. *—Bill Dahl*

• **Hi Heel Sneakers** / 1964 / Checker ♦♦♦♦♦
A dozen of his best blues and soul outings for producer Herb Abramson, including the two hits, the grinding soul rockers "Just for a Day," "I Don't Want 'Cha" and "I Warned You About Him" (oodles of Ray Charles influence on all of 'em), and an absolutely stunning "Come Rain or Come Shine." [The 1995 CD reissue adds eight bonus tracks from the mid-'60s that were not on the original LP, including the single "Alimony," effectively making it a Tommy Tucker best-of.] *—Bill Dahl*

Mother Tucker / 1974 / Red Lightnin' ♦♦♦
These are leftovers from deep in the Abramson archives. A precious few tracks—"Lean Greens," "Drunk"—possess the same gritty charm that invested Tucker's greatest hit, "Hi-Heel Sneakers" (here in longer, unedited form with Tucker's faltering organ solo intact).

Most of the 16-song LP is comprised of demo tapes and other flotsam that doesn't present the keyboardist in the best light. *—Bill Dahl*

The Turbans

f. 1955, Philadelphia, PA
Group / Doo Wop, R&B

The Turbans were among the first Philadelphia-based R&B outfits to achieve national recognition. They emerged in 1955 out of a local R&B scene that had previously been dominated by such tenor-led groups as the Castelles, the Capris, and the Dreams. The Turbans' distinctive trait (apart from their headgear) was the soaring falsetto lead singing of 17-year-old Al Banks (born July 26, 1937), supported by the backup harmony of Matthew Platt, baritone Charlie Williams, and bass Andrew Jones; all four were schoolmates when stardom beckoned.

They headed to New York and signed to Al Silver's Herald Records, where they cut their first record late in 1955. It was the B-side, the uptempo "When You Dance," that caught on with DJs and ended up charting nationally, thus giving the Turbans the opportunity to tour the East Coast. Their second single had a similar fate, the B-side, "Sister Sookie," supplanting the more mellow A-side, "I'll Always Watch Over You," on radio station turntables and play lists and becoming a regional hit. This proved to be the high point for the group—their next four records never matched the first two, and their Herald contract ended after the release of "Congratulations" in 1957. The group moved to Imperial and then to Roulette Records, undergoing numerous personnel changes in the process, with Banks remaining the lead singer throughout. Before his death in the late '70s, Banks became a member of one of the lineups of Drifters playing the oldies and club circuits, and "When You Dance" remained a part of his repertory. *—Bruce Eder*

Greatest Hits / 1973 / Collectables ♦♦♦

● **The Best of the Turbans** / 1985 / Collectables ♦♦♦♦♦
Anyone who thinks "When You Dance" was the Turbans' best song will think again after hearing this 18-song CD. The gorgeous, soaring "Three Friends"—showcasing Banks' gorgeous falsetto at its best and the richness of the group's harmony singing—is worth the price of the CD all by itself. Add on some great dance numbers, fast ("B.I.N.G.O.," "Sister Sookie") and slow ("I'm Nobody's"), and this becomes more than just a curiousity for doo wop collectors. The sound is astonishingly good and very close; the sax-combo solos seemingly right up against the speakers, the bells of the saxes on the microphones. Not all of it works—"I Won't Be Your Fool Anymore" is too busy to really pull together as a song. But this is a fine anthology of the best work by this beloved vocal outfit. *—Bruce Eder*

Big Joe Turner

b. May 18, 1911, Kansas City, MO, **d.** Nov. 24, 1985, Inglewood, CA
Vocals / Jump Blues, Urban Blues, R&B, Swing, Rock & Roll

The premier blues shouter of the postwar era, Big Joe Turner's roar could rattle the very foundation of any gin joint he sang within—and that's without a microphone. Turner was a resilient figure in the history of blues—he effortlessly spanned boogie-woogie, jump blues, even the first wave of rock & roll, enjoying great success in each genre. Turner, whose powerful physique certainly matched his vocal might, was a product of the swinging, wide-open Kansas City scene, hooking up with boogie piano master Pete Johnson during the early '30s. Theirs was a partnership that would endure for 13 years. Atlantic picked up his recording contract in 1951, and Big Joe Turner's heyday commenced with a gorgeously world-weary reading to the moving blues ballad "Chains of Love" that restored him to the uppermost reaches of the R&B charts. From there, the hits came in droves: "Chill Is On," "Sweet Sixteen," and "Don't You Cry" were all done in New York, and all hit big. Big Joe Turner had no problem whatsoever adapting his prodigious pipes to whatever regional setting he was in: in 1953, he cut his first R&B chart-topper, the storming rocker "Honey Hush," in New Orleans, and before the year was through, he stopped off in Chicago to record with slide guitarist Elmore James' considerably rougher-edged combo and hit again with the salacious "T.V. Mama."

Prolific Atlantic house writer Jesse Stone was the source of Turner's biggest smash of all, "Shake, Rattle and Roll," which proved his second chart-topper in 1954. Suddenly, at the age of 43, Big Joe Turner was a rock star. His jumping follow-ups—"Well All Right," "Flip Flop and Fly," "Hide and Seek," "Morning, Noon and Night," "The Chicken and the Hawk"—all mined the same goodtime groove. They called him "the Boss of the Blues," and the appellation was truly a fitting one: When Big Joe Turner shouted a lyric, you were definitely at his beck and call. *—Bill Dahl*

☆ **Boss of the Blues** / Mar. 6, 1956-Mar. 7, 1956 / Collectables ♦♦♦♦♦
During an era when Big Joe Turner recordings were often surprise hits with rock & roll fans (particularly "Shake, Rattle and Roll"), he occasionally recorded no-nonsense blues-oriented jazz dates too. This reissue album matched Turner for one of the last times with the veteran boogie-woogie pianist Pete Johnson and also includes a variety of top swing players: trumpeter Joe Newman, trombonist Lawrence Brown, altoist Pete Brown, tenor saxophonist Frank Wess, guitarist Freddie Green, bassist Walter Page, and drummer Cliff Leeman. It is not surprising, considering the number of Basie-ites on the date, that the band often sounds like a Count Basie combo. Turner is in top form on remakes of some of his early tunes (including "Cherry Red," "Roll 'Em Pete," and "Wee Baby Blues"), a few traditional blues, and a couple of swing standards. This music should appeal to many listeners. *—Scott Yanow*

Things That I Used to Do / Feb. 8, 1977 / Pablo/OJC ♦♦♦♦♦
This is one of Big Joe Turner's best albums of his last period. Turner is in fine form and joined by some superb blues and jazz musicians. Altoist Eddie "Cleanhead" Vinson (pity that he didn't have a vocal duet with Turner) and trumpeter Blue Mitchell get some solo space as does the veteran R&B tenor Wild Bill Moore, pianist Lloyd Glenn and guitarist Gary Bell. Mitchell can be heard on many of the tunes setting hot ensemble riffs. There are some loose spots but the spirit is definitely there and Turner's voice can be heard still in its prime on such tunes as "Jelly Jelly Blues," "Shake It and Break It" and "St. Louis Blues." Fun music. *—Scott Yanow*

★ **Big Joe Turner's Greatest Hits** / 1989 / Atlantic Jazz ♦♦♦♦♦
Big Joe Turner's music is the aural equivalent of a rare Porterhouse steak—oversized, juicy, and a glorious overload for the senses, and if isn't always good for you, that's just part of the fun. Whether what he was singing was billed as jazz, swing, rhythm & blues, or rock & roll, Turner pretty much always did things the same way, rolling with the big beat and shouting with carnal joy on the subjects of wine, women, and song (even his hurtin' songs were pretty lively), and to this day his rollicking Atlantic sides are an ideal way to get the party started. *Big Joe Turner's Greatest Hits* pulls together most of Turner's best-known tunes for Atlantic (fleshed out to a full 21 songs on its CD re-release), and while Turner recorded an awful lot of music over the course of a career that spanned five decades, this CD does a surprisingly good job of serving up the best stuff from his most fruitful and satisfying period, and if you can listen to "Shake, Rattle and Roll," "Flip, Flop and Fly," "Honey Hush," "Boogie Woogie Country Girl," or "Well All Right" without getting up to dance (or at least tapping your foot), maybe you shouldn't be bothering with this music stuff in the first place. Historically invaluable, and more importantly a whole lot of fun, *Big Joe Turner's Greatest Hits* pretty well lives up to its billing and is a superb place to introduce yourself to the music of one of the great wildmen of the blues. *—Mark Deming*

☆ **Big, Bad & Blue: The Big Joe Turner Anthology** / 1994 / Rhino ♦♦♦♦♦
This three-record anthology shows how Turner, without really ever changing his style, moved from strict Kansas City swing to pioneering rock & roll and back to basic jazzy blues. It contains 62 songs, everything from treasured hits to slow, sweltering ballads, strident uptempo wailers, moaning blues, novelty tunes, and fiery pieces with lyrics and sentiments that wouldn't make it in today's environment. A comprehensive, well-written, and lavishly prepared and illustrated booklet with numerous anecdotes and remembrances is the icing on a superb cake. *—Ron Wynn*

☆ **Jumpin' With Joe: The Complete Aladdin & Imperial Recordings** / Jan. 11, 1994 / EMI America ♦♦♦♦♦
Big Joe Turner's remarkable recordings for Atlantic and Decca have been frequently reissued and evaluated. But his singles for other labels haven't gotten similar treatment, which makes this 18-cut single-disc anthology of Aladdin and Imperial material so welcome. These were recorded in the late '40s and early '50s and were closer to the Kansas City swing Turner had done earlier in his career; there was more emphasis on lyric interpretation, swing, and timing than sheer volume and volcanic, non-stop hollering. Although these songs aren't remembered as fondly as the landmark Atlantic numbers, they're just as important a part of Turner's legacy. *—Ron Wynn*

Have No Fear, Big Joe Turner Is Here / Jul. 18, 1995 / Savoy ♦♦♦♦
Producer Herb Abramson's first encounters with Big Joe Turner weren't at Atlantic, but for the National logo, where Turner paused from 1945 to 1947 and cut the 26 swinging numbers on this collection. For once, the CD format limits the amount of selections rather than enlarging it; the original two-LP version of this package boasted a few more cuts. Pete Johnson returns to run the 88s on the first seven numbers (including a two-part cover of Saunders King's "S.K. Blues"), and familiar names like saxman Wild Bill Moore and drummer Red Saunders also turn up. "Sally Zu-Zazz," "I Got Love for Sale," and "My Gal's a Jockey" capture the peerless shouter at his ribald best. *—Bill Dahl*

★ **Very Best of Big Joe Turner** / Feb. 3, 1998 / Rhino ♦♦♦♦♦
After Rhino Records began their series of reissues of classic blues and R&B material from the Atlantic Records vaults, they did a snappy edit, shuffle, and augmentation of Atlantic's fine *Big Joe Turner's Greatest Hits*, and the result was the equally superb *The Very Best of Big Joe Turner. The Very Best of Big Joe Turner* features 12 of the tunes which appeared on the earlier album, while adding another four (mostly leaning toward the more rollicking side of Turner's musical personality, including the gloriously lascivious "TV Mama"). While *Big Joe Turner's Greatest Hits* covered a bit more ground, *The Very Best of Big Joe Turner* is even more consistent and offers one of the great pioneering shouters of hard-rockin' R&B at his wild and raving best. Sounding at once loose and thoroughly committed, this collection is a glorious summation of what Turner did best, and these 16 recordings are the soundtrack for a memorable after-hours party just waiting to happen. If you don't already have "Shake, Rattle and Roll," "Flip, Flop and Fly," or "Honey Hush" in your collection, than *The Very Best of Big Joe Turner* is one disc you need to add to your library posthaste, and the typically excellent remastering and packaging from Rhino only add to the value of this disc. *—Mark Deming*

Ike Turner & His Kings of Rhythm

b. Nov. 5, 1931, Clarksdale, MS
Vocals, Guitar (Electric), Songwriter, Piano, Guitar, Producer / Soul-Blues, R&B, Soul, Electric Memphis Blues

Ike Turner is certainly one of the most dehumanized figures in rock history. Mention his name and the first association that comes to most anyone's mind is "abusive husband," not "soul star" or "rock & roll pioneer." According to legend, Turner was a tyrannical ogre who used physical violence and psychological intimidation to control his infinitely more talented wife Tina, while indulging his own appetites for cocaine and women at every turn. That's not entirely accurate, although by most accounts Turner did quite a bit to earn that reputation; he spent time in prison due to his drug problems, and his own refutations of Tina's allegations of abuse have been inconsistent at best over the years. Still, this view of Turner as villain does a disservice to his very real musical legacy as an instrumentalist and bandleader. As a pianist in the early '50s, Turner helped lay the groundwork for rock & roll; he was also a distinctive guitarist with a biting, nasty tone, and was one of the first to make the whammy bar an integral part of his sound. It's true that he was nowhere near the singer Tina was, and it's probably also true that she was his ticket to stardom; moreover, his songwriting, while sometimes inspired, often possessed a generic quality that made consistent chart appearances difficult. But as a bandleader, his disciplinarian approach—when it wasn't manifesting itself in darker fashion, that is—resulted in undeniably tight, well-drilled ensembles and some of the most exhilarating live shows the R&B world ever saw—centered around Tina, yes, but spectacles nonetheless. If Turner isn't exactly the most defensible character around, in the end his musical strengths and weaknesses deserve the same objective appraisal as anyone.

Izear Luster Turner Jr. was born November 5, 1931, in Clarksdale, MS, the heart of the segregated South. His father was beaten to death by a mob of angry whites, and growing up in a hostile environment unquestionably hardened Turner. He found his calling in music from an early age; he learned boogie-woogie piano firsthand from his inspiration, Pinetop Perkins, and as a teenager talked himself into a DJ slot on the local radio station, where he played everything from the jump blues of Louis Jordan to country & western. He formed his first band while still in high school, and by the late '40s had assembled an outfit dubbed the Kings of Rhythm. In 1951, the Kings of Rhythm traveled to Memphis to record at Sam Phillips' Sun studio. Their original tune "Rocket 88" (actual authorship is still disputed) was recorded with a lead vocal by sax player Jackie Brenston, and as a result was released under the name Jackie Brenston & His Delta Cats, not Ike Turner & His Kings of Rhythm. "Rocket 88" zoomed to the top of the R&B charts and is today regarded by many critics as being quite possibly the first true rock & roll record.

During the mid-'50s, Turner moved the Kings of Rhythm to East St. Louis, where they rose to the top of the local R&B circuit. Adopting a revue format for their live performances, the Kings of Rhythm worked with a revolving group of vocalists during this period. One was a teenage singer originally from Tennessee named Anna Mae Bullock, who met Turner in 1956. She joined the revue, and moved into Turner's house after becoming pregnant by the band's sax player; soon, she and Turner began their own relationship and had a child of their own, marrying in 1958. Renamed Tina, Turner's new (and latest) wife got her first chance to sing lead on a recording in late 1959, cutting "A Fool in Love" for the Sue label. Released the following year, the song was a runaway smash on the R&B charts, peaking at number two. Turner realized he'd discovered a potential breakout star, and reshaped the band into the Ike & Tina Turner Revue, with Tina now the centerpiece of the act.

In 1969, Ike & Tina were invited to open for the Rolling Stones, and Turner realized that changing times had made the Revue's rough, nasty brand of soul music more palatable to white rock audiences. Accordingly, Turner incorporated contemporary rock & roll covers into the Revue's repertoire, giving them a whole new lease on life. Versions of "Come Together," "I Want to Take You Higher," and "Proud Mary" revived Ike & Tina's chart fortunes. However, Turner's off-stage problems were taking their toll on the act; 1973's "Nutbush City Limits," a song written by Tina, would be their last major hit, and Tina walked out on him in the middle of a 1975 tour. The Turners' divorce was finalized the following year, and Ike never quite recovered from the loss. —*Steve Huey*

Ike Turner & the Kings of Rhythm / 1963 / Sue ✦✦✦✦✦

Ike Turner Rocks the Blues / 1963 / Crown ✦✦✦✦✦

Ike Turner's Kings of Rhythm, rocking the blues in 1954, with a 23-year-old Turner performing some astonishing guitar acrobatics only a couple of years after taking up the instrument, including the legendary "All the Blues, All the Time." The only pity is that this 1950s material only exists on this incredibly expensive import from Japan, when it ought to be out at an affordable price over here. The late Lester Bangs called it "one of the greatest albums ever made, if not the absolute certifiable Greatest Guitar Album of All Time," and understandably so. —*Bruce Eder*

Bad Dreams / 1971 / United Artists ✦✦✦

Blues Roots / 1972 / United Artists ✦✦✦

Trailblazer / 1991 / Charly ✦✦✦✦✦

During 1956 and early 1957, Ike Turner's Kings of Rhythm recorded for the Cincinnati-based Federal label—the group's personnel included Raymond Hill and Eddie Jones on tenor sax, Jackie Brenston on baritone sax, Annie Mae Wilson and Fred Sample on piano, Jessie Knight Jr. on bass, Eugene Washington on drums, and Turner on guitar, with vocalists including Brenston and Billy Gayles. This is some of the most solid material in Turner's output, with a rich, soulful sound, more polished than most of the group's output on Cobra. Some of the music is derivative—in seeking chart success, the group at various times sought to emulate the Coasters, Bill Justis, et al., but they almost always put their own spin on these numbers. Billy Gayles' impassioned vocals on "No Coming Back," Jackie Brenston's boisterous rendition of "The Mistreater," and the rest are all worth the price of admission, which is fairly low on this mid-priced import—but, surprisingly, some of the best stuff on here is by the Kings of Rhythm backing the vocal group the Gardenias ("Miserable," one of the best tracks among these 20, remained unreleased until 1991). And the real treat here is Turner's guitar pyrotechnics. He could strum along like most band guitarists, and occasionally did this, but he preferred to step out front and, having discovered the use of the tremelo arm on his guitar, he fairly tortures the instrument on several of these sides (check out the break on "No Comin' Back," and his accompaniment on "She Made My Blood Run Cold," itself an R&B track deserving of legendary status), and even gets a Hawaiian sound out of his instrument on "Trail Blazer." Fans of rock & roll guitar must own this record. —*Bruce Eder*

1958–1959 / May 13, 1993 / Paula ✦✦✦✦✦

Ever the hustler, Ike Turner found himself picking up some extra money on a road trip through Chicago recording for Cobra Records both as a bandleader and sideman. After contributing the sparkle to several Otis Rush classics (an alternate of one of them, "Keep on Loving Me Baby" is found here) and some early Buddy Guy sides, Turner also recorded a handful of sides, scant few of them seeing release until now. This CD collects them all up, including surviving alternate versions, and is a delightful fly on the wall invite to a 1950s Chicago blues session. —*Cub Koda*

● **I Like Ike! The Best of Ike Turner** / Nov. 15, 1994 / Rhino ✦✦✦✦✦

Here are 18 songs spotlighting Turner's work as a bandleader, guitarist, and solo artist from 1951 to 1972, concentrating heavily on his work in the 1950s and early '60s. Leading off with Jackie Brenston's classic "Rocket 88," it includes rare singles featuring Turner by Dennis Binder, the Sly Fox, Willie King, and others, along with rare Turner solo recordings, some under the pseudonym Icky Renrut, and a 1958 45 with Tina, then known as Anna Mae Bullock, on backing vocals. These singers are usually journeymen, frankly, and the material is rather standard-issue R&B; better are the instrumentals, which give Ike a chance to really strut his distinctive tone. —*Richie Unterberger*

Rhythm Rockin' Blues / Nov. 1995 / Ace ✦✦✦✦✦

This is the definitive early Ike Turner collection, at least until someone comes out with a box that assembles *everything*. The 21 tracks here are mostly drawn from Turner's early-'50s sessions with the Kings of Rhythm at the Clarksdale studio, done under the auspices of the Bihari Brothers' Modern, RPM, and Flair labels. Apart from a few well-known numbers like the classic "Rocket 88," much of the material here isn't in other collections, nor has it been assembled in one place before—some of it has shown up on vinyl, but never together on CD. It consists of Turner working with the Kings of Rhythm, evolving his guitar and piano technique and pumping up the volume and beat on R&B, pushing it toward rock & roll. The highlight for completists is the medley "All the Blues, All the Time," on which Turner, newly confident on the guitar, goes through an extended instrumental medley of B.B. King, Elmore James, Muddy Waters, and John Lee Hooker material. Also included is some hard R&B-cum-rock & roll by the Kings of Rhythm fronted by J. W. Walker, Little Johnny Burton, Dennis Binder, Lonnie "The Cat," and Billy Gayles. The interesting thing is that "Rocket 88," for all of its renown, is just one of the good tracks here—"Early Times" by Dennis Binder could just as easily have caught the public's fancy with its beat. The sound is somewhat compressed on some of the early material (and, especially, the Johnny Wright/Ike Turner orchestra numbers, although Turner's guitar is real sharp on "The World Is Yours"), but generally it is equal or superior to any other digital incarnation of the individual tracks, and the notes are extremely thorough. —*Bruce Eder*

Ike's Instrumentals / 2000 / Ace ✦✦✦

Taken from a variety of sources, this collects 22 of Ike Turner's instrumentals from 1954-1965, none of them vocals, none of them recorded with Tina Turner, and all of them highlighting his guitar work. Turner's really wild and uninhibited for much of this set, especially in his ferocious string-bending and use of the whammy bar. While the tunes themselves are mostly generic R&B with a touch of rock & roll, it's also fair to say that generic instrumental rock rarely sounds this good, mostly because Turner's guitar work is so much more inventive and passionate than the nominal songs to which they're tethered. About half of this consists of the tracks on his 1962 Sue album, *Dance With Ike & Tina Turner & Their Kings of Rhythm Band*, a good showcase for his crackling axework on a batch of mostly self-imposed wordless workouts. There are also a couple of numbers he cut in the late '50s under the pseudonym Icky Renrut; a 1965 single with brass that has a more soul-oriented arrangement than anything else here, albeit soul of a gutbucket kind; and a smattering of items dating back to his mid-'50s R&B days with Flair. There's also an odd nine-minute medley of instrumental blues covers, "All the Blues All the Time," which wound up on a 1963 Crown LP, *Rocks the Blues*. —*Richie Unterberger*

Here and Now / May 22, 2001 / Ikon ✦✦✦

Back in the '80s, you would have been forgiven if you'd thought Tina Turner would prove to be the lasting half of one of music's notoriously volatile marriages. Back then, it seemed that Ike would be consigned to footnote status, forever a static signpost on a musical back road. Funny how things change. Now it's Tina's later music that sounds embarrassingly overdone and synth-drenched and it's Ike's blend of soul and blues that sounds, well, timeless. Stepping out on guitar and keyboard, Turner snarls and stomps through several roadhouse chestnuts with the vigor and swagger of a much younger man. If, in context, several of the lyrical choices here still sound like tangential swipes at his wife and—given their history—uncomfortable swipes at that, it's easy to forget on many of these tracks that this guy probably should have shuffled off to the dust heap years ago. The caveat to this record is the artificial drum overdubs that threaten to turn some of these tracks into exercises of techno embarrassment. —*Rob Ferrier*

The Sun Sessions / Jun. 26, 2001 / Varese Sarabande ✦✦✦✦✦

The early recordings of Ike Turner & His Kings of Rhythm (also sometimes known as the Kings of Rhythm featuring Ike Turner) are scattered all over the map, mostly owing to the sheer number of labels for which they recorded from 1951 until 1958. Astonishingly, given their reputation, Turner's Sun Records sides have always been a lot tougher to get hold of than the stuff he did for the RPM and Federal labels, which are downright ubiquitous on CD. Varese has fixed that problem with this 19-song disc covering his work for Sam Phillips between 1951 and 1958, working in every idiom from mournful blues ballads such as "You Can't Be the One for Me" (featuring Tommy Hodge) and "When My Baby Left Me" (sung by Billy "The Kid" Emerson) to the bouncy jump blues of "Love Is a Gamble," featuring his then-girlfriend Bonnie Turner on vocals. A couple of instrumentals, "The Snuggle" and "Bourbon Street Jump," also make this worth hearing as a cross-section of the band's sound and output, and some of the sides also present Turner's guitar, up close and personal—indeed, the best track on the album is arguably "Ugly Woman," one of the funniest songs in Turner's output and one that shows off the bandleader/guitarist/singer Johnny O'Neal working on all cylinders in overdrive. Tommy Hodge is the most consistent singer here, though the disc is also worth hearing for Bonnie Turner's work—whatever their other attributes, Turner evidently did choose the women around him at least partly on the basis of their vocal skills. The sound is excellent and the annotation by Bill Dahl is thorough and very well detailed. —*Bruce Eder*

Ike & Tina Turner

f. 1959, **db.** 1976

Group / R&B, Soul, Pop-Soul

As husband and wife, Ike & Tina Turner headed up one of the most potent live acts on the R&B circuit during the '60s and early '70s. Guitarist and bandleader Ike kept his ensemble tight and well-drilled while throwing in his own distinctively twangy plucking; lead vocalist Tina was a ferocious whirlwind of power and energy, a raw sexual dynamo who was impossible to contain when she hit the stage, leading some critics to call her the first female singer to embody the true spirit of rock & roll. In their prime, the Ike & Tina Turner Revue specialized in a hard-driving, funked-up hybrid of soul and rock that, in its best moments, rose to a visceral frenzy that few R&B acts of any era could hope to match.

Effusively praised by white rock luminaries like the Rolling Stones and Janis Joplin, Tina was unquestionably the star of the show, with a hugely powerful, raspy voice that ranks among the all-time soul greats. For all their concert presence, the Turners sometimes had problems translating their strong points to record; they cut singles for an endless succession of large and small independent labels throughout their career, and suffered from a shortage of the strong original material that artists with more stable homes (Motown, Atlantic, Stax, etc.) often enjoyed. The couple's well-documented marital difficulties (a mild way of describing Ike's violent, drug-fueled cruelty) eventually dissolved their partnership in the mid-'70s. Tina, of course, went on to become an icon and a symbol of survival after the resurgence of her solo career in the '80s, but it was the years she spent with Ike that made the purely musical part of her legend.

Izear Luster "Ike" Turner Jr. was born in Clarksdale, MS, in 1931; initially a pianist, he formed his first band in high school and put together the Kings of Rhythm in the late '40s. In 1951, that group cut the pivotal "Rocket 88," a tune often pinpointed as the first ever rock & roll record; however, since sax player Jackie Brenston took the vocal, the song was credited to Brenston & His Delta Cats rather than Turner & the Kings of Rhythm. Not long after, Turner switched from piano to guitar, and he and his band became a prolific session outfit in Memphis, backing various Sun artists and bluesmen during the early '50s. Turner moved the Kings of Rhythm to East St. Louis in the mid-'50s, where they became kingpins of the local R&B circuit. In 1956, he met a teenage, gospel-trained singer from Nutbush, TN, named Anna Mae Bullock, and promised her a chance to sing with his band. That chance kept failing to materialize, until one night Bullock simply grabbed the microphone and started belting. Impressed, Turner made her a part of his revue, changing her name to Tina. After Tina became pregnant by the band's saxophonist, Raymond Hill, she moved into Turner's house, an arrangement that led to their own relationship; the two were married in 1958 and soon had a child of their own.

In late 1959, Turner's band entered the studio to cut a song called "A Fool in Love" for the Sue Records label. The scheduled male vocalist failed to show up for the session, and Tina was pressed into service. Released in 1960, "A Fool in Love" shot to the number-two spot on the R&B charts, also making the pop Top 30. Tina was now clearly the focal point of the act, which Turner rechristened the Ike & Tina Turner Revue; with a large, horn-filled ensemble and a group of leggy backup singers dubbed the Ikettes (who complemented Tina's short-skirted, uninhibited gyrating), the Revue eventually developed a reputation for putting on one of the most exciting live shows in R&B. The R&B-chart hits came fast and furious during the early '60s: 1961's "I Idolize You" (number five) and "It's Gonna Work Out Fine" (number two), 1962's "Poor Fool" (number four) and "Tra La La La La" (number nine). It was an impressive run, but the well went dry over the next several years; Ike supplied much of the band's original material, and although he was responsible for many of the early successes, he simply wasn't a world-class songwriter who could deliver hit-caliber tunes with regularity. Much of the Revue's repertoire consisted of bluesy, chitlin circuit R&B that wasn't exceptionally memorable. Ike & Tina branched out from Sue Records and spent the next few years issuing records on additional labels, including Kent, Modern, and Loma. While they had some undeniable high points and several chart entries, none reached the level of their initial run of Top Ten hits.

In 1966, the Turners worked with legendary producer Phil Spector, who was seeking a way to restore his artistic and commercial standing at the forefront of pop music in the wake of advances by the Beach Boys and Beatles. The powerful instrument that was Tina's voice appealed to Spector's sense of grandeur, and he conceived of a massive-scale production framing that voice that would rank as his greatest masterpiece. Ike already had a reputation for demanding control, and Spector struck his deal accordingly: Although the records would be fully credited to Ike & Tina Turner, Ike would not be allowed to enter the studio or alter the finished recordings (in effect, Spector was paying him not to meddle). The centerpiece of Spector's collaboration with Tina was "River Deep—Mountain High," a monumental pop symphony that cost over $22,000 to produce (in 1966, this was a whopping sum for an album, let alone a single). The single represented Spector's so-called Wall of Sound style at its most gloriously excessive, and Tina's was one of the few voices in popular music strong enough to cut through the monolithic orchestral backing. With the high cost and his own slipping stature, Spector was betting the farm on "River Deep—Mountain High," and although it rocketed into the British Top Five and made Tina a star in the U.K., it flopped in America, where its mixture of black and white musical aesthetics was still slightly ahead of its time. A crushed Spector retreated from the music business not long after, and his Philles label yanked the accompanying album of the same name from American release (Spector wound up producing only five of the 12 cuts). Although some critics dismiss "River Deep—Mountain High" as overproduced bombast, many still consider it one of rock's greatest singles; George Harrison famously described it as "a perfect record from start to finish."

After the Spector deal fell through, Ike & Tina returned to their somewhat mercenary recording habits, cutting songs for Modern and Innis, then moving to Minit and Blue Thumb in 1969. That year, they went on the road as the opening act for the Rolling Stones, and Ike slightly retooled the Revue's sound to appeal to white rock audiences in addition to their core black following. In 1970, they signed with Liberty/United Artists and recorded *Come Together*, which incorporated contemporary rock & roll covers into their repertoire; versions of the Beatles' title track and Sly & the Family Stone's "I Want to Take You Higher" made the R&B Top 30. Released later that year, *Workin' Together* became the most popular album of their career, making the Top 25 on the strength of a storming reinterpretation of CCR's "Proud Mary." Featuring a notorious spoken intro by Tina, the "nice... and rough" version of "Proud Mary" gave Ike & Tina their first Top Five hit on the pop charts, and returned them to the same heights on the R&B side as well; it also won them a Grammy. The covers gimmick couldn't last forever, though, and their formula soon grew predictable; their last major success was 1973's "Nutbush City Limits," a semi-autobiographical song written by Tina that made the R&B Top 20 and just missed that placing on the pop side. By that point, Tina had grown increasingly uninterested in the duo's well-established act, and was tiring of the largely unchallenging material she continued to perform.

Unfortunately, the music itself wasn't the only factor in Ike & Tina's downturn. As a bandleader, Ike had long been a disciplinarian, but during the '60s he developed severe addictions to alcohol and, especially, cocaine. Wanting to maintain control over the star of his show at any cost, Turner kept his wife in line through an increasingly violent pattern of emotional and physical abuse; often drug-related, his flights of rage could result in severe beatings or burns that pushed Tina to attempt suicide in 1968, according to her autobiography. She continued to endure Ike's dominance through the early '70s, and her performances were clearly weary by the end; finally, she walked out on her husband and generally declined to pursue claims for financial compensation from their work together. Their divorce became official in 1976. After a long period of struggle, Tina re-emerged triumphantly in the '80s as a superstar solo act; Ike, meanwhile, ran his own recording studio for a time, but his drug problems worsened, resulting in several arrests. Sadly, and perhaps fittingly, he was serving prison time when he and his former wife were jointly inducted into the Rock and Roll Hall of Fame in 1991, and was unable to attend the ceremony. *—Steve Huey*

The Soul of Ike & Tina Turner / 1960 / Collectables ✦✦✦

The first early-'60s Ike & Tina Turner album, with Tina sounding tentative at times, and other times gaining confidence as the song progressed. They were far from a finished, polished act, especially in the studio. Tina was still determining how much power and sensuality she had in her voice and was developing her delivery and presentation, while Ike was honing the backdrop, and his band learning when to push and when to lay out behind Tina. *—Ron Wynn*

Sound of Ike & Tina Turner / 1961 / Sue ✦✦✦

Dance With Ike & Tina Turner & Their Kings of Rhythm Band / 1962 / Sue ✦✦✦

Although the 14 tracks on this album are very typical early-'60s rock/R&B instrumentals in their tunes and arrangements, Ike Turner's guitar work is sparkling, lifting the LP out of the generic realm. All but one of the songs were written by Turner, and are mostly uptempo, dance-oriented workouts, probably intended to cash in on the twist craze, as titles like "Twist-a-Rod," "Trackdown Twist," "Potato Mash," and "Prancing" indicate. Ike Turner really squeezes the last drop of invention out of these run-of-the-mill backdrops, though, relentlessly bending notes, wangling the whammy bar, and letting loose with some unpredictable runs and aggressive chording. Tina Turner does not sing on the album (nor does anyone), despite what the title might lead you to believe, but it does include an instrumental version of the duo's big hit "It's Gonna Work Out Fine." All of the songs are included on the Ace CD reissue compilation *Ike's Instrumentals*, which collects an assortment of Ike Turner instrumentals spanning the mid-'50s to mid-'60s. *—Richie Unterberger*

Festival of Live Performances / 1962 / United ✦✦✦✦✦

A great album that needs to be reissued immediately. Early Ike & Tina Turner in concert, long before things became so formulaic that even the Turner dance routines and sexy costumes became predictable and tiring. They were still a hungry, eager, galvanizing band then, and even performed with energy and fire on mundane filler. If you ever spot this one, grab it immediately. *—Ron Wynn*

Dynamite / 1963 / Collectables ✦✦

The first of three Ike & Tina Turner albums issued in 1963 had its moments, but overall was rather listless from a material standpoint. There wasn't a standout track among the batch; only Turner's shattering vocals and some good funky backdrops by Ike Turner's band saved things from total disaster. *—Ron Wynn*

It's Gonna Work Out Fine / 1963 / Collectables ✦✦✦

Please Please Please / 1963 / Kent ✦✦✦✦✦

Don't Play Me Cheap / 1963 / Collectables ✦✦✦

An early-'60s album from the formative days of the Ike & Tina Turner Revue. They were still developing the formula, but would soon begin striking soul gold. In the meantime, Turner was operating as an R&B and soul diva, although she later said that she hated singing these tunes. In this instance, what she was doing was mostly second-level material, but her husky, powerful voice sounded convincing. *—Ron Wynn*

Live! The Ike & Tina Tuner Show / Jan. 1965 / Warner Bros. ✦✦✦✦

In late 1964, Kent Records released the live album *The Ike & Tina Turner Revue Live*, which gave the group its first placing on a national LP chart in January 1965. Warner Bros. Records, which had just acquired rights to a similar recording by the label-hopping duo, quickly countered with this similarly titled album, which did even better than the Kent release, placing in the Top Ten of the R&B charts in February 1965. The recording is primitive and raw, with considerable distortion, but that only adds to the excitement as Tina Turner shouts and screams her way through standards like Sam Cooke's "Good Times" and the Isley Brothers' "Twist and Shout." Just to add to the confusion, in 1966 Warner put out another Ike and Tina Turner live album under the same title on its Loma subsidiary. *—William Ruhlmann*

Live! The Ike & Tina Turner Show, Vols. 1 & 2 / 1966 / Warner Bros. ✦✦✦✦✦

River Deep—Mountain High / Sep. 1966 / A&M ✦✦✦✦✦

These sessions, recorded in 1966, were produced by Phil Spector. Spector's production chops and Tina's voice were a match made in heaven. Tina possesses one of the strongest voices ever committed to wax; Spector envelops it in the grandest version of his Wall of Sound that he ever conceived. Besides the title track, Spector cut the Turners redoing their first three chart hits, "A Fool in Love," "I Idolize You," and "It's Gonna Work Out Fine." Although it's a sacrilege to say so, these versions are better than the originals. Finally, Turner's performance of the obscure Holland-Dozier-Holland ditty "A Love Like Yours" is another phenomenal highlight. *—Rob Bowman*

Ike & Tina Turner's Greatest Hits / 1967 / Warner Bros. ♦♦♦
This CD reaches back in time to a year when America was poised on the threshold of so many political and social changes. That year was 1967, and one of the hottest acts in the music business was the Ike & Tina Turner Revue. The incredible voice and energy of Tina Turner, backed by her husband's band, the Kings of Rhythm, had turned the R&B world upside down with their electrifying shows. Their influence on the evolving genre of rock & roll was huge. This was soul music at its best. It burned hot with Tina Turner's sensual persona. Though largely overshadowed by his wife's stage presence, Ike Turner holds a place in rock & roll history, often credited with recording its first tune, "Rocket 88," in 1950. But it was in the '60s that the Ike & Tina Turner Revue ruled. This CD compiles some of the best songs recorded by the band, one of the top revenue groups of all time, with 25 hits on the charts in the tumultuous decade of the '60s. The recording includes the song that catapulted Ike & Tina Turner to fame in 1960: the chart-topping "Fool in Love." "Poor Fool," "It's Gonna Work Out Fine," and "Tra La La La La" are among the others. Perhaps the title of another work of the Turners describes the music best: "Too Hot to Hold." *—Rose of Sharon Witmer*

Cussin,' Cryin' and Carryin' On / 1969 / Pompeii ♦♦♦

Get It Together / 1969 / Pompeii ♦♦
An amazing eight Ike & Tina Turner albums came down the pike in 1969, on every label from A&B to Blue Thumb to Minit. The glut resulted in the ludicrous situation of Ike & Tina competing en masse against themselves. It also doomed the prospects of most of the albums before they were even out of the chute. Yet amazingly, half made the pop charts, although this wasn't one of them. It was a decent album of routine soul and R&B, sung with Turner's usual sizzling energy, but otherwise lacking in distinction. *—Ron Wynn*

Her Man His Woman / 1969 / Capitol ♦♦

The Hunter / 1969 / Blue Thumb ♦♦♦
Released just a few years after the epochal Phil Spector-produced *River Deep Mountain High* and close to six years before their breakup, Ike & Tina Turner's *Hunter* often gets lost in the duo's long and stormy existence. And while the album certainly is not on the same plane as the Spector album or later work like *Workin' Together*, Hunter still boasts several fine blues workouts in the inimitably electrifying Ike & Tina mode. The Stax sound figures prominently here, with producer Bob Krasnow (Captain Beefheart) keeping things nice and uncluttered to better frame Tina's intense vocal workouts. Maybe not the best first-disc choice, but still a worthwhile title for Ike and Tina fans. *—Stephen Cook*

Outta Season / Jun. 1969 / Blue Thumb ♦♦
One of eight albums that were issued in this landmark year; this one is among the lesser-known or noticed. It contained routine soul and R&B numbers sung with little variety or emotion by Turner, and produced and arranged with almost no variety or flair. It was more a collection of singles than an actual album, but was rushed out among the raft of Ike and Tina product that glutted the market. It has since been deleted, and deservedly so. *—Ron Wynn*

Ike & Tina Turner in Person / Oct. 1969 / Minit ♦♦♦
An interesting, although quite erratic, album from their wealth of late-'60s releases. The Revue was featured in various concert performances ranging from inspired to ragged and loose. Tina Turner was at her rampaging, husky best, and at times Ike Turner had the band whipped to a frenzy behind her. At other times they sounded completely unrehearsed and awkward, while Tina just kept plowing on ahead, undeterred by the chaos behind her. *—Ron Wynn*

On Stage / 1970 / Valiant ♦♦

Come Together / Aug. 1970 / Liberty ♦♦♦

'Nuff Said / 1971 / United Artists ♦♦
This is an odd album, one of two the duo did in 1971. This one yielded no hits, but included an interesting version of "Baby (What You Want Me To Do)" and a remake of "Tell The Truth," from their first album. It was otherwise prototype Ike & Tina, but Tina didn't sound so enthused and Ike wasn't generating much magic behind her. *—Ron Wynn*

What You Hear Is What You Get / 1971 / EMI ♦♦♦
The duo were at their peak of popularity when this hour-long performance was recorded in New York on April 1, 1971. Of course Turner's volcanic stage presence can't be fully translated onto disc, and the set list goes heavy on predictable covers like "Sweet Soul Music," "Honky Tonk Women," "I've Been Loving You Too Long," "Respect," and a ten-minute-plus "Proud Mary." And the opening two numbers are sung not by Tina, but by the Ikettes. You'd be a real sourpuss, though, to let your rock critic microscope keep you from enjoying this smoky set. Tina drains every last bit of emotion from the material, especially on the bluesy "I Smell Trouble" and the drawn-out covers of "I've Been Loving You Too Long" and "Proud Mary," and the band offers a cookin' stew of R&B-soul-rock, paced by Ike's reverberating guitar. *—Richie Unterberger*

Workin' Together / Feb. 1971 / One Way ♦♦♦♦♦
Released early in 1971, a few months after *Come Together*, their first album for Liberty Records, *Workin' Together* was the first genuine hit album Ike & Tina had in years; actually, it was their biggest ever, working its way into *Billboard*'s Top 25 and spending 38 weeks on the charts. They never had a bigger hit (the closest was their Blue Thumb release, *Outta Season*, which peaked at 91), and, in many ways, they didn't make a better album. After all, their classic '60s sides were just that—sides of a single, not an album. Even though it doesn't boast the sustained vision of such contemporaries as, say, Marvin Gaye and Al Green, *Workin' Together* feels like a proper album, where many of the buried album tracks are as strong as the singles. Like its predecessor, it relies a bit too much on contemporary covers, which isn't bad when it's the perennial "Proud Mary," since it deftly reinterprets the original, but readings of the Beatles' "Get Back" and "Let It Be," while not bad, are a little bit too pedestrian. Fortunately, they're entirely listenable and they're the only slow moments, outweighed by songs that crackle with style and passion. Nowhere is this truer than on the opening title track, a midtempo groover (written by Icky Renrut, Ike's brilliant inverted alias) powered by a soulful chorus and a guitar line that plays like a mutated version of Dylan's "I Want You" riff. Then, there's the terrific Stax/Volt stomper "(Long As I Can) Get You When I Want You," possibly the highlight on the record. Though they cut a couple of classics over the next few years, most notably "Nutbush City Limits," the duo never topped this, possibly the best proper album they ever cut. *—Stephen Thomas Erlewine*

Feel Good / Jun. 1972 / United Artists ♦♦
Things were beginning to unravel with the Turners domestically, although they were still packing them in at various shows. But this album wasn't among their more inspired, as the formula was now wearing quite thin and Tina sounded less and less interested. The backing, arrangements, and production were equally uninspired, and everyone involved just punched the clock and ground this one out. *—Ron Wynn*

Let Me Touch Your Mind / Feb. 1973 / United Artists ♦♦
One of the final albums in the Ike & Tina Turner saga, and things had almost evaporated by this time. The Turners would score one more big hit with their next album, but it was evident that Tina had little interest in continuing to do soul and R&B ballads, and that their domestic problems were causing professional havoc. Her voice hadn't lost its power or resilience, but she had absolutely no energy or conviction in her vocals. The band was now on cruise control, and the entire operation was near its end. *—Ron Wynn*

Nutbush City Limits / Nov. 1973 / United Artists ♦♦♦♦♦
The album that marked the end of the Ike & Tina Turner alliance, although it wasn't their last album. But the turmoil that they were undergoing off-stage would soon shatter their personal and professional union. They scored a major international hit with the title cut, and also told their life story, although it turned out that this tale was a fantasy. Here's one of the few Ike & Tina Turner albums that deserves to be back in print. *—Ron Wynn*

It's Gonna Work Out Fine (The Best of the Sue Years) / 1986 / EMI America ♦♦♦
Tina sounds like a veteran on these early recordings, spitting lyrics, screaming, and phrasing like a seasoned studio pro. The Ikettes' stirring vocals, the big Kings of Rhythms band, and Ike's fast-handed guitar no doubt provided the motivation. "It's Gonna Work Out Fine" shuffles along, aided by Ike's incredulous quips and Tina's sexy speak-singing. Ike's formula meshes well on the gritty "A Fool in Love," an excellent combination of R&B and big band; Tina could place that scream in the pocket as effectively as Wilson Pickett. "Foolish" is a bluesy number reminiscent of Etta James. The lovestruck "I Idolize You" is a matter-of-fact statement by Tina to her man. Lloyd Price's "Stagger Lee" sounded humorous, but there's nothing funny about Ike & Tina's spinoff "Stagger Lee and Billy." This time, Billy busts Stagger hitting on his wife in a bar. Incensed and betrayed, Billy administers a brutal beating that Tina graphically describes. The 13 songs ranged from R&B, blues, and dated (even for the '60s) band selections that remind you of Ike's historic "Rocket 88." *—Andrew Hamilton*

Golden Classics / Apr. 20, 1990 / Collectables ♦♦♦
The legend of Tina Turner begins with these recordings, made with then-hubby Ike Turner for Juggy Murray's Sue Records in the early '60s. They're crudely produced sides, and sometimes Tina is handed some downright flabby material by producer-songwriter Ike ("Tra La La La La" and "You Can't Blame Me" are weak in the extreme), but the formula also brought the duo their first hits in tracks like "A Fool in Love," "It's Gonna Work Out Fine" (with Ike's voice over played by Mickey "Guitar" Baker of Mickey & Sylvia fame), "I Idolize You," and "Poor Fool." Also aboard are alternate takes of "Poor Fool" and "I Idolize You." All in all, a solid collection of this duo's earliest sides. *—Cub Koda*

● **Proud Mary: The Best of Ike & Tina Turner** / Mar. 18, 1991 / EMI ♦♦♦♦♦
Proud Mary: The Best of Ike and Tina Turner is a fine 23-track collection that looks at the Turners' career at the beginning and the end. Their early-'60s hits on Juggy Murray's Sue label are included, as are their early- and mid-'70s successes on Liberty and United Artists. The mid- and late-'60s recordings for Kent, Loma, Modern, Innis, Blue Thumb, and Minit are not here, unfortunately. Superior liner notes round out a fine package. *—Rob Bowman*

40 Rare Recordings/Proud Mary / Jul. 1, 1992 / Sound Solutions ♦♦♦
40 Rare Recordings/Proud Mary is the most comprehensive of many similar collections of Ike and Tina rarities, if only for the sheer volume of songs included; there are good reasons why a lot of this material is not more widely known, but enough of these performances are worthwhile to make the set necessary for fans. *—Jason Ankeny*

Bold Soul Sister: The Best of the Blue Thumb Recordings / Jul. 15, 1997 / Hip-O ♦♦♦♦♦
Make no mistake about it, this 16-track collection culled from their two albums recorded for the Blue Thumb label in 1969 (*Outta Season* and *The Hunter*) is as much Ike's show as it is Tina's—truly the other half of the equation, the blues part of rhythm & blues. His stinging guitar matches Tina's voice lick for nasty lick, and the blues song choices ("Dust My Broom," "Three O'Clock Blues," "Please Love Me," "Five Long Years," "You Don't Love Me," "Mean Old World," "Rock Me Baby," "Honest I Do," "Reconsider Baby") were undoubtedly tunes he and the Kings of Rhythm knew in their sleep, playing them since they were new hits on the charts. These were the last truly pure R&B albums the two of them would ever make, and even the then-current stabs at R&B trends (the title track is little

more than Ike's version of a James Brown groove with Tina babbling in true JB incomprehensibility in spots) shine brightly in the spotlight of hindsight. Subtitled *The Best of the Blue Thumb Recordings*, this makes a great document of what they must have sounded like in the clubs that dotted the landscape of the chitlin circuit way back when. *—Cub Koda*

The Kent Years / May 16, 2000 / Kent ♦♦♦♦
This compilation features 26 of the duo's 1964-1967 recordings (five previously unissued) for the Kent and Modern labels. Note, however, that this is just a partial retrospective of their mid-'60s work, since during this time the Turners were also releasing sides on several different other labels. It remains, though, a good sampling of their sound during this era, when their soul tracks still betrayed much of their blues/R&B roots, and before the arrangements had gotten as heavy and beefy as they would in the late '60s and early '70s. Tina Turner's vocals are unflaggingly enthusiastic and committed, if perhaps not as nuanced as they could be. What keeps this from the top rank of mid-'60s soul, however, is the largely average, occasionally below average material (mostly written by Ike Turner). It's often a collision of blues, chitlin circuit R&B, and brassy pop-soul that sounds a bit dashed off. There are some ace moments along the way, of course, like the infectious "I Can't Believe What You Say," the down-and-bluesy "Hurt Is All You Gave Me," and the swaggering soul-swing shuffle of "Chicken Shack." Ike Turner's twangy guitar seems underutilized for much of the set, and there's very little of the vocal sparring that would be such a big part of their act by the early '70s. Tina Turner goes into a big rap on the previously unissued "All I Could Do Was Cry" where she really overdoes the raspy breast-beating; Etta James' more famous version has a big edge. "Give Me Your Love" is minor-keyed blues/R&B that's not too far from Otis Rush territory; at the other extreme, "Makin' Plans Together" has gossamer strings typical of the New York pop-soul on the Scepter/Wand labels. *—Richie Unterberger*

Ruby Turner

b. Handsworth, Birmingham, England
Vocals / Urban
Ruby Turner sang a duet with Jonathan Butler in 1986: "If You're Ready (Come Go With Me)." This Jamacian singer has a solo career singing songs by Cecil/Linda Womack among others. *—AMG*

The Motown Songbook / 1988 / Jive/Novus ♦♦♦
British songstress Ruby Turner showed her range and power on this collection of Motown classics. Unfortunately, she didn't get the attention she deserved or the praises she merited for her wondrous, soulful interpretations. But the gospel-tinged stylist turned in a standout performance, and showed that it was possible to bring fresh life to shopworn classics. Sadly, this has now been deleted. *—Ron Wynn*

Paradise / 1989 / Jive/Novus ♦♦♦
In the early '90s, veteran *Los Angeles Times* rock critic Robert Hilburn visited London and wrote a long article on England's R&B explosion. As Hilburn saw it, another British Invasion was in progress—only this time, the invaders were urban contemporary artists instead of rockers. And Hilburn had good reason to be excited; in the late '80s and early '90s, British neo-soulsters like Lisa Stansfield, Soul II Soul, Karen Wheeler, the Brand New Heavies, and the Chimes could hold their own against any of the urban contemporary that was coming from the U.S. Ruby Turner was also a product of the British R&B scene, but in the U.S. she didn't enjoy nearly as much attention as Stansfield or Wheeler. *Paradise* (1990) wasn't a big seller in the U.S., and the problem may have been insufficient promotion. Another possible reason for the CD's unimpressive sales is the fact that the material, although pleasant and enjoyable, is not fantastic. But then, many urban contemporary releases that had a lot less to offer did much better in 1990. At any rate, Turner shows a fair amount of promise on this album. The songs that producers Loris Holland and Jolyon Skinner wrote for Turner (or co-wrote with her) aren't exceptional, but the album is generally decent—and one hears the singer's potential on urban/neo-soul items like "Sexy," "Leaves in the Wind," and the single "It's Gonna Be Alright." The CD's strongest track, however, is the mysterious "See Me," which unlike most of *Paradise* was written and produced by Cecil & Linda Womack. Again, *Paradise* isn't a bad album. But Turner was capable of much more—both commercially and creatively. *—Alex Henderson*

● **The Other Side** / 1991 / Jive/Novus ♦♦♦
On 1991's *The Other Side*, Ruby Turner works with two different producing/songwriting teams. One is Cecil & Linda Womack (Bobby Womack's relatives), and the other is the team of Hula & K. Fingers. Regrettably, neither team was able to give the under-exposed Turner the big North American hit she needed—in the U.S., this CD was a commercial disappointment and was totally ignored by urban radio. *The Other Side*, in fact, received even less U.S. attention than her previous album, *Paradise*. However, *The Other Side* isn't a bad album. Although slightly uneven, the disc is decent more often than not. The more memorable tracks range from the seductive "Provoking (Love Strokin')" and the melancholy "Merry Go Round" (both Womack & Womack offerings) to the sleek "A Little Bit More," which Turner co-wrote with Hula & K. Fingers and which has a Soul II Soul-ish appeal. Like Soul II Soul leader Jazzie B., Hula & K. Fingers obviously have a healthy appreciation of Chic and know how to put a high-tech, hip-hop-influenced spin on the influential Nile Rodgers/Bernard Edwards sound—there are traces of Chic on "Thinking About Your Love" as well as "A Little Bit More" and "Put Your Trust in Me." The catchy title song even samples Chic's 1979 hit "I Want Your Love." Back in the late '70s and early '80s, many rock critics wrongly dismissed Chic as a pedestrian, run-of-the-mill disco act and didn't give Rodgers & Edwards nearly enough credit, but Hula & K. Fingers—much like Jazzie B.—are a perfect example of how influential Chic continued to be long after the '70s ended. *The Other Side* contains a few weak, forgettable tracks, but all things considered, it isn't a bad album to have in your collection. *—Alex Henderson*

Sammy Turner

b. Jun. 2, 1932, Paterson, NJ
Vocals / R&B, Soul
Smooth R&B singer Sammy Turner's classy remakes of the standards "Lavender Blue" and "Always" lit up the pop charts in 1959. Signed to Big Top Records and given lush production by Jerry Leiber & Mike Stoller, Turner also hit with "Paradise" in 1960. He turned up on Motown later in the decade. *—Bill Dahl*

Lavender Blue Mods / 1962 / Big Top ♦♦♦

Lavender Blue: Golden Classics / Nov. 12, 1993 / Collectables ♦♦♦♦♦
This is lushly produced R&B-styled versions of venerable pop standards; from the late '50s/early '60s. *—Bill Dahl*

● **Lavender Blue: The Very Best of Sammy Turner** / May 8, 2001 / Collectables ♦♦♦♦♦
Sammy Turner is a classy pop singer who's often mislabeled R&B, which is perplexing because there aren't many traces of rhythm or blues in his music. Turner is MOR, easy listening, and pop, but hardly R&B. This best-of presents 19 of Turner's best, executed in his laid-back methodical style, including his signature piece, "Lavender Blue"—a title that aptly describes his voice. Turner's vocal approach worked well during the pioneering '50s but dated badly when the '60s rolled around. If you enjoy crooners like Nat King Cole, Johnny Hartman, Billy Eckstine, Johnny Mathis, etc., you will love this CD, because Sammy Turner's in that class. *—Andrew Hamilton*

Spyder Turner (Dwight Turner)

b. 1947, Beckley, WV
Vocals / Soul
Born Dwight Turner in 1947 in Beckley, WV, he grew up in Detroit, MI. As a teenager, Turner sang in doo wop groups and in glee clubs. Producer/engineer Clay McMurray submitted a demo of Turner performing "guess-timating" imitations of Jackie Wilson, David Ruffin, Billy Stewart, Smokey Robinson, and Chuck Jackson singing "Stand By Me" to MGM Records. MGM issued the demo as a record. Spyder Turner's cover of "Stand By Me went to number-three R&B, number-12 pop on *Billboard*'s charts in February 1967. MGM released a 1967 album, *Stand By Me*, which reached number-14 R&B/number-158 pop in spring 1967. The follow-up single, "I Can't Make It Anymore," charted number-95 pop that same year. In 1996, the Collectables label reissued the album as Golden Classics Edition: Stand By Me.

Turner stayed active in the business, doing concerts and working behind the scenes. The singer/songwriter's "Do the Dance" was a number-four R&B/number-39 pop smash for Rose Royce on former Motown producer Norman Whitfield's (the Temptations' '70s hits) Warner Bros.-distributed label Whitfield Records. In 1998, Detroit-based Turner had a regional hit on an independent release. *—Ed Hogan*

Stand By Me / 1967 / MGM ♦♦
Dwight "Spyder" Turner's only hit came with a song he didn't like and one he never expected to released as a single—his remake of Ben E. King's "Stand By Me," which included vocal impressions of David Ruffin, Eddie Kendricks, James Brown, Chuck Jackson, Billy Stewart and others. The demo was intended to show how others would sing King's classic. Executives at MGM disagreed with Turner's assessment and released an edited version that zoomed to number-12 pop in February of 1967. The novelty really wasn't that good; Spyder's impressions were weak and the production was poor, yet record buyers loved it. MGM followed with the very ordinary "I Can't Make It Anymore," a below-average song that only managed to dent the pop 100 chart at #95. The rest of the songs are weak remakes and even weaker fillers. Turner sings in his natural voice throughout the LP; his second tenor lacks bite, however, and becomes unbelievably boring after a few songs. *—Andrew Hamilton*

Music Web / 1978 / Warner Bros. ♦♦
Spyder Turner had a 1967 hit with a cover of Ben E. King's "Stand By Me" from 1961. The singer/songwriter wrote "Do the Dance," pop smash for Rose Royce on former Motown producer Norman Whitfield's Warner Bros. Records-distributed label, Whitfield Records. Because of that success, turner got an artist deal with the label and his *Music Web* was released in summer 1978. Produced by former Motown producer Norman Whitfield, who also had a hand in the Temptations' '70s era hits, this album has stellar orchestral arrangements by Dave Blumberg and Gene Page, as well as some of the top talent of the day: bassist Keni Burke, guitarist Wah Wah Watson, drummer James Gadson, keyboardist Mark Davis, and background vocals by Turner's labelmates Stargard on "Which Way Is Up." Turner's wide, engaging vocal range recalls a gruff Edwin Starr and a soft Eddie Kendricks. The somewhat cramped mix contributes to the "live show" sound of the LP. Standouts are the first single, the thumpin' bass-laced "Get Down," the midtempo jazz sprinkled cut "Is It Love You're After," the gritty "I've Changed," the dynamic "I've Been Waitin'," the dramatic ballad "Tomorrow's Only Yesterday," and the sly, solid groover "You Never Had This Before." Three singles were issued from *Music Web*: "Is It Love You're After," "I've Been Waitin'," and "Tomorrow's Only Yesterday." *—Ed Hogan*

● **Stand by Me: Golden Classics** / 1996 / Collectables ♦♦♦
CD technology does wonders for this old Spyder Turner album. Originally released on vinyl in 1967, it comes to life on disk. The sound is crisp, and you can hear the grooves they heard in the studio. Turner's earnest delivery, while hardly unique, displays true passion. There are no bonus tracks (a disappointment), but just the original 12, which includes Spyder's reworking of Ben E. King's "Stand By Me," where he imitates Eddie Kendricks, David Ruffin, Billy Stewart, Chuck Jackson, and James Brown; "I Can't Make It Anymore" (popular with the Northern soul crowd); and renditions of "Hold on, I'm Coming," "Moon River," "Dream Lover," "I Don't Want to Cry," and "For Your Precious Love." *—Andrew Hamilton*

Tina Turner (Anna Mae Bullock)

b. Nov. 26, 1938, Nutbush, TN

Vocals / Pop/Rock, Adult Contemporary, Soul

The most dynamic female soul singer in the history of the music, Tina Turner oozed sexuality from every pore in a performing career that began the moment she stepped on-stage as lead singer of the Ike & Tina Turner Revue in the late '50s. Her gritty and growling performances beat down doors everywhere, looking back to the double-barreled attack of gospel fervor and sexual abandon that had originally formed soul in the early '50s. Divorced from Ike in the mid-'70s, she recorded only occasionally later in the decade but resurfaced in the mid-'80s with a series of hit singles and movie appearances; her high-profile status was assured well into the '90s.

Born Anna Mae Bullock near Brownsville, TN, she began singing as a teen, and joined Ike Turner's touring show as an 18-year-old backup vocalist. Just two years later, Tina was the star of the show, the attention-grabbing focal point for an incredibly smooth-running soul revue headed by Ike and his Kings of Rhythm. The couple began hitting the charts in 1960 with "A Fool in Love," and notched charting singles throughout the '60s, though the disappointing position of "River–Deep–Mountain High"—cited by Phil Spector as one of his best productions—was very hard to take. All expectations were filled in 1971 with "Proud Mary," a number-four hit which became the capstone of Ike & Tina's Revue. Frustrated by Ike's increasingly irrational behavior, though, Tina walked out just three years later.

She celebrated her new-found freedom in 1975 with a role in the film version of the Who's *Tommy*. Playing the Acid Queen, she delivered an outrageous, all-too-brief performance in an otherwise forgettable mistake of a movie. Several albums were recorded for United Artists during the late '70s, but she appeared to be washed up by the turn of the decade. Surprisingly, Tina returned in 1983, first teaming with a Heaven 17 project named BEF on a remake of the Temptations' "Ball of Confusion." Tina's vocal offering was understandably apocalyptic, and she gained a solo deal with Capitol that same year. Her first single, a cover of Al Green's "Let's Stay Together," hit the Top 30 early in 1984. Second single "What's Love Got to Do With It" became one of the year's biggest hits, spending three weeks at number one. Her album *Private Dancer* included two more Top Ten singles, the title track and "Better Be Good to Me." With another movie role in 1985 (*Mad Max: Beyond Thunderdome*), she found a number-two hit with its theme, "We Don't Need Another Hero." Her next big hit followed in 1986 ("Typical Male"), after which Tina began to decline, still charting occasionally and selling respectably with albums including 1989's *Foreign Affair*, 1996's *Wildest Dreams*, and 2000's *Twenty Four Seven*. *—John Bush*

Rough / 1978 / United Artists ✦✦✦

Love Explosion / 1979 / United Artists ✦✦✦

● **Private Dancer** / Nov. 16, 1984 / Capitol ✦✦✦✦✦

In 1984, a 45-year-old Tina Turner made one of the most amazing comebacks in the history of American popular music. A few years earlier, it was hard to imagine the veteran soul/rock belter reinventing herself and returning to the top of the pop charts, but she did exactly that with the outstanding *Private Dancer*. And Turner did so without sacrificing her musical integrity. To be sure, this pop/rock/R&B pearl is decidedly slicker than such raw, earthy, hard-edged Ike & Tina classics as "Proud Mary," "Sexy Ida" and "I Wanna Take You Higher." But she still has a tough, throaty, passionate delivery that serves her beautifully on everything from the melancholy, reggae-influenced "What's Love Got to Do With It" to the gutsy "Better Be Good to Me" to heartfelt remakes of the Beatles' "Help," Al Green's "Let's Stay Together" and David Bowie's "1984." A reflection on the emptiness of a stripper's life, the dusky title song is as poignant as it is depressing. Without question, this was Turner's finest hour as a solo artist. *—Alex Henderson*

Break Every Rule / 1986 / Capitol ✦✦✦

Because it contains its share of memorable and inspired material—and even a few gems—it seems inappropriate to call *Break Every Rule* a disappointment. But because *Private Dancer* was so incredible a comeback, one greeted this anxiously awaited follow-up with such high expectations that anything less than outstanding would have been disappointing. And the album isn't outstanding—it's generally quite enjoyable and far from weak, but not outstanding. Be that as it may, there's a lot to savor here. "Two People" is forgettable, but Turner definitely has some gems in the power ballad "I'll Be Thunder," the driving rocker "Back Where You Started" and the haunting David Bowie piece "Girls." While *Private Dancer* would be a much better introduction to Turner's work as a solo artist, this has more plusses than minuses. *—Alex Henderson*

Tina Live in Europe / 1988 / Capitol ✦✦

Foreign Affair / Sep. 13, 1989 / Capitol ✦✦✦

Turner's last studio album for Capitol was produced by the late Dan Hartman of "Instant Replay" disco fame; however, this was not a retro '70s-style album. This set was comprised of 12 mature, middle-range, adult rock and pop songs. Turner tackled rock on "Steamy Windows" and "The Best," the latter a universal hit. She created fine club tracks such as "Falling Like Rain," "I Don't Wanna Lose You," and "Look Me in the Heart." Still, she cooled down long enough for a couple of gutbucket ballads in "Be Tender With Me Baby" and "Ask Me How I Feel." The most interesting cut was the scorching return to Turner's Delta roots on the flawless "Undercover Agent for the Blues," one of the finest pop-blues performances since B.B. King's "The Thrill Is Gone." Despite the slight musical style variations, the whole project was wrapped in an enticing pop style that gave it buoyancy and synthesis. *—Bill Carpenter*

Simply the Best / 1991 / Capitol ✦✦✦✦✦

A solid greatest-hits collection culled from her solo Capitol albums. Includes "Typical Male," "Steamy Windows" (written and produced by Tony Joe White), "I Can't Stand the Rain," and a duet with Rod Stewart on "It Takes Two." *—Cub Koda*

What's Love Got to Do With It / Jun. 15, 1993 / Virgin ✦✦✦

This is the soundtrack for the Tina Turner film that got Angela Bassett and Lawrence Fishburne Oscar nominations. There's little here that you couldn't get elsewhere in better versions, but if you only want a hint of the music Tina Turner made in various contexts, with and without Ike, this would be a serviceable purchase. Otherwise, get the film and hear the music in the correct setting. *—Ron Wynn*

The Collected Recordings—Sixties to Nineties / Nov. 15, 1994 / Capitol ✦✦✦

Over the course of three discs, *Collected Recordings—Sixties to Nineties* runs through most of Tina Turner's biggest hits, both with and without Ike Turner. However, the third disc comprises nothing but obscurities, making the collection a bit too much for anyone but the most devoted fans. *—Stephen Thomas Erlewine*

Wildest Dreams / Sep. 3, 1996 / Virgin ✦✦

Dues Paid, Vol. 1 / Aug. 24, 1999 / Frank Music ✦✦

As the title suggests, *Dues Paid, Vol. 1* contains a selection of early, little-heard recordings from Tina Turner. They're not that early, when you consider that she had sung with Ike for a number of years before going solo, but the key to this collection is that it's filled with lesser-known material. Some of this is very good, but the problem with the compilation is that it's shoddily assembled and has poor sound. This material is worthy, but it deserves better presentation than this. *—Stephen Thomas Erlewine*

Twenty Four Seven / Dec. 7, 1999 / Virgin ✦✦✦

The album is actually credited to just Tina, and no one has earned the right to a single moniker more than the former Mrs. Turner. Now over 60, Tina has picked a suite of songs about survival, a topic she knows well, and imbued them with as much soul as she can muster. Tina still puts Mariah Carey and Celine Dion to shame. But unfortunately, on *Twenty Four Seven*, the famous Turner passion is often submerged in glossy production that virtually defines "adult contemporary." In some transcendent moments, Tina reminds us of the woman who sang "River Deep—Mountain High"—like when she spits out "I've never been a winner but I still play the game" in "All the Woman," or during the powerful coda to "I Will Be There." As Tina sings in "Absolutely Nothing's Changed," she's lived to fight another day, and that's proof she ain't been broken. *—Mark Morgenstein*

Titus Turner

b. May 1, 1933, Atlanta, GA, **d.** Sep. 13, 1984, Atlanta, GA

Vocals / R&B, Jump Blues, East Coast Blues

Although he recorded regularly during the 1950s and 1960s, R&B singer Titus Turner today remains best known as a composer, authoring such perennials as "Leave My Kitten Alone," "All Around the World," and "Sticks and Stones." Born in Atlanta, GA, in 1933, Turner made his recorded debut for OKeh in 1951, in all recording nine singles for the label including "Got So Much Trouble." None made much commercial impact, however, so he moved to Mercury's Wing imprint, where chart success continued to elude him; in 1955, however, Little Willie John scored a major hit with Turner's "All Around the World," later covered by Little Milton under the title "Grits Ain't Groceries." Turner and John also collaborated on the single "Leave My Kitten Alone," subsequently covered by everyone from the Beatles to Elvis Costello. While recording for the King label in 1959, Turner scored his first hit with "The Return of Stag-O-Lee," an answer song to the Lloyd Price classic "Stagger Lee"; his vocal similarity to Price was again exploited for the follow-up, "We Told You Not to Marry," a response to the recent Price smash "I'm Gonna Get Married." Ray Charles' smash rendition of the gospel-inspired "Sticks and Stones" preceded the 1961 release of Turner's biggest hit "Sound Off," the title track from his lone studio LP; follow-ups like "Party Train" and "Miss Rubberneck Jones" failed to maintain the momentum, however, and he spent the remainder of the decade recording little-heard sides for a series of labels including Enjoy, Columbia, Atco, Murbo, Philips, and Josie. "His Funeral, My Trial" (1969) was Turner's recorded swan song; he died in Atlanta in 1984. *—Jason Ankeny*

Sound Off / 1961 / Jamie ✦✦✦

Soulville: Golden Classics / 1990 / Collectables ✦✦✦✦✦

This underrated veteran R&B vocalist is finally enjoying a reissue disc of his vintage efforts. *—Bill Dahl*

● **Sound Off: The Jamie Masters** / 1994 / Bear Family ✦✦✦✦✦

Titus Turner's complete masters for the Jamie label (plus a few previously unreleased cuts) are collected on this single import CD. Compared to his bluesy R&B recordings for the OKeh label in the '50s, Turner's Jamie recordings are quite different, in more of a teen-oriented Bill Haley-rock & roll vein, including several novelties and twist numbers, as well as rocked-up versions of such standards as "Sweet Georgia Brown" and "Day in Day Out." The approach works well on many tracks, including "Me and My Lonely Telephone" and "I Bet You Shut Your Big Mouth Now," and the excellent should-have-been-hit recording of "Beautiful Stranger." The title track was a minor hit for Turner, and the rest were either album tracks or non-hit singles, all of which were recorded in 1961. Although *Sound Off* is ultimately a collection of obscure recordings by an artist better known for his songwriting than his singing, there are several gems that will reward the inquisitive. *—Greg Adams*

Tweet

Vocals / Urban, Hip-Hop, Contemporary R&B, Neo-Soul

The successful duo of Missy Elliott and Timbaland presented Tweet in early 2002, a soulful vocalist with hip-hop savvy and unrestrained sexuality. Like Sparxxx's debut album, Tweet's debut, *Southern Hummingbird*, featured production by Timbaland and vocals by Elliott, most notably on the lead single, "Oops (Oh My)." The single became an overnight hit, and a remix for the song featuring Fabolous garnered even more spins on urban radio, helping her cross over to the rap audience and setting the stage for her album's awaited release date. Before debuting with "Oops (Oh My)," Tweet had appeared alongside

Elliott on "Take Away" (a single also featuring Ginuwine from *Miss E... So Addictive*) and "X" (an album track from Ja Rule's *Pain Is Love*). *—Jason Birchmeier*

- **Southern Hummingbird** / Apr. 2, 2002 / Gold Mind/Elektra ♦♦♦♦

Prior to her debut album, *Southern Hummingbird*, Tweet made her name as a protégée of Missy Elliott, appearing as a backing/guest vocalist on a few tracks with Elliott and, naturally, Elliott's producer, Timbaland. It should come as no surprise that those are the two dominant personalities on *Southern Hummingbird*, even if Tweet produces and co-writes several cuts here, since this whole axis has one sound that has served them well. Served them so well, it's given them critical and chart hits, along with a host of imitators, so there is no reason to abandon it now, even if the skeletal rhythms and endlessly looped riffs are beginning to wear a bit thin. This formula depends more on the overall sound of the track than the charisma of the singer—but, ironically enough, it works best when its fronted by somebody with personality, like Elliott. Tweet fades into the mix. She's attractive and is sweetly sexy, but isn't forceful. That works to her advantage on the lead single, "Oops (Oh My)," where she's so taken by a seduction she can barely speak, or even name who's taking her. Driven by a clever Casio-bass clarinet loop, it's the hottest thing on the record, punctured slightly by Elliott's disarming murmur, "I was feeling so good I had to touch myself," but it's good enough to withstand that. The rest of *Southern Hummingbird* sustains the essential feel of that track, occasionally forcing a *Sign o the Times*-era Prince to the forefront (which is welcome), and it does have a few songs that distinguish themselves, such as "Smoking Cigarettes," but it all blends together a little bit too much to be distinctive and, as such, it has a faint feel of product, a slow seduction record for the Timbaland-worshipping hipster set. A feel that is only enhanced by the end of the record, when Tweet actually *records* her thank you shout-outs as a full track, then, as a bonus, there are two uncredited Missy Elliott tracks that don't seem to have a trace of Tweet to them. Their inclusion is puzzling, unless you consider them the overdue payment of distinctive hip-hop for those hardcore fans who sat through the even-handed, stylish but samey urban soul that is *Southern Hummingbird*. *—Stephen Thomas Erlewine*

24-Carat Black

Group / Funk, Soul

Classically trained Detroit arranger Dale Warren got his start with the famed Motown label and, from the late '60s throughout the early '70s, composed the majority of string scores for soul artists on Stax Records (arranging for such artists as Billy Eckstine, Eddie Floyd, Isaac Hayes, Albert King, and the Staple Singers, among others). During this time, Warren befriended an up-and-coming Cincinnati soul outfit called the Ditalians. After he convinced them to change their name to 24-Carat Black, he took them under his wing—both composing and producing their lone album, 1973's *Ghetto: Misfortune's Wealth*, a conceptual work that focused on life in the inner city. The album went unnoticed and fell through the cracks shortly thereafter, as 24-Carat Black never issued any other recordings. But over the years, *Ghetto: Misfortune's Wealth* became a sort of cult classic among hip-hop artists, as such acts as Heal, Young Disciples, and Digable Planets used samples from the album for their own tracks. Long out of print, *Ghetto: Misfortune's Wealth* was finally issued on CD in 1995. The members of 24-Carat Black would later turn up in the group Shotgun. *—Greg Prato*

- **Ghetto: Misfortune's Wealth** / 1973 / Stax ♦♦♦

The Tymes

f. 1960, Philadelphia, PA

Group / Soul, Beach, R&B

The Tymes began as the Latineers in 1956. This Philadelphia ensemble's founding members were Donald Banks, Albert Berry, Norman Burnett, and George Hilliard. After a four-year apprenticeship on the city's club circuit, they changed their name to the Tymes in 1960 and added lead singer George Williams. They were signed by Cameo-Parkway in 1963 following a successful appearance at a talent show sponsored by Philly radio station WDAS. The group scored its biggest hit with its debut single, "So Much in Love," a Williams composition rearranged by Roy Stragis and producer Billy Jackson. Their first LP, *So Much in Love*, contained both the title cut and follow-up hit, a cover of Johnny Mathis' "Wonderful, Wonderful." Those two songs were both crossover smashes as well as R&B winners, with "So Much in Love" topping the pop charts. But after a third hit, "Somewhere," the next year, the group faded.

The Tymes tried issuing albums on their own label, Winchester, but had to fold it after two releases. They signed with MGM, but were dropped after two flops. They enjoyed a brief comeback on Columbia in 1968 with another remake; this time they covered "People" from the musical *Funny Girl*. But CBS also dropped them in 1969. They spent three years retooling their sound, while Hilliard departed. Their longtime producer, Billy Jackson, financed some sessions at Gamble & Huff's Sigma Sound studios in an attempt to get them on the Philadelphia International roster. Gamble & Huff passed on the unfinished demos, but RCA signed them. They scored three more hits from 1974-1976, the biggest being "It's Cool" in 1976, which reached number three on the R&B charts and number-18 pop. Various aggregations using the name have remained active on the oldies/cabaret circuit in the '80s and '90s. *—Ron Wynn*

So Much in Love / 1963 / Parkway ♦♦

Sound of the Wonderful Tymes / 1963 / Parkway ♦♦♦

- **Best of Tymes** / 1974 / ABKCO ♦♦♦♦♦

Great Soul Hits / Nov. 18, 1997 / Koch International ♦♦♦♦♦

A well-assembled and -mastered live collection of hits from the smooth pop-sounding Tymes from Philadelphia, PA. They should have released a collection like this during their heyday in the '60s. Their studio recordings were more pop than R&B, but live, their melodic voices and seasoned harmonies are more vibrant and soulful. Unlike most R&B groups, the material is all Tymes', not remakes of other people's hits with some originals thrown in for authenticity. The only substantial Tymes recording omitted is their remake of Johnny Mathis' "Wonderful, Wonderful," a number-seven pop hit for them in 1963. Includes excellent live versions of "It's Cool," a smooth "Sha-La Bandit," and the soulful "Ms Grace" (which bombed in the States, but was number one in the U.K.). The compilation concludes with their biggest record, the doo wop-ish, melodic "So Much in Love," a number-one pop hit. *—Andrew Hamilton*

Tyrese

Vocals / Urban, Contemporary R&B

R&B singer Tyrese began his career at the age of 14, performing in local talent shows around his home in Los Angeles' Watts section; his big break came when he starred in a commercial for Coca-Cola, shortly followed in 1998 by his self-titled debut album for RCA. He followed three years later with *2000 Watts*. *—Jason Ankeny*

Tyrese / Sep. 29, 1998 / RCA ♦♦♦♦

- **2000 Watts** / May 22, 2001 / RCA ♦♦♦♦

It would be easy to dismiss Tyrese as just another pop pretty boy. Looking at his previous work as a model and VJ, it's hard not to classify him as a musician more concerned with commercial success than any real musical artistry. Listening to *2000 Watts*, even the most cynical of R&B fans would have to admit that Tyrese has real talent. Flanked by a series of heavyweight producers such as Rodney Jerkins and Jermaine Dupri, Tyrese delivers a series of ballads and uptempo numbers that are bound to appeal to fans of BET and *TRL*, respectively. His first single, "I Like Them Girls" is a bouncing homage to women. Equally impressive is "There for Me (Baby)," a melodic ballad produced by Babyface. After a relative successful debut album, *2000 Watts* demonstrates that Tyrese is a legitimate R&B talent with a lot more skills than a lot of people expected. *—Jon Azpiri*

U

The Undisputed Truth

f. 1970, **db.** 1981

Group / Soul, Funk, Motown, Psychedelic Soul

It's not exactly fair to peg the Undisputed Truth as a one-hit wonder, because they did have a few hits for Motown in the first half of the 1970s (albeit only one big one), as well as made half-dozen albums for the label. Still, it's not that far from the truth. Nothing else they did matched the strength of "Smiling Faces Sometimes," which made number three in 1971. Crafted by Norman Whitfield, Motown's most adventurous producer of the time, it employed the funk-psychedelic guitars and ominous, socially aware lyrics that were also characteristic of his work with the Temptations during the period.

The Undisputed Truth came into being after Bobby Taylor brought Billie Rae Calvin and Brenda Joyce to Motown as part of the Delicates. When the Delicates broke up, the pair kept busy doing background vocals for the Four Tops, Diana Ross, and Edwin Starr. Whitfield teamed them up with Joe Harris of the Preps, laying the groundwork for the male-female vocal interplay that would typify their Motown sessions. It's fair to say that the Undisputed Truth were little more than a mouthpiece for Whitfield. He wrote most of their material (sometimes in association with Barrett Strong), and used their sessions as a laboratory to devise funk rhythms and psychedelic guitar effects. He was doing the same thing with the Temptations, and the Undisputed Truth's records couldn't help but suffer in comparison. As vocalists they weren't in the same league as the Temptations, and Whitfield was most likely reserving his real killer songs for the more famous group.

The group never approached the success of "Smiling Faces Sometimes" again, although they racked up a series of modest R&B hits through the mid-'70s. The best of these were "You Make Your Own Heaven and Hell Right Here on Earth" (which perhaps recalled "Smiling Faces" a little too closely) and the original version of "Papa Was a Rollin' Stone," which Whitfield would quickly redo with the Temptations for a much more definitive (and massively successful) version. Little else in the Undisputed Truth discography demands attention, though Motown scholars will find their work worth a listen to investigate some of the ideas rattling around Whitfield's head in the 1970s. *—Richie Unterberger*

The Undisputed Truth / 1971 / Gordy ✦✦✦✦

This sparkling debut, fueled by "Smiling Faces Sometimes," a number-three pop hit, zoomed to number 43 on *Billboard*'s Top 200 albums chart. Lead singer Joe Harris had recorded as a teenager with Little Joe & the Moroccos and later with the Fabulous Peps, and logged a brief, unsuccessful stint with the Ohio Players. Additionally, Brenda Joyce and Billie Rae Calvin had done background work and sung in the Delicates. Producer Norman Whitfield brought one original song to the session, "You Got the Love I Need"; every other cut was previously recorded by others (Holland-Dozier-Holland's "We Got a Way Out Love" was originally done by the Originals, and so on). Whitfield had the creative juices flowing on "Ball of Confusion," which bounces along for more than ten minutes and is true bliss; the arrangement is totally different from the Temptations blockbuster. The monster "Smiling Faces Sometimes" has a dead serious beat and some strong comments about people who show their teeth all the time. The tracks, with a couple of exceptions, follow a pattern: Harris sings lead, sounding Jerry Butler-ish, and Joyce and Calvin sweeten the tracks with their sugary, two-part harmonies. On Bob Dylan's "Like a Rolling Stone," Whitfield experiments with the trio by testing the pop/psychedelic waters, an indication of a new direction for Undisputed Truth. *—Andrew Hamilton*

Face to Face / 1972 / Gordy ✦✦✦✦

Face to Face peaked at number 114 on the charts, 71 slots lower than their self-titled debut, yet overall it's artistically more satisfying. Side one is straight-ahead music, all remakes, but arranged totally different from their predecessors. "You Make Your Own Heaven and Hell Right Here on Earth" had all the biting commentary of "Smiling Faces Sometimes," and then some. Originally done at a faster tempo by the Temptations, Norman Whitfield slowed the pace for the Truth. Joe Harris sang with perfect diction, making the stark lyrics even more riveting, while Brenda Joyce and Billie Calvin chirped like songbirds. Likewise for "Ungena Za Ulimengu (Unite the World)," another Temptations cut that Whitfield slowed and transformed into a psychedelic mind bender. You won't recognize the arrangement of "Friendship Train," a hit for Gladys Knight & the Pips; and Marvin Gaye's classic "What's Going On" may come off a bit too esoteric for most. Norman Whitfield never produced a song the same way twice, and that's the undisputed truth. *—Andrew Hamilton*

Down to Earth / 1974 / Gordy ✦✦✦

Lead singer Joe Harris was the only constant in the Undisputed Truth lineup. This LP bears no resemblance to the group's first two sets on Gordy. The sounds run the spectrum from rock ("Brother Louie") to pop ("Our Day Will Come") to a jazzy version of the Temptations' "The Girl's Alright With Me." A couple of singles charted from this diverse collection. *—Andrew Hamilton*

Cosmic Truth / 1975 / Gordy ✦✦✦

Fans of the Undisputed Truth's first two albums were shocked when they purchased *Cosmic Truth*. On their previous album, *Down To Earth*, they had combined older tracks featuring original members Billie Rae Calvin and Brenda Joyce Evans' pretty two-part harmonies with harder-edged tracks by new members. The group consisted of Calvin Stephenson, Tyrone Douglas, and Virginia McDonald. Stevens and Douglas had been members of the Magictones, a third-tier Detroit R&B group. The threesome joins Joe Harris for some spacy, rock-influenced, funky sounds. "UFO's" skips along with an infectious beat, a futuristic sound, and incredulous vocals from Joe Harris. Neil Young's "Down By the River" gets a soul injection, as if it needed one. Their version of "(I Know) I'm Losing You" is sung by one of the newer male members, and producer Norman Whifield allows him to cut loose—unusual for Whitfield, who usually demanded that his singers stick close to the melody. "Earthquake Shake" and "Got to Get My Hands on Some Lovin'" are pure heavy metal. "1990" has a strutting beat and is more subtle than the Temptations' version, with Dennis Edwards' in-your-face vocals. If you like howling and chattering guitars, this one is for you. *—Andrew Hamilton*

Higher Than High / 1975 / Gordy ✦✦✦✦

Higher Than High expands on the spacy vibes first exhibited on *Down to Earth*, expanded on via *Cosmic Truth*, and maximized on this, their exit album from the Gordy/Motown family of labels. Members, Joe Harris, Calvin Stephenson, Tyrone Berkeley, Tyrone Douglas, and Virginia McDonald bend your mind on a set that's comparable to critically acclaimed Funkadelic albums of the same period. "Life Ain't So Easy," asung by Joe and Virginia, is a haunting ballad about the perils of big city life; "Poontang" probably shocked Berry Gordy Jr. out of his mansion—the risqué chorus goes "I used to hate it, til I ate it." "Help Yourself" is the best rocker on the set; this version is different from an earlier version they recorded. And I can't imagine what type of dance you would do to "Boogie Bump Boogie," a psychedelic groover performed at laser speed. "I Saw You When You Met Her" is an eerie ballad about a woman who caught her man cheating; nice, but I like David Ruffin's version off the *Me & Rock 'n' Roll Are Here to Stay* album better. "I'm In the Red Zone" compares sexual frustration to a jonesing junkie. A nice parting shot for the group and Norman Whitfield. *—Andrew Hamilton*

The Best of Undisputed Truth / 1977 / Motown ✦✦✦✦✦

Undisputed Truth's initial lineup of Joe Harris, Billie Calvin and Brenda Evans were easily accessible; a later edition with Harris, Tyrone Berkeley, Tyrone Douglas, Calvin Stephenson and Virginia McDonald was an acquired taste. This 20-song compilation contains tracks from each lineup. From the stalking "Smiling Faces Sometimes," to the psychedelic "Overload," they're here, including their original rendition of "Papa Was a Rolling Stone," that stiffed months before the Temptations' version received so much love it won a Grammy. Contains many unsung heroes, like the rocking "Mama I Got a Bring New Thing," the stompin' "Big John Is My Name," and acid influenced mutha's "UFO's," and "Spaced Out." Plus Billie and Brenda's cooing two part harmonies above Joe's clear-as-a-bell baritone on "Save My Love For a Rainy Day," and the thought provoking "You Make Your Own Heaven and Hell Right Here on Earth." *—Andrew Hamilton*

● **Milestones: The Best of the Undisputed Truth** / Aug. 8, 1995 / Motown ✦✦✦✦✦

Milestones collects all of the Undisputed Truth's hit singles, as well as a significant number of their album tracks. Although the album is certainly definitive, it may be a bit too much for anyone but devoted fans. *—Stephen Thomas Erlewine*

The Unifics

f. 1966, **db.** 1972

Group / Soul, Pop-Soul, R&B

A late-'60s and early-'70s soul group, the Unifics formed at Washington, D.C.'s Howard University. Their lead singer was Al Johnson, with tenors Michel Ward and Grek Cook and baritone Harold Washington. Their biggest hit was 1968's "Court of Love," which mixed narrative, mock courtroom proceedings, and Johnson's passionate vocals. It peaked at number three and also made it to number 25 on the pop charts. A second single, "The Beginning of My End," also cracked the R&B Top Ten at number nine. They enjoyed two other mild hits in 1969, "It's a Groovy World" and "Toshisumasu," but were never again major players in the soul arena. Ward and Washington left in 1970, and were replaced by Marvin Brown and Tom Fauntleroy. The Unifics moved from Kapp to the Fountain label in 1971, making a few more records before disbanding. Johnson enjoyed some success as a lead singer and producer in the late '70s, '80s, and '90s. *—Ron Wynn*

Sittin' in at the Court of Love / 1968 / Kapp ♦♦♦
The Unifics formed in Washington, D.C. This CD contains their entire debut LP on Kapp, plus a slew of remakes. Lead singer Al Johnson sang in an aching tenor and had less range than an electric car; their two hits, however, fit his voice. "Court of Love" was akin to a dramatic skit with music and harmony; people's faces would light up at the end when Al sang, "I got justice in the court of love." For a split second, one actually thought he was vindicated in a court of law for his ex-lover's misdeeds. The follow-up, "The Beginning of My End," is an extremely morbid tale about a guy's girlfriend getting killed that almost equals "Court of Love" in popularity. "Tables Turned" was a good midtempo ballad, while "It's All Over" grooved along, complemented by some funky drums. The rest of the LP consists of below-average soul tracks and tired remakes like "Harper Valley P.T.A.," "Little Green Apples," "It's a Hard Day's Night" and the Rascals' "People Got to Be Free." *—Andrew Hamilton*

● **Sittin' in at the Court of Love: A Golden Classics Edition** / 1996 / Collectables ♦♦♦

Universal Robot Band

f. 1976

Group / Club/Dance, Disco

Yet another member of the underground disco family overseen by Patrick Adams and Greg Carmichael, Universal Robot Band cut a pair of full-length albums in the late '70s (both for Carmichael's Red Greg label) and re-emerged in the '80s, most notably for the classic 1982 boogie cut "Barely Breaking Even." URB's debut release was the "Dance and Shake Your Tambourine" single, a midtempo groove with a number of female background vocalists highlighted by the wild, indelible synth work of Adams. In 1977, the single became the title track of URB's first LP, which included a jokey rendition of *The Flintstones'* theme and a great track penned by Kleeer's Woody Cunningham ("You're My Music"). *Freak in the Light of the Moon*, the second and final LP, followed in 1978. "Disco Trek" followed in the footsteps of "Flintstone Disco" as a bit of a novelty jam, this time putting a dancefloor spin on the *Star Trek* theme.

A small number of URB recordings were scattered during the '80s, after most of the group's touring members defected to form Kleeer. "Let's Get This Thing Together," recorded with Debbie Hayes, was issued in 1980. And in 1982, the Caliber label funded the spectacular "Barely Breaking Even" single, a lengthy slice of boogie featuring one of LeRoy Burgess' finest lead vocal turns. Unidisc has kept both URB LPs in print throughout the years, and several rare groove and disco compilations have kept their legacy alive as well. *—Andy Kellman*

Dance and Shake Your Tambourine / 1976 / Red Greg ♦♦♦
Featuring more darting and swooping trails of synths than you can shake a stick at, Universal Robot Band's *Dance and Shake Your Tambourine* is nonetheless a surprisingly unmemorable album when compared to the other disco works bearing the stamp of Greg Carmichael and Patrick Adams. The album opens with the nine-minute "Flintstone Disco," a dancefloor-fitted version of *The Flintstones'* theme song, yabba-dabba-dos and all. "Space Disco" is similarly light in spirit and long in length, and uses high-pitched, multi-tracked vocals similar in fashion to the ones heard on Bumblebee Unlimited's "Love Bug" (another Carmichael/Adams product). "Dance and Shake Your Tambourine" and "You're My Music" are the two top cuts. The former, while not spectacular, has a sticky chorus and a pleasant boogie drift. The latter, penned in part by future Kleeer leader Woody Cunningham (actually, most of the players on this record would later become that group), is closer to smooth but funky soul than anything else and deserved to be a radio staple. This is not a bad record by any stretch of the imagination, but it looks that way when stacked against the group's 1982 single, "Barely Breaking Even" (though it did feature a drastically different lineup), and other flashes of timeless brilliance from Carmichael and Adams. Originally issued by Carmichael's Red Greg label in 1976, Unidisc reissued it for CD in the '90s and added a single edit of the title track. *—Andy Kellman*

● **Freak in the Light of the Moon** / 1978 / Red Greg ♦♦♦

Unlimited Touch

f. Brooklyn, NY

Group / Urban, Club/Dance

Unlimited Touch was an R&B group with club leanings from Brooklyn. They weren't disco, and they weren't exactly straight-up R&B; like their Prelude labelmates D Train, Unlimited Touch combined the two forms into what is often referred to as post-disco. They enjoyed minor success on the R&B charts, but they were embraced more by DJs—such as the Paradise Garage's Larry Levan—and became one of the countless inspirations behind house music. Their singles were often full-blow songs, with verses and a chorus, and they were often made with the dancefloor in mind.

The group's formation was sparked from the efforts of Crown Heights Affair's William Anderson and Raymond Reid. The sextet—bassist Sandy Anderson, drummer Tony Cintron, guitarist Phil Hamilton, vocalist Stephanie James, keyboardist Lenny Underwood, and vocalist Audrey Wheeler—broke out on Prelude in 1980 with "I Hear Music in the Streets," a single that didn't do much commercially but fared much better in U.K. and U.S. clubs. A handful of other singles were issued, including the number-29 U.K. chart hit "Searching to Find the One," prior to the release of a self-titled LP that packaged the singles together. The less successful *Yes We're Ready* followed in 1983, and the group dissolved shortly thereafter. Unidisc would later issue the *Searching to Find the One* compilation in the early '90s. *—Andy Kellman*

Unlimited Touch / Jun. 20, 1981 / Prelude ♦♦♦

Yes We're Ready / 1983 / Prelude ♦♦♦

● **Searching to Find the One** / 1993 / Unidisc ♦♦♦♦♦
Serving up most of the tracks from Unlimited Touch's two Prelude albums, plus a single-only release, this collection is a worthy investment for fans of the group who can't locate the original LPs. The invigorating rhythm arrangement and fun vocal melodies of 1980's "I Hear Music in the Streets" (the core of which was later reworked into rapper Rampage's 1997 hit "Take It to the Streets") and the slower, but just as groovy "Searching to Find the One," blending heavy keyboards with a fine electric guitar solo, are the outfit's most successful kinetic endeavors. Both numbers are from the self-titled 1981 album and find vocalists Audrey Wheeler and Stephanie James in top form. Cuts like "Love Explosion" and "Yes I'm Ready" from 1983's *Yes We're Ready* LP are not as convincing, as a lot of the live instrumentation had become drenched by synths at this point. The group had downsized from six to three, meaning that session musicians substituted for the initial group chemistry. Still, the overall selection is consistent and it's a definite party-pleaser for fans of the early-'80s "post-disco" dance scene. *—Justin Kantor*

U.N.V.

f. 1991

Group / Urban, Contemporary R&B

John "J-Ski" Powe and his brother Shawn grew up singing together in Lansing, MI. They added John "J.C." Clay and Demetrius Peete (aka Peete) in high school and college; the quartet formed and began to write songs and rehearse. Moving to Detroit to record their contemporary R&B-based a cappella compositions, U.N.V. soon found "Something's Goin' On" receiving airplay on local station WJLB. The song became a local hit, prompting Maverick Records to sign the band and release the single. It topped the R&B charts, forcing U.N.V. to quickly record an album. *Something's Goin' On* was released in 1993; *Universal Nubian Voices* followed two years later. *—John Bush*

Something's Goin' On / 1993 / Maverick/Sire ♦♦♦

● **Universal Nubian Voices** / 1995 / Maverick/Warner Bros. ♦♦♦♦

Phil Upchurch

b. Jul. 19, 1941, Chicago, IL

Guitar, Bass / Fusion, Jazz-Pop, Jazz Blues

A prolific guitarist who is comfortable playing blues, soul, R&B, and jazz, Phil Upchurch has been a prominent figure in Chicago music circles since the mid-'50s. He initially did freelance sessions with such musicians as Jerry Butler before becoming house guitarist for Chess. Upchurch's sensitive, often funky chording, riffs, and licks were heard on numerous releases by such artists as the Dells, Howlin' Wolf, Gene Chandler, and Muddy Waters. He frequently teamed with drummer Maurice White, who later headed Earth, Wind & Fire. He formed the Phil Upchurch Combo in the early '60s, and had a hit with the instrumental "You Can't Sit Down" in 1961. They did some follow-up singles, but none equaled the initial record's success. Upchurch did several soul-jazz and funk dates for such labels as Sue and Cadet in the mid- and late '60s. He signed with Blue Thumb in the '70s and split his time between sessions with the Crusaders and Ben Sidran and making his own albums.

Tommy LiPuma produced *Darkness, Darkness* and *Lovin' Feelin* in 1972 and 1973. Upchurch did one LP for Creed Taylor's Kudu label in 1975, *Upchurch Tennyson*, with pianist/vocalist Tennyson Stephens. He returned to studio work, but recorded as a leader for Palladin in 1985, Ichiban in 1991, and Ridgetop in 1995 and 1997. He returned in 1999 with *Rhapsody & Blues* and again with *Tell The Truth* in 2001. *—Ron Wynn*

Twist the Big Hit Dances / 1961 / United Artists ♦♦

You Can't Sit Down, Vol. 1 / 1961 / Boyd ♦♦

You Can't Sit Down, Vol. 2 / 1961 / United Artists ♦♦

The Way I Feel / Nov. 1969 / Cadet ♦♦♦

Upchurch / 1969 / Cadet ♦♦

● **Darkness, Darkness** / 1972 / Blue Thumb ♦♦♦♦♦
Recorded in 1971, shortly after he departed Cadet Records in Chicago where he served as a prime sideman to both Curtis Mayfield and Jerry Butler, guitar king Phil Upchurch headed for the West Coast and Blue Thumb Records. Produced by Tommy LiPuma, Upchurch's *Darkness, Darkness* is his quintessential (double) album, full of laid-back funky grooves, elegant, mind-blowing guitar work, and in-the-pocket string and horn arrangements (as well as some fine Fender Rhodes work) from Donny Hathaway with legendary session bassist Chuck Rainey and smooth jazz piano great Joe Sample in the house. Upchurch is one of the rare guitarists who can walk the line of jazz, blues, rock, soul, and funk and fold them all into one another without sacrificing anything in the process, and that is displayed on countless occasions here. On the cover of the Youngbloods on the title track, Upchurch leaves all the fuzz tone and distortion of his early work behind him for the shimmering cleanliness of the West Coast sound. He gets the dirty grooves through the notes, not the effects, bringing out a funkier side of the Jesse Colin Young tune than its author ever knew existed. Hathaway's spare, tasty muted horn arrangements follow in counterpoint to the melody, creating an extended harmony that acts almost as another voice. On "Fire and Rain," the James Taylor nugget that was a current hit, Upchurch begins tenderly, wringing the melody slowly and purposefully from the guitar before the keyboards and strings reach in and grab hold of it. Forced to respond, he chunks up with large Wes Montgomery-styled chords and knotty fills for the piano and horn lines, cascading like water in the background. He increases the tempo and turns it out as a funky soul tune, resonating with the haunting melodic invention that brings it back to its rooted, poignant lyric. And while these tunes signify Upchurch as capable of turning even the most melancholy of folk tunes into funk-driven boogaloos, it's on the soul tunes where he shines brightest. His covers of James Brown's "Cold Sweat," Percy Mayfield's "Please Send Me Someone to Love," and Marvin Gaye's "Inner City Blues" carry the record into the pop stratosphere. While the rock music was danceable and inspiring to begin with and was reinvented both structurally and emotionally by Upchurch's playing, it's when he digs into classic R&B material that things really start to happen. He

plays with so much soul and sticky groove that he wrings every sweat-drenched ounce of emotion from these songs and turns them into anthems of funky transcendence. There isn't anything extra in his silky approach, but there is a profound knowledge of when to move and when to slip, slide, and groove through these charts that is a trademark for Upchurch. No one could take a raw tune like "Cold Sweat," smooth it out, an still give it the tough, minimal, feeling read that Upchurch does here. His fingers are flying all over the place but are never outside the reach of the rhythm section. Never. *Darkness, Darkness* is the soul-jazz album of 1971 to beat, and one of the finest albums of its genre ever released. Upchurch is a genius and this album proves it beyond doubt. *—Thom Jurek*

Lovin' Feeling / 1973 / Blue Thumb ♦♦♦♦♦
Phil Upchurch's sophomore date for Blue Thumb is a move away from the heavy, fuzzed-out distorted funk of his Cadet sides, and a decidedly more direct move toward the laid-back West Coast sound. Having left Chicago a year earlier, he recorded *Darkness, Darkness* with Tommy Li Puma and a host of Cali musicians. The texture and easy groove of the music on that album must have agreed with him, because here, he shines by indulging in the smooth grooves with a funkier hand on his fretboard. The mood is decidedly a jazzy one with chunky bits of funk and groove thrown into a smooth, silky mix. Upchurch is a master guitarist, and his sidemen for this date were chosen with great care; he even replaced his own bassist Lucky Scott from the Curtis Mayfield band. This date also marks the first appearance in Upchurch's band of future longtime collaborator, pianist and songwriter Tennyson Stephens. Plainly put this is easily of Upchurch's finest recorded moments. With the fuzz tones and other noise boxes sidelined, the guitarist has a new opportunity to showcase his deep melodic sensibilities and the chromatic lyricism in his soloing and chord work-without, as he did on *Darkness, Darkness,* giving up the soulful funkiness that makes his style so unique. Standouts include a massively souled-out read of "You've Lost That Lovin' Feelin'" (that challenges any vocal version including the Righteous Bros. as definitive) and "Another Funky Tune," an Upchurch standard. Where strings and sparse horn arrangements frame certain tunes, like the back drop in "I Still Love You," and "Sitar Soul," the rhythm section still propels Upchurch into feats of dizzying in the cut groove, and in the more up tempo numbers, where strings are relegated to a back seat for a more keyboard driven approach, such as in "Washing Machine," and the album's closer "You've Been Around Too Long, Upchurch takes his playing into wah-wah saturated overdrive, creating funk inside of soul and soul inside of funk, then turning them both inside out with raving arpeggios as dirty grooves comes off as clean sensual fills and cascading skeins of sexy ringing lines of pure, easy, club night vibe. *Lovin' Feelin'* is truly amazing from start to finish, a high point in a career filled with them. *—Thom Jurek*

Phil Upchurch / 1977 / Marlin ♦♦♦
Chicago guitarist Phil Upchurch was comfortable in most genres; his plucky style can be heard on many sessions, including those of George Benson, who often sought him out. This self-titled LP contains seven cuts, four produced by John Tropea (instrumentals of familiar hits) and three by Benson (Phil Upchurch originals). Upchurch displays fingering dexterity and funkability on Shuggie Otis' "Strawberry Letter 22," made famous by the Brothers Johnson. "Free" is even better, bubbling along as Upchurch fills every space with adroit notes, playing the lilting ballad as sensitively as Deniese Williams' vocal. He does a marvelous job on "Good Times," an underappreciated Jacksons tune written by Kenny Gamble & Leon Huff, again showing the ability to phrase like a voice on his guitar. Tropea saves his best production for last; the stalking, tempo-changing "Church Street Station" is as commercial as anything here. Some of New York's best session players accompany Upchurch, including Steve Gadd, Richard Tee, Will Lee, and Tropea himself on rhythm guitar. The Upchurch originals are more elastic and abstract. You get a good earful of contemporary jazz with "It's Almost Five," a bender that hits the spot. Benson achieves a warm tone from Upchurch's guitar that's totally different from the Tropea sides. The sidemen are different too, studio rats the likes of Harvey Mason, Chuck Rainey, Jorge Dalto, and Henry Gibson, a master percussionist. Longer than its listed 3:56 time, "Fooling Around" features superb playing by all involved; it takes you there, then brings you back, and you feel better for the experience. Upchurch plays the guitar like it was a keyboard on the vibrant "Cyrenna," a hill-and-valley delight that's slightly marred by an intrusive synthesizer. *—Andrew Hamilton*

Love Is Strange / 1995 / Go Jazz ♦♦♦♦
One of the most remarkable things about guitar hero Phil Upchurch's output from 1961 to the present day is that it's remarkably consistent. No matter the style, whether it is R&B, soul, jazz, blues, funk, rock, or smooth jazz, he's on it and in it. This date from 1995 is no exception. Upchurch teams up with Ben Sidran—who acts as both producer and vocalist—for a remarkably tasty and mellow date of shimmering jazz and contemporary soul. The opening track, "Winds of Change," features a stunning vocal performance from Chaka Khan. Her voice, heading for the rafters, is allowed to break and crack naturally (thank God Quincy Jones didn't produce this; he would have had her sounding like she was doing an ad for satin sheets); it blends nicely with Upchurch's understated, graceful playing. Khan delves deep into the lyric for meaning and puts in front of the band, who floats it out transcendentally. On the funked up blues of "It's My Thing," Upchurch pops notes with a greasy fury. His vocals, limited though they are in range, are perfectly suited to the arpeggiated funk-blues. In the title track Upchurch slips in for the voodoo blues kill with Khan once again using her smoky, alluring voice to bring home a dark, sensual lyric. Upchurch uses both acoustic and electric guitars to bring in an undertow of conflicting, sexual emotions. The finest track on the album, however, is "It Was Groovy in There," with Sidran on vocals. It's actually a remake of Charlie Parker's "Relaxin' at Camarillo" with lyrics. Upchurch glides through the knotty, angular melody with Sidran doing his best Jack Kerouac. The matching arpeggios, the long, staccato melody lines, and Upchurch's burning, slippery solo offer a large tapestry for Sidran to sing from, and place his accents and diction in the right spaces. While it's true that *Love Is Strange* may be among Upchurch's slickest records, it's nonetheless a rewarding one. *—Thom Jurek*

Tell the Truth! / Jun. 12, 2001 / Evidence ♦♦♦♦♦
The world-renowned guitarist Phil Upchurch plays 13 great songs on *Tell the Truth.* This CD is a gem. Playing blues, soul, R&B, and jazz, Upchurch shows his remarkable versatility on such great songs as "Jive Samba," "La Costa," the title track, and "St. Louis Blues." He performs a flamenco version of "La Costa" with beauty and style, and flaunts his "stride guitar" technique on a solo rendition of "St. Louis Blues." His inimitably smooth and soulful phrasing shines on "Manhattan," and he doubles on harmonica on his original composition "She's Alright." However, the highlights of this great program are "Tell the Truth," a song Upchurch wrote with Ray Charles in mind, and his great arrangement of Dave Brubeck's "Take Five," which he plays much in the same way as he did on George Benson's smash hit "Breezin'." Joined by David Arnay on piano, Kevin Axt on bass, Vince Wilburn Jr. on drums, and Mike Smith on percussion, this great CD comes 40 years after Upchurch's first recording as a leader, and it's priceless. *—Paula Edelstein*

Usher (Usher Raymond)

b. 1979, Atlanta, GA
Vocals / Urban, Hip-Hop, Club/Dance
After being spotted by a LaFace record executive at a talent show in his hometown of Atlanta, GA, it took no time for hip-hop crooner Usher Raymond's career to take off. The 14-year-old auditioned for LaFace Records co-founder L.A. Reid, who signed the gospel choir boy to a recording contract. Raymond was introduced to the world simply as "Usher," and released his debut album of the same name in 1994, which featured co-executive producer Sean "Puffy" Combs. The first single, "Think of You," gained Usher notoriety and reached gold status. From that initial exposure, Usher was approached to do other projects. In 1995, he recorded a national holiday jingle for Coca-Cola. He also joined several top male R&B vocalists to form Black Men United for the single "You Will Know," featured on the *Jason's Lyric* soundtrack. He also teamed with teen singing sensation Monica for a duet remake of Latimore's "Let's Straighten It Out."

After graduating from high school, Usher graduated as well to his sophomore release, *My Way,* in 1997. In an attempt to display his maturity and songwriting abilities, Usher co-wrote six of the nine songs and enlisted the help of producers Jermaine Dupri, Babyface, and, again, Sean "Puffy" Combs. The album's first single, "You Make Me Wanna," re-established Usher as one of R&B's hottest artists, and also made him a crossover sensation; it topped the R&B charts for 11 weeks, hit number-two pop, and eventually went double platinum. Both of the follow-up singles, "Nice & Slow" and "My Way," also went platinum; the former stayed at number one on the R&B charts for eight weeks and became his first number-one pop single. In the meantime, Usher launched an acting career, appearing in the 1998 horror spoof *The Faculty* and the 1999 urban high-school drama *Light It Up.* To tide fans over, he issued a concert recording titled simply *Live* in 1999. Usher returned with his third proper album, *All About U,* toward the end of 2000. His third album, *8701* (2001), moved Usher from a teen pop star to a sultry R&B singer. *—Lynda Lane*

Usher / 1994 / LaFace ♦♦♦

● **My Way** / Sep. 16, 1997 / LaFace ♦♦♦♦
Usher proved that he had a strong, soulful voice with his self-titled debut, but he fulfilled his potential on his second record, *My Way.* What makes Usher distinctive from his urban lover-man peers is the fact that he doesn't oversing; he simply delivers his songs soulfully. Unfortunately, he falls prey to uneven material, just like any of his peers, but there are more strong songs on *My Way* than many contemporary R&B albums from the late '80s. Both Jermaine Dupri and Babyface contribute seamless productions and fine songs; respectively, "You Make Me Wanna . . ." and "Bedtime" are their best ballad contributions. Even if the ballads are usually seductive and romantic, cuts like the funky "Just Like Me," which features a cameo from Lil' Kim, might make you wish Usher didn't play it cool all of the time. And while it's refreshing to hear a hip-hop/urban R&B album clock in at a reasonable running time, it would have been nice if the tenth track was something other than a remix of "You Make Me Wanna." Nevertheless, it's a strong second effort that showcases Usher at his best. *—Stephen Thomas Erlewine*

Live / Mar. 23, 1999 / LaFace ♦♦
Usher broke big in 1997 with his second record, *My Way* and there was no looking back. After it rocketed up the charts, Usher capitalized on his good looks and sweet charms, attempting to break into movies and pushing his celebrity status. All of which meant, of course, that there was little time for him to concentrate on a sequel to *My Way.* Nevertheless, in pop music it's imperative to stay in the public eye, so *Live* was released a year and a half after *My Way.* Live albums often feel like a way to buy time while an artist figures out what to do, and there's no question that Usher's entry is part of that time-honored tradition, since there's no real reason for him to release a live album as his third record. And *Live* does feel like filler, since the only real evidence of his charismatic performances are the continual shrieks from the teenage audience. As a matter fact, he sounds tired and weary on many tracks, even his signature tunes "You Make Me Wanna" and "My Way." Hardcore fans will find his Bobby Brown medley of interest, since it doesn't appear on either studio record, but the live performances here all fall flat. The remixes that are tacked on to the end are better, especially Jermaine Dupri's reworking of "My Way," but they don't necessarily improve an unnecessary album. *—Stephen Thomas Erlewine*

8701 / Aug. 7, 2001 / Arista ♦♦♦
Usher has the reputation as a lover-man, largely because he fits the bill so well. He looks good, his material is smooth and seductive, and he has a nice voice, even if he tends to favor miasma. This has been true throughout his career, and remains true on his third

album, *8701*, a classy, seductive affair masterminded by Usher, Jermaine Dupri, and Antonio "L.A." Reid. There's not much new here, but Usher does move further in both directions—the ballads are lusher, the dance numbers hit a bit harder—but not so much so that it's really noticeable. Overall, the record is probably his strongest yet, but he still suffers from a lack of really memorable material (the singles usually are pretty good, but the album tracks are filler) and a tendency to oversing. Because of these two things, *8701* is more mood music than anything else, and while it does work fairly well on that level, it's not memorable outside of that mood. *—Stephen Thomas Erlewine*

V

The Valadiers

f. 1959, Detroit, MI, **db.** 1964

Group / R&B, Soul, Motown, Doo Wop

The Valadiers formed in Detroit, MI, in 1959; Stuart Avig (lead), Martin Coleman (lead, bass, baritone), and Art Glasser (second tenor) went to Oak Park High, and Jerry Light (bass, baritone) attended Detroit Mumford. Early influences include Jerry Butler & the Impressions, the Dells, the Flamingos, and Jackie Wilson. They auditioned at Hitsville USA one day after high school, secured a three-year contract, and became Motown's first white group.

Their initial recording session produced "Nothing Is Going to Change It," and "Somebody Help Me Find My Baby," which Motown shelved. Nothing happened until their next session that produced the self-written "Greetings, This Is Uncle Sam," and "Take a Chance," the B-side. According to Avig, "the sessions took one or two hours for both the vocals and the music." The Valadiers wrote "Greetings," but everyone wanted a piece of the songwriters' credits, the 45 listed only P. Bennent—who nobody knew—as the songwriter. When it appeared on a compilation album, the credits listed Robert Bateman, Brian Holland, and Ronnie Dunbar. B.M.I. lists Bateman, Holland, Dunbar, and the Valadiers as the writers. "Greetings" was popular in the East and the Midwest, but never sold enough copies to classify as a hit.

The Valadiers appeared in Pittsburgh, Syracuse, Flint, Baltimore, Washington, and other cities with the top names in R&B. On a memorable show at the Cleveland Arena with Marv Johnson, the Isley Brothers, and Wilbert Harrison, the blue-eyed soul singers received a louder ovation than the Isleys. They enjoyed playing hometown spots like the 20 Grand Lounge and the Graystone Ballroom. Lead, Stuart Avig, a 5'4" dynamo, had voice that was a cross between Jackie Wilson and Smokey Robinson; his showstopping voice and demeanor wowed audiences.

The Valadiers' next recordings appeared on the Gordy label. "When I'm Away" (released the summer of 1962) and "I Found a Girl" (January 1963) received little promotion and there were no other releases, and they disbanded by 1964. The Monitors redid "Greetings" on Soul Records and out-charted the original. The Isley Brothers also cut a version that remained in Motown's vaults until the mid-'80s. Stuart cut some solo tracks at Golden World Records as Stuart Ames. He tried to bring Marty Coleman along but the owner, Ed Wingate, only wanted Stuart and squashed the record in its promotional stage. He recorded some tracks, uncredited, with the Reflections ("Just Like Romeo and Juliet") on Golden World. After that experience Stuart sang around town in various clubs solo, or as the Valadiers, when he could assemble a group. Coleman concentrated on songwriting; B.M.I. lists 38 songs by him, but he wrote more. His biggest was "If This Is Love (Than I'd Rather Be Lonely)" by the Precisions on Drew Records. He wrote and arranged for Detroit's Top Dog label, owned by Artie Fields, and remain with the company until it folded after 11 single releases.

One of Marty's Top Dog songs, "Together We Can Make Such Sweet Music," was redone by both the Spinners and the Supremes & the Four Tops on Motown; Joe Towns recorded the original on Top Dog. When Motown absorbed Top Dog, Coleman fell in as a staff writer, placing tunes with the Originals, Gladys Knight & the Pips, and others. Britisher Ian Levine recorded the Valadiers in the late '80s. Stuart Avig was the sole original member, the other spots were filled by stand-ins. The material ran the gamut and included remakes of the Spinners' "Love Don't Love Nobody," the Isley Brothers' "I Guess I'll Always Love You," and the Miracles' "Ooh, Baby, Baby" with Stuart sounding as good as ever. *—Andrew Hamilton*

The Valentinos

f. 1961, **db.** 1965

Group / Soul, Chicago Soul, Northern Soul, R&B

Friendly Womack Sr. dreamed of fathering five gospel-singing sons before Friendly Jr., Bobby, Harry, Curtis, and Cecil were conceived. When they arrived, the hard-working laborer/preacher groomed them to praise the Lord and audiences watched the Womack Brothers perform at churches with Bobby standing on a crate because he was so small. They lived in the East 85th & Quincy area, one of the roughest neighborhoods in Cleveland in the late '50s and early '60s; a dubious honor that housing projects claimed in the '70s and '80s. If not for a strict father, they could have succumbed to their tumultuous surroundings. They attended Quincy Elementary, Rawlings Jr. High, and East Technical High School and were regular guys with classmates and acquaintances. Friendly took his name seriously and you won't hear one bad word about him. He married a girl named Shirley before the recordings, worked at a furniture store on Euclid Avenue, and as security at Karamu House, a landmark African American theater that features live plays.

They met Sam Cooke on a gospel tour with the Soul Stirrers in the mid-'50s. The brothers had a row with their father some years later for singing the devil's music and were thrown out of the house. Cooke had started SAR Records, discussions had begun for the brothers to sign, and there was no better time than right then. A call to Cooke in Los Angeles produced 3,000 dollars to wire as an advance on future royalties. They brought an old Cadillac and motored precariously to California to record for SAR Records, saying goodbye to 85th and Quincy and its cast of nefarious characters forever.

Their first record was credited as the Womack Brothers in 1961. The two gospel sides "Somebody's Wrong" b/w "Yield Not to Temptation," pleased their father, but didn't sell many copies. For their second SAR release, they changed to the Valentinos and instead of singing about the Lord, they wailed about love, lust, and life. SAR stood for letters in Sam Cooke, J.W. Alexander, and Leroy Crume's names; Crume sang with the Soul Stirrers and like Alexander, Cooke's manager, had a stake in the company. SAR's roster included Johnny Taylor, Johnny Morrisette, the Sims Twins, and the Soul Stirrers. Housing for the Womacks' was initially at the Dunbar Hotel, where the characters exceeded the ones on Quincy Avenue.

SAR issued "Looking for a Love" (March 1962); it became a popular rocker on urban radio, particularly in their hometown where many were stunned to hear Reverend Womack's sons singing rock & roll. They followed with "I'll Make It Alright" b/w "Darling Come Back Home," January 1963, both sides composed by Curtis Womack. "I'll Make It Alright" was a rousing gospel number with secular lyrics and "Darling..." was a loping beat ballad with Bobby's longing lead and a striking falsetto voice accenting the chorus. A third release, "She's So Good to Me" b/w "Baby Lots of Luck" (July 1963), sank without a whimper. The fourth single, "It's All Over Now," was released in August 1964 and was more country-rock than soul and wasn't their most beloved R&B tune because you couldn't do any of the popular dances to it and if you did, you looked stupid. But lo and behold, the Rolling Stones redid the song and introduced it to millions; the J. Geils Band also updated "Looking for a Love."

Their last SAR single surfaced in 1964, the same year Sam Cooke was killed at a motel. "Everybody Wants to Fall in Love" stiffed and SAR was wobbling. After Cooke's death, J.W. Alexander and Leroy Crume lost interest in the label, so in 1965, Barbara, Cooke's widow, dissolved the company. Bobby Womack married Barbara, some say too soon after Cooke's death, and started testing the solo waters. The Valentinos surfaced uncredited in 1965 on Bobby's Checker Records recording "I Found a True Love" b/w "A Lonesome Man." A year later, Chess released "What About Me" with Bobby on lead. A final Chess single, "Sweeter Than the Day Before," surfaced in October 1966 and has become a Northern soul favorite. Jubilee Records issued two singles, one in 1968 and another in 1969, but neither left a mark. Around the same time, Mary Wells signed with Jubilee too; she had also divorced Herman Griffin and married Cecil Womack. Before Jubilee, she recorded a few sides for Atco Records with Carl Davis producing and they developed a relationship that nearly led to marriage.

Bobby's solo career was accelerating, plus he played on sessions and wrote songs for everybody from Gabor Szabo to Wilson Pickett, carving a career that should merit Hall of Fame consideration. When Cecil and Wells divorced, brother Curtis and Wells lived together for years but never married. Wells had kids by both Cecil and Curtis. In the '90s, the offspring formed a group called Wells that consisted of Cecil Womack Jr., Harry James Womack, Nicole Womack, and Stacy Womack. To complicate matters, Cecil married Linda Cooke, Sam Cooke's daughter, and the two performed and recorded as Womack & Womack. Harry was murdered in California, it's believed a popular Bobby Womack recording entitled "Harry Hippie" was a dig at his lethargic brother. Cecil's songwriting career took off with "Love T.K.O." for Teddy Pendergrass, "Your True Heart (A Shining Star)," for the O'Jays, songs for the Dramatics, and others. *—Andrew Hamilton*

Luther Vandross

b. Apr. 20, 1951, New York, NY [The Bronx]

Vocals / Urban, Quiet Storm, Soul

In R&B music, Luther Vandross ranked with Prince, Stevie Wonder, and Michael Jackson as one of the most successful singer/songwriters and producers of the '80s. Amazingly, unlike those peers, for the most part he did not cross over to widespread pop appeal, a situation that finally began to change at the end of the '80s. Vandross had an elastic tenor that made him a natural for backup singing and commercial work in the early '70s, when he became a top session vocalist. In the second half of the '70s, he recorded under a variety of guises, cutting two albums for Cotillion under the name "Luther," recording with the session groups Roundtree and Change, and singing on hits by Chic.

In 1981, Vandross signed with Epic and released his debut album, *Never Too Much*, which topped the R&B charts and sold two-million copies. The title track was also an R&B number-one hit single and reached the pop Top 40. Vandross went on to produce albums for Aretha Franklin and other female singers, while maintaining his own career through the '80s. His albums *Forever, for Always, for Love* (1982), *Busy Body* (1983), *The Night I Fell in Love* (1985), *Give Me the Reason* (1986), and *Any Love* (1988) were all million-sellers that spawned major R&B hits, but Vandross' pop success was spotty until 1989, when Epic released *The Best of Luther Vandross... The Best of Love*, a greatest-hits album containing the new track "Here and Now," which became Vandross' first Top Ten pop hit. That proved his breakthrough, and Vandross' next album, *Power of Love* (1991), another million-seller, featured two pop hits, "Power of Love/Love Power" and "Don't Want to Be a Fool." Vandross returned to the pop Top Ten in 1992 with "The Best Things in Life Are

Free" from the movie *Mo' Money*, a duet with Janet Jackson. His next album, *Never Let Me Go* (1993), marked a slight falloff in sales, but *Songs* (1994), an all-covers album, restored his commercial standing, featuring a gold-selling pop Top Ten remake of "Endless Love," a duet with Mariah Carey. *This Is Christmas* (1996) and *Your Secret Love* (1996) were million-sellers. *One Night With You: The Best of Love, Vol. 2* (1997) compiled Vandross' hits from 1991 to 1996. He returned in 1998 with *I Know*. *Smooth Love* ollowed two years later and a self-titled release on J-Records appeared in spring 2001. *—William Ruhlmann*

Never Too Much / 1981 / Epic/Legacy ♦♦♦♦

The debut solo album from Luther Vandross featured one outstanding song after another. Vandross concocts a bouncy, vibrant flow on his uptempo numbers and an intimate, emotional connection on his moderate grooves and his lone ballad. The title track stormed up the *Billboard* R&B charts to number one where it remained for two weeks. The mellow groove of "Don't You Know That," which checked in at number ten, was the second single. "Sugar and Spice" had less of an impact on the charts due to its short stay of six weeks. However, this feverish number gets all the juices flowing as does the unreleased "I've Been Working." Also featured on this set is the sentimental number "You Stopped Loving Me." The song was written by Vandross but initially released by Roberta Flack; both versions stand tall. "A House Is Not a Home" is the only ballad, and an elegant one it is, written by Burt Bacharach & Hal David and originally sung by Dionne Warwick nearly 20 years prior. Vandross orchestrates a contemporary masterpiece with this vintage number. Though it was never an official release by the label, it's a quiet storm jewel. In addition to his many music credits, Vandross was a featured guest vocalist with the progressive band Change. The same vocal savvy and smooth styling that the New York City native exhibited on songs like "Searching" and "Glow of Love" resurface here. This is one of the better R&B albums of the early '80s. *—Craig Lytle*

Forever, For Always, For Love / 1982 / Epic/Legacy ♦♦♦♦

New York City native Luther Vandross did not generate any number-one hits with his second effort for the Epic imprint. Nonetheless, he presents another solid album. The smooth crooner has demonstrated a keen ability to attractively arrange remakes with such beauty and suspense as he did with three of the four featured releases. On the vintage ballad "If This World Were Mine," Vandross teams up with Cheryl Lynn. The single peaked at number four on the *Billboard* R&B charts. He lays his signature on a jammin' medley remake of "Bad Boy/Having a Party." The chandelier-swinging number stepped in at number three. He concludes with the Temptations' gem "Since I Lost My Baby." Penned by Smokey Robinson and Warren Moore, this mournful midtempo number tipped in at 17. "Promise Me," "Once You Know How," "She Loves Back," and the other selections are supreme compositions. Luther Vandross' dominance of the R&B arena was beginning to surface. *—Craig Lytle*

Busy Body / 1983 / Epic ♦♦♦♦

Luther Vandross has acquired a reputation for releasing solid, quality albums. Whereas some artists, whether intentional or unintentional, release albums with one or two good songs, Vandross makes every recording count regardless if every song is released. This project falls in line with one superb composition after another. From the alluring arrangements to the striking melodies, every song glitters with a delightful spirit. The New York native did a remarkable job on the medley "Superstar/Until You Come Back to Me (That's What I'm Gonna Do)." Showing his appreciation for the Carpenters ("Supertar") and Aretha Franklin ("Until You Come Back to Me"), Vandross created a masterpiece with the combination of these two songs. It was a number-five single on the *Billboard* R&B charts. "How Many Times Can We Say Goodbye," a duet with Dionne Warwick, is another work of art by the serenading tenor. It peaked at number seven. With a hurdling groove, "I'll Let You Slide" pranced its way to number-five on the *Billboard* R&B charts. From a supernatural lyric to a suspenseful string arrangement, "Make Me Believer" summed up the four releases cresting at 48. Only three selections remain, and all three could have easily charted. This is a splendid album. *—Craig Lytle*

The Night I Fell in Love / 1985 / Epic ♦♦♦♦

His fourth album under the Epic banner, and Luther Vandross still retains that freshness that is fulfilling to his audience and rightly so. This album spawned four *Billboard* R&B singles in "Til My Baby Comes Home," "It's Over Now," "Wait for Love," and "If Only for One Night." However, as superb as these songs are, any one of the remaining selections could have achieved comparable chart status. For starters, "The Other Side of the World" has that suspenseful rhythm and engaging lyric; "My Sensitivity" has a balmy arrangement enhanced with a bashful, yet mature, lyric. As for the title track and the remake of the Stevie Wonder classic "Creepin'," Vandross is witty with his vocal stylings. "If Only for One Night" was also a remake; it was written by Brenda Russell and covered by both her and Roberta Flack. The production skills of Vandross are commendable as he exhibits patience and acumen to know his boundaries. *—Craig Lytle*

Give Me the Reason / 1986 / Epic/Legacy ♦♦♦

Luther Vandross was riding high in the 1980s, dominating the R&B charts and slowly, but steadily, increasing his pop exposure. This was his fourth consecutive platinum smash and second straight double-platinum winner, but beyond that was a superbly sung, expressive triumph. "Stop to Love" and "Give Me the Reason" were beautifully produced, arranged, and performed numbers and huge R&B hits (the latter a chart topper), and deserved a better pop fate. *—Ron Wynn*

Any Love / 1988 / Epic ♦♦♦♦♦

There were some who felt that Vandross suffered a slight slump when this album only reached the platinum level after two consecutive double-platinum winners. But "Here and Now" was a huge smash, and by now the pop crowd was fully aware of Vandross' vocal charms and allure. "She Won't Talk to Me" was a bit on the posturing side, but still managed to do decently, while there were also fine album cuts like "I Wonder" and "Are You Gonna Love Me." *—Ron Wynn*

★ **The Best of Luther Vandross . . . The Best of Love** / Sep. 1989 / Epic ♦♦♦♦♦

By the time this way-overdue double-record hits collection came out, Vandross had done many more R&B singles than could fit on it, so *The Best of Luther Vandross... The Best of Love* is inadequate to encompass him. It does, however, contain "Here and Now," which broke Vandross through to the pop Top Ten long after most people had given up hope that he'd ever cross over. *—William Ruhlmann*

Power of Love / Apr. 23, 1991 / Epic/Legacy ♦♦♦

Power of Love finds Luther Vandross at his peak, crafting immaculate urban R&B hits that are seductive and soulful. The singles "Power of Love / Love Power," "Don't Want to Be a Fool," "The Rush" and "Sometimes It's Only Love" are the high points, but the album is filled with songs that are nearly as powerful, including a wonderful cover of Ben E. King's "I (Who Have Nothing)." *—Stephen Thomas Erlewine*

Never Let Me Go / Jun. 1, 1993 / Epic ♦♦

Songs / Sep. 27, 1994 / Epic ♦♦

Greatest Hits 1981–1995 / Jan. 1996 / Epic ♦♦♦♦♦

Greatest Hits 1981-1995 is an adequate single-disc overview of Luther Vandross' biggest hits for Epic Records, but the double-disc *The Best of...* is a richer collection that makes a stronger case for his talent as a smooth soul vocalist and a songwriter. *—Stephen Thomas Erlewine*

Your Secret Love / Oct. 1, 1996 / Epic ♦♦♦

Luther Vandross' tenth new studio album has much in common with its predecessors. It is filled with midtempo love ballads in which Vandross emotes over tasteful R&B gospel arrangements, mostly writing his own songs, but also finding room for a couple of pop favorites—in this case, Stevie Wonder's "Knocks Me Off My Feet" and the old Little Anthony & the Imperials hit "Goin' Out of My Head." As steeped as he is in the nomenclature of R&B vocal expressionism, Vandross as usual sounds more self-involved than romantically devoted. His references have always seemed not so much real emotions as other love songs, which makes him something of an anomaly: a formalist in a field at least nominally defined by excess of feeling. Of course, that's always been something of a conceit, which may be why the traditional R&B audience faithfully takes Vandross to its bosom each time out, while his relationship to the pop audience, after a flirtation in the early '90s, remains largely unconsummated. He may profess "Endless Love," but pop fans are only willing to believe him when he's singing with a diva like Mariah Carey. Give Vandross credit, he wants to be taken on his own terms, which is why he released his own songs, the title track and "I Can Make It Better," as the singles instead of going for a trendy R&B hit with "I Can't Wait No Longer (Let's Do This)," which features a rap by Deidra "Spin" Roper of Salt-N-Pepa, or trying to make "Goin' Out of My Head" a pop hit for the third time. Such integrity is probably what kept the album from selling beyond Vandross' existing fan base; lucky for him, there were a million of them. *—William Ruhlmann*

One Night With You: The Best of Love, Vol. 2 / Sep. 30, 1997 / Epic ♦♦♦♦♦

One Night With You picked up where Luther Vandross's first hits collection left off, including the R&B/pop Top Ten hits "Power of Love/Love Power," "Don't Want to Be a Fool," "The Best Things in Life Are Free," and "Endless Love," as well as the R&B Top Ten hits "Little Miracles" and "Your Secret Love." Also included was the Grammy-winning "Love the One You're With." Fans may have found the omission of some R&B hits in favor of Vandross' interpretation of Rodgers & Hammerstein's "My Favorite Things" questionable, and the four new songs, despite boasting the hot songwriting pens of Diane Warren, R. Kelly, and Jimmy Jam & Terry Lewis, did not generate any new hits of the kind that propelled Vandross' first hits album to triple-platinum status. Indeed, this second set was a sales disappointment. Maybe Vandross' fans already had these songs on the original albums. (More likely, the album marked the end of his sometimes stormy relationship with Epic, and the company didn't push it.) *—William Ruhlmann*

I Know / Aug. 11, 1998 / Virgin ♦♦♦♦

Playing the role of R&B love god has always come naturally to Luther Vandross. On his Virgin debut, he eases into his groove once again. Whether he's dealing in the easy, gospel-inflected pop of album opener "Keeping My Faith in You" or the jazzy hooks of the title track (with Stevie Wonder guesting on harmonica), Vandross is in command. While the faux hip-hop of "Get It Right" (with rap by Precise) seems a bit forced, the disc is strong overall. R&B doesn't get any glossier. *—Tim Sheridan*

Always & Forever: The Classics / Sep. 22, 1998 / LV/Epic ♦♦♦♦

The title of *Always & Forever: The Classics* implies that its a collection of Luther Vandross' greatest hits of the mid- to late '90s. That's not the case. *The Classics* truly means classics, with each one of the featured songs (with an exception or two) ranking as a true pop classic. Since Vandross is an excellent, peerless contemporary R&B vocalist, this is an excellent opportunity for him to shine, and he does, particularly on "A House Is Not a Home," "Anyone Who Had a Heart," "Going Out of My Head" and "I (Who Have Nothing)." Occasionally, the production is a little too polished or smooth, but Vandross shines throughout the entire album, making it another treasure in his catalog. *—Leo Stanley*

Greatest Hits / Nov. 16, 1999 / Epic ♦♦♦♦♦

Greatest Hits from 1999 may not be as generous as 1989's *The Best of Luther Vandross*, which contained 20 tracks on two discs, but it's a good, concise 14-track collection that includes many of his very best songs. There is a lot of overlap with *The Best of*—it shares no less than nine tracks with that collection—but it also has such '90s hits as "Don't Want to Be a Fool" and "Power of Love/Love Power." It is a tight, single-disc collection, which may make it preferable to some listeners. However, *The Best of* does cover Vandross' prime period better, and since *Greatest Hits* covers much of that same territory while missing several big '90s hits, it isn't quite all it could be. Essentially, it's for casual fans that want all the big hits on one disc—serious listeners will want to stick with *The Best of*. *—Stephen Thomas Erlewine*

Luther Vandross / Jun. 19, 2001 / J-Records ♦♦♦♦
Luther Vandross made a return to form, of sorts, with his 2001 self-titled album, and his first bow for former Arista chief Clive Davis' new label, J-Records. *Luther Vandross* ranks as the singer's best since 1991's critically and commercially lauded *Power of Love*, and it produced the single "Take You Out," which proved to be the velvet-voiced crooner's first Top 40 pop hit since "Endless Love," his drippy hit duet with Mariah Carey from 1994's covers collection *Songs*. *Luther Vandross* employs a bevy of the day's hottest producers and songwriters, in an effort to bring Luther back into the mainstream, and for the most part it works, although it infuriated more than a few old-school purists. Luther effortlessly brings on the funk on stellar uptempo tracks, such as "Grown Thangs," the neo-disco of "Say It Now" (which recalls his classic "Never Too Much"), and the fabulous "How Do I Tell Her," the latter two utilizing a long standing trademark of Vandross' stellar female background vocals that nearly steal the show. The album also includes the classic ballads—lush, romantic quiet storm numbers such as "Hearts Get Broken All the Time," the melodic "I'd Rather," "Any Day Now," and "Love Forgot." Additionally, Vandross delivers an inspired cover of the Burt Bacharach/Hal David classic "Are You There (With Another Guy)," The album's second single, "Can Heaven Wait," is a lush ballad that was destined to become a massive hit, but, unfortunately, due to the overly melodramatic nature of the song, which recalls R. Kelly at his schlockiest, the single stiffed. Nonetheless, *Luther Vandross* is the singer's most engaging, exciting, and compelling album in years, and shows Vandross in step with changing times, all the while still managing to hold on to the essence of what made him so famous in the first place. *—Jose F. Promis*

The Ultimate Luther Vandross / Aug. 7, 2001 / Epic ♦♦♦♦♦
Fans who prefer a little bit more material and/or Vandross' earlier era might be more satisfied sticking with the 20-song *The Best of Luther Vandross*, which only goes up to the late '80s in its coverage. However, *The Ultimate Luther Vandross* is his best single-disc compilation, with 17 songs from 1981-1994, 13 of which were Top Ten R&B hits. Naturally, his big Top Ten pop hits, "Here and Now," "Power of Love/Love Power," and "Don't Want to Be a Fool," are here. *—Richie Unterberger*

Earl Van Dyke

b. Detroit, MI, **d.** Sep. 18, 1992, Detroit, MI
Keyboards, Organ / Soul, Motown, R&B
Nicknamed the "Chunk of Funk," Earl Van Dyke was the keyboardist/bandleader for the Motown studio band of the '60s affectionately dubbed the Funk Brothers. The band can be heard on 22 number-one pop hits and 48 number-one R&B hits, generating sales of over 300 million records. With support from his parents (his father was a classical violinist turned Ford Motors factory worker), Van Dyke started playing piano when he was five years old. He took lessons at the Detroit Conservatory of Music. He began playing professionally as a teenager hanging out with the likes of Barry Harris, Yusef Lateef, Tommy Flanagan, Roland Hanna, Kenny Burrell, and Hank Jones, getting a gig here and there. While touring with Lloyd Price, Van Dyke met fellow Detroiter James Jamerson in Rockville, NY, in 1959. The phenomenal bassist was backing another Detroiter, singer Jackie Wilson. Jamerson had been recording for an upstart label called Motown Records headed by a young songwriter/producer named Berry Gordy. Gordy had written or co-written all of Wilson's hits to that point. Jamerson enthusiastically encouraged Van Dyke to move back to Detroit and become part of something that was going to be big.

When original pianist Joe Hunter left Motown in 1963, producer William "Mickey" Stevenson named Van Dyke the bandleader for the Funk Brothers. Based around Van Dyke, bassist Jamerson, and drummer Benny Benjamin, other key members were guitarists Robert White, Eddie Willis, and Joe Messina; percussionist Eddie "Bongo" Brown; vibist/percussionist Jack Ashford; and later, "replacement" drummers Uriel Jones and Richard Pistol Allen. Once the march of the Motown hits began, Van Dyke and the rest of the band were on call 24 hours a day, every day of the week. All-day recording sessions became common with a few scant hours left to maintain family and personal relationships, relax, or keep their chops up by playing jazz at the Twenty Grand Club, Phelp's Lounge, and their favorite after-hours haunt, the Chit Chat Club. The band became so tight that the label would have them record rhythm tracks (no singers, not even an actual song) and would later add vocals to them after a song had been written to fit the tracks. In some instances, a band member would have a part that he created replaced and recreated by a vocal line or riff.

With Motown having hit after hit, you'd think that the pay scale of the Funk Brothers would've increased. But that wasn't the case. Though the musicians were paid well for their services, they were still well below union scale. This being a commonly known fact in the Detroit music community, several music entrepreneurs, local and otherwise, took advantage of the situation and offered the band more money, leading to the Funk Brothers being heard on a lot of backdoor sessions. For the local Golden World and Ric-Tic labels owned by Twenty Grand Club owner Ed Wingate, the band can be heard on "Agent Double-O Soul" and "Stop Her on Sight" by Edwin Starr, "I Just Wanna Testify" by the Parliaments, and for Ollie McLaughlin's Karen label, "Cool Jerk" by the Capitols. The band can be heard on records issued by the numerous labels that sprang up in lieu of Motown's phenomenal success. Making the trips to nearby Chicago, they also cut several hits for producer Carl Davis and Jackie Wilson.

1969 was the year that some issues came to a head. Motown made it known, if not by words but certainly by action, that they wanted Van Dyke and company to remain in the recording studio, laying the foundation for the label's many hits. But the Funk Brothers long wanted to release an album of their own and somewhat got their wish granted, with *That Motown Sound* (1965) and *The Earl of Funk* (1970), both released on Motown's subsidiary label Soul. Neither release was what they really wanted, though, which was a straight-ahead jazz album. On *That Motown Sound*, Van Dyke played organ lines over existing Motown tracks.

Jamerson and Van Dyke moved to California separately at different times during the '70s. A couple of years later in the mid-'80s, Van Dyke moved back to Detroit after not adjusting well to the California lifestyle. He got a job with the Detroit Board of Education at Osborne High School, gigged locally with the Jimmy Wilkins Band and his own ensembles, and did advertising jingle recording sessions, the occasional record dates, and local festivals. 1991 was the year that marked the end of his playing days as he succumbed to the debilitating carpal tunnel syndrome. The following year in September of 1992, at the age of 62, Van Dyke died of prostate cancer at Harper Hospital in Detroit. *—Ed Hogan*

That Motown Sound / 1965 / Motown ♦♦

● **The Earl of Funk** / 1970 / Soul ♦♦
Earl Van Dyke was a Funk Brother, the name given to the rhythm section of Motown's studio musicians, along with cohorts James Jamerson (bass), Robert White (guitar), and Benny Benjamin (drums). Their names will be forever etched in history for being the backbone of Berry Gordy's popular sound. The four were essential cogs in Motown's assembly line. That said, you can imagine how much promotion went into Van Dyke's solo recording efforts: zilch! Gordy obviously recorded the mammoth keyboardist as an appeasement, a stroke, a perk. A hit by Earl would have been great for him but a disaster for Hitsville U.S.A.; Gordy needed Earl in the studio, period. This LP, like his first, consists largely of remakes; only four of the 12 selections are originals, the best being "The Flick," where Van Dyke warms the airwaves with his busy organ. The remakes cover the gamut from Steams' "Na Na Hey Hey (Kiss Him Goodbye)" to Brook Benton's remorseful "Rainy Night in Georgia." Frankly speaking, there's nothing here to make a programming DJ listen more than 15 seconds. *—Andrew Hamilton*

The Van Dykes

f. 1964, **db.** 1968
Group / Soul, Southern Soul, R&B
The Van Dykes were a Texas soul trio whose sound, harmonies, and style were closely patterned after Curtis Mayfield and the Impressions. Lead singer Rondalis Tandy formed the group in 1964, teaming with tenor vocalist Wenzon Mosley, bass singer James Mays, and falsetto artist Eddie Nixon. But Nixon left before they cut their signature song, "No Man Is an Island," in 1964. Both this and subsequent singles revolved around Tandy's sweeping, pained falsetto leads and the trio's keen, tight interaction and harmonizing. They folded when Tandy left for California in 1968. *—Ron Wynn*

Tellin' It Like It Is / 1967 / Bell ♦♦♦
Rondalis Tandy's haunting falsetto defines the Van Dykes' sound. This, their sole LP, contains their biggest single, "No Man Is an Island," a virtual showcase for Tandy's weeping falsetto. The groups' smoldering two-part harmonies compete with sustained organ chords for wallpapering honors. Its successor, "Hey Mr. Lonesome," recaptures the magic everywhere but on the charts. Their rendition of "Never Let Me Go" clones the Impressions' early '60s version. An unrequited love theme permeates the album as some of the titles—"What Will I Do (If I Lose You)," "You're Shakin' Me Up," and "I've Got to Go on Without You"—indicate. *—Andrew Hamilton*

No Man Is an Island / 1982 / Solid Smoke ♦♦♦♦

● **Tellin' It Like It Is: The Mala Sessions** / Jul. 18, 2000 / Sundazed ♦♦♦♦
This is, in fact, a CD reissue of their 1966 Bell album *Tellin' It Like It Is* with bonus tracks. Yet it also serves as a simultaneous best-of and an "everything you need to hear by" comp, since the group was active for such a short time, and that LP contained most of their recordings. The Van Dykes were unabashedly derivative of the Impressions and were imitating the kinds of records the Impressions had done two or three years before the Van Dykes cut their own sides, at that. That made them a bit anachronistic even in their own time, and like most such imitative artists, not nearly as significant as their prototypes. That doesn't mean that this isn't good, if somewhat second-tier, soul. Rondalis Tandy had one of the highest and most resonant falsettos in soul music and had a good knack for penning Curtis Mayfield-like tunes. The four bonus cuts include the non-LP B-sides "Save My Love for a Rainy Day" and "A Sunday Kind of Love," as well as a couple of previously unreleased cuts that have an old-school harmony soul aura similar to the rest of their output. *—Richie Unterberger*

Vanity 6

f. Minneapolis, MN
Group / Dance-Pop, Urban, Club/Dance
Known for its trashy, pornographic image and its sexually exploitive lyrics, Vanity 6 was a short-lived female vocal trio that came out of Prince's funk-rock empire in 1982. Vanity 6 was formed in Prince's hometown of Minneapolis, where singer/actress Vanity (whose real name is Denise Matthews) got together with fellow singers Brenda (a native of Boston) and Susan. Backed by the Time, Vanity 6 recorded its self-titled debut album for Warner Bros. in 1982. The single "Nasty Girl" became a major hit, and like Prince's albums, *Vanity 6* successfully bridged the gap between R&B/funk and rock/pop/new wave. Vanity 6's first album was also its last; in 1984, Vanity left the group and signed with Motown as a solo artist. Susan and Brenda, meanwhile, hooked up with singer Apollonia (another Prince disciple) and formed a new group called Apollonia 6. That trio recorded a self-titled album for Warner Bros. in 1984 and had a hit with "Sex Shooter," which was heard in Prince's film *Purple Rain*. Apollonia 6 also turned out to be a one-album act; in 1985, the group broke up. As a solo artist, Vanity didn't get very far commercially; none of her Motown albums were big sellers. And when she became a born-again Christian in the 1990s, Vanity gave up secular music for good. *—Alex Henderson*

● **Vanity 6** / 1982 / Warner Bros. ♦♦♦♦
No one ever accused the members of Vanity 6 of being great singers; if you wanted to hear female vocalists with great chops in the early '80s, you listened to Teena Marie, Alicia Myers, or Evelyn "Champagne" King. Nor did the female trio have the depth of its mentor Prince. But then, Vanity 6 wasn't supposed to be about depth or vocal prowess. Its mission was to entertain, and if you accept this self-titled debut album for what it is—wild, decadent, trashy entertainment—Vanity and her colleagues are insanely fun. Prince's stamp is all over this 1982 release, which finds Vanity, Brenda, and Susan backed by the Time. The raunchy lyrics reflect Prince's obsession with all things sexual, and like Prince, Vanity 6 manages to bridge the gap between funk/R&B and rock/pop/new wave. Even if the sexually exploitive lyrics become predictable after awhile, this LP is quite diverse and unpredictable musically. The hit "Nasty Girl" and the hilarious rap tune "If a Girl Answers (Don't Hang Up)" are irresistibly funky, and new wave audiences were drawn to more rock-minded tracks like "Bite the Beat," "Make-Up," and the Go-Go's-influenced "He's So Dull." As it turned out, Vanity 6's first album was also its last. In 1984, Vanity went solo, and Brenda and Susan formed the very similar Apollonia 6 with singer Apollonia. That group only recorded one album, which is probably just as well—Vanity 6 and Apollonia 6 certainly weren't without their limitations. But despite those obvious limitations, *Vanity 6* is a highly entertaining footnote in the history of Prince's Minneapolis funk-rock scene. —*Alex Henderson*

Melvin Van Peebles

Producer / Blaxploitation, Soul, Urban
Melvin Van Peebles' status as a pioneering African-American filmmaker likely obscures the fact that he also busted barriers and blazed trails as one of the forebears of rap music. If there's anyone who can draw from a large pool of life experiences, it's Van Peebles, a supremely creative individual who can also list Air Force bombardier, cable car driver, postal worker, portrait painter, journalist, novelist, playwright and actor in his resumé. Not only that, but he has lived in several locations throughout the U.S., Mexico, France and Holland. Most of the attention aimed at Van Peebles throughout the years has been through the films he has written, directed and scored—including *The Story of a Three Day Pass* (1968), *The Watermelon Man* (1970) and *Sweet Sweetback's Baadasssss Song* (1971)—but he also revolutionized black music with several albums that combined rapping with out-there jazz and funk.

Just after Van Peebles completed his direction of *The Story of a Three Day Pass*, he signed a recording contract with A&M. The first result was 1968's *Br'er Soul*; with its back cover sleeve work simply stating "Free Huey," the grooves within consisted of the artist's street-wise raps with free jazz accompaniment. *Ain't Supposed to Die a Natural Death* (1971), a Broadway production helmed by Van Peebles, yielded an Original Broadway Cast double LP—like *B'rer Soul*, it was released on A&M. That same year saw the release of the revolutionary *Sweet Sweetback's Baadasssss Song*, which also featured a soundtrack recording with each track penned by the director. One of his finest recording moments without ties to cinema or Broadway came that same year; *As Serious as a Heart-Attack* took his eclectic mish-mash of soul, funk, jazz and rapping even further and featured backing from Doug Carn, Albert Hall and Tom Scott.

Van Peebles' prolific run continued with the double album for 1972's *Don't Play Us Cheap*, which was a little lighter in tone than its predecessor. The director wasn't able to get it on the big screen, so he took it to Broadway. He landed on Atlantic for 1974's *What the... You Mean I Can't Sing*, another studio album that built on his prior non-film/ non-stage work. Then, 20 years went by until he returned to recording. *Ghetto Gothic*, released in 1995 by Capitol, was a characteristically Van Peebles record, filled with stylistic curveballs, Broadway-like compositions, and his animated verbal delivery. —*Andy Kellman*

Br'er Soul / 1969 / A&M ♦♦♦

As Serious as a Heart-Attack / 1971 / A&M ♦♦♦

Sweet Sweetback's Baadasssss Song / Apr. 1971 / Stax ♦♦♦

Don't Play Us Cheap / 1972 / Stax ♦♦♦

Ghetto Gothic / 1995 / Capitol ♦♦♦
These days, Melvin Van Peebles may be best known to later generations as the father of actor/director Mario Van Peebles of *New Jack City* film fame. But Van Peebles helped to ignite the gritty urban genre known as blaxploitation with his hit 1971 film, *Sweet Sweetback's Baadasssss Song*. Van Peebles also influenced a lot of rap's forefathers (Gil-Scott Heron, the Last Poets, as well as Tom Waits) through his style of story-songs, starting with 1967's *Brer Soul*. On this, his ninth release and his first for Capitol Records, he breaks a nine-year recording hiatus. His sing-speak delivery is at once reminscent of both Louis Armstrong, the comedy albums of Bill Cosby from the '70s, and the wild antics of cartoon voice artists Mel Blanc and Hans Conreid. The opening track, "Blinded By Your Stuff," begins with a grand choir and classical kettle-drum hits sounding like something out of *Fantasia*; it has a scorching, mid-song sax solo and is both funny and melancholy. "My Love Belongs to You" has Van Peebles delivering dry, drawling bluesy vocals over a pumping hip-hop track. The lightest track on the album is the mostly instrumental, catchy slide reggae number "Greasy Lightin'." Only a Van Peebles through his years of experience could compose a song like "Just Don't Make Sense," that lists the everyday contradictions of the African-American experience. Some songs on *Ghetto Gothic* may be more suited for inclusion in musical stage plays, but Van Peebles started recording when such offbeat releases were commonly released by mainstream labels. As it stands, this is an idiosyncratic recording from an artist who has been doing cutting-edge work in film, theater and music for four decades. —*Ed Hogan*

● **The Melvin Van Peebles Collection** / Oct. 26, 1999 / Stax ♦♦♦♦
A double CD that combines the soundtrack to Van Peebles' 1971 movie *Sweet Sweetback's Baadasssss Song* and the original cast recording of his 1972 Broadway production *Don't Play Us Cheap*. *Sweet Sweetback's Baadasssss Song* was an important film that paved the way for black filmmakers in American cinema in general, and the 1970s blaxploitation genre in particular. Van Peebles is not nearly as well-known a musician as he is a filmmaker, but he did compose the soundtrack, which was performed by Earth, Wind & Fire, who had then just released their first album. Heard on its own, the soundtrack is, unlike *Superfly* or *Shaft*, not a significant musical achievement. It's serviceable period funk-soul, both instrumental and vocal, sprinkled with some dialogue from the film, although it did make number 13 on the soul album charts. "Hoppin' John" is an obvious James Brown-inspired tune, though sung with considerably less heat than Brown himself would have mustered. "Come on Feet Do Your Thing" is the cut most like Van Peebles' pre-rap excursions on A&M Records, which is unsurprising, as he had already recorded it on his A&M album *Ain't Supposed to Die a Natural Death*. *Don't Play Us Cheap* was originally intended as his follow-up film to *Sweet Sweetback's Baadassss Song*. Although the film was completed, it could not find a distributor, and Van Peebles ended up staging it on Broadway. This is the original cast recording of that production, the music entirely composed by Van Peebles himself. A much more lighthearted endeavor than *Sweet Sweetback's*, *Don't Play Us Cheap* featured music centered around gospel, its cast including bass singer George McCurn (who was in the Pilgrim Travelers), Joshie Jo Armstead (an ex-Ikette who wrote soul songs with Nick Ashford & Valerie Simpson), and famed actress Esther Rolle. It's good-natured, varied, unexceptional contemporary gospel mixed with Broadway, light jazz, and soul, some of the brief tracks serving mostly to move the performance along rather than standing up as musical pieces noteworthy on their own merit. —*Richie Unterberger*

The Velours

f. 1956, Brooklyn, NY, **db.** 1961
Group / R&B, Doo Wop
The Velours were originally from the Bedford-Stuyvesant section of Brooklyn and although they never scored any major chart hits, they are fondly remembered for their variety of vocal group romantic ballads, novelty numbers, and uptempo jump and rockin' songs. Original members tenor Jerome "Speedo" Ramos," John Cheetom (first tenor), Donald Heywood (second tenor), Kenneth Walker (baritone), and Marvin Holland (bass) came together in the mid-'50s and began recording for the newly formed Onyx label in June of 1956. Their first single, "My Love Come Back," (1956) failed to hit. In the spring of 1957, the group issued their biggest record, a ballad called "Can I Come Over Tonight." Other singles included during the late '50s included "Blue Velvet," "This Could Be the Night," "Romeo," "Remember," and "Crazy Love."

In 1957, Holland and Walker left; they were replaced by Charles Moffitt and baritone John Pearson. This new lineup carried the Velours through their Onyx days. From 1958 on to 1961, the group moved over to Cub and added either Troy Keyes or Keith Williams as an additional tenor, making them a sextet. One album was issued by the group: *Remember With the Velours* (Onyx 201). The Velours recorded into 1961 before disbanding, only to reform as the R&B-flavored Fantastics in 1968. This act continued into the early '70s before calling it quits. —*Bryan Thomas*

● **Remember With the Velours** / 1958 / Onyx ♦♦♦♦♦

The Velvelettes

f. 1963, Detroit, MI, **db.** 1970
Group / Motown, Soul, Girl Group, Pop-Soul
The Velvelettes had three small chart hits for Motown in the mid '60s, including "He Was Really Sayin' Somethin'," revived with great success in Britain by Bananarama in the early '80s, and "Needle in a Haystack," which almost made the pop Top 40. Very much in the Motown girl-group mold shared by the Marvelettes, Martha & the Vandellas, and the Supremes, they never broke out as those other groups did. In part, this was because they didn't carve as identifiable a sound as any of those other acts had, and in part it was because the group's personnel changed rapidly before they disbanded around 1970. The Velvelettes were formed by Bertha Barbee at Western Michigan University in the early '60s, with Cal Gill ending up as the lead singer, although she was only 14 years old when she joined. With encouragement from one of Berry Gordy's nephews, they auditioned for Motown and released their first single on the label in 1963.

Several of Motown's biggest guns wrote and produced for the group between 1963 and 1967, including Norman Whitfield, Mickey Stevenson, and Sylvia Moy, although one original member (Betty Kelly) left to join Martha & the Vandellas for several years in 1964. However, the Velvelettes only did about a half-dozen singles for Motown in the '60s, and although an album was scheduled for release, it never came out. Cal Gill brought in two new singers to keep the group going at the end of 1967, but they broke up shortly afterwards. A reformed version of the Velvelettes began playing in 1984, and a compilation of their '60s Motown material finally came out on CD in 1999. —*Richie Unterberger*

The Velvelettes Meet the Royalettes / 1999 / Marginal ♦♦♦
This Belgium import lost its luster when Motown released *The Very Best of the Velvelettes* in 1999. Before that, this was the only collection by the Velvelettes, who scored with "Needle in a Haystack" and "He Was Really Saying Something." The inclusion of the Royalettes' sides doesn't help this CD's viability; you could always find their tracks on various albums and compact discs. They scored with "It's Gonna Take a Miracle," but never had a run of hits despite recording goodies like "He Is My Man," "Lonely Girl," and "It's a Big Mistake," all included here. Skip this one, and go with these groups' other recordings that use more modern mastering techniques. —*Andrew Hamilton*

● **The Very Best of the Velvelettes** / Mar. 23, 1999 / Motown ♦♦♦♦
Here are 11 songs from their 1963-1966 singles, plus four previously unreleased tracks. The swaggering "He Was Really Sayin' Somethin'" and the handclapping soul dance stomper "Needle in a Haystack" are the undoubted highlights; another single that grazed the charts, "These Things Will Keep Me Loving You," is also on hand, and a young Stevie Wonder—then still "Little" Stevie Wonder—plays harmonica on their first single, "There He

Goes"/"That's the Reason Why." This is pleasant and competent mid-'60s Motown girl-group soul, but it often variously recalls other, bigger Motown acts—the Temptations on "Lonely Lonely Girl Am I," Martha & the Vandellas on "I Know His Name (Only His Name)," Mary Wells on "Think of the Time," the Miracles on "A Bird in the Hand (Is Worth Two in the Bush)"—more than it does the Velvelettes themselves. The generic Motown sound of the '60s was a lot better than the best sound achieved by lots of other labels, though, and the disc fills a long-standing gap in the Motown reissue discography. *—Richie Unterberger*

The Velvet Angels

f. 1961, Detroit, MI, **db.** 1964

Group / Doo Wop, R&B

It's with groups like the Velvet Angels that doo wop music gets really interesting, as well as frustrating. The very fact that they left behind at least 19 first-rate songs puts them in the front ranks of early-'60s singing groups. On the other hand, the reality that they never charted a record nationally, coupled with the fact that nobody seems to know precisely what finally happened to them, indicates just how ephemeral even the best doo wop music could be, outside of the ranks of the most fanatical hardcore collectors. The Velvet Angels—Robert Calhoun, Willie Hunter, Jay Johnson, and Cy Iverson—first got together in Detroit. Somehow, despite being a startlingly talented group in a city with an alert, watchful label like Motown, they never caught the notice of Berry Gordy and company. Instead, they struggled for recognition for a year or two before deciding that the East Coast was more inviting. They made a name for themselves in and around Jersey City, NJ, performing at local clubs, where their a cappella singing—mixing gospel, doo wop, and early soul—and very lively stage act quickly caught on.

The group's first recordings, cut at a time when Detroit-based tenor/falsetto Nolan Strong was probably in their ranks, came about when an admirer taped them performing in a hotel room. He brought the results to record store owner and doo wop fanatic Eddie Gries, who promptly purchased the rights to their tapes for release on his Medieval Records label. "I'm in Love" b/w "Let Me Come Back" was their first release and a local hit, selling very well, and was followed by their versions of "Blue Moon" and "Fools Rush In," which were issued as singles (and also appeared later on one of the first serious collectors doo wop showcase LPs ever assembled, *The Best of A Cappella*). The group also made a number of informal studio recordings during this period in association with their then-manager.

The group itself scarcely survived long enough to avail themselves of the beginning of a recording career—they broke up sometime around 1964, with two members heading back to Detroit. Around this same time, Fortune Records, a Detroit-based label which had Nolan Strong under contract, claimed ownership of all Velvet Angels masters, and began threatening Medieval with legal action, none of which was ever forthcoming. To add to the confusion, additional tapes surfaced, and others were thought to have existed in the hands of their one-time manager and his family, although many were destroyed in the course of time as the interest and value of such music waned in the late '60s, even in the local doo wop haunts of North Jersey. By that time, all whereabouts of the Velvet Angels' members had disappeared from the music business. All that was left began surfacing in the 1970s on various doo wop compilations and a group retrospective album. *—Bruce Eder*

● **I'm in Love** / Jul. 1, 1994 / Relic ✦✦✦✦✦

Forget the fact that you probably never heard of them, or heard their records—this is one of the greatest R&B and doo wop collections that you can buy. Years before the Persuasions made a career out of a cappella singing, the Velvet Angels were there, with some awesome accomplishments that, alas, seldom got heard outside of North Jersey. This 19-track CD, running over 40 minutes, is an amazing document to the majesty and beauty of this unheralded group. Made up partly of studio recordings and partly of tapes cut in a hotel room in Jersey City, it's all amazing—just when it seems like another exquisite layer of harmony singing is beyond the reach of the room, there it is, wafting out of the speakers like the sweetest perfume. Worth the price of admission for their versions of Johnny Mercer's "Fools Rush In," and Robert Calhoun's gospel-driven version of "Ol' MacDonald," the Cy Iverson-Willie Hunter original "Mary," and the luscious title track (by Calhoun, Iverson, and Hunter), though almost everything here, whether from the studio or the hotel room, is pretty much up to that same standard. *—Bruce Eder*

The Velvets

f. 1959, Odessa, TX, **db.** 1961

Group / Doo Wop, R&B

The Odessa, TX-based Velvets are best remembered for their violin-enriched 1961 Top 40 hit "Tonight (Could Be the Night)," during which the group chanted "doo wop" behind lead singer Virgil Johnson. It was one of the first uses of the phrase in a song (the Turbans' use of the phrase on the 1955 "When You Dance" predates it by a few years). Johnson was a high school English teacher who recruited four of his students—Clarence Rigsby (lead tenor), Robert Thursby (tenor), William Solomon (baritone), and Mark Prince (bass)—to form the Velvets in 1960. They were soon spotted by Roy Orbison, who helped get them signed to the Nashville-based Monument label (he later cut "Lana" a song of theirs, while at the label).

The Velvets' recording career started with a catchy revival of "That Lucky Old Sun," but despite the presence of Nashville's finest session players on their releases, only the uptempo "Tonight (Could Be the Night)," which was penned by Johnson, would score a U.S. Top 40 hit (number-26 pop, May 1961). This song tells of a guy trying to get his nerve up to ask his girl to marry him. Their next release, the spirited Roy Orbison/Joe Melson-penned "Laugh," became their last chart entry. The group released another six singles before going back to teaching and studying. *—Bryan Thomas*

Tonight (Could Be the Night) / 1989 / Sony Special Products ✦✦✦✦

This Texas R&B vocal quintet shares Orbison's trademark musical approach, with soaring lead vocals by Virgil Johnson and sumptuous string-drenched arrangements. *—Bill Dahl*

● **Tonight Could Be the Night: The Very Best of the Velvets** / Mar. 23, 1999 / Collectables ✦✦✦✦

The Velvets, a '60s R&B/doo wop group from Odessa, TX, recordings featured Floyd Cramer's honky tonk piano, Boots Randolph's frantic saxophone, and other exemplary Nashville musicians. The African-American quintet were championed by Roy Orbison, and while not the most dynamic doo wop group (you won't find them listed on many Top Ten or 20 favorite doo wop groups' surveys), they appeared to be having fun. Lead singer Virgil Johnson's classic tenor isn't really employed to its fullest potential because of the songs' so-so arrangements. And despite having the accompaniment of the *Grand Old Opry's* best, these recordings lack depth and that heart-on-my-sleeve conviction demanded by doo wop purists. Featured are the shining moments "Tonight Could Be the Night," "Lana," and "Laugh," written by Orbison and Joe Melson; a rendition of "That Lucky Old Sun"; and six by Johnson that represent the Velvets' true identity better than the other songs. *—Andrew Hamilton*

Billy Vera (William McCord)

b. May 28, 1944, Riverside, CA

Compilation Producer, Songwriter, Vocals / Blue-Eyed Soul, Soul

Not only is Billy Vera (born William McCord Jr.) a rock historian, he's made some rock history himself over the last quarter century. Vera wrote for the likes of Barbara Lewis and Rick Nelson during the mid-'60s before recording his "Storybook Children" as an R&B duet with Judy Clay in 1967 for Atlantic. It proved a solid hit, as did their 1968 follow-up "Country Girl—City Man." Vera surfaced as a solo artist in 1987 when "At This Moment," a song he'd cut in 1981 with his band, Beaters, was featured on the popular TV sitcom *Family Ties* and topped the pop charts on Rhino. Vera recently returned to a soulful duet format, this time with ex-LaBelle belter Nona Hendryx, for "You Have to Cry Sometime" on Shanachie. Vera has also compiled and annotated many CD reissue projects, notably the *Legends of Specialty* series. *—Bill Dahl*

With Pen in Hand / 1968 / Atlantic ✦✦

Billy & the Beaters / 1981 / Alfa ✦✦

● **By Request: The Best of Billy Vera & the Beaters** / 1987 / Rhino ✦✦✦

By Request: The Best of Billy Vera & the Beaters is a short nine-track best-of album, but is the best introduction to Billy Vera commonly out there. His own major hit, "At This Moment," is included as are eight other tracks. This was the album on which the song (first heard on *Family Ties*) was available. Sadly, none of them are from his song writing days for Rick Nelson or Barbara Lewis. This album also does not include any of Billy Vera's work with Judy Clay, with whom he formed the first interracial, coed singing duo in the late 1960s. Recommended for those looking for a good, non-overplayed 1980s song like "At This Moment." The "by request" and "best-of" titles are both misleading because this non-live compilation is hardly exhaustive. *—JT Griffith*

At This Moment: A Retrospective / Feb. 27, 1992 / Collectables ✦✦✦

Considering that Billy Vera had written a ton of liner notes in the years preceding the release of this retrospective (for which he penned the notes himself) and presumably cares about such things as dates and recording sources, the track listing and notes for this compilation are surprisingly vague about some such details. Certainly much of it comes from a 1995 live performance. And certainly a few of the remaining cuts come from the soundtracks to *Blind Date, Rainbow Drive, Baja Oklahoma, Desperate for Love,* and *Ride the Wind* ("Desperate Frame of Mind" was in fact used for both of the latter two movies). As for the version of "At This Moment," the number-one hit that will certainly be the song to attract most interest on the collection, it's a studio version made for the picture *Starstruck*, though in the notes Vera seems to imply the CD includes a live recording of the tune (it doesn't). Whatever the discographical minutiae, these are journeyman blends of rock, pop, soul, R&B, and adult contemporary music (and even a bit of country at times, as on "Desperate Frame of Mind"), done by a man who obviously cares deeply about classic roots forms but is only an adequate singer. The Beaters are only serviceable as backers, sounding like a television house band with more funk than most. *—Jimmy James*

Billy Vera & Judy Clay

db. 1968

Group / Soul

Billy Vera & Judy Clay were less notable for their music than for their historical importance: certainly the first interracial recording duo in soul music, this late-'60s team may have been the first interracial recording duo of any sort. Vera was a New York songwriter with some minor successes (Ricky Nelson's "Mean Old World," Barbara Lewis' "Make Me Belong to You") when he brought his composition "Storybook Children" to Atlantic executive Jerry Wexler. Vera initially tried to record it with Nona Hendryx (then with Patti LaBelle & the Blue Belles), but when that idea didn't pan out, he teamed up with Clay. Born Judy Lee, Clay had joined the gospel group the Drinkard Singers (who also featured Cissy Houston) in the late '50s, and had recorded soul singles throughout the '60s without notable success.

"Storybook Children," interpreted by some listeners as a fable of interracial romance (although Vera insists it is about adultery), became a modest R&B and pop hit in early 1968, as did the follow-up single, "Country Girl—City Man (Just Across the Line)." Clay was by far the stronger vocal partner on their material (much of it written by Vera and and noted producer/songwriter Chip Taylor), which was solid (though not great) easygoing soul with heavy pop, at times middle of the road, overtones. Failing to land another hit single, the duo recorded an album, *Storybook Children*, in 1968 before going their own ways. Clay recorded for Stax and Atlantic in the late '60s, making the R&B charts as William Bell's duet partner in 1968 with "Private Number," and landing her only R&B chart single, "Greatest Love," in 1970. Vera eventually formed the Beaters in L.A., hitting number one in 1986 with "At This Moment," and remained very active as an R&B historian, liner note writer, reissue compiler, and member of the Rhythm & Blues Foundation into the 2000s. *—Richie Unterberger*

- **Storybook Children** / 1967 / Atlantic ♦♦♦

The Versalettes

f. 1961, **db.** 1968

Group / Soul, Girl Group, Chicago Soul, R&B

The Versalettes were an exciting Chicago female group of the mid-'60s whose records never amounted to anything. Forming at Marshall High School in 1961, Theresa Legg, Kathleen Spates, Vera Rugolis, and Viola Floyd built a reputation doing talent shows and community functions. Personnel at Cortland/Witch Records caught wind of the Versalettes' buzz and signed them in 1963, while they were still in high school. Donald Jenkins worked with them and imprinted his doo wop sound on their recordings, which, supposedly, they hated.

At the urging of their manager, Bobby Mason, they added Helen Greenfield before cutting their first single, "Shining Armor" b/w "True Love Is a Treasure," in 1963 on Bill Erman's Witch label; the Blenders ("Daughter") recorded the B-side a year earlier. Disc jockeys Lucky Cordell and Herb Kent gave it perfunctory hometown spins; for this favor, the Versalettes did free record hops for them. Around this same time, Erman released "The Fisherman" b/w "Nobody but You" on his Cortland imprint and credited it to the Trinkets, who were really the Versalettes. Again, sales were virtually nonexistent. A third single, "Don Juan in Town," a dated doo wop, floundered as well; the Witch recordings never captured the group's essence. The song was an answer to "Don Juan," which was recorded by Donald Jenkins and Ronnie Strong as the Starr Brothers. Cortland also issued the song by the Ideals on the B-side of "Gorilla." Jenkins (Delighters) got them ready to record, but Bob Catron, the A&R man, got the production credits.

Cortland/Witch stopped making records in 1964, and the original Versalettes took the opportunity to axe Greenfield, whom they considered a wayward outsider anyway. After graduating from high school in 1965, they continued the community gigs but didn't record again for awhile. A final single surfaced in 1968 on OKeh Records. The nondescript sides "So Glad Your Love Don't Change" b/w "Love Made to Order" didn't have a chance. The group never even knew OKeh released the single until the '90s because nobody bothered to tell them; OKeh credited it to the Little Foxes. Bill Erman is reclusive about his Cortland/Witch recordings, which is why they aren't found compiled on any albums, cassettes, or discs. *—Andrew Hamilton*

The Vibrations

f. 1960, Los Angeles, CA, **db.** 1976

Group / Soul, Northern Soul, R&B

Though never major hitmakers, the Los Angeles-based Vibrations were consistent performers through the '60s. The lineup included James Johnson, Carl Fisher, Richard Owens, Dave Govan, and Don Bradley. They began recording as the Jayhawks, then scored a couple of novelty hits performing as the Marathons. Neither "The Watusi" nor "Peanut Butter" were particularly triumphant, but each managed to chart in both the R&B and pop markets. When they became the Vibrations in 1964, they gradually turned to more romantic material, although their first hit, "My Girl Sloopy," was closer to their previous cuts. They had their last brush with glory in 1968 with the OKeh song "Love in Them There Hills." Although Richard Owens was briefly in the Temptations in 1971, the Vibrations continued on until 1976, closing out their career as a nightclub act. *—Ron Wynn*

Watusi / 1961 / Checker ♦♦♦♦

Misty / 1965 / OKeh ♦♦♦♦

Think again if you thought *The Temptations in a Mellow Mood* (an album of standards) pioneered this concept by a '60s soul group; this smooth set preceded the Temptations' album by a couple of years and probably inspired the Motown classic. The dancing, exciting Vibrations shocked their fans with this early-'60s release of standards sung in modern but soulful harmony. It was before its time and wasn't really appreciated until years later when it was out of print. "Misty" charted, but the California natives also serve up excellent renditions of "The Days of Wine and Roses," "I Wish You Love," "What Kind of Fool Am I," and "Gina." The Vibrations' OKeh albums are excellent but rare, each deserves reissuing on CD, and why this hasn't happened is a mystery. *—Andrew Hamilton*

Shout / 1965 / OKeh ♦♦♦♦

This is a live set based around the Vibrations' 1964-1965 OKeh recordings. OKeh tried everything but never did break this excellent group into the big time. Emulated by everybody from the Contours and the Five Du-tones to the O'Jays and Temptations, the Vibrations—Ricky Owens, Carlton Fisher, James Johnson, David Govan, and Donald Bradley—were a five-tool group who could sing, dance, entertain, write, and produce when allowed. An extremely visual act, a live recording by them helps but isn't the same as being there. Still, the Los Angeles group (who began as the Jayhawks) struts their stuff and drives the audience zany with live renditions of "Misty," "Watusi Time," "Finding Out the Hard Way," "Sloop Dance," "Keep on Keeping On," and more. *—Andrew Hamilton*

New Vibrations / 1966 / OKeh ♦♦♦

OKeh Records issued this album dominated by pop standards by the Vibrations a year before Gordy Records unleashed *In a Mellow Mood* by the Temptations, which featured the Tempts' signature harmonies on standards. This wasn't the Vibrations' first attempt at crooning easy listening favorites; they had a little success with "Misty" during the winter of 1965. "Soul a Go Go" is the only deviant from the middle-of-the-road theme. Deserving of glass case display are silky renditions of "Secret Lover," "Canadian Sunset," "For Your Love," and the sentiment-laced "And I Love Her." *—Andrew Hamilton*

- **The Very Best of the Vibrations** / Nov. 14, 2000 / Collectables ♦♦♦♦

The Vibrations first recorded as the Jayhawks in 1956 and hit anonymously with "Peanut Butter" as the Marathons on Argo Records in 1959; so 20 songs may seem like a lot, but is hardly definitive of an 18-year recording career. Still, it's a good compilation for what it is. The CD is chock full of tracks from a lengthy stint with Checkers Records, starting with their debut there, "So Blue" (1961), which first dropped on Bet Records. Their OKeh years (1964-1967) are represented well and "My Girl Sloopy," from an Atlantic stint, adds variety to the set. Depending on the genre, a different sound emanated from these guys. When rocking and souling, a raspy lead took the spotlight, excelling on the novelty/dancers but flattening out on midtempo and uptempo soul tunes that needed blasting à la Levi Stubbs and Dennis Edwards. On the modern harmony arrangements, falsetto Ricky Owens takes over and they exude a smooth, bathing sound that washes you away in harmony. Nothing they recorded after an obscure Epic tune—"Cause You're Mine" (1968), produced and written by Kenny Gamble & Leon Huff—is included; they recorded until 1974. *—Andrew Hamilton*

Doo Wop Delights / 2002 / Black Tulip ♦♦♦♦

Doo Wop Delights is a cornucopia of early Vibrations recordings, beginning with "So Blue," a 1960 release on Bet Records, and continuing through their Marathons sides and 1960-1963 releases on Checker Records. Later recordings on OKeh, Neptune, etc., didn't make this one, nor did the group's debut Jayhawks platters from 1956 to 1957. The 31 tracks showcase them at their energetic best. They redo "Stranded in the Jungle," a song they first did as the Jayhawks on Flash Records, and liven up the party with a slew of dance songs: "Watusi," "Let's Pony Again," "New Hully Gully," "Doin' the Slop," "Dancin' Danny," and "Peanut Butter" (recorded as the Marathons). The multi-talented Los Angeles natives croon deliciously on "Over the Rainbow," "Since I Fell for You," and "Time After Time." The Vibrations hung tough for a long time. They had a handful of sporadic hits but few real chart-busters despite recording exciting music. This CD will start new fans off on the right foot and will bring back fond memories to those who remember these songs from the early '60s. *—Andrew Hamilton*

Village People

f. 1977, New York, NY

Group / Disco

Part clever concept, part exaggerated camp act, the Village People were worldwide sensations during disco's heyday and keep reviving like the phoenix. Producer Jacques Morali in 1977 assembled a group designed to attract gay audiences while parodying (some claimed exploiting) that same constituency's stereotypes. Songwriters Phil Hurtt and Peter Whitehead were tabbed to compose songs with gay underpinnings, and roles and costumes were carefully selected; among them were a cowboy, biker, soldier, policeman, and construction worker complete with hard hat. The group clicked first in England with the single "San Francisco (You Got Me)" in 1977, then reaped stateside honors with "Macho Man" in 1978. "Y.M.C.A." and "In the Navy" were worldwide smashes, both peaking at number two on the pop charts. After two more successful singles, "Go West" and "Can't Stop the Music," the group's fortunes plummeted, in large part due to their participation in the ill-fated film also titled *Can't Stop the Music*. *—Ron Wynn*

Village People / 1977 / Casablanca ♦♦♦

In spite of looking like village idiots, the Village People surprised everybody with this popular four-song album. Phil Hurtt, a good friend of Thom Bell, and the writer of "I'll Be Around" arranged, and coauthored three songs. Produced by Henri Belolo and Jacques Morali (Ritchie Family) Village People exploits and promotes gay liberation, in a little over 20 minutes of music. The vocals slap you in the face, the beats nonstop, but it's hard to fully enjoy because visions of clowns dressed in every Halloween costume imaginable keep dancing in your head. The four energetic tracks: "San Francisco (You've Got Me)," "In Hollywood (Everybody Is a Star)," "Fire Island," and "Village People" practically clone each other with the lyrics the only distinguishing difference. *—Andrew Hamilton*

Cruisin' / 1978 / Casablanca ♦♦

Revved up after the success of *Macho Man*, the Jacques Morali-produced Village People unleashed their biggest ever hit upon an eager public with the November 1978 release of their third LP, *Cruisin'*. Having already become symbols of the outrageous hedonism of the disco movement, the band now thrust their high camp into the mainstream, and what was once intended to draw people to the clubs now brought an entire nation to the milieu. The band's shining, defining moment, "Y.M.C.A.," gave the Village People a number-two hit, and from late 1978 into the next year, that song was seemingly everywhere as it rampaged off the dancefloor and into middle America's living rooms. Catchy, hooky, and sing-alongable, the song tongue-in-cheek-ily espoused the many, and often surprising benefits of paying a visit to that now immortalized club/hostel. It even spawned a dance complete with calisthenic arm movements—clubbers were doing it, kids were doing it, even their parents were doing it. The only question was, did anybody actually ever listen to the lyrics? You haven't lived until you've seen your grandmother going to the Y.M.C.A. As smashing as "Y.M.C.A." was, the album, sadly, couldn't live up to the same standards, although it did hit the Top Five on the strength of the single. Whereas the Village People had turned in some quite good performances across their first two outings, the rest of this album is nothing more than light disco filler, and even the talents of lead vocalist Victor Willis didn't help the situation across the medley "The Women/I'm a Cruiser" and the dismally boring and self-explanatory "Hot Cop." Equally light, but worth one spin for kicks is the pill-popping ode "Ups and Downs." Bottom line, buy the 45 and let the rest slip through. *—Amy Hanson*

Macho Man / 1978 / Casablanca ♦♦♦

Assembled by French producer Jacques Morali, who also struck gold with the outrageous Ritchie Family, the Village People took high camp and good spirits even farther over the top with their overtly gay-oriented disco. Masters of exploitation or attraction was always the debate as the band cruised through songs that were immediate club staples during the late '70s. But despite the inevitable, and often ridiculous controversies, what is important is that this band, no matter how plastic fantastic or politically incorrect they may have appeared, still turned in some classic performances. The sextet, fronted by the talented vocalist Victor Willis, had already made a splash on the disco scene with their self-titled 1977 debut. With that LP clocking in under 30 minutes, Morali ensured that there was still room for more. One of two Village People albums to appear in 1978, *Macho Man* hit the stores in the spring to immediate success. A punchy, driving disco flanked by Willis' funk vocals marks the consistent keynote of this LP—one that was all but crushed under the dominance of "Macho Man." And OK, the costume party image was the gimmick, it was the distracting fascination that brought the band so much attention. But there are interesting moments buried here as well. "I Am What I Am" may not have been subtle, but it certainly was a well-constructed slab of groove. And as for the gospel-tinged "Sodom and Gomorrah," there's a good reason why it was buried at the end of the album. Also of note, for the preservation of history, is the throwaway "Just a Gigolo/I Ain't Got Nobody" medley. This particular coupling was devised by Louis Prima in 1956 and, of course, the classic 1985 rendering by a top-hatted and be-suited David Lee Roth is now nearly a camp classic. In terms of hot pop shenanigans, however, the lesson here is that the Village People did it first. *—Amy Hanson*

Go West / 1979 / Casablanca ✦✦
Capitalizing on the success of past glories, which included "Macho Man" and "Y.M.C.A.," Village People hoped to breach those disco peaks once more. Iconographic darlings of the discotheques, the band found themselves becoming middle America's new favorites in the wake of 1978's *Cruisin'* LP, so it was no surprise that the release of *Go West* saw the band reach the Top Ten for the second time in Spring 1979. The cheekily tongue-twisted "In the Navy," which chronicled, via disco of course, all the wonderful things that particular branch of the armed forces had to offer, not only gave humorous advertisement to seamen everywhere, but probably gave their superiors at least a pause for thought, as the endorsement fluttered down in a heap of chaps and boots, Indian feathers, and cowboy hats. The song proved a massive hit, reaching number three on the pop charts. The title track, meanwhile, weighed anchor with the full-chorused exhortation to "go west"—beckoning listeners to the beach, to the west, to the sun and spray of an unencumbered life. Innocent to its extreme, the song became a gay-club anthem and would be completely revitalized with the Pet Shop Boys' over-the-top update in 1993. Unfortunately, those two songs really are the dominant forces behind *Go West*. Even though Village People tried to rally with "Manhattan Woman," which contained some interesting, James Brown-inflected vocalizations, ultimately the rest of the songs on the LP sound like a rehash of the band's already released finest. The album's worthwhile, though, for the two aforementioned songs and the typically outrageous Technicolor cover. Cops and cowboys and bikers, oh my. *—Amy Hanson*

Live and Sleazy / 1979 / Casablanca ✦✦

Renaissance / 1981 / Rock Bottom ✦

Greatest Hits / 1988 / Rhino ✦✦✦✦✦
Rhino's *Greatest Hits* is a comprehensive overview of the Village People's biggest-hits, featuring 13 of their best-known songs, plus two bonus "disco mixes" of "Y.M.C.A." and "In the Navy." Not only are crossover hits like "Macho Man," "Go West," "Ready for the '80s" and "Can't Stop the Music" included, but so are key club hits like "Sodom and Gomorrah," "San Francisco (You've Got Me)," "My Roommate" and "Hot Cop," making it a near-definitive collection. *—Stephen Thomas Erlewine*

• **The Best of Village People** / Mar. 22, 1994 / Casablanca ✦✦✦✦✦
With an earlier, very similar Rhino anthology now out of print, Casablanca's 14-track *The Best of Village People* stands as the clear-cut choice for disco and camp fanatics who want a detailed portrait of the group's career. This collection includes both the 7-inch and 12-inch versions of their two Top Five pop hits, "Y.M.C.A." and "In the Navy," plus the 12-inch version of their other signature tune, "Macho Man." There's also a generous selection of lesser-known club hits, including their debut single, "San Francisco (You've Got Me)," "Go West," "Can't Stop the Music," and "Ready for the '80s," plus B-sides like "Key West" and "In Hollywood (Everybody Is a Star)." Self-explanatory cuts like "Fire Island" and "Hot Cop" don't really bother disguising the Village People's target audience, although the Rhino inclusion "Sodom and Gomorrah" is missing here. Even so, it's hard to imagine anyone being dissatisfied with such a generally thorough retrospective, and it's probably more than some casual fans will need in the first place. *—Steve Huey*

The Vocals

f. 1963, **db.** 1965
Group / Soul, R&B
The Vocals stayed together less than a year, but six months was spent touring with Ray Charles. They were a quartet consisting of Lamonte McLemore, a photographer; Marilyn McCoo, a recent beauty contest winner; Harry Elston; and Floyd Butler. Forming in Los Angeles, CA, in 1963, the melodious foursome got lucky with the Charles connection, signing with his Tangerine label for a single in 1964 entitled "Lonesome Mood" b/w "Look Out For Love." They also appeared with Margie Hendrix on her April 1964 Tangerine release, "Let No One Hold You" b/w "A Lover's Blues," credited as Margie Hendrix and the Vocals. Hendrix, a Raelet, previously sang with the Cookies ("Don't Say Nothing Bad About My Baby").

Problems compelled Elston and Butler to leave; they owned and operated a clothing store in Los Angeles before forming the Friends of Distinction with Jessica Cleaves and Barbara Love, scoring high on the hog with "Grazing in the Grass" and "Going in Circles." McLemore returned to photography and landed a dream job snapping bronze beauties clad in bathing suits for *Jet* magazine's centerfold; McCoo got a position at a department store. McLemore and McCoo later joined forces with Florence LaRue, a school teacher and former beauty contest winner; Ron Townsend; and Billy Davis, a gospel/soul singer from St. Louis, MO, to form the Fifth Dimension. The pop-ish sounding quintet surfaced before the Friends of Distinction and scored many pop hits including "Up, Up and Away," "One Less Bell to Answer," and "Aquarius (Let the Sunshine In)." *—Andrew Hamilton*

The Voice Masters

f. 1959
Group / Soul, R&B
The Voice Masters evolved from the Five Jets and the Five Stars and were one of the first groups that Berry Gordy used on sessions. Core members Crathman P. Spencer, Walter Gaines, and Henry Dixon were led by the dynamic leads of David Ruffin, Ty Hunter, Joe Charles aka Joe Murphy, and Lamont Dozier. Melvin Franklin's booming bass is heard on early releases, and female voices are as prominent as males on some recordings. The Five Jets recorded on Deluxe Records from 1953-1954 and released one single as the Five Dollars on Fortune Records in 1957; the Five Stars emerged in 1957, cutting at least four singles on as many labels. By 1959 they were the Voice Masters and signed to Gwen Gordy and Billy Davis' Anna Records. Anna's first two singles were by them. "Oops I'm Sorry" with "Hope and Pray" didn't do any better than the Five Jets' or Five Stars' efforts. "Needed," the second single, did a little better but not much; Melvin Franklin's powerful 14-year-old bass growl awakens like caffeine on the opening refrain. "Needed" features an Eddie Holland-ish, operatic lead.

Ty Hunter handles lead on the next two singles: "Orphan Boy" and "Everytime." A flute mocking Hunter's quivering falsetto plays a sweet melody to introduce "Everytime" featuring Hunter and credited as Ty Hunter and the Voice Masters; the floater is one of the groups' finest moments. Subsequent releases featured Lamont Dozier and David Ruffin with the Voice Masters supplying uncredited vocal help. Dozier leads "Lets Talk It Over" (1960), the song that set the foundation for Holland, Dozier, & Holland's "Darling Baby," a modest hit for the Elgins; and Ruffin's magnificent on "I'm in Love" (1961), a turbulent, gospel-inspired ballad.

When Billy Davis, aka Roquel and sometimes Tyran Carlo, left Anna to form Checkmate Records, the Voice Masters followed. The first release features Dozier on the romping "I Didn't Know," which gets better with each listen. It was billed as Lamont Dozier & the Voice Masters, and it was the last single that they received label credit. They accompanied Ty Hunter on "Memories," which is almost as crucial as "Everytime," and David Ruffin on two smokers: "Action Speaks Louder Than Words" and "Mr. Bus Driver." "Lonely Baby" was first issued on Checkmate but was licensed to Chess in 1963 to become a decent R&B hit and Hunters' biggest solo release.

Davis closed Checkmate, which like Anna was distributed by Chess, and became Chess' Artist and Repertoire Director. Spencer, Gaines, and Dixon united with Freddie Gorman, and as the Originals they hit with "Baby I'm for Real" and "The Bells"; Joe Stubbs sang with the first Originals lineup. Lamont Dozier, who previously recorded with the Romeos, allied with the Hollands (after original partner Freddie Gorman left to work for Golden World Records) to form the crack Holland-Dozier-Holland production machine. Like Dozier, Ty Hunter sang with the Romeos, soloed, joined the Glass House, then replaced C. P. Spencer in the Originals. David Ruffin, who recorded as Little David Bush, struck gold when the Temptations axed Elbridge Bryant and eased him in the lineup. The Temptations' first number-one record "My Girl" featured Ruffin's, rough, hair-raising tenor; they went on to become the world's most popular vocal group. Joe Charles later sang with Lorri Rudolph as Loe & Joe on Harvey Records. Davis left Chess in the late '70s and became a force in the commercial jingle business. Hunter died February 24, 1981. *—Andrew Hamilton*

The Voices of East Harlem

Group / Soul, Contemporary Gospel
An often stirring 20-member ensemble whose music was better suited for devotional and inspirational material than commercial R&B or soul, the Voices of East Harlem included lead vocalists Gerri Griffin and Monica Burress. Producers Leroy Hutson and Curtis Mayfield worked with the group, whose ages ranged from 12 to 21, and cut some material on the Just Sunshine label that didn't generate any chart action. But their 1973 LP, *The Voices of East Harlem*, was a superbly performed release nonetheless, and the single "Cashing In" was a cult favorite. The single "Wanted Dead or Alive" was later reissued as a 12-inch remixed cut and got some international dance attention. *—Ron Wynn*

Right on Be Free / 1970 / Elektra ✦✦✦

Brothers & Sisters / 1972 / Elektra ✦✦✦

• **The Voices of East Harlem** / 1973 / Vinyl Experience ✦✦✦✦

Can You Feel It / 1974 / Vinyl Experience ✦✦✦

Voices of Theory

Group / Urban
Heavily influenced by fellow Philadelphians Boyz II Men, Voices of Theory is an urban contemporary group that combines R&B/pop crooning with hip-hop production. All five members of the group—Mechi, James, Hector, David, and Mike G—are Latino men who grew up in North Philly, a tough area of the city that has often been compared to the South Bronx. Formed in the early 1990s, Voices got its first major break in 1993, when the quintet opened for Mariah Carey on a 12-city American tour. It was also in 1993 that Voices recorded a cover of "Why Do Fools Fall in Love" for the soundtrack to the film *Calendar Girl*. Not long after that, Voices suffered a major setback when their manager and mentor, Melvin Wallace, was murdered. But the quintet found new management and continued, and in 1997, was signed to producer Jellybean Benitez's H.O.L.A. Recordings (H.O.L.A. stands for Home of Latino Artists). Voices' self-titled debut album was released in 1998. *—Alex Henderson*

• **Voices of Theory** / 1997 / H.O.L.A. ✦✦
When this self-titled debut album came out in 1998, Voices of Theory was often described as a Latin Boyz II Men. The comparisons were inevitable—both groups came out of Philadelphia, and Boyz member Michael McCarey produced and co-wrote four tunes on the R&B/pop effort CD: "I'll Give My Love to You," "It's Been Awhile," "Wherever You Go"

and "If I Knew." In fact, Boyz II Men's influence is hard to miss even on the songs that McCarey *didn't* produce. The thing that's missing from this less-than-memorable collection of mostly ballads and slow jams is originality. Apart from some Spanish lyrics on a few tracks, there's little to distinguish Voices from countless other Boyz II Men disciples who were all over urban contemporary radio in the 1990s. *—Alex Henderson*

The Volumes

f. 1960, Detroit, MI

Group / R&B, Doo Wop

Fronted by Ed Union, the Volumes cut their only hit in 1962, "I Love You," for the tiny Chex label. The Latin-beat R&B tune was written by bass singer Ernest Newsom and manager Willie Ewing. Follow-ups on Chex and American Arts failed to click despite their soulful grooves. *—Bill Dahl*

I Love You: Golden Classics / Aug. 30, 1994 / Collectables ♦♦♦

The Collectables set *I Love You: Golden Classics* is a brief look at the Volumes' short career on the Chex label during the early '60s. Including about one-third of the group's three-dozen-track career, the set includes their only chart entry, the 1962 Top 40 hit "I Love You," along with fair period material like "Roly Poly," "Miss Silhouette," and "Angel." Most R&B one-hit wonders are best-heard on various-artist compilations, and the Volumes are a perfect example. This one *is* a cheap disc though, good for the type of fan more intrigued by average material from a certain era than the classics of any other. *—John Bush*

● **From Doo Wop to Northern Soul** / 2002 / Chex ♦♦♦♦♦

The energetic Volumes were a doo wop group in a soul era. The Detroiters' stark, uncluttered recordings have always been large among R&B/soul purists because their voices ring out loud and sweet. The 34 tracks include songs recorded on Chex, Jubilee, Old Town, American Arts, and Inferno Records. Only "The Trouble I've Seen" b/w "The Same Old Feeling," an obscure single on Impact Records, is missing from this, the most comprehensive collection of Volumes' tunes to date. Their signature clear-as-a-bell piercing falsetto lead and high-end backing fills will have your dog scratching at the door to get out of the house. But you'd be trying to doo wop and blow along with this always interesting group who spent as much time on background-vocal trappings as they did on the lead. Included here are "I Love You," the Volumes' first and biggest hit at number-22 pop; "Gotta Give Her Love," one of their better non-hits, recorded on American Arts, a small label out of Pittsburgh, PA; and "Come Back Into My Heart," on which Lamont Dozier plays drums. *—Andrew Hamilton*

The Vondells

f. 1964, **db.** 1965

Group / Soul

Lowrell Simon, Jessie Dean, Glen Murdock, William McCoy, and James Neely began as the LaVondells while all attended high school on Chicago's South Side. Simon, Murdock, and McCoy attended Philips High, and Neely and Dean, Dunbar High. By the time they debuted on Marvello Records they had dropped the "La" and were simply the Vondells. "Errand Boy" b/w "Then I'll Know" released early in 1964 didn't do much business but established them as school stars. After all, they had a record out. In July 1964, Marvello issued their second and final record "Lenore" b/w "Valentino." Both sides, like the previous single, were written by Jessie Dean, Alton Curtis, and James P. Johnson and published by Duncan & Johnson Publishing owned by Johnson and Harrison Duncan. "Lenore" was something of a local hit; it sold more than 25,000 copies but never broke outside of Chicago. The group was managed by Bill Coday who was responsible for teaming them (uncredited) with Ruby Stackhouse for one Kellmac Records release "Please Tell Me Why" b/w "Waiting" (1965). It only got a little local play and Stackhouse became Ruby Andrews who scored on Zodiac Records with "Casanova."

The Vondells disbanded when Dean was drafted. Murdock teamed with Joyce Kennedy to form a hot duet act that transformed into Mother's Finest. When Dean's tour of duty ended, Simon formed Lost Generation with his brother Fred Simon, Dean, and Larry Brownlee, the ex-lead singer of the C.O.D.'s ("Michael the Lover"). Lost Generation recorded "The Sly, Slick & the Wicked," "Talking the Teenage Language," and "Wait a Minute," among others. They disbanded because of problems with Brunswick Records, who stiffed them on royalties and claimed their name; undaunted, Lowrell Simon regrouped as Lowrell with Simon, Dean, and others and cut a series of good records in the late '70s, including "Mellow, Mellow Right On." *—Andrew Hamilton*

The Vontastics

f. 1965, **db.** 1967

Group / Soul, Chicago Soul

The Vontastics' career mirrors that of the Ideals, another Chicago group, in that each had three records that achieved some popularity outside of Chicago. They even recorded for the same label, St. Lawrence Records though the Cortland label released "Gorilla," "Mo Gorilla," and "Mo Jo Hanna," the Ideals most popular recordings. The latter, about a voodoo lady from Louisiana was first recorded by Henry Lumpkin (Motown 1962). Powered by two lead singers, Kenneth Gholar & Jose Holmes, a prolific songwriter, Bobby Lee Newsome, and Raymond Penn, the Vontastics' sound was fresh and emotional and only lacked the proper exposure. In 1965, they receive some local love with their first release "I'll Never Say Goodbye" b/w "Don't Mess Around," on Satellite Records, but few heard it outside of Chicago.

"No Love For Me" b/w "Peace of Mind," issued in October of 1965 began an encouraging time on St. Lawrence Records. While it didn't light up the charts, the follow-up "I Need You" b/w "Keep Rollin' On" (March 1966) were two equally good sides that received dual play in some cities. The next release "Day Tripper" (September 1966) is curious because the songwriter credits say Bobby Newsome, though it's the same song that John Lennon & Paul McCartney wrote. The jam became their biggest record; St. Lawrence followed with "You Can Work It Out" b/w "Never Let Our Love Grow Cold," February 1967; the A-side strutted like "Day Tripper," the B-side groove was similar but the lyrics more meaningful. Subsequent one off releases on Moonshot, Chess, and Ernest Leaner's Toddlin' Town Records didn't do much of anything and the guys left the music business. *—Andrew Hamilton*

W

Narada Michael Walden

b. Apr. 23, 1952, Kalamazoo, MI

Producer, Drums, Percussion, Synthesizer / Urban, Adult Contemporary, Disco, Dance-Pop, Soul

Drummer/songwriter/producer/vocalist Narada Michael Walden's career spans over three decades and is threaded with gold, platinum, and multi-platinum awards. He's produced and/or (co) written number one hits by Whitney Houston, Mariah Carey ("Vision of Love"), Aretha Franklin ("Freeway of Love"), and Lisa Fischer ("How Can I Ease the Pain"). His proficient drumming skills have made him a first-call session musician playing on countless recording sessions. Walden has played on all kind of sessions from rock, jazz, pop, R&B, to fusion, sharing the recording and concert stage with the likes of John McLaughlin, the Mahavishnu Orchestra (a 21-year-old Narada replaced drumming legend Billy Cobham), and Jeff Beck (his *Wired* album) to name a small few. His own career as a recording artist is showcased on Rhino's *Ecstasy's Dance: The Best of Narada Michael Walden*. Walden's eclecticism is threaded throughout his recordings in varying degrees. In the '80s, he became a Grammy-winning mega-producer: Producer of the Year in 1987, Album of the Year for the 1993 movie soundtrack *The Bodyguard* (Narada Michael Walden, producer), and the Song of the Year award in 1985 for writing Aretha Franklin's "Freeway of Love." The song helped the Queen of Soul land her first platinum album. Walden was named one of the Top Ten Producers With the Most Number One Hits by *Billboard* magazine. Narada produced the Temptations' "Stay," the group's first number one record in 25 years from their platinum-plus Grammy-nominated *Phoenix Rising*. He also produced tracks for their follow-up album, *Ear-Resistable* issued by Motown/Universal on May 16, 2000.

Born April 23, 1952, in Kalamazoo, MI, Walden was given the name Narada by guru Sri Chinmoy. After college graduation, he trekked to Miami, FL, playing in various rock bands. Signing with Atlantic Records, his debut album, *Garden of Love Light*, included the midtempo "Delightful," which charted at number-81 R&B in spring 1977. His next LP, *I Cry, I Smile*, boasted the sweet "So Long" and the radio-aired LP tracks the languid "I Need Your Love," the delicious "I Remember," and the charming "Better Man." Even though these top-notch tracks received airplay in Chicago and other markets, other than "Better Man," none were released as singles. Instead, the label picked "Soulbird" and "Manago Bop," which worked well as album tracks, but not singles.

The Awakening proved to be his breakthrough album, going to number-15 R&B in spring 1979 on the strength of the brassy "I Don't Want Nobody Else (To Dance With You)." Awakening radio-aired LP tracks were the airy "Listen to Me" and the jubilant album opener "Love Me Only" (also arranged by Patrick Adams). *Awakening* also featured top session bassist Keni Burke, formerly of the Five Stairsteps and best known for his own "Risin' to the Top."

His second highest charting single, "I Shoulda Loved Ya," hit number-four R&B in late 1979. It was on his *The Dance of Life* (number-nine R&B, late 1979), which included the gentle ballad "Why Did You Turn Me On." "You're #1" and "Summer Lady" were both on his *Confidence* LP from summer 1982. Walden's cover of the Four Tops' "Reach Out I'll Be There," "Reach Out," a huge dance hit, was listed on *Looking at You, Looking at Me*, which charted in spring 1983. Switching to Warner Bros., his duet with Patti Austin, the Motown-ish pop confection, "Gimme Gimme Gimme," issued as Narada Michael Walden with Patti Austin, went to number-39 R&B in early 1985 and was listed on his *The Nature of Things* album. His single "Divine Emotions" on the Warner Bros. imprint Reprise Records appeared in the Michael J. Fox movie *Bright Lights, Big City*. *The Divine Emotion* LP included the charting mellow single "Wild Thing" and the smooth, chugging, radio-aired LP track "That's the Way That I Feel About Cha." His 1995 Toshiba/EMI album was titled *Sending Love to Everyone*.

In late 1985, Walden opened Tarpan Studios, a state-of-the-art recording studio located near San Francisco. Walden's work appears on releases by Stacy Lattisaw ("Let Be Your Angel"), Al Green ("Your Heart's in Good Hands"), Shanice Wilson ("I Love Your Smile," "I Hate to Be Lonely"), Ray Charles, Diana Ross, George Michael, Wild Orchid, Tevin Campbell, Angela Bofill, Diana Ross, MyTown, Steve Winwood, Phaze II, Regina Belle-Passion ("Baby Come to Me"), Andy Vargas, Debelah Morgan, Jai, Jermaine Stewart ("We Don't Have to Take Our Clothes Off"), Natalie Cole ("Good to Be Back"), Clarence Clemons, Puff Johnson, Eddie Murphy ("Put Your Mouth on Me"), and Carl Carlton ("The Bad CC"), among many many others.

Other Narada Michael Walden-related releases are Stacy Lattisaw and Johnny Gill (*Perfect Combination*), Lisa Fischer (*So Intense*), and the movie soundtracks to *Beverly Hills Cop II, Perfect, Waiting to Exhale, License to Kill, The Bodyguard, Jason's Lyric, 9 1/2 Weeks, Crooklyn, Free Willy*, and *The Associate*. *—Ed Hogan*

Garden of Love Light / May 1977 / Atlantic ✦✦

I Cry, I Smile / 1978 / Atlantic ✦✦✦

Awakening / 1979 / Atlantic ✦✦

On *Awakening*, Narada Michael Walden placed aside the jazz fusion leanings of his early albums in favor of a more radio-friendly sound. The strategy worked, with Walden having his first Top Ten R&B single, "I Don't Want Nobody Else (To Dance With You)," which also charted number 47 on the pop charts in early 1979 and *Awakening* breaking into the R&B Top 15. The follow-up single, the midtempo groover "Give Your Love a Chance" featured grand arrangements by Patrick Adams. Walden displays his hyperkinetic drumming skills on "They Want the Feeling." Other standouts are "Love Me Only," the beautiful radio-aired album track "Listen to Me," and the tender "Will You Ever Know." *—Ed Hogan*

The Dance of Life / 1979 / Atlantic ✦✦

Narada Michael Walden had seen the light, and it was a swirling disco ball. The multi-talented Michigan native saw that the way to the top of the charts was by way of the dancefloor. For *The Dance of Life*, the follow-up LP to his *Awakening* ("I Don't Want Nobody Else (To Dance With You)"), Walden square took aim at "dancing feet." The result was that the effervescent "I Shoulda Loved Ya" went to number four on the R&B charts and mid-charted pop in late 1979, while the album broke the R&B Top Ten. Its follow-up was the bright, brassy Top 40 R&B hit "Tonight I'm Alright." Other highlights are the acid rock-ish "You're Soo Good," "Crazy for Ya," "Carry On," and the wistful ballad "Why Did You Turn Me On." *—Ed Hogan*

Victory / 1980 / Atlantic ✦✦

The Nature of Things / 1985 / Warner Bros. ✦✦

For *The Nature of Things*, Michigan native Narada Michael Walden went back to his musical roots when he lent a strong Motown vibe to "Gimme Gimme Gimme," his rousing duet with Patti Austin, which recalls the romantic upbeat hits of Marvin Gaye & Tammi Terrell. It was a Top 40 R&B hit in the spring of 1985. That same year, the '60s Motown sound worked very well for producer Walden and singer Aretha Franklin on "Freeway of Love," a Top Three R&B/pop smash from *Who's Zoomin' Who?* Other standouts are the airy "High Above the Clouds" and the hopeful, reggae-ish "Wear Your Love." Both "Gimme Gimme Gimme" and "High Above the Clouds" appear on Rhino's *Ecstasy's Dance: The Best of Narada Michael Walden*. *—Ed Hogan*

● **Ecstasy's Dance: The Best of Narada Michael Walden** / Nov. 19, 1996 / Rhino ✦✦✦

There's no denying Narada Michael Walden's drumming chops, but he's also a very talented hitmaker as well. Since the '70s, he's scored several R&B hits as a solo artist, and is a top session musician to this day. He's played with the best (Jeff Beck, Kenny G, Mariah Carey, and Aretha Franklin) and has dabbled in just about every musical form—dance, rock, fusion, soul, etc. Rhino has compiled the best of Walden's solo work, entitled *Ecstasy's Dance: The Best of Narada Michael Walden*, which showcases his many talents. Highlights include his two Top Ten R&B hits, "I Don't Want Nobody Else (To Dance With You)" and "I Shoulda Loved Ya," as well as the outstanding album tracks "Delightful" and "The Awakening." Other minor hits are also represented, such as "The Real Thang," "Divine Emotions," and a disco-fied version of the Holland-Dozier-Holland classic "Reach Out." Also included are nicely assembled and informative liner notes, as well as a message from Walden himself. *—Greg Prato*

Junior Walker (Autry DeWalt Mixon)

b. Jun. 14, 1931, Blytheville, AR, **d.** Nov. 23, 1995, Battle Creek, MI

Saxophone, Vocals / Motown, Soul, Pop-Soul, Rock & Roll

Motown's skilled but mostly anonymous instrumentalists very rarely stepped out on their own. The lone exception to the rule was tenor saxman Junior Walker, whose rough-and-ready, old-school R&B was a marked contrast with the label's typically smooth, polished product. Walker's squealing gutbucket style was inspired by jump blues and early R&B, particularly players like Louis Jordan, Earl Bostic, and Illinois Jacquet. Possessed of a raspy, untrained voice, Walker's singing nonetheless complemented the energy of his sax playing, and he cut a wealth of danceable, party-hearty R&B for Motown during his heyday in the second half of the '60s.

Junior Walker was born Autry DeWalt II on June 14, 1931 (even though Motown gave his birthdate as 1942) in Blytheville, AR. (Some accounts list his birth name as Oscar G. Mixon, which was then changed at some point during his early childhood.) DeWalt grew up in South Bend, IN, and began playing the saxophone in high school; he was soon performing in local jazz and R&B clubs with his first band, the Jumping Jacks, under the name Junior Walker. He next joined a trio led by drummer Billy "Stix" Nicks, which also featured organist Fred Patton; they soon added backing vocalist and guitarist Willie Woods, and played around northern Indiana and southern Michigan. Walker took over the group after Nicks joined the Army; in the late '50s, he relocated to Battle Creek, MI, and formed a band billed as Junior Walker & the All-Stars. Initially, they featured Patton, Woods, and drummer Tony Washington; Patton was later replaced by Victor Thomas, and Washington by Jack Douglas and, finally, James Graves. The All-Stars continued to play around the area, and took up a residency in Battle Creek's El Grotto club. There they were discovered by singer Johnny Bristol, who recommended them to his friend, ex-Moonglow

Harvey Fuqua. Fuqua signed the group to his Harvey label in 1961; they made their first recordings in 1962, and the following year Fuqua's labels were absorbed by Motown. Walker & the All-Stars ended up on their Soul subsidiary, debuting for the label in 1964. In early 1965, they scored their first big hit with the dance tune "Shotgun," which marked Walker's vocal debut; in fact, the only reason he sang the song was that the vocalist he'd hired didn't show up for the session, and he was somewhat flabbergasted by the label's decision to leave his vocal intact. Berry Gordy's instincts proved right, however, when "Shotgun" topped the R&B charts and hit the pop Top Five. A steady stream of mostly instrumental R&B chart hits followed, including "Do the Boomerang," "Shake and Fingerpop," and "How Sweet It Is (To Be Loved by You)" (Walker was, naturally, encouraged to record instrumental versions of Motown hits). In 1966, Graves left and was replaced by old cohort Billy "Stix" Nicks, and Walker's hits continued apace with tunes like "I'm a Road Runner" and "Pucker Up Buttercup." Toward the end of the '60s, seeking to diversify their approach, the All-Stars began recording more ballad material, complete with string arrangements and Walker vocals. That approach resulted in the group's second Top Five pop hit, the R&B number one "What Does It Take (To Win Your Love)," which helped refuel Walker's career. He landed several more R&B Top Ten hits over the next few years, with the last coming in 1972.

Walker resurfaced as a solo artist during the disco era, working with producer Brian Holland beginning in 1976 with the single "Hot Shot"; a pair of albums followed. In 1979, Walker joined up with another former Motown mainstay in 1979, signing with producer Norman Whitfield's Whitfield label, though without much success. Walker returned to the spotlight in 1981 with a well-publicized (and well-executed) guest solo on Foreigner's Top Five hit "Urgent." Two years later, he re-signed with Motown and recorded *Blow the House Down*; by that time, his melodic style was being absorbed into a new generation of R&B-flavored jazz instrumentalists. Walker continued to tour through the '80s and '90s, sometimes with his son Autry DeWalt III playing drums. Unfortunately, in 1993 his activities were severely curtailed by cancer, which claimed his life on November 23, 1995. In the wake of his death, Billy "Stix" Nicks continued to tour with a version of the All-Stars. *—Steve Huey*

Shotgun / 1965 / Motown ✦✦✦✦✦

Junior Walker's debut remains highly explosive decades after it first detonated. The seductive "Cleo's Mood" and the syncopated "Cleo's Back" reveals a musical, funky fascination with a fickle chick name Cleo. On "Shotgun" an opening gun blast grabs your attention. Junior's gritty vocal alternates leads with his torrid tenor sax play. He kicks it up another notch on "Shake and Fingerpop," the screeching sax and the opening lyrics are hookers: Put on your wig woman, we're going out to shake and fingerpop. The swaying "Do the Boomerang" finds Walker relaxed and shadowed by All Star, Willie Woods on vocals. The biggest surprise: Holland-Dozier-Holland's "I'm a Road Runner"; on paper, the collaboration seems ridiculous, but in the studio the combo created industrial strength soul. An uncredited baritone sax player plays soulful low riffs countering Junior's sharper, more emphatic sax squeals. With so much going on, "Shoot Your Shot" got overlooked by many, and that's too bad; it's a dancer, with instructions, featuring Walker's tenor blowing on top an organ flavored rhythm bed. Only his greatest hits' compilations and *Road Runner* reign supreme over this scorcher. *—Andrew Hamilton*

Roadrunner / 1966 / Motown ✦✦✦✦✦

Motown had to reissue this one. Junior Walker's *Shotgun* LP failed to crack *Billboard*'s Top 100 albums, despite being one of Motown's finest releases. This does better, number 64 but still failed to obtain the lofty rungs it should have. The three rockers: "Road Runner," and exciting updates of Marvin Gaye's "How Sweet It Is," and Barrett Strong's "Money" should have punted this sucker into the Top 20, but for some reason Walker didn't get the type of promotion accorded other Motown artists. Four hits exploded from this LP, the three mentioned, and "Pucker Up Buttercup." On the softer side, "Ame Cherie (Soul Darling)" is one of Junior's sweetest instrumentals. But, if you like the All-Stars' harder sound, a remake of Harvey Fuqua's "Anyway You Wanna," "Last Call," and "Baby You Know It Ain't Right" are full of Junior's earthy vocals and sax assaults. *—Andrew Hamilton*

Soul Session / 1966 / Soul ✦✦✦

Released to ride "Shotgun"'s back *Soul Session* is uncut, polyunsaturated Junior Walker & the All-Stars waxed prior to Motown on Harvey Fuqua's Harvey label. The original line up consisted of Junior Walker, Willie Woods (bass), Vic Thomas (organ), and Billy Nix (drums). Motown session players' don't play behind Junior on these tracks like they do on his Motown recordings. Motown rarely used the All-Stars in the studio. And no vocals. Sorry! Junior didn't display his vocal prowess until "Shotgun." "Brainwasher" the groups' second Harvey single is an upbeat groove driven by Walker's tenor and Thomas' impressive organ, Junior excitedly shouts "wind it up" near the end. Jock's flipped it, however, for the seductive "Cleo's Mood." "Good Rockin'" their third and final Harvey single is aggressive, roadhouse R&B. Motown omitted their Harvey debut "Twist Lackawanna" but stuck it on another album. *Soul Session*'s loaded with tight grooves composed mostly by Walker, with some collaboration with Willie Woods. Vic Thomas contributed "Hewbie Steps Out" and Fuqua provides "Three Four Three," and "Decidedly." *—Andrew Hamilton*

Live / Jan. 1967 / Soul ✦✦✦

Without the studio reverb, the background singers, and the ability to reset if you suck, Junior Walker still holds his own live. The songs with vocals suffer, since Junior isn't a singer. He never wanted to sing on his records anyway; the guy scheduled to sing "Shotgun" (Junior's first recorded vocal) didn't show, so Berry Gordy had Walker chant the lyrics. "I'm a Road Runner" and "Shotgun" are shells of the studio versions, but when he blows that big tenor sax, it doesn't matter whether he's a singer or not. Junior's sax riffs, like B.B. King's guitar licks, mesmerize. Blowing hard or sweet, he manages to tantalize the ears with arresting notes sequenced and bent as only he can. His rendition of "Moonlight in Vermont" is simply beautiful; Junior shows he got skills. The funky "Cleo's Back" displays Walker's sax at its sassiest. Motown's keyboardist Earl Van Dyke provides the finale, a rocking "Heartbeat"; stepping up the tempo considerably, Earl pumped that Hammond like a crazy man—it's amazing he didn't break one of the pedals. *—Andrew Hamilton*

Gotta Hold on to This Feeling / 1969 / Motown ✦✦✦✦✦

Initially, Motown released this as *What Does It Take to Win Your Love*, then reissued it as *Gotta Hold on to This Feeling* when the love-struck single of the same name started its chart ascension. "What Does It Take" originally appeared on the *Home Cooking* album, but Motown stuck it here, along with other previously released tracks. "Gotta Hold on to This Feeling" features lovely, flowing backing voices, and a sincere vocal from Walker. The only new songs are two remakes, the lovely "These Eyes," and "Proud Mary," and two in-house productions: "I Got to Find a Way to Win Maria Back," and "Clinging to the Thought That She's Coming Back." Vintage Walker "How Sweet It Is (to be Loved by You)," "Cleo's Mood," "Hot Cha," and "Sweet Soul" spices this potent collection. *—Andrew Hamilton*

Home Cookin' / 1969 / Motown ✦✦✦

This is a solid, mostly uptempo album, featuring some of his biggest late-'60s hits: "What Does It Take (To Win Your Love)," "Come See About Me," and "Hip City." Among the other tracks, the bittersweet instrumental "Sweet Soul" is a highlight. As with many Motown albums, the most noteworthy tracks are featured on best-of compilations. *—Richie Unterberger*

A Gasss / 1970 / Soul ✦✦✦✦

There's nothing weak or mediocre about Junior Walker's albums—all have a high standard and feature his winning gusto sax screams and sauced vocals. He cut some of the tightest tracks laid at Motown's Studio A—aka the Snake Pit. The insidious "Do You See My Love for You Growing" explodes for more than three blasting minutes. His deep-fried update of Stevie Wonder's "I Was Made to Love Her" is off the hook and as gritty as sandpaper. He dusts off Johnny Bristol & Jackey Beavers' "Carry Your Own Load," outshining the duo's nondescript original. On Neil Diamond's "Holy, Holy," Walker's sax cries like a mourning dog. "Shut Up, Don't Interrupt Me" didn't endear Junior to women libbers, but "Groove and Move" elevated his funk/psychedelic stock. *—Andrew Hamilton*

Moody Jr. / 1971 / Soul ✦✦✦✦

A less intense Junior Walker still makes splendid music on a collection of updates salted with some new sides. The sax man remakes "Way Back Home," originally done by the Crusaders; Gladys Knight & Johnny Bristol wrote lyrics for Wilton Felder's composition: Walker's version did a respectable number-24 R&B, and number-52 Pop. "Walk in the Night" with its stalking beat and diverse rhythms scaled to number-ten R&B and number-46 Pop, his last substantial release on Motown. The psychedelic-influenced "Groove Thang" went to number-46 R&B, but missed the bus to the Pop chart, despite a tight groove, and tough, rough neck runs from Junior over a def track. Junior's sax measures up to the vocals on the original versions of "I Don't Want to Do Wrong," popularized by Gladys Knight & the Pips, and the Jackson Five's "Never Can Say Goodbye." *—Andrew Hamilton*

Rainbow Funk / 1971 / Soul ✦✦✦

"Take Me Girl I'm Ready" has Junior Walker singing more lyrics than he probably cared to remember, the midtempo jaunt didn't crack the Pop Top 40, but did scoot to number 18 on *Billboard*'s R&B chart. A heavier, funkier groove rocks "Right on Brothers and Sisters" but Motown hid it on the back of "Take Me Girl," a waste of an obvious A-side. Walker sounds like a country preacher on the Crusaders' "Way Back Home" and does an adequate job delivering Johnny Bristol and Gladys Knight lyrics. "Psychedelic Shack" gets a blistering update, and he sounds sweet as sugar on a remake of the Velvelettes' "These Things Will Keep Me Loving You." A rare Walker LP in that he sings more than he plays. *—Andrew Hamilton*

Peace & Understanding Is Hard to Find / 1973 / Soul ✦✦✦

This ranks as one of Junior Walker's poorest selling albums. "Gimme That Beat, " bubbly beat and all, only charted at number-101 Pop and number-50 R&B. However, it exceeded "I Don't Need No Reason, " and "Peace and Understanding"—both non charting singles. Motown wrings all it can from "I Don't Need No Reason, " done smooth and jazzy by Walker, it also reigns supreme on the Miracles underrated *Renaissance* album. "Peace and Understanding" has a weird off-the-beat bass drum hit that's up front in the mix. He does credible remakes of Carole King & Johnny Nash's "It's Too Late, " and "I Can See Clearly Now." The spirited "Soul Clappin'" appeared as the B-side on both "Peace and Understanding," and "I'm So Glad" from the *Hot Shot* album. *—Andrew Hamilton*

Sax Appeal / 1976 / Soul ✦✦✦

Smooth / 1978 / Soul ✦✦

Back Street Boogie / 1979 / Whitfield ✦✦

Blow the House Down / 1983 / Motown ✦✦✦

Junior Walker's signifying sax cries are showcased on eight explosive tracks. Walker's songs are usually about dancing or romance, but these deal with sex and lust. Titles like "Sexpot," "Ball Baby," and "In and Out" are self-explanatory. *—Andrew Hamilton*

Nothing But Soul: The Singles / 1994 / Motown ✦✦✦✦✦

This 40-song double CD includes virtually every Walker track of significance, and then some. Walker is a great player and hits a great groove, but that groove can get tiring over the course of several dozen tracks, especially the similar-sounding early instrumental cuts. Also, the post-'60s selections that take up much of disc two are hampered by material that is inferior to the best output of his '60s heyday. It has excellent package and liner notes, but most listeners should be satisfied with the single-disc *Greatest Hits*, leaving this one for the collectors and specialists. *—Richie Unterberger*

● **The Ultimate Collection** / Oct. 7, 1997 / Motown ✦✦✦✦✦
The Ultimate Collection nearly lives up to its billing, featuring 25 tracks on a single disc, including all of Junior Walker & the All-Stars' Top Ten pop and R&B hits ("Shotgun," "Do the Boomerang," "Shake and Fingerpop," "Cleo's Back," "(I'm A) Road Runner," "How Sweet It Is (To Be Loved By You)," "Come See About Me," "Hip City, Pt. 2," "What Does It Take (To Win Your Love)," "These Eyes," "Gotta Hold on to This Feeling," "Do You See My Love (For You Growing)," "Walk in the Night"). For most casual fans, those who just want the hits, this will be the definitive collection. *—Stephen Thomas Erlewine*

Ronnie Walker

Vocals / Soul
Between 1966 and 1975, Philadelphia soul singer Ronnie Walker released nine singles on almost as many labels. In the late '60s, a couple of his singles—1967's "Really, Really Love You" and 1969's "It's a Good Feelin'"—did well enough locally to make the charts of Philadelphia soul radio stations, without making noise on a national level. Like a number of other male Philly soul singers of the time, Walker, still in his teens when he began making records, had a rich falsetto voice. The records, like many other Philadelphia soul singles famous and obscure, boasted full, sumptuous production, and echoing doo wop in some aspects of the harmonies and song construction. However, they were quite modern in the textural arrangements, combining horns, strings, organs, female backup singers, and such in a polished manner. His singles were not top-level Philly soul in the manner of Brenda & the Tabulations, the Delfonics, Eddie Holman, and so on, but were respectable, and worth finding by fans of the aforementioned artists who want more in the same vein.

All but one of the songs from Walker's seven 1966-1972 singles, along with ten previously unreleased songs, were issued by Philly Archives on the 2000 CD *Someday*. Walker, incidentally, also wrote or co-wrote songs that were recorded by several other artists, ranging from a 1966 single by the Agents to some material in the late '70s, including one song by Esther Phillips. His most famous songwriting credit, however, is attached to a song that has little to do with his own Philly soul recordings: Charo's "Cuchi Cuchi." *—Richie Unterberger*

● **Someday** / Oct. 14, 2000 / Philly Archives ✦✦✦
Someday includes all but one of the songs on the seven singles released between 1966-1972 by the obscure Philly soul vocalist (somehow the 1970 cut "Didn't We" went missing), padded with ten previously unreleased tunes. Walker was a solid falsetto singer, and his work on these sides is all the more impressive considering he was still of high school age when he made his first 45. It's also impressive that he wrote or co-wrote most of the tracks on the CD, yet in the end it's just good journeyman Philadelphia soul. That's a good thing, not a mediocre thing, but you can't really say that any of the numbers were so outstanding that they should have demanded national attention. Walker did vary the program to include uptempo sweet soul as well as ballads. But it was the slow and sad tunes on which he was at his best, particularly the local 1967 hit "Really, Really Love You" and "I'm Saying Goodbye," which have that sad, late-night smoochy vibe so peculiar to Philadelphia soul of the era. On the later sides, he got into a slightly slicker, more groove-oriented direction that could strongly echo Motown; it's easy to imagine Smokey Robinson doing some of this as album filler, for instance, and "Now That You're Gone" sounds like a late-'60s Supremes cut with a high-pitched male singer. This review might be making the disc sound less attractive than it is; although Walker's not a standout, this is certainly above average by the standards of little-known soul from the time being excavated for the collector's market. *—Richie Unterberger*

The Wallace Brothers

f. 1963, **db.** 1968
Group / Soul, Funk
Cleveland Warnock gave the Wallace Brothers their start but can't remember all the members' names. But that's understandable: Warnock is 71 years old and still works in building and construction while caring for a brother afflicted with Alzheimer's. It didn't help that his house caught fire some years ago, destroying master recordings, pictures, and other mementoes. A guy named Wallace, no kin to the brothers, brought the six-piece band to Warnock's attention in 1963. Promoted as a duet, the Wallace Brothers were actually a six-man band with cousins John Simon and Ervin Wallace on lead vocals. Other Wallaces, Cooky and Earnest, played in the band. Calling the outfit ragtag is being kind. Simon doubled on a saxophone that was in such bad shape that Warnock had to have it repaired. The drummer supported his drum kit with broomsticks. Ervin played the guitar, and Earnest the organ.

Warnock wrote songs with Billy Bardon in the '40s and '50s for movie cowboy Jimmy Wakely, and never strayed far from the music business. He liked the Wallace Brothers and their potential. Simon in particular had a flair for showmanship, and was handsome and smart. Their members ranged from 14 to 16 years of age and all attended Archer High School in Atlanta. Warnock transported them from Atlanta to his East Point, GA, home for basement rehearsals. "Faith" b/w "I'll Let Nothing Separate Me," written by Earnest, was their first single. The words are biblical but the omission of the Lord's name made them secular. Cleveland's newly founded Royal label launched the Wallace Brothers in 1963. A copy of "Faith" on Royal Records is a nice collector's item. Now recording artists, the Wallace Brothers stepped up their gigging. Nashville disc jockey John R. Richbourg of WLAC played "Faith" on his popular radio program and generated some interest. A deal was struck with Russell Sims, and subsequent copies of "Faith" and the Wallace Brothers' future recordings bore the Sims Records logo. Warnock received percentage points from Sims and co-publishing rights to the Wallace Brothers' songs. With Richbourg touting "Faith," many R&B stations east of the Mason-Dixon line added the single to their rotations.

Their second single, "Precious Words" b/w "You're Mine," released in the spring of 1964, opened more doors. It spent six weeks on the *Cash Box* black music survey, but never climbed higher than number 31. Claudia Robinson, a blue-eyed soul singer/writer listed as Claud Robinson by B.M.I., wrote the song. Cleveland managed Claudia, who sung in a female group when he met her. He took her to Nashville, but nothing happened for her except the few songs she composed for the Wallace Brothers.

The Wallace Brothers' last gem was their third single, "Lover's Prayer." Released in the fall of 1964, it squeaked into *Billboard*'s Hot 100, stopping at number 97. At the time, *Billboard* didn't have a black music survey, but the record did make the *Cash Box* black survey. Written by Earnest and Cooky Wallace, it followed the same format as the previous singles, two-part harmonies sung over a simple rhythm bed, accented by a rolling organ. While nothing hit with much authority, their crude recordings were added to R&B play lists in the South and the North. Sims released their only LP, *Soul, Soul and More Soul*, in 1965. Sims took them to Muscle Shoals, AL's famed Fame Studios to cut additional tracks for the album, which included both sides of the first three singles. Sims Records released one more song off the album in 1965, but "One Way Affair" b/w "Go on Girl" sunk without a trace. Two additional singles issued in 1966, "I'll Stay Aside" and "No More," added to the doldrums.

The United Kingdom division of Sue Records issued three Wallace Brothers singles, with the last being "I'll Step Aside," in 1967; Sue also dropped a compilation album of Wallace Brothers tracks called *Soul Connection* in 1968. Back in the States, Russell Sims issued the last Wallace Brothers single, "Thanks a Lot," on Sims in 1967. When it bombed, Sims and the band parted ways. They signed with Jewel Records in 1968, releasing three singles that 99.9 percent of the world's population have yet to hear. Simon joined the Naturals, who enjoyed one release on Calla Records, "I Can't Share You"; they faded when Calla's owner, Nate McCalla, was murdered at his home in Florida.

According to Warlock, the Wallace Brothers' biggest problem was their mom, who at one time inked them to six different contracts. Each time she signed them to a production or record company she received money. This led to contractual problems, and hard feelings which contributed to the group's demise. *—Andrew Hamilton*

Soul, Soul and More Soul / 1965 / Sims ✦✦✦
The Wallace Brothers had two records that achieved a fair amount of air play on Southern, Eastern and Midwestern R&B stations: *Faith* and *A Lovers Prayer*. Both were recorded on primitive equipment (sounds like two-track to me) and featured two part harmony leads. Inspired by gospel influences, the innocent, down-to-earth lyrics and delivery overcame the skimpy instrumentation and unsophisticated equipment. "Precious Words" is similar to the their two hits, but didn't do quite as well, I guess the formula had played out. Lovers of simple, heartfelt soul will love this collection, there's nothing jive or slick about the Wallace Brothers, they're the real deal, and this recording accomplished in Florence, AL, at the famous Fame Recording Studios attests to that. *—Andrew Hamilton*

● **Lover's Prayer: Their Complete Sims Recordings** / Feb. 27, 1996 / Excello ✦✦✦✦✦

The Wanderers

f. 1952
Group / Doo Wop, R&B
The Wanderers were a popular East Coast doo wop group who went through numerous name changes during their decade-long career, and despite various label-related shuffling and stylistic changes, national success eluded them at each turn. They are best known for their cover material, and had minor East Coast hits with "For Your Love" and "Thinking of You." They began their career in 1952 as the Barons. The original group members—Ray Pollard (lead), Frank Joyner (tenor), Robert Yarbrough (baritone), and Sheppard "Shep" Grant (bass)—came to the attention of the Newark, NJ-based Savoy Records and were signed to a recording contract in mid-October, 1953. Their first release was "Hey Mae Ethel," which earned enough airplay in the New York area to attract booking agents who began to get them regular appearances in clubs, including an opening slot for Big Maybelle (who was already waxing huge R&B hits for Columbia's OKeh subsidiary) at Harlem's Club Baby Grand. The group then went on tour and Savoy issued a single by Dolly Cooper, "Love Can Be Blind," which featured their backing vocals. No further Barons singles were issued, however.

By the middle of 1954, the group had left Savoy and were signed to Decca Records. For a time, they were calling themselves the Larks (not to be confused with either the Eugene Mumford-led gospel act nor the L.A.-based Don Julian-led group from the early '60s). They ultimately decided there were too many bird-named groups, and changed their name to the Singing Wanderers for the release of a new single in July, "Say Hey Willie Mays." The single was an obvious attempt to gain a new audience by singing about the great baseball player then making news, but it didn't help much. Their follow-up, "Three Roses," fared little better. Meanwhile, the group was still performing strong, appearing with non-R&B acts and even making the rounds of TV shows like *Ed Sullivan's Toast of the Town* in 1955.

By 1957, the group—now simply called the Wanderers—began releasing singles on the Onyx label. They tried broadening their material, even recording a pop single called "Thinking of You," which was already familiar to New Yorkers as the Honeydreamers had recorded it as the theme song to Brad Phillips' radio show *Battle Royal*. The audience response to the Wanderers' version provided them with some hope and began to clearly define the outlines of a smooth pop vocal career. Unfortunately, Onyx was then absorbed by the larger major MGM, and so they moved over to Orbit Records, a label run by Onyx's Jerry Winston. That label changed names a month later (in April of 1958) because of the proliferation of small labels using the name Orbit, becoming Cub Records.

The first release on Cub was "Teenaged Quarrel" (it had been issued on Orbit, then withdrawn, making it a rare 45 today). Unfortunately, the single failed to connect, as did further efforts from the group throughout the rest of the '50s. By 1961, the group had been performing for nearly a decade without much success outside the East Coast. They went through another stylistic change to keep with the times, focusing on a more commercial R&B sound for their cover of Ed Townsend's 1957 classic ballad "For Your Love." The single rose up the national pop charts in the summer of 1961 and was a favorite of East Coast vocal group fans. The follow-up—a ballad version of Frank Sinatra's early '40s hit "I'll Never Smile Again"—failed to connect, however. Their last effort, an original called "Somebody Else's Sweetheart" performed well and moved up the charts. Unfortunately, once again, the group had been switched by the successful Cub over to their parent label, which was also MGM, who failed to promote the group. The were eventually dropped by MGM in 1962.

Not to be undone just yet, the Wanderers then signed to the United Artists label, who issued two singles by the group, 1962's "After He Breaks Your Heart" and 1963's "You Can't Run Away From Me," but neither did well and they were soon dropped from UA. The Wanderers continued to perform in the Northeastern U.S. until lead vocalist Ray Pollard landed a role in the Broadway musical *Purlie*. He dropped out of the group, who disbanded soon thereafter. After the musical ran its course, Pollard continued to make club appearances as a solo artist, performing in a wide variety of styles. —*Bryan Thomas*

● **The Best of the Wanderers** / Onyx ✦✦✦✦✦

Dexter Wansel

b. Philadelphia, PA

Keyboards, Synthesizer, Producer / Urban, Soul

Keyboardist/arranger/producer/recording artist Dexter Wansel can be heard throughout the catalog of Kenneth Gamble & Leon Huff's Philadelphia International Records. His skills can be heard on non-PIR sides like Jermaine Jackson's "Where Are You Now" from his gold LP *Let's Get Serious* and "Tonight" from Junior's *Acquired Taste* LP. His frequent songwriting partners were Cynthia Biggs, Bunny Sigler, and T. Life. A synth pioneer, Wansel's first LP arranging assignment was several tracks on Carl Carlton's 1975 LP, *I Wanna Be With You*, produced by Bunny Sigler. A Biggs/Wansel song, "The Sweetest Pain," a duet between Wansel and Jean Carn, originally a 1979 single from Wansel's *Time Is Slipping Away* LP, was a popular radio-aired LP from Loose Ends' *Zagora* LP. Two of Carn's LPs, *When I Find You Love* (entirely produced by Wansel) and *Sweet and Wonderful*, and *Jean Carn* and *Happy to Be With You* were issued on a two-album single CD by U.K. label Westside Records in early 1999.

When Wansel was 12 years old, he got the job of a gofer for the Uptown Theater in Philadelphia, going to get sandwiches and clothes out of the cleaners for the various acts that performed at the venue like Stevie Wonder and Patti LaBelle. Many years later, Wansel would co-write a number-one R&B hit for LaBelle. In 1975, Wansel met Kenneth Gamble & Leon Huff when he was a member of a band called Yellow Sunshine, which also boasted guitarist Roland Chambers who would later become a part of MFSB, the house band for Gamble & Huff's Philadelphia International Records. Becoming a part of the staff creative collective, Wansel began arranging, playing keyboards, and writing songs for the label's acts including the O'Jays, Teddy Pendergrass, and the Intruders, among others.

When Patti LaBelle signed with PIR, she recorded Wansel's "Shoot Him on Sight," a song Wansel intended for Jackson Browne, on her 1981 album *The Spirit's in It*. A song Wansel co-wrote with Kenneth Gamble and Cynthia Biggs, the lovely unrequited love ballad "If Only You Knew," held the number-one R&B spot for four weeks in early 1984. It was on her *I'm in Love Again* LP, which went gold, hitting number-four R&B.

A partial list of Wansel-associated sides would include Jean Carn's popular radio-aired LP tracks "I'm in Love Once Again," "You Are All I Need" (music by Instant Funk), "Where Did You Ever Go," "Free Love," and the dance classic "Give It Up"; Shirley Jones' "Last Night I Needed Somebody" and "She Knew About Me"; The Jacksons' "Keep on Dancin'," "Living Together," "Do What You Wanna Do," and "Jump for Joy"; The Stylistics' "Hurry Up This Way Again,"; keyboardist Patrice Rushen covered "Hurry Up This Way Again"; The O'Jays' dreamy ballad "I Really Need You Now"; Phyllis Hyman's radio-aired track "Living All Alone"; The Jones Girls' "We're a Melody", the exotic "Nights Over Egypt," "Love Don't Ever Say Goodbye," and "Why You Wanna Do That to Me"; Archie Bell and the Drells' "Old People"; and Evelyn "Champagne" King's "Till I Come Off the Road" and the radio-aired LP track ballad "The Show Is Over."

Wansel's own charting LPs were *Life on Mars* from summer 1976 (includes two tracks with Instant Funk, "Life on Mars" and "You Can Be What You Wanna Be"), *What the World Is Coming To*, *Voyager* (with its great space-age oriented graphics) from spring 1978, and *Time Is Slipping Away* from 1979. Several tracks from his LPs were radio-aired LP tracks (the lushly orchestrated "Theme From the Planets," the spacy, funky "Disco Lights") and some songs—"Together Once Again," "One Million Miles From the Ground," and "Holdin' On"—are still in singers' repertoire today. "Holdin' On" was a radio-aired LP track from actor Lawrence Hilton-Jacobs' self-titled album produced by Lamont Dozier. "Global Warming" from the 1991 PIR/Zoo/BMG CD *Universe Featuring Dexter Wansel* received some airplay on smooth jazz radio stations. During the '90s, Wansel continued to work with the reactivated Philadelphia International Records and occasionally toured. Dexter Wansel-related releases are Grover Washington Jr. *Ultimate Collection, Heaven & Earth-That's Love, Best of MFSB: Love Is the Message*, and *Best of the Intruders*. —*Ed Hogan*

Life on Mars / 1976 / Philadelphia International ✦✦✦

Science fiction was big in the 1970s. So from a marketing standpoint, it made sense when, in 1976, Dexter Wansel went for a sci-fi theme on his debut album, *Life on Mars*. Not that the Philadelphia producer/keyboardist needed a gimmick to get over—if you're good enough to work with heavyweights like the O'Jays, the Stylistics, and the Intruders, you don't need a gimmick. Even without the sci-fi theme, *Life on Mars* would have been a memorable debut for Wansel, who produced the album and wrote or co-wrote all of the material. This diverse LP is far from predictable; if you bought *Life on Mars* for its title song (a haunting piece of space funk that employs members of Instant Funk), you quickly learned that the record also includes mellow quiet storm offerings ("One Million Miles From the Ground," "Together Once Again") as well as Curtis Mayfield-influenced funk ("You Can Be What You Wanna Be") and pop-jazz/crossover instrumentals ("A Prophet Named K.G.," "Theme From the Planets"). In fact, one of the musicians Wansel employs is saxophonist Bob Malach, a jazzman who is heavily influenced by Michael Brecker but is more Grover Washington-influenced on this album. Ranging from decent to excellent, *Life on Mars* is arguably Wansel's strongest album. —*Alex Henderson*

What the World Is Coming To / 1977 / Philadelphia International ✦✦✦

Dexter Wansel's second album, *What the World Is Coming To*, found the Philadelphia-based producer/keyboardist/vocalist temporarily ditching the sci-fi imagery that his debut album, *Life on Mars*, was known for. But other than that, *What the World Is Coming To* isn't a radical departure from its predecessor. Like *Life on Mars*, this 1977 LP is a diverse outing that was recorded at Philly's famous Sigma Sound Studios and ranges from mellow quiet storm material ("Holdin' On," "Dreams of Tomorrow") and sleek disco-funk ("Dance With Me Tonight") to instrumental pop-jazz ("First Light of the Morning," "Ode Infinitum," and the title track). The only tune on this album that is unlike anything on *Life on Mars* is "Going Back to Kingston Town," a reggae number with a strong Bob Marley influence. Except for Wansel's unexpected detour into reggae, this album isn't quite as strong as its predecessor—creatively, Wansel experiences a bit of a sophomore slump. But while *What the World Is Coming To* isn't a masterpiece and isn't the Philadelphian's most essential album, it is a decent record that his die-hard fans will enjoy. —*Alex Henderson*

Voyager / 1978 / Philadelphia International ✦✦✦

After employing a lot of sci-fi/space travel imagery on his first album, *Life on Mars*, Dexter Wansel got away from the outer space theme on his second album, *What the World Is Coming To*. But as it turned out, that was only temporary—the cover of Wansel's third album, *Voyager*, finds him dressed like an astronaut. In the late '70s, Wansel wasn't known for recording one-dimensional albums—and he lives up to his reputation for diversity on this decent 1978 outing, which ranges from funk ("All Night Long," "I Just Want to Love You") and smooth Philadelphia soul ("I'm in Love") to instrumental pop-jazz ("Time Is the Teacher") and fusion ("Voyager"). Most of the instrumentals that Wansel provided in the late '70s were more pop-jazz/NAC than fusion, but *Voyager*'s title track is the sort of hard, aggressive fusion that one would have expected from Chick Corea's *Return to Forever* or John McLaughlin's *Mahavishnu Orchestra* in the 1970s. And that's ironic because one of the players who is featured on that track is Philly saxman George Howard, who went on to become a NAC/smooth jazz favorite in the 1980s but had yet to provide any albums of his own back in 1978. *Voyager* falls short of mind blowing, but it's a likable record that deserves credit for its unpredictable nature. —*Alex Henderson*

Time Is Slipping Away / 1979 / Philadelphia International ✦✦✦

Some artists are quite happy being redundant and predictable; they become known for a particular style and dare not stray from it. But Dexter Wansel isn't like that; when the producer/composer/keyboardist/vocalist recorded four albums for Philadelphia International in the late '70s, he made certain that all of them were diverse and unpredictable. True to form, Wansel keeps listeners guessing on 1979's *Time Is Slipping Away*, which was the last of the four. The LP gets off to a Chic-influenced start with the lush, glossy disco number "I'll Never Forget (My Favorite Disco)," but most of the other material isn't disco. *Time Is Slipping Away* also contains everything from Parliament-minded P-Funk ("Funk Attack") to sophisticated quiet storm music ("The Sweetest Pain") to instrumental jazz-funk ("One for the Road"). Occasionally, this album is excellent—"The Sweetest Pain," which features female vocalist Terry Wells, is a caressing gem that quickly became a favorite on quiet storm formats. But for the most part, *Time Is Slipping Away* is merely decent. Unlike Stevie Wonder, Marvin Gaye, or Earth, Wind & Fire, Wansel didn't record a lot of albums that were superb from start to finish. Nonetheless, his Philadelphia International output was generally likable, and this LP is no exception. —*Alex Henderson*

● **Very Best of Dexter Wansel** / Dec. 1, 1999 / Recall ✦✦✦✦✦

Dexter Wansel deserves classification in two genres: rock and jazz. He jumps from bag to bag, style-wise, and you never know what to expect. These 32 songs chronicle his recording career on two discs; a multifaceted artist, he wore the hats of producer, writer, arranger, musician, and singer. Disc one begins futuristic, incorporating jazz and urban and some funky vibes for the dancefloor freaks. Disc two encompasses jazz, funk, disco, urban, pop, and reggae. Favorites, and for different reasons, include "You Can Be What You Wanna Be," "Theme From the Planets," "Sweetest Pain," "It's Been Cool," "Holdin' On," and "Ode Infinitum." Jean Carn, Terri "Brandi" Wells, and Herb Smith contributes vocals on some selections. —*Andrew Hamilton*

War

f. 1969, Long Beach, CA

Group / Funk, Brown-Eyed Soul, Latin Rock, Soul

One of the most popular funk groups of the '70s, War was also one of the most eclectic, freely melding soul, Latin, jazz, blues, reggae, and rock influences into an effortlessly funky whole. Although War's lyrics were sometimes political in nature (in keeping with their racially integrated lineup), their music almost always had a sunny, laid-back vibe emblematic of their Southern California roots. War kept the groove loose, and they were given over to extended jamming—in fact, many of their studio songs were edited together out of longer improvisations. Even if the jams sometimes got indulgent, they demonstrated War's truly group-minded approach: no one soloist or vocalist really stood above the others (even though all were clearly talented), and their grooving interplay placed War in the top echelon of funk ensembles.

The roots of War lay in an R&B cover band called the Creators. Guitarist Howard Scott and drummer Harold Brown started the group in 1962 while attending high school in the Compton area, and three years later, the lineup also featured keyboardist Leroy "Lonnie" Jordan, bassist Morris "B.B." Dickerson, and saxophonist/flutist Charles Miller (all of them sang). The group had an appetite for different sounds right from the start, ranging from R&B to blues to the Latin music they'd absorbed while growing up in the racially mixed ghettos of Los Angeles. Despite a two-year hiatus following Scott's induction into the service, they released several singles locally on Dore Records (their first, "Burn Baby Burn," was with singer Johnny Hamilton), and backed jazz saxophonist Jay Contreli, formerly of the psychedelic band Love; they also went by the names the Romeos and Señor Soul during this period. In 1968, the band was reconfigured and dubbed Nightshift; Peter Rosen was the new bassist, and percussionist Thomas Sylvester "Papa Dee" Allen, who'd previously played with Dizzy Gillespie, came on board, along with two more horn players. B.B. Dickerson later returned when Rosen died of a drug overdose. In 1969, Nightshift began backing football star Deacon Jones (a defensive end for the L.A. Rams) during his singing performances in a small club, where they were discovered by producer Jerry Goldstein. Goldstein suggested the band as possible collaborators to former Animals lead singer Eric Burdon, who along with Danish-born harmonica player Lee Oskar (born Oskar Levetin Hansen) had been searching L.A. clubs for a new act.

After witnessing Nightshift in concert, Burdon took charge of the group. He gave them a provocative new name, War, and replaced the two extra horn players with Oskar. To develop material, War began playing marathon concert jams over which Burdon would free-associate lyrics. In August 1969, Burdon and War entered the studio for the first time, and after some more touring, they recorded their first album, 1970's *Eric Burdon Declares War*. The spaced-out daydream of "Spill the Wine" was a smash hit, climbing to number three and establishing the group in the public eye. A second album, *The Black Man's Burdon*, was released before the year's end, and over the course of two records it documented the group's increasingly long improvisations (as well as Burdon's growing tendency to ramble). It also featured War's first recorded vocal effort on "They Can't Take Away Our Music." Burdon's contract allowed War to be signed separately, and they soon inked a deal with United Artists, intending to record on their own as well as maintaining their partnership with Burdon. However, Burdon—citing exhaustion—suddenly quit during the middle of the group's European tour in 1971, spelling the beginning of the end; he re-joined War for a final U.S. tour and then left for good.

War had already issued its self-titled, Burdon-less debut at the beginning of 1971, but it flopped. Before the year was out, they recorded another effort, *All Day Music*, which spawned their first Top 40 hits in "All Day Music" and "Slippin' Into Darkness"; the album itself was a million-selling Top 20 hit. War really hit their stride on the follow-up album, 1972's *The World Is a Ghetto*; boosted by a sense of multicultural harmony, it topped the charts and sold over three-million copies, making it the best-selling album of 1973. It also produced two Top Ten smashes in "The Cisco Kid" (which earned them a fervent following in the Latino community) and the title ballad. 1973's *Deliver the Word* was another million-selling hit, reaching the Top Ten and producing the Top Ten single "Gypsy Man" and another hit in "Me and Baby Brother." However, it had less of the urban grit that War prided themselves on; while taking some time to craft new material and rethink their direction, War consolidated their success with the double concert LP *War Live*, recorded over four nights in Chicago during 1974.

Released in 1975, *Why Can't We Be Friends* returned to the sound of *The World Is a Ghetto* with considerable success. The bright, anthemic title track hit the Top Ten, as did "Low Rider," an irresistible slice of Latin funk that became the group's first (and only) R&B chart-topper, and still stands as their best-known tune. 1976 brought the release of a greatest-hits package featuring the new song "Summer," which actually turned out to be War's final Top Ten pop hit; the same year, Oskar released his first solo album, backed by members of Santana. A double-LP compilation of jams and instrumentals appeared on the Blue Note jazz label in 1977, under the title *Platinum Jazz*; it quickly became one of the best-selling albums in Blue Note history, and produced an R&B-chart smash with an edited version of "L.A. Sunshine."

Yet disco was beginning to threaten the gritty, socially aware funk War specialized in. Later in 1977, the band switched labels, moving to MCA for *Galaxy*; though it sold respectably, and the disco-tinged title track was a hit on the R&B charts, it fizzled on the pop side, and proved to be the last time War would hit the Top 40. After completing the *Youngblood* soundtrack album in 1978, the original War lineup began to disintegrate. Dickerson left during the recording of 1979's *The Music Band* (which featured new female vocalist Alice Tweed Smith), and not long after, Charles Miller was murdered in a robbery attempt. After *The Music Band* was released, the remaining members attempted to refashion their image to fit the glitz of the era, and added some new personnel: bassist Luther Rabb, percussionist Ronnie Hammon, and saxophonist Pat Rizzo (ex-Sly & the Family Stone). *The Music Band 2* flopped, and the group was thrown into disarray; Smith exited, and the follow-up took an uncharacteristic three years to prepare. Released in 1982, *Outlaw* was a moderate success; the title track was a Top 20 R&B hit, and "Cinco de Mayo" became a Latino holiday standard. Yet it didn't restore War's commercial standing. Rizzo left later in the year; Harold Brown followed in 1983, after *Life Is So Strange* flopped; and Rabb was replaced with Ricky Green in 1984. In the years that followed, War was essentially a touring outfit and nothing more. Papa Dee Allen collapsed and died onstage of a brain aneurysm in 1988, leaving Jordan, Hammon, Oskar, and Scott as the core membership (Oskar would finally leave in 1992). Interest in War's classic material remained steady, however, thanks to frequent sampling of their grooves by hip-hop artists. 1992's *Rap Declares War* paired the band with a variety of rappers, paving the way for the 1994 comeback attempt *Peace Sign*; for that record, Brown returned on drums, and Jordan (now on bass), Scott, and Hammon were joined by saxophonists Kerry Campbell and Charles Green, percussionist Sal Rodriguez, harmonica player Tetsuya "Tex" Nakamura, and Brown's son, programmer Rae Valentine (plus guests Lee Oskar and José Feliciano). The album failed to chart, however, and the group returned to the touring circuit. Brown and Scott left the lineup in 1997. *—Steve Huey*

War / Jan. 1971 / Rhino ✦✦

War laid the groundwork for future developments on their debut album without Eric Burdon. The intriguing "Sun Oh Son," with its nice vocal arrangement, and "Lonely Feeling" were close-but-no-cigar singles. Still, they did what they had to do: establish an identity without Burdon and begin to blend their diverse elements. *—Ron Wynn*

All Day Music / Nov. 1971 / Rhino ✦✦✦✦✦

As controlled as their self-titled debut was loose, War's sophomore effort, *All Day Music*, appearing a little over six months later in November 1971, was packed with subtly understated grooves. A hit with the fans, the LP peaked in the Top Ten, ultimately spending a massive 39 weeks on the charts. Side one is a gorgeous slab of mellow grooves and jazzed funk highlighted by both the title track and "Get Down," while "That's What Love Can Do" is an outstanding, textured, sleepy love affair revolving around the band's superior vocal harmonies and a tenor sax solo. The light, spare rhythm is like a warm treacle binding. With just three songs picking up the second half, War steps up the pace across the Latin-influenced jam "Nappy Head," the funky, bass-laden "Slipping Into the Darkness," and the all-out electric blues jam that rips through the prototype "Baby Brother." The latter was recorded live on June 30, 1971, at California's Hollywood Bowl and would, in revised and seriously edited form, be reborn as the monster "Me and Baby Brother" on War's *Deliver the Word* opus. Not nearly as fiery (with the exception of "Baby Brother," of course) as either their live performances or later albums, *All Day Music* is still one of this band's best-ever efforts. At times mellow enough to border on horizontal, the songs are filled with such texture and such rich intent that even in the band's quietest breath there is a funky resonance that fulfills Lee Oskar's vision fully. *—Amy Hanson*

The World Is a Ghetto / 1972 / Rhino ✦✦✦✦

War hit its peak with this 1972 album, the only one they ever released that topped the pop charts. The title track was a triumphant blend of great exchanges and unison vocals, plus concise and spirited musical contributions all around. It also contained the delightful "Cisco Kid" and elaborate "City, Country, City," plus the curious "Beetles in the Bog." Harmonica player Lee Oskar and percussionist Papa Dee Allen were at their best, as were keyboardist Lonnie Jordan and saxophonist/flutist Charles Miller. *—Ron Wynn*

Deliver the Word / 1973 / Rhino ✦✦✦✦

Focusing in part on their softer side, War unleashed *Deliver the Word* in fall 1973. A smooth blend of the band's more progressive jazz-rock fusion, the LP shot to the top of the R&B charts, their second of four number one records in a row. It was a perfect tonic to the mediocre MOR music rampaging its way through the early part of the decade. The opening "H2 Overture" is a restrained jazz jam that gives way to "In Your Eyes," which keeps the progressive momentum going but adds unexpected vocal twists that vary from interesting spoken pleasures to full vocal harmonies—it's sex on a groove. Both "Southern Part of Texas" and a long-awaited studio recording of "Baby Brother—now titled "Me and Baby Brother"—swing the band back to their alter ego cutting-edge funk stomp. "Gypsy Man," meanwhile, is a near-12-minute mantric, tantric opus whose blues riffs are pinned down only by the song's low, unyielding rhythm. It's a memorable slab of pure prog passed through Lee Oskar's stroboscopic brain. An outstanding album split between War's two definitive styles, *Deliver the Word* ultimately delivers a vibe, a groove, and an intent that are hard to resist. A magical ride with plenty of surprises to keep the listener on his or her toes, this set is a perfect example of the band at their genre-fusing best. *—Amy Hanson*

War Live / 1973 / Rhino ✦✦

Radio Free War / 1974 / United Artists ✦✦✦

Why Can't We Be Friends? / 1975 / Rhino ✦✦✦✦

Cut from the same cloth as the band's 1973 *Deliver the Word* LP, War's 1975 *Why Can't We Be Friends?* is a masterpiece in its scope and breadth. And, emerging as the last work the band would do for its longtime label, United Artists, it became a fitting swan song, powering up the charts and giving War its fourth and final number-one hit. In recent years, the album has been overshadowed by the monstrously popular bass-beating and bright brass of its singular hit, "Low Rider." Indeed, the song would become the band's signature theme, as the Latino street-cruiser jam quickly became a live set staple and, much later, was reinvigorated through sampling on songs by the Beastie Boys, Stereo MC's, and Offspring. However, that one track, iconographic as it is, is by no means the only treat onboard *Why Can't We Be Friends?* There are far more interesting and superb treats roiling in the wake of "Low Rider." The snappy title track, which poses the question of the decade and, oddly, closes the album, is a feel-good thumper. Its bright brass punctuation and rakish vocals are wonderfully combined with an absolutely contagious reggae beat. Then, add the doesn't-get-much-better-than-that medley "Leroy's Latin Lament." Divided into four "songs," the music swings from the smart vocal opening "Lonnie Dreams" to the effervescent Latin jam of "La Fiesta." And, of course, where there's War, there's funk—this time on the seven-plus minute "Heartbeat." Wrap it all up with the poignant ballad "Lotus Blossom," and the result is pretty much perfection. *Why Can't We Be Friends?* remains one of War's truly outstanding efforts, and has become an integral part of the funk genre's landscape. It also remains the nightcap of their finest hour. War's ill-timed move to MCA changed the energy and focus of the band forever. *—Amy Hanson*

Love Is All Around / 1976 / ABC/Paramount ✦✦✦

When War debuted as Eric Burdon's backing band in the late '60s, they were on ABC/Paramount. The group was still hot in 1976, and ABC reissued vault material from their early days in a deceptive package trying to coast on the band's hitmaker status. The album deservedly flopped, and ABC's clumsy attempt failed. *—Ron Wynn*

Galaxy / 1977 / Rhino ✦✦

There wasn't much that the emergent *Star Wars* culture didn't touch in the latter part of the 1970s, and War's 1977 LP, *Galaxy*, was no exception. As the band moved further and further from the funk that drove its earliest grooves through to its street-savvy "Low Rider" alter ego, War's core audience was co-opted by a new crop of fans just looking for a groove. *Galaxy* filled that gap well. On paper, the LP should have been driven by the title track—a wonderful eight-minute frenzy that glories in compulsive hooks and weaves in some super-stellar *Star Wars* lyric riffing, all the while pounding the beat home underneath a rhythm borrowed from los Chakachas' "Jungle Fever." It's an outstanding opener. Unfortunately, the band drizzled downhill all the way through the rest of the set, across lightweight and uninspired material that couldn't even be redeemed by the sassy "Hey Señorita." Even the ballad "Sweet Fighting Lady" wasn't up to their usual down-tempo stuff, and any achievements were wiped right off the slate by the closer, "The Seven Tin Soldiers," which is an unending, unyielding 14-minute instrumental. One song, no matter how marvelously executed, does not an album make, and at the end of the day *Galaxy* couldn't pull the band out of its rut. *—Amy Hanson*

Platinum Jazz / 1977 / Avenue Jazz ♦♦♦

An often overlooked and underrated part of War's legacy was its instrumentals, many of which were quite imaginative. War's members loved jazz, and they expressed that passion not because they had any illusions of trying to compete with Miles Davis or Joe Henderson (or even Charles Earland and Grover Washington Jr.), but simply for the enjoyment of it. Initially released as a two-LP set and reissued as a single 78-minute CD in 1992, *Platinum Jazz* gathered War's previously released instrumentals with fine results. Jazz-fusion material ranging from the unpredictable "City, Country, City" (arguably the band's best instrumental ever, and certainly its best known) and the salsa-influenced "Nappy Head" to the mellow "H2 Overture" and the congenial "Smile Happy" show just how effective War's members could be without vocals. And when saxman Charles Miller and keyboardist stretch out, it's clear that as improvisers, they weren't half bad. *—Alex Henderson*

Youngblood / 1978 / United Artists ♦♦

War got decent mileage from the soundtrack for this B-movie, which premiered near the end of the first blaxploitation era. They ended with two R&B hits, and while they were perturbed that United Artists, the label they had left, reaped the benefits, it at least kept them active and in the R&B hunt. *—Ron Wynn*

The Music Band / 1979 / MCA ♦

Adding vocalist Alice Tweed Smith to their lineup, and jumping ship to the MCA label, were occasions that only furthered War's slide into a decisive end-of-decade malaise as they followed their hit label debut, *Galaxy*, with *The Music Band* in spring 1979. The lackluster start to a series of three loosely connected albums, *The Music Band* revealed a late-decade War not as the fierce funkers they once were, but as the purveyors of a lite jazzy disco that occasionally scraped the bottom of a now well-worn barrel in a fruitless search for some classic rhythms. Jumping straight into the fray with the title track, War delivered a midtempo tribute to their fans that would have been more at home on the stage of some rock opera than on what one hoped would be a funk album. This experience is repeated at the end, too, as the band drops the curtain with the oddly reggae-inflected "All Around the World." However, there is some redemption, as War finally remember what they do best across the jazzy jam of "Millionaire" and the disco fusion of "Good Good Feelin'." But those are the high points in what is, overall, a disappointing set and a horrific precursor to two more volumes of self-gratifying concept rock, as War shifted gears and tried to figure out where their politicized funk belonged in an age without substance. *—Amy Hanson*

The Music Band 2 / 1979 / MCA ♦

The second in a loose trilogy of late-'70s LPs, 1979's *The Music Band 2* picks up where *The Music Band* left off, filling the empty spaces with a light jazz-funk that's a long, long way from the masterful early-/mid-'70s grooves that War are renowned for. But although critics resoundingly hammered it, the album crept into the R&B Top 40 at the end of the year, allowing the band to limp into a new, and hopefully more promising, decade. Unfortunately, though, there's not much here to recommend *The Music Band 2*. It's competent, it's slick, but it just isn't very interesting. Of the two minor hit singles spawned by the album, one is vaguely memorable—"Don't Take It Away" took the band into lite disco waters and does have some interesting vocal work behind it. Unfortunately, "I'll Be Around" is nothing more than a benevolently smooth ballad, with sax solo and not much else. Elsewhere, War reinvented their late-1972 hit "The World Is a Ghetto" into a new, 13-plus minute instrumental riffer that stripped any lingering goodness from the original, and only the closing title track, with its remarkably punchy Latin-tinged jazz/disco, is even slightly interesting. War is a far finer funk band than this album would have you believe. Stick to the classics with which they gifted the scene in both their early, and, surprisingly, occasional late-era material, and overlook this self-indulgent mid-period morass altogether. *—Amy Hanson*

Outlaw / 1982 / RCA ♦♦♦

With the utterly dismal and critically hammered *Music Band* trilogy thankfully behind it, War ground to a halt in the wake of the death of former saxophonist Charles Miller. After a time out of the spotlight, and shrugging off the shadows, a rejuvenated War reappeared on RCA in 1982 sporting bright '80s-hued bandannas. Learning from (recent) past failings and leaving them behind, *Outlaw* saw the band taking tentative steps back toward its roots across a solid if at times slightly flat set. Both the punchy, funky opener, "You Got the Power," and the older-styled title track propelled the band back into the Top 20, while leaving plenty of room for the reggae-rhythmed "Just Because" and the outstanding "Baby, It's Cold Outside" to muscle in. But where War proved that it was back on track was across the muscular medley "The Jungle," which combined classic funk across bass and horns with politicized patter and surprisingly placed vocal harmonies. *Outlaw*, then, became a triumphant trumpet, a heralding battle cry—War was returning to form. It was a strong comeback that not only brought the band back to its old fans, but also sowed the seeds for the themes and grooves that would be so prevalent on the following year's *Life (Is So Strange)* LP. *—Amy Hanson*

Life (Is So Strange) / 1983 / RCA ♦♦

War kept battling in the mid-'80s, switching labels and trying different producers in an attempt to maintain their viability. This was the second of two albums they recorded for RCA, and they were unable to sustain the comeback begun with the previous album. The title track was a moderate success, but by now they sounded weary and uninspired. The same was true for their production, arrangements, and compositions, as well as past strengths like group interplay, musical support, and solos. *—Ron Wynn*

The Best of War . . . And More / 1991 / Rhino/Avenue ♦♦♦♦

It's not a perfect compilation by any means—there's no "The World Is a Ghetto" and a bad remix of "Low Rider," for starters—but it's an important release from this influential band. The original vinyl was definitive. *—Stephen Thomas Erlewine*

Peace Sign / 1994 / Rhino/Avenue ♦♦

When War reunited in 1994 and recorded *Peace Sign*—its first album since 1983's *Life (Is So Strange)*, the band's sound hadn't changed very much. Instead of going high-tech and trying to appeal to urban contemporary tastes, the influential Angelenos continued to offer the type of slow and relaxed yet gritty soul and funk they'd been playing 20 years earlier. The results is a decent album that's hardly in a class with *All Day Music*, *The World Is a Ghetto* or *Why Can't We Be Friends*, but has its moments. War had long commanded an intensely devoted following in the Mexican-American community, and it's hard to miss the Latin influence on such enjoyable numbers as "Wild Rodriguez" (a fun ode to the "low rider" or "vato loco" culture) and "East L.A." The CD's strongest offering, however, is "Homeless Hero," a poignant and rightly angry reflection on homeless Vietnam veterans. But despite its strong points, *Peace Sign* is an album that only War's more devoted followers should invest in—more casual listeners would be much better off with a collection of the band's '70s recordings. *—Alex Henderson*

Anthology (1970–1994) / Oct. 18, 1994 / Rhino/Avenue ♦♦♦♦♦

For some reason, there still isn't a truly comprehensive single-disc War collection on the market. Rhino's *Grooves and Messages* easily comes the closest, although its unnecessary remix disc kicks up the price a bit (and one could argue about a couple of omissions in favor of latter-day tracks). That makes Rhino's own double-disc *Anthology (1970-1994)* even more valuable—it might be too much for casual fans who just want War's biggest hits, but there's absolutely nothing missing here. All the hits are included, of course, as well as some overlooked singles and fine album tracks; plus, *Anthology* does fans a service by gathering the highlights from their uneven later work, which is more disco-tinged and less distinctive. A concise overview this is not; what *Anthology* illustrates instead is the full scope of War's versatility, and their loping, easygoing way with a groove. War's eclectic, Latin-spiked sound was tremendously distinctive, and if a few tracks get a little too mellow and start to drift, the band's interplay usually redeems the extended jams. *Anthology*'s extensiveness does illustrate that, aside from their big singles, War was often more about musicianship than tight songwriting; thus, two discs' worth will probably be most enjoyable for funk aficionados looking for a different, lighter sort of groove to get lost in. Casual fans are better off with *Grooves and Messages*, but *Anthology* is a definitive War package, containing everything most fans will ever need. *—Steve Huey*

The Best of War and More . . . Vol. 2 / Sep. 3, 1996 / Rhino ♦♦♦♦

Since Avenue botched War's *The Best of War . . . And More* by neglecting to put on hit singles like "The World Is a Ghetto" and "Gypsy Man"—although there was plenty of room for both songs, among others—the company needed to assemble a second compilation to take care of all the leftover singles and songs that didn't make the first volume. But, they managed to botch *The Best of War and More . . . Vol. 2* as well. Sure, "The World Is a Ghetto," "Gypsy Man," "L.A. Sunshine," "Good, Good Feelin'," and several other R&B hit singles made the cut this time around, but the album is baited by an unnecessary remix of "Spill the Wine" by Junior Vasquez, plus selections from their latter-day albums (such as "Peace Sign") that could have been replaced by more first-rate album tracks in the vein of the killer "Don't Let No One Got You Down." Still, if you want to supplement the first collection, the second volume is necessary. However, if you're going to spring for just two discs of War, you might as well go with the comprehensive double-disc collection, *Anthology*. *—Stephen Thomas Erlewine*

The Music Band, Vols. 1-2 / Feb. 2, 1999 / Rhino ♦♦♦

● **Grooves & Messages: Greatest Hits of War** / Jun. 15, 1999 / Rhino ♦♦♦♦♦

Grooves & Messages is another compilation from Rhino that recycles War's greatest hits and, like the previous collections, it contains most of the hits, but not all of them. The difference is, it actually has all the Top Ten pop hits and the majority of the Top Ten R&B hits (only "L.A. Sunshine" is missing), and it's sequenced in chronological order—two important elements that were absent on *The Best of War* and its sequel, *The Best of War and More . . . Vol. 2*. Sounds perfect, doesn't it? The problem is, *Grooves & Messages* contains a bonus disc of remixes. There are a couple of big-name mixers here, including Armand Van Helden and Ganja Kru, but none of the mixes are of any interest. Furthermore, the casual fans that will want the first disc will have little use for the second. Still, that first disc is the best, most concise collection of War hits on the market, and *Grooves & Messages* is a specially priced double-disc set, so it may be worth the time of some casual fans, those willing to spend a little bit more to get a good hits collection. However, it would have been nicer if the first disc was available individually. *—Stephen Thomas Erlewine*

Anita Ward

b. 1957, Memphis, TN

Vocals / Disco, Urban, Soul

Perhaps more so than any other genre in the history of popular music, the '70s disco scene was littered with countless one-hit wonders, including Anita Ward. Born during 1957 in Memphis, TN, Ward developed an interest in music at an early age, although it was gospel and not the uptempo dance style she'd become synonymous with years later. Ward went on to sing with the Rust College A Cappella Choir (which included recording alongside renowned Metropolitan Opera vocalist Leontyne Price), as well as issuing an obscure album recorded by her own gospel quartet. But after graduation, Ward didn't automatically set out to pursue a career in music and instead became a substitute teacher in the Memphis elementary school system. It wasn't long before Ward realized music was too much a part of her life to ignore and her manager put her in contact with singer/songwriter Frederick Knight (who had scored a substantial hit on his own in the summer of 1972 with "I've Been Lonely for So Long"). Knight signed on to help produce a three-song demo session with Ward, but once the tape was rolling, Knight became so taken by Ward's singing ability that the sessions soon produced an album's worth of material.

Upon listening back to their work, both agreed that they were still one song short, which resulted in Knight digging up an old track titled "Ring My Bell" that he had originally penned for a young teenybopper singer, Stacy Lattisaw (who would later score several hits in the early '80s). The song's original lyrics dealt with teens chatting away on the phone and even though Knight gave the track a quick lyrical overhaul, Ward was less than enthusiastic about the song. Still, she agreed to record it (with Knight providing most of the musical accompaniment himself, including one of the first uses of synth drums on a record), which only took a total of two days to record. "Ring My Bell" turned out to be the best track of the bunch, resulting in a recording contract with the TK label, and the release of Ward's debut album, *Songs of Love*, in 1979. It didn't take long for "Ring My Bell" to scale the charts and it peaked at number one during the summer (out-gunning such other future disco-classics as Donna Summer's "Hot Stuff" and "Bad Girls," plus Sister Sledge's "We Are Family," all of which were in the Top Five) and remained on the charts for five months solid.

Since the song was a fluke to begin with, there weren't any other tracks on the album that really resembled "Ring My Bell" (most were ballads and midtempo songs), resulting in the album disappearing from the charts soon after. A follow-up single, "Don't Drop My Love," could only make it as far as number 87 on the charts in December of the same year, signaling that Ward's 15 minutes had come and gone, delegating her to one-hit wonder status. Although Ward only scored a lone hit during her brief recording career, a 12-track best-of set was released in 1998, unsurprisingly titled *Ring My Bell*; a remix of the track, "Ring My Bell 2000," was issued shortly thereafter. *—Greg Prato*

● **Songs of Love** / 1979 / TK ♦♦♦

An aptly titled album originally released in 1979 on TK Records. The soaring "Ring My Bell," included here, sold a million copies but if you're looking for similar smashes you won't find them. Majestic ballads and midtempo tracks sung in Ward's squeamishly lush soprano are what you'll find on this menu with "Spoiled By Your Love" and "There's No Doubt About It" as the choice picks. Though labeled a Southern singer, Ward was more like Anita Baker than Betty Wright. *—Andrew Hamilton*

Billy Ward & the Dominoes

b. Sep. 19, 1921, Los Angeles, CA

Vocals / R&B

The Dominoes (also sometimes known as Billy Ward & the Dominoes) had one of the finest musical pedigrees of any R&B vocal group of the 1940s, at least based on its founder's training and experience. A lot of R&B acts came out of a gospel background, and Bo Diddley even studied violin as a boy, but rare is the R&B vocal group whose founder was trained at Juilliard. Billy Ward (born September 19, 1921, Los Angeles) had a minister father and a musician mother, and was a musical prodigy as a child, schooled in classical music theory and composition as well as performance. Before he was in his teens, Ward was good enough on the organ to play at his father's services and he won a composition award at age 14 from Walter Damrosch, the celebrated New York music educator, composer, and administrator. Following his military service during World War II, Ward studied at the Art Institute of Chicago and at the Juilliard School of Music in New York, where he later became a voice coach; he also began working on Broadway during the late '40s. It was from the ranks of his ex-students that he recruited the original members of the Dominoes: Clyde McPhatter as lead singer, Charlie White (tenor), Joe Lamont (baritone), and Bill Brown (bass). The Dominoes won a series of talent contests, including a competition on the television show *Arthur Godfrey's Talent Scouts*, which got them a lot of engagements and an audition with Ralph Bass, the head of the newly established Federal Records label, part of Syd Nathan's King Records, during the final months of 1950.

The Dominoes, with McPhatter's high tenor lead, had a startlingly fresh sound and enjoyed a number-six R&B hit in early 1951 with one song from their first session, "Do Something for Me." It was in May of that year that the group broke through to the top of the R&B charts with "Sixty Minute Man," which also established them as one of the leading crossover acts between gospel and blues. Riding the wave of demand for their performances off of that hit—one of the first great double entendre records of the '50s, and a very early example of what would be considered a "rock & roll" record—the group spent the next seven months on the road, building up a lot of public good will and a reputation as one of the top R&B acts of the era.

What made the Dominoes special, besides the excellent arrangements and McPhatter's unique voice, was their appeal beyond the usual racial lines of demarcation. They were huge in the black community, but they were also one of a relative handful of R&B acts that developed a small but fiercely loyal following younger white listeners as well during the early '50s, which didn't matter a lot at the time—and, as things worked out, was only incidental to their fate—but helped plant a seed that blossomed into the full-blown rock & roll boom four years later. The Dominoes' star seemed poised only to rise, but there was already trouble within the lineup as early as 1951, when Charlie White quit and was succeeded by James Van Loan, followed by Bill Brown, who was replaced by David McNeil, formerly of the group the Larks. White (who later joined the Clovers) and Brown passed through a short-lived vocal group called the Checkers, while the reconstituted Dominoes continued scoring hits with "I Am With You" and "That's What You're Doing to Me," before scaling the top of the R&B charts again with "Have Mercy Baby," which was number one for two and a half months in 1952.

Amid these successes, and the constant touring and occasional recording, there was rising dissension within the ranks of the group over the way that Ward had it organized, musically and financially. Nobody disputed that Ward had the musical training to run the group on that level, and his ruling it with an iron hand where arrangements and repertory were concerned was understandable; the problem was that the ticket-buying and record-buying public was enamored of the singing itself, especially that of lead tenor Clyde McPhatter, and the singers were seeing very little of the money that the group was earning. McPhatter himself was being paid barely enough to live on, which was bad enough, but to add insult to injury, he often found himself billed as Clyde Ward in order to fool fans into thinking that he was Billy Ward's brother. In the spring of 1953, it all hit the fan at once as McPhatter exited the lineup in April. Under the encouragement of Atlantic Records chief Ahmet Ertegun, he quickly organized a new group of his own called the Drifters. McPhatter's exit from the Dominoes hit the group's core audience within the black community like news of an earthquake, so beloved was the lead singer among their fans. The group and the singer enjoyed the adulation appropriate to a pop/R&B outfit, but they also evoked deep passions that were more akin to those elicited by a gospel outfit, and his departure from the Dominoes should have derailed the group.

Ward must have sensed that there was trouble coming, however, because during the prior year he had approached a young boxer-turned-singer named Jackie Wilson, who had a voice that, if anything, was better than McPhatter's. A high tenor similar to McPhatter, he moved right into the fold with the latter's departure and the Dominoes picked right up with their performances and their contract at King/Federal. Wilson's singles with the group included "You Can't Keep a Good Man Down" and "Rags to Riches," which kept their demand reasonably high for the next year. The Dominoes seemed to be on track once more, despite more lineup shifts, including the departure of David McNeil for military service. The new Dominoes lineup was Jackie Wilson (lead), James Van Loan (second tenor), Milton Marle (baritone), and Cliff Givens (bass), with Billy Ward still in charge. In 1954, Ward decided to forego renewing the group's contract at King Records—it seemed as though they hardly ever saw anything from their work in the studio, despite having sold so many records that, at one point, Nathan had put his pressing plant on overtime just to meet the demand for the group's records. Ward made his move in 1954, taking the group to Jubilee Records that August, where they lasted through two singles. Finally, in early 1955, the Dominoes moved to Decca Records, where they enjoyed that long-sought national hit with "St. Teresa of the Roses." The group was unable to replicate that success over the next year, however, and in late 1956, Wilson quit to begin a solo career that would make him a star.

Ward tried to keep the franchise going with the addition of ex-Lark Eugene Mumford as lead singer, and got the group a new contract with California-based Liberty Records. The new incarnation of the Dominoes suddenly found themselves with a major hit in the form of "Star Dust," which rode the pop charts for 24 weeks and got as high as number 13 nationally. This proved to be their last serious assault on the charts, however, and the group went hitless despite singles issued on the ABC label into the late '50s. Despite their lack of chart success, the Dominoes continued to perform into the 1960s and LPs—mostly exploiting Clyde McPhatter's and Jackie Wilson's name and work—did appear periodically. Today the group is principally remembered in the context of their respective careers, though "Sixty Minute Man" does occupy an exalted place in its own right as a breakthrough R&B record. *—Bruce Eder*

Billy Ward & His Dominoes / 1956 / Federal ♦♦♦

Clyde McPhatter With Billy Ward and His Dominoes / 1957 / King ♦♦♦♦♦

Sea of Glass / 1957 / Liberty ♦♦♦

Yours Forever / 1958 / Liberty ♦♦♦

Featuring Clyde McPhatter and Jackie Wilson / 1961 / Deluxe ♦♦♦♦♦

★ **Sixty Minute Men: The Best of Billy Ward & His Dominoes** / Nov. 16, 1993 / Rhino ♦♦♦♦♦

Billy Ward was neither a flamboyant vocalist nor a great instrumentalist; his success came directly from his ability to spot and nurture talent. Unfortunately, Ward was also a taskmaster and couldn't hold onto singers very long after discovering and recruiting them for his groups. But for a short period in the 1950s, Ward & the Dominoes ruled R&B by featuring two of its premier vocalists, Clyde McPhatter and Jackie Wilson. Neither stayed long, but were in the band enough time to make some seminal hits, included in this 20-cut anthology. Ironically, the song the group is remembered for the most featured bass vocalist Bill Brown doing the lead on the title track. *—Ron Wynn*

14 Hits, Vol. 1 / 1995 / King ♦♦♦♦♦

One of R&B's great pioneering groups sparkles on these early-'50s hits featuring three great lead singers: Clyde McPhatter, bass singer Bill Brown, and McPhatter's replacement Jackie Wilson. Brown boasts of his sexual prowess on "Sixty Minute Man" and fronts the equally infectious "Pedal Pushin' Papa." Clyde McPhatter shows his versatility on stirring ballads and jumps including the terse "I Am With You," the handclapping, sax blowing "That's What You're Doing to Me," and the pleading "Have Mercy Baby." Jackie Wilson's biggest Dominoes' hit "Rags to Riches" features a devastating opening operatic note. McPhatter's last Dominoes release, a remarkable version of "These Foolish Things," features Brown's low groaning bass under McPhatter's probing tenor embellished by imaginative backing vocals that made every Dominoes recording special. *—Andrew Hamilton*

The Dominoes Meet the Ravens / Feb. 21, 1995 / Sequel ♦♦♦♦♦

Here is a 20-song collection featuring two groups, drawn from Jubilee (and licensed from EMI), all unified by their chronology and the fact that their respective lead singers, Jackie Wilson of the Dominoes and Jimmy Ricks from the Ravens, became successful solo artists. Otherwise, peculiarly enough, these aren't among the best-selling or best-known sides by either group (a fact acknowledged in the notes). However, they do superbly showcase the singing of each group's most famous member, Jackie Wilson opening the disc with a near-operatic performance on "Take Me Back to Heaven," while the Ravens open with a wonderfully subtle, swinging rendition of "Green Eyes" that harkens back to the Mills Brothers. Ricks' baritone is a magnificent instrument throughout this collection, which features a trio of previously unissued songs ("Rockin' at the Record Hop" among them). At the same time, Wilson delivers a gloriously frenzied lead performance on the Dominoes' previously unissued "Stop!... You're Sending Me." The sound is a match for the best reissues from Rhino or Ace, and the notes are a treasure trove of information on the Ravens, in particular. *—Bruce Eder*

The Best of the 50's Masters: 1957–1959 / Mar. 21, 2000 / Varese ♦♦♦♦♦
This 19-song anthology covers Ward & the Dominoes' stint with Liberty. Although this was the period that saw them land two of their biggest hits—both "Star Dust" and "Deep Purple" made the Top 20—it's not remembered or written about nearly as much as are their recordings during the first half of the 1950s. That's because their late-'50s material was far less R&B-oriented than their discs for Federal and King, and also because the Dominoes' two best lead singers, Clyde McPhatter and Jackie Wilson, had departed the lineup. Indeed, by this time the group was walking pretty close to the middle of the road, covering numerous pre-rock popular standards and using lots of orchestration. There are still some doo wop and R&B elements involved, but it's far closer to pop than it is to rock & roll. Half a dozen different singers are on lead vocals, though most often taking lead is Eugene Mumford, the voice on "Star Dust" and "Deep Purple." It's not bad as far as harmonized pop vocals go, but often it's rather a throwback to the Ink Spots and the Mills Brothers, and certainly not as innovative as the group's earlier efforts. At times, there's a resemblance to the Platters (they even do "Smoke Gets in Your Eyes"), and for just one moment they turn into a straight R&B/rock group on an unexpected cover of the Jan & Arnie hit "Jennie Lee" that made the middle of the pop charts. Incidentally, five of the tracks (including an earlier vocal take of "Star Dust") were previously unreleased; on one of them, "These Foolish Things (Remind Me of You)," they totally lose the beat going into the second bridge. *—Richie Unterberger*

The Very Best of Billy Ward and the Dominoes / Jan. 22, 2002 / Collectables ♦♦♦♦
Even though there are a number of reissues featuring the best of the original Billy Ward & the Dominoes output on Federal and King Records, this collectables reissue gathers more tunes on a single disc. Both Clyde McPhatter and Jackie Wilson are heard over these 25 tracks, including the original versions of "Sixty Minute Man," "Can't Do Sixty No More," "Rags to Riches," and "The Bells." *—Al Campbell*

Leon Ware

b. Detroit, MI

Producer, Songwriter, Vocals / Urban, Smooth Soul, Motown, Soul

A Detroit native, songwriter/singer/producer/arranger Leon Ware first met Motown founder Berry Gordy while a teenager. Gordy produced some sides on Ware but was also busy writing hits for singer Jackie Wilson ("Lonely Teardrops," "That's Why I Love You So") and the group the Gaylords. Being an impatient youth, Ware became involved in other things. Throughout the '60s and '70s, the songwriter worked on and off for Motown. His first hit as a songwriter was the Isley Brothers' Motown single "Got to Have You Back" (co-written by Ware with Stephen Bowden and Ivy Hunter) from spring 1967. Other Motown artists recorded his songs: Michael Jackson, Martha Reeves & the Vandellas, Kim Weston, and Junior Walker. The Miracles recorded the joyous "I Don't Need No Reason" (Ware/Pam Sawyer) on their first post-Smokey album, *Renaissance*, released on Tamla/Motown in 1973. "What Is a Heart Good For" (Ware/Ross) was the album's opener and its first single and it was included on their next LP. Ware's "Give Me Just Another Day" was the group's first single from their second album, *Do It Baby*.

Quincy Jones' 1974 A&M album, *Body Heat*, has three Ware songs, the title track (Ware/Jones/Bruce Fisher/Stanley Richardson), "If I Ever Lose This Heaven" (Ware/Sawyer), "One Track Mind." The *Body Heat* LP went gold and peaked at number-six pop in summer 1974. The Average White Band's cover of "If I Ever Lose This Heaven" went to number-25 R&B in summer 1975. The tune has also be recorded by Sergio Mendes, Nancy Wilson, Maxine Nightingale, Stanley Turrentine, Jonathan Butler, and Marta Sanchez. "Body Heat" was later covered by Rufus & Chaka Khan and was sampled by Tupac for "How Do You Want It." Another album that did well for Ware was Minnie Riperton's 1975 Epic album, *Adventures in Paradise*, produced by Stewart Levine and featuring the Crusaders (with Larry Carlton). Ware, Riperton, and her husband Richard Rudolph co-wrote the single "Inside My Love," "Baby This Love I Have," "Feelin' That Your Feelin's Right," and the LP's opening track, "Can You Feel What I'm Sayin'." Trina Broussard covered "Inside My Love" on the soundtrack of the 1997 New Line movie *Love Jones*. Also on the CD were the Ware tunes "Sumthin' Sumthin" by Maxwell, and Riperton's original version of "Inside My Love" is on the soundtrack of the 1997 Pam Grier/Quentin Tarentino/Miramax movie *Jackie Brown*.

On Marvin Gaye's mega-selling 1076 *I Want You* album, two of Ware's songs became instant classics. The title track single (Ware/Arthur Ross), originally to be part of a Ware Motown LP, hit number-one R&B in spring 1976. Gaye recorded the whole album with Ware and it peaked at number-four pop. Billy Griffin, former lead singer of the Miracles, covered "If I Ever Lose This Heaven" on his 1985 Columbia LP *Systematic*, and Ware co-wrote the title track with James Ingram. Other Ware songs include Melissa Manchester's "Don't Cry Out Loud." "Trust Your Heart" (Ware/Womack/Don Davis) was the first single from Bobby Womack's 1977 Columbia album *Pieces*. More songs that Ware wrote or co-wrote are Carl Anderson's "How Deep Does It Go," Instant Funk's "Kinky," Vesta Williams' "It's You," Donny Hathaway's "I Know It's You," Melissa Manchester and Peabo Bryson's "Lovers After All," Jeffrey Osborne's "Forever Mine," Chicago's "Baby Don't Stop Me," Johnny Mathis' "Priceless," Teena Marie's "My Dear Mr. Gaye," Nancy Wilson and Ramsey Lewis' "Slippin' Away," Deodato's "Just This One Night," Parliament's "Fantasy Is Reality," Marlena Shaw's "Sweet Beginnings," and Lulu's "Independence."

Ware's songs have been ample material for rappers/urban artists who've sampled his songs for their hits, such as 2Pac, A Tribe Called Quest, Montell Jordan, EPMD, Da Youngstas, Nefretiti, Ice Cube, Zhane, Aliyah, and Prince. Popular in the U.K., Ware has collaborated with Mica Paris, Carl McIntosh of Loose Ends, Labi Siffre, Pauline Henry, and Omar. *—Ed Hogan*

● **Musical Massage** / 1976 / Expansion ♦♦♦♦♦
Leon Ware's classic Motown offering from 1976 came about as the result of another classic recording done by Marvin Gaye. Ware had written the single "I Want You" for a demo recording to score T-Bone Ross a recording contract with Motown. Berry Gordy heard it and told Ware he had to have the song for Marvin Gaye's next single. He took it to Gaye, who also loved it. Later, as Ware finished the tracks and orchestrations for his own album, he was playing it back for friends at Gaye's home when Gaye came out of a bedroom to inquire about what it was. He asked for—and received—all the tracks from Ware for the legendary *I Want You* album. This left Ware no choice but to compose an entirely new set of songs for his own record; the result is *Musical Massage*. (It should be noted that, according to Ware, Gordy, Gaye, and others felt he should also give this album away as a follow-up to *I Want You*, but Ware refused.) *Musical Massage* is the perfect mix of soul, light funk, jazz, and what was about to become the rhythmic foundation for disco. Picture the Motown song orchestrations with arrangements by Barry White for the Salsoul Orchestra and you get a bit of the picture. The disc opens with two smooth soul wonders in "Learning How to Love You" and "Instant Love." Strings dominate the melodic arrangement and Ware croons directly to them as Ray Parker Jr. fills the lines with a silky but chunky guitar. Ware's mellifluous tenor is deep in the swell of strings and guitars as the rest of the band provides a shimmering backbeat for his soul crooning. On a re-recording of the track "Body Heat"—which Ware had recorded as a duet with Minnie Riperton for Quincy Jones' album of the same name a year earlier—Parker and bassist Chuck Rainey set a groove for Bongo Brown, Gary Coleman, and Bobbye Hall's percussion orgy. Ware's vocals, augmented by a three-piece female choir, cover the tune with dripping, seductive, sexual energy. Bobby Womack guests on the title track and "Holiday," while Gaye also lends a hand on the latter. Both tracks are spurious soul-funk workouts with fat, smooth grooves underlying Ware's gorgeous voice that melts the heart strings like butter, sounding like the whispering of satin sheets. Produced by Ware with Hal Davis and engineer Cal Harris, the disc has the same sweet, swaying feel as Gaye's *I Want You* but is a bit tougher, a little funkier in the breaks. The string arrangements by Dave Blumbery and Coleridge Taylor Perkinson are among the best the Motown studios issued to date. Ultimately, *Musical Massage* is a little-known classic from the supposedly twilight years of Motown. This record reveals Ware as a talented but under-celebrated visionary; he envisioned the evolution of soul and went about to bring it to fruition. *Musical Massage* is a watermark not only for Ware, but for Motown as well. The CD reissue features excellent sound and balance, and includes five bonus tracks from the sessions, including the stellar "French Waltz" and "Best of Both Worlds." *—Thom Jurek*

Inside Is Love / 1979 / Expansion ♦♦♦♦
Writer and producer Leon Ware has been responsible for some of R&B and pop's most lush and romantic tracks. Ware produced Marvin Gaye's 1976 classic *I Want You*. He also co-wrote songs like Michael Jackson's "I Wanna Be Where You Are," Marlena Shaw's "Sweet Beginnings," and the Main Ingredient's "Rollin' Down a Mountainside" to name a few. This album is the follow-up to his 1976 Gordy release *Musical Massage* and was released shortly after he was behind the controls for nine of the ten tracks of Melissa Manchester's *Don't Cry Loud*. *Inside Is Love* has the intelligent and melody rich work fans expect from Leon Ware. Produced by Ware and Ron Roker, this has arrangements from David Blumberg, Gene Page, and Sonny Burke. Although he's not the world's strongest vocalist, his methodical, light tenor gives these songs a personal stamp. The first track, "What's Your Name" has Ware playing his naïve lothario act to the hilt. The magnificent "Love Is a Simple Thing," co-written by Chicago member Robert Lamm, possesses a chorus that is both poignant and uplifting. Throughout *Inside Is Love*, Ware has some of his best lyrics and a batch of players to pull it off. The fanciful "Club Sashay," co-written by Manchester, has a gentle rhythm that's a perfect match for the phonetically pleasing words. The last track, "Hungry" has Ware mixing his classic style with the disco-fied chorus. Despite a couple of tracks that miss the mark, *Inside Is Love* is an absolute necessity for fans of emotional and brainy R&B/pop. *—Jason Elias*

Rockin' You Eternally / 1981 / Elektra ♦♦♦♦
This 1981 set was the follow-up to Ware's 1979 classic *Inside Is Love*. This effort gave him more of a commercial opportunity with a bigger label. The good news here is that Ware didn't change his style that much and served as sole producer. Although one would expect Ware to pull out all of the stops, *Rockin' You Eternally* features the same likeable and spare band who offers smooth support throughout. Although *Rockin' You Eternally* is another great effort from Ware, it doesn't start off with a "classic." The first track, "A Little Boogie (Never Hurt No One)," is an odd dance request coming from someone who's known for begging for something else. The synth hook-laden "Baby Don't Stop Me" co-written by Laudir De Oliveira and Peter Cetera has Ware helping himself on backing vocals. On the pleading "Sure Do Want You Now," Ware's vocals are especially impassioned and polished. The hypnotic title track has Ware wanting an extended relationship as he sings, "Don't you know I'm rocking/For the rest of time." On this effort's best track, the instrumental "Don't Stay Away" possesses an intricate melody and a soaring string arrangement from Gene Page. The only bumble here is the final track. "In Our Garden" has Ware tackling the "big issues" about the suffering in this land. It's commendable but you'd just as soon hear him singing about romance. Luckily, the majority of *Rockin' You Eternally* has Ware doing just that. *—Jason Elias*

Leon Ware / 1982 / Elektra ♦♦♦
This is the follow-up to 1981's much loved *Rockin' You Eternally*. While that effort had Ware engaged and willing to do rich and melodic work with no commercial consideration, *Leon Ware* more often than not seems to be overly concerned with making a big hit. *Leon Ware* was co-produced by Ware and the legendary Marty Paich. Although Paich had everyone from young Ella Fitzgerald to Boz Scaggs on his resumé, there wasn't much he could do with Ware. Paich also arranged the rhythm here, which is undoubtedly Ware's forte. That's not to say *Leon Ware* is a dismal failure—far from it. The first track "Slippin' Away" is Ware's best track here but it's reminiscent of a so-so track from Earth, Wind & Fire's *Faces*. In fact, *Leon Ware* employs some of the same players and writers from that effort. The oddly peppy "Lost in Love With You" was no doubt aiming for the charts but it possesses little or nothing of what makes Ware musically special. The track that comes

closest to Ware's style is "Deeper Than Love" despite its smoldering sax solos from Gato Barbieri; the song is a little overdone. Perhaps the most telling is the duet with Flora Purim, "Somewhere." The track's promise seems to evaporate with the intro. If Purim wasn't going to light a fire under the proceedings, no one could. Throughout this effort, Ware's sounds wan and hemmed in. Given the fact that this didn't include many great songs, *Leon Ware* isn't the best way to get acquainted with the artist. *—Jason Elias*

Taste the Love / May 17, 1995 / Kitchen ✦✦✦✦
Leon Ware is a perfect example of a vocalist who is much better known for his songwriting, producing and arranging than his singing. As a songwriter/producer, he's truly a heavyweight, but Ware's own albums haven't given us a lot of major hits. If you're a serious soul collector, chances are that you have a lot of Ware's songs in your collection—even if you don't have any of Ware's own LPs or CDs. It was in 1995 that Ware released the pleasing *Taste the Love* on his Kitchen label. Seductive, smooth offerings like "I Got Your Recipe," "Cream of Love" and "Come Live With Me, Angel" recall Marvin Gaye's romantic 1970s recordings (as opposed to his sociopolitical songs such as "Inner City Blues" and "What's Going On" or a party tune like "Got To Give It Up"), and that's no coincidence—Ware co-wrote Gaye's sexy 1976 hits "I Want You" and "After the Dance." You won't find a lot of fast, uptempo numbers on this CD; Ware maintains a lush, romantic atmosphere and gives us an enjoyable collection of R&B/pop mood music. For those who have savored the romantic side of Gaye and the Isley Brothers, *Taste the Love* is definitely worth hunting for. *—Alex Henderson*

Dee Dee Warwick

b. 1945
Vocals / Soul, Pop-Soul, Uptown Soul
Like Darlene Love and Cissy Houston, Dee Dee Warwick's considerable gifts as a soul singer were mostly confined to session work. And like Aretha Franklin's sisters, Dee Dee had to struggle with the shadow of a superstar sibling, Dionne Warwick. Certainly she had the talent to compete as an artist in her own right, but she only had a sporadic run of small hits in the 1960s and early '70s, and benefited from neither frequent recording opportunities nor substantial promotion from her labels.

Dee Dee began singing with her older sister Dionne as a teenager in the 1950s. They formed the Gospelaires, who sometimes sang with the Drinkard Singers, a long-running gospel outfit that their mother Lee had helped found, and that also featured their aunt, Cissy Houston. Like many gospel singers, Dee Dee moved into secular soul in the early '60s. Along with Dionne, Cissy, Doris Troy, and the Sweet Inspirations, she was one of New York's most in-demand session vocalists during the era, contributing to numerous pop/soul records by the likes of the Drifters, Chuck Jackson, Garnet Mimms, Aretha Franklin, Nina Simone, and Wilson Pickett. During her early career, Dee Dee was content to make a comfortable living as a backup singer. She began making her own records in 1963, however, cutting the original version of "You're No Good," which Betty Everett covered for a hit (and which Linda Ronstadt took to number one in 1975). It was produced by Jerry Leiber & Mike Stoller, who tried one more time with her in 1964 on "Standing By"; a single for the small Hurd label also flopped. She began treating her solo career more seriously in the second half of the 1960s, during which she released almost a dozen singles for Mercury, as well as a couple of albums.

Dee Dee's '60s recordings, while much less successful than Dionne's, were good New York pop/soul with a more pronounced R&B influence than her sister's. Some of these were actually substantial R&B hits; "I Want to Be With You," "Foolish Fool," and "I'm Gonna Make You Love Me" all made the R&B Top 20. The Supremes and the Temptations, however, would steal some of Dee Dee's thunder when their duet cover of "I'm Gonna Make You Love Me" made number two on the pop charts. Warwick signed to Atco at the beginning of the 1970s, getting a Top Ten R&B single right off the bat with "She Didn't Know (She Kept on Talking)." Over the next couple of years she'd make several other singles and an album, all of which comprised her earthiest work to date, sometimes with help from the Dixie Flyers rhythm section and backup vocals by the Sweet Inspirations. Only "Cold Night in Georgia" made a little commercial noise, however, and she returned to Mercury in 1973 (she has since claimed that Atlantic was throwing most of its promotional weight for female soul singers behind Aretha Franklin and Roberta Flack). She continued to record for various labels in the 1970s, but only "Get Out of My Life" (1975) dented the R&B charts. Since the mid-'70s, she has done backup vocals for Dionne Warwick, and recorded sporadically on her own. Long overdue, Soul Classics compiled her best Atco recordings for compact-disc reissue in 1996, and a Mercury reissue appeared in 2001. *—Richie Unterberger*

I Want to Be With You / 1967 / Mercury ✦✦✦✦✦
It's not too easy to find, but a strong album that features the original versions of "I'm Gonna Make You Love Me" (which would reach number two as a duet between the Supremes and the Temptations), "Gotta Get a Hold of Myself" (covered by the Zombies), and the Latin-tinged "House of Gold," which sounds like a super-soulful cover of a Jay & the Americans tune. *—Richie Unterberger*

Foolish Fool / 1969 / Mercury ✦✦✦✦✦

Turnin' Around / 1970 / Atco ✦✦✦

She Didn't Know: The Atco Sessions / Feb. 1996 / Ichiban/Soul Classics ✦✦✦✦✦
In the early '70s, Warwick recorded for Atco with limited success, reaching the R&B Top Ten with "She Didn't Know (She Kept on Talking)," and gaining a couple of smaller R&B hits with "Cold Night in Georgia" and a cover of "Suspicious Minds." She did quite a bit of recording for Atco between 1970 and 1972 in a fairly down-home vein, sometimes with backing by the esteemed Dixie Flyers rhythm section, and backup vocals by the Sweet Inspirations, Cissy Houston, and Judy Clay. These sessions sounded something like a poppier variation on the Stax sound, though none of the songs had the arresting qualities necessary to break her to the pop audience. This 22-track compilation of her Atco work is a typically high-class Soul Classics production, including all the hits, non-LP singles, tracks from her 1970 LP *Turning Around*, and seven unreleased songs that are just as impressive as her official performances from the era. Dee Dee, incidentally, sounds nothing like her famed sister Dionne here, favoring far gutsier vocals, material, and arrangements. It's good late-period vintage soul, and more evidence that Warwick was one of the more unjustly neglected soul performers of her time. *—Richie Unterberger*

The Sixties / 1998 / Marginal ✦✦✦✦✦
The sound and packaging on this 25-song collection leave something to be desired, yet it plugs a big gap in the lost '60s soul catalog by assembling a wealth of material by one of the decade's most underrated artists into one place. Leading off with all ten songs from her decent 1966 Mercury album, it also has the great original version of "You're No Good" (which even predates Betty Everett's small hit with the tune); the 1969 R&B Top 20 hit "Foolish Fool"; a strange but effective cover of "I (Who Have Nothing)"; a couple good Van McCoy-penned pop-soul numbers from 1964 ("Standing By" and "Don't Think My Baby's Coming Back"); and the outstandingly moody "Don't Call Me Anymore" (written by "You're No Good" author Clint Ballard). Unfortunately, this anthology is not definitive: some '60s singles are missing, and the six tracks from her 1970-1971 stay at Atco are a waste of space considering they are on the much more easily obtainable *She Didn't Know: The Atco Sessions* CD. There's nothing in the way of useful liner notes, and the sound seems partially or wholly dubbed from disc (without any major foul-ups). However, until such time as U.S. labels decide to give vintage artists like Warwick who didn't have big hits the respectful, cross-licensed treatment they deserve, there will continue to be a need for compilations of dubious origin such as this one. *—Richie Unterberger*

● **I Want to Be With You: The Mercury/Blue Rock Sessions** / Jun. 5, 2001 / Hip-O ✦✦✦✦✦
It wasn't for lack of talent that Dee Dee Warwick never approached the mainstream superstardom of her more famous older sister. As a sort of companion to *She Didn't Know: The Atco Sessions*, this generous 26-track collection compiles everything she recorded for the titular label from 1965-1969, with two tracks from a later 1973 session. The younger Warwick's rawer approach was closer to Aretha's but, when she slides into the high notes, the similarities to sister Dionne are obvious. Although revered by soul authorities as a great talent, when listening to these tracks it's easy to hear why she never clicked with the general public. For all her obvious vocal talents, there aren't enough great songs that draw attention to her fabulous gospel-driven voice. Additionally, like Dusty Springfield, her best assets are often buried behind a fussy and overbearing production that does neither her, nor these tunes, any favors. Ranging from pop-soul to R&B, the various producers add strings, backing vocals, horns, and at times everything short of Phil Spector in an effort to bolster some of these weak songs, but the results generally don't justify the effort. Even the great Philadelphia team of Gamble & Huff can't create sparks on the few tracks they are involved with. That said, there are enough gems scattered throughout to justify this disc's existence, especially since it marks the first CD appearance of many of these heretofore rare songs. Warwick lays into the bluesy "That's Not Love" like Etta James, causing distortion as she hauls off and wails with soul-searing power. The obscure Goffin & King tune "Yours Until Tomorrow," best-known from Gene Pitney's version, is a should-have-been hit, as is the original version of "I'm Gonna Make You Love Me," later a smash when the Temptations and the Supremes took it to the charts. Ultimately, Warwick was a substantial talent who didn't find her niche, or land songwriters of the Bacharach/David stature to guide her. This worthy collection—predominantly taken from the original masters but still sounding thin and sometimes shrill—is an important historical item for die-hard '60s soul fans, but disappointing for the casual listener. *—Hal Horowitz*

Dionne Warwick

b. Dec. 12, 1940, East Orange, NJ
Vocals / Pop-Soul, Brill Building Pop, Pop, Soul
It is easier to define Dionne Warwick by what she isn't rather than what she is. Although she grew up singing in church, she is not a gospel singer. Ella Fitzgerald and Sarah Vaughan are clear influences, but she is not a jazz singer. R&B is also part of her background, but she is not really a soul singer, either, at least not in the sense that Aretha Franklin is. Sophisticated is a word often used to describe her musical approach and the music she sings, but she is not a singer of standards such as Lena Horne or Nancy Wilson. What is she, then? She is a pop singer of a sort that perhaps could only have emerged out of the Brill Building environment of post-Elvis Presley, pre-Beatles urban pop in the early '60s. That's when she hooked up with Burt Bacharach & Hal David, songwriters and producers who wrote their unusually complicated songs for her aching, yet detached alto voice. Warwick is inescapably associated with those songs, even though she managed to build a career after leaving Bacharach & David that drew upon their style for other memorable recordings, such that she remains a unique figure in popular music.

Marie Dionne Warrick was born into a gospel-music family. Her father was a gospel record promoter for Chess Records and her mother managed the Drinkard Singers, a gospel group consisting of her relatives. She first raised her voice in song at age six at the New Hope Baptist Church in Newark, NJ, and soon after was a member of the choir. As a teenager, she formed a singing group called the Gospelaires with her sister Dee Dee and her aunt Cissy Houston (later the mother of Whitney Houston). After graduating from high school in 1959, she earned a music scholarship to the Hartt College of Music in Hartford, CT, but she also spent time with her group recording background vocals on sessions in New York. The Gospelaires are said to be present on such well-known recordings as Ben E. King's "Spanish Harlem" and "Stand By Me." They were at a Drifters session working on a song called "Mexican Divorce" composed by Burt Bacharach when Bacharach, attending the session, suggested Warwick might do some demos for him. She did, singing songs he had written with lyricist Hal David. Bacharach & David pitched one of the songs to Florence Greenberg, head of the small independent Scepter Records label, and Greenberg liked the demo singer enough to sign her as a recording artist. Bacharach

& David wrote and produced her first single, "Don't Make Me Over," in 1962. When the record was released, the performer credit contained a typo; it read "Dionne Warwick" instead of "Dionne Warrick," and she kept the new name. (Her sister Dee Dee eventually became Dee Dee Warwick as well.)

"Don't Make Me Over" peaked in the Top 20 of the pop charts in early 1963, also reaching the Top Five of the R&B charts. Warwick's subsequent singles were not as successful, but in early 1964, she reached the pop and R&B Top Ten and the Top Five of the easy listening charts with "Anyone Who Had a Heart," which was also her first record to reach the charts in the U.K. (There, such singers as Cilla Black and Dusty Springfield sometimes would cover her records before her own versions had a chance to become hits.) "Walk on By" followed it into the Top Ten of the pop, easy listening, and U.K. charts in the spring of 1964, and it hit number one on the R&B charts. By then, the Beatles had arrived on the American scene, followed by the British Invasion, and for a while, pop artists like Warwick took a beating on the charts. Nevertheless, the singer continued to place singles and LPs in the rankings over the next couple of years and in the spring of 1966, she returned to the Top Ten of the pop charts and the Top Five of the R&B charts with "Message to Michael." Other, more modest hits followed, including the most successful U.S. recording of the title song from the movie *Alfie*, which reached the R&B Top Five and the pop Top 20 in the spring of 1967. That summer, Warwick topped the R&B LP charts with her gold-selling *Here Where There Is Love* album and by the fall, Scepter had amassed enough chart singles to issue *Dionne Warwick's Golden Hits, Pt. 1*, her first album to reach the pop Top Ten.

Curiously, Warwick's career reached a new level with a single not written by Bacharach & David, although they produced it. It was "(Theme From) Valley of the Dolls," written by André & Dory Previn and issued at the end of 1967. The record reached the Top Five of the pop, R&B, and easy listening charts. Its B-side, Bacharach & David's "I Say a Little Prayer," reached the Top Five of the pop and R&B charts, helping the single become a gold record and the *Valley of the Dolls* LP also made the Top Five of the pop and R&B charts and went gold. With that, Warwick was on a roll. Her next single, "Do You Know the Way to San José," reached the pop Top Ten and the R&B and easy listening Top Five in the spring of 1968 and won the Grammy Award for Best Contemporary Pop Vocal Performance, Female. In the winter of 1969, her version of "This Guy's in Love With You," re-titled "This Girl's in Love With You," made the pop and R&B Top Ten and the easy listening Top Five and in early 1970, "I'll Never Fall in Love Again" from Bacharach & David's score for the Broadway musical *Promises, Promises* made the pop Top Ten and topped the easy listening charts, bringing her another Grammy Award for Best Contemporary Vocal Performance, Female.

In 1971, Warwick added an "e" to the end of her name on the advice of a numerologist, retaining the new spelling until 1975. She also left Scepter Records and signed a deal with the major label Warner Bros. that included Bacharach & David as her writer and producer. The team produced the 1972 album *Dionne*, which was a modest seller, but then Bacharach and David split up in the wake of the critical and commercial failure of their work on a musical remake of the film *Lost Horizon* in 1973. Due to her contractual commitment, Warwick was forced to sue her old partners. A settlement was reached, but they would not work together again for many years and Warwick's career suffered.

Warwick bounced back with "Then Came You," a song she recorded with the Spinners, which topped the pop and R&B charts and reached the Top Five of the easy listening charts in October 1974, going gold in the process. It proved to be a one-off success, but Warwick (now without the "e") signed to Arista Records in 1979 and returned to the Top Five of the pop adult contemporary (formerly easy listening) charts with "I'll Never Love This Way Again," produced by labelmate Barry Manilow and featured on her first platinum-selling album, another LP simply titled *Dionne*. "Deja Vu," also from the album, was a Top 20 pop and number one adult contemporary hit. "I'll Never Love This Way Again" won Warwick her third Grammy for Best Pop Vocal Performance, Female; "Deja Vu" won her her fourth for Best Rhythm & Blues Vocal Performance, Female.

Warwick topped the adult contemporary charts in 1980 with "No Night So Long," but her next across-the-board hit did not come until she hooked up with the Bee Gees for her 1982 album *Heartbreaker*. Barry Gibb produced the gold-selling LP and the three Gibb brothers wrote the title song, which made the pop Top Ten and topped the adult contemporary charts. In 1985, Warwick was reconciled with Bacharach and she organized a charity recording of his and Carole Bayer Sager's song "That's What Friends Are For" to benefit AIDS, featuring Elton John, Gladys Knight, and Stevie Wonder, in addition to herself. The record topped the pop, R&B, and adult contemporary charts in the winter of 1985-1986, the album *Friends* on which it was included went gold, and the song earned Warwick her fifth Grammy for Best Pop Performance by a Duo or Group with Vocal. In 1987, Warwick topped the adult contemporary charts and reached the Top Five of the R&B charts with "Love Power," a duet with Jeffrey Osborne that was another Bacharach/Sager composition.

Warwick enjoyed less commercial success after the late '80s. She parted ways with Arista Records after her 1995 album *Aquarela Do Brazil*. In 1998, she issued *Dionne Sings Dionne*, an album consisting largely of re-recordings of her hits, on River North Records. *—William Ruhlmann*

Presenting Dionne Warwick / 1963 / Scepter ✦✦✦✦✦

This is an excellent debut, nine of the 12 songs being Bacharach-David compositions. Some of these count among the most durable achievements of the careers of both Warwick and the songwriting team, including "Don't Make Me Over," "Wishin' & Hopin'," "This Empty Place," and "Make It Easy on Yourself." Most of the songs are available on the domestic '60s Warwick compilations on Rhino and Soul Classics. [In Britain, Sequel has reissued the album on CD on a two-fer that also includes her second LP, *Anyone Who Had a Heart*.] *—Richie Unterberger*

Anyone Who Had a Heart / 1964 / Scepter ✦✦✦

Dionne Warwick was in her most vulnerable-sounding, pop/soul best on this mid-'60s album. The title cut was among her first smash hits and would reappear on later albums. She found in the Bacharach/David writing team the lyricists and composers that would give her magical hits throughout the 1960s. *—Ron Wynn*

Make Way For / 1964 / Scepter ✦✦✦

Make Way For is Dionne Warwick's third long-player for Scepter Records. The album would eventually be her first to make the charts and was undoubtedly propelled by the hits "Walk on By," "You'll Never Get to Heaven," and "Wishin' & Hopin'"—all of which became key components of Warwick's performance repertoire. Interestingly, the latter track as well as "I Smiled Yesterday" had also been included on Warwick's debut album, *Presenting Dionne Warwick*. However, that didn't seem to deter listeners eager for new tunes. Warwick's musical mentors and collaborators Burt Bacharach & Hal David also presented the singer with several additional compositions that would become signature songs for other performers in the ensuing years. "(They Long to Be) Close to You" became synonymous with the Carpenters, while Dusty Springfield shared some of Warwick's notoriety with her own hit version of "Wishin' & Hopin'." The trio of tracks *not* derived from the voluminous Bacharach/David catalog include Jules Styne's "People," from *Funny Girl*, as well as a few numbers from a pair of other well-known Brill Building teams of pop songwriters. Gerry Goffin & Carole King serve up "Make the Night a Little Longer," while the arguably lesser-known pairing of Howard Greenfield & Helen Miller offer the somewhat antiquated "Get Rid of Him." In 1995, Sequel Records began a restoration campaign of Warwick's classic Scepter Records output. [*Make Way For* was paired along with the follow-up, *The Sensitive Sound of Dionne Warwick* LP, onto one CD with recently penned liner notes from Hal David biographer Adam White.] *—Lindsay Planer*

The Sensitive Sound of Dionne Warwick / 1965 / Scepter ✦✦✦✦✦

Things were just beginning to explode for Dionne Warwick in the mid-'60s. This album shows her sound maturing, the Bacharach/David team beginning to write the patented anguished laments and sophisticated soul tunes that were her forte, and Warwick gradually weaning the gospel out of her voice and smoothing out her delivery. While she actually didn't fare that well commercially, you can hear the groundwork being laid on such songs as "Who Can I Turn To" and "You Can Have Him." *—Ron Wynn*

Here I Am / Dec. 1965 / Scepter ✦✦✦✦

Dionne Warwick's early- and mid-'60s Scepter Records catalog stands as some of her finest and most prolific work in conjunction with the songwriting team of Burt Bacharach & Hal David. By the time of *Here I Am* in 1966, the superhuman nature of the trio's relationship had resulted in five long-players in three years—not counting soundtracks and live albums, which would bring the total to seven during the same time. Although some of their most successful collaborations were still ahead of them, the marriage of the duo's well-crafted and distinct pop songs with Warwick's light, supple vocals again resulted in several masterpieces. "Are You There (With Another Girl)," "Window Wishing," "Don't Go Breaking My Heart," and "Long Day, Short Night" are but a few of the hits and listener favorites on this album. In addition to the eight Bacharach/David pieces, Warwick truly demonstrates her versatility as an interpreter on the inimitable cover of the Gershwin standard "I Love You, Porgy." Her voice conveys the noir tale with haunting resonance. In direct contrast is the joyous "This Little Light," which furthers the evidence supporting her skills as a performer and features Warwick's solo piano accompaniment. In 1995, U.K.-based Sequel Records paired *Here I Am* with the 1967 follow-up *Here Where There Is Love* on a single CD. The latter would continue the hit parade with "Alfie" and "What the World Needs Now" and is also notable for the cover of Bob Dylan's "Blowin' in the Wind." *—Lindsay Planer*

Dionne Warwick in Paris / 1966 / Scepter ✦✦✦

Outside of a brilliant live version of "A House Is Not a Home," this album was more politely sung than most of what Dionne Warwick turned in regularly throughout the 1960s. It was a nice departure and did reasonably well, but wasn't a showcase or definitive concert album. It's long gone now, but might be worth it if you come across it in an auction. *—Ron Wynn*

Here Where There Is Love / 1967 / Scepter ✦✦✦

Here Where There Is Love was a big album for Dionne Warwick, a very respectable adult contemporary creation featuring three Top 30 hits: "Trains and Boats and Planes," "I Just Don't Know What to Do With Myself," and the classic theme from the film of the same name, "Alfie." The problem here is a double-edged sword, part of which is the packaging that Scepter Records wrapped this beautiful music in. The photo of two lovers on a beach under off-pink skies at sunset looks like something Ray Coniff might have been happy with. If Warwick were on a Columbia Records-sized label, she might not have had the string of hits she enjoyed with this smaller record company, but her albums, like those of Johnny Mathis, might have had significantly more catalog value just from the promotion and packaging side of things. Side one is completely composed by her ace producers, Burt Bacharach & Hal David, with Bacharach listed as the arranger and conductor on both sides. However, Bob Leeman and O.B. Mastingill get arranging credits on side two under certain titles, and the feel is distinctly different. The Bacharach/David material has elegance and that superb resonance that made this trio so powerful, and some of that is absent from the material not written by the core team. The work of Warwick/Bacharach and David was to adult contemporary pop what Phil Spector was to the Wall of Sound; listen to the absolute tension in "Alfie"—it's a soft rock version of Shirley Bassey's "Goldfinger," the minor chords exploding in a calmer setting. Mastingill's arrangement of Lionel Bart's "As Long As He Needs Me" plays like an early-'60s Johnny Mathis record. It really doesn't sound like Burt Bacharach is involved in this track—same for Bob Leeman's arrangement of his own co-write "(I Never Knew) What You Were up To." O.B. Mastingill also arranges "I Wish You Love" and the cover of Dylan's "Blowing in the Wind," and as pretty and nice as the titles are, there's no denying the album has gone in a different direction. What began as powerful adult contemporary album with stunning sounds evolves into a cabaret-style recording that was the basis for many other middle-of-the-road artists from before, artists who eventually found themselves singing songs Warwick made famous. In other words, *Here Where There Is Love* feels like it was pieced together to get some product out there to benefit from the singles chart action. But it all somehow works, a credit to Dionne Warwick, who is absolutely on no matter who the composer, no matter what song she's given. A tremendously underrated talent, the liner notes by *Cash Box* magazine's Rick Bolsom tell listeners absolutely nothing about the LP. Like the album jacket failing to have the star front and center, the wonderful voice within had to find an audience through hit singles—and did. *—Joe Viglione*

On Stage and in the Movies / 1967 / Scepter ✦✦✦
A nice collection of show tunes and movie songs, one of her best non-greatest hits or anthology albums. Warwick's brand of sophisticated, soft pop/soul translated well to the stage and film song arena, even if she didn't always get quality numbers. But these songs were expertly chosen and brilliantly performed. *—Ron Wynn*

The Windows of the World / Aug. 1967 / Scepter ✦✦✦✦✦
This proved both one of Warwick's strongest albums and a solid commercial LP as well. It included such hits as "I Say a Little Prayer" and "(There's) Always Something There to Remind Me," and had some fine album cuts as well. The title track had the kind of haunting refrain and anguished lyrics that became a Warwick specialty. *—Ron Wynn*

The Valley of the Dolls / 1968 / Scepter ✦✦✦
The biggest hit album of her career, even though it was far from her greatest music. Warwick stayed on the charts for almost a year with his release. The theme song just missed topping the charts, while "Do You Know the Way to San Jose" rivals "Promises, Promises" and "I Say a Little Prayer" as Warwick's best uptempo number. *—Ron Wynn*

Promises, Promises / Nov. 1968 / Scepter ✦✦✦
Dionne Warwick was still rolling along in the late '60s, as the Bacharach/David axis hadn't yet disintegrated. While the material was getting safer and more pop-centered, it retained its lyrical quality and production sheen. Both the title song and "This Girl's in Love With You," the distaff version of the Herb Alpert hit, were superly crafted and wonderfully sung. Warwick hadn't yet encountered the demons that would make the early '70s such a turbulent time. *—Ron Wynn*

Alfie / 1969 / Scepter/Pickwick ✦✦✦✦
A budget repackaging of some current and past Dionne Warwick hits, this collection sort of underlines the fact that her releases were not very well coordinated. Generally, whenever Dionne had a hit (which, of course, was often), Scepter usually made that the lead track of an album and threw together the remainder from several other past (and released) hits. This tended to diffuse any illustration of her evolution as an artist. It was, however, an era when singles were king, so it has to be looked at as a release of the time. In addition to the gorgeous "Alfie," this record contains some of Dionne's finest performances ever, with the sterling "Always Something There to Remind Me," "Don't Make Me Over" and "Message to Michael." One surprise is her version of "Wives and Lovers," which had been covered by Jack Jones as well as Frank Sinatra. Overall, though, this is a too-short nine-song collection, and the mastering and sound leave a bit to be desired. *—Matthew Greenwald*

Freewheelin' / 1969 / Pye ✦✦✦

Greatest Motion Picture Hits / 1969 / Scepter ✦✦✦✦✦
A fine collection of film themes and show tunes, Dionne Warwick did well with these types of songs, whether she had outstanding numbers or weak ones. "As Long As He Needs Me," "Look of Love," and "One Hand, One Heart" were only some of the highlights. This was by far Warwick's best set devoted to cinematic material. *—Ron Wynn*

Soulful / 1969 / Scepter ✦✦

Decade of Gold / 1970 / Scepter ✦✦✦

I'll Never Fall in Love Again / 1970 / Scepter ✦✦✦
While Herb Alpert had a number-one hit with his version of the title track, Dionne Warwick captured the real contradictory flavor and irony in the theme. It was one of her last albums for Scepter, and her relationship with the Bacharach/David team had soured. But she turned in some good album cuts for a change, and such songs as "Let Me Go To Him" and "Paper Mache" were nice follow-up numbers. *—Ron Wynn*

Very Dionne / 1970 / Scepter ✦✦✦
Dionne Warwick was in the midst of a transitional phase that would ultimately see her leave Scepter, split with the Bacharach/David team, and even change her last name to Warwicke. Some of the effects could be heard in this material; there were a few misguided numbers, like "Green Grass of Home," and she even recycled "I Just Don't Know What To Do With Myself." *—Ron Wynn*

Then Came You / 1975 / Warner Bros. ✦✦✦✦
After being a premier vocalist in the '60s, Warwick seemed to have hit a stylistic wall by the early '70s. By the time she signed with Warner Bros. in 1970, Warwick attempted many styles and producers. *Then Came You*, released in 1975, has her teaming with both Jerry Ragovoy and, for one track, Thom Bell. Jerry Ragovoy was a successful producer who had Garnet Mimms and Howard Tate among his credits. For this effort, Ragovoy assembled a strong New York session band, including John Tropea, Leon Pendarvis, and Bob Babbitt. The first track, "Take It From Me," has Warwick getting a more R&B styled production rather than MOR. That was perfect since her voice had matured, attaining an effortless warmth and ease. Here she wasn't so much an interpreter of "great material," her voice and charm were the primary draw. Ragovoy's track "Move Me No Mountain" has a Barry White-styled backing, and Warwick got a chance to be more sensual. "How Can I Tell Him," a skilled, song about exiting a relationship, written by Ragovoy and Jacob Brackman, incorporates a slick arrangement that perfectly matches the feeling of person exiting a relationship. Warwick perfectly sung the lyrics with a sense of cautiousness, but also a little bit of happiness to be leaving. The title track is the duet with the Spinners. The song, produced by Thom Bell, was a number-one pop single and her biggest hit in close to four years. *Then Came You* is mostly an innovative effort of New York R&B/pop that should make anyone's short list of albums that truly capture the style. *—Jason Elias*

Track of the Cat / 1975 / Warner Bros. ✦✦✦
After leaving Scepter, Dionne Warwick floundered for a while as she sought the production and arranging assistance she needed to return to her past heights. She didn't get it on this 1975 release, as songs like "Love Me One More Time" and "Jealousy" were tentatively sung, burdened with unimpressive lyrics or poorly produced. Warwick was also experiencing personal problems and experimenting with adding an "e" to her last name, neither of which helped the situation. *—Ron Wynn*

Only Love Can Break a Heart / 1977 / Musicor ✦✦✦

Love at First Sight / 1979 / Warner Bros. ✦✦✦
Produced by the hit production team of Steve Barri and Michael Omartian (Rhythm Heritage's number-one pop hit "Theme From S.W.A.T"), Dionne Warwick's 1979 Warner Bros. LP *Love at First Sight* came closest in pop ethic to her earlier sides on Sceptor. Serving as a reminder of those days is the wispy ballad "Do I Have to Cry" and the perky "Early Morning Strangers," which were co-written by Hal David who co-wrote Warwick's '60s/early-'70s hit classics with Burt Bacharach. The upbeat first single, "Do You Believe in Love at First Sight," was one of the more catchier tracks of the singer's '70s records. However, the cornerstone of the LP was the atmospheric "Don't Ever Take Your Love Away," co-written by Issac Hayes. The Barry Mann/Cynthia Weil charmer, "Long Way to Go," is closest in theme to Warwick's favorite song, "Windows of the World." [*Love at First Sight* was reissued on CD on June 13, 2000 by WEA International.] *—Ed Hogan*

Dionne / May 1979 / Arista ✦✦
Dionne Warwick's career was revived when she teamed with Barry Manilow on this 1979 LP. Manilow's production of such heavily orchestrated numbers as "I Know I'll Never Love This Way Again" put Warwick back in the spotlight, as she once again sounded confident and compelling. It was the first platinum album of her career, and also her first album in ten years to crack the Top Ten on the pop album chart. Warwick scored another hit with "Déjà Vu" and was back on track. *—Ron Wynn*

Hot! Live and Otherwise / 1981 / Arista ✦✦
This was one of those "product" releases satisfying contractual obligations. Arista trotted out three sides of decent-to-boring live sets and padded it with a fourth studio side. The results were forgettable, although the song "Some Changes Are For Good" was a decent track and generated a little noise on the R&B end. *—Ron Wynn*

Heartbreaker / Oct. 1982 / Arista ✦✦✦
Barry Gibb took his shot at producing Dionne Warwick and had quite a bit of success with this early-'80s album. While the title track sounded awkward and forced, it cracked the Top Ten. Warwick was squarely back in the mainstream, and although she wasn't making transcendent hits, she was making creditable ones. *—Ron Wynn*

How Many Times Can We Say Goodbye / 1983 / Arista ✦✦✦✦
In the early '80 Warwick experienced a career renaissance thanks to "Déjà Vu" and her singing to Arista, a label seemed to be more sympathetic to her needs. This 1983 album pairs her with producer Luther Vandross. Vandross, who also produced Aretha Franklin's *Jump To It* in 1982, is a much better teaming of singer and producer. Although "Got a Date" and "I Do It 'Cause I Like It" are both disposable pop-based filler, this album has phenomenal versions of some of Vandross' unsung gems. The poignant title track is a duet with Vandross and Warwick, and finds their voices blending extremely well. The gentle "So Amazing" and the gossamer and touching "What Can a Miracle Do" have Warwick's all-encompassing and raspy vocals cohering in Vandross' trademark lush surroundings. She also tackles Michael McDonald's grade A weeper "I Can Let Go Now" and brings a deeper sense of longing and hurt than the great original. In the same vein, "Will You Love Me Tomorrow" shows up as a reflective ballad featuring the Shirelles. This album features arguably Vandross' best players, including Nat Adderley Jr. on keyboards, drummer Yogi Horton, bassist Marcus Miller, and great emotive synth work by Skip Anderson. While a few tracks fall short of the mark, the best here makes *How Many Times Can We Say Goodbye* an absolute necessity for fans of Warwick and Vandross. *—Jason Elias*

Finder of Lost Loves / 1985 / Arista ✦✦
This one-season television program featured Dionne Warwick doing the title track, and spawned this album. Neither the song nor the LP were much better than the show. "You Made Me Want to Love Again" wasn't bad, nor were "It's Love" or "Love Doesn't Live Here Anymore," but weren't strong enough to salvage the album. *—Ron Wynn*

Friends / 1985 / Arista ✦✦
The huge chart topper "That's What Friends Are For" ensured that this would be a big hit album for Dionne Warwick. The song has become a signature piece, even though it's not as compelling as "Walk on By," and Warwick's vocal isn't as gripping as that of either Gladys Knight or Stevie Wonder (or even Elton John). But it was the perfect tune for the times and made everything else on the album insignificant (which it was anyhow). *—Ron Wynn*

Reservations for Two / 1987 / Arista ✦✦✦
Dionne Warwick's aptly-titled LP *Reservations for Two* is a collection of smooth pop duets, some of which reunite the singer with Burt Bacharach. The first single, "Love Power," sung with Jeffrey Osborne, is as mild as a warm cup of coffee and made the Top Five on the R&B and Top 20 on the pop charts. The track is on Osborne's *Ultimate Collection* and Warwick's own *Definitive Collection*. The title track duet with Kashif was a Top 20 R&B hit in late 1987 can also be found on Kashif's own *Definitive Collection*. *—Ed Hogan*

★ **The Dionne Warwick Collection: Her All-Time Greatest Hits** / 1989 / Rhino ♦♦♦♦♦
Rhino's *The Dionne Warwick Collection: Her All-Time Greatest Hits* is the best Warwick collection on the market, culling 24 tracks from her '60s prime. Although it doesn't cover her entire career, it does feature nearly all of her very best material, and it's all in the style that made her famous; top to bottom, it's a stronger, more consistent listen than anything else out there. This was the period when she established herself as the premier interpreter of Burt Bacharach's music, and pulled off the neat trick of appealing to both R&B and easy listening audiences. Warwick was soulful without necessarily singing soul music per se; her smooth, light delivery and polished technique meshed very well with the sophisticated pop of the Bacharach/Hal David team, who co-composed all but one of the songs included here. No other singer navigated Bacharach's deceptively tricky compositions with such effortless grace; the ease she projects on the rhythmically complex "I Say a Little Prayer" and "Promises, Promises" is startling. It's no wonder her versions of Bacharach's songs often became the definitive ones. This compilation doesn't cover Warwick's later hits, like the Spinners' duet "Then Came You," "That's What Friends Are For," or her late-'70s/early-'80s adult contemporary fare; for those, look to Arista's *The Definitive Collection*, which touches on every phase of her career, or the more specific *Greatest Hits (1979-1990)*. But for a sparkling demonstration of everything that made Warwick great, there's no better buy than *The Dionne Warwick Collection*. *—Steve Huey*

Greatest Hits (1979–1990) / Oct. 1989 / Arista ♦♦♦
Dionne Warwick enjoyed a career revival in the late '70s and 1980s when she teamed with such producers as Barry Manilow, Barry Gibb, and even Luther Vandross. They returned her to the elaborately arranged and structured soul-tinged pop that had marked her finest hits, although the lyrics and compositions weren't as consistent as they were during the Burt Bacharach/Hal David period. This album collects the biggest hits from this second phase of Warwick's career, including such triumphs as "Déjà Vu" and "I Know I'll Never Love This Way Again"; it also introduced a new tune, "Take Good Care of You And Me." *—Ron Wynn*

Sings Cole Porter / Jul. 1990 / Arista ♦♦♦
It was a grand idea, but Warwick didn't meet the challenge as magically as she might have in the 1960s or '70s. Instead, she sounded almost prim and stiff instead of engaging and confident. It was a surprise, given how wonderful Warwick sounded doing similar (though certainly not as well constructed) material from Barry Manilow. It was still worth hearing, but far from the anticipated triumph. *—Ron Wynn*

☆ **Anthology (1962–1969)** / 1991 / Rhino ♦♦♦♦♦
Rhino's *Anthology (1962-1969)* was an excellent 24-track retrospective of Dionne Warwick's prime period, and has since gone out of print. Why? Because it contained exactly the same track listing as Rhino's *The Dionne Warwick Collection: Her All-Time Greatest Hits*, which had been released just two years prior—and still remains available. The reason *Anthology* was issued, under a different title and with different artwork, is now lost in the mists of time. *—Steve Huey*

Hidden Gems: The Best of Dionne Warwick, Vol. 2 / Mar. 24, 1992 / Rhino ♦♦♦♦♦
Turning the spotlight on various rarities, B-sides, and album cuts, *Hidden Gems* reminds us that some of Dionne Warwick's best work with the prolific Burt Bacharach/Hal David team received little or no radio airplay. In retrospect, it's hard to believe that Warwick's versions of "What the World Needs Now Is Love," "The Look of Love" (also recorded by Isaac Hayes, Anita Baker, and countless others), and "Make It Easy on Yourself" (a smash for Jerry Butler) weren't major hits. They certainly deserved to be, as did the hauntingly pretty "Any Old Time of the Day" ("Walk on By"'s B-side) and "They Long to Be (Close to You)." For those who might have overlooked this fine material, *Hidden Gems* is quite a revelation. *—Alex Henderson*

Friends Can Be Lovers / 1993 / Arista ♦♦♦
Here lies the pleasant balance between Dionne-esque pop anthems ("Age of Miracles" and "I Sing at Dawn"), ballads (Sting's "Fragile" and a duet with Whitney Houston on "Love Will Find a Way"), down-right funk on "Much Too Much" and shameless lust on "Where My Lips Have Been." Also included is Warwick's glorious reunion with Bacharach/David on "Sunny Weather Lover." Certainly one of her best-produced, best-sung and well-packaged albums since joining the Arista roster. *—Bil Carpenter*

Presenting Dionne Warwick/Anyone Who Had a Heart / 1995 / Sequel ♦♦♦♦♦
This is the first in a series of releases—featuring two LPs on one CD—aimed at reissuing the classic Scepter Records catalog of pop vocalist Dionne Warwick. *Presenting Dionne Warwick* and *Anyone Who Had a Heart* are her first and second long-players and almost immediately established the young singer as the perfect vehicle for the noir love songs of Hal David & Burt Bacharach. The songwriting duo's prolific nature is instantaneously evident as two-thirds of the 21 songs that comprise these two long-players bear not only their names, but more importantly their distinct sound. From right out of the box, this artist/composer team began having hits. However, the union was much closer to *not* occurring than their track record might suggest. The record label's co-founder, Florence Greenberg, despised the first tune that the combo recorded. She hated it so much, legend has it that she became quite upset that the label's money was being spent on such. It wasn't until "Don't Make Me Over" began to outperform the single's A-side, "I Smiled Yesterday," by racing up the pop and R&B charts that Greenberg changed her own tune. In short order, it became Warwick's first national hit as well as one of her signature songs. Although the first, it was far from the only hit that these discs produced. "Wishin' and Hopin'" not only predates Dusty Springfield's version, it was admittedly the blueprint and inspiration behind Springfield choosing to cover it. "Make It Easy on Yourself" and the title track to Warwick's second album, *Anyone Who Had a Heart*, were also radio hits and became concert performance staples. There are a few non-Bacharach/David tunes that are worthy of mention. Foremost is the upbeat and Latin-tinged Doc Pomus & Mort Shuman tune "Shall I Tell Her"—which would have made a great Supremes cover. Then there is the oddly hip version of "Zip-A-Dee-Doo-Dah." The lead electric guitar and Shirelles-like vocal arrangement make this reading a keeper. *—Lindsay Planer*

From the Vaults / Oct. 1995 / Ichiban/Soul Classics ♦♦♦
An anthology of 24 fairly obscure tracks, drawn from Warwick's 1963-1966 albums and B-sides. Although it has the look of something that would appeal primarily to serious fans and collectors, this is hardly any less satisfying than the greatest hits collections covering the same era. It's also just as good as Rhino's *Hidden Gems*, another anthology of little-known Warwick recordings from the '60s; what's more, it doesn't repeat any selections from that previous compilation. The first half of the CD (covering 1962-1964) shows Dionne at her most girl group-ish and soulful, with arrangements that often recall those of her labelmates, the Shirelles (who in fact recorded their own versions of a few of these songs). "It's Love That Really Counts" and "Get Rid of Him" are highlights; "Mr. Heartbreak" is a wrenching, stately ballad, easily up to the standard of her hits of the period. The last half of the program covers material from 1965 and 1966, all of which (like most of the songs she sang in the late '60s) was penned by Bacharach/David. These show her going in a smoother, adult pop-oriented direction, and while the somewhat gutsier earlier sides are preferred, there are some good tunes that are impossible to come by otherwise, except on long out-of-print LPs. *—Richie Unterberger*

Dionne Sings Dionne / Oct. 6, 1998 / River North ♦♦♦
As one of the premier pop/R&B singers with a singular voice, Dionne Warwick's list of hits includes "Are You There (With Another Girl)," "Once You Hit the Road," and the often nerve-racking "Heartbreaker." As she racked up the singles, Warwick fans also realize she has also released fulfilling albums through the years, including 1975's *Track of the Cat* and her 1979 comeback effort, *Dionne*. *Dionne Sings Dionne* is also a strong effort. While including new tracks, the bulk of *Dionne Sings Dionne* consists of reconfigured versions of her '60s work with Burt Bacharach and lyricist Hal David. Although many talented singers have come up empty when reviewing their classics, Warwick seems to be having fun here and deftly reexamines her oeuvre like only a handful of artists could. The '80s Earth, Wind & Fire-styled production values boost "Reach Out for Me." The song also features the Emotions, DeBarge, and the talented El DeBarge, who has some great chemistry with Warwick. "Say a Little Prayer" gets a casually elegant quiet storm reworking, with the rasp of Warwick's voice coming through loud and clear. Along the same lines, the always sweet Bacharach & David gem "All Kinds of People" is just as steady, with Warwick now bringing a sense of wisdom to the lyric where there once was hope. A new track, "Be My Neighbor," features Tyrese. With a lyric expressing that Warwick is desired by Tyrese as a surrogate mother who can offer advice, it comes off apt and sweet. Although at first this does seems haphazard, *Dionne Sings Dionne* is a fun and skilled effort. *—Jason Elias*

Definitive Collection / Apr. 13, 1999 / Arista ♦♦♦♦
Although the title might be stretching it a bit, *The Definitive Collection* is nevertheless a solid overview of Dionne Warwick's storied career; its greatest strength is that it encompasses the full breadth of the singer's catalog, assembling material not only from her peak-era Scepter tracks but also from her later hits on Arista. The vintage Burt Bacharach/Hal David-composed smashes have lost none of their lustre in the passing years, and many—"Walk on By," "Do You Know the Way to San Jose," "Don't Make Me Over" and "Anyone Who Had a Heart"—are presented here in their definitive readings; Warwick's subsequent recordings can't help but suffer in comparison, although hits like "I'll Never Love this Way Again" and the Barry Gibb duet "Heartbreaker" possess a certain charm. *—Jason Ankeny*

The Very Best of Dionne Warwick / May 23, 2000 / Rhino ♦♦♦♦♦
Rhino's *The Very Best of Dionne Warwick* collects 16 of the singer's classic singles from 1962-1974, the heyday of her collaboration with songwriters Burt Bacharach & Hal David. "Walk on By," "Alfie," "I Say a Little Prayer," and "This Girl's in Love With You" are some of the hits that define Warwick's soulful, orchestral sound from that era, along with "(Theme From) Valley of the Dolls," "Do You Know the Way to San Jose" and "Then Came You," which also features the Spinners. A must for Warwick fans and worthwhile for anyone interested in classic singing and songwriting. *—Heather Phares*

Martha Wash

b. San Francisco, CA

Vocals / Dance-Pop, Hi-NRG, Club/Dance, Urban

An exuberant singer with a huge voice and booming, declarative sound, Martha Wash originally teamed with Izora Rhodes. They were known as Two Tons of Fun when they backed Sylvester and later recorded for Fantasy. They changed their name to the Weather Girls and recorded for CBS. Wash then began doing session work as a solo singer. She was in the midst of a big flap in the early '90s, as she claimed that the C&C Music Factory didn't credit her for vocals on its huge hit "Gonna Make You Sweat (Everybody Dance Now)." It was Wash's rich, shattering voice that turned "Everybody Everybody" into a smash for Black Box, but she wasn't featured in the video, something else that didn't make her very happy. Wash signed with BMG in 1991. *—Ron Wynn*

● **Martha Wash** / Jan. 1993 / RCA ♦♦♦♦
Martha Wash's work with the Weather Girls and Black Box was so strong that one couldn't help but greet this debut solo album with high expectations—perhaps so high that a generally enjoyable album came as a slight disappointment. Anyone familiar with the big-voiced diva's history couldn't help but hope for a soul/disco/house extravaganza, and this CD, for all its strong points, doesn't fit that description. There are a few dancefloor gems on the album (including "Things We Do for Love," "Leave a Light On" and the soaring "Carry On"), but most of the tracks fall under the heading of decent but not outstanding. And after hearing Wash belt it out on the Weather Girls' "It's Raining Men" and

Black Box's "Everybody Everybody," it's impossible to expect less than consistent excellence from her. This album has more going for it than most of the faceless, sound-alike releases flooding the urban contemporary market in 1992, but Wash is capable of so much more. *—Alex Henderson*

The Collection / Jun. 3, 1997 / Logic ✦✦✦✦
While a collection of Martha Wash's assorted hits is a great idea, *The Collection* is likely to leave most listeners wanting more. While most of Wash's hits—which she typically performed anonymously for studio projects including C&C Music Factory and Black Box—are included, many are in newly recorded renditions which pale next to the originals; for every vintage track like the C&C chart-topper "Gonna Make You Sweat (Everybody Dance Now)," there's another like "It's Raining Men… The Sequel," which substitutes the original Weather Girls camp classic for a tired retread featuring RuPaul. Also subpar are the three new tracks—"God Bless the Road," "Come" and "Catch the Light" (presented in both "East Coast" and "West Coast" mixes). *—Jason Ankeny*

Baby Washington (Justine Washington)

b. Nov. 13, 1940, South Carolina
Vocals / Soul, Uptown Soul, R&B, Pop-Soul
Her sultry delivery earned Justine "Baby" Washington R&B chart bows in four different decades, most notably on the delectable uptown soul classic "That's How Heartaches Are Made" for Sue Records in 1963. Born in South Carolina but raised in Harlem, Washington was a member of the Hearts in 1956 before tallying her first R&B hit in 1959 with "The Time" for Neptune. Billed occasionally as Jeanette or Justine Washington, she scaled the soul charts into the mid-'70s with hits still hot from the '60s, such as her nugget "Only Those in Love." *—Bill Dahl*

That's How Heartaches Are Made / 1963 / Collectables ✦✦✦
Baby Washington cut her finest songs for Sue in the early '60s. Although few made the charts, all were delivered with conviction, sung in an earnest and riveting manner, and produced with minimal gimmicks. While the title track is perhaps her best cut, this album thankfully covers many lesser-known tracks and avoids the singles that have frequently popped up on numerous anthologies. "Careless Hands" and "Standing on the Pier" are superior to material that did get airplay; even the always troublesome Collectables sound quality can't override the importance of this release. *—Ron Wynn*

Only Those in Love / 1965 / Collectables ✦✦✦
The title track is an understated ballad that sets the stage for a dozen prime Baby Washington tracks, many of which sound dated for 1965 (the original release date of this CD reissue). "Go On" owes its soul to doo wop and "Money's Funny" to R&B; both are fine examples of each style. "Hey Lonely" and "Run My Heart" are the most contemporary tracks (along with the two Christmas Songs, "White Christmas" and "Silent Night"). But nothing here can compete with what Motown and other companies were raising the bar with. *—Andrew Hamilton*

With You in Mind / 1968 / Veep ✦✦✦

● **The Best of Baby Washington** / 1987 / Collectables ✦✦✦✦✦
Baby Washington could sound like a hard-edged, no-nonsense wailer one moment and a wounded sparrow the next. She never enjoyed much pop attention, but equaled Dionne Warwick and Maxine Brown among female light soul singers. This 12 tracks on this collection cover her late-'50s and early-'60s songs for Neptune and Sue, including "The Bells," "The Time" and the classic "That's How Heartaches Are Made." *—Ron Wynn*

● **The Sue Singles** / 1996 / Kent ✦✦✦✦✦
Excellent 28-track compilation of her work for the Sue label in the '60s leaves the domestic Collectables anthologies in the dust in terms of quantity and quality. Has all of the significant R&B hits she recorded for the company, including "That's How Heartaches Are Made," "Handful of Memories," "Who's Gonna Take Care of Me," "It'll Never Be Over for Me," "Only Those in Love," and "No Time for Pity." It's also the best showcase for her versatility, going from near-gospel to string-laden uptown pop/soul, and even a bit of blues, straight pop, and jazz-inflected numbers. Her influence on Dusty Springfield can easily be detected on "I Can't Wait Until I See My Baby's Face" and "Doodlin'," both of which Springfield covered in the '60s. *—Richie Unterberger*

Dinah Washington (Ruth Lee Jones)

b. Aug. 29, 1924, Tuscaloosa, AL, **d.** Dec. 14, 1963, Detroit, MI
Vocals / Vocal Jazz, Traditional Pop, Standards, Ballads, Jump Blues
Dinah Washington was at once one of the most beloved and controversial singers of the mid-20th century: beloved to her fans, devotees, and fellow singers; controversial to critics who still accuse her of selling out her art to commerce and bad taste. Her principal sin, apparently, was to cultivate a distinctive vocal style that was at home in all kinds of music, be it R&B, blues, jazz, middle-of-the-road pop—and she probably would have made a fine gospel or country singer had she the time. Hers was a gritty, salty, high-pitched voice, marked by absolute clarity of diction and clipped, bluesy phrasing. Washington's personal life was turbulent, with seven marriages behind her, and her interpretations showed it, for she displayed a tough, totally unsentimental, yet still gripping hold on the universal subject of lost love. She has had a huge influence on R&B and jazz singers who have followed in her wake, notably Nancy Wilson, Esther Phillips, and Diane Schuur; and her music is abundantly available nowadays via the huge seven-volume series *The Complete Dinah Washington on Mercury*. *—Richard S. Ginell*

Dinah Jams / Aug. 15, 1954 / EmArcy ✦✦✦✦✦
Recorded at the start of Dinah Washington's climb to fame, 1954's *Dinah Jams* was taped live in front of a studio audience in Los Angeles. While Washington is in top form throughout, effortlessly working her powerful, blues-based voice on both ballads and swingers, the cast of star soloists almost steals the show. In addition to drummer Max Roach, trumpeter Clifford Brown, and other members of Brown and Roach's band at the time—tenor saxophonist Harold Land, pianist Richie Powell, and bassist George Morrow—trumpeters Maynard Ferguson and Clark Terry, alto saxophonist Herb Geller, and pianist Junior Mance also contribute to the session. Along with extended jams like "Lover Come Back to Me," "You Go to My Head," and "I'll Remember April"—all including a round of solos—there are shorter ballad numbers such as "There Is No Greater Love" and "No More," the last of which features excellent muted, obbligato work by Brown. Other solo highlights include Land's fine tenor solo on "Darn That Dream" and Geller's alto statement on the disc's standout Washington vocal, "Crazy." And even though she's in the midst of these stellar soloists, Washington expertly works her supple voice throughout to remain the star attraction, even matching the insane, high-note solo blasts trumpeter Ferguson expectedly delivers. A fine disc. Newcomers, though, should start with more accessible and more vocal-centered Washington titles like *The Swingin' Miss D* or *The Fats Waller Songbook*, both of which feature top arrangements by Quincy Jones. *—Stephen Cook*

In the Land of Hi-Fi / Apr. 1956 / EmArcy ✦✦✦✦✦
As with most Dinah Washington records, *In the Land of Hi-Fi* includes an eclectic program of ballads and swingers, all of which become prime vehicles for the singer's dramatic, blues-tinged vocal stylings. Framed by Hal Mooney's mix of string-laden arrangements and big-band charts, Washington imparts both tenderness and passion to slow numbers like "I've Got a Crush on You" and "Say It Isn't So," while getting into some charged vocal buildups on swingers like "Our Love Is Here to Stay" and "If I Were a Bell." In addition to the gospel-imbued number "There'll Be a Jubilee," Latin-tinged cuts like the beautiful bolero-style "Let Me Love You" and the lounge mambo "Nothing Ever Changes My Love for You" provide nice contrast to this jazz and pop set. Topped off with fine contributions by alto saxophonist Cannonball Adderley and pianist Junior Mance, *In the Land of Hi-Fi* is yet another impressive set among the many fine EmArcy records Washington cut in the '50s. *—Stephen Cook*

The Fats Waller Songbook / Oct. 1957 / EmArcy ✦✦✦✦✦

What a Diff'rence a Day Makes! / 1959 / Mercury ✦✦✦✦✦
One of the more notorious albums in the history of vocal music, *What a Diff'rence a Day Makes!* is the lush session that bumped up Dinah Washington from the "Queen of the Blues" to a middle-of-the-road vocal wondress—and subsequently disenfranchised quite a few jazz purists. Washington had been praised in the same breath as Holiday and Fitzgerald for more than a decade, but Mercury nevertheless decided to back her with mainstream arrangements (by Belford Hendricks), heavy strings, and wordless vocal choruses similar to the radio hits of the day. Apparently, the mainstream backings didn't faze Washington at all; she proves herself with a voice as individual and evocative as ever. To be honest, the arrangements are quite solid for what they're worth; though it's a bit jarring to hear Washington's voice wrapped in sweet strings, the effect works well more frequently than not. Most of the songs here are familiar standards ("I Remember You," "I Thought About You," "Cry Me a River," "Manhattan," "Time After Time"), but they've been transformed by Washington as though they'd never been sung before. The Top Ten title track is by no means the best song on the album, but its title proved prophetic for Washington's career. Though her vocal style hadn't changed at all, one day she was a respected blues singer; the next, according to most of the jazz cognoscenti, she had become a lowbrow pop singer. Thankfully, the evidence against Washington's "transformation" is provided right here. *—John Bush*

Unforgettable / Nov. 1991 / Mercury ✦✦

Back to the Blues / 1963 / Roulette ✦✦✦✦✦
Prior to her 1959 hit "What a Diff'rence a Day Makes," nearly every Dinah Washington recording (no matter what the style) was of interest to jazz listeners. However, after her unexpected success on the pop charts, most of Washington's sessions for Mercury and Roulette during the last four years of her life were quite commercial, with string arrangements better suited to country singers and Dinah nearly parodying herself with exaggerated gestures. Fortunately, this 1997 CD reissue brings back an exception, a blues-oriented collection that features Washington returning to her roots, backed by a jazz-oriented big band (although with occasional strings and background voices); in addition to the original program, there are previously unreleased versions of "No One Man" and "Me and My Gin." Eddie Chamblee and Illinois Jacquet have some tenor solos, guitarist Billy Butler is heard from and the trumpet soloist is probably Joe Newman. In general, this is a more successful date than Dinah Washington's earlier investigation of Bessie Smith material, since the backup band is more sympathetic and the talented singer is heard in prime form. Dinah Washington clearly had a real feeling for this bluesy material. *—Scott Yanow*

★ **The Complete Dinah Washington on Mercury, Vol. 1 (1946–1949)** / 1987 / Mercury ✦✦✦✦✦
All of Dinah Washington's studio recordings from 1946-1961 have been reissued in definitive fashion by Polygram on seven three-CD sets. *Vol. 1* finds the youthful singer (who was 21 on the earliest sessions) evolving from a little-known but already talented singer to a best-selling R&B artist. Ranging from jazz and spirited blues to middle-of-the-road ballads, this set (as with the others in the *Complete* series) includes both gems and duds but fortunately the great majority fall into the former category. The backup groups include orchestras led by Gerald Wilson, Tab Smith, Cootie Williams, Chubby Jackson, and Teddy Stewart and there are a dozen strong numbers with just a rhythm section. The first five volumes in this series are highly recommended. *—Scott Yanow*

☆ **The Complete Dinah Washington on Mercury, Vol. 2 (1950–1952)** / 1987 / Mercury ✦✦✦✦✦
Dinah Washington was a best-selling artist on the R&B charts during this period but she was also a very versatile singer who could easily handle swinging jazz, schmaltzy ballads,

blues, and novelties with equal skill. The second of these seven three-CD sets in Mercury's *Complete* program mostly finds Washington being accompanied by studio orchestras although the Ravens join her on two numbers and drummer Jimmy Cobb heads a couple of jazz groups (including one with both Ben Webster and Wardell Gray on tenors). Not every selection is a classic but the quality level is quite high and the packaging is impeccable. Recommended. *—Scott Yanow*

Slick Chick: R&B Years / Oct. 17, 1990 / EmArcy ✦✦✦✦✦
This double LP has the cream of Dinah Washington's early recordings. She recorded extensively for Mercury and EmArcy and all of the performances are available on multidisc sets but, for those listeners who want just a sampling of Dinah Washington at her best, this two-fer is the one to get. All 16 of her R&B hits from 1949-1954 are here plus her very first recording session (which is highlighted by the original version of "Evil Gal Blues") and seven other selections. Whether backed by the Gerald Wilson Orchestra, Tab Smith, Cootie Williams, an all-star unit headed by drummer Jimmy Cobb or studio orchestras, she is in superb form. *—Scott Yanow*

☆ **The Complete Dinah Washington on Mercury, Vol. 3 (1952–1954)** / Jul. 1991 / Mercury ✦✦✦✦✦
Of the seven three-CD sets in Mercury's *Complete* series of Dinah Washington recordings, this is the most jazz-oriented one. The versatile singer participates in a very memorable jam session with an all-star group (featuring Clifford Brown, Maynard Ferguson, and Clark Terry on trumpets), meets up with Terry and tenor saxophonist Eddie Lockjaw Davis on another spontaneous date (highlighted by uptempo romps on "Bye Bye Blues" and "Blue Skies"), and has several classic collaborations with the warm Lester Young-ish tenor of Paul Quinichette. There are a few commercial sides with studio orchestras that are included (since they took place during the same period) but those are in the great minority on this essential volume. *—Scott Yanow*

☆ **The Complete Dinah Washington on Mercury, Vol. 4 (1954–1956)** / Jul. 1991 / Mercury ✦✦✦✦✦
The fourth of seven three-CD sets in Mercury's *Complete* series alternates between strong swinging jazz with the likes of trumpeter Clark Terry, tenor saxophonist Paul Quinichette, pianist Wynton Kelly, and altoist Cannonball Adderley, and middle-of-the-road pop performances with studio orchestras. The third volume is the strongest in this series but the first five sets all contain more than enough jazz to justify their purchase. *Vol. 4* really attests to Dinah Washington's versatility. *—Scott Yanow*

★ **The Definitive Dinah Washington** / Sep. 24, 2002 / Verve/Blue Note ✦✦✦✦✦
This 20-track compilation released as a joint venture by Verve and Blue Note, covers a lot of ground—from 1943 to 1962—but then, so did Dinah Washington. She sang down-and-dirty blues, lush ballads, romantic standards, sophisticated R&B, swinging jazz, and even country, and this disc gives a taste of each style. Her earliest recordings were rooted in the blues and are represented by 1943's low-down and nasty "Evil Girl Blues," 1951's "New Blowtop Blues," and the filthy and funny "Big Long Slidin' Thing" from 1954. By the mid-'50s Washington had segued into a more sophisticated jazz style. Her version of "Teach Me Tonight" from 1954 featuring Hal Mooney's orchestra is seminal, her recording of "White Gardenia" from 1955 nothing short of heartbreaking. She also did an incredible cover of Hank Snow's country hit "I Don't Hurt Anymore" in 1954. A nice inclusion is a live recording of "All of Me" from the 1958 Newport Jazz Festival that finds Washington commandeering Terry Gibbs' vibraphone and banging out a solo. By time the late '50s rolled around, Washington had begun recording R&B and pop under the guidance of Belford Hendricks. In 1959 he teamed her up with Brook Benton and they had an R&B hit with the sassy "Baby, You've Got What It Takes." Washington had a hit on her own with a silky and very smooth version of "What a Diff'rence a Day Makes" in 1960. She jumped to Roulette in the early '60s and recorded pop songs, three of which are included here. Washington was an unforgettable singer and *The Definitive Dinah Washington* shows just why that is so. Highly recommended. *—Tim Sendra*

Ella Washington

Vocals / Soul, Southern Soul
An outstanding Southern soul vocalist, Ella Washington was another performer whose style was so raw and intense that it had little chance of attracting any attention outside the R&B world. She also recorded for various small labels who were never able to break her songs, even within the soul arena. Her best material was done in the late '60s and early '70s, much of it produced by legendary disc jockey John Richbourg, for Monument's Sound Stage 7 label. Washington had one single, "The Grass Is Greener," leased to Atlantic from Octavia, but her 1969 self-titled LP didn't fare well, although she got good response from the single "He Called Me Baby/Stop Giving Your Man Away." *—Ron Wynn*

● **Ella Washington** / 1969 / Sound Stage 7 ✦✦✦✦✦

Geno Washington & the Ram Jam Band

b. Evansville, IN
Vocals / Soul, Pop-Soul, Northern Soul
Initially stationed in England for the Air Force during the early '60s, American soul shouter Geno Washington fronted a British group known as the Ram Jam Band for a series of moderate U.K. chart hits during 1966-1967. Though he was born in Indiana, Washington had the grit of a deep soul testifier like Wilson Pickett or Don Covay. While stationed in East Anglia, Washington became known as a frequent stand-in at gigs around London. When guitarist Pete Gage saw him at a club in 1965, he asked Washington to join his new group with bassist John Roberts, drummer Herb Prestige, organist Jeff Wright, Lionel Kingham on tenor sax, and Buddy Beadle on baritone.

Geno Washington stayed in England after his release from the Air Force, and the band earned notice around the Southeast for an infectious live show that packed dozens of uptempo R&B/soul nuggets into a half-hour. Signed to Piccadilly by early 1966, the group just broke into the Top 40 with "Water." Though it was their highest-charting single, Geno Washington & the Ram Jam Band hit the charts three times in the next year with "Hi-Hi Hazel," a cover of "Que Sera Sera," and "Michael." The band's first two LPs— *Hand Clappin' Foot Stompin' Funky-Butt... Live!* and *Hipsters, Flipsters, Finger-Poppin' Daddies!*—were much better documents of the band at work, and both hit the British Top Ten. Still, Geno Washington recorded only two more albums with the Ram Jam Band before splitting by 1970. Gage went on to join Vinegar Joe, while Washington returned in 1976 with *Geno's Back!* Four years later, Washington earned his only number-one hit (of a sort), when Dexys Midnight Runners took the tribute track "Geno" to the top of the charts. He recorded another LP (*Put Out the Cat*) in 1981, and continued to tour sporadically during the '80s, '90s, and 2000s, often incorporating a blues stance as well as a hypnotism act. *—John Bush*

Hand Clappin' Foot Stompin' Funky-Butt... Live! / Dec. 1966 / Piccadilly ✦✦✦

Hipsters, Flipsters, Finger-Poppin' Daddies! / Sep. 1967 / Piccadilly ✦✦✦

Geno Washington & Jimmy James / Oct. 25, 1994 / Castle ✦✦✦

● **My Bombers My Dexy's My Highs: The Sixties Studio Sessions** / Nov. 14, 2000 / Castle ✦✦✦✦
Geno Washington wasn't a great soul singer and the Ram Jam Band weren't a spectacular soul group. They didn't do the greatest songs and the production isn't very imaginative. What Geno Washington & the Ram Jam Band had going for them was energy. Tracks like "Que Sera Sera" and "She Shot a Hole in My Soul" succeed because of the sheer amount of sweat that Washington sheds as he pushes his band along in a whirlwind of dancefloor-filling mania. This two-disc set covers all the group's studio records of the 1960s, the first collecting singles and the second the entire *Shake a Tail Feather Baby!* record plus eight previously unissued bonus tracks. Most of the best tracks are uptempo groovers. "Michael (The Lover)" is a highlight with its singsong melody, "Different Strokes" is a hard and funky jam finding Washington in fine tonsil-shredding voice, and "Water" is a fine slice of Stax-sounding soul. A few of the tracks—including the strange "Would You Believe (My Little Chickadee)" and the surprisingly soulful take on "Que Sera Sera"—are almost bubblegum soul, with chugging rhythms and a lighthearted delivery. The ballads aren't very successful, as Washington's somewhat rigid voice can't carry a tune with a slow tempo; he needs the Ram Jam Band clattering away behind him. His inept take on "Tell It Like It Is" is the low point of the collection. For some strange reason, Castle includes six songs from the 1970s. Apart from the lame supper-club soul of "Each and Every Part of You," the tracks are OK. The second disc is less successful than the first. The *Shake a Tail Feather* album is made up mostly of derivative covers of soul standards ("Knock on Wood," "I'm Your Puppet," "Three Time Loser") and several songs from the first disc are repeated. Of more interest to Washington fans are the previously unissued tracks that close the disc. There are tracks that sound like nothing else Washington recorded: the dramatic, Four Tops-influenced "If This Is Love (I'd Rather Be Lonely)"; "Careful Not to Break the Spell," a psychedelic country-folk soul tune replete with fuzztone guitar and female backup singers straight off a Glen Campbell record; the ska instrumental "I Was Kaiser Bill's Batman"; the pedal steel-driven country bubblegum tunes "Boomerang" and "She's All I've Got"; and the reggae-influenced cornball novelty number "Summer Fever." While the collection is a vital piece of the Geno Washington story that should be in every fanatic's collection, casual fans and soul aficionados would be much better served by a single-disc collection that combines the best of Washington's studio work and the best of his incendiary live albums. *—Tim Sendra*

Gino Washington

Vocals / Soul, Rock & Roll, R&B
In 1962, homegrown Detroit R&B was at its apex. As the music of Nolan Strong, Nathaniel Mayer, the Volumes, the Falcons and a gaggle of early Motown hits filled the airwaves, so did the music of Gino Washington. Gino scored two local back to back hits in "Out of This World" and "Gino Is a Coward" in 1963 and 1964 while breaking down racial barriers by working the white teen club circuit with a Caucasian backing band, the fire-breathing Jeff & the Atlantics. Gino, known in those days as "Jumpin' Gino," was a mesmerizing live performer who was equal parts James Brown and Wilson Pickett if both of those artists had also decided to sing music that drew equally from the wells of rock & roll and R&B. After being drafted in the Army at the peak of his early success, he found his bit of micro-fame being usurped by a British-based soul singer named Geno Washington, who released several dance albums while our hero was cooling his heels in the service of Uncle Sam. He returned to recording in 1967, releasing old stockpiled material and new sides on local labels into the 1970s when he hosted his own television variety show on a local Detroit station. A collection of the best of Washington's early sides is available on Norton's *Out of This World*, a marvelous souvenir of a time in Detroit rock & roll history when the possibilities seemed endless. *—Cub Koda*

● **Out of This World** / Jul. 24, 2000 / Norton ✦✦✦✦
Here is a rip-snorting collection of Gino Washington tearing it up on 15 classics that run the gamut from early R&B to rock & roll to Northern soul. On most of the tracks he's accompanied by Jeff & the Atlantics, a local Detroit combo who also played on the Reflections' "Just Like Romeo and Juliet," the Shades of Blue's "Oh How Happy" and Edwin Starr's "Agent Double-O Soul." Jeff Williams' guitar breaks on "Out of this World" and "Gino Is a Coward" are worth the price of admission alone, while Washington's performances on the frantic "Come Monkey With Me," the soulful and smooth "Puppet on a String" and "I'll Be Around (When You Want Me)," "Like My Baby" (here in a faster alternate take), "Romeo" and the seldom-heard screamer "Baby Be Mine" make this collection a lost chapter in Detroit rock & roll history well worth owning. *—Cub Koda*

Grover Washington Jr.

b. Dec. 12, 1943, Buffalo, NY, **d.** Dec. 17, 1999

Sax (Soprano), Sax (Tenor), Sax (Alto) / Crossover Jazz, Soul-Jazz, Quiet Storm

One of the most popular saxophonists of all time (even his off records had impressive sales), Grover Washington Jr. was long the pacesetter in his field. His roots were in R&B and soul-jazz organ combos, but he also fared very well on the infrequent occasions when he played straight-ahead jazz. A highly influential player, Washington was sometimes blamed for the faults of his followers; Kenny G largely based his soprano sound on Grover's tone. However, most of the time (except when relying on long hit medleys), Washington pushed himself with the spontaneity and chance taking of a masterful jazz musician.

Grover Washington Jr., whose father also played saxophone, started playing music when he was ten and within two years was working in clubs. He picked up experience touring with the Four Clefs from 1959-1963 and freelancing during the next two years, before spending a couple years in the Army. He moved to Philadelphia in 1967, becoming closely identified with the city from then on, and worked with several organists, including Charles Earland and Johnny "Hammond" Smith, recording as a sideman for the Prestige label. His biggest break occurred in 1971, when Hank Crawford could not make it to a recording date; Washington was picked as his replacement, and the result was *Inner City Blues*, a big seller. From then on he became a major name, particularly after recording 1974's *Mister Magic* and 1980's *Winelight*; the latter included the Bill Withers hit "Just the Two of Us."

Although some of his recordings since then found him coasting a bit, Washington usually stretched himself in concert, being almost overqualified for the R&B-ish music that he performed. He developed his own personal voices on soprano, tenor, alto, and even his infrequently-used baritone. Grover Washington Jr. recorded as a leader for Kudu, Motown, Elektra, and Columbia and made notable guest appearances on dozens of records ranging from pop to straightforward jazz. He died of a sudden heart attack on December 17, 1999 while taping an appearance on CBS television's *The Saturday Early Show*; Washington was 56. The posthumous *Aria* was issued early the following year. *—Scott Yanow*

Inner City Blues / Sep. 1971 / Motown Jazz ✦✦✦✦✦

Grover Washington Jr.'s debut as a leader is a classic of its kind. Straddling the boundary between soul jazz and R&Bish crossover, Washington on alto and tenor (under the direction of Creed Taylor and utilizing the arrangements of Bob James) puts plenty of feeling into his soulful versions of "Mercy Mercy Me," "Ain't No Sunshine," "Georgia on My Mind" and "I Loves You Porgy." It is obvious from listening to this music alone that he was destined to be a star. *—Scott Yanow*

All the King's Horses / May 19, 1972-Jun. 1972 / Kudu ✦✦✦✦

Grover Washington Jr.'s second album as a leader once again utilizes Bob James arrangements for a string orchestra and a notable horn section. The backup group includes James' electric piano, organist Richard Tee and guitarist Eric Gale. Not as many high points are reached as on his debut but Washington is typically soulful on such numbers as "Where Is the Love," "Lean on Me" and "Lover Man," alternating quite effectively between tenor and alto. *—Scott Yanow*

☆ **Soul Box** / Mar. 1973 / Kudu ✦✦✦✦✦

The early work of alto saxophonist and composer Grover Washington Jr. is a rare and beautiful thing to behold. His entire Kudu period, marked by the albums *Inner City Blues, All the King's Horses, Soul Box, Mister Magic*, and *Feels So Good*, is brilliant, solid urban groove jazz played with grace, mean chops, and slippery funkiness. *Soul Box*, a double LP recorded in 1973, has Creed Taylor's production enhanced by a symphony orchestra and full-blown jazz band arranged and conducted by Bob James. Some of the session men include Ron Carter, Billy Cobham, Eric Gale, Idris Muhammad, Airto, and Richard Tee. *Soul Box* only contains seven cuts. Among them are truly innovative reads of Weather Report's "Taurian Matador," Stevie Wonder's "You Are the Sunshine of My Life," a side-long jam on Marvin Gaye's "Trouble Man" (the album's centerpiece and masterpiece), and the deep funk of Norman Whitfield's "Masterpiece." "Trouble Man," however, is the cut on which all the contradictions of the session come to bear and are resolved due in large part to Washington's deeply lyrical improvising and James' ability to layer an orchestra into a groove. There are cadenzas written in after choruses that bring the orchestra in to accent the sketchy funk in the tune and bring out its deep blue hues. When Washington gets to the front of it all, he lets go like he's crying from the heart. On other tracks, the orchestra adds the right drama or sweetness—as it does on Wonder's cut—but Washington makes them grittier, with soloing that sidles up to the melody before reinventing it. For its length, *Soul Box* is a modern classic for its instrumental and arrangement invention and for its deeply emotional bounty. *—Thom Jurek*

Mister Magic / Nov. 1974 / MoJazz ✦✦✦✦✦

This is one of Grover Washington Jr.'s best-loved recordings and considered a classic of R&Bish jazz. All four songs (which includes Billy Strayhorn's "Passion Flower") are quite enjoyable but it is "Mister Magic" that really caught on as a major hit. Bob James provided the colorful if somewhat commercial arrangements, there are spots for guitarist Eric Gale, and Washington (mostly on tenor and soprano) is heard in particularly creative form. Highly recommended. *—Scott Yanow*

A Secret Place / Oct. 1976 / Kudu ✦✦✦

Grover Washington Jr. (on soprano and tenor) is in typically soulful form on this Kudu set but the material (even with the inclusion of Herbie Hancock's "Dolphin Dance") is less interesting than usual. Washington is joined by a relatively small group that includes pianist Dave Grusin, an all-star rhythm section (with guitarist Eric Gale), two horns (arranged by David Matthews) and no strings; this was his first date as a leader without Bob James' charts. A decent but not essential effort by the pacesetter among modern soul jazz saxophonists. *—Scott Yanow*

Live at the Bijou / 1978 / Motown ✦✦✦

Grover Washington Jr. always put on exciting shows, and this performance from the Bijou Cafe in Philadelphia is a good example of his repertoire in 1977. It does not reach the heights of his best studio recordings or concerts, but there are some fine moments. Utilizing his octet of the time (with violinist John Blake, keyboardist James Simmons, and flutist Leslie Burrs), this CD (a straight reissue of the original LP) mostly features Washington playing lesser-known tunes that would not stay in his repertoire for long (other than a medley that includes "Mr. Magic"), but Washington (heard on tenor, alto, and soprano) consistently uplifts the material. *—Scott Yanow*

Paradise / 1979 / Elektra ✦✦✦

Grover Washington Jr. made his mark early on with hit recordings for Kudu and Motown. After he switched to Elektra, the soulful saxophonist debuted on the label with Paradise, a decent but not overly memorable effort. Washington (on soprano, tenor, flute and baritone) plays quite well as do the members of his septet (which include violinist John Blake, guitarist Richard Steacker and bassist Tyrone Brown) but the material (seven group originals) failed to include any really catchy melodies or strong hits. This date is therefore more for Grover Washington completists than for general fans of the idiom. *—Scott Yanow*

Skylarkin' / Oct. 1979 / Motown ✦✦

Come Morning / 1980 / Elektra ✦✦

Winelight / Jun. 1980 / Elektra ✦✦✦✦✦

Grover Washington Jr., has long been one of the leaders in what could be called rhythm & jazz, essentially R&B-influenced jazz. *Winelight* is one of his finest albums, and not primarily because of the Bill Withers hit "Just the Two of Us." It is the five instrumentals that find Washington (on soprano, alto and tenor) really stretching out. If he had been only interested in sales, Washington's solos could have been half as long and he would have stuck closely to the melody. Instead he really pushes himself on some of these selections, particularly the title cut. A memorable set of high-quality and danceable soul jazz. *—Scott Yanow*

Anthology / 1981 / Motown ✦✦✦

The Best Is Yet to Come / 1982 / Elektra ✦✦✦

On *The Best Is Yet to Come*, the title cut was a major R&B hit, with Patti LaBelle doing vocals. The rest, unfortunately, is formulaic fusion. *—Ron Wynn*

Inside Moves / Mar. 1984-Jun. 1984 / Elektra ✦✦

Anthology / 1985 / Elektra ✦✦✦

Anyone who's seen Grover Washington Jr., live can attest to the fact that whether he's playing electric jazz/funk or going acoustic on Billy Strayhorn's music, the Philly resident is a masterful saxman who has as much technique as he does soul and charisma. However, the distinctive saxman's studio recordings (which range from outstanding to watered down) haven't always demonstrated just how commanding an improvisor he can be. *Anthology*, a 1985 CD focusing on his work for Elektra, contains more hits than misses. Well worth hearing are jazz/R&B/pop instrumentals like the congenial "East River Drive" and the seductive "Let It Flow" and the R&B numbers "The Best Is Yet to Come" (which boasts a heartfelt vocal by Patti LaBelle) and Washington's major hit with Bill Withers "Just the Two of Us." Unfortunately, Elektra made the mistake of including Washington's pointless version of reggae king Bob Marley's "Jammin'" (which is more of a pop cover than a genuine jazz interpretation), the insipid "Jet Stream" and the pleasant but not very memorable "In the Name of Love." *—Alex Henderson*

House Full of Love (Music from *The Cosby Show*) / 1986 / Columbia ✦✦

Strawberry Moon / 1987 / Columbia ✦✦✦

Grover Washington Jr.'s first album in three years (and debut for Columbia) did not yield any major hits but found him playing in prime form. Switching between his distinctive soprano, alto and tenor, Washington is joined by bassist-producer Marcus Miller, a large rhythm section and guest vocalists B.B. King ("Caught a Touch of Your Love") and Jean Carne (on two songs). Highlights include "Strawberry Moon," "The Look of Love," "Maddie's Blues" and "Summer Nights." *—Scott Yanow*

Time Out of Mind / 1989 / Columbia ✦✦✦

One of the most electrified of Grover Washington Jr.'s albums, this Columbia set features the popular saxophonist (who plays soprano, alto and tenor) joined by oversized rhythm sections and plenty of keyboards on a variety of funky and danceable material. Not one of Washington's more essential releases (his Columbias overall have not been that memorable), the pacesetter among R&Bish saxmen is actually in fine form; if only the material were better. *—Scott Yanow*

All My Tomorrows / 1994 / Columbia ✦✦

● **Ultimate Collection** / Nov. 2, 1999 / Hip-O ✦✦✦✦

Grover Washington Jr.'s *Ultimate Collection* collects 11 of the saxophonist's greatest hits, including "Just the Two of Us" with Bill Withers, "Bright Moments," "Black Frost," and his interpretation of Marvin Gaye's "Inner City Blues." "Mister Magic" and "Summer Song" are also featured on this concise collection of Washington's jazz/soul/pop performances. *—Heather Phares*

Aria / Mar. 7, 2000 / Sony ✦✦✦

This legend of urban jazz-funk left way too soon at age 56, but listeners can at least take heart in the fact that before he departed, he lived out a career-long dream by recording an album pairing his inimitable saxophone style with classic opera pieces. While the album may hit many of his fans as an unexpected departure, it actually completes a circle that began when Washington first studied music—classical music—at Buffalo's Wurlitzer School of Music. Even as he inspired a generation of saxmen with his amazing blend of jazz and soul, his first love remained classical music. Performing here on soprano, alto, tenor, and baritone saxes, he draws upon his artistry as a melodist to capture the emotional spirit of a dozen of opera's most beautiful arias, from Puccini's "O Mio Babbino Caro" to Delibes' "Flower Duet," all with a sensibility that is very much of our day. The Orchestra of St. Lukes is most effective wrapping its lushness around the tenor on a dramatic rendering of Puccini's "Donna Non Vidi Mai." Bassist Ron Carter and pianist Billy Childs complete a beautiful trio. This isn't Grover at his most inventive or exciting, but like everything he did, it's full of pure heart. *—Jonathan Widran*

Discovery: The First Recordings / Aug. 28, 2001 / Prestige ✦✦✦✦

While it's true that Grover Washington Jr.'s first album as a leader was the wonderful *Inner City Blues* album on Creed Taylor's Kudu label, the sessions included here predate it and feature Washington Jr. in the role of sideman to Charles Earland, Johnny "Hammond" Smith, Boogaloo Joe Jones, and Leon Spencer Jr. The nine cuts included here were recorded between September 1970 and August 1971. Most of them are straight-ahead blowing B-3 dates where the emphasis on groove and grit is equal and pervasive. While there isn't a weak track here and Washington's playing is deeper in the register than in his later material, there is one irritating factor about the assemblage of the album. Rather than place all of Washington's work with a particular leader in one place, such as all the Boogaloo Joe Jones tracks in one place, the producers have elected to go with the timeworn path of least resistance and arrange them chronologically. While there is an argument that can be made for a player's development over time, there is another to make for the work a musician does with a particular leader. And this is where the disparity comes in here. While the scorching funk and groove of "No Way," with Jones, gets the disc off to a hot start (with Bernard Purdie on drums, Sonny Phillips on organ, and Jimmy Lewis on bass) with its rolling eights, it is contrasted on the follow-up with "Between the Sheets," with Smith leading the date (and James "Poppa" Clark on guitars, Lewis on bass, and Eddie Gee on skins). While Washington's solo is notable here for its smoother and silky delivery, it stands in sharp contrast to the previous track, and on and on. Thankfully, the Earland track "Killer Joe," with its wailing counterpoint between the leader and his saxophonist, is saved for last since there is simply no other track to follow it. This is a small complaint, however, as the material here is strictly top-shelf, full of sweat, raw groove, and greasy funk. This isn't a package job for quick cash, but a revealing portrait of an amazingly soulful and talented soloist who walked in the door in 1970 in full possession of his voice with clear directions on how to get around on his instrument. *—Thom Jurek*

Keith Washington

b. Detroit, MI

Vocals / Urban, Smooth Soul

Among the up-and-coming ballad stylists in the '90s urban contemporary generation, Keith Washington rode to fame with his 1991 LP *Make Time for Love.* The song "Kissing You" was an R&B smash, and later was heard as background music on an NBC soap opera. Washington issued the follow-up LP *You Make It Easy* in 1993. After a lengthy absence, he resurfaced in 1998 with *KW.* *—Ron Wynn*

● **Make Time for Love** / 1991 / Qwest ✦✦✦✦

Although it seems like Keith Washington was an overnight success, the truth is that he was busy many years prior trying to find his way to the music charts as an artists. Finally, that ambition has come to fruition and the result is resplendent. The Detroit native's first single was the captivating "Kissing You." The soft, mellow intro bows to a dynamic pre-hook string arrangement before returning to an affectionate chorus. The ballad stayed on the *Billboard* R&B charts for 20 weeks, peaking at number one. The second single was "Are You Still in Love With Me." The lyric expresses much concern and Washington conveys that message in his urgent cry; the single topped off at number 15 on the *Billboard* R&B charts after 14 weeks. The third release was the more romantic title track "Make Time for Love." Unlike the prior two singles, "Make Time..." settles into a gentle rhythm. Washington, however, exerts his energy as the song gradually builds momentum. It climaxed at 22 after 15 weeks on the charts. "When You Love Somebody" sizzles with a feverish rhythm accented by a spirited bridge and Washington's convincing delivery. This is a superb song. It only managed to crack the top 30 at number 26 after a mere 11 weeks. The production on this album is excellent as are Washington's vocals as he utilizes his vibrato on most of the selections. It was anticipated that Washington's emergence onto the music scene was to be followed by chart dominance but contractual problems stifled that possibility. Notwithstanding, this album will be revered for years to come for its many gems. *—Craig Lytle*

You Make It Easy / 1993 / Qwest ✦✦✦

KW / Mar. 10, 1998 / MCA ✦✦✦

After 1993's successful *You Make It Easy,* five years passed before Keith Washington came out with another album. The passionate singer re-emerged on Silas Records (an MCA-distributed label owned by MCA urban contemporary exec Louis Silas Jr.) in 1998 with his third album, *KW.* Containing mostly ballads and slow jams, the CD is very much in the late 1990s neo-soul vein—the production is high-tech and hip-hop-ish, but the singing is classic R&B. Washington often brings to mind Alexander O'Neal, and he also shows an awareness of Luther Vandross and Freddie Jackson. A few of the tracks are excellent, including the silky "I Love You" (a duet with Chanté Moore), the remorseful "You Let Me Down" and a sexy remake of Marvin Gaye's "You Sure Love to Ball." Most of the other material, however, is decent, although not remarkable. But while *You Make It Easy* isn't the all-out gem that Washington is quite capable of providing, it was still nice to see him recording again. *—Alex Henderson*

Crystal Waters

Vocals / Urban, Dance-Pop, Club/Dance

A New Jersey vocalist who majored in computer science at Howard, Crystal Waters had one of 1991's surprise left-field hits with "Gypsy Woman (She's Homeless)." The song had both a potent message and wonderful vocal that smartly mixed anger, irony, and humor. None of Waters' other songs were quite that inspired, but her debut LP, *Surprise,* got her in the hunt. *Storyteller* followed in 1994, and in 1997 Waters returned with a self-titled effort. *—Ron Wynn*

Surprise / 1991 / Mercury ✦✦✦

In 1991, Crystal Waters made it clear that house music could be as socially aware as rap with her wildly infectious treasure "Gypsy Woman (She's Homeless)"—a poigant and moving reflection on a homeless woman's struggle that makes its point without preaching. The nasal-voiced neo-disco/R&B diva doesn't have a great range, but proves that a vocalist doesn't need one in order to be expressive and convincing. While nothing else on *Surprise* is as outstanding as two mixes of "Gypsy Woman"—clearly, the CD's greatest asset—Waters has highly addictive and enjoyable house/neo-disco (neo by 1991 standards) fare in "Makin' Happy" and "Good Lovin'." *Surprise's* greatest weakness is an uneventful version of jazz saxophonist Wardell Gray's "Twisted." Embracing singer Annie Ross' zany lyrics to the bebop classic, Waters isn't terribly confident or assured. But in the dance and R&B realms, she showed much promise—and lived up to it on her 1994 follow-up *Storyteller.* *—Alex Henderson*

● **Storyteller** / 1994 / Mercury ✦✦✦✦✦

On *Storyteller,* Crystal Waters demonstrates the flexibility and insights that characterized *Surprise,* her remarkable hit debut. Her tone and voice are light and supple, and she seldom sounds intense or animated during a song, even on a number where the lyrics would seem to require a more heated approach. But she can stun, alert and inform with her range and subject matter. "Storyteller" and "Daddy Do" aren't frilly numbers; the former describes a relationship gone sour in literate, emotionally compelling terms, while the latter is a hard-hitting attack on wife abuse. Waters scores lots of points through delivery and inflection, and her CD is much more than a dance/disco diva's outpourings. *—Ron Wynn*

Crystal Waters / Jun. 24, 1997 / Mercury ✦✦✦

● **The Best of Crystal Waters** / Aug. 11, 1998 / Mercury ✦✦✦✦✦

Jody Watley

b. Jan. 30, 1959, Chicago, IL

Vocals / Urban, Dance-Pop, Club/Dance

Jody Watley got her start as a dancer on the TV show *Soul Train.* From 1977 to 1984, she was a singer in the group Shalamar. Her debut solo album, *Jody Watley* (1987), sold a million copies and produced three Top Ten hits—"Looking for a New Love," "Don't You Want Me," and "Some Kind of Lover." As a result of its success, Watley won the Grammy Award for Best New Artist of 1987. Her second album, *Larger than Life* (1989), went gold and contained the number-two pop hit "Real Love" as well as the Top Tens "Friends" and "Everything." *You Wanna Dance With Me?,* released at the end of that year, contained dance remixes of her hits. Watley's third album, *Affairs of the Heart,* was released at the end of 1991; *Flower* followed in 1998. *—William Ruhlmann*

Jody Watley / 1987 / MCA ✦✦✦✦

After achieving considerable success as a dancer and member of popular R&B/rock group Shalamar, Jody Watley staged a spectacular debut as a solo artist with her self-titled album. This set not only scored five hit singles, but also a Grammy for Best New Artist. For a few years, Jody Watley was almost as hot as Madonna, scoring major pop, R&B, and dance hits. Of all her albums, her debut was the most successful (and the most dance-oriented), and produced some of the most memorable dance hits of the decade. Included here is "Lookin' for a New Love," which spent four weeks perched at number two on the U.S. pop charts, as well as the Top Ten hits "Don't You Want Me" and "Some Kind of Lover." However, both those songs were remixed when released as singles—hence, the versions on this album are inferior to the single mixes (but those versions can be found on her *Greatest Hits*). Also on this set is the stunning second single, "Still a Thrill," which wasn't a big pop hit, but featured Watley singing in her lower register, and ranks as one of the funkiest and oddest dance tunes of its time. This album also contains another minor pop/R&B hit, "Most of All," as well as a forgotten duet with George Michael (who was also at the top of his game at the time), "Learn to Say No." This album really doesn't possess any duds (or ballads), with other album tracks like "Love Injection" proving almost as infectious as the singles. This album clearly ranks among the artist's best, but if one desires the hit versions of most the singles, then one would be better off with *Greatest Hits.* *—Jose F. Promis*

Larger than Life / 1989 / MCA ✦✦✦✦✦

The former Shalamar member and goddaughter of Jackie Wilson followed her hit debut album with a solid second entry, although it was much more uptempo and dance-dominated. Watley secured a huge pop and R&B hit with "Real Love," and "Friends" was a new jack swing number with rap contributions from Eric B. & Rakim. "Everything" was another Top Ten pop and R&B success. While the thinness of Watley's vocals and the preponderance of predictable beats seemed to indicate that trouble lay ahead, she happily took the gold record certification for the album. *—Ron Wynn*

You Wanna Dance With Me? / 1990 / MCA ✦✦

Affairs of the Heart / 1991 / MCA ✦✦✦✦

Watley's sorely overlooked junior opus is the standout of all her '80s and '90s output. Combining the best of both of the artist's musical worlds, *Affairs of the Heart* supplies a handful of energetic dance numbers and a plentiful selection of quiet storm ballads. The result is a set that's much thicker and deeper than 1987's *Jody Watley* and 1989's *Larger Than Life*, while free of the lagging that occurred on 1993's *Intimacy* and 1995's *Affection*. Watley goes from etchy R&B-funk ("I Want You"), to classy house ("I'm the One You Need"), to inspirational pop ("It All Begins With You"), to 1960s Motown-inspired soul ("Stolen Moments"), all the while sounding enthusiastic and engrossed in the material. Co-writing nine of the album's 11 cuts, she is equally impressive in her lyrical scope: The moving honesty of "Until the Last Goodbye" centers around a troubled relationship on the verge of breaking up a family, while the core message of the distinctive title track is achieving peace and humility through the power of music and listening to one's heart. Additionally, *Affairs of the Heart* is notable for the fact that, even with five producers on board (including Watley herself), it maintains a solid consistency in its entirety. Nearly every song on the album stands strong on its own, too, making *Affairs of the Heart* the singer/songwriter/producer's finest effort. *—Justin Kantor*

Intimacy / 1993 / MCA ♦♦♦
Jody Watley, who was one of the biggest American music stars at the end of the 1980s, saw her streak come to an abrupt end with the release of her fourth solo album, *Intimacy*, which, years later, still manages to sound fresh and undated. She toned down the rhythms (a little bit) which had made her so famous, and instead recorded an album ripe with midtempo, jazz-influenced grooves, which shine on the set's first single, "Your Love Keeps Working On Me," which peaked at an embarrassing number 100 on the American pop charts. *Intimacy*, which is quite a varied album, begins with the harmonica-enhanced summer jam "Workin' on a Groove." The album's second track is the set's second single, "When a Man Loves a Woman," which is a seductive, meandering, spoken word, early-1990s anthem which, among other things, warns of the dangers of AIDS. A couple of overly long and unremarkable ballads weigh *Intimacy* down towards the end, but, other than that, the album is a definite treat. Other highlights include the house track "Ecstasy," the funky, riff-laden "Are You the One?," the slow burning R&B jam "To Be With You," and the gorgeous, soaring ballad "Too Shy to Say." Who is to say why this album, and Watley's fabled career, floundered so badly—perhaps this style of music didn't vibe with the grunge and hip-hop that ruled American pop music in the early 1990s, or perhaps it was due to lousy marketing. In any case, *Intimacy* is a fine, well-rounded album that has managed to stand the test of time. *—Jose F. Promis*

Affection / Jul. 11, 1995 / Avitone ♦♦♦

● **Greatest Hits** / Feb. 13, 1996 / MCA ♦♦♦♦
When Jody Watley was at the top of her game, she was truly a force to be reckoned with. Equipped with superior dancing skills, a keen sense of fashion, great looks, sultry vocals, and some of the catchiest pop/dance tunes of her time, Watley scored an impressive string of hit singles in the late '80s and early '90s. Unfortunately, her descent was just as dramatic as her success, and within a few years her hit parade completely stopped. This collection does a great job in compiling all of the singer's essential hits, and a few—including "Don't You Want Me" and "Some Kind of Lover"—are included in their beefed-up single versions that weren't available on the original albums. Included here is the album-length version of her signature hit "Looking for a New Love," the unstoppable runaway smash "Real Love," the hip-hop club track "Friends" (which featured Eric B. & Rakim), the ballad "Everything," and "I'm the One You Need" (albeit in its original album version as opposed to the single mix). Minor hits, save for "Precious Love," also appear, including the guttural, bass-heavy dance hit "Still a Thrill," the jazzy, sophisticated "Your Love Keeps Working on Me" (which amazingly peaked at an embarrassing number 100), the R&B cut "I Want You," and the pop track "Most of All." Her largely spoken-word single "When a Man Loves a Woman" is also included, but in remixed form—the album version was much better. Finally, this compilation includes a sleek house remix of the album track "Ecstasy." For fans of late-'80s/early-'90s dance/pop/R&B, this stellar collection of irresistible songs is a must, and for new fans it provides a perfect introduction and summary of Jody Watley at her peak (since this album's release, Watley scored another minor hit with "Off the Hook" from the album *Flower*). *—Jose F. Promis*

Flower / Mar. 31, 1998 / Atlantic ♦♦♦
Jody Watley's popularity dipped drastically in the '90s, forcing her into the position of making her Atlantic debut, *Flower*, something of a comeback record. Watley decided to go all the way with the record, hiring an all-star cast of producers—Malik Pendleton (SWV, Mary J. Blige), Phil Galdston (Vanessa Williams), Masters at Work, Dwayne Wiggins (Tony! Toni! Toné!), Derek Edmondson, Bryce Wilson (Groove Theory)—that help bring her sound into the mainstream of the late '90s. *Flower* presents a more mature Watley, one more concerned with well-crafted, seductive urban soul than dance-pop. It's an attractive sound and, surprisingly, her vocals are rich and nuanced, giving the music the treatment it deserves; she's never sounded better or more assured. Since Watley and the production are both alluring, it's a shame that the songs aren't deserving of such loving treatment. Only a handful of cuts, such as the Pendleton-produced single "Off the Hook," are actually strong, memorable songs, but that doesn't hurt the album considerably because the sound of the record is appealing on its own terms. *—Stephen Thomas Erlewine*

Johnny "Guitar" Watson

b. Feb. 3, 1935, Houston, TX, **d.** May 17, 1996, Yokohama, Japan
Guitar, Vocals / Modern Electric Texas Blues, Electric Texas Blues, Soul-Blues, Funk, R&B
"Reinvention" could just as easily have been Johnny "Guitar" Watson's middle name. The multitalented performer parlayed his stunning guitar skills into a vaunted reputation as one of the hottest blues axemen on the West Coast during the 1950s. But that admirable trait wasn't paying the bills as the 1970s rolled in. So he totally changed his image to that of a pimp-styled funkster, enjoying more popularity than ever before. His first sides for the King subsidiary found him tinkling the ivories, but by 1954, when he dreamed up the absolutely astonishing instrumental "Space Guitar," the youth (he was two days short of his 17th birthday!) had switched over to guitar. "Space Guitar" ranks with the greatest achievements of its era—Watson's blistering rapid-fire attack, done without the aid of a pick, presages futuristic effects that rock guitarists still hadn't mastered another 15 years down the line. Watson moved over to the RPM label in 1955 and waxed some of the toughest upbeat blues of their timeframe. He scored his first hit in 1955 for RPM with "Those Lonely Lonely Nights." Watson's first released version of "Gangster of Love" emerged in 1957 on Keen; singles for Class ("One Kiss"), Goth, Arvee (the rocking introduction "Johnny Guitar"), and Escort preceded a hookup with Johnny Otis at King during the early '60s. He recut "Gangster" for King, reaching a few more listeners this time, and dented the R&B charts again in 1962 with his impassioned, violin-enriched blues ballad "Cuttin' In." Still, little had been heard of this musical chameleon before he returned decked out in funk threads during the mid-'70s. He hit with "I Don't Want to Be a Lone Ranger" for Fantasy before putting together an incredible run at DJM Records paced by "A Real Mother for Ya" in 1977 and an updated "Gangster of Love" the next year. *—Bill Dahl*

Listen / 1973 / Fantasy ♦♦♦
When Johnny "Guitar" Watson recorded *Listen* for Fantasy in 1973, he was three years away from the major comeback he would enjoy with 1976's *Ain't That a Bitch*. The singer/guitarist still had some very devoted fans, who remembered him for his blues output of the 1950s. But Watson was going after young R&B audiences in 1973, which is why *Listen* is a soul/funk album and not a blues album. You won't find another "Gangster of Love" or "Hot Little Mama" on *Listen*, an LP that was produced and arranged by Watson himself and makes it clear that he was paying close attention to what black radio (or "soul radio," as it was called) was playing at the time. Black radio, of course, was playing very few 12-bar blues numbers in the early 1970s; nonetheless, R&B still had plenty of blues feeling, and Watson knew that soul and funk (just like rock) were very much an outgrowth of the blues. So he sounds quite comfortable on soul items like "You're the Sweetest Thing I've Ever Had," "It's All About You," and the sentimental "You Stole My Heart." However, *Listen* isn't a great record—decent, but not great and not in a class with subsequent DJM gems like *Ain't That a Bitch* and 1977's *A Real Mother for Ya*. This LP, although likable, is only recommended to serious Watson collectors. *—Alex Henderson*

I Don't Want to Be Alone, Stranger / 1975 / Fantasy ♦♦♦
It isn't easy to reinvent yourself when you're in your late thirties, but Johnny "Guitar" Watson was among the artists who was able to pull it off. In the 1950s, the singer/guitarist became well known in the blues world for classics like "Gangster of Love" and "Hot Little Mama"; some blues fans would have been happy if he had remained a blues singer for the rest of his life. But in the 1970s, Watson was determined to change with the times and appeal to young R&B audiences. So he reinvented himself as a funk-soul artist, and that stylistic makeover paid off in a major way when 1976's *Ain't That a Bitch* went through the roof commercially. Released in 1975, *I Don't Want to Be a Lone Ranger* isn't in a class with *Ain't That a Bitch* or 1977's *A Real Mother for Ya*, but it's still a decent record. Although Watson turned 40 in 1975, this LP (which was his last album for Fantasy) is hardly the work of someone who was stuck in the past. Enjoyable soul items like "It's Way Too Late," "Tripping," and "You Make My Heart Want to Sing" are definitely relevant to what young soul audiences were demanding in 1975—and they weren't demanding the type of 12-bar blues recordings that put Watson on the map back in the 1950s. *I Don't Want to Be a Lone Ranger* falls short of essential, but it's a respectable effort that's worth hearing if you're among Watson's hardcore fans. *—Alex Henderson*

Ain't That a Bitch / 1976 / Collectables ♦♦♦♦
Coming out of Houston's fertile blues scene with Albert Collins and Johnny Copeland, Johnny "Guitar" Watson tread the same route to fame that his peers did in the latter half of the '50s and for most of the '60s. Unlike Collins and Copeland, though, Watson found his biggest success as a funkster in the '70s. And lest one thinks of an aging blues legend embarrassing himself aping the innovations of George Clinton and Sly Stone, Watson found a singular groove by slicking up his already urbane blues style with lots of tasty horn arrangements, plenty of fat basslines, and wah-wah-issue guitar licks. The latter element, of course, was to be expected from a virtuoso such as Watson. And whether reeling off one of his subtle solos or blending in with the band, the reborn blues star was never less than compelling. *Ain't That a Bitch*, from 1976, heralded Watson's new funk era with plenty of guitar treats and one of the best batch of songs he ever cooked up. The variety here is stunning, ranging from the calypso-based blues swinger "I Need It" to the quiet storm soul ballad "Since I Met You Baby." In between, Watson goes wide-screen with the comic book funk of "Superman Lover" and eases into an after-hours mood on the organ-driven jazz and blues gem, "I Want to Ta-Ta You Baby." Besides the fine Watson roundups on the Rhino and Charly labels, *Ain't That a Bitch* works beautifully as a first-disc choice for newcomers, especially those who want to hear the '70s funk material. *—Stephen Cook*

A Real Mother for Ya / Jan. 1977 / Collectables ♦♦♦
Obviously, the storming funk workout that gives this 1977 gold album its title is the album's principal draw (it's been covered countless times, but never duplicated). As was his wont by this time, the multitalented Watson plays everything except drums and horns. *—Bill Dahl*

Funk Beyond the Call of Duty / Feb. 1977 / Collectables ♦♦♦
Less consistent than its immediate predecessors but still a reasonably good funky time, as Johnny "Guitar" Watson once again displays his streetwise humor on "It's About the Dollar Bill" and "Barn Door" on the 1977 set. *—Bill Dahl*

Love Jones / 1980 / Collectables ♦♦♦♦
From 1974 through 1980, Johnny "Guitar" Watson was on a tear no one, including George Clinton or Bootsy Collins, could equal. While the P-Funk machine began to run out of

steam by 1978—with the exception of the Brides of Funkenstein—Watson kept churning out the weird, kinky funk well into the era of Rick James. *Love Jones*, his last fine record for quite awhile, had all the trademarks in place: the choppy, heavily reverbed and wah-wahed guitar that had made Watson a blues sensation, the sci-fi keyboards, the handclap that Nile Rodgers & Bernard Edwards ripped off for Chic, the expandable horn section that intertwined with the guitar riffs, and the punched up basic basslines that kept the funk a simple but ultimately moving thing. It's true that some of the crazy lyrics that graced *Ain't That a Bitch* had given way to chanted clichés by this time, but it hardly mattered since Watson was making music for discos and clubs, and not for radio play any longer. He got hip to the fact that if you wanted to break a record you had to get a club DJ to play the hell out of it. Here, the standouts are "Booty Ooty," the truly weird and wonderful "Goin' Up in Smoke," "Telephone Bill," and the hilarious—and extremely funky—"Lone Ranger." This may have been the last real winner in Watson's catalog for a long time, but there is plenty of magic still present in these grooves. *—Thom Jurek*

The Very Best of Johnny Guitar Watson / 1981 / DJM ♦♦♦♦

Culled from the fine run of bluesy funk sides Watson cut between 1976-1980, DJM's *The Very Best Of...* doesn't really qualify as a complete hits package—"Superman Love" and "Tarzan" are missing, for starters—but sports an attractive mix of solid tracks all the same. Featuring plenty of Watson's P-Funk-inspired grooves and inflation-era commentary, the 14 tracks include such highlights as "Ain't That a Bitch," "Lover Jones," "A Real Mother for Ya," and "I Need It." Equally heavy on the funk, but a bit off the quality radar, more obscure album tracks like "Booty Ooty," "Mother-in-Law," and "Miss Frisco" still come through with an abundance of Watson's irresistible guitar licks and wry vocals. Also adding to the fine stock here are progressive funk sides like "What The Hell Is This" (reminiscent of P-Funk experiments like "Hydraulic Pump"), the after-hours blues ballad "I Want to Ta-Ta You Baby," and the gospel-tinged "Strung Out"—and that's not too mention the incredible arrangements and seamless blend of styles Watson pulls off. Even without all the hits, this DJM package is quality all the way. *—Stephen Cook*

Hot Just Like TNT / 1996 / Ace ♦♦♦♦♦

This generous serving of 28 tracks focuses on Watson's mid-'50s recordings (both released and unissued) for RPM, throwing in some songs by singers Devonia Williams, Jeannie Barnes, and Crodella de Milo (on whose songs he was accompanist); a couple of 1957-1958 singles for Keen; and some previously unavailable tracks he recorded for Johnny Otis, probably dating from the late 1950s and early 1960s. This is worthwhile for fans of Watson in particular as well as fans of the R&B-blues crossover sound of the '50s in general. It's a patchy set, however, in which Watson and his associates try on several different styles for size, but not always with memorable success. Watson's stinging guitar is satisfying on cuts like "Hot Little Mama," and one can tell that it was probably played at a volume that challenged the limitations of 1950s engineering technology; but his playing is sometimes less to the fore in the arrangement than is desirable. For the most part, the material is adequate but not exciting. Sometimes it follows the lead of Watson's avowed hero Ray Charles, while other times it is shaded with doo wop and New Orleans R&B. On the Keen tracks he ventures into Larry Willliams-styled rock; on "Gangster of Love" (one of the standouts on the disc), he accomplishes swinging and boasting first-person-narrative blues. The tunes certainly aren't as impressive as the instrumental skills of Watson and the RPM/Modern house bands overseen by Maxwell Davis. Among the tracks, one will find the 1956 single "Three Hours Past Midnight"—a slow blues that, according to the liner notes, the teenaged Frank Zappa considered "his number one record which had a big influence on his own guitar playing." *—Richie Unterberger*

The Very Best of Johnny "Guitar" Watson: In Loving Memory / 1996 / Collectables ♦♦♦♦♦

Watson had been in the business for over 20 years before he began to amass a large following and achieved gold albums with his first two efforts for DJM. Despite the sad title, *The Very Best of Johnny "Guitar" Watson in Loving Memory* is a great overview of his 1976 to 1980 work. He quietly started on his hit-making path on Fantasy with 1975's "I Don't Want to Be Lone Ranger." This set ignores that work but offers a healthy sampling from his commercial peak. By 1976 Watson had his sound down pat, his great "band" was essentially him on keyboards, guitar, and bass with drummer Emery Thomas and a three-piece horn section augmenting the patently laid-back sound. The great "Ain't That Bitch" found his caustic yet smooth style refined to perfection. His biggest hit, "A Real Mother for Ya," has great melodic changes and proved that as a "bluesman" Watson had more in common vocally with Leroy "Sugarfoot" Bonner and Mick Jagger, than, say, Bobby "Blue" Bland. "Tarzan," despite the silly title, has Watson doing great work on electric piano and, of course, the guitar. Shortly after, the tracks "Love That Will Not Die" and "What the Hell Is This?" well-addressed the disco and dance concerns; this effort proves that Watson did run out of ideas. The ballad "Love Jones" is a dispiriting rewrite of the Emotions' "Don't Ask My Neighbors." The laugh-proof "Telephone Bill" is an embarrassing stab at rap with an inane premise. The best work here proves that Watson was one of the more influential artists and is still enjoyable to listen to. *—Jason Elias*

★ **The Very Best of Johnny "Guitar" Watson** / Apr. 20, 1999 / Rhino ♦♦♦♦♦

Johnny "Guitar" Watson was a blues/R&B/funk pioneer, both in sound and music, and this 18-track collection zeroes in on his bluesiest and earliest sides. Watson a true multi-talent and this set shows it off to great advantage while still staying firmly in the blues mode throughout; he was a blazing boogie woogie pianist (check him out on the earlier version with Chuck Higgins of "Motorhead Baby"), a futuristic guitarist who influenced Bo Diddley and Ike Turner in the instrument-as-noisemaker department (1954's "Space Guitar") and a soulful singer who was both uptown and as gutbucket as you could possibly ask for (1962's "That's the Chance You've Got to Take" and 1955's "Three Hours Past Midnight" which also sports one mean and spare guitar solo), an artist who understood low-down blues and bebop jazz and came up with his own melding of it. Watson is the lost genius of the blues and this set is a long overdue tribute to a true pioneer visionary. *—Cub Koda*

Watts Prophets

Group / Poetry, Fusion

The West Coast's answer to the Last Poets, Watts Prophets didn't get quite the same recognition for their contributions to raising black consciousness and laying the foundations for rap. The group was formed at the Watts Writer's Workshop, an organization started by screenwriter Budd Schulberg designed to provide a creative outlet in the wake of the 1965 Watts riots. Father Amde Hamilton (an Ethiopian Orthodox priest, born Anthony Hamilton), Otis O'Solomon, and Richard Dedeaux met in the workshop circa 1967, and soon began performing together as Watts Prophets, setting their socially and politically conscious poetry to spare, often jazzy musical backing. They won second place in an inner-city talent show, which led to a residency at John Daniels' Maverick's Flat club in South Central L.A.; they also performed at fundraisers, in prisons, and around their community whenever possible.

In 1969, Watts Prophets debuted with *The Black Voices: On the Streets in Watts*. Two years later, the group released *Rappin' Black in a White World* on ALA, with accompaniment by ex-Motown pianist DeeDee McNeil. The radical, incendiary tone of their work fit right in with the emerging black power movement, and attracted unfavorable notice from the government; the home of the Watts Writers Project was destroyed by fire in 1975 after having been infiltrated by an FBI informant. Record deals were hard to come by, and were continually falling through (including one with Bob Marley's home, Tuff Gong, that evaporated with Marley's premature death). Still, they remained sporadically active as performers, and were rediscovered by the hip-hop generation as their records were sampled frequently; additionally, O'Solomon's "Hey World" was covered by Ziggy Marley. In 1997, Watts Prophets released an album of new material with pianist Horace Tapscott, *When the 90's Came*, on ffrr, which also reissued their two original LPs. The Prophets remain dedicated community activists today, promoting creative self-expression and the arts to young people around Southern California and beyond. *—Steve Huey*

● **The Black Voices: On the Streets in Watts** / 1969 / ffrr ♦♦♦♦

The obvious comparison for this group is the Last Poets. Like those guys, the Prophets deliver politically charged poetry over African drums. Unlike them though, the mood here is a tad more relaxed, if the polemic certainly isn't. While each member steps to the mike to deliver his message, the others can be heard in the background, adding a "right on" or "preach it" to the proceedings. Over most of the tracks a saxophone screeches and yowls, adding a nails-against-the-chalkboard tension to the proceedings. This caustic cup of tea isn't for every taste, but those hooked on the Last Poets will get a blast from the Left Coast side of things. Those into the movement, or the '60s in general, will find this a valuable document. *—Rob Ferrier*

Rappin' Black in a White World / 1971 / ffrr ♦♦♦

When the 90's Came / Mar. 11, 1997 / ffrr ♦♦♦

The Weather Girls

f. 1982

Group / Urban, Soul, Hi-NRG

The Weather Girls, Martha Wash and Izora Rhodes, started out in the gospel group NOW (News of the World) before becoming backup singers with Sylvester in the '70s. They formed the duo Two Tons of Fun, later changing their name to the Weather Girls and recording in the early '80s. Wash later went on to do session singing and was the uncredited lead vocalist on "You're My One and Only (True Love)" by Seduction, "Everybody Everybody" by Black Box, and "Gonna Make You Sweat (Everybody Dance Now)" by C&C Music Factory. Wash, who is overweight, was invariably replaced in the songs' videos by lip-syncing models, and was forced to resort to legal action to get a proper share of the royalties for her work. *—Steve Huey*

Success / 1983 / Columbia ♦♦♦♦♦

It was fun while it lasted for Martha Wash and Izora Rhodes, better known as Two Tons of Fun. The single "It's Raining Men" was one of the better left-field hits of 1982, and it helped make their debut album a mild success, although it lacked either a suitable follow-up single or consistently strong material. It also failed to show how strong the women's voices were or exploit their gospel roots. *—Ron Wynn*

Big Girls Don't Cry / 1985 / Columbia ♦♦♦

The final Columbia vehicle for Martha Wash and Izora Rhodes; things had soured for the duo with the label. They began as a novelty act, but were truly a gospel-tinged soul unit who could also score with the dance crowd. They never really were allowed to showcase their real personalities or styles, and by the time this album was issued, they were doing formula pop/soul and dance filler. *—Ron Wynn*

● **Weather Girls** / 1988 / Columbia ♦♦♦♦♦

The third and final Weather Girls album was a disappointment, as it was evident that the major labels weren't willing to take the duo of Martha Wash and Izora Rhodes seriously enough to get them capable producers and find them suitable material. Instead, they struggled through another collection of clichés, weak tracks, and uninspired production and arrangements. The former backup singers for Sylvester never got as a lead act the kind of label support their late ex-boss received at Fantasy. *—Ron Wynn*

Brandi Wells

b. Philadelphia, PA

Vocals / Urban

Philadelphia vocalist Brandi Wells formerly backed "Fat" Larry James and his various groups, as well as serving as lead singer for Breeze and Slick. Her debut solo project was released in 1981 on the WMOT/Fantasy label, and in 1982 the single "Watch Out" became her only Top 30 R&B hit. *—Ron Wynn*

• **Watch Out** / 1981 / WMOT ✦✦✦✦
A finely crafted selection of easygoing midtempo funk numbers and soul ballads, Philadelphia vocalist Brandi Wells' debut album is one of the strongest in the WMOT catalog. The Top 40 R&B hit "Watch Out" is good, but there's a lot better in the moody swayer "I Hate to See You Go"; the bright, Motown-influenced track "Falling in Love"; and the album's second single, "What Goes Around Comes Around." Wells' gliding style combines influences of Deniece Williams' soprano tenderness with Phyllis Hyman's alto tenacity, but the phrasing and tone are distinctly her own. She conveys power without needing dramatic belting, with sensitivity barring excessive delicacy. Unfortunately, the masters were not preserved well, as CD reissues by both Unidisc and Hot Productions lack a certain crispness. Unidisc's is superior, though, for the inclusion of the extra track "Standing on the Outside Looking on the Inside" and 12-inch mixes of "Watch Out" and "What Goes Around Comes Around." Any fans of Philly soul and solid '80s soul, in general, will want to delve into this overlooked gem. *—Justin M. Kantor*

21st Century Fox / 1985 / Omni ✦✦✦✦
21st Century Fox is a competent follow-up to Wells' stellar *Watch Out*. Placing more emphasis on electro-pop/R&B grooves than its understated predecessor, the selections range from the mystical title track to the funky "Midnight Dancer" and vibrant "S." On "21st Century Fox," an uncanny back-alley groove gives way to Wells' calm delivery of intriguing lines like, "Picture the streets filled with seven-foot freaks/Dressed like outer-space Indian maidens/Leather and feathers completely together/They'll be totally dominating." She even gets a bit of her trademark scatting in during the song's fade, providing another unexpected element to the track's curiosity value. Meanwhile, she lets loose with impassioned belting and delayed attacks (à la Phyllis Hyman) on the emotive ballad "Why Can't We Be Lovers." Loyal listeners of Wells' previous album may at first be taken aback by the presence of more street-savvy, urban-contemporary aspects in place of restrained, smooth-groove stylings. But as far as effectively carrying out musical themes goes (with a number of fun ones here), *21st Century Fox* is every bit as solid and enjoyable as *Watch Out*. *—Justin M. Kantor*

Mary Wells

b. May 13, 1943, Detroit, MI, **d.** Jul. 26, 1992, Los Angeles, CA
Vocals / Motown, Soul, Pop-Soul, Girl Group
Time and legions of other soul superstars have obscured the fact that for a brief moment, Mary Wells was Motown's biggest star. She came to the attention of Berry Gordy as a 17-year-old, hawking a song she'd written for Jackie Wilson; that song, "Bye Bye Baby," became her first Motown hit in 1961. The full-throated approach of that single was quickly toned down in favor of a pop-soul sound. Few other soul singers managed to be as shy and sexy at the same time as Wells (Barbara Lewis is the only other that springs to mind), and the soft-voiced singer found a perfect match with the emerging Motown production team, especially Smokey Robinson. Robinson wrote and produced her biggest Motown hits; "Two Lovers," "You Beat Me to the Punch," and "The One Who Really Loves You" all made the Top Ten in the early '60s, and "My Guy" hit the number-one spot in mid-1964, at the very height of Beatlemania.

Mary turned 21 years old as "My Guy" was rising to the top of the charts, and left Motown almost immediately afterward for a reported advance of several hundred thousand dollars from 20th Century Fox. The circumstances remain cloudy years later, but Wells and her husband-manager felt Motown wasn't coming through with enough money for their new superstar; she was also lured by the prospect of movie roles through 20th Century Fox (which never materialized). It's been rumored that Wells was being groomed for the sort of plans that were subsequently lavished upon Diana Ross; more nefariously, it's also been rumored that Motown quietly discouraged radio stations from playing Wells' subsequent releases. What is certain is that Wells never remotely approached the success of her Motown years, entering the pop Top 40 only once (although she had some R&B hits). Motown, for their part, took care throughout the rest of the '60s not to lose their big stars to larger labels.

Wells' departure from Motown was so dramatic and unsuccessful that it has tended to overshadow the quality of her later work, which has almost always been dismissed as trivial by critics. True, it didn't match the quality of her Motown recordings—Smokey Robinson could not be replaced. But her '60s singles for 20th Century Fox (whom she ended up leaving after only a year), Atco, and Jubilee were solid pop-soul on which her vocal talents remained undiminished. She wrote and produced a lot of her late-'60s and early-'70s sessions with her second husband, guitarist Cecil Womack (brother of Bobby), and these found her exploring a somewhat earthier groove than her more widely known pop efforts. She had trouble landing recording deals in the '70s and '80s, and succumbed to throat cancer in 1992. *—Richie Unterberger*

Bye, Bye Baby, I Don't Want to Take a Chance / 1961 / Motown ✦✦✦
Mary Wells wasn't yet a polished vocalist when she first signed with Motown in the early '60s, and she later became the first performer to score a number one single and Top Ten pop hit for the label. But that didn't happen with these songs, although they have an edge, toughness and spark that wasn't always evident in the slicker hits that Wells made. *—Ron Wynn*

Two Lovers / 1962 / Motown ✦✦✦✦✦

The One Who Really Loves You / Jun. 1962 / Motown ✦✦✦
This is a fairly solid effort, with most of the songs penned by Motown mainstays like Smokey Robinson, Berry Gordy, and Mickey Stevenson. It includes the Top Ten hits "The One Who Really Loves You" and "You Beat Me to the Punch," as well as one of the few Wells originals she recorded while at Motown, "Drifting Love." But considering that seven of the ten songs appear on *Looking Back*, only Wells collectors need to pick this up. *—Richie Unterberger*

Live on Stage / Sep. 1963 / Motown ✦✦✦
This is a fine, but unfortunately deleted, album featuring Mary Wells in concert during her peak years. She was a shouting, triumphant vocalist in the early '60s, one whose delivery and manner were alternately seductive, defiant, and vulnerable. Motown should get this back into print immediately. *—Ron Wynn*

Two Lovers and Other Great Hits / Dec. 1963 / Motown ✦✦✦
Smokey Robinson's paradoxical composition "Two Lovers" rides shotgun on a Mary Wells LP designed to cross genres. The beautiful floater is about Smokey's wife Claudette, a Gemini, the astrological sign of the split personality. The harmonic "Operator," also written by Robinson, is one of Mary's most commercial efforts; it would have scored if Motown hadn't stamped it on the back on "Two Lovers"—what a waste. Wells is backed by the Love Tones, the most unheralded group in Motown's history; the three young men's claim to fame is backing Wells in the studio, the most famous coupling being "The One Who Really Loves You." You won't find Mary singing with more pain then she does on "Laughing Boy," where once again the Love Tones shine. Motown had big hopes for this ballad, pressing hundreds of thousands of copies in advance, something unheard of in the '60s for an R&B artist. The normal procedure was to press as you sold, hoping you could keep the distributors supplied with enough copies to satisfy their clients; though the record charted and was technically a hit, Motown manufactured far more copies then they sold. An attempt to spotlight Wells' versatility is evident in remakes of "Guess Who" and "Goody, Goody." A dark horse here is "My 2 Arms—You Equals Tears," but unfortunately its only exposure was on this LP. *—Andrew Hamilton*

Together / Apr. 1964 / Motown ✦✦✦
Motown mogul Berry Gordy Jr. decided to increase his chances for sales by recording his male and female stars together, and the public went for it too. *Together* trekked up the pop charts, finally stopping at number 42, a good showing for an R&B album in 1964. A two-sided hit and the only single released, "Once Upon a Time" and "What's the Matter With You Baby," helped the cause by charting in the upper echelons of the R&B and pop charts. The former is a slow, floating ballad, while the latter is an accusing, jump-beat number. A rendition of Sam Cooke's "(I Love You) For Sentimental Reasons" doesn't measure up to their talents or the song involved, while "Deed I Do" fits the mold of songs done by male/female duos of the early '60s. For the most part, the material is different than what Mary or Marvin normally cut; Marvin probably felt more comfortable with these songs than Mary, since they were closer to the MOR tunes that he preferred doing—at the time—anyway. *—Andrew Hamilton*

Greatest Hits / Apr. 15, 1964 / Motown ✦✦✦✦✦
Since Mary Wells left Motown in 1964, this 12-song compilation, released at the time, contains all her successful singles for the label, from "Bye Bye Baby" to "My Guy," with the exception of "I Don't Want to Take a Chance." As such, it is just about all the Mary Wells anyone reasonably needs. *— William Ruhlmann*

Mary Wells Sings My Guy / Jun. 1964 / Motown ✦✦✦✦✦
On this album, Smokey Robinson demonstrated his ability to craft and hone great material for female acts, something he would later repeat with the Marvelettes. Besides the title track, which became Motown's first Top Ten and number-one pop hit, there were other strong tunes, such as "He's the One I Love" and "At Last," that weren't hits but certainly should have been. *—Ron Wynn*

Love Songs of the Beatles / 1965 / 20th Century ✦✦✦

Mary Wells / 1965 / 20th Century ✦✦✦
Mary Wells' first non-Motown outing made a little noise, but it was clear that she wouldn't be getting the kind of songwriting, production, supporting performances, or instrumental backup she had previously received. *—Ron Wynn*

Two Sides Of . . . / 1966 / Atco ✦✦✦

Vintage Stock / Nov. 1966 / Motown ✦✦✦✦
Basically it's four of Wells' best-known hits (i.e., "My Guy," "Two Lovers") plus some previously unreleased tracks, some of them whose quality ranks with that of her classic hits (Good examples are "Honey Boy," "Everybody Needs Love" and "He's the One I Love"). This combination makes this album more than a curiosity. *—John Lowe*

Servin' Up Some Soul / 1968 / Jubilee ✦✦✦
The success of "The Doctor" and its flip, "Two Lovers History," prompted Jubilee Records to rush-release *Servin' Up Some Soul*, an album consisting of six originals, written by Mary Wells-Womack and Cecil Womack, and some bland remakes. The bluesy, deep soul inspired "Woman in Love," is saddled with brazen Memphis horns that nearly overpower her lead. "Two Lovers History" is better, more mainstream R&B, Mary's vocal is self assuring and alluring, and the horns aren't intrusive. "Bye Bye Baby," her first Motown release, gets an appreciated update, but lacks the stark, rawness of the original. A rendition of Bettye Swann's "Make Me Yours" is as creamy as whipped butter, but schlock versions of "Sunny," and "Stag-o-lee" are unimpressive. Womacks' soulful guitar introduces "The Doctor," a pleasant midtempo number that reached number 65 on *Billboards*' pop 100 Chart and number-22 R&B—her biggest Jubilee single. Unfortunately, it was the last time a Mary Wells single would crack the pop 100. Cecil, now known as Zekkariyas, plays guitar and supplies backing vocals. *—Andrew Hamilton*

In and Out of Love / 1981 / EPK ✦✦
What happened to Mary Wells was one of Motown's greatest disgraces. She was way past her prime on this early-'80s album, and was also hampered by poor material and unimaginative production. Someone who had made such marvelous music for Motown in its formative years shouldn't even have been working at that point, and certainly shouldn't have suffered the humiliation of churning out unrepresentative material to earn a living. *—Ron Wynn*

Keeping My Mind on Love / 1990 / Quality ♦♦♦

Mary Wells battled valiantly in the late '80s against the throat cancer that finally killed her in 1992. She clearly was singing strictly on emotion, desire, and willpower throughout this session, which was recorded in 1987 and issued in 1990 by Ian Levine. It should be regarded more as a final testament rather than judged, since Wells was in no shape to even be singing at that point. Levine deserves thanks for giving her one last shot, and any fan hearing it will be saddened that she's no longer around. *—Ron Wynn*

Complete Jubilee Sessions / 1993 / Sequel ♦♦♦♦♦

More proof that Wells still had what it took after leaving Motown. This 26-song collection assembles everything she recorded for the Jubilee label in the late '60s and early '70s: her 1968 LP *Servin' Up Some Soul*, a couple non-LP B-sides, and the entirety of a scrapped follow-up album (although some of the songs from that unreleased LP appeared on singles, seven were unreleased before this reissue). This is Wells' gutsiest period, with the majority of the material penned by her and husband Cecil Womack, who provides some excellent bluesy guitar licks. Wells is in top voice on both the fairly strong originals and a variety of well-done covers. The earlier *Servin' Up Some Soul* sessions have the edge over the later, slicker tracks, but almost all of it is well worth hearing. *—Richie Unterberger*

☆ **Looking Back 1961–1964** / Sep. 7, 1993 / Motown ♦♦♦♦♦

This two-CD, 43-track box set is the most comprehensive retrospective of Motown's biggest female star before Diana Ross. Although her first hit, "Bye Bye Baby," presented Wells as a blues belter, she quickly settled into a sly and sassy groove. Subsequent hits like "You Beat Me to the Punch," "Two Lovers," and "My Guy" (all included here) made the most of her shy, seductive voice by teaming her with some great songs and production by Smokey Robinson. Although many of these tunes were relegated to B-sides, album tracks, or even the can (11 were previously unreleased), the material—written by Motown stalwarts like Berry Gordy, Holland-Dozier-Holland, and Mickey Stevenson when Smokey was unavailable—is not far below the hits in quality. This is as much a testimony to Motown's overflow of prolific talent as Wells', but doesn't detract from the consistency of this set, which includes her duets with Marvin Gaye (as well as a previously unreleased duet with Smokey Robinson). Includes a comprehensive essay in the photo-packed booklet, although the mysterious absence of the excellent "Was It Worth It" is a notable loss. *—Richie Unterberger*

Ain't It the Truth: The Best of Mary Wells 1964–1982 / Aug. 30, 1994 / Varese Sarabande ♦♦♦

It doesn't have anything from her 1965-1967 years with Atco (those tracks are compiled on a separate collection), but otherwise this does a good job of assembling the highlights of her post-Motown career. The focus is on her handful of minor mid-'60s hits for 20th Century Fox (which were conscious or half-conscious attempts to emulate her Motown sound) and her grittier 1968-1970 recordings for Jubilee (which she co-wrote and co-produced with guitarist and husband/producer Cecil Womack). A couple of unimpressive tracks from her 1981 Epic album round out the collection; Wells is in fine form throughout. *—Richie Unterberger*

Dear Lover: The Atco Sessions / Jan. 1995 / Ichiban/Soul Classics ♦♦♦

In his autobiography, Jerry Wexler characterized Wells' tenure with Atlantic from 1965-1967 as a failure for all parties concerned, but he's being too harsh. Commercially, it was certainly a fallow period; only the title track (a Top Ten R&B hit) paid off. But actually, her Atco singles were solid mid-'60s soul, usually recorded in Chicago and bearing the influence of that city's noted soul producer, Carl Davis (who produced some of these tracks). This collection includes both sides of all four of her Atco singles, five covers from her sole Atco LP, and a couple of decent previously unreleased tracks. *—Richie Unterberger*

You Beat Me to the Punch / Mar. 14, 1995 / Motown ♦♦♦

Never, Never Leave Me: The 20th Century Sides / Feb. 1996 / Ichiban/Soul Classics ♦♦♦

If Wells' brief stint with 20th Century had been a total misdirected failure, it would be easier to dismiss. It wasn't, though. Wells continued to deliver pop-flavored soul in just as good a voice as ever, and in fact had a few small hits. The problem is not so much approach as quality. Her material, though not bad, lacked the special magic of her best Motown classics; the production was somewhat thinner as well. This 18-track anthology assembles her best 20th Century performances, including her singles (some of them previously unavailable on album), songs from her first 20th Century LP, and three previously unreleased songs. Though it's principally of interest to Wells fans, it's better than you might expect, worth hearing for the pleasure of Wells' voice if not the average material. *—Richie Unterberger*

● **The Ultimate Collection** / Feb. 10, 1998 / Motown ♦♦♦♦♦

Motown is notorious for recycling their catalog as endless hit collections, but *The Ultimate Collection* is one of the finest series of greatest-hits CDs they have ever assembled. Each disc contains all of the major hits from an artist, plus important B-sides, album tracks and minor hits. Mary Wells' entry in the series is no exception to the rule, boasting all her Top Ten pop and R&B hits. Not only are the familiar Motown singles here—"Bye Bye Baby," "I Don't Want to Take a Chance," "The One Who Really Loves You," "You Beat Me to the Punch," "Two Lovers," "Laughing Boy," "Your Old Stand By," "What's Easy for Two is So Hard for One," "You Lost the Sweetest Boy," "My Guy"—but also her Top Ten hit for Atco, "Dear Lover," a pair of singles from 20th Century and several minor Motown hits and B-sides, resulting in a total of 25 tracks. For anyone who wants a definitive hits collection but is hesitant to invest in the double-disc *Looking Back*, *The Ultimate Collection* is an ideal choice. *—Stephen Thomas Erlewine*

Fred Wesley

b. 1944, Mobile, AL

Trombone, Arranger / Funk, Soul, Jazz-Funk

Fred Wesley has played with Count Basie's orchestra. During the '60s and '70s, he was a pivotal member of James Brown's bands, serving at times as musical director. His slippery riffs and pungent, precise solos, contrasting with those of saxophonist Maceo Parker, gave Brown's R&B, soul, and funk tunes their instrumental punch. He later left Brown and spent several years playing with George Clinton's various Parliament/Funkadelic projects, even recording a couple of albums as a spin-off group, the Horny Horns. He later cut an album as a leader on Antilles, working with many young-lion types, who remember his music with Brown and are interested in finding common ground between improvisatory and funk/R&B territory. *—Ron Wynn*

● **A Blow for Me, A Toot for You** / 1977 / Atlantic ♦♦♦♦♦

In the 1990s, former James Brown sidemen Fred Wesley and Maceo Parker concentrated on instrumental jazz. But back in the late 1970s they were both part of George Clinton's empire and focused on P-Funk. Having been in Brown's employ, trombonist Wesley and saxman Parker were obvious choices for Clinton's various projects. The Godfather of Soul was a major influence on Clinton and gave Wesley and Parker a first-class education in funk and soul that served them well when they hooked up with Clinton. In 1977, Clinton and Bootsy Collins produced *A Blow for Me, A Toot for You*, the debut album by Fred Wesley and the Horny Horns—a group that boasted Wesley on trombone, Parker on tenor and alto sax, and Rick Gardner and Richard "Kush" Griffith on trumpet. Clinton and Collins did a lot of the writing, and not surprisingly, much of this vinyl LP is pure P-Funk. The album gets off to a gritty start with a remake of Parliament's "Up for the Down Stroke," and the Parliament influence is equally strong on "Between Two Sheets." As for the instrumentals, "Four Play" blends funk and jazz, while Wesley's moody "Peace Fugue" isn't unlike something you word have heard on a CTI recording in the 1970s. "Peace Fugue," in fact, is the least Clinton-sounding thing on the LP. *A Blow for Me, A Toot for You* isn't in a class with Parliament's *The Mothership Connection*, Collins' *Ahh… The Name is Bootsy, Baby!* or Funkadelic's *One Nation Under a Groove*, but it's a generally likable, if uneven, record that die-hard P-Funk collectors should be aware of. *—Alex Henderson*

Say Blow by Blow Backwards / 1979 / Sequel ♦♦♦

Released in 1979, *Say Blow by Blow Backwards* is the second of two albums that Fred Wesley and the Horny Horns (which employed Maceo Parker on tenor and alto sax) recorded for Atlantic in the late 1970s. Wesley produced this album with George Clinton and Bootsy Collins and it comes as no surprise that "We Came to Funk Ya" and shadowy "Half a Man" are straight-up P-Funk. But some of the time *Say Blow by Blow Backwards* doesn't sound all that much like a Parliament or Funkadelic project. Side two of this LP is entirely instrumental and Wesley's appreciation of jazz comes through on the instrumentals "Mr. Melody Man," "Just Like You," and "Circular Motion." These tracks aren't straight-ahead jazz—something that Wesley and Parker are both quite capable of playing—but they do offer a pleasant, if unremarkable, blend of R&B, jazz, and pop. Like the Horny Horns' first album, *A Blow for Me, A Toot for You*, this LP is uneven, and unlike Parliament's *The Clones of Dr. Funkenstein* or Funkadelic's *Maggot Brain*, it isn't an album that's thrilling all the way through. Nonetheless, *Say Blow by Blow Backwards* has more ups than downs and is worth searching for if you fancy yourself a serious P-Funk collector. *—Alex Henderson*

The J.B. Horns / 1990 / Mesa Blue Moon ♦♦

New Friends / 1990 / Antilles ♦♦♦

Comme Ci Comme Ca / Aug. 1991 / Antilles ♦♦♦♦

Trombonist Fred Wesley has spent much of his career either in the R&B groups of James Brown or Brown's sidemen but he has long been a closet bebopper. This CD offers several fine examples of Wesley's J.J. Johnson-inspired style. Using a superior group of associates (including altoist Maceo Parker, Karl Denson on tenor and trumpeter Hugh Ragin), Wesley is quite unselfish in delegating solo space. The selections (originals plus "On Green Dolphin Street" and "Moose the Mooche") all fall into the hard bop realm; Teresa Carroll chips in a couple of decent vocals. In general the music is consistently predictable and safe but enjoyable, one of Fred Wesley's better dates as a leader. *—Scott Yanow*

Amalgamation / Feb. 1994 / Minor Music ♦♦♦♦

Jazz purists have long argued that jazz and funk are incompatible—that the minute you bring in funk or soul elements, you're no longer playing jazz. But that myth has been exploded time and time again by everyone from Lou Donaldson, Eddie Harris, David Sanborn, and Grover Washington Jr., to Charles Earland, the Crusaders, and Herbie Hancock. Fred Wesley is another musician who has demonstrated how compatible jazz and funk/soul can be. In fact, the two complement one another beautifully on *Amalgamation*, a German release that unites the trombonist with trumpeter Hugh Ragin, saxman Karl Denson, keyboardist/organist Peter Madsen, bassist Dwayne Dolphin, and drummer Bruce Cox. Although groove-oriented accessibility is the rule on such funky jams as "Peace Power" and "No One," jazz considerations are not sacrificed. Spontaneity prevails, and there's still plenty of room for improvisation and blowing. The CD detours into Afro-Caribbean territory on the festive "My Neighborhood," while Wesley's romantic side asserts itself on Wham's "Careless Whisper." When Wesley was backing the James Brown, he had to do things Brown's way, but on this 1994 date, he maintains the driver's seat with engaging results. *—Alex Henderson*

Kim Weston (Agatha Natalie Weston)

b. Dec. 30, 1939, Detroit, MI

Vocals / Motown, Soul

Best known as a duet partner of Marvin Gaye, Kim Weston also charted with some of her own solo sides during the '60s, although she never had the breakout success of a

Martha Reeves or Diana Ross. Born Agatha Natalie Weston in Detroit in 1939, she started singing in her church choir at age three, and by her teenage years had joined a touring gospel group called the Wright Specials. She signed with Motown during the company's early days, scoring a minor R&B hit in 1963 with "Love Me All the Way." The following year, she recorded her first duet with Gaye, "What Good Am I Without You," but made the tactical error of turning down a chance to record "Dancing in the Street," which subsequently became a smash hit for Martha & the Vandellas. She enjoyed her biggest solo hit in 1965 with "Take Me in Your Arms (Rock Me a Little While)" and followed it up in 1966 with the equally soulful "Helpless," both of which helped make her reputation among soul collectors. Also in 1966, she cut an entire album of duets with Gaye, *Take Two*, which produced the Top Five R&B classic "It Takes Two." By the time it was peaking on the charts in early 1967, however, Weston had already left Motown; she and her husband, producer William "Mickey" Stevenson, moved to MGM, but a pair of albums there (*For the First Time* and *This Is America*) proved to be commercial failures.

Weston subsequently recorded for Volt (*Kim Kim Kim*), People (*Big Brass Four Poster*, an album of jazz standards with the Hastings Street Jazz Experience), and Johnny Nash's Banyan Tree, all without much success. She did, however, chart with her version of the anthem "Lift Ev'ry Voice and Sing" in 1970. Weston largely disappeared from the music industry during the '70s; in 1987, Weston became the first of many Motown artists to work with British producer Ian Levine on the Motorcity label, re-recording many of her old hits for the Northern soul market; her two albums for Motorcity, 1990's *Investigate* and 1992's *Talking Loud*, also featured some new material. *—Steve Huey*

For the First Time / 1967 / MGM ✦✦✦

Kim Kim Kim / 1970 / Volt ✦✦✦

● **Greatest Hits & Rare Classics** / 1991 / Motown ✦✦✦✦✦
All her singles (including many of her B-sides) are on this collection, though some of her best duet work with Marvin Gaye is missing ("It's Got to Be a Miracle (This Thing Called Love)" is one such example). Had Weston got the major promotional push that many of her counterparts at Motown received, she would have been a much bigger star than she was. *—John Lowe*

The Very Best of the Motorcity Recordings / Feb. 20, 1996 / Hot Productions ✦✦✦
Hot Productions' *The Best of Kim Weston* contains 18 tracks the singer recorded for Motorcity Records in the '70s, including "Somebody's Eyes," "Helpless," "You Hit Me Where It Hurt Me," "Signal Your Intention," "Case of Too Much Lovemaking," "Just One Man for Me," "Riding on the Crest of a Wave" and "Restless Feet." While there are some good songs on the record, Weston's Motorcity recordings are not among her best, and should only be explored by hardcore fans. *—Stephen Thomas Erlewine*

The Whatnauts

f. Baltimore, MD
Group / Soul
A Baltimore vocal group whose heartache tunes were admired by the '70s soul hardcore, though they didn't usually register enough with the general R&B audience to be hits. Lead vocalist Billy Herndon teamed with Garrett Jones and Gerald Pinkney for several memorable singles on Stang, although their best topical cut, "Message From a Black Man" in 1970, was on A&M. Their best known song was "I'll Erase Away Your Pain," which reached number-14 R&B in 1971. They also teamed with the Moments for "Girls," which peaked at number 25. *—Ron Wynn*

● **Introducing the Whatnauts** / 1970 / Stang ✦✦✦✦
This Baltimore, MD, quartet's skills are displayed on nine of the 11 selections, all exemplary sweet soul. Confusion existed because two instrumentals are included: "Souling With the Whatnauts" and "Dance to the Music." The former became popular; it was featured on many '70s R&B radio programs as theme or intro music, causing many to think the Whatnauts were an instrumental group. "Souling" is driven by a deliberate lead guitar, jangling percussion, and a gruff, baritone sax that honks out the beat the entire track. Sly Stone's "Dance to the Music" has spirited horns and a scratching guitar. The Temptations provide the inspiration for "Just Can't Leave My Baby" and "Message from a Black Man"; A&I Records released the latter prior to the group's signing with Stang Records as being by the Whatnauts & the Whatnauts Band. Garrett's falsetto was the heart of the group; his leads on "Just Can't Lose Your Love," the painful "She's Gone to Another," and "I'll Erase Away Your Pain" are legendary. "I'll Erase" became their biggest hit, outdistancing sales and chart positions of previous efforts "Please Make the World Go Away," and "What's Left to Give." George Kerr, Sylvia Robinson, and Nate Edmonds handled productions, while Kerr did the lion's share of the writing. *—Andrew Hamilton*

Reaching for the Stars / 1971 / Stang ✦✦✦
While less compelling then their first, this still has enough good moments to please sweet soul freaks. "Friends By Day (Lovers by Night)" has an unusual arrangement and ranks with their best. Cronies Harry Ray, Al Goodman, and Billy Brown wrote "Alibis and Lies," and it sounds more like them than the Whatnauts; either a fast one was pulled or Garrett is able to mimic Harry Ray to perfection. The uptempo "I Dig Your Act" is led by Herndon's gritty tenor. "You Gave Me True Loving" has the Ponderosa Twins Plus One written all over it. The performance and track are tight, but the lyrics and arrangement are too juvenile for the Whatnauts; Garrett sounds like he's trying to imitate Mickey Mouse. "World" is a chugger and is typical of the message songs of the times; at five minutes, 18 seconds, it's the longest tune on the album. "My Thing" has to be the most recorded copyright in the All Platinum/Stang Records catalog, and the Whatnauts' version doesn't sound any different than, or any more compelling than, versions by Sylvia or the Moments. Despite the criticism, though, this is a fine release overall. *—Andrew Hamilton*

Whatnauts on the Rocks / 1972 / Stang ✦✦✦

The Definite Whatnauts Collection / 1997 / Deep Beats ✦✦✦✦
For a group that never had a Top 40 pop hit and only five Top 40 R&B hits, a double-disc set seems a little indulgent, and the Whatnauts' *The Definitive Colelction* proves that theory to be true. The Whatnauts were a strong vocal group, and their smooth, early '70s soul is silkily seductive—in small doses, that is, such as on the singles "Girls," "Message from a Black Man," "I'll Erase Away Your Pain," "We're Friends By Day (And Lovers By Night)" and "Instigating Trouble Making Fool." However, spread out over two discs—which contains all of three of their albums, plus rarities and outtakes—it becomes a little numbing. Soul fetishists will fined *The Definitive Collection* fascinating, but for any one else, it's simply too much of a pretty good thing. *—Stephen Thomas Erlewine*

I'll Erase Your Pain / Mar. 23, 1999 / Collectables ✦✦✦
Garrett Jones oozes tears by the bucket on "I Just Can't Lose Your Love," Ellie Greenwich's "Please Make the Love Go Away," the Miracles' "Ooo Baby Baby," and "What's Left to Give (After Giving It All)"—all superb examples of heartache soul. This is the first of two compilations by the Baltimoreans on Collectables. It's titled after their debut on Sylvia & Joe Robinson's A&I label, *Message From a Blackman*; that single's B-side, Sly Stone's "Dance to Message," is on the second collection. It's almost as if somebody at Collectables put the A&I single and the tracks from their three Stang albums in a hat, closed their eyes, and randomly selected these 16 songs and saved the rest for the second CD, necessitating purchasing both to get all their goodies—or shelling deeper in your pockets for the 38-track, two-disc Deep Beats package. *—Andrew Hamilton*

Caron Wheeler

b. Jan. 19, 1963, London, England
Vocals / Urban, Dance-Pop, Hip-Hop, Soul
An excellent vocalist in either dance or urban contemporary settings, Caron Wheeler first gained fame singing with Soul II Soul. She initially sang in such reggae bands as Brown Sugar and Afrodiziak before doing sessions with Phil Collins, Erasure, and Elvis Costello. Her leads on the songs "Keep on Movin'" and "Back to Life" were featured on Soul II Soul's smash LP *Keep on Movin'* in 1989. The album sold two-million copies and "Back to Life" was a Top Ten pop and R&B hit. Wheeler left in 1990, and her solo debut was *U.K. Blak* on EMI. Her most recent release was *Beach of the War Goddess* in 1993. *—Ron Wynn*

U.K. Blak / May 1990 / EMI America ✦✦✦✦
Caron Wheeler showed a great deal of promise when she was with Soul II Soul, but the earthy diva made it especially obvious just how much depth she was capable of when she launched her solo career with the individualistic *U.K. Blak*. Like albums by other British R&B and dance music acts of the late '80s and early '90s—including Soul II Soul, the Chimes and Lisa Stansfield—this sleek yet gritty album contains up-to-date (by 1990 standards) hip-hop elements, yet draws heavily on soul music's rich gospel heritage. The fact that *U.K. Blak* has so much more warmth and substance than most of the formulaic '90s R&B recorded on this side of the Atlantic is evident on riveting neosoul ("neo" for 1990) treasures ranging from "Blue (Is the Colour of Pain)" and the moving "Livin' in the Light" to the haunting and introspective a cappella number "Somewhere." Reggae has been long enjoyed tremendous popularity in the Afro-British community, and Wheeler focuses on reggae's lighter side with the very likable results on "Jamaica" and "Proud." *—Alex Henderson*

● **Beach of the War Goddess** / 1993 / EMI ✦✦✦✦✦
The overall tone of Wheeler's ambitious second solo effort mirrors the singer's newfound vocal assurance, confidently fusing hip hop with Afro-pop and seemingly everything in between. Among the highlights is the jazzy soul of "Wonder," and the grinding R&B of "Land of Life," and the charged pop/rap of the title cut. *—Jason Ankeny*

The Whispers

f. 1964, Los Angeles, CA
Group / Urban, Soul, Pop-Soul
The Whispers are a veteran R&B quintet with an impressive 23-year legacy of R&B hits. Formed in Los Angeles by twins Walter and Wallace "Scotty" Scott, Nicholas Caldwell, Marcus Hutson, and Gordy Harmon (who left in 1973), the Whispers turned up on the Dore label in 1964 with "I Was Born When You Kissed Me." In 1969, the quintet climbed the soul charts for the first time with "The Time Has Come" on Soul Clock, and they cracked the R&B Top Ten the next year with "Seems Like I Gotta Do Wrong." They've remained hitmakers ever since for the labels Janus, Soul Train, and Solar, with smashes like the solid gold chart-topper "And the Beat Goes On" in 1980 and another number-one urban contemporary hit, "Rock Steady," in 1987. Twin lead vocalists Walter and Wallace Scott recorded as a duo under the name Walter & Scotty for their 1993 album *My Brother's Keeper*, but remained a part of The Whispers as well. The following year marked The Whispers 30 year anniversary. *Toast to the Ladies* followed in 1995 and in 1997 they released *Songbook, Vol. 1: The Songs of Babyface*. *—Bill Dahl*

Whispers Love Story / 1972 / Janus ✦✦✦

Bingo / 1974 / Janus ✦✦✦✦
Arguably one of the Whispers' best LPs, this went virtually unsung due to poor promotion. It was the L.A. natives' first foray outside of California to record. Norman Harris, along with Allan Felder, Bunny Sigler, and Ron Baker presented them with a treasure chest of tunes. The title track cut a groove from the first note, as the uptempo number was a perfect vehicle for the Whispers; "Mother for My Children" did all right, rising up the charts, then like a pricked balloon fell even faster. The romantic "Someone is Waiting" has the deft harmonies favored by the fellows. "Little Red Riding Hood" languished on the LP, but deserved a better fate; Sigler and Felder took the fairy tale and concocted a melodic love song. Writers Hawes, Jefferson, and Simmons' bouncy "Where There Is Love" is similar to what the Spinners were doing, though their arrangement differs from

a Thom Bell chart. "Once More With Feeling" scored on the disco chart; written by bassist Ron Baker, the guys sing the throbbing rump-shaker with gusto. A good mixture of slow jams and booty movers. *—Andrew Hamilton*

Whispers Greatest Hits / 1975 / Janus ✦✦✦✦
These songs encompass the Whispers' Janus recordings that chronicle the second phase of their recording career; they cut their teeth with Dore Records. A larger recording budget and better songs make this a sweeter package then the primitive sounding Dore tracks. Unlike the Dore tracks, these recordings got played outside of California and established the group as more than just regional phenoms. "I Only Meant to Wet My Feet" has to be their first recording to air East of the Mississippi River. The cleverly conceived ballad, featuring the twin leads of Walter and Scotty had Midwesterners wondering, "who are these Whispers?" "Seems Like I Gotta Do Wrong" had some insightful lyrics that bordered on reverse psychology, seems this lad had to do wrong for people to notice him; he wanted to be noticed, so he did wrong. As exciting and as relevant as "Planets of Life" was, it dealt with astrological signs, it didn't achieve the same success as the previous two songs. Solid choices from the underrated *Bingo* LP are included, including the excellent title track, and the poignant "A Mother for My Children." *—Andrew Hamilton*

One for the Money / 1976 / Soul Train ✦✦

Open up Your Love / 1977 / Soul Train ✦✦✦
This eight-song recording first appeared on Soul Train Records in 1978. From the festive remake of "Make It With You" to the lovely Lionel Richie-influenced "I'm Gonna Make You My Wife," the LP is prime Whispers. An ebullient "I Fell in Love Last Night (At the Disco)" has the same happy feel as the Bread remake, and there are a few ballads to satisfy the quiet storm lovers. *—Andrew Hamilton*

Headlights / 1978 / Solar ✦✦✦
The Whispers had scored a couple Top Ten hits prior to his album, but most of their songs, in spite of their quality, floundered throughout the latter half of the Top 100. However, this album houses two singles that graced the *Billboard* R&B Top Ten and 20. "(Let's Go) All the Way" was the first release. With a modest midtempo groove paced by an uncanny bass rhythm and a spriteful horn section, Walter and Scotty inflict their wholesome vocal appeal which is enhanced by the group's harmonious background vocals. The beat was too funky for disco, and not funky enough for funk. Notwithstanding, it is a solid number. It sealed the *Billboard* R&B Top Ten. On a slower, yet moderate note, "(Olivia) "Lost and Turned Out" illuminates with sensuality in spite of the song's message, which laments a young lady's life on the streets. It tipped in at number 13 on the charts after 22 weeks. "(You're a) Very Special Part of My Life" was never a release but a beautiful number it is. From Walter and Scotty's unwavering delivery to the song's soulful flow, it is reminiscent of the Natural Four's "Can This Be Real." It has become a standard on the quiet storm format. The title track is a funky selection as is "The Planets of Life." *—Craig Lytle*

Imagination / 1981 / Solar ✦✦✦✦
The Whispers scored big with the number-two *Billboard* R&B hit "It's a Love Thing." The rapidly paced single, seasoned with all the intangibles of a dance anthem, found a welcome mat on the pop charts as well, peaking at number 28. The second and only other single to chart was "I Can Make It Better." Co-written by two members from Lakeside, this dance cut showcases Walter and Scotty urgently delivering sympathetic lyrics supported by a funky groove. It only managed to hold on at number 40 after ten weeks. This album retains three splendid ballads ("Say You," "Girl I Need You" and "Fantasy") that never showed themselves on the charts. "Imagination," like the rest of this album, presses on in that uptempo vein with one appealing groove after another. *—Craig Lytle*

This Kind of Lovin' / 1981 / Solar ✦✦✦

Love Is Where You Find It / 1982 / Sequel ✦✦✦
Released after 1981's *This Kind of Lovin'*, *Love Is Where You Find It* finds the group continuing its hitmaking style and boasts the production work of Leon F. Sylvers III and the Solar sound. While the group's albums were never necessities, like the Temptations or to a lesser extent the Dramatics, the worth of the ballads and dance tracks often made the Whispers worth seeking out. *Love Is Where You Find It* is no exception. The album's biggest hits—the polished and kinetic "In the Raw" and "Emergency"—quickly joined the pantheon of Whispers dance classics. The near-brilliant "Turn Me Out" arguably beats them both for sheer sonic value and the witty lyrics. Unlike many of the Whispers' albums of the time, the ballads here diminish the set. The radio staple "Say Yes" may be too smooth and cloying even for Whispers devotees. *Love Is Where You Find It* isn't an especially strong album, but "Turns Me Out" makes it worth looking for. *—Jason Elias*

Love for Love / 1983 / Capitol ✦✦✦
The bouncy, irresistible "Tonight" gets this reissue off and flying. Originally released in 1983, *Love for Love* dissects, analyzes, and emotes on relationships via a solid set of love songs. These nine meaty tunes include the spunky "Keep on Lovin' Me," a staple of their live show, and "Do They Turn You On," a scintillating ballad written by Caldwell. Here's a tip: Go straight to the songs penned by Caldwell on Whispers' albums, the guy writes gems; a Whispers album featuring Caldwell songs only is overdue. The title track, "Had It Not Been for You," and "Try It Again" are jazzy, piano-tinkling torchers that are even more enjoyable with your boo, a glass of wine, and soft lights. *—Andrew Hamilton*

More of the Night / Jul. 23, 1990 / Capitol ✦✦✦✦✦
More of the Night was the Whispers' debut for Capitol Records after having a string of hits for Dick Griffey's Solar Records. Working with up-and-coming producers, several of the album's tracks are in the new jack swing vein. The Robert Brookins-produced "Innocent" went to number three on the R&B charts in the summer of 1990. Troop's Steve Russell helmed the midtempo cut "Misunderstanding." Still, it was the tracks that were more in line with the Whispers' classic sound that are the cornerstones of this album and gave the group two more Top Ten R&B hit singles. Produced by Gary Taylor, the smooth "My Heart Your Heart" is sprinkled with the group's doo wop harmonies. Tsuyoshi Takayanagi's Latin-tinged "I Wanna Make It Good to You" was given an extended remix, a name change ("Is It Good to You"), and received massive radio play. No doubt these two tracks pushed *More of the Night* to gold status. *—Ed Hogan*

30th Anniversary Anthology / Jan. 24, 1994 / Castle ✦✦✦✦✦
Different labels have issued this same batch of songs, but the results are always the same—the best assembly of Whispers' songs ever! The festivities span from 1970 to 1988, and thankfully omits their pioneering years on Dore Records, beginning with "Seems Like I Gotta Do Wrong" and concluding with "Special F/X," a Leon Sylvers production. The cream between those two cookies include "I Only Meant to Wet My Feet," "Bingo," Van McCoy's "Living Together in Sin," "(Olivia) Lost and Turned Out," "A Song for Donny," "Lady," and all their significant *Soul Train* dance ditties. The songs aren't in strict chronological order, but a finer overview of the Whispers' amazing career—they began recording in 1964—hasn't been released. *—Andrew Hamilton*

Greatest Slow Jams / Jun. 11, 1996 / Capitol ✦✦✦✦
Put this with your make out CDs, it qualifies as an aphrodisiac. Some lip smacking, delicious sounds from the Whispers that includes forgotten gems like the late Van McCoy's "Living Together (In Sin)," a lush, romantic tune that you'll never tire of, and the soft and lovely "Chocolate Girl." "Song for Donny" is one of their signature songs, a bigger than life adaptation of Donny Hathaway's classic. Some of their trademark scat singing is featured on "Love Is Where You Find It." Member Nicholas Caldwell is responsible for many of their most popular slow jams, check out "Lady," "Say Yes," "Are You Going My Way" and the churning "Do They Turn You On," all scrumptious ditties. The memorable melody and sensuous lyrics of Babyface's "In the Mood," coupled with the amazing twin leads of Walter and Scotty, plus the understated harmonies of Nicholas and Leavil Degree equals masterpiece. *—Andrew Hamilton*

● **Greatest Hits** / Jun. 3, 1997 / Capitol ✦✦✦✦
By the time this was released in 1997, the Whispers had a few compilation albums on the market, but this was better. *Greatest Hits* covers the group's stint on Dick Griffey's Solar Records during the years 1974-1992 in a coherent fashion. Although this misses the classic "What More Can a Girl Ask For," *Greatest Hits* makes up for it by including both "Living Together in Sin" and "(Olivia) Lost and Turned Out." The heart of *Greatest Hits* is the Whispers' 1979-1987 work with Solar. The first big hit, "And the Beat Goes On," written and produced by Leon Sylvers, was a perfect song to bridge the gap between disco and the synthesizer R&B of the coming decade. That style is apparent on the best tracks of *Greatest Hits*. Other Sylvers-produced tracks, "It's a Love Thing," "In the Raw," and the perfect "Keep on Lovin' Me," more than retain their punch and danceable appeal. Later tracks "Contagious" and "Tonight" suffer from synth overload. Unlike many greatest-hits sets, this has the group gaining momentum near the end of the effort. The innovative "Rock Steady," produced by L.A. Reid and Babyface, gave the group its biggest hit. By the late '80s, the Whispers eased into a more pronounced balladic approach. Gary Taylor's melodic "My Heart Your Heart" and smooth "Is It Good to You" boast the smooth production values of the group's trademark romantic early-'90s sound. Despite a few omissions, *Greatest Hits* more than works as a substantial overview. *—Jason Elias*

Songbook, Vol. 1: The Songs of Babyface / Nov. 25, 1997 / Interscope ✦✦✦
The Whispers' latter-day recordings were uniformly solid, but it took an album like *Songbook, Vol. 1: The Songs of Babyface* to remind many listeners what a valuable soul institution they were. The idea behind any "songbook" collection is to showcase a particular songwriter, as well as the skills of the interpretive artist. Choosing the songs of Babyface, one of the most successful and respected composers of contemporary urban soul, was a savvy move for the Whispers, since it proves that the group is hip enough to know what's what in the urban universe and by focusing on Babyface's songs, the album assumes that he's one of the great soul songwriters of his time. *Songbook, Vol. 1* doesn't necessarily prove that last point—simply put, he's not as good as Stevie Wonder or Smokey Robinson—but it remains a fine, fine record, featuring terrific versions of "You're Makin' Me High," "Two Occasions," "For the Cool in You," "Whip Appeal," "As Soon As I Get Home," "My, My, MY" and "Exhale (Shoop Shoop)." *—Stephen Thomas Erlewine*

Greatest Slow Jams, Vol. 2 / Jan. 23, 2001 / Capitol ✦✦✦✦
More enjoyable than the wonderful *Vol. 1*, this second set of Whispers slow jams features their earlier career-defining sounds, such as "Seems Like I Gotta Do Wrong" (their first national R&B hit and "I Only Meant to Wet My Feet"—a song on the favorite list of every old school fan, it prompted Midwest and Eastern region tours where the Whispers amazed crowds expecting a laid-back ballad singing group, but got five fireballs running on-stage turning somersaults, carrying each other, forming human pyramids, and stepping their butts off. But ballads were their forte and this CD will bring back fond memories. It contains the long version of "(Olivia) Lost and Turned Out," "Somebody Loves You," "Just Gets Better With Time," and other evergreens revered by early connoisseurs. *—Andrew Hamilton*

Barry White

b. Sep. 12, 1944, Galveston, TX
Vocals, Keyboards, Arranger / Smooth Soul, Soul, Disco, Urban
Say the name Barry White and you'd be hard pressed to follow it with the name of any other recording artist with such a huge, cross-sectional following. He's at home appearing on *Soul Train*, guesting with a full band on *The Today Show*, and appearing in cartoon form in various episodes of *The Simpsons*. During the '70s, Dinah Shore devoted a full hour of her daily syndicated *Dinah!* show to White. While there was a period where Barry White wasn't releasing records or making the pop charts, he did stay active touring and appearing on other artists' records including Quincy Jones' "The Secret Garden

(The Seduction Suite)," Regina Belle, and rap star Big Daddy Kane's "All of Me." It's surprising to find out that such an illustrious career almost didn't happen because White wasn't interested in being a recording artist.

White made his first record when he was 16 with a group called the Upfronts. The song was called "Little Girl" on a local L.A. label called Lummtone Records. Later he worked for various independent labels around Los Angeles, landing an A&R position with Bob Keene, the man who first recorded Sam Cooke. His label, Keen Records, was hot at the time with a group called the Bobby Fuller Four in 1966. White was hired for 40 dollars a week to do A&R for Keene's other labels, Mustang and Bronco. During this time, White flirted with the idea of being a recording artist, making a record for Bronco called "All in the Run of a Day." But he chose to stick with his A&R duties. One of the first groups he worked with was the Versatiles who later changed their name to the 5th Dimension. White's first big hit came from an artist familiar to dancefloor denizens—Viola Wills, whose "Lost Without the Love of My Guy" went Top 20 R&B. His salary went up to 60 dollars a week. White started working with the Bobby Fuller Four. Bob Keene and Larry Nunes—who later became White's spiritual advisor and true friend—wanted to cut a female act. White had heard about a singer named Felice Taylor. They had three hit records, "It May Be Winter Outside," "I'm Under the Influence of Love," and "I Feel Love Coming On." They were huge hits in England. White started making 400 dollars a week.

When Bronco went out of business, White began doing independent production. Those were some lean times for White. Veteran arranger Gene Page, who would later arrange or co-arrange White's hits, helped him out, giving him work and non-repayable loans. Then three years later, Paul Politti, who also worked at Bronco, contacted him to tell him that Larry Nunes was interested in starting a business with him. Nunes had started cutting tracks for a concept album he was working on. Meanwhile, White had started working with this girl group who hadn't done any singing professionally. They rehearsed for almost a year. White wrote "Walkin' in the Rain (With the One I Love)" with lyrics that were inspired by conversations with one of the singers, Glodean. White christened the group Love Unlimited.

Larry Nunes took the record to Russ Regan, who was the head of the Uni label owned by MCA. Love Unlimited's *From a Girl's Point of View* became a million-seller. Soon after, Regan left Uni for 20th Century Records. Without Regan, White's relationship with Uni soured. With his relationship with Uni in chaos and Love Unlimited contract-bound with the label, White decided he needed to work with another act. He wanted to work with a male artist. He made three song demos of himself singing and playing the piano. Nunes heard them and insisted that he re-record and release them as a recording artist. They argued for days about it. Then he somehow convinced White to do it. White was still hesitating up to the time the label copy was made. He was going to use the name "White Heat," but the record became the first Barry White album. That first album was 1973's *I've Got So Much to Give* on 20th Century Records. It included the title track and "I'm Gonna Love You Just a Little More Baby."

White got a release from Uni for Love Unlimited and they joined him over at 20th Century Records. Then he had a brainstorm for another concept album. He told Regan he wanted to do an instrumental album. Regan thought he had lost it. White wanted to call it the Love Unlimited Orchestra. The single, "Love's Theme," went to number-one pop, was a million-seller, and was a smash all over the world. The song earned him a BMI award for over three-million covers. For the next five years, from 1974 to 1979, there was no stopping the Barry White Hit Train—his own *Stone Gon'*, *Barry White Sings Love Songs for the One You Love* ("It's Ecstasy When You Lay Down Next to Me," "Playing Your Game Baby"), *Let the Music Play* (title track, "You See the Trouble with Me"), *Just Another Way to Say I Love You* ("I'll Do for You Anything You Want Me To," "Love Serenade"), *The Man* ("Your Sweetness Is My Weakness," "Sha La La Means I Love You," "September When We Met," a splendid cover of Billy Joel's "Just the Way You Are"), and Love Unlimited's *In Heat* ("I Belong to You," "Move Me No Mountain," "Share a Little Love in Your Heart," and "Love's Theme," with lyrics). He also scored a soundtrack for the 20th Century Fox film *The Together Brothers*, enjoying a resurgence on home video.

His studio band included such luminaries as guitarists Ray Parker Jr. (pre-Raydio, co-writer with White on "You See the Trouble With Me"), bassist Nathan East, Wah Wah Watson, David T. Walker, Dean Parks, Don Peake, bassist Wilton Felder of the Crusaders, Lee Ritenour, drummer Ed Greene, percussionist Gary Coleman, and later keyboardist Rahn Coleman. His hit streak seemed, well, unlimited. Then it all derailed. Russ Regan and another ally, Hosea Wilson, left 20th Century Records and White was left with management that he thought of in less than glowing terms.

White left after fulfilling his contract with two more album releases, Love Unlimited Orchestra's *My Musical Bouquet* and his own *I Love to Sing the Songs I Sing*. White signed a custom label deal with CBS Records. At the time it was touted as one of the biggest deals ever. He started a label called Unlimited Gold. The roster included White, Love Unlimited, the Love Unlimited Orchestra, Jack Perry, and a teenaged singer named Danny Pearson who charted with a song called "What's Your Sign Girl." He also did a duet album with Glodean called *Barry & Glodean*. Aside from the gold album *The Message Is Love*, most of the albums weren't huge sellers. After eight Barry White albums, four Love Unlimited albums, four Love Unlimited Orchestra albums, constant touring, and dealing with the rigors of the music industry, White decided to take a break.

Then in 1992, White signed with A&M, releasing the albums *The Man Is Back*, *The Right Night & Barry White*, and *Put Me in Your Mix* (which contains a duet with Issac Hayes, "Dark and Lovely"). *The Icon Is Love* became his biggest-selling album since the '70s releases, going multi-platinum. It includes the platinum single "Pratice What You Preach." The production lineup includes Gerald LeVert and Edwin "Tony" Nicholas, his godson Chuckii Booker, Jimmy Jam & Terry Lewis, and White and his longtime friend Jack Perry. While some later efforts buried his vocals in whiz-bang electronic effects, on *The Icon Is Love*, White's deep steam engine baritone pipes are upfront in the mix. *Staying Power* followed in 1999, showcased in the best tradition of soul music where the focus is the singer and the song. White's thankful for a career that has taken him from the ghetto to international success with 106 gold and 41 platinum albums, 20 gold and ten platinum singles, with worldwide sales in excess of 100 million. —*Ed Hogan*

I've Got So Much to Give / 1973 / 20th Century ♦♦♦

It was no real surprise when Barry White's 1973 debut LP, *I've Got So Much to Give*, rocketed to the top of the R&B charts in April. The sound of whispered voices, half-empty champagne bottles, and rumpled satin sheets, its seamless blend of lush instrumentals and rich, deep vocal numbers was delivered with a suave coolness that shook up the mores of traditional '60s-style soul and turned it into something so sexy that blush and groove vied for the same space. The album is built around the massive "I'm Gonna Love You Just a Little More Baby," which scored White both his first charting single and his first ever number one—and remains, for many, the song to which White's style is indelibly inked. With just a little funk behind the strings and keys, it's White's quietly-spoken declaration of love-without-innuendo that completes the mood, long before he turns to verse and chorus. Silly, perhaps; thrilling, definitely; and titillating—it depended on who you spoke to. "I've Got So Much to Give," the follow-up hit, follows that format—of course it does. But the novelty of White's approach, coupled with the universality of his subject matter, ensured that there was no sense of having heard it all before. Indeed, even with two such groundbreaking songs to lead the way, the three remaining tracks only maintain the mood and prolong the pleasure, completing a concerto that spans the full gamut of romantic emotion—an astonishing "Standing in the Shadows of Love," the yearning "Bring Back My Yesterday," and the absolutely joyful "I Found Someone." Together, too, they amount to some of the purest, easiest material White ever recorded. —*Amy Hanson*

Stone Gon' / 1973 / 20th Century ♦♦♦♦♦

Stone Gon' was the second release in an incredible run of sensually charged titles White produced during the first half of the '70s. His patented mix of love monologues and rich vocal dynamics would come to mark the best songs of the period, including the two chart-toppers here, "Honey Please, Can't Ya See" and "Never, Never Gonna Give Ya Up." Of course, White's inventive arrangements and crack band only add to the stock of these soulful pop excursions. And beyond the hits, tracks like "You're My Baby" and "Hard to Believe That I Found You" maintain the high standard, compliments of mesmerizing backdrops and more vocal seduction; with wine and candlelight already casting a spell, it's just a matter of time before White's supremely tranquil delivery and blissed-out wash of strings and saxophone will cause the amatory to completely lose it. Bringing things back to earth, White displays unerring sensitivity on "Girl It's True, Yes I'll Always Love You," a love song as sincere and sanctified as any he's made. Essential listening. —*Stephen Cook*

Rhapsody in White / 1974 / 20th Century ♦♦♦♦

Together Brothers / 1974 / Mercury ♦♦♦

Barry White's soundtrack to the 1974 blaxploitation film *Together Brothers* doesn't match the quality of classic efforts like Curtis Mayfield's *Superfly*, Isaac Hayes' *Shaft*, or Marvin Gaye's *Trouble Man*, but it is an appealing and welcome release all the same. Mayfield's and Gaye's soundtracks, in particular, benefited from solid material throughout, whereas White's soundtrack does suffer from some plodding moments; "You Got Case" and "Stick Up" recycle past funk grooves, while the main theme "Somebody Is Gonna Off the Man" is ineffectively reconfigured throughout. An eerie, Morricone-style whistling and harp interlude on "Killer's Lullaby" intrigues at first but falters with a thin arrangement. The lightness of tone and many string-laden numbers on *Together Brothers* shouldn't be a surprise, though, since they reflect White's romantic soul style: ghetto streets flowing with champagne. In fact, on a majority of the tracks, White's spacious and silky arrangements and the Love Unlimited Orchestra's adroit backing are substantial enough to offset the album's weaker moments. The vocal version of "Somebody Is Gonna Off the Man" and the soundtrack's one hit "Honey, Please Can't You See" are classic examples of White's pop-soul style, while mood numbers like "So Nice to Hear" and "Can't Seem to Find Him" benefit from strong and varied arrangements; the latter features an effective three-way collage of funk, noir ambience, and orchestral bombast. *Together Brothers* is a must for dedicated White fans and a respectable title in the blaxploitation soundtrack catalog. —*Stephen Cook*

Can't Get Enough / Feb. 1974 / 20th Century ♦♦♦♦

The third in White's mostly stellar run of albums on the 20th Century label, *Can't Get Enough* finds the bedroom alchemist coming up with another solid batch of lush, proto-disco gems. White went from strength to strength during the '70s, collaborating with co-arranger Gene Page on some of the most sophisticated and seamless charts in popular music (Philly soul architects Leon Huff, Kenny Gamble, and Thom Bell also deserve recognition in this regard). And thanks to an amazing succession of hits, White not only impressed the music cognoscenti, but repeatedly scored with the radio faithful, too—*Can't Get Enough* features two of his biggest chart toppers, "You're the First, the Last, My Everything" and "Can't Get Enough of Your Love, Babe." And besides the hits, it's not just all padding here: "I Can't Believe You Love Me" and "Oh Love, Well We Finally We Made It" qualify as two of White's most fetching slow burners, while "Mellow Mood (Pts. 1 & 2)" shows off his knack for layered instrumentals. Another highlight from White's prime. —*Stephen Cook*

Barry White's Greatest Hits / 1975 / Casablanca ♦♦♦♦♦

Just Another Way to Say I Love You / 1975 / 20th Century ♦♦♦

With his 1973 debut, *I've Got So Much Love to Give* White redefined the R&B and pop with his grand arrangements and pursuit of studio excellence. The frothy "Love's Theme" from his Love Unlimited Orchestra is considered influential early disco. By the time this was released, the sound was slightly on the wane. With his demanding schedule of cranking out an album or more a year, as well as work from Love Unlimited and Love Unlimited Orchestra This effort shows the strain. The album kicks off with "Heavenly, That's What You Are to Me," and despite its great intro, it ultimately pales in comparison to earlier tracks. On "I'll Do for You Anything You Want Me To" finds White in ragged voice throughout and the onslaught on his grunts and groans didn't help him not be a parody of himself. *Just Another Way to Say I Love You* seems to cautiously plod along, but White had something innovative planned here. "Love Serenade" has him throwing all caution to the wind with lines like "I don't wanna feel no clothes," followed by the even better, "And take off that brassiere, my dear." As for regular ballads, "Let Me Live My Life Lovin' You Babe" clocks in at a sleep-inducing 10:29. This album closes out with "Love Serenade (Pt. 2)," a bass heavy, libidinous instrumental. This is not a horrible effort, but he no doubt could do much better. *—Jason Elias*

Is This Whatcha Wont? / 1976 / 20th Century ♦♦♦

After an incredible three-year run of topflight material and several chart-toppers, Barry White's star began to dip a bit with this 1976 release. Though not as disappointing as later albums like *Sheet Music*, *Is This Whatcha Wont?* still wears thin at times because of some weak tracks—"Don't Make Me Wait Too Long" and "Now I'm Gonna Make Love to You" find White recycling past glories and stretching his proto-disco magic a wee thin. Maybe he was just opting for a lighter production approach than before, but even taken more as pop ephemera and less like some dancefloor classics, these tracks still falter, especially under the weight of White's preferred extended-mix mode. Nevertheless, there's a lot of quality stuff to be had, especially sensual slow burners like "I Wanna Lay Down With You Baby" and "Your Love—So Good I Can't Take It" (the latter featuring fine work by White's guitarist at the time, Ray Parker Jr.). Also included here is the uptempo hit and Philly bump sound-alike "I'm Qualified to Satisfy You." There are plenty of White and Gene Page's top-notch arrangements, too; during the disco era, who did strings better than these two? Those who want to explore White's output from the latter half of the '70s should first check out the excellent *Let the Music Play*. White fans, though, could certainly do a lot worse than picking up this highly enjoyable record. *—Stephen Cook*

Let the Music Play / 1976 / 20th Century ♦♦♦♦

In between his run of gold in the first half of the '70s and a pre-comeback sabbatical in the '80s, Barry White produced this top-notch album in 1976 as one of a long line of releases on the 20th Century label. While not full of any Top Ten pop hits, the six tracks do feature minor successes in "Baby, We Better Try to Get It Together," "You See the Trouble With Me" (co-written with White's guitarist at the time, Ray Parker Jr.), and the title track. White's proto-disco arrangements are of the highest order here, full of sophisticated orchestrations and silky but solid funk-lite rhythm tracks. The lyrical content, though, does not speak of the endless nights of lovemaking and blossoming relationships addressed in earlier songs, but instead focuses on the hurdles and downside of love. White expertly couples his subtle vocal delivery with just the right amount of pathos to highlight the lover on the outs. Something of an overlooked gem, *Let the Music Play* is a must for Barry White fans and qualifies as a fine choice for listeners looking for something beyond the singer's base of hits. *—Stephen Cook*

Barry White Sings for Someone You Love / 1977 / 20th Century ♦♦♦♦

This was Barry White's first bona fide success in close to two years. It is due in part to the slight change of his music formula. After albums such as the Love Unlimited Orchestra's *Music Maestro, Please* and 1976's *Is This Whatcha Wont?* disappeared without a trace, White ended his over the top musical extravagance and returned with a sleeker more relaxed style. *Barry White Sings for Someone You Love* is often so laid back, it's almost reclining. This album biggest hit was "It's Ecstasy When You Lay Down Next to Me." That song more than anything else here typified White's new and improved production style and offered one of his drollest vocals. The amazing "Oh What a Night" has him effortlessly capturing the drama of R&B from a decade or two earlier and it is both sensual and romantic. The sleeper of the album, "I Never Thought I'd Fall in Love With You," is lush, confident, and assured. If it appeared on an album before this, it's doubtful White could have gotten the subtle musical nuances or the plaintive vocal. As for pure ballads, "You Turned My Whole World Around" and "Of All the Guys in the World" are good, but with their interchangeable dirge-like paces, they practically cancel one another out. *Barry White Sings for Someone You Love* in essence restarted White's career and contains some of his best work. *—Jason Elias*

Barry White the Man / 1978 / 20th Century ♦♦♦

Barry White Sings to Someone You Love (1977) put him back on the right side of the charts. He shed the pomposity that landed him in the cutout bins by as early as 1976. In contrast to this albums' predecessor, *Barry White Sings for Someone You Love*, there's more of a balance between the dance tracks and ballads. "Look at Her," "You're Sweetness Is My Weakness," and "Sha La La Means I Love You" all employ Latin flourishes and tough horn charts. Although his Latin seemed closer to Ricky Ricardo than Tito Puente, White's good spirits and the crack backing band make it all worthwhile. The sensual "It's Only Love Doing Its Thing" does its business in under five minutes with White saying, "Let me put my hand right there/Lord have mercy." On the ballads he seems a little more reflective than usual. As they somewhat diminished *Barry White Sings for Someone You Love*, the ballads enrich *The Man*. On his cover of Billy Joel's "Just the Way You Are," he gives the lyrics complete seriousness and somehow makes them bittersweet. "Early Years" has a flamenco-styled guitar and an autumnal arrangement. The track gives him to a depth beyond "relationships," even though it was clear from his disconsolate delivery that his reminiscing didn't exactly make him feel any better. With such rich and varied songs, *The Man* might be the only album one might need from Barry White, but it will make you seek out even more of his catalog. *—Jason Elias*

I Love to Sing the Songs I Sing / 1979 / 20th Century ♦♦

I Love to Sing the Songs I Sing was issued as the same time as Barry White's CBS Records debut *The Message Is Love*, with most of the attention going towards the latter. It's a shame because its one of The Maestro's best albums. The title track single was his homage to Motown. There are several sweet ballads—"Girl, What's Your Name," "Once Upon a Time," and "Oh Me, Oh My, (I'm Such a Lucky Guy)." The delicious uptempo tracks "I Can't Leave You Alone," "Call Me Baby," and "How Did You Know It Was Me" are jams and feature horns, a rarity on White tracks. Thankfully, this album was reissued as a 1996 Polygram CD. The White-produced *My Musical Banquet* from Love Unlimited Orchestra met a similar undeserved overlooked fate. *—Ed Hogan*

The Message Is Love / 1979 / Priority ♦♦♦

Sheet Music / 1980 / Priority ♦♦♦

This 1980 release came out half a decade after Barry White's hot run of bedroom soul hits and during a time when the silky, compact production style of disco had left its mark on much of modern R&B music. *Sheet Music* reveals the downside of the situation with a slew of well-below-the-grade numbers and feeble, redundant grooves. The title track starts things off in desperate fashion as White interjects anesthetized Earth, Wind & Fire horn riffs over a perfunctory "Rock the Boat" beat. Influence works both ways, though, since Beck used the nasal vocal vamp from the end of this song to comedic effect on his *Midnite Vultures* cut "Hollywood Freaks." The disappointments continue on *Sheet Music* as White warms to "The Theme From Love Boat" on "Lady, Sweet Lady," turns the already repetitive "I Believe in Love" into an extended mix, and gives calypso a disco turn on "Rum and Coke." The latter cut does contain one of White's irresistible, sexual-advisory monologues, and infectious grooves do pop up sporadically, but these moments are rare. Barry White is a great soul artist; *Sheet Music* just happens to be a low point in his strong catalog. For those interested in White's music, pick up his *Greatest Hits, Vol. 1* on Casablanca or check out any of his fine, early-'70s releases on the 20th Century label. *—Stephen Cook*

Barry & Glodean / 1981 / Priority ♦♦♦♦

Barry and Glodean White combined for a delightful LP that got overlooked. After the dark, moody opening "Our Theme" the husband and wife team gets busy on the infectious "I Want You," and the Motown-ish "You're The Only One For Me." On tracks 4, 5, and 6 they beg the pop/easy listening audience . . . maybe a bit too much, for fans of White's satiny brand of soul. They get back on track with "You," but fall back off with the disjointed "You Make My Life Easy Livin'." Simply lovely is "Didn't We Make It Happen," a Barry White, Danny Pearson composition and one of the CD's four strongest tunes. It begins with White's traditional rap, and fans into a beautiful midtempo floater. The slow, erotic "Baby," concludes a fine effort. *—Andrew Hamilton*

Greatest Hits, Vol. 2 / 1981 / Casablanca ♦♦♦♦

The Man Is Back! / 1989 / A&M ♦♦♦

Although Barry White's sales had long since decreased by the time he recorded *The Man Is Back*, the influential soul veteran continued making worthwhile albums. *Man* isn't in a class with either his classic albums of the '70s or his superb comeback album of 1994, *The Icon Is Love*, but is a likable and decent (though not outstanding) effort demonstrating that he hadn't lost his touch as a vocalist, composer or producer. With the black music charts dominated by rap and new jack swing in 1989, White remained artistically viable not by emulating the aggression of younger artists (many of whom were sampling his '70s hits left and right), but by being true to himself. Though White goes for a more high-tech, urban-contemporary-influenced production style that's indeed a departure from his lavish orchestral approach of the '70s, noteworthy cuts like the addictive "L.A. My Kinda Place," the plea for unity "Follow That and See (Where It Leads Y'all)" and an inspired remake of the doo wop classic "Goodnight My Love" are essentially the type of smooth, classy and sophisticated "uptown soul music" that put him on the map. *—Alex Henderson*

Just for You / Nov. 17, 1992 / Casablanca ♦♦♦♦♦

With 1970s nostalgia being quite the rage in the early '90s, Mercury set out to cash in on the trend with this three-CD box set by one of the top soul/disco men of that decade. Though three CDs is a bit much for novices (who would be better off with the 1995 single-CD anthology *All Time Greatest Hits*), more seasoned White devotees will find that there's a lot to admire about this comprehensive package. Essential '70s hits like "I'm Gonna Love You Just a Little More, Baby," "Can't Get Enough of Your Love, Babe" and "It's Ecstasy" are included along with gems he produced for the female group Love Unlimited (including the sexy "Walking in the Rain With the One I Love" and the sweet "I Belong to You") and his instrumental-oriented Love Unlimited Orchestra ("Love's Theme" and "Satin Soul," among other hits). And the set also contains some of White's more recent work, such as 1989's "L.A. My Kinda Place" and a remake of Lisa Stansfield's "All Around the World" that finds him forming a memorable duo with the British singer. Despite the fact that some of the newer selections aren't essential, *Just for You* does a fine job of summarizing White's many post-1971 accomplishments. *—Alex Henderson*

The Icon Is Love / 1994 / A&M ♦♦♦♦

Barry White has been to the top of the charts an admirable number of times, but only one of his hits was a ballad (a studio effort for the Quincy Jones album *Back on the Block* that included El DeBarge, James Ingram and Al B. Sure!). However, as a solo artist, White has never had a ballad usurp the number-one spot on the *Billboard* charts. This album's featured release fills that void. "Practice What You Preach," which unites the maestro with producers Gerald LeVert and Edwin "Tony" Nicholas, has a simmering arrangement, evocative lyric and White's brawn delivery. The catchy melody and sensuous female backing vocals enhance this already stellar single. It stayed on the *Billboard* R&B charts for 30 weeks and had a consecutive three-week run at number one. White showcases his seductive, bassy baritone with romantic rap introductions on most of the selections. There is a balance of uptempo and balladic songs. The other two featured releases were "Come On" and "There It Is." The former is reminiscent of his days as the king of disco-swing, and the latter is a contemporary funky ballad. Respectively, they tipped in at numbers 12 and 54. White, who is credited as producer and writer on every selection, embraces the savvy writing talents of industry veterans Barry Eastmond & Michael Lovesmith, and the keen production skills of Chuckii Booker (his godson), Jam & Lewis, and Jack Perry. *—Craig Lytle*

★ **All Time Greatest Hits** / 1995 / Mercury ♦♦♦♦♦
It took quite a while for a definitive Barry White compilation to hit the market, but *All-Time Greatest Hits*—part of Mercury's Funk Essentials series—finally filled the bill in 1995. Boasting a full 20 tracks from White's heyday of 1973-1978, more than half of which made the R&B Top Ten, *All-Time Greatest Hits* is easily the most generous single-disc White collection on the market. It includes the edited single versions, not the full-length album tracks, which actually makes for a more digestible introduction to White's achievements. Like his forebear Isaac Hayes, White was not just a deep-voiced crooner, but a talented producer and arranger who'd spent years honing his craft behind the scenes in the industry. And like Hayes, White spent a great deal of time setting up moods on his albums, using lush, sweeping orchestrations to build very gradually to climaxes. (Actually, that probably explains a good deal of his effectiveness.) But White was not simply a Hayes disciple; his swirling productions were less complex than Hayes', but more in tune with the emerging disco sound, which certainly boosted his popularity. Plus, he took full advantage of R&B's new lyrical permissiveness in the wake of Marvin Gaye's *Let's Get It On*. If his voice was limited, it was also a tremendous asset for the kind of music he recorded—deep, resonant, caressing, but always suggestively masculine. The total package made White an R&B love-man icon not just for the disco era, but all time. For all but the most dedicated fans, *All-Time Greatest Hits* is one-stop shopping. *—Steve Huey*

Under the Influence of Love: The Very Best of Barry White / Jan. 5, 1998 / Collectables ♦♦
The phrase "very best" in the title of *The Very Best of Barry White: Under the Influence of Love* is a little disingenuous. This ten-track compilation is not a collection of his biggest hits; it's an overview of his earliest recordings with the Love Unlimited Orchestra. While there aren't any big hits here, and many of the songs are underdeveloped, White's seductive, string-drenched style can be heard in embryonic form on this disc, which makes it of interest to hardcore collectors. *—Stephen Thomas Erlewine*

Boss Soul: The Genius of Barry White / Aug. 4, 1998 / Del-Fi ♦♦♦
In 1966-1967, long before he attained '70s superstardom as a growling bedroom funkster, Barry White gained valuable experience as an A&R man for the Del-Fi label in Los Angeles. This compilation has 16 tracks that he was involved with as producer, engineer, songwriter, and/or session musician, the results appearing on Del-Fi's Bronco and Mustang subsidiaries; note, however, that only five of the cuts are by White himself (including one instrumental and a pre-Del Fi 1965 single released under the pseudonym of Lee Barry). At this time, White was very much under the spell of Motown both as producer and songwriter (he wrote or co-wrote all but two of these tunes). The material, whether by White or other Mustang/Bronco artists Felice Taylor, Viola Wills, and Johnny Wyatt, consists for the most part of very derivative, but nonetheless enjoyable and professional, Motown variations. Felice Taylor's "It May Be Winter Outside," a number-42 pop hit in 1966, is the most accurate mid-'60s Supremes imitation bar none, both for Taylor's uncanny Diana Ross-like vocals and the dead-on Motown-esque arrangement. Her only slightly less Supremish "Under the Influence of Love," though unreleased in the U.S., was a number-11 hit in the U.K. in 1967; an instrumental version (credited to White) is also on the CD. As for White's own performances, it's a shock to hear that familiar hoarse voice applied to much lighter, poppier songs than we're accustomed to hearing from the singer, and though they're OK efforts, it's easy to see why they may not have been considered commercial properties in the '60s. An interesting document of White's little-heard formative years, and a decent pickup for aficionados of little-heard '60s soul in general. *—Richie Unterberger*

Staying Power / Jul. 27, 1999 / Private Music ♦♦♦
By the late '90s, Barry White was primarily known as an icon. His music was well-known, but his voice was known better, as it stood for the epitome of sultry, sexy soul. And, befitting his icon status, he could still support a large audience in concerts, which led to new recordings—recordings that were minor hits upon their release, but never eclipsing his classic hits. *Staying Power*, his first album since 1994's *The Icon Is Love*, fits neatly into that category. It certainly is an enjoyable album, since White's voice is aging remarkably well and the production is uniformly appealing, but it's never a memorable one. Like most contemporary albums by veterans, it's littered with cameos that are designed to broaden his audience and increase chances of airplay. With the exception of the Bone Thugs-N-Harmony duet "Thank You"—which is the worst track on the album—they all work pretty well, and the Chaka Khan & Lisa Stansfield showcase "The Longer We Make Love" is very good indeed. However, the record sounds the best when the spotlight is on White. Nevertheless, once the album is completed, it's hard to remember any of it, even if it was enjoyable as it spun. Which means *Staying Power* is a standard-issue iconic release—it's classy and entertaining, but doesn't add to the legacy. *—Stephen Thomas Erlewine*

The Ultimate Collection / Jan. 25, 2000 / Mercury ♦♦♦
The Ultimate Collection gathers two discs' worth of Barry White's greatest hits and definitive tracks, as selected by White himself. Along with the title track from his 1999 album *Staying Power*, the set collects '70s hits like "I'm Gonna Love You Just a Little More Baby," "Can't Get Enough of Your Love Babe," "You're the First, the Last, My Everything," and "Never, Never Gonna Give You Up" and highlights of his work with the Love Unlimited Orchestra such as "My Sweet Summer Suite," "Midnight and You," and "Love's Theme." Later tracks like "Sho' You Right," "Put Me in Your Mix," and "Practice What You Preach" round out this worthwhile overview of White's career highlights. *—Heather Phares*

Karyn White

b. Oct. 14, 1965, Los Angeles, CA
Vocals / Dance-Pop, Pop-Soul, Urban, Soul, Club/Dance
Contemporary pop/R&B singer Karyn White was born in Los Angeles, where her father played trumpet and her mother was a church choir director. White gained experience singing in choir and also in local talent shows and beauty pageants. She sang with local band Legacy and then toured with R&B vocalist O'Bryan in 1984. A lead vocal on instrumentalist Jeff Lorber's "Facts of Life" led to Warner Bros. signing her. The self-titled debut, released in 1988, featured "The Way You Love Me," "Love Saw It," and "Superwoman"; the album sold two-million copies. Her gold follow-up, *Ritual of Love* (1991), featured production by Jimmy Jam & Terry Lewis. Karyn White later married Lewis and together they had a daughter, Ashley. Jam & Lewis also contributed production help on 1994's *Make Him Do Right*. *—John Bush*

● **Karyn White** / 1988 / Warner Bros. ♦♦♦♦♦
Photogenic session vocalist Karyn White scored a hit in 1987 by lending her vocals to the Jeff Lorber track "Facts of Love." Not long after, her self-titled solo debut propelled her to pop stardom, and was one of the first albums to solidify Babyface and L.A. Reid as top-notch songwriters. The album was lush, state-of-the-art pop R&B at its finest, and scored no less than three pop Top Ten hits for the burgeoning songbird. "The Way You Love Me" and "Secret Rendezvous," which were also big dance hits, were groove-heavy, melodic, and sophisticated, and their success was no doubt aided by White's striking good looks. However, the song that White will probably be best remembered for is the anthemic ballad "Superwoman," a song that touched a chord with working women everywhere, and, likes its predecessors, shot to the pop Top Ten and the top of the R&B charts. The song wasn't whiny, nor was it male bashing, it was simply of statement of reality. Other notable tracks on this set are the slow-burning "Slow Jam" and the Babyface duet "Love Saw It," which, although not a pop hit, was huge on the R&B charts. This album is sophisticated, late-'80s pop/dance/R&B at its finest, before the genre took an angry turn in the early to mid-'90s. *—Jose F. Promis*

Ritual of Love / Sep. 10, 1991 / Warner Bros. ♦♦♦♦♦
Jimmy Jam & Terry Lewis' production is the real star of White's sophomore album. And while the results aren't nearly as stunning as similar work they did with Janet Jackson around the same time (many of these songs sound like *Rhythm Nation* leftovers), there is a uniformity to the tracks that makes *Ritual* a more consistent and enjoyable listen than it should be. Highlights are "Romantic," "The Way I Feel About You," "Walkin' the Dog," and "Do Unto Me." *—Michael Gallucci*

Make Him Do Right / 1994 / Warner Bros. ♦♦♦

Barrence Whitfield & the Savages

Vocals / Soul, R&B, Rock & Roll
A Boston-based singer of what one might refer to as "traditional" R&B (i.e., '50s- and '60s-style), Barrence Whitfield is the owner of one incredible pair of lungs and limitless energy and enthusiasm for his music. A soul screamer in the spirit of Little Richard, Wilson Pickett, Solomon Burke, and early Don Covay, Whitfield & the Savages, though never breaking big nationally, are a great cult act, a triumph of substance over style, with a bunch of terrific records to boot.

Whitfield (real name Barry White, no joke!) came to Boston from New Jersey in the late '70s to attend Boston University. Prior to college, he'd spent time singing in an assortment of ill-fated hard rock, disco, and even progressive rock bands, never really singing the soul music he grew up loving. His move to Boston was a way of putting (at least temporarily) his musical past behind him. He had no intention of starting another band; his focus was on college. That was until he fell in with a bunch of Boston musicians led by ex-Lyres guitarist Peter Greenberg, who shared Whitfield's love of raging soul and R&B. After hearing Whitfield sing, Greenberg was convinced they'd found the best voice in the city and Barrence Whitfield & the Savages were born. For a while, they were the toast of the town, and without a doubt one of the best live acts in Boston. It was a hopeful sign too—an African-American man working with a bunch of white guys in a city not known for its racial hospitality. After some dues-paying at college frat-house parties, the Savages were ready for the local club scene, and they tore it up. Whitfield was a dervish on-stage, working himself into such a frenzy of screaming and running around that he would occasionally black out. The band, especially Greenberg and drummer Howie Ferguson, were raucous and rough, in high gear from the moment they hit the stage.

Their debut LP was released to much acclaim (some of it national) in 1984, but the Savages' brand of old R&B, and the fact that they relied almost exclusively on covers, didn't help them get beyond their status as enthusiastic archivists. By the time the third album was released, the Savages had been replaced by a whole new band, and while the mania remained intact, there was a concerted effort for smoother soul songs designed to show off Whitfield's voice. While America was being apathetic to the Savages, England was going wild for them. BBC disc jockey Andy Kershaw fell in love with the band, taped a gig in Boston for air in Britain, and brought the Savages over for a tour. Among their English fans were Robert Plant (who showed up at some gigs) and Elvis Costello, who was supposedly writing a song for them.

Unfortunately, English success didn't translate back into big sales in America, and the band soldiered on with a few more personnel changes, but remained a cult act, touring in their strongholds and releasing fewer and fewer records. In 1997, Whitfield began working with the Movers, a Boston-based blues octet. *—John Dougan*

Barrence Whitfield and the Savages / 1984 / Rounder ♦♦♦
It clocks in at under 30 minutes, so these days it qualifies as an EP, but the Savages' debut record is a scorcher. A 100-mph rave-up from the moment Barry screams his way through Don Covay's "Bip Bop Bip" to the go-for-broke "Ship Sails at Six." Peter Greenberg's garage grunge guitar sounds great propelling these tracks, and the whole thing just screeches party. *—John Dougan*

Dig Yourself / 1985 / Rounder ♦♦♦
Better produced than their debut, *Dig Yourself* picks up where the mania of the first album left off. Again, Barry sounds great, as does the band, ripping it up with a wild-eyed exuberance that you could go months without hearing these days. Contains one of the

best Savages tracks, "Juicy Fruit." Caveat emptor: this was recorded in the vinyl era and is only 30 minutes long. *—John Dougan*

Call of the Wild / 1987 / Demon/Rounder Europa ♦♦♦

● **Ow! Ow! Ow!** / 1987 / Rounder ♦♦♦♦♦

Is it the best Savages album ever made? This was the first record with the "New" Savages, and the turn is to more original material. Guitarist Milton Reder's "Madhouse" is a wonderful fit for Barry's voice, as is sax player David Scholl's "I Don't Dig Your Noise." But the payoff is the Reder-penned "Girl From Outer Space," which Barry sings in a falsetto scream that is dazzling (he even riffs on Sun Ra at the end of the song). What makes this the strongest Whitfield/Savages album is its variety, and the fact that Barry's voice is strong and versatile enough to bring more nuance and emotion to the material. Why this wasn't a big hit for them remains a mystery; it's a fine, fine record. *—John Dougan*

Live Emulsified / 1989 / Rounder ♦♦

Cowboy Mambo / 1993 / East Side Digital ♦♦♦♦♦

Fans of *Hillbilly Voodoo*, the fine first collaboration between country-soul singer Barrence Whitfield and folkie Tom Russell, will not be disappointed by this follow-up. Once again, Russell skillfully handles production chores, and once again, he leaves the spotlight to Whitfield, who turns in a dozen high-spirited, live-in-the-studio-sounding performances. The inspired program of tunes taps writers ranging from the Band's Robbie Robertson ("Daniel and the Sacred Harp") to Nashville outlaws like Steve Earle ("The Devil's Right Hand") and Gram Parsons ("Brass Buttons"). There are also several contributions from Russell, including the title cut and the affecting "Home Before Dark." *—Jeff Burger*

Hillbilly Voodoo / 1993 / East Side Digital ♦♦♦♦

It's appropriate that soul singer Barrence Whitfield has his mouth wide open and folkie Tom Russell has his closed in the cover photos of both this album and its follow-up, *Cowboy Mambo*. Throughout each disk, Whitfield holds the spotlight; Russell joins in the fun and also contributes some songs, but his main role seems to be as producer and fan: he clearly loves Whitfield's music and seems determined to help popularize it. And no wonder—Whitfield's music is terrific stuff. If you had to slap a label on him, it would be country-soul singer, but he's soaked up far too many influences and turned them into something far too special for that tag to do him justice. The material—alternately playful and emotional—is uniformly first-rate, with highlights including Lucinda Williams' "I Just Want to See You So Bad," and Bob Dylan's "Blind Willie McTell," Van Morrison's "Cleaning Windows," Jesse Winchester's "Mississippi, You're on My Mind," and Russell's own "The Cuban Sandwich." *—Jeff Burger*

Ritual of the Savages / Jul. 4, 1995 / Ocean Music ♦♦♦♦

If you think that cult acts become bitter as they get older and release records that are pale copies of their (albeit fleeting) glory days, it's not the case with the Savages. *Ritual of the Savages* may not be as totally berserk as, say, *Dig Yourself*, but Barry and band still make fine records, alternately energetic and soulful; their repertoire has expanded, and Milton Reder's writing chops (e.g., "Got Your Love Right Here" and "House of Love") have become a valuable asset to the sound. Since the late '80s, the Savages have had a relationship with Ben Vaughn, and his presence and songwriting contributions have helped them continue to refine their sound without loosing the sense of manic energy that made their earlier releases so important. Now a decade-plus on, Barrence Whitfield & the Savages are clearly no the same band they were in 1984, but they're still a fine band. *—John Dougan*

Norman Whitfield

b. 1943, New York, NY

Producer, Songwriter / Motown, Soul, Psychedelic Soul

Norman Whitfield was one of the major architects of the Motown sound, almost from its inception as a national label up through its waning days of major chart success. More than that, however, Whitfield and his personal drive became an important part of the psychological dynamic of the label, often pushing Motown founder Berry Gordy to try out songs and sounds that he didn't fully appreciate himself, to their mutual benefit.

Born in New York in 1943, Whitfield wasn't yet in his teens when R&B began exerting itself as a major force. He learned very fast, however, and before he was 20, he'd gained some experience as a staff producer at Detroit's Thelma Records. He was also a working session musician in Detroit, even playing tambourine with the band Popcorn & the Mohawks on some 1959 vintage recordings on which they backed the Distants, the precursors to the Temptations. He was to see sides and potential in the group's sound that would enhance both their careers in the decade to follow.

In late 1962, Whitfield became part of the early boom era at Motown Records, joining the ranks of Harvey Fuqua, Mickey Stevenson, and the Holland-Dozier-Holland songwriting team. Whitfield was originally brought into Motown as a songwriter, and among his early successes was "I Couldn't Cry If I Wanted To," written in collaboration with Eddie Holland and cut by the Temptations in late 1962. It soon became clear to Berry Gordy that Whitfield's talents extended to arranging and production, and it was in the latter capacity that he came to prominence at the label. Whitfield enjoyed some success as a composer with "Too Many Fish in the Sea" by the Marvelettes and "Needle in a Haystack" by the Velvelettes, but it was his drive—and his vision as a producer—that allowed him to take over the helm of the Temptations' records.

From 1963 onward, Whitfield had produced most of their recordings of his own songs, and by 1966, he'd completely taken over producing the Temptations in the wake of their huge hit "Ain't Too Proud to Beg," as well as "Beauty Is Only Skin Deep" and "I Know I'm Losing You." For the next few years, Whitfield or his protégé, Frank Wilson, produced virtually all of the Temptations' recordings, although as Gordy recalled in his autobiography, Whitfield was ambitious enough to extend his influence as a producer far and wide; he still wrote songs as well, and he was always looking for different ways of presenting the same composition. Whitfield's approach to music resembled that of the record producers of a bygone era in that he would treat the same song differently with a variety of artists, looking for new permutations of the song's appeal to put before the public. Had he worked for a label like Columbia or RCA, with a roster of artists spanning the musical spectrum, Whitfield might have been cutting R&B, country, pop, and rock & roll versions of his songs, looking for versions that clicked with himself and the public.

His enthusiasm was infectious and Gordy marveled at the moments when Whitfield was hooked on an idea. Even when one of his songs was a hit, he would try the song in a different way. Gordy also soon learned to trust Whitfield's bouts of seemingly reckless enthusiasm. When the record label chief vetoed a single release of Whitfield's "I Heard It Through the Grapevine" that had been cut by Marvin Gaye, opting instead for a more romantic song, Whitfield refused to let the matter drop. He turned around and annoyed Gordy intensely, finally cajoling him into okaying another attempt at the song by Gladys Knight & the Pips. Their version, almost a gospel rendition, was a huge hit; in its wake, the Marvin Gaye version, much more raw sounding (and also produced by Whitfield), was issued and became a second hit version. The song became one of the most valuable copyrights owned by Motown, as it was covered by hundreds of artists, most notably Creedence Clearwater Revival, both on an edited single and as an epic-length jam on their perennially popular LP *Cosmo's Factory*.

Whitfield became the company's spark plug as music entered the psychedelic era, taking to the new sound and, especially, the use of sound effects, more easily than most of the rest of the label. The Temptations were his instrument, their singles and albums his canvas, as Whitfield began creating more involved and ambitious works. Beginning with the single "I Wish It Would Rain"—written in collaboration with lyricist Eddie Holland, who became Whitfield's songwriting partner—he moved the group and the company into this new era, which opened up the subject matter as well as the sound of their songs. "I Can't Get Next to You," "Ball of Confusion," and "Cloud Nine" were among the best records to come out of the label during the turn of the '60s into the '70s. When Whitfield wasn't producing the albums himself, his protégé, Frank Wilson, using techniques and approaches he'd learned from Whitfield, was in charge. By way of Wilson's contemporary work with the Four Tops, Whitfield's influence extended to other corners of the Motown stable during this era.

Whitfield kept moving with the times, and had other songs and outlets for his compositions in mind. Edwin Starr had been with Motown for several years without scoring a major hit, but in 1970, he scored the biggest hit of his career with "War," co-written by Whitfield and Holland. The song was so well-known that 22 years later, its lyrics ("War, what is it good for") figured in a key joke (involving Tolstoy's *War and Peace*) at the center of an episode of *Seinfeld*. He also put together a new group around this time, the Undisputed Truth, out of the ruins of a failed Motown act called the Delicates and one ex-member of a group called the Preps. With Whitfield putting Billie Rae Calvin, Brenda Joyce, and Joe Harris together and calling all of the shots for the group as far as songs and recordings, they became one of his two principal vehicles for musical expression. The group hit right out of the box with another Whitfield song that managed to capture its time and place, "Smiling Faces Sometimes," which became a number-three hit in 1971. The song itself may have said more than it meant to about the time in which it was written, recorded, and released, with a slow tempo and an ominous mood. They never hit again as big as they did with that song, as Whitfield concentrated most of his efforts on the Temptations, but he used the Undisputed Truth to try out funk and psychedelic experiments, both with his own songs (including the first version of "Papa Was a Rolling Stone") and covers of other writers' songs.

The dawn of the '70s and the success of albums such as Marvin Gaye's *What's Going On* and Stevie Wonder's *Innervisions* saw the company enter a last, great flowering in its recordings. Whitfield created his greatest effort, *Masterpiece*, by the Temptations during this period, but its critical notices were better than its sales and he soon found himself, like most of the label's other producers, being discouraged from further recordings as ambitious as that, particularly as Motown's fortunes declined. The company had started the '70s in healthy enough condition, but by the middle of the decade had taken huge losses, not only on many recordings but on several dubious film-related projects.

In 1975, Whitfield left Motown to start his own label, Whitfield Records (its emblem, a W, was virtually an inverted Motown M with a different color scheme), taking the Undisputed Truth with him. He recruited new members, most notably Taka Boom (aka Yvonne Stevens, the sister of Chaka Khan) (later with the Glass Family), to work with Joe Harris, and saw some hits from this version of the group with "You+Me=Love" and "Let's Go Down to the Disco." Whitfield's big success with his own label, however, and his last big commercial hit came in 1976 with the group Rose Royce, which he had discovered during their time as Edwin Starr's backup band (known as Magic Wand). Beginning with their soundtrack to the movie *Car Wash*, the group enjoyed a series of three hit albums and accompanying hit singles for Whitfield's label. Since the beginning of the '80s and the decline of disco, however, Whitfield has been virtually unheard as either a producer or songwriter, except for the omnipresent reissues of his 13 years of Motown productions. *—Bruce Eder*

Marva Whitney

Vocals / Funk, Soul, Deep Funk

Although she's not a household name, Marva Whitney is fondly remembered by funk devotees as one of the rawest, brassiest, most powerful divas the music ever produced. Along with fellow funk belters Lyn Collins and Vicki Anderson, Whitney made her name singing with the James Brown Revue for a few years, and her limited, much-sampled recordings for Brown-associated labels now fetch astronomical sums on the collector's market. Born in Kansas City, Whitney began performing at the age of three with her family's touring gospel group, the Manning Gospel Singers. She studied music in college and caught on as lead singer of the R&B group Tommy Gadson & the Derbys. In 1967, she signed on with the James Brown Revue as a featured female vocalist, meaning that she would perform her own small set every night while Brown took a break. Whitney accompanied Brown on his late-'60s tour of Vietnam, and made other international appearances with him as well. In 1969, Whitney made her first solo recordings for King, Brown's label at the time. She scored a Top 20 hit on the R&B charts with "It's

My Thing (You Can't Tell Me Who to Sock It To)," a rewrite of the Isley Brothers hit; the follow-up, "Things Got to Get Better (Get Together)," just missed the R&B Top 20. Far too gutsy and funky to cross over to the pop charts, Whitney remained with the Revue until 1970, without scoring any more significant hits on her own. Still, cuts like "Unwind Yourself" (now very recognizable through several hip-hop samples) and the duet "You Got to Have a Job (If You Don't Work)" helped cement her reputation among record collectors. Her only studio LP, *It's My Thing*, was released in 1969 and has been heavily bootlegged and sampled by numerous DJs; her *Live and Lowdown at the Apollo* LP also commands hefty price tags. Whitney went on to record for the Isley Brothers' T-Neck label, as well as Nashboro, but her prime material is from the James Brown years. Seven of those tracks were compiled on the Polydor collection *James Brown's Original Funky Divas*. Whitney has reunited sporadically with Brown for live performances over the years. *—Steve Huey*

● **It's My Thing** / 1969 / Soul Brother ✦✦✦
Like any disc produced by James Brown and featuring the mighty J.B.'s as a backing group, *It's My Thing* is a stone-cold funky record. Marva Whitney sang in the James Brown Revue from 1967 to 1969, and in 1969 she released this record. Not only did Brown produce but he wrote or co-wrote most of the tracks and it basically sounds like a James Brown record with a female singer. A tough, aggressive female singer. Marva sounds like she could take any comers and leave them shaking in their go-go boots. From the opening blast of "It's My Thing, Pt. 1 and "Pt. 2," a rewrite of the Isley Brothers' "It's Your Thing, she shouts, exhorts, wails, and basically lets it all hang out as the band lays down groove after groove. Thankfully after four exhausting tracks, Marva slows it down with "If You Love Me," an Otis Redding-style broken-hearted ballad. After an instrumental break she jumps right back into the funky fray with "Unwind Yourself," which features a classic horn line and some gritty vocalizing from Marva. The rest of the record follows this pattern of a couple of stompers and a ballad. The highlight of the record is "I'm Tired I'm Tired I'm Tired (Things Better Change Before It's Too Late)," a funky (yes, every track on this disc is funky) lament that details just how tired Marva is of society putting her down. Check out Brown going wild in the background about halfway through the song. The disc has five bonus tracks added to the original album, including the slow-burning "I Made a Mistake Because It's Only You, Pts. 1 & 2" and a duet with James Brown on "Sunny." This is a great record and it is a pity that it is on such a tiny label and not one of the major reissue labels because Marva deserves wider recognition. By all means seek this one out. *—Tim Sendra*

Wild Cherry

f. 1974, Steubenville, OH, **db.** 1981

Group / Funk, Disco

One-hit wonders Wild Cherry was led by Rob Parissi (singer, guitarist, songwriter), who originally formed the group in 1970. Influenced by the likes of the Yardbirds and Sly & the Family Stone (and named after a flavor of cough drops), the group played around their hometown of Steubenville, OH, and even inked a recording contract with Brown Bag Records (led by former Grand Funk Railroad manager Terry Knight). But the group never issued any albums for the label and split up in 1975. Understandably dejected, Parissi turned his back entirely on music, selling all the band's equipment and for a while, managing a local steakhouse. But it wasn't long before Parissi's interest in music returned and he formed a new version of Wild Cherry with a whole new lineup, including Mark Ausec (keyboards), Bryan Bassett (guitar), Allen Wentz (bass), and Ronald Beitle (drums).

The group was still mostly rock-based and with the public's attention shifting to more dance-oriented styles (namely disco), the group was accosted nightly between sets by fans who wanted them to "Play that funky music." It wasn't long before Parissi took heed and penned a song under the same title, an infectious ditty that merged funk and rock together. The quintet entered a studio shortly thereafter to record the track (although they felt that a cover of the Commodores song "I Feel Sanctified" stood more of a chance of becoming a hit). A friend of an engineer at the studio overheard the track, eventually bringing it to the attention of Epic Records, which in turn signed the group.

"Play That Funky Music" became a monster hit in 1976, peaking at number one on both the *Billboard* R&B and pop charts, while both the single and Wild Cherry's self-titled debut obtained platinum certification. Wild Cherry was rewarded with a number of accolades shortly thereafter, including being named Best Pop Group of the Year by *Billboard*, receiving an American Music Award for Top R&B Single of the Year, and even earning a pair of Grammy nominations for Best New Vocal Group and Best R&B Performance by a Group or Duo. But Wild Cherry proved to be susceptible to the dreaded sophomore jinx and as their follow-up recording, 1977's *Electrified Funk*, failed to spawn any hits and sunk from sight shortly after its release, as did such further releases as 1978's *I Love My Music*, plus 1979's *Only the Wild Survive* and *Don't Wait Too Long*; Wild Cherry split up the same year (with Parissi eventually turning up later as a disc jockey in Wheeling, WV). Wild Cherry's lone hit remains a favorite in dance clubs to this day, as a pair of collections were issued after their split: *Play the Funk* and *Super Hits*. *—Greg Prato*

● **Wild Cherry** / 1976 / Epic ✦✦✦✦
The debut album from the foursome from Ohio. It featured the ferocious single "Play That Funky Music." Robert Parissi's animated vocals were complemented by the soulful chimes of the guitar, a smokin' bassline, and some hyped backing vocals. It peaked on the *Billboard* R&B and pop charts at number one. They received rave reviews considering that the band was all white conveying such a funky message. (The arrangement and lyrical phrasing are very similar to that of Stevie Wonder's "You Haven't Done Nothing" found on his *Fulfillingness' First Finale* album that was released two years prior.) No other singles came from this album. However, there were funk jams and smokin' numbers including remakes of "No Where to Run" and "99 1/2." Still, nothing compares to the featured single. *—Craig Lytle*

Electrified Funk / 1977 / Epic ✦✦✦
Wild Cherry was the epitome of a one-hit wonder. Anyone who is seriously into 1970s soul/funk is familiar with "Play That Funky Music," but a lot of the people who know Cherry for that wildly infectious number-one hit probably wouldn't be able to name any of their other songs. That's regrettable because while "Play That Funky Music" was Cherry's only major hit, it wasn't the only worthwhile song the band recorded. *Electrified Funk*, Cherry's second album, wasn't a huge seller but it's a generally respectable collection of rock-influenced funk and blue-eyed soul. The LP gets off to an unimpressive start with "Baby, Don't You Know," which is nothing more than a poor man's "Play That Funky Music." However, when Cherry rips into "Dancin' Music Band," "Are You Boogieing Around on Your Daddy" and the Commodores-influenced "Hot to Trot," this album wins listeners over, reminding them that there was more to Cherry than "Play That Funky Music." Also appealing is Cherry's remake of "Hold On," a ballad that they had previously recorded for their self-titled debut album of 1976 (which was the only Cherry album ever reissued on CD). Unfortunately, *Electrified Funk* has long been out of print, and considering Cherry's one-hit-wonder status, it's hard to imagine Epic reissuing the album. *—Alex Henderson*

I Love My Music / 1978 / Epic ✦✦✦
In the late 1970s, Wild Cherry took a hint from the Ohio Players and favored LP covers that depicted young women in sexy poses. *I Love My Music*, Cherry's third album, depicted a scantily clad woman with the band's name tattooed on her derriere—if that isn't right out of the Ohio Players' school of LP-cover erotica, nothing is. But those sexy LP covers didn't do much for Cherry commercially. More than titillating covers, the band needed a really strong single, and no such thing was to be found on *I Love My Music*. Nothing on this album is in a class with "Play That Funky Music," the gem to which all of Cherry's late-'70s output would inevitably be compared. Still, it's a decent, if unspectacular, soul/pop/rock release, and the band is likable enough on material that ranges from the driving, Commodores-influenced funk of "Don't Stop, Get Off" to melodic blue-eyed soul offerings like "Fools Fall in Love," the ballad "Try One More Time," and the Motown-ish "1 2 3 Kind of Love." Cherry's appreciation of 1960s Motown also asserts itself on covers of the Isley Brothers' "This Old Heart of Mine" and the Four Tops' "It's the Same Old Song," both of which are competent but definitely fall short of the excellence of the original versions. Like *Electrified Funk* and *Only the Wild Survive*, *I Love My Music* has long been out of print, and the chances of it ever being reissued on CD are slim. *—Alex Henderson*

Only the Wild Survive / 1979 / Epic ✦✦
Fair or unfair, everything Wild Cherry recorded in the late '70s was destined to be compared to "Play That Funky Music." Ideally, Cherry would have come out with a second smash single that was totally different but equally successful. That never happened, though, and one could say that while "Play That Funky Music" had millions of admirers, Cherry itself had only a small following. *Only the Wild Survive* was Cherry's fourth album and it would also be their last. Like *I Love My Music* before it, *Only the Wild Survive* is a decent but uneven and unremarkable soul/pop/rock LP that lacked the really strong single that Cherry desperately needed. The Ohio outfit tries a variety of things, and the results are enjoyable on tunes that range from the ballsy "Hold on to Your Hiney" (which has a Rare Earth-meets-the Commodores sort of appeal) and the Motown-flavored "Take Me Back" to the dramatic, pop-minded "Starlight." But in 1979, decent wasn't enough to save Wild Cherry. *Only the Wild Survive* was ignored by both pop and R&B radio; the only people who bought the long out-of-print LP were Cherry's small group of die-hard fans. At that point, Cherry's breakup seemed inevitable. *—Alex Henderson*

Don't Wait Too Long / 1979 / Epic ✦

The Wild Magnolias

f. 1973

Group / Funk, Ceremonial, New Orleans R&B

Though more a ceremonial group than a performing or touring band, the New Orleans Mardi Gras "Indian Tribe" the Wild Magnolias issued a critically acclaimed LP for Polydor in 1974. Bo Dollis, Monk Boudreaux, June Johnson Jr., Crip Adams, Tobias Johnson, Bubba Scott, and James Smothers brought the rich, fervent flavor of New Orleans to vinyl, backed by Willie Tee's band. The LP wasn't a huge seller, but it attracted so much media interest the Magnolias appeared at Carnegie Hall that year, as well as the Capitol Center in Washington, D.C. *—Ron Wynn*

The Wild Magnolias / Dec. 1974 / Polydor ✦✦✦
This debut marked a milestone for New Orleans music as it was one of the first major label record for a Mardi Gras Indian tribe; this was soon to be followed by another great tribe band, the Wild Tchoupitoulas. Not to be confused with Native American tribes, the Mardi Gras Indians are part of an African-American gang-land tradition going back decades that started out as brawls and developed into more civilized costume and song contests (much like the hip-hop style wars later on). Beginning as a practice group formed by leader/Big Chief Theodore "Bo" Dollis and Joseph "Monk" Boudreaux of the Golden Eagles tribe, the Wild Magnolias caught the eye of local promoters and were recorded in 1973 with the New Orleans Project featuring keyboardist Willie Tee and fiery guitarist Snooks Eaglin. Dollis and Boudreaux lead the group through gospel-ish call-and-response chants that become funky mantras as Tee and Eaglin kick up driving grooves to go along with it. Along with inspired originals like "Handa Wanda" and "Two Way Pak E Way," they cover traditional numbers that go way, way back like "Saints" ("come marching in") and "Shoo Fly" ("don't bother me"). The 1993 reissue on Polydor is especially fine as it includes a number of unreleased songs from the same session and a B-side that go along well with the original album. *The Wild Magnolias* is an exciting non-stop dance fest and an excellent introduction for any interested in the music of the Big Easy. *—Jason Gross*

They Call Us Wild / May 3, 1994 / Polydor ✦✦✦

● **Life Is a Carnival** / Mar. 9, 1999 / Metro Blue ✦✦✦✦
The Wild Magnolias are one of the 20 or so tribes of "Mardi Gras Indians" (Social Clubs) that swarm the streets on Mardi Gras Day in African-American neighborhoods searching for other tribes so that they can show off their incredibly spectacular suits. These suits are sometimes worked on for more than a year, consisting of feathers, plumes, sequins, rhinestones and more. This disc is probably the finest example of New Orleans funk and roll that has crossed this changer in many years. Other purveyors of this genre will not be insulted as they are probably represented on this disc. Represented here, and playing some of this genre's most exciting music, are members of the Neville Brothers, the Meters, Dr. John, Davell Crawford, Wardell Quezergue and many more. Suffice it to say, this is a summit meeting of musicians organized by the Big Chiefs to work together and display what they are about, rather than stay separate and compete. The Wild Magnolias are led by Big Chief Bo Dollis, and with this disc (it has been recorded for the second time in 25 years), its traditional call-and-response street chants fused with the incendiary rhythm and blues indigenous to the area are blended further with the funk of the Brass Band. This disc successfully fuses the different styles into one of the most infectious and danceable discs of the late '90s. Aside from the luminaries of the New Orleans music scene listed above Robby Robertson, Bruce Hornsby, Rockin' Dopsie Jr., June Yamagishi, Marva Wright and so many more are also thrown into the fray. What comes out of the kettle for your aural pleasure is a stew that is considerably superior to the individual pieces of the mixture, and that is what this disc is all about: the drawing together of the diverse parts into a harmonious whole. *—Bob Gottlieb*

Wild Orchid

Group / Dance-Pop, Adult Contemporary
Wild Orchid is a teen-oriented dance-pop group that gained a small following in the mid-'90s. The three members of Wild Orchid—Stacy Ferguson (born March 27, 1975, Whittier, CA), Stefanie Ridel (born May 17, 1973), and Renee Sandstrom (born February 15, 1974, Worchester, MA)—met as children, and decided to form a group after they acted together in the Nickelodeon show *Kids Incorporated* and sang backup for Martika. The group signed with RCA, and their A&R rep, Ron Fair, co-produced the band's eponymous 1996 debut, drafting in such session musicians, collaborators, and writers as Jerry Hey's Horns, David Frank, Abraham Laboriel Sr., Junior Vasquez, Bob Brockmann, and Matthew Wilder. *Wild Orchid* was greeted with generally positive reviews and was a moderate hit; *Oxygen* followed in 1998. *—Stephen Thomas Erlewine*

Wild Orchid / Oct. 29, 1996 / RCA ✦✦✦

● **Oxygen** / Sep. 29, 1998 / RCA ✦✦✦✦

The Wild Tchoupitoulas

f. Louisiana
Group / New Orleans R&B, Funk, Ceremonial
The Wild Tchoupitoulas—Spy Boy (Amos Landry), Trail Chief (Booker Washington), Big Chief Jolly (George Landry), Flag Boy (Carl Christmas), the Third Chief (Thomas Jackson), and Second Chief (Norman Bell)—are a Mardi Gras ceremonial parade group and "Black Indian tribe" based in New Orleans. George Landry is an uncle to the Neville Brothers. *The Wild Tchoupitoulas* is their only album. *—William Ruhlmann*

★ **The Wild Tchoupitoulas** / 1976 / Mango ✦✦✦✦✦
The Wild Tchoupitoulas—a group of Mardi Gras "Indians" headed by George "Big Chief Jolly" Landry—only released one album, but that one record caused a sensation upon its initial 1976 release. It was one of the first records of the album-rock generation that captured the heady gumbo of New Orleans R&B and funk. Landry may have fronted the Wild Tchoupitoulas, but the key to the record's success was his nephews, Charles and Cyril Neville, who headed the rhythm section. They drafted in their brothers, Art and Aaron, to harmonize, and thereby unwittingly gave birth to the band that became the Neville Brothers. Still, the fact that *The Wild Tchoupitoulas* ranks among the great New Orleans albums isn't because of the Nevilles themselves, but the way the Tchoupitoulas lock into an extraordinary hybrid that marries several indigenous New Orleans musics, with swampy, dirty funk taking its place in the forefront. There are only eight songs, and they are all strung together, as if they're variations on the same themes and rhythms. That's a compliment, by the way, since the organic, flowing groove is the key to the album's success. *—Stephen Thomas Erlewine*

Eugene Wilde (Ron Broomfield)

b. Miami, FL
Vocals / Urban, Soul
Ron Broomfield, aka Eugene Wilde, seemed ready to become a megastar in the mid-'80s. The Miami-based vocalist, who had formerly been with Life, had a resonant, authoritative voice and very confident manner. He scored number-one R&B hits in 1984 and 1985 recording for Philly W. Records. "Gotta Get You Home Tonight" and "Don't Say No Tonight" were lyrically predictable, but expertly produced and sang with plenty of suggestiveness and sentimental appeal. Wilde scored one more Top Ten hit with "Diana" in 1986, but switched to MCA and soon lost his momentum. Wilde later sang lead vocals for Cabo Frio on their Zebra/MCA LP before trying again in vain with *I Choose You Tonight* in 1989. *—Ron Wynn*

How About Tonight / 1992 / MCA ✦✦✦
With hip-hop dominating the charts, Wilde attempted to fit in among the many, even though that's not what his forte had been with his previous projects. This was evident with "How About Tonight," and the only single to chart from the album. With its progressive R&B rhythm, Wilde intensely conveyed the lyric. But in spite of the single's buffed texture, it is not what fans and radio expected from the talented vocalist. Nonetheless, the number still peaked at number 17 after 13 weeks on the *Billboard* R&B charts; it also didn't enjoy the recurring air play of its predecessors ("Gotta Get You Home Tonight" and "Don't Say No Tonight"). Although Babyface wasn't credited as a producer, "Angel" sounds very much like one of his compositions. The only tune to come close to Wilde's charismatic touch is "Special Feelings," and it has a Freddie Jackson aura. These songs were all produced quite competently, but they did nothing to complement Wilde's urban, romantic appeal. Moreover, it appeared more like the producers intentionally refrained from embracing the sound that made Wilde an R&B favorite. *—Craig Lytle*

Eugene Wilde / Jul. 2, 1996 / Hot Productions ✦✦✦

● **The Greatest Hits** / Feb. 5, 2002 / Empire Musicwerks ✦✦✦✦

Alyson Williams

b. New York, NY
Vocals / Urban, Quiet Storm, New Jack Swing
An immensely talented vocalist able to sing new jack swing tunes or old-time soul ballads with equal skill, Alyson Williams spent awhile on the edge of stardom. The daughter of trumpeter and bandleader Bobby Booker, Williams did background vocals for Curtis Hairston, Melba Moore, B.B. & Q., Ca$hflow, Unlimited Touch, Bobby Brown, and Barbara Mitchell before joining High Fashion in 1982. Williams also sang with the Affair before going solo in 1986 with a cover of the Pointer Sisters' "Yes We Can Can." She joined Def Jam in 1987, and the scorching duet "Make You Mine Tonight" with Chuck Stanley established her credentials with urban audiences. Williams also did a duet with Oran "Juice" Jones, "How to Love Again," that was featured on his LP *G.T.O.: Gangsters Takin' Over.* Her Def Jam debut was *Raw* in 1989. Williams did another duet, this time with Tashan, in 1989, and the two later toured England together. She returned in 1991 with a self-titled release for the OBR/Columbia label, but it was her last. *—Ron Wynn*

● **Raw** / 1989 / Def Jam ✦✦✦✦
This album introduced this classy singer to a vast audience that welcomed her versatile style. The first release was the energized number "Sleep Talk." The revealing lyric and symphonic arrangement are accentuated by Williams' colorful delivery. There is also a cameo by Oran "Juice" Jones. It was a top three hit on the *Billboard* R&B charts. On the same burnin' note and with an even catchier hook and change up, "My Love Is so Raw" peaked at number 12 inside 14 weeks. The New York native displays her affection on the ballad "Just Call My Name." Seasoned with a spellbinding arrangement, Williams patiently cuddles the lyric with her seductively enthralling vocals. It tipped in at number four. "Not on the Outside" is a melodious number basted with a sweet string arrangement and the stellar vocals of the songstress. The chic vocalist comes with one outstanding effort after another as she covers the spectrum of R&B, jazz, dance and rap. *—Craig Lytle*

Alyson Williams / 1991 / Columbia ✦✦✦

Andre Williams

b. Nov. 1, 1936, Chicago, IL
Vocals, Guitar, Producer / R&B, Detroit Blues, Soul
Multitalented Zeffrey "Andre" Williams has worn many musical hats during his long career: recording artist, songwriter, producer, road manager, among others. The R&B legend is best known for co-writing and producing "Twine Time" for Alvin Cash & the Crawlers, "Shake a Tailfeather" by the Five Du-Tones, and a greasy solo recording "Bacon Fat," where Andre talked over a funky, crude rhythm. Andre starting talking instead of singing because he knew he couldn't compete vocally with the Nolan Strongs, Clyde McPhatters, Little Willie Johns, Jackie Wilsons, and others. He created a new style that was later adapted by Harvey Fuqua ("Any Way You Wanna"), Jerry-O, Shorty Long, Bootsy Collins, and others. He originally ventured to Detroit in his late teens and befriended Jack and Devora Brown, the owners of Fortune Records. At Fortune, Andre started singing with the Don Juans and became adept at putting songs together.

In 1956, Fortune issued seven singles by Andre Williams, all but two with co-billing with the Don Juans: "Going Down to Tia Juana," "It's All Over," "Bacon Fat," "Mean Jean," "Jail Bait," "The Greasy Chicken," and "Country Girl." Andre later sang with the Five Dollars who released records on Fortune from 1956 to 1957, and were billed as Andre Williams & the Five Dollars on a 1960 release. After Fortune, Andre languished with Berry Gordy and Motown from 1961 to 1965. By 1965 he left Motown for good to sign with Chicago's Chess Records and had a string of R&B releases including "The Stroke," "Girdle Up," "Humpin' Bumpin' & Thumpin'," and "Cadillac Jack." His biggest period as an artist was around 1960 when Fortune released the LP *Jail Bait.* However, the cocksure attitude, winking innuendos and hip style that Williams carried throughout his career made him a cult favorite with appeal that reached beyond typical soul and R&B fans. By the 1990s, a surge of interest in Williams' music created a mini-revival that led to several reissues and enough new recordings to eclipse his meager catalog from the previous four decades several times over. *—Andrew Hamilton*

● **Jail Bait** / 1960 / Fortune ✦✦✦✦✦
Jail Bait collects ten of the early sides that Williams recorded for Fortune between 1956 and 1959. Backed by the Don Juans, Williams rips through his most famous songs, including "Jail Bait," a notorious tale of forbidden love and the often hilarious and definitively hip contrition of the protagonist pleading before the judge, all related with the smart syncopation that helped earned Williams the nickname "Mr. Rhythm." However, before the novelty R&B of "Jail Bait" and "Greasy Chicken" that earned Williams a consistent, if marginal, existence in the music world, he penned some fine R&B, including the mambo-rock of "Going Down to Tia Juana" as well as "It's All Over," "You Know I Can't Refuse," and "I Just Want a Little Love, Love, Lovin'." All of the songs here are essential, and while it's not quite complete—"Bacon Fat" is a glaring omission—it's a great look at a soul legend before the full-time hustle and permanent poker face was in place. *—Wade Kergan*

Silky / Feb. 10, 1998 / In the Red ✦✦✦
After spending most of the '80s and '90s out of music and living on the streets thanks to a severe drug problem, Andre Williams cleaned himself up and cut a new album in 1996,

in which he dusted off some of the classic tunes he cut for Fortune Records in the '50s and '60s. But Williams dove head first into the present day with 1998's *Silky*. Working with Mick Collins and Dan Kroha (formerly of the Gories, now respectively recording with the Dirtbombs and the Demolition Doll Rods), Williams merged his wild and greasy R&B style with Collins and Kroha's noise-spattered, stripped-down, roots-punk assault, and the results are flat-out nuts. On "Agile, Mobile, and Hostile," "I Wanna Be Your Favorite Pair of Pajamas," and "Looking Down at You Looking Up at Me," Williams sounds like the world's most spectacularly dirty old man as a squadron of Detroit alt-rock all-stars kick up a wall of rockin' din behind him, and the two side-closers, "Bring Me Back My Car Unstripped" and "Everybody Knew," are *Twilight Zone* psychodramas so bizarre they defy conventional description. Vintage soul purists will doubtless be horrified by *Silky*, but anyone wanting to hear the wildest man in '50s R&B getting even wilder 40 years on ought to give *Silky* a spin at their next stag party or parole hearing. —*Mark Deming*

Red Dirt / 1999 / Bloodshot ✦✦✦✦
Sure, it's sloppy and it sags in the middle, but the jumping snarl of "She's a Bag of Potato Chips" alone warrants the purchase of this disc. Williams mines the darker, funkier side of the country ethos, tossing out a truly creepy stalker ballad, "I Can Tell," with such twanging covers as "Pardon Me (I've Got Someone to Kill)" and "Psycho." Backing by the Sadies is first-rate, and if you get enough beers in you even the weaker spots start to sound right pretty. —*Tim Sheridan*

Rib Tips & Pig Snoots: Rare & Unreleased Au-Go-Go Soul, 1965–1971 / 2000 / Soul-Tay-Shus ✦✦✦✦
The sound of a soulful, leering swagger. That's what you want in an Andre Williams record, and *Rib Tips & Pig Snoots* delivers the mother lode. This collection of rare and unreleased soul from small labels, covering 1965-1971, finds Williams moving and grooving, showing and proving. Known for his greasy R&B of the 1950s, Williams had already scored hits in the early '60s writing and producing for Alvin Cash & the Crawlers ("Twine Time") and the Five Du-Tones ("Shake a Tail Feather"). *Rib Tips & Pig Snoots* finds Williams complementing his grooves with the occasional flute or string arrangement, all to a positive effect. "Pearl Time" and "Do It," among other vocal numbers, show that Williams still had his game uptight, working the ladies and starting new dance steps at the same time. A strong, long-overdue collection that showcases Williams at the top of his game as a performer and producer. —*Kurt Edwards*

The Black Godfather / May 2, 2000 / In the Red ✦✦✦
After recording one of the sleaziest albums of recent memory, 1998's *Silky*, what was Andre Williams supposed to do for an encore? Well, with *The Black Godfather*, Mr. Rhythm brings sleaze rock to new heights (or depths, depending on how you look at it). On *Silky*, producer and general co-conspirator Mick Collins (of the Gories and the Dirtbombs) rounded up an impressive team of Detroit-area grit-rock all-stars to back up Williams, but for *The Black Godfather*, Collins and Williams went nationwide, with the Jon Spencer Blues Explosion, the Compulsive Gamblers (formerly the Oblivions), the Cheater Slicks, and the Countdowns all kicking up a fuss as Williams wails on "Whip That Booty," "Nasty Women" "I Hate Cha," and "The Dealer, the Peeler, and the Stealer." While *Silky* sounded somewhat more unified, *The Black Godfather* rocks a good bit harder, and while the previous album featured the occasional moment of (relatively) subtle calm, this time out Williams is firing on all cylinders at once and sounding as nasty as he wants to be. *The Black Godfather* is loud, it's wild, and my, but it's in poor taste; if that sounds like a bad thing to you, you're best off leaving this be, but if that description sounds like fun, pick this up and have a party as Andre Williams shows you how to Sling That Thing. Points added for the cover, a hilariously accurate parody of a typical No Limit Records package. —*Mark Deming*

Fat Back & Corn Liquor / Jun. 23, 2000 / St. George ✦✦✦
Andre Williams, the man who was rappin' three decades before they had a name for it, is back after a much too long sabbatical, with the kind of comeback album that would do any R&B legend proud. With a tight little band and the El Dorados providing crackerjack support, producer George Paulus has managed to restoke some of the fires that burned so brightly on a spate of brilliant, creative singles for Fortune and Checker in the '50s and '60s. The big plus here is that Williams can still deliver that deadpan badass turn of the phrase better than anybody. Although I personally find the recuts here of his old Fortune classics like "Jail Bait" ill-advised (to quote Rocky, the Flying Squirrel, "That trick never works!"), there's just so much great stuff on this biscuit that it's a minor niggling point at best. By far and away, my favorite track on here is one simply titled "Gin." Recalling one of his legendary Fortune sides, "Please Pass the Biscuits," without Xeroxing it, this is four minutes plus of Williams at his nutzo best. A winner. —*Cub Koda*

Whip Your Booty! / 2001 / Soul-Tay-Shus/Tuff City ✦✦✦
The long and twisted tale of Andre Williams is far too, well, long and twisted to get into here. If you don't know about him, check the bio. What's here are three tracks recorded in 1967 in Detroit with many of the Motown session players and ten tracks recorded in 1977 in Chicago with a band Williams put together called the Velvet Hammer. The Detroit songs are smooth, soulful ballads, with Williams oozing some of his unique charm, "The Velvet Groove: Blue" being an especially nice instrumental. The Chicago session marks Williams' foray into the world of disco and, as usual, he does it his way. "Whip Your Booty" is a nasty and funny dancefloor-filler; "I Don't Need Mary (Juana)" an ode to Williams' newly clean lifestyle. Williams sings lead on that track and "Betcha Gonna Like It" only; the rest he gave to the other members of the group. A highlight of the set is Karl Tarleton's soaring vocal on the sweet ballad "Impossible." The tracks were originally slated to be released on the Susie label, which Williams started with a Chicago-area restaurant-owner, but the plans fell through and the tracks were in limbo for many years. Fans of Andre Williams will find this disc to be fun, but not essential. For anyone else, you won't miss much if you pass this one by. —*Tim Sendra*

Bait and Switch / Jun. 12, 2001 / Norton ✦✦✦✦
Another irreverent, punkish set from the king of sleaze rock, *Bait and Switch* contains almost no surprises for fans of Andre Williams' predictably wild and raucous R&B. Backed by a garage band featuring the aggressive guitar of Matt Verta-Ray and the greasy, growling tenor sax of Lonnie Youngblood, Williams belts his tales of double-standard misogyny with the same enthusiasm as his early singles back in the 1950s. Fans of music that denigrates women will find "Sling It, Bang It and Give It Cab Fare Home" appealing, but Williams also goes far enough to balance the tables with the hilarious "Put That Skillet Away" (his lover is not cooking with it, but threatening to beat him). Long-lost brother to the late Screamin' Jay Hawkins or thug rapper born 40 years too early, Williams is still a treasure of the American rock underground. —*John Duffy*

Deniece Williams

b. Jun. 3, 1950, Gary, IN
Vocals / Quiet Storm, Contemporary Gospel, Soul, Dance-Pop
Deniece Williams grew up singing in a Pentecostal church, which was strict on the congregation listening only to gospel music. During the late '60s, she was a candy striper in a Chicago hospital. Outside of wanting a 1959 Thunderbird, she had no serious ambitions. Nontheless, she still had interest in listening to music. Her favorites were Carmen McRae for her diction and Nancy Wilson, who, for Williams, exemplified class and elegance. However, her mother, also a singer, was her idol. The Gary, IN, native was also fond of Stevie Wonder, Earth, Wind & Fire, Minnie Riperton, and Patti LaBelle. (The latter two she tried to emulate before her introduction into the music industry.)

In need of employment and with college on the back burner, the fledgling singer was introduced to Wonder by John Harris, her cousin from Detroit, who happened to be on tour as a valet for Wonder (and was also his childhood friend). Her cousin arranged for Williams to meet Wonder backstage at a concert. Six months later, the gifted vocalist was flown into Detroit by Wonder for an audition. Among the 26 who auditioned, Williams, who sang "Teach Me Tonight," was only one of three who was hired by Wonder. The three became known as Wonderlove. Williams being hired by Wonder was a big surprise. Soon after the audition, she toured with Wonder, who was the opening act for the Rolling Stones at the time. Her touring with Wonder lasted for several years. Though her stint with Wonder was a great experience and opportunity, it was also difficult considering Williams had to make many adjustments professionally and personally (she had two sons prior to taking the gig: one four months old, the other 18 months).

Williams left Wonderlove in 1975 and teamed up with producer Maurice White, the leader of Earth, Wind & Fire. Under White's direction, Williams learned the business of music and was able to unwind and express herself musically. Under the Columbia banner, Williams released her first album entitled *This Is Niecey*. It featured the *Billboard* R&B number-two single "Free," which also sealed the Top 25 on the pop charts. The song was personal to Williams, who felt restricted while with Wonderlove. The album also featured "Cause You Love Me Baby" and "That's What Friends Are For." In 1977 the album *Song Bird* was released, and it featured the number-13 single "Baby, Baby My Love's All for You." The following year the dynamic singer scored her first number-one song on both the R&B and pop charts with "Too Much, Too Little, Too Late," which was a duet with the legendary Johnny Mathis. The follow-up single, "You're All Need to Get By," was also recorded with Mathis and it was a Top Ten single.

Still under White's tutelage, Williams moved over to White's American Recording Company (ARC) and stumbled a few times with several releases before scoring the smash hit "Silly." Written by Williams and produced by famed producer Thom Bell, she sang this song from her own personal experience as well. The single became a Top Ten gem. In 1982 Bell returned the sweet songstress to number one with the single "It's Gonna Take a Miracle." Always writing from her own experience, Williams wrote the Top Ten single "Do What You Feel" based on the ordeals of someone else. (A believer in the song at the time, she no longer employs those beliefs.) In 1984 Williams recorded the number-one hit "Let's Hear It for the Boy." Featured on the *Footloose* soundtrack, the single was produced by music virtuoso George Duke, who initially thought the song was too pop-ish and would not work. However, Duke's production savvy proved to be as paramount as Williams' vocals.

In 1984 the sensational singer recorded "Black Butterfly." From a African-American perspective, Williams immediately bonded with the song. The song would become a prelude to the uplifting gospel material Williams would record a few years later. With her label, Columbia, uninterested, Williams released the gospel album *From the Beginning* on Sparrow Records. The album featured the Grammy award-winning single "They Say." The same year she also won a Grammy for "I Surrender" and another for "I Believe in You" in 1987.

Never a big fan of touring, Williams remains a homebody. She enjoys the creative side of music (writing and singing), her family (four boys), and her home. On occasion she may perform or make a public appearance. —*Craig Lytle*

This Is Niecey / 1976 / Columbia ✦✦✦✦
This was Deniece Williams introduction to the national charts as a solo artist. Under the direction of Maurice White and Charles Stephney, much of this production has Earth, Wind & Fire undertones and that's a good thing. The featured release was the number two *Billboard* R&B single "Free." With its symphonic intro, rhythmic beat and cooing background vocals, Williams cradles the affectionate number with her gracefully flowing soprano. The second and only other release was the "Cause You Love Me Baby." With its delightful, melodic structure, the former Lovelites member (known then as Deniece Chandler) embraces the lyric with such warmth and beauty. The EW&F influence is manifested on the inspirational "Watching Over," "It's Important to Me" and "Slip Away." Deniece Williams gives a vocal workshop with her precision and agility. As all the selections are credible, "That's What Friends Are For" and "If You Don't Believe" are two meaningful numbers that blossom with love and understanding. —*Craig Lytle*

Song Bird / 1977 / Columbia ♦♦♦

My Melody / 1981 / Columbia ♦♦♦♦♦

Deniece's heavenly soprano is as impressive as ever under the guidance of producer Thom Bell. The sweet Philly sound architect keeps Williams' expressive, high-range vocals under wraps, transforming her into a bel canto singer on eight delightful selections. Highlights include the R&B hit "Silly," "Strangers," and the lovely Stylistics-inflected "You're All That Matters." Bell departs from signature sound on the reggae-drenched "Suspicious," but Williams handles the jerk groove as well as she does the ethereal "Sweet Surrender." *—Andrew Hamilton*

Niecy / 1982 / Columbia ♦♦♦♦♦

Williams enlisted Philly soulmeister Thom Bell as her co-producer (and primary co-writer) a second time on this mellow 1982 release. Building upon the lush balladry of 1981's *My Melody*, this set inevitably bears a few similarities to its predecessor, but manages a more diverse soundscape. The rock-influenced "Love Notes"; the soft opening verse and subsequently alternating degrees of percussive intensity on "How Does It Feel"; the moody "Waiting"; and the marching rhythm and glorious melodic structure of "Now Is the Time for Love" almost defy classification. Vocally, Williams is in top shape here and seems completely in sync with the material and arrangements. *Niecy* also gave the songbird her second Top Ten pop hit in a cover of the Royalettes' 1962 hit "It's Gonna Take a Miracle," which she delivers capably, but not as intuitively as the original selections (all of which she co-wrote). *Niecy* is an essential addition to any Deniece Williams collection. *—Justin Kantor*

Let's Hear It for the Boy / 1984 / Columbia ♦♦♦♦♦

Hot on the Trail / 1986 / Columbia ♦♦♦

Probably Williams' least-known album, *Hot on the Trail* came shortly after her gospel debut, *So Glad I Know*. On this secular outing, Williams assumed greater involvement in the writing process, co-writing all but one of the songs. However, she stepped back from producing, which she took part in prominently on 1984's *Let's Hear It for the Boy*. The set suffers from a slight lack of musical direction, but boasts several noteworthy cuts. The metaphorical "Video" is a Latin-esque groover with a smooth sax solo by Tom Scott, and the breezy, midtempo "He Loves Me, He Loves Me Not" has a feel-good vibe. The problem with some of the selections is musical arrangements that get settled too soon. Fortunately, Williams' pensive lyrics, flowing melodies, and top-notch vocal performances rise over the dry areas, making this an enjoyable listen, if not the most memorable. *—Justin Kantor*

Water Under the Bridge / 1987 / Columbia ♦♦♦♦

Deniece Williams' incredible high-octane soprano soars over ten tracks. Songs like "Never Say Never" will keep every nerve on red alert. The title track was a victim of lackadaisical promotion, and the unusual "Love Finds You," sung in a delicious soprano-falsetto, never got picked as a single. Her passion for ballads hasn't diminished and she gives "Not by Chance" and "Baby This Is Love" sensuous workouts. Equally as effective is the bouncy "One Less Lonely Heart" and "I'll Believe in You," a building thriller. *—Andrew Hamilton*

So Glad I Know / 1988 / Sparrow ♦♦

Deniece Williams raised some eyebrows when she decided to begin splitting her focus between urban contemporary and contemporary gospel. The results have thus been quite mixed, and this first gospel venture not only wasn't a major success, but didn't even get widespread exposure in the gospel ranks. It was likewise ignored by pop and R&B audiences. The vocals were competent, the production dull and the material surprisingly timid. *—Ron Wynn*

Lullabies to Dreamland / Nov. 12, 1991 / Word ♦♦♦

Deniece Williams seemed out of answers as she moved into the 1990s. Her light, airy voice had once seemed charming and enticing, but was now older and less wide-ranging and alluring. There was also a shortage of quality material and a split focus between gospel and pop. The result was this rather dismal early-'90s outing, with no hits and not even a memorable single. The vocals and production were barely passable; Williams was now floundering in search of a concept. *—Ron Wynn*

Love Solves It All / 1996 / P.A.R. ♦♦

The Songbird has returned to the recording studio for the first time in six years and she even owns the record label. Unfortunately, the whole project seems like a hurried demo record, a series of uninteresting, hookless, programmed songs. "Stop a Tear From Falling Down" and "One More Kiss" are juvenile, but the traditional a cappella gospel hymn "Great Is Thy Faithfulness" suits the singer well. "Why You Wanna Do Me" is funky and fast-paced track, while "Love Don't Even Live Here No More" is a ballad done in Williams' distinctive style, but other than those exceptions, much of the material is of average quality—nothing special, nothing particularly memorable. *—Bill Carpenter*

● **The Best of Deniece Williams: Gonna Take a Miracle** / Mar. 12, 1996 / Columbia/Legacy ♦♦♦♦♦

This 16-track, 72-1/2-minute compilation contains Deniece Williams' two number-one pop/R&B hits, "Let's Hear It for the Boy" and "Too Much, Too Little, Too Late" (a duet with Johnny Mathis), as well as her remake of "It's Gonna Take a Miracle," an R&B number one and Top Ten pop hit, and "Free," which just missed the top of the R&B chart and made the pop Top 40. Otherwise, the collection is a somewhat idiosyncratic, compilation producer Leo Sacks' idea of Williams's best, rather than her greatest hits. Her success on the R&B singles chart, where she scored 18 Top 40 hits, is shortchanged, as the set fails to contain such major R&B hits as "Never Say Never" and "You're All I Need to Get By." At the same time, Sacks finds room for the eight-minute album track "If You Don't Believe" and Williams' early gospel composition, "God Is Amazing." Such tracks serve to emphasize the diversity in Williams' catalog, but R&B fans may find the set wanting. *—William Ruhlmann*

Love Songs / Jan. 18, 2000 / Columbia/Legacy ♦♦♦

Among these 14 songs of ardor cut by Williams between 1976 and 1983, several were big hits, like "Free," "It's Gonna Take a Miracle," and "Too Much, Too Little, Too Late." In fact, nine of them also appear on Williams' Columbia greatest hits collection. This is not an acceptable substitute for that disc, particularly as it is missing the number-one single "Let's Hear It for the Boy." There's also too much overlap for this to serve as a good supplement. The only one of the five songs not found on the best-of collection that made the charts was 1981's "What Two Can Do" (number-17 R&B). The version of "I Found Love" here, by the way, is the "special disco version." *—Richie Unterberger*

Larry Williams

b. May 10, 1935, New Orleans, LA, **d.** Jan. 7, 1980, Los Angeles, CA

Vocals, Saxophone, Keyboards, Songwriter, Piano / Rock & Roll, R&B, Pop-Soul, Soul, Funk

A rough, rowdy rock & roll singer, Larry Williams had several hits in the late '50s, several of which—"Bony Maroney," "Dizzy, Miss Lizzy," "Short Fat Fannie," "Bad Boy," "She Said Yeah"—became genuine rock & roll classics and were recorded by British Invasion groups; John Lennon, in particular, was a fan of Williams, recording several of his songs over the course of his career. As a child in New Orleans, Williams learned how to play piano. When he was a teenager, he and his family moved to Oakland, CA, where he joined a local R&B group called the Lemon Drops. In 1954, when he was 19 years old, Williams went back to New Orleans for a visit. During his trip, he met Lloyd Price, who was recording for Specialty Records. Price hired the teenager as his valet and introduced him to Robert "Bumps" Blackwell, the label's house producer. Soon, the label's owner, Art Rupe, signed Williams to a solo recording contract.

Just after Specialty signed Larry Williams, Specialty lost Little Richard, who had been their biggest star and guaranteed hitmaker. Little Richard decided to abandon rock & roll for the ministry shortly after Williams cut his first single, a cover of Price's "Just Because," with Richard's backing band; "Just Because" peaked at number 11 on the R&B charts in the spring of 1957. After Richard left the label, the label put all of its energy into making Williams a star, giving him an image makeover and a set of material—ranging from hard R&B and rock & roll to ballads—that was quite similar to Richard's hits.

Williams' first post-Little Richard single was the raucous "Short Fat Fannie," which shot to number one on the R&B charts and number five on the pop charts in the summer of 1957. It was followed in the fall by "Bony Maronie," which hit number four on the R&B charts and number 14 on the pop charts. Williams wasn't able to maintain that momentum, however. "You Bug Me, Baby" and "Dizzy Miss Lizzy," his next two singles, missed the R&B charts but became minor pop hits in late 1957 and early 1958. Despite the relative failure of these singles, Williams' records became popular import items in Britain; the Beatles would cover both sides of the "Dizzy Miss Lizzy" single (the B-side was "Slow Down") in the mid-'60s. However, Williams' commercial fortunes in America continued to decline, despite Specialty's release of a constant stream of singles and one full-length album.

In 1959, Williams was arrested for selling narcotics, which caused Specialty to drop him from the record label. He drifted through a number of labels in the early '60s, recording songs for Chess, Mercury, Island, and Decca. By the mid-'60s, he had hooked up with Johnny "Guitar" Watson and the duo cut several sides for OKeh Records, including the Top 40 R&B hits "Mercy, Mercy, Mercy" (spring 1967) and "Nobody," which was recorded with Kaleidoscope (early 1968). Williams also became a house producer for OKeh Records in 1966, although very few of his productions became hits. Between 1968 and 1978, Williams was inactive, recording nothing and performing very little. In 1978, he released a funk album, *That's Larry Williams*, for Fantasy Records that sold poorly and received bad reviews. In 1980, Williams was found dead in his Los Angeles home; he died of a gunshot wound to his head. The medical examiners called the death a suicide, but rumors persisted for years after his death that he was murdered because of his involvement in drugs, crime and—allegedly—prostitution. A compilation of Williams' biggest hits and best-known songs entitled *Bad Boy* was released on Specialty Records in 1989. *—Stephen Thomas Erlewine*

Here's Larry Williams / 1959 / Specialty ♦♦♦♦♦

One of the great R&B long-players of the '50s, *Here's Larry Williams* collects nearly all of the Los Angeles-based singer/songwriter's key work ("Bad Boy" and 1967's "Mercy Mercy Mercy" are the only truly essential tracks missing), and a bunch of smokin' obscurities besides. Listening to these tracks, it's clear why John Lennon was such a huge Larry Williams fan; his rough-and-ready no-bull voice is elastic enough to move from a Little Richard trill to a Ray Charles growl, and songs like "Dizzy Miss Lizzy" and "Short Fat Fannie" are raucous enough to be punk rock nearly a full two decades before the concept was even in existence. Of the lesser-known tracks, the giddy Buddy Holly-meets-Richard Berry "You Bug Me, Baby" and the salacious "Little School Girl," featuring a good and greasy sax solo, are the highlights; on the downside, "Ting A Ling" is as slight and tossed-off as its title, and the intrusive female chorus that sounds like it made the wrong turn from the Rosemary Clooney session down the hall is just plain awful. *—Stewart Mason*

Larry Williams Show With Johnny Guitar Watson / 1965 / Edsel ♦♦♦

Larry Williams' Greatest Hits / 1967 / OKeh ♦♦♦♦♦

Unreleased Larry Williams / 1986 / Specialty ♦♦♦

☆ **Bad Boy [LP]** / 1992 / Specialty ♦♦♦♦♦

This is 45 minutes of nigh-unto-awesome rock & roll hailing from the '50s, and the only reason it gets knocked at all is that it's 45 minutes spread out over four sides of black plastic. Mind you, it makes for good dynamic range—but then again, 45 minutes on a *single* album doesn't exactly stretch things, either. Who is Larry Williams? Well, he was, in some respects, a replacement for Little Richard when Little Richard went off to the ministry. He certainly has some of the same qualities, but doesn't get anywhere near as hypertense as Little Richard, which makes for a more interesting listening experience in some respects.

Williams was also the guy who popped up with "Short Fat Fannie," which manages to quote every popular rock & roll number from the time without once missing a beat, mussing its hair, or sounding contrived. Williams also gave listeners "Dizzy Miss Lizzy" and several songs that were staples of the Beatles and the Rolling Stones—"She Said Yeah" and the aforementioned "Dizzy Miss Lizzy" amongst them, elements of which you could hear in the work of the Beatles at least for years. There's something intensely nostalgic about this release—the label design, simple yellow and white, the fact that it's on black vinyl and you have to drop the needle, the fact that there's obvious distortion in the original recordings (digital remastering doesn't always help, either, because here there's a lot of hashing on sibilants and cymbals; treble cut is recommended), and the lack of gloss, glitter, and polish. These guys sound like they're having a *great* time, and the hell with slips here and there. Compare William's cut of "Iko Iko" against later versions—it's a nonsense song, and the version here sounds like it was a ball to do. Having to take a foot-wide plastic platter and do all those manual things with it feels absolutely right. If you can stand the fact that it's 45 minutes on two vinyl analog discs, this is a great album to have. The other significant note is that it won't be available in this form on compact disc—this version has all the versions that were released and became hits. The compact disc sports additional tracks, and also uses alternate versions of many of the songs on the vinyl version. It's an interesting way of approaching things. —*Steven McDonald*

★ **Bad Boy [CD]** / Apr. 6, 1992 / Specialty ✦✦✦✦✦

Bad Boy compiles 23 tracks Larry Williams recorded between 1957 and 1958. The core of the collection are his hit singles—"Bony Maronie," "She Said Yeah," "Lawdy Miss Clawdy," "Just Because," "Dizzy Miss Lizzy," "Short Fat Fannie," "Bad Boy," "Slow Down"—many of which became standards. —*Stephen Thomas Erlewine*

Bad Boy of Rock N' Roll / Feb. 19, 1999 / Ace ✦✦✦✦✦

This is essential late '50s R&B by one of rocks' most nefarious characters. Specialty Records released Williams from his contract in 1959 after he was sent to prison for drug dealing. The singer/pianist expired from a gunshot in 1980 that was rumored a hit but ruled self-inflicted. Bad career choice aside, Williams uncorks with unbridled fury on his classic musical caricatures: "Short Fat Fannie," "Bony Moronie," "Dizzy Miss Lizzy" and 21 others. He recorded these in New Orleans with some of the city's finest young musicians—Art Neville (piano), Leo Morris b.k.a. Idris Muhammad (drums) and Lee Allen (tenor sax). Early, raw R&B at its best. —*Andrew Hamilton*

Lee Williams & the Cymbals

Group / R&B, Soul, Northern Soul

This Harlem vocal group was discovered Hollywood style. The guys were singing in the backyard of a brownstone on 127th Street where they lived when Joe Evans, the owner of Carnival Records, heard them practicing as he walked by. Carnival, a tiny operation in Newark, NJ, had three employees, with Evans being one of them. At the time of the discovery Evans was in Harlem on a promotional mission for his label. Excited by what he heard, he persuaded the landlady to let him in so he could see the warblers. Evans conducted an audition for the singers and the guys gave it their all. Liking their blend and the powerhouse lead of Lee Williams, Evans signed them on the spot. When he got back to Newark he made up a tape of songs for the group to learn. Ronnie McCoy, who had a group called the Topics, wrote one of the songs, "I Love You More." He had been sending Evans songs and bugging him to record his group. McCoy wanted the song for his group but Evans thought it would be better served to have his new discoveries record it. As a consolation Carnival released "She's So Fine"/"I Don't Have to Cry" on the Topics.

"I Love You More" sold substantially in many cities including Baltimore, Washington, Cleveland, Philadelphia, and Chicago. It was so popular in Chicago the group did a stint at the city's Regal Theater. The record barely missed entering *Billboard*'s R&B Top 40, stalling at number 41 in 1967. It would be the group's biggest record ever. Carnival followed with "Peeping Through the Window," another McCoy composition, which didn't do as well but was their second most popular waxing. Four more singles followed: "Shing a Ling USA," "Please Say It Isn't So," "I Need You Baby," and "Til You Come Back to Me." All were good records but they only attracted local and spot interest. The group left Carnival though they were the label's second most popular act (next to the Manhattans) and recorded for some even smaller labels. One was Black Circle Records in Pittsburgh, PA, where they had a few releases that stiffed due to the same problem that afflicted Carnival Records—lack of promotion. —*Andrew Hamilton*

● **Golden Carnival Classics, Pt. 2** / Jun. 25, 1994 / Collectables ✦✦✦✦

Thanks to this CD, you no longer have to be satisfied with 30-year-old scratchy and worn 45s of Lee Williams & the Cymbals; they never recorded an album, and due to limited promotion, their recordings aren't well-known. People who remember the songs haven't a clue who sang them. Six of their Carnival recordings appear on this compilation, which includes other even more obscure sides by Carnival artists. Williams sang in a warm, excitable tenor that slid into heart-stopping falsetto squalls. "I Love You More" barely missed making the national R&B Top 40; it's one of the coolest R&B records ever made. For a few seconds, the opening melody stalks and tantalizes, then the backing croons, and Williams reiterates "Two lips to kiss you/Two arms to hold you/One heart that needs you/One mind that believes in you/'Cause I, I love you more than anyone ever loved anyone." "Peeping Through the Window" had potential, but didn't fare as well; it's the familiar tale of a guy coming home and finding someone else with his girlfriend. Ironically, their best vocal performance, the excellent "Til You Come Back to Me," a Joe Evans composition, is not available. A good supporting cast completes this worthy set. The Lovettes never got any run and it's unfortunate. Four of their girly efforts appear and all rate well, especially the lovely, matter-of-fact, syncopated "I Need a Guy." The self-doubting "I'm Afraid to Say I Love You" is innocent and arresting; the backing reminds you of the early no-hit Supremes. Sides by Barbara Brown, Norma Jenkins, the Symphonies, the Turner Brothers, and Kenny Ruffin are pure deep soul. Two versions of "Need Someone to Love" appear, Norma Jenkins' original and the Symphonics' remake. Phil Terrell's "Baby Doll" is a cult item among international soul fanatics. It's a blessing to have these hard-to-find 45s on CD. —*Andrew Hamilton*

Lenny Williams

b. Feb. 6, 1945, Little Rock, AR

Vocals / Quiet Storm, Urban

Although Lenny Williams has had a long solo career, he is still best-known for his three years as the lead singer of Tower of Power, one of the top funk/soul bands of the '70s. But Williams was pursuing a solo career before joining Tower of Power, and he resumed his solo career after leaving that famous Oakland outfit in 1975. Born in Little Rock, AR, on February 6, 1945, Williams was only a child when he started singing in church (the place where so many great R&B singers got their start). Williams, who moved to Oakland, CA, when he was 14, planned to become a Christian minister but ended up changing his mind and decided to pursue a career as a secular R&B singer. In 1969, Williams signed with Fantasy and recorded his first single, "Lisa's Gone," a soul ballad that was far from a big hit, but did receive some airplay in the Bay Area. After providing a second single for Fantasy, Williams was signed to Atlantic by Jerry Wexler and recorded a version of the Thom Bell/Linda Creed gem "People Make the World Go Round." Williams' version might have been a hit—had it not been for the Stylistics, that is. Unfortunately for Williams, the Stylistics' famous version of "People Make the World Go Round" came out as a single and soared to the top of the charts before Atlantic had a chance to release Williams' version. (Michael Jackson also recorded the tune in the early '70s, although not with the same set of lyrics that the Stylistics embraced). But that setback was hardly the end of Williams' career; in 1972, he was hired as the new lead singer of Tower of Power. Because the band's previous lead singer, Rick Stevens (best-known for his soaring performance on the hit ballad "You're Still a Young Man") had recently been convicted of murder, a replacement was needed, and Williams was definitely the man for the job.

Williams' three years with Tower of Power established him as a big name in soul and funk and he became famous for his lead vocals on major hits like "What Is Hip?," "Don't Change Horses (In the Middle of a Stream)," "This Time It's Real," and the ballad "So Very Hard to Go." But while Tower of Power was a big break for Williams, he only stuck around for three years; in 1975, the Bay Area resident left the band and became a full-time solo artist. His first few solo albums (recorded for Motown) didn't do much, but his solo career took off in a big way when he recorded *Choosing You* for ABC. That 1977 release (which contains the major hit "Shoo Doo Fu Fu Ooh!") almost went gold in the U.S. (meaning that it sold close to 500,000 units). Williams next solo effort, *Spark of Love* (also on ABC), became his first gold solo album and boasted the hit ballad "Cause I Love You." After providing a few albums for MCA, Williams recorded for the independent Rocshire label in 1983 and 1984; when that company folded, he was deprived of a 50,000 dollar advance he said he was owed. Disgusted with music industry, Williams considered giving up singing and devoted a lot of his time to real estate investments. But in 1986, Williams ended up signing with Knobhill, a short-lived indie that was distributed by Fantasy. Williams' 1986 LP, *New Episode*, wasn't a blockbuster, although the single "Ten Ways of Loving You" became a minor hit and reached number 67 on *Billboard*'s R&B singles chart. But while Williams wasn't as big in the '80s and '90s as he was in the '70s, he still had a loyal following. In 1994, he recorded *Chill* for Bellmark; Williams' next album, *Love Therapy*, came out on Volt/Fantasy in 2000. —*Alex Henderson*

Lenny Williams / 1974 / Warner Bros. ✦✦✦

Rise Sleeping Beauty / 1975 / Motown ✦✦✦

Choosing You / Jul. 1977 / ABC ✦✦✦✦

Lenny Williams was a product of a pre-MTV era, in which talent and chops counted for more than image in R&B. Although the former Tower of Power singer was considered attractive and could drive women wild—especially when he was belting out a romantic Tower of Power ballad like "So Very Hard to Go" or "Willing to Learn"—it was Williams' amazing vocal range that ultimately won over '70s soul audiences. One of the best solo albums that Williams recorded after leaving Tower in 1975 was 1977's *Choosing You*, a generally excellent LP that was produced by Frank Wilson. Most of the time, this is a very optimistic record—Williams' optimism is hard to miss on upbeat offerings like "Shoo Doo Fu Fu Ooh!," "Look Up With Your Mind," and the funky title song (which boasts an addictive groove that won't quit). *Choosing You* isn't a disco album, although its positive outlook reflects the feel-good mentality of the disco era. This isn't to say that the lyrics aren't substantial—on "Please Don't Tempt Me," for example, Williams portrays a married man who is battling the urge to commit adultery. Regrettably, *Choosing You* went out of print when ABC folded—and when the 20th century came to an end, it had yet to be reissued on CD. —*Alex Henderson*

Spark of Love / Jul. 1978 / ABC ✦✦✦✦

Originally released on ABC Records in 1978, this compilation succeeded *Choosing You*, which spawned Lenny Williams' biggest solo hit, "Shoo Doo Fu Fu Ooh!" (included here). The tunes run the gamut from disco, ballads, and the sociopolitical whoop 'em up "Changes." "I Still Reach Out" has a stalking beat, and Lenny's in-your-face vocals, accented by an ear piercing rock guitar. Producer Frank Wilson snatches a piece of "Backstabbers" for "Have Past Love." Theatrical love ballads like "Cause I Love You," "Think What We Have," and "Love Came and Rescued Me" are better appreciated live. [The disc contains two industrial strength disco tracks: "Midnight Girl" and the infectious "Free Fall (Into Love)."] —*Andrew Hamilton*

Cause I Love You: The Best of Lenny Williams / Nov. 21, 1995 / SCL ✦✦✦✦

While he's best-remembered for his three-year stint as the lead singer for Oakland, CA's longtime R&B legends Tower of Power, Lenny Williams had an interesting solo career before and after his stay with the band, earning a reputation as a polished but powerful vocalist who could convincingly approach both ballads and uptempo dancefloor-fillers. *Cause I Love You: The Best of Lenny Williams* is an 18-song compilation that features highlights from Williams' post-Tower of Power recordings for ABC and MCA; memorable tunes include "Shoo Doo Fu Fu Ooh!," "People Make the World Go Round," "Midnight Girl," and a fine cover of the Five Stairsteps' "O-o-h Child." If not startlingly original, *Cause I Love You: The Best of Lenny Williams* is a fine set of solid, professional R&B from a singer who invariably made the most of his material; it's a nice overview for fans and a good introduction for the curious. *—Mark Deming*

Love Therapy / Jun. 6, 2000 / Volt ♦♦♦

In the 1990s, Lenny Williams wasn't as visible or as popular as he was in the 1970s. But he still had an enthusiastic following and was still quite capable of providing a worthwhile album. Williams was 55 when he entered the 21st century with 2000's *Love Therapy*, his first album since 1994's *Chill*. With Preston Glass doing most of the producing and Williams doing most of the writing, the former Tower of Power singer delivers a CD that is solid and enjoyable even though it isn't in a class with solo favorites like 1977's *Choosing You* or 1978's *Spark of Love*. Those who know Williams for his 1970s work will find that he's more restrained on *Love Therapy*, which tends to favor a very laid-back approach. The vocalist doesn't belt as much as he used to, and he doesn't get into as much aggressive funk as he once did. But then, he doesn't have to belt to get his points across. Williams still has plenty of charisma, and it serves him well on relaxed, smooth, Isley Brothers-minded slow jams like "Next Door Neighbor," "Jody" and "Oh Oh Oh." Slow jams, in fact, are the main focus of *Love Therapy*, which falls short of essential but is a solid album that Williams' diehard followers will enjoy. *—Alex Henderson*

● **The Ultimate Collection** / Jul. 17, 2001 / Hip-O ♦♦♦♦♦

The Ultimate Collection boasts a generous 16 tracks of Lenny Williams, covering the best of the ex-Tower of Power singer's solo career (and tacking four Tower of Power tunes on at the end). Williams was capable of both upbeat, disco-flavored dance tracks and smooth, romantic ballads, and this compilation makes the best case for his talents. *—Steve Huey*

Maurice Williams & the Zodiacs

b. 1940, Lancaster, SC

Vocals / Doo Wop, R&B

Maurice Williams is one of the most extraordinarily durable figures in the history of classic R&B and rock & roll, despite the fact that, as a performer, he only ever racked up one major national hit on the pop charts. That song, "Stay," became one of the classic singles in the history of rock—a number-one hit upon its release in 1960 on Al Silver's Herald label, and a popular favorite for decades since, revived in 1987 with its prominent use in the movie *Dirty Dancing*. Maurice Williams & the Zodiacs recorded only two more minor pop hits before they disappeared from the charts, but Williams has remained active as a performer and, periodically, as a recording artist and songwriter ever since.

Williams was born in Lancaster, SC, in 1940 (one source indicates April 26, 1938), and showed himself musically inclined from a very early age—he started learning the piano from his older sister in the late '40s, practicing daily so that by the time he was ten years old he was having friends from elementary school over for informal jam sessions at his house. Williams had sung in church, but his interest lay more in popular music, and in 1953, he and his friends were ready to form a group that they called the Royal Charms. The group's original membership, in addition to Williams, included Earl Gainey (tenor, guitar), Willie Jones (baritone), William Massey (tenor, baritone, trumpet), and Norman Wade (bass). They played school events and talent shows, winning several and acquiring a local following, before they finally got a paying gig at the local Veterans of Foreign Wars post. The year they'd started out, 1953, Williams had also written two songs that were to have a pivotal effect on his life and career, and the group's history: "Little Darling" and "Stay."

The Royal Charms loved performing, and were popular locally, but working the area around Lancaster, they found their prospects limited. The group's first real break took place in 1956 when a Nashville disc jockey hooked them up with Ernie Young, the head of Excello Records—Williams, then only 16, bluffed his way into an audition over the phone and then had to raise money from friends and local merchants in Lancaster to make the trip to Nashville in December of 1956. "Little Darling" impressed Young, although he altered it somewhat, giving the song a calypso beat that it didn't originally have. He also insisted on the group changing its name—it seemed as though every R&B vocal group (the word "doo wop" hadn't been invented yet) had either "Royal" or "Charms" in its name, and bird-named groups were too common as well. Young happened to like flowers, and selected the name the Gladiolas. "Little Darling" by the Gladiolas was released by Excello in January of 1957 and was a hit on the R&B charts, rising to number 11 in a four-week run in the early spring of that year. It had a more muted presence on the pop charts, lingering there for 11 weeks but never getting higher than number 41.

What happened next is a matter of interpretation. In some historians' eyes, the Gladiolas' version of the song was undercut by a competing rendition, recorded for Mercury by a white Canadian group called the Diamonds, which rose to number one on the pop charts and sold more than a million copies, even becoming a definitive "doo wop"-type single. On the other hand, some listeners, comparing the two versions, say that the Diamonds' version is more fully realized than that by the Gladiolas, not only with a more ambitious arrangement and greater vocal virtuosity, but a better sound; the Gladiolas' single, by contrast, almost seems like a demo, only partly realized in technical terms.

Regardless of the virtues of either, Williams, for his part, never minded the Diamonds' version, because Young—in an example of honesty all too rare in the record business in those days—told him that, as writer of the song, all he should care about is that it sells and gets played, not whose version sells. Young had also left him with full rights as songwriter, rather than trying to buy them away from him, which Williams admits he could've done for practically no money at all in those days. It was a decision that was to earn Williams a vast amount of money at the age of 17 and beyond, and educated him painlessly and well about the business side of the music business.

Williams was a serious high school student, and he earned a music scholarship to Allen University in Columbia, SC, that he had to turn down—he was simply doing too much in music to interrupt his career, tempting as it was. The Gladiolas kept performing, touring the West once before returning to South Carolina, where they became a heavy favorite among fraternities, especially at the University of South Carolina. At the end of 1958, the group decided against re-signing with Excello, which meant they had to give up their name, which Young owned. This could have been a disaster, forcing them to reestablish themselves in a new incarnation, but a name and a song, courtesy of Williams, made that easy. According to Williams, it was group member Bobby Gore who saw a German car called a Zodiac, and immediately seized on the name—Maurice Williams & the Zodiacs became the group's new identity.

Over the next year, the original Zodiacs' lineup expanded to nine members, including two saxmen (Calvin McKinnie, Harold Alexander). In 1960, the band hooked up with Al Silver of Herald Records in New York, by way of producers Phil Gernhardt and Al McCullough. The group was supposed to provide demos, and Williams retrieved a song he'd written back in 1953—strangely enough, to the same girl for whom he'd written "Little Darling"—called "Stay" and present it to Silver. The group signed with Herald and "Stay," sparked by a stunning falsetto performance by Shane Gaston, became their debut on the label during the summer of 1960. It hit number one that fall and easily topped a million sales at the time, also becoming the biggest hit in the history of Herald Records. Williams & the Zodiacs never had another record nearly as big as "Stay," which came out at just the right moment and seemed to sell in subsequent years at the drop of a hat, as a romantic and nostalgia favorite—by some estimates, their record has topped ten-million sales internationally. Additionally, other artists, including the Four Seasons, Jackson Browne, and Rufus & Chaka Khan, all made the Top 20 or better with their respective versions of the song, and the Hollies cut it as a single at the outset of their career.

The Zodiacs didn't fare as well as the song. "I Remember," also released on Herald, never made it past number 86 on the pop charts and didn't appear on the R&B charts at all. Neither did "Come Along," which was released in the spring of 1961 and only climbed to number 83 on the pop charts. During the mid-'60s, the group hooked up with the New Orleans-based production team of Marshall Sehorn & Allen Toussaint. With their guidance, the group cut a passionate, soulful recording of Williams' "May I," a dazzlingly beautiful song that held a lot of promise. Unfortunately, they chose to license it to Vee-Jay, which was then the most successful black-owned record company in the world. But Vee-Jay went into bankruptcy within days of the record's national release, and "May I" never recovered—the record did get out on the Dee Su label in New Orleans, which rescued it physically from oblivion, and it found an audience on the radio. It has been certified a million-seller by the RIAA, despite never managing to appear on either the pop or R&B charts. Five years later, it became a modest Top 40 hit in a smoother version by Bill Deal & the Rhondels, a white dance-rock and R&B-based band from the Virginia-Carolinas area who'd been doing it on-stage for years. The group subsequently released records on Atlantic, Sea-Horn, and Scepter, including a fine single, "Return," with Gladys Knight & the Pips singing behind them. Williams saw minimal chart action from any of this, but remained active—Maurice Williams & the Zodiacs were still a major draw in the South, especially in their native state, and in 1965 cut a live album at Myrtle Beach, SC.

Throughout the 1970s and 1980s, Williams led various incarnations of the Zodiacs on oldies tours, primarily on the beach music circuit on the U.S. East Coast. In the wake of *Dirty Dancing*, which yielded sales of another eight-million copies of "Stay," he re-emerged as a recording artist on the Ripete label, based in Columbia, SC, which specializes in beach music (they've also got a best-of the Swinging Medallions out on CD). Ripete has since released the impossible-to-find 1965 live album on CD, and an excellent career anthology of Maurice Williams & the Zodiacs. *—Bruce Eder & Stephen Thomas Erlewine*

At the Beach / 1965 / Snyder ♦♦♦♦

The original vinyl version of this concert recording is one of the rarer releases in Maurice Williams' output, which makes the CD reissue from Night Train intrinsically welcome. And the 39-minute live album is a good representation of what concerts of this kind were like—"Stay" is the only one of Williams' own hits represented on this set, which mostly consists of covers of then-current hits such as "Stubborn Kind of Fellow," "It's Not Unusual," "Something You Got," and "You've Lost That Loving Feeling," as well as rock & roll standards such as "Twist & Shout." The sound is surprisingly good for a show recorded live in Myrtle Beach, SC in 1965, when the art of concert recording was decidedly primitive—it's a little flat in the recorded ambience itself, and there's been no touching up; the occasional wrong notes do stand out; the balances are a little off; and there are leakages every so often—but overall, this is a decent testimony to the kinds of sets that Maurice Williams & the Zodiacs used to play. "Stay" gets the best performance of anything on the CD, but nothing else here will give offense, and the instrumental version of "Soldier Boy" has a beguiling innocence all its own, while "It's Not Unusual" and "You've Lost That Loving Feeling" could have each been great singles for Williams and company, with the band really cooking from the former's opening bars, and Williams rising to the occasion as a singer on the latter. *—Bruce Eder*

The Best of Maurice Williams & the Zodiacs / 1991 / Collectables ♦♦♦♦

● **Maurice Williams & the Zodiacs Anthology** / 1992 / Ripete ♦♦♦♦♦

One would have expected Maurice Williams & the Zodiacs to have their work represented by a good Rhino anthology, but they don't. Instead, Ripete Records out of Columbia, SC, for which Williams has recorded in recent years, has released this 25-song compilation, which includes material going back to "Little Darlin'" by the Gladiolas (which appears here in an alternate take) and the original demo version of "Stay." There are very few stones left unturned here, as the disc features a mixture of rare outtakes ("Stay" with punchier rhythm instruments and an organ) and brilliant Williams originals, of which the most fascinating is "May I," produced by Marshall Sehorn and Allen Toussaint. One of Williams' most beautiful songs, buried by the bankruptcy of Vee-Jay Records, "May I" never charted, but Bill Deal & the Rhondells later had a hit with it. Williams' version is slower, more passionately and compellingly performed, if a little less smooth in its tempos and choruses than Deal's version. The overview provided by this anthology doesn't include background notes on every track, but the tracks justify themselves—"Return," which features Gladys Knight & The Pips on backing vocals, being a case in point, an elegantly soulful 1964 song mixing Williams' and the other voices very delicately. Four numbers from a 1965 live album cut at Myrtle Beach, SC, show off Williams and company doing superb covers of other peoples' songs ("The In Crowd," "Sherry," "Stubborn Kind of Fellow," "It's Not Unusual"), the mix of band and backing vocals startlingly good for what should be one of the great mid-'60s live soul albums. The big surprise, however, is the quality of Williams' 1987 recordings-he still has the same gift for rich, memorable melodies, and inventive, clever lyrics, when he doesn't fall into the nostalgia trap, that he had in the late '50s, a voice that's even more expressive if not quite as rich, and a great sense of how to phrase a lyric; coupled with tasteful arrangements, the results are as compelling as anything in Williams' output. *—Bruce Eder*

Otis Williams & the Charms

b. Oct. 30, 1939, Cincinnati, OH

Vocals / R&B, Doo Wop

A Cincinnati vocal group, Otis Williams & the Charms landed a number-one R&B hit for almost ten weeks in 1954 with "Hearts of Stone," a song that remains among the most enduring doo wop anthems. Otis Williams, Richard Parker, Donald Peak, Joe Penn, and Rolland Bradley first recorded for Rockin' in 1953, but did "Hearts of Stone" for Deluxe the next year. They had several other hits, among them "Ling, Ting, Tong," "Two Hearts," "Ivory Tower," and "United," all of which made the Top Ten on the R&B charts between 1955 and 1957. Their songs were issued as Otis Williams & His Charms in 1956 and 1957. Williams later tried his hand at country. *—Ron Wynn*

This Is Otis Williams & the Charms / 1959 / King ✦✦✦✦

● **The Original Rockin' and Chart Masters** / Dec. 1, 1995 / Ace ✦✦✦✦✦

This 28-track CD contains the early Rockin' label recordings Otis Williams made with the original Charms. Their 1954 Top 15 pop hit "Hearts of Stone" was a significant achievement for an R&B group at that time, and "Two Hearts" was covered by Pat Boone and became his first hit. The Charms left Williams to record for Chart before he made "Ivory Tower" (his biggest hit), and those recordings sans Williams, including alternate takes, are here as well. "Ivory Tower" is not included, nor is "Ling, Ting, Tong" or "Bazoom (I Need Your Lovin')." Ace records released this CD for the European market, and although the track listings on the two versions are the same, the U.S. version has only a brief excerpt from the liner notes of the Ace release. Unfortunately, the abbreviated essay is entirely inadequate for those wanting to understand the tangle of labels and litigation behind these recordings. A more hit-oriented collection would provide a better overview, but collectors will appreciate the thoroughness and specific focus of *The Original Rockin' & Chart Masters*. *—Greg Adams*

Vanessa Williams

b. Mar. 18, 1963, Tarrytown, NY

Vocals / Dance-Pop, Adult Contemporary, Urban

When Vanessa Williams began her singing career, she was known chiefly as the Miss America pageant winner who'd been forced to renounce her title for posing in *Penthouse* magazine. Williams not only put the scandal behind her, she all but obliterated it, turning out a series of slick, sophisticated hits that made her one of the most popular adult contemporary R&B singers of her time. In addition to her broad crossover appeal, she established a parallel acting career in both film and television, ending the '90s as a highly successful all-around entertainer.

Vanessa Lynn Williams was born March 18, 1963, in the upstate New York town of Millwood to parents who were both music teachers. She loved performing musical theater as a teenager, and won a scholarship to study it at Syracuse University in 1981. In the meantime, she began entering beauty pageants, with considerable success; in 1983, she represented New York in the Miss America pageant and became the first African-American woman ever to be crowned the winner. Unfortunately, her triumph was short-lived. Williams had posed for a series of nude photos for *Penthouse* prior to her historic victory, and when the magazine published them in 1984, the ensuing scandal forced her to resign as Miss America. Undaunted, Williams began to pursue her first love, singing; she backed George Clinton on his 1986 album *R&B Skeletons in the Closet*, including the single "Do Fries Go With That Shake?" Williams also returned to acting, making her feature film debut with a small role in *The Pickup Artist* in 1987; the same year, she married her manager, Ramon Harvey. All the renewed exposure eventually helped land her a record deal with Mercury/Polygram subsidiary Wing.

Williams' debut album, *The Right Stuff*, was released in 1988, featuring a mix of urban dance-pop and adult contemporary balladry. The title track was a decent-sized hit, and the ballad "Dreamin'" became Williams' first Top Ten single, going all the way to number one on the R&B charts. *The Right Stuff* went gold, and Williams subsequently appeared in several TV movies. Her 1991 sophomore set *The Comfort Zone* was a star-maker; it spawned another R&B chart-topper in "Running Back to You," but the real story was the ballad "Save the Best for Last," a ubiquitous across-the-board smash that became Williams' first number-one hit on the pop charts. The title track solidified Williams' growing reputation for smooth, sexy adult pop, and the album went on to sell over two-million copies. In 1993, Williams' duet with Brian McKnight, "Love Is," became another huge hit when it was featured on the soundtrack of *Beverly Hills 90210*.

In 1994, Williams returned to her roots by accepting her first starring role on Broadway, taking over the lead in *Kiss of the Spider Woman*; she also appeared on a re-recorded version of the cast album. Late that year, she also released her third album, *The Sweetest Days*, which found her branching out into jazzy pop and torch songs in addition to her usual urban and adult contemporary fare. It also featured material by Babyface and Sting, and its upscale, sophisticated ambience gave Williams her second platinum album. In 1995, Williams was tabbed to sing the commercial version of "Colors of the Wind," the theme to the Disney film *Pocahontas*; not only was it a huge hit, it also won an Academy Award. In 1996, she got a divorce from manager Harvey, and the holiday album *Star Bright* came out; most notably, Williams landed her biggest feature film role to date when she starred opposite Arnold Schwarzenegger in that year's *Eraser*, and she followed it with an appearance in the ensemble drama *Soul Food* in 1997. Her fourth proper album, *Next* (1997) didn't attract quite as much attention as its predecessors. After the release of *Greatest Hits: The First Ten Years* in late 1998, Williams remained relatively quiet on the musical front, save for the occasional live performance event; she concentrated more on her acting career, and was prominently featured in *Dance With Me* (1998), *Light It Up* (1999), and the remake of *Shaft* (2000). In 1999, Williams remarried to L.A. Lakers basketball player Rick Fox. *—Steve Huey*

The Right Stuff / Feb. 1988 / Wing ✦✦✦✦✦

The disc is evenly divided between dancefloor fodder and AOR fluff, and it ain't half bad. Despite the fact that Williams works with six producers and eight songwriters, the disc has a consistent feel, and while Vanessa doesn't have a voice suited to belting out raunchy R&B, she's smart enough to stay within her limitations and let her personality take up the slack. *—J. Poet*

The Comfort Zone / Aug. 20, 1991 / Wing ✦✦✦✦

Typically, Vanessa Williams' albums are mixed bags. She's at her most exciting when taking chances and coming from the heart, and at her worst when recording frightfully dull material that is designed strictly for commercial radio airplay. This is certainly true of her sophomore effort, *The Comfort Zone*. Williams is at her best on the sexy, alluring title song and a striking remake of the Isley Brothers' "Work to Do," and at her worst on the hit adult contemporary ballad "Save the Best For Last." The song isn't genuinely romantic, only corny and insipid. One wishes Williams would stick to songs that are worthy of her, but when artists are under pressure from labels to sell as many albums as possible, artistic considerations easily fall by the wayside. *—Alex Henderson*

Sweetest Days / 1995 / Wing ✦✦✦

More diverse than Vanessa Williams' two previous albums, *The Sweetest Days* finds the singer exploring jazz-influenced songs without giving up the type of boring, radio-minded fluff that had enabled her to sell millions of albums. The CD's standout track is "Ellamental," an irresistible R&B/jazz/hip-hop tribute to Ella Fitzgerald. (Much to her credit, Williams was insightful enough to praise the jazz legend while she was still alive instead of waiting until after her death.) She's almost as appealing on "Sister Moon" (a torchy Sting gem) and the Babyface contributions "You Can't Run" (which has a Sade-ish quality) and the haunting "Betcha Never." But sadly, Williams doesn't hesitate to waste her talent on such contrived, hopelessly dull adult contemporary fluff as the title song—a song that's every bit as cliched and insipid as "Save the Best For Last." *—Alex Henderson*

Star Bright / Nov. 5, 1996 / Mercury ✦✦✦✦

Next / Aug. 26, 1997 / Mercury ✦✦✦

Although it relies a little too heavily on ballads, *Next* finds Vanessa Williams in fine form. Williams has grown into a strong singer, capable of wringing emotion out of even banal adult contemporary tracks. She can turn the relatively empty songs into impressive showcases for her vocal talents, and when she has a good song, like the sultry "Someone Like You," the results are first-rate. There could have been more uptempo dance numbers like "Happiness" to give *Next* more depth, but it's still a worthwhile effort from Williams. *—Leo Stanley*

● **Greatest Hits: The First Ten Years** / Nov. 17, 1998 / Wing/Mercury ✦✦✦✦✦

When former Miss America/*Penthouse* poser Vanessa Williams picked up a microphone in 1988 with *The Right Stuff*, her managers did the business-smart, and expected, thing: They buried her beneath a coat of glossy production and dancefloor beeps and bips to disguise whatever vocal shortcomings this walking mannequin might have. But a funny thing happened within a few years. It turned out that Williams, when given the right material, could actually sing. And when handed torch songs that emphasized her natural slow burn—like on the glorious ballad "Save the Best For Last"—Williams was a genuinely sexy and capable performer. *Greatest Hits: The First Ten Years* gathers the biggest 13 songs from her first decade. The club tunes are generic and could be served just as well by anyone, but the finest tunes here ("Save the Best For Last," "Love Is," and "Colors of the Wind") are smoldering slices of R&B that certify Williams is more than just a pretty face. *—Michael Gallucci*

Willie & the Mighty Magnificents

Group / Funk, Soul, Deep Funk

Willie & the Mighty Magnificents were a New Jersey-based funk ensemble led by guitarist/vocalist Willie Feaster, who recorded for Joe and Sylvia Robinson's All Platinum label family. Initially completed by bassist/keyboardist Val Burke and drummer Arnold Ramsey, the group had a harder, deeper, more Southern-tinged sound than the smooth soul artists who tended to dominate the label's output. Willie & the Mighty Magnificents issued their first single, "Check It Baby," in 1968 and followed it the next year with the cult funk classic "Funky 8 Corners." Further single releases over 1969-1970 included "Play That Funky Beat" (originally titled "Concerto in F"), "Make Me Your Slave" b/w "Soulin'," and "Think Funky." Their first full-length album, *On Scene '70*, featured some of those previous singles. Saxophonist Tyrone Johnson became a member of the group, and Skip McPhee and Ronnie Pace also filled the drum chair at various points. A second LP, *Very Soulful*, was released in 1972. The group also issued records under the name Willie & West, including the single "Get Away From Me Girl"; there was also a Willie & West LP, *At Their Best*. *—Steve Huey*

On Scene '70 / 1970 / Sequel ✦✦✦

Very Soulful / 1972 / All Platinum ✦✦✦✦

● **Play That Funky Beat** / 2000 / Sequel ✦✦✦✦

Chick Willis (Robert Willis)

b. Sep. 29, 1934, Cabiness, GA

Vocals, Guitar / Modern Electric Blues, R&B, Soul-Blues, Dirty Blues

Cousin to the late blues ballad singer Chuck Willis, Robert "Chick" Willis is primarily beloved for his ribald, dozens-based rocker "Stoop Down Baby." The guitarist cut his original version in 1972 for tiny La Val Records of Kalamazoo, MI, selling a ton of 45s for the jukebox market only (the tune's lyrics were way too raunchy for airplay).

The Atlanta-born Willis left the military in 1954, hiring on as valet and chauffeur to cousin Chuck, then riding high with his many R&B hits for OKeh Records. At that point, Chick's primary role on the show was as a singer (he made his own vinyl debut in 1956 with a single, "You're Mine," for Lee Rupe's Ebb Records after winning a talent contest at Atlanta's Magnolia Ballroom), but he picked up the guitar while on the road with his cousin (Chick cites Guitar Slim as his main man in that department).

When Chuck died of stomach problems in 1958, Willis soldiered on, pausing in Chicago to work as a sideman with slide guitar great Elmore James. A few obscure 45s ("Twistin' in the Hospital Ward," cut for Alto in 1962, sounds promising) preceded the advent of "Stoop Down Baby," which Willis has freshened up for countless sequels ever since (he developed the song by teasing passersby with his ribald rhymes while working in a carnival variety show). Risqué material has remained a staple of Willis' output in recent years. He cut several albums for Ichiban, notably 1988's *Now!*, *Footprints in My Bed* in 1990, and *Back to the Blues* in 1991. Willis has continued to tour and record for a number of small labels into the new millennium. *—Bill Dahl*

● **Stoop Down Baby . . . Let Your Daddy See** / 1972 / Collectables ♦♦♦♦♦
Here's the signifyin' original "Stoop Down Baby" in its long, unexpurgated version as issued on the tiny La Val label in 1972. "Mother Fuyer" travels the same salacious route, but Chick Willis has a serious side too—a pair of Guitar Slim covers spotlight Willis's stinging guitar and sturdy singing. *—Bill Dahl*

Now! / 1988 / Ichiban ♦♦

Footprints in My Bed / 1990 / Ichiban ♦♦♦♦
One of the few real blues LPs to post a warning about explicit lyrics, though it seems pretty tame in these rap-hardened times. Nevertheless, "Jack You Up," "Nuts for Sale," and "Big Red Caboose" are firmly in the best risqué Willis tradition—and very well produced and played to boot. *—Bill Dahl*

Back to the Blues / 1991 / Ichiban ♦♦♦
Willis takes things a little more seriously than usual, concentrating largely on covers of material by Percy Mayfield, Howlin' Wolf, Clarence Carter, and Guitar Slim. His own contributions include "I Ain't Jivin' Baby" and "Bow-Legged Woman" (he couldn't resist the raunchy stuff entirely!). *—Bill Dahl*

Holdin' Hands With the Blues / 1992 / Ichiban ♦♦
Thanks to a weak selection of songs and an indifferent production, *Holdin' Hands With the Blues* is one of Chick Willis' lesser efforts. Occasionally, he works up a nice lascivious snarl and spits out a couple of good solos, but for the most part, the record falls into predictable, uninspiring, dirty-minded shuffles and boogies. *—Thom Owens*

Nasty Chick / 1992 / Ichiban ♦♦♦

I Got a Big Fat Woman / 1994 / Ichiban ♦♦

Chuck Willis (Harold Willis)

b. Jan. 31, 1928, Atlanta, GA, **d.** Apr. 10, 1958, Atlanta, GA

Vocals / R&B

There were two distinct sides to Chuck Willis. In addition to being a convincing blues shouter, the Atlanta-born Willis harbored a vulnerable blues balladeer side. In addition, he was a masterful songwriter who penned some of the most distinctive R&B numbers of the 1950s. He can't be granted principal credit for his 1957 smash adaptation of "C.C. Rider," an irresistible update of a classic folk-blues, but Willis did write such gems as "I Feel So Bad" (later covered by Elvis Presley, Little Milton, and Otis Rush), the anguished ballads "Don't Deceive Me (Please Don't Go)" and "It's Too Late" (the latter attracting covers by Buddy Holly, Charlie Rich, and Otis Redding) and his swan song, "Hang Up My Rock and Roll Shoes."

Harold Willis (he adopted Chuck as a stage handle) received his early training singing at YMCA-sponsored "Teenage Canteens" in Atlanta and fronting the combos of local bandleaders Roy Mays and Red McAllister. Powerful DJ Zenas "Daddy" Sears took an interest in the young vocalist's career, hooking him up with Columbia Records in 1951. After a solitary single for the major firm, Willis was shuttled over to its recently reactivated OKeh R&B subsidiary. In 1952, he crashed the national R&B lists for OKeh with a typically plaintive ballad, "My Story," swiftly encoring on the hit parade with a gentle cover of Fats Domino's "Goin' to the River" and his own "Don't Deceive Me" the next year and "You're Still My Baby" and the surging Latin-beat "I Feel So Bad" in 1954. Willis also penned a heart-tugging chart-topper for Ruth Brown that year, "Oh What a Dream."

Willis moved over to Atlantic Records in 1956 and immediately enjoyed another round of hits with "It's Too Late" and "Juanita." Atlantic strove mightily to cross Willis over into pop territory, inserting an exotic steel guitar at one session and chirpy choirs on several more. The strategy eventually worked when his 1957 revival of the ancient "C.C. Rider" proved the perfect number to do the "Stroll" to; *American Bandstand* gave the track a big push, and Willis had his first R&B number one hit as well as a huge pop seller (Gene "Daddy G" Barge's magnificent sax solo likely aided its ascent).

Barge returned for Willis's similar follow-up, "Betty and Dupree," which also did well for him. But the turban-wearing crooner's time was growing short—he had long suffered from ulcers prior to his 1958 death from peritonitis. Much has been made of the ironic title of his last hit, the touching "What Am I Living For," but it was no more a clue to his impending demise than its flip, the joyous "Hang Up My Rock and Roll Shoes." Both tracks became massive hits upon the singer's death, and his posthumous roll continued with "My Life" and a powerful "Keep A-Drivin'" later that year. *—Bill Dahl*

Chuck Willis Wails the Blues / 1958 / Epic ♦♦♦

The King of the Stroll / 1958 / Atlantic ♦♦♦♦♦
Willis began recording for Okeh before moving to Atlantic. These numbers are Willis' rousing Okeh hits, which displayed his dynamic sound and energetic style. They've been reissued on some other compilations, so this may no longer be around. *—Ron Wynn*

A Tribute to Chuck Willis / 1960 / Epic ♦♦♦

I Remember Chuck Willis / 1963 / Atlantic ♦♦♦♦♦

His Greatest Recordings / 1971 / Atco ♦♦♦

My Story / 1980 / Columbia ♦♦♦♦
Not as exhaustive as Legacy's subsequent look at Willis' early- to mid-'50s hitmaking stint at OKeh, but this 14-tracker still gets the job done with the smooth ballads "Going to the River," "Don't Deceive Me," and "My Story" and Willis' surging, Latin-tempoed original "I Feel So Bad." *—Bill Dahl*

Let's Jump Tonight! The Best of Chuck Willis: 1951–1956 / 1994 / Epic/Legacy ♦♦♦♦♦
Before his brief turn as a rock & roll star with Atlantic, Willis cut a lot of material for OKeh in much more of an R&B/jump blues vein. This 26-cut collection includes all of his early and mid-'50s R&B hits—"My Story," "Goin' to the River," "Don't Deceive Me," "You're Still My Baby," and his most famous number from this period, "I Feel So Bad" (revived by Elvis Presley, among others). The influence of Joe Turner, Charles Brown, early Lloyd Price, and similar performers is strongly felt; Willis could shout competently, but was much better on the emotional R&B ballads. Not as strong or distinctive as his Atlantic material, this includes several cuts that were previously unreleased or previously unavailable in the U.S. *—Richie Unterberger*

★ **Stroll On: The Chuck Willis Collection** / Oct. 19, 1994 / Razor & Tie ♦♦♦♦♦
Here are all 25 of the versatile Atlanta-bred singer's Atlantic Records sides, presented beautifully (every R&B reissue on CD should be packaged so well, with plenty of brilliant stereo). Willis really hit his stride at Atlantic, doing the Stroll with his easy-going "C.C. Rider" and "Betty and Dupree" (both boasting darting sax breaks from Gene Barge), baring his tender soul on a devotional "What Am I Living For," and taking R&B into fresh directions with a jumping "Kansas City Woman," the relentless "Keep A-Drivin'," and a buoyant "Hang Up My Rock and Roll Shoes." *—Bill Dahl*

I Remember Chuck Willis/The King of the Stroll / Nov. 13, 2001 / Collectables ♦♦♦♦
This reissue from Collectables combines two classic Chuck Willis albums: one for OKeh and the other from Atlantic. These are *I Remember Chuck Wills* and *The King of the Stroll*, released in 1963 and 1958, respectively. The disc features 25 tracks, including a number of jump blues, early R&B, and tender, yearning ballads. This is a sure-bet purchase and also sports the addition of the original LP track sequence that highlights obscure cuts that are just as enjoyable as the hits. *—Al Campbell*

Chuck Willis Wails! The Complete OKeh Recordings 1951–56 / Feb. 25, 2003 / Sundazed ♦♦♦♦♦

The Willows

f. 1955, New York, NY

Group / Doo Wop

The Willows bloomed in 1950 from Harlem as the Dovers: Richie Davis, John Steele, Ralph Martin, Joe Martin (twins), and Bobby Robinson. Tony Middleton replaced Robinson who left in 1952 to open a record shop on 125th Street that became Fury Records. The Dovers built a reputation battling other groups; they often practiced with Gloria Lynne's group, the Dell-Tones; Lynne later recorded on Premium with the Wheels before going solo. Pete and Goldie Doraine became their managers and financed the groups' 1953 debut, "Love Bells," on their own Pee Dee label, as the Five Willows. Three singles followed on Allen Records in 1953 that balm egos but did nothing for their bank accounts. After two flops on Herald in 1954, they hit as the Willows (dropping the "Five" for booking purposes) on Melba in 1956 with "Church Bells May Ring," featuring Neil Sedaka on chimes. It blasted to number-11 R&B but died at number-62 pop due to the Diamonds' number-14 pop cover. The Cadets and Sunny Gale also played the cover game.

They didn't have any more hits but hung tough until 1965. Platters on Eldorado and Gone in 1957-1958 credited to Tony Middleton & the Willows went unnoticed; ditto for singles as the Willows on Club and Warwick Records. The Martin twins, Freddie Donovan, and Dotty Martin (Joe's wife) were the Willows for two nonstarters on Heidi Records in 1964. And a lineup featuring Tony Middleton and Richie Davis appeared in the '70s to work the doo wop revivals; but by the '90s, the Willows wept no more. *—Andrew Hamilton*

● **Rockin' Doowops** / Oct. 25, 1994 / Castle ♦♦♦

Jackie Wilson

b. Jun. 9, 1934, Detroit, MI, **d.** Jan. 21, 1984, Mount Holly, NJ

Vocals / R&B, Soul, Uptown Soul, Chicago Soul, Pop-Soul

Jackie Wilson was one of the most important agents of black pop's transition from R&B into soul. In terms of vocal power (especially in the upper register), few could outdo him; he was also an electrifying on-stage showman. He was a consistent hitmaker from the mid-'50s through the early '70s, although never a crossover superstar. His reputation isn't quite on par with Ray Charles, James Brown, or Sam Cooke, however, because his records did not always reflect his artistic genius. Indeed, there is a consensus of sorts among critics that Wilson was something of an underachiever in the studio, due to the sometimes inappropriately pop-based material and arrangements that he used.

Wilson was well-known on the R&B scene before he went solo in the late '50s. In 1953 he replaced Clyde McPhatter in Billy Ward & the Dominoes, one of the top R&B vocal groups of the '50s. Although McPhatter was himself a big star, Wilson was as good as or better than the man whose shoes he filled. Commercially, however, things took a downturn for the Dominoes in the Wilson years, although they did manage a Top 20 hit with

"St. Therese of the Roses" in 1956. Elvis Presley was one of those who was mightily impressed by Wilson in the mid-'50s; he can be heard praising Jackie's on-stage cover of "Don't Be Cruel" in between-song banter during the *Million Dollar Quartet* session in late 1956. Wilson would score his first big R&B (and small pop) hit in late 1956 with the brassy, stuttering "Reet Petite," which was co-written by an emerging Detroit songwriter named Berry Gordy Jr. Gordy would also help write a few other hits for Jackie in the late '50s, "To Be Loved," "Lonely Teardrops," "That's Why (I Love You So)," and "I'll Be Satisfied"; they also crossed over to the pop charts, "Lonely Teardrops" making the Top Ten. Most of these were upbeat, creatively arranged marriages of pop and R&B that, in retrospect, helped set the stage both for '60s soul and for Gordy's own huge pop success at Motown. The early Gordy-Wilson association has led some historians to speculate how much differently (and better) Jackie's career might have turned out had he been on Motown's roster instead of the Brunswick label.

In the early '60s, Wilson maintained his pop stardom with regular hit singles that often used horn arrangements and female choruses that have dated somewhat badly, especially in comparison with the more creative work by peers such as Charles and Brown from this era. Wilson also sometimes went into out-and-out operatic pop, as on "Danny Boy" and one of his biggest hits, "Night" (1960). At the same time, he remained capable of unleashing a sweaty, uptempo, gospel-soaked number: "Baby Workout," which fit that description to a T, was a number-five hit for him in 1963. It's true that you have to be pretty selective in targeting the worthwhile Wilson records from this era; 1962's *At the Copa*, for instance, has Jackie trying to combine soul and all-around entertainment, and not wholly succeeding with either strategy. Yet some of his early Brunswick material is also fine uptown soul; not quite as earthy as some of his fans would have liked him to sound, no doubt, but worth hearing.

Wilson was shot and seriously wounded by a female fan in 1961, though he made a recovery. His career was more seriously endangered by his inability to keep up with changing soul and rock trends. Not everything he did in the mid-'60s is totally dismissible; "No Pity (In the Naked City)," for instance, is something like *West Side Story* done uptown soul style. In 1966, his career was briefly revived when he teamed up with Chicago soul producer Carl Davis, who had been instrumental in the success of Windy City performers like Gene Chandler, Major Lance, and Jerry Butler. Davis successfully updated Wilson's sound with horn-heavy arrangements, getting near the Top Ten with "Whispers," and then making number six in 1967 with "Higher and Higher." And that was really the close of Wilson's career as either a significant artist or commercial force, although he had some minor chart entries through the early '70s.

While playing a Dick Clark oldies show at the Latin Casino in New Jersey in September 1975, Wilson suffered an on-stage heart attack while singing "Lonely Teardrops." He lapsed into a coma, suffering major brain damage, and was hospitalized until his death in early 1984. *—Richie Unterberger*

He's So Fine / 1958 / Brunswick ✦✦✦✦

In 1957, Jackie Wilson left the Dominoes and released this debut album on Brunswick Records a year later. The new songwriting team of Berry Gordy Jr. & Tyran Carlo (aka Billy Davis) wrote six of the 12 songs. Backed by a big band, Wilson belts out "Reet Petite" like it's an Olympic event, displaying his irresistible vocal gymnastics; "Etcetera" treads the same path, but lacks the dynamics. "To Be Loved" and "Danny Boy," the old standard, are heartfelt, stately ballads. Wilson wrote "Come Back to Me," a rather bland jump tune. An overblown big band sound mars all but the most crafted creations, and there's no denying Wilson's fantastic takes, but the Brunswick sound may be a bit too full for die-hard soul lovers. *—Andrew Hamilton*

Lonely Teardrops / 1959 / Brunswick ✦✦✦✦✦

Jackie Wilson's big beautiful voice outshines Dick Jacobs' bombastic big-band sound on his second solo album. His voice-of-plenty makes two hopelessly MOR tunes ("Hush-A-Bye" and "By the Light of the Silvery Moon") tolerable, and contributes two compositions himself ("You Better Know It" and "Singing a Song"). Berry Gordy and Billy Davis, with help from Gwendolyn Gordy-Fuqua, contribute the most commercial songs, including the hit "That's Why I Love You So," "Each Time I Love You More," and "We Have Love." This marked the final time Gordy and Davis worked with Wilson; the hitmaking combo split because Gordy objected to Brunswick's dogmatic refusal to put their songs on the flip side of their hit A-sides. (He resented other writers' songs riding the coattails of their hits and cutting their mechanical income in half; he also wanted a share of the publishing. Regent Music published all the songs Gordy and Davis wrote for Wilson, and still holds the copyrights.) *—Andrew Hamilton*

So Much / 1959 / Brunswick ✦✦✦

Jackie Sings the Blues / 1960 / Brunswick ✦✦✦✦✦

My Golden Favorites / 1960 / Brunswick ✦✦✦✦✦

Night / 1960 / Brunswick ✦✦✦

A Woman, A Lover, A Friend / 1960 / Brunswick ✦✦✦

Try a Little Tenderness / 1961 / Brunswick ✦✦✦

You Ain't Heard Nothin' Yet / 1961 / Brunswick ✦✦✦

Body & Soul / 1962 / Brunswick ✦✦✦

Jackie Wilson at the Copa / 1962 / Brunswick ✦✦✦

The only live album of Wilson's career was recorded in the early '60s at New York's famous Copacabana nightclub. It was an almost obligatory rite of passage for early soul stars breaking into the mainstream, one also enacted by Sam Cooke and several Motown stars. As you'd expect, the cirumstances don't exactly lend themselves to showing Wilson at his greatest advantage, particularly if you're principally a fan of Wilson the soul singer, not Wilson the all-around entertainer. He sounds like an over-the-top lounge lizard throughout much of the proceedings, zipping through standards like Leonard Bernstein's "Tonight," "Body and Soul," "St. James Infirmary," and Cole Porter's "Love for Sale," occasionally pausing for some corny between-song patter. He does interject a few of his R&B hits ("That's Why," "Doggin' Around," "To Be Loved," "Lonely Teardrops"), but these too get the casino band treatment, complete with strings and strident female backup vocalists. No, it's not what you play as exhibit A to showcase Jackie Wilson, Rock and Roll Hall of Famer. But taken on its own terms it's enjoyably cheesy entertainment, Wilson's astounding vocal prowess always in evidence. [Out of print since 1967, it was reissued on CD in 1995.] *—Richie Unterberger*

Baby Workout / 1963 / Brunswick ✦✦✦

The World's Greatest Melodies / 1963 / Brunswick ✦✦✦

Soul Time / 1965 / Brunswick ✦✦✦✦✦

Soul Galore / 1966 / Brunswick ✦✦✦

A connoisseurs' package of 24 Jackie Wilson sides, and an indispensable treat, because other than the obvious hit, "Whispers (Getting Louder)," the rest were chosen with no regard to chart action or popularity, though many did chart R&B. Some of these will be new to you if you didn't purchase any of the many albums Brunswick Records flung on the market by Wilson. Check his version of the Holland-Dozier-Holland's hit on the Supremes, "You Keep Me Hanging On." If Brunswick hadn't held Wilson under contract you would have got a taste of the artist cutting HDH tunes at Motown, but Wilson's management never let it happened, for Wilson signing with Brunswick was akin to joining a gang—blood in, blood out. His version of "Love Uprising"—also recorded by Otis Leavill and the Chi-Lites—is the best, ditto for "You Got Me Walking," also done (unreleased when recorded) by Cicero Blake, and a rip snortin' rendition of Darrell Banks' "Open the Door to Your Heart." The CD also contains some nice midtempo as well as some grittier sounds from the talented singer/entertainer whose career suffered from some horrific circumstances that he couldn't get out from under. *—Andrew Hamilton*

Whispers / 1966 / Brunswick ✦✦✦

Higher and Higher / Nov. 1967 / Brunswick ✦✦✦✦

Driven by Jackie Wilson's biggest latter-day hit, "(Your Love Keeps Lifting Me) Higher and Higher," this 1967 LP offers great performances (from vocalist and band) and a variety of material. Though original LPs surely aren't the best place to start for Wilson, fans of the nearly irresistible Brunswick sound will find much here to like, from the propulsive "You Can Count on Me" and "Open the Door to Your Heart" to the classy Impressions-style "When Will Our Day Come" and the ballad "Those Heartaches." Wilson's performances are excellent as usual, making *Higher and Higher* one of the better original albums of his career. *—John Bush*

I Get the Sweetest Feeling / Feb. 1968 / Brunswick ✦✦✦

The Greatest Hits of Jackie Wilson / 1969 / Brunswick ✦✦✦✦

This Love Is Real / 1970 / Brunswick ✦✦✦

By the time of the release of *This Love Is Real*, it seemed that Chicago soul producer Carl Davis had the hit formula for Jackie Wilson down pat. He'd recruit Motown's James Jamerson, Earl Van Dyke, Benny Benjamin, and the rest of the Funk Brothers and combine their dynamic interplay with a top-notch song from his stable of talented songwriters. It had worked with Wilson's comeback hit "Higher and Higher and was still working some three years later. The effervescent single "(I Can Feel Those Vibrations) This Love Is Real" charted on *Billboard* in late 1970, becoming a steppers classic. The pop ballad "Love Is Funny That Way" broke the R&B Top 20. Wilson's impressive vocal prowess is showcased on "Let This Be a Letter (To My Baby)" and "Love Uprising," both written by the Chi-Lites' Eugene Record. The ethereal "Think About the Good Times" features an outstanding instrumental break that features fluid wah-wah guitar, dazzling bass runs, and otherworldly sound effects supplied by engineer Bruce Swedien. [*This Love Is Real* was reissued with another great Davis/Wilson LP, *You Got Me Walking*, on a fine 1999 single CD *This Love Is Real/You Got Me Walking* from U.K. label Edsel Records.] *—Ed Hogan*

It's All a Part of Love / 1971 / Brunswick ✦✦✦

You Got Me Walking / 1971 / Brunswick ✦✦✦✦

Produced by Chicago soul producer Carl Davis, *You Got Me Walking* was one of Jackie Wilson's best albums. As usual with Davis/Wilson collaborations, Motown's studio band the Funk Brothers were on hand to lay down their tight grooves. Written by the Chi-Lites' Eugene Record, the funky, loping single "You Got Me Walking" strutted up to number-22 R&B on *Billboard*'s charts in early 1972. An earlier single, the tender "Love Is Funny That Way," charted in late 1971. Wilson's gospel roots are on full display on Record's rollicking, honking "The Fountain." Other standouts are the majestic "Forever and a Day," the swinging, brassy "Hard to Get a Thing Called Love," and the charting single "The Girl Turned Me On." [*You Got Me Walking* was paired with *This Love Is Real* on a superb 1999 single CD *This Love Is Real/You Got Me Walking* from U.K. label Edsel Records.] *—Ed Hogan*

Beautiful Day / 1973 / Brunswick ✦✦✦

Produced by Chicago soul stalwarts Carl Davis and arranger Sonny Sanders with musical direction by Willie Henderson, *Beautiful Day* is Jackie Wilson's last commercially viable album and finds the phenomenal singer in fine form. Songwriter/producer Jeffree Perry (known for the steppers classic "Love's Gonna Last") co-wrote all of the songs. The standouts are the inspiring title track, the peppy "Pretty Little Angel Eyes," and the sensitive renderings Wilson gives on "Go Away," "I Get Lonely Sometimes," and the splendid "This Love Is Mine." What makes this track even more endearing is that you can hear the last part of a count-off (as in "1-2-3, go!") just before the music begins. Despite the LP's rich consistency, the only single to chart was the effervescent "Because of You," which just missed the R&B Top 40 in spring 1973. [*Beautiful Day* was included with another Jackie Wilson LP *Nobody but You* on the single CD *Beautiful Day/Nobody But You* issued by Edsel Records on September 29, 1999.] *—Ed Hogan*

Nobody but You / 1976 / Brunswick ♦♦♦

Produced by Carl Davis and Sonny Sanders, *Nobody but You* was Jackie Wilson's final and possibly his finest album. Originally issued in late 1976, it was recorded in Detroit and had top-notch arrangements by Sanders and David Van De Pitte. One charting single was the wise and exuberant "Don't Burn No Bridges," which featured his Brunswick labelmates the Chi-Lites. Other highlights are the reflective "Where Is Love"—similar in tone to another Wilson track, "Beautiful Day"—the buoyant "It Only Happens When I Look at You," the footstomper "Satisfy My Soul," and the Sam Dees ballad "Just As Soon As the Feeling's Over." It's bittersweet that the LP ends with the steadfast "I've Learned About Life"—by the time of its release, the great singer had succumbed to the effects of an on-stage heart attack from which he'd never recover. [*Nobody but You* is on the splendid 1999 two-LP single Edsel CD *Beautiful Day/Nobody ut You*.] *—Ed Hogan*

The Jackie Wilson Story / 1983 / Epic ♦♦♦♦♦

If there's anyone in the history of R&B who deserved a better hand than they were dealt when it came to making records, it was Jackie Wilson. Wilson had boundless energy, unbeatable charisma, and a frankly astounding voice; just listen to "Reet Petite" and be awestruck at the rapid-fire array of vocal effects Wilson reels off with casual ease. But while he was among the finest singers of his generation, Wilson was usually saddled with second-rate songs, dunderheaded arrangements, and lame backing vocalists whose presence is the musical equivalent of putting mayonnaise on hot pastrami. Wilson's recorded career is dotted with disasters and miscalculations, but the man was simply too talented to not strike lucky every once in a while, and part of his genius was that he could make something out of the most unlikely material; it's hard to imagine why Wilson's A&R man thought it was a good idea to cut "Danny Boy," but the artist actually finds a way to make it sound soulful. And on the rare occasions when he got the right song (such as "Lonely Teardrops," "To Be Loved," "You Don't Know What It Means," or ("Your Love Keeps Lifting Me) Higher and Higher," he was unbeatable. Longtime fans Joe McEwin and Gregg Geller sorted through 15 years worth of Wilson's recordings to compile *The Jackie Wilson Story*, a superb two-record set that brings together most of Wilson's hits and adds a number of top-quality also-rans, obscurities, and oddities (including that version of "Danny Boy"). The flaws that pock-marked many of Wilson's recordings are evident throughout, but his voice shines like a diamond on every cut, and if you want to know the artist was a top draw on the R&B circuit for close to two decades, one listen to this set will show you—no one could sing quite like Jackie Wilson. *—Mark Deming*

Through the Years / 1987 / Rhino ♦♦♦

Mr. Excitement / Nov. 10, 1992 / Rhino ♦♦♦♦♦

A three-CD box from the experts of reissue at Rhino, *Mr. Excitement* takes Wilson's career from his first sides with Billy Ward & the Dominoes in 1956 through his final recordings in the early '70s. The former Detroit boxer hit either the R&B or pop chart over 50 times, making him one of the most successful R&B artists ever, in chart terms at least. Every one of those recordings is contained in this set, including such classics as "Reet Petite," "Lonely Teardrops," and "(Your Love Keeps Lifting Me) Higher and Higher." Wilson had an explosive falsetto and a downright weird sense of phrasing that made him utterly unique. Some of his productions were a little overwrought but even in the most extreme cases, that voice was a gift from God. Seminal. *—Rob Bowman*

☆ **The Very Best of Jackie Wilson** / Feb. 4, 1993 / Ace ♦♦♦♦♦

This is similar to the U.S. greatest-hits collection of the same name (on Rhino), but with substantially more tracks. This 24-song anthology has all the familiar big singles on the Rhino compilation, but goes into his late-'60s/early-'70s material in greater depth. His best stuff was recorded before that, though, so you're not much (if at all) worse off by sticking to the cheaper, more easily available domestic collection. *—Richie Unterberger*

★ **The Very Best of Jackie Wilson** / Jan. 18, 1994 / Rhino ♦♦♦♦♦

Rhino's *The Very Best of Jackie Wilson* is not to be confused with Brunswick's own compilation of the same title; each has its own advantages, and it's difficult to go wrong with either. Rhino's collection offers fewer tracks (16 versus Brunswick's 24), but concentrates exclusively on the singer's prime period, and also boasts the typically excellent remastering and sound quality that have become the label's hallmark. Rhino also paints a more complete picture of his career by allowing a bit more space for Wilson's MOR pop leanings, which were—soul fans' tastes notwithstanding—a significant part of his repertoire. Not only did they help him maintain a white audience and a presence on the pop charts, they also gave him a chance to show off the near-operatic range and power of his elastic, swooping voice. Of course, that voice was also a pivotal instrument in transforming R&B into soul music, and after an early spate of hits co-written by a pre-Motown Berry Gordy, Wilson continued to alternate R&B tunes with pop ballads for the supper-club set. And any lingering skepticism about Wilson's soul credentials ought to be obliterated by his incredible performance on album closer "(Your Love Keeps Lifting Me) Higher and Higher," one of the purest fusions of secular romance and gospel transcendence ever committed to wax. Unfortunately, the Rhino set has gone out of print, leaving Brunswick's the only top-notch single-disc currently on the market; still, if *The Very Best of . . .* can be found used, it's certainly an excellent choice as well. *—Steve Huey*

Higher and Higher / Jan. 1, 1997 / Charly ♦♦♦♦

Charly Records did a good job narrowing the selection down to these 25 songs when you considered the many albums Wilson recorded. Some diligent person took the time to wade through a lot of stuff to pick these jewels. Picking the hits was easy, but coming up with "Tear of the Year," "You Don't Know What It Means," "Am I the Man" and "Why Can't You Be Mine" deserves some praise. Jackies' full, honey-throated tenor is as numbing as any voice in pop music. Wilson could sing addresses from the white pages and pull it off. The stuttering, vocal gymnastics used by Wilson on "Reet Petite" is amazing. I always wanted Stevie Wonder to redo this one, it has the same big band sound Wonder used on "Sir Duke" and "Deed I Do." If the collaboration had continued, Berry Gordy and Tyran Carlo (Billy Davis) would have done for Jackie what Holland-Dozier-Holland did for the Supremes: write hit on top of hit for him. Their songs "Reet," "Lonely Teardrops," "That's Why (I Love You So)" and "I'll Be Satisfied" are some of the best he ever recorded. Just as comfortable with fast songs, Jackie let it all out on "Shake, Shake, Shake," and "Baby Workout." The late '60s produced a Motown-ish Wilson; the infectious "Whispers (Getting Louder)" and the frantic "(Your Love Keeps Lifting Me) Higher and Higher" showed that Jackie didn't have a problem flowing with the times. *—Andrew Hamilton*

Titan of Soul / Oct. 27, 1998 / Demon Duplicate ♦♦♦♦♦

After a stint with Billy Ward & the Dominoes, Jackie Wilson recorded solely for Brunswick Records. He wanted out several times, but legal and physical threats prevailed and kept Wilson in contract hell. One good thing about the scenario is that Brunswick recorded J.W. all the time—he could have covered his living, dining, and bedroom walls with his album covers without using the same one twice. The label locked him down because they felt that Wilson's overwhelming talent would eventually take him to the top, and, voila—payback. It never happened to that extent, but the wheels behind him didn't stop rollin' until the singer became comatose. He cut R&B, soul, pop, pop operas, jazz—the works. These 66 tracks spread over three discs are the pearls of an extensive recording career; the most comprehensive package to date, it includes the best of his solo work, plus imaginative duets with Linda Hopkins, LaVern Baker, the Chi-Lites, tracks with Count Basie, and a book. *—Andrew Hamilton*

This Love Is Real/You Got Me Walking / Jun. 29, 1999 / Edsel ♦♦♦♦

Uptown and Upnorth (Floorsnapper, Floaters and Floorshakers) / Sep. 15, 1999 / WestSide ♦♦♦

Other than "Your Love Keeps Lifting Me (Higher and Higher)," not included, and "Whispers (Getting Louder)," which is, Jackie Wilson's later Brunswick recordings produced mainly by Carl Davis suffer from underappreciation—which is a shame because he recorded some good sides during this era. Check out "Love Uprising" (made popular by Otis Leavill), "You Got Me Walking" (an obscure Chi-Lites tune), a yearning rendition of Darrell Banks' "Open the Door to Your Heart," and two songs by the guitar-playing Reed brothers (Danny and Bernard Reed), "My Heart Is Calling" and "Just Be Sincere." Soul fans would be wise to investigate this and other groupings of mid-'60s Brunswick recordings. This set includes the light and melodic "I Get the Sweetest Feeling" and a chilling update of Holland-Dozier-Holland's "You Keep Me Hanging On." Unlike Wilson's early Brunswick recordings, these aren't marred by syrupy strings and Ray Coniff-ish arrangements—this is bumpin' uptown soul, baby. *—Andrew Hamilton*

Beautiful Day/Nobody But You / Sep. 27, 1999 / Edsel ♦♦♦♦

Nancy Wilson

b. Feb. 20, 1937, Chillicothe, OH

Vocals / Traditional Pop, Vocal Jazz, Pop-Soul, Standards, Ballads

Diva Nancy Wilson was among contemporary music's most stylish and sultry vocalists; while often crossing over into the pop and R&B markets—and even hosting her own television variety program—she remained best known as a jazz performer, renowned for her work alongside figures including Cannonball Adderley and George Shearing. Born February 20, 1937, in Chillicothe, OH, Wilson first attracted notice performing the club circuit in nearby Columbus; she quickly earned a growing reputation among jazz players and fans, and she was recording regularly by the late '50s, eventually signing to Capitol and issuing LPs including 1959's *Like in Love* and *Nancy Wilson With Billy May's Orchestra*. Her dates with Shearing, including 1960's *The Swingin's Mutual*, solidified her standing as a talent on the rise, and her subsequent work with Adderley—arguably her finest recordings—further cemented her growing fame and reputation.

In the years to follow, however, Wilson often moved away from jazz, much to the chagrin of purists; she made numerous albums, many of them properly categorized as pop and R&B outings, and toured extensively, appearing with everyone from Nat King Cole and Sarah Vaughan to Ruth Brown and LaVern Baker. She even hosted her own Emmy-winning variety series for NBC, *The Nancy Wilson Show*, and was a frequent guest performer on other programs; hits of the period included "Tell Me the Truth," "How Glad I Am," "Peace of Mind," and "Now, I'm a Woman." Regardless of how far afield she traveled, Wilson always maintained her connections to the jazz world, and in the 1980s, she returned to the music with a vengeance, working closely with performers including Hank Jones, Art Farmer, Ramsey Lewis, and Benny Golson. By the 1990s, she was a favorite among the "new adult contemporary" market, her style ideally suited to the format's penchant for lush, romantic ballads; she also hosted the *Jazz Profiles* series on National Public Radio. *—Jason Ankeny*

Like in Love / 1959 / Capitol ♦♦♦

Swingin's Mutual / Jun. 29, 1960-Jan. 7, 1961 / Capitol ♦♦♦♦

Something Wonderful / 1960 / Capitol ♦♦♦♦

Nancy Wilson & Cannonball Adderley / Sep. 1, 1962 / Capitol ♦♦♦♦♦

Yesterday's Love Songs/Today's Blues / Dec. 1963 / Blue Note ♦♦♦

A Touch of Today / 1966 / Capitol ♦♦♦

A Touch of Today is another of Nancy Wilson's contemporary dates, comprised of standards from Broadway, Motown, the Beatles, and Bacharach, among other '60s sources. Though her voice is as strong and pliable as ever, Wilson isn't always right for this material, as her attempt to sound exuberant on Stevie Wonder's "Uptight (Everything's Alright)" displays. Most of the others work just fine though, and Wilson stamps her versions of familiar pop songs like "The Shadow of Your Smile," "Call Me," "And I Love Her" (naturally adjusting the lyrics and title to read "And I Love Him"), "Yesterday," and "Goin' out of My Head." The arrangements, handled either by Oliver Nelson or Sid Feller, are occasionally too reliant on period clichés, but *A Touch of Today* is a solid album adrift in a period of lesser efforts by great singers. [A 1999 two-fer reissue by Capitol/EMI paired *A Touch of Today* with Wilson's 1964 LP *Today, Tomorrow, Forever.*] *—John Bush*

Nancy: Naturally / 1967 / Capitol ♦♦♦

Nancy Wilson displays all her talents on this 1967 Capitol release. On the blues end of things, she turns the lights down low with a smoldering cover of Lil Green's classic "In the Dark" and swings it hard and brass-heavy on the Joe Williams/Count Basie number "Alright, Okay, You Win." And for some of her patented ballad heaven, there are stunners like Michel Legrand's "Watch What Happens" and Lil Armstrong's forlorn standard "Just for a Thrill." To flesh out this relatively traditional program, Wilson keeps up with the times on mod pop reworkings of the Willie Dixon-penned Little Walter hit "My Babe" and another Joe Williams favorite, "Smack Dab in the Middle." Foreshadowing Oliver Nelson's fine blues and swing charts for Wilson's excellent *Welcome to My Love* recording, veteran arranger and Sinatra-alumnus Billy May provides nicely lubed charts full of organ pop and drum-kit power. Whether going full throttle, chilling after hours, or hinting at a bit of the old lowdown, May is adept with all the album's many moods. *Nancy: Naturally* may not be essential Wilson listening, but it still makes for a very enjoyable trip around the turntable. *—Stephen Cook*

Lush Life / May 13, 1967-May 16, 1967 / Blue Note ♦♦♦

Welcome to My Love / 1968 / Blue Note ♦♦♦♦

Most of Nancy Wilson's late-'60s releases contained four or five good tunes and the rest would be filler from the day's batch of B-grade pop material. Her 1967 date *Welcome to My Love*, though, is an exception. It offers a consistent selection of high-quality standards and strong contemporary material impressively set off by Oliver Nelson's soulfully urbane arrangements. On the subdued end there are straight-ahead ballads like "May I Come In" and "It Never Entered My Mind" as well as more soul-tinged numbers such as "Welcome to My Love" and "Let's Make the Most of a Beautiful Thing." Wilson's smoky, whispered voice imparts just the right amount of tender drama here while Nelson's dark and restrained string charts keep things from getting syrupy. Balancing out the set are a series of bluesy big-band numbers including "In the Heat of the Night," "I'm Always Drunk in SF" and an amazing version of "Ode to Billy Joe." This classic Bobbie Gentry tune gets a funked up, backwoods treatment à la Etta James with Wilson in full swagger. Eddie "Lockjaw" Davis effectively echoes the intensity with his back in the mix, burning tenor solo while drummer Shelly Manne and bassist Buster Williams anchor the proceedings with driving intensity. The set is rounded out by fine renditions of "For Once in Life" and the classic Ray Charles hit "You Don't Know Me." On *Welcome to My Love*, Wilson successfully straddled the jazz/soul divide and in the process produced one of her best albums of the '60s. *—Stephen Cook*

Now I'm a Woman / 1970 / Capitol ♦♦♦♦

Wilson spent the late '60s doing her fair share of cover material and pop-oriented work that often betrayed her jazz roots and the beauty and intelligence in her voice. After an extended period of albums with producer David Cavanaugh, Wilson did this 1970 album with Gamble & Huff productions, featuring producers/arrangers including Thom Bell, Bobby Martin, and arranger-conductor Lenny Pakula. Cavanaugh was the executive producer. Around this time the Philly production team was best known for their work with artists like Jerry Butler, Billy Paul, and the Delfonics, among many others. Wilson falls right into the production style. The title track is a customary strong outing from Kenny Gamble & Leon Huff. The beautiful "Joe" has the sound of a prime Thom Bell production, and Wilson gives an amazing performance and a particularly emotional note that might go through a listener. Wilson shines on "Lonely, Lonely" and "Let's Fall in Love Again"; both benefit from Bobby Martin's patently brassy and sweeping Philly production. While some might be hard-pressed to understand why *Now I'm a Woman* didn't earn more raves, the answer lies in the covers. Even Wilson in great voice couldn't withstand the triple whammy of "They Long to Be (Close to You)," "Long and Winding Road," and "Make It With You." Despite a few missteps, *Now I'm a Woman* is an important album in Wilson's oeuvre and the Philly sound. *—Jason Elias*

All in Love Is Fair / 1973 / Capitol ♦♦♦

Greatest Hits / 1979 / CEMA ♦♦♦♦♦

To the extent that the phrase "greatest hits" equates to "highest-charting pop singles," this Nancy Wilson *Greatest Hits* album, released by the budget division of Capitol Records, is definitive. Not counting a couple of holiday songs, Wilson hit the pop singles charts nine times between 1963 and 1971 on Capitol Records, and every one of those singles is here. They include such performances as Wilson's treatment of "I Want to Be With You" (from the Broadway musical *Golden Boy*) and her covers of the Stevie Wonder classic "Uptight" and the Frankie Valli standard "Can't Take My Eyes Off You." These are the recordings of a middle-of-the-road '60s pop singer with elements of rock and R&B. Of course, those who consider Wilson an R&B singer will note the omission of her many R&B chart singles that didn't cross over to the pop charts, and those who think of her as a jazz singer will be left out entirely. But that's the dilemma of an artist with a multi-genre appeal. However, this album does capture one aspect of Nancy Wilson's work succinctly. *—William Ruhlmann*

Life, Love and Harmony / 1979 / Capitol ♦♦

Forbidden Lover / Jan. 19, 198787 02 / Columbia ♦♦♦♦♦

Lady With a Song / 1990 / Columbia ♦♦♦

● **Anthology** / Jun. 6, 2000 / Capitol ♦♦♦♦

Wilson is a vexing artist to summarize with a best-of compilation, due both to her versatility and her prolific discography. This two-set CD concentrates on her pop- and R&B-influenced recordings for Capitol in the 1960s and '70s. While that means that her jazziest and most standard-inclined sides are relatively lightly represented (although not ignored), it does mean that this is the material most likely to be familiar to the general audience. In truth the soul influence is quite light; this is really pop material, not R&B, soul, or rock, even as it might show some traces of those genres (as well as jazz and cabaret). As a whole, this easy-listening soul music was light fare, but Wilson was probably better at it (and certainly more successful at it) than anyone else. The first disc, covering 1962-1970, is the better of the pair, with the big 1964 hit "(You Don't Know) How Glad I Am" and a couple of nice non-LP singles in 1963's bluesy "Tell the Truth" and 1965's "Where Does That Leave Me." Her reading of Stevie Wonder's "Uptight" is actually respectable, and some of her better mid-'60s singles show the influence of New York uptown soul production. The second disc charts the decline of pop-soul as a whole, even if it does lead off with a couple of 1970 Gamble & Huff-affiliated tracks. Much of the rest marks Wilson as one of the mothers of adult contemporary music, which is not the highest badge of honor one can bear. Is this *the* anthology you should have if you only get one Wilson collection? If your tastes run to pop rather than jazz, it probably is, though it should be cautioned that it's uneven and does not reflect the full scope of her repertoire. *—Richie Unterberger*

The Essence of Nancy Wilson: Four Decades of Music / Feb. 12, 2002 / Capitol ♦♦♦♦♦

Nancy Wilson has recorded a lot of material in several different styles, so an accurate summary is hard to achieve—even on a collection the size of the four-disc *The Essence of Nancy Wilson*. Perhaps realizing this, the compilers have ditched the traditional chronological progression of a box set and instead dedicated each disc to a specific theme. The first disc is "Spanning the Decades," containing "rare singles and charted hits"; the second is a collection of 23 previously unreleased cuts, including an entire unreleased *Live at the Sands* album from August 1968, dubbed "From the Vaults"; each of the 22 selections on the third disc were selected by the artist herself on a disc appropriately called "Nancy's Choice"; the fourth is "Hidden Gems," featuring 18 tracks finding their first U.S. release on CD here. This is an idiosyncratic approach, to say the least, and it does have its charms, especially since the *Live at the Sands* is nicely done (albeit a little supper-clubby), and there are good moments peppered throughout the rarity-filled collections, moments that hardcore collectors will cherish. That doesn't mean that this is the definitive Nancy Wilson set, or that it truly captures her "essence," either, especially since it often leans toward the pop side and does favor the obscure to the basic canon (which essentially is on disc one and much of disc three). That doesn't make this a bad box, since it does have a lot of good Nancy Wilson in one place, plus a lot of interesting material for collectors, but it falls short of being truly definitive. *—Stephen Thomas Erlewine*

The Winans

f. Detroit, MI

Group / Contemporary Gospel, Urban, Black Gospel, CCM

These four brothers hail from Detroit, MI. Their contemporary gospel style reflects traditional black gospel roots. They sang gospel all their lives and began their professional careers in the '80s. Marvin, Carvin, Ronald, and Michael have performed several times with the likes of Michael McDonald, Anita Baker, and Vanessa Bell Armstrong. *—Bil Carpenter*

Introducing the Winans / 1981 / Light ♦♦♦

Tomorrow / 1984 / Platinum ♦♦♦♦♦

Let My People Go / 1985 / Qwest ♦♦♦

Return / 1990 / Qwest ♦♦

The frustrating truth about a lot of R&B and soul that's being made today is that everything tends to be so identical that it's difficult to tell one label from another, one act from another. A soul act on Motown sounds like one on Epic sounds like one on Qwest—all twinkling synthesizers, obnoxious drum machines doing the same programmed beats, all low smooth bass, all the same neatly arranged vocal harmonies. It's all very professional, all very formal, and one wonders, even with gospel acts like the Winans, whether there's any soul left after the gloss has leeched out the interesting wrinkles. It's a sad truth that most of the technology that's been developed since the introduction of MIDI has wound up backing up either R&B acts or new age performers. That major gripe aside, what about this new Winans album, *Return*? Well, it's a nice enough affair, despite the fact that they open the album with one of those mutant rap songs that's also meant to be a forceful number about it being time to stand up and be counted. After that it's a not-too-obnoxious mix of standard-sounding modern R&B and Isley-flavored ballads in which the floating harmonies of the Winans are a constant key. They're just about rough-edged enough still, and forceful enough, that the vocals carry through the synthesizer barrages. On the whole, though, the best numbers here are probably the ballads, such as "When You Cry" and "Together We Stand," in which a real human band interacts nicely with the voices. It's an interesting example, in fact, to listen to the juxtaposition of "Together We Stand" and the following track, "This Time It's Personal"—the latter is a cool, ticking number that does a fair bit of bible-thumping, and has the voices buried under or fighting against a harsh backing track. It's a rather annoying example; the song itself isn't particularly inspiring, and the way in which the performances end up struggling against each other is something of an indictment of the technology in use. The same problem crops up with just about all the tracks produced with machinery—the high end is harsh and brittle, and the rhythm arrangements, never mind anything else, are extremely irritating. Musically, trying to mix gospel with modern R&B is tricky at best, frustrating at worst, and the half-and-half mix here is truly annoying. One hopes that the next time will see the Winans taking their admittedly solid songs into the studio with altogether more flexible performers. Gospel is very much a music of the spirit, and there's very little spirit evident in most of the music on *Return*. *—Steven McDonald*

● **The Very Best of the Winans** / Apr. 16, 2002 / Rhino ♦♦♦♦

This collection covers material stemming from this landmark group's 1981 Light Records debut, *Introducing the Winans*, to their 1993 release *All Out*. Included are such favorites as "The Question Is," "Tomorrow," "Let My People Go," "Ain't No Need to Worry," "It's

Time," "A Friend," and "Payday," among others. This release truly shows why the Winans are considered one of the artists responsible for bridging the gap between gospel and mainstream urban contemporary music. *—Tim A. Smith*

BeBe & CeCe Winans

f. Detroit, MI

Group / Contemporary Gospel, Black Gospel, Urban

Detroit-born brother and sister BeBe (Benjamin) and CeCe (Priscilla) Winans are part of the gospel-singing Winans family that also includes the Winans, their four brothers. As a duo, BeBe & CeCe maintain the gospel message, although their records have the production values and style of contemporary R&B. They released their major label debut album, *BeBe & CeCe Winans,* in 1987 and scored a moderate hit (number 49) on the R&B charts with the single "I.O.U. Me" scoring on the R&B and adult contemporary charts. This earned them three Grammy nominations and one award (gospel). Their second album, *Heaven*, came in 1988 and found them scoring three R&B hits with the title track, "Lost Without You," and "Celebrate Life." The album reached the R&B Top Ten (number 95 in the pop chart) and went gold. 1991's platinum-selling *Different Lifestyles* was their biggest hit yet, topping the R&B album chart and featuring the R&B number ones "Addictive Love" and "I'll Take You There." *— William Ruhlmann*

Lord Lift Us Up / 1985 / PTL ✦✦✦✦✦

BeBe & CeCe Winans / 1987 / Capitol ✦✦✦

Heaven / Sep. 1988 / Capitol ✦✦✦✦✦

If you listen carefully, the songs *are* about Jesus rather than love sweet love, but even a casual hearing lets you know this is one of the most soulful duos to come along since Marvin Gaye & Tammi Terrell. Keith Thomas gives the production a contemporary R&B sheen. *— William Ruhlmann*

Different Lifestyles / Jun. 24, 1991 / Capitol ✦✦✦

On *Different Lifestyles,* BeBe and CeCe Winans employ hip-hop, R&B, jazz and soul sounds to impart their messages of faith and worship; they even bring in rapper Hammer as well as Mavis Staples (for a cover of the 1972 hit "I'll Take You There") for more crossover appeal. It's this same pandering to mainstream tastes that sinks the record; the Winans' spiritual messages simply don't jibe in these secular and pop-oriented settings, and come off stilted and shallow. *—Jason Ankeny*

Relationships / 1994 / Capitol ✦✦✦

The duo's first outing without the involvement of producer Keith Thomas finds them heading toward more down-tempo, ballad-heavy R&B, with Cedric Caldwell and BeBe himself at the producer helm, along with mainstream-heavyweights Arif Mardin and David Foster. *— Thom Granger*

● **Greatest Hits** / Nov. 12, 1996 / Sparrow/EMI ✦✦✦✦✦

Greatest Hits contains 12 of BeBe and CeCe Winans' biggest hits, covering nearly every one of their R&B Top 40 hits, including "Lost Without You," "Addictive Love," "I'll Take You There," "It's O.K.," and "Heaven." In addition to the well-known songs, the collection features two new tracks, one of which—"Feels Like Heaven (With You)"—became a hit single upon the album's release. It's an excellent retrospective of one of contemporary gospel's finest groups. *—Rodney Batdorf*

CeCe Winans

b. Detroit, MI

Vocals / Contemporary Gospel, Black Gospel, Urban

The eighth of ten siblings in the musical Winans family, CeCe Winans (born Priscilla) performed most often with her brother, BeBe, in a duo which recorded gospel material with R&B settings and proved to be the most commercially successful of the Winans groupings (which also includes her older brothers Marvin, Carvin, Ronald, and Michael in the Winans and her parents in Mom & Pop Winans). Born in Detroit, she worked with BeBe in a duo called the PTL Singers until 1987, when they released their self-titled debut album (with vocal contributions from nine members of the family). Four albums followed during the next seven years (two of which hit gold) plus 1991's platinum *Different Lifestyles.* The duo's success increased as they added more contemporary forms of production—their two number-one R&B singles, "Addictive Love" and "I'll Take You There," both treated spiritual love in fuzzy terms just as conducive to the physical.

After 1994's *Relationships*, CeCe began recording her very first solo album. Released in 1995, *Alone in His Presence* found her working her way back to traditional gospel, singing standards like "Great Is Thy Faithfulness," "Blessed Assurance," and "I Surrender All." *His Gift* followed in 1998, and a year later Winans returned with *Alabaster Box.* *—John Bush*

Alone in His Presence / Oct. 10, 1995 / Sparrow ✦✦✦

The R&B grooves of her earlier recordings with The Winans' give way to a more string-oriented traditional gospel sound (exemplified by "Blessed Assurance" and "Great Is Thy Faithfulness") on her solo debut. *—John Bush*

● **Everlasting Love** / Mar. 17, 1998 / Pioneer ✦✦✦✦✦

For her second solo album, CeCe Winans decided to record a full-fledged urban R&B/soul album, enlisting an impressive array of guest artists and collaborators—including Keith Crouch, Tony Rich, Lauryn Hill, Diane Warren, Daryl Simmons and Tommy Sims—to record *Everlasting Love.* All of the guest stars do nothing but enhance Winans' talents. There is no doubt this is her record, and she breathes life even into the weaker material. Fortunately, there isn't much that's weak on *Everlasting Love.* The songwriting is consistently classy, the production is polished without being slick, and Winans' voice simply soars. The only gospel inflections that remain are in her singing, as all of the songs, with the exception of Hill's direct, affecting "On That Day," have a distinct contemporary flavor. It's to Winans' credit that she flourishes in this setting and makes the album as personal as her gospel album *Alone in His Presence.* *— Stephen Thomas Erlewine*

CeCe Winans / Jun. 19, 2001 / Sparrow ✦✦✦✦

After eight years of performing as a duo with brother BeBe Winans, 1995 saw the beginning of CeCe Winans' solo career, a move that only served to further the artistry and ministry of this singer/songwriter. In 2001, Winans' self-titled release marked her second album from Wellspring Gospel. The follow-up project to her 1999 gold-certified album, *Alabaster Box,* the release combines a variety of styles, including CCM, pop, urban, R&B, inspirational, and gospel. Winans had no doubt as to the direction and purpose of the self-titled release. In fact, with it she desired for "people to feel encouragement and passion." And the album does just that. Upbeat, energy-filled, and enthusiastic, the project is not only musically diverse but offers hard-hitting messages. The song "It's Gonna Get Better" was written with teen suicide prevention programs in mind, while "Bring Back the Days of Yea and Nay," a duet with brother Marvin Winans, challenges parents to take responsibility for training their children. A definite highlight on the album is the song "Looking Back at You." It is an inspirational track, leaning toward a ballad, that speaks of God's unfailing and unconditional love. *—Ashleigh Kittle*

Angela Winbush

b. St. Louis, MO

Vocals, Keyboards, Synthesizer / Urban, Quiet Storm, Dance-Pop

Singer/songwriter/keyboardist/producer Angela Winbush's credentials include her own solo hits such as her number-one R&B hit, "Angel"; hits as one-half of the singing duo Rene & Angela and their hits "Save Your Love (For #1)" and "Your Smile"; and her hits by Stephanie Mills and the Isley Brothers. One Rene & Angela hit, the 1983 ballad "My First Love," was covered by Avant on his spring 2000 debut CD, *My Thoughts.* Winbush's own albums are *Sharp, Angela Winbush,* and *It's the Real Thing.* Besides Rene Moore, Winbush's early collaborators were Moore's brother, Rufus, bassist Bobby Watson, engineer/producer Bruce Swedien, and George Duke.

Born in St. Louis, MO, Winbush grew up singing gospel music in the church choir and learned to play piano as a child. She had no intentions of pursuing a professional music career when she began attending Washington, D.C.'s Howard University majoring in architecture. To earn money to pay expenses, she began singing on recording sessions and formed a singing trio that opened for Van McCoy and Al Jarreau. She became interested in the music business and changed her major to music education.

Around 1977, Winbush sent a demo tape to New York DJ Gary Byrd. He played it over the phone for his friend Stevie Wonder. He called Winbush and invited her to Los Angeles. While singing in Wonder's backup band Wonderlove, Winbush learned about writing and producing by sitting in on sessions with Wonder. In 1980, she met singer/songwriter Rene Moore through Wonderlove vocalist Carolyn Dennis and they began writing songs together, eventually forming the duo Rene & Angela. In 1978, former Tower of Power lead singer Lenny Williams recorded one of their songs, "Changes." A friend introduced the duo to Dr. Cecil Hale, a Capitol Records executive who signed the duo to the label. Two LPs were issued, *Wall to Wall* and *Rise.* Another Rene & Angela song, the ballad "I Have Learned to Respect the Power of Love," was recorded by Alton McClain and Destiny on their self-titled 1978 Polydor LP. It can be found on Polygram's *Power of Love: Best of Soul Essentials Ballads.* In 1985, Rene & Angela signed with Polygram and were assigned to their Mercury imprint. Their label debut, *Street Called Desire,* went gold, yielding the number one hits "Save Your Love (For #1)," which featured a rap by Kurtis Blow, and "Your Smile." An earlier Rene & Angela song would resurface in a big way. The first single from Stephanie Mills' 1985 *Stephanie Mills* album was "Stand Back"; on its flip side was her passionate cover of "I Have Learned to Respect the Power of Love." Because of its massive radio play as an album track, Mills' version, produced by Philly Soul keyboardist Ron Kersey, was reissued as an A-side and held the number-one spot for two weeks in spring 1986.

By 1987, Winbush was solo and got her first production job on the Isley Brothers' *Smooth Sailing* LP after the group's lead singer, Ronald Isley, mentioned to Warner Bros. records executive Benny Medina that he wanted to work with the group who did "Your Smile." After working together, Isley became the singer's manager. Becoming romantically involved, Winbush married Ronald Isley on June 26, 1993. She produced and wrote the bulk of his solo debut, *Spend the Night,* credited as the Isley Brothers Featuring Ronald Isley. Winbush's other credits include the platinum Isley Brothers album *Mission to Please,* Body, Lalah Hathaway, the 1982 self-titled debut of Plush, Klymaxx, Sheena Easton's *The Lover in Me,* and the 1993 Warner Bros. various artists set, *A Tribute to Curtis Mayfield.* *—Ed Hogan*

● **Sharp** / 1987 / Mercury ✦✦✦✦

It's the Real Thing / May 1989 / Mercury ✦✦✦

In the late 1980s, thin-voiced females who couldn't sing were quite prevalent in the urban contemporary arena. But thankfully, singers like Meli'sa Morgan, Vesta Williams and Angela Winbush were around to remind us that big-voiced belters still had a place in R&B. Originally part of the duo Rene & Angela, Winbush went solo in 1987 and formed a lucrative partnership with husband-to-be Ronald Isley. Winbush's input proved beneficial on the Isley Brothers' albums, and vice versa. Although Winbush (whose emotive singing is along the lines of Chaka Khan and Alicia Myers) does all of the composing, producing and arranging on her second solo album, *The Real Thing,* Isley serves as executive producer. And his influence is very noticeable on the electro-funk of "No More Tears" and "It's the Real Thing," as well as softer, more relaxed cuts like "Please Bring Your Love Back," "Precious" and "Menage A Trois" (which isn't an ode to kinky sex, but a call for monogamy and fidelity). For all its slickness and high-tech production gloss, this is an album with plenty of soul and grit. *—Alex Henderson*

Angela Winbush / Mar. 15, 1994 / Elektra ✦✦✦

Angela Winbush has seductive, entrancing tracks like "Treat U Rite," "Keep Turning Me On," and "Hot Summer Love." A singer's singer, Winbush's intense, sinewy vocalizing can turn the most mundane arrangement into the sweetest ear candy. The only disappointment is her ballyhooed remake of Marvin Gaye's "Inner City Blues (Make Me Wanna Holler)." *—Andrew Hamilton*

- **Ultimate Collection** / Jan. 23, 2001 / Hip-O ✦✦✦✦

While the title of *The Ultimate Collection* may be overstating the matters somewhat, this 17-track compilation does come very close to fulfilling the title's promise. This compilation concentrates on Angela Winbush's late-'80s recordings for Mercury, dipping into the early '80s and early '90s on occasion, so some may complain that it's too focused on a particular era, yet that helps the collection, since that's when Winbush was at her best. Relying on single versions, radio mixes, and edits (though there are several album versions here, as well), this gives a good portrait of what Winbush was all about—smooth urban soul, graced with exceptional vocals. Her material may not always be first-rate, but her performances are usually impassioned, and this collection makes an excellent case for her talents. *—Stephen Thomas Erlewine*

The Winstons

f. Washington, D.C.

Group / R&B, Soul, Beach, Pop-Soul

A Washington, D.C.-based soul act led by Richard Spencer, the Winstons signed to Curtom in early 1968 and lasted there for one single, the rousing "Need a Replacement." They had a sound that was somewhat similar to the Impressions, but were unfortunate enough to have signed with Curtom before the label had national distribution, and the single never got the play it should have. A year after leaving Curtom, they hit for the Metromedia label with a huge single called "Color Him Father," which became a Top Ten R&B and pop hit, just missing number one on the R&B list, and also earned a Grammy for Best R&B Song. It was both a great tribute number and outstanding lead vocal from Richard Spencer, along with Ray Maritano, Quincy Mattison, Phil Tolotta, Sonny Peckrol, and G.C. Coleman. Mattison and Coleman were veterans of Otis Redding's band. The Winstons eventually toured as the backup band for the Impressions, but never again made any noise on the charts. *—Ron Wynn & Bruce Eder*

- **Color Him Father** / 1969 / Metromedia ✦✦✦

Ruby Winters

Vocals / Soul, R&B

Vocalist Ruby Winters recorded several energetic soul singles for tiny labels throughout the late '60s and early '70s, but never could break out beyond regional status. Winters was born in Kentucky, but raised in Cinncinnati. She had her first chart hit in 1967, teaming with Johnny Thunder for a duet remake of Jo Stafford's 1954 single "Make Love to Me." Their version peaked at number 13 on the R&B charts. She had another Top 20 hit with "I Don't Want to Cry" in 1969 for Diamond, and one final Top 20 single in 1969 with "Guess Who." Subsequent releases on Polydor, Playboy, and Millennium through the '70s failed to generate much interest. *—Ron Wynn*

Ruby Winters / 1978 / Creole ✦✦✦

- **I Will** / 1980 / Millennium ✦✦✦

Ruby Winters is cut from the same mold as Dorothy "Misty Blue" Moore: She sings stately Southern soul and contemporary country ballads with an easy, smoldering passion. "I Will" made some waves overseas, and even did some business in the States. Her rendition of "Neither One of Us," originally done by Gladys Knight & the Pips, is a moving experience and, along with the title track, the best song here. She motors down country roads on "For the Good Times," "I Won't Mention It Again," and "I Can't Fake It Anymore," all strong ballads. The gospel-tinged "If This Is Our Last Time" is the only song she breaks a sweat on. *—Andrew Hamilton*

Bill Withers

b. Jul. 4, 1938, Slab Fork, WV

Vocals / Soul, Smooth Soul, Urban

Songwriter/singer/guitarist Bill Withers is best remembered for the classic "Lean on Me" and his other million-selling singles "Ain't No Sunshine" and "Use Me," but he has a sizable cache of great songs to his credit. Al Jarreau recorded an entire CD of Withers' songs on *Tribute to Bill Withers* (Culture Press 1998). His popular radio-aired LP track from *Still Bill*, "Who Is He? (And What Is He to You?)," was a 1974 R&B hit for Creative Source. Born July 4, 1938, in Slab Folk, WV, Withers was the youngest of six children. His father died when he was a child and he was raised by his mother and grandmother. After a nine-year stint in the Navy, Withers moved to Los Angeles to pursue a music career in 1967. He recorded demos at night while working at the Boeing aircraft company where he made toilet seats. His recording career began after being introduced to Clarence Avant, president of Sussex Records.

Stax Records stalwart Booker T. Jones produced his debut album, *Just As I Am* (with some co-production by Al Jackson Jr.), which included his first charting single, "Ain't No Sunshine" that went gold and made it to number-six R&B and number-three pop in summer 1971 and won a Grammy as Best R&B Song. Its follow-up, "Grandma Hands," peaked at number-18 R&B in fall 1971. The song was later covered by the Staple Singers and received airplay as a track from their 1973 Stax LP *Be What You Are*. "Just As I Am" featured lead guitar by Stephen Stills and hit number-five R&B in summer 1971.

Withers wrote "Lean on Me" based on his experiences growing up in a West Virginia coal mining town. Times were hard and when a neighbor needed something beyond their means, the rest of the community would chip in and help. He came up with the chord progression while noodling around on his new Wurlitzer electric piano. The sound of the chords reminded Withers of the hymns that he heard at church while he was growing up. On the session for "Lean on Me," members of the Watts 103rd Street Rhythm Band ("Express Yourself," "Loveland") were used: drummer James Gadson, keyboardist Ray Jackson, guitarist Benorce Blackman (co-wrote with Withers "The Best You Can" from *Making Music*), and bassist Melvin Dunlop. His second gold single, "Lean on Me," landed at number-one R&B and number-one pop for three weeks on *Billboard*'s charts in summer 1972. It was included on his *Still Bill* album which went gold, holding the number one R&B spot for six weeks and hitting number-four pop in spring 1972. "Lean on Me" has became a standard with hit covers by U.K. rock band Mud and Club Nouveau. "Lean on Me" was also the title theme of a 1989 movie starring Morgan Freeman. *Still Bill* also included "Use Me" (gold, number-two R&B for two weeks and number-two pop for two weeks in fall 1972) .

Withers' Sussex catalog also included *Bill Withers Live at Carnegie Hall*, *'Justments*, and *The Best of Bill Withers*. Withers contributed "Better Days" to the soundtrack of the Bill Cosby 1971 western *Man And Boy*, released on Sussex. There was a duet single with Bobby Womack on United Artists, "It's All Over Now," from summer 1975. After a legal battle with Sussex, Withers signed with Columbia Records. Columbia later bought his Sussex masters when the label went out of business. Withers was briefly married actress Denise Nicholas (ABC-TV's *Room 222* and the 1972 horror film *Blacula*) in the early '70s. His releases on Columbia were *Making Music* ("Make Love to Your Mind," number-ten R&B), which hit number-seven R&B in late 1975; *Naked and Warm*; *Menagerie* ("Lovely Day," a number-six R&B hit), which went gold in 1977; and *'Bout Love* from spring 1979.

Teaming with Elektra Records artist Grover Washington Jr., Withers sang the crystalline ballad "Just the Two of Us," written by Withers, Ralph MacDonald, and William Salter. It went to number-three R&B and held the number-two pop spot for three weeks in early 1981. "Just the Two of Us" was redone with hilarious effect in the Mike Myers movie *Austin Powers: The Spy Who Shagged Me*, released in summer 1999. Withers teamed with MacDonald for MacDonald's Polydor single "In the Name of Love" in summer 1984. Withers' last charting LP was *Watching You, Watching Me* in spring 1985. He occasionally did dates with Grover Washington Jr., during the '90s. His songs and recordings have been used as both the source of numerous covers (Aaron Neville's "Use Me") and sampled by a multitude of hip-hop/rap groups. *—Ed Hogan*

Just as I Am / 1971 / Sussex ✦✦✦✦✦

☆ **Still Bill** / 1972 / Sussex ✦✦✦✦✦

Bill Withers came into his own on his third album, *Still Bill*. Released in 1972, the record is a remarkable summation of a number of contemporary styles: the smooth soul coming out of Philly, smoky, late-night funk via Bobby Womack, bluesy Southern soul, and '70s singer/songwriterism. It's rich, subtly layered music, but its best attribute is that it comes on easy, never sounding labored or overworked. In fact, it takes several spins of the album to realize just how versatile Withers is on *Still Bill*, to hear how he makes intricate, funky rhythms sound as effortless and simple as the album's best-known song, the gospel-tinged inspirational anthem "Lean on Me." That's the genius behind Withers' music: it's warm and easily accessible, but it has a depth and complexity that reveals itself over numerous plays—and, given the sound and feel of the music, from the lush arrangements to his comforting voice, it's easy to want to play this again and again. Then there's the quality of the songwriting, which is as assured on the grooving "Lonely Town, Lonely Street" as it is on the suspicious, paranoid "Who Is He (And What Is He to You)?" or "Use Me," where he happily submits to being used by his object of affection. This high level of songwriting is sustained throughout the record, making this the greatest testament to his considerable gifts. [The 2003 reissue contains two bonus tracks from his *Live at Carnegie Hall* album.] *—Stephen Thomas Erlewine*

Live at Carnegie Hall / 1973 / Columbia/Legacy ✦✦✦✦

A wonderful live album that capitalizes on Withers' trademark melancholy soul sound while expanding the music to fit the room granted by a live show. Lovely versions of "Grandma's Hands" and "Lean on Me" are balanced by heartfelt downbeat numbers like "Better Off Dead" and "I Can't Write Left-Handed," the latter being an anti-war song with a chilling message. The set finishes off with the lengthy "Harlem/Cold Baloney," with lots of audience-pleased call-and-response going on. It's one of the best live releases from the '70s. *—Steven McDonald*

Making Music / 1975 / CBS ✦✦✦

Naked & Warm / 1976 / Columbia ✦✦✦

Menagerie / 1977 / CBS ✦✦✦✦✦

Following the twin peaks of *Still Bill* and *Live at Carnegie Hall* in the early '70s, Bill Withers had a little trouble sustaining his peak of creativity, along with his chart positions. He still made good music and had hits, but had trouble delivering a consistent album that brought him back to the heights of his Sussex work. Finally, in 1977, he delivered *Menagerie*, an assured return to form by one of soul's greatest singer/songwriters of the '70s. If *Menagerie* doesn't have the earthiness or consistent brilliance of *Still Bill*, it nevertheless has a solid set of songs and an easy, relaxed charm that is thoroughly winning. Where his Sussex material was slyly eclectic, touching on a number of different styles, this album is more cohesive, a smooth album that points the way toward quiet storm while retaining a warm soulfulness, largely due to Withers' wonderful voice. Even when the tempo gets sprightly, as on "Lovely Night for Dancing," there's a relaxed vibe and a nice sheen to the production that keeps things even-handed and easy. As such, those listeners who preferred the darker undercurrents that ran through such songs as "Use Me" and "Who Is He (And What Is He to You)?" may find this a little too amiable, but that's just a matter of taste—this is an easy record to like, after all, with a consistent tone and a soothing vibe, plus a good set of songs. If it's not as distinctive as his Sussex records, it's nevertheless an undeniable high point in his catalog. [The 2003 reissue contains three bonus tracks: a previously unreleased demo of "Rosie," a single version of "Lovely Night for Dancing," and an instrumental of "Let Me Be the One You Need."] *—Stephen Thomas Erlewine*

'Bout Love / 1979 / CBS ✦✦

Bill Withers collaborated with keyboardist/arranger/songwriter Paul Smith on this engaging set issued. *Still Bill* offers his usual mellowness and down-home sincerity on such cuts as "All Because of You," "Dedicated to You My Love," and the brotherly love-themed "Look to Each Other for Love." There are surprising uptempo tracks like the horn-punctuated Top 30 R&B lead single "Don't Make It Better," and the back-alley funk of its follow-up, "You Got the Stuff," with its squishy, cartoonish vocoder-generated background vocals. "Love Is" and "All Because of You" are on *Ain't No Sunshine* issued by BMG International on February 29, 2000. "Love Is" was covered by dance artist Gino Soccio on his *S Beat* LP. *—Ed Hogan*

The Best of Bill Withers / 1980 / CBS ♦♦♦

Greatest Hits / 1981 / Columbia ♦♦♦♦

Lean on Me: The Best of Bill Withers / Aug. 9, 1994 / Columbia/Legacy ♦♦♦♦♦
Here are 18 tracks, from the early '70s to the mid-'80s, including his early Top Ten singles, but also minor hits like "Grandma's Hands," "Kissing My Love," and "Lovely Day." Those who admire songs like "Lean on Me" and "Ain't No Sunshine" are advised to approach this best-of with caution; from the mid-'70s onward, Withers forsook his folky singer-songwriter soul for more anonymous, slick MOR soul and urban contemporary. His early sound was far more distinctive, and his early-'70s Sussex albums are recommended alternatives to this compilation. *—Richie Unterberger*

● **The Best of Bill Withers: Lean on Me** / May 30, 2000 / Columbia/Legacy ♦♦♦♦♦
Collectors note: This is *not* the same as the very similarly titled *Lean on Me: The Best of Bill Withers*, a 1994 best-of that also came out on Columbia/Legacy. Each disc has 18 tracks and includes his biggest and best hits, yet only 13 of the songs are found on both CDs, and the 2000 compilation has a new set of liner notes by David Ritz. This is still too light on his earliest Sussex material, which is his best work and is represented by just seven of the tunes. It's also messily sequenced, with six less impressive and poppier mid-1970s Columbia outings leading off the program before you get to the early '70s goodies, including "Ain't No Sunshine," "Lean on Me," and "Use Me." Still, this would have to get the nod over the 1994 best-of just for the inclusion of one of those Sussex tunes alone, the uplifting and earthily bluesy 1971 cut "Harlem." *—Richie Unterberger*

Jimmy Witherspoon

b. Aug. 8, 1923, Gurdon, AR, **d.** Sep. 18, 1997, Los Angeles, CA
Vocals / Urban Blues, Jazz Blues, Jump Blues

One of the great blues singers of the post-World War II period, Jimmy Witherspoon was also versatile enough to fit comfortably into the jazz world. Witherspoon was born on August 8, 1923, in Gurdon, AR. As a child, he sang in a church choir, and made his debut recordings with Jay McShann for Philo and Mercury in 1945 and 1946. His own first recordings, using McShann's band, resulted in a number-one R&B hit in 1949 with "Ain't Nobody's Business, Pts. 1 & 2" on Supreme Records. Live performances of "No Rollin' Blues" and "Big Fine Girl" provided 'Spoon with two more hits in 1950.

The mid-'50s were a lean time, with his style of shouting blues temporarily out of fashion; singles were tried for Federal, Chess, Atco, Vee Jay, and others, with little success. *Jimmy Witherspoon at the Monterey Jazz Festival* (HiFi Jazz) from 1959 lifted him back into the limelight. Partnerships with Ben Webster or Groove Holmes were recorded, and he toured Europe in 1961 with Buck Clayton, performing overseas many more times in the decades to follow; some memorable music resulted, but Witherspoon's best 1960s album is *Evenin' Blues* (Prestige), which features T-Bone Walker on guitar and Clifford Scott on saxophone. As the '70s began, Witherspoon decided to take a short break from live performances, settled in Los Angeles, took a job as a disc jockey, and continued making records. In 1971 Witherspoon teamed up with former Animals vocalist Eric Burdon for the album *Guilty*. Unfortunately it sold poorly.

By 1973 his short retirement from live performances was over. Witherspoon was ready to get back on the road and assembled an amazing band featuring a young Robben Ford on lead guitar. Those live shows had received positive reviews, rejuvenating Witherspoon's move toward a definite rock/soul sound. He traveled to London in 1974 to record *Love Is a Five Letter Word* with British blues producer Mike Vernon. Vernon had produced critically acclaimed British blues albums by John Mayall, Fleetwood Mac, and Ten Years After. By the early '80s, Witherspoon was diagnosed with throat cancer. Although he remained active and was a popular concert attraction, the effect of the disease on his vocals was obvious. Witherspoon passed away on September 18, 1997, at the age of 74. *—Bob Porter, Scott Yanow & Al Campbell*

Singin' the Blues / 1959 / Blue Note ♦♦♦♦♦
Jimmy Witherspoon is heard in superior form throughout the two Pacific Jazz sessions included here. With fine backup and short solos from either Harry "Sweets" Edison (in top form) or Gerald Wilson on trumpet, both Teddy Edwards and Jimmy Allen on tenors, Henry McDode or Hampton Hawes on piano, rhythm guitarist Herman Mitchell, bassist Jimmy Hamilton and drummer Jimmy Miller, 'Spoon digs into such numbers as "When I've Been Drinkin'," "Then the Lights Go Out," "There's Good Rockin' Tonight" and a remake of his big hit "'Tain't Nobody's Business." The closing "Midnight Blues" is an instrumental, giving the band a chance to stretch out a bit. Recommended. *—Scott Yanow*

Roots / 1962 / Reprise ♦♦

Baby Baby Baby / Mar. 6, 1963 / Bluesville/Original Blues Classics ♦♦♦
Veteran singer Jimmy Witherspoon is in good voice on this CD reissue, performing a dozen two- to four-minute songs that include such blues standards as Duke Ellington's "Rocks in My Bed," "Bad Bad Whiskey," "One Scotch, One Bourbon, One Beer" and "It's a Lonesome Old World." He is joined by a quintet featuring altoist Leo Wright and guitarist Kenny Burrell on the first eight numbers and a background septet (with trumpeter Bobby Bryant and Arthur Wright on harmonica) for the remainder of the set. The music is enjoyable if not classic, and should please Witherspoon's many fans. *—Scott Yanow*

Evenin' Blues / Aug. 15, 1963 / Prestige/Original Blues Classics ♦♦♦♦
A good, relaxed (but not laid-back) session, and one of his bluesier ones, with organ, Clifford Scott (who played on Bill Doggett's "Honky Tonk") on sax, and T-Bone Walker on guitar. Nothing too adventurous about the song selection, including well-traveled items like "Good Rockin' Tonight" and "Kansas City," but Witherspoon sings them with ingratiating soul, reaching his peaks on his cover of "Don't Let Go" (perhaps better than the hit version by Roy Hamilton) and the late-night ambience of the title track. [The CD reissue adds previously unissued alternate takes of four of the songs.] *—Richie Unterberger*

Blues Around the Clock / Nov. 5, 1963 / Prestige/Original Blues Classics ♦♦♦

Blue Spoon / 1964 / Prestige ♦♦♦
Blue Spoon was one of Witherspoon's jazzier sessions, still retaining his characteristic jazz-blues blend, but lighter on the soul, pop, and shouting R&B elements of some of his other releases. The jazzy flavor was guaranteed by his backup quartet of Kenny Burrell on guitar, Eddie Kahn on bass, Gildo Mahones on piano, and Roy Haynes on drums. Dominated by ballads, it's on the mellow side, with a pleasant yet unadventurous selection of covers. These include Cecil Gant's "I Wonder," "Nobody Knows You When You're Down and Out," "It's All in the Game," and "Baby Please Don't Go" (here retitled "Back to New Orleans," with the writing credits given to Brownie McGhee & Sonny Terry). Kenny Burrell contributed one composition, "Blues in the Morning." [The album was combined with a quite different 1965 session, *Spoon in London*, on a 2001 single-CD reissue.] *—Richie Unterberger*

Spoon in London / 1965 / Prestige ♦♦♦♦
Spoon in London is an uncharacteristic entry in the Witherspoon catalog. Recorded in London in June 1965, there's a definite soul-pop slant to the production, with backup women singers that wouldn't have been out of place at a Ray Charles session; brassy, bright arrangements; and lean blues-rock guitar backup that leads one to suspect that an ace U.K. session man like Jimmy Page or Big Jim Sullivan might have been responsible (the personnel, unfortunately, is not documented). The orchestra was arranged and conducted by Benny Golson, and there's a definite sense of trying to cross Witherspoon's habitual classy soul-jazz over into the soul and rock markets. Purists, of course, will probably be offended, but, in fact, this deviation from the usual format makes this one of Witherspoon's more interesting and, yes, fun releases. He's more than up to the task of broaching this territory, sounding rather like a cross between Ray Charles and Brook Benton at times (yet closer to Benton). Tracks like "Free Spirits" swing in a more traditionally jazz manner; "Room for Everybody" has a sing-along country-folk feel; and "Two Hearts Are Better Than One" is decorated by odd Dixieland touches. [The album was combined with a quite different 1964 session, *Blue Spoon*, on a 2001 single-CD reissue.] *—Richie Unterberger*

★ **The 'Spoon Concerts** / Jul. 11, 1989 / Fantasy ♦♦♦♦♦
This single CD (which reissues all of the music from an earlier two-LP set) includes the high point of singer Jimmy Witherspoon's career. On October 2, 1959, he appeared at the Monterey Jazz Festival and created such a sensation that it caused his career to go through a renaissance. Heard at the peak of his powers, Witherspoon holds his own with a mighty group of veterans (trumpeter Roy Eldridge, both Ben Webster and Coleman Hawkins on tenors, clarinetist Woody Herman, pianist Earl Hines, bassist Vernon Alley, and drummer Mel Lewis). Although the five-song set only lasted 25 minutes, Witherspoon's performance was the hit of the festival. The other half of this CD features Witherspoon romping through ten mostly traditional blues songs two months later with Webster, baritonist Gerry Mulligan, pianist Jimmy Rowles, bassist Leroy Vinnegar, and drummer Mel Lewis; the performance is equally exciting. Highly recommended, this CD is the one truly essential Jimmy Witherspoon release. *—Scott Yanow*

☆ **Blowin' in from Kansas City** / 1993 / Flair ♦♦♦♦♦
These 20 tunes pair the great Mr. Witherspoon with the finest jazz, jump, and blues talents around. Jay McShann, Maxwell Davis, Tiny Webb, and Chuck Norris are only a few of the first-rate sessionmen and arrangers who grace the tracks of this essential CD. A special mention must be made of tenor sax legend Ben Webster, whose solo on "I'm Going Around in Circles" is simply magnificent. This is quintessential Kansas City blues. Of all the shouters, Witherspoon is perhaps the greatest singer. *—Larry Hoffman*

Ain't Nobody's Business / Oct. 1, 1996 / Jazz Hour ♦♦♦♦♦
It is unfortunate that the recording dates and personnel are not given on this budget CD, for the performances (although not always that well-recorded) are excellent. Singer Jimmy Witherspoon is heard near the beginning of his career. Five songs (the third through the seventh) are taken from a Pasadena concert on May 9, 1949. Backed by pianist Gene Gilbeaux's quartet (with Donald Hill featured on alto), Witherspoon is in extroverted form entertaining the enthusiastic crowd; on "New Orleans Woman," a few unidentified horns honk away to the audience's enjoyment. Of the other five songs, two are from 1950 ("I Done Found Out" and "Fickle Woman") and have Witherspoon backed by a nonet including pianist Jay McShann and tenor saxophonist Maxwell Davis. "Good Jumpin'" is with the Buddy Floyd sextet in 1948, and two others are not listed in discographies. But details aside, the enjoyable music straddles the boundary between blues, early R&B, and jazz. *—Scott Yanow*

● **Jazz Me Blues: The Best of Jimmy Witherspoon** / May 6, 1998 / Prestige ♦♦♦♦♦
Whether this is truly the "best" of Witherspoon is debatable—there's nothing predating 1956—however, it's a good 20-track sampling of 1956-1966 material, favoring (but not limited to) his sessions for Prestige. Witherspoon puts his imprint on a lot of blues/R&B classics—"Good Rockin' Tonight," "Bad Bad Whiskey," "One Scotch, One Bourbon, One Beer," "C.C. Rider," "Money's Gettin' Cheaper, "T'Ain't Nobody's Bizness"—and while not everyone will find these to be his definitive versions, they *are* all good ones. The roster of jazz luminaries heard at one point or another over the course of the disc is staggering, including Coleman Hawkins, Woody Herman, Gerry Mulligan, T-Bone Walker, Kenny Burrell, and Pepper Adams. Never do they overshadow the singer, and on the whole this is one of the better jazz/blues vocal collections available, displaying his skill in both small combos and big bands. *—Richie Unterberger*

Blue Spoon/Spoon in London / 2001 / Prestige/Original Blues Classics ✦✦✦✦
This CD combines two chronologically close, but stylistically different, LPs onto a single-disc reissue. *Blue Spoon*, from 1964, was one of Witherspoon's jazzier sessions, still retaining his characteristic jazz-blues blend, but lighter on the soul, pop, and shouting R&B elements of some of his other releases. The jazzy flavor was guaranteed by his backup quartet of Kenny Burrell on guitar, Eddie Kahn on bass, Gildo Mahones on piano, and Roy Haynes on drums. Dominated by ballads, it's on the mellow side, with a pleasant yet unadventurous selection of covers. These include Cecil Gant's "I Wonder," "Nobody Knows You When You're Down and Out," "It's All in the Game," and "Baby Please Don't Go" (here retitled "Back to New Orleans," with the writing credits given to Brownie McGhee & Sonny Terry). Kenny Burrell contributed one composition, "Blues in the Morning." *Spoon in London* is an uncharacteristic entry in the Witherspoon catalog. Recorded in London in June 1965, there's a definite soul-pop slant to the production, with backup woman singers who wouldn't have been out of place at a Ray Charles session; brassy, bright arrangements; and lean blues-rock guitar backup that leads one to suspect that an ace U.K. session man like Jimmy Page or Big Jim Sullivan might have been responsible (the personnel, unfortunately, are not documented). The orchestra was arranged and conducted by Benny Golson, and there's a definite sense of trying to cross Witherspoon's habitual classy soul-jazz over into the soul and rock markets. Purists, of course, will probably be offended, but in fact this deviation from the usual format makes this one of Witherspoon's more interesting and, yes, fun releases. He's more than up to the task of broaching this territory, sounding rather like a cross between Ray Charles and Brook Benton at times (yet closer to Benton). Tracks like "Free Spirits" swing in a more traditionally jazz manner; "Room for Everybody" has a singalong country-folk feel; and "Two Hearts Are Better Than One" is decorated by odd Dixieland touches. *—Richie Unterberger*

Womack & Womack

f. 1982
Group / Soul, Urban, R&B
Cecil Womack (born 1947) and his wife Linda (born 1952) had a long history before the release of their first duo album in 1983. Cecil was one of the gospel-singing Womack Brothers who became the Valentinos and toured with Sam Cooke in the early '60s; Linda was Cooke's daughter. Both Womacks were successful songwriters for such performers as Teddy Pendergrass, Wilson Pickett, and Aretha Franklin prior to hooking up as a performing team. The focus is on songwriting in their collaboration; they began with *Love Wars*, which featured the Top 40 R&B hit "Baby I'm Scared of You." *Radio M.U.S.I.C. Man* (1985) contains unfinished Sam Cooke songs completed by the duo. It was followed by *Conscience* in 1988 and *Family Spirit* in 1991. *—William Ruhlmann*

● **Love Wars** / 1983 / Elektra ✦✦✦✦✦
Womack & Womack are steeped in the early-'60s style of Cecil's Valentinos and Linda's father, Sam Cooke, but they have updated the style. Nevertheless, this is contemporary soul likely to be embraced by fans of Cooke, Otis Redding, and others of the genre. *—William Ruhlmann*

Radio M.U.S.I.C. Man / 1985 / Elektra ✦✦✦

Conscience / Jun. 13, 1988 / Island ✦✦✦

Transformation to the House of Zekkariyas / May 25, 1993 / Warner Bros. ✦✦

Bobby Womack

b. Mar. 4, 1944, Cleveland, OH
Guitar, Vocals, Producer / Soul, Smooth Soul, Blaxploitation, Quiet Storm
A veteran who paid his dues for over a decade before getting his shot at solo stardom, Bobby Womack persevered through tragedy and addiction to emerge as one of soul music's great survivors. Able to shine in the spotlight as a singer or behind the scenes as an instrumentalist and songwriter, Womack never got his due from pop audiences, but during the late '60s and much of the '70s, he was a consistent hitmaker on the R&B charts, with a high standard of quality control. His records were quintessential soul, with a bag of tricks learned from the likes of Sam Cooke, Wilson Pickett, and Sly Stone, all of whom Womack worked closely with at one time or another. Yet often, they also bore the stamp of Womack's own idiosyncratic personality, whether through a lengthy spoken philosophical monologue or a radical reinterpretation of a pop standard. An underrated guitarist, Womack helped pioneer a lean, minimalist approach similar to that of Curtis Mayfield, and was an early influence on the young Jimi Hendrix. Additionally, his songs have been recorded by numerous artists in the realms of both R&B and rock, and the best of them rank as all-time classics.

Bobby Dwayne Womack was born in Cleveland on March 4, 1944. His upbringing was strict and religious, but his father Friendly also encouraged his sons to pursue music as he had (he sang and played guitar in a gospel group). In the early '50s, while still a child, Bobby joined his siblings Cecil, Curtis, Harry, and Friendly Jr. to form the gospel quintet the Womack Brothers. They were chosen to open a local show for the Soul Stirrers in 1953, where Bobby befriended lead singer Sam Cooke; following this break, they toured the country as an opening act for numerous gospel groups. When Cooke formed his own SAR label, he recruited the Womack Brothers with an eye towards transforming them into a crossover R&B act. Learning that his sons were moving into secular music, Friendly Womack threw them out of the house, and Cooke wired them the money to buy a car and drive out to his Los Angeles offices. The Womack Brothers made several recordings for SAR over 1960 and 1961, including a few gospel sides, but Cooke soon convinced them to record R&B and renamed them the Valentinos. In 1962, they scored a Top Ten hit on the R&B charts with "Lookin' for a Love," and Cooke sent them on the road behind James Brown to serve a boot-camp-style musical apprenticeship. Bobby eventually joined Cooke's backing band as guitarist. The Valentinos' 1964 single "It's All Over Now," written by Bobby, was quickly covered by the Rolling Stones with Cooke's blessing; when it became the Stones' first U.K. number one, Womack suddenly found himself a rich man.

Cooke's tragic death in December 1964 left Womack greatly shaken and the Valentinos' career in limbo. Just three months later, Womack married Cooke's widow, Barbara Campbell, which earned him tremendous ill will in the R&B community; many viewed him as a shady opportunist looking to cash in on Cooke's legacy, especially since Campbell was significantly older than Womack. According to Womack, he was initially motivated to look after Campbell in an unstable time, not to tarnish the memory of a beloved mentor. Regardless, Womack found himself unable to get his solo career rolling in the wake of the scandal; singles for Chess ("I Found a True Love") and Him ("Nothing You Can Do") were avoided like the plague despite their quality. The Valentinos cut a couple of singles for Chess in 1966, "What About Me" and "Sweeter Than the Day Before," which also failed to make much of a splash. To make ends meet, Womack became a backing guitarist, first landing a job with Ray Charles; he went on to make a valuable connection in producer Chips Moman, and appeared often at Moman's American Studio in Memphis, as well as nearby Muscle Shoals, AL. In the process, Womack appeared on classic recordings by the likes of Joe Tex, King Curtis, and Aretha Franklin (*Lady Soul*), among others. He recorded singles for Keymen and Atlantic without success, but became one of Wilson Pickett's favorite songwriters, contributing the R&B Top Ten hits "I'm in Love" and "I'm a Midnight Mover" (plus 15 other tunes) to the singer's repertoire.

Womack had been slated to record a solo album for Minit, but had given Pickett most of his best material, which actually wound up getting his name back in the public eye in a positive light. In 1968, he scored the first charting single of his solo career with "What Is This?" and soon hit with a string of inventively reimagined pop covers—"Fly Me to the Moon," "California Dreamin'," and "I Left My Heart in San Francisco," the former two of which reached the R&B Top 20. A songwriting partnership with engineer Darryl Carter resulted in the R&B hits "It's Gonna Rain," "How I Miss You Baby," and "More Than I Can Stand" over 1969-1970. A series of label absorptions bumped Womack up to United Artists in 1971, which proved to be the home of his greatest solo success; in the meantime, he contributed the ballad "Trust Me" to Janis Joplin's masterpiece *Pearl*, and the J. Geils Band revived "Lookin' for a Love" for their first hit. He also teamed up with jazz guitarist Gabor Szabo on the LP *High Contrast*, which debuted Womack's composition "Breezin'" (which, of course, became a smash for George Benson six years later). Most importantly, however, Womack played guitar on Sly & the Family Stone's *There's a Riot Goin' On*, a masterpiece of darkly psychedelic funk that would have an impact on Womack's own sound and sense of style.

Womack issued his first UA album, *Communication*, in 1971, which kicked off a string of excellent releases that ran through the first half of the decade. In addition to several of Womack's trademark pop covers, the album also contained the original ballad "That's the Way I Feel About 'Cha," which climbed all the way to number two on the R&B chart and became his long-awaited breakout hit. The 1972 follow-up *Understanding* spawned Womack's first chart-topper, "Woman's Gotta Have It," co-written with Darryl Carter and stepdaughter Linda (Womack divorced Barbara Campbell in 1970). The follow-up "Harry Hippie," a gently ironic tribute to Womack's brother, also hit the R&B Top Ten. Later that year, Womack scored the blaxploitation flick *Across 110th Street*; the title cut was later revived in the 1998 Quentin Tarantino film *Jackie Brown*. *The Facts of Life* (1973) had an R&B number-two hit in a rearrangement of the perennial "Nobody Knows You When You're Down and Out," and the following year's *Lookin' for a Love Again* found Womack revisiting his Valentinos hit; the re-recorded "Lookin' for a Love" became his second number-one R&B single and his only Top Ten hit on the pop charts. Follow-up single "You're Welcome, Stop On By" made the R&B Top Five.

Womack was by this time a seasoned veteran of the rock & roll lifestyle, having befriended the likes of the Rolling Stones, the late Janis Joplin, and Sly Stone. After his brother Harry was murdered by a jealous girlfriend in 1974 (in Bobby's own apartment), the drug usage began to take a more serious turn. Womack scored further R&B Top Ten hits with 1975's "Check It Out" and 1976's "Daylight," the latter of which seemed to indicate a longing for escape from the non-stop partying that often masked serious depression. Despite Womack's new marriage to Regina Banks, the song was a sign that things were coming to a head. Womack pushed UA into letting him do a full album of country music, something he'd always loved but which the label regarded as commercially inadvisable (especially under the title Womack reportedly wanted to use: Step Aside, Charley Pride, Give Another Nigger a Try). They eventually relented, and when *BW Goes C&W* met with predictably minimal response, UA palmed the increasingly difficult Womack off on Columbia. A pair of albums there failed to recapture his commercial momentum or reinvent him for the disco age, and he moved to Arista for 1979's *Roads of Life*, which appeared not long after the sudden death of his infant son.

At a low point in his life, Womack took a bit of time off from music to gather himself. He appeared as a guest vocalist on Jazz Crusader Wilton Felder's 1980 solo album *Inherit the Wind*, singing the hit title track, and subsequently signed with black entrepreneur Otis Smith's independent Beverly Glen label. His label debut, 1981's *The Poet*, was a critically acclaimed left-field hit, rejuvenating his career and producing a number-three R&B hit with "If You Think You're Lonely Now." Unfortunately, money disputes soured the relationship between Womack and Smith rather quickly. *The Poet II* was delayed until 1984, and featured several duets with Patti LaBelle, including another number-three R&B hit, "Love Has Finally Come at Last." Beverly Glen released a final LP culled from Womack's previous sessions, *Someday We'll All Be Free*, in 1985, by which time the singer had already broken free and signed with MCA. Another hit with Wilton Felder, "(No Matter How High I Get) I'll Still Be Looking Up to You," appeared that year, and his label debut *So Many Rivers* produced a Top Five R&B hit in "I Wish He Didn't Trust Me So Much." *Womagic* (1996) reunited Womack with Chips Moman, and he also backed the Rolling Stones on their remake of "Harlem Shuffle." By the following year he'd christened himself *The Last Soul Man*, which proved to be his final recording for MCA.

In the years since, Womack has made high-profile returns to the music business only sporadically. 1994's *Resurrection* was recorded for Ron Wood's Slide label and featured an array of guest stars including Wood, Keith Richards, Rod Stewart, and Stevie Wonder. In 1999, he fulfilled a long-standing promise to his father (who passed away in 1981) by delivering his first-ever gospel album, *Back to My Roots*. *—Steve Huey*

The Womack Live / 1967 / Liberty ♦♦♦

Fly Me to the Moon / Jan. 1969 / Minit ♦♦♦

My Prescription / Feb. 1970 / Minit ♦♦♦

Bobby Womack's second album on Minit Records rivals his first, *Fly Me to the Moon*. He establishes himself firmly in the mold of his contemporaries: Wilson Pickett, Don Covay, Johnnie Taylor, and other top soul men. An accomplished writer, Womack's never handicapped by poor material, but never hesitates to redo popular songs by other writers. He scores with a funky rendition of "Fly Me to the Moon" (taken from his debut Minit LP), and with poorer results (chart-wise), "I Left My Heart in San Francisco," though aesthetically it's as funky as a bowl of hardened grits. He takes both easy listening songs far from their original molds. "How I Miss You Baby," "More Than I Can Stand," and Sam Cooke's "I'm Gonna Forget About You" made the rotations at R&B stations across America for good reason—they rock. Bobby Womack fills this prescription and has you hankering for a refill. *—Andrew Hamilton*

Communication / Sep. 15, 1971 / The Right Stuff ♦♦♦♦

A CD reissue of a Bobby Womack album originally released in 1971 on United Artists Records that yielded the solid "That's the Way I Feel About 'Cha" and across-the-tracks remakes of Ray Stevens' "Everything Is Beautiful," James Taylor's "Fire & Rain," and a monologue-dressed, nearly ten-minute-long rendition of Hal David & Burt Bacharach's "Close to You." Released intact with the original eight tracks; fine, for 1971, they did it like that then, but skimpy for the '90s where 14 tracks and more CDs became commonplace. *—Andrew Hamilton*

Understanding / May 30, 1972 / The Right Stuff ♦♦♦♦♦

As compelling as Bobby Womack's lacerating baritone may be, it still has that uncanny ability to be an engaging voice. This album has that timeliness appeal. It features the chart-buster in the midtempo number "Woman's Gotta Have It." It was a number-one single on the *Billboard* R&B charts. In addition to the aforementioned song, Womack also features a host of other granite numbers like "Ruby Dean" and "I Can Understand It." The latter, penned by Womack, was also covered by New Birth. Both versions are excellent. However, Womack's version has a soothing effect as it employs a sensuous string arrangement while New Birth's rendition is rather funky, retaining a spirited horn arrangement. Womack's version was never a release. "Harry Hippie" is a narrative about his brother and former bandmate Harris Womack. It checked in at number eight. The Ohio native's unique trait to calm a song with his blistering baritone re-surfaces on "Sweet Caroline," the album's third and final release. For a song to be so sweet and gentle, Womack enhances the flavor of this sentimental number with a heartfelt, soulful approach. It slipped into the Top 20 at 16. By all standards, this album is stirring. *—Craig Lytle*

Across 110th Street / Dec. 16, 1972 / Charly ♦♦♦

The soundtrack to a relatively little-known 1972 blaxploitation film featured songs written and performed by Bobby Womack, as well as a musical score by J.J. Johnson. Although the inconsistency of the approach precluded a musical statement along the lines of *Superfly*, it's an interesting find for those looking for little-heeded early-'70s soul with funk and rock influences. Womack's cuts count among his better material, and even if the title track cops much of its attitude from *Superfly*, it has a satisfyingly tough soul-rock groove of its own. "If You Want My Love" is a good grainy ballad, "Quicksand" a propulsive number well-suited for action scenes, and "Do It Right" in the mold of James Brown, but more rock-oriented. Johnson's instrumental contributions, while not as interesting, set a nice period soul-jazz mood, and there are nifty periodic washes of electronic effects in both composers' contributions. *—Richie Unterberger*

The Facts of Life / Jun. 8, 1973 / The Right Stuff ♦♦♦♦♦

Womack is one of the most prolific and influential acts in R&B and rock. With songs like "I Can Understand It," "Harry Hippie," and "Woman Got to Have It," Womack often displayed a depth, candor, and an expert turn of phrase that helped him outpace his contemporaries. *Facts of Life* is the follow-up to the 1971 classic *Communication*. This album is even better. Womack is known for his often uncomfortably real takes on love, life, and relationships, and *Facts of Life* expertly deals with a myriad of subjects. The only released single is his revamped take of the standard "Nobody Wants You When You're Down and Out." The song has been done *ad infinitum*, but Womack put a nasty edge on it that made it sound like a song he wrote himself. "I'm Through Trying to Prove My Love to You" is punctuated by his great guitar riffing and plaintive vocal and lyrical gems like, "See when you take my heart/I can't let you take my soul." "He'll Be There When the Sun Goes Down" benefits from more witticisms and a strong string arrangement from Womack and Rene Hall. Perhaps the most surprising thing about *Facts of Life* is that Womack is so adept at taking others' material and making it his own. "Natural Man," a cover of "You Make Me Feel Like a Natural Woman," is the biggest shock here. Where Aretha Franklin's version had her skillfully shouting from the rooftops, Womack brings tenderness to the lyric and is believable. Produced by Womack and recorded in Muscle Shoals with its renowned players, *Facts of Life* is an album of undeniable craft. *—Jason Elias*

Lookin' for a Love Again / Jan. 11, 1974 / The Right Stuff ♦♦♦♦

Bobby Womack is one of the best soul singers of all time, bringing his songs to life with testimonial pleas and lacerating deliveries. The title track from 1974's *Lookin' for a Love Again* gave the Cleveland native his second number-one song. It held that position on the R&B charts for three consecutive weeks and scaled the Top Ten on the pop charts as well. (His other number-one song was "Woman's Gotta Have It.") "You're Welcome, Stop on By" was the second single. As with most of this soulman's numbers, this one has that irresistible, percolating rhythm augmented by Womack's wailing delivery. Whether Womack is strokin' country & western rhythms, burnin' a blues melody with his guitar, or expressing a painful confession with his trademark baritone, rest assured that the outcome is going to be nothing short of sizzlin'. *—Craig Lytle*

I Can Understand It / 1975 / United Artists ♦♦♦

I Don't Know What the World Is Coming To / Mar. 28, 1975 / United Artists ♦♦♦♦♦

Safety Zone / Oct. 27, 1975 / United Artists ♦♦♦

During the early '70s, Womack was one of the most prolific and talented artists. With albums like *Communication* and *Lookin' For a Love Again*, Womack quickly became one of the most prolific and talented singers in R&B/pop. This album's predecessor, *I Don't Know What The World Is Coming To*, did show a slight decline in his Muscle Shoals sound and his writing skills. *Safety Zone* finds Womack getting a sonic overhaul whether he needed it or not. Produced by David Rubinson who was behind the boards for everyone from the Pointer Sisters to Herbie Hancock, it creates a slick, up-to-the minute style that may be too "perfect" for Womack's core fans. The album's first track, "Everything's Going to Be Alright," meanders and sets the standard for this album's pursuit of style over substance. The two covers, "Something You Got" and "I Wish It Would It Rain," both feature eccentric arrangements but Womack's vocals seem facile around the edges. As an album like the *Facts of Life* scored on his honesty throughout, *Safety Zone* only has two instances that come within striking distance. "Trust in Me," a self-written gem first recorded by his friend Janis Joplin, has Womack's gritty and wry vocal finally breaking free from the Rubinson's glossy production and arranging style. "Daylight" is one of Womack's best tracks. As Womack sings "The real set don't get started/'Til every one else is in," you hear him conflicted, but not bothered enough to stop. For the track, Rubinson's offhanded grace made the song even stronger. The main problem with *Safety Zone* is that it doesn't possess the earthy and challenging productions of Womack's earlier '70s albums. He too often seems straitjacketed in an attempt to curb his eccentric nature. Fans of Womack no doubt will love the great tracks but will have little or no need for the rest. *—Jason Elias*

Pieces / 1977 / Columbia ♦♦♦

Produced by Don Davis (Johnnie Taylor, the Dramatics), Bobby Womack's *Pieces* was released during disco's peak. Aside from a couple of tracks aimed in the direction of the dancefloor, the album sticks closely to the singer's soul music roots. Womack is joined by fellow soul veterans on a couple of tracks: David Ruffin (Davis produced his *So Soon We Change* and *Gentleman Ruffin* LPs) on the chugging single "Trust Your Heart" and Candi Staton on the ethereal ballad "Stop Before We Start." Womack has a way with songs about infidelity ("I Wish He Didn't Trust Me So Much"); this skill is put to good use on the swaying "Caught Up in the Middle" and "When Love Begins Friendship Ends." [Some of the album's tracks are on the Columbia CD *At Home in Muscle Shoals*, which was issued in August 1998.] *—Ed Hogan*

Save the Children / 1979 / Solar ♦♦

Save the Children was Bobby Womack's sole release for Dick Griffey's Solar Records. Produced by Womack, Keg Johnson, keyboardist Frank Hamilton, and Cecil and Kevin Womack, it was a pretty good attempt to update Womack's '60s soul-based sound while reflecting the influences of late-'80s hip-hop and pop. Highlights include the snappy "Baby I'm Back," "She's My Girl," and the torchy duet "Now We're Together," but it's on "Too Close For Comfort," a ballad co-written with H.T. Payne, that Womack comes closest to rekindling the kind of sound found on some of the best-known tracks. The title track (not to be confused with similarly named songs by Marvin Gaye and the Intruders) managed to chart R&B in late 1989. Of special note is the title track of Eddie Murphy's 1985 music album, *How Could It Be*, redone as the socially conscious "How Can It Be," a version of which can be found on the 1998 Sequel CD *Soul Sensation*. [*Save the Children* was reissued on CD by U.K. label Sequel in October 1999.] *—Ed Hogan*

The Poet / 1981 / Razor & Tie ♦♦♦♦

Eschewing the orchestrated sound that dominated much of his 1970s output, the *Across 110th St.* soundtrack being the definitive example, with *The Poet* Womack stays in that slick vein, but this time does so with a soft jazz feel. Workouts like "Where Do We Go From Here" contain long intros and codas with Womack's gruff vocal style trading off with the silky voices of a female choir; on "So Many Sides of You," one of the more rollicking songs on the record, the piano, drums, and Nathan East's bass are as crisp as a new dollar bill. A bonus, aside from the songs, is the great cover art, which shows Womack decked out in a lavender sportcoat and a pair of sunglasses, which only someone of his soulful grace could pull off. *—Steve Kurutz*

Bobby Womack & the Valentinos / 1984 / Chess ♦♦♦♦♦

It was a travesty when Bobby Womack and his brothers split—the sum was better than the individuals. If they had stayed together, they might be Rock and Roll Hall of Fame candidates. They possessed soulful voices and good songwriting skills, and produced themselves. This is a collection of their Chess recordings; the brothers went their separate ways after the tenure. "What About Me" got considerable play in some markets but failed to make an impact, though it was top-notch and Southern-fried. Northern soul favorite "Sweeter than the Day Before" is even further down soulville and garnered little notice in the States, but it is well known to Northern soul collectors. Womack recorded "I Found a True Love" later as a solo; it was also cut by Wilson Pickett, who cut quite a few of Womack's creations. While bred and buttered in Cleveland, the Valentinos had a gritty deep soul sound that was magical on the right material. *—Andrew Hamilton*

Poet II / 1984 / Razor & Tie ♦♦♦

Though Womack's in great voice, there's only one major thing wrong with *The Poet II*: it's an inferior follow-up to *The Poet*, which successfully executed ideas Womack had been tinkering with since 1979's *Roads of Life*. This seeks the success *The Poet* got by surprise. Womack's skill is his pragmatic take on relationships but on *The Poet II*, his aim is a little off. "Love Has Finally Come at Last" is the first of three duets with Patti LaBelle. The song is OK, but a fan might want to hear him sing all by himself. The duet idea works better on "It Takes a Lot of Strength to Say Goodbye"; it sounds better suited for two singers, and the dramatic arrangement and chemistry between Womack and LaBelle are strong but not that exciting. *The Poet II* also features some over-produced though skillful dance tracks. "Tell Me Why" is effective and has Womack asking why his relationship is failing and uses his children as pawns when he sings, "You don't have to do it for me/But do it for the sake of the kids." By the end of the album, Womack's lack of winning premises starts to catch up with him. "I Wish I Had Someone to Come Home To" has him sounding a little phony with lyrics like "Ain't no way this lonely man can seem to win." Fans of Womack know he'd think up something to do. The effort's last track "American Dream" features snippets of Martin Luther King's Jr.'s "I Have a Dream" speech. With its so-so lyrics and plodding arrangement, it just falls apart within the first two minutes. *The Poet II* is no doubt a good Bobby Womack album, but it is clear that he can do much better. *—Jason Elias*

Somebody Special / 1984 / EMI ✦✦✦✦✦
Bobby Womack's career takes in most of soul music history. After recording solo sides with the help of Sam Cooke and scoring hits with his brothers in the vocal group the Valentinos, Womack penned songs for Wilson Pickett and played guitar and bass on albums by Aretha Franklin and Sly Stone, among many others. His solo career, while maybe not as high profile as some, includes a healthy string of records full of the many top-notch and unique sides he's penned since the early '60s. Still going strong after an early-'80s comeback, Womack is probably best known for his late-'60s and early-'70s sides for United Artists. This fine 15-song collection brings together period highlights like "I'm a Midnight Mover" and "I'm in Love" (both hits for Pickett), "That's the Way I Feel About Cha," and "Lookin' for a Love." The sessions are split between late-'60s sides recorded in Memphis by Chips Moman and early-'70s tracks cut at Muscle Shoals. With Womack's guitar lines snaking their way through most of the songs, the set shifts into high gear on the last seven numbers; tracks like "I Can Understand It," "If You Don't Want My Love, Give It Back," "You're Welcome, Stop on By," and "If You Want My Love, Put Something Down on It" (recast as "Do Ya Think I'm Sexy" by Rod Stewart) figure right alongside other pinnacles of soul music by the likes of Curtis Mayfield and Marvin Gaye. And while EMI's two-disc *Midnight Mover* set is the collection to get for newcomers, this less comprehensive package is still a very good buy and covers pretty much all the prime sides. *—Stephen Cook*

So Many Rivers / 1985 / MCA ✦✦✦

Last Soul Man / 1987 / MCA ✦✦✦

Womack Winners: The Best of Bobby Womack 1968-75 / 1989 / Charly ✦✦✦✦✦

Greatest Hits / 1990 / Liberty ✦✦✦✦

● **Midnight Mover: The Bobby Womack Collection** / Feb. 1993 / EMI America ✦✦✦✦✦
Midnight Mover: The Bobby Womack Collection is a double-disc set offering 44 tracks from Womack's 1968-1976 stint with United Artists and its related labels. Early selections like "I'm a Midnight Mover," "I'm in Love," and "Broadway Walk" have Womack feeling his way with producer Chips Moman. After parting ways with Moman, Womack himself became one of the more skilled and inventive producers in the Muscle Shoals tradition. "That's the Way I Feel About 'Cha" and "I Can Understand It" both have plaintive melodies and are punctuated by Womack's guitar skills plus his ever-broadening vocals. Disc two covers the years 1973-1976, during which time he had become an even bigger star with albums that were sagacious ruminations on love and life. From an effortlessly revamped and rock-fueled "Nobody Wants You (When You're Down and Out) to his perfect cover of Sam Cooke's "That's Heaven to Me," Womack's interpretive skills were only matched by his rootsy yet polished productions. After the frisky "Check It Out," Womack seemed preoccupied with the darker side of love with a little religion on the side to confuse things. Tracks like "Jealous Love" and "Interlude #1/I Don't Know" have the message and meaning slipping through his fingers. *Midnight Mover* is a flawless anthology. *—Jason Elias*

Lookin' for a Real Love: The Best of Bobby Womack / 1994 / Razor & Tie ✦✦✦✦✦
At 14 tracks, Razor & Tie's *Lookin' for a Real Love: The Best of Bobby Womack* isn't particularly comprehensive, and it does miss some excellent, even important tracks, but as a sampling, it still works very well since it contains such classics as "That's the Way I Feel About 'Cha," "Woman's Gotta Have It," "Harry Hippie," "It's All Over Now," and "Across 110th Street," while whetting the appetite to hear more. So, while it might not be the definitive word on Womack's great solo career, it does work as an effective introduction. *—Stephen Thomas Erlewine*

The Soul of Bobby Womack: Stop on By / Oct. 29, 1996 / The Right Stuff ✦✦✦✦✦
Whether you love him or hate him, Bobby Womack is one hell of a soul singer. Mentored by Sam Cooke, Womack became one of the true stylists of his generation, and one of the few with staying power. Only Barry White and the late Curtis Mayfield could make the same claim. This 1996 compilation features 15 tracks from Womack's most creative period, 1970-1975, and features one unreleased demo version of the classic "Across 110th Street." Here is Womack the funk/soul poet digging deep into the longer jams like "I Can Understand It," "Jealous Love," and "Communication," along with his more conventional singles like "Nobody Wants You When You're Down and Out," "That's the Way I Feel About 'Cha," "You're Welcome, Stop on By," and others, all of which charted on both the R&B charts and the pop charts. These tracks are culled form such memorable albums as *Understanding, Facts of Life, What the World Is Coming To, Lookin' for a Love Again, Communication,* and others. All of them were made with musicians of the caliber of Herbie Hancock, Chuck Rainey, Jimmy Johnson, Leon Ware, Wah Wah Watson, Willie Weeks, and singers like Pam Grier (really, that one), the Pointer Sisters, Bill Withers, and many more. Such is the depth of this compilation, listeners will be tempted to play it twice just to believe what they just heard. The tunes groove, shimmy, streak, sway, and pump along, one after another, in a blissfully funky mix that kicks ass on most soul comps by various artists from the same era. *—Thom Jurek*

Fly Me to the Moon/My Prescription / Jan. 28, 1998 / Charly ✦✦✦
Fly Me to the Moon and *My Prescription*—Womack's second and third LPs, respectively—are assembled on this two-fer, which hints at the peaks reached a few years later on such outings as "Across 110th Street." *—Jason Ankeny*

At Home in Muscle Shoals / Feb. 17, 1998 / Columbia/Legacy ✦✦✦✦
The first CD hits package to focus on Bobby Womack's Muscle Shoals recordings of the late '70s and '80s, *At Home in Muscle Shoals* is a 15-track collection including "Trust Your Heart" and "Stop Before We Start," a duet with Candi Staton. *—John Bush*

Back to My Roots / Jul. 27, 1999 / The Right Stuff ✦✦✦✦✦
Soul/R&B legend Bobby Womack is definitely a man who's paid his dues—as the writer of such classics as "It's All Over Now" (covered by the Stones), "Lookin' for a Love" (covered by J. Geils) and the guitarist on Sly Stone's chestnut "Family Affair" and Wilson Pickett's mover "Funky Broadway," he has all the prerequisites for a spot in the Rock and Roll Hall of Fame. After leaving his strictly religious father's home in the late '50s, (with a car bought for them by Sam Cooke) Bobby and the Womack Brothers set out to conquer popular radio, using their church-bred voices and down-home, bluesy stylings to twist and change genres they hadn't even heard of yet. *Back to My Roots* finds Womack doing just that, singing some of his favorite gospel numbers, while retaining some of that old fire that made him so popular with the white youth of America and Britain in the '60s. Enlisting the aid of J. W. Alexander (Sam Cooke's partner and a former member of the Pilgrim Travelers gospel group) to introduce and close the album, Womack dedicated this work to his father, who unfortunately died before he got a chance to hear the finished product, as did Alexander. With versions of "Rug" (one of his '60s hits), "Motherless Child" and the Staple Singers' classic "Oh Happy Day," this album showcases Womack's love of all styles and genres, from country pickin' to funky, bluesy breakdowns, to choir-esque, baptismal über-joy. The opening lines of the first track, "Rug," say it all: "Now I'm sitting here reminiscing about the good old days/Singing gospel music with my brothers/We called ourselves the Womack Brothers/Before we were ever born, my father prayed for five sons, he said, "God, if you bless me with them, I will teach them to sing your praises"/Well, he got his wish, not knowing that we would want the material things in life/I remember the first time I told my father I was going to sing rock and roll; that's the first time I saw my daddy cry/I remember him saying, "What does it profit a man to gain the world, and lose his soul?/And I know now, absolutely nothing." *—Tom Hallett*

● **Greatest Hits** / Oct. 5, 1999 / The Right Stuff ✦✦✦✦✦
Compiling virtually all of Bobby Womack's best recordings, this 19-track expansion of Capitol's 1990 *Greatest Hits* is a solid, though slightly flawed, alternative to the occasionally exhaustive two-disc set *Midnight Mover.* The disc spans most of his career—from the late '60s through his '70s breakout and on into the '80s—though nearly all of it dates from the '70s, his brilliant period recording for United Artists. Few songs better exemplify Womack's raw, straining delivery and funky, forthright songwriting than his big R&B hits "That's the Way I Feel About 'Cha" and "Woman's Gotta Have It," while the tough rocker "It's All over Now" illustrates his enviable range. An extended live track, "The Preacher/More Than I Can Stand," shows how Bobby Womack the songwriter, sessionman, or recording artist could occasionally be upstaged by Bobby Womack the testifying live performer, and his proficiency at interpreting standards ("Nobody Wants You When You're Down and Out" and "Home Is Where the Heart Is") is assured as well. The only failure of *Greatest Hits*—and it's a big one—is that it doesn't include Womack's blaxploitation nugget "Across 110th Street," not a big hit but one of his best performances and a song he's become increasingly identified with (after its reuse in the 1997 film *Jackie Brown*). Also, there are a few other can't-miss tracks not heard here that the two-disc *Midnight Mover* wisely included: "I'm a Midnight Mover," "What Is This?," "It's Gonna Rain," and "Arkansas State Prison." Here's the upshot: for those who don't need two discs of Bobby Womack, *Greatest Hits* is an acceptable substitute. *—John Bush*

The Legends Collection / Apr. 24, 2001 / Dressed to Kill ✦✦✦✦
A compilation of the six earliest years of Womack's solo career from 1969 to 1975 of tracks recorded for Minit and United Artists Records; the collection is pretty definitive for that period, making it a must for Womack fans. Employing a gritty, storytelling tenor, the Cleveland-spawned soul singer, writer, producer, and guitarist does his thing on 38 tracks, all full-length, making this work even more essential. If not a big fan, Bobby's grits-and-sausage delivery becomes samey after six or seven tracks; he doesn't punctuate with screams, à la Wilson Pickett, or change range as more fluid singers do, but smokes the right material. A blue-collar singer, Bobby Womack appeals to lovers of the raw, though many will argue that point as his tracks are usually lavish for the brand of soul he sings; Bobby, however, has the ability to dumb down the most sophisticated string or horn arrangement to no nonsense takes, as in "Woman Gotta Have It," a soulful "Fly Me to the Moon," "I Can Understand It," "That's the Way I Feel About 'Cha," "You're Welcome, Stop on By," a bumpin' update of "Looking for a Love," a remake of the Temptations' "Just My Imagination," "Harry Hippie," an ode to his late brother, and "Across 110th Street" from the movie of the same name. *—Andrew Hamilton*

Stevie Wonder (Steveland Hardaway Judkins)

b. May 13, 1950, Saginaw, MI
Vocals, Piano, Piano (Electric), Keyboards, Harmonica, Drums, Guitar / Soul, Motown, Pop-Soul, Smooth Soul, Psychedelic Soul, Funk, Pop/Rock, Album Rock, Urban
Stevie Wonder is a much-beloved American icon and an indisputable genius not only of R&B, but popular music in general. Blind virtually since birth, Wonder's heightened awareness of sound helped him create vibrant, colorful music teeming with life and ambition. Nearly everything he recorded bore the stamp of his sunny, joyous positivity; even when he addressed serious racial, social, and spiritual issues (which he did quite often in his prime), or sang about heartbreak and romantic uncertainty, an underlying sense of

optimism and hope always seemed to emerge. Much like his inspiration, Ray Charles, Wonder had a voracious appetite for many different kinds of music, and refused to confine himself to any one sound or style. His best records were a richly eclectic brew of soul, funk, rock & roll, sophisticated Broadway/Tin Pan Alley-style pop, jazz, reggae, and African elements—and they weren't just stylistic exercises; Wonder took it all and forged it into his own personal form of expression.

His range helped account for his broad-based appeal, but so did his unique, elastic voice, his peerless melodic facility, his gift for complex arrangements, and his taste for lovely, often sentimental ballads. Additionally, Wonder's pioneering use of synthesizers during the '70s changed the face of R&B; he employed a kaleidoscope of contrasting textures and voices that made him a virtual one-man band, all the while evoking a surprisingly organic warmth. Along with Marvin Gaye and Isaac Hayes, Wonder brought R&B into the album age, crafting his LPs as cohesive, consistent statements with compositions that often took time to make their point. All of this made Wonder perhaps R&B's greatest individual auteur, rivaled only by Gaye or, in later days, Prince. Originally, Wonder was a child prodigy who started out in the general Motown mold, but he took control of his vision in the '70s, spinning off a series of incredible albums that were as popular as they were acclaimed; most of his reputation rests on these works, which most prominently include *Talking Book*, *Innervisions*, and *Songs in the Key of Life*. His output since then has been inconsistent, marred by excesses of sentimentality and less of the progressive imagination of his best work, but it's hardly lessened the reverence in which he's long been held.

Wonder was born Steveland Hardaway Judkins in Saginaw, MI, on May 13, 1950 (he later altered his name to Steveland Morris when his mother married). A premature infant, he was put on oxygen treatment in an incubator; likely it was an excess of oxygen that exacerbated a visual condition known as retinopathy of prematurity, causing his blindness. In 1954, his family moved to Detroit, where the already musically inclined Stevie began singing in his church's choir; from there he blossomed into a genuine prodigy, learning piano, drums, and harmonica all by the age of nine. While performing for some of his friends in 1961, Stevie was discovered by Ronnie White of the Miracles, who helped arrange an audition with Berry Gordy at Motown. Gordy signed the youngster immediately and teamed him with producer/songwriter Clarence Paul, under the new name Little Stevie Wonder. Stevie released his first two albums in 1962: *A Tribute to Uncle Ray*, which featured covers of Stevie's hero Ray Charles, and *The Jazz Soul of Little Stevie*, an orchestral jazz album spotlighting his instrumental skills on piano, harmonica, and assorted percussion. Neither sold very well, but that all changed in 1963 with the live album *The 12 Year Old Genius*, which featured a new extended version of the harmonica instrumental "Fingertips." Edited for release as a single, "Fingertips, Pt. 2" rocketed to the top of both the pop and R&B charts, thanks to Wonder's irresistible, youthful exuberance; meanwhile, *The 12 Year Old Genius* became Motown's first chart-topping LP.

Wonder charted a few more singles over the next year, but none on the level of "Fingertips, Pt. 2." As his voice changed, his recording career was temporarily put on hold, and he studied classical piano at the Michigan School for the Blind in the meantime. He dropped the "Little" portion of his stage name in 1964, and re-emerged the following year with the infectious, typically Motown-sounding dance tune "Uptight (Everything's Alright)," a number-one R&B/Top Five pop smash. Not only did he co-write the song for his first original hit, but it also reinvented him as a more mature vocalist in the public's mind, making the similar follow-up "Nothing's Too Good for My Baby" another success. The first signs of Wonder's social activism appeared in 1966 via his hit cover of Bob Dylan's "Blowin' in the Wind" and its follow-up, "A Place in the Sun," but as Motown still had the final say on Wonder's choice of material, this new direction would not yet become a major facet of his work.

By this time, Wonder was, however, beginning to take more of a hand in his own career. He co-wrote his next several hits, all of which made the R&B Top Ten—"Hey Love," "I Was Made to Love Her" (an R&B number one that went to number-two pop in 1967), and "For Once in My Life" (another smash that reached number-two pop and R&B). Wonder's 1968 album *For Once in My Life* signaled his budding ambition; he co-wrote about half of the material and, for the first time, co-produced several tracks. The record also contained three more singles in the R&B chart-topper "Shoo-Be-Doo-Be-Doo-Da-Day," "You Met Your Match," and "I Don't Know Why." Wonder scored again in 1969 with the pop and R&B Top Five hit "My Cherie Amour" (which he'd actually recorded three years prior) and the Top Ten "Yester-Me, Yester-You, Yesterday." In 1970, Wonder received his first-ever co-production credit for the album *Signed, Sealed & Delivered*; he co-wrote the R&B chart-topper "Signed, Sealed, Delivered I'm Yours" with singer Syreeta Wright, whom he married later that year, and also scored hits with "Heaven Help Us All" and a rearrangement of the Beatles' "We Can Work It Out." In addition, two other Motown artists had major success with Wonder co-writes: the Spinners' "It's a Shame" and the Miracles' only pop number one, "Tears of a Clown."

A turning point in Wonder's career came in 1971. On his 21st birthday, his contract with Motown expired, and the royalties set aside in his trust fund became available to him. A month before his birthday, Wonder released *Where I'm Coming From*, his first entirely self-produced album, which also marked the first time he wrote or co-wrote every song on an LP (usually in tandem with Wright) and the first time his keyboard and synthesizer work dominated his arrangements. Gordy was reportedly not fond of the work, and it wasn't a major commercial success, producing only the Top Ten hit "If You Really Love Me" (plus a classic B-side in "Never Dreamed You'd Leave in Summer"). Nonetheless, it was clearly an ambitious attempt at making a unified album-length artistic statement, and served notice that Wonder was no longer content to release albums composed of hit singles and assorted filler. Accordingly, Wonder did not immediately renew his contract with Motown, as the label had expected; instead, he used proceeds from his trust fund to build his own recording studio and to enroll in music theory classes at USC. He negotiated a new deal with Motown that dramatically increased his royalty rate and established his own publishing company, Black Bull Music, which allowed him to retain the rights to his music; most importantly, he wrested full artistic control over his recordings, as Gaye had just done with the landmark *What's Going On*.

Freed from the dictates of Motown's hit-factory mindset, Wonder had already begun following a more personal and idiosyncratic muse. One of his negotiating chips had been a full album completed at his new studio; Wonder had produced, played nearly all the instruments, and written all the material (with Wright contributing to several tracks). Released under Wonder's new deal in early 1972, *Music of My Mind* heralded his arrival as a major, self-contained talent with an original vision that pushed the boundaries of R&B. The album produced a hit single in the spacy, synth-driven ballad "Superwoman (Where Were You When I Needed You)," but like contemporary work by Hayes and Gaye, *Music of My Mind* worked as a smoothly flowing song suite unto itself. Around the same time it was released, Wonder's marriage to Wright broke up; the two remained friends, however, and Wonder produced and wrote several songs for her debut album. The same year, Wonder toured with the Rolling Stones, bringing his music to a large white audience as well.

For the follow-up to *Music of My Mind*, Wonder refined his approach, tightening up his songcraft while addressing his romance with Wright. The result, *Talking Book*, was released in late 1972 and made him a superstar. Song for song one of the strongest R&B albums ever released, *Talking Book* also perfected Wonder's spacy, futuristic experiments with electronics, and was hailed as a magnificently realized masterpiece. Wonder topped the charts with the gutsy, driving funk classic "Superstition" and the mellow, jazzy ballad "You Are the Sunshine of My Life," which went on to become a pop standard; those two songs went on to win three Grammys between them. Amazingly, Wonder only upped the ante with his next album, 1973's *Innervisions*, a concept album about the state of contemporary society that ranks with Gaye's *What's Going On* as a pinnacle of socially conscious R&B. The ghetto chronicle "Living for the City" and the intense spiritual self-examination "Higher Ground" both went to number one on the R&B charts and the pop Top Ten, and *Innervisions* took home a Grammy for Album of the Year. Wonder was lucky to be alive to enjoy the success; while being driven to a concert in North Carolina, a large timber fell on Wonder's car. He sustained serious head injuries and lapsed into a coma, but fortunately made a full recovery.

Wonder's next record, 1974's *Fulfillingness' First Finale*, was slightly more insular and less accessible than its immediate predecessors, and unsurprisingly imbued with a sense of mortality. The hits, however, were the upbeat "Boogie On, Reggae Woman" (a number-one R&B and Top Five pop hit) and the venomous Richard Nixon critique "You Haven't Done Nothin'" (number one on both sides). It won him a second straight Album of the Year Grammy, by which time he'd been heavily involved as a producer and writer on Syreeta's second album, *Stevie Wonder Presents Syreeta*. Wonder subsequently retired to his studio and spent two years crafting a large-scale project that would stand as his magnum opus. Finally released in 1976, *Songs in the Key of Life* was a sprawling two-LP-plus-one-EP set that found Wonder at his most ambitious and expansive. Some critics called it brilliant but prone to excess and indulgence, while others hailed it as his greatest masterpiece and the culmination of his career; in the end, they were probably both right. "Sir Duke," an ebullient tribute to music in general and Duke Ellington in particular, and the funky "I Wish" both went to number-one pop and R&B; the hit "Isn't She Lovely," a paean to Wonder's daughter, became something of a standard, and "Pastime Paradise" was later sampled for the backbone of Coolio's rap smash "Gangsta's Paradise." Not surprisingly, *Songs in the Key of Life* won a Grammy for Album of the Year; in hindsight, though, it marked the end of a remarkable explosion of creativity and of Wonder's artistic prime.

Having poured a tremendous amount of energy into *Songs in the Key of Life*, Wonder released nothing for the next three years. When he finally returned in 1979, it was with the mostly instrumental *Journey Through the Secret Life of Plants*, ostensibly the soundtrack to a never-released documentary. Although it contained a few pop songs, including the hit "Send One Your Love," its symphonic flirtations befuddled most listeners and critics. It still made the Top Ten on the LP chart on Wonder's momentum alone—one of the stranger releases to do so. To counteract possible speculation that he'd gone off the deep end, Wonder rushed out the straightforward pop album *Hotter Than July* in 1980. The reggae-flavored "Master Blaster (Jammin')" returned him to the top of the R&B charts and the pop Top Five, and "Happy Birthday" was part of the ultimately successful campaign to make Martin Luther King Jr.'s birthday a national holiday (Wonder being one of the cause's most active champions). Artistically speaking, *Hotter Than July* was a cut below his classic '70s output, but it was still a solid outing; fans were so grateful to have the old Wonder back that they made it his first platinum-selling LP.

In 1981, Wonder began work on a follow-up album that was plagued by delays, suggesting that he might not be able to return to the visionary heights of old. He kept busy in the meantime, though; in 1982, his racial-harmony duet with Paul McCartney, "Ebony and Ivory," hit number one, and he released a greatest-hits set covering 1972-1982 called *Original Musiquarium I*. It featured four new songs, of which "That Girl" (number-one R&B, Top Five pop) and the lengthy, jazzy "Do I Do" (featuring Dizzy Gillespie; number-two R&B) were significant hits. In 1984, still not having completed the official follow-up to *Hotter Than July*, he recorded the soundtrack to the Gene Wilder comedy film *The Woman in Red*, which wasn't quite a full-fledged Stevie Wonder album but did feature a number of new songs, including "I Just Called to Say I Love You." Adored by the public (it was his biggest-selling single ever) and loathed by critics (who derided it as sappy and simple-minded), "I Just Called to Say I Love You" was an across-the-board number-one smash, and won an Oscar for Best Song.

Wonder finally completed the official album he'd been working on for nearly five years, and released *In Square Circle* in 1985. Paced by the number-one hit "Part Time Lover"—his last solo pop chart-topper—and several other strong songs, *In Square Circle* went platinum, even if Wonder's synthesizer arrangements now sounded standard rather than groundbreaking. He performed on the number-one charity singles "We Are the World" by USA for Africa and "That's What Friends Are For" by Dionne Warwick & Friends, and returned quickly with a new album, *Characters*, in 1987. While *Characters* found Wonder's commercial clout on the pop charts slipping away, it was a hit on the R&B side, topping the album charts and producing a number one hit in "Skeletons." It would be his final release of the '80s; he didn't return until 1991, with the soundtrack to the Spike Lee film *Jungle Fever*. His next full album of new material, 1995's *Conversation Peace*, was a commercial disappointment, despite winning two Grammys for the single "For Your Love." That same year, Coolio revived "Pastime Paradise" in his own brooding rap smash "Gangsta's Paradise," which became the year's biggest hit. Wonder capitalized on the renewed notoriety by cutting a hit duet with Babyface, "How Come, How Long," in 1996. Since then, Motown has released a number of remasters and compilations attempting to define and repackage Wonder's vast legacy. His far-reaching influence was felt in the neo-soul movement that came to prominence in the late '90s, and he also remained a composer of choice for jazz artists looking to incorporate harmonically sophisticated pop/R&B tunes into their repertoires. That only scratches the surface of Wonder's impact on contemporary popular music, which is why he was inducted into the Rock and Roll Hall of Fame in 1989, and remains a living legend regardless of whatever else he does. *—Steve Huey*

The Jazz Soul of Little Stevie / Sep. 1962 / Motown ♦♦♦
More than any single LP, this album showed how much pure talent Stevie Wonder possessed. He was a gifted drummer, fantastic chromatic harmonica player, engaging vocalist and exceptional composer. All these skills were highlighted throughout this record, and Wonder's youthful, exuberant voice had a maturity suggesting that greatness was around the corner. *—Ron Wynn*

Tribute to Uncle Ray / Oct. 1962 / Motown ♦♦
"Little Stevie Wonder, Tamla's 11-year-old musical genius, is blind, a similarity he shares with a famed musician and vocalist of today," shamelessly announce the liner notes of this album. Unfortunately, Wonder at 11 does not share much of Ray Charles' vocal abilities, even when he is singing Charles' songs (others are "originals in the style of his idol") and, since he doesn't play on the record, there's no similarity there either. Today, listening to a child emote his way through songs like "Drown in My Own Tears" is a curiosity at best, and the album is only for hard-core Wonder fanatics. *—William Ruhlmann*

Workout Stevie, Workout / 1963 / Tamla ♦♦♦

The 12 Year Old Genius / May 21, 1963 / Motown ♦♦♦
Recorded live, this includes the full seven-minute version of his number-one hit "Fingertips." The rest of the album shows him as a young prodigy fixated on Ray Charles; indeed, the final three songs are covers of the early Charles tunes "Hallelujah I Love Her So," "Drown in My Own Tears," and "Don't You Know." A couple jams and a cover of "(I'm Afraid) The Masquerade Is Over" fill out this seven-song LP. *—Richie Unterberger*

With a Song in My Heart / Dec. 28, 1963 / Motown ♦♦♦
Having tried to turn Little Stevie Wonder into Big Ray Charles, then broken him through with "Fingertips—Pt. 2," and Motown now gave us Steve Wonder, Lounge Lizard. At least, that's what you'd think listening to this string-filled crooning session, in which the 13-year-old earnestly makes his way through the likes of Johnny Mercer's "Dream," "Get Happy," "Without a Song," and other supperclub standards. Berry Gordy's wish for all his artists may have been to play the Copacabana, but this one was far below the legal drinking age, and, although Wonder brought his usual willingness to the project, it was years beyond his abilities. *—William Ruhlmann*

Stevie at the Beach / Jun. 23, 1964 / Tamla ♦♦♦
Stevie Wonder once described this period in his musical development as embarrassing. He particularly spoke of "Harmonica Man" in this regard; an early single release, it featured a barking male backing chorus, a zippy beat, and some spirited harmonica playing and vocalizing by Stevie. "Red Sails in the Sunset" and "Beachstomp" have the same feel as "Harmonica." The slower "Castles in the Sand" also failed to scale the charts, as it's a rather dull attempt to appeal to surfers and beach hangers; the instrumental version (included) is more appealing then the vocal, since the lyrics were just too wimpy. Not one of Stevie's most sterling efforts, but it's not the embarrassment he claims either. Well... maybe for him. *—Andrew Hamilton*

Uptight / May 4, 1966 / Motown ♦♦♦♦♦
Stevie Wonder began demonstrating his production skills and compositional acumen on his first of two albums in 1966. Although still just a teenager, Wonder was already anxious to do more than simply grind out love tunes. He covered Bob Dylan's "Blowin' in the Wind" and also contributed "Pretty Little Angel" alongside the monster hits "Nothin's Too Good For My Baby" and the title song. It was also a signal Wonder had moved beyond simply paying homage to Ray Charles and now wanted to establish his own musical identity. *—Ron Wynn*

Down to Earth / Nov. 16, 1966 / Motown ♦♦♦
Stevie Wonder's third album signaled more artistic growth, but was the first of his career that didn't make much commercial headway. It didn't contain a single big hit, something that wouldn't happen again to Wonder for many, many years. There were moments of uncertainty and awkwardness on such songs as "Angel Baby (Don't You Ever Leave Me)" and "Lonesome Road." Wonder was laying the groundwork for numerous classics that routinely came throughout the 1970s and '80s; his voice was losing its cuteness and beginning to gain the richness and edge that punctuated many of his future albums. *—Ron Wynn*

I Was Made to Love Her / Aug. 27, 1967 / Motown ♦♦♦
This album was rushed out to capitalize on the success of the title song, which was Wonder's biggest pop hit since "Fingertips—Pt. 2" and would not be bettered until "Superstition" in 1972. Other than the hit, it's all filler, but not uninteresting for that. There are several contributions from the Wonder team at Motown, covers of other Motown hits, and stabs at sounding like Ray Charles, James Brown, and Otis Redding. At 17, Wonder was becoming both a remarkable mimic and an original talent on his own. *—William Ruhlmann*

Someday at Christmas / Nov. 27, 1967 / Motown ♦♦♦

Greatest Hits / Mar. 25, 1968 / Motown ♦♦♦♦
When it was released, Stevie Wonder's first hits collection, a 12-track disc tracing his work from 1963 to 1967, served a common function of compilations: It gathered together stray, disparate pieces, from "Fingertips—Pt. 2" to "I Was Made to Love Her," and focused attention on the artist. Wonder had a spotty singles record: five Top Ten hits, but only two of them in succession over the four-and-a-half years, yet *Greatest Hits* made him seem like a consistent hitmaker with an astounding range, from those early harmonica instrumentals to soulful wailers like "Uptight (Everything's Alright)" and even oddball ballads like "A Place in the Sun." By now this set has long since been eclipsed, notably by the *Looking Back* album, but as a demonstration of Wonder's early promise, it is notable. *—William Ruhlmann*

Eivets Rednow . . . Alfie / Nov. 20, 1968 / Motown ♦♦♦
By 1968, Motown had Wonder pegged as a soul-pop shouter, so his harmonica instrumental of "Alfie," and the movie theme that had been a Top 15 hit for Dionne Warwick in 1967, was released under another name—his own spelled backwards—and on a different record label. This album, issued after that single made number 66 on the pop chart, consists of more harmonica instrumentals, everything from "A House Is Not a Home" to "Grazing in the Grass," and is enough to convince you that Wonder, who, after all, broke through playing harmonica, is a tuneful player of the instrument, more a Larry Adler than a Bob Dylan. Nevertheless, this is a minor item in the Wonder catalog. *—William Ruhlmann*

For Once in My Life / Dec. 6, 1968 / Motown ♦♦♦
Rather than rushing out an album in the spring of 1968, when "Shoo-Be-Doo-Be-Doo-Da-Day" (number-nine Pop, number-one R&B) hit, Motown waited, through the modest summer success of "You Met Your Match" (number 35 Pop, number-two R&B) until "For Once in My Life" (number-two Pop and R&B) became Wonder's next mammoth single, to release an album. As a result, this album contained all three hits, making it one of Wonder's more consistent albums of the '60s, even with filler like "Sunny" and "God Bless the Child." The real find, however, is the driving "I Don't Know Why," which, when placed on the B-side of Wonder's next single, "My Cherie Amour," became a hit on its own, going number-39 pop, number-16 R&B. *—William Ruhlmann*

My Cherie Amour / Aug. 29, 1969 / Motown ♦♦♦
Notable for containing Wonder's then-most recent Top Ten hit, the title track, and its follow-up, "Yester-Me, Yester-You, Yesterday," this album otherwise contains contemporary filler like "Light My Fire," plus a peculiar arrangement of "Hello, Young Lovers" from *The King and I* that makes it sound like "For Once in My Life." *—William Ruhlmann*

Live at the Talk of the Town / 1970 / Motown ♦♦♦
A strong record, this live album captures Stevie just before he turned 21 and assumed complete creative control at Motown. Wonder turns in solid performances of "Bridge Over Troubled Water" as well as his own hits "For Once In My Life" and "My Cherie Amour." The treat of the album, though, is hearing Stevie introduce his brand new single, "Signed, Sealed, Delivered I'm Yours," before launching into a blistering rendition of the now-classic song. *—Steve Kurutz*

Signed, Sealed & Delivered / Aug. 7, 1970 / Motown ♦♦♦
Stevie Wonder was beginning to rebel against the Motown hit factory mentality in the early '70s. While he certainly hadn't lost his commercial touch, Wonder was anxious to address social concerns, experiment with electronics and not be restricted by radio and marketplace considerations. Still, he gave the label another definitive smash with the title track, while sneaking in a cover of the Beatles' "We Can Work It Out" and penning more intriguing tunes like "I Can't Let My Heaven Walk Away" and "Never Had a Dream Come True." *—Ron Wynn*

Where I'm Coming From / Apr. 12, 1971 / Motown ♦♦♦♦♦
One month before he turned 21, Stevie Wonder released *Where I'm Coming From*, the most distinctive record of his young career, and one that looked forward—in its breadth of material as well as its futuristic production aesthetic—to his many successes later in the '70s. There's a fabulous song here for nearly every type of fan; the soothing love ballad ("Think of Me as Your Soldier"), a gritty, apocalyptic funk extravanganza ("Do Yourself a Favor"), a kinetic, refreshing nod to the pop charts (the Top Ten hit "If You Really Love Me"), and an agonizing piece of heartache soul ("Never Dreamed You'd Leave in Summer" (slightly reworked for "Superwoman" on his next album *Music of My Mind*). Still, there are a few echoes of his occasionally pedestrian '60s work, and a pair of songs on the flip side sound especially anachronistic. The first is a piece of inspirational fluff called "Take up a Course in Happiness" with an odd arrangement pitched halfway between Sammy Davis Jr., and *Sgt. Pepper's*, the second a jokey pick-up number named "I Wanna Talk to You" (complete with leering old-man vocals). Those two however, are the exceptions; the rules are uniformly excellent. The set closers "Never Dreamed You'd Leave in Summer" and "Sunshine in Their Eyes" are bravura performances, Stevie summoning his purest register to convey heartbreak and hopefulness, respectively, in equal measure. For all the great material included, there was little chance of these songs hanging together as a proper album, and Berry Gordy's misgivings about releasing a record like this on a Motown label were, temporarily, well-placed. Still, *Where I'm Coming From* was a frequently astonishing album from Motown's new genius of the recording studio. *—John Bush*

Greatest Hits, Vol. 2 / Oct. 21, 1971 / Motown ♦♦♦
Stevie Wonder's second hits collection, gathering together his singles from 1968 to 1971, traces his development into a virtuoso talent, from upbeat Motown numbers like "For Once in My Life" to the emergence of Wonder's own style in songs like "Never Dreamed You'd Leave in Summer" and "If You Really Love Me." Along the way, he demonstrates an amazingly broad pop sensibility that allows him to handle soul, pop/rock, and ballads, all with equal ease. And, of course, the remarkable thing is that this set was obselete the day it came out, the summing up of what turned out to be only the first phase of Wonder's remarkable career. This album has been superseded by the *Looking Back* compilation. *—William Ruhlmann*

Music of My Mind / Mar. 3, 1972 / Motown ♦♦♦♦♦
With a new contract from Motown in his hand, Stevie Wonder released *Music of My Mind*, his first truly unified record and, with the exception of a single part on two songs, the work of a one-man-band. Everything he had learned about musicianship, engineering, and production during his long apprenticeship in the Snakepit at Motown Studios came together here (from the liner notes: "The sounds themselves come from inside his mind. The man is his own instrument. The instrument is an orchestra.") *Music of My Mind* was also the first to bear the fruits of his increased focus on Moog and Arp synthesizers, though the songs never sound synthetic, due in great part to Stevie's reliance on a parade of real instruments—organic drumwork, harmonica, organs and pianos—as well as his mastery of traditional song structure and his immense musical personality. The intro of the vibrant, tender "I Love Every Little Thing About You" is a perfect example, humanized with a series of lightly breathed syllables for background rhythm. And when the synthesizers do appear, it's always in the perfect context: the standout "Superwoman" really benefits from its high-frequency harmonics, and "Seems So Long" wouldn't sound quite as affectionate without the warm electronics gurgling in the background. This still wasn't a perfect record, though; "Sweet Little Girl" was an awkward song, with Stevie assuming another of his embarrassing musical personalities to fawn over a girl. *—John Bush*

★ **Talking Book** / Oct. 27, 1972 / Motown ♦♦♦♦♦
After releasing two "head" records during 1970-1971, Stevie Wonder expanded his compositional palate with 1972's *Talking Book* to include societal ills as well as tender love songs, and so recorded the first smash album of his career. What had been hinted at on the intriguing project *Music of My Mind* was here focused into a laser beam of tight songwriting, warm electronic arrangements, and ebullient performances—altogether the most realistic vision of musical personality ever put to wax, beginning with a disarmingly simple love song, "You Are the Sunshine of My Life" (but of course, it's only the composition that's simple). Stevie's not always singing a tender ballad here—in fact, he flits from contentment to mistrust to promise to heartbreak within the course of the first four songs—but he never fails to render each song in the most vivid colors. In stark contrast to his early songs, which were clever but often relied on the Motown template of romantic metaphor, with *Talking Book* it became clear Stevie Wonder was beginning to speak his mind and use personal history for material (just as Marvin Gaye had with the social protest of 1971's *What's Going On*). The lyrics became less convoluted, while the emotional power gained in intensity. "You and I" and the glorious closer "I Believe (When I Fall in Love It Will Be Forever)" subtly illustrate that the conception of love can be stronger than the reality, while "Tuesday Heartbreak" speaks simply but powerfully: "I wanna be with you when the nighttime comes/I wanna be with you till the daytime comes." Ironically, the biggest hit from *Talking Book* wasn't a love song at all; the funk landmark "Superstition" urges empowerment instead of hopelessness, set to a grooving beat that made it one of the biggest hits of his career. It's followed by "Big Brother," the first of his directly critical songs, excoriating politicians who posture to the underclass in order to gain the only thing they really need: votes. With *Talking Book*, Stevie also found a proper balance between making an album entirely by himself and benefiting from the talents of others. His wife Syreeta and her sister Yvonne Wright contributed three great lyrics, and Ray Parker Jr. came by to record a guitar solo that brings together the lengthy jam "Maybe Your Baby." Two more guitar heroes, Jeff Beck and Buzzy Feton, appeared on "Lookin' for Another Pure Love," Beck's solo especially giving voice to the excruciating process of moving on from a broken relationship. Like no other Stevie Wonder LP before it, *Talking Book* is all of a piece, the first unified statement of his career. It's certainly an exercise in indulgence but, imitating life, it veers breathtakingly from love to heartbreak and back with barely a pause. *—John Bush*

☆ **Innervisions** / Aug. 3, 1973 / Motown ♦♦♦♦♦
When Stevie Wonder applied his tremendous songwriting talents to the unsettled social morass that was the early '70s, he produced one of his greatest, most important works, a rich panoply of songs addressing drugs, spirituality, political ethics, the unnecessary perils of urban life, and what looked to be the failure of the '60s dream—all set within a collection of charts as funky and catchy as any he'd written before. Two of the highlights, "Living for the City" and "Too High," make an especially deep impression thanks to Stevie's narrative talents; on the first, an eight-minute mini-epic, he brings a hardscrabble Mississippi black youth to the city and illustrates, via a brilliant dramatic interlude, what lies in wait for innocents. (He also uses his variety of voice impersonations to stunning effect.) "Too High" is just as stunning, a cautionary tale about drugs driven by a dizzying chorus of scat vocals and a springing bassline. "Higher Ground," a funky follow-up to the previous album's big hit ("Superstition"), and "Jesus Children of America" both introduced Wonder's interest in Eastern religion. It's a tribute to his genius that he could broach topics like reincarnation and transcendental meditation in a pop context with minimal interference to the rest of the album. Wonder also made no secret of the fact that "He's Misstra Know-It-All" was directed at Tricky Dick, aka Richard Milhouse Nixon, then making headlines (and destroying America's faith in the highest office) with the biggest political scandal of the century. Putting all these differing themes and topics into perspective was the front cover, a striking piece by Efram Wolff portraying Stevie Wonder as the blind visionary, an artist seeing far better than those around him what was going on in the early '70s, and using his astonishing musical gifts to make this commentary one of the most effective and entertaining ever heard. *—John Bush*

Fulfillingness' First Finale / Jul. 22, 1974 / Motown ♦♦♦♦♦
After the righteous anger and occasional despair of the socially motivated *Innervisions*, Stevie Wonder returned with a relationship record: *Fulfillingness' First Finale*. The cover pictures his life as an enormous wheel, part of which he's looking ahead to and part of which he's already completed (the latter with accompanying images of Little Stevie, JFK and MLK, the Motor Town Revue bus, a child with balloons, his familiar Taurus logo, and multiple Grammy awards). The songs and arrangements are the warmest since *Talking Book*, and Stevie positively caresses his vocals on this set, encompassing the vagaries of love, from dreaming of it ("Creepin'") to being bashful of it ("Too Shy to Say") to knowing when it's over ("It Ain't No Use"). The two big singles are "Boogie on Reggae Woman," with a deep electronic groove balancing organic congas and gospel piano, and "You Haven't Done Nothin'," an acidic dismissal of President Nixon and the Watergate controversy (he'd already written "He's Misstra Know-It-All" on the same topic). As before, *Fulfillingness' First Finale* is mostly the work of a single man; Stevie invited over just a bare few musicians, and most of those were background vocalists (though of the finest caliber: Minnie Riperton, Paul Anka, Deniece Williams, and the Jackson 5). Also as before, the appearances are perfectly chosen; "Too Shy to Say" can only benefit from the acoustic bass of Motown institution James Jamerson and the heavenly steel guitar of Sneaky Pete Kleinow, while the Jackson 5 provide some righteous amens to Stevie's preaching on "You Haven't Done Nothin'." It's also very refreshing to hear more songs devoted to the many and varied stages of romance, among them "It Ain't No Use," "Too Shy to Say," "Please Don't Go." The only element lacking here, in comparison to the rest of his string of brilliant early-'70s records, is a clear focus; *Fulfillingness' First Finale* is more a collection of excellent songs than an excellent album. *—John Bush*

☆ **Songs in the Key of Life** / Sep. 28, 1976 / Motown ♦♦♦♦♦
Songs in the Key of Life was Stevie Wonder's longest, most ambitious collection of songs, a two-LP (plus accompanying EP) set that—just as the title promised—touched on nearly every issue under the sun, and did it all with ambitious (even for him), wide-ranging arrangements and some of the best performances of Wonder's career. The opening "Love's in Need of Love Today" and "Have a Talk With God" are curiously subdued, but Stevie soon kicks into gear with "Village Ghetto Land," a fierce exposé of ghetto neglect set to a satirical baroque synthesizer. Hot on its heels comes the torrid fusion jam "Contusion," a big, brassy hit tribute to the recently departed Duke Ellingon in "Sir Duke," and (another hit, this one a Grammy winner as well) the bumping poem to his childhood, "I Wish." Though they didn't necessarily appear in order, *Songs in the Key of Life* contains nearly a full album on love and relationships, along with another full album on issues social and spiritual. Fans of the love album *Talking Book* can marvel that he sets the bar even higher here, with brilliant material like the tenderly cathartic and gloriously redemptive "Joy Inside My Tears," the two-part, smooth-and-rough "Ordinary Pain," the bitterly ironic "All Day Sucker," or another classic heartbreaker, "Summer Soft." Those inclined toward Stevie Wonder the social-issues artist had quite a few songs to focus on as well: "Black Man" was a Bicentennial school lesson on remembering the vastly different people who helped build America; "Pastime Paradise" examined the plight of those living in the past with little hope for the future; "Village Ghetto Land" brought listeners to a nightmare of urban wasteland; and "Saturn" found Stevie questioning his kinship with the rest of humanity and amusingly imagining paradise as a residency on a distant planet. If all this sounds overwhelming, it is; Stevie Wonder had talent to spare during the mid-'70s, and instead of letting the reserve trickle out during the rest of the decade, he let it all go with one massive burst. (The similarly gargantuan but largely instrumental soundtrack *Secret Life of Plants* was his only subsequent record until 1980.) *—John Bush*

★ **Looking Back** / Nov. 30, 1977 / Motown ♦♦♦♦♦
Between 1963 and the end of 1971, Stevie Wonder placed 25 songs on *Billboard*'s charts, and 24 of those—including such radio staples as "Fingertips—Pt. 2," "Uptight (Everything's Alright)," "I Was Made to Love Her," "For Once in My Life," "My Cherie Amour," and "Signed, Sealed, Delivered, I'm Yours"—appear on *Looking Back*. Wonder's recordings in the '60s stand apart from most Motown acts partially because he was paired with producers and writers who very rarely worked with the Temptations, Supremes, et al. In the beginning Wonder was often produced by Clarence Paul and/or William Stevenson; during the golden years, Henry Cosby was usually manning the controls. Then in 1970, Wonder started producing himself, beginning with "Signed, Sealed, Delivered." Most of Wonder's singles were written by Wonder himself in tandem with a variety of others, or by Ron Miller. The hits alternated between stomping barn-burners and midtempo, understated ballads. *—Rob Bowman*

Journey Through the Secret Life of Plants / Oct. 30, 1979 / Motown ♦♦♦
Perhaps the most curious album in Stevie Wonder's career, this was ostensibly a soundtrack for a film few people saw (if indeed it was ever released). These were mostly instrumentals, plus a few oddball vocals, but most observers didn't know what to make of it at the time. Wonder was so hot that the record peaked at number four on the pop albums chart, despite the lack of any real singles and confounding almost everyone who heard it. Though "Send One Your Love" and "Outside My Window" both made the pop charts, the R&B community ignored the entire album. *—Ron Wynn*

Hotter Than July / Sep. 29, 1980 / Motown ♦♦♦♦♦
Four years after the pinnacle of Stevie Wonder's mid-'70s typhoon of classic albums, *Hotter Than July* was the proper follow-up to *Songs in the Key of Life* (his *Journey Through the Secret Life of Plants* concept record was actually a soundtrack to an obscure movie that fared miserably in theaters). It also found Wonder in a different musical climate than the one that savored his every move from 1972 to 1977. Disco and new wave had slowly crept their way into the mainstream record-buying public, and hindered the once-ample room for socially and politically charged lyrics. However, Wonder naysayed the trends and continues to do what he did best. Solid songwriting, musicianship, and production are evident in the majority of *Hotter Than July*. Wonder also carries on his tradition of penning songs normally not associated with his trademark sound, from the disco-tinged "All I Do" (originally planned to be released by Tammi Terrell almost ten years previously) to the reggae-influenced smash "Master Blaster (Jammin')," which went straight to the top of the R&B charts. While admittedly there are a few less-than-standard

tracks, he closes the album on an amazing high note with one of the most aching ballads in his canon ("Lately") and a touching anthem to civil rights pioneer Martin Luther King Jr. ("Happy Birthday"). While most definitely not on the same tier as *Innervisions* or *Songs in the Key of Life*, *Hotter Than July* is the portrait of an artist who still had the Midas touch, but stood at the crossroads of an illustrious career. *—Rob Theakston*

★ **Original Musiquarium I** / May 4, 1982 / Motown ✦✦✦✦✦
Released in 1982, the double-album *Original Musiquarium I* summarizes Stevie Wonder's classic period of the '70s, concentrating primarily on the hits, but adding a few album tracks to hint at the depth of his albums, as well as four new songs (one for each side, all pleasant, none particularly remarkable). Though there could be some dispute about the album tracks, this does wind up as an excellent overview of Wonder's period of greatest activity, and it's a terrific listen to boot—any record that sports such hits as "Superstition," "You Haven't Done Nothin'," "Living for the City," "You Are the Sunshine of My Life," "Higher Ground," "Sir Duke," "Boogie on Reggae Woman," and "I Wish" is guaranteed to be a great listen, and it is. Wonder remains a quintessential album artist, but this record is a terrific snapshot of the highlights. *—Stephen Thomas Erlewine*

The Woman in Red / Aug. 28, 1984 / Motown ✦✦✦
Stevie Wonder's career in the 1980s was a source of frustration to the fans he had earned in the '60s and '70s. In 1982, there were a few new songs on a greatest-hits album and a duet with Paul McCartney. Then came this soundtrack to a Gene Wilder film comedy that was simultaneously more of a pop vocal album than most soundtracks and yet less than a full-fledged Wonder record. The gold-selling number-one hit that resulted was the sappy "I Just Called To Say I Love You," a formulaic TV commercial-in-the-making. "Love Light in Flight" also hit, and the album featured Dionne Warwick on two duets and one solo. This was a pleasant record, but slight, and after four years, Wonder fans wanted more than that. *—William Ruhlmann*

In Square Circle / Sep. 13, 1985 / Motown ✦✦✦
Although it went platinum, nothing stands as better evidence of how cyclical the pop experience is than the response to *In Square Circle*. Wonder actually wrote some superb songs, and several, like "Overjoyed" and "I Love You Too Much," were superior to the hit single "Part-Time Lover." But that one zoomed to the top spot and became the album's definitive tune in the minds of many. *—Ron Wynn*

Characters / Nov. 6, 1987 / Motown ✦✦✦
Wonder shocked fans by taking only two years to release his next new non-soundtrack studio album, *Characters*. Unfortunately, it had long since become clear that Wonder was willing to settle for good pop music without challenging himself to make great pop music. And by now, a big chunk of his formerly mass audience had gotten the message: this was Wonder's first new album to miss the pop Top Five in 15 years. (The black music audience, however, responded far more favorably, as the album topped the R&B charts for seven weeks.) The biggest single was the "Superstition"-like dance track "Skeletons" (number-19 pop, number-one R&B), and Wonder also charted with the pretty "You Will Know" and an uptempo duet with Michael Jackson, "Get It." *—William Ruhlmann*

Jungle Fever / May 22, 1991 / Motown ✦✦✦
Despite all of the hype surrounding it, the soundtrack to *Jungle Fever* is Stevie Wonder's best work in years. Although it can't compare to Wonder's glory days, *Jungle Fever* is a considerable improvement from his bland late-'80s albums. Wonder still borders on saccharine on his ballads, although even the sappiest of them ("These Three Words") is never as sickening as "I Just Called to Say I Love You." While the keyboard funk of "Chemical Love," "Gotta Have You" and "Queen in the Black" doesn't sound new, it does sound alive, which is better than Wonder has sounded in years. *—Stephen Thomas Erlewine*

Conversation Peace / Mar. 21, 1995 / Motown ✦✦✦
Stevie Wonder's albums have not caught the public's attention since the mid-'80s, and *Conversation Peace* did not change that, although it wasn't for lack of trying. Wonder's gift for melody is still in place, and he incorporates understated hip-hop rhythms into his music well, yet he isn't able to make music that fits into the rigid playlists of '90s urban contemporary radio. *—Stephen Thomas Erlewine*

Natural Wonder / Nov. 21, 1995 / Motown ✦✦✦
Following the relative commercial failure of *Conversation Peace*, Stevie Wonder rushed out this double-disc live album drawn from an international tour during which he was backed by different symphony orchestras, his older songs featuring string parts in place of the synthesizer lines. He introduced several new songs—"Dancing to the Rhythm," and the instrumental "Stevie Ray Blues," "Stay Gold," and "Ms. & Mr. Little Ones"—which demonstrated that his melodic muse was still with him and that he remained an awkward lyricist when he was more interested in the political stance than the poetical scansion. But for most of the running time, he acted as a human jukebox, pumping out his hits with enthusiasm and humor before an audibly enthralled audience. That made *Natural Wonder* entertaining, but inessential. *—William Ruhlmann*

Song Review: Greatest Hits / Dec. 10, 1996 / Motown ✦✦✦✦✦
While it's not quite the definitive compilation it could have been, the double-disc *Song Review: Greatest Hits* is still a good overview of Stevie Wonder's long, prolific career. Skipping over "Fingertips, Pt. 2" and picking up with "Uptight (Everything's Alright)" and "I Was Made to Love Her," *Song Review* runs through the next three decades, hitting most of his biggest hits along the way, including "Signed, Sealed, Delivered I'm Yours," "Superstition," "You Are the Sunshine of My Life," "Higher Ground," "Living for the City," "I Wish," "Master Blaster (Jammin')," "Ebony and Ivory," "I Just Called to Say I Love You," and "Part-Time Lover." Unfortunately, none of the songs are presented in chronological order. It begins in the '80s, switches to the '70s, hits the '80s again before going back to the '60s—in other words, it's not really coherent. Nevertheless, most of Wonder's best-known and a good cross-section of his very best songs are included, making *Song Review* a fine, but not perfect, introduction to his career. *—Stephen Thomas Erlewine*

☆ **At the Close of the Century** / Nov. 23, 1999 / Motown ✦✦✦✦✦
He's been called one of the most influential performers and songwriters of the century, but until 1999 Stevie Wonder didn't even have a box set to call his own. Such was the reissue campaign at Motown that, until very recently, some of the best pop music of the '60s sounded poorer in reissue form than when it was first played on AM radio. In 1996, the long-awaited Stevie Wonder digital-age hits package *Song Review* reached the shelves, but it didn't even follow compilation etiquette (that is, chronological order). Finally, *At the Close of a Century* made everything right—complete with digital remastering, near-perfect sound, complete coverage of his epic career, an attractive design, and copious liner notes and pictures. The box, a four-disc set spanning 1962 to 1996, debuts with "Fingertips, Pts. 1 & 2," the long-unheard seven-minute version of his first hit. The first disc includes every hit that fans can remember, including great-sounding versions of "Uptight (Everything's Alright)" and "Hey Love," plus plenty of moderate hits they may not remember, like his definitive cover of the Beatles' "We Can Work It Out." Disc two features more than a dozen of his biggest hits, including "Superstition," "You Are the Sunshine of My Life," "Living for the City," "Higher Ground," and "Boogie on Reggae Woman." Disc three begins with no less than nine tracks from *Songs in the Key of Life*, his standout double album from 1976. Right into the '80s and '90s, Stevie Wonder remained at the top of the charts, with hits like "Rocket Love," "Master Blaster (Jammin')," "Happy Birthday," "I Just Called to Say I Love You," and "Part-Time Lover." It took far too long, but Motown finally issued a box set worthy of Stevie Wonder's continuing artistry. *—John Bush*

Definitive Collection / Oct. 29, 2002 / Motown ✦✦✦✦✦
When you're putting together a 21-song collection of a major artist who's had more than 40 Top 40 hits, inevitably there's going to be a lot of good stuff left out. Stevie Wonder's long and varied career (not over when this anthology appeared) really needs more than one disc to even adequately summarize the highlights. But this single-disc comp does squeeze in most of his best-known songs, from 1963's "Fingertips, Pt. 2" to the mid-'80s number-one hits "Part-Time Lover" and "I Just Called to Say I Love You." Along the way there's "Uptight (Everything's Alright)," "I Was Made to Love Her," "For Once in My Life," "My Cherie Amour," "You Are the Sunshine of My Life," "Superstition," "Higher Ground," "Living for the City," "You Haven't Done Nothin'," "Boogie on Reggae Woman," "I Wish," "Sir Duke," and more. There is a sharp decline in quality following "Masterblaster (Jammin')," but at least that only lasts five songs. Of course, there's a lot missing too: "A Place in the Sun," "Shoo-Be-Doo-Be-Doo-Da-Day," "If You Really Love Me," and "Don't You Worry 'Bout a Thing," to pick only some obvious candidates. Why exactly the 1967 single "Hey Love" (a Top Ten R&B single that barely made the pop charts) is included is a mystery, though at least it breaks up the predictability. For casual fans it's a decent career-spanning overview, though, and even the most casual fan will sense the musical genius and enormous artistic growth that shines through most of the selections. *—Richie Unterberger*

Brenton Wood (Alfred Jesse Smith)

b. Jun. 26, 1941, Shreveport, LA
Vocals / Soul, Pop-Soul, Beach
Brenton Wood's charmingly unpredictable phrasing and his infectious sense of good times made the smooth uptown soul of "The Oogum Boogum Song" and "Gimme a Little Sign" into hits in 1967. Despite his skill as a pop-soul vocalist, Wood was never able to match such heights again, yet those two songs became genuine R&B classics of their era. Born Alfred Jesse Smith in Shreveport, LA, Brenton Wood moved west to San Pedro, CA, as a child. After learning how to play piano, he began forming vocal groups, inspired by Sam Cooke and Jesse Belvin. One of these groups, Little Freddie & the Rockets, recorded a single in 1958. While he was studying at Compton College, he assumed the name Brenton Wood, naming himself after his home county. Wood formed the Quotations during college, but soon after graduation he became a solo act. Signing with Double Shot Records, Wood had a hit single in the spring of 1967 with "The Oogum Boogum Song," which reached number 19 on the R&B charts and number-34 pop. It was quickly followed by "Gimme a Little Sign," which climbed to number-nine pop and matched its predecessor's R&B position. It was a promising start to a career, but Wood wasn't able to follow it through. "Baby You Got It" stalled in the bottom reaches of the pop and R&B Top 40 in early 1968 and "Some Got It, Some Don't" failed to make the pop charts later that year. Wood continued to perform and even recorded a duet with Shirley Goodman, but he wasn't able to reach the charts again until 1977, when "Come Softly to Me" registered in the lower reaches of the R&B Top 100. Following its release, Wood became part of the oldies soul circuit. In 2001, he finally returned with an album of new material, *This Love Is for Real*. *—Stephen Thomas Erlewine*

Baby You Got It / 1967 / Double Shot ✦✦✦✦
Getting it while the getting was good, Double Shot records issued this LP the same year they dropped *Oogum Boogum*. "Gimme a Little Sign," which was also included on *Oogum Boogum*, exploded worldwide and "Baby You Got It" had the same potential. An organ is the most dominant instrument on these half-baked but likable tracks. The songs are bubblegum-ish lyrically and musically but are not nearly as inane as the idiocy Buddah records was releasing on Ohio Express, 1910 Fruitgum Company, and others; besides, you can't help but admire Wood's vocal aerobics. Cuts to hear include: "Catch You on the Rebound," "Me and You," and "Three Time Loser." *—Andrew Hamilton*

Oogum Boogum / 1967 / Double Shot ✦✦✦✦
Brenton Wood's first LP for Double Shot records (or anybody, for that matter), it followed fast on the heels of his chart smash "The Oogum Boogum Song," an infectious ditty where Wood's elastic, charming vocals made you overlook the songs' Mickey Mouse production. As enticing is Wood's sincere delivery of "I Think You Got Your Fools Mixed Up." Also featured are a rendition of Count Five's (labelmates) "Psychotic Reactions" and his

follow-up chartbuster "Gimme a Little Sign." A simplistic but arresting—due solely to Wood's unpredictable vocalizing—album. But at 23 minutes total running time, it's over before you can get your groove on. Out of print, but the best cuts are available on various best-of Brenton Wood CDs. *—Andrew Hamilton*

Come Softly / 1977 / Cream ♦♦♦

The Best of Brenton Wood / 1986 / Rhino ♦♦♦♦♦

• **Brenton Wood's 18 Best** / Jun. 5, 1992 / Original Sound ♦♦♦♦♦
It's hard not to hear Brenton Wood's biggest hit "Gimme a Little Sign" and not be convinced that it very well might be the greatest single ever cut. It relies on no one thing—the song is slinky, surprising and seductive, blessed with a perfect production (the organ break in the middle is positively, eerily beautiful) and a wonderful, understated performance by Wood, who proves with his smooth, sure-handed delivery that he is one of the finest soul singers of his generation. Apart from "Gimme a Little Sign" and the cheerful, infectious "Oogum Boogum," he had few blockbusters, but those were two of the best singles of the '60s, and the rest of his canon was uniformly enjoyable, even if lacking songs as undeniable as that pair. Sadly, his catalog still lacks a truly convincing overview of his career, but, in a pinch, *18 Best* will have to do. Doggedly non-chronological, lacking liner notes or cohesion, and not necessarily spotlighting his best, it still does make a strong case for Wood's talents as a singer and even the weaker material is enjoyable, thanks to his voice and production. It may not be perfect, but it does have a perfect single, one nearly as good, and a bunch of other songs that prove Wood was at the forefront of uptown soul in the '60s. *—Stephen Thomas Erlewine*

18 More of the Best, Vol. 2 / Oct. 5, 1999 / Original Sound ♦♦♦♦
Brenton Wood's biggest hits were covered on Original Sound's first collection, *18 Best*, which leaves this collection without any easy hook into its treasures. But, make no mistake, even with this shoddy packaging, indifferent mastering, and haphazard sequencing (including some songs that might not have made the cut in a more carefully considered collection), this still has a number of wonderful, easygoing, classy pop-soul gems that offer convincing evidence that Wood is one of the most underrated soul singers of his time. And, considering that so little of his material is easily available on CD, you take these kind of pleasures wherever you can find them. *—Stephen Thomas Erlewine*

Better Believe It / Mar. 7, 2000 / WestSide ♦♦♦
Nine of these 15 tracks originally surfaced on Wood's 1977 Cream Records album, *Come Softly*. The songs are structured better and the recordings are of a much higher quality than his run of hits for Double Shot Records. But it's obvious that Wood's uniqueness works better when the arrangements aren't as tight and he has room to twist and curl notes as he pleases. On these, he's more mellow and predictable. There aren't any bust-out hits but there are some good sounds. On "Just Like the First Time," he sounds like Sam Cooke; "Love Is Free" is Smokey Robinson-esque; "You're Everything I Need" and "Better Believe It" bring out the Marvin Gaye. In fact, he sounds like everybody but the "Oogum Boogum Song" man who millions loved and supported via record purchases. But this isn't a negative, just a surprise; he displays a much wider range of skills—reggae, jazz, pop—than the young man who charmed the world with his elastic voice. The last cut, "Watchin' Johnny Carson Thru' My Toes," is as cute as its title. *—Andrew Hamilton*

This Love Is for Real / Apr. 10, 2001 / Varese ♦♦
On his first collection of all-new recordings in a decade, Brenton Wood presented mostly new songs, along with remakes of "Boogum Boogum Boogum/The Oogum Boogum Song" and "Baby You Got It." It's always a bad sign on comebacks by soul veterans when you see keyboard programmers credited on most of the songs. True to suspicions, this is mellow soul updated with contemporary arrangements, with synthesizers and ultra-sweet backup vocals. Whether intentionally or not, the impression is that of songs calculated to pick up adult contemporary radio airplay. The best that can be said is that Wood's voice is good, and still expert at hitting the high silky notes. But the material is dull, and the production worse. *—Richie Unterberger*

Bernie Worrell

b. Apr. 19, 1944, Long Beach, NJ
Keyboards, Piano, Synthesizer, Organ / Funk
Raised in Plainfield, NJ, Bernie Worrell was a classically trained pianist at three years old. Throughout his childhood he played with symphonies and orchestras, and even wrote his own concerto at the age of eight. Slowly, he listened to the radio and discovered sounds other than classical, and when he went to college, he played with a number of bar bands, including the Tavares (who were known as Chubby & the Turnpikes back then). It was also around this time that Worrell met George Clinton, who was the vocalist for a Motown-influenced group called the Parliaments. The Parliaments soon split up and moved to Detroit, where Clinton re-formed them into a new group, called Parliament. Clinton then formed another side band, called Funkadelic, several of whose members had been in Parliament but were now performing under the new name due to contractual glitches. Worrell joined Funkadelic in 1970, beginning with their album *Free Your Mind and Your Ass Will Follow*. He was an essential part of the P-Funk mob and continued to play with them right up until the early '80s. He then joined the Talking Heads as a session man and went on tour with them throughout the '80s, basically working with David Byrne and the band right up to their split in early 1992. Besides his solo career, Worrell continues to work with members of the P-Funk, including Bootsy Collins. His work on such songs as "Flashlight," "(Not Just) Knee Deep," and "Cosmic Slop" influenced not only other R&B/soul artists but also many rap groups, who continue to sample his work in their own songs. *—John Book*

All the Woo in the World / 1978 / Arista ♦♦♦
Parliament/Funkadelic keyboardist Bernie Worrell's first LP is more Funkadelic than Parliament, and with the exception of one tune, less exciting than either. The keeper is "Insurance Man for the Funk," 12 minutes and 39 seconds of pure P-Funk; it has everything: layered sounds, a toe-tapping midtempo beat, and some incredible horns. The chorus has a great hook—"Insurance Man for the funk/Take some insurance out on your romp/You are the beneficiaryyyy"; it also has some side-cracking lines like "Leroy's (Lloyd's) of London," and a great synthesizer solo by Bernie. Not to knock Bernie's rendition, which is great, but if George had cut this with Parliament or Bootsy's Rubber Band, it would have blown up. Unfortunately, nothing else here measures up to "Insurance Man"; the other selections have a weird feel to them. Bernie does most of the lead vocals, and Junie Morrison plays a significant role. You get the feeling that most of these tracks were first slotted for other artists under George Clinton's umbrella of stars. "Woo Together" features Bernie and Junie on a funk number; Morrison leads the rather dull "I'll Be Here." The concept is supposed to be something called Woo, which is not adequately explained. *—Andrew Hamilton*

B.W. Jam (Rock the House) / 1990 / Rhino ♦♦♦

• **Funk of Ages** / Feb. 1991 / Gramavision ♦♦♦♦♦
Keyboardist Bernie Worrell was one of the key members of George Clinton's "Parlaifunkadelicment Thang" and he later went on to work as a sideman with everyone from Talking Heads to Keith Richards, as well as a long series of projects with producer and Material mastermind Bill Laswell. But outside of *All the Woo in the World*, a tossed-off project which got lost in the glut of P-Funk-related product released in the late '70s, it wasn't until 1991 that Worrell applied his estimable talent to an album with himself as headliner. *Funk of Ages* is a glossy set of funk workouts and jazz-influenced side trips with an impressive list of guest stars (including David Byrne, Keith Richards, Vernon Reid, Herbie Hancock, Sly Dunbar, Robbie Shakespeare, and Maceo Parker), and while Worrell certainly gives himself plenty of room to show off his estimable skill at the keyboard, he also has the good sense to make room for his friends and collaborators, giving the album the sound and feel of a group effort rather than a declaration of musical independence. In fact, if the album has a flaw, it's that it lacks a central presence giving the material an anchor; this eternal sideman certainly has the skills to take the reins on an album, but this set suggests he lacks the ego to do so (and he's not much of a lead singer). But his years with Clinton and Laswell have taught Worrell more than a little about the fine art of getting a groove on, and *Funk of Ages* serves up thick, juicy rhythms topped with smart and flavorful melodic support; it's a more ambitious and enjoyable album than anything George Clinton cooked up on his own in the 1990s. *—Mark Deming*

Blacktronic Science / 1993 / Rhino ♦♦♦
His status as a great team player (Parliament, Funkadelic, Talking Heads) is irrefutable, but as a solo artist, Worrell is strictly hit-or-miss. For all the moments that *Blacktronic Science* meshes and hits undeniable grooves, it's undone by bad ideas and a tendency to be too eclectic. Worrell has surrounded himself with a superb band (Bootsy, Mudbone Cooper, Maceo Parker, Fred Wesley, Tony Williams), but what they need is to follow a leader with a vision like George Clinton (who makes an appearance here) or James Brown. Worrell tries hard, but comes up with pseudo-soundtrack sludge like "Revelation In Black Light" or fake jazz like "Blood Secrets..." The P-funkin' of "Dissinfordollars" really takes off and gives you the impression that, had this been a Clinton project, it might have been meatier, more fun and more focused. *—John Dougan*

Da Bomb / Jan. 26, 1999 / Vanguard ♦♦♦
The new wave-flavored funk of this forgotten band is most notable for the participation of P-Funk keyboardist Bernie Worrell. The obvious debt to George Clinton is a bit too strong to ignore, though, and rather than evoking the abandon of Funkadelic, this disc is a bit too disco for funk comfort. That is not to say there aren't some good moments, such as this guitar frenzy on "Love Slave (Nose Job)" and the cozmik debris of "Your Mother" (with lyrics like "Your momma comes from Tokyo/She loves to rollerskate, you know"). A fun diversion. *—Tim Sheridan*

The Wrens

f. 1954, **db.** 1956
Group / Doo Wop, R&B
The Wrens were one of the best of the dozens of R&B vocal groups who recorded in the mid- to late '50s for George Goldner, signed to his Rama and Gee labels in the wake of his success with "Gee" by the Crows. Lead singer Bobby Mansfield, George Magnezid (tenor), Francis "Frenchie" Concepcion (tenor), and James "Archie" Archer (bass) first started singing together in 1954 at a community center in the Bronx, NY. There they were spotted by Fred Johnson, a promoter who organized local talent shows, and he offered to manage the quartet. The Wrens were known best for their smooth, elegant harmony singing, which elevated both their ballads and their jump numbers above much of the competition. They sang R&B, but it tended more toward mature ballads and serious jump songs, rather than teen novelties.

Johnson got the group an audition with George Goldner's Rama Records and a recording contract followed late in 1954, with the group's first session taking place on November 21 of that year. Fred Johnson played piano behind them on that session and Goldner produced; in later recordings, legendary saxman Jimmy Wright led the band that backed them up. The group's first released single was "Love's Something Made for Two" b/w "Beggin' for Love," featuring Mansfield and Concepcion, respectively. It was their second single, "Come Back My Love," however, that achieved some local popularity in New York early in 1955 and put the Wrens on the map for R&B vocal fans. At their best, the Wrens sounded a lot like the Moonglows—Mansfield's singing at times bore a striking resemblance to Harvey Fuqua of the latter group, and both outfits were at their best doing mid-tempo jump numbers and ballads, though the Wrens' records also had a hard edge from Wright's sax and the bold sound of the Rama house band under his leadership.

Goldner issued a total of six singles by the Wrens, but they never enjoyed a bigger hit than "Come Back My Love," which became their signature song despite competition from a cover version done by the Cardinals on Atlantic that same year. By 1956, however, Bobby Mansfield had split off from the group for a solo career, during which he made some records for Goldner with the Supremes (the male R&B vocal group, not the Motown trio) backing him. The Wrens disappeared into the mists of R&B vocal group history, while Mansfield remained active into the 1990s, even recording with a new group of "Wrens" in the middle of the decade. The original Wrens all lived long enough to see themselves inducted into the United Group Harmony Association's Hall of Fame in 1998. Collectables Records issued a collection of the Wrens' recordings in the early '90s and England's WestSide label followed this up in 2000 with *Strictly for the Birds*, compiling the Wrens' and the Crows' material on one CD. —*Bruce Eder*

● **The Best of the Wrens** / Nov. 25, 1991 / Collectables ♦♦♦♦♦

Bernard Wright

b. 1963, Miami, FL

Keyboards, Synthesizer / Urban, Funk, Fusion

Keyboardist Bernard Wright seemed like a coming fusion and urban star when he toured with Lenny White at 13 and played with Tom Browne in 1979. He got such strong response that he was signed to GRP in 1981. But the LP *'Nard* stalled, though there was good reaction among R&B and fusion fans to the single "Just Chillin' Out." It was followed by *Funky Beat* for Arista and *Mr. Wright* for Manhattan/EMI. Wright also co-wrote and sang with La La on "We'll Keep Strivin'." He has recorded with Cameo, Bobby Brown, Pieces of a Dream, and Charles Earland, among others. —*Ron Wynn*

● **'Nard** / 1981 / BMG ♦♦♦♦

Like Tom Browne and Lenny White/Twennynine, Bernard Wright was part of Jamaica, Queens' R&B/funk scene of the late '70s and early '80s, which gave us such major hits as Twennynine's "Peanut Butter" and Browne's "Funkin' for Jamaica." Browne and White were both talented jazz musicians, but R&B/funk was their main focus at that time. Similarly, keyboardist/pianist Wright occasionally flirts with instrumental jazz on his debut album, *'Nard*, but pays a lot more attention to vocal-oriented soul and funk. The only instrumentals on this out-of-print LP are the jazz-funk smoker "Firebolt Hustle," the Rodney Franklin-ish "Bread Sandwiches," and a relaxed interpretation of Miles Davis' "Solar," which finds Wright forming an acoustic piano trio with bassist Buster Williams and drummer Roy Haynes. Otherwise, this is an R&B album that is defined by such impressive funk as "Spinnin'," "Master Rocker," and the goofy but wildly infectious "Haboglabotribin'." Recorded when the keyboardist/pianist was only 16, *'Nard* was expected to be a big hit, but surprisingly, didn't fare as well as albums by Browne and White. —*Alex Henderson*

Funky Beat / 1983 / Arista ♦♦♦

Retaining the services of veteran producers Dave Grusin, Larry Rosen, Lenny White and Wright himself, this album explores several subgenres of music. Being as gifted as he is, Wright obviously did not want to limit himself by recording just one style of music. With the popularity of breakdancing and the rise of video arcades, Wright's pioneering vision is witnessed on "Funky Beat" and "Video Generation." The former made the *Billboard* R&B charts, peaking at number 39, but the latter was never a release. These compositions are not breathtaking recordings, but do offer a alternative to the routine rhythms normally used; they verge on pre-techno. Wright slows it down with a more contemporary sound on "Keep on Doing That Right Thing" and "Won't You Let Me Love You." The latter is a skillfully written, highly underrated song that made the *Billboard* R&B charts at number 88 after only a two-week run. Wright further displays his versatility on a remake of the Clifford Brown jazz classic "Joy Spring," a melodious, soft and easy jazz composition that features Lenny White on drums. However, no selection is more noteworthy than "Mr. Clean," a funky, jazzy, souful instrumental driven by improvised keyboard solos and a pulsating, electric bass. —*Craig Lytle*

Betty Wright

b. Dec. 21, 1953, Miami, FL

Vocals / Soul, Quiet Storm

Singer Betty Wright proved to be a consistently strong presence on the Miami music scene, primarily throughout the '70s and '80s, although she continues to record. Born on December 21, 1953, in Miami, FL, Wright began her singing career early on as a member of her family's own gospel group the Echoes of Joy. By the age of 13, Wright had begun appearing on other artists' recordings as a backup singer and two years later was issuing her own solo singles (scoring a Top 40 hit the same year with "Girls Can't Do What the Guys Do") and albums (*My First Time Around*). It would be several years, however, before Wright would enjoy her next substantial hit, but it would prove to be worth the wait when 1972's "Clean Up Woman" (notable for its prominent guitar riff and Wright's swaggering lead vocal) peaked at number two on the R&B and number six on the pop charts. In 1974, Wright received a Grammy Award for the song "Where Is the Love?" (not to be confused with the renowned Roberta Flack/Donny Hathaway tune of the same name); Wright steadily continued to issue albums throughout the decade, including such standout titles as 1975's *Danger High Voltage* (which spawned three R&B hits, "Shoorah! Shoorah!," "Where Is the Love?," and "Tonight Is the Night") and 1978's *Betty Wright Live*.

In 1981 her hit collaboration with Stevie Wonder, "What Are You Gonna Do With It?," proved to be Wright's last substantial hit. Wright continued issuing albums throughout the '80s and '90s, in addition to trying her hand as a television talk show hostess and contributing backing vocals to a wide variety of other artists such as Erykah Badu, Regina Belle, David Byrne, Jimmy Cliff, Gloria Estefan, Inner Circle, Millie Jackson, Jennifer Lopez, Johnny Mathis, etc. The early 21st century saw the release of Wright's first all-new studio album in several years, 2001's *Fit for a King*, as well as the fine 16-track career overview *The Very Best of Betty Wright*. —*Greg Prato & Christine Ohlman*

My First Time Around / 1968 / Atco ♦♦♦

I Love the Way You Love Me / 1972 / Alston ♦♦♦

Hard to Stop / 1973 / Alston ♦♦♦

Danger High Voltage / 1975 / Alston ♦♦♦♦♦

Danger! Hi-Voltage is an apt title for Betty Wright's finest hour. It contains three R&B hits—"Shoorah! Shoorah!," "Where Is the Love," and "Tonight Is the Night"—but also features an array of other tasty tracks, including the heart-tugging "That's When I'll Stop Loving You." Out of print, but available on CD with another Wright album as a two-for-one. —*Andrew Hamilton*

Betty Wright Live / Feb. 1978 / Rhino ♦♦♦♦♦

When *Betty Wright Live* was first released in 1978, there was some speculation on whether or not it was really a live album or simply a studio recording with canned applause. To be sure, the applause doesn't sound authentic, and the original LP's liner notes listed neither a recording date nor a location. But whether it was recorded on-stage or in the studio, this album (reissued on CD in 1992) provides much evidence of Wright's vitality as a singer. *Live* became best known for its version of "Tonight Is the Night," a moving account of a young woman losing her virginity to her first true love. But the gritty Miami soulster is equally expressive on Leon Russell's "A Song for You" and versions of her hits "Where Is the Love" and "Clean Up Woman" (which is performed as the main song in an 11-minute medley). Even if the title *Betty Wright Live* is an example of false advertising, this is a recording that fans of gritty, emotionally direct Southern soul would do well to experience. —*Alex Henderson*

Betty Travelin' in the Wright Circle / 1979 / Alston ♦♦♦

Betty Wright produced this final Alston release herself, and it's easy to understand why Henry Stone (Alston's owner) shelved it until the end of his association with the singer. Wright, who, as a teen, belted out "Clean Up Woman" like a bona fide tramp, brings none of that intensity to these sessions. A coupling of Darrell Banks' "Open the Door to Your Heart" and the O'Jays' "Love Train" falls flat. Like Wright's vocals, the songs lack conviction, passion, and depth. The lilting ballad "Thank You for the Many Things You've Done" is the most satisfying cut—which isn't saying much, considering the quality of the other songs. "Listen to the Music (Dance)" attempts to reach the disco market, but instead will have listeners reaching for the off switch. —*Andrew Hamilton*

Back at You / 1983 / Epic ♦♦♦♦

This Marlon Jackson production recorded in Jamaica hits on all cylinders. "Burning Desire," a Marlon and Tito Jackson song exploits the disco groove in an infectious way, the rhythm track, and trappings including Luther Vandross on backing vocals will set you right. I'm down with "She's Older Now," with its subtle reggae groove, Betty's sweet vocal, and the squalls that I never heard her do before; Vandross, again contributes behind the groove. "Be Your Friend," the third straight winner, shuffling beat and poly rhythms invite your best dance moves. Marlon duets with Betty on "I Promise You," a floater, accented by a strident sax, and romantic lyrics. An enthusiastic "Live, Love, Rejoice" continues the winning tradition, the title is sung like a cheerleading chant, with a tight guitar adding seasoning. Marlon, Randy, Tito, and Jackie Jackson wrote "Special Love," which Betty starts in an airy falsetto like Jackie Jackson's; the reggae rhythms' makes this work, and Wright's singing toughens as the tape rolls. "Show Me," "Gimme Just Another Try," and "Reggae This Way, " meshes American soul with Jamaican reggae. —*Andrew Hamilton*

Golden Classics: Clean Up Woman / 1988 / Collectables ♦♦♦

Mother Wit / 1988 / Vision ♦♦♦

4U2Njoy / 1989 / Vision ♦♦♦

Betty Wright's second album for Vision Records features a stunning picture of her decked out in a white outfit topped with a wide-brim, white hat. She had a hand in writing all nine songs, all of a consistent quality, but none of which are really essential. While competently done, the whole shebang reeks of another session; the lyrics are a series of clichés and street sayings, some marrying better than others. Just as any artist shouldn't put an album out every year just to keep his or her name out there (because if it's mediocre or average it won't enhance their career or get heard anyway), neither should Wright. She could likely put out killer albums every three or four years, but one per year, or every two years is a bit much at the stage of her career during which *4U2Njoy* was recorded. The best of the lot includes the title track, "Keep Love New," "Valley of Lonely," and "It's Been Real." Notable is the contribution of former Rose Royce lead Gwen Dickey on backing vocals. —*Andrew Hamilton*

Passion & Compassion / 1990 / Vision ♦♦♦

The cover of Wright's final CD on Vision Records emulates the first two by depicting Wright dressed like a high-fashion model, this time in purple. The music, however, is much better than her previous Vision releases. This one is smooth and mellow, and caters to the urban/quiet storm crowd. The first cut "Help Is on the Way," is a superb Wright composition. The title track "Passion & Compassion" continues the urban love fest, which gets even better on "Deep Water," a torcher accented by a crying sax. She duets with a male vocalist on "Search 4 Love Is Over," written with Angelo Morris who plays an essential role on this CD as a musician. One of Wright's finest releases in sometime. —*Andrew Hamilton*

The Best of Betty Wright / Sep. 29, 1992 / Rhino ♦♦♦♦♦

An excellent collection, covering the years between 1968 and 1978; it's 20 tracks of Betty Wright at her best. —*Stephen Thomas Erlewine*

The Best of Betty Wright: The TK Years / 1995 / Sequel ♦♦♦

The TK years were lucrative for Ms. B; this was Stage 2 of Betty Wright's career, sandwiched by early hits on Alston Records, e.g., "Girl's Can't Do What The Guys Do" and "Clean Up Woman," and career winders on various labels. The TK years cuts came in Wright's prime, past the teen years—though this set does include "Tonight Is The Night" a tune about a virgin losing her virginity—and before middle-age spread. These tracks are more elaborate than the sparse Alston recordings and they include crossovers:

"Shoorah! Shoorah!," Slip And Do It," a remake of Brainstorm's "Lovin' Is Really My Game" and "Where Is The Love." The 18-track disc also features slow Southern burners like "That's When I'll Stop Loving You," "If I Ever Do Wrong" and "You Can't See For Looking"; Wright co-wrote many of the songs. *—Andrew Hamilton*

Betty Wright Live/Travelin' in the Wright Circle / Mar. 3, 1999 / WestSide ✦✦✦✦✦

● **The Very Best of Betty Wright** / Jun. 20, 2000 / Rhino ✦✦✦✦✦
Rhino's *Very Best of Betty Wright* collects some of the soul diva's definitive tracks, including her first Top 40 hit "Girls Can't Do What the Guys Do," her 1971 Top Ten hit "Clean Up Woman," "Let Me Your Lovemaker," her 1974 Grammy winner "Where Is the Love," and "I'm Gettin' Tired Baby." Though it's not as extensive as the label's earlier compilation *The Best of Betty Wright*, this album does present most of her major singles as well as a few representative album tracks. *—Heather Phares*

Billy Wright

b. May 21, 1932, Atlanta, GA, **d.** Oct. 27, 1991, Atlanta, GA
Vocals, Fiddle / Jump Blues, R&B, Soul-Blues
A prime influence on Little Richard during his formative years, "Prince of the Blues" Billy Wright's hearty shouting delivery was an Atlanta staple during the postwar years. Wright was a regular at Atlanta's 81 Theatre as a youth, soaking up the vaudevillians before graduating to singing and dancing status there himself. Saxist Paul "Hucklebuck" Williams caught Wright's act when they shared a bill with Charles Brown and Wynonie Harris at Atlanta's Auditorium, recommending the teenaged singer to Savoy Records boss Herman Lubinsky.

Wright's 1949 Savoy debut, "Blues for My Baby," shot up to number three on *Billboard*'s R&B charts, and its flip, "You Satisfy," did almost as well. Two more of Wright's Savoy 78s, "Stacked Deck" and "Hey Little Girl," were also Top Ten R&B entries in 1951. The flamboyant Wright set his pal Little Richard up with powerful WGST DJ Zenas Sears, who scored the newcomer his first contract with RCA in 1951. It's no knock on Richard to note that his early sides sound very much like Wright. Wright recorded steadily for Savoy through 1954, the great majority of his sessions held in his hometown with hot local players (saxist Fred Jackson and guitarist Wesley Jackson were often recruited). After he left Savoy, Wright's recording fortunes plummeted—a 1955 date for Don Robey's Peacock discery in Houston and sessions for Fire (unissued) and Carrollton in 1959 ended his discography. Wright later MCed shows in Atlanta, remaining active until a stroke in the mid-'70s slowed him down. He passed away at the age of 59 on October 27, 1991 in his hometown of Atlanta. *—Bill Dahl*

Stacked Deck / 1980 / Route 66 ✦✦✦✦
The title track was a major R&B hit for Wright in 1951, and there are 13 more gems by the animated blues shouter on this import piece of vinyl. Everything's from the Savoy vaults except for an ultra-rare Wright cover of Billy Ward & the Dominoes' "Do Something for Me" that was cut live at Atlanta's Harlem Theatre in 1952. *—Bill Dahl*

Goin' Down Slow (Blues, Soul & Early R 'n' R, Vol. 1) / 1984 / Savoy ✦✦✦✦✦

● **Billy Wright** / 1994 / Savoy Jazz ✦✦✦✦✦
Here are 15 of the Atlanta jump blues shouter's very best outings for Savoy, spanning 1949-1954. Wright's pleading style, a large influence indeed on a developing Little Richard, is irresistibly spotlighted on "After Awhile," "I Remember," and the romping "Billy's Boogie Blues." *—Bill Dahl*

Charles Wright & the Watts 103rd St. Rhythm Band

b. 1942, Clarksdale, MS
Vocals, Guitar / Funk, Soul
Charles Wright headed one of the great funk groups of the late '60s and early '70s, the Watts 103rd Street Rhythm Band. Wright, who was born in Clarksdale, MS, was a singer, pianist, guitarist, and leader of the eight-member band, which had been recruited from Watts in Los Angeles. They were originally known as the Soul Runners. Bill Cosby helped get the band off the ground by giving them appearances at his gigs. They began recording for Keyman in 1967, then moved to Warner Bros. in 1969. While "Do Your Thing" and "Till You Get Enough" were Top 20 R&B hits, their finest selection was "Express Yourself," a song that expressed the urge for freedom as adroitly as the Isley Brothers' "It's Your Thing" had in the '60s. It has also been among the most sampled funk tracks for hip-hop and rap groups. "Your Love (Means Everything to Me)" was their final R&B hit in 1971, peaking at number-nine R&B and number-12 pop.

The group's best ballad, "Love Land," did better among pop fans than R&B ones, many of whom saw it as a bit soft. They continued recording for Dunhill in 1973 before disbanding. Drummer James Gadson and guitarist Al McKay, who later joined Earth, Wind & Fire, were among the instrumental corps of the Watts 103rd Street Rhythm Band. *—Ron Wynn*

Watts 103rd St. Rhythm Band: Hot, Heat and Sweat Groove / 1967 / Warner Bros. ✦✦✦
Hot, Heat and Sweat Groove is the debut album by the funky band led by the charismatic Charles Wright. The Wright brood moved to Los Angeles when Charles Wright was 12. In Watts, Wright befriended doo woppers and balladeers like Jesse Belvin, the Hollywood Flames, the Youngsters, and others who lived in the area. Propped by stars like Bill Cosby and publicized by two and a half years of sold-out crowds at the Haunted House (a local club), along with an unexpected local hit, the band was able to secure a contract with Warner Bros. Records. Nothing major came from this set that displayed a choppy rhythmic approach similar to Dyke & the Blazers. But this surprisingly hard-to-find album produced by James Carmichael, who went on to great success with the Commodores, features some thick funk: "Fried Okra," "Brown Sugar," and reworkings of "Yellow Submarine," "The Girl From Ipanema," and "Bring It on Home to Me." While not the most cohesive set, you can't knock the hot SoCal energy exhibited by Wright and his crew of young hopefuls, including future Earth, Wind & Fire member Al McKay, along with James Gadson, Melvin Dunlap, Big John Rayford, Bill Cannon, Gabriel Flemings, and Joe Banks. The LP's most popular track, "Spreading Honey," charted at number-44 R&B and number-73 pop in 1967. The Watts 103rd Street Rhythm Band didn't even record the song. Wright cut the track with Bobby Womack, Leon Haywood, James Carmichael, and others as the theme song for DJ Magnificent Montague's radio show. But it smoked so much that Warner Bros. signed them on the dotted line and credited the single to the Watts 103rd Street Rhythm Band; this album followed, and the rest is history. *—Andrew Hamilton*

Together / 1968 / Warner Bros. ✦✦✦

In the Jungle, Babe / 1969 / Warner Bros. ✦✦✦✦
Charles Wright & the Watts 103rd Street Rhythm Band were near the peak of their popularity on this, their third Warner Brothers LP featuring three chart singles. Artistically, they are right there. The rough unevenness of LP number one is gone, and it flows smoother than their second album—which spawned "Do Your Thing." "Till You Get Enough," a heavy dose of funk, charted at number-68 pop and 12 R&B in 1969; the slow, sensuous "Love Land" faired much better overall at number-ten pop and number-20 R&B in 1969. A final single, "Must Be Your Thing" (1970), charted at number-67 pop and 12 R&B. The band also affix their disjointed rhythmic approach to remakes of Edwin Starr's "Twenty Five Miles," the Doors' "Light My Fire," and Wilson Pickett's "I'm a Midnight Mover." *In the Jungle, Babe* is easily the most satisfying album of the bands' career. *—Andrew Hamilton*

Express Yourself / 1970 / Warner Bros. ✦✦✦✦✦
The quintessential Charles Wright & the Watts 103rd Street Rhythm Band record, *Express Yourself*, displays the purposefully sloppy rhythms and shout vocals that would make this band a legend in soul circles. Every track on this album is a classic, from the oft-sampled and highest-charting pop single "Express Yourself" to the first of many readings of "I Got Love" that would appear on the band's records—and even Wright's solo works for years to come. The aching balladry of "Tell Me What You Want Me to Do" and the complex compositions "High as Apple Pie, Slice 1" and "High as Apple Pie, Slice 2" showcase a versatility found in other West Coast collectives such as War. Perhaps the treasure of this album is the opener, "Road Without an End," a charming, stepping groover punctuated by choppy horns and snapping drums that blend beautifully with one of Wright's best vocals of his career, all accented by sweeping strings. *Express Yourself* is '70s soul at its most creative and satisfying. *—Douglas Siwek*

You're So Beautiful / 1971 / Warner Bros. ✦✦
Following the success of their most popular album ever, Charles Wright & the Watts 103rd Street Rhythm Band seem to be running out of ideas on *You're So Beautiful*. Kicking off the festivities is a re-working of their big hit, "Express Yourself." Steeped in call-and-response revivalism, "Express Yourself II" brings the funk, but is repetitive and lacks focus. Elements of the band's unbridled yet controlled soul are still evident, but the songs themselves are without structure and seem to ramble. A prime example is the spaced-out "Let's Make Love Not War." A Tribe Called Quest and Brand Nubian have plucked juicy lines from "What Can You Bring Me," with its chicken-scratch guitar licks and ebbing horn patterns. Sadly, this album is not available on CD and is ultra-rare on the crate-digging vinyl circuit. *—Douglas Siwek*

Rhythm and Poetry / 1972 / Warner Bros. ✦✦✦

Doin' What Comes Naturally / 1973 / Dunhill ✦✦✦
After leaving the fading Watts 103rd Street Rhythm Band, Charles Wright released this sprawling double LP full of roof-burning funk grooves, tender soul serenades, and new interpretations on his patented brand of messed-up R&B. Scoring a mild chart hit with the album's title track, Wright wasn't satisfied with rehashing the past successes of his work with his old band. The longing midtempo reflection on lost love of "You & Me" holds its own neatly next to the baroque soul vibrations of "A Mother's Love." As evidenced by his previous work with the Watts 103rd Street Rhythm Band, Wright excels at balladry, and they flow thick on *Doin' What Comes Naturally*. The sublime keys that tickle throughout "1, 2, 3, 4, 5,?" blend sweetly with its instrumental counterpart, "1, 2, 3 You & Me," later on. Only keen quiet storm radio show hosts will acknowledge the beauty of "You Threw It All Away," with its pleading chorus and lush string arrangements, a treasure. The tracks stretch out in length throughout the course of two slabs of wax; unfortunately, the entire fourth side is occupied by the track "Nonsense," which, after one listen, can be described as just that. This solo debut is an intensely pleasurable listening experience. *—Douglas Siwek*

Ninety Day Cycle People / 1974 / Dunhill ✦✦

Lil' Encouragement / 1975 / ABC ✦✦

● **Express Yourself: The Best of Charles Wright and the Watts 103rd Street Rhythm Band** / 1993 / Warner Archives ✦✦✦✦✦
Express Yourself: The Best of Charles Wright collects 16 tracks by this underappreciated L.A. funk outfit. By this point, everyone recognizes the oft-sampled title track, but most of their other work is still mainly the province of specialists. That's too bad, because there's a lot for more general funk fans to discover here. Some members of the Rhythm Band had previously played on several Dyke & the Blazers sessions, and there's a definite parallel between those sides and the loose, messy, off-the-cuff brand of funk that Wright and his cohorts lay down. But even if both groups worked out most of their songs through jamming, there's a great deal more variety here. Wright led the band through laconic grooves like "Express Yourself," "Your Love (Means Everything to Me)," "Doin' What Comes Naturally," and the tripped-out "Ninety Day Cycle People"; hard-driving funkers like "The Joker (On a Trip Through the Jungle)" and "One Lie (Leads to Another)"; lean, spare grooves like "Do Your Thing" and "Till You Get Enough"; and mellower, soul-flavored offerings like "Keep Saying," "Tell Me What You Want Me to Do," "Comment

(If All Men Are Truly Brothers)," and the hit ballad "Love Land." As a vocalist, Wright could play the soulful shouter or do a bit of crooning, but more often he'd just ride the groove, chanting along or throwing out hip interjections. This collection neglects the group's nuttier, druggier side a bit—it might have been nice to have evocatively titled outings like "High As Apple Pie," "Fried Okra," or "Gimme That Sammich" on board. Still, it's hard to expect anything more generous than this, and there's more than enough here for the uninitiated. An intriguing and underrated listen. *—Steve Huey*

In the Jungle, Babe/Express Yourself / Apr. 8, 1997 / Warner Bros. ✦✦✦✦✦

Going to the Party / Aug. 18, 1998 / A Million Dollars Worth of Me ✦✦✦

After going for more than a few years without recording, Charles Wright & His 103rd St. Rhythm Band made an unexpected return to the studio in 1998 with *Going to the Party.* Wright had enjoyed some major hits in the 1960s and 1970s, but in the 1980s and 1990s, the singer wasn't nearly as visible (although his signature tune, "Express Yourself," and had been sampled by N.W.A and other rappers). This CD's front cover boasts that it was "played by human beings, not by machines," and Wright speaks the truth. *Party* sounds like it was played by a real band, not just one guy with a drum machine, sequencers and synthesizers. Instead of trying to appeal to urban contemporary tastes of the late '90s, Wright sticks with a 1970s-type sound on gritty funk smokers like "Groove It" and "She Don't Believe," as well as silky slow jams such as "I'll Give You Time" and "Is It Real." In fact, much of the material sounds like it could have been recorded 20 or 25 years earlier. Wright doesn't have the voice he did in his heyday, and *Party* isn't in a class with his outstanding Warner Bros. output of the 1960s and 1970s. But it's a competent and sincere effort from someone who knows what a real R&B band sounds like. It was nice having Wright back in the studio. *—Alex Henderson*

Edna Wright

b. 1944, Los Angeles, CA

Vocals / Soul, Pop-Soul

The sister of Darlene Love, Edna Wright first gained fame as the lead singer of the Honey Cone in the early '70s. Wright had been a member of the Blossoms and Bob B. Soxx & the Blue Jeans before joining the Honey Cone. Her surging leads helped make such songs as "Want Ads" and "Stick-Up" R&B chart-toppers in the early '70s, as the Honey Cone scored three Top Ten R&B singles, two number-one R&B hits, one number-one pop single, and two other Top 20 pop tunes before disbanding in 1973. *—Ron Wynn*

● **Oops! Here I Go Again** / 1976 / RCA ✦✦✦

Jaguar Wright

Vocals / Neo-Soul, Hip-Hop, Contemporary R&B

Philadelphia-based singer/songwriter Jaguar Wright's name can be added to the list of such Philly-based neo-soul talents as Grammy award-winning rap band the Roots and multi-platinum hitmakers Jill Scott and Musiq Soulchild. She grew up in a household where secular music was forbidden, so her earliest musical influence came through attending church events, social gatherings, and weddings where her father would sing. Still, Wright got her fill of such favorites as Stevie Wonder, Marvin Gaye, and Minnie Riperton by attending parties and listening to music while her parents were away. She started performing as a rapper in a group called Philly Blunts and later began doing background vocal work for artists in Philly, New York, and New Jersey. After impressing Scott Storch of the Roots, she was added to the lineup of the Black Lily, an acclaimed performance showcase held at the Five Spot in Philly, and later toured with the group on the Okayplayer Tour. Wright also earned rave reviews for her background vocal stint at Jay-Z's MTV *Unplugged* appearance in December 2001, and and released her debut album (*Denials Delusions and Decisions*) early the following year through the Roots' Motive label. *—Ed Hogan*

● **Denials Delusions and Decisions** / Jan. 29, 2001 / MCA ✦✦✦✦

Jaguar Wright's debut album, *Denials Delusions and Decisions*, arrived at a perfect time, just as the early-2000s neo-soul movement led by similar female vocalists such as Jill Scott and Mary J. Blige was at its peak. A few years earlier, Wright probably wouldn't even have been given a major-label contract; however, she debuted in early 2002 with not only a substantial major-label marketing push courtesy of MCA, but also a stellar roster of producers—Scott Storch, James Pyser, and Ahmir "?uestlove" Thompson—and a high-profile appearance on Jay-Z's MTV *Unplugged* broadcast, where she sang backup vocals, just as her album was hitting the streets. And while it's easy to compare her to all the other early-2000s neo-soul divas, she's no Erykah Badu (she's a bit more street-orientated), she's no Aaliyah (she has more attitude), and she's no Alicia Keys (she isn't nearly as radio-ready); instead, Wright lives up to her "Jaguar" persona, being sexy and seductive but still vicious and somewhat of a femme fatale (for instance, in her liner notes she addresses her "enemies," "x-boyfriends," and "old sex partners"). And though it's difficult to look past her alluring image and persona and focus exclusively on her music, you don't really want to; it only adds an additional dimension, being incredibly analogous—again, sexy, seductive, and vicious. However, even when you do focus exclusively on her music, you can't help but be effected by her overall aura. It's not just how she sings, what she sings, or the music she sings over; it's the synthesis. She exudes sassy soulfulness and sensuality. And her producers are the perfect match, all of them laying down smoked-out beats that are as informed by hip-hop as they are by '70s soul—the most hip-hop-informed moment being her collaboration with Black Thought, "Ain't Nobody Playin'," clearly the album's crossover single; the most soul-informed moment being her cover of Patti LaBelle's "Love Need and Want You," clearly an ode to her Philly soul roots. So just when you thought the early-2000s neo-soul movement was starting to get a little marketing-driven, albums like this come along and remind you that soul music never died with the rise of hip-hop in the early '80s; it just took a decade or two to rediscover itself and be embraced by a new generation. *—Jason Birchmeier*

Milton Wright

Vocals / Disco, Funk

The brother of soul singer Betty Wright (of "Clean-Up Woman" fame), Milton Wright made some underappreciated records for the disco-oriented Miami label TK (specifically its Alston subsidiary). Blending smooth, rich vocals with disco-tinged funk and a strong electronic flavor (often courtesy of Moog synthesizers), Wright issued his debut album *Friends & Buddies* in 1975. His single "Keep It Up" became a cult classic among funk and disco collectors, and he followed it with another LP, *Spaced*, after which he faded from view. *—Steve Huey*

● **Friends & Buddies** / 1975 / Alston ✦✦✦

Norma Jean Wright

b. Elyria, OH

Vocals / Disco, Dance-Pop, Funk

Singer Norma Jean Wright recorded both under her own name and as Norma Jean—not to be confused with the same-named country singer.The Elyria, OH, native first came to fame as a vocalist with Chic. Chic leaders Nile Rodgers & Bernard Edwards produced her debut single "Saturday" in summer 1978. Her self-titled LP, produced by Rodgers & Edwards, was released by Bearsville Records in July 1978. The follow-ups were a cover of Sam Cooke's "Having a Party" and the title track single from her next LP, *High Society*, from late 1979.

Norma Jean Wright related releases are Sister Sledge (*We Are Family* (Rhino)), Randy Crawford (*Abstract Emotions*), Nick Scotti (*Nick Scotti*), Nelson Rangell (*Nelson Rangell*), Madonna (*Madonna*) and Luther Vandross (*Never Too Much/Forever, for Always, for Love*). *—Ed Hogan*

● **Norma Jean** / 1978 / Bearsville ✦✦✦

O.V. Wright (Overton Vertis Wright)

b. Oct. 9, 1939, Leno, TN, **d.** Nov. 16, 1980

Vocals / Soul, Southern Soul, Memphis Soul, Deep Soul

A truly incendiary deep soul performer. O.V. Wright's melismatic vocals and Willie Mitchell's vaunted Hi Rhythm Section combined to make classic Memphis soul during the early '70s. Overton Vertis Wright learned his trade on the gospel circuit with the Sunset Travelers before going secular in 1964 with the passionate ballad "That's How Strong My Love Is" for Goldwax in Memphis. Otis Redding liked the song so much that he covered it, killing any chance of Wright's version hitting. Since Wright was already under contract to Houston-based Peacock as a gospel act, owner Don Robey demanded his return, and from then on, Wright appeared on Robey's Backbeat subsidiary. Wright's sanctified sound oozes sweet soul on the spine-chilling "You're Gonna Make Me Cry," a 1965 smash, but it took Memphis producer Willie Mitchell to wring the best consistently from Wright.

Utilizing Mitchell's surging house rhythm section, Wright's early-'70s Back Beat singles "Ace of Spades," "A Nickel and a Nail," and "I Can't Take It" rank among the very best Southern soul of their era. No disco bandwagon for O.V. Wright—he kept right on pouring out his emotions through the '70s, convincing his faithful that "I'd Rather Be (Blind, Crippled & Crazy)" and that he was "Into Something (Can't Shake Loose)." Unfortunately, he apparently was—drugs have often been cited as causing Wright's downfall; the soul great died at only 41 years of age in 1980. *—Bill Dahl*

If It's Only for Tonight / 1965 / Back Beat ✦✦✦

An earlier album by this Memphis soul great, it includes the sublime "You're Gonna Make Me Cry." *—Bill Dahl*

Eight Men, Four Women / 1967 / MCA ✦✦✦✦✦

Memory Blues / 1968 / MCA ✦✦✦

Nucleus of Soul / 1968 / Back Beat ✦✦✦

A Nickel & a Nail & Ace of Spades / 1971 / Back Beat ✦✦✦✦✦

Since no domestic CDs yet exist of this gospel-drenched soul great, seek out this classic Memphis-soul album, which drips passion. *—Bill Dahl*

Memphis Unlimited / 1973 / Back Beat ✦✦✦✦✦

This is hard-driving soul produced by Willie Mitchell. *—Bill Dahl*

Bottom Line / 1978 / Hi ✦✦✦

Pledging My Love / 1978 / MCA ✦✦✦

We're Still Together / 1979 / Hi ✦✦

Released at the peak of disco fever in 1979, *We're Still Together* is a product of its era. Willie Mitchell's production is slick and overpowering, with dense string arrangements and vocal choruses that flatten everything around them. Although the material, including a cover of Aretha Franklin's "Baby Baby Baby," is strong and Wright is in fine voice throughout, it's tough to consider *We're Still Together* anything more than an ambitious failure. *—Jason Ankeny*

Gone for Good / 1984 / Charly ✦✦✦✦✦

That's How Strong My Love Is / 1991 / Hi ✦✦✦✦

● **The Soul of O.V. Wright** / Dec. 22, 1992 / MCA ✦✦✦✦✦

The Soul of O.V. Wright isn't fancy, but it gets the job done. In that way, this solid 18-track compilation is just like its subject, one of the most underrated deep soul singers of his era. Although the Houston-based Wright had the grit of Otis Redding (minus Redding's occasional tendency to oversing) and the spiritual grace of Sam Cooke's pre-secular work, Wright only managed a couple of major hits on the R&B charts, and not even his best single, 1965's startling, Ray Charles-like ballad "'You're Gonna Make Me Cry,'" crossed over to the pop charts. Regardless, all 18 tracks here are sublime deep soul, from the testifying swing of his first single "'I Don't Want to Sit Down'" to his remarkable work with Willie Mitchell in the '70s. ("I'd Rather Be Blind, Crippled and Crazy" is every bit the equal of any of Mitchell's better-known work with Al Green from the same period.) There is plenty more to savor where this came from, but *The Soul of O.V. Wright* is a terrific introduction to this amazing performer. *—Stewart Mason*

Hi Masters / Sep. 15, 1998 / Hi ✦✦✦

The *Hi Masters* compiles 15 studio recordings, all from 1977 and 1978 with the exception of the two songs that comprised O.V. Wright's first release on Hi, the 1976 single "Rhymes" (which charted in the R&B Top 100 that year) and it's B-side, "Without You." The collection kicks off strong with the gospel-drenched delivery, decidedly secular subject, and driving momentum of "Into Something (Can't Shake Loose)," his sole hit in 1977 (it reached the Top 50). The following year brought the last two songs by Wright to hit the charts, "Precious, Precious" (R&B Top 50, early 1978) and "I Don't Do Windows" (Top 100). Besides the inclusion of his last four hits, the *Hi Masters* is a collection of the lesser-known material from late in Wright's career. It's not his prime period, but the soft-moving numbers and ballads from this time, including standouts "I Don't Know Why" and "Your Good Thing Is About to End," make *Hi Masters* a relaxed listen that is second priority—but a nice complement—to O.V. Wright's key earlier recordings. *—Joslyn Layne*

The Complete O.V. Wright on Hi Records, Vol. 1: In the Studio / Aug. 24, 1999 / Hi ✦✦✦✦✦

The first volume of the two-disc set *The Complete O.V. Wright on Hi Records* concentrates on *In the Studio*, which means this is the stuff that hit the charts and the stuff that made the albums. Wright was one of the gutsiest vocalists on the tight, smooth, soulful Hi label, as this collection proves, and he often had material to match his talents, thanks to such fine songwriters as the Mitchell/Randle team. It is true that 30 tracks may be a bit much for a certain breed of listener, since there are some cuts that are merely good genre pieces, but for the soul aficionado, this is a welcome addition to the library. *—Stephen Thomas Erlewine*

The Complete O.V. Wright on Hi Records, Vol. 2: On Stage / Oct. 26, 1999 / Hi ✦✦✦✦

O.V. Wright was a hell of a performer, one of the highlights of Hi's roster, but that doesn't necessarily mean that the second volume of *The Complete O.V. Wright on Hi Records* is necessary for anyone outside of the hardcore. The reason for this? It's because it concentrates entirely on live performances he cut for the label. He was a fine live performer, as several of these selections prove, but these recordings are primarily for the dedicated—especially because the disc has a rather abbreviated running time. They will find this collection pleasing, but it's likely too specialized for anyone outside of the devoted. *—Stephen Thomas Erlewine*

God Blesses Our Love / Mar. 15, 2000 / Suzie Q ✦✦✦

O.V. Wright sang genuine Southern soul, not blues-Southern or soul-Southern, but true, sweltering heat, mosquitoes, roaches, stank-breath, grits, biscuits, and gravy Southern with no apologies. He stamps an unshakable earthiness on every track, and his compilation CDs are all buyers and keepers that don't need titles like "best-of" or "greatest hits" because O.V. took care of business every time he went in a recording studio, gutting out nothing but potential A-sides. *God Blesses Our Love* contains many tracks you won't find on similar CDs by Wright, so it's a good pickup even if you have two or three discs by the late singer already. He wallops your heart on an assortment of updates, songs originally attributed to Aretha Franklin, Jackie Moore, Bobby Womack, Mabel John, and others, while dazzling on three-heart tangles like "Into Something I Can't Shake Loose" and whisky-inspired declarations. *—Andrew Hamilton*

X

Xscape

f. 1990, College Park, GA

Group / Club/Dance, Urban

The female R&B quartet Xscape debuted singing at producer Jermaine Dupri's birthday party in 1991, and were the recipients of a platinum album just two years later. The quartet was formed around sisters LaTocha and Tamika Scott, who had grown up in the church—their father, Rev. Randolf Scott, performed in the R&B group the Scott Three during the early '70s. Rev. Scott began training the girls at an early age, and they eventually made the jump from the church to working talent shows around the area. While attending Tri-City High School in the Atlanta suburb of College Park, the sisters met Kandi Burruss and Tameka "Tiny" Cottle, forming Xscape in 1990.

After the group appeared at Dupri's birthday party, he signed them to his So So Def record label and recorded their debut album, *Hummin' Comin' at 'Cha*. The LP broke into the Top 20 thanks to the number two hit "Just Kickin' It," and later hit platinum. The second Xscape effort also made platinum, though the group smoothed out their sound for their third album, *Traces of My Lipstick*. Besides singing with the group, Tamika is also an ordained minister, and has recorded a solo gospel album. *—John Bush*

Hummin' Comin' at 'Cha / Oct. 12, 1993 / Columbia ✦✦✦✦✦

Xscape's debut had some intriguing variations that distinguished it from others in the ever-crowded distaff end of the urban contemporary circuit. Their shared leads were more gospel-edged than those of En Vogue or SWV; their first hit, "Just Kickin' It," had a bawdy undercurrent that made it genuinely appealing, and Xscape demonstrated grit and energized harmonizing rather than over-rehearsed polish. But Xscape's most captivating quality, at least on this CD, was their spontaneity, something that can't be faked. *—Ron Wynn*

● **Off the Hook** / 1995 / So So Def ✦✦✦✦✦

Xscape's follow-up to their hit debut *Hummin' Comin' at 'Cha* is an improvement on their first record, demonstrating gains both in terms of music and lyrics. Before, Xscape were part of the large bigrade of sexually-obsessed R&B groups, selling a number of copies of their carnal single, "Just Kickin' It." While they are still sexual on their second album, *Off the Hook*, it doesn't overwhelm the music as it did on their debut. Recording with producers Dupri, Daryl Simmons, and Organized Noize on various tracks, the group has developed into a impressive musicians, with a thorough grasp of slow, seductive soul and slick funk. *Off the Hook* may run a little long—the 12 songs clock in at well over an hour—but the record proves that Xscape has staying power. *—Stephen Thomas Erlewine*

Traces of My Lipstick / May 12, 1998 / So So Def ✦✦✦

On their third album, *Traces of My Lipstick*, Xscape pretty much follows the cue of their two earlier efforts, with only slightly diminished results. The group sounds as good as ever, bringing real soul and passion to their performances, but unfortunately much of their record consists of average, unremarkable material. There are enough strong songs (primarly the singles) to make the record enjoyable, but it simply doesn't have the same resonance as their two earlier efforts. *—Leo Stanley*

Y

Yarbrough & Peoples

f. Dallas, TX

Group / Urban, Funk

The singing duo of Yarbrough & Peoples burst onto the music scene with the million-selling single "Don't Stop the Music," a sinewy slab of synth-based R&B/funk that was ahead of its time and had a far-reaching influence in the years following. The sizzling track held down the number-one R&B spot for five weeks and hit number-19 pop on *Billboard*'s charts in the spring of 1981. Calvin Yarbrough and Alisa Peoples first met when they were small children, growing up in Dallas, TX; he was six years old and she was four. They were both taking lessons from the same music teacher and attended the same neighborhood church, where both sang solos in the church choir. After their college years, Peoples worked a regular job while Yarbrough played keyboards and sang in a band called Grand Theft. Tulsa, OK, musicians Robert, Ronnie, and Charlie Wilson were in the audience for one of the band's shows and offered the keyboardist/singer a background vocals job on the Leon Russell tour that they were a part of. Once the tour was over, Yarbrough returned to Dallas, playing local gigs with Grand Theft.

Around 1977, Peoples sang a song with the band during one of their club dates. Everyone there knew it was the beginning of musical magic. The Wilson brothers, now known as the Gap Band, were having hit after hit ("Shake," number-four R&B, spring 1979, "Steppin' (Out)," number-ten R&B, late 1979, "I Don't Believe You Want to Get Up and Dance (Oops, Up Side Your Head)," number-four R&B, early 1980). When the group came to Dallas to perform, Yarbrough had them listen to an audio tape he and Peoples had recorded. Impressed, Charlie Wilson enthusiastically woke up their manager/producer Lonnie Simmons in his hotel room. Wilson, followed by the singing duo, entered the room and stayed while Simmons listened to the tape. Simmons was taken by the couple's humble, genteel manner and good attitudes. Exchanging phone numbers, he bid them all a good night. One day while in the lobby of his Los Angeles-based label Total Experience Records, Simmons was surprised to see Yarbrough and Peoples. He suggested that the duo make a record demo and teamed them with staff producer Jonah Ellis. They recorded seven songs, the last of which was "When the Music Stops." Ellis felt the song was a filler; if they had enough studio time left, they would record it on the demo, if not it was no big deal. Yarbrough liked the song, so Ellis recorded a track with both a drum machine and drummer Jonathan Moffett. Retitled "Don't Stop the Music" and co-written by Peoples (producers Jonah Ellis and Lonnie Simmons, issued on Mercury), the song inherited the number-one R&B spot from the Gap Band's "Burn Rubber (Why You Wanna Hurt Me)" during February 1981.

Their debut album *The Two of Us* went gold, peaking at number 16 on *Billboard*'s album charts. The follow-up, "The Third Degree," peaked at number-74 R&B, summer 1981. The next LP, *Heartbeat*, was issued on Total Experience as part of a distribution deal producer Simmons had with Polygram in spring 1982. Two singles were released with strong "Don't Stop the Music" leanings, "Heartbeats" (number-ten R&B, late 1982) and "Feels So Good" (number-20 R&B, spring 1983). Their next album, *Be a Winner*, produced by Yarbrough, Ellis, and Oliver Scott, and released spring 1984, yielded another number-one R&B single. Mixed by Nick Martinelli and David Todd (who co-mixed Evelyn "Champagne" King's "Shame" with Al Garrison), "Don't Waste Your Time" clocked in at number-one R&B, spring 1984. The LP's title track climbed to number-20 R&B in summer 1984. *Guilty* was the name of Yarbrough and Peoples' best album, issued in late 1985. The title track "Guilty"—not to be confused with the Alexander O'Neal hit—went to number-two R&B around the time of the LP's release. The track was written and produced by Jimmy Hamilton and Maurice Hayes of the band Prime Time, who had a hit on Total Experience with "I Owe It to Myself," number-21 R&B, fall 1984. The Hamilton/Hayes follow-up, the percolating "I Wouldn't Lie" went to number-six R&B in spring 1986. The gentle ballad "Wrapped Around Your Finger" peaked at number-46 R&B, summer 1986.

Although they're known for their uptempo hits, "Guilty" proved that Yarbrough and Peoples could handle ballads. Listen to the airy, ethereal ballad "I'll Give Anything to Have You Back." Another standout track is the Oliver Scott-produced "Anytime," with its rumbling, tumbling, comin'-to-get-ya funk groove. The duo worked with the other acts signed to Total Experience including the Gap Band and Penny Ford. On the singer's *Pennye* LP, the singing duo co-wrote and produced the heart-tugging ballad "Never Let Go." Ford was featured on the Gap Band's "I Found My Baby," number-eight R&B, spring 1985 (available on *Smooth Grooves: Vol. 1-New Jack Ballads*, Rhino, 1998), and was the lead vocalist on Snap's 1990 multi-platinum worldwide hit "The Power" and its gold follow-up "Ooops Up." Yarbrough and Peoples sang "Christmas Dreams" on the 1984 multi-artist LP *A Total Experience Christmas* on Total Experience/RCA. Sometime during the '80s, Yarbrough and Peoples became a married couple. Total Experience folded in the late '80s and the couple returned to Texas. PGD/Polygram Pop/Jazz issued *Best of Yarbrough & Peoples* (which includes the 12-inch version of "Heartbeats") in May 1997, and "Don't Stop the Music" is on the label's compilation *Dance Funk*, released November 1997. *—Ed Hogan*

The Two of Us / 1980 / Mercury ♦♦♦

This marked the debut release from the male/female duo, and their presence was immediately felt with the smash hit "Don't Stop the Music." Centered around dance lyrics, Alisa Peoples pushes the verse while Carvin Yarbrough sounds off the chorus with the help of an electronic vocalizer supported by some animated backing vocals. Though probably considered a disco track, it does not have the rapid rhythm that disco songs are known for. Discovered by the Gap Band, Yarbrough & Peoples savored the success of this album due to this one song, since the second release, "Third Degree," did not have much chart action (*Billboard* number 74, five weeks). "Don't Stop the Music" reached the ultimate apex and retained that position for five consecutive weeks inside of number 27 on the *Billboard* R&B charts. *—Craig Lytle*

Guilty / 1985 / Total Experience ♦♦♦♦

Guilty was Yarbrough & Peoples' best album. Issued in late 1985, the LP was ample proof that the duo could come through on both dance cuts and slow jams. The gritty funky title track, not the Alexander O'Neal hit, was a number-two R&B hit and has one of Alisa Peoples' best vocals. Produced and co-written by labelmates Jimmy Hamilton and Maurice Hayes of Prime Time (the number-22 R&B-charting "I Owe It To Myself"). Hamilton and Hayes did the follow-up, the rousing number-six R&B smash, "I Wouldn't Lie." The third single was the delicate ballad, "Wrapped Around Your Finger." Other highlights were the breezy ballad, "I'll Give Anything to Have You Back" and the snarlingly funky "Anytime." [Some of *Guilty*'s tracks are on the 1997 Polygram CD, *The Best of Yarbrough & Peoples*.] *—Ed Hogan*

● **The Best of Yarbrough & Peoples** / May 20, 1997 / Mercury ♦♦♦♦♦

Alisa Peoples and Calvin Yarbrough's music is like a breath of fresh air—a perfect fusion of soul, disco, and pop. Their manager and producer Lonnie Simmons never lets the sound get too heavy or too light. The pleasantries include "Don't Stop the Music," "Heartbeats," "Be a Winner," and "Come to Me." A scrumptious compilation that will spin for hours on your CD player. *—Andrew Hamilton*

Young-Holt Unlimited

f. 1966, Chicago, IL, **db.** 1974

Group / Soul, Pop-Soul, Chicago Soul, Soul-Jazz

Bassist Eldee Young and drummer Isaac "Red" Holt attended the American Conversatory of Music in Chicago together, and played together in a dance orchestra called the Cleffs, where they met pianist Ramsey Lewis and formed a popular jazz trio in 1956. After a decade as Lewis' rhythm section, Young and Holt split to form their own act in the wake of the trio's breakout pop hit "The 'In' Crowd." Hiring pianist Hysear Don Walker and christening themselves the Young-Holt Trio, they scored a quick Top 20 R&B hit with the infectious and silly "Wack Wack." Most of their material, recorded on several LPs for Brunswick, cut an invigorating soul-jazz groove that explored the territory between Jimmy Smith and Junior Walker, with dour bass, Ray Charles-inspired keyboards, faint scat vocals, and a live party ambience.

In 1968, Walker was replaced by Ken Chaney as Young and Holt tightened up their sound, added some funky rhythms, and renamed the group Young-Holt Unlimited. They scored a left-field smash with the instrumental "Soulful Strut," which was actually the backing track from Brunswick soul singer Barbara Acklin's "Am I the Same Girl." Although the actual Young-Holt group was rumored not to have even played on the track, it went all the way to number three in 1969, driven by a bright, indelible horn riff. Attempts to duplicate its success met with indifference, and although Young-Holt Unlimited remained a popular concert attraction on both the R&B and jazz circuits (sometimes with pianist Bobby Lyle in place of Chaney), their recording career was on the wane. They cut LPs for Atlantic (1972's *Oh Girl*) and Paula (1973's *Plays Superfly*) which failed to restore their commercial momentum, and disbanded in 1974. Both Young and Holt reunited with Ramsey Lewis in 1983. *—Steve Huey*

Wack Wack / 1966 / Kent ♦♦♦♦

Like an amoeba, the Ramsey Lewis Trio split into two virtually identical units in 1966, with bassist Eldee Young and drummer Isaac "Red" Holt forming their own soul-jazz piano trio. Then known as the Young-Holt Trio, this may have been the only major trio to feature the bassist and drummer, but not the pianist (!), in the group's name, probably to capitalize on their recently lucrative association with Lewis. In any case, the pianist was Hysear Don Walker, who basically labors in a pleasing Lewis vein on their debut album, which winningly continues the Lewis formula of translating recent pop hit material ("Monday, Monday," "Sunny," "Strangers in the Night," etc.) and a few jazz standards like "Girl Talk" and "Song for My Father" into the Chicago soul piano trio groove. Although Walker can't help but be the dominant melodic and sole harmonic force here, the irrepressible Young nevertheless manages to steal the spotlight whenever he can, with sly pizzicato and arco bass leads, occasional casual vocals, and blithe-spirited scatting (his "You Know That I Love You" amounts to an homage to Slam Stewart). Their first single, "Wack Wack," a number-40 pop hit, is a funny, blues-based riff with the band honking out the title words on cue—and the flip side of the single, the spiritual "This Little Light of Mine," is an irreverently joyful scatted takeoff. A highly enjoyable debut, worth combing through the bins for. *—Richard S. Ginell*

Soulful Strut / Dec. 1968 / Brunswick ✦✦✦✦

It's unclear how much actual playing the Young-Holt Trio does on their debut LP, *Soulful Strut.* The title track happens to be the instrumental track of "Am I The Same Girl," by Barbara Acklin, with Acklin's vocal removed and the piano raised in the mix. Likewise for "Please Sunrise," "Love Makes a Woman," and "Just Ain't No Love," all songs that Acklin recorded. The trio consisted of Ken Chaney (piano), and Eldee Young (bass, cello, vocals), and Isaac "Red" Holt (drums), formerly of the Ramsey Lewis Trio. Whether a fast one got pulled or not, the ten tracks make for enjoyable and delightful listening. It's excellent old school, smooth jazz. *—Andrew Hamilton*

Just a Melody / Aug. 1969 / Brunswick ✦✦

Fresh off the unexpected smash of the "Soulful Strut" hit single and album of the same name in the fall of 1968, Eldee Young and Isaac "Red" Holt tried to do it again in 1969, only to fall far, far short of the mark. Only 26 minutes and a few seconds long, this record sounds almost desperate—forced, rushed, poorly recorded, and unimaginatively arranged, with the strangely unidentified piano soloist having to work on an out-of-tune instrument. Producers Eugene Record and Carl Davis, the composers of "Soulful Strut," came up with four new songs; the title track is OK, managing to inch up to number 49 on the R&B charts, but the magic touch was gone on the others. "Young and Holtful," co-written by Holt, is actually the best copy of "Soulful Strut," but that didn't get anywhere. Except for that track, the whole enterprise concedes defeat on side two as YHU lights the Doors' fire, picks Marvin Gaye's grapevine, and drifts with Jim Webb down to Phoenix for the umpteenth time that decade. *—Richard S. Ginell*

● **The Best of Young-Holt Unlimited** / Jun. 6, 1995 / Brunswick ✦✦✦✦

Here are 12 of their most famous cuts, including the hits "Soulful Strut" and "Wack Wack, " a live medley, and some neat obscurities (like "Give It Up" and the propulsive "Dig Her Walk"). It's not quite as comprehensive, however, as the 16-track British import *Wack Wack* (on Kent), which is still the better collection to pick up if you can find it. The only song here that's not on *Wack Wack* is their version of "Light My Fire." *—Richie Unterberger*

Young Jessie (Obediah Jessie)

b. Dec. 28, 1936, Lincoln Manor, TX

Vocals / R&B, Doo Wop

The Los Angeles R&B vocal group scene of the 1950s was a fairly incestuous one—members flitted from one aggregation to the next, often sporting several connections at the time. Young Jessie was a member of the Flairs, Hunters, and Coasters, as well as scoring a solo West Coast hit with his 1955 rocker "Mary Lou." Obediah Jessie was a Los Angeles high-school classmate of Richard "Louie Louie" Berry. The two put together the Flairs and debuted on the Bihari Brothers' Flair label in 1953 with "She Wants to Rock." The Flairs recorded steadily for the firm, but solo status awaited Jessie, who cut a cover of Big Mama Thornton's Leiber/Stoller-penned "I Smell a Rat" for Modern (the Biharis' flagship logo) in 1954. "Mary Lou," arranged by saxist Maxwell Davis, emerged the next year; its unusual minor-key arrangement must have appealed to rockabilly wildman Ronnie Hawkins, who hit the pop lists with it in 1959 for Roulette.

Platters manager Buck Ram took over Jessie's career in time to pen his torrid 1956 rocker "Hit, Git & Split" under the sobriquet of Lynn Paul. Both that cut and its follow-up, "Oochie Coochie," stemmed from a New York date that backed Jessie with Mickey Baker on guitar and saxman Sam "The Man" Taylor. Jessie reverted to his vocal-group roots in 1957, joining the Coasters to sing harmonies on their smashes "Searchin'" and "Young Blood" for Atco. The same firm issued a solo Jessie 45, "Shuffle in the Gravel," before moving him to Atlantic for "Margie."

Later singles for Capitol and Mercury did little to rekindle Jessie's career, though the Mercury 45s sported some impressive credits. "Be-Bop Country Boy" was produced by ex-Little Richard/Sam Cooke cohort Bumps Blackwell, while a remade "Mary Lou" found Jessie collaborating with a trio of Phil Spector associates: Jack Nitzsche arranged, and Lester Sill and Steve Douglas co-produced. *—Bill Dahl*

● **I'm Gone** / Feb. 1996 / Ace ✦✦✦

This overview of Young Jessie's Modern recordings has a bunch of his mid-'50s singles, the 1953 "Rabbit on a Log"/"Down at Hayden's" single he did as part of the Hunters (which also included Richard Berry), and a few leftovers that weren't issued until subsequent compilation LPs, as well as a couple of unissued tracks that make their debut here. *I'm Gone* offers fun, witty, sometimes wise-guy R&B that should appeal to fans of Richard Berry, the Robins, and the early Coasters. Young Jessie had a lower, throatier voice than many of his peers, (but not a worse one), which meshes well with the typically accomplished Modern house band backups led by Maxwell Davis. As is the case with many such compilations of minor R&B/early rock & roll singers from the time, the material could stand to be more diverse. The original version of "Mary Lou," Young Jessie's best and most famous recording, is here in a version that is notably cheerier in melodic structure and delivery than Ronnie Hawkins' subsequent rockabilly hit cover. Leiber-Stoller fans will want to check this out for three of their more obscure tunes: "I Smell a Rat" (originally written for Big Mama Thornton), "Hot Dog" (also done by Elvis Presley, though the Young Jessie version didn't come out until 1982), and "Here Comes Henry" (which Leiber-Stoller co-wrote with G. Motola). *—Richie Unterberger*

Z

Zapp

f. 1978, Dayton, OH, **db.** 1991

Group / Funk, Urban, Quiet Storm

One of the most underrated funk groups of the 1980s, Zapp revolutionized the computer pop of electro with their trademark vocoder talk boxes and bumping grooves, emulating the earthier side of Prince and Cameo, with a leader in Roger Troutman who was more than efficient at polished production. The family group, with brothers Roger, Lester, Larry, and Tony Troutman, grew up in Hamilton, OH, influenced by hometown heroes the Ohio Players as well as Parliament and other funk groups. Tony was the first to begin recording, with an obscure single for Gram-O-Phon Records, "I Truly Love You," which scraped the R&B charts in 1976. Joined by his brothers (with Roger on vocals and guitar, Lester on drums, Larry on percussion, and himself contributing bass) and christened Zapp, the group played around the Midwest and gradually picked up backing vocalists (Bobby Glover, Jannetta Boyce), keyboard players (Greg Jackson, Sherman Fleetwood) and a horn section (Eddie Barber, Jerome Derrickson, Mike Warren).

Zapp's following quickly gained notices, and Bootsy Collins himself was hired on to work with the group on their debut album. Released in 1980, *Zapp* hit the Top 20 on the pop charts, thanks to the single "More Bounce to the Ounce." The following year, Roger worked on Funkadelic's *The Electric Spanking of War Babies* and released his solo debut album, *The Many Facets of Roger*. His special cover of "I Heard It Through the Grapevine," complete with vocoderized talk box, pushed the album into gold territory (as *Zapp* had done). *Zapp II* appeared in 1982 and proved just as popular as the group's first, including Zapp's only number-one R&B single, "Dance Floor."

Zapp III barely made the Top 40 pop charts upon release in 1983, and Roger's second solo album, *The Saga Continues*, was also a disappointment, though his cover of "Midnight Hour" featured the Mighty Clouds of Joy. *The New Zapp IV U* fared slightly better after release in late 1985 (thanks to the single "Computer Love"), but in 1987, Roger's third solo album, *Unlimited!*, featured the group's biggest hit yet, "I Want to Be Your Man," a chart-topper on the R&B lists and a respectable number-three pop. Though Roger and/or Zapp hit the R&B charts frequently during the rest of the late '80s, the unit had effectively halted recording with the 1991 Roger LP *Bridging the Gap*. Roger continued to produce and play with other artists, and it was his talk box that graced Dr. Dre & 2Pac's Top Ten 1996 single "California Love." The 1993 Roger & Zapp collection *All the Greatest Hits* sold well, earning the collective their first platinum record. The Zapp story ended in tragedy on April 25, 1999, when Roger was shot to death by Larry, who then turned the gun on himself. *—John Bush*

Zapp / 1980 / Warner Bros. ✦✦✦✦

Released in 1980 just as George Clinton's P Funk empire had reached the brink of its existence, Bootsy protégé Roger Troutman proved himself a worthy successor with Zapp's self-titled debut album and its subsequent two follow-ups. In actuality, Zapp originally was a branch of the Parliament/Funkadelic collective, as group leader Roger Troutman was originally signed to Clinton's short-lived CBS subsidiary, Uncle Jam Records. After Troutman completed the album with CBS' money, Clinton's help, and Bootsy's production, Warner Bros. stepped in, offered Roger a considerable sum of money, and slyly bought the album—leaving a distressed Clinton with no Zapp album for his shaky boutique label. Propelled by the dancefloor smash "More Bounce to the Ounce," the album quickly became a considerable hit. It was here that Troutman first defined the vocoder-laden funk aesthetic that would become his trademark for the remainder of his career. In addition to the near ten-minute "More Bounce," the album also featured "Be Alright," another epic jam that slowed down the funk to a smoked-out, almost ballad-like tempo (both songs would later fuel numerous early-'90s West Coast rap hits via sampling). Of the remaining four songs, "Funky Bounce" and "Brand New Player" also stand as perennial standouts, further affirming Troutman's dense funk aesthetic. Later Zapp albums would have their moments, but this debut is absolutely solid from beginning to end, in addition to being the foundation from which Troutman would base all later work, and with "More Bounce to the Ounce" and "Be Alright," it houses two of the best moments in '80s funk. *—Jason Birchmeier*

Zapp II / 1982 / Warner Bros. ✦✦✦

Building upon the unprecedented success of Zapp's self-titled debut and group leader Roger Troutman's solo debut, *The Many Facets of Roger*, along with those two album's hit singles—"More Bounce to the Ounce" and "I Heard It Through the Grapevine," respectively—Troutman returned in 1982 with *Zapp II*, a strong album again propelled by a mammoth single, "Dance Floor." Outside of the infectious single, which topped the R&B singles chart, Troutman stuck to his patented formula of vocoder-laden funk on each of the album's other songs. There isn't anything new here that wasn't on *Zapp* or *The Many Facets of Roger*, just more of the same; of course, this isn't exactly a bad thing, as Troutman retreads familiar ground effectively. At this point in his career, Troutman wasn't short on ideas and was able to inventively lay down dense, carefree funk with ease—in sum, there's literally no filler here, impressive when you consider his prolific output during this era. Not quite as fresh as the first Zapp album but still a great album for its era. *—Jason Birchmeier*

Zapp III / 1983 / Warner Bros. ✦✦✦

Where the first two Zapp albums were nearly flawless with their beginning-to-end knee-deep funk, *Zapp III* showed slight symptoms of becoming derivative. You are still strained to find any filler here, but the album's second side does pale considerably in relation to its first side, alluding to the possibility that group leader Roger Troutman may have finally begun struggling for new ideas at this point. These latter songs such as "Spend My Whole Life" aren't necessarily bad, just uninspired. The album's first side features two mammoth jams—"Heartbreaker, Pt. 1 & 2" and "I Can Make You Dance"—that weren't as successful commercially as "More Bounce to the Once" or "Dance Floor" yet were nearly as effective in terms of dancefloor utility. With both clocking near ten minutes in length, these songs never sound monotonous or dull in their entirety, as Troutman kept the grooves grooving and the hooks catchy, while forever focusing on the funk. In the end, though, these two wonderful songs end up carrying much of this album's weight, mostly because of their epic stature and their obvious dancefloor emphasis. The remaining songs are just that—songs—rather than jams. Still, even though this album may often get overshadowed by its predecessors, it has aged well and remains one of the best early-'80s funk albums. *—Jason Birchmeier*

The New Zapp IV U / 1985 / Warner Bros. ✦✦✦

Though *Zapp III* was far from a failure or even a disappointment, it wasn't quite on par with previous Roger Troutman efforts, being a little uneven and less of a commercial success. So when Troutman resurfaced in 1985, he shook up his formula a bit, focusing on an even collection of succinct songs rather than an album driven by epic anthems and filled out with shorter songs. To further communicate the concept that he was shaking things up, Troutman blatantly titled his album *The New Zapp IV U*. On the one hand, things really didn't change as much as Troutman would have you believe. *The New Zapp IV U* is still immersed in bouncy, carefree funk, and he still has a monster anthem with "Computer Love." The main change seems to be an emphasis on tighter song structures rather than loose, epic dancefloor jams. Yet on the other hand, these tiny changes are all Troutman really needed to do. The previous three Zapp albums were all stellar, and it would have been a shame for him to abandon a winning formula. In the end, the new approach to songwriting here proves just enough change to make this a fresh-sounding album. Had Troutman returned with yet another Zapp album propelled by one or two epic, ten-minute dancefloor jams and a few shorter funk exercises, it would have seemed incredibly trite—after three albums, it was time for a change to keep things fresh. *—Jason Birchmeier*

Zapp V / Sep. 12, 1989 / Reprise ✦✦

● **All the Greatest Hits** / 1994 / Warner Bros. ✦✦✦✦✦

This Dayton, OH, band came to typify swinging, effervescent, and melodic funk in an era when Parliament, Funkadelic, and other outfits were getting bogged down and burned out. Zapp, unlike the other P Funk units, had their own personality divorced from George Clinton, so much so a listener might not get the connection unless they read the album notes. While both Zapp and Roger had enough hits to make separate greatest hits compilations, *All the Greatest Hits* works well due to the song inclusions and the level of skill. Zapp's first hit, "More Bounce to the Ounce" with it's hard-hitting funk with jazzy underpinnings, set the template. Tracks from Roger Troutman's solo debut, like the great "Do It Roger" and a cover of "Heard It Through the Grapevine," seemed to sap the strength from the Zapp name, although the band was on them too. Zapp's 1983 near-classic "Heartbreaker 1 and 2" still amazes with its minimal, lean sound. The synth-based sound also served Troutman well on the mid-'80s solo hit "In the Mix" and Zapp's ballad "Computer Love." As the Zapp never did regain its commercial footing by the late '80s, Roger fared better solo and turned in the romantic ballad and surprise hit "I Wanna Be Your Man." *All The Great Hits* diminishes its appeal by adding disposable tracks like "Curiosity '93 (Remix)" and the live "Midnight Hour-Live '93 (Remix)." While the hits are indeed here, a fan could just as easily obtain a 1980-1984 album of Zapp or Roger to get a better sense of the importance of the music. *—Jason Elias*

Compilation: Greatest Hits, Vol. 2 & More / Nov. 19, 1996 / Reprise ✦✦✦

Greatest Hits 2 & More collects Zapp's lesser-known singles and album tracks like "Play Some Blues" and "It Doesn't Really Matter," adding four rare songs from Roger Troutman, including the newly-recorded cover of Stevie Wonder's "Living for the City" and his contributions to the soundtrack of *A Thin Line Between Love and Hate*. Though there aren't any hits on *Greatest Hits 2*, the album does a good job of collecting all of the highlights from Zapp's frequently uneven albums. *—Leo Stanley*

We Can Make You Dance: The Zapp & Roger Anthology / Jan. 15, 2002 / Rhino ✦✦✦✦
Weighing in at two discs and 29 songs, this is easily too much for the average listener, but for those with the inclination, dedication, or patience, *We Can Make You Dance: The Zapp & Roger Anthology* is clearly the ideal retrospective on Zapp & Roger. What makes it so successful is that it doesn't stick to recordings released under the name Zapp—there are solo cuts from Roger, selections from his early recordings with the Human Body, even a cut from H-Town to close the collection. Along the way, all of the hits are present, many in their single versions, and it's all bolstered by a fine, 32-page booklet with notes by Tom Vickers and plenty of photos. Much of this is very, very good funk; some of it is great, but the comprehensiveness of the set and the fact that the majority of the greatest cuts sit nicely on more comprehensive single-disc collections pretty much guarantees that this is just for the serious funkateer—who will not be disappointed, mind you. *—Stephen Thomas Erlewine*

Zhané

f. 1993, Philadelphia, PA
Group / Urban, Contemporary R&B, Club/Dance
Given a high-profile spot on the all-star compilation *Roll Wit tha Flava* as their first recording opportunity, Zhané lived up to the pressure and came away with one of the hip-hop party anthems of all time, "Hey, Mr. DJ." Jean Norris and Renee Neufville initially met while both were studying music at Philadelphia's Temple University (Norris is originally from Rhode Island, Neufville from Jamaica). After meeting Naughty by Nature's Kay Gee, Zhané impressed the producer enough to go right into the studio to record for *Roll Wit tha Flava*. When "Hey, Mr. DJ" was released as a separate single as well, it hit number six on the pop charts and earned the group a contract with Motown in 1994. Their debut album, *Pronounced Jah-Nay*, produced two further Top 40 hits ("Groove Thang," "Sending My Love") and went gold by the end of the year.

Zhané kept busy during 1995-1996 with spots on tracks by Busta Rhymes and De La Soul as well as new songs of their own on the *NFL Jams* and *NBA 50th Anniversary* compilations and the soundtracks to *Higher Learning* and *A Low Down Dirty Shame*—the latter, "Shame," became their fourth Top 40 hit. Norris and Neufville returned with a new LP in 1997, co-produced by Kay Gee, Eddie F., and themselves. It peaked just outside the Top 40. *—John Bush*

● **Pronounced Jah-Nay** / Feb. 15, 1994 / Motown ✦✦✦✦
In late 1993, the R&B vocal duo Zhané scored a Top Ten pop hit with the '70s Philly soul meets disco meets '90s hip-hop R&B smash "Hey Mr. DJ," a sleek slice of earthy, sophisticated soul that stands as one of the best R&B/pop hits of the '90s. Several months later the duo issued its highly anticipated debut, *Pronounced Jah-Nay*, on Motown, and the album yielded hit single after hit single for the better part of a year. Melding classic soul with honey-sweet vocals, hip-hop beats, jazz, disco, and pop, the duo stood out from the onslaught of manufactured R&B acts that dominated the airwaves and pop charts in the early to mid-'90s. The duo scored a Top 20 pop hit with its follow-up single, "Groove Thang," which, although still smooth and infectious, sounds like "Hey Mr. DJ" part two. Other singles included the glorious, elegant, and sleek "Sending My Love," which also managed to crack the pop Top 40, the funky R&B hit "Vibe," and the ballad "You're Sorry Now." The duo seems to shine brightest when tackling jazz ballads, such as the Sade-ish "La, La, La" and "Off My Mind," two songs that were never hits but easily rank as the album's overlooked treasures. *Pronounced Jah-Nay* is definitely one of the better R&B albums of the '90s—unfortunately, this album's success was never repeated, and that was most likely due to lousy marketing and single choices for the duo's sophomore outing, *Saturday Night*. *—Jose F. Promis*

Saturday Night / Apr. 22, 1997 / Motown ✦✦✦
More textured and funkier than their debut album, Zhané's second record *Saturday Night* is an infectious set of percolating funk, club beats, and new jack harmonies. The songs aren't always as strong as the performances, but Zhané's vocal charisma makes such shortcomings forgivable. *—Leo Stanley*

Zingara

Group / Urban
Motown alumnus Lamont Dozier produced Zingara's R&B ballad single "Love's Calling," which featured lead vocals by James Ingram. The Los Angeles-based quartet included guitarist/singer Wali Ali, violinist Karen Coleman, drummer Minor Williams, and bassist Rick Jones (who also played on Carl Carlton's 1981 gold LP *Carl Carlton*, which listed the million-selling single "She's a Bad Mama Jama"). Released on the independently distributed Wheel label, "Love's Calling" went to number-29 R&B in late 1980. Dozier produced the group's self-titled LP, which was issued in June 1981. *—Ed Hogan*

● **Zingara** / 1981 / Castle ✦✦✦
Much to the pleasure of soul aficionados, Zingara's self-titled debut record was finally reissued by Castle in 2001. Its 1981 release was highly sought after due to lead singer James Ingram's voice on the chart hit "Love's Calling." Fans of Ingram's highly polished solo productions would be well served by a listen to this record, as it demonstrates the versatility of Ingram's voice depending on what the material calls for. Motown alumnus Lamont Dozier brings out the very gritty, raw qualities to Ingram's voice, and the songs run from traditional quiet storm ballads to upbeat '80s contemporary R&B. Zingara was a promising group primed for future success until its label ran out of money and folded, and Ingram was promptly signed to Quincy Jones' Qwest label. *—Rob Theakston*

Zulema (Zulema Cusseaux)

b. Tampa, FL
Vocals / Urban, Soul
Zulema was a pioneer of sorts in that she was a '70s black R&B singer who wrote much of her own material, and was able to assume some of her own production chores. The records themselves were average forerunners of urban contemporary music, occasionally reaching the lower parts of the R&B charts, Zulema's vocals betraying a strong Aretha Franklin influence.

Born Zulema Cusseaux in Tampa, FL, she was a member of the Lovelles in the late '60s and early '70s. A Van McCoy-produced Lovelles single ("So Much Love") became a Top 20 R&B hit in 1971, but Zulema went solo shortly afterwards, recording a couple of albums for Sussex. She assumed her highest profile with a series of LPs for RCA in the mid-'70s, reaching the middle of the R&B charts in 1975 with "Wanna Be Where You Are." Her recording career ended after an album for Le Joint in the late '70s. *—Richie Unterberger*

Zulema / 1972 / Sussex ✦✦✦

Z-Licious / 1978 / Le Joint ✦
Producer Van McCoy never was able to get Zulema past first base. On this, her last known LP, the former original member of Faith, Hope & Charity shares production credits with McCoy on nine jams, 11 if you include the "Prologue" and "Epilogue." This has plenty of disco, but the ballads "I'm Not Dreaming" and "What Do I Do Now" are the most arresting. None of the singles, including "Change," a mild disco offering, did anything. Other pleasant but non-essential items include "Higher Plane," "See," and "You've Got Something for Me." *—Andrew Hamilton*

● **The Best of Zulema: The RCA Years** / Apr. 1996 / Ichiban/Soul Classics ✦✦✦✦✦
Competent but unremarkable mid-'70s soul on the verge of fusing with adult contemporary into urban contemporary music. This collection assembles 18 tracks from the three LPs that she cut for RCA in the mid-'70s, emphasing the singer-songwriter's original material. *—Richie Unterberger*

Various Artists

'70s Soul Revue / 1997 / Warner Black Music-ol' ♦♦♦
'70s Soul Revue does feature a lot of big names, from Chaka Khan, Rose Royce and Dionne Warwick to Sly & the Family Stone, Graham Central and Charles Wright. However, none of these artists—with the exception of Khan, whose "I'm Every Woman" is included—is represented by their best-known work. Instead, the compilation is comprised entirely of near-misses and forgotten singles largely from the latter half of the decade—in other words, this is music by artists past their prime. A few of the songs are worthwhile, yet the majority of the record is not quite there. The production is good and the vocals are strong, but the material is unmemorable, and the artists and songs aren't quite obscure enough to make *'70s Soul Revue* appealing to fetishists. It's simply a missed opportunity. *—Stephen Thomas Erlewine*

16 #1 Hits from the Early 60's / 1982 / Motown ♦♦♦
The budget-priced *16 Early 60's #1 Hits* assembles chart-topping hits from Motown's formative years, including familiar favorites like Martha & the Vandellas' "(Love Is Like a) Heat Wave," Little Stevie Wonder's "Fingertips, Pt. 2," the Temptations' "My Girl," the Supremes' "Where Did Our Love Go" and Junior Walker & the All-Stars' "Shotgun." Despite decades of incessant airplay, each song is a classic, and in tandem with its sequel *16 Late 60's #1 Hits*, the disc offers an easy and inexpensive way to collect some of the biggest and most enduring hits of the era (although as many of Motown's finest hours never topped the charts, you can't stop here). *—Jason Ankeny*

16 #1 Hits from the Late 60's / Oct. 17, 1990 / Motown ♦♦♦
The budget-priced *16 Late 60's #1 Hits* assembles chart-topping hits from Motown's creative pinnacle, including familiar favorites like Stevie Wonder's "Uptight (Everything's Alright)," the Temptations' "Get Ready," the Supremes' "You Keep Me Hangin' On" and Smokey Robinson & the Miracles' "I Second That Emotion." Despite decades of incessant airplay, each song is a classic, and in tandem with its prequel *16 Early 60's #1 Hits*, the disc offers an easy and inexpensive way to collect some of the biggest and most enduring hits of the era (although as many of Motown's finest hours never topped the charts, you can't stop here). *—Jason Ankeny*

18 Soul Hits from the '60s / 1996 / JCI ♦♦♦
There are better and more extensive '60s soul collections around, but sticking just to the contents at hand, this is first-rate stuff by any measure. Includes major hits by James Brown, Wilson Pickett, the Isley Brothers, Sam & Dave, Otis Redding, Carla Thomas, and Johnnie Taylor, as well as big singles by minor performers like the Capitols, Archie Bell, Fontella Bass, Don Covay, Robert Parker, and James & Bobby Purify. *—Richie Unterberger*

1942–45: The R&B Hits / Nov. 5, 1997 / Indigo ♦♦♦♦♦
Yet another excellent collection from British blues and R&B label Indigo, *1942-45: The R&B Hits* chronicles the heady period when small and big band swing morphed into jump blues in major cities across the U.S. Featuring 44 cuts spread over two discs, the mix takes in most of the major players, including Louis Jordan, Lucky Millinder, Wynonie Harris, Joe Turner, Jimmy Rushing, the Count Basie band, and Jimmy Liggins. Also on hand are such smooth crooners as Nat King Cole, Ivory Joe Hunter, and Helen Humes. Mighty contributions are also heard from vintage blues picker Tampa Red, R&B-hewn jazz diva Dinah Washington, rock & roll forefather Arthur "Big Boy" Crudup, and vibraphone master Lionel Hampton. Crucial cuts abound on an album that consistently rocks the house. *—Stephen Cook*

1949: The R&B Hits / Jan. 1, 2000 / Indigo ♦♦♦♦♦
The defining year for music in general was 1949, the first year back in full force after World War II and the musician union's ban on recording in 1948. It was also the first year that African-American record charts were called "rhythm & blues" instead of "race" charts. It was the end of the big band era; Louis Jordan was at his peak, and the resurgence of old Delta-styled blues played electrically was making inroads on small labels across America. This 48-track, two-disc set gives a real feel, through its very nice cross-section, of what was actually popular with R&B listeners that important year—and does it with nice, clean transfers on most of the material. Along the way, we're treated to the diverse sounds of John Lee Hooker "Boogie Chillen"), Paul Williams ("The Hucklebuck"), Louis Jordan ("Saturday Night Fish Fry"), Ruth Brown ("So Long"), Larry Darnell ("For You My Love"), Charles Brown ("Trouble Blues"), Amos Milburn ("Roomin' House Boogie"), Tampa Red ("When Things Go Wrong"), Lionel Hampton ("Lavender Coffin"), Big Jay McNeely ("Deacon's Hop"), Robert Night Hawk ("Annie Lee Blues") and Stick McGhee ("Drinkin' Wine Spo-Dee-O-Dee"). A diverse and quite listenable collection, this tips the scale rightly with a nice balance of hits and important music. *—Cub Koda*

1950: The R&B Hits / Mar. 27, 2001 / Indigo ♦♦♦♦
This is a two-CD, 48-track compilation of, as the no-frills title suggests, songs that were R&B hits in 1950. Jump blues, piano boogies, and bluesy ballads form virtually the entire program, much of which consists of contributions from well-known pioneers such as Louis Jordan, Ivory Joe Hunter, Wynonie Harris, Little Esther, Lowell Fulson, Amos Milburn, Roy Brown, Tiny Bradshaw, Ruth Brown, Johnny Otis, Floyd Dixon, Fats Domino, John Lee Hooker, and Lightnin' Hopkins. Some of these are famous classics: Hunter's "I Almost Lost My Mind," Clarence Garlow's "Bon Ton Roula" (the first zydeco-influenced song to be a big hit), Joe Liggins' "Pink Champagne," Percy Mayfield's "Please Send Me Someone to Love," and Amos Milburn's "Bad Bad Whiskey." For the most part, though, these aren't going to be overly familiar to anyone but R&B collectors, for whom the most unusual items will be the occasional selections by obscure performers, like Ray-O-Vacs' reading of "Besame Mucho" and Nellie Lutcher and Nat King Cole's duet on "For You My Love." It's a good overview of where R&B was at in 1950, though perhaps not diverse enough to compel those who aren't devotees of jump blues and boogie. It would be good to have more thorough liner notes than the perfunctory annotation given on the sleeve, as well as the actual chart positions of these songs, as they were (one assumes) selected on the basis of their popularity. *—Richie Unterberger*

20 Classic Doo-Wop Hits / AMC ♦♦♦♦
A lot of great doo wop came out of Chicago in the years between 1954 and 1965, the year when soul music took over the R&B charts. The majority of the great ones came out on Chess and Vee-Jay Records, and this 20-track collection samples some of the very best. Kicking off (the disc runs chronologically) with 1954's "Goodnight, Sweetheart, Goodnight" by the Spaniels—who also appear on "You Painted Pictures"—the set features two tracks each by the Flamingos ("The Vow" and the absolutely gorgeous "I'll Be Home"), Lee Andrews & the Hearts ("Teardrops" and "Long Lonely Nights"), the Dells (the original "Oh What a Night" and the 1965 set-closing "Stay in My Corner") and three from the Moonglows ("Ten Commandments of Love," "Twelve Months of the Year" and "In My Diary"). This would make a formidable enough backbone for a comp, but add the El Dorados' "At My Front Door," Gene Chandler's "Duke of Earl," the Students' "I'm So Young," Johnnie & Joe's "Over the Mountain, Across the Sea," the Magnificents' "Up on the Mountain," the Pastels' "So Far Away" and the Sensations' "Let Me In" to the mix and you've got a healthy chunk of some of this genre's greatest music in one quick history lesson. *—Cub Koda*

20 #1 Hits From 20 Years / 1990 / Motown ♦♦♦
20 #1 Hits From 20 Years focuses almost exclusively on the Motown of the 1970s—a period less anthologized than the label's 1960s commerical heyday, it nevertheless gave rise to many of the company's finest moments, among them the creative renaissances of both Marvin Gaye and Stevie Wonder as well as the introductions of the Jackson 5 and the Commodores. And while such highlights as "You Are the Sunshine of My Life" and "What's Going On" are still best represented within context of the brilliant albums which spawned them, the enduring greatness of smashes like "I Want You Back" and "Papa Was a Rolling Stone" serve as a reminder that Motown's days as the definitive singles label of the pop era were far from over. *—Jason Ankeny*

20 Sweet Soul Classics / Nov. 17, 1998 / Double Play ♦♦♦♦♦
A CD chock full of hits and only the hits, most from the '60s and early '70s, with the sole exception being Atlantic Starr's "Secret Lovers," which seems out of place stuck between Joe Tex's "Hold On to What You Got" and Aaron Neville's "Tell It Like It Is." A good sampling of the soul experience with solid charters from Jimmy Ruffin, the Shirelles, Jewel Aikens, Chuck Jackson, Jerry Butler, and others. *—Andrew Hamilton*

2000 Volts of Stax / Jan. 18, 1996 / Stax ♦♦♦♦
Perfect for the Stax completist, the 18-tracks include many you probably don't have by artists like the Astors ("Come Out Tonight"), the Tonettes ("Please Don't Go"), the Mad Lads ("She's The One"), and Deanie Parker ("How About You"). A few familiar sounds: William Bell's "You Don't Miss Your Water," Albert King's "Crosscut Saw," and Otis Redding's "Try A Little Tenderness," and the mournful "Pain in My Heart," offers soul with no apologies. Johnnie Taylor gives his take of Sam & Dave's "You Don't Know Like I Know," and Rufus Thomas stamps his M.O. on Lee Dorsey's "Ride Your Pony." Features an assortment of treats by stellar but unheralded soulsters, and known artists doing unfamiliar sides. The list includes Ruby Johnson, Eddie Kirk, Eddie Floyd, the Mar-Keys, Carla Thomas, and Booker T. & the MG's—every selection carries that patented Stax sound: horns on the chorus, tight simplistic rhythms, and spontaneous, earthy singing. *—Andrew Hamilton*

25 All-Time Doo Wop Hits / May 7, 2002 / Varese ♦♦♦♦♦
These are not the *best* 25 all-time doo wop hits—whether because of licensing restrictions or not, there's no "The Great Pretender," "Tears on My Pillow," "Maybe," "Searchin'," "Gee," "Stay," "A Teenager in Love," "I Only Have Eyes for You," "Why Do Fools Fall in Love," "Book of Love," "Silhouettes," or numerous other smashes that might be reasonably

championed as among the cream of the cream. As doo wop comps go, though, it's pretty good, and a good disc if you want a few anthologies in the genre without fussily building a systematic collection. To start with, it does have several core doo wop classics: the Silhouettes' "Get a Job," the Five Satins' "(I'll Remember) In the Still of the Nite," the Penguins' "Earth Angel," the Capris' "There's a Moon out Tonight," Don & Juan's "What's Your Name," the Crests' "16 Candles," the Earls' "Remember Then," Johnnie & Joe's "Over the Mountain; Across the Sea," and the Skyliners' "Since I Don't Have You." There are also a number of low-charting singles that nonetheless got a lot of regional airplay and may be well-remembered even by non-doo wop specialists, like the Willows' "Church Bells May Ring," the Genies' "Who's That Knocking," the Jive Five's "What Time Is It?," and Robert & Johnny's "We Belong Together." And, surprisingly, five of these didn't make the national charts at all, though the Eternals' witty "Babalu's Wedding Day," Tony Allen & the Champs' sillier "Nite Owl," and the Harptones' "A Sunday Kind of Love" were heard by many in their day and remain on the play lists of doo wop-oriented radio shows. It's a good mix of the classic and the less familiar, though the classics are still better than the less familiar. This CD marks, incidentally, the first time the Casuals' "A Casual Look," a big hit in 1956, has been on CD in the U.S. *—Richie Unterberger*

25 Years of R&B: 1971 / 2000 / Flashback ✦✦✦
This budget compilation from Rhino's Flashback division collects ten tracks from seven record labels that were Top Ten R&B hits in 1971 and 1972. (Despite the single year cited in the title, Millie Jackson's "Ask Me What You Want" dates from the first quarter of 1972, not 1971.) The biggest hit here is Jean Knight's chart-topper "Mr. Big Stuff," which went double platinum, while four of the other tracks went gold. The music reflects the mixed state of black music in the early '70s, starting with Curtis Mayfield's solo debut single, the socially conscious and deeply cynical "(Don't Worry) If There's a Hell Below We're All Going to Go" and continuing with lush pop tunes like Joe Simon's "Drowning in the Sea of Love," funky workouts like Rufus Thomas' "The Breakdown," and revivals of '60s favorites "Where Did Our Love Go?," by Donnie Elbert, and "Spanish Harlem," by Aretha Franklin. Clearly, the music was in transition, and even in only these ten representative recordings the changes are noticeable. *— William Ruhlmann*

25 Years of R&B: 1972 / 2000 / Flashback ✦✦✦✦
The year 1972 in soul music is represented well (if concisely) on this budget-priced collection assembled by the Rhino subsidiary Flashback Records. Eight different label imprints issued these recordings originally, among them Atlantic and Curtis Mayfield's Curtom. Mayfield leads things off with the indelible "Superfly," one of six gold records to be included. He is followed by Aretha Franklin, whose buoyant "Day Dreaming" hit number one on the *Billboard* soul chart in 1972, as did four other tracks here. (A sixth chart-topper, the Spinners' "Could It Be I'm Falling in Love," though released in late 1972, didn't top the chart until February 1973.) The collection provides a good cross-section of popular black music in 1972, from its grittier aspects (whether they be the streetwise "Superfly" or Joe Tex's funky "I Gotcha") to its more lush moments, such as the Stylistics' "Betcha By Golly, Wow." The album does not provide a full-length portrait of the era, but, as a snapshot, it captures an accurate glimpse. *— William Ruhlmann*

25 Years of Soul: 1970 / 1997 / Flashback ✦✦✦✦
Flashback, a division of Rhino devoted to budget collections, has a winner with this sampling of the soul music of 1970. All ten tracks were Top Ten soul hits, five of them reaching the top of the *Billboard* chart and seven going gold. Six originated with Atlantic Records (one of which, Brook Benton's "Rainy Night in Georgia," was issued on its Cotillion subsidiary); two with Holland-Dozier-Holland Productions, which the songwriter/producers established after leaving Motown (the Chairmen of the Board's "Give Me Just a Little More Time" on Invictus and 100 Proof (Aged in Soul's) "Somebody's Been Sleeping" on Hot Wax); one with Stang Records (the Moments' "Love on a Two-Way Street"); and one with Chimneyville (King Floyd's "Groove Me"). The tracks trace the development of soul music in the '70s, the expressive pop/R&B of Aretha Franklin and Wilson Pickett combining with the Motown-styled Chairmen of the Board and the forward-looking funk of King Floyd. And then there are indelible hits like Clarence Carter's rural survival tale, "Patches." This collection is short, but it has been well chosen. *— William Ruhlmann*

4000 Volts of Stax & Satellite / 1995 / Stax ✦✦✦✦
This *Volts of Stax* volume features some obscure solo artists and groups that recorded for Stax and Volt Records. The Del-Rios (featuring William Bell) do "Pop-Eye the Sailor Man," a novelty released in the labels' embryo days. Bell also does "Any Other Way," one of many male solos; others by Prince Conley, Oscar Mack, Bobby Marchan, Otis Redding, and Eddie Kirk are fine, if not well-known, examples of Stax's sound. The Astors crank out two tunes, and other unheralded groups—the Drapels, the Chips, the Canes, the Cobras, and the Vel-Tones—get one song apiece. Wendy Rene, who sung with the Drapels, knocks out "I Wish I Were That Girl" with youthful exuberance. In sum, this is a fantastic import of some hard-to-get tunes. *—Andrew Hamilton*

60's Girl Groups / 1998 / Warner Bros. ✦✦✦✦
Overshadowed by Motown biggies who ruled the '60s airwaves, these girl groups represent the many vital pockets of black female harmonizers found across the U.S., especially in the East. And going even further afield into fringe terrain, the people at Warner's have chosen a potent mix of obscure sides and minor hits by such golden contingents as the Chiffons, the Three Degrees, the Apollas, and the Cookies. No "He's So Fine" here (a huge smash for the Chiffons)—*60's Girl Groups* packs it in with such angelically disguised R&B highlights as the Royalettes' "There He Goes" and the Blossoms' "Good, Good Lovin'." A fine sampler for all those astute girl group fans. *—Stephen Cook*

ABC's of Soul, Vol. 1: Classics from the ABC Records Catalog 1961–1969 / Sep. 9, 1996 / Hip-O ✦✦✦✦
A various artists compilation that's slanted toward Southern soul and blues with the Impressions' doo wop-flavored "Gypsy Woman" and the Marvelows' harmony gem "I Do" added for variety. B.B. King's "The Thrill Is Gone" and O. V. Wright's "Eight Men, Four Women" are blues and deep soul classics. Ike and Tina Turner are represented on two selections: "The Hunter" and their erotic rendition of "I've Been Loving You Too Long." Songs the magnitude of Eddie Holman's "Hey There Lonely Girl," and Joe Hinton's "Funny" defy labeling. Maxine Brown, Bobby "Blue" Bland, and the Tams tracks are *pièces de résistance*. The Marvelows and the Impressions provide more ear treats with "In the Morning" and "We're a Winner," respectively. It's a good party CD. *—Andrew Hamilton*

ABC's of Soul, Vol. 2: Classics from the ABC Records Catalog 1969–1974 / Sep. 9, 1996 / Hip-O ✦✦✦✦
The second volume in the *ABC's of Soul* series covers the late '60s, the era which laid the groundwork for funk and disco. The collection features Ike and Tina Turner ("Bold Soul Sister") and B.B. King (performing Howard Tate's "Ain't Nobody Home"), along with the Four Tops, the Pointer Sisters, Bobby "Blue" Bland, the Crusaders and Rufus with Chaka Khan. *—Jason Ankeny*

ABC's of Soul, Vol. 3: Classics from the ABC Records Catalog 1975–1979 / Sep. 9, 1996 / Hip-O ✦✦✦✦
The evolution of soul into funk and disco is the subject of Vol. 3, which includes the Dramatics' "Me and Mrs. Jones" and Harold Melvin & the Blue Notes' "Reaching for the World" and "After You Love Me, Why Do You Leave Me," along with songs from the Pointer Sisters, O.V. Wright, Lenny Williams, Al Hudson & the Partners, and Denise LaSalle. *—Jason Ankeny*

Absolutely: The Very Best of Prelude Records / Apr. 22, 1997 / Deep Beats ✦✦✦
Similar to Deep Beats' electro collection, the Prelude volume in the *Absolutely* series covers the disco and proto-house label with tracks by Jocelyn Brown, Sharon Redd, D Train, France Joli and Musique, among others. The contributors aren't quite as essential as the remixers, however; no less a collection of production all-stars than Shep Pettibone, François Kevorkian, Larry Levan and Tony Humphries contribute extended remixes, all of them contemporary with the original Prelude release. The result is a compilation which charts the changeover from '70s disco to '80s house, though with much greater depth than is needed. *—John Bush*

Absolutely: The Very Best of Disco / May 6, 1997 / Deep Beats ✦✦✦
A mammoth box of disco—three hours and 45 minutes of music—and while it might not be the absolute best, it may be the most extensive compilation available. None of these songs scaled very high on the pop chart, but most are dead-on dancing grooves that will boost your party a couple of notches. The most familiar tracks are the Main Ingredient's "Happiness Is Just Around the Bend," Frankie Smith's only hit "Double Dutch Bus," Jocelyn Brown's disco turnaround of "Ain't No Mountain High Enough," and Dynasty's "I Don't Want to Be a Freak," which got good exposure on the *Soul Train* television show. The collection also features two songs by Sylvester among the 33 tracks, and some good movers by the likes of Hamilton Bohannon (two songs), D Train, Positive Force, La Rita Gaskins, and Pam Todd & Love Exchange. *—Andrew Hamilton*

Ace Story, Vol. 1 / 1979 / Ace ✦✦✦✦✦
With five separate volumes, *Ace Story* is the most comprehensive portrait of the seminal New Orleans R&B record label. Over the course of the series, each of the label's hits are featured, including "Sea Cruise," "Rockin' Pneumonia," "Pop Eye," among others, as well as many lesser-known gems. During the late '50s and early '60s, Ace's roster featured such R&B giants as Huey "Piano" Smith, Eddie Bo, Joe Tex, Lightnin' Hopkins, Charles Brown, Amos Milburn, and Earl King; each artist is featured on at least one disc of *Ace Story*, along with several acts that didn't have hits, but recorded some outstanding tracks. Start with the first volume, then proceed to the other discs; every one is filled with timeless R&B. *—Stephen Thomas Erlewine*

Across 110th Street / 1997 / Rykodisc ✦✦✦
The soundtrack to a relatively little-known 1972 blaxploitation film featured songs written and performed by Bobby Womack, as well as a musical score by J.J. Johnson. Although the inconsistency of the approach precluded a musical statement along the lines of *Superfly*, it's an interesting find for those looking for little-heeded early-'70s soul with funk and rock influences. Womack's cuts count among his better material, and even if the title track cops much of its attitude from *Superfly*, it has a satisfyingly tough soul-rock groove of its own. "If You Want My Love" is a good grainy ballad, "Quicksand" a propulsive number well-suited for action scenes, and "Do It Right" in the mold of James Brown, but more rock-oriented. Johnson's instrumental contributions, while not as interesting, set a nice period soul-jazz mood, and there are nifty periodic washes of electronic effects in both composers' contributions. *—Richie Unterberger*

Across the Tracks, Vol. 1: Nashville R&B and Rock 'N' Roll / 1996 / Ace ✦✦✦
Nashville is now firmly cemented in the collective consciousness as a country capital. But in the '50s and '60s, it did harbor a reasonably active R&B/blues/soul scene. Of the Nashville-based R&B labels, Excello had the highest profile; this compilation gathers 28 late '50s and early '60s tracks from several smaller local competitors (the Champion, Cherokee, Kit, Calvert, Poncello, Spar, and Valdot labels). Few of the performers are even known on a cult level; Gene Allison (who had a hit with "You Can Make It If You Try," not included here) is about the only one with even modest name recognition value. It's decent but generic early R&B, a bit of gospel, pure soul, or out-and-out Little Richard-like rock & roll thrown in, recommended only if early R&B/soul if your main bag. Which

isn't to say it's mediocre; there is not, however, a clearly identifiable Nashville R&B sound, as there is for, say, Memphis. The highlights are the most soul-oriented outings from the early '60s (by Lucille & the Strangers, Herbert Hunter, Leevert Allison, and Roscoe Shelton), if only because the tunes are more sophisticated and the production a bit more ambitious. *—Richie Unterberger*

Across the Tracks, Vol. 2: More Nashville R&B and Doo Wop / 1997 / Ace ✦✦✦
Like volume one of the series, this documents the nearly forgotten Nashville R&B scene of the 1950s and 1960s, on 30 obscurities issued on small local labels. It's similar in content to its predecessor: smoky, often raw sides, sometimes sparsely (even crudely) produced, the approaches varying from bluesy stuff and raunchy rock to doo wop and '60s soul. There's even a 1959 gospel side by the Fairfield Four, who wouldn't reach the peak of their fame until almost four decades later. It's like an encyclopedia of black popular music styles from the time, the caveat being that while they're representative examples, they're not outstanding. The standouts are the most modern-sounding cuts at the end: Earl Gaines and Lucille Johns' duet on "You Are My Sunshine," and the uptown soul of Gene Allison's "Stay a Little Longer," and the previously unissued, Stax-like "It's Almost Sundown" by Roscoe Shelton. Allison's version of "You Can Make It If You Try" (covered by the Rolling Stones) on this disc, by the way, is not the original, but a 1968 remake. *—Richie Unterberger*

Africafunk: The Original Sound of 1970's Funky Africa / Jan. 19, 1999 / Harmless ✦✦✦✦
Africafunk collects contemporary African music from artists like Tony Allen, Peter King, Vecchio, and Ice. Manu Dibango's "Weya," Oneness of Juju's "African Rhythms," Mombasa's "African Hustle," and Fela Ransom Kuti's "Expensive Shit" are among the standout tracks on the album, which shows off Africa's up-to-date mix of tradition and pop. *—Heather Phares*

The Aladdin Records Story / 1994 / EMI ✦✦✦✦✦
The *Aladdin Records Story* box set collects '50s and '60s R&B hits from the label's roster, including Floyd Dixon's "Telephone Blues," the Cookies' "Don't Let Go (Hold Me, Hold Me, Hold Me)," the Sharps' "Our Love Is Here to Stay," and Thurston Harris' "Little Bitty Pretty One." Songs by Marvin & Johnny, the Five Keys, the Jivers, Gene & Eunice, and Shirley & Lee round out this comprehensive collection of Aladdin's definitive singles. *—Heather Phares*

All Night Boogie: The Great Atlantic Vocal Groups, Vol. 2 / 1996 / Rhino/Collectors' Choice Music ✦✦✦
Another two-CD, 50-track collection of R&B vocal group (usually doo wop) rarities from the Atlantic vaults, recorded in the 1950s and early '60s. None of these are familiar hits, except for the Coasters' "Yakety Yak" and "Charlie Brown," presented in previously unreleased stereo mixes. It's not recommended if you're not heavily into the genre, but if you're a doo wop specialist, this is one of the best packages of its kind available, with sides (many hard to find) by the Clovers, Cardinals, Penguins, Bobbettes, Sensations, Skyliners, and others. There are also previously unreleased items by the Chords and the Drifters (from both the Clyde McPhatter and Ben E. King lineups), and the original version of "Twist and Shout" (by the Top Notes). *—Richie Unterberger*

All Platinum Funk / Apr. 25, 1995 / Charly ✦✦✦
While better known for quiet storm staples performed by the Moments, the Whatnauts, Sylvia Robinson, and George Kerr, All Platinum Records wore many hats. On a handful of labels they cut all facets of soul music, including the funky tracks on this collection by a number of the long list of artists who ventured into their Englewood, NJ, recording studios. Sounding better than ever on CD are funky concoctions by Dallas, TX, native Bobby Patterson, the Rimshots, saxman Lonnie Youngblood, First Class, Mother Freedom Band, and more. Brother to Brother's warmer-than-room-temperature "In the Bottle" is also onboard, along with four tracks by Eddie "Juni" Fisher. Even the sexy Moments funk in with "Stay." *—Andrew Hamilton*

Am I Black Enough for You / Oct. 31, 1995 / Sony ✦✦✦
Am I Black Enough for You is a thoroughly entertaining collection of early-'70s soul with a black power message that's either explicit or implicit in the music itself. Since it's limited to a single disc and the Sony vaults (which include Columbia, Epic, and Philadelphia International), the collection isn't quite definitive, but it is an excellent sampler, containing underappreciated gems from Sly & the Family Stone ("Thank You for Talkin' to Me Africa"), the O'Jays ("Big Gangster," "Don't Call Me Brother"), Harold Melvin & the Blue Notes ("Ebony Woman," "Where Are All My Friends"), the Isley Brothers ("Freedom," "Brother, Brother," "Go for Your Guns"), the Intruders ("Save the Children"), the Jacksons ("Man of War") and Billy Paul ("Am I Black Enough for You"). *—Stephen Thomas Erlewine*

American Roots of the British Invasion / Jul. 16, 2002 / Varese ✦✦✦✦✦
These are the original versions of 20 American songs, mostly but not all rock & roll, covered by British Invasion bands in the mid-'60s, usually but not always for hits. To do a comprehensive survey of original versions of British Invasion classics, you'd need a few shelves of CDs. But this does have many of the better ones, and even if the stylistic threads connecting them are thin other than the British Invasion connection, it's a pretty great listen, taking in various strands of high-grade American rock & roll from the 1950s and first half of the 1960s. Although just about all of this stuff appears on more than one compilation (and sometimes on many compilations), there are still many listeners who know the British Invasion covers of many of the songs, but not the originals. For instance, there is Chan Romero's "Hippy Hippy Shake" covered by the Swinging Blue Jeans (and the Beatles, though their version didn't come out officially until the 1990s); the Shirelles' "Boys," done on the Beatles' first album; the Donays' girl group classic "Devil in His Heart," done on the Beatles' second album; Barbie Gaye's peppy 1957 rock & roller "My Boy Lollipop," covered by Millie Small; Bessie Banks' soul-pop ballad "Go Now," a hit for the Moody Blues; and Dr. Feelgood's "Mr. Moonlight," covered by the Beatles. And more: Bobby Day's "Over and Over" was done by the Dave Clark Five, Evie Sands' fetching girl group-ish "I Can't Let Go" by the Hollies, and Del Shannon's dramatic ballad "I Go to Pieces" by Peter & Gordon. Getting more obscure, Little Willie John's "Leave My Kitten Alone" was indeed recorded by the Beatles in 1964, but that cover wasn't released for three decades. Getting less obscure, the Isley Brothers' "Twist and Shout," Maurice Williams & the Zodiacs' "Stay," Little Richard's "Long Tall Sally," and John Lee Hooker's "Boom Boom" were all big hits in the United States before being taken up by British bands. There are also a couple of interesting detours outside of rock in Buck Owens' Bakersfield country classic "Act Naturally," done by the Beatles, and Buffy Sainte-Marie's "Universal Soldier," which gave Donovan an American hit. For the original versions of Beatles songs specifically, there are actually a few more on the 1986 Rhino LP *Beatle Originals*, including some important songs that don't appear on this CD, like Buddy Holly's "Words of Love" and Arthur Alexander's "Anna (Go to Him)." Still, a very fun CD this is, whether you're looking for the original versions or not. It seems kind of suspect, though, that Gene Pitney's "Pretty Flamingo" was the "original" for Manfred Mann's cover; Manfred Mann recorded that tune in March of 1966, the same year Pitney put it on an album. *—Richie Unterberger*

The Arock & Sylvia Soul Story / Aug. 9, 2002 / Kent ✦✦✦
In the mid-'60s, veteran saxophonist Al Sears ran the Arock & Sylvia labels, which put out a couple dozen or so obscure New York soul records. Typically, Kent manages to make a CD out of its catalog, the 28 tracks split about half between 1962-1966 singles and previously unissued sides. In fact, much of the unreleased material was sung by unidentified demo singers, and although Kent has identified a few of these with confidence, three cuts are for the time being ascribed to "unknown." Often this kind of thing is something that only die-hard genre specialists can hear in one sitting, but though it'll be those collectors that comprise this disc's listenership, it's better than the average such archival anthology. You have to stare long and hard at the track listing for any of these names to ring bells, though some might recognize two of the "demo singers," Marie Knight (who did the original of "Come Tomorrow," covered by Manfred Mann for a British Invasion hit) and Sam Hawkins (who had a 1965 Top Ten R&B hit with "Hold on Baby"). Sterling Magee, represented by pretty straight soul tunes, might be better known to latter-day listeners as half of the blues duo Satan & Adam, who had some indie success in the 1990s. The name of Van McCoy pops up too, as the singer and songwriter of "Too Much," a 1964 single credited to the DC Playboys. Still, despite the relative anonymity of the other contributors, there's some good period pop-soul here, sometimes with a gospel feel. The Corvairs sound halfway between the Drifters and Gene Pitney on "A Victim of Her Charms"; Tutti Hill sounds a lot like Mary Wells on the original version of "He's a Lover," which Wells herself covered in 1965; two of Joan Moody's tracks are pretty accurate Supremes imitations; Gene Burks sounds like an early Stax artist on "Can't Stand Your Fooling Around"; and Garrett Saunders' "A Day or Two" is an upfront imitation and rewrite of Chuck Jackson's "Any Day Now," if an enjoyable one. The numerous demos are as a whole considerably inferior to the singles in both production and the quality of the songs, but it's interesting to hear a sparse piano-voice-dominated demo of Knight's "Come Tomorrow," though the single from which Manfred Mann learned the song isn't here, as it came out on a different label. The Larks, who do the 1964 single "For the Love of Money" here, by the way, are a different Larks than the group who did the hit "Cool Jerk," though "For the Love of Money" isn't a bad tune all the same. *—Richie Unterberger*

At the Club / Jun. 22, 1999 / Kent ✦✦✦✦✦
These songs seem to be packaged as soul cuts ideally suited for clubs, either in the 1960s when they were originally released, or later, when the perennial soul cult among the British still thrives. For those of us who are just regular old soul fans without a particular yen for club culture, it's better to think of it as a fine collection of 1960s soul from Atlantic Records, most of it not very easy to get on reissues. A few hits dot the 25-track program, like the Mar-Keys' "Last Night," Doris Troy's "Just One Look," and the Coasters' "Poison Ivy." There are also relatively underexposed items by a good number of Atlantic and Stax stars like Booker T. & the MG's, Carla Thomas, Rufus Thomas, Wilson Pickett, Solomon Burke, and Ben E. King. The real pleasure of this set for collectors, though, are the numerous rarities, chief among them Richie Barrett's Ray Charles-ish "Some Other Guy," the original version of the song covered live and on the BBC by the Beatles; the Soul Brother Six's "Some Kind of Wonderful"; Ray Sharpe's weird "Help Me (Get the Feeling) Pt. 1," which is like a soul version of Van Morrison's "Gloria"; Tami Lynn's maddeningly catchy "I'm Gonna Run Away From You," which was only a fluke hit in the U.K. six years after it was recorded; the Goodtimers' jazz-soul instrumental version of "Chain of Fools"; and King Curtis' cover of "Green Onions." There's even the rare and good 1965 white R&B single "He Don't Love You (And He'll Break Your Heart)" by Levon & the Hawks, who would soon change their name to the Band. Mel Tormé's "Comin' Home Baby" might seem like an odd choice in this company, its inclusion explained by its long-time status as a fave dance cut in English soul clubs. Some greater detail about the individual tracks in the liner notes would have been nice, but this is a fine investment for those who want soul as good as it is rare. [This U.K. import is not available for sale in North America.] *—Richie Unterberger*

Atlantic Hit 45's '58–77 / 1988 / Atlantic ✦✦✦
From Bobby Darin's bathroom hijinks to England Dan & John Ford Coley's Malibu Rum-lathered balladry, this Atlantic pop-hits roundup resuscitates the songs that were branded on youthful ears via millions of car radios. And while the label might be best

regarded for their milestone R&B recordings from the '40s-'60s, this 20-track set shows that house producers Jerry Wexler and the Ertegun brothers knew what the youth from both sides of town wanted to shimmy to. Such omnipresent cultural artifacts as the Rascals' "Good Lovin'" and Stephen Stills' "Love the One You're With" still ring with freshness, while '70s blips like Blue Image's "Ride Captain Ride" and Hot's "Angel in Your Arms" provide some difficult listening of the pleasant variety. A late-nite treat for all those tongue-in-cheek revelers. *—Stephen Cook*

Atlantic Honkers: Rhythm & Blues Sax Anthology / Aug. 12, 1950-Dec. 14, 1970 / Atlantic ✦✦✦✦
In the shadow of the label's headline-grabbing R&B and rock & roll stars, Atlantic's honking hornmen not only fired up many a vocal chart-topper, but they also helped lay the foundation for the mid-'50s rock revolution with their own jump swinging instrumentals from the decade before. In lieu of probable figures like Big Jay McNeely and Bill Doggett making this Atlantic two-fer of mad R&B blowers, though, such other A-list players as Willis Jackson, King Curtis, and jazzer Arnett Cobb take center stage for the course of the collection's 28 tracks. In addition, key honkers are featured on cuts by the jazz and R&B bands of pianist Jesse Stone (Sam "The Man" Taylor), guitarist Tiny Grimes (Red Prysock), and drummer Joe Morris (Johnny Griffin). A solid affair through and through, as the mix does heavy time in the prime late-'40s and early-'50s stretch, then reveals the enduring quality of all that bar walkin' with several late-'60s boogaloo revisions by Curtis, including his "Memphis Soul Stew" and a go at Led Zeppelin's behemoth "Whole Lotta Love." *—Stephen Cook*

Atlantic Jazz: Soul / 1947-1986 / Atlantic ✦✦✦✦
The *Atlantic Jazz* series continues with this slice of mostly '60s jazz-soul treats. Fittingly, the 11-track disc includes a side by one of the prime progenitors of soul, Ray Charles: He and MJQ vibraphonist, Milt Jackson, stretch out on the canonized "How Long Blues." Further expounding on the soul-jazz trajectory, the collection spotlights work by organist Shirley Scott (the Aretha Franklin hit "Think"), Les McCann and Eddie Harris (their classic Montreux Festival cut "Compared to What"), Yusef Lateef ("Russell and Elliot"), and Hank Crawford ("You're the One"). And there's even a bit of boogaloo-enhanced bossa, compliments of trumpeter Nat Adderley ("Jive Samba"). The soundtrack to your next retro-cool shindig. *—Stephen Cook*

Atlantic Records 50 Years: The Gold Anniversary / Feb. 17, 1998 / Atlantic ✦✦✦✦
Adequately covering the rich legacy of Atlantic Records' first 50 years over only two CDs is an impossible task, even concentrating only on rock and R&B, so it would be difficult to expect *Atlantic Records 50 Years: Gold Anniversary* to offer anything more than a cursory overview. The compilation does illustrate the incredible depth and diversity of talent that the label has maintained over the years, even if it doesn't come anywhere near a coherent presentation of that talent. Instead, *50 Years* skims a sampling of some of the best and best-known songs from throughout the company's history. The first disc concentrates primarily on Atlantic's rich catalog of R&B and soul music from the '50s and '60s (a greater portion of which easily filled a hugely entertaining nine-CD box set) and moves into seminal rock legends like Cream, CSNY, Led Zeppelin, and the Rolling Stones—all represented by only one song apiece. The second disc is wildly varied, featuring prog-rock from Yes, a couple of disco hits, and mainstream pop/rock from the '80s, as well as a few selections from Atlantic's most popular '90s artists (Tori Amos, Hootie & the Blowfish, Brandy, Jewel). So the problem certainly isn't with the quality of the music; it's just that there are so many different musical styles represented here that the set can't present them in any sort of context. Nearly all of these artists have a great deal more quality material out there, certainly enough that having one cut from each is hardly a satisfying proposition; moreover, there are various-artists compilations covering most of these styles in more coherent fashion. However, even if it isn't at all unified, *Atlantic Records 50 Years* undeniably possesses a wealth of great music. *—Steve Huey*

☆ **Atlantic Rhythm & Blues 1947–1974** / 1991 / Atlantic ✦✦✦✦✦
This eight-CD set should be a part of any collection that presumes to take American music—not just rock & roll or R&B—seriously. Atlantic Records was one of dozens of independent labels started up after the war by neophyte executives and producers, but it was different from most of the others in that the guys who ran it were honest and genuinely loved music. Coupled with a lot of luck and some good judgment, the results trace a good chunk of the history of American music and popular culture. Disc one opens with cuts which slot in somewhere midway between jazz, bop, and "race" music (as the term was used then). Disc two is pure, distilled R&B, the stuff filling the airwaves of black radio and the jukeboxes in the "wrong" parts of town in 1952-1954. Surprisingly, the material on disc three, covering 1955-1957, isn't very different in content or character from disc two, despite the fact that it covers the period when white teenagers were starting to listen to and buy these records in large numbers. It's only with Disc four that one sees the consequences of the late '50s—Ray Charles in his final days with the label, juxtaposed with the Drifters in their post-1958 incarnation and the start of the company's relationship with Stax/Volt Records. Disc six (1965-1967) is practically a mini-tribute to Stax/Volt, filled with the best-known sides of Eddie Floyd, Otis Redding, Sam & Dave, and Booker T. & the MG's. Discs seven and eight run from the late '60s and the heyday of Aretha Franklin to some great early-'70s soul, including Roberta Flack and the Spinners. The booklet, with a full sessionography and biographical notes on each artist, would be worth 20 bucks on its own. *—Bruce Eder*

Atlantic Sisters of Soul / 1992 / Rhino ✦✦✦✦✦
A fine collection of lesser-known female soul artists on Atlantic, including artists that aren't normally associated with the label, like Mary Wells and the Pointer Sisters. All of the songs were recorded in the late '60s and early '70s, and only three of the disc's 23 tracks scratched the R&B Top 20, although most the tracks were good enough to be hits. While the songs may not be familiar, their sweet sound is, making the disc a worthwhile purchase for fans of early-'70s soul. *—Stephen Thomas Erlewine*

Baadasssss Cinema / Aug. 6, 2002 / TVT ✦✦✦✦
As a compilation of blaxploitation soundtrack selections, *Baadasssss Cinema* certainly gets the job done. Mixing standards like Curtis Mayfield's "Pusherman" with welcome obscurities like Lonnie Liston Smith's "Expansions," the set provides superb, classic funk and soul recorded between 1971 and 1976 from often neglected sources. Bonus points for passing up Isaac Hayes' overplayed "Shaft" in favor of his equally great, if not as revered, "Truck Turner." It's especially fascinating to hear some of the more obscure but first-class selections such as Edwin Starr's "Big Papa" (which proves he had more than just his biggest hit "War" in him) or the heavily Latin-influenced cuts by War and the Blackbyrds. So while the set has no duds, there are a couple of caveats. For one thing, the liner notes are extraordinarily unhelpful, detailing nothing about which movie contains which song. For another, the disc is less than one hour long, which leaves plenty of room to be more thorough. A compiler savvy enough to include Gil Scott-Heron and Roy Ayers could have included "Brothers Gonna Work It Out" by Willie Hutch (from *The Mack*) or Melba Moore's "Black Enough" (from *Cotton Comes to Harlem*). Their absence means this is not quite as conclusive as it wants to be. Still, these are minor flaws, and *Baadasssss Cinema* works as either a worthy companion to *Pimps, Players & Private Eyes* (which many consider the definitive blaxploitation sampler) or as an excellent primer in its own right. *—Victor W. Valdivia*

Back to Stax: Memphis Soul / Jun. 25, 2002 / Music Video Distributors ✦✦✦
Stax Records issued countless classic soul and R&B hits from a variety of artists during the '60s—all of which were backed in the studio by the label's famous house band, Booker T. & the MG's. In January of 1990 (at the Palais De Festivale in Cannes, France), the surviving members of Booker T. & the MG's (keyboardist Booker T. Jones, guitarist Steve Cropper, and bassist Donald "Duck" Dunn) and fill-in drummer Danny Gottlieb were joined by a variety of Stax hitmakers on-stage, documented on the 2002 home video/DVD *Back to Stax: Memphis Soul*. While the members of Booker T. & the MG's remain on the stage for the show's duration, such artists as Sam Moore (of Sam & Dave), the Memphis Horns, Carla Thomas, Eddie Floyd, and Phil Upchurch join the backing band for mini-sets of their hits. Booker T. & the MG's prove to still be a viable and sturdy R&B instrumental outfit all these years later, as proven by a fine version of their biggest hit, "Green Onions," which opens the video. Other highlights include Sam Moore's "Hold on I'm Coming," the Memphis Horns' "Last Night," Carla Thomas' "Lovey Dovey," Eddie Floyd's "Knock on Wood," and Phil Upchurch's "Love and Peace," among others. *Back to Stax: Memphis Soul* proves to be a fun and surprisingly effective overview of Stax's most renowned artists, who remain in fine voice all these years later. *—Greg Prato*

Bad, Bad Whiskey (The Galaxy Masters) / 1994 / Specialty ✦✦✦✦✦
A subsidiary of Fantasy, the Galaxy label recorded a diverse assortment of soul and R&B in the 1960s and early '70s. This is a 26-track compilation of highlights from the company's output, covering 1962 to 1972. Landing the occasional minor R&B chart hit, Galaxy couldn't be said to have an especially distinctive label sound, though their efforts were on the whole bluesier than much soul of the era. But this is still a decent grab bag of odds and ends from soul's vintage period, with obscure sides by well-known performers like Betty Everett, Little Johnny Taylor, Lenny Williams, Charles Brown, Johnny "Guitar" Watson, Merl Saunders, and a host of unknowns. Especially good are the three sides by Rodger Collins, whose 1966 single "She's Looking Good" (which leads off the CD) was one of the better regional soul hits of the '60s, and was covered by Wilson Pickett for a Top 20 smash a couple of years later. *—Richie Unterberger*

Baddest Love Jams, Vol. 1 / Oct. 1995 / Motown ✦✦✦
Often the recycled packagings of Motown hits fail to meet expectations; not so with *Baddest Love Jams, Vol. 1*, which is all that and then some. All renditions are full versions, not radio edits. "Zoom" by the Commodores is 7:05 of bliss. A full 7:47 "Quiet Storm" spotlights Smokey Robinson's tenor in an apparent cutting contest with the flutist. The Miracles "A Fork in the Road" off their *Going to a Go Go* LP defines their harmony; the lush ballad also served as the flip to "Tracks of My Tears," and was a favorite at blue light basement parties. Eddie Kendricks sings "Intimate Friends" in an aching falsetto; Kendricks was famous for booty shakers, so this ballad will deliver a pleasant surprise for first time hearers. One of Ashford & Simpsons' best creations, "Shoe Shoe Shine," by the Dynamics Superiors, along with the lush "I Wanna Be Closer," written by Jermaine Jackson, and performed by Switch, are worth the price alone. You're gonna love "Young Love," by Tina Marie; she sounds like a female Smokey Robinson, phrasing as he would on the firey ballad. There's more sensuous tracks from Rick James, Marvin Gaye, David Ruffin, and others. This CD more than lives up to its boasting title. *—Andrew Hamilton*

The Ballad Era: Harlem, N.Y., Vol. 2 / Nov. 30, 1992 / Collectables ✦✦✦✦
Sweet, seminal doo wop from groups mainly from Harlem, NY. Other than skimpy liner notes, doo wop lovers won't find a thing about this collection to complain about. Certainly not the music. Even newcomers to the pioneering style will appreciate the bell-clear, untouched voices and heartfelt efforts from legendaries like the Avons (from Newark, NJ), the Dubs, the Heartbeats, the Harptones, the Flamingos (a Chicago-based group), the Cadillacs, the Rainbows, and more, including Tiny Tim & the Hits (with Tiny Tim being Timothy Wilson, who later sang with the Serenaders alongside George Kerr and Sidney Barnes). *—Andrew Hamilton*

Bar-B-Que Soul-A-Bration / May 5, 1998 / Rhino ✦✦✦✦
Generally sounding like the soundtrack to a black house party or outdoor BBQ of the 1960s, this gem-laden two-CD set focuses primarily on the soul music of that era, but

isn't without some very R&B-minded jazz and organ-combo selections. Much of the package (which spans 1952 to 1989) falls into the Southern soul category, and anyone who's seriously into Southern-style R&B will be familiar with such classics as Aretha Franklin's "Respect," Sam & Dave's "Soul Man," Booker T. & the MG's' "Green Onions" and Wilson Pickett's "Land of 1000 Dances." Meanwhile, the sleeker approach of Northern R&B is represented by Billy Stewart's "Summertime," Brenton Wood's "The Oogum Boogum Song," the Capitols' "Cool Jerk" and Archie Bell & the Drells' "Tighten Up." The jazz that Rhino has included fits right in because it's groove-oriented and R&B-minded—Jack McDuff's "Hot Barbecue," Mongo Santamaria's take on "Watermelon Man" and the Ramsey Lewis Trio's hit version of "The 'In' Crowd" are a long way from the cerebral offerings of Ornette Coleman, Jackie McLean and Charles Mingus. And while this collection takes its key inspiration from the 1960s, it doesn't exclude black party music of the 1950s (the Clovers' "One Mint Julep"), the 1970s (Betty Wright's "Clean Up Woman" and the Spinners' "Rubber Band Man") or the 1980s. It's highly recommended. *—Alex Henderson*

Baton Label: Sol's Story / Nov. 18, 1997 / Ace ♦♦♦
The Baton label, run by Sol Rabinowitz, was a small New York R&B indie that had some modest successes in the 1950s, most notably with the original version of "Got My Mojo Working," by Ann Cole (included here). This has 28 sides from 1953-1959, three of them previously unissued, presenting a solid if occasionally generic mix of period R&B styles, particularly doo wop and jump R&B. Highlights include the dreamy doo wop of the Rivileers' 1953 single "A Thousand Stars," Baton's first release and first success; the Hearts, whose "Lonely Nights" (from 1955) is one of the best examples of the fairly infrequently recorded female doo wop group genre; and the Lonely Ones' "My Wish," which sounds a little like Little Anthony & the Imperials. Much of the doo wop material has a rather poppier flavor than the typical stuff from the style, which actually makes it stand out from the pack a bit. Blues collectors will be most interested in the nine tracks by Ann Cole; none of them match "Mojo Working" ("I've Got Nothing Working Now" is a blatantly similar-sounding follow-up), and some of them have no relation to the blues, but "Each Day" is a pretty good cut that sounds like a minor-keyed variation of Little Walter's "My Babe." *—Richie Unterberger*

Battle of the Blues, Vol. 1 / 1959 / Deluxe ♦♦♦♦
This first volume of King's *Battle of the Blues* series features two of the label's biggest acts: Roy Brown and Wynonie Harris. Having already made their names in the late '40s as premier blues shouters on the R&B and jump blues circuit, both singers migrated to the Cincinnati independent and reached even loftier chart heights. Brown takes up the first side with seven sides of his animated and gospel-fired vocals, including the classic "Boogie at Midnight." For his part, Harris indulges his rougher-hewn vocal cords for an update of his big smash, the Brown-penned "Good Rockin' Tonight," and one of his all-time King highlights, "Bloodshot Eyes." For some whiskey-soaked R&B nostalgia, this fine collection is hard to beat. *—Stephen Cook*

The Beach Music Anthology / 1992 / Ripete ♦♦♦♦
A four-CD, 90-track "beach-music anthology" with not a hint of Jan and Dean or the Beach Boys? The official explanation is that this is beach music from the other coast, specifically from the Carolinas. But this collection's definition of Southern beach music is loose, to put it mildly. It extends beyond records created in the South (there's at least one track by a British group), beyond tunes popular during the summer (some of these hit the charts in mid-winter), and way beyond the subjects of sun and surf (there is a smattering of songs on the subject, but most have nothing to do with it). So what is the theme? It appears that any R&B-spiced rock that got played on Carolina beaches from the mid-'50s to the early-'90s, no matter where it came from or what it was about, was fair game. One suspects a more honest title for this package would be *90 Songs the Label Could License Rights To.* That said, the anthology holds together well musically, the quality level is rather consistently good, and the collection includes quite a few national hits and regional obscurities that are difficult or impossible to find elsewhere. Among the many highlights: Jackie Wilson's "Lonely Teardrops," Chuck Jackson's "Any Day Now," the Corsairs' "Smoky Places," the Foundations' "Build Me Up Buttercup," and Billy Stewart's "Sitting in the Park." This may not all be what you'd call "beach music"; it may not even contain much of what you would call beach music. Still, you could do a heck of a lot worse for a soundtrack for your next beach party. *—Jeff Burger*

Beach Music Anthology, Vol. 2 / Mar. 23, 1999 / Ripete ♦♦♦♦
The Beach Music Anthology, Vol. 2 doesn't contain nearly as many hits as the first anthology, but the quality is still rather consistently good, although perhaps a cut below *Vol. 1. —Jeff Burger*

Beat Goes On... Atlantic's Dance Through the 50's, 60's & 70's / Dec. 12, 2000 / Import ♦♦♦♦
Hearing this CD is like wading through an eccentric, imaginative tape that a friend has made of vintage Atlantic R&B and soul, mixing hits, flops, and star-sung obscurities over almost a quarter of a century, from the early '50s to the mid-'70s. Because it is a mix of hits and non-hits, it's hard to envision exactly who the intended audience is, but that doesn't mean it's not a pretty cool CD anyway. The hits include Dr. John's "Right Place, Wrong Time," the Clovers' "One Mint Julep," Sonny & Cher's "The Beat Goes On," Aretha Franklin's "(Sweet Sweet Baby), Since You've Been Gone," and Archie Bell & the Drells' "(There's Gonna Be A) Showdown." If you're interested in old Atlantic material in the first place, chances are you know about those, and will be more impressed by the less overexposed tracks. There are plenty of those, many of them very good, like the Coasters' "Shoppin' for Clothes," which is just as witty as their more famous hits, Ray Charles' sly 1953 cut "It Should've Been Me," the Drifters' 1963 effort "One Way Love," the Mar-Keys' instrumental "Philly Dog," and Wilson Pickett's debut Atlantic single, "I'm Gonna Cry." The prize oddity has to be Solomon Burke's cover of Bob Dylan's "Maggie's Farm," which was actually released as a single in 1965, and is an unusual, fairly effective match of a soul great with an early folk-rock song. Some of the other big-name efforts here are far more mundane; LaVern Baker's "You'd Better Find Yourself Another Fool," for instance, is an obvious attempt to simulate the sound of Don Gardner & Dee Dee Ford's gospel-rock crossover hit, "I Need Your Loving." [This U.K. import is not available for sale in North America.] *—Richie Unterberger*

Before They Were Hits or We Did It First, Vol. 2 / 2001 / Triple Crown ♦♦♦
As the title suggests, this is the second installment in a collection featuring original versions of songs that became hits for others. Did you know that "Message to Michael," a hit for Dionne Warwick, first appeared as "Message to Martha" by Lou Johnson? Or that Judy Harriet's "Tall Paul" preceded Annette's? Betty Everett's "Shoop Shoop Song" was first recorded by Ramona King. How about "Suspicious Minds," the Elvis Presley hit that first entered the fray by a singer name Mark James, or the Dells' first take of "Higher and Higher," which Jackie Wilson recut with chart success? On most tunes there's not much difference between the original and the hit covers, with the only exceptions being renditions done years after the originals, such as Bill Medley's "Don't Know Much," a hit for Linda Ronstadt and Aaron Neville. *—Andrew Hamilton*

Beg Scream & Shout: The Big Ol' Box of '60s Soul / Aug. 5, 1997 / Rhino ♦♦♦♦
Six CDs, and 144 songs, of classic '60s soul, including selections by every major performer in the idiom (except for Sam Cooke and Sly Stone, who were unavailable for licensing reasons), as well as numerous influential minor performers, one-shot artists, and just plain unknowns. The music is classic, and the packaging is an event in itself, with the discs enclosed in a mock briefcase for carrying 45 singles, and trading cards for each song on the volume that have photos and trivia questions on front, and mini-essays on the back. Yet it ultimately occupies a rather perplexing space on the collector's shelf. Anyone who's enough of a soul lover to fork over the dough for this production will no doubt have a good many of the tunes already, particularly the Hall of Fame hits like "Sweet Soul Music," "(I Know) I'm Losing You," "Don't Make Me Over," and "La-La-Means I Love You." There are numerous great rarities here—Jay Wiggins' magnificent melancholy ballad "Sad Girl," and the rare original versions of "Shake a Tail Feather" (the Five Du-Tones), "Tainted Love" (Gloria Jones), "Mustang Sally" (Sir Mack Rice), and "Piece of My Heart" (Erma Franklin). Yet the tracks used to represent some superstars—"You've Been in Love Too Long" for Martha & the Vandellas, or "Fly Me to the Moon" for Bobby Womack—seem almost deliberately idiosyncratic, even though this method also yields underrated off-the-beaten-tracks by Ray Charles ("In the Heat of the Night"), Al Green ("Back Up Train"), and others. It's almost as if some guys stayed up several nights running trying to make the ultimate '60s soul party tape—one which demonstrated both their impeccable taste and the depth of their record collection—and got so carried away with the idea that a box set resulted. Like all well-made party tapes, the content is excellent, but the sum is neither a definitive '60s soul box (an impossible task in any case), nor one which offers quite enough lost classics to justify its hefty price tag for those who already have half or more of the tunes. *—Richie Unterberger*

Ben Lee's Philadelphia Story / Feb. 26, 1999 / Kent ♦♦♦
In the 1960s, musician-producer-songwriters Frank Bendinelli and Leroy Lovett formed a production company, Ben-Lee Music, that generated tracks that were leased to other labels, as well as sides that were put out on their own small Philadelphia labels, like Benn-X and Sonata. The exact routes (whereby each side got placed where) are painstaking to trace nowadays; all the lay fan needs to know is that the Ben-Lee umbrella produced obscure Philadelphia soul throughout the decade. There are 24 of their 1963-1968 efforts are collected on this disc, half of them previously unissued. As was usual for small-label soul, the songs are often derivative of larger trends. It's less generic than the usual collection of items that were resuscitated by the Northern soul graveyard in Britain, however, due to the Philadelphia feel of its doo wop-influenced harmonies and peppy horn arrangements. Gamble & Huff freaks will want to pick this up since Leon Huff has a hand in several tracks as pianist and songwriter; Gamble & Huff wrote two of the better tracks: Patty & the Emblems' "He Said, She Said" and Kenny Gamble's own "What Am I Gonna Say to My Baby," which are both tuneful and emotional ballads. There aren't any lost treasures here, but the best tracks are pretty fair pop-soul. The Inspirations' "I'm Cuttin' In" sounds like a missing Drifters B-side; Joyce Bennett's "The New Boy" (actually produced by Tony Luisi, who ran studios that Ben-Lee usually used) has a bouncy uptown girl-group production feel; and the Symbals' "Don't Go, He Don't Love You" is an ingenious inversion of Jerry Butler's "He Will Break Your Heart." *—Richie Unterberger*

The Best of Ace Records, Vol. 1: The Pop Hits / 1992 / Scotti Bros. ♦♦♦
In the late '50s and early '60s, Ace was one of the most successful New Orleans-based rock & roll labels, recording hits by Huey Smith, Frankie Ford, and Jimmy Clanton. This 14-song compilation isn't the best way to hear the Ace catalog, though. Ford and Smith, both of whom have tracks here, are better represented by full compilations of their work; Ford's magnificent "Sea Cruise" is here, but Smith's only big hit, "Don't You Just Know It," is strangely missing in favor of a couple much less renowned tracks. Clanton recorded some nice hits in the teen idol style ("Just a Dream," "Venus in Blue Jeans," and "Go, Jimmy, Go"), all of which are here. But these sound misplaced next to Ford and Smith, and the other Clanton cuts are weak. There's also a rare early single by Joe Tex, "Charlie Brown Got Expelled," an answer record to the Coasters' "Charlie Brown." *—Richie Unterberger*

● **Best of Ace Records, Vol. 2: The R&B Hits** / 1993 / Scotti Bros. ♦♦♦♦♦
Scotti Brothers' two volumes of highlights from Ace Records' roster are the best available sampler of the label's late-'50s/early-'60s R&B and pop hits, featuring such stars as Huey "Piano" Smith, Frankie Ford, Joe Tex, and Jimmy Clanton. Both volumes have

detailed liner notes and great songs; both are essential for comprehensive rock and R&B collections. —*Stephen Thomas Erlewine*

The Best of Candlelite Records, Vol. 1 / 1993 / Juke Box Treasures ♦♦♦
This is the original installment in this landmark series, collecting 28 obscure doo wop tracks that were originally issued on Wayne Stierle's Candlelite label. The original "Why Don't You Write Me" by the Feathers is here, along with Jesse Belvin sitting in with them on "Love Song." The crude and crazed "Jeannie" by the Thrashers also makes its first CD appearance, along with the teenage bop of "Come on Baby" by the Five Discs and the dreamy teen sentimentality of "Lost Lover" by the Cameos and "Romance in the Spring" by the Five Roses. An excellent compilation covering the super-obscure side of the genre, and great listening every note of the way. —*Cub Koda*

The Best of Candlelite Records, Vol. 3 / 1994 / Juke Box Treasures ♦♦♦
Another installment of obscure doo wop singles from Wayne Stierle, this time featuring the El Domingos, the Original Sonics, the Sensation Owls (their track taken from a live '50s gospel radio broadcast), and the Delacardos. But the true winner here is the out of tune, surreal ballad "Empty Hours" by the Melodees, which must be heard to be believed. —*Cub Koda*

The Best of Charly Groove / Apr. 25, 1995 / Charly ♦♦♦♦
Two meaty discs packaged together in a sturdy slipcase, *The Best of Charly Groove* is a fine overview of the more R&B-oriented releases by the venerable U.K. reissue label Charly Records. A nice mixture of funk classics (Ohio Players' "A Little Soul Party," Funkadelic's "One Nation Under a Groove"), early disco gems (Joe Tex's "Ain't Gonna Bump No More (With No Big Fat Woman)"), New Orleans voodoo from Lee Dorsey and the Meters, plus not one but two sweaty James Brown live workouts, these 30 tracks show an impressively varied concept of the groove. There's even room for Mongo Santamaria's jazz fusion "Mambo Mongo," and it fits perfectly. There are few tracks here unfamiliar to devotees of the groove, but neither is it devoted solely to the usual suspects, which makes *The Best of Charly Groove* perfect for those people who are ready to move on up from their George Clinton and Sly & the Family Stone discs into the wider world of '60s and '70s R&B. —*Stewart Mason*

The Best of Chess R&B, Vol. 2 / 1990 / MCA ♦♦♦♦
Standing in the shadows of soul bigwigs Motown and Stax, Chicago's Chess label found a way to translate their blues catalog success of the '50s into a tidy and very respectable line in soul records during the '60s; this short but potent mix provides some very enjoyable insights. The key to the whole thing rested on huge hits by Fontella Bass ("Rescue Me"), the Ramsey Lewis Trio ("The 'In' Crowd"), Etta James ("Tell Mama"), and Billy Taylor ("Summertime"). And far from just qualifying as filler, the relatively less-popular fare by the likes of Tony Clarke, Jackie Ross, and the Radiants provides some of the collection's best moments. And one can't forget such blues-fueled classics as the Dells' "Stay in My Corner" and Little Milton's "If Walls Could Talk." A fine sampler for those soul newcomers looking to dig a little deeper. —*Stephen Cook*

☆ **The Best of Chess R&B, Vol. 1** / 1990 / MCA ♦♦♦♦♦
After many mutations, the two volumes of *The Best of Chess R&B* series certainly deserve to be combined into a single-disc edition, ideally with some extra tracks. As it stands, though, the 24 tracks are still broken up, languishing in various independent record-store bins. That said, the music on this initial volume is solid, ranging from vocal harmony cuts (the Moonglows) to blues diva gems (Etta James, Sugar Pie DeSanto). Also included are fine sides by the amazingly versatile singer Billy Stewart ("I Do Love You"), uptown-blues great Little Milton ("We're Gonna Make It"), and the hushed-toned Jan Bradley ("Mama Didn't Lie"). Hits, misses, and a whole lot of prime R&B. —*Stephen Cook*

The Best of Chess Rock & Roll, Vol. 1 / 1987 / Chess ♦♦♦♦
The Best of Chess Rock & Roll, Vol. 1 charts some of the most crucial developments in the music, from blues-based romps to vocal harmony gems. Rightfully needing to be teamed with volume two on one disc, the slim but potent mix here takes in both key figures like Chuck Berry and Bo Diddley and such delightful dark horses as Dale Hawkins and New Orleans' Eddie Bo. So, whether your mood calls for street-corner symphonies by the Flamingos or some grizzled R&B from Clarence "Frogman" Henry, this collection will make for a fine night by the record player. —*Stephen Cook*

The Best of Chess Rock & Roll, Vol. 2 / 1987 / Chess ♦♦♦♦
While this and the first volume of Chess' vintage rock & roll series should really be combined on one disc, *The Best of Chess Rock & Roll, Vol. 2* still delivers enough in the way of '50s gems to provide a satisfying listening experience. This time out, though, the fare is decidedly more pop, erring on the doo wop side and mostly eschewing the gritty end of the spectrum. Save for a song apiece by Chuck Berry and Bo Diddley, the majority here is in the dreamy vein of such album cuts as the Jaynetts' "Sally, Go 'Round the Roses" and the Monotones' "The Book of Love." It's more inspiration point than sock-hop rumble. —*Stephen Cook*

The Best of Chess Vocal Groups / 1988 / Chess ♦♦♦♦♦
Rounding out the trilogy of Chess sampler albums, this one features "Long Lonely Nights" by Lee Andrews & the Hearts, the highly influential "Every Day of the Week" by the Students, and the Southern soul of the Knight Brothers "Temptation 'Bout to Get Me." —*Cub Koda*

The Best of Chess Vocal Groups, Vol. 1 / 1988 / Chess ♦♦♦♦♦
This features classic doo wop from the Moonglows, the Flamingos, etc. —*Cub Koda*

The Best of Chess Vocal Groups, Vol. 2 / 1988 / Chess ♦♦♦
This slim but potent mix of vintage harmony vocal sides spotlights Chess' roll in a market that was often dominated by the Atlantic and Mercury labels. Cut before and during Chess' run of electric blues hits, the mix here takes on such legends as the Moonglows ("In My Diary"), the pre-fame Flamingos ("Dream of a Lifetime"), and the post-fame Ravens ("Give Me (A Simple Prayer)"). Also on hand, a young Four Tops poised for Motown gold, the Students, and the Chess brothers' first signing, the Dozier Boys. Better doo wop collections are out there, but at a bargain price, this album could be the perfect introduction to all that '50s fun. —*Stephen Cook*

The Best of Chess/Checker/Cadet Soul / 1989 / Chess ♦♦♦♦♦
The Best of Chess/Checker/Cadet Soul contains 16 solid Billy Davis productions for a variety of artists who recorded for the Chess conglomerate of labels in the '60s. There's everything from the late Billy Stewart's stuttering, syncopated "Summertime" to deep soul classics like Mitty Collier's "I Had a Talk With My Man" to the light, cool, jazzy sounds of the Ramsey Lewis Trio on "The 'In' Crowd" and "Wade in the Water." This is loaded with gems like the Radiants' Impressions-like three-part harmonies on "Voice Your Choice" and Tony Clarke's introspective "The Entertainer," easily the finest record of the late Detroiter's career. When Clarke lived in Detroit, he wrote songs for Billy Davis' Checkmate label, plus other local labels, as Ralph Thomas Williams. The fire of Sugar Pie DeSanto is featured on the scorching "Soulful Dress," written by Radiant Maurice McCallister. Fontella Bass does three numbers, one a rocking duet with Bobby McClure on "Don't Mess Up a Good Thing" that sounds like a Memphis recording. McClure's "Peak of Love" is not included, but would have been a welcome addition ditto for DeSanto's "In the Basement." Jackie Ross, the Dells, and Gene Chandler are also represented. These excellent recordings, with few exceptions, never achieved the success they should have. —*Andrew Hamilton*

The Best of Chess: Sisters of Soul / 1984 / Chess ♦♦♦
Chess Records compilations always satisfy. The label's post-'50s output never achieved the acclaim or sales it merited. They had hits, but nothing like Motown, and with the exception of Etta James and Koko Taylor, most of their main artists faded decades ago. Taylor, whose career got resurrected later by Alligator Records, cut "Wang Dang Doodle" on Chess; it didn't light up the charts, but did all right, and remains her signature tune thanks to her spine-tingling, soulful growl. Jackie Ross hit with "Selfish One," a soft number done in her sexy voice, and scored with Trade Martin's "Take Me for a Little While." Ross and Etta James are the only artists with more than one track. The tough-sounding James does three R&B soap operas: "Two Sides to Every Story," "Only Time Will Tell," and "Lovin' You More Everyday." Mitty Collier's waltz-paced "I Had a Talk With My Man," an adaptation of Reverend James Cleveland's "I Had a Talk With God," did well. But the Jaynetts' "Sally Go 'Round the Roses" broke the bank, and it wasn't even a Chess production; it came out on Tuff Records, which Chess distributed. "Rescue Me" by Fontella Bass sold more copies and charted higher than anything here, and deservedly so—the track smokes, and so does Bass' energetic vocal. —*Andrew Hamilton*

Best of Chicago Trax / May 26, 1998 / M.I.L. Multimedia ♦♦♦
The two-disc *Best of Chicago Trax* assembles 26 tracks from the Windy City-based dance label best known for its affiliation with Frankie Knuckles, whose "Baby Wants to Ride" and "Your Love" are among the highlights here. Other featured tracks include Liz Torres' "Can't Get Enough" and Mr. Fingers' "Can You Feel It." —*Jason Ankeny*

The Best of Disco One Hit Wonders / Feb. 20, 1996 / Hot Productions ♦♦♦♦♦
This collection includes unedited recordings from the disco era (some disco, some not) like William DeVaughn's "Be Thankful for What You Got" and the Independents' epic "Just as Long as You Need Me." Four songs represent the work of Sylvia & Joe Robinson's All Platinum label: "Shame, Shame, Shame," by Shirley & Co., Sylvia's "Pillow Talk," the Moments & the Whatnauts' "Girls," and Donnie Elbert's "Where Did Our Love Go." The many good-to-hear-again tracks include New York City's smash "I'm Doing Fine Now," as well as songs by Ultra High Frequency, John Travolta, and South Side. A fine collection with a misleading title, as most of the songs on this album aren't traditional disco, nor are all the artists bona fide one-hit wonders. —*Andrew Hamilton*

☆ **Best of Doo Wop Ballads, Vol. 2: Golden Archive Series** / 1991 / Rhino ♦♦♦♦♦
The Best of Doo Wop Ballads, Vol. 2: Golden Archive Series is an excellent supplement to the first volume, featuring 14 classic doo wop songs, including the Flamingos' "I Only Have Eyes for You," the Cadillacs' "Gloria," the Clovers' "Devil or Angel," the Heartbeats' "A Thousand Miles Away," Shep & the Limelites' "Daddy's Home," Lee Andrews' "Tear Drops," the Jive Five's "What Time is It?," and the Skyliners' "Since I Don't Have You." It's an excellent single disc, but doo wop connoisseurs may prefer to invest in Rhino's excellent pair of doo wop boxes instead of this collection. —*Stephen Thomas Erlewine*

☆ **Best of Doo Wop Ballads** / 1989 / Rhino ♦♦♦♦♦
The companion volume to Rhino's *Best of Doo Wop Uptempo* checks out the ballad side of the aisle and comes up with 18 smoothies in the bargain. Highlights include Dion & the Belmonts' "Where or When," the Five Satins' "In the Still of the Nite," the Cadillacs' "Gloria," the Moonglows' original of "Sincerely," the Velvetones' "Glory of Love," the Crests' "16 Candles," the Flamingos' evocative "I Only Have Eyes for You," and Lee Andrews & the Hearts' "Teardrops." Selections from the Pastels, the Skyliners, the Jive Five, the Dells, the Blue jays, the Penguins, the Spaniels, and the Heartbeats complete the set. —*Cub Koda*

☆ **Best of Doo Wop Uptempo** / 1989 / Rhino ♦♦♦♦♦
Part of a two-volume set, this brings together 18 classic performances from rock & roll's ground floor era. in addition to mega hits like "Gee," "Come Go With Me," "Speedo," "I Wonder Why," "Blue Moon," "Book of Love," and "Why Do Fools Fall in Love," the collection also features some more obscure sides like "Denise" by Randy & the Rainbows, "I Love You" by the Volumes, "Hushabye" by the Mystics, and "Foot Stomping-Part 1" by the Flares. Although this material gets recycled quite a bit on other compilations,

this one's a nicely assembled set and a fine addition to anyone's rock & roll collection. *—Cub Koda*

☆ **Best of Doo Wop Uptempo, Vol. 2: Golden Archive Series** / 1991 / Rhino ♦♦♦♦♦
The Best of Doo Wop Uptempo, Vol. 2: Golden Archive Series is a good supplement to the first volume, containing a number of classic doo wop singles, but true collectors would be better served by Rhino's pair of doo wop boxes. *—Stephen Thomas Erlewine*

Best of Ecko, Vol. 1 / Aug. 12, 1997 / Ecko ♦♦♦♦♦
Gutbucket Southern soul at its absolute best, with the distinct aftertaste of cornbread and molasses. The outrageous titles tell it all, including Chuck Roberson's bawdy "Whisky Glass and a Woman's Ass," Barbara Carr's "Make Me Feel It Like You Feel It Too," the late Ollie Nightingale's insidious "I'll Drink Your Bath Water Baby," and Bill Coday's "Her Love Is Good Enough to Put in Collard Greens." This is hard-nosed, adult-theme soul, old school style, with an underlying thread of broad humor. The perfect ice breaker for those backyard barbecues or late-night card games. *—Andrew Hamilton*

☆ **The Sound of the Swamp: The Best of Excello, Vol. 1** / 1991 / Rhino ♦♦♦♦♦
The Nashville-based Excello label specialized in obscure blues, R&B, and rock & roll from the '50s and early '60s. This first volume of *Sound of the Swamp: The Best of Excello Records, Vol. 1* covers the best from Crowley, LA, producer Jay Miller's blues, rockabilly, and swamp-pop sides. *—John Floyd*

The Southern Rhythm 'n' Rock: The Best of Excello, Vol. 2 / 1991 / Rhino ♦♦♦♦♦
The Best of Excello Records, Vol. 2 doesn't have the high percentage of classics and interesting obscurities that made the first volume essential, but it does have some fine cuts that will be of interest to fans of swamp R&B, including the Gladiolas' "Little Darlin'," Rudy Green's "My Mumblin' Baby," Louis Brooks & His Hi-Toppers' "It's Love Baby (24 Hours A Day)," Ray Batts' "Stealin' Sugar," Robert Garrett's "Quit My Drinkin'," Arthur Gunter's "Baby Let's Play House," the King Crooners' "Now That She's Gone," Hooks Coleman's "Fine Young Girl," and Shy Guy Douglas' "Long Gone." *—Stephen Thomas Erlewine*

The Best of Excello Records / 1995 / Excello ♦♦♦♦♦
Although several overviews of the Excello label exist (including Rhino's two-volume set), this single-disc thumbnail collection may be the most digestible and therefore the best of the bunch. With a generous 30 tracks on a single disc to recommend it for openers, this collection tries to hit virtually all popular strains that the label dabbled in, from big city blues to doo wop to rockabilly to R&B to its best known swamp blues offerings. With hits aboard like Slim Harpo's "Raining in My Heart" and "Baby, Scratch My Back," the Gladiolas' original version of "Little Darlin'," Lillian Offitt's "Miss You So," the Marigolds' "Rollin' Stone," and Guitar Gable's "Congo Mombo," this collection delves far further into collectors' favorites, including "Hey! Baby" by rockabilly Al Ferrier, "Wild Cherry" by Leroy Washington, "Now That She's Gone" by the King Crooners, and the original version of "This Should Go on Forever" by Guitar Gable. The blues quotient inherent in the label's output is also well represented with the inclusion of "Rooster Blues" by Lightnin' Slim, "Baby Let's Play House" by Arthur Gunter, "My Next Door Neighbor" by Jerry McCain, "My Home Is a Prison" by Lonesome Sundown, and "I Hear You Knockin'" by Lazy Lester. All in all, a collection that's hard to beat, especially if your budget doesn't extend to multi-disc retrospectives. *—Cub Koda*

The Best of Impact Records / Jan. 5, 1998 / Collectables ♦♦♦
The Best of Impact Records is a 25-track collection that features a selection of rare singles released by the Detroit-based indie label. The collection is approriately balanced between garage-rock and soul singles, with the most familiar group being the Detroit Wheels. Other artists on the collection are the Human Beings, Mickey Denton, the Boss Five, the Shades of Blue, the Classmen, the Sheppards, the Inner Circle, Sincerely Yours, the Lollipops, the Sixpense and Rod Riguez. Some of these songs are absolute dynamite, while others are recommended only because of thier sheer rarity, but the disc should be of interest to hardcore '60s rock collectors. *—Stephen Thomas Erlewine*

The Best of King Federal & Deluxe Doo Wop, Vol. 1 / Jul. 27, 1999 / Collectables ♦♦♦♦
This is a solid 20-track collection of vocal group and R&B offerings from Sid Nathan's stable of labels. In addition to classics from the Dominoes, Hank Ballard & the Midnighters, Otis Williams & the Charms, and the Checkers, the set also features rarities and hits from the Chanters ("No No No"), the Swallows ("It Ain't the Meat, It's the Motion"), the Platters ("Voo-Vee-Ah-Bee"), the Guytones ("She's Mine"), Donnie Elbert ("Hear My Plea"), the Hurricanes ("Pistol Packin' Mama"), Little Willie John ("Leave My Kitten Alone"), and Wynonie Harris ("Loving Machine"). An excellent blend of obscure material and R&B hits. *—Cub Koda*

The Best of Loma Records: Rise and Fall of a 1960s Soul Label / Nov. 14, 1995 / Warner Bros. ♦♦♦♦♦
It's fair to say that Loma Records was one of the most misunderstood records labels of its time. An R&B subsidiary of Warner Bros., Loma existed in a vacuum, fronted by a record company that was embracing the progressive trends in rock and pop with varying degrees of success. Add that to the fact that Warner really didn't quite know what to do in the R&B market, and it's a wonder the label lasted as long as it did (1964-1968). But the music was another story, and the fifty tracks collected on *The Best of Loma Records* reveal that the records were made with an incredible degree of care and class. Although they were obviously attempting to ape the success of labels like Motown, Stax and others, the talent on these quality sides (Ike & Tina Turner, J.J. Jackson, the Enchanters) and the producers (Jerry Ragovoy, Lenny Waronker) produced excellent and original results. Highly recommended for any fan of '60s soul, this is the real thing. *—Matthew Greenwald*

The Best of Melron Records: The Early Philly Sound / Jul. 24, 2000 / Philly Archives ♦♦♦
Melron Records was a tiny, independent Philly label that put out several dozen singles, mostly in the 1960s. This is a compilation of 25 tracks recorded there in the early- to mid-'60s (some, most likely, previously unreleased; the liner notes are indefinite on that point; at any rate, a number of the cuts did not come out on Melron singles). There aren't any hits among them, but Melron, along with numerous other low-profile Philly labels, were doing their bit to move the Philadelphia R&B sound from its roots in doo wop, girl groups, and twist music to more modern forms of soul. As such, this record might find most favor with scholars who appreciate the hidden links in musical history that lead to the full-fledged expression of a genre—in this case, Philly soul. That's not to say, though, that much of this isn't nice to hear on its own terms, even if the songs aren't brilliant and the styles are derivative. In fact, the all-over-the-place nature of the tracks, as they stumble around for something that might be hit-bound, is a big part of the fun. There are raucous dance tunes, smooth group vocal harmonizing, Latin rhythms, decent girl group tunes (by Lori Ann), and humorous novelties. What's missing is top-level material, but there's an engaging unself-conscious enjoyment to the delivery, the production usually being no-frills and competent (although some of the cuts are rough). Colly Williams' "We'll Make It Someday," with its cheesy organ and soulful backup female vocals, comes the closest to sounding like a hit that never made it to hit status. The liner notes speculate that the Pheasants' introduction to "Out of the Mist" might have been lifted for the Beatles for "This Boy." Although the melodies are similar, it is likely just a coincidence, as the Pheasants' single was so obscure, and the melody line a basic variation on progressions often found in Latin and Hawaiian music. *—Richie Unterberger*

The Best of Motorcity Records, Vols. 1-3 / 1994 / MotorCity/Hot Productions ♦♦♦♦♦
This three-volume set was partially the result of efforts of British songwriter/producer and Motownphile Ian Levine to record Motown artists who were left behind when Motown moved to Los Angeles in the early '70s. Much of the major and minor artists are represented by performances of new and original disco-based dance tracks, which proves to suggest that there's still life in the once-vibrant Detroit recording scene. *—John Lowe*

★ **The Best of New Orleans Rhythm & Blues, Vol. 1** / 1988 / Rhino ♦♦♦♦♦
The Best of New Orleans Rhythm & Blues, Vol. 1 is an incredible collection of 18 of the greatest Crescent City R&B singles ever released. Divided equally between classics ("Mother-In-Law," "It Will Stand," "I Hear You Knocking," "I'm Gonna Be a Wheel Someday," "Lipstick Traces (On a Cigarette)," "A Certain Girl," "One Night," "Ooh Poo Pah Doo (Pt. 1)"), and terrific but frequently underappreciated singles from the likes of the Spiders, Irma Thomas, Aaron Neville, Earl King, and Dave Bartholomew, the collection is a concise and utterly intoxicating overview of New Orleans R&B, one that appeals not only to neophytes, but also to collectors. *—Stephen Thomas Erlewine*

☆ **The Best of New Orleans Rhythm & Blues, Vol. 2** / 1988 / Rhino ♦♦♦♦♦
The Best of New Orleans Rhythm & Blues, Vol. 2 is just as thrilling as its predecessor, featuring 18 tracks of classic, funky R&B from the likes of Frankie Ford ("Sea Cruise"), Shirley & Lee ("Let the Good Times Roll"), Lee Dorsey ("Ride Your Pony," "Working in a Coal Mine"), the Meters ("Cissy Strut"), Irma Thomas ("Ruler of My Heart," "It's Raining"), the Dixie Cups ("Iko Iko"), Lloyd Price ("Just Because," "Lawdy Miss Clawdy"), Barbara George ("I Know (You Don't Love Me No More)"), Guitar Slim ("The Things That I Used to Do"), Chris Kenner ("I Like It Like That") and Clarence "Frogman" Henry ("Ain't Got No Home"). There are no bad cuts here, and nearly every song is a classic, making it an essential edition to any library, as well as one of the definitive overviews of New Orleans R&B. *—Stephen Thomas Erlewine*

The Best of Red Top Records, Vol. 1 / 1999 / Red Top ♦♦♦
Here are 30 obscure tracks from Philadelphia's Red Top Records, a local company that recorded some of the city's young hopefuls between 1957 and the early '60s. The Quin-Tones' "Down the Aisle of Love" charted nationally, but most of these selections were rarely if ever heard outside Philly. Outtakes, unreleased tracks, and sides recorded under Red Top's umbrella and leased to other companies pad the track listing. Vol. 1 includes three rare ones by Donnie Elbert ("Mommie's Gone," "For Sentimental Reasons," and "Someday," released on Jalynne Records in 1961); "Blue Star" by Harold Melvin (later of the Blue Notes, a 1961 release on 20th Century Records; and Joe Tex's ultra-rare blues ballad "Goodbye My Love." The Four Naturals' tracks are pure pop. *—Andrew Hamilton*

The Best of Red Top Records, Vol. 2 / 1999 / Red Top ♦♦♦
Here are 29 more tracks from Philadelphia's Red Top Records, a local label which helped cover the doo wop and R&B scene from the late '50s to the early '60s. None of these selections made any noise nationally and were strictly local successes; outtakes, unreleased tracks, and Red Top productions leased to other companies flesh out the track total. The Blue Notes' (an early edition of Harold Melvin & the Blue Notes) biggest single prior to Philadelphia International ("My Hero") is on board, as well as super rarities by Joe Tex and the outrageous Screamin' Jay Hawkins. The Four Naturals' pop songs are the only deviants from the doo wop/R&B stew. *—Andrew Hamilton*

The Best of Sue Records / Feb. 15, 1990 / Collectables ♦♦♦♦♦
As much as any 18 song collection could, this single CD presents a decent cross-section of the New York-based label's biggest hits. The range of material includes the biggest or best-known hits by Ike & Tina Turner ("It's Gonna Work Out Fine," "A Fool in Love"), Inez Foxx ("Mockingbird"), Baby Washington ("A Handful of Memories," "That's How Heartaches Are Made"), Bobby Hendricks ("Itchy Twitchy Feeling"), the Poets ("She Blew a Good Thing"), Wilbert Harrison ("Let's Work Together"), and Jimmy McGriff ("I've Got a Woman"), among others. There will be a few surprises here, including the degree to which Bobby Hendricks sounded like Jackie Wilson, and how much Tina

Britt's 1965 hit "The Real Thing" (issued on Eastern Records) was imitative of "Heat Wave" by Martha & the Vandellas. The sound is excellent, probably derived from the same body of masters that EMI assembled to put together its own *Sue Records Story* box that same year, and the annotation is decently detailed, at least where the major acts are concerned, if a little unstructured. *—Bruce Eder*

The Best of the Girl Groups / 1987 / Rhino ♦♦♦♦♦
This Rhino collection makes for the perfect introduction to the '60s heyday of Brill Building-issue girl groups. In fact, many of the 18 cuts here were cut for BB associates Leiber & Stoller's Red Bird label and come from the pens of such Brill mainstays as Carole King, Gerry Goffin, Jeff Barry, and Ellie Greenwich: while Barry/Greenwich can be credited with such landmarks of the genre as the Shangri-Las' "Leader of the Pack" and the Dixie Cups' "He's So Fine," Goffin/King share the same rarefied songwriting air for gems like the Shirelles' "Will You Still Love Me Tomorrow" and the Chiffons' "He's So Fine" (actually a King solo composition). There's even a stellar example of the work of Brill kings Bacharach & David: the Shirelles' "Baby It's You." Beyond the hits and the prestige, though, the disc also packs in more obscure highlights by the likes of the Exciters, Claudine Clark, Evie Sands, Skeeter Davis, and Cher (an early, Spector-esque cut produced by Sonny Bono); and don't not forget the work of Red Bird producer George "Shadow" Morton, who oversaw many of these sessions. A last taste of innocence before the youth "tuned in" during the Summer of Love. *—Stephen Cook*

The Best of the King Tut Record Company / 2000 / King Tut ♦♦♦
Here are 20 selections from New York's R&B/doo wop label King Tut, which didn't have many hits but recorded some prominent names (or at least acquired their masters). The list of tracks include obscure label hoppers Ike Perry & the Lyrics, whose rare "Please Don't Send Me Away" is included here. Many of these tunes were unreleased, though all these artists enjoyed documentable releases on other labels, including the Five Pennies, the Sheppards, Earl Lewis & the Channels, the Solitaires, the Ly-Dells, and the Four Intruders. *—Andrew Hamilton*

Best of United Records 1958–1972 / Sep. 9, 1996 / Stardust ♦♦♦♦
Choice selections from United Artists Records archives. Includes early Berry Gordy productions on Marv Johnson ("You Got What It Takes," and "(You've Got To) Move Two Mountains"), and two killers from Cornelius Brothers & Sister Rose ("Treat Her Like a Lady," and "Too Late to Turn Back Now"). Easy Listening lovers can reminisce with Steve Lawrence's "Portrait of My Love," and Don Costa's "Never on Sunday." Patty Duke, a '60s television star, sings "Say Something Funny," and country is represented with Bobby Russell's "Sunday Morning Confusion." The Exciters' rock the house with "Tell Him" (their female lead singer, Barbara Reid, is the mother of R&B mogul L.A. Reid. Tasty numbers by Garnet Mimms, the Clovers, the Magnificent Seven, and the Highwaymen are also included in the package, and all appear in true stereo. *—Andrew Hamilton*

Best of Wally-O-Productions / Feb. 6, 2001 / Philly Archives ♦♦♦
Producer Wally Osborne is not a household name, even to students of Philadelphia soul, but he did involve himself in numerous Philly soul records, as producer, songwriter, and musician. This anthology collects 22 of his productions from 1964-1973 (all but three from the 1960s); none of 'em hits even on a large local scale, let alone a national one. There wasn't a Wally Osborne sound, and the material here (some previously unreleased)—by obscure artists like Herb Johnson, the Topics, the Four Thoughts, and Bobby Holland—wasn't of such high quality that it demanded airplay. The CD has its value, though, as further evidence of just how incredibly prolific the Philly soul scene was, years before it peaked commercially in the early '70s, with entrepreneurs like Osborne hustling to get whatever they could together. And even if these have a somewhat generic quality, these are very professional, good-sounding records, displaying the tight arrangements, horn sections, creamy lead vocals, funky guitars (at least on the uptempo numbers), and effective backup harmonies for which the region was renowned. Some of the better cuts include the previously unreleased "Cement, Plaster & Gold" by the Natural Soul Brothers LTD, which has a very 1970 expansion of the soul format in its jazzy flutes, swelling organ, and looser grooves, and the Passionettes' "My Life Depends on You," with haunting doo wop-indebted harmonies that were very retro (yet appealing) for 1969. The sound quality is usually excellent, although a few tracks seem to have been transferred from acetates and the like. *—Richie Unterberger*

☆ **The Big Chill** / 1983 / Motown ♦♦♦♦♦
Motown scored big with this album, which contains ten 60s hits, from Marvin Gaye's "I Heard It through the Grapevine" to Procol Harum's "A Whiter Shade of Pale," just the sort of thing the yuppie thirtysomethings in the movie loved, and music rediscovered by the audience that saw the film. *—William Ruhlmann*

Big City Soul, Vol. 2 / 1994 / Goldmine/Soul Supply ♦♦♦
The second in Goldmine's *Big City Soul* series features soul tracks released on Verve and its subsidiary labels. The listing includes some early solo Wilson Pickett material, on which he doesn't sound as wicked as he later became, and a lot of surprises, including a solo side from Nick Ashford, a Poindexter Brothers jam, one by Terri Bryant, and a good Superiors track. Collectors will gravitate toward songs by Garnet Mimms, Howard Tate, and the forgotten Howard Guyton. For variety, Clara Ward (a gospel singer) checks in with "My Right Direction" and Bessie Banks (a blues singer) with "I Can't Make It (Without You Baby)." *—Andrew Hamilton*

Big City Soul, Vol. 3 / Goldmine/Soul Supply ♦♦♦♦
This collection from the MGM vaults offers a solid cross-pollinated look at soul in the early to mid-'60s from Detroit, New York, Philly, and even Texas. Comprised of 27 tracks, this collection of rare soul from MGM features performers usually associated with other labels, such as Millie Jackson ("My Heart Took a Licking"), Kim Weston ("I Got What You Need" and "You're Just the Kinda Guy"), and Johnny Nash ("You Never Know"). But there are also stellar tracks by the likes of Detroit's obscure but truly amazing Spyder Turner ("I'm Alive With the Love Feeling" and "I Can't Make It Anymore") and Roy Hamilton ("You Can Count on Me" and "The Panic Is On"). Some of the other performers included here are Dean Courtney, Tony Middleton, and Lou Roberts. Among the groups are the amazing Velours, who hail from the '50s originally and came straight from doo wop, the Broadways, an obscure and highly refined quartet, the Charades, the Solitaires, the Formations, and the Superiors, and there is one track from Marlina Mars. What these tracks have in common is the restlessness and vision of the MGM A&R department staff, who were interested in trying to capture anyone and everyone capable of landing them on the singles charts. While it didn't exactly translate into that *en masse*, there were more than enough contenders and this is just a small sampling of the best the label had to offer. Soul collectors and fans would be well advised to scarf this one up. *—Thom Jurek*

Big in Wigan / 1996 / Kent ♦♦♦
The *raison dêtre* of this disc needs some explanation to North American audiences. Subtitled "collection of shameless oldies played in the golden era of Northern soul," it's an anthology of 20 obscure soul tracks from the mid-'60s to the mid-'70s that have found favor with the cult of obsessive soul listeners in Northern England. There's no real thread connecting the tracks, other than that each one has been selected to represent one of the DJs that spins rare 45s for the dancers who still go to British clubs to hear this music. It's easy to see why these numbers are dancefloor favorites—most have a solidly thumping pop-soul groove conducive for dancing, especially if you're one of those old-fashioned fogies who doesn't want to get blasted into the English Channel with synth-driven rave and techno. It's also, to be harsh, easy to see why they made a beeline for the collector bins rather than the AM airwaves—the material wasn't arresting enough to capture the ears of the masses. Judged solely as a stone-cold home listening experience, it's definitely not an A-list choice for the soul compilation library, even if you're a soul fan. If you're a specialist collector, you may well find it to your liking, populated as it is by obscure names such as Flower Shoppe and the Lovettes, obscure singles by minor soul notables like Bobby Freeman, Millie Jackson, and Leon Haywood, and the primo mod soul of Mickey Lee Lane's "Hey Sah-Lo-Ney," probably the rawest and most compelling track here. *—Richie Unterberger*

Big Top Soul Cellar / Goldmine/Soul Supply ♦♦♦♦
This collection brings together 30 sides from New York's premier independent soul label, Big Top, begun in 1959 and closely affiliated with similar sounds from pre-Motown labels in Detroit. They also registered a hit with the original recording of "Runaway" by Del Shannon. While that smash isn't included here, it doesn't matter a whit. Here are two-and-a-half-dozen classic underground soul singles by the great Lou Johnson, Joann Courcy, the Volumes, the Dynamics, Sarah Cooke, Buddy & Stacey, and plenty of others. The sound is decidedly in the Motown vein, very urban, a bit on the sweet side, but full of a rawness in the mix that belies the pop edges of these tunes. One listen to Courcy's "I Got the Power," Bobbie Smith's "Wanted," or even Gerri Grainger's "Breakdown" offers a scintillating portrait of a label loaded with talent, great songs, and killer production techniques, but without the distribution to make it happen on the same scale that Motown cracked—which is not to say that all of these Northern soul masterpieces weren't heard in their day, because they were (at least regionally). The exuberant soulful swing of "Are You Putting Me on the Shelf" by Don & Juan prefigures Mel & Tim's "Backfield in Motion" by at least a decade; it also features heavily in the arrangements of early rollicking sides by Marvin Gaye and the Four Tops. The band Danny Wilson formed its entire sound based on the vocals and arrangements from Lou Johnson singles. In all these tracks is the revelation of soul music's power to remain timeless in a dark and cynical age. Guaranteed to have you swinging it with your honey on the dancefloor and in your heart, if not your basement. *—Thom Jurek*

Bill Haney's Atlanta Soul Brotherhood / Jun. 23, 1998 / Kent ♦♦
Bill Haney was an all-around entrepreneur—producer, label owner, occasional songwriter—whose Down South Productions generated a bunch of soul recordings in the 1960s and early '70s. Some were released on his own Chant label, some were leased to other companies, and some were unreleased. This 24-song compilation combines all of the above categories; indeed, half of it was previously unreissued. It's acceptable period Southern soul, varying from sweet romantic stuff to gritty son-of-Otis Redding-or-James Brown tunes, but it doesn't stand up to even the better unknown soul of the era. The only names familiar to general fans are Dee Clark, Roy Hamilton, and Arthur Alexander, all represented by unreleased songs, none recorded when the artists were at their peaks; Alexander's tune, "You Better Listen to Me," and is nice but way too derivative of his famous "You Better Move On." The same lack of originality afflicts even the better cuts on this collection. Jarvis Jackson's "Something I Ain't Never Had," for instance, is a cop (and a rather good one) of the style Otis Redding used on "I've Been Loving You Too Long," and Staxy riffs also surface on things like the Dino and Doc male-female duets. A less clichéd source was plundered for Charlie Thomas' "Don't Let Me Know," whose melody is uncomfortably similar to Gerry & the Pacemakers' "Don't Let the Sun Catch You Crying." *—Richie Unterberger*

Bill Haney's Atlanta Southern Soul Brotherhood, Vol. 2 / Aug. 10, 1999 / Kent ♦♦
As with Vol. 1, this is taken from holdings of producer, writer, and label owner Bill Haney, who had a hand in a lot of soul tracks recorded in Atlanta in the 1960s and 1970s. Some of the material on this 26-song compilation appeared on labels huge (Capitol) and tiny ones (Haney's own Chant); eight of them were previously unissued. There's exactly one well-known name here, Arthur Alexander, represented by a previously unreleased

mid-'60s cut, "You Ain't for Real," that hardly matches up to his better work. On the whole it's journeyman Southern soul, sometimes close to the Stax sound, as on Randolph Walker's "Pride and Soul," which can't fail to recall Otis Redding with its pleading vocals, sharp blues-soul guitar, and punctuatin' horns. Jerry Woodard's "Something I Never Had" gets even deeper into the Otis trench, its slow tempo and spare guitar reminiscent of tracks like "I've Been Loving You Too Long." Gay Meadows, on the other hand, is trying for a Ben E. King thing on "Only One," probably the earliest track (dating from 1962), while Charlie Thomas gets into a candlelit Sam Cooke mood on "Why'd You Have to Make the Little Girl Cry." Overall, the disc is inoffensive and inessential. *—Richie Unterberger*

Billboard Hot R&B Hits 1980 / Feb. 27, 1996 / Rhino ♦♦♦♦♦
Billboard Hot R&B Hits 1980 features some of the year's most popular contemporary R&B singles, including the Isley Brothers' "Don't Say Goodnight (It's Time for Love) Pts. 1 & 2," Fatback's "Backstrokin'," and Teddy Pendergrass' "Love T.K.O." Gladys Knight & the Pips' "Landlord," the Manhattans' "Shining Star," and Twennynine's "Peanut Butter" are some of the other standouts on this album, which reaffirms that 1980 was one of the decade's strongest years for R&B singles. *—Heather Phares*

Billboard Hot R&B Hits 1981 / Feb. 27, 1996 / Rhino ♦♦♦♦♦
Billboard Hot R&B Hits 1981 features some of the year's most popular contemporary R&B singles, including Earth, Wind & Fire's "Let's Groove," the Four Tops' "When She Was My Girl," and the Gap Band's "Burn Rubber (Why You Wanna Hurt Me)." Chaka Khan's "What Cha' Gonna Do for Me," Evelyn King's "I'm in Love," and Ray Parker Jr.'s "A Woman Needs Love (Just Like You Do)" are some of the other standouts on this album, which also features songs by Grover Washington, Roger, and Yarbrough & Peoples. While it doesn't always flow together as cleanly as one might hope, this collection still offers a clear and concise look at the year in R&B. *—Heather Phares*

Billboard Hot R&B Hits 1982 / Feb. 27, 1996 / Rhino ♦♦♦♦♦
One of the best volumes of the *Billboard Hot R&B Hits* series, *1982* features Marvin Gaye's classic "Sexual Healing," Ray Parker Jr.'s "The Other Woman," and Aretha Franklin's "Jump to It" in addition to strong tracks by Evelyn "Champagne" King, Zapp, and Junior. Deniece Williams' "It's Gonna Take a Miracle," Atlantic Star's "Circles," and Hall & Oates' surprise R&B chart hit "I Can't Go for That (No Can Do)" complete this entertaining and too-brief look back at 1982's hottest R&B hits. *—Heather Phares*

Billboard Hot R&B Hits 1983 / Feb. 27, 1996 / Rhino ♦♦♦♦♦
Billboard Hot R&B Hits 1983 gathers a funky and eclectic collection of the year's most popular R&B hits, including George Clinton's "Atomic Dog," the Gap Band's "Outstanding," Rufus' "Ain't Nobody," and Donna Summer's "She Works Hard for the Money." Aretha Franklin's "Get It Right," Mtume's "Juicy Fruit," and Gladys Knight & the Pips' "Save the Overtime (For Me)" are some of the album's other standout tracks. Songs by Klique and Evelyn "Champagne" King are also worthwhile, reaffirming that 1983 was one of the '80s' best years for R&B singles. *—Heather Phares*

Billboard Hot R&B Hits 1984 / Feb. 27, 1996 / Rhino ♦♦♦♦♦
Perhaps the best volume in the *Billboard Hot R&B Hits* series, *1984* features five of the '80s' contemporary R&B classics: Ashford & Simpson's "Solid," Shannon's "Let the Music Play," Kool & the Gang's "Joanna," Chaka Khan's "I Feel for You," and the Pointer Sisters' "Automatic." The rest of the collection is strong as well, with Cameo's "She's Strange," Patti LaBelle's "If You Only Knew," and Cheryl Lynn's "Encore" among its other highlights, proving that 1984 was an unusually good year for R&B singles. *—Heather Phares*

Billboard Hot R&B Hits 1985 / Nov. 21, 1995 / Rhino ♦♦♦
Billboard Hot R&B Hits: 1985 features some of the year's most popular contemporary R&B singles, including modern classics like Aretha Franklin's "Freeway of Love" and the Commodores' "Nightshift." Freddie Jackson's "Rock Me Tonight (For Old Times' Sake)," DeBarge's "Rhythm of the Night," and Kool & the Gang's "Cherish" are some of the other standouts on this album, which does an adequate job of collecting the year's biggest R&B hits. *—Heather Phares*

Billboard Hot R&B Hits 1986 / Nov. 21, 1995 / Rhino ♦♦♦
Billboard Hot R&B Hits: 1986 presents the year's most popular contemporary R&B singles, including Billy Ocean's "There'll Be Sad Songs (To Make You Cry)," Gregory Abbott's "Shake You Down," and El DeBarge's "Who's Johnny." Nu Shooz' "I Can't Wait" and Timex Social Club's "Rumors" are two of the other standouts from this collection, which also features tracks from Freddie Jackson, Ready for the World, Rene & Angela, and Meli'sa Morgan. The quality of these collections varies with the quality of the year's singles, and unfortunately 1986 wasn't the most memorable year for R&B, but die-hard fans of the style will probably find a lot to appreciate here anyway. *—Heather Phares*

Billboard Hot R&B Hits 1987 / Nov. 21, 1995 / Rhino ♦♦♦
Billboard Hot R&B Hits 1987 features some of the year's most popular contemporary R&B singles, including Jody Watley's "Looking for a New Love," Lisa Lisa's "Head to Toe," and Freddie Jackson's "Have You Ever Loved Somebody." Tracks by Angela Winbush, Cameo, Force MDs, Stephanie Mills, and LeVert complete the album; though it's a somewhat uneven collection, it does an adequate job of collecting the year's biggest R&B hits. *—Heather Phares*

Billboard Hot R&B Hits 1988 / Nov. 21, 1995 / Rhino ♦♦♦
Billboard Hot R&B Hits 1988 features some of the year's most popular contemporary R&B singles, including Bobby Brown's "My Prerogative," Al B. Sure's "Nite and Day," and Pebbles' "Girlfriend." Ziggy Marley & the Melody Makers' "Tumblin' Down" and Tony! Toni! Toné!'s "Little Walter" are some of the other standouts on this album, which also features tracks by Teddy Pendergrass, Freddie Jackson, LeVert, and Boys. Though it's not an especially well-focused collection, it does a fine job of collecting the year's biggest R&B hits. *—Heather Phares*

Billboard Hot R&B Hits 1989 / Nov. 21, 1995 / Rhino ♦♦♦
Billboard Hot R&B Hits 1989 features some of the year's most popular contemporary R&B singles, including Soul II Soul's "Keep on Movin'," De La Soul's "Me, Myself and I," and the Gap Band's "All of My Love." Regina Belle's "Baby Come to Me," Jody Watley's "Real Love," and Maze's "Can't Get Over You" are some of the other standouts on this album, which also features songs by Surface, Skyy, Eric Gable, and Miki Howard. While this set lacks a unified musical outlook, it does offer an accurate cross-section of the year's biggest R&B hits. *—Heather Phares*

Billboard Hot Soul Hits: 1970 / Jul. 18, 1995 / Rhino ♦♦♦♦
A perfect gift for that musically precocious niece or nephew who doesn't care if there are ten or 20 songs to listen to. And what better way to introduce them to the wonderfully rich world of '70s soul than ten of the best radio hits from the beginning of the decade. While James Brown and Sly Stone lay down a little history lesson in burgeoning funkology, Aretha Franklin, the Delfonics, Tyrone Davis, and the Jackson 5 will light up the high road of soul power and harmony. And to cap off the youngsters' night of musical scholarship, B.B. King can be counted on to bring the roots with a modern blues classic. *—Stephen Cook*

Billboard Hot Soul Hits: 1971 / Jul. 18, 1995 / Rhino ♦♦♦
Rhino continues on with their excavation of top soul hits from the '70s. This edition takes in 1971 with ten classics from the vaults of Stax, Motown, Atlantic, and Brunswick, among others. After starting off with two often unsung but amazing sides by Honey Cone ("Want Ads") and the Undisputed Truth ("Smiling Faces"), the mix hits the top of the pile with perennials by Aretha Franklin, Johnnie Taylor, the Chi-Lites, the Persuaders, and James Brown. And while the "Hot Pants" are coolin' down, you can join Rufus Thomas for one of his ever-pleasing dance grooves, "(Do the) Push and Pull, Pt. 1." A fine soul roundup best suited for casual listeners. *—Stephen Cook*

Billboard Hot Soul Hits: 1972 / Jul. 18, 1995 / Rhino ♦♦♦
As 1972 saw the rise of funk, so too did it witness a bevy of slick soul, replete with lush string charts and heavenly harmonies. Philly International producers Gamble & Huff cut some of the best of these easy R&B grooves, notably Harold Melvin & the Blue Notes' "If You Don't Know Me by Now," which is featured here. Rhino's ten-track survey of 1972 soul spotlights the work of another Philly contributor, Thom Bell, who cut both the Stylistics' "Betcha By Golly Wow" and the Spinners' "I'll Be Around." Sticking to the smooth harmonies and lush production mode, the compilation also includes quality smashes by the Chi-Lites and the Dramatics; even the relatively more rough-hewn Al Green and Aretha Franklin are featured on some mellow gems. But to make sure they don't forget the funk, the disc closes out with one of the music's pinnacle cuts, James Brown's "Talkin' Loud & Saying Nothing," and a rather obscure but still very solid clavinet jam by Billy Preston. *—Stephen Cook*

Billboard Hot Soul Hits: 1973 / Jul. 18, 1995 / Rhino ♦♦♦♦
Other collections may offer more for the money, but Rhino's *Billboard Hot Soul Hits* discs deliver the perfect dose for all those top-of-the-charts trainspotters. With 1973 in focus, these ten tracks chart the period's fertile mix of Stax and Motown roots (Four Tops, Staple Singers), nascent funk (Fred Wesley), and proto-disco strains (Harold Melvin & the Blue Notes' Philly bump). As usual, gospel fervor fuels the ride, whether in smoldering (Gladys Knight), sanctified (Al Green), or revival fashion (Pop Staples and company). And the typically elastic nature of that musical wellspring is demonstrated quite impressively, too, notably on Timmy Thomas' lithe organ and drum machine groove, "Why Can't We Live Together," and the Isley Brothers' Hendrix-in-a-quiet-storm jam, "That Lady, Pt. 1." *—Stephen Cook*

Billboard Hot Soul Hits: 1974 / Jul. 18, 1995 / Rhino ♦♦♦
This is another bargain roundup of soul hits compliments of Rhino. The ten tracks here may be too familiar for many listeners, but the song quality has certainly not diminished over the years. Ranging from Philly soul (MFSB & the Three Degrees) to template funk (James Brown), the mix also takes in the one-hit wonder (Blue Magic's "Sideshow"), a bit of bedroom soul (Barry White), and the Queen herself, Aretha Franklin. So, whether your tastes run to the Philly bump alchemy of the Spinners or Gladys Knight's always-stunning vocal talents, this slim-yet-potent mix should satisfy. *—Stephen Cook*

Billboard Top Dance Hits: 1976–1980 / 1976-1980 / Rhino ♦♦♦♦
Covering the disco years in detail, Rhino's five-volume *Billboard Top Dance Hits* series is a worthwhile budget retrospective. It isn't as complete or definitive as the label's *Disco Years* series, but it features several tracks that didn't make that series, as well as songs that aren't easily available on other compilations, making it necessary for disco fans. Ten of the top dance hits for each year from 1976 to 1980 are featured on each disc, including such hits as "You Should Be Dancing," "Love Hangover," "Ring My Bell," "You Make Me Feel (Mighty Real)," "Funkytown," "Got to Give It Up," and "Call Me" in their original single form. Unlike the other *Billboard* series, *Top Dance Hits* actually has liner notes about the songs, not trivia about a particular year. *—Stephen Thomas Erlewine*

Billboard Top R&B Hits: 1955 / 1989 / Rhino ♦♦♦♦♦
Despite its faults, Rhino's *Billboard Top R&B Hits* is one of the finest retrospectives of R&B from 1955 to 1974 ever assembled. The song selection was sometimes puzzling, the liner notes nonexistent, and each disc only had ten tracks, frequently lasting under half an hour. However, the 20-disc series featured most of the major artists and singles of each individual year, as well as providing a rough sketch of the evolution from R&B to soul to disco. For beginners, such an affordable introduction was invaluable; for collectors, the brevity may have been frustrating, but they couldn't argue with the fidelity or

the fact that many of these songs were appearing on disc for the first time. Legends like Clyde McPhatter, Little Richard, Jackie Wilson, James Brown, Ben E. King, Brook Benton, Marvin Gaye, Temptations, Supremes, Aretha Franklin, Smokey Robinson, Isley Brothers, Sly Stone, and Curtis Mayfield are featured. *—Stephen Thomas Erlewine*

Billboard Top R&B Hits: 1956 / 1989 / Rhino ✦✦✦✦✦
No wonder R&B woke up teenage America, with Little Richard, the Cadillacs, Clyde McPhatter, and the Five Satins producing classics like these. *—Jeff Tamarkin*

Billboard Top R&B Hits: 1957 / 1989 / Rhino ✦✦✦✦✦
It was a good year for good-time rockin'. Fats and Little Richard rule; The Dell-Vikings, Mickey & Sylvia, and Bobby "Blue" Bland bring it all home. *—Jeff Tamarkin*

Billboard Top R&B Hits: 1958 / 1989 / Rhino ✦✦✦✦✦
Very similar in style and packaging to their successful *Billboard Rock 'n' Roll* series, this volume brings together ten classics from the year 1958. Big ticket items are Jackie Wilson's "Lonely Teardrops," Bobby Day's "Rockin' Robin," the Johnny Otis Show's "Willie and the Hand Jive," the Monotones' "Book of Love," and Fats Domino's "Whole Lotta Loving." Also aboard are big hits from the Chantels, Bobby Freeman (the original "Do You Want to Dance"), Little Anthony & the Imperials, and instrumental charters from Cozy Cole and Ernie Freeman. Almost anything in this series is worth picking up, and the transfers are delightfully clear. *—Cub Koda*

Billboard Top R&B Hits: 1959 / 1989 / Rhino ✦✦✦✦✦
Fine R&B from the Falcons, Dee Clark, Jackie Wilson, and James Brown gives this set staying power. *—Jeff Tamarkin*

Billboard Top R&B Hits: 1960 / 1989 / Rhino ✦✦✦✦✦
Headin' uptown with Brook Benton, Jerry Butler, and Dinah Washington—this is a classy collection. *—Jeff Tamarkin*

Billboard Top R&B Hits: 1961 / 1989 / Rhino ✦✦✦✦✦
The roots of soul? The Miracles top the list; Ben E. King, Lee Dorsey, and the Jive Five round it out. *—Jeff Tamarkin*

Billboard Top R&B Hits: 1962 / 1989 / Rhino ✦✦✦✦✦
Motown and Stax make their entries, while James Brown and a host of hot ladies give 'em a run. *—Jeff Tamarkin*

Billboard Top R&B Hits: 1963 / 1989 / Rhino ✦✦✦✦✦
Featuring the Impressions, Jackie Wilson, Marvin Gaye, Mary Wells—we are talking fine. *—Jeff Tamarkin*

Billboard Top R&B Hits: 1964 / 1989 / Rhino ✦✦✦✦✦
Here is the complete Motown invasion—Four Tops, Temptations, Martha, and the Supremes. Non-Detroiters may as well have sat this one out. *—Jeff Tamarkin*

• **Billboard Top R&B Hits: 1965** / 1989 / Rhino ✦✦✦✦✦
It's 1965, and soul is hitting its stride with the Godfather on the rise, Motown heavily in the black, and independent labels producing some gems. Rhino delivers the dancefloor goodies on another edition of their generally fine yet slim *Billboard Top R&B Hits* discs. This time around, the ten cuts are primarily taken over by Berry Gordy's Motor City Hit Factory. Whether hearing Marvin Gaye, the Four Tops, the Miracles, or the Supremes, the dance-pop genius of Gordy's crew is made very clear; and that's not to overlook more raw gems from Motown's bar walkin' sax master Junior Walker & the All-Stars ("Shotgun") and Chess' overshadowed soul diva Fontella Bass ("Rescue Me"). Not the thorough collection for discerning fans, but still a potent sampling of some of soul's marquee moments. *—Stephen Cook*

Billboard Top R&B Hits: 1966 / 1989 / Rhino ✦✦✦✦✦
This is the summit of soulsville—"Going to a Go-Go," Wilson Pickett, Joe Tex. *—Jeff Tamarkin*

Billboard Top R&B Hits: 1967 / 1989 / Rhino ✦✦✦✦✦
It has another batch of soul beauts. This one includes Aretha, Aaron Neville, and more Motown. *—Jeff Tamarkin*

Billboard Top R&B Hits: 1968 / 1989 / Rhino ✦✦✦✦✦
This has black pride anthems from James Brown and the Impressions; great love songs from the Delfonics and Smokey Robinson—plus six more. *—Jeff Tamarkin*

Billboard Top R&B Hits: 1970 / 1990 / Rhino ✦✦✦✦✦
The names were the same—Temptations, James Brown—but no doubt about it, a new decade was dawning. *—Jeff Tamarkin*

Billboard Top R&B Hits: 1971 / 1990 / Rhino ✦✦✦✦✦
J.B. said "Make It Funky" and Marvin wondered "What's Going On." And everyone was ready to do some dancing. *—Jeff Tamarkin*

Billboard Top R&B Hits: 1972 / 1990 / Rhino ✦✦✦✦✦
Tougher times, tougher tunes. Al Green made it all sound sweeter, and Curtis Mayfield put out a warning. It was a good year for getting spiritual. *—Jeff Tamarkin*

Billboard Top R&B Hits: 1973 / 1990 / Rhino ✦✦✦✦✦
The gospel-bred Staple Singers topped the charts, and Harold Melvin and the Isleys took it to the discos. *—Jeff Tamarkin*

Billboard Top R&B Hits: 1974 / 1990 / Rhino ✦✦✦✦✦
The mid-'70s was a rich period for R&B, what with funk, Philly bump, proto-disco, and the updated strains of raw soul all making an appearance on the charts. Rhino brings on the potent variety with ten top-drawer cuts. Complaints of a stingy offering aside, the riches flow early on with such stellar sides as James Brown's latter-day masterpiece "The Payback," Kool & the Gang's jazz and funk classic "Hollywood Swinging," and Gladys Knight & the Pips' entry for all-time-great soul ballad "Best Thing That Ever Happened to Me." And there's more sophisticated fare, including fine tracks by Benny Latimore, Al Green, and Tavares. Turn the clock back and hit the floor. *—Stephen Cook*

Birth of Soul / 1996 / Kent ✦✦✦✦✦
Here are an ingenious mix of 28 pivotal tracks from 1957-1965, mostly from the early '60s, that helped lay the groundwork for soul music. Some heavy-duty collectors may have wished these were all rarities, rather than a blend of hits and rarities. But it must be said that several of the hits here don't turn up on many compilations, like the ones by Inez & Charlie Foxx ("Mockingbird"), the Tams ("Hey Girl Don't Bother Me"), Joe Henderson ("Snap Your Fingers"), Bobby "Blue" Bland ("Ain't Nothing You Can Do"), and the Marvelows ("I Do"). And there are plenty of nifty collector items as well: outtakes by Otis Redding and Wiliam Bell, "answer" records by Thelma Kilgore and Gloria Lynne, and early Southern soul by Jimmy Hughes. A special treat is the rabble-rousing city soul of Derek Martin's "Daddy Rollin' Stone," which became one of the Who's most obscure tracks when they covered it on the B-side of their second British 45 in 1965. The compilation may fall between the cracks of general soul listeners and soul specialists. But if you don't have most of the tracks yet, it's a good survey of early soul, with an all-encompassing diversity that includes many regional styles, and embraces both "down-home" and "uptown" productions. *—Richie Unterberger*

Birth of Soul, Vol. 2 / Feb. 10, 1998 / Kent ✦✦✦✦
A soul smorgasbord, containing big hits as well as hard-to-find gems by under promoted artists like the Diplomats, here represented by the thrilling "Here's a Heart"; the Falcons, featuring a teenaged Wilson Pickett, on the soulful "I Found a Love;" and "Standing in the Shadows" by Kenny Gamble & the Romeos. (Gamble later founded Philadelphia International Records with Leon Huff and Thom Bell). Producer/writer George Kerr started his career in the Serenaders, who explain why "Two Lovers Make One Fool." Major Lance's "Um, Um, Um, Um, Um, Um," Ray Charles' "What I Say," the Drifters' "There Goes My Baby" and Maxine Brown's "All in My Mind" were major crossover hits, while Gene Chandler's "Man's Temptation," Theola Kilgore's "This Is My Prayer" and Betty Harris' "Cry to Me" did well on R&B charts and stations. Other picks include the rambling "Call Somebody Please," an early recording by the Manhattans, and the deep soul two part harmonies of "Lovers' Prayer" by the Wallace Brothers. A good, well-rounded collection, and the 28 selections feature something for everybody. *—Andrew Hamilton*

Birth of Soul, Vol. 3 / May 2001 / Kent ✦✦✦
This compilation presents a potent if scattershot look at the early years of the soul music revolution. There's little in the way of a common thread; everything from the Impressions' obscure "Shorty's Gotta Go" (recorded on Bandera Records) to Richard Berry & the Pharoahs' pulsating "Have Love Will Travel" is featured. With few exceptions (i.e., the Spinners' "That's What Girls Are Made For," Ike & Tina Turner's "It's Gonna Work Out Fine," and Wilson Pickett's "It's Too Late"), most of these tracks are hard to find on CD. The set includes rare Motown tracks: Jimmy Ruffin's "Don't Feel Sorry for Me" (his first recording), the Miracles' "If Your Mother Only Knew" (the flip side of "Way Over There"), and Carolyn Crawford's "When Someone Is Good to You" (her final and least-known Motown single). Also included are Don Gardner & Dee Dee Ford's "I Need Your Loving," two from Garnet Mimms & the Enchanters, rarities from the Superbs, and other soulful expressions that will make this a strong addition to your collection. *—Andrew Hamilton*

Birth of the Groove / Jul. 13, 1971-Mar. 1976 / CTI ✦✦✦✦
Funky jazz was not born on the CTI label in the early '70s (making the title of this sampler CD a bit silly), but the ten selections on this reissue do contain a great deal of worthwhile grooving music. Some of the performances (such as George Benson's "I Remember Wes") are quite rare, and many of the songs have not yet been otherwise reissued on CD. Suitable as dance music, for backgrounds or for close listenings, this is an enjoyable if not essential set. Among the artists featured are Deodato, Joe Farrell ("Canned Funk"), Esther Phillips, Johnny Hammond Smith, Hank Crawford, Stanley Turrentine ("Storm"), Milt Jackson, Dave Matthews, Idris Muhammad and Benson; among the sidemen are Grover Washington Jr. and David Sanborn, both captured early in their careers. *—Scott Yanow*

Black Gold / Disky ✦✦✦✦✦
A box set CD comprising 61 tracks of quality soul from Philly, New Jersey, the South, and points elsewhere for your delight. The bulk of the tracks were recorded by Philadelphia International Records, with the All Platinum family of labels running a distant second. Chicago soul from the Chi-Lites and the Dells, and tracks from Michael Henderson, Melba Moore, Ruby Turner, Joe Tex, and others make this a good addition to your CD collection, featuring a wealth of great songs in one package. *—Andrew Hamilton*

Blaxploitation, Vol. 1 / 1996 / Global TV ✦✦✦
This title of this generous two-CD anthology is a bit of a misnomer: While it includes several blaxploitation film themes, it is much more than just a strict genre compilation. Although there are the expected soundtrack picks like "Shaft" by Isaac Hayes and "Superfly" by Curtis Mayfield, this album also includes plenty of non-soundtrack items to create a convincing urban atmosphere. The producers wisely layer in some interesting obscurities along with the obvious choices, and this helps to keep things fresh and interesting. Some of the unexpected highlights in the soul arena include Esther Phillips' intense but controlled reading of the Gil Scott-Heron message song "Home Is Where the Hatred Is" and Bootsy Collins' "I'd Rather Be With You," a lovely ballad that reins in his tendency for cartoon wackiness to create a moody and genuinely romantic atmosphere. There are also plenty of extended jazz-funk selections like "Expansions" by Lonnie Liston Smith and Deodato's famous remake of "Also Sprach Zarathustra," which keep

the good grooves rolling as they enhance the compilation's soundtrack feel. If there is a downside to the compilation, it is that the different styles of music it contains are not mixed together in a balanced fashion. For instance, three lengthy jazz fusion cuts all play out back to back on the first disc; they might have been more effective if interspersed with some of the vocal-oriented tracks. Just the same, this an admirable package that effectively blends favorites and left-field choices to create a distinctive musical experience. A slick booklet, which mixes pictures of the artists with cheeky yet informative liner notes and photos designed to resemble blaxploitation film stills, rounds the package out nicely. Anyone with an interest in the classic soul sounds of the 1970s should definitely check *Blaxploitation*. *—Donald Guarisco*

Blaxploitation, Vol. 2: The Sequel / 1997 / Global TV ♦♦♦
Since the first volume of *Blaxploitation* used most of the obvious picks for this kind of compilation, the compilers of this volume are left free to make plenty of fresh choices. As a result, *Blaxploitation, Vol. 2: The Sequel* boasts plenty of enticing rarities like "Let's Clean Up the Ghetto" by the Philadelphia All-Stars, a funky message tune voiced by a collection of the stars from the Philadelphia International label (including Lou Rawls and Teddy Pendergrass). Another fine rarity is the album-length version of the Temptations' classic "Papa Was a Rollin' Stone": At 11-plus minutes, this slickly orchestrated slice of ghetto realism plays out like an urban symphony. Ample room is also given to instrumental excursions with a jazz-funk twist, two of the standout choices being the Herbie Hancock classic "Chameleon" and the more obscure "24 Carat Black Theme" by the Stax Records album group 24 Carat Black. Another notable track in this instrumental vein is Grover Washington's epic reinterpretation of the Temptations' classic "Masterpiece," which effectively pits a wordless chorus and a lush orchestral arrangement against an unrelenting groove laid down by the rhythm section. Like the first volume of this series, *Blaxploitation, Vol. 2: The Sequel* could use better sequencing: If the vocal and instrumental cuts were alternated with greater frequency, they might pack a stronger punch. This volume also lacks the fun liner notes that graced the first one. These caveats aside, *Blaxploitation, Vol. 2: The Sequel* remains a fine collection of soul tracks that will find favor with hardcore soul music enthusiasts. *—Donald Guarisco*

Blaxploitation: The Payback, Vol. 3 / 1998 / Global TV ♦♦♦♦♦
Strictly speaking, the double-disc collection *Blaxploitation: The Payback, Vol. 3* isn't solely a blaxploitation collection, since it features just as many early-'70s soul hits that were never in films as movie music. That ultimately leads to a better compilation, since forgotten gems like Bobby Womack's incredible "Across 110th Street" can sit next to hits like the O'Jays' "Back Stabbers," as well as artists like Curtis Mayfield, James Brown, Isaac Hayes and Marvin Gaye. There are a few dull moments scattered throughout the collection, but even those will be of interest to fans of this stylish, funky sound, which makes *Blaxploitation: The Payback, Vol. 3* necessary for collectors of this sound and style. *—Stephen Thomas Erlewine*

Blue '60s: Blue Note Strikes a Radical Chord / 1995 / Blue Note ♦♦♦♦
Blue Note joins the picket lines and protesters with 11 slices of radical bop from circa 1970. One of the more obscure collections from the label, the disc still features such stable greats as Bobby Hutcherson, Lou Donaldson, Stanley Turrentine, and Lee Morgan. The mix ranges from the political (Herbie Hancock's M.L.K. homage "I Have a Dream") to the recreational (Morgan's "Psychedelic"), with Horace Silver taking the prize for his to-the-point contribution, "Acid, Pot and Pills." Whether it's Vietnam (Grant Green's "Cease the Bombing") or a cultural edict in the spotlight (Turrentine's "Blowing in the Wind"), *Blue '60s* keeps up the vigil in fine fashion. *—Stephen Cook*

Blue 'N' Groovy, Vol. 1: Blue Note Connects with the Good Vibes / Aug. 31, 1999 / Blue Note ♦♦♦♦
Blue 'N' Groovy, Vol. 1 is an excellent 11-track sampler of the funkiest soul-jazz and hard-bop in the Blue Note catalog, containing calssic moments from Duke Pearson ("Chili Peppers"), Jack Wilson ("On Children"), Stanley Turrentine ("Meat Wave"), Don Wilkerson ("Dem Tambourines"), Art Blakey ("Ping Pong"), Tina Brooks ("True Blue"), Bobby Hutcherson ("8/4 Beat"), Wayne Shorter ("Tom Thumb"). While a couple of these moments are familiar—Herbie Hancock's "Cantaloupe Island" and Lee Morgan's "The Sidewinder," for instance—there's a number of rarities previously unavailable on CD, as well, making this of equal interest to collectors and casual fans. *—Stephen Thomas Erlewine*

Blue 'N' Groovy, Vol. 2: Mostly Modal / Feb. 9, 1999 / Blue Note ♦♦♦
Blue Note Records hit its creative peak in the late '60s, a time when jazz was being flooded with influences from across the musical spectrum and around the world. *Blue 'N' Groovy 2* captured the crackling energy of this time, and shows the funk, soul, and Latin infused grooves of artists like the Jazz Messengers, McCoy Tyner, Lee Morgan, and Art Pepper. *—Stacia Proefrock*

Blue 45s: Ultimate Jukebox / Apr. 13, 1999 / EMI ♦♦♦♦
Taking in some prime hard bop real estate, *Blue 45s: Ultimate Jukebox* finds its theme in the low-profile yet potent singles sideline Blue Note pursued while making its name mostly off of their LPs. With incredible artwork and photography, not to mention superb sound by Rudy Van Gelder, the Blue Note catalog of LPs forms a cornerstone of jazz history. But the '60s were also a time when the rise of rock & roll and soul made 45s a lucrative business. And doing their best to keep up with the kids, even Blue Note cashed in to a small extent with several soul-jazz releases, many of which are included here. Along with popular sides by Lee Morgan ("The Rumproller"), Horace Silver ("The Jody Grind, Pt. 1"), and Lou Donaldson ("Alligator Boogaloo"), this 21-track import boasts equally ripe boogaloo from the relatively obscure likes of tenor saxophonist Don Wilkerson, organist Freddie Roach, and flutist Bobbi Humphrey. A generous and tasty slice of hard-boppin' grooves. *—Stephen Cook*

Blue '70s: Blue Note Got Soul / Mar. 28, 2000 / Blue Note ♦♦♦
On the surface, *Blue '70s: Blue Note Got Soul* is packaged as a Blue Note funk compilation, but the selected music is closer to what would become "smooth jazz" in the '80s and '90s. These tracks were recorded by the Blue Note label at a time when it intentionally embraced the synthesizer, R&B, and disco hybrids tailor-made for pop radio exposure. While the majority of this material was recorded between 1975 and 1977, it does contain two excellent soul jazz blowouts from Lonnie Smith and Grant Green, both from 1970, and totally unlike everything else represented here. Most would agree that the '70s would not symbolize the epitome of what is known as the Blue Note sound. *—Al Campbell*

Blue Break Beats, Vol. 1 / 1992 / Blue Note ♦♦♦♦
Blue Note released the two volume *Blue Break Beats* compilation in the early '90s. The music on *Blue Break Beats* dates from the late '60s and early '70s, when a large portion of Blue Note's soul-jazz artists began experimenting with funk and rock, creating dense electric fusions that concentrated on rhythm, not improvisation. None of this music has ever received much critical praise from jazz purists, but in the late '80s and early '90s, scores of hip-hop and dance DJs discovered these old records and began sampling the original tracks to use in new rap and dance songs. By the early '90s, this jazz/rap/funk fusion had become hip and profitable, which led Blue Note to assemble the *Blue Break Beats* compilations. All of the tracks on the two discs are rare tracks from out-of-print late '60s and early '70s albums, featuring multi-layered percussion, organs, and guitars. Every song on the two discs—which are sold separately—is hot, with a deep funky groove, and there are no dull spots on the albums. Though it's designed to appeal to fans of contemporary funk and rap, fans of rock-influenced soul-jazz will find *Blue Break Beats* a necessary purchase. *—Stephen Thomas Erlewine*

Blue Break Beats, Vol. 2 / 1993 / Capitol ♦♦♦
Publishing can be an incredibly lucrative field. Whenever a rapper sampled a recording in the '80s and '90s, the person who owned the publishing stood to make some big bucks—that is, if the rapper had permission. Some MCs made the mistake of sampling tunes without permission, which resulted in major lawsuits. When Blue Note/Capitol assembled this collection of soul-jazz and jazz-funk in 1993, it encouraged hip-hop, urban contemporary, and acid jazz artists to sample the recordings (which span 1967-1975). But it also stressed that legal clearance would be required—unless, of course, you wanted to face a lawsuit. And asking for permission is most definitely the right thing to do; as many dues as veteran jazz artists have paid, they certainly deserve monetary compensation whenever their work is sampled (assuming they kept their publishing). Not everything on *Blue Break Beats, Vol. 2* is a masterpiece, but overall, it's an enjoyable collection of soul-jazz and jazz-funk. Most of the tunes are from the Blue Note vaults, although Gerald Wilson's infectious, Latin-flavored "Viva Tirado" (which became a big hit for El Chicano in 1970) was actually recorded for Pacific Jazz. None of this material is for jazz purists or bop snobs; *Blue Break Beats, Vol. 2* is strictly for those who like their jazz laced with a lot of R&B, and listeners who fit that description are the ones who can appreciate funky, groove-oriented numbers like Lou Donaldson's "The Caterpillar," Grant Green's "Ain't It Funky Now," and Donald Byrd's "Beale Street." Make no mistake: what you hear on this CD is a commercial approach to jazz. But commercial doesn't necessarily mean bad, and for the most part, *Blue Break Beats, Vol. 2* demonstrates that jazz can be accessible and still have integrity. *—Alex Henderson*

Blue Break Beats, Vol. 3 / 1997 / Capitol ♦♦♦
Blue Note's *Blue Break Beats* series spotlights songs from their vaults that have been sampled for various hip-hop and techno tracks. As a result, it's been one of their most popular and entertaining series of the '90s, and for good reason—this funky soul-jazz lends itself to compilations much easier than bop, since the groove is the only thing that matters. Unfortunately, the compilers of *Vol. 3* don't always keep that in mind. Much of the collection is weighed down with vocal cuts like Shirley Bassey's "Light My Fire" and Jackie McLean's "Soul," which intercuts nearly free bop with beat poetry. While these are interesting in their own right, they stop the momentum of the disc cold. However, the remainder of *Blue Break Beats, Vol. 3* is on par with its two predecessors, featuring funky soul-jazz from the likes of Cannonball Adderley and Lou Donaldson. These are the tracks that can be sampled effectively, and they make for excellent listening in their own right. *—Stephen Thomas Erlewine*

Blue Break Beats, Vol. 4 / Feb. 9, 1999 / Blue Note ♦♦♦
While this collection contains some of the most memorable hooks in the history of jazz and R& B, with classic tracks from Gene Harris, Buddy Rich, Herbie Hancock, Ike & Tina Turner, and others, its main appeal may be to fans of dance music and hip hop. These songs have provided fodder for samplers throughout the '80s and '90s, showing up on tracks by De La Soul, Gang Starr, and Deee-Lite. Funky, catchy, and groovy, this compilation will get you moving. *—Stacia Proefrock*

Blue Eyed Soul / Apr. 18, 2000 / Mars ♦♦
The emphasis is more on "blue-eyed" than "soul" on this 14-track compilation—how else to explain the inclusion of the Standells' garage-rock anthem "Dirty Water," John Cafferty's Springsteen-lite "Tough All Over," and Jeff Healey's blues-rock workout "Angel Eyes"? It's a shame *Blue Eyed Soul* is so haphazardly compiled, because there are some great songs here—the Spencer Davis Group's propulsive "Gimme Some Lovin'," the Foundations' faux-Motown classic "Build Me Up Buttercup," and Mitch Ryder's incendiary "Devil With a Blue Dress On/Good Golly, Miss Molly" among them—but the set's inherent clumsiness, combined with some seriously questionable material, like the Clarence Clemons/Jackson Browne duet "You're a Friend of Mine" and Bruce Willis' "Respect Yourself," make it easy to pass up. *—Jason Ankeny*

Blue Magic, Major Harris, Margie Joseph Live! / 1976 / WMOT ✦✦✦✦
When R&B went high-tech in the '80s, many urban contemporary artists became so reliant on studio technology that they sounded inept in a live setting. But back in the '70s, when R&B was still played instead of programmed, artists who excelled in the studio were just as likely to excel on-stage. Unfortunately, many '70s soulsters never provided live albums, but Blue Magic gave their fans a treat when they joined forces with Major Harris and Margie Joseph for this live two-LP set. Recorded at the Latin Casino in Cherry Hill, NJ, in 1975 and released the following year, this album is a pleasing, if imperfect, document of these artists on-stage. Blue Magic is the main attraction, and the Philly group is in fine form on performances of hits like "Sideshow" and "Stop to Start." Harris, also from Philly, is quite memorable on the smooth "Loving You Is Mellow" and his smash hit "Love Won't Let Me Wait." The only non-Philadelphian on the bill is Joseph, who soars when she joins forces with Blue Magic on the dreamy "What's Come Over Me." Joseph stumbles on Morris Albert's sappy "Feelings"—even someone as soulful as Joseph cannot salvage one of the most insipid hits of 1975. But Joseph fares much better when she gives Paul McCartney's "My Love" a Northern soul makeover. Although uneven, this double-LP has more ups than downs and is worth searching for if you're a serious collector of '70s soul. *—Alex Henderson*

Blue Note Rare Grooves / 1996 / Blue Note ✦✦✦✦✦
Balancing previously unreleased tracks with obscure gems from out-of-print albums, *Blue Note Rare Grooves* is an excellent collection of extremely funky soul-jazz. All of the tracks were recorded between 1967 and 1971, with the majority dating between 1968 and 1969. Though some of the tracks on the disc have been featured on other Blue Note collections, none of the albums they were pulled from are easily available, which makes *Blue Note Rare Grooves* all the more valuable. A good cross-section of artists—featuring John Patton, Richard "Groove" Holmes, Larry Young, Stanley Turrentine, Jack McDuff, Jimmy McGriff, Donald Byrd, Candido, Reuben Wilson, and several others—are included and every single track has a raw, intoxicating groove. *Blue Note Rare Grooves* may not be for jazz purists, but for listeners looking for a first-rate jazz-funk sampler, it's essential. *—Stephen Thomas Erlewine*

Blue Note Salutes Motown / Nov. 3, 1998 / Blue Note ✦✦✦
The name of the game here is easy versions of Motown's biggest hits by Blue Note artists like Stanley Turrentine, John Patton, Earl Klugh, Ray Barretto and Dianne Reeves, among others. Motown's many inclinations toward jazz make these hits work quite well in an instrumental context; witness "What's Goin' On" by Barretto or "Ain't That Peculiar" by Patton. Still, these versions don't really stretch the songs at all. The album is much more suited to Motown fans who want soft-toned versions of their favorites than a jazz fan looking for music of real depth. *—John Bush*

The Blue Note Years, Vol. 3: Organ & Soul 1956–1967 / May 4, 1999 / Blue Note ✦✦✦
This two CD collection was originally released as part of *Blue Note's 60th Anniversary* boxed set. Jimmy Smith, who was signed by Alfred Lion after he saw just one of Smith's shows, sets the pace for this chronicle of the organ fever of soul jazz. Other great organists featured include John Patton, Larry Young, and Freddie Roach. Aggressive and funky, this CD documents a sound that borrowed heavily from the blues and would influence jazz and rock well into the next decade. *—Stacia Proefrock*

The Blue Note Years, Vol. 4: Hard Bop & Beyond 1963–1967 / May 4, 1999 / Blue Note ✦✦✦
Many people associate the sounds of hard bop with Blue Note—the music from a time when jazz was at its creative peak and the label issuing gem after gem. This two CD collection, which was originally part of the *Blue Note 60th Anniversary* boxed set, documents this high point in the history of the label. Freddie Hubbard, Joe Henderson, Herbie Hancock, Tony Williams, and Wayne Shorter are all featured here, making for a highly listenable compilation. *—Stacia Proefrock*

The Blue Note Years, Vol. 6: New Era 1975–1998 / May 4, 1999 / Blue Note ✦✦✦
Originally part of the *Blue Note 60th Anniversary* boxed set, this collection spans music recorded at the label after the death of Alfred Lion in 1971. Contained here is the work of Donald Byrd, Earl Klugh, and Ronnie Laws from the period before the label folded in 1981, as well as material from the new era that began in 1985 when it was resurrected. One of the most interesting additions during that era was US3, who added hip-hop sensibility to jazz music; songs from Dianne Reeves, Cassandra Wilson, and Stanley Jordan show that the label still has a sense of tradition. *—Stacia Proefrock*

Body & Soul: Quiet Storm / Nov. 23, 1999 / Time Life ✦✦✦✦
Body & Soul: Quiet Storm collects soulful, sensual R&B ballads by masters of the genre like Earth Wind & Fire, Regina Belle, and the Manhattans. Marvin Gaye's "Sexual Healing" and Billy Paul's "Me and Mrs. Jones" are two of the definitive quiet storm songs included on the album, and Peabo Bryson & Roberta Flack's "Tonight, I Celebrate My Love," the O'Jays "Let Me Make Love to You," and Freddie Jackson's "Rock Me Tonight (For Old Times Sake)" round out this overview of some of the biggest quiet storm hits. *—Heather Phares*

Bongo Bop / 1996 / Hip Bop ✦✦✦
This is an interesting if rather unfocused tribute to the jazz organ. Organists Joey DeFrancesco, Reuben Wilson, Doug Carn and Lonnie Smith appear in different combinations; Carn's interpretation of Max Roach's "Raoul" is a highlight. Carn has two individual features, and Smith plays an unusual version of Herbie Nichols' "The Lady Sings the Blues." In addition, there are organ duets by DeFrancesco and the long obscure Reuben Wilson, by Wilson and Smith, and by Carn with DeFrancesco. Drummer Idris Muhammad and Papo Pepin (on bongos) are on every track, and there are guest appearances by trombonist Josh Roseman, violinist Michal Urbaniak (who steals solo honors every time he appears), clarinetist Bob Franceschini and altoist Jorge Sylvester. In addition, DeFrancesco plays two short and inconclusive versions of "Bongo Bop" that find Roseman doing a close impression of J.J. Johnson. Overall, this is a bit of a hodgepodge collection, but organ fans and those listeners who wonder whatever happened to Reuben Wilson and Doug Carn will certainly want to acquire it. *—Scott Yanow*

Breaks Sessions / Jun. 25, 2002 / Sessions ✦✦✦
Possibly infuriating the blurry-eyed crate-diggers and wannabe DJs who have spent hours finding some of these proverbial needles in the haystack at garage sales and record fairs, *Breaks Sessions* spreads 30 rare, no-longer-rare, and never-were-rare cuts from the R&B vaults that time (or label catalog departments) forgot across two discs. Enticing the consumer on its cover with a laundry list of rap artists who appropriated elements of each selection contained within, the compilation delivers the goods by curating an extensive set of songs that will leave many a rap fan exclaiming, "Oh, so *that's* where..." over and over and over. For the most part, this compilation stands up on its own without the theme, with plenty of should-be and already-are classics scattered throughout. And, in some cases, there's a good reason why some of them remained obscurities until they had their drum breaks, basslines, keyboard tones, vocal warblings, and guitar flicks filched by DJs and production teams: they weren't all that great to begin with. Semi-infamous favorites like Bob James' "Nautilus" and Skull Snaps' "Tres-passin'" mix it up with universally known songs like the Meters' "Same Old Thing," Isaac Hayes' "Joy," and the Dramatics' "Get Up and Get Down," so it's hardly a "rarities only" deal. One amusing thing to consider is how ripe some of these songs have been for the picking: for example, if you subtracted each element from the Last Poets' "Tribute to Obabi" that has been appropriated throughout the years, only a lonely, distant shaker would remain. All things considered, *Breaks Sessions* is a valuable package, throwing together an impressive, multi-hued set of R&B-derived nuggets from the '60s and '70s. Not only does it demystify key elements of numerous rap cuts, but each selection is accompanied in the liner notes by informed commentary spiked with anecdotes. *—Andy Kellman*

Bring in 'da Noise Bring in 'da Funk / Jul. 29, 1996 / RCA ✦✦✦✦✦
Savion Glover's smash Broadway hit *Bring in 'da Noise Bring in 'da Funk* took critics by storm, and this album is a live recording of a performance of the show. The album progresses through five main movements of black history and tap. "In 'da Beginning" pertains to the slave era. "Urbanization" portrays the Chicago black scene. "Where's the Beat" deals with the progression of dancing. "Street Corner Symphony" deals with the new urban era, and "Noise/Funk" is a demonstration of the prowess of Glover and his comrades in hittin', the new style of tap created by Glover, which involves less of the visual show associated with dance, and serves primarily to create music with the sounds of the tap shoes, as well as associates on various objects (paint buckets, chains, fencing, etc.). In truth, stripped of the costuming and visual effects, the album becomes a large work of poetry, sounding at times like *Stomp*, with orchestral accompaniment and vocalists. The work can seem like *musique concrète* at times, but retains a large musical interpretation of black culture, as well as some impressive percussion pieces, in the "Noise/Funk" section. The music is exceptional, but for the full power of the show, one really needs to see Savion Glover at work. *—Adam Greenberg*

Broken Hearted Soul Essentials, Vol. 1 / Nov. 2, 1999 / Polygram ✦✦✦✦
Broken Hearted Soul Essentials is a great collection of 17 heartbreak soul songs. The compilers nicely balance '60s and '70s material, and the end result is always entertaining, thanks to such classics as "Have You Seen Her," "The Tracks of My Tears," "When a Man Loves a Woman," "What Becomes of the Broken Hearted," "Going in Circles," and "I Wish it Would Rain," plus such lesser-known gems as "Make it Like it Was," "Ask the Lonely," "Just Once," "How Could I Let You Get Away," "I'm Going Down," "My Whole World Is Falling Down," and "I Wouldn't Treat a Dog (The Way You Treated Me)." *—Stephen Thomas Erlewine*

Brown Eyed Soul: The Sound of East L.A., Vol. 1 / Sep. 16, 1997 / Rhino ✦✦✦
Rhino's three-disc series *Brown Eyed Soul* intends to document the underappreciated Chicano soul scene of East Los Angeles in the '60s. Although many of the artists featured on *Brown Eyed Soul* are indeed Hispanic, many of the cuts on the series are by artists, such as Brenton Wood, that were simply popular in East L.A. and weren't Chicano. Throughout the late '50s and '60s, East L.A. was vibrant, filled with excellent R&B, soul and rock & roll that was rarely heard outside of the city. Regrettably, *Brown Eyed Soul* is not sequenced chronologically—on this first volume, it jumps from 1956 to 1980 to 1971 to 1954—but there's a wealth of terrific music scattered throughout the series, even if none of the volumes make for cohesive listening. On this first volume, there are cuts from War ("All Day Music"), the Penguins ("Hey Senorita"), Tony Clarke ("The Entertainer"), Van McCoy ("Mr. D.J."), Brenton Wood ("Me and You"), Chuck Higgins ("Pachuko Hop"), and the Five Satins ("Our Anniversary"). *—Stephen Thomas Erlewine*

Brown Eyed Soul: The Sound of East L.A., Vol. 2 / Sep. 16, 1997 / Rhino ✦✦✦
Since *Brown Eyed Soul: The Sound of East L.A.* doesn't follow any chronological order, *Vol. 2* doesn't really pick up where its predecessor left off. Instead, it simply follows the pattern of *Vol. 1*, compiling forgotten singles from the '50s, '60s, '70s, and '80s with no particular rhyme or reason. There are a few familiar songs on *Vol. 2*—including Ritchie Valens' "We Belong Together," War's "Why Can't We Be Friends?," and the Premiers' "Farmer John"—but its main strength is that it gathers regional soul, R&B, and rock & roll hits from the likes of the Blendells ("La La La La La"), McKinley Travis ("Baby, Is There Something on Your Mind"), the Gallahads ("I'm Without a Girl Friend"), Cannibal & the Headhunters ("Please Baby Please"), Brenton Wood ("Baby You Got It"), and Hank Jacobs ("East Side"). *—Stephen Thomas Erlewine*

Brown Eyed Soul: The Sound of East L.A., Vol. 3 / Sep. 16, 1997 / Rhino ♦♦♦♦
An enjoyable compilation of diverse R&B recordings released between 1959 and 1975 which earned plenty of airplay on East Los Angeles radio stations. Many were also hits elsewhere, like the Olympics' "Mine Exclusively," a hard, bouncy R&B vocal that proved they could do more than just dance tunes. The little-known ballad "I Fooled You This Time" (by Gene Chandler) and "Forever" (by the Marvelettes) (a popular song at weddings) were R&B chart-dwellers that never crossed over to pop. Smashes like "Land of 1,000 Dances" by Cannibal & the Headhunters, Leon Haywood's "It's Got to Be Mellow," and "Natural High" by Bloodstone are balanced by local favorites such as Brenton Wood's "Catch You on the Rebound," El Chicano's "Tell Her She's Lovely," and Rosie & Ron's "Bring Me Happiness. *—Andrew Hamilton*

Brunswick Records Greatest Hits, Vol. 1-3 / 1994 / Brunswick/Score ♦♦♦♦
Brunswick was a pivotal Chicago soul label, becoming the city's primary outlet for black performers after Vee-Jay's demise. It featured the superb harmonizing of the Chi-Lites, plus other emerging performers like Barbara Acklin, the Artistics, Young-Holt Unlimited, and veterans from other companies like Gene Chandler and Tyrone Davis. Most of all, they had Jackie Wilson. This three-disc set, starting in 1957 and ending in 1980, includes one disc that's virtually all Wilson. The second disc moves through the 1960s and into the early '70s; the final disc contains essential numbers from the Chi-Lites and Tyrone Davis, dividing 14 of its 15 selections between them. *—Ron Wynn*

The Brunswick Years, Vol. 1 / 1995 / Brunswick ♦♦♦♦
In the 1960s and early '70s, the Brunswick label recorded some of the best soul to come out of Chicago. This two-disc, 40-song collection would have ranked higher if the organization was a little less scattered. The cuts by Jackie Wilson, Gene Chandler, Tyrone Davis, Young-Holt Unlimited, and the Chi-Lites are mostly good, but are better heard in the context of those artists' own compilations. Collectors will welcome the presence of rarer items by Barbara Acklin, Billy Butler, the Artistics, Otis Leavill, and Erma Franklin (Aretha's sister), though these tracks are pleasant period fare, not obscure classics. This isn't a bad anthology for those who prefer their vintage soul on the sweet side, but it's probably only worthwhile for specialists. *—Richie Unterberger*

Bubblegum Classics, Vol. 5 / Feb. 10, 1998 / Varese ♦♦♦♦
Bubblegum Classics, Vol. 5 is a retitled reissue of Varese's *Soulful Pop* collection. This is the kind of compilation that doesn't attract much critical attention, but is a pretty nifty concept: 17 songs from 1966-1976 that are soul-pop at its poppiest and most commercial, running the scale from R&B-grounded cuts to near-bubblegum. It's a good mix of classics of the micro-genre (the Foundations' "Build Me Up Buttercup" and "Baby, Now That I Found You," Jay & the Techniques' "Keep the Ball Rollin'," Maxine Nightingale's "Right Back Where We Started From"), minor half-forgotten hits (James & Bobby Purify's "Let Love Come Between Us," Chairmen of the Board's "You've Got Me Dangling on a String"), singles that were only big in England (Blue Mink's "Melting Pot," the Love Affair's cover of Robert Knight's "Everlasting Love"), and total flops (by the Groove and the People's Choice). Especially ingratiating are the Five Stairsteps' "O-oh Child" and Chee-Chee & Peppy's "I Know I'm in Love," a forgotten Jackson 5 imitation (and minor hit) from 1971. *—Richie Unterberger*

Can You Dig It? The '70s Soul Experience / Oct. 16, 2001 / Rhino ♦♦♦♦♦
Like other super-ambitious genre overviews on Rhino, this six-CD box set is documenting a style so large and diverse that the track selection is not going to completely satisfy everybody, even with 136 songs. There are many good things to say about this release, though. To start with the positive, most of the major soul stars of the '70s are represented with at least one track, and sometimes with a couple cuts. In addition, there are lots of fine hits by dozens of artists who only had a few (or only one) big records, from the Winstons' "Color Him Father" and Jean Knight's "Mr. Big Stuff" to Cornelius Brothers & Sister Rose's "Too Late to Turn Back Now" and Sylvia's "Pillow Talk." Rather than be strict about the chronological boundaries of the project, there are a half-dozen 1969 singles in the '70s soul vein to lead off disc one, as well as a solitary cut from the early '80s (Rose Royce's "Golden Touch," which could have been left off without any tears shed). Room is made for some non-African-American soul by whites and Latinos, and plenty of big-but-not-huge hits. Sensibly, the first half of the '70s is heavily represented, all but one of the post-1975 cuts getting shunted onto disc six. On the other hand, there is no way to boil down, say, the output of Al Green, Marvin Gaye, Curtis Mayfield, Sly & the Family Stone, and other superstars to just one or two representative songs, and some might quibble with the ones selected, though generally the compilers wisely played it safe by targeting big hits. In addition, some superstars are not present at all—the Jackson 5, Diana Ross, Aretha Franklin, and Stevie Wonder, for instance. There's nothing that might be considered rare, with nearly every one of the tracks having been a substantial hit single, even if some of those—the Fuzz's "I Love You for All Seasons," the 8th Day's "She's Not Just Another Woman," and Brighter Side of Darkness' "Love Jones," for instance—aren't exactly over-represented on compilations. The final disc might round out the chronology of the decade, but also is far inferior to the rest of the set, often illustrating soul's decline into pop slickness. But you know what? It's still a very good, intelligent overview of '70s soul, guaranteed to please someone who doesn't collect this stuff obsessively, but wants a lot of it around, sequenced in a manner that ensures variety and quality. The packaging is, as is always the case with major Rhino box sets, quite imaginative, with a 78-page information booklet and an outer cover that simulates a rack of eight-track tapes. *—Richie Unterberger*

The Carnival Day: The Essential Recordings of New Orleans / Apr. 24, 2001 / Indigo ♦♦♦♦
This anthology of New Orleans R&B is a little undersold by the packaging, which lists the song titles on the back cover, but not the artists. The track listings on the inner sleeve do at least give the personnel on each recording, leaving the hapless consumer to make the final, intuitive leap of logic to deduct that the vocalist is the actual performer. At any rate, it's a decent 24-track grouping of very early New Orleans R&B performances, spanning 1947-1950, laying some important groundwork for early rock & roll before rock & roll had a name. Aside from Fats Domino's "The Fat Man" and Professor Longhair's "Mardi Gras in New Orleans" and "Bald Head," it's doubtful that any of these tunes are instantly familiar to many rock and blues fans, though Archibald's "Stack-A-Lee" is the first R&B adaptation of a folk song that also provided the basis for Lloyd Price's huge pop hit "Stagger Lee." Overall it's solid, if sometimes generic and lo-fi, New Orleans R&B with more of a blues/boogie/jazz base than the more widespread New Orleans rock sounds of the last half of the 1950s, also including tracks by noted Crescent City figures Paul Gayten, Roy Brown, Dave Bartholomew, and Smiley Lewis. Professor Longhair, whether under the name of Roy Byrd or his *nom de plume*, is the most frequent contributor, with nine songs. Those looking for something more obscure may be satisfied by the inclusion of efforts by Joseph August, Chubby Newsome, and Jewel King. *—Richie Unterberger*

Carnival of Soul, Vol. 1: Wishes / Nov. 8, 1994 / Kent ♦♦♦
Two record companies, Collectables and Kent, have taken it upon themselves to reissue everything cut by Joe Evans' Carnival Record label. Collectables have the best idea musically—they include six or eight tracks by one known artist and fill the rest of the CD with cuts by the real unknowns. However, Collectables doesn't include songwriters' credits, and the liner notes and artist information are either skimpy or missing. Kent's discs have more than 20 cuts each and extensive annotation, but no more than two or three by any artist, so you get a potpourri of unfamiliar tracks that are average at best. *Vol. 1* of Kent's Carnival Records compilation consists of 24 tracks and one lone R&B hit: Lee Williams & the Cymbals' "I Love You More." Two Manhattans tunes made the cut—the unreleased "Til You Come Back to Me" and "All I Need Is Your Love," an obscure album track. Northern soul fans will love the inclusion of Phil Terrell's "Love has Passed Me By"; the song went unnoticed in the States, but is considered a collector's item in Europe. A female group called the Pets has the most interesting track here, an early production by George Clinton entitled "I Say Yeah," originally released and forgotten in 1965. Tracks by the Metrics, the Topics, and the Lovettes are interesting, and the Pretenders cuts always demand attention, but the rest is subpar. *—Andrew Hamilton*

Carnival of Soul, Vol. 2: Feelin' Good / Apr. 21, 1995 / Kent ♦♦♦
Vol. 1 of this Carnival Records anthology contained one lone R&B hit; this second volume doesn't include any at all. The Manhattans' second record, "There Goes a Fool," is a good little number, but nothing special. Lee Williams & the Cymbals' second-biggest record, "Peepin' Through the Window," still sounds good, and was one of the few Carnival Records releases to get played outside of New Jersey. The Symphonies' "That's What Love Will Do" is a heart-rending girl group ballad and a bona fide tear-jerker, while The Lovettes' "I'm Afraid (To Say I Love You)" is another good slice of female group soul. The Metrics and the Topics sides are always interesting; Joe Evans (Carnival Records' owner) should have taken them in the studio more. Sides by Barbara Brown and Norma Jenkins may have been recorded in New Jersey, but they're deep soul. *—Andrew Hamilton*

Carnival of Soul, Vol. 3: I Wanna Be / Nov. 21, 1995 / Kent ♦♦♦
Many labels and label owners have been given unofficial sainthood by fans (all petitions to the Vatican are pending), but in the world of independent soul perhaps one of the most deserved of this massive praise is Joe Evans and his Carnival imprint. Spanning most of the '60s and taking occasional forays into the '70s and even the indie soul tundra of the '80s, Carnival quietly issued soul-blues rockers, somber ballads, Northern classics, disco anthems, and crossover classics before most of those designations had been invented. Among the legends here are Lee Williams & the Cymbals' classic "I Need You Baby" (imagine Marvin Gaye singing lead with the Impressions), Phil Terrell and his fantastic "I'll Erase You (From My Heart)," Wilber Bascombe's bona fide funk anthem "Groove in G," and the sophisticated '80s surprise of New Jersey Connection's "Love Don't Come Easy." This is the third and final volume in Kent Records' reissue series that presents the entire catalog of Carnival, including previously unissued material. If you really want the whole story, though, you'll have to check out all three volumes; exhaustive notes and photos are provided in sequence throughout the thick booklets accompanying each disc. *— Wade Kergan*

Casablanca Records Story / 1994 / Casablanca/Mercury ♦♦♦♦♦
Even though it includes four discs, *The Casablanca Records Story* ignores the record label's biggest success, Kiss. But that doesn't matter; Kiss didn't fit into the rest of the label's roster. Driven by the massive success of Donna Summer, Casablanca was arguably the definitive disco label in the late '70s, scoring a string of hit singles that have become classics of the era. Featuring four discs of original single versions and 12-inch mixes, *The Casablanca Records Story* features most of the best music the label released, even though it probably could have been more effectively compiled on two or three discs. Nevertheless, there is plenty of fine, even seminal, music here, which makes it essential for serious disco collectors. *—Stephen Thomas Erlewine*

Celebration of Soul, Vol. 1 / Jul. 5, 1994 / Varese ♦♦♦♦
This set compiled two CD's worth of Carl Davis' Chi-Town productions. Davis produced these same artists in the '60s for Brunswick, OKeh, and Constellation Records; Davis' early productions received critical acclaim, but these later '70s/'80s productions were often overlooked. Davis had a bigger budget at Chi-Town (distributed and marketed by 20th Century Fox Records), and the sound is a little slicker, lacking the edge that some soul aficionados crave. Gene Chandler's "Does She Have a Friend" is bouncy and infectious; it made noise on the R&B charts but failed to equal the Duke of Earl's biggest

Chi-Town recording, "Get Down," a disco smash that is also included. The Dells cut some stunners on Chi-Town; they even updated "Stay in My Corner." The floating "Passionate Breezes," and "I Touched a Dream," are scrumptious, both featuring Johnny Carter's soaring falsetto countering Marvin Junior's blustering baritone. The original Chi-Lites regrouped and scored with the hiccupping "Hot on a Thing." An updated "Have You Seen Her," is delightful, but not as charismatic as the original. Producer, Carl Davis recorded updates of everyone's biggest recordings, including Walter Jackson's. In addition to new thriller: "What Would You Do," and "Baby I Love Your Way," he dusts off Jackson's lamenting "It's All Now." "Feelings," and the probing "An If I Had," are two ritzy ballads. The reorganized Impressions do some serious harmonizing on three tunes, the best being the classy "Maybe I'm Mistaken." It's a good collection for uptown soul lovers. *—Andrew Hamilton*

☆ **A Cellarful of Motown!** / May 28, 2002 / Universal International ♦♦♦♦♦

Motown can certainly be taken to task for issuing the same old stuff over and over again—no matter how great it is, how many versions of Marvin Gaye's "What's Goin On" or of Motown's Top 20 singles does anybody really need?—even if it is as important as Beethoven's *Fifth Symphony* (or anybody else's, for that matter). Not so in this case. *Cellarful of Motown* is a double CD chock-full of soul classics that have remained virtually unheard since they were first recorded—or, in some cases, relegated to the cutting room floor—by Motown's front-line artists, and many that should have been. We can thank the Northern soul underground in the U.K. for this issue in a sense, due to their constant demand for rare Motown soul issues and the massive bootlegging that goes with it—and a collector's market that was out of control price-wise at the dawn of the 21st century. Here are 40 tracks that were recorded in the glory days of the Detroit soul scene, but never issued at the time due to Berry Gordy's near-fascistic quality control. Track titles include "My Sugar Baby" by Frank Wilson, "I Wish I Liked You" by Marvin Gaye, "Baby a Go Go" by Barbara McNair, "If You Ever Get Your Hands on Me" by Gladys Knight & the Pips, "How Can I" and "All Your Love" by Brenda Holloway, "He Was Really Sayin' Somethin'" by Earl Van Dyke, "Until You Came Along" by Carolyn Crawford, "Before It's Over" by Sammy Ward, "Long Gone Lover" by Velvelettes, "Lucky Lucky Me" by Jimmy Ruffin, "You Made Me Feel Like" by Syreeta, "Don't Let Me Down" by Kim Weston, "Don't Put Off Till Tomorrow What You Can Do Today" by the Monitors, and "It Must Be Love Baby" by Chuck Jackson & Yvonne Fair. And this is just a sampling. There are solid notes giving recording origins and personnel wherever possible, and some cool photos in the package with liner notes by Northern soul aficionado DJ and editor Paul Nixon, but the music is the treat here. When Holloway sings "All Your Love," the emotion in her voice is underscored by the giant string section and cracks the mix in two, wrenching every ounce of emotion from Frank Wilson's words. When Chris Clark's pathos-ridden "Do I Love You (Indeed I Do)" cuts loose from the heart of a huge horn section and brings the message home in a raw, direct way; the feet will be two-steppin' even as the sultry need of the track moves deep into the solar plexus. That this is followed by the stomp and swagger of the Contours' "Baby Hit and Run," with it's gospel chorus and the funk rhythms is almost too much to take. It's seriously enough to take your breath away. There is one theory as to why these tracks weren't issued at the time of their recording despite their obvious high and enduring quality. Emotionally and/or production-wise, many of these singles were just too raw for the Motown squeaky-clean machine. If one gives a solid listen to Holloway's material in particular, the deep, unruly, sexy nature of the material is not one that is usually associated with Motown. The Contours could have recorded for Stax they were so raw, and Jimmy Ruffin's various performances give his voice the workout it never got on the officially released material. Simply put: This is the most essential Motown collection release since the first singles box, and, in a sense, since that material is available in a number of ways, it is perhaps more so—and not merely academically. This is as great an introduction to Detroit soul music as anything you are likely to come across. This is the most important—and thoroughly enjoyable—soul reissue in years. *—Thom Jurek*

Chess Club Rhythm & Soul / Jun. 11, 1996 / Kent ♦♦♦♦♦

This compilation is a good but peculiar British import of 25 Chess tracks from the 1960s, with the anachronistic exception of Little Walter's 1955 classic "My Babe." It's mostly soul, but sometimes blues, and sometimes a mixture of the two. There's not a solid concept linking the selections, except perhaps that they were (and are) considered good songs to dance to at English clubs. For the most part these are fairly obscure cuts that aren't that easy to pick up in the States, though a few—"My Babe," Little Milton's "Grits Ain't Groceries," Billy Stewart's "Summertime," Sonny Boy Williamson's "Help Me," and Tommy Tucker's "Hi Heel Sneakers"—are apt to already be in the collections of soul and blues fans who are likely to be interested in a CD like this. The choosy buyer would probably want this more for the lesser-known items, and there are some good ones here, such as Etta James' robust, brassy 1964 outing "Mellow Fellow," Muddy Waters' blues-with-horns "Messin' with the Man," Don & Bob's raucous rock version of "Good Morning Little Schoolgirl," the Kolettes' girl-group-soul "Who's That Guy," and soul-jazz from Lou Donaldson, Ramsey Lewis, Brother Jack McDuff, and Bobby Moore. You won't find cuts by Fred Hughes, Marlena Shaw, Kip Anderson, and Jamo Thomas on many other anthologies, Chess-only or otherwise. There are a lot of Ace/Kent compilations geared toward soul specialists that are pretty scattered in focus; although this is one of them, it's one of the best. The tracks are very respectable at worst, and excellent at best. The source label put out so much quality stuff, and this is a good supplement to the libraries of those looking to fill out their Chess sections. *—Richie Unterberger*

Chess New Orleans / Apr. 25, 1995 / MCA ♦♦♦

The Chicago-based Chess label isn't often associated with the New Orleans rock and R&B scene of the '50s, but its dalliances there produced a handful of hits including Clarence "Frogman" Henry's "Ain't Got No Home" and Bobby Charles' "See You Later Alligator" and "Time Will Tell." *Chess New Orleans* is a two-disc set that collects 44 hits, misses, album tracks, and previously unreleased recordings from the Chess vaults, including cuts from the subsidiary labels Checker and Argo, and distributed sides like Rod Bernard's hit "This Should Go On Forever." Certain artists, such as Bobby Charles, Clarence Henry, Sugar Boy Crawford (maker of the first version of "Iko Iko," titled "Jock-A-Mo"), and Paul Gayten, are well represented with up to a half-dozen tracks each. The selections run the gamut from straight rock and R&B to Clifton Chenier's accordion-driven Cajun sides to regional novelties like the Hawketts' "Mardi Gras Mambo." *Chess New Orleans* is not a representative regional or hits anthology but revives many worthwhile rarities for collectors. *—Greg Adams*

Chess Rhythm & Roll / 1994 / MCA ♦♦♦♦♦

A four-disc set chronicling the more rockin' sides in this landmark label's catalog. Here we have the landmark early recordings by Chuck Berry, Bo Diddley, the Moonglows, the Flamingos, marvelous one-shot hit artists like the Monotones ("Book of Love"), Dale Hawkins ("Susie-Q"), the Sensations ("Let Me In"), as well as seminal soul sides from Etta James, Billy Stewart and Tommy Tucker's original "High Heel Sneakers." Essential doesn't even begin to describe this box; music from a landmark label that changed the world. *—Cub Koda*

Chess Soul: A Decade of Chicago's Finest / Aug. 26, 1997 / MCA ♦♦♦♦♦

While Chess made numerous legendary contributions to the fields of blues and rock & roll, its reputation as a major mover and shaker in the soul field from 1961 to 1971 is unassailed. This 2-CD, 45-track compilation is another excellent entry in the *Chess 50th Anniversary Series* and shows why the label had the Windy City almost sewn up when it came to brand-name artists and material. Whether the tracks were master purchases from a smaller Chicago or Southern label (Jan Bradley's "Mama Didn't Lie," Cookie & the Cupcakes' "I've Been So Lonely," the Kolettes' "Who's That Girl?," Big Maybelle's "Don't Pass Me By" or Denise LaSalle's "A Love Reputation") or in-house productions from Billy Davis and Leonard Caston, next to Stax or Atlantic, no one stood for soul music in the 1960s like Chess Records. Featuring the label's strong hitmakers and soul shouters Etta James (the devastating "Only Time Will Tell"), Billy Stewart (the scat classic "Summertime"), Fontella Bass ("Rescue Me"), Gene Chandler ("I Fooled You This Time"), Mitty Collier ("I'm Satisfied") and Sugar Pie DeSanto ("Soulful Dress") alongside isolated moments of Chi-Town brilliance (the Radiants' "Voice Your Choice," the Knight Brothers' "Temptation 'Bout to Get Me" and Tony Clarke's "The Entertainer") with early Muscle Shoals productions thrown in to give the big picture (Laura Lee's "Dirty Man," Maurice & Mac's "You Left the Water Running"), this is one very potent two-disc anthology and an essential addition to anyone's soul collection. *—Cub Koda*

The Chess Story: 1947–1975 / Feb. 2000 / MCA International ♦♦♦♦♦

First the good news, which is really good: the sound on this 340-song set is about as good as one ever fantasized it could be, and that means it runs circles around any prior reissues; from the earliest Aristocrat sides right up through Muddy Waters' "Going Down to Main Street," it doesn't get any better than this set. The clarity pays a lot of bonuses, beginning with the impression that it gives of various artists' instrumental prowess. In sharp contrast to the past efforts in this direction by MCA, however, the producers of this set have not emasculated the sound in the course of cleaning it up. When the rock & roll era dawns at Chess as depicted on disc five, the sound is nice and dirty, just really sharp. The contents of the set are largely "limited"—if that's the word for any 340-song collection—to Chess' blues, R&B, rock & roll, and soul output, although Ramsey Lewis gets a nod, as does comedian Pigmeat Markham. What's more, the care lavished on the songs is virtually universal—there was time spent getting all of it right. One wishes that the same could be said for one of the featured bonuses on this set, the CD-ROM that comprises the 15th disc. First, there are the skimpy film clips, misspellings ("Arether Franklin") and incorrect dates. There also would have been enough room to put a complete Chess discography on the CD-ROM, rather than just the MCA reissues of Chess' material. The CDs themselves are conveniently assembled in three fold-out volumes in a slipcase, but identifying individual tracks and artists means constantly referring back to the booklets glued into those volumes; additionally, it would've been nice to have had a sessionography on the songs, or at least the release dates, or even release years. *—Bruce Eder*

Chess Uptown Soul / Mar. 25, 1997 / Kent ♦♦♦

If you're trying to differentiate what was specifically "uptown" about these '60s Chess soul sides, you're getting into a game of serious hairsplitting. Basically this 24-track comp offers material—mostly non-hits—from 1963-1967 that leans toward sophisticated, brassy soul borrowing much from Motown and Curtis Mayfield, but not matching the peaks of either. It's still pretty enjoyable, if sometimes generic, material, including efforts by some stars (Gene Chandler, Billy Stewart, Etta James, Ramsey Lewis, Little Milton, the Dells, Fontella Bass), Jan Bradley's great one-shot "Mama Didn't Lie," Tony Clarke's fine Top 40 ballad "The Entertainer," and barely heeded names like Jackie Ross, the Radiants, and Marlena Shaw (there's also an early non-hit by Johnny Nash). There's also the occasional song that deserved a much wider hearing than it got, like Nash's "Love Ain't Nothin'," the Radiants' infectious "It Ain't No Big Thing," and Mitty Collier's "I Had a Talk With My Man," which was covered by Dusty Springfield. *—Richie Unterberger*

Chess/Checkers Group, Vol. 1 / 2001 / Chess/Checkers ♦♦♦

Here is a compilation (released in Spain) with 24, many hard-to-find, recordings from Leonard and Phil Chess' Chess and Checkers labels, based in Chicago, Illinois. This CD is loaded with rare nuggets like the Coronets' "It Would Be Heaven"; "Could It Be You," a pre-Motown Four Tops recording; "When I Look At You" by the Encores; the Ideals' "Knee Socks"; and two by the Students. The collection also features a hard-to-find early track by the Miracles, "Bad Girl," which Berry Gordy leased to Chess prior to Motown's commercial success. *—Andrew Hamilton*

Chi Sound: Soul from the Windy City / Sep. 29, 1998 / Southbound ✦✦✦✦
Carl Davis' Chi Sound productions, distributed by 20th Century Fox, don't get the acclaim that his OKeh, Constellation, and Brunswick's sides do—unfortunate, because these are some smooth, classy soul sounds. The Chi-Lites four selections—"Heavenly Body," an updated "Have You Seen Her," "Me and You," and the group's only Chi-Sound hit "Hot on a Thing (Called Love)"—are comparable to their Brunswick sides. Gene Chandler smokes on "Get Down," Chi-Sound's biggest hit, and "Does She Have a Friend for Me." Also among the 15 tracks is Manchild's "Especially for You," whose lineup included Kenny "Babyface" Edmonds. In addition, there are tracks by the Impressions, Walter Jackson, Sidney Quails, and the Windy City Orchestra. *—Andrew Hamilton*

Chicago House '86-'91: The Definitive Story / 1997 / PRD ✦✦✦✦
Including three discs of classic Chicago house (though the final disc is a Marshall Jefferson megamix encompassing singles already on the first two), *Chicago House '86-'91* distills only the best and most influential tracks from producers like Jefferson, Farley Jackmaster Funk, Phuture and Larry Heard. All of the most familiar tunes are here—"Move Your Body," "Love Can't Turn Around," "Acid Trax," "No Way Back," "Can You Feel It," "You Used to Hold Me," "Your Love"—and with a few arguable exceptions, only the best is included. *—John Bush*

Chicago Radio Soul / 1996 / Kent ✦✦✦
The title might be *Chicago Radio Soul*, but it's really a 26-track compilation of soul that was released on Chicago-based Chess Records during the 1960s. Only one of the songs was a big hit (Fontella Bass' "Rescue Me"), though Jackie Ross' "Selfish One" and Mitty Collier's "Sharing You" did well on the R&B charts. There are also little-known singles by Etta James, Little Milton, Billy Stewart, and Denise LaSalle, as well as names that will only be familiar to serious soul fanatics, like the Gems, the Radiants, and Bobby McClure. Chess wasn't as much of a presence in soul as it was in blues, although by the '60s, it was concentrating much more on the soul market. On the whole this is decent if unremarkable '60s soul, showing the influence of both Motown and the crosstown Chicago sound of the OKeh label. High points worth noting by any soul fan are the girl group-tinged "I Can't Help Myself" (the Gems) and Jackie Ross' "Take Me for a Little While," a rare example of a black soul cover of a single by a white female singer (Evie Sands). *—Richie Unterberger*

Chicago Soul Uprising! The Real Sound of Chicago 1967–1975 / 1987 / Charly ✦✦✦
These sides, released between 1967 and 1975, are neither Brunswick's most successful nor unsuccessful releases. The only song here that failed to chart nationally is Jackie Wilson and the Chi-Lites' forgotten collaboration "Don't Burn No Bridges," a good song that wasn't well promoted. The most successful record is Jackie Wilson's "Since You Showed Me How to Be Happy," a jubilant jitterbugger that went to number-32 pop. Willie Henderson & the Soul Explosion's "Funky Chicken" is a delight; thankfully, the compilers included Pts. 1 & 2. Two numbers by the underrated Lost Generation are worth the price alone: "Wait a Minute" and "The Sly, Slick & Wicked." On "SS&W," the fellows warn young girls about the three kinds of guys alluded to in the title. The most pleasant surprise is Barbara Acklin's "Am I the Same Girl"—it only went to number-33 R&B and number-79 pop, but the song's instrumental track shot up the charts as "Soulful Strut" by the Young-Holt Trio. Barbara's version is an exhilarating piece of music and should have been a monster; her vocals are powerful and urgent. Otis Leavill, Erma Franklin, Tyrone Davis, the Artistics, and Gene Chandler also contribute to the 16-song collection. *—Andrew Hamilton*

Chitlin Circuit Soul! The Best of Today's Southern Blues / May 15, 2001 / Rhino ✦✦✦✦✦
This is the soul record people have been looking for for a long time, but may not have known it. Alongside the Stax/Volt and Motown compilations that keep selling, and every rarities collection from the soulful '50s and '60s that's issued in Europe or Japan and disappears upon release, exists a soul music every bit as vital and pure as those venerable recordings have offered us. Apparently, soul music is now a secret music in America, where in urban centers, on weekends, large groups of folks get together and clap, shout, and dance for their favorite performers—some of whom have been making music for decades and some younger people who are making vital, exciting soul music now because it's the only music that moved them when they were coming up. This compilation aims to showcase a number of these current artists by juxtaposing their music against some of the genre's greats. The folks at Rhino, who do some of the best reissues in the world, are also committed to new explorers. The set opens with the illustrious silver-tongued angel Bobby "Blue" Bland with his deeply moving "Members Only," cut for Malaco in 1985 (and reached number 43 in the R&B chart). Bland is the consummate soul singer, and the arrangement is classic Chicago gospel croon à la Curtis Mayfield. When Bland sings "Members only, it's a private party/don't need no money to qualify/don't bring your checkbook, bring your broken heart/cause it's member's only tonight/say you lost your woman, say you lost your man/you got a lot of problems in your life/they're throwin' a party for the broken hearted/it's members only tonight," the melody is straight from "People Get Ready," and the strings swirl into the spare horn arrangements as the female vocals enter at the chorus. With a flute solo in the bridge, it's as deep and moving a song as there exists today. Johnnie Taylor, Bobby Rush, Clarence Carter (forget about "Patches"; his "Strokin'" is a racy, sensual extrapolation of "Givin' It Up for Your Love," Little Milton, Shirley Brown—whose "Woman to Woman" is as marvelous, feminine, and tough a ballad as any ballad ever recorded), Betty Wright, and Millie Jackson are among the legends on the 16-track set. And so what—right, these are all stalwarts who are the current soul dudes and divas that carry the torch for a music that seems impossible to make in the current cultural climate. OK. First of all, there's the remarkable Sterling Harrison & the New Breed doing the classic "There's a Rat in My House"—given such a stinging wrangling guitar treatment by Buddy Guy in the '80s that the song was lost—is a blues that comes from the Magic Sam School of Blues & R&B. His growling, roaring gospel-preacher moans open the door for the backbone to slip on out the back door. Newcomer Ronnie Lovejoy's chitlin' circuit jukebox hit (remember those), the cocky "Still Wasn't Me," is a deeper-than-blue study in romantic denial and deceit. His mix of righteous indignation and soulful pleading are infectious and reaching. The drums are a bit thin, but the tune's story, his killer voice—Solomon Burke meets Wilson Pickett—with Philly soul production and a huge chorus of female backing vocals are convincing evidence that deep soul is still alive and kicking. Sterling Meadows, whose spoken beginning is another tale of denial: the protagonist's former woman is hanging out steady with someone else, and he's refusing to buy it as authentic. When he croons with the backbeat: "She can fool her friends, that's the easy part/Just wait she can't fool her heart/You're still my love . . . You can't turn it off when you want to/Love don't work that way/For eyes that weep, there's a heart that yearns/And soon he'll learn/She's still my love. . . ." Echoes of Al Green, Brook Benton, Cecil Womack, and David Ruffin slip through the mix unabashedly, but the tune has it all anyway. The delivery could be anyone because the groove is so deep. There isn't a dog in this 16-track collection. *—Thom Jurek*

Christmas Time with Motown / Apr. 16, 1995 / PSM ✦✦✦
Listening to *Christmas Time with Motown*, it comes as something of a surprise to realize that the label never launched a truly classic seasonal hit—the ten tracks which make up this disc, while engaging, just never reach the peaks associated with holiday perennial status. Still, fans of the fabled Motown Sound will enjoy this budget-priced collection, which spans the company's history to assemble performances ranging from Stevie Wonder's "The Christmas Song" to the Jackson 5's "The Little Drummer Boy" to Johnny Gill's "Give Love on Christmas Day." *—Jason Ankeny*

Cinemaphonic: Electro Soul / May 16, 2000 / Emperor Norton ✦✦✦
The quest for all things rare and grooving from the '60s and '70s finds audio hounds trudging through the music libraries of TV and film production houses. Your captain this time out, appropriately enough, is former U.S. sitcom actor David Hollander, who played *Little Earl* on the '70s show *What's Happening*. There's no sight of Henry Mancini's infectious *What's Happening* theme, but *Cinemaphonic: Electro Soul* does contain plenty of other hits and misses from tube and screen's endless reels of incidental music. The template takes in soul-jazz, blaxploitation, and celluloid tunes of old; the nuts and bolts include large doses of electric piano, primitive synths, flutes, harpsichords, and sundry other devices endemic to cinematic soul. And while Walter "A Fifth of Beethoven" Murphy's noirish grooves, Mario Nascimbene's clavinet-fueled funk, and Earl Salisbury's atmospheric panoramas hit the mark, the remainder often falls victim to stale beats and thin dressing; in other words, it's music that screams out for images of Mannix chasing punk hoods or Rerun and Raj concocting another hair-brained scheme at Mama's Cafe. *—Stephen Cook*

Classic 60s Soul / Sep. 30, 1997 / BMG Special Products ✦✦✦
BMG Special Products' *Classic 60s Soul, Vol. 1* is a fairly entertaining sampler of familiar hits and cult singles from the decade. Although the song selection appears random, the ten-track compilation does have a number of good moments, such as Aretha Franklin's "Respect," Wilson Pickett's "In the Midnight Hour," the Friends of Distinction's "Going in Circles," James & Bobby Purify's "Let Love Come Between Us," Otis Redding's "Try a Little Tenderness," Tyrone Davis' "Is It Something That You Got" and the Masqueraders' "I Ain't Got to Love Nobody Else." There's no reason why these were chosen for this compilation, but the end result is a reasonably enjoyable listen. *—Stephen Thomas Erlewine*

Classic 70s Soul / Sep. 30, 1997 / BMG Special Products ✦✦✦
Like its *'60s* companion piece, BMG Special Products' *Classic 70s Soul, Vol. 1* is a fairly entertaining sampler of familiar hits and cult singles from the decade. Although the song selection appears random, the ten-track compilation does have a number of good moments, such as the Spinners' "Could It Be I'm Falling in Love," George McCrae's "Rock Your Baby," Gladys Knight & the Pips' "On and On," the Main Ingredient's "Just Don't Want to Be Lonely," the Moments' "Love on a Two Way Street," Sylvia's "Pillow Talk," the Friends of Distinction's "Love or Let Me Be Lonely" and the Chi-Lites' "A Letter to Myself." Though this collection seems to have been compiled with little rhyme or reason, you can't argue with the quality of the music on board. *—Stephen Thomas Erlewine*

Classic Jazz-Funk, Vol. 1 / 1991 / Mastercuts ✦✦✦✦
The Mastercuts label's great *Classic Jazz-Funk* series kicked off in 1991, and like the remainder of volumes released in its wake throughout the '90s, the first volume more or less concentrates on the '70s end of jazz-funk, as opposed to the form's beginnings during the '60s. Jazz artists were incorporating more potent and often easily danceable backbeats and were also allowing for the R&B of the time to infiltrate their sound, causing purists to shriek in horror at the break from tradition and—just as importantly—the crossover appeal. Though this series was aimed at the rare groove crowd in the U.K. that was at full boil during the '90s, many of these cuts have always been valued in the underground clubs of the U.S.—from David Mancuso's earliest New York Loft parties in the '70s and on through the gatherings that have featured roots-conscious house DJs from Chicago, Detroit, New York, and New Jersey. Not only that, but rap DJs have constantly visited the jazz-funk well for prime sample material. Featured on *Classic Jazz-Funk, Vol. 1* are Donald Byrd's "Change" (perhaps *the* classic jazz-funk song), Gil Scott-Heron's "The Bottle" (a cautionary, gloriously flute-inflected jam with a thick bottom), Johnny

Hammond's "Los Conquistadores Chocolates" (a Latin-tinged delight featuring scratchy guitars, crazy key work, gauzy strings, and just a little flute), and Lonnie Liston Smith & the Cosmic Echoes' "Expansions" (a brilliant, typically soaring keyboard number with endlessly rolling percussion and—of course—some sprightly flute). Other selections from Harvey Mason, Dizzy Gillespie, Ronnie Laws, and Spyro Gyra round out the disc. As with the other volumes in the series, it's a valuable history lesson and an uplifting listen that packs a mighty wallop. *—Andy Kellman*

Classic Rare Groove Mastercuts, Vol. 1 / 1993 / Mastercuts ✦✦✦
Mastercuts' three-volume *Classic Rare Groove* series provides a sampling of the early-'90s U.K.-based phenomenon curated by Norman Jay, the DJ behind London's pirate radio station Kiss FM. The term "rare groove," as defined by Jay through his play lists, encompasses late-'70s and early-'80s dance musics that take in disco, R&B, jazz, funk, and all hybrids of those genres. While each volume has some true treasures, not everything can be expected to be earth-shattering. The first volume features Eighties Ladies' "Turned on to You," Leon Ware's "Why I Came to California," Breakwater's "Say You Love Me Girl," Roberta Gilliam's "All I Want Is My Baby," and Patrice Rushen's "Number One." *—Andy Kellman*

Classic Salsoul Mastercuts, Vol. 1 / 1993 / Mastercuts ✦✦✦✦
Like Salsoul's *Original Salsoul Classics* double-disc set and Charly's three-volume *Salsoul Essentials* series, Mastercuts compiles an impressive batch of Salsoul nuggets for both volumes of *Classic Salsoul Mastercuts*. Included on this first volume: Candido's thumping, blazing "Jingo," Instant Funk's "I Got My Mind Made Up" (one of Larry Levan's hottest remixes for 12-inch), Salsoul Orchestra's kitschy "You're Just the Right Size," the great Leroy Burgess' "Heartbreaker," First Choice's monumental "Let No Man Put Asunder," Double Exposure's "Ten Percent" (the first commercial 12-inch single, remixed by Tom Moulton), and Joe Bataan's excellent, horn-drenched take on Gil Scott-Heron's "The Bottle." Although *Classic Salsoul Mastercuts* wasn't the first to highlight some of the label's output, it's still an invaluable and timeless document of some of the finest dance music recorded. *—Andy Kellman*

Club Africa, Vol. 1: Hard African Funk, Afro-Jazz, & Original Afro-Beat / 1999 / Strut ✦✦✦✦✦
One of a handful of Afro beat/Afro jazz compilations put out by British promoter and DJ Ross Dewbury, *Club Africa* features an infectious blend of '70s cuts informed by Fela's groundbreaking Afro roots and jazz blend. High profile moments come courtesy of Mandingo, Peter King, and Miriam Makeba, revealing the collection's cross-cultural bent in the process. In fact, a good amount here is global, coming from the likes of Columbia's Wganda Kenya, the New York-African group Buari (featuring jazz drummer Bernard Purdie), and the U.S. session band behind Chakachas' funk hit "Jungle Fever." And, yes, there is plenty of Africa here too, not only in all the music of course, but more directly in the Fela-meets-Sunny Ade side "Jungle Funk" by Nigeria's Nkengas and the Afro-Cuban cut "Kenia" by Kenya's Mombasa. The grooves are incredible throughout, making it easy to believe, as Dewbury purports in the liner notes, that this music is "the flavor of '99 with cutting edge DJs." Save for the Gaytones' lifeless rendition of the Manu Dibango hit "Soul Makossa" and the Ashantis' Afro-Allman Brothers jam "Everybody's Groove," it's not hard to see why the hipsters of Dance Nation are getting down to cuts like these. *—Stephen Cook*

Club Soul / Kent ✦✦✦✦
This is soul & R&B from the Scepter/Wand Records catalog that features a few absolute gems among the 16 selections. Jack Montgomery only recorded a few rare singles, and "Dearly Beloved," Montgomery's best, features a once-in-a-lifetime vocal battling a scintillating track. Lee Charles, who appeared on many labels as well, delivers "I Never Want to Lose My Sweet Thing," with spine-tingling passion. Nella Dodds' best recordings were Motown remakes, and "Honey Boy," originally done by Mary Wells is no exception. Chuck Jackson's warm baritone on "Two Stupid Feet," and "Hand It Over," will have you wanting more. The Esquires' "You've Got The Power," led by Gilbert Moorer's crystal shattering falsetto is a sweet, syncopated, *tour de force*. As solid are Candy & the Kisses' "Let Love Win," Big Maybelle's "Oh Lord What Are You Doing to Me," Maxine Brown's "Since I Found You," and Brenton Wood's "Mr. Schemer." A tight package that makes cherry picking individual tracks difficult. *—Andrew Hamilton*

Collection of 16 Big Hits, Vol. 2 / 1982 / Motown ✦✦✦✦
Motown Records released these 16-track compilations from November 1963 until October 1969 (11 volumes); these trendsetters set the bar high for compilation albums. While every song here isn't a smash, they all have that patented Motown sound, which makes for a cohesive package. It originally came out in July 1964 (mono); dropped again in August 1966 (stereo); and was burned on a CD in the '90s. It features quality local and regional songs like the Valadiers' "Greetings This Is Uncle Sam," the Supremes' "Buttered Popcorn," and Eddie Holland's "Leaving Here," along with smashes like "Heat Wave," "Fingertips 2," "I Gotta Dance to Keep From Crying," and "Hitch Hike." *—Andrew Hamilton*

Collector's Choice / Apr. 1996 / Rounder ✦✦✦
An excellent collection in the New Orleans' piano blues style, featuring tracks from various artists with Professor Longhair as the dominant figure, cranking out ten of the 19 songs. Longhair's recordings are from the same era as Fats Domino; Domino scored worldwide with a long list of hits and Longhair became a cult figure, but it's easy to understand the accolades—Longhair's a stone groove to listen to. Vocally, he's similar to Domino, but less colorful; however, the accompanying blues/R&B arrangements, with some charts apparently written for a whistler, even the score. The disc's other nine tracks are performed by Al Johnson, a young Irma Thomas on "Don't Mess With My Man," Joe Jones yakking out "You Talk Too Much," Eddie Bo, and others. Longhair's tracks alone make this an essential item for '60s big easy piano blues lovers. *—Andrew Hamilton*

Come Together: Motown Sings the Beatles / 1994 / Razor & Tie ✦✦
Motown artists covered Beatle songs fairly often during the 1960s, but the results were among neither the better Motown recordings nor the better Beatle covers. This 15-song compilation has renditions of Lennon-McCartney songs (and George Harrison's solo hit "My Sweet Lord") by most of Motown's biggest stars, including the Supremes, Marvin Gaye, Stevie Wonder, the Four Tops, the Temptations, and Gladys Knight. Most of these were used as album filler in the late '60s and early '70s, and favor the too-syrupy style of "sweet soul" production; the Four Tops (who do "Michelle" and "Got to Get You into My Life") fare about the best. In this context, the Supremes' sloppy but energetic 1964 covers of "Can't Buy Me Love" and "A Hard Day's Night" sound better than they really are. This does have the only Beatle song to become a Motown hit (Stevie Wonder's 1971 version of "We Can Work It Out"), another of the highlights on this generally uninspiring collection. *—Richie Unterberger*

☆ **The Complete Stax-Volt Singles 1959–1968** / 1991 / Atlantic ✦✦✦✦✦
At nine discs and 244 tracks, *The Complete Stax-Volt Singles: 1959-1968* is far too exhaustive for casual fans, but that's not who the set is designed for—it's made for the collector. Featuring every A-side the label released during those nine years, as well as several B-sides, the set is a definitive portrait of gritty, deep Southern soul. Many of the genre's major names—Otis Redding, Sam & Dave, Carla Thomas, Booker T. & the MG's, William Bell, Rufus Thomas, the Bar-Kays, Albert King—plus many terrific one-shot wonders are showcased in terrific sound and augmented with an in-depth booklet. For any serious soul or rock collector, it's an essential set, since Stax-Volt was not only was a musically revolutionary label, their roster was deep with talent, which means much of the music on this collection is first-rate. But if you only want the hits, you'll be better off with a smaller collection, since too much of this set will sound too similar, and sorting through the nine discs will be a monumental task if you only want to hear Otis, Rufus, Carla and Sam & Dave. *—Stephen Thomas Erlewine*

The Complete Stax-Volt Soul Singles, Vol. 2: 1968–1971 / 1993 / Stax ✦✦✦✦✦
The first Stax-Volt box was a monolith, standing as the definitive document of the labels and, therefore, gritty Southern soul. Its sequel, *The Complete Stax-Volt Soul Singles, Vol. 2: 1968-1971* is considerably more problematic. Covering only four years compared to its predecessor, which showcased nine years, *Vol. 2* contains 216 tracks, including all of the A- and B-sides released during that era. Most critics consider these four years to be substantially less interesting than Stax's earlier years, and in a sense, they're right. There's no Otis Redding or Sam & Dave, and the music doesn't have the same innovative, kinetic spark of the early years. There's still a lot of great, great music here, but it's difficult to sort it out among these nine discs. About three or four discs' worth of material is truly essential, and it might have been better to boil this era down to a smaller box set, since that would have made for a necessary purchase. As it stands, it's too sprawling and comprehensive to be an essential purchase for anyone other than soul fetishists and hardcore collectors, but those listeners should find much of this fascinating. *—Stephen Thomas Erlewine*

The Complete Stax-Volt Soul Singles, Vol. 3: 1972–1975 / 1994 / Stax ✦✦✦
As the last installment in the three-volume document of the complete Stax-Volt singles, *Vol. 3: 1972-1975* is by far the weakest of the series. During those four years, the label was winding down, since it was unable to successfully make the transition from gritty soul to smoother soul and disco. Their older artists couldn't handle the newer sound, and the newer artists were generally saddled with undistinguished songs. In other words, there weren't many great singles from this era, which is what makes listening to *The Complete Stax-Volt Soul Singles, Vol. 3: 1972-1975* such a chore. While the sound of the set is pleasant, evoking both the funky and smooth soul of the early '70s quite well, the songs and the performances aren't particularly noteworthy. There's about a disc and a half worth of prime material scattered across this set, and only die-hard collectors and fetishists will have the patience to find them. Still, those dedicated listeners will find the box a nice way to conclude the series, since it is a well-produced and comprehensive set, even if the music itself is uneven. *—Stephen Thomas Erlewine*

Constellation of Soul, Vols. 1-2 / Apr. 22, 1997 / Collectables ✦✦✦
Although active for only three years during the mid-'60s, Chicago's Constellation label scored with a few soul hits, most coming from their two big acts: Gene Chandler and Dee Clark. This wrap-up of the Constellation sound includes only four from Chandler and none from Clark—since they're represented on their own collections—so its value immediately slips a bit. The songwriting and production values don't rate too high either, but the level of performances from the artists make a much stronger bid for immortality. The opener (and the best track, hands down) is the full version of Chandler's hit "Rainbow '65," during which one of Chicago's best testifiers spends six minutes expertly teasing a largely female audience into hysterics with the most playful of pleadings. New Orleans legend Lee Dorsey is represented with a pair of average sides, while Nolan Chance (who replaced Chandler in the Dukays) scored a regional hit with the countrified "She's Gone (And She Won't Be Back)." The rest are period soul sides, capable of placing any listener squarely in the sound of 1965 but certainly lacking the timeless qualities of classic soul music. *—John Bush*

The Cream of Vintage Soul, Vol. 1 / May 1998 / Life On Mars ✦✦✦✦✦
This three-CD compilation from Mars Records is loaded with familiar artists doing unfamiliar songs. Known tunes are the Parliaments' "I Wanna Testify," Eddie Holman's "This Can't Be True," and Bob & Earl's "Harlem Shuffle." The rest—like Frank Beverly's "Love (Your Pain Goes Deep)," the Dynamics' "Bingo," David Ruffin's "You're Still in My Heart," and the Flirtations' "Settle Down"—will be strangers to most ears. L.J. Reynolds

& the Relations weigh in with "We're in the Middle," recorded prior to Reynolds' association with the Dramatics. There are also tracks by J.J. Barnes, Darrell Banks, and many others. *—Andrew Hamilton*

☆ **Creole Kings of New Orleans** / 1992 / Specialty ✦✦✦✦✦
Creole Kings of New Orleans is a splendid 26-track sampler of Specialty Records' numerous R&B legends, including Professor Longhair, Percy Mayfield, Lloyd Price, Joe Liggins, and Guitar Slim. Although only a couple of big hits are included, the material is consistently strong, making the disc an excellent purchase. *—Stephen Thomas Erlewine*

Creole Kings of New Orleans, Vol. 2 / 1993 / Specialty ✦✦✦
Here are 25 New Orleans R&B/rock/blues sides from the 1950s, taken from the vaults of Specialty, Ebb, and Regal Records. There aren't any big hits here (though some did well on the R&B charts), and despite the presence of names like Lloyd Price, Professor Longhair, Guitar Slim, Clifton Chenier, and Larry Williams, there are several other vintage Crescent City R&B collections that you should pick up before getting to this one. It's sort of generic, if on the whole quite acceptable. Its appeal will primarily lie in the R&B collector crowd, due to obscure tracks by the above-mentioned names (including Price's follow-up singles to his famous "Lawdy Miss Clawdy") and unknowns like Willie Johnson, Roy Montrell, and Ernest Kador (who became Ernie K-Doe of "Mother-In-Law" fame). There are also curious demos of "Good Golly Miss Molly" (by Bumps Blackwell) and "All Around the World" (Li'l Millet), which are much more renowned via the versions cut by Little Richard. *—Richie Unterberger*

☆ **Crescent City Soul: The Sound of New Orleans** / Apr. 2, 1996 / EMI ✦✦✦✦✦
This is the new king of the hill as far as retrospectives of early New Orleans R&B/rock go. This four-CD, 119-song box has hits by all of the major artists and hits and misses by most of the important minor ones as well. The standards for inclusion are flexible and reasonable: Although New Orleans residents usually carry the day, important records that were recorded in New Orleans by non-natives are also featured. Fats Domino, Little Richard, Irma Thomas, Lee Dorsey, Smiley Lewis, Chris Kenner, Barbara George, Ernie K-Doe, Clarence "Frogman" Henry, Lloyd Price, Aaron Neville, Professor Longhair, Shirley & Lee, and Dr. John are all here, as are one-shots and regional figures like the Showmen, Earl King, Benny Spellman, Dave Bartholomew, and the Spiders. There are plenty of hits, but also plenty of fine songs that most listeners won't be aware of: the original versions of "My Ding-A-Ling" (two of them!), "I'm Gonna Be a Wheel Someday," and "One Night," for instance, which were covered for huge smashes by Fats Domino, Chuck Berry, and Elvis Presley. It's not perfect: the absence of Frankie Ford's "Sea Cruise" is absolutely inexcusable, and the omission of hits like "Blueberry Hill," "Ya Ya," and "Rocking Pneumonia" only slightly less mystifying. It's still the best chunk of New Orleans rock/R&B in one place, with more than enough variety to make the lengthy set a pleasure all the way through. *—Richie Unterberger*

Crooklyn / 1995 / MCA ✦✦✦✦✦
Spike Lee's *Crooklyn* is a touching coming-of-age film, set in the early '70s. Appropriately, the soundtrack is crammed with an abundance of smooth soul and gritty R&B from the era. *—Stephen Thomas Erlewine*

Crooklyn, Vol. 2 / 1995 / MCA ✦✦✦
The second collection of songs from Spike Lee's *Crooklyn* is nearly good as the first, featuring a wealth of first-rate '70s soul and R&B. *—Stephen Thomas Erlewine*

Cruisin' With Porky Chedwick / Dec. 16, 1995 / Increase ✦✦✦✦
A compilation of heavyweight doo wop groups including the Flamingos, the Spaniels, the Del-Vikings, the Skyliners, Harvey & the Moonglows, and Joe Turner—artists played by Porky Chedwick back in the day when he was Pittsburgh's hottest DJ. A short CD consisting of only 12 tracks (ten if you don't count "Porky's Intro" and "Porky's Theme"). One small hiccup, "Those Oldies but Goodies (Remind Me of You)," is not the most popular version by Little Caesar & the Romans but a good-to-go rendition by Nino & the Ebbtides. The airwave jewels include the Moonglows' "The Ten Commandments of Love," Joe Turner's "Flip, Flop and Fly," and the Marcels' incredible "Blue Moon." *—Andrew Hamilton*

CTI Records: The Birth of Groove / Sep. 2, 1997 / Sony ✦✦✦✦
CTI Records: Birth of Groove is a budget-priced, ten-track sampler that was designed to promote Sony's 1997 reissue of the CTI catalog. During the '70s, CTI was one of the leading fusion and jazz-rock labels, boasting a roster full of big names like Stanley Turrentine, George Benson, Milt Jackson, Esther Phillips and Deodato. All of those musicians, plus several others, are showcased on *Birth of Groove*, which offers an excellent portrait of the smooth, laidback, vaguely funky jazz that was the label's trademark. For the curious, it's a neat way to become acquainted with the label. *—Stephen Thomas Erlewine*

Curiosities: The Ace '70s Singles and Sessions / Jul. 11, 2000 / WestSide ✦✦✦✦
A two disc set of Johnny Vincent's Ace Records releases from the '70s. This double-disc collection is a curious mixture of new vocals pasted on old recycled band tracks, plus blues, soul, and rock & roll from folks like Little Shelton, George "Cryin' in the Streets" Perkins, Guitar Reed, Bobby Marchan, Mack Allen Smith, Dicky Williams, Earl Gaines, and Bobby Jay, even a stray track from Willie Dixon. No hits were forthcoming from this second resurrection of Vincent's Ace imprint, but some interesting music emerged nonetheless. *—Cub Koda*

● **The Curtom Story** / 1996 / Charly ✦✦✦✦✦
Charly Records' 51-song double-CD *Curtom Story* is the perfect companion volume to Rhino's Curtis Mayfield triple-CD set, with surprisingly little overlap-more than 30 artists are represented, not only Curtis Mayfield (two songs) and the Impressions (five songs), and the expected stars like the Stairsteps, Leroy Hutson, the Natural Four, and Linda Clifford, but also Gene Chandler, Jamo Thomas (who was on Eddie Thomas's self-named label), the Fascinations, June Conquest, Donny Hathaway, Major Lance, Cash McCall, the Amazers, the Winstons, the Symphonics, the Stridells, Baby Huey, Bobby Franklin's Insanity, Moses Dillard & the Tex Town Display, Jesse Anderson, Freddie Waters, the Triplett Twins, the Notations, the Staple Singers, Mavis Staples, and Fred Wesley. What's more, there's hardly a weak track anywhere on this set, which is also annotated with extraordinary thoroughness by Trevor Swaine. Additionally, in contrast to some Charly reissues of the 1980s, *The Curtom Story* boasts stunning sound. The hits by each of these artists are here, from Jamo Thomas' 1966 "I Spy (For the F.B.I.)" to Fred Wedley's "House Party," from 1980, a range and a time-span that speak volumes about Curtom Records' importance in the R&B field-even the non-hits such as the Mayfield Singers' "I've Been Trying" show off a level of style and sophistication in its arrangement that pointed toward Curtis Mayfield's ambitious early '70s solo work; and even where the material isn't groundbreaking in some respect, as in the case of June Conquest's "What's This I See," the Amazers' "Without a Warning," the Symphonics' "Guilty" (with a delicious baritone sax solo that comes out of nowhere), or the Winstons' gloriously harmonized "Need a Replacement," it's so eminently listenable and enjoyable on its own terms, that the set is irresistiable, especially the first disc, covering the earlier history of the company. The disco era material may be a little hard to absorb for those attuned to the label's earlier sound, but the assembly of tracks is so careful, that one more or less eases into that period, and there are so many hard-to-find singles included here, that it should be a part of any serious soul CD collection. *—Bruce Eder*

Dance Like the Devil: Pye Northern Soul, Chapter 1 / Nov. 24, 1998 / Sequel ✦✦✦
As time marches on and proper recognition has started coming toward Brit soulsters like Dusty Springfield, this collection is the first entry in reassessing the Northern soul movement in England in the mid-'60s and how the British attempted to come up with their own version of it. This fat-cat, 30-track collection brings together artists black and white, British, West Indian and American, all cutting soulful sounds for the British Pye label. Rather than carbon copies of the legendary soul hits, what we have here—with a few notable exceptions—is a collection of strong original material performed in a solid approximation of an American style. Highlights are numerous, including Jimmy James' "This Heart of Mine," Jason Knight's "Our Love Is Getting Stronger," Ebony Keyes' "If You Knew," Kenny Roberts' poppish "Run Like the Devil," Lorraine Silver's "Lost Summer Love," and Petula Clark's "A Sign of the Times," the biggest hit on here. Interesting covers also abound in Sounds Orchestral's 100-mph rendition of "Black Is Black," Geno Washington's "She Shot a Hole in My Soul," Helen Shapiro's "Take Me for a Little While," Jackie Trent's "You Baby" and Tammy St. John's "Nobody Knows What's Going On." The other side of the British Invasion that didn't make it to American shores. *—Cub Koda*

Dancing 'til Dawn / Nov. 20, 1995 / Kent ✦✦✦
There are numerous 1960s soul compilations on the Kent label that seem geared for the Northern soul crowd in the U.K.: soul music with a danceable tempo—a trait to be prized above all others, including content. This assemblage of 25 tracks from the 1960s and early 1970s, all originally issued on the Scepter/Wand label and subsidiaries, is average or maybe a bit below average as far as such collections go. Much of Scepter's output epitomized the poppy, uptown New York soul sound, which is heard often here. Though the stomp-beats might be reliable, the songs are run-of-the-mill, and sometimes derivative, particularly of Motown. Some of Scepter's best acts are here—the Shirelles, Maxine Brown, Chuck Jackson, and Tommy Hunt—but they're not represented by their best tracks. If you really like those singers and/or the Scepter sound in general, you're far better off getting into their single-artist compilations. But of course that's not the point; those comps would be too diverse for nonstop, dancefloor action. Among this reissue's highlights is the big 1967 hit "Get on Up" by the Esquires, for the soul fan who somehow doesn't have that. There's also some competent blue-eyed soul from unexpected sources: Ronnie Milsap's 1966 single "Ain't No Soul (Left in These Ole Shoes)," produced by Huey Meaux, who also did B.J. Thomas' "I Don't Have a Mind of My Own" (also here) in that same year. There's a smattering of cuts by singers known for things other than their Scepter work (Al Wilson, all-around entertainer Leslie Uggams, and Eartha Kitt, who imitates the Supremes on "There Comes a Time"). A reissue like this is not all it should be, though, when it's more interesting rattling off the oddities from the track listings than it is describing the music. *—Richie Unterberger*

● **Dangerous Doo Wop, Vol. 1** / 198 / DDW ✦✦✦✦✦
One of the most enjoyable of R&B vocal collections, this first volume of the *Dangerous Doo Wop* series not only offers a first-rate entrée into the music, but should intrigue collectors as well. The familiar sounds of the Chords' "Sh-Boom" and the Robins' rendition of "White Cliffs of Dover" are included along with such marginalia as the Blisters' "Shortnin Bread" and the Poets' "Vowels of Love." Full of hits or not, the 20 numbers here are high quality, spanning the range of straight a cappella to combo R&B. The rich vocal tradition born in black churches is given secular wings throughout, informing both the Velvet Angels' utterly transcendent "I'm in Love" and King Odom 4's sublimely terrestrial "All of Me." And adding to the fun are the Larks' Ink Spots-inspired "Lucy Brown," the Monograms' malt shop bit of innocence "My Baby Dearest Darling," and Flamingos' rock & roll jumpin' "Let's Make Up." A record that never gets old. *—Stephen Cook*

Dave Godin's Deep Soul Treasures: Taken From Our Vaults, Vol. 1 / May 20, 1997 / Kent ✦✦✦✦
Dave Godin is a big name, perhaps the biggest in British soul scholarship. He was a writer and critic in *Blues & Soul* magazine in the 1960s and 1970s, and an all-around promoter and collector who was instrumental in getting much American soul released in the U.K. This is his personal selection, accompanied by almost 10,000 words in liner

notes, of 25 of his favorite "Deep Soul" tracks (a term that, according to his notes, he coined himself) from the 1960s and early 1970s. There are no songs by Otis Redding, Aretha Franklin, or the like here, so presumably the cuts were also chosen with an eye toward how undeservedly unknown they are. Irma Thomas, represented by the original 1964 mono single version of "Anyone Who Know What Love Is (Will Understand)," is the sole name likely to be familiar to non-fanatics. The main qualification for inclusion is the intensity of the vocal performances, and on that grounds this disc certainly delivers; the life-dependent emotion puts this, in some senses, closer to gospel than pop. As far as this anthology representing the alpha and omega of the best rare "deep soul," it's been a little overhyped. It's certainly leagues above the average soul rarity compilation (including many done by the same Kent label), in part because it licenses from so many sources, rather than just one or two labels as such collections are apt to do. It also doesn't focus exclusively on soloists, adding group vocal performances with more of a pop and doo wop influence here and there. The songs and singers, though, aren't as striking as they are on the records made by the best soul stars. Is it the best compilation of rare deep soul, then? Well, it's up there, although some of the tunes are more generic than Godin seems willing to admit, and the slow-to-midtempo churchy arrangements can get a bit stifling all at once. As for songs that should definitely be better known, Kenny Carter's almost apocalyptically operatic "Showdown," actually written for (and turned down by) the Moody Blues as a possible follow-up to "Go Now," is certainly a lost classic. Zerben R. Hicks' "Lights Out" features a taut drama that crosses from the simply intense to the haunting. Raw Spitt's "Songs to Sing" has a specific social consciousness missing from most of the tracks here; it is comparable to the material Swamp Dogg put on his early-'70s albums, which is no surprise as Swamp Dogg produced Mr. Spitt (aka Charlie Whitehead). *—Richie Unterberger*

Dave Godin's Deep Soul Treasures: Taken From Our Vaults, Vol. 2 / Feb. 12, 1999 / Kent ✦✦✦✦✦

Here are 25 "deep soul" (the term used to refer to soul music that has a generally slow tempo and is seriously emotional) tracks from 1964-1975. There are a few stars here and there (Otis Redding, Carla Thomas, Ben E. King, Arthur Conley and Irma Thomas, although none of them do hits) and even a couple of cuts that have appeared on widely circulated compilations (Bessie Banks' original version of "Go Now," which was covered for a hit by the Moody Blues, and Toussaint McCall's "Nothing Takes the Place of You"). Generally, though, it's the kind of obscure material that the average Joe can't get access to without getting some rabid soul collector to make a tape for him. Dave Godin is such a collector, and his compilations have received glowing press notices in the U.K., though they don't match the summit of soul compilations (various ones on Rhino are better) that include better-known material. It's a decent assembly of good obscure soul, not much of which screams "overlooked masterpiece," and the constant slow grooves can get dull at times. It *is* better (and more craftily sequenced and annotated) than most obscure soul compilations (including some on the Kent label) that compilers trumpet as killer discs even though they're just anthologies of average soul tracks that happen to be very rare. If you're not a completist but are on the lookout for good cuts that have escaped your attention, check out Conley's "Let Nothing Separate Us," which didn't make it onto his Ichiban best-of comp; Ruby Johnson's "I'll Run Your Hurt Away," a 1966 Volt single that stands up to Redding's better tracks, albeit with appealingly raw female vocals; the Premiers' "Make It Me," which like the Johnson cut is a good mid-'60s Stax production written by David Porter and Isaac Hayes; George Perkins' quizzical "Cryin' in the Streets"; and Lisa Richards' "Let's Take a Chance," which is like '60s soul accented with the feel of doo wop groups like Rosie & the Originals. *—Richie Unterberger*

Dave Godin's Deep Soul Treasures: Taken From Our Vaults, Vol. 3 / Oct. 31, 2000 / Kent ✦✦✦✦

The third installment of this well-respected series of (mostly) rare and (mostly) 1960s deep soul maintains the high standards of the previous two releases. The compiler bends just a little in the direction of greater accessibility here by including more names and songs that might actually be known to people with less than a few hundred soul records in their collections. Not that there are any songs that you'll hear on the average oldies radio show, but names like Carla Thomas, James Brown, Bobby Womack, the Impressions, and Bobby "Blue" Bland are pretty well-known to many Joe Q. Publics. And songs like Irma Thomas' "Wish Someone Would Care," Etta James' "I'd Rather Go Blind," and Maxine Brown's "All in My Mind" (the original 1961 hit version that usually eludes reissue anthologies, not a remake) are actually familiar, though not exactly overplayed. Far from being a sellout, this actually enhances the listenability of the disc, which is still largely populated by rarities, some excellent, some just alright. Highlights this time around include Baby Washington's "Breakfast in Bed," more famous as sung by Dusty Springfield; Bessie Banks' Brill Building-flavored "It Sounds Like My Baby," the flipside of the original "Go Now"; Syl Johnson's "Is It Because I'm Black," which adds some much-needed blues-funk grit and social conscience; and Betty Lavette's "Let Me Down Easy," a classic of anguished soul. Rick James' 1983 single "Ebony Eyes" has no business being here, though—far from being "deep soul," it's shallow as a puddle. *—Richie Unterberger*

Dave Hamilton's Detroit Dancers / Mar. 10, 1998 / Kent ✦✦✦

Dave Hamilton's Detroit Dancers compiles mostly obscure material to which the Detroit session guitarist contributed his funky, grooving licks, including sides from Hamilton himself, Little Ann, Tobi Lark, Priscilla Page, and JT Rhythm. *—Steve Huey*

Dave Hamilton's Detroit Dancers, Vol. 2 / Dec. 14, 1999 / Kent ✦✦✦

Dave Hamilton was a producer, session musician, and songwriter on the Detroit soul scene starting in the 1960s. You can't really tell that from the liner notes, which basically say nothing about Hamilton's role in this music other than that the CD was compiled from his collection of tapes. It can be presumed, though, that Hamilton was involved in all of these records in some capacity, and he does have songwriter and production credits on some of the tracks. Most of them date from the mid- to late '60s, although some were done as late as the early '80s; some were unreleased demo-type tracks, and several came out on the Topper and TCB labels, indicating that Hamilton might have been involved with those companies. So, the music? It's acceptable, and not exceptional, period Detroit soul. As was the case with several small Detroit-area soul labels of the time, it often sounds like a minor-league Motown (indeed, Hamilton played on some Motown sessions himself). Motown is a good model, but nonetheless, adhering to a role model does not, in fact almost always does not, mean the resultant product stands up to the prototype, and that's the case here. Sometimes the micro-model is obvious; Tobi Lark's "Challenge My Love" sounds a lot like a Mary Wells song, "Ain't That Groovy" (an instrumental by the Dave Hamilton Band) like a Marvin Gaye backing track, Dottie & Millie like an amalgam of the Marvelettes and early Supremes—you get the picture. It's not bad, but there's the nagging feeling that the musicians involved were just below the standard good enough to get involved with Motown itself. As is the case with several Kent/Ace compilations, the decision to sprinkle in a few disco- and urban contemporary-influenced cuts from a decade or later than the end of the 1960s disrupts the groove as surely as a hoseful of cold water in the face. *—Richie Unterberger*

The Dawn of Doo-Wop / May 7, 2002 / Proper Box ✦✦✦

England's Proper label issued this 100-track attempt to sum up the state of black harmony groups between 1940 and 1952. Though there's a lot of incredible music from the era, this four-disc set overly concentrates on slow ballads instead of uptempo numbers. The first disc, "Digging the Roots," begins right where it should, with tracks by the forefathers of doo wop: the Mills Brothers and the Ink Spots. Unfortunately, instead of a swinging track like "Tiger Rag" or even "The Glow Worm," *The Dawn of Doo-Wop* programs the Mills Brothers' "Paper Doll" and "You Always Hurt the One You Love" and the Ink Spots' "When the Swallows Come Back to Capistrano." Following hot on their heels are a variety of groups influenced by either (or both) of the above, including the Four Vagabonds, the Toppers, the Syncopaters, the Deep River Boys, and, best of all, the Ravens. Most of these are ballads too, with only a pair of good-time, uptempo songs: "Shorty's Got to Go" by Bill Johnson & His Musical Notes and "Boogie Woogie on a Saturday Night" by Steve Gibson & the Red Caps. The second disc, "Birdland," has 25 tracks, all by "bird" groups (the Orioles, the Larks, the Swallows, the Ravens, the Robins, etc.), while the third, "Doo-Wop Dreamin'," slows the tempo even more. Finally, the set gets moving a bit on the final disc ("Doo-Wop Dancin'"), with swinging novelties from the Swallows ("It Ain't the Meat"), the Royales ("Too Much of a Little Bit"), the Dominoes ("Sixty Minute Man"), the Treniers ("Go Go Go"), and the Clovers ("Fool Fool Fool"). Fans of doo wop will undoubtedly discover many new groups on this set, but wading through all the down-tempo material is quite a chore. *—John Bush*

Dead Presidents / Oct. 1995 / Capitol ✦✦✦✦✦

The soundtrack to the Hughes Brothers' tribute to early-'70s blaxploitation gets the sound of the era right, featuring hits by the O'Jays, the Spinners, Isaac Hayes, Al Green, and Harold Melvin & the Blue Notes, among others. The inclusion of Danny Elfman's instrumental theme interrupts the flow of the album, but for the most part, *Dead Presidents* is a first-rate collection of prime soul. *—Stephen Thomas Erlewine*

Deep Grooves/Prelude / Oct. 24, 1994 / Sequel ✦✦✦✦✦

A British CD compilation pieced together in 1993, *Deep Grooves* functions effectively as a succinct summation of Prelude's influential contribution to electronic dance music, bridging the gap between disco and garage/house. While the tracks aren't sequenced chronologically, the liner notes do provide dates, allowing the listener to map out the New York label's evolution from Sine's "Just Let Me Do My Thing" from 1977 to Unique's "What I Got Is What You Need" from 1983. Along the way, the sounds get increasingly reliant on synthesizers rather than traditional instrumentation, alluding to the rise of electronic dance music. It's hard to pinpoint exact highlights on the album, since every song here was an underground anthem and few crossed over to mainstream success. Strictly from an aesthetic standpoint, Saturday Night Band's "Come on Dance, Dance" may be the best song here while Hi-Gloss' "You'll Never Know" is the album's most poetic moment, a true disco ballad. True to the spirit of Prelude, each of the songs feature prominent use of female diva vocals that tend to focus on various romantic themes, peaking during the uplifting choruses. In fact, little electronic dance music was ever able to duplicate the Prelude sound, which didn't follow a specific musical template in terms of specific sounds and was highly reliant on its verse-chorus-verse vocals to carry the weight of the song. *—Jason Birchmeier*

Deep in the Philly Groove / 1995 / Kent ✦✦✦✦

In line with the company's generally excellent R&B compilations, Kent's *Deep in the Philly Groove* does right by the stellar legacy of Stan Watson's '70s soul label, Philly Groove. Along with Thom Bell, Kenny Gamble, & Leon Huff's Philly International Records, Philly Groove helped define the '70s soul sound and set the stage for a wide range of R&B and pop hits to come—Gamble & Huff's Philly bump rhythm certainly had an impact on disco. Featuring two of the biggest hits from the label's most successful group, the Delfonics ("La-La (Means I Love You)" and "Didn't I (Blow Your Mind This Time)"), the 24 tracks spotlight equally worthy harmony groups like First Choice (the female trio was the label's other success story, thanks to smashes like "Armed and Extremely Dangerous" and "Smarty Pants") and Nat Turner's Rebellion, featuring Major Harris, a future Delfonic, and Phil Spratley, the singer who would replace Harold Melvin after his split from the Blue Notes. And this is not to forget several excellent cuts by Ben Aiken (a past beneficiary of Jerry Ragovoy's stellar production work at Roulette and Loma) and a few shots from the underling likes of Broadway Express and the Coup de

Villes. Topped off with those choice Philly Groove charts (lush strings and vocals anchored by smooth soul-funk grooves) by Watson & Bell, *Deep in the Philly Groove* gives air to one of the best labels cutting sides during that fertile transition from early soul to high-tech funk and disco—be sure to also check out the equally impressive sequel, *Deeper in the Philly Groove*. —*Stephen Cook*

Deep Note: Music of 1970's Adult Cinema / Jan. 22, 2002 / Ost ♦♦♦
If you've ever wondered what '70s porn movies sounded like, this would be a prime example, containing highly obscure, warbled funk instrumentals by anonymous musicians laced with all the typical sexy trimmings of muted flutes, salty organs, wah-wah guitars, and plenty of heavy moaning. This is best represented by *Orgasmatron 75*'s "Boob Tube," which epitomizes the sexy porno sound of a decadent decade—a slow, watery funk groove crackles with dusty organs and seedy horns, culminating in a detective-like theme finale. Further conjuring a grainy time-period haze, "Love Dance," "My Cousin Hanne," "Psychedelic Orgy," and "On the Prowl" also display satisfying variations of the suggestive genre. What's unfortunate, though, is that the majority of these selections are merely short snippets of explicit disjointed dialogue that would be routinely fast-forwarded on videotape and instead fill in for where music could be. Nostalgia-seekers may find *Deep Note: Music of 1970's Adult Cinema* interesting, but casual listeners will discover that it's never as good the second time around and perhaps best left for those who lived it. —*Craig Curtice*

Deeper in the Philly Groove / May 12, 1999 / Kent ♦♦♦
A sequel to the Kent compilation *Deep in the Philly Groove*, this goes pretty far into the vaults of the Philly Groove soul label, which was most noted for hits by the Delfonics and First Choice. A few tracks by each of those acts are on this 23-track disc, but most of the names will be unfamiliar even to many soul experts, e.g. Nat Turner Rebellion (great name), Tapestry, Mary Holmes, the Finishing Touch, Major Harris, and the Quickest Way Out; five of the selections were previously unreleased. As you'd expect, the production is super-lush almost without exception. Even when a song wasn't a hit, or obviously wasn't going to be a hit, the producers and arrangers certainly seemed to pull no punches with the budget, especially with the creamy harmonies and strings (and discoish rhythms on the later numbers). It's that *sound*, rather than the songs, which will attract some sweet soul fans to the compilation, because there aren't any obvious overlooked classics or hits-that-should-been. Indeed all at once it's rather too sweet for easy digestion, but if you like the style, it's like tuning into a vintage soul station and suddenly hearing lots of songs that fit the format like a glove, yet are mostly or entirely unfamiliar. Ones to listen for are the Delfonics' previously unreleased "You'll Get Enough," co-written by Thom Bell; "Merry-Go-Round" by David Lasley, who would later be in Chic; and First Choice's "Gotta Get Away (From You Baby)," which sounds like a disco hit despite its modest number 64 showing on the R&B charts. —*Richie Unterberger*

Deepest Soul, Vol. 2: Soul Confessions from the 70's / 1997 / Goldmine/Soul Supply ♦♦♦
A true blue Northern soul compilation, loaded with obscure tunes performed by obscure artists; if you didn't tune in to the right AM stations back in the day, you missed these songs entirely. Truth's "Come Back Home" reminds you of the O'Jays, and for good reason, Bobby Massey (an O'Jays member at the time) produced and co-wrote the track. Detroiter Bobby O' Brown's "I Can Feel My Love Growing" ably represents this album's theme—slow, dramatic soul, as does, Clevelander Jessie Fisher's "I Can't Stop Loving You," and Betty Fykes wailing "Glory of Love." —*Andrew Hamilton*

Del-Fi Doo-Wop, Vol. 3: Honey for Sale / Feb. 17, 1998 / Del-Fi ♦♦
The least impressive entry in Del-Fi's doo wop series has fair but undistinguished obscurities, some of which (as in the series' other installments) lean closer to rock & roll or even early soul than classic doo wop. There's an early-'60s, pre-Motown effort by Brenda Holloway, and Earl Nelson (later half of Bob & Earl of "Harlem Shuffle" fame) has a couple of sides under the moniker Chip Nelson. Prentice Moreland definitely chalks up the weirdest tracks, with his R&B-Charlie Chan fusion on "Chinese Junk," and an exotica-tinged R&B ballad with "Looking for Your Heart." —*Richie Unterberger*

Del-Fi Girl Groups: Gee Baby Gee / Apr. 20, 1999 / Del-Fi ♦♦♦
Overall, Del-Fi's version of the girl group sound leans closer to the Shangri-Las and the early Motown side of the equation than the Spector or more well known Brill Building sounds. But this 21-track collection of singles from Bob Keane's various labels truly has its own flavor, and a tasty one at that. With the Chicano trio known as the Sisters establishing the core of this compilation doing the title cut and six others in a East L.A. variant of the formula, noteworthy tracks from Desda (a version of "Splish Splash" that skirts the outer edges of melody), and a 16-year-old Mary Sawrey make this a nice addition to anybody's girl group collection. —*Cub Koda*

Delicious Doo-Wop and Tasty Treats, Vol. 1 / 2000 / Itzy ♦♦♦
This zany concept CD about "eats" never strays, running for 30 tracks from appetizers to entrees. Novelty lovers will relish the Genie's "Chicken Necks," Andre Williams & the Five Dollars' "Bacon Fat," "A Chicken Ain't Nothing But a Bird" by the Echos, Marvin & Johnny's "Butterball," Lil Joe & the Thrillers' "Peanuts" (in two versions, no less), and dozens of other scrumptious morsels. —*Andrew Hamilton*

Delicious Doo-Wop and Tasty Treats, Vol. 2 / 2000 / Hot Dog ♦♦♦
The second in a series of compilations consisting of edibly-themed doo wop tunes insures the concept is well done with morsels like "Rock and Egg Roll" by the Four Tunes, "Sweet Potato" by Marvin & Johnny, the Castletones' "No Pork in the Beans," and the Rays' "Moo Goo Gai Pan." The CD's 31 tracks include three bonus numbers by Danny Overbea, Billy Love, and Rusty Isabelle, plus two takes of the Chips' "Rubber Biscuit." —*Andrew Hamilton*

Detroit Soul Music Rarities / Jan. 16, 1996 / Starr Digital ♦♦♦♦
This 30-song collection of recordings from Detroit's Lupine label includes the Primettes' (later to become the Supremes) "Tears of Sorrow," and "Pretty Baby." Wilson Pickett's screams on "I Found a Love" will give you shivers. Falcons members Joe Stubbs and Eddie Floyd both fly solo; Stubbs is impressive on "Part Time Love" and "You Must Know I Love You," but if Floyd's tracks hadn't been labeled, you'd never guess it was Mr. "Knock on Wood," as he approaches a totally different sound. Lupine's crude, unpolished recordings are treasures, and prime cuts like Betty Lavette's "You Killed the Love," and the Ohio Untouchables "I'm Tired" (the group would later become the Ohio Players) are spine tingling. —*Andrew Hamilton*

Diggin' in the Crates for Beats Y'all / Apr. 9, 1996 / Hot Productions ♦♦♦♦
Hot Productions' collection of early-'80s electro goes beyond the average to include a few lesser-known tracks from the seminal era. Beside the easily available classics ("Planet Rock," "Jam on It," "Set It Off," "Electric Kingdom," "Hip Hop Bee Bop (Don't Stop)"), obscure acts like Quadrant 6, George Kranz (with the original "Din Daa Daa") and Key-Matic (the hilarious "Breaking in Space") make *Diggin' in the Crates* more enjoyable than the average electro compilation. —*John Bush*

Disco 54: Funkin' on the Floor / Apr. 21, 1998 / Hip-O ♦♦♦
Hip-O's second entry into their vintage disco collection starts heading into mainstream hits with more emphasis on name artists as well. Hits aboard on this 12-track collection include the Dramatics' "Shake It Well," the Crusaders' "Street Life," Bootsy's Rubber Band's "The Pinocchio Theory," the Bar-Kays' "Holy Ghost," Parliament's "Flash Light" and Rufus featuring Chaka Khan's "Dance Wit Me." This compilation also includes some great one-off sides by Mass Production ("Firecracker"), Tom Browne ("Funkin' for Jamaica (N.Y.)"), Rose Royce ("Put Your Money Where Your Mouth Is"), GQ ("Disco Nights (Rock Freak))," Stargard ("Theme Song From "Which Way Is Up") and Vaughan Mason & Crew ("Bounce, Rock, Skate, Roll—Pt. 1") to fill things out. —*Cub Koda*

Disco 54: The AVI Collection / Mar. 24, 1998 / Hip-O ♦♦♦
This is one strong compilation of '70s disco material from the vaults of AVI Records. This was the period in the music's history when independent producers could get a record out and into clubs for pennies a serving, starting a whole scene in the clubs that proliferates to this day and did much to rejuvenate the independent side of the record industry. Dance-worthy highlights include Sweet Potato Pie's "Hot Disco Night (Are You Ready?)," and El Coco's "Cocomotion," "Caravan," and "Let's Get It Together," Dave Williams' Inner Circle with "Come on Down, Boogie People," and Eastbound Expressway's "Never Let Me Go." Tracks by Davis Import ("I'm Glad You're Mine"), James Wells ("True Love Is My Destiny"), Rinder & Lewis ("Lust") and Captain Sky ("Super Sporm") round out the package. —*Cub Koda*

Disco 54: The Studio Collection / Mar. 11, 1997 / Hip-O ♦♦♦
This features 14 disco cuts from the genre's prime (1976 to 1979), including selections from Chic, the Brides of Funkenstein, Cameo, Rose Royce, Rufus, Quincy Jones, and Dr. Buzzard's Original "Savannah" Band. Disco lovers will dig this, but it's far from the best survey available, especially due to its total lack of liner notes. —*Richie Unterberger*

Disco 54: Where We Started From / Apr. 21, 1998 / Hip-O ♦♦♦
The third volume in Hip-O's vintage collection of vintage disco material includes sides from the Dramatics ("You're Fooling You"), B.T. Express ("Do It ('Til You're Satisfied))," Tavares ("It Only Takes a Minute"), Blue Magic ("Welcome to the Club"), Ace Spectrum ("Don't Send Nobody Else") and Maxine Nightingale's title track.This also features sides from R&B artists attempting to make the switch over to the disco beat, including Eddie Kendricks ("Girl, You Need a Change of Mind"), the Four Tops ("Catfish") and the wildly thumping "Shame, Shame, Shame" from Shirley & Company. Tracks from S.O.U.L. ("This Time Around"), Don Downing ("Dreamworld"), Maryann Farra & Satin Soul ("Stoned Out of My Mind"), Lonnie Liston Smith & the Cosmic Echoes ("Expansions") and First Choice ("Armed and Extremely Dangerous," presented here in a previously unreleased extended version) complete the package. —*Cub Koda*

Disco Boogie, Vol. 1 / Sep. 17, 1996 / Salsoul ♦♦♦♦♦
The only compilation that actually translates the transcendent feel of a disco club onto wax, *Disco Boogie, Vol. 1* is quadruple-sided LP mix set featuring Salsoul classics mixed with help from Tom Moulton and Walter Gibbons, among others. Though it's a shame that individual mixes last under 20 minutes, the chunky beats and warm vibes of tracks by Claudja Barry, First Choice, Double Exposure, the Salsoul Orchestra and Loleatta Holloway make mainstream hits like *Saturday Night Fever* sound like soulless sellouts. After years of cult status among club fans, *Disco Boogie* was re-released as a double-CD set on The Right Stuff's line of old-school classics. —*John Bush*

Disco Breaks Mastercuts / 2001 / Beechwood ♦♦♦♦
The real extended mix party that was disco is essayed here on this import collection of original 12-inch cuts. Unfortunately, not all is extended ecstasy. Fans of A Taste of Honey's "Boogie Oogie Oogie," Carrie Lucas' "Dance With You," and Musique's "Keep on Jumpin'" will sadly discover that these are, in fact, not the original 12-inch mixes. And adding to the party downer, "Let's Lovedance" by Gary's Gang is not the original mix of any kind but rather a '90s update. These qualms aside, *Disco Breaks Mastercuts* still delivers a solid dancefloor soundtrack with lengthy gems from Sylvester, Loose Joints, the Jacksons, and Black Ivory, among others. A disco party on wax that leaves most of the Top 40 competition in the dust. —*Stephen Cook*

Disco Juice / 1997 / Counterpoint ♦♦♦♦
As with the histories of rock & roll and R&B, disco's glorious past is riddled with underground legends that never got their due. Patrick Adams and Peter Brown are two such figures—two arrangers, producers, and musicians who teamed up to run a series

of independent labels during the late '70s and early '80s. Sounds of New York, Queen Constance, Sound of the Universe, Heavenly Star, Golden Flamingo, and—most notably—P&P were the names of some of the labels the formidable duo helmed. None of these label names prickle the ears of the average disco fan like Casablanca, Salsoul, or even Prelude or West End (labels for which both auteurs did exceptional work), but to hardcore devotees, these labels bring to mind low-budget (*not* necessarily lo-fi), raw, spine-tingling gems by the likes of Cloud One, Paper Doll, Clyde Alexander, and Johnson Products. Released by the U.K.-based Counterpoint, *Disco Juice* is the first in a multi-volume series dedicated to giving new life to the catalogs of Adams and Brown's labels. Since the producers were doing this work for themselves and were only answering to themselves, the freedom enabled them to try things they wouldn't normally do with their freelance work. The combination of their freed-up approach with the spirited drive of the uncommercial artists on their roster resulted in some brilliant, exciting, and occasionally wild-sounding dance music that stands up to this day. The obvious standout is Cloud One's midtempo "Disco Juice," a dizzy 1977 single that brims with giddiness throughout its duration. Based on a highly repetitive rhythmic structure and the uplifting melody that rides it, it's one of those songs that cloaks you in its joyous glow. The remainder of the disc follows suit with another dozen tracks that range from good to spectacular. *—Andy Kellman*

Disco Juice, Vol. 2 / May 28, 2002 / Counterpoint ♦♦♦

The second volume of Disco Juice shows that the first volume, though stronger overall, hardly ransacked all the goods from the catalogs of the labels run by Patrick Adams and Peter Brown during the late '70s and early '80s. The prolific producers' quietly pioneering work largely went unrecognized in the reissue world until Counterpoint came along to release these crucial documents of underground dance music. However, referring to the lovingly assembled *Disco Juice* compilations as mere documents would be grossly limiting, as they offer plenty of disco, soul, and old school rap that—for the most part—sounds terrific decades after original release. Where the first volume of *Disco Juice* stuck primarily to disco, the second volume opens things up to incorporate soul (Florence Miller's "The Groove I'm In," Cloud One's "Dust to Dust") and rap (Margo's Kool Out Crew's "Death Rap," Willie Wood & Willie Wood Crew's "Willie Rap," Super-jay's "Super-jay Love Theme"; as a side note, the latter two incorporate Johnson Products' "Johnson Jumpin'"). Hot disco isn't in short supply, either. "New York Moving" by Ahzz, "Roller Rink Funk" by Shift (a great roller jam that slightly resembles Michael Jackson's "Workin' Day and Night"), and "The Guardian Angel Is Watching Over Us" by Golden Flamingo Orchestra (a great cross between the Staple Singers and Sister Sledge) highlight the more floor-friendly selections. Despite their strength, the most astonishing aspect of the *Disco Juice* compilations is that they hardly exhaust the career highlights of the producers/label heads they spotlight. Putting together retrospectives of their freelance work would be a monstrous task. *—Andy Kellman*

Disco Not Disco / 2000 / Strut ♦♦♦♦♦

Is it disco? Well, not completely. Just look at the title—it sounds confused. And the title was inspired by one of the groups featured here, and that group, Was (Not Was), was not disco. Most of these songs came from the post-punk era, and like the material by a lot of the bands that easily fit in that category, they blur the line between punk (in attitude) and dance (in rhythm). But only one or two of the artists here could honestly be classified as post-punk. Furthermore, how could anyone say with a straight face that a compilation with the Steve Miller Band's 17-minute long "Macho City" is a post-punk one? So what is it then? It's *Disco Not Disco*, a compilation of songs suitable for the dancefloor. Less ambiguously, what binds these strange bedfellows together is the fact that they were popular on the dancefloors of New York City clubs in the late '70s and early '80s. *Disco Not Disco* digs deep—real deep—into the play lists of DJs like Larry Levan, who kept club patrons moving with oddball choices from the likes of pub rock icon Ian Dury ("Spasticus Autisticus"), leftfield jazz legend Don Cherry ("I Walk"), and Yoko Ono ("Walking on Thin Ice"), along with relatively expected fare from Liquid Liquid ("Cavern") and the wild mind of producer/auteur Arthur Russell, who was behind a handful of the key selections found here (including Dinosaur's "Kiss Me Again" and Indian Ocean's "Tree House/School Bell (Pt. 1)"). Ably compiled by noted house producer Joey Negro and Kiss FM DJ Sean P., this compilation seemingly does a great job at conveying the spirit behind this era of cultural collisions. Not only does the music stand on its own (there's a reason why thousands of young DJs and vinyl hounds collapsed in confoundment upon finding out that these rare gems were being issued together), but the liner notes provide a story behind each song, only adding to the mystique. *—Andy Kellman*

Disco Not Disco 2 / Mar. 19, 2002 / Strut ♦♦♦♦

The Strut label and two of their trusty compilation assemblers, Joey Negro and Sean P., return for a second installment in the *Disco Not Disco* series, two years after the inaugural edition. Like its predecessor, *Disco Not Disco 2* offers should-be classics from the underground disco vaults, focusing on dance tunes—some of which came from unlikely sources—that were spun by New York club DJs in the late '70s and early '80s. While the stuffiest dance music fanatic might sniff at the fact that the Clash's "This Is Radio Clash," Yello's "Bostich," and Alexander Robotnick's "Problemes D'Amour" haven't exactly been tough to locate throughout the years, the songs in question have hardly been as ubiquitous as the average classic rock staple or new wave chart smash. More importantly, the three above-mentioned songs were as crucial to the scene/period being documented here as their harder-to-find counterparts, and they act as fine signposts for curious novices who wonder what they're getting into with a compilation like this. The highlights amongst highlights: the electro zap and tickle of Laidback's brilliant "White Horse," with its cautionary anti-drug sentiment (see Monifah's "Touch It" for one example of the song's lasting value); Material's fat-bottomed funk in "Ciguri," which showcases New Yorker Bill Laswell's revolving-door supergroup at their early best; the Coach House Rhythm Section's "Timewarp," which is little more than an infectious rhythm extended ad infinitum by its sole creator, Eddy Grant; and then there's Arthur Russell's "Let's Go Swimming," a delightfully odd twist of psych-disco refracted through a cracked fun house mirror. Despite all the advances made in dance music in the decades that followed the greatness featured here, the lasting value is undeniable. If you want the picture to become more complete, it would also behoove you to track down Larry Levan's *Live at the Paradise Garage*, another priceless snapshot from this great era released by Strut. *—Andy Kellman*

Disco Queens: The '80s / Jul. 8, 1997 / Rhino ♦♦♦

The '80s version of the *Disco Queens* series predictably includes a bunch of offshoots of disco itself: house, electronic, club. In the end, it all amounts to dance music, and, with this set, dance music that also happened to score big on the pop charts: Kim Wilde's "You Keep Me Hangin' On," Jody Watley's "Looking for a New Love," Pebbles' "Mercedes Boy." Best, though, are the more subtle forays into disco: "Straight Up" (Paula Abdul), "The Glamorous Life" (Sheila E.), and "Let's Hear It for the Boys" (Deniece Williams). *—Michael Gallucci*

Disco Queens: The '90s / Oct. 28, 1997 / Rhino ♦♦♦

Disco Queens: The '90s is a 16-track collection that rounds up some of the biggest dance diva hits of the '90s. Every one of the tracks was a hit, and many of these are among the greatest dance singles of the decade, including Soul II Soul's "Back to Life (However Do You Want Me)," the KLF's "Justified and Ancient," Black Box's "Strike It Up," Nicki French's "Total Eclipse of the Heart," Snap!'s "Rhythm Is a Dancer," Technotronic's "Move This" and DJ Miko's "What's Up." It's an excellent, intelligently compiled collection that is a necessary addition to any basic dance collection. *—Stephen Thomas Erlewine*

Disco Spectrum 1 / 1999 / BBE ♦♦♦♦

The same injustices classic hits and oldies radio have inflicted on rock, pop, and R&B history have undermined disco as well—as myopic play lists determine what is and is not a part of the accepted canon, more and more great music falls prey to the whims of selective memory. Disco was so much more than the Bee Gees and the Village People, although you'd be hard pressed to realize it by picking up any major-label retrospective or listening to any all-'70s format radio broadcast, which in its way makes the BBE label's two-disc *Disco Spectrum* collection as essential as Rhino's *Disco Box* or any other similar collection. Compiled by Joey Negro, the set assembles 19 long-forgotten classics which may have electrified clubfloors but failed to translate to commercial radio; while unmistakably the product of their times, each track holds up brilliantly—because highlights like Ramona Brooks' "I Don't Want You Back" or Omni's stellar "Out of My Hands" aren't as immediately familiar as bigger hits of the era, they also haven't fossilized like their more campy counterparts. It's unlikely even the most superb material here will strike a chord of recognition, but given the amount of sex, drugs, and debauchery that energized the moment in question, then what they say about Woodstock probably holds true of disco as well—if you remember it, you weren't really there. *—Jason Ankeny*

Disco Spectrum 2 / 2001 / BBE ♦♦♦

More stunning *Real Disco for Real People*, like its predecessor compiled with insight and authority by Joey Negro; the names are more familiar this time out—Patti LaBelle, George Duke, the Main Ingredient, Eddy Grant (!)—even if the material itself is ripe for rediscovery. Several tracks, including Don Ray's brilliant opener "Standing in the Rain," spotlight the great French producer Cerrone, who at his best rivaled the legendary Giorgio Moroder, while Cloud One & the Universal Robot Band's spacy "Don't Let This Rainbow Pass Me By" shifts the focus to Patrick Adams, another of the era's most prolific and groundbreaking studio svengalis. Where so much disco has grown stale over the decades, all 22 of *Disco Spectrum*'s choice cuts sound as fresh today as one imagines they did back in their day; BBE can do no wrong. *—Jason Ankeny*

Disco Spectrum 3 / Apr. 30, 2002 / Urban Theory ♦♦♦

The third installment in Barely Breaking Even's *Disco Spectrum* series adds Sean P. to the track selection committee. Joey Negro took on the duties of curating the first two volumes, and now he's joined by P., who has previously teamed with Negro on the spectacular *Disco Not Disco* compilations released by Strut. Once you get past the garish artwork of this double-disc set, featuring an open-mouthed vixen bedecked in a silver body suit with space dust sprinkled around her, there's a fair amount of rare to not-so-rare disco to enjoy. The majority focuses on the tail end of the '70s and the early '80s, when disco's popularity was waning in the mainstream. However, this late period of the style was fertile, providing plenty of fodder for club DJs that has often translated to the present much better than their gold and platinum counterparts. What can be found here stylistically is what directly fed into early house, as late-period disco morphed into it. A light shines on Motown, thus proving that the label had something going for it after its exodus to the West Coast. Eddie Kendricks' sweet but sour "Goin' Up in Smoke," Mandre's cheesy but funny "Solar Flight," and Syreeta's effortlessly infectious "Can't Shake Your Love" are strung together. Other bright spots include Idris Muhammad's "Could Heaven Ever Be Like This," Blair's "Night Life," Denise LaSalle's "I'm So Hot," Dazzle's "Reaching," and the Universal Robot Band's "Let's Get This Thing Together." All in all, *Disco Spectrum 3* has plenty to please obscurantists, but it's far from the best entry point. *—Andy Kellman*

Disco Tech, Vol. 2 / 1975 / Motown ♦♦♦

Motown's *Disco Tech* series was badly conceived and, thankfully, short-lived; labeling a dozen upbeat tracks disco doesn't make them true to the genre. The only saving grace of this volume is the inclusion of some obscure tracks that you might not have in your collection (e.g., G.C. Cameron's "No Matter Where," the Undisputed Truth's "I'm a Fool for You," the Miracles' "What Is a Heart Good For," and Willie Hutch's "You Sure Now

How to Love Your Man"). But none of the aforementioned has much to do with disco, nor does the rest of the album, which is comprised of more familiar tracks such as the Jackson 5's "Dancing Machine." The first volume in this series didn't pain as much because it was crammed with some of Motown's most lovable uptempo hits, though they still weren't disco—and were even further removed from the genre than these tunes (time and style-wise). —*Andrew Hamilton*

☆ **The Disco Years, Vol. 1: Turn the Beat Around** / 1990 / Rhino ♦♦♦♦♦
A comprehensive series featuring many of the greatest disco songs ever recorded, Rhino's five-volume *Disco Years* set accurately chronicles *the* pop music sensation of the mid-'70s. The first two volumes are the places to start; the other three are necessary for devoted disco fans and pop music historians. —*Stephen Thomas Erlewine*

☆ **The Disco Years, Vol. 2: On the Beat** / 1990 / Rhino ♦♦♦♦♦
Disco Years, Vol. 2: On the Beat continues the fine tradition of its predecessor, offering 16 classic disco singles, plus a handful of interesting obscurities. Of course, there are more hits than rarities here, and the hits are what make this one of the handful of definitive disco compilations. Among the highlights are "I Want Your Love," "Ring My Bell," "I Will Survive," "Ain't No Stoppin' Us Now," "Funkytown," "Celebration," "YMCA," "Heart of Glass," "Last Night a DJ Saved My Life" and "Got to Be Real." They're all songs that defined an era, and there's no better place to hear them than this collection. —*Stephen Thomas Erlewine*

☆ **The Disco Years, Vol. 3: Boogie Fever** / 1992 / Rhino ♦♦♦♦♦
Disco Years, Vol. 3: Boogie Fever isn't quite as consistent as its two predecessors, but it has enough seminal singles—"Rock the Boat," "Get Down Tonight," "Boogie Fever," "I Love the Nightlife (Disco 'Round)," "Macho Man," "Dancing Machine," "Soul Makossa," "Le Freak," "We Are Family," "Knock on Wood," "Bad Girls"—to make it an essential disco collection. —*Stephen Thomas Erlewine*

The Disco Years, Vol. 4: Lost in Music / 1992 / Rhino ♦♦♦♦♦
This is another good installment in Rhino's comprehensive five-volume overview of the disco era. For disco fans, each volume is worth purchasing. —*Stephen Thomas Erlewine*

The Disco Years, Vol. 5: Must Be the Music / 1992 / Rhino ♦♦♦♦♦

The Disco Years, Vol. 6: Everybody Dance / Jul. 18, 1995 / Rhino ♦♦♦♦
Rhino's six-volume *The Disco Years* is the best, most comprehensive overview of disco's late-'70s heyday, featuring all of the genre's biggest hits with the exception of the Bee Gees' singles from *Saturday Night Fever.* The first four volumes—*Turn the Beat Around, On the Beat, Boogie Fever,* and *Lost in Music*—are essential additions to any comprehensive pop library, since they contain the biggest and best hits: "The Hustle," "Never Can Say Goodbye," "That's the Way (I Like It)," "Car Wash," "Disco Inferno," "Love Hangover," "Turn the Beat Around," "Boogie Oogie Oogie," "You Make Me Feel (Mighty Real)," "Ring My Bell," "I Will Survive," "Funkytown," "Celebration," "Y.M.C.A.," "Heart of Glass," "Get Down Tonight," "Macho Man," "Le Freak," "We Are Family," "Bad Girls," "Hot Stuff," "He's the Greatest Dancer," "In the Bush," and "Good Times," among others. The next three—*Must Be the Music, Everybody Dance,* and *The Best Disco in Town*—aren't nearly as consistent, but for listeners with a deep interest in disco, they have enough obscurities and interesting tracks to make them worthwhile. Still, the first four volumes of *The Disco Years* are what's really necessary for most listeners, since that's where all the true classics are. —*Stephen Thomas Erlewine*

The Disco Years, Vol. 7: The Best Disco in Town / Jul. 18, 1995 / Rhino ♦♦♦
The Weather Girls, Hot Chocolate, and Chic all pop up on the seventh volume of this disco collection. Also included in the glitter of the disco ball are Kool & the Gang, Evelyn King, and Ashford & Simpson. —*Jonathan Ball*

Disco-Trek / 1976 / Atlantic ♦♦♦♦
This is a compilation of 1972-1975 singles from Atlantic and its related labels. Despite the title, the lengthened tracks, added congas, and other sound effects, most of the tracks were cut before disco was even a viable genre. That being said, *Disco-Trek* is an accurate set that spotlights Philly-produced songs as well as Southern R&B, two styles partly responsible for disco's success. The Philly sound, of course, gets the nod for its rhythmic innovations. Blue Magic's "Look Me Up" with Norman Harris producing and Vince Montana arranging, has a melodic, smooth, and effortless sound. It's a track that was made for another musical interpretation, but the Spinners; "I'll Be Around" might have been even better. *Disco-Trek* also has a few of the more obscure tracks to come out of Philadelphia. Compared to the standard set by Blue Magic, the tracks from Sons of Robin Stone and early Sister Sledge are less of the same. Oddly enough, the song that benefited most from the re-edit and exposure was Clyde Brown's "You Call Me Back." A perfect match of standard-issue lyrics and anonymous but competent vocals, it's likable despite the fact that Brown sings both the title and "Thank ya" over 20 times. Side two features the Southern dance music style from producers like Dave Crawford and Brad Shapiro. Jackie Moore's "Time" and the Sweet Inspirations' cover of "This World" both have more languid rhythms than their Philly counterparts. But again, they aren't "disco," either, despite the remixing. Atlantic meant serious business with this effort. All of the eight tracks were skillfully mixed and edited by Tom Moulton and remixed at Sigma Sound Studios in Philadelphia and then mastered at New York's Media Sound. While the tracks here are more like prized finds in someone's B-plus singles collection, *Disco-Trek* is one of the best and earliest albums to cash in on the disco craze. —*Jason Elias*

Doing the James Brown / Aug. 14, 2001 / Harmless ♦♦♦♦
An entire album of J.B. covers sounds initially like a project which has got up on the bad foot, but this long-player from Harmless, subtitled "in the footsteps of the godfather of funk" by its compiler (respected journalist James Maycock) works on so many levels that it adds up to an essential purchase for funk aficionados. While some tracks pay homage others, like the Daktaris' "Give It Up or Turn It Loose," stray far from the original, as the bongo-rocked spoken word of the Last Poets vision encapsulates not the material of James Brown, but the man himself. Of course, despite the effort of some superb performers (Otis Redding, Aretha Franklin, and Lou Pride amongst them), there is nothing quite like the man himself with the highlight taking the form of a spectacular 12-minute live performance of "Cold Sweat." Clyde Stubblefield and Nate Jones provide the super tight rhythm section, whipping the number-one soul brother into a twisting dervish—breathtaking. —*Kingsley Marshall*

The Domino Records Story / Apr. 21, 1998 / Ace ♦♦♦♦
Back in the late 1950s, Domino was the first record label out of the now burgeoning musical scene of Austin, Texas. Formed by 11 adults taking a business night course, the company only lasted for about three years, issuing 16 singles before closing up shop in 1961. But the label found themselves leasing product to a bigger label (Liberty) with their first release and having one big hit with the original recording of "You Cheated" by their number one group, the Slades. This 30-track compilation is pretty much a tribute to the local Austin singing group, collecting up all 12 sides of their original six singles (including "The Waddle," a rockabilly scorcher that was the flip side of "You Cheated") and tacking on six more goodies from a previously unreleased rehearsal tape of the group doing a cappella runthroughs of top-40 faves like "Little Star" and "Ling-Ting-Tong." But equally compelling are five entries from blues belter Joyce Harris, who turns in a scorching rockabilly version of "I Got My Mojo Working" done up more Ann Cole-style than the better known Muddy Waters arrangement. Harris' backup band, the Daylighters (featuring a young Sonny Rhodes), made one single ("I'll Never Let You Go" and "Something Is Wrong") which is here as well. Rounding things out is Joyce Webb, who sang on the Slades' "Baby." They return the favor on both sides of her single, "After You've Gone" and "Right Here." There's a marvelous innocence to all of the tracks collected here; some are so crude as to not even feature drums on what are supposedly rock & roll records! But the sweetness of the Slades' harmonies, the unabashed enthusiasm of Joyce Webb, the unbridled squawling power of Joyce Harris and the shake-and-stomp fervor of the Daylighters make this a collection loaded with charm. —*Cub Koda*

Don't It Sound Good: The Great Atlantic Vocal Groups / 1995 / Rhino/Collectors' Choice Music ♦♦♦♦♦
There are 50 doo wop cuts from the Atlantic vaults on this double CD, all but one from the 1950s. Divided between hits and rarities, there's no getting around the fact that, due to the factors of both familiarity and quality, the hits are far more interesting to the non-collector. There are quite a few of those here by both the Drifters and the Clovers, as well as the Robins' "Smokey Joe's Cafe," and the Chords' "Sh-Boom," and the Cardinals' "Wheel of Fortune." After that it's collector territory, with outfits like the Diamonds (no relation to the White group that had a hit with "Little Darlin'"), the Regals, the Pearls, the Raiders, the Royal Jokers, the Sensations, and others. Characteristically well-done vocal arrangements don't disguise the truth that the material is not as memorable as the hits. Nevertheless, doo wop fans will certainly dig this, as the Atlantic imprint ensured a basic standard of quality. —*Richie Unterberger*

Doo Wop 50 Live! / Nov. 7, 2000 / Rhino ♦♦♦
Recorded in Pittsburgh on May 11 and May 12 of 1999, this is the soundtrack to the PBS special on the 50th anniversary of doo wop, featuring performances by Gene Chandler, the Del-Vikings, the Penguins, the Cadillacs, the Moonglows, the Skyliners, the Flamingos, the Jive Five, and other doo wop hitmakers. Most of the groups were fronted by their original lead singers, according to the liner notes, and they sound pretty good considering that four decades or so had passed since their commercial prime. There's no personnel listing that might enable you to figure out how much the lineups have been altered, though, and "The Great Pretender" is done by Herb Reed rather than his group, the Platters (for which Reed was not even lead singer). The house band backs them competently, modernizing the arrangements with the sheen of nostalgia that you would expect from such an endeavor (and such a PBS broadcast). No, it isn't the same or as good as hearing the original singles; for those, you can turn to the *Doo Wop Box Set* series, which like this soundtrack is also issued by Rhino. The arrangements stick close to those heard on the original classic studio versions, though there's an extended vocal and instrumental break on the Cadillacs' "Speedoo." The group must be going through some dance routines while the backing musicians vamp repeatedly, judging from the crowd response; heard without the accompanying visuals, the interpretation doesn't make much sense. In fact, a two-volume video of these performances is also available on Rhino, and might be a preferable investment than the audio soundtrack alone. —*Richie Unterberger*

Doo Wop 51 Live! / Aug. 21, 2001 / Rhino ♦♦♦
Doo Wop 51: Live! isn't for everybody, nor is it for every doo wop fan, either. It's for the fan who loves the singing and loves nostalgia—the kind who wants to hear the great groups reunite, in some form, and sing their hits years later. This isn't necessarily the same thing as being a doo wop fanatic, since there are plenty of ravenous doo wop fans—the kind who seek out rare singles, arguing the merits of Philadelphia vs. New York—who will not be interested in this simply because it is a latter-day recording. Similarly, this will not find an audience among listeners who just want to hear nothing but the best doo wop. Instead, this is solely a nostalgia trip and, on that level, it's pretty good. No, the groups don't sound as good as they used to, and while there are good vibes, the recording isn't as warm as the atmosphere, but for those looking for a reunion record—looking to hear these groups reunite and sing the old songs another time while basking in sweet memories—this fits the bill. —*Stephen Thomas Erlewine*

☆ **Doo Wop Box** / 1994 / Rhino ♦♦♦♦♦
Rhino's four-disc collection *The Doo Wop Box* may not contain every classic doo wop single ever recorded, but it comes damn close. Featuring a hundred tracks, superb

sound, and amazingly detailed liner notes, the set is one of the best various-artist box sets ever assembled; although these four discs will be all the doo wop some listeners will ever need, hopefully the set will make most listeners want to investigate the genre even further. —*Stephen Thomas Erlewine*

The Doo Wop Box, Vol. 2 / Oct. 1, 1996 / Rhino ✦✦✦✦✦
Rhino's first box set of doo wop classics was obviously successful enough to bring about this second, four-CD set. This time around, with all of the hits covered on the first box, the compilers have dug deep into the genre's history to put together a selection of some of the music's great sides, lesser-known hits, and rarities. Highlights on disc one include "Fool, Fool, Fool" by the Clovers, "A Thousand Stars" by the Rivileers, "I Love You So" by the Crows, "I'll Be Forever Loving You" by the El Dorados, "Smokey Joe's Cafe" by the Robins, "Life Is But a Dream" by the Harptones, and "Ling Ting Tong" by the Five Keys. Disc two covers a two year period (1955-1957) and features "Eddie My Love" by the Teen Queens, "Ruby Baby" by the Drifters, "Zoom" by the Cadillacs, "Ka-Ding Dong" by the G-Clefs, "The ABC's of Love" by Frankie Lymon & the Teenagers, "Guided Missiles" by the Cuff Links, "Glory of Love" by the Velvetones, and "Mr. Lee" by the Bobettes. Disc three covers sides from 1957 to 1960, including "Could This Be Magic" by the Dubs, "Zoom Zoom Zoom" by the Collegians, "We Belong Together" by Robert & Johnny, "You're So Fine" by the Falcons, "Island of Love" by the Sheppards, "Bad Girl" by the Miracles, and "Love Potion No. 9" by the Clovers. The final disc covers 1960 to 1963, when doo wop had its last great renaissance on the pop charts, with "Valarie" by the Starlites, "Those Oldies But Goodies (Remind Me of You)" by Little Caesar & the Romans, "Pretty Little Angel Eyes' by Curtis Lee, "I Love You" by the Volumes, "Duke of Earl" by Gene Chandler, "What Time Is It?" by the Jive Five, and "Rip Van Winkle" by the Devotions. A sumptuous booklet also provides much important info on the artists, the sound and the style. This is an important addition to anyone's doo wop or '50s music collection. —*Cub Koda*

Doo Wop Box, Vol. 3: 101 More Vocal Group Gems from the Golden Age of Rock-N-Roll / Aug. 1, 2000 / Rhino ✦✦✦✦
The first two Rhino doo wop box sets were straightforward anthologies of the best music in the style, concentrating on big and small hits and the best overlooked rarities. The third installment is also a worthy chunk of the genre's better moments, yet it is definitely a notch or two below its predecessors. Part of the reason is that, as many doo wop records as there were, the lion's share of the great hits were already used up on the first two boxes. Thus, Rhino took a different strategy for this four-disc set, devoting the first CD to hits (many of which weren't *that* big, or have certainly escaped oldies rotation); disc two to "should-have-been hits"; disc three to "celebrity picks" of the favorite doo wop tunes by star musicians, comedians, and record executives; and disc four to modern doo wop postdating the early '60s. Overall, it's still a nice package, but it's probably an idea that has finally come to the end of its line. —*Richie Unterberger*

Doo Wop Delights: The Boston Groups / 1995 / Relic ✦✦✦✦
Assembled by Relic Records engineer Walter DeVenne (a lifelong Boston resident), this hour-long retrospective has a very personal slant, encompassing many of his favorite records of the late '50s and early '60s, drawn from decades of working with these acts and their music. The G-Clefs (who are still performing in the 1990s) open this collection with the rousing, soaring "Cause You're Mine" (and provide a killer dance number, "Ka-Ding Dong"), followed by the Majestics gentle ballad "Sweet One." The Syndicates' tribute to Gene Chandler's "Duke of Earl," called "The Duke," is a beautiful, passionate record in its own right. Other groups featured include the Love Notes, the Uniques, the Supremes (no, not the girl trio), the Del-Tones (doing a doo wop version of "Misty" that's pretty cool, and a gloriously romantic ballad called "Lonely Drifter"), the Delphonics, Bobby Mathis & the Sevilles, the C-Quins and the Estelles (with a coyly passionate number called "Merry-Go-Round"). The variety is fairly impressive, and the sound is generally good to excellent, with some of these groups captured in good stereo. —*Bruce Eder*

Doo Wop Delights: The Hartford Groups / 1992 / Relic ✦✦✦✦✦
This is an unusual collection, even for Relic—16 previously unissued songs by acts that include Gene Pitney at the outset of his career. Drawn from the roster of John Rys' Recording Co. Associates in Hartford, CT, the songs include stunning performances by the Five Bel Aires, featuring John Hall ("Wedding Bells," "Come on Home") and Henry Hall ("House of Love," "My Friends," "I'm So Happy"), the Embers featuring Larry Lee ("Winter's Romance," "Tremble") and Gene Pitney ("Darkness," Victory," "Runaway Lover," "So Tired"), and the Serenaders featuring Larry Lee ("Too Young," "Dreams of Heaven"). Pitney's voice during this era (1957-1960) sounds uncannily like that of Clyde McPhatter, and the songs, authored by Pitney, are first-rate as well. The fact that not one of the songs on this album ever got issued is astonishing—the Five Bel Aires were at least a match for the likes of the Five Satins and the Nutmegs, both doo wop acts from Connecticut that made it, and could rock out as well as harmonize in elegant fashion. Apparently Rys was never able to conclude the deal that he needed with an active record label (there may have been a missed chance with Old Town Records), and the tapes languished for 30 years, until Relic got hold of them. Apart from Pitney, none of the artists featured here ever made it in the music business, but they deserve to be heard, which this release at least assures. The sound, incidentally, is excellent, and half of the material is in good quality true stereo. —*Bruce Eder*

Doo-Wop from Dolphin's of Hollywood, Vol. 1 / 1992 / Specialty ✦✦✦✦✦
This mid-'50s Los Angeles doo wop was produced by John Dolphin. Groups include the Turbans, the Voices, the Gassers, Bobby Relf, the Turks, Gaynell Hodge & the Blue-Aires, Bobby Byrd, and the Jaguars. —*AMG*

Doo-Wop from Dolphin's of Hollywood, Vol. 2 / 1991 / Specialty ✦✦✦✦✦
Dolphin was a pretty casually run R&B label back in the '50s, and these tapes from the vaults reveal a wealth of vocal group treasures with little, if any, documentation. With names of obscurity, like the Hollywood Arist-O-Kats, the Turks, aka Hollywood Flames (two different versions of this West Coast one-shot group), Grady Chapman & the Suedes, the 5 Bars, the Ebonaires, Bobby "Baby Face" Byrd and the Birds, and Clyde "Thin Man" Tillis, this is no hit fest by any stretch. But the music, as unknown as it is, is all top-drawer, and if raw West Coast doo wop is your cup of tea, then this set is heartily recommended. —*Cub Koda*

Dootone Rock N' Rhythm & Blues / Apr. 23, 2002 / Ace ✦✦✦
Dootone was one of many notable Los Angeles independent labels releasing R&B and early rock & roll in the mid-'50s, though it wasn't on the same level, musically or commercially, as Specialty and Modern. This gathers 28 Dootone cuts from the mid- to late '50s that generally lean toward the jump blues and jazzy R&B end of things, though there's some honkin' sax rock & roll too. In fact, most of the artists were pretty important figures in the scene, though many would contend that their best work was done for other labels: Roy Milton, Helen Humes, Chuck Higgins, and Joe Houston (though the last is represented by just one track, the 1958 single "Shindig"). These kind of styles were passing their peak by the mid-'50s, and while the artists hadn't lost their energy or skills, the songs do sound on the routine and samey-sounding side. Miss Mickey Champion fronts two songs by Roy Milton's orchestra, and these stand out a little due to her saucy, slightly raunchy vocals. The duo of Lorenzo Holden & Ernie Freeman also contributes to variety with their two organ instrumentals. Overall it's one for those who just can't get enough of the urbane-to-rough 1950s Los Angeles R&B sound, and not among the best anthologies of the style. —*Richie Unterberger*

DooWoppin' with King, Federal and Deluxe Vocal Groups / Dec. 15, 1998 / WestSide ✦✦✦✦
Although they never had the success of other R&B indie labels of the 1950s, there's no doubt that King Records (and its subsidiaries, Federal and Deluxe) recorded more doo wop than anybody, hoping to get its fair share of the market nonetheless. This first entry into a multi-volume series is subtitled "Volume 1: Dynamite Darling," and brings together 21 tracks from some of the most obscure groups to record for the Cincinnati imprint. The only name of any import on here are the two Deluxe sides by Otis Williams and the Charms (the title track and "I'd Like to Thank You, Mr. DJ" which open and close this compilation), but from a musical standpoint, this is some of the best stuff ever issued on the label. Great one-off singles abound from groups like the Buckeyes ("By Only You" and the slow grinder "Dottie Baby"), the Van Dykes ("The Bells Are Ringing" and "Meaning of Love"), the Chanters (the Frankie Lymon sound-alikes "No, No, No" and "Over the Rainbow"), the Guytones ("I Don't Care" and "You Won't Let Me Go"), the Five Chances ("Tell Me Why"), the Swingin' Phillies ("L-O-V-E"), the Cats (the swingin' "I Don't Care No More") and three astounding tracks from the totally unknown Carpets (two takes of "Lonely Me" and "Why Do I"), making this a keeper to any doo wop collection you'd care to add it to. Like the best music in any genre, there's always a pile of great ones by a bunch of people you never heard of, and here's a motherlode of just that. —*Cub Koda*

Dot Records Cover to Cover... Hit Upon Hit / Jun. 20, 1995 / Ace ✦✦✦✦
In the mid-'50s, as rock & roll was getting launched, it was a common practice for white artists to cover R&B and rock records (usually by black musicians) in tamer versions that were targeted for the pop market. For a couple of years this succeeded in tallying wider sales than the gutsier originals. Dot Records was one of the most active practitioners of this sly art, although this methodology died out around 1957, when the real rock & roll article had conquered the pop market. This has 30 singles of Dot "covers" issued from 1954-1957, including seven alone by Pat Boone, and others by artists like Gale Storm, the Fontane Sisters, Jim Lowe, the Hilltoppers, and even the Mills Brothers and Pat Boone's brother, Nick Todd. "Far from locking out the original R&B versions," claims Rob Finnis in the liner notes, "which weren't likely to garner much airplay on pop stations anyway, Dot's clearly enunciated and immaculately balanced interpretations helped to prepare the way for the eventual acceptance of black rock & roll by the white media in those fast-changing musical times." Well, that's a highly debatable contention that could be argued well into the 21st century. What *is* clear from this compilation is that these cover versions, now forgotten but usually more popular than the originals at the time of their release, are audibly inferior to the real deal. They are not as ghastly as some historians have made them out to be, although tracks like Boone's whitewashed "Long Tall Sally," Gale Storm's stiff reading of "Why Do Fools Fall in Love," and Tab Hunter's "Young Love" are pretty horrid. Most of the performances on this disc would be more accurately characterized as drab rather than awful, with little or no grasp of the spirit motivating the original performers and songwriters, and by extension little or no grasp of rock & roll as a whole. If you'd rather hear these than the originals, you need to have your head examined. A lot of these discs have been hard to find (or hear on oldies radio) since the 1950s, though, so this does perform a valuable archival service for serious rock & roll historians. Not all of these were successful hits or even copies of black artists, by the way, as was the case with Jim Lowe (famous for "Green Door") and his hopeless attempt to outdo Carl Perkins and Elvis Presley with "Blue Suede Shoes." —*Richie Unterberger*

Down & Out: The Sad Soul of the Black South / 1998 / Trikont ✦✦✦✦✦
This volume in Trikont's wonderfully eclectic, well-researched, American music series should have been called "Dogged Again, the Dirty Blue Soul of the Deep South." Never has a collection of obscure, raging heartbreak songs like these been issued. These are "done wrong" songs, but they have an edge missing in so much of the period's R&B and blues. These songs believe in a love so pure, it can only be consummated by murder, suicide, or an act of divine intervention such is its emotional intensity. Even where the protagonist begs, such as Johnny Copeland on "Down on Bended Knees," there is a rage in

his hurt, an anger barely hidden in the cage of his heart. And then there's the suicidal—literally—"Dead" by Ede Robin, who sings: "And then there's me along, with a razor in my hand/I remove my watchband." There's a B-3 blazing in the background and Illinois Jacquet blasting out the blues on his tenor before Robin comes back in, begging her lover not to do her "like that." When her spoken vocal whispers out at the end of the tune, we know how it ends. There is just so much bad-assed material here, almost all of it B-sides, discarded tracks, or singles played only on jukeboxes in the bars south of the Mason-Dixon Line. Shouters like Virgil Griffin come out and beg the Lord to abate his loneliness that has reached the pitch of anger. Only a power higher than himself can relieve his fear and misery. Elsewhere, Bill Brandon, Ella Brown, Betty Lavette, James Kelly Duhon, Ella Washington, Geater Adams, Juke Boy Bonner, Percy Mayfield, and even Gashead—with his underground classic "Why Do You Treat Me Like a Tramp"—weigh in with tales of domestic problems, and the attempt to survive them. Perhaps nowhere is the desire to transcend these circumstances more evident than O.V. Wright's "Everybody Knows (The River Song)," where he sings, "God, I'm so sad and so scared/I want to go to heaven/but I'm scared to fly." When Joe Medwick follows this will, a gospel blues called "I Cried" with a chorus answering his testimony, trying to hold him up the whole record comes undone, it spills rivers of tears and rage and pain into the listener's space; it would be overwhelming were it not for the powerful groove and roll of the rhythms and arrangements. This is deep soul as it hasn't been presented in a long, long while, if ever. Unadorned, raw, immediate, *Down & Out* tells a truth so simple and all-encompassing it will be unfathomable to many. *—Thom Jurek*

☆ **Duke-Peacock's Greatest Hits** / 1992 / MCA ♦♦♦♦♦

Don Robey, something of an infamous figure even in the rough-and-tumble world of 1950s R&B labels, owned one of the first successful black-owned labels in the country, and his output was rich and varied. *Duke-Peacock's Greatest Hits* offers a revealing overview of his operation, beginning with major hits by two of the company's humongous female belters, Big Mama Thornton's "Hound Dog" and Marie Adams' "I'm Gonna Play the Honky Tonks." Johnny Ace, Bobby "Blue" Bland, and Junior Parker are represented by a few of their biggest hits, but it's the relatively unknown "Pack Fair and Square" by San Antonio pianist Big Walter Price that wields a knockout punch. Vocal groups aren't forgotten, with sides by Norman Fox & the Rob Roys and the El Torros, and a foray into rockabilly is recalled by the Original Casuals' "So Tough." *—Bill Dahl*

Dynamite Soul Harmony, Vol. 3 / 2000 / Dynamite ♦♦♦♦

Dynamite Soul Harmony, Vol. 3 continues the tradition of the previous volumes by presenting obscure harmony groups of the '60s and '70s that failed to ignite commercially, but were burning with artistic merit. The 22 selections here dash madly between the two decades; the liner notes are brief but do provide the year and label of each release. The result is a stylistic roller coaster that reveals the depth of artistic possibilities within this untapped pocket of soul. From the group-charged garage soul of Little Mr. Lee & the Cherokees' "Will My Baby Come Back," which admirably captures the regret of lost love, to the steamy, window-fogging smoothness of Bunny Sigler's early PIR single "Picture Us," the *Dynamite Soul Harmony* series provides a unique window into a fascinating world of lost soul. Other bright moments include an early version of Tavares recording here as Chubby & the Turnpikes and their beautiful "I Didn't Know the Inside Story," the Naturals' doo wop update "Different Girls," the uptempo cheer of the Embracer's "Stop and Let Yourself Go," and a young Carl Carlton's "So What." It should be noted that some of the selections here have been mastered from vinyl sources and some crackle and hiss is apparent, but it's only a minor setback to a great set of music. *—Wade Kergan*

East Side Story, Vol. 3 / Nov. 18, 1997 / East Side ♦♦♦

The third volume in the East Side label's ongoing series of oldies collections is highlighted by the Delfonics' "La La Means I Love You," the Shirelles' "Dedicated to the One I Love" and Barbara Lewis' "Hello Stranger." *—Jason Ankeny*

East Side Story, Vol. 5 / Mar. 30, 1999 / East Side ♦♦♦♦

It may not contain many big hits, but that's the reason why *East Side Story, Vol. 5* is a wonderful collection of '60s R&B and soul. Brenton Wood is the most familiar name here, but he's represented by lesser-known singles like "Baby, You Got It" and "Me & You"—which are very close to being as good as his hits. And that's the key to this disc and the whole *East Side Story* series. The compilers have found a number of great obscurities that sound new and exciting. Yes, some of the featured songs aren't as sublime as the acknowledged classics, but there's not a loser in the bunch and it's enjoyable from beginning to end. It's a great choice, not only for Northern soul and Uptown soul fanatics, but for old-school soul, pop and R&B fans looking for something that sounds familiar, but feels fresh. *—Stephen Thomas Erlewine*

East Side Story, Vol. 7 / May 19, 1998 / East Side ♦♦♦

Strange mix of early-'50s to mid-'70s R&B, juxtaposing Gene Chandler ("Duke of Earl"), Billy Stewart ("Cross My Heart"), the Five Satins ("In the Still of the Night"), the Escorts ("Look Over Your Shoulder"), and Johnny Ace ("Pledging My Love") on the same CD, with no notes, explanations, or accounts of music or careers. There are some forgotten hits, such as "Talk to Me" by Sunny & the Sunliners, a cover of the Little Willie John song that became a number-11 hit in 1963. The better sides here include salsa star Ralphi Pagan's falsetto version of David Gates' "Make It With You," Yvonne Carroll & the Roulettes' "Gee What a Guy," Brenda & the Tabulations' "Dry Your Eyes" (a number-20 pop hit in 1967), and the Incredibles' hit "Heart and Soul." The sound is decent if not exactly state-of-the-art on most of this (though the Incredibles' track has definite surface noise from a disc source), but the selection mixes the familiar and the unusual in an engaging and entertaining fashion. More anthologies should follow this lead, but this disc should also have included one or two more cuts and some notes, to really be of value to its purchasers. *—Bruce Eder*

East Side Story, Vol. 8 / May 19, 1998 / East Side ♦♦♦

Philadelphia R&B, '70s Chicago soul, and '60s folk-rock harmony meet East Los Angeles on this volume, covering the 1950s through the 1970s. The Defonics' "Didn't I Blow Your Mind" shares space with the Premiers' "Duffy's Blues," and a couple of generations of R&B and soul rub shoulders with them. Billy Stewart ("Do I Love You"), the Moonglows ("Sincerely"), the Mello Kings ("Tonite, Tonite"), the Shells ("Baby Oh Baby") and Eddie Holman ("Hey There Lonely Girl") are all here, representing 15 years of great music. The mix is surprisingly compelling, considering the divergence of styles and periods, the Casinos' 1967 Association-style cover of John D. Loudermilk's "Then You Can Tell Me Goodbye" alongside Holman's falsetto-textured "Hey There Lonely Girl" and the Elgins' 1966 Motown debut "Darlin' Baby." It's hard to tell the meaning or the links between the material, as the disc's programming is more akin to what a good oldies DJ would play than to anything that should sell to the public in big numbers, which is why this CD deserves to sell—or, at least, it would if it had more than a dozen songs and maybe some sleeve notes, or a slightly lower list price. But it isn't bad as a fairly serious oldies collection. *—Bruce Eder*

The Ebb Records Story, Vol. 1: The Group Era (1957–1959) / Jan. 30, 2001 / Specialty ♦♦

Ebb Records, run by Lee Rupe (the ex-wife of Specialty Records' owner Art Rupe), was a minor Los Angeles rock and R&B label of the late '50s. Its biggest hit was the infectious Hollywood Flames' uptempo doo wop tune "Buzz-Buzz-Buzz," which leads off this collection of R&B vocal group releases on the label between 1957-1959. And, as is often the case on these kinds of collections, the one familiar hit is the best and most memorable song by far. The 30 tracks are almost wholly routine doo wop, with a decent balance between fast numbers and ballads, and pretty hackneyed chord progressions throughout. One thirsts for a bit of unexpected innovation, a bit of outstanding quality, and is largely left dry, ears perking up at the slightest differentiation, like the Ebbtones' calypso-influenced "Trinidad Woman." The Twilighters, with future funkster Charles Wright as leader, put some exaggerated Elvis Presley inflections into the delivery of "Live Like a King"; the Zion Travelers, who close the CD with both sides of a 1957 single, were (in contrast to the other artists on the disc) gospel. Eleven of the songs were previously unissued, a logical enough bonus considering that the compilation's allure is limited to doo wop collectors. *—Richie Unterberger*

The Ebb Records Story, Vol. 2: Blues N' Rhythm & Rock N' Roll (1957–1959) / Jan. 30, 2001 / Specialty ♦♦♦

This disc contains a grab bag of R&B, early rock & roll, a bit of rockabilly, and pop-R&B vocal works from the vaults of Ebb, a minor Los Angeles indie label of the late '50s. There aren't any great moments here, but it's serviceable and energetic period fare, the interest heightened by the presence of some sides by recognized artists. In particular, these include four 1957 songs by Professor Longhair, one of them previously unreleased, all of them good-time New Orleans R&B/rock. There's also a 1957 single by Floyd Dixon, but otherwise we're getting into names that no one who is not acquainted with the small print of collector's manuals will know. The influence of Sam Cooke can be felt here and there on the poppier numbers, and Earl Nelson's "Come On" in particular is like a bridge between early Cooke and the early Motown soul sound of Marv Johnson. Tony Harris offers Little Richard-styled rock, while Smokey Hogg comes off rather like a raw Professor Longhair on "Good Mornin' Baby," which sounds more like a studio warm-up than a finished take. Incidentally, this has a different focus than its companion volume, *The Ebb Records Story, Vol. 1: The Group Era 1957-1959*, and is better than that volume, due both to greater diversity and a higher grade of material. *—Richie Unterberger*

Eighteen Soulful Ballads / May 14, 1996 / JCI ♦♦♦♦

A soulful potpourri dominated by hard-edged R&B, with a dash of deep soul and a few featherweights thrown in. Some tunes you may love but not have include the Jive Five's "My True Story," Garnet Mimms & the Enchanters' "Cry Baby," Don & Juan's "What's Your Name," and Maurice Williams & the Zodiacs' "Stay." Hard stuff like Otis Redding's "Try a Little Tenderness" is balanced by the fluffy soul sounds of Deon Jackson's "Love Makes the Round" and the Drifters' "Save the Last Dance for Me." A highly representative collection of '60s R&B. *—Andrew Hamilton*

Esquire Soul Classics / Sep. 8, 1998 / K-Tel ♦♦♦♦

Esquire: Soul Classics accomplishes the nigh-impossible mission of filling a compilation with a broad range of soul hits that never let up and work well together. Including hits from the 1950s, '60s and '70s, the album includes the Temptations' "Get Ready," the Isley Brothers' "Twist and Shout," Sam & Dave's "Soul Man," Ike & Tina Turner's "Proud Mary," the Delfonics' "Didn't I (Blow Your Mind This Time)," B.B. King's "The Thrill Is Gone" and the Main Ingredient's "Everybody Plays the Fool." *—John Bush*

The Essential Detroit Soul Collection / 1992 / Goldmine/Soul Supply ♦♦

This collection of 23 obscure soul tracks, recorded for small time Detroit labels during the '60s, will intrigue collectors, but offers little for interest for casual fans. The Masqueraders, Tony Clarke, and Steve Mancha are the most familiar artists, notwithstanding Rosey Grier, the football player turned actor turned reverend, who also sang a bit. Two tracks by Jackey Beavers, who began with Johnny Bristol as Johnny & Jackie, are also on deck. If you like Detroit soul, you've probably been panting for this CD, but less devoted soul enthusiasts will not be especially excited by this. *—Andrew Hamilton*

Essential Funk Classics, Vol. 1 / Oct. 25, 1994 / Deep Beats ♦♦♦

They may not be essential as most funk fans understand the word, but this collection compiled by Deep Beats includes 14 great tracks—most of which are rarely heard except by collectors sporting high-end turntables. It doesn't sound quite essential from the track listing—"Hustle Bus Stop" by Mastermind, "Hypertension" by Calender, "The Message" by Cymande, "Every Way But Loose" by Plunky & the Oneness of Juju (remixed by disco legend Larry Levan), and "Waterbed, Pts. 1-2" by LTG Exchange—but the grooves are deep and *Essential Funk Classics* is a great place to turn for listeners who think they've run out of great listening. *—John Bush*

Essential Modern Soul, Vol. 1 / Goldmine/Soul Supply ✦✦✦✦
Compiled by noted British soul DJ and discographer Kev Roberts, *Essential Modern Soul* presents little-heard examples of dance-friendly soul in the '70s and early '80s. As this collection is geared to deep soul fans, rarity is the primary concern and there is a minimal amount of background noise on selections mastered from secondary sources. About half of the 16 tracks are disco or disco-influenced, like Aaron Neville progeny Ivan Neville's minimal, Latin-influenced "Dance Your Blues Away" and the full-on hi-hat attack of the Patrick Adams-produced Four Below Zero's "My Baby's Got (ESP)." There are uptempo Southern soul numbers as well, like Bill Brandon's anti-drug lament "The Streets Got My Lady" and the Clarence Carter-reminiscent "Gettin' Ready for the Getdown" by ZZ and Company. The Leroy Hutson-produced "Trying to Get Next to You" by Arnold Blair and Dee Edwards' "I Can Deal (With That)" are the standouts here; two midtempo songs with appeal on and off the dancefloor, making this collection worthwhile to hardcore '70s soul fans and less-obsessed thrill-seekers, too. *– Wade Kergan*

Essential Slow Groove Dancefloor Classics, Vol. 1 / Oct. 25, 1994 / Deep Beats ✦✦✦✦
Smooth waves of soul including obscure slow grinds and crawlers. Full versions of "Sexy Mama," "Be Thankful for What You Got," and Tamiko Jones' sensuous rendition of Marvin Gaye's "I Want You" makes this a serious contender. Jim Gilstrap's "Love Talk," Norman Connor's "You Are My Starship," and Pam Todd & Love Exchange's "Making Love" are just a few examples of the classy tunes cherry-picked for this collection. *—Andrew Hamilton*

Essential Sweet Soul Selection / 1998 / Goldmine/Soul Supply ✦✦✦✦✦
A tremendous collection of ballads by one- and two-record wonders, mostly recorded for short-lived labels. Harmony lovers will drool over stellar cuts like "A Lovely Way to Meet," by True Movement, and "Young Hearts Get Lonely Too" by the New Younghearts. An early Dynamics tune, "We're Gonna Be Together," highlights the unheralded Detroit natives' sweet vocal blend. The East Coast's Shock Tricky Dick delivers "Why Should I Forgive You," a Ronald McCoy composition. Cleveland natives the Imperial Wonders display high and low-end harmonies on "Turned Around Over You"; member Al Boyd later wrote "Shaky Ground" for the Temptations. The mellow grooves keep coming; check out obscure romancers and lamenters by Natural Resources, Final Chapter, Four Tracks, Sweet Berry, California Malibu's, Norfolk, and others for your pleasure. *—Andrew Hamilton*

The Evolution of Soul / Apr. 4, 2000 / Collectables ✦✦✦✦✦
Nothing but heavyweights on this six-decade chronicle, featuring everybody from the Ohio Players to Sammy Davis Jr. What makes this one special is the inclusion of two obscure tunes by jazz/blues singers Billie Holiday and Ella Fitzgerald; if you've never heard Holiday's "Gimme a Pigfoot (A Bottle of Beer)" or Fitzgerald's "Stone Cold Dead in the Market," here's your chance. Plus, you have familiar chart-toppers such as the Temptations' "Papa Was a Rolling Stone," Marvin Gaye's "What's Going On," and Etta James' fantastic rendition of "At Last." *—Andrew Hamilton*

Excello Story, Vol. 2: 1955–1957 / Feb. 9, 1999 / Hip-O ✦✦✦✦
The end of the period covered on the second installment of this Excello retrospective saw the label start to record the Louisiana swamp blues artists for whom it is most famed: Slim Harpo, Lazy Lester, Lightnin' Slim, Lonesome Sundown. While each of those artists is represented here by a cut or two (including Harpo's classic "I'm a King Bee"), much of it's devoted to more urban mid-'50s blues/R&B crossover, most of it recorded in Nashville. A couple of these were big hits: the Marigolds' "Rollin' Stone" made the R&B Top Ten in 1955 (and was covered for a pop hit by the Fontane Sisters), while Louis Brooks made number-two R&B that same year with "It's Love Baby (24 Hours a Day)" (covered with success by Ruth Brown). Jerry McCain does raw, early electric blues with "Courtin' in a Cadillac;" Guitar Gable does blues with a Mardi Gras rhythm on "Congo Mambo"; a young Johnny Copeland plays "chicken licking" guitar on Clarence Samuels' "Chicken Hearted Woman"; and there are a couple of lowdown blues by Little Al (Arthur Gunter's brother). There's also some rockabilly by Johnny Jano, whose "Havin' a Whole Lot of Fun" is attractively over-the-top, and Al Ferrier, whose "Hey! Baby" is a transparent derivation of "Baby Let's Play House." Like *Vol. 1* of this fine series, it's a good collection of a variety of sounds on the cusp of becoming rock & roll, though by this point the line was sometimes being crossed into bona fide early rock. *—Richie Unterberger*

Excello Story, Vol. 3: 1957–1961 / Apr. 6, 1999 / Hip-O ✦✦✦✦
Excello was hitting its prime as a good R&B, blues and rock label in this era. This has swamp-blues by Slim Harpo (just one song, but that's okay as he's well-represented by single-artist anthologies), Lightnin' Slim, Lonesome Sundown and Lazy Lester, who's represented by the great "I Hear You Knockin'" and the original version of "I'm a Lover, Not a Fighter" (covered by the Kinks in the '60s). There's more than Louisiana blues, though. For doo wop, there's the Gladiolas' original version of "Little Darlin'" (covered for a big pop hit by the Diamonds), and the one-shot smash "Oh Julie" by the Crescendos. Carol Fran's "Emmitt Lee" is top-notch, early New Orleans soul that will find favor with any Irma Thomas fan, so close is the arrangement to the sound of Thomas' early records. The sound strays closer to straight rock & roll with Lattimore Brown's "Somebody's Gonna Miss Me" and two early sides by swamp pop legend Warren Storm. *—Richie Unterberger*

The Excello Story, Vol. 4: 1961–1975 / Apr. 6, 1999 / Hip-O ✦✦✦
Just from the large chronological span of the final volume of this series, it's obvious that Excello's momentum started to peter out in its later years. Still, over half of this is fine, rock-solid blues that saw the label keep the flame of raw & funky blues with a soul/R&B influence alive better than almost any other company did in the '60s. There are good cuts by Excello, swamp blues stalwarts Slim Harpo (his hits "Baby, Scratch My Back" and "Tip on In"), Lonesome Sundown, Lightnin' Slim and Silas Hogan, but also some decent tracks by less famed bluesmen like Tabby Thomas, Little Sonny and Charles Sheffield (whose "It's Your Voodoo Working" has a snaky modern New Orleans feel). The last 40 percent of the compilation is given over to more modern sounding soul from the '60s and the first half of the '70s, and this isn't nearly as enjoyable, the last few selections in particularly boasting a generic "sweet soul" feel. It's obvious Tiny Watkins is trying to emulate the feel of Percy Sledge's early material with "Soldier's Sad Story," one of the better soul songs here. *—Richie Unterberger*

Fantastic Funk, Vol. 1 / 1999 / Goldmine/Soul Supply ✦✦✦✦
Goldmine/Soul Supply is the U.K. label that put together the stellar *Sound of Funk* series, compiling a host of terrific deep funk rarities for the groove-obsessed collector. *Fantastic Funk, Vol. 1* is a worthy addition to that legacy, gathering 16 more obscure, infectious funk singles from what seems like an inexhaustible supply. Unlike many deep funk comps, there's a hefty preponderance of vocal performances on this one, which helps give it a bit more personality. Many, many bonus points are awarded just for the inclusion of deep funk legend Lee Fields' "Funky Screw," a would-be dance craze every bit as priceless as its title suggests. Elsewhere, Julia DeWitt gets into an endearingly involved monologue on the cheating tale "If You Want Your Man," which features the oughta-be-a-classic line "Now who in the world ever heard of a nurse's aide convention?!" There's also a solo cut by Sam Moore of Sam & Dave, "Can You Dig It," which interpolates a bit of "Soul Man" in what seems like a desperate bid for recognition. Terrific grooves abound throughout the set, supporting lyrics about love, philosophy, and just plain dancing. More proof that Goldmine is perhaps the most reliable deep funk reissue label around. *—Steve Huey*

Fat! Fat! Fat! / Blubba ✦✦✦
A whole compilation devoted to songs about fat people? While this 18-track collection will certainly win no awards for political correctness, it nonetheless contains a fine selection of R&B and '50s rock & roll tunes all singing about the virtues of the calorically challenged, and usually in a positive, lovestruck manner. Although the cover does depict a 1950s vintage photo of a hugely obese, smiling African-American woman holding a bloody butcher knife, there's certainly no gender bias in the song selection, as Big John Greer's "I'm the Fat Man," Slim Dortsch's "Big Boy Rock" are evenly matched in cholesterol content by Joe Ron and George's "Half Ton Mama," Bill Mack's "Fat Woman" and Bobby Rutledge's "Go Slow Fatso." As single-subject compilations go, this is a pretty insane idea—and a subject matter that some people find disgusting and tasteless—that nevertheless works out fine from a musical standpoint. Love songs for the high-calorie crowd. *—Cub Koda*

☆ **Finger Poppin' and Stompin' Feet: 20 Classic Allen Toussaint Productions for Minit . . .** / Mar. 12, 2002 / Capitol ✦✦✦✦✦
Allen Toussaint is a giant of American popular music, but his work was primarily behind the scenes as a songwriter, producer, arranger, and sessionman. Even as a leader, his songs and recordings became better-known through interpretations and assimilations from such artists as Glen Campbell, Lowell George, and Bonnie Raitt, instead of his darkly sensual, funky records of the '70s. That's why a collection like *Finger Poppin' and Stompin' Feet: 20 Classic Allen Toussaint Productions* is so welcome—it shines a spotlight on Toussaint's most influential work as a producer and songwriter, all from the vaults of Minit Records. This is hardly the totality of Toussaint's contributions—not only are his solo recordings nowhere to be seen, such brilliant work as his collaborations with Lee Dorsey are nowhere to be heard on this disc—but it's an exuberant celebration of a musician at the top of his game. Plus, it's just a hell of a good listen, nearly a greatest-hits collection of New Orleans R&B as a whole, thanks to such classics as the Showmen's "It Will Stand"; Ernie K-Doe's "Mother-in-Law," "A Certain Girl," and "I Cried My Last Tear"; Aaron Neville's "Over You"; Jessie Hill's "Ooh Poo Pah Doo, Pt. 1"; Benny Spellman's "Fortune Teller" and "Lipstick Traces (On a Cigarette)"; and Irma Thomas' "Ruler of My Heart" and "It's Raining." In addition to those, there are lesser-known gems from the same artists, plus cult artists like the Del Royals and Allen Orange, which add seasoning to a collection already bursting with flavor. Even if you already know Allen Toussaint's work and reputation, it's a revelation and a joyous listen. And, needless to say, it's also essential to any pop or R&B collection. *—Stephen Thomas Erlewine*

Finger Poppin' Time: Best of Ocean Drive / Jan. 27, 1998 / Ripete ✦✦
Ripete Records are America's greatest exponents of beach music, a broad term which encompasses a variety of dance-friendly soul sounds popular in the South. Despite the diverse collection of artists on this set—everybody from Jimmy McCracklin to Freda Payne—you don't get the feeling you're listening to different genres because all these tunes have the same bouncing beat (or seem like it anyway). The music has plenty of energy, but after a few tracks the redundant arrangements become boring for listening purposes. But if you're dancing in the sand with your shoes off, these are as good as any to shag to. *—Andrew Hamilton*

The Fire and Fury of Bobby Robinson / Aug. 1, 2000 / RPM ✦✦✦✦
In the late '50s and early '60s, Bobby Robinson produced a good share of interesting rock, blues, and R&B for his Fire and Fury labels, often mixing the forms together for music approximating a blues-soul blend. This disc has 22 Fire and Fury recordings from 1957-1964, and is not the ideal introduction to the peak of Robinson's achievements,

though it's musically respectable and contains a good number of rare performances. Several of the label's biggest and best singles are absent: there's no "Kansas City" (Wilbert Harrison), "Fannie Mae" (Buster Brown), "I Need Your Loving" (Don Gardner & Dee Dee Ford), or "Shake Your Moneymaker" (Elmore James), although all of those artists are represented by other songs. There *are* a couple of the biggest Fire/Fury hits: Bobby Marchan's "There's Something on Your Mind" (the weird R&B-cum-spoken narrative, presented in both parts, not just part two, which was the hit) and Gladys Knight & the Pips' "Every Beat of My Heart." The rest is a fairly interesting yet erratic bag, including little-known outings by famous acts (King Curtis, Lee Dorsey, Jack Dupree); rockabilly-influenced blues (Tarheel Slim's "Number Nine Train"); a strutting talking jazz-blues by Dr. Horse, "Jack That Cat Was Clean"; an instrumental by brilliant blues guitarist Jimmy Spruill; doo wop by the Charts ("Desiree") and a few other groups; June Bateman's ballad "Believe Me Darling," with some extraordinary tremolo guitar by Spruill; and Wilbert Harrison's "Let's Stick Together," to be reworked in 1970 as his comeback hit "Let's Work Together." Fire/Fury worked the rawer end of the R&B/early soul sound in interesting ways, but this is too odds 'n' end-ish to be a completely successful listen. *—Richie Unterberger*

Fire/Fury Records Story / 1993 / Warner Bros. ✦✦✦✦✦
Although the sequencing is a little too scholarly to be truely compulsive listening, the 51-track, double-disc box set *The Fire/Fury Records Story* contains the majority of the major songs recorded for the seminal blues and R&B label. Apart from Elmore James, Wilbert Harrison, Lightnin' Hopkins, Gladys Knight and Lee Dorsey, King Curtis and Mighty Joe Young, there aren't too many big names here, nor are there many hit singles; only James, Harrison and Dorsey are represented by their best-known songs. Still, the absence of big hits makes the consistently high quality of the set all the more impressive, and serious R&B and blues fans will find it well worth their time. *—Stephen Thomas Erlewine*

The Fish That Saved Pittsburgh / 1979 / Lorimar ✦✦✦✦✦
Appearing on many writers' Top Ten worst sports movies of all time, *The Fish That Saved Pittsburgh* might have been an air ball at the box office, but the music for the movie is nothing but net. This fairly obscure album features music arranged and conducted by Thom Bell, with many guests appearing throughout. Fans of the Spinners, the Sylvers, and the Four Tops are treated to deep, rich, textured vocals as well as full funky instrumentation. "Moses Theme," sung by Frankie Bleu, showcases a laid-back '70s groove with an emotional string arrangement coupled with strong bass and percussion. The Four Tops' instantly singable "Chance of a Lifetime" features catchy lyrics that pop over a funk string hook and infectious rhythm. William Hart's falsetto vocals on "Follow Every Dream" serve as a smooth ride over more outstanding arrangements reminiscent of Bell's work with the Spinners. Other standout tracks include "(Do It, Do It) No One Does It Better," "Mighty Mighty Pisces," and the title song. It's a shame that only a limited quantity of "promotional only" records made it to stores in 1979, probably due to the poor attendance at movie theaters. This soundtrack is overlooked as a fitting addition to the soul masterpieces of the '70s, filled with hope, hard work, and dreams. *—Craig Curtice*

Flip Doo Wop, Vol. 1 / Dec. 13, 2001 / Ace ✦✦✦
Originally released on Max and Lillian Feirtags' Flip Records (hence the title), *Flip Doo Wop, Vol. 1* features seminal West Coast doo wop recorded by some of Los Angeles' finest warblers. The label enjoyed an eight-year reign from 1955 to 1963 before ceasing operations. Artists featured are Richard Berry & the Pharaohs, the Six Teens, the Bel-Aires (later Donald Woods & the Velaires), the Rhythm Masters, the Flippers, Candy Rivers & the Falcons, and ex-major-leaguer Arthur Lee Maye, who could sing and hit a baseball. The 22 sides embody many of Flip's finest efforts, including the Six Teens' number 25 pop hit, "A Casual Look," and the Velaires' hurting "Death of an Angel" and "White Port and Lemon Juice," the latter titled after the popular mixed drink of L.A.'s hipsters. *—Andrew Hamilton*

For Connoisseurs Only / Jul. 31, 2001 / Kent ✦✦✦
There are no less than 28 soul rarities from the Modern and Kent labels on this compilation, all dating from the mid-'60s to the mid-'70s, mostly from the last half of the 1960s. Such an anthology is by definition something that's going to appeal to virtually no one but lovers of the genre. But within that guideline, it's satisfactory enough, though short on moments of stunning beauty, as such discs usually are. Z.Z. Hill, Johnny Copeland, Ike & Tina Turner, Lowell Fulson, the Marvellos, and the Ikettes are the well-known or reasonably known names, though none are represented by any of their most famous cuts. Otherwise the names will flash by like the small print in a price guide or auction list. For the most part it's middleweight soul, getting the job done without leaving an indelible mark for a lifetime or even a few days. It's mostly in the more or less mainstream soul mold, though some of these artists (like most of the ones mentioned above) have kept a foot in the blues scene as well. Some above-average efforts, in the context of this compilation at any rate, are Bobby White's "Just Another Week Behind," with echoes of the Impressions (with weaker vocals); Johnny Copeland's "Soul Power," a fine blues-soul shouter from a performer far more talented than most of the surrounding artists; Ike & Tina Turner's "I Need a Man," if only because Tina Turner's vocals create so much more heat than the average track here; the Other Brothers' "I Got Love," which has a Major Lance-like arrangement; and Johnny Williams' "You've Got It," a good mix of bluesy swing with Motown-ish female backup singers. *—Richie Unterberger*

Freestyle Explosion, Vols. 1-5 / May 2, 2000 / Thump ✦✦✦✦✦
Thump's *Freestyle Explosion* compilation series was an excellent, definitive overview of the Latin-influenced dance-pop style born and bred in the clubs of Miami. Thump repackaged all five volumes of the series into a limited-edition slipcased box set, giving devoted freestyle fans a handy way to pick them all up at once. While some of the artists here scored bigger pop-chart successes with ballads, these collections concentrate only on the dancefloor; some of those artists include Stevie B, TKA, Sweet Sensation, the Cover Girls, Exposé, Taylor Dayne, Sa-Fire, Lisette Melendez, Lisa Lisa & Cult Jam with Full Force, Dino, Will to Power, Nu Shooz, and Pretty Poison. *—Steve Huey*

From Chicago to Shreveport: Deep Soul, Vol. 1 / Sep. 18, 2001 / Varese ✦✦✦✦
From Chicago to Shreveport: Deep Soul, Vol. 1 attempts to round up some of the style's more remembered practitioners along with some of their better songs. It's disappointing not to see some of the more popular crossover artists like Aretha Franklin or Otis Redding featured. However, there's no shortage of highlights here despite the lack of big names. You get classic songs like "C.C. Rider" and classic performers like Little Johnny Taylor. Furthermore, by eschewing more obvious deep soul artists like Franklin and Redding, this collection goes out of its way to familiarize you with some of the more obscure artists from the golden age of deep soul. An educational listen sure to inspire further investigation. *—Jason Birchmeier*

From Philly with Love: Rhythm and Soul / 1995 / Legacy/Epic ✦✦✦✦
From Philly with Love: Rhythm and Soul is a fine 14-track collection that features many of the best Philly soul ballads of the early '70s, including "Ooh Child," "When Will I See You Again," "Stay with Me," "Wanna Know Your Name" and "Me and Mrs. Jones." It's not a definitive overview of the genre, but it's a strong sampler. *—Stephen Thomas Erlewine*

Funk Ballads / Nov. 18, 1997 / Polygram Chronicles ✦✦✦
To some the term "funk ballads" may seem an oxymoron—after all, isn't funk supposed to be uptempo dance music?—but if the disco, funk and quiet storm ballads on *Funk Ballads* are anything to judge by, it's term that makes some sense. It basically stands for smooth, slow numbers by soul, R&B, funk and disco artists in the late '70s—essentially, it's the roots of what became known as quiet storm. Although the album isn't definitive, since it draws from only one label, the entertaining *Funk Ballads* captures its era well, featuring hits by Love Unlimited Orchestra ("Midnight and You"), Cameo ("Why Have I Lost You"), Gap Band ("Yearning for Your Love"), Marvin Gaye ("Distant Lover"), Smokey Robinson ("Quiet Storm") and Rose Royce ("Love Don't Live Here Anymore"), among many others. *—Stephen Thomas Erlewine*

Funk Box / Nov. 21, 2000 / Hip-O ✦✦✦✦
At four discs and 55 tracks, Hip-O's *Funk Box* seems to want to be the last word on funk, and while it's a pretty good set, it ends up more representative than definitive of its chosen genre. Virtually all of funk's most important artists are featured, but not always by their most significant singles—sometimes the collection gets it right, and sometimes it's disappointing (leaving out Curtis Mayfield's "Superfly," the Average White Band's "Pick Up the Pieces," War's "Low Rider" and "Why Can't We Be Friends," and the Ohio Players' "Fire" and "Love Rollercoaster" in favor of alternate selections). Still, the *Funk Box* does have a generous helping of full-length funk classics, including several rare 12-inch versions; moreover, it's been digitally remastered, and it features a 48-page booklet. It's just too bad the set doesn't completely hit the mark. *—Steve Huey*

Funk Funk: The Best of Funk Essentials, Vol. 2 / 1994 / Mercury ✦✦✦✦
Picking up where *Funky Stuff* left off, the next installment in the *Funk Essentials* series, 1994's *Funk Funk: The Best of Funk Essentials, Vol. 2*, pumps up the energy and pulls out every stop before finding a few more to grab on this absolutely outstanding compilation that showcases this genre's finest. While the songs on *Funk Funk* won't be surprising to aficionados, what will be pleasing is the inclusion of often hard-to-find 12-inch versions of several favorites—Parliament's "Aquaboogie," Kool & the Gang's slightly mellower "Get Down on It," and the Gap Band's infectious, bass-looped "You Dropped a Bomb on Me" are club classics, well worth hearing in all their extended glory. More importantly, though, is the appearance of the 12-inch version of Orange Crush's "Action." Recorded by Kurtis Blow's own band (Blow's also here solo with his groundbreaking fusion of funk and rap, "The Breaks"), "Action" is a powerful reminder of just how smoothly rap, funk, and soul grew up together across this stunning clash of breakbeat and James Brown guitars. With these three songs priming the groove, it's an easy vibe straight into some of the genre's best-loved songs. Cameo pokes fun at their first hit, "Rigor Mortis," on their mothership-meets-*Star Trek* epic, "Funk Funk," leaving the Bar-Kays' "Let's Have Some Fun" to temper the humor with classic style, and Barry White to smooth the moves with his instrumental "Just a Little More, Baby." Well planned and executed, *Funk Funk* probably couldn't have been better. A mighty ride, this compilation—like its 1993 counterpart—teaches in the gentlest way just how easily the fusion of so many musical styles was able to create a vibrant sound all of its own. *—Amy Hanson*

The Funk Project: How Good Is Good? Vol. 2 / 2001 / Goldmine/Soul Supply ✦✦✦
The quality of the music on this comp is high, and had there been a real package to go with the contents, *The Funk Project: How Good Is Good? Vol. 2* would deserve an even higher rating. In other words, in uncharacteristic fashion, Goldmine/Soul Supply offers absolutely no information about any of the artists presented here. Usually, there are more artists' blurbs and song session details than one can shake a stick at on Goldmine Northern soul compilations, but when it comes to Northern funk, apparently it's a different story. All you can do is praise this record for the consistent quality of its songs and wonder in aggravating mystery as to how many (if any) other cuts these artists are responsible for. As it stands, there are 16 illustrious tracks on *Vol. 2.* Many of them—Walt Jenkins' "Funky Walk," Good Time Charlie's "Rover or Me," Clarence Jackson's "Party Time"—are dyed in the James Brown & the J.B.'s methodology of a hypnotic rhythm with over-the-top effects such as high, echoplexed guitars, slippery yet constant basslines, and grooved-out punchy horns. Others, however, were influenced by the "soul brother" movement of the 1960s, such as the killer, Meters-like funk of "Get Down Brother" or

the Sly Stone-inflected "Trust Your Child, Pt. 1" by Patrizia & Jimmy. In all, though, derivative or not, there isn't a weak cut in the bunch. It's all slam, all stomp, all the time. A killer set of grooves for whatever your next occasion is. *—Thom Jurek*

Funk Sessions / Oct. 30, 2001 / Sessions ♦♦♦♦♦
From the same folks who brought you the *Soul Sessions* compilation comes this badass double-CD set of pure, greasy funk bliss. These discs are chock-full of the hits (30 in all) that defined this music in an era when the funk had not yet been betrayed by disco. There is nothing fancy about the packaging, as Union Square—from Cowley, England—is strictly a licensing operation. The discs are in a slim-line jewel box inside a cool but unremarkable slipcase. Which is fine, because you aren't gonna have them in the box much anyway. For proof, try *starting* things with Funkadelic's "One Nation Under a Groove" (!) and slipping immediately into the Fatback Band's "Do the Bus Stop," drifting into the Isleys' "It's Your Thing." Beginning to get the picture of how these tracks were compiled? Yeah, right, they're all mid-'70s groove jockeying for position on the dancefloor jams. Roy Ayers picks it up from there with "Everybody," before Herbie Hancock's "Fat Mama" and Johnny "Guitar" Watson's "A Real Mother for Ya" turn it up. And that's only half of disc one. It's true, you've heard it all before, but perhaps not like this in a while. On top of having the good taste to jam all these tracks together for maximum groove, the slick juke-savvy producers used the long versions of these cuts whenever possible. Disc two kicks it with Charles Wright's "Express Yourself," before seguing into Maceo Parker's "Got to Get Cha" and the O'Jays' "For the Love of Money." In addition, the set includes the relatively unheard Toney Lee's "Reach Up" (a classic) and the 24-Carat Black's signature tune. The Meters' "Look-Ka Py Py" precedes Aaron Neville's only bona fide funk classic, "Hercules," the Bar-Kays' "Son of Shaft" makes an all-too-rare compilation appearance, and Watson, Fatback, and Funkadelic return, as the set closes with "(Not Just) Knee Deep." Say what you will and argue away, but for sure this pack o' wax tracks should be blarin' out the box at your next soirée y'all. *—Thom Jurek*

Funk Soul Sisters / Jul. 17, 2001 / Metro ♦♦♦♦
Spreading itself thick across three decades of funk, soul, and smooth R&B, Metro's *Funk Soul Sisters* not only covers a fair amount of stylistic ground, but it also mixes chart hits with rare groove, and in turn serves up a compilation that plugs gaps in one's collection while remaining a great listen from front to back. Though the focus is obviously on the women who made these songs what they are, the graceful touch of Roy Ayers is felt on four highlights of the disc's 16 cuts: Bobby Humphrey's "Baby Don't U Know," Eighties Ladies' "I Knew That Love," and two songs from Eighties Ladies' vocalist Sylvia Striplin's solo album ("All Alone" and "Will We Ever Pass This Way Again"), which were released on Ayers' Uno Melodic label in the early '80s. These four songs represent the smoother side of the album, while the remainder—such as Betty Wright's Top Ten hit "Clean Up Woman," the Jones Girls' "Will You Be There" and "I Turn to You," Betty Harris' "There's a Break in the Road," Betty Davis' "No Good at Falling in Love," and Deniece Chandler's "It's You I Need"—are a shade grittier and a bit funkier in comparison. It goes without saying that these songs are uplifting, empowering, and emotionally resonant for those who have gone through the experiences that these artists sing about. Like its counterpart, *Funk Soul Brothers* (seems a bit odd that a compilation focusing on male artists would be necessary, doesn't it?), *Funk Soul Sisters* has plenty to offer. *—Andy Kellman*

Funk Spectrum: Real Funk for Real People / Apr. 5, 1999 / Import ♦♦♦♦
Compiled by Josh Davis (aka DJ Shadow) and Keb Darge, *Funk Spectrum* is yet one more addition to the stable of essential BBE label collections, a virtual primer in old-school funk that assembles 20 tracks likely familiar to only the most diligent of rare groove collectors. According to Davis' liner notes, the omission of artist credits from the sleeve is in homage to the code of B-boy secrecy, although it makes the disc damn hard to critique; that said, the opening "Party Time" conjures the spirit of James Brown to uncanny perfection, "Let's Do It Today" could be a lost Charles Wright & the Watts 103rd Street Band track, and "Clap Your Hands" imagines an alternate reality where the Jackson 5 comprised sisters, not brothers. Darge's ten selections are excellent as well, most of them slavish in their devotion to the genius of James Brown—some are actual covers (Lou Pride's uptempo reading of the perennial "It's a Man's Man's Man's World") and some are just mirror images (Ricky Caloway's "Tell Me," with its "Good God!" interjections), but all boast the funk in spades. *—Jason Ankeny*

Funkgasm / Oct. 21, 1997 / Relativity ♦♦♦♦♦
Crank the volume and clear some dance space when you cue this explosive disc. Trumpeter Tom Browne kicks off this rocket-fueled collection with his bombastic "Funkin' for Jamaica," and *Funkgasm* closes with the eight-minute "The Jam" by Graham Central Station. Sandwiched between are kicking tracks such as "Bootzilla," "For the Love of Money," "Dazz," "Wanna Make Love (Come Flick My Bic)," and other live wires. "Slide" by Slave broke new ground and, like the other selections, is included whole and pure—no radio edits here. An ice breaker for parties, and a must for funk lovers. *—Andrew Hamilton*

Funkin' on the 1 / Jun. 5, 2001 / Simply The Best ♦♦♦
The no-frills *Funkin' on the 1* box set gives you plenty of bang for your buck by dishing out 90 tracks spread across five discs. By no means definitive, the nonetheless highly serviceable box bounces between the well-known and not-so-known, providing a snapshot of all things soul, funk, and proto-disco produced between the mid-'60s and early '80s, with a heavy emphasis on the first half of the '70s. Put the entire set on rotation during a party and put your worries about keeping things fun and varied to rest. There's little overlap here with the myriad funk compilations that were released in the late '90s. For instance, you don't get Parliament's ubiquitous "Flash Light," but you do get the Parliaments' "Breakdown," "Funky Woman," and "Good Ole Music," among others. And while you don't get the Ohio Players at their most familiar, you do get all 113 rough seconds of 1968's Sam & Dave-influenced "Trespassin'." For every classic known by the general populace, like Curtis Mayfield's "Superfly" or Average White Band's "Pick Up the Pieces," you get a handful of relatively (!) unknown gems, such as Donald Byrd's "Change," and Gil Scott-Heron's "The Bottle." Repetition with groups like the Meters (one song per disc), Ripple (three songs), and Average White Band (enough to choke a large farm animal) can be forgiven with the representation of some of the lesser-documented acts of the genres. Housed in a compact box, its cheap import price is good for an impulse purchase. Unless you're a die-hard collector and have all of this (not very likely), the content should please just about anyone. *—Andy Kellman*

Funkology / Oct. 9, 2001 / Wea International ♦♦♦♦♦
After rappers began sampling old-school funk tracks from the 1970s, plenty of record companies started knocking out funk compilations to cash in on the newfound popularity of these sampled gems. *Funkology* is an above-average (and quite generous) version of this kind of collection. Though it runs in to some of the licensing and programming problems that plague similar compilations, it remains a very impressive and diverse sampling of classic funk tunes. Of course, there are plenty of classic jams from the acknowledged masters of the genre: James Brown logs in with "Sex Machine" and "Make It Funky," while George Clinton's P-Funk legacy is represented by such gems as "P-Funk (Wants to Get Funked Up)," "One Nation Under a Groove," and "Atomic Dog." There are also plenty of one-shot hits, like Yarbrough & Peoples' sizzling synth funk classic "Don't Stop the Music" and Charles Wright & the Watts 103rd Street Rhythm Band's jazzy, horn-laden "Express Yourself." The poppier tracks on the album are balanced with some sizzling jazz-funk tracks like Billy Cobham's percussion-driven "Stratus (Pt. 1)" and Herbie Hancock's rap/electronic synthesis "Rockit." Rounding out the package are some lesser-known tracks by familiar artists: Bootsy Collins' gleefully goofy funk epics are passed over in favor of "I'd Rather Be With You," a surprisingly sultry ballad laced with some fluid wah-wah guitar licks, and Fred Wesley and the J.B.'s more rootsy tracks are downplayed in favor of "Blow Your Head," a wild funk jam whose squiggly synthesizer leads paved the way for synth funk artists like Zapp. *Funkology* manages to cover an impressive amount of ground during its generous running time and this makes one of the best compilations for a novice funk fan to pick up. *—Donald A. Guarisco*

Funkology, Vol. 1: Got to Give It Up / Sep. 12, 1995 / Motown ♦♦♦♦
This excellent first volume of Motown's *Funkology* series features songs recorded between 1974 and 1983, some previously unreleased or alternate LP versions. All unedited, including 11:48 seconds of Marvin Gaye's "Got to Give It Up." Twelve inch mixes rule: the Commodores' "Brick House," Rick James' "Busting Out," Bobby Nunn's "She's Just a Groupie," Dazz Band's "Let It Whip," and "Gigolette," by Ozone will have you bouncing around the room. So will an extended "Square Biz" the underrated funk/rap by Tina Marie, the Commodores' "Machine Gun," and two sultry jam-ons from the Mary Jane Girls. *—Andrew Hamilton*

Funkology, Vol. 2: Behind the Groove / Sep. 12, 1995 / Motown ♦♦♦♦
The groove never stops on *Funkology, Vol. 2*, a collection of bottom heavy Motown tracks recorded between 1976 and 1984. Dancefloor jams by Teena Marie, the Commodores, Diana Ross, and Stevie Wonder will rock any house. Lesser-known tracks such as "Strutt My Thang," by Ozone, "We Like To Party," by Switch, and the Dazz Band's "Keep It Live (On the K.I.L.)" keep the funk flowing. *—Andrew Hamilton*

The Funky 16 Corners / Nov. 1, 2001 / Stones Throw ♦♦♦♦♦
This outstanding collection of funk singles compiled by Stones Throw Records includes 16 songs recorded between 1968 and 1974 by obscure underground groups from America. One of the strongest crossover funk labels of the last decade, Stones Throw pays due respect to modern music's forgotten grandfathers on this most grooving recorded history lesson of impeccable quality. Anchored by the Highlighters' classic "The Funky 16 Corners," whereby the Indianapolis group upped the ante in 1969's craze for bands counting "corners" (read: hit me three times!) by breaking the recorded benchmark with 16, this compilation leans heavily on the James Brown sect and celebrates the lesser-known groups of the genre, who with high talent and low budget put to tape some of the most raw funk ever captured to date. Representative modernist Cut Chemist of Jurassic 5 even gets an interpretation slot with "Bunky's Pick" on one of two bonus tracks. Every track is essential to the record and every groove a lost gem. An informative 16-page booklet with full-color photos is included. *—Nic Kincaid*

Funky Broadway: Stax Revue Live at the 5/4 Ballroom / 1992 / Stax ♦♦♦♦♦
Nearly an hour of previously unreleased Stax soul recorded at a Los Angeles venue in August 1965, including cuts by Booker T. & the MG's, Carla Thomas, Rufus Thomas, William Bell, and the Mar-Keys; a couple of relatively little-known Stax vocal groups, the Mad Lads and the Astors, round out the program. This isn't just of interest to soul completists. Good live mid-'60s soul records, in decent fidelity, are fairly rare items. This is genuinely galvanizing stuff, with a rawer, more party-oriented feel than the classic Stax studio sides of the same era. Especially good are Booker T. & the MG's, who really burn through classics like "Green Onions" and "Soul Twist," and Rufus Thomas, who clowns his way through a nine-minute version of "Do the Dog." *—Richie Unterberger*

Funky Soundtracks, Vol. 1 / 1997 / Sound Score Corporation ♦♦♦♦
The soundtrack music created for various types of action films or television shows has proven to be like some kind of artifact of archaeology: not considered all that valuable when it was originally buried, but creating much interest once unearthed. Between the rapidly growing fandoms of soundtrack music and vintage funk, this series should be able to keep winding out volumes well into the future. Running out of good material is even doubtful, since there's almost as much of this music as there is action entertainment produced each year. Not every soundtrack is going to be genius; in fact, the actual water level seems more along the lines of functionally groovy. This is music created efficiently to fill a demand. Some of the soloists sound like they have their eyes shut when

they are blowing; the producer surely had his wide open, staring at the time clock. Professional players are invariably called in to make sure the finished job is both quick and beefy, with the resulting musical efforts often contrasting sharply depending on what city's film scene produced them: New York, Los Angeles, Rome, London, and Paris are among the many options. The introductory set in this series spans the decade beginning in the mid-'60s, the music bearing the inescapable stamp of that era's creative tumult. Psychedelia, raw funk, and out jazz are just a few of the ingredients in the salad, but prepare for it to be mixed as if it was a bag of groceries that Detective Bullit ran over in a high-speed chase. Lalo Schifrin was the fellow responsible for that soundtrack, one of several Hollywood composers who was adept at utilizing both intense jazz and weird rock elements. Other creators of action music featured here include Quincy Jones, Les Baxter, and J.J. Johnson. Although not as big a name, Johnny Harris gets a bigger chunk of time, with more than five minutes building up a perfect background for a twisted, corrupt, fuzz box solo, a soundtrack excerpt from the forgotten film *Fragments of Fear.* With this type of music the compilation concept is preferable to investing in full soundtracks, even if one was able to find them. The superb, inventive sequencing and editing make these collections real winners. Speaking of which, this "funky" thing combines two previously released mini-LPs that were known as *Funky Soundtracks* and *Funky Soundtracks 2*, plus a couple of extra tracks. *—Eugene Chadbourne*

Funky Soundtracks, Vol. 3 / 1996 / Sound Score Corporation ♦♦♦♦
This collection of soundtrack music walks through the same neighborhoods as previous *Funky Soundtrack* collections, but checks out some different street corners. The eerie sleaze of New York's 14th Street was captured like never before or after in *Taxi Driver,* and fans of the film probably don't need to be reminded that the Bernard Hermann soundtrack was one of the main reasons such a chilling effect was created. Souped-up rockabilly can also have a place in the action film genre, a fact that means this particular compilation is especially fun, following up the bleached-out Wayne Cochran with Quincy Jones' theme from *Ironside.* Of course there is lots of Jones, as is par for the course with this series. Despite his efforts to be the great American composition genius, Jones really seems at his best when hacking out quick bits of exploitative trash. It is really a misuse of that word, since a garbage scavenger would probably die in shock coming across high-powered music such as this, played by chopsy pals of Jones out for vengeance as well as extra cash. Another familiar participant is Lalo Schifrin, who created some of the most interesting scores for action films and television shows. There are also tracks from Roy Budd, Neil Hefti, and even Manfred Mann. An excerpt from *The Odd Couple*'s soundtrack might not be a place one expects to find the funk, but in the post-*Sanford and Son* era, the situation comedy genre actually did become a stronghold for bass poppers. It is another aspect of that familiar period in wise-ranging musical anarchy beginning in the mid-'60s and drinking deep of the washed-out but still funky '70s. Something or somebody called the Tri-Lateral Committee is responsible for the sequencing and editing, and really deserves the *Dirty Harry* 45-magnum salute. The album is so well thought out in terms of programming that it almost plays like an extended composition, which if it was would represent one of the greatest musical compositions in history. There are many fantastic performances, however, heard here in a compilation context that actually makes each track sound more interesting than it is. Perhaps some of the material isn't even all that good, so mightily enhanced it is by this faultless production. Forget the "perhaps" part when it comes to Tom Scott's music for *Starksy and Hutch.* *—Eugene Chadbourne*

Funky Tales / 1996 / Ace ♦♦♦♦♦
Although the Nashville-based Excello label is primarily known for its recordings of Louisiana swamp blues with Slim Harpo, Lazy Lester, and Lightnin' Slim, it moved into soul music pretty aggressively in the late '60s and early '70s. This 24-song compilation of tracks that were cut for the label between 1967 and 1976 offers yet more evidence of how many vital, little-known soul sides were issued during the era by small companies. This is the greasy stuff, too, with no relationship to either "sweet soul" or proto-disco. If you like the sound of the James Brown band circa 1969, or the hardest elements of Stax/Volt, and want more of the same by acts that you never heard on the radio, this is a good investment. Aside from Slim Harpo (represented by a funkish number) and Marva Whitney and Maceo Parker (both of whom recorded for Excello after leaving the James Brown road show), few of these names will ring any bells for all but the most seasoned soul collectors. It's mostly quality, gritty fare, including quite a few percolating instrmentals (the underwater Booker T.-like groove on the Solicitors' "Music for the Brothers" is a highlight). For some quality imitation James Brown arrangements, check out the two previously unissued tracks by the mysterious Little Royal. *—Richie Unterberger*

The Further Adventures of Funk Soul Brothers / May 14, 2002 / Metro ♦♦♦
With the exception of the Meters' "Cissy Strut," this is for the most part lesser-known '60s/'70s funk. But obscurity doesn't mean poor quality. This CD's treats include Cymande's "Bra," Lonnie Smith's "Lean Meat," Pee Wee Ellis' "Moon Walk," and Curtis Mayfield's "You're So Good to Me." Other hard-to-find treasures include Baby Huey & the Baby Sitters' "Hard Times," Lightnin' Rod's "Sport," and Maceo Parker & All the King's Men's drivin' "Got to Getcha"—not to mention Bobby Womack's plea to a resisting woman, "(If You Want My Love) Put Something Down on It." *—Andrew Hamilton*

George Goldner Presents The Gone Story: Doo-Wop To Soul 1957–1963 / Nov. 23, 1999 / WestSide ♦♦♦♦
Here are 65 songs representing a dead-perfect cross-section of the singles output of one of New York's great R&B labels of the late '50s and early '60s. The opening cut, the Dubs' slow, romantic "Don't Ask Me (To Be Lonely)," shows just how far George Goldner's conception of R&B had come in the four years since he'd founded Rama Records in 1953. Gone Records, starting in 1957, featured a more sophisticated output, oriented toward elegant, impassioned ballads rather than the dance numbers that had gone over so big in the mid-'50s. The label's sound was very polished, although Goldner and company found room for an occasional hard rocker like "Love Is Dynamite" by would-be rockabilly star Gary Dale or lady rock & roller Jo-Ann Campbell's "Wait a Minute." A few of the harmony groups turn in rousing, rocking performances—the Willows' rendition of "Let's Fall in Love" is a delight, a bright, glowingly fresh rendition of an old chestnut that, if it isn't in the league of "I Only Have Eyes for You" by the Flamingos, is still worth owning. Other noteworthy items include the Channels and their soaring "Altar of Love," and the Isley Brothers, whose "Everybody's Gonna Rock 'n Roll" is a lost jewel out of their early history. Even Cab Calloway rose to the occasion with a solid piece of rock & roll, "Tomorrow Night," showing that the '30s entertainer could have cut it with the kids if they'd given him a listen. Another oddity worth giving more than one listen is Jackie DeShannon (billed as Jackie Dee) doing a Brenda Lee/Wanda Jackson turn on the countrified rock & roll ballad "I'll Be True to You." The notes are reasonably thorough, and the sound is state-of-the-art. *—Bruce Eder*

Get Down Tonight: Best of T.K. Records / 1990 / Rhino ♦♦♦♦♦
A fine collection of the best tracks from the seminal '70s disco label, including tracks by KC & the Sunshine Band, George McCrae, Gwen McCrae, Betty Wright, Benny Latimore, and Little Beaver. *—Stephen Thomas Erlewine*

Get Low Down!: The Soul of New Orleans, '65–'67 / Feb. 2001 / Sundazed ♦♦♦♦
Although it wasn't the most renowned phase of his career, in the mid-'60s Allen Toussaint did a great deal of arranging, producing, and songwriting for the Sansu label. This double CD has 50 songs that came out on Sansu, and occasionally on Bell and Tou-Sea, during that era, including four previously unreleased tracks. Of all these tunes, just two, Lee Dorsey's "Ride Your Pony" and "Holy Cow," were sizable national hits, and indeed other than Dorsey none of the performers are that famed, though Benny Spellman, Betty Harris, Earl King, and Art Neville all made some noted marks on the R&B scene. This is the sound of early New Orleans rock and R&B turning into full-fledged soul music, although New Orleans soul would never became as successful and identifiable a brand as Detroit, Memphis, Philadelphia, or New York soul. While it's fairly strong stuff with a distinctively New Orleans pre-funk beat and some bluesy licks, it lacks the classic melodies and hooks of the best 1960s soul, and there's some sameyness to much of the material, a little over half of which was penned by Toussaint. It does much to fill in an under-documented part of New Orleans rock history, though, since many of these releases, by such obscure singers as Curly Moore, Eldridge Holmes, Diamond Joe, and Willie Harper, have rarely or never been reissued. While it might seem that Dorsey and Harris are under-represented by this compilation (with just two songs each), note that each is well represented by single-artist anthologies should you want to take a deeper dive. *—Richie Unterberger*

Get on the Bus / Oct. 8, 1996 / Interscope ♦♦♦
The soundtrack *Get on the Bus*, Spike Lee's tribute to the Million Man March of 1995, is comprised of new songs from soul and hip-hop artists as diverse as Curtis Mayfield, D'Angelo, Stevie Wonder, Doug E. Fresh, Blackstreet, the Neville Brothers, Guru and Earth, Wind & Fire. Nearly every song is loosely tied into the film's theme of black empowerment and social liberation. Even with an explicit political agenda on hand, the music rarely sinks into dogma, simply because these musicians are too talented for that. Much of the music here is first-rate, and the album holds together *because* of its diversity, not in spite of it. One complaint: Though the advertisements mention it prominently, the song Michael Jackson wrote explicitly for *Get on the Bus* is left off the soundtrack, per the King of Pop's orders. *—Stephen Thomas Erlewine*

☆ **Girl Group Greats** / Feb. 27, 2001 / Rhino ♦♦♦♦♦
There are two ways of looking at Rhino's *Girl Group Greats.* First, you could argue that it's unnecessary, since every one of its 20 cuts is known (and probably owned) by girl group collectors. Second, you could argue that it's absolutely necessary, since every one of its 20 tracks forms the essential foundation for a girl group collection. And that's probably the best way to view the collection, since it summarizes all the girl group hits from the early '60s, including cuts from Motown and solo cuts that fit the musical definition, even if they aren't by groups. So, this turns out to be a nearly impeccable collection of early-'60s pop, as not one of these 20 songs could qualify as anything less than indispensible (with the possible exception of Joanie Sommers' "Johnny Get Angry," which still stands as a great artifact of its times). Ultimately, this isn't an album for collectors, but rather something for a listener wanting an immediate immersion into the best of girl groups, and this functions flawlessly. *—Stephen Thomas Erlewine*

Girl Group Sound: 25 All Time Greatest Hits From Red Bird Records / Jun. 26, 2001 / Varese ♦♦♦♦
Varese Sarabande's *Girl Group Sound: 25 All Time Greatest Hits From Red Bird Records* comes ten years after Charly Records released the four-disc *Red Bird Story.* This single disc whittles the previous 96 tracks down to 25, and the result feels like a sampler more than a stand-alone hits collection. *Girl Group Sound: 25 All Time Greatest Hits From Red Bird Records* is a disc that falls somewhere between an introduction for newbies and a treat for serious girl group collectors. Half the disc consists of well-known songs that charted in the Top 50 (e.g., "The Boy From New York City" by the Ad Libs), whereas the rest are lower-charting (but memorable) tracks or B-side cuts, like "I Wonder" by the Butterflys (with great production by Phil Spector). All the rare, non-hit tracks were part of the four-disc set, so ardent fans would be unlikely to choose it. *Girl Group Sound: 25 All Time Greatest Hits From Red Bird Records* is probably designed for the newer girl group fan who is familiar with the famous songs but may be hesitant to dive headfirst into larger box sets. If nothing else, *Girl Group Sound: 25 All Time Greatest Hits From Red Bird Records* proves the

strength and depth of the girl group genre. Standout tracks include the original version of "Go Now" by Bessie Banks and an alternate version of "The Kind of Boy You Can't Forget," made famous by the Raindrops but here recorded by the Jellybeans. Since the complete *Red Bird Story* is unavailable, this is a great intro to the Jerry Leiber & Mike Stoller label which employed Jeff Barry & Ellie Greenwich. *—JT Griffith*

Girl Zone / 1986 / Impact ✦✦

Here are 16 tracks in the girl group style (although usually performed by solo singers, not groups), originally released on Decca in the 1960s. Alas, this acts as evidence of how generally inferior British girl group records were to ones being produced across the Atlantic, with occasional exceptions. Much of this is average pop, with decorative flourishes of '60s production the only factors that really distinguish this from pop of any era. Some sparks are kicked up by Beverly (aka Beverly Martyn), Marianne Faithfull's "The Sha La La Song" (one of her better early tracks), and Lulu's smoking cover of Goffin-King's "I Can't Hear You No More," though each of these cuts is available on better compilations. Trainspotter types might want to note the presence of Vashti's "Some Things Just Stick in Your Mind" (one of the least impressive songs that Mick Jagger and Keith Richards donated to other artists), the Orchids' "Mr. Scrooge" (an early Shel Talmy production), and the Vernons Girls' "Only You Can Do It," covered to greater effect by French singer Françoise Hardy. *—Richie Unterberger*

Girls Girls Girls, Vols. 1-14 / Marginal ✦✦✦✦✦

If you're pretty much done with your bedrock "classic" rock collection and are looking for genres to plumb in greater depth, you should be aware that the girl group style provides a surprisingly deep well of undiscovered recordings. In comparison to, say, rockabilly, doo wop, and garage rock, there have been relatively few reissues of obscure, non-hit early- to mid-'60s girl group singles. That's beginning to change, with an increasing number of rarity collections. The *Girls Girls Girls* anthologies comprise the most extensive series in this line by far, sort of the *Pebbles* of girl groups—14 volumes' worth by the end of 1995, with more no doubt to come. The focus is not on girl groups per se, but early to mid-'60s female performers who sang in the style; in fact, most of the tracks are by solo female singers, not actual groups. Now, you've got to be pretty committed to go for a complete set of these, as they sell at import prices. If you do want to take the plunge, you won't be disappointed at the quantity—each volume has 20 tracks (the earliest have 25), meaning that if you get every installment so far, you'll have about 300 rarities. Quality is a different story—like many garage or rockabilly compilations, it's erratic, mixing gems with the routine and humdrum. There *are* some gems, though, which very few people have heard, by the likes of Barbara Dane, Vicki Salee, Ann Cole, Patty Walsh, and Nancy Adams. What is most astonishing, aside from the sheer quantity of material unearthed, is the considerable range the series encompasses. Extremely Catholic in their tastes, the compilers include just about every permutation of the classic girl group/early '60s female-sung pop-rock sound imaginable: quasi-Spector productions, dippy White teen idols, supper-club ballads, novelties, hard R&B, smoldering near-blues, Motown imitations, New Orleans R&B, Italian and British girl singers, TV/movie celebrities, and early soul. Most of the performers are no-names, but there are also some choice rarities by stars like Mary Wells, Carole King, and Betty Everett, as well as flops by one-hit wonders like Diane Renay, Peggy March, and Dodie Stevens. Which volumes you like the best, and even which tracks strike your fancy, depends on your very individual or idiosyncratic tastes—no one's going to like every cut on any given volume, but the amazing variety is also going to keep most girl group fans from being bored for too long. Oddly, the later volumes seem to feature better material than the first ones; it usually works in exactly the reverse for these sorts of series. Unfortunately, there are no liner notes, though the sound (probably remastered from vinyl copies) is usually pretty good. *—Richie Unterberger*

Girls Got Soul / Jul. 4, 2000 / Kent ✦✦✦✦✦

This 25-track compilation consists solely of Atlantic female-sung soul from the 1960s, concentrating largely on cuts that weren't hits, even when the performers were famous (and not all of these singers were). The only hugely successful Atlantic woman of the 1960s was, of course, Aretha Franklin, and although she has a couple of songs here (the 1967 LP track "Save Me" and the 1968 B-side "Ain't No Way"), they're not among her more familiar ones. Still, the talent aboard this anthology is enough to fill a wing of the Rock and Roll Hall of Fame: Mary Wells, LaVern Baker, Ruth Brown, the Sweet Inspirations, Patti LaBelle & the BlueBelles, Barbara Lynn, and Doris Troy, for starters. It's true that if you've been collecting soul CDs diligently for more than a decade, you might have a good deal of this, particularly on the Soul Classics label. Even if that's the case, though, this is a tremendous listen, just below the top cut of soul anthologies of any sort, and certainly one of the very best CD various-artist collections of obscure '60s soul. The brilliant producers and songwriters enlisted by Atlantic throughout the decade ensure a consistent high quality as do the talents of the vocalists themselves. Among the neglected treasures here are Doris Troy's West Indian-influenced "Whatcha Gonna Do About It" covered by the Hollies; LaVern Baker's ebullient original version of "Bumble Bee" covered for a hit by the Searchers; the Ikettes' sultry 1962 Top 20 hit "I'm Blue (The Gong-Gong Song)"; and the lush Bert Berns production of Baker's 1964 flop single "Go Away." As far as insanely rare things that will even whet the appetite of maniac collectors, there's the solid, somewhat Motown 1965 pop-soul single by the unknown Rozetta Johnson and Ann Mason's "You Can't Love Me (In the Midnight Hour)," a strange but impassioned "answer" record to "In the Midnight Hour." Barbara Lynn's version of "You'll Lose a Good Thing" on this disc, incidentally, is a 1967 remake, not her original 1962 hit; if you're disappointed by her merely OK reworking of that classic, as compensation there's a previously unreleased 1968 outtake, "Unloved, Unwanted Me." *—Richie Unterberger*

Girls With Guitars / 1989 / Impact ✦✦

Despite what the title might imply, this is not a compilation of self-contained female rock groups (which were a real rarity in the 1960s). It's a selection of 16 of the gutsier mid-'60s British tracks that were sung by U.K. women, usually in a girl group-type style. It's a good concept for a reissue compilation. The problem was that there isn't a great depth of material to choose from in this arena, most British girl group records being rather timid copies of the American prototypes. Certainly much of the songs here are energetically performed, but the material just isn't very arresting. Goldie & the Gingerbreads (actually an American group based in Britain) were one of the few all-woman bands from the era that played their own instruments, but the two cuts on offer here aren't that special. Lulu, as is often the case on British '60s female rock compilations, takes the honors with her soulful "I'll Come Running Over." A more unlikely highlight is the Vernons Girls' zany update of Bizet-Hammerstein's "Dat's Love." *—Richie Unterberger*

Go Girl!: Soul Sisters Tellin' It Like It Is / Oct. 15, 1996 / Rhino ✦✦✦✦✦

The concept here is made plain in the title: tough female soul singers, singing about the hard bumps of romance with toughness and independence. If that's what you want, there's plenty of straight talking here. If you're primarily after good late-'60s/early-'70s soul, it delivers that as well. Aside from Aretha Franklin's "Respect," none of these were big pop hits; many of them didn't even make a splash in the R&B world. It's a good mix of lesser-known tracks by Ann Peebles, Irma Thomas, Betty Wright, and Mable John with ones by singers who are hardly known at all outside of soul aficionados, like Janice Tyrone, Priscilla Price, Jeane & the Darlings, and James Brown protégée Lyn Collins. It also has the Velvelettes' "Needle in a Haystack," one of the least frequently anthologized mid-'60s Motown singles. *—Richie Unterberger*

Go Go Power: Classic Chess Soul / 196 / Charly ✦✦✦✦

Culled from the deep vaults of Chicago's Chess Records, *Go Go Power: Classic Chess Soul* takes its name from a fantastic slice of gritty Chicago R&B groove by pint-sized soulster Sugar Pie DeSanto. The songs here were not chart hits in the U.S., but were popular in the U.K., where clubs devoted to soul music continue to thrive. Marlena Shaw's excellent "Wade in the Water" shows that she wasn't restricted to jazz recordings, and Billy Stewart surprises with the funky rendition of the blues standard "Everyday (I Have the Blues)." As if they weren't potent enough by themselves, Sugar Pie DeSanto and Etta James team up for "In the Basement" and ask you to "stop and check yourself" on "Do I Make Myself Clear." It's also nice to see lesser-known names make stellar appearances here, like the Knight Brothers—best known for their 1965 ballad "Temptation 'Bout to Get Me"—turn in a Memphis burner with "That'll Get It," while Chicago staple Bobby McClure proves he knows what he wants with the pulsing "Peak of Love." A thoroughly consistent selection that makes for a fine downtown diversion when the uptown gloss and polish of Motown seems too genteel. *—Wade Kergan*

Going Back: A Collection of Rhythm & Blues / Aug. 15, 2000 / Specialty ✦✦✦

What unites these 26 tracks? They're all black vocal group sides from 1960-1970, originally released on the Galaxy, Fantasy, 4-J, Riverside, and Specialty labels. That might be a fragile thread to tie a compilation around, but basically it's a way for Fantasy, which now distributes Specialty, to round up a bunch of doo wop, R&B, and soul rarities that it has license to. It's an agreeable though not great listen, illustrating in a modest way the transitional links between doo wop and soul music. It mixes some late-period doo wop sounds—some as late as 1964, as with the Showcases' "(This Love) Was Real"—with other '60s records that went into soul and a bit of girl group music, the harmonies retaining links to the doo wop era. Only one of these, the Sevilles' rollicking 1960 single "Charlena," made the national charts (and only at number 84, for that matter), so for both doo wop and soul fans, this is bound to include some damned hard to find sides. As for cuts that make the leap from OK to noteworthy, the Serenaders' 1963 single "Adios, My Love" is a superbly arranged, energetic cut that (according to the liner notes) included original Temptations Eddie Kendricks and Eldridge Bryant; the Playgirls' "Donnie" is rare and slightly raw girl group soul; and Lonnie Russ' "Something Old, Something New" has the kind of orchestration that you might associate with a group like the Skyliners. As for a big name, there's a pre-Motown single by the Four Tops, 1962's "Pennies From Heaven" (on Riverside). As for a big price tag, there's Eugene Knox's "Miss You"/"Carmelita," pairing a smoocher with a Latin-influenced uptempo tune, originally issued by Galaxy in 1962, and so rare that it reportedly is worth up to four figures on the collector's market. *—Richie Unterberger*

Gold Soul / 1970 / Stax ✦✦✦

A misleading title, since only a few of these 13 tracks went gold, and a couple are downright weak. David Porter's "Can't See You When I Want To" simply takes up space. Mavis Staples' "A House Is Not a Home" fails to excite, and besides, the song has been redone to death. However, "I Like What You're Doing to Me," by Carla Thomas, and the Emotions' "So I Can Love" represent Stax's soft side well. And the melodic "I Never Found a Girl," by Eddie Floyd, and William Bell & Judy Clay's "Private Number" are excellent midtempo shufflers. The Soul Children's dramatic "Sweeter He Is," Rufus Thomas' "Do the Funky Chicken," and Johnnie Taylor's "Who's Making Love" are definitive Stax. Goodies by Booker T. & the MG's, Isaac Hayes, Albert King, and William Bell complete the collection. *—Andrew Hamilton*

★ **Golden Age of American Rock 'n' Roll, Vol. 1** / 1991 / Ace ✦✦✦✦✦

For many years, Original Sound's *Oldies But Goodies* series was acknowledged as the best source for catching up on the many great early rock & roll hits by artists who had only one (or two, or three, or even a few more) classics to offer. Ace's *Golden Age of American Rock 'n' Roll* series, however, has surpassed *Oldies But Goodies* as the series of choice in the CD age. Even at an import price, they offer better value (with 30 songs each!); they use the best possible available source tapes for remastering; they also offer lengthy, intelligent liner notes and some photos, where Original Sound have historically offered none. Most important, they offer a wealth of great hits from rock & roll's first decade as a widespread phenomenon (1954-1963), some of which are very difficult to find on other recordings, CD or not. There are some huge hits represented, but an equal amount of attention is paid to lower-charting items that have fallen out of rotation at oldies stations, as well as some slight/regional hits that you might not have heard even if you grew up during the era. *Vol. 1*, like each installment, reflects the incredible diversity and excitement of rock's first decade: doo wop, primitive rockabilly, girl groups, instrumental rock, proto-soul, pop/rock, and more, ranging from famous one-shots (the Jaynetts' "Sally Go 'Round the Roses," the Penguins' "Earth Angel") to semi-forgotten treasures like the Fendermen's "Mule Skinner Blues" and Toni Fisher's "The Big Hurt." —*Richie Unterberger*

★ **The Golden Age of American Rock 'n' Roll, Vol. 2** / 1993 / Ace ♦♦♦♦♦
No volume of the *Golden Age of American Rock 'n' Roll* series is more essential than any other one. As all have a good range of styles, and a mix of big and small hits, none is particularly recommended more than others; all are worth acquiring if you want to build a serious rock & roll collection. *Vol. 2* has plenty of classics (the Silhouettes' "Get a Job," Maurice Williams' "Stay," Lonnie Mack's "Memphis," the Rivieras' "California Sun," Link Wray's "Rumble") to go along with some neat one-shots (the Bell Notes' "I've Had It," Barbara George's "I Know," Harold Dorman's "Mountain of Love"). Just as interesting are the minor hits, like the Eternals' ridiculous "Rockin' in the Jungle" (uptempo doo wop with side-splitting bird calls) and the Gladiolas' original version of "Little Darlin'" (covered with much bigger success by the Diamonds). —*Richie Unterberger*

★ **The Golden Age of American Rock 'n' Roll, Vol. 3** / 1994 / Ace ♦♦♦♦♦
This is full of more good, classic stuff. Everyone will have different favorites according to their tastes, which is an advantage of having such a diverse collection on CD—you can skip around as you like. The roll call here includes many classic one-shots, by Wilbert Harrison ("Kansas City"), Bill Parsons ("The All American Boy," sung by Bobby Bare, although Parsons got the label credit), the Teddy Bears ("To Know Him Is to Love Him," Phil Spector's first classic), the Turbans ("When You Dance"), Skip & Flip ("It Was I"), the Olympics ("Western Movies"), and the Castells ("Sacred"). —*Richie Unterberger*

★ **The Golden Age of American Rock 'n' Roll, Vol. 4** / 1994 / Ace ♦♦♦♦♦
Another reliably well-packaged collection of major and minor pre-Beatles rock hits. Besides the hits by stars like Dion, Gary "U.S." Bonds, Jan & Dean, and Buddy Knox, you have plenty of one-shots by the likes of the Edsels ("Rama Lama Ding Dong"), Little Caesar & the Romans ("Those Oldies but Goodies"), Barbara Lynn ("You'll Lose a Good Thing"), and Ray Sharpe (the classic R&B/jump rocker "Linda Lu"). The further the series goes, the deeper it gets into the lower rungs of the charts, so even rock scholars may not have previously heard cuts by the likes of Nat Kendrick, Nappy Brown, or the Royaltones. Others you may have only heard once or twice, like the ones by Tommy Facenda, the Rip Chords, and Billy & Lillie. —*Richie Unterberger*

★ **The Golden Age of American Rock 'n' Roll, Vol. 5** / 1995 / Ace ♦♦♦♦♦
It's been said before, but it bears repeating: much of the history (and soul) of early rock & roll resides not only in the recordings of giants like Elvis, Little Richard, Chuck Berry, and Buddy Holly, but in the literally hundreds of acts who managed to produce one or two great singles, in an incredible variety of styles. You can't claim to have a comprehensive rock & roll collection without seeking these out, and you'll have a surprising amount of fun doing so. The fifth volume of the *Golden Age of American Rock 'n' Roll* series shows no signs of flagging in its mission to document these important sounds. Big hits by stars (Freddie Cannon, Jan & Dean, Gene Chandler); huge one-shot hits like Dale & Grace's "I'm Leaving It Up to You," and Johnnie & Joe's "Over the Mountain, Across the Sea," and Jimmy McCracklin's "The Walk"; treasured cult classics by the Showmen ("It Will Stand") and Eddie Fontaine ("Nothin' Shakin'," covered by the Beatles on *Live at the BBC*); all are here, and more. —*Richie Unterberger*

The Golden Era of Doo-Wops: Herald Records / 1994 / Relic ♦♦♦♦♦
Herald Records existed for a good deal longer than most independent R&B labels, 1953 through 1963. Founded by Freddie Mendelsohn, the company started off with a pair of hard blues recordings by Eddie Boyd and Little Walter Jacobs, but soon after, pressing plant owner Al Silver came aboard with another new partner—later buying out Mendelsohn—and transformed Herald into an R&B specialty label. The company began recording R&B harmony groups, including the Rocketeers and the Five Willows; it was in 1955 that they had their first success with the Nutmegs' "Story Untold," and later that year scored a major hit with "When You Dance" by the Turbans. Later acts included the Mint Juleps, Little Butchie Saunders & His Buddies, and the Debonaires. Beginning in 1958, the company began courting the rock & roll market with acts such as the Mello Kings, the Desires, and the Loungers, but it was Maurice Williams and the Zodiacs with "Stay," a monster hit in 1960, who did the best for the label. This 28-song collection includes all of Herald's biggest R&B and rock & roll hits, starting with the mid-1950s doo wop classic "Story Untold," driven by Leroy Griffin's impassioned lead singing. The Debonaires sing well enough on "Darling," but the most notable attribute of the pleasant midtempo ballad is the searing guitar solo by arranger Wesley L. Jackson. The Heralds, formed out of the Billy Dawn Quartet and the Four Dukes, offer more of a bluesy sound, complete with a raunchy band sound on "Gonna Love You Everyday," which, properly speaking, belongs on a blues rather than a doo wop anthology. From later in he label's history, "Teenage Bells" by the Loungers is a surprise, a lively and pleasing number that might easily have been a hit, but went unreleased until now. "Betty My Own" by the Dynamics is another diamond in the rough, a soaring, impassioned ballad with a gentle, unobtrusive orchestral accompaniment. "I Wanna Holler" and "Lindy Lou" by Little Butchie Saunders and His Buddies were well-intentioned attempt to treads on Frankie Lymon territory, and the latter, in particular, was a pretty fair rock & roll number, and rather catchy. The sound on this collection is, as with most of Relic Records' releases, extraordinary. —*Bruce Eder*

The Golden Era of Doo-Wops: Ember Records / 1994 / Relic ♦♦♦♦♦
Forget about other doowop collections, the Relic compilation is the end (oops, that was another label). The 25 songs here, including hits and obscurities by The Silhouettes and lost tracks by the Five Satins, and work by the Barries, the Boptones, the Smoothtones, the Camelots, the Fabulons, and the Skarlettones, among others, are mastered so beautifully that many listeners may do a double-take. Master tapes were located, or very clean copies were digitized very carefully, so that this release will prove a revelation, even on hearing old chestnuts like "Get a Job." The notes are thorough as well—real work went into this CD, and it shows; it's also a great tribute to its subject, each song having something new and different to offer. —*Bruce Eder*

The Golden Era of Doo-Wops: Lupine Records / Oct. 1, 1996 / Relic ♦♦♦♦♦
Motown collectors take note—Lupine Records was one of several outfits controlled by Robert West, one of Detroit's more ambitious music entrepreneurs in the years before Berry Gordy founded Motown Records. Other labels with which West was associated included Flick, Kudo, Contour, and Bumble Bee, all of which are represented on this 25-song collection—future Motown songwriting mainstay Eddie Holland sang on Kudo's release of "(Where Is the Joy) In Nature Boy," while Marv Johnson cut "Once Upon a Time," both of which show up here. This disc has a rich mix of fast-paced rock & roll ("Bill Is My Boyfriend" by the Conquerors, "Lonely Night" by Jimmy Von Carl) and broad ballads ("This Heart of Mine" and "You're So Fine" by the Falcons, whose members included Levi Stubbs' brother Joe, and Eddie Floyd) with dreamy a cappella harmony cuts ("Please Let It Be" by the Bumble Bees). There are also some real pieces of choice ephemera here, such as the Conquerors' answer to Gene Chandler's "Duke of Earl," called "Duchess Conquers Duke." —*Bruce Eder*

The Golden Era of Doo-Wops: Angletone Records / Feb. 15, 1996 / Relic ♦♦♦
Angletone was a subsidiary of Atlas Records, one of a myriad of New York indie labels in the '50s recording doo wop groups literally right off the street. This 25-track collection brings together a nice brace of vocal group obscurities and true rarities like the Chandeliers' "Blueberry Sweet," the Lincoln Quintet's "Dream of Romance," and the Original Charmers' "For Sentimental Reasons." If you like Frankie Lymon "kiddie" vocals, you'll flip for Little Butchie & the Vells' "Sometimes Little Girl," "Please Tell the Angels," and "Over the Rainbow." Tracks by the Fabulous Fabulaires, Dougie & the Dolphins, Rickie & Vickie, the Casinos, & Rudy & the Tradewinds complete this overview. —*Cub Koda*

The Golden Era of Doo-Wops: Apollo Records, Pt. 4 / Jul. 2, 1996 / Relic ♦♦♦
This excursion into the vaults of Apollo Records yields some marvelous doo wop moments. The Delroys' "Bermuda Shorts" features "rap" slang some 50 years before it came into vogue, and the Cellos' "Rang Tang Ding Dong (I Am the Japanese Sandman)" is one of the great nonsense vocal-group recordings of all time. The balance of the set shines the spotlight on lesser-known acts like the Vocaltones, the Tonettes, La Fets & Kitty, the Chesters (with Little Anthony), the Casanovas, the Claremonts, Armanda & the Jays, the Brochures, and the Admirations. No big names on this volume, but a ton of great doo wop, which is exactly what you're looking for. —*Cub Koda*

The Golden Era of Doo-Wops: Atlas Records / Feb. 15, 1996 / Relic ♦♦♦♦♦
Tommy Robinson's Atlas Records, originally based on 125th St. in New York's Harlem, was one of the first culturally significant record labels founded and operated by a black owner. From 1951 until the early 1970s, the company specialized in R&B, evolving from urban blues and jazz in the beginning to doo wop music in the late 1950s—their first release in December of 1951 was "Rock H-Bomb Rock" by H-Bomb Ferguson. In 1953, he started recording vocal groups, which heralded his entry into the doo wop field with the Caverliers Quartet. Other harmony groups and a cappella outfits that came aboard included the Revels, the Travelers, the Fi-Tones (the reorganized Caverliers), the Parakeets, the Gypsies (who had more of a jump sound), the Five Dukes, and the Lincolns, all of whom—along with many others—are represented on this 29-song collection. None of Atlas' releases ever charted nationally—the company was essentially a one-man operation, and lacked the promotional clout and money to push songs that high nationwide—but their artists were fixtures on local and regional charts. As for the diversity of material here, it runs the gamut from raunchy, heavily R&B-flavored numbers like the Caverliers' "Dynaflow" (a great unheralded car song with a real cool sax solo) and the Gypsies' jumping "Young Girl to Calypso," to smooth near-pop like "Lenora" by the Travelers. This collection also includes a pair of unreleased numbers by the Travelers and the Fi-Tones. The sound is generally good, and the notes are exceptionally detailed, as well. —*Bruce Eder*

The Golden Era of Doo-Wops: Flash Records / Apr. 16, 1995 / Relic ♦♦♦♦♦
Flash Records existed for only four years, from 1955 until 1959, an outgrowth of the Flash Record Shop in south central Los Angeles, owned by Charlie "Flash" Reynolds. The Georgia-born Reynolds recognized that there was a vast array of talent in the neighborhood who had the potential for success but no chance to be recorded, and he changed that in June of 1955 when he cut his first three singles, by Sidney Maiden, B. Brown & the McVouts, and Haskell Sadler—none of their blues sides (none of which are on this collection) ever came close to charting, but they didn't have to. Reynolds had set up his operation so that he could make back his costs with only a few hundred sales, and as he had confidence in the product and could recommend it, he did that over his own counter. His entry into R&B harmony vocals came with signing the Jayhawks—he later added

the Poets and Emanon 4 to his stable, and the Cubans. All of these acts, although they emphasized vocals, had a fairly hard rock sound by doo wop standards, and they gave Flash a tougher sound than a lot of the usual releases in this field. *—Bruce Eder*

The Golden Era of Doo-Wops: Glory Records / Jun. 6, 1995 / Relic ✦✦✦✦✦
Glory Records was founded by Phil Rose, a former executive of Derby Records and Coral Records, in 1955. In contrast to a lot of other labels known for their doo wop recordings, Glory (which was based not in Harlem but on West 57th, at the north end of New York's midtown entertainment district) also released a wide variety of recordings in both pop and R&B, and at one point even had Sidney Poitier on the label, with the album *The Poetry of the Negro*, in 1956. The label folded in 1959, but Rose subsequently found success as the producer of the Lorraine Hansberry play *A Raisin in the Sun*, and also *Purlie* and *Shenandoah*. This 27-song collection shows the range of musical styles embraced by the label, from the soulful, impassioned balladeering of the Leaders ("Stormy Weather") to the dance-novelty sounds of the Dusters ("Teenage Jamboree," which has a most impressive guitar break) and the smoother-sung sounds of the Four Fellows ("Take Me Back Baby," "You Don't Know Me"). The range is greater than one typically finds in any doo wop collection, demonstrating just how wide the definition of the music could become in the right hands. *—Bruce Eder*

The Golden Era of Doo-Wops: Grand Records / Jan. 1, 1996 / Relic ✦✦✦
The sound of Philadelphia begins with these recordings. Grand Records was a very important label in the history of R&B harmony. Between 1953 and 1956, the label set the tone for the early doo wop group sound, featuring mournful ballads loaded with great harmonies and soaring tenor leads. This 22-track set brings together jewels from the Marquees (whose kickoff track, "The Rain," is worth the price of admission alone), the Cherokees, the Castelles, the Belltones, the Angels, the Dreamers, the Carter Rays, and the Castroes. Another winner in this great series. *—Cub Koda*

The Golden Era of Doo-Wops: Holiday Records / Apr. 16, 1995 / Relic ✦✦✦✦
Holiday Records, founded by Danny Robinson, the younger brother of Fire/Fury Records founder Bobby Robinson, existed for only two years, a period in which it cut music by such groups as the Bop Chords ("Castle In the Sky," "When I Wake Up This Morning"), Jimmy Jones & the Pretenders ("Tonight," "I Love You So"), and the Ladders ("Counting the Stars"), the latter two from New York's Harlem, plus lesser-known acts like the Harmonaires ("Lorraine") and the Lower Manhattan-based Love Notes ("United," "Tonight"), fronted by Johnny Hicks and featuring Lucy Cedeno (for 30-plus years the wife of Gary "U.S." Bonds). The sounds here are all solid '50s doo wop with an edge—the Bop Chords rock out really well on "When I Woke Up This Morning," which has an infectious beat and a solid band accompaniment, while Jimmy Jones & the Pretenders have a more romantic ballad style, with soaring harmonies and deeply passionate lead singing. The sound is excellent, and the history of the label (which only existed from 1956 until 1958) is well detailed. *—Bruce Eder*

The Golden Era of Doo-Wops: Johnson Records / Jul. 1, 1994 / Relic ✦✦✦
Hiram Johnson ran a small R&B label that, in the late '50s, recorded some of the best of the Chicago's doo wop groups. Although he only had hits with the Shells' "Baby Oh Baby" and the Dubs' "Don't Ask Me to Be Lonely," this 29-track collection reveals that Johnson Records was a haven for obscure vocal acts. Groups like the Cordovans, the Carribians, the Arcades, Little Nate & the Chryslers, the Cameos, the Marvels, Bobby Capri & Velvet Satins, and Cleo & the Crystaliers show that the label had a sound—a crude one, to be sure—which permeated all the releases on this interesting collection. *—Cub Koda*

The Golden Era of Doo-Wops: Klik Records / Dec. 5, 1994 / Relic ✦✦✦
Klik was a short-lived New York label that never really had much in the way of hits but nonetheless cranked out a small batch of absolutely great doo wop sides before the payola scandal of 1959 closed its doors. This voluminous 30-track compilation brings together obscure gems from the Nobles, the Dreamtones, the Rajahs (early Nutmegs), the Passionettes, the Syncopates, the Berets, the Avalons, the Pyramids, and Five Satins lead singer Fred Parris in various group configurations. No big hits aboard, but a chunk of great vocalizing, all well worth the price of admission. *—Cub Koda*

The Golden Era of Doo-Wops: Len Records / Oct. 17, 1995 / Relic ✦✦✦
Len was a short-lived subsidiary of the Philadelphia based V-Tone label and this 18-track collection rounds up all of the important vocal-group sides that were issued on the label. This is late-'50s to early-'60s Philly music, full of street-corner promise—not soul by any means, but with one foot still firmly in doo wop territory. Strong sides from Herb Johnson, the Dreamlovers, the Four Bars, the Masters, Little Jimmy & the Tops, Nelson Dupree, and the Parliaments make this another solid entry in the series. *—Cub Koda*

The Golden Era of Doo-Wops: Lummtone Records / Jun. 6, 1995 / Relic ✦✦✦✦✦
Lummtone was a doo wop label founded in Los Angeles at the tail end of the 1950s, in the remnants of the R&B boom. During the early 1960s, in the wake of Alan Freed's arrival at radio station KDAY, which he turned into an R&B outlet, this music once more became big business locally. As Donn Filetti points out in his notes, Freed's presence, and the counter-programming of other stations in response, turned South Central L.A. briefly into an R&B mecca amid the otherwise relatively undefined musical years of the early 1960s—even local hits could earn a small label considerable profits, and there was the chance of being picked up nationally. Lummie Fowler was a postal worker (who also had formal musical training) from the Crenshaw district in South Central Los Angeles who formed Lummtone in 1959, releasing 36 songs on 18 singles through 1965. Fowler recognized not only that he understood music better than any of the competition, but could produce records with a distinctive sound. The company started out creating pure doo wop music highlighted by unusually complex harmonies, although by the end it was trying to compete in the more sophisticated soul market. One of his major groups, the Upfronts, featured a young Barry White in its lineup—other artists on the label were the Elgins, George Powell & the Troopers, the Five Ramblers, and the Colognes. The music here is a mix of pure doo wop (the Upfronts' "It Took Time"), beautifully sung in an ethereal ballad style, and a more commercial rock & roll sound ("Benny Lou and the Lion," also by the Upfronts), with a harder, fuller backing band and a more emphatic beat. The late-'50s stuff by George Powell & the Troopers, or the Colognes, is all heavily influenced by the Platters and other sophisticated harmony acts of the era, all well sung with a lean piano accompaniment (played by Fowler), but Lummtone's early-1960s material shows the clear influence of early Motown sides such as the Contours' "Do You Love Me" and the Miracles' "Shop Around"—the Upfronts could have been a Motown act in a different reality, and one of the songs here, "I Lost My Love in the Big City," even got picked up by Motown for some of its artists. "Baby For Your Love," by the Upfronts, even sounds like a Motown release. There are some beautiful sides here, and even an answer record that Bear Family has managed to miss, the Upfronts' "I Stopped the Duke of Earl," which also manages to parody "The Book of Love." The mastering is very clean and the annotation is detailed and engrossing. *—Bruce Eder*

The Golden Era of Doo-Wops: Parrot Records / Apr. 14, 1994 / Relic ✦✦✦✦✦
Among the rarest R&B labels ever based in Chicago, Parrot Records, which existed from 1953 until 1956, was essentially a one-man operation, the dream-child of concert promoter and sometime DJ Al Benson. Operated mostly out of Benson's home, Parrot never had any serious distribution outside of the Chicago area. The highlight of this collection is the four songs cut by the Flamingos, who came to Parrot after a stay with Chance Records and cut their first Parrot release, "Dream of a Lifetime," in late 1954. The group's stay on Parrot only lasted for two singles, after which they jumped to Chess-Checker—the CD is worth the price just for their sultry-yet-jumping "Get With It," one of the best numbers that the group ever cut; it's so good that it's worth hearing just for the band's break. The rest of this collection is just as alluring—the Rockettes' smooth, sultry R&B was almost retro for the 1950s, based in a post-big band sound with some '40s pop and jazz influences (they toured with jazz saxman Illinois Jacquet in 1953 and '54); their "Rockin' at Midnight" (a rewrite of "Good Rockin' Tonight") bridges the gap between the '40s- and '50s-style R&B. Their work had a good beat and was extremely catchy, however, and is nicely dressed up by the soaring sax of Paul Bascomb—Benson knew how to recruit a backing band. And then there are the Orchids, led by Gilbert Warren, a doo wop outfit that must rate as one of the most soulful and rocking vocal ensembles of the period, melding R&B with more teen-oriented rock & roll themes. The sound is superb throughout. *—Bruce Eder*

The Golden Era of Doo-Wops: Relic Records, Vol. 1 / Oct. 17, 1995 / Relic ✦✦✦
Here's the early story of R&B reissue label Relic Records as told by collectors Donn Fileti and original founder Eddie Gries, from their humble beginnings hustling old, forgotten doo wop masters from a store in Hackensack, NJ to the releases of those very first singles on their fledgling label. There are some pretty raw sides here by obscure, one-off groups like the Unique Teens, the Levees, the Zircons, the Academics, and the Four Most. The story of a very important reissue label—one of the very best at doing what they specialize in—begins right here. *—Cub Koda*

The Golden Era of Doo-Wops: Times Square Records / Mar. 22, 1995 / Relic ✦✦✦✦✦
This 28-song collection is made up mostly of masters that Times Square—the first oldies label in history—owned outright, including "In My Heart" by the Timetones, "Did It" by the Laddins, "Hello" by the Nutmegs, the Crests' "No One to Love" and "Wish She Was Mine," or stuff that the label head regarded as so good but so obscure, that it was simply pressed at his discretion. The stuff is first-rate, and there are pleasant discoveries to be made at every turn, including Frankie & the C-Notes' "Forever and Ever" and "Go Back Where You Came From" by the Summits. With a few notable exceptions, the audio quality is good to excellent, which is near-miraculous considering that master tapes were difficult, if not impossible, to trace in all instances. *—Bruce Eder*

The Golden Era of Doo-Wops: Whirlin' Disc Records / Jan. 10, 1996 / Relic ✦✦✦✦
Before Bobby Robinson had Fury Records (and its offshoot, Fire), he was the proud cofounder (with Jubilee Records owner Jerry Blaine) of Whirlin' Disc Records, which cut some of the best doo wop music to come out of New York City during the mid-'50s. Beginning with the Channels' "The Closer You Are," which charted locally and ended up getting covered by acts associated with major labels, the company showed a lot of promise. The acts that Robinson signed and produced all demonstrated highly sophisticated, polished sounds, and as late as 1957 the company was competitive in the burgeoning rock & roll field. The Channels were the best act on Whirlin' Disc, but the Continentals and the Whirlers all treated their songs memorably—only the Empires, who seem somewhat crude and unsophisticated, break this pattern, and they only lasted on the label for one single. Robinson folded Whirlin' Disc in early 1957 over his disillusionment with the accounting practices of his partner, Jerry Blaine, and moved his newest discovery, Lewis Lymon & the Teenchords, from their intended birth at the old label into a new venture, Fury Records, which was to prove the most successful recording venture of Robinson's career in music. This collection of 26 songs (including outtakes—Whirlin' Disc only issued 20 total sides) is beautifully mastered from what sound like first-generation tapes, and the annotation is all anyone could want on a lot of these acts. And the music is among the finest doo wop material that one can buy. *—Bruce Eder*

The Golden Era of Doo-Wops: Fury Records / May 16, 1994 / Relic ✦✦✦✦✦
Now this is a collection with staying power, and not just for doo wop enthusiasts. Bobby Robinson, who cut Elmore James and a lot of other top veteran blues and R&B talent for his Fury Records label, also tried his hand at doo wop music. In fact, it was R&B vocal acts like Lewis Lymon & the Teenchords that occupied his time far more than bluesmen

such as James and Lightnin' Hopkins, even though the latter two—thanks to recent reissue boxes—are now more closely associated with Robinson and Fury. Located on 125th Street in Harlem, right in the heart of an ocean of musical talent, Fury Records ended up with an extraordinary roster. The acts represented here, including the Brooklyn-based Du Mauriers ("All Night Long," "Baby I Love You"), the Newark-based Kodaks ("Runaround Baby"), Lewis Lymon & the Teenchords, Jackie & the Starlites ("Valerie"), the Federals ("While Our Hearts Are Young"), and the Scarlets ("Truly Yours"), not to mention the early hit sides of Gladys Knight & the Pips ("Every Beat of My Heart"), all have a degree of professionalism in their presentation and production that stands them ahead of most of the rival doo wop outfits of the era. Indeed, listening to the material on this collection, one appreciates that Fury was one of the biggest and best rivals to George Goldner's legendary End and Gone labels, with its nationally known acts like the Teenagers and the Flamingos. *—Bruce Eder*

The Golden Era of Doo-Wops: Swingin' Records / Feb. 18, 1997 / Relic ✦✦✦
Los Angeles disc jockey Hunter Hancock was the Alan Freed of the West Coast scene, so it was logical that he would eventually start his own label and Swingin' Records was the result. This 20-track collection spotlights the doo wop side of the label's output, centering on Rochell & the Candles, the Hollywood Saxons, the Calendars, the Williams Brothers, Art Wheeler, and Buddy Gibson & the Vanguards. It's all solid West Coast doo wop, sporting strong harmonies and sometimes crude production methods. *—Cub Koda*

Golden State Soul: San Franciscan Dancers & Smoochers / Mar. 21, 2000 / Kent ✦✦✦
Even by the benchmark of obscure soul compilations, the music on *this* soul anthology is really arcane. Previously unreleased, were 17 of the 24 tracks, and what *was* released only appeared on tiny local labels. What it has in common was that it was all done at Leo Kulka's Golden State Recorders in San Francisco, mostly in the late '60s (although some was cut in the early '70s). The San Francisco area was not known as a beachhead of great soul music, and given that virtually all of these musicians are unknown and released little that saw the light of day, you might be suspicious that the results were distinctly minor-league. Yet this is actually one of the better collections of its kind (outclassing, for instance, numerous other obscure soul comps on the Kent/Ace labels themselves). While there was not a distinctly original top-gear soul sound for either the Bay Area or the acts on this disc, it's pretty enjoyable, and quite well-produced and well-arranged, period late-'60s soul music. Nothing really classic, just a pretty solid listen, and rather more pop-soul (in a good sense) than might be expected from San Francisco soulsters, who were often in a more blues/R&B-hued vein. The San Francisco TKOs' "Make Up Your Mind" and George & Teddy's "Lover," for instance, are both tight polished swingers, while Blondell Breed & the Imports' "When I See My Baby" has slight girl group and Jamaican influences. One future name of note does appear: white soul-rock singer Lydia Pense, known mostly as lead vocalist of Cold Blood, is heard on two previously unreleased items by one of her previous bands, the Generation. In fact she would record Barbara Lynn's "I'm a Good Woman" (one of the two Generation numbers, and one of the highlights of the CD) again with Cold Blood. Did the San Francisco TKOs really think their thin cover of the Miracles' "Ooh Baby Baby" (actually released as a 1971 single) was going to make anyone forget the original, though? *—Richie Unterberger*

The Goldwax Story, Vol. 1 / Dec. 11, 2001 / Kent ✦✦✦✦
The Memphis '60s soul label Goldwax is most known for its lengthy series of singles (many of them R&B hits) with James Carr, but also recorded several other artists during the decade. Three of the 24 tracks on this anthology belong to Carr, including his most famous song, "The Dark End of the Street." Otherwise, though, most of these names will draw blanks, except for O.V. Wright (who did just one single for the label) and Timmy Thomas (whose jazzy 1967 organ instrumental, "Liquid Mood," with some scat singing, preceded his big vocal hit "Why Can't We Live Together" by five years). Deep Southern soul fans will enjoy this release mightily, as it has so many of the stocks-in-trade of Southern soul in general and Memphis soul in particular: tight soul backup, urgent, pleading vocals, and a leaning toward slow, emotional balladry in the songwriting (with some uptempo tunes thrown in). It isn't, though, on the same level as the somewhat similar and much more famous soul being done in the same town at the same time at Stax Records. The vocalists are too often derivative of Otis Redding and Sam Cooke; the Ovations' Louis Williams sounds like a Sam Cooke clone, so close are his vocals and so obvious is his role model. The George half of George & Greer, heard on their light-hearted, uptempo 1966 single "You Didn't Know It, But You Had Me," was well-known songwriter George Jackson. For some variety, you get the instrumental "Here It Is Now" by Gene "Bowlegs" Miller, which strongly recalls the work of Stax instrumental groups Booker T. & the MG's and the Mar-Keys. The Lyrics' "Darling," the first Goldwax release in 1964, is the most doo wop-indebted cut, with some ludicrously over-the-top crying at the cut's outset. *—Richie Unterberger*

Got a Good Thing Going / 1996 / Sequel ✦✦✦✦✦
Subtitled "25 R&B Radio Hits of the 60s," Billy Vera compiled this with the intention of giving listeners some prime soul singles that weren't huge hits, but also not selected simply on the basis of obscurity. Besides J.J. Jackson's "But It's All Right" and Freddie Scott's "Hey Girl," however, you'd be hard-pressed to recognize any of these, unless you listened to soul stations all the time in the '60s. The attention to quality over rarity, however, has resulted in the one of the finest anthologies of semi-obscure and very obscure '60s soul that you're likely to come across, with lots of diversity, ranging from gospel-tinged shouters to uptown New York productions to exquisite ballads. Almost all of this is very good, and some of it's a lot better than that—the original version of "You're No Good" by Dee Dee Warwick (covered by Betty Everett in the '60s and Linda Ronstadt in the '70s) is a stunner. Little Buster has a fine Sam Cooke sound-alike, Jimmy Ricks has a deep croon that sounds like a 45 playing at 33 RPM, Mary Wells offers an overlooked bluesy cut from the late '60s, and Valerie Simpson & Nick Ashford are heard on a rare 1965 single attributed simply to Valerie & Nick. And the mysterious Mighty Hannibal's "Hymn No. 5" is a must-hear for any '60s soul/rock fan, its creepy gospel/soul moan offering one of the best understated protests against the Vietnam War ever recorded. *—Richie Unterberger*

Grazing in the Trash, Vol. 1 / Jan. 23, 2001 / Soul Fire ✦✦✦✦
When the funk revival label Desco dissolved, co-founders Gabriel Roth and Phillipe Lehman split to form their own separate imprints: Dap-Tone and Soul Fire, respectively. Lehman conceived of Soul Fire as a vehicle for his personal taste in production: raw, lo-fi, and intentionally amateurish. That's the sound that dominates Soul Fire's first singles compilation, *Grazing in the Trash, Vol. 1*. It follows in the footsteps of Desco's *Spike's Choice* collections, which gathered the company's limited-edition 45 rpm records for CD release. This one features the A- and B-sides of six singles, plus one "educational" release featuring drum tracks to be imitated; aside from stalwart Lee Fields—weighing in with his trademark James Brown homages—there are no holdovers from the Desco days. Two groups here went on to cut their own full-length albums not long after; Calypso King & the Soul Investigators offer strong J.B.'s/Meters grooves on "Compin' and Smokin'," while JD & the Evil's Dynamite Band conjure a blunted, psychedelic feel on "Haaa-Sheesh." Of the more obscure groups, Speedometer and the Soul Command share that J.B.'s/Meters fixation, with the latter throwing in a cover of Eddie Bo's classic "Hook and Sling"; the Third Point, meanwhile, offer a more relaxed, jazzy style. These groups won't make you forget their influences, but they definitely know how to groove, and funk fanatics with a taste for things on the raw side will likely enjoy this collection quite a bit. *—Steve Huey*

Great R&B Duets / Oct. 31, 2000 / Ace ✦✦✦✦✦
The R&B duets that this 25-track anthology emphasizes are those from the early days of rock & roll, spanning 1954-1960. The song selection is a bit quirky and uneven, but generally it's a pretty good sampling of some hits and choice obscurities from the era, emphasizing male-female duets most often, but also including male duos and a solitary female duo (the Teen Queens, with their doo wop hit "Eddie My Love"). A number of these tunes are familiar hit classics: Mickey & Sylvia's "Love Is Strange," Brook Benton & Dinah Washington's "Baby (You've Got What It Takes)" and "A Rockin' Good Way (To Mess Around and Fall in Love)," Ike & Tina Turner's "It's Gonna Work Out Fine," Shirley & Lee's "Let the Good Times Roll," Johnny & Joe's "Over the Mountain, Across the Sea," among others. More intriguing for those in search of something they might have seldom or never heard are cuts like Tarheel Slim & Little Ann's splendid "It's Too Late," a minor-key haunter with scarifying blues/gospel overtones. Also on hand are a number of original versions of songs that became more famous via subsequent white cover versions: Gene & Eunice's "Ko Ko Mo (I Love You So)," Marvin & Johnny's "Cherry Pie" (later a hit for Skip & Flip), Don & Dewey's "I'm Leaving It (All) Up to You" (later a huge hit for Dale & Grace), and most enticingly of all Willy & Ruth's original 1954 version of Leiber & Stoller's "Love Me" (covered in 1956 by Elvis Presley). Some of the other relatively unknown selections are on the forgettable side, but overall this is a good alternation of familiar and unfamiliar performances in this early rock & roll subgenre. *—Richie Unterberger*

Great R&B Instrumentals / Oct. 9, 2001 / Ace ✦✦✦✦
The title *Great R&B Instrumentals* suggests a category wide enough to include a lot more than the 25 songs, spanning the late '40s to the mid-'60s, heard on this disc. You wouldn't turn to this CD as the ultimate gathering of the cream of the crop, as it excludes a number of classics, like Bill Doggett's "Honky Tonk Pt. 2." Some of those, admittedly, are not here because Ace chose not to overlap with other compilations on its label, particularly in the *Teen Beat* series, which had already included cuts like "Honky Tonk" and others. What you end up with is a mix of big hits and things that are mostly the province of specialty oldies radio shows. It's still a pretty respectable collection, if a little spotty. Among the familiar tunes, some of those are unquestioned classics, like Jimmy Forrest's 1952 number-one hit, "Night Train," Joe Liggins' "The Honeydripper" (though it's a 1950 remake and not the 1945 original), Pee Wee Crayton's "Blues After Hours," Paul Williams' "The Huckle-Buck," Joe Houston's astonishingly athletic sax showcase "All Night Long," Ernie Freeman's "Jivin' Around" (both parts are included), and Booker T. & the MG's' 1965 single "Red Beans and Rice" (not a hit, but one of their great grooves anyway). Much of the rest is of also-ran quality, however, even if some of the names (Rene Hall, Maxwell Davis, Plas Johnson) were important session men and arrangers. Of the numbers that might be known to a few, perhaps the best is "Hard Grind," with the biting blues-rock guitar of Wild Jimmy Spruill, famous as the soloist on Wilbert Harrison's huge hit, "Kansas City." Big Bob Dougherty's "Honky" is also worthy of mention as a sax showcase of exceptional urgency. *—Richie Unterberger*

Groove On!, Vol. 1 / 1996 / DCC ✦✦✦✦
DCC's *Groove On!, Vol. 1* contains a selection of ten seductive or stylish soul, disco and urban-pop tunes from the '70s. There's not much rhyme or reason behind the featured tunes, but with the Emotions' "Best of My Love," the Spinners & Dionne Warwick's "Then Came You," Tavares' "It Only Takes a Minute" and the Isley Brothers' "Harvest for the World," there's really nothing that would qualify as weak. Since there's nothing tying the songs together outside of their era, *Groove On!* winds up being nothing more than a sampler. But it's a really enjoyable sampler, nonetheless. *—Stephen Thomas Erlewine*

Groove On!, Vol. 2 / 1996 / DCC ✦✦✦
Like its predecessor, DCC's *Groove On!, Vol. 2* contains a selection of ten seductive or stylish soul, disco and urban-pop tunes from the '70s. There's not much rhyme or reason behind the featured tunes, but there are no weak songs either, thanks to such highlights

as the Main Ingredient's "Everybody Plays the Fool," the Emotions' "Don't Ask My Neighbors," Deniece Williams' "Free," Earth, Wind & Fire's "Can't Hide Love," Natalie Cole's "I've Got Love on My Mind" and Ashford & Simpson's "Is It Still Good to Ya?" Since there's nothing tying the songs together outside of their era, *Groove On!* winds up being nothing more than a sampler. But it's a really enjoyable sampler, nonetheless. *—Stephen Thomas Erlewine*

Groove On!, Vol. 3 / 1996 / DCC ♦♦♦
Like its two predecessors, DCC's *Groove On!, Vol. 3* contains a selection of ten seductive or stylish soul, disco and urban-pop tunes from the '70s and early '80s. There's not much rhyme or reason behind the featured tunes, but there are no weak songs, either, thanks to such highlights as Brick's "Ain't Gonna Hurt Nobody," the Isley Brothers' "That Lady," Marvin Gaye's "Sanctified Lady," Rebbie Jackson's "Centipede," Ashford & Simpson's "It Seems to Hang On," Harold Melvin & the Blue Notes' "Wake Up Everybody" and the Three Degrees' "When Will I See You Again." Since there's nothing tying the songs together outside of their era, *Groove On!* winds up being nothing more than a sampler. But it's a really enjoyable sampler, nonetheless. *—Stephen Thomas Erlewine*

Groove Station, Vol. 1 / Dec. 15, 1998 / WestSide ♦♦♦
The WestSide compilation *Groove Station* includes jazz-groove classics from Al Sears ("Baltimore Bounce," "Groove Station," "Nell Don't Wear No Button Up Shoes"), Preston Love ("Strictly Cash," "Like a Ship at Sea," "September Song"), Wild Bill Moore ("Hey Spo-Dee-O-Dee," "Neck Bones and Collard Greens," "Balancing with Bill"), and Fats Noel ("Applejack," "Feelin' the Blues," "Rocket Flight"). *—Earl Simmons*

Groove Story: R&B from the Radio Corporation, Vol. 2 / Nov. 10, 1998 / WestSide ♦♦♦♦
RCA Victor started up their Groove subsidiary in 1954 after watching indie labels like Specialty, Chess, Modern, Savoy, Atlantic, King and others dominate the R&B market. Actually, the label was relaunched on two separate occasions after that, but this 28-track collection is pulled from its original 1950s incarnation. As a companion volume to WestSide's *Honkin' 'N' Hollerin': R&B From the Radio Corporation, Vol. 1*, there's some marginal duplication with the previous entry (Beatrice Reading's "I'd Gladly Do It Again" is inadvertently repeated, and Arthur "Big Boy" Crudup's cover of Professor Longhair's "She's Got No Hair" is listed but is an audio no-show), but this equals the rockin' and bluesy quotient of its predecessor with consummate ease. From the deep blues of Big John Greer ("Bottle It Up and Go"), Melvin Smith ("You Can't Stay Here") to the jump novelties from the Nitecaps ("Tough Mama"), Buddy Lucas ("High Low Jack") and the Five Keys ("Lawdy Miss Mary") to the straight-ahead jump instrumentals of Big Al Sears ("Here's the Beat") and King Curtis ("Moving On"), it's obvious that the Groove label had more than its share of high-quality R&B releases, and this disc brings together some of the very best of them. *—Cub Koda*

Groovesville Review / 1997 / Goldmine/Soul Supply ♦♦♦♦♦
Here is one of the great grails of Detroit soul, 24 rare tracks that have been traded on tenth-generation bootleg tapes for decades until these masters were unearthed in 1996. And no, we are not talking Motown; check the title, folks: *Groovesville Review*, the name should say it all. Dig the names: Edwin Starr ("Has It Happened to You Yet" and "You're My Mellow"), Steve Mancha ("Let's Party," plus four more, including a killer duet with Melvin Davis on "I Need My Baby"), Barbara Mercer ("Happiness Is Here"), Joyce Vincent ("Solid as a Rock"), Robert Ward ("Pigfeet"), Darrell Banks ("I'm the One Who Loves You"), David Ruffin, ("Still in My Heart"), Andrea Henry ("Time Fades Away"), Spyder Turner ("Trying to Forget You"), and way, way more by acts such as the Professionals, J.J. Barnes, the Parliaments (yeah, those guys), and some in the groove instrumentals as well. There are few compilations that can touch this one for raw beauty, urban sophistication, and sheer verve. Listing a few of the cuts included is review enough. You shouldn't be reading this; you should be out beating on your CD shop's door to get a stack of these in the bins. *—Thom Jurek*

Groovy, Vol. 1: A Collection of Rare Jazzy Club Tracks / Jul. 5, 1996 / Irma ♦♦♦♦
Of the many multi-volume collections released in the '90s by Irma, the Italian label's *Groovy* collection is one of the most engaging. The collection is subtitled *A Collection of Rare Jazzy Club Tracks* and indeed lives up to its name, compiling obscure jazz records that are lively enough—either in terms of funk or soul—to warrant play in a dance club setting. The collection goes all the way back to the '50s and up to the '80s, compiling a little bit of everything, from traditional jazz to non-traditional jazz-inflected styles of music. Highlights of the first volume include Milt Jackson's "The Metal Melter," Patti Austin's "That's Enough for Me," Deodato's "Super Strut," Steve Stills & Al Kooper's "Season of the Witch," and Boz Scaggs' "Hercules." *—Jason Birchmeier*

Groovy, Vol. 2: A Collection of Rare Jazzy Club Tracks / Jan. 14, 1997 / Irma ♦♦♦♦
Of the many multi-volume collections released in the '90s by Irma, the Italian label's *Groovy* collection is one of the most engaging. The collection is subtitled "A Collection of Rare Jazzy Club Tracks" and indeed lives up to its name, compiling obscure jazz records that are lively enough—either in terms of funk or soul—to warrant play in a dance club setting. The collection go all the way back to the '50s and up to the '80s, compiling a little bit of everything, from traditional jazz to non-traditional jazz-inflected styles of music. Highlights of the second volume include Billy Paul's "East," Donovan's "Barabajagal," Marc Dorsey's cover of the Stylistics' "People Make the World Go Round," and Ray Barretto's cover of Stevie Wonder's "Pastime Paradise." *—Jason Birchmeier*

Groovy, Vol. 3: A Collection of Rare Jazzy Club Tracks / Jan. 26, 1999 / Irma ♦♦♦
This Irma collection includes the funkier side of jazz and Latin-jazz, featuring excellent tracks like "Mambero" by Cal Tjader, "Song Sung Long" by Carla Bley, "Aht Uh Mi Hed" by Shuggie Otis, "About Love" by Ben Sidran, and an excellent cover of "Give Peace a Chance" by Lonnie Liston Smith. *—Keith Farley*

Growin' Up Too Fast: The Girl Group Anthology / Jun. 18, 1996 / Polygram ♦♦♦♦♦
A two-CD, 50-song collection of girl group hits and misses originally released on the MGM, Smash, Philips, Fontana, 20th Century Fox, and Mercury labels in the early and mid-'60s. It's nice to have some of these rarities easily available in state-of-the-art fidelity, but it's not one of the best girl group compilations around, in terms of either thematic coherence or consistent quality. The hits by the Shangri-Las, Lesley Gore, Dusty Springfield, the Angels, and the Royalettes are good to great, but are better heard in the context of their own compilations. Much of the rest—by obscure singers like Ginny Arnell, the Pixies Three, and Beverly Washburn—is pleasant but rather forgettable. There are some really neat one-shots and lost classics here, though, like Diane Renay's Top Ten hit, "Navy Blue," and her flop follow-up, "Watch Out, Sally!," is one of the toughest white girl group records ever. Also cool are the Secrets' "The Boy Next Door" (an Angels sound-alike) and the two songs by Sadina, which are among the best unknown Wall-of-Sound-type productions ever. *—Richie Unterberger*

Gumbo Stew / 1993 / Ace ♦♦♦
In the early '60s, arranger and multi-instrumentalist Harold Battiste (who had done some A&R for Specialty) formed the New Orleans-based AFO label with the intention of giving local artists a fairer deal via a black-owned company. Only one true hit resulted, Barbara George's "I Know" (included here), but some solid New Orleans R&B was recorded during its brief time in operation. This is the first of three compilations of AFO material, including a couple of obscure performances by the young Dr. John, sides by second-tier Crescent City artists like Eddie Bo and Alvin Robinson, and several names known only to record collectors. Most of it's from the early '60s, although a few from the late '60s (when Battiste was a successful arranger on the West Coast) also sneak in. This disc isn't up to the level of the classics you'll find on the best vintage New Orleans R&B anthologies, but if you're the kind who plans your vacations around New Orleans music festivals, you won't be disappointed by what's on offer here. *—Richie Unterberger*

★ **Hardcore Doo-Wop: In the Hallway—Under the Street Lamp** / 1993 / Specialty ♦♦♦♦♦
This compact disc collects 25 doo wop collector's classics from a variety of small West Coast R&B labels who dabbled in the genre. The California version of the streetcorner vocal group phenomena had stronger leanings toward bluesier harmonies and vocal performances bordering on madness. As best exemplified here by groups like Arthur Lee Maye & the Crowns and Byron "Slick" Gipson & the Sliders, the West Coast doo wop movement definitely had a sound all its own. *—Cub Koda*

Harlem Shuffle: 60s Soul Classics / 1999 / Charly ♦♦♦♦♦
The title suggests Harlem Shuffle features only upbeat, dancers from the '60s. But a closer look reveals a mixture of fast, ballads, and midtempo numbers. Bob & Earl's "Harlem Shuffle," and "Backfield In Motion," by Mel & Tim exemplifies soulful midtempo grooves with sliding beats. The Soul Survivors' "Expressway to Your Heart," the Capitols' "Cool Jerk," and "Dancin' Holiday," by the Olympics are speed demons. "Hello Stranger," by Barbara Lewis, "Oh How Happy," by the Shades of Blue, and Deon Jackson's "Love Make the World Go Round" represent the sweetness of the soul ballad. You get Brenton Wood's two biggest singles: "Oogum Boogum Song," and "Gimme a Little Sign." And check out Fred Hughes' "Oo Wee Baby I Love You"; Hughes sounds like Eddie Holland, the Motown singer turned Hall-of-Fame Songwriter. There are 16 songs in all and not a loser in the bunch. *—Andrew Hamilton*

Harlem Shuffle: The Sound of Blaxploitation / Jun. 1, 1999 / Plastic ♦♦♦♦
This above-average collection showcases deep grooves from classic blaxploitation flicks circa 1969-1977. During its heyday, the blaxploitation film provided an outlet for adventurous composers in the funk and soul genres. For mainstream audiences, Isaac Hayes and Curtis Mayfield exemplified this spirit of remarkable creativity, elevating the musical moods of textures of the inner city into mass popular consciousness. It is therefore fitting that *Harlem Shuffle: The Sound of Blaxploitation* kicks off with cuts from both artists and features several more cuts from their soundtrack work. The anthology goes on to prove there was a lot more to the genre than "Shaft" and "Superfly," both of which are conspicuously absent. Highlights include the Bar-Kays' gritty funk workout "Son of Shaft," the wah-wah-inflected acid jazz of "Harlem Clavinet" from the classic soundtrack *Across 110th Street*, and Melvin Van Peebles' demented chase rap, "C'mon Feet," layered over frantic accompanying music by Earth, Wind & Fire from the cult film *Sweet Sweetback's Baadasssss Song*. Purists might lament the exclusion of tracks from seminal films like *Coffy* and *Black Caesar*. Nevertheless, *Harlem Shuffle: The Sound of Blaxploitation* provides a steady workout of funky stone-cold grooves. *—Joe Pettit Jr.*

● **Have a Nice Decade: The 70s Pop Culture Box** / Jun. 16, 1998 / Rhino ♦♦♦♦♦
For anyone who grew up during the last days of AM radio, anyone who remembers gas shortages, disco scarves and feathered hair, this mammoth seven-disc box set will be a holy grail of nostalgia. First of all, the discs themselves contain a staggering 164 tracks. Basically, if you remember the song, it's probably included: from enduring chestnuts even today's teenagers can sing ("Fire and Rain," "Fly Like an Eagle") to obscure gems of kitsch like "The Night Chicago Died" and the supremely maudlin "Billy Don't Be a Hero." If you were born in the 1960s, you'll probably find this stuff enjoyable rather than embarrassing to the degree that you can think back on your adolescence without cringing. But don't let the music distract you from the packaging, either. The box is covered in avocado-green shag carpeting (embroidered with a happy-face pattern), and the booklet contains photos of all the artists, essays on the politics and culture of the period and capsule references to notable events, fads and people. Only

Rhino Records could have put out a reissue package of music, images and text this perfect. *—Rick Anderson*

Have a Nice Night: Romantic Hits of the '70s / May 19, 1998 / Rhino ♦♦♦
Since *Have a Nice Day: Super Hits of the '70s* is Rhino's best-selling series, it isn't surprising that the label has created a number of spin-offs and sequels designed to cash in on its good name. What it is surprising is how they continue to find new ways to recycle the series and its mainstream '70s pop, discovering new themes within the same songs every few months. *Have a Nice Night: Romantic Hits of the '70s* appeared just a few months after the gargantuan *Have a Nice Decade* box set, but the twist is, this is a collection of adult contemporary and MOR love songs, many of which didn't make the box at all. Granted, five of the 11 tracks ("I'd Really Love to See You Tonight," "Lead Me On," "Midnight at the Oasis," "Dancing in the Moonlight," "Help Me Make It Through the Night") were on various volumes of *Have a Nice Day*, and three of them were on the box, but there are more new songs to the *Have a Nice*... series than ever before. The best of them, "I Love a Rainy Night," didn't chart until 1981, but it fits into the mellow, late-night vibe of the compilation. The remaining new numbers—"Let Me Love You Tonight," "This Night Won't Last Forever," "Ships," "Don't Tell Me Goodnight" and "Night Hours," which has never been available on another various-artists '70s collection—are pleasant, but not essential. The same thing could be said for this album—it's entertaining enough, but it's not really necessary. *—Stephen Thomas Erlewine*

HDH Solid Gold, Vol. 1 / Aug. 17, 1999 / Fantasy ♦♦♦
Fantasy Records has not always done well in reissuing the Invictus, Hotwax, and Music Merchant tracks produced by Holland-Dozier-Holland, but this collection helps make up for past errors. Crushing productions on Chairmen of the Board's "Give Me Just a Little More Time," 100 Proof (Aged in Soul)'s proverbial "Don't Scratch Where It Don't Itch," the 8th Day's "She's Not Just Another Woman," the Flaming Ember's "Westbound #9," and Honey Cone's "Want Ads" say it all. The compilation also includes spine-tingling songs by HDH, the Glass House, and Freda Payne among the 16 stunning tracks. *—Andrew Hamilton*

Heart and Soul / Dec. 11, 1997 / Crimson ♦♦♦♦♦
This box set of soul tracks is a step above the others thanks to its blend of familiar favorites and collectable rarities, like the British-made sides from the Real Thing and Ruby Turner, New York City's "I'm Doing Fine Now," the Jaki Graham numbers, and the Southern delights from Ann Peebles. The marathon begins with Percy Sledge's "When a Man Loves a Woman" and ends with the Average White Band's scot-soul rendition of "Walk on By." In between are creamy fillings from the Chi-Lites, William DeVaughn, Timmy Thomas' only hit "Why Can't We Live Together," plus light soul from Shalamar, old-school rollicking with "Harlem Shuffle" by Bob & Earl, and jazzy sounds from Dinah Washington and Nina Simone. This is a real something-for-everybody set and a great box for outings and gatherings—just pop the discs in, let the 54 tracks play randomly, and forget about it. *—Andrew Hamilton*

The Heart and Soul of Philadelphia: A Collection of Soulful Love Songs / Jan. 18, 1999 / Music Club ♦♦♦♦
Here are 17 romantic songs from the crack crew of writers, producers, musicians and singers at Philadelphia International Records at the height of their powers. Opening with Teddy Pendergrass' "Close the Door" and ending with the O'Jays' heart-tugging "Lovin' You," this collection also contains some sentimental journeys you might not own, like Dee Dee Sharp's "Trying to Get the Feeling Again," Billy Paul's "Without You," Jerry Butler's "Best Love I Ever Had," and Phyllis Hyman's "Slow Dancin'." Other excellent choices include Teddy Pendergrass' "Love T.K.O.," Shirley Jones' "Do You Get Enough Love," and Jean Carn's "Don't Let It Go to Your Head." With the material that Music Club has to select from, the label could release ten more volumes of *The Heart and Soul of Philadelphia* of this quality. *—Andrew Hamilton*

The Heart of Southern Soul, Vol. 2 / 1996 / Ace ♦♦♦
Stax and Hi weren't the final words in deep Southern soul in the late 1960s; Excello also recorded some solid efforts in the vein. This 24-track compilation accumulates material that appeared on the label and its offshoots from the mid-'60s to the mid-'70s (concentrating on the late '60s) that's known only to serious soul hounds. The Wallace Brothers, Kip Anderson, and Mava Whitney are the most well-known names, to give you an idea of the level of specialization we're talking about here. A lot of this has the churchy, bluesy feel you expect from prime Southern soul, though little if any is truly among the classic cream of the genre. Certainly the swamp blues duet of Dee & Don and the gospel harmonies of the Wallace Brothers are worth hearing by listeners who want to build a large soul collection. Inspirational lyric (from Jerry Washington's "Right Here is Where You Belong"): "He told me I have something worse than cancer. He told me what I have was a very, very bad case of the blues!" *—Richie Unterberger*

Heart of Southern Soul: From Nashville to Memphis and Muscle Shoals / 1995 / Excello ♦♦♦♦♦
Nashville's Excello label recorded pure Southern soul—the good stuff, authentic, rootsy, passionately executed dramas and proclamations that touch the heart and soul. This is drinking and moaning music, the perfect company for love's pains or joys. Kip Anderson's "I Went Off and Cried," Tiny Watkins' "A Soldier's Sad Story," and Johnny Truitt's "Your Love Is Worth the Pain," are the real deals. Even on the happy tunes the underlying strain of maintaining a relationship is evident. The 24-tracks include selections by the Wallace Brothers, Marva Whitney, the Kelly Brothers, the Interpreters, and Dee & Don. *—Andrew Hamilton*

Heavy Soul / 1971 / Atlantic ♦♦♦♦
As the title implies, this is a substantial collection of soul with extra helpings of grit and pain thrown in for good measure, corralling tracks you probably don't own, making it ultimately a good catch. Included among the 20 selections: King Floyd's "Groove Me," Little Sister's "Somebody's Watching You," Dee Dee Warwick's "Suspicious Minds," Beginning of the End's "Funky Nassau," and King Curtis' "Changes," as well as evergreens from the Persuaders, Jackie Moore, Aretha Franklin, Betty Wright, and Tyrone Davis. A good buy, one you can't go wrong with, and a good fit for most musical collections. *—Andrew Hamilton*

Here Come the Girls, Vol. 5: Sisters from the City / Oct. 24, 1994 / Castle ♦♦♦♦
Subtitled *Sisters From the City, Vol. 5* in the consistently wonderful *Here Come the Girls* series isn't a girl group collection per se, at least not in the conventional Shangri-Las/Chiffons/Ronettes sense of the phrase. The subject is instead soul sides dating from between 1963 and 1974, relative light years in musical terms that encompass everything from the primal R&B of Betty Harris' deep-soul ballad "Cry to Me" to the insistent Philly proto-disco of Ecstasy, Passion & Pain's "I Wouldn't Give You Up"; although the set consequently lacks the focus and clarity common to the remainder of the *Here Come the Girls* series, the quality of the assembled material is nevertheless high throughout. Five of the disc's 20 tracks (mostly drawn from the Roulette and Calla vaults) spotlight the unjustly neglected Jean Wells, whose incendiary gospel-inspired vocals combined with the slinky production of the great Clyde Otis to yield a series of strong singles like "I Feel Good" and "Have a Little Mercy," all of which earned little notice during the Summer of Love. Other highlights: the Fuzz's beatific "I Love You for All Seasons," Betty Lavette's Northern soul perennial "Let Me Down Easy," and Oohna Truth's funky "If It Feels Good, Do It." *—Jason Ankeny*

Here Come the Girls, Vol. 7: The Trouble with Boys / Sep. 5, 1995 / Sequel ♦♦♦♦
Where most compilation series run out of material over the course of their first few volumes, Sequel's *Here Come the Girls* maintains an uncommon consistency from start to finish—*Vol. 7*, subtitled *The Trouble With Boys*, is arguably the best of the bunch, a superb 24-track set that, despite its reliance on minor hits and obscurities, deserves consideration alongside the finest girl group collections ever compiled. The one-two punch of the opening "Baby Baby (I Still Love You)" and "Please Don't Wake Me," which together constitute the A- and B-sides of the lone offering of the Cinderellas (really the Cookies in disguise), is alone worth the price of admission, a brilliant approximation of Phil Spector's Wall of Sound aesthetic at its most dramatic and grandiose. Equally magical is the Jewels' "Opportunity," a classic fusion of teen-dream innocence and R&B swagger capturing the girl group sound at its most soulful and street-smart. Lesser-known recordings from hitmakers like the Toys, the Essex, Shelley Fabares, and Little Eva round out the set—essential stuff for collectors and casual fans alike. *—Jason Ankeny*

The Hi Records Story / 1989 / Hi ♦♦♦♦♦
This 24-song compilation isn't exactly comprehensive, jumping over Hi records' first success, Carl McVoy's 1957 rockabilly single "Tootsie" b/w "You Are My Sunshine," to start with Bill Black's Combo and Ace Cannon, and then moving on to Murray Kellum's goofy "Long Tall Texan," roots rock legend Gene Simmons (perhaps better identified as Jumpin' Gene Simmons) with "Haunted House," and Charlie Rich. From there, it's on to more familiar names such as Willie Mitchell, Ann Peebles, Al Green, Otis Clay, et al., and the soul sounds for which Hi became known at the end of the 1960s and the beginning of the 1970s. Sandwiched between those two sides of the label's history is Jerry Jaye's "My Girl Josephine," a piece of rockabilly that was ten years out of its time and still managed to make the Top 30, with a sound that Creedence Clearwater Revival would soon perfect. The mastering is excellent, even for a release going back to 1989; the combination of sounds is as fascinating as the songs are extraordinary; and only the somewhat unfocused annotation is a slight disappointment. *—Bruce Eder*

Hi Records: Early Years, Vols. 1 & 2 / May 11, 1999 / HI ♦♦♦
Hi Records is usually identified with such R&B artists as Al Green and Ann Peebles, but this 57-track double-CD reveals the early pop, country, rockabilly, and rock & roll roots of the label. Drawn mainly from the late-'50s and '60s, *Hi Records: The Early Years* includes contributions by such recognizable names as Ace Cannon, Narvel Felts, Gene Simmons (whose 1964 hit "Haunted House" is here), and the Bill Black Combo. Other interesting items include seven tracks by the Johnny Cash-influenced Tommy Tucker, seven tracks by one-hit wonder Jerry Jaye (whose "My Girl Josephine" charted in 1967 and is included on this compilation), and a handful of recordings by Carl McVoy, one of Jerry Lee Lewis' many musical cousins. Much of this music is marginal but enjoyable, and the compilation is clearly aimed at collectors and specialists. Enthusiasts of country, rock, and rockabilly from this period might look for *Hi Records: The Early Years* in the R&B racks, where it will inevitably be misfiled. *—Greg Adams*

Hi Records: River Town Blues / May 11, 1999 / Cream-Hi ♦♦♦♦
This two-disc set examines the bluesier part of the label's output and bookends it with another disc subtitled "the R&B Sessions + The Soul Years." Although Hi's brand of blues was much further away from their Delta roots than other labels', some good down-home results were still produced on artists like Donald Hines, Big Amos Patton, Big Lucky Carter and Joe Lee Carter. Selections from Willie Mitchell, Gene "Bowlegs" Miller and Don Bryant complete the first disc. Disc two collects up the R&B sessions of Mitchell, Miller, Bryant, Norm West, Janet & the Jays, James Fry & the Five Royales, while also collecting up soul sides from Al Green, Syl Johnson, O.V. Wright, Otis Clay, Bobo Mr. Soul, Phillip Mitchell, the Masqueraders, Ann Peebles, Joint Venture and George Jackson. It's another great slab of Memphis musical history. *—Cub Koda*

Hi Records: The 45's Collection Vols.1-2 / May 11, 1999 / Cream-Hi ♦♦♦
Hi Records became famous for a brace of Southern soul recordings by folks like Al Green and Ann Peebles, both produced by Willie Mitchell and expertly played by the Hi

house band. This is a two-disc set of rarities from that same Hi soul team, simply loaded with breathtakingly raw but elegant soul gems. In addition to stray tracks from Peebles, O.V. Wright, and Otis Clay, we're also treated to true rarities from James Fry, David Duke, Eddie McGee, Norm West, Syl Johnson, Bobo Mr. Soul, T-99, Willie Walker, George Jackson, Erma Coffee, Phillip Mitchell, the Masqueraders, and Teacher's Edition. It's an important chunk of Memphis musical history. *—Cub Koda*

Hi Times: Hi Records R&B Years / Feb. 21, 1995 / Capitol ✦✦✦✦✦
Hi Times: Hi Records R&B Years is a superb three-disc box set covering all of the label's greatest hits, plus a number of forgotten gems. Al Green understandably dominates the set, since he not only was Hi's biggest artist, he also defined the label's sound with producer Willie Mitchell. As a result, the music on these three discs can sound a little similar at times, but the songwriting and performances from the likes of Green, Ann Peebles, and Joe Clay is first-rate, making *Hi Times* a necessary addition to any serious soul collection. *—Stephen Thomas Erlewine*

Hi Times: The R&B Years Sampler / 1995 / The Right Stuff ✦✦✦✦✦
Along with other Memphis labels like Stax, Goldwax, and American, Hi helped expose the world to Southern soul music. While the company didn't strike gold in the '60s along with its rivals, it did hit its stride in the '70s thanks to Al Green. Launched in 1959, the label first moved into the spotlight with Bill Black's Top 20 hit "Smokie, Pt. 2." Focusing on the honking R&B formula of that instrumental, Hi rode out most of the '60s with a steady stream of moderately successful releases. With veteran Memphis jazz musician Willie Mitchell coming on board as A&R director in the late '60s, however, the company found its sound and went on to become one of the most successful of all Memphis labels. The elegant, but earthy soul Mitchell preached can be ideally heard on Al Green hits like "Can't Get Next to You" and "Simply Beautiful," both of which are included on this substantial Hi sampler (the collection comes out of a three-disc set covering all the label's hits as well as a selection of minor gems). Along with other high-profile moments like Otis Clay's "Trying to Live My Life Without You," Ann Peebles' "I'm Gonna Tear Your Playhouse Down," and Syl Johnson's cover of Green's "Take Me to the River," there are plenty of lesser-known prizes from Erma Coffee, O.V. Wright, Ace Canon, and Quiet Elegance. Also on display, the superb Hi Rhythm Section comprised of drummer Al Jackson and the brother team of Teenie, Charles, and Leroy Hodges on guitar, organ, and bass, respectively. A perfect introduction to at least one side of the fertile sound of Southern soul. *—Stephen Cook*

☆ **Highlights from the Mercury R&B Story** / Sep. 24, 1996 / Polygram ✦✦✦✦✦
There are 20 early R&B hits from the Mercury stable collected on this sampler (a teaser to the label's eight-disc box set), featuring Dinah Washington, Jimmy Witherspoon, Lightnin' Hopkins, Big Bill Broonzy, Memphis Slim & His Orchestra, Arthur Prysock, Johnny Otis and Eddie "Cleanhead" Vinson. *—Jason Ankeny*

The Hip Walk: Jazz Undercurrents in 60s New York / May 7, 2002 / BGP ✦✦✦✦
It's hard to get a keen grasp of what the concept or unifying thread might be behind this compilation, other than that it's all 1960s New York jazz, and was mostly issued on the Riverside, Prestige, and Milestone labels. If the idea was to simply make an anthology of 1960s New York jazz, that's as impossible to adequately reflect in a single CD (and for that matter a box set) as 1960s London rock would within a single disc. The music itself, though, isn't any the worse for the thematic vagueness. It's a good (and, at 76 minutes, long) disc for those who aren't diligently building a thorough jazz collection, but want some reasonably wide-ranging samplers of quality sounds around. Tenor saxophonists Gene Ammons (on "Ca'purange (Jungle Soul)") and Willis Jackson (on "Nuther'n Like Thuther'n") dovetail with soul-jazz; vibraphonist Johnny Lytle seems to be making an exotica homage with "The Village Caller," and lays down some downright infectious and danceable "Milestones"-like riffs on "Selim." When that's followed by the R&B-informed jazz of Phil Upchurch's "Muscle Soul," you might begin to suspect this is aimed toward listeners with inclinations toward the more accessible pop spectrum of jazz. But actually this contains its share of straight-ahead contemporary and even somewhat experimental sounds with Art Blakey's Jazz Messengers' "Ping Pong," Yusef Lateef's "Love Theme From Spartacus," Joe Henderson's "The Kicker," and Cannonball Adderley's cover of Lateef's "Brother John" tribute to John Coltrane. George Braith and Joe Dukes aren't well-known names, but organ jazz fans will have heard of accompanists John Patton and Grant Green, who play on Braith's "Cantaloupe Woman," and Jack McDuff and George Benson, who play on Dukes' "The Soulful Drums." *—Richie Unterberger*

Hipsters' Holiday: Vocal Jazz & R&B Classics / 1999 / Rhino ✦✦✦✦✦
Featuring the heppest of the hepcats (and kittens), this'll jingle your jangle with Big John Greer's "We Want to See Santa Do the Mambo" and Pearl Bailey's "Five Pound Box of Money." The inimitable Babs Gonzales lays "Bebop Santa Claus" on you, and you'll "Jingle All the Way" with Lena Horne. *—Dennis MacDonald*

☆ **History of New Orleans R&B, Vol. 1** / 1987 / Rhino ✦✦✦✦✦
It's simply the best sounding and most enjoyable series (two discs/three cassettes) of the bouncy, piano-driven sound that could only come from a goodtime town like New Orleans. Lots of star power—Art Neville, Lee Dorsey, Irma Thomas, Frankie Ford, Shirley & Lee, Lloyd Price, Guitar Slim, Earl King, and many more. *—Myles Boisen*

☆ **Hitsville USA: The Motown Singles Collection 1959–1971** / 1992 / Motown ✦✦✦✦✦
Instead of following Stax/Volt's pattern and delivering an exhaustive box set containing all of their singles, Motown decided to limit their singles box, *Hitsville USA: The Motown Singles Collection 1959-1971*, to four discs that concentrated on the hits. There are a handful of wonderful lesser-known songs here, such as the Contours' "First I Look at the Purse," but the main strength of the 103-track box is that it features all of the biggest songs from Motown's golden era in one place. Collectors could have used a more comprehensive set, and the box itself could have been packaged with a little more care (there are no artists listed on the back of the individual discs, only songs), but *Hitsville USA* stands as a definitive overview and introduction to one of the most groundbreaking labels in pop music history. *—Stephen Thomas Erlewine*

Hitsville USA, Vol. 2: The Motown Singles Collection 1972–1992 / Oct. 19, 1993 / Motown ✦✦✦
Hitsville USA was such a success that it was little wonder that Motown decided to issue the sequel, *Hitsville USA, Vol. 2: The Motown Singles Collection 1972-1992*. Certainly, these four discs couldn't help but suffer in comparison to their predecessor—the first volume contained some of the greatest pop singles in history—since Motown was following trends during these 20 years instead of setting them. Nevertheless, there are a surprising number of classic singles here, from "Papa Was a Rolling Stone," "Let's Get It On," and "Dancing Machine" to "Easy," "Brick House," and "Super Freak." Unfortunately, there are too many mediocre songs on this set to make searching for these gems a pleasurable experience. If the compilers had limited themselves to a two-disc set, they would have been able to fit all the highlights on a consistent, listenable collection. As it stands, *Hitsville USA, Vol. 2* simply contains too much middling music to make it useful for anyone but dedicated Motown fans. *—Stephen Thomas Erlewine*

Honkin' 'N' Hollerin': R&B from the Radio Corporation, Vol. 1 / Nov. 10, 1998 / WestSide ✦✦✦✦
RCA Victor was one of the very few majors who actually had an R&B division that could keep pace with labels like Chess, Modern, Savoy, Atlantic, King and others. This opening volume of an ongoing series comes up with 28 terrific performances illustrating that the corporate giant at least had their pulse on what actually constituted R&B in the early '50s, and then some. From the out-and-out wildness of Mr. Bear and the Bearcats' "Mr. Bear Comes to Town," Big Al Sears' "Great Googa Mooga," Milt Trenier's "Day Old Bread" and the Jackson Brothers' "There's No Other Way," this collection also plumbs some deep blues with the unissued Larry Dale tracks "Midnight Hours," "Please Tell Me" and "Down to the Bottom," all three featuring some stellar guitar work from Mickey Baker. Other highlights include Louis Jordan's "Chicken Back," Big Al Sears' "Rock 'n' Roll Ball," Beatrice Reading's bluesy "I'll Do It All Again," an 11-year-old George Benson's first record ("She Makes Me Mad"), Eartha Kitt's uncharacteristic R&B outing "My Heart's Delight," and Big Connie's "Mumbles Blues." A nice chunk of seldom-anthologized American music. *—Cub Koda*

House of Soul: House of Blues / Goodman Group ✦✦✦
A mammoth 64-song compilation featuring urban Chicago soul and gritty traditional blues. Priscilla Bowman, the lone female, offers one track. Only three groups are represented: the Dells, the El Dorados, and the Spaniels. Early Jerry Butler sides and tracks by Gene Chandler, Major Lance, and Dee Clark highlight a smorgasbord of urban soul. Jimmy Reed and John Lee Hooker dominate the blues cuts with quality tracks like "Big Legs, Tight Skirt," "Big Boss Man," "Baby What You Want Me to Do," and "Dusty Road." Otis Rush, Elmore James, Gene Allison, and Wade Flemons perform as well, along with a host of others. *—Andrew Hamilton*

How Stella Got Her Groove Back / Aug. 11, 1998 / Flyte Tyme/MCA ✦✦✦✦
By the time they assembled the soundtrack for the film adaptation of Terry McMillan's acclaimed novel *How Stella Got Her Groove Back*, Jimmy Jam & Terry Lewis were no longer the hippest names in urban soul, but they hadn't lost their groove. They still knew what worked and what didn't within the context of urban R&B, they could still write strong songs, and they had a keen eye for talent. All of which is a complicated way of saying that *How Stella Got Her Groove Back* is an exceptional soundtrack—a well-constructed, consistently entertaining collection that manages to be cohesive despite its eclecticism. Or maybe, it's successful because of its diversity—it's great to hear the music slyly shift from updated Soul II Soul grooves to reggae to hip-hop to urban ballads. Everything is tied together by a classy, stylish attitude and sultry production that makes even the weaker songs sound alluring. Boasting highlights from Stevie Wonder & Wyclef Jean, Shaggy & Janet, Mary J. Blige, Big Punisher & Beenie Man, Me'Shell NdegéOcello, Maxi Priest and K-Ci & JoJo, *How Stella Got Her Groove Back* comes close to matching the dazzling heights of *Waiting to Exhale* and *Soul Food*; and that's good company indeed. *—Stephen Thomas Erlewine*

Hush Productions Music Makers, Vol. 1 / Oct. 22, 1996 / Hush ✦✦✦
Mellow offerings from Hush Productions. Twelve creamy tracks. Everything from the urban jazz sounds of Alex Bugnon's "Piano in the Dark," and Najee's "Sweet Love," to Sarah Dash's & Patti LaBelle's fire and brimstone duet, "You're All I Need to Get By." Freddie Jackson is a prime player on three bedroom staples: "You Are My Lady," "Rock Me Tonight (For Old Time Sakes)" and "Little Bit More," a duet with Melba Moore. Ray, Goodman & Brown shines on what is arguably their finest waxing, the romantic and sensual "Take It to the Limit." A quality compilation that gets better every play. The other players are suave singing Lillo Thomas, Ashford & Simpson and Meli'sa Morgan. *—Andrew Hamilton*

I'll Always Love My Mama / May 12, 1998 / Sony ✦✦✦✦
A whole album of "mama" songs. A good idea, but the selections could have been better. Etta James' "Tell Mama," and Koko Taylor's "Come to Mama" are smokers but they don't fit, as the mama in those songs refers to a man's woman, not his mother. However, more appropriate songs by the Intruders, Maze, Soloman Burke, Shirley Caesar and others, make up for the less than appropriate tracks. Major Lance's tender "That's What Mama Say," Arthur Prysock's "My Mother's Eyes," Buddy Guy's bluesy "My Mother," and the Intruders' "I'll Always Love My Mama," are as good as it gets. *—Andrew Hamilton*

If Loving You Is Wrong: 20 Cheatin' Heartbreakers / Mar. 12, 2002 / Kent ✦✦✦✦✦
This actually isn't the first soul compilation devoted to cheating songs; there were a couple on Ichiban/Soul Classics in the mid-'90s. The genre's fertile enough that there's no repetition between those and this 20-song disc, which spans 1967 to 1982, and generally (though not exclusively) mines the earthy, deep soul end of things. With some exceptions (Shirley Brown's "Woman to Woman," James Carr's "Dark End of the Street"), these aren't automatically familiar to general listeners. And while the artist roster includes some big soul names—Johnnie Taylor, Irma Thomas, Carla Thomas, Isaac Hayes—it's filled out with more cultish and journeymen artists like Denise LaSalle, the Soul Children, Eddie Floyd, and Jackie Moore (and even collectors may have heard nothing by Phillip Mitchell, Sam Dees, or Rozetta Johnson). As music, it's mostly emotional ballads that might be suitable for slow dancing or making out if not for the somewhat salacious lyrical content. Because of such content, these songs have more wit than many a soul slowie, and they're generally above average, though the lugubrious tempos tend to draw down your disposition after a while. The concept of an uptempo cheating song seems to have been rather foreign, and thus it's a relief when Carla Thomas hits a danceable groove on "Some Other Man (Is Beating Your Time)" or Mel & Tim's chirpy hit "Backfield in Motion" comes on. Some of the more surprising or interesting entries include Lloyd Price's 1971 single "Mr. and Mrs. Untrue," from a time when the '50s rocker had long been out of the sales spotlight; an obscure 1972 effort by Irma Thomas, "She'll Never Be Your Wife," penned by Jerry Williams (aka Swamp Dogg); Ann Peebles' steamy "Breaking Up Somebody's Home"; and Jackie Moore's 1969 single "Loser Again," which is a little more uptown in its production mood than much of what's here. The low spot is certainly Candi Staton's cover of "Suspicious Minds," not made any more palatable by the fact that it was a moderate hit in Britain. *—Richie Unterberger*

Impressed!: 24 Groups Inspired by the Impressions & Curtis Mayfield / Feb. 19, 2002 / Kent ✦✦✦
Stars inspire imitation, and you don't have to be a musicologist to be familiar with a lot of songs and artists that have imitated singers and genres like Elvis Presley, the Beatles, Motown, Bob Dylan, and so forth. It's not always remembered, though, that some smaller-scale stars also inspired a surprising wealth of, if not exactly imitations, recordings that certainly owed a lot to a definite source. That's the concept behind this intriguing compilation, devoted to a couple dozen songs from the 1960s and early '70s that were blatantly or subtly influenced or inspired by the Impressions. None of the groups on this anthology were huge names, though some—like the Astors, Larks, Detroit Emeralds, Manhattans, and Mad Lads—had hits and were reasonably popular. Most, though, were no-names on indie labels big and small, creating smooth, group-vocalized soul that approximated the feel of familiar radio hits. What was missing? The vocals of Curtis Mayfield and the like, of course, but more importantly, songs as strong and immediately distinctive as "People Get Ready" or "We're a Winner." Still, if you're a fan of well-organized soul vocals and arrangements that fall on the slicker side of 1960s soul, this material is always competent, and sometimes (though not always) pretty respectable on its own grounds. And different phases of the Impressions are emulated, too: the Astors do a nice 1963 cut in the spirit of early Mayfield-Impressions Latin-tempoed efforts, "Just Enough to Hurt Me," while entries like the Marvellos' "In the Sunshine" are lush late-'60s productions. The Poets, represented by a 1965 single, would eventually evolve into the Main Ingredient. If the compilers had really wanted to be adventurous, they could have licensed a 1960s Jamaican reggae cut or two from the Wailers or others who showed a definite debt to the Impressions. The liner notes are a big plus since most of these groups (and certainly most of these cuts) are barely known. It seems like the 1962 date given for the Brilliants' track, though, has to be wrong: as the liners properly note, it bears similarity to "People Get Ready," a song that wasn't a hit until 1965. *—Richie Unterberger*

Invictus Club Classics / 1999 / Sequel ✦✦✦✦✦
This disc collects tracks suitable for club dancing taken from Eddie Holland, Lamont Dozier, & Brian Holland's Hotwax, Invictus, and Music Merchant labels. A good buy for serious collectors, *Invictus Club Classics* features a wealth of lesser-known material; HDH had their share of hits and misses, but their quality was consistent. It contains Freda Payne's first single on Invictus, "Unhooked Generation," and Lee Charles' soulful take of "Sittin' on a Time Bomb," a hit for the Honey Cone. Laura Lee does "Crumbs Off the Table," a hit for the Glass House. The Jones Girls are represented here on "Taster of the Honey (Not the Keeper of the Bee)." Chairmen of the Board's psychedelic/rock side blares on two cuts and on member Harrison Kennedy's solo shot "Sunday Morning People." Also included are tracks by Parliament, Eloise Laws, Raynel Wynglas, the Politicians, Tyrone Edwards, Smith Connection, and Holland Dozier's lovely "Why Can't We Be Lovers." *—Andrew Hamilton*

It Takes Two / 1996 / Columbia/Global/Sony TV ✦✦✦✦
As the title suggests, *It Takes Two* is a collection of R&B duets, including a whopping 40 tracks (though "If You Don't Know Me By Know," by Harold Melvin & the Blue Notes, "Midnight Train to Georgia," by Gladys Knight & the Pips, and "Kiss" by Tom Jones and The Art of Noise fudge the concept a bit). The many pairings of music superstars makes *It Takes Two* that much more interesting. The pleasant surprises include "Relight My Fire," by Lulu & Take That, one of Ian Levine's best compositions. Mica Paris pairs with Will Downing and delivers a powerful rendition of "Where Is the Love." Traditional pairings include the classics "You've Lost That Lovin' Feeling," by the Righteous Brothers, "Every Time You Go Away," by Hall & Oates, and "I Got You Babe," by Sonny and Cher, which seems out-of-place on this collection. Odd ball match-ups include "Don't Let the Sun Go Down on Me," by George Michael & Elton John, "Easy Lover," by Phil Collins & Phillip Bailey, "There's Nothing Better Than Love," by Luther Vandross & Gregory Hines, and "Don't Know Much," by Linda Ronstadt & Aaron Neville. Pricey, but excellent for them cozy winter nights with that special person. *—Andrew Hamilton*

It's a Deep Soul Thing / Black Cats ✦✦✦✦
Here is a semi- or illegal compilation of obscure soul, dating from the early '60s through the mid-'70s. There are liner notes (written by someone or something called "Musashimaru"), and they discuss with a fan's abandon many of the performers included here, but there is literally no discographical information other than artists and track titles. For fans of deep soul, this is a source of frustration, but for the folks who put this out in Vancouver, it protects their asses. Nonetheless, the music itself is ultimately what matters, and these 21 tracks are strictly top-notch. The masters are no big deal in terms of quality, but it seems likely that there are fewer than a couple of handfuls of the original singles on the planet, so what are you going to do? These are definitely mastered from records, not session tapes. Included here are Paul Kelly's "Nine Out of Ten Times" and a couple of numbers he produced, including Janice Tyrone's "I'm Gonna Make It" and Winfield Parker's "A Fallen Star." Also included is Sonny Fishback's monster jukebox smash from 1965, "I Won't Take Back These Words," and Luther Ingram's version of "You Don't Miss Your Water." And while there isn't a weak second on the entire set, perhaps its defining moment is late in the disc with Otis Williams' "Begging to You," followed by James Lewis Fields' "I Really Love You," followed by, at the end, Betty Harris' "Can't Last Much Longer," which will either send chills up and down your spine or you have sawdust for blood. This collection is symptomatic of a genre of music that was widely recorded—like doo wop before it—and barely documented. While it's true that this is for the most part only a bootleg, it is perhaps the only source for music that deserves to be studied, disseminated, and—most of all—played for perpetuity. *—Thom Jurek*

It's OKeh Up North / Mar. 13, 2001 / Goldmine/Soul Supply ✦✦✦✦✦
This magnificent compilation comes from OKeh Record sides, the Windy City company that produced some of the best soul music of the '60s. Offering over 20 tracks, the CD is top heavy with seven Major Lance songs. The romantic "Call Me Tomorrow," an early track by Major "Love Won't Let Me Wait" Harris, is also featured, along with contributions from the hard-singing Tommy Tate with the aching "I'm Taking on Pain," and Larry Williams and Johnny "Guitar" Watson, who wail on two saucy duets: "Too Late," and "A Quitter Never Wins." Included as well are Billy Butler's most famous song "Right Track," the Artistics' biggest OKeh release "This Heart of Mine," a soulful Little Richard on "I Don't Want to Discuss It," two tearjerkers from Walter Jackson, and more. *—Andrew Hamilton*

Jackie Brown—Music from the Motion Picture / Dec. 9, 1997 / Warner Bros. ✦✦✦✦✦
Quentin Tarantino established himself as one of the few filmmakers to effectively use pop music with his first film *Reservoir Dogs*, a movie where the music was integral to the success of the film yet also worked well as a collection of songs. *Jackie Brown*, Tarantino's long-awaited third feature, finds him exploring new territory, creating an homage to blaxploitation flicks as well as a surprisingly subtle character study and love story, and its soundtrack appropriately finds him in new territory as well. The soundtrack still features snippets of dialogue, which simply aren't as effective separated from the film as those from *Pulp Fiction*, but the unified collection of '70s soul and funk is refreshing. He has wisely selected a batch of songs that haven't been worn out by oldies radio, building the bulk of the album with cult favorites like Bobby Womack's "Across 110th Street," Bill Withers' "Who Is He (And What Is He To You?)," Randy Crawford's "Street Life," Minnie Riperton's "Inside My Love," the Vampire Sound Inc.'s "The Lions and the Cucumber" and Pam Grier's "Long Time Woman." Only "Didn't I Blow Your Mind This Time," "Strawberry Letter 23" and "Natural High," as well as the Grass Roots' "Midnight Confessions," are familiar oldies items, but they play an integral part in the film itself and help make the soundtrack a thoroughly enjoyable, compulsively listenable experience. *—Stephen Thomas Erlewine*

Jackie Robinson Tribute: Stealing Home / Sep. 23, 1997 / Sony ✦✦✦✦
This CD pays a heartfelt tribute to Jackie Robinson, the African-American baseball star who broke the major league color barrier when he signed on with the Brooklyn Dodgers in 1947. Choice selections include Sly & the Family Stone's "Stand!," Billy Paul's "Brown Baby," poetess Nikki Giovanni's "Stealing Home for Jackie Robinson" and Luther Vandross singing the trumpeting "Ain't No Stopping Us Now." Collectively, these songs celebrate the long struggle for racial equality, and the pride of the African-American community. The 13 tracks represent a soul music smorgasbord incorporating hip-hop, spoken word, urban, and rap, and the result is an uplifting tribute to the emotional power of music in times of trouble as well as triumph. *—Andrew Hamilton*

Jammin' Oldies / Feb. 20, 2001 / Rhino ✦✦✦
Rhino's 2001 collection *Jammin' Oldies* contains 20 soul and disco hits from the '70s, occasionally dipping into the '60s (Aretha Franklin's "Chain of Fools") or '80s (Patrice Rushen's "Forget Me Nots"). There's nothing unexpected here—when Redbone's "Come and Get Your Love," Evelyn "Champagne" King's "Shame," Cornelius Brothers & Sister Rose's "Treat Her Like a Lady," and Chaka Khan's "I Feel for You" seem obscure to their company ("Let's Stay Together," "Pick Up the Pieces," "Let's Get It On," "We Are Family," "I'll Take You There," "Mr. Big Stuff," "Superfly," the sublime "I'll Be Around," etc.), you *know* you're on familiar ground. Still, it's hard to fault the song selection, the sound is good, the packaging is well done (complete with nice notes by Denise Sullivan), which means that this isn't a bad choice for someone who just wants the familiar. *—Stephen Thomas Erlewine*

Jazz Dance Classics, Vol. 4 / Apr. 16, 1995 / Luv N' Haight ✦✦✦✦
Another in Luv N' Haight's series of rare-groove jazz retrospectives culled from the Fantasy vaults, *Jazz Dance Classics, Vol. 4* spans the years 1961-1973 with a mix ranging

from early, organ-free sides by alto saxophonist Prince Lasha and tenor legend Eddie "Lockjaw" Davis to meaty soul jams baked up by the likes of B-3 maestro Charles Kynard and guitarist Boogaloo Joe Jones. In addition to some Latin funk by Pucho & the Latin Soul Brothers and a bit of swamp blues from Little Sonny, this mostly instrumental collection of soul jazz highlights is further augmented by vocal turns by Funk Inc. and Linda Lyndell (her Stax hit "What a Man"). Breakbeat fanatics will be pleased to see drummer Bernard Purdie on the bill—he practically steals the show on Kynard's "Sweetheart"—while jazz musos will salivate upon seeing the names of guitarist Melvin Sparks, tenor saxophonist Houston Person, bassists Ron Carter and Jimmy Lewis, and drummer Idris Muhammad, among many other heavyweights. Those already in awe of Blue Note's similarly disposed *Blue Break Beats* series will not want to miss this quality collection. *—Stephen Cook*

The Jewel/Paula Records Story: Blues, Rhythm & Blues and Soul Recordings / Apr. 13, 1993 / Warner Brothers ♦♦♦

Jewel and Paula were started by Stan Lewis, a record store owner and mail-order operator specializing in the kind of vital R&B, blues, soul and gospel tunes that many people enjoyed, but were highly undervalued by most major record labels. Lewis moved into the record business during the mid-'60s, signing raw artists who made music light-years away from slick pop fare. This two-disc anthology features prime Jewel and Paula acts from the 1960s, '70s and '80s. The first disc includes urgent soul tunes from Toussaint McCall and Ted Taylor, Delta blues from Frank Foster, classic shouting R&B from Joe Turner, the smoother R&B sound of Charles Brown, Lightnin' Hopkins, John Lee Hooker, and others. The second disc is just as distinguished, featuring Little Johnny Taylor, Fontella Bass, Ike & Tina Turner, Buster Benton and Ted Taylor, then-budding stars Bobby Rush and Artie "Blues Boy" White, plus other regional attractions. *—Ron Wynn*

Jiving Jamboree, Vol. 2 / May 12, 1999 / Ace ♦♦♦♦♦

Some would argue that this is a slapdash collection of jump blues, R&B, and early rock from the late '40s through the late '50s, not held together by any style or even label, save having a good jump or swing beat for dancing. They'd be right, but on the other hand it's refreshing to come across compilations like these that are obviously geared toward collectors, and unafraid to bend genre lines in the service of creating an enjoyable (as opposed to completist or scholarly) program. Indeed some of these aren't rock or R&B at all, but rather swing music with a jumpy edge (Louis Prima's "Be Mine"), or somewhat square-sounding pop or jazz acts desperately trying to sound in line with the rock craze (the Deep River Boys' cover of Bill Haley's "Rock-A-Beatin' Boogie"). So you get hot sax-driven jump blues (Jack McVea's "Wine-O"); really strange R&B-verging-on-rock novelties (Rene Hall's "Twitchy," Vernon Green's "Buick '59"); little-known cuts by well-known New Orleans R&B figures Fats Domino, Smiley Lewis, and Dave Bartholomew; prime R&B boogie from the Treniers ("Go! Go! Go!"); bona fide early rock & roll from Larry Williams ("Slow Down," the only famous cut on the collection); rock-tinged swing jazz by Anita Tucker ("Hop, Skip and Jump"); and even danceable near-a cappella vocal group jive from the Prisonaires. If nothing else, it's a good sample of how many rock & roll roots lay in obscure swing, blues, R&B, and even pop songs that got to the verge of a genuine rock & roll sound, but stopped just short of the line. *—Richie Unterberger*

Jiving Jamboree, Vol. 3 / Sep. 17, 2002 / Ace ♦♦♦♦

Taken from the catalog of the King label, this has 24 tracks that generally fall into the dance R&B-jump blues-jazz crossover style of the early '50s, though a few of these post-date the mid-'50s (with one straggler from as late as 1964). There are cuts by a bunch of names who were big in their day, though they're relatively forgotten by all but dedicated enthusiasts now: Wynonie Harris, Bullmoose Jackson, Lucky Millinder, Mabel Scott, Tiny Bradshaw, Jimmy Rushing, Roy Brown, Boyd Bennett, Lula Reed, and Moon Mullican. And there are about as many by figures who wouldn't even be familiar to some genuine early R&B enthusiasts. Still, what's more important is that this is pretty high-quality music for the genre, with a lot of humor and verve, though as is the norm for said genre, diversity isn't its highest attribute. Some of the items that stand out for quality or relatively unusual flavor include Zeb Turner's "No More Nothin'," which has a much stronger hillbilly country flavor than most of the program; Pete "Guitar" Lewis' instrumental "Louisiana Hop," which has a much stronger blues guitar presence than most of the surrounding material; the Platters' "Voo-Vee-Ah-Bee," from 1954, which is far more playful and uptempo than their subsequent hits; H-Bomb Ferguson's "Midnight Ramblin' Tonight" (from 1960), in which '60s soul starts to creep into the arrangement; and Jesse Powell's "The Walkin' Blues" (featuring singer Fluffy Hunter), which has an instantly memorable catchy refrain. Those on the lookout for rare Jerry Leiber & Mike Stoller songs might want to hear Little Esther's "Hollerin' and Screamin'," an early collaboration of theirs from a 1953 single. *—Richie Unterberger*

Just Keep on Dancing: Chess Northern Soul / 1996 / Kent ♦♦♦

Here are 24 slices of mostly upbeat, dance-oriented soul cuts released on Chess between 1961 and 1971, though all but two date from 1964-1969. It's peppy, well-produced stuff that, like most of Chess' soul, bears the influence of both Motown and the Windy City productions of Curtis Mayfield and Carl Davis. It'll please Northern soul collectors, though it's more pleasant than compelling. It includes performances by a few big names (Gene Chandler, Billy Stewart, Etta James, the Dells), though most of them are only known to serious soul hounds, and some of the best tracks (James' "Seven Day Fool," Stewart's "A Fat Boy Can Cry") have been readily available on those artists' own compilations. Among the obscurities, Doug Banks' "I Just Kept on Dancing," on which he sounds like he's trying to become the Black Gene Pitney, is worth noting for its sheer oddity value. The Radiants' upbeat sweet soul harmonies on "Hold On" gave them a small R&B hit in 1968, though it has enough pop appeal to sound like a lost Top Ten hit of the late '60s. *—Richie Unterberger*

The K-Tel Presents Greatest Male R&B Groups: The 60's / Apr. 28, 1998 / K-Tel ♦♦♦

Top songs, but a tired compilation; something about this one just doesn't jell, despite obscure inclusions like the O'Jays' "I'll Be Sweeter Tomorrow" and the Soul Brothers 6's Southern-flavored "Some Kind of Wonderful." The Dells' "Stay in My Corner," the Delfonics' "La, La Means I Love You," and the Impressions' "It's All Right" are featured as well, but they're readily available on other collections. "My True Story" by the Jive Five is also in this mix; this classic R&B/doo wop beauty is always a pleasure. *—Andrew Hamilton*

The K-Tel Presents Greatest Male R&B Groups: The 70's / Apr. 28, 1998 / K-Tel ♦♦♦♦

Far more pleasing than 1960s' edition in this series, this compilation begins with Chairmen of the Board's bombastic "Pay to the Piper," and ends with the Tymes' melodic "It's Cool." In between, you'll find creamy, soulful '70s classics like the Persuaders' "Thin Line Between Love and Hate" and the Moments' enduring "Love on a Two-Way Street." Also included is Curtis Mayfield & the Impressions' "Finally Got Myself Together," and many fond memories from New York City, the Main Ingredient, the Dells, the Four Tops, and Blue Magic. *—Andrew Hamilton*

Kent's Magic Touch / Jun. 24, 1997 / Kent ♦♦♦

Here are 27 fairly obscure soul tracks spanning the mid-'60s to the early '70s, all originally recorded for the affiliated Musicor/Dynamo labels; three cuts were previously unissued. Some of these names are known to soul and pop fans, like Eartha Kitt, the Toys, the Jive Five, Tommy Hunt, Inez Foxx, Melba Moore, and the Platters, although they're not represented by any famous hits; most of the performers, indeed, may not ring a bell even with listeners who consider themselves soul collectors. It's all competent soul with pop-conscious, East Coast-flavored production, mostly dancefloor-ready, even if the only dancefloors moving to the sounds these days are found on the Northern soul scene. As is often the case on these compilations, there's little to complain about, but little that makes a deep impression. Exceptions might include the young Melba Moore's "The Magic Touch," unissued when it was recorded in 1966, though it served as a demo for an excellent rock single by Bobby Fuller; there's also a nifty 1965 version of "This Diamond Ring" (by Sammy Ambrose) that's far more soul-oriented than the famous hit rendition by Gary Lewis. *—Richie Unterberger*

KentStax / 1989 / Kent ♦♦♦

There are 16 Stax sides featured on this collection, most produced by Detroiter Don Davis. The bounty includes United Image's rare "Love's Creeping Up on Me" (the same group renamed themselves Double Exposure and scored some disco hits on Salsoul Records; two toughies from Steve Mancha ("I Don't Wanna Lose You" and "Just Keep on Loving Me"); selections by J. J. Barnes, Major Lance and Little Sonny, and Southern shaded tracks from the feminine perspectives' of Kim Weston, Barbara Lewis, and Margie Joseph. Don Davis' gutbucket uptown sound meshed perfectly with Stax's Southern groove, as this set makes clear. *—Andrew Hamilton*

King New Breed Rhythm & Blues / 2002 / Kent/Ace ♦♦♦♦♦

This collects 24 R&B sides from the esteemed King label cut between 1956 and 1967, though the emphasis is on the brands of R&B that preceded the golden age of soul music. The aim, and very successfully realized too, was to capture the poppier side of King's R&B, often mixing together varying amounts of blues, rock, soul, and pop. Many vault compilations of labels such as King—and Kent/Ace has been as guilty as anyone in this respect—are genre exercises, pleasing for completist collectors but just too homogenous to maintain interest for less-specialized tastes. In contrast, *King New Breed Rhythm & Blues* is not just varied, but almost unerringly good to excellent, in large part because so many of the songs do fall a bit outside the party musical lines expected or demanded of many a blues or soul purist. For one thing, many of the songs boast minor, moody tunes that just weren't the norm in much blues or soul. If it's true that several of the songs are explicitly derivative of "Fever" (with which Little Willie John had a huge hit on King in the mid-'50s), it's also true that tons of blues songs from this era stick to a 12-bar formula, and at least this was a different formula. Yet most of these tracks don't refer specifically to "Fever" (though Joe Tex's 1956 single "Pneumonia" certainly does), and some aren't even moody. They're just different from the norm, usually with edgy, exciting performances. Tiny Topsy's 1959 single "Just a Little Bit" is a true monster, too strange in construction to be a hit perhaps (and similar to but almost not quite the same as Rosco Gordon's "Just a Little Bit"), but brimming with sullen energy. Albert King's excellent "Had You Told It Like It Was (It Wouldn't Be Like It Is)" is downbeat soul-pop, but just as passionately performed as his more standard blues classics and a good deal more melodic. Other big names here include Little Willie John (with one of his better singles, "I'm Shakin'"), Freddie King (who duets with Lula Reed on "It's Easy Child," covered by the Moody Blues on the B-side of their hit "Go Now"), James Brown's right-hand man Bobby Byrd, Johnny Watson, the 5 Royales (whose "Think" isn't rare, but is an R&B classic with great guitar), and Ike Turner (whose 1957 single "She Made My Blood Run Cold" is a weird Screamin' Jay Hawkins-like slice of ghoul rock). Yet some of the no-name performers (and there are a lot of them) here offer tracks of the same caliber, whether it's Mike Pedicin's "Burnt Toast and Black Coffee," Bobby King's minor-keyed "Thanks Mr. Postman" (an answer record to "Please Mr. Postman"), Mary Johnson's girl group-influenced "Hard Forgetting Memories," or the peppy, upbeat 1963 dance soul of Hannibal's "My Kinda Girl." There's got to be more stuff around from this era that breaks boundaries a bit, whether on King or other labels, and Kent/Ace is to be applauded for compiling R&B-soul cuts that mine grooves that have not often been covered by other reissues. *—Richie Unterberger*

King Northern Soul / Jul. 27, 2000 / Kent ♦♦♦

In the last half of the 1960s, the King label was most known for the explosive soul-funk of its one superstar, James Brown. It is not so well known that King also released a wealth of soul music by other performers, not all of who were following soul brother number one's path. Indeed, as this 24-track compilation of 1963-1971 sides demonstrates, many of King's soul artists were pretty normal, mainstream soul singers. That's an interesting thing to discover, but it does not, alas, make for music that's nearly as interesting as James Brown's. Nor, actually, does it even make for music that's even as interesting as the King projects done by Brown's sidemen, associates, and protégés. Kent made a conscious decision to steer clear of product with ties to Brown (such items are available on some other compilations), resulting in a disc of agreeable but ordinary period soul, even if such rare 45s, like rare soul 45s of almost any kind, have found favor on England's Northern soul circuit. There are some mild standouts, like the high (indeed womanish) wails of Junior McCants on "Try Me for Your New Love" or Pat Lundy's quite Aretha Franklin-like "Prove It" (no surprise as Franklin did the original). As in much rare soul from the time, often it's derivative of trends in Motown and Chicago; the Expressions' "You Better Know It" is a blatant cop of the Impressions (down, of course, to the similar group names). As it ends up, there are a couple of things here with James Brown connections. Marva Whitney is represented by a 1968 single that predates her association with Brown. Brown himself produced the Determinations' "Bing Bong Goes My Heart" and co-wrote the Brownettes' ballad "Never Find a Love Like Mine," though both of those numbers are more normal sounding than Brown's usual bag. Also, the very young Bootsy Collins and Phelps "Catfish" Collins were in the group of Charles Spurling, represented by the 1967 single "She Cried Just a Minute." *—Richie Unterberger*

King Northern Soul, Vol. 2 / Oct. 9, 2001 / Kent ♦♦♦
Like *Vol. 1*, this assembles King soul records, mostly of the uptempo variety, that you've probably never heard of unless you spend a great deal of your time collecting old soul 45s. The chronological reach is 1957-1973, though most of the cuts come from the late '60s and early '70s; three of them were previously unreleased. The only artist that most listeners will know is Freddie King, represented by his 1962 single "One Hundred Years." Those formalities out of the way, this is a pretty average soul compilation, acceptable but unexceptional in the quality of the material and the distinction of the artists. There's some funk chops in the beats and arrangements, but it's not particularly James Brown-indebted for the most part. There's not much here that demands attention as a neglected gem, and indeed some is forgettable, though at its best it's pleasant soul of various stripes, from mild funk to girl group-dipped soul to Aretha Franklin imitations. The Solars seem to be doing their damnedest to cross the Impressions with Mel & Tim on "Here's My Heart," and Charles Spurling's "Mr. Cool" has a waltz-like beat that's pretty unusual for soul of the era. Freddie King's "One Hundred Years" is a standout in his catalog in that it doesn't bear blues influence, but sounds rather like the New York soul of the Drifters. The King Pins' "It Won't Be This Way (Always)," which sounds like Sam Cooke's lightest efforts, was actually a Top 20 R&B hit in 1963. If it sounds like this all still doesn't add up to anything substantial, that's correct, but it'll fill in some gaps for die-hards. *—Richie Unterberger*

King's Serious Soul: Too Much Pain / Jan. 1, 2000 / Kent ♦♦♦
There aren't a whole lot of King soul records that are well-known beyond the massive catalog James Brown assembled at the label. This 24-track compilation goes into King's vaults for numerous other soul records released by the company between 1964 and 1973. Actually much of this was not produced by King itself, but leased from other sources, such as Boblo in Macon, GA. In any case, most of it has a deep Southern soul feel. Not a single song made the charts, and not a single performer is widely known even by cult standards. It's ordinary soul music, which doesn't mean it's bad or ill-produced; it's just the kind of thing that will appeal exclusively to serious collectors. Sometimes the influence of Brown can be felt, but it's the balladeering Brown, not the funkified one, as heard on cuts like Eugene Evans' "Too Much Pain" and Thomas Bailey's "Wish I Was Back (In Your Arms Again)." Among the better tracks are Nancy Butts' (that's her real name) "Letter Full of Tears," an early-'70s recording of a Don Covay composition (popularized in the 1960s by Gladys Knight) that has an early-'60s retro feel. Jeb Stuart's "I Don't Want to Leave You Darling" and Jimmy Braswell's "I Can't Give You My Heart" have the smoldering ballad-with-bluesy-guitars-and-horn feel typical of some '60s Stax products. *—Richie Unterberger*

King's Serious Soul, Vol. 2: Counting Teardrops / Mar. 12, 2002 / Kent ♦♦♦
This anthology of rare soul on the King label from the '60s and early '70s might be only middle-of-the-pack as such things go. But you've gotta say this: Even if you have a wall full of these kinds of soul compilations, it's unlikely you'll recognize any of the artists behind these 24 tracks, with the exception of Oscar Toney Jr. (himself not exactly a household name). Junior McCants, Allison, Elaine Armstrong, Pat Lundy, James Duncan, Oscar Irvin, and the other names that fill out this disc are largely confined to the pages of price guides to rare 45s. As for the music, it's diverse but only fair soul, often in the emotional bluesy ballad mode, lacking the prime material or exceptional personalities needed to get the motors into highest gear. "Fair" is not synonymous with "bad," and a few of the songs are a little above the ordinary. Toney Jr. as it happens, has that indefinable bit of extra urgency and commitment in his gospel-soaked uptempo 1967 single "I've Found a True Love." Reuben Bell adapts the anguished, minor-key "I Hear You Knocking (It's Too Late)" to a more elaborate double-timing scenario with drawn-out spoken parts and crooning female backup vocals. LH & the Memphis Sounds do a good retro (by 1968 standards, anyway) job on the creamy slow tune "I'm a Fool in Love," with its doo wop-like vocals. And Oscar Irvin does a worthwhile cover of Bobby "Blue" Bland's "Cry, Cry, Cry." One of the songs, Junior McCants' high-pitched ballad "She Wrote It I Read It," was previously unissued. *—Richie Unterberger*

KRIS Records . . . Los Angeles' Showcase of Soul / Oct. 27, 1998 / Kent ♦♦♦
The Kris label, founded by Mel Alexander in 1963, put out soul and R&B records over the next few decades without finding any wide success. This 24-song compilation concentrates on the company's 1960s soul singles, though there are half a dozen post-1970 sides, one from as late as 1994. Los Angeles as a whole did not have an especially strong soul identity, something you could also say of the soul issued by Kris (much of which was written or co-written by Alexander). Often it sounds like it was trying to create a Motown groove; not a bad thing to aspire to and a quest in which Kris was hardly alone, but not a path conducive to branding your mark on history, either. If Lee Harvey's "Prove It" and the Del-Reys' "Walk Proud" thought they weren't trying their damnedest to sound like early Marvin Gaye, the artists and producers were only fooling themselves; BB Carter wants very much to be Mary Wells on "My Lover." By contrast, Fay Cooper tries hard to sound like early Atlantic-era Aretha Franklin on "Don't Hang Yourself (Talk Too Much)," and Harvey competently emulates the Major Lance/Curtis Mayfield Chicago sound on "My Assurance." Harvey (who also recorded as Lee Jones) is the most heavily represented artist, contributing six tracks, and claimed to have taught Sam Cooke how to sing, which is dubious. But as a singer he wasn't bad, coming up with this anthology's best cut, "I'm Gonna Make It (Up to You)," a sort of early funk take on the kind of riffs Gaye sang in the "Hitch Hike" days. The tracks from 1988-1994 are horrible urban contemporary soul, totally out of place given that the audience for soul compilations such as this is totally geared toward the early soul style. And, those aberrations aside, that audience will probably like this collection, though there's nothing particularly outstanding or original about the material or performances. *—Richie Unterberger*

Lafayette Soul Show / Jun. 7, 1996 / Kent ♦♦♦
Lafayette, LA, is not a large town, but its location in the midst of Cajun Louisiana means that a lot of musicians have come from the area, including soul and R&B acts as well as Cajun and zydeco ones. In the 1960s, the local La Louisianne label and its sister company Tamm recorded a good number of soul musicians, and about a couple dozen of their efforts comprise this CD. Swamp-pop and New Orleans R&B influences show up in the music sometimes, which gives this a regional flavor that distinguishes it somewhat from numerous other regional soul scenes around the U.S. However, this ain't no soul-Cajun hybrid. Much of it's just plain ordinary soul music, not too special or too bad, getting into a number of subgenres. Lil' Buck, for instance, does a credible James Brown/Dyke-style soul-funk instrumental on the 1969 single "Monkey in a Sack"/"Cat Scream"; Don Fredericks does quaintly emotional soul ballad covers in which the swamp-pop feel comes to the fore; King Karl uses a garage-rock organ on the previously unissued "Got the Fever Child." Raful Neal, better known as a bluesman than as a soul singer, contributes a couple of the stronger outings, both taken from a 1968 single, and both with a blues-soul crossover vibe, like Slim Harpo in a modern soul bag. Lynn August's "Little Red Rooster" credits Willie Dixon as songwriter, which seems like a mistake; with its frenetic dance beat, organ, and wholly unrelated lyrics, it's an entirely different song than the Dixon classic that was interpreted by Howlin' Wolf and the Rolling Stones. Certainly the most renowned track is Lil' Bob & the Lollipops' original version of "I Got Loaded," covered in the mid-'80s by Los Lobos. Not a brilliant compilation, but a little better than the norm for such specialized soul anthologies, due both to the regional idiosyncrasies and the decent variety of approaches. *—Richie Unterberger*

Last Days of Disco / May 28, 1998 / Sony ♦♦♦
The soundtrack to Whit Stillman's epic *The Last Days of Disco* is an excellent balance of predictable disco classics ("I Love the Nightlife (Disco 'Round)," "Got to Be Real," "Good Times," "He's the Greatest Dancer," "More, More, More"), plus a couple of cult items ("Doctor's Orders," "Everybody Dance," "Shame," "I'm Coming Out") and soul numbers ("The Love I Lost," "The Oogum Boogum Song," "Love Train") for good measure. The result may be a soundtrack that's heavily nostalgic, but it's a soundtrack that's enormously entertaining because it gets its era right and throws in some worthy surprises with the familiar. *—Stephen Thomas Erlewine*

Last Soul Company / Oct. 5, 1999 / Malaco ♦♦♦♦
To celebrate their 30 years in the soul and blues business, the Jackson, MS-based Malaco label released a six-disc box set covering the years 1969-1999. Luckily for the less keen lovers of Southern soul, the company has put together this two-disc, 30-track collection from the larger set. And while most of the big hits found on the multi-CD box are missing here (Jean Knight's "Mr. Big Stuff," Anita Ward's "Ring My Bell," King Floyd's "Groove Me," Dorothy Moore's "Misty Blue," and Z.Z. Hill's "Down Home Blues"), there's still plenty of quality material from the label's bountiful vaults. Besides many established stars who found a home at Malaco during the funk, disco, and hip-hop decades (Little Milton, Denise LaSalle, Tyrone Davis, Johnnie Taylor, and Bobby "Blue" Bland), the collection also features the more obscure talents of Latimore, Ruby Wilson, Bobby Rush, blues great Fred McDowell, G.C. Cameron, and many others. This was the sound of urbane, blues and gospel-soaked soul—the kind of music adults could still enjoy while their kids were going crazy for the latest acts on Def Jam, Tommy Boy, and Bad Boy. *—Stephen Cook*

Legacy's Rhythm & Soul Revue / 1995 / Legacy/Epic ♦♦♦♦♦
This is a bombastic party courtesy of Legacy Records. The festivities begin with an unedited "Wake Up Everybody" by Harold Melvin & the Blue Notes, flows into Isley, Jasper, Isley's "Caravan of Love," and then switches to adult theme ballads, the stature of "Me & Mrs. Jones," "Kiss and Say Goodbye," and Bill Withers' "Ain't No Sunshine." Brenda & the Tabulations' breezy but despairing "One Girl Too Late" is delightful. The Intruders' "Cowboy to Girls" and Major Lance's calypso-ish "Hey Little Girl" are irresistible. Includes LaBelle's potent "Lady Marmalade" and MFSB's contagious, six-plus minute "Love Is the Message." *—Andrew Hamilton*

Let's Crossover Again / 1999 / Kent ♦♦♦♦♦
Now *this* is a soul collection. Concentrating on the evolution of the music from its early raw dynamic in both its bluesier and R&B incarnations at Stax and its beat-conscious

dance rhythms at Motown during the early '60s, the music on these 24 tracks is decidedly different. The groove began to change in Memphis as it did in Detroit in the late '60s. Along with the somewhat excessive psychedelic experimentation that some artists would begin to employ in their productions, there came a period with more layered and textured arrangements, slower tempos, more polished vocals, and a widening and deepening of the dimensions of the sound of soul. These cuts epitomize that shift, as the "crossover" where soul's past met its present and future. With full discographical information and killer liner notes by U.K. Northern soul DJ and expert Ady Croasdell, *Let's Crossover Again* is an absolutely righteous and necessary compilation, one in which every track sheds some new light on the genre in general and in some cases offers a completely different view of an established artist. Great examples here would be the two opening tracks, "That's All" by Eddie Floyd and Johnnie Taylor's "Please Let Me In." Here are midtempo burners where the stomp and slam of the Stax rhythm section and the funky front-line work of Booker T. Jones and Steve Cropper are tempered with flowing horn lines and vocal lines that stress more than lyrics and become instruments in the mix. Later, in the Charmels' "I've Done It Again," the slow-tempo Stax ballad style is augmented by stunning chorus work—both male and female—and a muted horn section playing the accents at the end of the lines. Other highlights on this stunning set are Carla Thomas' "Closer to You," Cynthia & the Imaginations' "Nine Times Out of Ten," and the previously unreleased "City of Fools" by Colette Kelly. But it's all deeply moving, fully delightful, and so marvelous, feminine, and tough. *—Thom Jurek*

Live at the Apollo / 1990 / JCI ♦♦♦♦♦

This CD reissue features live performances by artists from the Atlantic Records roster (or Stax/Volt in the case of the Falcons & Rufus Thomas) This disc is essential for the two Falcons tunes "I Found a Love" and "Alabama Bound"; the songs may be the only live recordings of the Falcons in existence. The Coasters enact the slow, comedic "Taint Nothing to Me" and the rousing "Speedo's Back in Town," featuring Earl "Speedo" Carroll on lead. A young Otis Redding sounds insecure and tentative on "Pain in My Heart" and "These Arms of Mine," but Thomas is as confident as ever on "Walking the Dog" and "Rockin' Chair." Doris Troy, Ray Charles, and Apollo favorite Ben E. King give sterling performances, with King doing a three-song set of "Groovin'," "Don't Play That Song," and "Stand By Me." *—Andrew Hamilton*

Living the Nightlife / Nov. 20, 1995 / Kent ♦♦♦♦

Kent Records has set the standard for various-artists CDs in the U.K., displaying as much care with the packaging as they do compiling the songs, and this compilation features another sterling line-up of soul rarities and classics. Jack Montgomery's excellent "Dearly Beloved," for instance, is worth a fortune on 45, and you'll search long and hard to find a copy of Walter Johnson's obscure "Love Keeps Me Crying." Fred Hughes' "Send My Baby Back" was a mild R&B hit and Maxine Brown's "It's Torture" should have been. Big Maybelle is always magic, and the Shirelles' "Groovy Guy" is one girl group gem that you've probably never heard, featuring some male group sounds too. *Living the Nightlife's* 24 tracks offer plenty for the ears, and the packanging is easy on the eyes as well. *—Andrew Hamilton*

Lost & Found: The Blue Rock Records Story / Jul. 21, 1998 / Polygram ♦♦♦♦

Mercury R&B subsidiary Blue Rock Records had offices in Chicago and New York, and recorded in both cities. These 30 tracks compiled on two discs are a good, if not thorough, overview of the label's soulful offerings. No hits, but that was due to promotion, timing, and other unmeasurables, not the product. The music runs the gamut from uptempo finger-snappers to ballads to Southern soul. There's more than enough here to make a collector's mouth water: many of these tracks are difficult to find on 45 rpm, and Blue Rock never issued an individual album on any artist. There are two early pre-hit tracks from the Chi-Lites (recorded as the Hi-Lites for Daran Records); "She's Mine" and the dreamy "Never No More" are treasures. So is Sir Mack Rice's original version of "Mustang Sally," possibly Blue Rock's best-selling record along with "To Be or Not to Be" by Otis Leavill. Rice's baritone can also be heard on "You Can't Lose," but Leavill's four songs are the cream of the crop, enough to merit a solo CD. "To Be . . ." received scattered airplay, and the Impressions-sounding "Let Her Love Me" was a staple on Chicago's R&B stations; Leavill, a childhood crony of Curtis Mayfield and Major Lance also blows "Reason to Be Lonely" and "Let Me Live." Johnnie Mae Matthews, credited with recording the first incarnation of the Temptations (the Distants), displays her aggressive sound on "Baby What's Wrong" and "My Man." Other familiar voices include Dee Dee Warwick (Dionne's sister) on two tracks, the Shirelles, and Johnny Moore (Drifters). They're balanced by many unknowns, including Chuck & Cleo, Roy Hytower, Cynthia & the Imaginations, the Fads, the Lancers, Brenda Duff, and the Cat-Keys. *—Andrew Hamilton*

Lost Chicano Oldies, Vol. 2 / Jun. 27, 2000 / Lost Soul ♦♦

It wasn't immediately apparent from the first volume that a second would be warranted, but *Lost Chicano Oldies, Vol. 2* does reissue some incredibly rare tracks from Latin soul acts of the late '60s and early '70s. Most of these songs don't even rate for the one percent of collectors especially interested in the period, but a few tracks do rise above the soup. "She's My Woman, She's My Girl" by the Four Singing Avalons and "Wait Till I Find Her" by the not-so-fabulously named Fabulous Filtrations are the best here; they could've competed on the charts in Chicago during the late '60s or early '70s as Chi-Lites/Impressions sound-alikes. *—John Bush*

Lost Deep Soul Treasures, Vol. 1 / 2001 / Sounds of Soul ♦♦♦♦♦

This series commences to provide a well-needed service to fans of '60s soul: provide rare tracks by well-known artists alongside the work of lesser known performers of equal value. Here you get Otis Clay's extremely rare "You Hurt for the Last Time" (previously only available as the B-side of "Baby Jane") and Sam Dees' wonder "It's All Wrong (It's All Right)." But in addition are Willy McDougal's steamy wailer "I Can't Wait," Eddie Billups' heartbreakingly raw "No Love Have I," and Bobby Parker's pumped-up pleadfest "Don't Drive My Love Away." And that's just the beginning. In all there are 25 tracks here, and no lapse in quality. From the well known to the obscure, this is raw soul, lovemaking soul, tear-my-heart-out-a-piece-at-a-time soul. Where the South was cranking out the Stax/Volt side and Atlantic had a virtual factory of hitmakers, there were many of these cats and kittens who were making records for no other reason than to get them on the juke at the corner bar or perhaps in a neighboring county so they could get a gig or a radio appearance to perform their tracks before disappearing into the oblivion of day jobs forever. For a few years at least, these folks and their art get to live again on compilations like this one that rescue those treasures, package them well with reasonable liner notes, and place them out there for the fanatics, the curious, and the lovelorn to seek out the only kind of music that came from the spiritual human body: soul. And this is deep soul at that. *—Thom Jurek*

Lost Deep Soul Treasures, Vol. 3 / 2001 / S.O.S. ♦♦♦

The *Lost Deep Soul Treasures* series continues with another volume of absolutely necessary, indispensable music. The anonymous producers of these compilations are to be commended for bringing these tracks to the light of day again after decades in obscurity. But since there is no documentation (not even songwriting credits), it is safe to assume that these tracks were not issued legally. Here are 24 more killer cuts of the deepest of Southern soul, featuring well-established artists such as Sam & Dave ("Living It Up"), O.V. Wright ("To You Shall I Cling"), and Reuben Bell ("Asking for the Truth"). In addition, there are stunning works by lesser known or unknown soul artists such as Delilah, Pete Cook, and Mary Holmes (whose "After I Shed a Tear" will have you weeping buckets), an unreleased cut by Tommy Louis, and the killer "Talk to Me" by Inez Foxx. The consistency of the material is one thing—all of it is top-notch—but the emotional transference that happens in taking in more than an hour of these songs is remarkable. *—Thom Jurek*

Love Jones [Original Soundtrack] / Mar. 11, 1997 / Sony ♦♦♦♦

The soundtrack to the film *Love Jones* is arguably one of the best soundtracks of the 1990s. This neo-soul gem features a myriad of the decade's most prolific R&B acts, including Lauryn Hill, Dionne Farris, Groove Theory, Maxwell, Xscape, Brand New Heavies, Kenny Lattimore, and Me'Shell NdegéOcello, as well as tracks from jazz maestros Cassandra Wilson, Duke Ellington, and John Coltrane. The whole album flows like a classy, smooth set of perfect soul songs before shifting gears into jazz for the last several tracks. Lauryn Hill's "The Sweetest Thing" is just what its title implies, and stands as one of the hip-hop chanteuse's most lovely recordings, with her warm, melancholy vocals set against an acoustic backdrop courtesy of the Refugee Camp All-Stars. Dionne Farris' "Hopeless" is an intelligent, timeless gem of a ballad, and Xscape's version of "In the Rain" is just dripping with pure, unadulterated soul. Maxwell's hit "Sumthin' Sumthin'" is turned into an oozing, ultra-smooth ballad, highlighted by his signature falsetto, and long-absent neo-soul favorites Groove Theory provide a sexy and understated hip-hop cut with "Never Enough," which features Amel Larrieux's always welcome vocals. Trina Broussard's "Inside My Love" makes one feel as though they were watching her sing in an intimate club, and Cassandra Wilson's sublime "You Move Me" is the album's five-star track, with endless emotion packed into her brilliant, low-key performance. Finally, Brand New Heavies lend a welcome dose of uptempo funk with "I Like It." At the time of this album's release, most soundtracks included one or two new songs sandwiched between a bunch of filler and recycled tracks. *Love Jones* is a rare example of a flawless soundtrack album, and, dare we say, ranks as one of the best R&B albums of the 1990s, period. *—Jose F. Promis*

Love's Train: The Best of Funk Essentials Ballads / Nov. 1995 / Mercury Funk Essentials ♦♦

Some multiple-artists compilations satisfy more than others. On some you enjoy a few cuts, while others are use to accentuate romantic encounters—the kind you lay on the CD player, push "repeat all," and go for it, knowing the music is set. This collection is like that. It begins soft and slow with "Baby Blues" by the Love Unlimited Orchestra featuring Barry White; it kicks into second with Con Funk Shun's "Love's Train" and hits high gear on Stephanie Mills' electrifying closer "Feel the Fire." The different styles offer a cornucopia of love jams. Everything from Randy Brown's deep soul romp "I Wanna Make Love to You" to Kool & the Gang's jazzy, synthesized "Summer Madness." You won't find any disappointing edited versions, either; seven minutes and twenty seconds of "Heaven Must Be Like This" by the Ohio Players attest to that. *—Andrew Hamilton*

Lowrider Oldies, Vols. 1-9: Cruisin' Chrome Series / Nov. 13, 2001 / Thump ♦♦♦

Lowrider Oldies, Vol. 1-9: Cruisin' Chrome Series features a multitude of classic soul and R&B recordings that are intended to inspire memories of long-past days of cruising down the strip. Some of the featured performers include Mary Wells ("The One Who Really Loves You"), Aaron Neville ("Tell It Like It Is"), Delfonics ("La La Means I Love You"), the Dells ("Oh What a Night"), and Gene Chandler ("Duke of Earl"), in addition to countless others spread across these nine volumes. And though the majority of these recordings come from the '60s, there are a few '70s songs here as well, such as Kool & the Gang's "Ladies Night" and the Love Unlimited Orchestra's "I Belong to You." This multi-volume set is also available individually for those who don't want to make such a large investment. *—Jason Birchmeier*

Male Groups of the Motorcity / 1990 / Motorcity ♦♦♦

A handful for former Motown acts—the Valadiers, the Satintones, the Miracles, the Contours, the Lovetones, the Originals and the Fantastic Four—were rescued from recording limbo in the '80s by Ian Levine to record these tracks. The results, however, are uneven. The Satintones' new productions with Levine bear no resemblance to their original sound. Two songs, "Perfect Combination" and "Half a Man," sound like the work of a much younger group. Levine does much better with the Miracles' sound—the reproduction of "Love Machine," while not as riveting as the original, isn't half bad. The Contours' sides, "Ready or Not Here I Come" and "Look at the Stop Sign," will not remind you of the group who recorded dance dittys like "Can You Do It" or "Do You Love Me." The Bobby Taylor & the Vancouvers sides work better, as Taylor still has that magnificent, emotional tenor that mesmerized record buyers in the '60s. The Fantastic Four contribute a reworking of "I'll Be Doggone," popularized by Marvin Gaye, as their sole track, but it's a good one. The Lovetones, former backing vocalists for Mary Wells, are also only represented by one side, "Fire Alarm." Levine had a knack for getting a good authentic sound from the Originals; listening to the beautiful ballad, "Love Still Lives in My Heart," you know immediately that it's the "Baby I'm for Real" group. If you're looking for the old Motown sound from these old Motown groups you might be disappointed. But, if you want to hear familiar voices return to the spotlight, this will be a pleasurable experience. —*Andrew Hamilton*

Mark Lamarr's Ace Is Wild / Oct. 17, 2000 / WestSide ♦♦♦♦
And just *who* is Mark Lamarr, an American audience asks? Well, Lamarr is a highly successful comedian/presenter/emcee from Britain who also happens to be a record collector of renown in that country. This collection of his favorite Ace recordings is the British equivalent to Jay Leno professing to be an expert on Sun Records and putting together a compilation for Rhino. Besides having excellent taste, Lamarr also writes a great set of liner notes, full of wisecracks and off-kilter humor and a sense that you're sitting around spinning records with the guy in his living room. Although there's a couple of hits aboard from Huey "Piano" Smith (how can you resist?), Lamarr in the main sticks to obscuros from Joe Tex, Frankie Ford, Frankie Lee Sims, the Blue Dots and the Supremes. The blues side of the catalog is well represented, with sides from Sammy Myers, Earl King, H-Bomb Ferguson and Floyd Dixon, while the rockabilly side of the equation gives us rare opuses from the Phaetons, Hershel Almond, Eddy Seacrest and Danny Ray. Not a greatest-hits package by a long shot, but a compilation that instead gives a much better idea of what the label was *really* all about, and one that's well worth seeking out. —*Cub Koda*

Marvin Is 60: A Tribute Album / Jun. 22, 1999 / Motown ♦♦♦
Like most tribute albums, *Marvin Is 60: A Tribute Album* serves as a reminder of the greatness of the featured artist, not because the music is so strong, but because nothing on the record is as good as the original. That's not to say that *Marvin Is 60* is a bad album—given the caliber of Gaye's songs, it would be hard to make a bad album with them—but it's a pointless one. Motown assembled a strong roster of contemporary urban soul artists (many of which, it has to be said, are signed to Motown) and had them cover familiar Gaye songs, mostly from the '70s and early '80s. In other words, it's Marvin the Loverman, even on selections from *What's Goin' On?* That interpretation isn't surprising, since Gaye laid the groundwork for contemporary urban soul with his '70s music, but it makes the album sound a little monotonous. The real problem with *Marvin Is 60*, however, is the fact that almost nobody takes chances or attempts to make the songs their own. Only the Grenique & Tony Rich duet on "If This World Were Mine" offers a significant rearrangement and modernization and, not coincidentally, it's the most captivating song on the record. The rest of the album is always listenable and always predictable—even the promising Erykah Badu and D'Angelo duet on "Your Precious Love." It's as if all of the artists are trying so hard to be respectful, they can't help but deliver a fascimile of his performance. Since most of the featured artists are fine performers, it's a pleasant listen, but it never delivers any revelations about the songs, Marvin or the performers. Which means that it's hard not to finish *Marvin is 60* and wonder why it was even made. [*Marvin is 60* was also released as a limited edition, containing a bonus disc featuring the original versions of all 13 songs on the tribute album. The disc just confirms that nobody does Marvin like Marvin.] —*Stephen Thomas Erlewine*

Mercury Blues 'n' Rhythm Story 1945–55: Midwest Blues / Jun. 24, 1997 / Polygram ♦♦♦♦
Midwest Blues chronicles the best of the Mercury Records blues and R&B sessions that took place in Chicago from 1945 to 1952. If the entire *Mercury Blues 'n' Rhythm Story* box set is out of your reach and you're especially partial to Chicago blues, then you can settle for this two-disc volume. While it was no Chess Records in the down-home blues department, Mercury still attracted its share of Chicago-area talent in Memphis Slim, Sunnyland Slim, St. Louis Jimmy Oden, Robert Jr. Lockwood, and Big Bill Broonzy (who is represented here both as an electric guitar-wielding bandleader and as a solo folky songster). Most of the Chicago-style blues sides fill up disc two, while disc one offers a mix of swing, boogie-woogie, and R&B by a cast of recording stars that includes Dinah Washington, Julia Lee, T-Bone Walker, Sippie Wallace, and Albert Ammons. Whether or not all these styles fall under "Midwest blues" is probably subject to debate, but that hardly matters when all the music is uniformly this good. —*Ken Chang*

Messing With the Blues / Sep. 2000 / Ace ♦♦♦♦
Atlantic did not record a great deal of blues records, focusing even on its outset on more urban music that could be more comfortably classified as R&B (and later rock and soul). It did its share of worthwhile, though not classic, blues from the late '40s to the early '60s, and 25 examples are collected on this CD. Overall, the Atlantic blues sound, as heard here anyway, was usually smoother and more polished than that of more blues-oriented big indie labels like Chess and Modern. Of the famous figures on this anthology, Ray Charles is represented by three early cuts, the standout being "Losing Hand," with its unusual (for blues) minor jazz-tinged melody. T-Bone Walker is heard on a couple of OK 1955 singles; Jack Dupree does slightly jazz piano blues on two songs from a 1958 LP. John Lee Hooker's two characteristically biting, scabrous 1953 tracks were actually waxed for DeLuxe in 1953, though the masters were later bought by Atlantic. Joe Turner's sole cut is his 1954 Top Ten hit "TV Mama," which featured guitar by Elmore James. James also plays guitar on the five sides by his pianist, Little Johnny Jones, who does acceptable journeyman Chicago blues. The other performers who fill out the disc—Tiny Grimes, Frank Culley, Jimmy Earle, Lucky Davis, Chuck Norris (no, *not* the famous actor), Jimmy Griffin, Odelle Turner, and Hal Paige—do passable songs only of note to collectors, though Larry Dale does a nice 1961 cover of the standard "Drinkin' Wine Spo-Dee-O-Dee." [This U.K. import is not available for sale in North America.] —*Richie Unterberger*

MGM Soul Cinema, Vol. 1 / Jan. 8, 2002 / Beyond ♦♦♦
The first of two volumes, *MGM Soul Cinema, Vol. 1* compiles songs exclusively from 1970s Metro-Goldwyn-Mayer films that coincide with a series of soundtracks finally debuting on compact disc. Labeled indecorously as "blaxploitation flicks," these movies were often low-budget action films with thinly veiled messages revolving around violent ghetto themes. Driving the genre was distinctive music that featured top black artists developing proud soulful rhythms, adrenaline-pumping percussion, sexy horn work, and inspired, self-affirming lyrics. Highlights of *Vol. 1* include Isaac Hayes' hot buttered vocals on the emotional "Give It to Me," Lyn Collins' funk attitude during "Mama Feel Good," and James Brown's calculated down-low groove for "The Boss." Disappointing, however, is the lack thereafter of choice cuts on a disc less than 38 minutes long, and mediocre album artwork including back cover text that's laborious to read. Although this material is somewhat diluted over two albums, curious listeners may enjoy either volume, but those passionate about the genre should explore the individually released soundtracks. —*Craig Curtice*

MGM Soul Cinema, Vol. 2 / Jan. 8, 2002 / Beyond ♦♦♦♦
One of the finest elements of the blaxploitation genre was its music, which allowed gifted African-American performers like Curtis Mayfield and Isaac Hayes to underscore the action with music that was both funky and socially aware. Several interesting cuts from this era are captured on *MGM Soul Cinema, Vol. 2*, a compilation that collects a series of cuts from Beyond's blaxploitation soundtrack reissue series. Fans of this genre will be familiar with cuts like "Across 110th Street" and "Down and Out in New York City," both of which are staples of blaxploitation music compilations, but *MGM Soul Cinema, Vol. 2* remains of interest to genre connoisseurs because it unearths plenty of rarities. For instance, "Friday Foster" is a gently funky title song from a Pam Grier vehicle driven by lovely female harmony vocals and analog synthesizers. Another rare gem is "Black Enough," a quietly moving song about racial unity with stirring vocals from Melba Moore. *MGM Soul Cinema, Vol. 2* also uncovers some lesser-known delights from familiar performers: Isaac Hayes' "Main Title From Truck Turner" is a relentlessly grooving theme song that feels like a sequel to "Theme From Shaft," and James Brown's "People Get Up and Drive Your Funky Soul" is a hard-grooving delight worthy of his best early-'70s funk epics. In the end, *MGM Soul Cinema, Vol. 2* isn't as definitive a collection as *Pimps, Players, and Private Eyes*, but it is well worth a spin for the blaxploitation soundtrack aficionado. —*Donald A. Guarisco*

Modern New Orleans Masters / 1998 / Rounder ♦♦♦
This is an excellent budget compilation from Rounder, featuring modern New Orleans blues, soul, jazz, and funk. Even though some of the artists represented here have recorded for other labels over the years, Rounder has consistently championed excellent sessions from these key players in the Crescent City. Irma Thomas, the Dirty Dozen Brass Band, Johnny Adams, and Walter "Wolfman" Washington are all represented. An unreleased soulful outtake of "Amen" from James Booker's *Classified* sessions is the bonus ingredient in this enjoyable musical stew. —*Al Campbell*

The Modern Records Story / May 29, 2001 / Ace ♦♦♦♦
The Modern label was one of the top R&B indies of the late '40s and '50s, continuing to release some soul, blues, and rock of note throughout the '60s as well. This 28-song anthology serves as a sampler and Ace promo of sorts, since the Ace label reissues many Modern products. On its own terms, though, it's a good collection of 1947-1967 R&B-based music. Jump blues, raw blues, early rock, doo wop, and early soul are all heard over the course of the disc, with enough commonality in approach to make it a well-flowing listen. About half of these tunes were big R&B hits, sometimes crossing over to the pop charts as well, including classics like Lowell Fulson's "Tramp," Ike & Tina Turner's "I Can't Believe What You Say," the Cadets' "Stranded in the Jungle," Jesse Belvin's "Goodnight My Love," Marvin & Johnny's "Cherry Pie" (covered for a hit by Skip & Flip years later), John Lee Hooker's "In the Mood," and the Teen Queens' "Eddie My Love." The non-charters are important, too, however, as heard in entries such as Elmore James' "Dust My Blues," Young Jessie's "Mary Lou" (later covered by white rockers like Ronnie Hawkins), B.B. King's "Three O'Clock Blues," and Joe Houston's classic, rocking sax instrumental "All Night Long." It's a better compilation than most that focus on R&B of this era, due both to the high level of the material and the pretty varied approaches within the R&B umbrella. —*Richie Unterberger*

Modern Vocal Groups, Vol. 1 / Feb. 12, 1999 / Ace ♦♦♦♦♦
These two dozen smooth modern harmony tracks incorporate '50s R&B sounds and arrangements suitable for cocktail jazz lovers. Many tracks feature intrusive, boisterous sax and piano solos; particularly interesting are the tracks by the Five Hearts, each accented by an overeager pianist. Arthur Lee Maye & the Crowns' tracks are classy affairs, and the Original Jubalaires' takes are awesome. Some choice cuts include "Let Me Be Your Man," "Fine One," and "Please Please Baby" by Five Hearts; "Set Me Free" by Arthur Lee May & the Crowns; "Tell Me You Love Me" by the Flairs; and "Love Only You" by the Meadowlarks. —*Andrew Hamilton*

The Mood Mosaic, Vol. 2: Barnie's Groove / 1997 / Stone ♦♦♦♦
After an interesting but inconsistent first volume, the *Mood Mosaic* lounge compilation

series made a noticeable improvement on its second installment. *Mood Mosaic, Vol. 2: Barnie's Grooves* succeeds because it delivers a solid mix of soundtrack and easy listening cuts (plus the occasional soul track) that blend together nicely because they all have strong funk and jazz elements. Several of the tracks are studio-band covers of popular film and television themes: Henry Mancini takes the already-potent *The Streets of San Francisco* theme and transforms into a relentlessly grooving monster that switches back and forth between horn-driven funk and keyboard jazz without missing a beat, and Bobby Forrester does an interesting jazz version of the theme from *Sanford & Son* that uses the original theme's melody as a springboard for some tasty keyboard improvisations. There are also several strong original soundtrack cuts: Sammy Davis Jr.'s classic "Baretta's Theme" finds that usually elegant crooner getting down over a surprisingly funky track driven by horns and a disco-ish bassline, while Alexandro Jodorowsky's "The Desert Is a Circle" is an epic, multi-part instrumental that covers everything from easy listening to jazz-funk as it restates its central, Ennio Morricone-styled theme in a variety of ways. *Mood Mosaic, Vol. 2: Barnie's Grooves* also features the occasional straightforward soul cut; the best of these is Jimmy Smith's "Root Down," a classic jazz instrumental whose throbbing bassline and scratching rhythm guitar riffs were later sampled by the Beastie Boys. This diverse batch of tracks hangs together nicely thanks to their similar reliance on jazz and funk mannerisms, making the disc a fun and consistently engaging listen from start to finish. As a result, *Mood Mosaic, Vol. 2: Barnie's Grooves* is one of the best volumes in this series and a treat for lounge fans who like their lounge music funky. *—Donald A. Guarisco*

The Mood Mosaic, Vol. 5: Supervixens—A '70s Modal Collection / 1997 / Stone ✦✦
After putting out four volumes of lounge-oriented music, the compilers of the *Mood Mosaic* compilation series did an abrupt about-face on their fifth installment. *Mood Mosaic, Vol. 5: Supervixens—A '70s Modal Collection* is radically different from its predecessors because it abandons lounge entirely to concentrate on disco. However, this doesn't mean it features tracks like "Heart of Glass" and "Y.M.C.A."; instead, *Mood Mosaic, Vol. 5: Supervixens—A '70s Modal Collection* focuses on a series of obscure, lengthy tracks that will probably be known only to veteran clubgoers. Sadly, obscure doesn't always mean lost gem and this is the case with the often-inconsistent track listing of this compilation. The first half of the album is loaded down with run-of-the-mill disco tracks: Marta Acuna's "Dance Dance Dance" suffers from a repetitive melody and a weak, wobbly-sounding lead vocal, while Hiroshima's "Lion Dance" is a snoozy bit of jazz-disco that relies too much on the novelty overdubbing koto solos over a throbbing dance beat. Despite these frequent dull spots, patient listeners will be rewarded with a few solid disco gems if they can make it to the second half: Black Devil's "Follow Me" combines rhythmic programmed synthesizer and live drums in a way reminiscent of Giorgio Moroder, and Sylvia's "The Lollipop Man" is a sexily voiced and charmingly over-the-top tribute to television detective *Kojak*. Unfortunately, choice moments like these pop up too infrequently on this compilation and are surrounded by too much dancefloor filler. As a result, *Mood Mosaic, Vol. 5: Supervixens—A '70s Modal Collection* can only be recommended to disco completists and will probably leave the lounge fans who bought the series' other volumes cold. *—Donald A. Guarisco*

The Mood Mosaic, Vol. 9: The Sound Bullett / 2000 / Partners In Crime ✦✦✦
After covering a variety of lounge styles over eight previous volumes, the *Mood Mosaic* compilation series returned to the "cop show music" style explored on *Mood Mosaic, Vol. 2: Barnie's Grooves*. As a result, *Mood Mosaic, Vol. 9: The Sound Bullett* dishes out a strong series of tracks with a strong emphasis on soulful grooves and frenetic jazz rhythms. Of course, plenty of film and television themes are present: "Ironside" by Quincy Jones mixes the composer's trademark orchestral jazz with some whooping synthesizer sounds and Rudy Ray Moore & Soul Rebellion Orchestra's "Mayor's Get Away" is a gritty slice of ghetto funk driven by cymbal-heavy drum work and percolating clavinet riffs. There are also some covers of film themes by easy listening groups: the London Royal Orchestra turns in an instrumental rendition of "The Man With the Golden Gun" that bolsters its jazzy, brass-heavy attack with some snarling fuzz guitar and John Schroeder turns in a particularly fierce rendition of "Blowin' Your Mind" (originally from *Shaft's Big Score*) that mixes orchestral funk with explosive brass arrangements and tight wah-wah guitar riffs. There are also some soul tunes that aren't soundtrack cuts but fit in just fine thanks to their funky style: "Broasted or Fried" by Saint Vincent Latinaires is a gritty instrumental that layers swinging horns over a huge, echoed percussive backdrop and General Crook's "What Time It Is" is a snarling funk rock track with social commentary lyrics in the vein of the Temptations' message-oriented hits. Despite this array of solid tracks, *Mood Mosaic, Vol. 9: The Sound Bullett* is undone by one huge flaw: poor sound quality. The majority of the tracks feature audible snaps and crackles that make it obvious much of this material was transferred directly from beat-up vinyl. This often makes it tough to enjoy the music and sonic purists may want to think twice before picking this album as a result. However, *Mood Mosaic, Vol. 9: The Sound Bullett* remains a solid collection of funky and jazzy mood music for those who can brave its indifferent sound quality. *—Donald A. Guarisco*

More New Orleans Party Classics / Jan. 19, 1999 / Rhino ✦✦✦
More New Orleans Party Classics collects rousing, soulful oldies from artists like Robert Parker, Reggie Hall, the Party Boys, and Frankie Ford. Parker's "Barefootin'," Huey "Piano" Smith's "Rocking Pneumonia and the Boogie Woogie Flu," Chris Kenner's "Land of 1000 Dances," and Fats Domino's "When the Saints Go Marching In" are some of the danceable highlights from this fun compilation. *—Heather Phares*

Most Beautiful Soul Album on Earth / Nov. 17, 1997 / Telstar TV ✦✦✦✦
A grandiose 40-song collection, Alex Records boasts that this is the most beautiful soul album on earth. That may be debatable, but quibbling with the selections is a losing argument, as this set is overflowing with great soul tunes. These ballads come from all angles of soul, including Smokey Robinson, the Isley Brothers, Rose Royce, Al Green, Champaign, Luther Vandross, Mary J. Blige, the Three Degrees, and many others. It's perfect for the shuffle play mode on CD players, and for music lovers who like songs the way they remember them from the radio (no song rolls over five minutes, not even Marvin Gaye's "Sexual Healing"). *—Andrew Hamilton*

Motor City Memories, Vol. 1 / 1991 / Motor City ✦✦✦✦
Obscure recordings of mostly Detroit artists on some of the city's many labels, including early Motown sides by the Satintones, their first male vocal group. Also on board are the Distants, the Voice Masters (with Ty Hunter and Lamont Dozier as lead singers), and a hard-to-find Nolan Strong & the Diablos tune, "Someday You'll Want Me." Some of these sides should have done much better, particularly the "Charlie Brown"-sounding "Got to Get to School on Time," by the Five Quails. It's a collector's dream. *—Andrew Hamilton*

Motor City Memories, Vol. 2 / 1991 / Motor City ✦✦✦✦
Vol. 2 of *Motor City Memories* has more to offer than *Vol. 1*. Some interesting stuff—the Falcons, with Joe Stubbs singing lead, do a rousing "Just For Your Love." Ty Hunter & the Voice Masters shine on "Lonely Baby," which was later licensed to Chess Records for national distribution. Members of the Downbeats later became the Elgins ("Heaven Must Have Sent You") on Motown's VIP label; they're represented here with the Berry Gordy Jr.-penned "My Baby's Back." "Been Such a Long Time," by the Five Quails (Cleveland natives), is a gorgeous ballad, beautifully led by a Bobby Lester- (Moonglows) sounding tenor; it was originally released on Harvey Fuqua's Harvey label. The most interesting sound here is an early David Ruffin side, "I'm In Love"; the song is so gospel-laden you'd think he cut it in church. *—Andrew Hamilton*

Motor City Memories, Vol. 3 / 1991 / Motor City ✦✦✦
The tracks on *Vol. 3* of *Motor City Memories* are even more obscure than ones on the previous two. Here you meet early Detroit groups like the Royal Jokers, Five Emeralds, the Fresandos, the Flints, the Five Scalders, and others. Ty Hunter, leading the Voice Masters, puts his quivering falsetto to good use on "Everytime," which still sounds good. Ty later sang solo for Chess, and with the Glass House, before replacing C.P. Spencer in the Originals. Some of the songs are downright corny, like "Going to the Hop" by the Satintones; one listen and it's easy to see why it failed to chart. For serious collectors only. *—Andrew Hamilton*

Motorcity Blue-Eyed Soul / 1990 / Motor City ✦✦
British Motown fanatic Ian Levine recorded nearly 900 tracks by former Motown artists in the late '80s. While it's a joy to hear the old voices again, many of the productions are uninspiring; you have to wade though lots of mediocrity to arrive at the few nuggets Levine and his crew produced. This particular 16-song collection is one of the few Motor City compilations worthy of recommendation because with the exception of Rare Earth (and its lead singer, Pete Hoorelbeke), they didn't record much and this gives you the opportunity to hear some artists best known from reading Motown discographies. The Lewis Sisters, touted as the Singing School Teachers, perform three tunes: "Just Walk in My Shoes," "Baby, Baby," and "Dance With Danger." And Kay Lewis' daughter, Leeza Miller (Little Lisa at Motown), does "Tomorrow May Never Come" and "Sign of a Heartache." Mike & the Modifiers, led by Mike Valvano, perform two as does the obscure PJ; Mickey Denton does one, and the Valadiers, led by Stuart Avig, impress on two sizzlers. Hoorelbeke sings solo, and with Rare Earth on two cuts, including a rock-ish remake of the Supremes' "Love Is Here and Now You're Gone." *—Andrew Hamilton*

The Motortown Revue Live / 1970 / Motown ✦✦✦
This last released live *Motortown Revue* recording should have been inspiration for continuation, but sadly no more followed this one; these performances were recorded at the Fox Theater in Detroit at an annual Christmas show. Little-known Blinky Williams is featured on two numbers, her should-have-been-a-hit single release "I Wouldn't Change the Man He Is," written by Ashford & Simpson, and a rousing rendition of Otis Redding's "I Can't Turn You Loose." Bobby Taylor does three numbers, Johnnie Taylor's "Who's Making Love" and two numbers he recorded with the Vancouvers, "Does Your Mama Know About Me" and the charming, lilting "Malinda." The most powerful performance is delivered by the Temptations, who are introduced as special guests; they turned the Fox Theater out with a rousing version of "Cloud Nine." Gladys Knight & the Pips and Stevie Wonder serenaded the crowd with three songs each, surprisingly coming off rather lackluster. *—Andrew Hamilton*

The Motortown Revue Live at the Apollo / 1963 / Motown ✦✦✦
MC Bill Murray introduces the Contours and the show begins with these dancing fools doing their first Motown record, "Whole Lotta Woman." The Supremes follow with Florence Ballard leading a rousing "Let Me Go the Right Way," which features high-energy support from Diana Ross and Mary Wilson, especially on the fade, where Ballard snaps off lyrics over their shrieking and chirping. Ballard sounds so much like Diana Ross you wonder if she's actually singing lead, as she did on the studio recording. Marvin Gaye's two-song set begins with "What Kind of Fool Am I," one of those standards he loved doing. While he sings beautifully, it's not what the audience expected. He fulfills their needs, however, by throwing down on "Stubborn Kind of Fellow." The Marvelettes—who were more popular than the Supremes at the time—carry on with a medley of "Strange I Know" and "Someday, Someway," charming everybody in attendance. Little Stevie Wonder does major damage with a spirited rendition of Ray Charles' "Don't You Know," sounding older than his young teen years. Unassuming, likable Mary Wells performs two of her hits, "Two Lovers" and the harder-edged "Bye Bye Baby," with the audience singing along with her. The Miracles finish with an ultra soulful "You Really Got a Hold on Me," seguing into Sam Cooke's "Bring It on Home to Me" before closing the show with their great call-and-response song, "Way Over There." *—Andrew Hamilton*

The Motortown Revue Live, Vol. 2 / 1964 / Motown ♦♦♦

Berry Gordy's second live *Motortown Revue* recording is more pleasing than the first. The Temptations and some vintage Martha & the Vandellas help matters tremendously. Opening the show, the Temptations perform two of their early regional hits, "Dream Come True" and "I Want a Love I Can See." David Ruffin hadn't joined yet, so Paul Williams and Eddie Kendricks handled the lead vocals, and Williams' earthy, gritty baritone was a crowd-pleaser. Martha and her girls did three well-received numbers, Curtis Mayfield's "It's All Right" and their rousers "Quicksand" and "Heatwave"; the Vandellas, Annette Beard and Rosalind Ashford, worked well together, with Martha's Southern twang whipping the crowd into a frenzy. Young but talented Little Stevie Wonder's harmonica shines on "I'll Call It Pretty Music" and "Moon River." Mary Wells comes off sweet and innocent warbling "What's Easy for Two" and more like Dear Abby on the uptempo "You Lost the Sweetest Boy." Both Marvin Gaye and Kim Weston appear to be trying to distance themselves, arrangement-wise, from the other acts. Weston's two ballads are pleasant but don't flow with the show; she refused to sing uptempo numbers at this point in her career. The Marvelettes ran through a medley as if they had a bus to catch. The Miracles only had one number to display their wares—a subdued, jazz-flavored "Mickey's Monkey." —*Andrew Hamilton*

Motown Chartbusters, Vol. 4 / Sep. 4, 2001 / Polygram International ♦♦♦

Much like the several albums in the series, *Motown Chartbusters, Vol. 4* features a number of the chart-topping soul label's biggest hits. There's a fair amount of diversity in this collection when it comes to performers. No one performer steals the show, which makes for a much more eclectic mix of music. Some of the featured acts include the Jackson 5, Marvin Gaye, Stevie Wonder, the Supremes, the Temptations, and a few others. There isn't an overabundance of favorites here. Though all of these songs were hits in their day, only a few were some of Motown's bigger successes. You really can't go wrong with any of the volumes in this series, even if some are a little more thin than others—they're all filled to the brim with great songs. —*Jason Birchmeier*

Motown Chartbusters, Vol. 7 / Sep. 4, 2001 / Polygram International ♦♦♦

Motown Chartbusters, Vol. 7 follows the precedent set by preceding volumes in the series. Of course, Motown had no shortage of chart-toppers, and many are featured here, but by the seventh volume, the hits have become fairly minor. Still, even if these hits were all small hits for the featured performers, the big names here more than compensate: the Supremes, Gladys Knight and the Pips, Michael Jackson, the Temptations, the Four Tops, Stevie Wonder, Diana Ross, Martha Reeves and the Vandellas, Mary Wells, and more. It's also nice to see the album stacked full of songs—16 in total. You're better off beginning with the earlier volumes in this series of compilations first, but if you've heard those and want more, *Vol. 7* should satisfy you. It's loaded with great music. —*Jason Birchmeier*

Motown Special, Vol. 1 / 1962 / Motown ♦♦♦

From the beginning, Berry Gordy Jr. was light years ahead of others in the record business in the area of marketing. Gordy always piggybacked lesser-known artists with his hitmakers in an effort to increase their popularity. This LP and the preceding *Tamla Special, Vol. 1* were precursors to the popular *A Collection of 16 Big Hits* series, though their scopes are different. The Tamla/Motown *Special* albums contained only five artists and ten songs. Each artist is represented by the A- and B-sides of a past recording: Mary Wells' "The One Who Really Loves You," Eddie Holland's "Jamie," the Miracles' "What's So Good About Goodbye," the Marvelettes' "Twistin' Postman," and the blue-eyed soul sounds of the Valadiers' "Greetings This Is Uncle Sam." These A-sides are familiar to all. Of the flips, the Miracles' "I've Been Good to You" is a bawling, bluesy ballad that stands above the rest; Smokey Robinson sings it in a lower register than normal and you can definitely feel his pain. The Marvelettes' flip "I Want a Guy" was later redone by the Supremes for their first Motown recording; neither version merits much attention. The Valadiers display deep-seated doo wop roots on "Take a Chance on Me." The hard-to-find sides by the Valadiers and Eddie Holland make this a worthy collection for the Motown fanatic. —*Andrew Hamilton*

Motown Year By Year: The Sound of Young America, 1968 / Jun. 13, 1995 / Motown ♦♦♦♦

The symbiotic relationship between the Motown Sound and the young American culture it claimed to represent was never deeper than in the landmark year of 1968, a year which saw the sweeping changes throughout the country reflected in microcosm by the sweeping changes which hit Berry Gordy's recording empire. Most crucial was the defection of the Holland-Dozier-Holland production trio; in their absence the Motown Sound turned earthy and gritty under the supervision of producer Norman Whitfield, with real-world concerns the subject of sophisticated new hits like the Temptations' "Cloud Nine" (their first record to feature David Ruffin's replacement Dennis Edwards) and the Supremes' "Love Child." Whitfield also helmed 1968's Marvin Gaye chart-topper "I Heard It Through the Grapevine," arguably the label's absolute creative peak and the obvious highlight of this 16-track collection, which also includes hits from Stevie Wonder ("For Once in My Life") and Gladys Knight ("The End of Our Road"). —*Jason Ankeny*

Motown Year By Year: The Sound of Young America, 1970 / Aug. 22, 1995 / Motown ♦♦♦♦

Not only one of the greatest years in Motown history, 1970 was also one of the most pivotal—the turn of the decade brought with it not only new stars (the Jackson 5 and "ABC"), it also heralded new solo careers (Diana Ross and "Ain't No Mountain High Enough") and the continued evolution of some of the label's headlining attractions (Stevie Wonder and "Signed, Sealed, Delivered I'm Yours," the Temptations and "Ball of Confusion"). Like its predecessors, this entry into Motown's ongoing *Year By Year* does an effective job of placing the label's 1970 output in its proper historical perspective, highlighting not only the aforementioned smashes but also favorites like the Spinners' "It's a Shame" and Edwin Starr's "War," lesser-known gems such as Marvin Gaye's "How Can I Forget," and even rarities like Kiki Dee's "The Day Will Come Between Sunday and Monday." —*Jason Ankeny*

Motown Year By Year: The Sound of Young America, 1973 / Jun. 13, 1995 / Motown ♦♦♦

While 1973 unquestionably belonged to Stevie Wonder—who in the space of those 12 months delivered not only one of the era's all-time great love songs ("You Are the Sunshine of My Life") but also one of its most potent social commentaries ("Living for the City")—the remainder of the Motown stable acquitted itself admirably that year as well, as this 16-track collection amply proves. In addition to Wonder—both of whose hits are included here—there was Marvin Gaye, who with "Let's Get It On" delivered one of the most seductive come-ons ever committed to vinyl, as well as the Temptations, who distilled their 14-minute epic "Masterpiece" into a superb single clocking in well under five minutes, and even former group member Eddie Kendricks, who topped the charts with "Keep on Truckin'." Of most interest to collectors, however, will be the inclusion of ex-Temptation Paul Williams' previously unreleased "Feel Like Givin' Up," a title which proved all too prophetic when the singer committed suicide just weeks later. —*Jason Ankeny*

Motown Year By Year: The Sound of Young America, 1982 / Aug. 22, 1995 / Motown ♦♦

The year, 1982 was far from one of the truly banner years in Motown history, with legends like Stevie Wonder and Smokey Robinson past their creative primes and with new roster additions like Bobby Nunn, Betty Lavette and Jean Carn failing to pick up the slack. This 16-track entry into the label's *Year By Year* series sifts through the rubble to assemble the year's highlights, and the results are shockingly paltry—the novelty value of José Feliciano's "I Second That Emotion" aside, the only really distinctive single here is the Dazz Band's club smash "Let It Whip"; the remaining cuts are unmemorable, some of them best left forgotten altogether. —*Jason Ankeny*

Motown Year By Year: The Sound of Young America, 1985 / Jun. 13, 1995 / Motown ♦♦♦

While conventional wisdom holds that the Motown hit machine had essentially run out of gas by the middle of the '80s, this 16-track collection reveals that at least in 1985 the label was still capable of delivering its share of memorable records. Granted, "Part-Time Lover" is far from the best single Stevie Wonder ever cut, and the Mary Jane Girls' "In My House" is unlikely to erase the memory of classic girl groups like the Supremes or Martha & the Vandellas, but taken on their own terms, these are songs which deserve to bear the proud Motown imprint, in particular the Commodores' "Nightshift," an affecting tribute to the memories of Marvin Gaye and Jackie Wilson. (The "I had a dream, I had an awesome dream" passage from Lionel Richie's "Say You, Say Me" is still one of the most ridiculous lyrics ever written, however.) —*Jason Ankeny*

Music City Soul / May 19, 1998 / Kent ♦♦♦

This is Nashville soul from the mid-'60s through the early '70s, all released on labels partly or wholly owned by Ted Jarrett: Ref-O-Ree, Spar, and Poncello. It's not often acknowledged that Nashville, known almost exclusively for its country music, also had an active black music scene, which makes this 26-track compilation archivally important. The fact still remains, though, that Nashville, and certainly these labels, did not develop an outstanding or distinctive soul style. It's easy to play spot-the-influences here, whether it's the gritty Motown of the Temptations, the smooth soul of the Northeast or the midtempo gospel-flecked blues-soul of Stax. In fact, Jimmy Tig's "Foolish Lover" sounds like an attempt at a mathematical fusion of "Love Is Strange" and "Stay," while Herbert Hunter's "Isn't It Wonderful to Dream" is unabashedly derivative of classic Ben E. King sides, and Thomas Henry's "Is It Love" rips a page from Major Lance's book. You're not going to recognize any of the performers, with the possible exception of the well-traveled Gene Allison, whose bluesy "It's Almost Sundown" (with a vocal delivery reminiscent of Sam Cooke) is one of the best cuts. There are some nice oddities here and there, like the Jades' moving, moody ballad "My Loss, Your Gain," and Wendell Watts' super-lush "You Girl," with its bouncy strings, rhumba-ish beat, and lounge-lizard vocals. —*Richie Unterberger*

● **MVP Vintage Rhythms, Vol. 1** / Aug. 6, 1996 / MVP ♦♦♦♦

A dozen deadly R&B classics some together on this compilation, including good grooves such as Fontella Bass' "Rescue Me", Edwin Starr's "Twenty-Five Miles" and Shorty Long's "Function at the Junction." But there's more: King Curtis' pulsating "Memphis Soul Stew," the Isley Brothers' classic booty shaker "It's Your Thing," and Wilson Pickett's throbbing, chugging "Engine, Engine Number 9," a hypnotic Kenny Gamble & Leon Huff collaboration sounding as relentless as hungry lions. The Supremes' "Love Is Like an Itching in My Heart" must have had Motown's Studio A on fire. If this CD doesn't cure wallflower-itis, nothing will; even if you can't dance, you'll want to move when these grenades, with pins already pulled, explode from your speakers. —*Andrew Hamilton*

Natural High: 2-Step Soul, Boogie Fusion & Rare Groove / 2001 / Warner Music UK ♦♦♦♦

Sometimes lost in the wake of the disco tidal wave, it is easy to forget that people were still making soul records. *Natural High* combs the vaults of Atlantic, Elektra, and Warner Bros. and lays down 16 examples of smooth soul between the years 1975 and 1982. The sound is influenced by disco but also by funky jazz and the silky R&B flowing out of Philly. Some of the artists collected here were huge in the '60s: Ben E. King and Dionne Warwicke (yes, that is spelled correctly; her numerologist told her she needed to add the extra "e" at the end of her name). Some of the artists made great music in the '60s and early '70s, but weren't as well known: Terry Callier, Leroy Hutson, the Undisputed Truth. Even jazz great Donald Byrd shows up. Highlights of the disc include Leon Ware's funky ode to the Golden State, "That's Why I Came to California," featuring Janis Siegel of Manhattan Transfer; Faze-O (who were an alter-ego of the Ohio Players) and their blissed-out ballad "Riding High"; Patrice Rushen's sensual ballad "Remind Me"; and Eugene Record's "Overdose of Joy," which bubbles and pops like a classic Chi-Lites track (many of which Record wrote). From beginning to end, *Natural High* delivers nothing but high-quality smooth soul. If you think soul music just rolled over and died in the face of disco, you need to check this disc out. Though the sound had changed, soul was still alive. If you really don't care about the academic debate, this is still a great disc, perfect for late nights and mellow mornings. *—Tim Sendra*

☆ **Naughty Rock & Roll** / May 11, 1999 / Sugar Tit ✦✦✦✦✦
The 25 tracks compiled on this single-disc compilation have been issued under a plethora of titles since the '80s—most notably in the digital domain as *Raunchy Rock & Roll* (1995). Many of these dirty ditties have become legendary in frat houses and barrooms across the world, despite their initial obscurity due to excruciatingly poor under-the-counter circulation. A more sociological vantage point reveals a broad scope of musical styles, ranging from doo wop ("Don't Fuck Around With Love") to redneck country & western twang ("Pussy Cat Song"). However, there are a few pop music genres that seem to artistically lend themselves to the unadulterated and overtly sexual intonations—some intentional, others quite serendipitous. Among the most authentic are the '50s R&B and doo wop styles which inform tracks such as "Derby Town" and "The Rotten Cock Suckers Ball"—both of which became infamous platters for the Clovers. The latter title was revived by Frank Zappa as "Cock-Suckers' Ball" and issued on his live *Does Humor Belong in Music?* multimedia project from the mid-'80s. Likewise, there are '50s sock-hop ballads such as "It's So Hard to Say I Love You" and "Sit on My Face," and even rockabilly ("Yo Yo"). There are also garage rockers ("Baby, Let Me Bang Your Box") and a funky (literally!), randy reggae reading of Rare Earth's hit "Get Ready," which is subtitled "French Style." More modern rock & roll contributions include "Fuck Off" by, appropriately enough, the Dildos, as well as David Trout's double entendre-laden "Fast Food Song." Other notable inclusions are Screamin' Jay Hawkins' R&B hoodoo "Bite It" and "Constipation Blues," as well as the incendiary coupling of Jackie Wilson and LaVern Baker on a wild take of "Think Twice," which was decidedly toned down for the legit 45 rpm (b/w "Please Don't Hurt Me") for Brunswick in 1965. Also in the mix are a few sides—such as "Did He Eat Your Titty" and "Stickball"—that defy category. *For Adults Only* is a refreshingly self-indulgent artifact that reflects the decidedly more carnal and base aspects of popular music. Potential enthusiasts should be aware of the sound quality, which vacillates from track to track. While not unlistenable, there is copious surface noise to deal with on a majority of the recordings. *—Lindsay Planer*

Never Before Released Masters: From Motown's Brightest Stars / 1986 / Motown ✦✦✦
Motown's vaults have been known to harbor unheard goodies, and a few appear on this collection. One track, "Mind Over Matter," was released under the name the Pirates (who were actually the Temptations) on Berry Gordy's Melody label; it was a cover of a Nolan Strong & the Diablos' tune and featured Eddie Kendricks bragging about his brain power above a jangling rhythm. The Supremes' "Stay in My Lonely Arms" had been done by the Four Tops and the Elgins, and the Supremes' version treads no new ground. "Tears," a mesmerizing ballad, illustrates the Supremes' soulful sound before it became homogenized by Holland-Dozier-Holland. "Knock on My Door" by the Marvelettes is so ordinary that it's no mystery why it was never released. Smokey Robinson & the Miracles' "Stuck on You" stands as one of Robinson's cleverest songs; it's a beat ballad, the kind the Miracles excelled on. There are 12 songs featured here, including unheard cuts by Junior Walker & the All Stars, the Four Tops, Mary Wells, Stevie Wonder and Martha Reeves & the Vandellas. *—Andrew Hamilton*

New Breed R&B / Aug. 14, 2001 / Kent ✦✦✦
To ask the question that might be asked by soul fans sitting at the table for a Passover dinner: Why is this soul compilation different from all other soul compilations? Particularly when it's comprised of Kent/Modern '60s singles on a reissue label that has issued dozens of obscure '60s soul anthologies and already heavily raided the Kent/Modern vaults? Well, as the subtitle—"soulful '60s blues for today's dancers"—indicates, it draws more heavily from blues and roots R&B than much soul does, although it's definitely much more a soul disc than a blues or R&B one. Frankly it's a little more interesting than other rare '60s soul comps, not just because of the blues/R&B factor, but also because the material is often a little moodier and less predictable than much soul played at England's Northern soul clubs. It's a mixture of pretty seldom-traveled cuts by stars (B.B. King, Lowell Fulson, Ike & Tina Turner, and Bobby "Blue" Bland), fairly well-known singers (Z.Z. Hill, Big Mama Thornton, and Jimmy McCracklin), and no-names, at least to those who don't hang out at Northern soul venues. There are a good number of above-average items here, like Little Joe Hinton's unusually passionate early blues/R&B/soul hybrid "Tired of Walkin'"; Jackie Shane's sultry "Stand Up Straight and Tall" (cool organ groove here); the Newports' minor-key "Dixie Women"; Frank Armstrong's percolating soul-funk instrumental "Stuffed Peppers (Aka Humpin')"; Jimmy McCracklin's "I Got Eyes for You," which is actually Muddy Waters-derived blues recorded in 1955 and not issued until 1962; and Jimmy Holiday's "The New Breed," an acceptably urgent alteration of "Shake." As for the rest, even the rather generic stuff is listenable, and the rhythmic pace varies all over the map instead of sticking to the cheery midtempo so many soul anthologies do. *—Richie Unterberger*

New Orleans Party Classics / 1992 / Rhino ✦✦✦✦✦
The lazy, rolling piano sounds that open this album are not played by Fats Domino, who never whistled like this. It's Professor Longhair, who blazed trails for Domino and generations of other Crescent City musicians, with his definitive version of "Go to the Mardi Gras." The legendary Professor returns later with "Big Chief" and Fats checks in with an affable "Jambalaya." Pianists, especially those with a strong left hand, dominate many songs as this generous 18-track CD reissue lets us relive Mardi Gras year round. We might expect "Iko Iko" by Dr. John, "Hey Pocky Way" by the Neville Brothers, "Don't You Just Know It" by Huey "Piano" Smith and the Clowns and even "Sea Cruise" by Frankie Ford. But a reggae-influenced gem like "Meet de Boys on the Battlefront" by a self-described band of N'awlins "Indians" helped by the Nevilles and calling themselves the Wild Tchoupitoulas is a delightful surprise. The Dirty Dozen Brass Band and the Rebirth Brass Band cover the Dixieland segment of the broad New Orleans musical spectrum. A Little Richard tune might have made this disc perfect. *—Mark Allan*

New York Soul Serenade / 1997 / Kent ✦✦✦
Here are 28 rare '60s New York soul cuts, mostly from the vaults of the Scepter and Musicor labels. There are a few recognizable minor soul stars here (Maxine Brown, Chuck Jackson, Big Maybelle, Walter Jackson, Judy Clay, Johnny Maestro), as well as selections by performers on the downhill commercial slide (the Platters and Jive Five). The Scepter and Musicor discs were characterized by grand, melodramatic songs and production, and while these are not lost classics, they do boast some good tunes and arrangements. This is recommended above most of Kent's other soul rarities collections for that reason: there's a good deal of variety and range of emotion, not just the standard uptempo happy music so beloved on Northern soul dancefloors. And if you're looking for curiosities, there are plenty: an obscure Bacharach-David tune from 1962 (Jimmy Radcliffe's "(There Goes) The Forgotten Man"), blue-eyed soul from future country star Ed Bruce, social realism from football star Roosevelt Grier on "In My Tenement," the Dionne Warwick-produced side by the Gentlemen Four, and Big Maybelle's version of the superb ballad "Oh Lord, What Are You Doing to Me," better known as sung by Dionne Warwick. *—Richie Unterberger*

North of Watford: 24 Rare Pop & Soul Classics, Vol. 1 / Mar. 13, 2001 / Goldmine/Soul Supply ✦✦✦
A twist on the usual Northern soul compilation, this one is top heavy with obscure R&B and pop tracks produced in the United Kingdom. The U.K. productions, other than Real Thing's "You to Me Are Everything," never crossed the Atlantic Ocean. Tunes like Jimmy James' "A Man Like Me," the Sharonettes' rendition of "Going to a Go Go," Jimmy Radcliffe's "Long After Tonight Is All Over," and Wayne Gibsons' "Under My Thumb" will be new sounds to most listeners outside of Europe. The collection contains three genuine pop hits: the Chiffons' innocent "Sweet Talking Guy," the Newbeats' high energy "Run Baby Run," and Mel Carter's "Hold Me, Thrill Me, Kiss Me." The few obscure American R&B shots include Roy C's "Shotgun Wedding," "I Get the Sweetest Feeling," by Jackie Wilson, an early Barry White production on Felice Taylor's "I Feel Love Coming On," and Dobie Gray's "Out on the Floor." *—Andrew Hamilton*

The Northern Side of Philly Soul / Aug. 28, 2001 / Jamie/Guyden ✦✦✦
The Northern Side of Philly Soul is a grab-bag of 18 rare 1960s Philly soul tracks cut for the Phil-L.A. of Soul, Jamie, Dionn, Arctic, Frantic, and Guyden labels. Most, though not all, date from the latter half of the decade (and at least a couple are from the early '70s); four were previously unreleased. And like many a compilation with the tag "Northern soul" attached somewhere, it's competent but a little generic, and primarily of interest to collectors who are trying to find almost anything they can in the style. Generally, it favors the upbeat and uptempo face of the early Philly soul sound, with just a few names here and there that can be picked out by those not buried neck-high in rare soul 45s. Artists include Kenny Gamble, with his 1966 single "The Joke's on You," done before he'd become established as a star producer with Leon Huff; Benny Sigler, brother of Bunny Sigler; Dee Irwin; and the Temptones, a blue-eyed soul group that included a young Daryl Hall. Some of the better bets to click include the Volcanos' "A Lady's Man," which recalls the Temptations' harder-rocking sides; some of the members (the liner notes don't say which ones) later became the Trammps. Douglas Banks' "Ain't That Just Like a Woman," a 1963 single that's one of the earliest songs here, strongly recalls the stoic uptown pop-soul of Chuck Jackson. Dee Irwin's "Linda" has the slightly frantic string-laden soul of some of the late-'60s Dells sides; Kenny Gamble's "The Joke's on You" is one of the more downbeat and melodically sophisticated offerings. In all, it's rather slim on the excitement meter but, even at its least memorable, there are heavy streaks of the vibes, strings, and lush harmonies that would be characteristic of Philly soul as it attained greater prominence in a slightly later era. *—Richie Unterberger*

The Best Northern Soul All Nighter . . . Ever! / Jan. 8, 2002 / EMI ✦✦✦
While this collection is more accessible than most Northern soul packages—it features at least three instantly recognizable hits (Edwin Starr's "25 Miles," the Isley Brothers' "This Old Heart of Mine," and Jackie Wilson's "(Your Love Keeps Lifting Me) Higher and Higher") and a few other popular dusties (the Contours' "Just a Little Misunderstanding," "Wade in the Water" by the Ramsey Lewis Trio, "Move on Up" by Curtis Mayfield, the Chiffons' "Sweet Talkin' Guy," and Darrell Banks' "Open the Door to Your Heart.")—it's a tough sell for those not committed to the Northern soul genre. But whatever the label, this is a good gathering of '60s and '70s soul music that's balanced with both crossover and obscure recordings. (What's obscure? Try disc one, track 12—Wynder K. Frog's "Green Door"). *—Andrew Hamilton*

Northern Soul Fever, Vol. 3 / 1993 / Goldmine/Soul Supply ✦✦✦
Here are two bountiful disks of obscure soul from a myriad of artists recorded all over the United States. Disc one contains hard-to-find tracks like the Imperial Wonders' "Just a Dream," Joyce Kennedy's "Misunderstood," Little Ben & the Cheers' "I'm Gonna Get Even With You," and obscure, short-lived Cleveland duo Taurus & Leo's "I Ain't Playing

Baby." Disc two unearths L.J. Reynolds & Chocolate Syrups' "The Penguin Breakdown," A.C. Jones & the Atomic Aces' "Give Me Your Love," the Founders' "Don't Turn Your Back on Me," and the Prophets' "My Kind of Girl." Not a hit record in the bunch, which will please purists. *—Andrew Hamilton*

The Northern Soul of Chicago, Vol. 1 / 2000 / Goldmine/Soul Supply ♦♦♦♦
Blessed with an abundance of recording companies in the '60s, this disc features a healthy dose of soul tracks from Chicago whose quality outstripped their public recognition. Two songs escaped city limits—Otis Leavill's "I Got a Right to Cry" and the Ideals' "Go Gorilla Go"—but most were just local hits. This interesting compilation includes Wade Flemons' "Two of a Kind," the C.O.D.s' "Coming Back Girl," Geraldine Hunt's "Cheaper Than One," and Lee "Shot" Williams' "Love Now Pay Later." A satisfying compilation and a good indicator of the quality of soul music emanating from Chicago at the time. *—Andrew Hamilton*

Northern Soul Spectrum / Apr. 22, 1997 / Kent ♦♦♦♦
Taken from the vaults of EMI Records, *Northern Soul Spectrum* brings together soul styles from the vaults of many of the company's small label holdings, including classics from Roulette, Jubilee, Josie, Port, J2, Satin, Calla, and Rust. With 28 tracks covering the years 1962 to 1968 with a stray track from the '70s (Magic Night's soul-disco "If You and I Had Never Met") that atmospherically fits in, this is no mere R&B hodgepodge compilation, but instead a well-programmed and diverse selection of a wide variety of Northern soul styles. From the pop-flavored offerings of Annabelle Fox's "Lonely Girl" and Frankie & the Classicals' "What Shall I Do" to the minor-key Motown-on-fire romp of Brenda Lee Jones' "You're the Love of My Life" to the classic soul balladry of Scotty Williams on "I've Got to Find Her (and Tell Her)," the sheer emotionalism, musicality, and danceability of the genre is here for the listening. For those who want to investigate further than the hit packages of Motown and Stax/Atlantic material, here's a big chunk to digest in one sitting that's grade-A soul music from the classic era. *—Cub Koda*

Northern Soul's Classiest Rarities / Aug. 28, 2001 / Kent ♦♦♦
Kent might actually be underselling itself by titling this collection *Northern Soul's Classiest Rarities*. That leads listeners to expect yet another anthology of generic midtempo mid-'60s American soul singles that have somehow come to be worshiped as choice rarities in England's Northern soul scene. These couple of dozen tracks are from the '60s (and occasionally from the early '70s), they are rare, and they do go for absurdly high prices among Northern soul collectors. Actually, however, these form a more diverse CD than the usual Northern soul anthology, with a good number of decent, lushly produced ballads and harmonized soul-pop efforts along with the expected dancefloor filler. Some of the songs from the early half of the '60s have pleasing traces of doo wop and girl group sounds, too. Listeners are still not going to know who many of these people are unless they're one of those collectors, with some exceptions: there's a 1962 single by Joe Simon, a rarity by the Delfonics, and items by cult soul vocalists Clifford Curry and Bettye Swann. More surprisingly, there are a couple of blue-eyed soul ringers by Charlie Rich (whose "Don't Tear Me Down" is a fine and convincing cut with unexpected chord changes) and Jimmy Seals, the latter the same dude who was half of Seals & Crofts. The singles were done all over America, and although there's an absence of lost classics, it's pleasurable listening. Sometimes it's more than that, as with Karmello Brooks' "Tell Me, Baby," with its jazzy hue and dense but rocking strings; Clifford Curry's "Ain't No Danger," which holds up well when stacked next to the Temptations' tougher, late-'60s cuts; Pat Powdrill's infectious uptempo "Do It"; and the Joytones' "This Love That I'm Giving You," with its dreamy harmonies and uptown orchestration. *—Richie Unterberger*

Northern Soul: Cream of 60's Soul / 2001 / Pilot ♦♦♦♦♦
For this two-CD, 32-track compilation, the concept is Northern soul: rare, dance-oriented '60s soul that has developed an enduring cult following in England, that is. You'll find some artists here who had hits, though you won't find their big hits on the disc themselves: Eddie Holman, the O'Jays, the Manhattans, Martha Reeves, Bobby Womack, the Olympics, Jackie Lee, the Ad-Libs, David Ruffin, and Edwin Starr. A couple of these actually *were* hits: the Parliaments' "I Wanna Testify," with a young George Clinton, and Bob & Earl's oft-covered "Harlem Shuffle." And some of them, like Timothy Wilson's "Hiding in Your Heart," are luscious ballads, not uptempo tunes. Most of this stuff, though, is pretty rare, or certainly not heard on oldies radio anymore even if they were low-charting R&B hits or got some regional action. There are many Northern soul compilations (almost all of them, unsurprisingly, from the U.K.), and judged by the basis of track selection, this is one of the better ones. The songs have the kind of hooks, energy, disciplined harmonies, and thoughtful production that put them into the league of records that at their best should have been at least small hits, and at their worst would be enjoyable filler on the average '60s soul broadcast. In its disfavor, however, the liner notes do not give original release details on most of the tracks, though they do give reasonable background information on the performers. The sound is okay but has obviously, in at least some instances, been taken from vinyl, and often has a harsh, brittle high end. It still sounds better than the average tape of such stuff would if you got someone to make it from a private collection. And, it would cost you a bunch to buy these in different formats, whether on other CD reissues (if you could even find them on reissues) or the rare original 45s. The best obscurity is the Flirtations' "Settle Down," which is midtempo female-sung harmony soul with an outstanding melody. *—Richie Unterberger*

Northern Soul: Lost & Found, Vol. 1 / 1997 / Goldmine/Soul Supply ♦♦♦
Goldmine presents another 20-track-plus various-artists anthology focusing on obscure classics of the American soul and R&B scene of the 1960s. The first volume in a series of rare finds titled *Northern Soul: Lost & Found* includes future Chairmen of the Board member Danny Woods on "90 Days in the County Jail," Herman Griffin's "Dream Girl," Theola Kilgore's "It's Gonna Be Alright," and Kenny Carlton's theme track, "Lost and Found." *—Andrew Hamilton*

Northern Soul: Lost & Found, Vol. 2 / 1998 / Goldmine/Soul Supply ♦♦♦
Goldmine keeps churning out these 20-track-plus various-artists albums specializing in obscure American R&B and soul music. This one features near-impossible-to-find recordings like Jimmy Norman's "Family Tree," "The Girls With the Big Black Boots" (the Paramounts), Raeletts, Margie Hendrix's "Restless," and Charles Hodges' "I'll Never Go to a Party Again." The only song casual fans will recognize is Mary Wells' "Use Your Head," which seems out of place amongst these rare soul joints. *—Andrew Hamilton*

OKeh: A Northern Soul Obsession, Vol. 1 / 1995 / Kent ♦♦♦♦
A great R&B/Soul label, OKeh Records didn't get the recognition it deserved in the '60s. Under the guidance of production kings like Carl Davis, OKeh released some excellent records, many of which made the charts. This CD contains obscure OKeh tracks, featuring such artists as the Triumphs, the Seven Souls, Johnny Robinson, the Opals, the Carstairs, Jimmy Church, the Little Foxes, and the Autographs. The only real hits are the Artistics' "This Heart of Mine," and Walter Jackson's "It's an Uphill Climb to the Bottom." Billy Butler & the Chanters does "My Heart Is Hurtin'," and the Vibrations' "Gonna Get Along Without You Now," both chart strangers. The Carstairs "He Who Picks a Rose," previously done by both the Temptations and Edwin Starr, is as scorching as the Motown originals. In addition, there's two pre-"Love Won't Let Me Wait" sides from Major Harris, as well as tracks by Little Richard and Tommy Tate. There are 23 interesting tracks, with strong liner notes enhancing the unfamiliar music. *—Andrew Hamilton*

OKeh: A Northern Soul Obsession, Vol. 2 / 1997 / Kent ♦♦♦
Here are second-division Chicago '60s soul from the genre's pre-eminent label, OKeh. No big hits on this 24-track mix of mid-level names (Larry Williams, Johnny Watson, Major Lance, Walter Jackson, Billy Butler, a 1967 single by Little Richard) and unknowns (Tan Geers, Cookie Jackson, Joyce Davis, and several others). Like most compilations of this nature, it's not recommended unless you're deeply into the genre at hand. If you like the Smokey Robinson-meets-Curtis Mayfield nature of much Chicago soul, and want an intelligently annotated collection of some of the style's harder-to-find sides, this disc does a fine job. *—Richie Unterberger*

Old School Harmony / Apr. 20, 1996 / Sequel ♦♦♦♦
An import compilation of obscure releases by American artists, ranging from the mundane to the brilliant. Two tracks by the Escorts, "I'll Be Sweeter Tomorrow," and "Look Over Your Shoulder," are sub-par O'Jays covers, but they redeem themselves on the falsetto-led "Lets Make Love At Home Sometimes." Brilliance comes from Black Ivory and their shimmering "Will We Ever Come Together," possibly the New Yorkers' best single; Leroy Burgess crystal shattering lead will have you worrying about his well-being. Robert Winters & Fall's "Magic Man" is another masterful piece of music (the underrated group does three more), and lest not forget "What Am I Guilty Of," performed by the New Cymbals (formerly Lee Williams & the Cymbals). The 21 songss also include memorable sides from the Continental Four, the Carstairs, Richmond International, Reggie Sadler, Silk, and 9th Creation. *—Andrew Hamilton*

On the Modern Soul Side / 1990 / Goldmine/Soul Supply ♦♦♦♦
These 18 soulful sides from the '70s illustrate how strong local and regional records were at the time. Only two tracks received any national exposure: Prince Phillip Mitchell's boastful "Once I've Been There," and Eddie Holman's escalating "This Will Be a Night to Remember." Pleasant surprises abound, especially Mandrill's melodic soul trip "Too Late," and left-handed guitarist Beloyd's "Get You Into My Life." (Beloyd played with the O'Jays before this single release, and with Earth, Wind & Fire afterwards.) It includes the socio-political "Getting Together," by Brothers Guiding Light, Randolph Brown's "It Ain't Like It Used to Be," and Jesse James's lilting "If You Want a Love Affair." *—Andrew Hamilton*

On the Real Side: New Jersey Soul / Oct. 3, 1995 / Sequel ♦♦♦♦
This is a sweet Sequel import featuring All Platinum Records' male artists. George Kerr's "3 Minutes 2 Hey Girl" and Donne Elbert's "Where Did Our Love Go" charted the highest, followed by Chuck Jackson's "I've Got the Need" and "Needing You, Wanting You." Unsung ditties by the late Philippe Wynne, Larry Saunders' "On the Real Side," and Derek Martin spice up this 16-track collection that's further highlighted by Chuck Jackson's makeover of his classic "Any Day Now." *—Andrew Hamilton*

Original Players of Love / Feb. 24, 1998 / Simitar ♦♦♦♦
A scrumptious compilation of 20 soul-drenched love jams, with contributions by everyone from Barry White to Latimore. Group vocal sounds are mingled with solo performers, along with mellow music from self-contained bands like the Gap Band and the Ohio Players. Most of these tracks are familiar to soul enthusiasts, but it is good to hear Al Wilson's classic "Show and Tell," Leon Haywood's "I Wanta Do Something Freaky to You" and Johnny Bristol's "Hang on in There" again, since they are not as readily available as some of the other selections. *—Andrew Hamilton*

● **Original Salsoul Classics: The 20th Anniversary** / 1992 / Salsoul ♦♦♦♦
This features two smoking uncut disks courtesy of Salsoul Records, the home of Philadelphia disco. Inner Life's update of "Ain't No Mountain High Enough" runs 10:27 and Loleatta Holloway's "Hit And Run," 11 minutes. The all-encompassing 20 tracks include Joe Bataan's salsa makeover of Gil Scott-Heron's "In the Bottle"; over 19 minutes of Double Exposure, "My Love Is Free" and "Ten Percent"; three sultry steppers from First Choice; Instant Funk's "I Got My Mind Made Up"; Love Committee's jubilant "Just as Long as I Got You"; and Eddie Holman's explosive "This Will Be a Night to Remember." An essential collection that will transform disco haters into lovers. *—Andrew Hamilton*

Our Turn to Cry / Jan. 1, 2000 / Atlantic ✦✦✦✦✦
Like its companion volume, *Sanctified Soul*, this scours the Atlantic vaults for obscure soul ballads of the 1960s and early '70s. Although this in no way should be construed as a sampler of the best Atlantic had to offer in that category, for those who have digested all the famous classic soul by Atlantic stars and are ready for more, this is highly recommended. No big stars are found on this 26-track anthology, with the exception of the Isley Brothers, whose exquisite 1964 heartbreaker, "The Last Girl," is hardly something (unfortunately) that you're likely to hear on oldies stations. A few other singers here had mid-level success and fairly strong cult status, such as Baby Washington (who does "Breakfast in Bed," more famous as rendered by Dusty Springfield), Dee Dee Warwick, Dee Dee Sharp, Doris Troy, Bettye Swann, Mighty Sam, Johnny Adams, Lou Johnson, Benny Latimore, and Alvin Robinson. You don't see many of the other names anywhere unless you own singles price guides, but there are some real goodies. It's a long list. The Soul Brothers Six's "What Can You Do When You Ain't Got Nobody?" is churchy, pleading soul at its best. Bobby Marchan sounds a heck of a lot like a woman on "What Can I Do (Pt. 1)" (and he *is* a he, not a she). Mike Williams' "Lonely Soldier" is a moving, if subtle, commentary on the anguish of serving in Vietnam. Benny Latimore's "I'm Just an Ordinary Man," from 1969, is far more satisfying than his more well-known subsequent output. Alvin Robinson does a good approximation of Ray Charles on "Let Me Down Easy." Dee Dee Sharp breaks out of her novelty dance mold with the Dan Penn/Spooner Oldham song "Help Me Find My Groove." Bobby Harris does a cool tribute to the late Sam Cooke with "We Can't Believe You're Gone." Billy Mashburn does a perhaps inadvertently humorously overdone tribute to doo wop on "Don't It Sound Good (Pt. 1)." N.A. Allen does an obscure, soulful Goffin/King composition, "No Easy Way Down." Some of the early-'70s cuts are slicker and less interesting than those of the prior decade, but overall this sits very high on the ladder of obscure soul collections. [This U.K. import is not available for sale in North America.] *—Richie Unterberger*

People Get Up: Original House Party Funk & Get Down Jazz / Aug. 14, 2001 / Harmless ✦✦✦✦
In 1970 R&B and soul was developing into funk, but the synthesizer sounds of P-Funk were still in the future. *People Get Up* is a compilation of songs which all appeared in one single radio show by Jerry McRuth in March 1970. The subtitle is "Original House Party Funk & Get Down Jazz" and the album is filled with almost only uptempo songs and energetic solos. It's wave your hands in the air and dance like a maniac music, with good beats. Maybe it's a bit too intense for using as background music at home, but that is hardly its purpose. But it is not funk. Or rather, the only pure funk song included is James Brown's 12-minute "Make It Funky"; instead, much of the rest is high-energy R&B with a New Orleans feel, meaning blasting horns and organs. The melodies have not yet been swallowed up, and like in James Duncan's "I Got It Made (In the Shade)" the gritty guitars often have heavy reverb. This album can serve as a party record, and will do so with honor. Read the transcription of Jerry McRuth's introduction to the program, included in the booklet, and your mood will rise. So even more when you hear the hilarious "I'm Mister Big Stuff" by Jimmy Hicks, an answer to Jean Knight's similarly named song. If you don't feel like partying, see it as a document of the time when funk was just about to take over. *—Lars Lovén*

The Perfect Beats, Vol. 1 / Sep. 8, 1998 / Tommy Boy ✦✦✦✦
The subtitle of *The Perfect Beats* series, *New York Electro Hip-Hop & Underground Dance Classics 1980-1985*, pretty much sums it up. Gathering 14 songs from the seminal days of club-hopping electronica (not necessarily born in the Big Apple, just raised there), *Vol. 1* focuses on the genre's pioneers (Kraftwerk, Afrika Bambaataa & Soulsonic Force), as well as some early stabs at replicating the robofunk sound via a disco aesthetic: Planet Patrol's "Play at Your Own Risk," Peech Boys' "Don't Make Me Wait," Imagination's "Just an Illusion" and Nick Straker Band's "A Little Bit of Jazz." Subsequent volumes cover similar ground, occasionally veering toward old-school ancestors and the rare chartbuster. All four volumes should be heard; they document a consequential period in dance music that's influenced clubtrotters from Madonna to Goldie. Best cuts: Bambaataa's history shaping "Planet Rock" and Yaz's Europoppy, synth burp, "Don't Go." *—Michael Gallucci*

The Perfect Beats, Vol. 2 / Sep. 8, 1998 / Tommy Boy ✦✦✦✦
Vol. 2 of *The Perfect Beats* lands the four-part series squarely in the middle of its lengthy subtitle, *New York Electro Hip-Hop + Underground Dance Classics 1980-1985*. If *Vol. 1* is the launching point of the collection, and *Vol. 4* is the summing up, the middle chapters represent what the club-based movement was all about. In its post-disco reconstruction, the culture got a boost from the streets (which never really abandoned it in the first place)—electronic powered funk gave birth to hip-hop and the first seeds of the union are prominently displayed here. The series' (and the music's) first significant Top Ten hit is on *Vol. 2* (Shannon's "Let the Music Play") as are a handful of crucial, but semi-obscure, tracks from the era. And cuts by Freeze ("I.O.U."), Loleatta Holloway ("Crash Goes Love"), Man Parrish ("Hip Hop Be-Bop") and New Order ("Confusion") are the basis for many R&B electrobeats to come. *—Michael Gallucci*

The Perfect Beats, Vol. 3 / Sep. 8, 1998 / Tommy Boy ✦✦✦✦
The third volume in Tommy Boy's *Perfect Beats* series balances electro standards that many dance fans have heard (Shannon's "Give Me Tonight," Hashim's "Al Naafiysh," Heaven 17's "Let Go," Aleem's "Release Yourself") with quite a few neglected classics of the early-'80s garage/electro period like "Renegades of Funk" by Afrika Bambaataa, "If This Ain't Love" by Jay Novell, "Din Daa Daa" by George Kranz, and "99 1/2" by Carol Lynn Townes, among others. *—Keith Farley*

The Perfect Beats, Vol. 4 / Sep. 8, 1998 / Tommy Boy ✦✦✦✦
Unlike the previous three volumes in the series, the final chapter of *The Perfect Beats* strays a bit from its subtitle, *New York Electro Hip-Hop + Underground Dance Classics 1980-1985*, by tracing the R&B roots of club culture and offering up some of the genre's ancestral beats (from the likes of Blackbyrds' "Rock Creek Park," Lonnie Liston Smith's "Expansions" and Herman Kelly + Life's "Dance to the Drummer's Beat") for dissection. They add historical perspective to the series, but it's the solid futuristic electrofunk that anchors *Vol. 4*. C-Bank's "One More Shot," Quadrant Six's "Body Mechanic," Jonzun Crew's "Pack Jam" and Cybotron's "Clear" are pillars of the club community. Perfect finale: wrapping up the *The Perfect Beats* with Afrika Bambaataa's "Looking for the Perfect Beat," the mantra and objective of this exceptional series. *—Michael Gallucci*

Philadelphia Roots / 2001 / Soul Jazz ✦✦✦
Soul Jazz's releases tend to be groove-oriented, putting a premium on funky, rhythmic grooves—all the better to sample you with, my dear. Consequently, their loving reissues of obscurities are aimed at third- or fourth-generation listeners mining these recordings for sounds, not people who were there at the time, or collectors looking for great forgotten songs and singles. That's not to discount the material on their recordings, but it's to put them in the proper perspective—this is minutiae, collectors items only of interest to the die-hard, or those who are only interested in arcania, since it'll provide great unheard beats for their own recordings. This doesn't make for bad listening, and for record collectors, compilations like *Philadelphia Roots* are interesting, since they present largely unknown cuts from a familiar style (you may recognize the horns of Slipp Nobles & Co.'s "The Horse," but you're unlikely to spot anything else, unless you're from Philadelphia). Are there any lost treasures? No. And that is an unequivocal statement, because nothing here deserved to be as well-known as the best and biggest Philly soul singles, since they don't have the hooks, the melodies, the flair to have scaled the charts. But they do have the sound, and they often have the groove, which is why anybody would buy this record—it sounds like a famous sound, only with unknown songs and grooves, some of which are pretty engaging. Not all of it, though, and it's only for specialists—but for those specialists, this is a collection that will not disappoint. (And if you find this disappointing, well, you've realized that you're not a specialist.) *—Stephen Thomas Erlewine*

Philadelphia Uncovered / 1999 / Philadelphia International ✦✦✦
Now this is a great idea. Released in 1999, *Philadelphia Uncovered* actually offers songs people want to listen to as well as boasting a genuine rare quotient. It didn't come easily, though. Since the late '80s the Philadelphia International masters have been split between Sony and The Right Stuff. The result has caused years of haphazard and unsatisfying compilations. Again due to contractual deals, *Philadelphia Uncovered* starts at 1976 and stops at the early '90s. The tracks from MFSB are past their peak. For a label, if not genre, that often was wanting in the way of female vocalists, *Philadelphia Uncovered* finds the best tracks coming from them. Dee Dee Sharp's "I Love You Anyway" and Jean Carn's "Was It All It Was" are two of the strong 1979-1987 offerings. The true find of this compilation, Patti LaBelle's phenomenal "I Can't Forget You," is worth the price of the set. The best-known song from this is perhaps the O'Jays' 1987 "comeback" hit; "Lovin' You" proved that the label did have a great knack at going back to its classic sound at will. Despite the P.I. insignia on the CD's cover, *Philadelphia Uncovered* also features productions for artists on other labels. Given those facts, truly rare songs from the Temptations, 1978-1981 Trammps, and even commercial duds from Carl Carlton and ABC-era Harold Melvin & the Blue Notes could have made the cut. For true fans this will remain a good idea, but one that deserves a better sense of the sound and catalog of the genre. *—Jason Elias*

Philadelphia: Underground Anthems of Philadelphia Soul, 1973–1981 / 1998 / Harmless ✦✦✦✦
Compilations from the Philadelphia International archives seem to pop up on a weekly basis, but given the consistent quality of the music, there hasn't been a dud yet. This collection is especially sweet since it contains some outstanding lesser-known tracks. Nice to see the O'Jays' "The Big Gangster," a dynamite track from the forgotten *Lets Clean Up the Ghetto* LP. The group also shines on "Give the People What They Want," "Darlin' Darlin' Baby (Sweet Tender Love)," and the ecological "The Air I Breathe." You'll also like Lou Rawls' funky "See You When I Git There," the Jacksons' "Blues Away," and the Futures' "Ain't No Time Fa Nothing." You may never have heard Anthony White's "Where Would I Be Without You," the Trammps' "Trusting Heart," Norman Harris' "In Good Faith," or "Bump de Bump," by Monk Montgomery, but they're worth a listen. Also included are some ear-pleasing selections from Archie Bell & the Drells, Billy Paul, Teddy Pendergrass, the Jones Girls, MFSB, and Jean Carn. *—Andrew Hamilton*

Philly Favorites / Sep. 14, 1999 / Collectables ✦✦✦✦✦
Here is an apple and oranges compilation of Philly hits, spanning from Frankie Avalon to Harold Melvin & the Blue Notes. Most were major hits, but it includes a few tracks litle known outside the Philly/tri-state area like Anthony & the Sophomores' "Play Those Oldies Mr. DJ," the Dreamlovers' "You Gave Me Somebody to Love," and the Majors' "A Wonderful Dream." The oldies but goodies include Chubby Checker's "The Twist," the O'Jay's "I Love Music," Danny & the Juniors' "At the Hop," and many more, 21 in all. The price is more than reasonable, and the music is great. *—Andrew Hamilton*

Philly Soul Girls, Vol. 1 / 1999 / Philly Archives ✦✦✦
B&L Productions, formed by songwriter Frank Bendinelli and arranger Leroy Lovett, recorded quite a bit of music in Philadelphia in the 1960s for either their own small labels or for lease to other companies. Much of it typified the city's transition from R&B, doo wop, twist, and girl group music to early Philadelphia soul, and this 30-song compilation of rare singles and unreleased material focuses on the women vocalists they recorded during the mid-'60s. Most of the anthology bridges girl groups and soul, and while it's competently produced and representative of the period, it's also derivative

of certain styles and better songwriters. It could not be said, for instance, that the Persianettes (whose two songs were co-written by "Huff," presumably a young Leon Huff) were not trying to sing like the Supremes, and that the rhythm on Ann Byers' "Dead End" isn't heavily indebted to Martha & the Vandellas. Yes, Motown was an inspiration for many of the songs, but that's not the worst thing in the world; at least the model is good, and the execution of these facsimiles is fairly pleasing. Certainly the standout cut is Patty & the Emblems' "Mixed Up Shook Up Girl," with its swaggering horns and confident girl group-styled vocal. It was a big hit in Philly in 1964, and had the potential to be a big hit everywhere. Other highlights include Joyce Bennett's "New Boy," a good sassy girl group tune with an uptown sound, and Kim Brown's "Listen to My Heartbeat," a yearning ballad with a complex melody and such elaborate production (down to the booming orchestral drums) that it's puzzling it was not released at the time. Incidentally, the five cuts by Honey & the Bees are by an entirely different group than the more popular Honey & the Bees that recorded for Arctic/Josie. For listeners worried about duplication, only four of the songs also appear on Ace's compilation of B&L Productions sides, *Ben Lee's Philadelphia Story*. *—Richie Unterberger*

Philly Soul, Vol. 1 / Jul. 24, 2000 / Philly Archives ♦♦♦♦

This volume contains two gems and many choice goodies. If you're not touched by the Emanons' "One Heart," you need a checkup. The Temptones' "Goodbye Baby," done falsetto by Darryl Hall, sizzles. Hall (who later exploded with Hall & Oates) sings it sweet like Eddie Kendricks, but for some reason it stayed shelved for more than 30 years. The Ballads' "It's Magic," the Enkays' "Say Yes," and the Agents' "You're Everything," are nearly as magical. The talents of Ronnie Walker (who also recorded as Fletcher Walker III) are showcased on nine tracks, including "Really, Really Love You," "Thanks to You," "I Believe in You," "Precious," "Guess I'll Understand," "In Search of Love," and "Didn't We." *Philly Soul, Vol. 1* also features tracks by Clarence Williams, the Exceptions, and the Royal Five. An informative booklet with rare pictures completes the package. *—Andrew Hamilton*

Pittsburgh Favorite Oldies / 2000 / Itzy ♦♦♦

If you slapped a Northern soul title on this two-disc set, nobody would know the difference. These tunes are as obscure as any of the stuff Goldmine, Ace, West End, or other companies specializing in rare sounds crank out; even when the artists are familiar, the tunes are not (i.e., Harold Melvin & the Blue Notes' "You May Not Love Me" and Brenton Wood's "I Want Love"). The Jive Five's "Kiss, Kiss, Kiss" and Jay Wiggins' "Sad Girl" are the most identifiable tracks, while others like Ben Iverson's "Love Me" and Utmost's "I Need You" never got out of the chute. Though a sweet dedication to the memory of Mad Mike, this is for collectors and die-hards who will appreciate the whopping 54 hard-to-find tracks. *—Andrew Hamilton*

Pittsburgh's Favorite Oldies / Jul. 15, 1997 / Itzy ♦♦♦♦

The ongoing chronicle of Pittsburgh's music scene of the 1950s and '60s takes a slight detour from spotlighting the local talent and puts the spin on a fairly obscure batch of tunes that were hits in Steeltown (and sometimes nowhere else in the country) way back when, thanks to a handful of pioneering disc jockeys. One of those disc jockeys was Porky Chedwick, and it's his "Bongo Blues" theme that kicks off this third installment of Itzy's "At the Hop" series. These 24 tracks show the love affair the city had (and still does) with no-frills doo wop ("Those Three Little Words" by the Delcos, "Keeper of Dreams" by the Gallahads, "The Gift of Love" by the Van Dykes, "Oo Wee Baby" by the Ivy Tones) and hard '50s/'60s R&B ("Wizard of Ah's" by Count Ferrell, "Munch" by the Aladdins), and just plain greasy rock & roll ("Wine Wine Wine" by the Nightcaps, "Harlem Nocturne" by the Viscounts, "Hidi Hidi Hidi" by Mickey Hawks, "Chumba" by Gabriel & the Angels, "Gismo" by Jimmie Heap). Making ultra-rare compact disc appearances are several tracks from the Los Angeles-based Flip label, including a pair from Richard Berry (the original "Louie Louie" and "Have Love—Will Travel"), "White Port & Lemon Juice" by the Bel-Aires, "Uncle Sam's Man" by the Elgins, "A Casual Look" by the Six Teens and "Death of an Angel" by Donald Woods & the Vel-Aires. Definitely more "hit-laden" (and therefore more accessible to the novice collector who wants to dive a little deeper into the nether regions of early rock & roll) than the other volumes in the series, this is a solid winner all the way. *—Cub Koda*

Pop-A-Groove: 70's Rare Soul & Funk Collide on the Dancefloor / 2001 / Goldmine/ Soul Supply ♦♦♦♦♦

Usually compilations don't rate this highly, but this one is special for a number of reasons, not the least of which is the uncharacteristic *lack* of documentation by the usually scholarly Goldmine label. While the tracks and artists are listed along with producers in most cases, there is no other information provided—the inside booklet is blank. While this would be a detriment for most collectors and fans, it actually serves to make the collection more beguiling. Indeed, the Harry Smith *Anthology of American Folk Music* is considered to be a document that preserved the legacies of dozens of obscure artists who would have passed into oblivion, and this is the same idea. Here are cuts by Otis Jackson, Spaceark, the VIP Connection, Soul Band, Future Shock, Milton Hamilton Crystalized, and many others (14 in all) that offer a solid portrait of a particular place in time, with popping basslines, open jazz chords, double-timed drums, and killer vocals accenting groove over melody for the first time in the history of soul. Tracks are staggered to offer more groove-heavy funk numbers in alternate sequencing with more straight-ahead deep soul balladry, though all of these tracks are steeped in similar arrangements and a sound that screams the decade's name they came from. One needs only to get to track three, "The Stranger," by the C. Henry Woods Troupe (anyone ever hear of 'em?) to understand that Motown, Sly, the Parliaments, and Curtis Mayfield gave birth to an entirely new sound that none of them would embody individually yet would contribute to universally. This is essential music from a time that has yet to gets its due for the contributions it made to soul music. *—Thom Jurek*

Power of Love: Best of Soul Essentials Ballads / Feb. 6, 1996 / Polygram ♦♦♦♦

This gets high marks for the inclusion of obscure, and underappreciated gems like "Love Seasons," by Zoom; this marvelously produced ballad features a heart-piercing falsetto, a meaty tenor, creative backing vocals, some mighty fine rhythms and a gold star arrangement. Another rarity is Yvonne Elliman's "Hello Stranger," which is not as charming as the original by Barbara Lewis, yet Yvonne does a creditable job with one of the most lovable melodies ever created. Alton McClain & Destiny's original rendition of "I've Learned to Respect the Power of Love," will peak the ears accustomed to Stephanie Mills' version. Other class obscurities include "Hey There Lonely Girl," by Gerry Woo, "Let Me into Your Life," by Creative Source and "Love Song," by Mandrill. Lyn Collins gives a female perspective to "If You Don't Know Me By Know," a hit for Harold Melvin & the Blue Notes, and adds a Denise LaSalle-like rap to the mix. Ray, Goodman & Brown's romantic "Inside of You" features Brown's tough-as-nails falsetto, finger snapping and seasoned harmonies. Issac Hayes' version of "This Time I'll Be Sweeter," ranks with Angela Bofill's earlier recording as the best this song gets. A jazzy "You Sure Like To Ball," by Fred Wesley & the J.B.'s is more than four minutes of laid-back ecstasy; a tantalizing guitar is the lead player on an erotic instrumental of Marvin Gaye's song, with Fred's bossy trombone appearing mid-song. An intriguing compilation that stands a head above similar releases of this type. *—Andrew Hamilton*

Prelude Mastermixes, Vol. 1 / Aug. 1, 1989 / Unidisc ♦♦♦♦

This classic Prelude mastermix includes tracks by France Joli ("Gonna Get Over You"), D Train ("You're the One for Me"), Sharon Redd ("Can You Handle It") and Empress ("Dyin' to Be Dancin'"), among others. *—Keith Farley*

Prelude Mastermixes, Vol. 2 / Feb. 28, 1996 / Unidisc ♦♦♦

A second edition of classic Prelude mastermixes includes tracks by D Train, Indeep, Visual, Wuf Ticket, Musique and Sharon Redd. *—Keith Farley*

Prelude's Greatest Hits, Vol. 2 / Feb. 28, 1996 / Unidisc ♦♦♦♦

The second in the *Prelude Greatest Hits* series includes several seminal dance tracks like "Keep on Jumpin'" by Musique, "Searching to Find the One" by Unlimited Touch and "A-Freak-A" by Lemon. *—Keith Farley*

Prelude's Greatest Hits, Vol. 3 / Feb. 28, 1996 / Unidisc ♦♦♦♦

The third in the *Prelude Greatest Hits* series includes several seminal dance tracks like "D Train Dub" and "Tryin' to Get Over" by D Train, "Hot Summer Night" by Vicki Sue Robinson, "Somehow Someway" by Visual and "Check Out the Groove" by Bobby Thurston. *—Keith Farley*

Pure Funk, Vol. 2 / May 4, 1999 / Polygram ♦♦♦♦

Like *Pure Disco* before it, *Pure Funk* was a success, so there was only one thing for Mercury to do—release *Pure Funk, Vol. 2*. Since the *Pure* series is surprisingly enjoyable, the sequel was welcome and thankfully, it doesn't disappoint. Although some could argue that Queen's "Another One Bites the Dust" isn't real funk, most of the album delivers the goods, splitting the diffrence between the familiar and cult favorites. And that's the reason why *Pure Funk, Vol. 2* works—it has "Let It Whip," "Cut the Cake," "I Gotcha," "It's Your Thing," "I'm Gonna Love You Just a Little More, Baby," "You Sexy Thing," "Use Me," "Got to Give It Up" and "Keep on Truckin'," but also "Lovergirl," "You're the One for Me," "Get Down on It," "Mama Used to Say," "She's a Bad Mama Jama," "Street Life" and "Outstanding." The blend keeps the momentum going for both casual and hardcore funk fans and helps make *Pure Funk, Vol. 2* another winner in Mercury's ongoing series. *—Stephen Thomas Erlewine*

Rainy Day Doo Wops / Nov. 2000 / Rainy Day ♦♦♦♦

This compilation gets a high mark for the rarity of many of the selections, including "Lonely Rain" by the Mascots (later known as the O'Jays), released by King Records in 1961. Other obscurities include the Globetrotters' "Rainy Day Bells" and "Rain," "Another Rainy Day" by the Jive Five, Dee Clark's "Raindrops," "It Had to Rain" by the Catalina Six, and Eddie Delmar's "Garden in the Rain." Get the picture? Every song has rain or a form of the word in the title except "Drip Drop" by the Dodgers, "Cloudburst" by the Orlandos, and the Videos' "Trickle, Trickle." *—Andrew Hamilton*

Rama Story / Mar. 2, 1999 / WestSide ♦♦♦

This two-disc set brings together 61 tracks from this early George Goldner run label. Although Rama only had a three year run as a label, they made significant inroads, especially as a doo wop specialist with seminal tracks from the Crows ("Gee"), the Wrens ("Come Back My Love"), the Valentines ("Lily Maybelle") and the Heartbeats ("A Thousand Miles Away"). But there's also some errant pop sides and some fine rockabilly aboard as well from Don "Red" Roberts, Little Billy Mason (a white Frankie Lymon sound-alike with guitar band backing), and Roc LaRue. A delightful two-disc set that shows off the many sides of this interesting label. *—Cub Koda*

Rare Collectable and Soulful, Vol. 2 / Dec. 9, 1997 / Kent ♦♦♦♦

Sam Cooke to the contrary, RCA wasn't known as a soul powerhouse in the 1960s, but it did issue its share of recordings in the style. This 24-track compilation doesn't have any hits, although there are little-known outings from Johnny Nash, the Exciters (long after the "Tell Him" days), Roy Hamilton, and ex-Oriole Sonny Til; in fact, about half of it was previously unreleased. A lot of it was produced in New York and Detroit (the Motor City outings largely generated by the Pied Piper production team), and it's largely upbeat, mid- to uptempo, acceptable but unexceptional soul. That's the kind of style, of course, which is so beloved by Northern soul mavens, who will want this for the sheer rarity of the material if nothing else. The average soul fan should pass. If you find yourself in between, you may find it useful to know that the better tracks include Lorraine

Chandler's gutsy version of "You Only Live Twice" (yes, the same James Bond theme that was a hit for Nancy Sinatra), Hamilton's version of Bacharach-David's "Reach Out for Me," and Nash's Drifters-type go at his own composition "What Kind of Love Is This" (which would be a hit for Joey Dee). *—Richie Unterberger*

Rare Funk Liberation, Vol. 1 / Dec. 20, 1999 / Goldmine/Soul Supply ♦♦♦♦
Yet another excellent deep funk compilation from the folks at Goldmine/Soul Supply, who set the standard for obscure funk reissues with their ten-volume *Sound of Funk* series, and just keep on going. *Rare Funk Liberation, Vol. 1* offers no sign that the label has exhausted its supply of hard, high-energy funk rarities—in fact, it features 18 tracks instead of the usual Goldmine 16. The title might be taken to imply that the tracks here have some sort of continuous black-pride theme, but that's not the case—it's just the singles themselves that are being set free into the marketplace after decades of neglect. There is, however, a welcome skew toward female funksters in the selections, and there's even one immediately familiar name—Little Eva, singing a sassy "The Wind" and sounding not as little as in her "Loco-Motion" days. Joyce Williams' "The First Thing I Do in the Morning" and Kim Tomango's "Not by Bread Alone" are collector favorites, and Pearl Dowell serves up a fine leadoff track in "Good Things"; meanwhile, the bands Union ("Strike") and London Fog & the Continentals featuring Brenda Lee Jones ("Easy Mover") both sport tough, confident female lead singers. Elsewhere, Yesterday Today & Tomorrow make the inspired choice to write lyrics about playing their "D Minor Vamp," while Busey's Soulblenders puree their way through a crazed "Soul Power, Pt. 2" (terrible pun, but they do). The Blenders Ltd. and Lee Fields & the Devil's Personal Band both offer classic deep funk instrumentals in "You Got It All, Ain't No More" and "The Bull Is Coming," respectively, and it's well nigh impossible to resist James Fountain & the Soul Chargers' exhortations to dance the "Soul Charge, Pts. 1 & 2." Deep funk fans have another Goldmine comp to add to the collection. *—Steve Huey*

Rare Preludes, Vol. 1 / Feb. 3, 1994 / Unidisc ♦♦♦
The first volume in the *Rare Preludes* series includes contributions from Unique, Black Gold, Visual, Elektrik Funk and Visual. *—Keith Farley*

Rare Preludes, Vol. 2 / Mar. 4, 1994 / Unidisc ♦♦♦
The second volume in the *Rare Preludes* series includes contributions from D Train, U.N., Rosko Recites, Center Stage, Sticky Fingers and Kumano. *—Keith Farley*

Rare Preludes, Vol. 3 / Mar. 4, 1994 / Unidisc ♦♦♦
The third volume in the *Rare Preludes* series includes contributions from Daybreak, Next Movement, Gerald Mallory, Dianne Marie and Wuf Ticket. *—Keith Farley*

Rare Preludes, Vol. 4 / Mar. 4, 1994 / Unidisc ♦♦♦
The fourth volume in the *Rare Preludes* series includes contributions from Conquest, D Train, Unique, Jazzie Ladies, Sine and Passion. *—Keith Farley*

Rare Preludes, Vol. 5 / Mar. 4, 1994 / Unidisc ♦♦♦
The fifth volume in the *Rare Preludes* series includes contributions from Strikers, Nanette, Enchantment, Paulette, CD III and Wardell Piper. *—Keith Farley*

Rare Stax Vocal Groups of the 60s & 70s / 1992 / Stax ♦♦♦
A much better collection than the previously issued *The Stax Groups*, which had 13 tracks compared to the 21 here. Detroit's Dramatics are featured on three tracks: the oddly arranged "Highway to Heaven," a nondescript "Since I've Been In Love" and "Your Love Was Strange," where lead William "Wee Gee" Howard mimics David Ruffin. The zany Mad Lads were all bred in Memphis, TN; unfortunately, their four selections aren't their most memorable. Ditto for the Temprees, known for sweet ballads. The Newcomers selections are representative of their fine, underappreciated recordings. "Open Your Heart (And Let Love Come)" is a lilting beauty, and the chirpy "Girl, This Boy Loves You" displays the Newcomers' youthful innocence and energy. The Epsilons are represented on the doo wop-flavored, harmony-filled "The Echo," one of the best cuts here. Philly's United Image is represented by "Love's Creeping Up on Me" (the group later became the disco group Double Exposure). On "Anyone Can," the Leaders feature an airy falsetto and a pop sounding tenor. The Stringers' only track is a gem, the determined "I Refuse to Be Lonely." "All Because of You" by the Limitations is vibrant, a stinging tenor backed by flitting harmonies that are mixed too low; the groups' energy level is better than the song. *—Andrew Hamilton*

Rhythm & Roll / Mar. 2, 1999 / Nostalgia ♦♦♦
An 18-track collection of rare and very good jump blues sides from the pre-rock & roll era. With tracks aboard from T-Bone Walker, the Trenier Twins, Jay McShann, Rex Stewart, Louis Jordan, Roy Milton, Freddie Slack, and Albert Ammons, the quality is as high as this music gets. Nice, clean transfers of the material makes this set a joy to listen to and a better swing party collection would be mighty hard to find. *—Cub Koda*

Rock, Rhythm and Doo Wop, Vol. 1: The Greatest Songs From Early Rock 'n' Roll / Nov. 6, 2001 / Rhino ♦♦♦♦♦
This three-CD box set contains 66 tracks taken from various schools of the first decade (or so) of rock & roll: doo wop, girl group, rockabilly, early soul, light pop/rock, New Orleans R&B, and more. For the most part they were big hits, though one or two things you'll rarely if ever hear on oldies radio are thrown in, like Little Richard's "True, Fine Mama" or Shep & the Limelites' "Our Anniversary." Sometimes songs that were released after the British Invasion started, but owed much to doo wop or girl group sounds, are included. Well, how else would you explain the presence of songs like Jay & the Americans' "Cara, Mia" or the Casinos' "Then You Can Tell Me Goodbye," the latter of which didn't come out until 1967? But why opt for this particular collection, when there are so many other oldies anthologies that either opt for the absolutely most familiar huge smashes if buyers want just the biggest hits, or far narrower, specialized focuses like rockabilly and doo wop if the buyer's choosier and more knowledgeable? You certainly couldn't call a box that has nothing by Elvis Presley, Gene Vincent, Fats Domino, Jerry Lee Lewis, Sam Cooke, Carl Perkins, or Brenda Lee (just for starters) a definitive response to the gauntlet thrown down by the subtitle *The Greatest Songs From Early Rock 'n' Roll*. Generally, the compilation targets the kind of warm, romantic songs that nostalgic viewers of the PBS pledge drive perennial Doo Wop 50 special might be apt to buy (or submit a pledge in exchange for) on an impulse right after the credits roll. That's not a purely flip remark: The box was co-presented by Rhino with WQED, the Pittsburgh station that originated the Doo Wop 50 program. Any box that has classics like "Twist and Shout," "He's So Fine," "Cathy's Clown," "Do You Love Me," "Hello Stranger," "Will You Love Me Tomorrow," "Runaway," "Up on the Roof," "Stand By Me," "What'd I Say," and many others of similar quality has a lot going for it, but it's certainly not the best you could do if you're looking for starting points for collecting late-'50s/early-'60s rock. Basically, it's the equivalent of those all-over-the-map collections of oldies that have been hawked on TV for decades, assembled with considerably greater taste and much better liner notes. *—Richie Unterberger*

Rock, Rhythm and Doo Wop, Vol. 2: More of the Great Songs From Early Rock 'n' Roll / Dec. 20, 2001 / Rhino Handmade ♦♦♦
As with the first volume, this is a three-CD, 66-box set grab bag of all sorts of singles, most of them hits, from the first decade or so of rock & roll. And as with the first volume, you can stare at the track listing and package for hours without getting a handle on exactly why this specific grouping of songs was chosen, and who exactly this box would appeal to other than the random (very random, considering the expense of a box set) indiscriminate record buyer who's in a hurry to get several dozen oldies at once. There are girl group hits, early soul songs, instrumentals, pop-oriented hits by Bobby Darin and Trini Lopez, early Stax soul by Carla Thomas & Rufus Thomas, silly pop from James Darren, doo wop from the Duprees, and more. By and large (with some gaffes like the Darren track) the songs chosen are good and often classic; only a very few, like the Jewels' "Opportunity" and Eddie Platt's weird instrumental "Cha-Hua-Hua," are low-charting Top 100 entries that are seldom anthologized. But again: why splash out for a box that doesn't either focus on the very biggest hits of the time or focus on a more specific subgenre? It's different from the first box in this series, somewhat, in that the third disc is devoted primarily to non-hits, some of them rare. (In addition, unlike the prior box, you can only get this through the website of the Rhino Handmade imprint at www.rhinohandmade.com.) Yet, again, it's hard to see what makes that third disc special in a reissue world that's crowded with expert, fine-tuned thematic packages. Like the other two discs, it's a smorgasbord of doo wop, rockabilly, novelty, and early R&B-pop crossover, and while some of these are good—like the Spaniels' "Stormy Weather" and Rosco Gordon's oft-covered "Just a Little Bit"—most are only okay, and not the tunes you would choose for a compilation of the ultimate great little-heard early rock & roll. Some of the songs on disc three, to make matters more confusing, *were* fairly big hits, like Little Eva's "Keep Your Hands off My Baby," the Regents' "Runaround," and Ral Donner's "Girl of My Best Friend." There's a lot of good music on this set, but to what avail when the concept and organization are so screwy? *—Richie Unterberger*

The Roots of Elvis Presley / Apr. 24, 2001 / Catfish ♦♦♦♦♦
This multi-artist compilation is essential listening to any real devotee of Elvis Presley, and can also be highly recommended to any casual fan. The 22 songs here represent various songs made famous by Presley in the versions that he would have known them from. Apart from the overall quality of the analog-to-digital transfers, the most striking element of this CD is the sheer diversity of sounds embodied here: the gospel of Sister Rosetta Tharpe ("Down By the Riverside") and the Golden Gate Quartet ("Precious Lord"), the jaunty Western swing of Bob Wills ("Faded Love"), the blues of Arthur "Big Boy" Crudup ("That's All Right," "My Baby Left Me," "So Glad You're Mine") and postwar jump-style singer Wea Bea Booze ("See See Rider"), the country blues of Johnny Lee Wills ("Milk Cow Blues"), the country-based popular sounds of Gene Autry ("Blueberry Hill"), and forgotten country stars like the Shelton Brothers ("Just Because," "Aura Lee"). It's all evidence of one attribute of Elvis' that is often overlooked—that apart from his talent, he came to his career knowing more songs, in more different styles and genres, than any teenager rightfully ought to have known. The result here is a supremely diverse body of music by artists ranging from some of the most exalted to some of the most obscure performers of the mid-20th century. The annotation is reasonably thorough, though some of what's here begs for a real musicologist to address its content and true origins. In the meantime, it's great fun and an enlightening listen the first time or the 20th time. *—Bruce Eder*

Roots of Rhythm & Blues / Oct. 16, 2001 / Fremeaux & Associes ♦♦♦♦
Spread over two discs and a total of 36 tracks, *Roots of Rhythm & Blues* profiles rock & roll's predecessor with a potent and key mix of blues, swing (combo and big band), and jump blues from mostly the '40s. And the variety is never lacking, as T-Bone Walker delivers his dirty-guitar blues alongside Charles Brown's congenial piano-bar musings. The mix is a dizzying—yet still cogent—array of musical genius, taking in a the likes of Billy Eckstine, Arthur "Big Boy" Crudup, Louis Jordan, Sister Rosetta Tharpe, Joe Liggins, Dinah Washington, Lionel Hampton, and Wynonie Harris, among many others. Whether your vote for most important figure is Big "Joe" Turner or maybe even Johnny Otis, this R&B primer will go a long way in getting you up to speed on one of modern music's most vital eras. *—Stephen Cook*

Roulette Rock & Roll, Vol. 2: Everybody's Gonna / Oct. 24, 1994 / Castle ♦♦♦
The second entry in the series heads in a far more R&B direction than the raw rockabilly of the previous volume, but there's certainly nothing to complain about, as this 22-track collection sports no less than a half dozen sides by Wynonie Harris, a hot recut of his old hit "Bloodshot Eyes," and "Sweet Lucy Brown," along with four previously unissued sides from a 1960 session, "Spread the News," "Josephine," "Did You Get the

Message" and "Saturday Night." Along with stellar contributions from Screamin' Jay Hawkins ("The Whammy" and "Strange"), the Isley Brothers (both sides of their two singles for Mark X and Gone), and dynamite one-offs from the Duponts ("Screamin' Ball at Dracula Hall"), the Gone All-Stars (the storming instrumental "7-11"), the Cookies ("Hippy Dippy Daddy"), the Emanons ("Hindu Baby"), the Echoes ("Ding Dong"), the Valentines ("Woo Woo Train"), the Chaperones ("Dance With Me"), Jesse Powell & the Caddies ("Ain't You Gonna") and Mabel King ("Alabama Rock and Roll"), this is another hitherto unexplored side of the label that had more than its share of hard-rocking offerings by both sides of the color barrier. *—Cub Koda*

Sampled / Oct. 9, 2000 / Virgin ♦♦♦♦

Gotchyer! Caught with their hands in the sampled cookie jar, chart mega-weights have to fess up to their clever camouflage—and often outright thievery—of vintage disco, soul, jazz, and blues records. Which means this quite entertaining compilation piles on all types of original recordings that have remade their way into popular consciousness via the circuitous route of record-box revisionism. Want to know where that reggae break in Prodigy's "Out of Space" came from? It's here (Max Romeo and the Upsetters' "Chase the Devil"). Care to have someone show you where Fatboy Slim lifted the surf-guitar hop "Rockafeller Skank" from? Here, too (The Just Brothers' "Sliced Tomatoes"). And so it goes for 40 tracks, exposing the sampledelic smoke and mirrors with understated viciousness. Even when it sometimes highlights the superiority of the updates—Patti Page's "Cape Cod," for instance, lacks the teary comedown luster of Groove Armada, Lonnie Liston Smith's "Expansions" misses its helium-funk mark that Stetsasonic nails, and Herbie Hancock's "Bring Down the Birds" doesn't even get within hip-shaking distance of the uninhibited glee of Deee-Lite's "Groove Is in the Heart." But as you can guess, most of these exposés show the ransacking hacks for what they are; it's well-known that MC Hammer, Robbie Williams, and Eminem were stretching the definition of songwriting. The latter of which does nothing new in his Labi Siffre-induced "My Name Is" except nasal karaoke. Extremely convenient, brutally unsympathetic, and—at the very least—educational, *Sampled* is terrific fun. The perfect compilation for transforming into the "Pish posh, my good man, you want to hear who *really* wrote that?" plague of any party. *—Dean Carlson*

Sanctified Soul / Mar. 28, 2000 / Kent ♦♦♦♦

Both this and another Kent compilation, *Our Turn to Cry*, dig deep into the Atlantic vaults for a lot of slow soul from the 1960s and early '70s that's pretty hard to find, either in its original form or on reissue. *Sanctified Soul*, as the title would lead you to expect, is more oriented toward churchy, pleading songs than its companion volume is. The constant, emotionally wrought, deliberate pace of the tracks does make you wish for a little wider canvas of moods over the course of a 26-track compilation. It remains, however, a good group of tunes from one of the powerhouse soul labels, populated by unknowns and higher-profile singers with cult followings, like James Carr, Don Covay, Arthur Conley, Otis Clay, Judy Clay, and Bettye Swann. Relative heavyweights Wilson Pickett and Solomon Burke are also represented, with 1964 singles; there's also the only Atlantic solo single by Drifters lead vocalist Rudy Lewis, 1963's "I've Loved You So Long." The Soul Clan, the temporary soul supergroup of Arthur Conley, Ben E. King, Burke, Covay, and Joe Tex, lead off with their 1968 single "That's How It Feels." It's all reasonably satisfying, but not much is so outstanding that you'll be tempted to put it on selective tapes of rare soul gems. One interesting derailment from the hand-wringing love songs so common to the genre is Sam Dees' 1973 single "Signed, Miss Heroin," a look at drug use at a time when Curtis Mayfield's *Superfly* had opened up soul to such subjects. You don't find many soul covers of Bob Dylan songs, either, and J.P. Robinson's interpretation of "George Jackson" (from a 1972 single) is one. [This U.K. import is not available for sale in North America.] *—Richie Unterberger*

Say It Loud! A Celebration of Black Music in America / Sep. 18, 2001 / Rhino ♦♦♦

There's little question that Rhino's six-disc box *Say It Loud! A Celebration of Black Music in America* is well-intentioned and even educational, presenting a musical history (interspersed with spoken excerpts from famous speeches) of the 20th century, from Scott Joplin's "Maple Leaf Rag" to Coolio's "Fantastic Voyage." That's a lot of ground to cover, not just in terms of history, but in sheer terms of music, since a lot happened during those 100 years. Of course, that's the set's point—it WANTS to be overwhelming, to hit you in the face with the sheer vibrancy and creativity of black music, and to show how it evolved while remaining at the center of American culture. All well and good, and it even accomplishes its task quite well; even if it misses such stalwarts as Stevie Wonder and Public Enemy, it still gives the overall arc of history, which is no small feat. So, why doesn't *Say It Loud!* warrant a more enthusiastic recommendation? Because it never intoxicates with its music, never lets the listener get lost in the music itself, since it prefers to preach instead of cajole. The end result is a box that feels like the cornerstone of a thorough, yet rather dull, collegiate music history course—you'll learn a lot, possibly discover some great music (since there is almost nothing but great music here, even if some of the inclusions on the last two discs are a little questionable, such as Quincy Jones' "Sanford and Son" or Living Colour's "Elvis Is Dead"), but it feels more like an obligation than a passion. *—Stephen Thomas Erlewine*

Shag Spectacular / Jan. 2, 1996 / Ripete ♦♦

This compilation features British-produced latter-day tracks featuring a number of former Motown artists. Originally released on Motor City Records, these sides aren't bad, they just aren't the real deal; and they're pricey—an authentic CD of originals cost less. But Motown aficionados will enjoy listening to these vocalists prove that they've still got the goods. Includes James Ellis soloing on "If You Don't Want My Love," Edwin Starr's "Release This Love," and Ivory Joe Hunter's "Running Through My Fingers." There are also tracks by Pat Lewis, Frankie Gaye, Marv Johnson, Johnny Bristol, Jean, Sherri, & Lynda of the Supremes, and others. *—Andrew Hamilton*

Shag Spectacular, Vol. 2 / May 19, 1998 / Orion ♦♦

Shag music is the most dubious term going, nobody knows what it means. It includes every form of music from Bill Deal & the Rondells to Willie Tee. You can now add British Motown remakes to the shag controversy. The second of two volumes include aged-in-soul Motown artists' on "This Old Heart of Mine" (Contours), Mary Wells' "You Beat Me to the Punch" (the original is much better), and the Originals' "Please Mr. Postman" (member Freddie Gorman co-wrote the classic made famous by the Marvelettes). The selections make this more interesting than *Vol. 1*. Check out "Since I Lost My Baby" by Carolyn Crawford, "More Love" by the Fifth Dimension, Betty Lavettes' "Jimmy Mack," and "Ooh Child" by Mary Wilson. Also includes two duets by Johnny Bristol & Liz Lands: "Someday We'll Be Together" and "Hang on in There Baby," and "How Sweet It Is," a Lands solo. *—Andrew Hamilton*

Shake Me, Wake Me: A Tribute to Holland-Dozier-Holland / Aug. 30, 1994 / Hot Productions ♦♦♦♦

It's got the latter-day versions of groups like Martha Reeves & the Vandellas and the Contours, not to mention Levi Stubbs leading the "Motorcity All-Stars," but that shouldn't stop anyone from picking up this 20-song collection of new recordings. The artists have held together well, and they do their best to forge a compromise between their early-'60s sounds and mid-'90s expectations; "Heatwave" has a prominent harp arpeggio ornamenting its verses, but the arrangement is good and the singing is a good match for what we remember. Most of the rest matches up, from Kim Weston's version of "Helpless" to Rare Earth and their version of "Love Is Here and Now You're Gone." A couple of recent Supremes are here, and they hold their own, though the sound of the drums throughout most of this stuff is a little too up front. Other acts include Rose Banks ("You Keep Me Hangin' On"), Sherri Taylor ("Love Is Like an Itching in My Heart"), Syreeta ("Reflections"), and the Velvettes ("Come See About Me"). *—Bruce Eder*

● **Shakin' Fit!** / 1992 / Candy ♦♦♦♦

Soul music wasn't just Motown in the '60s. There were earnest gospel-filled ballads, and dancefloor rabble-rousers. There were also quite a few soul performers who treated the music as fun, first and foremost, taking a somewhat looser and goofier approach than the stars that had long careers. This 29-track CD is a good document of soul music as pure fun, by singers who never had a hit (Don & Dewey are the only marginally recognizable names here), and who owed stronger debts to the honking R&B music of the '50s than most other soul performers. Some of these are downright funny novelties (the Five Du-Tones' "The Chicken Astronaut," Emanual Laskey's "Welfare Cheese"); a great deal of these are novelty-tinged dance tunes that verge on silly, in the best sense of the word ("The Frog," "Skin the Cat," "Sticky Pig Feet," "The Cow," "The Chicken Scratch"). This could have done with some decent liner notes (there are virtually none), but it's a good deal for soul fans looking for some totally overlooked and fun-filled rarities. *—Richie Unterberger*

Shreveport Southern Soul / 2000 / Kent ♦♦♦

Based in Shreveport, LA, the Murco label didn't record soul music exclusively, but it did concentrate heavily on Southern soul in the late '60s and early '70s. There were no national hits, with the marginal exception of Eddy Giles' "Losin' Boy" (the first track on this CD), which registered briefly in the *Cashbox* Hot 100. In fact, none of the singers on this 26-track compilation of Murco sides (some of which came out on various subsidiaries, and a couple of which were previously unreleased) will be familiar even to most soul collectors. Still, operating under the direction of Dee Marais, the label produced deep soul that was well recorded and a cut above the soul done by many other small non-hit labels (of the sort anthologized on numerous other Kent compilations, for instance), although it was usually derivative. The churchy, bluesy, and brassy aspects of the Stax sound, for instance, are all echoed strongly here, sometimes very strongly, as on Charles Crawford's "A Sad Sad Song," which takes the pleading aspect of the Otis Redding school to town and back. And don't anyone try to claim that Ann Alford's "Got to Get Me a Job" was recorded after Sly Stone's "Thank You." Alford's "If It Ain't One Thing (It's Another)" is reminiscent of James Brown's ballads, while Dori Grayson's "Try Love" is a 1967 throwback to the Mary Wells Motown sound. Nonetheless, the arrangements and vocals show a degree of care and passion uncommon on many non-hit records, soul or otherwise. Certainly the most interesting of the several performers on this collection is Reuben Bell, whose high-pitched vocals can be mistaken for those of a woman. His 1967 single "It's Not That Easy," with its mesmerizing minor-key melody and tense arrangement, is easily the disc's standout. *—Richie Unterberger*

Shrine Records: Rarest Soul Labels / Aug. 25, 1998 / Kent ♦♦♦

Shrine Records was a record label run by Eddie Singleton and his new bride, Raynoma Liles Gordy, who was Berry Gordy's second wife and later wrote *Berry, Me and Motown.* Despite Gordy's groundbreaking success with Motown, the 18 singles released by Shrine received little, if any, airplay, and none ever made the charts. On the evidence of this collection of rare Shrine recordings, the label's product was spirited and energetic but the productions were sub par. Highlights include the Cairo's "Stop Overlooking Me," which may be Shrine's most commercial effort; the falsetto lead and enthusiastic harmony blends makes for a nice stepping piece of downtown soul. Ray Pollard's "No More Like Me" is a classy ballad popular among European collectors. On Traci's "Take It from Me," Shrine tries for a similar sound to what Smokey was doing with Mary Wells. Recordings by Eddie Daye, J. D. Bryant, Jimmy Armstrong and the Cairo's are the most sought after Shrine recordings. The first three male singers had a hard R&B sound that bordered on deep soul. Little Bobby Parker's "I Won't Believe It Til I See" borrows heavily from "In the Midnight Hour," and "Mystery" by Jimmy Armstrong is fast and furious, featuring a sax solo influenced by Thomas Bowles from the Motown session band, all in a minute and forty seconds. This compilation is a worthy item for historians and die-hard soul music fans, but nothing here would interest the casual fan. *—Andrew Hamilton*

Shrine: The Rarest Soul Label Ever, Vol. 2 / Dec. 12, 2000 / Kent ✦✦✦
In conjunction with the first volume of Kent's overview of the Shrine label, this rounds up all the remaining releases by this small mid-'60s Washington, DC-based soul record company, adding five previously unreleased tracks as well. Like the first volume (simply titled *Shrine: The Rarest Soul Label Ever*), it has well-produced, upbeat (usually), yet rather generic mid-'60s period soul music, with none of the performers being names of any notoriety. Motown, Curtis Mayfield, and New York uptown soul are ably echoed at various points, without much distinction or originality being thrown into the mix. This isn't to sneeze at a compilation that brings together some incredibly rare sides that are avidly sought by serious soul collectors, but it's a caution that it's not going to bowl over non-specialists. For those who like hearing enjoyable knockoffs of other formulas, there's plenty on order here, well-annotated as is Kent's wont. The DC Blossoms' "Hey Boy" sounds much like Motown's more energetic girl groups, and Bobby Reed's previously unreleased "Caldonia Brown" is in the style of the mid-'60s Impressions. In fact there are enough nods to famous harmony groups that it sometimes feel like a gig where the Temptations, the Impressions, and the Miracles had to cancel and the local promoter had to come up with the best similar-sounding substitutes. Some of the source material was so scarce that a few tracks had to be dubbed from the best available discs, but the sound quality is pretty good, and not too bad even on the ones when it's apparent the original tapes were unavailable. *—Richie Unterberger*

Slow 'n' Moody, Black and Bluesy / Nov. 20, 1995 / Kent ✦✦✦
Including a truckload of the grittiest bluesy soul cuts from Z.Z. Hill, Clay Hammond, Jackie Day, Jeb Stuart, Little Richard, Tommy Youngblood and Mary Love, this compilation is quite solid. *—Keith Farley*

Slow Jams: The Timeless Collection, Vol. 2 / 1994 / The Right Stuff ✦✦✦✦
A wallowing, self-pitying collection that includes the Unifics' "The Beginning of My End," with its funeral setting; "Cry Together," the O'Jays' dramatization about a couple with serious issues; Tina Marie's teary "Dear Lover"; Patti LaBelle's pleading "If Only You Knew"; Enchantments' sad realization "Where Do We Go From Here"; and the Isley Brothers' shameless, begging "Let Me Down Easy." Furthermore, Shirley Brown and Barbara Mason want to whip their men's outside women for messin' up their homes. So in the end, it almost seems as if Debra Laws' "Very Special" must be a mistake—it's the only happy tune. *—Andrew Hamilton*

Smooth Grooves: A Sensual Collection, Vols. 1-9 / 1995 / Rhino ✦✦✦✦✦
Rhino's *Smooth Grooves: A Sensual Collection, Vols. 1-9* is an excellent overview of late-'70s and early-'80s urban R&B ballads; in other words, it features the biggest hits and best-known quiet storm songs. Each disc contains 12 tracks, some presented in their 12-inch mixes never before available on CD. But the primary strength of *Smooth Grooves* is that it proves there were many classic soul songs released during this often-overlooked era. While there are a few tediously bland cuts on nearly every volume, there are more keepers than throwaways, including such classics as "Shining Star," "Sexual Healing," "Float On," and "Something He Can Feel." The curious should start with the first volume, which gives an accurate idea of what the series is about, but any quiet storm fan will find every volume worth acquiring. *—Stephen Thomas Erlewine*

Smooth Slow & Easy Soul Gems / 2000 / Triple R ✦✦✦
This collection of rare '60s, '70s, and '80s soul harmony obscurities brings the listener a complete record-listening experience, right down to hiss, crackle, and que-burns. Which is really fine, because the intended audience for *Smooth Slow & Easy Soul Gems* knows that many of these recordings are as rare as fabled Robert Johnson 78s from the '20s and that the noise apparent here is just part of the experience. However, in editing some of these tracks, greater care should have been taken; there are few things as unsettling as the dramatic, dead silence of a song cut short. Beyond these production foibles lies a collection of songs that are incredible documents of the weird and the beautiful, often within the same song. The Jaguars' "Wanda Why" blends a smoky Viscounts-like instrumental behind a great harmony that suddenly erupts in a crash of echo, and this might be the only place you can hear the El Roys' "I Crave Your Love" with its incongruous drum-machine backing and heartfelt, slightly fractured vocal. In fact, almost all of the 25 selections here have moments that suspend belief as they take uncharted paths along the edges of independent soul. *— Wade Kergan*

So Soulful 70's / Nov. 9, 1999 / Kent ✦✦✦
A pleasing collection of underexposed soul sounds from the '70s. Only two bona fide hits are included among the 24 tracks: the Persuaders' chilling "Thin Line Between Love and Hate" and Ben E. King's "Supernatural Thing." Elsewhere, kudos to Kent Records for unleashing some real nuggets like Vivian "Bubbling Brown Sugar" Reed's "Save Your Love for Me"; she's not bubbly on this tearjerker but so soulful she'll have you in tears before the fade. Sam Dee's "Fragile, Handle With Care" shows where the man was at (cutting hard-edged Southern soul music) before embarking on a more successful career as a hit songwriter. The T.S.U. Tornadoes (of "Tighten Up" fame) are represented by "What Good Am I," a change-of-pace (for them) floater. Dee Dee Warwick's rendition of Elvis Presley's "Suspicious Minds" proves that in some cases a Queen beats a King. Also included are two songs from the great, unheralded Betty Lavette. The liner notes make for insightful and interesting reading as this thoughtfully compiled disk spins. *—Andrew Hamilton*

Solid Gold Soul Inspiration / Apr. 17, 2001 / Time Life ✦✦✦✦
Time Life in the soul reissue business? That just can't be right. Well, by the looks of this fine mix and others, the answer is an enthusiastic yes. The theme this time out is inspiration, and there's plenty of it to be had. Whether in the gospel mode by Edwin Hawkins ("Oh Happy Day") and Smokey Robinson & the Miracles ("Abraham, Martin, and John") or by way of the black power vein compliments of the Impressions ("Keep on Pushing") and Sounds of Blackness ("Hold On (Change Is Comin')"), the grooves are solid and the charts are top-notch throughout. And with 14 more cuts to go and not just a few hits by the likes of the Staple Singers, Johnny Nash, Little Milton, the Commodores, and Harold Melvin & the Blue Notes, this inspiring disc is the perfect soul entrée for fans who like a little purpose in their gettin' down. *—Stephen Cook*

Soothers and Movers / 1996 / Goldmine/Soul Supply ✦✦✦✦✦
This is one of the best of many fine Northern soul releases on the Goldmine/Soul Supply label. As the title implies, the disc features a lively and urbane mix, with the emphasis being on the "Groovers." This collection of overlooked, '60s soul is brimming with some of the most slick, in-the-pocket grooves around, especially on standout cuts like J.R. Bailey's "Love Won't Wear Off" and the Impalas' "Speed Up." Other obscure gems include Leon Haywood's smoky toned "Consider the Source," Freddie Terrell's tasty, horns-a-plenty "You Had It Made," and Tommy Hunt's impassioned "I'll Make You Happy." On the more recognizable end, there are also fine contributions by Bobby Womack, Lou Rawls, the O'Jays, and Little Anthony, with the spirit of Sam Cooke being expertly invoked by Willie Hightower on his rousing "Because I Love You." And to keep the testosterone in check, the female persuasion is well represented by fine cuts from Doris Troy, Clydie King, and Bettye Swann. Straight from the vaults of Capitol, Imperial, Calla, and Mint Records, these 24 top-notch soul tracks are sure to satisfy. *—Stephen Cook*

Soul Ballads, Vol. 1 / Nov. 17, 1998 / Soul Disciples ✦✦✦
Traipsing through the '50s, '60s, and '70s, *Soul Ballads, Vol. 1* makes for a flimsy and unfocused after-hours soundtrack. Bookended by the now-calcified Percy Sledge hit "When a Man Loves a Woman" and Sam & Dave's still provocative "When Something Is Wrong With My Baby," the ten-track set both misses the mark badly (the Drifters' "Under the Boardwalk" and Dobie Gray's "Drift Away") and hits it spot-on (Billy Paul's "Me and Mrs. Jones" and the Chi-Lites' "Oh Girl"). After you get tired of skipping cuts, cue up Marvin Gaye's *Let's Get It On* or Barry White's *Greatest Hits* and select repeat mode. *—Stephen Cook*

The Soul Box / Mar. 19, 2002 / K-Tel Entertainment ✦✦✦
Leaving out most of the biggest stars from Motown and Stax, K-Tel has combed the '60s and early-'70s soul terrain to bring you some of the era's key sides. The package logic may be fuzzy (30 tracks on three discs?), but the budget price is certainly right. From Sam & Dave's "Soul Man" to Jean Knight's "Mr. Big Stuff," the dancefloor fillers here are consistently top-notch if more than a tad well-worn. But for those seeking a fairly good survey of the era's soul charts, *Soul Box* will make for a very enjoyable introduction. *—Stephen Cook*

Soul Classics Quiet Storm: The 70's / Apr. 16, 1995 / Rebound ✦✦
This 12-song collection of ballads contains practically every R&B style: from the deep soul grippers such as "If Loving You Is Wrong (I Don't Want to Be Right)" to the urban, Chi-town soul of Jerry Butler and Brenda Lee Eager's "Ain't Understanding Mellow." Jazzier tones like Marvin Gaye's melodic and floating "After the Dance," and Bobby Caldwell's "What You Won't Do for Love" mesh well with Dorothy Moore's stately, mature but sorrowful "Misty Blue" and Jeffery Osborne's passionate lead on "Love Ballad," recorded with L.T.D. A good cross-section of soul. *—Andrew Hamilton*

Soul Classics: Best of the 60's / Mar. 30, 1998 / Rebound ✦✦
I don't mean to be picky, but shouldn't a best-of-the-'60s-CD only include songs from the '60s? Last time I checked, "Lonely Teardrops" came out in 1958, and "Only You," by the Platters, was released in 1955. Despite the errors, this collection, which is an assortment of soul from all corners, makes for good listening. The smooth baritone of Jerry Butler makes the message of "Only the Strong Survive" that much more real. Billy Gordon wails like a crazed man on "Do You Love Me," the Contours' most successful record. The delightful rhythms of "I Can't Help Myself" by the Four Tops, will make you want to boo-ga-loo. And when will record companies start crediting "I Sold My Heart to the Junkman" to the Starlets, who actually recorded the song, and not Patti LaBelle & the Blue Bells? *—Andrew Hamilton*

Soul Classics: Best of the 70's / Mar. 30, 1998 / Rebound ✦✦
All the songs on this set are from the '70s, which is a big improvement from Rebound's '60s collection, which contained two songs from the '50s. These selections run the gamut, everything from Marvin Gaye's ecology warning "Mercy, Mercy Me," to Parliament's relentless "Up for the Downstroke," where the bass player rides the beat into the sunset. Other movers include Stevie Wonder's "Signed, Sealed and Delivered" and B.T. Express' enticing "Do It (Til You're Satisfied)." Romance makes frequent appearances in the form of Barry White's "I'm Gonna Love You Just a Little Bit More," and the Commodores' "Just to Be Close to You." The Temptations, Billy Preston, and Gladys Knight & the Pips are all also represented. *—Andrew Hamilton*

Soul Classics: Best of the 80's / Mar. 30, 1998 / Rebound ✦✦
Soul Classics of the '80s is dominated by female vovalists, with the ladies taking the lead on seven of the 12 songs. Jocelyn Brown's "Somebody Else's Guy" is one of the better pure disco tunes recorded, and Aretha Franklin's "Jump to It," written by Luther Vandross, is a prime piece of urban soul. When you hear Mica Paris' lovely voice on "My One Temptation," you know you're in for a good time. The men hold court with Rick James exhorting his lover to "Give It to Me Baby," over a funky beat, while the Gap Band's "Early in the Morning" is a smoker with a positive message for lovers on the rebound. It's a good CD for people looking for the hits. *—Andrew Hamilton*

Soul Classics: Best of the 90's / Mar. 30, 1998 / Rebound ✦✦
Rebound's final volume of the *Soul Classics* series follows the same pattern of the pre-

vious three—12 soul songs from a single decade randomly picked and compiled on CD. At least the music is authentic, everything from Salt-N-Pepa's naughty "Shoop," to R. Kelly's seductive "It Seems Like You're Ready." Zhane's melodic, two-part harmonies, Johnny Gill's passionate baritone and Brian Knights' tenor, along with Shanice's enthusiasm, will keep you listening. If you like the hits, then this CD is for you. *—Andrew Hamilton*

Soul Classics: Solid Soul, Vol. 1 / May 28, 2002 / Solid Soul ♦♦♦
This compilation plays like an obscure Northern soul collection, only these tunes are mostly familiar. This is soul music with varying styles, from Joe Tex's "Hold on to What You Got" to cult favorite Paul Kelly ("Nine Times out of Ten") to Toots & the Maytals' reggae interpretation of Shep & the Limelites' "Daddy's Home." The radio edit of William DeVaughn's "Be Thankful for What You Got" is no prize, but overall the selections are good, with many cuts not readily available elsewhere (e.g., the Jive Five's "Sugar (Don't Take Away Candy)," the Sandpebbles' "Because," and Charles Brimmer's version of the Southern soul classic "That's How Strong My Love Is"). *—Andrew Hamilton*

Soul for Sale / Nov. 24, 1998 / Sequel ♦♦♦
This set collects U.K.-produced pop and soul music that will doubtless be unfamiliar to most folks outside the U.K. Originally released on Pye Records, these 30 tracks features rehashes of American soul like Leonard Whiting's "That's What Mama Say" (Walter Jackson); Bobby Rio's "Ask the Lonely" (the Four Tops); Jimmy James' "Ain't No Big Thing" (the Radiants); Doni Collins & the Showband's "I Can't Help Myself" (the Four Tops); and Felder's Orioles' "Back Street" (Edwin Starr). Petula Clark's the only household name, and many of the artists fall in the blue-eyed soul category. The original songs are interesting, but not enough so to capture fans in the States. *—Andrew Hamilton*

Soul Hits of the 70's / Mar. 30, 2000 / Sony ♦♦♦♦
Here's proof that it's possible to do a budget compilation (almost) exactly right. Sony Music Special Products' *Soul Hits of the 70's* surveys a decade in which what was then known as CBS Records practically had the market cornered on great soul music. In addition to boasting stars like Earth, Wind & Fire on its flagship Columbia Records label and Sly & the Family Stone on its Epic subsidiary, CBS maintained a manufacturing and distribution deal with Gamble & Huff's Philadelphia International Records, bringing in a raft of hits from its roster. And a sampling of some of the biggest of those hits is here, ten gold or platinum records out of 12 selections, eight of them R&B chart-toppers and three of the others Top Five hits. (And note that "Fight the Power," "T.S.O.P.," and "Bad Luck" are all presented in longer edits than were issued on the original singles.) The only ringer on the album is Earth, Wind & Fire's "Reasons," an LP track from the band's *That's the Way of the World* soundtrack album that was never issued as a single. It's a good song, but why is it here? If the compilers had just used, say, "Shining Star" instead, this would be a great collection for the money. As it is, it's just very good. *—William Ruhlmann*

Soul Men of Detroit / 1991 / Motorcity ♦♦♦
Another flawed but interesting collection of former Motown singers brought back to the studio under the watchful eye of Ian Levine and his Motorcity Records crew. The 36 tracks include one by Herman Griffin (Mary Wells' first husband), Billy Eckstine, Ivory Joe Hunter, Richard "Popcorn" Wylie, and a voice you've never heard before (and with good reason), Billy Reeves, Martha's brother. Top marks go to the late blues/soul singer Sammy Ward, whose gritty interpretations of "You Really Got a Hold on Me" and "Try It Baby" prove he was one of the genre's unheralded voices. *—Andrew Hamilton*

Soul of a Woman: 20 Soulful Ballads / Oct. 10, 1995 / Griffin Music ♦♦♦♦
This 20-song compilation explores female singers from Britisher Mica Paris to the jazzy Maria Muldaur. Shirley Brown's "Woman to Woman," Millie Jackson's heartfelt "(If Loving You Is Wrong) I Don't Want to Be Right," and a stinging rendition of "I'd Rather Go Blind" by Ruby Turner provide a good representation of Southern soul. Fallen Miss America Vanessa Williams displays flexible and charismatic pipes on "Dreamin'," and Dionne Warwicke's "Walk On By" sounds as majestic as ever. Mica Paris displays her undisputed talent on two selections: her hit "My One Temptation" and "Where Is the Love," a duet with Will Downing. Patti LaBelle, Minnie Ripperton, Aretha Franklin, Randy Crawford, and Dorothy Moore are also among the featured artists. The only prominent male voices are duet partners—Peabo Bryson, Downing, and James Ingram—and the Pips crooning behind Gladys Knight on "You're the Best Thing That Happened to Me." *—Andrew Hamilton*

The Soul of Detroit / 1992 / Relic ♦♦♦
The Soul of Detroit is 16 slices of the more energetic productions for Bob West's Lupine label. The late Joe Stubbs' two soulful rantings, "What's My Destiny," and "Hey, Hey," shows why companies sought him out to front groups; Joe sang with the Falcons, 100 Proof (Aged in Soul), the Contours, and the Originals. Eddie Floyd scored big at Stax records, but you won't recognize him on these early sides. Eddie sounded completely different when he sang with the Falcons, and on his pre-Stax singles. The Primettes' (later the Supremes) distinct voices can be heard on Gene Martin's "Lonely Nights" and Don Revel's "The Return of Stagger Lee." Betty Lavette's "You Killed the Love" is a haunting blues number; the Falcons add some flavorful backing vocals. Sir Mack Rice, who charted with "Mustang Sally" (later made popular by Wilson Pickett) does "Baby I'm Coming Home." The T. J. Fowler Combo shines on all the tracks. An essential item for collectors. *—Andrew Hamilton*

The Soul of Money Records / Jun. 11, 2002 / Kent ♦♦♦
Based in Los Angeles, the Money label issued a fair amount of soul music without getting much national exposure or pioneering a notable house sound, though they did have some success with the Larks and Bettye Swann. Those are the only two names (along with Ted Hawkins, more noted for his post-1980 recordings) from this 24-song compilation that will be reasonably well-known even to major soul fans (the Johnny Adams who has two songs was apparently an obscure local singer, not the same as the more famous Adams from New Orleans). Even Swann and the Larks are better represented by their own compilations on Ace. Here they're heard amidst some pretty average if pleasant and well-produced period soul music, most of it from the 1960s, and some from the early to mid-'70s. Los Angeles may be in southern California, but this sounds much like the urban soul of the northern U.S., with Motown as a notable influence for sure, though there are some similarities with the sounds of Chicago, New York, and Philadelphia. This is far from the least impressive of such collector-oriented anthologies, but it's a struggle to come up with any descriptive zest, positive or negative, for the sounds. Nothing's close to a lost gem; it's usually good-natured romantic soul, sometimes getting into dance-themed songs like the Larks' "The Temptation Walk" and the M&M's & the Peanuts' (that's their real name) "The Phillie." Ted Hawkins' 1966 Sam Cooke-like single, "Baby," might seem like a real rare find since he didn't become well-known until playing folky blues-soul as an album-oriented artist in the 1980s and 1990s, but actually it had already been reissued on his Rhino best-of, *The Ted Hawkins Story: Suffer No More*. Three of the tracks are previously unreleased, and actually include some of the best material here: the Question Marks' "Don't Drop It (That's My Love You've Got)" has a nice minor-keyed groove and doo wop harmonies, while Ted Walters' "If We All Were Rich" features his rich near-falsetto vocals and fine pop-soul production. *—Richie Unterberger*

Soul of Science: Compiled by Ian O'Brien & Kirk Degiorgio / Dec. 19, 2000 / BMG International ♦♦♦♦
Fortunate are the musicians whose knowledge and musical taste run so deep that the very presence of their names on a record sleeve is indicative of the quality within. *The Soul of Science* opens with a pleasing synth/jazz ambient piece by Ian O'Brien, but that is hardly the point of this compilation. Rather than showcase their own talents, O'Brien and fellow techno-jazz muso Kirk Degiorgio present a well-thought-out collection of jazz-funk numbers that spans the 30-year history of electronic soul music. Included are much-lauded names like Lonnie Liston Smith, David Axelrod, and Shuggie Otis, all artists whose unrestrained funk sound would become the template for modern computer music. This is a 400-level musical course, with Degiorgio digging up ultra-rarities like Herbie Hancock's "The Spook Who Sat by the Door," a never-released gem from the legendary composer that was taken directly off of a promotional flexi-disc. He also includes the godfather of electronic soul, Stevie Wonder, playing the world's largest custom synthesizer on the freakishly raw "I Love Every Little Thing About You," a much-sought-after record that Wonder recorded with his wife, Syreeta. More than a trip through the basement record bins, the curators highlight the modern relevance of these dusty discs. Degiorgio's own "Kaleidoscope" perfectly demonstrates his modern revision of electronic soul, with the primal urgency of the forerunners digitally locked into a synthetic loop that keeps the jazz roots perfectly preserved far into the future. Seiji's "Into the Now" does just that, revisiting the sounds and rhythms of the past to create a jazz-breakbeat groove that has gained much favor with contemporary listeners. No single compilation can claim to offer a definitive lesson in a music as diverse and wide reaching as electronic jazz, but O'Brien and Degiorgio have assembled a flawless collection that effortlessly triggers the music fan's number one weakness: the desire to seek out more of this stuff. *—Joshua Glazer*

The Soul of Vietnam / 1994 / Sony Music Special Products ♦♦
The topic is Vietnam and wars in general on this compilation. The album includes "Christmas in Vietnam," by Johnny & Jon, as well as "Marching Off to War," by William Bell. The best-known cuts are Martha & the Vandellas' "I Should Be Proud," and the Impressions' "Choice of Colors," which doesn't seem to have anything specifically to do with Vietnam, war or soldiering. This could have been better, musically, as Sony left off so many better and more appropriate songs. How could they have missed "He'll Be Back" and "I'm So Glad You Waited," by the Players, or "Greetings! This Is Uncle Sam," by the Monitors? Most puzzling, however, is the omission of "War" and "Stop the War Now," by Edwin Starr. *—Andrew Hamilton*

Soul Power / May 29, 2001 / Dome ♦♦♦
An alternative to rap: freestyle, contemporary R&B tailored for those seeking songs dealing with heart checks and love/relationship quagmires. The voices outshine the material, but that's because the voices are so superb, everyone's a singer's singer, and the vocalists are some of music's brightest lights. Feel Mica Paris' soul on "I Wish I Never Met You"—a sumptuous duet with Bobby Womack, Rahsaan Patterson's "Treat You Like a Queen," Beverlei "the Body" Brown's "Best Friend," Coolys Hot Box's smokin' "Friend of Mine," and others, including Denetria Chance, who holds a baptismal on the wrenching ""I Will Always Remember You," sounding uncannily like Aretha Franklin. Slide it in, select shuffle, and forget about it, cause all 16 tracks are together. *—Andrew Hamilton*

Soul Satisfaction: The Motown Connection / 2001 / Motown ♦♦♦♦♦
Soul Satisfaction: The Motown Connection is a compilation tailor-made for people who love the Motown sound but can't stand hearing the same old songs over and over. There are no hits or even familiar tunes, just 24 floor-filling Northern soul stompers. There are plenty of big names like Tammi Terrell, Junior Walker, Smokey Robinson & the Miracles, the Temptations, Marvin Gaye, Gladys Knight & the Pips, and Edwin Starr as well as some less familiar like the Monitors, Carolyn Crawford, and the Fantastic Four. Some of the highlights are Carolyn Crawford's dramatic "Forget About Me," the Fantastic Four's finger-poppin' "Can't Stop Looking for My Baby," Edwin Starr's urgent "Running Back and Forth," and Gladys Knight's show-stopping version of Bill Withers' "Who Is She (And What Is She to You?)." Although they all sound like they should have

been hits, most of the tracks compiled here were first issued as B-sides or tucked away as album tracks until Northern soul fanatics plucked them from obscurity. Two tracks that are of special note to devotees of the unusual are Stevie Wonder's string-filled and jaunty take on the Doors' "Light My Fire" (why so many artists chose to cover this mostly tuneless and pretentious tune is a bit of a mystery) and bop pioneer Billy Eckstine's foray into the Motown sound," (I Wonder Why) Nobody Loves Me," which is a surprisingly non-embarrassing venture. This disc plays like an alternative greatest hits of Motown. Anyone who loves that instantly recognizable sound will find this disc a joy from beginning to end. *—Tim Sendra*

Soul Sessions / May 28, 2002 / Giant Step ✦✦✦
Giant Step's *Soul Sessions* is a compilation, not a mix album, spotlighting tracks from a diverse cast of artists inspired by soul. (Anyone troubled by the nebulous definition of the word circa 2002 will find one from each of the artists in the liner notes, like this one from Donnie: "It neither hungers, breathes, fights, has color, race or gender.") The music is far better than the liners, pursuing the same earnest fusion of acid jazz, house, and contemporary R&B that's united global concerns from Tokyo to Munich to London to San Francisco. Ultra Naté, one of the finest contemporary R&B vocalists, opens with the lush, largely acoustic "Twisted." Working with Jonathan Maron as Atlantis, Giant Step regular Ron Trent delivers the highlight: "Future Love," an earthy fusion of Lonnie Liston Smith atmosphere and Roy Ayers' groove. Joe Claussell's house remix of "The Essence" features Herbie Hancock with Chaka Khan. The producer tracks account for roughly half of the compilation, though vocalists Carl Hancock Rux and Jody Watley both acquit themselves nicely. With deep grooves but a largely acoustic setting, *Soul Sessions* succeeds in pulling fans from all manner of genres: dance music, acid jazz, even vocal music. *—John Bush*

Soul Spectacular! The Greatest Soul Hits of All Time / Feb. 19, 2002 / Rhino ✦✦✦✦
If you've been collecting records for any length of time—from two months to two decades—chances are you already own a good chunk of the 88 songs on Rhino's 2002 four-disc box set, *Soul Spectacular! The Greatest Soul Hits of All Time.* If you're just assembling your collection, you may only have a handful of the songs here, so this cornucopia of classic singles, ranging from Ray Charles' "What'd I Say" to the Manhattans' "Kiss and Say Goodbye," may be a good foundation for your soul collection, since most songs here are stone-cold classics (although it must be said that it loses steam toward the end of the set, as it gives way to second-tier songs and artists). That said, if you have a record collection that's fairly large (at least 100 CDs) and an interest in soul, you WILL have almost everything you're interested in; if not, you know them well enough and you might not need them in your collection. This isn't necessarily a bad thing, but the entire collection is so predictable it's hard not to wonder what the point of this collection is. After all, this collection is so predictable that even the great songs seem sorta blah, because this plays as the most predictable oldies station ever. Again, if you're just looking for these hits, it's not a bad choice—these are good, clean masters and great songs—but otherwise there's not much use to this collection for seasoned collectors, since the liner notes aren't particularly detailed and you know pretty much every song by heart. *—Stephen Thomas Erlewine*

Soul Spectrum, Vol. 1: Compiled by Keb Darge and Dr. Bob Jones / 1998 / BBE ✦✦✦✦
Best-known for his compilations of obscure funk, Scottish DJ/record collector extraordinaire Keb Darge teams up with Dr. Bob Jones, his cohort in Britain's soul club scene, to deliver *Soul Spectrum*, a collection of equally rare soul sides. Much like Darge's *Legendary Deep Funk* and *Funk Spectrum* series, this is a hugely entertaining listen even if you're not an obsessive collector, thanks to Darge and Jones' superb taste and a sure sense of how to get a club audience moving. Following the same format that *Funk Spectrum* later would, Darge and his co-compiler each select ten of their favorite tracks. Most of these cuts are on the sweeter side of '70s soul, the sort of thing that Britain's Northern soul crowd prizes above all else. There's also some deeper, Southern-style material, and a few sides date from the '60s or the '80s, but for the most part, this is highly arranged, Motown- and Philadelphia-influenced soul, packed with horns, strings, and/or electric piano. Most of it comes from smaller independent labels, so it's not as slickly produced, even on the more disco-flavored tracks. Surprisingly, given his hard-core funk stance, Darge favors that disco-ish sound quite a bit, and his taste proves just as accurate in this area; Jones is more given to unearthing lost gems of female soul, including sides by Ronn Feaster, Kim Tamango, Patti Jo, and Jeanie Tracy, as well as a solo side by Zapp sideman Tony Troutman ("What's the Use"). The whole thing is remarkably consistent, making it an excellent purchase for '70s soul fans interested in digging for lost treasure. *—Steve Huey*

Soul Spectrum, Vol. 2: Compiled by Keb Darge / 1999 / BBE ✦✦✦✦
Soul Spectrum, Vol. 2 takes a different approach than its predecessor—instead of splitting up track-selection duties with a partner, as he did on the first volume and the entire companion series, *Funk Spectrum*, compiler Keb Darge goes it alone, culling all 20 tracks from his own vast collection of rare 45s. Darge does include some incredibly hard-to-find sides, but thankfully he has the good sense to pick appealing, danceable tunes. The result is a highly listenable compilation designed for the avid soul *fan*, not just the collector with a rarity fetish. There are no big—or even recognizable—names here save for the Whispers, who are present with the highly obscure single "As I Sit Here." But that's not the point; the point is to reclaim high-quality music that, for whatever reason (usually financial), didn't get a fair shake in its day. In this case, its day was probably the '70s, when the vast majority of these tracks were recorded. As such, most of them have the sort of sweet, smooth arrangements popular with British soul club patrons, but their origins—generally smaller independent labels—mean that they don't sound like processed studio creations. They're loaded with horns, strings, wah-wah guitars, keyboards, and funk or disco rhythms, in the best traditions of Gamble & Huff, Curtis Mayfield, and Earth, Wind & Fire. Both the style and quality are pretty consistent throughout, making *Soul Spectrum, Vol. 2* just as worthy a purchase as its predecessor for '70s soul fans looking to unearth some surprisingly good obscurities. *—Steve Huey*

Soul Weekender Anthems / Mar. 23, 1999 / Crimson ✦✦✦✦
This bouncy, 18-song compilation is filled with momentous grooves like McFadden & Whitehead's "Ain't No Stopping Us Now," the Whispers' "It's a Love Thing," Edwin Starr's "Contact," Gene Chandler's "Get Down," and other classy steppers including Patrice Rushen's "Forget Me Nots" and Quincy Jones' "Stuff Like That." *—Andrew Hamilton*

Soul Years of Minit Records: Struttin' & Flirtin' (1966–1969) / 1986 / EMI America ✦✦✦
For three years, from 1966 to 1969, Minit Records made a serious run for recognition on the soul charts. They made a fine effort, despite less than expected sales, and artists like Bobby Womack, the O'Jays and Ike & Tina Turner went on to bigger and better things elsewhere. The Young Hearts' "I Got Love for My Baby," made a big splash on the charts; it has a Far East-type opening and features Ronnie Preyer's sweet falsetto complemented by James Moore's rough, soulful tenor/baritone; it was their biggest hit and did quite well in many markets. Bobby Womack's "What Is This" and "How I Miss You" were well received by soul jocks but neither set the world on fire. The Players' track, "Get Right," is not their finest moment at Minit; why "He'll Be Back" or "I'm So Glad You Waited," superior pieces, were omitted is baffling. Homer Banks deep soul saga, "60 Minutes of Your Love," is a classic but fails to ignite his singing career. Other notables include Jimmy Holiday, Gloria Jones, Gene Dozier & Brotherhood, Alder Ray and Junior Parker. *—Andrew Hamilton*

Soulful Pop / Aug. 27, 1996 / Varese ✦✦✦✦✦
This is the kind of compilation that doesn't attract much critical attention, but is a pretty nifty concept: 17 songs from 1966-1976 that are soul-pop at its poppiest and most commercial, running the scale from R&B-grounded cuts to near-bubblegum. It's a good mix of classics of the micro-genre (the Foundations' "Build Me Up Buttercup" and "Baby, Now That I Found You," Jay & the Techniques' "Keep the Ball Rollin'," Maxine Nightingale's "Right Back Where We Started From"), minor half-forgotten hits (James & Bobby Purify's "Let Love Come Between Us," Chairmen of the Board's "You've Got Me Dangling on a String"), singles that were only big in England (Blue Mink's "Melting Pot," the Love Affair's cover of Robert Knight's "Everlasting Love"), and total flops (by the Groove & the Peoples Choice). Especially ingratiating are the Five Stairsteps' "O-oh Child" and Chee-Chee & Peppy's "I Know I'm in Love," a forgotten Jackson 5 imitation (and minor hit) from 1971. *—Richie Unterberger*

The Sound of Funk, Vols. 1-10 / Goldmine/Soul Supply ✦✦✦✦✦
Assembled by the U.K. label Goldmine/Soul Supply, *The Sound of Funk* is the most exhaustive deep funk compilation series on the market, spanning a total of ten volumes containing 16 tracks apiece. The vast majority of this material is taken from incredibly rare 45 rpm singles, often by groups too obscure to have recorded a full-length LP. It's a collector's dream, but these comps don't play like dusty archival pieces—the music is teeming with energy and enthusiasm, no matter how derivative of its influences it may be. Sure, there are plenty of James Brown knockoffs, but they're *fun* James Brown knockoffs, and if you're hard-pressed to name a style of music more infectious than funk, this stuff will grow on you at an alarming rate. It doesn't necessarily take great songwriting to make a great funk single, just a great groove and a little inspiration. The seemingly endless supply of obscure bands who could capture those ingredients is what makes *The Sound of Funk* such an addictive listen for devoted funk fans, even if they've never heard of the songs or artists present (and most people haven't). There's a whole lost chapter of grassroots musical history here, waiting to be rediscovered. At ten volumes, and with no liner notes, *The Sound of Funk* isn't the best introduction to deep funk; for that, go to *The Funky 16 Corners* or one of Keb Darge's more concise series (*Legendary Deep Funk* or *Funk Spectrum* are both excellent). But this series was the original chronicle; once you're hooked, snap up as many as you can while they're still available. *—Steve Huey*

Spike's Choice, Vol. 1: Desco Funk 45 Collection / Nov. 10, 1998 / Desco ✦✦✦✦✦
Classic '70s-style funk enjoyed a massive resurgence in popularity during the '90s, not only providing the basis for the vast majority of hip-hop recorded during the decade, but also becoming a party music of choice on college campuses otherwise dominated by politically correct alternative rock; moreover, funky jazz acts like Medeski, Martin & Wood moved into the good graces of neo-hippie, jam-band audiences, and even most alternative metal bands bore some semblance of the music's stamp, thanks to predominantly rock-oriented acts like Faith No More and the Red Hot Chili Peppers. So it's somewhat surprising, even with the advent of sampling technology, that a full-scale funk revival movement, centered around old-school bands who played live instruments, never quite took shape. Thankfully, the New York-based Desco Records, founded by Philippe Lehman and Gabriel Roth, moved in to fill that vacuum in 1997, releasing a series of 45 rpm records devoted to funk of every flavor. The company moved into the CD market in 1998, and anyone who missed out on those vinyl issues can easily catch up with *Spike's Choice: The Desco Funk 45 Collection*, which collects the A and B sides of the company's first 12 singles. The dominant influence here is James Brown, both in the straight-ahead, late-'60s-style funk of singers like Sharon Jones, Joseph Henry, and the masterful Lee Fields, and the J.B.'s-derived instrumentals by the Other Side and the label's house band, the Soul Providers. Elsewhere, the groundbreaking Ravi Harris and the Prophets deliver a trancey, sitar-driven variation on the sound, and the Sugarman Three proffer a greasy brand of soul-jazz boogaloo

reminiscent of artists like Lou Donaldson. It's all performed live, and it all sounds astoundingly authentic and organic, which makes this already enjoyable music even more infectious. Whether the singles collected on *Spike's Choice* prove to be the start of something big or not, they stand on their own as some of the funkiest of the decade. *—Steve Huey*

Spike's Choice, Vol. 2 / Jan. 18, 2000 / Desco ♦♦♦♦
Spike's Choice, Vol. 2 is the second CD collection of funk-revival label Desco's terrific limited-edition 45s, featuring the A- and B-sides of eight singles (all tracks are making their CD debuts). Aside from the Sugarman Three (who cover Lou Donaldson's "Turtle Walk") and Joseph Henry (who guests as lead vocalist for the otherwise instrumental, Meters-influenced Mighty Imperials), none of the acts were present on the first volume of *Spike's Choice*. The Daktaris open the collection with their brand of Fela Kuti-style Afro-funk, and there's old-style Southern soul from Naomi Davis and the Knights of 41st Street, who welcome guest organist Cliff Driver. Perhaps the most intriguing discovery, though, is the insane energy of the Unstoppable S. Robinson & His Marvelaires. The collection is highly recommended for old-school funk fans hungry for new material in the genre, especially those who enjoyed the first volume. *—Steve Huey*

The Spotlite on Colpix Records, Vol. 1 / 1995 / Collectables ♦♦♦
Part of Collectables' 1995 series, this brings together 13 tracks issued on the Colpix label, with one unreleased track ("Her Love" by the Alvans) thrown in to round things out. As such, it's an interesting set, with tracks from the Marcels ("Blue Moon" and "Goodbye to Love," both here in true stereo) bookending the set, and rarities from Tony & the Twilights, the Skyliners, Eddie Friend & the Empires, and Ronnie & the Relatives (an early incarnation of the Ronettes) completing the collection. There are no liner notes or recording information—typical of early Collectables packaging—but this is a nice chunk of great music nonetheless. *—Cub Koda*

Spotlight on Rama Records, Vols. 1-4 / Feb. 13, 2001 / Collectables ♦♦♦♦
Music industry legend George Goldner started Rama Records in 1953 as an outlet for R&B releases. Spread out over four discs, the 56 tracks here are a foot-tapping, heart-string-tugging look at the early days of R&B vocal groups. Tracks by the Crows, Wrens, and Valentines give the listener a history lesson and a rockin' good time. Some all-time classic vocal group tracks are here, like the incredible "Gee" by the Crows, "Woo Woo Train" by the Valentines, "Oo Wee Baby" by the Harptones, but mostly you get lots of solid songs performed with a lot of soul. Of special note to collectors are two rare tracks: a previously unreleased version of "The Bells" by the Pretenders and an outtake version of "Falling for You" by the Valentines. *—Tim Sendra*

Spotlite on Apollo Records, Vol. 1 / Jul. 25, 1995 / Collectables ♦♦♦
Apollo Records was an East Coast bastion of doo wop and R&B in the late '40s and early '50s, and this entry in Collectables' *Spotlite* series is the first volume examining the goodies found in their vaults. Big-ticket items here are the Cellos' "Rang Ting Ding Dong," the Delroys' insanely great "Bermuda Shorts," and the 5 Royales' "Laundromat Blues." But tracks like "My Heart's Desire" by the Opals, "A Star" by the Keynotes, "Angel of Romance" by the Claremonts, and the closer "Darling" by the Vocaltones, are just as emblematic of a sound and style as anything else on here. More street-corner classics from the Charmers, the Ambassadors, and the Larks complete the set. *—Cub Koda*

Spotlite on Apollo Records, Vol. 2 / Jul. 25, 1995 / Collectables ♦♦♦
This is the second volume in Collectables' *Spotlite* series focusing on doo wop and R&B treasures from the vaults of Apollo Records. Among the 14 tracks are a combination of tunes by familiar names like the 5 Royales, the Larks, and the Keynotes, along with obscurities including "The Fires Burn No More" (the Chesters), "Thrill of Romance" (the Gaytunes), and "Girlie That I Love" (the Cellos). Even though some of these tracks never gained national attention, they deserved to. *—Al Campbell*

Spotlite on Apollo Records, Vol. 3 / Feb. 27, 1996 / Collectables ♦♦♦
Rare doo wop and R&B classics from the archives of Apollo Records are the focus of this compilation, the third in the Collectables' *Spotlite* series. Among the 14 tracks are tunes by familiar names like the 5 Royales, the Larks, and the Keynotes, and obscurities including "Tired of You" by the Gentlemen, "The Night Has Come" by Billy Austin & the Hearts, and the novelty "The Be-Bop Mouse" by the Cellos. Lots of excellent doo wop rarities here, which certainly deserve wider circulation. *—Al Campbell*

Spotlite on Apollo Records, Vol. 4 / Feb. 27, 1996 / Collectables ♦♦♦
The final volume in Collectables' *Spotlite* series collecting rarities from the catalog of Apollo Records, this set features hard-to-find doo wop and R&B selections. Among the 14 tracks are tunes by familiar names like the Larks, the 5 Royales, and the Casanovas, along with obscurities including "Zup Zup (You Dance So Nice)" by the Keynotes, "Love Me" by the Romeos, and "The Juicy Crocodile" by Cellos. A fine package for doo wop enthusiasts looking for top-shelf rarities. *—Al Campbell*

The Spotlite on Capitol Records, Vol. 1 / 1995 / Collectables ♦♦♦
This compilation features assorted 1950s sounds originally released under the Capitol Records umbrella, including novelty, straight doo wop, and R&B from early pioneers, with Sammy Hagan & the Viscounts looming large on "Out of Your Heart," a romantic, deep "wop" accented by "shab-ba-da-dooms." Furthermore, Johnny Otis & Group does "In the Dark," which features a dynamic female lead. Nonsensical, rhythmic harmonies from the Five Keyes on "Ling Ting Tong" and tracks by a cast of crooners including the Passions and Norman Fox & the Rob Roys makes this an oldie delight. Note, though, that the Spinners, who do "Love's Prayer," are not the more famous Detroit Spinners of Motown and Atlantic Records fame. *—Andrew Hamilton*

The Spotlite on Capitol Records, Vol. 2 / 1995 / Collectables ♦♦♦
Part of Collectables' 1995 series, this brings together 14 tracks originally issued by Capitol Records. Although not particularly noted for their doo-wop releases, the label *did* venture into R&B waters from time to time, with tracks by the Five Keys, the Fascinators, the Edsels, the Notes, Sammy Hagan & the Viscounts, and Norman Fox & the Rob Roys (the moronic "Pizza Pie" must be heard to be believed) to show for their efforts. Selections from Paul Williams, Johnny Otis, Frank Polk, Anita Tucker, and Mel Williams—all with vocal-group backings—complete the collection. As usual, there are no liner notes or recording information—typical of early Collectables packaging—but the transfers are squeaky clean, emblematic of this label's devotion to top-notch product. *—Cub Koda*

Spotlite on Carlton Records, Vol. 1 / Sep. 24, 1996 / Collectables ♦♦♦
Carlton Records was an East Coast indie that delved into R&B and rock & roll in the '50s and early '60s, and this entry in Collectables' *Spotlite* series is the first volume to examine the goodies found in the Carlton vaults. Big-ticket items here are "Prince of Players" by Tommy Fredericks & the Hi-Notes, "Tell Me Little Girl" by the Spices, "Faithfully Yours" by the Imperials, "Simple Simon" by Chip & the Quartertones, and "Heaven" by the Alcoves. More street-corner classics from the Impacts, plus two tracks each from the Capitols, the Strollers, Morry Williams & the Kids, and the Royal Holidays complete the set. *—Cub Koda*

Spotlite on End Records, Vol. 3 / Oct. 25, 1994 / Collectables ♦♦♦
The third volume of *End Records* puts together an enjoyable program of original doo wop from the '50s. Some of the genre's most revered names are featured: the Flamingos, Little Anthony & the Imperials, and the Chantels, along with obscure material from the Uniques, the Tunemasters, and the Classmates. This reissue series from Collectables should please both doo wop collectors and novices alike. *—Al Campbell*

Spotlite on End Records, Vol. 4 / Oct. 25, 1994 / Collectables ♦♦♦
The final volume of the *End Records Spotlite* series is a great program of classic doo wop from the key labels of the vocal group sound of the '50s. Some of the genre's most revered names are featured: Little Anthony & the Imperials, the Chantels, the Flamingos, and Lymon Lewis & the Imperials. Also featured are obscure tracks from the Tunemasters, the Tunedrops, and the Classmates. A solid set which should please doo wop collectors as well as listeners dabbling in the genre. *—Al Campbell*

Spotlite on Gee Records, Vol. 3 / Oct. 25, 1994 / Collectables ♦♦♦♦
Another entry in their label "Spotlight Series," this is the third volume digging into the vault of New York's Gee Records. Big ticket items here include "Paper Castles," "I'm Not a Juvenile Delinquent," and a vastly different alternate take of "I Want You to Be My Girl" by Frankie Lymon & the Teenagers, "Earth Angel" and "Hey Babe" by the Cleftones, "Laura My Darling" by the Regents, "Strange As It Seems" by the Quintones, and "Change of Time" by the Emanons. No liners, but loads of great and rare doo wop sides make this a set worthy to add to any vocal group collection. *—Cub Koda*

Spotlite on Gee Records, Vol. 4 / Oct. 25, 1994 / Collectables ♦♦♦
This fourth volume in Collectables' *Spotlite* series still finds goodies galore from the vaults of George Goldner's Gee Records. Kicking off with the Cleftones' "Little Girl of Mine," the set also includes the Heartbeats' follow-up to their "A Thousand Miles Away," "500 Miles to Go," Frankie Lymon's "Goody Goody," and the Regents' original version of "Barbara Ann." Selections from the Vatones, the Emanons, the Mellokeys, the Clippers, and Carol Blades & the Harptones fill out the track lineup. Another solid entry, despite the lack of—like all the others in the series—any liner notes, recording or publishing information, but a pile of great doo wop anyway. *—Cub Koda*

Spotlite on Goldisc / Feb. 28, 1995 / Collectables ♦♦♦
Spotlite on Goldisc is an enjoyable compilation highlighting the golden age of doo wop. Included on this 20-song collection from the vaults of Goldisc are lost treasures by the Dreamers, the Three Ducanes, Cleo & the Crystaliers, Orlandos, the Five Stars, Mickey Toliver & the Capitols, and the Universals. This compilation is highly recommended for doo wop fans who want to go deeper into that genre. *—Al Campbell*

The Spotlite on Gotham Records, Vol. 1 / 1995 / Collectables ♦♦♦
Part of Collectables' *Spotlite* series, this collects 13 tracks originally issued by Philadelphia's Gotham Records, plus one unreleased outtake. Gotham was a hotbed for great, crude early doo wop, and this set does not disappoint, kicking off with the beautiful "God Only Knows" by the Capris and including such obscure gems as the Whispers' "Fool Heart," the Captans' "I Love You So," the Dreamers' crude "I Need a Girl," and the Gazelles' rocking "Pretty Baby Baby." Like the other volumes in this series, there are no liner notes or recording information—typical of early Collectables packaging—but the transfers are surprisingly clean, especially considering that most of the original Gotham masters are missing in action. *—Cub Koda*

Spotlite on Gotham Records, Vol. 2 / 1995 / Collectables ♦♦♦
Gotham Records was an East Coast bastion for doo wop and R&B in the late '40s and early '50s, and this entry in Collectables' *Spotlite* series is the second volume examining the goodies found in their vaults. Big ticket items here are "Just Suppose" by Lee Andrews & the Hearts, "Are You Sorry" by the Whispers, and "It's a Miracle" by the Capris. But tracks like "Have You Seen My Baby" by the Ballenaires, "Honest" by the Gazelles, and "Goodby Bella" by the Dreamers are just as emblematic of the label's sound and style as anything else on here. More street corner classics from the Cap-tans, the Kings, and Doris Browne complete the set. *—Cub Koda*

Spotlite on Hull Records, Vol. 1 / Oct. 25, 1994 / Collectables ♦♦♦
This is an excellent compilation from Collectables featuring New York-based doo wop and R&B. Even though some of the artists represented here never recorded huge hit records, Hull had consistently championed excellent performances nevertheless. The Avons, Sparks, the Beltones, and the Carousselles are represented. Also included are out-

takes of "Book of Love" by the Monotones and "True Love Affair" by the Elegants. This compilation should appeal to both collectors of the genre and those discovering the music for the first time. *—Al Campbell*

Spotlite on Hull Records, Vol. 2 / Oct. 25, 1994 / Collectables ♦♦♦
Part of Collectables' 1995 series, this brings together 12 tracks originally issued on the Hull label, along with two unissued outtakes. The big hit aboard is the Heartbeats' "A Thousand Miles Away," but gems like Jackie & the Starlites' "I Cried 100 Tears" the Elegants' "Getting Dizzy," Shep & the Limelites' "Our Anniversary" and "It's All Over Now," and the Avons' "Our Love Will Never End" and "You Are So Close to Me" are equally as fine. Selections from the Pastels, the Sparks, the Avons, Rockin' Bradley & the Rockers, the Monotones (including an outtake of "Legend of Sleepy Hollow") and an unissued side from the Desires complete the collection. As usual, no liner notes or recording information—typical of early shoddy Collectables packaging—but the transfers are very clean, many of them in real stereo. *—Cub Koda*

Spotlite on Josie Records, Vol. 1 / Jan. 14, 1994 / Collectables ♦♦♦
Vol. 1 in the compilation series *Spotlite on Josie Records* includes 14 tracks taken from the vaults of this East Coast label. Josie was a premier label for early doo wop. Highlights include original versions of Teardrops' "The Stars Are Out Tonight," Cadillacs "Wishing Well," and the Five Notes "You Are So Beautiful." If you're curious about doo wop beyond the tried-and-true hits, this compilation is a good place to start your investigation. *—Al Campbell*

Spotlite on Josie Records, Vol. 2 / Mar. 21, 1994 / Collectables ♦♦♦
The second volume in the *Spotlite on Josie Records* series includes 14 tracks taken from the vaults of the influential East Coast label, a key outlet for pioneering doo wop acts. Highlights include original versions of the Starlings' "Ebb Tide," the Teardrops "Ooh Baby," and an alternate take of the Chips' "Rubber Biscuit," a track that was revived in the '80s by the Blues Brothers. If you're curious about the more obscure sidestreets of doo wop, this compilation is a fine place to start expanding your listening horizons. *—Al Campbell*

Spotlite on Jubilee Records, Vol. 1 / Apr. 24, 1995 / Collectables ♦♦♦
The first volume of the *Spotlite on Jubilee Records* series is an enjoyable program of original doo wop from the '50s. Some of the genre's most revered names are featured: the Orioles, the Ravens, the Sultans, and the Dominoes. Also featured are obscure tracks from the 4 Tunes, the Marylanders, and the Enchanters. This reissue series from Collectables should please both doo wop collectors and novices alike. *—Al Campbell*

Spotlite on Jubilee Records, Vol. 2 / Apr. 24, 1995 / Collectables ♦♦♦
This is a nice collection of obscure tracks from Jubilee Records, with the spotlight on many of the vocal-group treasures lurking in their vaults. Unfortunately, as is usually the case with Collectables, there's no recording information or liner notes of any kind to illuminate when or where or how these incredible recordings were created. That aside, there are great sides aboard from the Marylanders, the Orioles, the 5 Sharps (their legendary recording of "Stormy Weather"), the Ray O Vacs, the Top Notes, the Ravens, the Bob Knight Four, the Dominoes (with a previously unissued version of "Take Me Back to Heaven"), and the Crows backing up trumpeter/singer Fat Man Humphries. Final verdict: great music with cheap, shoddy packaging. You make the call. *—Cub Koda*

Spotlite on Melba Records, Vol. 1 / Apr. 24, 1995 / Collectables ♦♦♦
Spotlite on Melba Records, Vol. 1 collects 14 tracks from the golden era of doo wop. Instead of providing a retread biggest-hits collection, this package goes much deeper, providing lost treasures from the Melba label by the Willows, the Rocketones, the Monarchs, the Legends, the Nutmegs, and the Tokens. This reissue series from Collectables is the perfect place for the curious doo wop novice to dig deeper into the genre. *—Al Campbell*

Spotlite on Port Records, Vol. 1 / Apr. 24, 1995 / Collectables ♦♦♦♦
These are obscure regional recordings from the vaults of the Port label. These doo wop and R&B sides received some regional attention, but never achieved the national successes initially hoped for. Among the 16 gems in this collection are two are early rare Impressions tracks, "Shorty's Got to Go" and "Listen." Also featured are tunes from the long-forgotten Suburbans, Eboniers, Dreamers, and Chancellors. Any fan of early rock & roll will want to search this out. *—Al Campbell*

Spotlite on Rama Records, Vol. 1 / Jan. 14, 1994 / Collectables ♦♦♦
Spotlite on Rama Records, Vol. 1 collects 14 tracks from the vaults of Rama Records. Instead of providing a re-treaded biggest-hits collection, this package goes much deeper by dusting off lost treasures from the Valentines, the Joytones, Jimmy Jones & the Pretenders, the Wrens, the Buccaneers, and the Rainbows. *—Al Campbell*

Spotlite on Rama Records, Vol. 2 / Mar. 21, 1994 / Collectables ♦♦♦
Spotlite on Rama Records, Vol. 2 collects 14 rare sides from the archives of Rama Records. Avoiding radio-worn oldies, this set digs in deep by dusting off obscure dusties from the Valentines, the Bells, the Pretenders, the Harptones, the Crows, and the Heartbeats. This reissue series from Collectables is a good start for doo wop fans eager to dig deeper into the genre. *—Al Campbell*

Spotlite on Roulette Records, Vol. 1 / Jan. 14, 1994 / Collectables ♦♦♦
Spotlite on Roulette Records, Vol. 1: Doo-Wop includes some of the more obscure songs from Roulette's vast catalog. One of the problems with doo wop compilation discs is they tend to feature the same well-known tracks over and over again. That isn't the case with this first volume in the series. Among the 14 tracks are lost treasures by the Martiniques, Darrell & the Oxfords, the Ly-Dells, Tiny Tim & the Hits, and the Domineers. There is a wealth of rare doo wop material just as enjoyable as the hits. On this compilation, the listener gets a second chance to discover some of them. *—Al Campbell*

Spotlite on Roulette Records, Vol. 2 / Mar. 21, 1994 / Collectables ♦♦♦
Spotlite on Roulette Records, Vol. 2: Doo-Wop collects more hard-to-find tunes from Roulette's achives. Most doo wop compilation discs tend to repeat the same well-known tracks ad nauseum, but even obsessives will find selections they're not likely to have heard before. Among the 14 tracks are lost treasures by the Devotions, the Shells, the Edsels, the Duponts, and the Turbans. There is a wealth of rare doo wop material just as enjoyable as the hits, and you can sample a handful of lesser-known classics on this disc. *—Al Campbell*

Spotlite on Sun Records, Vol. 1 / Aug. 27, 1996 / Collectables ♦♦♦
While many of the artists who recorded for Sam Phillips' Sun studio wouldn't obtain the legendary status as Elvis, Jerry Lee Lewis, or Carl Perkins, every tune recorded at that Memphis studio is worth hearing. The multitude of early- to mid-'50s gospel, R&B, and blues tracks recorded at Sun stand up to any classics of those genres. Among the many rediscovered treasures included in this package are songs by the Prisonaires, Five Tinos, Four Dukes, and the Jones Brothers. "Just Walkin' in the Rain" by the Prisonaires is the original version that Johnnie Ray would have a hit with around the same time. *—Al Campbell*

Spotlite on Warwick Records, Vol. 1 / Sep. 1, 1995 / Collectables ♦♦♦
By rights, this CD shouldn't get as high of a rating as it does; its 15 songs scarcely take up 35 minutes and there is zero annotation, the interior of the insert given over instead to promoting other parts of this series. But the sound is good, and the quality of the music coupled with the relatively low price make this a handy and enjoyable collection of R&B harmony vocal recordings. Included among the highlights are "Always" by the Distants, the precursors to the Temptations, which Warwick Records licensed from their Detroit company; the Genies' rocking and exquisitely danceable "Crazy Love," "Little Young Girl," and "Twistin' Pneumonia" from their final year together on Warwick and the alluring, ethereal ballad "No Greater Miracle"; "Hep Teenager," a hot dance track by the Harptones; and the early Tokens single "Tonight I Fell in Love." Dean Barlow, whose "Friendly People" is also included, calls to mind a young Tommy Hunt. And it's hard to quibble with a CD that ends on so gloriously upbeat a number as "Today" by the Eternals, which leaves a radiant glow in the room long after the disc has ended. More information on Warwick would've been nice, but this is still one cool collection. *—Bruce Eder*

Stax Gold / Nov. 8, 1998 / Stax ♦♦♦
Here are 15 reasons why Stax remains one of the great R&B/soul labels of the 1960s. Big ticket items aboard include Isaac Hayes' "Theme From Shaft," Otis Redding's "Try a Little Tenderness," Johnnie Taylor's "Who's Making Love," Jean Knight's "Mr. Big Stuff," the Dramatics' "What You See Is What You Get," and Booker T. and the MGs' "Time Is Tight." Rounding things out are top-notch selections from the Temprees, Shirley Brown, Frederick Knight, Albert King, Judy Clay and William Bell, the Bar-Kays, and the Emotions. *—Cub Koda*

Stax of Funk, Vol. 2: More Funky Truth / Aug. 9, 2002 / BGP ♦♦♦
This 21-track collection focuses on some of the more obscure and funk-oriented music Stax put out in the first half of the 1970s. There are a few big names here and there, though not represented by famous tracks, such as the Staple Singers, the Bar-Kays, Albert King, and Rufus Thomas, and more moderately famous performers like Sir Mack Rice, Inez Foxx, the Emotions, the Sweet Inspirations, and Jimmy McCracklin. But a lot of the music is by artists most won't have remembered as being on the Stax roster, or on any other for that matter. On the whole it's OK, but not first-division period soul-funk crossover, sometimes recalling other, bigger artists too obviously, as Bernie Hayes does James Brown on "Cool Strut" (complete with "hit it!" exhortations). The Emotions' "From Toys to Boys" certainly sounds influenced by the kind of very early-'70s Motown production heard on some Jackson 5 records, as do to a lesser degree a couple of the other songs. As for the better moments, the blues-tinged "Big Leg Woman" by Israel "Popper Stopper" Tolbert was an actual 1970 R&B Top 20 hit that doesn't show up on many compilations, and the Bar-Kays' "Cold Blooded" is a cool, largely instrumental James Brown-like tune whose arrangement bears influences from both Philly soul and Santana. There's also Albert King's curious 1974 funk remake of "Crosscut Saw." The one previously unissued track is Rufus Thomas' "Do the Side Saddle." *—Richie Unterberger*

The Stax Soul Sisters / 1988 / Stax ♦♦♦
These fourteen slices of Southern soul from Stax feature some of the legendary label's many female vocalists, with Linda Lyndell's poppin' "What a Man" (later redone into a mega hit by Salt-N-Pepa) as the most interesting cut. Memphis Queen Carla Thomas is ultra soulful on "Guide Me Well," which begins with a spoken narrative; and Mavis Staples emotes as only she can on the classic "Since I Fell for You." With three cuts, Jean Knight is the most represented artist; her million-selling "Mr. Big Stuff" heads a trio of tunes that includes "You Think You're Hot Stuff" (alias "Mr. Big Stuff 2"). A creative horn arrangement colors Mabel John's "Running Out" and Inez Foxx's no-nonsense delivery of "The Time"—the old Baby Washington hit strikes as deep as the original. If you like Southern soul, you'll enjoy this set; if you're just a casual Southern fan, go for a compilation with more hits. *—Andrew Hamilton*

Steppin Across the U.S.A., Vol. 2 / May 28, 2002 / Steppin Muzak ♦♦♦
Steppin Across the U.S.A., Vol. 2 balances the work of known names with songs true to the stepping style. Contributions from the Temptations figure in here, even though they aren't often synonymous with stepping. The '80s work of several former Temptations—Dennis Edwards' great solo debut, "Don't Look Any Further," and David Ruffin and Eddie Kendricks' 1987 duet "Don't Know Why You're Dreaming"—show up here. Even better is 1992's "The Jones" from the Temptations, which is a perfect stepping record and one of the group's best early-'90s efforts. *Steppin Across the U.S.A., Vol. 2* also offers some truly innovative and vital music from lesser-known artists, like Loose Change's "Rising

Cost of Love," and bona fide classics of the genre, such as Jeffree's "Love's Gonna Last" and "Mr. Fix It." One of the later entries, Identity Crisis' cover of "Sing a Simple Song," is bass heavy and Soul II Soul-styled and very stepping-friendly. Despite all of the great songs included, there's little cohesion, but this compilation is a great place to find some rare songs, even if the overall selections seem scattershot. *—Jason Elias*

Steppin Across the U.S.A., Vol. 3 / May 28, 2002 / Steppin Muzak ♦♦♦
Steppin Across the U.S.A., Vol. 3 seems to zero in on the late '70s and '80s, featuring songs that will actually get stepping aficionados on the floor. Like the other volumes, this is not sequenced in chronological order and often spans decades at a time. The oldest track, Gabor Szabo's "Keep Smiling," produced by Bunny Sigler, is itself worth the admission. Hubert Laws' "Family" may give credence to the fact that the most elegant stepping music did indeed come from the late '70s. Like the other sets, *Steppin Across the U.S.A., Vol. 3* throws in a few rare tracks to please collectors. The rarest gem here has to be Hinton Battle and his 1984 song "Super Cautious Girl." Bernard Wright's "Won't You Let Me Love You" is right behind it. Believe it or not, those aren't the biggest surprises here. Ray Parker's ambient instrumental flip side from his 1987 Geffen album *After Dark*, "After Midnight," is a brilliant addition; it is well loved and always garnered lots of radio play. One of the better and interesting volumes of the series, *Steppin Across the U.S.A., Vol. 3* should appease stepping fans and collectors alike with its rare finds. *—Jason Elias*

Steppin Across the U.S.A., Vol. 4 / May 28, 2002 / Steppin Muzak ♦♦♦
Unlike the previous volumes, *Steppin Across the U.S.A., Vol. 4* goes back to the '60s for the majority of its songs. While that does seem like a prudent idea on the surface, a lot of this music isn't for the faint of heart, with depressing qualities that aren't conducive to cutting a rug. By far the best of the lot, the Monitors' "Say You," with its lead by Richard Street, has the automatic charge of lesser-known though potent Motown. While the Isley Brothers certainly had their fair share of songs good for stepping, *Steppin Across the U.S.A., Vol. 4* gets in the way-back machine for its Isley Brothers entries. Both "Standing on the Dancefloor" and "Write to Me" are shout 'n' shimmy ditties that would only appeal to hardcore R&B fanatics. Tracks like Jan Bradley's "I'm Over You," "Oh Cindy" from the Vibrations, and Bertha Tillman's "Oh My Angel" seem a bit slow and depressing to be stepping faves. It hardly matters. *Steppin Across the U.S.A., Vol. 4* won't make many listeners hit the dancefloor, but it's a fair set of little-known (though potentially grating) R&B songs. *—Jason Elias*

Steppin Across the U.S.A., Vol. 5 / Jun. 25, 2002 / Steppin Muzak ♦♦♦
Sure, some of the previous volumes of the *Steppin Across the U.S.A.* series missed the mark, but that's no reason to discount this set. This collection is close to the skill of the third volume and brings more rare essentials to the table. The opening track, "Da Backseat" mix of Bobby Brown's "Good Enough," is a good way to start things off. Of course, that track and Lil' Louis' "Nyce & Slo" pale in comparison to the more genuine songs that fit into the stepping zone. James Brown's 1975 hit "Super Bad, Super Slick, Pt. 1" has the perfect beat and all but makes this volume worthwhile. Like the other volumes, this includes some tracks that are more balladic than dance-friendly. Pharoah Sanders and Phyllis Hyman's classic "As You Are" and Dee Dee Sharp's cover of 10cc's "I'm Not in Love" seem incongruous for this compilation, but they certainly sound great. On the other hand, two duds from the Moonglows and the Supremes really should have been replaced by a strong '70s song like Ben Vereen's "I'll Keep My Light in My Window." Vicious' "Nika" holds up the end of the newer tracks. *Steppin Across the U.S.A., Vol. 5* isn't comprehensive or consistent, but it does offer several worthwhile tracks. *—Jason Elias*

Still Paying Our Dues / 1999 / Kent ♦♦♦♦♦
Another sparkling Kent compilation; most of the 25 tracks are from the Atlantic/Atco family of labels,with a few from Stax/Volt. The cross section of tunes features a mixture of good and bad, like the Ambassadors' "I've Got to Find Happiness," a bad Motown imitation, and Wendy Rene's "Bar-B-Q," a lackluster Michael Jackson-styled novelty. Worthwhile tracks includes the Pointer Sisters' "Send Him Back," Al Perkins' "Nothing's Impossible," Ben E. King's "What Can a Man Do," Archie Bell & the Drells' "Here I Go Again," and "Please Operator" by Tony & Tyrone. Kent CDs always contain colorful, informative booklets that enhance the listening. *—Andrew Hamilton*

Stone Soul: San Francisco's Loadstone Label / May 11, 1999 / Kent ♦♦♦
Loadstone, run by bus driver Walter Curry Stone, issued sporadic soul singles in the 1960s and 1970s without getting any strong sellers, although "Country Woman" by the Cals (which is not on this anthology) saw some regional action in 1962. This is a 24-track collection of the label's output, with just one effort by the relatively well-known singer Jean Knight (whose 1976 cut was done long after her sole big hit "Mr. Big Stuff"). Sly Stone to the contrary, the San Francisco area did not have a large or notable soul scene. This collection would not hold water as part of a convincing argument that the Bay Area contained its share of lost soul nuggets. It's average-to-below-average period soul, stepping from girl group, doo wop-styled efforts by the Chandeliers (some of the highlights, actually) and mid-'60s soul to somewhat more funky, bluesier-edged outings from the early '70s and partial-disco tunes from the mid- to late 1970s, some of which are pretty mediocre. There's a mild chuckle to be had, perhaps, from Charles Leonard's "A Funky Driver on a Funky Bus," written by Walter Curry Stone and based on his experiences as an employee of San Francisco's public transit system. Jacqueline Jones does a decent job with her Southern-flavored, early-'70s soul outings (a couple of which were likewise penned by Stone), and Paula Lamont's previously unissued "Swimming Partners" has a nice bluesy moodiness. On the other hand, Herman H. Harper II's "Inseparable"—from the late '70s, according to the liner notes, although it sounds like urban contemporary crud of a much later vintage—is as lousy a cut as any that have graced Kent compilations, which is really saying something given how many of them there have been. By the way, the sole Loadstone single by Sly Stone, "I Can't Turn You Loose"/"I Ain't Got Nobody" (actually licensed from 1967 demos made at Golden State Recorders), is not included. *—Richie Unterberger*

Stoned Alchemy / 1989 / Charly ♦♦♦
Here's an interesting idea for a collection: the original versions of 27 R&B songs that were covered by the Rolling Stones in the studio or on-stage. This is more than just a clever gimmick for a compilation, however. In addition to providing insight into the development of the Rolling Stones' music, this is also a first-rate collection of classic blues, soul, and early rock & roll. Highlights include "The Red Rooster," a slow blues number featuring Howlin' Wolf's legendary guttural moan; Gene Allison's soul ballad "You Can Make It If You Try"; and Bo Diddley's "Pretty Thing," which inspired British guitarist Dick Taylor to form the Pretty Things. Note that a couple selections are not the actual original versions of the songs, including Muddy Waters' "Got My Mojo Working" (first recorded by Ann Cole) and Bobby Womack's "It's All Over Now" (a re-recording of a song he wrote). *—Todd Kristel*

Street Corner Essentials / Oct. 23, 2001 / Hip-O ♦♦♦♦
Hip-O's 2001 release, *Street Corner Essentials*, intends to showcase many of the greatest doo wop singles of the genre's classic period—namely the late '50s and early '60s. This doesn't mean just the biggest hits; as a matter of fact, the compilers divide this 50-track, double-disc collection down the middle, devoting the first disc to "The Hits" and the second to "The Rare Sides." Since it primarily draws from the Universal vaults, this doesn't contain every great doo wop side, and there are several songs, such as "Happy Happy Birthday Baby" and "Little Darlin'," that aren't represented by the biggest hit versions. And if you want to get technical about it, a bunch of songs toward the end of disc one (and some of disc two) aren't strictly doo wop either, at least by the most rigid definition of the style. That doesn't mean this is a con, though. Hardly. While Rhino's *The Doo Wop Box* remains the classic summary/introduction to this music and its two sequels get nearly all the other great songs, this is where a lot of listeners—those who love this music dearly, but aren't obsessive—should turn next, since even if there is some duplication with that set, it's not that much and the singles on disc one are by and large very good. Then, there's that glorious second disc, which will please those aforementioned fans and the obsessive, since it is song-for-song stronger or equal to the first, and it has the added bonus of all the songs making their U.S. debut on CD. There may not be anything here that is a flat-out knockout, but every one of these rather obscure sides—some by names as familiar as the Crests with their "16 Candles" sequel "You Blew out the Candles"; some by names quite obscure; and some just plain curiosities, like an early single by Jimmy Castor (later known for such gonzo-funk anthems as "Bertha Butt Boogie" and "Trogolodyte")—provides great listening for the ferociously dedicated and casual doo wop lover alike. That might not quite make it essential, but *Street Corner Essentials* still would be welcome in any collection of classic R&B. *—Stephen Thomas Erlewine*

Street Grooves / Sep. 3, 2002 / Fantasy ♦♦♦♦
This is a solid, top-to-bottom compilation of the crossover jazz that blossomed in the 1970s, also known as groove jazz. Different than the soul-jazz of the 1960s it grew out of, the groove jazz that came out of the '70s and '80s was deeply entwined in funk and R&B—in many cases inseparable from it. Perhaps the best case for this is on the album's opener, "Happy Music" by the Blackbyrds, a group who grew out of Donald Byrd's album by the same name and was led by trombonist George Bohannon and saxophonist Ernie Watts and featured Merry Clayton on vocals. "Happy Music" was a smash 12-inch that was played on dancefloors all over the country and in Europe, but also featured enough of the jazz idiom in its rhythmic sophistication to not be called a straight funk number. On the following "Black Byrd" by Donald Byrd, we can see just how far the trumpeter was willing to take his integrated vision of jazz, funk, and soul. Produced by Larry Mizell, "Black Byrd" is the most quintessential Detroit jazz funk track, rooted in a step-down groove, with killer piano fills by Joe Sample (one of two electric pianos on the cut) and Byrd's trumpet providing an in-the-pocket groove mode for hand percussion and Harvey Mason's slip-beat drumming. Byrd's trumpet is placed through layers of effects bleats like Miles Davis' on *Bitches Brew*, but carries the outside melodic fringe the whole way. Other cuts here are also classics of the genre: Patrice Rushen's awesome "The Hump," with its off-kilter bassline; Stanley Turrentine's "Hope That We Can Be Together Again Soon"; the Hank Crawford/Jimmy McGriff collaboration "The River's Invitation," built on Percy Mayfield's original vocal number; and McGriff's excellent read of Fats Domino's "I'm Walkin'," which is drenched in funky soul power. The album closes with the Three Pieces' Philly-drenched "I Need You Girl," a vocal track with a harmony chart that is as sophisticated as any in jazz. The music here may be commercial music, or at least it was then, but it is full of a quality of presentation and musical sophistication that keeps it well within the jazz family album. *—Thom Jurek*

Street Jams: Back 2 the Old Skool / Feb. 16, 1999 / Rhino ♦♦♦♦
This essential box set contains all three volumes of *Street Jams: Back 2 Old School* that Rhino previously issued as single discs, plus another disc of mostly '50s and '60s oldies that includes Frankie Lymon & the Teenagers' "I Want You to Be My Girl," the Drifters' "Up on the Roof," and the Cadillacs' "Speedo." Also featured are songs you know and love but may not have, like Vaughn Mason's "Bounce, Rock, Skate, Roll," Bootsy Collins' underrated "Body Slam," with its wicked bass and lead guitar lines, Twennynine's "Peanut Butter," and Tom Browne's "Funkin' for Jamaica"—and that's the short list. There's much more. This amazing set contains 52 full-strength jams, commencing with "Dazz" by Brick and ending with "Superfly" by Curtis Mayfield. *—Andrew Hamilton*

Sugar Hill Club Classics / Apr. 20, 1999 / Import ♦♦♦♦♦
Sequel's impressive *Sugar Hill Club Classics* collection focuses less on the label as a

hip-hop pioneer and more on how Sugar Hill fit into the fraternal, interconnected club culture around New York City during the early '80s. After the disco era lost steam amidst a wave of commercial imitations, the dance scene splintered and went underground. At the same time, hip-hop began moving downtown from the South Bronx and gradually assimilated into all the other dance styles then current, from go-go to electro to R&B to funk to the last remnants of disco. Even though *Sugar Hill Club Classics* includes all the obvious hip-hop must-hears—"Rapper's Delight," "The Adventures of Grandmaster on the Wheels of Steel," "White Lines (Don't Do It)," "The Message," and "Monster Jam"—it also features a raft of more obscure, club-oriented cuts like the bomb-dropping "Spoon'nin Rap" by Spoonie Gee, "Pump Me Up" and "Drop the Bomb" by Trouble Funk, "Mosquito (aka Hobo Scratch)" by West Street Mob, and "We Got the Funk" by Positive Force (none of which appear on Rhino's massive five-disc box *The Sugar Hill Records Story*). *—John Bush*

The Summer of Sam / Jun. 29, 1999 / Hollywood ♦♦♦♦
Spike Lee has never shied away from controversy, but *Summer of Sam* seems like one picture that didn't warrant the undue attention it received. Labeled as exploitation before it even hit the theaters, the film captured the frenetic, paranoia that infused New York during 1977, when the serial killer David Berkowitz was loose. *Summer of Sam* was about the summer of 1977, so it's only appropriate that his soundtrack was filled with songs from that summer. True, he bends the rules a bit, but only by including oldies (besides, it's hard to argue that the Who's "Baba O'Riley" was not used effectively in the film). And although he does have a punk rocker as a central figure in the film, there's no punk on the record, which is for the best, since this blend of disco, funk, pop, and rock (including such unheralded chestnuts as Roy Ayers' "Running Away," Machine's "There but for the Grace of God Go I," and Peter Brown's "Dance With Me") makes for a coherent, enjoyable record. Yes, many of these songs do appear on a number of other soundtracks—"Best of My Love" and "Fooled Around and Fell in Love" were indelibly used in Paul Thomas Anderson's '70s epic, *Boogie Nights*, for instance—but they are also integral to Lee's film. Besides, they help make *Summer of Sam* an entertaining listen. Considering the film's subject matter, that may be a little ironic, but it's hard to deny that as a record, *Summer of Sam* is fun. *—Stephen Thomas Erlewine*

Superbad!: The Soul of the City / May 7, 2002 / Time Life ♦♦♦♦
If you are looking for a rock-solid collection of superfly '70s funk and soul, you could do a lot worse for yourself than picking up *Superbad!: The Soul of the City*. So many of the big hits are here: Isaac Hayes' "Theme From Shaft," War's "Low Rider," James Brown's "The Big Payback," and the O'Jays' "Back Stabbers." Plus there are a couple of less well-known artists who contribute great songs: Joe Simon with "Theme From Cleopatra Jones" and William DeVaughn with "Be Thankful for What You Got." Listeners are most definitely in for a funky good time when they slide this into their CD player. A complaint one might have is that there is not a single female artist in sight. Here are a few names: Betty Wright, Lyn Collins, Laura Lee, and Aretha Franklin. It seems a crime not to have included at least one of these funky females. Another complaint would be that instead of having two tracks by James Brown and two by the Temptations, the compilers could have found a spot for another worthy funk artist—like Lyn Collins, for example. Still, if you want some funk this is a good place to start. Just make sure you get some Betty Wright too. *—Tim Sendra*

SuperFunk2. / Mar. 13, 2001 / BGP ♦♦♦♦
BGP scoured far and deep for the 20 funk rarities (three previously unissued), spanning the mid-'60s to the late '70s, that comprise this CD. None of these artists made a notable splash as funk or soul artists, although a few—Pee Wee Crayton, Preston Epps, Johnny Otis, and Joe Houston—had early R&B/blues/rock hits in the 1950s and are represented by obscure and highly atypical ventures into funk. Given how many rarity compilations in all genres aren't as musically exciting as they are rare, it's a nice surprise to find much excellence on this anthology, which can be heartily dug by most rock listeners, not just funk devotees. If nothing else, it's a testament to just how wide and serious James Brown's influence was during this period. Billy Garner's "Brand New Girl," Granby Street Development's "Jelly Roll" (with the incredibly lewd female spoken interjection "that cat looks so good to me/he can have his jelly roll free!"), and Jackie Harris' "Do It, Do It" all kick up a funk fuss, much like what Brown and the J.B.'s did during their prime, and Freddy Wilson's "Promised Land" is one of the most accurate vocal imitations of Brown you'll find. Still, the grooves are so intense and compelling that you don't really mind that these tracks are quite derivative of the soul/funk godfather. Although many of the cuts are instrumental, also on hand are some fair female vocal numbers by the likes of Brenda George, Thelma Jones, and Irene Reid, though it are the wordless numbers that generate the most heat. For some variation, there are some wah-wah, fuzz and phasing effects in Sidney Pinchback's "Soul Strokes" that show the influence of psychedelia, while Willard Burton's "Warm the Pot ('Til It's Good and Hot)" has the sort of more jagged rhythms and warped textures that came into vogue with Stevie Wonder and Rufus. Joe Houston, known for his blues/R&B playing, blows as athletically as anyone in the J.B.'s horn section on "Mr. Big H," which bears a 1977 date but sounds much more like a 1969-1970 recording. It's a very cool collection that should be at the top of the list for those who've exhausted the major funk icons and are looking for undiscovered nuggets. *—Richie Unterberger*

SuperFunk3. / Jun. 11, 2002 / BGP ♦♦♦♦
The previous *SuperFunk* volumes have not been stuffed with many (or indeed have had hardly any) household names, and *SuperFunk3.* upholds the series tradition of super-rare and pretty high-quality late-'60s and early-'70s funk. Lowell Fulson and maybe Preston Love will be reasonably familiar names to learned soul fans, but otherwise you have to be pretty in with the funk collecting in-crowd to have heard any of these artists or particular tracks before. (Indeed, three of the tracks are previously unreleased.) It's true enough that some of this blends together in the songs' resemblances to more famed early funk work by the likes of James Brown (as does Preston Love's "Cissy Popcorn"), Dyke & the Blazers, and various blaxploitation soundtrack contributors. But it's still a pretty high-class assortment, guaranteed to impress friends if they're into this sort of thing, yet also reasonably pleasing to more fly-by-night listeners. As for some of the more interesting cuts, Cat Scream's "Li'l Buck" has some real slick high-speed jittery funk guitar, Dave Hamilton's "Take Care of Your Own Business" has a welcome bluesy harmonica and mildly Howlin' Wolf-like vocal delivery, Chico & Buddy's "Ain't It a Groove" has a more AM play list-friendly sound than most (with those Philadelphia-like vibraphones), and the Soul Senders' "Soul Brothers Testify" has some scorching Jimi Hendrix-influenced guitar. *—Richie Unterberger*

Sweet Soulful Chicago / 1987 / Kent ♦♦♦
This collection is the type of album soul music fanatics drool over, but casual fans have little interest in. Otis Leavill's chirpy, skippy "I Love You" is the only song that made any significant impact on the charts (number-ten R&B and number 64 pop), while many of these selections are virtually impossible to find on 45 rpm. Most of the artists here made few recordings, so various-artists collections like these are the only place to find these songs. "You Got Me Walking," an excellent example of Chicago soul by little-known Cicero Blake, was recorded in 1967 but never saw daylight until this release; an obscure Gene Chandler side, "My Baby's Gone," didn't escape the vaults until 1986 via his *Sixties Soul Brother* LP on Kent Records. Die-hard Esquire fans didn't know about "The Feeling's Gone" until this release because the 1968 recording was buried on the B-side of the inferior "Why Can't I Stop." Other goodies include former Artistic lead singer Marvin Smith's final solo release for Brunswick, "Hold On," and Billy Butler's "Help Yourself." Erma Franklin, Barbara Acklin, LaVern Baker, Walter Jackson, Tyrone Davis and others are represented on the 16 underexposed tracks. *—Andrew Hamilton*

Sweet Sound of Success / 1995 / Kent ♦♦
This Kent Records reissue of many of Sceptor's and Wand Records' minor soul numbers from the '60s makes a nice companion to Capricorn Records' more ambitious, three-disc collection of the New York-based label's big soul and pop hits. Even without many of the chart toppers from the Shirelles, Dionne Warwick, and—less disturbingly—B.J. Thomas, there is a large store of solid soul gems here by the Esquires, Brooks O'Dell, the Diplomats, and Chuck Jackson. Jackson's classic performances on "Hand It Over" and "Look Over Your Shoulder" provide some of the collection's high points, but more askew tunes like Lenny Miles' bubblegum and soul number "Invisible" and Timmy Shaw's R&B-surf workout "If I Catch You" provide obscurities not generally found on hit collections. The songs here, in fact, fall somewhere between the slick productions of Motown and the rougher yet more intriguing output from smaller soul labels like Groovesville and Calla; the gap is bridged explicitly by the appropriation of Martha & the Vandellas' "Dancin' in the Streets" on Freddie Hughes' earthy and loose "He's No Good." Add some more quality well-known (Big Maybelle) and not so well-known (Roscoe Robinson) contributions, and you've got a solid collection of soul material in this Kent compilation. *—Stephen Cook*

Sweet Stuff: New Jersey Soul / Oct. 24, 1994 / Sequel ♦♦♦
Sequel named this baby right, 17 sweets from All Platinum/Stang Records with eight tracks from Baltimore, MD's, Whatnauts, including their creamy "I'll Erase Your Pain," "Please Make The Love Go Away," and "Friends By Day (Lovers By Night)," all essentials, with "What's Left to Give" and "He's Gone to Another" the only omissions from their repertoire. Includes Brother to Brother's great version of Gil Scott-Heron's "In the Bottle" and two by Candi Staton: "Hurry Sundown" and "Suspicious Minds." First Class, a Baltimore-based group like the Whatnauts, does "Count on Me" in typical D.C./Baltimore style. The O'Jays' "Peace" features an opening intro by the late William Powell, followed by a freedom marching vocal from Ed LeVert on a song they first recorded on Saru Records prior to the Philadelphia International phenomenon. *—Andrew Hamilton*

Sweet Taste of Sin: Sensual Breakbeat Soul / 2001 / BGP ♦♦♦
Although the packaging markets this to collectors, producers, and DJs looking for samples to plunder, to the layperson it might be better described as a compilation of obscure sweet soul from the mid-'70s to the early '80s. (Phillip Mitchell's "I'll See You in Hell First" bears a 1990 date, but sounds as if it was recorded considerably earlier.) There are a few hitmakers here, like Betty Everett, Shirley Brown, Isaac Hayes, Johnny "Guitar" Watson, the Detroit Emeralds, and Millie Jackson, but none are represented by hits, and most of the other names will challenge the memory banks even if you were avidly listening to black radio at the time. It's just average soul of the period, though, distinguished from many other compilations by its focus on a later era than most, and by an unabashed willingness to treat soul productions with sweet strings and slick arrangements as worthy of reinvestigation. Some tracks are better than others, like Coffey's "Sweet Taste of Sin," with his trademark funky guitar licks; Mitchell's "I'll See You in Hell First," which has a vibe akin to 1970s Curtis Mayfield; and Jackson's "It Hurts So Good," which plays it straighter than the risqué material for which she's known. This washes down easier than many sweet soul records if only because it's not overly familiar, but it can't be denied that it also reflects an era in which the soul genre itself became more saccharine and less interesting. *—Richie Unterberger*

Swingin' Talkin' Verve / Nov. 10, 1998 / Polygram ♦♦♦♦
Verve was never much of a label for the kind of music that would sound familiar to those looking for a good swing-revival compilation. Still, the label scoured its vaults and came up with *Swingin Talkin Verve*, a variant on their usual series of proto-acid jazz (read: soul-jazz, Afro-Cuban, jazz-funk, etc.). The results aren't bad at all, although several of the tracks don't date from the '40s golden age of swing. Included are Gene Krupa's "Let

Me Off Uptown," Buddy Rich's "Jumpin' at the Woodside," Quincy Jordan's "Air Mail Special" and Harry James' "Back Beat Boogie." *—Keith Farley*

Tamla Motown Connoisseurs / 1994 / Spectrum ♦♦♦
This is the real deal, a variety of rare and obscure tracks recorded at Hitsville USA (with the Funk Brothers laying down the rhythms), most of which first appeared on albums or as B-sides, while others like the Contours' "It's Growing" and Tammi Terrell's "Long Lonely Town" were never issued at all in the States. Stevie Wonder's "Hey Love," a loping pearl of a beat ballad, is the most arresting song onboard; with the Originals' "Don't Stop Now," Chris Clark's rendition of Frank Wilson's "Do I Love You (Deed I Do)," and Junior Walker & the All-Stars' gutsy "Ain't That the Truth" almost as compelling. You may not be familiar with the songs, but most of these voices are instantly recognizable. Even non-connoisseurs will enjoy having this fine collection around. *—Andrew Hamilton*

Tamla Special No. 1 / 1962 / Motown ♦♦♦
This album marks Motown's first collection of different artists. Nine songs makes for a slim set, but it's an item for collectors because of three scarce recordings. The sole 45 featuring Singin' Sammy Ward and Sherri Taylor, "Oh Lover"/"That's Why I Love You So Much" is certainly rare enough. Motown never released any other sides by Taylor; while Ward had more releases, none were hits, and he's unknown to casual music fans. The other rare bird is the flip of Barrett Strong's "Money," "Oh I Apologize"; though "Money" charted for Barrett, Motown never released an album by him. "Apologized" is a bluesy, begging ballad written by Smokey Robinson and Berry Gordy that suited Strong's rough tenor. The other tracks aren't hard to find and have been stuck on innumerable compilations. *—Andrew Hamilton*

Tamla Motown Early Classics / 1996 / Motown ♦♦♦
This sweet assemblage doesn't live up to its title, but is still a good one to add to your collection, since it contains several had-to-find Motown titles. "Wait 'Till My Bobby Gets Home" by Martha & the Vandellas, Michael Jackson's "People Make the World Go 'Round," and Mary Wells' "He's the One I Love" were all latter-day album cuts which never saw release as singles. Only the Supremes' "Come See About Me," the Four Tops' "Baby I Need Your Loving," and to a lesser extent Marvin Gaye's "Can I Get a Witness" truly classify as early classics. The rest—tunes by Edwin Starr, the Isley Brothers, the Jackson 5, the Miracles, and Jimmy Ruffin—are seminal Motown tracks, but are they really early classics? Get past the grandiose title and you have a good disc for cruising. *—Andrew Hamilton*

Teenage Party/Pajama Party / Oct. 13, 1998 / WestSide ♦♦♦♦
Another two albums on one compact disc affair from WestSide, this one combining an album originally issued on George Goldner's Gee imprint in 1958 and its follow-up, which eventually came out on Roulette in the early '60s. *Teenage Party* is often cited as the first "oldies" album, even though the songs were only a couple of years old at the time of this LP's debut. Its follow-up, *Pajama Party,* didn't come out until Gee was absorbed by Roulette in the following decade. But either way, the music couldn't be better, bringing together hits and turntable faves from the stars of Goldner's doo wop stable of talent like the Crows ("Gee," "I Love You So"), the Harptones ("Three Wishes," "You're Driving Me Mad"), the Valentines ("Lily Maybelle," "Nature's Creation," "Don't Say Goodnight"), Frankie Lymon & the Teenagers ("Out in the Cold Again," "Little White Lies"), the Cleftones ("Little Girl of Mine," "String Around My Heart," "Can't We Be Sweethearts"), the Wrens ("Come Back My Love") and bandleader Jimmy Wright ("Move Over"). A solid chunk of New York City vocal group music during its peak of creativity, and a reissue well worth adding to anyone's doo wop collection. *—Cub Koda*

Teenagers in Love / 1998 / Razor & Tie ♦♦♦♦
These 40 tracks will delight lovers of the sweet, innocent rock songs of the '60s and bring back fond memories to those who lived the times. To list even the most significant tracks would be monotonous since there so many, but suffice to say this compilation is very comprehensive. It includes tracks from everyone from the Dells, the Drifters, Conway Twitty, and Connie Francis, to one-hit wonders like Paul & Paula, the Poni Tails, the Regents, and the Penguins (but what a one-hit wonder in the rock classic "Earth Angel"). *—Andrew Hamilton*

Thelma's Detroit Collective / 2000 / Goldmine/Soul Supply ♦♦♦♦
This is the second volume on the Thelma Records story issued by Northern soul freaks Goldmine/Soul Supply. The 24 selections here focus mainly on releases from the cult labels Thelma and Ge Ge, with a couple from Apollo. Here is the place to hear the demo version of "Hit and Run" by a very young Martha Reeves, the inimitable Joey Kingfish covering the Professionals' "Did My Baby Call," the three A-sides from Martha Starr, a few from Billie Kennedy, and, of course, Emanual Laskey and the early O'Jays. Tom Storm is in the house, as is Joe Matthews himself. In addition, there are rare singles by the Fabulous Peps, the Fabulous Playboys, Mancha, the Professionals, Eddie Hill, the San Remo Golden Strings, the Holidays, and the Thelma All Stars. Perhaps more than anything else, this gives yet another side of the Thelma story, a label considered even by Northern soul fans to be as collectible or as aesthetically valuable as Motown. Those points are arguable of course, but one listen to the material here offers a solid view of all things Detroit soul in the 1960s. Ingeniously arranged and produced sessions, great songs, and phenomenal singers are what gave Motown its moniker, and the Thelma, Ge Ge, and Apollo labels were no exception. This, the sound of the 1960s, marked a time of great promise, a musical terrain in which anything was possible as long as you had the chops and the opportunity to cut a single. The music here is timeless, savvy, and sexy as hell. *Thelma's Detroit Collective* is essential listening for any fan and/or collector of soul music. *—Thom Jurek*

There Is a Thin Red Line Between Doo Wop & Soul / 1999 / Presto Bar ♦♦♦
These 24 tracks explore the musical blood ties between doo wop and soul. Most are obscure releases from hole-in-the-wall recording companies all across America; none sound like blockbusters, but several of these artists have developed passionate followings among soul fans. Fannie & the Varcells tell you about "The Guy," Ronnie Love & Group heat it up with "Judy," and Sly, Slick & Wicked croon "Confessin' a Feeling" as if serenading a newborn. The Franciscans deliver on "Mother Please Answer Me," the Four Grand do the throwback "Lost Legend," and the Sunlovers' "This Love of Ours" is as smooth as ever. There are some nifty uptempo tracks as well, including "Tillie" by the Earles, the Superbs' "Only for Lovers," the Stoppers' "Come Back Baby," and Armonda & the Jays' 1959 release "Present of Love." *—Andrew Hamilton*

This Is Northern Soul! A Collection of 24 Tamla Motown Northern Soul, Vol. 1 / 1997 / Debutante ♦♦♦♦
Devoted fans of Motown Records will drool over this late-'90s compilation. The artists are familiar but many of these 24 tracks are obscure and unreleased songs by great Motown singers, writers, and producers. The only real hits onboard are the Marvelettes' soulful "I'll Keep Holding On," the Contours' "Just a Little Misunderstanding," and Brenda Holloway's "When I'm Gone." But the real treats here are the rarities, many of which fetch high prices as collectable singles (e.g., Frank Wilson's "Do I Love You (Deed I Do)," Linda Griner's "Goodbye Cruel Love," the Andantes' "Like a Nightmare," Frances Nero's "Keep on Loving Me," and Virgil Henry's un-Motownish "You Ain't Saying Nothing New"). The Temptations' "Gotta Find a Way to Win You Back," a barnstormer from their 1969 *Cloud Nine* album, was also thoughtfully included, as was Marvin Gaye's "This Love Starved Heart of Mine." *—Andrew Hamilton*

This Is Northern Soul! A Collection of 24 Tamla Motown Northern Soul, Vol. 2 / 1998 / Debutante ♦♦♦
This Is Northern Soul! A Collection of 24 Tamla Motown Northern Soul, Vol. 2 is Motown's attempt to get its share of the ever-growing market of Northern soul reissues, thereby curbing the profit of potential bootleggers. These tracks are primarily for Northern soul and Motown enthusiasts only, but those craving something deeper than Motown standards would be well served at giving this compilation a try. Tammi Terrell's previously unreleased solo take of "Two Can Have a Party" is just as stellar of a performance of the song as her rendition with Marvin Gaye. Never-before-heard re-masters of long-lost classics and more unreleased tracks are sure to satiate even the most rabid of soul collectors. Complete with well-written liner notes by Motown scholar Chris King, this compilation is a solid treasure chest of pure soul riches. *—Rob Theakston*

TK Deep Soul: Sunshine Girls / May 30, 1995 / Sequel ♦♦♦♦
Five female Southern soul artists tell it like it is, was, and is gonna be on a slew of salty love sagas. Jackie Moore cranks out eight of the 15 tracks, warming them with her golden alto and no-nonsense approach. Ann Sexton does only one track ("Loving You, Loving Me"), which is a shame since her distinctive, sexy soprano is an ice-breaker. Paulette Reeves smokes on four tracks, including "Jazz Freak," a song about her love of jazz music; it has a Southern feel, and it's also the only album track that's not about relationships. Reeves' jazzy, soulful rendition of "Your Good Thing Is About to End" is classy and well-done. Brandye contributes "One Woman's Trash Is Another Woman's Treasure," a song where the music and the lyrics don't equal the title. Ruby Wilson contributes "I'll Be Right Here (When You Return)" (with help from the Blue Chips) and "Man and a Baby Boy." *—Andrew Hamilton*

TK Disco 45 Collection, Vol. 1: 1976–1978—Dance to the Drummer's Beat / 1999 / TK/WestSide ♦♦♦
This sprawling double-disc compilation covers a selection of songs, mostly in their 12-inch versions, that were issued by the prolific TK Records during 1976 and 1978. The track listing divides its time nicely between songs that were big on the disco charts and obscurities that only devoted disco fanatics would remember. On disc one, the most memorable hits are "Do What You Wanna Do," a funky dance classic that blends Temptations-style harmonies with plenty of keyboard hooks over a thumping bass line, and "Do You Wanna Get Funky With Me?," a track that layers percolating synthesizers and percussive background chants over a hypnotic rhythm guitar riff. This disc also contains a major cult favorite in "Superman," a swirling, synthesizer-laden disco favorite from Celi Bee & the Buzzy Bunch that pays tribute to the famous superhero over a pulsating beat. The second disc includes "Get Off," a track from Foxy that mixes a funky beat with some surprisingly metallic guitar riffs, and the title track, a frenetic Herman Kelly and Life cut whose insistent rhythms made a breakbeat favorite for DJ's during hip-hop's early days. It also sports a memorable oddity in "Bertha Butt Encounters Vadar," a Jimmy Castor Bunch track that pays tribute to *Star Wars* in disco form. A few of the cuts fail to impress (Foxy's "The Way You Do the Things You Do" is undone by silly background vocal chants), but the majority of the cuts offer a reliable combinations of insistent beats and strong hooks. The package is rounded out by an informative set of liner notes that give plenty of information about the often-elusive studio players behind these cuts. In the end, *The TK Disco 45 Collection, Vol. 1: Dance to the Drummer's Beat* is too cultish for the casual listener, but offers a generous array of worthwhile hits and rarities for the hardcore discophile. *—Donald A. Guarisco*

Tom Joyner's Old School Mix / Mar. 16, 1999 / Rhino ♦♦♦
Around 1994, urban contemporary DJ Tom Joyner hired Steve "Silk" Hurley to provide "old school mixes" for his popular *Tom Joyner Morning Show*; and by old school, he meant the classic soul, funk, and disco of the late '70s and early '80s. To be sure, Hurley was perfect for the job; he had played an indispensable role in house music, and his credentials as a mixmaster were undeniable. The type of mixing that Hurley has done on his show is what he does for *Old School Mix,* which spans 1976-1982 and boasts a non-

stop mix of 18 major hits from that period. One gem segues right into another; just as Gwen McCrae's "Funky Sensation" is starting to fade out, Hurley comes right in with One Way's "Cutie Pie." And just as Peter Brown's "Dance With Me" is starting to end, Anita Ward's "Ring My Bell" makes its presence felt. The CD is full of gems that defined the disco era, such as Chic's "Le Freak," Sister Sledge's "He's the Greatest Dancer," and Foxy's "Get Off." But Joyner's mix has as much to do with hardcore funk and soul as it does with disco; Funkadelic's "One Nation Under a Groove," Slave's "Slide," and Zapp's "More Bounce to the Ounce" soared to number one or two on the R&B charts, but didn't fare nearly as well on the pop charts. In fact, *Old School Mix* is pretty much the type of soul/funk/disco blend you could have expected to hear on the mix shows that graced black radio in the late '70s and early '80s. Even if you're not familiar with Joyner's show and Hurley's contributions to it, this is a CD to savor. *—Alex Henderson*

Tom Joyner's Old School Mix Returns / Mar. 5, 2002 / Rhino ♦♦♦
There's a few songs that aren't entirely familiar here, which is to the credit of the compilers, since without those, *Tom Joyner Presents: The Old School Mix Returns* would be nothing more than a stroll down an oldies radio station, albiet one with good taste. Of course, everybody should be aware that the word "mix" is not a synonym for "compilation" in this case. No, it means that all the songs are mixed into the next, with seamless segues that truly are a real bitch if you're just looking for a clean copy of the original hit. This approach does lend the album the feeling of a DJ spinning each song, which could be welcome according to the circumstance—if you're throwing a party, it's acceptable, but as straight listening, it's a bit irritating. But, if you can ignore that, this is a collection with good taste and sharp sequencing, resulting in a party album that pretty much delivers party. But it very well might not be good for anything but a party. *—Stephen Thomas Erlewine*

Top Ten With a Bullet!: Motown Male Groups / 1987 / Motown ♦♦♦♦
If your antennae weren't fully extended, you probably missed this series of mid-'80s compilation albums that Motown released on the down low. Yet another vehicle for the company to market its most successful tracks, this volume spotlights male groups—a good concept, especially for variety lovers. Featured are contributions from Smokey Robinson & the Miracles, the Temptations, the Jackson 5, the Contours, the Four Tops, the Originals—and Junior Walker & the All-Stars (?); well, they didn't say vocal groups, just male groups, so presumably Junior Walker & the All-Stars qualify. *—Andrew Hamilton*

Top Ten With a Bullet!: Motown Girl Groups / 1987 / Motown ♦♦♦♦
If you blinked, you probably missed this series of mid-'80s compilation albums that Motown slipped onto the market ever so quietly. Yet another vehicle for the company to market its most successful tracks, this volume spotlights Motown's chart-busting female groups: Martha Reeves & the Vandellas, Diana Ross & the Supremes, and the Marvelettes. The concept gets stretched so thin it breaks—the other participants are Mary Wells (she's not a group!) and Gladys Knight & the Pips (one female and three guys—that's some female group). Still, this is a marvelous compilation filled with songs you've heard a thousand times, and they still sound amazingly fresh. *—Andrew Hamilton*

A Treasure Chest of Northern Soul / 1995 / Goldmine/Soul Supply ♦♦♦
A virtual cornucopia of gutsy, uptown soul which includes hard to find tracks from Tony Hester, Timothy Wilson, J. J. Barnes, Lester Tipton, Candi Staton, and the Masqueraders, most highly collectable in their original 45 rpm format. The two best-known selections are Bobby Womack's "What Is This" and the O'Jays' "I'll Never Forget You," co-written by Edwin Starr and designated for a Motown deal, which the O'Jays' nixed. These tunes are mostly for devoted Northern soul fans eager to uncover good singers, writers, and producers who never got the exposure they deserved. *—Andrew Hamilton*

A Tribute to Ashford & Simpson / Sep. 17, 1996 / Hot Productions ♦♦♦
This collection features 14 songs written by Ashford & Simpson and performed by various combinations of ex-Motown artists, as recorded for the Motor City label and initially compiled on the *Motor City Hits* and *The Sounds of Motorcity* collections. Despite the lackluster productions, this is an interesting disc. The Andantes were Motown's favorite female voices, appearing as backing vocalists on countless tracks, yet only had one Motown release, "Like a Nightmare." Here they redo "The Boss," and for 5:41 show why their glorious voices and the Motown sound were inseparable. Pat Lewis sang with the Andantes, but gets an opportunity to solo on "Remember Me." Louvain Demps, another Andante and sister of the Dramatics' Larry Demps, solos on "Reach Out and Touch Somebody's Hand." Scherrie Payne, who sang with Glass House and the Supremes, solos on "Ain't No Mountain High Enough." Syreeta redoes her first Motown recording, "I Can't Give Back the Love I Feel For You," which comes off better than the original. Some unique duet combinations spice things up: Martha Reeves & G.C. Cameron, Marv Johnson & Carolyn Gill, Kim Weston & Frankie Gaye, and the most obscure, Frances Nero & Geno Parks. Nero, who had one Motown release, is represented by two solo numbers, and holds the distinction of being the most successful Motor City artist. *—Andrew Hamilton*

Tribute to Berry Gordy / Sep. 17, 1996 / Hot Productions ♦♦♦
A fitting tribute to Berry Gordy, the mastermind of Motown Records. All of the songs, except "We Couldn't Get Along Without," "It's So Hard to Say Goodbye," and "Did You Know," are Gordy compositions. The collection comprises new and previously unreleased recordings, plus some old hits. The best of the former is a rousing version of the Contours' "Do You Love Me" by the Temptations; Ali Woodsen's lead is better than the one on the original version. The Temptations also supply backing vocals on Stevie Wonder's remake of one of their earlier ballads, "Dream Come True"—dreamy stuff. Gordy's two biggest Jackie Wilson hits, "To Be Loved" and "Lonely Teardrops," are included, along with the song that got the Motown machine rolling, "Money" by Barrett Strong. *—Andrew Hamilton*

A Tribute to Curtis Mayfield / Feb. 15, 1994 / Warner Brothers ♦♦♦
A fabulous assortment of artists from different areas of the rock genre gives a glorifying tribute to Curtis Mayfield in a sparkling 17-song package. Stevie Winwood does a partying rendition of "It's All Right"; a version of "Let's Do It Again" is performed by Mayfield and Repercussion that mimics the Staple Singers' original; Mayfield does Pop Staples' parts. Bruce Springsteen tackles an early Impressions classic, "Gypsy Woman," and makes the mystical song even more eerie. The number of producers equals the artists on this fine production, so the sound changes from track to track. Rocker Lenny Kravitz does "Billy Jack" in a surprising Mayfield-like falsetto. Phil Collins' dead-slow reading of "I've Been Trying" is a subdued dandy. The album's two best performances are pulled off by the Isley Brothers ("I'm So Proud") and Tevin Campbell ("Keep on Pushing"). Ron Isley outdoes himself on Mayfield's pretty classic redefining soul with his emotive phrasings, and Campbell's taking-you-to-church performance of "Keep on Pushing" could inspire the homeless; the cut will make you a T.C. fan if you're not already. The revised Impressions do a remake of their own "I'm a Fool for You" accompanied by Branford Marsalis' jazzy riffs. For blues lovers, B.B. King rocks the house with an uptempo, jumping "Woman's Got Soul." Stevie Wonder sings an old obscure Impressions recording, "I'm the One Who Loves You," in the sassy style he exhibited when he was Little Stevie Wonder. Eric Clapton does a rousing version of "You Must Believe Me." *—Andrew Hamilton*

Tribute to Norman Whitfield / Sep. 17, 1996 / Hot Productions ♦♦
The Motor City label—which specializes in new recordings featuring former Motown vocalists—pays tribute to producer and songwriter Norman Whitfield on this well-meaning but uneven collection. That's Frankie Gaye singing "I Heard It Through the Grapevine," sadly proving he has only a smidgen of the charisma, power and phrasing ability of his late brother Marvin. The Velvelettes' three sides are not as compelling as the originals; still, they sound good, singing with vigor on "Needle in a Haystack," "He Was Really Saying Something," and "Lonely, Lonely Girl Am I." Ex-Spinner G.C. Cameron's three sides are decent "Too Busy Thinking About My Baby," "Just My Imagination," and "Run Away Child", and his versatile, impressive voice transcends the unimpressive productions. The Undisputed Truth, the Marvelettes, Richard "Popcorn" Wylie, Kim Weston, Billie Calvin and little-known Vee Allen all perform one song each. This tribute to Norman Whitfield falls a little short, to say the least—no bag of tricks here. Hearing these classic voices again is a rush, but if you're expecting to hear James Jamerson's wicked basslines, Robert White's shimmering guitar, Benny Benjamin's remarkable drums, or Earl Van Dyke's gifted keyboarding, you will have to look elsewhere. *—Andrew Hamilton*

Tribute to Smokey Robinson / Feb. 20, 1996 / Hot Productions ♦♦♦
These tracks were originally released on Motorcity Records in the United Kingdom (a label which is devoted to producing new recordings by former Motown singers), and later compiled to pay homage to Smokey Robinson. Wanda Young-Rogers of the Marvelettes is enjoyable on "The Hunter Gets Captured by the Game," "Don't Mess With Bill," and "My Baby Must Be a Magician." While Young-Rogers was down on her luck when she cut these sessions, she delivers a commanding performance. Darrell Littlejohn leads the Monitors, but it's no wonder their renditions of "Tears of a Clown" and "Going to a Go Go" sound like the Miracles—Littlejohn is Robinson's nephew. The Contours dish a tasteful "Tracks of My Tears" with a slightly different arrangement; Sammy Ward lights a warm fire on "You Really Got a Hold on Me"; Bobby Taylor obviously loves singing "Get Ready"; and Linda Griner updates her "Goodbye Cruel Love" with a spoken part. Mary Wells does four of her biggest hits satisfactorily, and Carolyn Crawford shines on two efforts. For an added treat, a bunch of ex-Motowners jam on "The Way You Do the Things You Do." *—Andrew Hamilton*

Twinight's Chicago Soul Heaven / 1996 / Kent ♦♦♦
The Twinight label was a small, Chicago-based soul indie of the late '60s and early '70s that experienced most of its success with singles by Syl Johnson (before Johnson moved to Hi Records). This has 24 tracks issued by the label between 1967 and 1972, although only two of them are by Johnson (who produced a few of the tracks by other acts). Johnson is also the only name you're apt to recognize, unless you've got a knee-high stack of *Soul Survivor* back issues. The Notations, the Radiants, Elvin Spencer, Jimmy Jones, Renaldo Domino, and a host of other unknowns offer brassy, upbeat soul in the Chicago style, usually dancefloor-ready. There are a few surprises that keep one's attention—the country harmonica on Johnny Williams' "Maggie," the enchanted-island phrasing of Renaldo Domino on "Nevermore," the Hawaiian guitar on George McGregor's "Temptation Is Hard to Fight"—though on the whole the material is pleasantly average. *—Richie Unterberger*

Twisted Wheel Story / 1995 / Goldmine/Soul Supply/Vital ♦♦♦♦
This collection celebrates the Twisted Wheel, an English nightclub that played Northern soul music—mostly obscure R&B singles that were produced in the States by small companies and little known artists. The only real hits on this 27-song package are Chuck Jackson's R&B smash "Any Day Now" and Darrell Bank's "Open the Door to Your Heart." It has a few minor players, such as "Karate Boogaloo" by Jerry O, and plenty of blue-eyed soul on this compilation—Ronnie Milsap, Charlie Rich, Bill Black's Combo, and Mitch Ryder offer astonishing straight-soul takes. A good collection of '60s soul music and its many hues. *—Andrew Hamilton*

UK Stax Singles, 1968–1975: Magical Moments in Soul Music History / Jul. 31, 2000 / Stax ♦♦♦♦
British Stax singles, including some of the 23 assembled here, sometimes differed from

the label's U.S. release schedule in selection of tracks and designated A-sides. Really, though, this CD is just an excuse to bring together a couple of dozen or so tracks from Stax's later years, most of them not too well known; only Isaac Hayes' "Walk on By" and the Staple Singers' "If You're Ready (Come Go With Me)" should be familiar to the casual fan. Many of Stax's bigger names are represented—the Staple Singers, Johnnie Taylor, William Bell, Booker T. & the MG's, the Dramatics—alongside lower-profile artists like Shirley Brown, the Emotions, and the Rance Allen Group, and a bunch of singers that you might not even remember were on the label (Johnny Daye, Margie Alexander, the Newcomers, Darrell Banks, J.J. Barnes, Frederick Knight). It's a decent, though not stunning, cross-section of sounds from a time when Stax was losing its identity, but still putting out respectable late-period Southern soul with encroaching shades of funk and disco. As for some of the better lesser-known items, J.J. Barnes' "Baby Please Come Back Home," actually first released in 1967 as a single on Revilot (for which it made the R&B Top Ten), is a good emulation of the tougher sound of late-'60s Motown. Shirley Brown's "It Ain't No Fun," from Stax's last gasp in 1975, is a good lush-yet-tortured ballad (complete with spoken testimony in the middle), showing there was more to her than her famous hit "Woman to Woman." [This U.K. import is not available for sale in North America.] *—Richie Unterberger*

Ultimate Motown Rarities Collection, Vol. 1 / Sep. 22, 1998 / Motown ♦♦♦♦
Ultimate Motown Rarities Collection essentially posits a kind of bizarro-world take on the sound of young America, an alternate reality where familiar favorites like "I Want You Back," "I Heard It Through the Grapevine," and "Stop! In the Name of Love" were popularized not by the Jackson 5, Marvin Gaye, and the Supremes but by David Ruffin, Smokey Robinson, and Kim Weston instead. This eye-opening compilation unearths some 21 tracks from the Motown vaults, each the result of a musical assembly line that saw songs pass through any number of artists and producers before all the pieces finally fell into place. The pairing of familiar compositions and familiar artists yields most unfamiliar results, and while it's no doubt jarring to hear the Isley Brothers tackle "How Sweet It Is (To Be Loved by You)" or the Supremes take on "Can I Get a Witness," it's equally difficult to understand just why some of these recordings were rejected outright, the songs themselves then moving on to the artists who made them famous. As a glimpse into the label's creative process, *Ultimate Motown Rarities Collection* is invaluable, but on a less academic level, it's a consistently engaging set that takes overplayed classics and gives them new and entirely different life. *—Jason Ankeny*

Ultimate Rarities Collection, Vol. 1: Motown Sings Motown Treasures / 1998 / Motown ♦♦♦♦
Spiced with 18 previously unreleased recordings, this 21-track compilation from Motown's mighty vaults is basically a self-indulgent exercise in label backslapping. But what backslapping it is. Unearthing sparkling performances from Marvin Gaye, Smokey Robinson & the Miracles, Diana Ross & the Supremes, the Spinners, Stevie Wonder and the Temptations, among others, *The Ultimate Rarities Collection 1: Motown Sings Motown Treasures* has a pretty simple premise: Motown artists cover Motown artists. So, the Jackson 5 tear through the Miracles' "You've Really Got a Hold on Me," the Originals slip on the Supremes' "Come See About Me," the Spinners cruise through the Temptations' "The Girl's Alright with Me," etc. Best are Gaye's starry-eyed "My Girl" (which is also found on 1990's *Marvin Gaye Collection*) and Wonder's thrilling workout on "I Hear a Symphony" (from 1966 sessions). It's Prime stuff. *—Michael Gallucci*

Underground Oldies, Vol. 3 / Oct. 6, 1998 / ITP ♦♦♦♦
Compilation albums of R&B singles from the '60s and '70s usually contain either familiar hits, or recordings so obscure that nobody has heard of them. *The Underground Oldies* collections are different. While rare and little known, these tunes got played on local radio stations, and are slicker and better produced than the rare birds you find on most Northern soul collections. *Vol. 3* covers the same fertile ground as the first two. For many, Linda Jones' operatic "That's When I'll Stop Loving You" defines soul, and it maybe her most breathtaking performance. "One Life To Live" is a fine early release by the Manhattans featuring their original lead, George Smith. The Ethics' "Farewell" featuring Ron Tyson is sweet Philly magic. "Friends By Day (Lovers By Night)" by the Whatnauts is an early example of the blowing into the microphone technique that Luther Vandross uses to wow audiences. Also on board are cuts from Barbara Mason, Brenton Wood, the Variations, Mike & the Sensations, and Vivian Copeland. Sixteen substantive tracks for sweet soul lovers. *—Andrew Hamilton*

Underground Oldies, Vol. 4 / Mar. 16, 1999 / ITP ♦♦♦♦
Another fine installment in the *Underground Oldies* series, which compile outstanding vintage soul sides which were regional hits but missed the nationwide charts. *Vol. 4* has many memorable moments: the Manhattans teary "It's Gonna Take a Lot to Bring Me Back"; Little Anthony sound-a-like Timothy Wilson performs two tracks, and Lost Generation displays vocal sharpness on the wispy "I Can't Help You." Linda Jones' dramatic voice electrifies "It Won't Take Much," and she does further damage on a breathtaking remake of Ben E. King's "I Who Have Nothing." Sunny & the Sunliners' flow on the soft, rolling "Should I Take You Home," and "Let Me Love You." Choice cuts by Gene Chandler, Eddie Holman, and others rounds out another delightful package from ITP Records. *—Andrew Hamilton*

Up From the Vaults, Vol. 1 / Oct. 1, 2002 / Soul Fire ♦♦♦♦♦
Following on the heels of Soul Fire's two *Grazing in the Trash* singles comps, *Up From the Vaults, Vol. 1* continues the task of collecting the down-and-dirty funk revival label's limited-edition 45 rpm records for CD release. It's the best various-artists collection the label has yet offered, boasting a wider, more colorful range of carefully re-created vintage funk sounds. Where the shadow of the J.B.'s and Meters once loomed large over most of Soul Fire's output, their 45s have exhibited considerable growth, as this collection demonstrates. Of course, there's still some great classic-style funk courtesy of returning '70s veterans the Herb Johnson Settlement and the Detroit Sex Machines, but the fun comes from the changes of pace. There are Latin boogaloo-style grooves from Bronx River Parkway, bubbling Hammond-organ funk from WQLJ, revivalist Afro-beat by Massak, a perky rap (in the pre-hip-hop sense of the term) from female soul singer Mauri Bailey, and some groovy trumpet and sax soloing courtesy of the El Michels Affair. Add to that the label's increasing penchant for borderline stoner grooves, both laid-back (the Fabulous Three) and stompingly heavy (the Whitefield Brothers' excellent "Chokin'"), and you've got a document that bodes extremely well for the future of Soul Fire and of the deep funk revival in general. *—Steve Huey*

Uptown Down South / 1995 / Excello ♦♦♦♦
The title implies that these are recordings cut south of the Mason-Dixon Line, but with an uptown sound; the concept is flawed. Just as you can't make a silk purse out of a sow's ear, if you use Southern musicians and producers, the product is going to sound likewise. If Diana Ross used these same hookups, she would sound like Ann Sexton or Betty Wright. However, the compilation deserves kudos despite its gray area because its selections are so scarce. To have them accessible on one CD is a musical godsend. Highlights among the 24-tracks include Roger Hatcher's glorious "Sweetest Girl in the World"; Marva Whitney's tumultuous "Don't Let Our Love Fade Away"; Skip Mahoney & the Casuals' "Running Away From Love"; Bits 'N' Pieces' "Keep on Running Away"; the Wallace Brothers' "Thanks a Lot"; and Z.Z. Hill's "Our Love Is Getting Better." Other saucy entrées include tracks by the Kelly Brothers, the Avons (a little-known female group), and Lucille Mathis. *—Andrew Hamilton*

The Very Best of the King/Federal/Deluxe Years, Vol. 1 / Apr. 16, 2002 / Collectables ♦♦♦♦♦
This is the real deal. Raw and ready to rock, all the artists compiled here put the pedal all the way to the metal and let it rock. And when they aren't rocking, they are tearing your heart out with a sobbing ballad. Kicking off with the original version of "The Twist" by Hank Ballard & the Midnighters and ending an hour later with the Drivers' rock-boppin' "Smooth, Slow and Easy," there is not a single weak track to be found. Big names like Billy Ward & the Dominoes, the Platters, Wynonie Harris, and Percy Mayfield leave no doubt why they are big names, and the no-names like Pete "Guitar" Lewis and Lil Greenwood don't let down the side one bit. Classic tracks include Freddie King's landmark "Hide Away," the Swallows' slightly nasty "It Ain't the Meat, It's the Motion," and Rudy Ray Moore's "Step It Up and Go." If you are a fan of early R&B, you must own this record. It's that good. *—Tim Sendra*

VH-1 8-Track Flashback: Classic 70's Soul / 1998 / Rhino ♦♦♦
Like its predecessor, *VH-1 8-Track Flashback: One-Hit Wonders, VH1 8-Track Flashback: Classic '70s Soul* is a compilation that distills several of Rhino's multi-volume series—this time, *Didn't It Blow Your Mind: Soul Hits of the '70s* and *In Yo Face: The Roots of Funk*—to a single-disc compilation. A few of these songs, such as the Jackson 5's "Never Can Say Goodbye" and the Temptations' "Papa Was a Rollin' Stone," weren't on either series, but the majority of the 15 tracks have been on other Rhino discs, and while that doesn't necessarily make the comp unnecessary, it's nevertheless frustrating to collectors who already own the multi-volume series. On its own terms, it's pretty entertaining, featuring such classics as "Get Up (I Feel Like Being Like A) Sex Machine," "Tear the Roof Off the Sucker (Give Up the Funk)," "Fire," "I'll Be Around," "Midnight Train to Georgia," "Can't Get Enough of Your Love, Babe," "Ain't No Woman (Like the One I've Got)" and "Betcha By Golly, Wow." In fact, it's a better, more consistent collection than *One-Hit Wonders*, capturing the feeling of the era as well as some of its best sounds, which makes it ideal for casual fans of '70s soul and funk. *—Stephen Thomas Erlewine*

Voodoo Soul: Deep and Dirty New Orleans Funk / Aug. 28, 2001 / Metro ♦♦♦♦
A terrific collection of late-'60s/early-'70s funk singles that barely scraped the local charts, *Voodoo Soul* unearths a pile of gold in its 16 tracks. The Meters and Lee Dorsey loom large, but samples from the bygone careers of Clemon Smith, Skip Easterling, and the Backyard Heavies are every bit as great. There's barely a hit listed among these songs, and that's exactly the point; as *Voodoo Soul* proves, New Orleans was a hotbed of great music from the ground up. *—Jim Smith*

We're a Lover: Brunswick/Dakar's Brothers of Soul / WestSide ♦♦♦♦♦
Names like Jackie Wilson, Tyrone Davis, and Gene Chandler are established enough in the music world to at least garner a nod of recognition from most parties, but Sidney Joe Qualis, Wales Wallace, and Mighty Doug Haynes aren't as lucky. Which is why *We're a Lover: Brunswick/Dakar's Brothers of Soul* is such a welcome sight, as it brings together the cream of Chicago's soul crop, both known and otherwise forgotten singers. Most of the tracks here were produced by Carl Davis, and as such, there are lush strings and booming horns throughout the 24 tracks here. Highlights from some of the lesser-known artists here include sweet soul group Channel 3 with the appropriately titled "The Sweetest Thing" and the bombastic progressions of "Suddenly" by Tony Drake. Surprisingly, the heavily documented superstar of the Brunswick camp, Jackie Wilson, turns in an inspired song, "I Still Love You," which has been unavailable since the time of its release in 1969. And although not everything here holds universal appeal, the consistency is remarkable and makes this a great addition to any soul collection. *—Wade Kergan*

We're All in the Same Gang / Jun. 12, 1990 / Warner Bros. ♦♦♦
In 1988, violence at rap concerts and Black-on-Black crime inspired Boogie Down Productions leader KRS-One to found the Stop the Violence Movement and produce the all-star single "Self Destruction." That project was dominated by East Coast rappers, and some Californians wondered why more West Coast rappers hadn't been asked to participate. They reasoned that because black-on-black crime was as serious a problem in

L.A. and Oakland as it was in New York, more West Coast MCs should have been part of Stop the Violence. So in 1990, some of California's top rappers formed the West Coast Rap All-Stars and recorded *We're All in the Same Gang*, which became California's equivalent of Stop the Violence. The list of participants is impressive—Dr. Dre, Quincy Jones III (son of the famous Quincy Jones) and Bilal Bashir are among the producers, and the rappers include Ice-T, Tone Loc, MC Hammer, King Tee, Young MC, Def Jef and members of N.W.A., Digital Underground, Oaktown's 3.5.7 and Above the Law. Though some of the material is fun and escapist, the CD's overriding theme is a sociopolitical one—inner-city residents are encouraged to unite and put an end to black-on-black crime. The most compelling tracks include the title song, the South Central Posse's "Livin' in South Central L.A." and M.C. Supreme's "Black in America." Although generally enjoyable, the album on the whole isn't the all-out gem it could have been—some of the songs are excellent, while others are merely decent. But while *We're All in the Same Gang* isn't perfect, its historic value is undeniable. *—Alex Henderson*

The West End Story, Vol. 1 / 1981 / West End ✦✦✦✦✦
As the first volume of an excellent four-disc series, this album features several of the late-disco classics released by the New York label West End. Along with Prelude and Salsoul, West End represents one of the few disco labels that endured over time as the poor commercial strains of disco eventually disappeared and the better records became hard-to-find anthems with a seemingly timeless allure. What makes this series so impressive is the fact that the songs thankfully appear in unedited, DJ-friendly form, quite often surpassing ten minutes in length. Furthermore, while the featured artists on West End—Taana Gardner, Sparque, Raw Silk—may not seem overly familiar or important in retrospect, the producers who helped shape these tracks into such timeless form—Larry Levan, Tom Moulton, François Kevorkian—have definitely become hallowed names in the history of electronic dance music as pioneering artists who helped bridge the gap between proto-disco and electronic dance music without ever falling into the generic pitfalls that plagued most disco producers. This volume in particular features many of the label's early releases and is highlighted by Taana Gardner's "Heartbeat," arguably the label's most well-known hit, along with Brenda Taylor's "You Can't Have Your Cake and Eat It Too," another track that has aged well. Overall, there aren't many weak moments on this album or with this album relative to others in the series, since practically everything West End released has enduring quality attributes. *—Jason Birchmeier*

The Westbound Sound of Detroit: Sensational Motor City Groups 1969–1975 / 1995 / Westbound ✦✦✦✦
Lovers of vocal groups, R&B, and soul— make it your business to seek this sucker out. Loaded onto this bombastic CD are 25 tracks of great, underpromoted music from some of the thousands of fame-seeking male vocal groups that popped up in Detroit like dandelions. The exuberant sounds of Unique Blend occupy tracks one through five; UB's songs are good, top-shelf stuff, and their spirited vocals even better—check out "Mommy & Daddy" and "Old Fashion Woman." The Superlatives' "Don't Walk Away" is among the gems; Carl Carlton covered this midtempo stepper on Duke Records—his is cool, but this is the one. The Detroit Emeralds and the Fantastic Four are the only really known groups on board. Both are well represented with five songs between them. The FF's "I'm Falling in Love" and DEs' "That's All I Got" are clear highlights. Five sides are by the Magictones, who went on to become a second generation of the Undisputed Truth. The two standouts are by two totally unknown groups: the Houston Outlaws and the Mighty Elegants. "I'm Finding Myself Falling In Love With You" is a sweet falsetto-led ballad that grows on you with every play; the Houston Outlaws' "What Am I Gonna Do" is also a falsetto-led ballad that will have you standing in front of the mirror lip-synching. *—Andrew Hamilton*

What More Can a Woman Do? Brunswick & Chi-Sound Sisters of Soul / Oct. 26, 1999 / WestSide ✦✦✦✦
Chicago's female recording artists never got the same attention as their male counterparts; the scenario usually consisted of one or two hits, then a slide into obscurity. Barbara Acklin and Jackie Ross each scored a few R&B hits, a crossover success, and then disappeared. Acklin sounds strong on "Fool, Fool Look in the Mirror," "Love, You Are Mine Today," and the scorching "Love Makes a Woman." Ross' Chess Records hits aren't featured, but her Brunswick offering "Love Is Easy to Lose" isn't bad. Highlights include sassy Sugar Pie DeSanto's "The One Who Really Loves You," Della Reese's "Nothing But a True Love," and Lynn Roman's "I Don't Need No Sympathy." Linda Hopkins, Erma Franklin, LaVern Baker, and others also contribute. The only clunker is the Promises' "Living in the Footsteps of Another Girl." *—Andrew Hamilton*

When a Man Cries / Nov. 9, 1999 / Kent ✦✦✦
The soul music issued by the Scepter/Wand and Musicor/Dynamo labels tended to be the most pop-oriented, "uptown" sort of 1960s New York soul, as sung by stars on their roster like Dionne Warwick, Chuck Jackson, Maxine Brown, and the Shirelles. However, from the mid-'60s through the early '70s, these labels did license material from other sources (often from the South) that was in much more of a "deep soul" or "sweet soul" style, with gospel-derived vocals and brassy production. *When a Man Cries* collects 27 of those releases from 1965-1973. A lot of these names are unknown; with the exception of Lloyd Price, even the recognizable artists are minor ones, such as Jackie Moore, Judy Clay, L.C. Cooke (Sam Cooke's brother), and Johnny Copeland. Like so many of these collector-targeted anthologies, this represents the second or third tier of the genre, not the cream. The imprint of the Stax ballad approach (with horns, bluesy guitars and organs), as well as fainter echoes of the Philadelphia and Chicago "sweet soul" vibe, is audible on many of the cuts. By and large they're emotionally sung and well produced, but not possessed of that special something (particularly that special songwriting) needed to elevate the cut to major durability. There are occasional lifts from more famous songs (let's not try to pretend these don't exist) such as Murge's "How Long Must This Fool Pay," whose opening piano is pretty close to Brenda Holloway's classic "Every Little Bit Hurts." Guess what the punchline of Marvin Preyer's previously unissued "You Don't Have to Be Crazy to Love Her" is? (Yep: "But it sure helps a lot.") *—Richie Unterberger*

Where It's At: Soul in the Midnight Hour / Sep. 14, 1999 / Kent ✦✦✦✦✦
This collection of hard edge Southern soul features artists from the Atlantic family of labels spotlighting the works of Clarence Carter, Aretha Franklin, Percy Sledge, Sam & Dave, Wilson Pickett, and other giants. The treasure chest is full of gems like the Isley Brothers' "Your Old Lady," "Gee Whiz," by Carla Thomas, Sam & Dave's "You Don't Know Like I Know," "My Girl Sloopy," by the Vibrations, and Herbie Mann's funky "Philly Dog." *—Andrew Hamilton*

Where the Girls Are / 1997 / Ace ✦✦✦
Here are 24 girl-group rarities from all over the place, released between 1961 and 1968 (the track by Reparata & the Delrons was previously unissued). This will have pretty limited appeal beyond the hardline girl group collecting market. The level of production expertise is high—indeed, there are little-known efforts by Leiber & Stoller, David Gates, Goffin-King, and future early Byrds producers Terry Melcher and Allen Stanton. Yet the songs aren't really too special, with a higher innocuousness quotient than is the norm in an already innocuous genre. It does have a couple of semi-forgotten classics (though they actually hit the Top 40) in Ruby & the Romantics' 1963 original of "Hey There Lonely Boy" (which would be reworked into a number-two hit by Eddie Holman in 1970 as "Hey There Lonely Girl"), and Patty & the Emblems brassy 'n' sassy "Mixed-Up, Shook-Up Girl" (co-written by Leon Huff). Curiosity seekers, it must be said, will find plenty here, including barely known girl group-style singles by Joey Heatherton, Doris Day, and Dolly Parton; a 1961 single by Erma Franklin, Aretha's sister; and a 1962 single by Idalia Boyd, sister of Little Eva of "Loco-Motion" fame. *—Richie Unterberger*

A Whiter Shade of Doowop / 1995 / Sequel ✦✦✦✦
It might come as a revelation to a lot of people at this late date, but before the release of "I Wonder Why" by Dion & the Belmonts in the spring of 1958, white doo wop recordings were considered little more than a poor relation to their black cousins, at least by purists. That's all true, as presented by Dave Marosoli in his excellent notes to this collection, though the distinction seems little more than academic a half century on. Still, that doesn't diminish the instrinsic value of this enjoyable 25-song compilation, skimming what the producers purport to be the best examples of white doo wop from the Roulette, Gone, End, Gee, Colpix, and Josie labels. The material varies widely, however, from familiar fare such as the Regents' version of "Barbara Ann" to genuine obscurities by the Four Seasons, and the exquisite vocalizing of the Del Satins to the silliness of "Little Eva" by the Locomotions, a novelty record that's more of a curiosity than anything else. Some of these acts sound so realistically "black"—especially the Del Satins—that they can make even listeners in the 21st century do double takes; others offer more of a hybrid sound, and among the rarities in the latter category featured here are "Bermuda" and "Spanish Lace," a pair of tracks cut by the Four Seasons (in their debut under that name) for Gone Records in 1961; the B-side, in particular, offers the patented Frankie Valli falsetto in all of its glory and is only lacking the influence of producer Bob Crewe to slot in seamlessly with their classic material. Even the well-known tracks are balanced out by worthwhile obscurities, so that, in the case of the Regents, "Barbara Ann" is followed by a previously unissued cut of "Over the Rainbow" and the frantic, delightfully goofy "Runaround." And for some of the acts featured, this CD is their only moment of enduring glory—the Long Island-based Chaperones (who sounded a lot like the Elegants) performed all over the New York area, but not one of their singles on the Josie label ever made an impact much beyond their own immediate neighborhood; this is a chance to take in their smoothly beguiling "Shining Star," among other tracks. It's is all finely crafted, although some of what is here veers very close to the pop music of the period—the Skyliners, out of Pittsburgh, manage to straddle the line on "I'll Close My Eyes" and "The Door Is Still Open," and nearly fall over on the pop side. Neil Sedaka's fans and devotees of the Tokens may also want to make special note of this CD for its inclusion of four fine sides by Darrell & the Oxfords, an offshoot of the original Tokens formed by Hank Medress and Sedaka in 1956, after the latter's departure from the fold, and prior to Medress' forming the more familiar Tokens. The sound is excellent throughout, and the disc is one of the more enjoyable and enlightening in its field, for the neophyte or the serious listener. *—Bruce Eder*

Whole Lotta Soul 1966–1967 / Jan. 15, 1999 / Eclipse Music Group ✦✦✦
A compilation of soul recordings from 1966-1967, running the gamut from Toussaint McCall's deep soul classic "Nothing Takes the Place of You" to more elaborate productions such as Dionne Warwick's "I Say a Little Prayer." Other highlights include Motown offerings from the Elgins, Brenda Holloway, and the Marvelettes, as well as soft soul from Brenda & the Tabulations and Peaches & Herb. An apt title for a collection of winning tracks that will bring back fond memories. *—Andrew Hamilton*

Yo Philadelphia, Look What I Found / Aug. 31, 1999 / Heritage ✦✦✦✦✦
This is an extraordinary 26-song collection, mostly of R&B, and all of which is associated with Philadelphia and with Heritage Records founder Jerry Ross as producer or composer (although not all of the material appeared on Ross' Heritage label). It's devised to give a CD airing to a lot of rare R&B that hasn't previously been available in digital audio, and it does that job magnificently, as well as restoring to availability some small parts of the Cameo/Parkway catalog (still buried by ABKCO Records), which licensed several of these titles. The disc opens with one of the sweetest records ever to come from the city of brotherly love, "These Will Be the Good Old Days" by the Dreamlovers. Fans of the Cyrkle will be delighted with the soft, harmony-based, folk-like "Don't Say That You Love Me" and the Beach Boys-style, teen slice-of-life "Parking in the Kokomo," cut by the band under their original name, the Rhondells. Some of

what's here will be surprising on several counts, starting with Keith's "I Can't Go Wrong," a gloriously seductive and soulful non-soul record built on one of the best songs that Jerry Ross ever signed his name to; then there's the magnificent 1964 soul ballad "You Don't Know What You Got Until You Lose It" by Kenny Gamble, who was still a little ways away from success but fully deserving of it based on the evidence here. The real discovery on this CD for most listeners will be "Let Me Down Easy" by Chapter One, a brilliant, soaring, ethereal piece of mid-'70s soul. Kenny Gamble and Thom Bell turn up together as Kenny & Tommy on the 1963 single "I'll Get By." The fact that the songs tend to jump around, out of chronological order and across the decades, matters less than one would think, because the quality of Ross' work was consistent across the two decades or so covered by this anthology, even as R&B gave way to soul and then to disco. *—Bruce Eder*

Muscle Shoals, Vol. 3: You Better Believe It / May 21, 1996 / Overture ♦♦♦♦
The grinding sound of the Muscle Shoals soul factory is captured with depth and force on this collection of songs by four of its chief headliners, Tony Borders, Z.Z. Hill, Bill Brandon, and Don Varner. Both the raw funk and the earnest ballads are performed equally well, and for a program that offers a whole side's worth of unreleased songs, this is a surprisingly good listen, the occasional misstep excused. *—Jim Smith*

You Didn't Say a Word / 2000 / Goldmine/Soul Supply ♦♦
A glance at the artists listed on the cover of this CD might have you believe you're buying a collection of unreleased tracks from Motown's vaults. But that's not quite the case here; these are Ian Levine productions featuring former Motown artists, recorded in the late '80s and originally released on Motorcity. The release includes tracks by non-Motown artists as well, including the Watts 103rd Street Strings, Archie Bell & the Drells, Tammi Lavette, Gary the Master Blaster, Eddie Holman, Rocq-E-Harrell, and Shaydes of Harmony. But the rest are by ex-Motowners: Brenda Holloway, the Lovetones, the Andantes, David Ruffin and the Monitors. *—Andrew Hamilton*

You Must Remember These, Vol. 2 / 1972 / Bell ♦♦♦
This out-of-print 12-song hit collection covers many styles of the rock genre. Contains two selections each by the Box Tops and the Delfonics: "The Letter," "Cry Like a Baby," and "Didn't I Blow Your Mind," and "La, La Means I Love You," respectively. The bubble-gummy "G.T.O." by Ronny and the Daytonas, tracks alongside the heavier "Gimme, Gimme Good Lovin'" by Crazy Elephant. James & Bobby Purify and Lee Dorsey's soulful tracks and Merrilee Rush's folksy "Angel of the Morning," emphasizes the contrast in styles. Includes chart toppers by Joey Powers, Edison Lighthouse, and Syndicate of Sound. *—Andrew Hamilton*

Essays

Early Rhythm & Blues

When rhythm & blues began in the mid-'40s, it didn't even have a name. When the term caught on, though, it caught on in a big way. Right up until the present day, R&B has come to refer to the entire world of black popular music, although it's mostly identified as R&B—rather than rap, soul, or urban contemporary—by specialized audiences and music industry insiders, not general fans.

In its earliest form, rhythm & blues was among the most important precursors of rock & roll, if not *the* most important. Early rock & roll is basically R&B blended with country & western and pop influences. R&B wasn't only a crucial bridge between blues and rock & roll, but between blues and soul, R&B's longest-lived and most important offshoot.

The blues, of course, was a big part of rhythm & blues, but jazz was nearly as important. The earliest rhythm & blues artists emerged from the big-band and swing-jazz era. Before World War II, jazz, much more so than today, was a dance-oriented music, often featuring vocalists. Around World War II, many major jazz players began developing bebop and cool jazz, a decidedly less danceable (though equally worthy) style; economic factors, as well as the draft and wartime restrictions on travel, made big bands less viable. Audiences, especially the rapidly growing metropolitan African-American communities, still wanted dance music. The musicians accomodated them by playing louder, more electric instruments, and accentuating riffs, boogies, and vocals.

The first popular style of rhythm & blues is often referred to as "jump" blues. From jazz, jump blues took its horn-driven lineup and swing rhythms; from blues, it took its general riffs and chord structures. Cab Calloway was perhaps the most important precursor of the style, but in jump blues, the vocals were harsher, the rhythms faster. The instrumentation was different, too; the pianos pounded harder, and, most important, the saxes didn't just blow, but honked and squealed.

The most important and popular jump blues star was Louis Jordan, whose records, unusually for the era, enjoyed success with both black and white audiences; he was a particularly big influence on Chuck Berry. Many of the early jump blues performers emerged from Los Angeles, where a large black community had been growing during the Depression and the war; most other big cities had jump blues stars of their own by the end of the 1940s. Independent labels such as L.A.'s Specialty and Aladdin jump-started their success with the jump blues sound, filling a demand that the majors were basically unaware of. Joe Liggins, Tiny Bradshaw (the original performer of "The Train Kept A-Rollin'"), Amos Milburn, Camille Howard—all are largely forgotten except by record collectors, but all had huge R&B successes in the jump blues style, and ranked among the most popular black musicians of their time.

Jump blues itself came in several different styles. There were the vocalists that came to be known as the "shouters," adding energy, soul, and gospel to the more restrained brand of big-band singing. Big Joe Turner, who got his start with Kansas City jazz bands, was the most legendary link between the eras, shifting into the R&B era with ease, and even scoring some early rock & roll hits. Wynonie Harris, Roy Brown, Roy Milton, and Nappy Brown were a few of the most popular "shouters" of the late '40s and early '50s, although they aren't nearly as well remembered by history as Turner. There were also showmen, usually saxophonists, whose appeal was primarily instrumental: Big Jay McNeely, Illinois Jacquet, and Joe Houston with strong roots in jazz, drove dance crowds crazy with their acrobatic honking. And there were smoother, more urbane singers, like Charles Brown, Percy Mayfield, and Cecil Gant, who were as adept at ballads as uptempo material.

By the time the '50s started, "race" music, as it was known within the industry, had been renamed the more appropriate "rhythm & blues" by *Billboard* magazine staff member Jerry Wexler. As an A&R man at Atlantic Records, Wexler helped shape jump blues into something with more appeal to pop listeners and teenagers. The recordings by early Atlantic stars like Ruth Brown, LaVern Baker, the first incarnation of the Drifters, and Chuck Willis (who actually began at the OKeh label) retained a strong jump blues flavor, but their rhythms, riffs, and lyrics point more clearly toward rock & roll. Indeed, Baker, and Willis managed to enjoy some success in the early rock & roll era with material that was tailored toward a younger audience. As rock & roll began to emerge in the early and mid-'50s, several distinct branches of R&B had developed that would each exert a large influence on popular music in their own rights: doo wop groups, electric blues, and New Orleans rhythm & blues. All of these subgenres are examined in greater depth in this book in essays of their own, and all would prove to have a greater and more lasting impact on rock & roll than the earlier, jazzier forms of R&B.

Still, there were quite a few performers who survived through the 1950s, and sometimes thrived, recording music that could not be called anything but R&B. Ike Turner, Ivory Joe Hunter, Faye Adams, Wynona Carr, Big Mama Thornton, Big Maybelle—none of these were straight blues artists, but their music wasn't rock & roll either. Blues singers like Bobby "Blue" Bland, Junior Parker, and Little Milton bridged electric blues and soul, but they couldn't be pigeonholed as straight rock & roll singers. Occasionally R&B performers like Johnny Otis, Screamin' Jay Hawkins, and Wilbert Harrison crossed over to the rock & roll audience with their most hook-savvy songs; Harrison's *Kansas City* is largely jump blues with a shuffle beat, at least until it gets to the searing electric guitar break.

Several 1950s singers began as more or less straight R&B performers, but added an earthier, more pronounced gospel and church influence than had ever been heard before. Today, we recognize the greatest of these vocalists—Ray Charles, James Brown, Jackie Wilson, Little Willie John, Johnny Ace, Jessie Belvin, and Clyde McPhatter—as the forefathers of soul. Some of them, like Charles and Brown, would indeed become soul superstars in the '60s. Others, like McPhatter and John, were unable to make the transition, due to a combination of inability to grow with the times and personal problems that proved insurmountable. R&B, though it has changed greatly since its birth, remains a crucial part of rock, soul, and rap, just below or very much above the surface.

For all of its monumental significance, and the vast critical acclaim it has belatedly received, early R&B recordings can be tough to swallow in large lumps for the neophyte. The R&B performers and labels of the '40s and '50s were concerned with entertaining, not establishing diverse artistic oeuvres, and the similar chord patterns and arrangements can be wearing on a compact disc rather than a juke box or dancefloor, which is where the songs were often played in their heyday. Those investigating the genre in-depth for the first time are advised to start with some general various artist samplers, and move on from there according to their degrees of interest.

Recommended Recordings:

Various Artists, *Blues Masters, Volume 5: Jump Blues Classics* (Rhino). The best jump blues introduction, with key cuts by Joe Turner, Wynonie Harris, Roy Brown, Tiny Bradshaw, Big Jay McNeely, Big Mama Thornton, Ruth Brown, and others.

Various Artists, *Blues Masters, Volume 14: More Jump Blues* (Rhino). Up to the same level as Jump Blues Classics, with tracks by Louis Jordan, LaVern Baker, Big Maybelle, Faye Adams, and many more.

Big Joe Turner, *Big, Bad & Blue: The Big Joe Turner Anthology* (Rhino). As mammoth as the man himself, this three-disc set encompasses several decades, reflecting R&B's evolution from the days of big-band jazz through rock & roll. Too extensive for the casual fan; as alternatives, there are other Turner anthologies that focus on specific phases of his career.

Louis Jordan, *The Best of Louis Jordan* (MCA). Jordan recorded a great deal of material in the 1940s and 1950s, and no collection satisfactorily encompasses all of his classics; this one is the best.

Various Artists, *Atlantic Rhythm & Blues Vol.1-4* (Atlantic). The most important label in the development of modern R&B, this is part of a seven-volume series that goes up to 1974. There's a whole box set of them if you want to go whole hog, but the first four cover 1947-1962, before R&B had been fully renamed rock and soul.

Various Artists, *Specialty Story* (Specialty). At five discs, this is too much for non-specialists, if you'll pardon the pun. But it does offer a comprehensive survey of one of early R&B and rock & roll's most important labels, with tracks by such greats as Joe Liggins, Percy Mayfield, Roy Milton, and Lloyd Price up through early rock stars like Little Richard and Larry Williams.

Ruth Brown, *Rockin' in Rhythm: The Best of Ruth Brown* (Rhino). The singer on whom much of Atlantic's early fortune was built, this double disc contains her most popular 1950s sides.

LaVern Baker, *Soul on Fire: The Best of LaVern Baker* (Rhino). One of the most important singers to lead the transition from R&B to rock & roll.

The Drifters, *Let the Boogie-Woogie Roll: Greatest Hits* (1953-1958) (Atlantic). The first lineup of the Drifters, featuring Clyde McPhatter, could be called a doo wop group as well, but also had strong early R&B/jump blues influences.

Ike Turner, *I Like Ike: The Best of Ike Turner* (Rhino). Before joining Tina, Ike was an important talent scout, sideman, and bandleader. This collection of odds 'n' ends is mostly from the 1950s, and often walks the edge between R&B and electric blues.

Ray Charles, *Birth of Soul* (Rhino). Aptly titled three-disc box of Charles' work for Atlantic in the 1950s.

Johnny Otis, *The Capitol Years* (Capitol). An enormously popular figure in R&B as a bandleader, musician, and talent scout, Otis crossed over to success in the rock market in the late '50s by adding a Bo Diddley beat. Although Otis himself preferred straight R&B, this collection of late-'50s sides is his best.

Little Willie John, *Fever: The Best of Little Willie John* (Rhino). One of R&B's most versatile vocalists and a huge influence on James Brown.

Clyde McPhatter, *Deep Sea Ball: The Best of Clyde McPhatter* (Rhino). His biggest hits for Atlantic in the late '50s, after he left the Drifters.

James Brown, *Roots of a Revolution* (PolyGram). A double-CD retrospective of 1956-1964 recordings, bringing us from hardcore R&B to the verge of the birth of funk.

—*Richie Unterberger*

Music Map

R&B Through Soul and Funk to Urban and Contemporary R&B

Jump Blues
Louis Jordan • Joe Liggins
Amos Milburn • Wynonie Harris
Roy Brown • Big Joe Turner

Gospel
The Soul Stirrers • The Swan
Silvertones • Mahalia Jackson
Golden Gate Quartet • The Five
Blind Boys of Mississippi

'50s R&B
The Coasters • The Drifters
Fats Domino • Ruth Brown
LaVern Baker • Little Richard
Bo Diddley • Johnny Otis

'60s Soul
Ray Charles • Sam Cooke
Jackie Wilson • Solomon Burke
Otis Redding • The Supremes
Marvin Gaye

Late-'60s Funk
James Brown • Sly & the Family
Stone • The Isley Brothers
Charles Wright & the Watts
103rd Street Rhythm Band
Dyke & the Blazers

'70s Funk
Kool & the Gang • The Meters
Parliament-Funkadelic
Earth, Wind & Fire • War
The Ohio Players
The Commodores

Disco (Mid- to Late '70s)
Chic • Donna Summer
The Bee Gees • Barry White
Village People
KC & the Sunshine Band
Larry Levan • Sylvester

'70s Soul
Aretha Franklin • Stevie Wonder
Al Green • The O'Jays
Diana Ross • Bobby Womack
Harold Melvin & the Blue Notes
Donny Hathaway

The '80s
Michael Jackson • Prince • Janet
Jackson • Whitney Houston
George Michael • Gloria Estefan

The '90s
Mariah Carey • Boyz II Men
Aaliyah • Toni Braxton • TLC
D'Angelo • Lauryn Hill
Erykah Badu • Macy Gray

Independent Labels: The 1940s and 1950s

In many respects, 1945 was an incredibly scary time to be in America. World War II finally finished, and the country prepared to adjust from a wartime economy to a peacetime one that would need to reintegrate millions of returning veterans. The atomic bomb cast a cloud over the future of the planet; the rise of communism in the Soviet Union and Eastern Europe was sowing seeds of fear and paranoia. Many wanted to do nothing more than resume life as normal, but the fact was that changing geopolitics, new technology, and developing mass media meant that life could never be the same.

But at the same time, life had never been more exciting. The United States had finally recovered from the effects of the Depression, and those who had survived the war with their families and health intact were ready to relax and, to a degree, party. Music was needed, and with the end of wartime rationing of certain materials, the record industry could resume full-scale operations after years of manufacturing restrictions. It was in this uncertain yet intoxicating climate that a boomlet of independent labels helped lay the foundation for the recording and distribution of postwar blues music.

Historically, the music business has always been dominated by about a half-dozen "major" labels. Their names and initials change according to corporate transactions and mergers, but in the middle of the 1940s they were Columbia, Victor, Decca, Capitol, Mercury, and MGM. Ever since the blues began to be recorded, the major labels had paid some attention to the music, often placing the artists on subsidiary companies that were geared toward the "race" (i.e., black) audience. Hence the appearance of so many CD reissues of ancient blues on huge labels like Sony and BMG.

An independent label formed in the 1940s faced enormous obstacles in competing against the majors, but also had enormous opportunities. Blues, R&B, and hillbilly artists were still recording for big companies in the 1940s, but not in great numbers; the labels focused their energies on pop music that was oriented towards white Americans. This, naturally, left a vacuum in the marketplace, and several million disenfranchised listeners. Blues, R&B, and country were exploding as live, regional phenomenons, but weren't adequately represented on record. Demand necessitates supply, and numerous independent labels emerged to fill the gap.

There were no rule books for the new upstarts to adhere to, and one imagines that day-to-day life for these fledgling operations was both nerve-wracking and tremendously exciting. They didn't have the funds, state-of-the-art studios, or massive distribution networks that gave the Columbias of the world such huge advantages. All of them had to do things the hard way, driving from town to town to push their latest singles from the trunks of their cars, collect payments from shaky distributors and retailers, and chat up the local DJs in hopes of getting their releases on the air. What they usually had, above all, were ears to the ground: a real feel for what the communities of minority audiences—blacks, Southern whites, and teenagers—were listening to, on the regional radio stations (itself an exploding phenomenon of the time), the jukeboxes, and the dance halls. This was true whether the label owners were black or, as they were in many cases, white, sometimes being minorities of sorts themselves with Jewish and/or immigrant backgrounds.

Out of this crazy-quilt milieu came the labels so near and dear to the hearts of millions of blues, rock, and R&B fans: Chess, Sun, Specialty, Aladdin, Modern, King, Atlantic, Imperial, Vee-Jay, Duke/Peacock, and others. None of them focused on the blues exclusively: indeed, few of them even focused on black music exclusively. All of them, however, wanted in on the R&B market, to varying degrees. And thus it was that most of the best blues artists of the 1940s and 1950s recorded for these labels.

As far as establishing a label or "house" sound, Chess and Sun were probably the most distinctive of these operations, and their histories are outlined in separate pieces. While other prominent indies of the period may not have developed a production style as immediately distinctive, several made especially noteworthy contributions to blues and R&B history, and usually made a mark on rock & roll as well. In the mid-'40s, several companies sprouted up in Los Angeles, where the record and entertainment industry (which was then centered in New York) was truly beginning to establish roots. These labels also did a great deal to develop styles of blues/R&B that became identified with the West Coast, particularly jump blues.

One of the most important L.A. operations was Specialty, founded in 1945 by Art Rupe; that same year, it had one of the first truly monster independent R&B hits, Roy Milton's "R.M. Blues." Milton was one of the label's biggest stars, scoring nearly 20 R&B hits in a jump blues style; Camille Howard (Milton's pianist), Jimmy Liggins, Joe Liggins, and Floyd Dixon also had hits for the label, employing the boogie-woogie pianos and honking saxes that were early R&B staples. Specialty was also one of the first companies to scout the burgeoning New Orleans R&B scene, recording hugely influential hits in the early half of the 1950s by Lloyd Price and Guitar Slim.

Specialty was not solely devoted to R&B; it had an extensive gospel line as well, the jewel in the crown being the Soul Stirrers, who featured the young Sam Cooke. They also landed one of the biggest original rock & roll stars, Little Richard, and also had some success in the rock field with Larry Williams and Don & Dewey. Yet by the late '50s, Specialty was winding down its activities; Art Rupe was finding lucrative economic opportunities outside of the record business. It's also been suggested that he was discouraged by the success of Sam Cooke, who became a huge pop star after Rupe, frightened of tampering with the gospel singer's track record, refused to release secular material by Cooke on Specialty, giving both Cooke and producer Bumps Blackwell their walking papers in the bargain. Numerous well-packaged Specialty reissues have appeared on the market since the label sold its catalog to Fantasy in 1990.

Aladdin, also formed in L.A. in 1945, was a virtual storehouse of West Coast jump blues/R&B pianists, recording Amos Milburn, Floyd Dixon, and Charles Brown. The "honking" element of West Coast jump blues was provided by saxophonist Big Jay McNeely. In the mid-'50s, like some other labels, they got a cut of the New Orleans R&B/rock scene with the vocal duo of Shirley & Lee.

Modern, yet another L.A. company formed in 1945 (by the Bihari brothers), also had some tentacles into the West Coast blues/R&B scene, with a roster including Floyd Dixon (who recorded for several labels during his prime), Etta James, and saxophonist Joe Houston. In comparison with Aladdin and Specialty, however, they had a greater taste for guitar-focused, grittier blues, releasing sides by Jimmy McCracklin, Johnny "Guitar" Watson, and Pee Wee Crayton. They were also aggressive in scouting talent outside of their region, distributing some of the first nationally popular recordings by blues legends John Lee Hooker, B.B. King, and Elmore James, all of whom were based east of the Mississippi. In the '50s, they formed active subsidiary labels, RPM and Flair; when times became leaner, however, they focused on budget LP compilations for another of their subsidiaries, the Crown label.

A final L.A. giant was Imperial, founded in the late 1940s. Although it made significant contributions to West Coast blues by recording guitarists T-Bone Walker and Jimmy McCracklin, it will be mainly remembered for its forays into New Orleans R&B. No other label based outside of New Orleans (and maybe none within New Orleans) had as much success with Crescent City music, principally with Fats Domino, who spun out a never-ending series of hits for about a decade. Dave Bartholomew was an instrumental factor in many of Imperial's New Orleans hits as a producer and arranger, for Domino and others; the label also recorded some blues-oriented singers in New Orleans, like Roy Brown, Pee Wee Crayton, and Snooks Eaglin, in attempts to give them a commercial direction more in line with rock & roll's burgeoning popularity. The label's days as a major power came to end with its sale to Liberty in 1963, when Domino's never-ending chart success had finally ceased, and the company's biggest star, Rick Nelson, had been lured away to a major label.

Chicago blues was considerably rawer and more guitar-based than the kind usually issued by the West Coast labels, and Chess, though the giant in the field, wasn't the only game in town. Vee Jay, also based in the Windy City, had two of the most commercially successful bluesmen of the era, Jimmy Reed and John Lee Hooker (it should be noted that Hooker recorded for quite a few labels in his early career, often for several simultaneously, and occasionally under pseudonyms). Lesser-known but great sides were also recorded for Vee-Jay by harmonica player/singer Billy Boy Arnold and Eddie Taylor, who was Jimmy Reed's guitarist. In the early '60s, it had huge successes in the pop market with early recordings by the Four Seasons and the Beatles, but went belly-up in the mid-'60s.

A Chicago R&B label that flamed briefly and brightly was Cobra, who lured Chess bassist/arranger/songwriter Willie Dixon away for a brief time in the late '50s. If for nothing else, the label gained a niche in blues history for waxing classic early sides by Otis Rush that rate among the best and most chilling electric blues ever recorded. Magic Sam also recorded notable early sides for the label, although he wouldn't truly reach his peak until the '60s.

King, based in Cincinnati, was one of the most versatile independent labels of the time: R&B may have been its bread and butter, but it also made a great deal of key hillbilly records. But it certainly had an impressive roster of both blues shouters (Wynonie Harris, Bullmoose Jackson, Eddie "Cleanhead" Vinson) and instrumental-oriented honkers (Big Jay McNeely, organist Bill Doggett, Tiny Bradshaw, Earl Bostic, and others). In the 1960s it also had claim to one of the decade's most commercially successful blues guitarists, Freddie King. By that time, though, it was heavily reliant upon the empire of Soul Brother Number One, James Brown. King was sold to Polydor in the early 1970s; in recent years compilations of important King R&B/blues artists have appeared on Rhino.

A major outpost of Southern blues was Duke/Peacock, founded by legendary micro-manager Don Robey in Houston. In addition to recording Big Mama Thornton and Texan guitarists like Clarence "Gatemouth" Brown, Duke did its part to point the way for soul by recording two of the leading soul-bluesmen, Bobby "Blue" Bland and Junior Parker. The label seemed comfortable with both guitar-focused material and sophisticated horn arrangements that played off the gospel-influenced vocals of Bland in particular.

Excello, though founded in Nashville, really made its mark on blues history through its Louisiana-based artists, including Slim Harpo, Lightnin' Slim, and Lazy Lester. These are the singers who, aided by producer Jay Miller, were the key exponents of "swamp blues." By lending the musicians sympathetic production and the freedom to more or less be themselves, Miller was one of several producers who cultivated a characteristic sound, Sam Phillips (at Sun) and Leonard Chess (at Chess) being two of the most notable others.

New York is not noted as a groundswell of down-home blues, and it may be that the key contribution of Atlantic was in tilling the field for R&B, rock & roll, and soul, rather than developing straight blues. The company can't be overlooked, however, due to its crucial role in midwifing blues-derived R&B into more urbanized forms with a greater appeal to a younger audience. Joe Turner, Ray Charles, Sticks McGhee, Chuck Willis, Ruth Brown, and LaVern Baker were just some of the most prominent players with Atlantic contracts. And the label did record some straight-up blues, even if much of it tended to be with artists that made their most significant music for other operations.

A smaller notable independent based in New York City was Bobby Robinson's Fire label, with the active Fury and Enjoy subsidiaries. Robinson recorded some of the rawest guitar blues of the era, including some of Elmore James' best work. Buster Brown's "Fannie Mae" was one of the most undiluted blues records ever to make the Top 40. And Fire was also responsible for Wilbert Harrison's number-one hit "Kansas City," which may be the ultimate example of shuffle blues transposed into rock & roll, one of the key ingredients being Jimmy Spruill's scintillating guitar solo.

This roundup, it should be noted, has only encompassed some of the most active independent companies that recorded blues music between 1945 and 1960. Others made significant contributions, such as Savoy, which recorded a good deal of jump blues by

Johnny Otis and others, and Trumpet, which released some primeval Southern blues in the early '50s by Sonny Boy Williamson and others. In the 1990s, Capricorn Records dedicated a series of box sets to such labels, including ones for Cobra, Fire/Fury, Jewel/Paula, and Swingtime. Charlie Gillett's *The Sound of the City*, a history of rock & roll's first two decades, does an excellent job of detailing the many influential independent early rock and R&B labels, and is recommended further reading.

There were numerous tiny companies that released regional singles in small quantities; some lasted for only one or two 45s. Many of these can now only be enjoyed on small-run import reissues (if they even made it that far). But their deep obscurity, and the relatively raw production values employed on some of them, doesn't mean that they can't be just as enjoyable as sides produced on the "big" indies.

Independent rock and R&B labels, by and large, were reducing their blues rosters by the dawn of the 1960s. This was not necessarily, as some might charge, a reflection of lack of interest in the blues by the label owners, or ingratitude towards the artists that had helped put them on the map in the first place. The independents, it must be remembered, were not PBS; they were commercial enterprises that needed chart hits and cash flow. In focusing their energies elsewhere, they were usually responding to trends in the overall marketplace, most notably the increasing success of rock & roll. And a lot of the biggest independents didn't even survive the competition of the era, going under or selling their catalog to other companies; Atlantic, which is still thriving today, is more the exception than the rule.

R&B itself was loosening its ties to the blues, and looking forward to soul music. Some artists, like Bobby "Blue" Bland, Little Milton, Albert King, and Freddie King, were well-suited for adapting to the new era; unfortunately, most of the blues stars of the '40s and '50s blues stars were left out in the cold. It should be noted that a lot of indies didn't give up on the blues completely; Motown, the most successful of the whole lot, made little-noticed recordings with Amos Milburn and Earl King in the 1960s. But the commercial momentum of American pop had shifted away from blues and hardcore R&B, leaving the blues in the hands of a devoted but more specialized audience.

And the needs of that audience would be addressed from the 1960s onwards by independent companies. These, however, were independent companies that were not as concerned with commercial chart success as satisfying the tastes of a niche market that included increasingly younger, more affluent, and white listeners. The prime medium would not be the 45 single, but the long-playing record and, much later, the compact disc. The stories of those independents—Arhoolie, Delmark, Alligator, Fat Possum, and others—is told in a separate sidebar. The legacy of the earlier generation of independents is readily available for today's audience, however, on a plethora of CD reissues, several of which provided thematically linked (and sometimes, truth to tell, haphazard) overviews of the labels' valuable contributions to American music.

5 Recommended Albums:

Various Artists, *Chess Blues* (Chess)
Various Artists, *A Sun Blues Collection* (Rhino)
Various Artists, *The Specialty Story* (Specialty)
Various Artists, *Atlantic Blues Box* (Atlantic)
Various Artists, *The Cobra Records Story* (Capricorn)

—Richie Unterberger

Doo Wop

"Doo wop"—the words bring smiles to the faces of most knowledgeable rock listeners. In some cases, they're smirks of derision, from those who feel that the form exemplifies rock & roll at its most innocuous, silliest, and embarrassingly quaint. From those who grew up during the '50s, it's more likely a smile of pleasure from someone who treasures the exquisite vocal harmonies and mourns the loss of the utter lack of pretension and guile that characterized great doo wop recordings.

Love it or hate it, doo wop is a major part of rock & roll's lexicon. The R&B ballads and uptempo numbers of doo wop are characterized by those harmonies, of course, but also by the nonsense syllables that often formed the backbone of the backup vocals. "Doo wop" was just one of those common phrases; "bop-bop, dip-dip," "bomp-a-bomp-bomp-bomp, buh-dang-a-dang-dang," "wah wah, shoop shoop," "dooby dooby doo," and "yip-yip-yip-yip-yip-yip-yip-yip" were just a few of the others. Usually they were love songs, but often they were outrageous comic novelty tunes as well. They were early rock & roll at its most sentimental and humorous. Doo wop—like all great African-American music—has much of its roots in the harmonies and emotive phrasing of gospel. The more pop-oriented side of the equation was provided by the first popular American black vocal groups, the Ink Spots and the Mills Brothers. Adding a R&B flavor to this blueprint, as well as a strong "church" feel, the Orioles had a number-one R&B hit in 1948 with "It's Too Soon to Know," which is often cited as the first doo wop (and sometimes, even the first rock & roll) record.

Several groups followed in the Orioles' style over the next few years, including the Ravens the Cardinals, and the Larks (many of the early doo wop acts named themselves after birds). The Clovers drew more explicitly from rhythm & blues, and the snappier rhythms and saucier lyrics of jump blues infiltrated the form in recordings by the Dominoes (featuring Clyde McPhatter) and Hank Ballard & the Midnighters.

By 1954, singles by the Crows ("Gee"), Dominoes, Orioles and Hank Ballard had crossed over from the R&B market to become bona fide pop chart hits. Numerous urban vocal groups sprang up—a lot of them probably did start on the street corner, as legend would have it—and numerous record companies rushed to get a piece of the action. As rock & roll gained momentum, doo wop become brassier, with more honking sax solos, outrageous stuttering vocal interplay, and more explicitly teenage and young adult themes.

There were probably over a thousand groups that eventually cut a doo wop record over the next decade, leading to a vociferous collector community that probably ranks as the most devoted of its kind in rock & roll. A great many of the records originated in New York, though Los Angeles and Philadelphia were also active centers, and scattered doo wop acts were active, in the studio and otherwise, across the country.

Most of the doo wop groups, if they made it onto the charts at all, were one or two-shot acts, quickly fading into obscurity after failing to secure followups. The Penguins, the Five Satins, the Monotones, the El Dorados, the Dell Vikings, the Silhouettes—these are just a few of those glorious names, though in some cases they recorded some non-hit efforts that were nearly as fine as their smashes.

There were also a few groups that managed to maintain a presence on the R&B and pop charts for a few years running, sometimes with numerous personnel changes. The Clovers, the Flamingos, Little Anthony & the Imperials, and the Moonglows were a few of the best. With the Teenagers, Frankie Lymon pioneered a brand of pre-teen soul that was rightfully pinpointed as an influence on Michael Jackson when the Jackson 5 emerged many years later. Before Clyde McPhatter left to become a solo act, the first incarnation of the Drifters was one of the most popular R&B acts of the mid-'50s.

At the top of the pyramid was a couple groups that ranked among the most popular early rock & rollers. The Platters were one of the most pop-oriented of all of the doo wop groups, and appealed to the adult audience more than almost any of the early major rock & roll acts. The Coasters were among the wittiest rock groups of any era, courtesy of Jerry Leiber & Mike Stoller who penned and produced many classic songs for the singers, including "Searchin'," "Young Blood," "Yakety Yak," and "Poison Ivy."

As the '50s progressed, more and more white performers sang doo wop, sometimes in integrated ensembles (such as the Dell Vikings and the Impalas), sometimes as all-white groups (the Mystics, Dion & the Belmonts). Often Italian-American in origin, by the time the '60s began, these white singers were a major part of the form, which was becoming less of a commercial force.

But before doo wop vanished from the charts altogether, it underwent a revival of sorts in the early '60s, which saw huge doo wop hits by the likes of the Marcels, the Capris, Maurice Williams and Shep & the Limelites. By the time of the British Invasion, though, there was barely a ripple of pure doo wop to be found on the charts.

Doo wop did not vanish so much as become permanently absorbed into rock and soul. Early soul giants like the Miracles and the Impressions owed huge debts to doo wop; indeed, their early records pretty much are doo wop. A lot of doo wop could be heard in the girl groups of the early '60s. Many hits by the Four Seasons and Dion were doo wop in construction, if not always in production. In vocal surf music, there's no doubt that doo wop was a prime influence on the ensemble singing of the Beach Boys and Jan & Dean. You can also hear it in the early records by the Beatles and several other British Invasion groups, as well as many of Frank Zappa's satirical efforts. And right on up to Boyz II Men soul music has built upon the harmonies and vocal arrangements of doo wop music.

12 Most Essential Doo Wop Recordings:

Various Artists, *The Doo Wop Box, Vol.1-2* (Rhino)
Billy Ward & the Dominoes, *Sixty Minute Men: The Best of Billy Ward & His Dominoes* (Rhino)
Hank Ballard & the Midnighters, *Sexy Ways: The Best of Hank Ballard & the Midnighters* (Rhino)
The Drifters, *Let the Boogie Woogie Roll—Greatest Hits (1953-1958)* (Atlantic)
The Platters, *Magic Touch: An Anthology* (Mercury)
Frankie Lymon & the Teenagers, *Best of Frankie Lymon & the Teenagers* (Rhino)
Dion & the Belmonts, *Everything You Always Wanted to Hear by Dion & the Belmonts* (Laurie)
The Coasters, *50 Coastin' Classics* (Rhino)
The Clovers, *Down in the Alley: The Best of the Clovers* (Atlantic)
The Moonglows, *Blue Velvet: The Ultimate Collection* (Chess)
Various Artists, *The Best of Doo Wop Uptempo, Vol. 1, The Best of Doo Wop Uptempo, Vol. 2* (Rhino)
Various Artists, *The Best of Doo Wop Ballads, Vol.1, The Best of Doo Wop Ballads, Vol.2* (Rhino)

Books:

Doo Wop: *The Forgotten Third of Rock 'N Roll*, by Dr. Anthony Gribin & Dr. Matthew Shiff (Krause Publications, 1992)
They All Sang on the Corner, by **Phillip Groia** (Phillie Dee Enterprises, 1983)

—Richie Unterberger

New Orleans R&B

When it comes down to naming which American city contributed most to the birth of rock & roll, it really only comes down to two: Memphis and New Orleans. New Orleans, of course, already occupied a rarefied place in the legacy of American popular music for its crucial role in the birth of jazz music. Its contribution to rock & roll was nearly equal in stature, supplying the music with many of its bedrock rhythms, as well as much of its playful humor. Its population, a vibrant mix of Creole, Cajun, black, and white cultures, cultivated precisely the kind of melting pot of music that led to the early styles of rock & roll.

The early New Orleans sound was characterized by boogie piano, honking saxes, and relaxed, unfettered performances. Pianist Professor Longhair embodies the true sound of New Orleans for some listeners, but it wasn't established as a major commercial force until the emergence of Fats Domino. His 1950 single "The Fat Man" is one of the dozens of performances routinely cited as one of the first rock & roll records. It took a while for Fats to cross over to the pop audience, but once he did, starting with 1955's "Ain't That a Shame," he became one of the most popular early rock & roll performers, rolling off hit after hit for the next half-dozen years.

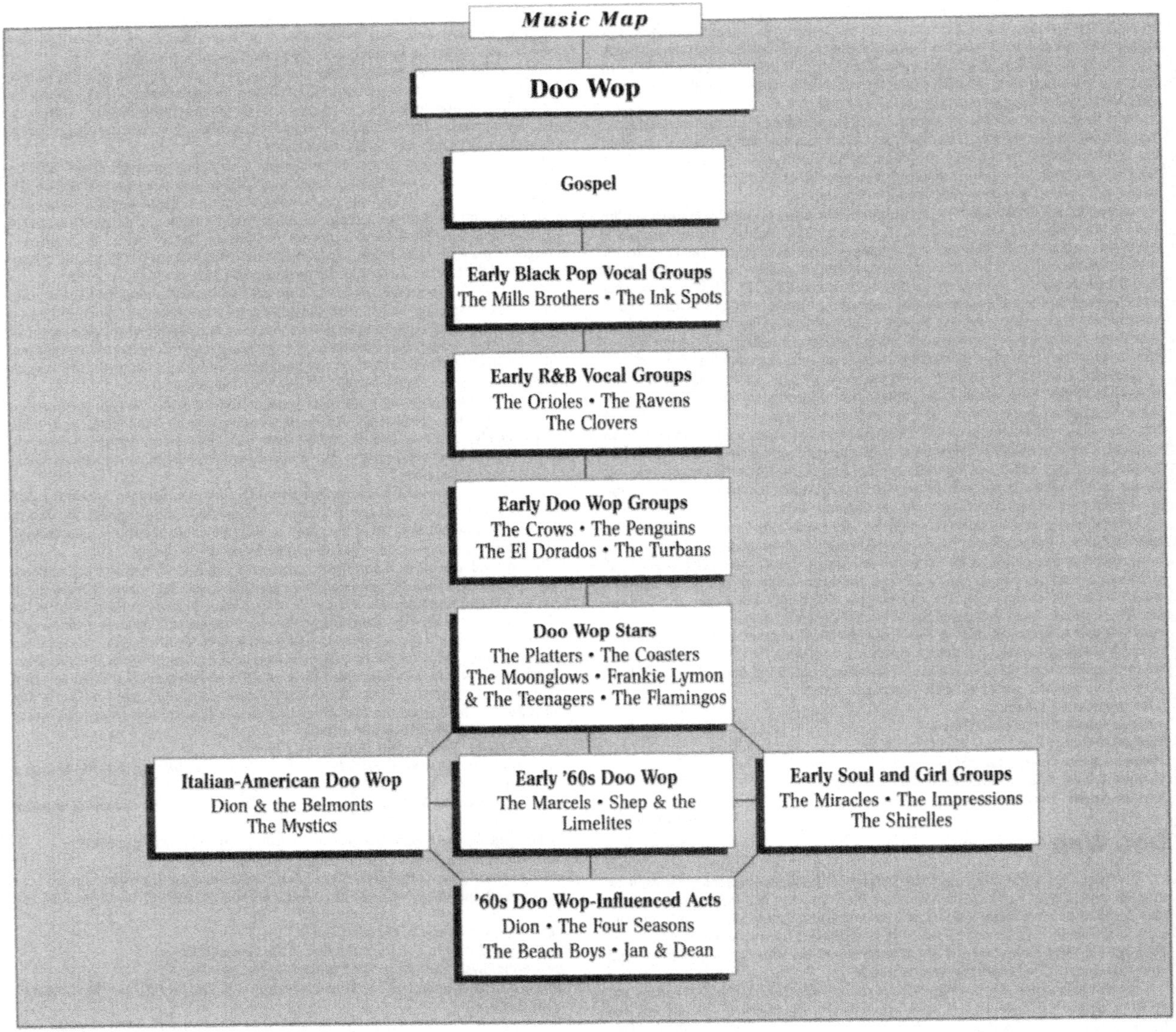

Another Crescent City candidate for the title of first rock & roll record was Lloyd Price's "Lawdy Miss Clawdy," a 1952 number-one R&B hit. Price's late-'50s hits had a much more commercial sound, but his early work was much rawer and influenced his label, the Los Angeles-based Specialty Records, to move its focus from jump blues to rock & roll. Their biggest star was Little Richard, a Georgia native who didn't find his groove until he started recording in New Orleans, reeling off a batch of hugely influential hit singles in the mid-'50s that helped define early rock & roll with their wooly vocals, pounding piano, and shrieking horns.

The chief behind-the-scenes architect of the New Orleans sound was Dave Bartholomew, a trumpeter, songwriter, and producer who graced many early classic New Orleans R&B/rock sessions, not the least of which were those of Fats Domino (whose hits Bartholomew co-wrote). Session players like drummer Earl Palmer and saxophonists Alvin "Red" Tyler and Lee Allen also played on numerous sessions, and were instrumental in putting the stamp on the early New Orleans sound.

Little Richard and Fats Domino were the only superstars to emerge from the city's rock & roll scene in the 1950s, but there were also many artists with only one or two national hits that recorded a wealth of fine material (much of which gave them sizable regional hits). Shirley & Lee ("Let the Good Times Roll"), Huey "Piano" Smith ("Rocking Pneumonia & the Boogie-Woogie Flu"), and Clarence "Frogman" Henry ("Ain't Got No Home"), all recorded classics which continue to live at the heart of the rock & roll repertoire. Most of the music was recorded by blacks, but Bobby Charles ("See You Later Alligator") and Frankie Ford ("Sea Cruise") proved that whites could also rock convincingly in the New Orleans style.

In the early '60s, the New Orleans sound updated slightly to reflect trends in the still-young soul scene. Pianist, songwriter, and producer Allen Toussaint inherited Dave Bartholomew's crown as the city's chief rock & roll visionary. Again, while there were no stars of the magnitude of Fats Domino or Little Richard, there were many classic hits and non-hits by the likes of Ernie K-Doe ("Mother-In-Law"), Chris Kenner ("I Like It Like That"), the Showmen ("It Will Stand"), Barbara George ("I Know"), and Benny Spellman ("Fortune Teller").

Some of the New Orleans performers emerging during this period proved to be durable, though not superstars. Irma Thomas may be the finest female New Orleans R&B singer of all time, not to mention one of the finest soul-R&B singers of any kind; in addition to her classic early New Orleans ballads, she also recorded great pop/rock sides in L.A. and "deep soul" tracks with the Muscle Shoals rhythm section. Lee Dorsey had charming novelty-tinged hits with "Ya Ya," "Working in a Coal Mine," and "Ride Your Pony." Clarence "Frogman" Henry roared back into the charts in the early '60s with several singles in a sort of updated Fats Domino style. The Dixie Cups ran off several great girl group singles in the mid-'60s, one of which, "Iko Iko," was a variation on a traditional Mardi Gras Indian chant. Barbara Lynn recorded many early soul singles, although only one, "You'll Lose a Good Thing," was a big national smash.

After the mid-'60s, national New Orleans R&B hits were relatively rare, although the city continued to house a lively music scene. The most influential latter-day Crescent City performers were the Meters, who mixed New Orleans rhythms with funk; Dr. John, a session player with extensive roots in the New Orleans scene dating back to the late '50s, who created a sort of mystic voodoo-tinged updating of the vintage New Orleans sound;

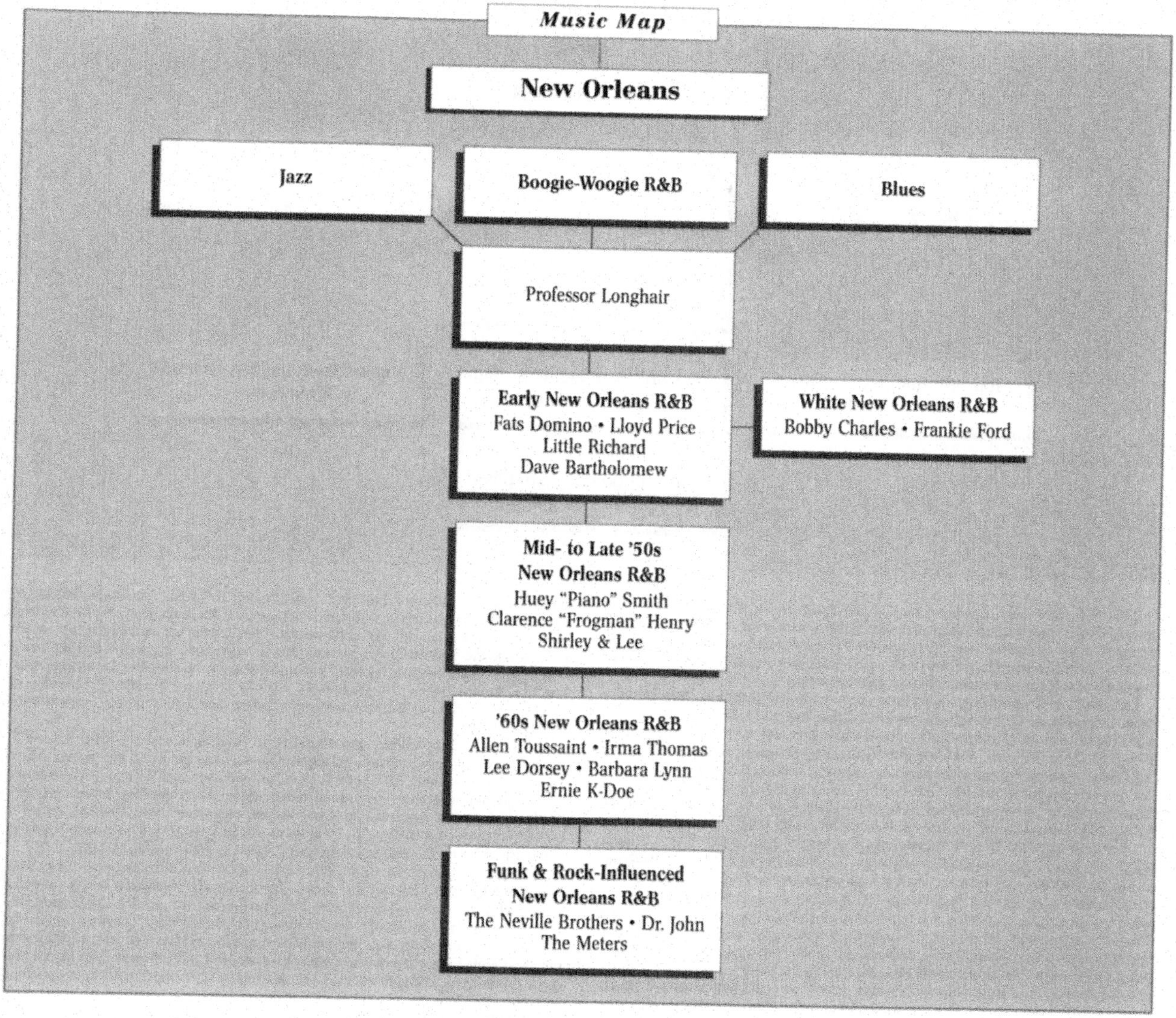

and the Neville Brothers, a prodigously talented family who had been releasing fine R&B and soul records, together and separately, since the mid-'50s.

The New Orleans sound may not be a big commercial presence nowadays—the Neville Brothers are the only big touring act associated with the sound, and they've never delivered the classic record that critics expect of their talents. But truth to tell, the city can carry on its traditions with little help from the rest of the nation, as many R&B musicians continue to base themselves in New Orleans and play to a regional audience. The city also continues to feature dozens of its R&B, blues, and rock performers in the massive New Orleans Jazz festival, which attracts huge crowds from around the world every year.

13 Most Essential New Orleans R&B Recordings:

Various Artists, *A History of New Orleans Rhythm & Blues Vol. 1-3* (Rhino)
Fats Domino, *My Blue Heaven: Best of Fats Domino* (EMI)
Little Richard, *18 Greatest Hits* (Rhino)
Lee Dorsey, *Holy Cow!: Best of Lee Dorsey* (Arista)
Dr. John, *Anthology* (Rhino)
Irma Thomas, *Time Is on My Side (The Best Of Irma Thomas), Vol. 1* (EMI)
Lloyd Price, *Lawdy!* (Specialty)
The Neville Brothers, *Treacherous—A History of the Neville Brothers (1955-1985)* (Rhino)
The Meters, *Funkify Your Life: The Meters Anthology* (Rhino)
Professor Longhair, *Fess: Professor Longhair Anthology* (Rhino)
Dave Bartholomew, *Spirit of New Orleans* (EMI)
Huey "Piano" Smith, *Rock & Roll Revival* (Ace, UK)
Various Artists, *Crescent City Soul: The Sound of New Orleans* (EMI)

—Richie Unterberger

Brill Building Sound

Rock & roll is usually thought of as a hybrid of several types of American roots music—the blues, country & western, R&B, gospel, and others. The influence of mainstream American popular songwriting, embodied by the conglomerate of professional composers and publishers dubbed Tin Pan Alley, on rock's early development is sometimes overlooked. While rock & roll was to a significant degree a reaction against the overly professional, sentimental, and sterile conventions of pre-rock American pop, the best of Tin Pan Alley's melodic and lyrical hallmarks were incorporated into rock & roll to raise the music to new levels of sophistication.

The songwriters most crucial to this process congregated in the early '60s in a New York block known as the Brill Building. Home to leading music industry publishers, it also bred a stable of young songwriters who were just as steeped in rock & roll and R&B as Tin Pan Alley, if not more so. Several of the most prominent worked for Aldon Music, a publishing firm headed by Al Nevins and Don Kirshner, the same Don Kirshner who would later mastermind the Monkees' hits and act as a legendarily bland master of ceremonies for network TV rock specials.

Many pop/rock songwriters worked in the Brill Building in the early '60s, but several teams carved a legendary legacy, including Gerry Goffin & Carole King, Barry Mann & Cynthia Weil, Jerry Leiber & Mike Stoller, Jeff Barry & Ellie Greenwich and Doc Pomus & Mort Shuman. Responsible for literally pages worth of hits in the late '50s and first half of the '60s, they matched Tin Pan Alley's highest standards of inventive melodies and lyrics, but they were clearly different from their predecessors. The rock & roll market demanded tunes targeted at teenagers, with earthier concerns than the classics of the '30s

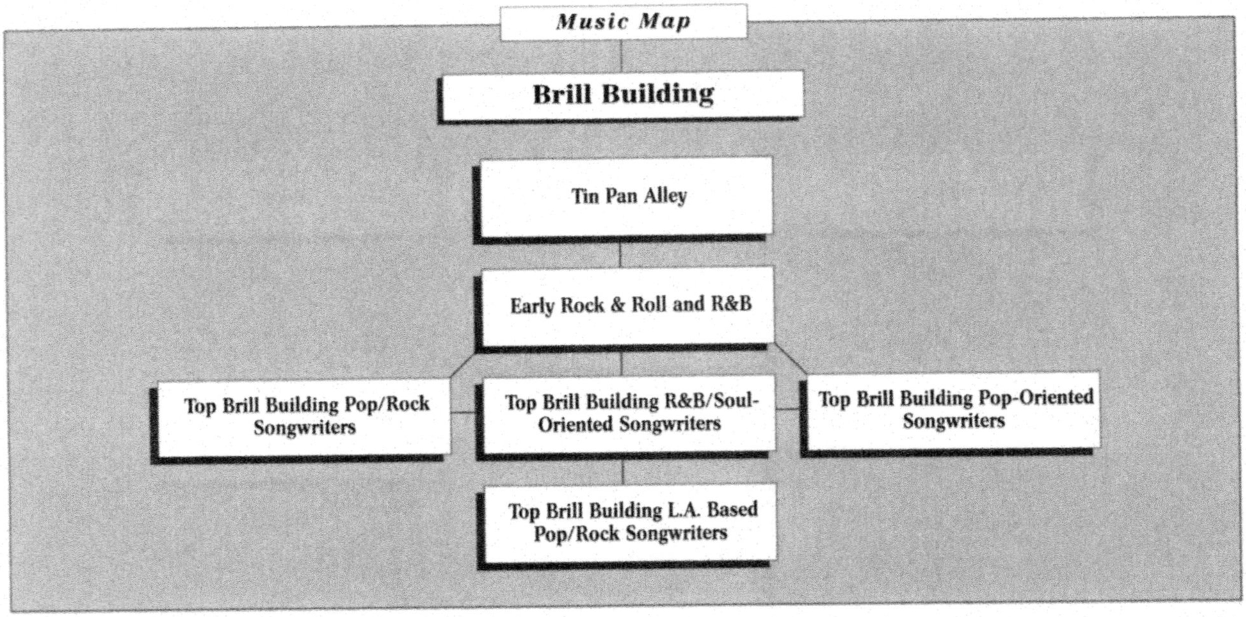

and '40s. For many of these songwriters, the task hardly required an adjustment; they were barely out of (or even still in) their teens, and they were going through the pangs of young love and searches for identity themselves. For good measure, Goffin-King, Mann-Weil and Barry-Greenwich were married to each other, infusing their work with a passion that was actually grounded in their real-life romances.

Brill Building compositions were placed all over the pop/rock map, but had their greatest impact and success with girl groups. It was a heavenly match: girl groups sang about young love with forlorn and passionate innocence, and were largely based near New York City, but very few were songwriters, and they needed suitable material; young Brill Building songwriters wrote about young love with forlorn and passionate innocence, and were largely based near New York City, but needed suitable performers. Most of the classic hits by the Ronettes, Chiffons, Shangri-Las, Dixie Cups and Little Eva originated at the Brill Building, as well as a few classic one-shots and misses.

Other prime outlets for Brill Building material were teen idols like Connie Francis, Bobby Vee, James Darren and Neil Sedaka (the last of whom was one of the most successful Brill Building songwriters himself, often in collaboration with Howard Greenfield). These tended to be the most lightweight Brill Building confections, at times even approaching disposable, as a listen to a James Darren greatest hits compilation confirms. Uneven quality couldn't be helped; the songwriters were under tremendous pressure to deliver tunes in a near-assembly-line fashion, and couldn't be expected to come up with "Will You Love Me Tomorrow" or "On Broadway" every time out.

Leiber-Stoller and Pomus-Shuman however, usually wrote for pop-flavored R&B and early soul acts. Leiber-Stoller wrote (and produced) most of the Coasters' classic comic vignettes, and Pomus-Shuman penned several of the Drifters' hits. Both teams also wrote some of the greatest Elvis Presley songs of the late '50s and early '60s; Goffin-King and Mann-Weil for their part, would supply songs for the Drifters and Phil Spector's great productions with the best blue-eyed soul act of the '60s, the Righteous Brothers.

Other notable Brill Building mainstays included Phil Spector, a great songwriter and even greater producer; Bert Berns, who also wore both songwriting and production hats, though he worked in a more of a pop-soul vein; and Bacharach-David, who probably owed the most to Tin Pan Alley classic traditions, although that didn't prevent them from writing some great pop/rock songs for the Shirelles, Dionne Warwick and others. And for every Goffin-King it must be remembered, there were dozens of much less successful hopefuls scuffling around the edges of the Brill Building crowd, including future folk-rock stars Paul Simon and Jim McGuinn, and future disco king of the "hustle," Van McCoy.

Though Phil Spector is by far the most legendary producer with Brill Building assocations, most of the great Brill Building songwriters were also great producers, although they weren't always credited on the label. Several of them were also great performers, and it has been said that the demos they cut were often as good or better than the versions recorded by the performers to whom they were given. Barry Mann, Carole King and Jeff Barry & Ellie Greenwich (the latter pair as the Raindrops) actually had some hit records on their own, though they much preferred to run things behind the scenes.

There were also quite a few Los Angeles-based songwriters who, though not based at the actual Brill Building, operated in an almost identical fashion. David Gates, Jackie DeShannon, Randy Newman and Nilsson were some of the best; eventually, each of them would become singing-songwriting stars in their own right.

The British Invasion turned the focus of rock & roll on performers that wrote their own material, and while that didn't spell the end of the success of the great Brill Building songwriters, it meant some adjustments were in order. Girl group records were still hugely successful in 1964, the first year of the British Invasion, but it was soon obvious that their time was coming to an end. The irony was that John Lennon and Paul McCartney owed a great deal to the Brill Building, openly declaring Goffin and King as their greatest songwriting influences, and covering Brill Building classics by the Shirelles, Cookies and Isley Brothers. Manfred Mann ("Do Wah Diddy Diddy"), Herman's Hermits ("I'm into Something Good"), and other British Invasion groups also took Brill Building covers into the top of the charts.

Occasionally Brill Building songwriters actually managed to supply fresh material to British Invasion groups, as Mann-Weil did with the Animals and Bert Berns did with Them and Lulu. But inevitably, the proliferation of self-contained rock groups, not to mention soul songwriters who wrote their own material, meant less of a need for professional tunesmiths. And the fact was, both the world and the songwriters were changing as fast as everything else was in the '60s; the composers wanted to express more mature concerns, and much of the rock audience had progressed beyond adolescent love affairs.

The principal architects of the Brill Building coped with these changes in varying fashions. Some became jingle writers; some (Ellie Greenwich) eventually wrote musicals; some (Jeff Barry) wrote and produced bubblegum for the Archies; some (Phil Spector) retired; some (Bacharach-David) moved from pop/rock to MOR pop. The most resourceful became singer/songwriter stars themselves; not only the aforementioned L.A. composers, but also Carole King who became a superstar as a solo act. The legacy of the Brill Building was enormous, setting the standard for pop/rock songwriting that has been emulated ever since, by everyone from the Beatles on down.

Ten Most Essential Brill Building Albums:
Various Artists, *Brill Building Sound* (Era)
Phil Spector, *Back to Mono* (ABKCO)
The Drifters, *All-Time Greatest Hits & More: 1959-1965* (Atlantic)
The Coasters, *50 Coastin' Classics* (Rhino)
Various Artists, *The Colpix-Dimension Story* (Rhino)
The Shangri-Las, *Golden Hits of the Shangri-Las* (Polygram)
Neil Sedaka, *All-Time Greatest Hits* (RCA)
Various Artists, *The Red Bird Story* (Charly, UK)
Various Artists, *The Best of the Girl Groups, Vol. 1* (Rhino)
Various Artists, *The Best of the Girl Groups, Vol. 2* (Rhino)

—Richie Unterberger

Girl Group

The story of the "girl group" sound—which reached its commercial and artistic peak in the early and mid-'60s—is not just the story of the performers. More than any other style in rock & roll, it was the product of more or less equal partnerships between the singer/performers, songwriters, and producers. The result was one of the most vital links between the birth of rock & roll and the British Invasion, the arrival of which gradually eroded the presence of girl groups on the charts even as it acknowledged enormous debts to the genre.

Girl groups were more polished than the early rock & roll pioneers, more innocent than the soul music that was originating at the same time, and as firmly planted in Tin Pan Alley as rhythm and blues. While it wasn't the rawest or most artistically expressive pop music, few forms of rock were as affecting, romantic, and tuneful. They also provided

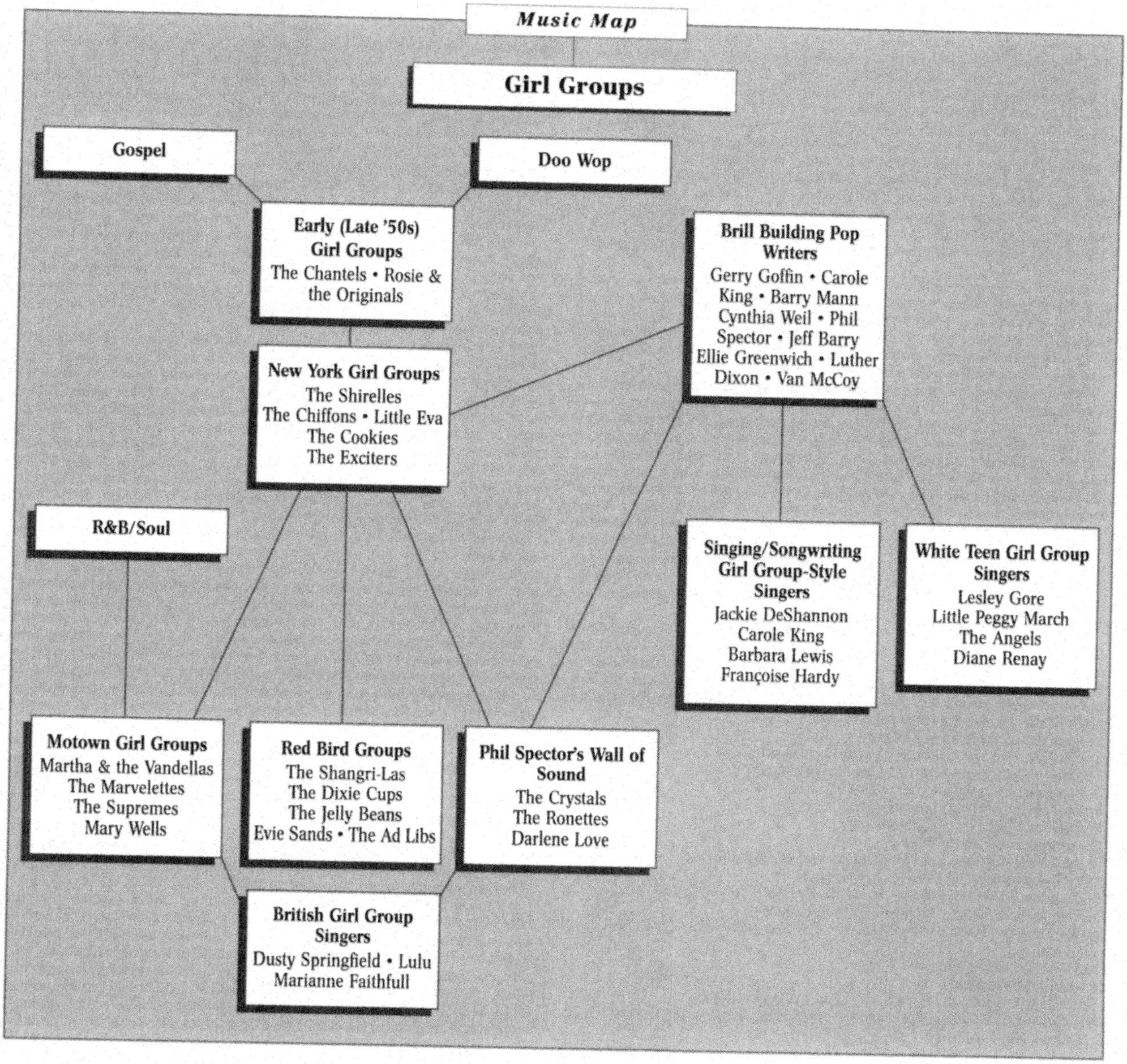

the forums and mouthpieces for some of pop/rock's most talented songwriting teams, as well as laying the foundation for groundbreaking orchestral production that lent an increased sophistication to rock & roll.

The Chantels led by the heart-wrenching vocals of Arlene Smith are generally acknowledged as the first girl group. Their Top 20 hit "Maybe" (1958) had obvious roots in gospel and doo wop, but also displayed yearning, innocent, and vulnerable qualities not apparent in the suaver male doo wop outfits.

It was the Shirelles however, who really established girl groups as a major force with their number one hit, "Will You Love Me Tomorrow?," in 1960. Significantly, that hit also featured many of the classic girl group trademarks—sweeping orchestral strings, full background harmonies, and a lead vocal that projected soul, warmth, hope, and uncertainty. The Shirelles scored a half-dozen Top 20 singles in the next couple years (along with several memorable lesser hits), and ranked as the most successful female vocal group of the era.

The song was written by Gerry Goffin & Carole King who would go on to write many girl group classics in the next few years, and were one of the hottest songwriting teams of the "Brill Building" sound. Named after a complex of music publishing offices on Broadway in New York, it also gave birth to the partnerships between Jeff Barry & Ellie Greenwich and Barry Mann & Cynthia Weil. These teams were responsible for the lion's share of the best girl group recordings, investing rock & roll with the best melodic and lyrical qualities of classic pop, while retaining a feel for the rhythm and blues roots of the performers. Less celebrated writers like Luther Dixon (who wrote several songs for the Shirelles) and a pre-disco Van McCoy also contributed classics to the genre.

It took Phil Spector to launch the girl group sound to its pinnacle. The producer set material from the cream of the Brill Building crop (as well as his own original compositions) to grandly majestic, orchestral arrangements that achieved an unheard-of density without sacrificing any of the music's passion and melody. The Crystals, the Ronettes, and Darlene Love (who sang uncredited vocals on some of the Crystals' biggest smashes) were the most talented pilots of Spector's grandoise "Wall of Sound" productions, most of which were released on his own label, Philles.

While the Shirelles and Phil Spector's acts were the most prominent girl groups in the years preceding the British Invasion, the sound was emulated by several one- or two-shot groups, and less-celebrated producers, with great success. The Chiffons, Claudine Clark the Cookies, the Jaynetts, Little Eva, and the Exciters all contributed timeless classics. And there were dozens—if not hundreds—of worthy singles in the style that, for one reason or another, didn't become blockbusters, although they had most or all of the essential elements.

Most of the great girl groups were black, with clear affinities for R&B and doo wop, but the most innocent qualities of the sound (and occasionally the most soulful ones) were projected in many records by white teen girl singers as well. Lesley Gore was the most renowned of these performers, who also included the Angels, the Raindrops (with Ellie Greenwich on lead vocals), and one-shot artists like Diane Renay and the Murmaids.

While the arrival of the Beatles in 1964 is often thought of as the beginning of the end for the girl groups, girl group records were actually as successful as ever during that year. The rise of the Red Bird label, featuring the Dixie Cups and the Shangri-Las (who both scored number-one hits in 1964), did much to boost the style's commercial fortunes.

Although financial problems caused the Red Bird label to fold within a few years of its founding, the years 1964 and 1965 saw the label shine brightly indeed, and found songwriters like Jeff Barry, Barry Mann, Ellie Greenwich, Jerry Leiber & Mike Stoller overseeing most of its output from the producer's booth. Producer and songwriter Shadow Morton—almost as idiosyncratic a talent as Phil Spector—created some of the greatest girl group records with the Shangri-Las. These tough-talking but tender-hearted Queens Teens may have made the sassiest and most heart-wrenching girl group mini-operas of all.

Although the burgeoning Motown empire wasn't heavily rooted in the girl group sound, 1964 saw the release of breakthrough discs by Mary Wells, the Supremes, and Martha & the Vandellas that owed heavy debts to the style. Relying heavily on the production and songwriting talents of Smokey Robinson and Berry Gordy Jr. (among others), their sound was nonetheless grittier and bluesier than the New York school, and their personas (on record and in performance) more distinctive.

There's no doubt that girl groups were among the British Invasion groups' chief influences. John Lennon has stated for the record that he and Paul McCartney hoped to duplicate the success of Goffin & King with their songwriting partnership, and the Beatles' early albums included covers of hits by the Shirelles, the Cookies, and the Marvelettes. Manfred Mann, despite their R&B roots, scored their biggest U.S. hits with covers of songs by the Exciters ("Do Wah Diddy Diddy") and the Shirelles ("Sha La La"), and several other British groups, ranging from Herman's Hermits and the Searchers to the Mindbenders also made it big with girl group covers. However, the most successful British groups—the Beatles first and foremost among them—were those that relied primarily upon their own material. And it was this shift in emphasis toward self-contained rock groups that played their own instruments that spelled the end of the girl groups as a major force, although singers like Jackie DeShannon, Dusty Springfield, Lulu, Evie Sands, Barbara Lewis and others continued to produce classic recordings (and sometimes score major hits) in the girl group vein throughout the '60s.

The girl group sound, though, never really went away. You can hear it in many female vocal groups, self-contained and otherwise, through the present day. In the case of some soul groups (such as the Pointer Sisters) or new wave bands (the Bangles, Blondie and the Go-Go's), the influence is worn quite cheerfully on the sleeve. More subtly, its echoes are heard in all rock that relies upon orchestral production, harmonies, and/or crafty, melodic compositions to send its message.

12 Most Essential Girl Group Albums:

The Shirelles, *The World's Greatest Girl Group* (Tomato/Rhino)
The Shangri-Las, *The Best of the Shangri-Las* (PolyGram)
The Ronettes, *Best of the Ronettes* (ABKCO)
The Crystals, *Best of the Crystals* (ABKCO)
The Chiffons, *Best of the Chiffons* (Laurie)
The Supremes, *Anthology* (Motown)
Martha & the Vandellas, *Live Wire! The Singles 1962-1972* (Motown)
Mary Wells, *Looking Back 1961-1964* (Motown)
Lesley Gore, *It's My Party: Mercury Anthology* (Mercury)
The Marvelettes, *Deliver: The Singles 1961-1971* (Rhino)
Various Artists, *The Best of the Girl Groups, Vol.1, The Best of the Girl Groups, Vol.2* (Rhino)
The Exciters, *Tell Him* (EMI)

Recommended Reading:

Girl Groups: The Story of a Sound, by Alan Betrock (Delilah, 1982)
Will You Still Love Me Tomorrow? Girl Groups From the '50s On . . ., by Charlotte Greig (Virago, 1989, UK)

—Richie Unterberger

Soul

More than almost any other genre of the rock era, soul is a wide-ranging and immensely diverse style that can only be delineated in the sketchiest manner in a few paragraphs. Peaking in the 1960s, it helped define the African-American experience in America with a passion, pride, and optimism rare in any art form.

Broadly speaking, soul was the combination of R&B, gospel, and pop. The gospel ingredient was most evident in the supremely emotional, pleading, and jubilant vocals and harmonies. Rock-solid rhythm sections, punchy horn arrangements, and tight instrumental and vocal ensemble work were also frequent hallmarks of the classic soul sound.

The forefathers of soul were veterans of 1950s rhythm & blues. Ray Charles was perhaps the first to merge gospel, pop, and rhythm and blues in a style that we recognize as a direct ancestor of soul with his 1954 hit "I Got a Woman." Other important pioneers were Jackie Wilson, Sam Cooke, and James Brown. They came from somewhat different backgrounds—Wilson from the R&B vocal group tradition, Cooke from straight gospel as the lead singer of the Soul Stirrers, Brown from the "chitlin" circuit—but they shared an appetite for constantly modernizing their sound with both pop crossover material and R&B-based work that put their emotions at the fore with an arresting grit, naked emotion, and increasingly mature lyrical concerns.

As R&B grew into soul in the early '60s, the arrangements became more intricate, as did the harmonies (though they were often rooted in doo wop, as is obvious from listening to the early work of the Miracles and the Impressions). Romance was usually the subject, but it often was a more complex, adult, and bittersweet form of love than the adolescent fare of much early rock & roll and R&B. Songwriter/performer/producers like Smokey Robinson and Curtis Mayfield put a greater personal stamp on their product than was customary in the 1950s. The session players at labels like Stax/Volt and Motown, though sometimes uncredited on the releases, set a level of instrumental discipline and virtuosity that remains among the benchmark standards of musical excellence in contemporary popular music. Starting with the Drifters, strings were often used to tastefully embellish the material without detracting from the performers' gutsy power.

There were literally hundreds of soul performers who laid down bodies of work that endure several decades later. In many cases, the artists themselves grew enormously over the course of their career, and cannot be conveniently pigeonholed into a certain subgenre or peak output—Marvin Gaye, Aretha Franklin, Curtis Mayfield, and Stevie Wonder are only a few of those. There were certain regional styles that developed, although soul was such a nationwide, overlapping phenomenon that these too cannot be categorized too rigorously, and great acts like the Isley Brothers couldn't be conveniently pigeonholed into any certain school.

By far the most successful style of soul was the kind that came to be identified with Motown Records in Detroit. Emphasizing melodic hooks, bright, clear production, and an extraordinary roster of talented vocalists, Motown was the most successful independent label of its era, crossing over to the pop charts for literally hundreds of Top 20 hits during the 1960s. Instrumental in bringing the sounds of black America into mainstream American life, Motown has been disdained by some latter-day critics for a formulaic approach, and for appealing to whites, teenagers, and pop listeners more than other kinds of down-home soul music. These are fairly ridiculous assertions. Motown was if anything more popular with black audiences than white ones, and its legendary performers—Smokey Robinson, the Temptations, Martha & the Vandellas, Marvin Gaye, Stevie Wonder, the Supremes, Mary Wells, the Four Tops, the Jackson 5, and many others—released an astonishingly large and diverse body of classic work in the 1960s and beyond.

Motown's most serious rival for soul supremacy was the Stax/Volt label, based in Memphis. With Booker T. & the MG's (stars in their own right) usually providing the backing, these records offered a funkier, rootsier brand of soul, with generally rawer vocals and a heavier reliance on horn riffs. Otis Redding, Wilson Pickett, Carla Thomas, and Sam & Dave were the biggest stars to emerge from the Stax/Volt label, which was absorbed into Atlantic in the late '60s. Atlantic Records itself was one of the most influential soul labels, with gritty soul sensations like Solomon Burke and Percy Sledge. A great deal of soul with a similarly down-home Southern sensibility also emerged from the legendary studios in Muscle Shoals, AL; Muscle Shoals players backed Aretha Franklin on many of her greatest sides.

In Chicago, performers like the Impressions, Jerry Butler, Betty Everett, Major Lance, and Gene Chandler established their own distinctive regional sound, prominently featuring blaring horn charts and smooth harmonic interplay. New York had a somewhat more pop-oriented, "uptown" sound, typified by Chuck Jackson and Maxine Brown, although as always there were rootsier exceptions like Garnett Mimms, and artists who combined the best of both worlds, like Ben E. King (both as lead singer of the Drifters and as a solo artist). Philadelphia soul records leaned toward doo wop-like group harmonies, eventually evolving into a serious rival to Motown's production machines with the ascendance of Gamble & Huff and Thom Bell.

By the late '60s, soul was changing with the times. Motown-producer Norman Whitfield expanded the label's lyrical scope into psychedelia and social consciousness with songs like the Temptations' *Cloud Nine*. James Brown pioneered funk music with his incredible churning rhythms backing increasingly assertive statements of black pride. Sly & the Family Stone merged hippie concerns and funk on a string of hit singles and albums. In the early '70s, Motown veterans Marvin Gaye and Stevie Wonder broke free of the label's hit-oriented production process to issue vastly influential, album-length statements. The Philadelphia sound, string-drenched and impeccably produced and harmonized, took soul to another level of slickness. In Memphis, Al Green established himself as an heir to Otis Redding with Hi Records and the Memphis Horns.

Soul diminished as a commercial presence in the mid-'70s, as funk and disco began to put more emphasis on danceable rhythms than songwriting and the singing. Al Green, seen by some fans as the standardbearer of the classic soul sound, turned to gospel; the once-thriving Stax/Volt empire collapsed in a confusing mess. Much black soul music became increasingly middle-of-the-road, leading to the new genre of urban contemporary music. Soul is still very much alive, of course, in the harmonies and production that continue to inform contemporary African-American popular music, whether in funk, disco, dance-pop, or rap. The "classic" soul style lives on in different ways—old stars continue to release and record new material for a specialized audience, and veteran performers like Tina Turner and Patti LaBelle have achieved new levels of superstardom with their updated brand of contemporary soul.

15 Most Essential Soul Recordings (omitting Motown releases, listed in separate music map):

Various Artists, *Soul Shots* series (Rhino)
Various Artists, *The Complete Stax-Volt Singles 1959-1968* (Atlantic)
James Brown, *Star Time* (PolyGram)
Otis Redding, *Otis! The Definitive Otis Redding* (Rhino)
Aretha Franklin, *Queen of Soul: The Atlantic Recordings* (Rhino)
Curtis Mayfield & the Impressions, *Anthology 1961-1977* (MCA)

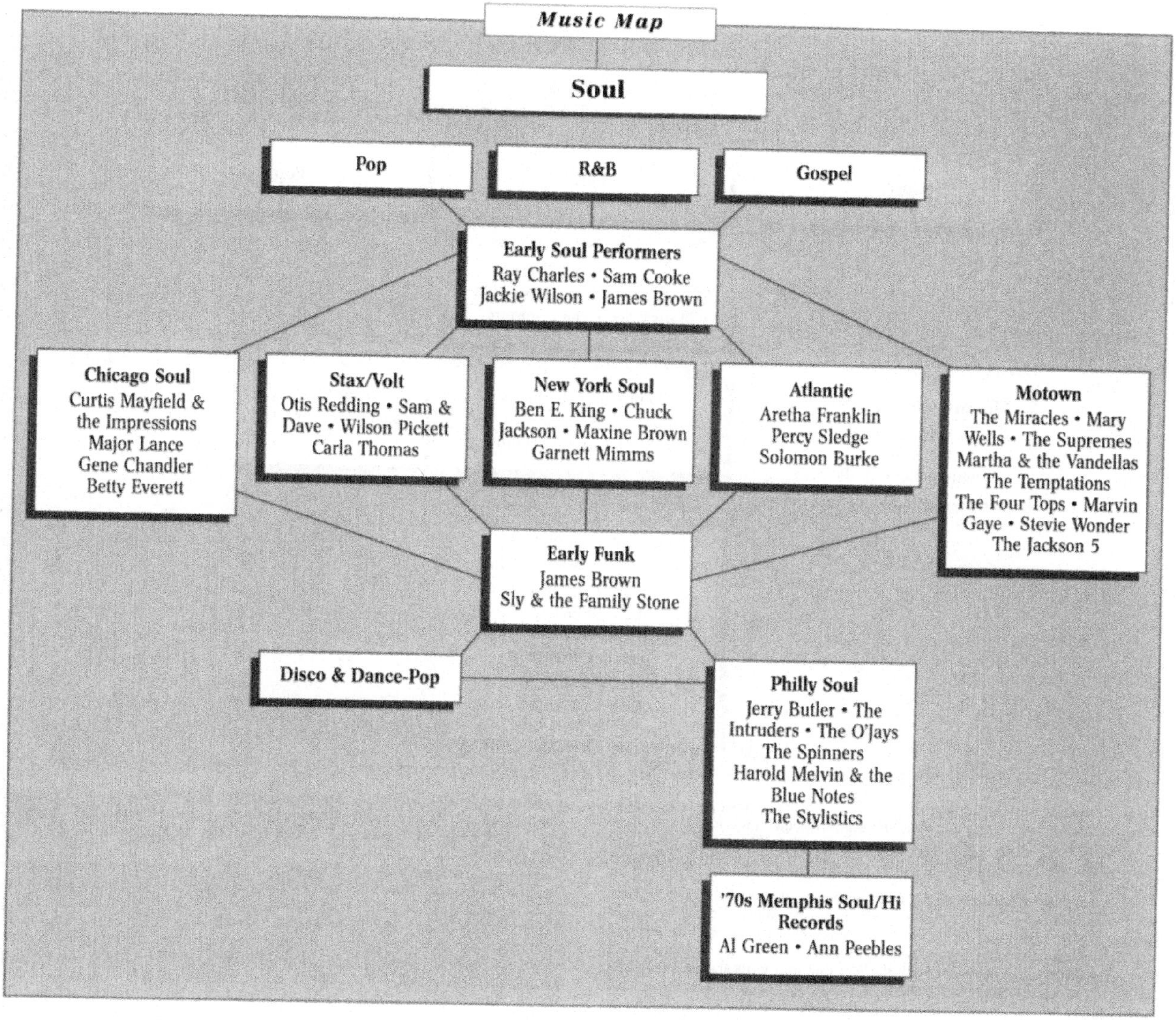

Sam Cooke, *Man & His Music* (RCA)
Ray Charles, *Birth of Soul* (Rhino)
Ben E. King, *Anthology* (Rhino)
Sly & the Family Stone, *Anthology* (Epic)
Al Green, *Al Green's Greatest Hits* (Hi)
The Isley Brothers, *The Isley Brothers Story, Vol.1* (Rhino)
Wilson Pickett, *A Man and a Half: The Best of Wilson Pickett* (Rhino)
Jackie Wilson, *Mr. Excitement* (Rhino)
Solomon Burke, *Home in Your Heart* (Rhino)

Books:

The Blackwell Guide to Soul Recordings, edited by **Robert Pruter** (Blackwell, 1993)
Where Did Our Love Go? The Rise and Fall of the Motown Sound, by **Nelson George** (St. Martin's Press, 1985)
Sweet Soul Music, by **Peter Guralnick** (Harper & Row, 1986)
Nowhere to Run: The Story of Soul Music, by **Gerry Hirshey** (Times Books, 1984)

—Richie Unterberger

Motown

Many labels have left their mark on rock & roll—Sun, Atlantic, Chess, Stax/Volt, Stiff, and lots of others left a permanent imprint on the music's legacy by honing distinctive styles and attitudes. Only one label, however, is immediately identified as a genre of its own. And not just by scholars and record collectors—Motown, to anyone who's listened to popular music since 1960, is not just a label in the middle of a record, but a sound that ranks among the most distinctive in rock history.

In its heyday, the Detroit label was home to the most commercially successful synthesis of R&B and pop ever produced. Motown developed many superstars, but performers were only part of the story. Equally important were the songwriters, including such masters as Smokey Robinson and the Holland-Dozier-Holland team; producers (who often doubled as songwriters); the (often uncredited) backing musicians, like bassist James Jamerson and drummer Benny Benjamin who gave the music its rock-solid foundation; and the vision of owner Berry Gordy Jr. You could almost always identify a Motown Record: instantly hummable melodies, pulsing basslines, punchy tambourines and handclaps, rousing horns and violins, and vocals that evoked a gospel flavor with the call-and-response lines between the lead and backup singers.

The Motown empire, which eventually grew into the biggest black-owned business in America, was a success story as unlikely as those of Elvis or the Beatles A former boxer and failed jazz record-store owner, Gordy was a struggling hustler on the edges of the R&B music business in the late '50s, writing some hits for Jackie Wilson In 1959, he borrowed money from his family to start an independent production company. After leasing hits by Marv Johnson and Barrett Strong to other labels, Gordy formed his own labels. The releases would appear both on Motown and other imprints like Tamla, Gordy, and Soul.

Motown quickly established itself in the early '60s with hits by the Miracles, the Marvelettes, and Mary Wells. It was Gordy's increasingly refined and systematic production techniques, however, that would ensure that the label continued to succeed and grow. The Motown sound has often been compared to an assembly line, drawing upon the influence of Detroit's automobile plants, with performers, songwriters, producers, and musicians embellishing a basic tried-and-true blueprint. If it were indeed true that

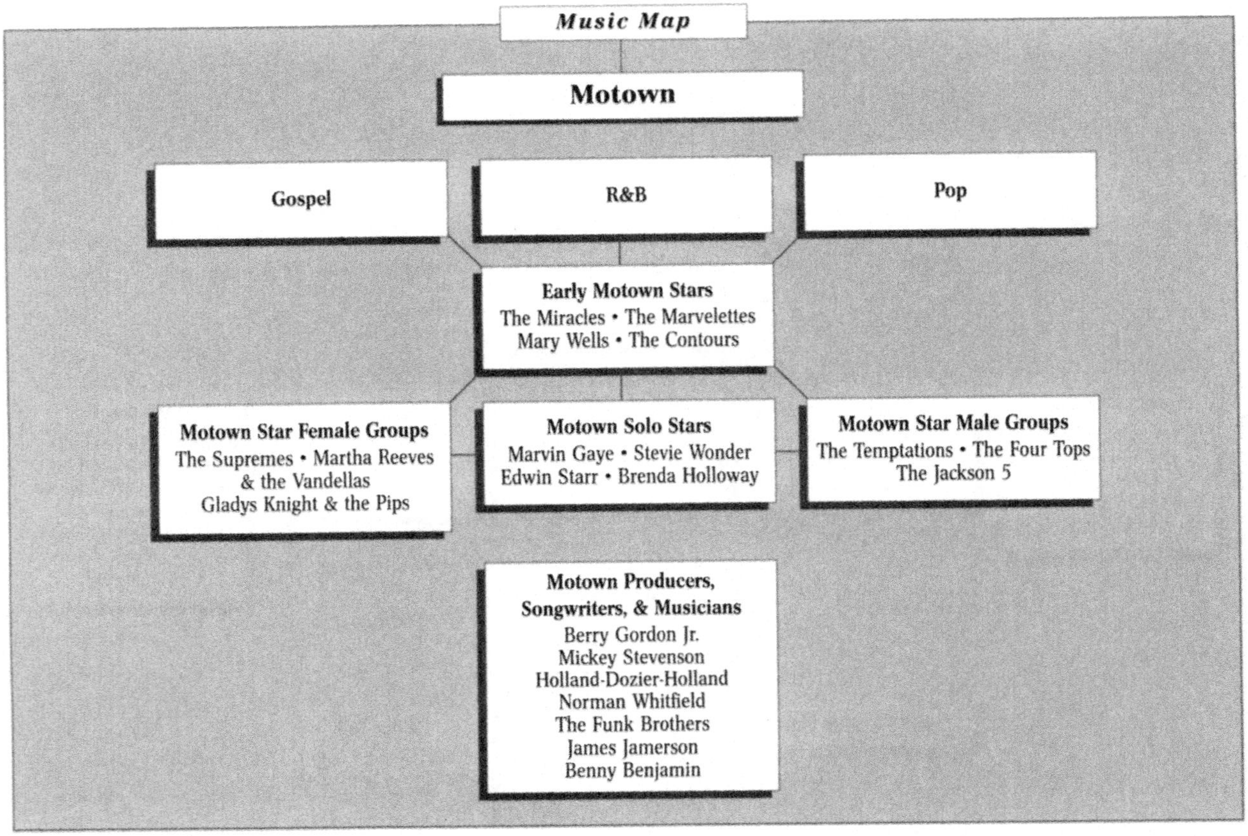

Motown's formula was nothing more than an assembly line, it most likely would have exhausted itself quickly. Gordy and Motown's genius was that it was able to spin almost infinite variations on its hugely appealing recipes, while still retaining an instantly recognizable sound, endearing itself to millions of listeners through both innovation and familiarity.

Motown releases might have shared many general similarities, but in time its superstars would develop strong identities of their own. The Miracles paced by Smokey Robinson (who wrote many of Motown's best songs, both for the Miracles and other artists), handled both romantic ballads and uptempo dance tunes; the Temptations were the most polished soul group of their day; the Four Tops were gritty and emotional; Mary Wells and the Marvelettes recorded the most soulful girl group singles around; child prodigy Stevie Wonder developed into a magnificently gifted songwriter and instrumentalist; Martha Reeves & the Vandellas were Motown at its most feverish and gospel-influenced; Diana Ross & the Supremes were, aside from the Beatles, the most successful pop group of the '60s; Marvin Gaye along with Stevie Wonder would prove to be the most eclectic and innovative singer/songwriter on the Motown roster, not even reaching his maturity as an artist (like Wonder) until the 1970s; Junior Walker cut the label's earthiest, most party-oriented R&B.

These were the superstars; there were other fine performers who recorded a notable body of work for Motown in the 1960s, including Gladys Knight, Brenda Holloway, Edwin Starr, Kim Weston, Tammi Terrell and the Contours. The label's roster was so deep, in fact, that some illustrious artists were neglected; the Spinners didn't do much of anything until they left Motown in the early '70s, the Isley Brothers had only one big hit during their several years there (perhaps because of their inability to truly adapt to the Motown formula), and early-'60s soul star Chuck Jackson had only minimal success after moving to Motown.

Even the stars sometimes expressed dissatisfaction about how they were promoted and directed by Motown, but they most likely knew that their success was at least equally attributable to the label as to their own talents. The point was underscored by Mary Wells' surprise decision to leave Motown in 1964 just after her number-one hit, *My Guy*. Lured away by a big contract and the promise of a movie career, Wells never had another big hit; without the estimable Motown team, she was just another soul singer.

The loss of Wells was covered by the burgeoning careers of other Motown stars, but Gordy faced a much more serious problem in late 1967, when the songwriting and production team of Brian Holland, Lamont Dozier & Eddie Holland demanded an accounting of their royalties. After initiating a suit against Motown, the trio left the label to establish a company of their own. For a few years, Motown's fortunes were unaffected; they launched the Jackson 5 as superstars, and producers such as Norman Whitfield infused Motown with contemporary funk, psychedelia, and social commentary on tracks like the Temptations' "Cloud Nine," "Psychedelic Shack," and Ball of Confusion."

Motown's golden age truly ended, however, in 1971, when the company moved from Detroit to Los Angeles. Around this time, the careers of some of Motown's mainstays, such as Martha Reeves and the Marvelettes had petered out; Diana Ross had already left the Supremes, Marvin Gaye, and Stevie Wonder recorded some stupendous album-length statements in the 1970s that showed their full gifts as songwriters and performers for the first time, as well as expanding their lyrical concerns beyond the romantic themes that Motown had largely stuck to. But Motown no longer bred scads of stars, or honed a distinctive sound; they were simply a soul/R&B record label, albeit a very big and successful one.

When people talk about the Motown sound, they're referring to those 1960s and early '70s recordings. The most successful label of its day, and the most successful independent label of all time (it's now part of MCA), it was the most influential factor in establishing African-American music as an integral part of mainstream U.S. culture.

15 Most Essential Motown Recordings:

Smokey Robinson & the Miracles, *Anthology*
Mary Wells, *Looking Back 1961-1964*
Martha & the Vandellas, *Live Wire! The Singles 1962-1972*
The Marvelettes, *Marvelettes' Greatest Hits*
Marvin Gaye, *Anthology*
Stevie Wonder, *Looking Back*
The Supremes, *Anthology*
The Temptations, *Emperors of Soul*
The Four Tops, *Anthology*
The Jackson 5, *Anthology*
Junior Walker, *Greatest Hits*
Gladys Knight & the Pips, *Anthology*
Brenda Holloway, *Greatest Hits & Rare Classics*
Edwin Starr, *Motown Superstar Series Vol.3*
Various Artists, *Hitsville USA: The Motown Singles Collection 1959-1971*

Book:

Where Did Our Love Go?: The Rise and Fall of the Motown Sound, by **Nelson George** (St. Martin's, 1985)

—Richie Unterberger

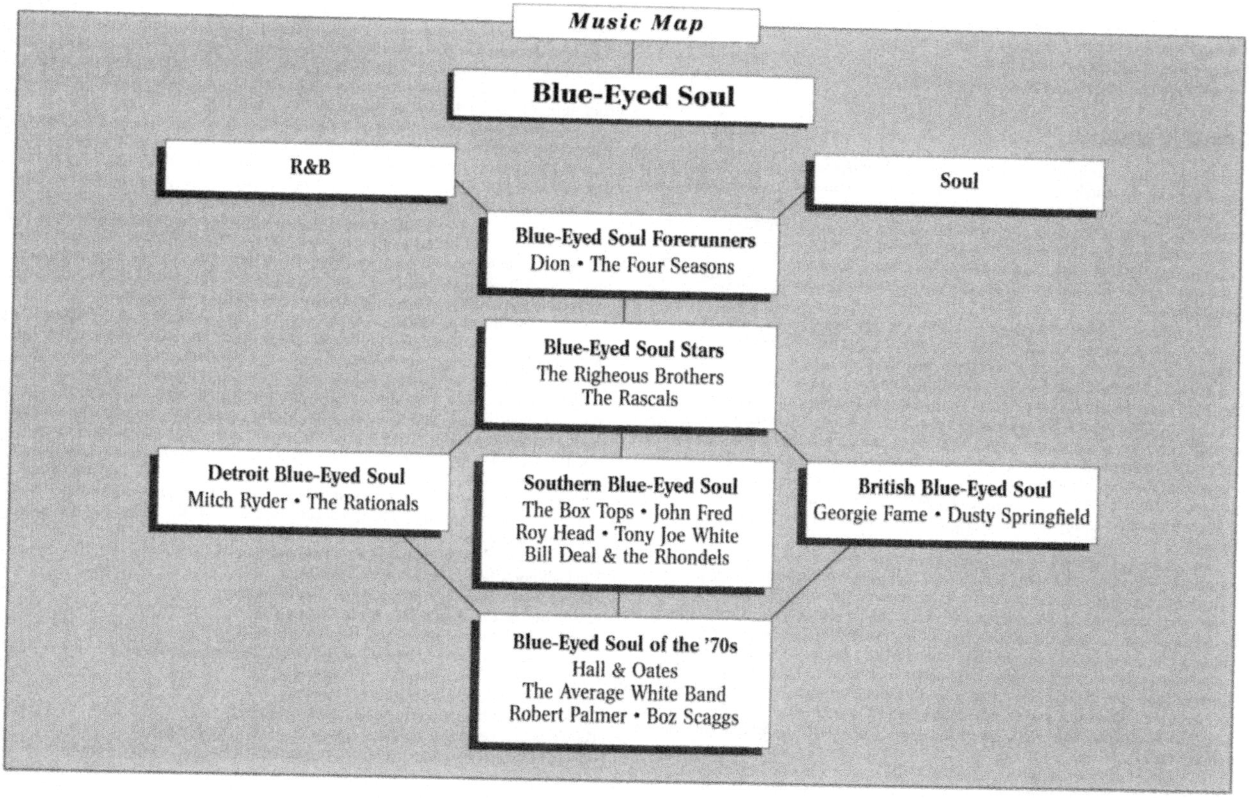

Blue-Eyed Soul

"Can white men sing the blues?" That's been a point of contention in the worlds of rock and soul since white musicians began singing music with heavy debts to R&B. White attempts to sing African-American-derived music have often been embarrassing (if sometimes touching in their naivete). But at the same time, some whites have crossed into the world of R&B and soul with a natural ease that proves that music, like all good things in life, is color-blind. During soul music's heyday, a handful of whites handled the challenge with confidence, giving rise to the relatively small but important subgenre of soul music called blue-eyed soul.

The roots of blue-eyed soul could probably be traced back as far as Elvis Presley's legendary Sun singles, on which he masterfully interpreted a handful of blues and R&B classics. It can also be detected in the many Italian-American doo wop singers during that music's last phase, as well as early '60s acts like Dion and the Four Seasons who borrowed heavily from R&B phrasing and harmonies.

The first of the classic blue-eyed soul acts, and one which was instrumental to defining the genre, were the Righteous Brothers. Hailing from Orange County, CA, of all places, Bill Medley and Bobby Hatfield looked very white, but sounded black. After teaming up with Phil Spector in the mid-'60s, they reeled off a brief string of huge hits that were as soaked with gospel feeling as any African-American soul, but were unable to maintain their artistic or commercial momentum after their association with Spector ended.

The most successful blue-eyed soul group of the '60s were the Rascals. Young veterans of New York's Italian-American rock & roll scene, they flavored their strong (and mostly original) material with horns, harmonies, and a touch of British Invasion energy. Although they worked within the self-contained rock band format, playing their own instruments and writing their own songs, their sound owed as much, if not more, to soul as '60s rock trends. They were also one of the relatively few blue-eyed soul acts to successfully change with the times, writing increasingly reflective and sophisticated material, culminating with the rabble-rousing anthem "People Got to Be Free" in 1968.

Blue-eyed soul acts tended to spring up in the proximity of regions with active soul scenes. Detroit's biggest contribution to the genre were Mitch Ryder and the Detroit Wheels, who served up some of the sweatiest soul-rock hybrids ever waxed. Motown couldn't help but influence a lot of the city's white rock and garage bands, and the Motor City sound is reflected in fine regional Michigan rock hits of the time by the Rationals and the early singles of Bob Seger.

White Southern performers also absorbed the inflections of deep soul into their own earthy sounds. John Fred and Tony Joe White displayed the influence of New Orleans and Louisiana R&B and soul in their brand of swamp pop; Bill Deal & the Rhondels played a kind of soul frat-rock that drew from the "beach music" cult of the Carolinas; Roy Head drew upon the melting pot of Texas blues and R&B for one of the mid-'60s best one-shot hits, "Treat Her Right." In Memphis, Dan Penn, a white Alabaman who helped write many great deep soul records, produced hits by the Box Tops; teenage lead singer Alex Chilton's vocals were so unnaturally gravelly that many listeners were convinced he was black. In Los Angeles, there were several Latin soul-rock-R&B acts, the best of which were Thee Midniters (although the group also played convincing Rolling Stones-styled garage rock).

The line between R&B-influenced rock & roll and blue-eyed soul is a thin one that was skirted by many of the British Invasion's finest performers. Certainly Eric Burdon (of the Animals), Stevie Winwood (of the Spencer Davis Group and Traffic), and Van Morrison were extremely soulful singers, even if their material and the sound of their backing groups were more rock-oriented than classic soul grooves. Georgie Fame probably fit the classic blue-eyed soul mold more than any other British Invasion performer, although he also owed quite a bit to Mose Allison's brand of jazz. Dusty Springfield was the best female blue-eyed soul singer of the '60s, though she also sang girl group, rock, and pop ballad material; at the end of the '60s, she traveled to Stax studios in Memphis to cut *Dusty in Memphis*, considered by many listeners as one of the finest white soul albums of all time.

It's worth pointing out that many classic soul records of the '60s by black performers featured white musicians. Booker T. & the MG's, an integrated ensemble featuring the economic, biting licks of white guitarist Steve Cropper played on most of the great Stax/Volt soul hits of the '60s, as well as cutting a lot of instrumental soul smashes on their own. Stax/Volt's strongest rival in the field of deep Southern soul was the Muscle Shoals Studio in Alabama, which also featured white musicians on many of their sessions, backing soul greats from Aretha Franklin on down. Duane Allman may be mostly known for helping to found Southern rock with the Allman Brothers but he also played guitar on sessions by Franklin, Wilson Pickett, Clarence Carter and King Curtis.

The heyday of blue-eyed soul, like soul music itself, was in the 1960s; after that decade, it was a more scattered presence, although acts like Hall & Oates, the Average White Band, Boz Scaggs, Robert Palmer, David Bowie (in one of his many phases), the latter-day Bee Gees and Billy Swan all carried the blue-eyed soul torch to large degrees. Contemporary acts like Michael Bolton and George Michael have also been labeled as blue-eyed soul, although their material owes more to classic MOR pop than the original pioneers of the style.

Ten Most Essential Blue-Eyed Soul Albums:
Various Artists, *Soul Shots Vol. 6: Blue-Eyed Soul* (Rhino)
The Righteous Brothers, *Anthology 1962-74* (Rhino)
The Rascals, *Anthology (1965-1972)* (Rhino)
Mitch Ryder, *Rev-Up: The Best of Mitch Ryder & the Detroit Wheels* (Rhino)
The Box Tops, *Ultimate Box Tops* (Warner Brothers)
Dusty Springfield, *Dusty in Memphis* (Rhino)

John Fred & the Playboys, *The History of John Fred & the Playboys* (Paula)
Tony Joe White, *The Best of Tony Joe White* (Warner)
Georgie Fame, *20 Beat Classics* (RSO)
Thee Midniters, *The Best of Thee Midniters* (Rhino)

—Richie Unterberger

Philly Soul

The last major movement of the classic soul era to make a wide impact, Philadelphia soul represented the style at its sweetest, and soul production at its most sophisticated. Its severest critics would contend that much of the genre was overly slick, the most lightweight of which helped set the ground for the more mechanized elements of disco and urban contemporary. Others would praise the music for almost exactly the same reasons, seeing the Philly sound as soul at its most romantic, ushering in an era of elaborate instrumental and vocal arrangements that continue to play a large part in black pop music today.

The hallmarks of Philadelphia soul—the lush, buoyant strings and horns, the smooth group harmonies with a touch of street corner a cappella, the insistent danceable rhythms and smoldering ballads—were often the handiwork of an extremely small clique of producers. Most of the classic Philly soul recordings of the late '60s and first half of the '70s were devised by the producers Kenny Gamble & Leon Huff (who worked as a team), as well as producer Thom Bell (who sometimes arranged material for Gamble & Huff). Their extremely prolific output, maintaining enough diversity to ensure continuing public interest while stamping each record with distinctive Philly soul qualities, was reminiscent in some respects of Motown's production line during their 1960s glory days. Gamble & Huff, like Motown, also used a house band of sorts, a core group of musicians that contributed mightily to establishing a sound that could be identified with their records.

None of this could have been accomplished without first-rate singers, both soloists and groups, and the Philly soul stars, like those of Motown, were distinctive talents in their own right. They did differ from their counterparts in that while Motown's stars were largely tapped from their Detroit base, the Philadelphia performers were often (though not by any means always) transplants. Indeed, after the Philly sound had become a major industry force, established soul stars like Wilson Pickett, Dionne Warwick, and Lou Rawls would travel to the city specifically to record with top producers. There was generally less grit involved in the Philadelphia studios, and though it's a matter of conjecture whether the performer's role was more or less limited than it was at Motown or other soul centers, there's no doubt that production was just as important, if not more, as material or performance.

Gamble & Huff were young veterans of the Philly music scene who began scoring their first big national hits in the late '60s with smooth vocal groups like the Intruders and Delfonics and more raucous, dance-oriented records with Archie Bell & the Drells. It was a long-running association with Jerry Butler, already a star with many popular Chicago soul recordings under his belt, that really got them on a roll. The team rode high through the mid-'70s with hits by the aforementioned acts and Joe Simon, Harold Melvin & the Blue Notes (featuring Teddy Pendergrass), and above all the O'Jays, who may have done more than any other act to define the Philadelphia soul sound.

Thom Bell oversaw a smaller roster, and generally pursued a smoother (though only slightly smoother) sound. His big acts were the Stylistics, whose creamy harmonies sailed on top of the frothiest Philly soul hits, and the Spinners, who found massive success in Philadelphia studios after years of recording as also-rans for Motown and other labels.

While Gamble & Huff and Bell dominated the Philly scene, they didn't produce every last hit of the era by any means. In particular, Bunny Sigler helped produce some successes for Gamble & Huff's Philadelphia International label, and Peter DeAngelis (who cut his teeth with, of all people, Frankie Avalon and Fabian) arranged and produced Philly soul records for Eddie Holman that both recalled and stood up to the best that Gamble & Huff were churning out at the same time.

Philadelphia soul hits occasionally boasted strong, socially aware lyrics, especially on some of the O'Jays hottest sellers; "Back Stabbers" in particular is often cited as one of the hardest-hitting reflections of urban street life in soul music. By and large, though, they focused on the joys and sorrows of romance, not civil rights or expanding consciousness. That didn't affect commercial sales in the least, but did perhaps limit their impact upon the world of rock at a time when the pressure for lyrical significance was high. David Bowie, always looking for something new to sink his teeth into, brought a lot of Philadelphia soul into his work in the mid-'70s when he unpredictably terminated his arty glam rock phase and traveled to Sigma Sound Studios, where many classic Philly soul hits were recorded, to cut some of his most commercially (though not critically) successful work.

With a rhythmic and elaborate production line already in place, the Philadelphia sound was more equipped than any other soul scene to face the disco era. Indeed, the mid-'70s saw many of the biggest early disco hits emerge from Philadelphia, including recordings which found stalwarts like the O'Jays adapting to the new trend, and new disco acts like the Trammps. Not as critically esteemed as the earlier Philadelphia soul productions, they were nonetheless extremely successful in the marketplace. But the Philadelphia sound, as practiced by Gamble & Huff and their brethren, had spent most of its power as a major artistic force by the end of the '70s, much as Motown lost most of its impetus after the '60s. Unlike Motown, though, the Philadelphia producers didn't maintain a respectable sales profile, largely dropping from sight after the early 1980s. Philadelphia soul lingers, however, in almost all urban contemporary soul and R&B, both by veterans like Patti LaBelle and newcomers like Jill Scott.

Ten Recommended Philadelphia Soul Recordings:
The Delfonics, *Best of the Delfonics* (Arista)
The Intruders, *Super Hits* (Philadelphia International)
Archie Bell & The Drells, *The Best Of* (Rhino)
Jerry Butler, *Iceman: The Mercury Years* (PolyGram)
The O'Jays, *The O'Jays in Philadelphia* (Philadelphia International)
Eddie Holman, *I Love You* (Varese Sarabande)
The Stylistics, *Best of the Stylistics* (Amherst)
The O'Jays, *Greatest Hits* (Philadelphia International)
The Spinners, *One of a Kind Love Affair—The Anthology* (Atlantic)
Harold Melvin & the Blue Notes, *Collector's Item* (Philadelphia International)

—Richie Unterberger

Psychedelic Soul

Bridging the divide between the classic soul sound of the mid-'60s and the funk and disco that dominated the 1970s, psychedelic soul represented the full flowering of the musical, social and racial diversity born of the hippie counterculture. Marrying traditional R&B with fuzzed-out, wah-wah guitars, hallucinatory production innovations and epic, improvisational arrangements, psychedelic soul enjoyed a relatively brief period of vogue, but it endures among the most provocative and influential music of its time, challenging long-held stylistic and cultural assumptions while shattering color lines and stereotypes. At the peak of the civil rights movement, psychedelic soul introduced a

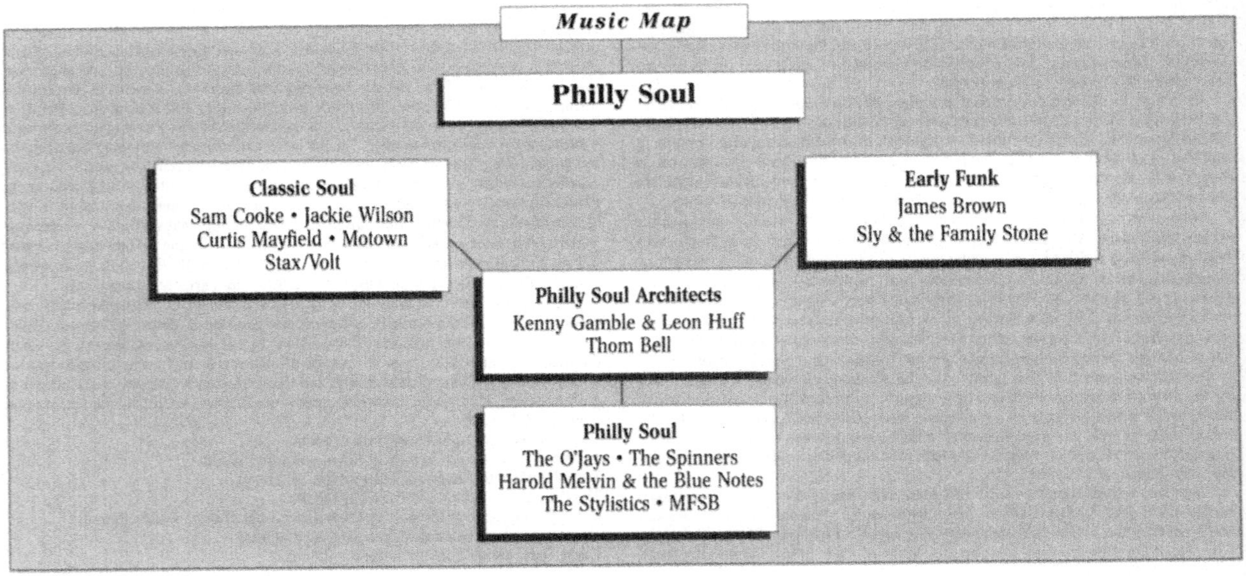

sociopolitical immediacy long suppressed in black popular music, but where most mainstream (read: white) psychedelia sought to expand the higher consciousness of listeners with messages of peace, tolerance and love, psych-soul elevated a different kind of consciousness, articulating the anger, unease and paranoia snaking its way through black America, transmitting not flower-child platitudes but grim, haunted dispatches from a culture torn apart by racism, poverty, war, drugs and in-fighting. Ultimately, the arc of psychedelic soul—from hopeful euphoria to bleak dissolution—mirrors the rise and fall of the counterculture itself.

The father of psychedelia in all its myriad forms and evolutions is Jimi Hendrix, arguably the most gifted and influential guitarist in rock and roll history. Hendrix was born and raised in Seattle, apprenticing on the R&B circuit backing artists including Little Richard, the Isley Brothers and King Curtis before gaining notoriety in early 1967 as a headliner in London, England, fronting his power trio the Jimi Hendrix Experience. Cutting and pasting elements of R&B, electric blues, pop, soul, jazz, folk-rock and lord knows what else, Hendrix created an alchemical sound simply unlike anything that had come before—making his triumphant return to America with a now-legendary performance at the Monterey Pop Festival, his 1967 debut LP *Are You Experienced?* ranks alongside the Beatles' *Sgt. Pepper's Lonely Hearts Club Band* as the foundation of psychedelia and the soundtrack of the Summer of Love, and he remained an avatar of the counterculture far past his 1970 death.

Hendrix was arguably the first true African-American rock icon—to be certain, black music innovators ranging from Chuck Berry to Sam Cooke to Marvin Gaye had enjoyed massive pop success well before Hendrix's arrival on the scene, but none were more representative of their times nor as completely embraced by audiences of all races and creeds. Hendrix singularly captured the zeitgeist of the late '60s: he not only created visionary, groundbreaking music, but with his wiry Afro, feather boas and dayglo-dandy, neo-Victorian wardrobe, he defined the colorful cutting-edge of psychedelic fashion. Moreover, he made rock & roll dangerously sexy, stroking and pumping his guitar with an onanistic fervor that bordered on obscenity. But most importantly, Hendrix helped obliterate racial divides—not only were Experience bassist Noel Redding and drummer Mitch Mitchell both white, but their music was never marginalized for audiences of one color or another. Hendrix was a rock & roller, no different from John Lennon, Bob Dylan or Mick Jagger—a message that impacted audiences on both sides of the color line. Musical mutations like psychedelic soul—a virtual oxymoron before Hendrix's ascendance—were now a reality in his wake.

If Jimi Hendrix birthed psychedelic soul, then Sly & the Family Stone defined and expanded its possibilities. No less eclectic than Hendrix but more clearly a product of their R&B origins, the San Francisco-based group annihilated more than a few stereotypes of its own—a multi-racial unit comprised of both men and women, Sly & the Family Stone was the first truly integrated act in rock history. The messages implicit in their personnel makeup were made daringly explicit in frontman Sly Stone's provocative lyrics—no other mainstream group was as outspoken in its political and social sloganeering. Along with the inimitable James Brown, the Family Stone not only popularized the street-smart funk that was bubbling under the surface of the polished soul created by labels like Motown and Atlantic, but they also set to music the messages of black power and entitlement that were gaining strength and momentum throughout urban America. And for better or worse, their career embodies the trajectory of psychedelic soul, from its joyous, mind-expanding beginnings to its dark, sinister denouement.

Sly & the Family Stone first attracted national attention in early 1968 with the celebratory "Dance to the Music," an anthemic call for democracy that cracked the Top Ten on both the pop and R&B charts. Later that year they returned with "Everyday People," a deceptively simple call for racial harmony that was all the more resonant in a year that witnessed the assassinations of Dr. Martin Luther King Jr., Robert Kennedy and Malcolm X. The follow-up LP, *Stand!* was an unqualified masterpiece—while the title track implored the masses to rise up against their oppressors and assert their independence, "Don't Call Me Nigger, Whitey" took an unflinching look at American race relations that were growing increasingly strained as Richard Nixon assumed the presidency. There were songs of unbridled joy ("I Want to Take You Higher"), heartfelt optimism ("You Can Make It If You Try") and creeping paranoia ("Somebody's Watching You")—in short, *Stand!* captured the exhilarating highs and gut-wrenching lows of the counterculture experience as the 1960s entered their final year with Vietnam still raging and America's inner cities still engulfed by fires both literal and metaphorical. The album's messages pinballed through the hardest-edged, most hallucinatory funk yet committed to vinyl, yet the Family Stone's finest moment—the watershed of psychedelic soul—was still to come.

But first, a status check. By now, psychedelia had wended its way into virtually every corner and pocket of the R&B and soul community—in 1968, the previously unheralded West Coast unit the Chambers Brothers scored a major radio hit with their 11-minute acid-soul epic "Time Has Come Today," while in Chicago, the perennially underrated producer and arranger Charles Stephney installed singer Minnie Riperton to lead his psych-soul protégés the Rotary Connection. Other Chicago acts that married psychedelia with soul include the renowned Curtis Mayfield and the under-appreciated folk-jazz mystic Terry Callier. However, some 300 miles east in Detroit, Midwestern psychedelic soul truly took root—not only were there intriguing obscurities like Fugi's mind-bending 1969 cult classic "Mary Don't Take Me on No Bad Trip," but one George Clinton assembled two bands, Parliament and Funkadelic, to explore the outer reaches of the funk experience. The self-styled P-Funk collective reconfigured the teachings of both Jimi and Sly, fusing funk, rock and psychedelia to forge a style and sound as bi-polar as the bands themselves—while Parliament laid down uplifting, ass-shaking funk, Funkadelic was the vehicle for Clinton's socio-political commentary and otherworldly preaching (although truth be told, the lines between the two groups were rarely that distinct). In part due to their unique vision and in part to their longevity—some lineup of P-Funk All-Stars is almost undoubtedly on the road even as you read these words—Parliament/Funkadelic is the bridge between psychedelic soul and the acid-rap of contemporary artists like OutKast and Common: Clinton was never an innovator on par with Hendrix or Stone, but his influence on successive generations of black artists is immeasurable.

However, the most commercially successful psychedelic soul to emerge from Detroit came from the most unlikely yet perfectly logical source of them all: Motown Records. Throughout the 1960s, Motown virtually defined soul music, creating sweeping, sophisticated classics that put the "urban" in "urbane"—the label was a hit machine nonpareil, and its impact remains incalculable. However, Motown was defiantly apolitical, at least on the surface—the political undercurrents in a handful of smashes like Martha & the Vandellas' "Dancing in the Street" are undeniable, yet they were coded messages for black listeners that went for the most part undetected by white audiences. But by 1968, Motown staff producer and arranger Norman Whitfield had had enough with pussyfooting around—after defining soulful paranoia with Marvin Gaye's landmark "I Heard I Through the Grapevine," Whitfield assumed full studio control of another of the label's premier acts, the Temptations, with the hit "I Wish It Would Rain." Stripping away the spit and polish to reveal the raw, muscular power of the group's renowned harmonies, with the follow-up "Cloud Nine" Whitfield led the Tempts' plunge into psychedelic soul—their music became gritty and funky, the title alone as explicit a drug reference as Motown had yet dared to acknowledge. As Woodstock gave way to Altamont and the counterculture grew more and more disenfranchised, the Temptations and Whitfield charted the fallout—the radio hits "Run Away Child, Running Wild," "Psychedelic Shack," "Ball of Confusion (That's What the World Is Today)" and the epic masterpiece "Papa Was a Rolling Stone" all followed, each darker, more political and funkier than the last.

The Temptations were not the sole Motown act now making politicized, psychedelicized statements—Edwin Starr's Whitfield-produced "War" remains as potent an anti-war screed as any ever waxed. Arguably Whitfield's crowning psychedelic soul achievement, however, was the Undisputed Truth's 1971 opus "Smiling Faces Sometimes"—amidst swirling, claustrophobic strings, guitars thick as milkshakes and metronome-like percussion, the group (Joe Harris, Billy Rae Calvin and Brenda Joyce Evans) railed against the white establishment with more resignation than fury: "Smiling faces sometimes pretend to be your friend/Smiling faces show no traces of the evil that lurks within...Beware of the handshake that hides a snake/Beware of the pat on the back/It just might hold you back." In a provocative, insightful essay in the January 2001 issue of the British music magazine *The Wire*, Peter Shapiro wrote of "Smiling Faces Sometimes," "After centuries of betrayals and lies, the smile, handshake and pat on the back are no longer ways of sealing a social contract. Instead, they become things to fear, temporary placations mollifying race and resentment until the inevitable u-turn, retraction and cutback comes. For African-Americans in the early '70s, the Cheshire Cat grin was all that was left of the promises of the '60s." The list of contemporary soul hits echoing "Smiling Faces Sometimes'" themes of suspicion and misanthropy is long and distinguished: the Staple Singers' "I'll Take You There," War's "Get Down," the Four Tops' "Are You Man Enough?," the Persuaders' "Thin Line Between Love and Hate" and, perhaps most notably, the O'Jays' one-two punch of "Don't Call Me Brother" and their classic "Back Stabbers." Both O'Jays efforts attacked not whites but traditional notions of black masculinity and fraternity, a hot button topic as the increasingly militant Black Power movement became a growing and divisive force within the Afro-American community.

And that brings us back to Sly & the Family Stone. By 1970, Sly Stone had descended into drug addiction, and he became notoriously unreliable, regularly missing live dates and studio appointments. There were even rumors that black nationalist leaders were coercing him to make his music more radical. When the much-delayed *There's a Riot Goin' On* finally appeared in late 1971, the lyrical optimism, buoyant melodies and radiant harmonies of past Family Stone records were no more, replaced by a brittle, scattershot sound equal parts entropy and irony. Stone created narcotic, hazy grooves that damned everything and nothing—"(You Caught Me) Smilin'," his own addition to the "Smiling Faces" hit parade, even heaped scorn on the listeners that still expected the up-with-people celebrations of past efforts. *There's a Riot Goin' On* remains the most brilliant and potent music of Stone's career if not psychedelic soul as a whole, but it's also a dead end—musically, spiritually and intellectually. And with the man responsible for the greatest humanist anthems of the 1960s finally giving up the good fight, psychedelic soul—at least as an exemplar of the counterculture dream in microcosm—was for all intents and purposes over.

But the influence of psychedelic soul remains vast. As the 1970s surged forward, psych-soul helped spawn both the funky blaxploitation grooves of Isaac Hayes and Willie Hutch as well as the gloriously silky Philly Soul sound, which itself begat disco; it also crossed over into jazz, yielding bizarre yet compelling records like Eugene McDaniels' much-sampled *Headless Heroes of the Apocalypse*, Bobbi Humphrey's *Blacks and Blues* and Horace Silver's *Human Response*, and even traveled the globe to influence African-based acts like the little-known but brilliant Blo. And there was still the offhand masterpiece of soulful psychedelia, like Shuggie Otis' 1974 underground classic *Inspiration Information*. In the early 1980s, Prince—who often seemed musically and even physically the reincarnation of Jimi Hendrix—honed his own brand of sprawling, genre-smashing music, drawing heavily on psychedelia and soul (and sometimes their sum) for groundbreaking albums including *1999*, *Purple Rain* and *Sign O' the Times*. Last but certainly not least, there's hip-hop, which has assumed psych-soul's mantle as the means for communicating the voice of urban society—once dubbed "Black America's CNN" by Public Enemy's Chuck D., hip-hop dominated commercial radio and record sales in the 1990s and beyond, elevating African-American culture to unprecedented heights of influence and dominance. As Sly Stone once sang, "Different strokes for different folks."

—Jason Ankeny

Funk

Bridging the classic soul era and the dawn of disco, funk was R&B at its most rhythmic, earthy, and (occasionally) wild and experimental. Not as hugely successful with the masses as soul or disco, it has proven to be about as influential, strongly affecting not just all post-1970 R&B, but also contemporary rap and alternative rock music.

What exactly puts the "unk" into "funk" can be hard to pigeonhole, but there are some basic traits which distinguish it from mainstream soul and rock music. The emphasis, above all, is on the rhythm, and on the bass and drums of the rhythm section. The accent is often placed on the downbeat, or the first and third beats of 4/4 patterns. The function of the guitar becomes more rhythmic than melodic, often employing what has been called "scratch" or even "chicken scratch" staccato bursts of percussive strings; the horns also take a stronger rhythmic role than traditional soul music, used for percussive riffing and punctuation as well as taking solos or providing harmonic support.

The rhythms, though, are often anything but simple, building upon each other and playing in counterpoint to build a polyrhythmic drive. Both the lead and backup singers often do their part to add to the excitement with chants, grunts, and screams. The lyrics have at times been quite sophisticated and socially conscious, but more often are principally concerned, like the music itself, with stream-of-consciousness grooves, built around slogans and exhortations to dance and party. Adding to the ferment are unpredictable influences from psychedelic and hard guitar rock, Latin music, doo wop, and other elements of the melting pot of American rock, soul, and pop.

Few would dispute that James Brown is not only the Godfather of Soul, but the Godfather of Funk as well. The ignition of the funk explosion can for most intents and purposes be boiled down to his landmark mid-'60s singles "Out of Sight" and especially "Papa's Got a Brand New Bag," the first smashes to incorporate the syncopated horns, stream-of-consciousness lyrics, and staccato guitars that would become funk trademarks. Although it would be a few years before the music began to be called funk, in the last half of the '60s Brown would continue to lay the funk prototype with workouts like "Cold Sweat" and "There Was a Time" that grew increasingly polyrhythmic, jazzy, and improvisational, pushing the melody to the background in favor of the churning beat and Brown's inimitable screams and groans.

The word "funk" itself began to enter the R&B/soul vocabulary with Dyke & the Blazers' R&B dance hit "Funky Broadway." Several theories and explanations of the origins of the actual word "funk" have been offered, the most likely consensus being that, like rock & roll and jazz, it was a euphemism for sexual activity, though "funk" often stood for smelly, gritty, or earthy stuff within the African-American community. By the end of the 1960s, it had come to stand for the greasiest and earthiest variant of soul music.

Although James Brown's early-'70s work was not nearly as commercially successful with the pop audience as the recordings of his 1965-1969 peak (though they remained huge R&B sellers), with time they have come to be viewed as nearly as important and influential. These discs found him getting deeper and deeper into the polyrhythmic funk groove, with increasingly basic workouts that in time came to resemble one continuous (if often compelling) performance. His backup band of the era, the J.B.'s, are now recognized as some of funk's greatest musicians, particularly guitarist Jimmy Nolen and horn-players Fred Wesley, Pee Wee Ellis, Maceo Parker, and St. Clair Pinckney; they also cut many underappreciated instrumental funk workouts on their own.

Another influential Brown sideman, although he was only with the band for about a couple years, was bassist Bootsy Collins, who was instrumental in boosting his instrument's importance in the funk mix. After leaving Brown in the early '70s, Bootsy teamed up with George Clinton to become a vital cog in what many funk fans regard as the finest exponents of the genre, Parliament/Funkadelic. Clinton was a veteran R&B/soul performer who changed gears radically around 1970, constructing elaborate funk heavily influenced by the acid rock of Jimi Hendrix, as well as touches of jazz and psychedelia. Almost anything went with Clinton and his troops, including extended spacy jams, inscrutable self-mythologizing and unfathomable concept opuses about spaceships and funk itself, though the bands never lost their slightly absurd sense of humor.

The Parliament/Funkadelic family tree is among the most twisted and difficult to follow in rock history, with a revolving door of musicians who often played in both Parliament and Funkadelic (for tangled contractual reasons, Clinton led similar groups recording under both names, sometimes simultaneously). It grew more complex when Bootsy Collins became a solo star in his own right with a similarly (perhaps even more excessive) cosmic vision, as a solo act and leader of Bootsy's Rubber Band. Both Clinton and Collins remain active and influential musicians to this day, as both individual artists and collaborators with other heavyweights.

Although they are usually categorized as a soul act rather than funk one, Sly & the Family Stone also did a great deal to cross-fertilize soul and psychedelia to come up with some of the most adventurous funk of the early '70s. Larry Graham's distinctive finger-popping bass sound has become perhaps *the* most single identifying characteristic associated with funk, and Sly Stone's commentaries on racial injustice and people power rank as some of the genre's most sophisticated lyrics. While their early, more soul- and

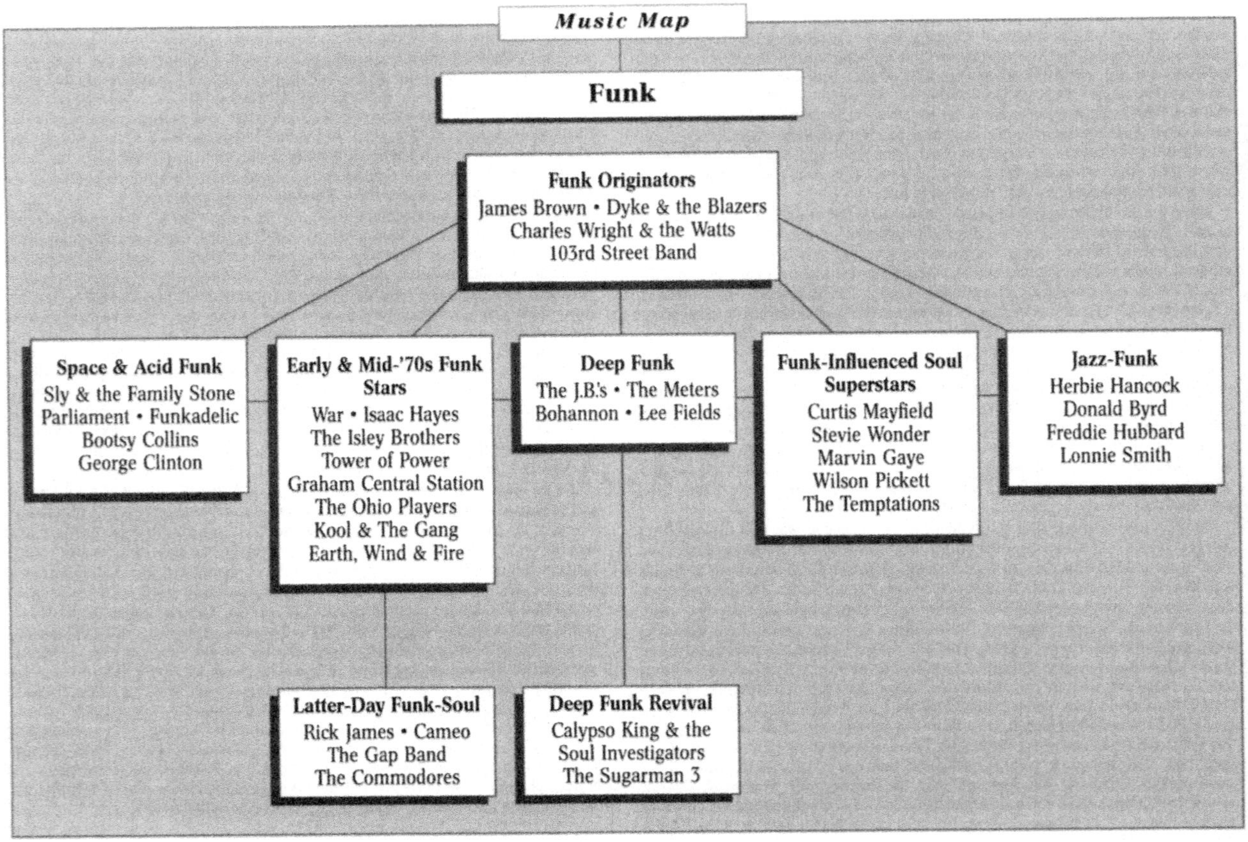

pop-flavored work of the late '60s is equally important, their 1971 album *There's a Riot Goin' On* is their deepest foray into hardcore funk, and remains one of the few funk LPs that hits as deep with its words as its grooves.

The late '60s and early '70s saw several other less important but interesting groups make their mark in the funk parade. Dyke & the Blazers and the Charles Wright & the Watts 103rd Street Rhythm Band (most famous for "Express Yourself") were among the style's earliest practitioners. After an apprenticeship with Eric Burdon, War stormed the charts in the early and mid-'70s with a series of hits that incorporated Latin rhythms, loose, jazzy grooves, and vague social pontifications. The Meters took the sound of New Orleans R&B, already a bedrock of much post-1950 R&B, soul, and rock, into the funk era, largely on instrumentals (at least at first). Isaac Hayes took endless bubbling funk monologues onto both album and single charts, as his *Shaft* took the wah-wah guitar signatures often found in funk to their limit.

There were also quite a few funk classics in the early '70s committed to vinyl by performers who are really best categorized as soul musicians, but were deeply influenced by the funk groove. These years certainly saw some of the best work of soul giants Curtis Mayfield, Stevie Wonder, Wilson Pickett, and Marvin Gaye, all of whom drew heavily upon the expanded lyrical and musical grooves opened up by funk. The Isley Brothers, always one of soul's most eclectic stars, became close to an out-and-out funk band after beefing up their guitars and arrangements under the influence of Jimi Hendrix and Sly Stone. Even more traditional soul vocal groups like the Temptations and O'Jays delved quite heavily into funk for a time to come up with some of their most memorable hits.

Opinions differ on the matter, but it could be argued that the early '70s saw funk at its peak. The music remained extremely popular through the mid-'70s, though, with less sophisticated acts who either concentrated on the dance-and-party element (Kool & the Gang, the Ohio Players, Graham Central Station) or the slicker, more soul- and harmony-influenced variants (Earth, Wind & Fire, Tower of Power). As for the original innovators, James Brown had seemingly run out of fresh ideas by the middle of the decade, accused even by his backup musicians of not only repeating himself but copying his imitators. Sly Stone fell victim to well-documented substance abuse and financial problems, and the Parliament/Funkadelic clan, while continuing to churn out music at the top of their game, were just too eccentric to truly catch on with the masses.

Disco, although it owed a great deal to funk in its dance rhythms, overran its ancestor in popularity in the mid- and late '70s. Some pop- and dance-oriented acts that owed a considerable debt to funk did enjoy great success in the late '70s and '80s, though, including Rick James, Cameo, the Gap Band, and the Commodores. The influence of funk was also felt in the jazz world with the advent of fusion, particularly in the work of Herbie Hancock, Donald Byrd, Freddie Hubbard, and Lonnie Smith.

If anything, funk underwent a bit of a renaissance in the '90s which continued into the 2000s. Bootsy Collins and George Clinton are both venerated pioneers who continue to record critically respected albums and draw huge crowds on the club circuit, although they don't chart like they did at their peak. Funk was a big element in the mix of the '80s biggest black superstars, Michael Jackson and Prince, and funk classics are sampled constantly (some would say excessively) by contemporary rappers. And even some of the biggest white alternative rock acts of the '90s, such as the Red Hot Chili Peppers, Faith No More, and Primus, drew heavily on funk's rhythms and in-your-face attitudes, if not delivering as much soul as its original progenitors.

17 Recommended Funk Recordings:

Various Artists, *In Yo' Face! The Roots of Funk, Vol. 1/2* (Rhino) [Note: this is volume one-half, or the "prequel" to the *In Yo' Face History of Funk Series* listed below.]
Various Artists, *In Yo' Face! The History Of Funk, Vol. 1-5* (Rhino)
James Brown, *Love Power Peace: Live at the Olympia Paris 1971* (PolyGram)
Various Artists, *James Brown's Funky People Parts1 & 2* (PolyGram)
The J.B.'s, *Funky Good Time* (PolyGram)
Dyke & the Blazers, *Dyke's Greatest Hits* (Original Sound)
Charles Wright & the Watts 103rd Street Band, *Express Yourself: The Best Of* (Warner Brothers)
Sly & the Family Stone, *There's a Riot Goin' On* (Epic)
Parliament, *Tear the Roof Off* (Casablanca)
Funkadelic, *Music for Your Mother* (Westbound)
Bootsy Collins, *Back in the Day: The Best Of* (Warners)
War, *Anthology (1970-1994)* (Rhino)
The Meters, *Funkify Your Life: The Meters Anthology* (Rhino)
Curtis Mayfield, *Superfly* (Curtom)
James Brown, *Foundations of Funk: A Brand New Bag: 1964-1969* (Polydor)
James Brown, *Funk Power 1970: A Brand New Thang* (Polydor)
James Brown, *Make It Funky: The Big Payback: 1971-1975* (Polydor)

—Richie Unterberger

Northern Soul

Throughout the 1960s, Motown's celebratory tagline "The Sound of Young America" wasn't so much hyperbole as it was simple fact—the company's groundbreaking, era-defining soul music dominated white and black radio alike, sparring throughout the decade with the British Invasion pop of the Beatles and the Rolling Stones for chart supremacy. As an African-American-owned label operating out of industrial Detroit, MI, during the formative years of the civil rights movement, Motown's commercial breakthroughs were unprecedented, and its musical achievements unparalleled; accordingly, the company's influence ran deep—small, independent labels began sprouting like weeds in virtually every major U.S. city, each striving to emulate the sweeping, ebullient Motown sound to varying degrees of success. And for every left-field hit that rode Motown's coattails to the upper reaches of the charts, there were hundreds if not thousands of resounding failures, some released only in pressings of 100 or 200 copies and virtually unknown outside of their respective geographic markets.

By the mid-'70s, however, the classic Motown Sound was increasingly falling out of favor on native shores, and despite the continuing popularity of black music in its myriad forms (chief among them funk, disco and later hip-hop), Motown—its copycat competitors long since relegated to obscurity—seemed increasingly out-of-touch with the times. The 1983 release of the hit film *The Big Chill* gave soundtrack classics from Marvin Gaye, the Temptations and Smokey Robinson & the Miracles new prominence, but also cemented the fabled Motown sound as a relic of the baby-boomer era. Moreover, the myopia of oldies radio further fostered the myth that Motown, and in fact the vibrant Detroit R&B scene as a whole, produced nothing worthy of playlist consideration outside of the acknowledged canon of chart blockbusters—a fallacy that Motown's own remarkably short-sighted and seemingly endless campaign of CD reissues has for the most part done little to rectify.

So it is the great irony of Britain's Northern soul club scene that a subculture obsessively committed to preserving in amber the sound and spirit of a bygone musical moment has at the same time invigorated that moment with altogether new life and meaning. The most clearly definable and enduring phenomenon born of the eternally vibrant British club culture, Northern soul—a catch-all term for the obscure American records of the 1960s that scenesters spin and revere—is the catalyst behind the rediscovery and reevaluation of untold numbers of little-known soul singles now viewed as lost classics: tireless archivists have plumbed the nooks and crannies of the Motown vaults for the kind of propulsive rare bits guaranteed to set clubs afire, valuing obscurity almost as much as the almighty groove. But Motown is not the only label that Northern soul DJs and collectors have mined and resurrected—the brilliant Southern-fried soul of the Stax imprint is a perennial crowd-pleaser, as are familiar names like Atlantic, OKeh, Cadet and Chess. Nevertheless, it is the hundreds of obscure regional labels that Motown both spawned and overshadowed that have come to best embody the scene, their derivative but undeniably potent melodies and arrangements fueling the all-night parties—events equal parts archaeological digs and Bacchanalian rites of passage—that are themselves intrinsic to the Northern soul experience, an experience that more than three decades on shows no signs of drawing to a halt.

A definition: "Northern soul" connotes not the geographic origins of the music itself but the general locale of the British clubs that first forged the culture in question. The earliest and most legendary Northern soul venues—the Twisted Wheel, Blackpool Mecca and Wigan Casino among them—emerged in northern England, a historically industrial, rough-and-tumble region that by no means coincidentally resembles the American cities (Detroit, Chicago, Philadelphia, etc.) that produced the original records. In essence, Northern soul constitutes a British working class obsession with American working class music, and the obvious national, racial and even temporal differences between the clubgoers and the often-obscure singers they idolize matter little. The hallmarks of the Northern soul experience are immediately recognizable, and have changed little over the decades—massive crowds of sweaty, drug-fueled club kids of all ages packing dancefloors until the wee hours of the night, grinding and gyrating to the relentless backbeats and soaring vocals of an era long since passed. In one form or another, Northern soul has consistently endured since the mid- to late '60s, and its influence as the archetype for subsequent clubgoing subcultures cannot be overstated.

According to legend, the term "Northern soul" was coined by *Blues and Soul* magazine journalist Dave Godin, who in June 1970 devoted his regular column to documenting the evolving rare soul collecting community. Noting the number of Northern-based customers frequenting his London record store Soul City, Godin wrote about the "Up-North soul Groove," inadvertently giving a genre, scene and subculture its name. But the roots of Northern soul date back some years prior to Godin's christening: the acknowledged ground zero of Northern soul's birth is the Twisted Wheel, opened in 1963 on Manchester's Brazennose Street. In the first few years of its existence, the club played a mish-mash of soul, blues and jazz, but upon relocating to nearby Whitworth Street in 1967 adopted a strict uptempo soul music policy. Led by DJs Roger Eagle and Bob Bellars, the Twisted Wheel popularized records like Gladys Knight's "Just Walk in My Shoes," Archie Bell & the Drells' "Here I Go Again" and Earl Van Dyke's "All for You," all virtually unknown in their native U.S. The club was also the first to import records from American retailers—technically an illegal activity in Britain prior to 1972—and welcomed live acts including the Drifters, the Crystals, Jimmy Ruffin and Jamo Thomas. The Twisted Wheel was rewarded for its diligence with a devoted clientele among the so-called Mods—young, mostly white Brits noted for their hipper-than-thou fashions, Italian motor scooters and love of amphetamines. Unfortunately, the drug culture ultimately spun out of control, and the Manchester city council revoked the Twisted Wheel's entertainment license. On January 31, 1971, the club closed its doors for good.

By then, however, the nascent Northern soul culture was reaching critical mass: a growing collective of underground clubs were devoting their energies solely to spinning American soul records, and as their numbers grew, so did rivalries among DJs. Knowledge and ownership of rare records was a mark of distinction in Mod circles, emblematic of the cutting-edge tastes and sensibilities the culture strived to define and maintain; consequently, many DJs covered up the labels on their most coveted, crowd-pleasing vinyls, often changing the artist and title to throw rivals off the trail. As the DJs burned through the catalogs of high-profile labels like Motown, Stax and Atlantic, they dug deeper and deeper to unearth records that barely registered during their initial American release, scouring second-hand stalls and jumble sales for something—anything—ripe for rediscovery. The Wolverhampton club Catacombs and its DJ Farmer Carl Dean were particularly renowned for their ability to unearth and popularize unknown gems—Doris Troy's

"I'll Do Anything (He Wants Me To)," an unqualified Northern soul classic, began as a Catacombs favorite, and Dean's cheerleading even propelled Tami Lynn's "I'm Gonna Run Away from You" and the Tams' "Hey Don't Bother Me" into the upper reaches of the U.K. pop charts without any kind of conventional radio airplay or promotion.

The Catacombs could have supplanted the Twisted Wheel as the premier Northern soul club of the early '70s, but closed so early—midnight each night—that its impact was blunted; other notable venues of the period included Sheffield's the King Mojo, Crewe's the Blue Orchid, Bradford's the Queen's Hall, Burnley's the Cats Whiskers, Bolton's VaVa's, York's the Holgate, Rotherham's Clifton Hall and Blackburn's King George's Hall. Perhaps the most pivotal, however, was the Torch, located in Stoke-on-Trent. Previously the Golden Torch, the building was constructed circa 1824 as a church, but later housed a cinema and skating rink. New owner Chris Burton converted the space to a club in 1965; middle-of-the-road pop acts like Billy J. Kramer and the Dakotas were the order of the day until late 1967, when the first soul act ever booked, Charlie & Inez Foxx, brought in a record gate and convinced Burton he could make a living booking soul music exclusively. Torch DJs Keith Minshull and Tony Jebb proved formidable tastemakers, introducing now-classic sides like Sandi Shelton's "You're Gonna Make Me Love You," and the club slowly but surely earned notice as a perennial hot spot, reaching its apotheosis on December 9, 1972 when Major Lance recorded his cult-classic *Major Lance Live at the Torch*, considered by many the greatest Northern soul live set ever documented.

But like the Twisted Wheel before it, the Torch was doomed by its patrons' drug use, and closed in 1973. It then fell to a pair of emerging rival clubs, the Blackpool Mecca and the Wigan Casino, to push Northern soul to new heights of popularity. The Blackpool Mecca opened in 1965; complete with a revolving stage, free coach service and a capacity approaching 3500, the club was briefly the most popular nightclub of its day, but as the decade closed, smaller, more intimate venues became the vogue, and the larger dancehalls generally fell into disrepair. However, nestled within the Blackpool Mecca was a smaller hall, the Highland Room, located above the main arena; in 1971 the Highland Room opened as a Northern soul venue, hosting acts ranging from Isaac Hayes to Edwin Starr to the Chi-Lites and boasting arguably the scene's greatest one-two punch in DJs Ian Levine and Colin Curtis. Levine regularly accompanied his businessman father on overseas trips, scouring American record stores, junk shops, warehouses and even recording studios to acquire music simply unavailable anywhere outside the U.S. Restricted by conservative licensing laws, the Blackpool Mecca also earned renown for introducing all-dayers, essentially all-nighters beginning at noon and ending at midnight. Soon all-dayers were *de rigueur* for all clubs, even those exempt from similar licensing constraints.

If the Blackpool Mecca represented Northern soul culture at its most musically progressive and socially far-ranging, from its 1973 launch onward Wigan Casino maintained the traditionalist hardline, rarely deviating from Motown originals and I-can't-believe-it's-not-Motown sound-alikes. (Tensions between the two clubs were so great that some club-goers even sported "Levine Must Go" T-shirts.) But even if its playlists lacked daring, Wigan Casino captured the Northern spirit at its most hedonistic, with all-nighters that are now the stuff of legend. A massive post-Victorian theatre-cum-snooker hall, its environment was ideal for dancing, with a sprung wooden floor instead of the concrete flooring common to other clubs; Wigan Casino also held about 2000 patrons, although at its peak card-carrying membership totaled a staggering 100,000-plus members. Spearheaded by DJs Russ Winstanley, Kev Roberts and Richard Searling, Wigan Casino broke more new records than any other club (the Velvets' "I Got to Find Me Someone," Willie Hutch's "The Duck" and Don Ray's "Born a Loser" were signatures), and in 1978 was named by *Billboard* magazine "Best Disco in the World," beating even New York's renowned Studio 54 at the peak of its own influence and notoriety. When city leaders closed Wigan Casino on December 6, 1981, to build a civic center that never even materialized, an era truly came to an end; a few months later, the derelict venue burned to the ground.

Shortly after the demise of Wigan Casino, Blackpool Mecca was shuttered as well, and Northern soul spent much of the 1980s clinging to life, its pulse resuscitated only by smaller, much less noteworthy clubs in areas like Morecambe and Stafford. Even as the original club scene struggled to remain afloat, however, Northern soul exerted a new-found influence on the popular culture at large—the Gloria Jones classic "Tainted Love," a longtime house favorite at Wigan Casino, was updated by synth-pop duo Soft Cell, whose re-imagined version boasted a sleazy, kinky sound far removed from the original. Purists blanched, but Soft Cell's single emerged as the best-selling British single of 1982 and a worldwide blockbuster, and remains one of the definitive records of the decade. Another British music press darling of the period, Dexy's Midnight Runners (of "Come On, Eileen" fame), borrowed their name, look and early, soul-influenced sound from Northern soul. Other club rats got into the mix as well: Pete Waterman, a onetime Northern soul DJ and promoter, subsequently emerged as one third of the Stock-Aitken-Waterman production team that helmed massive pop hits for Bananarama, Rick Astley and other chartbusters. Even Blackpool Mecca's influential DJ Ian Levine recast himself for a new era as the production mastermind behind boy-band sensations Take That and Boyzone. (Levine more recently reinvented himself yet again, this time as a documentary filmmaker—his film *The Strange World of Northern Soul*, containing some 124 new performances from the some of the greatest if most obscure names in music history, was released on video in early 2003.)

But the most auspicious development of the 1980s was the introduction and widespread popularity of the compact disc format, which exploded in the decade to follow. Thanks to reissue labels like Kent, Goldmine and countless others, the rarest Northern soul records, once exclusive to only the most diligent and deep-pocketed DJs and collectors, were now readily and cheaply available on CD retrospectives and compilations, often digitally remastered and sounding better than ever before. Although the exclusivity factor once such a critical component of Northern soul culture has waned as a result, CDs are credited with rejuvenating interest in the music, bringing in new fans and luring back some of the original club denizens now well into their middle age. Goldmine's *The Wigan Casino Story* sold 20,000 copies, and in 1997 Telstar's double-disc set *Soul Survivors* shifted 120,000 units; even Motown was getting into the act, in 2002 issuing *A Cellarful of Motown!*, a two-disc compilation of unreleased material from the label's vaults. The CD boom has not totally killed off the collectors market, however: in 1998, Scottish fan Kenny Burrell paid an astounding £15,000 for one of two known promotional copies of Frank Wilson's unreleased Motown effort "Do I Love You? (Indeed I Do)." (As of this writing, the record is believed to be the world's rarest seven-inch vinyl release, and Burrell's purchase reportedly the most ever paid for a 45 rpm single.)

After the introduction of the CD forever changed how fans collect music, the Internet changed everything yet again—now listeners from across the globe can purchase and download music previously limited to only the largest and most eclectic record shops, and the rise of collector websites like eBay and GEMM have fostered an entirely new market for the rarest grooves. And where news of Northern soul events once spread by word of mouth, there are now dozens upon dozens of rare soul websites exchanging information, fan recommendations and MP3 files, as well as old-school print magazines like the excellent *Togetherness*. This exchange of information has been pivotal in making the world a much smaller place, and there are now tiny but thriving Northern soul scenes in Australia, Canada, Germany, Italy and—yes—even the U.S. Somewhat ironically, the longest-running U.K. Northern soul venue, the 100 Club, is located on Oxford Street in central London—its southern locale aside, the 100 Club has regularly hosted all-nighters since 1980, and still presents Northern soul showcases each month. Nowhere do modern-day crowds reach the capacity and fever pitch of the Wigan Casino at its peak, but in an era where fads and trends seem shorter-lived than ever before, the devotion of the Northern soul die-hards nearly four decades on since the scene's inception is most impressive indeed.

Recommended Listening:

Various Artists, *This Is Northern Soul! Vol.1* (Debutante)
Various Artists, *This Is Northern Soul! Vol.2* (Debutante)
Various Artists, *Wigan Casino 25th Anniversary* (Goldmine)
Various Artists, *The Golden Torch Story* (Goldmine)
Various Artists, *The In Crowd: The Story of Northern Soul* (Castle)
Various Artists, *The Best Northern Soul All-Nighter ... Ever!* (Virgin)
Various Artists, *A Cellarful of Motown!* (Universal)
Various Artists, *The Best of Soultime* (Sony)
Various Artists, *Keep The Faith: The Northern Soul Generation* (Sanctuary)
Various Artists, *Big In Wigan* (Kent)

—Jason Ankeny

Go-Go

Throughout the '80s, go-go was supposed to become the "next big thing" in African-American music. Go-go's more optimistic supporters kept insisting that it was only a matter of time before it became as big as rap. And in Washington, D.C., where go-go was created, it was, in fact, as big as hip-hop at one time—in the '80s, go-go favorites like Chuck Brown & the Soul Searchers, Rare Essence, EU and Trouble Funk were as popular in Washington's black neighborhoods as Run-D.M.C., the Fat Boys, Whodini and LL Cool J. During that decade, go-go was huge in the nation's capitol. But regrettably, go-go only had a small cult following outside of Washington, D.C.

What exactly is go-go? It's hardcore funk, pure and simple—not electronic funk or synth-funk, but horn-powered funk that is played instead of programmed. Go-go owed a lot to '70s funk favorites like the Ohio Players, Parliament/Funkadelic, Bootsy Collins, the Bar-Kays and Cameo, but go-go had its own beat and involved a distinctive style of percussion playing. When soul music evolved into urban contemporary and R&B became increasingly high-tech in 1983 and 1984, Washington, D.C.'s go-go artists refused to go electronic and remained faithful to the spirit of '70s funk. One could say that go-go artists stubbornly refused to change with the times when it came to technology—they felt that drum machines, sequencers and samplers would water their funk down. And that refusal to go high-tech no doubt explains why go-go was, for the most part, rejected by urban contemporary radio outside of Washington, D.C.

To fully understand how go-go came about, one has to understand the history of funk—which started with James Brown in the '60s. Were it not for the Godfather of Soul's innovations, go-go never would have existed. Brown, after all, was the first true, honest-to-God funk artist. He wasn't the first person who was funky-some of the swing that Louis Jordan, Count Basie, Lionel Hampton and Cab Calloway provided in the '30s and '40s was funky. Duke Ellington's original 1932 version of "It Don't Mean a Thing (If It Ain't Got That Swing)" was mostly definitely funky-it was one of the funkiest party songs of the Great Depression, but being funky doesn't necessarily mean that one is providing funk. James Brown's '50s output (such as "Chonnie-on-Chon" and the hit "Please, Please, Please") was funky, but it wasn't funk-it wasn't until the '60s that the Godfather unveiled what came to be called funk. "Papa's Got a Brand New Bag," "Cold Sweat," "I Got You (I Feel Good)" and other Brown hits of the '60s are early examples of funk, and they had a major impact on Sly & the Family Stone and countless others.

If Brown was the first funk singer, Sly Stone was the second. Sly & the Family Stone hits like "Simple a Simple Song" and "Thank You (Falletin Me Be Mice Elf Again") (both of which are examples of late '60s funk) also helped pave the way for go-go. Then, in the early '70s, many more great funksters made their mark, including Tower of Power, Earth, Wind & Fire, Parliament/Funkadelic, Mandrill, War and Kool & the Gang (who played instrumental jazz before they became famous for funk classics like "Jungle Boogie" and "Funky Stuff"). The Ohio Players, the Bar-Kays and the Isley Brothers didn't start out playing funk—the Bar-Kays, in fact, were originally an instrumental Memphis soul group along the lines of Booker T. & the MG's—but in the '70s, those bands took the funk plunge in a major way.

The late '70s found a lot of popular funk bands doing their thing, including Rick James, Slave, Brick, the Gap Band, the Average White Band, Cameo, Con Funk Shun and Lakeside. And it was around that time that Washington, D.C.'s go-go scene got started; go-go was very much a product of the '70s funk explosion. The person who is often credited with getting the go-go ball rolling is singer Chuck Brown, leader of Chuck Brown & the Soul Searchers. Brown, who is known as "the Godfather of Go-Go," provided his debut album, *Bustin' Loose*, for the Source label in 1979. The title track became a national hit—one of go-go's few national hits, in fact—and the LP went down in history as a go-go classic. *Bustin' Loose*, which is considered the first important go-go album, let listeners know exactly what kind of funk go-go was. It wasn't the smooth, polished, sophisticated funk of the Brothers Johnson or Dynasty, and it wasn't disco-funk à la Chic—go-go was hard, aggressive, tough, sweaty, uncompromising funk. It was obvious that Chuck Brown and similar artists identified with the most extroverted sounds that Parliament/Funkadelic, the Bar-Kays, James Brown and pre-J.T. Taylor Kool & the Gang had to offer. (When Taylor's became Kool & the Gang's new lead singer in 1979, they softened their sound considerably and became much sleeker).

In the late '70s and early '80s, a lot of go-go bands followed the lead of Chuck Brown & the Soul Searchers and made their mark on the Washington, D.C. scene—people like EU (which stood for Experience Unlimited), Rare Essence and Trouble Funk. In America's capitol, those bands became local stars. Rare Essence, EU and Trouble Funk never headlined Madison Square Garden in New York or the Inglewood Forum in Los Angeles, but they never had a problem drawing a sizable crowd in their home town. In Washington, D.C., a go-go concert could be a big event in the '80s—a Chuck Brown, Trouble Funk, EU or Rare Essence show was, for D.C. residents, every bit as big an event as a visit by Run-D.M.C., New Edition or the Time.

Go-go artists didn't escape the influence of rap, but they acknowledged it on their own terms. Instead of embracing hip-hop's electronic beats, go-go artists would rap over real bass, real guitar, real drums and real horns. D.C. Scorpio, a rapper who was active in Washington, D.C. in the '80s, was willing to be accompanied by a go-go band instead of using a DJ like rappers in other cities.

Sadly, one of the things that had an adverse effect on Washington, D.C.'s go-go scene in the '80s was the drug PCP, which is known as angel dust in other cities but was called "love boat" in Washington street slang. When crack cocaine was plaguing New York, Chicago and Los Angeles, angel dust was assaulting D.C.'s inner-city neighborhoods—and much to the dismay of many go-go artists, drug dealers saw go-go shows as an opportunity to sell "love boat." That fact wasn't lost on local concert promoters, who were well aware of the problems that PCP was causing at go-go concerts. It's important to stress that the artists themselves were not to blame for the PCP plague in D.C.—go-go lyrics never promoted the use of angel dust in any way, shape or form. But drug dealers knew that there was money to be made from selling PCP, and they really didn't care how much they harmed the go-go scene.

But as tragic as the PCP plague in Washington, D.C. was, that wasn't the thing that hurt go-go on a national level. Outside of D.C., go-go's problem was—from a commercial standpoint—its refusal to connect with changing tastes in African-American music. Most of the urban contemporary and rap that has been recorded since 1984 has been extremely high-tech—the very thing that go-go is not. In contrast to Cameo-which started out as a horn band in the '70s but downsized and went high-tech in the '80s-go-go bands weren't about to replace their horn sections with synthesizers. To many urban radio programmers of the mid- to late '80s, go-go was too '70s-sounding; they felt that go-go was stuck in the past. Nonetheless, a go-go song did manage to become a national R&B hit in 1988, when EU's "Da Butt" was heard in the Spike Lee film *School Daze*. The success of "Da Butt" led some go-go enthusiasts to think that perhaps their dream was coming true—that perhaps go-go was on the verge of a big national breakthrough and would become more than just a local phenomenon in Washington, D.C. But "Da Butt" was an anomaly, and go-go never received the national success that its admirers kept hoping for.

Some go-go veterans, including Chuck Brown, continued to perform and record in the '90s and remained active when 21st century arrived. But most go-go fans would admit that go-go reached its peak in the '80s and wasn't nearly as plentiful in the '90s or early 2000s. Nonetheless, go-go was a lot of fun during its heyday, and go-go's lack of national success doesn't make it any less valuable.

Recommended Recordings:
Chuck Brown & the Soul Searchers, *Bustin' Loose* (Source)
Chuck Brown & the Soul Searchers, *Your Game: Live at the 9:30 Club* (Raw Venture)
Trouble Funk, *Saturday Night: Live from Washington, D.C.* (Island)
Trouble Funk, *Drop the Bomb* (MCA)
Rare Essence, *Greatest Hits, Vol. 1* (Liaison)
EU, *EU Live: Two Places at the Same Time* (Island)

—*Alex Henderson*

New Jack Swing

In the late '80s and early '90s, urban contemporary radio was obsessed with new jack swing—a style of high-tech funk that was heavily influenced by hip-hop. The new jack swing era lasted about half a decade or perhaps as long as six years; arguably, new jack swing started in 1987, and by 1993, its popularity was seriously declining. But new jack swing was incredibly popular at one time, and for a few years—especially in 1989, 1990 and 1991—it was inescapable if you listened to urban radio at all. In fact, the urban contemporary market became so saturated with new jack swing recordings that in 1993, there was inevitably a backlash. By that point, urban fans had grown tired of all the faceless Bell Biv DeVoe (BBD) clones and Guy wannabees who had been getting signed to major labels. But the best new jack swing—which included BBD, Guy, Bobby Brown and Keith Sweat—was an exciting, creative part of urban music.

New jack swing was hardly the first time that R&B singers acknowledged hip-hop in some way. As early as 1979, funk band Fatback embraced rapping on their hit "King Tim III." In 1981, soul/urban singer Teena Marie gave hip-hop a big shout out when she included a rap section on her hit "Square Biz." And although Blondie and Deborah Harry were primarily a pop-rock/new wave act, they found their way to a lot of black stations when she praised New York's hip-hop culture on "Rapture"—a 1980 gem that was way ahead of its time. These days, a lot of alternative rock artists are very cognizant of rap—many of them grew up listening to it—but in 1980, it was surprising to hear a major pop-rock star like Harry rapping and telling her listeners about Grandmaster Flash (one of rap's pioneers). So there was a long history of R&B, dance and pop artists acknowledging hip-hop long before the first new jack swing recordings were made.

What made new jack swing different from much of the hip-hop-influenced R&B that came before 1987? It really comes down to just how much hip-hop the singers decided to incorporate. Countless urban singers flirted with hip-hop before 1987, but new jack swing was more than just hip-hop-tinged—it was hip-hop-drenched. Soul goddess Chaka Khan flirted with hip-hop on her hit 1984 version of Prince's "I Feel for You," which featured rapper Melle Mel; but for Guy, Bell Biv DeVoe and Bobby Brown, it was more than a flirtation—it was an obsession. Hip-hop was an integral part of what jack swing artists did—not only in terms of the rapping that they incorporated, but also, because of their beats and production style. New jack swing wasn't neo-soul, although it certainly proved beneficial for Mary J. Blige and other hip-hop-minded neo-soulsters who emerged in the '90s.

R&B historians generally agree that new jack swing got started in 1987, when Keith Sweat provided his debut album, *Make It Last Forever* and had a big hit with the funky "I Want Her." That song was the first major new jack swing hit, and *Make It Last Forever* demonstrated that an urban artist could be a serious hip-hop head as well as a soul singer—not classic soul, but neo-soul. Again, new jack swing isn't part of neo-soul, but that doesn't mean that a singer couldn't embrace neo-soul one minute and new jack swing the next—which is exactly what Sweat did on *Make It Last Forever.* While "I Want Her" got the ball rolling for new jack swing, other parts of Sweat's album were romantic neo-soul. The hit title track and a fine remake of the Dramatics' early '70s hit "In the Rain" underscored Sweat's love of classic soul, but they weren't a carbon copy of it—rather, Sweat combined a passion for pre-'80s soul with a hip-hop-influenced production style. So in more ways than one, *Make It Last Forever* was a very progressive album for 1987.

The man who co-produced *Make It Last Forever* with Sweat was Teddy Riley, a major player in the new jack swing field. In 1987, Riley founded the trio Guy, whose other original members included Timmy Gatling, aka Tim-Tim, and singer Aaron Hall. Guy combined a hip-hop mentality with a strong Gap Band influence; in fact, Gap Band singer Charles Wilson was a major influence on Hall. But Guy were hardly Gap Band clones—they were quite distinctive themselves, and their self-titled debut album of 1988 went down in history as one of new jack swing's most important releases. Sweat's "I Want Her" made people aware of new jack swing, but the success of Guy's first album caused urban radio to become downright obsessed with it. Before long, countless singers were trying to emulate "Teddy's Jam," "Groove Me" and other major hits from that disc.

But the most valuable new jack swing artists weren't the automatons who tried to sound exactly like Guy; they were the people who brought something original to the table. And that's exactly what New Edition's Bobby Brown did when he recorded his second solo album, *Don't Be Cruel.* That 1988 release, which went down in history as Brown's best and most essential solo effort, found him embracing new jack swing on his own terms. The hit "My Prerogative" and the title song are clearly new jack swing, and they're also distinctively Bobby Brown. *Don't Be Cruel* was to Brown what *Control* was to Janet Jackson: a tougher, sexier, more aggressive project that let him shed his teen-oriented image and brought him to another level (both commercially and creatively).

One of the producers on *Don't Be Cruel* was Gene Griffin, who was Guy's manager before he had a falling out with that group in 1989. After parting company with Riley, Griffin supervised a new jack swing group called Basic Black, whose self-titled debut album of 1990 (a Motown release) was criticized for sounding contrived and formulaic—many rock critics saw Basic Black as a poor man's Guy.

Guy wasn't Riley's only group; the producer also had a rap group called Wreckx-N-Effect, which not surprisingly, was heavily influenced by new jack swing. But while Guy was an urban/funk group that incorporated hip-hop, Wreckx-N-Effect was essentially a pop-rap group that incorporated urban contemporary and new jack swing. Wreckx-N-Effect didn't appeal to rap purists, although they were responsible for some of the more enjoyable pop-rap of the early '90s.

One of new jack swing's most important releases came In 1990, when MCA put out Bell Biv DeVoe's triple platinum debut album, *Poison.* BBD was comprised of three New Edition members—Ricky Bell, Michael Bivins and Ronnie DeVoe—but the trio didn't sound anything like New Edition, whose main influences included the Jacksons and the Sylvers. Instead, BBD went for a tough, hard-edged sound that reflected their interest in hip-hop. The teen-friendly New Edition was also influenced by hip-hop, but not to the degree that BBD was. Bell, Bivins and DeVoe didn't sound like R&B singers who had only a casual interest in hip-hop—they sounded like R&B singers who lived and breathed it. Lyrically, BBD hits like "Poison" (which reached number three on *Billboard*'s R&B singles chart), "Do Me!" and "B.B.D. (I Thought it Was Me)" favored the sort of bluntness and directness that rap was known for. Unlike Public Enemy, Boogie Down Productions, Ice-T and N.W.A—four of the most compelling hardcore rap acts of the '80s and early '90s—BBD didn't inundate listeners with sociopolitical commentary or spend a lot of time describing the problems of the inner city. Their lyrics were about sex and romance, but like the hardcore rappers of that era, BBD didn't mince words. They had a way of getting right to the point and doing so without apology.

Another thing BBD had was a distinctive sound. At a time when other new jack swing groups were content to become clones of Guy, BBD insisted on doing their own thing. *Poison* was a breath of fresh air for new jack swing.

In 1991, Boyz II Men's infectious "Motownphilly" became one of the year's top new jack swing hits. But the Philadelphia-based vocal group didn't put all of their eggs in one basket—new jack swing was only part of what they did on their debut album, *Cooleyhighharmony*. So Boyz II Men had no problem surviving new jack swing's downfall in 1993. The anti-new jack backlash was inevitable; there were so many cheap imitations of BBD and Guy that people couldn't help becoming tired of new jack swing and burning out on the style. But those cheap imitations don't make BBD, Guy, Brown or Sweat's contributions any less valuable—those were the heavyweights of new jack swing, and their contributions to the style should not be forgotten.

Recommended Recordings:
Bobby Brown, *Don't Be Cruel* (MCA)
Guy, *Guy* (MCA)
Keith Sweat, *Make It Last Forever* (Elektra)
Bell Biv DeVoe, *Poison* (MCA)
Wreckx-N-Effect, *Wreckx-N-Effect* (Motown)
Boyz II Men, *Cooleyhighharmony* (Motown)

—Alex Henderson

British Soul

Since the rise of the Beatles in the early '60s, England has had no problem giving the United States a serious run for its money in the rock department. It is hard to imagine rock music without the contributions of Great Britain, which has given us everyone from the Rolling Stones and Led Zeppelin to the Sex Pistols—not to mention Black Sabbath, the Clash, the Who, Judas Priest, Oasis and countless others. British rock has been the subject of numerous articles and essays, but one subject that hasn't been discussed nearly as much is British R&B. Perhaps England's contributions to rock have been so great that the country's contributions to soul, funk and urban contemporary have been overshadowed, and perhaps R&B is so closely identified with the United States that American listeners usually don't give much thought to the subject of non-American R&B. After all, R&B is still dominated by the U.S., and it probably always will be.

But England is, in fact, the world's second largest market for R&B—historically, British listeners have spent more money on soul and urban contemporary than any other country except the United States. From the Temptations to Anita Baker to Mary J. Blige, American R&B singers have enjoyed a great deal of support in England over the years. Great Britain has also been highly supportive of rap, but that's the subject of another essay. The main focus of this essay is British R&B singing—soul, funk, urban, disco and otherwise.

The list of R&B-based (or at least R&B-minded) artists who have come from England over the years is a long one; it's a list that includes, among many others, Sade, Lisa Stansfield, Hot Chocolate, Imagination, Junior, Loose Ends, the Brand New Heavies, Soul II Soul, Caron Wheeler, Mica Paris, Billy Ocean, Cathy Dennis, Five Star, the Style Council, David Grant, Jamiroquai and Rick Astley. How do British R&B artists differ from American R&B artists? In most cases, their phrasing isn't all that different; people who speak with British accents don't necessarily sing with British accents. If any one thing separates British R&B singers (some of them, anyway) from their American counterparts, it is a tendency to be more eclectic. In the U.S., urban radio formats can be extremely rigid and unforgiving; consequently, many American urban artists are likely to avoid being too experimental (which isn't to say that American risk-takers like Erykah Badu, the Fugees and Macy Gray haven't beaten the odds). In England, America's urban radio formats are less of a consideration for R&B artists—British radio plays a lot of things that American stations won't touch.

Another big difference between British and American R&B artists is the reggae factor—a lot of British soul and urban singers have grown up listening to reggae. In England, reggae has been mainstream for a long time, whereas reggae has more of a cult following in the U.S. It should be noted that in London's black community, the Afro-Caribbean culture is quite strong; so it isn't uncommon for a British soul or urban singer to show some reggae, Caribbean or Afro-pop influence even if R&B is his/her main focus.

In 1975, Americans got a taste of British R&B when Hot Chocolate's "You Sexy Thing" because a big hit in the U.S. Hot Chocolate, a soul/funk band with rock and pop influences, was never huge in the U.S.; their only big hits on the American side of the Atlantic were "You Sexy Thing" and 1978's "Every 1's a Winner." Nonetheless, they had a strong following in the U.K. and went down in history as the finest British soulsters of that era. The '70s also gave us Hi-Tension, a British funk outfit whose influences included Kool & the Gang, Earth, Wind & Fire and Brass Construction. Although little known in the U.S., Hi-Tension recorded a noteworthy self-titled LP for Island in 1978.

The early to mid-'80s was when England's R&B scene really exploded—that was the era that gave us major hits by Junior, Imagination, Billy Ocean, Loose Ends and Sade. Americans who listened to urban radio during that time are likely to remember Junior for "Mama Used to Say," Imagination for "Just An Illusion" and Loose Ends for "Hanging on a String." Comparing Ocean and Sade really underscores the diversity of British R&B in the '80s; Ocean had Caribbean influences, while Sade brought jazz sensibilities to hits like "Smooth Operator" and "The Sweetest Taboo"—and yet, both of them are part of British R&B.

One of the most risk-taking British urban/pop groups of the '80s was the Style Council, a band that was founded by punk icon Paul Weller. Before the Style Council's formation in 1983, Weller was part of the Jam—a famous British punk band of the late '70s and early '80s. Influenced by soul, pop and jazz, the Style Council was a radical departure from Weller's work with the Jam (just as Public Image was a serious departure from singer John Lydon's work with the Sex Pistols). The Style Council weren't soul purists and never claimed to be, but they were certainly unpredictable and ambitious. In fact, some British rock critics felt that they could be too ambitious and eclectic for their own good—that creatively, they sometimes bit off more than they could chew. Another frequent complaint about the Style Council was that their sociopolitical lyrics could be preachy, but all things considered, Weller's band built an impressive catalog in the '80s.

Although the Style Council had their share of British hits, urban stations in the U.S. were generally unreceptive to their eclectic approach. Not that the Style Council was unique in that sense—many of England's urban, dance-pop and neo-soul artists of the '80s and '90s were probably too eclectic for urban radio in the U.S. Nonetheless, American listeners have heard a fair amount of British R&B and dance music on the radio—gems like Princess' "Say I'm Your Number One" in 1986, Rick Astley's "Never Gonna Give You Up" in 1987, Soul II Soul's "Keep on Movin'" in 1989 and Lisa Stansfield's "All Around the World" in 1990.

The '80s also gave us plenty of British artists who were more pop than R&B but still had a definite soul influence, including Wham!, George Michael, Culture Club, the Eurythmics, Everything But the Girl, Swing Out Sister and Simply Red. Culture Club's Motown-influenced "Church of the Poison Mind," the Eurythmics' "Missionary Man," Simply Red's "Holding Back the Years" and Wham!'s "Careless Whisper" aren't the work of soul purists, but they are the work of pop artists who have a healthy appreciation of American R&B.

In the early '90s, veteran Los Angeles Times rock critic Robert Hilburn traveled to London and wrote an article about a "new British invasion"—and this time, the "invaders" that he was describing were R&B-oriented instead of rock-oriented. Hilburn was inspired to write the article by the wave of British R&B artists who emerged in the late '80s and early '90s—a wave that included, among others, Soul II Soul, Caron Wheeler (who was a Soul II Soul participant before she became a full-time solo artist), Mica Paris, the Brand New Heavies, Cathy Dennis and Lisa Stansfield (who has often been described as the most convincing white R&B singer to come along since Teena Marie). Many of the British artists who emerged during that period had a neo-soul outlook and were able to blend influences from different eras. Stansfield, for example, combined a strong Barry White influence with a high-tech urban/hip-hop production style on her debut album, *Affection*, which included her breakthrough hit "All Around the World." Soul II Soul leader Jazzie B., meanwhile, was influenced by Chic but was also influenced by everything from hip-hop and house to African music.

While Soul II Soul, Paris and Stansfield were the essence of neo-soul, the Brand New Heavies favored a totally retro approach on their '90s albums. If you didn't know for a fact that their self-titled debut album was recorded in the early '90s, it would be easy to assume that it was recorded in the '70s—their sound was right out of the era that gave us Tower of Power, Rufus/Chaka Khan and the Average White Band (who came from England's neighbor Scotland). The Brand New Heavies were never innovative or groundbreaking, but they were still great at what they did and had a jewel of a lead singer in N'Dea Davenport (who was featured on the U.K. hits "Dream Come True" and "Stay This Way"). Davenport, an American vocalist who had moved to England, subsequently left the band and pursued a solo career.

Elements of soul continued to appear in British music throughout the '90s with groups like Massive Attack and Portishead evoking elements of R&B without ever falling directly into it's bloodline. At the end of the decade—and century—new voices could be heard that were of more direct Brit-soul lineage, none clearer than Craig David. David stormed the U.K. two-step/garage club scene in the late-'90s and proceeded to do the same to British and U.S. charts in the 2000s with his debut, *Born To Do It*, paving the way for a new generation of British soul stars.

Recommended Recordings:
Lisa Stansfield, *Affection)* (Arista)
Sade, *Diamond Life* (Epic)
Junior, *Ji* (Mercury)
Brand New Heavies, *The Brand New Heavies* (Delicious Vinyl)
Soul II Soul, *Keep On Movin'* (Virgin)
Soul II Soul, *Vol. II: 1990, A New Decade* (Virgin)
Imagination, *Like It Is* (RCA)
Hot Chocolate, *Hot Chocolate* (Big Tree)
Caron Wheeler, *U.K. Blak* (EMI)
Mica Paris, *Contribution* (Island)
Samantha Siva, *Rhythm of the Voices* (Genie)
Cathy Dennis, *Move to This* (Polydor)
Princess, *Princess* (Next Plateau)
Hi-Tension, *Hi-Tension* (Island)
Rick Astley, *Whenever You Need Somebody* (RCA)
David Grant, *Anxious Edge* (4th & Broadway)
Billy Ocean, *Suddenly* (Arista)
The Style Council, *My Ever Changing Moods* (Geffen)

—Alex Henderson

The Minneapolis Sound

Minneapolis isn't the only northern location that is identified with a particular R&B sound. In the '60s and '70s, Philadelphia, Chicago and Detroit all had their own distinctive brands of Northern soul. And Ohio's various cities were known for having a lot of aggressive, sweaty funk bands in the '70s—the Ohio Players, Lakeside, the Dazz Band (originally known as Kinsman Dazz), Bootsy Collins and Slave were among the many hardcore funksters who came from the Buckeye State. But the Minneapolis sound of the '80s was unique—it was quite different from the sophisticated soul of Philly and Chi-Town or the gutbucket funk of Dayton, Cleveland and Cincinnati. The Minneapolis sound of the '80s wasn't pure R&B; it was a hybrid mixture of funk, rock and pop, and it was a sound that made Prince both a funk/urban star and a rock/pop star.

The person who invented the Minneapolis sound was Prince. He was the innovative leader of a scene that, in the '80s, also gave us the Time, Morris Day, Vanity 6, Apollonia 6, Ta Mara & the Seen, Sheila E. and Jesse Johnson's Revue as well as lesser known Minneapolis residents like the Family and Mazarati. All of these artists were heavily influenced by Prince's work, and Prince's followers—like Prince himself—were not R&B purists. They had funk appeal, but they also had rock, pop and new wave appeal. Consequently, the Minneapolis sound attracted very integrated audiences. Parliament/Funkadelic and Gap Band fans attended concerts by Prince and his disciples; so did fans of Blondie, the Police and Duran Duran.

Although the Minneapolis scene reached its peak in the '80s, Prince actually got the ball rolling in the late '70s. The singer/composer started building a national following in 1978, when Warner Bros. Records released his debut album, *For You*, and he had a hit with the bouncy "Soft and Wet." In 1979, Warner released Prince's self-titled sophomore album, which contained the hits "Why You Wanna Treat Me So Bad?" and "I Wanna Be Your Lover." *For You* and *Prince* were enjoyable soul-pop albums, but they offered little evidence of the visionary, wildly ambitious work that was just around the corner (although Prince's second album does contain the funk-rock jewel "Bambi," which addresses the subject of lesbianism). In 1980, however, Prince took the gloves off—all the way off—on his third album, *Dirty Mind*. Both musically and lyrically, *Dirty Mind* was a major step forward for Prince and the Minneapolis sound. Without abandoning funk and soul, Prince became a lot more rock-minded. And *Dirty Mind*'s lyrics pulled no punches; parts of the album are downright explicit, especially Prince's references to oral sex on "Head" and incest on the shocking "Sister." But if *Dirty Mind* demonstrated that Prince could be great for shock value, it also demonstrated that he was an artist of considerable depth and vision. The fact that *Dirty Mind* was able to win over rock and new wave audiences without alienating the R&B base Prince had acquired with his first two albums is certainly impressive. And he acquired even more followers with equally risk-taking albums like 1981's *Controversy*, 1982's *1999* and 1994's *Purple Rain*.

For the most part, 1981 was a banner year for Minneapolis funk-rock—not only because of *Controversy* but also, because it marked the recording debut of the Time, a colorful, often humorous band that was heavily influenced by Prince but still quite distinctive. Sadly, 1981 was also the year in which Prince was booed off stage when he opened for the Rolling Stones at the Los Angeles Coliseum—some people in the audience still had the death-to-disco mentality and saw Prince as a disco artist even though he was using a lot of loud, rock-conscious guitar at that point. However, some of L.A.'s Stones fans were appalled and disgusted by the incident; they knew how much Mick Jagger and Keith Richard loved R&B and were sad that other Stones fans could be so narrow-minded. The people who booed Prince at the L.A. Coliseum seemed to forget how mindful of soul and funk the Stones had been on "Hot Stuff" and their 1978 smash "Miss You."

But times change, and if Prince had opened for the Stones in 1984 instead of 1981, he probably would have received a standing ovation. By that time, the death-to-disco mentality was a thing of the past, and a lot of younger rock fans were getting into rap, urban and dance-pop. That was not only a good thing for Prince—it was also a good thing for the Time and Vanity 6, a Minneapolis-based female trio that reflected Prince's obsession with sex and his ability to combine funk, rock and pop. Like Prince and the Time, the short-lived Vanity 6 (which evolved into Apollonia 6 after Vanity left to pursue a solo career) appealed to an interracial audience. So did the projects that former Time members Morris Day and Jesse Johnson recorded after the Time's breakup in 1984. When Johnson wasn't leading his post-Time band, Jesse Johnson's Revue, he was producing the Minneapolis-based Ta Mara & the Seen. That very Minneapolis-sounding outfit recorded two albums for A&M in the '80s and is best remembered for their 1985 hit "Everybody Dance."

During 1984, the year of the Time's breakup, singer/percussionist Sheila E. made her mark with her Warner Bros. album *The Glamorous Life* and the hit title song. Sheila E.'s association with Prince, however, was hardly her first experience in the music industry—before she joined forces with Prince and started hanging out in Minneapolis, the Bay Area native was a busy session player on the West Coast. Her real name is Sheila Escovedo; she is the daughter of percussionist Pete Escovedo and the niece of the late percussionist Coke Escovedo.

Two of the lesser known bands that came out of the Minneapolis school of funk-rock were the Family and Mazarati, whose self-titled debut album was released on Prince's Paisley Park label (distributed by Warner Bros.) in 1986. Mazarati was expected to become the next major band out of Minneapolis, but surprisingly, their album (which was produced by Prince sideman Brown Mark) fell through the cracks—and Mazarati broke up without ever recording a second album. Similarly, the Family also turned out to be a one-album wonder—despite the fact that the band included three ex-members of the Time: singer/keyboardist St. Paul Peterson, drummer Jellybean Johnson and percussionist Jerome Benton. Rounding out the lineup were saxophonist Eric Leeds and lead singer Susannah Melvoin, the daughter of jazz pianist Mike Melvoin and twin sister of Wendy Melvoin (who was with Prince's '80s band the Revolution before she became half of the Wendy & Lisa duo).

In the '80s, one didn't have to be from Minneapolis to embrace the Minneapolis sound. Scottish star Sheena Easton became very Minneapolis-minded when Prince wrote "Sugar Walls" for her in 1984, and Flint, MI's Ready for the World was heavily influenced by Prince and the Time. So was Le Klass, an obscure but noteworthy band from Augusta, GA. And Los Angeles resident Janet Jackson was among the many artists who worked with producer/songwriters Jimmy Jam & Terry Lewis, who formed a partnership after leaving the Time. Some of the albums that Jam/Lewis produced were more Minneapolis-sounding than others—it all depended on what a particular project called for. And the Janet Jackson albums that the Jam/Lewis duo worked on (including 1986's *Control* and 1989's *Rhythm Nation 1814*) were among their more Minneapolis-minded projects. The Prince/Time influence is impossible to miss on "Nasty," "Escapade," "What Have You Done for Me Lately" and other hits that they produced for her in the '80s. The Jam/Lewis team also produced Alexander O'Neal (another ex-member of the Time), Cheryl Lynn, the S.O.S. Band, the Human League and others.

The Time recorded an excellent reunion album, *Pandemonium*, for Paisley Park in 1990, and it was also in the early '90s that Prince formed a new band called the New Power Generation (which he unveiled on his 1990 release *Diamonds and Pearls*). By the mid-'90s, however, the popularity of the Minneapolis sound had decreased. Morris Day and Jesse Johnson weren't as visible in the mid- to late '90s as they were in the '80s, and Apollonia and Ta Mara weren't heard from at all. Meanwhile, Vanity (who didn't have much commercial success after she parted company with Prince and became a solo artist) proclaimed herself to be a born-again Christian and gave up secular music altogether. But while some of Prince's associates faded into obscurity after the '80s, Prince himself continued to command a huge international following and was still keeping busy when the 2000s arrived.

Recommended Recordings:
Prince, *Dirty Mind* (Warner Bros.)
Prince, *Controversy* Warner Bros.)
Prince, *Purple Rain* (Warner Bros.)
Prince, *1999* (Warner Bros.)
The Time, *Ice Cream Castle* (Warner Bros.)
The Time, *What Time Is It?* (Warner Bros.)
Vanity 6, *Vanity 6* (Warner Bros.)
Ta Mara & the Seen, *Ta Mara & the Seen* (A&M)
Janet Jackson, *Control* (A&M)
Janet Jackson, *Rhythm Nation 1814* (A&M)
Jesse Johnson's Revue, *Jesse Johnson's Revue* (A&M)
Morris Day, *The Color of Success* (Warner Bros.)
Apollonia 6, *Apollonia 6* (Warner Bros.)
Sheila E., *The Glamorous Life* (Warner Bros.)
Le Klass, *School of Cool* (AVC)

—*Alex Henderson*

Neo-Soul

In the '90s and early 2000s, the term neo-soul has been used to describe urban contemporary artists who have one foot in the past and one foot in the present—the past being the classic soul of the '60s and '70s, the present being urban and hip-hop. Although neo-soul is part of urban music, not all urban artists are neo-soul—in fact, the majority of them are not. The list of singers who have been part of the neo-soul movement in the '90s and 2000s has included, among others, Mary J. Blige (who has been dubbed "the Queen of Hip-Hop Soul"), Lauryn Hill, D'Angelo, Alicia Keys, Macy Gray, Jill Scott, Erykah Badu, Rahsaan Patterson, Maxwell, Jaguar Wright, Angie Stone, Jill Scott and India.Arie. All of these singers have been able to show a strong appreciation of '60s and/or '70s soul without being accused of sounding dated—they have enough of an urban/hip-hop influence to keep them from being totally retro-sounding. But upon careful examination, it becomes clear that the neo-sound trend didn't actually start with the influential Blige in the early '90s. If one thinks of neo-soul (which has often been called "hip-hop soul") as post-'70s soul music with hip-hop and urban elements, it is easy to argue that certain artists were providing neo-soul in the '80s—people who ranged from the Force M.D.'s to Keith Sweat to Alexander O'Neal.

When the Force M.D.'s started recording for Tommy Boy Records in 1984, they asserted that their music was meant to combine influences from different eras. Hip-hop was an influence on the New York-based vocal quartet, but so were '60s and '70s soul and '50s doo wop. The members of the Force M.D.'s were into LL Cool J, the Fat Boys, Whodini and Run-D.M.C., but they were also into '50s doo wop groups like the Five Satins and the Penguins—groups that were around before they were even born. To say that the Force M.D.'s were way ahead of their time is no exaggeration; they were providing hip-hop-minded neo-soul at least eight years before Mary J. Blige was exalted as "the Queen of Hip-Hop Soul" and at least six years before En Vogue's first album, *Born to Sing*, came out. For 1984, the Force M.D.'s were certainly an anomaly—back then, there weren't many R&B vocal groups who dressed like rappers while they were praising the Five Satins, and it took guts for Tommy Boy to sign them. But as the '80s progressed, it became increasingly clear that the Force M.D.'s weren't so crazy after all.

The Force M.D.'s were a perfect example of what music journalist Nelson George (a former *Billboard* columnist and the author of *The Death of Rhythm & Blues*) termed "retro-nuevo" in the '80s—retro in that they were quite cognizant of pre-'80s R&B, nuevo (which means "new" in Spanish) in that they also had hip-hop and urban influences. By retro-nuevo, George meant neo-soul; in George's mind, retro-nuevo artists were really soulsters at heart, but they knew they needed to make some urban contemporary moves if they wanted to be successful in the black music market of the '80s. Luther Vandross, Anita Baker and Freddie Jackson—three of the top quiet storm singers of that decade—are also examples of people George considered retro-nuevo. They weren't hip-hop-obsessed like the Force M.D.'s, but they did combine a soul vocal style with slick, high-tech urban contemporary production gloss. In fact, Baker's *Rapture* was sometimes described as neo-soul when it came out in 1986.

Similarly, Alexander O'Neal's mid- to late-'80s work fit George's definition of retro-nuevo and could easily be described as neo-soul. The producing/songwriting team of Jimmy Jam & Terry Lewis (who, like O'Neal were ex-members of the Time) saw to it that his Tabu/Epic releases were relevant to urban contemporary tastes yet faithful to his soul roots. From sweaty funk to sentimental ballads, the gritty, big-voiced Minneapolis native surrounded himself with synthesizers and drum machines but always gave the impression that he was really a soul man at heart. And unlike a lot of urban singers of the '80s, O'Neal wasn't obsessed with crossing over to the pop market—he was an R&B artist first and foremost, and he felt that pop stations had to accept him on his own terms.

Other noteworthy neo-soulsters who came along in the '80s included Oran "Juice" Jones (best known for his 1986 hit "The Rain") and Keith Sweat, whose 1987 debut, *Make It Last Forever*, was fresh-sounding and cutting-edge in more ways than one. Produced by Guy's Teddy Riley, that triple platinum release not only helped to popularize new jack swing—it also convinced a lot of people that being a hip-hop head and a soul singer were not mutually exclusive. The funky hit single "I Want Her" is an early example of the hip-hop-drenched style known as new jack sing, which isn't part of neo-soul; however, the album's romantic ballads and slow jams (including the hit title song and an excellent remake of the Dramatics' "In the Rain") clearly have a neo-soul perspective. The terms neo-soul, hip-hop soul and retro-nuevo certainly describe many of the '80s and '90s recordings of LeVert, a Cleveland trio that included two sons of long-time O'Jays singer Eddie LeVert: Gerald and Sean LeVert. Gerald LeVert sounded a lot like his father, and the group had a strong O'Jays influence. But LeVert was far from a carbon copy of the O'Jays, and they had no problem combining a love of classic soul with hip-hop and urban elements.

The rise of two of neo-soul's most important artists: the female vocal quartet En Vogue and British singer Lisa Stansfield came about in 1990. Uniting urban and hip-hop sensibilities with a strong appreciation of classic female groups like LaBelle, the Pointer Sisters and Martha & the Vandellas, En Vogue's debut album, *Born to Sing*, did a lot to bring female vocal groups back to R&B. Stansfield, meanwhile, had an obvious '70s influence and a definite love of Barry White, although her superb debut album, *Affection*, had enough urban/hip-hop production gloss to keep her from sounding dated. Many of Stansfield's admirers asserted that she was the most convincing white R&B singer to come along since Teena Marie.

Although Mary J. Blige didn't single-handedly invent the idea of neo-soul or hip-hop soul, she certainly did her part to make '90s R&B safe for soul singers—male or female. Like Keith Sweat, LeVert and En Vogue before her, Blige had one foot in classic soul and the other in the hip-hop culture. As the decade progressed, she developed into one of the decade's most expressive R&B singers.

Blige enjoyed the commercial success she deserved, but one cannot say that about the innovative yet underexposed G.A.T. The obscure vocal group's name stood for Gangstas And Thugs, and they looked like a West Coast gangsta rap group. But the Los Angeles-based G.A.T. were actually neo-soul singers whose material combined a passion for classic '70s soul with thugged-out, gangsta rap-minded lyrics—reviewers used phrases like "N.W.A meets the Chi-Lites" and "the Geto Boys meet the Dramatics" to describe G.A.T.'s unorthodox approach. In 1993, the group D.R.S. had tried something similar on their Capitol release *Gangster Lean*, but G.A.T. clearly had a style and vision of their own. One minute, G.A.T. was singing about gang violence and drive-by shootings; the next minute, they were belting out a smooth soul ballad or providing a remake of the Persuaders' "Thin Love Between Love and Hate." MCA released G.A.T.'s promising debut album, *Just Another Day*, in 1995; regrettably, it didn't sell, and G.A.T. never resurfaced on another label.

Although G.A.T.'s lack of commercial success was a big loss for neo-soul, there were many reasons for neo-soul enthusiasts to feel optimistic in the mid- to late '90s—a time that found promising artists like D'Angelo, Lauryn Hill (of Fugees fame), Macy Gray, Rahsaan Patterson, Erykah Badu, Adriana Evans (the daughter of jazz singer Mary Stallings) and Maxwell making their presence felt. From a neo-soul standpoint, the early 2000s were also very encouraging thanks to Alicia Keys, India.Arie, Jill Scott, Syleena Johnson (the daughter of Chicago soul great Syl Johnson) and Jaguar Wright, among others.

It's important to know the difference between neo-soulsters and artists who are 100 percent retro. If Badu and India.Arie fit Nelson George's definition of retro-nuevo, one could describe Mary Ann Redmond (an excellent soul-rock singer who has been active in the Washington, D.C., area in the '90s and 2000s) as a perfect example of "retro-viejo." (Viejo is the Spanish word for old). Lauryn Hill is semi-retro; Redmond is totally retro. While the neo-soul of Badu and India.Arie updates soul music, Redmond's outlook is straight-up old school—her '90s and 2000s albums sound like they could have been recorded in the '60s or '70s. The retro-viejo approach, unlike neo-soul, doesn't appeal to urban radio, although artists like Redmond tend to do well on the blues circuit.

Many music critics have often complained that they find a lot of '80s and '90s R&B to be very homogenized and formulaic—certainly more so than the R&B of the '50s, '60s and '70s. But the best neo-soulsters of the '80s, '90s and 2000s have indicated that we can't close the book on R&B just yet—that a more earthy and organic style of R&B singing still has its place. Soul music isn't as prevalent as it was in the '60s and '70s, but Blige, Keys and others have demonstrated that it can still be found if one knows where to look.

Recommended Recordings:

Erykah Badu, *Baduizm* (Universal)
Mary J. Blige, *Share My World* (MCA)
Mary J. Blige, *My Life* (MCA)
Lauryn Hill, *The Miseducation of Lauryn Hill* (Ruffhouse)
Alicia Keys, *Songs in A Minor,* (J Records)
Macy Gray, *How Life Is* (Epic)
India.Arie, *Acoustic Soul* (Motown)
Jaguar Wright, *Denials Delusions and Decisions* (MCA)
Lisa Stansfield, *Affection* (Arista)
En Vogue, Born to Sing (Atlantic)
En Vogue, Funky Divas (East West)
Adriana Evans, *Adriana Evans* (RCA)
Force M.D.'s, *For Lovers and Others: The Force M.D.'s Greatest Hits* (Tommy Boy)
G.A.T., *Just Another Day* (MCA)
Syleena Johnson, *Chapter 2: the Voice* (Jive)
Alexander O'Neal, *Alexander O'Neal* (Epic)
Keith Sweat, *Make It Last Forever* (Elektra)

—Alex Henderson

Gospel

Gospel music has rarely been a significant presence in the commercial mainstream, and indeed its fervent religious concerns will most likely always limit it to a specialized audience. Rock and pop fans often find pure gospel rough going, both due to its intensely spiritual focus and its melodic and compositional strictures. Yet even for those rock fans who never develop a passion for the form, it's worth appreciation as one of rock and soul's bedrock influences. There are strong gospel traditions, reaching back through several centuries, in both the black and white populations of America. The black tradition, a combination of indigenous African music with Western religious influences, found its expression in both "work songs" and the church, one of the few places where the black community could openly express itself in the days of segregation. When black gospel traditions began to mix with the music of the secular world, the combinations that resulted were pivotal in the birth of R&B and soul.

The groaning, moaning, pleading, and supplicating qualities of gospel are easy to hear in the vocals of jump blues artists like Percy Mayfield, Roy Brown and Wynona Carr as well as early soul pioneers like Ray Charles, James Brown, Clyde McPhatter and Little Willie John even if they may be singing about raucous and romantic joys. Likewise, the harmonies and call-and-response interplay of the classic doo wop groups, from the Orioles through the early work of the Impressions, were refined in the chapel as well as on the street corner.

The connection between gospel and soul, however, is often far more direct. A few of soul's greatest singers, including Wilson Pickett and Little Johnnie Taylor got their starts in gospel quartets. Taylor had been in the Soul Stirrers, also the breeding ground for Sam Cooke, the most famous singer to cross over to pop after establishing himself as a gospel star. Gospel fans were outraged when Cooke abandoned the circuit for pop stardom in the late '50s, but pop and rock fans were enriched immeasurably, as Cooke's work until his death in 1964 was immensely important in paving the road for modern soul music.

Notable female soul and pop singers who began as gospel vocalists include Dionne Warwick and Whitney Houston, whose mother Cissy directed the Sweet Inspirations, who sang backup vocals on some of Aretha Franklin's early hits. Franklin herself was the daughter of noted preacher and gospel singer C.L. Franklin, and recorded some gospel as a teenager. When she reached superstardom with a burst of soul smashes in 1967, listeners were responding to a voice letting loose the unbridled passion of gospel on contemporary pop-R&B. Franklin's vision is really too wide to be categorized as a gospel offshoot, but she has always remained cognizant of her roots, occasionally immersing herself in them, as on her acclaimed 1972 live album, *Amazing Grace*.

Other notable gospel-soul crossovers include the Chambers Brothers, who were one of the few black groups to become favorites with the psychedelic crowd; the Edwin Hawkins Singers, who landed a surprise Top Five hit in 1969 with "Oh Happy Day"; and the Staple Singers, whose Memphis soul-gospel approach yielded some of the most inspirational hits of the early '70s. Also from Memphis is Al Green, the most famous singer to travel in the reverse direction, abandoning pop superstardom for gospel. The music world was shocked when Green embraced gospel in the late '70s after a reign of five years or so as soul's most popular performer, and though he's largely a memory for the masses, he's been very active in the studio and as a performer in the gospel world.

In the world of white rock & roll, gospel has been a less prominent but nevertheless important influence. The church was a focal point of white Southern rural culture, and often offered the easiest place to sing and play music, as it did in the early African-American community. Most of the first white rock & rollers were Southern, and they were also schooled in gospel harmonies and spiritual standards. Many early country acts, like the Carter Family, Bill Monroe and Tennessee Ernie Ford, took a large part of their repertoire from gospel. The close harmonies of acts like the Delmore Brothers often derived from, and were sometimes actually used on, sacred songs, in turn influencing early rock & rollers who didn't actually perform gospel, the Everly Brothers being the most famous example.

Many early rockabilly stars may have been set on raising hell on-stage and in the studio, but gospel was a big part of their background, even in the most unlikely of cases—Jerry Lee Lewis, for instance, is Jimmy Swaggart's cousin, and can be heard debating spiritual matters with Sam Phillips on a famous outtake from Sun Studios. When Lewis, Elvis Presley, Carl Perkins and others gathered in the same studio in 1956 for the famous *Million Dollar Quartet* session, they jammed on the songs they all shared and knew by heart—many of which, to the surprise of some latter-day listeners, were gospel tunes. Elvis counted gospel groups like the Statesmen and the Blackwood Brothers among his biggest influences, and employed a gospel group, the Jordanaires, to harmonize and sing backing vocals on most of his biggest hits. He also recorded a good deal of straight gospel himself, from 1957 on through to the 1970s.

Rock stars without direct gospel influences have occasionally called on gospel singers to record appropriate embellishments to particular recordings; Paul Simon was never one to let a good ethnic flavor pass unnoticed, and his use of the Dixie Hummingbirds on the 1973 hit "Loves Me Like a Rock" is one of the most famous examples. Occasionally, rockers have embraced religion long after establishing themselves as secular pop stars, recording gospel-influenced albums that have by and large not been well received, Bob Dylan being the most famous of these. Dylan was outraged at the audience for, as he saw it, dismissing his music because of its religious values; this may have been partly true, but the audiences were also turning a cold shoulder to the records because spiritual music was not his strongest suit, and because they didn't enjoy being hammered over the head with a message, fundamentalist or otherwise. When Violent Femmes leader Gordon Gano recorded a gospel album with his side group the Mercy Seat, the reaction was not so much hostility as indifference, partly because Gano wasn't nearly as mythological a figure as Dylan.

In contemporary music, gospel usually isn't a visible factor, not because its influence is negligible, but because it permeated the rock and soul mainstream so deeply that it's become permanently absorbed into its structure. It continues to permeate urban contemporary R&B in the smooth harmonies and lead vocals, even if the singers are no longer as directly steeped in the church as they were in the 1950s and 1960s. And there are still instances of singers moving from spiritual music to secular pop/rock, as Amy Grant has done on a superstar level, and singer/songwriter Sam Phillips has done as a cult alternative rock favorite.

12 Recommended Recordings:

Various Artists, *Jubilation Vol.1-3* (Rhino). Anthologies of classic gospel. The first two volumes cover black artists like the Soul Stirrers, the Swan Silvertones, Aretha Franklin, Mahalia Jackson, the Staple Singers, and the Five Blind Boys; the third focuses on white country gospel, with sides by the Carter Family, the Louvin Brothers, Kitty Wells, George Jones and Tammy Wynette, Bill Monroe, Johnny Cash and Hank Williams.

The Soul Stirrers, *The Gospel Soul of Sam Cooke, Vol. 2* (Specialty). An entire disc of Cooke's sides with the gospel group during the first half of the 1950s. Other Soul Stirrers discs, if you want to go further, include performances by Johnnie Taylor and other noteworthy singers who took the leads when Cooke wasn't in the group.

Various Artists, *Something Got a Hold of Me* (RCA). Classic country gospel by the Carter Family, Bill Monroe, the Blue Sky Boys, Uncle Dave Macon and other less celebrated acts.

Elvis Presley, *The Million Dollar Quartet* (RCA). Actually Elvis, Carl Perkins and Jerry Lee Lewis plus a few other musicians (Johnny Cash was present for the photo but not for the recording, apparently), jamming on rock, R&B, and not a little gospel. The double-CD *Amazing Grace* is the most wide-ranging compilation of Presley's gospel recordings, but will have considerably less appeal for the rock fan.

Mahalia Jackson, *Gospels, Spirituals & Hymns* (CBS). Often rated as the best gospel singer of all.

Various Artists, *Sam Cooke's SAR Records Story 1959-1965* (ABKCO). Cooke acted as label owner and frequent producer and songwriter for SAR, recording gospel, soul, and combinations of the two by performers like the Womack Brothers, Johnnie Taylor, and the Valentinos.

The Chambers Brothers, *Time Has Come: the Best of the Chambers Brothers* (Columbia). An erratic group whose funk and psychedelic excesses never hid their gospel roots.

The Staple Singers, *Greatest Hits* (Fantasy). A compilation of early-'60s material that gives listeners a sampling of their gospel roots as it was being tempered by contemporary influences. No Staple Singers collection surveys their entire career, which stretches across several decades; try Vee-Jay compilations for their earliest and purest gospel material, and *The Best of the Staple Singers* (on Stax) for their soul hits.

Aretha Franklin, *Amazing Grace* (Atlantic). Her 1972 gospel album, also featuring James Cleveland and the Southern California Community Choir.

The Dixie Hummingbirds, *Live* (MCA). A 75-minute live set from the mid-'70s.

Al Green, *The Belle Album* (Hi). His last album (from 1977) before his conversion to full-time gospel, catching him bridging secular soul music with personal spiritual concerns.

Sweet Honey in the Rock, *Live at Carnegie Hall* (Flying Fish). Not purely a gospel group, though heavily gospel-influenced, this all-woman African-American a cappella group is proof that music can both draw on gospel traditions and comment on contemporary political, social, and personal concerns. Active since the mid-'70s, with various lineups under the leadership of Bernice Reagon, this is a 1988 concert recording.

—Richie Unterberger

Soul Jazz

The most popular jazz style of the 1960s was not bebop, hard bop or free jazz; it was the much-maligned soul jazz idiom. While many young jazz musicians were attempting to redefine jazz as an "art form" suitable for concert halls, soul jazz thrived in small black bars and clubs. Largely ignored by the jazz media during the era (but not by record buyers), soul jazz has still yet to be properly discussed in a full-length book or to gain the respect that it deserves.

Soul jazz differs from bebop and hard bop in that the emphasis is on the rhythmic groove. Although soloists follow the chords as in bop, the basslines (often played by an organist if not a string bassist) dance rather than stick strictly to a four-to-the bar walking pattern. The musicians build their accompaniment around the bassline and, although there are often strong melodies, it is the catchiness of the groove and the amount of heat generated by the soloists that determine whether the performance is successful. Since the goal is to be as catchy and as rhythmic as possible, it is little surprise that soul jazz has usually had a large audience and been one of the most accessible of jazz styles.

When bebop emerged in the mid-'40s, a valid criticism was that its players sometimes sacrificed feeling in favor of virtuosity and speed. In the 1950s cool jazz generally slowed down the tempoes and smoothed out some of bop's rougher edges but it took hard bop to add a wider range of emotions to straight-ahead jazz. Soul jazz was an outgrowth of hard bop and one can trace its roots to pianist Horace Silver. Although also a fine hard bop-based player, Silver had his own style from as early as when he was discovered by Stan Getz in 1950. By 1954 he was recording with Miles Davis (sounding quite unlike the dominant pianist of the era Bud Powell) and the following year Silver co-founded the Jazz Messengers with Art Blakey. Horace Silver, who started leading his own quintet in 1956, has the main talent of all soul jazz players: the ability to turn every song into the blues.

Silver's prominence as a pianist, a popular bandleader and a major composer largely launched the soul jazz movement. Other pianists followed in his wake including Bobby Timmons (who starred with Blakey and Cannonball Adderley before leading his own trios), Junior Mance, Les McCann, Gene Harris (with his Three Sounds) and Ramsey Lewis. These funky stylists were not shy to infuse jazz with gospel, blues and soul influences and each became popular stylists. Their playing also affected the mainstream of jazz so that other pianists (such as Oscar Peterson and Herbie Hancock) felt free to play funky when the spirit moved them.

The next major event in soul jazz history was the discovery of organist Jimmy Smith in 1956. Although there had been jazz organ players in earlier times (including Fats Waller in the 1920s, Milt Buckner, Bill Doggett, Wild Bill Davis and occasionally Count Basie), the organ was thought of as a novelty instrument until Jimmy Smith emerged. Over four decades later Smith remains his instrument's dominant force. His Blue Note recordings of 1956-1963 (which were often jam sessions with top soloists) found Smith not only holding his own with other players but being the consistent star. Although Jimmy Smith has been called "the Charlie Parker of the organ" since he was its first modern soloist and he is capable of playing bop standards, it is Smith's mastery of the blues and his melding together of bop's sophistication with the feeling of the blues that makes him most significant.

By the late '50s organ combos started becoming common, usually utilizing a tenor saxophonist, guitarist, drummer and an occasional bassist (at least on records). The repertoire of such bands tended to have blues at several tempos, soulful ballads and some well-known melodic standards. Smith's all-encompassing influence resulted in most organists sounding like a close relative but the best ones also displayed their own soulful approach. Among the top organists of the 1960s were Brother Jack McDuff (who played with Willis Jackson before launching his own bands), Shirley Scott (who had powerful bands with first Eddie "Lockjaw" Davis and then her husband Stanley Turrentine on tenors), Jimmy McGriff, Charles Earland, Richard "Groove" Holmes, Big John Patton, Johnny Hammond Smith, Don Patterson and Lonnie Smith among others. Only Larry Young, who explored modal and avant-garde jazz after the mid-'60s, managed to eventually escape from Smith's influence.

While organists were usually the bandleaders, they were not the only colorful soloists. Among the guitarists were the great Grant Green, George Benson (who first played with Jack McDuff), the young Pat Martino, the underrated Boogaloo Joe Jones and such part-time soul jazz players as Wes Montgomery and Kenny Burrell.

Many of the tenor saxophonists who appeared with soul jazz groups had experience both in jazz and early R&B where emotion (and the ability to honk) were highly valued. Stanley Turrentine, whose every note drips soul (and whose unchanging sound through the decades is surprisingly flexible), was always the perfect soul jazz tenor but he was far from alone. Willis "Gator" Jackson, Eddie "Lockjaw" Davis, David "Fathead" Newman, Gene "Jug" Ammons (great nicknames!), Houston Person, Jimmy Forrest, King Curtis (best-known for his R&B and pop recordings), Red Holloway and Eddie Harris (whose "Listen Here" was a soul jazz hit) were only a few of the thick-toned saxophonists who helped to keep the idiom alive and creative. All of the above (plus Hank Crawford, the definitive soul jazz altoist) inspired such later R&B-influenced stars as Grover Washington Jr. (who picked up early experience playing with organ groups) and David Sanborn.

Soul jazz, although not well publicized by the jazz press, was very well documented on recordings from the late '50s up until the early '70s. With such a large roster of viable players and a core of dedicated fans, why did soul jazz start to drop in popularity during the latter half of the 1960s? The competition had become a lot stronger with the rise of rock and the emergence of fusion. Electric keyboards were much easier to move around than organs and some of the top soul jazz organists in the 1970s switched to the lighter instruments although few were able to retain their own musical personality on the Fender Rhodes. Motown had made inroads with the black audience and when disco in the mid-'70s became the main dance music, soul jazz was greatly eclipsed and seemed to disappear.

However the tide turned by the mid-'80s. The young Joey DeFrancesco emerged as the first important new jazz organist in a decade, playing in a style nearly identical to Jimmy Smith. The surviving organists gradually reappeared on records, playing in an unchanged style and showing that they had lost none of their soul or fire. In addition, with the rise of acid jazz in the 1990s, there has been a great demand for the reissuance of groove-oriented soul jazz organ records of the 1960s and many of the earlier sessions are once again available, leading to the rediscovery of such veterans as Baby Face Willette, Mel Rhyne and Big John Patton in addition to the still powerful Jimmy Smith.

Now that all styles of jazz are able to co-exist, soul jazz has a bright future as one of the more likable areas of creative music.

22 Essential Recordings:
Horace Silver, *Finger Poppin'* (Blue Note)
Cannonball Adderley, *Live in San Francisco* (Original Jazz Classics)
Bobby Timmons, *This Here Is Bobby Timmons* (Original Jazz Classics)
Les McCann, *Swiss Movement* (Rhino/Atlantic)
Gene Harris, *Brotherhood* (Concord Jazz)
Jimmy Smith, *House Party* (Blue Note)
Jimmy Smith, *Midnight Special* (Blue Note)
Jimmy Smith, *Back at the Chicken Shack* (Blue Note)
Jack McDuff, *Live!* (Prestige)
Shirley Scott, *Soul Shoutin'* (Prestige)
Jimmy McGriff, *Right Turn on Blues* (Telarc)
Charles Earland, *Black Talk* (Original Jazz Classics)
Richard "Groove" Holmes, *Soul Message* (Original Jazz Classics)
Grant Green, *Grantstand* (Blue Note)
Grant Green, *Idle Moments* (Blue Note)
George Benson, *The New Boss Guitar* (Original Jazz Classics)
Willis Jackson, *Please Mr. Jackson* (Original Jazz Classics)
Gene Ammons, *Brother Jack Meets The Boss* (Original Jazz Classics)
Stanley Turrentine, *Let It Go* (Blue Note)
Eddie Harris, *The Electrifying Eddie Harris* (Atlantic)
Houston Person, *Stolen Sweets* (Muse)
Hank Crawford, *Soul Survivors* (Milestone)

—Scott Yanow

Reggae

As a rule, one is more likely to read about reggae in a world music book than an R&B-oriented book. That's because reggae was created on the Caribbean island of Jamaica; quite often, music historians have been inclined to lump it in with Afro-Caribbean and African pop—discussions of Bob Marley can easily accompany discussions of South Africa's Ladysmith Black Mambazo or Trinidad's the Mighty Sparrow. But reggae has always been quite close to R&B—more so, in fact, than any other Afro-Caribbean genre. From doo wop, soul, funk and disco to urban and hip-hop, African-American music has long had a major impact on the Jamaican music scene.

One could easily spend hours talking about hip-hop's influence on dancehall or how urban contemporary has affected reggae singing in the '80s, '90s and 2000s; the primary focus of this essay, however, is soul's impact on reggae. And any discussion of the reggae/soul connection should include some mention of ska and mento, both of which preceded reggae in Jamaica. In the '50s, Jamaica's music scene was dominated by mento, which has a lot in common with calypso and soca. But in the early '60s, mento's popularity decreased, and a new style became popular in Jamaica—a style called ska. Mento was an influence on ska, but so were R&B, jazz and rock & roll. According to one version of Jamaican musical history, ska came about when Kingston-based musicians were able to pick up a New Orleans R&B station and were influenced by what they heard. Musicologists have often asserted that when Jamaicans tried to play R&B in the early '60s but didn't quite get the beat right, the result was ska. At any rate, there is no getting around the fact that African-American soul music was a major influence on early ska artists like the Skatalites, Derrick Morgan, Laurel Aitken and the famous Prince Buster. Some of those artists went on to embrace reggae, although the Skatalites have always been a ska band first and foremost.

By about 1965 or 1966, ska had given way to rocksteady, which was the first type of reggae just as Dixieland was the first type of jazz. What was the difference between ska and early reggae? In a nutshell, reggae was slower and less jazz-influenced; the ska beat and the reggae beat aren't identical, but they're definitely similar. One of the things that rocksteady/reggae inherited from ska (which is still being recorded in the 21st century) was a strong soul influence; Bob Marley & the Wailers, Toots & the Maytals, the Paragons, the Heptones, the Gaylads, Desmond Dekker and countless others who embraced rocksteady in the mid- to late '60s were heavily influenced by soul. And the interesting thing is how, in the '60s and '70s, different reggae artists used the soul influence in different ways.

Anyone who appreciates the tough, rugged, sweaty Memphis soul that Stax Records was famous for in the '60s should have no problem getting into Dekker or Toots & the Maytals, a band that embraced reggae but never forgot its ska roots. Dekker and Toots Hibbert (Toots & the Maytals' expressive lead singer) were obviously well aware of the Southern-style soul that heavyweights like Sam & Dave, Wilson Pickett, Rufus Thomas, James Brown and the late Otis Redding gave us in the '60s. For those who are seriously into both reggae and soul, it isn't hard to see the parallels between Toots & the Maytals' "Funky Kingston" and Pickett's "In the Midnight Hour" or the common ground that Dekker's passionate "Warlock" shares with Redding's original version of "Respect."

In England—where reggae has long been much more mainstream than it is in the United States—people who have a lot of Stax recordings in their collections have tended to be very receptive to Toots & the Maytals and Dekker (who was also quite capable of incorporating Northern soul influences). Meanwhile, British reggae fans who crave a sweeter type of soul singing have often been drawn to the Paragons and the Heptones, which are two examples of reggae groups with Northern soul leanings. In the '60s, the Paragons and the Heptones were to rocksteady what groups like the Delfonics, the Four Tops, the Miracles, the Impressions and the Spinners were to were to Northern soul. And the Paragons' importance wasn't lost on pop-rock/new wave superstars Blondie, who covered their '60s hit, "The Tide Is High," in 1980.

Jimmy Cliff is another reggae singer who has been quite popular with British soul fans; in England, many of the people who acquired Marvin Gaye's *What's Going On* album and Curtis Mayfield's *Superfly* soundtrack were equally receptive to the soundtrack of the 1973 movie *The Harder They Come*, which is dominated by Cliff's songs but also contains Dekker's hit "007 (Shanty Town)." Most of Cliff's '70s and '80s releases are worth owning, but *The Harder They Come* is widely regarded as his most essential album.

No discussion of the reggae/soul connection would be complete without some mention of the late Bob Marley, who was the most famous reggae singer of all time. Marley, a Rastafarian, was best known for fiercely sociopolitical songs. His best protest songs—which range from "Them Belly Full" to "War" to "Get Up, Stand Up"—could easily be compared to Marvin Gaye's "Inner City Blues," the O'Jays' "Rich Get Richer" or Curtis Mayfield's "Freddie's Dead" (not to mention much of Gil Scott-Heron's extremely sociopolitical work). But Marley also recorded some excellent lovers rock; "Waiting in Vain" and "No Woman, No Cry" are among his best romantic songs.

For the uninitiated, the term lovers rock (which was coined in the '70s) refers to apolitical reggae—arguably, lovers rock is to reggae what quiet storm is to soul music, and the parallels between quiet storm and lovers rock are not hard to miss. Gregory Isaacs' "Night Nurse" and Jimmy Riley's version of Marvin Gaye's "Sexual Healing" are two examples of early '80s lovers rock that are oozing with quiet storm appeal. In fact, isn't uncommon for British quiet storm fans to be lovers rock fans—in London, Manchester and Liverpool, people who crave Teddy Pendergrass' ballads are also likely to appreciate Gregory Issacs and the late Dennis Brown. That isn't to say that Brown or Isaacs were strictly romantic singers in the '70s or '80s; like Marvin Gaye and Curtis Mayfield, they had no problem fighting the power one minute and getting into lover-man mode the next.

Again, reggae has been mainstream in Great Britain for many years; while Peter Tosh and Dennis Brown had a small cult following in the U.S., they were superstars in England. And British reggae fans know that reggae artists can use their soul influence in many different ways. While Third World's '70s and '80s recordings incorporated funk and disco-soul in a slick fashion, Burning Spear's classic '70s work is the epitome of rawness. Spear's sociopolitical, Rastafarian-oriented '70s hits (which included "Slavery Days" and "Old Marcus Garvey") have little in the way of pop gloss; those who like soul music at its most raw and basic tend to appreciate those gems' lack of slickness.

When a reggae recording is described as a hit in this essay, it usually means that the song was a hit in Jamaica or England rather than the United States. In the '70s and '80s, getting American R&B stations to play reggae was a major battle—most of them resisted it. But there were rare exceptions to that rule. In 1980, Stevie Wonder's reggae-influenced "Master Blaster" enjoyed heavy airplay on American R&B stations, which were also receptive to Third World's 1978 recording of "Now That We Found Love" (a Gamble & Huff song that had been recorded by the O'Jays). Third World had a lot more hits in Jamaica and Great Britain than they did in the U.S.; however, they did have more luck reaching American R&B audiences than most reggae bands, and "Now That We Found Love" is a rare example of a reggae single (albeit crossover reggae) that managed to penetrate *Billboard*'s R&B singles chart in the late '70s.

One could on and on about soul's impact on reggae—everyone from Mutabaruka to Black Uhuru to the Mighty Diamonds has been affected by American soul music in some way. Similarly, Jamaican dancehall (a generally harder, more abrasive version of '70s dubwise) has been greatly influenced by hip-hop in the '80s, '90s and 2000s. Many of today's reggae singers (as opposed to dubwise or dancehall toasters) will incorporate dancehall as well as urban and hip-hop. Nonetheless, the interest in classic soul remains in some reggae circles. And it is safe to assume that wherever reggae goes in the future, it will continue to be affected by trends in African-American music.

Recommended Recordings:
Desmond Dekker, *Rockin' Steady: The Best of Desmond Dekker* (Rhino)
Jimmy Cliff, *The Harder They Come* (Island)
Toots & the Maytals, *The Very Best of Toots & the Maytals* (Island)
Toots & the Maytals, *Live* (Island)
Paragons, *On the Beach With the Paragons* (Jet Set)
Bob Marley, *Rastaman Vibration* (Island)
Bob Marley, *One Love: The Very Best of Bob Marley* (Universal)
Black Uhuru, *Chill Out* (Island)
Black Uhuru, *Liberation: The Island Anthology* (Mango)
Dennis Brown, *Some Like It Hot* (Heartbeat)
Burning Spear, *Marcus Garvey* (Island)
Third World, *Journey to Addis* (Island)
Gregory Isaacs, *The Best of Gregory Isaacs: One Man Against the World* (VP)
Heptones, *The Meaning of Life: The Best of the Heptones 1966-1976* (Trojan)

—Alex Henderson

House

It isn't hard to understand why a novice who is trying to learn about the dance music of the '80s, '90s and 2000s might feel intimidated. Since the early '80s, countless styles of dance music have surfaced—some radical and extreme, some very melodic, accessible and pop-friendly. There are many styles and variations of techno, trance and tribal, and the term "house music" can also mean a wide variety of things. Some of the more underground house music has appealed to the rave subculture; some of the more commercial house recordings have enjoyed heavy exposure on Top 40 radio. House music runs the gamut—it could be as mainstream as Madonna's "Vogue" or as radical and left-of-center as Moonfou's "Shut Up."

The main focus of this essay is house music as it relates to soul music. Some of the more rave-friendly house has little, if any, soul influence, but some of the more melodic recordings that have been called "deep house" or "garage-house" (which has nothing at all to do with '60s garage rock) are really soul music with a dance beat. Ten City, Chanelle, Jeanne Harris, Adeva, Black Box and other deep house artists who emerged in the '80s or

'90s have their roots in the disco-soul of the '70s—their work is an extension of '70s favorites like the Trammps, Chic, Loleatta Holloway and Gloria Gaynor. And to understand where Ten City or Adeva were coming from in the '80s and '90s, one needs to know some things about the '70s disco-soul artists who preceded them.

Hardcore disco lovers could spend hours telling one another what they think the very first disco records were and why they feel that way; suffice to say that Isaac Hayes, Barry White and Philadelphia producer/songwriters Kenny Gamble & Leon Huff were among the people who helped bring about what came to be called disco. By the mid-'70s, the term disco (which is short for discotheque) had at least two meanings: (1) it referred to the sort of places that are now called dance clubs, and (2) it referred to a genre of music. And by 1975, it was clear that two different schools of disco had emerged. One was Euro-disco, which evolved into the European style that was called hi-NRG in the '80s and '90s. The other was disco-soul, which paved the way for deep house. An early example of the disco-soul sound is Jerry Butler's 1972 recording of Gamble & Huff's "One Night Affair," a gem that was originally recorded by the O'Jays in 1969. In Philadelphia, some soul and disco fans insist that Butler's ultra-danceable version of "One Night Affair" was the first real disco single. And even though it would be going overboard to give Butler and Gamble & Huff all the credit for disco—Barry White and Isaac Hayes were certainly important—Butler's single does sound like a blueprint for so much of the disco-soul that came out in the mid- to late '70s, not to mention the more soul-minded house recordings of the '80s and '90s. Butler's version of "One Night Affair" was definitely a progressive, cutting-edge single for 1972, and many disco-soul and deep house artists owe him a creative debt.

In the mid- to late '70s, many rock critics were vehemently critical of disco. One of their complaints was that disco wasn't soulful enough—that it lacked the grit and toughness of '60s R&B. But in fact, some '70s disco was extremely soul-minded. Gloria Gaynor, Loleatta Holloway, Double Exposure and the Trammps were the sort of disco-soul artists who brought plenty of soulful grit to the dance floor, and they paved the way for the more soul-minded house music that developed after the '70s.

House music started in the early '80s, when New York DJ/producer Frankie Knuckles moved to Chicago and made his mark on the Windy City club scene. Another important figure in early house was Marshall Jefferson, who has produced numerous house recordings. Before long, the beat that Knuckles and Jefferson embraced was being called house, and what started out as a Chicago phenomenon quickly spread to New York and Europe (although some New Yorkers claim that house really started in the Big Apple). By the mid-'80s, it was clear that radically different styles of house music were emerging. Some house has a rave mentality—in other words, it favors the sort of amelodic approach one would hear at the underground dance gatherings known as raves. A perfect example of that sort of extreme house is Moonfou's obnoxious, abrasive '80s single "Shut Up," which doesn't have a melody or a real song structure—it's basically a beat, a track and a soundbite. From a rave standpoint, "Shut Up" is a lot of fun, but it has nothing to do with soul singing.

Deep house, on the other hand, is quite faithful to the spirit of '70s disco-soul—it is highly melodic and adheres to a standard verse/chorus/verse/chorus structure. The production is usually a lot more high-tech; '80s and '90s deep house can be totally electronic, whereas '70s disco-soul often used elaborate horn and string sections. But when you get down to it, deep house artists like Ten City, Adeva, Xaviera Gold, Jeanne Harris, Vicky Martin, Inner City and Chanelle are really disco-soul artists. Ten City's roots are the Trammps, the O'Jays, Double Exposure and the Philadelphia sound; Adeva, Gold and Chanelle are an extension of Gloria Gaynor, Linda Clifford, Loleatta Holloway, Thelma Houston and similar '70s divas.

Those who are into house music may or may not be familiar with the term deep house, which was used in the '80s and early '90s and is basically a synonym for garage-house. The term garage-house comes from the Paradise Garage, a famous New York dance club—and again, garage-house has nothing to do with '60s garage rock. One of the problems with dance music in general is an excess of terminology; numerous terms come and go, and it is difficult to keep up with all of them. To complicate matters, the same dance music term can easily mean different things to different people. But whether or not a serious house fan is familiar with the term deep house—whether he/she refers to soul-minded house as deep house, garage-house or something else—he/she knows the sound. And the gems that have epitomized that soul-minded approach to house include Ten City's "That's the Way Love Is," Jeanne Harris' "Just Another Man, " Chanelle's "One Man," Black Box's "Strike It Up," Inner City's "Good Life," Ru Paul's "Supermodel (You Better Work)" and Coldcut's "People Hold On" (which features British neo-soul goddess Lisa Stansfield). Those gems were to the '80s or '90s what disco-soul classics like the O'Jays' "I Love Music," Gloria Gaynor's "I Will Survive," the Trammps' "Disco Inferno," Linda Clifford's "Runaway Love" and Sister Sledge's "He's the Greatest Dancer" were to the '70s—they were dance singles that emphasized vocal personality and realized the value of soul power and blues feeling. The fact that one of Adeva's best known clubs hits was a house interpretation of Otis Redding's "Respect"—which was a huge hit for Aretha Franklin in 1967—speaks volumes about her musical outlook. It tells you that her work is really uptempo soul music with a dance beat.

One of the most famous examples of the soul-drenched deep house style is Crystal Waters' 1991 hit "Gypsy Woman (She's Homeless," which was more than just a club favorite—it was a major hit on urban and pop/Top 40 radio. By the early '90s, house music—certain types of house, anyway—had become mainstream. Madonna's 1990 smash "Vogue" employed a house beat, and dance-pop doesn't get any more mainstream than Madonna. For the dance music underground, the fact that the more R&B-friendly and pop-friendly house recordings were enjoying mainstream acceptance in the early '90s was problematic—people in the underground often pride themselves on their outside-the-mainstream status and don't want to be mainstream in any way, shape or form. So the early to mid-'90s saw a new wave of underground house (some of which was termed "progressive house") that wasn't as harsh as techno but was much more rave-friendly than "Vogue" or "Gypsy Woman (She's Homeless)." Nonetheless, Jomanda, Ultra Naté, Dajae, Martha Wash and others continued to provide a melodic, soul-minded style of house (which isn't to say that Jomanda or Wash have recorded house music exclusively).

Of course, the rave-friendly approach to house isn't something that ever went away—even when "Vogue" was burning up the pop charts in 1990, there were plenty of underground producers and DJs who catered to ravers and distanced themselves from the mainstream. House music has always had its melodic recordings and its not-so-melodic recordings, both of which have their place. It all depends on what the listener is looking for—and if one is looking for house music that has a soul mentality and a lot of melody, singers like Ten City, Inner City and Adeva certainly did their part to make house music safe for disco-soul fans in the '80s and '90s.

Recommended Recordings:

Black Box, *Dreamland* (RCA)
Inner City, *Big Fun* (Virgin)
Inner City, *Fire* (Virgin)
Ten City, *Foundation* (Atlantic)
Adeva, *Adeva* (Capitol)
Adeva, *Love or Lust* (Capitol)
Various Artists, *The Best of House Music, Vol. 1* (Profile)
Various Artists, *Gotta Have House: The Best of House Music, Vol. 2* (Profile)
Various Artists, *House Music All Night Long: The Best of House Music, Vol. 3* (Profile)
D-Mob, *A Little Bit of This, A Little Bit of That* (PolyGram)
Slam, *Free Your Feelings* (MCA)
49ers, *49ers* (4th & Broadway)
RuPaul, *Supermodel to the World* (Tommy Boy)

—Alex Henderson

Essential Artists

Beach

- The Casinos
- ● General Johnson
- The O'Kaysions
- Billy Stewart
- ● The Tams
- Willie Tee
- ● Brenton Wood

Blaxploitation

- Blowfly
- James Brown
- Earth, Wind & Fire
- Marvin Gaye
- ● Isaac Hayes
- ● Willie Hutch
- ● Curtis Mayfield
- Rudy Ray Moore
- ● Melvin Van Peebles
- Bobby Womack

Blue-Eyed Soul

- David Bowie
- ● The Box Tops
- Paul Carrack
- Culture Club
- ● Fine Young Cannibals
- Flaming Ember
- John Fred
- ● Hall & Oates
- Dan Hartman
- ● Roy Head
- The Ides of March
- Bill Medley
- ● Robert Palmer
- Rare Earth
- ● The Rascals
- ● The Righteous Brothers
- ● Dusty Springfield

Brill Building Pop

- Bert Berns
- ● The Chiffons
- The Cookies
- Ben E. King
- Little Eva
- The Raindrops
- ● The Righteous Brothers
- ● The Shangri-Las
- ● The Shirelles
- ● Phil Spector
- The Toys
- ● Dionne Warwick

Brown-Eyed Soul

- ● Jesse Belvin
- ● Bloodstone
- Cannibal & the Headhunters
- Gene Chandler
- El Chicano
- ● Leon Haywood
- Chuck Higgins
- ● Van McCoy
- The Paradons
- ● The Penguins
- Tierra
- ● War
- ● Brenton Wood

Chicago Soul

- Barbara Acklin
- The Artistics
- Fontella Bass
- ● Jerry Butler
- Barbara Carr
- ● Gene Chandler
- ● The Chi-Lites
- Carl Davis
- Tyrone Davis
- The Dells
- The Esquires
- Donny Hathaway
- ● The Impressions
- Walter Jackson
- Major Lance
- ● Curtis Mayfield
- Minnie Riperton
- Jackie Ross
- ● Jackie Wilson
- Young-Holt Unlimited

Contemporary R&B

- India.Arie
- ● Erykah Badu
- ● D'Angelo
- Terence Trent D'Arby
- Ginuwine
- ● Macy Gray
- ● Lauryn Hill
- Imajin
- ● Wyclef Jean
- Kelis
- ● Maxwell
- ● Me'Shell NdegéOcello
- Rahsaan Patterson
- ● The Tony Rich Project
- Jill Scott

Country-Soul

- ● Arthur Alexander
- William Bell
- ● Solomon Burke
- ● James Carr
- ● Ray Charles
- ● Dobie Gray
- Jimmy Hughes
- ● Percy Sledge
- O.C. Smith
- ● The Staple Singers
- Candi Staton
- Eddie Bo
- ● Bohannon
- Bobby Byrd
- Lyn Collins
- ● Dyke & the Blazers
- The Gaturs
- Hot Chocolate
- ● The J.B.'s
- Kay-Gee's
- Sir Joe Quarterman & Free Soul
- Sound Experience
- ● Southside Movement
- Marva Whitney
- ● Willie & the Mighty Magnificents

Deep Soul

- Arthur Alexander
- Solomon Burke
- ● James Carr
- ● Clarence Carter
- ● Arthur Conley
- ● Don Covay
- Aretha Franklin
- ● Garnet Mimms
- ● Wilson Pickett
- ● Otis Redding
- Sam & Dave
- ● Joe Simon
- Percy Sledge
- Johnnie Taylor
- ● O.V. Wright

Disco

- ● The Bee Gees
- ● B.T. Express
- ● Chic
- Earth, Wind & Fire
- ● Gloria Gaynor
- Thelma Houston
- ● KC & the Sunshine Band
- Evelyn "Champagne" King

● Indicates top pick in that category.

- Larry Levan
- Love Unlimited Orchestra
- ● Van McCoy
- ● Giorgio Moroder
- ● Vicki Sue Robinson
- Nile Rodgers
- Rose Royce
- ● The Salsoul Orchestra
- ● Sister Sledge
- ● Donna Summer
- ● Sylvester
- Sylvia
- Tavares
- ● The Trammps
- The Andrea True Connection
- ● Village People
- ● Anita Ward

Doo Wop

- The Cadets
- ● The Cadillacs
- The Capris
- The Cellos
- ● The Chords
- ● The Clovers
- The Coasters
- The Crests
- Bobby Day
- ● The Del-Vikings
- The Dells
- ● Dion
- ● The Drifters
- The Duprees
- The Edsels
- ● The Five Satins
- ● The Flamingos
- The Hollywood Flames
- The Impalas
- The Jive Five
- ● Little Anthony & the Imperials
- Little Caesar & the Romans
- ● Frankie Lymon & the Teenagers
- The Marcels
- The Monotones
- ● The Moonglows
- ● The Orioles
- ● The Penguins
- ● The Ravens
- Shep & the Limelites
- ● The Skyliners
- The Spaniels

Funk

- The Bar-Kays
- Brick
- ● James Brown
- Cameo
- The Jimmy Castor Bunch
- ● Chic
- Bootsy Collins
- The Commodores
- Con Funk Shun
- Dazz Band
- ● Earth, Wind & Fire
- ● Funkadelic
- The Gap Band
- Isaac Hayes
- ● The Isley Brothers
- Rick James
- The J.B.'s
- ● Kool & the Gang
- ● Curtis Mayfield
- ● The Meters
- ● The Ohio Players
- ● Parliament
- ● Prince
- Slave
- ● Sly & the Family Stone
- Joe Tex
- The Time
- ● War
- ● Stevie Wonder
- ● Zapp

Girl Group

- ● The Angels
- The Bobbettes
- The Chantels
- ● The Chiffons
- ● The Cookies
- ● The Crystals
- The Essex
- The Exciters
- The Jaynetts
- The Jelly Beans
- Little Eva
- ● Darlene Love
- Martha & the Vandellas
- The Marvelettes
- ● The Ronettes
- Rosie & the Originals
- ● The Shangri-Las
- ● The Shirelles
- Phil Spector
- ● Dusty Springfield
- The Supremes
- ● The Toys

Go-Go

- Chuck Brown & the Soul Searchers
- ● E.U.
- Rare Essence
- ● Trouble Funk

Memphis Soul

- ● Bill Black
- Don Bryant
- Ace Cannon
- ● Otis Clay
- ● Al Green
- George Jackson
- Syl Johnson
- ● Willie Mitchell
- ● Ann Peebles
- ● Carla Thomas
- ● Rufus Thomas
- Tommy Tucker
- ● O.V. Wright

Motown

- ● The Four Tops
- ● Marvin Gaye
- ● Berry Gordy Jr.
- Eddie Holland
- Brenda Holloway
- ● The Jackson 5
- ● Michael Jackson
- Eddie Kendricks
- Gladys Knight
- ● Martha & the Vandellas
- ● The Marvelettes
- ● The Miracles
- ● Smokey Robinson
- ● Diana Ross
- David Ruffin
- Jimmy Ruffin
- Edwin Starr
- Barrett Strong
- ● The Supremes
- ● The Temptations
- Tammi Terrell
- The Velvelettes
- ● Junior Walker
- ● Mary Wells
- Kim Weston
- ● Stevie Wonder

Neo-Soul

- Sunshine Anderson
- ● India.Arie
- ● Erykah Badu
- ● D'Angelo
- ● Macy Gray
- ● Lauryn Hill
- ● Alicia Keys
- Lucy Pearl
- Maxwell
- ● Musiq
- ● Rahsaan Patterson
- D.J. Rogers Jr.
- ● Jill Scott
- Tony! Toni! Toné!
- Tweet
- Jaguar Wright

New Jack Swing

- Another Bad Creation
- ● Bell Biv DeVoe
- Blackstreet
- ● Boyz II Men
- ● Bobby Brown
- Tevin Campbell
- Color Me Badd
- En Vogue
- Force M.D.'s
- Johnny Gill
- ● Guy
- Michael Jackson
- ● New Edition

New Orleans R&B

- Johnny Adams
- ● Dave Bartholomew
- Eddie Bo
- Dr. John
- ● Fats Domino
- ● Lee Dorsey
- Frankie Ford
- Jessie Hill
- Ernie K-Doe
- ● Earl King
- ● Smiley Lewis

- Barbara Lynn
- ● The Meters
- ● The Neville Brothers
- Aaron Neville
- ● Lloyd Price
- ● Professor Longhair
- Shirley & Lee
- The Showmen
- ● Huey Piano Smith & the Clowns
- Benny Spellman
- The Spiders
- ● Irma Thomas
- ● Allen Toussaint

Northern Soul

- ● J.J. Barnes
- Bobby Freeman
- Major Harris
- Leon Haywood
- Loleatta Holloway
- Walter Jackson
- Marv Johnson
- Gloria Jones
- ● Major Lance
- Denise LaSalle
- Barbara Lynn
- Gloria Lynne
- The Manhattans
- Bobby McClure
- Garnet Mimms
- ● The Showmen
- Billy Stewart
- ● The Tams

Philly Soul

- ● The Delfonics
- Major Harris
- Norman Harris
- ● Eddie Holman
- Hues Corporation
- The Intruders
- ● Harold Melvin & the Blue Notes
- MFSB
- ● The O'Jays
- ● Billy Paul
- Lou Rawls
- Dee Dee Sharp
- ● The Spinners
- ● The Stylistics
- ● The Three Degrees

Pop-Soul

- Fontella Bass
- Maxine Brown
- Jerry Butler
- The Delfonics
- The Dells
- The 5th Dimension
- The Foundations
- Dobie Gray
- ● The Impressions
- ● The Jackson 5
- ● Chuck Jackson
- Ben E. King
- Gladys Knight
- ● Major Lance
- ● Barbara Lewis
- Martha & the Vandellas
- The Marvelettes
- Aaron Neville
- The O'Jays
- James & Bobby Purify
- ● The Supremes
- ● The Temptations
- ● Dionne Warwick
- Mary Wells
- Jackie Wilson
- ● Stevie Wonder
- Brenton Wood

Psychedelic Soul

- The Chambers Brothers
- ● The Chi-Lites
- Earth, Wind & Fire
- ● Funkadelic
- The Isley Brothers
- ● Curtis Mayfield
- ● Parliament
- Rotary Connection
- ● Sly & the Family Stone
- Edwin Starr
- ● The Temptations
- Norman Whitfield
- Stevie Wonder

Quiet Storm

- ● Ashford & Simpson
- Atlantic Starr
- Babyface
- ● Anita Baker
- Natalie Cole
- ● The Commodores
- The Delfonics
- The Dramatics
- Roberta Flack
- ● Marvin Gaye
- Stacy Lattisaw
- LeVert
- Curtis Mayfield
- Stephanie Mills
- The O'Jays
- ● Teddy Pendergrass
- ● Smokey Robinson
- The Spinners
- The Stylistics
- ● Luther Vandross
- ● Grover Washington Jr.
- Deniece Williams

R&B

- ● LaVern Baker
- Hank Ballard & the Midnighters
- Dave Bartholomew
- Brook Benton
- Jackie Brenston
- ● James Brown
- Roy Brown
- ● Ruth Brown
- Jerry Butler
- ● Ray Charles
- ● The Clovers
- ● The Coasters
- ● Sam Cooke
- ● Fats Domino
- ● Lee Dorsey
- ● The Drifters
- The 5 Royales
- Wynonie Harris
- Ivory Joe Hunter
- The Isley Brothers
- ● Etta James
- ● Little Richard
- ● Little Willie John
- ● Percy Mayfield
- Clyde McPhatter
- Roy Milton
- The Moonglows
- ● The Orioles
- ● Lloyd Price
- The Treniers
- ● Big Joe Turner
- Ike Turner & His Kings of Rhythm
- ● Billy Ward & the Dominoes
- Larry Williams
- Chuck Willis
- ● Jackie Wilson

Retro-Soul

- ● Johnny Adams
- Kip Anderson
- Bobby Blue Bland
- Barbara Carr
- Willie Clayton
- ● Z.Z. Hill
- Eddie Hinton
- ● The Holmes Brothers
- Millie Jackson
- Mighty Sam McClain
- The Memphis Horns
- Poonanny
- ● Bobby Rush
- Peggy Scott-Adams
- Marvin Sease
- ● Johnnie Taylor

Smooth Soul

- ● The Chi-Lites
- Tyrone Davis
- ● The Delfonics
- The Dells
- The Dramatics
- The Emotions
- ● Marvin Gaye
- ● Al Green
- ● Harold Melvin & the Blue Notes
- New York City
- The Persuaders
- Minnie Riperton
- ● The Spinners
- The Stylistics
- Barry White
- ● Bill Withers

Soul

- Arthur Alexander
- William Bell
- ● James Brown
- Solomon Burke
- Jerry Butler
- James Carr
- Clarence Carter

- ● Ray Charles
- ● Sam Cooke
- Don Covay
- ● The Four Tops
- ● Aretha Franklin
- ● Marvin Gaye
- ● Al Green
- ● The Impressions
- The Isley Brothers
- ● Curtis Mayfield
- Harold Melvin & the Blue Notes
- The O'Jays
- ● Wilson Pickett
- ● Otis Redding
- ● Smokey Robinson
- ● Sam & Dave
- Percy Sledge
- ● Sly & the Family Stone
- ● The Spinners
- Johnnie Taylor
- ● The Temptations
- Joe Tex
- Carla Thomas
- Junior Walker
- ● Jackie Wilson
- Bobby Womack
- ● Stevie Wonder

Soul-Blues

- Johnny Adams
- ● Bobby "Blue" Bland
- Lowell Fulson
- Ted Hawkins
- ● Z.Z. Hill
- ● Etta James
- Jimmy McCracklin
- Junior Parker
- Johnnie Taylor
- Ike Turner & His Kings of Rhythm

Southern Soul

- ● Arthur Alexander
- ● Booker T. & the MG's
- ● Solomon Burke
- ● James Carr
- Clarence Carter
- Otis Clay
- Arthur Conley
- ● Don Covay
- King Curtis
- Laura Lee
- Garnet Mimms
- ● Wilson Pickett
- ● Otis Redding
- ● Sam & Dave
- Joe Simon
- ● Percy Sledge
- ● Johnnie Taylor
- ● Carla Thomas
- Rufus Thomas
- The Van Dykes
- O.V. Wright

Uptown Soul

- P.P. Arnold
- ● Maxine Brown
- Jerry Butler
- ● The Impressions
- ● Chuck Jackson
- Major Lance
- ● Barbara Lewis
- Curtis Mayfield
- Jackie Wilson

Urban

- Ashford & Simpson
- ● Babyface
- ● Anita Baker
- Mary J. Blige
- ● Boyz II Men
- ● Toni Braxton
- Peabo Bryson
- ● Mariah Carey
- Natalie Cole
- DeBarge
- Destiny's Child
- Aretha Franklin
- Marvin Gaye
- Guy
- ● Whitney Houston
- ● Janet Jackson
- ● Michael Jackson
- ● R. Kelly
- Chaka Khan
- Kool & the Gang
- George Michael
- ● New Edition
- Jeffrey Osborne
- Teddy Pendergrass
- ● Prince
- Lionel Richie
- ● Smokey Robinson
- Patrice Rushen
- ● Sade
- ● TLC
- Usher
- Luther Vandross
- ● Stevie Wonder

Essential Songs

Beach

"Then You Can Tell Me Goodbye," The Casinos
"Carolina Girls," General Johnson
"It Will Stand," General Johnson
"Beach Fever," General Johnson & the Chairmen of the Board
"What Kind of Fool (Do You Think I Am?)," The Tams
"Teasin' You," Willie Tee
"Gimme Little Sign," Brenton Wood
"The Oogum Boogum Song," Brenton Wood

Blaxploitation

"The Payback," James Brown
"Trouble Man," Marvin Gaye
"Theme from Shaft," Isaac Hayes
"Brother's Gonna Work It Out," Willie Hutch
"Theme of Foxy Brown/Overture of Foxy Brown," Willie Hutch
"Freddie's Dead," Curtis Mayfield
"Superfly," Curtis Mayfield
"Sweetback's Theme," Melvin Van Peebles
"Across 110th Street," Bobby Womack

Blue-Eyed Soul

"Cry Like a Baby," The Box Tops
"Soul Deep," The Box Tops
"The Letter," The Box Tops
"Church of the Poison Mind," Culture Club
"She Drives Me Crazy," Fine Young Cannibals
"Westbound #9," Flaming Ember
"Rich Girl," Hall & Oates
"She's Gone," Hall & Oates
"I Can Dream About You," Dan Hartman
"Treat Her Right," Roy Head
"Vehicle," The Ides of March
"A Beautiful Morning," The Rascals
"Good Lovin'," The Rascals
"Groovin'," The Rascals
"You've Lost That Lovin' Feelin'," The Righteous Brothers
"Son of a Preacher Man," Dusty Springfield
"You Don't Have to Say You Love Me," Dusty Springfield

Brill Building Pop

"One Fine Day," The Chiffons
"Spanish Harlem," Ben E. King
"The Loco-Motion," Little Eva
"Unchained Melody," The Righteous Brothers
"You've Lost That Lovin' Feelin'," The Righteous Brothers
"Dedicated to the One I Love," The Shirelles
"Will You Love Me Tomorrow," The Shirelles
"The Look of Love," Dusty Springfield
"A Lover's Concerto," The Toys
"I Just Don't Know What to Do With Myself," Dionne Warwick
"Walk on By," Dionne Warwick

Brown-Eyed Soul

"Goodnight My Love," Jesse Belvin
"How Does It Feel," Bloodstone
"Natural High," Bloodstone
"Headhunters Dance Party," Cannibal & the Headhunters
"Land of 1000 Dances," Cannibal & the Headhunters
"Viva Tirado, Pt. 1," El Chicano
"It's Got to Be Mellow," Leon Haywood
"Pachuko Hop," Chuck Higgins
"Low Rider," War
"Spill the Wine," War
"The World Is a Ghetto," War
"Why Can't We Be Friends?," War

Chicago Soul

"Love Makes a Woman," Barbara Acklin
"Rescue Me," Fontella Bass
"He Will Break Your Heart," Jerry Butler
"There Was a Time," Gene Chandler
"(For God's Sake) Give More Power to the People," The Chi-Lites
"Turn Back the Hands of Time," Tyrone Davis
"Oh, What a Night," The Dells
"Stay in My Corner," The Dells
"Get on Up," The Esquires
"Gypsy Woman," The Impressions
"I'm So Proud," The Impressions
"It's All Right," The Impressions
"The Monkey Time," Major Lance
"Um, Um, Um, Um, Um, Um," Major Lance
"Soulful Strut," Young-Holt Unlimited

Contemporary R&B

"On & On," Erykah Badu
"Brown Sugar," D'Angelo
"Untitled (How Does It Feel)," D'Angelo
"Pony," Ginuwine
"I Try," Macy Gray
"Doo Wop (That Thing)," Lauryn Hill
"Gone Till November," Wyclef Jean
"Ascension (Don't Ever Wonder)," Maxwell
"If That's Your Boyfriend (He Wasn't Last Night)," Me'Shell NdegéOcello
"Nobody Knows," Tony Rich

Country-Soul

"Detroit City (I Wanna Go Home)," Arthur Alexander
"In the Middle of It All," Arthur Alexander
"You Better Move On," Arthur Alexander
"Just Out of Reach," Solomon Burke
"I Can't Stop Loving You," Ray Charles
"You Are My Sunshine," Ray Charles
"Loving Arms," Dobie Gray
"Watch Out for Lucy," Dobie Gray
"Steal Away," Jimmy Hughes
"Little Green Apples," O.C. Smith
"The Son of Hickory Holler's Tramp," O.C. Smith

Deep Funk

"Foot Stompin' Music," Bohannon
"I Know You Got Soul," Bobby Byrd
"Funky Broadway, Pt. 1," Dyke & the Blazers
"We Got More Soul," Dyke & the Blazers
"Gimme Some More," The J.B.'s
"Pass the Peas," The J.B.'s
"(I Got) So Much Trouble in My Mind," Sir Joe Quarterman
"Funky 8 Corners," Willie & the Mighty Magnificents

Deep Soul

"Pouring Water on a Drowning Man," James Carr
"The Dark End of the Street," James Carr
"Slip Away," Clarence Carter
"Sweet Soul Music," Arthur Conley
"Mercy Mercy," Don Covay
"Cry Baby," Garnet Mimms
"In the Midnight Hour," Wilson Pickett
"I've Been Loving You Too Long," Otis Redding
"Mr. Pitiful," Otis Redding
"When Something Is Wrong With My Baby," Sam & Dave
"The Chokin' Kind," Joe Simon
"Testify (I Wanna)," Johnnie Taylor
"Who's Making Love?," Johnnie Taylor
"Trying to Live My Life Without You," O.V. Wright

Disco

"Stayin' Alive," The Bee Gees
"Good Times," Chic
"Le Freak," Chic
"Boogie Wonderland," Earth, Wind & Fire
"I Will Survive," Gloria Gaynor
"Don't Leave Me This Way," Thelma Houston
"(Shake, Shake, Shake) Shake Your Booty," KC & the Sunshine Band
"Funkytown," Lipps Inc.
"The Hustle," Van McCoy
"Turn the Beat Around," Vicki Sue Robinson
"Car Wash," Rose Royce
"We Are Family," Sister Sledge
"Hot Stuff," Donna Summer
"You Make Me Feel (Mighty Real)," Sylvester

"Disco Inferno," The Trammps
"More, More, More," Andrea True
"Y.M.C.A.," Village People
"Ring My Bell," Anita Ward

Doo Wop

"Speedoo," The Cadillacs
"There's a Moon Out Tonight," The Capris
"Sh-Boom," The Chords
"Devil or Angel," The Clovers
"A Teenager in Love," Dion & the Belmonts
"Rama Lama Ding Dong," The Edsels
"In the Still of the Night," The Five Satins
"I Only Have Eyes for You," The Flamingos
"Those Oldies But Goodies (Remind Me of You)," Little Caesar & the Romans
"I Want You to Be My Girl," Frankie Lymon & the Teenagers
"Why Do Fools Fall in Love?," Frankie Lymon & the Teenagers
"Blue Moon," The Marcels
"Book of Love," The Monotones
"Crying in the Chapel," The Orioles
"Earth Angel (Will You Be Mine)," The Penguins
"Daddy's Home," Shep & the Limelites
"Get a Job," The Silhouettes
"Since I Don't Have You," The Skyliners
"Stay," Maurice Williams & the Zodiacs

Funk

"Dazz," Brick
"Cold Sweat," James Brown
"Get Up (I Feel Like Being A) Sex Machine," James Brown
"Papa's Got a Brand New Bag," James Brown
"Atomic Dog," George Clinton
"Brick House," The Commodores
"(Not Just) Knee Deep," Funkadelic
"One Nation Under a Groove," Funkadelic
"Theme from Shaft," Isaac Hayes
"It's Your Thing," The Isley Brothers
"Super Freak," Rick James
"Jungle Boogie," Kool & the Gang
"Superfly," Curtis Mayfield
"Cissy Strut," The Meters
"Love Rollercoaster," The Ohio Players
"Flash Light," Parliament
"Give Up the Funk (Tear the Roof off the Sucker)," Parliament
"Family Affair," Sly & the Family Stone
"Thank You (Falettinme Be Mice Elf Agin)," Sly & the Family Stone
"Low Rider," War
"Superstition," Stevie Wonder
"Express Yourself," Charles Wright & the Watts 103rd Street Rhythm Band

Girl Group

"My Boyfriend's Back," The Angels
"Maybe," The Chantels
"He's So Fine," The Chiffons
"One Fine Day," The Chiffons
"Da Doo Ron Ron," The Crystals
"Then He Kissed Me," The Crystals
"Tell Him," The Exciters
"Sally Go Round the Roses," The Jaynetts
"The Loco-Motion," Little Eva
"He's a Rebel," Darlene Love
"Be My Baby," The Ronettes
"Leader of the Pack," The Shangri-Las
"Remember (Walking in the Sand)," The Shangri-Las
"Dedicated to the One I Love," The Shirelles
"Mama Said," The Shirelles
"Will You Love Me Tomorrow," The Shirelles
"To Know Him Is to Love Him," The Teddy Bears
"A Lover's Concerto," The Toys

Go-Go

"Bustin' Loose, Pt. 1," Chuck Brown & the Soul Searchers
"Da' Butt," E.U.
"Drop the Bomb," Trouble Funk
"Pump Me Up," Trouble Funk

Memphis Soul

"The Call of Distress," Don Bryant
"Blues Stay Away from Me," Ace Cannon
"That's How It Is (When You're in Love)," Otis Clay
"Trying to Live My Life Without You," Otis Clay
"Call Me (Come Back Home)," Al Green
"Here I Am (Come and Take Me)," Al Green
"Let's Stay Together," Al Green
"Take Me to the River," Syl Johnson
"Soul Serenade," Willie Mitchell
"Tramp," Otis & Carla
"I Can't Stand the Rain," Ann Peebles
"I'm Gonna Tear Your Playhouse Down," Ann Peebles
"Trying to Live My Life Without You," O.V. Wright

Motown

"I Can't Help Myself (Sugar Pie, Honey Bunch)," The Four Tops
"Reach Out (I'll Be There)," The Four Tops
"Ain't Nothing Like the Real Thing," Marvin Gaye
"I Heard It Through the Grapevine," Marvin Gaye
"Pride and Joy," Marvin Gaye
"Leaving Here," Eddie Holland
"(Love Is Like A) Heat Wave," Martha & the Vandellas
"Dancing in the Street," Martha & the Vandellas
"Nowhere to Run," Martha & the Vandellas
"Please Mr. Postman," The Marvelettes
"Tears of a Clown," Smokey Robinson & the Miracles
"The Tracks of My Tears," Smokey Robinson & the Miracles
"Stop! In the Name of Love," Diana Ross
"Where Did Our Love Go," Diana Ross & the Supremes
"You Can't Hurry Love," Diana Ross & the Supremes
"My Girl," The Temptations
"The Way You Do the Things You Do," The Temptations
"Shotgun," Junior Walker & the All-Stars
"My Guy," Mary Wells
"It Takes Two," Kim Weston
"Signed, Sealed, Delivered I'm Yours," Stevie Wonder
"Uptight (Everything's Alright)," Stevie Wonder

Neo-Soul

"Video," India.Arie
"Brown Sugar," D'Angelo
"I Try," Macy Gray
"Doo Wop (That Thing)," Lauryn Hill
"Fallin'," Alicia Keys
"Halfcrazy," Musiq
"It's Alright Now," Rahsaan Patterson
"A Long Walk," Jill Scott

New Jack Swing

"Do Me!," Bell Biv DeVoe
"Poison," Bell Biv DeVoe
"Motownphilly," Boyz II Men
"My Prerogative," Bobby Brown
"On Our Own," Bobby Brown
"I Wanna Sex You Up," Color Me Badd
"My Lovin' (You're Never Gonna Get It)," En Vogue
"Tender Love," Force M.D.'s
"Rub You the Right Way," Johnny Gill
"I Like," Guy
"Sensitivity," Ralph Tresvant

New Orleans R&B

"Check Mr. Popeye, Pt. 1," Eddie Bo
"Right Place, Wrong Time," Dr. John
"Blue Monday," Fats Domino
"I'm Walkin'," Fats Domino
"Ride Your Pony," Lee Dorsey
"Working in the Coal Mine," Lee Dorsey
"Sea Cruise," Frankie Ford
"Ooh Poo Pah Doo," Jessie Hill
"A Certain Girl," Ernie K-Doe
"I Hear You Knockin'," Smiley Lewis
"One Night," Smiley Lewis
"You'll Lose a Good Thing," Barbara Lynn
"Look-Ka Py Py," The Meters
"Tell It Like It Is," Aaron Neville
"Mardi Gras in New Orleans," Professor Longhair
"Tipitina," Professor Longhair
"Let the Good Times Roll," Shirley & Lee
"It Will Stand," The Showmen
"Rockin' Pneumonia and the Boogie Woogie Flu," Huey "Piano" Smith
"Lipstick Traces (On a Cigarette)," Benny Spellman
"Time Is on My Side," Irma Thomas

Northern Soul

"Don't Mess Up a Good Thing," Fontella Bass
"There Was a Time," Gene Chandler
"Love Won't Let Me Wait," Major Harris
"I Want'a Do Something Freaky to You," Leon Haywood
"Tainted Love," Gloria Jones
"Trapped By a Thing Called Love," Denise LaSalle
"What Kind of Fool (Do You Think I Am?)," The Tams

Philly Soul

"Didn't I (Blow Your Mind This Time)," The Delfonics
"Hey There Lonely Girl," Eddie Holman

"If You Don't Know Me By Now," Harold Melvin & the Blue Notes
"T.S.O.P. (The Sound of Philadelphia)," MFSB
"Back Stabbers," The O'Jays
"Love Train," The O'Jays
"Me and Mrs. Jones," Billy Paul
"Could It Be I'm Falling in Love," The Spinners
"Mighty Love," The Spinners
"One of a Kind (Love Affair)," The Spinners
"Betcha By Golly, Wow," The Stylistics
"You Make Me Feel Brand New," The Stylistics
"Maybe," The Three Degrees
"When Will I See You Again," The Three Degrees

Pop-Soul

"Rescue Me," Fontella Bass
"Only the Strong Survive," Jerry Butler
"Didn't I (Blow Your Mind This Time)," The Delfonics
"Build Me Up Buttercup," The Foundations
"Drift Away," Dobie Gray
"The 'In' Crowd," Dobie Gray
"It's All Right," The Impressions
"I Want You Back," The Jackson 5
"Any Day Now (My Wild Beautiful Bird)," Chuck Jackson
"Stand By Me," Ben E. King
"The Monkey Time," Major Lance
"Baby I'm Yours," Barbara Lewis
"Love Train," The O'Jays
"I Hear a Symphony," Diana Ross & the Supremes
"My Girl," The Temptations
"I Say a Little Prayer," Dionne Warwick
"My Guy," Mary Wells
"(Your Love Keeps Lifting Me) Higher and Higher," Jackie Wilson
"Yester-Me, Yester-You, Yesterday," Stevie Wonder
"You Are the Sunshine of My Life," Stevie Wonder

Psychedelic Soul

"Time Has Come Today," The Chambers Brothers
"(For God's Sake) Give More Power to the People," The Chi-Lites
"Maggot Brain," Funkadelic
"Move on Up," Curtis Mayfield
"Stand!," Sly & the Family Stone
"Thank You (Falettinme Be Mice Elf Agin)," Sly & the Family Stone
"War," Edwin Starr
"Ball of Confusion (That's What the World Is Today)," The Temptations
"Papa Was a Rollin' Stone," The Temptations

Quiet Storm

"I'll Be There for You," Ashford & Simpson
"Solid," Ashford & Simpson
"Giving You the Best That I Got," Anita Baker
"Sweet Love," Anita Baker
"Easy," The Commodores
"Sexual Healing," Marvin Gaye
"I Feel Good All Over," Stephanie Mills
"Love T.K.O.," Teddy Pendergrass
"Cruisin'," Smokey Robinson
"Quiet Storm," Smokey Robinson
"Here and Now," Luther Vandross
"Just the Two of Us," Grover Washington Jr.

R&B

"Tweedle Dee," LaVern Baker
"Let's Go, Let's Go, Let's Go," Hank Ballard & the Midnighters
"Rocket 88," Jackie Brenston
"Please, Please, Please," James Brown
"Good Rocking Tonight," Roy Brown
"(Mama) He Treats Your Daughter Mean," Ruth Brown
"Hallelujah, I Love Her So," Ray Charles
"What'd I Say," Ray Charles
"One Mint Julep," The Clovers
"Searchin'," The Coasters
"Another Saturday Night," Sam Cooke
"Blueberry Hill," Fats Domino
"Money Honey," The Drifters
"Baby Don't Do It," The 5 Royales
"Good Rockin' Tonight," Wynonie Harris
"Since I Met You Baby," Ivory Joe Hunter
"Twist and Shout," The Isley Brothers
"At Last," Etta James
"I Hear You Knockin'," Smiley Lewis
"Tears on My Pillow," Little Anthony & the Imperials
"Fever," Little Willie John
"Please Send Me Someone to Love," Percy Mayfield
"A Lover's Question," Clyde McPhatter
"Crying in the Chapel," The Orioles
"Willie and the Hand Jive," Johnny Otis
"Lawdy Miss Clawdy," Lloyd Price
"Stagger Lee," Lloyd Price
"Let the Good Times Roll," Shirley & Lee
"Don't You Just Know It," Huey "Piano" Smith
"Shake, Rattle and Roll," Big Joe Turner
"A Fool in Love," Ike & Tina Turner
"Sixty Minute Man," Billy Ward
"Bony Moronie," Larry Williams
"C.C. Rider," Chuck Willis
"Lonely Teardrops," Jackie Wilson

Retro-Soul

"Down That Lonely Lonely Road," Johnny Adams
"A Knife and a Fork," Kip Anderson
"Somewhere Between Right & Wrong," Bobby "Blue" Bland
"Good Woman Go Bad," Barbara Carr
"Three People (Sleeping in My Bed)," Willie Clayton
"Everybody Knows About My Good Thing," Z.Z. Hill
"Please Don't Let Our Good Thing End," Z.Z. Hill
"I'll Come Running Back to You," Eddie Hinton
"Start Stoppin'," The Holmes Brothers
"Up Above My Head," The Holmes Brothers
"Hot! Wild! Unrestricted! Crazy Love," Millie Jackson
"What You Want Me to Do?," Mighty Sam McClain
"Poonanny Be Still," Poonanny
"Making a Decision," Bobby Rush
"What's Good for the Goose Is Good for the Gander," Bobby Rush
"I'm Getting What I Want," Peggy Scott-Adams
"Candy Licker," Marvin Sease
"Everything's Out in the Open," Johnnie Taylor
"I Found a Love," Johnnie Taylor

Smooth Soul

"Have You Seen Her?," The Chi-Lites
"Oh Girl," The Chi-Lites
"Didn't I (Blow Your Mind This Time)," The Delfonics
"Give Your Baby a Standing Ovation," The Dells
"Whatcha See Is Whatcha Get," The Dramatics
"Let's Get It On," Marvin Gaye
"Let's Stay Together," Al Green
"If You Don't Know Me By Now," Harold Melvin & the Blue Notes
"I'm Doin' Fine Now," New York City
"A Thin Line Between Love and Hate," The Persuaders
"Could It Be I'm Falling in Love," The Spinners
"One of a Kind (Love Affair)," The Spinners
"Betcha By Golly, Wow," The Stylistics
"I'm Gonna Love You Just a Little More, Baby," Barry White
"Ain't No Sunshine," Bill Withers

Soul

"You Don't Miss Your Water," William Bell
"I Got You (I Feel Good)," James Brown
"The Dark End of the Street," James Carr
"What'd I Say," Ray Charles
"A Change Is Gonna Come," Sam Cooke
"Didn't I (Blow Your Mind This Time)," The Delfonics
"Knock on Wood," Eddie Floyd
"Respect," Aretha Franklin
"I Heard It Through the Grapevine," Marvin Gaye
"What's Going On," Marvin Gaye
"Let's Stay Together," Al Green
"Gypsy Woman," The Impressions
"Stand By Me," Ben E. King
"Freddie's Dead," Curtis Mayfield
"If You Don't Know Me By Now," Harold Melvin & the Blue Notes
"Back Stabbers," The O'Jays
"In the Midnight Hour," Wilson Pickett
"(Sittin' on) The Dock of the Bay," Otis Redding
"The Tracks of My Tears," Smokey Robinson & the Miracles
"Soul Man," Sam & Dave
"When a Man Loves a Woman," Percy Sledge
"Everyday People," Sly & the Family Stone
"I'll Be Around," The Spinners
"Who's Making Love?," Johnnie Taylor
"Ain't Too Proud to Beg," The Temptations
"B-A-B-Y," Carla Thomas
"Just One Look," Doris Troy
"Shotgun," Junior Walker & the All-Stars
"Lonely Teardrops," Jackie Wilson
"Uptight (Everything's Alright)," Stevie Wonder
"Gimme Little Sign," Brenton Wood

Soul-Blues

"Cry Cry Cry," Bobby "Blue" Bland
"Turn on Your Love Light," Bobby "Blue" Bland
"Reconsider Baby," Lowell Fulson
"Tramp," Lowell Fulson
"Down Home Blues," Z.Z. Hill
"I'd Rather Go Blind," Etta James

"Tell Mama," Etta James
"Cheaper to Keep Her," Johnnie Taylor

Southern Soul

"Green Onions," Booker T. & the MG's
"If You Need Me," Solomon Burke
"Pouring Water on a Drowning Man," James Carr
"The Dark End of the Street," James Carr
"Slip Away," Clarence Carter
"Trying to Live My Life Without You," Otis Clay
"Sweet Soul Music," Arthur Conley
"Mercy Mercy," Don Covay
"Memphis Soul Stew," King Curtis
"Tramp," Otis & Carla
"In the Midnight Hour," Wilson Pickett
"Mustang Sally," Wilson Pickett
"Try a Little Tenderness," Otis Redding
"Hold On! I'm Comin'," Sam & Dave
"Soul Man," Sam & Dave
"When a Man Loves a Woman," Percy Sledge
"Who's Making Love?," Johnnie Taylor
"Gee Whiz! (Look at His Eyes)," Carla Thomas
"Walking the Dog," Rufus Thomas

Uptown Soul

"All in My Mind," Maxine Brown
"He Will Break Your Heart," Jerry Butler
"Only the Strong Survive," Jerry Butler
"Let It Be Me," Betty Everett
"I'm So Proud," The Impressions
"It's All Right," The Impressions
"Any Day Now (My Wild Beautiful Bird)," Chuck Jackson
"I Don't Want to Cry," Chuck Jackson
"The Monkey Time," Major Lance
"Um, Um, Um, Um, Um, Um," Major Lance
"Baby I'm Yours," Barbara Lewis
"Hello Stranger," Barbara Lewis
"(Your Love Keeps Lifting Me) Higher and Higher," Jackie Wilson
"Lonely Teardrops," Jackie Wilson

Urban

"Solid," Ashford & Simpson
"Whip Appeal," Babyface
"Sweet Love," Anita Baker
"Poison," Bell Biv DeVoe
"Real Love," Mary J. Blige
"End of the Road," Boyz II Men
"Un-Break My Heart," Toni Braxton
"My Prerogative," Bobby Brown
"Honey," Mariah Carey
"Shining Star," Earth, Wind & Fire
"My Lovin' (You're Never Gonna Get It)," En Vogue
"Sexual Healing," Marvin Gaye
"I Wanna Dance With Somebody (Who Loves Me)," Whitney Houston
"Nasty," Janet Jackson
"That's the Way Love Goes," Janet Jackson
"Billie Jean," Michael Jackson
"Human Nature," Michael Jackson
"I Believe I Can Fly," R. Kelly
"I Feel for You," Chaka Khan
"Love T.K.O.," Teddy Pendergrass
"1999," Prince
"Truly," Lionel Richie
"Being With You," Smokey Robinson
"Shoop," Salt-N-Pepa
"Waterfalls," TLC
"Here and Now," Luther Vandross

Index

A

.Arie, India **14**, 15, 584
AACM 535
Aaliyah **1**, 75, 209, 221, 222, 386, 686, 696
Aaron, John 497
ABBA 67, 201
Abbatiello, Sal 168
Abbey, John E. 692
Abbott, Gregory **1**, 2, 369, 527, 785
Abbott, Peter 23
ABC 139, 140, 312, 605
Abdul, Paula **2**, 6, 168, 213, 233, 291, 444, 529, 622, 695, 796
Abdul-Jabbar, Kareem 350
Abel, Frank 405
Abner, Ewart 266, 402
Abney, Jimmy 412
Above the Law 833
Abrams, Colonel **2**, 3
Abramson, Herb 94, 167, 700, 701
AC Black **3**
Ace of Base 499
Ace Spectrum **3**, 795
Ace 119
Ace, Buddy 3
Ace, Johnny **3**, 70, 193, 280, 307, 333, 487, 799, 836
Acierno, Vinnie 525
Acklin, Barbara **3**, 4, 126, 127, 137, 178, 414, 528, 567, 600, 773, 774, 789, 830, 834
Action 408
Acuff, Roy 309
Acuff, Roy & His Smokey Mountain Boys 309
Ad Libs **4**, 457, 803
Adam, George 235
Adams, Arthur 60, 171, 369, 693
Adams, Bob 173, 693
Adams, Bryan 150
Adams, Clifford 400
Adams, Crip 746
Adams, Ernie 13
Adams, Faye **4**, 464, 836
Adams, Gayle **5**
Adams, George 236
Adams, Greg 695
Adams, Jeff 556
Adams, Johnny **5**, 6, 63, 293, 447, 815, 825
Adams, Justin 475
Adams, Leonard 53
Adams, Marie 514, 799
Adams, Mark Antone 20, 622, 623
Adams, Nancy 804
Adams, Oleta **6**, 44
Adams, Patrick 53, 147, 280, 317, 337, 395, 488, 609, 623, 670, 709, 720, 795, 796, 799
Adams, Pepper 105, 759
Adams, Ritchie 240, 418, 571
Adams, Stanley 60
Adams, Walter 206
Adams, Wesley 691, 692
Adamski 605
Adaritha 159
ADC Band **6**, 54
Adderley, Cannonball 7, 23, 24, 54, 86, 168, 195, 375, 442, 732, 733, 755, 787, 810, 857, 858
Adderley, Nat 24, 54, 109, 376, 391, 780
Addison, Larry 57, 259, 260
Addrisi, Don 497
Ade, King Sunny 792
Adefumi, Shango Njoko 535
Adeva **6**
Adler, Larry 764
Admirations 805
Adonis 383, 399
Adu, Sade 596
Aerosmith 41, 73, 484, 695
Affair 312, 747
Affleck, Ben 428
Afra, Tybee 184, 185
African Music Machine **6**, 7
Afrodiziak 740
After "7" **7**, 27, 217, 225
Agee, Tawatha 485
Agent, David 149
Aguilera, Christina 77, 190, 205, 509, 538, 664, 689
Aiken, Ben 794
Airbus 134
Aitken, Laurel 687
Aitken, Matt 464
Akens, Jewel 7
Akwaaba 383
Aladdins 821
Alaimo, Steve 411, 459
Alan, Buddy 4
Albano, Paul 242
Albert 120
Albert, Morris 788
Albin, Rudy 650
Albright, Gerald 3, **7**, 8, 30, 202, 213, 289, 666
Alcivar, Bob 239
Aleem 553
Aleem, Taharqa 99
Aleem, Tunde-Ra 99
Aleems 99
Ales, Barney 461, 559
Alexander, Arthur **8**, 9, 238, 475, 582, 779, 784
Alexander, Clyde 795
Alexander, Fred Jr. 406
Alexander, Harold 751
Alexander, James 34, 36, 685
Alexander, Larry 328
Alexander, Mel 813
Alexander, Rudell 497
Alexander, Texas 261
Alexander, Willie "Loco" & the Confessions 557
Alexander, Willie 636
Alford, Ann 823
Ali, Bardu 514
Ali, Muhammad 121, 167, 440
Ali, Tatyana **9**, 234, 367
Ali, Wali 776
All 4 One **9**
All Saints **9**, 205, 407
All Star 721
Allan, Gene 202
Allbut, Barb 13
Allbut, Phyllis "Jiggs" 13
Allen, Barbara 3
Allen, Bill 421
Allen, Charles "Scoop" 34, 35
Allen, Daevid 474
Allen, Deborah 195
Allen, Donna 234
Allen, Esau 10
Allen, Fred 260
Allen, Henry "Red" 638
Allen, Jeff 474
Allen, Jimmy 759
Allen, Johnny 190
Allen, Lee **10**, 38, 69, 94, 102, 199, 310, 360, 361, 421, 424, 518, 574, 475, 613, 694, 750, 840
Allen, Marc 376
Allen, Papa Dee 724
Allen, Paul 615
Allen, Rance 10, 36, 462
Allen, Rance Group **10**
Allen, Richard Pistol 262, 263, 714
Allen, Rick 72
Allen, Ronald 577
Allen, Rusty 34, 624
Allen, Timmy 127, 374, 412, 472, 502
Allen, Tom 10
Allen, Tony & the Champs 778
Allen, Vee 832
Allen, William 26
Alley, Kirstie 551
Alley, Vernon 759
Allison, Ben 541
Allison, Gene 778, 779, 810, 817, 829
Allison, Leevert 779
Allison, Luther 369, 593
Allison, Mose 558, 847
Allison, Vern 187, 188, 540
Allman Brothers 93, 792, 847
Allman, Duane 256, 537, 600, 847
Allure **10**, 422
Almight Gee 270
Almond, Hershel 815
Alpert, Herb 256, 616, 694, 730
Alpert, Herb & the Tijuana Brass 599
Alston, Barbara 171, 172
Alston, Gerald **10**, 11, 441, 442, 529
Alvarez, Jesus 613, 614
Always, Billy 647
Amato, Buzz 453
Amazers 793
Ambassadors **11**
Ambrose, Sammy O. 812
Ambrosia 666
American Breed 388, 592
Amerie **11**
Ames Brothers 251, 409, 577
Ames, Joe 125, 367, 369, 575, 646
Ames, Roy C. 297
Ammons, Albert 815, 822
Ammons, Gene 24, 102, 558, 810, 857, 858
Amoo, Chris 566
Amoo, Eddie 427, 566
Amos, Tori 780
Amy, Curtis 25
Andantes 446, 670, 831, 832, 835
Anderson, Adrian 698
Anderson, Alfa 138
Anderson, Bill 326
Anderson, Carl 727
Anderson, Carleen 105
Anderson, Casey 572
Anderson, Deborah 642, 643
Anderson, James 18
Anderson, Jesse 361, 793
Anderson, Jon 523
Anderson, Katherine 447
Anderson, Kenny 623
Anderson, Kip **11**, 790, 809
Anderson, Lynn 400, 699
Anderson, Paul Thomas 830
Anderson, Ron 237
Anderson, Sandy 709
Anderson, Sunshine **11**
Anderson, Vicki 86, 91, 105, 313, 745
Anderson, William 170, 206, 709
Andes, Mark 688
Andrews Sisters 167, 326
Andrews, Dennis 553
Andrews, George 665
Andrews, Inez 36
Andrews, James 695
Andrews, Lee 11, 12, 13, 782
Andrews, Lee & the Hearts **11**, 12, 13, 124, 400, 777
Andrews, Michael 289
Andrews, Reggie 182, 383
Andrews, Roger 533
Andrews, Ruby **13**, 15, 82, 719
Andy, Bob 325, 606
Angelettie, Deric 331
Angelou, Maya 18
Angels **13**, 320, 808, 844
Anglin, Jack 747
Animals 72, 162, 191, 249, 259, 599, 696, 724, 759, 842, 847
Anka, Paul 374, 442, 577
Another Bad Creation **13**, 41, 599
Ant, Adam 383
Anthoni, Mark 335
Anthony & the Sophomores 820
Anthony, C.J. 69
Anthony, Lamont 202
Anthony, Marc 427, 688
Anthony, Mark 573
Apollas 778
Apollonia 213, 715
Apollonia 6 279, 666, 715
Apostol, John 114
Apple, Fiona 284, 483
Applebaum, Stan 207
Appleby, Kim 464
Appleton, Natalie 9
Appleton, Nicky 9
Aquarian Dream **13**, 14, 160, 219, 647
Aquatones **14**
Arbex, Fernando 37
Archer, Mark 14
Archer, Tasmin **14**
Archia, Tom 297
Archibald 789
Archies 240, 537, 842
Arcipowski, Ken 559
Ardoin, Chris 427
Areas, Chepito 151
Arena, Neil 464
Argent, Rod 639
Arlen, Harold 152, 504
Armato, Tony 525
Armor, Laythan 183
Armstead, Jo **15**, 184, 331
Armstead, Joshie 92, 231, 331, 349, 372, 660
Armstrong, Billy 259, 260
Armstrong, Harry 222
Armstrong, Louis 378, 379, 515, 555, 603, 715
Armstrong, Moses 222, 402
Armstrong, Sam 161, 222, 241, 606
Armstrong, Tyrone 260
Armstrong, Vanessa Bell **15**, 369, 756
Arnay, David 710
Arnell, Ginny **15**, 808
Arnell, Richard 15
Arnold 657
Arnold, Billy Boy 191, 371, 838
Arnold, Eddy 131, 462
Arnold, Joe 569
Arnold, Larkin 225, 274, 657
Arnold, P.P. **15**, 16
Arnold, Robert 652
Arrested Development **16**, 235
Arrington, Barbara 437
Arrington, Steve 20, 81, 226, 293, 488, 622, 623
Art Ensemble of Chicago 39, 151, 727
Art of Noise 270, 811
Art 494
Artful Dodger 177

Arthur, Joseph 76
Arthur, Rob 319
Artis, Ray 176
Artis, Ron 205
Artistics **16**, 17, 103, 125, 219, 789, 791, 811, 819
Arvizu, Ersi 140, 621
Arvizu, Mary 621
Arvizu, Rosella 621
Ashanti **17**, 478, 700
Ashby, Irving 433
Ashford & Simpson 15, **17**, 18, 26, 211, 252, 273, 290, 313, 337, 383, 388, 398, 416, 430, 472, 531, 580, 587, 593, 613, 619, 640, 644, 656, 662, 680, 785, 797, 810, 816, 832
Ashford, Arthur 545
Ashford, Jack 262, 468, 714
Ashford, Nickolas 15, 17, 92, 231, 271, 348, 349, 430, 586, 600, 619, 660, 663, 664, 807
Ashford, Rosalyn 445, 446
Ashley, Tyrone **18**
Ashton, Floyd 667
Askey, Gil 145, 328, 334, 372, 548
Association 509, 540
Assunto, Frank 447, 664
Assunto, Fred 428
Astley, Rick 464
Aston, Jay 166
Astors **18**, 19, 498, 777, 778, 802
Atkins, Cholly 107, 266
Atkins, Mickey 263, 522
Atkins, Roger 206
Atkinson, Sweet Pea **19**
Atlantic Starr **19**, 20, 184, 358, 471, 621, 777
Atlantis 825
Atley, Harold 601
Atmosfear **20**
Atom Heart 640
Attwood, Thomas 241
Audio Two 9
Auger, Brian 280
August, Lynn 813
Aurra **20**, 21, 70, 127, 622
Ausec, Mark 746
Austin, Billy & the Hearts 827
Austin, Claire 599
Austin, Dallas 168, 258, 478, 599, 666, 667, 691
Austin, Danny 4
Austin, Johnta 1
Austin, Larry 614
Austin, Patti **21**, 22, 336, 720
Austin, Sil 73
Autographs 369
Autry, Gene 134, 822
Avalon, Frankie 176, 318, 400, 438, 557, 579, 820, 848
Avalons 242, 806
Avant **22**, 316
Avant, Clarence 136, 629, 758
Avant, Myron 22, 629, 757
Average White Band **22**, 23, 60, 81, 88, 217, 227, 298, 341, 392, 444, 466, 536, 560, 607, 622, 648, 669, 695, 727, 801, 809, 847
Averne, Harvey 517
Avery, James 698
Avig, Stuart 712
Avons 577, 780, 827, 833
Axelrod, David **23**, 24, 25, 563, 564, 565, 825
Axt, Kevin 710
Axton, Hoyt 442
Ayers, Roy 20, **25**, 26, 29, 53, 74, 142, 159, 219, 230, 234, 324, 418, 485, 556, 559, 594, 647, 671, 801, 802, 825, 830
Ayers, Roy Ubiquity 25
Ayers, Virginia 142
Aykroyd, Dan 62, 169, 598
Ayre, Tom 177
Az Yet 27, 72
Aznavour, Charles 375, 640
Azoff, Irving 155
Azteca 213, 227

B

B 52's 102, 139, 676
B Two K **27**
B, Stevie 27, 686
B., Angie 606
B., Jon **27**, 29, 492, 686
B., Stevie **27**
Babbitt, Bob 202, 263, 730
Baby Face 575
Baby Ford 773
Baby Huey **27**, 28, 793
Baby Huey & the Baby Sitters 803
Bacchus, Brian 109
Bach, Johann Sebastian 88, 696, 697
Bacharach, Burt 16, 98, 104, 132, 152, 175, 238, 244, 252, 256, 260, 276, 283, 284, 295, 321, 326, 348, 359, 388, 397, 399, 404, 405, 420, 422, 472, 543, 579, 589, 592, 612, 613, 639, 666, 682, 713, 728, 729, 730, 731, 755, 761, 818, 821
Bacharach/Bayer Sager 640
Bacharach/David 19, 186, 239, 655, 728, 729, 731, 784
Bachelors 148
Bachman, Randy 358
Backstreet Boys 155, 332, 374, 499, 689
Backus, Gus 184, 185
Bad Boy Bill 150, 606
Bad Brains 102
Badham, John 40
Badu, Erykah 14, **29**, 175, 284, 388, 451, 487, 509, 525, 646, 768, 815
Baermann, Carl 142
Baez, Joan 360
Baeza, Andre 140, 689
Bahamadia 483
Bailey 107, 259
Bailey, J.R. **29**, 824
Bailey, James 107
Bailey, John 148
Bailey, Maureen 430
Bailey, Pearl 810
Bailey, Philip **29**, 30, 62, 214, 215, 216, 259, 387, 394, 450, 582, 645
Baillergeau, Gerald 584
Bailon, Adrienne 688
Bain, Carl 450
Baird, Tom 560
Baker, Anita 7, 8, **30**, 31, 44, 129, 225, 266, 297, 311, 349, 442, 483, 486, 527, 600, 726, 731, 756
Baker, Arthur 202, 317
Baker, Bea 31
Baker, Bill 243
Baker, Chet 127
Baker, Glenn A. 636
Baker, James 499
Baker, LaVern **31**, 95, 172, 409, 480, 562, 755, 804, 818, 830, 836, 838
Baker, Lennie 176
Baker, Mickey **31**, 32, 52, 56, 208, 298, 301, 309, 326, 378, 470, 613, 614, 774, 810
Baker, Ron 240, 296, 317, 318, 319, 468, 677, 697, 740, 741
Baker, Ronnie 468
Baker, Yvonne 606
Baldwin, John Jr. 481
Balgobin, Rupert 361
Balin, Marty 309
Ball 23
Ball, Kimberly 436
Ball, Marcia 402, 684
Ball, Roger 22, 23
Balladeers 616
Ballads **32**, 274
Ballard, Florence **32**, 403, 404, 548, 549, 586, 653, 654, 656, 663, 674, 816
Ballard, Glen 182
Ballard, Hank 32, 33, 85, 87, 90, 167, 343, 365, 514, 635, 688, 839
Ballard, Hank & the Midnighters **32**, 33, 135, 219, 345, 360, 647
Ballard, Robert 773
Ballen, Ivin 115
Baluyut, James 166, 234, 279, 307, 339, 444, 499, 634, 692
Bambaataa, Afrika 85, 218, 281, 317, 402, 820
Banana Splits 240
Bananarama 331, 715
Banashak, Joe 694
Band 129, 130, 192, 193, 694
Bangles 844
Bangs, Lester 124, 702
Banks, Al 701
Banks, Bessie 779, 784, 794, 803
Banks, Bryan 243, 244
Banks, Buddy 659
Banks, Darrell **33**, 34, 36, 37, 114, 410, 439, 754, 755, 768, 792, 808, 818
Banks, Dave 225
Banks, Donald 707
Banks, Doug 812, 818
Banks, Harvey 556
Banks, Homer **34**, 55, 233, 337, 826
Banks, James 95
Banks, Joe 769
Banks, Larry 468
Banks, Mad Mike 821
Banks, Richard "Shiadi" 556
Banks, Ron 79, 203, 204, 243, 244
Banks, Rose **34**, 823
Bar-Kays **34**, 35, 36, 81, 99, 110, 111, 170, 269, 279, 303, 308, 443, 456, 466, 500, 568, 614, 652, 792, 795, 801, 802, 808, 828
Baraka, Amiri 383
Barbara & the Uniques **36**, 209
Barbee, Bertha 715
Barber, Chris 196
Barber, Eddie 775
Barbieri, Gato 159, 555, 558, 728
Barbosa, Chris 407, 609
Barclay 123
Bare, Bobby 279, 692, 805
Barefield, Eddie 627
Barge, Gene 11, **36**, 37, 65, 152, 515, 753
Barker, Danny 195
Barker, George 325
Barker, Guy 312
Barksdale, Chuck 186, 187, 266, 480, 540
Barlow, Dean 828
Barlow, Lou 575
Barnes, Alan 380, 607
Barnes, Eddie 172
Barnes, J.J. **36**, 37, 692, 792, 808, 812
Barnes, James 533
Barnes, Jerry 380
Barnes, John 203, 289, 351
Barnes, Katreese 380
Barnes, Kevin 542
Barnes, Prentiss 266, 479, 480
Barnes, Raymond 409
Barnes, Reggie 237
Barnes, Sidney 247, 589, 607, 780
Barnett, Carl 423
Barnum, H.B. **37**, 80, 312, 334, 443, 505, 508, 564, 628
Baron, Sandy 309
Barons 722
Barrabás **37**
Barranco, John 58
Barrett, Marcia 66
Barrett, Richard 128, 129, 687
Barrett, Ronald 380
Barrett, Vinnie 296, 332
Barretto, Ray 140, 141, 577, 788
Barri, Steve 57, 252, 572, 573, 730
Barrier, Herman 3
Barrio 124
Barrow, Geoff 136
Barrow, Keith **38**, 436
Barry, Claudja **38**, 609, 795
Barry, Jeff 4, 196, 208, 367, 405, 415, 430, 558, 585, 608, 639, 784, 803, 841, 842, 843, 844
Barry, Joe 434
Barry, Kevin 456
Barry, Len 433, 602, 615
Barsalona, Joe 242
Bart, Lionel 729
Bartee, Claude Jr. 13
Bartee, Pete 13
Bartholomew, Dave **38**, 39, 56, 94, 115, 195, 198, 199, 249, 393, 421, 425, 475, 518, 547, 548, 574, 613, 636, 694, 783, 789, 793, 812, 840, 841
Bartholomew, Simon 74
Bartley, Chris **39**, 457, 546
Bartley, Dallas 378
Barton, Dee 136
Bartz, Gary 25, 106, 159, 485
Bascomb, Paul 806
Bascombe, Stuart 53
Bascombe, Wilber 789
Base, Rob 455
Base, Rob & DJ E-Z Rock 155
Bashir, Bilal 833
Basie, Count 24, 48, 131, 230, 263, 375, 376, 392, 512, 559, 562, 610, 627, 658, 668, 701, 739, 755, 777, 857
Basie, Count Big Band 48, 131
Basie, Count Orchestra 48, 430, 515, 610
Basile, Tony 242
Baskerville, Charles 611
Bass, Fontella 6, 36, **39**, 172, 188, 214, 242, 457, 525, 529, 576, 777, 782, 786, 790, 791
Bass, Lance 689
Bass, Martha 36, 529
Bass, Martha and Fontella 39, 529
Bass, Ralph 153, 461
Bassett, Bryan 746
Bassett, Clarence 611
Bassett, Johnnie 611
Bassey, Shirley 729, 787
Bassoline, Cholly 545, 546
Bataan, Joe 92, 517, 597, 792, 819
Bateman, June 800
Bateman, Robert 537, 600, 712
Batiste, Alvin 808
Batiste, Russell 466
Batt, Mike 419
Battiste, Harold 196, 277, 372, 808
Battle, Hinton 828
Battle, Phyllis 238
Battlecat 577, 578
Batts, Ray 783
Baughan, David 207
Baughn, David 206, 208
Baumann, Peter 310
Baylor, Bobby 629
Baylor, Helen 223
Baylor, John 336, 337
Baynard, James 170
Bayyan, Khalis 400, 401
Bayyan, Royal 575
BBC Radiophonic Workshop 589
Beach Boys 45, 49, 413, 414, 450, 559, 571, 635, 703, 781, 834, 839
Beal, Earl 616
Beal, Michael 214
Beale Streeters 3, 280
Bear, Booga 136
Beard, Annette 445, 446, 816
Beard, Joe 222
Beard, Michael 34, 35
Beard, Nidra 212
Beard, Stephanie 408
Beard, Van 408
Bears 313, 368
Bears, Sandra 313, 368
Beasley, David 216, 217
Beastie Boys 227, 634, 724
Beat 239, 240
Beaters 716
Beatles 8, 24, 34, 36, 37, 40, 47, 49, 50, 54, 65, 68, 73, 81, 92, 99, 113, 114, 115, 128, 132, 134, 135, 149, 150, 152, 162, 177, 178, 191, 198, 214, 215, 239, 244, 252, 255, 256, 261, 287, 292, 303, 309, 310, 311, 316, 319, 330, 340, 354, 362, 371, 381, 392, 397, 406, 407, 414, 418, 420, 424, 425, 467, 487, 514, 520, 536, 537, 542, 545, 546, 549, 554, 555, 558, 561, 564, 570, 579, 583, 612, 635, 653, 663, 697, 703, 704, 706, 728, 729, 749, 750, 755, 763, 764, 766, 779, 783, 792, 805, 838, 839, 842, 844, 845, 846
Beatmasters 15
Beaton, Keith 61
Beau Brummels 624
Beaubian, Susan 219
Beaumont, Jimmy 621
Beavers, Jackey 80, 721, 799
Beck Family 665
Beck, Alan 626
Beck, Billy 486, 502, 583
Beck, Jeff 50, 169, 320, 442, 605, 720
Beck, Joe 376
Beckett, Barry 314
Beckett, Wilson 384
Becton, Shelton 399
Bee Gees 31, **40**, 41, 118, 119, 125, 145, 182, 212, 220, 221, 236, 245, 278, 316, 366, 384, 444, 457, 509, 560, 582, 592, 650, 653, 658, 668, 669, 700, 729, 796, 797, 847
Bee, Jimmy **41**

Beedle, Ashley 99
Beeks, Morris 634
Beenie Man 548, 810
Beethoven, Ludwig van 88, 790
BEF 706
Beginning of the End **41**, 809
Beitle, Ron 746
Bel-Aires 801
Belafonte, Harry 135, 413, 490
Belcher, Linnie 10
Belfield, Dennis 592
Belgrave, Marcus 131
Bell Biv DeVoe 13, **41**, 72, 82, 369, 496, 497, 698
Bell Notes **41**, 42, 408, 805
Bell 185, 268, 497, 649
Bell, Al 36, 58, 248, 498, 641
Bell, Archie 42, 723, 777, 848
Bell, Archie & the Drells **42**, 44, 268, 460, 540, 820, 829, 835
Bell, Bernard 692
Bell, Chris 72
Bell, Gary 701
Bell, Kevin 384
Bell, Larry 117
Bell, Lee 42
Bell, Norma Jean **43**
Bell, Norman 747
Bell, Pedro 265
Bell, Reuben 814, 823
Bell, Ricky 41, 82, 496, 497, 698
Bell, Robert 277, 400, 401, 402
Bell, Robert "Kool" 401
Bell, Ronald 384, 400, 402
Bell, Sam 223, 473
Bell, Steve 439
Bell, Thom 21, 42, **43**, 60, 64, 78, 104, 122, 142, 185, 186, 268, 277, 292, 319, 328, 338, 348, 381, 423, 465, 497, 506, 527, 600, 610, 620, 631, 636, 637, 638, 639, 649, 650, 677, 717, 730, 741, 748, 749, 785, 786, 794, 795, 801, 834, 848
Bell, Tony 637
Bell, William 5, **43**, 44, 96, 143, 248, 359, 660, 716, 777, 778, 786, 792, 802, 804, 825, 828
Bellaire, Lloyd 475
Bellamy, Howard 203, 670
Belle, Bernard 45
Belle, Regina 11, **44**, 45, 96, 129, 195, 225, 442, 486, 671, 742, 768, 785, 788
Bellmon, Johnny 195
Bellotte, Pete 484, 617, 650, 651
Bells 828
Bellson, Louie 102
Belmonts **45**, 46, 193, 194
Belolo, Henri 717
Beltones 827
Belushi, James 62
Belushi, Jim 62
Belushi, John 62, 169, 181, 598
Belvin, Jesse **46**, 247, 434, 448, 461, 532, 669, 766, 769, 782, 815, 836
Ben Israel, Yackov 214
Ben Israel, Yehudah 535
Ben, Jorge 448
Ben-Ari, Miri 367
Benatar, Pat 562
Benet, Eric **47**, 230, 366, 602
Benford, Vassal 6, 358
Benitez, Jellybean 383, 718
Benjamin, Bennie 714, 845
Benjamin, Benny 262, 263, 360, 714, 754, 832
Benjamin, Von Elle 222
Bennett, Boyd 70, 332, 812
Bennett, Estelle 584
Bennett, Nedra 584
Bennett, Ronnie 584
Bennett, Tony 559
Bennett, Veronica 172, 584, 635
Bennett, Wayne 57, 58, 102, 456
Benson, Al 153, 219, 436, 806
Benson, George 21, 25, 26, **47**, 48, 92, 98, 159, 168, 257, 377, 383, 444, 513, 536, 555, 594, 666, 684, 710, 760, 793, 810, 857, 858
Benson, Jo Jo 602, 603
Benson, John 9
Benson, Obie 273
Benson, Renaldo 251
Benson, Ricci 585
Benson, Yvette 296
Benton, Brook 5, **48**, 49, 56, 57, 91, 95, 255, 302, 379, 458, 462, 480, 621, 733, 759, 760, 785, 786, 791, 807
Benton, Carla 296
Berg, Bob 540
Berg, Joakim 690
Berger, Ernest 308
Bergeron, Shirley 378, 688
Bergman, Alan 21
Bergman, Marilyn 21
Berkeley, Tyrone 708
Berlin, Irving 132, 197, 272, 342, 573, 658
Berliner, Jay 47
Berlmon, Joni 430
Bernard, Rod 790
Bernhard, Sandra 662
Berns, Bert **49**, 100, 208, 258, 296, 340, 343, 364, 405, 418, 438, 473, 557, 804, 842
Bernstein, Leonard 21, 256, 276, 754
Berry, Albert 707
Berry, Bill 281, 426, 558
Berry, Chuck 31, 33, 39, **49**, 50, 51, 52, 56, 73, 80, 102, 108, 113, 114, 135, 162, 167, 178, 191, 192, 198, 207, 340, 361, 379, 390, 425, 480, 487, 494, 495, 782, 790, 793, 805, 836
Berry, John 167
Berry, John [Country] 558
Berry, Richard **51**, 52, 279, 360, 516, 518, 749, 774, 801, 821
Best, Beatrice 368
Best, Michael 574
Best, Nathaniel 505
Best, Skeeter 131
Beverly & Duane **52**
Beverly, Frankie 30, 74, 444, 455, 456, 652
Bewley Brothers 660
Bickerton, Wayne 247
Biddu 134, 135, 362
Biddu Orchestra 135
Big Apple Band 138, 497, 582
Big Black 448
Big Boi 221
Big Bopper **52**, 427
Big Boys 688
Big Brother & the Holding Company 438, 557, 654
Big Bub 692
Big Chief 179
Big Daddy Kane 61, 98, 223, 227, 304, 377, 482, 742
Big Ella 692
Big Joe 297
Big L 628
Big Maybelle 31, **52**, 296, 722, 790, 792, 814, 818, 830, 836
Big Miller 307
Big Punisher 17, 810
Big Star 71, 72
Big Taylor 518
Big Willie 436
Biggs, Cynthia 405, 723
Biggs, Howard 52, 242, 562, 627
Biggs, Travis **52**
Bihari Brothers 300, 774
Bihari, Joe 345
Bilal 141
Bilk, Acker 391
Billingslea, Joe 160
Billington, Scott 5, 6, 69, 95, 684
Billops, Quincy Clifton Jr. 508, 516
Billups, Sandy 76
Billups, Viola 247
Billy & Lillie 805
Binder, Dennis 702
Bingham, Dinky 127
Binns, Leroy 135
Birch, Gaylord 83
Bird, Ronnie 31, 160, 413, 773
Birdsong, Cindy 403, 404, 586, 602, 653, 654, 655, 656
Birdsong, Edwin **52**, 53
Birkin, Jane 650
Biscoe, Joey 185
Biscuit 317
Bisi, Oye "Nalls" 535
Bivins, Edward "Sonny" 441
Bivins, Michael 13, 41, 72, 73, 82, 496, 497, 698
Biz Markie 98
Bizet, Georges 804
Bjork 9, 407
Black Box 2, 317, 731, 732, 737, 796
Black Crowes 179, 391
Black Eyed Peas 284, 366
Black Gold 822
Black Ivory **53**, 99, 337, 426, 488, 795, 819
Black Men United 175, 710
Black Merda **53**, 261
Black Nasty **53**, 54
Black Oak Arkansas 166
Black Satin 243
Black, Bill **54**, 113, 809
Black, Bill Combo 113
Black, Carlton 206
Black, Cilla 729
Black, James **54**, 63
Black, Jay 559
Black, Marion 251
Black, Robert 259
Blackbyrds **54**, 55, 541, 829
Blackfoot, J. **55**, 56, 280, 603, 630
Blackfoot, J.D. 56
Blackmon, Larry 2, 82, 110, 111, 112, 290, 628
Blackstreet **56**, 278, 290, 316, 351, 359, 367, 426, 575, 583, 661, 803
Blackwell, Bumps 162, 425, 749, 774, 793, 838
Blackwell, Chris 179, 280, 290
Blackwell, George 18, 688
Blackwell, Otis **56**, 375
Blackwood Brothers 856
Blaine, Hal 555, 640
Blaine, Jerry 107, 512, 806
Blair 796
Blair [1] 54
Blair, Arnold 800
Blair, John 303
Blake, Barbara & the Uniques 36
Blake, Cicero 402, 754, 830
Blake, Holly 205
Blake, John 734
Blake, William 24
Blakely, William 185
Blakey, Art 55, 70, 105, 282, 787, 857
Blakey, Art & the Jazz Messengers 648, 810
Blanc, Mel 715
Bland, Billy **56**
Bland, Bobby "Blue" 3, 56, **57**, 58, 90, 93, 161, 179, 280, 302, 318, 350, 361, 369, 372, 426, 456, 458, 487, 503, 520, 525, 545, 601, 638, 668, 673, 684, 692, 737, 778, 786, 791, 799, 836, 838, 839
Blandon, Richard 209
Blane, Marcie **58**, 191
Blank, Bob 99, 337
Blast, C.L. 184
Blasters 10, 425
Blatt, Melanie 9
Blazers 83
Bledsoe, Fern 235
Blendells 788
Blenders 172, 717
Blenders [Soul] 160
Bleu, Frankie 801
Bley, Carla 442, 808
Bley, Paul 241, 386, 606
Blige, Mary J. 11, 28, **58**, 59, 75, 77, 100, 225, 230, 240, 244, 259, 300, 317, 357, 367, 417, 460, 470, 519, 547, 572, 575, 585, 646, 661, 700, 736, 810, 816
Blisters 793
Blocker, Joe 383
Blondie 606, 612, 844
Blood, Sweat & Tears 182, 316, 330, 507, 559
Bloodstone 3, 22, **59**, 60, 444, 615, 626
Bloom, Bobby 555
Bloom, Rube 48
Bloomfield, Michael 196
Blossoms **60**, 172, 279, 319, 430, 634, 770, 778
Blount, Carlton 437
Blow, Kurtis 305, 357, 521, 572, 698, 757, 801
Blowfly **60**, 61, 458, 482, 572, 685
Blu, Peggi 472
Blu, Peggie 578
Blue Chips 831
Blue Diamonds 382
Blue Jays **61**
Blue Magic 60, **61**, 62, 84, 186, 235, 296, 332, 338, 379, 380, 423, 438, 448, 626, 633, 649, 669, 785, 787, 788, 795, 797, 812
Blue Mink 826
Blue Notes 322, 465, 466, 530
Blue Oyster Cult 342
Blue Sky Boys 857
Blue Zone U.K. 640
Blue 463
Blue, Andrew 463
Blue, Barry 308
Bluebelles 405
Bluebells 403, 404
Bluebirds 250
Bluegrass Cardinals 768
Blues Brothers **62**, 67, 141, 169, 487, 598, 828
Blues Brothers Band 248
Blues Rockers 436
Blues, Elwood 62
Blues, Jake 62
Blumberg, David 380, 727
Blunt, Robbie 320
Bo, Eddie 54, **62**, 63, 195, 612, 778, 782, 792, 807, 808
Boatwright, Grant 290
Bob & Earl **63**, 103, 150, 180, 318, 414, 415, 792, 795, 808, 809
Bob B. Soxx & the Blue Jeans 60, 279, 430, 634, 635, 636, 770
Bobbettes **63**, 779
Bobo, Willie 517
Bocage, Frank 475
Bocage, Peter 62
Body 757
Bofill, Angela 21, **64**, 159, 304, 600, 664, 720
Bogan, Anne 266, 447, 495, 496
Bogart, Neil 244, 339, 430, 472, 498
Bogen, Joel 359
Boggs, Tom 72
Bohannon **64**, 65, 414
Bohannon, George 383, 594, 829
Bohannon, Hamilton 35, 64, 65, 778
Bolan, Marc 374
Bolian, Jesse 16
Bolick, Earl 63, 674
Bolin, Tommy 43
Bolland, Bob 645
Bolland, Ferdi 645
Bolton, Michael 1, 150, 336, 484, 695, 847
Bomb Squad 227
Bonafide 27
Bond, Angelo 279, 313, 320, 509
Bond, James E. 13
Bond, Kevin 486
Bond, Maceo 513
Bonds, Gary "U.S." 36, **65**, 135, 145, 210, 547, 680, 805, 806
Bone Thugs-N-Harmony **66**, 359, 744
Boney James 22
Boney M **66**, 67
Bonfa, Luiz 686
Bongiovi, Tony 202, 276
Bonham, Vincent 566
Bonne Villes **67**
Bonner, Juke Boy 798
Bonner, Leroy "Sugarfoot" 502, 503, 504, 737
Bono, Sonny 199, 443, 784
Bonura, Carl 41
Boogie Down Productions 66, 833
Booker T. & the MG's 67
Booker T. & the MG's 34, 36, 44, **67**, 68, 113, 139, 166, 169, 371, 442, 443, 458, 466, 467, 469, 515, 568, 569, 598, 641, 644, 671, 682, 780, 792, 802, 844
Booker, Chuckii 30, **69**, 300, 573, 742, 743
Booker, James 54, **69**, 70, 197, 815
Boom, Taka **70**, 79, 205, 414, 745
Boomerang 389
Boone, Debby 117
Boone, Larry 667, 688
Boone, Pat 93, 198, 424, 798
Booth, Henry 32
Bop Chords **70**, 806
Borden, David 484
Borders, Tony 834
Borodin, Alexander 188
Borowiak, Tony 9
Borrell, Craig 177, 606
Bostic, Earl **70**, 71, 720, 838
Boston, Russell 166
Bottrell, Bill 355

Boudreaux, Monk 746
Bouknight, Nate 611
Boulanger, Nadia 375
Boulton, Nigel 652
Boulware, Will 313
Bounty Killer 366
Bourelly, Jean-Paul 222
Bowden, Al 491
Bowden, Stephen 727
Bowen, Jeffrey 124, 544, 580, 677
Bowen, John 144
Bowers, David "Boots" 409
Bowes, Tom 695
Bowie, Bahnamous Lee 39
Bowie, David **71**, 136, 139, 177, 308, 321, 407, 418, 419, 465, 571, 582, 706, 847, 848
Bowie, Lester 39
Bowlegged Lou 575
Bowles, Thomas "Beans" 579
Bowles, Thomas Sr. 823
Bowman, Priscilla 810
Bowman, Rob 69, 266
Bowman, Wayne 413
Box Tops **71**, 72, 128, 150, 362, 466, 835, 847
Boxtel, Ben 496, 499
Boy George 15, 124, 125, 172, 173, 466, 539, 646
Boy Howdy 417
Boy, Bobby 405
Boyce & Greene 414
Boyce & Hart 414
Boyce, Jannetta 775
Boyce, Tommy 414, 600
Boyd, Al 332, 333, 633, 700, 800
Boyd, Eddie 805
Boyd, Joe 69
Boyd, Skip 70
Boyd, Steve 244
Boyd, Tony 546
Boyer, Charles 473
Boyer, Greg 313
Boyfriends 242
Boykins, DeAndre 386
Boys 691
Boyz II Men 9, 13, 28, 41, **72**, 73, 112, 115, 116, 155, 176, 209, 323, 337, 359, 368, 383, 390, 492, 496, 497, 498, 499, 510, 573, 574, 617, 666, 718, 719, 839, 848
Brackman, Jacob 730
Bradford, Alex & the Bradford Singers 31
Bradford, Carmen 48
Bradford, Janie 653
Bradley, Carter 622
Bradley, Charlie 622
Bradley, Don 443, 717
Bradley, Jan 782, 790, 829
Bradley, Louis 219
Bradley, Owen 309
Bradley, Rolland 752
Bradshaw, Tiny **73**, 74, 491, 492, 777, 812, 836, 838
Bragg, Johnny **74**, 552, 553
Brahms, Johannes 88
Brailey, Jerome 488, 556
Braily, Jerome "Bigfoot" 488
Brainstorm **74**, 769
Braith, George 810
Braithwaite, Wayne 374
Bramble, Derek 308
Bramlett, Delaney 101
Brand New Heavies 23, **74**, 75, 140, 381, 483, 705
Brand Nubian 25, 358, 668, 769
Brandon, Bill 798, 799, 834
Brandy 73, **75**, 76, 190, 367, 478, 492, 525, 629, 666
Brantley, Johnny 502
Brashear, Oscar 76, 77, 142, 383, 384, 594
Brass Construction **76**, 98, 170, 312, 338, 449, 450, 473, 622
Brass Fever **76**, 77
Brass, Bob 688
Braxton, Tamar **77**
Braxton, Toni 27, 28, 29, **77**, 78, 128, 358, 367, 481, 492, 573
Braxton, Towanda 77
Braxton, Trina 77
Braxtons 77
Bread 30, 256, 379, 438, 517, 639, 657
Breakwater 792
Bream, Julian 192
Breathe 525
Brecker Brothers 154
Brecker, Michael 23, 38, 540, 723
Brecker, Randy 23, 30
Breedlove, Jimmy 172, 562
Breeze 737
Brel, Jacques 375
Brenda & the Tabulations **78**, 448, 722, 799, 813, 834
Brenston, Jackie **78**, 421, 702, 703
Breslau, Andy 319
Brewer, Alma 367
Brick **78**, 79, 157, 394, 829
Brickell, Edie 444
Bricker, Gene 443
Brickley, Audrey 512
Brickley, Shirley 512
Bricusse, Leslie 639
Brides 79
Brides of Funkenstein 20, 26, **79**, 98, 215, 269, 306, 522, 795
Bridges, Alicia **79**
Bridges, Fred 82, 572
Bridges, Gil 559, 560
Bridges, Lloyd 582
Bridges, Willie 475
Bridgewater, Joe 130, 131
Brigadier Jerry 380
Brigati, Eddie 218, 226, 561, 571
Briggs, Anne 692
Briggs, Fred 33, 379, 692
Briggs, Kimberly 692
Briggs, She'kspere 189
Bright, Jeryl 74
Bright, Larry **79**, 80
Brighter Side of Darkness **80**
Brimmer, Charles 824
Brincos 37
Brines, Phil 263
Brinsley Schwarz 150
Brinson, Ted 492
Briscoe, Jimmy 80
Briscoe, Jimmy & the Little Beavers **80**
Bristol, Dee 183
Bristol, Johnny **80**, 168, 201, 227, 266, 272, 397, 580, 591, 601, 610, 645, 647, 668, 669, 670, 720, 721, 799, 823
Britt, Tina 15, 783
Brittnam, Marion 96
Broadways 784
Brocco, Joe 242
Brockmann, Bob 747
Bronski Beat 662
Brookins, Robert 47, 513, 741
Brooklyn Bridge 169, 239, 341, 436
Brooks & Dunn 107, 268, 279
Brooks, Arthur 103, 333
Brooks, Billy 545
Brooks, Charles 107
Brooks, Garth 259
Brooks, Hadda 218
Brooks, La La 171, 172
Brooks, Louis 268, 800
Brooks, Orville 409
Brooks, Patti 430
Brooks, Ramona 796
Brooks, Richard 103, 333
Brooks, Tina 787
Broomfield, Ronald 747
Broonzy, Big Bill 810, 815
Brother to Brother **81**, 779
Brotherly Love 279
Brothers Johnson **81**, 82, 156, 308, 376, 377, 474, 515, 542, 572, 710
Brothers of Soul **82**
Brothers 81
Broussard, Trina 727
Broven, Jon 450
Browder, Stony 196, 389
Brown Dots 337
Brown Sugar 740
Brown, Aaron 525
Brown, Al 519
Brown, Barbara 750, 789
Brown, Bertram 55
Brown, Bill 726
Brown, Billy 477, 478, 565, 566, 688, 740
Brown, Bobby 28, 41, 59, **82**, 83, 277, 290, 323, 369, 430, 464, 496, 497, 659, 698, 747, 768, 785, 829
Brown, Buster 800, 838
Brown, Charity 83
Brown, Charles **83**, 84, 130, 133, 415, 480, 514, 518, 520, 753, 769, 778, 780, 812, 822, 836, 838
Brown, Charlie 555
Brown, Chuck 84, 698
Brown, Chuck & the Soul Searchers **84**, 699
Brown, Clarence "Gatemouth" 130, 392, 553, 838
Brown, Clifford 55, 105, 732, 733, 768
Brown, Clifford [Jazz] 375
Brown, Clyde 797
Brown, Cordell 209
Brown, Doug 402
Brown, Douglas 219
Brown, Earl 261
Brown, Eddie "Bongo" 262, 263, 714
Brown, Ella 798
Brown, Errol 320, 321
Brown, Garnett 76, 294
Brown, Gary 400, 671
Brown, Gerald 607, 632
Brown, Harold 723, 724
Brown, Henry "Pucho" 554
Brown, Jack 246
Brown, James 7, 32, 47, 48, 58, 62, 63, 67, 69, 71, 74, **85**, 86, 87, 88, 89, 90, 91, 110, 114, 122, 125, 127, 134, 138, 140, 149, 150, 151, 153, 154, 155, 162, 168, 177, 189, 198, 200, 211, 222, 225, 235, 237, 238, 243, 250, 251, 256, 260, 266, 288, 289, 294, 298, 299, 301, 303, 308, 312, 313, 319, 320, 336, 341, 348, 362, 365, 366, 368, 369, 371, 377, 383, 400, 407, 413, 423, 425, 437, 449, 456, 466, 471, 476, 487, 491, 514, 517, 520, 522, 525, 538, 547, 550, 554, 555, 556, 560, 569, 601, 606, 616, 619, 624, 630, 643, 650, 680, 681, 685, 697, 705, 709, 715, 718, 739, 745, 746, 753, 754, 760, 764, 767, 777, 778, 782, 784, 785, 786, 787, 794, 797, 801, 802, 803, 804, 807, 812, 813, 815, 820, 823, 826, 828, 829, 830, 836, 838, 844, 850, 851, 856
Brown, Jimmy 78, 94
Brown, Jocelyn **91**, 92, 135, 147, 195, 335, 337, 488, 597, 778
Brown, John 497
Brown, Josephine 259
Brown, Kenji 585
Brown, Kim 820
Brown, Koffee 45
Brown, Lawrence 701
Brown, LeNard 161
Brown, Marty 712
Brown, Marvin 708
Brown, Maxine **92**, 326, 348, 349, 546, 557, 732, 778, 786, 792, 793, 794, 814, 818, 834, 844
Brown, Mel 530
Brown, Michael 309
Brown, Milton 647
Brown, Morris 98, 393
Brown, Nacio Herb 208
Brown, Nappy **93**, 107, 255, 345, 480, 805, 836
Brown, Norman 202
Brown, Ollie E. 277
Brown, Oscar Jr. 334, 335, 371
Brown, Owen 314
Brown, Paul 22
Brown, Pete 210, 701
Brown, Peter **93**, 147, 488
Brown, Raphael 488
Brown, Ray 30, 222, 376
Brown, Rodney 5, 567, 689
Brown, Roy 85, 90, **93**, 94, 294, 297, 320, 424, 475, 514, 520, 627, 781, 789, 812, 836, 838, 856
Brown, Ruth 4, 5, 31, 63, **94**, 95, 130, 172, 360, 367, 409, 462, 647, 753, 755, 777, 800, 804, 836, 838
Brown, Samuel "Little Sonny" 339
Brown, Shirley **95**, 96, 153, 280, 457, 530, 791, 824, 825, 828, 830
Brown, Stanley 209
Brown, Terry 632, 698
Brown, Tom 324
Brown, Tyrone 734
Brown, Valerie 532
Brown, Veda **96**
Brown, William C. III 436, 477
Browne, Jackson 65, 144, 347, 348, 642, 723, 751, 787
Browne, Tom 21, 768, 795, 802, 829
Brownlee, Archie 428
Brownlee, Larry 428, 719
Brownmark 183
Brownstone **96**, 224, 390, 609
Brubeck, Dave 710
Bruce, Ed 818
Brumbach, John 70
Bruno, Gioia 231, 232
Brunson, Frank 532
Brunson, Frankie 533
Brunson, Tyrone 485, 513
Bruson, Frankie 533
Bryant, Al 220, 548
Bryant, Bobby 759
Bryant, Don **96**, 311, 529, 530, 809
Bryant, Eldridge 674, 804
Bryant, Jason 629
Bryant, Lecoy 449
Bryant, Marty 649, 650
Bryant, Randolph 463
Bryant, Sharon 19, 20
Bryant, Terri 784
Bryant, William 94
Bryson, Peabo 44, 45, **96**, 97, 100, 129, 152, 245, 324, 328, 349, 472, 473, 531, 657, 727, 825
BT Express **97**, 98, 450, 457, 548, 622, 795
Bubba Sparxxx 706
Buccaneers 828
Buchanan, Robbie 609
Buchanan, Wallis 364
Buckethead 488
Buckeyes 798
Buckingham, Steve 413
Buckley, Jeff 141, 690
Buckner, Milt 857
Buckwheat Zydeco 200
Budd, Arthur 185
Buffalo Springfield 24, 362
Buford, Ross 135
Buggles 134, 605
Bugnel, Jim 246
Buie, Charles 497
Bull & the Matadors **98**, 508
Bullock, Ernest 557
Bullock, Mitchell 557
Bullock, Tommy 238
Bumblebee Unlimited 488, 709
Bunn, Allen 408, 409
Burch, Charlene 129
Burch, Vernon 34, **98**, 99
Burden, Ricky 635
Burdon, Eric 259, 340, 513, 582, 724, 759, 847, 851
Burgee, Daryl 121, 309
Burgess, LeRoy 53, **99**, 337, 426, 553, 709, 792, 819
Burke, Alohe Jean 99, 244
Burke, Betty 99, 244
Burke, Byron 679
Burke, Chris 339, 614
Burke, Clarence 99, 244
Burke, Clarence Jr. 99, 244, 339
Burke, Cubie 53, 244
Burke, Dennis 99, 244
Burke, James 99, 244
Burke, Keni **99**, 100, 244, 373, 584, 705, 720
Burke, Kenneth 244, 373
Burke, Laddie 614
Burke, Osaze 100
Burke, Pat 250
Burke, Solomon 49, 62, **100**, 101, 102, 143, 158, 162, 167, 296, 348, 537, 553, 614, 630, 631, 658, 660, 744, 791, 844, 845
Burke, Sonny 109, 509, 580, 581, 727
Burke, Stanley 183
Burke, Val 752
Burnett, Chester Arthur 161
Burnett, Donald 161
Burnett, Norman 707
Burnett, Paul 364
Burnette, Dorsey 296
Burnette, Johnny 460
Burnette, Johnny Trio 480
Burnette, Smiley 192
Burns, Dick 177
Burns, Ralph 48, 131, 256

Burrage, Harold **102**, 179, 180
Burrell, Kenny 52, 133, 256, 288, 298, 714, 759, 760, 857
Burrs, Leslie 734
Burruss, Kandi 772
Burruss, Monica 718
Burston, Keith 479
Burton, James 114
Burton, Lori 405
Burton, Michael 81
Burton, Willard 830
Burvick, Jacques 13, 160
Bus Boys **102**
Busby, Jheryl 691
Bush, Kate 407, 451
Bushnell, Yvonne 307, 365
Busta Rhymes 351
Butera, Sam **102**
Butler, Antonia 108, 261, 540, 541, 718
Butler, Artie 365, 608
Butler, Billy [1] 42, 391, 453, 511, 732
Butler, Billy [2] **102**, 103, 178, 198, 266, 333, 451, 789, 819
Butler, Bobby 241
Butler, Bruce 562
Butler, Charlotte 612
Butler, Floyd 261, 718
Butler, Henry 69
Butler, Jerry 43, 84, 102, **103**, 104, 105, 108, 117, 126, 169, 190, 223, 231, 248, 268, 272, 297, 299, 302, 303, 322, 333, **334**, 335, 380, 395, 400, 407, 414, 451, 452, 453, 476, 505, 527, 533, 570, 588, 618, 619, **681**, 684, 687, 692, 708, 709, 731, 754, 777, 781, 786, 809, 810, 824, 844, 848
Butler, Jerry & the Impressions 103, 179, 375, 473, 692, 712
Butler, Jonathan 202, 705, 727
Butler, Joseph 475
Butler, Larry [Country] 688
Butler, Larry [Rock] 53
Butler, Wanda Nero 53
Buttacavoli, Ronnie James 405
Butterfield, Paul 129
Butterfield, Paul Blues Band 455
Butterflys 803
Buzz, Niki 652
By All Means 11
Byard, Jaki 70
Byers, Ann 820
Bykowski, Ron 218, 219, 264, 306, 523
Bynum, Mark 34
Byrd, Bobby 63, 85, 87, 89, 90, 91, **105**, 365, 366, 798, 812
Byrd, Byron 652
Byrd, Donald 25, 54, 55, **105**, 106, 275, 288, 383, 541, 558, 787, 788, 791, 802, 817, 829
Byrd, Gary 757
Byrd, Henry Roeland 553
Byrd, Robert 318
Byrd, Roy 789
Byrd, Roy & His Blues Jumpers 553
Byrd, Tony 4, 105
Byrds 330, 448, 834
Byrne, David 140, 154, 310, 515, 767, 768
Byron, Dennis 40

C

C & C Music Factory 127, 383, 422, 731, 732, 737
C Note 689
Cabo Frio 747
Cachao 577
Cadets **107**, 149, 345, 423, 508, 674
Cadillacs 29, **107**, 108, 149, 206, 219, 241, 288, 443, 479, 497, 530, 602, 780, 782, 785, 797, 827, 829
Caesar, Shirley 189, 323, 436, 810
Cafferty, John 787
Cahn, Sammy 528
Cain, Randy 185, 186, 296
Cairo 823
Cake 697
Caldwell, Ben 251
Caldwell, Bobby 30, 97, 152
Caldwell, Cedric 757
Caldwell, Happy 73
Caldwell, Nicholas 432, 740, 741
Caldwell, Ronnie 34
Caldwell, Steve 512
Cale, John 419
Calhoun, Andrew 181
Calhoun, Charles E. 647
Calhoun, Michael 394
Calhoun, Moon 592
Calhoun, Robert 716
Calhoun, Roy 12
Callahan, Charles 148
Callender, Red 492
Callier, Terry 103, **108**, 109, 110, 589, 645, 817
Calloway **110**, 470, 471
Calloway, Blanche 94
Calloway, Cab 62, 94, 196, 201, 389, 402, 803, 836
Calloway, James 99, 337, 426
Calloway, Joe 552
Calloway, Reggie 110, 398, 417
Calloway, Vincent 110, 398, 417, 470, 471
Calvin, Billie Rae 708, 745
Calvin, John 402
Calypso King & the Soul Investigators **110**, 807
Calypso Rose 127
Cam'ron 116
Camelots 805
Cameo 2, 20, 81, 82, 102, **110**, 111, 112, 159, 210, 259, 269, 290, 338, 443, 450, 504, 512, 556, 614, 622, 629, 652, 665, 698, 768, 775, 785, 795, 801, 851
Cameron, G.C. **112**, 533, 637, 663, 796, 832
Cameron, Timothy 617
Camillo, Tony 217, 396, 397, 571, 631
Camp Lo 621
Campbell, Alton 123
Campbell, Choker 390, 547
Campbell, Glen 157, 694, 733
Campbell, Jo-Ann 108
Campbell, Kerry 724
Campbell, Luther 482
Campbell, Tevin **112**, 113, 230, 366, 377, 525, 551, 720, 832
Can 264
Candido 399, 788, 792
Candy and the Kisses 268, 325, 792
Canibus 366, 367
Cannady, Darryl 491
Canned Heat 54, 298
Cannibal & the Headhunters **113**, 140, 584, 788
Cannon, Ace **113**, 809, 810
Cannon, Bill 769
Cannon, Freddy 45, 65, **113**, 114, 135, 176, 805
Cantrell, Blu 75, **114**, 696
Capehart, Jerry 7
Capers, Steven Jr. 574
Capitols **114**, 203, 263, 418, 714, 777, 781, 808, 827
Capris **114**, **115**, 839
Captain Beefheart 301
Captain Sky 795
Cara, Irene 453, 484
Caravans 324
Caravans 317
Carbo, Chuck **115**, 636
Carbo, Hayward [see Carbo, Chuck]
Carbo, Leonard "Chick" 115, 636
Cardenas, Billy 621
Cardigans 690
Cardinals 129, 219, 409, 779, 797, 839
Carey, Bill 635
Carey, Jake 246
Carey, Mack 698
Carey, Mariah 6, 10, 11, 28, 72, 73, 75, 77, **115**, 116, 168, 189, 190, 210, 223, 323, 369, 383, 478, 483, 484, 499, 547, 595, 609, 706, 713, 718, 720
Carey, Zeke 246
Carla 792
Carlin, George 585
Carlisle, Belinda 232
Carlisle, Cliff 697
Carlo, Tyran 266, 557, 718, 754, 755
Carlson, Charles 222, 418, 718
Carlton, Carl 15, 70, **117**, 184, 328, 615, 665, 720, 723, 776, 799, 820, 834
Carlton, Larry 170, 171, 640, 727
Carltons **117**, 395
Carlucci, Tony 332
Carlwell, Carl 259
Carman, Paul 125
Carman, Pauli 125
Carmichael, Arnell 521, 566
Carmichael, Darren 521, 566
Carmichael, Greg 99, 337, 395, 426, 709
Carmichael, Gregory 426
Carmichael, Hoagy 131
Carmichael, James Anthony 11, 20, 156, 157, 338, 769
Carmichael, Steve 373
Carn, Doug 117, 715, 788
Carn, Jean 26, **117**, 118, 136, 159, 160, 230, 310, 572, 723, 809, 817, 820
Carnations 107
Carne, Jean 117, 309, 734
Caron, Danny 83
Carousels 827
Carpenter, Karen 14
Carpenter, Richard 263, 693
Carpenters 103, 290, 661, 729
Carr, Barbara **118**, 151, 783
Carr, James **118**, 119, 179, 350, 356, 619
Carr, Jesse 658
Carr, Leroy 131
Carr, Pete 205
Carr, Robert H. 578
Carr, Wynona **119**, 836, 856
Carrack, Paul **119**, 120
Carriere, Linda 212, 427
Carrol, Gregory 512
Carroll, Diahann 416
Carroll, Earl "Speedo" 107, 108, 149
Carroll, Greg 562
Carroll, Porter Jr. 19
Carson, Johnny 413, 668
Carter Brothers **120**
Carter Family 856, 857
Carter, Albert 120
Carter, Benny 70, 415
Carter, Betty 131, 134, 228, 296, 389
Carter, Big Lucky 809
Carter, Blanche 148
Carter, Bruce 688
Carter, Calvin 402, 635
Carter, Carlene 120
Carter, Charles 20, 622
Carter, Chuck 233
Carter, Clarence 118, **120**, 121, 124, 299, 350, 545, 590, 753, 791, 799, 834, 847
Carter, Darryl 760
Carter, Ed 463
Carter, Goree 297
Carter, Helen 687
Carter, James 106
Carter, Jerry 120
Carter, Jimmy 241
Carter, Joe Lee 809
Carter, Joe 187
Carter, John [1] 402
Carter, John [2] 187
Carter, Johnny 186, 187, 219, 246
Carter, Kenny 794
Carter, Leslie 614
Carter, Mel **121**, 164, 818
Carter, Melvin 157
Carter, Roman 120
Carter, Ron 25, 29, 47, 159, 245, 256, 295, 561, 603, 611, 735, 811
Carter, Roy 308
Carter, Sam 622
Carter, Stephen 226
Carwell, Sue Ann 259
Casale, Suzanne 421
Casanovas 827
Cascades **121**
Casey, Brandon 359
Casey, Brian 359
Casey, Harry Wayne "K.C." 384, 385, 458, 572
Casey, John 41
Cash, Alvin **121**
Cash, Alvin & the Crawlers 121, 747, 748
Cash, Andrew 628
Cash, Fred 235, 244, 333, 334, 335, 408
Cash, Johnny 74, 100, 102, 132, 134, 195, 458, 809, 857
Cashflow 747
Cashmere **121**, 309
Casinos **121**, 799, 805
Cason, Buzz 173
Cason, Richard 96
Casserine 367
Cassidy, David 689
Castaways 696
Castelles **121**, 122, 438, 512, 557, 701, 806
Castells 805
Castillo, Emilio 353
Caston, Leonard 36, 387, 450, 451, 557, 790
Caston, Victor 557
Castor, Jimmy 122, 123, 829
Castor, Jimmy Bunch **122**, 416
Casuals 437
Cat Daddy 629
Catfish 263, 522
Cauley, Ben 34
Cavaliere, Felix 561
Cavaliers 606, 700
Cavanaugh, David 415
Cave, Claude 440, 441
Cayre, Joe 338, 597
Cayre, Ken 597
Cayre, Stan 597
Cecil, Malcolm 365, 603
Cellos **123**, 577, 805, 827
Cenas, Bundie 440
Ceniceros, Jacob 500
Center Stage 822
Cephus, Van 129
Ceroni, Ray 41
Cerrone 92, **123**, 170, 255, 317, 321, 796
Certain Ratio 20
Cetera, Peter 727
Chairmen of the Board **123**, 124, 202, 279, 315, 320, 331, 370, 415, 509, 614, 658, 789, 809, 811, 812, 819, 826
Chakachas **124**, 724, 792
Challengers 266
Chalmers, Charles 326, 476
Chambers Brothers **124**, 125, 488, 857
Chambers, Gordon 545
Chambers, Joe 125
Chambers, Karl 297, 468
Chambers, Paul 391
Chambers, Roland 468, 639, 723
Chamblee, Eddie 732
Champaign **125**
Champion, Miss Mickey 798
Champs 124, 390
Chan, Leo 383
Chance, James 389
Chance, Larry 213, 214
Chance, Nolan **125**, 209, 210, 228, 792
Chancler, Leon "Ndugu" 142, 413, 594
Chandeliers 805, 829
Chandler, Barbara 696
Chandler, Chas 3, 209, 210
Chandler, Gene 3, 102, 125, **126**, 127, 167, 178, 209, 228, 317, 334, 358, 371, 407, 414, 451, 452, 453, 464, 619, 709, 754, 777, 782, 786, 788, 789, 790, 791, 792, 793, 797, 798, 799, 805, 810, 812, 826, 830, 833, 844
Chandler, Lorraine 821
Chaney, Ken 773, 774
Change 92, **127**, 139, 140, 312, 416, 712, 713
Changing Faces **127**, 128
Channel Three 833
Channel, Bruce **128**
Channels 70, **128**, 246, 464, 803, 806
Channey, Walter 332
Chantels **128**, 129, 170, 201, 340, 367, 368, 549, 609, 653, 687, 786, 827, 843
Chanters **129**, 783, 798
Chanteuses 179
Chants 566
Chaperones 822, 834
Chapman, Grady 578
Chapman, Romell 13
Chapman, Thomas 32
Chapman, Tracy 14
Chapter Eight 30, **129**, 190, 423
Chapter One 834
Charades 784
Charlene **129**
Charles, Bobby 5, **129**, 130, 310, 790, 840
Charles, Denis 339, 628
Charles, Jimmy 220, 244
Charles, Joe 718

Charles, Lee 792, 811
Charles, Ray 5, 15, 17, 32, 33, 36, 57, 62, 81, 85, 92, 95, 101, **130**, 131, 132, 133, 134, 143, 153, 186, 243, 255, 256, 258, 261, 269, 277, 283, 293, 299, 307, 336, 340, 341, 348, 349, 369, 375, 376, 377, 378, 388, 390, 418, 420, 426, 430, 454, 455, 461, 520, 535, 546, 560, 565, 570, 574, 596, 611, 619, 623, 632, 647, 666, 694, 697, 700, 706, 710, 718, 720, 737, 749, 753, 754, 756, 759, 760, 763, 764, 770, 773, 780, 781, 786, 814, 816, 836, 838, 844, 845, 856
Charles, Sandra 479
Charles, Sonny 136
Charles, Sweet 91
Charles, Teddy 70
Charles, Tina **134**, 135, 362
Charlie & Ray 251, 464
Charmels 683, 813
Charmettes 367
Charo 597, 722
Charters, Samuel 108
Charts **135**, 165
Chase 330
Chase, Lincoln 222
Chase, Peter 523
Chasez, JC 689
Chatman, Christine 52
Chea, Alvin 666
Cheap Trick 358
Cheatham, Doc 135
Cheatham, Jeannie & Jimmy 115
Cheatham, Keith 652
Cheatham, Oliver **135**
Checker, Chubby 32, 33, 43, 63, 65, 88, **135**, 167, 205, 222, 238, 443, 558, 612, 635, 688, 820
Checkmates Ltd. **136**
Chee-Chee and Peppy 826
Cheech & Chong 670
Cheek, Callie 384
Cheek, Michael 384
Cheeks, Julius 164
Chen, Phil 361, 419
Chenier, Cleveland 153, 722
Chenier, Clifton 790, 793
Cher 277, 309, 416, 430, 784
Cherebin, Curtis 295
Cherelle **136**, 309, 511, 529
Cheren, Mel 270
Cherokees 806
Cherries 136
Cherry, Ava **136**
Cherry, Don 136, 796
Cherry, Eagle-Eye 690
Cherry, Neneh 9, **136**, 137, 385, 478, 690
Chess, Leonard 49, 129, 192, 266, 360, 480, 645, 790, 838
Chess, Phil 50, 480, 790
Chessler, Deborah 511
Chestnuts 500
Chi-Lites 3, 4, 120, **137**, 138, 178, 187, 237, 414, 416, 428, 436, 468, 510, 567, 754, 755, 785, 786, 789, 790, 809, 814, 817, 824
Chic 14, 30, 38, 42, 71, 79, 81, 100, 127, **138**, 139, 140, 170, 234, 312, 336, 374, 375, 428, 432, 497, 513, 522, 540, 582, 583, 587, 603, 619, 620, 621, 622, 623, 629, 631, 686, 698, 705, 712, 723, 770, 795, 797, 831
Chicago 182, 269, 507, 521, 727
Chicago Gangsters **140**
Chicano El **140**, 141, 254, 621, 689, 787
Chiffons **141**, 172, 584, 778, 784, 809, 818, 842, 843, 844
Child, Desmond 144
Child, Jane 290
Childs, Barney 234
Childs, Billy 307, 735
Childs, Wallace 234
Chilli 691
Chilton, Alex 71, 72, 529, 847
Chimes [1] **141**, 307, 631, 740
Chimes [2] 381
Chin, Brian 385
Chinmoy, Sri 145, 720
Chips **141**, 795, 828
Chocolate Genius **141**
Chocolate Jam Co. **142**
Chocolate Milk **142**, 694
Chocolate Syrup 203
Chocolate Watchband 374, 561
Choice Four **142**, 395, 437
Chong, Tommy 669, 670
Chopin, Frederic 69
Chords **142**, 779, 793, 797
Chosen Gospel Singers 314, 563
Chrisman, Gene 211, 466
Christian, Arlester "Dyke" 211
Christian, Charlie 47, 170
Christian, Earl 364
Christian, Tim 692
Christie, Lou 13
Christopher, Gavin 260, 593
Christopher, Gretchen 247
Chubby & the Turnpikes 669, 767, 799
Church, Eugene 46
Church, Jimmy 819
Church, Ralph 234
Churchill, Tony 495, 499
Cinderellas 809
Ciner, Al 592
Cintron, Tony 709
Cita, Raoul 295, 296
City, Mike 11, 316
Clan 166
Clanton, Ed "Mickey" 225
Clanton, Jimmy 108, 781
Clapton, Eric 22, 28, 29, 51, 95, 176, 196, 202, 220, 243, 390, 392, 452, 573, 699, 832
Clapton, Eric Band 221
Clark Sisters 286
Clark, Charles 102, 247, 248
Clark, Chris **142**, 143
Clark, Chris 142, 143, 642, 670, 790
Clark, Claudie "Nicky" 241
Clark, Claudine 784, 843
Clark, Dave Five 52, 180, 779
Clark, Dee 56, **143**, 219, 369, 402, 463, 784, 786, 792, 810, 821
Clark, Dick 1, 32, 113, 114, 135, 161, 176, 336, 400, 464, 473, 532, 547, 616, 668, 685, 754
Clark, Doug & Hot Nuts 60, 61
Clark, James "Poppa" 107, 241, 735
Clark, Jimmy 217
Clark, John "Sonny Boy" 241
Clark, Margie 313, 368
Clark, Mattie Moss 15
Clark, Mike 294, 307
Clark, Petula 68, 412, 825
Clark, Robin 136
Clark, Roderick 686
Clark, Roy 80
Clark, Rudy 566
Clark, Shellie 319, 320, 432
Clarke, Stanley 188, 311, 376, 388, 389, 558
Clarke, Tony [1] 788, 790
Clarke, Tony [2] 362, 782
Clarke, Willie 423, 458
Clash 191, 200, 226, 416, 628, 796
Class Action 99, 488
Classics 489
Classmates 827
Claudette 579
Claunch, Quinton 118
Claussell, Joe 383, 416, 825
Clay, Andrew Dice 264
Clay, Joe 809
Clay, John 709
Clay, Judy 43, 44, 96, **143**, 341, 479, 660, 716, 728, 804, 818, 828, 834
Clay, Otis 96, 102, 118, **143**, 144, 179, 311, 457, 476, 809, 810
Clay, Richard 159
Claypool, Les 154
Clayton, Buck 31, 759
Clayton, Harold 629
Clayton, Lee 63, 728
Clayton, Merry 52, 459, 572, 829
Clayton, Willie **144**
Clearmountain, Bob 202
Cleaves, Jessica 214, 215, 261, 718
Cleaves, Slaid 261
Clefs 773
Cleftones 123, **144**, 577, 827, 831
Clement, Denise 195
Clemons, Clarence **144**, 145, 257, 640, 720, 787
Cleopatra **145**
Cleveland, Al 293
Cleveland, James 153, 255, 256, 258, 583, 584, 857
Clickettes 226
Cliff, Jimmy 104, 150, 241, 490, 768
Clifford, Linda 6, 96, **145**, 146, 173, 304, 317, 321, 328, 397, 453, 457, 602, 679, 793
Cline, Patsy 682
Clinton, George 18, 34, 37, 69, 70, 79, 81, 84, 98, 102, 103, 124, 140, **146**, 147, 153, 154, 165, 181, 187, 214, 215, 224, 241, 260, 263, 264, 265, 266, 269, 299, 306, 310, 338, 348, 363, 366, 381, 411, 437, 486, 488, 517, 520, 522, 523, 524, 525, 535, 550, 551, 571, 583, 624, 625, 690, 699, 736, 739, 752, 767, 775, 782, 785, 850, 851
Clinton, Larry 409
Cliques 46
Clivilles & Cole 422
Clivilles, Robert 422
Clooney, George 427
Clooney, Rosemary 749
Cloud One **147**, 488, 795, 796
Cloud, Vanette 475
Clouden, Juan 450
Clovers 107, 121, 131, **148**, 149, 172, 295, 480, 647, 779, 781, 782, 784, 794, 797, 798, 818, 839
Clowney, David 166, 557
Clowns 626, 627
Club Nouveau **149**, 224, 690, 758
Coach House Rhythm Section 796
Coakley, Kirkwood 665
Coakley, Theophilus "T" 665
Coasters 46, 51, 52, 107, 108, 123, 148, **149**, 176, 179, 206, 207, 238, 242, 246, 293, 318, 336, 380, 390, 400, 415, 508, 509, 532, 535, 539, 578, 626, 629, 634, 702, 774, 779, 781, 814, 839, 842
Coates, Maurice 78
Cobb, Arnett 128, 780
Cobb, Ed 374, 416
Cobb, Jimmy 71, 733
Cobb, Joe 277
Cobb, Joyce 686
Cobb, Margaret 128
Cobham, Billy 25, 47, 376, 383, 648, 720
Cocco, Lenny 141
Cochran, Eddie 7, 108, 176, 480, 518
Cochran, James "Dimples" 635
Cochran, Todd 289, 434
Cochran, Wayne 63, **149**, 150, 293, 307, 365
Cochran, Wayne & the C.C. Riders 150
Cochrane, Todd 289
Cocker, Jarvis 354
Cocker, Joe 62, 79, 130, **150**, 582, 694
Coconuts 390
Coday, Bill **150**, 151, 719, 783
Codish, Chris 179
CODs 428, 436, 818
Coe, David Allan 130
Coffee, Erma 809, 810
Coffey, Dennis 234, 263
Cogbill, Tommy 211, 520, 692
Coggins, Danny 479, 480
Coghill, Phil 700
Cohen, Leonard 150, 194, 494, 635
Cohen, Ted 235
Cohran, Phil 535
Cohran, Philip & the Artistic Heritage Ensemble 535
Coko 661
Colbert, Chuck 592
Colbert, Godoy 259
Colbert, John 35, 55
Cold Blood **151**, 807
Coldcut 38, 640
Coldten, Melvin 408
Coldwater Stone 33, 379, 692
Cole, Ann 583, 781, 797, 804, 829
Cole, Cozy 786
Cole, David 422
Cole, Nat King 11, 46, 47, 48, 49, 50, 83, 86, 87, 130, 133, 151, 152, 172, 206, 272, 277, 293, 326, 358, 369, 433, 462, 463, 477, 563, 571, 755, 777
Cole, Nat King Trio 83
Cole, Natalie 30, 36, 96, 97, 100, **151**, 152, 153, 212, 229, 244, 336, 470, 471, 515, 519, 583, 657, 720
Coleman, Andrew 546, 712
Coleman, David 577
Coleman, Duke 120
Coleman, G.C. 758
Coleman, Gary 25, 428, 727, 742
Coleman, Gary B.B. 271
Coleman, Hooks 783
Coleman, Karen 776
Coleman, Martin 545, 712
Coleman, Ornette 527, 781
Coleman, Paul 562
Coleman, Rahn 742
Coleman, Tony 560
Coles, Chris 4
Coles, Johnny 4, 294
Collette, Buddy 76
Collier, Mitty **153**, 255, 589, 782, 790, 791
Collier, William 194
Collins Kids 202, 422, 473, 601
Collins, Aaron 107, 247, 345
Collins, Albert 421, 736
Collins, Betty 107, 345
Collins, Bootsy 28, 79, 85, 87, 89, 90, 91, 98, 110, 146, 147, **153**, 154, 155, 168, 222, 263, 264, 306, 310, 319, 366, 411, 470, 504, 517, 520, 522, 523, 524, 583, 637, 671, 698, 739, 747, 767, 775, 786, 813, 829, 850, 851
Collins, Bootsy Rubber Band 79, 153, 154, 520, 652, 767, 795
Collins, Phelps "Catfish" 85, 89, 90, 153, 154, 263, 365, 522, 583, 637, 813
Collins, Clarence 422
Collins, Dennis 337
Collins, Dorothy 195, 462
Collins, Everett 340
Collins, Frances 172
Collins, Judy 245, 559
Collins, Lewis 466
Collins, Lyn 89, 90, 91, **155**, 366, 745, 804, 815, 830
Collins, Mel 15
Collins, Peter 646
Collins, Phil 7, 29, 30, 66, 202, 214, 403, 664, 740, 811
Collins, Ray 532
Collins, Rodger 780
Collins, Rosie 107, 345
Collins, Shad 73
Collins, Tom Big 460
Collins, William "Bootsy" 89, 153, 365
Collins, Willie 460
Colon, Johnny 517
Color Me Badd 27, **155**, 230
Coltrane, Alice 561
Coltrane, John 7, 70, 108, 109, 159, 160, 202, 448, 527, 603, 604, 605, 810
Columbo, Chris 378
Combs, Sean "Puffy" 59, 112, 116, 210, 230, 427, 431, 460, 509, 510, 529, 631, 686, 693, 710
Comden, Betty 21
Commissioned 369
Commodores 11, 81, 98, 111, **155**, 156, 157, 161, 308, 450, 573, 574, 625, 652, 677, 746, 769, 777, 780, 785, 802, 824, 851
Common Ground 602
Communards 662
Como, Perry 74, 206, 462
Compton & Batteau 365
Compulsive Gamblers 748
Con Funk Shun 55, **157**, 158, 248, 259, 436, 456, 527, 529, 660
Concords 629
Condon, Eddie 94
Congo Ashante Roy 70, 185, 228, 324, 325, 497, 515, 541, 615, 638, 642, 666, 667, 719
Coniff, Ray 729, 755
Conley, Arthur 101, **158**, 159, 167, 525, 570, 630, 631, 657, 794
Conley, Cheryl 259
Conley, David 290, 352, 657
Conley, Prince 778
Connick, Harry Jr. 5, 54, 69
Conniff, Ray Singers 555
Connor, Tony 320
Connors, Bill 117
Connors, Norman 13, 14, 117, **159**, 160, 309, 310, 328, 363, 373, 567, 647
Conover, Willis 94
Conquerors 805
Conquest 822
Conquest, June **160**, 299, 793
Conried, Hans 715
Conservative Manor 2

Constandinos, Alec R. 428
Continental Four **160**, 819
Contours **160**, 161, 217, 247, 248, 263, 426, 500, 508, 509, 579, 626, 653, 674, 717, 790, 806, 810, 814, 816, 818, 823, 830, 831, 832, 846
Contrera, Al 489
Controllers **161**
Convertion 99, 337, 426
Conway, Don 255
Conway, Gerry 419
Cooder, Ry 388, 392, 578, 642, 668
Cook, Charles 577
Cook, Cheryl 606, 646
Cook, Delphine 612
Cook, Dinell 612
Cook, Gregory 708
Cook, L.C. **161**, 437
Cook, Little Joe **161**, 162
Cook, Roger 201, 636
Cooke 46, 161, 712
Cooke, L.C. 160, 164
Cooke, Sam 5, 14, 26, 28, 46, 85, 100, 101, 119, 121, 130, 152, 158, 160, **161**, 162, 163, 164, 201, 207, 208, 222, 238, 246, 248, 255, 256, 271, 284, 285, 293, 294, 302, 305, 327, 335, 337, 342, 356, 370, 375, 385, 390, 391, 418, 422, 425, 430, 437, 441, 451, 453, 457, 458, 462, 463, 473, 490, 494, 495, 516, 539, 543, 563, 565, 568, 569, 570, 584, 588, 621, 632, 653, 654, 671, 673, 682, 703, 712, 742, 753, 754, 760, 761, 762, 766, 770, 774, 781, 785, 799, 807, 813, 816, 817, 821, 824, 825, 834, 838, 844, 845, 856, 857
Cooke, Sam & the Soul Stirrers 164
Cookie & the Cupcakes **165**, 790
Cookies **165**, 192, 718, 778, 779, 809, 822, 842, 843, 844
Cool Riddims 695
Cool, Ricky 320
Cooler, Whey 547
Cooley, Cheryl 395
Cooley, Eddie 56
Coolidge, Rita 130
Coolio 147, 763, 823
Cooper, Bernadette 395
Cooper, Craig T. 300
Cooper, Deborah 127
Cooper, Gary 153, 154
Cooper, Ian 596
Cooper, Leroy 261
Cooper, Les 135, **165**, 390, 391
Cooper, Michael 157, 158
Cooper, Pat 559
Cooper, Ryan 431
Cooper, Ted 358
Cooper, Wayne 111
Copas, Cowboy 491
Copeland, Greg 585
Copeland, Johnny 736, 798, 800, 801, 834
Copeland, Kenny 585
Copeland, Rudy 101
Copeland, Ruth **165**
Coppola, Francis Ford 354
Coque, Oliver de 652
Corbett, Denie 219
Corbin, Warren 144
Cordell, Lucky 717
Cordells **165**
Cordes, Attrell 541
Cordes, Jarrett 541
Cordo, Ricky 438
Corea, Chick 30, 295, 388, 389, 594, 723
Cornelious, Eve 160
Cornelius Brothers & Sister Rose **166**, 784, 811
Cornelius, Don 468, 501, 607, 632, 633, 652, 653, 687
Cornelius, Eddie 166
Cornish, Gene 561
Coronets 790
Corporation 348, **166**, 533
Corsairs **166**, 781
Cortez, Dave "Baby" 122, **166**, 557
Corvairs 779
Coryell, Larry 413, 536
Cosby, Bill 159, 294, 376, 427, 486, 527, 533, 586, 642, 715, 758, 769
Cosby, Hank 579
Cosby, Henry 307, 308, 316, 571, 765
Cosper, Kina 96, 390
Costa, Don 784
Costandinos, Alec R. 428
Costello, Elvis 14, 34, 100, 102, 195, 581, 656, 694, 706, 740, 744
Costner, Kevin 322
Cotsworth, Simon 335
Cottle, Tameka "Tiny" 772
Cotton, James 487, 520
Cottonwood 177
Couch, Tommy 57, 545
Couch, Tommy Jr. 545
Counts **166**, 167
Coup de Villes 794
Courtney, David 635
Courtney, Dean 784
Courtney, Lou 693
Covay, Don 33, 101, 158, **167**, 326, 360, 425, 537, 558, 630, 631, 645, 682, 700, 744, 761, 777, 813
Covay, Don & the Goodtimers 167
Cover Girls **168**, 801
Cox 239
Cox, Andy 239
Cox, Bruce 739
Cox, Bryan-Michael 211
Cox, Dave 239
Cox, Deborah **168**, 323
Cox, Herbie 144
Cox, Terry 419
Cracolici, Albee 489
Cracolici, Phil 489
Craft, Morty 293, 295, 500
Craftys 293
Craig, Carl 383
Craig, Denise 409
Craig, Marvin 407
Craig, Mikey 646
Crain, Roy Sr. 632
Cramer, Floyd 310, 311, 716
Crawford, Carolyn 64, 65, 129, 307, 308, 325, 460, 546, 786, 790, 823, 825, 832
Crawford, Charles 823
Crawford, Dave 481, 644, 645
Crawford, Davell 95, 747
Crawford, Denise Dunning 621
Crawford, Hank 7, 95, 520, 555, 734, 780, 786, 829, 857, 858
Crawford, James 86, 313
Crawford, Randy **168**, 169, 171, 770, 811, 825
Crawford, Shep 666
Crawford, Sugar Boy 198, 790
Crawford, Traverse 188
Cray, Robert 51, 167, 250
Crayton, Pee Wee 39, 514, 830, 838
Crazy Elephant 835
Cream 71, 576, 589
Creative Source 61, **169**, 758, 821
Creatore, Luigi 342
Creators 4
Creed, Linda 21, 64, 277, 328, 381, 413, 610, 620, 649, 650
Creedence Clearwater Revival 100, 192, 654, 703, 745
Cregan, Jim 418, 419
Creme DCocoa 217
Crenshaw, Marshall 8, 142
Creole, Kid 196, 389, 390
Creque, Neal 555
Crescents 621
Crests **169**, 436, 778, 782, 806, 829
Crew Cuts 142, 409, 462
Crewe, Bob 113, 190, 191, 195, 392, 403, 697, 834
Crier, Arthur 293
Crier, Keith 281
Crimes, Russell 366
Croasdell, Ady 813
Croce, Joseph 141
Crocker, Frankie 108
Crockett, Gary 670
Crook, General 144
Cropper, Steve 18, 62, 67, 68, 140, 151, **169**, 220, 243, 248, 306, 369, 442, 469, 476, 515, 537, 568, 569, 641, 642, 677, 682, 780, 813, 847
Crosby, Bing 11, 45, 60, 94, 340, 378, 559, 629
Crosby, Gary 183
Cross, Joe 42
Cross, Reuben 393, 665
Crouch, Andrae 10
Crouch, Keith 168, 412, 666, 757
Crouch, Kenneth 412
Crow, Sheryl 552
Crowl, Charles 365
Crown Heights Affair 98, **170**, 449, 645, 709
Crowns 241
Crowns of Joy 217
Crows **170**, 206, 562, 629, 767, 768, 827, 828, 839
Crudup, Arthur "Big Boy" 144, **170**, 777, 822
Cruise, Tom 570
Crume, Leroy 632, 712
Crusaders 166, 168, 169, **170**, 171, 282, 358, 383, 401, 428, 515, 541, 558, 615, 709, 721, 727, 742, 795
Crutcher, Bettye 34
Crutchfield, Jerry 638
Crutchfield, Paul 395
Cruz, Celia 229, 366, 688
Crystal Mansion 122
Crystal, Billy 698
Crystals 60, 115, 168, **171**, 172, 196, 367, 430, 558, 579, 584, 635, 843, 844
Cuba, Joe 577
Cuber, Ronnie 295
Cues **172**, 562
Cuff Links 798
Culley, Frank 148
Culley, Sam 194
Culture Club **172**, 173, 444, 646
Cunningham, Bill 71, 72
Cunningham, Carl 34
Cunningham, Larry 247
Cunningham, Roy 34
Cunningham, Woody 395, 709
Cuoghi, Joe 475
Cuomo, Sal 571
Cups, Dixie 196
Curless, Ann 231, 232
Curry, Allen 413
Curry, Clifford **173**, 268, 307, 413, 500
Curry, Eugene 319, 615
Curry, Helen 336
Curry, Lige 517
Curry, Nelson 413
Curry, Thomas "Butch" 11
Curtain, Richard 606
Curtis, Bill 235, 236
Curtis, Catie 629, 693
Curtis, Clem 250
Curtis, Eddie 123, 124
Curtis, Herman 629
Curtis, Larry 283
Curtis, Rodney 517
Curtis, Ruby Nash 590
Cusseaux, Zulema 776
Custus, Eddie 124
Cutfather 145
Cutler, Carl 307
Cybotron 218
Cymande **173**, 174, 803
Cymone, Andre 279
Cypress Hill 366
Cyrkle 834

D

D Train 3, 127, 159, **175**, 383, 440, 567, 568, 709, 778, 821, 822
D., Chuck 147, 351, 411, 552
D'Angelo 14, 29, 141, **175**, 176, 313, 451, 646, 803
Da Brat 210, 211, 221, 359
D'Abo, Michael 250
Dabon, Robert 142
Da Costa, Anthony 500
Da Costa, Paulinho 159, 610
Daddy Cleanhead 312
Dahl, Bill 45, 58, 186, 702
Dahrouge, Ray 478, 647
Dailey, Albert 70
Dailey, William 70
Dakota Moon **176**
Dale & Grace 199, 805, 807
Dale, Eric Allan 250
Dale, Larry 210, 460, 810
D'Aleo, Angelo 45
Daley, Winston 13
Dallon, Miki 350
Dalto, Jorge 710
Dalyrimple, Brian 631
Dalyrimple, Christopher 631
Dalyrimple, Desiree 631
Dalyrimple, Jason 631
Damage 177
Damone, Vic 326
Dana, Vic 247
Dance Theatre of Harlem 64
Dancho, Dante 365
Dandrieu, Jean-Francois 233, 400
Dane, Barbara 804
Danelli, Dino 561
Daniel, Jeffrey 311, 608
Daniels, Billy 7, 607
Daniels, Eddie 7
Daniels, Jeffrey 607, 608
Daniels, Jerry 337
Daniels, Jesse 249
Daniels, Marvin 488
Daniels, Roy 647
Daniels, Warren 555
Danko, Rick 129, 130
Danleers **176**
Danner, Mike 179
Danny & the Juniors **176**, 820
Danny Wilson 784
Dant, Charles Bud 283
Dante & the Evergreens 368
Dante, Ron 240, 328
D'Arby, Terence Trent **177**, 451, 525, 605
Darge, Keb 802, 826
Darin, Bobby 56, 142, 176, 249, 255
Dark City Sisters 621
Darnell, August 196, 389
Darnell, Larry 277, 777
Darnells 447
Darren, James 532, 842
Dartells **177**
Dash, Sarah 310, 403, 404, 405, 565
Daughtry, Eugene 338, 339
Davenport, John 56
Davenport, N'Dea 74, 75
Davenport, Sonny 337, 426, 553
David, Craig **177**, 178, 640
David, Hal 98, 104, 132, 175, 244, 276, 283, 321, 348, 405, 422, 472, 589, 613, 713, 728, 729, 730, 731, 761
David, Timothy 698
Davidson, Lenny 61
Davie, Hutch 566
Davies, Ray 267
Davies, Ruth 83
Davis, Alia 10
Davis, Andrea 36, 576
Davis, Betty **178**, 331, 802
Davis, Bill 508, 516
Davis, Billy 207, 208, 266, 480, 645, 790
Davis, Billy Jr. 121, 238, 457
Davis, Blind Gary 162
Davis, Blind John 190
Davis, Bob 332
Davis, Carl [1] 3, 16, 102, 126, 138, 187, 206, 358, 407, 408, 414, 428, 511, 528, 712, 739, 754, 812
Davis, Carl [2] 126, 127, 137, 138, **178**, 180, 360, 567, 714, 755
Davis, Charles 160
Davis, Charles [Jazz] 209
Davis, Chester 698
Davis, Clifford 511
Davis, Clifton 276, 655
Davis, Clive 64, 168, 214, 276, 322, 323, 388, 552, 577, 578, 604
Davis, Delissa 607, 608
Davis, Dewayne 43
Davis, Don 33, 36, 37, 187, 203, 299, 410, 439, 457, 461, 505, 572, 642, 672, 682, 761, 812
Davis, Eddie "Lockjaw" 198, 733, 756, 811, 857
Davis, Ethel 307, 365
Davis, Gary 162
Davis, Geater **178**, 179
Davis, Hal 142, 273, 322, 327, 727
Davis, Huey 160
Davis, Jean 233
Davis, Joe 56, 209
Davis, Kenny 566
Davis, Larry 338, 378, 400
Davis, Leonard 200
Davis, Lloyd 237

Davis, Mac 101, 378
Davis, Mark 643, 705
Davis, Marlena 512
Davis, Martha 624
Davis, Mary 629, 630
Davis, Maxwell 297, 345, 360, 380, 421, 454, 458, 492, 737, 759, 774
Davis, Melvin 218, 219, 439, 808
Davis, Miles 14, 21, 25, 47, 55, 111, 112, 127, 159, 178, 245, 294, 307, 309, 310, 370, 375, 376, 377, 408, 437, 485, 526, 610, 666, 725, 768, 829, 857
Davis, Milton 235
Davis, Ray 525
Davis, Raymond 18, 522, 525
Davis, Rob 203
Davis, Roquel 251, 281
Davis, Ruth 36
Davis, Sammy Jr. 1, 21, 327, 572, 610, 653, 800
Davis, Skeeter 784
Davis, Spanky 95
Davis, Spencer **179**
Davis, Spencer Group 62, 71, 179, 316, 475, 560, 787, 847
Davis, Theresa 223
Davis, Thornetta **179**
Davis, Timothius 698
Davis, Trumaine 302
Davis, Tyrone 102, 178, **179**, 180, 184, 233, 255, 280, 370, 414, 601, 605, 648, 785, 789, 791, 809, 830, 833
Davis, Virginia 299
Davis, Warren 479
Davis, Wild Bill 198, 378, 379, 857
Davis, Willie 345
Dawes, Charles 218
Dawg, Ken 417
Dawn, Sandra 539
Dawson, Johnny 220
Day, Allen 161
Day, Bobby 15, 63, **180**, 318, 518, 779, 786
Day, Doris 46, 266, 490, 645, 834
Day, Graham 670
Day, Jackie 824
Day, Michael 125
Day, Morris 26, **181**, 370, 510, 666, 689, 690
Day, Mysti 20
Day, Otis & the Knights **181**
Daybreak 822
Daye, Cory 196, 389
Daye, Eddie 823
Daye, Johnny 626
Daylighters 797
Dayne, Taylor 319, 323, 578, 801
Dazz Band **181**, 182, 394, 400, 436, 652, 802
Dazzle 337, 488, 796
De La Soul 173, 265, 383, 542, 776, 785, 787
Dead Boys 636
Dead or Alive 38
Deal, Bill 182, 847
Deal, Bill & the Rhondels **182**, 751
Deal, Fred 311
Deal, Kelley 1, 160
Dean & Jean 700
Dean, Aki 428, 571, 719
Dean, James 461, 546
Dean, James [Actor] [1] 193
Dean, James [Producer] [2] 492
Dean, Joe 176
Dean, John 606
DeAndrade, Mario 242
DeAngelis, Peter 318, 848
DeBarge **182**, 183, 352, 499, 660, 661, 667, 785
DeBarge, Bobby 182, 660
DeBarge, Bunny 182, 183
DeBarge, Chico 182, **183**
DeBarge, El 182, **183**, 481, 660, 743, 785
DeBarge, Eldra 182, 183
DeBarge, James 182, 183, 351
DeBarge, Mark 182
DeBarge, Randy 182
DeBarge, Tommy 182, 279, 660
DeBrest, Spanky 159
Debussy, Claude 102, 188
DeCaro, Nick 48
DeCosta, Abel 172
DeCoteaux, Bert 437, 571, 623
Dedeaux, Richard 737
Dee Dee 270
Dee, Jay 29
Dee, Joey 173, 174, 183, 821
Dee, Joey & the Starliters **183**, 342, 561
Dee, Kiki 817
Dee, Sam 824
Deee Lite 153, 383, 823
Deele 28, **183**, 184, 470, 471
Deep Purple 37, 342, 542, 699
Deep River Boys 794
Dees, Rick 40, 487
Dees, Sam 126, 144, **184**, 317, 398, 755
Def Jef 833
Def Leppard 116
DeFrancesco, Joey 788, 857
DeFranco Family 689
Degiorgio, Kirk 825
DeGrate, Dalvin 368
DeGrate, Donald Jr. 368
Degroat, Dale 486
Deja 20, 575
Deja Groove 369
DeJohnette, Jack 47
Dekker, Desmond & the Aces 490
Deknight, Rene 188
Del Capris 403
Del Rios 43, 778
Del Satins 436, 834
Del-Phis 445, 571
Del-Vikings **184**, 185, 348, 786, 797, 839
Delaney & Bonnie 424, 699
Delaney, Jack 577
DeLaurentiis, Dino 429
DelBarrio, George 512
Delcos 821
DelDin, Robert 213
Delegates 143, 402
Delfonics 43, 61, 98, **185**, 186, 205, 225, 226, 292, 297, 320, 331, 333, 364, 428, 436, 438, 448, 498, 529, 542, 626, 649, 679, 688, 689, 722, 785, 786, 794, 795, 799, 812, 835, 848
Delicates 708, 745
Delilah 814
Dells 36, 108, 126, **186**, 187, 188, 204, 266, 271, 362, 381, 414, 418, 432, 439, 464, 465, 480, 511, 530, 540, 576, 578, 645, 646, 647, 692, 709, 712, 777, 781, 782, 786, 789, 790, 810, 812, 818, 831
Delmore Brothers 856
Delroys 499, 805, 827
Delta Rhythm Boys **188**, 562
Deltones 340
DeLuna, John 140
DeMell, Shena 361
Demery, Fred 235
Demps, Larry 79, 203, 204, 832
Demps, Louvain 832
Dempsey, Bill 295
Demudd, Pierre 181, 394
Denby, Al 243
Denby, Herman "Junior" 657
Deniro, Robert 688
Denman, Paul S. 596
Dennis, Carolyn 757
Dennon, Jerry 247
Denny, Sandy 694
Denson, Karl 288, 289, 739
Dent, Cedric 666
Denton, Mickey 783, 816
Denver, John 283, 302
Deodato Eumir **188**, 380, 380, 383, 400, 401, 402, 643, 671, 727, 786, 793
DeOliveria, Laudir Soares 727
DePasse, Suzanne 143
Depeche Mode 383
DePrisco, Pat 141
Derek & the Dominos 51
Derrickson, Jerome 775
Des'ree **188**, 390
DeSanto, Sugar Pie **188**, 189, 360, 361, 450, 557, 782, 790, 804
DeSario, Teri 385
DeShannon, Jackie 120, 239, 315, 397, 584, 682, 803, 842, 844
Desideros 137
Desires 805, 827
Destiny's Child 10, 45, 145, **189**, 190, 317, 366, 404, 698
Detroit Emeralds 129, **190**, 247, 309, 834
Detroit Symphony 581
Deupree, Taylor 4, 176, 601, 633
DeVaughn, William **190**, 339, 782, 809, 824, 830
DeVeaux, Gary 646
DeVenne, Walter 295
Devilles 71
Devo 200, 310, 694
DeVoe, Ronnie 41, 496, 497
DeVol, Frank 132
Devotions 828
Dewbury, Russ 792
DeWitt, Julia 800
Dexter, Dave Jr. 433
Dexter, Terry **190**
Dey, Tracey 58, **190**, 191
Diablos 367, 368, 463, 647, 648
Diamond D 621
Diamond Joe **191**, 803
Diamond, Greg 92, 699, 700
Diamond, Keith 482, 651
Diamond, Neil 49, 277, 362, 364, 721
Diamonds 185, **191**, 340, 751, 797, 805
Diante, Denny 498
Dibango, Manu 92, 440, 779, 792
Dibbs, J. 412
Dickenson, Vic 31, 415
Dickerson, B.B. 723, 724
Dickey, Gwen 157, 412, 585, 768
Dickson, Derek 129
Dickson, Jim 448
Diddley, Bo 31, 49, 52, 56, 130, **191**, 192, 193, 242, 262, 271, 313, 318, 361, 368, 469, 470, 579, 645, 646, 737, 782, 790, 829, 836
Difosco 340
Diggs, Benny 279
Digital Underground 146, 264, 523, 693, 833
Dillard, Moses 96
Dillard, Varetta 3, **193**
DiMucci, Dion 193, 194
Dinosaur 796
Dinosaur L 440
Dion 45, 46, **193**, 194, 206, 207, 436, 443, 635, 638, 805, 839, 847
Dion & the Belmonts 46, 176, 194, 242, 834
Dion, Celine 28, 115, 386, 706
Diouf, Zak 307
Diplomats **194**, 786, 830
Direct Current **195**
Dirty Dozen 195
Dirty Dozen Brass Band 63, **195**, 815, 818
Disco Tex & the Sex-O-Lettes **195**, 395
Dismuke, Phlanoid "Jay Dee" 628, 629
Distants 386, 479, 548, 674, 745, 814, 828
Dixie Belles **195**
Dixie Cups **196**, 415, 430, 783, 784, 840, 842, 844
Dixie Flyers 256, 466, 481, 599, 728
Dixie Hummingbirds 11, 345, 602, 857
Dixon, Ben 650
Dixon, Bill 126, 209, 326, 718
Dixon, Darryl 488, 556
Dixon, Floyd 415, 514, 777, 779, 799, 815, 838
Dixon, George 636, 637
Dixon, Hank 511
Dixon, Henry 511
Dixon, Kenny Jr. 43
Dixon, Luther 254, 326, 540, 612, 680
Dixon, Popsy 318, 319
Dixon, Reather 63
Dixon, Richard 400
Dixon, Willie 50, 51, 68, 102, 189, 250, 262, 360, 361, 365, 436, 543, 544, 575, 700, 793, 813, 838
Dixon, Wylie 619
DJ Cam 24
DJ Jazzy Jeff 686
DJ Jazzy Jeff & the Fresh Prince 602, 628, 686
DJ Kool 173
DJ Miko 796
DJ Minutemix 541
DJ Premier 176
DJ Quik 395, 700
DJ Rogers 584
DJ Shadow 24, 25, 515, 802
DJ Smash 288, 289
DJ U Neek 66, 646
DJ Yella 470
DJon, Paris 498
DMX 230, 313, 478, 619
Dobyne, Robert 16
DOC 470
Doctor Buzzard's Original Savannah Band 79, **196**, 270, 389, 795
Doctor Demento 163
Doctor Dre 59, 66, 77, 78, 147, 211, 264, 305, 368, 386, 523, 700, 775, 833
Doctor Feelgood 779
Doctor John 5, 69, 70, 115, 129, 195, **196**, 197, 198, 256, 309, 311, 372, 421, 450, 466, 475, 553, 570, 684, 694, 747, 793, 808, 818, 840, 841
Dodd, Aaron 535
Dodgers 821
Dodson, Anne 638
Dodson, Larry "D" 34, 35
Dogg Pound Posse 470
Dogg, Nate 211, 460, 578
Doggett, Bill 54, 70, **198**, 243, 378, 390, 643, 668, 759, 780, 838, 857
Dolby, Thomas 21, 146, 383
Dolemite 60
Dollar, Beau 91
Dollis, Bo 746
Dolphin, Dwayne 739
Dolphin, John 380, 798
Domino, Fats 10, 38, 39, 54, 63, 69, 90, 94, 113, 129, 130, 135, 165, 185, 197, **198**, 199, 249, 295, 310, 311, 382, 388, 393, 421, 427, 450, 475, 495, 518, 547, 548, 553, 613, 626, 627, 694, 753, 777, 786, 789, 792, 793, 812, 816, 818, 829, 839, 840, 841
Domino, Renaldo 832
Dominoes 93, 107, 148, 206, 409, 462, 726, 753, 754, 794, 839
Dominos 828
Don & Bob 790
Don & Dewey **199**, 296, 508, 518, 807, 823, 838
Don & Juan **199**, 497, 555, 778, 784, 799
Don, Rasha 235
Donable, Donny 405
Donaldson, Ernest Frank 562
Donaldson, Lou 200, 287, 289, 520, 650, 694, 739, 787, 790, 826
Donaldson, Pat 419
Donays 779
Donner, Ral 56
Donnie 825
Donovan 779
Doobie Brothers 69, 77, 341, 439
Doors 13, 182, 261, 645, 654, 769, 825
Dootones 463, 508
DoReen 631
Dorn, Joel 493, 495
Dorsey Brothers 559
Dorsey, Glenn 631
Dorsey, Jimmy 210, 597
Dorsey, Lee 114, **199**, 200, 255, 296, 307, 311, 382, 393, 450, 466, 467, 493, 685, 694, 777, 782, 783, 786, 792, 793, 800, 801, 803, 810, 833, 835, 840, 841
Dorsey, Thomas A. 102, 131, 141, 375, 632
Double Exposure 110, **200**, 317, 338, 476, 615, 679, 792, 795, 812, 819, 822
Doucet, Michael 198
Doucette, Salvadore Jr. 39
Douglas, Alan 410
Douglas, Carl 134, **200**, 201
Douglas, Carol 138, **201**, 202, 457, 567
Douglas, Charles 635
Douglas, Jack 720
Douglas, Kevin 449
Douglas, Mike 668
Douglas, Robert 649
Douglas, Shy Guy 783
Douglas, Steve 144, 774
Douglas, Tyrone 708
Douglass, Jimmy 622, 623
Doulphin, Edward 128
Dowd, Tom 208, 444, 639
Downbeats 220
Downchild Blues Band 179
Downing, Al 202
Downing, Big Al 458
Downing, Don **201**, 202, 795
Downing, Will 8, **202**, 234, 359, 519, 520, 811, 825
Downliners Sect 80
Downs, Bobby 495

Downs, Geoff 134
Dozier Boys 782
Dozier, Eddie 446
Dozier, Gene 629
Dozier, Holland 811
Dozier, Lamont 184, **202**, 203, 218, 220, 253, 266, 279, 281, 314, 315, 319, 320, 340, 354, 379, 380, 415, 439, 445, 446, 447, 502, 509, 511, 521, 527, 572, 642, 653, 654, 657, 704, 718, 719, 723, 739, 776, 811, 816, 846
Dozier, Tim 622
Dozier, Ugene 615
Drake, Laverne 107
Drake, Nick 109, 239
Drake, Pete 602
Drake, Tony 833
Drakeford, Lee 691, 692
Dramatics 60, 79, 186, **203**, 204, 205, 225, 243, 244, 266, 299, 309, 310, 333, 350, 410, 457, 461, 511, 546, 572, 615, 659, 668, 712, 741, 761, 778, 785, 788, 792, 795, 828, 832
Dranes, Earl 436
Drapels 683, 778
Drayton, Victor 267
Drea 373
Dream Machine **205**
Dream **205**
Dreamers 12, 60, **205**, 279, 827, 828
Dreamlovers 12, 61, **205**, 206, 339, 820, 834
Dreams 701
Drells 42
Drew, Patti **206**, 391
Drew-Vels 206
Drifters 11, 12, 31, 48, 49, 56, 67, 80, 107, 148, 165, 172, 185, **206**, 207, 208, 241, 255, 282, 294, 295, 345, 359, 363, 364, 391, 392, 404, 415, 457, 462, 463, 479, 508, 534, 539, 547, 548, 549, 577, 600, 635, 647, 660, 688, 701, 728, 779, 780, 786, 797, 824, 836, 839, 842, 844
Driftin' Slim 255
Drinkard Singers 143, 660, 716, 728
Drinkwater, Skip 183
Drivers 833
Dru Hill 189, **208**, 209, 210, 278, 488, 489, 499, 558, 619
Drue, John 552
Drumgole, James 449
Du Droppers **209**, 500
Duarte, Peter 384
Duarte, Tito 37
Dubs **209**, 345, 780, 798, 803, 806
Ducanes 635
Duchess 191, 192, 193
Duchin, Eddy 246, 528
Duda, Marty 222
Dudley, Cordell 178
Dudley, Theodore Jr. 324
Duettes **209**, 242
Duhe, Robin 455
Dukays 125, 126, 127, **209**, 210, 792
Duke, David 809
Duke, Doris **210**
Duke, George 26, 30, 55, 117, 142, 159, 213, 259, 311, 376, 377, 399, 481, 490, 512, 513, 515, 581, 592, 594, 608, 620, 667, 748, 757, 796
Duke, Patty 784
Dukes, Dwight Ronnell 121, 309
Dukes, James 309
Dukes, Joe 121, 810
Dukes, Terry 97
Dumas, Martin L. Jr. 562
Dumas, Tony 413
Dunbar, Richard 117, 395
Dunbar, Ron 522, 527
Dunbar, Ronald 279, 320
Dunbar, Ronnie 509, 712
Dunbar, Sly 310, 374, 767
Duncan, Cleveland "Cleve" 532
Duncan, Helen 686
Duncan, Malcolm 22, 23
Duncan, Phyllis 686
Dunham, Eric 279
Dunlap, Melvin 769
Dunn, Bob 62, 442, 585, 649
Dunn, Donald "Duck" 10, 62, 67, 68, 442, 469, 780
Dunn, Franklyn 312
Dunn, Freddie 585
Dunn, Homer 577
Dunn, James 205, 649
Dunn, Larry 214
Dunning, Bonny 621
Dunning, Delores 621
Dupónts 422, 828
Dupree, Champion Jack **210**, 390, 460
Dupree, Cornell 31, 361, 390, 391, 565, 648
Duprees 45, **210**
Dupri, Jermaine 1, 77, 116, 189, **210**, 211, 258, 359, 431, 481, 577, 578, 666, 710, 772
Duran Duran 2, 23, 139, 140, 255, 312, 407, 518
Durante, Jimmy 557
Durham, Norman 395
Durr, Phil 179
Dury, Ian 796
Duvals 241
DXT 488
Dyke & the Blazers **211**, 525, 769, 830, 850, 851
Dylan, Bob 36, 49, 65, 67, 72, 77, 93, 101, 102, 110, 125, 150, 153, 162, 194, 280, 300, 318, 319, 337, 340, 341, 367, 392, 420, 490, 494, 507, 534, 578, 641, 708, 729, 745, 763, 764, 857
Dynamic Superiors **211**, 437
Dynamics 203, **211**, 784
Dynasty 81, **212**
Dyson, Ronnie **212**, 336, 438

E

E., Sheila 158, **213**, 217, 227, 666, 796
Eager, Allen 103
Eager, Brenda Lee 103, 104
Eagles 96, 286, 354, 361
Eaglin, Snooks 39, 553, 574, 694, 746, 838
Earl, Raymond 338, 616
Earl, Ronnie 93
Earland, Charles 55, 320, 725, 734, 735, 739, 768, 857, 858
Earle, Steve 745
Earls **213**, 214, 778, 831
Earth, Wind & Fire 13, 14, 29, 30, 35, 43, 55, 62, 81, 88, 98, 106, 111, 112, 117, 123, 142, 154, 156, 169, 181, 188, 211, **214**, 215, **216**, 223, 231, 259, 261, 269, 275, 312, 315, 363, 367, 383, 384, 394, 398, 401, 403, 412, 420, 421, 432, 440, 441, 450, 456, 504, 513, 527, 535, 542, 583, 594, 597, 598, 611, 633, 642, 643, 645, 646, 652, 668, 699, 709, 715, 723, 727, 748, 769, 785, 788, 803, 808, 819, 826, 851
Easley, Toriano 686
East Coast Band 290
East, Nathan 428, 742, 761
Easterling, Skip 833
Eastmond, Barry 412, 513, 743
Easton, Sheena 28, 358, 757
Eastwood, Clint [Actor] 68
Eastwood, Clint [Reggae] 245
Eaton, Bobby 82
Eaton, Cleveland 420, 421
Eaton, John 566
Eaves, Hubert III 159, 175, 328
Eazy E 66, 469, 470
Ebonys **216**, 217, 325, 665
Echoes 795, 822
Echols, John 621
Echos 173
Eckstine, Billy 46, 49, 148, 251, 253, 294, 375, 425, 460, 563, 822, 825
Eckstine, Ed 460
Ecstasy, Passion & Pain 91, **217**, 615, 809
Eddy, Duane 532, 577
Eden's Crush **217**
Edison Lighthouse 835
Edison, Harry "Sweets" 287, 759
Edmonds, Ben 275
Edmonds, Kenneth "Babyface" 7, 27, **28**, 29, 59, 77, 82, 83, 112, 168, 183, 184, 217, 224, 229, 230, 277, 278, 323, 343, 347, 367, 373, 386, 414, 417, 470, 488, 492, 494, 538, 666, 686, 710, 741, 752, 764
Edmonds, Kevon 7, **217**
Edmonds, Melvin 7, 217
Edmonds, Nate 740
Edmonds, Tracey E. 28
Edmunds, Dave 194
Edmunds, Kenny 183
Edsels **217**, 805, 827, 828
Edwards, Bernard 127, 138, 139, 140, 228, 313, 335, 497, 522, 582, 583, 587, 620, 621, 623, 648, 686, 705, 770
Edwards, Bob 647, 648
Edwards, Carolyn 234
Edwards, Chico 112, 637
Edwards, Dee 800
Edwards, Denise 488
Edwards, Dennis 112, 160, 161, **217**, 218, 387, 560, 590, 633, 674, 675, 676, 677, 678, 679, 700, 717, 817, 828
Edwards, Earl 209, 210
Edwards, Esmond 77
Edwards, Gordon 591, 648
Edwards, J. Vincent 498
Edwards, Jackie 179
Edwards, James 601
Edwards, John 637, 638
Edwards, Millard 228
Edwards, Raymond 616
Edwards, Ricky 142
Edwards, Robert 338
Edwards, Sandra 220
Edwards, Skye 482, 483
Edwards, Teddy 25, 70, 71, 297, 759
Edwards, Tommy **218**, 251, 252
Efford, Bob 25
Egan, Willie **218**
Egyptian Lover **218**, 402
Eighth Day 202, **218**, 219, 279, 439, 509, 809
Eighties Ladies 53, **219**, 647, 792, 802
Eitzel, Mark 141
Eko, Ray Alan 312
El Capris 422
El Chicano 652, 689, 789
El Dorados 16, **219**, 402, 748, 777, 797
El-Rays 187
El Torros 799
Elbert, Donnie 33, **219**, 220, 782, 783
Eldridge, Roy 475, 759
Electras 693
Electric Light Orchestra 179
Electric Prunes 23, 24
Electrifying Mojo 43
Elegants **220**, 489, 827, 834
Elements 332, 573
Elfman, Danny 794
Elgin Park 289
Elgins **220**, 315, 386, 548, 654, 806, 821, 834
ElHadi, Suliaman 411
Eli, Bobby 38, 61, 276, 296, 319, 332, 468, 498, 600
Elizondo, Rene 351
Elliman, Yvonne 40, **220**, 221, 533
Ellington, Duke 45, 74, 84, 95, 108, 117, 131, 152, 188, 197, 309, 316, 389, 420, 422, 493, 512, 527, 543, 559, 572, 647, 759, 763, 838
Ellington, Robert 203
Elliot, Chad 189
Elliott, Melissa 221
Elliott, Mike 250
Elliott, Missy 59, 189, **221**, 222, 323, 488, 489, 530, 666, 667, 686, 693, 706, 707
Ellis, Alfred 366
Ellis, Barbara 247
Ellis, Bill 246
Ellis, Billy Pat 629, 630
Ellis, James 600, 823
Ellis, Jay 276
Ellis, Jimmy 165, 697
Ellis, Jonah 773
Ellis, Pee Wee 47, 85, 86, 90, **222**, 365, 366, 520, 803, 850
Ellis, Ralph 536
Ellis, Ray 536
Ellis, Shirley **222**, 396
Ellis, Terry **222**, 224
Ellis, Tinsley 93
Ellis, Tinsley & the Heartfixers 93
Ellison, John **222**
Ellison, Lorraine **223**, 405, 438, 557
Elston, Harry 261, 718
Embers 577, 606
Emerson, Billy "The Kid" 409
Emerson, Lake & Palmer 207
Emilio 229
Eminem 221, 823
Emmanuel 1
Emmons, Bobby 211, 466, 520, 692
Emotions 44, 179, 214, 215, **223**, 224, 230, 259, 315, 358, 372, 519, 737, 828
Empires 135, 165, 806
Empress 821
En Vogue 28, 149, 222, **224**, 358, 399, 432, 572, 612, 629, 661, 698, 772
Enchanette 224, 225
Enchanters 102, 473, 668, 783, 828
Enchantment **225**, 436, 545
Encores 790
Energetics **226**
English Beat 239
English, Barbara Jean **226**
Englund, George 260
Eno, Brian 71
Ephraim, Willie 176
Epics 161
EPMD 727
Epps, James 234
Epps, Kena 535
Epps, Nathaniel 141
Epps, Preston 830
Epsilons 459
EQ 1
Equals **226**
Eramus Hall **226**
Erasure 383, 740
Eric B & Rakim 105, 304, 520
Errico, Greg 178, 624
Ertegun, Ahmet 1, 49, 94, 148, 206, 207, 245, 284, 391, 392, 462, 553
Ertegun, Nesuhi 49, 206
Ervin, Difosco 339
Ervin, Frankie 3, 46
Escalera, Evelyn 168
Escorts **226**, 227
Escott, Colin 49, 54, 208, 250
Escovedo, Alejandro 227
Escovedo, Coke **227**
Escovedo, Pete 213, 227
Escovedo, Thomas 227
ESG 20, **227**
Eskridge, Ralph 80
Espinosa, Bobby 140
Esposito, Larry 464
Esquerita **227**, 228
Esquires Combo 623
Esquires **228**
Essex **228**, 809
Essex, David 566
Estefan, Emilio Jr. 229, 427
Estefan, Gloria 9, **228**, 229, 606, 768
Estefan, Gloria & Miami Sound Machine 229
Estes, Sleepy John 189, 229
Estes, Toni **229**
Estus, Deon 74
Eternals 805
E.U. 84, **230**, 231, 560, 699
Eubanks, Quentin 647, 648
Eugene, Jane 427
Europa 422
Eurythmics 257, 269, 484
Evans, Adriana **230**
Evans, Belton 391
Evans, Bill 230, 294, 392, 521, 547, 590, 693, 750
Evans, Brenda Joyce 708
Evans, Danny 693
Evans, Faith 27, 47, 177, **230**, 323, 470, 547, 558, 584, 686
Evans, Gil 376
Evans, Janice 522
Evans, Jerome 463
Evans, Joe 547, 750, 789
Evans, Joe 693
Evans, Keith 320
Evans, Nate 333, 334
Evans, Richard [1] 420
Evans, Richard [2] 109
Evans, Sticks 31
Evans, Terry 392
Eve 478, 700
Everett, Betty 15, 92, 104, 122, **230**, 231, 272, 372, 419, 626, 728, 780, 781, 804, 807, 830, 844
Everett, Ronald "Omar" 121
Everette, Ed 185
Everly Brothers 231, 292, 293, 317, 856
Ewing, Willie 719

Excellents 367
Exciters 3, **231**, 364, 373, 784, 821, 843, 844
Executive Suite **231**
Experience Unlimited **231**
Exposé **231**, 232

F
F., Eddie 776
Fabares, Shelley 809
Fabian 318, 438, 557, 848
Fabolous 706
Fabulous Peps 831
Fabulous Playboys 233, 831
Fabulous Thunderbirds 525
Facenda, Tommy 805
Faces 50
Facts of Life **233**
Faddis, Jon 450, 540
Fagen, Donald 587
Fagin, John 479
Fagin, Maurice 479
Fagin, Sandra 479
Fair, Ron 747
Fair, Yvonne 585, 790
Fairburn, Werly 61
Fairfield Four 779
Faison, Ruben 647
Faith No More 826, 851
Faith, Gene 697
Faith, Hope & Charity 142, 457, 591, 776
Faith, Jack 117, 338, 378, 564
Faithfull, Marianne 803
Fakir, Abdul 251
Falcons **233**, 248, 502, 509, 511, 536, 537, 538
Falls, Vernon 129
Falomir, Steve 689
Faltermeyer, Harold 484
Fambrough, Henry 636
Fame, Georgie 259, 309, 640, 847, 848
Fame, Herb 528, 533
Family **233**
Family Stand **233**, 234
Famous Flames 63, 85, 105, 491
Fania All Stars 517
Fann, Leroy 590
Fannie & the Varçels 831
Fantastic Four **234**, 309, 814, 825, 834
Fantastic Johnny C. **234**, 468
Fantastics 141
Fantasy 139
Fantasy **234**
Farag, Henry 635
Fargo 14
Farian, Frank 66, 67
Farley Jackmaster Funk 791
Farmer, Art 123, 375, 755
Farmer, Peggy 296
Farnon, Robert 48
Farra, Maryann & Satin Soul 795
Farrell, Bobby 66
Farrell, Joe 40, 48, 294, 540, 561, 786
Farrell, Kevin 440
Farrell, Wes 190, 497, 600
Farris, Dionne **235**, 390, 664
Farrow, Mikki 42, 380
Fascinations **235**, 247, 571
Fassert, Chuck 571
Fat Boys 98, 135
Fat Joe 17
Fat Larry's Band **235**
Fat Larry's Band 235
Fatback 122, 235, 236, 237
Fatback Band **235**, 236, 237, 785, 801, 802
Fatboy Slim 284, 822
F.A.T.E. **237**, 692
Fatone, Joey 689
Faussart, Celia 500
Faussart, Helene 500
Faze O 817
Fearing, Charles 521, 566
Fearman, Eric 181
Feaster, Claude 142
Feaster, Willie 752
Feathers 107, 345, 782
Federals 806
Fekaris, Dino 276, 528
Felder, Allan 100, 217, 240, 244, 297, 564, 616, 740
Felder, Wilton 166, 170, 171, 203, 252, 277, 428, 515, 721, 742, 760
Feldman, Lee 13
Feldman, Victor 377, 573
Feliciano, Jose 227, 229, 254, 344, 724
Felix, John 345
Felix, Ric 499
Felix, Steve 102
Fell, Terry 298
Feller, Sid 132, 755
Felton, Leslie 614
Felts, Narvel 809
Fendermen 804
Fennell, Skip 84
Ferbee, Willie 206
Ferguson, Charles "Little Jazz" 421
Ferguson, Doug 687
Ferguson, H-Bomb 805, 815
Ferguson, Helena 502
Ferguson, Howie 744
Ferguson, Jay 62, 664
Ferguson, Larry 320
Ferguson, Maynard 732, 733
Ferguson, Robert 339
Ferguson, Sheila 687
Ferguson, Stacy 747
Ferone, Steve 60
Ferrante, Bob 489
Ferrante, Russell 595
Ferrell, Flash 439
Ferrell, Rachelle 202
Ferrier, Al 783, 800
Ferrone, Steve 22, 23, 60, 100, 388, 512, 578
Ferrrell, Edward 373, 657
Ferry, Bryan 298, 582
FF 575
Fi-Tones **237**, 805
Field, John 151
Field, Philip 20
Field, Tim 638
Fields, Artie 712
Fields, Bobby 443
Fields, Brandon 331
Fields, Ernie 473, 518
Fields, Frank 39, 69, 613
Fields, Johnny 10, 241
Fields, Larry 151
Fields, Lee **237**, 238, 378, 800, 807, 822, 826
Fields, Phil 485
Fields, Richard "Dimples" 504
Fiestas **238**
Fifth Avenue 696
Fifth Dimension 12, 121, 206, **238**, 239, 259, 322, 327, 413, 436, 457, 655, 718, 742
Figueiredo, Larry 213
Fileti, Donn 122, 296, 307, 806
Finch, Richard 384, 385, 458, 572
Fine Young Cannibals **239**, 240
Fingers Inc. **240**, 383, 399, 440
Finished Touch 416
Finnerty, Barry 171
Finnie, Lance 233
Finnis, Rob 798
Fioravanti, Frank 190
Fire Fox 311
Fireflies **240**
First Born 12
First Choice 59, 79, 135, 217, 224, **240**, 241, 297, 313, 317, 416, 597, 612, 615, 617, 792, 794, 795, 819
First Class 660
First Family 365, 366
Fischer, Andre 592, 593, 595
Fischer, Clare 593
Fischer, Lisa 136, 720
Fishburne, Larry 55, 706
Fisher, Andre 300, 388
Fisher, Bruce 727
Fisher, Carl 443, 717
Fisher, Jessie 795
Fisher, Richard 548
Fisher, Toni 804
Fisher, Tony 698, 699
Fiske, Guy 533
Fitch, John 393, 665
Fitze, Gregory 556
Fitzgerald, Ella 21, 30, 102, 152, 198, 309, 377, 378, 500, 527, 727, 728, 732, 752, 800
Five Blind Boys 107, 857
Five Blind Boys of Alabama **241**
Five Blind Boys of Mississippi 382
Five Chances 798
Five Crowns 107, 206, 207, **241**, 391
Five Discs **242**, 782
Five DuTones 3, 121, **242**, 508, 555, 717, 747, 748, 781, 823
Five Echoes 246, 326, 671
Five Jets 718
Five Keys 11, 107, **242**, 611, 779, 797, 808, 827
Five Notes 827
Five Pennies 173, 307, 784
Five Quails 266, 816
Five Royales 32, 93, 96, **243**, 491, 812, 827
Five Satins 73, 121, **243**, 318, 332, 423, 464, 497, 500, 571, 601, 682, 778, 782, 785, 788, 798, 799, 805, 806
Five Sharps 611
Five Special **243**, 244
Five Stairsteps 53, 80, 99, 100, **244**, 300, 334, 339, 341, 488, 720, 751, 789, 826
Five Star **245**, 427
Five Thousand Volts 134
Five Tinos 828
Five Wings 3, 70, 345
Fizer, Charles 508
Flack, Roberta 21, 54, 92, 96, 97, 138, 160, **245**, 299, 310, 379, 397, 459, 485, 513, 520, 526, 540, 548, 610, 642, 646, 713, 728, 768, 780
Flairs 51, 52, 149, 246, 247, 774
Flames 63, 85, 105, 318
Flaming Ember **245**, 279
Flamingos 104, 142, 186, 206, 226, **246**, 326, 367, 480, 382, 464, 611, 658, 694, 712, 777, 782, 790, 793, 797, 803, 806, 827, 839
Flanagan, Tommy 714
Flares 107, **246**, 247, 782
Flash Cadillac & the Continental Kids 176
Flavor Flav 147
Flea 60
Fleetwood Mac 152, 425, 482, 543, 759
Fleetwood, Sherman 775
Fleetwoods **247**, 571
Fleming, Don 240
Fleming, Jimmy 628
Fleming, Leroy 84
Fleming, Robert 220
Fleming, Rochelle 240, 241
Flemming, Gabriel 475
Flemons, Wade 56, 187, 214, 598, 810, 818
Flippers 801
Flippin, Johnny 235
Flirtations **247**
Float Up CP 136
Floaters 35, 190, **247**, 248
Flournoy, Kevin 629
Flower Shoppe 784
Flowers, Anthony 665
Floyd, Aaron 16
Floyd, Buddy 759
Floyd, Eddie 43, 62, 68, 120, 223, 233, **248**, 249, 408, 476, 537, 549, 645, 682, 685, 777, 780, 795, 804, 805, 813, 825
Fluellan, Eddie 660
Flying Burrito Brothers 118, 546
Fogerty, John 136, 192, 277, 392
Fol, Hubert 413
Foley, Ira 463
Follow for Now 235
Fonda, Peter 448
Fontaine Sisters 798, 800
Fontaine, Eddie 805
Forbes, West 243
Force M.D.'s **249**, 339, 496
Ford, Dee Dee 270
Ford, Donald 533
Ford, Frankie 39, 196, **249**, 250, 259, 626, 627, 781, 783, 793, 810, 815, 816, 818, 840
Ford, Pee Wee 159
Ford, Penny 632, 773
Ford, Robben 759
Ford, Willie 203, 204, 333
Foreigner 418, 609, 721
Forest, Earl 3
Forester Sisters 480
Forester, Kim 464, 692
Formations 267, 784
Forrest, Jimmy 86, 287, 390, 857
Forrester, Bobby 94, 95
Forsten, Def Jeff 593
Forster, Christoph 185
Forster, Robert 185
Fortune, Jesse **250**
Fortune, Sonny 23, 25, 47
Foster, Curtis 241
Foster, David 77, 155, 216, 217, 224, 277, 283, 323, 324, 417, 757
Foster, Denzil 149, 222, 224, 629
Foster, Frank 48, 812
Foster, Paul 164, 632
Foster, Ronnie 48, 217, 328, 490
Foundations **250**, 781, 787, 789, 826
Founders 818
Fountain 241
Fountain, Clarence 241
Fountain, Eli 44, 273
Fountain, James 822
Fountain, Pete 197
Four B's 391
Four Below Zero 799
Four Blazes **250**, 251, 382
Four Bluebirds 578
Four Buddies 121
Four Coins **251**
Four Evers 489
Four Fellows **251**, 805
Four Freshmen 251, 253, 658
Four Hero 109
Four Jokers 307
Four Knights 172
Four Lads 409, 437
Four Mints **251**
Four Most 806
Four Non Blondes 538
Four Pennies 141, 307
Four Seasons 45, 161, 236, 408, 559, 637, 675, 697, 751, 834, 838, 839, 847
Four Sonics 648
Four Tops 32, 43, 80, 82, 100, 117, 124, 160, 190, 200, 202, 203, 211, 219, 236, 250, **251**, 252, 253, 257, 261, 263, 273, 276, 280, 281, 309, 310, 315, 327, 328, 368, 378, 384, 385, 446, 461, 477, 480, 509, 511, 544, 572, 644, 653, 654, 655, 668, 675, 691, 708, 712, 720, 733, 745, 746, 778, 782, 784, 785, 786, 790, 792, 795, 801, 804, 812, 818, 824, 825, 831, 844, 846
Four Tunes 795, 828
Four Vagabonds 794
Fowler, Gregory 244
Fowler, Mike 13
Fox, Michael J. 720
Fox, Norman 799, 827
Fox, Rick 752
Fox, Samantha 575
Foxworth, Margaret 279, 700
Foxx, Inez 95, 153, 254, 783, 812, 814, 828
Foxx, Inez and Charlie 95, 217, **254**, 786
Foxx, Jamie 457
Foxx, Redd 60, 291, 482
Foxy **254**, 255
Frampton, Peter 530, 546, 699
Fran, Carol **255**, 413
Franceschini, Bob 788
Francis, Connie 176, 434, 831, 842
Francis, Dean 251
Frank, David 509, 664, 747
Frank, Edward 115
Frank, Joe 481
Frankie Goes to Hollywood 255, 375, 605
Franklin, Aretha 6, 15, 28, 33, 48, 62, 69, 73, 85, 94, 96, 100, 103, 117, 118, 119, 130, 134, 136, 139, 143, 144, 151, 152, 155, 167, 175, 188, 210, 211, 225, 226, 233, 241, 243, 245, 253, **255**, 256, 257, 258, 271, 282, 284, 290, 299, 309, 314, 317, 321, 322, 324, 327, 371, 375, 376, 379, 380, 390, 400, 403, 405, 420, 430, 431, 444, 453, 457, 458, 466, 469, 472, 489, 502, 519, 521, 530, 536, 537, 547, 555, 558, 568, 575, 592, 595, 596, 599, 642, 646, 653, 655, 660, 682, 688, 690, 692, 712, 713, 720, 728, 760, 761, 762, 770, 776, 780, 785, 786, 793, 797, 804, 809, 811, 812, 813, 825, 830, 834, 844, 847, 856, 857
Franklin, C.L. 119, 257, 644
Franklin, Carolyn 255, 256, 257, **258**, 642

Franklin, Erma 49, 206, 255, 257, **258**, 259, 557, 789, 791, 830, 834
Franklin, Farrah 189
Franklin, Kirk **259**
Franklin, Kirk & the Family 233, 259
Franklin, Melvin 220, 226, 267, 332, 333, 386, 387, 479, 548, 562, 674, 675, 676, 677, 718
Franklin, Rodney 768
Franklin, William 400
Frazier, Al 577
Frazier, Ben 519
Frazier, Joe "Speedo" 332
Frazier, Richard 161
Frazier, Sam 408
Frazier, Skipper Lee 42
Fred & New J.B.'s 365, 366
Fred, John **259**, 847
Frederick, Kevin 181
Fredericks, Fred 361
Fredrix, Randy 652
Free Life **259**
Free Movement **259**
Free, Mickie 607, 608
Freed, Alan 31, 46, 49, 50, 102, 107, 108, 123, 172, 176, 184, 237, 249, 266, 301, 340, 370, 400, 422, 433, 479, 480, 806
Freed, Arthur 208
Freedom **259**, 260
Freeman, Bobby **260**, 624, 626, 784, 786
Freeman, Ernie 514, 798
Freeman, George 320
Freeman, Jim 243
Freeman, Lee 408
Freeman, Marston 3
Freeman, Morgan 322, 758
Freeman, Rich 243
Freeway 116
French, Nicki 796
Fresh **260**
Fresh Prince 628
Fresh, Doug E. 100, 213, 227, 244, 260, 803
Frey, Alan 496
Frey, Glenn 169
Fricke, Janie 132
Fridle, Lenny Jr. 122
Fried, Gerald 377
Friends of Distinction **261**, 477, 583, 718
Fripp, Robert 639
Frith, Fred 322
Fritts, Donnie 314
Frog, Wynder K. 818
Frontiere, Dominic 68
Frusciante, John 284
Fry, Barbara 686
Frye, Alan 495
Frye, David 479
Frye, Drake 261
Frye, Joe 450
Fuentes, Miguel 468
Fugees 173, 313, 366, 367, 500
Fugi **261**
Fukumura, Hiroshi 558
Full Force 90, 291, 353, 422, 575, 689
Fullbright, J.R. 218
Fuller, Anthony 574
Fuller, Bobby 812
Fuller, Bobby Four 742
Fuller, Curtis 282
Fuller, Jerry 628
Fuller, Johnny 3
Fuller, Karl 157
Fuller, Sam 296
Fulson, Lowell 130, **261**, 262, 458, 480, 520, 777, 801, 815, 818, 830
Fulson, Martin 261
Fulton, Paul 141
Fulwood, Ramon Tiki 263, 264, 306, 522
Funches, Johnny 186, 187
Funderburgh, Anson 93
Funicello, Annette 92
Funk Brothers **262**, 263, 266, 273, 360, 600, 714, 754, 830
Funk, Inc. 24, **263**
Funkadelic 6, 14, 34, 53, 54, 79, 81, 85, 88, 110, 111, 112, 124, 146, 147, 153, 155, 165, 166, 167, 170, 195, 219, 226, 248, 261, **263**, 264, 265, 266, 290, 295, 299, 306, 308, 348, 363, 381, 403, 437, 440, 488, 505, 509, 513, 517, 520, 522, 523, 524, 525, 535, 540, 554, 556, 560, 583, 622, 624, 625, 633, 637, 665, 673, 690, 693, 698, 699, 708, 739, 767, 775, 782, 801, 802, 831, 850, 851
Fuqua, Charlie 266, 337, 479
Fuqua, Gwen 112, **266**, 312, 480
Fuqua, Harvey 80, **266**, 271, 272, 274, 281, 360, 415, 426, 439, 445, 479, 480, 495, 497, 499, 637, 721, 745, 747, 767
Fury, Billy 135, 577
Futures 186, **266**, 267, 820
Fuzz **267**, 437, 809

G

G-Clefs 797
G Wiz, Gary 441
G, Kenny 76, 257, 429, 490, 720, 734
G, Nappy 289
G, Warren 225
G. Love 98, 261, 466
G., Kelly 558
Gable, Eric 785
Gable, Guitar 783, 800
Gabriel & the Angels 821
Gabriel, Peter 141, 241, 318, 582
Gadd, Steve 591, 648, 710
Gadson, James 68, 99, 705, 758, 769
Gainer, George 600
Gaines, Billy and Sarah 718
Gaines, Earl **268**, 779, 793
Gaines, Roy 57, 58
Gaines, Walter 511, 718
Gainey, Earl 751
Gaining, Cub 107
Gainors 473, 668
Gainsbourg, Serge 650
Gaither, Tommy 511, 512
Galbraith, Alastair 173
Galbraith, Rob 173
Galdo, Joe 254
Galdston, Phil 736
Gale, Eric 94, 294, 376, 413, 591, 648, 734
Gale, Sunny 209
Gale, Trevor 426
Galfo, George 489
Gallagher, Jimmy 525
Gallahads **268**, 788, 821
Gallery 373
Galliano 411, 554
Gallo, Joey 20
Gallo, Renard 660
Galloway, A. Scott 586
Galloway, Jim 295
Galuten, Albhy 40
Gambale, Frank 80
Gamble 42, 103
Gamble & Huff 42, 43, 84, 96, 98, 104, 105, 117, 140, 155, 167, 168, 216, 217, 240, 267, 296, 312, 313, 317, 319, 322, 325, 338, 339, 346, 347, 350, 372, 373, 381, 460, 465, 466, 505, 507, 526, 528, 533, 537, 543, 556, 563, 564, 567, 615, 616, 617, 618, 620, 632, 638, 639, 652, 665, 679, 687, 689, 707, 723, 728, 756, 781, 785, 794, 826
Gamble, Clifton 532
Gamble, Kenneth 11, 42, 43, 103, 104, 105, 117, 204, 205, 231, 266, 267, **268**, 292, 319, 325, 338, 339, 346, 372, 378, 405, 465, 468, 476, 499, 505, 506, 507, 530, 533, 563, 564, 565, 593, 600, 610, 615, 618, 632, 650, 660, 687, 723, 786, 794, 818, 834, 848
Gamble, Renaldo 400, 601, 602
Gamble, Terry 431
Gammond, Peter 337
Gane, Tim 515
Gang Starr 75, 136, 621, 787
Gangsters 140
Ganja Kru 725
Gano, Gordon 857
Ganser, Marge 608
Ganser, Mary Anne 608
Gant, Cecil 94, 759, 760, 836
Gant, Dean 100
Gant, Kenneth 470
Gap Band 22, 70, 81, 98, 170, **268**, 269, 270, 275, 290, 293, 338, 583, 622, 773, 785, 801, 851
Gapuz, Andrew 383
Garcia, Frank 113
Garcia, Jerry 493
Gardner, Billy 217
Gardner, Carl 149, 578
Gardner, Charles 463
Gardner, Don 270
Gardner, Don & Dee Dee Ford **270**, 413, 786, 800
Gardner, Joe 647
Gardner, Rick 739
Gardner, Taana **270**, 271, 416, 834
Garduno, Max 140
Garland, Judy 697
Garlow, Clarence 777
Garner, Al 549
Garner, Erroll 585
Garner, Henry 585
Garnes, Sherman 433
Garnett, Carlos 159
Garnett, Gale 565
Garnier, Laurent 43
Garrett, Amos 129
Garrett, Bobby 63
Garrett, Joanne **271**
Garrett, Kenny 105
Garrett, Robert 783
Garrett, Siedah 22, 75, 81, 217, 218, 354, 377
Garrett, Vernon **271**
Garrison, Al 665, 773
Garrison, Michael 476
Garvin, Rex 307
Gary's Gang 795
Gaskins, Ray 92
Gaston, Pat 629
Gaston, Steve 648
Gates, David 261, 279, 613, 799, 834, 842
Gates, Jennifer 259
Gates, Jimmy Jr. 617
Gathers, Helen 63
Gathers, Ronald 438
Gatling, Timmy 290, 291
Gaturs **271**
Gaudio, Bob 190, 191
Gautreau, Ernie 5
Gay, Rudy 3
Gaye, Anna Gordy 266, 271, 272, 274
Gaye, Ellie 558
Gaye, Frankie 823, 832
Gaye, Marvin 15, 16, 17, 23, 29, 33, 37, 44, 55, 80, 92, 99, 106, 108, 112, 137, 156, 157, 161, 166, 167, 175, 186, 192, 225, 234, 247, 263, 266, **271**, 272, 273, 274, 275, 276, 280, 281, 284, 285, 305, 309, 310, 313, 315, 320, 327, 328, 334, 338, 339, 345, 349, 353, 359, 360, 365, 369, 371, 374, 380, 384, 386, 394, 396, 410, 415, 416, 426, 427, 434, 435, 439, 444, 445, 447, 451, 452, 453, 455, 471, 474, 480, 481, 488, 492, 503, 509, 511, 520, 521, 525, 542, 549, 558, 568, 571, 573, 578, 579, 580, 584, 586, 587, 588, 604, 611, 616, 619, 644, 645, 646, 647, 648, 655, 657, 660, 663, 670, 673, 675, 680, 687, 688, 704, 708, 709, 720, 721, 723, 727, 728, 734, 735, 739, 740, 742, 745, 757, 758, 761, 762, 763, 770, 777, 780, 784, 785, 786, 787, 788, 789, 790, 792, 794, 800, 801, 802, 813, 814, 816, 817, 824, 825, 831, 833, 844, 846, 851
Gaye, Marvin & Tammi Terrell 408, 655
Gaye, Nona **275**
Gayle, Charles 168
Gayles, Billy 702
Gaylords 727
Gaynor, Gloria 6, 23, 38, 96, 175, 201, 202, **275**, 276, 277, 297, 317, 321, 397, 460, 533, 600, 609, 683, 686, 687
Gayten, Paul 102, **277**, 310, 789, 790
Gaytunes 827
Geddins, Robert 261, 300
Gee, Eddie 735
Geils, J. 762
Geils, J. Band 448, 601, 712, 760
Geller, Gregg 755
Geller, Herb 528, 732
Geller, Lorraine 206
Gems 36, 575, 576, 791
Gene & Eunice 779, 807
General Public 239
Genesis 120, 214
Genie 795
Genies 497, 589, 590, 778, 828
Gentile, Mickey 143, 580
Gentlemen 827
Gentry, Bobbie 283, 756
Gentry, Melvin 470
Gentry, William 614
Gentrys 72, 696
Gents 691
George & Teddy 626
George, Barbara 198, **277**, 579, 783, 793, 805, 808, 840
George, Langston 539
George, Lowell 419, 694
George, Sam 114
Georgia Mass Choir 323
Gerard, Don 47, 283
Gerran, Gregory 84
Gerrard, Donny **277**
Gerrard, Matthew 217
Gerry & the Pacemakers 85, 784
Gershwin & Gershwin 49, 588, 729
Gershwin, George 5, 88, 129, 132, 188, 337, 359, 416, 487, 504, 645
Geter, Gus 611
Getz, Stan 857
Giambalvo, Lenny 41
Gianatos, Rick 145
Gianolio, Paolo 127
Gibb, Andy 9, 40, 41, 189, 190, 592
Gibb, Barry 40, 220, 729, 730, 731
Gibb, Maurice 40
Gibb, Robin 40, 220, 592
Gibbons, Walter 200, 383, 795
Gibbs, Darryl 647
Gibbs, Derek 173, 174
Gibbs, Georgia 31
Gibbs, Mike 420
Gibbs, Terry 733
Gibson, Charlene 261
Gibson, Debbie 689
Gibson, Deborah 77
Gibson, Don 131, 456
Gibson, Elmer 159
Gibson, Henry 452, 710
Gibson, Michael 553
Gibson, Steve & the Red Caps 794
Gift, Roland 239, 240
Gilbeaux, Gene 759
Gilbert, Bill 251
Gilbert, Cary 322, 339, 465, 526
Gilberto, Astrud 188
Giles, Attala Zane 578, 660
Gill, Caldin "Cal" 715
Gill, Carolyn 371, 832
Gill, Johnny 7, 28, 82, 225, **277**, 278, 412, 417, 431, 492, 496, 497, 573, 609, 698, 720
Gillespie, Dana 230
Gillespie, Dizzy 195, 375, 376, 377, 389, 433, 544, 555, 610, 724, 763, 791
Gilley, Mickey 132
Gilliam, Barbara 267
Gilliam, Roberta 792
Gilliom, Robert 647
Gilmore, Dennis 545, 546
Gilstrap, Jim 466, 800
Ginuwine 221, **278**, 628
Giovanni, Nikki **278**, 279, 811
Girlfriends **279**
Girls **279**
Giscombe, Junior 381
Givings, Charles 560
Gladiators 293
Gladiolas 191, 751, 783, 805
Glasper, Robert 219
Glass House 219, **279**, 655, 718, 809, 811, 816, 832
Glass, Alan 381
Glass, Eugene 438
Glass, Preston 186, 317, 751
Glasser, Art 712
Glazer, Barry 679
Gleason, Jackie 149, 391
Gleeson, Patrick 55
Glenn, Garry 223, 617
Glenn, Lloyd 261, 701
Glover, Bob 775
Glover, Corey 234
Glover, Don 671
Glover, Henry 56, 183, 297, 488
Glover, Leroy 227
Glover, Savion 488, 788

Go Go's 715, 844
Goddard, David 14
Goddard, Pelham 14
Godfrey, Arthur 184, 511
Godfrey, Paul 483
Godfrey, Ross 483
Godin, Dave 793
Goetzman, Gary 581
Goffin & King 80, 165, 640, 728
Goffin, Gerry 92, 141, 165, 172, 208, 231, 256, 392, 423, 424, 574, 580, 610, 613, 639, 729, 784, 803, 834, 841, 842, 843, 844
Goings, Jimmy 599
Goins, Glen 488, 556
Goins, Herbie & Soultimers 418
Goins, Kevin 556
Gold, Jack 398
Gold, Ken 566
Goldberg, Whoopi 257, 376
Golden Eagles 746
Golden Gate Quartet 209, 409, 822
Golden Smog 525
Golden, Quinn **279**, 280
Goldentones 143
Goldie & the Gingerbreads 636, 804
Goldner, George 128, 129, 170, 185, 205, 246, 307, 367, 433, 464, 767, 803, 821, 827
Goldsboro, Bobby 126, 168, 356
Goldsmith, Cliff 63, 508, 673
Goldstein, Jerry 13, 724
Goldtones 618
Golson, Benny 70, 71, 282, 376, 755, 759, 760
Gomez, Leroy 599
Gomez, Ray 38
Gomez, Tony 250
Gonsales, Pablo 173
Gonsalves, Paul 74, 131
Gonsalves, Renell 74
Gonzales, Andy 295
Gonzales, Babs 810
Good Fellas 234
Good Girls 691
Gooden, Sam 103, 235, 333, 334, 335, 408
Gooding, Cuba **280**, 437, 438, 486, 541
Gooding, Cuba Jr. 437
Goodman, Al 349, 477, 478, 565, 575, 688, 740
Goodman, Benny 433, 567
Goodman, Benny Sextet 563
Goodman, Dickie 185
Goodman, John 62
Goodman, Mark 307
Goodman, Shirley 349, 613, 614, 766
Goodtimers 167
Goosly, Ronnie 365
Gordon, Billy 160, 824
Gordon, Bob 413
Gordon, Jim 555
Gordon, Mack 169
Gordon, Marc 30, 33, 143, 238, 322, 324, 331, 332, 413, 416, 417, 573
Gordon, Ron 34
Gordon, Rosco **280**, 684, 812
Gordy, Barry 656
Gordy, Berry Jr. 112, 121, 142, 143, 157, 160, 166, 183, 235, 250, 251, 253, 262, 263, 266, 268, 271, 272, 273, 274, 275, **280**, 281, 312, 315, 316, 327, 340, 346, 348, 352, 360, 369, 370, 396, 397, 426, 431, 433, 445, 447, 461, 472, 479, 480, 492, 500, 511, 527, 533, 537, 549, 559, 578, 579, 580, 581, 582, 584, 592, 643, 647, 648, 653, 654, 663, 675, 677, 679, 691, 714, 715, 716, 721, 738, 739, 754, 755, 763, 764, 784, 786, 790, 805, 818, 823, 831, 832
Gordy, George 266
Gordy, Iris 80, 581
Gordy, Kerry 677
Gordy, Robert 340
Gore, Lesley 15, 375, 376, 808, 844
Gorelick, Kenny 429
Gorham, Jimmy 408
Gories 748
Goring, Sonia 128
Gorman, Fred 511, 571, 600, 718
Gorrie, Alan 22, 23
Gospel Keynotes 646
Gospelaires 728
Gossett, Lou 377, 577
Gottehrer, Richard 13
Gotti, Irv 17
Gottlieb, Danny 780
Gourdine, Anthony 422, 423
Govan, Dave 443, 717
GQ **281**, 293, 795
Grace, Fredi 630
Graf, Hakon 80
Graham Central Station 81, 259, 260, 282, 283, 625, 684, 698, 777, 802, 851
Graham, Bill 151, 695
Graham, Billy [Country] 151
Graham, Jaki **281**, 308, 809
Graham, John 214
Graham, Larry 178, 184, 257, 260, 282, 283, 341, 393, 624, 684, 850
Graham, Larry & Graham Central Station **282**
Graham, Leo 180, 441
Graham, Willy 463
Grainger, Gary 542
Grainger, Gerri 784
Granahan, Gerry 13, 45
Grand Funk Railroad 35, 222, 746
Grand Puba 59, 75
Grand Theft 773
Grandmaster Flash 210, 399, 698
Grandmaster Flash & the Furious Five 259, 260
Grandmaster Melle Mel 388, 411
Grant, Amy 10, 857
Grant, Arthur 633
Grant, Cornelius 546, 547, 560
Grant, Darrell 235
Grant, Earl **283**
Grant, Eddy 226, 796
Grant, Eric 505
Grant, George 121, 122
Grant, Jim 53, 688
Grant, Noel 367, 368
Grant, Pete 535
Granz, Norman 132
Grass Roots 811
Grate, Tommy 209
Grateful Dead 493, 523
Graves, Alexander 266, 480
Graves, Carl **283**
Graves, James 720, 721
Gray, Andrew 284
Gray, Bruce 318
Gray, Diva 312
Gray, Dobie **283**, 284, 357, 818, 824
Gray, George 542
Gray, Macy 1, 14, **284**, 388, 390
Gray, Wardell 733, 735
Graydon, Jay 277, 509
Grayson, Alltrinna 64
Grayson, Dori 823
Grayson, Miles 673
Grayson, Rhonda 430
Graziano, Lee 592
Grease Band 150
Great Society 624
Greaves, R.B. **284**
Green, Adolph 21
Green, Al 15, 44, 96, 143, 144, 162, 150, 175, 190, 279, 281, 282, **285**, 286, 287, 293, 311, 368, 369, 371, 372, 379, 386, 409, 410, 425, 444, 445, 451, 455, 469, 475, 476, 499, 526, 529, 530, 535, 596, 601, 605, 606, 607, 632, 645, 659, 663, 700, 704, 706, 720, 771, 781, 785, 786, 791, 794, 809, 810, 816, 844, 845, 856, 857
Green, Bobby 225
Green, Cal 32
Green, Carl 448
Green, Charles 724
Green, Doc 208, 241, 577
Green, Freddie 701
Green, Garland 15
Green, Grant 13, **287**, 288, 787, 810, 857, 858
Green, Greg 510
Green, Jerome 191, 192, 193
Green, Jimmy 463
Green, Julius 436
Green, Leo 332, 633, 700
Green, Linda "Peaches" 528, 533
Green, Maxine 463
Green, McLauren 450, 557
Green, Ricky 724
Green, Rudy 783
Green, Sandra 266
Green, Tommy 16
Green, Toni 408
Green, Vernon & the Medallions **288**, 463, 464, 812
Green, Willie 185
Green, Willie Jr. 493
Greenaway, Roger 201
Greenberg, Chuck 326, 499
Greenberg, Florence 326, 612, 728, 731
Greenberg, Jerry 499
Greenberg, Peter 744
Greenburg, Larry 621
Greene, Carlos 183
Greene, Ed 428, 742
Greene, Larry 217
Greene, Mark 477
Greene, Marlin 314
Greene, Michael 384
Greene, Susaye **288**, 655, 656
Greenfield, Howard 717, 729, 842
Greenwich, Ellie 4, 144, 196, 208, 367, 415, 430, 558, 585, 639, 657, 784, 803, 841, 842, 843, 844
Greer, Big John 297, 800, 808, 810
Gregory, Byron 635
Gregory, Gerald 634, 635
Grey, Zane 98
Greyboy 288, 289
Greyboy Allstars **288**, 289
Grider, Robbin 395
Grier, David 185
Grier, Joseph 135, 165
Grier, Pam 185, 727, 811, 815
Grier, Roosevelt 818
Grier, Rosey 799
Gries, Eddie 648, 716, 806
Griffey, Dick 212, 406, 432, 607, 632, 633, 652, 653, 741, 761
Griffin, Billy **289**, 474, 475, 580, 727
Griffin, Don 474
Griffin, Donald 289
Griffin, Gene 290, 575
Griffin, Gerri 718
Griffin, Herman 266, 712, 819, 825
Griffin, Johnny 780
Griffin, Leroy 500, 805
Griffin, Lindsey 307
Griffin, Mary **289**
Griffin, Melvin 601
Griffin, Paul 31
Griffin, R.L. 369
Griffin, Reggie 28, 439
Griffin, Rick 296
Griffith, Johnny 262, 263
Griggs, Johnny 366
Grimes, Howard 286, 311
Grimes, Tiny 301, 780
Griner, Linda 831, 832
Groia, Phil 307
Groove Armada 823
Groove Collective **289**, 290
Groove Theory 409, 736
Grooverider 102
Grossman, Stefan 32
Group 321
Groves, Lani 466
Grudge, Mickey 76
Grusin, Dave 21, 64, 572, 734, 768
Grusin, Don 21
Guaraldi, Vince 24, 48
Guenther, Ian 686
Guerra, Joey 689
Guess Who 654
Guest, Annette 240, 241
Guest, William 539
Guida, Frank 36, 65
Guillaume, Jephte 383
Guishard, Jeffrey 312
Guitar Shorty 426
Guitar Slim [Alec Seward] 255, 783
Guitar Slim [Eddie Jones] 63, 90, 130, 392, 393, 434, 626, 753, 792, 793, 810, 838
Guitar, Johnny 736
Gulliver 292
Gummoe, John 121
Gunter, Arthur 783
Gunter, Cornell 149, 246
Gunter, Shirley 539
Guralnick, Peter 52, 314, 552
Guru 25, 373, 803
Gurvitz, Adrian 259
Guthrie, Gwen **290**, 419, 571
Guthrie, Scott 129
Guthrie, Woody 208, 416, 582, 619
Gutierrez, Juan 647
Guy 41, 56, 59, 82, 270, **290**, 291, 293, 355, 369, 506, 575, 631, 659, 661
Guy Called Gerald 698
Guy, Billy 149
Guy, Buddy 78, 250, 702, 791, 810
Guy, Jasmine **291**, 575
Guy, Sherman 34
Guy, Vernon 610
Guytones 783, 798
Guzman, Pablo 441

H
H Town 574
Hackford, Taylor 51
Hackman, Gene 687
Haffkine, Ron 565
Haggard, Merle 132, 356
Hailey, Cedric "K-Ci" 368, 382
Hailey, Joel "Jo Jo" 382
Hairston, Curtis 747
Hairston, Kenni 623
Hakim, Omar 25
Hale, Andrew 596
Hale, Jack 466
Hale, Traci 659
Hale, Willie Beaver 423
Haley, Bill 50, 129, 378, 408, 697, 706, 812
Haley, Bill & His Comets 4, 172, 647
Hall & Oates 7, 109, 120, 212, **292**, 293, 444, 591, 636, 667, 668, 669, 785, 811, 821, 847
Hall, Aaron 230, 290, 291, **293**, 575, 659
Hall, Albert 715
Hall, Arsenio 291
Hall, Barbara 184
Hall, Bobbye 727
Hall, Carl 662
Hall, Clarence 421
Hall, Damion 290, 575
Hall, Darryl 821
Hall, Daryl 231, 292, 563, 679, 818
Hall, David 412
Hall, Delores 662
Hall, Fred 188
Hall, Gerry 627
Hall, Jack 324
Hall, James 496, 499
Hall, Jim 376, 527
Hall, Joe 54
Hall, Joseph III 55
Hall, Reggie 816
Hall, Rene 518, 761, 812
Hall, Rick 8, 11, 143, 326, 350, 360, 415, 463, 555, 644, 645
Hall, Tony 493
Hall, Wesley 97
Hall, Willie 34, 685
Halloran, Jack Choir 131
Halos **293**
Hamilton, Andrew 692
Hamilton, Arthur 689
Hamilton, Bob 142, 571
Hamilton, Chico 25
Hamilton, Dave 794
Hamilton, Frank 761
Hamilton, Jimmy 759, 773
Hamilton, Larry **293**, 294
Hamilton, Milton 821
Hamilton, Phil 709
Hamilton, Roy 172, **294**, 304, 647, 759, 784, 821
Hamilton, Roy "Royalty" 660
Hamlin, Rosie 586
Hamlin, Rosie "Rosalie" 586
Hamlisch, Marvin 125
Hammer, Jack 56
Hammock, Cleveland 205
Hammond, Beres 294
Hammond, Clay **294**, 824
Hammond, John Jr. 196
Hammond, John Sr. 255
Hammond, John [Drums] 241
Hammond, Johnny 791
Hammond, Roy 589, 590

Hammond, Walter 508
Hampden, Larry 128
Hampton, Carl 233
Hampton, Lionel 25, 54, 70, 263, 351, 375, 512, 514, 520, 777, 822
Hampton, Michael 154, 263, 266, 306, 517, 523
Hampton, Mike 265
Hampton, Riley 358, 360
Hancock, Butch 307, 633
Hancock, Herbie 25, 47, 84, 159, 160, 210, 227, 287, 288, **294**, 295, 307, 308, 376, 377, 389, 390, 420, 474, 485, 488, 490, 543, 566, 594, 666, 671, 672, 734, 739, 761, 767, 787, 788, 801, 823, 825, 826, 851, 857
Hancock, Larry 333, 633, 700
Hand, K 43
Handy, Charles 535
Handy, John 558
Handy, Sylvester 315
Handy, W.C. 546
Haney, Bill 784
Hankerson, Barry 397
Hanks, Len Ron 98
Hanna, Jerome 368
Hanna, Roland Trio 714
Hannett, Martin 227
Hannibal 812
Hannibal, Chauncey 56, 290, 575
Hansen, Barret 163
Hanson 145, 689
Hardcastle, Paul 281
Harder, Eddie 213
Hardesty, Herbert 199, 421, 613
Hardin, Eddie 179
Hardin, Mel 464
Hardin, Tim 251, 321
Hardman, Bill 73
Hardsty, Herb 86
Hardy, Francoise 804
Hardy, Ron 399
Hare, Pat 57, 58, 520
Harem 430
Hargrove, Roy 29, 176
Harlem Boys Choir 385
Harlem River Drive **295**
Harley, Sanchez 486
Harley, Steve 419
Harmon, Gordy 740
Harmonica Slim 218
Harmonizing Four 473
Harold, Lyndon 434
Harp 443
Harp, Cornelius 443
Harp, Everette 30
Harper, Ben 241, 319
Harper, James 402
Harper, Vaughn 44
Harper, Willie 803
Harpo, Slim 62, 192, 783, 800, 803, 813, 838
Harps 295
Harptones 123, 242, **295**, 296, 332, 778, 780, 797, 827, 828, 831
Harralson, William Scott 601
Harrell, Andre 368, 657
Harrell, Paul 157, 158
Harrell, Rocq E 835
Harrell, Tom 30, 540
Harrell, Vern 299
Harris, Barbara 696, 697
Harris, Barry [1] 59
Harris, Barry [2] 400
Harris, Barry [3] 714
Harris, Beaver 632
Harris, Betty **296**, 365, 466, 694, 786, 802, 803, 809
Harris, Beverly 247
Harris, Bill 148
Harris, Bobby 181, 182, 394
Harris, Cal 727
Harris, Cortez 324, 510
Harris, Damon 42, 309, 332, 674, 676, 677
Harris, Dave 235
Harris, Dennis 697
Harris, Don Sugarcane 199, **296**
Harris, Eddie 7, 109, 420, 444, 739, 780, 857, 858
Harris, Frank 226
Harris, Gene 787, 857, 858
Harris, Hugh 4
Harris, James 630
Harris, Joe [1] 205, 479, 745
Harris, Joe [2] 200, 708
Harris, Lawrence "Big L" 628, 629
Harris, Lois 128
Harris, Louise 307
Harris, Major 185, 186, 212, **296**, 364, 688, 787, 788, 794, 795, 819
Harris, Michael 535
Harris, Muscle Shoals 762
Harris, Norman 62, 166, 190, 200, 217, 231, 240, 253, 276, **296**, 317, 318, 319, 338, 380, 387, 453, 468, 534, 597, 615, 618, 632, 633, 677, 697, 740, 797, 820
Harris, Peppermint 107, **297**
Harris, R.H. 164, 632
Harris, Richard 368
Harris, Sonny 577
Harris, Steve 244
Harris, Thurston 7, 56, 63, 180, **297**, 518, 577, 779
Harris, Tim 250
Harris, Tony 799
Harris, Warren 479
Harris, Webster 368
Harris, Wynonie 93, 94, 251, **297**, 298, 460, 514, 627, 769, 777, 781, 783, 812, 822, 833, 836, 838
Harrison, George 68, 99, 141, 244, 269, 566, 635, 699, 703, 792
Harrison, Jerry 240
Harrison, Keith 181
Harrison, Rich 11
Harrison, Spencer 160
Harrison, Sterling 791
Harrison, Wilbert **298**, 712, 783, 800, 801, 805, 836, 838
Harriston, Ernest 70
Harsch, Eddie 179
Hart, Bobby 600
Hart, John 697
Hart, Lorenz 649, 656
Hart, Wilbert 185, 186
Hart, William 160, 185, 186, 296, 348, 801
Hartford, John 256
Hartman, Dan 92, **298**, 299, 317, 639, 706
Hartman, Johnny 5
Harvey & the Moonglows 266, 480, 793
Harvey, Aston 415, 439
Harvey, Connie 14, 337
Harvey, Daddae 631
Harvey, P.J. 359, 690
Harvin, Martha 313, 368
Haskins, Clarence "Fuzzy" 264, 265, **299**, 522, 523, 525
Haslip, Jimmy 595
Hassan, Umar Bin 410, 411
Hatch, Tony 660
Hatcher, Roger **299**, 643, 833
Hatfield, Bobby 464, 574, 575, 847
Hathaway, Donny 14, 29, 47, 97, 104, 160, 231, 245, **299**, 300, 320, 327, 328, 334, 485, 520, 540, 598, 646, 682, 709, 727, 768, 793
Hathaway, Lalah 69, 299, **300**, 394, 670, 757
Hatim, Lee 449
Haught, Brian 3
Haukkala, Erno 110
Hauser, Fay 623
Hawes, Bruce 649
Hawes, Hampton 24, 25, 558, 759
Hawketts 466, 493, 495, 790
Hawkins, Coleman 603, 647, 759
Hawkins, Dale 782, 790
Hawkins, Edwin **300**, 302, 376, 824
Hawkins, Edwin Singers 300
Hawkins, Elizabeth 302
Hawkins, Gus 633
Hawkins, James 553
Hawkins, Roger 89, 314
Hawkins, Ronnie 774, 815
Hawkins, Rosa Lee 196
Hawkins, Roy **300**, 301
Hawkins, Sam 779
Hawkins, Screamin' Jay **301**, 340, 748, 783, 812, 818, 822, 836
Hawkins, Steve 634
Hawkins, Ted 294, **301**, 302, 825
Hawkins, Tramaine **302**
Hawkins, Walter 302
Hayden 521
Hayden, Shirley 522
Hayes, Bernie 828
Hayes, Bonnie 98, 773
Hayes, Chanelle 698
Hayes, Debbie 337, 709
Hayes, Edgar 70
Hayes, Isaac 10, 18, 22, 23, 34, 36, 52, 95, 96, 106, 145, 146, 175, 223, 273, 276, 290, **303**, 304, 305, 320, 326, 340, 357, 358, **369**, 371, 379, 380, 401, 444, 449, 533, 545, 555, 567, 598, 599, 601, 617, 630, 647, 660, 682, 685, 731, 742, 763, 786, 787, 788, 794, 804, 808, 815, 828, 830, 851
Hayes, Jimmy 534, 535
Hayes, John 485
Hayes, Kenneth 145
Hayes, Maurice 773
Hayes, Milton 98
Hayes, Paul 548
Hayes, Roger 601
Hayes, Willie 634
Haynes, Douglas 833
Haynes, Roy 759, 760, 768
Haywood, Kitty 257
Haywood, Leon 117, **305**, 336, 378, 769, 784, 788, 824
Hazel 263
Hazel, Eddie 14, 124, 147, 165, 263, 264, 265, 266, **306**, 517, 522, 523, 535, 677
Head, Roy **306**, 307, 458, 847
Headhunters 294, 295, **307**
Headliner 16
Healey, Jeff 787
Heap, Jimmy 821
Heard, Larry 240, 399, 791
Heart 79, 640
Heartbeats 123, 206, 271, **307**, 479, 611, 828
Heartbreakers 584
Hearts 12, **307**, 365, 577, 611, 732
Hearts of Stone **307**, 308
Heartsman, Johnny 361, 618
Heath Brothers 485
Heath, Albert "Tootie" 294
Heath, Jimmy 288, 485
Heath, Rhonda 617
Heatherton, Joey 834
Heatwave 81, 156, **308**, 622
Heaven & Earth 121, **309**
Heaven Seventeen 392, 484, 706, 820
Heavy D 127, 657, 693
Heavy D & the Boyz 216, 368, 373, 478
Hebb, Bobby 66, 198, **309**
Hebb, Hal 309
Hector, Hex 59
Height, Donald 318
Heller, Bobby 12
Heller, Eddie 12
Helm, Carl 318, 597
Helms, Jimmy 699
Henderson, Bernard 324
Henderson, Billy 636
Henderson, Buddy 20
Henderson, Eddie 159, 366, 485, 650
Henderson, Harvey Joe 35
Henderson, Horace 73, 102
Henderson, Joe 25, 105, 227, 287, 294, 388, 389, 485, 594, 659, 725, 786, 810
Henderson, Michael **309**, 310
Henderson, Mike 136, 159, 190, 309, 310, 329
Henderson, Scott 322
Henderson, Wayne 26, 84, 170, 171, 324, 358, 508, 541, 615
Henderson, Wes 670
Henderson, Willie 4, 180, 414, 754
Hendricks, Belford 732, 733
Hendricks, Bobby 206, 207, 241, 658, 783
Hendrix, Jimi 18, 29, 34, 53, 102, 146, 167, 170, 183, 191, 194, 231, 261, 263, 264, 265, 266, 306, 340, 341, 342, 343, 344, 376, 424, 425, 437, 462, 515, 546, 561, 576, 583, 605, 668, 670, 718, 760, 785, 830, 850, 851
Hendrix, Margie 134, 718
Hendryx, Nona 112, 298, **310**, 390, 403, 404, 405, 716
Henley, Don 168
Hennant, Jimmy 507
Henneghan, Greg 431
Henning, Doug 214
Henry, Andrea 808
Henry, Clarence "Frogman" 129, **310**, 311, 782, 783, 790, 793, 840
Henry, Errol 373
Henry, Joe 101, 102
Henry, Joe 100
Henry, Pauline 727
Henry, Virgil 831
Henson, Ronnie 431
Henson-Conant, Deborah 21
Herbert, Elyse 367
Herbert, Maxine 367
Herbert, Vincent 1, 369
Herman, Woody 102, 299, 759
Herman's Hermits 842, 844
Hernandez, Andy "Coatimundi" 196, 389
Hernandez, Felix 267
Hernandez, Patrick 196
Herndon, Billy 740
Heron 603, 604
Herring, Ursula 240, 241
Herron, Cindy 222, 224
Hesitations **311**
Hester, Carolyn 203
Hester, Eloise 331
Hester, Tony 203, 204, 468, 540, 832
Hewett, Howard 8, **311**, 353, 607, 608, 633
Hewitt, Lonnie 325
Hey, Jerry 747
Heyward, Dubose 562
Heyward, Louis 562
Heywood, Donald 715
Heywood, Leon 117
Hi Fi's 261
Hi Five 230, 575, 686
Hi Lites 137, 814
Hi Lo's 437, 658, 666
Hi Rhythm 231, 285, 286, **311**, 530
Hi Tension **312**
Hiatt, John 2, 5
Hibbler, Al 610
Hickman, Hargis 78
Hicks, Colin 250
Hicks, Joe 508
Hicks, Mark 622
Hicks, Marva 219
Hicks, Ulysses K. 242
Hicks, Valerie 237
Higginbotham, Robert 700
Higgins, Beau 412
Higgins, Bertie 3, 145
Higgins, Christine 145
Higgins, Chuck **312**, 737, 788, 798
Higgins, Cleopatra 145
Higgins, Monk 3, 209
High Fashion 139, **312**, 483, 747
High Frequency 99
High Inergy **312**, 313, 652
High, Martha **313**
Hightower, Johnnie 532
Hightower, Rossetta 512
Hightower, Willie 824
Highway QCs 161, 563, 632, 672, 673
Highwaymen [Country] 466
Highwaymen [Rock] 784
Hill, Billie 228
Hill, Don 759
Hill, Eddie 831
Hill, Fairest 161
Hill, Jessie **313**, 621, 694
Hill, Lauryn 59, 175, 176, 258, **313**, 314, 323, 366, 388, 470, 554, 572, 602, 646, 757
Hill, Mark 177, 178
Hill, Marvin 408
Hill, Matt 314
Hill, Raymond 78, 702, 703
Hill, Z.Z. 293, 294, **314**, 350, 369, 409, 418, 545, 673, 801, 813, 818, 824, 834
Hilliard, George 707
Hills, Chris 540
Hilltoppers 409
Hilton-Jacobs, Lawrence 202
Hinds, Jimmy 39
Hines, Ann 55
Hines, Donald 809
Hines, Earl 148, 360, 759
Hines, Gary 634

Hines, Gregory 1, 671, 698, 811
Hinsley, Harvey 320
Hinton, Eddie **314**, 660
Hinton, Joe **314**, 481, 778
Hirt, Al 197, 694
Hoagland, Jaheim 359
Hobbs 241
Hobbs, Elsbeary 207, 208, 241
Hochberg, Eric 109
Hodge, Gaynell 532, 798
Hodge, Tommy 702
Hodges Brothers 311, 476
Hodges, Charles 311, 372, 476, 810, 819
Hodges, Fred 311
Hodges, James & Smith **315**
Hodges, Johnny 287
Hodges, Leroy 311, 476, 810
Hodges, Mabon "Teenie" 286, 476
Hodges, Pat 315
Hodges, Teenie 311, 810
Hoffman, Steven 51
Hogan, Carl 378, 379
Hogan, Don 205, 206
Hogan, Silas 800
Hogg, Billy 160
Hogue, Liz 365
Holden, Lorenzo 798
Holiday 687
Holiday, Billie 29, 94, 95, 130, 152, 162, 258, 284, 324, 360, 388, 487, 527, 586, 587, 588, 662, 732, 800
Holiday, Eddie 439, 509
Holiday, Jimmy **315**, 826
Holiday, Valerie 687
Holidays 37, 439, 525
Holland Dozier Holland 123, 124, 142, 166, 200, 202, 218, 219, 226, 251, 252, 253, 266, 273, 279, 281, **315**, 320, 340, 346, 372, 413, 430, 445, 447, 484, 497, 509, 511, 521, 524, 527, 579, 598, 641, 642, 653, 654, 655, 656, 663, 697, 712, 721, 745, 754, 755, 817, 845
Holland Skin Tunnel 527
Holland, Bernie 418
Holland, Bobby 784
Holland, Brian 112, 218, 226, 279, 315, 319, 340, 354, 387, 414, 415, 430, 446, 447, 497, 509, 527, 600, 642, 653, 654, 655, 657, 663, 674, 677, 712, 721, 811, 846
Holland, Eddie 202, 226, 253, 279, 281, **315**, 316, 319, 320, 325, 340, 342, 415, 426, 430, 439, 445, 446, 447, 461, 509, 527, 560, 600, 642, 654, 655, 657, 677, 704, 718, 739, 745, 805, 808, 811, 817, 846
Holland, Jools 240
Holland, Loris 705
Holland, Willie 533
Hollans, Timmy 652
Holley, Major 376
Holliday, Jennifer 202, **316**, 583
Hollies 330, 340, 367, 699, 751, 779, 804
Hollimon, Clarence 57, 58, 255, 413
Hollis, George 247
Hollister, Dave 56, 290, **316**, 575, 659
Holloway, Brenda 3, 142, 179, 186, 225, **316**, 317, 461, 513, 790, 795, 831, 834, 835, 846
Holloway, Loleatta 6, 59, 96, 184, **317**, 318, 321, 338, 397, 398, 416, 597, 609, 615, 679, 687, 795
Holloway, Loretta 819
Holloway, Patrice 316, 414
Holloway, Red 94, 95, 246, 330, 857
Holloway, Ron 513
Holly, Buddy 52, 121, 135, 191, 414, 480, 749, 753, 779, 805
Holly, Buddy & the Crickets 176, 340
Hollywood Beyond 519
Hollywood Flames 63, 180, **318**, 769, 798, 799
Holman, Eddie 279, 297, 317, **318**, 590, 626, 674, 722, 778, 792, 799, 819, 833, 834, 835, 848
Holmes Brothers 294, **318**, 319, 385
Holmes, Cecil 237
Holmes, Eldridge 803
Holmes, Jennifer 216, 217
Holmes, Jose 319
Holmes, Richard "Groove" 217, 759, 788, 857, 858
Holmes, Sherman 318, 319
Holmes, Wendell 318, 319
Holroyd, Bob 383
Holt, Ednah 416, 440
Holt, Isaac "Red" 773, 774
Holt, Pat 602
Holt, Redd **319**, 420, 421
Honey & the Bees **319**, 820
Honey Cone 79, 124, 202, 224, 279, 315, **319**, 320, 415, 509, 770, 785, 809
Honeycombs 655
Honeydrippers **320**, 421
Hood, David 89, 314
Hooker, Earl 192, 421
Hooker, John Lee 54, 62, 179, 191, 259, 282, 296, 418, 685, 702, 777, 779, 810, 815, 838
Hooks, Curtis 652
Hooks, Robert 646
Hooper, Nellee 9, 407, 631
Hooper, Stix 170, 171
Hope-Taylor, Randy 335
Hopkins, Lightnin' 189, 194, 297, 777, 778, 801, 806, 810
Hopkins, Linda 755, 834
Hopkins, Sy 243
Hoppen, Lance 414, 511
Hopson, Sonny **320**
Horn, Jim 361
Horn, Ozie 475
Horn, Trevor 134, 374, 375, 605
Horne, Cleveland 234
Horne, Lena 728, 810
Horne, Sheila 20
Hornets 206
Hornsby, Bruce 747
Horny Horns 154, 523, 524, 739
Horton, Big Walter 250, 700
Horton, Bill 616
Horton, Gladys 447
Horton, McKinley 121, 309
Horton, Yogi 81
Hoskins, Ollie 508
Hot Band 662
Hot Buttered Soul Unlimited 304
Hot Chocolate 312, **320**, 321, 381, 573, 797
Hot 356
House, Son 642
Houston, Cissy 1, 97, 143, 245, **321**, 322, 479, 660, 688, 699, 716, 728, 856
Houston, Joe 798, 815, 830, 836, 838
Houston, Marques 332
Houston, Thelma 277, **322**, 352, 397, 398, 430, 465, 466, 609, 687
Houston, Whitney 1, 6, 7, 28, 72, 73, 77, 82, 83, 115, 116, 168, 175, 184, 229, 230, 245, 257, 321, **322**, 323, 350, 353, 366, 367, 388, 457, 472, 531, 609, 610, 660, 720, 728, 731
Howard, Adina **323**, 324, 629
Howard, Camille 218, 473, 836, 838
Howard, George 7, 100, 244, 277, 490, 723
Howard, Harlan 131, 618
Howard, Linda 312
Howard, Miki 26, 234, **324**, 352, 417, 615, 785
Howard, Oliver 636
Howard, Richard 12
Howard, Robert 12
Howard, Simon 670
Howard, William "Wee Gee" 203, 204
Howe, Bones 238, 239
Howell, Alphonso 606
Howell, Angela 488
Howlin' Wolf 93, 191, 192, 361, 371, 426, 487, 520, 682, 709, 753, 813, 829, 830
Hubbard, Freddie 47, 105, 376, 388, 389, 444, 485, 788, 851
Huber, Eric 30
Hudson, Al 135, **324**, 489, 510, 545, 628, 634, 635
Hudson, Al & the Soul Partners 187, 324, 489, 510
Hudson, Harold 157
Hudson, Lafayette 405
Hudson, Lavine 427
Hues Corporation **324**, 360
Hueys 627
Huff, Eric 338
Huff, Leon 11, 42, 43, 103, 104, 105, 204, 216, 231, 266, 267, 268, 292, 319, 324, **325**, 338, 339, 346, 372, 374, 378, 465, 468, 476, 505, 506, 507, 526, 530, 532, 533, 563, 565, 593, 600, 602, 610, 615, 616, 618, 632, 677, 687, 710, 717, 723, 781, 786, 794, 817, 818, 820, 834
Huff, Steve 22, 316
Huff, Terry **325**, 437
Hugh, Grayson **325**
Hughes, Brian 422
Hughes, Charlie 209, 241
Hughes, Fred 814
Hughes, Freddie **325**, 326, 830
Hughes, Gene 121
Hughes, Jimmy 293, **326**, 360, 534, 786
Hughes, Leon 149
Hughes, Michael 422
Hugo, Chad 492
Hull, Danny 151
Human Beinz 340, 783
Human League 177, 544, 690
Humble Pie 699
Humes, Anita 228
Humes, Helen 228, 777, 798
Hummons, Dean 652
Humphrey, Bobbi 112, 787
Humphrey, Paul 252
Humphries, Lex 159
Humphries, Tony 416, 778
Hunt 246, 263
Hunt, Carlton 506
Hunt, Cecil 263
Hunt, Geraldine 818
Hunt, Mary 195
Hunt, Tommy 246, **326**, 793, 812, 824, 828
Hunter, Charlie 176
Hunter, Deborah 327, 395
Hunter, Fluffy 812
Hunter, Herbert 779, 817
Hunter, Ian 298, 543, 636
Hunter, Ivory Joe 90, 95, 172, 252, 262, 266, 273, 296, **326**, 342, 396, 445, 468, 514, 600, 602, 714, 727, 777, 823, 836
Hunter, Lloyd 430
Hunter, Tab 798
Hunter, Ty 279, 467, 511, 718, 816
Hunter, Willie [1] 716
Hunter, Willie [2] 647, 648
Hunters 774
Huntsberry, Howard **327**, 395, 545
Hurd, Francine "Peaches" 528
Hurley, Earl 657, 658
Hurley, Steve "Silk" 224, 399, 588, 600
Hurst, Mike 15
Hurt, Philip 597
Hurtt, Phil 231, 318, 338, 339, 481, 615, 717
Hutch, Willie 140, 201, **327**, 380, 474, 796
Hutcherson, Bobby 105, 287, 787
Hutcheson, Susan 79
Hutchins, Sammie 449
Hutchinson, Jeanette 223
Hutchinson, Pam 223
Hutchinson, Sheila 223
Hutchinson, Wanda 223
Hutchison, Larry 218
Hutson, Leroy **327**, 328, 333, 334, 335, 372, 452, 479, 491, 718, 793, 799, 817
Hutson, Marcus 740
Hyde, Bob 169
Hyman, Phyllis 43, 44, 159, 160, 253, 309, 310, **328**, 329, 427, 485, 723, 738, 809, 829
Hyper Go Go 6
Hytower, Roy 814

I

I Threes 366
Ian, Janis 608, 640
Ice Cube 146, 147, 330, 583, 667, 727
Ice T 22, 330, 482
Ice 405
Iceberg Slim **330**
Icehouse 293
Ideals 790, 818
Ides of March **330**
Idol, Billy 44
If 418
Iglesias, Enrique 229, 323
Iglesias, Julio 229, 587
Ikettes 15, 279, 319, 320, **330**, 331, 475, 703, 704, 801, 804
Imagination 121, **331**
Imaginations 367
Imajin **331**, 332
Immature 189, **332**
Impact **332**
Impalas **332**, 368, 824, 839
Imperial Wonders **332**, 333, 700, 800, 818
Imperials 34, 422, 423, 635
Impressions 42, 103, 104, 117, 126, 146, 180, 190, 235, 244, 256, 299, 327, 328, **333**, 334, 335, 341, 358, 394, 407, 408, 414, 428, 434, 437, 438, 451, 452, 453, 454, 464, 477, 479, 491, 511, 557, 657, 679, 692, 693, 714, 758, 778, 786, 789, 791, 793, 794, 801, 812, 814, 824, 828, 839, 844
Incognito **335**
Incredibles **335**, 626
Indeep **336**, 821
Independents 36, **336**, 458
India [Latin] 688
India [Rap] 59
Indian Ocean 796
Inglot, Bill 561
Ingram, Ashley 331
Ingram, Barbara 296, 318
Ingram, Bobby 660
Ingram, Butch 449
Ingram, Gregory 614
Ingram, James 21, 22, 43, 117, 129, 202, 305, **336**, 377, 512, 608, 684, 727, 743, 776, 825
Ingram, Luther 57, 121, 242, **336**, 337, 684
Ingram, Phillip 660
Ingram, Raphael 242
Ingram, Ripley 242
Ingui, Charles 632
Ingui, Richard 632
Ink Spots 74, 121, 122, 148, 251, 162, 198, 242, 266, **337**, 409, 426, 479, 512, 552, 553, 562, 633, 648, 688, 727, 793, 794, 839
Inner Circle 768, 783, 795
Inner City 2, 399
Inner Life 92, 317, **337**, 416, 488, 567, 819
Insane Poetry 541
Instant Funk 117, 195, **338**, 378, 539, 601, 615, 616, 665, 723, 727, 792, 819
International Sweethearts of Rhythm 52
Intertains 700
Intrigues **338**
Intro 574
Intruders 127, 140, 200, 205, 268, 281, 283, 292, 325, **338**, 339, 460, 476, 528, 547, 626, 665, 679, 689, 723, 761, 779, 848
Invisible Man's Band **339**
Invitations 141
INXS 139
Iovine, Jimmy 298
Irby, Joyce "Fenderella" 395, 599
Irons, Eddie 78
Irving, Kevin 149
Irwin, Big Dee **339**, 340, 424
Isaac, Elliot 3
Isaak, Chris 247
Islam, A. Haqq 489
Islam, Afrika 488
Isles, Bill 505
Isley Brothers 1, 22, 23, 49, 68, 127, 167, 183, 260, 269, 305, 315, 320, 326, **340**, 341, 342, 343, 344, 347, 365, 431, 438, 453, 487, 540, 572, 579, 583, 638, 657, 670, 675, 697, 703, 712, 727, 728, 746, 751, 752, 757, 769, 777, 779, 785, 786, 801, 816, 817, 818, 822, 824, 829, 831, 832, 833, 834, 842, 844, 845, 846, 851
Isley Jasper Isley 340, 342, **344**, 365
Isley, Ernie 340, 341, 342, 343, **344**, 365, 475
Isley, Marvin 340, 341, 342, 344, 365
Isley, OKelly 340, 341, 342, 344
Isley, Ronald 22, 327, 340, 341, 342, 343, 344, 546, 659, 757
Isley, Rudolph 340, 341, 342, 344
Isley, Vernon 340
Iverson, Cy 648, 716
Ivey, Leon 70
Ivey, Michael 70
Ivory, Jennifer 20
Ivy 623
Ivy, Quin 623

J

J-Boog 27
J., Stevie 510, 666, 686
J.J. Fad 470
Ja Rule 17, 82, 359, 478, 707
Jabara, Paul 472, 650
Jackie & the Starlites 209, **345**, 806

Jacks 107, **345**, 508, 577, 674
Jackson Five 2, 13, 41, 115, 116, 129, 145, 156, 166, 182, 244, 276, 281, 286, 327, 332, **345**, 346, 347, 348, 350, 351, 352, 353, 354, 355, 358, 412, 428, 430, 433, 496, 497, 498, 528, 533, 620, 653, 657, 661, 668, 670, 691, 698, 721, 723, 777, 785, 796, 802, 817, 826, 828, 833, 839, 844, 846
Jackson, Adam 367, 368
Jackson, Al 369, 458, 469, 810
Jackson, Al Jr. 10, 34, 44, 67, 68, 69, 311
Jackson, Andy 242
Jackson, Anthony 388
Jackson, Bernard 352, 657
Jackson, Bill 212
Jackson, Billy 12, 707
Jackson, Bo 191
Jackson, Brian 603, 604
Jackson, Bull Moose 838
Jackson, Carol 600
Jackson, Caroline 168
Jackson, Charles 36, 348, 349
Jackson, Chuck 11, 92, 103, 151, 152, 185, 321, 326, 336, **348**, 349, 457, 525, 619, 621, 705, 728, 732, 779, 781, 790, 818, 834, 844, 846
Jackson, Deon 53, **349**, 410, 418, 799, 808
Jackson, Don 184, 185
Jackson, Eddie 78
Jackson, Eugene 556, 623
Jackson, Fred 350, 769
Jackson, Fred [Sax] 109
Jackson, Freddie 234, 327, **349**, 350, 374, 412, 460, 482, 483, 490, 510, 513, 684, 735, 747, 785, 788, 810
Jackson, George 58, 118, 184, 233, **350**, 809
Jackson, Gerald 582
Jackson, Glenmore 135
Jackson, Greg 775
Jackson, J.J. 247, 248, **350**, 783, 807
Jackson, Jackie 346, 347, 358, 768
Jackson, James Jr. 421
Jackson, Janet 2, 9, 56, 69, 75, 82, 213, 275, **350**, 351, 352, 354, 358, 378, 405, 481, 583, 622, 634, 689, 698, 713, 744
Jackson, Jermaine 166, 322, 323, 346, 347, 351, **352**, 353, 358, 410, 430, 472, 580, 582, 660, 663, 723, 780
Jackson, Jerome 437
Jackson, Jesse 103, 257, 336
Jackson, Johnny 346
Jackson, Joyce 307
Jackson, LaToya 311, 346, **353**, 358, 501
Jackson, Linda 606
Jackson, Mahalia 25, 546, 642, 644, 857
Jackson, Marlon 346, 347, 351, 358, 408, 768
Jackson, Maureen 358
Jackson, Maurice 336
Jackson, McKinley 203, 334, 373, 380
Jackson, Michael 21, 35, 69, 73, 80, 81, 96, 166, 177, 229, 278, 280, 290, 292, 308, 322, 323, 327, 345, 346, 347, 348, 351, 352, **353**, 354, 355, 357, 358, 366, 375, 376, 377, 386, 390, 399, 420, 433, 475, 487, 494, 499, 517, 533, 573, 575, 582, 583, 586, 588, 661, 689, 712, 727, 766, 796, 803, 839, 851
Jackson, Millie 89, 95, 145, 210, 233, 303, **356**, 357, 409, 410, 415, 459, 646, 663, 768, 784, 791, 825, 830
Jackson, Milt 130, 131, 133, 376, 392, 780, 786, 793
Jackson, Milt Quintet 780
Jackson, Nannette 279
Jackson, Oliver 390, 391
Jackson, Paul Jr. 47, 213, 307, 393
Jackson, Pervis 636
Jackson, Randy 346, 347, 358, 768
Jackson, Ray 758
Jackson, Raymond 34
Jackson, Rebbie **357**, 358, 657, 664
Jackson, Ricky 519
Jackson, Robert 499
Jackson, Ronald Shannon 590
Jackson, Samuel L. 303
Jackson, Thomas 747
Jackson, Tito 166, 346, 347, 358, 768
Jackson, Walter 178, 334, **358**, 407, 453, 789, 791, 811, 818, 819, 824, 830
Jackson, Wanda 803
Jackson, Wayne 442, 443, 466, 568, 569
Jackson, Wesley 769
Jackson, Willie 421, 634, 635
Jackson, Willis "Gator" 94, 810, 857, 858
Jacksons 182, 277, 346, 347, 353, 354, 358, 779, 795, 820
Jacobs, Adolph 149
Jacobs, Dick 754
Jacobs, Hank 788
Jacobs, Larry 542
Jacobs, Perk 54
Jacobucci, Don 571
Jacquet of Mantua 611
Jacquet, Illinois 198, 297, 461, 611, 720, 732, 798, 806, 836
Jadakiss 489
Jade **358**, 359
Jagged Edge 211, **359**, 412
Jagger, Mick 15, 139, 196, 241, 346, 347, 366, 568, 582, 737, 803
Jah, Titiyo 690
Jaheim **359**
Jai 359, 360
Jake 62
Jakes, T.D. 77, 486
Jalal 411
Jam 41, 629, 634
Jam, Jimmy 21, 30, 41, 59, 127, 136, 181, 249, 277, 278, 340, 343, 351, 352, 395, 434, 435, 474, 481, 496, 497, 510, 629, 630, 634, 689, 698, 713, 742, 744, 810
Jam, Jimmy & Terry Lewis 73, 145, 358, 630, 744
Jamal, Ahmad 413
Jamerson, James 202, 227, 262, 263, 273, **360**, 457, 654, 714, 754, 832
Jamerson, James Jr. 845
Jamerson, James Sr. 217
James Boys 468
James, Bill 532
James, Bob 21, 376, 734
James, Charlie 144
James, Chris 491
James, Clifton 189
James, Denita 315
James, Elmore 350, 516, 701, 702, 753, 800, 801, 806, 810, 815, 838
James, Etta 51, 63, 94, 130, 153, 189, 214, 281, 293, 317, 357, **360**, 361, 403, 480, 487, 514, 518, 536, 570, 575, 576, 683, 694, 704, 705, 728, 756, 782, 790, 791, 794, 800, 804, 810, 812, 838
James, Fanita 60, 279, 634
James, Fred 268
James, Glodean 428, 429
James, Harry 475, 500
James, Jesse 234, **361**, 499, 518
James, Jesse [1] 468
James, Jesse [2] 188
James, Jimmy **361**, 362, 818, 825
James, Joni 210
James, Josie 594
James, Kenny 559
James, Larry 737
James, Linda 428, 429
James, Mark 781
James, Rick 35, 81, 82, 84, 98, 104, 154, 170, 260, 269, 275, 308, 319, 338, **362**, 363, 364, 381, 444, 445, 483, 486, 504, 553, 614, 622, 652, 677, 780, 794, 802, 824, 851
James, Stephanie 709
Jamiroquai **364**
Jamison, Roosevelt 118
Jan & Arnie 727
Jan & Dean 408, 805, 839
Jano, Johnny 800
Jans, Tom 283
Jansen, Linda 13
January, John 491
Jaramillo, Joe 113
Jaramillo, Robert 113
Jarmels **364**, 489
Jarmusch, Jim 684
Jarreau, Al 48, 169, 218, 582, 620, 666, 757, 758
Jarrett, Keith 268
Jarrett, Ted 268, 817
Jasper, Chris 340, 341, 342, 344, **365**
Jay & the Americans 45, 210, 489, 608, 728
Jay & the Techniques 53, **365**, 789, 826
Jay Hawks 345, 443, 508
Jay-Z 116, 209, 222, 313, 386, 770
Jay, Bobby 793
Jay, Martin 134
Jay, Michael 446, 643
Jay, Norman 792
Jaye, Jerry 809
Jayhawks 107, 345, 508, 717, 805
Jaynetts 166, 307, **365**, 782, 804, 843
Jays 155
Jazz Crusaders 84, 106, 171, 541, 760
Jazz Messengers 159, 282, 857
Jazz 208, 619
Jazzanova 383
Jazzie B. 373, 444, 631, 632, 705
J.B. Horns 366
J.B.'s 47, 85, 88, 89, 91, 105, 110, 151, 153, 155, 214, 222, 289, 319, **365**, 366, 378, 467, 523, 556, 562, 694, 746, 801, 807, 833, 851
J.B.'s All Stars 521
JD & the Evil's Dynamite Band 807
Jean, Wyclef 112, 189, 313, 323, **366**, 367, 488, 489, 578, 628, 810
Jefferson Airplane 484
Jefferson, Claude 259
Jefferson, Eddie 307
Jefferson, Joe 296, 649
Jefferson, Joseph B. 789
Jefferson, Marshall 139, 170, 331, 393, 399, 679, 791
Jefferson, Tyrone 222
Jeffre, Justin 498
Jelly Beans **367**, 803
Jellybean 383
Jemmott, Jerry 390
Jenkins, Andrew 717
Jenkins, Chico 481
Jenkins, Fred III 367
Jenkins, Gary 617
Jenkins, Harold 400
Jenkins, Johnny 568
Jenkins, Norma 750, 789
Jenkins, Tomi 110, 111
Jennings, Bill 378
Jennings, Morris 420
Jensen, Harry 122
Jerkins, Rodney 77, 189, 354, **367**, 499, 707
Jesse, Amelia 181
Jessie, Obie 149
Jesters **367**, 368, 519
Jestofunk 399
Jesus & Mary Chain 636
Jeter, Claude 15, 658, 659
Jeter, Genobia 374
Jets 318
Jett, Joan 636
Jewels 86, **368**, 809
Jhene 27
Jive Five 61, **368**, 548, 626, 778, 782, 786, 797, 798, 799, 812, 818, 821, 824
Jivin' Gene 128
Jobe, Lequeint 585
Jobim, Antonio Carlos 159, 188, 639, 640
Jodeci 28, 209, 217, 221, 278, **368**, 382, 661
Joe Public **369**
Joel, Billy 134, 269, 304, 636, 742, 743
Johansson, Tore 690
John, Elton 43, 150, 177, 192, 257, 269, 277, 321, 322, 358, 465, 468, 469, 595, 687, 695, 729, 730, 811
John, Lee 331
John, Leee 331
John, Mable 151, **369**, 563, 804, 828
John, Robert 53
Johnnie & Joe 107, 777, 778, 805
Johnny & Jackey 266, 654
Johnny Hates Jazz 525
Johns, Eric 308
Johns, Glyn 600
Johnson Products 147
Johnson, Al 325, 395, 689, 708, 709
Johnson, Alan 443
Johnson, Albert 129, 463
Johnson, Alonzo 372
Johnson, Alphonso 376, 594
Johnson, Aubrey 3
Johnson, Augie 26, 324, 615
Johnson, Billy 480
Johnson, Bud 129
Johnson, Budd 298
Johnson, Buddy 113, 209
Johnson, Carl 190
Johnson, Charles 141
Johnson, Clarence 137, 309
Johnson, Claude 199, 497
Johnson, Corinthian "Kripp" 184, 185
Johnson, Cornelius 502
Johnson, Curtis 84
Johnson, Cynthia 422
Johnson, Danny 137
Johnson, David 423
Johnson, Delores 331
Johnson, Dennis 157
Johnson, Donald 370
Johnson, Earl 392, 393, 601
Johnson, Emanuel "E.J." 225
Johnson, Ernie 70, **369**
Johnson, Frank O. 144
Johnson, Freddy 443
Johnson, Frederick 657
Johnson, General 19, 123, 124, 320, **369**, 370, 509, 571, 614, 615, 658, 694
Johnson, George "Happy" 515
Johnson, George 81, 377
Johnson, Hiram 209, 806
Johnson, Howard 98
Johnson, Hubert 160
Johnson, J.J. 376, 739, 778, 788
Johnson, James P. 717, 719
Johnson, Janice Marie **370**, 389, 667
Johnson, Jay 648, 716
Johnson, Jellybean 510
Johnson, Jerry 173
Johnson, Jesse 26, 181, 351, **370**, 413, 510, 624, 666, 689, 690
Johnson, Jesse Revue 666
Johnson, Jimmy 314, 371, 372, 443, 578, 648
Johnson, Joan Marie 196
Johnson, Johnnie 51
Johnson, Johnny 49
Johnson, Karen 535
Johnson, Keg 761
Johnson, Kevin 622
Johnson, L.J. 18, 683
Johnson, LaMont 74
Johnson, Larry 16, 178
Johnson, Laurence 16
Johnson, Lester "Lammy" 638
Johnson, Lou 694, 781, 784
Johnson, Louis 81, 341, 377, 474, 512, 515, 658, 659
Johnson, Marv 46, 202, 220, 266, **370**, 371, 675, 689, 712, 784, 799, 805, 823, 832, 845
Johnson, Mary 812
Johnson, Milton 634
Johnson, Norman 368
Johnson, Pete 701
Johnson, Phil 293
Johnson, Plas 80, 361, 518
Johnson, Puff 720
Johnson, Ralph [1] 428
Johnson, Ralph [2] 335
Johnson, Ray 485
Johnson, Raymond 650
Johnson, Rick 647
Johnson, Robert 376, 520, 642
Johnson, Robert A. 58
Johnson, Robert P-Nut 153
Johnson, Rozetta 184
Johnson, Ruby **371**, 777
Johnson, Rudolph 228
Johnson, Rudy 228
Johnson, Smokey 54
Johnson, Steve 54
Johnson, Syl 96, 144, 150, 311, **371**, 372, 476, 588, 809, 810, 832
Johnson, Terry 442
Johnson, Toby 746
Johnson, Tommy 81
Johnson, Troy 3
Johnson, Tyrone 752
Johnson, Victor 102
Johnson, Virgil 716
Johnson, Wallace **372**
Johnson, Walter 700, 814
Johnson, Willie 793
Joint Venture 809
Jojo 28, 368
Joli, France 170, 778, 821

Jolley, Steve 331
Jolson, Al 131
Jones Boys 375
Jones Brothers 828
Jones Girls 77, 100, 145, 217, 244, 372, 373, 378, 453, 615, 723, 802, 811, 820
Jones, Allen 34, 35
Jones, Andrew 701
Jones, Andy 577
Jones, Billy [1] 476
Jones, Billy [2] 81
Jones, Bob [DJ] 826
Jones, Bob [Engineer] 144
Jones, Booker T. 18, 43, 67, 68, 369, 442, 466, 469, 476, 569, 660, 758, 780, 803, 813
Jones, Brenda 372, 378, 573, 700, 819
Jones, Carl 188
Jones, Chris 652
Jones, Creadel "Red" 137, 138
Jones, Curt 622
Jones, Curtis 20, 21
Jones, David 430
Jones, Deacon 724
Jones, Denise [see Lasalle, Denise]
Jones, Donell 27, 373
Jones, Doris 18, 373, 683
Jones, Douglas 235
Jones, Dwayne 574
Jones, E. Rodney 206
Jones, Earl 380
Jones, Eddie 702
Jones, Elvin 159, 287
Jones, George 52, 132, 134, 283, 494, 495, 857
Jones, George Jr. 217
Jones, Gerald 693
Jones, Glenn 160, 234, 373, 374, 412
Jones, Gloria 13, 60, 279, 374, 397, 472, 634, 781, 826
Jones, Grace 6, 139, 374, 375, 597
Jones, Hank 714, 755
Jones, Howard 444
Jones, James Earl 201, 630
Jones, Jamie 9
Jones, Janet 687
Jones, Jennifer 416
Jones, Jerome 332
Jones, Jerry 78
Jones, Jill 646
Jones, Jimmy 367, 832
Jones, Jimmy "Handyman" 56, 375
Jones, Joe "Boogaloo" 735, 857
Jones, Joe 242
Jones, Joyce 240
Jones, Kelvin 3
Jones, Kenny 50, 513
Jones, Kipper 412
Jones, Larry 405
Jones, Lawrence 393
Jones, Lee 449, 813
Jones, Linda 226, 299, 375, 607, 692, 833
Jones, London 390
Jones, Marshall "Rock" 502
Jones, Maxine 222, 224
Jones, Michael [Nuage] 97, 98
Jones, Mike 102
Jones, Ollie 172, 562
Jones, Oran "Juice" 375, 747
Jones, Orville "Hoppy" 337
Jones, Paul 72
Jones, Pearl 279
Jones, Peggy 70
Jones, Phalon 34
Jones, Quincy 7, 21, 22, 34, 48, 81, 82, 112, 113, 130, 131, 133, 134, 183, 269, 308, 313, 336, 353, 354, 355, 375, 376, 377, 378, 515, 527, 546, 575, 592, 651, 666, 710, 727, 732, 741, 743, 776, 795, 823, 826, 833
Jones, Randolph 380, 532
Jones, Raymond 513, 611
Jones, Raymond [Piano] 138
Jones, Rena 125
Jones, Rodney 95
Jones, Sam 391
Jones, Sharon 43, 377, 378, 826
Jones, Shirley 209, 372, 373, 378, 615, 723
Jones, Simon 415, 416, 428, 719
Jones, Spike 301
Jones, Tamiko 80, 800
Jones, Thad 94
Jones, Thelma 830
Jones, Tom 130, 367, 699
Jones, Tony 513
Jones, Tyrice 478, 479
Jones, Uriel 262, 263, 714
Jones, Valerie 372
Jones, Valorie 378
Jones, Walter 500
Jones, Will "Dub" 107, 149, 345
Jones, Willie 751
Jonzun, Michael 650
Joplin, Janis 119, 151, 223, 258, 438, 473, 474, 557, 636, 668, 703, 760, 761
Joplin, Scott 668, 823
Jordan, Carl 217
Jordan, Darnell 532, 533
Jordan, Eric Benet 47
Jordan, Lonnie 723, 724
Jordan, Louis 39, 74, 86, 90, 95, 197, 198, 277, 370, 378, 379, 448, 516, 547, 627, 697, 702, 777, 822, 836
Jordan, Montell 379, 498, 686, 727
Jordan, Stanley 788
Jordan, Steve 51, 68
Jordan, Taft 31, 627
Jordanaires 228
Joseph, David 312
Joseph, Ken 312
Joseph, Kirk 195
Joseph, Margie 80, 184, 296, 379, 380, 674, 692, 787, 788, 812
Joseph, Quinton 468, 498
Josie & the Pussycats 316
Journey 116, 500
Joy Division 227
Joyce, Barbara 98
Joyce, Brenda 708
Joyner, Bruce 507
Joyner, Frank 722
Joytones 828
Judas Priest 342, 485
Judds 200, 694
Judkins, Michael 6
Juicy 380
Julian, Don 380, 381, 408, 722
Julian, Don & the Meadowlarks 380, 381
Junie 381
Junior 381, 723
Junior, Marvin 186, 187, 188, 465, 530, 578, 789
Jurado, Jeanette 231, 232
Justice, Robert 500
Justis, Bill 195, 310, 702
Justman, Paul 263
Juston, Sidney 607

K

K-Ci 28
K-Ci & Jo Jo 217, 368, **382**, 628
K-Doe, Ernie 60, **382**, 383, 636, 694, 793, 840
K., Francois **383**, 488
Kaegi, Adriana 389
Kahn, Eddie 759, 760
Kahn, Ken 515
Kai **383**
Kain **383**
Kain, Gylan 383
Kajagoogoo 364
Kalyan 665
Kamoze, Ini 271
Kane, Pete 41
Karisma 147
Karma **383**, 384
Kashif 98, 234, 312, 363, 373, 393, 482, 483, 510, 525, 684
Kass, Art 244
Katz, Bruce 456
Katz, Gary 587
Kay Gee 776
Kay-Gee's **384**
Kay, Connie 131, 133
Kay, Jason 364
Kay, Jay 364
Kay, John 361
Kaye, Barry 184, 185
Kaye, Carol 25
Kayli, Bob 549
Kazanoff, Mark 574
KC & the Sunshine Band 60, 254, **384**, 385, 458, 503, 572, 803
Keane, Bob 80, 795
Keaton, Diane 482
Keaton, Josh 499
Kee, John P. 15
Keel, Howard 208
Keenan, Brian 125
Keene, Bob 428, 532, 742
Keene, Tommy 742
Keith & Darrell 479
Keith 834
Keith, Tommy 478, 575
Kelis **385**
Kelley, Ann 324
Kellum, Alphonso "Country" 90
Kelly Brothers 809, 833
Kelly, Agnes 449, 450
Kelly, Betty 445, 446, 715
Kelly, Carey 386
Kelly, Colette 814
Kelly, Eban 629
Kelly, Kenny 441, 442, 574
Kelly, Paul **385**
Kelly, R. 1, 22, 59, 77, 127, 128, 177, 259, 278, 343, 355, 385, 386, 451, 502, 554, 578, 584, 593, 617, 637, 659, 698, 700, 713
Kelly, Sam 173, 174
Kelly, Tim 666
Kelly, Tonya 358
Kelly, Wells 515
Kelly, Wenzell 204
Kelly, Wynton 391, 733
Keltner, Jim 578, 601
Kemp, Johnny 575
Kemp, Thomas 340
Kendall, Alan 40
Kendrick, Nat 805
Kendricks, Eddie 38, 42, 175, 202, 217, 263, 272, 289, 332, **386**, 387, 440, 451, 457, 462, 534, 548, 549, 591, 592, 607, 665, 674, 675, 676, 677, 678, 679, 705, 780, 795, 796, 804, 816, 817, 818, 821, 828
Kennedy, Bap 388
Kennedy, Errol 331
Kennedy, Harrison 123, 124, 811
Kennedy, Hershall 178, 282
Kennedy, Jerry 602
Kennedy, Joyce 234, **387**, 388, 428, 484, 485, 719, 818
Kennedy, Leon Isaac 269
Kennedy, Steve 485
Kenner, Chris 39, 63, 96, 113, **388**, 466, 579, 612, 694, 783, 793, 816, 840
Kennibrew, Dee Dee 171
Kenny, Bill 337, 415, 553
Kensey, Willie 137
Kent 690
Kent, Herb "Kool Gent" 402
Kenton, Stan 23, 295
Kermode, Richard 439
Kern, Jerome 40, 675
Kerr, Anita 226, 607
Kerr, Anita Singers 682
Kerr, George 32, 226, 227, 477, 505, 607, 740, 779, 780, 786, 819
Kersey, Ron 501, 618, 697, 757
Kershaw, Andy 302, 744
Kessee, Kelton 332
Kessel, Barney 70
Kevorkian, Francois 92, 175, 383, 416, 488, 567, 778
Key Notes 827
Key, Horace 667
Keyes, Bert 463
Keyes, Jimmy 142
Keyes, John 437
Keyes, Johnny 161
Keyes, Troy 715
Keys, Alicia 17, 114, 303, **388**, 478, 696, 700
Keys, Bobby 51
Khan, Chaka 17, 20, 23, 28, 59, 70, 77, 79, 81, 134, 151, 156, 205, 218, 234, 300, 322, 358, 365, 377, 379, **388**, 389, 399, 414, 444, 483, 491, 519, 592, 593, 600, 602, 609, 646, 648, 666, 710, 744, 757, 778, 785, 795, 811, 826
Khan, Rufus 156
Khan, Steve 450, 540, 565
Khoury, George 165
Kibble, Joey 666
Kibble, Mark 666
Kid Creole & the Coconuts 196, **389**, 390
Kid N Play 332
Kid Rock 179
Kid, Joey 407
Kilgore, Theola 786, 819
Kilgoreola 5
Killen, Buddy 385, 680, 681
Killgo, Keith 54, 55
Kina **390**
Kincaid, Jan 74, 75
Kinchen, Marc 474
King Biscuit Boy 466
King Crimson 419
King Crooners 783
King Curtis 135, 144, 149, 165, 256, 299, **390**, 391, 466, 470, 476, 554, 555, 558, 561, 612, 760, 780, 800, 801, 808, 809, 817, 857
King Floyd 293, **391**, 394, 398, 809, 813
King Hannibal 471
King Karl 813
King Tee 833
King, Albert 34, 43, 67, 69, 95, 256, 262, 293, 525, 694, 777, 792, 804, 812, 828, 839
King, B.B. 3, 46, 50, 54, 57, 58, 69, 93, 120, 171, 191, 250, 256, 261, 262, 271, 280, 300, 301, 366, 379, 392, 410, 425, 516, 568, 583, 668, 684, 702, 706, 734, 778, 785, 815, 818, 832, 838
King, Ben E. 22, 49, 56, 101, 103, 136, 158, 167, 207, 208, 241, 283, 290, 348, 356, 367, 371, **391**, 392, 415, 462, 592, 603, 607, 630, 631, 688, 705, 713, 728, 779, 784, 785, 786, 794, 814, 817, 824, 829, 833, 844, 845
King, Bobby **392**
King, Carole 31, 92, 104, 116, 141, 165, 167, 171, 172, 175, 182, 207, 208, 225, 231, 245, 256, 287, 303, 313, 325, 341, 380, 392, 403, 423, 424, 446, 573, 574, 580, 584, 610, 613, 639, 649, 721, 729, 784, 803, 804, 834, 841, 842, 843, 844
King, Chris 831
King, Clydie 824
King, Earl 39, 63, 93, 197, 369, **392**, 393, 466, 467, 553, 626, 694, 778, 783, 793, 803, 810, 815, 839
King, Evelyn 412, 785
King, Evelyn "Champagne" 98, 373, **393**, 394, 582, 665, 684, 715, 723, 773, 797
King, Freddie 125, 179, 305, 390, 442, 570, 593, 812, 833, 838, 839
King, Gary 652
King, James 266
King, Jay 149, 690
King, Jean 60
King, Jewel 789
King, Jimmy [1] 34
King, Jimmy [2] 476
King, John [Producer] 266
King, Johnny 235
King, Mabel 822
King, Marcel 660
King, Mark 688
King, Martin Luther Jr. 68, 762
King, Maurice 31, 190
King, Peter 779, 792
King, Ray 174
King, Robbie 670
King, Saunders 701
King, Stephen 430
King, Terry 294, 683
King, Will 702
King, William 155
Kings of Rhythm 702, 703, 704
Kingsmen 51, 574
Kinks 560
Kinney, Fern **394**
Kinsman Dazz 181, 182, **394**, 652
Kipling, Rudyard 11
Kipner, Steve 664
Kipps, Charles 397, 648
Kirby, George 676
Kirk, Alan 362
Kirk, Eddie 777, 778
Kirk, Rahsaan Roland 376, 380, 526
Kirk, Robie 172
Kirkland, Leroy 52, 298
Kirkland, Mike James **394**
Kirkpatrick, Chris 689

Kirshner, Don 62, 423, 558, 841
Kiss 789
Kitt, Eartha 793, 812
Kittens **394**
Kitty & the Haywoods 453
Kizart, Willie 78
Kleeer **395**, 709
Klein, Alan 135
Klein, Gary 397, 472
Klein, Howie 500
KLF 796
Klique 327, **395**, 785
Klugh, Earl 47, 48, 595, 788
Klymaxx **395**, 471, 757
Klymaxx Malsby, Lynn 395
Knauss, Dick 443
Knechtel, Larry 239
Knickerbockers 575
Knight Brothers 117, **395**, 782, 790, 804
Knight, Boobie **395**
Knight, Brenda 539
Knight, Bubba 397, 539
Knight, Cheri 1, 539
Knight, Frederick 58, 161, 184, 385, **395**, 548, 725, 726
Knight, Gladys 1, 6, 17, 28, 100, 120, 134, 136, 167, 225, 229, 255, 317, 321, 346, 356, 357, 375, 379, **395**, 396, 397, 398, 452, 453, 457, 459, 470, 472, 521, 529, 539, 579, 646, 653, 666, 682, 721, 729, 730, 745, 785, 792, 801, 813, 817, 825, 846
Knight, Gladys & the Pips 38, 57, 80, 184, 316, 396, 397, 398, 430, 457, 472, 496, 500, 533, 539, 579, 618, 647, 648, 655, 669, 708, 712, 721, 751, 752, 758, 785, 786, 790, 800, 806, 811, 816, 824, 825, 846
Knight, Jean 293, **398**, 399, 813, 820, 824, 828, 829
Knight, Jerry 152, 521, 566
Knight, Marie **399**, 779
Knight, Merald "Bubba" 539
Knight, Richard 82
Knight, Robert 117, **399**, 789, 826
Knight, Suge 470, 691
Knight, Terry 746
Knocturnal 700
Knopfler, Mark 392
Knowland, James 266, 480
Knowles, Beyonce 189, 222
Knowles, Errol 227
Knowles, Mathew 189
Knox, Buddy 94, 805
Knuckles, Frankie 6, 224, 331, 383, **399**, 416, 426, 434, 588, 782
Kodaks **399**, 400, 479, 602, 806
Koehler, Ted 528
Kohan, Mark 499
Kolax, King 70, 246
Kolettes 790
Kon Kan **400**
Kool & the Gang 20, 40, 69, 81, 188, 277, 308, 312, 324, 338, 384, **400**, 401, 402, 406, 421, 489, 504, 522, 541, 547, 562, 567, 572, 575, 576, 630, 671, 699, 785, 786, 797, 801, 851
Kool Gents 143, 219, **402**
Kool Keith 686
Kool Moe Dee 290, 377, 521
Kooper, Al 151, 192, 193, 223, 418, 515, 688
Korduletsch, Jurgen S. 38
Kornegay, Bob 209
Kornegay, Kenny "K-Smoove" 127
Kowalski, Tedd 191
Koz, Dave 47, 490
Kraftwerk 140, 218, 359, 383, 402, 484, 699, 820
Kranz, George 795, 820
Kravitz, Lenny 53, 235, 288, 381, 390, 646, 832
Kris Kross 210, 211, 583
Krisley, Ernie 652
Kristofferson, Kris 130, 285, 326, 396, 618, 623
Krivit, Danny 383, 416
Kroha, Dan 748
KRS One 260, 313, 628
Krukowski, Damon 332, 698
Krystal Generation 619
Kulka, Leo 626, 807
Kunze, Michael 617, 618, 623
Kupka, Stephen "Doc" 695
Kut Klose 659
Kuti, Fela 25, 448, 500, 792, 826
Kynard, Charles 811
Kyoto Jazz Massive 383
Kyper **402**

L
La La 352, 768
La Lupe 688
La Rue 345
LaBelle 138, 260, 271, 310, 390, **403**, 404, 405, 450, 466, 493, 502, 544, 642, 694, 716, 723
LaBelle, Patti 47, 285, 310, 375, 378, 403, **404**, 405, 417, 487, 519, 527, 538, 602, 615, 616, 621, 642, 643, 653, 662, 716, 723, 734, 748, 760, 761, 785, 796, 820, 824, 825, 844, 848
LaBelle, Patti & the Bluebelles 403, 404, **405**, 804, 824
LaBes, Larry 235
Laboe, Art 211, 243, 380
Laboriel, Abe Jr. 747
Lachey, Drew 498
Lachey, Nick 498, 499
Laddins 806
Ladies of the '80s 219
Lads 436
Lady B 195
Lady Soul 256
Lady T 445
Lafayette Afro Rock Band 405
Lafayettes 458
Laidback 796
Laine, Cleo 132
Laine, Denny 367
Laine, Frankie 11, 83, 94, 216
Lake, Ray 566
Lakeside 259, **406**, 407, 432, 470, 471, 607, 622, 632, 652, 741
Lala, Joe 575
LaMarr, Mark 814
Lambchop 483
Lambert & Potter 668
Lambert, Dennis 157, 218, 251, 252, 280, 506, 668, 669, 677
Lambert, Jennie Lee 143
Lambert, Kit 403
Lamm, Robert 727
Lamond, George **407**
Lamont, Darryl 80
Lampkin, Tyrone 264
Lamplighters 297, 577
Lamya **407**
Lance, Major 16, 17, 36, 102, 103, 167, 178, 293, 358, 371, **407**, 408, 414, 451, 453, 511, 579, 754, 786, 793, 801, 810, 811, 812, 813, 814, 817, 819, 844
Lancers 814
Land, Harold 23, 421, 732
Landau, Michael 578
Lander, Austin 499
Landis, Karl 365
Landreth, Sonny 130, 198
Landry, Amos 466, 747
Landry, George 493, 747
Landry, Jackie 128
Lands, Hoagy 49
Lands, Liz 64, 65
Lane, Herb 281
Lane, Jeff 14, 76, 97, 98
Lane, Mickey Lee **408**, 784
Lane, Preston 238
Lang, Fritz 484
Lang, Jonny 248
Lanier & Co. **408**
Lanier, Allen 408
Lanier, Farris Jr. 408
Lanier, Marlon 408
Lanois, Daniel 493, 494
Lanson, Snooky 49
LaPread, Ronald 155
Larados 606
Laredo, Joseph F. 471
Larkins, Percy 370
Larks 12, 380, **408**, 409, 611, 693, 722, 779, 793, 825, 827, 839
Larrieux, Amel **409**
Larrieux, Laru 409
Larson, Mel 474
LaRue, Florence 238, 718
LaRue, Roc 821
LaSalle, Denise 125, 150, 151, 184, 280, 350, 357, 408, **409**, 410, 411, 415, 481, 545, 606, 607, 778, 790, 791, 796, 821
Lasha, Prince 811
Laskey, Emanual **410**, 831
Lasley, David 795
Lassiter, Kevin 384
Last Poets 383, **410**, 411, 421, 603, 737, 788, 797
Last Word 365
Lastie, Dave 313
Lastie, Mel 561
Lastie, Melvin 277
Laswell, Bill 295, 310, 322, 403, 411, 767, 796
Lateef, Yusef 54, 714, 780, 810
Latimer, Emile 419
Latimore **411**
Latimore, Benny 95, 350, 411, 418, 710, 786, 803
Latimore, Ernest 614
Latineers 707
Lattimore, Kenny **411**, 412
Lattimore, Stacey 553
Lattisaw, Stacy 277, 278, 311, **412**, 457, 720, 726
Lauderdale, Jack 133, 261
Lauper, Cyndi 1
Laurels 63
Laurence, Lynda 586, 602
Laurence, Paul 349, **412**, 413, 472, 482, 684
Laurie, Annie 277
Laurnea 229
Lavette, Betty 220, **413**, 794, 795, 798, 809, 824
Lawes, Wayne 373
Lawes, William 185, 539
Lawrence, Linda 656
Lawrence, Ron "Amen-Ra" 331
Lawrence, Steve 784
Laws, Clifford 481
Laws, Debra **413**, 824
Laws, Eloise **413**, 811
Laws, Hubert 25, 47, 48, 170, 188, 376, 413, 561, 594, 603, 828
Laws, Ronnie 84, 214, 380, 615, 788, 791
Lawson, Doyle 688
Lawson, Floyd 307
Lawson, Herb 679
Lawson, Jerry 534, 535
Lawyer, Andrew 635
Lazy Lester 783, 800, 803, 838
Le Klass **413**
Leadbelly 511
Leaders 805, 822
Leak, Maysa 335
Leake, Danny Ray 683
Leake, Lafayette 50, 51, 192, 250
Leavell, Chuck 51
Leavill, Otis 103, 407, **413**, 414, 511, 567, 754, 755, 789, 791
Leavitt, Phil 191
LeBlanc, Emmanuel Rahiem 281
Lebon, Gerald 621
Lecuona, Ernesto 227
Led Zeppelin 49, 207, 320, 400, 484, 485, 506, 780
Ledesma, Ish 254, 255
Ledet, Rosie 586
Lee & the Leopards **414**
Lee, Arthur 589, 621
Lee, Bob 313, 368
Lee, Brenda 434, 590, 803
Lee, Byron 392, 490
Lee, Curtis 293, **414**, 635, 798
Lee, George 415, 590
Lee, Jackie 63, **414**, 415, 508
Lee, Jimmy 235
Lee, Johnny 176
Lee, Julia **415**, 815
Lee, Larry 18, 798
Lee, Laura 124, 279, 315, 320, 410, **415**, 683, 790, 811, 830
Lee, Leonard 613, 614
Lee, Nathaniel 488
Lee, Peggy 49, 375, 425
Lee, Rahm 535
Lee, Richard 395
Lee, Rosa 196
Lee, Spike 17, 98, 173, 291, 324, 763, 793, 803, 829
Lee, Toney 802
Leech, Mike 466
Leeds, Alan 91, 154
Leeds, Eric 213
Leeman, Bob 729
Leeman, Cliff 701
Left Banke 251, 252
Leftenant, Nathan 110, 111
Legends 828
Leiber & Stoller 31, 33, 51, 136, 149, 280, 392, 398, **415**, 437, 807, 834
Leiber, Jerry 4, 148, 149, 206, 207, 231, 293, 296, 298, 301, 348, 367, 391, 392, 415, 608, 685, 705, 728, 774, 803, 812, 839, 841, 842, 844
Leiber, Oliver 666
Lemon Drops 749
Lemon Pipers 36
Lemon 821
Lennear, Claudia 699
Lennon, John 13, 50, 71, 128, 136, 200, 244, 269, 277, 334, 354, 406, 420, 530, 560, 586, 635, 719, 749, 792, 842, 844
Lennon, John & the Plastic Ono Band 192
Lennon, Julian 51
Lennox, Annie 285, 287, 664
Leo's Sunship **415**
Leonard, Glenn 674, 677
Leonard, Harlan 514
Leonetti, Andy 242
Leopards 414
Lerchey, David 184, 185
Les Nubians 409
Lespron, Mickey 140
Lester, Bobby 266, 479, 480, 816
Lester, Ketty **416**
Lester, Robert "Squirrel" 137, 138
Lester, Wally 621
Lester, Willie 5, 393, 567, 689
Lesure, Nelson 508
Letta 24
Levan, Larry 92, 227, 270, 337, 338, 383, 399, **416**, 426, 468, 709, 778, 792, 796, 834
Levant, Oscar 559
Levay, Silvester 617, 618, 623
Level Forty Two 20
Levell, Joanne Boswell 235
Leverett, Charles 600
LeVert 30, 324, 332, **416**, 417, 431, 471, 485, 505, 506, 785
LeVert, Eddie 226, 324, 325, 416, 417, 418, 505, 506, 507, 657, 692
LeVert, Gerald 30, 47, 263, 324, 416, **417**, 418, 431, 505, 573, 584, 659, 742, 743
LeVert, Sean 416, 417, 505
Levine, Ian 18, 37, 112, 160, 220, 231, 289, 316, 371, 373, 426, 439, 447, 462, 479, 492, 571, 600, 602, 644, 670, 683, 712, 739, 740, 783, 811, 814, 816, 825, 835
Levine, Irwin 688
Levine, Stewart 203, 727
Levister, Dick 464
Levy, Andrew 74
Levy, Marcy 592
Levy, Morris 598
Levy, Ron 261, 314, 530
Lewis Sisters 816
Lewis, Anthony 41, 474, 598, 629
Lewis, Barbara 221, 277, **418**, 432, 457, 462, 716, 738, 799, 808, 812, 821, 844
Lewis, Bobby **418**, 480
Lewis, Chuck 266
Lewis, David 19, 20
Lewis, Denise 590
Lewis, Donald 368
Lewis, Earl 128, 246
Lewis, Earl & the Channels 784
Lewis, Eddie 508
Lewis, Elliot 23
Lewis, Freddie 626
Lewis, Furry 442
Lewis, Gary 114, 408, 812
Lewis, Helen 317
Lewis, Huey 695
Lewis, Huey & the News 547
Lewis, Jerry 345, 486
Lewis, Jerry Lee 52, 56, 93, 165, 191, 195, 200, 340, 460, 547, 809, 828, 856, 857
Lewis, Jimmy **418**, 603, 735, 811
Lewis, Jonathan 20
Lewis, Kay 317, 816
Lewis, Keri 77, 474, 545

Lewis, Larry 626
Lewis, Linda **418**, 419
Lewis, Mel 94, 759
Lewis, Melvin 368
Lewis, Michael 128
Lewis, Pat 823, 832
Lewis, Pete "Guitar" 514, 812, 833
Lewis, Ramsey 108, 214, 283, 319, **419**, 420, 421, 437, 646, 727, 755, 773, 790, 857
Lewis, Ramsey Trio 214, 319, 420, 598, 774, 782, 818
Lewis, Rick 616
Lewis, Ricky 161
Lewis, Robert 590, 693
Lewis, Rudy 207, 208, 462
Lewis, Shaznay 9
Lewis, Smiley 38, 39, 63, 392, **421**, 518, 626, 694, 789, 793, 812
Lewis, Stan 7, 118, 120, 261, 297, 673, 811
Lewis, Ted 670
Lewis, Terry 21, 30, 41, 59, 127, 136, 181, 249, 277, 278, 340, 343, 351, 352, 395, 434, 474, 481, 496, 497, 510, 629, 630, 634, 689, 690, 698, 713, 742, 744, 810
Lewis, Wayne 19, 20
Lewis, Webster 610
Liberace 428
Liebman, Dave 413
Life, Theodore 665
Ligertwood, Alex 23
Liggett, Mark 407, 609
Liggins, Jimmy **421**, 547, 777, 838
Liggins, Joe 113, **421**, 777, 792, 822, 836, 838
Light of The World 335
Light, Jerry 712
Lightnin' Rod 411, **421**
Lightnin' Slim 297, 800, 803, 838
Ligon, Joe 645
Lil Bow Wow 211
Lil Bud 659
Lil Fizz 27
Lil Joe 795
Lil Kim 128, 230, 538, 577, 578, 619, 710
Lil Louis 383, 829
Lil Suzy **421**
Lil' Louis 383
Lil' Mo 659
Lincoln, Abbey 500
Lincoln, Shedrick 141
Lincolns 805
Lind, Bob 256
Lind, Jon 520
Lindley, David 241
Lindsay, Steven 494
Lindsey, Bill 107
Lindsey, James 633
Lins, Ivan 21, 48, 377
Linx 308
Linzer, Sandy 502, 696, 697
Lion, Alfred 788
Lipps Incorporated **422**
Lipscomb, Belinda 470, 471
LiPuma, Tommy 21, 48, 97, 197, 648, 709
Liquid Liquid 227, 796
Lisa Lisa 422, 575, 785
Lisa Lisa & Cult Jam 10, **422**, 696
Lister, Hovie & the Statesmen 856
Lit, Hy 12
Little Al 800
Little Ann 794
Little Anthony 422, 423, 459, 490, 607, 635, 698, 805, 824, 833
Little Anthony & the Imperials 13, 141, 186, 219, 276, **422**, 423, 505, 559, 670, 579, 590, 607, 687, 713, 781, 827, 839
Little Beaver **423**, 803
Little Buster 807
Little Caesar & the Romans **423**, 508, 793, 805
Little Esther 514, 535, 562, 777, 812
Little Eva 141, 340, **423**, 424, 809, 821, 834, 842, 843
Little Feat 518, 519, 601, 694, 695
Little Jimmy 806
Little Joe & the Thrillers 161, 340
Little Lisa 816
Little Milton 36, 39, 57, 161, 179, 188, 262, 369, 426, 457, 462, 706, 753, 782, 790, 791, 813, 824, 836, 839
Little Richard 4, 10, 50, 51, 63, 73, 85, 86, 89, 93, 102, 143, 162, 167, 191, 198, 199, 227, 228, 325, 378, 408, **424**, 425, 433, 450, 476, 514, 518, 546, 547, 568, 615, 626, 627, 632, 680, 744, 749, 769, 774, 778, 779, 785, 786, 793, 799, 805, 811, 818, 819, 824, 836, 838, 840, 841
Little Royal 547, 803
Little Shelton 793
Little Sister **425**
Little Sonny 339, 800, 811, 812
Little Walter 65, 153, 361, 582, 790
Little Willie John 56, 87, 90, 340, 369, **425**, 426, 491, 514, 525, 570, 673, 706, 779, 783, 799, 812, 836, 856
Little, David 434
Little, Levi 56, 290, **426**, 575
Littlefield, Little Willie 298
Littlejohn, Darrell 479, 832
Littlejohn, Johnny 479
Littles, Hattie **426**, 447
Live 483
Liverbirds 191
Livin' Joy 578
Living Colour 141, 460, 491, 823
Livingston, Joe 600
Livingston, Ulysses 433
LL Cool J 10, 66, 73, 140, 227, 431, 478, 574
Lloyd Webber, Andrew 15, 220
Lloyd, Alvin 635
Lloyd, George 365
Lo, Billy 43
Lockett, Anthony 111
Lockett, Tom 20, 622
Lockwood, Robert Jr. 642, 815
Loewe, Frederick 546, 615
Logan, Andrew 176
Logan, Craig 176
Logan, Ed 466
Logan, Harold 547
Logg 53, 99, 337, **426**
Loggins, Kenny 357
Lomas, Barbara Joyce 97, 98
Lomax, Jackie 699
Lombardo, Guy 647
London, Julie 689
London, Mel 78, 436
Lonely Ones 781
Lonesome Sundown 783, 800
Long, Avon 393
Long, Jerry 580
Long, Pam 693
Long, Richard 416
Long, Shorty 266, **426**, 427, 747
Long, Teddy 219, 402
Longo, Mike 650
Lookofsky, Harry 377
Loose Ends 15, 195, 381, **427**, 498, 566, 723, 727
Loose Joints 795
Loose Touch 407
Loper, Ramon 242
Lopes, Joe 184, 185
Lopes, Lisa "Left Eye" 222, 529, 690, 691
Lopez, Carmen 502
Lopez, Jennifer 367, **427**, 428, 606, 768
Lopez, Lillian 502
Lopez, Lisa 489
Lopez, Louise 502
Lorber, Jeff 47, 393, 664, 744
Lord 233, 234, 422
Lord, Peter 2, 233, 234
Lord, Tracy 422
Lords of the Underground 621
Loren, Bryan 47
Loren, Londee 495, 496
Lorenz, Trey 115
Lorenzo, A.C. 383
Los Bravos 123
Los Lobos 813
Lost Generation **428**, 567, 626, 719, 791, 833
Loudermilk, John D. 799
Lounge Lizards 141
Louvin Brothers 857
Love 239, 589, 621, 724
Love Affair 826
Love and Kisses 317, 321, **428**, 665
Love Center Young Adult Choir 302
Love Committee 297, 317, 318, 819
Love Notes 242, 798, 806
Love Peace & Happiness 495, 496
Love Tones 142
Love Unlimited **428**, 429, 529, 742
Love Unlimited Orchestra 42, 428, **429**, 430, 468, 742, 743, 744, 801
Love, Airrion 649, 650
Love, Andrew 443, 466, 568, 569
Love, Barbara 129, 261, 718
Love, Billy 795
Love, Darlene 60, 172, 196, 279, 319, **430**, 579, 634, 635, 728, 770, 843
Love, Mary **430**, 824
Love, Milton 629
Love, Preston **430**, 808, 830
Love, Rudy 534
Lovejoy, Ronnie 791
Lovelace, Bobby 470
Lovelites **430**, 748
Lovelle, Herb 648
Lovesmith, Michael 280, 352, **430**, 431, 743
Lovett, Lee 633
Lovett, Leroy 339, 781, 820
Lovett, Lyle 287, 570
Lovett, Skitch 488
Lovett, Winfred "Blue" 441
Lovettes 784
Lovin' Spoonful 376
Lowe, Chris 638, 639
Lowe, Helen 615
Lowe, James 209, 210
Lowe, Jim 798
Lowe, Nick 100, 102, 120
Lowe, Robert 545
Lowe, Sam 87
Lowe, Sammy 255, 477
Lowrell 428, 719
Lowry, Roame 455
LSG 230, 417, **431**
LTD 48, 166, 382, **431**, 512, 513, 695
LTG Exchange **432**
Lubinsky, Herman 52, 93, 298, 461, 769
Lucas, Buddy 298, 808
Lucas, Carrie **432**, 462, 795
Lucas, Cassandra 127, 128
Lucas, George 185, 354
Lucas, Harold 148
Lucas, Ray 245
Lucas, Reggie 159, 328, 472, 485
Lucas, Stan 337, 488
Lucien, Jon 64, 328, 412
Luckett, LeToya 189
Luckey, Warren 32, 52
Lucy Pearl **432**
Ludacris 211, 221
Lukather, Steve 601
Lulu 49, 340, 727, 803, 804, 844
Lumet, Sidney 376
Luna, Rico 500
Lunceford, Jimmie 263, 697
Lundy, Antoine 249
Lundy, Carmen 249
Lundy, Pat 812
Lundy, Rodney 249
Lundy, Stevie D. 249
Lunt, Stephen Broughton 643
Lupper, Kenneth 258, 352
Lutcher, Joe **433**
Lutcher, Nellie 95, **433**, 777
Luvah, Bryce 409
Ly Dells 828
Lyle, Bobby 773
Lyles, Gerald 129
Lymon, Frankie & the Teenagers 80, 122, 129, 228, 340, 346, 399, 400, 422, **433**, 434, 480, 505, 522, 525, 586, 588, 601, 602, 621, 670, 683, 687, 698, 798, 805, 821, 827, 829, 839
Lymon, Louie & the Teenchords 400, **434**
Lynch, David 539
Lyndell, Linda 811, 828
Lyndon, Frank 45, 46
Lynn, Barbara 399, 409, 434, 602, 804, 805, 807, 840
Lynn, Cheryl 427, **434**, 435, 713, 785
Lynn, Clyde 627
Lynn, Loretta 89
Lynne, Gloria **435**, 786
Lyres 500, 744
Lyrics 784
Lytle, Johnny 810

M

M People 483
M., Eddie 213
Mabern, Harold 47
Mabon, Willie 5, 95, **436**
Mabry, Lynn 79, 213
Mac Band 234, 670
Mac, Marc 109
Macaulay, Tony 250, 397
MacBeth, Peter 250
MacColl, Ewan 245
MacDonald, Doug 758
MacDonald, Ralph 48, 758
Machine 389
Machito 577
Macho, Joe 600
Mack Ten 691
Mack, Bill 800
Mack, James 180, 453
Mack, Lonnie 121, 306, 805
Mack, Oscar 778
Mack, Sam 600
Mackey, David 665
MacLellan, Gene 699
MacLeod, John 250
Macon, Uncle Dave 857
Mad Dogs & Englishmen 150
Mad Lads 211, **436**, 439, 508, 802
Madara, John 176, 602
Madayag, Phillip 689
Maddox, James 219
Maddox, Walt 443
Madison Street 559
Madison, Irving 542
Madness 239
Madonna 2, 28, 93, 139, 140, 145, 213, 292, 312, 350, 383, 389, 407, 444, 446, 469, 491, 492, 499, 582, 631, 686, 696, 770, 820
Madsen, Peter 739
Maestro, Johnny 169, 341, **436**, 818
Maestro, Johnny & the Crests 169
Maffei, Frank 176
Maffitt, Rocky 125
Magee, Sterling 779
Magic Lady **436**, 437
Magic Sam 102, 371, 372, 458
Magictones 438
Magness, Brian 140
Magnificent Men 679
Magnificent Seven 784
Magnificents 161, **437**, 777
Magnum **437**
Mahavishnu Orchestra 412, 671, 720
Mahoaney, Skip & the Casuals 437
Mahones, Gildo 759, 760
Mahoney, Skip 437
Mahoney, Skip & the Casuals **437**
Maiden, Sidney 805
Maiden, Tony 592, 593
Main Ingredient 29, 280, **437**, 438, 494, 541, 623, 727, 778, 796, 807, 812
Main Source 75
Mainieri, Mike 48
Majestics 798
Majors **438**, 557, 820
Makeba, Miriam 448, 500, 792
Malach, Bob 723
Mallory, Gerald 822
Malloy, David 176
Malo 254, **438**, 439
Malone, Deadric 57
Malone, George 479
Mamas & the Papas 238, 239, 243, 252
Manardo, Bob 233
Mance, Junior 732, 857
Mancha 831
Mancha, Steve 36, 37, 218, 410, 436, **439**, 509, 799, 808, 812
Manchester, Melissa 96, 97, 157, 640, 727
Manchild 28, 183, 414, **439**, 440
Mancini, Henry 295, 791
Mancuso, David 416, **440**, 791
Mandel, Johnny 175
Mandingo 792
Mandre 796

Mandrell, Barbara 336
Mandrill 54, **440**, 441, 821
Mangione, Chuck 43, 671
Manhattan Transfer 4, 114, 122, 479, 579, 817
Manhattans 11, 44, 307, 338, **441**, 442, 668, 670, 750, 785, 786, 788, 833
Manigault, Bobby 122
Manilow, Barry 328, 389, 729, 730, 731
Maniquin 411, 412
Mann, Aimee 25
Mann, Barry 1, 97, 172, 309, 388, 537, 574, 585, 730, 841, 842, 843, 844
Mann, Herbie 23, 25, 37, 432, 834
Mann, Manfred 72, 231, 399, 612, 779, 842, 844
Manne, Shelly 76, 377, 756
Mansfield, Bobby 767, 768
Mantese, Mario 308
Mantronik, Kurtis 520
Mantronix 218, 409, 646
Manuel, Bobby 469
Manuel, John 559
Mar Keys 34, 67, 169, 303, 371, **442**, 443, 466, 682, 802
Marais, Dee 823
Marascalco, John 46
Marathons **443**, 508, 509, 717
Marcellino, Jerry 474
Marcels 185, 217, **443**, 793, 827, 839
March, Little Peggy 15
Marchan, Bobby 249, **443**, 444, 461, 626, 627, 778, 793, 800
Marco, Ken 485
Marcus, Greil 243
Marcus, Steve 4
Marcus, Wade 55
Mardin, Arif 22, 40, 48, 97, 256, 278, 292, 379, 380, 381, 388, 389, **444**, 572, 639, 757
Mardin, Joe 389
Maresca, Ernie 489, 571
Margouleff, Robert 99, 244
Margulies, Ben 115
Maria, Tania 444
Marie, Teena 23, 81, 104, 363, 364, 422, **444**, 445, 483, 500, 622, 640, 715, 727, 802
Marigolds 74, 107, 309, 345, 783
Marin, Cheech 670
Mariners 184
Marino, Frank & Mahogany Rush 484
Marion, Eddie 95
Maritano, Ray 758
Mark, Marky 317
Marketts 79
Markham, Pigmeat 790
Marks, Beau 177
Marl, Marley 224
Marley Marl 224
Marley, Bob 66, 280, 319, 366, 367, 381, 392, 490, 493, 604, 723, 734, 737
Marley, Rita 245
Marley, Stephen 29
Marley, Ziggy 737
Maron, Jonathan 289, 825
Marquees 266, 480, 645
Marr, Hank 86
Marsalis Family 54
Marsalis, Branford 26, 493
Marsalis, Ellis 54
Marsalis, Wynton 54
Marsh 513
Marsh, Dave 18
Marsh, Osiris 513
Marshall, Joi 358
Marshall, Larry 449
Marshall, Maithe 562
Marshall, Michael 690
Marshall, Paul 260
Marshall, Peter 142
Marshall, Sherman 497
Martha & the Vandellas 37, 141, 168, 224, 241, 281, 315, 319, 320, 385, 420, **445**, 446, 447, 533, 571, 600, 612, 655, 715, 716, 727, 740, 777, 781, 786, 816, 817, 820, 831, 844
Martika **446**, 525, 747
Martin, Barbara 32, 549, 586, 653
Martin, Billy 242
Martin, Bobby 217, 338, 431, 600, 668
Martin, Cedric 157, 158
Martin, Dean 210, 425
Martin, Debbie 240
Martin, Deborah 78
Martin, Derek 786, 819
Martin, Eddie 243
Martin, Gene 548, 549
Martin, Hearlon "Cheese" 366
Martin, Leslie 601, 602
Martin, Luci 139, 234
Martin, Max 499
Martin, Michelle 312
Martin, Milo 260
Martin, Porscha 20
Martin, Ricky 229, 499, 606, 628, 688
Martin, Sennie "Skip" III 181, 182, 400
Martin, Steve 62, 486
Martin, Trade 782
Martinee, Lewis 231, 232
Martinelli, Nick 195, 398, 472, 498, 585, 773
Martinez, Nancy **446**
Martinez, Ray 525
Martini, Jerry 282, 624
Martino, Pat 857
Martins, Vitor 21
Martyn, Beverly 803
Martyn, John 419
Marvelettes 37, 319, 426, **447**, 461, 481, 495, 511, 578, 600, 612, 653, 682, 696, 715, 738, 745, 788, 794, 816, 817, 818, 823, 831, 832, 834, 844, 845, 846
Marvellos **447**, 801
Marvelows **447**, 448, 626, 778, 786
Marvin & Johnny 218, **448**, 555, 779, 795, 807, 815
Mary Jane Girls 363, 802
Mascots 821
Mase 75, 547
Masekela, Hugh 203, 261, **448**, 499, 668
Masked Marauders 181
Mason 447
Mason, Ann 804
Mason, Barbara 95, 267, **448**, 449, 615, 682, 824, 833
Mason, Bobby 717
Mason, Dave 239, 348
Mason, Harvey 294, 295, 307, 710
Mason, Harvey Jr. 8, 791, 829
Mason, Little Billy 821
Mason, Melvin 447
Mason, Vaughan 795
Mason, Vaughn and Crew 407
Masqueraders 258, **449**, 626
Mass Production 98, 308, **449**, 450, 795
Massenburg, Kedar 29
Masser, Michael 48, 397
Massey, Bobby 321, 332, 505, 700, 795
Massey, Rodney G. 309
Massey, William 751
Massive Attack 9, 304, 359, 631, 632
Master Ace 173
Master P 210
Masterettes 231
Mastermind **450**
Masters 339, 806
Masters at Work 20, 92, 679, 736
Mastrangelo, Carlo 45, 46
Matadors 549
Matassa, Cosimo 199, 310, 350, **450**, 518, 636
Material 295, 310, 322, 323, 767, 796
Mathis, Johnny 43, 48, 103, 121, 139, 277, 423, 490, 529, 583, 657, 707, 727, 729, 748, 749, 768
Matias, Ivan 224
Matichak, Robert 669
Matta, Gregory 615
Matthew, Eric 525, 567, 568
Matthewman, Stuart 451, 596
Matthews, Artwell Jr. 54
Matthews, Audrey 6, 54
Matthews, Dave 54
Matthews, David 48, 88, 734
Matthews, Johnnie Mae 54, 360, 539, 814
Matthews, Kaiya 6
Matthews, LaSalle 500
Matthews, Sharon 559
Mattis, David 3
Mattison, Quincy 758
Matute, Raul 151
Mauldin, Michael 210
Maunick, Jean-Paul "Bluey" 335
Maupin, Bennie 294, 295, 307
Maurice & Mac **450**, 451, 555, 557, 790
Maxon, Joe 636
Maxwell 175, **451**, 509, 525, 596, 693, 727
Maxwell, Larry 392
May, Billy 756
Mayall, Gaz 296
Mayall, John 150, 199, 296, 390, 759
Maye, Arthur Lee & the Crowns 514, 801, 808, 815
Mayer, Nathaniel & the Fabulous Twilights 648
Mayes, Lenny 203, 204, 333
Mayfield, Curtis & the Impressions 4, 27, 28, 44, 55, 80, 100, 102, 103, 105, 106, 108, 109, 120, 125, 126, 136, 137, 145, 146, 151, 160, 167, 174, 175, 190, 224, 228, 234, 235, 241, 244, 248, 256, 257, 261, 273, 277, 280, 287, 289, 293, 294, 299, 302, 303, 317, 319, 320, 327, 328, 333, 334, 335, 338, 341, 358, 371, 378, 380, 384, 387, 394, 401, 405, 407, 408, 414, 418, 448, 449, **451**, 452, 453, 454, 468, 491, 505, 511, 517, 534, 554, 562, 615, 641, 642, 684, 709, 714, 718, 723, 742, 760, 762, 785, 786, 787, 790, 791, 793, 801, 802, 803, 808, 812, 813, 814, 815, 816, 818, 819, 821, 826, 829, 830, 832, 844, 851
Mayfield, Percy 5, 132, 134, 256, 266, **454**, 455, 520, 709, 753, 777, 792, 798, 829, 833, 836, 856
Mayo, Elaine 260
Mayo, Gary N. 441
Mayo, John 260
Mayorga, Lincoln 416
Mays, James 714
Mays, Odeen 400, 671
Mays, Roosevelt 176
Maze 74, **455**, 456, 513, 652, 665, 785
Mazelle, Kym 92
Mazza, Jim 370
Mbulu, Letta 377
MC Hammer 4, 73, 157, 214, 216, 583, 757, 823, 833
MC Lyte 45, 98, 431, 628, 667
MC Serch 75
MC Solaar 173
MC Trouble 691
McAlister, Maurice 450, 557
McArthur, Larry 161
McArthur, Reginald 161
McCain, Jerry 783, 800
McCain, Larry 691, 692
McCall, C.W. 402
McCall, Cash 143, 520, 793
McCall, John 219, 402
McCall, Louis 157
McCall, Toussaint **456**, 812, 834
McCann, Les 245, 563, 780, 857, 858
McCant, James 140
McCant, Leroy 140
McCant, Sam 140
McCants, Christopher 140
McCarter, Lisa 47
McCarthy, Gene 14
McCarthy, Tommy 499
McCartney, Linda 553
McCartney, Paul 13, 23, 244, 269, 277, 334, 353, 354, 355, 406, 420, 424, 450, 466, 467, 487, 553, 635, 653, 675, 719, 763, 766, 788, 792, 842, 844
McCarty, Ernest Jr. 535
McCary, Michael 72
McClain, Alton & Destiny 80, 402, 638, 696
McClain, Howard 402
McClain, John 351
McClain, Marlon 181
McClain, Mighty Sam **456**, 692
McClain, William 144
McClary, Thomas 155, 157
McClinton, Delbert 128, 130, 466, 570
McClure, Bobby 39, 150, 188, **456**, 457, 782, 791, 804
McConnell, Tommy 621
McCoo, Marilyn 136, 238, 239, 413, **457**, 572, 718
McCoo, Marilyn & Billy Davis, Jr. 360
McCord, Kevin 135, 324, 489, 510
McCormick, Charles 60
McCormick, Maureen 416
McCoy 528, 546, 693, 719, 750
McCoy, Gregory 449
McCoy, Ronald 693, 800
McCoy, Rose Marie 52
McCoy, Van 39, 78, 142, 231, 245, 258, 277, 325, 338, 358, 366, 395, 397, 398, 407, 412, 435, 447, 457, **458**, 463, 511, 528, 546, 591, 612, 648, 649, 728, 741, 757, 776, 779, 788, 842, 843
McCoy, William 719
McCoys 13, 49
McCracken, Hugh 197, 245
McCracklin, Jimmy 261, 305, 458, 800, 805, 818, 828, 838
McCrae, George 384, **458**, 459, 803
McCrae, Gwen 281, 439, **458**, 459, 567, 572, 685, 803, 831
McCraw, Lloyd 107, 345
McCune, Nat 176
McCurn, George 715
McDaniel, Chris 430
McDaniel, Elias 193
McDaniel, Willard 454, 492
McDaniels, Eugene 397, 459
McDaniels, Gene **459**
McDode, Henry 759
McDonald, Ian 419
McDonald, Michael 77, 336, 403, 404, 405, 587, 756
McDonald, Ralph 21
McDonald, Virginia 708
McDougall, Ian 686
McDuff, Jack 48, 110, 159, 287, 350, 650, 781, 788, 810, 857, 858
McDuffie, Joanne "Jojo" 368
McEachern, Bill 502
McElroy, Solly 246
McElroy, Thomas 149, 222, 224, 629
McEntire, Reba 152
McFadden & Whitehead 42, 268, **459**, 460, 616, 826
McFadden, Gene 381, 459, 460, 465
McFadden, Ruth 296
McFarland, Bill 634
McFarland, Gary 94
McFarlane, Fred 426
McGee, Pennington 109
McGhee, Brownie 56, 210, 460, 759, 760
McGhee, Howard 297, 610
McGhee, Jacci 233, 234
McGhee, Johnny T. 431
McGhee, Stick **460**
McGhee, Sticks 460, 777, 838
McGilberry, Harry 678
McGill, Lucius 186
McGill, Michael 188
McGill, Mickey 186, 187, 511, 540
McGinnis, Carl 532
McGlown, Betty 32, 548, 549
McGowan, Jim 251
McGregor, George 832
McGriff, Edna 512
McGriff, Jimmy 783, 788, 829, 857, 858
McGuire Sisters 480, 634
McGuire, Barry 176
McGuire, Pat 141
McIntosh, Carl 22, 427, 727
McIntosh, Robbie 22
McIntosh, Tom 47
McIntyre, Onnie 22, 23
McJohn, Goldy 362
McKay, Al 142, 211, 214, 769
McKay, James 601
McKay, Lennie 367, 368
McKee, Lonette 453
McKee, Sandy 151
McKeever, Steve 602
McKenzie & Condon's Chicagoans 332
McKenzie, Derrick 364
McKenzie, Don 549
McKenzie, Lester "Jelly" 332
McKinney, Al 542
McKinney, James 205
McKinney, Joseph 408
McKinney, Sami 47, 300
McKinney's Cotton Pickers 47
McKinnon, Catherine 400
McKinnon, Pearl 400, 602
McKissack, Perri 529
McKnight, Brian 30, 116, 426, 460, 547, 752
McKnight, Claude V. III 666
McKnight, Dewayne Blackbird 517

McLagan, Ian 50
McLaren, Malcolm 153
McLaughlin, John 720, 723
McLaughlin, Ollie 114, 167, 349, 418, 714
McLean, Jackie 159, 781, 787
McLean, Lalisha 10
McLean, Paul 312
McLean, Penny 617
McLemore, Lamonte 238, 718
McLeod, Vincent 590
McMichael, Julius 519
McMillan, Terry 22, 810
McMullen, Craig 452
McMurray, Clay 472, 546, 705
McNair, Barbara **461**, 790
McNeely, Big Jay 46, 102, 305, **461**, 514, 777, 780, 836, 838
McNeely, Bob 461
McNeely, Cecil 461
McNeil, David 408, 409
McNeil, Dee Dee 546
McNeil, Leroy 500
McNeir, Ronnie 253, **461**, 462, 591
McPhatter, Clyde 11, 12, 31, 32, 56, 176, 206, 207, 208, 242, 295, 369, 375, 391, 425, 439, **462**, 463, 480, 534, 648, 692, 726, 727, 753, 779, 785, 798, 836, 839, 856
McPhee, Skip 752
McPherson, Donald 280, 437, 438
McPherson, Tim 464
McQuater, Matthew 148
McQueen, Mike 497
McQueen, Tim 497
McRae, Carmen 748
McRae, George 459
McRae, Gwen 459
McRaney, Edna 78
McShann, Jay 49, 415, 759, 822
McTell, Blind Willie 167
McVea, Jack 461, 812
McVey, Cameron 9, 136
McVoy, Carl 809
McWilliams, Paulette 592
Meadowlarks 184, 381, 408
Meadows, Jonathan "Corky" 510
Meadows, Marion 159, 160
Means, Rick 129
Meaux, Huey P. 306, 398, 434, 602
Mechi 718
Meco 202, 487
Medallions **463**, 464
Medeiros, Glenn 82, 83, **464**
Medeski, John 141, 195
Medeski, Martin & Wood 141, 826
Medina, Benny 390, 757
Meditation Singers 36
Medley, Bill 191, **464**, 574, 575, 590, 781, 847
Medlin, Joe 562
Medress, Hank 834
Medwick, Joe 799
Meeks, Gary 47
Meeting 594
Mel & Kim **464**
Mel & Tim 57, 126, 242, 459, **464**, 619, 784, 808
Melanie 300
Melcher, Terry 834
Melendez, Lisette 801
Melky Sedeck 366
Mellencamp, John Cougar 224, 491
Mellett, Coleman 650
Mello Kings **464**, 805
Mello Moods 629
Melson, Joe 716
Melvin, Harold & the Blue Notes 43, 165, 200, 267, 268, 322, 325, 338, 339, 460, **464**, 465, 466, 468, 476, 531, 539, 573, 597, 669, 687, 779, 783, 785, 786, 794, 820, 821, 824, 848
Memphis Boys **466**
Memphis Horns 43, 391, 409, 410, 442, 443, 458, **466**, 481, 607, 641, 780, 844
Memphis Slim 90, 261, 487, 815
Men at Large 555, 628
Mendell, James 610
Mendelsohn, Fred 52, 298
Mendes, Sergio 727
Mendez, Akissa 10
Mendez, Annie 10
Mendez, Judy 10
Mendez, Linda 10
Mensah, Paapa 312
Mercado, Richard 141
Mercer, Barbara 808
Mercer, Johnny 48, 716, 764
Mercer, Pat 78
Merchant, Jimmy 433
Mercury, Daniela 249
Merenstein, Lewis 123
Merrit, Victor 584
Mesa, Omar 440
Mesner, Eddie 242, 297, 518
Messina, Joe 262, 273, 360, 714
Meters 25, 54, 63, 74, 110, 196, 197, 200, 234, 271, 296, 321, 403, **466**, 467, 493, 494, 495, 518, 519, 553, 562, 694, 747, 782, 783, 788, 801, 802, 803, 807, 833, 841, 851
Metheny, Pat 30
Method Man 176, 221, 222
Metro 71
Metronomes 222
Metros **468**
Meyers, Bill 519
MFSB 38, 40, 117, 135, 185, 190, 217, 240, 268, 296, 297, 317, 325, 338, **468**, 469, 499, 533, 597, 615, 687, 723, 785, 820
MG's 43, 67, 68, 110, 311, 443, **469**, 495
Miami Sound Machine 42, 228, 229
Miami **469**
Micale, Tony 571, 606
Michael, George 257, 323, **469**, 542, 720, 811, 847
Michaels, Lisa 399
Michel'le **469**, 470
Michel, Prakazrel "Pras" 313
Mickens, Robert "Spike" 400, 401
Mickey & Sylvia 31, 32, 309, 434, **470**, 477, 528, 613, 663, 786, 807
MicKinley, Ray 102
Mickle, Dale 196
Middlebrooks, Ralph "Pee Wee" 502
Middleton, Herb 412
Middleton, Mark 56
Middleton, Max 419
Middleton, Tony 784
Midler, Bette 92, 188, 277, 444, 493, 529, 567, 595, 662
Midnight Band 604
Midnight Star 35, 121, 152, 182, 402, **470**, 471
Midnight, Charlie 298
Midnighters 11, 32, 33, 93, 205, 491, 548
Mighty Clouds of Joy 583, 645, 673, 775
Mighty Flyers 582
Mighty Hannibal **471**, 807
Mighty Imperials 826
Mighty Marvelows 626
Mike + the Mechanics 119, 120
Milburn, Amos 218, 369, 458, **471**, 518, 547, 777, 778, 836, 838, 839
Miles, Buddy 80, 365, 488, 555
Miles, John 558, 605
Miles, Lenny 830
Milestone 217
Milira 691
Millar, Robin 239, 596
Miller, Bernard 530
Miller, Bobby 186, 187, 557, 645
Miller, Charles 724, 725
Miller, Cleo 220
Miller, Floyd 622, 623
Miller, Gene 326, 408, 409, 529, 568
Miller, Glenn 48, 324
Miller, Helen 729
Miller, Jake 209
Miller, Jay 783, 838
Miller, Jimmy 759
Miller, Kim 338
Miller, Leeza 816
Miller, Leo 142
Miller, Marcus 152, 666, 678, 734
Miller, Mulgrew 105
Miller, Rice 189
Miller, Roger 283
Miller, Ron 461, 765
Miller, Scotty 338
Miller, Steve 463, 600, 796
Miller, Tommy 247
Miller, Walt 122
Miller, William 400, 611
Milli Vanilli 2, 66, 67, 77, 500, 557
Millinder, Lucky 94, 198, 297, 777, 812
Milliner, Michael 525
Millionaires 399
Mills Blue Rhythm Band 73
Mills Brothers 74, 562, 648, 726, 727, 794, 798, 839
Mills, Allen 757
Mills, Eleanore 159, 160
Mills, Gordon 134
Mills, Stephanie 47, 195, 290, 396, 412, 417, **472**, 473, 485, 531, 608, 757, 785
Mills, Ted 62, 160, 387, 649
Milsap, Ronnie 144, 793, 832
Milstein, Alec 47
Milton, Roy **473**, 514, 547, 798, 822, 836, 838
Mimms, Garnet 34, 49, 302, 438, 473, 474, 557, 660, 668, 728, 730, 784, 844
Mimms, Garnet & the Enchanters 161, **473**, 786
Mincelli, Mike 114
Mind, Heart & Soul 430
Mindbenders 403, 405, 844
Miner, Tim 286
Ming, Leslie 97
Mingle, Brent 513
Mingo, Carrie 368
Mingus, Charles 781
Mink DeVille 636
Minogue, Kylie 464
Mint Condition 3, 77, **474**, 545
Minus, Rene 128
Miracles 37, 166, 192, 220, 225, 226, 275, 281, 289, 348, 370, 371, 426, 445, 448, 461, **474**, 475, 477, 479, 480, 526, 528, 533, 548, 557, 578, 579, 580, 581, 582, 600, 616, 655, 712, 721, 727, 763, 780, 786, 790, 796, 798, 807, 814, 816, 817, 818, 831, 832, 839, 844, 845, 846
Miranov, Jeff 202
Mirettes **475**
Mister Biggs 340
Mister Complex 483
Mister Fingers 240, 782
Mister Malik 478
Mister Rogers 422
Mitchell, Arthur 468
Mitchell, Barbara 312, 313, 747
Mitchell, Billy 148, 150, 279, 607
Mitchell, Blue 70, 71, 701
Mitchell, Blue Richard 114
Mitchell, Bobby 39, 310, 475
Mitchell, Bobby & the Toppers **475**
Mitchell, Brandon 290
Mitchell, Dwain 417
Mitchell, Herman 759
Mitchell, James 190, 247, 286, 466, 476, 607
Mitchell, John 578
Mitchell, Joni 194, 351, 542, 601, 605, 657
Mitchell, Keith 7, 217
Mitchell, Larry 279
Mitchell, Liz 66
Mitchell, Paul 44, 248
Mitchell, Phillip 159, 809, 830
Mitchell, Ralph 247, 248
Mitchell, Tiny 84
Mitchell, Vernessa 312
Mitchell, Willie 96, 143, 144, 150, 243, 285, 286, 287, 311, 371, 372, 409, 458, **475**, 476, 520, 529, 530, 601, 607, 684, 770, 771, 809, 810
Mitchum, Robert 582
Mizell, Don 108, 109
Mizell, Fonce 106, 166, 346, 348, 533, 644, 667
Mizell, Jason 108
Mizell, Larry 55, 106, 667, 829
Mobb Deep 129, 664
Mobley, Hank 287
Moby Grape 125
Modeliste, Joseph "Ziggy" 54, 466, 467, 785
Modern Jazz Sextet 170
Moffett, Jonathan 773
Moir, Monte 21, 510
Mojo Men 624, 625, 626
Molly Hatchet 484
Moman, Chips 5, 71, 118, 119, 294, 442, 449, 682, 683, 692, 760, 762
Mombassa 792
Moment of Truth **476**
Moments 60, 226, 349, 375, 412, 428, 438, **477**, 478, 565, 575, 607, 626, 647, 649, 740, 779, 812
Mona Lisa 1
Monaco, Bob 117
Monarchs 649, 828
Monardo, Meco 202, 276
Mondo Grosso 597
Monét, Jerzee **478**
Monette, Ray 263
Money, Eddie 636
Moneymaker, Kelly 232
Monica 75, 190, 367, **478**, 599, 710
Monie Love 6
Monifah **478**, 479, 796
Monitors 275, 439, **479**, 712, 790, 825, 829, 835
Monk, Thelonious 83, 123, 389, 400, 659
Monkees 7, 841
Monotones 400, **479**, 782, 786, 790, 827
Monroe, Bill 856, 857
Monroe, Marilyn 651
Montana, Vince 190, 468, 615, 797
Montana, Vincent Jr. 597
Montclairs **479**, 525
Montenegro, Hugo 45
Montereys 571
Montgomery, Barbara 331
Montgomery, Bob 168
Montgomery, Jack 792, 814
Montgomery, John Michael 9
Montgomery, Little Brother 277
Montgomery, Monk 820
Montgomery, Robbie 331, 475
Montgomery, Wes 47, 48, 139, 188, 288, 376, 709, 857
Montgomery, William 123, 345
Montiero, June 696, 697
Montrell, Roy 197, 518, 793
Montrose, Ronnie 298, 493
Moods 697
Moody Blues 779, 794, 812
Moody, James 30, 377
Moodymann 43
Mooney, Hal 732, 733
Moonglows 11, 186, 206, 228, 246, 266, 271, 295, 318, 360, 381, 382, 391, 415, 439, 443, 445, **479**, 480, 497, 539, 611, 720, 767, 777, 782, 790, 793, 797, 799, 829, 839
Moore, Ben 555
Moore, Bobby 790
Moore, Bobby & the Rhythm Aces **481**
Moore, Chanté 202, 358, **481**, 735
Moore, Curley 627
Moore, Dorothy 184, 249, 394, **481**, 813, 825
Moore, Henry 86
Moore, Jackie 89, **481**, 482, 506, 602, 797, 809, 831, 834
Moore, Johnny [Three Blazers] 83, 84, 326
Moore, Johnny [Drifters] 83, 84, 206, 207, 208, 314, 326
Moore, Larry 468, 481
Moore, Lee 414
Moore, Melba 47, 98, 269, 349, 412, 457, 460, **482**, 600, 684, 747, 786, 810, 812, 815
Moore, Melvin 634
Moore, Merrill 167
Moore, Michael 585
Moore, Oscar 83, 84
Moore, Pete 289
Moore, Phil 31
Moore, Ray 95
Moore, Raymond 233, 280
Moore, Rene 572, 757
Moore, Rudy Ray 60, **482**, 833
Moore, Sam 385, 598, 599, 800
Moore, Scotty 54
Moore, Warren "Pete" 289, 474, 475, 579, 580
Moore, Wild Bill 701, 808
Moorer, Alvis 228
Moorer, Betty 228
Moorer, Gilbert 228, 792
Morales, David 399, 578, 588
Morales, Miguel 37
Morales, Ricky 37
Morali, Jacques 717, 718
Moran, Tony 168
Morcheeba **482**, 483
More, Mike 176
Moreira, Airto 734
Moreland, Prentice 345, 795
Morgan, Brian Alexander 300
Morgan, Debelah **483**, 720

Morgan, John 366
Morgan, Lanny 25
Morgan, Lee 282, 287, 787
Morgan, Meli'sa 412, **483**, 484, 486, 757, 785
Morgan, Melissa 810
Morgera, Fabio 289
Morisette, Johnnie 162
Morissette, Alanis 385, 390
Moroder, Giorgio 35, 123, 147, 182, 283, 321, 402, 406, 416, **484**, 617, 645, 650, 651, 661, 796
Morrero, Ricardo 64
Morricone, Ennio 599
Morris, Angelo 768
Morris, Billy 128
Morris, Charlie 380
Morris, Eddie 238
Morris, Idella 438
Morris, Joe 4
Morris, Kenneth 632
Morris, Leo 750
Morris, Nathan 72
Morris, Richard 549, 580
Morris, Walter 349, 477, 565, 575
Morris, Wanya 72, 73, 510
Morrison, Dorothy 440
Morrison, James 686
Morrison, Jimmy 13
Morrison, Van 49, 102, 123, 130, 197, 222, 239, 306, 364, 491, 536, 601, 640, 658, 660, 745, 847
Morrison, Walter "Junie" 146, 381, 502, 517
Morrison, Willi 686
Morrissey 71
Morrow, George 732
Morton, George 558, 784
Morton, Jelly Roll 197
Morton, Shadow 608, 844
Mos Def 75, 602
Mosely, Chuck 422
Moses, Pirkle Lee Jr. 219, 402
Mosley, Ronald 590
Mosley, Wenzon 714
Moss, Bill 251
Mosson, Cordell 264, 523
Mostel, Raphael 47
Moten, Wendy **484**
Mother Freedom Band 779
Mother's Finest 234, 428, **484**, 485
Motherlode **485**
Mothers of Invention 532, 584
Motiv Eight 92
Motorhead 312
Mott the Hoople 71, 608
Mottola, George 46
Mottola, Tommy 115, 116, 292
Moulton, Tom 98, 338, 374, 385, 518, 697, 699, 700, 792, 795, 797, 834
Mouzon, Alphonse 25
Movers 744
Moy, Sylvia 446, 479, 715
Mtume 328, 380, **485**, 486, 664, 785
Mtume, James 26, 328, 472, 540
Mtume, Mindbender 485
Muhammad, Idris 750, 796
Muldaur, Maria 360, 530, 541, 825
Muldrow, Gail 282
Muller, Randy 76, 338, 473, 621
Mullican, Moon 812
Mulligan, Gerry 759
Mumba, Samantha **486**
Mumford, Eugene 408, 409
Mundi, Coati 389
Mundy, Jimmy 198
Mundy, Ronald 443
Munford, Jimmy 263
Munich Machine 321, 416, 665
Murdock, Glenn 388, 484, 485
Murdock, Shirley 484, **486**, 547, 719
Muriel, Linda 75
Murmaids 844
Murph, Randolph 80
Murphy, Bernard 78
Murphy, Eddie 73, 77, 102, 278, 282, 291, 351, 374, 381, 482, **486**, 487, 527, 664, 684, 720, 761
Murphy, Floyd 487
Murphy, Joe 718
Murphy, Kevin 388, 592, 593
Murphy, Matt "Guitar" 62, **487**
Murphy, Mic 47, 291, 664
Murphy, Phil 539
Murphy, Walter 40, **487**
Murphy, Walter & the Big Apple Band 138
Murray, Bill 285
Murray, Juggy 298, 704
Murray, Mickey 487
Murray, Roy 439
Murrell, Hadley D. 607
Murrell, Herb 649, 650
Muscle Shoals Horns 256, 356, 409
Muscle Shoals Sound Rhythm Section 255, 314
Music Explosion 36
Music Machine 338
Music Makers 468
Musical Youth 353
Musiq Soulchild 487, 488, 647, 770
Musiq (Talib Johnson) 487
Musique 92, 337, 374, 383, **488**, 567, 778, 795, 821
Musselwhite, Charlie 241
Mustangs 525
Mutantes 515
Mutiny **488**
Mya 366, **488**, 538
Myers, Alicia 324, **489**, 510, 715, 757
Myers, John 307, 308
Myers, Mike 189, 758
Myles, Billy 464
Myles, Willie 437
Mynah Birds 362
Myrick, Don 142, 214, 215, 535, 610
Mysterme 13
Mystic Merlin 349
Mystical 418
Mystics 155, 364, **489**, 839
Mystique 333, 338, 665

N

N cole 665
N Sync 155, 498, 499, 500, 538, 689
Nabors, Sylvia 615
Naftalin, Mark 455
Nails 136
Najee 7, **490**, 565
Nakamoto, Derek 289
Nakamura, Tetsuya 724
Nance, Allen E. 129
Nanette 822
Napier, Bruce 502
Narcardo, Vinny 114
Nas 10, 210
Nascimbene, Mario 791
Nash, Graham 47
Nash, Johnny 2, 183, **490**, 491, 721, 740, 790, 821, 824
Nash, Michael 585
Nash, Ruby 590
Nat Turner's Rebellion 296, 794
Nathan, David 18, 97, 256, 328, 456, 473, 486
Nathan, Pete 372
Nathan, Syd 425, 462, **491**, 658
Natural Four 327, **491**, 741, 793
Naturals 415, 416, 722, 799
Naughton, Naturi 688
Naughty by Nature 776
Navarrete, Bobby 689
Navarro 107
Navarro, Esther 107
Nazty 54
NdegeOcello, Me'Shell 263, **491**, 810
N'Dour, Youssou 136, 137, 367
NDR Big Band 222
Neal, Raful 813
Neal, Rochester 508, 516
Neal, Russell 686
Neely, Sam 719
Negro, Joey 796
Negroni, Joe 433
Neil, Fred 194, 555
Neilson, John 108
Nelson, Billy "Bass" 263, 306, 517, 522
Nelson, Chip 795
Nelson, Earl 63, 318, 415, 795, 799
Nelson, George 511, 512
Nelson, Jimmy **492**
Nelson, Marc 72, **492**
Nelson, Mercury 249
Nelson, Nate 246, 539
Nelson, Oliver 379, 536, 755, 756
Nelson, Phyllis **492**
Nelson, Ricky 49, 93, 121, 716
Nelson, Tracy 684
Nelson, Willie 104, 130, 133, 134, 272, 285, 314, 481, 570, 650, 653
Neons 12
Neptunes [1] 689
Neptunes [2] 189, 492
NERD **492**
Nero, Frances **492**, 831, 832
Nervous Norvus 102
Neto, Renato 213
Neufville, Renee 776
Nevarez, Alfred 9
Neville Brothers 197, 366, 450, 466, **493**, 494, 495, 747, 803, 818, 841
Neville, Aaron 5, 277, 437, 466, 492, 493, **494**, 495, 634, 694, 695, 747, 758, 777, 781, 783, 786, 793, 799, 802, 811
Neville, Art 466, 467, 493, **495**, 747, 750
Neville, Charles 54, 466, 493, 494, 747
Neville, Cyril 466, 493, 494, 747
Neville, Ivan 493, 799
Neville, Naomi 694
Nevins, Al 841
New Birth 266, 333, 457, **495**, 496, 499, 655
New Breed 791
New Direction 328
New Edition 13, 41, 82, 83, 155, 277, 332, **496**, 497, 533, 650, 657, 698
New Jersey Connection 789
New Kids on the Block 2, 155, 317, 496, 533, 689
New Power Generation 549, 551
New Seekers 699
New York City 138, **497**, 582, 688, 782, 809, 812
New York Community Choir 278, 279
New York Dolls 608, 688
New York Philharmonic Orchestra 366
New York Port Authority 315, **497**
Newbeats 219, 349
Newberry, Booker III **497**, 498
Newborn, Phineas 25
Newbury, Mickey 72
Newcomers 18, 19, **498**, 822
Newley, Anthony 639
Newman, David "Fathead" 7, 130, 131, 133, 171, 198, 256, 261, 392, 857
Newman, Floyd 568
Newman, Herb 7, 416
Newman, Joe 294, 701, 732
Newman, Randy 72, 361, 639, 640, 684, 842
Newmark, Andy 624
Newsom, Ernest 719
Newsome 789
Newsome, Ernest 234
Newsome, Tony 218
Next 359, 577
Next Movement **498**, 822
Nice, Rich 691
Nichol, Steve 427
Nicholas, Big Nick 73
Nicholas, Edwin 417, 743
Nicholas, J.D. 156, 157, 308
Nicholas, Tony 742
Nichols, Billy 98
Nichols, Herbie 788
Nichols, Jay 431
Nichols, Red 415
Nickens, Richard 219
Nickerson, Rod 413
Nicks, Stevie 298
Nicole 227
Nicoletti, Mike 434
Night Train Clemons 302
Nightcaps 821
Nightingale, Maxine **498**, 727, 789, 795, 826
Nightingale, Ollie 508, 783
Nightingales 516, 668
Nilsson, Harry 608
Nimoy, Leonard 309
Nine Inch Nails 451
Ninety Eight Degrees **498**, 499
Ninety Four East 2
Ninth Creation 819
Nirvana 354
Nite Liters 468, 495, 496, **499**
Nitzsche, Jack 774
Nix, Don 442
Nix, Kenton 270, 271
Nixon, Eddie 714
Nixon, Emmett 698
Nixon, Hammie 714
Nixon, Lynn 14
No Authority **499**
No Question **499**
Nobles, Cliff 68, 468, **499**, 500
Nocentelli, Leo 466
Noel, Carl 361
Noel, Fats 808
Nokio the N-Tity 208, 209
Nolan, James 90
Nolan, Kenny 403
Noland, Andrew 502
Nolen, Jimmy 85, 91, 312, 366, 514
Nolte, Nick 486
Nomad, Naz 181
NORE 209
Norma Jean 770
Norman, Don And the Other Four 114
Norman, Jimmy 295
Norris, Charlie Eldridge "Chuck" 84, 454, 492, 759
Norris, Jean 776
Norris, Jerry 117
Northern Lights 134
Norvo, Red 415
Norwalt, Rose 585
Norwood, Brandy 75
Notations 173, 428, **500**, 626, 793, 832
Notorious BIG 17, 66, 230, 470, 547, 693
Novell, Jay 820
Now 737
NPG 551
NRBQ 51
Nu Flavor **500**
Nu Shooz 785, 801
Nubians **500**
Nugent, Ted 54, 484
Numan, Gary 518
Nunes, Clara 428, 742
Nunes, Larry 428, 742
Nunn, Bobby [1] 817
Nunn, Bobby [2] 578
Nuriddin, Jalaluddin Mansur 410
Nurse, Bobby 611
Nutmegs 464, **500**, 798, 805, 806, 828
Nuyorican Soul 440, 597
NWA 66, 469, 470
Nyasuma, Mamadi 431
Nyro, Laura 25, 238, 239, 322, 403, 404, 444, 582, 588, 590, 655
Nytro **500**

O

Oak Ridge Boys 694
Oakenfold, Paul 416
Oakes, Bill 220
Oakley, Isiah "Ike" 366
Oasis 292, 293, 679
Oates, John 292, 563, 668, 679
Obiedo, Ray 213
O'Brian, Bobby 795
O'Brien, Brendan 638
O'Brien, Ian 825
O'Brien, Matt 179
O'Bryan **501**, 744
Ocean Colour Scene 196
Ocean, Billy 336, 353, 381, 399, **501**, 502, 785
O'Connor, Sinead 366, 551
Octavius, Anthony 121, 122
O'Day, Alan 640
Odds & Ends 53, 688
O'Dell, Brooks 830
Oden, Saint Louis Jimmy 815
Odyssey 202, 203, **502**, 560
O'Farrill, Chico 441
Offitt, Lillian 783
Offspring 724
Ogden, Robert 94
Ogermann, Claus 48, 288
O'Hagan, Sean 515
Ohio Players 23, 42, 76, 81, 98, 110, 111, 154, 170, 175, 269, 327, 381, 384, 406, 407, 450, 455, 457, 486, 500, 502, 503, 504, 540, 614, 622, 625, 652, 690, 708, 746, 775, 782, 800, 801, 802, 814, 817, 819, 851
Ohio Untouchables 233, 502

O'Jays 43, 47, 55, 84, 100, 103, 120, 141, 166, 186, 204, 211, 225, 226, 267, 268, 318, 321, 325, 332, 338, 339, 356, 378, 403, 405, 416, 417, 418, 422, 460, 468, 498, **505**, 506, 507, 512, 533, 539, 571, 597, 607, 615, 616, 628, 638, 649, 668, 669, 697, 700, 712, 717, 723, 768, 779, 788, 794, 795, 802, 809, 812, 820, 821, 824, 830, 831, 848, 851
O'Kaysions **507**
O'Keefe, John 434
Ol' Dirty Bastard 116, 385, 621
Oldham, Alan 415
Oldham, Andrew Loog 15, 635
Oldham, Spooner 72, 129, 159, 314, 405, 450, 456, 555, 623, 683, 684
Olive, Pat 320
Oliver, Clarence 575
Oliver, David **507**, 508
Oliver, Gwen 319
Oliver, Jimmy 206, 207
Oliver, Troy 278
Ollie & the Nightingales **508**
Olympics 63, 199, 368, 423, **508**, 509, 519, 561, 562, 788, 805
Omar 203, **509**, 664, 727
Omarion 27
Omartian, Michael 57, 572, 573, 651, 730
Onderlinde, Johnny 338
100 Proof (Aged in Soul) 37, 124, 202, 218, 219, 233, 248, 279, 415, **509**, 511, 809
One O One North 259
One Twelve 10, **509**, 510, 558
One Way 135, 324, 489, **510**, 628
O'Neal, Alexander 136, 399, 496, **510**, 511, 735, 773
O'Neal, Brian 102
O'Neal, Johnny 702
O'Neal, Kevin 102
O'Neill, Tina 282, 331, 704
Oneness of Juju 231, 779
Ono, Yoko 796
Onyx 235
Opals 453, **511**, 615, 819, 827
Oquendo, Manny 295
Orange, Walter 155, 156, 157
Orb 440
Orbison, Roy 128, 247, 285, 716
Orchids 803
Ordettes 403, 404, 602
Organized Noize 529, 772
Origin 289
Original Casuals 799
Originals 7, 37, 64, 275, 279, 281, 415, 492, **511**, 571, 586, 592, 600, 712, 814
Orioles 11, 12, 33, 107, 121, 148, 206, 255, 395, 409, 479, **511**, 512, 539, 562, 611, 634, 657, 794, 828, 839, 856
Orlando, Tony 169, 559
Orlons **512**
Ortiz, Diana 205
Orton, Beth 108, 109
Orzabal, Roland 6
Osborne, Billy 431, 512
Osborne, Jeffrey 157, 166, 388, 431, 450, **512**, 513, 620, 729, 730
Osborne, Joan 263, 318, 319
Osborne, Kell 386, 548, 549, 635, 674
Osibisa 441, 552
Osiris **513**
Oskar, Lee 283, 295, 325, 413, **513**, 724
Osmond, Donny 689
Osmonds 80, 350, 661
Ostrow, Leib 534
Otis & Carla 459
Otis, Clyde 48, 49, 332, 414, 458, 809
Otis, Johnny 3, 32, 38, 70, 94, 188, 189, 192, 198, 296, 297, 360, 397, 430, 461, 473, **514**, 515, 516, 535, 736, 737, 777, 810, 822, 827, 830, 836, 839
Otis, Johnny Band 578
Otis, Johnny Show 41, 515
Otis, Shuggie 430, 514, **515**, 516, 710, 808, 825
Ouimette, Tim 392
Ousley, Curtis 390
Out Front 365
OutKast 28, 154, 210, 221, 313, 481
Outsiders 340
Outta Control 400
Ovations 350, 508, **516**
Overbea, Danny 795
Overton, Chuck 74
Owens, Buck 658, 779
Owens, Kevin 136
Owens, Monte 629
Owens, Paul 658, 659
Owens, Richard 443, 717
Owens, Ricky 42, 717
Owens, Robert 240, 399
Oxfords 828
Oyewole, Abiodun 383, 410, 411
Ozark Mountain Daredevils 546
Ozen, Gonzales 660
Ozuna, Sunny 42

P

P-Funk All Stars 34, 98, 146, 153, 154, 214, 264, 265, 266, 381, 411, 488, **517**, 522, 523, 524, 527, 535, 571, 624, 625, 699, 767
P. Diddy [see Puff Daddy] 59, 230, 278
Pace Won 483
Pace, Ronnie 752
Pace, Sam 228
Pacheco, Johnny 517, 577
Packers 442
Padro, Charles 440
Pagan, Ralfi **517**
Page, Bobby & the Riff Raffs 517, 529
Page, Gene 97, 334, 428, 429, 529, 633, 705, 727, 742, 743
Page, Hot Lips 52
Page, Jimmy 150, 320, 484, 699, 759, 760
Page, Martin 216
Page, Patti 142, 210, 823
Page, Richard 578
Page, Walter 701
Paich, Marty 46, 131, 727
Paige, Fred 129
Paige, Sharon 465, 466
Pakula, Lenny 468, 616
Palmer, Bruce 362
Palmer, Clarence 47
Palmer, Earl 24, 25, 38, 39, 69, 70, 198, 424, 475, 514, **518**, 555, 613, 840
Palmer, Reese 480, 558
Palmer, Robert 133, 139, 466, 467, 493, 507, **518**, 519, 694, 847
Palmieri, Charlie 295
Palmieri, Eddie 295
Palumbo, Larry 213
Pam & Dodi **519**
Pangelinan, Frank 500
Papa Don 117
Paper Doll 795
Paperclip People 383
Paradons 61, **519**
Paragons 242, 367, **519**
Paramounts 399
Paris Sisters 635
Paris, Mica 202, **519**, 520, 727, 811, 825
Parissi, Rob 746
Park, Paisley 112
Parker, Alan 484
Parker, Charlie 70, 102, 312, 389, 526, 710
Parker, Christopher 648
Parker, Corey 313
Parker, Deanie 683, 777
Parker, George 325
Parker, Graham 150, 543
Parker, Herman "Little Junior" 520
Parker, Jimmy 366
Parker, Johnny 312
Parker, Junior 57, 487, **520**, 684, 799, 826, 836, 838
Parker, Junius 408
Parker, Maceo 7, 85, 87, 88, 89, 90, 91, 110, 147, 154, 222, 313, 365, 366, 517, **520**, 521, 522, 523, 524, 583, 739, 767, 802, 803, 850
Parker, Maceo & All the King's Men 520
Parker, Maceo & the Macks 365, 366
Parker, Melvin 520
Parker, Ray Jr. 97, 380, 496, 509, **521**, 566, 587, 645, 828
Parker, Robert 39, 69, **521**, 777
Parker, Roger 622
Parkes, Lloyd 460
Parks, Dean 428, 742
Parks, Gino 492, 648
Parks, Lloyd 466
Parks, Van Dyke 98, 239
Parlet **521**, 522
Parliament 6, 14, 18, 37, 43, 53, 70, 79, 81, 85, 88, 110, 111, 112, 124, 146, 147, 153, 154, 155, 156, 167, 170, 182, 195, 219, 236, 248, 261, 263, 264, 265, 266, 269, 290, 299, 306, 308, 338, 381, 400, 437, 440, 466, 488, 502, 509, 517, 520, 521, **522**, 523, 524, 525, 540, 556, 560, 585, 606, 622, 625, 637, 643, 646, 665, 673, 693, 699, 723, 727, 739, 767, 775, 795, 801, 802, 850, 851
Parliaments 263, 264, 306, 522, **525**, 714, 767, 802, 806, 808, 821
Parris, Fred 243, 601, 806
Parris, Wayne 76
Parrish, John 559
Parrish, Man 218, 820
Parrish, Theo 43
Parritt, Barbara 696, 697
Parsons, Bill 805
Parsons, Gram 745, 805
Parsons, John 69
Parton, Dolly 152, 157, 277, 322, 379, 572, 834
Partridge Family 689
Pasadenas **525**
Passion **525**
Passionettes 267
Passions 364, 489, **525**
Pastels 777
Pastorius, Jaco 150, 295, 558
Pate, Johnny 333, 334, 394, 407, 447
Paterson, Alex 36, 184
Patrick, Charles 479
Patrick, James 479
Patrick, Jimmy 400
Patten, Edward 471, 539
Patterson, Berman 144
Patterson, Bobby 6, 7, **525**, 779
Patterson, Don 857
Patterson, Lover 107, 207, 241
Patterson, Mark 54
Patterson, Patrick 173
Patterson, Rahsaan **525**, 526, 825
Patterson, Russell 53
Patterson, Samuel 184
Patterson, Teddy 263
Patterson, Tim 209
Patti Jo 826
Patton, Big Amos 809
Patton, Big John 287, 788, 810, 857
Patton, Charley 640, 642
Patton, Louis 615
Patty & the Emblems 325, **526**, 820, 834
Paul & Paula 272, 831
Paul, Billy 43, 44, 84, 268, 350, 435, 449, **526**, 527, 564, 687, 779, 788, 809, 811, 820, 824
Paul, Clarence 243, 426, 445, 461, 653, 763, 765
Paul, Les Trio 188
Paul, Lyn 774
Paul, Wilbur "Yunkie" 241
Pauling, Lowman 243
Paulson, Charlie 14
Paulus, George 748
Pavement 599
Pawelski, Cheryl 665
Paxton, Tom 194
Payne, Darryl 202
Payne, Freda 1, 124, 135, 202, 279, 315, 320, 415, 509, **527**, 528, 800, 809, 811
Payne, Hazel 370, 667
Payne, Lamorris 500
Payne, Scherrie 279, 527, 586, 655, 656, 657, 832
Payton, Brenda 78
Payton, Eric 22
Payton, Larry 76
Payton, Lawrence 251, 252, 253, 572
Peachena 556
Peaches & Herb 166, **528**, 533, 567, 834
Peak, Donald 752
Peake, Donald 166, 428, 742
Peake, Sam 616, 665
Pearce, Earnestine 247
Pearce, Shirley 247
Pearls 166, 797
Pearnell, Zola 473
Pearson, Carlton 577
Pearson, Danny **528**, 529, 742, 743
Pearson, Darryl 190, 488
Pearson, Delroy 245
Pearson, Deniece 245
Pearson, Doris 245
Pearson, Duke 787
Pearson, Eugene 208, 577
Pearson, Gene 144
Pearson, John 715
Pearson, Lorraine 245
Pearson, Stedman 245
Pearson, Trisco 249
Peaston, David 39, 129, 269, 387, 486, **529**
Pebbles (Perri McKissack) 28, 29, 136, 183, 230, **529**, 785
Peckrol, Sonny 758
Pedicin, Mike 812
Pedziwiatr, Wayne 320
Peebles, Ann 96, 311, 371, 476, **529**, 530, 804, 809, 810
Peech Boys 416
Peek, Paul 228
Peel, John 670
Peeler, Gary 177
Peels, Leon 61
Peeples, Lewis 243
Peeples, Nia 6
Peete, Demetrius 709
Peil, Rich 177
Pela, Mike 596
Pello, Gene 166
Pendarvis, Leon 730
Pendergrass, Larry 129
Pendergrass, Teddy 2, 3, 32, 44, 84, 110, 218, 268, 309, 322, 325, 338, 359, 383, 417, 465, 466, 470, 471, 472, 473, 498, **530**, 531, 532, 534, 573, 578, 665, 712, 723, 760, 785, 787, 809, 820, 848
Pendleton, Malik 646, 736
Penguins 46, 206, 380, 480, 496, **532**, 539, 562, 778, 779, 782, 788, 797, 804, 831
Peniston, Ce Ce **532**
Penn, Dan 5, 71, 72, 95, 100, 101, 118, 119, 159, 294, 314, 405, 415, 450, 456, 525, 555, 570, 623, 660, 683, 684
Penn, Joe 752
Pennington, Barbara 683
Penny, Hank 297
Pense, Lydia 151, 807
Pentagons **532**
Pentangle 419
People's Choice **532**
People's Choice 325, 532, 533, 789, 826
Peoples, Alisa 773
Peoples, Dottie 773
Peoples, Theo 252, 678
Pepin, Papo 788
Pepper, Art 46, 787
Peppers 247
Peretti, Hugo 342
Perfect Gentlemen **533**
Perkins, Al 489
Perkins, Carl 74, 113, 828, 856, 857
Perkins, Joe Willie 409
Perkins, Pinetop 702
Perkins, Roy 517
Perkins, Walter 527
Perkinson, Coleridge Taylor 583, 727
Pernell, Willie 42
Perren, Freddie 166, 277, 289, 346, 348, 474, 475, 528, **533**, 644, 661, 668, 669, 670
Perrey, Al 448
Perri 100
Perriera, Joe 140
Perrilliat, Nat 54
Perry, Barney 54, 55
Perry, Gregg 320
Perry, Jack 742, 743
Perry, Jeffree 529, 754
Perry, Linda 538
Perry, Phil 21, 479
Perry, Richard 182, 198, 322, 463, 543, 571, 678
Persianettes 820
Person, Houston 5, 21, 83, 811, 857, 858
Persuaders **533**, 534, 626, 824
Persuasions **534**, 535, 716
Pet Shop Boys 195, 383, 605, 638, 639, 718
Peter & Gordon 779
Peter, Paul & Mary 113, 162
Peterik, Jim 330
Peters, Jerry 106, 432, 583

Peterson, Ed 5
Peterson, Gilles 335
Peterson, Lucky 53, 642
Peterson, Oscar 62, 474, 857
Peterson, Ray 414, 558
Petillo, Mike 244
Petrus, Jacques Fred 127, 312
Pettaway, Bill 77
Pettibone, Shep 337, 513, 778
Pettiford, Oscar 130, 131, 133
Pettis, Fred 16
Pettus, Kenny 181, 394
Petty, Norman 430
Pha, Jazze 190, 316
Phaetons 815
Phajja **535**
Pharaohs **535**
Pharcyde 75
Pharoahs 259
Pharr, Kelsey 188
Philidor, Andre Danican 747
Phillinganes, Greg 388, 432, 587
Phillips, Anthony 46, 448
Phillips, Doug 177
Phillips, Esther 8, 514, **535**, 536, 658, 684, 722, 732, 786, 793
Phillips, John 238
Phillips, Joseph 20
Phillips, Jud 165
Phillips, Marvin 46, 218, 448
Phillips, Paul 312
Phillips, Phil 165, 320
Phillips, Robert 107, 436
Phillips, Sam [Producer] 54, 74, 78, 280, 450, 552, 553, 702, 838
Phillips, Sam [Singer] 165, 280, 685, 828, 856, 857
Phillips, Sandra 210
Phillips, Sonny 735
Phoenix Horns 214, 535, 611
Phreek 488
Phuture 791
Phyrework **536**
Piaf, Edith 446
Piano Red 102, 627
Piccirillo, Mike 581
Pickett, Wilson 67, 100, 113, 143, 144, 158, 167, 169, 185, 195, 211, 233, 248, 267, 297, 309, 314, 327, 336, 346, 348, 350, 392, 525, **536**, 537, 538, 547, 549, 562, 583, 591, 599, 600, 630, 631, 658, 660, 685, 704, 712, 728, 744, 760, 761, 762, 769, 777, 780, 781, 784, 786, 791, 795, 817, 825, 834, 844, 845, 847, 848, 851, 856
Picone, Vito 220
Pieces of a Dream 110, 470, 768
Pierce, Dick 46
Pierce, Jason 198
Pierce, Les 47
Pierce, Marvin 502
Pierce, Maryland 242
Pierce, Nat 31
Pierce, Oji 412
Pierce, Webb 302
Pilate, Felton C. II 157, 158
Pilgrim Travelers 259, 563
Piller, Eddie 108
Pilot, Felton 157, 158
Pinchback, Sidney 830
Pinckney, St. Clair 85, 87, 89, 91, 366
Pink **538**
Pink Floyd 367, 699
Pinkney, Bill 206, 207, 241, 462
Pinkston-Mayo, Valerie 129
Piper, Wardell 822
Pips 395, 396, 397, 398, **539**
Pirates 648, 818
Pitney, Gene 15, 56, 218, 247, 293, 635, 728, 779, 798, 812
Pitt, Eugene 368
Pitter Pats 627
Pittman, Fred 186, 317
Pittman, Wayne 507
Pitts, Charles 304
Pixies Three 808
Pizzarelli, John 245
Planets 41
Plant, Robert 320, 744
Platt, Matthew 701
Platters 141, 172, 206, 209, 242, 246, 247, 318, 375, 422, 480, **539**, 540, 541, 559, 633, 727, 774, 783, 797, 806, 812, 818, 833, 839
Platypus **540**
Players Association **540**, 541
Pleasure **541**
Plunk, Jerry 246
PM Dawn 30, **541**
Pockets 259, **542**
Poco 330
Poets 141, 411, 793, 805
Pointer Sisters 2, 151, 178, 179, 200, 307, 313, 327, **542**, 543, 544, 612, 617, 642, 643, 694, 747, 761, 778, 780, 785, 829, 844
Pointer, Anita 542, 543, 544
Pointer, Bonnie 220, 542, 543, **544**
Pointer, June 542, 543, 544
Pointer, Noel 21, 202
Pointer, Ruth 542, 544
Poitier, Sidney 333
Poke 10
Police 230, 374
Politti, Paul 742
Pollard, Lisa 723
Pollard, Ray 722, 723, 823
Pollution 283
Pomus, Doc 5, 207, 208, 392, 489, 570, 684, 841, 842
Pomus, Doc & Mort Shuman 731
Ponder, Jimmy 5
Ponderosa Twins Plus One 740
Poole, Ashley 205
Poonanny **544**, 545
Poonanny, Joe 544, 545
Pop, Iggy 167, 374
Pope, Charles 667
Pope, Joseph 667
Poppies 307, 394, 684
Popwell, Pops 171
Porcaro, Jeff 361, 587
Poree, Anita 583
Porter, Art 47
Porter, Bob 263
Porter, Cole 32, 136, 272, 276, 433, 528, 579, 588, 754
Porter, David 10, 34, 95, 96, 223, 303, 369, 371, 537, **545**, 598, 599, 601, 630, 660, 682, 794, 804
Porter, David Lee 545
Porter, George Jr. 466, 574
Porter, Lorena 395
Porter, Sam 455
Porter, Shirley 687
Portishead 136, 198, 290, 483
Positive Force **545**, 778, 829
Potter, Arthur 32
Potter, Brian 251, 252, 280, 668, 669
Potts, Gregory 566
Potts, Sylvester 160
Potts, Wardell Jr. 20
Pought, Emma 63
Pought, Jannie 63
Powe, John 709
Powe, Shawn 709
Powell, Archie 4, 546
Powell, Bobby **545**
Powell, Bud 129, 857
Powell, Chris 500
Powell, Jesse [1] **545**
Powell, Jesse [2] 812
Powell, Michael 258
Powell, Michael J. 30, 129, 224, 225
Powell, Richard 573
Powell, Richie 732
Powell, William 324, 505, 507
Power Station 139, 518, 519
Powers, Joey 835
Powers, Tony 558
Powers, William 519
Pras 366
Pratcher, Mildred 195
Prater, Dave 598, 599
Prater, David 598, 599
Pratt, Bill 260
Pratt, Richard 61
Pratter, Samuelle 149
Precisions **545**, 546, 712
Pree, Karen **546**
Prelude 337
Premiers 199, 296, 584, 788, 799
Preps 708, 745
Presencer, Gerard 75
Presidents **546**
Presley, Elvis 8, 14, 33, 49, 54, 56, 73, 74, 80, 88, 93, 101, 115, 128, 130, 131, 148, 170, 194, 195, 206, 227, 228, 255, 261, 297, 307, 326, 337, 345, 349, 389, 415, 421, 425, 430, 434, 454, 462, 466, 475, 480, 490, 495, 512, 552, 553, 636, 660, 728, 753, 754, 774, 781, 793, 798, 799, 805, 807, 822, 824, 828, 842, 845, 847, 856, 857
Pressure Cooker 322
Prestia, Rocco 695
Prestige All Stars 558
Preston, Billy 52, 81, 99, 100, 112, 134, 162, 164, 244, 282, 309, 319, 331, 376, 391, **546**, 583, 626, 644, 663, 664, 668, 695, 699, 785, 824
Preston, Jerry 105
Preston, Johnny 52
Preston, Wayne 394
Pretenders 375, 533, **547**, 827, 828
Pretty Boy 167
Pretty Poison 547, 801
Pretty Purdie 603
Pretty Russ 659
Pretty Things 191, 350, 829
Previn, Andre 729
Previn, Dory 729
Price, Big Walter 799
Price, Kelly 323, **547**
Price, Leo & Band 547
Price, Leontyne 725
Price, Lloyd 10, 38, 63, 69, 87, 258, 424, 475, 495, 518, **547**, 548, 626, 635, 668, 704, 706, 714, 749, 753, 783, 789, 792, 793, 810, 834, 836, 838, 840, 841
Price, Louis 674, 677
Price, Morris 76
Price, Priscilla 804
Price, Terry 118
Price, Vincent 353, 440
Pride, Charley 283, 302, 596
Pride, Lou 802
Priest, Maxi 245, 335, **548**, 810
Prima, Louis 102, 473, 718, 812
Primal Scream 198, 264
Prime Movers 670
Prime Time 773
Primes 386, **548**, 549, 674
Primettes 248, 548, **549**, 586, 653, 674, 795
Primus 264, 523, 851
Prince 2, 10, 26, 35, 43, 79, 102, 112, 116, 139, 140, 141, 146, 147, 154, 158, 175, 177, 181, 182, 213, 218, 227, 233, 234, 241, 264, 278, 279, 282, 289, 292, 301, 310, 312, 336, 351, 358, 364, 368, 370, 386, 388, 389, 390, 404, 412, 413, 437, 444, 451, 472, 473, 483, 492, 501, 510, 520, 542, 546, **549**, 550, 551, 552, 566, 573, 592, 608, 642, 646, 663, 664, 666, 689, 690, 691, 693, 707, 712, 715, 727, 763, 775, 851
Prince & the Revolution 183, 550, 551
Prince Be 541, 542
Prince, Mark 716
Prince, William Rodney 545
Princess **552**
Principle, Jamie 383, 399
Prine, John 444
Pringle, Keith 583
Pringle, Peter 583
Prisonaires 74, **552**, 553, 812, 828
Prisoners 670
Process & the Doo Rags **553**
Procol Harum 662, 784
Procope, Russell 73
Proctor, Jay 365
Prodigy 129, 822
Professionals 808, 831
Professor Longhair 62, 69, 196, 197, 310, 393, 433, 521, **553**, 626, 627, 694, 789, 792, 793, 799, 818, 839, 841
Proffer, Spencer 283
Profyle **553**, 554
Prophet, Billy 368
Pru **554**
Pruitt, Joseph 234
Pruitt, Ralph 234
Pruter, Robert 187, 405
Pryor, Richard 291, 482, 486, 585, 590
Prysock, Arthur 563, 810
Prysock, Red 73, 297, 780
Psychedelic Psoul 282
Psycho 541
Public Announcement 385, 386, **554**
Public Enemy 16, 41, 66, 147, 227, 351, 359, 405, 441, 823
Public Image Limited 227, 695
Pucho & His Latin Soul Brothers **554**, 577
Puckett, Jerry 398
Puente, Tito 140, 141, 577, 743
Puff Daddy 205, 210, 230, 258, 331, 386, 460, 470, 509, 510, 547, 686, 693
Pugh, Demetrius 13
Pugh, Marliss 13
Pukwana, Dudu 448
Pullen, Don 520
Pulp 354
Purdie, Bernard 295, 326, 554, 555, 735
Purdie, Bernard "Pretty" 31, 294, 376, **554**, 555
Purify, Bobby 555
Purify, James 555
Purify, James & Bobby **555**, 692, 777, 826
Purim, Flora 64, 513, 728
Push 605
Puzey, Leonard 562
Pyramids 806

Q

Q-Tip 10, 75, 146, 176, 323, 351
QNice 629
Quails 96
Qualis, Sidney Joe 833
Qualls, Sydney Joe **556**
Quarterman, Joe **556**
Quazar 488, **556**
Quebec, Ike 287
Queen 139, 140, 312, 821
Queen Latifah 1, 237, 385, 666
Queen Pen 128, 491
Queen Yahna 147
? & the Mysterians 52
?uestlove 29
Quezergue, Wardell 398
Quick, Clarence E. 184, 185
Quiet Elegance **556**, 810
Quiet Riot 485
Quin Tones 783
Quinichette, Paul 31, 733
Quinn, Lance 202
Quotations 766

R

Ra, Sun 266, 535, 745
Ra, Sun Arkestra 535
Rabb, Luther 724
Rabbitt, Peter 492
Rabin, Trevor 605
Rabinowitz, Sol 577, 781
Radcliffe, Jimmy 818
Radiants 36, 450, 451, **557**, 626, 679, 782, 790, 791, 812, 825, 832
Radiohead 141, 690
Rae, Fonda 99
Raekwon 10
Raelettes 132, 165, 369
Raffi 244
Ragin, Hugh 739
Ragland, Lou 321, 692
Ragovoy, Jerry 49, 122, 223, 258, 388, 438, 473, **557**, 558, 616, 668, 730, 783, 794
Ragtyme 679
Raiders 797
Rainbows 167, 271, 313, **558**, 645, 780, 828
Raindrops **558**, 803, 842, 844
Rainey, Chuck 31, 245, 361, **558**, 709, 710, 727
Rainey, Ma 14, 433
Rainge, Carl 635
Raitt, Bonnie 83, 95, 438, 558, 567, 642, 694, 695
Rakim 520, 700
Raleigh, Ben 558
Ram Jam Band 733
Ram Z **558**
Ram, Buck 172, 246, 539, **558**, 559, 774
Ramirez, Humberto 643
Ramirez, Louie 517
Ramone, Joey 636

Ramone, Phil 153, 308, 472
Ramones 635, 636
RAMP **559**
Ramsey, Arnold 752
Ramsey, Thurman "Ray" 437
Rancifer, Ronnie 346
Randazzo, Teddy 183, 422, 423, 590
Randell, Denny 502, 696, 697
Randi, Don 25
Randle, Bernadette 575
Randolph, Barbara 307, 539
Randolph, Boots 310, 311, 716
Randolph, Jimi 629
Randolph, Robert 241
Randy & the Rainbows **559**
Rangell, Nelson 21, 770
Rankin, Billy 279
Ranking Roger 239
Ranks, Shabba 278
Ransom, Ray 78
RaOof, Abdul 629, 630
Rapp, Danny 176
Rappin' Four Tay 364
Rare Earth 54, 142, 250, 260, 261, 383, **559**, 560, 644, 746, 816, 818, 823
Rare Essence 84, **560**
Rare Gems Odyssey **560**
Ras Kass 25
Rasboro, Jonathen "John John" 617
Rascals 71, 72, 119, 444, 509, **561**, 562, 640, 709, 847
Rashad, Phylicia 17
Rasputin's Stash **562**
Rasputin's Stash 562
Rationals 847
Ravan, Genya 636
Ravel, Maurice 188
Ravens 11, 12, 107, 148, 172, 337, 409, **562**, 563, 611, 634, 726, 733, 782, 828, 839
Raw Silk 834
Raw Soul 455, 456, 665
Raw Spitt 794
Rawls, Lou 5, 23, 24, 25, 80, 130, 134, 294, 309, 322, 347, 485, 503, **563**, 564, 565, 787, 820, 824, 848
Ray, Ada 307, 365
Ray, Andre 431
Ray, Danny 815
Ray, Don 796
Ray, Goodman & Brown 477, 478, **565**, 647, 810
Ray, Harry 160, 349, 477, 478, 565, 566, 575, 688, 740
Ray, Harvey 209
Ray, James **566**
Ray, Johnnie 74, 552, 828
Ray, Randy 177
Ray, Willie 209
Raydio 43, 428, 521, **566**, 742
Raye, Don 167
Raynor, JaKima 693
Rays 616, 795
Raz-B 27
Raze 173
Ready for the World **566**, 785
Reagan, Ronald 604
Real Thing 80, 427, **566**, 567, 660
Rebels 577
Rebennack, Mac 196, 197, 198, 249
Rebillot, Pat 202, 540
Record, Eugene 3, 4, 16, 36, 137, 138, 187, 414, 428, 517, 528, **567**, 754, 817
Red Hot Chili Peppers 60, 154, 264, 284, 503, 523, 826, 851
Red Rat 548
Red Top 783
Redbone 122, 123, 507
Redd, Gene 237
Redd, Sharon **567**, 568, 778, 821
Redding, Emmanuel 449
Redding, Noel 46
Redding, Otis 6, 27, 34, 36, 40, 43, 44, 46, 62, 67, 85, 92, 99, 100, 118, 119, 125, 158, 159, 162, 169, 185, 239, 240, 248, 256, 261, 262, 285, 293, 302, 303, 314, 349, 350, 356, 360, 369, 381, 385, 390, 391, 434, 456, 459, 466, 476, 487, 504, 510, 520, 525, 530, 536, 555, **568**, 569, 570, 582, 589, 590, 599, 602, 605, 630, 631, 641, 644, 645, 646, 682, 683, 684, 692, 746, 753, 758, 760, 764, 770, 777, 778, 780, 784, 786, 792, 793, 794, 797, 799, 814, 816, 823, 828, 844
Reder, Milton 745
Redman 176, 221, 316
Redman, Don 70
Redman, Izora 731
Redman-Armstead, Izora 737
Redmond, Gus 317, 428, 498
Redwoods 558
Reed, A.C. 203, 512
Reed, Al 198
Reed, Bernard 372, 755
Reed, Bill 191
Reed, Dalton **570**
Reed, Di 358
Reed, Francine **570**
Reed, Herb 539, 797
Reed, Jimmy 125, 256, 282, 318, 371, 434, 534, 583, 601, 634, 682, 700, 838
Reed, Johnny 511, 570
Reed, Larry 203
Reed, Lou 48, 122, 194, 700
Reed, Lula 95, **570**, 812
Reed, Marc 532
Reed, Michael 125
Reed, Robert 698
Reed, Taylor 698
Reed, Vivian 824
Reeder, Howard 125
Reese, Della 291, 445, 834
Reeves, Del 610
Reeves, Dianne 21, 442, 565, 788
Reeves, Herbert 610
Reeves, Jim 74
Reeves, Lois 445, 446
Reeves, Martha 4, 80, 112, 235, 263, 290, 317, 445, 446, 447, 546, **571**, 653, 682, 740, 831, 832, 846
Reflections **571**, 606, 712
Regalado, Hector "Rudy" 140
Regals 41, 107, 797
Regan, Julianne 428, 742
Regan, Russ 428, 742
Regents **571**, 834
Reggae Philharmonic Strings 632
Reginald 110, 470
Regney, Noel 15
Reichman, Joe 102
Reid, Bert 170
Reid, Brenda 231, 373
Reid, Clarence 60, 61, 458, 459, **571**, 572, 685, 692
Reid, David 312
Reid, Irene 830
Reid, L.A. 7, 28, 73, 77, 82, 183, 184, 217, 277, 347, 373, 529, 538, 691, 710, 741, 744, 784
Reid, L.A. & Babyface 278
Reid, Raymond 170, 645, 709
Reid, Terry 223
Reid, Vernon 141, 767
Reiner, Rob 185, 392
Reinhardt, Django 420
Reisdorff, Bob 247
Reklaw-Raheem, Derf 535
Relf, Bob 63, 798
REM 136, 137
Remains 309
Renaldo, Don 468, 597
Renay, Diane 804, 808, 844
Renda, Lenny 332
René & Angela 22, 383, **572**, 757, 785
Rene, Leon 63, 326, 421
Rene, Wendy 682, 778, 829
Renee, Nicole 202, **572**
Renfro, Prudensca 554
Renzetti, Joe 205
Reparata & the Delrons 834
Resch, Robert 614
Resnick, Art 208
Return to Forever 105, 159, 295, 389, 450, 536
Revolution 549, 550
Rey, Daniel 636
Reynolds, Burt 1, 168
Reynolds, Debbie 203
Reynolds, James 217
Reynolds, Jeannie **572**
Reynolds, L.J. 203, 204, 461, 572
Reynolds, L.J. & Chocolate Syrup 818
Reynolds, Sheldon 214
Reynolds, Tony 502
Rhoad, Herbert 534
Rhodes, Doris 279
Rhodes, Emitt 279
Rhodes, Izora 662, 737
Rhodes, Phyllis 597
Rhodes, Sonny 797
Rhodes, Todd 31
Rhodes-Chalmers-Rhodes 79
Rhone, Sylvia 176
Rhymes, Busta 431, 776
Rhyne, Mel 857
Rhythm Aces 41
Rhythm Heritage 360, **572**, 573, 730
Rhythm Kings 14
Rhythm Makers 281
Rhythm Method 436
Ribot, Marc 141
Ricardo, Ricky 743
Rice, Gene **573**
Rice, Bonny "Mack" 54, 223, 233, 508, 562, 781, 814, 825, 828
Rice, Tim 220
Rice, Tony 356
Rice, Verlie 121, 209
Rich, Buddy 787
Rich, Charlie 58, 511, 623, 753, 832
Rich, Eddie 657, 658
Rich, Tony 77, 278, **573**, 693, 757, 815
Richard, Cliff 260
Richard, Frank 142
Richards, Andy 639
Richards, Billy 578
Richards, Deke 166, 346, 348, 533, 580, 655, 670
Richards, Dwight 142
Richards, Keith 50, 51, 193, 241, 257, 310, 488, 493, 568, 760, 767, 803
Richards, Rod 559
Richards, Roy 578
Richardson, Allen 491
Richardson, Dennis 338
Richardson, Jerome 52, 376, 558
Richardson, Joe 391
Richardson, Johnnie Louise 307, 365
Richardson, Karl 40
Richbourg, John 618, 722, 733
Richie, Brenda 666
Richie, Lionel 155, 156, 157, 308, 353, 376, 450, 573, 574, 586, 741
Richmond, June 473
Ricks, Jimmy 172, 562, 726, 807
Ricks, Tommy 205
Riddle, Nelson 152
Ridel, Stefanie 747
Rideout, Rex 646
Ridgeley, Andrew 469
Ridgley, Tommy 39, **574**, 683
Riff **574**
Rigg, Diana 503
Righteous Brothers 63, 71, 72, 191, 199, 292, 294, 296, 464, 529, 561, 562, **574**, 575, 580, 590, 631, 635, 811, 847
Rigsby, Clarence 716
Riley, Ben 575
Riley, Billy Lee 67, 113
Riley, Cheryl Pepsii **575**
Riley, Markell 290
Riley, Melvin 566
Riley, Teddy 56, 82, 229, 290, 291, 316, 355, 367, 374, 478, 554, **575**, 619, 659, 661, 691
Rimshots **575**, 779
Ringling Brothers Barnum & Bailey Circus Band 693
Rip Chords 219, 805
Rip Rig & Panic 136
Riperton, Minnie 36, 188, 203, 230, 420, 444, **575**, 576, 589, 594, 609, 633, 645, 727, 748, 770, 811
Ripple **576**
Risbrook, Bill 97
Risbrook, Louis 97
Riser, Paul 190
Rison, Andre 691
Ritchie Family 312, 717
Ritenour, Lee 8, 21, 76, 77, 377, 380, 428, 481, 515, 594, 742
Ritz, David 258, 274, 275, 505, 759
Rivera, Hector **577**
Rivera, Pete 559
Rivers, Candy 801
Rivers, Johnny 80, 238
Rivers, Sam 159, 389
Rivieras **577**, 805
Rivileers 144, **577**, 797
Rivingtons 294, **577**
Rizzi, Tony 70
Rizzo, Pat 34, 513, 724
RL **577**, 578
Roach, Freddie 787, 788
Roach, Max 105, 420, 732, 788
Rob Roys 799
Robbins, Rockie 184
Roberson, Chuck 783
Roberson, Danny 628
Roberson, Doc 137
Roberson, Jeffrey "Jeff Tight" 628, 629
Roberson, Kevin 183
Roberson, Latavia 189
Robert & Johnny **578**, 778, 798
Roberts, Ed 590
Roberts, Howard 25, 94
Roberts, Juliet 427
Roberts, Kev 799
Roberts, Pete 80
Roberts, Solomon Jr. 621, 622
Robertson, Bernard 184
Robertson, Brian 184
Robertson, David 510
Robertson, Ken 234
Robertson, Robbie 745
Robeson, Paul 25, 301
Robey, Don 3, 57, 117, 271, 297, 514, 520, 602, 692, 769, 770, 799, 838
Robie, John 23
Robillard, Duke 5, 95, 280
Robins 51, 63, 149, 508, 514, 535, **578**, 793, 797
Robinson, Alvin 808
Robinson, Ann 320
Robinson, Bert 324, **578**, 738
Robinson, Bob 11, 209, 298, 434, 520, 666
Robinson, Bobby 200, 270, 298, 345, 390, 391, 400, 601, 800, 806, 838
Robinson, Claudette 579, 580, 581
Robinson, Claudia 722
Robinson, Curtis Jr. 383
Robinson, Cynthia 34, 282, 624, 625
Robinson, Danny 135, 165, 806
Robinson, Dawn 222, 224, 432
Robinson, Dutch 502
Robinson, Fenton 15, 297, 600
Robinson, James 127, 159
Robinson, Janice **578**
Robinson, Joe 478, 575, 663, 752, 782
Robinson, John "J.R." 592
Robinson, Johnny 819
Robinson, Kevin 373
Robinson, Neil 670
Robinson, R.B. 632
Robinson, Rex 692
Robinson, Roscoe 6, 525, 659, 830
Robinson, Sharon 549
Robinson, Smokey 44, 67, 80, 109, 110, 112, 122, 124, 142, 160, 161, 166, 176, 227, 228, 251, 253, 256, 263, 266, 272, 280, 281, 289, 316, 317, 327, 334, 342, 348, 349, 358, 363, 364, 370, 390, 426, 431, 433, 444, 445, 447, 449, 451, 461, 462, 463, 466, 474, 475, 479, 480, 484, 507, 517, 525, 533, 544, 546, 549, 560, 570, 573, **578**, 579, 580, 581, 582, 587, 592, 602, 626, 630, 646, 648, 653, 655, 656, 657, 663, 664, 667, 674, 675, 676, 677, 705, 712, 713, 722, 727, 738, 739, 741, 780, 785, 786, 801, 816, 817, 819, 831, 832, 833, 844, 845, 846
Robinson, Smokey & the Miracles 122, 226, 271, 345, 520, 535, 549, 554, 561, 578, 579, 580, 581, 582, 663, 777, 818, 824, 825
Robinson, Sylvia 32, 81, 233, 309, 349, 470, 477, 478, 517, 575, 613, 614, 646, 663, 740, 752, 779
Robinson, Tad **582**
Robinson, Vicki Sue 229, **582**, 665, 821
Robinson, William 579
Robles, Ralph 517
Robotnick, Alexander 796
Rocca, Rossilio 434
Roche, Guy 643
Rochell and the Candles 807

Roches 639
Rock, Chris 189, 260
Rock, Monti III 195
Rock, Pete 335
Rock, Raymond 170
Rocketeers 41, 805
Rocketones 828
Rockets 41
Rockin' Dopsie 372
Rockin' Sidney 398
Rockwell **582**
Rodgers & Hammerstein II 403
Rodgers & Hart 443, 655
Rodgers, Bill 532
Rodgers, Bobby 579
Rodgers, Jimmie 600
Rodgers, Nile 30, 71, 127, 138, 139, 140, 234, 310, 313, 320, 374, 375, 522, **582**, 583, 587, 603, 620, 621, 623, 686, 705, 770
Rodgers, Richard 656
Rodgers/Hart 272
Rodriguez, Douglas 178, 440
Rodriguez, Jay 289
Rodriguez, Sal 724
Roger **583**, 775
Rogers, Billy 171
Rogers, Bobby 289, 474, 475, 579, 580
Rogers, Ce Ce 661
Rogers, Claudette 578
Rogers, D.J. 52, 100, 244, 269, 466, **583**, 584
Rogers, D.J. Jr. **584**
Rogers, Jimmy 499
Rogers, Johnny 473
Rogers, Kenny 367, 403, 535, 573, 574, 583
Rogers, Lee 36
Rogers, Nat 422
Rogers, Tim 90
Rohlehr, Beverly 534
Roker, Ron 727
Roland, Carl 545
Rolling Stones 8, 15, 49, 50, 51, 63, 89, 100, 125, 136, 162, 167, 179, 191, 192, 203, 296, 345, 390, 403, 404, 424, 434, 438, 466, 467, 536, 543, 546, 550, 557, 568, 598, 635, 636, 683, 684, 685, 694, 699, 702, 703, 712, 748, 750, 760, 762, 763, 779, 780, 813, 829
Rollins, Henry 698, 699
Rollins, Sonny 105, 485, 558
Rollow, Champ 107
Romancers 260, **584**
Romani, David 127
Romano, Carman 220
Rome **584**
Rome, Richard 616
Romeo, Max & the Upsetters 822
Romeos 43, 202, 268, 279, 325, 827
Romero, Chan 779
Ronettes 136, 172, 183, 196, 309, 325, 430, 579, **584**, 585, 600, 608, 635, 636, 697, 809, 827, 842, 843, 844
Roney, Wallace 700
Ronnie & the Delinquents 198
Ronnie & the Relatives 827
Ronstadt, Linda 51, 118, 231, 336, 370, 493, 494, 495, 667, 728, 781, 807, 811
Rooftop Singers 682
Rooney, Corey 278
Rooney, Herb 231, 373
Rooney, Mark 183
Roosters 93, 103, 333
Roots 29, 603, 770
Roper, Deidra "Spin" 713
Rosanna 1
Rose Royce 157, 168, 412, 500, **585**, 586, 643, 705, 745, 768, 777, 795, 801, 816
Rose, Charisse 127, 128
Rose, Greg 309
Rose, Mike 173
Rose, Tim 72
Roseman, Josh 289, 788
Rosen, Larry 64, 768
Rosen, Peter 724
Rosie 794
Rosie & Ron 789
Rosie & the Originals **586**
Rosolino, Frank 23, 76, 376, 377
Ross, Annie 735
Ross, Arthur 727
Ross, Diana 17, 32, 79, 80, 100, 139, 156, 166, 210, 238, 251, 272, 274, 280, 281, 322, 346, 353, 358, 372, 374, 378, 383, 399, 433, 445, 446, 468, 472, 533, 540, 548, 549, 571, 573, 582, **586**, 587, 588, 653, 654, 655, 656, 657, 663, 674, 675, 682, 697, 708, 720, 738, 739, 740, 744, 802, 816, 817, 833, 846
Ross, Diana & the Supremes 80, 347, 445, 527, 653, 654, 655, 656, 675
Ross, Eugene 93
Ross, Fred 222
Ross, Jackie **588**, 589, 782, 790, 791, 834
Ross, Jerry 205, 309, 600, 614, 834
Ross, Lucius Tawl 263, 265, 306, 522
Rossman, Sonia 387
Rotary Connection 576, **589**
Rotations 332, 700
Roth, David Lee 718
Roundtree 712
Rowan, Peter 535
Rowe, Dennis 97
Rowe, Hahn 359
Rowland, Kelendria 189
Rowles, Jimmy 759
Roxy Music 119
Roy C 589, 590, 818
Roy, Barbara 91, 217
Royal Five 821
Royal Holidays 827
Royal Sons Quintet 243
Royal, Billy Joe 699
Royalettes **590**, 715, 749, 778, 808
Royals 32, 33, 243
Royaltones 242, 805
Royer, Peter 427
Rubber Band 154
Ruben & the Jets 181
Rubin, Alan 62
Rubinson, David 125, 543, 761
Ruby & the Romantics 457, **590**, 834
Rudd, David 698
Rude Boys 417, 628
Rudolph, Richard 444, 576, 589, 727
Rue, Jackie 209, 345
Ruff Ryders 478
Ruff, Nathaniel 364
Ruffin & Kendricks 462
Ruffin Brothers **590**, 591, 592
Ruffin, David 80, 117, 137, 142, 144, 160, 217, 266, 272, 293, 332, 349, 368, 387, 461, 590, **591**, 592, 672, 674, 675, 676, 677, 678, 679, 688, 705, 718, 761, 780, 791, 792, 808, 816, 822, 828, 833, 835
Ruffin, Grace 313, 368
Ruffin, Jimmy 80, 387, 396, 410, 498, 590, 591, **592**, 777, 786, 790, 831
Ruffin, Kenneth 688
Ruffino, Joe 553
Rufus & Chaka Khan 81, 260, 317, 390, **592**, 622, 727, 751
Rufus 28, 70, 117, 260, 308, 388, 389, 572, 592, 593, 757, 785, 795
Run DMC 210
Runarounds 571
Runaways 636
Rundgren, Todd 167, 253, 292, 298, 341, 518
Runnels, Rochelle 642, 643
RuPaul 732
Rupe, Art 46, 162, 393, 421, 425, 454, 463, 473, 547, 548, 613, 749, 799, 838
Rush 264
Rush, Bobby **593**, 791, 812
Rush, Donell 399
Rush, Merrilee 636, 835
Rush, Otis 78, 102, 250, 487, 702, 705, 753, 810, 838
Rushen, Patrice 26, 136, 159, 160, 307, 353, 583, **593**, 594, 723, 792, 811, 817, 826, 829
Rushing, Jimmy 297, 298, 514, 777, 812
Russ, Lonnie 804
Russaw, Todd 230
Russell, Arthur 440, 796
Russell, Bert 208
Russell, Bobby 784
Russell, Brenda 1, **595**, 713
Russell, Brian 595
Russell, Joe 534
Russell, Karl 324
Russell, Leon 48, 57, 114, 150, 212, 584, 640, 699, 768, 773
Russell, Luis 73
Russell, Patty 526
Russell, Robert 148
Russell, Robin 499
Russell, Steve 741
Russell, Tom 745
Ruth, Jay Ella 74
Ruth, Thurmon 408
Rutherford, Mike 120
Rux, Carl Hancock 826
Ryanes, John 479
Ryanes, Warren 479
Rydell, Bobby 612
Ryder, Mitch 169, 426, 561, 574, 787, 832, 847
Ryder, Mitch & the Detroit Wheels 783

S

S., Robin 328
Saadiq, Raphael 176, 340, 432, 647
Sabater, Louise "Angel" 168
Sabino, Robert 138
Sacks, Leo 673, 749
Sadane, Mark 202, 485
Sade 381, 409, 451, 500, 554, **596**, 752
Sadler, Reggie 819
Safire **596**
Safuto, Frank 559
Sager, Carole Bayer 152, 388, 405, 543, 729
Sahm, Doug 444, 602
Sain, Oliver 39, 95, 118, 457, 529
Saint James, Sylvia 324, 615
Saint Patrick's Cathedral Choir 1
Saint Victor, Sandra 2, 233, 234
Sainte-Marie, Buffy 779
Sakamoto, Kyu 370, 667
Salaam, Kalamu Ya 673
Salas, Jerry 140
Salas, Rudy 140, 689
Salas, Steve 140, 689
Salma, Doug & the Highlander 586
Salsoul Orchestra 92, 297, 317, 338, **597**, 792, 795
Salt-N-Pepa 190, 224, 529, **597**, 598, 606, 691, 713
Salter, William 758
Salty Peppers 214, **598**
Salutations **598**
Sam & Bill 555
Sam & Dave 34, 62, 63, 67, 105, 118, 150, 151, 169, 234, 261, 277, 303, 385, 457, 466, 502, 503, 545, 555, **598**, 599, 619, 634, 645, 777, 780, 781, 792, 800, 802, 814, 824, 834, 844
Sam, Robert 282
Samaad, Abdul 208
Sambora, Richie 538
Sammie **599**
Sample, Fred 702
Sample, Joe 8, 25, 170, 171, 203, 328, 666, 709, 829
Sampson, Dave 557
Sampson, Wallace 557
Samuel, Bill "Foots" 5, 101
Samwell, Ian 418, 419
San Remo Golden Strings 831
Sanborn, David 88, 129, 450, 540, 648, 666, 695, 739, 786, 857
Sanchez, Freddie 140
Sanchez, Marta 727
Sanchez, Poncho 141
Sanchez, Roger 335
Sandee 440
Sanders 307
Sanders, David 449
Sanders, Marcell 552
Sanders, Marcus 686
Sanders, Pharoah 55, 159, 411, 527, 603, 829
Sanders, Sonny 16, 537, 600, 754, 755
Sanders, Zell 307, 365, 577
Sandlin, Johnny 314, 658
Sandpebbles 824
Sandridge, Shawn 652
Sands, Evie 588, 779, 784, 791, 844
Sandstrom, Renee 747
Santa Esmeralda **599**
Santamaria, Mongo 140, 517, 604, 781, 782
Santamaria, Nick 114
Santana, Carlos 37, 140, 141, 151, 174, 178, 227, 284, 366, 388, 437, 438, 439, 440, 441, 493, 552, 604, 626, 695, 724, 828
Santana, Jorge 438, 439
Santiago, Herman 433
Santiago, Neftali 440, 441
Santiel, Terral "Terry" 585
Santiglia, Peggy 13
Sapphires **600**
Saraceno, Joe 79
Satan & Adam 779
Satchell, Clarence "Satch" 502
Satellites 180, 318
Satintones 307, 447, 537, **600**, 814
Satterfield, Louis 36, 535
Saturday Night Band 794
Saunders, Larry 819
Saunders, Merl 178, 695, 780
Saunders, Orville 54
Saunders, Red 701
Savage, Chantay **600**
Savages 744, 745
Savela, Eero 110
Savoy Bearcats 73
Savoys 375
Sawyer, Pam 358, 397, 405, 472, 474, 511, 727
Sawyer, Ray 727
Sawyer, Vernon 61
Sawyer, Wendall 61
Scaggs, Boz 80, 392, 404, **600**, 601, 694, 727, 847
Scales, Harvey **601**
Scarborough, Skip 61, 158, 328, 404, 527
Scarlets 243, 500, **601**, 806
Scarpantoni, Jane 141
Schatz, Warren 582
Scheff, Jerry 586
Schemers 251
Scher, Richard 643
Schifrin, Lalo 376, 565, 671
Schock, Harriet 636
Schoefield, Willie 537
Scholl, Bob 464
Scholl, Dave 745
Scholl, Jerry 464
Scholl, Robert 464
Schon, Neal 178
Schoolboys 161, **601**, 602
Schoolly D 330
Schroeder, Aaron 388
Schroeder, Papa Don 555, 692
Schultz, Alex 582
Schuur, Diane 732
Schwartz, Bob 489
Schwartz, Chris 499
Schwartz, Gene 242, 489
Schwarzenegger, Arnold 752
Scipio, Steve 173
Scorsese, Martin 14, 480
Scott, Barrington 678
Scott, Bobby 258
Scott, Bubba 746
Scott, Cindy 339, **602**
Scott, Clifford 86, 198, 759
Scott, David 3, 137
Scott, Dick 225, 378
Scott, Douglas "Smokey" 533
Scott, Dred 230
Scott, Freddie 34, 49, 307, 602, 807
Scott, George [1] 241, 311
Scott, George [2] 647, 648
Scott, Gloria 626
Scott, Harold 674
Scott, Harrison 115
Scott, Helen 687
Scott, Howard 723, 724
Scott, Jill 1, 15, 114, 340, 343, 554, **602**, 770
Scott, Jimmy 15
Scott, Joe 57, 58
Scott, Kenneth 500
Scott, Kimberly 366
Scott, Latocha 772
Scott, Mabel 812
Scott, Oliver 773
Scott, Peggy 602, 603
Scott, Peggy & Jo Jo Benson **602**
Scott, Raymond 435
Scott, Rena 310, 461, 485
Scott, Sherry 214

Scott, Shirley 780, 857, 858
Scott, Tamika 772
Scott, Tee 337
Scott, Tom 715, 749
Scott, Wallace "Scotty" 8, 740, 741
Scott, Walter 8, 740, 741
Scott, Winfield 56, 172
Scott-Adams, Peggy **603**
Scott-Heron, Gil 55, 81, 383, 404, 405, 482, 536, 592, **603**, 604, 605, 715, 786, 791, 792, 802, 819, 830
Scotti, Nick 770
Scrafton, Tim 145
Scroggins, Marie 227
Scroggins, Renee 227
Scroggins, Valerie 227
Seacer, Levi Jr. 11
Seal 14, **605**
Seals & Crofts 341, 343
Seals, Son 150
Seals, Troy 283
Searchers 149, 418, 692, 804, 844
Sears, Al 231, 779, 808
Sears, Big Al 808
Sears, Zenas 753, 769
Sease, Marvin **605**, 606
Sebastian, John 150, 214
Sebastian, Ricky 614
Sebesky, Don 47
Secada, Jon 229, **606**, 609
Second Verse 400
Secret Affair 248
Secrets 808
Sedaka, Neil 206, 239, 261, 408, 834, 842
Seduction 737
Seeger, Pete 582
Seger, Bob 143, 277, 350, 436, 543
Sehorn, Marshall 466, 694, 751
Seiji 825
Selah Jubilee Singers 408
Sellers, Chris 13
Sembello, Michael 529, 620
Seminoles **606**, 674
Sensations 408, 558, **606**, 777, 779, 790, 797
Sepe, Tony 529
Sequel 809
Sequence 357, **606**, 646
Sequins 150, **606**, 607
Serenaders 226, **607**, 786, 804
Sermon, Erick 316, 577, 578
Serreo, Peter 173, 174
Service, Paul 281
Servicemen **607**
Sessions, Angel 186, 204, 225
Setzer, Brian 320
Seven O Two 221, 373, 628
Severinsen, Doc 487
Sevilla, Mickey 196
Sewell, Marshall 217
Sex-O-Lettes 195
Sextants 307
Sexton, Ann 693, 831, 833
Seymour, Mary 488
Shad, Bob 297
Shades of Black 70
Shades of Blue 783
Shades 669
Shaffer, Paul 62, 320
Shaggy 548, 590
Shai 574, **607**
Shakespeare, Robbie 290, 374, 375, 767
Shalamar 20, 29, 121, 139, 234, 311, 383, 416, 470, 471, 498, **607**, 608, 632, 633, 646, 652, 735, 809
Shangri Las 168, 312, 408, 415, 527, 558, **608**, 609, 612, 784, 795, 808, 809, 842, 844
Shanice 278, **609**
Shanklin, Ray 18, 673
Shannon **609**
Shannon, Del 375, 414, 418, 779, 784
Shannon, Preston 476
Shannon, Ronnie 211, 212
Shante, Roxanne 363
Shapiro, Brad 89, 169, 233, 356, 797
Sharp, Alexander 511, 512
Sharp, Benny 610
Sharp, Dee Dee 512, 609, 610, 809, 820, 829
Sharp, Joel "Razor" 153
Sharp, Sylvester Logan 139
Sharpe, Ray 805
Sharpees **610**
Sharps 63, 297, 577, 779
Shaw, Artie 131
Shaw, Greg 415
Shaw, Marlena **610**, 611, 670, 727, 790, 804
Shay, Dorothy 416
Shayne, Gloria 15
Shearing, George 511, 755
Sheen, Bobby 430, 634
Sheffer, Jacob 542
Sheffield, Charles 800
Shelby, Lorena 395
Sheldon, Jack 46
Sheldon, Sandi 231
Shell, Ed 497
Sheller, Marty 517
Shells **611**, 828
Shelton Brothers 822
Shelton, Billy 148
Shelton, Dave 13
Shelton, Earl 235
Shelton, Louie 268
Shelton, Louis 166
Shelton, Roscoe 268, 779
Shep & the Limelites 70, 177, 206, 307, 352, **611**, 824, 827, 839
Shepp, Archie 159, 322
Sheppard, Andy 228, 307, 611
Sheppard, Bill 228
Sheppard, Buddy 45, 46
Sheppard, James 307, 611
Sheppard, Stan 11
Sheppard, T.G. 385
Sheppards **611**, 783, 784, 798
Sherrill, Billy 168, 195, 350, 407, 463
Sherrys 161, **612**
Sherwood, Motorhead 312
Shetler, Tom 233
Shider, Gary 146, 154, 264, 265, 306, 517, 523
Shields 46, 532
Shields, Brooke 573
Shift 796
Shipp, Horace Jr. 44
Shire, David 40
Shirelles 13, 58, 191, 224, 243, 279, 326, 348, 445, 457, 580, 584, 600, 608, **612**, 613, 674, 680, 682, 731, 777, 779, 784, 793, 799, 814, 830, 834, 842, 843, 844
Shirley & Lee 38, 39, 293, 443, 518, **613**, 614, 615, 779, 783, 793, 807, 810, 838, 840
Shirley and Company 613, **614**, 795
Shirts 636
Shocked, Michelle 695
Shocklee, Hank 41
Shocklee, Keith 41
Shockley, Stephen 406
Shore, Dinah 741
Shores, Landy 559
Shorter, Wayne 295, 787, 788
Shotgun **614**
Shoukichi, Kina 390
Shout 602
Show Stoppers **614**
Showaddywaddy 364
Showmen 123, **614**, 793, 805, 840
Shuman, Mort 207, 208, 392, 489, 842
Shur, Itaal 289
Side Effect 26, 84, 324, **615**
Sidran, Ben 709, 710, 808
Siegel, Janis 817
Sierra, Anibal 621
Siffre, Labi 727, 823
Sigel, Beanie 686
Sigler, Bunny 42, 117, 145, 184, 217, 231, 240, 297, 313, 317, 325, 338, 373, 378, 405, 416, 428, 453, 481, 506, 526, 539, 564, 601, 602, 615, 616, 665, 687, 723, 740, 799, 818, 828, 848
Sigler, Jack Jr. 405
Sigler, Jimmy 616
Sigman, Carl 218
Sigue Sigue Sputnik 484
Silas, Alfie 633, 678
Silas, Louis Jr. 545
Silhouettes 464, **616**, 617, 778, 805
Silk Tymes Leather 210
Silk 244, **617**
Sill, Lester 532, 774
Sills, Courtney 509
Silva, Dawn 26, 79, 269
Silver Condor 317
Silver Convention 79, 170, 321, **617**, 618, 623, 665
Silver, Horace 520, 787, 857, 858
Silver, Lee 532
Silvertones 659
Silvester, Tony 280, 437, 438, 571, 623
Simmons, Al 558, 773
Simmons, Chester 266, 480, 558, 649
Simmons, Daryl 77, 112, 168, 189, 258, 439, 454, 538, 757, 772
Simmons, David 620
Simmons, James 734
Simmons, Lonnie 269, 583, 773
Simmons, Luther Jr. 280, 437, 438
Simmons, Pete 635
Simmons, Ronald 619, 634
Simmons, Russell 375, 379
Simmons, Walter Simtec 619
Simms, Gerald 407
Simon & Garfunkel 145, 255, 645
Simon, Calvin 264, 265, 306, 522, 525
Simon, Carly 24, 135, 254, 444, 699
Simon, Fred 428, 719
Simon, Joe 234, 297, 408, 616, **618**, 619, 830, 848
Simon, John 130, 722
Simon, Lowrell 428, 567, 719
Simon, Paul 339, 375, 376, 448, 459, 489, 658, 694, 842, 857
Simone, Nina 25, 245, 284, 299, 426, 535, 536, 596, 728, 809
Simoneaux, Harry 517
Simply Red 190, 366, 465
Simpson, Ashford 654
Simpson, Brian 657
Simpson, Jessica 499
Simpson, John 629
Simpson, Paul 6, 217
Simpson, Valerie 15, 17, 92, 151, 211, 231, 271, 272, 273, 331, 348, 349, 376, 430, 580, 586, 587, 600, 613, **619**, 660, 663, 715, 807
Sims Twins 712
Sims, David Wm. 722
Sims, Frankie Lee 815
Sims, Gerald 16, 36
Sims, Jody 660, 661
Sims, Joyce 122
Sims, Larry 74
Sims, Russell 722
Sims, Tommy 757
Simtec & Wylie 126, **619**, 634
Sinatra, Frank 11, 37, 45, 46, 48, 62, 86, 141, 188, 206, 249, 296, 309, 326, 375, 376, 462, 615, 723, 730
Sinatra, Nancy 400, 821
Sinclair, Kenneth 508
Sine 822
Singer, Artie 176
Singer, Hal 297
Singletary, Larry 691, 692
Singleton, Eddie 492, 823
Singleton, James 95
Singleton, John 351
Singleton, Raynoma Gordy 370, 492, 823
Singleton, Shelby 5, 49, 602, 639
Sir Douglas Quintet 143, 177, 434
Sir Isaac & the Doo-Dads 303
Sir Joe Quarterman 556
Siraisi, Gengi 289
Sisqó 208, 209, 488, 558, **619**
Sista 221
Sista Teedy 695
Sister Sledge 5, 139, 219, 290, 338, 582, 619, 620, 621, 623, 657, 726, 770, 796, 797, 831
Sisters Love 327
Sisters **621**
Siva, Samantha 205
Six Teens **621**, 801, 821
Skinner, Jolyon 705
Skip & Flip 805, 807, 815
Skola 209
Skull Snaps 194, **621**, 788
Skylark 155, 277, 283, 495
Skylarks 295
Skyliners 404, **621**, 778, 779, 797, 834
Skyy 76, 98, 416, **621**, 622, 785
Slack, Freddie 167, 822
Slades 46, 797
Sladich, Joe 245
Slash 134
Slater, Andrew 284
Slaughter, Willie "Skip" 647
Slave 6, 20, 21, 226, 406, 455, 456, 488, 504, 614, **622**, 623, 652, 802, 831
Slay, Frank 113
Sledge, Debbie 413, 619, 620, **623**
Sledge, Joni 619, 623
Sledge, Kathy 619, 620, 623
Sledge, Kim 619, 623
Sledge, Percy 5, 8, 118, 184, 293, 314, 415, 456, 536, 541, 570, **623**, 624, 668, 809, 824, 834, 844
Slick Rick 155, 210, 284, 483
Slick 737
Slick, Darby 235
Slits 136
Sloan, P.F. 231
Slutsky, Al 263
Sly & Robbie 290, 374
Sly & the Family Stone 16, 34, 42, 43, 100, 124, 137, 140, 178, 192, 214, 216, 260, 261, 269, 282, 283, 284, 331, 347, 348, 363, 364, 396, 437, 466, 484, 502, 513, 560, **624**, 625, 626, 655, 693, 703, 724, 746, 760, 777, 779, 782, 811, 844, 845, 850, 851
Sly Fox 702
Sly Stone & the Mojo Men 141, 282, 361, 515, 517, 521, 762, 785
Sly, Slick & Wicked 281, **626**, 831
Small Faces 316
Small, Danny 611
Small, Millie 233, 490, 779
Smalls, Biggie 367
Smalls, Charlie 448
Smallz, Biggy 650
Smashing Pumpkins 289
Smith Connection 430
Smith, Alice Tweed 724, 725
Smith, Andrew 339
Smith, Annette 129
Smith, Arlene 128, 129, 843
Smith, Bernadine Boswell 235
Smith, Bessie 31, 178, 409, 662, 732
Smith, Bill 128
Smith, Bobbie 491, 636, 637, 692, 784
Smith, Charles 400
Smith, Danny 430
Smith, Darrell 307
Smith, Dave 566
Smith, Denise 632
Smith, Dickie 242
Smith, Eddie 310
Smith, Elliott 141
Smith, Floyd 16, 317
Smith, Fred 63, 508
Smith, George "Smitty" 307, 441, 442
Smith, Harry 821
Smith, Herb 723
Smith, Huey "Piano" 63, 197, 249, 313, 393, 421, 553, 626, 627, 636, 694, 778, 781, 815, 816, 840, 841
Smith, Huey "Piano" & the Clowns 124, 443, 612, **626**, 627, 636
Smith, James 649
Smith, James Oscar "Jimmy" 367, 368
Smith, James Herb 468
Smith, Jean 335
Smith, Jeffrey L. 233, 234
Smith, Jesse 447
Smith, Jessica 315
Smith, Jessie 331, 475
Smith, Jimmy 48, 76, 166, 263, 325, 788, 857, 858
Smith, John 479
Smith, Johnny "Hammond" 734, 735, 857
Smith, Lawson 32
Smith, Lloyd 34, 35
Smith, Lonnie Liston 159, 450, 786, 795, 808, 823, 825
Smith, Lonnie Liston & the Cosmic Echoes 791
Smith, Lonnie 5, 788, 851, 857
Smith, Lonnie Trio 48
Smith, Louis 430
Smith, Mabel Louise 52
Smith, Mack Allen 793
Smith, Marvin "Smitty" 16, 136, 219
Smith, Melvin **627**, 808

Smith, Mike 710
Smith, O.C. 80, **627**, 628
Smith, Otis 30, 760
Smith, Patti 602
Smith, Paul 758
Smith, Ray 259, 260, 364
Smith, Robert 667
Smith, Ron 455
Smith, Samuel 192
Smith, Stuff 648
Smith, Tab 732
Smith, Toby 364
Smith, V. Jeffrey 2, 554
Smith, Will 9, 367, 376, 386, 593, 602, **628**, 629
Smiths 383
Smithson, Daniel 500
Smoke 592
Smooth Approach 499, **628**, 629
Smothers, James 746
Smothers, Smokey 15
Smothers, Tom 533
Smythe, Danny 71, 72
Snap 773, 796
Snatch and the Poontangs 514, 515
Sneaker Pimps 483
Snell, Lester 55, 96, 449, 618
Snipes, Wesley 427
Snoop Dogg 153, 154, 269, 432, 577, 578, 583
Snoop Doggy Dogg 66, 210, 364, 574, 658
Snow, Hank 131, 733
Snow, Phoebe 2, 332, 633, 700
Snow, Tom 64, 97
Snow, Wally 70
Snyder, Eddie 121
So Plush 367
Soccio, Gino 123, 759
Soft Cell 374
Softones 437
Soldier Boys 167
Solid Senders 473
Solitaires **629**, 784
Solomon, Clifford 83
Solomon, William 716
Somerville, Dave 191
Somerville, Jimmy 662
Somethin' for the People **629**
Something Sweet 384
Sommers, Joanie 15, 803
Sondheim, Stephen 276
Sonics 209
Sonny & Cher 196
Sonotones 270
SOS Band 136, 387, **629**, 630, 690
Soul Brothers Six 222, **630**
Soul Children 34, 55, 157, 233, 303, 545, **630**
Soul Clan 101, 158, 167, **630**, 631
Soul for Real **631**
Soul Generation **631**
Soul II Soul 2, 75, 140, 312, 381, 399, 407, 444, 500, **631**, 632, 705, 740, 785, 796, 810, 828
Soul Notes 408
Soul Providers 237
Soul Runners 769
Soul Satisfiers 276
Soul Searchers 436
Soul Shakers 38
Soul Solution 578
Soul Stirrers 36, 107, 118, 161, 162, 163, 164, 457, **632**, 644, 671, 672, 673, 712, 760, 838, 844, 857
Soul Survivors 325, **632**, 808
Soul Train Gang **632**, 633
SOUL **633**, 700, 795
Soul, Jimmy **633**
Soul, Tommy 499
Soulciety 395
Sound Experience **633**
Soundgarden 690
Sounds of Blackness **634**, 824
Soussan, Simon 607
South, Joe 256, 371, 667, 699
Southern California Community Choir 255, 256, 258
Southside Johnny & the Asbury Jukes 162, 200, 636
Southside Movement 619, **634**
Soxx, Bob B. & the Blue Jeans 319, 430, **634**
Spampinato, Joey 51
Spandau Ballet 331, 541, 542
Spaniels 219, 464, 479, 480, 512, **634**, 635, 777, 782, 793, 810
Spanish Fly 59
Spann, Otis 191
Spann, Patricia 144
Spark, Mark 11
Sparkle 386
Sparks 827
Sparks, Melvin 811
Sparks, Willy 282
Sparrow, Woody 400
Spartans 558
Spears, Britney 205, 367, 499, 689
Special Delivery 325
Specter, Dave 250, 582
Specter, Dave & the Bluebirds 582
Spector, Abner 166, 365
Spector, Phil 13, 16, 31, 58, 60, 121, 136, 171, 172, 191, 194, 196, 279, 293, 325, 367, 391, 392, 414, 415, 430, 447, 558, 574, 575, 579, 584, 585, 608, 634, **635**, 636, 639, 703, 704, 728, 729, 774, 784, 803, 805, 809, 842, 843, 844, 847
Spector, Ronnie 1, 309, 584, 585, **635**, 636
Spedding, Chris 419
Speech 16, 235
Speedometer 807
Speight, Bruno 313
Spellbinders 39
Speller, Kino 405
Spellman, Benny 382, **636**, 694, 793, 803, 840
Spencer, Bobby 107
Spencer, C.P. 279, 511, 816
Spencer, Casey 368
Spencer, Elvin 832
Spencer, Jeremy 718
Spencer, Jon 650
Spencer, Kevin 212
Spencer, Leon 735
Spencer, Richard 758
Spice Girls 9, 145, 689
Spice, Irving 76
Spidel, Jim 507
Spiders 115, 613, **636**, 783, 793
Spielberg, Steven 376
Spindrift 114
Spinners 43, 44, 80, 112, 117, 122, 143, 166, 186, 200, 253, 266, 267, 296, 297, 309, 328, 332, 358, 468, 480, 491, 497, 505, 521, 559, 597, 633, **636**, 637, 638, 649, 655, 712, 729, 730, 731, 740, 780, 781, 794, 807, 817, 833, 846, 848
Spinners [Surf] 200, 266, 533, 600, 665, 763
Spirit of Memphis Quartet 314
Spiritual Concept 665
Spiritualized 196, 198
Spivey, Keisha 693
Spoonie Gee 829
Spradley, David 517
Spratley, Phil 794
Springers **638**
Springfield, Dusty 100, 105, 142, 153, 279, 309, 314, 326, 339, 444, 576, **638**, 639, 640, 728, 729, 731, 732, 790, 793, 794, 808, 844, 847
Springfields 638, 640
Springsteen, Bruce 65, 144, 145, 152, 153, 188, 277, 298, 452, 542, 543, 598, 640, 832
Springsteen, Bruce & the E Street Band 65, 144, 145
Spruill, Jimmy 166, 298, 800, 838
Spruill, Stephanie 24
Spyro Gyra 791
Squeeze 119, 120
Squier, Billy 167
Squires 199
Stackhouse, Houston 719
Stafford, Jo 210, 758
Stairsteps 98, 244, 793
Stakka Bo 690
Stallings, Mary 230
Stamm, Marvin 188, 540
Standells 374, 787
Stanley, Bob 640
Stanley, Chuck 160, 312, 747
Stanley, Pamala **640**
Stansfield, Lisa 29, 328, 381, 399, 520, 572, 631, **640**, 705, 740, 743, 744
Stanton, Allen 834
Stanton, Candi 644
Staple Singers 34, 38, 223, 299, 380, 396, 519, **640**, 641, 642, 758, 762, 785, 786, 793, 796, 824, 828, 857
Staples, Cleo 641
Staples, Cleotha 641, 642
Staples, Mavis 43, 44, 248, 257, 324, 530, 551, **641**, 642, 757, 793, 804, 828
Staples, Pervis 640, 641, 642, 682
Staples, Roebuck "Pops" 640, 641, **642**, 660, 785
Staples, Yvonne 641
Starfires 117, 395
Stargard **642**, 643, 795
Starks, John "Jabo" 90, 366
Starlets 403, 404
Starlighters 457
Starling, Jade 547
Starlings 828
Starliters 183
Starlites 345, 798
Starr, Brenda K. 115, 116, 407, **643**
Starr, Edwin 37, 80, 129, 166, 299, 394, 396, 427, 439, 447, 500, 533, 560, 585, 591, 638, **643**, 644, 647, 676, 698, 705, 708, 714, 733, 745, 769, 808, 817, 818, 819, 823, 825, 826, 831, 832, 846
Starr, Maurice 82, 496, 533, 650, 698
Starr, Ringo 69, 198, 269, 555, 699
Starship Orchestra 159
State of Art 513
Staton, Candi 350, 534, **644**, 645, 761, 762, 830, 832
Steacker, Richard Lee 734
Steals, Melvin 42, 334
Steals, Mervin 42, 334
Steele, David 239
Steele, Jeff 239
Steele, Tommy 250
Steels, Tyrone 614
Steely & Clevie 502
Steely Dan 9, 93, 159, 254, 289, 573, 587, 666
Stefani, Gwen 552
Steiger, Rod 376
Steinberg, Lewis 67
Stephens, Barbara 683
Stephens, Geoff 201
Stephens, Lascelles 168
Stephens, Mark 20
Stephens, Tennyson 152, 709
Stephenson, Calvin 708
Stephenson, Wolf 57, 96
Stepney, Charles 108, 186, 187, 214, 224, 420, 576, 589, **645**, 748
Steppenwolf 167, 169, 362, 484
Stereo MC's 724
Stereolab 515
Stereos 332
Sterling, Annette 571
Stern, Bert 52
Stetsasonic 823
Steve, Miami 65
Stevens, Andreas 288
Stevens, Bobby 136
Stevens, Cat 15, 403, 404, 418, 419, 548
Stevens, David 121
Stevens, Dodie 804
Stevens, Lona 365
Stevens, Mark [1] 389
Stevens, Mark [2] 70, 374
Stevens, Ray 123, 639
Stevens, Rick 695
Stevenson, B.W. 315
Stevenson, MacLean 94
Stevenson, Mickey 315, 316, 445, 446, 447, 675, 715, 738, 739, 745
Stevenson, Samuel 211
Stevenson, William "Mickey" 266, 315, 414, 426, 492, 571, 714, 740, 765
Steward, Herbie 309
Steward, Keith 121, 309
Stewart, Amii 80, 248, **645**
Stewart, Billy 36, 52, 103, 136, 167, 188, 214, 281, **645**, 782, 313, 368, 558, 626, 646, 689, 705, 781, 782, 790, 791, 799, 812
Stewart, Denise 160
Stewart, Freddie 624
Stewart, Jermaine **646**, 720
Stewart, Jim 436
Stewart, Jimmy 562
Stewart, Melvin 205
Stewart, Paul 379
Stewart, Ralph 569
Stewart, Rex 822
Stewart, Rod 15, 48, 58, 139, 140, 145, 352, 357, 419, 444, 533, 605, 695, 706, 760, 762
Stewart, Sandy 108
Stewart, Sylvester "Sly Stone" 6, 16, 105, 106, 146, 192, 214, 260, 263, 283, 288, 294, 319, 370, 371, 381, 468, 476, 513, 517, 522, 624, 625, 626, 658, 760, 781, 801, 821
Stewart, Teddy 732
Stewart, Thomas 313
Stewart, Tricky 77
Stewart, Wayne 372
Stewart, William 552
Stewart, Winston 34
Sticky Fingers 822
Stierle, Wayne 611, 782
Stigwood, Robert 40, 444, 582
Still, Cleveland 209
Stillman, Al 559
Stills, Stephen 256, 259, 340, 341, 365, 467, 543, 592, 641, 655, 657, 699, 758
Stillwell, Chris 289
Sting 178, 666, 731, 752
Stingily, Byron 662, 679
Stipe, Michael 136, 137
Stitt, Sonny 55, 73, 444
Stock, Aitken & Waterman 353, 464, 552, 644, 651, 661
Stock, Mike 464
Stockert, Ron 592
Stockman, Shawn 72
Stodghill, Charles 533, 693
Stokes 694
Stokes, Chris 332
Stokes, Linda 436
Stokes, Michael 38, 225, 436, 545
Stoller, Mike 1, 4, 148, 149, 207, 231, 293, 296, 298, 301, 348, 367, 391, 392, 415, 608, 685, 705, 728, 774, 803, 812, 839, 841, 842, 844
Stoltz, Brian 466
Stone City Band 363
Stone, Al 364
Stone, Angie 554, 606, **646**, 647
Stone, Freddie 34
Stone, Henry 60, 89, 93, 254, 298, 411, 423, 458, 571, 572, 598, 768
Stone, Jesse 148, 172, 206, 207, 558, **647**, 701, 780
Stone, Rose 624
Stone, Trey III 205
Stone, Wayne 485
Stoneground 151
Stooges 174
Stop the Violence Movement 833
Storball, Donald 114
Storch, Scott 770
Stories 320
Storm, Gale 421, 798
Storm, Warren 800
Stover, Don 415, 416
Stover, Elgie 415
Stover, Kenny 415
Strafe 227
Stragis, Roy 707
Strain, Sam 141, 422, 505, 506
Strangeloves 13, 49, 191
Strauss, Johann II 40
Strauss, Richard 188
Stray Cats 320
Strayhorn, Billy 734
Streep, Meryl 229
Street 479
Street People **647**
Street, Richard 410, 479, 674, 676, 677
Streisand, Barbra 323, 397, 486, 595, 651
Stretch, Eric 499
Strikers **647**, 822
Stringer, Bob 590
Striplin, Sylvia 13, 219, **647**, 802
Strollers 827
Strong, Barrett 187, 266, 281, 426, **647**, 676, 677, 708, 721, 830, 845
Strong, Jimmy 647, 648
Strong, Nolan 367, 545, 579, 647, 648, 716
Strong, Nolan & the Diablos 414, **647**, 648, 816, 818

Stroud, James 398, 449, 493, 500
Strozier, Gordon 566
Strunz, Jorge 420
Stuart, Hamish 22, 23
Stuart, Jeb 813, 824
Stuart, Marty 641
Stuart, Marv 642
Stubblefield, Clyde 85, 87, 89
Stubbs, Joe 36, 160, 233, 248, 439, 509, 511, 718, 795, 816
Stubbs, Levi 32, 124, 160, 190, 203, 251, 252, 253, 263, 272, 509, 655, 717, 823
Stubbs, Terry 506
Students 777, 782, 790
Stuff **648**, 649
Sturgis, Ted 157
Stylistics 60, 61, 84, 138, 142, 159, 160, 186, 200, 267, 292, 328, 329, 355, 372, 373, 448, 457, 468, 535, 618, **649**, 650, 660, 674, 696, 723, 785, 848
Sublime 366
Suburbans 828
Sue Ann 485
Sugar Hill 265
Sugarfoot 503
Sugarhill Gang 139, 236, 305, 312, 357
Sugarman Three **650**
Sugarman, Neal **650**
Suggs, Brad 113
Suleyman, Sunay 427
Sullivan, Denise 811
Sullivan, Ed 31, 191
Sullivan, Jim 759, 760
Sultans 828
Sumlin, Hubert 189, 456
Summer, Donna 38, 145, 146, 170, 201, 255, 275, 277, 311, 321, 428, 449, 472, 484, 486, 540, 560, 595, 609, 617, 650, 651, 652, 662, 686, 696, 700, 726, 785, 789
Summers, Bill 307
Summers, Bobby G. 183
Sumner, Bernard 400
Sun 622, **652**
Sun, Ahaguna G. 652
Sunbear **652**, 653
Sunday's Child **653**
Sunlovers **653**, 831
Sunny & the Sunliners 799, 833
Sunnyland Slim 189, 405, 815
Sunset Travelers 770
Superbs 786, 831
Supergrass 196, 198
Superiors 784
Supremes 17, 32, 54, 80, 81, 162, 202, 210, 219, 224, 227, 241, 248, 251, 253, 254, 277, 280, 281, 312, 315, 316, 331, 347, 369, 390, 396, 403, 404, 405, 414, 416, 429, 445, 446, 447, 461, 477, 530, 548, 549, 559, 571, 579, 580, 581, 586, 587, 588, 598, 600, 602, 612, 642, 646, **653**, 654, 655, 656, 657, 674, 675, 691, 697, 712, 715, 722, 728, 731, 744, 754, 765, 768, 777, 779, 785, 786, 792, 793, 798, 815, 816, 817, 818, 820, 823, 829, 831, 832, 833, 844, 846
Sure, Al B. 71, 230, 286, 287, 588, **657**, 743, 785
Surface 352, **657**, 785
Surprise Package 2
Sussewell, John 644
Suthers, Isaac 327, 395
Suttles, Warren 562
Sutton, Al 179
Sutton, Charles 32
Sutton, Mike & Brenda 26, 580
Sutton, Tyrone 533
Svensson, Peter 690
Swain, Tony 331
Swaine, Trevor 793
Swallows 107, 206, 246, 562, **657**, 783, 833
Swamp Dogg 13, 100, 101, **658**, 682, 794
Swan Silvertones **658**, 659, 857
Swan, Billy 462, 847
Swanee Quintet 107
Swanigan, Doug 263
Swann, Bettye 184, 293, 313, **659**, 825
Swans 562
Sweat Band 154
Sweat, Keith 47, 100, 209, 244, 290, 293, 332, 337, 343, 359, 369, 417, 431, 492, 554, 575, 617, 619, **659**, 660
Sweathog 697
Swedien, Bruce 48, 355, 572, 754, 757
Sweet Honey in the Rock 857
Sweet Inspirations 256, 257, 321, 326, 331, 479, **660**, 728, 797, 804, 828
Sweet Sensation **660**
Sweet Thunder 497, 498
Sweet, Matthew 383
Sweet, Rachel 582
Sweetback 409
Swing Out Sister 4
Swing, DeVante 127, 221, 368, 686
Swingin' Phillies 798
Swinging Blue Jeans 779
Swingle Singers 479
Swingsters 170
Switch 182, 430, 628, 629, **660**, 661
Swizz Beatz 489
SWV 127, 189, 260, 290, **661**, 736, 772
Sybil 127, **661**
Sydor, Bob 312
Sykes, Roosevelt 320, 520
Sylvers 166, 212, 277, 360, 412, 528, 533, **661**, 662, 668, 801
Sylvers, Angela 661
Sylvers, Charmaine Elaine 661
Sylvers, Edmund 661
Sylvers, Foster 661
Sylvers, James 661
Sylvers, Leon F. III 81, 212, 373, 388, 393, 398, 608, 661, 741
Sylvers, Olympia-Ann 661
Sylvers, Patricia 661
Sylvers, Ricky 629, 661
Sylvester 178, 255, 266, 383, **662**, 663, 696, 731, 737, 795
Sylvester, Andy 320
Sylvester, Jorge 788
Sylvia 349, **663**
Sylvia [Country] 478
Symphonics **663**, 750, 793
Syndicate of Sound 835
Syreeta 112, **663**, 664, 790, 796
System 30, 182, 216, 291, 389, 509, **664**
Szabo, Gabor 227, 616, 712, 760, 828

T

T Boz 691
T Connection **665**
T Life 393, 747
T Rex 374, 551
T. Life 393, 582, **665**, 723
T., Booker 68
Ta Mara & the Seen 413, **666**
Tabano, Ray 41
Tackett, Fred 601
Tacuma, Jamaaladeen 310
Tafolla, Noah 586
Taj 661
Takayanagi, Tsuyoshi 741
Take Six 460, 473, 534, **666**
Take That 498, 668, 689
Talbert, Billy 614
Talbert, Homer Alexander III 104
Talk Of The Town 460
Talk Talk 141, 484
Talking Heads 139, 310, 641, 767
Talley, Gary 71
Talmy, Shel 803
Tamar 77
Tamia 377, 492, **666**, 667
Tampa Red 120, 777
Tams 182, 437, 492, **667**, 778, 786
Tandy, Rondalis 714
Tangerine Dream 310, 484
Tapscott, Horace 737
Tarantino, Quentin 185, 380, 760, 811
Tardogono, Frank 220
Tarheel Slim 800
Tarheel Slim & Little Ann 409, 807
Tarleton, Karl 748
Tarnopol, Nat 418
Tarplin, Marvin 579
Tarsia, Joe 297
Tashan **667**, 747
Taste of Honey 166, 281, 370, 389, **667**, 795
Tate, Bruce 532
Tate, Buddy 577
Tate, Grady 30, 256, 376, 558
Tate, Howard 33, 223, 473, 547, 557, **668**, 730, 784
Tate, Joe 267
Tate, Pam **668**
Tate, Tommy **668**, 811, 819
Tatum, Art 62
Taupin, Bernie 446
Tavares 40, 80, 166, 277, 280, 497, 563, 566, 646, **668**, 669, 679, 767, 786, 795, 799
Tavares, Antone 668
Tavares, Arthur 668
Tavares, Feliciano 668
Tavares, Ralph Vierra 668
Taylor, Allan 295
Taylor, Angel 698
Taylor, Billy 420
Taylor, Bobby & the Vancouvers 143, 447, 546, 654, **669**, 670, 708, 814, 816
Taylor, Brenda 834
Taylor, Carmen 172
Taylor, Chip 358, 636, 716
Taylor, Creed 21, 47, 48, 159, 188, 283, 376, 536, 709, 734, 735
Taylor, Debbie 468, **670**
Taylor, Delburt 622
Taylor, Diane 367, 428, 429
Taylor, Don 652
Taylor, Eddie 838
Taylor, Elizabeth 318
Taylor, Felice 428, 742, 744, 818
Taylor, Gary **670**, 741
Taylor, Gina 488
Taylor, Jack [1] 621
Taylor, Jack [2] 670
Taylor, James 2, 176, 254, 299, 341, 375, 401, 564, 761, **670**, 671
Taylor, James "JT" 20, 45, 81, 400, 401, 402, 541, **671**
Taylor, John T. 4
Taylor, Johnnie 34, 95, 125, 151, 164, 179, 201, 303, 309, 410, 441, 545, 457, 572, 601, 605, 632, 642, **671**, 672, 673, 682, 761, 777, 785, 791, 804, 813, 816, 828, 857
Taylor, Johnny 162, 219, 233, 350, 370, 457, 605, 632, 673, 692, 712, 777
Taylor, Koko 36, 782
Taylor, Leroy 499
Taylor, Little Johnny 6, 7, 153, 293, 294, 525, 545, 672, **673**, 780, 812, 856
Taylor, Marvin 570
Taylor, Mick 546
Taylor, Red 475
Taylor, Richard 441
Taylor, Robbie 381
Taylor, Rodney 228
Taylor, Russell 609
Taylor, Sam "The Man" 52, 56, 93, 207, 208, 301, 774, 780
Taylor, Shawn 228
Taylor, Sonnie 652
Taylor, Ted 6, 7, 107, 345, 418, 525, 673, **674**
Taylor, Ty 176
Taylor, William 121, 122
Taylor, Zola 539
Teardrops 827, 828
Tears for Fears 6
Tease 69, 485
Technotronic 796
Teddy Bears 635, 805
Tedesco, Tommy 109
Tee, Richard 245, 377, 413, 565, 591, 648, 710, 734
Tee, Willie 63, 271, **674**, 746, 823
Teen Chords 434
Teen Queens 345, 797, 807
Teen Tones 303
Teenagers 122, 191, 400, 433, 434, 602, 806, 839
Temperton, Rod 21, 48, 308, 377, 520
Temple, Phil 646
Temprees **674**
Temptations 7, 18, 36, 60, 112, 117, 124, 127, 150, 160, 161, 204, 205, 211, 217, 218, 220, 225, 234, 251, 252, 253, 257, 263, 264, 266, 267, 280, 281, 285, 302, 306, 317, 318, 332, 333, 346, 349, 362, 363, 368, 381, 386, 387, 396, 418, 446, 447, 457, 461, 462, 479, 480, 491, 500, 507, 511, 521, 525, 534, 547, 548, 554, 559, 560, 562, 566, 578, 580, 581, 583, 585, 587, 590, 591, 592, 600, 607, 618, 628, 633, 643, 644, 645, 646, 647, 648, 652, 654, 655, 656, 666, **674**, 675, 676, 677, 678, 679, 684, 700, 705, 708, 713, 717, 718, 720, 728, 741, 745, 762, 765, 777, 785, 786, 787, 792, 800, 814, 816, 817, 818, 819, 820, 825, 828, 830, 831, 833, 844, 846, 851
Temptones **679**, 818
Ten CC 610, 829
Ten City 240, 662, **679**, 680
Ten Years After 759
Tenaglia, Danny 416
Tench, Bob 419
Tennant, Neil 638, 639
Terranova, Joe 176
Terrel, Freddie 824
Terrell, Dorothy 426
Terrell, Ernie 602
Terrell, Jean 653, 654, 655, 656, 657, 680
Terrell, Phil 441, 750, 789
Terrell, Tammi 17, 29, 80, 161, 266, 271, 272, 273, 274, 275, 276, 434, 435, 439, 602, 612, 619, 644, 655, **680**, 720, 757, 765, 825, 830, 831, 846
Terrell, Ty 578
Terry, Clark 376, 732
Terry, Dewey 199
Terry, Helen 173
Terry, John 208
Terry, Mike 15
Terry, Phil 338, 339, 526
Terry, Sonny 56, 759, 760
Terry, Sonny & Brownie McGhee 582
Tex, Joe 8, 85, 101, 158, 167, 196, 255, 266, 371, 372, 385, 463, 466, 525, 605, 630, 631, **680**, 681, 682, 692, 760, 777, 778, 781, 782, 783, 786, 812, 815, 824
Tharpe, Sister Rosetta 319, 822
Tharps, Gina 488
The Golden Tones 402
The The 136
The Wild Tchoupitoulas 747
Theberge, Chris 289
Thee Midniters 140, 584
Them 49, 179, 842
Thiele, Bob 527, 603
Thielemans, Toots 376, 377
Thigpen, Henderson 95
Thin Lizzy 269
Third Bass 75
Third Generation 437
Third World 506
Thirty Eight Special 298, 330
Thomas Bucknasty 665
Thomas, Alex 214
Thomas, Alton 345
Thomas, Andrew 447
Thomas, B.J. 134, 793, 830
Thomas, Bobby 123, 500
Thomas, Carl 230, 316, 578, 584
Thomas, Carla 13, 43, 44, 67, 92, 136, 248, 261, 262, 299, 303, 349, 379, 415, 530, 545, 568, 569, 570, **682**, 685, 777, 780, 792, 794, 802, 804, 813, 828, 834, 844
Thomas, Charles 241, 367
Thomas, Charlie 207, 208, 784, 785
Thomas, Cheryl 590
Thomas, Danny "Sweet Man" 157
Thomas, David 666
Thomas, Dennis "Dee Tee" 400
Thomas, Derrick 413
Thomas, Eddie 125, 793
Thomas, Eric 336
Thomas, Evelyn 18, 235, 552, **683**
Thomas, Fred 87, 366
Thomas, Gerry 122, 235, 236
Thomas, Grady 264, 265, 522, 523, 525, 547
Thomas, Harold 449
Thomas, Irma 63, 223, 293, 317, 438, 557, 570, **683**, 684, 694, 783, 792, 793, 794, 800, 804, 810, 815, 840, 841
Thomas, Jamo **684**, 790, 793
Thomas, Jenn 139
Thomas, Jerome 313
Thomas, Joe 225
Thomas, Keith 757
Thomas, Lillo 412, **684**, 810
Thomas, Marvell 682
Thomas, Mary 171
Thomas, Mary Ann 4

Thomas, Michael 697
Thomas, Pete 312
Thomas, Philip Michael 170, 453
Thomas, Rozonda 529, 690, 691
Thomas, Rufus 43, 442, 502, 503, 682, 684, **685**, 689, 777, 785, 792, 802, 804, 814, 828
Thomas, Shirley 195
Thomas, Stanley 532
Thomas, Tabby 800
Thomas, Timmy 384, 423, 685, 686, 785, 809
Thomas, Tony 339
Thomas, Truman 34, 546
Thomas, Vaneese 22
Thomas, Vic 721
Thomas, Victor 720
Thomas, Wayne 240, 455
Thomas, Will 700
Thompkins, Russell Jr. 387, 649, 650
Thompson Twins 139
Thompson, Ahmir Khalib 91
Thompson, Anthony "Packrat" 652
Thompson, Arthur 12
Thompson, Barbara 415
Thompson, Bobby 129
Thompson, Cedric 486
Thompson, Chucky 59
Thompson, Danny 241, 419
Thompson, David 532, 533
Thompson, Emery 737
Thompson, Frank "Captain Disaster" 34, 35
Thompson, Gina 686
Thompson, James 126, 334
Thompson, Linda 617
Thompson, Mack 371
Thompson, Marc Anthony 141
Thompson, Marshall 137, 138, 567
Thompson, Richard 98, 617
Thompson, Rick 97
Thompson, Sonny 570, 619
Thompson, Sonny 36, 570
Thompson, Syleena 371
Thompson, Tony 230, 582, **686**
Thompson, Tony [Drums] 138, 139
Thompson, Wayne Carson 72, 128
Thornhill, Claude 460, 697
Thornton, Alfonso **686**
Thornton, Big Mama 415, 514, 684, 774, 799, 818, 836, 838
Thornton, Fonzi 583, 686
THP Orchestra **686**
Thrasher, Andrew 206
Thrasher, Gerhart 206, 207, 241
Thrasher, Norman 32
Thrasher, Sibel 559
Threat, Dickie 242
Three Amigos 644
Three Chuckles 571
Three Degrees 79, 129, 201, 217, 241, 268, 313, 372, 468, 612, 617, 620, 642, **687**, 688, 778, 816
Three Dog Night 117, 250, 650, 694
Three LW **688**
Three Million **688**
Three Pieces 829
Three Reasons **688**
Three Sounds 857
Three Suns 539, 559
Thrillers 161, 612
Thunder 688
Thunder, Johnny **688**, 758
Thunderclap Newman 404
Thunderpuss 59
Thunderpuss Two Thousand 400
Thunders, Johnny 636, 688
Thunders, Johnny & the Heartbreakers 636
Thurman, Ed 552
Thursby, Robert 716
Thurston, Bobby **689**, 821
Thurston, L.C. 62
Tick Tocks 443
Ticket, Wuf 821, 822
Tierra 140, 254, **689**
Tiffany 689
Til, Sonny 332, 512, 821
Til, Sonny & the Orioles 32, 511, 512
Tillery, Calvin 227
Tillery, Donald 84
Tillery, Linda 227
Tilley, Sandra 445, 446
Tillis, Clyde "Thin Man" 798
Tillman, Floyd 131
Tillman, Ivory 190
Tilmon, Abrim 190
Tilmon, Cleophus 190
Tilmon, Raymond 190
Tim Dog 470
Timbaland 1, 221, 222, 278, 619, 686, 689, 691, 700, 706, 707
Timberlake, Justin 460, **689**
Time 181, 279, 351, 370, 413, 510, 629, 666, **689**, 690, 715
Timetones 806
Timex Social Club 149, **690**, 785
Timmons, Bobby 857, 858
Timmons, Jeff 498
Timmy & the Empires 339
Timmy & the Persianettes 339
Tiny Tim 222, 780
Tiny Tim & the Hits 607, 780, 828
Tiny Topsy 812
Tio, Mario G. 142
Tipton, Lester 832
Tisby, Dexter 532
Titelman, Russ 21, 48
Titiyo **690**
Tiven, Jon 538
Tjader, Cal 808
TKA 801
TLC 28, 77, 127, 189, 205, 210, 222, 224, 227, 304, 404, 481, 486, 489, 529, 538, 573, 617, 688, **690**, 691, 698
Tobin, George 581
Today 506, **691**, 692
Todd, David 665, 773
Todd, Nick 798
Tokens 559, 828, 834
Tolbert, Israel 828
Tolbert, Larry 521, 566
Toles, Michael 34
Tolliver, Charles 25, 692
Tolliver, Kim **692**
Tolotta, Phil 758
Tom Tom 2000 22
Tompkins, Carl 437
Tone Loc 833
Tonettes 683
Toney, Kevin 54, 55
Toney, Norma 449
Toney, Oscar **692**
Toney, Oscar Jr. 683, 692
Tony! Toni! Toné! **692**, 693
Too Short 316, 482
Tooley, Ron 313
Toots & the Maytals 77, 824
Top Notes 340, 779
Topics **693**, 750, 784, 789
Toppers 475
Torian, Reggie 333, 334, 335
Torme, Mel 131
Torres, Liz 782
Toscano, Eli 102
Tosches, Nick 148
Tosh, Peter 280, 290
Total **693**
Toto 695
Touch 177
Toussaint, Allen 54, 151, 196, 197, 199, 200, 294, 296, 310, 313, 314, 372, 382, 383, 388, 403, 404, 405, 419, 421, 450, 466, 467, 493, 494, 495, 518, 542, 543, 553, 601, 613, 636, 683, **693**, 694, 695, 751, 803, 840
Toussaint, Lee 219
Touzet, Rene 51
Tower 695, 750
Tower of Power 23, 55, 60, 79, 81, 105, 111, 151, 269, 308, 322, 383, 419, 450, 507, 521, 541, 593, 652, **695**, 696, 699, 750, 751, 757, 851
Towles, Fred 408
Towles, Nat 430
Townes, Carol Lynn **696**, 820
Townes, Jeff 602, 628
Townsend, Cliff 326, 657
Townsend, David 352, 358, 657
Townsend, Ed 326, 333, 334, 458, 655, 657, 722
Townsend, Ron 718
Townshend, Pete 220, 404
Townsmen 434
Townson, Gregory 222
Townson, Ron 238, 239
Toya 75, **696**
Toys 682, **696**, 697, 809, 812
Traci 823
Tracy, Jeanie 826
Traffic 179, 847
Tramaine 302
Trammps 110, 297, 317, 476, 501, 597, 669, 677, 679, **697**, 818, 820, 848
Trashmen 577
Travis, Betty 549
Travis, Donald 519
Travis, McKinley 788
Travis, Merle 672
Travis, Richard 339
Travolta, John 782
Traynor, Jay 489
Treadwell, George 206, 207, 241, 391, 462
Trees, Harvey 136
Trenier, Claude 697
Trenier, Cliff 697
Treniers **697**, 698, 794, 812
Trent, Ron 825
Tresvant, Ralph 82, 496, 497, **698**
Tribe Called Quest 25, 75, 383, 432, 646, 727, 769
Tribe, Tony 362
Tricker, Dave White 122, 176
Tricky 483
Trilark 170
Trin I Tee Five:Seven **698**
Trinidads 125
Triple Threat 693
Triplett, Willie 566
Triumphs 505
Troggs 114, 636
Trone, Roland 199
Troop 69, 417, 741
Tropea, John 188, 710, 730
Trouble Funk 84, 560, **698**, 699, 829
Troutt, Frank 438
Troutman, Larry 486, 583, 775
Troutman, Lester 583, 775
Troutman, Roger 365, 486, 583, 775
Troutman, Tony 583, 775, 826
Troxell, Gary 247
Troy, Doris 321, 325, 660, **699**, 728, 804, 814, 824
Trudell, Johnny 381
True Movement 700, 800
True, Andrea 699, 700
True, Andrea Connection **699**, 700
Truitt, Johnny 809
Truth Hurts 478, **700**
Truth 332, 633, **700**
TSU Toronados 42, 824
Tubbs, Hubert 695
Tubbs, Pierre 498
Tucker, Alonzo 32
Tucker, Anita 812, 827
Tucker, Bobby 499
Tucker, Ira 602
Tucker, Sundray 339, 602
Tucker, Tee 700
Tucker, Tommy 114, **700**, 790
Tuff Crew 405
Tufo, Rich 334
Tunedrops 827
Tunney, Dick & Mel 464
Turbans 36, 464, **701**, 716, 798, 805, 828
Turks 65, 318, 532, 798
Turner, Big Joe 31, 58, 63, 113, 172, 293, 295, 297, 421, 463, 647, **701**, 812, 822, 836
Turner, Charles 540
Turner, Dwight 705
Turner, Ike 31, 33, 78, 151, 243, 280, 330, 331, 350, 475, 684, **701**, **702**, 703, 704, 705, 706, 737, 812, 836
Turner, Ike & His Kings of Rhythm 49, 78, 702, 706
Turner, Ike & Tina 15, 31, 33, 179, 200, 242, 254, 270, 319, 389, 485, 592, 635, 655, 702, **703**, 704, 705, 706, 778, 783, 807, 818
Turner, Irving 657
Turner, Joe 39, 463, 480, 514, 753, 777, 793, 838
Turner, Linda 687
Turner, Lou Willie 647
Turner, Nakeisha 431
Turner, Ron 507
Turner, Ruby **705**, 786, 809, 825
Turner, Sammy **705**
Turner, Sonny 539, 540, 633
Turner, Spyder **705**, 784, 808
Turner, Tina 16, 33, 121, 136, 139, 151, 176, 331, 369, 379, 390, 530, 579, 592, 605, 701, 702, 703, 704, 705, **706**, 801, 844
Turner, Titus 56, 425, **706**
Turner, Zeb 812
Turrentine, Stanley 70, 133, 188, 261, 287, 288, 324, 727, 786, 787, 788, 793, 829, 857, 858
Turtles 231
Tuten, James 216, 217
TW Funkmasters 440
Tweedy, Jeff 525
Tweet **706**, 707
Twennynine 785
Twenty Four Carat Black **707**, 802
Twilighters 799
Twitty, Conway 307, 461, 543, 831
Two Friends 439, 555
Two Live Crew 60, 66, 482, 545
Two Pac 66, 230, 351, 382, 395, 583, 664, 727, 775
Two Tons 662
Two Tons O Fun 731, 737
Tyler, Alvin "Red" 5, 38, 69, 197, 198, 231, 249, 424, 613
Tyler, Bonnie 702
Tyler, Steven 41, 538
Tyler, West 519
Tymes 12, 169, **707**
Tympany Five 198, 370, 378, 379
Tyner, McCoy 287, 328, 329, 787
Tyree, Glenn 627
Tyrese **707**
Tyrone, Janice 804
Tyson, David 441
Tyson, Ron 42, 253, 318, 597, 618, 677, 678, 833
Tyson, Ronnie 453
Tyson, Sheila 387

U

U Two 177, 383, 631
UB40 130, 281, 362
Uballez, Max 584
Ubiquity 25, 26
Uggams, Leslie 793
UGK 211
Ultra High Frequency 782
Ultra Naté 825
Ultra Violet 177
Ultramagnetic MC's 470
Underwood, Lenny 709
Undisputed Truth 70, 205, 479, 560, 585, **708**, 745, 796, 817
Unifics 325, **708**, 709, 824
Union, Ed 719
Unique Attraction 72
Unique Blend 834
Unique 822
Uniques 798, 827
United Image 200, 812, 822
Unity 688
Universal Robot Band 99, 395, **709**, 796
Universals 827
UNKLE 24
Unlimited Touch 170, **709**, 747, 821
Unrest 227
Unto, Vincent 231
UNV 629, 709
Upchurch, Phil 47, 48, 109, 143, 299, 452, 490, 511, **709**, 710, 780, 810
Upchurch, Robert 697
Upsetters [R&B] 161
Upsetters [Reggae] 96
Upshaw, Gene 184
Urban Species 108
Urban, Margo 168
Urbaniak, Michal 788
Urena, Alvin 425
Urge Overkill 523
USA for Africa 353, 376, 573, 763
Usher 28, 210, 211, 230, 373, 478, 577, 578, 696, **710**
Usry, John L. 117
Utah Saints 644
UTFO 422, 575
Uzzell, Moses 166

V
V., Stevie 686
Vagabonds 361, 362
Valadiers **712**, 814, 816, 817
Valance, Ricky 558
Valdes, Vicentico 577
Vale, Jerry 420
Valens, Ritchie 52, 108, 518, 788
Valentine, Bobby 517
Valentine, Gerald 566
Valentine, Michelle 168
Valentine, Rae 724
Valentines 128, 687, 827, 828
Valentino & the Lovers 63
Valentino, Bobby 63
Valentinos 125, 162, 164, **712**, 760, 761, 762
Valli, Frankie 161, 309, 367, 566, 697, 756, 834
Valor, Tony 234, 235
Valvano, Mike 545, 546, 816
Vampire Sound Incorporated 811
VanBuskirk, Bill 136
Vance, Dick 122
Vance, Frank 121, 122
Vancouvers 346, 814
Vandals 437
Vandellas 4, 220, 263, 320, 446, 537, 546, 571, 816
VanDePitte, David 381, 755
Vandross, Luther 69, 77, 92, 97, 127, 136, 139, 169, 175, 182, 255, 257, 287, 349, 350, 351, 359, 363, 434, 435, 483, 498, 510, 588, 595, 665, 666, 678, 686, 688, 698, **712**, 713, 714, 730, 731, 735, 768, 770, 811, 816, 824, 833
VanDross, Patricia 169
VanDyke, David 297
VanDyke, Earl 37, 262, 263, 360, 426, 445, 600, **714**, 721, 754, 790, 832
VanDykes **714**, 798, 821
VanGelder, Rudy 787
VanHalen, Eddie 353, 355
VanHelden, Armand 725
Vanilla Ice 574
Vanity Six 279, 437, 666, **714**, 715
Vanity 213, 715
VanLoan, Joe 209, 562
Vann, Edgar Jr. 688
Vann, Joey 210
Vann, Teddy 688
Vannelli, Gino 428
Vannelli, Joe 578
VanPeebles, Mario 715
VanPeebles, Melvin 214, **715**, 808
VanZandt, Steven 65
Variations 574
Varner, Don 834
Varner, Jimmy 11, 678
Vasquez, Junior 59, 318, 578, 725, 747
Vaughan Brothers 139
Vaughan, Jimmie 193
Vaughan, Sarah 30, 94, 152, 206, 245, 328, 358, 375, 376, 377, 480, 527, 610, 666, 728, 755
Vaughan, Stevie Ray 14
Vaughn, Ben 745
Vaughn, Carla 26
Vaughn, Clarence 216, 217
Vaughn, Tony 178
Vee, Bobby 148, 688, 842
Vega, David 282
Vega, Little Louie 168
Vega, Tata 21, 112
Vegas, Lolly 122
Velaires 801
Velez, Lisa 422
Vells 446
Velours 141, 332, **715**, 784
Vels 445, 571
Velvelettes 307, 371, 445, **715**, 716, 721, 790, 832
Velvet Angels 648, **716**, 793
Velvet Hammer 748
Velvet Underground 174, 503, 716
Velvetones 782, 798
Velvets **716**
Velvettes 745
Venegas, Victor 295
Venet, Nick 563
Venosa, Arthur 220
Ventura, Charlie 102
Ventures 79, 671
Venuto, Joe 640
Vera, Billy 143, 425, **716**, 807
Vera, Billy & Judy Clay **716**
Vereen, Ben 829
Vernon, Mike 759
Versalettes **717**
Versatiles 185, 742
VerScharen, Joe 621
Verta-Ray, Matt 748
Vertical Hold 606, 646
Vesta 21, 47, 584
Vibrations 234, 414, 443, 487, 508, 509, 543, 679, **717**, 819, 829, 834
Viceroys 177
Vicious 829
Vicious, Johnny 317
Vick, Harold 288
Vickers, Carle 431
Vickers, Tom 524
Vickers, Walter 228
Victory, George 235
Vidal, Juan 37
Videls 141
Videos 611, 821
Vienneau, Jim 15
Villa-Lobos, Heitor 47
Village People 540, 662, 686, 700, **717**, 718
Villari, Guy 571
Villery, Louis 6, 7
Vincent, Gene 56, 177, 227
Vincent, Johnny 83, 144, 249, 393, 627, 793
Vincent, Joyce 808
Vincent, Leo 367, 368
Vincent, Rickey 283
Vincent, Stan 212, 244
Vinegar Joe 518
Vinnegar, Leroy 759
Vinson, Eddie "Cleanhead" 491, 514, 548, 558, 701, 810, 838
Violent Femmes 857
Violinaires 36
Viray, Errol 383
Virgo 383
Viscounts 821, 824
Visual 821
Vocaleers 629
Vocals **718**
Vogel, Janet 621
Vogues 210
Voice Masters 266, 279, **718**, 816
Voice, Roger 496, 499
Voices of East Harlem **718**
Voices of Theory **718**, 719
Volcanos 697, 818
Volumes **719**, 782, 784, 798
Vondells 428, **719**
Vontastics **719**
Voormann, Klaus 699
VSOP 295

W
Wachtel, Waddy 578
Waddy 153
Waddy, Frankie "Kash" 153, 517
Wade, Bluford D. 586
Wade, Bobby 408
Wade, Cory 93
Wade, Earl 107
Wade, Harold 697
Wade, Larry 108, 109
Wade, Norman 751
Wade, Stanley 697
Wagner, John 652
Wagner, Kurt 483
Wagner, Richard 332
Wahlberg, Donnie 317
Wahlberg, Mark 317
Wahls, Shirley 15
Wailers 280
Wain, Bea 409
Waits, Tom 100, 102, 141, 241, 318, 319, 715
Wake, Rick 643
Wakefield, Kathy 387, 580
Wakely, Jimmy 722
Wakeman, Rick 419, 523
Walden, Dana 125
Walden, Narada Michael 22, 43, 64, 100, 136, 257, 258, 328, 412, 454, 506, 520, 595, 609, 620, **720**
Walden, Phil 118, 314, 658, 692
Waldron, Mal 405
Wales, Ashley 509
Wales, Kevin 509
Walker, Albertina 317
Walker, Alice 376
Walker, David 34
Walker, David T. 80, 97, 166, 360, 428, 742
Walker, Don 319
Walker, Greg 238
Walker, Hysear Don 773
Walker, Jimmy 415, 575
Walker, Junior 122, 203, 334, 583, 618, **720**, 721, 727, 773, 825, 846
Walker, Junior & the All-Stars 80, 266, 315, 474, 720, 721, 722, 786, 830
Walker, Mel 514
Walker, Phillip 262
Walker, Randolph 784
Walker, Ronnie **722**, 821
Walker, Shirley 235
Walker, T-Bone 39, 57, 120, 251, 392, 411, 516, 601, 759, 815, 822, 838
Walker, T-Bone Jr. 300
Walker, Willie 809
Wall of Sound 809
Wallace Brothers 415, **722**, 786, 809
Wallace, Cooky 722
Wallace, Earnest 722
Wallace, Ervin 722
Wallace, Sippie 815
Wallace, Victoria 687
Wallace, Wales 833
Waller, Charlie 548
Waller, Don 139
Waller, Fats 542, 544, 857
Wallert, Charles 349
Walls, Van "Piano Man" 627
Walsh, John 365
Walter & Scotty 432
Walter, Robert 289
Walters, Ted 380, 825
Walton, James "Toy" 148
Walton, Mercy Dee 461
Wanderers 332, **722**, 723
Wansel, Dexter 15, 117, 347, 372, 373, 378, 381, 405, 468, **723**
War 6, 140, 174, 202, 295, 312, 325, 341, 420, 437, 441, 513, 514, 541, 554, 573, **723**, 724, 725, 769, 788, 801, 830, 851
Ward, Anita 184, 395, **725**, 726, 813, 831
Ward, Billy 90, 726, 769
Ward, Billy & the Dominoes 148, 206, 409, 462, **726**, 727, 753, 755, 833, 839
Ward, Carlos 97
Ward, Clara 39, 529, 784
Ward, Clara Singers 207, 645
Ward, Herb 320
Ward, Jesse 76
Ward, Michael 708
Ward, Robert [1] 93, 502, 582, 808
Ward, Robert [2] 233
Ward, Sammy 36, 369, 790, 825, 832
Ward, Walter 508
Ware, Bill 289
Ware, David S. 727
Ware, Leon 159, 227, 273, 289, 358, 437, 451, 474, 509, 591, **727**, 728, 792, 817
Ware, Martyn 300
Warlock 722
Warner, Alan 250
Warner, Eddie 115
Warnes, Jennifer 1, 150, 464
Waronker, Lenny 390, 783
Warp Nine 202, 647
Warren, Diane 1, 77, 150, 182, 224, 232, 488, 489, 494, 713, 757
Warren, Ernest 634, 635
Warren, Harry 169
Warren, Mervyn 21, 666
Warsinske, James 413
Warwick, Clint 117
Warwick, Dee Dee 210, 321, 326, 479, 660, 699, **728**, 729, 807, 809, 814, 824
Warwick, Dionne 3, 23, 92, 117, 175, 187, 201, 258, 271, 276, 277, 303, 304, 311, 315, 322, 326, 348, 357, 373, 397, 399, 472, 479, 512, 513, 536, 559, 637, 639, 655, 660, 679, 682, 688, 699, 713, **728**, 729, 730, 731, 732, 763, 764, 766, 777, 781, 817, 818, 830, 834, 842, 848, 856
Was (Not Was) 19, 796
Was, David 19
Was, Don 2, 19
Wash, Martha 201, 662, **731**, 732, 737
Washboard Willie 360
Washburn, Beverly 808
Washington, Baby 365, 682, **732**, 783, 794, 828
Washington, Booker T. 307, 747
Washington, Charles 450, 557
Washington, Chet 214
Washington, David 129
Washington, Denzel 284
Washington, Dinah 21, 48, 49, 91, 94, 95, 126, 186, 258, 375, 409, 526, 535, 536, 582, 610, 621, **732**, 733, 777, 786, 807, 809, 810, 815, 822
Washington, Ella 684, **733**, 798
Washington, Eugene 702
Washington, Fats 262, 369
Washington, Frank 186, 266
Washington, Geno 733
Washington, Geno & the Ram Jam Band **733**
Washington, Gino **733**
Washington, Grover Jr. 30, 118, 289, 490, 555, 648, 723, 725, **734**, 735, 739, 758, 785, 857
Washington, Harold 708
Washington, Jeanette "Baby" 732
Washington, Jerry 809
Washington, Justine 732
Washington, Keith 492, **735**
Washington, Larry 80, 468, 597
Washington, Leroy 783
Washington, Steve 20, 21, 622
Washington, Tom 498
Washington, Tony 211, 720
Washington, Tuts 392, 421, 553
Washington, Walter 5
Wasserman, Rob 495
Waterman, Paul 687
Waterman, Pete 464
Waters, Crystal **735**
Waters, Ervan 194
Waters, Freddie 793
Waters, John 94
Waters, Luther 572
Waters, Muddy 36, 49, 80, 162, 191, 192, 361, 365, 453, 480, 570, 702, 709, 790, 797, 818, 829
Waters, Oren 572
Waters, Shawn 249
Watkins, Alious 535
Watkins, Tiny 800, 809
Watkins, Tionne 529, 690, 691
Watley, Bobby 263
Watley, Jody 139, 140, 263, 311, 432, 483, 607, 608, **735**, 736, 785, 796, 826
Watson, Anthony 137
Watson, Betty 300
Watson, Bo 470
Watson, Bobby 572, 592, 593, 757
Watson, Deek 337
Watson, Joe 241
Watson, Johnny "Guitar" 46, 231, 312, 393, 505, 514, **736**, 737, 749, 780, 801, 802, 812, 819, 838
Watson, Stan 43, 240, 633, 794
Watson, Valerie 149
Watson, Wah Wah 106, 263, 295, 376, 428, 451, 705, 742
Watt, Dave 4
Watts 103rd Street Rhythm Band 211, 769
Watts Prophets **737**
Watts, Ernie 109, 377, 383, 420, 594, 829
Watts, Russell 332, 700
Wattsline Choir 376
Wayans, Marlon 698
Wayne, Edith 279, 320
We Three 34
Weakley, Steve 263
Weather Girls 575, 662, 731, 732, **737**, 797
Weather Report 215, 671, 734
Weatherly, Jim 397, 398, 534, 669
Weathers, Barbara 20
Weatherspoon, Danny 486
Weatherspoon, William 313, 461, 492
Weaver, Blue 40, 592
Weaver, Donny 507
Webb, Chick 378
Webb, Danny 176

Webb, Jimmy 43, 150, 159, 160, 238, 239, 245, 322, 467, 640
Webb, Joyce 797
Webb, Laura 63
Webb, Tiny 759
Webster, Ben 733, 759
Webster, Danny 622, 623
Webster, Gary 502
Weckl, Dave 320
Weems, Ted 12
Weil, Cynthia 64, 97, 172, 309, 388, 537, 574, 585, 730, 841, 842, 843
Weil, Kurt 48
Weinger, Harry 158, 275
Weintraub, Jerry 495
Weir, Alex 81
Weir, Bob 493, 535
Weiss, Betty 608
Weiss, Hy 237, 238, 409
Weiss, Mary 608
Weiss, Sam 426
Welch, Lenny 298, 420
Welding, Pete 133, 192, 514
Weldon, Chuck 519
Weller, Paul 109, 196, 198
Wellman, Ricky 84
Wells, Avon 332
Wells, Brandi 118, **737**, 738
Wells, Cory 332, 712
Wells, Ed 621
Wells, James 795
Wells, Jean 809
Wells, Junior 130, 371
Wells, Kitty 379, 857
Wells, Mary 126, 127, 178, 228, 271, 274, 275, 316, 339, 388, 396, 426, 445, 447, 461, 471, 549, 571, 578, 620, 630, 644, 645, 653, 693, 712, 716, **738**, 739, 779, 780, 786, 792, 794, 804, 807, 813, 814, 816, 817, 818, 819, 823, 825, 831, 832, 844, 845, 846
Wells, Mary Sue 307, 365
Wells, Milton 614
Welnick, Vince 535
Wenner, Jann 600
Wentz, Allen 746
Werner, Craig 105
Wesley, Fred 87, 89, 90, 91, 109, 147, 154, 198, 222, 289, 319, 365, 366, 440, 517, 520, 521, 522, 523, 524, **739**, 767, 785, 793, 850
Wesley, Fred & the Horny Horns 79
Wesley, Fred & the J.B.'s 91, 365, 366, 821
Wess, Frank 701
West 400
West Coast Vocaleers 260
West End 834
West Street Mob 541, 829
West, Bernie 242
West, Bob 233, 549
West, James 242
West, Kyle 529, 657
West, Matt 636
West, Norm 809
West, Ricky 400, 401
West, Robert 233, 235, 248, 805
West, Rudy 242
Weston, Jimmy 176
Weston, Kim 271, 272, 274, 307, 396, 445, 549, 568, 644, 655, 727, **739**, 740, 784, 790, 812, 816, 823, 832, 833, 846
Weston, Ruth 94
Wexler, Gerald 49
Wexler, Jerry 49, 101, 196, 206, 207, 255, 256, 360, 390, 392, 418, 444, 472, 598, 639, 658, 716
Whalum, Kirk 7, 30, 202, 666
Wham! 469
Whatnauts 227, 349, 437, 477, 478, **740**, 779
Wheeler, Alvin 635
Wheeler, Art 807
Wheeler, Audrey 709
Wheeler, Carl 632
Wheeler, Caron 427, 520, 631, 632, **740**
Wheeler, Cheryl 136
Wheeler, Karen 705
Whirlers 165
Whispers 8, 28, 81, 100, 183, 188, 316, 328, 329, 432, 470, 471, 597, 615, 632, 633, 652, 670, **740**, 741, 826, 827
Whitaker, Harry 159
Whitburn, Joel 67
White Heat 279
White Zombie 636
White, Adam 729
White, Alan 63, 211, 428, 429, 528, 529, 598
White, Anthony 820
White, Artie 812
White, Barry 42, 46, 63, 69, 101, 135, 275, 279, 304, 369, 377, 410, 417, 418, 428, 429, 430, 468, 487, 513, 523, 528, 529, 533, 566, 573, 617, 640, 663, 698, 727, 730, **741**, 742, 743, 744, 785, 801, 806, 814, 818, 819, 824
White, Carl 577
White, Charlie 148
White, Clifford 89
White, Dave [Engineer] 602, 612, 615
White, David [Producer] 122
White, Dennis 384
White, Fred 214, 223, 619
White, George 211
White, Glodean 428, 429, 743
White, Judy 341
White, Karyn 28, **744**
White, Lavelle 369
White, Lenny 388, 389, 450, 609, 768
White, Lynn 56
White, Maurice 36, 214, 215, 216, 223, 224, 259, 316, 398, 420, 421, 535, 542, 583, 584, 598, 621, 645, 709, 748
White, Peter 30
White, Robert 262, 263, 360, 714
White, Ron 289, 474, 475, 579, 580
White, Ronald 580
White, Ronnie 475, 578, 579, 763
White, Tommy 12
White, Tony Joe 5, 48, 306, 534, 639, 706, 847, 848
White, Verdine 214, 216, 223, 420, 542, 642, 643, 645
Whitefield Brothers 833
Whitehead Brothers 100
Whitehead, Charlie 794
Whitehead, Don 214, 598
Whitehead, John 465, 459
Whitehead, Peter 717
Whitfield, Barrence 205, 500, 585, 744, 745
Whitfield, Barrence & the Savages **744**, 745
Whitfield, Norman 59, 70, 205, 252, 263, 266, 273, 274, 281, 313, 396, 418, 447, 479, 500, 559, 560, 579, 583, 585, 591, 592, 642, 643, 644, 647, 674, 675, 676, 677, 679, 705, 708, 715, 721, **745**, 817, 832, 844, 846
Whitfield, Thomas 486
Whiting, Leonard 824
Whitley, Chris 141, 182
Whitley, Ray 182
Whitney, Marva 90, 377, **745**, 746, 803, 809, 812, 833
Whitsett, Carson 5, 469
Whitten, Jesse 308
Whittington, Chuck 200
Who 221, 403, 404, 474, 786, 830
Whodini 210, 667
Whyte, Cliff 90
Wickham, Vicki 403, 404, 405
Wiggins, DWayne 189, 692, 736
Wiggins, Jay 781, 821
Wiggins, Percy 311
Wiggins, Raphael 432, 692
Wiggins, Spencer 350
Wilber, Benjamin 500
Wilco 525
Wild Cherry 26, **746**
Wild Magnolias 271, 674, **746**, 747
Wild Orchid 664, 720, **747**
Wild Pair 2
Wild Sugar 235
Wild Tchoupitoulas 493, 494, 694, **747**, 818
Wilde, Eugene **747**
Wilde, Kim 281, **381**, 796
Wilder, Gene 763, 766
Wilder, Jerry 84
Wilder, Johnny 308
Wilder, Keith 308
Wilder, Matthew 595, 747
Wiley, Ed Jr. 479
Wiley, Isaac 181
Wiley, Michael 181, 394
Wilhoite, Orion 622
Wilkerson, Don 787
Wilkie, Corky 177
Wilkins, Elbert 203
Wilkins, Ernie 31
Wilkins, Jimmy 714
Wilkinson, Dianne 44
Will to Power 801
Willams, Paul "Tubbs" 335
Willette, Baby Face 857
Williams, Alvin 123
Williams, Alyson 312, 375, 667, **747**
Williams, Andre 80, 98, 121, 146, 209, 271, 387, 648, 675, **747**, 748, 795
Williams, Andy 108
Williams, Beau 460
Williams, Benny 499
Williams, Bernice 209
Williams, Billy 41
Williams, Blinky 644, 816
Williams, Buster 294, 756, 768
Williams, Byron 213
Williams, Charles [Percussionist] 338
Williams, Charles [Sax] 94
Williams, Charlie 701
Williams, Christopher 47, 230
Williams, Clarence 378, 821
Williams, Cliff 123
Williams, Clifford 479
Williams, Cootie 732
Williams, Curtis 532, 630
Williams, Curtis "Fitz" 46, 629
Williams, Dave 795
Williams, Dean 309
Williams, Deniece 26, 43, 214, 245, 259, 412, 466, 483, 519, 527, 572, 583, 590, 645, 738, **748**, 749, 785, 796
Williams, Dennis 693
Williams, Devonia 737
Williams, Dicky 793
Williams, Doc 266
Williams, Don 283
Williams, Dootsie 463
Williams, Duane 52
Williams, Earl 658
Williams, Eddie 83, 84
Williams, Eric 56
Williams, Erskine 235
Williams, Fleming 324
Williams, Geoffrey 69, 450
Williams, George 235, 236, 707
Williams, Gloria 445
Williams, Gregory 660
Williams, Hank 52, 74, 131, 132, 192, 285, 425
Williams, Hank Jr. 132, 245
Williams, Henry 60
Williams, Herbie 468
Williams, Hype 691
Williams, J. Mayo 460
Williams, James "Diamond" 502
Williams, James "D-Train" 3, 98, 175
Williams, Janice C. 642, 643
Williams, Jeff 733
Williams, Jerry Jr. 65, 101, 210, 658, 682
Williams, Jimmy 200
Williams, Jody 102
Williams, Joe 24, 456, 463, 563, 627, 668
Williams, John [Film Composer] 99
Williams, John [Soul Producer] Gary 436
Williams, Johnny 122, 207, 832
Williams, Jonathan 575
Williams, Joseph 217
Williams, Joyce 821
Williams, Kae Jr. 616, 617
Williams, Keith 233, 715
Williams, Kenneth 463
Williams, Kiely 688
Williams, Larry 261, 424, 495, 547, **749**, 750, 793
Williams, Lee "Shot" 818
Williams, Lee & the Cymbals **750**, 789
Williams, Lenny 434, 542, 572, 695, 696, **750**, 751, 757, 778, 780
Williams, Leroy 312
Williams, Little Jerry 658
Williams, Lloyd 205
Williams, Louis 350, 516
Williams, Lucinda 745
Williams, Maizie 66
Williams, Marcus 645
Williams, Maurice 182, 464, 675, 751, 752, 805, 839
Williams, Maurice & the Zodiacs **751**, 779, 799
Williams, McKinley 455
Williams, Mel 514, 827
Williams, Mentor 283
Williams, Michelle 189
Williams, Milan 155, 156
Williams, Minor 776
Williams, Oscar 426
Williams, Otis 386, 479, 548, 674, 675, 676, 677, 678, 700, 752
Williams, Otis & the Charms 220, **752**
Williams, Paul 127, 332, 386, 387, 548, 549, 674, 675, 769
Williams, Percy 468
Williams, Pharrell 492
Williams, Ralph 434, 512
Williams, Ric 13, 15
Williams, Ricardo 449
Williams, Robbie 177, 823
Williams, Ronnie 545, 630
Williams, Ronny 660
Williams, Samuel M. 449
Williams, Scotty 819
Williams, Stokley 474
Williams, Tom 647
Williams, Tony [Drums] 295, 767
Williams, Tony [Platters] 539, 540
Williams, Trudy 621
Williams, Tyrone 449
Williams, Val 267
Williams, Vanessa 69, 460, 667, 736, **752**, 825
Williams, Vernon 600
Williams, Vesta 486, 670, 727, 757
Williams, Walter 417, 505, 506, 507
Williamson, Fred 166, 533, 644
Williamson, Sonny Boy 189, 487, 520, 839, 601
Williamston, Wade 76
Willie & the Mighty Magnificents **752**
Willingham, Gus 107
Willingham, Theodore 500
Willis, Bruce 787
Willis, Carol 327
Willis, Carolyn 279, 319, 320, 634
Willis, Chick **753**
Willis, Chuck 36, 57, 90, 94, 242, 326, 515, 528, **753**, 836, 838
Willis, Eddie 262, 714
Willis, Greg 565
Willis, Harold 753
Willis, Kerry 628, 629
Willis, Larry 448
Willis, Marvin 247
Willis, Ralph 460
Willis, Victor 717, 718
Willows 70, 107, 191, 345, **753**, 778, 803, 828
Wills, Bob 261, 822
Wills, Viola 428, 742, 744
Wilmott, John 671
Wilson Phillips 232
Wilson, Al 201, 360
Wilson, Belinda 504
Wilson, Brian 49, 102, 450, 635, 636
Wilson, Bryce 409, 736
Wilson, Carlos 440, 441
Wilson, Cassandra 788
Wilson, Charles 269
Wilson, Charlie 268, 269, 270, 364, 773
Wilson, Clyde 37, 218, 439, 509
Wilson, Curtis "Sauce" 629
Wilson, David 121
Wilson, Flip 426
Wilson, Frank [1] 202, 430, 745
Wilson, Frank [2] 143, 252, 387, 461, 579, 654, 655, 831
Wilson, Frank [Producer] 33, 252, 273, 316, 457, 580, 655, 750, 790
Wilson, Gerald 24, 131, 140, 141, 732, 733, 759, 787
Wilson, Gerald Orchestra 25
Wilson, Henry 170
Wilson, Hosea 742
Wilson, J. Frank & the Cavaliers 150
Wilson, Jack 25, 238, 294, 409, 425, 462, 464, 539, 727, 787
Wilson, Jackie 3, 31, 32, 46, 56, 95, 108, 130, 156, 160, 178, 187, 202, 207, 242, 266, 281, 282, 285, 293, 294, 315, 327, 342, 348, 360, 369, 370, 395, 418, 422, 457, 463, 473, 480, 514,

545, 567, 586, 598, 705, 712, 714, 726, 727, 735, 738, **753**, 754, 755, 781, 783, 785, 786, 789, 791, 817, 818, 832, 833, 836, 844, 845
Wilson, Leslie 431, 495, 496
Wilson, Lou 440, 441
Wilson, Mary 32, 548, 549, 586, 653, 654, 655, 656, 657, 670, 674, 816, 823
Wilson, Melvin 495, 496
Wilson, Muki 170
Wilson, Nancy 30, 136, 258, 309, 527, 727, 728, 732, 748, **755**, 756
Wilson, Paul 246, 683
Wilson, Precious 552
Wilson, Reuben 788
Wilson, Ric 440, 441
Wilson, Rocky 577
Wilson, Ron 240
Wilson, Ronnie 269
Wilson, Ruby 831
Wilson, Shanice 720
Wilson, Timothy 607, 780, 832, 833
Wilson, Tony 320
Wilson, Turner 577
Wilson, Wallace 361
Wiltshire, Christine 488
Wiltshire, Kenneth 697
Winans 10, 30, 322, 369, 417, 575, **756**, 757
Winans, BeBe 7, 757
Winans, BeBe & CeCe **757**
Winans, Carvin 756, 757
Winans, CeCe 666, **757**
Winans, Mario 529, 666
Winans, Marvin 756, 757
Winans, Michael 756, 757
Winans, Mom & Pop 757
Winans, Ron 756, 757
Winbush, Angela 43, 300, 342, 472, 486, 572, **757**, 758, 785
Winchester, Jesse 745
Winchester, Lem 420
Winding, Kai 76, 376, 557
Windross, Rose 631, 632
Winfield, Willie 242, 295
Wingate, Ed 37, 360, 571, 712, 714
Wingo, Richard 359
Wings 379, 553
Winley, Harold 148
Winley, Paul 367
Winston, George 69, 633
Winston, Jerry 722
Winston, Walter 633
Winstons **758**, 793
Winter, Edgar 63
Winter, Edgar Group 298, 299, 668, 669, 687
Winter, Johnny 298
Winters, Ruby 688, **758**
Winwood, Muff 179
Winwood, Steve 62, 71, 130, 150, 179, 720, 847
Wise, James 42
Wise, Richie 397
Wisner, Jimmy 559, 600
Withers, Bill 2, 57, 100, 149, 155, 169, 171, 202, 222, 244, 270, 287, 303, 322, 341, 355, 374, 380, 397, 409, 490, 491, 493, 494, 604, 734, **758**, 759, 811, 813, 825
Witherspoon, Jimmy 57, 88, 167, 196, 350, 415, 454, 503, 627, **759**, 760, 810
Witnesses 102
Witt, Bill 519
Wizzard 484
Wobble, Jah 227, 440
Wolf & Epic 698
Wolf, James 607
Wolf, Peter 167
Wolf, Ramona 617
Wolfe, Colin 168
Wolfert, David 472
Wolinski, David 512, 593
Wolinski, Hawk 592
Womack & Womack 705, 712, **760**, 857
Womack Brothers 164, 712, 760
Womack, Bobby 11, 44, 48, 81, 95, 144, 162, 164, 167, 277, 280, 309, 315, 340, 356, 357, 364, 382, 418, 442, 462, 466, 495, 496, 517, 537, 582, 593, 594, 624, 631, 671, 677, 705, 712, 727, 738, 758, 760, 761, 762, 769, 778, 781, 787, 803, 811, 824, 826, 829
Womack, Cecil 506, 705, 712, 738, 739, 760, 761, 791
Womack, Curtis 712, 760
Womack, Friendly 760
Womack, Friendly Jr. 712, 760
Womack, Harry 712, 760
Womack, Linda 705, 760
Womack, Nicole 712
Womack, Stacy 712
Womack, Trenita 74
Wommack, Kevin 761
Wonder, Stevie 9, 15, 24, 28, 47, 53, 55, 56, 59, 64, 65, 74, 77, 80, 84, 86, 99, 106, 112, 117, 122, 129, 138, 141, 145, 161, 175, 177, 179, 202, 215, 219, 227, 234, 241, 253, 255, 256, 269, 271, 274, 280, 281, 284, 289, 290, 293, 295, 298, 308, 309, 310, 315, 327, 328, 335, 341, 345, 346, 352, 353, 355, 358, 364, 369, 373, 376, 377, 380, 381, 384, 386, 388, 394, 415, 420, 437, 438, 445, 447, 451, 452, 459, 471, 474, 487, 488, 490, 499, 509, 511, 521, 526, 542, 543, 549, 559, 564, 573, 576, 579, 580, 581, 583, 587, 592, 594, 602, 604, 633, 637, 638, 649, 653, 657, 663, 666, 686, 687, 712, 713, 715, 721, 723, 729, 730, 741, 745, 746, 748, 755, 756, 757, 760, **762**, 763, 764, 765, 766, 768, 770, 775, 777, 792, 802, 803, 810, 816, 817, 818, 823, 824, 825, 830, 832, 833, 844, 846, 851
Wonderlove 576, 602, 748
Woo, Gerry 821
Woo, Philip 455
Wood, Bobby 211, 466, 700
Wood, Brenton 316, **766**, 767, 781, 788, 799, 821, 833
Wood, Chris 141
Wood, Randy 508
Wood, Ron 167, 191, 193, 760
Woodard, Chester 341
Woodard, Jerry 784
Woodard, Lyman 218
Woodman, Britt 95
Woods 539, 653
Woods, Belita 74
Woods, Danny 123, 124, 370, 819
Woods, Donald 463
Woods, Maceo 36
Woods, Mark 406
Woods, Phil 376, 527
Woods, Ren 653
Woods, Robert 148
Woods, Sonny 32
Woods, Stu 515
Woods, Willie 535, 720, 721
Woodson, Ali "Ollie" 678
Woodson, Elbert 569
Wooley, Michael-Leon 544
Woolfolk, Andrew 214
Wooten, George 166
Wooten, William 74
World Class Wreckin' Cru 402
Worrell, Bernie 124, 154, 263, 264, 265, 266, 306, 411, 441, 488, 509, 517, 522, 523, 524, 601, **767**
Worth, Richard 289
Worthy, Dave 13
Wray, Link 805
Wreckx N Effect 290, 405
Wrens 562, **767**, 827, 828
Wright, Arthur 539, 560, 673, 674
Wright, Benjamin 669
Wright, Bernard **768**, 828
Wright, Betty 60, 358, 409, 410, 423, 458, 459, 571, 603, 686, 726, **768**, 769, 770, 781, 791, 802, 803, 804, 809, 830, 833
Wright, Billy 424, **769**
Wright, Charles 279, 320, 504, 769, 770, 777, 851
Wright, Charles & the Watts 103rd Street Rhythm Band **769**, 770, 802
Wright, Clifton 128
Wright, Dorsey 614
Wright, Edna 319, 320, **770**
Wright, Ernest Jr. 422
Wright, Gary 389
Wright, Gene 614
Wright, Jaguar **770**
Wright, James 4
Wright, Jimmy 767, 831
Wright, Johnnie 308
Wright, Johnny 702
Wright, Leo 759
Wright, Marva 153, 747
Wright, Milton **770**
Wright, Norma Jean 100, 138, 234, **770**
Wright, Norman 184, 185
Wright, O.V. 96, 118, 179, 409, 476, 529, 530, 582, 644, **770**, 771, 778, 798, 809, 810, 814
Wright, Orlando 372
Wright, Patricia 171, 172
Wright, Peter 206, 372
Wright, Phil 645
Wright, Philip Adrian 118
Wright, Ray 384
Wright, Richard 266, 686
Wright, Rita 663, 664
Wright, Robert C. 642, 686
Wright, Robert 542
Wright, Ruben 115
Wright, Sunshine 168
Wright, Syreeta 763
Wu Tang Clan 29, 66, 227, 249
Wulf, Ramona 617
Wyatt, Johnny 744
Wycoff, Michael 670
Wylie, Delores "Honey" 612
Wylie, Richard 540
Wynette, Tammy 259, 857
Wynn, Toby 431
Wynne, Kevin 400
Wynne, Philippe 112, 153, 309, 497, 636, 637, 638

X
X-Pensive Winos 493
Xscape 210, 359, 378, **772**

Y
Yamagishi, June 747
Yancey, Kym 652
Yancey, Mama 442
Yancy, Marvin 36, 152, 212, 336
Yanney, Yvonne 671
Yarbrough & Peoples **773**, 785
Yarbrough, Calvin 773
Yarbrough, Glenn 773
Yarbrough, Robert 722
Yardbirds 73, 191, 193, 340, 382, 613, 746
Yarian, Christine 474
Yaz 383
Yearwood, Trisha 493, 494
Yello 796
Yellow Sunshine 723
Yellowjackets 202, 213, 595
Yes 207, 402, 605, 780
Yokohura, Yutaka 21
Yonah 145
York, Peter 179
Young Disciples 105
Young Jessie 774, 815
Young MC 833
Young Rascals 183, 508, 561, 631
Young, Arthur 405
Young, Colin 250
Young, Dean "Cousin Sugar" 700
Young, Earl 11, 165, 190, 240, 297, 317, 318, 319, 468, 597, 677, 697
Young, Eldee 319, 420, 421, 773, 774
Young, Ernie 173, 751
Young, Howie 170, 647
Young, James 569
Young, Jesse Colin 709
Young, Jessie **774**
Young, Jimmy 202
Young, John 12
Young, Kathy & the Innocents 577
Young, Kenny 208
Young, Larry 166, 287, 288, 788, 857
Young, Lee 492
Young, Leron 84
Young, Lester 102
Young, Mighty Joe 801
Young, Mike 20
Young, Neil 67, 69, 130, 341, 362, 413, 467, 662
Young, Reggie 211, 466, 520
Young, Rusty 330
Young, Sheila 267
Young, Starleana 20, 21, 622
Young, Tommie 6, 525
Young, Wanda 447
Young, Weldon Dean 700
Young, William 20
Young-Holt Trio 4, 319, 773, 774, 791
Young-Holt Unlimited 3, 178, 319, 420, 421, **773**, 789
Youngblood, Lonnie 607, 748, 779
Youngblood, Tommy 824
Youngbloods 709
Younghearts 626, 631
Youngsters 769

Z
Zabo, Dave 121
Zachary, Zach 468
Zager, Michael 96, 97, 321, 700
Zander, Robin 358
Zane 10
Zant, Henry "Red" 3
Zap Mama 500
Zapp 127, 218, 328, 338, 486, 583, 622, **775**, 785, 826, 831
Zapp & Roger 583
Zappa, Frank 43, 146, 155, 199, 296, 312, 381, 532, 535, 584, 658, 737, 818, 839
Zavatsky, Danny 499
Zawinul, Joe 256, 377
Zender, Stuart 364
Zero, Mike 559
Zero, Sal 559
Z'ev 383
Zhané 593, 628, 727, **776**
Ziegler, Richard 240
Zigman, Aaron 152
Zingara **776**
Zion Travelers 382
Zircons 806
Zodiacs 751
Zombies 113, 728
Zulema **776**
ZZ Top 2

CPSIA information can be obtained at www.ICGtesting.com
Printed in the USA
BVOW09s1422080915

417068BV00011B/101/P